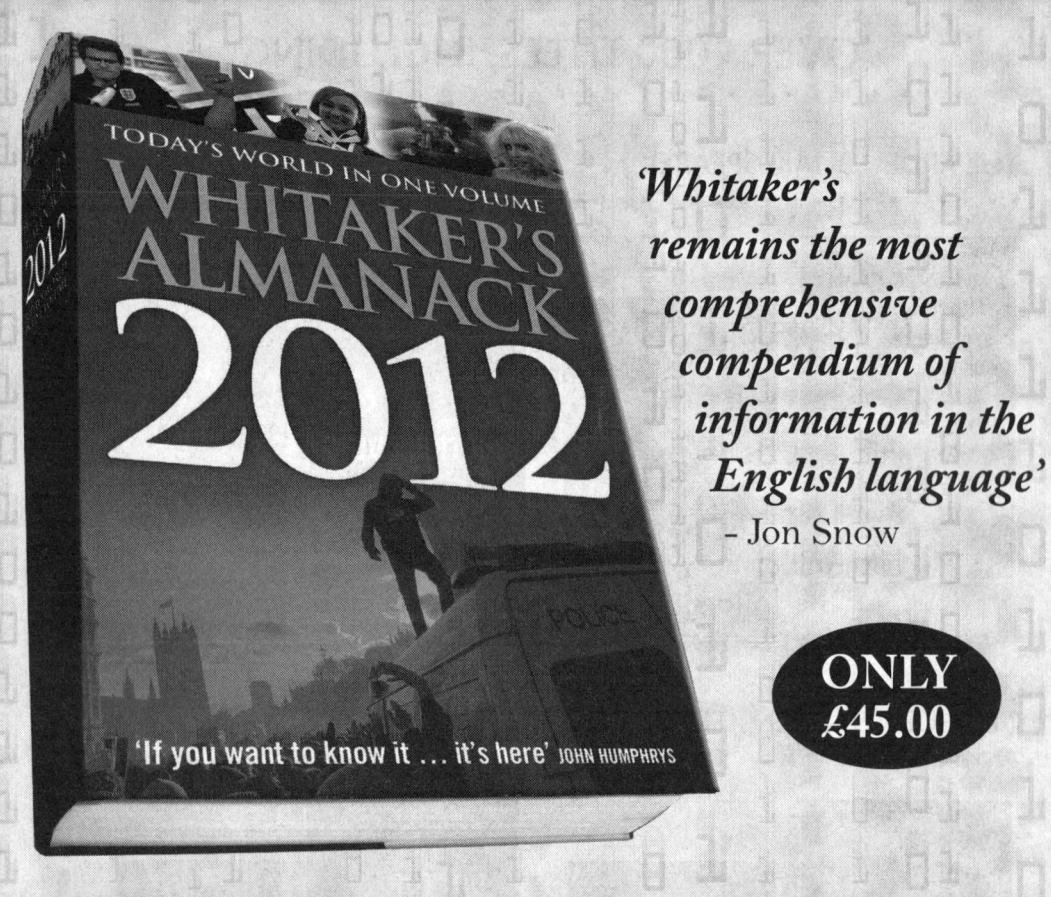

INDEPENDENT SCHOOLS YEARBOOK

2011–2012

Boys Schools, Girls Schools,
Co-educational Schools
and Preparatory Schools

Details of Schools in membership of one or more
of the following Constituent Associations of the
Independent Schools Council (ISC):

Heads
Headmasters' and Headmistresses' Conference (HMC)
Girls' Schools Association (GSA)
Society of Heads of Independent Schools (SHMIS)
Independent Association of Prep Schools (IAPS)
Independent Schools Association (ISA)

Overseas Schools
Council of British International Schools (COBIS)

EDITED BY
JUDY MOTT

A&C BLACK • LONDON

© 2011 A&C Black Publishers
an imprint of Bloomsbury Publishing Plc
50 Bedford Square
London WC1B 3DP

Tel: 020 7631 5600
e-mail: isyb@acblack.com
website: www.isyb.co.uk

A CIP catalogue record for this book is available from the British Library.

ISBN: 978-1-4081-5206-5

Typeset by AMA DataSet Limited, Preston PR5 6QE
Printed and bound by CPI Group (UK) Ltd, Croydon CR0 4YY

This book is produced using paper that is made from wood grown in managed, sustainable forests. It is natural, renewable and recyclable. The logging and manufacturing processes conform to the environmental regulations of the country of origin.

INDEPENDENT SCHOOLS YEARBOOK 2011–2012

CONTENTS

PART I: **HEADMASTERS' AND HEADMISTRESSES' CONFERENCE**
309 schools for pupils from age 11 to 18, whose Heads are members of HMC; 62 of these are international members. They are all-boys schools (some admitting girls to the Sixth Form), co-educational schools, "Diamond" schools (girls and boys taught separately in the 11–16 age range), and some are all-girls schools. Many of the schools also have a Preparatory/Junior School/Department.

PART II: **GIRLS' SCHOOLS ASSOCIATION**
168 schools for pupils from age 11 to 16/18, whose Heads are members of GSA. They are all-girls schools in the 11–16 age range (some admitting boys to the Sixth Form) and some are "Diamond" schools (girls and boys taught separately in the 11–16 age range). Some of the schools also have a Preparatory/Junior School/Department.

. . ./continued

PART III: SOCIETY OF HEADS OF INDEPENDENT SCHOOLS
91 schools for pupils from age 11 to 18 whose Heads are members of SHMIS. The majority are co-educational schools, but membership is open to boys and girls schools. Many of the schools also have a Preparatory/ Junior School/Department.

PART IV: INDEPENDENT ASSOCIATION OF PREP SCHOOLS
598 schools whose Heads are members of IAPS; 29 of these are overseas members. Most of the schools are co-educational; some cater for boys only or girls only. The preparatory school age range is 7 to 11/13, but many of the schools have a pre-preparatory department for children up to age 7.

PART V: INDEPENDENT SCHOOLS ASSOCIATION
267 schools in membership of ISA. Schools in this Association are not confined to one age range and can cater for any age range of pupils up to 18/ 19 years.

49 British Schools abroad that are members of COBIS and have undergone, or will undergo, an inspection by the Independent Schools Inspectorate. Members of this Association include primary, secondary, and all-through schools.

ISC

INDEPENDENT SCHOOLS COUNCIL

website: www.isc.co.uk

"Working with its members to promote and preserve the quality, diversity and excellence of UK independent education both at home and abroad"

The Independent Schools Council (ISC) is the representative body for eight UK independent schools Associations, with some 1,250 member schools that educate more than 500,000 children in the UK and select British schools overseas.

The Constituent Associations of ISC are:

Association of Governing Bodies of Independent Schools (AGBIS)
Council of British International Schools (COBIS)
Girls' Schools Association (GSA)
Headmasters' and Headmistresses' Conference (HMC)
Independent Association of Prep Schools (IAPS)
Independent Schools Association (ISA)
Independent Schools' Bursars Association (ISBA)
Society of Heads of Independent Schools (SHMIS)

ISC works to ensure that independent education is fairly and accurately represented to Government and to the media. It carries out research; gives advice to schools; provides advice to parents via its website and the Independent Schools Council information & advice service (ISCias); responds to Government legislation, regulations and consultations; and administers new teacher induction in independent schools.

The professionally independent inspection service, ISI (Independent Schools Inspectorate), inspects (under statute) schools in membership of the ISC's Associations in England and also schools abroad in membership of COBIS.

Acting Chairman
Toby Mullins

Chief Executive
(to be appointed)

Deputy Chief Executive
Matthew Burgess

Head of Research and Intelligence
Rudolf Eliott Lockhart

Head of Schools' Services
Judith Fenn

Head of Press
Alex Beynon

**Independent Schools Council
St Vincent House
30 Orange Street
London WC2H 7HH**

**Tel: 020 7766 7070 • Fax: 020 7766 7071
ISCias parental helpline: 0845 7246657
e-mail: office@isc.co.uk**

HMC

HEADMASTERS' AND HEADMISTRESSES' CONFERENCE

website: www.hmc.org.uk

The HMC dates from 1869, when the celebrated Edward Thring of Uppingham asked thirty-seven of his fellow headmasters to meet at his house to consider the formation of a 'School Society and Annual Conference'. Twelve headmasters accepted the invitation. From that date there have been annual meetings. Thring's intention was to provide an opportunity for discussion at regular intervals, both on practical issues in the life of a school and on general principles in education. He believed that his guests would discharge their practical business more effectively at a residential meeting where they could also enjoy being in the company of like-minded men. Annual Meetings of the HMC still combine formal debate on current educational questions with the second element of conversational exchanges in an agreeable environment. These gatherings, which up to 1939 were usually at individual schools, then took place at a University. Nowadays they are held in major hotels and Conference centres in the Autumn term. In addition to these annual conferences attended by all members, there are local meetings each term arranged by the ten branches or Divisions into which the country is divided.

Present full membership of the HMC is a total of two hundred and fifty one, which now includes headmasters and headmistresses of boys', girls' and co-educational schools. In considering applications for election to membership, the Committee has regard to the degree of independence enjoyed by the Head and his/her school. Eligibility also depends on the academic standards obtaining in the school, as reflected by the proportion of pupils in the Sixth Form pursuing a course of study beyond GCSE and by the school's public examination results, including A Levels, the International Baccalaureate and the Cambridge Pre-U.

The Constitution provides that the full membership shall consist only of heads of independent schools in the UK and Ireland. At the same time, it is held to be a strength that the Conference includes heads of schools of other status. There is provision therefore for the election of a small number of heads of maintained schools (Additional Membership).

In addition the HMC has a number of International members, who are heads of high quality schools from around the world. There is also a small number of Honorary Associates who have been elected to life membership on retirement.

The HMC is closely associated with the other independent sector associations that also belong to the Independent Schools Council (ISC), and with the Association of School and College Leaders (ASCL), which represents the Heads and senior staff of secondary schools and colleges in both the maintained and independent sectors.

The HMC Committee 2011–2012

Chairman	Kenneth Durham	University College School
Vice-Chairman	David Levin	City of London School
Chairman-Elect	Chris Ray	The Manchester Grammar School
Treasurer	Barry Martin	Hampton School
Chairman – East	Garry Bowe	Wellingborough School
Secretary – East	Philip John	Gresham's School
Chairman – Irish	David Carruthers	Coleraine Academical Institution
Secretary – Irish	Scott Naismith	Methodist College, Belfast
Chairman – London	Mark Hanley-Browne	Emanuel School
Secretary – London	Mark Steed	Berkhamsted School
Chairman – North East	Geoffrey Boult	Giggleswick School
Secretary – North East	Michael Gibbons	The Grammar School at Leeds
Chairman – North West	Robert Karling	King Edward VII & Queen Mary School
Secretary – North West	John Clark	Birkenhead School
Chairman – Scottish	David Gray	Stewart's Melville College
Secretary – Scottish	David Girdwood	St Columba's School
Chairman – South Central	Gregg Davies	Shiplake College
Secretary – South Central	Simon Williams	Churcher's College
Chairman – South East	Jonathan Gillespie	Lancing College
Secretary – South East	Peter Green	Ardingly College
Chairman – South West	Christopher Alcock	Queen's College
Secretary – South West	Martin Reader	Wellington School
Chairman – West	Paul Smith	Hereford Cathedral School
Secretary – West	Jonathan Lancashire	Dean Close School
Chairman – International	Steffen Sommer	British School of Paris

Co-opted Members

Chairman of Academic Policy	Chris Ray	The Manchester Grammar School
Chairman of Professional Development	Chris King	Leicester Grammar School
Chairman of Universities Sub-Committee	Tim Hands	Magdalen College School
Chairman of Inspection Sub-Committee	Stephen Cole	Woodbridge School
	Tony Little	Eton College

Secretary: William Richardson, BA, DPhil (Tel: 01858 469059)

Membership Secretary: Ian Power, MA (Tel: 01858 465260)

Headmasters' and Headmistresses' Conference
12 The Point, Rockingham Road, Market Harborough, Leicestershire LE16 7QU
Tel: 01858 465260 • Fax: 01858 465759 • e-mail: hmc@hmc.org.uk

GSA

GIRLS' SCHOOLS ASSOCIATION

website: www.gsa.uk.com

The Girls' Schools Association (GSA) is the professional association of the heads of independent girls' schools in the UK and overseas and is a constituent member of the Independent Schools Council (ISC).

GSA is a member-led organisation that facilitates mutual professional support whilst ensuring that it represents the views of practising heads of girls' schools in advising and lobbying educational policy makers. The Association is supported by a small dedicated team based in Leicester that facilitates and directs its work.

The aims of GSA are
- to promote high standards of education for girls
- to inform and influence national educational debate
- to raise awareness of the benefits of single-sex education for girls
- to support members through the provision of a broad range of services

GSA schools are widely recognised for their exceptional record of examination achievements. Education is, however, not only about success in exams. Girls' schools offer wider development opportunities, and are special for a number of reasons. They provide an environment in which girls can learn to grow in confidence and ability. In a girls' school, the needs and aspirations of girls are the main focus, and the staff are specialists in the teaching of girls. Girls hold all the senior positions in the school, and are encouraged by positive role models in the schools' teaching staff and management. Expectations are high. In GSA schools, girls do not just have equal opportunities, they have *every* opportunity. Members of GSA share a commitment to the values and benefits of single-sex schools for girls, and a belief that all girls, regardless of educational setting, deserve the opportunity to realise their potential, to be active and equal, confident and competent leaders, participants and contributors.

For further information about girls' schools visit the MyDaughter website – www.mydaughter.co.uk – the first website dedicated to providing a valuable source of up-to-date information, expert opinion and useful advice on all aspects of educating and raising girls which is brought to you by the Girls' Schools Association.

Officers 2011

President:	Helen Wright	St Mary's Calne
Vice-President:	Gillian Low	The Lady Eleanor Holles School
President Elect:	Louise Robinson	Merchant Taylors' Girls' School
Treasurer:	Sue Marks	Withington Girls' School

Officers 2012

President:	Louise Robinson	Merchant Taylors' Girls' School
Vice-President:	Helen Wright	St Mary's Calne
President Elect:	Hilary French	Central Newcastle High School GDST
Treasurer:	Sue Marks	Withington Girls' School

Committee Chairmen

Boarding:	Wendy Griffiths	Tudor Hall
Education:	Caroline Jordan	Headington School
Research brief:	Ruth Weeks	Edgbaston High School for Girls
Inspections:	Jenny Dwyer	Sherborne Girls
Membership:	Alun Jones	St Gabriel's School
Professional Development:	Alice Phillips	St Catherine's School Bramley
Sports:	Lesley Watson	Moira House Girls School
Universities:	Bobby Georghiou	Bury Grammar School Girls

Regional Representatives

East:	Elaine Purves	Ipswich High School for Girls GDST
London:	Marion Gibbs	James Allen's Girls' School
Midland:	Ruth Weeks	Edgbaston High School for Girls
North East:	Hilary French	Central Newcastle High School GDST
North West:	Lillian Croston	Westholme School
South Central:	Alice Phillips	St Catherine's School Bramley
South East:	Jayne Triffitt	Woldingham School
South West & Wales:	Isabel Tobias	The Red Maids' School
Scotland:	Michael Farmer	Kilgraston School

Secretariat

Executive Director:	Sheila Cooper
Membership Services Director:	Jane Carroll
Business & Events Manager:	Lindsey Hills
PA to Executive Director:	Jeven Sharma
Membership Services Assistant:	Emma Good
Web Manager:	Imogen Vanderpump
Communications Manager:	Rachel Kerr

Girls' Schools Association
130 Regent Road, Leicester LE1 7PG
Tel: 0116 254 1619 • Fax: 0116 255 3792 • e-mail: office@gsa.uk.com

SHMIS

SOCIETY OF HEADS OF INDEPENDENT SCHOOLS

website: www.shmis.org.uk

The Society is an Association of Heads of over 100 well-established independent schools. It was founded in 1961 at a time when the need arose from the vitality and growth of the independent sector in the 1950s and the wish of a group of Heads to share ideas and experience.

The Society continues to provide a forum for the exchange of ideas and consideration of the particular needs of the smaller independent school. These are frequently different from the issues and from the approach of the larger schools. All members value their independence, breath in education and the pursuit of excellence, particularly in relation to academic standards.

The Society's policy is to maintain high standards in member schools, to ensure their genuine independence, to foster an association of schools which contributes to the whole independent sector by its distinctive character and flexibility, to provide an opportunity for the sharing of ideas and common concerns, to promote links with the wider sphere of higher education, to strengthen relations with the maintained sector and with local communities.

Within the membership there is a wide variety of educational experience. Some schools are young, some have evolved from older foundations, some have behind them a long tradition of pioneer and specialist education, the great majority are now co-educational but we also have boys' and girls' schools. A good number of the member schools have a strong boarding element and others are day schools. Some have specific religious foundations and some are non-denominational. All offer a stimulating Sixth Form experience and at the same time give a sound and balanced education to pupils of widely varying abilities and interests.

The Society is one of the constituent Associations of the Independent Schools Council. Every Full Member school has been accredited through inspection by the Independent Schools Inspectorate and is subject to regular visits to monitor standards and ensure that good practice and sound academic results are maintained. The Society is also represented on many other educational bodies.

All members are in membership of the Association of School and College Leaders (ASCL) and Full Member schools belong to AGBIS.

There are also categories of Additional, Overseas and Conference Membership to which Heads are elected whose schools do not fulfil all the criteria for Full Membership but whose personal contribution to the Society is judged to be invaluable. They are recorded separately at the end of the entries.

The Society has a one-day meeting for members in the autumn and summer terms and organises a two-day residential conference in the Easter term.

Officers 2011–2012

Chairman: Andy Waters, Kingsley School
Vice-Chairman: Philip Cottam, Halliford School
Chairman Designate: David Boddy, St James Senior Boys' School
Hon Treasurer: David Vanstone, North Cestrian Grammar School

SHMIS Committee 2011–2012

Stephen Aiano, Bearwood College
David Boddy, St James Senior Boys' School
Philip Cottam, Halliford School
Damian Ettinger, Cokethorpe School
Gerry Holden, Dover College
Lynne Horner, Abbey Gate College
Toby Mullins, Seaford College
Isobel Nixon, Scarborough College
Richard Palmer, St Christopher School
Martin Priestley, Warminster School
John Walmsley, Sidcot School
Andy Waters, Kingsley School
Graham Wigley, Friends' School

Secretariat

General Secretary: Dr Peter Bodkin

12 The Point, Rockingham Road, Market Harborough, Leicestershire LE16 7QU
Tel: 01858 433760 • Fax: 01858 461413 • e-mail: gensec@shmis.org.uk

IAPS

INDEPENDENT ASSOCIATION OF PREP SCHOOLS

website: www.iaps.org.uk

Together, IAPS schools represent a multi-billion pound enterprise. Our schools educate more than 150,000 children and employ more than 15,000 members of staff.

As the voice of independent prep school education, IAPS has national influence and actively defends and promotes the interests of our members. We lobby the government on their behalf and promote prep school issues on a national and international stage. We work directly with ministers and national policy advisers to ensure the needs of the prep school sector are met.

IAPS only accredits those schools that can demonstrate they provide the highest standards of education and care. Our member schools offer an all-round, values-led, broad education, which produces confident, adaptable, motivated children with a lifelong passion for learning. In order to be elected to membership, a Head must be suitably qualified and schools must be accredited through a satisfactory inspection.

Our schools are single-sex and co-educational; boarding, day and mixed; situated in urban and rural areas. Sizes vary from more than 800 to less than 100 pupils per school, with the majority between 150 and 400. Most schools are charitable trusts, some are limited companies and a few are proprietary. There are also junior schools attached to senior schools, choir schools, those with a particular religious affiliation and those that offer specialist provision.

With more than 600 members, both in the UK and worldwide, IAPS offers excellent opportunities for fellowship and networking. We have one of the independent sector's top training programmes, which includes a broad range of professional development courses. New members are offered an experienced Head as a mentor and members are divided into district groups by geographical location, giving them the chance to meet with fellow heads on a regular basis.

A brand new website with dedicated members' area is packed with news, policy examples, advice and support. The site also actively promotes the prep sector to parents and the media.

The Council and Officers for 2011–2012

President: Stuart Thackrah

Chairman: Tim Johns

Chairman-Elect: Nicholas Allen

Immediate Past Chairman: Andy Falconer

Vice-Chairman: Penelope Kirk

Members of Council:

Robert Blake	Eddy Newton
Mark Brotherton	Andrew Potts
Chris Calvey	Andy Rathborne
Jonathan Carroll	Peter Tait
Paul Easterbrook	John Tranmer
John Greathead	Howard Tuckett
Matthew Lovett	David Westcombe
Richard Merriman	

Officials:

Chief Executive: David Hanson
Director of Education: Julie Robinson
Finance and Operations Director: Richard Flower
Courses and Conferences Manager: Larraine Curzon
Membership Officer: Jill Wharfe
Association Administrator: Christine McCrudden

IAPS
11 Waterloo Place, Leamington Spa CV32 5LA
Tel: 01926 887833 • Fax: 01926 888014 • email: iaps@iaps.org.uk

ISA

INDEPENDENT SCHOOLS ASSOCIATION

website: www.isaschools.org.uk

The Independent Schools Association, established in 1879, is one of the oldest of the Headteachers' Associations of independent schools that make up the Independent Schools' Council. It began life as the Association of Principals of Private Schools, which was created to encourage high standards and foster friendliness and cooperation among Heads who had previously worked in isolation. In 1895 it was incorporated as The Private Schools Association and in 1927 the word 'private' was replaced by 'independent'. The recently published History of the Association demonstrates the strong links ISA has with proprietorial schools, which is still the case today, even though the majority are now run by Boards of Governors.

Membership is open to any independent school Head or Proprietor provided they meet the necessary criteria, which includes the accreditation standards of the Independent Schools Inspectorate. ISA's Executive Council is elected by Members and supports all developments of the Association through its Committee structure and the strong regional network of Coordinators and Area Committees. Each of ISA's seven Areas in turn supports Members through regular training events and meetings.

ISA celebrates a wide ranging membership, not confined to any one type of school, but including all: nursery, pre-preparatory, junior, preparatory and senior, all-through schools, co-educational, single-sex, boarding, day, and performing arts and special schools.

Promoting best practice and fellowship remains at the core of the Association, as it did when it began 130 years ago. The 300 Members and their schools enjoy high quality national conferences and courses that foster excellence in independent education. ISA's central office also supports Members and provides advice, and represents the views of its membership at national and governmental levels. Pupils in ISA schools enjoy a wide variety of competitions, in particular the wealth of sporting, artistic and academic activities at Area and National level.

The Council and Officers for 2011–2012

President: B J Maybee, JP MA

Vice-Presidents:
C J Ashby, BSc PGCE
M Grant, CertEd
M J Milner-Williams, CertEd
M Hewitt, BA CertEd
A D Stranack, BA CertEd

Honorary Officers (2011):	*Honorary Officers (2012)*:
A G Bray, CertEd (*Chairman*)	J R Wood, MA PGCE (*Chairman*)
G R Gorton, BA PGCE (*Vice-Chairman*)	A G Bray, CertEd (*Vice-Chairman*)
J R Wood, MA PGCE (*Vice-Chairman*)	A Culley, CertEd (*Vice-Chairman*)

Elective Councillors:

D Odysseas-Bailey, BA PGCE	M K Savjani, BSc
C A Baker, BEd MA	D G Vanstone, MA PGCE
R H Brierly, BEd	R M Walden, MA CertEd MEd FCollP
C Brown, CertEd DipEd RSA DipSpLD	J T Wilding, BSc
B G Chittick, BEd CertEd	J R Wood, MA PGCE
P Moss, CertEd	J Stearns, MA BSc PGCE NPQH
Prof P Preedy, PhD MEd BEd CertEd	

Area Coordinators:

L Maggs-Wellings, BEd CertEd (*London West*)	A Hampton, BA LTCL MEd NPQH (*East Anglia*)
A Culley, CertEd (*London South*)	M A Denton, CertEd (*North*)
R A Fowke, BEd (*South West*)	P Soutar, BEd (*Midlands*)
A Evans, BA PGCE (*London North*)	

Officials

Chief Executive Officer: Neil Roskilly, BA PGCE NPQH FRSA FRGS
Membership Officer: Anne-Marie Hodgkiss, BSc PGCE
Professional Development Officer: Maggie Turner, BA
Marketing and Business Development Officer: Phil Rennie, BSc
Membership and Professional Development Coordinator: Gillian Herbert, BA MA
Secretary and PA to the CEO: Emma Prentice, BSc
Accountant: Ghavini Mistry

Independent Schools Association
1 Boys' British School, East Street, Saffron Walden, Essex CB10 1LS
Tel: 01799 523619 • e-mail: isa@isaschools.org.uk

COBIS

COUNCIL OF BRITISH INTERNATIONAL SCHOOLS

website: www.cobis.org.uk

COBIS is a proud global membership association with over 100 schools in more than 40 countries worldwide, serving British International Schools of Quality. COBIS exists to serve, support and represent its member schools – their leaders, governors, staff and students.

Membership at defined levels is open globally to British international schools of quality which satisfy specified criteria.

COBIS membership provides:
- Quality assurance.
- Representation with the British Government, educational bodies, and the corporate sector.
- A network of support through contacts, consultancies, information and marketing.
- A forum for discussion through conferences, seminars, and continuing professional development.
- Access to information about developments and trends in UK education.
- Support with the recruitment and retention of high-quality teachers and school leaders.
- CRB checks for COBIS member and non-member schools and support with safer recruitment practices.

COBIS holds an Annual Conference in London in May for Heads, Governors, and members of school Senior Leadership Teams. The Association also runs inset conferences for teachers and support staff at different international venues. COBIS aims to support its members and represent their interests in Britain and overseas in order to advance the interests of British schools outside the UK.

COBIS was founded in 1981 as COBISEC (Council of British Independent Schools in the European Communities). The Association is managed by an elected Executive Committee which includes both Heads and Governors. COBIS is a responsive organisation, open to current and to future opportunity. It has developed markedly since its foundation, changing to meet the needs and aspirations of its growing global membership.

COBIS Executive 2011–2012

Honorary Vice Presidents
The Rt Hon Lord Andrew Adonis
Sir Mervyn Brown KCMG OBE
Michael Cooper OBE
Lord Lexden OBE
The Rt Hon The Lord Macgregor OBE
Dame Judith Mayhew Jonas DBE
Sybil Melchers MBE
Jean Scott
Lord Sharman OBE

Secretariat
Executive Director: Colin Bell

Executive Committee
Dawn Akyurek, British Embassy Study Group, Turkey
John Bagust, Prague British School
Jennifer Bray MBE (*Inspections Officer*)
Nigel Fossey, St George's International School, ASBL, Luxembourg
Anne Howells, British International School of Stavanger
Simon O'Grady, The British International School, Cairo (*Treasurer*)
Trevor Rowell, Governor, British School of Alicante (*Chairman*)
Peter Simpson, The British School in The Netherlands
David Smith, St Julian's School, Portugal (*Secretary*)
Dr Steffen Sommer, British School of Paris (*Vice Chairman*)

Council of British International Schools
Pembroke House, 8 St Christophers Place, Farnborough, Hampshire GU14 0NH
Tel: 01252 513930 • Fax: 01252 516000 • e-mail: executive.director@cobis.org.uk

AGBIS

ASSOCIATION OF GOVERNING BODIES OF INDEPENDENT SCHOOLS

REGISTERED CHARITY NO. 1108756

website: www.agbis.org.uk

The Object of the Association is to advance education in independent schools and, in furtherance of that object, but not otherwise, the Association shall have power:

(a) to discuss matters concerning the policy and administration of such schools and to encourage cooperation between their Governing Bodies;

(b) to consider the relationship of such schools to the general educational interests of the community;

(c) to consider and give guidance on matters of general or individual concern to the Governing Bodies of such schools;

(d) to promote good governance in such schools;

and

(e) to express the views of the Governing Bodies of such schools on any of the foregoing matters and to take such action as may be appropriate in their interests.

Full Membership

The Governing Body of any independent school in the United Kingdom may apply for full membership of the Association, subject to conditions determined by the Board. Admission to full membership of AGBIS will be conditional upon the educational and other standards of the school and admission of the Head to membership of the Headmasters' and Headmistresses' Conference, The Girls' Schools Association, The Society of Headmasters and Headmistresses of Independent Schools, The Independent Association of Prep Schools or The Independent Schools Association within one year. COBIS Schools and others from outside the United Kingdom should have similar characteristics to those expected of UK applicants.

Associate Membership

Any Independent School in the United Kingdom which is not a charity but whose head is a member of one of the above listed Heads' Associations or is expected to become a member within one year, may apply for Associate Membership of the Association. Such schools must show evidence of the existence of the arrangements for governance which may be in the form of an advisory board or similar.

Any independent school within the United Kingdom which meets the requirements as above, apart from membership of an ISC Heads' Association, and is in membership of either SCIS or WISC, and schools outside the United Kingdom in membership of COBIS, BISW or similar organisations and which are inspected by ISI, at the discretion of the AGBIS Board, may also apply for Associate Membership.

Board

Chairman: Sam Alder (Lancing College)

Joint Deputy Chairmen:

Miss June Taylor (Godolphin & Latymer School, St Mary's Shaftesbury and Sherborne Prep)

Richard Green (Prior's Field School)

Honorary Treasurer: Charles Paull (Kimbolton School)

Jonathan Cook (Hordle Walhampton School & Lymington Infant School)
Revd Dr Martin Dudley (City of London School for Girls)
Anthony Eady (Sir William Perkins's School)
Tony Evans (Sevenoaks School)
Michael Fowle CBE (Rugby School)
Gordon Jack (The Glasgow Academy)
Michael Jeans MBE (Chairman Haberdashers' Company Education Committee)
Mrs Jane Richardson (Ipswich High School GDST & Norwich High School GDST)
Mrs Joy Richardson (Uppingham School)
Miss Margaret Rudland (Merchant Taylors' School, Northwood)
Thomas Wheare (Exeter School, Port Regis School & Dragon School)
Mrs Joanna Williams (Christ College Brecon)
Jerry Wooding OBE (Arnold School)

General Secretary: Stuart Westley

Association of Governing Bodies of Independent Schools
The Grange, 3 Codicote Road, Welwyn, Hertfordshire AL6 9LY
Tel: 01438 840730 • e-mail: gensec@agbis.org.uk

ISBA

INDEPENDENT SCHOOLS' BURSARS ASSOCIATION

website: www.theisba.org.uk

Membership
Full membership of the Association is open to Schools who are members of one of the constituent associations in membership of the Independent Schools Council. Bursars or other officials of other independent and state schools, such as city academies, may apply for Associate Membership provided that the school is recognised as an educational charity.

The Work of the Association
The Association provides first-class support to independent schools as businesses and charities. It assists members in their work by the sharing of best practice and information on matters of common interest and undertakes joint negotiation with Government Departments and other bodies where this is considered advisable. The ISBA is one of the eight constituent Associations of the Independent Schools Council (ISC) and works closely with the ISC and the other seven Associations, namely: the Headmasters' and Headmistresses' Conference (HMC), the Girls' Schools Association (GSA), the Society of Headmasters and Headmistresses of Independent Schools (SHMIS), the Independent Association of Prep Schools (IAPS), the Independent Schools Association (ISA), the Council of British International Schools (COBIS), and the Association of Governing Bodies of Independent Schools (AGBIS).

A full professional development programme is run that includes events such as an annual conference and new bursars' course. In addition to the Bursar's Review, the in-house journal, bulletins are circulated at intervals to all members containing notices about decisions of the Executive Committee, information received by the Secretary, and other matters of day to day interest, as well as contributions from members and digests of information collected by means of questionnaires. There is also an Annual Report. The Association has a very comprehensive and active website.

Schools Represented
The first meeting of the Association was held in London in 1932, and was attended by representatives of 47 Schools. There are now over 900 Schools in membership.

Management
The Executive Committee consists of the Chairman of the Association, Mrs A Martin, the Bursar of Warminster School and the bursars of eleven other leading independent schools.

The Independent Schools' Bursars Association is a Registered Charity, number 1121757, and a Company Limited by Guarantee, registered in England and Wales, number 6410037.

General Secretary: Mr Mike Lower

Registered Office: **Unit 11–12, Manor Farm, Cliddesden, Basingstoke, Hampshire RG25 2JB**
Tel: 01256 330369 • e-mail: office@theisba.org.uk

BSA

BOARDING SCHOOLS' ASSOCIATION

website: www.boarding.org.uk

The BSA is the UK Association promoting and serving boarding education.

Full school membership of the Association is only open
to schools which are members of a Participating Association
(COBIS, GSA, HMC, IAPS, ISA, SHMIS, SCIS or SBSA)
Academies with boarding are welcome to join SBSA

The BSA enjoys Associate Membership of the Independent Schools Council.

Aims
The BSA's aims are:
- To promote the qualities of boarding life provided by all types of boarding schools in membership of the Association
- To encourage the highest standards of welfare for boarding pupils in its member schools
- To provide information to parents and young people considering boarding education about boarding and boarding schools which are in membership of the BSA
- To organise a professional development programme for all staff and governors of boarding schools
- To produce appropriate publications on boarding issues and good practice in boarding
- To conduct and authorise appropriate research
- To work with other bodies concerned with boarding education
- To develop links with boarding associations and boarding schools worldwide
- To maintain a regular dialogue with appropriate Government Ministers and their departments, Members of Parliament, and Local Government Officers

Membership

Membership is open to all schools with boarders which are members of Associations within the Independent Schools Council (ISC), to schools in membership of the Scottish Council of Independent Schools (SCIS), and also to state-maintained boarding schools in membership of the State Boarding Schools' Association (SBSA). Membership may also be offered to boarding schools overseas at the discretion of the Executive Committee. Current membership comprises over 400 schools (fully boarding, weekly/flexi boarding, or day schools with boarding provision; co-educational or single-sex; preparatory or secondary).

Associate Membership is available to individuals, schools and other bodies at the discretion of the Executive Committee. They will be entitled to receive all Association mailings. Associate membership is open to former heads of member schools and anyone else interested in supporting the cause of boarding.

Support for Schools

The Professional Development Programme

In partnership with Roehampton University, the BSA has established a Professional Development Programme for all staff working in boarding schools. These BSA courses lead to university validated Certificates of Professional Practice in Boarding Education. There is a programme of Day Courses on a range of topics including Child Protection, Anti-Bullying strategies, the role of Gap Assistants, Boarding Legislation and Good Practice, Boarding Governance. There are also individual courses tailored to the particular needs of a school or group of schools.

BSA training is available to all staff who work in boarding schools and to the Governors of boarding schools.

BSA Training Programmes are also used by schools and boarding associations throughout the world.

Residential Conferences

Four conferences are held annually for:

Heads of Boarding Schools and representatives of their member associations
Deputy Heads
Housemasters and Housemistresses
Matrons and Medical Staff

The latter two conferences incorporate part of the BSA/Roehampton University Professional Development Programme.

Publications

These include:

* ***Good Practice in Boarding Schools – A Resource Handbook for all those working in boarding***
  Edited by Tim Holgate
* ***Duty of Care***
  By Dr Tim Hawkes (amended by Tim Holgate)
* ***World Class***
  By Christopher Greenfield and Philip Hardaker
* ***Running a School Boarding House – A legal Guide for Housemasters and Housemistresses***
  By Robert Boyd, Revised by Veale Wasbrough Lawyers 2009
* ***Parenting the Boarder***
  By Libby Purves
* ***Being a Boarder***
  By Rose Heiney
* ***Boarding School*** – the BSA magazine published twice a year
* ***The BSA Bulletin*** – published five times a year
* ***Boarding Briefing Papers*** – are published at regular intervals on matters concerning boarding legislation and good practice

National Boarding Standards

The Association liaises with the Department for Education, Ofsted, and the Independent Schools Inspectorate on the inspection of boarding schools under the National Minimum Standards for Boarding schools.

Liaison with National Bodies

The Association meets regularly with the Department for Education to discuss issues concerned with boarding. It also liaises with Local Government, ISI (Independent Schools Inspectorate), Ofsted (Office for Standards in Education), CEAS (Children's Education Advisory Service) and all the national educational organisations.

Organisation

At the Annual General Meeting, held at the Heads' Annual Conference, Officers of the Association are elected together with the Executive Committee. The Honorary Treasurer is usually a Bursar from a member school.

National Director
Hilary Moriarty, e-mail: director@boarding.org.uk

Director of Training
Alex Thomson OBE, e-mail: training@boarding.org.uk

The Boarding Schools' Association
Grosvenor Gardens House, 35-37 Grosvenor Gardens, London SW1W 0BS
Tel: 020 7798 1580 • Fax: 020 7798 1581

INDEPENDENT SCHOOLS INSPECTORATE

AND ISI CONSULTANCY LTD

website: www.isi.net

The Independent Schools Inspectorate (ISI) is the body approved by the Secretary of State to inspect schools in England in membership of Associations within the Independent Schools Council (ISC). Inspection is conducted in accordance with the Education Acts, the Childcare Act 2006 and the Children Act 1989 and under the professional scrutiny of Her Majesty's Inspectors (HMI) in the Office for Standards in Education, Children's Services and Skills (Ofsted) who monitor ISI's work on behalf of the Department for Education (DfE). ISI inspects schools according to a schedule agreed with the DfE at intervals of up to six years, and EYFS (Early Years Foundation Stage) and Boarding Welfare (National Minimum Standards) every 3 years. ISI also inspects schools in more than 30 countries worldwide, using a framework that takes account of the schools' international setting, and is approved to inspect schools under the UK government scheme for British Schools Overseas. Inspection reports are published to parents and made available, with other related material, on the ISI website, www.isi.net.

ISI inspections are led by professional Reporting Inspectors, who are mainly either former HMI or Ofsted Inspectors or are former head teachers who have qualified as Reporting Inspectors. The remainder of the inspection team is drawn from serving headteachers or other senior staff from ISC schools, and trained by ISI. This incorporation of peer review gives the teams the vital combination of professional rigour with an immediate understanding of the diverse character of the schools and an up-to-date grasp of current educational developments.

ISI also conducts inspection of private Further Education and English Language providers. Inspection under this voluntary educational oversight scheme for colleges satisfies the requirements for inspection necessary to apply for or renew a Tier 4 licence to sponsor international students under the UKBA Points Based System.

ISI also, through its subsidiary company ISI Consultancy Ltd, offers a range of seminars, INSET and consultancy services to schools in the UK and overseas on matters related to inspection and school improvement.

Chief Inspector/CEO: Christine Ryan

ISI Office: CAP House, 9–12 Long Lane, London EC1A 9HA
Tel: 020 7600 0100 • Fax: 020 7776 8849 • e-mail: info@isi.net

METHODIST INDEPENDENT SCHOOLS TRUST

website: www.methodisteducation.co.uk

Methodist Church House, 25 Marylebone Road, London NW1 5JR
Tel: 020 7935 3723

Chairman: Revd Dr David Deeks
Secretary: Mr Graham Russell, MA

Schools for Boys and Girls
Culford School, Bury St Edmunds, Suffolk • www.culford.co.uk
Farringtons School, Chislehurst, Kent • www.farringtons.org.uk
Kent College, Canterbury, Kent • www.kentcollege.com
Kingsley School, Bideford, North Devon • www.kingsleyschoolbideford.co.uk
Queen's College, Taunton, Somerset • www.queenscollege.org.uk
Shebbear College, Beaworthy, Devon • www.shebbearcollege.co.uk
Truro School, Truro, Cornwall • www.truroschool.com
Woodhouse Grove School, Apperley Bridge, West Yorks • www.woodhousegrove.co.uk

Schools for Girls
Kent College Pembury, Tunbridge Wells, Kent • www.kent-college.co.uk

OTHER METHODIST INDEPENDENT SCHOOLS

Schools for Boys and Girls
Ashville College, Harrogate, North Yorks • www.ashville.co.uk
Kingswood School, Bath, Somerset • www.kingswood.bath.sch.uk
The Leys School, Cambridge • www.theleys.net
Methodist College, Belfast • www.methody.org
Rydal Penrhos School, Colwyn Bay, North Wales • www.rydal-penrhos.com
Wesley College, Dublin • www.wesleycollege.ie

Schools for Girls
Queenswood School, Hatfield, Herts • www.queenswood.org

A School prospectus, together with particulars of fees, and other information may be obtained from the Headmaster or Headmistress.

In cases of need applications may be made to a Methodist Bursary Fund for financial help to enable Methodist children to attend these schools. This fund is available to day pupils as well as boarding pupils. Details are available from the Trust.

Information regarding other sources of assistance with fees may be obtained from The Independent Schools Council, St Vincent House, 30 Orange Street, London WC2H 7HH. Tel: 020 7766 7070.

THE GIRLS' DAY SCHOOL TRUST (GDST)

website: www.gdst.net

The GDST (Girls' Day School Trust) is the leading group of independent girls' schools in the UK, with nearly 4,000 staff, and 20,000 students between the ages of three and 18.

As a charity that owns and runs a family of 24 Schools and two Academies in England and Wales, it reinvests all its income in its schools. Founded in 1872, the GDST has a long history of pioneering innovation in the education of girls, and is the largest single educator of girls in the UK (and the UK's largest educational charity).

At the GDST our aim is not just to provide an outstanding education, but to help girls develop into rounded, confident people, happy and resilient, who can meet and overcome the demands life will make of them.

Our 24 schools and two academies are all individual, but this commitment to developing the whole person is part of our shared DNA. Because of this strength and depth, we are an extraordinarily effective network for sharing knowledge and for spreading best practice (whether it is excellence in hockey, supporting all our medical school applicants to obtain places, or maximising our girls' potential in public exams). We can also develop and promote talented teachers through our network.

We celebrate our girls' differences, reinforce their strengths, and help them overcome their challenges. And, because we're single-sex, girls can be themselves, and grow at their own pace. They're not cloistered – far from it – but their individual characters can take shape in a way that isn't possible in a mixed environment.

Our girls are great to talk to. In fact, they illustrate us better than anything we could write. They'll tell you how exhilarating it is. They'll tell you how much fun they have, and how much encouragement they're given. They'll almost certainly tell you how lucky they feel.

Every girl is different – good at some things, less good or less keen on others – but we make sure that, regardless, she is the best she can be, and that she tries things, reaches for things, achieves things she may have thought beyond her. And when she does this, she grows in confidence and maturity in a way that will stay with her forever.

GDST Schools and Academies

The Belvedere Academy, Liverpool	Notting Hill & Ealing High School
Birkenhead High School Academy	Nottingham Girls' High School
Blackheath High School	Oxford High School
Brighton & Hove High School	Portsmouth High School
Bromley High School	Putney High School
Central Newcastle High School	The Royal High School, Bath
Croydon High School	Sheffield High School
Heathfield School, Pinner	Shrewsbury High School
Howell's School, Llandaff, Cardiff	South Hampstead High School
Ipswich High School	Streatham & Clapham High School
Kensington Prep School	Sutton High School
Northampton High School	Sydenham High School
Norwich High School for Girls	Wimbledon High School

Information on the Schools can be found in the Yearbook or on the GDST website: www.gdst.net
The Girls' Day School Trust is a Registered Charity, number 306983.

100 Rochester Row London SW1P 1JP
Tel: 020 7393 6666 • e-mail: info@wes.gdst.net

INDEPENDENT SCHOOLS EXAMINATIONS BOARD
COMMON ENTRANCE EXAMINATIONS

website: www.iseb.co.uk

Chairman: M S Spurr, MA, DPhil

General Secretary: Mrs J Williams, BA, PGCE

Independent Schools Examinations Board, The Pump House, 16 Queen's Avenue, Christchurch, Hampshire BH23 1BZ

Telephone 01202 487538; Fax: 01202 473728; e-mail: enquiries@iseb.co.uk

The Common Entrance Examinations are used for transfer to senior schools at the ages of 11+ and 13+. The syllabuses are devised and regularly monitored by the Independent Schools Examinations Board which comprises members of the Headmasters' and Headmistresses' Conference, the Girls' Schools Association and the Independent Association of Prep Schools.

The papers are set by examiners appointed by the Board, but the answers are marked by the senior school for which a candidate is entered. A list of schools using the examination is given below. Common Entrance is not a public examination as, for example, GCSE, and candidates may normally be entered only if they have been offered a place at a senior school, subject to their passing the examination.

Candidates normally take the examination in their own junior or preparatory schools, either in the UK or overseas.

Dates

The 11+ examination is held in early November or mid-January.

The 13+ examination commences either on the first Monday in November, the last Monday in January or on the first Monday in June.

Entries

In cases where candidates are at schools in membership of the Independent Association of Prep Schools, it is usual for heads of these schools to make arrangements for entering candidates for the appropriate examination after consultation with parents and senior school heads. In the case of candidates at schools which do not normally enter candidates, it is the responsibility of parents to arrange for candidates to be entered for the appropriate examination in accordance with the requirements of senior schools.

Conduct of the Examination

Regulations for the conduct of the examination are laid down by the Independent Schools Examinations Board.

Fees

The Independent Schools Examinations Board decides the fees to be charged for each candidate. Schools are notified annually in the spring term of fees payable for the following three terms. Parents seeking information about current fees should look on the ISEB website or contact the ISEB office.

Correspondence

Correspondence about academic matters relating to the Common Entrance examinations and requests for further information about the administration of the examinations should be addressed (as above) to the General Secretary, ISEB.

SENIOR SCHOOLS USING THE COMMON ENTRANCE EXAMINATIONS
TO INDEPENDENT SCHOOLS

MEMBERS OF THE HEADMASTERS' AND HEADMISTRESSES' CONFERENCE

Abingdon School	City of London Freemen's School	Framlingham College
Aldenham School	Clayesmore School	Frensham Heights
Ampleforth College	Clifton College	Giggleswick School
Ardingly College	Cokethorpe School	Glenalmond College
Barnard Castle School	Colfe's School	Gresham's School
Bedales School	Cranleigh School	Haberdashers' Aske's School
Bedford School	Culford School	Haileybury
Berkhamsted School	Dauntsey's School	Hampton School
Bishop's Stortford College	Dean Close School	Harrow School
Bloxham School	Denstone College	Highgate School
Blundell's School	Downside School	Hurstpierpoint College
Bradfield College	Dulwich College	Ipswich School
Brighton College	Durham School	Kelly College
Bromsgrove School	Eastbourne College	Kimbolton School
Bryanston School	Ellesmere College	King Edward's School, Witley
Canford School	Eltham College	King's College, Taunton
Caterham School	Emanuel School	King's College School, Wimbledon
Charterhouse	Epsom College	King's School, Bruton
Cheltenham College	Eton College	King's School, Canterbury
Chigwell School	Felsted School	King's School, Chester
Churcher's College	Fettes College	King's School, Ely
City of London School	Forest School	King's School, Rochester

Kingston Grammar School
Kingswood School
Lancing College
Latymer Upper School
Leighton Park School
The Leys School
Lincoln Minster School
Lord Wandsworth College
Loretto School
Loughborough Grammar School
Magdalen College School
Malvern College
Marlborough College
Merchant Taylors' School,
Northwood
Merchiston Castle School
Millfield School
Mill Hill School
Monkton Combe School
Monmouth School
New Hall School
Norwich School
Oakham School
Oratory School
Oundle School
Pangbourne College
Plymouth College
Pocklington School
Portsmouth Grammar School

Prior Park College
Queen's College, Taunton
Radley College
Ratcliffe College
Reading Blue Coat School
Reed's School
Reigate Grammar School
Repton School
RGS Worcester
Royal Grammar School, Guildford
Royal Hospital School
Royal Russell School
Rugby School
St Albans School
St Bede's School
St Benedict's School
St Columba's College, Dublin
St Columba's College, St Albans
St Edmund's College
St Edmund's School
St Edward's School
St George's College
St John's School
St Lawrence College
St Leonards School, Fife
St Paul's School
St Peter's School
Seaford College
Sedbergh School

Sevenoaks School
Sherborne School
Shiplake College
Shrewsbury School
Stamford School
Stonyhurst College
Stowe School
Strathallan School
Sutton Valence School
Taunton School
Tonbridge School
Trent College
Trinity School
Truro School
University College School
Uppingham School
Wellingborough School
Wellington College
Wellington School
Wells Cathedral School
Westminster School
Whitgift School
Woodbridge School
Worksop College
Worth School
Wrekin College
Wycliffe College

MEMBERS OF THE GIRLS' SCHOOLS ASSOCIATION

Badminton School
Benenden School
Bruton School for Girls
The Cheltenham Ladies' College
Cranford House School
Downe House
Godolphin School
Haberdashers' Monmouth School
Headington School
Heathfield School, Ascot
Kilgraston School
Leweston School

Malvern St James
Moira House School
More House School, London
Moreton Hall School
Portsmouth High School
Princess Helena College
Queen Anne's School
Queen Margaret's School
Queenswood School
Roedean School
Rye St Antony School
St Gabriel's School

St George's School, Ascot
St Leonard's-Mayfield School
St Mary's School, Calne
St Mary's School, Shaftesbury
St Swithun's School
Sherborne School for Girls
Stonar School
Tudor Hall School
Westonbirt
Woldingham School
Wycombe Abbey School

THE FOLLOWING SCHOOLS USE THE COMMON ENTRANCE FOR SOME CANDIDATES

MEMBERS OF THE SOCIETY OF HEADS OF INDEPENDENT SCHOOLS

Battle Abbey School
Bearwood College
Bethany School
Box Hill School
d'Overbroeck's College

Ewell Castle School
Halliford School
Hampshire Collegiate School
Kingham Hill School
Langley School

Milton Abbey School
Portland Place School
Rendcomb College
St James Senior Boys' School

MEMBERS OF THE INDEPENDENT SCHOOLS ASSOCIATION

Chilton Cantelo School
Claires Court School
Heathfield School, Wolverley

Ibstock Place School
Lewes Old Grammar School
Sackville School

Sherfield School

OTHER SCHOOLS

Academic International School,
Africa
Ballard School
Cundall Manor School
Duke of Kent School

Gordonstoun School
Hampton Court House School
Harrodian School
Hillcrest Secondary School, Kenya
Lichfield Cathedral School

Old Swinford Hospital School
Peponi Secondary School, Kenya
St Andrew's School, Kenya

CATHOLIC INDEPENDENT SCHOOLS' CONFERENCE

website: www.cisc.uk.net

Objects

The CISC exists to:
- promote the work of 140 Catholic independent schools throughout the UK;
- give and coordinate support and advice to member schools;
- organise activities for member schools including an annual conference, retreats and study days;
- represent the interests of CISC schools as appropriate;
- provide a help line for those seeking a Catholic Independent School for their children.

Schools

There are 140 schools currently in membership of the CISC. Schools in membership include day and boarding schools, single-sex and co-educational, senior and junior schools and special schools.

Membership

There are two categories of Members: **Full Members** and **Associate Members**.

Full Members

Full Members may be invited by the Committee to take up membership. He/She will be the Head or Principal of a school which satisfies the following seven conditions:

(a) The school shall be recognised by the local Catholic bishop as being Catholic.
(b) The school shall have been recognised as a charitable foundation by the Charity Commissioners.
(c) The school shall be independent.
(d) The school shall be in the United Kingdom.
(e) The school will have been subjected to a nationally accredited inspection and found to be in good standing.
(f) The expectation is that the head of the school will be a practising Catholic. Where governors appoint a head who is not a Catholic CISC will expect governors to provide training and support for the head to enable the head to lead a Catholic school, and will assist them in so doing.
(g) Full members only attend the AGM.

Associate Members

Associate Members may be invited by the Chairman to take up membership, but do not attend the AGM.
The following are eligible for associate membership:

(a) Heads of proprietary-owned schools, which meet the conditions of Full Membership apart from not being recognised by the Charity Commissioners as a charitable foundation.
(b) Retired full Members.
(c) Catholics, and other Christians, who are in sympathy with the aims of CISC.
(d) Heads of Foundation or Voluntary-Aided Schools, which meet the conditions of Full Membership, apart from not being recognised by the Charity Commissioners as a charitable foundation.
(e) Heads of Catholic Independent Schools outside the United Kingdom.

Officers for 2011–12

Chairman: Mr Joe Peake, MA – St George's College
Vice-Chairman: Mr Chris Cleugh, MSc – St Benedict's School
Treasurer: Mr Christopher Lumb, BSc, MEd – Austin Friars St Monica's School

Committee:
Mrs Stephanie Bell, MA – Rydes Hill Preparatory School
Mr Clive Dytor, MC, MA, MA – The Oratory School
Fr Gabriel Everitt, MA, DPhil – Ampleforth College
Mrs Katherine Jeffrey, MA, BADiv, MA EdMgt – New Hall School
Mr Laurence McKell, MA – Mount St Mary's College
Mrs Lynne Renwick, BEd – Our Lady's Abingdon

General Secretary: Mr John Shinkwin, MA

Keepers Barn, Lenborough, Buckingham MK18 4BS
Tel: 01280 824401 • e-mail: johnshinkwin@cisc.uk.net

CHOIR SCHOOLS' ASSOCIATION

website: www.choirschools.org.uk

Patron: The Duchess of Kent

Committee:
Chairman: Roger Overend, King's Rochester Preparatory School
Vice-Chair: Mrs Elizabeth Cairncross, Wells Cathedral School
Treasurer: Robert Bacon, St Edmund's Junior School, Canterbury

Neil Blundell, Bristol Cathedral Choir School
Tim Cannell, Prebendal School, Chichester
Alex Donaldson, Minster School, York
Mrs Claire Moreland, Chetham's School, Manchester

Nick Robinson, King's College School, Cambridge
John Waszek, St Edward's College, Liverpool
Richard White

Administrator:

Information Officer:

Mrs Susan Rees, Wolvesey, College Street, Winchester, Hampshire SP23 9ND
Tel: 01962 890530, Fax: 01962 869978, e-mail: admin@choirschools.org.uk
Jane Capon, Tel: 01359 221333, e-mail: info@choirschools.org.uk

Blackburn Cathedral
Bristol Cathedral School
St Edmundsbury Cathedral, Bury St Edmunds
King's College School, Cambridge
St John's College School, Cambridge
St Edmund's School, Canterbury
St John's College, Cardiff
Carlisle Cathedral
St Cedd's School, Chelmsford
The Prebendal School, Chichester
Croydon Parish Church
The Chorister School, Durham
St Mary's Music School, Edinburgh
The King's School Junior School, Ely
Exeter Cathedral School
The King's School, Gloucester
St James' School, Grimsby
Lanesborough School, Guildford
Chapel Royal, Hampton Court
Hereford Cathedral School

Leeds Cathedral
Leicester Cathedral
Lichfield Cathedral School
Lincoln Minster School
Runnymede St Edward's School, Liverpool
St Edward's College, Liverpool
The Cathedral School, Llandaff
City of London School
The London Oratory School
St Paul's Cathedral School, London
Westminster Abbey Choir School, London
Westminster Cathedral Choir School, London
Chetham's School of Music, Manchester
St Nicholas Cathedral, Newcastle-upon-Tyne
Norwich School
Christ Church Cathedral School, Oxford

Magdalen College School, Oxford
New College School, Oxford
The King's School, Peterborough
The Portsmouth Grammar School
Reigate St Mary's Choir School
The Cathedral Choir School, Ripon
King's Preparatory School, Rochester
Salisbury Cathedral School
Sheffield Cathedral
The Minster School, Southwell
Polwhele House School, Truro
Queen Elizabeth Grammar Junior School, Wakefield
Wells Cathedral School
The Pilgrims' School, Winchester
St George's School, Windsor
St Peter's Church, Wolverhampton
The King's School, Worcester
The Minster School, York
Ampleforth College, York

CSA Full and Associate Members

Overseas Members:
St Andrew's Cathedral School, Sydney, Australia
St Patrick's Cathedral Choir School, Dublin
The Cathedral Grammar School, Christchurch, New Zealand
National Cathedral School, Washington DC, USA
St Thomas Choir School, New York, USA

The 45 choir schools in the UK are all attached to cathedrals, churches or college chapels and educate over 24,000 pupils, including 1,300 choristers. Westminster Abbey Choir School is the only school to educate choristers and probationers only. The Association's associate membership includes cathedrals and churches without choir schools.

Choir schools offer a very special opportunity for children who enjoy singing. They receive a first-class academic and all-round education combined with excellent music training. The experience and self-discipline choristers acquire remain with them for life. There is a wide range of schools: some cater for children aged 7–13, others are junior schools with senior schools to 18; most are Church of England but the Roman Catholic, Scottish and Welsh churches are all represented.

Most CSA members are fee-paying schools and nine out of ten choristers qualify for financial help with fees. Deans and Chapters provide fee assistance while Government support comes in the shape of the Choir Schools' Scholarship Scheme. Under the umbrella of the Music and Dance Scheme, funds are available to help those who cannot afford even the reduced school fees. The Government funding, along with other monies in its Chorister Fund, is administered by the CSA. Each application is means-tested and an award made once a child has secured a place at a choir school.

Each CSA member school has its own admissions procedure for choristers. However, every child will be assessed both musically and academically. A growing number of children are given informal voice tests which enable the organist or director of music to judge whether they have the potential to become choristers. Some are offered places immediately or will be urged to enter the more formal voice trial organised by the school. In some cases a family may be advised not to proceed. Alternatively, the child's voice may be more suitable for one of the other choir schools.

A number of special ingredients help make a good chorister: potential, a keen musical ear and an eagerness to sing. A clutch of music examination certificates is not vital – alertness and enthusiasm are! At the same time, school staff must be satisfied that a new recruit can cope with school work and the many other activities on offer as well as the demanding choir workload.

To find out more about choir schools please visit the CSA website: **www.choirschools.org.uk**
CSA members can be contacted or you can write, e-mail or telephone
for further information about choir schools and the Chorister Fund to:

Jane Capon, Information Officer, Village Farm, The Street, Market Weston, Diss, Norfolk IP22 2NZ
Telephone: 01359 221333; e-mail: info@choirschools.org.uk

The Association publishes a newsletter *Singing Out* – to receive a copy please contact Jane Capon.

website: www.woodard.co.uk

Woodard Schools form the largest group of Anglican schools in England and Wales. In addition to the above list of incorporated schools, over 20 schools in the independent and maintained sectors choose to be associated or affiliated. Woodard also sponsors academies. The schools are not exclusive and take pupils of all faiths and of none. In total some 30,000 pupils are taught in schools throughout the group. Three overseas schools also choose to be associated/affiliated.

This unique partnership of schools, independent and state, boarding and day, junior and senior, co-educational and single-sex, is united by a determination to provide a first-class holistic education within a distinctive Christian ethos. The schools were founded by Nathaniel Woodard in the nineteenth century and aim to prepare children from a wide variety of backgrounds for responsibility, leadership and service in today's world.

The schools seek to provide flexible, stimulating, demanding and appropriate schemes of academic study together with a rich variety of sporting, artistic and recreational opportunities. We encourage personal success, self-confidence and self-respect whilst also stressing the importance of responsible citizenship, high moral values and a commitment to use one's gifts in the service of others.

With the geographical spread and diversity of schools included in the group it is able to offer parents a wide range of educational options for their children. Woodard incorporated schools operate bursary and scholarship schemes including all classes of concession. Fees vary from school to school and are set locally.

The Woodard Corporation is a Registered Charity (No. 1096270) and Company (No. 4659710). The objects of the charity are to promote and extend education in accordance with the doctrines and principles of the Church of England/Church in Wales by directly or indirectly carrying on schools.

***Head Office*: Woodard Schools, High Street, Abbots Bromley, Rugeley, Staffordshire WS15 3BW**
Tel: 01283 840120 • Fax: 01283 840893 • e-mail: jillshorthose@woodard.co.uk

MONTESSORI SCHOOLS ASSOCIATION

website: www.montessori.org.uk

The Montessori Schools Association (MSA) was founded to support and represent all Montessori schools across the United Kingdom. The MSA works through 11 national regions each with its own Regional Chairman. The Montessori Schools Association currently has over 3,500 members and 600+ Montessori schools ranging in size from 15 to 400+ pupils covering the 0–11 age range.

It is supported and run by the Montessori St Nicholas Charity (founded in 1954). The charity today works to support Montessori across the UK in every way it can.

The mission statement of the Montessori St Nicholas Charity is to:

- facilitate the unification of the Montessori movement across the UK;
- make awards and finance initiatives that support the development of Montessori education in the fields of training grants for individuals, equipment and advice;
- fund research and development into the value and effectiveness of Montessori education.

In September 2008 the Montessori St Nicholas Charity set up the Montessori Evaluation and Accreditation Board (MEAB), a new national evaluation and accreditation scheme to raise standards within the Montessori Schools Association and put "*best practice*" at the heart of what it does. Montessori staff are generally more highly qualified than in many other settings. The MEAB scheme builds on Montessori's excellent track record in education. 88% of Montessori schools received a "*good*" or "*outstanding*" rating at their last Ofsted inspection. There are now over 100 MEAB schools.

18 Balderton Street, London W1K 6TG
Tel: 020 7493 8300 • Fax: 020 7493 9936 • e-mail: centre@montessori.org.uk

COUNCIL FOR INDEPENDENT EDUCATION (CIFE)

website: www.cife.org.uk

President:
Baroness Perry of Southwark

Vice President:
Hugh Monro, MA

Chairman:
Steven Boyes, BA, MSc, PGCE
Principal, MPW London

Vice-Chairman:
Mario Di Clemente, BA, PGCE
Principal, Cambridge Tutors College, London

Independent sixth-form colleges are extremely well placed to offer what is needed for students preparing for university and beyond. The best such colleges are members of CIFE, the Council for Independent Education, an organisation which was founded 38 years ago. There are 17 CIFE colleges, geographically spread across the country, each one offering individual features but all subject to high standards of accreditation. For example, there are some colleges that specialise in students wishing to retake in order to improve exam grades, some offering GCSE and pre-GCSE programmes as well as full A Level courses, which may be residential, homestay, day, or a mix of all three. Several colleges offer foundation programmes and are twinned with universities. In short, CIFE colleges offer a wide range of educational environments in which students can succeed.

Teaching in CIFE colleges really helps and supports students since teaching groups are small and teachers highly experienced and specialists in their subject. The 'tutorial' system derives directly from Oxbridge where it continues to be world famous. A student in a small group receives a greater degree of individual attention. Regular testing ensures that she/he maintains good progress, and the emphasis on study skills provides essential support for the AS/A2 subjects.

It is not surprising that a student gains confidence and self-belief within such an environment. Colleges engender a strong work ethic in their student communities. Many of the minor rules and regulations essential for schools are not necessary at CIFE colleges. Good manners and an enthusiastic attitude are every bit as important, but uniform, strict times for eating or homework, assemblies or games participation are not part of the picture. It can be seen from the large numbers of students going on to higher education from CIFE colleges that universities regard our students highly.

Increasing numbers of young people are deciding to move school at the age of 16, not because they are unhappy with their school, but because they see the need for a change at this stage. It may be that they wish to study a subject which their school does not offer, such as Accounting, Law, Psychology or Photography. Perhaps they are looking for a more adult environment or one where they can focus on their academic subjects to the exclusion of other things. However, it would be misleading to suggest that CIFE colleges are lacking in extra-curricular activities of all sorts, sporting, social and creative. All colleges recognise the need for enrichment. The difference is that activities are at the choice of the student.

As with schools, choosing a college calls for careful research. CIFE colleges undergo regular inspection either by the Independent Schools Inspectorate, Ofsted and/or the British Accreditation Council, recognised bodies which regulate the provision and standards of teaching, safety and pastoral care. While each college has its own individual character, all share the desire to provide each individual student with a superb preparation for higher education.

Members of CIFE
Ashbourne Independent Sixth Form College
Bales College
Bath Academy
Bosworth Independent College
Brooke House College
Cambridge Centre for Sixth-form Studies
Cambridge Tutors College, London
Chelsea Independent College
Collingham
DLD College
Duff Miller Sixth Form College
Exeter Tutorial College
Harrogate Tutorial College
Lansdowne College
Mander Portman Woodward, Birmingham
Mander Portman Woodward, London
Oxford Tutorial College

Further information can be obtained from:

CIFE
Tel: 020 8767 8666 • e-mail: enquiries@cife.org.uk

ISCO

ISCO is the independent schools careers service from The Inspiring Futures Foundation

www.inspiringfutures.org.uk

Chairman: M E Hicks, MSc, DPhil
Hon Treasurer: Ms J Middleton
Chief Executive: A R Airey, MA, MBA

Council 2011–2012

Advice on ISCO services:

Contacts

Who to ask for information and help
Contact your Regional Director (see below) or the Information Helpline on 01276 687515

Further information on The Inspiring Futures Foundation:
Chief Executive: Andrew Airey (e-mail: a.airey@inspiringfutures.org.uk)

Purpose and Aims

The Inspiring Futures Foundation is a not-for-profit, careers guidance organisation. It exists to help young people make decisions and develop skills which maximize their potential, enhance their employment opportunities and allow them to make a fulfilling contribution to the world in which they live.

In order to do this, Inspiring Futures works with like-minded people and organisations to provide expert careers guidance, innovative learning resources and personal skills training to young people from all backgrounds, particularly those entering higher education.

Each of these services is based around the ongoing needs of the young person and is delivered through a unique, integrated approach, which is practical, progressive and provides a foundation for lifelong learning.

The ISCO careers service for independent and international schools provides schools with a range of careers and higher education related services to complement and reinforce school programmes with impartial and professional expertise. Services include the Futurewise personalised careers guidance programme, Futurewise courses and training events for students and a range of professional services to support schools' careers staff.

ISCO Regional Directors
by area of operation

North East:	Gillian Binns (Tel: 01937 843569, e-mail: gillian.binns@isco.org.uk)
Oxfordshire & Berkshire:	Terry McDermott (Tel: 020 8429 1322, e-mail: t.mcdermott@isco.org.uk)
North London:	Steve Cane (Tel: 020 8447 3955, e-mail: steve.cane@isco.org.uk)
Sussex & Kent:	Helen Davison (Tel: 01342 317537, e-mail: helen.davison@isco.org.uk)
West Midlands:	Sarah Frend (Tel: 0121 705 5692, e-mail: sarah.frend@isco.org.uk)
South West:	Jonathan Hardwick (Tel: 01453 827761, e-mail: jonathan.hardwick@isco.org.uk)
Surrey & Hampshire:	Marilyn Hawkswell (Tel 01483 424241, e-mail: marilyn.hawkswell@isco.org.uk)
Shropshire, Staffordshire & Derbyshire:	Sally Hayward (Tel: 01952 210777, e-mail: sally.hayward@isco.org.uk)
South London:	Carey Irwin (Tel: 020 8544 9749, e-mail: carey.irwin@isco.org.uk)
Essex:	Linda Levett (Tel: 01621 783828, e-mail: linda.levett@isco.org.uk)
Dorset & Isle of Wight:	John MacArthur (Tel: 01252 661957, e-mail: john.macarthur@isco.org.uk)
Manchester, Cumbria, Lancashire, Cheshire & N Wales:	Rod Morley (Tel: 0161 428 1013, e-mail: rod.morley@isco.org.uk)
SW London & Surrey:	Helen Rogers (Tel: 01932 566224, e-mail: helen.rogers@isco.org.uk)
Scotland:	David Setchell (Tel: 01505 502685, e-mail: david.setchell@isco.org.uk)
East:	John Watson (Tel: 01572 823073, e-mail: john.watson@isco.org.uk)
North & Central Scotland:	Greta Weir (Tel: 01796 482318, e-mail: greta.weir@isco.org.uk)
Far East:	John Broadbent (Tel: 00 60 3894 11879, e-mail: john.broadbent@isco.org.uk)
Middle East:	Martin Minshall (e-mail: martin.minshall@isco.org.uk)
Europe:	Julia Watson (Tel: 01572 823073, e-mail: julia.watson@isco.org.uk)

ASSOCIATION FOR MARKETING AND DEVELOPMENT IN INDEPENDENT SCHOOLS (AMDIS)

FOUNDED 1993

website: www.amdis.co.uk

Objectives:
- To promote and develop good marketing practice in independent education
- To help increase the effectiveness of the marketing representatives of Member Schools
- To encourage personal development within the schools' marketing profession

Achieved through:
- Seminars and workshops on a variety of marketing-led subjects held throughout the year
- Annual residential conference
- Regional networking lunches
- Training – Diploma in Schools' Marketing & Certificate in Admissions Management
- Newsletters with articles from Member Schools and invited contributors
- Help Line
- Website
- On-line News bulletins throughout the year
- Speakers provided for conferences, inset days and similar

Membership:
- School Membership, renewable annually by subscription
- Associate membership considered on application
- Corporate membership considered on application

The Association is directed by a Chairman, Vice Chairman and Treasurer together with an Executive Committee. The Chairman, Vice Chairman and Treasurer together with members of the Executive Committee are selected (or re-elected) by prior nomination, annually at the AMDIS AGM.

General Secretary: **Tory Gillingham, 2 St Michael's Street, Malton, North Yorkshire YO17 7LJ Tel: 01653 699800 • e-mail: enquiries@amdis.co.uk**

ASSOCIATION OF REPRESENTATIVES OF OLD PUPILS' SOCIETIES (AROPS)

Founded in 1971

website: www.arops.org.uk

Founder and Past President: Mike Comer (Old Johnian)
Immediate Past President: Roy Elliott (Old Caterhamian)
President: Margaret Carter-Pegg (Old Crohamian)
Vice-Presidents: John Kidd (Old Portmuthian), Guy Cliff (Old Silcoatian), Roger Moulton (Old Pauline)

Committee
Chairman: Bill Gillen (Old Arnoldian and Old Instonian)
Secretary: Michael Freegard (Old Haileyburian)
Treasurer: Tim Neale (Old Radleian)
Registrar: Peter Booth (Lord Wandsworth College Sternians Association)
and 12 committee members
Administrator: Tristan Bradley (arops@arops.org.uk)

Aim: To provide a forum for the exchange of views and experiences between representatives of old pupils' societies.

Membership: Open to representatives of any old pupils' society.

Meetings:
Each May AROPS holds a whole day Conference. Venues vary from year to year and are chosen with regard to geographical location and differing type of school – day, boarding, co-educational or single sex.

Each Conference is divided into four sessions which aim to cover a wide range of topics that will be of assistance and interest to society representatives. Recent topics have been data protection, attracting younger members, society/school relations, subscriptions and charitable status. During the day there are ample opportunities for representatives to meet and talk with each other. The day always finishes with the conference dinner.

The AGM is held on a weekday evening in October at a school in the London area and is followed by a buffet supper.

The AROPS Committee meets five times a year to deal with the running of the Association, prepare for the Conference and AGM and to respond to correspondence from old pupils' societies. It also arranges surveys providing information on matters of current interest such as registers and life membership subscriptions.

AROPS works with the Independent Schools Council (ISC) and its constituent members whose officers are invited to attend AROPS conferences.

AROPS is a non-political body, but its interests are opposed to any threat to independent education. Changes in national policy are carefully considered on behalf of member societies.

Subscription: £18 per year. Societies interested in membership should write to: The Chairman, AROPS, via The Independent Schools Council office, St Vincent House, 30 Orange Street, London WC2H 7HH or e-mail arops@arops.org.uk.

MEDICAL OFFICERS OF SCHOOLS ASSOCIATION

FOUNDED 1884

website: www.mosa.org.uk

Objects
Mutual assistance of members in promoting school health, and the holding of meetings for consideration of all subjects connected with the special work of medical officers of schools.

Membership
Medical officers of schools and medical and dental practitioners and nurses especially concerned with the health of the schoolchild are eligible for membership, and members of the teaching profession, and those related to independent school management, for associate membership. The membership currently stands at 400.

The work of the Association
The Council meets three times a year and is chaired by the current President, Dr Neil Arnott, MO to Sevenoaks School, Kent. The Hon Secretary sends out three newsletters a year and is available for advice to members and non-members. Clinical meetings are arranged each year together with an annual summer visit to a school. Research projects are carried out individually and collectively. The Association strongly recommends that all independent schools appoint medical officers to carry out preventative medicine duties which are undertaken in maintained schools by the School Health Service.

Publications
The 18th edition of the Handbook of School Health, published in May of 1998, deals in detail with the administrative, ethical, public health and clinical aspects of the school medical officer's work and is widely accepted as the definitive guide to current practice. A Proceedings and Report are published annually. The Association also publishes appropriate guidelines for its clinical Medical Officers and these are updated regularly.

For further information about the Association and other related business enquiries should in the first instance be directed to:

The Hon Secretary: Dr Rebecca Pryse, MB BS, DCH, DRCOG, DFSRH
North End Surgery, High Street, Buckingham MK18 1NU
Tel: 01280 818600; Fax: 01280 818618
e-mail: rebecca.pryse@nhs.net

For administrative information and background please contact:
The Executive Secretary: Mrs Louise Fortune
e-mail: executive.secretary@mosa.org.uk

THE ENGLISH-SPEAKING UNION

website: www.esu.org

Secondary School Exchange scholarships to North America

"It was an amazing, life-changing year. Thank you!"

An SSE Scholarship offers a once in a lifetime opportunity to spend a year or six months in a private North American high school. Scholars gain opportunities to travel, to try new sports and to meet new people. Scholars learn new subjects and study with different teaching methods. Much is learnt in the classroom and through extra-curricular activities. More importantly, scholars learn much about themselves and about what they can achieve.

To be eligible for a scholarship students must be British, have taken their A Levels or equivalent, and not exceed the age of 19 years and six months when they take up the scholarship. The schools offer free board and tuition, worth approximately $40,000 each. All other expenses must be met by the scholar's family; we estimate these costs combined come to about £3,500. Scholars are responsible for making their own travel arrangements and obtaining their visas.

In addition each year UK boarding schools offer free board and tuition to senior students from North America.

For further information on either side of the programme please contact:

The English-Speaking Union, 37 Charles Street, London W1J 5ED
Tel: 020 7529 1550 • e-mail: education@esu.org

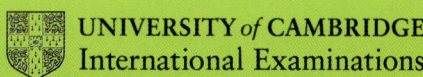

The Falcons
School for Boys
Preparatory Department
7-13 years

OPEN MORNING: Saturday 8th October 2011

41 Kew Foot Road, Richmond TW9 2SS
For further details please call:
020 8948 9490 or email: admin@falconsprep.co.uk
www.falconschool.com
If you would like to visit the school at another time,
please contact us to arrange a date.

Her future is an open book

As your daughter begins a new chapter
in her education, we'll help her to
prepare for the future in a happy, caring
and inspirational environment. With us
she will settle in quickly, make great
friends, develop confidence in her own
unique abilities, have fun learning and
achieve her potential.

The story begins here...

We are a leading independent day and boarding
school for girls aged 3-18. Please contact our
Registrar, Lynda Bevan, to arrange a private visit.

The Royal High School, Bath
Nursery • Junior School • Senior School • Sixth Form College

  Girls' Day School Trust

Lansdown Road, Bath BA1 5SZ   t: 01225 313877   e: royalhigh@bat.gdst.net   www.royalhighbath.gdst.net

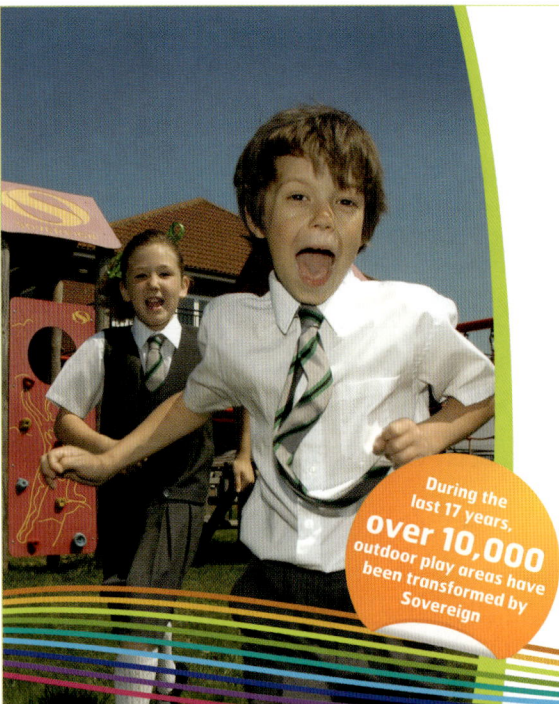

SOVEREIGN
Bringing imagination into play

PLAYGROUND EQUIPMENT
OUTDOOR FURNITURE
IMAGINATIVE PLAY
PLAYGROUND MARKINGS
BALL GAMES
ADVENTUROUS PLAY
SAFER SURFACING
FENCING
CANOPIES & SHADE
INSTALLATION & INSPECTIONS
FREE DESIGN & PLANNING SERVICE

During the last 17 years, **over 10,000** outdoor play areas have been transformed by Sovereign

Fun-filled
imaginative
play and learning

For a copy of our new brochure and a free no obligation consultation, contact us on **01702 291129** or why not visit us at
www.sovereignplayequipment.co.uk

T: 01702 291129
www.sovereignplayequipment.co.uk

Sovereign Design Play Systems Limited
40 Towerfield Road, Shoeburyness
Southend-On-Sea, Essex, SS3 9QT

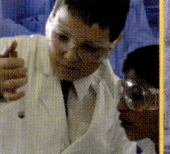

westridge

Hartnup Street, Maidstone
£6,100,000

Bexhill Museum, Bexhill
£1,500,000

Balfour School, Brighton
£2,300,000

Plumpton College, Plumpton
£4,500,000

Abbey House, Storrington
£1,000,000

Ringmer Surgery, Ringmer
£670,000

Contact us to find out how we can deliver your projects through either traditional procurement or on a design and build basis.

T: 01580 830600   **F**: 01580 830700
www.westridgeconstruction.co.uk
enquiries@wcluk.co.uk

Ruskin House, Junction Road, Bodiam, East Sussex, TN32 5UP

● **Speed** ● **Reliability** ● **Quality** ● **Cost** ● **Flexibility** ●

The **Manor** House Hotel **&** The **Ashbury** Hotel

www.sportsandleisurebreak.co.uk

0800 955 0358

The Manor House and Ashbury Hotels are two sister hotels located on the foothills of Dartmoor National Park. We are a Craft and Sport Hotel complex with indoor and outdoor facilities that are unrivalled anywhere in England.

TEAM SPORTS

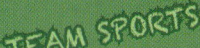

RACKET SPORTS

17 CRAFT ACTIVITIES

TEAM SPORTS
5-A-SIDE • BASKETBALL
ROUNDERS • VOLLEYBALL
CONTINUOUS CRICKET

RACKET SPORTS
10 TENNIS COURTS
UP TO 8 BADMINTON COURTS
2 SQUASH COURTS

CRAFT CENTRE
POTTERY • ENAMELLING
HOT PRESS PRINTING
WOODWORK • JEWELLERY
GLASS ENGRAVING

GAME ZONES + LEISURE
3 GAMES ZONES
6 SNOOKER TABLES
TEN PIN BOWLING
3 SWIMMING POOLS
WATER POLO • TABLE TENNIS

7 GOLF COURSES

TARGET SPORTS

12.5% GROUP DISCOUNT
STUDENTS UNDER 16
FROM £194 FOR 4 NIGHTS

OFF-SITE ACTIVITIES

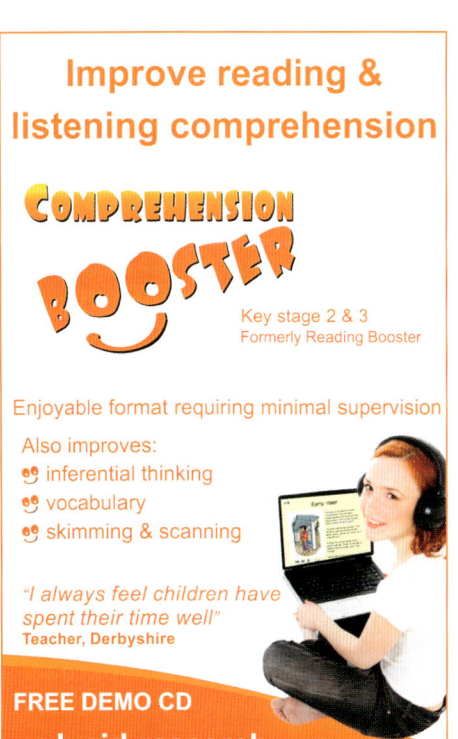 
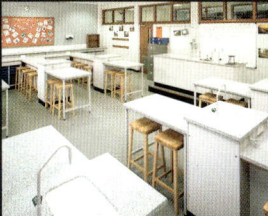
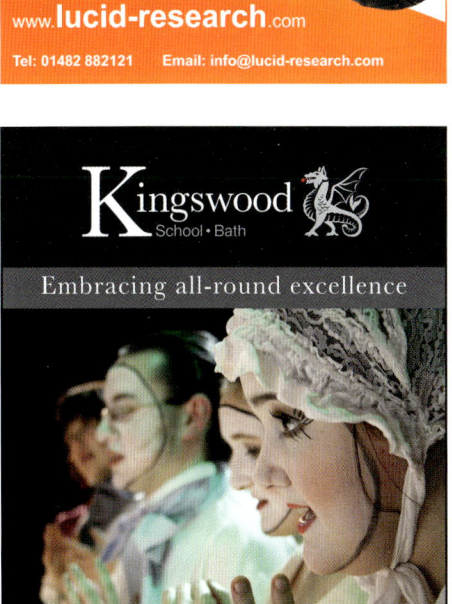
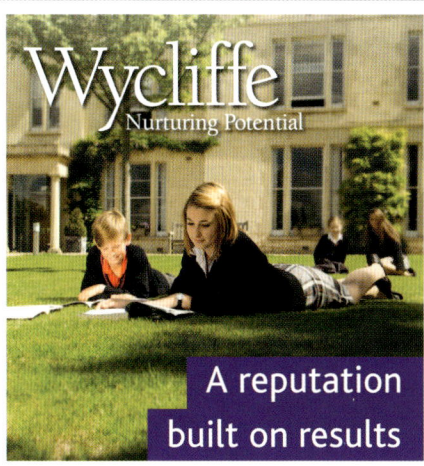

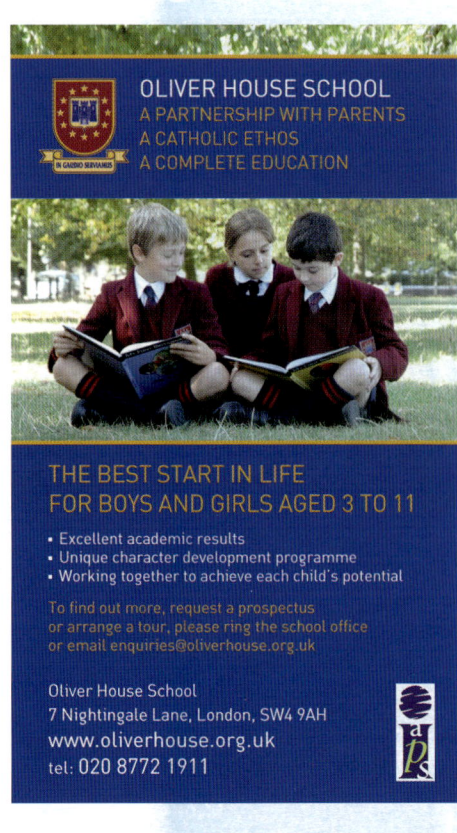

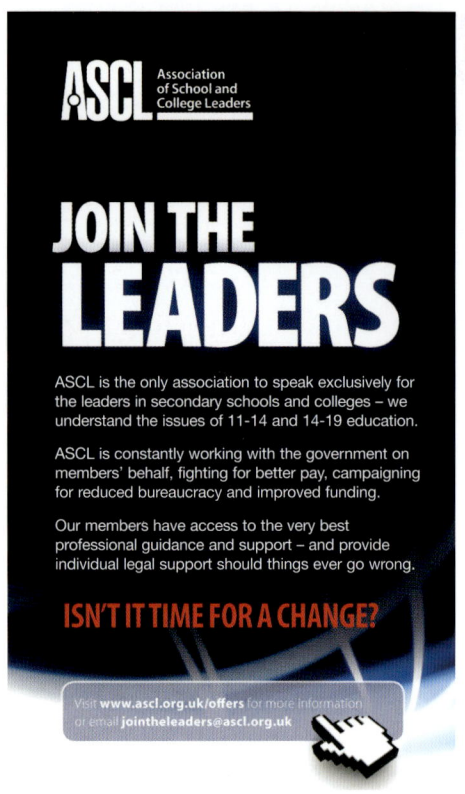

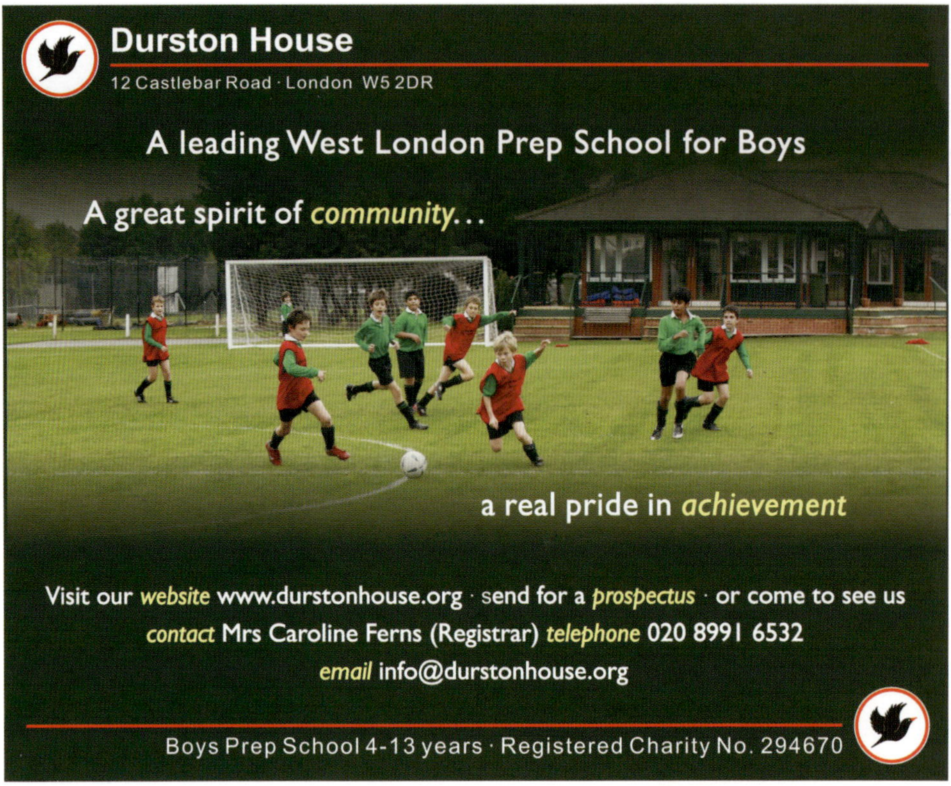
Durston House
12 Castlebar Road · London W5 2DR
A leading West London Prep School for Boys
A great spirit of community...
a real pride in achievement
Visit our website www.durstonhouse.org · send for a prospectus · or come to see us
contact Mrs Caroline Ferns (Registrar) telephone 020 8991 6532
email info@durstonhouse.org
Boys Prep School 4-13 years · Registered Charity No. 294670

UNIVERSAL SERVICES
Universal Services specialise in the supply, manufacture and installation of both 'fixed' and 'portable' sports equipment for the institutional market, including netting, basketball goals, games posts, climbing frames, trampolines, weight training equipment, sports matting etc. We provide a free technical advice service and our installations are carried out by our directly employed teams of engineers.
We can offer equipment for all your sports needs, and having over 30 years experience in this market you can be sure of good advice and a first class service.
Members of SAFEA, SAPCA and affiliated to the Youth Sports Trust.
Beckingham Business Park,
Tolleshunt Major, Maldon, Essex CM9 8LZ
Tel: 01621 868700 • Fax: 01621 860697
www.universalservicesuk.co.uk
info@universalservicesuk.co.uk

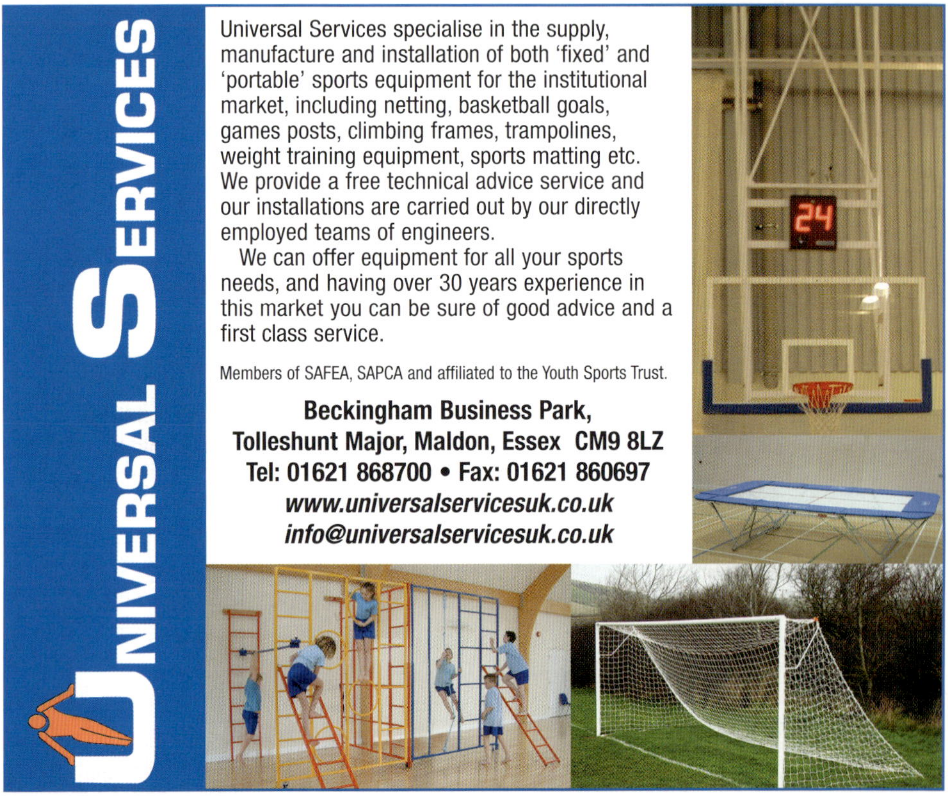

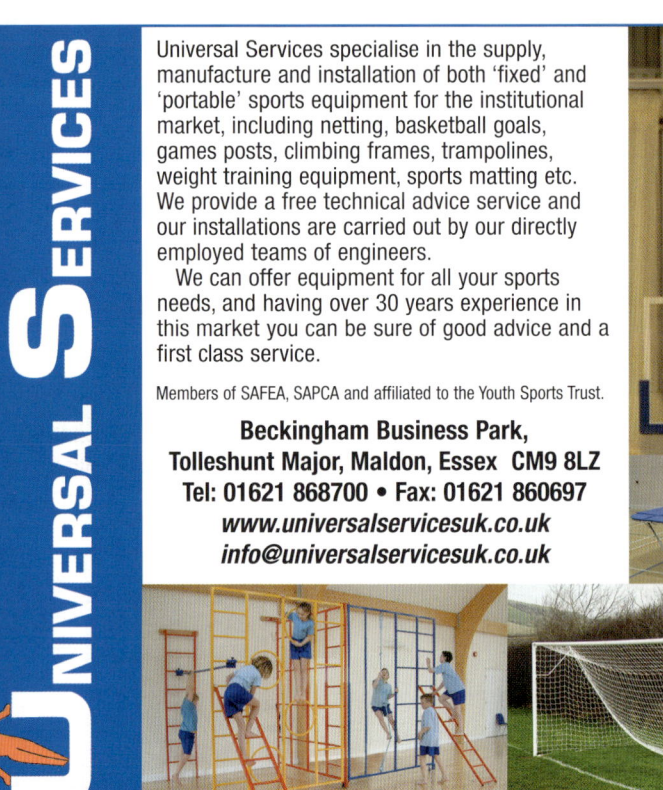

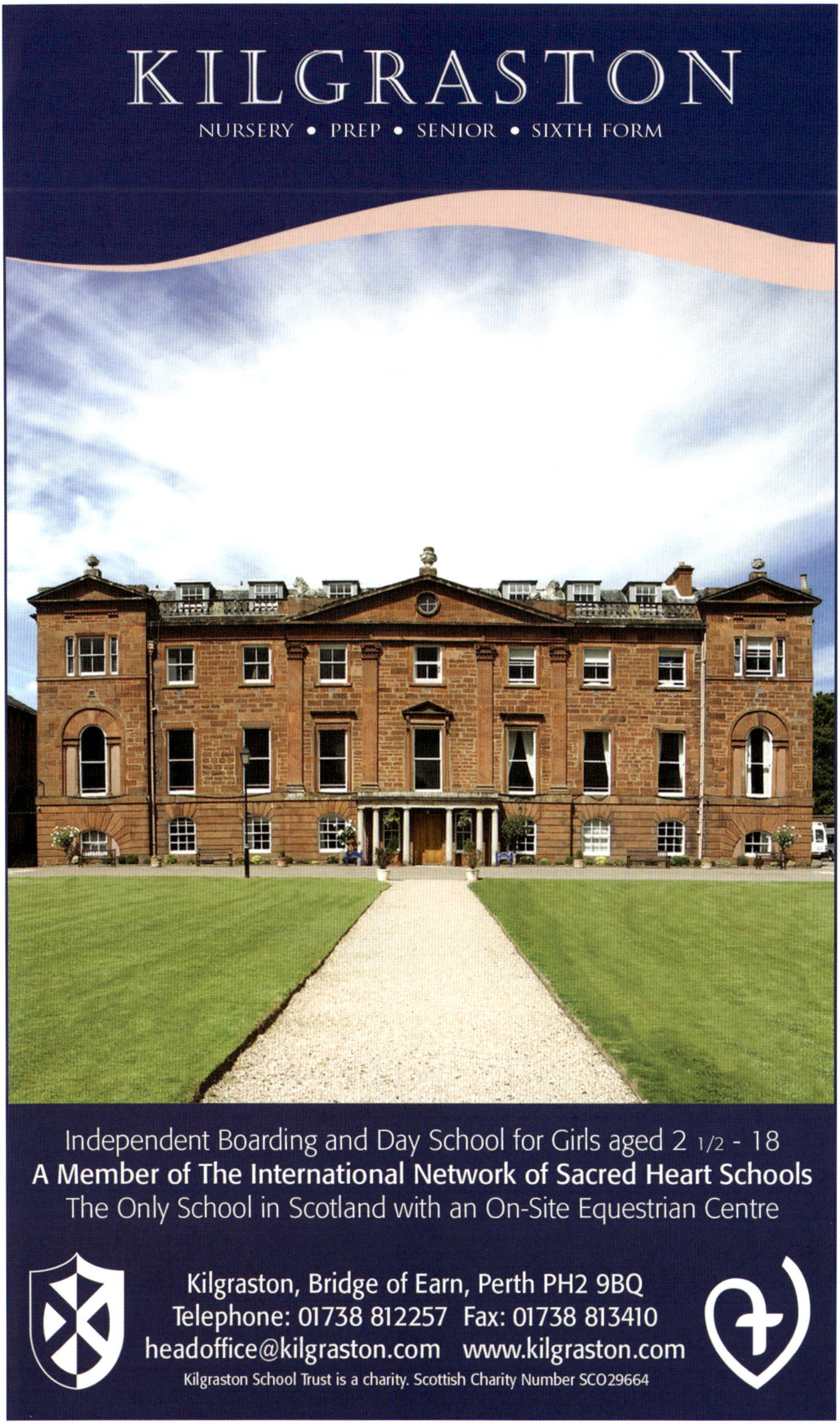

KILGRASTON

NURSERY • PREP • SENIOR • SIXTH FORM

Independent Boarding and Day School for Girls aged 2 1/2 - 18
A Member of The International Network of Sacred Heart Schools
The Only School in Scotland with an On-Site Equestrian Centre

Kilgraston, Bridge of Earn, Perth PH2 9BQ
Telephone: 01738 812257 Fax: 01738 813410
headoffice@kilgraston.com www.kilgraston.com
Kilgraston School Trust is a charity. Scottish Charity Number SCO29664

TOURS FOR SCHOOLS & YOUNG PEOPLE WITH POPPY TRAVEL

Poppy Travel is the official travel arm of The Royal British Legion. Our tours offer memorable historical and cultural experiences, enabling young people to learn about the realities of conflict.

- Suitable for primary and secondary school pupils and for youth groups
- Visits to battlefields, war cemeteries and memorials provide an understanding of Remembrance
- UK and overseas tours tailored to the aims and requirements of each group
- Every tour led by an experienced, fully trained, CRB checked guide
- Bursaries available to ensure tours are accessible to all

The Royal British Legion is recognised as the custodians of Remembrance.

POPPY TRAVEL
the experience of Remembrance

Registered Charity No: 219279

PART I
Schools whose Heads are members of the Headmasters' and Headmistresses' Conference

ALPHABETICAL LIST OF SCHOOLS
UK & Ireland

4

Symbols used in Staff Listings	
* Head of Department	§ Part Time or Visiting
† Housemaster/Housemistress	¶ Old Pupil

Individual School Entries
UK & Ireland

Abingdon School

Park Road, Abingdon, Oxfordshire OX14 1DE
Tel: 01235 521563 School
        01235 849041 Registry
        01235 849022 Bursar
Fax: 01235 849077 Head
        01235 849079 School
        01235 849085 Registry
e-mail: heads.pa@abingdon.org.uk
        admissions@abingdon.org.uk
        bursars.sec@abingdon.org.uk
website: www.abingdon.org.uk

The foundation of the School appears to date from the twelfth century; the first clear documentary reference occurs in 1256. After the dissolution of Abingdon Abbey, the School was re-endowed in 1563 by John Roysse, of the Mercers' Company in London. It was rebuilt in 1870 on its present site, and many further buildings have been added with the most recent £8m sports development newly completed. Abingdon Preparatory School, formerly known as Josca's, is situated close by at Frilford (*see entry in IAPS section*). The total establishment numbers about 1,100 boys.

Stewards:
N E Guiver
Mr and Mrs Q M E Hoodless
T A Libby
Mr and Mrs D Whibley

Governing Body:
D P Lillycrop, LLB, FCMI (*Chairman*)
J R Gabitass, MA (*Vice Chairman*)
A Saunders-Davies, MRICS, MBA (*Vice Chairman*)

The Mayor of Abingdon
The Master of Christ's Hospital, Abingdon
J M Bunce
Professor K M Burk, BA, MA, DPhil, FRHistS, AIWS
Miss J E Cranston
Dr O R Darbishire, MA, MSc, PhD
R S Farrant
Mrs J Forrest, CertEd
Mrs M T Hawley, BA
Miss E J C Hohler, MA
Dr E H T Lumsden, MA, MB BS, MRCGP, DRCOG
G R Morris, FCA
C J W Owen, MA
The Hon Sir Vivian Ramsey, KT, MA, DipLaw, CEng, MICE
Mrs O Senior, MSc
Professor C Stebbings, LLB, PhD, FRHistS

Clerk to the Governors: T R Ayling, MA

Head: Miss O F S Lusk, BMus

Second Master: D J Dawswell, BSc
Deputy Head, Academic: G May, MA
Deputy Head, Pastoral: D J Wickes, MA
Chaplain: Revd H L Kirk, BD, MA
Upper Master: J S Barker, BA
Middle Master: Revd P D B Gooding, MA, DipTh, DipMin
Lower School Housemaster: A J Jenkins, BA
Master of Scholars: Dr C J Burnand, MA, DPhil
Master i/c the Other Half: S A Evans, BA

Housemasters:
Boarders:
School House: D G Aitken, BA
Crescent House: A N J Tate, MA
Davies's House: E S Davies, BA

Dayboys:
D A Boyd, BA
A C Christodoulou, MSc, BEng
D J T Franklin, MA
N J O'Doherty, BSc
R Southwell-Sander, BA
M R Webb, BSc

Assistant Masters:
Miss H K Allcock, BA
Mrs D C Bennison, BSc
D J Bickerton, MSc
S E Bliss, BSc
J P G Brooks, BSc
Ms K E Byrne, BA
Miss S E Carey, BSc
K T Carson, MPhil
P J E Coke, BSc
J A Cotton, BA, MA
Mrs C Cross, CertEd
L F Dudin, MSc, PhD
A J P English, BA, MLitt
D Evans, BA
N Fieldhouse, BA
R M Fisher, BSc
I C Fishpool, BSc, FRGS
Mrs J E Fishpool, MA
C M Fletcher-Campbell, MA
M W Forth, MChem
Ms J Gardner, BSc, MA
Mrs L P Glenn-McKibbin, LLB, MEd
S J Grills, MSc
Dr T C Gunn, BA, PhD
A S Hall, BA
D Haworth, BSc, LRAM
Miss V E Hicks, BA
D M Hughes, BA
A T Hundermark, BSc
S James, MPhys
Dr R K Jeffreys, BSc, PhD
Mrs J P Jennings, MA
Miss T Katie, BA
Miss K Lee, BSocSc
M I Litchfield, BSc
O T Lomax, BA
A J Loughe, MA, MSc

Miss L Man, BSc
Mrs J A Mansfield, CAPES
Miss E A Marshall, BSc
Dr C J May, BA, PhD
D R McGill, BA
Mrs S C V McRae, BSc
I Middleton, MA
G R Moody, MA
H C G Morgan, MMath
Dr M J Murray, BSc, PhD
J P Nairne, BFA
Mrs E O'Doherty, MA
Miss R Papadopoulos, MA
Mrs V D Penrose, BSc
M D Perriss, MA
Miss N Petrov, BSc
B J L Phillips, BA
D J Pope, MA
Mrs M V Pradas Muños, BA
H F C Price, BA
N A F Pritchard, MA
N M Revill, BA
D C Shirazi, BA
Mrs E M-T Slatford, MA
M A Stinton, MA, ARCM, LRAM
A P Swarbrick, BA, MPhil
J H Taylor, BA
Mrs F R Tufnell, BA
S R Whalley, MA, MSt
M B Whitworth, BA
Dr J S Wiejak, MA, PhD
Mrs S Wigmore, BEd
P Willerton, MA
Dr A P Willis, BSc, PhD
J H Winters, MA
Miss R Yarrow, BA, MSc

Librarian: Mrs G J Cooper, BSc

Part-time:
Mrs J Bentley, BSc
Mrs V A Clark, BSc
J D E Drummond-Hay, BEd
A J Mansfield, BSc
Ms S A L Northey, BA, MSc

Mrs M Pringle, MMus, FTCL, LRAM
Mrs A K Quick, BA
Dr S J Ridd, MA, PhD
Miss N Spurling-Holt, BA
Mrs A M Streatfield, BEd

Bursar: J M C Webster, BSc, ACA
Registrar: Mrs J H Jørgensen, MA
Medical Officer: Dr M F Khan, MBChB, FRCS, DRCOG, DFFP

In the Senior School there are about 870 boys aged 11–18, of whom approximately 120 are boarders. Boarding starts from age 13.

Boarding is organised in three houses: School House (Mr D G Aitken), Davies's House (Mr E S Davies) and Crescent House (Mr A N J Tate). The School values its boarding element very highly and weekly boarding features strongly as part of a policy aimed at asserting a distinctive regional identity for the School.

Pastoral Care. The Lower School has a self-contained system of pastoral care, led by the Lower School Housemaster. All boys join a senior house on entering the Middle School. Within the house system there are distinct tutoring arrangements for Middle School and Upper School boys, which are coordinated by the Middle Master and Upper Master respectively. Special emphasis is placed on the value of parental involvement and also on the provision of careers guidance at appropriate points in a boy's development. Great importance is attached to pastoral care and the School's teaching philosophy is based on a tutorial approach.

Land and Buildings. The School is surrounded by 35 acres of its own grounds, yet is within a few hundred yards of the historic centre of Abingdon, which lies 6 miles down the Thames from Oxford. A further 30 acres of playing fields are located at the Preparatory School, three miles from Abingdon.

The last quarter-century has seen a considerable expansion in the School's stock of buildings. A major development in the 1990s was Mercers' Court, which celebrated the School's historical link with the Mercers' Company of London. In 2003 a £3m Arts Centre was opened providing purpose-designed facilities for music, art and drama.

Sports facilities have been greatly enhanced by a new £8m sports centre with a superb 8-lane swimming pool, fitness suites, classroom space, squash courts, climbing wall and a martial arts and fencing studio. This follows the opening in 2003 of a beautiful timber-framed boathouse situated on the River Thames a short distance from the School.

Courses of Study. The School is essentially academic in character and intention and levels of both expectation and achievement are high. Subjects taught include English, History, French, German, Spanish, Mandarin Chinese, Latin, Greek, Ancient History, Economics, Business Studies, Geography, Mathematics, Physics, Chemistry, Biology, Art, Religious Studies, Psychology, Music and Theatre Studies. Over the last few years there has been increasing collaboration with the School of St Helen and St Katharine with joint tuition particularly in Theatre Studies, Government and Politics and History of Art. The School is well equipped with computing facilities and audio-visual teaching aids.

All boys spend three years in the Middle School (13 to 16 year olds), in which many different subject combinations are possible, and there is no specialisation before the Sixth Form. In the Sixth Form many boys combine courses in arts and sciences; four subjects are normally taken at AS in the Lower Sixth, followed by three or four at A2 in the Upper Sixth. Classroom teaching at all levels is supplemented by a programme of specialist lectures and outside visits. In general terms, the curriculum aims to combine academic discipline and excellence with the fullest encouragement of a wide range of interests and pursuits.

Games and Activities. The School enjoys some 80 acres of playing fields and has its own sports centre, swimming pool, fitness suites, climbing wall, squash and tennis courts and a boathouse on the River Thames. The major sports are rowing, rugby, cricket, hockey, tennis, athletics and cross-country. Special success has been achieved recently in rowing, fencing, badminton and shooting. Other sports include sailing, golf, fives and football.

Importance is attached to the development of a sense of social responsibility, through voluntary membership of Community Service and the Duke of Edinburgh's Award

Schemes. There is a contingent of the Combined Cadet Force based on voluntary recruitment.

There are numerous societies catering for all kinds of interests and enthusiasms. Music is particularly strong, with over half the boys taking instrumental or vocal lessons in the School. In addition to the Chapel Choir, Choral Society and three orchestras, there are excellent opportunities for ensemble playing, including jazz.

Religion. The School is Anglican by tradition, but boys of other denominations are welcome, and normally attend by year group a short non-denominational service approximately once a week.

Health. The School has its own doctor and there is a well-equipped health centre in the school grounds. In cases of emergency boys are admitted to one of the local hospitals.

Admission. The normal ages of entry to the Senior School are 11, 13 and 16; there are occasionally vacancies at other ages. About half of each year's intake enter the School at age 11 and most of the rest at age 13. Registration at age 9 or 10 is recommended. Abingdon Preparatory School has its own entrance arrangements (*see entry in IAPS section*).

Details of the entrance examination procedures for 11 and 13 year old candidates are available from the Registry. Entry to the Sixth Form, at 16, generally depends on promising GCSE grades and written tests where it is appropriate, as well as on interviews and a report from the previous school.

Term of Entry. September is the usual date of entry and is preferred by the School. Boys may be accepted in any of the three terms, if vacancies occur in their age group.

Fees per term (2011-2012). The tuition fee, for dayboys, is £4,835. This includes the cost of lunches and textbooks.

For boarders, the total fee (including tuition and all extras except for instrumental music lessons and some disbursements directly incurred by individual boys) is £8,545 (weekly) and £9,915 (full).

Scholarships and Bursaries. (*See Scholarship Entries section.*) The School offers a number of means-tested scholarships and bursaries at ages 11, 13 and 16; full details are published in the spring of each year and are available, on application, from the Registry.

Honours. Numerous places are won each year at Oxford and Cambridge and on other highly selective university courses.

Old Abingdonian Club. Administrator: c/o Abingdon School.

Charitable status. Abingdon School Limited is a Registered Charity, number 1071298. It exists to provide educational opportunities which are open to talented boys without regard to their families' economic standing. Its curriculum is designed to promote intellectual rigour, personal versatility and social responsibility.

Ackworth School

Ackworth, Pontefract, West Yorkshire WF7 7LT
Tel: 01977 611401
Fax: 01977 616225
e-mail: admissions@ackworthschool.com
website: www.ackworthschool.com

This co-educational boarding and day school was founded in 1779 and occupies a large rural estate which surrounds the gracious Georgian buildings and spacious gardens and playing fields which form the School Campus. It is one of the seven Quaker Schools in England.

Governing Body:
Members appointed by The Religious Society of Friends

Clerk: Alison Tyas

Secretary and Bursar: John Lebeter, ICSA

Full time Teaching Staff:

Head: Mrs Kathryn Bell, BSc, PGCE

Deputy Head (Curriculum): Jeffrey D Swales, MA, PGCE

Deputy Head (Pastoral): William Yates, BSc Ed

Director of Marketing: Marion Mitchell, BA, PGCE

Head of Sixth Form: Andrew Ward, BSc, PGCE

Heads of Subject Departments:
Alistar Boucher, BA, MA, PGCE (*English*)
Rebecca Durham, BA, PGCE (*Drama*)
Lucinda Hamill, MA, BEd, BA (*Mathematics*)
Andrew Ward, BSc, PGCE (*Biology*)
Taras Anthony, MA (*Chemistry*)
Francis Hickenbottom, BSc, PGCE (*Physics*)
Helen Smith, MA, MA (*German*)
Elizabeth Rayner, BA Hons, PGCE (*French*)
Derek Wilkinson, BEd (*Design & Technology*)
David Palmer, BSc, PGCE (*Information Technology*)
Sarah Rose-Peirson, BA (*Art*)
Rhiannon Davies, MA (*Music*)
Thomas Plant, BA, PGCE (*History*)
Stephen Minihan, BA, PGCE (*Geography*)
Nicola Tod, BA, PGCE (*Business Studies*)
Jackie Hodgson, BSc, PGCE (*Physical Education*)

Heads of Boarding Houses:
Boys: Christopher Bailey, BSc
Girls: Claire Cougan, BSc, PGCE

Coram House (Junior School):
Head: Mary Wilson, BA Hons, PGCE

§Librarian: Erica Dean

Nursing Sister: Pamela Evans, SRN
Medical Officer: Gwenan Davenport, MBChB, MRCGP

There are 524 girls and boys aged from 4 to 18 years, 405 of whom are day pupils. Some of the pupils are from Quaker homes, but the School has long been open to boys and girls unconnected with the Society of Friends, and these pupils are now in the majority. The pattern of school life is based on the Quaker belief that religion and life are one: that spiritual conviction directly affects the way in which people behave toward each other and determines their attitude to life in general. However, while the life of the School is based on the Quakers' interpretation of Christianity, the approach is broad-based and open-minded, for the life of the community is enriched by contributions made by those of other denominations and faiths. Although all pupils attend school assemblies and Meetings for Worship, arrangements can generally be made for pupils to worship in their own churches and boys and girls can be prepared for confirmation.

Houses. Boys and girls live separately in two houses, with resident house staff and matrons responsible for their welfare.

Curriculum. Pupils follow courses leading to GCSE, IGCSE and Advanced level examinations. A wide range of subjects can be taken. The main foreign languages taught are French, German and Spanish. There is a strong Music department and group instrumental tuition is part of the First Year (Year 7) course; Design and Technology and Art are also very well provided for, and all of these subjects are integral parts of the core curriculum. The School also has a strong sporting tradition with many successful teams, thanks to excellent coaching and first-rate facilities. The large academic Sixth Form, which offers all of the traditional subjects as well as more recent additions such as Sport and PE and Drama, prepares students extremely well for university entry and for life beyond School.

The most recent addition to our provision is our flourishing International Centre. Here, intensive English coaching is offered to students of Sixth Form age who wish to go on to follow Advanced Level courses and a one-year GCSE course.

Leisure Time. The many clubs and societies on offer cater for all ages and all tastes. The facilities for crafts, art and music are freely available outside the teaching day, and pupils participate in a huge range of team and individual sports. There is a very full programme of weekend activities and visits.

Buildings. A policy of expansion and upgrading has been maintained over the years and within the last decade wide-ranging improvements have been made to the School's facilities. Study accommodation for Sixth Formers is large and modern and the science laboratories have been re-equipped. The modern Music Centre and Fothergill Theatre provide spacious facilities for individual and ensemble music making, together with an excellent venue for concerts and School productions. The Design and Technology Centre houses a thriving department and numerous creative after-school clubs, and the spacious, well-appointed study, reference and careers library caters for all age groups. The superb, modern Sports Centre and fully resourced Information Technology Centre are in constant use. The most recent changes have been to boarding accommodation – the girls have specially designed, purpose-built furniture, while the boys' rooms have been re-designed to include en-suite facilities.

Scholarships and Bursaries. (*See Scholarship Entries section.*) A number of awards are made each year to selected boys and girls entering the School who show high academic ability or exceptional talent in Music or Art. Bursaries are available to members of the Society of Friends and others according to need. Travel Scholarships are available to members of the Sixth Form.

Admission. Interested parents will be sent a prospectus upon application to the Head and visits can always be promptly arranged. There are also two Open Mornings during the year, at which parents and families are welcome to tour the School and to talk to staff and pupils. Pupils for entry at age 7 and above take the School's entrance test, while entry at age 4 is based on interview. The majority of children enter the Senior School at the age of 11, but there is also a sizeable entrance at 12, 13, 14 and 16+. Entry is always possible at other ages if places are available, and there is a direct entry into the Sixth Form for pupils who are able to take the full two-year A level course.

Coram House (Junior School). Coram House caters for day boys and girls aged 4 to 11, the majority of whom move on into the Senior School. In September 2002 a nursery opened catering for pupils aged 2 to 4 years.

Pre-prep classes are housed in new, spacious, purpose-built accommodation. From Reception onwards, emphasis is placed on a thorough understanding of the basic skills in reading, literacy, numeracy and science. In addition, a wide-ranging curriculum is provided to encourage creativity and physical ability through Art, Craft, Technology, Drama, Music and Sport.

In the Preparatory Department pupils work to a more structured timetable and are gradually introduced to specialist subject teaching. Staffing in Coram House is generous, so a thorough grounding can be given in the core subjects of English, Mathematics and Science. A broad curriculum is provided which includes French, Art and Crafts, Technology, Drama, Music and Sport – the children thus receive a rounded education and are able to develop their individual talents.

Before-school care from 8.00 am and after-school care until 5.30 pm are both available, at no extra charge. Extended care to 6.30 pm is also available on request.

Fees per term (2011-2012). Coram House: £2,435–£2,505 (day); Senior School: £6,545 (boarding), £3,920 (day); International Centre: £8,995 (boarding). The day pupil fees include lunch (and other meals if required).

The Ackworth Old Scholars' Association. This is a flourishing Association with a membership of over two thousand. Annual gatherings are held at Ackworth at Easter and there are Guild Meetings held in the regions at other times in the year. The General Secretary is Keith Daniel, 8 Derwent Court, Silsden, Keighley, West Yorkshire.

Charitable status. Ackworth is a Registered Charity, number 529280. It was established for the purpose of providing independent education.

Aldenham School

Elstree, Herts WD6 3AJ
Tel: 01923 858122
Fax: 01923 854410
e-mail: enquiries@aldenham.com
website: www.aldenham.com

The School was founded in 1597 by Richard Platt, 'Cytyzen and Brewer of London.'

Motto: *'In God is all our Trust.'*

Governing Body:
Chairman: J S Lewis, DL, FCIS
Governor Emeritus: Field Marshal The Lord Vincent, GBE, KCB, DSO (*OA*)

P J Easby (*OA*)	D T Tidmarsh
B Woodrow, OBE, DL	C J Hayfield
(*OA*)	Dr D Nicholes
S J B Redman	Mrs V Shah
J R Baugh (*OA*)	A Day (*OA*)
Revd Canon Dr M Sansom	Dr J Altree
H M Saunders	J T Barton (*OA*)
P Carr (*OA*)	S Nokes
J H Jones	

Headmaster: **J C Fowler**, MA

Deputy Head: A M Williams, BSc
Senior Master: N D Pulman, MA
Director of Studies: D S Watts, MA, CChem, MRSC
Head of Sixth Form & Careers: R P Collins, BA, MSc

Heads of Department:
Art: Miss G Nye, BA
Biology: Dr P J Reid
Business Studies: P S Green, BA
Chemistry: S P Williams, MA, BSc
Design Technology: Miss S E Nicholl, BSc
Drama: Ms J Bannister, BA
English: C R Jenkins, MA
Games and Physical Education: G Cornock, BA
Geography: M I Yeabsley, BSc
History: P A Wright, BA
Academic ICT: D J Michael, BSc
Learning Support: Mrs L V Jones, CertEd
Mathematics: D A Chorley, BSc
Languages: Mrs A Venter, MA
Director of Music: J R Wyatt, GRSM, LRAM, ARCO
Physics: R A C Pomeroy, BSc
Sciences: S P Williams, MA, BSc
Theology: C D Bembridge, BTheol

Head of Prep School: Mrs V Gocher, BA
Deputy Head of Prep School & Head of Foundation Stage: Mrs C J Watts, CertEd

Houses and Housemasters:

Boarding Houses:
McGill's: P M Dunstan, BA
Beevor's: S W Mainwaring, BEd
Kennedy's: W P N Pietrek, BA
Paull's: A O Dean, BA

Day Houses:
Paull's: A O Dean, BA
Leeman's: C S Irish, BSc
Riding's: A P Stephenson, BA
Martineau's: Mrs L Gall, BEd
Deputy: P S Turner, PhD, BSc

Chaplain: Revd D M Bond, BA
Librarian: A Nelson, MA, DLIS, ALA
Bursar: A W C Fraser, FCIS

Number in School. 700, of which there are 126 boarders and 574 day pupils. (There are 185 girls in the School including the Preparatory School.)

Aldenham is situated in its own beautiful grounds of more than 110 acres in the Hertfordshire green belt, with excellent access to London (First Capital Connect/Jubilee Line) and within the M25, close to the M1. Aldenham's particular reputation as a close knit, small and supportive community with a strong boarding ethos makes it the very best environment for a high-quality all-round education encouraging children to enterprise. The achievement of every child's academic potential remains central but the building of confidence comes too from sports, music and drama, and by living and working together within the disciplined and vigorous community that is Aldenham today.

Admission. The first step towards gaining a place is to visit the School. A fully illustrated prospectus is available on request from the Admissions Coordinator and prospective parents are encouraged to visit the School with their sons and daughters, either individually or at one of the school's 2 open days in June and October.

At 11, entry is by tests and interview, at 13 by interview and reference, and at 16 by interview and GCSE results. Every effort is made to meet parents' wishes as regards which House is chosen for their son. All girls enter Paull's House at 13.

Registration fee £50; Deposit £1,000.

Fees per term (2011-2012). Boarders £6,367–£8,860; Day Pupils £4,250–£6,083. These fees include most compulsory extras.

Scholarships and other awards. (*See Scholarship Entries section*.) Scholarships, Exhibitions and Bursaries are available at each point of entry.

Curriculum. From 11 to 16 the timetable closely reflects the National Curriculum. Boys and girls are prepared for GCSEs across a range of subjects including Maths, English, French, Science and a number of other Arts and language options. Care is taken that all pupils include Art, Music, Technology and Computing in their programme and there is a progressive course of Theology throughout the School with GCSE taken in Year 11. The aim is to ensure that subject choices affecting AS/A2 levels are made as late as possible and the ISCO programme of tests and interviews are used as a basis for career planning and AS/A2 level choice in Year 11.

Those in the Lower Sixth Form normally take 4 AS levels from a range of 25 subjects, which narrows to three choices at A2 in the Upper Sixth year. In combination with the extensive extra-curricular programme, work experience and UCAS advice, the curriculum in the Sixth Form continues to give pupils their best opportunities for university entry. The majority go on to degree courses at universities. There are regular successes at Oxford and Cambridge. All those in the Sixth Form attend an Introduction to Industry Conference, and Aldenham runs a European-wide Work Experience Scheme.

Games and Other Activities. Great value is placed on the participation of every pupil in Games and Activities. A programme integrated into the working week offers enormous variety across all ages. The School has a fine record in traditional team games. Soccer, Hockey, Cricket and Athletics are the major sports for boys, whilst girls benefit from a breadth of in and out of school activities including Hockey,

Tennis, Badminton, Dance, Squash, Netball, Trampolining, Aerobics and Sailing. In addition there is a full programme of House and School competitions in Squash, Eton Fives, Basketball, Tennis, Sailing, Fencing, Badminton, Table Tennis, Shooting, Swimming, and Cross-country. Volleyball, Horse Riding, Climbing, Judo and Golf are also available. The Sports Hall provides excellent facilities for expert and novice alike and incorporates a full size indoor hockey pitch, dance studio, martial arts room, gymnasium and a rifle range. Time is set apart for activities and societies; these include CCF, Adventure activities, the Duke of Edinburgh's Award Scheme, Community Service, Electronics, Chess, Computing, Motor Club, Photography and Model Railway. The Debating and Philosophy societies meet regularly throughout the year

Music and Drama. Music flourishes in the School. More than one third of the School has individual instrumental tuition. There is a Chapel Choir, School Orchestra and wind and brass groups. A spring concert is performed annually in the School Chapel. A number of boys and girls learn to play on the fine, modern, 3-manual pipe organ in the Chapel. A music school with practice and performance facilities was opened in September 2000.

A new school theatre opened in 2007 encourages a high calibre of Drama students. In addition to an annual School Play there are Senior and Junior House Play competitions and boys and girls have the opportunity to produce and design as well as to perform in the various productions. The School's proximity to London makes possible frequent visits to theatres and concerts. Theatre Studies is offered as a full A Level subject.

Organisation. Whilst the framework of the School is contemporary, it takes as its basis the long established 'House' system. Each House creates an extended family and provides the formal and social focus of the School. There are four boarding and three day Houses together with a distinct yet fully integrated Junior House for 11–13 year olds. Each has a Housemaster or Housemistress and a team of tutors so every pupil has a personal tutor. In the Boarding Houses the Housemaster, his family, Matron and tutors live at the centre of the community ensuring the well-being of each child.

Boarding. Aldenham's unique array of day and boarding options enables it to provide the educational benefits of a boarding school to Day and Day Boarding pupils and to offer real flexibility with its arrangements for boarders, the vast majority of whom live within 20 miles of the School. Boys and girls may board from entry at 11+.

Religion. Aldenham is a Church of England foundation and seeks to maintain a strong Christian ethos to which those of other faiths are warmly welcomed.

Old Aldenhamian Society. There is a thriving Old Aldenhamian Society. Further details from the Secretary at the School.

Charitable status. The Aldenham School Company is a Registered Charity, number 298140. It exists to provide high quality education and pastoral care to enable children to achieve their full potential in later life.

Alleyn's School

Townley Road, Dulwich, London SE22 8SU
Tel: 020 8557 1500
             Headmaster: 020 8557 1493
             Bursar: 020 8557 1450
Fax: 020 8557 1462
e-mail: enquiries@alleyns.org.uk
website: www.alleyns.org.uk

The School is part of the foundation known as 'Alleyn's College of God's Gift' which was founded in 1619 by Edward Alleyn, the Elizabethan actor.

Motto: '*God's Gift*'

The Governing Body:

Chairman: Prof the Lord Kakkar, BSc, PhD, FRCS
Mr I Barbour, BSc Econ Hons, ACIB
Dr E F Bowen, BSc, MBBS Hons, PhD, FRCP
Mrs A M Brownbill, LLB
The Lady Butler
Rt Revd C Chessun, Bishop of Southwark, BA
Mr M Fosten, BA
Mr T Franey, FIMI
Mr P George, FCA
Mr C Holloway, MA
Mr B Martin, MA, MBA, FCMI, FRSA
Mr J I K Murray, MA, FCA
Mr P Perry, BA Hons
Mr I Pulley

Headmaster: **Dr G J Savage**, MA Cantab, PhD, FRSA

Senior Deputy Head: Mr A R Faccinello, MA

Deputy Head: Mr J G Lilly, BA

Assistant Heads:
Mr A W A Skinnard, MA (*Head of Upper School; Religious Studies*)
Mr D C A Morton, BA (*Head of Middle School; Geography*)
Mr S E Smith, BA (*Headmaster of Lower School; Classics*)
Mrs A MacAuliffe, BA (*Assistant Head, Director of Studies; Modern Languages*)
Ms S P Chandler, BSc (*Assistant Head Co-Curricular; PE*)

Bursar: Mr S R Born, BA

Registrar: Mrs L Aldwinckle

Teaching Staff:
* *Head of Department*
† *Head of House*
§ *Part-time*

Dr M Abdalla (*Mathematics*)
Ms A K S Ackerman, MA (**Religious Studies, Philosophy, Induction Mentor*)
Mr D S Adkins, MA, MMus (§*Music*)
Mr R J Alldrick, BA (†*Brown's House, PE, DoE, Field Centre Coordinator*)
Mr B D Allen, BA (*Design Technology*)
Mrs G T Anderson, MA (*English*)
Mrs S E Arthur, BSc (§*Chemistry*)
Miss R A Barnes, BEd (*Religious Studies*)
Miss H Barton, BA (*History*)
Miss R H Baxter, BA (*Theatre Studies, Drama*)
Mr P Berman, BA (§*Religious Studies, History*)
Miss A J Blythe, BA (*Geography 2nd in Dept*)
Miss A L Boltsa, BA (*Head of Charities, Art*)
Mrs S C Bonnington, BA (**Politics, History*)
Mr A M Bruni, BSc, BEd (*Mathematics 2nd in Dept, Community Service*)
Revd A G Buckley, MA (*History, Chaplain*)
Miss J R Carlsson, MA (**Geography, International Links Coordinator*)
Dr A Choudhary, BSc, MSc (*Biology*)
Mrs C A Clift, BSc (*Girls' PE & Games*)
Mr P M Cochrane, BSc (†*Roper's House, Chemistry, Middle School Careers*)
Miss W L Collins, BSc (**Chair of Science,* *Chemistry)
Mrs R M Conway, BA, MA (*Religious Studies*)
Miss C V Copeland, MA (**Classics, Assistant Head of Upper School*)
Mrs J C Count, MA (§*Biology*)
Revd S C Dalwood, BA (*Examinations Officer, Mathematics*)
Mrs E-JC Doherty, MA (*Classics*)
Miss J Doley (*Music*)

Ms S M Dury, MA (*Psychology)
Dr S Dutta, MA (Classics)
Mrs H F Eagle, BSc (§Design & Technology)
Mr M D Eastmond, BA, MSc (Mathematics)
Mr G English, BA (PE)
Mr C M Fish, BA (Music)
Miss J H Fitzgerald, BEd (PE)
Mrs J Franco, MPhys (Physics)
Ms L Gardner, GRSM, LRAM, MSc (*Lower School Music)
Mr R L Geldeard, MA (†Spurgeon's House, Classics, Head of Philosophy)
Miss K A Goff, BA (Modern Languages)
Miss C M Goldsworthy, BA (*Art)
Miss S Gore, BA (Religious Studies)
Mrs K M Green, BSc (§Mathematics)
Mr N J Green, BEd (†Tyson's House, PE)
Mr M F Grogan, BA, MA (Media Studies)
Mrs K D Guy, BA (§Deputy Head of English)
Mrs P Hall, BA (Spanish)
Mr R G Halladay, BA, MA (English, Deputy Head Middle School)
Mr D J Harley, BSc (*History, Politics, Assistant Head of Upper School)
Mr P J Harper, BA (Modern Languages)
Dr D O Hawes, BA, MA, PhD (History 2nd in Dept, Politics)
Mrs M Heaton-Caffin, CertEd (§PE)
Miss J Hewitson, BSc (Geography)
Mr J Hodgkinson, MA (English)
Mr G L Jenkins, MA (English)
Miss M Jenney, BA (History)
Mrs M A Joel, BA (Modern Languages, Deputy Head of Middle School)
Mr B Jones, MSc (Physics)
Dr S P Kelly, BA, MA, PhD (*German, Head of Universities & Careers Centre)
Mrs S Kent, MA (History, General Studies 2nd in Dept)
Mr A T Kermode, MA (*Director of Music)
Miss S Khachik, BA (English)
Ms S Kingston, MA (Art)
Mr N R Kinnear, MA (Mathematics)
Miss G V Kirby, BA (English)
Miss S A Lane, MA, CertEd (Deputy Head of Upper School, PE)
Mrs H E Lawrence, BA (§Deputy Head of English, Learning Support)
Miss A M Legg, MA (*Media Studies, English)
Miss V A Lodge, BSc (PE)
Dr M Long, BSc, MA (§Learning Support)
Mr P M Macdonagh, BSc (*ICT)
Mr P A Mackie, MA (Head of Modern Languages)
Mr A Macmillan, BA (*Design Technology)
Mr E D Mann, BA (Mathematics)
Miss A E Marriott, BA (Biology)
Mrs S Mathieson, CertEd (*Food Technology)
Mr M McCaffrey, BA (*French)
Mr S G Milne, MA (Economics & Business Studies)
Miss R Millward, BSc (Biology)
Miss E M Nicoll, BA (Modern Languages, Deputy Examinations Officer)
Mrs E O'Donnell, BA, Grad Dip LIB Science(*Librarian)
Mr R N Ody, BEd (Head of Games and Boys' PE)
Miss R L Ottey, BSc (†Cribb's House, *Physics)
Miss K J Owens, BEd (Deputy Head of Lower School, Design Technology, Head of PSHE)
Mr R D W Payne, BSc (Information Technology)
Ms V A Penglase, BA (§Drama, Theatre Studies)
Mr C L Perez, BSc (Biology)
Mr J S S Piper, MA (*Drama)
Miss M M Pokorny, BSc (Psychology, Biology, PSHE 2nd in Dept)
Miss A M Poole, BSc (*Mathematics)

Mr N Price, MA (Art)
Mrs K Pryse-Lloyd, MSc (Physics)
Mr G Reid, MA (†Brading's House, Religious Studies)
Mr M Riedel, BSc (Mathematics)
Mr A W Robertson, BSc, MBA (*Economics & Business Studies)
Mr P J Ryder, BEng (Mathematics)
Miss A Schüller, MA (Modern Languages)
Mr J E Sheils, BSc (Physics)
Mr J G Shelton, BEd, RSA Dip IT (†Dutton's House, Information Technology)
Mr P R Sherlock, CertEd (†Tulley's House, PE)
Mrs G Silver, MA (*English)
Miss J M Sixsmith, BA (Modern Languages)
Mrs S C Smiddy, BSc (*Biology)
Mr P A Smith, BMus, ARCM, LRAM (*Instrumental Studies)
Mr V A Strain, BA (Modern Languages)
Mr T Strange, BA (Classics)
Ms C H Symes, BSc (Director of ICT)
Mrs J M Tait, BA (§Food Technology)
Mr P Thomas, BA (§Mathematics)
Mr J Thompson (Music)
Miss C M Tostevin, MSc (Chemistry)
Mr D Tuohey, BSc (Physics 2nd in Dept, Physics KS4 Coordinator)
Mrs J L van der Valk, BA (Learning Support Coordinator)
Miss M J Walker, BA (*Director of Sport & PE)
Mrs C L Wells, BSc (Deputy Director of Studies, Mathematics)
Miss H Williamson, BA, PG Dip Fine Art (Art)
Mr M Workman, MA (Chemistry)
Mr A Živanić, BA (Biology, Chemistry)

The School. Alleyn's is a co-educational day school for pupils aged 11 to 18 years, some 990 strong, of whom approximately 300 are in the Sixth Form. The Headmaster is a member of the Headmasters' and Headmistresses' Conference.

It is, with Dulwich College, the lineal descendant of "the School for twelve poor scholars" endowed by Edward Alleyn, the Elizabethan actor-manager, under a Royal Charter of 1619.

It was a Direct Grant school from 1958 until the abolition of this status in 1976. The Governors then opted for independence and at the same time opened the entry to girl pupils, making it London's first independent co-educational senior school. The School is fully co-educational.

Alleyn's Junior School, for ages 4 to 10 years, which opened in September 1992, is also on the site. (See entry in IAPS section.)

Entrance. A registration fee of £50 is charged for all applications.

Admission to the School is by competitive examination open to both boys and girls at age 11, the normal age for transfer from primary to secondary school; entrance is decided on the basis of the scholarship/entrance examination held in January for entry the following September. A report is requested from the Head of the applicant's school and, if they reach a satisfactory standard in the examination, boys and girls are invited for interview. Fee-paying places, and scholarships are awarded on the results of the entrance examination and interview. Means-tested bursaries are available for academically able children whose parents could not afford full fees. The examination consists of Reasoning papers, an English paper and a Mathematics paper. Candidates should be entered for the School before the end of November (slightly earlier for 16+), for admission the following September.

There is a smaller entry by examination open to both boys and girls at age 13. The procedure is similar to that for the 11-year-old entry, with the addition of papers in Languages and Science and the omission of Reasoning papers.

A similar procedure operates for entry at 16+, with an examination in November including subject papers and a general paper.

Opportunities for entry at other ages occasionally occur from time to time. At age 4, 7 and 9 Junior School places are awarded on the basis of an assessment held in January for entry the following September.

Fees per term (2011-2012). £4,867 (£14,601 per annum).

Scholarships and Bursaries. (*See Scholarship Entries section.*)

Curriculum. All pupils follow a broad and balanced curriculum in the first three years, including English, Mathematics, French, Latin and/or additional foreign languages (German or Spanish), Biology, Chemistry, Physics, Geography, History, Religious Studies, Art, ICT, Music and Design Technology. In Years 10–11, pupils take nine or ten GCSE subjects which will include English, English Literature, Mathematics, Biology, Chemistry and Physics. In addition they choose four option subjects. In Year 12, four main subjects are followed to AS Level and pupils may also take Critical Thinking to AS Level. In Year 13, three or four A Levels are taken. In addition to those subjects listed above, Business Studies, Classical Civilisation, Computing, Economics, Classical Greek, Italian (ab initio), Media Studies, Philosophy, Politics, Psychology, Physical Education and Drama are also available.

Pupils go on to universities, medical and dental schools, and Art Colleges. Almost all enter higher education each year. Selected pupils are prepared and entered for Colleges at Oxford and Cambridge, where a very good record of places is maintained each year.

Organisation. The Lower School (Year 7 and Year 8) has its own separate building and its own Head. Pupils in the Upper and Middle Schools have a Head of Upper School and a Head of Middle School, and belong to one of eight Houses. Each Head of House is responsible, not only for organised games, but also for the welfare of each of their pupils during their time in the School. This care is supplemented by a system of form tutors for supervision of academic progress and the giving of appropriate advice. Parents are invited to Open Evenings during the year, at which pupils' work and progress are discussed with the teaching staff.

Games. The School stands in its own grounds of 26 acres and offers a wide variety of sports and games including Soccer, Hockey, Cricket, Swimming, Athletics, Netball, Cross-Country Running, Rugby Fives, Water Polo, Gymnastics, Badminton, Fencing, Golf, Basketball, Tennis, Rounders, Trampolining, Aerobics, Fitness and Weight Training, Squash and Horse Riding.

Religious Education. The Foundation belongs to the Church of England. Religious Education of a non-denominational nature is given throughout the School, and pupils also attend regular worship in Assembly and once each term in the Foundation Chapel or in St Barnabas Church. The School Chaplain holds voluntary Holy Communion Services during term-time. Pupils may be excused from religious education if parents request.

Buildings. The main school building dates from 1887. The school has a fully-equipped sports hall, with cardio-vascular room, an indoor swimming pool, a technology centre, a music school, two digital language laboratories, an all-weather playing surface, a sports hall and pavilion, computer rooms, a library/resource centre and a new, RIBA Award-winning performing arts centre, containing the 350-seat Michael Croft Theatre, a Sixth Form study centre, classrooms, the Robert Laurie lecture theatre, and a studio for the National Youth Theatre. Some 800+ computers are networked on the school's site. The School has its own Field Centre near Buxton.

The **Fenner Library** is available to all pupils for private study. Library staff encourage reading for pleasure, with a variety of fiction and non-fiction books to borrow. Newspapers, periodicals, audio CDs and DVDs are also available.

Music, Drama and Art feature very strongly in the life of the School. There are 5 major concerts each year including the annual St John's Smith Square concert; the School runs 3 orchestras, 3 bands, 3 choirs and has over 30 Chamber groups, chosen by ability rather than age. 5 or 6 dramatic productions are staged each year. In Art, all pupils are taught to work in different media (Painting, Drawing, Sculpture and Ceramics).

There are many clubs and societies in the school; these include, in addition to Drama groups, Debating, Photography, Chess, Politics, Science and the Christian Union.

The Combined Cadet Force has long been one of the most flourishing in the country, containing Army, Navy and RAF sections and a band, and provides opportunities for such other activities as canoeing, rock climbing, sailing and flying. Pupils are encouraged to join at age 14 and serve for a minimum of 2 years. Pupils who do not join the CCF are expected to join either the Duke of Edinburgh's Award Scheme or the Volunteering group.

Career Guidance is given by specialised staff with the time and facilities for this important work. In Year 11 systematic aptitude testing is followed up by talks by parents themselves who give their time to talk about their own careers and who give help with offers of work experience to pupils.

An annual event, Year 12 Interview Day, is held in March. Students make a mock application for various and widely-ranging positions and university lecturers come in to help pupils to develop their skills.

A School Council, with members of all ages from Year 9 to Year 13, represents pupils' views to the Headmaster.

Relations with Parents. The Alleyn's Association is a dynamic and enthusiastic parent organisation which aims to nurture close links between parents and the School, and which raises considerable funds for the benefit of the School's Pupil Support Fund.

The Edward Alleyn Club. Past pupils are automatically members of the Edward Alleyn Club. This enables them to keep in touch with the school and their contemporaries, and also to take part in sporting activities if they wish. Communications should be sent to the Head of Alumni Relations, Mrs Susie Schofield, c/o Alleyn's School (alumni@ alleyns.org.uk).

Charitable status. Alleyn's College of God's Gift is a Registered Charity, number 1057971. Its purpose is to provide Independent Education for boys and girls from age 4 to 18.

Ampleforth College

York YO62 4ER
Tel: 01439 766000
Fax: 01439 788330
e-mail: admin@ampleforth.org.uk
website: www.college.ampleforth.org.uk

Ampleforth Abbey was founded in 1607 at Dieulouard in Lorraine by English Benedictine monks who had strong links with the mediaeval Benedictines of Westminster Abbey. After the French Revolution the monastic community was resettled at Ampleforth in 1802 and the present School was started there soon after.

The Community is dedicated, first to prayer, and then to religious and charitable works. Ampleforth College and St Martin's Ampleforth are the works of St Laurence Educational Trust. The other works of the Community include parishes in Yorkshire, Lancashire and Cumbria, St Benet's Hall in Oxford and pastoral involvement both at Ampleforth and elsewhere.

Motto: '*Dieu le Ward*'.

Governance: The Abbot of Ampleforth is elected by the Community for eight years at a time and presides over the Community and its works.

The Abbot is Chairman of the Ampleforth Abbey Trustees, which is the legal institute that owns and governs its foundation. St Laurence Education Trust is a separate limited company formed by the Abbey Trust. This also has charitable status and is responsible for both Ampleforth College and St Martin's Ampleforth.

The governance of these works is the responsibility of the Abbot who, with structured advice, appoints the officials, monastic and lay, who are in charge of their administration.

Governing Body:
The Abbot of Ampleforth is the Chairman of Governors acting with the Council and Chapter of Ampleforth Abbey. He is assisted by a lay Advisory Body.

Headmaster: Rev C G Everitt, OSB, MA, DPhil

Deputy Head: Mr J R Browne, BA
Director of Studies: Mr I F Lovat, BSc, MInstP
Director of Professional Development: Mr A S Thorpe, BSc, CChem, MRSC
Director of Admissions: Mrs R M A Fletcher, MA
Head of Sixth Form: Mr W F Lofthouse, MA
Head of Careers/Assistant Head of Sixth Form: Mrs J Campbell, BA
Guestmaster: Rev H Lewis-Vivas, OSB, MA

Academic Departments:

Christian Theology:
*Mr M B Fogg, BA
Rev C G Everitt, OSB, MA, DPhil
Mrs A M McNeill, BA
Mr J M Mishra, BA
†Mrs G M O McGovern, MA
Mr A J J Macdonald Powney, MA
Miss H E Jones, BA
Mr J D Rainer, BA

Christian Living:
Ms A Le Gall, MA (*Head of EAL*)
Mrs M B Carter, BSc

Classics:
*Mr J B Mutton, MA
Mr W F Lofthouse, MA
Mr J Layden, BA
Miss J Sutcliffe, BA

History:
*Mr P T Connor, MA
†Mr H C Codrington, BEd
†Rev C Boulton, OSB, BA
Mr G D Thurman, BEd
Dr E J Fern, MA, PhD
Miss B Fuller, BA
Miss M F Peterson-Johansson, BA

English:
*Mr A C Carter, MA
Mr D R Lloyd, MA (*Special Needs*)
Dr D Moses, MA, DPhil
Miss H R Brown, BA
Mr T A Barfield, MA
Mr D J Davison, MA
Miss L L Pearson, BA

Modern Languages:
*Mr S R Owen, MA
Mr J P Ridge, MA
Mr K J Dunne, BA
Mr M Torrens-Burton, BA (*EAL*)
Rev A McCabe, OSB, MA

Mrs F Garcia-Ortega, BA
Mrs C M T Olley, BA
Rev J Callaghan, MA
Miss A L Kimmerle, MA

Geography:
*Mrs C R M Dent, BSc
†Mr P M Brennan, BSc, FRMetSoc
Miss C Willey, BSc, MSc
†Mr A P Smerdon, BSc

Modern Studies:
*Mr M A Dent, BSc
Miss J M C Simmonds, BSc
Mrs J Stannard, BA
Mr J E McCullough, MSc

Mathematics:
*Dr H R Pomroy, BSc, PhD
Mrs P J Melling, BSc, BA
Dr R Warren, BSc, PhD (*Head of Middle School*)
†Mr D Willis, BEd, MEd
Mr C G O'Donovan, BSc
Dr J M Weston, BSc, DPhil
Dr J W Large, BSc, PhD
Mrs T M Jones, BSc

Physics:
*Mr J O Devitt, MPhys
Mr I F Lovat, BSc, MInstP
Dr L M Kessell, BSc, PhD
Miss K E Selby, BSc

Chemistry:
*Mr S J Howard, BSc
Mr A S Thorpe, BSc, CChem, MRSC
Dr D L Allen, MA, DPhil, CChem, MRSC (*Chemistry and Physics*)
Mr S J Howard, BSc
Dr M J Parker, BSc, PhD

Biology:
*Mr P W Anderson, BSc
Mr A J Hurst, BSc
Mrs J Hurst, BSc
Dr H Webster, MA
Miss R Beber, MSc

Music:
*Mr I D Little, MA, MusB, FRCO, ARCM, LRAM
Mr W J Dore, MA, FRCO
Mr D de Cogan, DipRCM, ARCM
Mr P J McBeth, MusB
Mr T M Foster, BMus

Design and Technology:
*Mr B W Gillespie, BEd
†Mr B J Anglim, BEng
†Mrs V Anglim, BEng

ICT:
*Mr M A Barras, BSc
Mrs L Canning, BSc

Art:
*Mr S G Bird, BA, ATC, DipAD
Mr T J W Walsh, MA
Mrs M A Young, BA
Miss L E Bolton, BA

Theatre Director:
Miss J Sutcliffe, BA

PE and Games:
*Mr G D Thurman, BEd (*Games Master*)
Mr G J Muckalt, BA (*Head of PE, Director of Rugby*)
Miss J N Horn, BA (*Head of Girls' Games*)
Mr J J Owen, BEd

Houses and Housemasters/Housemistresses:
St Aidan's (*girls*): Dr E V Fogg, MA, PhD
St Bede's (*girls*): Mr B and Mrs V Anglim, BEng
St Margaret's (*girls*): Mrs G M O McGovern, MA
St Cuthbert's: Mr D Willis, MEd
St Dunstan's: Mr B T A Pennington, BSc
St Edward's and St Wilfrid's: Mr A P Smerdon, BSc
St Hugh's: Mr H C Codrington, BEd
St John's: Dr D Moses, MA, DPhil
St Oswald's: Mr P J McBeth, MusB
St Thomas's: Mr P M J Brennan, BSc, FRMetSoc

Counsellor: Mr J G J Allisstone, BA

Procurator: Rev W Peterburs, OSB, MA, PhD

Medical Officers:
Dr Kaye Mechie, MBChB
Dr G Black, MBChB, MRCGP, DRCOG

Headmaster's Secretary: Mrs L M Featherstone

Number in School. There are 600 students, of whom 500 are Boarders, including 180 girls, 63 are Day Boys and 37 are Day Girls.

Our aims are:
* to share with parents in the spiritual, moral and intellectual formation of their children, in a Christian community with which their families may be joined in friendship and prayer for the rest of their lives.
* to educate the young in the tradition and sacramental life of the Church and to encourage each towards a joyful, free and self-disciplined life of faith and virtue.
* to work for excellence in all our endeavours, academic, sporting and cultural. We ask students to give of their best. We ask much of the gifted and we encourage the weak. Each is taught to appreciate the value of learning and the pursuit of the truth.
* to help Ampleforth boys and girls grow up mature and honourable, inspired by high ideals and capable of leadership, so that they may serve others generously, be strong in friendship, and loving and loyal towards their families.
Organisation. St Martin's Ampleforth, an independent preparatory school at Gilling Castle, educates boys and girls from 3 to 13 years old. (*For further details, see entry in IAPS section.*)

The upper school has 7 houses for boys aged 13 to 18 and three houses for girls aged 13 to 18. Houses are kept small and are home to no more than 60 boarders and there are some day students in each.

Each house has its own separate accommodation. All students eat their lunch in separate house refectories. They eat breakfast and supper in a central cafeteria with the House staff, chaplains and tutors.

The work and games of the whole school are centrally organised. At least five tutors are allocated to each house to supervise students' work and provide the appropriate guidance at each stage in their school career. The Head of Careers provides information and assistance and can arrange expert advice for pupils, parents and tutors. Some of the non-teaching life of the school is organised around the houses. House competitions help to create a strong house loyalty. We have a central school chaplaincy that acts as a social meeting place for the middle school and a sixth form social centre, the Windmill, just off the campus.

There has been over £20m invested in the school in the last 10 years.

Curriculum. The first year (year 9) provides a broad basis from which to make informed GCSE choices. In the second and third years a core of English, Mathematics, Science and Christian Theology is studied to GCSE together with a balanced selection from a wide range of subjects. In the first year of the sixth form (year 12) up to 5 subjects may be studied to AS level. One of those subjects may be AS level Christian Theology but, if not, students follow a Chris-tian Theology short course. Normally three subjects will be taken on to A level in the second year (year 13). A comprehensive health education programme is provided in all years.

Games and Activities. There are opportunities to play a wide variety of representative sports at all levels with excellent indoor and outdoor facilities. Many activities and games take place during the week and weekends, including drama, debating, outdoor pursuits, creative arts and a wide variety of sports. These sports range from lacrosse to rugby. The school has its own outstanding 9-hole golf course and has recently completed a new all-weather hockey surface and new tennis courts. In addition, the college has its own all-weather athletics track.

Music, which is a strong academic subject, plays a major part in the extra-curricular life of the school. The Schola Cantorum, our liturgical choir, sing for Mass in the Abbey and perform sacred music in Britain and abroad. They have been responsible for the production of several commercial CDs in recent years. The Schola Puellarum, our girls choir, sings with the Schola Cantorum on alternate Sundays and has its own repertoire. It has undertaken tours both at home and abroad and has also released its own CD.

Further enquiries may be made directly to the Games Master on 01439 766729 or the Director of Music on 01439 766730.

Admission. Applications may be made through the Admissions Office. Registration Fee: £75.

Fees per term (2011-2012). Boarders: £9,472; Day Boys/Girls: £6,095.

The fees are inclusive, the only normal extras being for individual tuition in Music: £30 per lesson, £28 for a second instrument; TEAL £800 per term.

Entrance Scholarships. (*See Scholarship Entries section.*) Academic, Music and All-Rounder scholarships are awarded at 13+ and for entry to the Sixth Form.

Charitable status. St Laurence Educational Trust is a Registered Charity, number 1063808. Its aim is to advance Roman Catholic religion.

Ardingly College
A Woodard School

Haywards Heath, West Sussex RH17 6SQ
Tel: 01444 893000
Fax: 01444 893001
e-mail: head@ardingly.com
website: www.ardingly.com

Ardingly is a co-educational school in the Woodard Family founded to teach the Christian Faith.

Our aim is to enable all boys and girls to develop their love of learning, academic potential and individual talents, in a caring community which fosters sensitivity, confidence, a sense of service and enthusiasm for life.

Motto: '*Beati Mundo Corde*'.

School Council:
J Sloane, Esq, BSc (*Chairman*)
The Rt Revd Lindsay Urwin, OGS, MA (*Provost*)
The Revd C Bennett
D F Gibbs, Esq
A A Holmes, Esq, FCA
Mrs A A Ivanec, LLB Hons
D Johnson-Poensgen, Esq
The Earl of Limerick, MA
G Turner, Esq, BSc, FCIOB
P C Ward, Esq
S C Ward, Esq, FRICS

***Headmaster*: Peter Green**, MA

Deputy Headmaster: Richard Bool, BA

Chaplain: Father David Lawrence-March, BA Hons

Head of the Prep School: Chris Calvey, BEd

Bursar: Paddy Jackman

Medical Officer: Dr B Lambert

History and development of the College. Ardingly College, the third of Nathaniel Woodard's schools, was founded in Shoreham in 1858 and moved to its present beautiful site in Mid Sussex, about halfway between Gatwick and Brighton, in 1870. The College now consists of a Pre-Prep day School and a weekly boarding and day Prep School, for boys and girls between the ages of 2½ and 13, and a boarding and day Senior School for boys and girls aged between 13 and 18.

In the Prep School, which has been co-educational since 1986, there are 240 pupils, of whom 141 are boys and 99 are girls; 4 are boarders. There are 109 boys and girls in the Pre-Prep.

In the Senior School, which became fully co-educational in 1982, there are 485 pupils of whom 204 are in the Sixth Form. There are 304 boys and 181 girls, and 248 are boarders.

For further details about the Ardingly Prep School and the Ardingly Pre-Preparatory School, see entries in the IAPS section.

Academic. Ardingly has an extremely good academic record in both arts and science subjects achieved by boys and girls who come from a wide spectrum of ability. The A level and IB percentage pass rate has been 100% for the past 3 years. Every year about four to six Ardinians gain entry to Oxford or Cambridge and overall 99% of the Upper Sixth go on to Higher Education. At GCSE the A*–C pass rate is 100% and most candidates take 9 subjects or more.

Curriculum. *First year*: A broad course in which all pupils do virtually everything: second Modern Language (German or Spanish); Expressive Arts; Design Technology and Information Technology for all.

GCSE (2nd and 3rd years): All take English and English Literature, Maths, Sciences, at least one Modern Language, and the usual wide range of options.

Sixth Form Curriculum: Standard choices in a highly flexible block system at AS/A2 or in the International Baccalaureate Diploma Programme. ICT skills are developed through AS/A2 and IB courses and AS students follow the ECDL qualification. All Lower Sixth students follow a development course which covers life skills, careers and HE study skills.

All Lower Sixth pupils receive a refresher course in Information Technology.

Pastoral. There are 7 Middle School Houses, four for boys and three for girls which contain everyone from the first year to the Lower Sixth. In the Upper Sixth all boys and girls transfer to a separate, integrated co-educational House, "Woodard" (opened in 1988), in which they are able to concentrate more fully on their studies and can be given greater responsibility for themselves and be better prepared for life at University or in the outside world. Each House has its own Housemaster or Housemistress, Assistant and House Tutors. In addition every boy and girl will have a Tutor who has responsibility for the work, progress, choices and many other aspects of the pupil's life. Tutorials are regular, one-to-one and usually weekly. Tutors work closely with careers staff including a professional adviser who comes in one day a week.

In Year 9 pupils study and discuss life topics in small mixed groups as part of a specially designed course called 'Learning for Life' and within the Religious Studies course in other years.

There is an efficient Medical Centre in the centre of the school with a residential Sister in charge. The School Doctor takes three surgeries a week in the School and is always on call.

Two Boys' Boarding Houses were opened in September 2003. The Girls' Houses were refurbished in 2009. A new Multigym and Business Studies Dept opened in June 2010. Since September 2005 School on Saturdays has been discontinued.

Expressive Arts. *Music*: Choir, Chamber Choir, Schola Cantorum, Jazz Singers, Orchestras, Concert Band, Jazz Band, Chamber Music. Instrumental lessons taken by about half the boys and girls.

Art: Painting, drawing, printing, ceramics, sculpture, fashion & textiles, photography, etching.

Design Technology: Real design problems solved in a variety of materials and forms.

Drama: Many productions in the course of the year for all ages. Large flexible theatre and a small workshop theatre.

All four of these expressive arts are studied in modular form in the first year, are options for GCSE and A Level and offer scholarships for talented candidates, at both 13+ and for the Sixth Form.

Sport. Boys play Football, Hockey, Rugby 7s, Cricket, Tennis; Girls play Hockey, Netball, Tennis, Rounders. (Football and cricket are also available for girls).

Also (for both boys and girls) there is Squash, Cross Country, Swimming, Shooting, Golf, Volleyball, Horseriding, Clay Pigeon Shooting, Basketball, Badminton (new Sports Hall opened in 1999), Karate, Croquet, Sailing, etc. The indoor pool is open to both Prep and Senior Schools and pupils who cannot swim are taught to do so.

Activities. Combined Cadet Force (Army based), Outward Bound (compulsory modular programme in first year), Duke of Edinburgh's Award, Cooking, Sewing, Stagework, Modern Dance, Photography, Computers, Fencing, etc.

Admission to the Senior School normally takes place at 13+ or directly into the Sixth Form at 16+. Admission is also possible at 14+ but is not advisable at the beginning of the years in which GCSE or A Levels are taken unless there are very special reasons.

At 13+ entry is by written assessments in English, Mathematics and Verbal Reasoning and satisfactory results at Common Entrance. We also require a report and reference from the pupil's previous school. The headmaster likes to interview prospective pupils if practicable. The selection of candidates for direct entry to the Sixth Form takes place in November of the year prior to entry. All candidates are interviewed and take an English paper and a Maths paper. A report from their Head is also required. Places will then be offered subject to the candidate gaining a minimum of 6 grade Bs or above at GCSE. Modifications of these procedures and of the timing for individuals at any stage are almost always possible.

The Prep School has entry at 7+ and 11+ or at any other time between the ages of 7 and 11. Transfer into the Senior School is by entrance assessments and Common Entrance.

Scholarships. A number of Scholarships are offered for annual competition at 13+ and 16+. They include Academic, Art, DT, Drama, Music and Sports Awards. Ashdown Awards for all-rounders are offered for those entering at 13+. The Prep School offers Academic, Art, Music and Sports Awards at 11+ with Academic Awards at 7+ and are tenable for the Prep School years only. Along with other HMC schools, the maximum value of a scholarship is 40% of the basic fees pa but all may be supplemented by a means-tested bursary if need can be shown.

A limited number of bursaries (value up to 50% of basic fees pa) are available for the children of the Clergy.

Please address all enquiries about admissions, scholarships and bursaries to the Registrar (Tel: 01444 893000; fax: 01444 893001; e-mail: registrar@ardingly.com).

Term of Entry. Main 13+ and Sixth Form intake in September. Intake at other ages and other times on an individual basis.

Registration. The School Prospectus may be obtained from the Registrar, and is sent whenever an enquiry about a vacancy is received. Registration (where a non-returnable fee of £100 is charged) can be made at any age subject to the availability of places. No separate registration is required for children transferring from the Prep to the Senior School.

Fees per term (2011-2012). Senior School: Boarding £8,710–£9,105, Day Pupils £6,530–£6,880. Casual Boarding: £46 per night. Prep School: Weekly Boarding (in addition to Day Fees) £430–£1,290 (1–5 nights); Day Pupils £3,430–£4,335; Casual Boarding £40 per night. Pre-Prep: £1,435–£2,395.

Fees are inclusive. There is a surcharge of £180 per term for those entering at the Sixth Form stage.

Further Particulars. For further information, application should be made to the Registrar.

Charitable status. Ardingly College Limited is a Registered Charity, number 1076456. It exists to provide high quality education for boys and girls aged 2½ to 18.

Arnold School
UCST

Lytham Road, Blackpool, Lancashire FY4 1JG
Tel: 01253 346391 Senior & Junior School
Fax: 01253 336250 Senior School
            01253 336251 Junior School
e-mail: Headmaster.Arnold@church-schools.com
            info@church-schools.com
            Katy.Wright@church-schools.com
website: www.arnoldschool.com

The foundation dates from 1896 when Frank Truswell Pennington opened a school with eight pupils in his rooms in Bright Street, South Shore, Blackpool. In 1903 he moved the school to the present site in Lytham Road and called it Arnold House after a school which had previously occupied the building.

In 1937 the School was reconstituted and in 1938 the School – now called Arnold School – was placed on the Direct Grant list where it continued to flourish before reverting to independent status in 1976. Arnold has been fully co-educational since September 1977 and is now a 3-form entry day school for 517 boys and girls (11–18 years) with a Junior School for 197 boys and girls (2–11 years).

The Governors are committed to an on-going capital development programme. The campus includes a Sports Complex, Performing Arts Studio, Languages Centre, Music Centre, Art and Design Centre, ICT suites, a large extension to the Junior School and an all-weather playing surface. All classrooms are networked to a centrally managed ICT facility and are equipped with the latest Promethean interactive whiteboards and associated technology.

In 2008 the school joined the United Church Schools Trust.

Motto: '*Honor Virtutis Praemium*'.

Local Governing Body:
Chairman: J M Wooding, OBE, BSc, CEng, FRAeS
Vice Chairman: ¶J C Armfield, CBE, DL

D Aird LLB
A E D Baines, BA, RIBA
¶M S Brennand
M C Brook, BA, FCA
Mrs S C Carr, OBE
Mrs G M Connolly, BSc, MA
W T Gillen, MA
P Maguire, ACA
¶P M Owen, ACIB

Mrs R Pigott, OBE, LLB
¶J R Taylor, LLB

Bursar and Clerk to the Council: Commander P McCarthy, RN

¶ *Old Arnoldian*
* *Head of Department*
† *Head of House*

Tutorial Staff:

Headmaster: J Keefe, BA

Deputy Head & Director of Studies: C W Jenkinson, MA
Senior Teacher (Higher Education, Careers & Administration): Mrs M A Thornton, BSc
Senior Teacher – Pastoral & Head of Sixth Form: A J McKeown, BSc
Senior Teacher – Pastoral & Head of Middle School: P E Hayden, BA
Head of Lower School: Mrs J A Nicholls, CertEd

Heads of House:
School: D G J Culpan, BSc
Howarth: G R McIntyre, BA
Pennington: L J Sobey, BSc
Liston: (*to be appointed*)

Archivist: K S Shenton
Admissions Secretary: Mrs J Follows

Biology:
*M S Downey, BSc (*Head of Science*)
Mrs J J Arnold, BSc
A J McKeown, BSc
Miss N Strino, BSc
A J Treharne, BSc, PhD, CBiol, MIBiol (*Examinations Officer*)

Business Studies & Economics:
*Mrs S P Donald, BSc
†G R McIntyre, BA
J E Keefe, BA

Chemistry:
*Mrs M A Thornton, BSc
P J Collinson, BSc
M B Kirkham, BSc, CChem, MRSC

Classics:
*I J Morton, MA

Art & Design:
*Mrs H R Caunce, BA
Miss C S Norris, BA

Drama and Theatre Studies:
Miss F E Horrocks, BA
Miss C S Norris, BA

English:
*J L Bridges, BA
D E Smyth, BEd, MA, MA Lit
P E Hayden, BA
J R Gardner, BA

Geography:
*N O'Loughlin, BSc
Miss J A Lamarra, BA
I R Winterflood, BSc

History:
*J R Davey, BA
R E Golding, MA, BA

†G R McIntyre, BA
Mrs J A Nicholls, CertEd

ICT:
*†D G J Culpan, BSc
D Hewitt, BA

Library:
Mrs J E Darkins, BSc

Mathematics:
D R Bruce, BSc
*†D G J Culpan, BSc
J M Rimmer, BSc
†L J Sobey, BSc
Mrs P J Taylor, BSc

Modern Languages:
*Mrs F M M Burnett, BA
C W Jenkinson, MA
Mrs D A Jenkinson, BA
Mrs D J Pailing, BA
*Miss R C Porritt BA

Music:
*D J Chandler, BMus
D Hewitt, BA

Physics:
Miss R Matheson, BSc
K D Bleakley, BSc

Physical Education:
*R L Jones, BEd
Miss A DeMiranda, BEd
M L Evans, BSc
Mrs J M Malin, BEd
Ms K E Preston, RAD, BTDA
Miss G Raby, CertEd
Mrs M Whorlton-Jones, BEd

Psychology:
*Miss L J Hanson, MA

Religious Education:
*M A Harding, BEd
Mrs J A Nicholls, CertEd

Instrumental Staff:
Mrs K Dangerfield
M Giudici
A Harrison
C Hodder
Miss R Holt
Mrs M Johnstone
T Reaney
Mrs A Rosser
D Usher

Careers and Higher
Education:
*Mrs M A Thornton, BSc

P E Hayden, BA
A J McKeown, BSc
†L Sobey, BSc

Learning Support:
*Mrs E J Luke, BEd

Combined Cadet Force:
CO: Maj A Treharne
SSI: WO1 T F Beck, MISM
Sub Lt S Downey
Lt W Chadwick
2nd Lt P Collinson
2nd Lt D Smyth

Junior School (including Infants and Kindergarten)

Head of Junior School: Miss K R Wright, BA
Head of Foundation Stage: Miss J Allen, BA
Head of Key Stage 1: Mrs D V Smith, BEd
Head of Key Stage 2: Mrs S E Knight, BA
Mrs A J Briggs, BSc
Mrs L Buck, BSc
Mrs L Cole, BEd
Mrs L C Fielder, BEd
Mrs G E Foster, BEd
Mrs M A Hecht, CertEd, DipSpLD
A R Hodgkinson, BSc
Mrs J Woodhead, CertEd
Teaching Assistant: Mrs M L Brooker, TA Dip
Teaching Assistant: Mrs H K Hine, BA
Teaching Assistant: Mrs L G Parkinson, NVQ3
Teaching Assistant: Mrs Y S Walsh, HLTA
Kindergarten Manager: Mrs K Hartley, NNEB
Kindergarten Supervisor: Miss N Metcalfe, BTEC
Senior Nursery Nurse: Mrs T Dagger, NVQ3
Senior Nursery Nurse: Miss J M Hamer, NVQ4
Senior Nursery Nurse: Mrs S McGivern, NVQ3
Senior Nursery Nurse: Miss C E Parkin, NVQ3
Senior Nursery Nurse: Miss R Starritt, NVQ2

Site and Buildings. The School lies on the south side of Blackpool, half a mile from the sea. The facilities include modern well-equipped laboratories, three ICT Suites, a modern Music facility, a Sixth Form Centre and the Memorial Hall. Recent additions include a Sports Complex, Performing Arts Studio and Languages Centre, Art & Design Centre, The Lawrence House Music Centre and an all-weather pitch, which is adjacent to our playing fields. The School also owns an Outdoor Pursuits Centre at Glenridding in Cumbria. An ambitious building programme is planned for the near future.

The Junior School (2–11 years) is situated on the same site as the Senior School and is therefore able to benefit from its facilities.

Curriculum. The School aims to give its boys and girls a broad education, and in particular to prepare them for public examinations and for entry to Universities (including Oxford and Cambridge) and other places of Higher Education. There are about 150 students in the Sixth Form, the vast majority of whom proceed to degree courses.

A period of work experience is arranged for all Year 11 pupils immediately after the GCSE examinations. The School has excellent links with Industry. Careers education is provided from Year 9 onwards.

Clubs and Activities. There is a very wide range of co-curricular activities: Academic Society, Art, Basketball, Community Service, Chess, Choir, Dance, Drama, Debating, Fencing, Greek, Orchestra, Photography, Swing Band, Outdoor Pursuits, Young Enterprise and the Duke of Edinburgh's Award Scheme.

Games. Organised Games and Physical Education periods play an important part in School life. Playing fields of 13 acres adjoin the School for Rugby Football and Hockey in the Winter and Spring terms and for Cricket, Tennis and Athletics in the Summer. Other Sports include Football, Basketball, Badminton, Netball and Fencing. There are dance classes for the girls.

Combined Cadet Force. Membership is open to all pupils from Year 9, and pupils may join the RAF, Naval or Army Section. The Contingent has a successful record and emphasis is placed upon Adventure Training.

Junior School. The Junior School pupils occupy buildings that have been built since 1970. Admission is at 2+, 4+ or 7+. Entry at other ages depends upon vacancies occurring. Pupils transfer to the Senior School at 11 years conditional upon maintaining suitable progress in Key Stage Two. The Junior School has its own separate buildings (including an ICT Centre) and a distinct corporate life, though it is situated alongside the Senior School whose facilities it also uses. The games played are Association Football, Rugby, Hockey, Netball and Cricket. Athletics and Swimming competitions are held annually. Music is encouraged and there is a flourishing Choir. There is a full range of co-curricular activities, including Chess, Choir, Dancing, Games, Gardening, Gymnastics, Horse-Riding, ICT, Orchestra, Science, Speech & Drama and Yoga. Recent developments have included the expansion of the Kindergarten and the addition of new changing rooms, Staff Common Room, classrooms, Art and Science Room and Resource Room.

Admission. Prospectus and Admissions forms can be obtained from the Admissions Secretary.

All entries to the Senior School are made through the Headmaster. Pupils are admitted to the Senior School on the basis of the School's own examinations in English, Mathematics and Non-Verbal Reasoning. The main intake to the Senior School is at 11, though entry at other times is possible depending on availability of places.

For entry at Sixth Form level, respectable GCSE grades in at least five subjects are normally expected in addition to a satisfactory report from the pupil's current Head.

Entry into the Junior School (2–11 years) is normally at the ages of 2, 4 and 7. Enquiries should be made to the Admissions Secretary.

Fees per term (2011-2012). Tuition (including books and stationery): Seniors £3,020 (Lunch £212); Juniors £2,311 (Lunch £199); Infants £2,311 (Lunch £192); Kindergarten (including lunch): Full Week £189 per week, Full Day £43 per day, Half Day £22 per half day, Short half day (lunch not included) £16.24 per session. Extras are minimal.

Entrance Scholarships. (*See Scholarship Entries section*.) Several scholarships (including those for Music, Art & Design, and Sport) are available for entry at 11+. Music, Sport, Art & Design and Drama scholarships are available in the Sixth Form.

Registration. Pupils may be registered at any time although this should be as early as possible if entry is requested at ages other than 2, 4, 7 or 11 years. Candidates will be called for examination in the year of entry, although those who live at a distance may have the papers sent to their schools.

Charitable status. The United Church Schools Trust (of which Arnold School is a member) is a Registered Charity, number 1016538. Its aims and objectives are to provide pupils with a sound education based on, and inspired by, Christian principles.

Ashford School
UCST

East Hill, Ashford, Kent TN24 8PB
Tel: 01233 625171
Fax: 01233 647185
e-mail: registrar@ashfordschool.co.uk
website: www.ashfordschool.co.uk

Chairman of School Council: Mr P Massey, MA
Vice-Chairman: Mr R I Henderson, JP, LLB

Council Members:
Mr R Coombe
Mrs A Cottrell, JP
Mr P Oldroyd
Mr W Peppitt, MRICS
Mr A J Rawlins
Mrs E Rose, MSc
Mrs L van der Bijl
Mrs J M Webb, BA

Head: **Mr Michael Buchanan**, BSc London

Head of the Prep School: Mr R Yeates, BA Exeter
Deputy Head, Director of the Senior School: Mrs Y
  Howard, BA Durham
School Business Manager: Mr I Williams, BEng
  Shrivenham

Senior School:
Deputy Head, Director of Teaching and Learning: Mrs C
  Allum, BA Durham, MPhil
Director of Studies: Miss L Allen, BA London
Director of Upper School: Mr T Wilding, BA Exeter
Director of Sixth Form: Miss H Semple, MA Edinburgh
Director of Co-curriculum and Community Relations: Mrs
  N Timms, BEng Loughborough

Prep School:
Deputy Head: Mrs P Willetts, BPrimEd

Ashford School was founded in 1898 as an independent, day and boarding school and provides education for boys and girls from 3 months to 18 years. There are over 420 students in the Senior School and over 350 in the Prep School (age 3–11). There are around 130 boarders in the school cared for by resident teachers and support staff in extensive accommodation that includes en-suite rooms for many. Forty nationalities are represented and specialist English tuition is provided for those who require it. There are no lessons on Saturdays.

Ashford School is a member of a group of independent schools run by the United Church Schools Trust which, together with its subsidiary charity the United Learning Trust, provides a first-class education for more than 25,000 pupils. The Trust aims to be at the forefront of educational development, bringing the very best resources, both human and physical, to the children in its schools.

The Senior School occupies a 25-acre site in a prominent position close to the centre of Ashford and near to the International Station. A green and secure haven in a busy and growing town, Ashford is 37 minutes from London by rail and also benefits from rapid access to Paris, Lyon, Brussels, Amsterdam, Cologne and Frankfurt on the Eurostar. With easy access to the M20 motorway and local train services, the central location and easy accessibility provides an ideally located school whether you live in the UK or anywhere across the globe.

With playing fields on site, two gyms, indoor swimming pool, floodlit Astroturf, tennis and netball courts, boarding houses and dining hall, the School enjoys all the specialist teaching facilities you would expect of an independent school and has embarked on a programme to refurbish and extend the facilities. The Pre-Nursery, Bridge House, is located on the Senior School site and the Prep School is located in the nearby picturesque village of Great Chart and has recently undergone major redevelopment to double its size and further improve facilities and opportunities for pupils at the school.

Almost half of the students entering the Senior School at 11+ join direct from the Prep School and the remainder from other primary and prep schools. There are then normally three classes per year through to GCSE with additional students joining other years and the Sixth Form. All Sixth Form students go on to take degree courses at leading universities in the UK and abroad. In 2010, around 75% of students leaving Year 13 achieved places at their first-choice university, with 24% gaining a place at one of the UK's top 10 universities.

The Senior School curriculum is broad and provides many opportunities in the classroom and in activities. The school has interactive whiteboards in every teaching room and modern facilities throughout. Pupils follow a broad curriculum to keep their options open and in addition to the core subjects of English, maths, the sciences and a language they may study additional languages, history, geography, classical civilisation, Latin, religious studies, information technology, art and textiles, music, drama and physical education. Throughout the Senior School, subjects are set by ability where possible and there is a strong pastoral system based around six Houses.

External Examinations. Most pupils take 9/10 subjects at GCSE. Many A Level combinations are available to the Sixth Form, all of whom go on to Higher Education before entering a varied range of careers including music, design, advertising, banking, engineering, journalism, law, management, the media, medicine and veterinary science. There is a consistently high external examination success rate and pupils are prepared for Oxbridge in all subjects.

Entry requirements. School report, tests and interview for the Sixth Form, supporting six or more A–C grades at GCSE. Written tests at Years 7 and 9. Places are generally available throughout the year in all other year groups.

Scholarships. (*See Scholarship Entries section.*)

Fees per term (2011-2012). Senior: £4,856 (day), £7,785 (weekly boarding), £9,075–£9,401 (full boarding); Prep: £3,644; Pre-Prep: £2,138–£2,458; Nursery: £428 (one full day per week), £2,138 (full-time).

Charitable status. Ashford School is a member of The United Church Schools Trust, which is a Registered Charity, number 1016538. Founded in 1883, UCST has a long and distinguished tradition in the provision of independent education and boarding and now operates 11 fee-paying independent schools across the UK with a subsidiary charity, ULT, operating 20 academies.

Ashville College

Green Lane, Harrogate, North Yorkshire HG2 9JP
Tel: 01423 566358
Fax: 01423 505142
e-mail: ashville@ashville.co.uk
website: www.ashville.co.uk

Ashville was founded in 1877 by the United Methodist Free Church, but has been strengthened by taking under its wing at different times two older non-conformist schools: Elmfield College, founded by the Primitive Methodists in 1864, which amalgamated with Ashville in 1932; and New College, which began in 1850 with strong Baptist connections and merged with Ashville in 1930.

Although a Methodist foundation a large proportion of its pupils come from non-Methodist homes, and the school welcomes pupils from overseas. Until 1976 Ashville was a Direct Grant school. When the Government decided to bring Direct Grant to an end, it was unanimously resolved that Ashville should revert to fully Independent status. In 1982 the school became co-educational.

Ashville College offers fully-integrated co-educational boarding and day opportunities for girls and boys from the age of 4 years to 18 years and was voted as one of the top 100 schools in the UK last year. In 2009 the GCSE results in government tables were also in the top 100.

Motto: '*Esse quam videri*'

Visitor: The President of the Methodist Conference

Governing Body:
Chairman: Mr P Holt
Deputy Chairman: Mr M Verity

Headmaster: Mr D M Lauder, MA Aberdeen

Deputy Heads:
Mr A T Johnson, BA Dunelm (*Head of Classics*)
Mrs E Fisher, BSc Strathclyde

Chaplain: Revd David Barker, BA Dunelm, BD, MPhil Manchester

Director of Studies: Mr G R Johnson, BSc Manchester

Year Heads:
Year 7: Mrs M Burrell, BA Hull
Year 8: Miss J Ellis, BA Brighton
Year 9: Mr D Grainger, BSc Edinburgh
Year 10: Ms E Ekstein, BA Leeds, MA Leeds
Year 11: Mr C Pearce, BEd Leeds
Head of Sixth Form: Mrs V Rumsey, BA East Anglia
Assistant Head of Sixth Form: Mrs K Rutter, BEd Leeds

Senior Housemaster: Mr N P Cornforth, BSc Wales

Heads of Departments:
Science: Mr M Finch, BSc Surrey
Physics: Mr C Davies, BSc Sussex
Chemistry: Mr D J Normanshire, BSc Bangor
Biology: Mr P D Forster, BSc Salford
Classics: Mr A T Johnson, BA Dunelm
Modern Languages: Mr I W Kendrick, MA Leeds, BA
French: Mrs J M Wilcocks, MA Leicester, BA London
German: Mr I A Popley, BSc Aston
Drama: Mrs J Normanshire, BA Wales
Director of Music: Mr J Dunford, GTC Hons, LTCL, ARCO, ALCM, AMusTCL
Head of Instrumental Studies: Mr R Simpson, BA Salford
English: Mr G Kurczij, BA, MA Leeds
Mathematics: Dr J Dekanski, BSc, PhD Leeds
Art: Mr S Brook, BA Canterbury
CDT: Mr C Pearce, BEd Leeds
Geography: Mrs V A Simpson, BSc Salford
History: Mr A J Barker, MA St Andrews
Director of Sport: Mr I Gould, BA Leeds
PE Academic: Mr J Goldthorp, BSc Loughborough
Home Economics: Mrs L Hayes, CertEd
EFL: Mr P Gilmore, MA York, BSc
Economics: Mr N P Cornforth, BSc Wales
Business Studies: Mrs C Guy, BA John Moores
AVCE: Mrs C Guy, BA John Moores
Religious Studies: Ms C Walker
ICT: Mr D Taylor, BSc Sheffield, MSc Manchester
Learning Support: Mrs M G Levey, BA Leeds, BDA Di

Junior School:
Head: Mr J D Dolman, BSc Swansea, PGCE Cantab
Deputy Head: Mr J Thompson, BEd Dunelm
Head of Junior School Music: Miss H J Dexter, BMus London, LGSM

Pre-Prep:
Head: Mrs C Berrie, BEd Hull
Deputy Head: Mrs J Hopkins, BA Liverpool

Bursar: Mrs E Sanderson, BA, MA, ACA

Registrar & Headmaster's PA: Mrs C Butcher

Medical Officer: Ms J Tate, MS

Numbers. There are over 500 boys and girls in the Senior School, 160 in the Junior School (aged 7–11), and approximately 100 in the Pre-Prep.

Site and Buildings. The Ashville estate consists of 60 acres of land on the south side of Harrogate.

The original house has been considerably extended to provide all the administrative accommodation and also houses the library and several of the arts faculties.

A programme of continuous building and improvement has taken place over the last 20 years. A successful appeal in 1989 provided a new Music and Drama Centre. In 1994 a magnificent Sixth Form Centre was opened, and at the same time, the Design Technology workshop was extended, a pottery room was created for the Art Department and an additional Biology Laboratory was built. A Pre-Prep was opened in 1995, and moved into its own purpose-built accommodation in September 2000. Twenty acres of land were purchased for hockey and rugby pitches in 1997. A four million pound refurbishment programme started in 2007 which included work on new classrooms for maths, geography, history and English as a foreign language. In 2009 the newly refurbished library and IT suite were opened and refurbishment of the boarding houses continues.

Curriculum. The Pre-Prep and Junior Schools aim to give a firm grounding in National Curriculum core and foundation subjects. French is introduced at 7+. All pupils are prepared for the General Certificate of Secondary Education at 16, and the Advanced Level GCE examinations two years later. From the age of 11 pupils spend five years on the GCSE course, which includes the study of English Language and Literature, History, Geography, Music, Art, Religious Education, French, German, Spanish, Latin, Mathematics, Physics, Chemistry, Biology, Design Technology, Home Economics, Business Studies, and Physical Education. At Advanced Level Economics, ICT, History of Art, English Language and Physical Education are also available. Guidance is given by the Careers Staff in the choice of Sixth Form studies and decisions are made after consultation with parents. Most pupils who complete the Advanced Level course go on to study at university or other institution of higher education. In addition to their specialist subjects all pupils continue their general education and most offer General Studies as a subject at GCE A Level.

Physical Education. Physical Education is a part of the curriculum for all pupils, and there are games afternoons for all during the week.

The main school games are Rugby and Cricket for the boys, Netball and Rounders for the girls but there are school fixtures also in Hockey, Cross-Country, Swimming, Athletics, Lawn Tennis, Squash and Badminton. Many students represent the school at County level.

Careers. Careers guidance is regarded as a very important part of the service provided by the school. Ashville is in membership of the Independent Schools Careers Organisation, and parents are encouraged to share with the careers staff the responsibility for giving appropriate guidance at the Fifth and Sixth Form stage. Pupils are helped in their choice of university and degree course, and arrangements are made for them to visit universities and go on careers courses.

Religious Life. All pupils attend Morning Prayers every weekday, and there is a school service for boarders on Sunday evening. Confirmation classes are held in the Spring Term each year, and boys and girls are prepared for Joint Confirmation in the Church of England and the Methodist Church. The School Chaplain is always glad to meet parents by appointment.

Leisure Activities. There are school societies which cater for a wide range of interests, and pupils are guided in the use of their free time in the early years. The school has no cadet corps, but boys and girls are enabled to take part in the Duke of Edinburgh's Award scheme. Drama has a strong following and the school play is a highlight of the year's programme.

Music is well provided for, and pupils are encouraged to take up the study of piano, organ or an orchestral instrument. The School Choir has acquired a high reputation by its contributions at the Harrogate and Wharfedale Festivals.

Admission. The school is prepared to admit pupils at any convenient time. Entry to the Pre-Prep is by means of interview. Entry to the Junior School is by means of an interview and test papers in English and Arithmetic.

Candidates for entry at the age of 11 are required to take the Ashville Entrance Examination in the January preceding the September of entry. The examination consists of papers in English, Mathematics and Reasoning.

Candidates at Preparatory Schools seeking entry at the age of 13 are required to sit a similar examination.

Candidates for entry at other ages and into the Sixth Form are considered on the evidence of a headmaster's report and interview.

Registration forms and prospectus are obtainable from the Registrar. There is a registration fee of £50.

Fees per term (2011-2012). Tuition: Senior School £3,760–£3,790, Junior School £2,665–£3,225, Pre-Prep £2,220. Boarding (in addition to tuition fees): Full £2,130–£3,630, Weekly £1,920–£2,970.

Scholarships and Bursaries. Discretionary Awards: Scholarships are awarded at the discretion of the Headmaster for excellence in academic performance or other disciplines, for example music. Scholarships are awarded to pupils for specific stages of their education at Ashville.

Financial Assistance: Bursaries are available at the discretion of the school and are means tested.

Forces Boarding Bursary: If a parent is serving in the armed forces and their children are boarding at Ashville, the bursary is 20% of tuition and boarding fees for junior school pupils and 10% for senior pupils.

Charitable status. Ashville College is a Registered Charity, number 529577, administered by Ashville College Trustee Ltd, company number 4552232. It aims to provide a boarding and day education for boys and girls.

Bablake School

Coundon Road, Coventry CV1 4AU
Tel: 024 7627 1200
Fax: 024 7627 1290
e-mail: info@bablake.coventry.sch.uk
website: www.bablake.com

Bablake School was originally part of the College of the same name founded by Queen Isabella in 1344. After the dissolution of the monasteries it was refounded in 1560 by the city; it is chiefly associated with the name of Thomas Wheatley, whose indentures of 1563 put its finances on a firm foundation.

The Governing Body is Coventry School Foundation, on which are represented Sir Thomas White's Charity, the Coventry Church Charities, Coventry General Charities, Oxford and Warwick Universities and the University of Coventry. There are also several co-opted governors.

Chairman of Governors: Mr B Connor

Headmaster: Mr J W Watson, MA

Deputy Heads:
Mrs G F Thomas, BA
Mr C R Seeley, BA, MPhil

Assistant staff:
* Head of Department

Mrs L J Alderson, LLB (*Head of Fifth Year*)
Mrs L B Alexander, BSc
Dr P B M Archer, PhD
Mr L Atwal, BSc
Mrs K Barnacle, BSc (*Psychology*)
Mrs H M Billings, MA (*German*)
Miss R M Blattner, BSc

Mrs D R Booth, BSc
Mr J M Bunce, MA
Mr R L Burdett, BSc (*Boys' Sport*)
Mr J G Burns, MA (*Assistant Head*)
Mrs A S Cassell, BA
Miss L R T Cheffings, MA
Mr A D Chowne, BSc
Mr P Cleaver, MA (*Art*)
Mr S Cooper, GLCM
Mr T Crompton, GBSM, ABSM (*Director of Music*)
Mrs C B Davey, BSc (*Home Economics*)
Mr J M Drury, BSc
Mr M Duerdin, BSc (*Physics*)
Miss K L Dzikowska
Mr S P Enstone, BSc
Ms K G Ewart, MA
Mrs M C Field, L-ès-L
Dr S E Foster, DPhil
Mrs L A French, BSc
Mrs C Friebe, CertEd (*Learning Support*)
Mr J M Grantham, BA
Mrs N D Green, BSc
Mr A M Hall, BSc (*Biology*)
Mrs S V Harris, BSc (*Director of Marketing & Admissions*)
Mrs A S Heath, BEd
Mrs S E Hill, BA
Mr J C Hobday, BSc
Mr A M Hopkins, BA (*Director of Studies*)
Mr T Hyde, BSc (*Head of Lower School*)
Mrs L J Jackson, CertEd
Mr S W Jackson, BSc (*Geography*)
Mrs A J Jones, BSc (*Head of Shells; First Year*)
Mr I S Kalsi, MA
Dr P J Knight, PhD (*Chemistry*)
Miss A H Learmont, MA, VetMB
Miss J E Kukucska, BA
Mrs P J Marchant, BEd
Mr M J Masters, BSc
Mr C Mellers, CertEd (*Religious Studies*)
Mr S Memon, BSc
Mr D C Menashe, BA (*Classics*)
Mrs C Mills, CertEd
Mr C W Mohamed, BSc
Mrs M O'Neill, MA (*Spanish*)
Mr P Nicholson, BEd
Miss K L Ormsby
Mr G L Park, BA (*English*)
Mr J R H Pease, BA
Mr A C Phillips, BSc
Mr D F Prescott, BA (*Director of Drama*)
Mrs M R Prowse, BSc
Mrs L J Reddish, BA
Mrs C A Rees, BA
Mr D M Rhodes, BSc
Miss E L Sara, BSc
Mrs C L Scott, BEd
Mrs C L Scott-Burt, DipTCL
Mr R G Sewell, BA (*Economics & Business Studies*)
Miss J L Simmons, MSc
Mrs H Skilton, MA (*History*)
Mrs S M Smith, BEd (*Head of Fourth Year*)
Mrs D A Thomas, BEd (*IT Manager*)
Mrs S L Thompson, BSc
Mrs G A Timothy, BA (*French*)
Mr S C R Timothy, MSc (*ICT*)
Mrs A J Tumber, BA (*Head of Sixth Form*)
Mr K J Tyas, BEd (*Mathematics*)
Mrs S L Webley, BSc
Mr C R West, BEd (*Design Technology*)
Mr S E Williams, BEng
Mr B G Wilson, BEd
Miss S L Wilson, BA (*Girls' Sport*)
Mr M G A Woodward, BA (*Careers*)

Mrs L A Yates, MPhil
Miss R F Young, BSc

Junior School

Headmaster: Mr N A Price, BA

Deputy Head: Mr A Bogyor, CertEd

Assistant staff:
Mr E Benfield, BSc
Miss G Davies, BA
Mrs K Francis, BEd
Mrs T Horton, BEd
Mrs J Legate, BSc
Miss K Love, BSc
Mrs M Mason, BEd
Mr S Norman, BEd
Mrs K Price, BA
Mrs A Reed, CertEd
Miss S Tatum, BA, QTS
Mrs A Thomas, BSc

Headmaster's Personal Assistant: Mrs R Mohomed

Number in School. There are about 850 Day Pupils (including 410 girls) and 190 in the Junior School. There is also a Pre-Preparatory school for 100 children aged 3 to 7 on a separate site.

Buildings. In the Home Field of 11 acres stand the main buildings which have been considerably extended to include a Sports Centre, heated indoor swimming pool and a purpose-built Modern Languages block. A purpose-built English, Music and Drama block was completed in July 2000. In 1993 Bablake Junior School was opened on the Home Field site for pupils aged 7–11. The school has its own nationally recognised weather station. At Hollyfast Road there are 27 acres of playing fields, a large pavilion and two all-weather hockey pitches. The school has a study centre in Fougères in the Normandy region of France and each pupil spends one week there during Year 8.

Curriculum. The Junior School is for children aged 7 to 11. There is a broad and balanced curriculum which encourages excellence and individual achievement. (*For further details, see Bablake Junior School entry in IAPS section.*)

Pupils take and must pass the Governors' Examination for entry to the Senior School. The Senior School provides courses leading to the GCSE examinations and GCE A Levels. Subjects available include: English, Mathematics, History, Geography, French, German, Spanish, Religious Studies, Latin, Classical Civilisation, Physics, Chemistry, Biology, Music, Art, Home Economics, Design and Technology, Information Technology and Textiles. Design Technology and Home Economics courses are followed by both boys and girls. The separate sciences or Science and Additional Science are taught up to GCSE. Most pupils study 10 subjects at GCSE, the majority progressing into the Sixth Form where 4 subjects and sometimes 5 are taken at AS Level. At A2 Level all students take a minimum of three subjects. Most of the subjects named are available up to AS Level and A2 Level. In addition several new subjects are available, including Business Studies, Economics, Geosciences, Psychology, Sports Studies and Theatre Studies. There is a wide range of Enrichment Studies options including Art, Astronomy, Chinese, Computing, Cookery, Design, Drama, Music, Photography and many others. Some pupils take the Extended Project Qualification. All pupils follow a structured programme of PE and Games.

Games and Activities. Rugby, Hockey, Netball, Basketball, Cross-Country Running, Athletics, Rounders, Tennis, Cricket, Soccer, Squash and Swimming. The school has an extensive artificial turf games area, used mainly for hockey, but providing in the summer an additional 24 tennis courts. A wide range of extra-curricular activities is offered, and there are approximately 50 societies and clubs. Drama and Music are strong features. All pupils are involved in the charity work of the school and there is a large Community Service programme for the Senior pupils in the Fifth and Sixth Forms.

Scholarships. The Governors award annually a number (not fixed) of Entrance bursaries each year. These are dependent on academic ability and on parental means. Academic, Art and Music scholarships are also available.

Academic, Sports and Music scholarships are available in the Sixth Form.

Fees per term (2011-2012). Senior School £3,056; Junior School £2,313.

Admission. Entry is via the School's own Entrance Examination held annually in January for entrance the following September. The normal age of entry is 11 but there are smaller intakes at 12 and 13. Entry to the Sixth Form is based on gaining at least 5 GCSE passes at Grade B or above and an interview with the Headmaster and Head of Sixth Form. Enquiries about admissions should be addressed to the Admissions Officer, Mrs L Baines.

Charitable status. Coventry School Foundation is a Registered Charity, number 528961. It exists to provide quality education for boys and girls.

Bancroft's School

Woodford Green, Essex IG8 0RF
Tel: 020 8505 4821
Fax: 020 8559 0032
e-mail: head@bancrofts.org
website: www.bancrofts.org

By the Will of Francis Bancroft (1727) all his personal estate was bequeathed on trust to the Worshipful Company of Drapers of the City of London to build and endow almshouses for 24 old men, with a chapel and schoolroom for 100 poor boys and 2 dwelling-houses for masters. The Foundation was originally situated at Mile End, but by a scheme established by the Charity Commissioners in 1884 the almshouses were abolished and the School transferred to Woodford Green, Essex. In 1976 the School reverted to independence, and became a fully co-educational day school, with a Preparatory School being added in 1990.

Motto: '*Unto God only be honour and glory*'

The Worshipful Company of Drapers

President: The Master of the Drapers' Company

Trustees and Governors:

Appointed by the Drapers' Company:
S P Foakes, TD, DL, FCIB (*Chairman*)
Mrs C G Bonnor-Moris
C S Tallents, BA, FCA
Dr C Bowe

Appointed by the London Borough of Redbridge:
R I Barden
M J Stark

Appointed by the Essex CC:
R Gooding

Co-opted:
Mrs R J Abbott
R J Priestley, BA
M B Jones
Dr A V Philp
Mrs A Papathomas
Mrs S Siddiqui
Dr P D Southern, MA, PhD

Head: Mrs M E Ireland, BSc, DipEd, CBiol, MBS

Deputy Head: M Mikdadi, MSc

Assistant Heads:
M Dixon, BSc
Mrs A H Taylor, BA
C A F Butler, BSc

Headmaster, Preparatory School: C M Curl, MA, BEd

Assistant Staff:
† *Housemaster/mistress*

†T R C Jones, MA	J Prole, BSc
C H Pearson, BA	Mrs E Tynan, MEng
N R Poore, BSc, MPhil	Mrs V Burn, BA
R F Tatam, MA	Mrs L Coyne, BA
C J Bates, PhD	G Ismail, BSc, PhD
A P Macleod, BEd	Miss I Ward, BA, MA
C N Taylor, BA	Mrs A Patel, BSc
L M Gibbon, MA, MPhil	S Oakes, PhD
Miss P Telford, BEd	M Piper, BA
J K Lever, Essex CCC &	Miss D Mardell, MA, MEd
England	Dr J Wunderle, MMath,
Mrs A M Scurfield, BSc	PhD
Mrs S P Thompson, BSc	Mrs K Yelverton, BA
S P Woolley, BSc	Mrs S Jones, BA
Mrs C Tootell, BA, MA	Mrs C Pluck, BEd
†Mrs P R Tindall, BA	Mrs H Chilvers, MA, BEd
†Miss J K Robbins, BA	Miss H Gartland, BA
Ms H M Andrews, BSc	S Hawkins, BA
Mrs C Lavender, BA	Mrs M Wright, BA
N A Jaques, BA	Mrs S O'Sullivan, BA, MA
Mrs C A Rampton, BA	L Brennand, BA
R M Bluff, MA, FRCO	Miss A Moor
Mrs R Porter, BA	Mrs K Dixon, Stadt Degree
Mrs J Colman, CertEd	M Capuano, BEd
G F Welstead, BA	R Faiers, BA
†R C de Renzy Channer,	R Bustin, BSc
BA	A Baum, BA
J C Pollard, BEd	Mrs A Carter, BSc
†Miss H J Prescott-Morrin,	Miss A Adams, BA
BSc	L Taylor, BA
S Burton, BA	Mrs L Life, BA
Miss J M Green, BA	Mrs E Norris, BA
S A Hunn, BA, DPhil	Mrs C Biston, BA
N Goalby, MEng	Mrs S O'Sullivan, BA
I Moore, MA, MTh	Ms H Barry, BA
Mrs N Doctors, BA	Mrs R Deniz, BSc
†Miss C G Edwards, BA	A Busch, BSc, MSc
†Mrs E F de Renzy	Miss C Pegram, BA
Channer, BA	Miss A Fryer, BSc
†Miss A M H Wainwright,	Mrs K Dean, BA, ACA
BA	Miss Phelps, BA
Mrs V Talbot, BA	J Choy, MSc
P A Caira, BSc	J Lees, MSc
Miss G R Abrams, MSc	Miss L Ellery, BSc
Mrs S Bhangal, BEd	Mrs S Strong, BA, MA
A J Smethurst, BA	Miss D Haynes, BA
K P Gallagher, BA	N Maloney, MA
Mrs A Hunter, MA	Mrs C Foster, BA
Mrs J M Hitching, BA	Miss E Middleton, BA
D J Argyle, BEd	J Raw, BA
J P Layburn, MA	N Thomas, BComm
N E Lee, BSc	Miss A Patterson, BJ
M Flaherty, MA	Mrs P Morton, BA
Mrs M Baker, BA	S Ahmed, MSci, PhD
R M Hitching, BA	

Bursar: M W Jackson

Matron: Mrs B Sharma

Bancroft's School is a co-educational day school of about 1,000 pupils. It stands in its own grounds with about five acres of playing fields and it has a further 16 acres of playing fields near Woodford Station. Its buildings have successfully combined the spacious style of the original architecture with the constant additions demanded by developing needs.

These include a swimming pool, enhanced science facilities and music resources. In 2006 a new building housing kitchens, additional teaching space and a new Sixth Form Centre were opened, and a new sports centre and performing arts studio were opened in 2007. A lecture theatre seating up to 120 people, digital language lab and a new ICT suite were added in 2009. 2011 has seen the addition of an enhanced Sixth Form study area, new Arts and Ceramics Workshops and additional science laboratories.

Meals are taken in a well-equipped central dining room, and there is a good variety of menu with self-service on the cafeteria principle.

Pupils are grouped in four Houses – North, East, West and School. Each of the Houses has its own Housemaster or Housemistress and a tutorial system.

The School offers a wide range of subjects at GCSE and A Level and has a strong record of academic success. Virtually all Bancroftians progress to university, with about 12 each year to Oxford or Cambridge.

The major sports for girls are hockey, netball, tennis and athletics. Rugby football, hockey and cricket are the main games for boys. Swimming, soccer, and basketball are also provided. The Physical Education programme includes gymnastics, trampolining, dance and badminton.

The School has a Contingent of the CCF, Sea Scout and Explorer Scout Units, a branch of the Duke of Edinburgh's Award Scheme, and a Social Service Group, each of which caters both for girls and boys. The School has enjoyed considerable success in the Engineering Education Scheme. The programme of concerts and plays through the school year offers opportunities for pupils of all age groups.

Preparatory School. The School opened in September 1990 occupying purpose-built accommodation on a separate site within the school grounds. There are 12 classrooms, a hall, a library, a performing arts studio and specialist rooms for art and science. Although self-contained, the Prep School makes extensive use of the Senior School's sports, music and drama facilities.

(*For further details, see Preparatory School entry in IAPS section.*)

Admission. 65 places are available each year for boys and girls wishing to enter the Preparatory Department at 7+; entry tests take place in the January. Transfer to the Senior School is automatic. At 11+ there are another 50 places available for children entering Bancroft's who take an examination in mid-January. A few places may be available for candidates at 13+; for candidates of other ages individual arrangements are made. Applications for 7+ and 11+ entry must be made before 1 December in the year prior to entry. There is a direct entry for boys and girls into the Sixth Form dependent upon GCSE results and performance in the School's 16+ entrance examination.

Scholarships. (*See Scholarship Entries section.*) Each year up to 15 Scholarships, worth typically one half, one third or one quarter of the full fees, are awarded to candidates at 11+ on the basis of performance in the 11+ Entrance Examination. Two will generally be awarded as Music Scholarships to children of outstanding musical talent. Academic and Music Scholarships, each worth up to 50% of the full fees, are available to external candidates entering the Sixth Form. Means-Tested scholarships are also available at 16+. A further three academic awards are available to internal candidates.

Five Francis Bancroft Scholarships are available at age 11, which are means tested and can cover the full fees. Two means-tested Francis Bancroft Scholarships are available for entrants to the Prep School at age 7; these only cover Prep School fees.

Fees per term (2011-2012). Senior School £4,396, Prep School £3,542. Fees include lunch and books.

Old Bancroftians' Association. Hon Secretary: Mrs A S Campbell, 46 Mayfair Gardens, Woodford Green, Essex IG8 9AB.

There is a strong Old Bancroftians' Association. The OBA also helps to organise work experience for members of the school.

Charitable status. Bancroft's School is a Registered Charity, number 1068532. It exists to provide an academic education to able children.

Bangor Grammar School

13 College Avenue, Bangor, Co Down BT20 5HJ, Northern Ireland
Tel: 028 9147 3734 (School)
           028 9146 5085 (Sports Pavilion)
Fax: 028 9127 3245
e-mail: info@bgs.bangor.ni.sch.uk
website: www.bangorgrammarschool.org.uk

Bangor Endowed School was founded in 1856 as a result of a bequest by the Rt Hon Robert Ward. The School is now known as Bangor Grammar School.
Motto: '*Justitiae Tenax*'.

Governors:
The Governing Body is composed of 10 representative Governors elected by Subscribers, 4 Governors nominated by the Department of Education, 2 Parent Governors and 2 Teacher Governors.

Chairman: J Adrain, BSocSc Econ, FCA

D G Gray, BSc Econ, LGSM, FCA (*Hon Secretary*)
W R T Dowdall
Mrs P Baird
K Best, MSc, RIBA
I G Henderson, OBE, MSc Econ
Mrs D Hutchieson, MA
J Gillvray, OBE, BSc, CEng, FICE, FIHT (*Hon Treasurer, Immediate Past Chairman*)
P Blair, MD, FRCS
W McCoubrey, LLB (*Hon Asst Treasurer*)
B McKee, LLB
S J Robinson, BSc, PGCE
S Smith, BAgr
G Stoops
D B Thompson, BSc Econ, FCA, MIMC
S J Wolfenden, BA, PGCE

Bursar and Clerk to the Governors:
Mrs Fiona Woods, BSc, FCA

Headmaster: S D Connolly, MA

Academic Vice-Principal: D Cairnduff, BA, MEd

Pastoral Vice-Principal: Mrs E P Huddleson, MSSc, BEd PQH NI

Senior Teachers:
C C J Harte, BA
A J Mackie, BA
S Robinson, BSc
J Wilson, BA, PQH NI
C M McDonald, MSc, PQH NI

Assistant Staff:
* Head of Department

Mrs M-C Allsopp, BA
Mrs P H Bates, BA
S A Beggs, BSc
   (*Geography*)
M Black, BEd
A Cardwell, BSc, BAgr
Miss C Champion, BA
Miss A Chapman, BA
Miss S Chapman, BA
   (*Politics*)
Mrs S Crawford, BTh
B S M Christy, BSc
Mrs M Cree, BA
W A Cree, BA, MEd
   (*German*)
J W Culbert, BSc
D P Cunningham, MA

M Dickson, BA
Miss C S Evans, BEd
Mrs M Faulkner, BSc, PhD
Mrs S Forbes, BSc
D Gallagher, BA
Mrs M E Garland, BA, MSc (*Computing*)
F Gilmour, BSc
A Gray, BA
G Greer, BEd, MA, Adv CertEd (*English*)
P K Hancock, BLS
Mrs L Henry, BA (*RE*)
D S Holley, BA
D G Kennedy, BSc (*PE*)
A I J McCrea, BA
Mrs R McKee, BSc
Mrs C McGilton, BSc
Mrs C McGrath, BEng, MSc
Miss C L Mills, BSc, PhD
D J Napier, CertEd
M S Nesbitt, BD
N Nowatarski, BSc, HRes (*Biology*)
Mrs J K Payne, BSc, ATD (*Drama*)

Mrs K Quinn, BSc (*Mathematics*)
J Rea, BA, LTCL (*Music*)
D Robinson, BSc Econ, MBA, MEd (*Business Studies*)
P Scullion, BA
Mrs R Shaw, BA
Mrs M C Sheeran, BA
S Sinclair, MA
B Smith, BSc, PhD (*Chemistry*)
Mrs C N Steele, BA (*Art*)
S W Stevenson, BA, PhD
W R Stevenson, BA, ATCL
Miss S Stockdale, BA
J T Titterington, BEng (*Design Technology*)
J S Todd, BSc
C H M Turner, BEd
A R Walker, BEng, MSc
Mrs I S Weir, BA (*French*)
J B Wilson, BA
S Wolfenden, BA (*History*)

Headmaster's PA: Mrs S Cordner, BA

Preparatory Department:
J L Ekin, BA (*Head of Connor House*)

Mrs M Baker, BEd
Mrs B Brittain, BA
Mrs J Alexander, BEd
Mrs A Ormsby
Miss C E Patterson, BEd
Mrs A Ruding, BSc

Mrs J Matthews, BA, MSc
Miss H West, BEd

Pre-Prep:
Mrs M Nelson
Mrs P Connolly (*Assistant*)

Secretary: Mrs D Young

There are 2 departments in the School: the Preparatory, with 150 boys and girls, and the Senior with 900 boys.

The Preparatory Department. Connor House is a self-contained unit with its own building adjoining the main campus. A full range of subjects is taught, including French. Sport is well catered for and mini-rugby, hockey, football and cricket are played against other schools.

There is a Pre-Prep in operation each morning in term-time for boys and girls of 3 and 4 years of age.

School Buildings. In the last decade there has been major development of new buildings and equipment. A new, full-sized Sports Hall and a new, three-storey Design Centre have been built. In addition, a new Sixth Form Centre, Library and Music Suite have been provided and 2 new fully-fitted Computer Laboratories were opened in December 1998. Six new classrooms have been added. A new Chemistry and Technology wing has been opened affording the most up-to-date facilities in both subjects. The oldest building in the school, the Crosby Building, was refurbished in summer of 2005.

Admission and Curriculum. Boys are admitted to the Senior School after the age of 11 as a result of their performance in the Department of Education transfer procedure. All boys follow a common curriculum for the first three years. The choice of subjects for the Fourth and Fifth Forms is kept as wide as possible to enable boys to keep their future options open right up to the GCSE examinations. The School's policy is to encourage boys to undertake a wide range of studies.

A Sixth Form of 200 plus makes possible a wide range of subjects from which boys normally take four AS Level and three or four A2 subjects.

Activities. School games include rugby football, cricket, sailing, tennis, squash, badminton, golf, hockey, swimming, athletics, basketball and cross-country running. There are numerous societies and clubs. Both drama and music flourish. There are two major play productions in the year with further smaller-scale productions in the Summer Term. Numerous opportunities are afforded for instrumental and choral performance throughout the year, both inside and outside school. Adventure training is catered for by a flourishing contingent of the Combined Cadet Force (with Army and Naval Sections) and the Duke of Edinburgh's Award Scheme. Boys are encouraged to gain an experience of social work through the active Community Service Group. Frequent continental visits are arranged and an expedition under the auspices of World Challenge takes place every other year.

The School has very high standards in sport. The rugby 1st XV dominated the Ulster Schools Rugby Cup in the Eighties, with seven appearances in the final, including four victories. Other teams have been successful in the Ulster Schools Golf Championship, the major Ulster Hockey cups, the Ulster and Irish Squash and Tennis Championships and in the major Ulster Cricket cups and the Ulster Badminton Championships. Recent foreign tours have included Zimbabwe and Canada (Rugby) and Australia (Cricket).

Careers. Extensive and continuous help is available to boys in connection with careers. There are five careers staff under the leadership of the Head of Careers. Careers courses, lectures, visits, interviews, work experience, work shadowing and a Challenge of Industry Conference are part of the regular careers structure for boys in Year 10 and above.

Honours. Boys from the School enter all the major universities in the British Isles. Places have been won regularly at Oxford, Cambridge and other universities.

Bangor Grammarians Association. *Hon Sec*: David Humphreys, 10 Alexandra Road, Donaghadee, BT21 0QD.

Barnard Castle School

Barnard Castle, Co Durham DL12 8UN
Tel: 01833 690222
Fax: 01833 638985
e-mail: secretary@barneyschool.org.uk
website: www.barnardcastleschool.org.uk

The St John's Hospital in Barnard Castle was founded in the 13th century by John Baliol, whose widow founded the Oxford College. By a Scheme of the Charity Commissioners, bequests under the will of Benjamin Flounders of Yarm were combined with the funds of the St John's Hospital and public subscriptions to build and endow the present foundation in 1883. Originally known as the North Eastern County School, the name was changed to Barnard Castle School in 1924.

Motto: '*Parvis imbutus tentabis grandia tutus*'.

The Governing Body:
Chairman: M McCallum
Vice-Chairmen:
D N Williams
Miss C Elgey, JP

J C Macfarlane, CBE	Cllr Mrs M Hamilton
D F Starr	D C Osborne
C Dennis	A Fielder
Mrs S Peat	Col N C T Millen
Dr N Thorpe	P Hodges
M H Crosby, JP	Cllr G M Richardson
Mrs R Dent, JP	S Crowe

Clerk to the Governors: M White

Headmaster: **A D Stevens**, BA, MA (*History*)

Second Master: D S Gorman, BA (*History*)
Senior Mistress: Mrs B Ellison, BA (*Modern Languages*)
Chaplain and Deputy Head (Academic): Revd S J Ridley, MA

Assistant Staff:
* *Head of Department*
† *Housemaster/mistress*

†G Bishop, BA (**Economics & Business Studies*)
C P Johnson, BA (**Modern Languages*)
S Kean, BSc (*Mathematics*)
D C S Everall, BEd (**PE, Mathematics, Head of Sixth Form*)
A M Waddington, JP, BA (**English*)
Mrs S R Cuthbertson, BA, ATC (**Art*)
R Child, BSc, PhD (*Biology*)
M N R Fuller, BEd (**Biology, Careers*)
J D N Gedye, BA (**Classics*)
M H Nicholson, BSc, BA (**Mathematics*)
Miss F Cover, BEd (*PE & Geography*)
Mrs C Shovlin, BA, ALA (*Librarian*)
†Mrs A Armstrong, BEd (*PE*)
†D W Dalton, MA, BA (**Geography*)
M Donnelly, CertEd, FLCM (*Music*)
†B C Usher, BSc (*Mathematics*)
Mrs A Gorman, BA (*English*)
C H Alderson, BSc (*Geography & History*)
M P Ince, BA (**History*)
M T Pepper, BA (**Director of Sport*)
N Toyne, BSc (*Mathematics*)
†A M Beaty, BSc (**Technology*)
Miss T C Broadbent, BA (*PE*)
Mrs A J Campbell, BA (*History & *Politics*)
†A J Allman, BA, MA (**Religious Studies*)
I M Butterfield, BSc, PhD (**Chemistry*)
A Jacobs, BA (*Modern Languages, *Spanish*)
Miss K Welsh, BA (*Art*)
A M Mawhinney, MA, ARCO CHM, ARCM, LTCL (**Director of Music*)
M L West, BSc (*Chemistry*)
Mrs E E Beaty, BA (*English*)
Miss J Brown, BSc, MSc (**ICT*)
M S Atherton, MA, FTCL (*Prep School Director of Music*)
L D Monument, BSc (*PE*)
†Miss L Shorthouse, BEd (*PE*)
P Everitt, BEng (*Physics*)
P C Oakley, BSc, MSc (*Technology*)
D G Goldberg, MA (*Mathematics*)
A Maude, BSc (*Mathematics*)
Mrs M Abela, BA, LLCM TD (*Music*)
C R Butler, MSc, MA (*Physics*)
N J Connor, BA (*Business Studies & ICT*)
J G Brettell, MA (*Classics & *Latin*)
Miss C E Hall, BSc (*Biology*)
†Miss A G Jackson, BA (*Geography*)
Mrs L Nicholson, Mgr, MCIL, DPSI (*ESL*)
Miss C J Snaith, LLB, LPC, MA (*Religious Studies*)
S J F Tomlinson, BA (*Modern Languages*)
Mrs S Butler, BA (*RS*)
A Dunn BSc, MSc (*Physics*)
T S Edwards, BA (*English & Theatre Studies*)
H W Fairwood, BSc (*ICT*)
Dr G Mancino, MSc, PhD (*Chemistry*)
Dr E McDermott, BSc, PhD (*Chemistry*)
Mrs M E Waddington, BEd (**Learning Support*)
Mrs E Hewlett, BA (*English*)
Miss E K McKenzie, BSc (*Sport*)
Mrs R M Mitchell, BA (*Modern Languages*)
A M Wade, BA (*English & History*)
D S Walton, BSc, PhD (**Physics*)

Combined Cadet Force:
Commanding Officer: Major C E Hall, BSc
SSI: WO1 M G Lewis

Preparatory School

Headmaster: C F Rycroft, BEd Hons

Deputy Head: N I Seddon, BEd
Joint Directors of Studies: Mrs R Robertson, BEd & Mrs L
    E Turner, BA, MA

A Dougherty, BEd, MEd, MPhil, FRGS
Mrs S M Seddon, BEd
Mrs H Brown, BEd
Mrs L Rowlandson, BA
Mrs F M Killeen, BA
Miss E Bennington, BA
Mrs G Wilson, BA, PG Dip SpLD
Mr S T Ayres, BA
B Wicling, BA
Mrs C Bale, BA
Mrs M Dickinson, BA
Mrs T Michelin, BA
Miss A White, BA

Bursar: S Dowson, MBA

Medical Officer: Dr M Welch
Medical Centre:
Mrs B Preece, RGN, BSc
Mrs L Thorman, RGN

Headmaster's Secretary: Mrs J A Ridley

Barnard Castle is a day and boarding school for boys and girls between the ages of 4 and 18.

Organisation and Numbers. There are 550 pupils aged 11–18 in the Senior School, of whom 188 are boarders. The Preparatory School comprises a Pre-Prep Department of 57 pupils between the ages of 4 and 7, and 150 pupils between the ages of 7 and 11, of whom 15 are boarders. (*See also Preparatory School entry in IAPS section.*) The Senior and Preparatory Schools are located on adjacent sites and operate separately on a day-to-day basis whilst enjoying the mutual benefits of being able to share a number of resources and facilities. Girls were first admitted in 1981 and the School has been fully co-educational since 1993.

Location. The School is situated in its own extensive grounds on the outskirts of an historic market town in an area of outstanding natural beauty. The area is well served by Durham Tees Valley and Newcastle airports and by Darlington railway station. The School also operates its own bus service for pupils from a wide area.

Curriculum. This is designed to provide a broad, balanced and flexible programme, avoiding undue specialisation at too early a stage. In the Prep School emphasis is given to literacy and numeracy skills, as well as Science, History, Geography, French (from age 8), Religious Education, Technology, Art, Music, Information Technology, Physical Education (including swimming) and Games. These subjects are developed further in the Senior School, with the addition of Latin or Classical Civilisation, Personal, Social and Health Education, and three separate sciences. German or Spanish is added at age 14, whilst Business Studies increases the list of GCSE options at age 15. There are some twenty A, AS or Pre-U Level subjects which give a wide choice in the Sixth Form. Almost all Sixth Form leavers go on to University or College courses. A Learning Support Department provides specialist help for those who need it in both the Preparatory and Senior Schools, and tuition is offered in English as a Second Language.

Religious Education. The School is a Christian foundation and the Chapel stands at the heart of the School in more than just a geographical sense. The School Chaplain, who plays an important role in the pastoral structure of the School as well as being responsible for Religious Studies

and Chapel worship, is an ordained member of the Church of England, but the School is a multi-denominational one which welcomes and supports pupils of all faiths and none. Pupils attend weekday morning assemblies in Chapel, and there is a Sunday service for boarders.

Boarding and Day Houses. There are eight single-sex Houses within the Senior School – three boarding and five day – each small enough for pupils to know each other well, but large enough to allow a mixture of interests, backgrounds and abilities, as well as opportunities for leadership. Housemasters and Housemistresses, each supported by a team of Tutors and Assistants, are responsible for the welfare and progress of each pupil in their charge.

Junior Boarders (boys and girls aged 7–11) and Senior Girl Boarders live in their own modern Houses in the School grounds, alongside their Houseparents, Boarding Tutors and Matrons. The two Senior Boys' Boarding Houses have recently undergone a major programme of restructuring and refurbishment, and offer comfortable accommodation within the main building of the School. The resident Housemasters are supported by resident boarding tutors and matrons, and by the School Sister in the School's Medical Centre. The School Doctor visits daily.

Cultural and other activities. The School has a flourishing music department in which the Chapel Choir, Orchestras, Wind and Jazz Bands and smaller ensembles perform regularly.

Drama is also prominent, with a regular programme of productions taking place throughout the year. There is a strong tradition of after-school activities; both day and boarding pupils take part in a wide range of clubs and societies, selecting from over 100 weekly activities.

Games. Lacrosse, Rugby, Hockey, Netball, Cricket, Athletics, Squash, Cross-Country Running, Tennis and Swimming are the main sports, and other options such as soccer, badminton, basketball and golf are available. The School has extensive playing fields, a modern Sports Hall, and Fitness Centre, squash and tennis courts, and a heated indoor swimming pool. A full-size, floodlit "astroturf-style" pitch is available for all to use. Regular inter-school matches are arranged at all levels.

Outdoor Activities. There is a strong emphasis on providing instruction, opportunity and challenge in a wide range of outdoor activities. Much of this takes place under the auspices of a flourishing Cadet Force (Army and RAF sections) or the Duke of Edinburgh's Gold and Silver Award Schemes.

Careers. The School works closely with the Durham County Careers Service. There is a well-equipped Careers Room, and a team of careers staff work together with the Higher Education Coordinator to provide pupils at all stages of the School with expert advice and help in decision-making and application procedures.

Admission. Pupils are admitted at all stages either via the School's own Entrance Assessments or via the Common Entrance Examination. There is also direct entry into the Sixth Form subject to satisfactory performance at GCSE level. Details of the application procedure are obtainable from the Headmaster's Secretary.

Scholarships and assisted places. (*See Scholarship Entries section.*) The School makes Entrance Awards on entry to the Senior School (including at Sixth Form level). In addition to academic awards, these may include awards for musical, artistic and sporting ability and potential. The School is also able to offer a small number of its own means-tested assisted places for able children whose parents would not otherwise be able to send them. Details are available from the Headmaster's Secretary.

Fees per term (2011-2012). Senior: £6,572 (Boarders), £3,660 (Day). Prep: £4,944 (Boarders), £2,557 (Day). Pre-Prep: £1,683. Fees are inclusive and subject to annual review.

Charitable status. Barnard Castle School is a Registered Charity, number 1125375, whose aim is the education of boys and girls.

Bedales School

Church Road, Steep, Petersfield, Hampshire GU32 2DG
Tel: 01730 300100
       Registrar: 01730 711733
       Assistant Registrar: 01730 711569
Fax: 01730 300500
e-mail: admissions@bedales.org.uk
website: www.bedales.org.uk

Governors:
D Alexander, QC, BA, LLM
Mrs F Bayliss, Froebel CertEd, FRSA
Dr B Ellis, BSc, PhD, MBA, MB BS, MRCGP, FRCP
Mrs S Ford, BA, PGCE
Dr T Hands, BA, AKC, DPhil
Ms A Hardie, BEd, JP
Professor B Johnson, FRS, FRSE, FRSC, FAcadEuropa
Mrs M Johnson, BA
Rear Admiral J Lippiett, CB, MBE
T Parker, MA, MSc
A Redpath (*Chairman*)
M Rice, BA
N Vetch, ARICS
C Watson, BA

Headmaster: K J Budge, MA University College Oxford

Clerk to the Governors and Bursar: R Lushington, BA, MCIPD

Director of External Relations: R T Reynolds, BSc, DipM
Registrar: Mrs J Jarman

Managing Head of Senior School: D Oliver, BA, MPhil

Assistant Head: J A Scullion, BA, MA
Assistant Head/Director of Co-curricular and Student Welfare: (*to be appointed*)
Director of Teaching and Learning: A McConville, MA, PGCE

Secretary to the Headmaster: (*to be appointed*)

Assistant Staff:
* *Head of Department*
† *Housemaster/Housemistress*

Mrs V E Alderson-Smart, BSc, PGCE (*Biology*)
†Mrs J Alldridge, AISTD, ALAM (*Dance*)
Mrs R Austen, BSc, PGCE (*Learning Support*)
G T H Banks, BA, PGCE (**English*)
J Barker, BLib, ARCM (*Bedales Arts Coordinator*)
†Mrs L Barnes, BSc, PGCE (*Chemistry*)
K Boniface (*Physical Education*)
C Bott, BA, PGCE (*History*)
†Mrs J Brittain, DipSpD (*Speech & Drama*)
P Brittain, BA, CertEd (*Librarian*)
Ms T Butcher (*Dance*)
C Burch, BA, PGCE(*Mathematics*)
Mrs R E Carpenter-Jones, BA, PGCE (*Spanish*)
Mrs S Cartwright, BSc, PGCE (**Physical Education*)
A Cheese, BA (*Art*)
P W Coates, BEd (**Outdoor Work, Mathematics*)
Ms K Connolly, BA, PGCE (*Art*)
Mrs H Crawford (*LAMDA*)
†G D Dale, HDE SA (*Physics*)
Ms L Fellingham, BA Brighton, PGCE London (*Design*)
Mrs C Gammon, BA Surrey, PGCE
S Gardner, BA (*Drama and Head of Sixth Form*)
Mrs K Gardner (*LAMDA*)

N E Gleed, MA, PGCE (**Director of Music*)
Miss C Grey, BA, MPhil (*Philosophy and Religious Studies*)
J Green, BA East Anglia (**Drama*)
Ms J C Greenwood, MA (*Theatre Technical Manager*)
C Grocock, BA, PhD (*Classics*)
M-P Hamard, MA, PGCE (**French*)
T A Hardy, BSc, MA, PGCE (**Physics*)
†Mrs G Harris, BA, PGCE, PGDip (**Learning Support*)
G J Hatton, BA, CertEd (**Art*)
Mrs M-E Houghton, BA, PGCE (*English and Classics*)
Mrs H Howarth, BA, ATC (*Design & Textiles*)
Mrs V Hunter, LRAM, LTCL (*Speech & Drama*)
S Inglis, BA, PGCE (*Learning Support*)
Ms C Jarmy, BA, MPhil (**Philosophy and Religious Studies*)
R N Jayatissa, BSc, MBA, PGDE (*Physics*)
P Jones, BSc (*Business Studies*)
S Kingsley-Pallant, BA (*English*)
Mrs J Kirby, BSc, MSc (*Librarian*)
M Lambert, BA, MA, PGCE (**Classics*)
Mrs K Layton, BSc, Dip HE, PGCE (**Geography*)
W Lithgow, Prof Cert Music RAM, PGCE (*Assistant Director of Music*)
Mrs C Lock, BSc, PGCE (*Biology and Head of Block 3*)
Mrs S Mabe, BA, PGCE, DipSpLD (*Learning Support*)
Mrs A Mason, BA, PGCE (*French, Spanish*)
A McNaughton, BSc, PGCE (*Design*)
N Meigh, BA, PGCE (*History*)
Ms R Nash, CDE (*Dance*)
M C Newman, BSc, PGCE (**Chemistry*)
Ms S Oakley, BA, PGCE (*Art*)
Mrs C Osborne, BSc, PGCE (*Biology*)
Ms Y Parkin, LISTD (*Dance*)
F Parton (*French and Philosophy*)
Ms H Parsons, MA (*English*)
†P C Parsons, BA, CertEd (*History*)
C W Prowse, BSc, MA, PhD (*Geography and Chemistry*)
Mrs S Robson, BSc, PGCE (**Information Technology*)
K A C Rowe, ARCM, LRAM (*Music*)
J A Scullion, BA, MA (**Economics*)
J K Selby, BA, PGCE (**History*)
†N Shannon, BA, PGCE (*French*)
B Shaw, BSc (**Design*)
R A Sinclair, BA, PGCE (**Biology, *Science*)
Ms E Stacy, BSc, MPhil (*Chemistry*)
Mrs J D Sueref, BA, PGCE (*Geography*)
Ms P Tribe, BEd (*Mathematics*)
M Truss, MPhys, PhD (**Mathematics*)
Ms F Vigars, BA, PGCE (*Art*)
Mrs D Wallsgrove, BA, MA, PGCE (*English*)
Ms J Watkins, BA, MA (*Mathematics*)
Mrs J L Webster, BEd (*Mathematics*)
A Wright, BA, PGCE (*Physical Education*)

Dunhurst (*Junior School*)

Head: Mrs J Grubb, BA
Deputy Head: R Morel, BSc
Senior Master and Boarding Housemaster: A Simmons, BA, CertEd
Head of Groups: Mrs K Olphert, BEd
Director of Teaching and Learning: Ms K Misson, BA, PGCE
Head of Assessment & Monitoring; Gifted & Talented Coordinator: D Kettle, BEd, DipEC

Secretary to the Head: Ms F Harris

Mrs L Banks, BEd (*Art*)
J Beatty, BA (*Mathematics*)
Mrs F Box, BEd, DipDysInst, AMBDA (**Learning Support*)
Mrs M Budge, BEd, DipSpLD (*Learning Support*)
Ms O Burnett-Armstrong, BA (*Careers Advice*)

Ms M Canter, BA (*English*)
Ms E Chilton (*French*)
Ms M Clark, BA, PGCE (*Group 2*)
Ms S Coates, BEd (*LAMDA Speech & Drama*)
M Collins, BEd (*Mathematics, Physical Education*)
Ms K Connolly, BA, PGCE (*IT*)
K Cope, Dip AD Bristol (*Creative Studies*)
D Ellis (*Physical Education*)
Ms G Graham, BEd, CertSpLD (*Learning Support*)
Miss R Hearnshaw, BA (*Physical Education*)
Mrs E Hewitt, BA (*Art and Design*)
Ms J de Jongh (*LAMDA Speech & Drama*)
D Kettle, BEd (*Mathematics*)
Mrs J Kingsley-Pallant (*Librarian*)
S Kingsley-Pallant, BA (*Drama and Performance*)
M Lambert, BA, PGCE (*Classics*)
N Maddocks (*Outdoor Work*)
Mrs A Mowat (*Librarian*)
Ms C Murphy, BSc, MEd (*Mathematics*)
Ms R Nash, CDE (*Dance*)
R Nice, PGCE (*Design Technology*)
Ms L Perry (*Textiles*)
Ms D Payne (*Group 1*)
Mrs J Peel, BEd, DipSpLD (*Learning Support*)
Ms E Pickett (*Latin and Greek*)
Mrs N Read (*Spanish*)
Ms H Retter (*Girls' Housemistress*)
Mrs C Reynolds, BA (*EFL*)
Ms N Scott-Charles, BA (*Music*)
A Simmons, BA, CertEd (*PSHE and Science*)
Ms L Suter, MA (*Music*)
Ms P Tribe, BEd (*Mathematics*)
Ms J Walker, MA (*Humanities, Librarian*)
R Walsh, BA (*Group 3, Physical Education*)
Ms M Watney, BSc, MA (*Group 2*)
Ms P Wilson, BA (*Learning Support, Mathematics*)
Mrs A Wilson-Smith (*Group 3*)

Dunannie (*Pre-Prep School*)

Head: Ms J Webbern, CertEd Froebel
Senior Teacher: Ms J Brown, BEd Froebel

Mrs D Adamson-Brattland, MA, PGCE (*Acting Director of Music*)
Mrs L Banks, BEd (*Sculpture*)
Mrs J A Brown, BEd (*Reception*)
Ms C Canter, CertEd, CertSpLD (*Learning Support, English*)
Ms E Chilton (*French*)
Mrs C Claasen, BA, MA (*Year 3*)
Mrs D Cooper (*Nursery*)
Mrs A de Courcy, BEd (*Year 1*)
Ms N Curry, BA, PGCE (*Reception*)
Mrs J Kingsley-Pallant (*Librarian*)
Ms B MacMillan, BEd
Mrs S Rose, BA, QTS (*Nursery*)
Mrs J Uttley, C&G (*Year 2, Art*)
(*A Teaching Assistant is assigned to each class.*)

School Physicians:
Dr A J H Holden, MB BS, DRCOG, DFFP
Dr F Jacklin, MB BS, DRCOG, DFFP, DipPaeds NZ, MRCGP, DA

Number in School. 460 in Senior School. Equal numbers of boys and girls. 70% boarders.

Bedales stands in an estate of 120 acres in the heart of the Hampshire countryside, overlooking the South Downs. Although only one hour from London by train, this is one of the most beautiful corners of rural England. Founded in 1893, Bedales is one of the oldest co-educational boarding schools. The community is a stimulating and happy one, in which tolerance and supportive relationships thrive at all levels.

The school has strong traditions in both the Humanities and the Sciences, in Art, Design, Drama and Music. The school estate supports a thriving 'Outdoor Work' programme, including the management of livestock and a variety of traditional crafts.

The school is known for its liberal values, the individualism and creativity of its students, and a sense that the students are generally at ease with who they are. The atmosphere is relaxed (first-name terms for staff and students; no uniform), but it is underpinned by a firm structure of values, some rules, guidance and support.

Admission. Entry to the School is from 3+ (see Dunannie), 8+, 9+, 10+, 11+ (see Dunhurst), 13+ and 16+ (Bedales). Once in the school, pupils are assessed before proceeding to the next stage.

Entry Tests. Entry for newcomers at 10+, 11+ and 13+ takes the form of residential tests in the January preceding the September entry. Entry at 16+ is by a series of interviews spread over a single day. Write in the first instance to the Registrar.

Senior School (13 to 18). Up to 100 in each year. A new curriculum in Blocks 4 and 5 (Years 10 and 11) was introduced in September 2006. In order to promote more stimulating, varied and wide-ranging work in these years, and to reduce prescriptive external assessment, students will typically take a combination of externally moderated Bedales Assessed Courses (BACs) alongside GCSE and IGCSE subjects. BACs are designed to give a strong basis for A Level study.

All current GCSE/BACs subjects (except Outdoor Work) are also offered in the Sixth Form at AS and A2 Level, together with Classical Civilisation, Dance (AS), Economics, Further Mathematics, Psychology and Theatre Studies. Sixth Form students can also opt for an assessed Extended Project in an area of interest. A programme of personal and social education runs in Years 9 and 10, and a general course covering a wide range of topical and personal issues is taught in the Sixth Form. Students are attached to a tutor in groups of mixed ages, and meet their tutor on a regular basis.

Year 9 students spend a week at the Outward Bound Centre at Ullswater, Geography and Biology departments run sixth form field courses, and there are special interest trips such as a History visit to Russia. IT facilities are well funded, each student having an email address and monitored access to the Internet. Students have access to desktop computers throughout the day, and those with their own laptops have wireless access to the school network across the campus. There are excellent recreational facilities including extensive playing fields, gymnasium, sports hall with multi-gym, indoor heated swimming pool and a floodlit astroturf pitch. The Outdoor Work project is centred on two eighteenth-century barns reconstructed in the school grounds by students. The Bedales Gallery and Olivier Theatre run public programmes of art, drama, dance and music, and distinguished speakers visit the school to give assemblies or as part of the 'Civics' programme. Evening assemblies ('Jaw') and other talks often have a religious or moral theme, but there is no chapel; the school is non-denominational.

There are no prefects, but students take responsibility for a wide variety of aspects of school life by running activities for younger students, taking part in committees and putting forward individual initiatives. A School Council of elected representatives provides a forum for discussion including all levels of the school. Until the final year, students sleep in small mixed-age dormitories; in the final year they move to a co-educational house with exceptional facilities. This arrangement fosters very good relationships across the age range.

Dunhurst (8 to 13). (*See entry in IAPS section*).

Dunannie (3 to 8). Entrance at 3+ is by date of registration, after this acceptances are made following informal assessments should vacancies arise. 90 pupils. Dunannie has six classes including a nursery. Its aim is for children to develop a lifetime's love of learning in a stimulating environment.

The school has bright airy classrooms, an extensive library and an excellent ICT room. There are fabulous music rooms, hall and dining room which are shared with Dunhurst. The children at Dunannie benefit from the indoor swimming pool, tennis courts, sports hall, pitches, art gallery, farm and theatre which are all close by on the Bedales estate. The outdoor play areas include a stunning orchard with a climbing frame, Sound Garden of outdoor instruments and a hill fort.

The children have many opportunities to thrive and flourish. Dunannie offers a rich and varied curriculum that allows for rigour in basic skills, but also embraces creativity. Children are encouraged to think and be independent in their response to cross-curricular activities. First hand experiences are an integral part of learning. All children from Nursery to Year 3 go on inspiring visits that enrich the classroom experiences. There are close links between Dunannie, Dunhurst and Bedales. Children in Year 3 can automatically transfer from Dunannie to Dunhurst unless there are exceptional circumstances. There are frequent visitors to the school too. Sport is a strength with a comprehensive programme of activities including swimming, gymnastics, netball, football and orienteering. Year 3 children have sport with Dunhurst Group 1 children and have the opportunity to play inter school matches. Dunannie is a very friendly school with happy, confident children who relish being at school. Staff and parents work in partnership together and we are always pleased to welcome visitors and prospective parents to Dunannie.

Scholarships and Bursaries. (*See Scholarship Entries section*.) Music scholarships are available at Dunhurst (10+ and older; exceptionally, 8+) and at Bedales (13+ and 16+). Other scholarships are available at 13+ and 16+.

Scholarships attract an automatic award of £750, which can be increased through means-tested bursaries.

Means-tested bursaries are also available to those of proven need.

For full details of scholarships, please apply to the Registrar.

Fees per term (2011-2012). Senior: Boarders £9,985 Day £7,850. Dunhurst: Boarders £6,860, Day £5,370, Year 4 £4,370. Dunannie: £1,235–£2,810.

Charitable status. Bedales School is a Registered Charity, number 307332. Its aims and objectives are to educate children as broadly as possible in a creative and caring environment.

Bedford Modern School

Manton Lane, Bedford, Bedfordshire MK41 7NT
Tel: 01234 332500
Fax: 01234 332550
e-mail: info@bedmod.co.uk
website: www.bedmod.co.uk

Bedford Modern School is one of the Harpur Trust Schools of Bedford, sharing equally in the educational endowment bequeathed for the establishment of a school in Bedford by Sir William Harpur in 1566. Bedford Modern School was a Direct Grant Grammar School which became independent in 1976. It became co-educational in September 2003.

Chairman of the School Committee: I McEwen, BPhil, MA, DPhil

Headmaster: **M Hall**, BA, MA

Senior Deputy: S Davis, MA, PGCE

Deputy Head Academic: M R Price, MA

Deputy Head Pastoral: I C Grainger, CertEd

Head of the Junior School: R Lynn, BA, PGCE, MA

Director of Sixth Form: J P White, BEd

Director of Marketing and Admissions: M Upton, DipSchMkt

Director of Sport: P L Jerram, BSc

** *Head of Faculty*
* *Head of Subject*

Faculty of Art, Design &
  Information Technology:
**S E Milton, BA, PGCE
Art:
S E Milton, BA, PGCE
P Edwards, BA, MA
J McGregor, BA, PGCE
Design Technology:
*P Kennington, CertEd
G Dudley, BA
I C Grainger, CertEd
A Rock, BSc
J P White, BEd
ICT:
*S Harris, MA, MSc, PGCE, CITP
A Rock, BSc
P J Smith, BSc

Faculty of English:
**S D Bywater, BA, MLitt
Dr J P Barnes, PhD, BA
J Chumbley, BA
A E Martin, BA
J P Sanders, BA
E P Sheldon, BA
J Ware, BA, MA
Film Studies:
*J P Sanders, BA

Faculty of Humanities:
**D J Kendall, BA, MA
Geography:
*N C Robinson, BSc, MA
B W Day, BSc
D R Mistrano, BA
M R Price, MA
I R D White, BA, MA
History:
*S E Wright, MA
S Baker, BSc, PGCE
S Boa, BA, PhD
A D Tapper, BSc, MSt
C Webb, BA
Religious Studies:
J Searle, BA, PGCE
D J Kendall, BA, MA

Faculty of Mathematics:
**N D Shackleton, BSc, PGCE
S A Brocklehurst, BA
I R Hay, BSc
N Hussain, BSc
S J Jacobs, BSc
R Kay, BSc
D M King, BSc
M Oxteby
P J Russell, BSc, MSc
A Slater, BEng

Faculty of Modern Foreign
  Languages:
**G A Watkins, BA

G Amoros, L-ès-L
M J Cooper, BEd
L Hendry, BA
R J Killen, BA (*German*)
L Sedeno, BA
Classics:
*J Newton, MA
T a Lomas
C W H Rees-Bidder, BA, MEd

Faculty of Music:
**J Mower, GRSM, ARCO, ARCM, Dip RAM
H D Shoukry, MA
Music Technology:
*H D Shoukry, MA

Faculty of Performance Arts:
**H Rees-Bidder, BEd
Drama:
*J Riddington-Smith, Adv Dip LAMDA, PGCE
H Rees-Bidder, BEd
N Rudd, BA, PGCE
Speech & Drama:
*M A Burgess
R E Cassell, BA
T Walsh, BA, MA
Dance:
*R Bradley

Faculty of Politics,
  Philosophy & Economics (PPE):
**A Pollard, BA, MA, PGCE
Economics & Business Studies:
*R Smith, BA, PGCE
J R Ryan, BA, PGCE
Government & Politics:
*S Baker, BSc, PGCE
Philosophy:
*A Rowley, BA, MA, PhD (*School Chaplain*)

Faculty of Science:
**N R Else, BEd, MA
Biology:
*R J Brand, BSc, MA
D Greenfield, BSc
D A Jenkins, BSc, MSc, DipEdTech
S Sanctuary, BSc
S Sumal, BSc, MSc, PGCE
Chemistry:
*Dr C M Catley, BSc, PhD, PGCE
N K Cordell, BE
N R Else, BEd, MA
L Emms, MSc

J P Fitton, BSc
J Sadler, BA
Physics:
*R J Turner, BSc, MA
S Bartlett, MPhys, PhD
W D Hallett, BA, MA
S S Harvey, BSc
T P Mullan, BSc
T E Rex, BEd
Psychology:
*H J Kelly, BSc, PGCE

Other Areas:
Careers: P Russell, BSC, MSc
Librarian: M S Brown, BSc, ALA
School Chaplain: Revd Dr A Rowley
Technical Theatre Manager: N Parker, BA

SpLD Academic Support:
**T Collins, BA, PGCE
D Costello, BA, MA
C Setchfield, BA, PGCE
M Tew, BA, PGCE

Houses:
Senior Head of House: P Edwards, BA, MA
Bell House: A G Higgens, BSc, QTS
Farrar House: S E Milton, BA, PGCE
Mobbs House: J Ware, BA, MA
Oatley House: H L Gilbert, BA, MA, PGCE
Rose House: B Day, BSc
Tilden House: N K Cordell, BE

Junior School

Head: R Lynn, BA, PGCE, MA

Deputy Head: J C Rex, BA

Head of Junior School Sports Development: T Bucktin, BSc, PGCE

H Avery, BEd
J Barlow, BEd
C Barrow, BEd
T Bucktin, BSc, PGCE
L Burton, BEd
G M Colling, CertEd
H Farrow, BA, MA, LRAM
M Fox, BA, PGCE
K Johnson, BA
J Leydon, BEd
S J Nicholls, BA
P Pacyna, BA
R Watson, BA
E Warren, BA

Bursar: A T Smyth
Admissions Registrar: J Foster
Marketing & Communications Officer: B Messina, BA Hons
Media & Communications Assistant: S Kendrick
Senior Marketing Officer: F Billington, BA Hons, DipM
Examinations Officer: P J Birch, BSc
SSI: Captain B Simpson, MInstLM
Senior School Nurse: M Jones, RGN

Number of Pupils. There are 224 pupils in the Junior School (aged 7–11) and 984 pupils in the Senior School (aged 11–18).

(*See also Bedford Modern Junior School entry in IAPS section*.)

Facilities. The School occupies an attractive forty-acre wooded site to the north of Bedford. The main buildings date from 1974 and there have been substantial additions

Faculty of Sport:
**P L Jerram, BSc
    (*Director of Sport*)
*A Brown
*R J K Hardwick
*P J Woodroffe, BA
*P R Bignell, BEd
*D Orton, BEd, DipML
*E Rumbold, BEd
H L Gilbert, BA, MA, PGCE
N J Chinneck, BEd
A G Higgens, BSc, QTS
N T Whitwham, BA, PGCE

since that time, most notably a new Assembly Hall, Performance Arena and classrooms to the Junior School (2002); a Sixth Form Study Centre and Refectory (The Rutherford Building – 2006) and new Library Resource Centre (2007). There are extensive facilities for Science, Technology and Information Technology. There have been recent extensions to the Music School and Performing Arts Centre. Each Year Group has its own Common Room as a pastoral centre.

The playing fields are all on the School site with extensive facilities for Rugby, Football, Cricket and Athletics. There is also a large swimming pool, a fitness suite, gym and sports hall. Recent additions include two large all-weather training areas and netball courts. The School shares a large and well-stocked Boathouse with the other Harpur Trust Schools on the River Ouse.

Admissions. Pupils are admitted between the ages of 7 and 16. The School conducts its own Entrance Assessments which are held in January of the year prior to September entry.

Registration fee is £100.

Fees per term (2011-2012). Tuition: Junior School £2,596, Senior School £3,561.

Assistance with Fees. The School offers The Modern Awards which are available to pupils joining the School from Year 7 (11+) upwards. All Awards are means-tested and are also dependent on a pupil's academic success in the Entrance Assessments. Further details may be obtained from the School.

Curriculum. The Junior School (ages 7–11) curriculum covers Mathematics, English, Science, Technology, Modern Foreign Languages, PE, History, Geography and RE (taught as Humanities), Art, PSHE and Games. Pupils benefit both from a purpose-built Practical Skills Centre containing Art and Science rooms as well as specialist computer and technology rooms, and from the Senior School Music, PE and Games facilities.

In the Senior School, the curriculum includes all the core subjects, as well as Technology, IT, RE, PE, Music, Art and Drama. All pupils experience French, German, Spanish and Latin in Years 7 and 8 before making choices. Pupils opt for ten GCSE subjects. For the Sixth Form, pupils select from a wide range of 29 subjects. In addition to all the traditional options, the choice of subjects also includes ICT, Government and Politics, Economics, Business Studies, Religious Studies, Philosophy, Systems & Control, Classical Civilisation, Theatre Studies, PE, Psychology, Film Studies and Music Technology. All subjects can be taken both to A2 and AS Level.

ICT Facilities. The School boasts a superb range of ICT facilities offering both staff and pupils an individual network account and e-mail address so that they are able to enjoy over 400 networked PCs across the School in addition to high-speed broadband Internet access, wireless classroom laptop sets, networked printing, and an extensive subject software library including a range of training courseware material.

All standard classrooms are equipped with a ceiling mounted data projector. A number of interactive whiteboards and additional presentation equipment are also available for use. The School's website can be viewed at www.bedmod.co.uk.

Religious and Moral Education. The School is multi-faith and multicultural, and religious and moral education is given throughout. The pupils learn about all major world religions and it is hoped that they can learn to be tolerant whilst accepting the place for firmly held beliefs. Personal, Social and Health Education is a fundamental and well-established part of the timetable.

Individual Care. Every pupil has a personal tutor, who supervises and takes an interest in his or her academic progress, co-curricular activities and sporting interests. Tutors meet with their tutees on a daily basis and there is at least one longer pastoral session each week. Each Year

Group has its own common room for use at break and lunch-times and other non-taught times with a study area and recreational facilities.

We believe that common sense and courtesy lie at the heart of pastoral care. We stress self-discipline and high standards of personal conduct. The tutorial system and the academic organisation are discrete, working in parallel to complement each other. Teaching class sizes are a maximum of twenty-four and often many fewer. We aim to provide a relaxed but purposeful environment; a culture in which all feel at ease and are ambitious to achieve their best.

Drama. There are several productions each year, as well as a House Drama Festival and several smaller events. There are also separate Drama and Dance Studios. Speech and Drama is offered throughout the School, leading to LAMDA examinations. Ballet, tap and modern dance lessons follow the ISTD syllabus.

Music. Pupils can learn all the orchestral and band instruments as well as piano, keyboard, guitar/electric guitar and singing. The School has a large variety of choirs, orchestra, bands and ensembles. Pupils can follow courses for GCSE and A Level Music as well as A Level Music Technology. Music accommodation includes an ICT suite with 10 Apple computers and state-of-the-art recording facilities.

Activities. There are many school societies and clubs catering for a variety of tastes and interests. The voluntary Combined Cadet Force is strong with Army, Navy, RAF and Marine sections. Pupils may learn flying, sailing and paragliding. Community Service and the Duke of Edinburgh's Award Scheme are very popular.

Sport. Rugby, football, cricket, rowing are major sports for boys; hockey, netball and rowing for girls. Additional activities include: table tennis, water polo, badminton, hockey (boys), equestrian, snowsports, cycling, cross-country, weights and fitness, fencing, fives, sevens, swimming, dance, basketball, athletics, softball, rounders, tennis, climbing, shooting, and gymnastics. Regular representation at national, divisional and regional levels.

Higher Education. In 2010, 108 pupils gained entry to a degree course.

Old Bedford Modernians' Club. Secretary: R H Wildman, Esq, Bedford Modern School, Manton Lane, Bedford MK41 7NT.

Charitable status. The Bedford Charity (The Harpur Trust) is a Registered Charity, number 204817. It includes in its aims the provision of high quality education for boys and girls.

Bedford School

De Parys Avenue, Bedford MK40 2TU
Tel: 01234 362200
Fax: 01234 362283
e-mail: admissions@bedfordschool.org.uk
website: www.bedfordschool.org.uk

A renowned boarding and day school for boys aged 7–18 that offers progressive and innovative education. The School is situated in an extensive 40-acre estate in the heart of Bedford and is just 40 minutes from London by train.

Established in 1552, the School has a national reputation for academic excellence with additional strengths in music, sport, drama and art. The highly qualified teaching staff are selected on their ability to communicate and inspire, and the School's facilities are virtually unrivalled. The School's academic success is demonstrated by a long history of impressive examination results at GCSE, A Level, and in the International Baccalaureate Diploma.

However, an education at Bedford School is about more than grades; students are encouraged to develop an awareness of the world, think independently and learn values to prepare them for life beyond the school gates. Within its genuinely caring community the School aims to find every boy's individual talent and help him to reach his full potential.

School Governors:

Chairman: Professor Stephen Mayson, LLB, LLM, PhD, Barrister, FRSA
Deputy Chairman: D G Dixon, BA Hons, MBA, FCA, AIB
Chairman of the Harpur Trust: Mrs S Peck
Cllr C Atkins, MBE
D Doran, MSc, BSc
P W Wallace, MA, FCA, FBRP
M Womack, MA, LLM

Co-opted Governors:
Dr A Egan
C Johnson
Air Chief Marshal Sir Clive Loader, KCB, OBE, FRAeS, RAF
A Malek, QC, MA, BCL Oxon
H Maltby
R G Miller, MA Cantab, DipEd, Dip HA, RAFVR(T)

***Head Master*: J S Moule**, MA Lady Margaret Hall Oxford

Vice Master: C Baker, BSc Manchester, CChem, FRSC

Deputy Head (Academic): I H Latif JP, BSc King's College London, CChem, FRSC

Bursar and Clerk to the Governors: Col J M W Stenhouse, OBE, MVO, MBA

Assistant Head (External Affairs): R J Midgley, BA Ed Exeter

Director of Admissions: R T Williams, BSc Dundee, DipEd

Director of International Baccalaureate: C L Marsh, MA St John's College Cambridge, MLitt Oxford

Senior Boarding Housemaster: M H Cassell, BSc Surrey

Senior Day Housemaster: Mrs F G McEwan-Cox, BA Worcester, DipTEFL, Cert SpLD

Undermaster: I B Armstrong, BSc Sunderland, MSc Leeds

Assistant staff:
* *Head of Department*

Academic Support (EFL & SpLD):
*Mrs F G McEwan-Cox, BA Worcester, RSA Dip, Cert SpLD

Art:
*R H Campbell, BA London, Camberwell School of Arts & Crafts
M Croker, BA Stourbridge College of Art
S Chance, BA Norwich

Biology:
*M A Beale, BSc Surrey, MEd
M J Gunn, BSc London, MIBiol, CBiol
Ms F Bell, BSc Edinburgh
C Palmer, BSc Southampton, MA Hughes Hall Cambridge
Miss C S Evans, BA Somerville College Oxford
M J Mallalieu, BSc Liverpool
F Laughton, BSc Exeter

Chemistry:
*I A Sheldon, MChem University College Oxford
C Baker, BSc Manchester, CChem, FRSC
A J Crowe, BSc, PhD Aston
C W Duckworth, BSc Liverpool
W G Suthers, BSc Durham, MSc Queen Mary Westfield College, PhD Reading
B Johnson, MA Gonville & Cauis College Cambridge, MSc, PhD Warwick
I H Latif JP, BSc King's College London, CChem, FRSC

Classics:
*A D Melvill, BA Durham
R H Palmer, MA Emmanuel College Cambridge, PhD East Anglia
Miss M E Ambler, MA St Hilda's College Oxford

Computing:
*P E Davis, BSc Imperial College London
R A Eadie, MA Trinity College Cambridge (*Computer Manager*)

Design Technology:
*I B Armstrong, BSc Sunderland, MSc Leeds
M Huddlestone, BA Loughborough
L Holt, BA Southampton
G J Waite, MEng Nottingham

Economics & Business Studies:
*H Taylor, BSc Loughborough
C J Bury, BA Leeds
M H Cassell, BSc Surrey
Mrs C M Medley, BA Leicester
R E Heale, BSc Loughborough

English:
*D G Ashton, BA Sydney
A W Grimshaw, BA Lampeter
Mrs L Di Niro, BA, MPhil De Montfort
R H Palmer, MA Emmanuel College Cambridge, PhD East Anglia
Ms S Van Heerden, BA Rhodes
Mrs A L M Smith, BA Swansea
S Adams, BA St Edmund's College Cambridge
Miss C Charlwood, BA, MPhil Sidney Sussex College Cambridge

Geography:
*R J Walker, BA Selwyn College Cambridge
Ms S Spyropoulous, BA Durham
W R Montgomery, BSc Nottingham
G M Strachan, BA Durham
M Gracie, BSc Loughborough

History:
*Ms E E Parcell, BA Churchill College Cambridge
J N W Fleming, MA Merton College Oxford
M W Graham, BA Trevelyan College, Durham, MA Durham
M Jamieson, BA Birmingham
C Walker, BA Northumbria

Library:
*Mrs L Harrison, BSc UWA

Mathematics:
*Mrs J C Beale, BSc Surrey, MA Nottingham
S A Adams, MPhys Bath
B J Burgess, BA Ed Exeter
N J Cox, MA Christ's College Cambridge
A Eames-Jones, BSc Liverpool, PhD Birmingham, CEng, CPhys
Mrs S Staincliffe, BSc Manchester
J B Watson, MA St Edmund Hall Oxford
P Sherwin, MEd Melbourne
Mrs R Down, BSc Leeds
Mrs T Harbinson, BSc Leicester
M T Hutchinson, BA St Catherine's College Cambridge
Mrs N Tekell-Mellor, BSc East Anglia

Modern Languages:
*F J G Inglis, BA Cardiff, MLitt Jesus College Oxford (*German*)
Ms C Geneve, MA University of Grenoble (*French*)
A J R Huxford, MA St John's College Cambridge (*Spanish*)
C L Marsh, MA St John's College Cambridge, MLitt Oxford
J E J O'Neill, BA Stirling, MCIL

J C Osman, BA University College London
Miss J C Law, BA Exeter
Ms E Calleja-Rubio, BA University of Oviedo
Dr A Chen, MBA Hertfordshire, PhD Cranfield
L S E Gearing, BA St Anne's College Oxford
A J Braithwaite, BA Exeter

Music:
*A W Morris, MA, BMus London, MEd Pembroke College Cambridge, GRSM, FTCL, ARAM, ARCO CHM, LRAM, ARCM
G V Bennett, GGSM
J A Rouse, MA Girton College Cambridge, FRCO
M C Green, GRSM, LRAM, ARCM, DipRAM
M Hughes, GRSM, ARCM
J Lark, MA Girton College Cambridge (*Composer in Residence*)
R Thompson, BMus, PGDip (*Pianist in Residence*)

Physical Education:
*G M K Fletcher, BEd Exeter, DipPhysEd Leeds
B J Burgess, BA Ed Exeter
R J Midgley, BA Ed Exeter

Physics:
*M A R Crisp, MEng Durham
P N Brough, BSc Southampton
D J Waugh, BSc Durham
R T Williams, BSc Dundee, DipEd
Dr E Palmer, MSc UCL, PhD Southampton
S James, MPhys Jesus College Oxford
G J Green, BSc Birmingham
L J Guise, BA Magdalene College Cambridge

Religious Education:
*A D Finch, BA New College Oxford, MA Hull
The Revd A S Atkins, MA St Peter's College Oxford, MA Selwyn College Cambridge (*Chaplain*)
Dr K Viswanathan, BSc University College London, MA Bristol, PhD Essex

Theatre Studies:
*Mrs S Swidenbank, MA East Anglia
J N Pharoah, BA Leeds

Houses and Housemasters:

Boarding Houses:
Sandersons: R J Midgley
Burnaby: R E Heale
Pemberley: P Sherwin
Redburn: C J Bury
Phillpotts: A W Grimshaw
Talbots: M H Cassell

Day Houses:
Ashburnham: B J Burgess
Bromham: A J R Huxford
Crescent: Miss J C Law
Paulo Pontine: A J Braithwaite
St Cuthberts: L M Holt
St Peter's: Mrs F G McEwan-Cox

Chaplain: The Revd A S Atkins, MA

Medical Officer: Dr D Fenske

Number in School. There are some 713 boys in the Upper School of whom some 253 are boarders and 460 day boys.

The Curriculum. Boys enter the Preparatory School from 7 and the Upper School at 13 years of age. The Preparatory School has its own Headmaster and specialist staff. (*See also Bedford Preparatory School entry in IAPS section.*)

A coordinated curriculum takes boys through the two Schools. The emphasis is on breadth of experience: as few doors as possible are closed at option stages. Boys are prepared for GCSE and for the new broader portfolio of AS and A Levels, and for Key Skills and General Studies. Boys also have the option to study the International Baccalaureate Diploma in the Sixth Form as an alternative to A Levels. Notably strong are Languages, Mathematics and the Sciences, and there has been heavy investment in Technology and Information Technology. Since September 2009, the School has adopted the IGCSE qualifications in the three Sciences and Design and Technology, adding English in 2010. Mandarin Chinese is also taught off timetable to those boys wishing to study the language. There is also a well-resourced Academic Support department providing valuable assistance to boys where necessary.

Boys are encouraged to make good use of non-teaching time. There are extensive departmental and central library facilities, and strong emphasis is placed upon Music, Art, Drama and IT. Clubs and Societies abound for both boarders and day boys. Concerts, plays, lectures and film performances are given in the Great Hall, the Recital Hall, the Erskine May Hall and the Theatre.

Facilities. The School's £3 million Music School is one of the largest in the country. The Recreation Centre incorporates a 250-seat theatre, new state-of-the-art fitness suite, large sports hall, squash courts and a 25-metre indoor swimming pool. Other facilities include an observatory and planetarium, twin astroturf pitches and a £1.8 million library.

Classes. In the Preparatory School boys are taught in forms until age 11, and are setted for most subjects. For all post-GCSE work, a generous block system is used which enables boys to study a variety of subjects at AS and A Level, combining, if desired, Arts and Science subjects. In addition a range of subsidiary teaching is provided including Citizenship.

Information Technology. Always at the forefront of ICT developments, the school has a site-wide fibre-optic network, including wi-fi access everywhere, enabling approximately 650 school computers, 350+ pupil-owned laptops, and several hundred 'mobile devices' (such as iPads, iPods and phones) to use the extensive facilities provided both within and external to the site.

The school Intranet is used as a daily information system for staff, pupils, and parents, and provides a access to our eLearning site, emails (for all staff and pupils), as well as information such as school reports. The library maintains an excellent range of online resources, including 'Clickview' that delivers teaching video clips to classroom projectors and Interactive Whiteboards.

There are 12 ICT suites with between 15 and 24 PCs each, including subject specific ones in Art, DT and Music, and three sets of classroom laptops. The school is also actively investigating mobile initiatives using iPods to deliver curriculum materials.

Key ICT skills are taught in the first year in the Upper School, which boys use in most, if not all, of their academic subjects as they progress through GCSEs to A Levels or IB in the Sixth Form.

Careers and Higher Education. The School is a member of the Independent Schools Careers Organisation. There is a team of Careers Staff who maintain close contact with the Services and professional bodies, and commercial and industrial undertakings. There are regular contacts with local industry and Institutes of Technology and Higher Education. Annual Careers Conventions are held in Bedford.

Annually almost all of the Upper Sixth enters Higher Education, with between 10 and 15 boys entering Oxford and Cambridge Universities every year.

Games. A great variety of sporting activities is offered, and senior boys in particular have a wide choice. The major sports are Cricket, Rugby, Rowing, Hockey; and there is ample opportunity also for Athletics, Swimming, Tennis, Association Football, Rugby Fives, Squash, Badminton, Fencing, Basketball, etc. In addition, there are regular PE classes. The Recreation Centre facilities include a new fit-

ness suite, large sports hall, squash courts and heated indoor swimming pool.

Services and Activities. The School offers a diverse programme of extra-curricular activities every evening between 4.15 pm and 6 pm, many of which involve girls from other Harpur Trust schools. Boys are expected to participate fully in this programme during their time at the School. Activities include the Combined Cadet Force (CCF), Duke of Edinburgh's Award Scheme, Community Service, fundraising groups, and more than 50 other clubs and societies from Astronomy to Young Enterprise.

Music. As well as the two Senior Symphony Orchestras, a Chamber Orchestra, a Concert Band and a large Choral Society, there is a Chapel Choir trained in the English Cathedral tradition, two Junior Orchestras, a Dance Band, Jazz Band, a large number of chamber music groups, and a Music Club. The Music department is situated in a £3million, state-of-the-art, purpose-built development, which includes a fine Recital Hall.

Drama. A range of formal and informal dramatic productions are performed annually by all age groups. The well-equipped School Theatre provides a venue for visiting touring companies, performing for the benefit of pupils and the general public. House Plays are also produced on an annual basis.

Association with The Harpur Trust Girls' Schools. A large variety of co-educational activities are organised in association with the girls at our sister schools. These include academic cooperation in minority subjects, joint seminars in major subjects, and involvement in concerts, debates, conferences and a wide range of more informal social events.

Pastoral Supervision. We have a highly developed Pastoral system. Upper School pupils are under the supervision of a Tutor within small Tutor Groups; these "family" groups are organised on a vertical structure in terms of age.

Boarders and Day Boys. In the Upper School a careful balance of Boarders and Day Boys is maintained. The organisation and tradition of the School is such as to promote mixing and to avoid any discrimination between the two groups. They are combined in work, games and all other School activities, and are equally eligible for positions of responsibility whether in House or School. There are six Senior Boarding Houses, each containing up to 51 boys; and one Junior Boarding House of up to 35. There is also a Sixth Form Boarding House.

Visits and Exchanges. Well-established language-exchanges occur annually between Bedford and schools in France, Spain and Germany. There are also plentiful opportunities for educational travel including outward-bound and adventure camps and expeditions, annual skiing holidays, cultural visits to a range of countries, and inter-continental sports tours.

Admission to the Upper School. Applications should be made to the Registrar. The Registration fee is currently £100. All applicants are expected to provide evidence of good character and suitability from their previous school. Year 9 applicants from Preparatory Schools wishing to enter the Upper School are assessed in Year 7 by an initial Pre-test and interview. Subject to performance, a computer-based test (designed to measure raw academic potential) is taken at the School during Year 8. Applicants from Maintained Schools sit tests in English and Mathematics together with the computer-based test as mentioned above.

Scholarships and Bursaries. (*See Scholarship Entries section*.) Bedford seeks to identify boys of outstanding talent and give them access to a Bedford School education regardless of background. The school offers Access Awards and Scholarships to boys with academic, sporting or music potential.

Awards are available for boys joining the School at our 11+, 13+ and 16+ entry points.

For more information, please visit www.bedford-school.org.uk.

Fees per term (2011-2012). Day Boys £5,264; Full Boarders £8,649; Weekly Boarders £8,364.

Fees are payable to The Clerk, Harpur Trust Office, Pilgrim Centre, Brickhill Drive, Bedford MK41 7PZ.

Old Bedfordians Club. *Director*: Mrs B Roberts, 2 Burnaby Road, Bedford MK40 2TT. Tel: 01234 362262.

Charitable status. The Bedford Charity (The Harpur Trust) is a Registered Charity, number 204817.

Belfast Royal Academy

Belfast, Co Antrim BT14 6JL, Northern Ireland
Tel: 028 9074 0423
Fax: 028 9075 0607
e-mail: enquiries@bfsra.belfast.ni.sch.uk
website: www.belfastroyalacademy.com

Board of Governors:
K A Knox, MSc (*Warden*)
P S Sefton, LLB (*Senior Vice Warden*)
Mrs J Weir, BSc, CMath, MIMA (*Honorary Secretary*)
T M A Baldwin, BSc, MIBiol, CBiol
N W Beggs, Esq
Miss K M Bill, MBChB, FFARCSI
E W Bleakley, TCert, BA, MSc, BPGCUT
Mrs K Burns, BA
Mrs A Clements, BA
R Connolly, BSc
Ms C Dillon, BA
Ms W E Graham, MA
J A Hill, FREng, FIAE, BSc, Hon DSc, CEng, FICE, FIStructE, FIEI, FIHT
J W Martin, FRICS
P S McBride, BSc, MInstP
B W McCormack, BSc Econ, FCA
S B Orr, LLB
S R Potts, MB, BCh, BAO, FRCSI
N Reid, LLB, FCA
Mrs C Scoffield, CertEd, DipEd
G Simon, FRICS
D Walsh, BSc, MBA, CEng, MIME
I Warke, BSc
S J S Warke, ACII, DipPFS, TEP
A J Wilkinson, FCA
M T Wilson, BSc
J M G Dickson, MA

Headmaster: **J M G Dickson**, MA

Deputy Head: L H Campbell, BSc, PhD

Vice-Principals:
A R Creighton, BEd, PQH
Ms C N Scully, BSc, PhD, ALCM, PQH

Senior Mistresses:
Ms W E Graham, MA, PQH
Mrs B Lomas, BA, MEd, PhD

Senior Masters:
G J N Brown, BA, PhD
R D Evans, BA

Senior House Master: T M A Baldwin, BSc, MIBiol, CBiol

Deputy Senior Masters:
R J Jamison, BSc
M T Wilson, BSc

Heads of Departments:
Mrs P Kerr, BA, ATD (*Art*)
Mrs E McMorran, BSc (*Biology*)
Mrs G McQuiston, BEd (*Business Studies*)
Ms J R Adams, BEd (*Careers*)
B T McMurray, BSc, PhD (*Chemistry*)

J D L Reilly, MBE, BA (*Classics*)
Ms W E Graham, MA (*English*)
C A Stewart, BSc (*Geography*)
J A McCombe, BA, PhD (*History*)
P Cupples, BSc (*ICT*)
G J N Brown, BA, PhD (*Mathematics*)
Miss S B Park, BA (*Modern Languages*)
Ms M McMullan, MA, MusB, LTCL, ALCM (*Music*)
W I McGonigle, BEd (*Physical Education and Boys' Games*)
R Budden, MSc (*Physics*)
Mrs V Heaslip, BEd (*Religious Studies*)
Mrs B Lomas, BA, MEd, PhD (*Social Science*)
N E Moore, BSc (*Technology*)

Senior Subject Teachers:
R D Evans, BA (*Drama and Theatre Studies*)
S W Graham, MA (*Mathematics*)
Miss T McBeth, MA (*English*)
J M Patterson, BSc Econ, MSSc, DCG (*Economics*)
D R S Nash, BSc, MEd, DASE (*European Studies*)
Miss R McCay, MA (*German*)
Mrs R F Morrison, BA (*Home Economics*)
Mrs C Leyden, BA (*Spanish*)
Miss M P McCullough, BA (*Special Needs*)

Heads of Year (Boys):	*Heads of Year (Girls)*:
A A W Bell, BSc, BAgrSc, PhD, AIEA	Mrs G C Morris, BEd
J Buchan, BEM, MA	Mrs M Gray, BSc
J Carolan, MA	Ms S R Ardis, BSc
M C W Harte, BA	Mrs K McIntyre, BSc
R K Lunn, BEd	Mrs R F Morrison, BA
M J Neill, MSc	Mrs A M Reynolds, BSc
M T Wilson, BSc	Mrs J Robb, BSc

Assistant Staff:	
Mrs C J Adair, BA, PhD	D Morrison, MSc
Mrs N J Allen, BA	Mrs D M Nicholl, BA
Mrs J C Bell, BSc	Mrs L I Nicholl, BSc
Mrs K Black, BA	Mrs N S Nicholl, BA
Ms C Burns, BSc, PhD, MRSC	Mrs R O'Donnell, BA, DipAD, ATD
R Carroll, BEd	Mrs L Patterson, BA
Miss V Carson, MA, ALCM	P Porter, BA, BD Comm
Mrs J M Cleland, BSc	Miss C E Prior, BMus
Mrs J A Connolly, BA	Mrs S S Roberts, BA
Mrs L Cowan, MSc	M R Shields, BA
Mrs C E Currie, BA	Mrs J Smyth, BA
P Dorman, BTh	W J W Spence, BEd, MA
A Forrest, BA	S C Springer, MSc
Mrs F A Gilmore, BSc	P T Stretton, BEd
S W Graham, MA	Mrs A P Terek, BSc
Mrs M L Gray, BA, MEd, DASE	Mrs M E M Thompson, BA
Miss J L Hamilton, BA	Miss S Tinman, BA
Mrs N Henry, BSc	Miss R C Wallace, BA
Mrs C Hughes, BSc	Mrs M N Wilson, BA
T Hughes, MSc	Miss J Winning, BSc
N Irwin, BEd	
Mrs P Kerr, BA, ATD	*Classroom Assistants*:
Miss H L Lavery, BSc	Miss L Armour
C P Little, BA	Mrs B Burtenshaw, BA, DipEd
Mrs I Lyttle, MSc	Miss S Muhtadi
P J Martin, BEd	Miss S Stewart
Mrs G McCadden, DipAD, ATD	Mrs K Tepe
C R McCarey, BSc	Mrs N Watson
Mrs B McCaughran, Dip PE	*Careers Advisers*:
Mrs J McGowan, MA	Ms J R Adams, BEd
Miss D McGuigan, BA	Ms D Keenan, MSc
Mrs H Miller, BA	A K Moles, BSc
Mrs S M Miller, BEng	S B Murphy, BEd
	J M Patterson, BSc Econ, MSSc, DCG
	Mrs H Tate, BA

Preparatory Department:

Principal: Mrs V M McCaig, BEd, DASE
Deputy Principal: W T Wilson, BEd, LTCL

Assistant Staff:

P J Ingram, BEd, MSc	Mrs A Phillips
S Johnston, BSc	Mrs E L Philpott
Mrs P Lennon, BEd	Mrs L Todd
Mrs B Marshall, CertEd	
Mrs S Sherrard, CertEd	*Pre-Prep & Daycare Staff*:
Mrs E N E Wilson, BEd	Miss J Bradley
Mrs R Wilson, BA, BEd,	Mrs L Kyle
LTCL	Mrs E Moorhead
	Mrs C Sempey

Classroom Assistants:
Miss H E Crossan, BA

Administration:
Bursar: Miss E Hull, BSc, DipAcc, FCA
Assistant Bursar: D W Ritchie, BSc Econ
Headmaster's Secretary: Mrs P McClintock
General Office Manager: Ms P Ferguson
Office Administrator: Mrs L D Oliver
Receptionist/Telephonist: Mrs A Foy
Bursar's Secretary: Miss G Boyd, BA
Librarian: Mrs T Corcoran, BA
ICT Manager: J R Cleland, BSc
Matron: Miss P McKenna, BSc
Alumni Officer: E G A McCamley, MA
Estates Manager: W J Thompson
Sixth Form Study Supervisor: Mrs C A Clyde
Supervisor of Grounds: T D Robinson
Swimming Pool Manager: Mrs E Alexander, BA

Belfast Royal Academy, founded in 1785, is the oldest school in the city. It moved to its present site, on the Cliftonville Road in North Belfast, in 1880, and the Gothic building erected at that time has been extensively modernised and refurbished. The fourteen Science Laboratories were opened in 1971, a 25-metre indoor heated Swimming Pool was completed in 1974, a new building for Art and Craft came into full use in 1982, and a Sports Hall was opened to mark the Bi-Centenary year. In 1989 a new Sixth Form Centre and Careers Suite were opened and a purpose-built four-room Technology Suite was completed in September 1991. An additional classroom block for English and Drama was opened in September 1994, and a new building to house the Mathematics department came into use in 1998. Since 2001 four new ICT Suites have been provided, and there is extensive provision throughout the school for teaching and learning through information technology.

The Academy is a co-educational day grammar school and there is also a preparatory and kindergarten department. The grammar school has some 1,400 boys and girls, between the ages of 11 and 19. The kindergarten and preparatory department, known as Ben Madigan, has some 160 children, aged from 3 to 11; it is situated at 690 Antrim Road.

The curriculum has a strong academic bias and former pupils of the school are among the members of almost every university in the United Kingdom.

The work of the junior and middle Forms is directed mainly towards the GCSE examinations of the Northern Ireland Council for the Curriculum Examinations and Assessment, the Assessment and Qualifications Alliance or OCR, with a minimum of specialisation, all the usual subjects being provided and careful attention being given to the requirements of the universities and the professions. Religious studies are taught on a non-denominational basis.

There are more than 380 pupils in the Sixth Forms, where GCE Advanced Level courses are available in English, English Literature, Drama and Theatre Studies, French, German, Spanish, Latin, Mathematics (incorporating Mechanics and/or Statistics), Further Mathematics, Physics, Chemistry, Biology, Geography, History, Classical Civilisation, Economics, Politics, Art, Music, Home Economics, Business Studies, ICT, Physical Education, Religious Studies, Sociology and Technology. Some Sixth Formers take an additional Certificate of Competence in Information Technology, or an OCR-accredited qualification in keyboard skills. Pupils are prepared for entry to Oxford or Cambridge in all the main subjects.

Much attention is given to careers guidance by the Careers Advisors, other senior members of Staff, and the Heads of Year.

The normal school day is from 8.40 am to 3.30 pm. There is no Saturday school but matches are played in the major sports on Saturdays. The school year runs from the beginning of September to the end of June, with holidays of about a fortnight at Christmas and at Easter.

There are some sixty different activities in the extra-curricular programme.

The principal games are, for boys, rugby, cricket, hockey, cross-country running, swimming and athletics; for girls, hockey, netball, tennis, swimming, cross-country running and athletics. Show-jumping, water polo, golf and skiing are also available.

There is an orchestra, senior and junior choirs, a wind band, a Jazz band, several string ensembles and an Irish traditional group. Individual tuition in orchestral instruments is also provided. School organisations include Societies for Music, Drama, Chess, Bridge, Photography and Debating, an Air Training Corps, an Amateur Radio Club, Community Service and Christian Union groups and the Duke of Edinburgh's Award Scheme.

Parents pay a capital fee of £140 each year and a voluntary contingency charge of £21 per month.

In Ben Madigan, the annual fee is £3,075 for Years 1 to 3 and £3,255 for Years 4 to 7.

BRA Old Boys' Association. Hon Secretary: Dr L Campbell, c/o Belfast Royal Academy.

BRA Old Girls' Association. Hon Secretary: Mrs C Scoffield, 15 Glenshane Park, Newtownabbey, BT37 0QN.

Berkhamsted School

133 High Street, Berkhamsted, Hertfordshire HP4 2DJ
Tel: 01442 358000
Fax: 01442 358040
e-mail: enquiries@berkhamstedschool.org
website: www.berkhamstedschool.org

In 1541 John Incent, Dean of St Paul's, was granted a Licence by Henry VIII to found a school in Berkhamsted, Incent's home town. Until the end of the nineteenth Century Berkhamsted School served as a grammar school for a small number of boys from the town but over the last century it has developed into a school of significance. In 1888 the foundation was extended by the establishment of Berkhamsted School for Girls. In 1996, these two schools formalised their partnership, offering the highest quality education to pupils from ages 3 to 19.

There are 320 pupils in the flourishing co-educational Sixth Form; between the ages of eleven and sixteen 440 boys at the Boys School (Castle) and 320 girls at the Girls School (Kings) are taught in single-sex groups; and 450 pupils from ages three to eleven attend the Preparatory School.

The Principal is a member of both HMC and GSA.

Patron: Her Majesty The Queen.

The Governors:
¶Mr P J Williamson (*Chairman*)
¶Mrs A F Moore-Gwyn (*Vice-Chairman*)

Mr J J Apthorp	¶Mr S Bourne

Dr Y A Burne
Mr P Burroughs
Mrs B Canham
Mrs C Green
Mr R G Groom
¶Mr M P Horton
¶Mrs E Jeffrey
Mrs J Laws
Mr A H Noel

Mr B Parker, Fellow of St
 John's College,
 Cambridge
Mr A N Reston
Mr S Rolland
¶Mr M Scicluna
Mrs S Tidey
Mrs S Turner
Mr W R Winfield

Miss A K Martin, MA
Mr P Matthews, MA, BSc
†Mr R D Matthews, BSc
†Mr H R Maxted, BA
Mrs H McCann, MA, MBA
†Miss R McColl, BA,
 MPhil
†Mr T Medaris, MSc, BA
†Mrs R E Miles, BSc
Mr R Moseley, BA
Ms C J Moss, BA
Mr R K Mowbray, MA
†Mr R F Newport, BA
Mrs S Nicholls
*Mr B Noithip, MMus, BA
†Mr P H Northcroft, BA
Miss J Osborn
†Mr D R Pain, BA,
 BComm
Mrs D D Pearson, BEd
†Mr M S Pett, BA
§Mrs J F Phillips, BA, MA
Mrs K M Pickles, BEd
*Mrs A M Pike, CertEd,
 RSA DipSpLD
†Dr S A Redman, BSc,
 PhD
Mr S J E Rees, BA
†Mr D G Richardson, BSc

*Mrs E A Richardson, BA
*Mr P T Riddick, MA,
 MSc
*Mr S C Robinson, BSc
Miss A M V Rust, BA
Mrs C G Ryder, BSc
*Mr C H Savill, BA
Mr B P Shepherd, BSc
†Mrs S M Shipton, DEUG
 Licence
*Mr D W Short, BA
Mrs V M D Sim, BA
Mrs J Simons, BA
*Mr M Sparrow, BA
Miss L Spray, BA
*Mr I R Stewart, BA, MA
†Mrs G S Swart, BA
Mr M J Thum, MA
Mrs K E Tomlin, BA, MA
†Mr D S van Noordwyk
*Mr A van Straten, BA
Mrs R H Warburton, BSc
†Mrs K Warde, BSc,
 DipSpLD
Mr W A Webb, BA, BEd,
 MEd
Mr S A Whyte, BSc, MSc
Mr D J Wiles, BSc, MEd

Principal: Mr M S Steed, MA Cantab, MA

Vice Principal (Education): Dr H Brooke, BSc, PhD
Vice Principal (Business Operations): Mr P Nicholls, MA
 Cantab, ACA
Headmaster Sixth Form: Mr J M P Walker, MA Oxon, MA
Head Berkhamsted Boys (Boys 11–16): Mr C Nicholls,
 CertEd
Head Berkhamsted Girls (Girls 11–16): Mrs A J R Clancy,
 BEd
Deputy Head (Sixth Form): Mr G W H Anker, BA
Deputy Head (Sixth Form): Ms J Potter, MPhil, BA
Deputy Head (Boys 11–16): Mr R C Thompson, BA
Deputy Head (Girls 11–16): Mrs K M Woodrow, BSc
Director of Studies: Mr W R C Gunary, BSc
Chaplain: Reverend J E Markby, BA

Teaching staff:

Miss S Afsar, BA, LLM
*Mr C Allam, BEd, BSc
*Miss A M Ashby, BA
Mr A J Atkinson, BA
Dr J W R Baird, BA, PhD
*Mrs A E Bamforth, BA
Miss N A Barker, BA
Mr M E Batchelder,
 CertEd, DipEd, MA
*Mrs K R Best, BA,
 CPhys, MInstP
Mr D Binnie, BSc
Mrs K M Bly, BA
Mrs S M Blythe, MA
 Cantab, OCR DipSpLD
Ms J D Bohitige, BA
†Miss R M Bradley, BA
Mrs L C Briand, BA,
 DipTESOL
Mr S E Bridle, BA
Miss J E Brodie, BA
Dr A L Brogden, PhD,
 MChem
Miss E Brown, BA
Mr G R Burchnall, BEd
*Ms H-C Burt, BTh
*Mr N J Cale, BA
*Mr F Charnock, CertEd
Mr P Chaundy, BA
Mrs L J Chinnock, BSc
Mrs S A E Clay, Dip
 CSSD, CertEd, MA
Mrs N L Cohen, BA
*Mr R W D Coupe, BA,
 MA
*Mr P C Cowie, MA
Mr S J Dight, BA, DipEd
*Mr P E Dobson, BSc,
 CChem, MRSC
*Miss L M Doggett, BA
Mrs S M Dolan, BSc
Mrs A Dunmall, BSc,
 DipSpLD
Dr C M J Dutton, BSc, PhD
†Mr C H Eaton, BSc
Mr A J R Esland, MA,
 MMus

†Mrs B Evans, MA Cantab
†Mr B P Evers, BA
*Mrs C M E Ferguson,
 MA, BA
Mr D L Foster, BA
Mrs S C Foster, BSc
†Mrs L J Francis, BA
Mr V Fung, BSc
Mr R B Garner, BA
Ms F M Garratt, BSc
Miss J Gateau
Miss E L Gent, BA, MA,
 ATC
Mr D J Gibson, BSc
Mrs K A Gilbertson, MA
†Mr T A Grant, MA
†Mrs H A A Green, BSc
*Mrs S B Gunary, BA, MA
*Mr S R Hargreaves, BEd
Dr A J Harker, BA, MA,
 PhD
†Mr P J Harvey, BA
Dr P Hatfield-Iacoponi,
 BA, PhD
Mrs A Hatton, BA
Mr P J Hopkins, BA,
 BMus, FRCO, ARCM
Miss J J Hughes, BSc, MEd
†Dr S P S Hundal, BSc,
 PhD
Mrs L J Instone, BA
Mrs S J James, BEd
*Mr D Jeffers, BSc
Ms S P Jennings, BSc
Mrs T A Kergon, BSc
Mrs P Kent, CertEd
Mr T C Kirby, BA
Mr A Lansdell, DipEd
Miss A L Y Lefrancois,
 Licence LLCE
†Mr T D Lines, BA, MA,
 MEd
Mr P R Luckraft, BA
Miss J M Lupton, BA
*Mr R I Mackay, BA Ed
Mr B R Mahoney, BEd
Mr R H Mardo, BSc

Additional Staff:

Music:
There are 30 visiting music staff offering instrumental
teaching in: acoustic guitar, bagpipes, bassoon, cello, clarinet, double bass, electric guitar, euphonium, flute, French
horn, harpsichord, jazz piano, oboe, organ, percussion
(including kit drumming), piano, recorder, saxophone,
trombone, trumpet, tuba, viola and violin.

Sports Centre Manager: Mr H Adler
Head of Learning Resources: Miss R Guy, BA, MA
Medical Officer: Dr N Ormiston, MB BS, MRCP, DRCOG

PA to Principal: Mrs N M Golder
(Tel: 01442 358002; Fax: 01442 358003)
PA to Vice Principal (Education): Mrs L Hornsey
(Tel: 01442 358109; Fax: 01442 358003)
PA to Vice Principal (Business Operations): Mrs N Murray
(Tel: 01442 358005; Fax: 01442 358006)
PA to Head Berkhamsted Boys: Mrs T Rawlings
(Tel: 01442 358031; Fax: 01442 358032)
PA to Head Berkhamsted Girls: Mrs S Watney
(Tel: 01442 358161; Fax 01442 358162)
PA to Headmaster Berkhamsted Sixth: Mrs P M Webb
(Tel: 01442 358052; Fax 01442 358053)

Aims. At Berkhamsted we believe that excellent academic results do not have to be won at the expense of the
wider attributes of a good education. The School seeks to
enable pupils to achieve their full potential. In addition to
the development of the intellect, social, sporting and cultural
activities play an important part within the framework of a
disciplined and creative community based on Christian values. It is important that pupils come to value both the individual and the Community through School life. The School
seeks to encourage spiritual and moral values and a sense of
responsibility as an essential part of the pursuit of excellence.

Location. The School stands in the heart of Berkhamsted,
an historic and thriving town only thirty miles from London.
It enjoys excellent communications to London, the airports,
to the Midlands and the communities of Buckinghamshire,
Bedfordshire and Hertfordshire.

Facilities. The original site has at its heart a magnificent Tudor Hall used as a Schoolroom for over 300 years. Other buildings are from late Victorian to modern periods and of architectural interest (especially the Chapel modelled on the Church of St Maria dei Miracoli in Venice). There are new Science laboratories, Library and Learning Resources Centres, Information Technology suites, Sixth Form centres, Careers libraries, Dining hall, Medical centre, House rooms, Deans' Hall (an Assembly Hall and Theatre) and Centenary Hall (a modern 500-seat Hall also used for concerts and theatre productions). Recreational and sports facilities include extensive playing fields, Fives courts, Squash courts, Tennis courts, Gymnasium, Drama studio, Music school and Art studios. A new Sports Hall and 25m indoor swimming pool were opened in 2004 and a state-of-the-art Design Centre in 2008.

Diamond Structure. The School has a "diamond" structure that combines both single-sex and co-educational teaching. Boys and Girls are taught together until the age of 11, separately from 11–16, before coming back together again in a joint Sixth Form.

Curriculum. The senior school curriculum includes: English, English Literature, Mathematics, Biology, Chemistry, Physics, History, Geography, Religious Studies, French/German/Spanish, Latin/Classics, Music, Art, Design and Technology. Up to eleven subjects may be taken for GCSE. In the Sixth Form, AS/A2 courses are offered in 27 subjects. Pupils are prepared for university entrance, including Oxbridge. All pupils are taught computer skills and have access to ICT centres. Careers guidance and personal tutoring are offered throughout.

Day and Boarding. Pupils may be full boarders, weekly/flexible boarders or day pupils. The two Boarding houses, accommodating boys and girls separately, are well equipped and within a few minutes walk of the main campus. There are up to 100 boarding places. Day pupils come from both Berkhamsted and the surrounding area of Hertfordshire, Buckinghamshire and Bedfordshire.

Pastoral Care and Discipline. The main social and pastoral unit is the House; the Head of House and House Tutors provide continuity of support and advice and monitor each individual pupil's progress.

The aim is to encourage self-discipline so that pupils work with a sense of responsibility and trust. Pupils are expected to be considerate, courteous, honest and industrious.

There is a Medical Centre with qualified staff. The School Medical Officer has special responsibility for boarders. A qualified Counsellor is available to all pupils for confidential counselling. The school also has a full-time Chaplain.

Sport and Leisure Activities. Major sports for Girls are Lacrosse, Netball and Tennis and for Boys, Rugby, Football, Hockey and Cricket. A number of other sports are also pursued including Athletics, Badminton, Cross-Country, Eton Fives, Fencing, Golf, Hockey, Judo, Rowing, Shooting, Squash and Swimming. Team games are encouraged and pupils selected for regional and national squads.

There is a flourishing Duke of Edinburgh's Award scheme at all levels. The CCF, community service, work experience and 'Young Enterprise' are offered, along with clubs for gymnastics, drama, computing and technology. Regular school theatre productions, orchestral and choral concerts achieve high standards of performance.

Careers. A team of advisors, internal and external, is directed by the Head of Careers who also arranges Careers Lunches, and an annual Careers, Universities and GAP Year Fair. Heads of House oversee pupils' applications for higher education, together with parents and Careers advisors. The great majority of leavers proceeds to university and higher education.

Entry. Entry to the Preparatory School from the age of 3 onwards and entry to the Senior School from 11. The School's Entrance Assessments and an interview are required. The minimum entrance requirement for the Sixth Form is 5B and 2C grades at GCSE, with A grades required to proceed to Mathematics, Science and Language A Levels, although competition amongst external candidates means that it is the norm that top grades are required.

Scholarships and Bursaries. (*See Scholarship Entries section.*) It is the Governors' policy to award Scholarships and Exhibitions on merit to pupils whom the Governors wish to attract to Berkhamsted because of the contribution that they are able to make to School life, be that academic, musical, sporting, creative or as potential leaders.

Bursaries are awarded for academic or other merit, taking into account parental income and pupils' needs.

More information about Scholarships and Bursaries may be obtained on application to The Director of External Relations.

Fees per term (2011-2012). Day Pupils: Nursery £2,490; Preparatory £2,930–£3,915; Senior £4,770–£5,600. Boarding Pupils: £8,920.

Old Berkhamstedians. President: Mr Stephen Bourne.

Charitable status. Berkhamsted School is a Registered Charity, number 311056. It is a leading Charitable School in the field of Junior and Secondary Education.

Birkdale School

Oakholme Road, Sheffield S10 3DH
Tel: 0114 266 8408
Fax: 0114 267 1947
e-mail: headmaster@birkdaleschool.org.uk
           admissions@birkdaleschool.org.uk
           enquiries@birkdaleschool.org.uk
website: www.birkdaleschool.org.uk

Birkdale School is a day school for 790 pupils, boys from 4 to 18 with a co-educational Sixth Form. The 4–11 Preparatory School is on a separate campus nearby. (*For further details see IAPS section.*) The Sixth Form was launched in 1988 and now has around 180 pupils, 95% of whom in recent years have entered university. The Governing Body is in membership of the Association of Governing Bodies of Independent Schools.

Motto: '*Res non verba*'

Chairman of Governors: Dr J R Goepel, MBChB, FRCPath
D F Booker, BA, FCA
M H Crosby, MA
A McKenzie Smith
J E Oliver
Mrs A M Rees, MA, BEd, FRSA
Dr R Richardson
Mrs M C Townsend, BSc, BDS, MA
J A Viner, MA, MBA, DipM, MCIM
Mrs K M Walker

Bursar and Clerk to the Governors: D H Taylor, BSc

Head Master: Dr P M Owen, MA, PhD

Deputy Head: A S Gloag, BA

Director of Studies: P R King, BA

Senior Tutors:
K D Brook, BSc
S H Kenyon, MA
Mrs A M Oliver, BA
Mrs H A Parsons, MA
Ms V Stolz, BEd

Assistant Staff:
G T AbouZeid, BSc, PhD   A J Alsop, BSc
*J D Allen, BSc   S Bacsich, MA

G Bish, BMus
A N Briggs, MSc, BSc
*Mrs S J Burt, BA
Mrs H D Clark, BSc
T W Clark, BSc
*M S Clarke, MA
C E Clifford, MSc, BSc
C J Cook, BSc
*R J Cottom, BEd
*D Craddock, BEng
*Mrs M A Daly, BA
N Deans, BA
A Gallagher
*S R Gordon, MA
Dr J Greenhalgh, MA, PhD
*R D Heaton, BEd
*Mrs K M Higham, BA, MEd
Mrs A-M Hinchliffe, BA
J C Hudson, MA
*A M Jordan, BMus
D B Julian, BA
Mrs R M Kemp, BA
M C Lidbury, BA
*Mrs M Linford, MEd
*Miss K J McDonnell, MA, BA
Miss K McKay, BA
Miss S D Miles, BA
M I Morton, BSc
Mrs S Mulcrone, MEd

*Dr P D Myatt, BSc, DPhil
*W M Newton, BSc, PhD
J R Nolan, BEng
B J O'Toole, BA
H Parker, BSc
*T J Pearson, BA
Mrs P Pickford, BA
Dr S Pitfield, PhD, BMus
M A Potter, BEd
Miss M C Randall, BSc
*Mrs M B Reynolds, BEd, Cert SocEd Studies, PGCert Dyslexia/Literacy
*M E Roach, BSc
C F Rodgers, BSc
*M H Rose, MA
*Mrs K Rose, MA
*Mrs F Rusling, BA
Mrs S L Ryan, BA
A M Sanderson, MA
Mrs J A Savage, BA
Miss R M Sever, MA
*Mrs H V Sherborne, MA
P C Snell, BSc
*S B Stoddard, BA
Mrs H J Thaw, BA
J J Turner, MEd
Mrs C Weeks, BA
Mrs J M White, BSc
A J Woodley, BEd

Librarian: Mrs J McQuillin

Preparatory School
Head of Prep School: C J Burch, BA, PGCE

Director of Studies: A J Oakey, MSc Ed, BA
Senior Mistress: Mrs J Witte, MA, BEd
Deputy Head: J R Leighton, BEd

Assistant Staff:
Mrs E J Arcari, BA
Miss J V Black, MSc, BEd
Mrs C Brewster, BA, DipSEN, PGDip Dyslexia
Mrs C A Carter-Shepherd, BA
J H Cooper, BSc
N Dymock, BSc
Mrs C Edge
Mrs H E Fletcher, BMus
Miss V Frewin, BA
Mrs C Grover, BA
Mrs N Hall, CertEd
D P Jones, GGSM

F G Kirkham, TD, BEd
Mrs J Kitchen, MEd, BEd
Miss R M Kitt, BEd
J M Lockwood, MPhil, BA
J Marsh, BSc
Mrs K J Massey, MA
Mrs H J Oakey, BEd
Miss V H Roberts, BEd
Mrs C Simpson, CertEd, DipSEN, DipSpLD Dys
Mrs J E Taylor, CertEd
Mrs G Vallance, CertEd, CertDys
Mrs F L M Walton, MA
Mrs M S Whitt, BA

Visiting Music/Speech and Drama Staff:
J Beatty, PPRNCM, PgDip (*Trombone*)
Miss L Beavers (*Clarinet, Saxophone*)
T Cannelli (*Percussion*)
T Collingwood, BMus (*Cello*)
Mrs Z Collingwood, BMus, MMus (*Piano*)
Ms J Dungworth (*Oboe*)
J Hackett, BMus, LGSM (*Flute*)
Dr L James, PhD, BA, ALCM (*Violin*)
T James (*French Horn*)
J A Kirwan, BMus (*Guitar*)
Mrs V Leppard, BMus, LRAM (*Flute/Piano*)
M Redfearn, BMus, LTCL (*Trumpet*)
Mrs S Slater, BA (*Flute*)
P Taylor, PgDip VS (*Singing*)
A Thompson, BMus, CertPG Perf Studies (*Trumpet*)
Mrs E Tipple, ARCM, BMus (*Violin/Viola*)
Mrs J Wright, ARMSC, GRSM (*Violin*)

Head Master's Secretary: Ms S van der Merwe, BSc

Registrar: Mrs C M Brown, BA

Set in a pleasant residential area near the University 1.5 miles from the city centre, and 5 miles from the Peak District National Park, the school has expanded in recent years to provide for Sheffield and South Yorkshire the only independent secondary school for boys, with a co-educational Sixth Form. Birkdale Preparatory School for 300 boys is on a separate campus half a mile from the Senior School. School coaches bring pupils from Worksop, Chesterfield, North Derbyshire, Rotherham and Barnsley.

Birkdale is a Christian school, reflecting its foundation in the evangelical tradition. There is nothing exclusive about this: entrance is open to all, and there is no denominational emphasis. We seek to develop the full potential of each individual: body, mind and spirit. Within a framework of high academic standards, pastoral care is given a high priority, balanced by an emphasis on sport and outdoor pursuits, music and drama with a range of extra-curricular activities available.

At 18, over 95% of pupils go on to university, with a good proportion each year gaining places at Oxford and Cambridge.

Admission. The main ages of admission are at 4, 7, 11 and 16, although it is possible to admit pupils at other ages if a place is available. Entrance examinations for candidates at 11 are held annually towards the end of January. Entrance to the co-educational Sixth Form is subject to interview and a satisfactory performance in GCSE examinations. In the first instance, enquiries should be addressed to the Registrar.

Academic Curriculum. Over 20 subjects are offered at AS and A level. A full range of academic subjects are offered to GCSE. All pupils study English Language and Literature, Mathematics, Double Award Science, at least one Modern Foreign Language (French, German, Spanish) and at least one of the Humanities subjects (Classical Studies, Geography, History, RE). Optional subjects include Art, DT: Electronic Products, DT: Resistant Materials, PE, Latin, Drama and Music. The wider curriculum includes ICT, Religious Education, Health Education, Careers and Economic Awareness. Latin, German and Spanish are compulsory subjects in the Lower School (11–13) in addition to the usual range of National Curriculum subjects.

Games and Outdoor Pursuits. The major games are Rugby, Soccer, Cricket and Athletics, with Cross Country, Hockey, Netball, Tennis, Squash, Basketball, Volleyball, Swimming and Golf also available. A £2 million sports pavilion was opened in 2006 at the playing fields which are a short bus ride away from the school. All members of the school play games weekly. Additional team practices take place on Saturdays or at other times, and there is a full fixture list in the major sports. The school enjoys regular use of the university swimming pool nearby. Additionally, we use two local international venues, Ponds Forge and the English Institute of Sport for basketball, netball, dance and athletics. Birkdale's Sports Hall is at the centre of the Senior School campus.

Outdoor Pursuits play an important part in the overall leadership training programme. All members of the school participate in regular training sessions leading in each age group to a major expedition. This programme culminates in the 4th Form camp held annually in Snowdonia: this includes a trek involving all participants in leadership training. Virtually all members of the Third Form take the Bronze Award of the Duke of Edinburgh's Award Scheme, and an increasing number progress to Silver and Gold awards.

Music and the Arts. Music, Art and Drama flourish both within and outside the formal curriculum. A full annual programme of dramatic and musical productions is arranged. Over 120 pupils receive weekly instrumental music lessons at school, and a wide range of orchestras and choirs provide opportunities for pupils to experience group musical activities at an appropriate level.

Extra-Curricular Activities. There is a broad range of clubs and societies which meet at lunchtime and outside the formal school day, providing opportunities for members of the school to explore and excel in activities such as Chess, Debating, Design and Drama, as well as in the usual activities such as sport, outdoor pursuits, art and music.

Careers. The school is a member of the Independent Schools' Careers Organisation, and there is a well equipped Careers Centre in the Grayson Building. A biennial Careers Convention is held in the school and regular visits are made by services liaison officers and others to give advice and help to individual members of the school under the guidance of the school's careers staff.

All members of the Lower Sixth participate in a Work Experience scheme for a week, placed in a work environment in line with their possible choice of career.

The school runs Young Enterprise companies each year which introduce Sixth Formers to the world of business and management, and awards are often won in local competition.

Information and Communications Technology. In addition to the main ICT Centre, the computer network extends throughout the Campuses of both the Senior and Preparatory schools. Each member of the school is able to access the system in every part of the school. ICT is incorporated in a variety of ways into teaching across the curriculum. All pupils have supervised access to the Internet.

Learning Support Unit. Both the Senior and Preparatory school have their own Learning Support Centres. Pupils with dyslexic difficulties are given expert help within the school context and in full consultation with subject staff and are encouraged to achieve their full potential in public examinations.

Fees per term (2011-2012). Senior School £3,559, Preparatory School £2,939, Pre-Preparatory Department £2,485, including lunches, textbooks and stationery (with the exception of Sixth Form textbooks).

Scholarships. (*See Scholarship Entries section.*) The following Scholarships are available: Academic Scholarships at 11 and 16; Music Scholarships at 11 and 16.

Most scholarships are worth up to 25% of fees, with Bursaries available up to 100% of fees in cases of need.

Charitable status. Birkdale School is a Registered Charity, number 1018973, and a Company Limited by Guarantee, registered in England, number 2792166. It exists to develop the full potential of its members within a Christian community.

Birkenhead School

58 Beresford Road, Oxton, Birkenhead, Merseyside CH43 2JD
Tel: 0151 652 4014
Fax: 0151 651 3091
e-mail: enquire@birkenheadschool.co.uk
website: www.birkenheadschool.co.uk

Birkenhead School was opened in 1860, with the object of providing a public-school education, both Classical and Modern.

Motto: *'Beati mundo corde'*

Visitor: The Rt Revd The Lord Bishop of Chester

President: The Rt Hon Lord Nicholls of Birkenhead, MA Cantab, LLB, Hon LLD Liverpool

Honorary Vice-Presidents:
S J Haggett
D I Mackay
J A Gwilliam

A G Hurton
Lord Wade of Chorlton
A Whittam Smith
A L B Thomson

Emeritus Vice-Presidents:
K J Speakman-Brown
H W McCready
D A Fletcher

Governors:
Chairman: A Sutton, MA, FCA
Vice Chairman: Dr J K Moore, OBE, FRCA, MBA
I G Boumphrey
A J Cross, LLB
Mrs L Dodd, BA, FSI
G E Jones, MA
E N Rice, FRICS, MCIArb
W D C Rushworth, BA
Mrs A Walsh, BEd, Dip EFL
A F Watson, FCA

Headmaster: **D J Clark**, MA Exeter College Oxford

Deputy Headmaster: D R Edmunds, BSc

Deputy Head (Academic): R A Barlow, BSc

Assistant Head: M Roden, BA

Assistant Head: C D McKie, MA (*Head of History*)

Bursar and Clerk to the Governors: C F Button, BSc, CDir

Assistant Teachers:
A M Aldred
Mrs L D Alford-Swift, BSc
P G Armstrong, BSc (*Head of Biology*)
D R Bell (*Head of ICT*)
A J Blain, BEd (*Head of Art*)
K M Britton, MA, MSc
Miss S E Burns, MSc
S W Clark, PGCE
A S Davies, MA (*Network Manager*)
G J Ellis, BEd (*Director of Music*)
J L Fox, MA
S M Gill, MA (*Head of Geography*)
Ms E A Grey, BA (*Head of Religious Education*)
S Guinness, BSc (*Head of Design and Technology*)
M J Hayward, BSc (*Head of Science*)
D A Hendry, BEd (*Head of Year 11*)
T M Higginbottom, BEng
D W Highcock, BSc
G R Hill, BA
Ms M L Holgate, BA (*Head of Modern Languages*)
S W Hope, BSc (*Head of Mathematics*)
G Hopkins, MA (*Head of Sixth Form*)
W A Hughes, MA, PhD (*Head of Year 9*)
P Lindberg, BSc (*Head of Chemistry, Assistant Head of Sixth Form*)
R E Lytollis, BSc (*Head of Physical Education and Games*)
Miss S N Mason, BA
Mrs A McGoldrick, BA (*Head of English*)
J McGrath, MA
Miss J H Moore, BA (*Special Educational Needs Coordinator*)
Mrs I Nolan, BA
S J Parry, BA (*Head of Year 10, Assessment Manager*)
C Rimmer, BA (*Assistant Head of Overdale, Assistant Head of Modern Languages*)
R A Rule, BA (*Head of Economics*)
A Rymer, BSc
C L Smale, MA
Ms L Smeaton, BA (*Head of Overdale*)
M A Turner, MA
Mrs M T Washington, BA (*Head of Classics*)
Mrs C Walker, MA
P M Webster, BEng (*Head of Physics*)

Ms E Wilday, BA

Houses and Housemasters:
Beresford House: C L Smale
Shrewsbury House: A W Rymer
Bidston House: A J Blain
Kingsmead House: Miss S E Burns

Learning Support
Mrs B Cederholm, MA
Mrs G M Tooley, CertEd
Mrs E M Kearney, BA
Mrs P J Dale, CertEd

Headmaster's PA: Mrs D Roberts
Chaplain: Mrs Lesley Rendle, BSc
Librarian: Mrs E Reeve, BA
SSI: Captain Alan Joseph, BEM
Nurse: Mrs J Pizer, RGN, RSCN

Prep School

Headmistress: Mrs J A Skelly, BEd

Assistant Staff:

Mrs V Belchier, CertEd	Mrs P J McDonald, CertEd
Miss C M Bennett, BA	Mrs S G Mills, BEd
Miss A C Bentley, BA	Mrs G A Mudge, BSc
T G Brand, BSc	Ms P Relph, BA
N J Corran, BEng	Mrs H J Sewell, BA
Miss A C Delaney, BA	Mrs S Sharman, CertEd
N J Frowe, BA	Mrs I Smith, CertEd
Mr R A Halpin, BSc	M G Stockdale, BA
Miss S J Harris, BA	Mrs E Thuraisingam, BSc
Dr S M Jarvis, BSc, PhD	Mrs N J Williams, BA
Mrs S J Keating, BA	Mrs C E Winn, BEd
Mrs J Mayers, BEd	

The School consists of a Nursery, a Pre-Prep, a Prep School and a Senior School including a Sixth Form. Previously an all-boys School, the Sixth Form became co-educational in 2000 and the remainder of the School in 2008. Heads of Year and Head of Sixth Form have direct responsibility for the pastoral welfare of pupils in their section of the School and each oversees and coordinates the work of a team of Form Tutors. Pupils in Years 7 and 8 are mostly taught in their own building, *Overdale*.

Pupils come from all areas of Wirral, North Cheshire and North Wales. Public transport is good and there is an extensive network of School buses.

The School buildings are grouped around a spacious campus in the residential area of Oxton, and a development programme in recent years has added very considerably to the School's already extensive facilities. The Prep occupies the whole of the Shrewsbury Road site, a new Pre-Prep was opened in October 2004 and a Nursery for children from 3 months to 3 years in 2006. A major extension to the Prep School, including ICT and Design and Technology suites together with general classrooms, was opened in September 2009. In the Senior School a new Sixth Form Centre was opened in January 2011, along with new classrooms for English and Economics. Other developments in recent years include a new Music Department, three fully refurbished Physics laboratories, substantial extension to facilities for Technology, and an indoor climbing wall. Separate recreational facilities exist for Years 7–11. A new extension to the Sports Pavilion at McAllester Field was opened in 2009.

Curriculum. All pupils follow a common curriculum in Years 7 and 8 with a choice of two languages from French, Latin, German or Spanish in Year 8. The wide spectrum of subjects means that pupils are then ideally placed to make GCSE option choices at the end of Year 9. As well as the compulsory subjects – Mathematics, English (including for most English Literature), and three Sciences – pupils choose four more subjects from Art, French, Design and Technology, Geography, German, Greek, Spanish, Religious Studies, History, Latin and Music. Almost all combinations are possible, but attention is given to ensuring at this stage that pupils opt for appropriate subjects which will not restrict their future career choices. The School has remained committed to the teaching of Biology, Chemistry and Physics as separate subjects, but also offers Dual Award Science for some pupils. A "Beyond the Curriculum" programme has been established in Years 7 and 10, which includes, for example, an Etiquette course, the Environment, Drama, Philosophy and Debating, and a Sports Leaders Award. A programme of Personal Social and Health Education is provided for all pupils from Year 7 to Year 11, drawing on external agencies, as well as the School's own expertise. Compulsory Games and PE lessons not only support our highly successful sports teams but are also based on a philosophy of "games for all" with students of all abilities encouraged to enjoy physical activity by specialist games teachers.

Most pupils move into an academic Sixth Form environment where their AS and A Level preparation is geared towards post-18 university openings. Lower Sixth pupils can choose AS Levels from Art, Biology, Chemistry, Classical Civilisation, Design and Technology (Product Design or Systems and Control), Economics, English Language, English Literature, French, Further Mathematics, Geography, German, History, ICT, Latin, Mathematics, Music, Physical Education, Physics, Religious Studies, Spanish and Theatre Studies. Students in the Sixth Form also have a "Beyond the Curriculum" programme, which includes the European Computer Driving Licence, Business Enterprise, Russian, Politics, Philosophy, Engineering, and our innovative outreach programme "Beyond the Curriculum" programme, which includes the European Computer Driving Licence, Young Enterprise, Sculpture, Russian and our innovative outreach programme "Science in the Community". Upper Sixth students continue with three or four A Levels. An important part of the curriculum for all Sixth Form pupils is the Friday Lecture given by guest speakers from a wide range of backgrounds. The Careers Department provides talks and individual preparation for university applications; for most pupils the careers staff will have been involved in their decision-making from as early as Year 9. Advice on direct employment is also offered, although in practice over 95% of leavers move into Higher Education.

School Chapel. The School has its own Chapel and close links with St Saviour's, the local parish church. There is an outstanding Chapel Choir which sings at daily services and at the regular Sunday Evensong. Each summer the Chapel Choir performs in cathedrals and churches both in Britain and abroad.

Parents' Association. There is an active Parents' Association which provides opportunities for parents to meet informally and organises social events, as well as being involved on a day-to-day basis in the life of the School and in the funding of special projects.

Societies. Involvement in extra-curricular activities is strongly encouraged and there is a wide range of clubs from which to choose, including scientific, cultural and recreational. There is a strong tradition of drama, with regular productions, and an annual House Drama and House Music competition. The School has an Orchestra, a Concert Band, Big Band and Brass Ensemble. The School has a fine reputation for choral music and for a number of years the Choral Society, consisting of pupils, parents and friends of the School, has performed a major choral work annually at the Philharmonic Hall in Liverpool.

Games. Competitive sports are rugby, hockey, netball and lacrosse during the winter terms and cricket, athletics, tennis, rounders and golf during the summer. There are representative teams at all levels and the playing fields cover about 40 acres on three different sites. At McAllester Field there is a floodlit astroturf surface for hockey and tennis. A large sports complex, including a squash court, two fitness suites and a climbing wall, provides a focus for the School's comprehensive 'Sport for All' programme.

CCF and Outdoor Pursuits. The School has Army, Navy and RAF sections. From Year 8 onwards pupils may join one of these sections. The School runs its own Duke of Edinburgh's Award Scheme. Outdoor Pursuits form part of the curriculum and from Year 6 upwards pupils spend time away from School each year on residential outdoor pursuits activities. Climbing is available as part of the PE curriculum and as a co-curricular activity.

Admission to Senior School at 11 is by progression from the Prep or by the School's own Entrance and Scholarship Examination held on a Saturday at the end of January. Entrance at other stages is through individual assessments and interview. Sixth Form entrants are also welcome and this selection is based on GCSE grades and interview. Prospective parents are always welcome to visit the School and the Headmaster is happy to meet parents and assist with queries over dates, methods of entry, SEN and learning support.

Fees per term (2011-2012). Senior School £3,069–£3,202; Prep £2,215–£2,444. The Birkenhead School Foundation Trust was established in 1998 to provide Bursaries and Funded Places. Scholarships are also available. Particulars may be obtained from the Headmaster's PA, Mrs Debbie Roberts.

Charitable status. Birkenhead School is a Registered Charity, number 1093419. Our charitable status means the School not only accepts fee paying pupils but can offer places to able children from less advantaged backgrounds.

Bishop's Stortford College

Maze Green Road, Bishop's Stortford, Herts CM23 2PJ
Tel: 01279 838575
Fax: 01279 836570
e-mail: admissions@bishopsstortfordcollege.org
website: www.bishops-stortford-college.herts.sch.uk

Bishop's Stortford College is a friendly, co-educational, day and boarding community providing high academic standards, good discipline and an excellent all-round education. We aim to equip our pupils with the vital qualifications, skills, adaptability and, above all, confidence to thrive as adults in a rapidly changing world. A flourishing Junior School and a Pre-Prep Department, sharing many facilities with the Senior School, give all the advantages of educational continuity whilst retaining their own distinctive characters.

When founded in 1868, it was intended that the College should provide "a liberal and religious education" acceptable to non-conformist families in the Eastern Counties. In practice, Bishop's Stortford College welcomes boys and girls of all denominations and faiths, and, while the majority of present pupils' homes are in the Home Counties and East Anglia, a substantial number of parents work and live overseas.

Motto: '*Soli Deo Gloria*'.

Governing Council:
P J Hargrave, BSc, PhD (*Chairman*)
C Havers, MA
Mrs S Jellis, MA
Sir Stephen Lander, KCB
L Lindop, ACMA
G E Baker, BSc, MRICS
Mrs I Pearman, MA, MRICS
M Farmer
G Brant, MA, BEd
A A Trigg
A M Nicholls, MA, PhD
G P R Bramley, LLB

Headmaster: **Jeremy Gladwin**, BSc Dunelm

Assistant staff:
* *Head of Department*
† *Housemaster/mistress*

Mrs K Adkins, CertEd
N P Alexander, MSc (*Mathematics)
Dr G Allcock, BSc, PhD (*Careers Manager*)
Ms G Anderson, BA
Miss J Arnott, BA
T Atkinson, BA
S Bacon, BSc (*ICT)
Mrs H G Bailey, BA (*German)
A H Baker, BSc (*Physics)
C S Bannister, MA (*Chemistry)
P Bashford
J Bauer, MA
Mrs L Bell
P Beston, MPhil
J N Birchall, MA (**Business Studies/Economics*)
T G S Borton, BA (*Head of Sixth Form*)
G R Brooks, BA (*Joint Deputy Head*)
Mrs R C Brown, MSc
Mrs S Brown, BA (**Religious Studies*)
A M Bruce, MA (*Director of College Music*)
C de Bruyn
Mrs P Bull
Ms E Chaplin, BA (†*Benson House*)
Mrs L G Dickinson, BA
M Drury, BSc (†*Hayward House*)
Miss J Ellis, BSc
Mrs M Essien, MSc
B Fearnley, BA (*English, †*Sutton House*)
Ms C Flynn, BA
Mrs F M Freckelton, MSc
Mrs M E P Garrett, MCILIP (*Librarian*)
P M Griffin, BSc (†*School House*)
Mrs K Griffiths (*Marketing Manager*)
T A Herbert, MA (*Examinations*)
Mrs C Hinge, BSc
R M Honey, MA (*Art, †*Robert Pearce House*)
Mrs T Hood, BEd
T G Hudson, MA (*Modern Languages)
K Irvine, BA
Mrs K King, BA
J Kirton, BSc
R D Kisby, BA, DPE (*PE)
Mrs W E Livingstone-Chambers
Mrs G Lynch, MA (*Latin, †*Collett House*)
Miss V Marriott, BA (†*Tee House*)
Mrs J Marshall, BSc (†*Tee House*)
Revd M D Marshall, BSc (*Chaplain*)
Mrs P Mullender, MA (*Senior Mistress*)
Ms C I Munck, BA
R Norman, BA (*Director of Drama*)
I Nunez, BMus, PGDip, MM GSMD
P W O'Connor, PhD (*Geography)
Ms E Oakley, MSc
Mrs J Oldfield, BSc
Mrs A Picton, BA
N J Prowse, BSc
Ms M Raven, BA
Mrs A Self, BA
Mrs H Sheehan, BA
Mrs L Shepherd, BEd (*Director of Sport*)
Mrs A N Sloman, CertEd (**Girls' Games*, †*Young House*)
T Stuart, MA (*History)
N Thompson
M A Tomkys, BA (*Media)
J H Trant, BA (**Design & Technology*)
Ms V Turner, BSc
Mrs E A Wheeler, BSc
C H Williams, BSc (*Director of Studies*)

Mrs F H M Williams, BA (*Librarian, ESL*)
Mrs J Williams, BSc
Dr D J Williams, PhD (**Science*)
Mrs S J Wilson, BA (*†Alliott House*)
Mrs J Windley
C J Woodhouse, BSc (*Joint Deputy Head*)
Mrs T Wright, MA
Mrs S Wyatt, BA

Learning Support:
Mrs R J Gearing, CertEd, DipSpLD
Mrs G Miller, CertEd, DipSpLD

Junior School
Head of Junior School: J A Greathead, BEd

S Bailey, CertEd	E C Jones, LLB
(**Geography*)	Mrs A Leith
A R J Barnard	Mrs A Livings, BA
Mrs A Barretto, BA	Miss L Maltby, HND
C Beckley, MChem	G Millard, BA
G Bennett, BA	C I Murchie, BA
Mrs R Borthwick, BA	Miss E J Neville, BA (**Art*)
Mrs K Brooks, BA	Miss K Perkins, BA
Miss B Callow, BEd	Mrs R A Pike, BA
Mrs C Coates, BA	(*Librarian*)
R J Clough, BA	N Prowse, BSc
N B Courtman, BA	M J Self, BSocSc
Mrs L Davies, BA	(**History*)
N R Eddom, BEd	Mrs W Sharman, MSc
(**Mathematics*)	I Silk, BA (*Deputy Head,*
G Frackowiak, MA	**English*)
Mrs L Fraser, BA	G Sloman, BA (**ICT*)
S Gunter	J Spackman, PhD
Ms C Hammerton	G Sutcliffe, BA
Mrs N P Hatchett, BEd	Miss N Swales, BA
†A J Hathaway, BEd	J Talbot Rice, BA
†Mrs A Hathaway	Mrs C Taylor, BSc
†D A Herd, BSc	Miss K Taylor, BA
M Ingham, BSc	Miss N Watson, BA

Pre-Preparatory Department:
Head: Mrs R Boon, BSc

Miss E Barfoot	Mrs P Hopkinson, BA
Mrs B J Birley, CertEd	Mrs C Martin, MA
Mrs A M Cullum, BA	Mrs S Pearson-Philips, BEd
Mrs M Fenlon	Mrs J Perkins, MEd
Mrs P Field	Mrs R Pradhan
Mrs A D Foy, RSA SpLD,	Mrs J Prowse, BA
CLANSA	Mrs S J Shepherd

Bursar: M P Hemingway

Senior School Admissions Officer: Mrs M-L Gough
Junior School Admissions Officer: Mrs F Brett

There are 585 boys and girls in the Senior School (boarders and day), 450 boys and girls in the Junior School and 120 in the Pre-Prep Department.

Location. Bishop's Stortford is almost mid-way between London and Cambridge and is quickly reached from Liverpool Street or via the M25 and M11 motorways. Stansted Airport is a ten minute drive. The College is situated on the edge of the town adjacent to open countryside. The gardens and grounds cover over 100 acres.

Facilities. Purpose-built Pre-Prep accommodation, Junior and Senior School libraries, extensive ICT facilities across the campus, outstanding sports facilities, well-resourced centres for Design and Technology, the Sciences, Languages, Music and Drama and a superb new Art Centre. The main school Library and state-of-the-art indoor Swimming Pool are notable features. All the Houses offer a welcoming, family-like environment with internet access throughout.

At the centre of the School stands the Memorial Hall, used daily for Assembly, which was erected in 1921 as a memorial to Old Boys who served and fell in the 1914–18 war.

Academic Organisation. The Curriculum is designed to give as broad a course of study as possible up to the inevitable specialisation at A and AS Level and Oxbridge entry.

In addition to the three Sciences, French, English, Maths, Geography and History, all new pupils joining the Fourth Form (Year 9) take Design and Technology, ICT, Art and Music as well as one period each of RE and PE/Swimming. Most also begin German and a significant number continue with Latin.

In the Lower and Upper Fifth Forms (Years 10 and 11), the 'core' subjects, taken by all, are English, English Literature, Maths and the three Sciences. Four other subjects, one of which must be a modern foreign language, are chosen from History, Geography, Design and Technology, Latin, French, German, Art and Design, Music, Drama, ICT and Religious Studies. Pupils also have one period each of RE, PE/Swimming and ICT. GCSE Spanish can also be taken as an additional subject outside the normal timetable.

At all stages, progress is carefully monitored by Housemasters, Housemistresses and Tutors, and in Staff Meetings.

The Sixth Form. Pupils will choose between three and five subjects at AS level in the Lower Sixth, before specialising in three or four in the Upper Sixth at A2 level. Some may take an extra AS level in the Upper Sixth, while others will take one of a variety of extension subjects such as Japanese or Spanish. Sixth Formers will select from the following subjects: Art, Biology, Business Studies, Chemistry, Classical Civilisation, Design and Technology, Drama and Theatre Studies, Economics, English Literature, French, Geography, German, History, Maths, Further Maths, Latin, Media Studies, Music, Physical Education, Physics, Politics, Psychology, Religious Studies.

An extensive PHSE programme operates throughout the school and there is a weekly Upper Sixth Form lecture.

Each Department organises visits and invites guest speakers to meetings of Societies, which are held in lunch hours or evenings. These, together with small group teaching, seminars and excellent resources, help to encourage students to develop their self-reliance, their analytical skills and their spirit of academic enquiry to equip them for Higher Education and beyond.

The progress of Sixth Formers is constantly assessed by House Masters/Mistresses and Academic Tutors, and in Staff Meetings under the overall supervision of the Head of Sixth Form. Parents are closely involved and regular Parents' Meetings are held.

Throughout the Senior School, grades for Effort and Attainment are given twice termly, and full written reports are sent home twice a year for each year group.

Careers. A purpose built Careers Centre is open daily and managed by specialist staff. The College has close ties with ISCO, local commerce and industry and the Hertfordshire Careers Service. Links with local business are strong and there is an extensive programme of Work Shadowing/Experience organised for pupils in the Upper Fifth and Lower Sixth Forms.

Worship. The Religious Instruction, Sunday Worship and occasional weekday services are inter-denominational. The opportunity of exploring faith and being prepared for adult membership of particular churches (including Confirmation) is offered each year through the Chaplain.

Activities. Whether as Boarders or Day Pupils, our young people are involved in an environment of wholehearted participation. A diverse range of extra-curricular activities alongside high academic standards provides the opportunity for every child to discover areas of interest and success that might otherwise lie untapped.

In addition to the meetings of Clubs and Societies, Wednesday and Friday sessions are set aside within the timetable for Activities, including those related to The Duke of Edinburgh's Award. We thus encourage pupils to pursue their own interests and introduce them to others, so that they will wish to carry these on into their spare time and beyond the confines of the School. Projects which promote a willingness to serve others are an important aspect of the breadth of activity offered.

Music and Drama. An interest in and appreciation of all kinds of music is encouraged throughout the school. In their 1st and 2nd Forms (Years 3 & 4), all pupils in the Junior School are taught an instrument in class and those who show promise are encouraged to continue individually in the Senior School.

There are numerous ensembles including Orchestra, Wind Band, guitar and string quartets, brass group, a Choral Society, and Choirs. Pupils are also encouraged to make music in small groups from the earliest stages. There is a fully equipped Recording Studio. The Music Staff includes 27 visiting teachers of singing and all the main instruments, together with the Director of Music, 2 Assistant Directors and a Musician in Residence. The House Music Competition is a major event in the school year, involving all pupils. Pupils have regular opportunities to perform in public at Pupils' Concerts and in School Assemblies. Overseas tours also provide excellent performing experience.

Drama is an area of strength with significant developments in recent years to the theatre facilities, curriculum and performing opportunities. There are numerous opportunities for all pupils to participate. AS and A level Theatre Studies are offered, as is GCSE Drama.

Sport. The College has an excellent reputation in all areas of sporting achievement. Physical Education is taught in the Fourth and Fifth Forms and facilities include a Sports Hall, an impressive indoor swimming pool, two floodlit all-weather surface hockey pitches, hard tennis courts and 100 acres of playing fields.

Health. The Medical Centre is staffed by a resident Sister and her SEN Assistant. Regular Surgeries are held by the School's Medical Officer.

Varied and wholesome meals are provided in the College central Dining Hall, with plenty of choice. All day pupils take lunch at School and the cost is included in the fees.

Junior School. The organisation of the Junior School (for pupils up to age 13+) is largely separate from that of the Senior School, but the curricula of the two Schools are carefully integrated. Pupils are able to share Senior School resources in Sport, Design and Technology, Music and Drama.

(*For further details see entry in IAPS section.*)

Admission. The main ages of admission are 4, 7, 11, 13 and 16, but entry at intermediate stages is possible. Entry to the Senior School at 13+ is based on school reference, interview and entry test results. Sixth Form Entry Interviews and Examinations are held in the November before year of entry.

Scholarships. (*See Scholarship Entries section.*) Academic, Art and Music Scholarships are awarded at three levels: (1) Sixth Form; (2) 13+ for Senior School Entry; (3) 10+ or 11+ for pupils entering the Junior School. All awards may be supplemented by Bursaries according to need.

Fees per term (2011-2012). Senior School: Full Boarders £7,192; Overseas Boarders £7,406; Weekly Boarders £7,121; Day £4,999.

Junior School: Full Boarders £5,011–£5,452; Overseas Boarders £5,159–£5,613; Weekly Boarders £4,961–£5,397; Day £3,569–£3,999; Pre-Prep £2,339.

Fees are inclusive except for individual music tuition.

Charitable status. The Incorporated Bishop's Stortford College Association is a Registered Charity, number 311057. Its aims and objectives are to provide high quality Independent Boarding and Day education for boys and girls from age 4 to 18.

Bloxham School
A Woodard School

Bloxham, Banbury, Oxon OX15 4PE
Tel: 01295 720222
          01295 724341 Headmaster
Fax: 01295 721714 Bursar
          01295 721897 Registrar
          01295 722962 Headmaster
e-mail: registrar@bloxhamschool.com
website: www.bloxhamschool.com

The School was founded in 1860 by the Revd P R Egerton. Since 1896 it has been a member of the Woodard Corporation.

Motto: '*Justorum Semita Lux Splendens.*'

The School Council of Governors:

Provost: The Rt Revd Lindsay Urwin

Chairman: N J E Bankes, Esq

Members:

P J P Barwell, MBE	M S Hedges, Esq, MA,
M R Deeley, Esq	FCA, FRSA
D J B Long, Esq, BA	Mrs E L Lewis-Jones
R E Towner, Esq, MA	R W Loades, Esq
Mrs M S Brounger, LLB	C E L Mann, Esq
Mrs R A H Needham	J E Spratt, Esq
Mrs F M Turner	R Gasson, Esq
Mrs P J Woodhouse, BMus	
Hons	

Headmaster: **M E Allbrook**, MA

Deputy Head: Miss E C Trigg, BA

Director of Studies: D A Cooper, BSc, BEd, MSc, MCollP

Chaplain: The Revd M G Price, MA, MPhil

Head of Lower School: G A Stindt, BSc

Teaching Staff:
* Head of Department

T I Hatton, BA (*Director of Sixth Form Studies; *History*)
C Newbould, BSc
S J Batten, MA (*Head of Scholars*)
T M Skevington, BEd (**Design & Technology*)
G P Cruden, BA
M Pye, DipFA (*Director of Art*)
C V Atkinson, BA (**Drama*)
J P Horton, CertEd (*Director of Sport*)
N StJ D Pigott, BA (**Geography*)
J F Berry, BSc (**Mathematics*)
H J Alexander, MA (*Head of Dyslexia Course*)
D F McLellan, BA (**Modern Languages*)
Mrs J H White, BEd
M J M Moir, BSc
Mrs B M Whitehead, BA
N E C Evans, BSc
D R Best, BA
R J Thompson, BSc (**Business Studies*)
Mrs A L Cooper, BA, BAdmin
Miss A Hickling, BA
Dr C E Evans, PhD, MSc
A M Goldsmith, BA
Miss G T Barbour, BA
Mrs C M McCaffrey, MA
Mrs N R A Patrick
R W F Hastings, BA
R J Longman, MEd, MA, FRSA, ARCO Dip CHD
   (**Director of Music*)
M G Noone, MA (**Biology*)

D K Jordan, BA
Miss E Hicks, BA
Mrs E Moyle, MA (*English*)
Miss N C Lister, BA
Mrs L J Lane, BSc
R Pyper, BSc
T W Tuthill, BA
D Dales, BEd (*PE*)
Dr D Herring (*RE*)
E J Heddon, MSc, MBA, FCIPD (*ICT*)
E F Bradley
R A Devesa

There are a number of visiting Instrumental teachers.

Houses and Housemasters/mistresses:

Boys' Houses:
Crake: D R Best
Egerton: R J Thompson
Seymour: D K Jordan
Wilson: T M Skevington

Girls' Houses:
Raymond: Mrs J H White
Wilberforce: Mrs A L Cooper

Lower School Weekly Boarders:
Park Close: Mr & Mrs A N Irvine

Headmaster's PA: Mrs H M Hill

Registrar: Mrs S H McClellan

Medical Officer: S A Haynes, MBBS, MRCGP, DFFP

State Registered Nurses:
Miss S Ashton, RGN
Mrs L A Deeley, RGN

Bursar: N Urquhart

Director of Marketing & PR: A N Irvine, CertEd, MCIPR

Organisation. There are approximately 240 boarders and 190 day boarders. There are 4 senior houses for Boys and 2 for Girls. Day boarders are full members of their boarding houses and are allocated house rooms, studies, etc according to seniority in the same way as full boarders. They have all meals except breakfast at the School and may stay for homework.

Lower School, for day or weekly boarding pupils aged 11–13, is an integral part of the School and has its own boarding house.

School Buildings and Grounds. The School is situated in a delightful conservation village on the edge of the Cotswolds and yet just 3 miles from Banbury and 4 miles from the M40 (J11). It is within easy reach of both Heathrow and Birmingham International airports.

The attractive local Hornton stone enriches the School and the village. The last decade has been one of major investment and the school's facilities are now comparable with even the largest of schools. The Raymond Technology Centre continues to offer first-class facilities and, as a further indication of Bloxham's intent to remain at the cutting edge of the use of technology in education, the school has invested in campus-wide wireless networking. Pupils are now given a laptop computer as they enter Year 10 which they may keep after their A Levels.

The boarding houses provide excellent accommodation for all with all Sixth Formers enjoying individual studies. Lower School weekly boarders are housed in Park Close which offers superb, homely facilities and space for the youngest pupils to enjoy. The school has two artificial grass hockey pitches, a fully-equipped sports centre including two glass-backed squash courts, and an indoor swimming pool. Equestrian sport is well catered for off campus.

An exciting new library building opened in 2006. Music, art and the performing arts have also benefited from recent additions to the Bloxham campus facilities.

The Sixth Form benefit from their own social centres which they manage themselves.

Admissions. We admit around 35 pupils each year at 11 (day pupils or weekly boarding pupils) by entrance examination set by the school.

At 13 (boarding and day). Those from prep schools are required to pass the Common Entrance Examination, while candidates from state schools are given an alternative examination specially designed to suit the National Curriculum.

At 16 (boarding and day). Those who wish to start a two-year A Level course are admitted to the Sixth Form on the basis of interview, school report and GCSE results.

There is a Dyslexia Course which takes up to six pupils each year, at age thirteen, with full scale IQs of 120+.

Applications should be made to the Headmaster.

Scholarships and Exhibitions. (*See Scholarship Entries section*.) Scholarships and Exhibitions are awarded at 11+, 13+ and for entry to the Sixth Form. Academic awards are made on the basis of a competitive examination. Awards for Art, Design Technology, Music (with free instrumental tuition) and Sport (not at 11+) are also made.

All the above awards may be up to 20% of fees according to merit.

Sir Lawrence Robson Scholarships and Exhibitions are awarded each year to Sixth Form entrants. The value of these will be up to 20% of fees.

Age limits for candidates on 1st September: 11+ under 12, 13+ under 14, Sixth Form under 17.

Further details of all scholarships may be obtained from the Headmaster.

Bursaries. Generous support is available to children of Armed Forces parents, Clergy and Teachers. Bursaries based on financial need are also considered on an individual basis.

The Roger Raymond Trust Fund sponsors the boarding education of outstanding pupils who would not otherwise be able to attend the school.

Details may be obtained from the Headmaster.

Fees per term (2011-2012). Boarders £9,255; Day Boarders £7,160, both inclusive and covering all meals (lunch, tea and supper) taken at School by day pupils. Lower School: Weekly Boarders £6,565; Day £5,055 (inclusive of lunch).

Information on the payment of fees by Insurance Schemes, and a School Fees Remission Scheme in case of absence, are obtainable from the Bursar.

Optional Extras. Private tuition in a particular subject, £38, £22, £17 and £14, according to the number of pupils in a group. Instrumental Music from £245 per term.

Curriculum. For the first three years pupils have a broad based curriculum which leads to nine or ten GCSEs. No choices need to be made in the Third Form and the full range of subjects is studied. In the Fourth and Fifth forms all pupils continue to study for GCSEs in English Language, English Literature, Mathematics, French, Physics, Chemistry, Biology, Religious Studies (short course), and in addition choose three other subjects from a range of options including History, Geography, Spanish, German, Art, Music, Design Realisation, Electronics and Business Studies. In the Sixth Form A Level Courses are available in Art, Biology, Business Studies, Chemistry, Design Technology, Economics, English, French, Further Mathematics, Geography, German, History, Mathematics, Music, Physics, Politics, Spanish, Theatre Studies, Physical Education and Psychology. A wide choice of combination is again offered. All pupils follow a comprehensive General Studies programme throughout the Sixth Form and the majority take General Studies A Level. Boys and girls are prepared for entrance to Oxford and Cambridge.

Tutorial System. In addition to the Housemaster or Housemistress, pupils have a House Tutor. Every Tutor looks after about 12 pupils and is thus able to give close personal attention to the development of each, both in and out of School. At regular intervals of three weeks the tutor reviews each pupil's Form Assessment which gives details of standard and approach to work in all subjects as well as information on extra mural activities.

Music. There is a wide range of instrumental and choral opportunities ranging from the School Orchestra and Concert Band to chamber ensembles and close harmony groups.

Games and Outdoor Activities. Boys and girls play the traditional major sports, rugby, athletics, hockey, cricket and netball according to season and in addition there are good facilities for badminton, basketball, squash, fives, sailing, shooting, equestrian activities including polo, swimming, canoeing, cross-country, fencing and tennis. Boys and Girls are strongly encouraged to develop their own particular talents. In the Third Form and below, pupils are expected to participate in major sports, but they have an increasing range of choices as they progress up the school. Boys and girls are also given the opportunity of participating in a flourishing Community Service Organisation.

CCF. All those in the Third Form undertake Duke of Edinburgh's Award Scheme type training. In their second year many join the CCF, to which there are various challenging alternatives. Adventure Training Camps are held annually at Easter as well as the usual CCF Summer Camps.

Societies. There is a large number of societies, academic and practical. All pupils are expected to participate in some of these activities according to their interest.

Old Bloxhamist Society. *Resident Secretary:* R L Stein.

Charitable status. Bloxham School Limited is a Registered Charity, number 1076484. Its aim is to provide high quality academic education in a Christian environment.

Blundell's School

Tiverton, Devon EX16 4DN
Tel: 01884 252543
Fax: 01884 243232
e-mail: info@blundells.org
website: www.blundells.org

The School, with its attendant connection to Balliol and Sidney Sussex Colleges, was built and endowed in 1604 at the sole charge of the estate of Mr Peter Blundell, Clothier, of Tiverton, by his executor the Lord Chief Justice, Sir John Popham. In 1882 the School was moved to its present site on the outskirts of Tiverton.

Governors:
E D Fursdon, DL, MA Oxon, FRICS (*Chairman*)
N Arnold, BA
R R A Breare, MA
M I R Bull, LLB
J F Bullock, BA, MA
C M Clapp, FCA
Revd H Dawson, BA, MA
Dr K C Hannabuss, MA, DPhil (*Representative of Balliol College, Oxford*)
Mrs E V Heeley, BA, CertEd
B J Hurst-Bannister, MA
P M Johnson, MA, FRSA
J Macpherson, BEd
Mrs J M A Mannix, MA
Mrs A C Mayes, MBE, BSc
Ms L J Smith, BA
His Hon Judge W E M Taylor
B W Wills-Pope, MBE, FInstD
Sir Christopher Ondaatje, OC, CBE (*Governor Emeritus*)

Clerk to the Governors and Bursar: D Chambers, FCA

Head Master: **I R Davenport**, BA Durham

Second Master: R W Thane, BA, FRGS

Senior Leadership Team:
Director of Studies: Mrs C V Sherwood, MA
Senior Master: P F Rivett, MA
Senior Mistress: Mrs N J Klinkenberg, BSc
Head of Junior Department (School House): *D P Marshman, BSc
Head of Boarding: *A J R Berrow, MA
Head of Science: Mrs G M L Batting, BEng
Director of Sport: E K G Saunders, BA

Chaplain: The Revd T C Hunt, MTh, BD, ARICS

Assistant Masters:

A J Deighton-Gibson, BSc	J M Trew, BA
T D Dyke, MA	B Wheatley, MA
A H Barlow, MPhil, MA, FRSA	Miss P J Black, CertEd
J G Pilbeam, BEd	A J Guy, BSc
S J Goodwin, BA	Miss H L Youngs, BTec
J S Shrimpton, BA	I R Chick, BA
P H Gordon, BA, BEd	D Rhodes, BSc
Mrs D Brigden, BEd	Ms D M Drew, BTec
M P Dyer, MSc	R J Turner, BA
Mrs S J Rumble, BA	Mrs L J Chick, BA
J T Balsdon, PhD, BSc	Mrs C E West, BEng
Mrs A J Frankpitt, BSc	Mrs T R Griffiths, BA
*Miss D J Hosking, BEd	B M Marsden, BA
Mrs A M Menheneott, BEd	G A Bucknell, BSc
Miss I G Scott, MA	Mrs A T Candler, BSc
Mrs K J Wright, BA	M J Hawkins, MA
*Mrs R J Crease, BEd	L Wynell-Mayow, BA
C L L Gabbitass, BEd	R J Holman, BA
R D J Matthew, MDes	Miss L R M Mimmack, BA
Miss S A Norman, BSc (*Careers*)	J Nelmes, BA
	Mrs J Olive, BA
*L Menheneott, BEd, MBA	Mrs A M Rhodes, BA
Miss F A Baddeley, MA	C Roberts-Jones, BSc
*C M Hamilton, BA	D J D Smart, BSc
C G Hedley-Dent, CertEd	Miss K Wilson, BSc
Mrs R E Milne, MA	Miss C A L Fordham, BA
S J Dawson, BA	Mrs E V Weaver, BSc
Miss C C G Rebuffet, MA	D E Morrison, MEng
Mrs S L Holman, BA	A J Mead, BSc
Mrs B A Nuttall-Owen, BSc	T E Candler, BA
	J C Hatton, BA
	D J Richards, BA

Director of Development: Mrs A Oliver, MInstF

Head Master's Secretary: Mrs J A Gale

Registrars:
*P J Klinkenberg, BEd
Mrs E Thane, BSc

Medical Officer: Dr F O'Kelly, MBE, MB BS, MRCGP, DA UK, DCH, DRCOG

Admission. Entry is at 11 or 13 for most pupils. This is via the Blundell's Entrance Test or the Common Entrance Examination. Most join the School in September, though a January entry is welcome.

Numbers. There are 570 pupils of whom 228 are girls. 208 board or weekly board, 158 flexi board. There are three boys' Houses and two girls' Houses for Years 9–12 and a separate Upper Sixth House which was opened in 2004. The Junior Department (Years 7 and 8) shares facilities but is taught and housed separately.

Fees per term (2011-2012). Full Boarding £6,095–£9,040; Weekly Boarding £5,515–£7,950; Day £3,635–£5,830. Flexi boarding is also available. A basic tuition fee is charged for those living within ten miles of Blundell's (over the age of 13).

Scholarships. (*See Scholarship Entries section.*) Blundell's offers a wide range of generous fee remissions at the age of 13, primarily for academic merit. Each March awards are made of up to 50% of the chosen designation fee (ie boarding, weekly, flexi, day) on the basis of set examinations. Music, Art and All-Round awards are also examined at the School in March. Sporting aptitude is also taken into account and may be acknowledged with its own award. A generous Services Package is in place for sons and daughters of serving officers and diplomats. There are also four Foundation Awards for candidates from the Ancient Borough of Tiverton or those who reside in Devon. These can be awarded at the age of 11. Full details of all scholarships and bursaries are available from the Registrars.

School Work. There are four forms at age 11 and five at age 13. During the first three years most pupils will study Art, Biology, Chemistry, Design and Technology, Divinity, Drama, English, French, Geography, History, Information Technology, Mathematics, Music (Class), Personal and Social Development, Physical Education and Physics. Latin, Greek, German and Spanish are also available.

During the GCSE years the range of subjects remains broad. Extensive advice is provided by the School to assist both GCSE and A Level choices. Parents are advised to enter their children for the Independent Schools' Careers Organisation Futurewise programme.

Sixth Form options enable a wide combination of subjects to be taken. Four of the following are taken to AS Level and three to A Level: Art, Biology, Business Studies, Chemistry, Classical Civilisations, Design Technology, Drama, Economics, English, Film Studies, French, Geography, German, History (Modern & Early Modern options), ICT (AS only), Latin, Mathematics and Further Mathematics, Music, Music Technology, Photography, Physical Education, Physics, Psychology, Religious Studies (Ethics) and Spanish.

Mark Orders, Tutorial System and Reports. Good communication is a central concept. Frequent Mark Orders and Staff Meetings are held to monitor each pupil's work. All pupils have academic tutors. Parents receive termly formal written feedback in addition to receiving Mark Order summaries every few weeks. There are regular parents' meetings and information forums.

Music and Drama. Blundell's music is excellent. Based in our own music school there are several choirs, an orchestra and varying musical ensembles. These range from a jazz band through a chamber choir to brass, woodwind and string groups. The Department has a good electronic section and in addition to School concerts there are visits from professional musicians. The Choir undertakes a European tour at Christmas; recent destinations have included Prague, Paris, Oslo, and Venice.

Similarly, Drama plays a key role in the School. There are three major School Plays each year, as well as House plays. The magnificent, purpose-built Ondaatje Hall offers the combined facilities of a theatre, a concert hall and an art studio. Frequent visits are made by theatre companies and Blundell's is a cultural venue for Mid-Devon.

Games and Physical Training. Boys play rugby football in the Autumn Term whilst girls play hockey. Lent Term sports include cross-country, squash, rugby fives, hockey, soccer, fencing, basketball, netball and rugby sevens. In the Summer Term cricket, tennis, swimming, athletics and sailing take place. Golf, clay pigeon shooting, canoeing and miniature range shooting are also available. The Sports Hall gives further scope to the range of sport, as does the all-weather floodlit pitch.

Computing and Technology. All Blundellians have access to the school IT network and will develop a range of skills during their time at school to support their studies.

Recent New Facilities. There have been extensive developments at Blundell's over the past two decades which include upgrading the Science Departments, provision of advanced technological and careers arrangements as part of

the resources included in the redesigned Library, a new Modern Languages block, an Upper Sixth pre-university year House and an ongoing refurbishment of all boarding houses. With the relocation of St Aubyn's School (now called Blundell's Preparatory School) onto the Blundell's site, the whole campus provides education from the age of 3 to 18 years. The Blundell's Foundation has been set up to advance plans for the future and a major development plan was started to coincide with 2004, the school's quatercentenary. Two imaginative projects, a music school and an academic centre, opened in September 2007and there are more exciting plans on the horizon.

Community Service. The School is involved in a wide variety of activities, both local and national.

Adventure Training. Blundell's is well placed to make full use of Dartmoor and Exmoor, the coast and rivers of the area, for academic fieldwork or adventure training. For many years the School has entered teams for the Ten Tors Expedition on Dartmoor and canoes the Devizes–Westminster race.

CCF. Everyone in Years 9 and 10 serves for a year in the CCF. Thereafter it is voluntary and comprises senior pupils who provide the NCO Instructors. There are links with the 18 Cadet Training Team, Derriford, and the Rifle Volunteers.

Boarding. Blundell's is built around the ethos of boarding and all pupils (full boarding, weekly, flexi-boarding and day) are accommodated in one of seven houses on the campus. A full range of weekend activities is offered including a Leadership Programme, Ten Tors, sport and a range of local trips and activities.

Religion. The School maintains a Christian tradition, while welcoming members of other faiths. All pupils are expected to attend weekday morning Chapel and boarders go to the School Service on Sundays. The Chaplain prepares boys and girls who wish to be confirmed; the Confirmation Service takes place annually in the Spring Term.

Accessibility. Blundell's is close to the M5, and is served by Tiverton Parkway Station, two hours from Paddington, London. Airports at Bristol and Exeter are close at hand.

Prospectus. Fuller details of School life are given in the prospectus, available from the Registrars. Prospective parents are invited to visit the School, when they will meet the Head Master, and a Housemaster or Housemistress and have a full tour of the School with a current pupil. The Blundell's website (www.blundells.org) is regularly updated throughout the academic year and as well as giving details of the school and academic departments, lists the main sporting, musical and dramatic events of each term and some match results.

Preparatory School. Blundell's Preparatory School for children aged 2½ to 11 years is on its own extensive site at Blundell's. For further information apply to the Headmaster, Mr N A Folland. (*See also entry in IAPS section*).

Charitable status. Blundell's School is a Registered Charity, number 1081249. It exists to provide education for children.

Bolton School Boys' Division

Chorley New Road, Bolton BL1 4PA
Tel: 01204 840201
Fax: 01204 849477
e-mail: seniorboys@boltonschool.org
website: www.boltonschool.org/seniorboys

Bolton School Boys' Division seeks to realise the potential of each pupil. We provide challenge, encourage initiative, promote teamwork and develop leadership capabilities. It is our aim that students leave the School as self-confident young people equipped with the knowledge, skills and attributes that will allow them to lead happy and fulfilled lives and to make a difference for good in the wider community.

We do this through offering a rich and stimulating educational experience which encompasses academic, extra-curricular and social activities. We provide a supportive and industrious learning environment for pupils selected on academic potential, irrespective of means and background.

Motto: *'Mutare vel timere sperno'*.

Chairman of Governors: M T Griffiths, BA, FCA

Headmaster: P J Britton, MBE, MEd

Deputy Headmaster: R D Wardle, BA
Assistant Head (Academic): D J Jones, BSc
Assistant Head (Activities): Dr F H Mullins, BSc, PhD

Teaching Staff:
* Head of Department

Art:
*M Frayne, BA
Mrs M A Ryder, BA
Miss L Turner, BA

Biology:
*Dr S Wastie, BSc, PhD
Dr J C Catterall, BSc, PhD
Miss R S Crowther, BSc
M Hobbiss, BA
Dr N Morgan, BSc, DPhil
Dr F H Mullins, BSc, PhD

Business Studies:
*Mrs C M Edge, BSc
D W Kettle, BA

Chemistry:
*Dr M Yates, BSc, PhD
Dr S P Cooper, BSc, MSc, PhD
Miss S J Gorner, BSc
Mrs E M Greenhalgh, BSc
Mrs J F Knibbs, BSc
Dr D Rogers BSc, DPhil
H H Schenk, BSc

Classics:
*Dr J E Reeson, MA, PhD
A E Jackson, BA
Mrs E D Watts, BA
Mrs K Wrathmell, BA, MA

Economics:
*A J Raitt, BA

English:
*R J Griffiths, MA
M A Bannister, BSc
N Cropper, BA
Dr S W Holland, BA, PhD
Miss J Kemp, BA
A Liptrott, BA, PG Dip RNCM
Miss N Lord, BA

French:
*A C Robson, BA
Mrs H M Baker, BA
A I McNeil, MA
M H J Prentki, BA

Geography:
*A C R Compton, BA
P D Jackson, BSc
J A Rutter, BSc
Miss H Tunstall, MSc
R D Wardle, BSc

German:
*R A Catterall, MA
K Brace, BA
K M Hiepko, MA

History:
*J W Rich, BA
B J Armstrong, MA
Miss S V Burgess, MA
Miss C L Dickinson, BA
C C Joseph, MA

ICT:
*P J Humphrey, BSc
Mrs E Fielding, BA

Mathematics:
*D N Palmer, BSc
Dr R Booth, BSc, PhD
P Costello, BSc
N C Holmes, BSc, CIMA
C Hunter, BSc
Mrs D Stevens, BSc
D L Stevens, BSc
J L Taylor, BSc

Music:
*S J Martin, BA
J Bleasdale, BA, LLCM
R Eastham, ABSM
Mrs A J Hampson, BMus

Physics:
*Dr J M Thatcher, BSc, PhD
A Altimeemy, BSc, PhD
E J Dawber, BSc
Mrs L J Dootson, BSc
Miss B Jones, BSc
D J Jones, BSc
Mr M Ormerod, BSc

Religious Studies:
Mrs C E Fox, BA

Russian:
*P G Davidson, BA
C A J Pownall, BA
Mrs V Tymchyshyn, BA

Spanish:
*Miss J Wardle, BA

Physical Education:
*P Fernside, BA (*Head of Games*)
*M Johnson, BSc (*Head of PE*)
T P Pledger, BA

K Branagan, UEFA A Grade
H Howard, BA
G N McMillan, FDA

Technology:
*C J Walker, BA
P A Brownrigg, BSc
G J Butchart, BEd
C Coffey, BA

Instrumental Music Staff:
Miss F J Berry, BMus, LRSM, LTCL, LLCM (*Clarinet, Saxophone*)
Mrs T A Coglan, ARCM
G Curtain, BMus, MA (*Brass*)
I C Dawkins, Kneller Hall (*Clarinet & Saxophone*)
I K Forgrieve, GMus, RNCM, PPRNCM (*Percussion*)
P Fowles, BA, LLCM, AMus TCL, BIHE (*Guitar*)
J Gjylaci, BMus, RNCM (*Guitar*)
Mrs C Hall-Smith, GBRSM, PGRNCM
A Lockett (*Brass*)
M J Pain, MA, FRCO, LRAM, ARCM, CertEd (*Pianoforte & Organ*)
Mrs J Pearse, LTCL, LRAM, LGSM, AMusTCL
G F Watton (*Percussion*)
Mrs M F Webb, LRAM, GRSM (*Violin & Viola*)
Mrs C Whitmore, BA, LRSM (*Voice/Singing*)
M Wildgust, GMus, ARCM, LTCL (*Brass*)

Junior School:
Head of Junior School: S Whittaker, BEd
Deputy Head: Mrs S A Faulkner, BA, MA

Mrs T Clarke, DipEd
T Dickinson, BEd
M Duxbury
A B Harrison, DipEd
Mrs A L Hough, BSc, DPS

C D Hough, BSc
Mrs P J Lockett, BEd
Mrs S J Ives, BA
Mrs H J Willis, BMus

Headmaster's Personal Assistant: Ms M M Leather

Headmaster's Secretaries:
Mrs M P Jones
Mrs S Yates

The School, founded ante 1516, was rebuilt and endowed by Robert Lever in 1641. It was re-endowed in 1915 by Sir W H Lever, Bart (later Viscount Leverhulme).

Situated in imposing sandstone buildings on a thirty-two acre site, Bolton School Boys' Division educates over 1,100 boys, all day pupils. Of these, 200 are members of the Junior School which is housed in an adjacent separate building close to the main site providing education for boys aged 7–11. In the Senior School of 900 boys, 220 are in the Sixth Form.

Curriculum. The GCSE programme comprises a core curriculum of English Language, English Literature, Mathematics, Biology, Chemistry, Physics and Sport. In addition, pupils select a further 4 options chosen from Art, Drama, French, Geography, German, Greek, History, Latin, Music, Philosophy and Ethics, RE, Russian, Science Enrichment, Spanish and Technology. One of these choices must be a foreign language. At A Level approximately 30 different subjects are currently on offer. Boys study four subjects to AS Level, with the majority reducing to three A2 Levels in Year 13. In addition all boys have the option of taking General Studies to A2 Level. While many boys elect to take standard combinations of either Arts or Science subjects in the Sixth Form, a high degree of flexibility ensures that any desired combination of subjects can be offered. Throughout both years of the Sixth Form, there is an additional and extensive programme of academic work which supports the GCE Advanced curriculum. Some boys will take the AQA Bacc qualification and all boys do an enrichment course and take part in community service.

Facilities and Organisation. The Boys' and Girls' Divisions of Bolton School are housed in separate buildings on the same site and, though the organisation of the two Divisions provides single-sex schools, there are many opportunities for boys and girls to meet and to cooperate in the life of the school community. In some subjects co-educational arrangements are in operation. The buildings of the Boys' Division include the Great Hall, two libraries, gymnasium, sports hall, swimming pool, laboratories, art rooms, sixth form common room and ICT learning centre, design technology centre, performing arts centre, MFL laboratory, classrooms and dining hall. The Junior School building has recently been extended and refurbished and contains eight form rooms and specialist rooms for ICT, art & design and science & technology together with a gymnasium, library and its own dining accommodation. Use of the sports hall, the adjacent 25-metre swimming pool and the arts centre is shared by all sections of the school.

Games and PE. The extensive playing fields which adjoin the School contain thirteen pitches. Principal games are football and cricket. Rugby, tennis, hockey, swimming, water polo, badminton, athletics, golf and orienteering are also all played at representative school level. Games and physical education feature in the timetable of all boys. The School is divided into four Houses for the purpose of internal competitions.

Art, Drama, Design, Music. In addition to timetabled sessions in each discipline there are many opportunities for extra-curricular activities in all these pursuits. Facilities in the art department include a pottery room with kiln; within the very active musical life of the School there are choral groups, orchestras and ensembles catering for all ages and abilities. In addition arrangements can be made for individual lessons on all orchestral instruments, piano, organ and in singing. Drama is an important part of the work of the English department and boys are encouraged to develop their talents in the drama studio and arts centre. The annual major school play, musical or opera is produced in cooperation with the Girls' Division. Design and technology features strongly in the curriculum in both Junior and Senior Schools with considerable success each year in the A level technology courses, many boys gaining industrial sponsorships as a result. In addition, a wide variety of extra-curricular opportunities exists in both the design technology base and the computer rooms. All boys are encouraged to take part in the extensive lunchtime programme when over 120 clubs, societies and practices are offered to different groups.

Outdoor Pursuits. All junior school pupils and all students up to and including Year 12 in the senior school undertake an annual period of outdoor education within curriculum time. In addition, camps, trips, exchanges and expeditions go to 63 destinations over two years, 17 of them abroad. The School has its own 60-bed Outdoor Pursuits Centre, Patterdale Hall in Cumbria, used by parties of boys regularly for curriculum, weekend, holiday and fieldwork expeditions. There is a large and active Scout Group with its own modern headquarters on school premises.

Religion. The School is non-denominational; all boys have periods devoted to religious education. In assemblies the basic approach is Christian although a great variety of readings and methods of presentation are adopted. Religious education is taught in a broad undogmatic style which encourages free discussion on many issues.

Careers and Higher Education. Careers education and guidance, and life-long learning are key elements of the curriculum. In Year 8 pupils take part in a Work Sampling Day. Careers Education is part of the Year 9 curriculum including a project marked by the Headmaster. As an aid to Sixth Form choices, the Morrisby Test with follow-up interviews and extensive feedback is undertaken in Years 10 and 11. All pupils take part in Work Experience placements at the end of Year 11 and throughout the Sixth Form.

In Year 12, all pupils attend a 3 day residential business training course at Patterdale Hall and take part in an e-business competition. Mock interviews are conducted on Interview Skills Evenings. Year 13 pupils are guided through UCAS procedures and careers advice is always available from two full-time Careers Assistants in the Careers Library.

The Head of Careers oversees all these events and can be consulted by all parents and pupils.

Transport. The School provides an extensive coach service which offers secure and easy access for pupils from a wide surrounding catchment area. Currently twenty-two routes are being operated by either the School's own fleet of coaches or by contract hire arrangements.

Admission. An entrance examination is held in January annually for boys over 7 and under 8 on August 31st of the year of admission and also for those over 8 and under 9 on the same date. Fifty places are available at 7+ and a few additional places thereafter. Admission to the first year of the Senior School (130 places) is by entrance examination held annually in mid-January. Boys who are over 10 and under 12 on August 31st of the year of entry are eligible. Entry to the Sixth Form is available to boys who have taken GCSE examinations elsewhere on the basis of interview and agreed levels of performance in these public examinations. Boys are also admitted at other ages when vacancies occur; in these cases admission is gained through satisfactory interview and test performances. There is a co-educational preparatory section – Beech House Infants' School – which has recently moved to new purpose-built, state-of-the-art premises. Admission is from the age of 4 and enquiries should be made to infants@boltonschool.org. There is also a nursery providing facilities for children from 3 months to 4 years old.

Fees per term (2011-2012). Senior School £3,290; Junior School £2,514. Fees include lunch which is compulsory.

Fee Assistance. Foundation Grants are available and one in six Senior School pupils receive assistance with fees.

Prospectus and Open Day. The School holds an annual Open Morning for the benefit of prospective candidates and their parents. This is normally in mid-October. Individual tours can be arranged on working days throughout the year. Further information concerning all aspects of the School is contained in the School Prospectus, copies of which may be obtained by writing to the Headmaster at the School, or telephoning the Headmaster's Secretary. More detail can be found on the School website: www.boltonschool.org/seniorboys. Enquiries concerning admission are welcome at any time of the School year.

Charitable status. The Bolton School is a Registered Charity, number 1110703. Under the terms of the Charity it is administered as two separate Divisions providing for boys and girls under a separate Headmaster and Headmistress.

Bootham School

York YO30 7BU
Tel: 01904 623261 (School)
          01904 623261 (Headmaster)
Fax: 01904 652106
e-mail: office@boothamschool.com
website: www.boothamschool.com

Bootham offers Full and Weekly Boarding and Day Education to both boys and girls from 11–18, together with day education from the age of 3 at Bootham Junior School. There are now over 480 pupils in the Senior School and 150 day pupils in the Junior School.

The School was founded in 1823 by Quakers, but pupils of all denominations or none are welcomed. All pupils attend Meetings for Worship and arrangements are made for pupils to be prepared for confirmation or membership of their own churches.

Head: **Jonathan Taylor**, MA Oxon, MEd

Deputy Head: Graham J Ralph, BA, MA

Head of Junior School: Sue Pattison, BEd, MEd

Assistant Heads:
Sarah Allen, BD, BEd
Suzanne Hall, BA, PhD
William Lewis, MA
Robert Tribe, BSc

Head of Boarding: Michael Shaw, BSc (*†Fox House*)

Bursar: Andy Woodland, BA, MA, MICE, MCIWEM

Assistant Staff:
* *Head of Department*
† *Housemaster/mistress*

Rachel Antill, BA (*Art*)
Mathew D Aston, BEd (*Mathematics*)
Joan Attwell, BA (*Drama*)
Richard M Barnes, BA, MA (*Art*)
Andrew Bell, BA (*Physical Education, English*)
Simon Benson, BA, MA (**Drama*)
Elizabeth Brown, BSc, PhD (**Geography*)
Paul K Burton, BTech, MInstP, CPhys (**Physics*)
Richard N Burton, BA (*Music*)
Carol L Campbell, BA (*French, Spanish, †Rowntree House*)
Judith Campbell, BEd (*Religious Studies, Music*)
Ben Coxon, BA (*Physical Education*)
Debbie Dawson, BSc (*Biology, Chemistry*)
Christopher Dobson, BSc (*Chemistry*)
Joanna Dowson, CertEd (*Physical Education*)
Margaret Drake, BA, CELTA (*EAL*)
Fiona Dunlop, BA, MA, PhD (*English*)
Harriet Ennis, BSc (**Psychology, Biology*)
Paul Feehan, BA (**Director of Music*)
Susanne Gair, MA (**Learning Support*)
Elizabeth Gallagher-Coates, BA (*English, Psychology*)
Robert Gardiner, BSc (**Biology*)
Emma Glover, BA (*English*)
Kirit Gordhandas, BSc (*Mathematics, †Evelyn House*)
Robert E Graham, BEd (*Physical Education, Geography*)
Sally Gray, BA (*Classics*)
James Harrison, BA (**Classics*)
Andrew Hedges, MEng, CEng (*Design & Technology*)
Elisabeth Hooley, BA (**Physical Education, Mathematics*)
Freya Horsley, BA, MA (*Art*)
Robert Hudson, BA (*History*)
Paul Irvine, BA (*Spanish, French*)
Leslie Jackson, BA, MSc (*Art*)
Clare Little, BMus (*Music*)
Elizabeth McCulloch, MA (**History*)
Eamonn Molloy, BEd (**Design & Technology*)
Catherine Morin (*French Language Assistant*)
Tracey Morley, BA (**Religious Studies*)
Russell Newlands, MSc, BEng (*Physics*)
Sarah O'Keeffe, BSc (**Economics & Business Studies*)
Christina Oliver, BA, MA (*French, German*)
Peter Rankin, BEng (*Information Technology, Physics*)
James Ratcliffe, BSc (**Mathematics*)
Mark Robinson, BA, MA (**Chemistry*)
Sarah Robinson, BA (*Classics*)
Catherine Rowell BSc, PhD (*Biology, Chemistry, Physics*)
Angela Singleton, BA, MEd (**English*)
David Swales, BA (**Art*)
Richard Taylor, BA, MA (**Modern Foreign Languages*)
Anne Whittle, BSc (*Mathematics*)
Angela Woods, BEd (*Geography, Physical Education*)

Development Director: Jane Peake, BA

Registrar: Jenny Daly

Librarian: Stephen Bosworth, BA, MSc

Curriculum. In Years 7–9 all pupils pursue a course of study which includes English (including Drama), History, Religious and General Studies, Careers, Geography, Latin, French, German, Spanish, Mathematics, the three separate Sciences, Music, Art and Craft, Physical Education, Design & Technology and Computer Studies.

In Years 10 and 11 pupils follow a curriculum leading to 10 or 11 subjects at GCSE.

The College Classes (Sixth Forms) are preparatory to university entrance. The majority of pupils remain at school until the age of 18 and each year there is a strong Oxbridge entry. A wide choice of subjects is offered. It is usual to study 4 or 5 examination subjects and to study subjects of wider interest.

The following subjects may be taken, in many combinations, to the AS & A2 and University Entrance levels: Mathematics, Further Mathematics, Physics, Chemistry, Psychology, Biology, English, French, German, Spanish, Modern History, Classical Studies, Geography, Economics, Business Studies, Music, Art, Design Technology, Religious Education, Drama and Theatre Studies, and Sports Studies. To counter-balance the effects of specialisation, pupils in the College classes are required to follow courses in Religious, Physical and General Education. In General Studies pupils follow a course in a wide range of topics such as English Literature, Political History, Music Appreciation and International Affairs, given by members of the staff and, from time to time, by specialists who visit the School for this purpose. Particular emphasis is placed on the study of personal relations and the structures of communities.

Site and Buildings. The School is situated close to York Minster. From the road it appears as an impressive line of Georgian houses but behind this is the spacious main school campus. There is a steady programme of development, and the buildings now include 8 well-equipped Laboratories, a Music School, 2 ITC Suites, 2 Workshops, an Astronomical Observatory, an up-to-date Physical Education Department with Sports Hall, Indoor Swimming Pool and Squash Courts, and a modern Assembly Hall, which received a national RIBA award. There are many facilities for leisure time pursuits which are an important feature of the lives of pupils at the School. The buildings are complemented by formal gardens and a beautiful Cricket Field, overlooked by the Minster. Another large Playing Field is situated nearby, in Clifton, which also houses Bootham Junior School in a new purpose-built complex.

Pastoral Care. As a Quaker School, Bootham places great emphasis on caring relationships within a friendly community. There are three boarding houses, under the special care of House staff. Each House has its own recreational facilities. Throughout the School, both boarding and day pupils are supervised and guided by form tutors. In College, pupils have Personal Tutors who are responsible for both academic and pastoral matters, and guidance towards Higher Education.

Admission. Pupils usually enter Bootham at the age of 11. Entry is also usually possible at 12, 13 and 14. The main entrance examination is held annually in January and this forms the basis of Scholarship and Bursary selection. Sixth form entry is welcomed and selection is on the bases of school report and GCSE performance. In special circumstances late entrants can be considered.

Leisure Time Activities. The School has long been recognised as a pioneer in the right use of leisure. The Natural History Society, founded in 1832, claims to be the oldest society of its kind with an unbroken history in this country. Other clubs and societies include Debates, Drama, Bridge, Chess, Cookery and Jazz. There are around 80 activities offered each week. Pupils follow the Duke of Edinburgh's Award scheme and are involved in Community Services.

Music. The Director of Music and his assistant are supported by 21 visiting teachers. Tuition is arranged in a wide variety of instruments and a strong tradition of music in the School is maintained. A recent leaver was named 'Young Composer of the Year' and there is a strong record of success in gaining Music College and University scholarships.

Games. Association Football, Hockey, Tennis, Fencing, Cricket, Swimming, Athletics, Netball, Basketball, Badminton, Squash, Rounders. There is no cadet force.

Fees per term (2011-2012). Boarding: £5,180–£8,600. Day: £4,770–£5,125.

Fees for instrumental music lessons are extra. Enquiries for up to date information are welcome.

Scholarships. (*See Scholarship Entries section.*) Honorary Academic Scholarships are awarded at 11+ and 13+. Music Scholarship awards of up to 50% fee remissions are also available at 11+ and 13+.

Bootham Old Scholars' Association. There is an annual Reunion in York during the second weekend in May. The Bootham Old Scholars Association has branches in all parts of the country and Eire. The Secretary may be contacted through the School.

Charitable status. Bootham School is a Registered Charity, number 513645.

Bradfield College

Bradfield, Reading, Berkshire RG7 6AU
Tel: General Enquiries: 0118 964 4500
        Headmaster: 0118 964 4510
        Bursar: 0118 964 4530
Fax: 0118 964 4513
e-mail: headmaster@bradfieldcollege.org.uk
website: www.bradfieldcollege.org.uk

Bradfield College was founded in 1850 by Thomas Stevens, Rector and Lord of the Manor of Bradfield.

We define our ethos by the outcome of our pupils as they leave Bradfield. We aim to inspire our pupils to become caring, contributing and confident members of the new global community. We build on our pupils' strengths. Bradfield excellence is defined as a combination of the personal development of the individual, providing an excellent academic education and preparing its pupils for real life by emphasis on extra-curricular pursuits and service in the wider community. The College is a co-educational boarding school dedicated to the provision of the highest possible care for all its pupils.

Motto: '*Benedictus es, O Domine: Doce me Statuta Tua*'. Blessed are you, our Lord; teach me your laws (from Psalm 119).

Visitor: The Right Revd The Lord Bishop of Oxford

Council:
M H Young (*Warden*)
Lady Ryder
P G F Lowndes
J M Layton
Mrs M Riall
M A Jones
A H Scott
D Shilton
P B Saunders

Lady Waller (*Child
    Protection Governor*)
Dr S Fane
G W P Barber
Professor D Paterson
I M Wood-Smith
P C H Burrowes
H P Gangsted

Clerk of the Council: T M Sills

Headmaster: S C Henderson, MA

Second Master: S P Williams, MA, MLitt

Deputy Heads:
K J Collins, MA
Mrs A M C Acton, BA

Bursar: T W Llewellyn, BA, FCA
Director of Development: J Wyatt
Registrar: Mrs A H Marshall, CertEd
Headmaster's PA: Ms J Delany
Admissions Secretary: Mrs N Williams

Chaplain: Revd R G Hilliard, MA, Dip Theol

Houses and Housemasters:
A – *Loyd*: J C Harding, MA
C – *Army*: A S Golding, BA
D – *House on the Hill*: S A Long, BEd
E – *Stone House*: P C Armstrong, BA
F – *Hillside*: C A Carlier, MA
G – *House on the Hill*: A R MacEwen, MA
H – *The Close*: G W S Masters, BA
I – *Palmer House* (*Girls*): Mrs D E Harrison, MA
J – *Armstrong House* (*Girls*): Mrs S K M Ronan, CertEd
K – *Stevens House* (*Girls*): Dr S C Beeson, BSc, PhD
M – *Stanley House* (*Girls*): Miss S R Duff, MA
L – *Faulkner's* (*Year 9*): Mr R J Wall, BA & Mrs F J C
        Wall, BA

Assistant Staff:
* *Head of Department*

Art:
*M Holmes, BA, MA
Miss A Cowan, BA
I P Dugdale, RAS Dip
Mrs M R Purcell, BA
Mrs R M Swainston, MA

Biology:
*F R Dethridge, BSc
    (*Science)
*Miss D A Entwistle, BSc
Miss W Bangay, BSc, MA
Mrs E H Barnes, BSc
Dr K J Ogbe, BSc, PhD
Miss C Pegg, BSc
A J Smith, BSc, MSc, MA

Careers:
*Mrs H L Allen, BSc, PG
    Dip, QCG

Chemistry:
*N M Burch, MSci
Miss J R Grimshaw, BSc
S T Lunt, MA
Dr D P Robinson, MEarth
    Sci, DPhil, FRAS
T J Ronan, BSc, MSc

Classics:
*Miss M E Staniforth, BA
    (*Acting Head*)
P C Armstrong, BA
W Fagg, MA

Design & Technology:
*D J M Lait, BSc
M K Goodwin, MA
Miss R Holloway, BA

*Economics & Business
    Studies*:
*T H Chaloner, MA
Mrs B A Eldridge, BA,
    MBA
Miss L C Marshall, BEd
M R Rippon, BA

English:
*Miss A L Hatch, BA
K J Collins, MA
Mrs E V Earnshaw, BA
A S Golding, BA
J C Harding, MA
Dr J Higgins, BA, MA,
    PhD
Ms M Lenehan, MA
B C Miller, MA

Miss S Pearson, BA, MA
Miss I G Power, BA
Miss A J Routledge, BA

EAL:
*Mrs H E Bebbington, BA,
    MA
Mrs D Bevan, TESOL Cert
Mrs J Kingston, BA
G Rush, Cert TEFL

Film Studies:
*R Keeley, MA

Geography:
*R Keeley, MA
Miss S R Duff, MA
M S Hill, BA
T J Kidson, BSc
R J Wall, BA

History:
*R J Veal, MA
C J Barnes, BA
Miss F D Martin, BA
Mrs R J Paynton, BA
D J Sullivan, MA

History of Art:
*T E Goad, BA
Mrs B H Bond, BA

ICT:
*G N Macleod, BA
J A Nalty, BA
Dr L S Vat, BSc, PhD

Mathematics:
*N J Taylor, BSc
Dr S C Beeson, BSc, PhD
C B Burgess, MA, MEng
T H K Burgess, BSc
Dr D J Doole, BSc, PhD
Miss M C Jenkins, BA
A M Maynard, BEd
Mrs C A Shaikh, CertEd
N A Taylor, MA
S N Whalley, BSc

Modern Languages:
*M M Etherington, BA
    (*French & German*)
Mrs A M C Acton, BA
    (*German*)
Mrs M E Ashcroft, BA
    (*Spanish*)
T Aucutt, BA (*Spanish*)
Mrs B Benito Lozano, BA
    (*Spanish*)

C A Carlier, MA (*French & German*)
Miss J Collot, Lic d'Anglais (*French & Spanish*)
Miss A E Davis, BA, MSt (*French*)
J C Hanbury, BA (*French & Spanish*)
Mrs C Jones, BA (*French*)
Miss J Lynam, MA (*Italian & French*)
Mrs A Nalty, BA (*French*)
Mrs K L Parker, BA (*Spanish*)
Mrs F J C Wall, BA (*French*)

Music:
*Ms A Wright, BA, FTCL
Miss V S Beattie, BA
Mrs R Frost, MA
Mrs F Laughton, BMus, MA, MTh
Ms A White, BMus, MMus
T O Anderson (*Music Technology*)

PE:
*D J Clark, BA
Miss C Bedford, BSc
S A Long, BEd
D J Mitchell, BSc
Mrs S K M Ronan, CertEd
Mrs K J Sanford, BA
Mr R P P Sanford, BSc

Physics:
*Mrs R B Clamp, MSci, CPhys, AMInstP
Mrs D E Harrison, MA
M A T Harrison, BSc, CPhys, MInstP
M H N Rigby, MPhys
D Rowley, BA

Librarian: Mrs J E Dyson, BA, MCLIP

Visiting Staff:
M Allen, PPRNCM Llb (*Percussion*)
B Arthey (*Guitar*)
Ms S Ashworth, ARMCM, LGSM MT (*Bassoon*)
K Bartlett, GGSM (*Percussion*)
P Border (*CCF Instructor*)
Mrs R Brown BMus (*Singing*)
N Charlton, LTCL (*Cello*)
C de Souza, BA (*Piano*)
Ms E Elliott (*Harp*)
M Frith, GGSM (*Clarinet, Flute & Saxophone*)
H Hetherington, BA (*Singing*)
C Hobkirk, BA, ARCO (*Singing*)
Mrs C Hultmark, BA (*Violin*)
P Johnson (*Squash*)
D Lane (*Tennis*)
S Lasky, BA, MA (*Jazz*)
Mrs A Law, GRSM, ARCM, Dip Rott (*Oboe*)
Miss M S Legg (*Dance*)
Miss E Lucas (*Dance*)
A Mosharrafa (*Electric Guitar*)
H Nelson, ARAM, LTCL (*Flute*)
T Osborne, LRAM, ARAM, CertEd, BACS (*Double Bass & Bass Guitar*)
L Phillips (*Tennis*)
Dr N Pyper, BA, PhD (*Portuguese and Economics*)
J Shaw (*Games*)
K Takhar (*Hockey*)

J van Es, BSc

Politics:
*C M Ashurst, BA
A R MacEwen, MA

PSHE:
*Mrs L K Shortland, BA
Mrs A H Marshall, CertEd

Psychology:
*Mrs R Hageman, BSc

Religious Studies:
*Mrs M Baynton-Campbell, BD
J P A Ball, MA
Mrs P M Donnelly, BA
Revd R G Hilliard, MA, DipTheol
G W S Masters, BA
S P Williams, MA, MLitt

Support and Study Skills:
*Mrs C Whittingham, BSc, MA, SENCO PGC, DipSpLD
Mrs P C Brims, MA, MPhil
Dr L C Hutchins, BSc, PhD
H McCartney, BSc
Mrs F McPherson, BA, DipSpLD
Mrs C Ponsonby, BA, DipSpLD
Mrs C Prior, BA, DipSpLD
Mrs I Smith, BEd
Mrs A Tibbs, CertEd, DipSpLD

Theatre Studies:
*Mrs J Crossley, BA
Miss S F Bernsten, BA
J Brough, BSc, LAMDA Dip
Mrs A M Hanbury, LAMDA Dip

E Tarrant, AGSM (*Brass*)
Ms L Taylor (*Tennis*)
J M Thompson (*Fencing*)
J Wood (*Cricket*)

Location. Bradfield College occupies the village of Bradfield, 8 miles west of Reading and 9 miles east of Newbury. It is 2 miles from Junction 12 of the M4 (the Theale access point). There are good road and rail communications with Reading, Oxford, London and Heathrow.

Organisation. The College is a fully co-educational boarding school with approximately 730 pupils, of whom about 115 are day pupils. At 13+ entry girls and boys spend their first year in Faulkner's, a purpose-built co-educational house with its own facilities and dining hall. Thereafter, the College is divided into 11 houses (7 for Boys and 4 for Girls), each with its own bedsit including studying and recreational facilities. Day pupils are full members of the boarding houses. The Housemaster/mistress is assisted by House Tutors and a Matron. Meals are served in the central Dining Hall. About sixty girls and boys join the large and vibrant Sixth Form through 16+ entry.

Admission. 13+ candidates qualify by taking either the Common Entrance Examination, the Common Academic or Bradfield College Scholarship Examination, or the Bradfield Entrance Examination (if not taking Common Entrance); candidates are interviewed by the Headmaster and school reports and references are required. Admission to the Sixth Form is by Assessment; this comprises a General Abilities test and interviews. In addition, school reports and references are required. Scholarships, Exhibitions and Awards are available.

A school prospectus and details of the entry procedure may be obtained from the Admissions Secretary or College website.

Fees per term (2011-2012). Boarders £9,845; Day pupils £7,876.

A fee is payable on registration. 20 months before the date of entry a Guaranteed Place fee of £1,000, which is later credited against the final account, is payable.

Entrance Scholarships. (*See Scholarship Entries section*.) Academic Scholarships and Exhibitions for all-rounders are awarded annually after competitive examinations in the Lent term. Music Scholarships up to 50% of the full fees are offered annually, as well as Drama, Sports, Art, Performing Arts and Design Awards. All awards are augmentable according to financial need. Full details may be obtained from the Admissions Office or College website.

Academic Organisation. Pupils enter the College in September and follow a three-year course to GCSE examinations, and then a two-year course to A Level.

In the first three years all the normal school subjects are taught in a core curriculum, but there is also opportunity to emphasise the linguistic or the aesthetic or the practical elements through a system of options.

In the Sixth Form GCE AS and A2 Level courses are offered in all subjects studied for GCSE with the addition of Economics, Politics, Philosophy and Ethics, History of Art, Theatre Studies, Psychology, Business Studies and Computing. Bradfield College is a candidate school for the IB Diploma Programme. It is pursuing authorization as an IB World School from September 2012. In addition, a Sixth Form Foundation Year will be offered from September 2011.

A brand new state-of-the-art and environmentally-friendly Science Centre opened its doors to pupils and the local community in September 2010. It includes ten sophisticated laboratories, a living grass roof, a conservatory and a biomass boiler providing an educationally and environmentally exciting space for the teaching of science.

Academic Staff. There are 117 members of the Academic Staff who cover all the main subjects. These are almost entirely graduates recruited from British universities, although there are also native speakers of German, French and Spanish in the Modern Languages department.

Careers. The Careers Department provides a wide range of careers education, information, advice and guidance to all year groups, particularly at key decision points. The College is a full member of ISCO and through them, all pupils in the Fifth Form (and new pupils in the Lower Sixth) undertake Futurewise (Morrisby) psychometric profiling, follow-up interviews and receive a detailed personal report to help them plan for the future. In the Sixth Form, pupils have opportunities to find out about various professions, industries and the Armed Services through talks, visits and courses. Specialist advice is available on University entrance in the UK and overseas, Gap Years and work-related learning.

Games. The main games for boys are football in the Michaelmas term, hockey in the Lent term and cricket and tennis in the Summer term. The main games for girls are hockey in the Michaelmas term, netball in the Lent term and tennis and rounders in the Summer term. Girls also have the chance to play competitive lacrosse, football and cricket. In addition, teams represent the College at squash, fives, cross country, fencing, athletics, golf, sailing, swimming, shooting, badminton, basketball, clay pigeon shooting and polo. There are also opportunities to take part in dance classes and aerobics.

There are 2 all-weather artificial grass pitches used for hockey, football and tennis, a 3-court indoor Tennis Centre, 6 other hard tennis courts, 5 netball courts, 4 fives courts, 4 squash courts and a very large and modern Sports Complex, including an indoor swimming pool. The College grounds extend to nearly 250 acres and include fine playing fields, a nine-hole golf course and fly fishing on the river Pang.

Recreation, Drama and Music. Every encouragement is given to pupils to develop their interests and talents in a wide variety of creative activities. There is a modern and well-equipped studio for art and sculpture, an Information Technology Centre, a purpose-built and very extensive Design and Technology Centre and a Music School with a Concert Hall and practice rooms. The Drama department stages a diverse number of productions each term and a classical Greek Play is produced every three years. In addition, there are about 30 Societies covering a wide range of other interests.

Religion. Chapel services are those of the Church of England, and Religious Education is part of the core curriculum in Year 9. Confirmation Services are held each year for Anglicans in the College Chapel and for Catholics in the local parish.

Combined Cadet Force. The College maintains a contingent of the Combined Cadet Force which all pupils have the opportunity of joining. There is a full range of alternative activities, including Community Service and The Duke of Edinburgh's Award. All pupils take part in a programme of Adventure Training.

Old Bradfieldian Society. The College values its links with its former pupils and a series of social and sporting occasions is held each year to enable friendships to be maintained and renewed. Address: Old Bradfieldian Society, Bradfield College, Reading, Berkshire RG7 6AU.

Charitable status. Bradfield College is a Registered Charity, number 309089.

Bradford Grammar School

Keighley Road, Bradford, West Yorkshire BD9 4JP
Tel: 01274 542492; Headmaster: 01274 553701
Fax: 01274 548129
e-mail: hmsec@bradfordgrammar.com
website: www.bradfordgrammar.com

Bradford Grammar School is known to have existed in 1548 and received a title of Incorporation as 'The Free Grammar School of King Charles II at Bradford', in 1662. It was reorganised in 1871, and the Scheme was revised in 1909, and again in 1973, amended by Order of the Charity Commission in 1974, 1980, 1994, 2004 and 2005.

Motto: '*Hoc Age*'

Corporate Trustee: Bradford Grammar School Trustee Limited.

Governors:
Chairman: Lady L Morrison, LLB
Vice-Chairman: Professor C Mellors, BA, MA, PhD
President: A H Jerome, MA

Ex-officio:
The Dean of Bradford, The Very Reverend D J Ison, BA, PhD
J E Barker, DL, MA
W Bowser, ACIB
Professor A W Boylston, BA, MD, FRCPath
Mrs A C Craig, DL, DCR
Professor A Francis, BSc, ACGI, FBAM, CCMI
Mrs C Hamilton-Stewart
His Honour Judge J A Lewis, LLB
Professor Sir Alexander F Markham, BSc, PhD, MB, BS, DSc, FRCP, FRCPath
T H Ratcliffe, MBE, LLB
J G Ridings, FCA
P T Smith, FRICS
C M Wontner-Smith, BA, FCA

Governor Emeritus:
P J M Bell, JP, FCIS, CText, FTI, FRSA
R G Bowers, BSc, CEng, FRSA
Mrs J D Fenton, MCSP, SRP
I Crawford, FCA

Bursar and Clerk to the Governors: I Findlay, BA, ACA

Headmaster: S R Davidson, DL, BSc

Deputy Head: M J Sharpe, BSc, PhD

Assistant Heads:
R I Page, BA, MSc
N R Smith, BSc, MEd
J D Boardman, BSc
D S Conroy, BSc

Department Staff:
* *Head of Department/Subject*
§ *Part-time*

Art:
*R I Walker, BA
Ms J Barraclough, BA
§Mrs L A Hepworth-Wood, BA
Mrs S E Horsfield, BA
H R Thornton, BA

Biology:
*Mrs P M A Dunn, BSc
Mrs M Bibby, BSc
Mrs D J Chalashika, BSc
S R Hoath, BSc
Miss E Comer, BSc

Business Studies:
*Mrs D M Hicks, BSc
D A Pullen, BSc

Chemistry:
*G C Fisher, BSc, MA
§Mrs G M Heywood, BSc
Mrs N S Nicholas, BSc
A B R Macnab, BSc
Mrs D J Mouat, BSc, PhD

Classics:
*Mrs M J Chapman, MA (*Asst Head Lower School*)
T C Bateson, MA
Dr J McNamara, BA, PhD
§R A West, MA

Design and Technology:
*M D McKay, BA
D Leake, BEd, MA
S G Taylor, BSc (*Asst Head Middle School*)
§N J Walker, BEd

Economics:
*R D Schofield, BA
Miss E Anthony, BSc

English and Drama:
*A P Johnson, BA
Miss S J Ball, BA (*Drama*)
Mrs S Brear, BA
Mrs P Buckham-Bonnett, BA, MA
Miss G D'Arcy, BA, MA
Miss A M Lancelot, BA, MA
S D Rees, BA
Miss S M Waring, BA
L W Hanson, BEd, MA

Geography and Geology:
*A G Smith, BSc (*Geology*)
Miss A C Hicks, BA
Mrs F R Handbury, BA
Miss H R Morgan, BA
N R Smith, BSc, MEd (*Asst Head*)

History:
*N A Hooper, MA, FRHistS
J D Devlin, BA, DPhil
J Reed-Purvis, BA, MA (*Head of Sixth Form*)
Mrs K E Wilde, BA (*Head of Lower School*)
§Mrs H J Baines, BA

Information Technology:
*Mrs C M Conroy, BSc
C R F Bright, BSc,
Mrs S E Palmer, BEd
§Mrs C Harvey, BA, MA (*Careers*)
D S Conroy, BSc (*Asst Head*)

Mathematics:
*D W Fishwick, BSc, PhD
§A B Baines, BSc
Mrs E C Boyes-Watson, BA
A Crabtree, BSc
Ms S Harris, MMath, PhD
P Merckx, BSc (*Head of First Year*)
M A Thompson, BSc (*Head of Middle School*)
P Watson, BSc, PhD
S L Denby, BSc
R I Page, BA, MSc (*Asst Head*)

Modern Languages:
*G P Woods, MA
R J Carter, BA
Ms M B Cuesta-González (*Spanish*)
§S B Davis, MA, LTCL, MIL (*Russian*)
§Mrs E J Kingsley, BA
Mrs C Jackson, BA, MA
Ms K Murach, MA
R A Salter, MA
Mrs S Woodhead, BA
Mrs A P Simmonds, BA
Miss V Martí-Fernández, BA
Mrs E Tomlinson, BA (*French*)
J Bove, BA

Music:
*N A Mann, ALCM
C J Brook, BA

§D G Roberts, LRAM, LGSM

Physics and Electronics:
*P Shepherd, BEng, PhD
T W Carman, BSc, PhD, ARCS, CPhys, MInstP
§J R Charlton, BSc
R W Morley, BSc, MA
J D Boardman, BSc (*Asst Head*)
I E Walker, BA

PE and Games:
*C W Lines, BA
§S Darnbrough (*Rowing Coach*)
A J Galley, BEd
Mrs M E Harling, BSc, MA
C E Linfield, BA
Mrs C A Taylor, BA (*Asst Head of Sixth Form,*)
§B Townsend (*Swimming Coach*)
M A Wilde, BA (*Asst Head of Middle School*)
Mrs H E Boughton, BSc
Miss G K Jones, BEd
S M Smith, BA

Politics:
*M P J Simpson, MA, DipSp
Miss A L Slater, BA

Psychology:
*Ms C J White, BSc

Religious Studies:
*R E Skelton, BD
B R Malley, BA

The Junior School:
Headmaster: N H Gabriel, BA, DipArch
Deputy Head: Mrs J Manning, BEd

Miss K L Howes, BSc, MSc
Mrs L Morris, BEd
C P Newsome, BA
J A Price, BA
P Smales, BEd, BA
G P Smith, BEd
N E Sykes, GLCM, ARCM
§C Thorpe, CertEd (*Sports Coach*)
Miss E D Clucas, BA
Mrs A H Tebbutt, BSc
J A Watts, BA

Visiting Music Teachers:
Ms A Brown, BMus (*woodwind*)
Mrs J Bryan, GMus, CT ABRSM, LRSM (*woodwind*)
A Cook, GLCM (*guitar*)
M Gaborak, LTCL, GCLCM (*guitar*)
J Griffett, ARCM (*singing*)
Ms J Harrison, GRNCM (*singing*)
Mrs P J Jordan, ARCM (*piano*)
Mrs E Kenwood-Herriott, ATCL (*double reed instruments*)
M McGuffie, BA (*clarinet*)
D Roberts, LRAM, LGSM (*brass*)
A J Sherlock, BA, ALCM (*piano, Instrumental Studies Coordinator*)
B G Stevens, BA (*percussion*)
Miss A Verity, MA (*lower strings*)
Ms C Walker, LTCL (*upper strings*)

Bradford Grammar School provides a stimulating and supportive environment in which bright boys and girls can work together to achieve their individual potential. There are currently 697 boys and 418 girls aged 6–18.

Situation and Buildings. The school stands in fine buildings and extensive grounds about one mile from the centre of Bradford. There are excellent road and rail links with Wharfedale, Airedale, Leeds City Centre, Calderdale and Huddersfield. The Junior School occupies Clock House, a seventeenth century Manor House within the school grounds, where it enjoys its own assembly hall, IT and DT facilities and teaching accommodation. Facilities available to both Senior and Junior Schools include the Hockney Theatre, the Library and Information Technology Centre, the School Debating Chamber, the Design and Technology Centre, Sports Hall, Sixth Form Centre, Music School and Swimming Pool. The Price Hall is the centrepiece of the main school building and provides a magnificent setting for assemblies, concerts and other major events.

Junior School Curriculum. All pupils study English, Mathematics, Geography, History, Science, Music, Art, IT, Design and Technology, Physical Education, Games, Religious Studies, PHSE and from Year 4 modern foreign languages – French, Spanish and German.

(*For further details about the Junior School, see entry in IAPS section.*)

Senior School Curriculum. In the First and Second Forms all pupils study English, Mathematics, French, German, Latin, Biology, Physics, Chemistry, Geography, History, Art, Music, Design and Technology, Information Technology, Religious Studies, Physical Education and Games.

In the Third Form, pupils follow a common core of English, Mathematics, Geography, History, Physics, Chemistry, Biology, Religious Studies, Physical Education and Games, a choice of French, German or Spanish and three subjects from German, Russian, Latin, Greek, Art, Music, Design and Technology, ICT and Spanish.

In the Fourth and Fifth Forms, all pupils take English, Mathematics, Biology, Chemistry, Physics, PE and Games, a core modern foreign language, choosing between French, German and Spanish, and three subjects from: Geography, History, German, Russian, Latin, Spanish, Greek, Art, Music, Design and Technology, ICT and Religious Studies. Pupils are entered for seven GCSEs and three IGCSEs. Pupils who have not chosen it as an option have one period per fortnight of ICT.

Sixth Form Curriculum. Pupils choose four Advanced Subsidiary Level subjects from Art, Biology, Business Studies, Chemistry, Classical Civilisation, French, German, Greek, Design and Technology, Economics, Electronics, English Language, English Literature, English Language & Literature, Geography, Geology, History, ICT, Latin, Mathematics and Further Mathematics, Music, Music Technology, Psychology, Physical Education, Physics, Politics, Russian, Religious Studies, Spanish and Theatre Studies. There is also a General Studies programme, which includes Japanese. There is the opportunity for senior pupils to sample Mandarin. In the Upper Sixth Form pupils take three or four A Level subjects. The school has a strong record of success at public examinations and university admissions; over the last nine years 133 pupils have gained places at Oxford or Cambridge. A comprehensive Career Service operates throughout the school.

Extra-Curricular Activities. There is a thriving culture of extra-curricular activities. Music and Drama are an important part of school life; Debating flourishes and there are active CCF units and Community Service groups. Most academic subjects have societies run by pupils, and religious interests are represented in the Christian Fellowship, Islamic Society and Inter Faith Forum. A wide variety of sporting activities is offered, including athletics, badminton, basketball, climbing, cricket, cross-country running, hockey, netball, rounders, rowing, rugby, sailing, squash, swimming, table tennis, tennis, water polo and The Duke of Edinburgh's Award Scheme. Senior pupils also take part in the biennial Outlook Expeditions scheme.

Pastoral Care. The Assistant Head (Pastoral) with his team of Year Heads and Form Teachers work closely with pupils and parents to ensure that support is available in school and at home. An extensive Peer Support scheme and a growing system of Year Group Councils are just two ways in which pupils are encouraged to take responsibility for each other and themselves in school.

Admission. Boys and girls can join the school at the ages of 6, 7, 8, 9, 10 in the Junior School or 11, 12, 13 in the Senior School. Pupils are admitted into the Sixth Form on the basis of interview and GCSE results. Candidates for entry at 6+, 7+ and 8+ are invited to spend an informal day in the Junior School. Admission for all other ages is by examination in Mathematics and English in January each year.

Bursaries. Bursaries are available each year on a means-tested basis for entrants at 11+, 13+ and 16+ to support the education of the successful candidates throughout their time at the school. Family circumstances will be reviewed annually and the value of any bursary adjusted accordingly.

Fees per annum (2011-2012). Senior School £10,490; Junior School £8,210.

Old Bradfordians Association. President: Dr G Craig, c/o Bradford Grammar School.

The Parents' Association (previously BGS Society). Chairman: Mrs S Rosborough, c/o Bradford Grammar School.

Charitable status. The Free Grammar School of King Charles II at Bradford is a Registered Charity, number 529113. It exists to provide education for children.

Brentwood School

Ingrave Road, Brentwood, Essex CM15 8AS
Tel: 01277 243243
Fax: 01277 243299
e-mail: headmaster@brentwood.essex.sch.uk
website: www.brentwoodschool.co.uk

Brentwood School was founded in 1557 and received its charter as the Grammar School of Antony Browne, Serjeant at Law, on 5th July, 1558. The Founder became Chief Justice of Common Pleas shortly before the death of Queen Mary, and was knighted a few months before his death in 1567. The Foundation Stone over the door of Old Big School was laid on 10th April, 1568, by Edmund Huddleston and his wife Dorothy, who was the step-daughter of the Founder. The Elizabethan silver seal of the School Corporation is still in the possession of the Governors. In 1622 Statutes were drawn up for the School by Sir Antony Browne, kinsman of the Founder, George Monteigne, Bishop of London, and John Donne, Dean of St Paul's.

Motto: '*Virtue, Learning and Manners*'.

Governors:
C J Finch, FRICS (*Chairman*)
Sir Michael Snyder, DSc, FCA (*Vice-Chairman*)
P C Beresford, FNAEA
Mrs S F Courage, DL
Professor B J W Evans, BSc Hons, PhD
H E Flight, MA, MBA
Lord Hanningfield of Chelmsford
Mrs J M Jones, BA, ARCM
M Lightowler, LLB, NP
The Venerable D Lowman, BD, AKC
Lady McAllister, BSc
R I McLintock, MSc, DMS, DipEd
J M May, MA, LLB
J H M Norris, CBE, DL
R W Owers
R E Ramsey, LLB, FRSA
Dr T J Stone, MA, PhD
R J Wilson, MA

Bursar and Clerk to the Governors: I F Bruton, BA Hons, MIoD

Headmaster: **D I Davies**, MA, FRSA

Second Master: D M Taylor, GRSM, LRAM, MTC, FRSA
Deputy Head: N J Carr, MA, MA EconEd, ACEM, FRSA
Deputy Head (Pastoral): S D Weale, MA

Heads of Year:
Sixth Form: Mrs K Beston, MA
Sixth Form Deputy Head (Curriculum): J D Williams, BSc
Sixth Form Deputy Head (Pastoral): Mrs L E Bengston, BSc
Sixth Form Deputy Head: I Foakes, MA
Fifth Year: Miss C Holding, BA
Fourth Year: I Wignall, BA
Third Year: Mrs M E Belsham, BSc
Second Year: L P Bishun, MSc, MIS
First Year: J R Brown, BA

Houses & Housemasters/mistresses:
East: J MCann, BEng
Hough: P Rees, BA & Mrs C Rees
Mill Hill: J Shipway, BSc & Mrs J Shipway
North: N S Crosby, BA
South: C M Long, BA
Weald: Mrs N Heelam, BSc
West: Dr G J Fisher, MA, PhD

* Head of Department

Art:
*Mrs M Parsons, BA
Miss N J Bixby, MA
Miss I Lumsden, BA
D McAuliffe, BA, MA
Ms N Poole
Mrs S J Wells, BSc

Biology:
*Dr P Tiffen, BSc, PhD
Mrs L E Bengston, BSc
Miss J P Byrne, BSc
Mrs P Ebden, BSc, MSc
H Gauntlett
K Gray, BSc
Miss H English, BSc
M McGowan, BSc
Miss V Rutter, BSc
J Shipway, BSc

Business Studies:
*Miss M Sorohan, BA, MA
N J Carr, MA, MA
  EconEd, ACEM, FRSA
C A Graves, BSc
Ms R Lees, BA
Mrs K Miller, BA
P Slater, MA

Chemistry:
*Dr A Hill, BSc, PhD
S L Gonsalves, BA
Mrs J Khush, MSc
A Pask, BSc
G Pye, BSc

Classics:
*Miss K Bryce, MA
Mrs L J Acton, BA
Mrs D Anand
Miss K Bryce, MA
Mrs K Beston, MA
Miss K L Crane, BA
Dr G J Fisher, MA, PhD
Revd David Gilchrist, MA
D Hodgkinson, BA
Ms J Moore, BA
D Paul, MA

Computing & ICT:
*J J McCann, BEng Hons
G M Kiff, BA (*Director of Design Centre*)
Mrs K Rajani, BSc
Mrs J Ryalls, BSc
D Wright, BSc

Design & Technology:
*A R Eckton, BSc Hons
R T Chapman, CertEd
S Harvey, BA
Mrs M Tyler, BA

Drama:
*L Jones, MA
P Cleaves, BA
Ms L West, BA

Economics:
*Mrs A Cox, BSc
N J Carr, MA, MA
  EconEd, ACEM, FRSA
C A Graves, BSc
Ms R Lees, BA
P Rees, BA
P Slater, MA

English:
*Dr S Evans, BA, PhD
Mrs H Barker, BA
Miss R Begum, BA
Miss M Blackwell, MA
D Dunn, MA
Mrs J Edwards
I Foakes, MA
Mrs C Gordon-Johnson, BA
Mrs S Hawkings, BA (*Director of Life Skills*)
Mrs S Heyn, BA
Miss E Holland, MA
Mrs L A Hurlock, BA
L Jones, BA
Miss H McMahon
S Taylor, LLB

EAL:
Mrs E Fisher, CELTA

Food Technology:
*Mrs B Daly, BEd
Mrs S Hardy, BSc, MIFST
D M Taylor, GRSM, LRAM, MTC, FRSA

Geography:
*N S Crosby, BA
Mrs R Barford
Mrs S Davis, BSc
M Golland, BA
C M Long, BA
Mrs F Wood, BSc

History:
*Mrs M E Belsham, BSc
C Berkley, BA
Miss N J Bixby, MA
J R Brown, BA
M Clark, BA
Miss R Fairfull, MA
Mrs C Harvey, BA, PhD
Mrs J Keylock, BA
S D Weale, MA
M V Willis, BA

Learning Development:
*Mrs S Heyn, BA
Mrs L Buck
Mrs S Knowles, BEd

Mathematics:
*A J Drake, MA
T Acton, BSc
Mrs C A Bear, BSc
L P Bishun, MSc, MIS
Mrs K Bowes, BSc
Mrs J J Coppin, BSc, MSc
Miss A Denniss, BA
Mrs R Hamborg, BSc
J L Killilea, BEd, AIST, MA
G J Little, MA
A Newby, BSc
Ms S Quinn, MA
I M Sanderson, BSc
Mrs P Sanderson, BSc
J D Williams

Modern Languages:
*Dr R M Storey, BA, PhD
R Pritchard, BA (*Spanish*)
Dr E Rowlands, BA, PhD (*French*)
I Walton, MA (*German*)
J Bowley, MA, Maître (*Gifted & Talented*)
Miss R Campbell, BA
Mrs L G M Dearmer-Decup, BA
L Herrera, MA
Miss A Leath, BA
Miss S Lloyd, BA
Mrs E Lusty, BA, MA
Ms A Moreno, BA
Miss I Penalver-Escamez, BA

Director of IB: M Taylor, MA, MA, MCIEA
Careers and University Entrance: I Foakes, MA
Admissions Registrar: Mrs M Henning
Headmaster's PA: Mrs P Scott
Chaplain: The Revd David Gilchrist, MA
School Medical Officer: Dr Nasif

Mrs S J Roast, BEd
D E G Saunders, BA
D Sheppard, BA
Mrs T Sheppard
Mrs M D Taylor, BA

Music:
Director of Music: D J H Pickthall, MA, FRCO
S R Rumsey, BA
D M Taylor, GRSM, LRAM, MTC, FRSA
Mrs H Khoo, GRSM (*Academic Music*)

Physics:
*A Robson, MEng
W M Gray, MA
Mrs N C Heelam, BSc
L C Jenkins, MSc, FRAS
R O'Rourke, BSc
Ms K Vassiliou, BSc, PhD
J Williams

Physical Education & Games:
*J Kayne, BSc Hons
W Castleman (*Rugby Coach*)
Miss J Farrow, BSc
B R Hardie, NCAAC
Miss C Holding, BA
Mrs W L Juniper, BEd
J L Killilea, BEd, AIST, MA
Mrs S Knightbridge, BSc
Miss J Saunders, BEd (*Girls' Games*)
Miss L Smith, BSc
I Wignall, BA

Politics:
*M V Willis, BA
J R Brown, BA
Mrs R Coppell, MA
Mrs C Harvey, BA, PhD

Psychology:
*Mrs A R Bailey, BSc
Mrs L E Bengston, BSc
Dr G Childs, MSc, PhD
M McGowan, BSc
Mrs J O'Connell, BSc

Religious Studies:
*B Clements, BA, MPhil
Mrs L J Acton, BA
Miss R Bishop, BA
D I Davies, MA, FRSA
Revd D Gilchrist, MA
Mrs S Hawkings, BA (*Director of Life Skills*)
R Jenkins, BA
M Monro, BA
S R Rumsey, BA

Science:
*Dr M Garstin, BSc, PhD

Brentwood School is a co-educational school with a total of 1,600 pupils including 143 in the Pre-Preparatory School and 242 in the Preparatory School. The Pre-Preparatory School and Preparatory School are fully co-educational as is the Sixth Form (of 330 pupils), but boys and girls are taught separately between the ages of 11 and 16. Boarding is available for boys and girls from 11.

Buildings and Grounds. The School occupies a 72-acre site on high ground at the northern end of the town some 20 miles north-east of London. Old Big School, the original school room, is still in regular use thus maintaining a direct link with the school's founder. Over recent years a major building programme has seen extensions to the Science and Modern Languages buildings and Dining Hall; refurbishment of the Preparatory School, Boarding Houses and Sixth Form accommodation; the building of the magnificent Brentwood School Sports Centre; a Performing Arts Centre, an all-weather pitch, an Art and Design Centre and an indoor heated swimming pool. The School is currently building a new Sixth Form Centre and Assembly Hall. The Sixth Form Centre will provide an exemplary educational environment for the International Baccalaureate Diploma programme, an assembly space for up to 400 students and staff, a performance venue for an audience of 300 and include 16 additional classrooms.

Organisation. The school is one community within which, for good educational reasons, girls and boys are taught separately from age 11 to 16. They are encouraged to participate together in all extra-curricular activities. The Senior School is divided into Year Groups. Each Year Group has a Head of Year and Deputy who oversee it. The vast majority of pupils join the school at 11 after successfully completing our Entrance Examination. A broad curriculum is followed through the first three years and this continues through careful choice of GCSE subjects to the end of the Fifth Year. Entry to the Sixth Form is conditional upon success in the GCSE examinations. In the Sixth Form students take either four of the 27 AS level subjects or follow the International Baccalaureate Diploma programme. Most go on to University. Pass rates at Advanced Level reach 100% and many pupils gain places at Oxford and Cambridge each year.

Religion. The School is an Anglican Foundation. There is a resident Chaplain and all pupils attend Chapel fortnightly. Regular Communion Services are held. Members of other faiths are welcomed and their views respected.

Boarding. There are two Boarding Houses, both of which have been thoroughly modernised. The boys reside in Hough House which can accommodate up to 48 students; the girls reside in Mill Hill House where 27 can be accommodated. The public rooms are spacious and both Houses generously staffed. Full and weekly boarding are available. A qualified Matron runs an efficient Sanatorium.

Pastoral Care. Brentwood School takes very seriously its pastoral responsibilities and provides two supportive systems. Responsibility for pastoral care is vested in the Form Tutors under the guidance of the Heads of Year and the Deputy Head, Pastoral. This system is complemented by a strong House system with Housemasters/Mistresses and House Tutors. Partnership with parents is regarded as essential and they are encouraged to join in activities and to visit regularly.

Music, Drama and Art. Music plays an important part in the life of the School, as do drama and art. There are 4 orchestras and several ensembles and jazz groups. The Big Band is internationally acclaimed. There are at least three dramatic productions each year, together with regular Art Exhibitions.

Careers. There is an excellent University Entrance and Careers Department where students receive advice and can obtain information about courses and/or careers. Aptitude Tests; Work Experience; visits to colleges, universities and places of work; visiting speakers are all part of the provision. A careers convention is held in March each year.

CCF and CSU. All pupils either join the Combined Cadet Force or, through the Community Service Unit, engage in a wide-ranging series of activities which bring them into contact with the Community. The Duke of Edinburgh's Award Scheme runs alongside these activities.

School Societies. There are many flourishing societies covering a wide range of interests, catering for all ages. The Sir Anthony Browne Society (SABS) at Brentwood School is a society for Sixth Form pupils, which provides them with an opportunity for intellectual discussion and cultural interest.

Sports Facilities. The playing fields are part of the School complex and provide ample space for soccer, cricket, hockey, rugby and tennis. There is a cinder athletic track. The Brentwood School Sports Centre includes an indoor soccer/hockey pitch, six badminton courts, indoor cricket nets, basketball courts and a fencing salle, as well as squash courts and a fitness suite. There is a heated indoor swimming pool and an all-weather pitch. Provision is made for golf, sailing and table tennis. The Astroturf and netball courts are floodlit for use in winter.

Preparatory and Pre-Preparatory Schools. *See entry in IAPS section for details.*

Entry. Entrance Examinations for both boys and girls aged 11 are held at the School in January each year. Entries are also accepted at 13 plus, following the Common Entrance Examination, vacancies permitting. Transfers at other ages are also possible. Sixth Form entry is through GCSE success, and interview.

Scholarships and Bursaries. (*See Scholarship Entries section.*) The school offers scholarships at 11+ and for entry to the Sixth Form for Music, Drama, Art, Sport and Choral in addition to Academic scholarships. Means-tested bursaries are also available.

Fees per term (2011-2012). Day £4,724; Boarding £8,481.

Old Brentwood's Society. There is a flourishing Society for pupils to stay in touch once they have left the school. The Secretary is Ian Pitwood, socobs@pitwood.com.

Charitable status. Brentwood School (part of Sir Antony Browne's School Trust, Brentwood) is a Registered Charity, number 310864. It is a Charitable Trust for the purpose of educating children.

Brighton College

Eastern Road, Brighton BN2 0AL
Tel: 01273 704200
          01273 704339 Head Master
          01273 704260 Bursar
          01273 704269 Prep School
Fax: 01273 704204
e-mail: admissions@brightoncollege.net
website: www.brightoncollege.net

The first of the Sussex public schools, Brighton College was founded in 1845 with the object of providing a 'thoroughly liberal and practical education for the sons of the local gentry in conformity with the principles of the Established Church'. With its Victorian Gothic buildings, the front quad, largely unchanged since then, has the appearance of a Cambridge court in the heart of the Kemp Town, whilst to the North of the main range many modern buildings have been added in recent years.

The college first admitted girls into the Sixth Form in 1973 and became fully educational in 1988. There are now some 830 in the Upper School and 100 pupils in the Lower School, of whom a third are boarders and 40% girls. Pupils are divided into 12 houses. Pupils aged 11 were admitted to the college for the first time in August 2009.

Motto: TO Δ 'EY NIKATΩ (*Let the right prevail*)

Patron and Visitor: The Right Revd The Lord Bishop of Chichester, DD

Council
President: Rt Hon Lord Renton of Mount Harry, PC, DL

Vice-Presidents:
S J Cockburn
The Rt Hon Sir John Chilcot
I W Dodd
R F Jones
Mrs J Lovegrove
P D C Points
L C W Rea
R J Seabrook, QC
Dr A F Seldon
Lady H Trafford, DSc, SRN
Dr J Wade, JP, MB, BChir

Chairman: Prof Lord Skidelsky, FBA

Vice-Chairman: I J White, FRICS

Governors:
N Abraham, CBE
Mrs J Aisbitt, JP
M Burgess
M D L Chowen, DL
Mrs J Deslandes
Ms L Hayman
P Jackson
Rt Hon F Maude, MP
G R Miller, MBE, FCIB
D A Nelson-Smith
A Pettitt
A J Symonds FRICS, MCI Ard
L Tomlinson, OBE

Head Master: R J Cairns, MA, FRSA

Second Master: S G R Smith, BA, FRSA

Director of Finance & Deputy Head: P Westbrook, BA, FCA

Deputy Head Master: M J Beard, MA

Deputy Headmistress: Mrs J A Riley, MA

Assistant Heads:
A R Bird, MA (*Sixth Form*)
J R Weeks, BA (*Middle School*)
Miss L Hamblett, MA (*Lower School*)
R A Nicholson, BEd (*Co-Curricular & Director of Sport*)
K A Grocott, MA (*Director of Boarding*)
J Carr-Hill, MSc (*Director of Studies*)

Director of Admissions: Mrs A Withers

Medical Officer: Dr Richard Gray, MB BS, MRCP, MRCS

Academic Staff:
R Alvers, BA
M D Bach, BA
Mrs K M Brown, MA
N Buoy, BSc (*Director of Rugby*)
N Carter, LTCL
S Chenery, MA (*Director of Music*)
Miss E T M J Cody, BA (*Housemistress, Chichester House*)
B Collie, BSc
Miss N Collins, BA (*Housemistress, Seldon House*)
J A Cornish, MSc
Mrs F M Cremona, BA (*External Exams Officer*)
D A Crichton, BA (*Head of History and Politics*)
Mrs N Davin, BA

A T Debney, BSc (*Head of Mathematics; Director of Curriculum*)
Ms G A Dore, BA
J W Dunn, BA
Ms J Dynes, BA (*Head of ESL*)
Revd R Easton, BA, MTheol (*Chaplain*)
Ms J A Elsom, BA
B M Frier, BSc (*Head of Academic PE*)
D Gabriele, MA (*Head of English*)
T L D Godber, MA
M Godfrey, BA (*Housemaster, School House*)
Dr T J Gravestock, MChem, PhD
G Hart, BSc (*Housemaster, Aldrich House*)
S Hawkes, BA (*Head of DT; Housemaster, Durnford House*)
Ms M L Holness, BA
Ms V Hulme, BSc
Mrs H C Jordan, BA
D Kerr, BA (*Director of Drama*)
B L Lambe, BSc (*Head of Information Technology*)
Ms J Langhorne, BEd (*Head of Girls' Games*)
R Law, MA, MPhil
M V Lewis, BSc
Ms M J Marsh
C Mayanobe, MA (*Librarian, Head of Careers*)
A Merrett, BSc
Mrs R Miller, BA
W Minter, BA
G Mitchell, BA (*Head of Modern Languages; Head of Spanish*)
C Morrissey, BA (*Tutor for Admissions*)
Mrs M A Murphy, BA (*Housemistress, Fenwick House*)
R A Nicholson, BA (*Director of Sport*)
J Pass, BEng
O E Peck, BSc (*Head of Biology*)
Ms K T Playfair, MA (*Head of Classics*)
Mrs M L Porter, BA (*Director of Dance*)
S Radojcic, BSc (*Proctor*)
L P Rao, MA
E Rees, BSc
M Reeve, BSc
D Roberts, BA, LSDC
D V Rosa, BA (*Head of French*)
R Ruz, MSc (*Director of IT*)
Ms J Scopes, BA
P J Smales, BEng
J Spencer, MA (*Head of Geography*)
Ms E Sturgeon, BA
Miss C M Szekely, BA (*Head of Mathematics*)
Mrs J Thomas, MA
E F Twohig, MA, NDipAD (*Director of Art*)
Miss B C Walsh, BA (*SENCO*)
M E Walsh, BSc, DPhil (*Head of Chemistry*)
Ms E Whipple, AGSM, CRD
Mrs A C Withers (*Housemistress, Williams House*)
J A St J Withers, BEd (*Housemaster, Hampden House*)
Mrs S A Woodmansey, BA (*Head of Business Studies; Housemaster, Ryle House*)
Ms J J Zhao, MA (*Head of Mandarin*)

There are twenty Part-time Academic Staff and thirty Visiting Music Staff.

Buildings. The College is situated in the fashionable Kemp Town district of Brighton. The original north range and Headmaster's House was designed by Gilbert Scott in 1847. The Chapel was added in 1858 and extended in 1923 as a memorial to the Old Brightonians who gave their lives in the First World War. The south and west range of boarding houses was completed to a design by Sir Thomas Jackson (an Old Brightonian) in 1886. The Great Hall (1913), Swimming Pool, Armoury, covered Miniature Range and Squash Courts are all early twentieth century additions. New Workshops for Technical Studies and two day boy Houses were added in September 1959. A Classroom Block was completed in 1972, and the Sports Hall in 1973. The Lester Building, for IT and Mathematics was built in 1986, and girls' day accommodation in 1990. The Hordern Room, a small theatre and concert hall was opened by Sir Michael Hordern, an Old Boy, in January 1995 as part of the College's 150th Anniversary Celebrations.

An extensive programme of development is currently taking place. A new 3 storey Performing Arts Centre, incorporating a Dance Studio, Café de Paris and Music practice classrooms, opened in Summer 2000; a new Music and Drama School was acquired in 2003; at the same time a major refurbishment and upgrade of the Library also took place together with the creation of The Rose Lecture Theatre, which also serves as a cinema. In March 2008 the Alexander Centre for the Visual Arts and a new language laboratory were opened. A new building to house the Lower School and 6 classrooms has recently been built. A new leisure facility for boarders is currently under way.

Admission. Pupils are admitted to the Lower Third at the age of 11 via assessments held at the college in January; to the Fourth Form between the ages of 13 and 14 via the Common Entrance examination, the Scholarship Examination, or by special Assessment and interview; and into the Sixth Form for a two-year A2 course, between the ages of 16 and 17, subject to a minimum of 12 points at GCSE (based on three points for an A* grade, two points for an A grade and one point for a B grade) and ideally an A grade in each subject to be studied at A Level. In all cases pupils must also produce evidence of good character and conduct from their previous school. The College Prospectus and registration form can be obtained from the Director of Admissions.

Entry for new Lower Third, Fourth Form and Sixth Form pupils is at the beginning of the Michaelmas term.

Houses. Hampden, Leconfield, Aldrich, Durnford, Ryle, Chichester and Williams and Seldon are Day Houses, each with their own premises. Head's House, School House, Abraham and Fenwick are Boarding Houses, which have recently had an extensive programme of refurbishment. From September a third of the pupils will be boarders in the school. Weekly boarding is increasingly popular. Pupils may go home on Friday afternoon and return either on Sunday evening or on Monday morning.

Dyslexia Centre. The specialist Dyslexia Centre enables children who are assessed as Dyslexic, but with high intelligence, to take a suitably adjusted GCSE course within the normal College curriculum with the opportunity to proceed to A Levels in the Sixth Form.

Health. There is a Central Health Centre with a team of qualified nurses, and the Medical Officer visits regularly.

Catering. There is self-service dining room, managed by a qualified Catering Manager.

Holidays. The usual School holidays are about 3 weeks each at Christmas and Easter, and 8 weeks in the Summer. There is a half-term holiday of 1 week in all three terms.

Religion. A short morning service is held in Chapel on 2 days a week: Friday's service aims to embrace all faiths. There are services for all pupils on some Sundays to which parents and visitors are welcome. Candidates are prepared by the Chaplain for Confirmation.

Curriculum. The School is divided into 6 Forms – Lower Third, Fourth, Lower Fifth, Upper Fifth, Lower Sixth and Upper Sixth. (This will become 7 forms from 2010.) In the Sixth Form some 28 subjects are available at AS or A2 Level, the latest additions being Psychology, Photography and Dance. For GCSE, pupils select their 9 subjects at the end of the Fourth Form. 95% of pupils proceed to university. Preparation for the UCAS process begins in the second term of the Lower Sixth, and pupils are guided towards appropriate choices by the Head of Sixth Form in conjunction with the individual pupil's tutor.

Sport. The College enjoys a strong record of excellence at most sports. The main playing-field (the Home Ground) is part of the College campus and there is another ground a mile away at East Brighton Park. All pupils take part in the College's extensive games programme. The main sports for boys are rugby and cricket and for girls, netball, hockey and cricket. In addition, a host of other options are available including Soccer, Squash, Tennis, Golf, Fencing, Biathlon, Aerobics, Yoga, Athletics and Cross-Country. There is also a flourishing Sailing Club. The College has its own indoor swimming pool.

Service. All pupils from the Lower Fifth onwards are expected to participate in a service activity on one afternoon a week. This may involve entering one of the 3 sections of the CCF, or joining the Duke of Edinburgh's Award Scheme. In addition, pupils may participate in charity work or, in the Sixth Form, Community Service.

Music. One in three pupils learns at least one musical instrument. There is a strong musical tradition and pupils reach a very high level of performance. The Choir, Chamber Orchestra, Symphony Orchestra, Concert Band and Swing Band perform regularly both inside and outside the College. There are several Chamber groups, and the Choral Society and Orchestra usually perform major works at the annual Brighton Festival.

Drama. The College has a strong tradition of excellence in drama. There are opportunities for anyone to be involved and the College stages plays ranging from Tudor Interludes through Shakespeare, Restoration comedy and twentieth century classics. In addition to the regular calendar of a musical, Sixth Form studio production, Sixth Form play, Fourth Form play, Lower School play and House Drama festival, there are also many productions mounted entirely by pupils. There is also a junior Drama Club.

Activities. Creative activities are encouraged both in and out of school time, and the College has its own Art School and Gallery where exhibitions by leading Artists are regularly staged. Dance is an increasingly popular activity.

Careers. Ms Cecile Mayanobe heads a team of tutors who advise pupils on careers. The College is a member of the Independent Schools Careers Organisation.

Entrance Scholarships. (*See Scholarship Entries section.*)

Fees per term (2011-2012). Full Boarders £9,525–£10,782; Weekly Boarders £8,243–£8,628; Day Pupils £4,227–£6,225. The Registration Fee is £75.

Old Brightonians' Association. The Old Brightonians' Association has annual Dinners and a number of flourishing sports clubs.

Preparatory School. The College has its own fully coeducational Prep School with a Pre-Preparatory department. (*For details see entry in IAPS section.*)

Brighton College Family Society. The society organises talks, outings and other social events and is open to all parents, Old Brightonians and friends of the College.

Charitable status. Brighton College is a Registered Charity, number 307061. It exists for the purpose of educating boys and girls.

Bristol Grammar School

University Road, Bristol BS8 1SR
Tel: 0117 973 6006
Fax: 0117 946 7485
e-mail: headmaster@bgs.bristol.sch.uk
website: www.bristolgrammarschool.co.uk

'The Grammar School in Bristowe' existed under a lay master in 1532 in which year, under a charter of Henry VIII, it was endowed with the estates of St Bartholomew's Hospital by the merchant and geographer Robert Thorne and others. The trust was placed in the care of the Corporation of Bristol and then the Trustees of the Bristol Municipal

Charities. In September 2004 the School incorporated as a company limited by guarantee with registered charitable status and is now governed under Memorandum and Articles of Association approved by the Charity Commission in 2004.

Co-educational since 1980, today BGS provides a wide-ranging and challenging education for boys and girls aged between 11 and 18, while BGS Infants and Juniors, based on the same site, caters for those in the 4–11 age range.

Motto: '*Ex Spinis Uvas.*'

Governors:
P Rilett, MBA, FCA (*Chairman*)
Mrs B Bates, BA, MA, FRSA
Mrs K Case, CertEd
N Dawes, BSc Hons
B R England, DL, ACIB (*Vice-Chairman*)
N Fitzpatrick, BA, FIA, ASIP, FRSA
D K Golledge, FCA
C J Haworth, BSc, FRICS
S A Lipfriend, BA Hons
Mrs C J Monk, JP, CertEd, BEd Hons (*Vice-Chairman*)
Mrs A Nosowska, CertEd, BEd Hons
N Reeve, FCA
J Symons, BSc Hons, MRICS
Prof D Stoten, BSc, PhD, DEng, CEng, FIMechE
Mrs A J Arlidge
M Hill, BSc, FCA

Headmaster: **R I MacKinnon**, BSc

Headmaster, BGS Infants and Juniors: P R Huckle, BA, MEd
Deputy Head: Ms L Carleton, BA
Deputy Head: P R Roberts, BSc, MSc
Deputy Head: G L Martyn, BA, MA
Bursar: J Berry

Assistant Head: Miss F A Ripley, BSc
Assistant Head: P Z Jakobek, BEd
Assistant Head: Dr A J Dimberline, BSc, PhD
Assistant Head: R M Sellers, BSc
Assistant Head: M Bennett, BSc
Assistant Head: Dr M G Ransome, BA, PhD
Assistant Head: J S Harford, BSc

* *Head of Department*

Art:
*J Lever, MA
Mrs S Cooper, BA
Ms J Estdale, BA, MA
Mrs B D Barnacle, BA
P Z Jakobek, BEd (*Head of House*)

Biology:
*M Bennett, BSc
Mrs R Cullen, BSc
Ms N A Diamond, BSc (*Head of House*)
N S Fuller, BSc, MSc, CBiol, MIBiol
A J Goodland, BSc
J S Harford, BSc (*Director of Sixth Form*)
Ms K Surry, MA

Careers:
*Mrs M L Guy, CertEd

Chemistry:
Miss A Conboy, BSc
A Nalty, MSc
Dr H Perrett, BSc, PhD
Mrs C M Phillips, BSc
*D J Stone, BSc
Dr J Stone, BSc, PhD (*Head of Year*)

Classics:
Mrs J Nesbit, BA (*Leader of the Honours Students*)
S R Holman, MA (*Senior Head of House*)

*A J Keen, BA
D Watkins, BA

Dance:
Miss K Aldred, BA

Design & Technology:
*P M Whitehouse, BSc
M Hilliard, BSc (*Acting Head of House and Head of SPD*)
Ms L-J Knights, BA
P Thomas, BA

Drama:
*Miss J Harbour, BA
G L Martyn, BA, MA
E S Levy, BA, MA

Economics/Business Studies:
A J Catchpole, BSc (*Head of House*)
*Mrs D Dutton, (*Acting Head*)
*J Williams, BSc (*Acting Head*)

English:
*D L Briggs, BA
R P Clare, MA
Mrs C V Maddock, BA, MEd
D S Mair, BA
D M Selwyn, BA, MMus
Mrs A Selvey, BA, MA
Mrs J Whitehead, BA
Ms E Yemenakis, BA

EPQ:
*Mrs R Atkins, BSc

Geography:
Mrs R Atkins, BSc
R A D Cox, BSc
Dr A J Dimberline, BSc, PhD
*Mrs J L Foster, BSc
L Goodman, BA
Miss R Martin, BSc

History:
*Dr R A Massey, BA, PhD
Ms S Bassett, BA
O R T Edwards, BA (*Head of House*)
Miss A Humphrey, BA
N W Haines, BA, MA
Miss P Worth, BA

Information Technology/Computing:
*G S Clark, BSc (*Head of Year*)
R S Jones, BSc
Miss A Henderson, BA

Learning Support:
*Dr M G Ransome, BA, PhD
Mrs J Benn

Mathematics:
*Miss S M Poole, BSc
J Carr
O L Chambers, BSc (*Head of Year*)
Miss C Dupont, BSc
G R Iwi, MSc
Mrs K H Jones, BSc (*Director of Activities*)
Miss S J McCrorie, BSc
Miss A L Nicholsby, BSc
P R Roberts, BSc, MSc
A Thackray, BSc
Miss J Wall, BSc

Modern Languages:
Dr M G Ransome, BA, PhD
Mrs R Allen, BA
S Alpine, BA
Ms L Carleton, BA
Miss E Corrigan, BA (*Head of French*)

G D Fellows, BA
Miss C M Hölzer, MA
Mrs J Hennessy, BA (*Acting Head of German*)
Mrs C Kent, BA (*Head of Year*)
Mrs A C Macro, BA (*Head of Spanish*)
Mrs D M G Swain, BA (*Head of Russian*)
Mrs L E Woodhead, BA

Music:
*R T Osmond, MA
Miss V Elcock, BA
Mrs N Pocock, BMus
N Sutton, BA

PE/Games:
*R M Sellers, BSc (*Director of Sport*)
K R Blackburn, BSc
P Z Jakobek, BEd (*Head of House*)
Mrs R E John, BA
Miss L Lewis, BA
Miss F A Ripley, BSc
Miss V L Ryan, BEd
B Scott, BEd (*Head of PE*)

Physics:
*J T Morris, BSc, MSc
R Jervis, MEng
E J Knoop, BSc
Dr C A Rosser, BSc, PhD
Miss L Glenn, BEng

Psychology:
*Mrs L Dilley, BSc
Mrs K E Alexander, BSc, BA

Religious Studies:
*R M Smith, BA
A Gunawardana, BA (*Head of House*)
Mrs J B Lewis, CertEd (*Head of Year*)
C P Wadey, MA

PA to Headmaster: Miss C Davies

Bristol Grammar School is a day school with c 1,000 students aged between 11 and 18. Students learn in an atmosphere that motivates them to enjoy their education and as a result BGS has a deserved reputation as one of the leading academic schools in the South West. The School has a friendly and lively environment and students are encouraged to make the most of the wide-ranging opportunities available to them. Students joining at age 11 have their form rooms in the Princess Anne Building. This helps ease the transition to senior school, as well as providing an important opportunity for the year group to bond socially. This continues up the School with each year group allocated form rooms, based in separate, self-contained buildings, although teaching is spread throughout the School's specialist facilities.

Close to the city centre and adjacent to the University, Bristol Grammar School is well placed to take advantage of the city's many amenities. It is also committed to a continuing programme of investment to ensure its own facilities continue to offer the best possible opportunities to its students.

The Houses. The School is divided into six Houses, each organised by a Head of House, with the assistance of a Deputy Head of House and House Tutors. Older students become leaders within their House, whilst social, theatrical, musical, sporting and other opportunities allow those from all year groups to work together in a friendly and cooperative atmosphere. As well as providing continuity of pastoral care and enhancing school/home links, the Houses operate as families within the school community, encouraging a real sense of belonging amongst students.

Curriculum. The school takes note of the National Curriculum but, in keeping with its academic ethos, a far wider range of subjects and opportunities is offered. Setting is used in some subjects, but there is no streaming. In the first two years all students follow a curriculum which includes English, Mathematics, Science, French, Spanish, History, Geography, Technology, Food & Nutrition, IT, Latin, Religious Studies, Art, Textiles, Music, Drama, Dance and Physical Education. Further up the School other subjects become available such as Russian, German, Greek and Business Studies. At the end of Year 11, most students take 10 GCSEs drawn from the core subjects of English, Mathematics, Science, a Humanities subject and a Modern Foreign Language, together with a selection of other subjects, chosen from a carefully balanced range of options. BGS currently offers the IGCSE in Mathematics, English, the Sciences, History and Food & Nutrition. The Sixth Form provides a flexible range of A Level options chosen from English, Mathematics and Further Mathematics, the Sciences, Technology, Modern Languages, Classics, History, Geography, Economics, Business Studies, Computing, IT, Psychology, Religious Studies (Philosophy and Ethics), Theatre Studies, Sports Studies, Art and Music. In addition, many students prepare for the Extended Project Qualification and Gold Duke of Edinburgh's Award; all students follow enrichment courses and attend a richly diverse programme of weekly lectures by visiting speakers; and many attend enrichment lessons to support university preparation in subjects such as Medicine, Veterinary Science and Law. Students from the Sixth Form proceed to a wide range of faculties at universities in the UK and abroad, with the majority securing places at their first-choice universities. 12 students gained places at Oxbridge in 2010.

There are frequent opportunities for parents to consult Form Tutors, Heads of Houses and Heads of Year and regular meetings are held for parents to meet the teaching staff.

The School also has two teachers to help students with SEN and a full-time careers advisor.

Games. The games options, which vary with different age groups, include Rugby, Hockey, Football, Cross-Country, Cricket, Athletics, Swimming, Golf, Tennis, Rounders and Netball. Facilities for Orienteering, Aerobics, Climbing, Dance, Judo, Fencing, Badminton and Squash are available. There is a Pavilion and extensive playing fields at Failand, which include an all-weather Hockey/Tennis area and two Astroturf hockey pitches. Below the Sixth Form, all students, unless excused for medical reasons, participate in School games; the full range of sports is available to the Sixth Form on a voluntary basis.

Activities and Societies. All students take part in a wide-ranging programme of activities one afternoon a week (as part of the curriculum) and there are many voluntary clubs and societies at lunchtimes and after school. There are flourishing choirs and orchestras; tuition can be arranged in a large number of instruments. Drama productions are regularly staged by different age levels of the School and by the Houses. Ski trips are offered each year. Regular excursions are made abroad, as well as cultural exchange visits, including Japan and Russia. Students may join the Duke of Edinburgh's Award Scheme in Year 10 and there is an active Community Service Unit. Overseas expeditions take place every two years and have recently visited Mongolia, Ecuador, India, Peru and Arctic Norway.

Admission. Entry to the School is normally in September at age 11+ following a satisfactory performance in the entrance examination held in the previous spring and a creditable school report or reference. An additional 20–25 places become available each year at ages 13+ and 16+. Students may be accepted into the school during any term subject to the availability of places.

Applications should be made to the Recruitment Office at the School. Prospective entrants and their families are always welcome to visit the School. Please see the website for information about Open Days, Tours and Taster Days.

Bursaries. The School's Assisted Places Scheme is able to offer substantial financial assistance towards the fees of able students whose parents have limited means. The scheme is kept under regular review by the Governors who constantly seek to extend it. The School became a member of the Ogden Bursary Scheme in 2000.

Scholarships. (*See Scholarship Entries section.*)

Fees per term (2011-2012). Senior School £3,711.50; Junior School: £2,456.75 (Years 3–6), £2,417.75 (Years 1 and 2), £1,997.75 (Reception). Fees include the cost of most textbooks and stationery. Infants fees are inclusive of Breakfast club and lunch.

BGS Infants and Juniors. The Junior School has now extended its provision to include infants, with its first Reception year class in Sept 2010. The School admits children from 4–11 and is housed in its own buildings on the same site as the Senior School. (*For further details see entry in IAPS section.*)

Old Bristolians Society. Close contact is maintained with former students through the Old Bristolians Society whose honorary secretary can be contacted at the School.

Charitable status. Bristol Grammar School is a Registered Charity, number 1104425. It has existed since 1532 to provide an education for Bristol children.

Bromsgrove School

Worcester Road, Bromsgrove, Worcestershire B61 7DU
Tel: 01527 579679
Fax: 01527 576177
e-mail: admissions@bromsgrove-school.co.uk
website: www.bromsgrove-school.co.uk

The date of the School's Foundation is unknown but it was re-organised by Edward VI in 1553 and was granted a Royal Charter 6 years later. It was refounded in 1693 by Sir Thomas Cookes, Bt, at the same time as Worcester College, Oxford (formerly Gloucester Hall). The link between School and College has been maintained ever since.

Motto: '*Deo Regi Vicino.*'

Patron: A Denham-Cookes

President: V S Anthony, BSc, Hon DEd, Hon FCP, FRSA

A Vice-President: J M Baron, TD, MA
A Vice-President: Prof Sir Michael Drury, OBE, FRCP, FRCGP, FRACGP
A Vice-President: J A Hall, FCA
A Vice-President: N J Birch, MIMechE
A Vice-President: Prof K B Haley, BSc, PhD, FIMA, CMath, FIEE, CEng
A Vice-President: T M Horton, BA
A Vice-President: G R John, CBE

Governing Body:
S Towe, CBE (*Chairman*)
Ms Alison Brimelow, BA, Hon LLD
R D Brookes, FRICS
Mrs R Heggett, LLB
A Hodge, LLM
Miss F Horden
R Lane, MA
Air Commodore S P J Lilley, MA (*RAF*)
R G Noake, FCA, FCCA
Prof J G Perry, BEng, MEng, PhD, FICE, MAPM
T D Pile, BA
Dr A Silk, PhD (*Vice-Chairman*)
G Strong
Dr N Venning, BSc, PhD, MBA
Dr P Walsh-Atkins, MA, DPhil
D Walters, MA, FCA

Company Secretary: J Sommerville, MA

Headmaster: C J Edwards, MA Oxon

Bursar: Mrs L Brookes, ACMA
Deputy Headmaster: P St J Bowen, BA, PGCE
Assistant Head: Miss R M Scannell, BA, PGCE
Second Deputy (*Academic*): P S Ruben, BSc, MPhil, MBA
Second Deputy (*Co-Curricula*): P S T Mullan, BA, PGCE
School Medical Officer: Dr D Law MA, MBChB Oxon, MRCGP, DRCOG, DFFP
Head of Foundation: Mrs J E Rogers, BA, MSc

Staff:
* *Head of Department*
† *Houseparent*

Mrs C P M Maund, BSc, PGCE (*Assistant Pastoral Head*)
D Langlands, BSc, CertEd (*i/c DofE*)
Mrs E A Langlands, BSc, CertEd
A W Burton, MA Cantab, PGCE (*Timetable Coordinator*)
M D Bowen-Jones, BSc, MEd, PGCE (*IB Coordinator*)
Mrs A M Bowen-Jones, CertEd, BPhil (*Ed*) (*i/c Activities*)
S J Kingston, BEd (*Examinations Secretary*)
Mrs P T Kenward, BA, PGCE
J Stateczny, BA, PGCE (**Politics*)
Mrs C E Turner, BA, PGCE
C A Dowling MA Cantab, PGCE (**Chemistry; Academic Database Coordinator*)
†Mrs R Al-Nakeeb, BEd, MA
Dr D A Wilson, BSc, PhD, PGCE
Dr A S Woollhead, BSc, PhD, PGCE (**Biology; Assessment Manager*)
Dr M R Werrett, GRSC, PhD, PGCE (*Senior Mistress*)
†M A Stone, BEng, ACGI, PGCE
Mrs H S Barnett, BSc, PGCE
R E W Stephens, BA, PGCE, MMus, ARCO, ARCM (*OC CCF*)
Mrs J A Holden, MA Oxon, PGCE
J Wingfield, BA, PGCE (**Economics and Business Studies*)
Mrs K Linehan, BA, MA, PGCE (**English*)
Miss S Dick, BSc, PGCE (*Head of Upper Fourth Form; Head of Pupil Monitoring*)
Dr A R Johns, BSc, PhD, PGCE (*Head of Sixth Form – Pupil Progress*)
R A C Barr, BA, MA, PGCE (*Head of Sixth Form; Careers and UCAS*)
Ms S J Cronin, BA, DMS, PGCE
Mrs F K Bateman, BSc, PGCE (*Head of Lower Sixth Form; *Sixth Form Enrichment Curriculum*)
Mrs C Bentham, BEd (*Coordinator, International Students; *EAL*)
J W B Brogden, BA, PGCE (**Media Studies*)
Mrs S E Ascough, BSc, PGCE
Miss K E Tansley, BA, MA, PGCE
†D G Wilkins, BA, SCITT (*Senior Day Houseparent*)
M A C Beet, MA Cantab, PGCE (**Modern Languages; i/c Oxbridge; President of the Common Room*)
†D N Perry, BA, PGCE (*Senior Boarding Houseparent*)
F A Quinn, CertEd, DipPhysEd, SSI
M R Webb, BSc (*ICT Development Manager*)
Miss F E Diver, BA, PGCE (*Head of Lower Fourth Form, *Geography*)
†S D Coates, BSc, PGCE
Miss E M O'Brien, BA, MA, PGCE
†Miss Z L Leech, BA (**PSHE, Careers Adviser*)
D C Howard, MA, BEd, CertEd
M D Ravenscroft, MA
N C J Riley, BSc, PGCE (**Mathematics*)
Mrs E L E Buckingham, BA (**Girls' PE & Games*)
Miss S A Franks, BSc, PGCE
Mrs M M Haycock, BA, PGCE (**Spanish*)
†Mrs T L Helmore, BA, PGCE
R O Knight, MA Oxon, ARCO (*Assistant Director of Music*)
A D Langlands, BSc, PGCE (**Academic PE, Master i/c Hockey*)

O A Matthews, BEng, PGCE (*Design and Technology*)
Dr M Thompson, BSc, PhD, MInstP, PGCE
  (*Science,*Physics*)
R Watkins, BA, PGCE (*French*)
Mrs T James, BA, PGCE (*Drama*)
Revd P Hedworth, BEd, BA (*Chaplain*)
Miss C Ellis-Owen, BA, PGCE (*History*)
Mrs J L Spearing, BA, PGCE (*Critical Thinking*)
Dr M K Ruben, BA, PhD, PGCE (*Gifted and Talented*)
Miss L E McCutcheon, BA
Miss S J McWilliams, BA, PGCE
Miss S Morgans, BA, PGCE, DipND (*Art*)
Mrs I Peric Crnko, BEd
Dr J Ogston, BSc, PhD, PGCE
Mrs M Deighan, BA, Adv Cert SpLD, PGCE (*Learning
  Support*)
J R Kingston, BMus, DipMusCh, PGCE, FRSA, (*Music*)
A C Merrick, BSc, PGCE
Ms J Comley, MSc, BA, PGCE
G N Delahunty, BA, PGCE
Ms E L Densem, BA, PGCE
†H Bell, MA, PGCE
G Bowmer, BA, PGCE
†A McClure, BA, PGCE (*Classics*)
Miss S Nelson, BSc, PGCE
Miss L McKee, BA, PGCE
Miss J Zafar, BA, PGCE
S Broadbent, BA, QTS
Mrs C Wedelich-Niedzwiedz, BMus, PGCE
L Falconer, BA, PGCE (*Head of Academic Transition*)
Ms K Garratt, MA
G George, BSc, PGCE (*Boys' PE & Games*)
M Giles, BSc, PGCE
Ms R Lambert, BSc, PGCE
D Tamplin, BSc, PGCE
D Whiting, BSc, GTP
†J D Jones, MA (*i/c Extended Project Qualification*)
J Hansford, BA, PGCE
Mrs M Parkinson, BA, PGCE
Miss A Williams, BA (*Head of Fifth Form*)
†Mrs T Tweddle, BSc, CertEd FE
Mrs K Hands, BA, PGCE (*Religious Studies*)
Mrs H Barton, BA, PGCE
Miss A Brereton, BSc, PGCE
D Fallows (*Director of Cricket*)
Miss R Fenn, BA, PGCE
Mrs J Golightly, BA
Miss R Keys, BA, PGCE
S Phennah, BEd
Mrs H Race, BSc, PGCE
Ms G Tyrrell, BA, PGCE
D Williams, BA, PGCE
Mrs A Andrews, BEng, PGCE SCIT
A Carrington-Windo (*Director of Rugby*)
S Cleary, BA, PGCE
Miss L Davenport, BSc, PGCE
Miss F J Hardy, BA, PGCE
Miss L I Lancett, BA, PGCE
Miss J Law, BSc, PGCE
S Noble, BSc, PGCE
N Philips, BSc, MResearch, QTS
Mrs Y Sharatt, BA, PGCE

Houses and Houseparents:
Boarding:
Elmshurst (*Boys*): D N Perry
Housman Hall (*Sixth Form*): J Jones
Mary Windsor (*Girls*): Mrs T Tweddle
Oakley (*Girls*): Mrs T L Helmore
Wendron-Gordon (*Boys*): H Bell

Day:
Hazeldene (*Girls*): Miss Z L Leech
Lupton (*Boys*): A L McClure

Lyttelton (*Boys*): S D Coates
School (*Boys*): M A Stone
Thomas Cookes (*Girls*): Mrs R Al-Nakeeb
Walters (*Boys*): D G Wilkins

Music Staff:
J R Kingston, BMus, DipMusCh, FRSA, PGCE (*Director
  of Music*)
Mrs C R Bayliss, MA, PGCE, LLCM
R O Knight, MA Oxon, ARCO (*Assistant Director of
  Music*)
Mrs E Edmonds, BA Cantab, PGCE (*Music, Preparatory
  School*)
Mrs M AMartin, BA

Visiting Music Staff:
Mrs J Ayres, ABSM (*Oboe*)
P Badley (*Voice*)
Miss S Balls, GBSM (*Percussion*)
N Barry, GGSM, LTCL (*Piano*)
Miss H Bool, GBSM, ABSM, BTechNat (*Percussion*)
M Broadhead, LTCL, DipTCL, (*Cello*)
R Bull (*Guitar*)
T Bunting, BA (*Bass & Bass Guitar*)
W Coleman, BA, LTCL (*Singing*)
Miss A M Dodd, BA, ABSM (*Violin*)
J Dunlop, BA, GBSM, ABSM (*Flute*)
A Gittens, BTec, HND (*Electric Guitar*)
Mrs J A Hattersley, CT ABRSM, LRSM (*Brass*)
C Hickman (*Trombone*)
Mrs J Hiles, GBSM, ABSM (*Flute*)
Ms A Kazimierczuk GBSM, ABSM, (*Singing*)
T Martin, BA, DipABRSM (*Saxophone*)
T Porter, BA (*Clarinet*)
M Roberts, BA Music (*Trumpet*)
D Scally, MA, BMus, LTCL, DipCSM (*Piano*)
Ms F Swadling, BA, ABSM, GBSM, (*Viola, Violin, Piano*)
A D C Thayer, BMus, PGDip, MA (*Piano*)
D J G Whitehouse, ABSM (*Bassoon*)

Preparatory School

Headmaster: J R Evans, BEd Hons, AdvDipEdMan

Deputy Head: Mrs M Purdy, BSc, PGCE
Assistant Head (*Pastoral*): S J P Loone, MEd, BA, BTheol,
  PGCE, NPQH (*Religious Education*)
Head of Junior Department: Mrs C M Leather, BSc, PGCE
  (*Staff Appraisal and Development*)
Director of Studies: Mrs K Ison, BEd (*Timetable
  Coordinator*)

Miss K Baker, BA, PGCE (*French, *Gifted and Talented*)
Miss N C Barton, CertEd, CertSpLD
Mrs P Barton, CertEd
Mrs C R Bayliss, MA, PGCE, LLCM
Mrs S M Bourne, BSc, PGCE (*Science*)
Mrs G Butler, BEd (*Head of Year 3*)
Miss S Cadwallader, BA, PGCE (*Head of Year 6*)
W R Caldwell, BA, MA, MEd, PGCE (*Senior Master,
  Latin & Library)
Mrs M L Caldwell, CertEd (*SENCO, *Learning Support &
  PSCHE*)
Miss S Cartwright, BSc, PGCE
G Clark, BEd (*Head of Year 7*)
N Cook, BSc, PGCE
Mrs J Danks, BMus, PGCE (*Girls' PE*)
Mrs K Edmonds, BA, PGCE (*Music*)
A Evans, BSc, BEd (*ICT*)
Mrs C Evans, BEd
M Faulkner, BA, PGCE
Ms N Gillett, BSc, PGCE
C F Harris, DipPE, CertEd
Mrs R Ivison, BA, PGCE (*Head of Year 4*)
G Jones, BA, PGCE (*Boys' PE*)
Mrs R Laurenson, BA, PGCE

Ms E Lightfoot BA, PGCE (*English*)
Mrs F Mack, MA, PGCE
J Marks, MA, BEd (*Drama*)
Miss R McRandal, BA, PGCE (*Spanish*)
†Mrs E Mullan, BEd (*Head of Year 8, *Girls' Boarding*)
†Mrs H Newton, CertEd
†R J Newton, BEd (*Boys' Boarding, i/c Activities*)
D Pover, BA, PGCE
Mrs A Purver, BA, PGCE (*History*)
Ms A Read, BTec, BA, PGCE (*Head of Year 5*)
Miss C Robinson, BA, PGCE
P Sutherland, HD Ed (*Design & Technology*)
Ms A Welke, BSc, PGCE (*German*)
†Mrs R Whiting, BA, PGCE
R Widdop, BA, DipSpPsy (*Geography*)
Miss V Ziar, MA, BA, PGCE, BIAD (*Art*)

Boarding Houses and Houseparents:
Cobham (Boys): Mr R & Mrs H Newton
Honeysuckle (Girls): Mrs E Mullan
Page (Junior boys and girls): Mrs R Whiting

Location. This co-educational boarding and day school is situated some 13 miles north of the Cathedral City of Worcester and an equal distance south of Birmingham. Birmingham International Airport and Station are a 20-minute drive by motorway. The M5, M6, M42 and M40 motorways provide easy access to the School.

The School stands in 100 acres of grounds on the south side and within walking distance of the market town of Bromsgrove.

Facilities. The school's £25 million building and development programme since 1994 has included all-weather, floodlit sports facilities, a state of the art Library and Resources Centre, extensions to the Maths and Modern Languages facilities, an award winning Art, Design and Technology Building and a new Humanities building. Boarding facilities have been enhanced by a 20-room Girls Sixth Form extension with single en-suite rooms and the opening of Housman Hall, the school's first mixed Sixth Form House. Eighteen new and refurbished Science laboratories were completed in 2010. Work has started on a major new sports complex including an eight badminton court sized sports hall, dance studios, gym, teaching rooms and hospitality suite / sports viewing room.

Boarding. Nearly half of Bromsgrove Senior School's pupil body is made up of boarders accommodated between six houses, one of which is in the town. Loyalty to House and the traditions attendant upon it are significant factors of life at Bromsgrove. The boarding environment is happy, stable, disciplined and nurturing. House competition, day and boarding, from sport to drama, music to debating is keen.

The stability and continuity that enable boarders to thrive are provided by resident houseparents (all academic members of staff) and their families, assistant houseparents, house mothers and a team of house-based tutors. All meals are taken centrally in the School except in the case of the evening meal at Housman Hall, the Sixth Form-only House sited in the town.

A huge upgrading of boarding facilities is currently under way with one House now totally en suite and others set to follow. A new girls' boarding house is currently being built and the second girls' boarding house is being totally refurbished.

Numbers. There are 890 pupils in the Senior School, of whom 490 are boys. The adjacent Preparatory School has a further 470 pupils aged 7 to 13. (*See also Preparatory School entry in IAPS section*.)

Curriculum. In the Preparatory School and throughout the first year in the Senior School a broadly based curriculum is followed. In addition to the usual academic subjects time is given to Art, Music, ICT, Drama, Design Technology and to a full programme of Physical Education. Languages on offer include French, German, Spanish and Latin.

As pupils move up the School other options become available and some narrowing of the curriculum is inevitable. 11 subjects is the norm at GCSE, with a broad core including the three separate sciences and a further three optional subjects chosen, including if a pupil wishes the AS Level Extended Project. The minimum qualification for entry for a full programme of study in the Sixth Form is eight B grades at GCSE. Pupils may study the IB Diploma or take the A Level route and a BTEC course in Sports Performance and Excellence is also on offer. Flexibility in timetabling aims to ensure that all pupils' subject choices are catered for whatever the combination. Many subjects are available including, Art, Biology, Business, Chemistry, Classics, Design, Drama, Economics, English, French, Geography, German, Graphics, ICT, Latin, Mathematics and Further Mathematics, Music, Physical Education, Physics, Politics, Religious Studies, Spanish and Textiles. Under the IB umbrella, Italian, Environmental Systems, Mandarin and Psychology are also on offer. About 90% stay on after Year 11 for the Sixth Form and virtually all of these pupils proceed to degree courses at university.

Music. Music flourishes as important and integral parts of the School's activities both within and outside the formal curriculum under the leadership of Jonathan Kingston. House Music Competitions fill four afternoons, Pop & Jazz Festival two evenings and Music Scholars hold concerts twice a year. There is plenty of scope for involvement in the School Orchestra and String, Wind and Brass Ensembles, Chamber Groups, Jazz & Swing Bands, a 50-strong Chapel Choir and large Choral Society. The Music School has three floors of practice, rehearsal and concert space along with a large soundproofed recording studio for drummers and rock musicians.

The timetable is sufficiently flexible to allow special arrangements to be made for outstanding musicians. The Chapel Choir are used for broadcasts and toured major venues in New York summer 2010. Visits to Lincoln Cathedral to sing Evensong and a Senior production of *The Threepenny Opera* were two main features of 2010-11. School musicians took part in the final gala concert of Bromsgrove Festival's 50th year at Worcester Cathedral, where they performed with the English Symphony Orchestra. The 120-strong Choral Society performed Haydn's Creation in the splendour of Birmingham Town Hall. The performing arts are well supported at Bromsgrove School and rightly thrive.

Careers. The school employs a fully qualified, full-time careers advisor and a comprehensive careers counselling programme is pursued for pupils of all ages.

Reports and Consultation. Pupils receive grades and tutor comments twice a term and there are regular reports and parents' evenings. Supervision is shared by Houseparents and House Tutors, whom parents may meet informally by appointment. There are regular parent-teacher evenings. Parents may arrange appointments to meet members of the Careers Department.

Extra-Curricular Activities. A wide range of sports and activities is offered, giving opportunities to participate at a competitive level in Rugby, Hockey, Netball, Athletics, Badminton, Basketball, Clay Pigeon shooting, Cricket, Cross-Country, Debating, Fencing, Golf, Rounders, Soccer, Squash, Swimming, Tennis and Young Enterprise.

The Saturday timetable, in conjunction with the weekday programme, allows the activities programme more flexibility to offer both recreational and academic choices. Pupils may select from a diverse range of recreational activities including Academic extension and support, Electronics AS Level, Revision for GCSE, AS and A2, Oxbridge, Biology, Chemistry and Physics Olympiad, Aerobics, Animation Creation, Art, Badminton, Chess, Corps of Drums, Design Technology, Drama, EPP (Economics, Politics and Philosophy) Engineering, Golf driving range, Handicrafts, Media Club, ICT, Military skills, Music, Outdoor pursuits (including climbing, high ropes, kayaking, orienteering, raft building, sailing), Mahjong, Photography, Plaster Modelling, School Magazine, Steel Pans, Table tennis, Website design and Weight training. There are opportunities to gain qualifications in Horse riding, Modern dance, Life saving, First Aid, RADA, LAMDA, Sport/Dance Leader Awards and Martial Arts. In addition to the activities programme, Year 9 pupils participate in Bromsgrove Badge, comprising a selection of activities that help to prepare them for the Bronze Duke of Edinburgh's Award and culminating in a four-day camp at the end of the year. There is a thriving Combined Cadet Force (Army and RAF), whilst approximately 100 pupils are currently involved in the Duke of Edinburgh's Award Scheme. The School's Community Action programme caters for large numbers of pupils and provides a wide range of activities; examples include working in local schools and charity shops, visiting residential homes, acting as Learning Mentors and Student Listeners, running a Fair Trade café, helping in animal sanctuaries and supporting conservation projects.

Admission. Entrance at 13 is by Common Entrance and/or Bromsgrove School Entrance Examinations. Boys and Girls may be admitted to the Preparatory School at any age from 7 to 12 inclusive. Entrance Tests take place in late January. Places are also available in the Sixth Form to boys and girls who have had their GCSE education elsewhere.

Although pupils are normally accepted into the School only at the start of the Michaelmas Term of the year in which they have reached their eleventh, thirteenth or sixteenth birthdays, the Headmaster considers sympathetically applications for admission at other ages and at other times of the academic year.

Entrance Scholarships. (*See Scholarship Entries section.*) Awards are made on the results of open examinations held at the school in January: a significant number of scholarships and bursaries for pupils of academic, artistic, musical, sporting and all-round ability are awarded at 11+, 13+ and 16+. All Scholarships may be augmented by means-tested bursaries.

Fees per term (2011-2012). Senior School (age 13+): £8,395 full boarding, £9,385 international boarders, £5,980 weekly boarding, £4,285 day. Preparatory School (age 7–13): £6,085–£7,500 full boarding, £4,225–£5,370 weekly boarding, £3,050–£3,985 day.

Charitable status. Bromsgrove School is a Registered Charity, number 1098740. It exists to provide education for boys and girls.

Bryanston School

Blandford, Dorset DT11 0PX
Tel: 01258 452411
Fax: 01258 484661
e-mail: head@bryanston.co.uk
website: www.bryanston.co.uk

Founded in 1928, Bryanston School aims above all to develop the all-round talents of individual pupils. A broad, flexible academic and extra-curricular programme together with an extensive network of adult support encourages pupils to maximise their particular abilities as well as to adapt positively to the demands of the society of which they are part. Creativity, individuality and opportunity are the school's key notes, but a loving community is the school's most important quality. Happy children growing up in a secure environment, aware of beliefs and values and confident of their own worth, will be well balanced 18 year olds. That is what we seek to produce.

Motto: '*Et Nova et Vetera*'.

Governors:
Chairman: R H Cox, BA

S F Bowes
Ms S A Buxton, MA, ACA
The Rt Revd S D Conway, MA, BA
M Davies, MA, BA
Mrs S Foulser, BA
G E T Granter, MA
J R Greenhill, MA
Mrs B Hollond, MA, FRSA
B M Irvani, MA, FCA
M A S Laurence
Mrs V M McDonaugh, MA
R A Pegna, MA
Dr H M Pharaoh, MBBS, DRCOG, MRCGP
A R Poulton, BA
Dr M L Reynolds, BA, PHD
Miss R Rogers, BMUS
Professor J F Smyth, MD, FRCP, FRCPE, FRCSE, FRCR, FRSE
D M Trick
P G E Walker, FRICS

Bursar and Clerk to the Governors: N P McRobb, OBE, MBA, BA

Head: Ms S J Thomas, BA

* *Head of Department*

Second Master: P J Hardy, JP, MA, PGCE (*Economics and Business*)
Director of Studies: P Simpson, MA (*History*)
Senior Mistress: Mrs E M Barkham, BA, MSc, PGCE (*Biology*)
Director of Academic Administration: N S Boulton, MA, PGCE (*Politics)

Staff:
* *Head of Department*
† *Housemaster/Housemistress*

C S Poole, BSc, CertEd, AFIMA (*Mathematics*)
B G Stebbings, BA, CertEd (*Senior Teacher; Geography; Geology*)
G Q Craddock, BSc, CertEd (*Mathematics*)
Mrs T J Doble, BSc, PGCE (*Mathematics*)
P A L Rioch, BMus, BA
†S R L Long, CertEd (**PE; Sports Studies*)
D C Bourne, MA, PGCE, FRGS (*Geography; Senior Tutor*)
D Boyle, BA, CertEd (*German)
Mrs S Stacpoole, BA (*History of Art)
G S Elliot, BA, PGCE (*Chemistry*)
M N Pyrgos, BSc, PGCE (*Economics and Business*)
Mrs F K Pyrgos, BSc, PGCE (*Careers)
†I R Haslam, CertEd (*Design and Technology*)
J N G Fisher, BEd, PGCE (*English*)
J L Jones, MA, PGCE (*Modern Languages*)
Mrs E M Long, CertEd (*PSE*)
†D Fowler-Watt, MA (*Classics*)
Mrs J Ladd-Gibbon, MA (*Design*)
Mrs M F Barlow, BA (*Economics and Business*)
Mrs R A Simpson, BA (*English*)
A J Marriott, BA, PGCE (*History*)
Mrs J S Le Hardy, BA, PGCE (*Spanish)
S J Richardson, BEd, MA, FRMetS, NPQH (*Geography; Academic Registrar*)
M T Kearney, MA, PhD (**Science; Physics*)
Mrs J A Price, BA, PGCE (*Music*)
Mrs J G S Strange, BA, PGCE (*History*)
M J Owens, MA, PGCE (*Art)
Mrs S M Haslam, CertEd (*Art*)
S J Turrill, BSc, PGCE (*Chemistry)
N J Davies, BEd (*Design Technology*)
L C Johnson, BA, LTP (*French)
Miss J F Quan, MA (*Director of Drama*)
Mrs D M Wellesley, MA (*Modern Languages*)

C T Holland, BA (*Classics*)
†Dr P S Bachra, MA (*Economics and Business*)
S H Jones, BSc, PGCE (*Biology*)
Mrs A J Gilbert, BA, PGCE (*Modern Languages*)
†Mrs L C Kearney, BEd (*Geography*)
†Mrs H E Dean, BA, PGCE (*Art*)
Ms L Boothman, BA, PGCE (*English*)
†Mrs C L Miller, BEd (*Sports Studies*)
R J Collcott, MEng, MSc (*Mathematics and Physics*)
A J Barnes, BA, CertEd (*Director of Technology*)
†Dr H L Fearnley, BA, PhD (*Classics*)
D J Melbourne, BSc, PGCE (*Mathematics*)
†S M Vincent, BA, PGCE (*History*)
G M Scott, BA, ARCO, LTCL, PGCE (*Assistant Director of Music, Keyboard*)
Miss C L Bentinck, BA (*English*)
A Day, BSc, PGCE (*Information Technology*)
L C E Blanco Gomez, BA (*Spanish*)
N M Kelly, BA, PGCE (*English*)
†W J Lockett, BA, PGCE (*Classics*)
†J J A Beales, BA, PGCE (*Economics*)
Mrs C S Scott, BMus, PGCE, FTCL, ARCM, LTCL (*Strings*)
J E J Sidders, MA, PGCE (*Physics*)
N Welford, BSc, PGCE (*Biology*)
Miss K J Witchell, BA, PGCE (*Drama, English*)
Miss N Morley, BSC, PGCE (*Physics*)
Miss C A Çava, MPhys (*Physics*)
Mrs C Gordon, BA, PGCE, AKC (*Spanish*)
D M Emerson, BMus, PGCE (*Director of Music*)
T W Sellers, BA, PGCE, AKC (*History*)
A K Tarafder, BSc (*Mathematics*)
†Mrs C L Bray, BSc, PGCE (*Sport Studies*)
B J Lawes, BSc (*PE, *Cricket*)
N C Davies, BSc PGCE (*Chemistry*)
Mrs S L Worrall, BEd (*Mathematics*)
Mrs L M Jones, MA (*Classics*)
Miss R Eales, BSc, PGCE (*IT, Economics*)
Revd A M J Haviland, BEd, DipCMM (*Chaplain*)
M S Deketelaere, BA, MSc, DIC (*Geography*)
Miss A J Granville, BSc (*Chemistry*)
Miss C R Evans, BA (*Fine Art*)
C J Mills, BA, PGCE, (*Design and Technology*)
M Bolton, BA, GTP (*Design and Technology*)
W P Ings, MA, ARCO, PGCE (*Assistant Director of Music, Academic*)
Mrs J M I Velasco, BA, PGCE (*French*)
T R Booth, MChem, PGCE (*Chemistry*)
R D Heal, BSc, PhD (*Biology*)
M S Christie, MA, PGCE (*Economics and Business*)
J Dickson, BA, PGCE (*Art*)
A C Hartley, MMath, PGCE (*Mathematics*)
R J Johnson, BSc, PGCE (*Chemistry*)
J M C Lyne, MA (*History of Art*)
I W McClary, MA, PGCE (*Head of Sixth Form*)
Dr S W S Openshaw, PhD, BSc, PGCE (*Biology*)
Miss J M Pike, BA, PGCE (*Modern Languages*)
L J Pollard, MA (*Religious Studies*)
A J Sanghrajka, BA, BPP (*Classics*)

Admissions Registrar: Mrs S J Birkill
Head's PA: Mrs F J Howard

Situation. Occupying a magnificent Norman Shaw mansion, the School is located in beautiful Dorset countryside near the market town of Blandford. There are 400 acres of grounds, which include a stretch of river used for rowing and canoeing, playing fields, woodland and parkland.

Numbers. There are approximately 385 boys and 290 girls in the School.

Admission. Boys and girls are normally admitted between 13 and 14 years of age on the results of Common Entrance or the School's own entrance exam. Sixth Form entrants are admitted after interview, conditional upon securing at least 40 points at GCSE.

Scholarships. (*See Scholarship Entries section.*)

Organisation. The School is organised on a House basis with 5 senior boys' houses, 5 girls' houses, and 2 junior boys' houses. All pupils have a personal tutor throughout their time in the School, with whom they meet on a one-to-one basis at least once a week. No tutor has more than 15 pupils. Feeding and medical care are organised centrally. All Sixth Form pupils in their final year have individual study-bedrooms. Lower Sixth Formers usually share study-bedrooms.

Religion. Religious instruction is widely based and is carried on throughout the School. There are two assemblies each week for the whole school. Pupils attend either assemblies or services on most Sundays during the term. Holy Communion is celebrated every Sunday and on some week days. A Chaplain is responsible for pastoral work and preparation for Confirmation.

School Work. The School aims at leading pupils, over a period of 5 years, from the comparative dependence on class teaching in which they join the school, to a state in which they are capable of working on their own, for a University degree or professional qualification, or in business. In addition to traditional class teaching, there is, therefore, increasing time given to private work as a pupil moves up the School. This is in the form of assignments to be completed within a week or a fortnight. Teachers are available to give individual help when required, and Tutors supervise pupils' work and activities in general.

Every pupil is encouraged to explore a range of opportunities. All pupils follow the same broad curriculum in Group D (the first year), if at all possible. This curriculum includes Latin, modern languages, three separate sciences, creative arts, technology and music. GCSE is taken after 3 years when a pupil is in Group B. There is a highly flexible choice of subjects at this level and subjects are setted independently. In the Sixth Form (Group A) pupils are expected to study up to five subjects at AS Level in the first year and to continue with three or four subjects to Advanced (A2) Level in the second year. 24 subjects are offered at AS Level and 22 at A2 Level and there are few restrictions on combinations. All Lower Sixth Formers follow a compulsory Personal and Social Education course and the Humanities programme provides supplementary courses to develop key skills and thinking techniques.

Music. Music plays a very important part in the life of the School. There are 2 Orchestras, a Concert Band, a Dance Band, a String Chamber Orchestra, five Choirs, a Choral Society and many informal ensembles: numerous professional and amateur concerts take place throughout the year. Lessons are given in all orchestral instruments and in piano, organ, guitar and singing. Class music is a compulsory part of the curriculum for all First Year pupils, who also receive introductory free tuition on an orchestral instrument. Well over half the pupils have regular instrumental lessons.

Drama. A well-equipped, modern theatre provides the venue for the many school productions which take place during the year and for touring professional companies. In addition to acting, pupils are involved in Stage Management, Stage Lighting and Sound, and front-of-house work. There is also a large Greek Theatre in the grounds.

Sport and Leisure. A wide variety of sports is on offer at the school, including Athletics, Archery, Badminton, Canoeing, Climbing, Cricket, Cross-Country, Fencing, Fives, Hockey, Lacrosse, Netball, Riding, Rowing, Rugby, Sailing, Shooting, Squash, Swimming and Tennis. Extensive playing fields between the School and the River Stour provide 46 tennis courts, 2 astroturf pitches, 9 netball courts, an athletics track and grass pitches for all major sports, an all-weather riding manège and cross-country course. A Sports Complex provides an indoor heated 25m Swimming Pool, Gymnasium, large Sports Hall, Squash courts and Fitness

Centre. Sailing takes place at Poole Harbour where the School has 6 dinghies at its own base. In addition to sport, a number of clubs and societies, catering for a wide range of interests, meet in the evenings and at weekends.

Additional Activities. To encourage a sense of responsibility towards the community, a growing self-reliance and a practical training in the positive use of leisure, all pupils take part in all or some of the following:

1. Community and Social Service.
2. Extra-curricular activities chosen from a wide range of options.
3. The Duke of Edinburgh's Award Scheme.
4. Adventure Training.

Dress. There is no school uniform but there is a dress code.

Careers. There is a well-resourced Careers Room and the school maintains close links with ISCO. A full time member of staff runs a careers programme which covers the pupils' five years in the school. All pupils undertake Work Experience after their GCSEs and specific advice is given to help with A Level and University degree choices. In the Sixth Form, a mock interview course and the teaching of presentation skills ensure that pupils are well-prepared for the future.

Further Education. The vast majority of pupils in the Sixth Form gain admission to Universities or other academies of further education.

Fees per term (2011-2012). Boarders £9,990, Day Pupils £8,192.

Charitable status. Bryanston School Incorporated is a Registered Charity, number 306210. It is a charitable trust for the purpose of educating children.

Bury Grammar School Boys

Tenterden Street, Bury, Lancs BL9 0HN
Tel: 0161 797 2700
Fax: 0161 763 4655
e-mail: info@bgsboys.co.uk
website: www.bgsboys.co.uk

The School, formerly housed in the precincts of the Parish Church of St Mary the Virgin, was first endowed by Henry Bury in 1634, but there is evidence that it existed before that date. It was re-endowed in 1726 by the Revd Roger Kay and moved to its current site in 1966. The school is a selective grammar school which aims to provide a first-class academic and extra-curricular education; to nurture the whole person in a safe, stimulating, challenging and friendly community in which each individual is encouraged to fulfil his potential; and to prepare each boy for an adulthood of fulfilling work, creative leisure and responsible citizenship.

Motto: '*Sanctas clavis fores aperit.*'

Governing Body:
Chairman: Mrs S T Henry
Deputy Chairman: L A Goldberg

B Allan	A C Murray
Dr G Brown	Mrs B Peachment
S N Brown	Mrs J D Pickering
M Entwistle	Dr J G S Rajasansir
The Revd Dr J C Findon	J A Rigby
Mrs D L Hampson	J H Spencer
A Marshall	Mrs S N Yule

Bursar and Clerk to the Governors: D A Harrison, BSc, FCA

Headmaster: **The Revd S C Harvey**, MA

Second Master & Deputy Head (Academic): R N Marshall, MSc (*Chemistry, Head of Science*)

Deputy Head (Administration & Pastoral): D P Cassidy, BSc (*Chemistry*)

Assistant Staff:
M Ahmad, BSc (*Physics*)
B Alldred, BSc (*Mathematics*)
D S Benger, MA (*Music*)
D A Bishop, BSc (*Head of Geology*)
M R Boyd, BA (*Head of French*)
Mrs R L Bradley, BA (*Classics*)
Mrs H M Brandon, MA (*Head of English*)
Mrs C A Brooks, BSc (*Geography*)
Mrs H Campion, BA (*Economics & Business Studies*)
Mrs S G Cawtherley, BA (*Religious Studies*)
A P Christian, BA (*History & Politics*)
M J Cooke, BEd (*CDT & Electronics*)
K M Cryer, BA (*French*)
P F Curry, BSc (*Physics*)
C A R Davidson, BSc (*Head of Physics*)
A E Dennis, BSc (*Mathematics*)
J Eastham, BA (*History*)
W Elf, BSc, MA (*Mathematics*)
G D Feely, MA (*Head of Classics*)
D A Ferguson, BA (*Computing*)
G A Ferguson, BSc (*Head of Biology, Head of Sixth Form*)
Mrs C Forsyth, MA (*Classics*)
Mrs A C Gill, BSc (*Biology*)
Miss K J Gittins, BA (*Art*)
Miss K A Gore, BA (*Head of Art*)
D Hailwood, BEd (*Head of CDT & Electronics*)
G Hall, BSc (*PE & Sport*)
M J Hone, MA (*Head of History & Politics*)
Mrs S J Howard, BA (*French & German*)
C N J Hyde, GRNCM (*Director of Music*)
D R Lee, BA (*Head of German*)
G R Lovgreen, BA (*Director of Sport*)
P Meakin, BSc (*Head of Computing*)
Miss C Meredith, BA (*English*)
D Morse, BSc (*Chemistry*)
D T Newbury, BSc (*Geography*)
T J Nicholson, BA (*Head of Mathematics*)
P O'Sullivan, BA (*Mathematics*)
N Parkinson, BA (*Head of Economics & Business Studies*)
L A Purdy, BSc (*PE & Sport*)
Mrs H C Shan, MChem (*Chemistry*)
M J Sherlock, BSc (*Mathematics*)
Miss J M Solomon, BSc (*Head of Chemistry*)
A L Stacey, BEd (*Head of Religious Studies*)
Miss E A Stansfield, BA (*English*)
Mrs T J Taylor, MA (*Head of Geography*)
A D Watts, BSc (*Biology*)
Miss N M Whittaker, BA (*English*)

Junior School:
D J Crouch, CertEd (*Head of Junior School*)
Miss F K Ackroyd, BA (*Deputy Head*)
Mrs T H Coward
Mrs J M Harrison, BEd
Mrs F M L Hartwell, BSc
Mrs C A Howard, BSc
N G Robson, BA
B J Shakespeare, BA
S H Sheikh, BA
Miss C L Wheeler, BA
S Williams, BSc

Headmaster's PA: Mrs A Cloke

Numbers of Boys. 632, aged 7 to 18.

Admission, Scholarships and Bursaries. Admission is by examination and interview. Most boys join the school at either 7 or 11, although, subject to places being available, admission is possible at other ages. A number of means-tested bursaries, based on academic performance and financial need, are awarded each year.

Fees per term (2011-2012). Senior School £2,912; Junior School £2,164.

Facilities and Development. This ancient grammar school, proud of its historic links with the town of Bury and the surrounding area, possesses a full range of modern facilities. These facilities enable the school to offer a broad and rich academic curriculum and extra-curricular programme. Since 1993 the Junior School has occupied its own site opposite the Senior School. Junior School pupils are able to take advantage of the additional specialist facilities and resources in the Senior School. A new Learning Resource Centre, consisting of a Library, extensive ICT provision and private study facilities, was opened in 2002, and a new Art Centre in 2004. A major redevelopment of the Science facilities began in Autumn 2008.

An Appeal was launched early in 2006 to raise funds for the new co-ed Kindergarten which has been built on the Girls' School site, opposite the Boys' School; for a new Sixth Form Centre, to provide study and recreational facilities for both boys and girls; and for bursaries to extend the school's ability to welcome able boys whose parents cannot afford the fees.

Pastoral Care. Each boy has a Form Tutor who has primary responsibility for his pastoral care and for oversight of his academic progress and his extra-curricular programme. Form Tutors are led by Heads of Year who also oversee a boy's academic progress. There is also a strong House system for a wide range of sporting, musical and cultural interhouse competitions.

Curriculum. The Junior School offers a balanced and enriched curriculum in a friendly, disciplined and caring environment in which the boys' all-round development is of paramount importance.

In the Senior School, First Form boys study English, Mathematics, French, Biology, Chemistry, Physics, Geography, History, Religious Studies, Music, Information Technology, Art and CDT. All Second Form boys are taught German and either Latin or Classical Civilisation. At GCSE, all boys study English, Mathematics, Biology, Chemistry and Physics (all boys take separate sciences) and at least one Modern Foreign Language, and choose from a wide range of option subjects. Most boys offer ten subjects at GCSE.

In the Sixth Form, students study four subjects to AS Level and have the option of reducing to three subjects at A2 Level. A Level subjects are chosen from: Biology, Chemistry, Physics, Systems and Control Technology, Mathematics, Further Maths, History, Politics, Economics, Business Studies, Geography, Geology, English Literature, English Language, French, German, Latin, Greek, Classical Civilisation, Psychology, Religious Studies, Music, PE, Art and Computing. All Sixth Form students take AS General Studies, with the option of A2 General Studies in the Seventh Form.

Art. The Art facility in the Senior School consists of two main studios and a separate sixth form studio. There is also a designated sculpture and pottery studio. In the first three years, all boys study Art and Pottery. Art is a popular choice at GCSE, AS and A2.

Music. Music is an important part of school life. As an academic subject it is offered at GCSE, AS and A2. At least three major musical events take place each year. Visiting peripatetic teachers teach over 180 pupils and also assist in running the wide range of extra-curricular music, including choir, orchestra, concert band, dance orchestra and several chamber groups.

Physical Education and Games. Boys participate in Games throughout the school and in Physical Education until the end of the Fourth Form. In addition, boys in the Junior School and in the First Form of the Senior School are taught swimming in the school's own pool. Indoor facilities include a sports hall, and outdoors there are extensive playing fields, a floodlit all-weather area and tennis courts. The major sports in the autumn and spring terms are Football and Rugby. In the summer term the major sport is Cricket. Other sports which are played at inter-school level are Athletics, Basketball, Cross-Country, Golf, Hockey, Swimming and Tennis.

Outdoor Education. In the Senior School, the Outdoor Activities programme includes a residential course for all First Form boys at the National Water Sports Centre at Plas Menai in Wales. A residential course at an outward-bound centre in the Lake District is offered to boys at the end of the Third Form. Boys in the Fifth, Sixth and Seventh Forms can choose Outdoor Activities as part of their Games programme. This includes a variety of activities and trips, including climbing, kayaking, dry-slope skiing and cycling.

CCF. Boys may join the CCF in the Third Form, and the school contingent is a strong one. The CCF helps the boys develop qualities such as self-discipline, resourcefulness and perseverance, a sense of responsibility and skills of man-management and leadership.

Careers. The Careers Department aims to provide all boys with access to the information and advice they need to make informed and sensible decisions about their futures. In addition to a very good Careers Library, guidance is provided by individual interviews. There are regular Careers Conventions. All boys are encouraged to complete a period of work experience after their AS examinations in the Sixth Form.

Religion. The school has a Christian foundation but is proud of its tradition of being an open and inclusive community which welcomes boys and staff from different religious faiths as well as those who belong to no faith community.

Bury Grammar School Old Boys' Association. Secretary: Martin Entwistle, 8 Greenmount Drive, Greenmount, Bury, BL8 4HA. Tel: 01204 882502.

Charitable status. Bury Grammar Schools Charity is a Registered Charity, number 526622. The aim of the charity is to promote educational opportunities for boys and girls living in or near Bury.

Campbell College

Belmont Road, Belfast, Co Antrim BT4 2ND, Northern Ireland
Tel: 028 9076 3076
Fax: 028 9076 1894
e-mail: hmoffice@campbellcollege.co.uk
website: www.campbellcollege.co.uk

Campbell College, which was opened in 1894, was founded and endowed in accordance with the will of Henry James Campbell, Esq (Linen Merchant) of Craigavad, Co Down.
Motto: '*Ne Obliviscaris*'.

Governors:
M E J Graham, BSc, MSc, FCIOB (*Chairman*)
G F Hamilton, BA, FIFP (*Vice-Chairman*)
A J Boyd, BSc Econ, FCA
Mrs F Chamberlain, MA
J Fetherston (*Parent Governor*)
Mrs G Hool, BA
T M Horner, QC
D M McKee, BA, PGCE, DipModLit (*Staff Governor*)
M A D Moreland, LLB, FCA
M C Nesbitt, MA Cantab, DBA
M D M Rea, OBE, BSc, DipEd
J I Taggart, ARICS
W B W Turtle, LLB
J F Young, MA

Headmaster: **J A Piggot**, MA

Vice-Principals:
D Johnston, BA, PGCE
A R Cluff, BSc, PGCE

W Keown, MA, PGCE

Senior Teachers:
W J McKee, BSc, DipEd
H J McKinney, BSc, CertEd
C G Oswald, BSc, PGCE, AdvCertEd, MEd

Assistant Teachers:
S D Quigg, BSc
D Catherwood, BMus, PGCE
C G A Farr, BA, DASE, AdvCertEd, MEd, CertPD
R J S Taylor, BSc, PGCE
D W D McDowell, BSc, PGCE
D M McKee, BA, PGCE, DipModLit
Ms B M Coughlin, BEd, PGCertComp
Mrs S Boyce, BA, PGCE (*Learning Support*)
Mrs K E Sheppard, MSc, BSc, PGCE
Mrs G E Wilson, BMus, MTD
D Styles, BA, PGCE, Dip IndStudies
Mrs K P Crooks, BA, ATD
B F Robinson, BA, PGCE, MSc
A W Templeton, BSc, PGCE
Mrs S L Coetzee, BMus, PCGE, PGCE Careers
N R Ashfield, BSc, PGCE
S P Collier, BA, PGCE
G Fry, BA, PGCE
D Walker, BEd
Mrs K-A Roberts, BA, PGCE
C McIvor, MA, PGCE
Mrs C Caldwell, BA, MA, PGCE, PG Dip FrLit
B Meban, BSc, PGCE
J McCurdy, BD, MA, PGCE
M P Cousins, BSc, PGCE
Mrs L Haughian, BA, PGCE
Miss D H Shields, MA, MSc, PGCE
M G Chalkley, BA, PGCE, MEd, PQH
N McGarry, BA, PGCE
Mrs M Debbadi, BA, PGCE, MSc
Dr J A Breen, BSc, PGCE, PhD
R D Hall, BSc, PGCE
Mrs E McIlvenny, BA, PGCE
A J Millen, MSci, PGCE
Mrs K Magreehan, BA, PGCE
Miss L F Sparkes, BEd
Mrs C E Woods, MA, BA, PGCE, PGH
Mrs F A Mottashaw, BA, PGCE
H H Robinson, BSc, PGCE
Mrs L Brown, BA, QTS
Miss J Mount, BA, PGCE
Mrs C A M Irwin, BSc, PGCE
P D A Campbell, BEd
T R Thompson, BSc, PGCE
A McCrea, BEng, PGCE
Mrs W Pearson, BEd
J H Rea, BSc, PGCE
Mrs K Murphy, BSc, PGCE
Ms V Reading, BA, PGCE
F N Mukula, BSc, AssDipTh PGCE
Miss J-A Taylor, BA, PGCE
Ms G Lamont, BEd, MSSc
G P Young, BEd
Mrs C M Crozier, BSc, PGCE, MSc
Miss E J Armstrong, BSc, PGCE
J P Cupitt, BSc, PGCE
Mrs W Shannon, BA, PGCE
Mrs R M McNaught, MA, PGCE
Mrs E L P Hogg, MA, PGCE
Mrs J L Hempstead, MA, PGCE
Mrs K McGarvey, MSci, PGCE
Mrs E Kennedy, BA, PG Dip ESL
Ms S Kirsh, BA, PGCE

Visiting Music Teachers:
Mrs M Fenn (*Woodwind*)
Mrs J Leslie (*Brass*)

M Wilson (*Brass*)
Mrs H Neale (*Upper strings and Piano*)
Mrs K Lowry (*Lower strings*)
M McGuffin (*Piano*)
Mrs L Molyneaux (*Guitar*)

Bursar: J M Monteith, FCA
Headmaster's Secretary: Mrs Y J Mallon
Medical Officer: Dr J M Bell, MB, BCh, DRCOG, MRCGP
Matron: Mrs E M Hoey, SRN
General Manager: S R Moody, MIOH
Marketing Manager: Miss A Johnston, BA
Facilities Manager: C W Harper

Junior School:
Head: Mrs H Rowan, BA, PGCE
Mrs E M Gwynne, BEd
A P Jemphrey, BEd, DASE
Mrs P McGarry, BEd Hons
Mrs V A Vance, BEd
Mrs F Mottram, BA, ATD
J S Anderson, BEd Hons
Mrs H M Jennings, BEd Hons, Dip PD
Mrs L M Leyland, BEd Hons
Mrs E Boyd, MA
Mrs L Wilson, BA Hons, PGCE

At Campbell College, an HMC school, we aim to promote all personalities, all talents and interests and to inculcate a culture of mutual trust. Academic and vocational study is vitally important to this school and we expect our students to reach for high grades, but Campbell's view of education celebrates the creative, physical and spiritual as well as the intellectual. Above all, we want our students to leave this school with an assured set of values; we want them to believe that they can make a difference in society; we want boys to leave this school with things that are going to matter to them for the rest of their lives.

Pastoral Care. Campbell places a high priority on the pastoral care of each boy in our community. We contend that boys flourish when they are known individually and feel valued within a supportive, encouraging ethos. To this end, our structure of Personal Tutors working alongside Heads of Year, Assistant Heads of Year and Housemasters is designed to ensure that boys are closely supported in all aspects of pastoral welfare, academic progress and across the total curriculum.

Smaller tutor groups of around eighteen boys help to create a sense of belonging that enables boys to feel secure and also gives parents a first point of contact with a Personal Tutor who understands their son's needs and values them as individuals.

There are eight Houses at Campbell and they form the focus for participation across the total curriculum. Boys are proud of their Houses and cultural and sporting pursuits are keenly contested.

At Campbell we view pastoral care as a whole school responsibility recognising that all staff have a duty of care for ensuring the well-being of every boy. High expectations, hard work and mutual respect are accordingly the recurring themes of our school life.

Boarding has always been central to the life of the College. Boarding requires a boy to take responsibility for his own life and to interact with a community of other people. It also provides him with a secure base and a focus of loyalty in a large school, as well as an opportunity for exercising responsibility and leadership in a community. School House is presided over by the Head of Boarding, Mr Bert Robinson, appointed from Haileybury School. Mr Robinson is responsible for the academic, pastoral and social welfare of his boys and for dealings with their parents.

The Head of Boarding is assisted by Mr Neil McGarry, appointed as Head of Middle School Boarding, and four

House Mothers, who look after the health of the boys and the domestic affairs of the House. Every boy is assigned to a House Tutor in School House whom he sees regularly, and has access to a range of medical, pastoral and counselling services. The House Tutor is the first point of contact for a boy.

As a boarding and day school, Campbell College is committed to providing a broadly-based education designed to enable all boys to discover their strengths, and to make the most out of their talents within Campbell and beyond. It is our belief that the experience of living in a boarding community engenders respect for individuality and the difference of others. In School House we seek to foster self-confidence, enthusiasm, perseverance, tolerance and integrity. Above all, however, we want all boarders to be happy during their time at Campbell.

Boarding at Campbell offers excellent value for money compared to other UK boarding schools; the accommodation facilities are of a very high standard. Middle School House boys (Years 8–10) board in dormitory style rooms and in a combination of 2, 4 or 5 boys per room; Senior boys (Years 11 to 14) have a single bedsit, with Year 14 students residing in a newly-built unit that was specifically built to ease the transition from school to university.

School House has full use of all the College's facilities, including squash courts, tennis courts, two sports halls, an indoor swimming pool, two all weather surfaces, the College library and ICT suite. School House also has designated kitchen areas and well-equipped TV, DVD and Games rooms.

Academic. At Campbell, we cherish the life of the mind, whatever a student's academic profile. Indeed, when we see a student, we do not see a grade, or a label: we see an individual, with potential, and it is our duty to add value by helping a student achieve academic success and appreciate the joy of becoming a lifelong learner. Prepare to be challenged, stretched and tested at Campbell.

Key Stage 3. Upon entry boys are banded into 6 classes and all take English, Mathematics, Science, Spanish, History, Home Economics, Geography, Drama, Religious Studies, Art, Music, Design and Technology, Information Communication Technology, Physical Education and Learning for Life and Work. Following an assessment some pupils will receive additional support in Literacy and Numeracy.

In Year 9 all boys take up German or French. Following an assessment some pupils will receive additional support in Literacy and Numeracy.

In Year 10 Science is studied as the three separate disciplines of Biology, Chemistry and Physics. During Year 10, pupils select their course of study for GCSE. Parents and pupils are encouraged to consult with subject teachers and Personal Tutors before any final decisions are made. Following an assessment some pupils will receive additional support in Literacy and Numeracy.

GCSE (Key Stage 4). In Years 11 and 12 a varied programme of GCSE subjects is offered within the requirements of the Northern Ireland Curriculum. The subjects, currently, offered include Additional Mathematics, Art and Design, Business Studies, Drama, English Language, English Literature, French, Geography, German, History, Hospitality, ICT, Journalism, Leisure and Tourism, Mathematics, Music, Physical Education, Product Design, Science (offered as either Double Award Science or the three separate Sciences), Spanish, Technology and Design, and Religious Studies as a short course. There is also some provision for pupils to vary the number of subjects they study for GCSE.

Sixth Form. Pupils in Year 13 (Lower Sixth) take three or four AS subjects chosen from a wide range which includes Applied Business, Leisure Studies, and Theatre Studies, Further Mathematics and Political Studies as well as the previously mentioned subjects. Pupils in Year 13 have the opportunity to select an Enrichment Programme from the range on offer.

At Year 14 (Upper Sixth) these entire subjects may be taken to A Level. There is ample opportunity for discussion between parents, teachers, Personal Tutors and Careers Advisors before the final programme is decided.

The Careers Department advises pupils throughout their time at the College with guidance available through a taught programme and individual interviews. Pupils also benefit from mock interviews, computer research, links with local industry and work experience.

In periods of non-class contact, students are in a supervised Study Hall.

Total Curriculum. At Campbell College we believe in a Total Curriculum. For us, education, like life itself, is about much more than the academic; students need to leave school with a range of knowledge and skills. Our duty is to identify the individual's strengths and then help foster their passion for those activities, be they in the classroom, the CCF, the drama studio, the music workshop, the sports field, the swimming pool.

We want every student at Campbell to find things to value, so that we can prepare him, both for the examinations he will sit within the College, and for the possibilities of the life beyond. That is why Campbell continues to invest so impressively in its campus and staff, to offer our students the broadest range of opportunities possible.

Drama. Every student takes Drama in Years 8 and 9 and those with aptitude and interest may take the subject through to A Level. The once tired Lecture Theatre has been transformed into an impressive Drama Studio providing a bright and modern learning environment: its virtues number a generous stage, tiered seating and a fully-kitted sound and lighting box. As a result, drama has prospered with lunchtime performances and a lunchtime theatre club where the boys script, direct and perform their own productions.

Music. Musical opportunities are readily available in the form of a Choir, the Junior, Senior and Full Orchestra, the Jazz Band, and the Pipe Band. Individual performances and ensemble playing take place at Family Services throughout the year and as part of the Easter Concert.

The Charity Committee. This is a group of staff and students (Years 11–14) who make a worthwhile contribution to the wider community. Two cherished events include, The Christmas Fair, which incorporates stalls from many international charities and raises a significant amount of money for the Committee's chosen projects; and the annual Daffodil Tea in March, which is popular with senior citizens. In addition, further events are organised with those who have care of children in need of special help.

Combined Cadet Force (CCF). All students in Year 10 join the Pioneers, which is led by the CCF staff. They will learn basic skills in First Aid, map and compass work and adventure training. From Year 11, students may join the Army, Navy or Air Force sections of the CCF where they are offered an exciting range of adventure training. They can explore a wide variety of rich opportunities and attend Field Days as well as Easter and Summer Camps. They may test themselves in competition, or join the bugles, pipes and drums of the Contingent's Pipe Band: a band that carries a valued history and tradition.

Members of the CCF, who have completed their training, may also choose to take a BTEC First Diploma in Public Services. This award is equivalent to 4 GCSEs and is recognised by employers and Universities as a worthwhile vocational qualification.

Duke of Edinburgh's Award. Boys have the opportunity to participate in the Award Scheme with Bronze, Silver and Gold Awards available throughout the year. At present, a maximum of 50 places for Middle School boys are available on the Bronze course. As this is a very popular activity, places are gained on a first-come, first-served basis.

Sport. We pride ourselves on offering an excellent selection of sporting opportunities and we are fortunate to accommodate most of them on-site. All students are encouraged to participate in some form of sport, whether it is in Inter-House Competitions or against other schools, and Campbell students are regularly selected to play representative sport at provincial and international level. Whatever the level of participation or ability, we strongly believe that sport is integral to the development of each individual.

Sports and Activities offered by the College are: Archery, Athletics, Badminton, Basketball, Chess, Cricket, Cross-Country, Fencing (there is an additional charge for this), Golf, Hockey, Rugby, Sailing, Soccer, Squash, Swimming, Tennis, Volleyball, Shooting.

Holidays. There are three annual holidays: two weeks at Christmas and Easter, and eight in the summer. In the Christmas and Easter terms there is a half-term break of one week, during which parents of boarders are required to make provision for their sons to be away from school.

Admissions. Campbell College welcomes students at all entry levels. Dayboys can begin in Kindergarten and stay through to Sixth Form; boarders may start at Year 8.The school structure is designed to offer our students easy transitions as they grow and mature; they begin in Junior School, then move at age 11 to Middle School, before progressing to Senior School to prepare for their public examinations (GCSE, AS and A2 Level).

There are approximately 914 students in the College, of whom 104 are boarders. The admission number following the Transfer Procedure has been set at 140 by the Department of Education (NI) and we also welcome admissions at all year groups, in particular at 16+ for A Level study.

Fees per annum (2011-2012). Tuition Fee: £2,200. Boarding (available from age 11): £8,751. Junior School: £3,400–£3,650. Students from non-EU countries will pay a tuition fee of £6,360.

Campbell College is a Voluntary B Grammar School and as such is allowed to charge fees to all students attending the College. Fees for the academic year commencing in September are set in the previous Summer Term by the Board of Governors and are charged equally in September and January. Prompt payment is expected and many methods of payment, including direct debit (over 10 months), may be used. Boarding fees are also charged twice yearly.

Discounts are available to those having three or more children at day school (two or more in boarding), members of the clergy or those in the armed forces. The Governors will consider assistance to those families who suffer severe financial hardship.

Scholarships and Bursaries. *Years 8 & 9*: Pupils who have sat the Association for Quality Education (AQE) examinations will be allocated to a Quintile that will reflect their achievement in those examinations. Pupils who have achieved a place in the first Quintile (top 20% academically) and the second Quintile (next 20% academically) will qualify to have their fees reduced in Years 8 & 9 by the following amounts: First Quintile £1000, Second Quintile £500.

Years 10, 11 and 12: Academic Bursaries are available. Year 10 bursaries are granted to pupils who achieve the required standard in their internal examinations at the end of Year 9.

Pupils in Year 10 wishing to be considered for Years 11 and 12 Bursaries must apply in writing to the Headmaster not later than 30th April and, in addition to the internal examinations, will have to sit 3 'special papers' (Maths, English and Science).

Years 13 and 14: Academic Bursaries are awarded as a result of high achievement in external examinations; in addition, Bursaries may be awarded to those pupils who are judged to have excelled in the fields of sport, music, the arts or a recognised vocational subject.

Music Scholarships and Exhibitions for Years 8 and 9 are awarded following examinations during Year 8, and awards

for Years 10, 11 and 12 following examination at the end of Year 9.

An *Art* Scholarship is awarded for Years 10, 11 and 12 based on continuous assessment throughout Year 9.

University Grants of up to £1,000 per annum will be made to boys who achieve Oxbridge entry.

The decisions of the Board of Governors are final and all awards are in the gift of the Board of Governors.

Prospectus. Further information is included in our prospectus which can be obtained from the College Office or you may download a copy from the College website.

Old Campbellian Society. Register, 1894–2000, Sixth Edition, 2000. (There is also a link from College website.)

Charitable status. Campbell College is registered with the Inland Revenue as a charity, number XN45154/1. It exists to provide education for boys.

Canford School

Wimborne, Dorset BH21 3AD
Tel: 01202 841254
Fax: 01202 881009
e-mail: admissions@canford.com
website: www.canford.com

Canford School was founded in 1923.
Motto: '*Nisi Dominus Frustra.*'

Governors:
Chairman: G F Page, CBE, DL, MA
R G A Baxter, MA
A W Browning, BSc, PGCE, MA Ed, CChem, MRSC
Mrs F Costa, ARCM
A J L Cottam, BSc, FCA
B Coupe, BA, DipArch, RIBA
R W Daubeney, BA
Rear Admiral J M de Halpert, KCVO, CB
M T Keats, MA
D R Levin, BEcon, MA, FRSA
J D McGibbon, FCA
B W Richards
A F Simmons
Dr K J Torlot, MB BS, FRCAnaes
G E Vardey, MA, MSI
Mrs E T Watson, BA

Secretary to the Governing Body: M B M Porter, MA

Headmaster: J D Lever, MA, PGCE

Deputy Head: R J Knott, MA, ARCM
Deputy Head (Pastoral): Dr H K Laver, BSc, PhD
Director of Studies: Dr S K Wilkinson, MSc, DPhil
Registrar: M A Owen, BA, PGCE
Bursar: D S B Phipps, BA

Assistant Staff:
* *Head of Department*
† *Housemaster/mistress*

English, History, Classics, Politics, Drama, Information Technology:
*Dr L J D Kennedy, BA, PhD (*English*)
*A C Fearnley, BA, MLitt, (*Politics*)
*C E Thomas, BA, MA, PGCE (*Drama*)
*C M S Rathbone, MA, PGCE (*History*)
*C A Wilson, BA, PGCE (*Classics*)
F T Ahern, MA
Miss C Barrett, BA, MA
Mrs L J Blake, MA
Mrs S Ellis, BA, PGCE
K D R Hay, BA, Cert Ed
Dr C E Ives, MA, PhD
Mrs P J Knott, MA, PGCE

Miss L H J McClelland, BA
Mrs K M Orpwood, BA, MA
M A Owen, BA, PGCE
†R M B Salmon, BA, PGCE
S Vandvik, MA
M H Walters, BA, MPhil
Ms K M Watts, BA, PGCE

Geography and Economics:
*Mrs K J Hoey, MA (*Geography*)
*Mrs C E Kilpatrick, BSc (*Business Studies/Economics*)
†N H Jones, BA, PGCE
S D Grant, BA
J R Orme, MA, PGCE
R S Raumann, MA, PGCE
P D A Rossiter, MA, PGCE
†Mrs J Smith, BA, PGCE
R B Woolwright, BEng, MSc

Mathematics and Science:
*R J Baldwin, BEng, MSc, PGCE (*Mathematics*)
*C L Fenwick, BSc, PGCE (*Physics*)
*Dr H K Laver, BSc, PhD
*G R Shaw, MChem, PGCE
D J Allen, BSc, MSc, PGCE
†H Bishop, BSc, ACMA
†Mrs C D Byng, BA Ed
Miss H L Chartres, BSc, PGCE
†L M Corbould, BSc, PGCE
†D P Culley, MA
S D Excell, BSc, PGCE
R H J Hooker, BSc
Dr F G Horton, MA, DPhil
C H Jeffery, BA, MEng
Miss A Jenner, MA, PGCE
Miss B E Keely, BA
R J Knott, MA, ARCM
Miss A L Mulley, BSc
A J Naden, BSc, BEng
Dr D Neill, BSc, PhD, PGCE
O T Parkin, BSc
B J Sparks, MSc, BA, PGCE
T J Street, BSc, PGCE
Mrs E C Thornburrow, BSc, PGCE
A J Tyndall, MChem
Dr S K Wilkinson, MSc, DPhil

Modern Languages:
*F Compan, Licenciado en Filología Inglesa (*French*)
*A Neame, BA, MBA (*Spanish*)
*R A Wilson BA, MA, PGCE (*German*)
W R Baugniet, LLB, Maîtrise en Droit, LLM
Mrs L Harding, BA, MA, PGCE
Mrs R Harris, BA
Miss V J Lethbridge, BA, PGCE
†Mrs M Marns, Maîtrise d'Anglais, PGCE
Mrs E Pellejero, BA, MA
Mrs C J G Stone, Licence ès Lettres, PGCE

Music:
*C C Sparkhall, MA, ARCO, PGCE (*Director of Music*)
Miss R F Partington, MusB (*Head of Woodwind*)
Miss F M McKinley, BA, LMusA (*Head of Strings*)
D A Warwick, MA, FRCO, ARCM

Art and Design:
*D H Wright, MA, PGCE (*Art*)
*N Watkins, BEd (*Design Technology*)
P A Effick, BEd, BSc
Ms J Jones, BA, PGCE
A Kirkby, BA, MA
†D F Lloyd, BA, PGCE
J V Martin, BEng, MSc, PGCE

Religious Studies:
*The Revd C Jervis, BEd, Cert Theol

J W G Boothby, MA

Physical Education:
*M S Burley, BSocSci, MA (*Director of Sport*)
†N R Baugniet, BA
B Edgell, BSc
Miss H C Morrell, BSc

Careers and Higher Education: D A Dodwell, MA, PGCE
Examinations Officer: Mrs V M Horwood
Archivist: F T Ahern, MA, PGCE

Houses & Housemasters/mistresses:

Boarding Houses (Boys):
Court: R M B Salmon
Franklin: H Bishop
Monteacute: D F Lloyd
School: L M Corbould

Boarding Houses (Girls):
Beaufort: Mrs J Smith
de Lacy: Mrs M Marns
Marriotts: Mrs C D Byng

Mixed Day Houses:
Lancaster: D P Culley
Salisbury: N H Jones
Wimborne: N R Baugniet

Medical Officers:
P J N Dickins, MA, MB BS, DCH, DRCOG, MRCGP
B L Lear, MB BS, MRCGP
H Sankson, MB, MRCGP
R Skule, MB BS, MRCP, MRCGP

Canford is a leading co-educational, boarding and day school for pupils aged between 13 and 18. Canford has a culture which encourages participation and hard work. There is a strong sense of community, teamwork, friendliness and integrity leading to mutual trust which in turn brings achievement. Pupils are offered a wide range of opportunities inside and outside the classroom. Our aim is to provide not only an academic but also a diverse cultural, social and spiritual environment in which pupils can flourish.

Situation. Canford School stands on the edge of Wimborne, Dorset, in an enclosed park of 300 acres which includes a stretch of the river Stour used for rowing, fishing and canoeing. The main building was designed by Blore in 1825 and remodelled by Sir Charles Barry in 1846. Since the foundation of the school in 1923 there have been numerous additions on the site to provide a full range of modern facilities.

Numbers. There are about 635 pupils of whom approximately 70% are boarders and 60% are boys.

Houses. There are 4 boarding houses for boys, 3 boarding houses for girls and 3 mixed day houses.

The Curriculum. There is considerable breadth in the lower school. In their Shell year pupils study the core subjects of English, Mathematics and Religious Studies. In addition they study Physics, Chemistry and Biology, French, German or Spanish, Latin and Classical Civilisation or Extra English, Music, Art, Design Technology, History, Geography, Drama, PE and General Studies. In the Fourth Form Business Studies is added to these non-core subjects, from which pupils are asked to choose seven to study for GCSE. At least two sciences must be taken to GCSE. PE is not available at GCSE. The compulsory RS course is non-examined; in addition pupils may choose a GCSE in Religious Studies.

A Level subjects offered are English, Latin, History, Religious Studies, Politics, Geography, Economics, Business Studies, French, German, Spanish, Mathematics, Physics, Chemistry, Biology, Music, Art, Design Technology, Theatre Studies, Classical Civilisation and Sports Studies. Combinations of subjects are as flexible as possible. All pupils in all year groups follow a General Studies course, which includes Personal and Social Education in the first two years.

University Destinations. 95%+ of pupils proceed to higher education, popular destinations recently include Bath, Bristol, Cambridge, Cardiff, Durham, Edinburgh, Exeter and Oxford. On average more than a dozen places are gained at Oxford and Cambridge annually.

Tutorial System. In addition to their Housemaster/mistress and House Tutor the pupils in the Sixth Form each have an Academic Tutor who is responsible with the Housemaster/mistress for academic progress, university entry, and careers guidance. There are monthly academic assessments throughout the school which are monitored by the tutorial staff and emailed to parents.

Religion. Chapel services are held in the Norman church of Canford Magna which stands in the school grounds, and also in the Music School and the Theatre. Arrangements can be made for those of different faiths and denominations to worship independently.

Music. Music is a compulsory subject for pupils in the Shell year, and an option for GCSE and A Level. 400 individual music lessons are taken each week and more than half of pupils learn an instrument. Larger ensembles include senior orchestra, string orchestra, 2 concert bands, jazz band, Chapel Choir, Chamber Choir, Junior Choir and Choral Society while there is also a wide range of chamber ensembles. The Music School has 2 large rehearsal rooms, practice rooms and a computer suite. Regular concerts, both formal and informal, are given in the 200-seat Concert Hall as well as in prestigious outside venues.

Drama. In their first year, pupils have the opportunity to study drama as part of the curriculum and beyond that Drama and Theatre Studies are offered at GCSE and A Level. The 300-seat Layard Theatre is home to the Drama Department and provides an exciting venue for a wide range of school productions as well as hosting work from professional companies.

Art and Design Technology. Art and Design Technology are compulsory for all pupils in their first year during which they are introduced to drawing, painting, printing, sculpture, metalwork, woodwork, plastics and CAD/CAM. They may also pursue these interests in their daily activities time and at weekends. Pupils may take GCSE and A Level.

ICT. In their Shell year all pupils follow the IAM Award which is a QCA level 2 award, equivalent to a B grade at GCSE. Thereafter the well-equipped Information Technology Centre provides cross-curricular induction courses to all, aiming to establish IT as a natural tool for learning and life, and enabling pupils to apply it to a range of academic and other work, from preps to projects, personal correspondence to school publications. Each department has a teacher assigned to the development of IT within its subject curriculum. There is open access to the centre for all pupils and staff throughout the day and in addition all houses are equipped with computers as is the library. Houses and most public areas have a wireless network for internet access.

Sport. All pupils participate in sport. The principal sports are: in the Christmas Term rugby for boys, hockey for girls; in the Easter Term hockey and rowing for boys, netball and rowing for girls; in the Summer Term cricket and rowing for boys, tennis and rowing for girls. The school also has representative teams in athletics, cross-country, sailing, swimming, golf, squash, badminton, lacrosse and royal tennis. There are other sports available. The school facilities include: a well-equipped sports centre incorporating double-sized sports hall, dance studio, physiotherapy room, two sports science classrooms and state-of-the-art fitness suite; two astroturf pitches used for hockey and tennis; three hard court areas suitable for tennis and netball; four squash courts; a royal tennis court; a nine-hole golf course, 12 grass pitches, and a new indoor 25m, 6-lane pool. There is also a climbing wall and a fully equipped boathouse on the adjacent River Stour. The school employs professional cricket, squash, royal tennis, rowing, hockey, rugby, golf and netball coaches.

Societies, Hobbies and Activities. Various societies meet on a regular basis including Debating, Literary, Science and Art. The school operates a comprehensive activity programme which is compulsory for all Shell and Fourth Form pupils. This takes place twice a week and offers a wide range of sporting, musical, drama, practical and recreational activities. There is also scope for further involvement in the senior part of the school.

Community Service. About 120 pupils work in the local community each week, teaching in schools, volunteering at National Trust properties and other charities, helping the elderly, the disabled, and visiting patients in hospices and respite care centres. They also help to give lessons in swimming and science and look after disadvantaged children. Each year parties of Canfordians help in orphanages in Southern India, Tanzania and Argentina.

Combined Cadet Force. Army, Navy and Marines sections make up a 240 strong cadet force staffed by 12 officers. About 90% of pupils join in their second year on a voluntary basis and remain in the CCF for two years. A number stay on until the end of their sixth form as NCOs. There are numerous opportunities for training exercises in the UK and abroad, including Norway and France.

Careers and Higher Education. The careers programme at Canford accelerates in the Fifth Form with testing and interviews. The whole year group has the opportunity to undergo testing for career directions and A Level choices. The Lower Sixth year starts the advice procedure for higher education applications with talks, lectures and one to one consultations. The Upper Sixth year completes these processes. A well-appointed careers room is always available and parental participation at all stages of the programme is encouraged.

Medical. The purpose-built Health Centre is staffed 24 hours a day by five fully-qualified nurses. A medical officer visits the Health Centre daily during the week and remains on call throughout and during weekends. The Health Centre also provides a physiotherapy and confidential counselling service.

Admission. Boys and girls may be registered at any time. Application should be made to the Admissions Office. The examination normally used for entry is the Common Entrance Examination, but the school uses its own entry tests for those who are not at preparatory schools. Pupils are usually admitted between their 13th and 14th birthdays or by a competitive examination at 16+.

Scholarships. (*See Scholarship Entries section.*) All Canford's scholarships are indexed as a percentage of the fees so that their relative value remains constant throughout the scholar's school career.

Scholarships at 13+. Scholarship examinations are held in February and March for the following awards: Academic, Music and Sport scholarships worth from 10% to 50% of the fees; Art, Drama and Design Technology scholarships worth from 10% to 20% of the fees; an academic Royal Naval scholarship worth 20% of the fees to the son/daughter of a serving Naval Officer. Candidates must be in Year 8 at the time of the examination. All scholarships are tenable with effect from the September of the year in which they are awarded. Candidates may enter for more than one scholarship.

Entrance Scholarships at 16+. Entrants to the school at Sixth Form level may apply for any combination of the following scholarships: Academic, Music, Assyrian (for extra-curricular excellence including sport). The examinations are held in the November prior to entry. Assyrian awards are offered for an extra-curricular contribution of excellent quality to school life and are worth from 10% to 40% of the fees; Academic and Music scholarships are worth from 10% to 50% of the fees.

Bursaries. Means-tested bursaries worth up to 100% of the fees are available from the school where the financial need of the prospective or current parents has been established.

Further details about any awards can be obtained from the Admissions Office.

Fees per term (2011-2012). Boarders £9,305; Day £7,245.

Composition Fee. At any time in advance a composition fee at special rates may be paid to cover the cost of a pupil's education for his/her career at the school. Details may be obtained from the Admissions Office.

Insurance. There is a fees insurance scheme also covering medical and operation expenses, at the option of the parents.

The Old Canfordian Society. Enquiries to The Old Canfordian Society, Canford School.

Charitable status. Canford School Limited is a Registered Charity, number 306315. It exists to provide education for children.

Caterham School

Harestone Valley Road, Caterham, Surrey CR3 6YA
Tel: 01883 343028
Fax: 01883 347795
e-mail: enquiries@caterhamschool.co.uk
admissions@caterhamschool.co.uk
website: www.caterhamschool.co.uk

Caterham was founded in 1811 by the Revd John Townsend to provide a boarding education for the sons of Congregational ministers. Logically it was named the Congregational School. By 1884, the School had outgrown its premises, and the 114 boys with their teaching staff moved to Caterham. In 1890, the school opened its doors to the sons of laymen and to day boys. In 1995, after 184 years as a boys' day and boarding school, it merged with Eothen School for Girls to create a new independent co-educational foundation. Girls had been coming to Caterham for Sixth Form education since 1981, but the merger integrated the schools and enabled co-education to be offered to pupils aged 3 years and upwards. In 1995 the School became an associate member of the United Church Schools Trust and benefits from the strength provided by this partnership.

Motto: *Veritas Sine Timore.*

Board of Trustees:
Chairman: J W Bloomer
Vice-Chairman: I R M Edwards
D P G Cade
D P Charlesworth
J Joiner
J E K Smith
R J S Tice
G M Walter
Mrs S M Whittle
Mrs P H Wilkes

Bursar and Clerk to the Trustees: J C L King, MBE

The School Staff:

Headmaster: J P Thomas, BSc Hons, MBA, FRSA

Deputy Head: Ms T B Ridge, MA
Deputy Head (Curriculum): T J Murphy, MA Oxon
Senior Teacher & Head of Boarding: J P Seymour, BSc Hons
Director of Learning and Teaching: K Wells, MA Cantab
Assistant Head: D Clark, BA, MPhil Cantab

Academic Staff:

Art and Design:
*Mrs M Kyle, MA, MEd
M Sherrington, BA Hons (*Head of Underwood, Head of Photography*)
Miss A Church, MA (*Head of Art, Head of Textiles*)
N Evans, MA
Miss C D Pateman, BA Hons
B Wilkinson, BA Hons (*Head of 3D Design*)

Biology:
*D Quinton, MA Oxon MSB (*Head of Science*)
S F Hayes, BSc Hons
A P Taylor, BSc Hons (*Head of Second Year*)
S Marlow, MBiochem Oxon
Miss A Henry, BSc Hons (*Assistant Head of Fifth Year*)

Chemistry:
*D Keyworth, MSc
J Burnside, PhD, MChem Hons (*Head of Lewisham*)
Mrs E Rivers, BSc (*Head of Fourth Year*)
S Gilbert, MA
Miss K Handford, PhD

Classics:
*K Waite, MA Oxon
M Owen, BA Hons Oxon
Mrs S Carpenter, BA Oxon

Drama & Theatre Studies:
*Miss L McMullin, BA Hons

Economics and Business Studies:
*C Smith, BA Hons, BEd
A Fahey, BA Hons (*Head of Lower Sixth*)
C James, BSc Hons, MBA (*Head of Upper Sixth, Head of Harestone*)
Mrs C Wallace, BA Hons, ACIB

English:
*G C Killingworth, MA Cantab, MA London
Miss A Cox, BA
Miss A O'Donnell, MA Hons
A Van Niekerk, BA (*Head of Townsend*)
M Broughton, BA Hons (*Head of Fifth Year*)
Mrs A L T Yankova, BA Hons
Miss H Killick, BA Hons
Mrs L Tapley, BA, DipSpLD, AMBDA (*Head of Lower School, Head of First Year*)

Geography:
*S Terrell, MPhil
A Van Niekerk, BA (*Head of Townsend*)
Mrs V Mesher, MA
Miss C Searl, MSc, MEd

History:
*R Salem, MA Oxon (*Pupil Data Coordinator*)
M Lesser, MA, MBA (*Director of Sixth Form*)
N Mills, BA Hons (*Head of Viney*)
Mrs S Carter-Esdale, BA Hons
T Cooper, MA (*Second in Department, Head of Ridgefield House*)

Information Technology:
*P R Hoad, BA (*Director of ICT Development*)
M G Bailey, BA Hons, BEd (*Head of Sixth Form ICT*)

Mathematics:
*W Jaundrill, MA Cantab, MSc
Mrs A Crook, BSc, MSc (*Second in Department*)
Miss N Dawrant, MA Oxon
Mrs R Stowell, MA (*Examinations Officer*)
J Ogilvie, BSc (*Examinations Officer*)
D R Todd, MA Oxon
S Lander, MA Oxon, MSc (*Assistant Head of Third Year*)
C Ware, BSc Hons
D King, BA Hons (*Head of Third Year*)

R Jones, BSc Hons (*Assistant Head of Second Year*)

Modern Languages:
*S Bird, MA (*Head of Modern Foreign Languages, Head of German*)
Mrs J Laverick, BEd Hons Cantab
*N Parker, MSc (*Head of Spanish*)
Mrs C M Clifton, BA Hons
*Mrs N McVitty, DEUG, Licence d'Anglais (*Head of French, Assistant Head of Sixth Form*)
K Wells, MA Cantab (*Director of Learning & Teaching*)
C Garcia, BA Hons
Mrs S Carpenter, BA Oxon
Mrs C Jackson, BA Hons
Miss E Harris, BMus

Music:
*S Thompson, GRSM, LRAM, ARAM, MBA (*Director of Music*)
Mrs H Richards, BMus Hons
Mrs C Aldren, Prof Cert Hons, LRAM, ALCM (*Head of Strings*)
J Marshall, ALCM (*Head of Wind & Brass*)
A Assen, BA Mus (*Assistant Director of Music*)
Mrs A Martin, MMus

Physical Education:
*R Clarke, BSc Hons (*Director of Sport*)
*Miss J Leach, BSc Hons (*Head of Examination PE*)
R Smith, CertEd (*Head of Cricket*)
*Mrs N Lomas, BA Hons (*Head of Girls' Games*)
A Patterson, MA (*Head of Hockey, Head of Aldercombe, Coordinator of Clubs and Societies*)
Miss R Hart, BA Hons

Psychology:
*D Kokott, BA
L Barnard, BSc Hons (*Assistant Head of First Year*)

Physics:
*L Dannatt, MEng
J P Armitage, BSc
J Miller, BSc, MA
Miss N Francis, BSc Hons
A Wood, MSc

Politics:
*T Cooper, MA (*Head of Ridgefield House*)
D Clark, BA, MPhil Cantab (*Assistant Head*)
T J Murphy, MA Oxon (*Deputy Head – Curriculum*)

Religious Education:
*Revd Dr R Mearkle, BA, MDiv, DMin (*Chaplain*)
Ms T B Ridge, MA (*Deputy Head*)
Miss H Trehane, BA Hons (*Examinations Officer*)
J Whyatt, BA, MA
Mrs S Carter-Esdale, BA Hons

Special Needs:
*Mrs L Tapley, BA, DipSpLD, AMBDA (*Head of Lower School, Head of First Year*)

EAL:
*Mrs S Dall'Oglio, BA Ed Hons
J P Seymour, BSc Hons (*Senior Teacher, Head of Boarding*)
Mrs S Fothergill, CELTA, DELTA

Careers: Mrs C Brown

Registrar: Miss R Fisher

Preparatory School

Head Teacher: H W G Tuckett, MA
(*For further information see IAPS section*)

Number in School. In the Senior School there are 825 pupils, of whom 168 are boarders. In the Preparatory School there are 279 pupils.

Aims. Our aim is to provide an excellent all-round education so that every pupil can achieve his or her full potential academically and socially.

We focus on developing the whole person, aiming to ensure that each pupil leaves here ready for the challenges of life at university and beyond. We believe that truly excellent education is about more than academic achievement alone: it is also about developing a passion for learning, moral values, self-confidence without arrogance and genuine interests that extend beyond the confines of the classroom.

We are a family school with Christian values. We believe that the virtues of tolerance, understanding, respect and courtesy really matter. We strive to ensure that Caterham pupils have an understanding of their place in society – locally and globally – and seek to make a positive impact upon it.

Situation. Caterham School is in a rural location in north Surrey just 22 miles from the centre of London. The 80-acre campus is in the beautiful, wooded Harestone Valley. We are less than a mile from the centre of Caterham, and only five minutes drive from Junction 6 of the M25. The journey by taxi to London Gatwick airport is 20 minutes and about 50 minutes to London Heathrow.

Caterham Railway Station is a 15 minute walk. The frequent trains into London (Victoria or London Bridge) make educational and cultural visits easy to organise.

There are separate boarding houses for boys (Townsend and Viney) and girls (Beech Hanger). Common rooms, dormitories (for younger pupils) and study-bedrooms are comfortably furnished, many with en-suite facilities.

In recent years there has been a substantial building and development programme. The boarding accommodation has been extended and refurbished. There is a new sports centre, a new theatre/assembly hall, a language laboratory and very extensive investment has been made in ICT. The new science labs and refectory were completed in 2007 and a new Sixth Form Centre and Health Centre were opened in 2008

The Preparatory School. This consists of 2 large houses in the school grounds. Mottrams contains the Pre-Prep department and the kitchen and dining rooms. Shirley Goss contains classrooms, assembly hall, a library, an IT room, separate art and craft rooms, and changing accommodation for the Prep department. (*For further information see IAPS section.*)

Continuity of education is provided as boys and girls move from the Preparatory School to the Senior School at the age of eleven.

Admission. Intake is by selection on academic merit and on assessment of a pupil's likely positive contribution through good behaviour to the aims, ethos and co-curricular life of the School. All candidates must sit our examinations.

For day pupils the main intake ages are 11+ years, 13+ years and for the Sixth Form. All day pupil candidates are required to attend an interview and a report from the pupil's current school will be required prior to an offer of a place being made.

Places in the Sixth Form are offered subject to a minimum of six GCSE passes (or equivalent) at Grade A. Additionally, pupils will be expected to meet the specific subject entry requirements for their AS and A Level choices. This is a pass at grade A or B (or equivalent) depending on the subject.

All international applicants for boarding places must pass our examinations which are usually taken at the offices of the British Council or one of our overseas agents. For all international applicants we require a school report at registration.

For further details please contact the Registrar, Miss R Fisher, Tel: 01883 335058, e-mail: admissions@caterhamschool.co.uk.

Details concerning the admission of pupils to the Pre-Preparatory and Preparatory School are published separately (*see entry in IAPS section*).

Term of Entry. Pupils are normally accepted for entry in September each year, but vacancies may be filled at other times.

Scholarships and Bursaries. (*See Scholarship Entries section.*) Academic, Art, Music and Sport scholarships are awarded at 11+, 13+ and 16+. In addition to these, pupils joining the school at 13+ may apply for All-Rounder scholarships, and pupils entering the Sixth Form may apply for Science scholarships. Scholarships are also awarded to boarding pupils judged to have the potential to make a significant contribution to the boarding community.

We wish to ensure that Caterham School is accessible to talented students, irrespective of parental income. Therefore, any prospective pupil from a low-income family is eligible to apply for a Caterham Bursary to obtain means-tested financial support in respect of day fees. A fully funded day place for a Sixth Form student is provided by a Wilberforce Bursary. Bursaries do not preclude pupils from holding a scholarship award. Bursaries are also available for the sons and daughters of URC Clergy, Regular Forces and FCO personnel.

Fees per term (2011-2012). Boarding £8,526–£8,988; Day £4,602–£4,817. Lunch for Day Pupils: £190.

Curriculum. Preparatory School: A wide range of subjects is provided following National Curriculum guidelines. (*For further details see entry in IAPS section.*)

Senior School: For GCSE the core curriculum is English Language and Literature, Mathematics, Physics, Chemistry, Biology and a Modern Language as well as PE and Games and RPSE. To this core is added three further subjects from Latin, Greek, Modern Languages (French, German, Spanish, Italian), Art, 3D Design, Music, Drama, GCSE PE, Economics and Business Studies, IT (AS), History, Geography and Religious Studies. All of the subjects offered at GCSE are available at A Level, as well as Further Mathematics, Economics, Business Studies, Photography, Psychology, Politics and Textiles. The curriculum is supplemented by an innovative, non-examined 'Forum' programme that includes expert led lectures and seminars designed to prepare students for the opportunities and responsibilities of adult life. Sixth Form students can also participate in the Caterham Award which recognises public speaking, community service and leadership development.

Music, Drama and Creative Arts. Music is an important feature of the life of the School. Individual lessons are given on the piano, in string, brass and wind instruments, and the organ. The Choral Society performs at least one major choral work each year. Each term there are several School concerts and a programme of recitals is arranged. Drama is also well-supported and popular. Each year there are three major productions which involve a large number of pupils both on and off stage. The expertise within the Art Department is broad, including painting, printmaking, textiles, fashion, ceramics, photography, digital media and sculpture and pupils are encouraged to pursue their interests in creative work, as diverse as ceramics, textiles, digital manipulation, drypoint etching and mixed media.

Societies and Hobbies. All pupils are encouraged to pursue a hobby or constructive outside interest, and there are a large number of active School Societies, including: Art, CCF, Chess, Amnesty International, Astronomy, Dance, Debating, Duke of Edinburgh's Award, Film, Greek, ICT Club, Jewellery, Kit Car Club, Moncrieff-Jones (Sixth Form Science), Music, Circus, Textiles, Young Enterprise. The School has an active charity committee and significant funds are raised annually to support partner schools in Tanzania and the Ukraine.

Games. Most of the playing fields adjoin the School including an 'all weather' synthetic grass pitch for Lacrosse, Hockey and Tennis. Overall there are 18 different sporting activities, but in each term at least one major game is played. For boys it is Rugby in the Autumn Term, Hockey in the Spring Term and Cricket in the Summer. Other options include Tennis, Football and Golf. The girls play Lacrosse, Netball, Rounders and Tennis. Pupils can also participate in Athletics, Fencing, Equestrian, Swimming, Badminton, Basketball, Cross-Country, Squash, Tae Kwon Do and, in the Summer Term, Sailing, Windsurfing and Canoeing.

Health. There is a well equipped Health Centre with a SRN Sister. The School Doctor attends regularly.

Careers. The Careers staff are available to give advice. The School has membership of the Independent Schools Careers Organisation and parents are encouraged to enter their sons or daughters for the ISCO Aptitude Test in the Sixth Form year. The School arranges Careers and Higher Education Forums and the Headmaster and Careers staff are available to discuss careers with parents.

Old Caterhamians' and Parents' Associations. The School has flourishing Old Caterhamians' and Parents' Associations. Information about these may be obtained from the School.

Charitable status. Caterham School is a Registered Charity, number 1109508. Its aim is to develop the academic and personal potential of each pupil in a Christian context.

Charterhouse

Godalming, Surrey GU7 2DX

Tel:	Admissions: 01483 291501
	Headmaster: 01483 291600
	Bursary and Enquiries: 01483 291500
Fax:	Admissions: 01483 291507
	Headmaster: 01483 291647
e-mail:	admissions@charterhouse.org.uk
website:	www.charterhouse.org.uk

Charterhouse is one of the great historic schools of England and among the most beautiful. Founded in London in 1611, the School moved to its impressive 200-acre site in the Surrey countryside near Godalming in 1872.

The School offers outstanding facilities. The boarding accommodation is divided into 11 houses and there is a new Sixth Form day house. There are over 740 pupils, including 100 girls in the Sixth Form. The School prides itself on the excellence of its all-round education and long tradition of distinguished teaching and academic success.

Motto: '*Deo Dante Dedi*'.

Governing Body:
Chairman: J L Walker-Haworth, MA

The Archbishop of Canterbury
M J Collins, MA, DPhil
G A Reid, PhD
Professor G A Parker, BSc, PhD, EurIng, CEng, FIMechE, Mem ASME
Lady Toulson, CBE, LlB
P J Drew
Mrs C M Oulton, MA
Professor K R Willison, BSc, PhD
W S M Robinson, BA
R A Henley, FCA
P M R Norris, MA
N J Kempner, BSc
D Jennings, MA, Dip Arch RIBA
K R Willison, BSc, PhD
M L Everett, MA
C W V Wright, MA
Mrs C Curran, BSc

Clerk to the Governing Body and Bursar: D A E Williams, BA, FCA

***Headmaster*: The Revd J S Witheridge**, MA

Deputy Headmaster: A J Turner, BA, LLM

Assistant Headmaster (*Academic*): M G Armstrong, MA

Assistant Headmaster (*Pastoral*): N T Cooper, BA, MBA

Head of Girls: Mrs M H Swift, BDS

Assistant Staff:

A Aidonis, MA, PhD
Miss P Aguado, BA
Mrs S C Allen, MA
S P M Allen, MA
Mrs A B Bailey, MA (*Head of Higher Education*)
M J Bailey, MA
S G Barker, BSc
Miss L F Batty, BSc
M J Begbie, BA
M Bicknell
M L J Blatchly, MA, FRCO
R A Bogdan, MA
S F C Brennan, BA
K D Brown
R A Brown, MPhys, PhD
The Revd C Case, BA, MTh
O W Choroba, PhD
Miss S Clarkson, MSt
Miss E J Clement-Walker, BA
Mrs C F Clive, DipTEFL
N L Coopper, BSc
M J Crosby
C J Ellis, BSc, PhD, MIBiol
M K Elston, BSc
O P Elton, BA
Miss E J Fox, BA
J D Freeman, BA (*Director of Drama*)
J P Freeman, MA
P Funcasta, BA, MSc
H D Gammell, MA
N S Georgiakakis, MSc
G H M Gergaud, L-ès-L
M R Gillespie, BA
Miss Z Green, MA
N Hadfield, MA
E Hadley, BA
T G Hager, BA
C R G Hall, MA (*Master of the Scholars*)
I J M Hamilton
The Revd S J Harker, MA
R W T Haynes, MA
J S Hazeldine, BA
S T Hearn, MSc, MInstP
Miss A L Hoek, MSci
I A Hoffmann de Visme, MSc
Mrs E H H Holloway, BSc, PhD
E J How, BA
A R Hunt, BA
S D James, MA
A G Johnson, MSc
D R H Johnson, BSc, DPhil
A Johnston, MA, PhD
J H Kazi, MA (*Director of Curriculum*)
M D Kinder, MChem
J J Knight, BA
D N Lancefield, CPhys, MInstP, MIEE, MIEEE
W J Lane, MA

P J Langman, BSc, PhD
Miss A M Lewis, BA
R V Lewis
P F Lewthwaite, BA (*Sculptor-in-Residence*)
M F D Lloyd, MA
C W D Marsh, BA
S P Marshall, MMath, DPhil
D P Martucci, BSc
D J McCombes, BA
R C D Millard, MA, MPhil
P Monkman, MA (*Director of Art*)
Miss A J Mulroy, BA
M W Nash, BA
Mrs E P Nelson, BSc, MSc
Mrs F C Noble, BEd
R P Noble, MA (*Director of Sport*)
S J Northwood, BA, MPhil, PhD
Mrs M D B Olive, ACL (*Librarian*)
The Revd C J B O'Neill, MA, PhD, DCH, Dip Psych, Cert Couns ECP
Mrs M H Orson, BA
Mrs D Osborn, BA
J N Parsons, BA, LRAM, ARCM
N S Pelling, MA
Miss H E Pinkney, BA
P A Price, MA
Miss J Puri, BA
P J Rand, BA, MPhil, PhD
Miss E J Rees, BSc
E J Reid, MMath (*Master of the Under School*)
A N Reston, BA, MSL
T E Reynolds, MA, MSc
I S Richards, MA
J M Richardson, BA
Miss C L Robinson, MA
S A Rowse, BA, MA, DipSpLD
R D Sarre, BSc, DPhil
J H B Schmitt, BA
J Sergison-Main, MSM
M N Shepherd, MA, FRCO, ARCM (*Director of Music*)
J M Silvester, BSc
P St H Stimpson, MEng
R W Smeeton, ARCM, LRPS, MLC
Mrs C R I Smith, BA, MArAd (*Archivist*)
B P Thurston, MA, MSt, DPhil
Miss J Tod, MSc
J C Troy, BSc
J Tully, BEng, FICS, FRGS
N P Wakeling, MA
F Wiseman, MA, CertTEFL
D G Wright, LTCL

M G Yeo, MA
E H Zillekens, BA, DPhil (*Senior Librarian and Archivist*)

Senior Chaplain: The Revd Clive Case, BA, MTh

Admissions Registrar: H D Gammell, MA
Assistant Registrar: Mrs S Stevens

Estate Bursar: L Dudas
Accountant: P G Hay

Medical Officer: Dr A Borthwick, MA, MB, BChir

Counsellors:
The Revd C J B O'Neill
Mrs V Gordon-Graham, MA

Cricket Professionals: M Bicknell, R V Lewis
Rackets Professional: M J Crosby

Houses and Housemasters
Saunderites: S P M Allen and Mrs S C Allen
Verites: N Hadfield
Gownboys: M L J Blatchly
Girdlestoneites: B P Thurston
Lockites: A Johnston
Weekites: K D Brown
Hodgsonites: D G Wright
Daviesites: J Tully
Bodeites: J S Hazeldine
Pageites: N S Pelling
Robinites: S T Hearn

Admission. Parents wishing to enter their sons for the School should contact the Registrar, Charterhouse, Godalming, Surrey GU7 2DX at least 3 years before they are due to come to the school.

Parents wishing their sons or daughters to enter Charterhouse in the Sixth Form should contact the Registrar at the beginning of the summer term in the year before the September entry.

At least one term's notice is required before the removal of a pupil from the School.

Details of the School's admissions policies can be found on the website.

Date of admission. Boys and girls are accepted for September entry only.

Fees per term (2011-2012). Inclusive fees: £10,178 for Boarders, £8,414 for Day Boarders, £7,227 for Sixth Form Day Pupils (Fletcherites). The Governing Body reserves the right to alter the School Fee at its discretion.

Scholarships, Bursaries and Exhibitions. (*See Scholarship Entries section.*) *For entry at 13+*: 10 Foundation Scholarships, 5 Exhibitions, a Benn Scholarship for Classics, up to 5 Music Scholarships and 2 Art Scholarships are offered annually. In addition 5 Peter Attenborough Awards are given annually to candidates who demonstrate all-round distinction. 2 Park House Awards are made annually to exceptional sportsmen. The Blackstone Award, for the sons of lawyers, is made two years before the winner joins the School.

For entry into the Sixth Form: 6 Sir Robert Birley Academic Scholarships, 7 Academic Exhibitions, 3 Music Scholarships and 2 Art Scholarships are offered.

All Awards (except Exhibitions) may be increased to the value of the full school fee in cases of proven financial need.

Music. A tradition of musical excellence at Charterhouse is maintained and enhanced with 6 full-time staff and 30 visiting staff. 400 music lessons a week are taught, and orchestral and choral standards are enviable. GCSE and Cambridge Pre-U are offered.

Art. The Studio offers excellent facilities to study painting, print-making, ceramics, sculpture, photography and film-making. GCSE and Cambridge Pre-U are offered. Life-drawing and the study of art history and architecture complement the practical work.

Design. The John Derry Technology Centre provides facilities for the teaching of GCSE, AS and A level Design and Technology. The Centre offers boys and girls the opportunity to work in a wide range of materials.

Drama. The School has its own modern Theatre which is used extensively by pupils in term time, as well as by the public in school holidays. AS and A Level Theatre Studies are offered.

Golf. A 9-hole golf course was given to the school in July 1988 by the Old Carthusian Golfing Society.

Sports Centre. A £3.8 million Sports Centre was opened by The Queen in February 1997. It includes a 25m x 6 lane Swimming Pool, a multi-purpose Sports Hall, Fitness Suite, an Activities Room and an internal Climbing Tower.

Athletics Track. An all-weather Athletics Track was opened during the autumn of 1996.

Old Carthusian Club. All enquiries should be made to Mrs M F Mardall, The Recorder, Charterhouse, Godalming, Surrey GU7 2DX.

Prospective parents and their children are warmly invited to visit Charterhouse where they normally meet the Headmaster or Registrar, other staff and members of the School.

Charitable status. Charterhouse School is a Registered Charity, number 312054. Its aims and objectives are the provision of education through the medium of a secondary boarding school for boys, and girls in the Sixth Form.

Cheadle Hulme School

Claremont Road, Cheadle Hulme, Cheadle, Cheshire SK8 6EF

Tel: 0161 488 3330
Fax: 0161 488 3344
e-mail: registrar@chschool.co.uk
website: www.cheadlehulmeschool.co.uk

Originally founded in 1855 as the Manchester Warehousemen and Clerks' School for Necessitous Children, today Cheadle Hulme School is one of the country's leading independent co-educational day schools offering both excellent academic teaching and outstanding extra-curricular opportunities.

Set in 83 acres of Cheshire countryside, the School nurtures motivated, happy pupils who take every opportunity to develop their talents, gaining the personal skills and confidence to shape their own futures in a rapidly changing world.

Motto: '*In loco parentis*'

Governing Body:
P R Johnson (*Chairman*)

J M Anderson	Dr D N Riley
Mrs C Boyd	C Roberts
Mrs A Bradley	D C Shipley
Dr S Butler	P Sidwell
P J Driver	R Simon
Mrs M Kenyon	Mrs J M Squire

Bursar and Clerk to the Governors: Mrs A Bolton, MA, MBA

Head: Miss L C Pearson, BA Oxon

Second Master: L H Carr, BSc

Deputy Heads:
A D Nolan, BSc (*Pastoral*)
S Pagan, MA (*Academic*)
L Richardson, BA (*Co-Curricular*)

Assistant Masters and Mistresses:
N Axon, MA (*Head of Politics*)
Miss R Baker, BA
Mrs J A Banks, NNEB
Mrs F Barber, BTechNN
Mrs L J Barfoot, BA
D Barnett, MSc
Mrs J Barton, BSc
Mrs K A Booth, BSc
Mrs B C Bottoms, BSc (*Head of Junior School*)
Mr D Brackenbury, BA
Miss R Y Breese, BA
Miss P Brogan, BA
Mrs J Brown, BA
Mrs K E Bruce, BSc
Miss N J Buckley, BA
P D Bullock, MA (*Deputy Head of Careers*)
S Burnage, BEd (*Head of Boys' PE*)
Mrs F J Buxton, BA
Mrs V Byrne, MSc
Dr A E Carlin, MSc, PhD
Mrs E E Carter, MA
Ms R Chakrabarti, BEd
I Chippendale, BA (*Head of Chemistry*)
Ms L Cleary, BA
Mrs S Cocksedge, MA, LTCL (*Deputy Director of Music*)
Mrs M Cookson, BEng
Miss S Craig, BA
Mr A Crook, MPhil (*Head of History*)
Mrs B Crothers, BSc
Miss C M Curtis, BSc
K Cuthbert, BEng
Mrs R Dalton-Woods, MSc (*Head of Food & Nutrition, Learning Enrichment Coordinator*)
Mrs S K Davies, BEd
Mrs C T Davis, MA
R S Davis, BA (*Head of Middle School*)
P Dewhurst, BA (*Director of Music*)
Mrs J Drennan, BMus, MEd
Mrs V R Ellison, BEd
Mrs S Evans, BMus
Mrs A H Firth, BA
Mrs A Foster, BA, MEd
K Foster, BEd
Mrs L Fowler, BEd (*Head of Year 11*)
Miss R E Fox, BA, NNEB
Miss S Gale, BSc (*Head Girls' PE*)
Mrs A Gardener, BA (*Head of Year 9*)
Miss R E Garrett, CertEd
Ms K M Gilbertson, BSc (*Head of Psychology, Staff CPD Mentor*)
Mrs H Giles, BA
Miss C Greenwood, BSc
M Hackney, BA (*Head of Lower Sixth*)
Mrs C Haffner, BA
Ms C J Harms, BA (*Head of Drama/Theatre Studies*)
Mrs K Haspell, Dip Theatre Arts (*PHSE Coordinator*)
Mrs L W Hayes, BA (*Head of IT*)
Mrs L Hodges, BSc
S Horsman, MA, FRGS (*Head of Geography*)
Mrs A Hoverstadt, MSc (*Head of Careers*)
D A Jackson, BSc
Mrs D L Jackson, NNEB
N Jeram-Croft, BSc
Mrs A M Johnson, BA (*Head of Classics*)
Dr J E Johnstone, MPhys, PhD (*Head of Physics*)
M Jones, BA
Mrs R Leonard, BSc
Mrs H C Lewis, BA
Mrs F Lucas, BA (*Head of French*)
Mrs D A Manton, BEd
Miss C Martinez-Elviras
Mrs D Masters, Licence d'Anglais

Mr G Matthews, BSc (*i/c General Studies*)
Mrs S M Matthews, BSc (*Learning Support Coordinator*)
C J McAllister, BA (*Head of Philosophy, Theology and Religious Studies*)
Dr J B McDouall, BSc
Mrs N Meredith, BA (*Head of German*)
F Morris, BA
Mrs G M Mutch, BA
Mrs B A Myers, BA
Mrs L Nelson, BA
Mrs S Norton, BA
Miss C Owens
Ms M Pakay, BA
S C Parkin, MA (*Head of Year 11*)
K Pearson, BSc, BEd
G C Peat, BSc, MBA, CBiol, MIBiol, Cert Health Ed (*Head of Biology*)
Mrs S E Petrie, BA (*Head of Lower School*)
Mrs H M C Phillips, BEd
Miss S Plimmer, BA
Miss K Purchase, BSc
Mrs A Pye, BSc (*Head of Infants*)
Mrs B Rawling, BSc
Mrs L Roberts, BA
Miss E Roskell, BSc (*Head of Mathematics*)
Mrs S E Sanders, BSc
Mrs S Sanders, BEd
Mrs K Sargent, BA
Mrs J D Shand, MA
Mrs S Sharples, BSc (*Second in Maths Dept*)
M P Sparrow, BSocSci
Mrs J Stafford, BSc
Mrs J Sym, BEd
P Tann, BA (*Head of Upper School*)
Miss L H Tarnowski, MSc
S D Taylor, BSc
D A Thomson, BA
S Treadway, BEd
Mrs K M Turner, BA (*Head of Upper Sixth and Deputy Head of Sixth Form*)
M Turner (*Deputy Head of Junior School*)
P Upton, BEd
Mrs A J Vernon, BEd
Mrs K L Vlastos, BA
Miss S Walsh, BA
Miss M J Webster, BA
N O Westbrook, BA (*Head of English and Library*)
Mrs B J Williams, BSc (*Head of Year 8*)
J K Wilson, MPhil (*Head of Spanish and ECA Coordinator*)
J C Winter, BA (*Head of Sixth Form*)
A Wrathall, BSc (*Coordinator of A Level PE*)
Dr P J B Wright, MA, PhD
K Yearsley, BA (*Head of Art and Design*)

Visiting Staff:
French Assistant
German Assistant
Spanish Assistant
Specialist Music Teachers

Number in School. 1,390 (751 boys, 639 girls) of whom 301 are in the Junior School and 278 in the Sixth Form.

Location. The School which is about 10 miles south of Manchester, 3 miles from the Airport and 10 miles from the Derbyshire Hills consists of the original and many new buildings in its own 83 acres of open land.

Admission. Pupils are admitted as a result of assessment at age 4, and examination at age 7, 8, 9 and 11; to the Sixth Form for A Level work; or at other ages when chance vacancies occur.

The entrance test, which is competitive because many more children apply than places exist, is designed to deter-

mine that the child can profit from the type of education provided.

Organisation and Curriculum. For pastoral care and administrative purposes the School is divided into Sixth Form; Upper (Years 10 and 11); Middle (Years 8 and 9); Lower (Year 7); Juniors and Infants. The curriculum is kept as broad as possible to the end of Year 11 and no vital choice has to be made between Arts and Sciences until this point. In the Sixth Form pupils choose their AS and A2 Levels or Cambridge Pre-U exams from a wide range of subjects. Special provision is made for those who wish to enter Oxford or Cambridge. Extensions classes are available in all subjects.

On leaving virtually all pupils progress to University.

Clubs and Societies. There are many extra-curricular activities. These include a variety of music groups such as Concert Band, Big Band, Rock School, Wind and Guitar ensembles, Sinfonia and choirs, and there are annual dramatic and musical productions. Among the societies and clubs catering for those interested are The Ezekiel Brown Society, Brain Aerobics, Multimedia ICT, CHS TV,Geography, Language clubs including Russian, Italian, Spanish and German, Eco Soc, Design Challenge, CSI Science, Chess, Minimus Latin club, Classics club, War Gaming society, Climbing, a wide range of Sports clubs, Dance and Fitness Clubs, Philosophical Society and JSoc, Amnesty International, Model United Nations, Young Enterprise, Think Tank, 'Diggers' History, Student Industrial Society, Volunteer and Community Groups and many others. Large numbers of pupils undertake the school's own 'Cheadle Hulme Challenge' which introduces them to a variety of new skills and expeditions to develop organisational and leadership abilities and many undertake the Duke of Edinburgh's Award Scheme. Newly introduced 'Student Leader schemes' in over 50 extra-curricular clubs give older pupils the opportunity to gain experience and skills working with and coaching younger pupils.

Games and Physical Activities. There is a full range of the usual field and team games, and, additionally, in Year 11 and Sixth Form, Yoga, Badminton, Volleyball and Basketball. Swimming is for all in the School's heated indoor pool.

Fees per term (2011-2012). (*See Scholarship Entries section.*) Subject to termly review: Junior School £2,281–£2,448; Senior School £3,158.

New parents, who are not already in membership of the Foundation Scheme, will automatically be enrolled in it. The aim of the scheme is to assist pupils to remain in the School in the face of financial difficulty following the incapacitation or the death of a parent. Benefits cannot be guaranteed, but in recent years no deserving case has been refused.

Charitable status. Cheadle Hulme School is a Registered Charity, number 1077017.

Cheltenham College

Bath Road, Cheltenham, Gloucestershire GL53 7LD
Tel: College: 01242 265600
        Admissions: 01242 265662
        Bursar: 01242 265686
Fax: College: 01242 265630
        Headmaster: 01242 265685
        Bursar: 01242 265687
e-mail: admissions@cheltenhamcollege.org
website: www.cheltenhamcollege.org

Situated in 72 acres of beautiful grounds in the heart of the Cotswolds, Cheltenham College is one of the country's leading co-educational independent schools for boarding and day pupils aged 13–18. Combining a strong academic record with a considerable reputation for sport, drama, music and outward-bound activities, College offers an outstanding all-round education. Founded in 1841, it was the first of the great Victorian schools.

Motto: *'Labor Omnia Vincit.'*

Visitor: The Rt Revd The Lord Bishop of Gloucester

The Council:
President: The Revd J C Horan
Deputy President: Colonel J C A Smith

Dr R Acheson	Mr C Smyth
Mr L Anderson	Mr W Straker-Nesbit
Mrs J Blackburn	Mr D Levin
Mr P Brettell	Ms K Sayer
Mrs B Hodson-Cottingham	Mr M Wynne
Mrs V Isaac	Mr P Bernhard
Professor la Velle	Ms R Lewis
Mr E L Rowland	

Headmaster: **Dr A L R Peterken**, BA Durham, MA London, EdD Surrey

Bursar & Secretary to Council: Mr J Champion, FCIB

Deputy Head (Pastoral): Ms K L Davies, BA Cambridge
Deputy Head (Academic): Mr D J Byrne, BA Cambridge, MA Cambridge
Chaplain: The Reverend Dr A J Dunning, BA Oxford, PhD Birmingham
Senior Tutor: Mr A J Gasson, MA Dundee
Director of Admissions and Marketing: Mrs C Wood, BSc Sheffield

Special Responsibilities:
Director of Learning: Dr M P Plint, BEd Johannesburg, MEd, PhD Gloucestershire
Head of Upper College: Mr J O M Pepperman, MA Cantab
Head of Lower College: Mrs J O'Bryan, MSc, Nottingham
Head of Third Form: Ms S L Proudlove, BA Durham, MA York
Scholarships Coordinator: Mrs C E Conner, BA Hons Southampton
Head of Higher Education and Careers: Dr R D A Woodberry, MA Oxon, MLitt, PhD Bristol, FRSA
Director of Activities: Mr D R Faulkner, BSc Imperial
Tutor for International Pupils: Dr G L Jardim, BA Johannesburg, MTh Potchefstroom, PhD
Coordinator for the most able pupils: Mr J L Jones, BSc Wales, MSc Surrey, CChem, MRSC
Head of Critical Thinking: Dr S J C Morton, MSc, PhD Birmingham
Coordinator of PSHCE: Mr T P F Carpenter, BSc Bristol
Head of Community Service & 2 i/c PSHCE: Mr J C Stubbert, BEng Cardiff
Examinations Officer: Mr M C Brunt, BEd Bristol
Induction Tutor Coordinator: Mrs C E Harrison, BSc Warwick
Development Director: Mr A J Harris, BA, MA Wales

Housemasters and Housemistresses:
Ashmead Girls: Mrs A V Cutts, BEd Middlesex (*English & Drama*)
Boyne House Boys: Mr S F Bullock, BA Exeter (*Economics*)
Chandos Girls: Mrs H Merigot, BA Nottingham (*Modern Languages*)
Christowe Boys: Mr N Nelson, BA East Anglia (*History of Art*)
Hazelwell Boys: Mr S E Conner, BSc Durham (*Geography*)
Leconfield Boys: Mr C L Reid, BA Portsmouth, MA Ed Anglia Ruskin (*History & Politics*)
Newick House Boys: Mr F Llewellyn, BA London (*English and Theatre Studies*)
Queen's Day Girls: Mrs W Bates, BA, MA Nanterre, Paris (*Acting Housemistress*)
Southwood Day Boys: Mr B J Lambert, BSc Brunel (*Design Technology*)

Westal Girls: Mrs S M Jackson, TTD Johannesburg, FDE South Africa

Common Room:

Art:
Mr M H Ward, CertEd Westminster College, Oxford (*Head of Art*)
Mr N Nelson, BA East Anglia (*Head of History of Art*)
Mr P J Lelliott, BA Coventry, MA RCA
Miss S L Millyard, BA Cheltenham & Gloucester College of Higher Education
Ms M Bradshaw, BTEC Gloucestershire

Classics:
Mr T A Lambert, BA, MPhil King's College Cambridge (*Head of Classics*)
Mrs S Reid, BA, Dip CLASS Newcastle, PGCE Cantab
Miss S McNee, BA Cambridge

Design Technology:
Mr G J Cutts, BA Sheffield City (*Head of Design Technology*)
Mr B J Lambert, BSc Brunel
Ms B M Kaja, BA Bretton Hall College, West Yorkshire
Mr C P M McKegney, BA Loughborough

Economics & Business Studies:
Mrs A Chapman, BA Nottingham, MA Open University (*Head of Economics and Business Studies*)
Mr S F Bullock, BA Exeter
Mrs Z la Valette-Cooper, BA London Guildhall
Dr S J C Morton, MSc, PhD Birmingham
Mr M Todd, BComm Natal, CA SA
Mr M J Evetts, BSc Bath

English and Drama:
Mr T E Brewis, BA Exeter (*Head of English*)
Ms J E Brodigan, BA Reading (*Second in Department*)
Mr F J Llewellyn, BA Royal Holloway
Mr K A Cook, BA Southampton
Mrs A V Cutts, BEd Middlesex
Miss P J Morris, BA Durham
Mrs S M McBride, BA, MA Warwick (*Teacher i/c Drama*)
Miss G J-M de la Bat Smit, BA Oxford
Miss N J Wofford, BA Wales, MA UCL

English for Academic Purposes:
Ms S L Proudlove, BA Durham, MA York
Mr A Endicott, BA, MA TEFL

General Studies:
Mr T P F Carpenter, BSc Bristol (*Coordinator of Department*)

Geography:
Mr R J Penny, BSc Swansea (*Head of Geography*)
Mr S E Conner, BSc Durham
Mr A J Gasson, MA Dundee
Mr M W Stovold, CertEd Loughborough
Mr W Bates, BA Exeter

History & Politics:
Miss J E Doidge-Harrison, BA, MA Cantab (*Head of History*)
Mr J O M Pepperman, MA Cantab
Dr M D Jones, MA Cantab, PhD London
Dr R D A Woodberry, MA Oxon, MLitt, PhD Bristol, FRSA
Mr R Moore, BA Mancheste (*Head of Politics*)r
Mr C L Reid, BA Portsmouth, MA Ed Anglia Ruskin
Mr G H Williams, BSc Cheltenham & Gloucester College of Higher Education, MA Gloucestershire

Information Technology:
Mr A H Isaachsen, BEd Deakin, Melbourne (*Director of ICT*)
Mr G J Stuckey (*Network Director*)
Mr P C Provins, BA Anglia Ruskin (*Systems Manager*)

Learning Support:
Dr M P Plint, BEd Johannesburg, MEd, PhD
  Gloucestershire
Mrs I T M Pemberton, BA Oxford Brookes

Library:
Mrs G Doyle, MCLIP (*Librarian*)
Ms C Bleakley, MCLIP
Mrs M Cluer, BSE MLQ University, Philippines
Miss A-K Muehlberg, Dip LIS Aberystwyth

Mathematics:
Dr B E Enright, BSc, PhD Hull (*Head of Department*)
Mr J R Card, BSc Birmingham, MEd Birmingham
Dr P D Chipman, BSc Leeds, PhD Manchester
Mr J S Morton, BEng Imperial
Mr D R Faulkner, BSc Imperial
Mr R Peacock, BSc Bristol
Mr J C Stubbert, BEng Cardiff
Dr G A Ward, MEng Durham

Modern Languages:
Mr S J Brian, MA (*Head of Department*)
Mrs S L Checketts, BA Cardiff (*Second in Department*)
Mrs W A Bates, BA, MA Nanterre, Paris
Mrs G Fryer, Baccalaureat Serie A2, Nantes (*French
  Assistant*)
Mrs H K Mérigot, BA Nottingham
Mrs I T M Pemberton, BA Oxford Brookes (*German
  Assistant*)
Ms A S Lopez Reyes (*Spanish Assistant*)
Mr P J Weir, BA Durham
Mr J Coull, BA Thames Valley
Mrs E Leach, BA UWE
Mrs A Radway, BA, MA Nantes, MPhil Birmingham, PhD
  Bristol

Music:
Mr G S Busbridge, BA East Anglia, MMus, FRCO CHM,
  ADCM, LRAM, ARCM (*Director of Music*)
Mr A J McNaught, GRSM, LRAM, ARCM (*Assistant
  Director*)
Mr A M M Ffinch, MA Oxon, ARCM

Physical Education and Sports:
Mr M K Coley, BSc Leeds (*Head of Physical Education*)
Miss R K Cannon, BSc Exeter
Mr A Deadman, SRA, LTA (*Sports Complex Manager*)
Mr R Shepherd (*Squash Professional*)
Mr M P Briers (*Cricket & Rackets Professional*)
Mr R Lane, BSc Birmingham (*Hockey Professional*)
Mr J Cload, ACHE Portsmouth (*Officer i/c Shooting*)
Mr G Williams, BSc, MA Cheltenham and Gloucester
  College of Higher Education, MA University of
  Gloucestershire (*Hockey Professional*)

Religious Studies:
Dr G L Jardim, BA Johannesburg, MTh Potchefstroom,
  PhD(*Head of Department*)
The Reverend Dr A J Dunning, BA Oxford, PhD
  Birmingham
Dr A L R Peterken, BA Durham, MA London, EdD Surrey
Mr A G Peacock, BA Oxford, MA Lancaster

Science:
Mr T R C Adams, MA Oxon (*Head of Science, Head of
  Physics*)
Mr J L Jones, BSc Wales, MSc Surrey, CChem, MRSC
  (*Head of Chemistry*)
Dr E R Chare, BA Oxon, DPhil Oxon (*Head of Biology*)
Mrs C E Harrison, BSc Warwick
Mrs S Ramsay, BEd Durban
Mr M Debenham, MSc Liverpool, BSc Leeds
Mrs C Goodman, BSc Manchester
Mr T Carpenter, BSc Bristol
Mr M G P Alderton, MPhys Southampton
Mrs J M O'Bryan, BSc Nottingham

Mrs J L Smith, BSc Nottingham
Miss N Cornwell, BSc Bristol

CCF:
Mr R J Penny, BSc Swansea (*Contingent Commander*)
Major S G Clark, MBE (*College Adjutant*)
Regimental Quartermaster Serjeant A Jones (*College
  Marshall, Assistant SSI*)

Archives:
Mrs C A Leighton, BA London, DAA Aberystwyth
  (*Archivist*)
Mrs J Barlow, BA Cardiff, MA Illinois (*Assistant
  Archivist*)

Location. Stunning buildings and first-class playing
fields provide a magnificent setting near the centre of
Regency Cheltenham. Situated in the heart of the beautiful
Cotswolds with excellent road and rail connections with
London and the major airports, Cheltenham College offers
all the advantages of life in a thriving town community,
whilst maintaining a separate campus life.

Numbers. Boys: 330 boarders; 60 day boys. Girls: 150
boarders; 70 day girls.

Admission. Entry to College is into Third Form at 13+ or
Lower Sixth at 16+. Able pupils may also be admitted into
the Fourth Form at 14. Entry at 13 can be secured in three
ways: Common Entrance, College Entrance papers or College Academic Scholarship papers. Entry at 16+ can be
secured by scholarship and entry tests in November or
March, good GCSE predictions and a testimonial from previous school. Full details, prospectuses and application
forms can be obtained from the Admissions Department
who will always be glad to welcome parents who wish to see
College. There is a registration fee of £75 and a final acceptance fee of £950 (for pupils aged 13–16) or £1,250 (for
Sixth Form entrants) which is deducted from the final term's
account.

Scholarships and Bursaries. Awards are available for
entry at 13+ and for those joining the College at Sixth Form
level. In addition to academic scholarships and exhibitions,
awards are also made for Music, Drama, Art, Sport, Design
Technology and All-round Potential. Discounts for Services
Families and bursaries are also available.

Fees per term (2011-2012). Boarders £9,909, Day pupils
£7,425. Sixth Form: Boarders £10,209, Day pupils £7,725.

Chapel. There is a ten-minute service in the Chapel each
weekday morning and a main service each Sunday. There is
a Confirmation service every year.

Houses. The 10 Houses, eight boarding and two day, are
at the heart of College life and all located around the College
campus. Girls are in four houses, with day boarding having
been introduced in 2010, and boys are in six houses. Accommodation and pastoral care is outstanding for both boys and
girls.

Planned Developments. College is now entering a new
phase of development with exciting plans for a new library,
performing arts centre, science buildings and an art and
design centre.

Curriculum. On entry at 13, pupils follow a broad course
for one year, before embarking upon GCSE in the Fourth
Form. The core of the curriculum comprises: GCSE
English, Language and IGCSE English Literature, IGCSE
Mathematics, and all three Sciences (examined as IGCSE
Dual Science Award). All then choose at least one Modern
Language (French, German, Spanish); and four options
from Art, Design Technology (Resistant Materials, Textiles),
Drama, Geography, Greek, History, Latin, Music, PE and
Religious Studies. In the Sixth Form, twenty-five AS and
full A Level subjects as well as EPQ are offered. Boys and
girls and given extensive preparation for entrance to Oxford,
Cambridge and other universities. Over 95% of leavers go
on to university.

Cultural Activities. The Arts are central to the life of College, with at least six plays being staged each year in the school's various theatres. Boys and girls are encouraged to attend concerts, plays, films and lectures not only in Cheltenham but in nearby Oxford, Stratford, Bristol and London. College is also significantly involved in Cheltenham's Jazz, Science, Literature and Music Festivals. Art is housed in Thirlestaine House, a beautifully elegant early nineteenth century mansion, with a Gallery that houses an exhibition of current Art and that also serves as an excellent chamber music concert hall, housing the superb Bösendorfer Imperial Concert grand pianoforte. The beautiful Chapel houses a magnificent 3-manual Harrison & Harrison organ. Music plays a vital part in College life, with pupils able to learn just about every orchestral instrument imaginable, even bagpipes. The Chapel Choir, Chamber Choir and Barbershop groups enable singers to reach very high standards and many achieve university Choral Scholarships. The numerous instrumental groups and ensembles, from the Orchestra, Chamber Orchestra and Wind Band to the Jazz Bands and String Quartets, regularly perform in Cheltenham Town Hall, the town's Pump Rooms, as well as in the College Chapel and other venues. Both the top Jazz Band 'JIG' and the Chamber Choir have recorded CDs in the last few years.

Sports. Cheltenham College is one of the strongest schools nationally in a wide cross section of sports and benefits from top-level sports professionals and coaches. The main boys' games are rugby, hockey, tennis, cricket and rowing. The main girls' games are hockey, netball, tennis, cricket and rowing. In addition to the two astroturf pitches, the Sports Hall and swimming pool, there are excellent facilities for other sports, which include rackets, squash, golf, basketball, athletics, cross country, badminton, basketball, polo, climbing and shooting.

Activities. On entry to College, a structured programme of outdoor pursuits, team building exercises and leadership initiatives are provided for one year. Following this, CCF is compulsory for one year at age 14, optional thereafter. The Duke of Edinburgh's Award Scheme operates at Bronze and Gold level and a wide range of expeditions is available, including an annual trip to Nepal. College offers a full range of activities in the period after GCSEs. Up to 30 clubs operate weekly, including shooting, dance, pottery, film making and drama.

Service. There is a strong Community Service scheme which serves the town, and an Industrial Link scheme enables all College Sixth-formers to experience the world of work. The College's Humanitarian Aid Project raises funds for building and refurbishment work in a number of orphanages and schools and the members of the group regularly visit Romania and Kenya to provide practical assistance. Wherever possible, all College facilities are made available to the town, especially the festivals, and other schools.

University entry and Careers. There is a full-time teacher in charge of Careers, and another responsible for University and Higher Education advice. In addition, every Sixth-former has a tutor who is charged with ensuring that he or she is fully aware of the opportunities and challenges available.

Cheltonian Association. Tel: 01242 265694.

Cheltenham College Junior School. *For details see entry in IAPS section.*

Charitable status. Cheltenham College is a Registered Charity, number 311720. As a charity it is established for the purpose of providing an efficient course of education for boys and girls.

Chetham's School of Music

Long Millgate, Manchester M3 1SB
Tel: 0161 834 9644

Fax: 0161 839 3609
e-mail: chets@chethams.com
website: www.chethams.com

Chetham's is a co-educational school for boarding and day students aged eight to eighteen. The School teaches a broad curriculum set within a framework of music. At the centre of every child's course is a 'musical core' of experiences rooted in a determination to educate the whole person. Originally founded in 1653, through the Will of Humphrey Chetham, as a Bluecoat orphanage, the School was reconstituted in 1969 as a specialist music school.

Governors:
Dame A V Burslem, DBE (*Chairman*)
R Bailey
Mrs S Berry
Councillor P Fairweather
The Very Revd Rogers Govender, Dean of Manchester Cathedral
Prof E Gregson, BMus, GRSM, LRAM, FRAM
Dr R Haylock
Professor G D Henderson
Dr D Hill
R Kiel
P Lee
Mrs J Pickering
Mrs R Pike, JP
P Ramsbottom, MusB, FCA
A Simpkin
J Wainwright, BA

Staff:

Head: Mrs Claire Hickman, MA

Director of Music: S Threlfall, GRNCM Hons, FRSA
Bursar: Mrs S C Newman, BSc Hons, FCA
Deputy Head, Pastoral: Ms C Rhind, BA
Deputy Head, Curriculum: C Newman, MA, MSc

Music:

Music Department Coordinator: I Mayer, BA
Concert Administrator: A Duncan, BA
Music Department Timetabler: Mrs J Stuckey

Key:
Chamber Music Tutor
(*Hallé*) *Member of Hallé Orchestra*
(*BBC*) *Member of BBC Philharmonic*
* *Tutor at Royal Northern College of Music*
(*O.North*) *Member of Opera North Company*
(*RLPO*) *Member of Royal Liverpool Philharmonic Orchestra*
X *Manchester Camerata*
(*CBSO*) *Member of City of Birmingham Symphony Orchestra*

Brass:
Head of Department: David Chatterton
Euphonium Tutors: Bill Millar #, David Thornton #*
Horn Tutor: Elizabeth Davis #*
Guest Tutor: Richard Watkins
Tenor Horn Tutor: Lesley Howie *
Percussion Tutors: Dave Walsh (*Kit*), Sophie Hastings (*Latin percussion and Kit*), David Hext (*Hallé*), Paul Patrick (*BBC*)#*
Trombone Tutors: Robert Burtenshaw #(*O.North*), Les Storey #, Philip Goodwin #
Guest Tutor: Andrew Berryman *(*Hallé*)
Trumpet Staff: David Chatterton #
Tutors: John Dickinson *#, Murray Greig *# (*O.North*), Tracey Redfern #X, Gareth Small (*Hallé*)#, Tom Osborne (*Hallé*)
Tuba Tutors: Brian Kingsley *#(*O.North*)

Keyboard:
Head of Department: Murray McLachlan *
Staff: Susan M Bettaney #, Simon Bottomley #, Peter Lawson *
Tutors: Pauline Alston, Alison Havard, Susan M Bettaney #, Simon Bottomley #, Hazel Fanning, John Gough, Marta Karbownicka, Helen Krizos *, Peter Lawson *, Murray McLachlan #, Jeffrey Makinson, Jonathan Middleton, Dina Parakhina *, Marie-Louise Taylor, Kathleen Uren #, Masa Tayama, Graham Caskie
Visiting tutors: Kathryn Stott #, John Lill, Peter Donohoe
Accordion Tutors: Murray Grainger
Harpsichord Tutor: Charlotte Turner
Jazz Piano Tutor: Les Chisnall, Visiting Tutor: Gwylim Simcock
Organ Tutors: Christopher Stokes, Andrew Dean, Jeffrey Makinson
Chamber Tutors: Benjamin Frith, Jeremy Young

Strings:
Head of Department: Nicholas Jones
Assistant: Cathrine Perkins
Senior Chamber Music Tutor: Graham Oppenheimer
Violin Staff: Cathrine Perkins
Tutors: Kristoffer Dolatko, Mikhail Gurevitch, Benedict Holland *, Eyal Kless, Adrian Levine #, Wen Zhou Li *, Marije Ploemacher #, Maciej Rakowski *, Jan Repko *, Cathy Studman, Xander Van Vliet #, Deirdre Ward, Connie del Vecchio (*RLPO*), Yumi Sasaki
Guest Violin Tutors: Alf Richard Kraggerud
Viola Tutors: Adrian Levine, Graham Oppenheimer #, Cathrine Perkins #
Cello Staff: Nicholas Jones # *, Stephen Threlfall #
Tutors: Barbara Grunthal X, Christopher Hoyle (*BBC*), David Smith #, Gillian Thoday
Double Bass Tutor: Yi Xin Salvage (*Hallé*), Steve Berry (*jazz*)
Guest Double Bass Tutor: Cathy Elliot
Harp Tutor: Gabriella Dall'Olio
Guitar Tutors: Wendy Jackson #
Lute Tutor: Hugh Cherry
Guest Chamber Music Tutors: Bruno Schrecker, Pavel Fischer

Woodwind:
Head of Department: Belinda Gough
Recorder/Baroque Ensembles Tutor: Alan Davis *, Chris Orton
Baroque Flute: Martyn Shaw
Oboe Tutors: Rachael Clegg X, Valerie Taylor *, Stephane Rancourt (*Hallé*)
Flute Tutors: Katherine Baker (*Hallé*), Rachel Forgreive *, Belinda Gough #, Laura Jellicoe #*, Linda Verrier #*, Peter Lloyd, Claudia Lashmore
Orchestral Tutor: Richard Davis (*BBC*)*
Clarinet Tutors: Rosa Campos-Fernandez (*Hallé*), Jim Muirhead (*Hallé*)#, Jo Patton (*CBSO*), Robert Roscoe #, Andrew Wilson #
Saxophone Tutors: Iain Dixon (*Jazz*), Jim Muirhead (*Hallé*), Andrew Wilson #
Guest Tutor: Rob Buckland *
Bassoon Tutors: Graham Salvage (*Hallé*), Anthea Wood
Contra-Bassoon Tutor: Steve McGee *(*Hallé*)

Vocal Department:
Tutors: Helen Francis #, Oliver White, Diana Palmerston
Consultant: Jane Highfield

Staff Accompanists:
Heads of Department: Brenda Blewett, Nicholas Oliver
Staff: Elena Namilova, Martyn Parkes, Hilary Suckling

Composition:
Head of Department: Dr Jeremy Pike
Staff: Dr Gavin Wayte

Music Technology:
Head of Department: Dr Jeremy Pike
Staff: Simon Chaplin, Adrian Horn

Big Band:
Directors: Richard Iles, Jim Muirhead (*Hallé*)

Improvisation:
Steve Berry *, Les Chisnall (*Keyboard*), Iain Dixon

Academic Music:
S King, BA, MA, MPhil, PhD
M Bussey, MA
Miss C Campbell Smith, MA
J LeGrove, BA
D Mason, BA
A Dean, MMus, FRCO, ARCM
Mrs S Noon, MC
Dr S Murphy

Languages:
C Law, PhD, MA
P Chillingworth, BA
Mrs S Clough, BA
Mrs M Potts, BA

English:
Miss G Simpson, MA
P Dougal, MA
I Little, BA
J Runswick-Cole, MEd

Drama:
P Dougal, MA

Special Needs/Compensatory Education:
Mrs B L Owen, BEd, RSA, DipSLD
Miss L Fogg, MA
Miss C Lynch, BA

Sciences:
P Przybyla, BSc
J Blundell, BSc
Mrs A Dack, BSc
A Henderson, BA
J Thomson, MSc

Mathematics & Information Technology:
C Crowle, BSc
C Bramall, BA
Mrs F Holker, BSc
E Kimber, PhD

Humanities:
A Kyle, BA
C Newman, MA
Mrs P Rigby, BA

Art:
Miss A Boothroyd, BA
Mrs J Jones, BA

Recreation:
Ms I Staszko, BEd, MA
Miss C Whittaker, BA

PSE & RE:
Miss H Woods, BA
A Poole, MA

Primary:
D Harris, BA

Librarian: Mrs R Jones, MA

Careers:
P G Lawson, GRSM, ARMCM (*Music Colleges*)
C Newman, MA (*Universities*)
Mrs R Jones, MA

Houses:
Mr & Mrs J Runswick-Cole (*Boys' House*)

Miss I Patel (*Girls' House*)
Mr G Taylor (*Victoria House*)

School Doctor: Dr J Tankel
Nurse: Mrs K Scott, RGN
Head's PA: Mrs L Haslam

The School numbers 296 students, of whom 153 are girls. There are 213 boarders. Admission is solely by musical audition, and any orchestral instrument, keyboard, guitar, voice or composition, may be studied. Each student studies two instrumental studies, or voice and one instrument, as well as following academic courses which lead to GCSE and A Levels and to university entrance and music college. The School stands on the site of Manchester's original 12th century Manor House adjacent to the Cathedral, and is housed partly in the fine 15th century College Building, around which are grouped Palatine Building (1846), Millgate Building (1870, formerly The Manchester Grammar School), the 'Chapel' (1878) and the classroom and laboratory block (1954).

Music. Instrumental tuition is guided and monitored by the advisers in each specialism, who visit regularly to survey students' work, conduct internal examinations and give Master Classes. Internationally renowned musicians hold residences at the School for string, wind, brass, percussion and keyboard players. The Director of Music has responsibility for the full-time Music Staff and also for about 100 visiting tutors. All students receive three sessions of individual instrumental tuition each week. Practice is rigorously set and supervised. Academic Music is normally studied at A Level.

Boarding. There are two boarding houses for girls and boys aged 13 to 18 and one for Juniors aged 8 to 13. Each House is run by Houseparents in residence, with resident assistants. All members of staff act as Tutors and are involved with pastoral care. In addition, when necessary, students have open access to the School Counsellors.

Recreation. Serious attention is paid to recreation, PE and games and the students' physical well-being. On-site facilities include an indoor swimming pool, gym, multi-gym and a squash court.

Applications, Visits. The Prospectus and application forms are sent on request and are available on the school's website: www.chethams.com. Preliminary assessment auditions are held throughout the year, with final auditions in the Christmas and Spring terms. Parents and prospective students are welcome to visit the School, by arrangement with the Head's PA.

Fees, Grants. (*See Scholarship Entries section.*) All entrants from the United Kingdom are eligible for grants from Central Government. Parental contribution to cost is calculated according to circumstances under the Department for Education Scheme.

Choristers. The School is a member of the Choir Schools' Association and Choristerships at Manchester Cathedral for day boys and girls are available under a separate scheme. Choristers' Fee: £9,480 pa (subject to Cathedral Bursaries).

Charitable status. Chetham's School of Music is a Registered Charity, number 526702. It exists to educate exceptionally gifted young musicians.

Chigwell School

Chigwell, Essex IG7 6QF
Tel: 020 8501 5700
Fax: 020 8500 6232
e-mail: hm@chigwell-school.org
website: www.chigwell-school.org

The School was founded in 1629 by Samuel Harsnett, Archbishop of York, "to supply a liberal and practical education, and to afford instruction in the Christian religion, according to the doctrine and principles of the Church of England". William Penn, founder of Pennsylvania, is the most famous Old Chigwellian.

Today the School welcomes boys and girls from all backgrounds and is a lively, happy community in which pupils are encouraged to develop all their talents to the full.

The School became co-educational in September 1997 and currently there are over 743 pupils, including 27 international boarders.

Motto: '*Aut viam inveniam aut faciam*', '*Find a Way or Make a Way*'.

Governing Body:
Chairman: C P de Boer, Esq
Vice Chairman: D Morriss, Esq, BSc, CEng, FIET, FBCS, CITP
Mrs P B Aliker, BA, MBA, ACMA
J Cullis, Esq, MBE, BA, MSc
Sir Richard Dales, KCVO, CMG, MA
N Garnish, Esq, BSc, MBA, MCMI
M Higgins, Esq
Mrs F T Jamieson, LLB, DipM
The Revd M Lambert, BSc, MA, MPhil
Dr A Pruss, BSc, PhD, MBBS
The Revd G R Smith, AKC
R H Youdale, Esq, MA

Clerk to the Governors: G Norman, Esq, BSc Econ

Bursar: D N Morrison, MA, PGCE

Headmaster: M E Punt, MA, MSc, PGCE

Deputy Head: D J Gower, BSc, PGCE

Head of the Junior School: S C James, BA, PGCE

Deputy Head of the Junior School: A Stubbs, BA

Assistant Staff:
* *Head of Department*
† *Housemaster/mistress*

Mrs A M Aitken, MA
E Aitken, MA (*Art and Design*)
Ms S Bell, BA
Mrs K S Bint, BSc (*PE & Girls Games*)
Ms L M Bloxsidge, BA, G DipEd
Mrs J M Botham, BSc
Mrs J M Boughton, BA
M L Bradley, BA, MMus, MLitt
Dr P F Burd, BSc, PhD (*Third Master*)
S M Chaudhary, MA (*Mathematics*)
GG Clapp, BEd
Dr P G Clayton, BSc, PhD
S Coppell, MA (*Modern Languages*)
Ms E Creber, BSc
Mrs S T Davies, MA
Miss S L Dick, BSc
W P Eardley, BSc (*Biology*)
H J G Ebden (*Music*)
Miss L M Edwards, BA
K Farrant, BEd (*Boys Games*)
Mrs E M P Feeney, L-ès-L
P R Fletcher, MA, DipTEFL
Mrs A L Gehrke, BA
S J Goodfellow, MA (*Religious Studies*)
D J L Harston, MA
D W Hartland, MA (*Geography*)
R J Hartley, BA
Miss A Hurribunce, DipEd (*†Lambourne*)
G S Inch, BA (*Senior Master*)
Mrs S Inch, BEd
Mrs V C James, BEd

Mrs N A Jermyn, MEd, BA (*Design & Technology*)
Mrs N J Jones, BA
Mrs L Joughin, BEd
C K Lawrence, BSc
Miss F M Leach, BMus
A Long, MSc (*Head of Sixth Form*)
R A F Lonsdale, MA
C J Lord, MA (*Classics*)
H J Lukesch, 1st & 2nd STEX (*German*)
J L Maingot, BA (*Drama*)
J H Martin, MA (*History*)
Dr T Martin, PhD (*Chemistry*)
A McKenzie, MA
F Meier, BA
Mrs V G Meier, BA
Dr B H Mistry, MMath, PhD
Miss J Mitchell, BEd
J P Morris, BSc (*†Penns*)
D N Morrison, MA
D J Morse, BA (*Academic IT*)
R C Ogle, BA (*†Caswalls*)
Ms J Osborne, BEd (*Learning Support*)
D I Patel, BSc
The Revd S N Paul, BA (*Chaplain*)
S B Pepper, BA
Mrs P Pewsey, BSEd, TEFL
Mrs R J Philip, BEd
J S Porter, BA (*†Swallow's*)
D P Rabbitte, BA, LLB
Mrs E R Rea, MA (*English*)
B Rees, CertEd
Ms P S Rex, BA
N M Saunders, BSc (*Director of Studies*)
M P Slocombe, BA
R S Spicer, BA (*Economics*)
J M Stedman, BA
Ms M C Teichman, BSc
Mrs C E Tilbrook, BEd, DipSEA
Miss S E Wales, BA
Miss M Weeks, BSc
Mrs S E Welsford, BEd
B Wille, BSc
S C Wilson, MEd, BSc

Admissions Registrar: Mrs J S Long

Medical Officer: Dr I Hussain, MBBS, MRCGP, DRCOG, DCH

Location. Chigwell School stands in a superb green belt location in 70 acres of playing fields and woodlands, midway between Epping and Hainault Forests and enjoys excellent communications. It is easily accessible from London (by Central Line Undergound network). Both the M25 and M11 motorways are close by, while Heathrow, Gatwick, City of London, Stansted and Luton Airports are all reachable from the School within the hour.

Buildings. The original building is still in use and houses the Senior School Swallow Library. There has been a considerable amount of building in the past years and all the older buildings have been modernised while retaining their character. New facilities include a Junior School classroom block, a new Junior School library, a state-of-the-art Drama Centre, new catering facilities, a Sixth Form coffee shop, upgraded boys' boarding houses and a superb floodlit all-weather pitch.

Organisation. The School is divided into the Senior and Junior Schools but is administered as a single unit with a common teaching staff.

The Head of the Junior School is responsible for all pupils between the ages of 7 and 13, although teaching from Year 7 upwards is coordinated by the Senior School. The Junior School is on the same site as the Senior School and all facilities and grounds are used by Junior pupils. Assembly, Games and Lunch are all arranged separately from the Senior School. (*For further details, see Junior School entry in IAPS section.*)

In the Senior School, all the day pupils and boarders are divided into four Day Houses. Each House has a large House room, studies for Senior pupils and a Housemaster's or Housemistress's study.

Curriculum. Pupils follow a broad based course leading to GCSE. Maths, English, Science and one modern language form the common core of subjects. Science is taken either as three separate subjects (Physics, Biology, Chemistry) or as Coordinated Science. In addition, a wide range of options is taken at GCSE including Art and Design, Graphic Design, Design Technology, French, German, Spanish, Latin, Greek, Geography, History, Religious Studies, Drama and Music.

Sixth Form. Students take 4 AS Level subjects in the first year and 3 or 4 A2 Level subjects in the second year. Subjects taken include, Latin, Greek, Classical Civilisation, French, German, Spanish, English, Economics, History, Geography, Maths, Further Maths, Physics, Chemistry, Biology, Music, Art, Design and Technology, Religious Studies, PE and Theatre Studies.

Games and Activities. Cricket, Football, Netball, Hockey (Boys and Girls), Athletics, Cross-Country Running, Swimming, Squash, Tennis, Golf, Basketball and Badminton. There are numerous School Societies and a Venture Scout Troop. Many pupils join The Duke of Edinburgh's Award scheme. There is a swimming pool, two Sports Halls and extensive playing fields on site.

Art & Design, Ceramics, and D & T. Art is taught throughout the School and there is excellent provision for Ceramics and D & T which form part of the curriculum for all pupils between the ages of 10 and 14.

Music. There are three Orchestras, two Wind Bands, one Swing Band and six Choirs. Many other ensembles flourish and perform at major concerts during the year, some of which take place in the local community. Pupils may learn any instrument (including the Organ).

Boarding. Boy Boarders are accommodated in Church House, run by Mr and Mrs Meier, and Harsnett's House, run by Mr and Mrs Saunders. Sandon Lodge, set in the middle of the beautiful School Grounds, accommodates Sixth Form Girl Boarders under the care of Dr and Mr Lord. Hainault House, under the supervision of Mr and Mrs McKenzie, lies adjacent to the Junior School and offers accommodation for girls.

Fees per term (2011-2012). Full boarding £7,665; Day pupils £3,330–£4,846. Fees vary depending on age. Fees are inclusive of all tuition, meals (lunch and afternoon tea), textbooks, societies and most clubs.

Admission. Pupils usually join Chigwell School at 7+, 8+, 11+, 13+ or 16+.

Scholarships and Bursaries. Academic scholarships are awarded each year, primarily at 11 and 16. They are awarded in recognition of academic merit, irrespective of financial means.

A competitive examination for Academic scholarships is held each year during the Lent Term for pupils aged 11+ and during the Michaelmas Term for pupils aged 16+.

Music scholarships are also awarded at age 11. Music, Art and Drama scholarships are available at age 16.

Chigwell has always tried to ensure that children who would benefit from an education at the School are not excluded for financial reasons. A number of means-tested Bursaries are offered.

Further details can be obtained from the Admissions Registrar (email: admissions@chigwell-school.org).

The Old Chigwellians' Association. c/o Development Office, Chigwell School, Essex.

Charitable status. Chigwell School is an Incorporated Charity, registration number 1115098. It exists to provide a rounded education of the highest quality for its pupils.

Christ College
Brecon

Brecon, Powys LD3 8AF
Tel: 01874 615440 (Head)
         01874 615440 (Bursar)
Fax: 01874 615475
e-mail: enquiries@christcollegebrecon.com
website: www.christcollegebrecon.com

Founded by Henry VIII, 1541. Reconstituted by Act of Parliament, 1853.
   Motto: '*Possunt quia posse videntur.*'

Visitor: Her Majesty The Queen

Governing Body:
The Revd Professor D P Davies, MA, BD (*Chairman*)
The Rt Revd The Lord Bishop of Swansea and Brecon
The Venerable The Archdeacon of Brecon
J Bartlett
W R M Chadwick, JP
D G Clarke, TD, OBE, DL
Prof R B Davies
M Gittins
Mrs S A E Gwyer Roberts, BA, MEd, NPQH, FRSA
R J Harbottle, BA
Mrs J James
Sir Roger Jones, OBE, BPharm, MSc
The Hon Mrs E S J Legge-Bourke, LVO, Lord Lieutenant
   of Powys
P Lewis
A L Price, CBE, QC, MA
Mrs K Silk
A Whittall
Mrs J M E Williams

Registrar: T J P Davenport, LLB

Head: Mrs Emma Taylor, MA Oxon

Deputy Head: S A Spencer, BA (*English*)

Director of Studies: J D Bush, MA (*English*)

Assistant Staff:
* *Head of Department*
† *Housemaster/mistress*

Mrs R E Allen, BA (**History*)
C Andras, BA (*Welsh/Modern Languages*)
The Revd S A Baker, BEd (*Chaplain*)
†Mrs E Blatt, BSc (*Biology*)
N C Blackburn, BSc (**Mathematics*)
P Chandler, BA (*EAL*)
J T Cooper, BA, ARCO (*Director of Choral Music*)
†A Copp, BSc (*Economics*)
P E Curran, BSc (*Information Technology*)
Mrs J K Curran (*Drama*)
P K Edgley, ARPS (*Photography*)
Mrs U Feldner, BA (*Art*)
Mrs C N Forde-Halpin, BA (*Mathematics*)
D R Grant, BSc (*Chemistry*)
†G Halpin, BSc (*Business Studies*)
Miss H J Havard, BA (*Modern Languages*)
Dr G Horridge, BA, PhD (*History*)
Mrs A Hefford, BA (**Art*)
G Hope, BEng, MSc (**Physics & Science*)
Mrs J Hope, MA (**English*)
†Mrs N C John, BSc (*PSHE*)
Miss S E Jones, BSc (*Biology*)
Mrs F Kilpatrick, BA, RSA DipSpLD, AMBDA
   (**Learning Support*)
D A Lyon, BA (*Geography*)
Mrs L McLean, BA (**Modern Languages*)

I J Owen, BSc (*Mathematics*)
Dr D Phelps, MA, PhD (**History*)
A Reeves, BSc (*Physics*)
R G Rogers, BA (**Design & Technology*)
†P Shannon, BSc (*Mathematics*)
†M P Sims, BSc (**Biology*)
R C Slaney, BA (**EAL*)
P W Smith, BSc, PhD, MRSC, CChem (**Chemistry*)
Miss M K E Tanner, MA (*English*)
C Thomas (*Physics*)
N E Thomas, BSc (**Geography*)
T J Trumper, BEd (*PE*)
Miss E Warren, BA (*Modern Languages*)
C J Webber, BEd (**PE*)
Mrs L Webber, CertEd, DipPsych, MEd Psych (*PE*)
R West, MSc (*Director of Music*)
G M Wolstenholme, BA (**Business Studies and Careers*)

Visiting Music Staff:
A S Davies, GWCMD
J C Herbert
G Hamlin
Ms S Fairplay
Mrs E Prosser
Miss E Priday, LRAM, ARAM
I Russell
Mrs D Taylor
T Cronin
Mrs C E Walker, MA Oxon, ARCM

Medical Officer: Dr M B J Heneghan, BSc, MB, BCh,
   MRCP, DRCOG

Bursar: K C Dempsey
Admissions Registrar: Mrs M L Stephens
SSI: WO2 M Bevan
OBA Liaison: H L P Richards
Development Director: S Maggs, BA, GCGI, PMICS

   Christ College, Brecon lies in a setting of outstanding natural beauty at the foot of the Brecon Beacons on the edge of the small market town of Brecon, two minutes walk away on the opposite side of the river. The River Usk flows alongside the playing fields providing good canoeing and fishing while the nearby Llangorse Lake is available for sailing and windsurfing.
   The school was founded by King Henry VIII in 1541 when he dissolved the Dominican Friary of St Nicholas. The 13th Century Chapel and Dining Hall are at the centre of school life and the school's mix of important, historic buildings and modern architecture represents the continuity of education at the school. In the last ten years additional boarding capacity has been added to a girls house, all of the houses have been refurbished, an Astroturf built as well as Fitness Suite, the Art School re-located and expanded while a Sixth Form Centre renovated as well as extensive landscaping of the school campus. Most recently, a £1.5m Science Centre has been opened. Most pupils in the last two years of school enjoy single study-bedrooms.
   Estyn, Her Majesty's Inspectorate for Education & Training in Wales, inspected the school in 2011 and rated the school's current performance as 'excellent' with 'excellent prospects for improvement'.
   Organisation. Christ College was a boys' only school until 1987 when girls were admitted to the Sixth Form. In 1995 the school became fully co-educational. There are 340 pupils in the school of whom 195 are boys and 144 girls. Approximately 66% of pupils board and there are three senior boys' houses, School House, Orchard House (about to be extended) and St David's House, two senior girls' houses, Donaldson's House and de Winton House (recently extended), and a junior house, Alway House, for 11–13 year old boys and girls. The school eats centrally in a Dining Hall dating from the 13th century but served by modern kitchens.

Chapel. Chapel services are conducted in accordance with the liturgy of the Anglican church, but entrance to Christ College is open to boys and girls of all faiths. The ownership of Chapel by the boys and girls, demonstrated through their participation in services and their singing, is a feature of the school. Pupils are prepared for Confirmation by the School's Chaplain who lives on site.

Curriculum. Up to the Fifth Form pupils follow a balanced curriculum leading to GCSE at which most pupils take 10 subjects. Options are chosen at the end of form 3 (Year 9).Current subjects taught include English Language, English Literature, Mathematics, French, Spanish, Physics, Chemistry, Biology, History, Geography, Latin, Religious Studies, Art, Music, Design & Technology, Business Studies, Physical Education, Photography, Drama, PSE, Information Technology and Welsh. Greek is sometimes available as an extra subject outside the timetable.

In the Sixth Form a similar range of subjects is taken at AS and A2 Level plus opportunities to take Economics, Further Mathematics and Philosophy. All pupils have timetabled tutorial periods and in the Sixth Form periods are set aside for Careers advice. The school has recently introduced the new 'Extended Project' for Sixth Form pupils.

Class sizes rarely exceed 20 up to GCSE and average fewer than 10 at A Level.

Games. The main school games are Rugby Football, Cricket, Hockey, Soccer, Netball, Cross-Country and Athletics. Tennis, Badminton, Squash, Volleyball, Basketball, Golf, Fishing, Swimming, Shooting, Mountain Biking, Canoeing, Fencing, Indoor Cricket, Climbing, Triathlon and Aerobics are also available. The playing fields are extensive and lie adjacent to the school. Christ College has entered into a corporate partnership with Cradoc Golf Club, two miles outside of Brecon, to encourage pupils of all ages and experience in the fundamentals of the game of golf. The opportunity to play at Cradoc Golf Club and receive professional instruction is also extended to all parents of pupils attending Christ College. A recent initiative with The Pony Club also means that equestrians now have access to a British Eventing standard course at the nearby Glanusk Estate.

Thursday Afternoons. On Thursday afternoons the CCF Contingent meets. There is a choice between Royal Navy, Army and Royal Air Force sections and the CCF has its own Headquarters, Armoury and covered 30m Range in the school grounds. Pupils take their proficiency certificate after two years and may then choose to continue as Instructors, undergo training for the Duke of Edinburgh's Award Scheme or leave the CCF and may become involved in community service.

Music. The Chapel Choir is large and enjoys a good reputation with radio and television broadcasts as well as overseas tours to its credit. As befits a school in Wales singing on all school occasions is committed, energetic and frequently with natural harmony. The school has a Jazz Band, a junior orchestra and its pupils play a prominent role in the South Powys Youth Orchestra. There are many other opportunities to play in ensemble groups throughout the school. Individual instrumental and singing lessons are delivered by visiting musicians.

Activities. In addition to sporting pastimes a wide range of activities are available to pupils including Sixth Form Film Society, Advanced Chemistry, Archery, Art, Ballet/ Dance, Badminton, Basketball, Brass Group, Canoeing, Chamber Choir, Chess, Choir, Climbing, Community Service, Disability Sport, Drama, Fencing, Fitness, Golf, Indoor Cricket, Jazz Band, Mandarin Chinese, Modern Language Film Society, Music Practice, Music Theory, Percussion Group, Shooting, Stage Management, String Group, String Quartet, Technology, Wado Kai Karate and Young Enterprise. The Duke of Edinburgh's Award Scheme has been popular for many years and the majority of pupils gain at least a Bronze award, and a significant number go on to achieve the Gold award.

Overseas Travel is frequent and extensive. In recent years tours, expeditions and exchanges have taken place to Beijing, Canada, Japan, Nepal, New York, Shanghai, Tibet and Barbados as well as a number of European destinations.

Careers. Three members of staff also serve in the Careers department which also enlists the help of the Independent Schools Careers Organisation as well as the local Careers organisations. Former pupils return annually for Careers evenings and in this the Old Breconian Association is very helpful.

Entrance. Pupils are admitted at the age of 11 and 13 following the school's own entrance papers in English and Mathematics plus an IQ test, school report and interview. These tests are usually held in Jan/Feb but individual arrangements can be made. The majority of 11 year old entrants come from local State Primary Schools, those at 13 from Preparatory schools when, instead of the Common Entrance examination, pupils face the same entrance procedures as at 11. Boys and girls also enter the Sixth Form on the basis of GCSE grade estimates, an IQ test and an interview.

Term of Entry. Pupils are accepted in the Michaelmas, Lent and Summer terms.

Scholarships. (*See Scholarship Entries section.*) The maximum value of scholarships is half fees. Scholarships are available for entry aged 11, 13 and 16. At 11 the scholarships are awarded for Academic, Music and Sporting prowess. At 13 additionally for all-rounders, Art and Science. At Sixth Form on the same basis as at 13.

Bursaries are available at all ages and are subject to a means-test. Fees remissions are available for sons and daughters of Clergy, children of Service Personnel and for the sons and daughters of those currently in the teaching profession.

Fees per term (2011-2012). Years 7 and 8: Day £4,150; Boarders £5,710. Years 9–13: Day £4,725; Boarders £7,300.

Charitable status. Christ College, Brecon is a Registered Charity, number 525744. Its aims and objectives are to provide a fully rounded education for boys and girls between the ages of 11 and 18.

Christ's Hospital

Horsham, West Sussex RH13 0LJ
Tel: 01403 252547
Fax: 01403 255283
e-mail: hmsec@christs-hospital.org.uk
website: www.christs-hospital.org.uk

Head Master: **John Franklin**, BA, MEd

Deputy Heads:
B Vessey, BA, MA (*History*)
Mrs J Thomson, BA (*English*)

Chaplain:
Revd S Golding, BA, MA (*Theology & Philosophy*)

Assistant Staff:
* Head of Department

P A Andersen, BA (*History*)
J Anderson, BA (*Geography*)
Dr P Attwell, PhD (*Biology*)
Miss J Azancot, BA (*Design & Technology*)
R S Baker, BEd (*Geography, Physical Education*)
A C Bawtree, BA (**Music*)
Dr R Brading, BA, MA, PhD (*English*)
Mrs E A Callaghan (*Theology & Philosophy*)
T J Callaghan, BMus, LRAM (*Music*)
J B Callas, BSc (**Biology*)
K Camburn, BA (*Economics & Mathematics*)
R M Castro, BSc (*Mathematics*)

G N Chandler, BA (*Computer Studies, Languages*)
J W Cherry, BA, MPhil (*Theology & Philosophy*)
Miss M Ciechanowicz, BA (*Languages*)
M Commander, BEng (*Physics*)
S A Cowley, BA (*Art*)
Mrs J Davey (*Housemistress*)
P Deller, BA (**Art*)
Miss L E Donald, BA, MA (*Art*)
P L Dutton, MA, ARCO (*Music*)
Mrs V C Dutton, BEng, MSc (*Physics*)
S T Eason, BA, MIL (*Languages*)
Mrs M A Fleming, BA (**Classics*)
N M Fleming, BA, DipArch, LRPS (**Archaeology*)
Mrs A K Franklin, BA, MA (*English*)
Miss S Gamba, BMus (*Music*)
A H Goddard, BA, MA, PhD (*History*)
Mrs M K Golding, BA, MA (*SEN*)
D Griffiths, BSc (*Mathematics*)
P H Hall-Palmer, BA (**Design & Technology*)
Dr K H Hannavy, BSc, DPhil (*Chemistry*)
E Hansen, BA (*Biology, Chemistry*)
E W G Hatton, BA (**Classics*)
P J P Heagerty, MA (**German*)
Mrs C M Hennock, MA (*Mathematics*)
A E Henocq, BSc (*Chemistry*)
J Herbert, BA, PhD (**English*)
H P Holdsworth, BA, CertEd (*English*)
P D Holland, BA (*Languages*)
V R Holme, BEd (*Design & Technology*)
I B Howard, MA (*Languages*)
Mrs C E Jacques, BSc (**Chemistry*)
P Jacques, BA (*History*)
M R Jennings, BA, PhD (*History*)
Dr E Keane, PhD (*History*)
D M L Kirby, BA (*English, Theology & Philosophy*)
S Last, BA, MA (*Mathematics*)
Miss H Lewis, BA (*Housemistress*)
J D Lewis, BSc (**History, SENCo*)
P C Lewis, BA (**Economics*)
Miss F Mackenzie, MA (*Librarian*)
Mrs C L Martin, BSc (*Biology*)
S Mason, BSc (**Physics*)
A Mayhew, BSc (*Mathematics*)
K McArtney, BA (*Computer Studies*)
Mrs D McCulloch, MSc (*Mathematics*)
F McKenna, BTech (*Computer Studies, Design & Technology*)
M I Medley, MSc, PhD (*Chemistry*)
D H Messenger, BA (**Director of Sport*)
Miss I Motyer, BA (*English*)
D Mulae, BSc (*Biology, General Science*)
Mrs K L Newson, BA (**Physical Education, Geography*)
S J O'Boyle, BSc, ARCS (*Mathematics*)
M J Overend, MA (**Languages/French*)
A R B Phillips, BA (*Languages*)
M J Potter, MBE, BEd (*History, PE*)
Mrs E A Robinson, BA (**Food & Nutrition*)
Miss C Rodger, BA (*Drama*)
Miss V Rowcroft, MA (*Music*)
Mrs H Rowland-Jones (*Asst Director of Sport*)
A Saha, MA, BA (*English*)
D P Saunders, BA (**Drama & Theatre Studies*)
A L Smith, BSc (**Mathematics*)
S Sookhun, BSc, PhD (*Physics*)
Mrs D J Stamp, BEd (*Mathematics*)
I N Stannard, BA (**Careers, Theology & Philosophy*)
R W Stuart, MA, PhD (*English*)
Miss A K Swain, BSc (*Geography*)
J Tamvarkis, BEd, (*Science, Mathematics*)
F J Thomson, BEd (*Geography*)
Miss L E A Thornton, MA (*History*)
S M Titchener (*Music*)
Miss M Waller, BSc (*Geography*)

S W Walsh, MA (*English*)
Miss G M Webster, BA PG Dip (*Music*)
T W Whittingham, BA, LTCL (*Music, Bandmaster*)
G P Whiteley, BA (*Art*)
Mrs S H Wilson, BSc (*Biology*)
A R Wines, MA, PhD (*History*)
Mrs L Wyld, MA (*Languages*)
Miss P Wynne, BA (*Classics*)
S C Young, MSci (*Chemistry*)

Clerk: Rear Admiral D Cooke
Operations & Commercial Director: K J Willder, MBE
Admissions Registrar: Mrs J Howard
Head Master's P.A: Mrs C Clark

Christ's Hospital was founded in the City of London by King Edward VI in 1552. In 1902 the boys moved to Horsham, where they were joined by the girls from their Hertford school in 1985.

Christ's Hospital is now a fully co-educational 11–18 boarding and day school for up to 850 pupils set in over 1000 acres of magnificent Sussex countryside.

Christ's Hospital has remarkable facilities for all aspects of its life. There are excellent boarding facilities, all recently updated, two Boarding Houses for occupation by Grecians (Year 13) and sixteen Houses, for boys or girls between 11 and 17. These facilities join an already well-provided school, with an exceptional theatre, an extensive sports centre with swimming pool, gym, sports hall, squash and fives courts, and an astroturf. The original 1902 buildings include a noble chapel and imposing Dining Hall and Big School, each of which can accommodate the entire school and staff.

The school has a distinguished academic record, numbering four former heads of Oxford colleges among its former pupils. Other Old Blues include Samuel Taylor Coleridge, Charles Lamb, Edmund Blunden, Constant Lambert, Barnes Wallis, Sir Colin Davis, Charles Hazlewood and Bernard Levin. Notable aspects of the school's life include its music, art, sport, drama and community action.

The academic programme is compatible with the National Curriculum but not constrained by it. Emphasis is placed on encouraging each pupil to become a confident and independent learner, assisted by an extensive ICT network and an excellent library. The normal day is a busy blend of lessons, activities, games, meals, rehearsals, tutorials, private study and social time. Pupils become responsible in the allocation and use of their time. In addition to the support of House staff, the two Chaplains and an active peer-support group, each pupil in Year 9 and above has an individual tutor to assist with academic advice, learning and life skills. The Chapel provides a blend of corporate and voluntary services during the week which form an important aspect of the life of the school community. An energetic programme of hobbies and adventurous activities, including Scouts, Duke of Edinburgh's Award and Cadet Force, which gives pupils extensive opportunities for involvement in holidays too, is seen as an integral part of the educational provision of the School. Pupils receive extensive career guidance and nearly all leavers go on to university.

The Boarding House is a major focal point for all pupils (both day and full boarders), who have generous personal space appropriate for study, as well as many social and recreational areas. The youngest boarders are in groups of four in House and the top years have individual study-bedrooms. Each House has a resident Housemaster or Housemistress, a tutor and a matron. The Health Centre is served by three qualified nurses and the school doctors visit daily. Every third weekend pupils are encouraged to visit parents or friends, but arrangements are made to look after those who choose to stay in School.

Admission. *Foundationer Boarding (Means-Tested)*: Its very substantial Foundation allows it to maintain the charitable purposes of its Founder so that currently the majority of pupils are subsidised in some degree; currently 16% are educated free of charge.

Direct Entry Places (Full-Fee): In addition to its assisted places, Christ's Hospital is offering a limited number of Direct Entry day and boarding places at age 11, 13 and 16. Direct Entry places are open to pupils whose parents wish to pay the full fee without the means-testing associated with the School's supported places. Candidates will be expected to meet the entry criteria, but will not compete for a place.

The majority of children enter at age 11 (into Year 7). There is an initial academic screening, plus for boarders, a two-day residential assessment in early January for entry in September that year. All candidates have to show they can respond positively to the academic challenges of a school which in due course will expect them successfully to take 11 GCSEs, followed by 4 AS Levels and 3 A2s, or the IB Diploma being offered alongside A Levels from September 2011. There is an entry into the Sixth Form, subject to assessment.

Details on Direct Entry (full-fee) and means-tested places can be obtained by contacting the Admissions Registrar on 01403 211293.

Fees per term (2011-2012). Direct Entry Full-Fee Places: Boarding £8,335; Day £4,500 (Years 7–8), £5,665 (Years 9–13).

Charitable status. Christ's Hospital School is a Registered Charity, number 1120090, supported by the Christ's Hospital Foundation, Registered Charity number 306975.

Churcher's College

Petersfield, Hampshire GU31 4AS
Tel: 01730 263033
Fax: 01730 231437
e-mail: enquiries@churcherscollege.com
website: www.churcherscollege.com

The College was founded in 1722 by a local philanthropist, Richard Churcher, who provided an endowment for boys to be taught English, Mathematics and Navigation in preparation for apprenticeships with the East India Company. The school relocated to more spacious grounds and accommodation in 1881. The College roll is 986 pupils. The Sixth Form totals 171 and the Junior Department (ages 4 to 11 years) totals 217.

The school is fully co-educational.

Motto: *'Credita Cælo'* – Entrusted to Heaven

Governing Body:
M J Gallagher, DipArch Hons, RIBA, MIOD, FIMgmt (*Chairman*)
F W Parvin, ACIB (*Vice-Chairman*)
S Beecham
Mrs J Bloomer, LLB
Mrs D Cornish, BA, MLitt
P Dacam, BA
S Flint, BSc, MBA
Mrs C Herraman-Stowers
M Leigh, BA, FCA
R May
A P Phillips, BDS
C J Saunders, MA
Ms A J Spirit, BA

Headmaster: S H L Williams, BSc, MA

Deputy Heads:
Mrs S M J Dixon, BSc (*Staff and Co-curricular*)
C D P Jones, MA (*Pastoral*)
R J Lynn, BA (*Academic*)

Head of Sixth Form: Mrs V A Godeseth, MA

Senior Teacher (*Pastoral*): Mrs J E Jamouneau, BEd, MSc (*Head of Collingwood House*)

Senior Teacher (*Public Relations*): Mrs J B Millard, BSc, ARCS

Academic Registrar: Dr R E Bowden, BSc Econ, MSc Econ, PhD, MRES, FIEA

Creative & Performing Arts Faculty:
Head of Art: A Saralis, BA, AT Cert
Head of Drama: Ms S Stokes, BA, BTEC
Director of Music: R Goodrich, BA, ABSM, LTCL
Miss C Dromey, BMus, MMus
M Grubb, BA
Mrs G Heath, BA
Mrs H J Purchase, BA (*Head of Instrumental Studies*)
Miss L Shore, BA
A R W Ward, BMus (*Assistant Director of Music*)

Sports Faculty:
Director of Sport: K F Donovan, CertEd
Director of Adventurous Activities: M A Eaton, BEd
D R Cox, BA, MSc (*Head of Boys' PE, Assistant Head of Sixth Form*)
J Daniel
Mrs C Eaton, CertEd (*Head of Girls' PE*)
Miss L Howe, BSc (*Head of A Level PE*)
Mrs D L Knight, BSc

English Faculty:
Head of Faculty: Dr D P Cave, BA, PhD
Miss S Brunner, MA
Mrs S Herrington, BA (*Head of Drake House*)
Mrs C Lilley, BA
Ms C Reynolds, BEd
Mrs L Wade, BA

Humanities Faculty:
Head of Faculty: Mrs J R Grill, BA MA, DMS (*Head of Religion & Philosophy*)
Head of Classics: J Hegan, BA
Head of Economics & Business Studies: P Ratinckx, BA
Head of Geography: D J Nighy, BSc
Head of History: J E Paget-Tomlinson, BA (*Assistant Head of Sixth Form*)
W Baker, BA (*Head of Grenville House*)
C M Best, BA (*Assistant Head of House*)
Mrs S M J Dixon, BSc (*Deputy Head Staff and Co-curricular*)
M Hill, BA
M Hoebee, MA
C D P Jones, MA (*Deputy Head Pastoral*)
Miss L Jenkinson, BA
Miss C Letherby, MA, BA (*Assistant Head of House*)
Mrs D J Link, BA
J Lofthouse, BA, MMus, PGDip
Mrs N Plewes, BSc (*Deputy Head of Sixth Form*)
Mrs D Pont, BA, DMS
Miss J A Rendell, BA

Mathematics Faculty:
Head of Faculty: Mrs T L Greenaway, BSc
Mrs B A Erith, BSc
Mrs H B G Groves, BA
Dr N Jackson, DPhil, MSc
Mrs A Ladbury-Webb, MA (*Assistant Head of Sixth Form*)
R J Lynn, BA (*Deputy Head Academic*)
H Parker, BSc
Mrs L Rona, BSc
J Seaton, BA
Mrs L J Selby, BSc

Modern Languages Faculty:
Head of Faculty: Mrs R P Smith, BA (*Head of French*)
Head of German: I M Crossman, BA (*Deputy Head of Sixth Form*)

Head of Spanish: Mrs A-M Giffin, BA
Mrs H Bond, BA
Mrs V A Godeseth, MA, PGCE (*Head of Sixth Form*)
Mrs S Schofield, BA
Mrs K A Shaw, BA
Mrs P Sykes, BSc (*Assistant Head of House*)

Science Faculty:
Head of Faculty: Mrs J B Millard, BSc, ARCS (*Senior Teacher Marketing & Public Relations; 5th Year Pastoral Coordinator*)
Head of Chemistry: D J Dunster, MA
Head of Physics: M C Kelly, BSc
Head of Biology: Ms M J Westwood, BSc
Mrs S L Cockerill, BSc (*Assistant Head of House*)
Dr T J K Dilks, BSc, BA Ed, DPhil, CBiol, MIBiol
R M Hoe, BSc (*Head of Nelson House*)
Mrs J E Jamouneau, BEd (*Senior Teacher Pastoral, Head of Collingwood House*)
Dr V Raeside, BSc, PhD
Dr G B N Robb, MPhys, MSc, PhD (*Assistant Head of House*)
Mrs F J Sefton-Smith, BSc
J G Yugin-Power, BSc (*Head of Rodney House*)

Technology Faculty:
Head of Faculty: M Parrish, BSc, DipArch (*Head of Design & Technology*)
Head of ICT and Computing: G Bradshaw, BSc
M J B Adams, BEd
Mrs C Lines, BA

Curriculum Support:
Mrs L Blackman, BEd, Dip SpLD

Junior School

Head of Junior School: Mrs S M Rivett, CertEd, Dip Drama
Deputy Head: Mrs P Yugin-Power, BSc, MA Ed, QTS
Head of Infant Department: Miss K M Humphreys, BEd (*Class 2*)
Senior Teacher Middle School: Mrs S J Moore, ARCM, GRSM (*Class 4M*)
Senior Teacher Upper School: A R Greenaway, BEd, MA Ed (*Class 6G*)
Senior Teacher Staffing: Mrs S Roberts, BEd (*Class 6R*)

Miss H Parry, BA (*Class R Teacher*)
C Taylor, BSc (*Class 1 Teacher*)
Mrs N J Munro, CertEd (*Class 3M Teacher*)
Mrs J Gillard (*Class 4G Teacher*)
M Forbes, BSc (*Class 4F Teacher*)
Mrs K Tkaczynska, BEd (*Class 5T Teacher*)
N Rushin, MSc (*Class 5R Teacher*)
Mrs S Bint, GMus RNCM (*Head of Music*)
Mrs R Cameron, CertEd, DipSpLD (*Learning Support*)
Mrs A C Chilton, BEd (*Head of PE*)
J Daniel (*Assistant Sports Teacher*)
Miss C Dromey (*Music Teacher*)
Mrs L M Eddy, BA (*English, Sport/PE*)
Mrs F Little (*Language Studies*)
Mrs S I Strike, Cert Ed (*ICT*)
Mrs P Clemens, BEd (*Sport, Drama*)

Librarians:
Mrs L M Robbins, BSc, MIEH (*Junior School*)
Dr R C Dunn, BSc, PhD
Mrs V Johnson, BSc

Bursar: D T Robbins, BSc, FCCA

Admission. The normal ages of admission to the Senior School are 11+ and 16+, and 4+ and 7+ in the Junior School after Churcher's assessment in the Spring Term. However, if vacancies exist, pupils are considered for admission at other ages.

A prospectus and application form, with details of fees, are available from the Headmaster.

The Sixth Form. Students are prepared for GCE A and AS Levels.

A wide combination of choices is offered from English, History, Geography, Economics, French, German, Spanish, Latin, Art & Design, Music, Drama, Philosophy & Ethics, Business Studies, Mathematics, Further Mathematics, Physics, Chemistry, Biology, Classical Civilisation, Design & Technology, Sport and Physical Education and Computing. All students take a course to prepare them for AS Level General Studies.

There is a fully-equipped Sixth Form Centre, for both study and recreation, a floor of the Library dedicated to Sixth Form private study, an excellent Careers Library and full-time Careers Officer and specialist Sixth Form teaching rooms and ICT facilities.

Years 1–5. From the 11+ entry all pupils follow a common academic programme comprising Mathematics, English, French, Physics, Chemistry, Biology, Latin, Classical Civilisation, Geography, Religion and Philosophy, Music, Art, Design & Technology, ICT, Drama and PE. In Year 2 an additional Modern European language (German or Spanish) is added to the programme. All pupils follow a broad curriculum and are not asked to specialise until they reach GCSE. All pupils follow GCSE courses in Mathematics, English, Science, a Modern Language, a Humanity and at least 2 additional optional subjects.

Pupils are tested and examined regularly with formal assessment procedures each half term and each end of term.

Facilities. Churcher's academic facilities include impressive purpose-built teaching accommodation, ICT suites, drama studios, art and design studios, design technology workshops, music centre and science block. Sports facilities include a swimming pool, sports halls and on-site tennis courts, netball courts, rugby pitches, all weather hockey pitches and cricket squares. Churcher's has the facilities and resources to support an extensive range of extra-curricular activities. The Sixth Form enjoys extensive recreational and teaching facilities. The Junior School is situated on its own spacious 10 acre site in Liphook, close to Petersfield.

Games and other Activities. The major sports played are Rugby, Hockey, Netball, Cricket and Rounders. There are also facilities for Badminton, Basketball, Volleyball, Tennis, Athletics, Aerobics and Cross-country, to name but a few. The School has a strong CCF unit with Army, Air Force and Naval Sections, and a flourishing Duke of Edinburgh's Award programme. Other activities include Mountain Biking, Canoeing, Gliding, Climbing, Adventurous Training, Young Enterprise Companies, Dance, Karate, Fencing, Football, Sailing, Horse-riding, Bridge, Chess, Debating, Drama and Photography.

Music, drama and dance are very strong in the school with School and House plays produced regularly and a wide range of out-of-school activities. The school also has a significant range of orchestras, wind bands and choirs and many more ensembles.

Careers. The College has a full-time Careers Adviser on the staff and regular visits are made by other professional Career Advisers. Talks are given to pupils in the Third Form and above, and individual interviews are arranged.

A **Parents' Association** was formed in 1967 and meetings are held each term.

Fees per term (2011-2012). Senior School £3,850; Junior School £2,450–£2,615. Fees include charges for examination fees and textbooks, but exclude lunches and individual music lessons.

Charitable status. Churcher's College, Petersfield, Hampshire is a Registered Charity, number 307320. Its aims and objectives are to provide a school for boys and girls between the ages of 4 and 18 in the Parish of Petersfield.

City of London Freemen's School

Ashtead Park, Surrey KT21 1ET
Tel: 01372 277933
Fax: 01372 276165
e-mail: headmaster@clfs.surrey.sch.uk
website: www.clfs.surrey.sch.uk

The City of London Freemen's School was founded at Brixton by Warren Stormes Hale in 1854. It is one of 3 schools governed and maintained by the City of London Corporation. It removed to Ashtead Park in 1926.
Motto: '*Domine dirige nos*'

The Board of Governors:

Chairman: J A Bennett
Deputy Chairman: (*to be appointed*)

Aldermen:
Miss A J Gowman
A C D Yarrow

Common Councilmen:
R A Eve, Deputy   Mrs V Littlechild
A C Graves   Ms S D Moys
Revd S D Haines, Deputy   Ms E Rogula
B N Harris   J L Simons
M Hudson   J H Spanner, TD
A Llewelyn-Davies   Mrs A M Starling

Co-opted:
F M Bramwell
J W Brewster, OBE
Sir Clive Martin
D J L Mobsby, MBE, Deputy
Councillor C Townsend

Clerk to the Governors: Gemma Goulding

Headmaster: P MacDonald, MA Oxon

Deputy Head: Mrs V E Buckman, BSc

Second Deputy Head: R J Alton, MA Cantab, MPhys

Head of Junior School: M J Beach, BA, MA Ed
Head of Upper School: Mrs E E Guest, BA
Head of Sixth Form: M D Close, BA, MSc

Assistant Staff:
* *Head of Department/Subject*

Art & Design:
*T J Rees, BA
Mrs R Houseman, BA
Ms G Humphreys, HD Fine Arts, Dip Theatre Design

Business Studies & Economics:
*Mrs P A Brooks, MBA
Mrs J Marvin, BSc
Mrs R Sullivan, BA

Classics:
*A Chadwick, BA
Miss R Gregory, BA
M G Hearne, MA

Computing & Information Technology:
*R Flook, BSc
Miss H L Crow, BSc, MEd

Design Technology:
*A D Kew, BEng
M J Collier, BEd (*Electronics & Technology*)
Mrs M A Smith, BEd (*Food Technology*)
D F Treloar, BEd

Drama:
*P M Tong, MA

Ms S M Chamberlain-Webber, BA

English:
*Miss S E Hearne, BA, MA Ed
C E Bloomer, BA
Miss R Butterwick, BA
Ms S Chamberlain-Webber, BA
Miss R Gregory, BA
Mrs E E Guest, BA
Mrs A M Sloper, BA
Mrs S A Stewart, BA, MA

Geography:
*A P McCleave, BA, MA
Mrs H Pennington, BA

History & Politics:
*A J Wright, MA Oxon, MA
J A Brooke, BA
Mrs K S Edwards, BA
Mrs R E Joss, BA
B J Lewis, BA

Mathematics:
*Mrs R M Hobbs, BSc, MEd
M J Belcher, BSc
E Bramhall, BSc
Mrs M A Cast, BSc
Mrs C A Inns, BA
Mrs E C Newhouse, MA (*Sixth Form Enrichment Studies*)
A Parkin, BSc (*Assistant Head of Sixth Form*)
R G Retzlaff, BSc, BEd, MPhil

Modern Languages:
*Mrs S E Hankin, BA (*German*)
Miss J T Desouches, MT (*French*)
Mrs L A Headon, BA
Mrs C J Leighton, BA
Mrs C A Salisbury, BA (*Spanish*)
Miss L R Vickers, MA
Mrs B C Wheatley, BA
Mrs M Willis-Jones, LFL

Music & Music Techology:
*P M Dodds, BA (*Director of Music*)
M J Bird, GNSM, MTC
Ms N Z Eaglestone, BMus

Physical Education:
*W T Deighton, BEd (*Boys Games*)
*Ms K Ridley, BA (*Girls Games*)
A Bird, BSc
Miss S L Bone, BEd
Mrs N C Clark, BSc
J G Moore, BA (*A Level Sports Studies*)
Mrs L J Shaill, BEd

Psychology:
*Miss J C Vinall, BSc, MSc

Religious Education:
*Revd D F Rutherford, BA
Miss R Gregory, BA
A N Illingworth, BA

Science:
*J D Hallam, BSc (*Physics*)
Mrs V E Buckman, BSc
Mrs J E Dickson, BA
Mrs R M Fox, BSc
Mrs J S Hawkes, BSc
Mrs H M Irwin, BEd
Mrs V I Judge, BSc
I G Knowles, BSc (*Biology*)
Mrs S Meek, BSc
Mrs S J Mitchell, BSc, MSc (*Chemistry*)
M A Newcome, BSc, MA Ed
P Norman, BSc

D F Parker, BSc
Mrs K S Standish, BSc

Junior School:

Miss N S Chambers, BA	Mrs M Restall, BA
Mrs J E Cooper, BEd	Mrs R S Samson, BA
S P Davies, BA	Mrs E C Smith, LLB
Mrs S J Gillespie, BA	Mrs V C Symonds, BSc
Mrs L J Jowitt, MA	M P Valkenburg, HDE
Miss R J Kempster, BA	Mrs P G Whiteley, BSc
R A Metcalf, BA	Mrs C A Williams, BEd
Ms F I Moncur, BEd	

Sixth Form Careers Advisor: A P McCleave, BA, MA

Learning Support Manager: A Illingworth, BA

Chaplain: Revd D F Rutherford, BA

Visiting Instrumental Staff:
Miss V Barnes, MMus, BA
Ms N Berg, BA, MA, ARCM
Mrs A Bishop, ARAM
Ms N Berg, BA, MA, ARCM
Miss R Chappell, AGSM
D Eaglestone, AdDip
G Gottlieb, BA, MMus
C Hurn, BA, MusEd, LGSM
Miss K Keay, BMus
Mrs M MacDonald, BA, Dip ABRSM
J O'Carroll, BMus
Miss E Pappalardo, BMus, MMus
N Perona-Wright, LRAM, LTCL, LLCM TD
Ms H Pritchard, BA, LTCL
P Smith
Mrs G Wallace, LRAM, GRSM
J Wallace
D Ward, AGSM

Music Department Administrator: Mrs S Grover

Cricket Professional: N M Stewart
Swimming Coach: D Cross

Bursar: Mrs Y Dunne, BA, ACA

Administrative Staff:
Assistant Bursar (Administration & Human Resources):
    Mrs A J Atkins, BCom, MCIPD
Finance Manager: Mrs G Bilsland
Marketing and Admissions Manager: M Holland, BSc, MA
Catering and Domestic Services General Manager: S Thorne
Housemistress, Girls' Boarding House: Mrs L J Retzlaff
Housemaster, Boys' Boarding House: B J Lewis, BA
Assistant Housemistress (Girls): Miss S Bone, BEd
Assistant Housemaster (Boys): C E Bloomer, BA
Assistant Housemaster (Boys): A G Bird, BSc
House Parent (Boys): Mrs P Lewis
Headmaster's Secretary: (to be appointed)
Senior Secretary: Mrs A Caprano-Wint
Deputy Head's Secretaries: Mrs S M Davis, Mrs L Ryckaert
Second Deputy Head's Secretaries: Mrs A Moss
Senior School Receptionist/Secretary: Miss E North
Junior School Secretary: Mrs G Anklesaria
Junior School Receptionist/Secretary: Mrs A Tindall
Admissions Secretary: Mrs H Choudhry
Bursar's Secretary: Mrs J Dalton-Sedgwick
Reprographics Officer: N Fairhurst
Reprographics Assistant: S Butcher
Finance Officer: Mrs A Thomas
School Doctor: Dr G Carver, MB, BCh
School Sisters: Mrs A Eversfield, SRN; Mrs J Clark, RGN; Mrs K Utchanah, BA Adult Nursing, RN
Senior Librarian: Mrs S Dawes, BLib, MCLIP
Assistant Librarians: Mrs L J Retzlaff, Mrs J Morris

There are 860 pupils in the School, approximately equal numbers of boys and girls, including up to 20 girl and 25 boy boarders. There are 491 pupils over the age of 13, including a Sixth Form of approximately 207.

The School stands in 57 acres of playing fields and parkland between Epsom and Leatherhead with easy access to Heathrow and Gatwick via the M25. Buildings include a central Georgian Mansion containing the Girls' Boarding House, Dining Hall and Music Department. Other facilities include a modern Assembly Hall and heated 6 lane swimming pool, a floodlit all-weather pitch and a Sports Hall complex completed in 1995. The School Medical Centre is attached to the Boys' Boarding House. The recent multi-million pound building programme includes the new Sixth Form Centre (opened 1997), a new Art and Design Centre (September 1998) and a new Science and Technology Centre (January 1999). New teaching facilities for all subject Departments were completed with the opening of the Haywood Centre in September 2000. This provides classrooms, a new Library/Resource Centre and multimedia facilities, as well as two Senior Computer Laboratories and the Careers Department. A new Studio Theatre was opened in October 2001, providing an auditorium for all productions, recitals, concerts and lecture facilities. An adventure playground for Junior School pupils was completed in 2003. In the same year, the swimming pool was refurbished and the all-weather pitch was replaced, bringing both up to modern national representative standards.

Junior School. Since September 1988 the Junior School, ages 7–13, has been accommodated in a new complex in Ashtead Park. (*See separate IAPS entry.*) This provides 18 classrooms with 3 classes of 20 pupils in each year group and therefore up to 360 pupils in total. The Junior School is fully integrated within the framework and policies of the whole school and other facilities include specialist rooms for Art and Design, Science, Music and an integrated Technology Centre as well as a large Assembly Hall and Library.
See also Junior School entry in IAPS section.

Organisation and Entry. The School is divided into 2 sections but is administered as a single unit. The Junior Department has its own specially trained staff and its own self-contained building, but otherwise all staff teach throughout the School.

Junior entry is by the School's own competitive examination at 7+ (normally in January).

Senior School entry is by passing the Common Entrance examination, normally at the age of 13+, or by the School's own 13+ examination. Screening tests for Senior School entry have been introduced for Year 6 and Year 7 pupils; these take place in January. CLFS Junior School pupils may expect to transfer satisfactorily to the Senior School at 13+ without sitting a special examination.

Sixth Form entry is by obtaining good GCSE grades with a minimum of 50 points from nine subjects, 55 points from 10 subjects with at least 8 passes at GCSE (grade C or better) including English and Mathematics. Grade B must be obtained in any subject to be studied at AS or A Level, with grade A needed in French and Mathematics and strongly preferred in Physics. At least four grade B passes must be obtained at GCSE in appropriate subjects if new subjects are being studied at AS level. (A*=8, A=7, B=6, C=5)

Foundation entry is open to orphan children of Freemen at any age from 7+ to 16+, subject to satisfactory academic potential.

(Except for Foundationers, it is not necessary for applicants to be children of Freemen of the City.)

Curriculum. The first four years (7+ to 10+ in Years 3 to 6) are largely taught by class teachers up to Key Stage 2 following the broad outlines of the National Curriculum. Up to the age of about 14 all pupils have substantially the same curriculum which comprises English, French/German/Spanish, Mathematics, Physics, Chemistry, Biology, History, Geography, Religious Education, Latin, Design Technology,

Information Technology, Food Technology, Art and Music. Thereafter, apart from a common core of English, French or German or Spanish, Mathematics and the 3 separate Sciences, selection is made for the course to GCSE from 15 other subjects including Spanish, German, French, Computer Studies, Drama, Electronics, Latin, Sociology and Design Technology so that the average pupil will offer 10 subjects. The principles of the National Curriculum are followed at all levels. Physical Education and Personal, Social and Health Education are included in the curriculum at all levels.

Sixth Form courses include the following main AS and A Level subjects: Mathematics, Further Mathematics, Physics, Chemistry, Biology, Electronics, History, Geography, Politics, Classical Civilisation, French, German, Spanish, Business Studies, Computing, Drama, Art, Music, Physical Education, Food Technology, Design Technology, Music Technology, Information Technology, Economics, Psychology and Philosophy and Theology. Pre-U courses are also offered in Literature In English and Art & Design. All pupils follow an Enrichment Curriculum which consists of Critical Thinking, an Extended Project and Physical Education.

The School has an excellent academic record. Recent GCSE results have been excellent, with more than 80% of examinations awarded A* or A grades. A Level results have been equally impressive with over 90% of examinations awarded A or B grades, and nearly all leavers go on to degree courses at universities or other higher education institutes.

Computer Studies is well equipped and established, with specialist rooms in each of the Junior and Senior Schools, as well as substantial departmental IT resources as appropriate.

Each pupil is allocated to a House comprising a cross-section of boys and girls, both day and boarding, throughout the School. House teams compete in all forms of sport as well as Music and Drama.

Games. *For Boys*: Principally Rugby, Cricket, Athletics and Swimming. Badminton, Basketball, Hockey, Squash, Tennis are also available.

For Girls: Principally Hockey, Tennis, Athletics and Swimming. Badminton, Netball and Squash are also available.

There is a very wide choice of extra-curricular activities throughout the School. The Duke of Edinburgh's Award Scheme is a very popular option in the Senior School.

Fees per term (2011-2012). Tuition: £4,866 (Senior School); £3,624–£3,828 (Junior School). Boarding: £2,880 (in addition to tuition fees). Instrumental Music lessons: £195.

Scholarships and Exhibitions. (*See Scholarship Entries section*.) Scholarships and Exhibitions valued at up to one half of tuition fees are awarded at the main entry points. These awards are open to both internal and external applicants.

City of London School

Queen Victoria Street, London EC4V 3AL
Tel: 020 7489 0291
Fax: 020 7329 6887
e-mail: headmaster@clsb.org.uk
website: www.clsb.org.uk

The City of London School occupies a unique Thameside location in the heart of the capital and has 925 day boys between the ages of 10 and 18 from all parts of the capital. It traces its origin to bequests left for the education of poor boys in 1442 by John Carpenter, Town Clerk of the City. The Corporation of London was authorised by Act of Parliament in 1834 to use this and other endowments to establish and maintain a School for boys. This opened in 1837 in Milk Street, Cheapside, and moved to the Victoria Embankment in 1883. In 1986 the School moved again, to excellent purpose-built premises provided by the Corporation on a fine riverside site in the City, to which a new Technology building was added in 1990. The School lies on the riverside next to the Millennium Bridge with St Paul's Cathedral to the north and the Globe Theatre and Tate Modern across the Thames to the south. The School's Board of Governors is a committee of the Court of Common Council, the Corporation of London's governing body and four independent co-opted members.

Chairman of Governors: Revd S Haines, MA

Headmaster: D R Levin, BSc, MA, FRSA

Second Master: G S Griffin, BA
Assistant Headmaster: C B Fillingham, BA, MA
Director of Studies: Miss N H Murphy, BA
Director of Admissions: D R Heminway, BD
Director of Staff Development: J B Cook, BSc

Head of Sixth Form: G J Dowler, JP, MA
Deputy Head of Sixth Form: Miss Z L Connolly, MA
Deputy Head of Sixth Form: N P McMillan, BEd
Head of Fifth Form: B L Jones, BA
Deputy Head of Fifth Form: G W Dawson, BSc
Head of Fourth Form: S S Fernandes, BSc, MA
Deputy Head of Fourth Form: Miss E M A Earl, BA
Head of Third Form: G P L Farrelly, BA
Deputy Head of Third Form: Mrs A C Stewart, BSc
Head of Second Form: J Norman, MA
Deputy Head of Second Form: Miss K A Saunt, BA
Head of First Form and OG: M P Kerr, BA
Deputy Head of First Form and OG: Miss C A Hudson, BSc

* *Head of Department*

Classics:
*W Ellis-Rees, MA
B L Jones, BA
Miss C L Rose, BA
Miss Z L Connolly, MA
J E G Pile, BA
S A Swann, BA, MPhil

Design & Visual Arts:
*R G Pomeroy, BA
G P L Farrelly, BA
Miss A E Gill, BA
Miss B Easton, BA
S R Lewington

Drama:
*M C Biltcliffe, BA
Miss S H Dobson, BA

Economics:
*L M Redit, BSc
N P McMillan, BEd
M Wacey, BSc

English:
*G Phillipson, MA
J B Keates, MA, FRSL
R S Blanch, MA
J Norman, MA
J S Williams, BA
Miss H M Sénéchal, MA
M Hilton-Dennis, BA

Geography:
*O J Davies, BSc, MSc
D C Pike, BSc
P S Marshall, MA
Miss V J Robin, BA

History and Politics:
*A J V McBroom, BA
G S Griffin, BA
Miss N H Murphy, BA
Miss F N Bennett, BA
Mrs V W Arnold, BA
A J Bracken, BA
P T Brooke, BA, MPhil
Miss K A Saunt, BA
S M Jones, BSc, MPhil
S J Brown, BA, MA

Information Technology:
*Mrs S L Ralph, BA
Mrs A M MacDonagh, BSc, BSc

Mathematics:
*D R Eade, BA
R P Hubbard, BSc
D J Chamberlain, BSc, MSc
Miss C A Hudson, BSc
S S Fernandes, BSc, MA
Mrs C S Musgrove, MA
Miss J C L Mesure, BA
Miss E L McCallan, MA
A D Blake, BSc
S J Dugdale, BSc, PhD

Modern Languages:
*R Edmundson, MA
A T Laidlaw, MA
(*French*)
P A Allwright, MA
G J Dowler, JP, MA
Mrs A J Heaf, BA, MA
Miss V Vincent, MA

Mrs A L Robinson, BA
C B Fillingham, BA, MA
Mrs E Morgan, BA
P R Eteson, BA
Ms M Ciechanowicz, MA
Miss M Kidwell, MA

Music:
*P Harrison, GLCM, MA
Miss J E Jones, BA
J Harrison, BA

Physical Education:
*N F Cornwell, BEd
M P Kerr, BSc, MSc
B J Silcock, BPE
J P Santry, BEng
C E Apaloo, BSc

Religious Education:
*J T Silvester, BA
D R Heminway, BD
Miss K E Wratten, MA, MA
Miss E M Earl, BA

Mrs A Giannorou, BSc, BA, MPhil

Science:
H R S Jones, BSc (*Physics, *Science)
N O Mackinnon, BSc, PhD (*Biology)
Mrs P C McCarthy, BSc (*Chemistry)
R F Davey, BSc, MSc
J Easingwood, CertEd, BA
J B Cook, BSc
N J Baglin, BSc
K Khand, BSc, PhD
R Mackrell, BSc
G W Dawson, BSc
Mrs A C Stewart, BSc
E Whitcombe, BSc
K P Rogers, MChem
P J Naylor, BSc
Miss R A Norman, BSc
Miss C Weller, BSc
Mrs J D Dobbin, BSc

There are Visiting Music Teachers for Bassoon, Cello, Double Bass, French Horn, Flute, Guitar, Jazz, Oboe, Organ, Percussion, Piano, Saxophone, Singing, Trombone, Trumpet, Tuba, Viola, Violin.

Learning Support:
*Miss A S Ross-Scott, BSc, Hornsby DipSpLD
*Miss P R Scott, BSc, Hornsby DipSpLD
D W Dyke, BA

Library:
*D A Rose, BA, Dip Lib, ALA
Ms J Grantham, MA
Miss R Stocks, BA

Finance Director: P J Everett, FCA, BSc Econ, MA
Headmaster's Secretary: Miss J Williams
Admissions Secretary: Mrs J Brown
Human Resources Manager: Miss S F Denbow, BA, PG Dip

Admissions. Pupils are admitted aged 10, 11 and 13 (as on 1st September of year of entry), on the results of the School's own entrance examinations held each year in January. Those admitted at 16 into the Sixth Form are selected by test and interview in November. Application forms for admission may be obtained from the Admissions Secretary at the School or from the website.

Fees per term (2011-2012). £4,350.

Entrance Scholarships. (*See Scholarship Entries section*.) At least 30 Academic, Music and Sports Scholarships, with a value of up to half of the school fees, and a number of minor awards, are awarded annually to candidates at all ages of entry. Candidates for entry to the School may also apply for Choristerships at the Temple Church or the Chapel Royal, St James's (the choristers of both choirs are pupils at the School). Choristers receive Choral Bursaries whose value is two-thirds of the school fee. Potential choristers may also take auditions and academic tests at the age of 8 or 9; successful applicants will be offered an unconditional place in the School for the year after their 10th birthday.

Sponsored Awards. The School offers a number of Sponsored Awards, up to full fees, to assist those parents of academically very bright boys, who otherwise could not contemplate private education. These awards are only available at 11+ and 16+.

Curriculum. All boys follow the same broad curriculum up to and including the Third Form. The First Form curriculum includes an introduction to the use of computers, and in the Third Form boys spend some eight afternoons throughout the year on educational visits to institutions and places of interest in and around the City. Latin and French are started by all in the First Form and two choices from Greek, Classical Civilisation, Drama, German and Spanish may be added as options in the Third Form. Fourth and Fifth Form boys take a core of English, Mathematics, three Sciences (the core subjects are all IGCSEs), and at least one Modern Foreign Language (which can include Russian), and choose three other subjects from a wide range of subjects available for study to GCSE/IGCSE. In the Sixth Form boys take a combination of AS or A2 Level subjects together with the ECDL. A majority of the Senior Sixth finish with four A Levels and usually over fifty per cent get four grade As. Virtually all boys leaving the Sixth Form proceed to their first or second choice of Russell Group University or Medical School.

Games. The School's 20 acres of playing fields, at Grove Park in south-east London, offer excellent facilities for football, cricket, athletics, and tennis. Sporting facilities on the School site include a sports hall, a gymnasium with conditioning room, three squash courts, a fencing salle, and a 25-metre swimming pool. Particular success has been achieved in football, water polo, fencing, table tennis, basketball and badminton.

School Societies. There is a large number of School Societies, catering for a very wide range of interests. Every encouragement is given to benefit from the School's central position by participation in the cultural and educational life of London and of the City in particular. The School has a strong musical tradition; tuition is available in any instrument, and membership of the School choirs and orchestras is encouraged. Choristers of the Temple Church and of the Chapel Royal are educated at the School as bursaried scholars provided that they satisfy the entrance requirements. There is much interest in Drama, and the staff includes a full-time Director of Drama: the School has a fully-equipped and recently refurbished Theatre and also a Drama Studio. There is a large CCF Contingent which boys may join from the age of 13 until 18, with Army, Navy and RAF Sections. There is also a successful Community Service programme. Boys frequently take part in the Duke of Edinburgh's Award Scheme.

Alumni Association. There is a flourishing Old Boys' Society known as the John Carpenter Club, website: www.jcc.org.uk. The Alumni Relations Officer can be contacted at the School.

Clayesmore School

Iwerne Minster, Blandford Forum, Dorset DT11 8LL
Tel: 01747 812122
Fax: 01747 813187
e-mail: hmsec@clayesmore.com
website: www.clayesmore.com

Developing the unique gifts of every girl and boy

Council of Governors:
Dr R Willis, MA, BM, BCh (*Chairman*)
J Andrews, LLB
A Beaton
C Campbell
P Dallyn, FRICS, FAAV
Mrs F Deeming, BA Hons, PGCE
Mrs D Geary
D M Green, MA Cantab (*Vice-Chairman, Education*)
R Morgan
R H C Phillips, BA Hons, CertEd, LGSM
Mrs R Stiven
Dr J Traill, BA, MMus, DPhil Oxon, FRSM

Headmaster: **M G Cooke**, BEd, FCollP

Deputy Head: J R Carpenter, BA

Assistant Head: Mrs E M Bailey, BA, PGCE

Director of Teaching & Learning: A R West, BA, MA, PGCE

Head of Sixth Form & Senior Master: R A Chew, MA

Bursar: M J M Dyer

Assistant Staff:
R J D Anderson, BMedSc, PGCE
Mrs A J A Balasingam, CertEd, OCRCertSpLD
B Brackstone, BA, OCRCertSpLD
Mrs H N Christmas, BA
Miss T S Cook, BA
Mrs E A Cooke, BEd, AdvDipECSN
Mrs D M Denning, BA, PGCE
C B A Didier, BEng, PGCE
Miss H A Edwards, BA, PGCE
Mrs H M Farley, BEd, RSASpLD
Mrs H B Forster, MA, PGCE
M S Fraser, BA
G M Glasspool, BSc
H J Gibbons, BSc, PGCE
A Hanson-Stewart, BSc, PGCE
Miss J E Hayes, BEd
D A Humphreys, BSc Tech
Mrs R M Hunter, CertEd, BA, RSACertSpLD
A Jancis, BSc, PGCE
Dr A P G Jancis, BA, PhD, MIBiol, PGCE
P K Jones, BA, PGCE
J J Kimber, BA, MA
Mrs J M Martin, Dip SteinerEd, RSADipSpLD
Mrs K R Mareau-Jones, BA
Mrs M May, BA, PGCE
C R Middle, BA
Mrs T J Mousalli, BA, PGCE
Mrs S-J Newland, BSc, PGCE
Miss K E O'Rourke, BA, PGCE
Mrs F Pattenden, BA, CertTEFL
Mrs V Peevor, CertEd, OCRDipSpLD
A G Pienaar, MSc, HDE
D K Pigot, BMus, ARCM, LTCL, CertEd
Revd J C E Pottinger, MA, MTh
P J Randall, BA, PGCE
J Reach, BEng, PGCE
Miss S-J Rhead, BSc, PGCE
K A Richards, BA, PGCE
D I Rimmer, MA
E R Robeson, MA, PGCE
H C Smith, BA, PGCE
S A Smith, BSc, PGCE
H P Stevenson, BA, PGCE
Miss C L Storey, BA, PGCE
Mrs S E Tew, CertEd, BA, OCRCertSpLD
Dr F M Thomason, BSc, PhD, OCNCertSpLD, PGCE
Mrs C Thompson, BA, PGCE
T P A Weaver, CertEd, AMBDA, OCRCertSpLD
A K P Young, BSc, PGCE

Administrative Staff:
Headmaster's Secretary & Registrar: Mrs M B McCafferty
Bursar's Secretary & Assistant Registrar: Mrs H de Bie
School Secretaries: Mrs R Rutherford, Mrs H Horley

House Matrons:
Mrs J Lilley (*Wolverton*)
Mrs W Everest (*Gate*)
Mrs A Goates (*King's*)
Mrs J Dalton (*Manor*)
Mrs J Williams (*Devine*)

Medical Officer: Dr N Berry, BM, BS, BMedSci, DRCOG, MRCGP, DFFP

Nurses:
Mrs D J Amphlett, RGN
Mrs J Morris, RGN, RSCN, HV
Mrs H Berry, RNLD
Mrs G Hakimzadeh RGN
Mrs M Sandiford, RGN
Assistant: Mrs H Sanger

Director of Sport & Enterprise: Mr C Humpage, BH, PGCE
Assistant Director of Sport & Enterprise: Mr R S Miller, BSc, PGCE
School Staff Instructor: Mr C Evans
Buildings & Estate Manager: Mr J Handley
Catering Manager: Mr N D'Allen, MCHIMA
Head Groundsman: Mr R Norris, BSc, DipEnv
Librarians: Mrs J-A Murphy, Mrs M-A McCrow

Clayesmore Prep School

Headmaster: R D H Geffen, BEd

Deputy Head: Mrs M Barnes, CertEd, RSA DipSpLD, AMBDA
Director of Teaching & Learning: Mrs S J Moulton, BA Hons, PGCE
Head of Pre-Prep & Nursery: Mrs J E Bolger, CertEd

Assistant Staff:
Mrs R Beal, BA Hons, PGCE, AMBDA
C Birchill, CertEd
Dr S Bragg, BA, PhD
D J Browse, BA
Mrs C Caiger, BA, PGCE, PGDip
Mrs S M Chinnock, BA, PGCE
Mrs J E Coplan, BMus, MA, PGCE
Mrs A Cowley, BSc Hons, PGCE, MEd SEN
D A Harrison, BSc
Mrs S Hart, CertEd
Mrs P-A Middle, BA, PGCE
N Moore, BEd
Mrs M M Oakley, CertEd
Mrs S Panton, BSc, MA, PGCE
Mrs E F Pogson, BEd
Mrs P Price, CertEd
Mrs C Ritchie, BA
Mrs I Rose, BA, PGCE
Miss N Rowse, BEd, RSACertSpLD
J Smith, BMus Hons, PGCE
Mrs J Warburton, CertEd, RSACertSpLD
Mr G Weaver, BA
Mrs C J Weeks, CertEd, RSACertSpLD
C Whytehead, BEd
R Wilson, BA
Mrs S L Wilson, BEd
S Wilson

Pre-Prep and Nursery School:
Miss G Ankers, BA Hons, PGCE
Mrs E A Anderson, BTech Hons, PGCE
Mrs J Findon
Mrs S L Hart, BA Hons Joint, PGCE
Miss N Hitt
Mrs H Martin
Mrs A Williams

Administrative & Pastoral:
School Office Manager: Mrs L Chaffey
Registrar: Mrs L Brown
School Secretary: Mrs H Young

Sister in charge: Mrs S Hilliard, RN
Deputy Sisters: Mrs S Millard, RGN; Mrs R Flute, RGN
Matrons: Miss J Foulger, BSc; Mrs H Galley; Mrs J Thorne

Librarian: Mrs H Bignold, BLib, MA, MCLIP

Clayesmore is a flourishing co-educational school with Senior (13–18) and Preparatory (2½–13) departments on one beautiful 62-acre site. There are 423 pupils in the Senior School, nearly two-thirds of whom are boarders, and another 250 at the Prep School, of whom 75 board. There is also a Nursery School.

The school was founded in 1896 (the Prep in 1929) and the two schools came together in 1975 when the Prep School joined the Senior School at Iwerne Minster, in its own, new, purpose-built accommodation. Clayesmore is very much one organisation yet with two schools, each with its own Headmaster, staff and separate teaching areas.

Buildings and Grounds. Facilities have been radically improved in recent years and generally are excellent. The main building functions very much as the school's headquarters. The upper floors are used entirely as a girls' boarding house – Wolverton – whilst on the ground floor may be found a fine library complete with up to the minute computer facilities for private study and research, as well as reception rooms which are used for a myriad of purposes throughout term time.

The magnificent prize-winning, three-storey high Jubilee Building provides eight science laboratories, two computer suites (networked to the library) and a lecture theatre as well as the highly acclaimed Learning Support Centre. The construction of the Jubilee Building allowed the school to improve the boys' boarding accommodation in Gate House.

Another new building, named The Spinney Centre after a former distinguished Chairman of Council, comprises superb, state-of-the-art classrooms for Careers, Geography, History and Business Studies. The Design and Technology Department has also been extended.

There is a superb Sports Centre complete with gymnasia, 25-metre indoor pool, squash courts, modern fitness suite, four badminton courts and indoor cricket nets. Outside, as well as the many pitches and netball courts we have a full-sized, floodlit, all-weather hockey pitch which provides 12 tennis courts for summer use.

There is an excellent Music School and Art School, as well as the Chapel, built in 1956 as a memorial to the 81 Old Clayesmorians who gave their lives in the two World Wars. The parkland grounds are quite outstanding, with excellent playing fields, a lake, and wonderful views towards historic Hambledon Hill with its Saxon fort.

Houses and Pastoral Care. In the Senior School, there are five houses (three for boys and two for girls) each with resident, married House Staff, and resident Tutor. It is an important element of our pastoral care that boarding pupils and day pupils are together – there are no day houses. All pupils have a Tutor to oversee academic progress and help with the important decisions at various points in a pupil's school career. Clayesmore is a school with a striking family atmosphere and the School's comparatively small size enables the Headmaster and the staff to get to know the girls and boys well. Great attention is paid to the pastoral care of the pupils, not only through the House and Tutor system, but through the full extra-curricular programme as well.

Entry arrangements. Entrance to Clayesmore School is at 13 with entrants from preparatory schools taking the usual Common Entrance examination. For those entering from maintained schools, there are tests in English, Mathematics, Science and French. Girls and boys may join Clayesmore earlier by becoming members of Clayesmore Preparatory School and it is quite normal for new pupils to arrive aged 11 and undertake Years 7 and 8 at the Prep School. Each year, between 10 and 20 young people join us as Sixth Formers, and the total number in the Sixth Form is roughly 140.

Scholarships. Means-tested scholarships are available in the usual way and information on these is available from the School.

Academic work. Academically, pupils follow the usual pattern. Year 9 serves as a useful foundation year prior to GCSE courses getting under way in Years 10 and 11. Sixth Form students pursue four AS Levels in the Lower Sixth, taking three of these on to A2 in the Upper Sixth. The trend at Clayesmore at present is for year groups of 90 or so pupils in Years 9–11 divided roughly into five groups of 18–20 pupils. There is setting in core subjects and French, Spanish and German are all offered through to A Level. There is much emphasis in the Sixth Form on preparing students for the world beyond Clayesmore both at university and in careers generally, and the Head of Sixth Form coordinates a highly structured and most effective group of Sixth Form tutors.

It is very much at the centre of Clayesmore's philosophy that we pay close attention to the needs of the individual boy or girl both academically and in other spheres of life. For many years, the School has had a strong reputation for helping pupils with dyslexia.

Clayesmore Preparatory School. Clayesmore is fairly unusual in having its Prep and Senior Schools together and this is an added strength for many parents, particularly of boarders, who are keen to keep their children together in one place. The opportunity for a seamless transition at 13 is one that pupils and parents value highly. The Prep School has its own main building containing many of the classrooms including a colourful, well-stocked library and an excellent Information Technology suite, as well as all the boarding and pastoral facilities. It has its own laboratories, Design Technology and Art studios, and shares use of the Music School, Sports Centre, Dining Hall and Chapel. The Pre-Prep and Nursery is housed in their own accommodation with its dedicated play area and they have their own teaching and support staff. In September 2008 a brand new state-of-the-art building was opened. This comprises five classrooms which accommodate Years 3 and 4 and two new science laboratories. Pupils in Years 3 and 4 have a form teacher, but enjoy specialist teachers and classrooms for music, French, art and ICT. Entrance to the Preparatory School may take place into any year group assuming a place is available, and is dependent upon interview with the Headmaster and a report from the present school.

See also Clayesmore Preparatory School entry in IAPS section.

The wider life at Clayesmore. Sport is very much a strength at Clayesmore. Rugby, Hockey, Cricket, Athletics, Netball, Swimming and Cross-Country, are the major sports in the Senior School, and badminton, squash, sailing and orienteering are also very popular and successful subsidiary sports.

Pupils in Years 10 and 11 can benefit from membership of the School's Combined Cadet Force with many enthusiasts continuing as NCOs into the Sixth Form. There is a strong link between the CCF and the Duke of Edinburgh's Award Scheme which is in operation at the School. There is a comprehensive and wide-ranging activities programme which operates throughout the week.

There is a high standard of music-making and drama throughout Clayesmore. Every encouragement is given to pupils of all ages to learn instruments, participate in group activities and sing in the choirs. There are all sorts of ensembles and new ones are formed to suit different pupil interests when necessary. The Theatre is a really practical, intimate space, and is used with great imagination not only for the various termly productions but also for the GCSE and A Level Theatre Studies. Some A Level performances were filmed by an exam board as exemplar material representing top grade work for other schools to see.

Fees per term (2011-2012). Senior School: £9,558 (boarding), £6,993 (day). Preparatory School: £6,340–£6,949 (boarding), £2,538–£5,161 (day).

Charitable status. Clayesmore School Limited is a Registered Charity, number 306214. It exists for educational purposes.

Clifton College

Bristol BS8 3JH
Tel: 0117 3157 000
        Preparatory School Headmaster: 0117 3157 502
Fax: 0117 3157 101
e-mail: admissions@clifton-college.avon.sch.uk
website: www.cliftoncollegeuk.com

Clifton College was founded in 1862, and is a Corporation by Royal Charter granted 16 March 1877.
    Motto: '*Spiritus intus alit.*'

Council:
President: D N Tarsh, OBE, BA
Chairman: T S Ross, MA
Vice-Chairmen: P L Howell-Richardson, BA; A Streatfeild-James, MA
Treasurer: C W Smith, FCA

C K Beale, PhD, MBA, FRAeS
N J B Cooper, MA, LLB
B J Hanson, CBE, FRICS
S R Lang, BSc, PhD
Mrs C Lear, BA
D Maggs
Mrs D A Moore, BA
A W Morgan, MA, MBA
R M Morgan, MA
C Pople, ACA, ATII
Reverend J Witheridge
B Worthington, MA

Secretary and Bursar: Mrs L K J Hanson, BSc, ACA

Head Master: M J Moore, MA

Deputy Head (Pastoral): J P Middleton, MA
Deputy Head (Academic): A Spencer, BA
Assistant Head: J H Greenbury, MA
Assistant Head: Miss A C Tebay, BSc
Chaplain: Revd K Taplin, BA, MTh, FRSA
Director of Admissions: P C Hallworth, MA, MEd
Director of External Relations: Mrs F J W Hallworth, MA

Heads of Department:
A J Wilkie, BA (*Art*)
D R B Barrett, BSc (*Biology*)
J Bobby, BA (*Boys' Games*)
T M Greene, BA, DPhil (*Chemistry & Science*)
W Huntington, MA (*Classics*)
M R Barnacle, BA (*Design & Technology*)
R Morris, BA (*Director of Drama*)
A Ballance, BSc (*Economics & Business Studies*)
Miss S A Clarke, MA (*English*)
Miss C Bloor, BA (*French*)
Mrs H J Mann, MA, MSc (*Geography*)
O G Lewis, MA (*German*)
Mrs L A Catchpole, BA (*Girls' Games*)
N Mills, BA (*History*)
D Dean, MA, PhD (*Information Technology*)
Ms E Cordwell, BA (*Mandarin*)
G E Simmons, BSc (*Mathematics*)
L Siddons, MA (*Modern Languages*)
J Hills, BA (*Director of Music*)
D Janke, BA (*Philosophy & Religious Studies*)
A Hasthorpe, MSci (*Physics*)
Mrs N D Bright, BA (*PSHE*)
Mrs V Bodger, MA (*Psychology*)
P G Lidington, BA (*Politics*)
Miss M Harris, BA (*Spanish*)
P Askew, BEd (*Director of Sport*)

Houses and Housemasters/mistresses:

Boys Boarding:
School House: J H Hughes, MA
Moberly's: A J O'Sullivan, BA
Wiseman's: W J Huntington, MA
Watson's: S Heard, BA

Girls Boarding:
Oakeley's: Mrs K A Jeffery, BSc
Worcester: Mrs A J Ballance, BSc
Hallward's: Mrs K J Pickles, BA

Boys Day:
North Town: D M Rodgers
South Town: J S Tait, BA
East Town: J H Thomson-Glover, BA

Girls Day:
West Town: Mrs L A Catchpole, BA Ed

Clifton College was founded in 1862, and incorporated by Royal Charter in 1877. It is situated in the City of Bristol, on the edge of Clifton Down and not far from open country. The School is well placed to take advantage of the many cultural and educational activities of the City, and to gain much else of value from its civic and industrial life. There are friendly links with the University and with other schools of various types.

Admission. Boy and girl boarders and day pupils are normally admitted in September between the ages of 13 and 14, and most are required to pass the Common Entrance examination, which can be taken at their Preparatory Schools. Credentials of good character and conduct are required. Registration Forms can be obtained from the Director of Admissions, 32 College Road, Clifton, Bristol BS8 3JH.

Houses. It is usual for a pupil to be entered for a particular House, but where parents have no preference or where no vacancy exists in the House chosen, the Head Master will make the necessary arrangements.

Day Pupils and Day-Boarders. Day boys are divided into Houses: North Town, South Town and East Town. Day girls enter West Town or Hallward's. The town Houses have the same status as Boarding Houses and day pupils are encouraged to take a full part in the various activities of the School. A small number of day-boarder places are available for boys and girls.

Catering is managed by our own experienced caterers and boarders take all meals in the School Dining Hall. Day pupils and day-boarders are required to have their midday meal at School, and arrangements are made for their tea and supper at the School when necessary.

Fees per term (2011-2012). Boarders £9,590–£9,750, Day Boarders £8,690–£8,950, Day Pupils £6,590–£6,790.

Scholarships. (*See Scholarship Entries section.*) All awards are limited to 25% of the fees on merit, but they may be augmented by means-tested bursaries. Candidates must be under 14 years of age on the 1st of September. Boys and girls under 14 already in the School may compete. The following Entrance Scholarships are offered each year:
    (a) Up to 20 Academic awards. (b) Awards for Music with free instrumental tuition. (c) Awards for Art. (d) A Birdwood Scholarship for sons or daughters of serving members of HM Forces. (e) Sports Scholarships for entry at 13+. (f) At least 6 scholarships a year for entrants at Sixth Form level (Academic, Music and Sport).
    Award winners are assured of places in the School. The Head Master distributes them to Houses, if possible in accordance with parents' wishes.

Academic structure. Boys and girls enter the School in the Third Form, following a general course for their first year. Most GCSEs are taken at the end of the Fifth Form.
    Thereafter boys and girls enter Block I (Sixth Form) and take an advanced course consisting of 4 subjects at AS Level, then 3 at A Level. A great many combinations of sub-

jects are possible. Boys and girls are prepared for entrance to Oxford and Cambridge.

Service. All pupils are given a course in outdoor pursuits and other skills in the Third Form. In the Fourth Form they are given more advanced training, which may include involvement in the Duke of Edinburgh's Award Scheme, and at the end of the year they decide whether to join the Army, Navy or Air Force sections of the CCF or to take part in Community Service. There is regular use of a property owned by the school in the Brecon Beacons for all these activities.

Societies. Voluntary membership of Scientific, Historical, Literary, Dramatic, Geographical, Debating and many other Societies is encouraged.

Music and Art. The Musical activities of the School are wide and varied, and are designed for musicians of all standards. They include the Chapel Choir, Choral Society and Chamber Choir, a full orchestra, 2 string orchestras, 2 wind bands, a jazz band, as well as numerous chamber music activities. Visiting concert artists regularly run masterclasses, and there are wide opportunities for performance. Teaching is available on virtually all instruments and in all styles. Instrumental and vocal competitions are held at House level and individually annually. The well-equipped and recently refurbished Music School include practice facilities, computers, recording studio, an extensive sheet music library and a large record/compact disc library.

Drawing, Painting, Sculpture, Pottery, Textiles and various Crafts are taught under the supervision of the Director of Art in the Art School. There is an annual House Art Competition and various exhibitions throughout the year.

Theatre. Drama plays an important part in the life of the School. The Redgrave Theatre is used for School Plays, the House Drama Festival, and for other Plays that may be put on (eg by individual houses, the staff or the Modern Language Society). Each House produces a play each year. It is also used for teaching purposes, and in addition for Concerts, Lectures and Meetings.

Information and Communication Technology. The ICT Centre at the heart of the school houses the most advanced Internet Facility of any school in the west.

Physical Education. Physical Education is part of the regular School curriculum and games are played at least twice per week by all age groups.

In the Michaelmas Term, boys play Rugby Football and girls play Hockey. There is a multi-sport option for seniors who are not in team squads. In the Lent Term, Hockey and Soccer are the main options for the boys whilst the girls mostly play Netball. Rowing, Running, Squash, Swimming, Shooting, Tetrathlon and Fives are among the alternative options for senior boys and girls. In the Summer Term, Cricket is the main sport for the boys and Tennis for the girls, with Tennis, Athletics, Rowing, Swimming and Shooting as alternatives for seniors. The Clifton College playing fields in Abbots Leigh include three floodlit all-weather hockey and football pitches, six floodlit tennis courts, a 3G artificial pitch for soccer and rugby, and a Real Tennis court. An indoor facility for tennis and netball is one of the best in the region.

Careers. Careers advice is the shared responsibility of the Head Master, Housemasters, Housemistresses, Heads of Departments and the Head of Sixth Form. The School is a subscribing member of the Independent Schools Careers Organisation and of the Careers Research and Advisory Centre at Cambridge. The proximity of the City of Bristol enables the Careers Department and other members of the staff to keep in close touch with Universities, business firms and professional bodies about all matters affecting boys' and girls' careers.

Clifton College Preparatory School. *Headmaster*: J Milne, BA, MBA

The Preparatory School has separate buildings (including its own Science laboratories, Arts Centre, ICT Centres and

Music School) and is kept distinct from the Upper School. The two Schools nevertheless work closely together and share some of the facilities, including the Chapel, Theatre, Sports complex, all-weather playing surfaces and swimming pool. Most boys and girls proceed from the Preparatory School to the Upper School. Pupils are also prepared for schools other than Clifton. There is a Pre-Prep School (Butcombe) for day pupils aged between 3 and 8. Older pupils are divided into ten houses, some boarding, some day and some mixed. Boys and girls are accepted at all ages and Scholarships are available at age 11.

For further details see entries for Clifton College Preparatory School and Butcombe in IAPS section.

Old Cliftonian Society. *Secretary*: S J M Reece, The Garden Room, 3 Worcester Road, Clifton, Bristol BS8 3JL (Tel: 0117 3157 156).

Charitable status. Clifton College is a Registered Charity, number 311735. It is a charitable trust providing boarding and day education for boys and girls aged 3–18.

Clongowes Wood College

Clane, Co Kildare, Ireland
Tel: 00 353 45 868202
Fax: 00 353 45 861042
e-mail: reception@clongowes.net
website: www.clongowes.net

Motto: '*Aeterna non Caduca*'

Clongowes Wood College was founded in 1814 in a rebuilt Pale castle – Castle Brown in North Kildare, about 25 miles from Dublin. A boarding school for boys from 12–18, the school has developed steadily ever since and now has 500 pupils on the rolls, all of whom are boarders.

Trustee of the School: Fr Tom Layden, SJ, Provincial of the Society of Jesus in Ireland

Chairman of the Board of Management: Dr Patrick Nolan

Headmaster: Fr Leonard Moloney, SJ, BA, HDip, MDiv, MPhil (Ecum)

Assistant Headmaster: Mr Martin Nugent, MA, HDipEd, HDip in Educational Management

Deputy Assistant Headmaster: Mr Frank Kelly, BComm, HDip

The College is situated on 150 acres of land, mostly comprising sports fields and a 9-hole golf course. It is surrounded by about 300 acres of farmland. Clongowes is listed as an historic building.

Admission. Application for admission should be made to the Headmaster. There is a registration fee of €50. An assessment day is held in early October prior to the year of entry and entry is determined by a variety of factors including family association, geographical spread including Northern Ireland and abroad, date of registration, and an understanding of the values that animate the College. Normal entry is at the age of 12; entry in later years is possible in exceptional circumstances if a place becomes available.

Curriculum. A wide choice of subjects is available throughout the school and pupils are prepared for the Irish Junior Certificate and the Irish Leaving Certificate. This latter is the qualifying examination for entry to Irish Universities and other third-level institutions. It is acceptable for entry to almost all Universities in the United Kingdom, provided the requisite grades are obtained. All pupils take a Transition Year programme following the Junior Certificate. This programme is recommended by the Department of Education in Ireland. Work experience modules, social outreach programmes, exchanges with other countries and opportunities to explore different areas of study are all included in this programme.

Religious Teaching. Clongowes is a Jesuit school in the Roman Catholic tradition and there are regular formal and informal liturgies. Boys are given a good grounding in Catholic theology and are encouraged to participate in retreats, prayer groups and pilgrimages (Taize, Lourdes). Social Outreach is part of the curriculum in Transition Year and is encouraged throughout the school. A small number of boys of other faiths are pupils in the school.

Sport. All boys play rugby in their first year in school. They then have the choice to continue in that game or to play other games. Rugby pitches, a golf course, tennis courts, soccer pitches, squash courts, a cross-country track, an athletics and cricket oval, a gymnasium and a swimming pool provide plenty of opportunity for a variety of activities. Athletics, Gaelic football and cricket are popular activities in the third term. Clongowes has a strong rugby tradition and has won the Leinster Championship twice in the last decade.

Other activities. Following the Jesuit tradition, the school has a fine reputation for debating and has won competitions in three different languages (English, Irish, French) in the last decade. A large school orchestra and school choir gives a formal concert at Christmas and another before the summer holidays. Drama productions take place at every level within the school. A large-scale summer project for charity has been undertaken each year. A residential holiday project for children with disabilities takes place in the school each summer and is animated by teachers and pupils. The College has recently created link programmes with schools in Hungary and Romania.

Pastoral Care. The school is organised horizontally into Lines. Two 'prefects', or housemasters look after each year within a Line, composed of two years, with a Line Prefect in charge of the Line itself. In addition, an Academic Year Head oversees the academic work of each of the 70 pupils within each year. A Spiritual Father or Chaplain is attached to each line. There is a strong and positive relationship with parents and a good community spirit throughout the school. The school seeks to foster competence, conscience and compassionate commitment in each of the boys in its care.

Fees per annum (2011-2012). €16,500. Parents are also asked to support the continuing development of the College through various fundraising activities.

Clongowes Union. This association of past pupils of the school can be contacted through: The Secretary, The Clongowes Union, Clongowes Wood College, Clane, Co Kildare. e-mail: development@clongowes.net.

Cokethorpe School

Witney, Oxfordshire OX29 7PU
Tel: 01993 703921
Fax: 01993 773499
e-mail: hmsec@cokethorpe.org
          admissions@cokethorpe.org
          admin@cokethorpe.org
website: www.cokethorpe.org.uk

Cokethorpe School, founded in 1957, is a vibrant and dynamic day school for around 660 girls and boys aged 4 to 18. It is set in 150 acres of parkland, two miles from Witney and ten from Oxford. There are 140 children in the Junior School and 520 pupils in the Senior School (including 140 Sixth Formers).

Motto: *Inopiam Ingenio Pensant*

Governing Body:
Chairman: Sir John Allison, KCB, CBE, FRAeS
Vice-Chairman: B Brown Esq, BA, DA, FCSD, FRSA
J Bond Smith Esq, FIMI

A C Burdall Esq, BEng, MICE
Mrs G Butt, MA
P Vaughan-Fowler Esq, MBA, BA
S K Dexter Esq, FCA
Mrs C Bartlett, MA
R Walker Esq, BSc, PGCE, CChem, CSci, MRSC, FRSA
Professor J Wood, CBE, FREng

Headmaster: **D J Ettinger**, MA, PGCE

Second Master: K Walton, CertEd
Director of Studies: J P Floyd, MA
Bursar: Mrs S A Landon, BA, ACMA
Head of Junior School: Mrs C A Cook, BEd
Senior Tutor: E J Fenton, BD, AKC, PGCE
Head of Sixth Form: Mrs S M L Copeland, BA, PGCE, AdvDipPsych

Deputy Head of Sixth Form: Mrs S Howells, BA, PGCE
Deputy Head of Sixth Form: J E Bown, BSc, PGCE (*Pastoral*)
Deputy Head of Sixth Form: Mrs H M Kenworthy BSc, PGCE (*Academic*)
Registrar: Mrs L M Berry, BA
Third Master: C Maskery, MSc, BA, PGCE, FBAPT
Third Mistress and Lower House Mistress: Mrs J L Pratley, MCertSpLD
School Nurse: Mrs L S Haste, RGN
Chaplain: Revd Canon R Humphreys, BA, CertEd

Housemasters and Housemistresses:
Feilden: Miss P S M Townsend, BA, MBA, PGCE
Gascoigne: G J Sheer, BA, PGCE
Harcourt: J Capel, MA, PGCE
Queen Anne: Miss F M M Hamon, BA, PGCE
Swift: M G Cooper, BA, PGCE
Vanbrugh: T J Walwyn, BA

Heads of Departments:
Miss M Bennett, BA, PGCE (*Modern Foreign Languages*)
T J Bostwick, BA, PGCE (*History*)
Mrs H V Brown, BA, PGCE (*Design Technology*)
Dr C Flaherty, PhD, MSc, BSc (*Science*)
R I Hardie, BA (*ICT*)
S R Henderson, BSc, PGCE (*Music*)
Mrs C Hooper, Dip Acting (*Drama*)
R D Hughes, BA (*Business Studies*)
Miss D C H Jackson, BEd, DipEFL (*English*)
Mrs S F Martin, CertEd, BEd (*Learning Support*)
Mrs M R Martindale, MA (*Geography*)
C Maskery, MSc, BA, PGCE, FBAPT (*Sport*)
Ms A S Rose, BA, PGCE (*Psychology*)
Mrs C S Scaysbrook, BSc, PGCE (*Mathematics*)
M Schofield, BA, MA, PGCE (*Philosophy, Religion and Ethics*)
Miss M M Taylor, BA, PGCE, NDDA, PGDC (*Art*)

74 full-time academic teaching staff, plus 16 part-time. 14 visiting teachers for Piano, String, Wind and Brass instruments, Timpani and Singing. 12 part-time sports coaches.

Curriculum. A curriculum is offered that gives pupils the chance to pursue individual abilities, with both traditional and modern subjects, those that are highly academic and others that are more practical. The National Curriculum is broadly followed up to GCSE. All pupils study core subjects of English, Maths and Science at GCSE and have a wide choice of subject options. There is also a full programme of personal, social and health education.

Sixth Formers typically choose four subjects to study at AS Level and continue with three of these subjects to A2 Level. The small size of teaching groups is particularly conducive to individual attention and encouragement. The usual courses are supplemented by Economics, Photography, Politics, Philosophy and Law.

The Junior School offers a fully balanced curriculum with the focus on developing high standards and providing intellectual challenges. Whilst the National Curriculum is followed, the freedom to offer breadth is embraced. (*See Cokethorpe Junior School entry in IAPS section.*)

Parents are kept closely informed of their pupils' progress and achievement, both academically and socially.

Facilities. There is a continuous building and upgrading programme. Recent developments include a new Dining Hall and Sixth Form Centre in September 2009 which created additional classrooms elsewhere in the School and gave the opportunity to relocate and expand the Art studios and Reception Class facilities.

Pastoral. The House system, personal tutoring (including day-to-day care, pastoral welfare and academic progress), year-group specific social and health programmes and a joint Anglican and Roman Catholic foundation creates an excellent support structure. Small classes and dedicated teachers help pupils champion their strengths and challenge their weaknesses.

Sport. The School has a strong and successful sporting tradition. Principal sports include rugby, hockey, netball, soccer, cricket, tennis, kayaking and clay pigeon shooting. A wide variety of subsidiary sports are also available including badminton, athletics, cross-country, golf, judo, squash, swimming and sailing, designed to suit all tastes and abilities. All pupils do PE as part of the curriculum. The 150 acres of parkland provide ideal playing fields and a 9-hole golf course. There are also two all-weather pitches, and a sports hall, fitness suite, climbing tower and clay-pigeon shoot. There are regular county, national and international successes. The most talented pupils will be considered for the School Sports Academy.

Other Activities. The extra-curricular programme (known as 'AOB') plays a prominent part in a pupil's timetable and includes over 30 clubs such as Design, Music, Cookery, Science, Drama, Social Service, Computing, History of Film, Chess, Debating, Young Enterprise, and The Duke of Edinburgh's Award Scheme. There is a strong tradition of fundraising. Other activities include language exchanges, ski trips and sports tours abroad, cultural trips to Africa and Greece.

Music, Drama and Creative Arts. The Arts are extremely important at Cokethorpe. All pupils are encouraged to learn a musical instrument and join the choir or one of the range of orchestras and ensembles, and the majority do so. Peripatetic teachers cover a very wide range of instruments, and there are regular concerts and recitals during the year. Drama flourishes with two to three whole-school productions and the inter-house competition annually, numerous GCSE and A Level performances, a programme of lunchtime recitals from all years and frequent trips to the theatre. Art, Textiles, Design Technology (Resistant Materials and Graphic Design) are all offered at GCSE and A Level, with Photography also offered at A Level. There is also a vibrant and varied range of art, design and craft activities as part of the extended curriculum.

Higher Education and Careers. All Sixth Form leavers go on to Higher Education, enrolling in a wide variety of foundation courses, degrees or apprenticeships. A careers programme is followed throughout the Senior School, including work experience, careers conventions and psychometric profiling. Help and advice is given by experienced Careers teachers and the latest literature is available in the Careers Library.

Admission. Pupils usually enter the Junior School at 4 or 7 (the latter based on an assessment day in January) and the Senior School either at 11, 13 or 16. There are occasionally vacancies at other ages. Candidates at 11 are required to sit assessments in Maths, English and Reasoning, at 13 either assessments or Common Entrance and at 16 GCSEs or equivalent. Places are offered on the basis of these, plus interviews and school reports. There is a registration fee of £75. Registration forms and details of entrance examination procedures are available from the Registrar.

Scholarships. Means-tested scholarships are assessed separately and awarded at Year 7, Year 9 and Sixth Form. Academic, All Round, Art and Design, Music, Sport, Drama and Modern Languages scholarships are available.

Bursaries. Financial assistance is available, through the award of means-tested bursaries, to those families entering the School from ages 11 through to 18 (occasionally into the Junior School). The value of the bursary can be up to 100% of fees.

Fees per term (2011-2012). Junior School Junior School £3,425; Senior School: £4,875 (Years 7 and 8), £4,975 (Years 9–13). Extras are kept to a minimum.

The Cokethorpe Society. c/o *Director of External Affairs*: Warwick Daniels, Cokethorpe School (society@cokethorpe.org).

Charitable Status. Cokethorpe Educational Trust Limited is a Registered Charity, number 309650. It aims to provide a first-class education for each individual pupil.

Colfe's School

Horn Park Lane, London SE12 8AW
Tel: 020 8852 2283
Fax: 020 8297 1216
e-mail: head@colfes.com
website: www.colfes.com

Colfe's is one of the oldest schools in London. The parish priest of Lewisham taught the local children from the time of Richard Walker's Charity, founded in 1494, until the dissolution of the monasteries by Henry VIII. Revd John Glyn re-established the school in 1568 and it was granted a Charter by Queen Elizabeth in 1574. Abraham Colfe, Vicar of Lewisham, became a Governor in 1613 and the School was re-founded bearing his name in 1652. Colfe declared that the aim of the School was to provide an education for "pupils of good wit and capacity and apt to learn", reflecting the School's emphasis on sound learning and academic achievement since the earliest times. Colfe's original vision was to educate the children of "the hundred of Blackheath" and although today our pupils travel to the School from all parts of London, a strong sense of local community remains, with most of the pupils coming from the four boroughs which surround the school. One of Abraham Colfe's wisest moves was to invite the Leathersellers' Company, one of the oldest of the city Livery Companies, to be the Trustee of his will. Links between the School and the company are strong.

Mottos: 'Soli Deo honor et gloria' (Leathersellers) 'Ad Astra per Aspera' (Colfe)

Visitor: HRH Prince Michael of Kent

Board of Governors:
Revd Scott Anderson, Vicar of Lewisham
Dr Angela Brueggemann, DPhil
Miss Serena Cheng, MA, LLB
Sir John Garnar Newton, Bt
John Guyatt, MA Oxon
Gregory Jones, MA Oxon, LLM Lond
Dr Sara Owen, DPhil
Ian A Russell, MBE (*Chairman*)
Nigel R Pullman, JP (*Master of the Leathersellers' Company*)
Simon W Polito, MA, LLB
Andrew B Strong, BSc
Anthony C L Thornton, QC
Sean Williams, MA Oxon, MPA Harvard
P J Winter, MA

Headmaster: **R F Russell**, MA Cantab

Deputy Head – Academic: Ms C Butler, MA Oxon
Deputy Head – Pastoral: Mrs A Cobbin, BA
Deputy Head – Administrative: J King, BSc, MA
Head of Sixth Form: S Drury, BA, MA
Head of Preparatory School: J Gallagher, BA, MBA
Bursar: Miss J Deacon, MA Cantab

Senior School:
* *Head of Department*

Art:
*Ms S Beetlestone, BA
Mrs J Burton, BA
S Zivanovic, BA

Biology:
*C Morriss, BSc
N Crowe, BEd, MA
Dr B Davies, MA Cantab, PhD
Dr J Lea, PhD, BSc
Mrs E Lyons, BEd
Mrs S O'Leary, BSc
Dr E White, BSc, PhD

Chemistry:
*J Worley, BSc
R Hazard, BSc
Miss L Mellor, BSc
Ms L Murphy, BEd

Classics:
*A Corstorphine, MA Cantab, MPhil
Ms C Butler, MA Oxon
Miss N Harris, MA Cantab
R Russell, MA Cantab

Design & Technology:
*D S Smith, BEd, MA
Miss C Humphries, BA
Miss C Quinton, BA

Drama:
*G Bruce, BA
Mrs R Medhurst, MA Cantab
Mrs J Vander Gucht, BA
S Zivanovic, BA

Economics & Business Studies:
*R Otley, BA
S Drury, BA, MA
J King, BSc, MA
Miss S Price, BA, MSc

English:
*R Thompson, PhD, MMus, LGSM
Miss N Cadwallender, MA
Mrs A Cobbin, BA
Miss H Dawson, MA Oxon
C Dunsmore, MA Oxon
Mrs E Karavidas, BA, MA
J Smith, BA

General Studies:
*C Foxall, BA

Geography:
*O Snell, BSc, MSc
Mrs F McAuliffe, BSc
A Newell, BSc
Miss E Taylor, BA,BSc

History:
*A Foster, MA Cantab
Miss L Lechmere, BA

J Patterson, BA
S Varley, BA, MA

IT:
*O Snell, BSc, MSc

Learning Support:
*Mrs P Turrent, OCR DipSpLD

Mathematics:
*Miss H Ball, BSc
Miss C Craciun, BSc, MA
Miss E Cross, BSc
Mrs O Hamidzadeh, BSc
A Pearson, BSc
Mrs C Stokes, BEd, BSc
Mrs J Toms, BSc
U Vijapura, BSc

Media Studies:
*C Foxall, BA
Miss H Dawson, MA Oxon
Miss Li-Sue, BA

Modern Foreign Languages:
Ms S Kuehl, BA (*French)
M Koutsakis, MA (*German)
A Seddon, BA, MIL (*Spanish)
Mrs E Biggs, BSc, MA
Miss S Brennan, BA
Mrs A Chapman, BA
Miss H Laurenson, BA, MA, PhD
Mrs J German, BA

Music:
Miss K Collinson, MA Cantab
Mrs M Metherell, BA
A Harper, BMus, LTCL

Outdoor Education:
*Major C Cherry, BSc

Physical Education:
N Miller, BSc (*Boys PE)
Miss R Hargrave, BEd (*Girls PE)
A Bateson, BA
A Brooker, DLC
Major C Cherry, BSc
Miss E Cross, BSc
Miss K Murray, BSc
Mrs J Pearson, BSc
Mrs N Rayes, BEd, MA

Physics:
*Mrs B Durkin, BSc
R Ashley, BSc
P Cummins, BSc (*Science)
J Fishwick, BSc
M Hillmer, BSME, MS

Politics:
*S Drury, BA, MA
R Otley, BA

Psychology:
N Crowe, BEd, MA
Dr J Lea, PhD, BSc

Religious Studies & Philosophy:
*J Chuter, MA
Mrs M Metherell, BA
D S Smith, BEd, MA
Mrs C Stokes, BEd, BSc

Director of Admissions: Mrs J German, BA
School Counsellor: Mrs K Kashif, BEd, MA
Examinations Officer: A Newell, BSc
Librarian & Careers: Mrs J Cardnell, BA, DipLib, MCLIP
Executive Assistant to the Headmaster: Mrs A Salmon, CSBM
Registration Secretary: Mrs S Walker

Preparatory School

Head of Preparatory School: J Gallagher, BA, MBA
Secretary to J Gallagher: Mrs E Benjamins, BEd
Deputy Head: Miss D Lempriere, BA
Director of Studies: M Heil, BEd
Deputy Head – Pre-Prep and Nursery: Mrs S Redman, BEd
Secretary to Mrs Redman: Mrs M Russo

Miss S Cabotage, BSc, BEd
P Donoghue, BEd
Mrs L Douglas, BA, DipSpLD
Mrs J Dunmore, BA
Mrs K Eggins, BSc
J Ford, BA
Mrs E Higgs, BA
Mrs H Lowth, BSc
Miss A Manning, BA

Mrs E Otley, CertEd, DipSpLD
Mrs J Pearson, BSc
Ms D Santos, BEd
C Stringfellow, CertEd
Miss C Tullis, BA, MA
Mrs S Watts, BEd, LTCL, Dip Perf Stds Opera
Mrs V Welch, BA, DipEd

Pre-Preparatory and Nursery Staff:
Mrs A Bradsley, NNEB
Mrs E Frost, BA
Ms S Grover, NNEB
Mrs S Gurr, BEd
Mrs R Hall, BA
Miss C Harknett, BTech
Miss L McNally, NNEB, NVQ2
Mrs M Moody, BEd, NNEB

Mrs L Mountford-Day, NVQ3
Mrs E Otley, TCert, DipSpLD
Miss H Ross, BA
Mrs C Russell, NNEB
Ms G Scala, NVQ3
Mrs S Smith, NNEB
Ms D Wheater, BEd
Miss N Williams, BA
Mrs S Williams, BSc

Admissions. There are 700 pupils in the Senior School, including 200 in the Sixth Form. The Preparatory School, incorporating the Nursery and Pre-Preparatory departments, caters for a further 330 pupils. All sectors of the school are fully co-educational. The main points of entry to the Preparatory School are 3+ and 4+ (Nursery and Pre-Prep) and 7+. The majority of the Prep School pupils transfer to the Senior School at 11. Approximately 65 pupils from a range of local state primary and Prep schools enter the Senior School directly at 11 and there are a limited number of places available to pupils wishing to join in the Sixth Form at Year 12.

Buildings. All the teaching accommodation is modern and purpose built. Specialist on-site facilities include the Leisure Centre, comprising sports hall, swimming pool, and fitness suite. The Leathersellers' Sports Ground, located less than a mile from the main school campus, provides extensive playing fields and related facilities. A new centre for the Visual and Performing Arts was built in 2003 and an extensive all-weather pitch was completed in 2006. The Preparatory School, including Nursery and Pre-Preparatory departments, is housed in a separate modern building on the main school site.

Curriculum. The curriculum follows the spirit of the National Curriculum in both Preparatory and Senior Schools. Fast track pupils are entered for the separate Sciences at GCSE and follow the IGCSE Maths course. A wide range of subjects is available at A Level, 26 in total, including Drama, Government and Politics, Media Studies, Physical Education, Psychology and Philosophy.

Physical Education and Games. Physical Education and Games are compulsory for all pupils up to and including Year 11. Full use is made of the wide range of facilities available on-site, including a fully-equipped Sports Centre, swimming pool and all-weather surface.

The main sports for boys are rugby, football and cricket. Girls play hockey, netball, tennis and athletics. Other sports available include badminton, basketball, cross-country running, squash and swimming.

Music and Drama. Music and Drama thrive alongside each other in the purpose-built Performing Arts Centre. The music department is home to a wide range of performance groups ranging from beginners to advanced ensembles in both classical and contemporary genres. There are regular performance opportunities given throughout the year, some held in the purpose-built recital hall and others in external venues. A team of 20 visiting instrumental teachers provide further opportunities for pupils to enjoy making music. Drama is a popular subject at both GCSE and A Level, with large numbers of pupils also involved outside the classroom. We recently staged a full-scale production of *One Flew Over The Cuckoo's Nest* at the Greenwich Theatre, London.

Careers. The Careers and Higher Education Department is staffed on a full-time basis. Regular events include University Information Evenings and Careers Fairs.

Fees per term (2011-2012). Senior School £4,371 (excluding lunch); Preparatory School £3,546 (excluding lunch); Pre-Preparatory £3,345 (including lunch); Nursery & Reception £3,054 (including lunch).

Scholarships and Bursaries. Academic Scholarships are awarded mainly on the basis of outstanding performance in the Entrance Examinations. The exams are designed to identify and reward academic potential, as well as achievement.

Means-tested bursaries are also available at 11+. Bursaries may, in exceptional circumstances, cover the total cost of tuition fees. Application forms are available from the Registrar.

A limited number of Music and Sports awards are also available at 11+. In the case of Music scholars, free instrumental tuition may accompany the award. Details of Music and Sports awards can be obtained from the Registrar.

A number of scholarships, bursaries and other awards are also available to candidates entering the school at 16+. Details can be obtained from the Registrar.

Preparatory School. The Preparatory School building, with splendid facilities, was opened by HRH Prince Michael of Kent in 1988. Specialist rooms of the Senior School are also used. While the curricular emphasis is on high standards in basic Mathematics and English, a wide range of other subjects is taught, including Science and French. There is also a range of activities similar to those enjoyed by the Senior School and all pupils are expected to participate. All pupils proceed to the Senior School if they achieve the qualifying standard. It is expected that virtually all pupils from the Prep school will proceed to the Senior school at 11. (*For further details see entry in IAPS section.*)

Nursery and Pre-Prep. A co-educational nursery and pre-preparatory school for pupils aged 3 to 7 is housed in modern accommodation adjacent to the Prep School.

Old Colfeians' Association. Enquiries to the Hon Secretary, Eltham Road, London SE12 8UE. Tel: 020 8852 1181.

Charitable status. Colfe's School is a Registered Charity, number 1109650. It exists to provide education for boys and girls.

Colston's School

Stapleton, Bristol BS16 1BJ
Tel: 0117 965 5207
Fax: 0117 958 5652
e-mail: enquiries@colstons.bristol.sch.uk
website: www.colstons.bristol.sch.uk

Colston's School, which is celebrating its 300th anniversary in 2010, is a co-educational day school for pupils aged 3 to 18. It is located on a spacious 32-acre site at Stapleton village in north Bristol, with the Lower and Upper Schools sharing the extensive facilities. The Governors of the school are The Society of Merchant Venturers, Merchants' Hall, Bristol BS8 3NH.

Motto: '*Go, and do thou likewise.*'

Governors:
D J Marsh (*Chairman*)
Mrs K Morgan, OBE, DL (*Vice Chair*)

Mrs A Bernays	D Mace
C A Booy, OBE	Professor J McGeehan,
M Broad, MBE	CBE
¶R Cotton	R Morris
Mrs K Curling	Mrs P Morris
¶S Davies	T Taylor
¶L Frewin	R Thornton
J Hunt	J Webb
T Kenny	

¶ *Old Colstonian*

Headmaster: P T Fraser, MA

Deputy Headmaster: P Goodyer, BA

Deputy Head Academic (*Acting*): R D Mardle, BSc

Staff:
* *Head of Department*

N Aspden, BSc
C Banning, BSc Hons
B Berry, BA
D J Betterton, BA (**Physics*)
G G Boyce, BA
Mrs J Brighton, BSc
Miss J Burke, BA
A Calder, BA Hons
Mrs A J Chisnall, BA
Mrs D S Currie, BA (**Modern Languages*)
Mrs G Dann, BA, DipCG, IPD
Dr K Dawson, BA, PhD
Miss O De Zarate, BA
Miss D Drake, BSc
N J Drew, BA (**History*)
M W Eyles, BSc (**Geography*)
Miss C Flay, BA Hons
R P Gash, BSc (**ICT*)
Miss K Goddard, BSc Hons
J Gwilliam, BA Hons
O Harris, BSc
Mrs C L Hambley, BA
J Harper, MA
Mrs A M Hart, BSc
Mrs R Johnson, BA (**Mathematics*)
P A Jones, BSc
D Kaye, BA Hons
Miss N Kendall, MA
Dr A D E Martin, BSc, PhD (*Acting *Science, *Biology*)
D L Mason, BSc
L Masters, BSci
Miss L McGregor, BSc
Mrs J Murray, BA

D Nichols, BSc Hons (*Business Studies*)
Mrs J L Poppy, BA
S Pritchard, MA (*Drama*)
C Pullen, BA
T Rounds, BA Hons (*Religious Studies*)
Miss K Snell, BA (*Design Technology*)
J Shooter, MA (*Director of Music*)
P Temple, BSc (*Chemistry*)
P T Thornley, BEd (*Director of Physical Education*)
Dr J A Tovey, PhD (*English*)
Miss S Victor, BEd
D Wall, BEd (*PE, Games*)
Miss L J Wight, BEd
T Williams
Ms C J Wyatt, BA
N C Y Yaxley, BEd (*Art*)

Lower School

Head of Lower School: Mrs C Aspden, MA

Deputy Head: M Weavers, BEd

Junior Department:

W J Barber, BSc	Mrs M May, BEd
Mrs J Barwell, BEd	K Watts, BEd
O J R Barwell, BA	Mrs P M Webley, BA
Mrs H Fitzpatrick, BSc	
T George, BSc	*Assistants*:
Miss V Hawkings, BSc	Mrs J Robinson
Miss K M Jones, BA	

Pre-Prep:
Head of Pre-Prep: Mrs R Wyles, CertEd

Miss H Dennehy, BSc	*Nursery*:
Mrs S Howlett, BEd	*Nursery and Foundation*
Mrs S Lake, CertEd	*Stage Coordinator*: Mrs
Mrs S Shafi, BA	T L May, BEd

Assistants:	Mrs C F Bastin, NNEB
Mrs R Butler, CACHE 3	Mrs W Gardiner, NNEB
Mrs R Nowak, NVQ3	Miss K Merchant, CACHE
Mrs S Powell, STA NOCN	3
Mrs S Quilter, LLB,	
CACHE 2	

Librarian:
Headmaster's PA: Mrs D Sollis
Lower School Head's Secretary: Mrs C Pullin
Director of Finance: Mrs N Prosser
Accounts Manager: Mrs S Ogden
Facilities Director: A Meakin
Catering Manager: Miss J Prichard
Officer Commanding CCF: Lt Col T Scarll, BEM
SSI CCF: WO2 S Sinar
School Administrator: Mrs D Thomas
Matrons: Mrs N Webb, Mrs D Drew
Receptionist: Mrs E Hughes

Organisation. There are approximately 830 pupils at Colston's, one third of whom are girls. The Lower School, catering for the 3–11 age range, is adjacent to the main site which accommodates the Upper School (11–18 years). Pastoral care is exercised through a house system and Sixth Form of some 160 boys and girls.
For details of the Lower School, see entry in IAPS section.

Admission. Pupils are admitted at 11+ through the school's own examination or at 13+ through the Common Entrance Examination or the school's own examination. Admission direct into the Sixth Form is also quite normal. Awards and bursaries are available including music, art, drama and sports scholarships. All awards are subject to means testing.

Work. The curriculum is broadly based, avoiding premature specialisation, and is in line with the provisions of the National Curriculum. German, Spanish, Religious Knowledge, Drama, Art, Music, Technology, Design Technology and ICT are optional subjects. There is a wide choice of A Level subjects in the Sixth Form.

Chapel. Colston's is a Church of England Foundation, and use is made of neighbouring Stapleton Parish Church for morning assembles and other services. Boys and girls of other denominations are also welcomed.

Games and Activities. Colston's has over 30 acres of playing fields surrounding the school. A continuous programme of improvement has recently provided a floodlit Astroturf pitch and newly-refurbished floodlit tennis and netball courts. Pupils have use of a sports hall, squash courts, fitness suite and heated outdoor swimming pool. Principal boys' games are rugby, hockey and cricket. Principal girls' games are tennis, hockey, netball and rounders. In addition all pupils can take part in athletics, cross country, swimming, squash, badminton and basketball. The Colston's Combined Cadet Force has grown to record levels with over 240 cadets and a new purpose-built headquarters building. A range of adventure activities are provided through CCF including flying, gliding, sailing, canoeing and camping. The school also encourages pupils to undertake social and community service in Bristol.

Music and Drama. With a new concert hall and a well-equipped theatre, music and drama play a very important part in the life of the school. There is a large element of devised work in drama, with all pupils having the opportunity to act and produce as well as helping with staging and lighting. Regular theatre visits are arranged. About half of all pupils learn musical instruments, and there is an orchestra, swing band and a variety of choirs.

Careers. There is ample opportunity for boys and girls to obtain professional advice on the choice of a career. Colston's is a member of the Independent Schools Careers Organisation whose services are available. The Head of Careers arranges a full week's work experience for all Year 10 pupils, and also arranges visits to Careers Conventions organised by employers and universities.

Fees per term (from January 2011). Full boarders £6,580; day pupils £3,445 (excluding lunches).

Modernisation. An extensive building programme has been carried out in recent years including a new concert hall and CCF headquarters. A full refurbishment of the library was completed in summer 2007, and the laboratories and Sixth Form facilities have been completely refurbished in the last year.

Situation. Colston's is located in Stapleton village which is within the city of Bristol, and enjoys the advantage of having all its playing fields and facilities on site. The school makes full use of Bristol's extensive cultural and sporting opportunities, particularly with theatre and concert visits. Road and rail communications are excellent, particularly because the school is less than a mile from Junction 2 of the M32. London Heathrow can be reached in one-and-a-half hours by road or rail.

The school is large enough to sustain a wide range of activities at a high level and yet small enough for each boy or girl to contribute actively and be known as individuals. Every effort is made to provide for and develop pupils' abilities in academic, cultural and other extra-curricular activities. The school aims to encourage a strong sense of community and service, and to fully develop and extend the talents of every boy and girl.

Charitable status. Colston's School is a Registered Charity, number 1079552. Its aims and objectives are the provision of education.

Cranleigh School

Cranleigh, Surrey GU6 8QQ
Tel: 01483 273666; 01483 276377 (Head)
Fax: 01483 267398; 01483 273696 (Head)
e-mail: enquiry@cranleigh.org
website: www.cranleigh.org

Cranleigh School was founded in 1865.
  Motto: '*Ex cultu robur*'

Visitor: The Rt Revd The Lord Bishop of Winchester

Governing Body:
Chairman: J A V Townsend, MA
Deputy Chairman: A J Lajtha, MA, FCIB

Dr R Chesser, MA, MB, BChir, MRCP
Mrs M M S Fisher, MA
J A M Knight, BA
Mrs A J Lye, BA
M J Meyer
Dr S Mockford, BSc, PhD, CEng, MIEE, FRSA
Mrs L A Muirhead, BA
The Revd Canon N P Nicholson, DL
Mrs H J O'Hagan, BA, ATII
A C Ramsay, AADipl, RIBA
R A Robinson, FCA, MBA
The Revd Dr T J Seller, BSc, PhD
Mrs E Stanton, BSc, ACA
Dr J Stevenson, MA, DPhil
J G M Wates, BA, MBA
O A R Weiss, MA
Dr T D Wilkinson, BEng, PhD, MIET
Mrs M J Williamson
J P G Wiseman, CMG

Bursar and Clerk to the Governors: P T Roberts, MBE

Head: **Guy Waller**, MA, MSc, PGCE, FRSA (Worcester and Wolfson Colleges, Oxford)

Deputy Head: A J Griffiths, BSc, MSc, DIC, CGeol, FGS, QTS
Director of Studies: I M Allison, MA, PGCE
Assistant Deputy Head: T I McConnell-Wood, BSc
Senior Master: J F G Thompson, MA, PGCE
Senior Teachers:
D R Boggitt, BEng, PGCE
Dr A P Saxel, BSc, PhD
Head of School Administration: Ms A J Russell-Price

Members of Common Room:
† *Housemaster/mistress*

Mrs M C Allison, BEd
R M Allon-Smith, MA, PGCE
D I Ardley, BEd, CNAA DT
Mrs L Ardley, M-ès-L, PGCE
Miss M Baffou, LLCE
T H J Barnett, MA, DipAD
J Bartlett, BA
S J Batchelor
S D Bird, BA (*†East*)
T R Boardman, MMath, PGCE
S A A Block, MA
C H D Boddington, BA, PGCE (*†Cubitt*)
J J Brookes, BA
M J Brookes, BA
B W Browne, BSc, PGCE
E M Burnett, BSc, PGCE (*†North*)
Mrs V J Burnett, BA, PGCE
Mrs H K E Burns, BEd
Mrs O Burt, BA, MA
R A Clarke, BA, BPhil, QTS

Mrs A P L Cooke, BA
S T Cooke, BA
J L Copp, BA
Mrs E G M Dellière, BA
Miss S C Diamond, BA, PGCE
Mrs E L Ellin, BA, PGCE
T R Fearn, BSc, PGCE
Mrs H B Fearn, BA
A P Forsdike, MA
Mrs R E Frett, MA, PGCE (*†South*)
D J Futcher, BSc
Miss S L Greenwood, BA Ed
D A W Hogg, MA, DPhil
W D Holloway, BA
A R Houston, BSc
R A C Humes, BA
Dr C M Jackson, BSc, PhD
R G H J Jackson, BA, MEd
Mrs E J Jenkins, BA, PGCE
R C E K Kefford, BSc, PGCE
Dr S L Kemp, BSc, PhD, PGCE
R Lailey, MA
P Leggitt, MA
A A G Logan, BA, PGCE (*†Loveday*)
P J Longshaw, MA
J C E Mann, BSc, PhD, CBiol, MIBiol, QTS
T J Marriott, BA
Mrs M Maunder, BEd
Mrs S E McLaughlin, BEd
P A McNiven, DipAD, QTS (*Director of Art*)
Miss R A Miller, BMus, PGDip, PGCert, PGCE
J C Monk, BA
Miss K T Morland, BA
Mrs C Neill, BA, PGCE (*†West*)
G J N Neill, BA, PGCE
Miss C E Nicholls, MA, PGCE
Ms R P F Nicholson, BA, PGCE
Mrs N L Odhams, BA, MEng
S M Owen
B E Page, BA, PGCE
The Revd P V Parker, BSc, BA, MA, PGCE, FRGS (*Chaplain*)
Mrs S R Parry, BA, PGCE
M C Pashley, BMus (*Director of Cranleigh Music*)
Miss S M Peers, BSc, MSc, PGCE
Mrs J A Pimm, BEd
Mrs O D Ravilious, BA, PGCE
Miss S E Roberts, BA, PGCE
J S Ross, MA, PGCE
R J Saxel, BA, DipRam, LRAM
P N Scriven, BA, MA, LRAM, MM (*Organist in Residence*)
Miss L E C Sturdee, MA, PGCE
Mrs N R Sutton, BA
Mrs S D Thomson, BSc
B R Tyrrell, MChem, DPhil
K W Weaver, BA Music, PGDip
Miss S L Webb, BA
R A Wilson, LTCL
J M Witcombe, BSc, PGCE
Mrs U C Yardley, BA, PGCE
S A H Young, BSc, MSc, PhD, PGCE

Medical Officer: Dr G Tyrrell, MB BS, DObstRCOG

Preparatory School
(*see entry in IAPS section*)

Head: M T Wilson, BSc University of Keele

Deputy Head: Mrs S D Gravill, BA, PGCE

Members of Common Room:
J Dale-Adcock, BA, PGCE
A J Artman, BA
E T Batchelor, BSc

Mrs C A Beddison, BMus, PGCE
D Britt, BA, PGCE
Mrs J Brown, HND
R B P Carne, MA, PGCE
B M Dixon, BA, CertEd
J Forster, BSc, PGCE
Mrs R Frett, MA, PGCE (*Chaplain*)
Mrs C Frölich, BA, PGCE
Miss C Gibson, BSc, PGCE
M J Halstead, BSc, PGCE
Miss K Hatfield, Dip Dance, ISTD
C D Henderson, BA, PGCE
D Hitchen, GRSM, ARMCM
M S F Howard, BA, CertEd
Mrs S Johnston, BSc, PGCE
Mrs A Jolly, BSc, PGCE
Mrs H Kitson, CertEd
D S Manning, EDE
Mrs J J Marriott, BA, PGCE
Miss L R Martin, BA, PGCE
Mrs H McNiven, BA
Mrs P R Meadows, BEd
Miss F Nutley, BEd
Mrs H L H Pakenham-Walsh, BA
Miss R Quinn, BEd
J S Simpson, BA
Mrs E Reed, BSc, PGCE
Mr P B Storey, DipEd
T M Stroud, BSc
Mrs T Thistlethwaite, BEd, CertEd
Miss L Thompson, BA
P G Waller, MA, PGCE
Dr M Ward, PhD
Mrs C J Wilson, BEd, RSA Dip SpLD

Head's PA: Mrs P Adams (Tel: 01483 542054)
Registrar: Mrs F M J Bundock (Tel: 01483 542051)
School Secretary: Mrs J M Cooke (Tel: 01483 542058)

Cranleigh School's principal aim is to provide an environment in which pupils can flourish, enabling them to capitalise on the diverse range of opportunities offered by the School and to achieve to the best of their ability within a framework of shared values and standards. The School's 240-acre site, situated eight miles from Guildford on the Surrey-West Sussex border, lies on the outskirts of Cranleigh Village and within 45 minutes of London. The School is fully co-educational, with some 200 girls and 400 boys between the ages of 13 and 18, including a Sixth Form of about 240. It is a predominantly boarding community, attracting boarders from both the local area and further afield; it also, however, welcomes day pupils, who are fully integrated into the Cranleigh community, playing their part in the activities of their respective Houses and benefiting from the advantages thereby offered.

Each House (separate for boys and girls) has a resident Housemaster or Housemistress, a resident Deputy, a Warden, two Matrons and a team of eight Lower School Tutors; Sixth Formers can choose their own Tutor from the whole of Common Room. There is also a strong and active partnership between parents and the School.

Cranleighans are encouraged to relish challenge, to feel they are known as individuals, and to become talented and wise adults with an inherent ability to adapt to a fast-changing world. Aligned with this, the School boasts an impressive record in academic achievement. Almost all pupils achieve three A2 Levels plus at least one additional AS Level, and in recent years more than 99% have gone on to university – 90% to their first-choice university.

Academic Patterns. Our aim is to act within the spirit of the National Curriculum, but to offer more, taking full advantage of our independence and the extra time available to a boarding school. We therefore retain a very broad curriculum in the Fourth Form, and have an options system in the Lower and Upper Fifth Forms which enables a pupil to take between nine and eleven GCSE subjects before moving on to AS Levels in the Sixth Form. We offer the opportunity to do Double or Triple Award Science, as well as giving good linguists the chance to take two foreign languages (with Latin if they wish). In the Sixth Form pupils can select from a wide choice of around twenty AS Level subjects.

Work on languages, with an emphasis on commercial and colloquial fluency, is encouraged for non-specialist linguists, and much use is made of the Language Laboratory. Exchanges take place with pupils in schools in France, Spain and Germany. We have comprehensive facilities for Science, with an emphasis on experimental work. All members of the Lower Sixth Form study a course in Critical Thinking, or attend a series of lectures on a variety of topics, to help broaden their education.

Information Technology is incorporated into the teaching of all other subjects, with each academic department having its own IT policy, coordinated by the Director of IT. There are several teaching rooms with networked PCs, and every House and academic department has PCs available for use, all linked to the School's network and the Internet.

Creative and Performing Arts. Cranleigh has maintained an enviable reputation for Music over many years, and the Merriman Music School offers pupils some of the finest facilities available. We send Choral Scholars to Oxford, Cambridge and major Music Departments and Colleges elsewhere; boys and girls of all ages successfully take part in national competitions and well over a third of the School learns a musical instrument. Keyboard players have access to a new Mander two-manual tracker organ, purposefully designed for versatility and teaching, and to two Steinway concert grand pianos. An exciting new Cranleigh Music initiative is now also in place, bringing together the Music Departments of Cranleigh School and Cranleigh Preparatory School under a single performing, management and administrative structure. Whilst facilities remain on separate sites (both sides of Horseshoe Lane), the ethos will be that of a single Music Faculty encompassing the full 7–18 age range, whose cohesive structure will help to nurture and progress talent from a very young age, so ensuring that all pupils are able to perform in an environment commensurate with their individual ability.

Cranleigh also boasts a strong Drama tradition. Regular large-scale productions take place in the Devonport Hall, to which is linked a studio theatre, the Vivian Cox Theatre, while a flourishing Technical Theatre department encourages the development of 'backstage' skills. The School's proximity to London allows for regular attendance at professional theatre, music and opera productions.

Art & Design have recently been brought together under one new Faculty, housing a talented mix of practising artists, teachers and designers. The spectacular Rhodes Art & Design School is spread over several buildings, with a mix of dedicated airy studios and manufacturing and prototyping areas. A comprehensive range of disciplines across drawing, painting, sculpture, textiles, printmaking, ceramics, graphics, product and industrial design, prototyping and CAD/CAM are delivered. The studios are open every day and appropriate use is made of the Faculty library, ICT and digital video and photo facilities. External visits are encouraged (both nationally and internationally). All students exhibit throughout the year.

Sport. Cranleigh provides an extremely diverse range of sporting activities for all pupils.

The School possesses an impressive array of sports facilities, including four full-size Astroturf pitches (one of which is floodlit), a 9-hole golf course, an Equestrian Centre with floodlit sand-school, 4 squash courts, 6 fives courts, 24 tennis courts, 8 netball courts and both indoor and outdoor swimming pools. The large Sports Hall complex (the Trevor Abbott Sports Centre) provides a popular venue for netball, tennis, badminton and basketball, and also includes an indoor cricket school, a separate dance studio and a fully equipped fitness suite. High standards are set for the numerous competitive teams, with an extensive programme of fixtures at all levels and for all ages. 'Sport for All' is a key philosophy at the School, supported by an experienced and talented team of coaches, many of whom have competed themselves at county, national and Olympic level. The School has witnessed some outstanding team and individual successes in recent years, including winning this year's Nationals in boys' hockey; having several current pupils picked for National representation in hockey, rugby and cricket; taking the National title in horse riding, and also seeing several recent Old Cranleighans continue to compete in the international arena, including in this year's Cricket World Cup, and as Olympic hopefuls.

In the Michaelmas Term the majority sports are hockey for girls and rugby for boys; in the Lent Term the majority sports are netball for girls and hockey for boys. During the winter terms, pupils can also compete in lacrosse, cross-country, golf, water polo, soccer, fives, rugby-sevens, basketball, riding and squash, plus badminton and canoeing for the Sixth Form. All pupils in the Fourth and Lower Fifth Forms take part in the majority sport, whilst an element of choice is gradually introduced for the older pupils. All pupils in the School take part in sport, even in the Sixth Form.

In the Summer Term, the main team sport for boys is cricket, whilst some boys compete in tennis, swimming, athletics and golf. For girls the main sport is tennis, with competitive swimming, athletics, rounders and cricket popular additional offerings.

Service Activities. There are opportunities for pupils to take part in a range of 'service' activities. Boys and girls may join the CCF or get involved with community service, ecology or first-aid training. Cranleighans help local elderly people in their homes and also have links with local schools for children with learning difficulties and with a home for adults with similar problems. Many Houses and the Fundraising Group raise money for various charities. Wider initiatives also include Amnesty and Environmental Awareness groups, and the School's new initiative, 'Beyond Cranleigh' – a key partnership between Cranleigh School and Beyond Ourselves, a London-based charity that works to improve the lives of disadvantaged young people in both London and in Zambia. This partnership will offer pupils various opportunities beyond Cranleigh – such as a Summer 2011 trip out to the Kawama School in the Copperbelt region of Zambia, to build much-needed classrooms. Such initiatives are designed to focus pupils' thoughts on life beyond the School.

Outdoor Education. Cranleigh operates a large Duke of Edinburgh's Award Scheme group, with many pupils completing the Gold Award before leaving school. By way of introduction, all Year 9 pupils undergo an Outdoor Education programme in order to improve their self-awareness and confidence. There are many other opportunities for Outdoor Education through the CCF, there is a well-attended climbing club (which has its own bouldering wall), and the School enters the annual International Devizes-to-Westminster Canoe Race (with both the boys' and the girls' team taking first place among Schools in the country in 2010).

Religion. The striking, neo-Gothic Chapel was built as a central point of the School, and Cranleigh maintains its concern to present the Christian way of life.

Developments. The latest in a line of major building projects, the Emms Centre houses the Modern Languages, Science and Mathematics Departments, while the new Faculty of Art & Design offers fabulous work spaces for these disciplines (*see Creative and Performing Arts section*). A timber-pole Workshop, designed using sustainable principles, was completed in February 2010. A premier 1st XV rugby pitch and additional cricket pitches are scheduled to be ready for play in September 2011.

Planning for our Pupils' Future. Cranleigh takes the future of its pupils very seriously. It maintains good contacts with the professions, industry and commerce, through links developed as part of the careers advice structure. All pupils are regularly assessed during their time at the School, and this process includes a period of Work Experience at the end of the Upper Fifth year. On a personal level, the Old Cranleighan Society enables current and past boys and girls to maintain lasting links with one another.

Admission and Registration. Parents wishing to enquire about places at the School or to request a copy of the detailed Prospectus should contact the Head of School Administration on 01483 276377, or visit the website at www.cranleigh.org. If you wish to visit the School, the Head would be delighted to welcome you: please telephone to make an appointment. Pupils between the ages of 13 and 14 are admitted in September, via the Common Entrance or the Scholarship examinations. There may be vacancies at other levels and there is a small intake at Sixth Form level. The entrance procedure at Sixth Form level includes a series of interviews and a written test for candidates for Academic Awards.

Awards. (*See Scholarship Entries section.*) The Master of the Scholars has a specific responsibility for all Scholars. They are members of their Houses and attend normal lessons, but also have an additional programme throughout their time at the School that covers a wide variety of academic, cultural, social and commercial areas beyond the syllabus and which encourages independent thinking and research.

At age thirteen, Academic, Music and Art Awards are available, along with Eric Abbott awards for candidates with at least one other clearly established area of excellence and the potential to have a positive impact on life at Cranleigh. In addition, Head's Awards are made, at his discretion, in recognition of attributes of a true Cranleighan – leadership, commitment and service. Music Awards include free musical tuition. In certain circumstances, additional consideration may be given to sons or daughters of public servants, members of the armed forces and the clergy of the Church of England.

At Sixth Form level, Academic, Music, Art and Eric Abbott Awards are offered.

All Awards are fees-linked and may be augmented in cases of proven financial need. Awards can be made to boys and girls already at the School if their progress merits it. Full details of Awards can be obtained by telephoning 01483 276377. In addition, enquiries are welcomed with regards to Foundation Awards.

Fees per term (2011-2012). Boarders £9,805, Day Pupils £7,990.

It is the policy of the School to keep extras down to an absolute minimum, and limited to such charges as individual music tuition. Textbooks are supplied until the Sixth Form, at which point pupils are encouraged to buy their own so that they may take them on to university. A scheme is available for the payment of fees in advance.

Preparatory School. The School has its own Preparatory School and boys and girls are normally admitted at seven or eight, but also at other ages. For further information, apply to the Head of the Preparatory School (*see entry in IAPS section*).

Charitable status. Cranleigh School is a Registered Charity, number 1070856. It exists to provide education for children aged 13–18 and the Preparatory School for those aged 7–13.

Culford School

Bury St Edmunds, Suffolk IP28 6TX
Tel: 01284 728615

Fax: 01284 728631
e-mail: admissions@culford.co.uk
website: www.culford.co.uk

Founded in 1881 in Bury St Edmunds, Culford School moved to its present site in 1935. The School is under the overall control of the Board of Management for Methodist Residential Schools, but is administered by a Board of Governors, to whom local control is devolved.

Motto: '*Viriliter Agite Estote Fortes*'

Visitor: The President of the Methodist Conference

Governors:
Chairman: Professor R Swanston, DSc, FRICS, FCMI

Air Cdre S Abbott, CBE, MPhil, BA	A P Crane
I H Angus, MA, HDipEd	M J Freeman, FRICS
Ms S A Blackmore, MA	J M Hammond, MA
N J Bristow, FCA	Mrs S E Kohl, MSR
Ms J M Broadbridge, BA	T C Matthews, BSc, FRICS
Mrs M G Browning, MBE, MA	G Russell, MA
	The Revd Canon G Thompson
The Rt Hon Viscount Chelsea	Mrs C Whight, FCIPD
	K Willimott

Headmaster: **J F Johnson-Munday**, MA, MBA

Deputy Heads:
Dr J Guntrip, BSc, PhD
J Williams, BA, PGCE

Director of Sport: D V Watkin, BEd

Chaplain: The Revd Simon Battersby, BTh

Members of the Common Room:
* *Head of Department*
† *Housemaster/mistress*

Ms R Ainscough, BSc, MBA	L Hoggar, BA
Ms C Alfaro, BA	*Dr A Hubbard, BSc, PhD
Mrs S L Antonietti, BSc	*Mrs B A Hunt, BA
†S Arbuthnot, MSc	*P M Jones, MA
Mrs H Baker, BSc	*Miss M Kane, BA
*M Barber, MA	Mrs K Kemp, BEd
D Bolton, DipMus	Ms J Loco, BA
D Bosworth, BSc, PhD	Mrs E Long
Miss P Buis, BSc	A H Marsh, CertEd
Dr A R Butler, BSc, PhD	Mrs L Martin, MA, MCLIP
Dr J M Byrne, MA, PhD	P Massey, BA
*†Mrs C Byrne, MA	*Mrs B Murray, TTHD, Dip SpLD
J Christopher, BSc	Revd Dr A G Palmer, MTh, PhD
Miss J Cooke, BA	
Mrs J Cope, BA, Cert SpLD	*Mrs A Parsons, BSc
	†Mrs B Recknell, MA
Mrs D A Copping, CertEd, Cert SpLD	*J D Recknell, MA, FRCO
R N Cox, BA	†G Reynolds, BEng
*A R Deane, BA	Mrs C Reynolds
R J Davie, BA, BSc, MEd, CPhys, MInstP	Mrs L Robinson
	R P Shepperson, BSc
*I C Devlin, BEd	B Thomas
†G E Draper, BA	*N J Tully, BSc
*A Edgar, BEng	*T Walsh, MPhil
*A P Fisk, MSc	D Watkin, BEd
Dr J Guntrip, BSc, PhD	D S Weyers, MMus
D Hall (*Director of Tennis*)	D M Williams, BSc
*E Hall, BA	Miss S Wood, BSc

Finance Manager: Mrs E Boardley, BA, FCCA

Operations Manager: C Muir, BSc, MRICS

Medical Officer: Dr N Harpur, MB BS, MRCGP, DRCOG

Headmaster's PA: Mrs C A Gordon

Registrar: Mrs K Tompkinson

Preparatory School
(*see entry in IAPS section*)

Headmaster: M Schofield, BEd

Deputy Head: Miss J Hatton, BEd

Director of Studies: N Hopton, MA, MEd

*Mrs C Alston, BA	Mrs L Matheson, MA
Mrs T Black	Mrs J Pineo, BA
Miss P Buis, BSc	*R Pineo, BSc
Mrs A Bunting, BA	Mrs E Rowlands
*Mrs H Carrington, BA	Mrs H Sceviour
Mrs C Currie	*Mrs L M Scott, BSc
D Dagnall, MA	Mrs R Stevens, Dip SpLD
*P Harrison, BEd	*T Walsh, MPhil
Mrs E Herd	D S Weyers, MMus
J Herd, BSc	Mrs S Whitcombe, Dip SpLD
*Mrs D Hollins, BA	
*S Jacubowski, BEd	*Mrs H Whiter, BA

Pre-Preparatory School:

Headmistress: Mrs S Preston, BA

Mrs E Grey, DPP	Mrs A Morrell, BEd
Mrs S Guntrip, BSc	Mrs R Ratcliffe, BEd
Miss C Hamilton, BEd	Miss N Rodwell, BTEC
Miss K Harrison, BEd	Miss K Trow, BTEC
Mrs A McEwen-Smith, DPP	Ms S Varley, BA
	Miss S Widger, BSc

Culford School is a co-educational boarding and day school of about 650 pupils aged 3–18 years. The Senior, Prep and Pre-Prep schools are all situated in a beautiful 480-acre landscaped park, four miles north of Bury St Edmunds, close to the university town of Cambridge and within easy reach of Stansted Airport.

The Senior School, for 13 to 18 year olds, has 360 pupils of whom half are boarders. There is a comprehensive programme of weekend activities on offer throughout each term. The Prep School for 7 to 13 year olds has over 220 pupils with a boarding community of some 50 children.

Culford believes education should be challenging, enriching and fun. There is a clear commitment to excellence in all areas of school life, and hard work in the classroom is complemented by full sporting and extra curricular programmes. Integrity and respect for the individual are encouraged along with a sense of responsibility towards the wider community. Pupils are given every opportunity to learn to take responsibility both for themselves and others. Well-founded House and tutorial systems ensure that the pastoral care is close and effective and this is made possible by a pupil/staff ratio of approximately 10:1. The School respects its Christian heritage as part of a Methodist foundation and is deliberately inclusive, welcoming pupils of all faiths and of none.

The Buildings and School Facilities. The main building is Culford Hall, an 18th century mansion formerly the seat of Marquis Cornwallis and Earl Cadogan. This building, with a blend of Robert Adam and Louis XVI interior design, has glorious views across Culford Park and houses the main reception, the Headmaster's study, the main Library and the Workman Library, and the newly-refurbished Music School, as well as additional classrooms and offices. A superb purpose-built Studio Theatre was constructed within the Hall in 2006.

Set in close proximity to Culford Hall and the Boarding Houses are the Hastings and Skinner Buildings, which are the main teaching blocks. Next to them lie the very well-equipped Bristol-Myers and William R Miller Science Centre. The School also has excellent Art, Design and Technology facilities in the Pringle Centre.

A new Sports Centre, comprising a 25-metre pool, Squash Courts, Fitness Centre, Dance Studio, Sports Hall and changing facilities, was completed in 2002 and a climbing wall was installed in 2006. A championship standard four-court Indoor Tennis Centre opened in 2009 enabling pupils to combine their education with a top-level tennis coaching programme.

A £2.5m refurbishment of the day and boarding houses began in February 2004. There are five Houses; two for day pupils and three for boarders. Boarders in their first year share study-bedrooms moving into single rooms in the Upper Sixth. There is internet access throughout each House and resource rooms for day pupils are similarly equipped. Cadogan House provides accommodation for boys and girls aged 7 to 13 years boarding at Culford Prep School.

The Pre-Prep School occupies its own area of the Estate in Fieldgate House. A combination of new and entirely refurbished buildings, it provides teaching for 80 boys and girls from Reception through to age seven in a delightful setting within the grounds. The Pre-Prep was extended in 1994 and in 2003 a multi-purpose assembly hall, the Weston Hall, was added. A purpose-designed Nursery opened in a separate building with its own well-equipped play area and garden in 2008.

A fully-equipped Medical Centre, supervised by a resident nurse, includes provision for residential care when necessary. The School also has a Tuck Shop.

Games. The School is set in a beautiful 480-acre park and there are ample facilities for physical recreation, including the Sports and Tennis Centre and Astroturf pitches. The 1st XI Cricket pitch has been described as one of the most beautifully sited in the country. A championship standard four-court Indoor Tennis Centre opened in 2009. The main games are Rugby, Hockey, Tennis and Cricket for the boys, and Hockey, Netball, Tennis and Rounders for the girls. However, many options are available to pupils including Athletics, Climbing, Swimming, Canoeing, Squash, Sailing, Sub-Aqua, Basketball, Golf and Riding. Pupils may also fish in our well-stocked lake.

Curriculum. The aim of the School is to provide a broad and balanced education in order to fulfil every pupil's academic potential. Core subjects at GCSE are English Language and Literature, Mathematics, the three sciences and a foreign language. Pupils choose additional subjects from a wide range of options. Their choice is guided by the Director of Studies, their teachers and House Tutor who, with the Housemaster or Housemistress, has responsibility for their academic and social progress. Information and Communication Technology is an integral part of the curriculum. Our pupil laptop scheme allows pupils to use ICT whenever and wherever they think it appropriate to support their learning. Pupils also experience PSHCE and PE. The Sixth Form offers a wide choice of subjects. Pupils usually study four subjects at AS Level, followed by three at A2. The Head of Scholars runs an enhancement programme for all Scholars and Exhibitioners, and which is open to all other interested pupils. Several pupils each year gain admission to Oxford and Cambridge.

Religion. The School is a Methodist foundation but children of all backgrounds are welcomed. All pupils attend Christian assemblies and all boarders attend a service on Sunday. Pupils are prepared for confirmation into both the Anglican and Methodist Churches in accordance with their parents' wishes.

Music. Music plays an important part in the life of the School which has strong links with the Cathedral in Bury St Edmunds. There are many choirs, orchestras and chamber ensembles. Regular concerts are held in order to give pupils of all ages opportunities to perform in public. Individual music tuition is offered in voice, piano, organ and all orchestral instruments. Pupils are also encouraged to form their own bands and perform to the school at its annual rock concert.

School Activities. There is an extensive range of clubs and societies from academic and creative through to sporting and outdoor pursuits. Many pupils participate in the

Duke of Edinburgh's Award Scheme or choose to join the CCF. Drama is very strong, including House plays and Concerts as well as major productions: these include regular musicals and plays for different sections of the school. The School arranges a varied programme of lectures and recitals of general interest. Pupils are encouraged to take part in Community Service Activities, which cover a wide range of services to the School and the local community. In addition, there are sponsored activities and events in support of local and national charities.

Members of staff regularly take pupils on visits and expeditions. Every summer a group of Sixth Formers and teachers spend 3 weeks in Malawi helping with various development projects. Other recent expeditions include China, Morocco and Venice, skiing in France, Switzerland and Italy, scuba diving in Egypt and sports tours in the United Kingdom and Europe.

Entry. The majority of pupils join in September at age 7+, 8+ and 11+ (Culford Preparatory School) and at 13+ and 16+ (Culford Senior School). Entrance examinations are held in the January and February of the year of entry or pupils may enter having passed Common Entrance in June. Entry to the Sixth Form is on the basis of GCSE performance or its equivalent for overseas candidates.

Entry to Culford Pre-Preparatory School is by informal assessment just prior to enrolment.

Applications are welcome from individuals throughout the year, subject to places being available.

Visits. If you wish to visit Culford, the Headmaster will be delighted to welcome you. Please contact the Admissions Office to arrange an appointment on 01284 385308 or to ask for a copy of the school prospectus. Open Mornings are held each term. Please visit www.culford.co.uk for more information.

Scholarships and Exhibitions. (*See Scholarship Entries section.*) The School holds its own scholarship examinations between November (Sixth Form Scholarships) and January/February for entry in the following September. Tennis and Rugby Scholarships are also now available.

Fees per term (2011-2012). Day £2,550–£5,285, Boarding £6,160–£8,555.

Charitable status. Culford School is a Registered Charity, number 310486. It exists to provide education for boys and girls.

Dame Allan's Boys' School

Fenham, Newcastle-upon-Tyne NE4 9YJ
Tel: 0191 275 0608 (School); 0191 274 5910 (Bursar)
Fax: 0191 275 1502 (School); 0191 275 1501 (Bursar)
e-mail: enquiries@dameallans.co.uk
website: www.dameallans.co.uk

The School was founded in 1705 by Dame Eleanor Allan and in 1935 was moved to Fenham on a site of 13 acres.

Governors:
Chairman: Mr E Ward
Vice-Chairman: Mr B W Adcock
Mrs S Banerjee
Mrs K Bruce
Mrs O Grant, OBE
Mr J Hargrove
Dr J A Hellen, MA, PhD
Prof P D Manning
Mrs M E Slater, MBE, JP
Mrs J Slesenger
Mr A M Stanley
Mr D Tait Walker
Mr T St A Warde-Aldam
Miss J Weatherall

Revd N Wilson

Ex officio:
The Lord Mayor of Newcastle upon Tyne
The Dean of Newcastle upon Tyne
The Vicar of the Parish of St John

Clerk to the Governors and Bursar: J Fleck, ACMA

Principal: J R Hind, MA Downing College, Cambridge, MEd Newcastle, PhD Durham

Vice-Principal: W J Lomas, BA, MA Newcastle
Assistant Head: P Wildsmith, BSc Birmingham, CBiol, MIBiol, MBES
Head of Sixth Form: D C Henry, BSc Heriot-Watt, FIMLS

J A Benn, BA Newcastle
H R Borland, MA Aberdeen
A C Chuter, BA Warwick
A H Davison, BDS, BA Newcastle MA, DCCI OU
J L Devine, BA Liverpool
J Downie, BA Durham
J C Downie, BSc Lancaster, MA Newcastle
M J Dutton, BA Huddersfield
J Etherington, BSc Manchester
M J Ford, BSc, MEd Newcastle
L J Friel, BA Hull
J P Gardner, MA Girton College, Cambridge
R Gates, MA New Hall, Cambridge
F Gold, BA Oxford
P Healey, BSc Newcastle
W P Hudson, BSc Loughborough
T Kingston, BA Leeds
K S Lewis, BA Goldsmiths College, London, ATD Leicester, CDT Trent
M V Lynch, BA Manchester
E Marsh, BSc Hull
B Nixon, BSc Northumbria
D F O'Connor, BSc Durham
R Oliver BA Manchester
L Phillips, MA University College, Oxford, BSc Middlesex
J P E Procter, BA York
C Pulford, BA Leeds
E Renshaw, BSc Nottingham
M J Salisbury, BA Swansea
G Sharp, BSc Durham
P Surrage, BSc Durham
C N Tuck, BSc, PhD Aston
H Walton, BA Leeds
S Watt, BA Newcastle
B J Whitehouse, BA Liverpool
K Wilkinson, MA, BA, PhD Sheffield
G J M Witney, BSc London
T J Wood, BA Newcastle
S E Wright, BA Northumbria

Junior Department:
Head: A J Edge, MA St Andrews
Assistant Head: D M Farren, BA Warwick
A Brown, BSc Northumbria
L P Cruickshank, BA Newcastle
J Loraine, BEd Newcastle
B Metcalf, BSc York
R Watson, BA Leeds

There are approximately 500 boys in the School, which has a three-form entry at 11+. With the Girls' School, which is in the same building, it shares a mixed Sixth Form and a mixed Junior Department (8+ to 10+).

The Main School follows the normal range of subjects, leading to examination at GCSE. German is introduced in Year 8 and Spanish is offered in Year 9.

Most boys stay on into the Sixth Form and from there normally go on to Higher Education.

Buildings. In recent years, developments have included additional classrooms, a new Library, Computer Resource Centre, Technology Centre, ICT network, a new Sixth Form Centre, and a Drama and Dance Studio.

School Societies. The current list includes: outdoor pursuits (including Duke of Edinburgh's Award scheme and orienteering), choirs, orchestra, drama, computing, art, chess, Christian Fellowship, Amnesty International, history, science, electronics, mathematics, dance, public speaking, and debating.

Pastoral. Each boy is placed in the care of a Form Teacher who oversees his progress and development. In the Sixth Form he has a Tutor who is responsible for both academic and pastoral care.

Careers. There is a structured programme, beginning in Year 9, with a significant contribution from Connexions.

Sixth Form. In 1989 the Sixth Form was merged with that of our sister School, giving both Schools the rare constitution of single-sex education (11–16) with a co-educational Sixth Form. The Head of Sixth Form is Mr D C Henry who will welcome enquiries concerning admission.

Games. The principal games are Rugby Football and Cricket. The School playing field adjoins the premises. Cross-Country, Swimming and Athletics are also available. Hockey and Tennis are introduced as options from Year 9 and older boys may also participate in a range of other sporting activities.

Admission. Governors' Entrance Scholarships are awarded on the results of the Entrance Examinations held annually in the Spring Term at all ages from 8+ to 13+. A limited number of Bursaries are available to pupils aged 11+ and over on entry.

Fees per term (2011-2012). Senior School £3,291; Junior Department £2,586.

Dame Allan's Allanian Association. President: Mr B Sanderson, c/o Dame Allan's Schools.

Charitable status. Dame Allan's Schools is a Registered Charity, number 1084965. It exists to provide education for children.

Dauntsey's School

West Lavington, Devizes, Wiltshire SN10 4HE
Tel: 01380 814500
Fax: 01380 814501
e-mail: info@dauntseys.org
website: www.dauntseys.org

"Friendly, down to earth, independent education with absolutely no snobbishness or arrogance. Fab." (Good Schools Guide). Founded in 1542 by Alderman William Dauntesey of the Mercers' Company. New School buildings erected in 1895 and extended regularly from 1919 to the present.

Governors:
Chairman: R G Handover, CBE
Vice-Chairman: Mrs S H Courth
R M Bernard, CBE
A G P Dudgeon, Esq
Mrs P L P Floyer-Acland, BSc
Prof L M Harwood, MA Oxon, BSc, MSc, PhD, CSci, CChem, FRSC
Air Chief Marshal Sir Richard Johns, GCB, KCVO, CBE
P L R Lane, Esq
M J H Liversidge, Esq, BA, FSA, FRSA
A S Macpherson, Esq, BA, ACA, JP
R P Matters, Esq
Dr R E L Quarrell, BA, MA, DPhil
Brigadier P P Rawlins, MBE
J A Rendell, Esq, BSc, FCA
Brigadier M S Rutter-Jerome, FCMI

F W Scarborough, Esq
N W Smith, Esq
Mrs L F Walsh Waring, BA
C E Whittington, Esq

Clerk to the Governors: P M A Nokes, Esq, MA, MPhil

Head Master: Stewart Roberts, MA

Deputy Head: Mrs J F E Upton, BSc

Second Master: M C B McFarland, BA

Director of Studies: M A C Neve, BSc

Head of Lower School: Mrs S J Corke, BSc

Heads of Department:
Art: N J Wingham, MA, RCA London
Careers: J J Hutchinson, BSc Kent
Design Technology: A Pickford, BA Wales
Drama and Dance: R M Jackson, BA Warwick
Economics and Business Studies: C V Wakefield, BA
  Newcastle
English: L Lloyd-Jukes, BA York
EFL: D A Whitchurch, BA Swansea, TESOL
Geography: A J Palmer, BSc London, FCIEA
History: J A Spencer, MA Bristol
Information Technology: G R Parry, BSc London
Language Development: C W W Wilson, BA Exeter, Dip
  SpLD
Mathematics: T A Bowley, BSc Manchester, MSc London
French: P J Harrison, BA Birmingham
German: V A H Wilks, BA Exeter
Spanish: A L Jackson, BA Nottingham
Music: C B Thompson, GMus Huddersfield
Physical Education: M D Collison, BSc Bath
PSE: A J Sheffield, BSc Leeds
Religious Studies: S B M Gifford, MA Exeter, BD Wales
Science: P K Wheatley, MA Cantab
Biology: W J Corke, BSc London
Chemistry: T J Parker, MA Oxon, MRSC
Physics: R V Lewis, BSc, PhD Wales, FRAS
Sailing: T R Marris, DTP, YME
A Level PE: S J Hardman, BEd Loughborough

Houses and Housemasters/Housemistresses:

Upper School:
Evans: Mr & Mrs N Yates
Farmer: Mr J F O'Hanlon
Fitzmaurice: Mr & Mrs R A Reid
Hemens: Miss E Conidaris
Jeanne: Mrs A L Jackson
King-Reynolds: Mrs E Crozier
Lambert: Ms A Willis
Mercers: Mr & Mrs P J Thomas

Lower School:
Manor: Mr T W Butterworth
Forbes: Mrs E C Gardiner
Rendell: Mr M Olsen
Scott: Mrs G S Ward

Chaplain: Revd D R Johnson, MA, BSc
Bursar: Air Cdr S Lilley, RAF Retd
Registrar: Mrs J H Sagers, BA
Head Master's Secretary: Mrs D Caiger

Medical Officers:
N Swale, MA, FRCS, DRCDG
C C Cowen, MA, FRCS, DRCDG

Sanatorium Sister: Sister S Crawford, RN, MSc

Number. 789 Pupils aged between 11–18 years: 447 boys, 342 girls, approximately 40% board.
Residence. On entering the School at 11 or 13 pupils are in the Lower School where they stay until they reach the end of the Third Form. They then move into the Senior School

Houses. Half the Houses are for boarders and the other half for day pupils.
Situation. The School is set in an estate of over 100 acres in the Vale of Pewsey in Wiltshire. The Manor House, a mansion with its own woodland and playing fields, is the co-educational Junior boarding house for pupils in the First to Third Forms.
Recent Developments. Dauntsey's recognises the importance of first-class boarding facilities and a dynamic and ongoing development programme has been under way since 2004. A new girls' boarding house opened in 2005, and since then an additional £5 million has been spent on boarding facilities. Sports facilities have been enhanced too with the opening of a second Astroturf pitch in 2008 and the levelling and landscaping of land behind the School has provided three additional rugby pitches, a cricket square and athletics track. September 2010 saw the completion of a new, purpose-built day house for over 100 senior day girls and building work began on the last stage of development of a fully-integrated Science Centre for completion by September 2011.
Curriculum. The School is modern in its outlook and affords wide facilities. Briefly the curriculum (i) provides a good general education which includes Religious Education, English, History, Geography, Economics and Business Studies, French, German, Latin, Spanish, Greek, Russian, Pure and Applied Mathematics, Physics, Chemistry, Biology, Information Technology, Music, Art, Craft, Design, Technology; (ii) prepares for the General Certificate of Secondary Education, Advanced Subsidiary and Advanced Levels and University Entrance.
Games. The major sports are Rugby, Football, Hockey, Cricket and Netball. Other games options include Tennis, Squash, Athletics, Swimming, Soccer, Water Polo, Fencing, Badminton and Basketball. In the Sixth Form further options include Triathlon training, Canoeing, Basketball, Rifle-shooting, Yoga, Cross-Country, Ballet, Dance, Conditioning and Riding. Sixth Formers can also choose to do volunteer work within the community. Special attention is given to Physical Education.
Societies and other Activities. Over 100 clubs and societies – from Mountaineering to Mandarin, Fashion Design to Fencing and Sub-Aqua to Symphony Orchestra. The Sailing Club provides ocean sailing and racing in the famous yacht Jolie Brise (class winner of the 2006 and 2008 Tall Ships' Races and the 'Round the Island' race in 2004, 2005 and 2007). In 2009 pupils took part in the Tall Ships' Transatlantic Challenge, racing to Bermuda, up the East Coast of America, and back across the ocean, from Halifax to Belfast. They were awarded several prizes at the end of the race.
All pupils in the Third Form are members of 'Moonrakers', an outward-bound programme culminating in a week's residential camp.
Fees per term (2011-2012). Boarders £8,755; Day Pupils £5,195; International Pupils £9,830. There are no compulsory extras.
Admission. Boys and girls are admitted at 11 on the result of a competitive examination; at 13 on the results of Scholarship and Common Entrance examinations; to the Sixth Form dependent upon academic record and reports, with a minimum of six GCSE passes, three at grade A and three at grade B.
Scholarships. (*See Scholarship Entries section.*) Scholarships open to boys and girls are awarded on examinations held each year. Awards for Music and Art are available. Scholarships are awarded on merit for entry to the First, Third and Sixth Form. Each year 40–45 new scholarships are offered. The school funds three new, 100% bursary places each year to pupils whose parents would otherwise be unable to fund any portion of the school fees. In addition, there is a fund to provide short-term bursarial support for current pupils whose parents or guardians who meet financial difficulties. Full particulars from the Registrar.

Charitable status. Dauntsey's School is a Registered Charity, number 1115638. It is dedicated to the education of boys and girls.

Dean Close School

**Shelburne Road, Cheltenham, Gloucestershire
GL51 6HE**
Tel: 01242 258000
Fax: 01242 258003
e-mail: registrar@deanclose.org.uk
website: www.deanclose.org.uk

The School was opened in 1886, in memory of Francis Close, DD, Rector of Cheltenham 1826–56 and later Dean of Carlisle. Sitting on a beautifully landscaped 50 acre site in the Regency town of Cheltenham, the School is an attractive mixture of old, traditional buildings and modern, hi-tech structures. Co-educational since 1967, Dean Close is a Christian school which believes that education is as much about building character and relationships as it is about gaining knowledge. An independent Preparatory School was established in 1949.

Motto: '*Verbum Dei Lucerna.*'

Visitor: The Rt Revd Michael Perham, The Lord Bishop of Gloucester

President: The Baroness Cox of Queensbury

Council of Members:
Sir John Adye, KCMG, MA
G W Barnes
¹N C J Bewes, BA
¶A R Bird, BA
¹Dr W E Bowring, BEd, ADB Ed, MEd
¹Dr T Brain, OBE, QPM, BA, PhD, FRSA
Air Cdre M Brecht, CBE, MA
Professor P Broadfoot, CBE, DSc, AcSS
¹A J Bruckland, BA
¶C J Buckett, FCA
¶Mrs N Cansdale, BA, MA
¹J M Carter
¹M J Cartwright, BA, FCA (*Treasurer*)
Mrs G A M Cocks, BA, DipEd
¹The Revd R M Coombs, BSc, MA
¹Mrs R Dick, BA, ACA
¹C R Evans, MA
¶Professor R J W Evans, MA, PhD, FBA
N V J Goodwin
Mrs L S M Hardy, OBE, JP
The Earl of Harrowby, MA, FRICS
Prof E Higginbottom, MA, DPhil, BMus, FRCO
¹S M Hill, MA
¹Mrs S L Hirst, BEd
¶H J Hodgkins, ACIB
¶The Revd Dr J M Holmes, MA, PhD, VetMB, MRCVS
A J Hunt
The Very Revd J D Irvine, MA
Mrs C M Lainé, BA, JP
P J Lawrence
¶C P Lynam, MA
I W Marsh, BSc
General Sir John McColl, KCB, CBE, DSO
¹Mrs P G Napier (*Chairman of Board of Trustees*)
C R H Rank
Mrs K Riding, LLB
¹¶The Lord Ribeiro, KT, CBE, FRCS
¶Major E T Taylor, BA, BA
¶The Rt Revd P St G Vaughan, MA
¹The Revd Canon T P Watson
¹The Rt Revd J S Went, MA

¶The Revd P C Youde, LLB

¹ *Member of Board of Trustees*
¶ *Old Decanian*

The Trustees are elected by the Members of Council and oversee the overall governance of the School. They carry a substantial burden of financial and legal responsibility on an entirely voluntary basis and the School is greatly indebted to them.

Headmaster: **J M Lancashire**, MA, ACA

Deputy Head: B J Salisbury, BA, PGCE
Senior Master: D R Evans, MA
Senior Mistress: Mrs J Davis, MA, PGCE
Deputy Head (Academic): M D Tottman, MA, MBA
Director of Studies: A J George, MA, PGCE
Common Room President: D J R Pellereau, MA, PGCE

Housemasters & Housemistresses:
Brook Court: J Slade (*2004*)
Dale: J P Watson (*2004*)
Fawley: Mrs J Abbott (*2011*)
Field: P S Montgomery (*2005*)
Gate: M D Tottman (*2008*)
Hatherley: Miss K E Miller (*2011*)
Mead: Mrs P S Watson (*2001*)
Shelburne: Mrs J D Kent (*2001*)
Tower: B W Williams-Jones (*2008*)

Assistant Staff:
* *Head of Department*

Miss S F Villiers, BA, PGCE
L S Allington, BA (*Drama)
Mrs H L Porter, BA, LRAM, PGCE (*Director of Music*)
D J R Pellereau, MA, PGCE
Mrs J D Kent, GDLM
P S Montgomery, MA, PGCE
Mrs F M Harris, MA, PGCE
Mrs C Allen, BMus, ALCM, LGSM, PGCE
Miss A E Ash, BDes, PGCE
P J P Anstis, MA, MEd, PhD, PGCE (*Examination Coordinator*)
J M Allen, MA, PGCE (*Classics)
D M Fullerton, MA (*Careers)
Miss I M Carames-Castelo, BA, PGCE
J P Watson, BA, CertEd
Mrs P S Watson
Mrs M Cormack, MEd, Cert TEFLA
A J George, MA, PGCE (*Director of Studies*)
Dr S Thomas, BEd, MPhil, PhD (*Learning Support)
Mrs L Chandler-Corris, BSc, FAETC, TEFL
C R Haslam, MA, PGCE (*Senior Tutor*)
J Slade, MA
S G Hamill, BA (*English)
P J J Garner, MA, PGCE (*Mathematics)
Miss R J Donaldson, BSc, PGCE (*Academic PE)
Mrs L A Mears, BA (**Religious Studies*)
A J Davies, FISTC
Mrs B J Edkins, CertEd
Mrs C J Evans, BA, PGCE (*Director of Art)
A R Needs, BSc, PGCE, AMRSC (*Chemistry)
Miss R M O Vines, BA, FVCM, LALAM, ALAM (**Speech & Drama*)
D D Evans, BSc (**Design Technology*)
P Davies, MA, PGCE (**History/Politics*)
A R Swarbrick, BSc, PGCE
G Tredgett
Miss K E Miller, BA
B W Nicholas, MA, ARCO (*Director of Choral Music*)
A A Groom, BA, PGCE
B P Price, BSc, PGCE
Mrs R S Rushton, BA, PGCE
The Revd E L Talbot, MA (*Chaplain*)
B W Williams-Jones, MA, PGCE

R Gwilliam, BA, PGCE (*Director of Sport*)
A G A Milne, BA, PGCE
C J Hooper, BA, PGCE (**Modern Languages*)
M D Jacobsen
Miss K S Roberts, BSc
Miss G Hildick-Smith, BA
J E Talbot, MA, PGCE (**Geography*)
J C Niblett, MA, PGCE (**Physics*)
Miss A Y Webb, MA, PGCE
Dr M Bradley, MBChem, DPhil, PGCE (**Biology*)
P J C Hicks, BSc, PGCE
Miss T L Williams, BSc, PGCE, GTP (**Psychology*)
I V McGowan, BCom, TDip (**Economics/Business Studies*)
Miss S Ellingford, BSc, PGCE
L A Kent, BSc, PGCE
J R B Stott, BSc
Mrs C H S Montgomery, BA,PGCE
Miss B Puig
Mrs F O'Neill
R P Wood, BSc, PGCE
J Mears, BA, PGCE
Miss K M O'Brien, MA, PGCE
J Hutter, BA
Miss F L Hildick-Smith, BA
J P Blair, BSc
Mrs L J Goodyear, BSc, PGCE
Mrs C M A Tufnell, BA, PGCE
G N Baber-Williams, BA, PGCE
B K Wilson, BA
Miss K Morgan, Dip TEFLA (**EAL*)
Mrs E Banks, Cert TEFLA
Mrs R E Tottman, MA
Mrs G M Fentum, MA, PGCE
Mrs K Brown
Mrs J E George, BSc, PGCE

Medical Officers (both Schools):
Dr J Wilson & Partners, MBBS, DRCOG, Dip Pall Med, FRCGP
Overton Park Surgery

SSI, CCF: WO2 B Lloyd

Preparatory School
(*see entry in IAPS section*)
Headmaster: The Revd Leonard J Browne, MA
Deputy Head: A S Brown, BEd
Deputy Head Academic: Mrs L Sorrell, BA
Senior Mistress: Miss E Krick, BSc, PGCE

Pre-Preparatory School
(*see entry in IAPS section*)
Headmistress: Dr C A Shelley, PhD
Deputy Head: J E Cowling, BA, PGCE
Early Years Foundation Stage Coordinator: Mrs D Atwick, BM, PGCE

Bursar: J K Ewbank, FCMI
Deputy Bursar (Finance): R G Perry, ACA
Deputy Bursar (Estates): P L Bray

Admissions Tutor: Mrs M-A McClaran, MA
Registrar (DCS): Mrs S F H Smith, BSc
Head of Marketing (DCS): Mrs T C Colbert-Smith, BA, MCIM
Admissions / Marketing (DCPS): Mrs R Chaplin, BSc

Headmaster's PA (DCS): Mrs J Lynton
Headmaster's PA (DCPS): Mrs T Raybould

Admission and Withdrawal. Admission to the Senior School at 13 is through Common Entrance or direct entrance tests in English, Maths and Verbal Reasoning. Sixth Form: examination and interview, 4 A/Bs and 2 Cs minimum at GCSE. Prospectus and application forms are available from the Registrar who is also happy to arrange a visit at a time to

suit. There is a non-returnable fee of £100 and a returnable deposit of £750 payable one year before entry. One term's notice is required before a pupil is withdrawn from the School.

Inclusive Fees per term (2011-2012). Boarders £9,615, Day Boarders £7,295, Day Pupils £6,790. The Governors normally set the fees in September and do not vary them during the year.

Term of Entry. We prefer to accept pupils in September but will make exceptions at any time of year, even in the middle of a term, if a good reason exists.

Scholarships. (*See Scholarship Entries section*.) The School offers scholarships, exhibitions and bursaries at age 13 and for entry into the Sixth Form. The six areas of talent which are recognised are academic, music, sport, drama, art and design technology. An all-rounder award is also available at 13. The size of award is set according to performance. A descriptive leaflet is available.

Number and Organisation. There are 510 in the Senior School (13–18). The Sixth Form comprises approximately 40% of the School. There are nine Houses: three for boarding boys, two for day boys, two for boarding girls and two for day girls. Housemasters take immediate responsibility for pupils' work, careers, applications for universities and further education. A tutorial system ensures that all pupils have a member of the teaching staff who takes a particular interest in them, both academically and pastorally. There is a Careers department. The Prep School (2½–13) has approximately 389 pupils of whom 163 are girls. There are scholarships available for entry into the Prep School.

Work. Pupils do not have to choose between science and arts until after GCSE and even then the choice of subjects for A Level is wide enough to allow a mixed course if desired. In the lower part of the School pupils are set rather than streamed. Included in the Lower School timetable is a Creative Studies course introducing pupils to a wide range of artistic and creative subjects, embracing DT, Art, Drama, Music and Physical Education. The language centre, high-tech seminar room, music school, art school, sports hall, modern laboratories, computer, electronics and creative workshops combine excellent teaching and leisure facilities which are available both in timetabled and extra-curricular time. Much of the accommodation has been built in the last twenty years and is modern and purpose-built. A professional 550-seat theatre houses an ambitious programme of productions. There is also an open-air theatre. As well as several orchestras, wind band, many ensembles and the Chapel Choir, the School has a Choral Society which performs a major work at least once a year. Tuition in any number of musical instruments is available as an extra. Free tuition is provided for music award holders and high-grade musicians. The theatre also affords first-class concert facilities.

Religious Education. The teaching and Chapel services are in accordance with the Church of England and the School's strong Evangelical tradition is maintained. The Chaplain prepares members of the School for confirmation each year. Most services are in the School Chapel. There is a fine pipe organ. There is a thriving Christian Union and each House hosts voluntary weekly bible studies groups.

Games. The School has a 25m indoor swimming pool and a £3m sports hall, both used all the year round. There are two astroturf pitches and a large number of tennis courts. Hockey, rugby, cricket, basketball, netball, rounders, badminton, athletics, tennis, squash and cross-country are the main sports.

Health. The School has three qualified Sisters with Assistants and visiting Doctors. There is a surgery and a sanatorium.

Outside Activities. A very active Combined Cadet Force with RN, RAF and Army sections trains every Wednesday afternoon and, for some, Silver and Gold Duke of Edinburgh's Awards can be pursued. There is an active outward bound club and a large Community Action group gets involved with projects on a local, national and international level.

Denstone College
A Woodard School

Uttoxeter, Staffs ST14 5HN
Tel: 01889 590484
Fax: 01889 591295
e-mail: admissions@denstonecollege.org
website: www.denstonecollege.org

Achievement, Confidence and Happiness are central to the College philosophy, through which girls and boys are always encouraged to aim high and so reach their full potential. Founded in 1868, the College is rich in tradition and history, but combines this with a forward thinking approach to education.

Denstone College offers a rounded education, where proper emphasis is placed on academic achievement and high standards are the top priority. A wide range of other opportunities, however, ensures that every individual finds and develops his or her own special talents. Denstonians emerge with a degree of self-esteem and confidence, possible only as a result of so much opportunity and challenge. They have the qualifications, skills and personality to make their mark in today's competitive world.

Motto: '*Lignum Crucis Arbor Scientiae.*'

Visitor: The Bishop of Lichfield

School Council:
Mrs P J Gee, DL (*Custos*)
The Revd Canon B D Clover MA, LTCL (*Senior Provost*)
R J Bokros
A D Coley
His Honour Judge R T N Orme, LLB
Miss E M Mullenger, BA, CertEd
J S F Cash, BSc, MRICS
J B Vinecombe (*Deputy Custos*)
G Gregory, MA, BA Hons Econ
Mrs B C Hyde, BA Hons, Dip MS, MBA
K Threlfall
C J Lewis
Mrs Z Raybould, BA

Headmaster: **D M Derbyshire**, BA, MSc

Second Masters:
B J Gillions, BEd
J Hartley, BA (*Registrar*)

Chaplain: The Revd R C M Jarvis, MA, MPhil, Cert Th

Masters and Mistresses:
A N James, BA
  (*†Shrewsbury*)
Miss J R Morris, GMus
  (*†Meynell*)
T P S O'Brien, DA
R C Menneer, BSc, CNAA
M P Raisbeck, BA, CNAA
  (*†Selwyn*)
Mrs S A Leak, BEd
Miss J H Plewes, BA
  (*†Woodard*)
A J Wray, BA
M J Porter, BA (*Head of Middle School*)
J M Tomlinson, BSc
  (*†Heywood*)
Mrs V A Derbyshire, BA

Mrs P A Provan
A C Bonell, BEd
R Ayton, BA
D T Önac, BSc
Mrs K Hood, BSc (*Senior Mistress*)
M S Skipper, BMus
J S Peel, BSc
Mrs F L T Porter, BSc
P D Brice, BA
N J Hill, BSc
Mrs M J Oakes, BA
Mrs S Parsons, BA, MA
C J Sassi, MA (*†Philips*)
J P Tuxford, BA
B J R Duerden, BSc
Mrs K Rylance, BSc

L J Cottrell, BSc
Dr J H Cocker, BSC, PhD
S R Francis, BSc
T J Bell, BA (*Director of Studies*)
C J Lush, MA
Mrs M Moore, BA
M R M Norris, BA (*Head of Senior School*)
Mrs M Silvey, BA
Mrs J A Teather (*†Moss Moor*)
Miss S Bach, BA

Mrs C Mathieson, BA, MSc
Miss C Stanley, BA
R D Waller, BSc
I A K Sherwani
J M Tyler, BA
Mrs C L Burrows, BA
Mrs C G Bailey, MA
P S Garcha, BSc
A D Pearson, BSc
Miss G Wright, BSc, MSc
Miss G K Brown, BSc
J I Young, BA

Visiting Music Staff:
Mrs A O'Brien, DRSAMD, PGDip RSAMD, ARCM (*Piano, Singing, Recorder*)
D Gore (*Guitar*)
Mrs S Stewart, GRNCM (*Violin*)
Mrs A Hardy, GBSM, ABSM (*Flute*)
R Shaw, BA, GRSM, PGDip, ARCM, ABSM (*Saxophone, Clarinet*)
S J Ryde, ARCM, ARCO (*Piano*)
Ms C M Thomson, LRAM, GRSM, PGCE, CDRS (*Piano, Flute, Singing*)
W Raffle (*Guitar*)
Ms L Kaniewski (*Cello*)
P Murfin, BA, BSc (*Percussion*)
Mrs R Theobald, LRAM, ALCM (*Voice, Piano, Oboe*)

Chapel Organist: G Walker, MA, ARCO, FRSA

Finance Bursar and Clerk to the School Council: D M Martin, ACIB

Operations Bursar: J S Peel, BSc

Headmaster's Secretary: Mrs T F Wedgwood, BA

Admissions Secretary: Mrs V J Carman

Preparatory School: Smallwood Manor

Headmaster: M Harrison

(*For further details about the Prep School, see entry in IAPS section.*)

Location. Denstone College is situated on the Staffordshire/Derbyshire border, 6 miles north of Uttoxeter in 100 acres of grounds. The site is located in magnificent countryside, but is well served by road, rail and air.

Organisation. The College is divided into the following units: Junior School (ages 11–14, Years 7, 8 and 9), Middle School (ages 14–16, Years 10 and 11), and Senior School (ages 17–18, Sixth Form which typically numbers around 170 pupils).

All girls and boys are in one of the six houses, each numbering about 90 members, with a total roll of 575. Weekly boarding is a popular option. Just over a quarter of our pupils board, and one third are girls, who have separate boarding accommodation. The College does not believe in vertical boarding.

Smallwood Manor, also a Woodard School, is 9 miles away. Age range 3–11.

Buildings. The main building contains classrooms, day and boarding areas, studies, Dining Hall, Chapel, Theatre and resident staff accommodation. A great deal of school life is thus centred in this main block, which also includes IT facilities, library, and a language laboratory.

The Sports Hall, laboratories, other classrooms, indoor heated swimming pool, Art Centre, Design and Technology Centre, and other buildings, such as the Medical Centre and School Shop, are elsewhere in the grounds.

A £2 million Music School and classroom block was completed in May 2010.

Recent and Future Developments. Over £7 million has been spent on improving our buildings and on building new facilities in recent years.

Most recent developments include a second Astroturf and £750,000 invested in the kitchens and dining area, and the updating of boarding facilities, including the development of a Sixth Form girls' boarding house.

A £2 million Music School and classroom block was completed in May 2010. Lessons have already begun in the Music School, which not only houses the Music department with state-of-the-art facilities but also has allowed the College to upgrade classroom provision. As well as practice rooms and two music classrooms with interlinking recording studio, there are also two History classrooms, a Psychology classroom and three IT classrooms in the building.

Curriculum. In the Junior School (ages 11 to 14, Years 7, 8 & 9) all follow roughly the same spread of subjects: English, Drama, French, Spanish, Mathematics, Physics, Chemistry, Biology, History, Geography, Art, Music, DT, Religious Studies, Information Technology, and PE.

Girls and boys enter the Middle School at the beginning of Year 10. Subjects are studied in option blocks. Mathematics, English Language and Literature, a Modern Language, RS and Science are core subjects, and three others are chosen from those listed above, along with Business and Economics GCSE.

Girls and boys then specialise in AS and A2 Levels, chosen in an option system appropriate to the current discussions regarding Sixth Form Curriculum nationally. Four AS Levels will normally be taken in the Lower Sixth. Subjects offered are Mathematics, Further Maths, Physics, Chemistry, Biology, English Language, English Literature, French, Spanish, History, Geography, Economics, Psychology, Politics, Art, Theatre Studies, PE, and DT. There will also be a minority who will study, in varying numbers from year to year, Music and Religious Studies. An extremely flexible timetable is possible and we aim to offer most combinations of subjects.

The vast majority of pupils take A Levels, with the aim of going on to University. Each year, some girls and boys are prepared for Oxford or Cambridge entrance. In 2010 half of the applicants were offered a place at an Oxbridge College. Around 50% of the Upper Sixth are typically accepted into one of the Russell Group Universities and almost all to their first-choice university.

The School is well-equipped with computer rooms, laboratories, and a 200-seat Theatre. Each department remains up-to-date with subject development and members of staff regularly attend courses and conferences.

Class sizes are small. Up to Year 11, 20 is an average class size, and in the Sixth Form sets vary from 6 to 14.

In addition to having a Head of School and Head of House each pupil has a Tutor with whom he or she meets regularly to discuss work and progress, and both half termly and end of term grades and reports are issued.

Pupils in both Junior and Middle School have a number of staff supervised Homework sessions incorporated into the school day. Boarding members of Fifth Form, Lower Sixth and Upper Sixth have shared or single studies.

Out of Class Activities. The aim is to provide as wide a variety of opportunities for pupils of differing aptitudes and inclinations as possible.

Games: The College has 2 full-size all-weather hockey pitches, one of which is floodlit and provides 9 tennis courts. A nine-hole handicap-standard golf course has been laid out to the west of the College. There is an indoor heated swimming pool, and the main Sports Hall accommodates indoor sports as well as a fitness room. The Drill Hall provides further games space.

The main sports in the Michaelmas Term are rugby for the boys and hockey for the girls, with opportunities for other games. In the Lent Term these change to hockey and football for the boys and netball for the girls, along with swimming, cross country, aerobics, and others. In the summer there is a degree of choice between cricket, athletics, swimming, golf, and tennis and rounders for girls.

In the course of the year there is opportunity for boys and girls to take part in a wide variety of sports, in which they can represent both their House and the School.

CCF and Pioneers: There is also a Combined Cadet Force with Army and Royal Air Force sections, a climbing group and The Duke of Edinburgh's Award Scheme.

The Arts: There are set times each week when priority is given to non-sporting clubs and activities, giving pupils opportunities in a wide range of experiences. Music plays a central role in College life. There is a School Orchestra, Swing Band, and Jazz Ensemble. There is a Girls chamber choir, and the Chapel choir sings at the main service each Friday. In addition, there are also other specialist ensembles and small instrumental groups. Music is included in the curriculum of Years 7-9 and in addition tuition in most instruments from both resident and visiting staff is available. A number of musical events takes place annually, including the Junior School Music concert, and the Summer Serenade, the showcase concert, held in May.

Traditionally there is a major play or musical at the end of the Michaelmas term. The College has a proud record of 104 Shakespearean productions. The 2010 School Play was *40 Years On* by Alan Bennett, in addition to which were the Junior School Play (*The Demon Headmaster*), the Junior Drama Festival and performances from GCSE Drama and A Level Theatre Studies students.

The DT Department is fully equipped with Art and Pottery centres. These facilities are housed in the Centenary Building and allow pupils to fulfil abilities in design, woodwork, metalwork, painting, drawing, ceramics, and printing.

Entrance. Pupils wishing to join Year 7 (age 11+) or Year 9 (age 13+) sit examinations at the College in January and February. Pupils wishing to join Year 9 (age 13+) from Independent Preparatory Schools sit the Common Entrance examination in June. There is also entry in the Sixth Form, an increasingly popular option for girls and boys after their GCSEs.

Occasionally pupils enter at other ages and times. They need to show that they have attained the necessary academic standard either by public examination results or by sitting papers set by the College.

The Registration Fee is £50 and the Entrance Fee is £200.

Scholarships. (*See Scholarship Entries section.*) Scholarships and Exhibitions are offered annually, of varying value up to 40%. They are competed for in three main age groups:

First, some are awarded to the best candidates in the January and February examinations referred to above; second, to candidates from Preparatory Schools (and internal College candidates) who are under 14 on 1 June of the year in which the examination is taken; and third for Sixth Form entry.

In all Scholarships, in addition to academic excellence, all-round ability and out-of-school activities and interests are taken into account.

Scholarships are offered annually for Music (instrumental and choral), Art, DT, Drama, Sport, Golf and All-Round ability. The Alastair Hignell Scholarship and the Governors' Award carry very significant financial benefits, and further details are available on the website or from the Admissions staff.

A number of bursaries may be awarded to those in genuine financial need. Special consideration is given to the children of Clergy, Old Denstonians and Service Children.

Fees per term (2011-2012). Boarding: £4,867 (Year 7), £6,451 (Years 8 & 9), £7,072 (Years 10–13) including items of board and education other than music lessons and extra tuition.

Day: £3,361(Years 7–9), £4,061 (Years 10–13).

The **Old Denstonian Club.** *Secretary*: Mr M S Smith, Denstone College, Uttoxeter, Staffs. Regional Clubs based in London, Manchester and at the College.

Charitable status. Denstone College is a Registered Charity, number 1102588. It exists to provide Christian education for children.

Dollar Academy

Dollar, Clackmannanshire FK14 7DU
Tel: 01259 742511
Fax: 01259 742867
e-mail: rector@dollaracademy.org.uk
website: www.dollaracademy.org.uk

The Academy, founded in 1818 and the oldest co-educational boarding and day school in Britain, is situated in forty acres of its own grounds on the southern slopes of the Ochil Hills, 30 miles from Edinburgh, 38 from Glasgow, 40 from St Andrews and 10 miles east of Stirling. The Academy is renowned for its academic reputation, for its inclusive international outlook, and for its range of co-curricular activities. In recent years, all the boarding houses have been extensively refurbished, and the quality of the facilities throughout the school campus is of the highest order; a new Sixth Form Centre was opened in 2010. The A-listed Playfair Building of 1821 is surrounded by a number of impressive modern buildings named after distinguished Scots.

Motto: '*Juventutis veho fortunas*'

Governors:
Chairman: J B Cameron, CBE, FRAgS, AIAgE

Vice-Chairmen:
Professor J McEwen, MBChB, FRCP, FFPH, FFOM, FDSRCS, FMEdSci
Professor R E Morris, MA, DPhil

Members:
D J Anderson, FCIBS
M W Balfour, BCom, CA
A T Black
K M Brown, MA
Mrs D A Burt, MCSP
Cllr A D Campbell, CA
D M Clark, MA, LLB, WS
Dr G B Curry, BA Mod, PhD, DIC
I C Glasgow, BSc, DipSurv, Dip IA, ASIP
R P S Harris, BCom, DipCom, CA
Mrs G K Hepburn, BSc, MCOptom
Dr M A Hogg, LLB, LLM, PhD, NP, FRSA
J McAslan, RIBA, FRSA, ARIAS
C J Milne, BSc
Mrs J M Smith, BA
A P M Walls, CA
Revd A H Ward, MA, BD
A G Webb, BCom

Bursar and Clerk to Governors: J StJ Wilkes, MA
Assistant Bursar: Mrs J Johnson, MA, ACA
Bursar's PA: Mrs M Campbell, BA

Rector: D J Knapman, BA, BSc, MPhil

Deputy Rector: G P Daniel, MA, MA

Assistant Rectors:
Dr J M Hendry, BSc, PhD, CPhys, MInstP
Mrs L H Hutchison, BA
S P Johnson, MA
Mrs A M Morrison, BA (*also Head of Prep & Junior School*)

Director of Music: J McGonigle, DipMus, RSAMD

* *Head of Department*
† *Houseparent*
‡ *Head of Year*

Prep & Junior School:
Deputy Head, Prep & Junior School: Mrs J G Adamson, BA, AUPE
Assistant Head, Junior School: Miss S Horne, BEd

Mrs L Barlow, MA	Mrs M Harewood, MA, BEd
Miss L L Beattie, BEd	Mrs L Hudson, BA
Ms K Cleghorn, MA, MLitt	Mrs N M Letford, BEd
Mrs V Currie, DipCE	†Mrs G A McFadyean, BA
T A Dann, BEd	A Mills, BEd
Mrs O Dunn, BA	Mrs J W Moffat, BEd
Ms L E Duncan, BEd	Mrs J Montgomery, BA, CertFPS
Miss R E Foster, MA	Miss L S Pollock, BEd, AVCM
Mrs M E Hamilton, BA, DipCE	

Mrs K Bunyan (*Prep Assistant*)
Mrs E Beveridge (*Prep Assistant*)
Mrs S Davis (*Prep Assistant*)

Senior School:
Art & Design:
*A K MacLean, DA
Mrs C L Kelly, BA
Ms S C Kennedy, BA
Mrs T L Livingstone, BA
Mrs C MacLean, DA
Ms E Scott, MA
Ms K A Watt, BA

Biology:
*C K Ainge, BSc
J B Fraser, BSc
Mrs F McDonald, BSc
Dr L A Payne, BSc, PhD
Mrs S Shakir, BSc

Business Education:
*M C Moore, BSc, IDMDip
*Ms T Spencer, BA
Mrs H M Duncan, BA
Mrs J Greenlee, BSc
Mrs A L Robinson, MA
J A Simpson, BA
Mrs M A Waddell, DipCom

Chemistry:
*Dr W Beveridge, BSc, PhD, CChem, MRSC
‡N F Blezard, BSc, MRSC
Mrs H Cook, MChem
‡Dr R Johnson, BSc, PhD
‡D J Lumsden, BSc
Dr S Scheuerl, BSc, PhD, MRSC
‡C Smith, BSc

Classics:
*D C Hall, MA, MPhil
Mrs H S Lumsden, MA
Dr E Macleod, MA, PhD
Miss J R Wightwick, BA, MA

Computing:
Ms R McGuinness, MSc

English:
*Mrs C Murray, MA, MPhil
Miss C Abel, BA, MLitt

Mrs K G du Vivier, MA
D A H Johnston, BA, MLitt, MPhil
Ms E M Langley, MA
Mrs S C Lindsay, MA
Mrs H K Moore, BA, MLitt
Mrs J Nozedar, MA
P G Russell, BA (**Drama*)
Mrs E A Taylor, MA

Engineering, Design & Technology:
*Dr D A Keys, BA, PhD
S W Cochrane, BEdTech
J Delaney, BEdTech
Mrs P Webster, BEdTech

Geography:
*A M McConnell, BSc
Mrs F M McBride, MA
Mrs S A Scott, BSc

History & Modern Studies:
*Miss M D Sharp, MA
R Lindsay, MA
N G McEwan, MA
†N J McFadyean, MA, MPhil (**World Studies*)
Miss G McCord, MA
†R W Welsh, MA

Home Economics:
Mrs C Maciver, DipHomeEc
Mrs N O'Donnell, BA
Mrs S Malcolm, DipDomSci

Mathematics:
*Dr J T Brooks, BSc, PhD
Miss S G Cannon, BSc
Mrs C M Childs, BSc
R W Durran, BA
Mrs L A Jeffrey, BA
I Mackenzie, BSc, CEng, MIET
Mrs M Pennie, BSc
Mrs F G Stewart, BSc

Modern Languages:
*D Delaney, MA

Miss C Bowie, BA,
Maîtrise FLE
Mrs S Brooks, MA
Mrs A R Bryce, BA
Dr J M Fotheringham, BA,
PhD
S K Young, BA
Mrs J Young, MA
(*staff to be appointed*)

Assistants:
Mlle C Amoric (*French*)
Herr J Topf (*German*)
Signor A Neri (*Italian*)
Señor J Folgado (*Spanish*)

Music:
*Mrs K Fitzpatrick, MSc,
BMus
D M Christie, BA, LLCM,
ALCM
Ms S A Herbert, BMus
Mrs M Leggatt, MusB,
DipMTh, LGSM, LLCM

Pupil Counsellor: Mrs L A Jeffrey, BA
Librarian: Mrs E McDonald, BA, MSc
Rector's PA: Mrs W M Pearson
Marketing & Liaison Manager: Mrs E Gunn, MA, Dip IDM
School Office Manager: Mrs E C Gallagher
Network Manager: J L Tracey
Network Consultant: R W Marchant, BSc
IT System Administrator: Ms E C Williamson
IT Support Assistant: A J Kenny
Music Technologist: F W Jackson, BA
Janitor: W Anderson
Groundsman: R W Meldrum
Piping Instructor: C Stewart
Pool Manager / Swimming Instructor: R W Kidd, FIOS, MSTA, TEAQ

Houseparents:
Argyll: Mr & Mrs R W Welsh
Heyworth: Mr & Mrs A Robson
McNabb/Tait: Mr & Mrs N J McFadyean

Organisation. The Academy is divided into the Senior School (ages 12–18, 848 pupils); the Junior School (ages 10–12, 176 pupils) and the Prep School (ages 5–9, 210 pupils). It is fully co-educational throughout, and has been from 1818.

Academic. Pupils follow a course of study based upon the Scottish Curriculum for Excellence. In the Senior School, pupils are also prepared for Scottish qualifications at Standard Grade or Intermediate 2 (generally in 7 or 8 subjects) and Higher Grades (usually in 5 subjects); and then afterwards for a range of Advanced Highers, further Highers or wider interest modules. These Scottish qualifications will be valid for entry to all world universities. Three Modern Languages are offered from age 10, besides co-curricular Japanese, and the separate sciences are available from 13. The timetable is created around the needs of the pupils rather than requiring them to slot into pre-arranged subject blocks.

Beyond Dollar. Senior staff offer advice on Careers and Higher Education to current and former pupils. In addition, all pupils are offered the services of a professional careers adviser, and both Planitplus and Centigrade programmes are used. The Academy has a flourishing Work Experience programme for seniors locally, and in France, Germany and Spain.

International links. Contact with other countries has increased notably in recent years. For example, Biology trips are organised in Malaysia; the Art department visits Paris,

Physical Education:
*S R Newton, BSc
Ms L Allan, BEd
‡Mrs E A Borrowman,
DipPE
J G A Frost, BEd, MSc
P N Gallagher, BEd
Mrs C C Galloway, BEd
M I Hose, BEd
R A Moffat, BEd
Mrs G M Robb, BEd
Mrs V A Smith, BA

Physics:
*J T A Fulton, BSc
Dr S Fulton, BSc, PhD
‡A N Johns, BSc, CPhys,
MInstP

Support for Learning:
*Mrs S Birrell, BA, MSc
Mrs W J Ainge, MA
Mrs A Gibson, DipCE
Mrs J Smith, BA

Berlin, London and Madrid; the Geography department visits Morocco, Iceland and the Swiss Alps; the Modern Languages department runs exchange programmes and trips to France, Germany, Spain and Japan, while sporting links are firmly established elsewhere in Europe, in Japan, Ireland, Australia and South Africa. The Pipe Band has toured in the Far East and mainland Europe. The boarding community includes boys and girls from throughout the world.

Games and Activities. The extensive playing fields and new all-weather playing surface are immediately adjacent to the school, as are the Games Halls, the Sports Centre with fully-equipped Fitness Suite, 25-metre indoor heated swimming pool and the rifle range.

Teams represent the school in rugby, hockey, cricket, tennis, athletics, swimming, skiing, shooting, curling, fencing, football, golf, badminton and basketball.

The Duke of Edinburgh's Award Scheme is widely supported at all three award levels. The Combined Cadet Force has equal numbers of boys and girls in a Royal Signals troop, an Infantry section, a REME section, an RAF section, an RN section and two Pipe Bands.

Dollar follows the principle of allowing pupils to opt into co-curricular activities as well as games, and an extraordinarily wide variety of clubs is on offer, from surfing and falconry to gardening, film making and child care.

The Arts. Music is taught as part of the curriculum, and tuition is offered as an extra in most orchestral instruments, besides bagpipes, guitar, drums and clarsach. There are six choirs, four orchestras and two Jazz bands. Junior and Senior Musical productions are performed annually. Drama productions and clubs are found throughout the age range; a range of performance spaces is used including the purpose-built Studio Theatre. Many Art Clubs take place outwith the timetabled lessons and exhibitions are held throughout the year. Dance – whether it be Scottish Country, Latin American, or Egyptian Belly Dancing – is taught at all levels. Debating and Public Speaking are popular and competitive activities both within Dollar and in national competitions, where success is regularly achieved.

Boarding. Boarding pupils are accepted from the age of nine. There is one Boys' and two Girls' Houses. Weekly or flexible boarding arrangements can be made to suit pupils' and parents' needs.

Fees per term (2011-2012). Tuition: £2,505 (Prep), £2,880 (Junior), £3,351 (Senior). Boarding fee: £4,296 (full), £3,885 (weekly).

Admission. This is by interview and/or test with the Head of the Prep and Junior School for ages 5–14; and by interview and current school report for ages 14–18. The biggest single intakes are at age 5, and at 10 and 11 to the Junior School; there are intakes in other years as vacancies occur.

Charitable status. The Governors of Dollar Academy Trust is a Registered Charity; it exists to provide education for boys and girls.

Dulwich College

London SE21 7LD
Tel:　　020 8693 3601
Fax:　　020 8693 6319
e-mail:　info@dulwich.org.uk
website:　www.dulwich.org.uk

Motto: '*Detur gloria soli Deo*'.

The Governing Body:

Chairman: Lord Turnbull, KCB, CVO

V P Bazalgette, MA
Sir Brian Bender, KCB
Ms V Flind, BA

R J Foster, BEd
W A Foster, MA, PhD
S Ghosh
Mrs J Hill, MA
J D Lovering
The Rt Hon P J R Riddell, MA, FRHistS
S A Taylor, FRICS
G N C Ward, CBE, FCA, FEI

Clerk to the Governors: Ms K Jones, LLB

Master of the College: **Dr J A F Spence**, BA Hons

Deputy Masters:
S R Northcote-Green, BA (*Pastoral*)
A J S Kennedy, BA (*Academic*)
R I Mainard, BA, MA Theol, MA Ed (*External*)

Chief Operating Officer: S J Yiend, MA
Director of Finance: N Prout, BA, ACA
Head of Learning Assessment: J P Devlin, BA, PhD
Head of Upper School: C S B Pyke, MA, PhD
Head of Middle School: N D Black, BA, PhD
Head of Lower School: I L H Scarisbrick, BSc
Head of Junior School: Mrs A Fleming, BA, MA
Head of DUCKS (*Kindergarten and Infants School*): Mrs H
   M Friell, DipEd
Registrar: Mrs S Betts
Archivist: Mrs C Lucy, BA, MCLIP
Head of Academic Administration: N P Young, BSc

Heads of Department:
R R S Baylis, MA, MA (*Modern Languages*)
A J Binns, BA (*Marketing*)
J D Cartwright, MA (*Computer Science*)
N T Croally, MA, PhD (*Head of Scholars and General and
   Liberal Studies*)
P J Cue, BSc, PhD (*Biology*)
W Dugdale, BA (*German*)
T Edge, BA (*History*)
D Flower, BA (*Politics*)
J H Fox, BA (*Religious Studies*)
N K M Fyfe, BA (*Economics*)
Jean-Michel Hulls, BA (*Classics*)
P V Jolly, BA, DipRSA (*Director of Drama*)
D Kent, BA (*PE*)
J Kinch, BA, BPhil, DPhil (*Critical Thinking*)
D King, BA (*Physics*)
J R King, BEd (*Director of Sport*)
N Mair, BA (*Director of Dulwich Modern Languages*)
Miss C Malloch, BA (*Physics*)
R G Mayo, MA, MusB, FRCO (*Music*)
M Nash, MA (*Spanish*)
C J Ottewill, BA, MPhil (*Mathematics*)
Miss L V A Rand, MChem (*Chemistry*)
Michael Ross, BA (*Design & Technology*)
A C Storey, BA, MSc, PhD (*Director of ICT*)
R F Sutton, BA (*English*)
R Weaver, BA, MA, FSA Scot (*Keeper of the Fellows'
   Library*)
H I L Williams, BSc (*Science Administrator*)
J Woolley, BA (*Geography*)

*DUCKS (Dulwich College Kindergarten and Infants
   School)*:
Mrs S Donaldson, NNEB (*Head of Kindergarten*)

Medical Centre Charge Nurse: Mrs P Heaton, RGN, RM,
   RSN, BSc Hons Specialist Community Practitioner, Dip
   Counselling
College Counsellor: Ms J De Heger, BEd, Dip Art Therapy
Medical Officer: R A Leonard, MBE, MA, MB, BChir,
   MRCGP, DRCOG
Master's PA: Mrs R Weavers

Dulwich College was founded by Edward Alleyn, the
famous Elizabethan actor-manager. On 21 June 1619 a
licence was granted for his 'College of God's Gift' at Dulwich. In 1857 the College was reconstituted by special Act
of Parliament and subsequently moved to its present 70-acre
site on the edge of Dulwich Village.

The College's principal aims for all its boys are:

• to offer an appropriate academic challenge which enables
  each pupil to realise his potential;
• to create an environment which promotes an independent
  work ethic and encourages all boys to acquire a love of
  learning;
• to provide a wide range of sporting, cultural and adventurous activities through which boys can learn to take the
  lead and to work cooperatively;
• to nurture a supportive community which encourages social responsibility and spiritual and personal development
  and in which boys from a variety of cultural and social
  backgrounds can feel secure and equally valued.

Dulwich is academically selective and the boys are generally in the top 20 percent of the national academic range.
They come from a wide range of backgrounds and have
diverse interests which enrich the life of the College. Almost
all students proceed to university with about a sixth of them
being accepted into Oxbridge or top American universities.

Organisation. The College, comprising some 1,450
boys, has four specific schools: Junior School, Lower
School, Middle School and Upper School. Each of these has
its own Head who is responsible to the Master for that part
of the College. Within each School there are Heads of Year
and form tutors who have daily contact with boys in their
care. These teams are responsible for overseeing the pastoral
and academic welfare of the boys and they ensure that close
links are fostered between parents and the College.

DUCKS, Dulwich College's Kindergarten and Infants
School, is the only co-educational element of the College
providing a secure foundation for future learning and development. Most children from DUCKS enter leading independent schools in south London, and many boys will pass the
entrance examination for the College.

Day House system. A thriving Day House system offers
boys the opportunity to take part in a wide range of competitive activities including art, chess, poetry, general knowledge, debating, drama and music. They can also compete in
a number of sports throughout the academic year, including
rugby, soccer, hockey, cricket and athletics.

Facilities. Over the years the College has developed its
complex of buildings to meet the needs of boys' education in
the twenty-first century, and this development continues.
The latest addition, which was completed in February 2009,
is the Lord George Building which houses a new Sixth Form
Centre with adjoining suites for economics and careers, a
cafe and a suite of changing rooms

Extensive IT facilities are available to all pupils. The IT
network gives pupils and staff access to a wide range of centrally stored learning resources through the College's own
virtual learning environment, 'MyDulwich'. Three separate
libraries, all staffed by professional librarians, cater to the
specific needs of different age groups. Exhibitions, drawn
from the College archive, are regularly mounted in the
Wodehouse Library.

The College has two separate dining areas which provide
a wide choice of foods, including a vegetarian option, on a
cafeteria basis for both pupils and staff. The College also has
its own shop, the Commissariat, where uniform, equipment
and stationery can be purchased. The Richard Penny Medical Centre provides professional nursing care on a round-
the-clock basis for boarders and day boys. The College
Counsellor, based in the Medical Centre, provides confidential consultation for pupils and parents.

Sport is integral to life at Dulwich College both within
the curriculum and as part of the wider co-curricular programme. There are over 60 acres of playing fields. The **PE
Centre** includes a substantial sports hall and a modern
indoor 25-metre swimming pool. The College owns a boat-

house on the Thames, accommodating the thriving Boat Club, and a Field Centre in the Brecon Beacons which is used for a variety of outdoor activities and residential courses. The sports programme provides a continuity and breadth of experience across the age range, with 24 different sports on offer, giving all boys the opportunity to reach their sporting potential.

Music and Drama. A professionally equipped, purpose-built Music School provides all pupils with the opportunity to study a musical instrument. More than 500 pupils receive individual tuition every week from 35 experienced specialist musicians, led by the Heads of Strings, Wind, Brass, Keyboard and Singing. The College Chapel Choir, an ancient foundation, leads regular services in the Foundation Chapel and also at other venues throughout the country. The Edward Alleyn Theatre is a fully rigged auditorium with a capacity of 250; over 50 events are staged annually and the facility includes rehearsal and teaching spaces, as well as dressing rooms.

Clubs and Societies. A wide variety of clubs and societies, many run by the boys themselves, take place during the lunch break and after school. These range from Lego for the younger boys to the Political Society which is responsible for inviting prominent public figures to speak. The College encourages boys to take part in expeditions as well as many community-based activities which can include membership of the Combined Cadet Force, Scouts, the Duke of Edinburgh's Award Scheme and Community Service. Academic, cultural and sporting excursions take place at various points throughout the school year.

Careers. Specialist careers staff, professional external advisors, dedicated IT facilities and an accredited library provide an up-to-date service assisting boys in planning higher education and careers. Boys and their parents attend the annual Courses and Careers Convention to consult with representatives from key employers, professional institutes and around 25 universities. Upper School boys receive guidance on how degree course choices might influence their future careers.

Boarding. There are three boarding houses in Dulwich College, all situated within or close to the campus. Each house has a Housemaster who is resident with his family. Younger boys (aged up to 16) live in The Orchard, sharing comfortable study-bedrooms. Boys in the Upper School live in Blew House and Ivyholme, where each boy has his own room with en-suite facilities. At present, there are around 120 boarders. Boarding at Dulwich is truly international with boys coming from all over the world and this adds to an atmosphere of cultural tolerance and intellectual curiosity.

Entry. Boys are admitted to the College as day boys, boarders or weekly boarders. Places are available at age 7, 11, 13 and 16. Casual vacancies occur from time to time at ages 8, 9, 10 and 12. At age 7 places are awarded on the basis of interview, report and practical assessment during the Lent Term. At age 11 places are awarded on the results of the Combined Entrance and Scholarship Examination held in the Lent Term. Candidates take papers in English and Mathematics and also a Verbal/Non-Verbal Reasoning test. At age 13 boys may take the College's own Entrance Examinations held in the Lent Term. Entrance is by examination and interview. At 16+ places are offered on the results from subject specific tests, interview and GCSE grades. Application should generally be in the year before desired date of entry. For further information please contact the Registrar, Mrs Sarah Betts, on 020 8299 9263 or by email: the.registrar@dulwich.org.uk.

Fees per term (2011-2012). The consolidated Day fee is £4,964. Boarding fees (in addition to Tuition fees): £5,249 Full Boarders; £4,706 Weekly Boarders.

Scholarships and Bursaries. (*See Scholarship Entries section.*) A significant number of academic scholarships are awarded each year up to one-third of the tuition fee. Scholarships can be enhanced by Bursaries in cases of financial need. There are also scholarships for music, art and sports. The College has a substantial Bursary Fund from which means-tested awards of up to 100% of tuition fees are made annually.

Alleynians. Founded in 1873, The Alleyn Club is a flourishing former pupils' association with over 7,500 Old Alleynian (OA) members. The club's name acknowledges the founder, Edward Alleyn, actor, theatre manager and contemporary of William Shakespeare.

Charitable status. Alleyn's College of God's Gift; Dulwich College is a Registered Charity, number 312755. It exists for the education of children.

The High School of Dundee

Euclid Crescent, Dundee, Tayside DD1 1HU
Tel: 01382 202921
Fax: 01382 229822
e-mail: enquiries@highschoolofdundee.org.uk
website: www.highschoolofdundee.org.uk

The present School traces its origins directly back to a 13th century foundation by the Abbot and Monks of Lindores. It received a Royal Charter in 1859. Various Acts of Parliament in the 19th Century were finally consolidated in an Order in Council constituting the High School of Dundee Scheme 1965, which was revised in 1987.

Motto: '*Prestante Domino*'.

Board of Directors:

The Board comprises, Chairman, 2 ex officiis Directors, viz, The Lord Dean of Guild and The Parish Minister of Dundee. The Guildry of Dundee, the Nine Trades of Dundee, the Old Boys' Club and the Old Girls' Club and the Parents' Association each elect one Director. Six Directors are elected by The Patrons' Association and 6 co-opted by the Board.

School Staff:

***Rector*: Dr J D Halliday**, BA Hons, PhD

Deputy Rector & Head of Senior School: P J Tinson, MA Aberdeen

Head of Junior School: Mrs G McLaren, MA, CEY

Bursar: C M Sharp, FCCA

Deputy Heads:
Mrs L A M Hudson, MA
Mrs V A Vannet, MA, DipEd
R W Illsley, MA
Mrs J Rose, BEd
Mrs K J I McIntosh, DipCE

Director of ICT: J Christie, BEng Hons

Junior School

Mrs P L Hourd, BSc (*Junior/Senior Transition Coordinator*)

Mrs L J Mooney, DipCE	Mrs I Goddard, BEd
Mrs L Docherty, DipCE	Mrs C Powrie, BSc
Mrs E D Cargill, DipCE	Mrs F S Wilson, BEd
Mrs M A Mordente, BEd	Miss G Alexander, BEd
Miss M Cardno, MA, PGCE	Mrs L Coupar, BEd
Mrs G M Wood, DipCE	Miss C Anderson, BEd
Mrs L Smith, BEd	Mrs S Fish, BEd
Miss C E Hulbert, MA, PGCE	Mrs M MacIntyre, BA, BEd
Mrs A Davie, BEd	Mrs S Gallagher, BEd
Mrs P J Halliwell, BEd	Miss K Reith, BEd, MA

Senior School
* Head of Department

English:
**Mrs J Phillips, MA
T F W Durrheim MA
Mrs D M Wilson, MA
Mrs D Keogh, MA
M Stewart, MA, MPhil
Mrs M Ovenstone Jones, MA
Ms L Dunn, MA
D Meechan, BA

Drama and Media Studies:
**Mrs L M Drummond, Dip Drama
I R Cowieson, BA

Modern Studies:
**G J Rennet, MA
G Fyall, BA

History:
**I E R Wilson, MA
Mrs L A Hudson, MA
G Fyall, BA
Miss K McKie, MA

Geography:
**Miss J A Stewart, BSc
C R McAdam, MA
Mrs S B Williams, MA
P J Tinson, MA
D Foulds, BSc

Religious Studies:
**D J Goodey, BA, MA
Ms B D Quigley, MTheol

Economics:
**Miss A L Laing, DipCom, DipEd
Mrs R M Crighton, DipCom

Classics:
**J Meehan, MA
E Faulkes, BA

Modern Languages:
**N A MacKinnon, MA
Mrs I M McGrath, MA
Mrs F Cram, MA
Mrs G A Mackenzie, BA
Mrs L Smith, MA
D A Summerville, BA
Mrs J Brown, BA
Ms A Aguero, BA, BEd

Mathematics:
**G A Mordente, BSc
A G Blackburn, BSc
Mrs M A Oliver, BSc
D J C Elgin, BSc, MSc
R C Middleton, BSc
Miss D MacDonald, BSc
Mrs L A Craig, BSc

Chemistry:
**D A Brett, BSc
Mrs C A Sinclair, BSc
Mrs G Spinks, BSc
Dr P Taylor, PhD

Biology:
**Dr E Duncanson, BSc, PhD
Mrs L A Woodley, BSc

Dr M W Fotheringham, BA, PhD
G M S Rodger, BSc

Physics:
**Mrs S H Fletcher, BSc, MSc
T Guild, BSc
Dr G MacKay, BSc, MSc, PhD
S Hill, BEd, MSc

Technology:
**C Rose, BA
D Preston, MA, BEd

Computer Studies:
**D Smith, BSc
C P Stuart, BSc
J Rainey, BSc

Art and Craft:
**G R Mackenzie, DipGrDes
Mrs M Angus, BA
Miss A Douglas, BDes
Miss J Campbell, MDes

Music:
**Mrs J F Melville, DipMusEd
Mrs S J Magill, BMus
D G Love, DipMusEd, DRSAMD
Mrs M Scott-Brown, LTCL
Ms G Simpson, DipMus, ALCM
S Armstrong, DRSAM
Mrs S Sneddon, LTCL, ALCM
Miss A Evans, BA, LTCL
J McAuley, BA
Ms S Morgan, BA

Learning Skills:
**Mrs P A Maxwell, BEd
Mrs D Burt, MA
Mrs M A Mordente, BEd

Physical Education:
**B Beckett, BEd
G W Spowart, BEd
Mrs J A Hutchison, DipPE
Mrs P Spowart, BEd
P N Gallagher, BEd
Miss V Bunce, BSc (Coach)
W Nicol (SSI/Instructor in Outdoor Activities)
E Jack, BEd
Mrs E Rudman, BA
Mrs L Christie, BA

Home Economics:
**Mrs G A Madden, DipHome Econ
Mrs L J Ross, MA

Guidance:

Principal Teachers:
C P Stuart, BSc
C R McAdam, MA
G W Spowart, BEd
Mrs P Spowart, BEd

Assistant Principal Teachers:
Mrs F Cram, MA
Mrs J Hutchison, DipPE
Mrs J Brown, BA
Mrs S Williams, MA

Careers Coordinators:
Mrs L J Ross, MA
G M S Rodger, BSc

Co-Curricular Activities:
**G J Rennet, MA
G Ross, BA (Outdoor Education Instructor)

Admission. The School comprises two sections: The Junior School – 333 pupils (Primary 1 to Primary 7). The Senior School – 684 pupils (Form 1 to Form 6).

The normal stages of entry are Primary 1 and Form 1. Entry to Primary 1 (age 4½ to 5½ years) is by interview held in January and to Form 1 (age 11 to 12 years) by an Entrance Examination held in January. Where vacancies exist entrance is usually available at all other stages subject to satisfactory performance in an entrance assessment.

Bursaries. A limited number of bursaries are provided to pupils entering Form 1.

Fees per term (2011-2012). Junior School: £2,360 (L1 to L2), £2,419 (L4 to L5), £2,756 (L6 to L7); Senior School £3,350.

Buildings. The 5 main school buildings are in the centre of the city and form an architectural feature of the area. Two excellent playing fields – Dalnacraig and Mayfield – are situated some 1½ miles to the east of the school. The Mayfield Sports Centre, comprising state-of-the-art games hall, dance studio, gymnasium and fitness suite, is adjacent to the playing fields.

Curriculum. The Junior School follows a wide-ranging primary curriculum. Subject specialists are employed in Physical Education, Art, Home Economics, Music, French, Information Technology.

In the Senior School, after two years of a general curriculum, some specialisation takes place with pupils prepared for the Scottish Qualifications Authority Examinations at Standard Grade, Intermediate 2, Higher and Advanced Higher which lead directly to university entrance.

Co-Curricular Activities. A wide range of activities is offered. There is a flourishing contingent of the Combined Cadet Force including a pipe band. Drama, Public Speaking and Debating, Chess and The Duke of Edinburgh's Award Scheme are examples of the wide variety of activities available.

Music plays an important part in the life of the school. Special tuition is provided in a wide variety of instruments.

Charitable status. The Corporation of the High School of Dundee is a Registered Charity, number SC011522. The school is a charity to provide quality education for boys and girls.

Durham School

Durham City DH1 4SZ
Tel: 0191 386 4783
Fax: 0191 383 1025
e-mail: d.woodlands@durhamschool.co.uk
website: www.durhamschool.co.uk

Motto: *Floreat Dunelmia – Let Durham Flourish*

Durham School is one of the oldest in England. It probably has a continuous history from Saxon times and has always been closely associated with the Diocese of Durham. As the Bishop's School it was re-organised and endowed by Cardinal Langley in 1414 and was re-founded in 1541 by Henry VIII as a Lay Foundation under the control of the Dean and Chapter of Durham. In 1995 it left the Cathedral Foundation to become a separate body. The school is now fully co-educational 3–18, incorporating Bow, Durham School (3–11).

Governing Body:
Mr A MacConachie, OBE, DL (*Chairman*)
Mr F Nicholson (*Deputy Chairman*)
Mr A B Anderson
Mr P S Bell
Canon S A Cherry
Mrs M Coates
Professor P Gilmartin
Miss G Kerr
Mr R A Langdon
Mr R Uttley
Mr D Welsh
Mrs H G Weston

Headmaster: **Mr E M George**, BA, MBA Ed

* *Head of Department*
† *Housemaster/mistress*

Deputy Headmaster: Mr D W Goodhew, BA, PGCE
Bursar: Mrs R Gardner
Deputy Head (*Pastoral*): Mrs F M Parker, BEd
Head of Boarding: Mr M J Bushnell, BSc (**Business
Studies & Economics*)
Senior Master: Mr H Dias, BA
Head of Bow, Durham School: Mr R N Baird, BA, PGCE
Marketing Director: Mrs A N McCann, Dip CIPR, MCIPR
Chaplain: Revd B Cooper, MA, BA
Headmaster's PA: Mrs S Spence
Registrar: Mrs D C Woodlands

Assistant Staff – Senior School:
Mr D B Aitken, BSc
Mr M P Alderson, BA, MA (*†School House, *Modern
Languages*)
Mr M C T Baldwin, BA (**Art and DT*)
Mrs K Barnett, MMath, PhD
Mr M Bedworth
Mr B Brownlee, BA (**Psychology*)
Mr E Bryant (**Boys Rowing*)
Mr M F Burke, BSc (**Biology, Junior† Poole House*)
Dr J M Burns, BA, PhD (*†Pimlico House*)
Mr I J Campbell, BEng (*Assistant† Caffinites House,
Physics)
Mrs L Chapman, MA
Mr M J Clayton, BA
Mr T A Davies, BA (*Director of Lower School Studies,
Classics)
Mr P Dias, BSc (*Junior† School House*)
Mrs K E Dougall, BA (**Girls' Games*)
Mr R J Duff, BEd (*†Poole House*)
Mrs C Eccleston, BA
Miss K Finch, BSc
Mr M B Fishwick
Miss F Fletcher (**Girls Rowing*)
Mr C S Fordyce, BSc (**Mathematics,†Caffinites House*)
Mr M A Gardner, BSc (**ICT*)
Mr P C Gerrard, BEd (*Director of Sixth Form Studies,*PE*)
Mrs E L P Hewitt, MA
Mr R N Hewitt, BEd
Miss L J Hinde, MA
Mr J G James, BSc (*Junior† Caffinites House*)
Mr K S Jones, BSc (**Chemistry*)
Mrs S Kerridge, BSc, BA
Miss K Lowery, BSc (**Chemistry*)
Mr B M Mason, BEd (**Games, Assistant† School House*)
Miss K McNicholas, BA
Mr R A Muttitt, BMus, ARCO, FRSA (*Director of Middle
School Studies, *Music*)
Miss L M Nicholson, BA (*Junior† MacLeod House*)
Mrs N Parker, MA, BA
Miss J Plummer, BSc
Mrs M F Proud, MA (**Religious Studies*)
Mr J C Renshaw, BA (**Geography*)
Ms E J Ross, BA, MA Ed (**Learning Support*)

Miss C Shepherd, BA, MA, PGCE
Mr A P Smith, BSc (**Physics*)
Mrs F Swan, BA (**English*)
Mrs N J Thompson, BA (*†MacLeod House*)
Mr S Thompson, BA
Mr D Tyreman, BA, MA (**History*)
Mr A R Wallace, BSc
Mr D Wiles, BSc, PhD
Mrs K L Wilkinson, BA
Mr D R Woodhead, BA (**Theatre Studies*)
Mr S Wright, BSc (*Mathematics*)
Mr M Younger, BA (*Assistant† Poole House*)

Location. The School is magnificently situated above the
steep banks of the River Wear, overlooked by the west towers of Durham Cathedral on the opposite bank, and has
occupied its present site since 1844. The School is physically compact – all the buildings are within 2 minutes' walk
of each other; the playing fields and the rowing are adjacent.
The School still has connections with Durham Cathedral
and all pupils attend Chapel on a regular basis and the cathedral once a term.

Aims. While pursuing the highest academic standards,
the School has an intellectual range which includes both
prospective Oxford or Cambridge entrants and pupils who
will succeed at A Level with the careful teaching and support the School provides. The School's main objective is to
bring out the best in every pupil. Everyone is expected to
contribute fully to the life of the School and thus to develop
all their talents to the full. The School provides the care, the
teaching and the facilities to do this in happy and attractive
surroundings.

Size. Numbers are relatively small, around 450, with an
excellent staffing ratio. Our Preparatory School (age 3–11)
currently caters for a further 130 day boys and girls.

The House System. The House system is one of the great
strengths of the School, enabling pastoral care of the highest
order. There are 5 Houses: three for boys (School House,
Poole House and Caffinites House) and two for girls (Pim-
lico House and MacLeod House). Junior House staff look
after the interests of Years 7 and 8 and in the boys' Houses
Assistant Housemasters are in charge of Years 10 and 11.
Although the majority of pupils are day pupils, the School
still offers full, weekly or part-time boarding and has some
100 boarders (girls and boys) and this number is likely to
increase in the short term. Day pupils enjoy all the benefits
of a "boarding style" education during the day (including
breakfast and supper, included in the fee), the same leisure
facilities as the boarders and space for private study.

Admission. Entry at age 11 is by way of the Durham
School 11+ Entrance Examination. Pupils joining at age 13
sit the School's 13+ Entrance Examination. It is also possible to join in the Sixth Form. Such admission is by interview,
testimonial and GCSE results, although there are also generous academic and non-academic awards. Entrance and
Scholarship examinations and interviews generally take
place in late January/early February (see scholarships
below). A prospectus with full details can be obtained on
application to the Registrar.

Academic. Academic courses are followed to GCSE, AS
and A2 Levels. A broad programme is pursued during the
years up to GCSE and there is a wide choice and flexible
programme for the Sixth Form, which numbers about 140.
There is a fully developed Careers Advisory Service.

Extra-Curricular Activities. A very wide and growing
variety of musical, dramatic, sporting and other activities is
available. Sports on offer include rugby, hockey, rowing,
cricket, netball, rounders, squash, swimming, athletics,
cross-country, tennis and water polo. The School has an all-
weather sports pitch. Various types of Adventure Training
are pursued through the CCF and pupils can take part in
World Challenge expeditions and the Duke of Edinburgh's
Award scheme.

Scholarships and Bursaries. (*See Scholarship Entries section.*) Generous academic and non-academic awards are available at 11, 13 and 16 (up to a maximum of 50% of fees). Financial support in the form of Bursaries is available at all ages where appropriate and these Bursaries can be held alongside academic and non-academic awards. There are generous concessions for brothers and sisters, children of clergy and the Armed Forces (in addition to the CEA Boarding allowance). The prestigious King's Scholarship award can be awarded to top performing candidates at 13+.

Fees per term (2011-2012). Years 7–8: £6,240 (full boarding), £5,490 (weekly boarding), £3,860 (day). Years 9–13: £7,425 (full boarding), £6,680 (weekly boarding), £5,000 (day).

Extras are kept to a minimum.

Bow, Durham School (formerly Bow School) is Durham School's Preparatory School and caters for 130 girls and boys from age 3–11. It is situated in its own beautiful grounds half a mile away from the Senior School and makes use of some of the Senior School facilities. (*For further details, see Bow, Durham School entry in IAPS section.*)

Charitable status. Durham School is a Registered Charity, number 1023407. It exists to provide a high quality education for boys and girls.

Eastbourne College

Old Wish Road, Eastbourne, East Sussex BN21 4JX
Tel: Headmaster: 01323 452320
         Bursar: 01323 452300
Fax: Headmaster: 01323 452327
         Bursar: 01323 452307
e-mail: hmsec@eastbourne-college.co.uk
website: www.eastbourne-college.co.uk

Founded 1867; Incorporated 1911.

Governing Body:
President: His Grace The Duke of Devonshire, CBE

Vice-Presidents:
The Bishop of London
The Earl of Burlington

¶ *Former Pupil*

Council:
¶Dr T Alfillé, MA, PhD
Ms A H Anderson, BSc, ACA (*Treasurer*)
¶Mr M T Barford, MA, FCA
¶Mr P A J Broadley, MA, FCA, FRSA (*Vice-Chairman*)
Dr C R Darley, MD, FRCP
Mr C M Davies, FRICS, ACIArb
Mrs N L Eckert, BA, PGCE
¶Admiral Sir Ian Forbes, KCB, CBE (*Chairman*)
¶Mrs V J Henley, BA
Mr G Marsh, MA Oxon
¶Sir Charles Masefield, MA Cantab, CEng, FRAeS, FIMechE
¶Dr R A McNeilly, MBBS, DCH, MRCGP, DOccMed, MBA
¶General Sir David Richards, GCB, CBE, DSO, ADC Gen
[Mr T S Richardson, FRICS
Mr A M Robinson, BA, ACA
¶Mr E G S Roose
¶Mr J H Ryley, BA Dunelm, AMP
Mrs A M Saunders, LLB
¶Dr D L Smith, MA Cantab, PhD, PGCE, FRHistS
¶Mr D Winn, OBE, MInstM
Mr A W L Wolstenholme, OBE, BSc, CEng, FICE
¶Mr S J D Yorke, MA Cantab

In attendance:
Mr S P Davies, MA Oxon
Mr S Severino, MA Oxon, PGCE
Mr M M Turnbull, BA, MA

Clerk to the Council: Ms C Meade, MA Cantab

Senior Management Team:

Headmaster: Mr S P Davies, MA

Deputy Head: Mr M M Turnbull, BA, MA
Bursar: Ms C Meade, MA
Assistant Head (*Curriculum*): Mr J M Gilbert, BSc, MRSC, CChem
Assistant Head (*Co-curricular*): Mr A T Lamb, BA
Assistant Head (*Teaching and Learning*): Mr D J Ruskin, BA
Registrar: Mr L Chu, BA
Marketing and Communications Director: Mrs J S B Lowden, BA
Foundation and Development Director: D A Stewart

* *Head of Department*
† *Housemaster/mistress*
§ *Part-time*
¶ *Former Pupil*

Art:
*Mrs S J Whiteley, BA
Mrs J L A Harriott, BA
Miss K M Hobden, MA
¶§Ms J Lathbury, DipFA

Classics:
*Mr H B Jourdain, BA
†Mr M J Banes, BA
§Mr S J Beal, BA
¶Miss J H Meakin, MA (*Greek)
¶†Mr I P Sands, MA
Mr A D B Smith, BA, MA

Design and Technology:
*Mr M B Wilders, BSc, DipArch
Mr N J Clark, BA
Ms Z B Cosgrove, BA, MA (*Textiles)
Mr G L McDonald, BEd
Mr W L Trinder, BEd
§Mrs A Young, MA

Drama:
*Mr T W Marriott, BA
†Mrs A F Marriott, BA, MA Ed
†Mrs L A Salway, BA, MA

Economics & Business Studies:
*Mr C I Bainbridge, BA
¶Mr L I Pearce, BSc
†Mr J P S Toy, MA, MSc
Mr A Wiscombe, BA

English:
*Mr O K Marlow, MA
¶Miss E M Boxer, BA (*Deputy HoD*)
Mr T S Fisher, BA, MA
Mrs L J Jourdain, BA
Mr P H Lowden, MA
Miss A E P Phelps, BA
†Mr N J Russell, MA

English as an Additional Language:
§*Miss K Briedenhann, BSecEd Sci, CELTA
§Mrs A F Maddock, BSc, MSc, CTEFLA
§Mrs G L Williams, BA, RSADip TEFL

General Studies:
*Mr J Thornley, BA

Geography:
*Mr R K Hart, BA
Mr G J L Kene, BSc
Mr A T Lamb, BA, FRGS
Mr W M Longdon, BA
Mr M M Turnbull, BA, MA

History:
*Mr J C Miller, BA
†Mr R H Bunce, MA
Mr S F Lomon, BA
Revd C K Macdonald, BA, DipTheo (*Chaplain*)
Mr B J Sadler, BA

Information and Communication Technology:
*Mr I R Shakespeare, BSc
Miss M A Smith, BSc

Learning and Thinking Skills and E-learning:
Mr S H K Maddock, BA, MTeach

Learning Support:
*Mr M L Saul, BEd
§Mr J M Tibbles, BEd, RSADip

Life and Learning Skills:
Mr E V Protin, MA

Mathematics:
*Mr J R Wooldridge, MA
¶Mr S E Beal, BA (*Deputy HoD*)
Mr O L Dennis, BA, PgDipMus

Mr R M Giles, MEng
Mr M J Green, BEng
Mr J J R Holliday, BA
¶§Mr L G Karunanayake, BA
†Mrs K F MacGregor, MA, MSc, MBA
¶Mr S F G Mattingly, BSc
†Mr J C Stevens, BEng
Mrs J C Wood, MA

Modern Languages:
*Mrs G A Webb, BA
Miss V E Burford, MA
Mr L Chu, BA
§Sra A G Del Angel, BA, MA
§Mlle A-L Lafargue, BA
Mr N G A Miller, BA
§Mrs H R Rünger-Field, BA
Mr D J Ruskin, BA
Miss M J Sheridan, BA
Mr J Thornley, BA
Mrs M C Tripp, BA, CMIL, DipTrans IoL (*Deputy HoD*)

Music:
*Mr G L Jones, BA
Mr D R S Force, BA
Mr J E Hughes, BMus, BA
Mr S W Parry, BMus

Physical Education:
*Mr S H K Maddock, BA, MTeach

Visiting Music Staff:
Ms E Blackshaw, ARCM (*Viola*)
Mrs A Boothroyd, MA, ARCM (*Piano*)
Miss S Carter, GMus (*Flute*)
Mr J Cruttenden, BA, ABSM (*Double Bass*)
Miss R Dines, ARAM, MMus, BMus, LRAM, ARCM (*Piano*)
Mr J Eady, BMus, PGDipMus, MMus, LRAM, LTCL, FRCO, AKC (*Cello, Organ*)
Mr P Edwards, MMus, GRSM (*Woodwind*)
Mrs R Elias, BMus, LRAM (*Oboe*)
Mr M A Elliott, MA (*Vocal Studies*)
Mr D Fuller, BMus, LGSMD (*Horn*)
Mr A Gilbert, ALCM TD, DipLCM (*Electric Keyboard*)
Mr K Goddard (*Guitar, Bass Guitar*)
Mr C Greenwood, BA (*Jazz Piano*)
Mr S Hollamby, ARCM, DipRCM (*French Horn, Trumpet, Trombone*)
Mr H Jones, AGSM, PgDipGSMD (*Bassoon, Percussion*)
Mrs J Lakin, GRSM, ARCM, LRAM (*Piano*)
Mr T Lees (*Guitar*)
Mrs J Mansergh, FTCL, LTCL, ARCO (*Piano*)
Mrs R Parry, BMus, PgDipPerf (*Violin*)
Mrs R Walker, LTCL, FTCL (*Keyboard*)
Ms L Wigmore, GRSM, ARCM (*Violin*)

¶§Mrs J M Kirtley, BA
Mrs J M Simmonds, BA
†Mrs G E Taylor-Hall, BA
Miss C Whiddett, BA
§Miss K L Wilson, BA

Religious Studies and Philosophy:
*Revd D J Peat, BA, MA
Miss C Travis, MTheol

Biology:
*Mr D J Beer, BSc
Miss C S Arnold, BSc
Mr C C Corfield, BSc
¶Mr P J Fellows, MBioMedSc

Chemistry:
*Miss A R Whitehead, BSc
Mr J M Gilbert, BSc, MRSC, CChem
Revd N H Green, MA, CertTh
¶Mr D C Miller, BSc, MRSC, CChem
§Ms J D Thornhill, MA

Physics:
*Mr D J Hodkinson, BSc (*also *Science*)
Dr A Ball, BSc, PhD
Mr J M Hall, BSc, CPhys, MInstP
§Dr G L Jones, MA, PhD
Mr D J Talbot, MPhys

Situation. The College is situated 400 metres from the sea in the prime residential part of the town of Eastbourne, adjacent to the national Tennis Centre at Devonshire Park, the Congress Theatre and the Cultural Centre. There is easy access to a wide range of cultural opportunities. The train to Gatwick Airport and London Victoria is under ten minutes walking distance; it is 1½ hours travel to London. The College links closely with the local community assisting people through its extensive S@S (Service at School) and PIPS (Pupils in Primary Schools) programmes, as well as providing opportunities for local musicians through its support of

the town's orchestra and choral society. There are a number of successful partnership schemes with local schools in the maintained sector.

Organisation and Pastoral Care. The College is a medium-sized boarding and day community where the ethos is of full boarding education. The College is co-educational with a ratio of girls to boys of 40:60. In 2010–2011 there were 632 pupils, of whom half were boarders. There are five boarding houses, three of which are for boys (Gonville, Pennell and Wargrave) and two are for girls (Nugent and School). There are five day houses, three of which are for boys (Craig, Powell and Reeves) and two are for girls (Blackwater and Watt). Day and boarding houses have similar facilities and are run on similar lines with resident house staff and full tutorial teams. All day pupils take supper at school and do prep in houses before returning home, some on school buses. There is great commitment from staff and pupils in all areas and there is strong system of pastoral care.

Curriculum. Pupils study the full range of subjects in their first year which includes the opportunity to study both Latin and Classical Greek along with a second modern language. For GCSE, pupils study biology, chemistry, English, French, mathematics and physics, as well as four other subjects from a choice of 14. At AS level, most pupils select four subjects from a choice of 23. Life and Learning skills are available in addition. Sixth Form students are encouraged to pursue individual research through extended projects, calling upon their teachers and tutors to support and encourage as needed. At A2 level most pupils study three subjects and all follow an extensive General Studies programme. ICT is central to the teaching and learning experience and the College is networked with its own Intranet.

Sport. A wide variety of sports is offered: major sports are cricket, hockey and rugby for boys; and hockey, netball and tennis for girls. Athletics, cross-country running, fencing, fives, football, golf, rowing, sailing, squash, swimming and tennis are also offered. All games pitches are within a short walking distance. Two Astroturf hockey pitches form 24 tennis courts in the summer. The school has its own 25-metre indoor swimming pool and a sports hall. Most major sports enjoy international tours at regular intervals (for example, hockey to South Africa in 2009, cricket and netball to Barbados in 2010 and rugby to Argentina/Chile in 2011).

Religion. The College is a Church of England foundation and the Chapel is at the heart of the school. All pupils experience regular Christian worship and religious education is compulsory in the first three years. There is a strong choral tradition and the Chapel or Chamber Choir leads the worship every Sunday in term time.

Development Plan. All boarding and day houses have been rebuilt or refurbished recently. A sizeable new extension to Nugent House now accommodates rising girl boarding numbers. An award-winning Science Centre was built in 2002; a new Design and Technology Centre and an ICT Centre were opened in 2003; and the Birley Centre, a whole-school facility to include a new music school, is being built with completion due by September 2011. Future plans include enlargement to the dining hall, a classroom block and a new sports hall.

Activities. A wide variety of activities are undertaken as part of the junior school programme and numerous and diverse clubs and societies flourish throughout the school. All pupils are encouraged to do something well and standards in art, drama, dance and music are all high. The Birley Centre (due to be opened in September 2011) will provide state-of-the-art facilities for the performing arts. The school has three other theatres: Big School Theatre, the Le Brocq Studio and the Dell Theatre for outdoor productions. The CCF, Duke of Edinburgh's Award Scheme and S@S (Service at School) all offer opportunity for leadership, initiative testing and service to the community. Regular College expeditions have recently visited Uganda, Bolivia, Borneo, Kyrgyzstan, Mongolia, Peru and India while a wide range of other outdoor activities thrive on the Sussex "Sunshine Coast".

Admission. Boys and girls are generally admitted between the ages of 13 and 14 years in Year 9 or for the Sixth Form in Year 12 after GCSE examinations. A prospectus and application form may be obtained from the Admissions Secretary. The website contains more information and parents and prospective pupils who wish to visit the school are welcomed. Early registration for a place is recommended, preferably a year in advance; a registration fee (£75) is charged and places are confirmed with a guaranteed place deposit (£750 for UK; a term's fees for overseas) within a year of entry. All pupils start in September, although exceptional cases are occasionally considered at other times.

Scholarships and Bursaries. (*See Scholarship Entries section.*) Academic, Art, Drama, Design & Technology, Music and Sports Scholarships are offered up to 50% to candidates of sufficient merit. Applicants must be under 14 on 1 September in the year they are due to enter the College. Academic Scholarships (including the Scoresby-Jackson Science Award and the Bernard Drake Award) and Music Scholarships are offered to pupils who join the school in Year 12 after GCSEs. A 10% boarding discount is available to HM Forces and Diplomatic Service families.

Fees per term (2011-2012). Boarding £9,105, Day £5,995 including meals and most extras.

Preparatory School. The charitable bodies governing Eastbourne College and the independent prep school, St Andrew's, have amalgamated to become one charity. Collaboration between the two schools has always been extremely close but until now, there has been no formal financial or governance links between them. This is a change of governance and not of the school. The schools will continue to operate independently and St Andrew's will prepare boys and girls for a variety of schools including the College.

The **Old Eastbournian Association** celebrated its century in 1995. Strong links are maintained with former pupils and a careers' directory links alumni and offers assistance to current pupils. The OEA runs a convention every year to support the careers and higher education programme.

The **Eastbourne College Society** is the friend-raising arm of the College and meets regularly to organise various events. It comprises all current parents and College employees, parents of former pupils, all former pupils, and other friends.

There is a thriving **Foundation and Development Office** to direct fundraising for bursaries and new developments.

The **Devonshire Society** (legacy club) meets annually.

Charitable status. Eastbourne College Incorporated is a Registered Charity, number 307071. It exists for the purpose of educating children.

The Edinburgh Academy

42 Henderson Row, Edinburgh EH3 5BL
Tel:　　0131 556 4603
Fax:　　0131 624 4990
e-mail:　enquiries@edinburghacademy.org.uk
website:　www.edinburghacademy.org.uk

Lord Cockburn, Leonard Horner and John Russell, WS, were chiefly responsible for the foundation of The Edinburgh Academy, which was incorporated by Royal Charter 5th Geo. IV. Sir Walter Scott, one of the original Directors, presided at the opening ceremony in 1824. The Academy is an independent School governed by a Court of Directors.

Court of Directors:

Chairman: S A Mackintosh

Extraordinary Directors:
Lord Cameron of Lochbroom
Professor J P Percy
J H W Fairweather
J B Leggat
A F Zegleman (*Chairman FGPC*)
Miss S J M Whitley (*Chairman PPC*)
M W Gregson

Elected Directors:
P I Bell
A M Duncan
Dr A E Gebbie
C Gillies
Dr B Hacking
G Hartop
Mrs F Houston
G N Hunt
Dr A Huntingdon
Ms T L LeBlanc
A N G Macdonald
Ms M McNeill
A J November
D H Scott (*Chairman Enterprises*)
F S D Spratt (*FGPC; Chairman PrC*)
Professor D J Webb

Co-opted Members:
The Rector
The Senior Deputy Rector
The Headteacher of Junior School

Secretary to Court and Bursar:
G G Cartwright, CA

FGPC = Finance & General Purposes Committee
PPC = Planning & Policy Committee
PrC = Property Committee

Rector: M G Longmore, MA Edinburgh, FRSA

Senior Deputy Rector: Mrs D K Meiklejohn, BSc Hons Edinburgh
Deputy Rector/Director of Studies: R T Wightman, BSc Edinburgh, PhD OU
Deputy Rector (Pastoral and Personnel): M Bryce, BSc Stirling

Senior School Staff:
* *Head of Department*

Classics:
*A K Tart, MA Cantab
Mrs P H Brignall, MA Edinburgh

English:
*J R Meadows, BA Dunelm
G M Trotter, MTheol St Andrews
S A Mair, MA Edinburgh
Ms C M Bannatyne, MA Glasgow
Miss J A Steele, MA St Andrews
Mrs J Cutress, BA Cambridge
D Holmes, BA Edinburgh

Drama:
*G M Trotter
Mrs J Cutress, BA Cambridge

Geography:
*Dr D J Carr, BSc Aberdeen, PhD Edinburgh
M Bryce, BSc Stirling (*Deputy Rector, Personnel & Pastoral*)
Mrs T L E Robinson, MA Dundee
Miss H Kilfeather, BA Ireland

History, Politics and Modern Studies:
*J Lisher, BA Hons Oxford
J E Miller, MA Oxon
C M Turley, BA Dunelm

S Carlin, BA Napier
Mrs S F Gray, BA Bristol

Mathematics:
*C A Brookman, BSc Edinburgh, PhD Edinburgh, GRSC, MInstP
M A L Shipley, BSc Heriot-Watt
Mrs R L Strudwick, BSc Edinburgh
Mrs F M McQuin, MA Aberdeen
Miss C Parsons, MA Glasgow
Mr C E Cooke, BSc Napier (*Head of Transition Years*)

Modern Languages:
*Mrs T J Irving, MA Heriot-Watt
Mrs S G S Heintze, MA, MPhil Glasgow, MIL
Mrs Y D Harley, LL Paris Sorbonne
Miss K A Haslett, MA Glasgow
Mrs F B Slavin, MA Edinburgh (*Head of Sixth Form*)
Mrs S McCredie, MA Aberdeen
Mrs Y Fortune, MA York
Mrs F Preston, BA Germany
Miss H L Duthie, MA Glasgow

Biology:
*A W MacPherson, BSc Edinburgh, MSc Birmingham, PhD Reading
Miss G Arbuthnott, BSc St Andrews
D M Lowe, BSc Edinburgh
Miss L Jackson, BSc Newcastle

Chemistry:
*Dr J R Coutts, BSc Dunelm, DPhil Oxon
T Blackmore, BSc, PhD Bristol, MRSC
K D Mitchell BSc Heriot-Watt, PhD Heriot-Watt
Miss H Kincade, BSc Edinburgh

Physics:
*N Armstrong, MA Oxon, CPhys, MInstP (*Deputy Director of Studies*)
R T Wightman, BSc Edinburgh, PhD OU (*Deputy Rector/ Director of Studies*)
K S Gilroy, BSc Manchester, PhD Cantab
J A Smith, BSc Heriot-Watt, PhD UMIST
A McCann, BSc Strathclyde (*Examination Officer*)

Computer Studies:
D G Stewart, BSc Heriot-Watt

Art:
*D L Prossser, BA
Mrs P E Prosser, BA London
C R Murray, BA Edinburgh College of Art (*Head of Middle Years*)
Ms E Mackinlay, BA London

Design & Technology:
*Miss S M Hennessy, BA Cardiff, MA Manchester Metropolitan
Miss J Kenwright, BA Wales

Business Studies:
*W J Turkington, BA Heriot-Watt
Miss A Koller, BA Germany

Music:
*P N Coad, MA, PhD Cantab, FRCO (*Director*)
P E Backhouse, BMus Edinburgh, ARCM, FRCO
L Morrison, DRSAM
Mrs M A Fergusson, DRSAM
A C Tully

Physical Education:
*M J de G Allingham, MSc
Miss L McWilliam, BEd Edinburgh
R W Sales, BSc Napier
M E Appleson, BA Leeds
Mrs H Dean, BEd Edinburgh

Support for Learning:
*Mrs B Bellis, MA St Andrews
Mrs S F Gray, BA Bristol
Mrs F Constable, BSc Glasgow
Mrs L McMillan, BA Hons Lancaster
Mrs H Dean, BEd Edinburgh

Religious Education:
*H Jarrold, M Theol St Andrews
M Hughes, BA Edinburgh

Careers: *Mrs Y D Harley

Librarian: Mrs S Phillips

OC CCF: Sqn Ldr S G S Heintze, RAF
CCF SSI: Captain E B Burnett, Hldrs

Junior School Staff:
Headteacher: G Calder, MA Edinburgh
Deputy Head: B Dean, BEd Hons

Assistant Heads:
Mrs L A Becher, DCE Dundee, INSC (*Head of Early Years*)
Mrs B Robertson, BEd Dundee, DPSE Moray House (*Head of Middle Primary*)
P Bertolotto, BEd Hons CREDL, PGCE (*Head of Upper Primary*)

Mrs E F Black, BEd Stirling, PGD, DipCE Moray House
Mrs S Boyd, MA Hons, MCIBS, PGDE
Miss A Thomson, BSc Napier, PGCE Paisley
Mrs C Petrie, BEd, HDNS Northern College
Mrs K L McLean, BEd Northern College
Mrs B E Mackie, CertEd Lancaster
Mrs C Chan, BEd Jord
Mrs S Walker, DCE Call Park
Mrs G A Wood, CELTA, MA Hons Glasgow, PGCE
S MacDonald, BA Napier, PGCE
C McCloghry, BA Moray House, HNC Telford, PGCE
R Tyrell, BSc
M Enos, MA Edinburgh, BA Strathclyde, PGCE (*PE & Games*)
Mrs L A Russell, BEd Hons (*Music*)
R Zbikowski, MA (*Science*)
Mrs C Bingham, BEd Hons 1st
Miss J Purves-Home, BEd Hons
Mrs V G Lewis, MA Hons, PGCE
Mrs S Taylor, BEd Primary Aus
Miss N Kelly, MA, PGCE
M Willis, BA, PGDE
Ms P Richardson, BA Hons, PGCE
Miss K Forster, BA Hons, PGCE
Mrs F H Penman, BA Hons, MSc, PGCE
Miss J Williams, BSc Hons, PGDE

Support for Learning:
*Mrs P Macnair, BA, MA Ed
Mrs M Marlborough, BSc, MEd Edinburgh
Mrs C Burke, BEd Hons

Nursery:
Mrs P Howden Thomson, BEd Hons 1st
Mrs A Addison, NNEB
Mrs K Thomson, NNEB
Mrs K Jones, NNEB
Mrs T A Sutherland, NNEB
Mrs F Ho, HNC
Mrs S Stewart, NNEB, SEN
Miss J Evans, NNEB
Mrs D Galbraith, NNEB
Miss E Hill, NNEB
Ms S Semple, NNEB
Miss A Hill, NNEB
Mrs G Scott, SVQ Level 3
Mrs M Byfield, SVQ Level 3
Mrs A Chambers, NNEB

Mrs R Morrow, NNEB
Mrs L Campbell, BA, DipEd
Mrs A Ramsay, Montessori Cert
J Saddler, HNC Early Education

The Edinburgh Academy became fully co-educational in August 2008. At present The Edinburgh Academy consists of a Senior School, containing about 405 boys and 165 girls (ages 10½ to 18), a Junior School containing about 250 boys and 100 girls (ages 4½ to 10½), and a Nursery Department of 100 pupils.

Site and Buildings. The Senior School occupies a site in Henderson Row, less than a mile from Princes Street and at the northern limits of the Georgian 'New Town', of which it was designed to be a part. The buildings there include a School Hall, Library, Music School, Dining Hall, Gymnasium, Miniature Rifle Range, Fives Courts, James Clerk Maxwell Science Centre and the Magnusson Centre for the Performing Arts completed in 2009. A further programme of development is currently being agreed, aimed at major improvements to the general facilities of the Senior School in the build up to the Bi-centenary of the School in 2024. The Playing Fields are about half a mile from the main buildings – Raeburn Place (8½ acres) (shared with the Old Boys), New Field in Inverleith Place (20 acres), and a further 5 acres, also at Inverleith, with a Running Track. There are Squash Rackets courts and all-weather Tennis Courts at Inverleith. A small all-weather pitch at Inverleith along with two full-sized all-weather pitches at New Field opened in October 2009. The Academy possesses its own Field Centre in the Highlands (Glen Doll, Angus). A new Sports Centre was built in 1997. A new purpose-built nursery and after-school facility was opened in August 2008.

Forms. (Senior School only). Seventh and Sixth Classes: by tutor groups studying either GCE A Levels or Highers. Seconds, Thirds, Fourths and Fifths: 4 Classes in sets for subjects. Geits (Firsts): 4 Classes. No teaching group consists of more than 24 pupils, and many are substantially smaller. In the Junior School class sizes are 20 (P1–P3) and 22 (P4–P6)

Scheme of Work. In the Junior classes of the Upper School all pupils do English, Drama, History, Geography, Latin, French, Mathematics, Sciences, Art and Design Technology, Electronics, Computing, Drama and Music. Either German, Spanish or Mandarin is started in the Seconds. In addition to the above Business Studies, Physical Education, and Religious & Moral Studies may be studied as full subjects in the Fourths. GCSE is taken in the Fifths. In the Sixths the majority of pupils take SQA Highers (whereby many achieve Scottish university entrance qualifications) and others do first year work in preparation for GCE A Level taken in the Sevenths. A wide choice of subjects is available: Art, Biology, Business Management, Chemistry, Computing, Design Technology, Drama, English, Economics, Geography, History, Latin, Mathematics, Modern Languages (French, German, and Spanish), Modern Studies, Music, Physical Education, Physics, Religious, Moral & Philosophical Studies. Pupils are prepared for University entrance. Places at Oxford, Cambridge and Russell Group Universities have been regularly won in all departments. In 2010 95% of our pupils went on to study degree courses, some 15% of those after a Year Out.

Divinity. An assembly for Prayers is held at 8.50 am each morning, and is attended by the whole school. In every class one period a week is devoted to Religious Education. School Services for the whole School are held on several occasions during each term.

Physical Education and Games. All pupils take Physical Education and Games (which are regarded as an integral part of the curriculum) unless they are exempt on medical grounds. Rugby Football and Hockey are played in the Autumn Term and during half of the Spring Term as are Hockey and Association Football. Cross-Country Running and other games occupy the first part of this Term. Hockey is the main sport for girls. In the Summer Term boys and girls choose from Cricket, Athletics, Hockey, Sailing, Shooting, Swimming and Tennis according to their year groups. Golf, Rugby Fives, Squash Rackets and Badminton are also played, and instruction in Fencing and Judo is available. The School has led the development of Rugby Football in Scotland for over a century. In recent years, School teams have regularly reached the National Schools Cup final, winning in both age categories (U18, U16).

Combined Cadet Force. All pupils over 14½ join the CCF (they may enter directly into either the Army or RAF sections) or The Duke of Edinburgh's Award Scheme unless exempt. All members of the CCF are required to attend at least the Annual Camp in their first year. After three terms of service pupils are free to leave the CCF. The Academy has a Pipe Band. Piping and Drumming classes are held for pupils in the Junior classes of the Upper School as well as for members of the CCF.

Duke of Edinburgh's Award and Outdoor Activities. Considerable importance is attached to outdoor education. In addition to The Duke of Edinburgh's Award Scheme there are residential trips for both 1st and 3rd year pupils. The Academy's Field Centre in Glen Doll, Angus, is ideally situated as a centre for Hill-Walking, Climbing, Skiing, Fishing, and for Geographical and Biological Field Studies.

Music, Drama, Art. A purpose-built Music School was opened in 1992. In addition to the full-time Music Staff, there are a number of visiting teachers for various instruments. Musical appreciation and Singing form part of the curriculum of the Junior Classes. Throughout the rest of the Senior School there are regular periods of Music Appreciation. Pupils are encouraged to learn a Musical Instrument and over 300 do. The Edinburgh Academy Chamber Choir won the BBC Songs of Praise School Choir of the Year 2011, cementing the great strength in choral and orchestral work at the School. There is a Choral Society, a Choir, and a special Chamber Choir, a School Orchestra, Junior Orchestra, and a Wind Band. Inter-Division Music Competitions, both Choral and Instrumental, are held annually. Also important are the Pipe Band and the Dance Band and Jazz Band.

The New Magnusson Centre for the Performing Arts was opened in 2009 and provides a modern and dynamic setting for the several Senior and Junior Dramatic productions each year, including a major Play, Opera or Musical. There are Drama Competitions involving all pupils in the Fourths classes and for Divisions (Houses). A major Choral work is performed each year, and a mix of formal and informal Saturday evening Concerts are given through the year.

Art and DT are included in the curriculum for the Junior Classes, and there are regular lessons in Art Appreciation throughout the School. Pupils are regularly prepared for GCSE and A Level or for SCE Higher in Music, Art, DT and Drama.

Other Activities. There are Arts, Model United Nations, Debating, History, Modern Languages, Photographic, Jazz, Jewellery, Politics, Computer and Electronic, Scientific and Mathematical Societies; Scripture Union and Video Club, Bridge, Chess, and Classes for the further study of Art and for Scottish Country Dancing. All pupils have an opportunity each week to devote some time to some creative art or craft, Music, Painting, Pottery, etc. for which good facilities are available.

Junior School. The Senior Department of the Junior School (ages 6½ to 10½) is in a building opened in 1960, close to New Field. The Early Years Department (ages 4½ to 6½) is in Denham Green House, built in 1987 on the same site. The work of the Junior School is arranged so as to ensure a smooth transition to the Senior School. All pupils in the Junior School have Physical Education. Rugby and Association Football, Hockey, Athletics and Cricket all have their place. For Music, there are 2 full-time teachers and a number of visiting teachers for various instruments. Musical Appreciation and singing form part of the curriculum and every encouragement is given to pupils to learn a Musical Instrument and to take part in the wide range of Musical Activities offered by various Choirs and Instrumental Groups.

Residence. No pupil may attend the Academy who does not live under the charge of his parents or legal guardian. Exemptions from this rule are rarely made by the Directors, and only in very exceptional cases.

Fees per term (2011-2012). Nursery £1,410–£2,215. Junior School P1–P6 £2,200–£2,737. Senior School: £3,012 (Geits), £3,740 (2nds–7ths).

When 3 or more brothers or sisters are in attendance at the School at the same time, a reduction of one-third of the tuition fees is made for each brother or sister after the first two.

Scholarships and Bursaries. (*See Scholarship Entries section*.) A number of external Scholarships are offered each year at various ages from age 11. The Examination takes place in January. Further details are available from the Senior Deputy Rector. Means-tested Bursaries are available to both new and existing pupils in cases of need which may arise.

Admission. The majority of new pupils are admitted at the beginning of the Autumn Term in late August, though they can be accepted at any time places are available. There are places each year at Sixth Form level in the Upper School, and also in the First to Seconds classes (10½–12½), where special provision is made for pupils who have previously done no languages; and there are possibilities for casual vacancies at other levels.

All candidates for admission to the Academy must first be assessed by the School. For admission in August, candidates for the Junior Department of the Junior School are assessed in January, along with those for the Senior Department, and for the Upper School. Pupils should be registered as candidates for entry as early as possible. Application forms are obtainable from the Admissions Secretaries at Senior and Junior Schools. There is a registration fee of £30.

Edinburgh Academical Club. There is a strong Academical Club, whose headquarters are at Raeburn Place, Edinburgh. *Secretary*: Mr Alan Fyfe, The Edinburgh Academy, 42 Henderson Row, Edinburgh EH3 5BL (Tel: 0131 624 4944).

Charitable status. The Edinburgh Academy is a Registered Charity, number SC016999. It exists to provide good quality education.

Elizabeth College

The Grange, St Peter Port, Guernsey, Channel Islands GY1 2PY

Tel: 01481 726544
Fax: 01481 714176
e-mail: secretary@elizabethcollege.guernsey.net
website: www.elizabethcollege.gg

Elizabeth College was founded in 1563 by Queen Elizabeth I in order to provide education for boys seeking ordination in the Church of England. It is one of the original members of the Headmasters' Conference and has Direct Grant status. It provides a broad education while maintaining the Christian aspirations of its Foundress. There are approximately 760 pupils in the College, of whom about 260 are in the Lower School. Girls are accepted into the Lower School. The Sixth Form is mixed through a partnership with nearby Ladies' College.

Motto: '*Semper Eadem*'.

Visitor: The Bishop of Winchester

Directors:
The Very Revd Canon Paul Mellor, Dean of Guernsey
  (*Chairman*)
Professor R Conder
Mr K M Hudson
Mr S Le Maitre
Mr N L Guillemette
Mrs M Wheatley
Advocate R Clark
Mr A Langlois
Mr J Perkins

Principal: G J Hartley, MA, MSc

Vice-Principal (*Academic*): R J W James, BA
Vice-Principal (*Pastoral*): J M Shaw, BA, MA
Head of Sixth Form: C R W Cottam, MA, CT ABRSM

Members of Teaching Staff:

B W Allen, CertEd	A Hale, BSc
B E H Aplin, BSc	M N Heaume, BSc
M A Buchanan, BA	Miss C F Hélie, Licence Lit
Mrs C S Buchanan, BA	D S Herschel, BSc
Mrs A J Brun, BA, MA	J J Hills, BA, MPhil
Mrs M Campbell, BA, MA	J R Hooker, BA
G S Cousens, BA	L Hudson, BA
Mrs P E Cross, BA, ARCM	S J Huxtable, BA
P Davis, BSc	D R L Inderwick, BA, MA
R Davis, BA	Miss K Labbé, Licence Lit
Miss A C M Demongeot,	R G Le Sauvage, BSc
BA, MA	R A Morris, BA
T R De Putron, BSc	D F Raines, BSc, DPhil
Miss P J Dudley, MSci,	Dr E Ryder, BSc, PhD
MA, MRSC	Mrs K M Shaw, BA
T Edge, BA, MA	T C Slann, Dip NEBSS
Miss J Flood, BA, MA	Mrs L Stephens, BA
M Garnett, BA	M A G Stephens, BA
A J Good, BSc	C C J Telfer, BSc
Miss H M Gordon, BA	C D van Vlymen, BSc, PhD
Mrs M Gordon, MA	M Wesley, BSc
Mrs C A Gribbens, BSc	

Chaplain: The Revd R G Harnish, BSc, DPhil, MA
Director of Music: P C Harris, GRSM, ARCM
Games and Physical Education: D Wray, BEd

Head of the Junior School: Mrs S Battey, CertEd
Deputy Head: C Veron, BEd

	Pre-Prep:
Mrs E J Brooker, BSc	Mrs J Atkinson, BEd
Mrs S Crittell, BA	Mrs C Bowden, BEd
Miss K Henry, BA	Miss E Carré, BA
Mrs D M McLaughlin, BSc	Mrs J Chauhan, BA
Mrs A M Pollard, BA	Mrs R Curtis, BA
Mrs K J Robinson, BEd	Miss C Gillman, BA
P Sargent, BA	L Purdue, BSc
R Sutton, BA	Miss L Wadley, BA
Miss D Wenman, BA	

Bursar and Clerk to the Directors: J M Willis, MCMI

Buildings and Grounds. The Upper School (for pupils over 11 years) is situated in imposing buildings dating from 1829 which stand on a hill overlooking the town and harbour of St Peter Port. The classrooms and laboratories, all of which are equipped with appropriate modern teaching aids, the Hall, Sports Hall and Swimming Pool are accommodated on this site. Recent improvements have included a new Sixth Form Centre, improved Design and Technology and ICT facilities and a Modern Languages computer suite. There are two large games fields, one of which includes an artificial pitch for hockey and soccer and a recently completed Pavilion. Elizabeth College Junior School comprises Beechwood, a prep school, and Acorn House, a pre-prep and nursery school. Beechwood has its own site some ten minutes' walk from Elizabeth College. It takes boys and girls from 7 to 11 years old. Acorn House accepts boys and girls from 4 to 7 years old and also has a pre-school facility for younger children.

Academic Curriculum. In their first three years in the Upper School boys follow a broad curriculum which is common to all – covering arts, sciences, creative and practical subjects. Information Technology is timetabled in all three years to develop the skills needed for the demands of GCSE and A Level courses. Opportunity is also afforded to boys to sample both Latin and a second Modern Foreign Language in addition to French. PSHE, RE, PE, Games and Drama are timetabled throughout. In Years 10 and 11 the aim is to produce a high level of achievement and choice at GCSE by offering flexibility wherever possible. Three separate sciences or Core and Additional Science are studied. At least one modern language must be taken, although two are available as an option. English Literature is studied within the English teaching groups, but is not compulsory for all. Other GCSE options combine the traditional with the contemporary. Art, Business Studies, Classics, Citizenship, Drama, Graphics, History, Information Technology, Latin, Music, PE and RS are currently offered. Alongside the GCSE courses PSHE and PE continue to be taught. The Sixth Form is run in partnership with The Ladies' College, with interchange of pupils between schools and shared teaching of many groups. The Sixth Form offers a very broad array of choices across the two schools enabling a wide variety of choices. Tutorial periods enable vocational, careers and pastoral guidance to be available.

Music. There is an orchestra, a brass band, a wind band and a number of chamber music groups. The College choir makes regular visits to the French mainland to sing in Cathedrals and at concerts. Instruction is available in all the usual orchestral instruments in addition to the piano and organ. The Junior School has its own choir, orchestra and recorder group. Each summer holiday the College hosts a week-long orchestral course when tuition is provided by eminent professionals to over two hundred and fifty boys and girls.

Games. The sports fields cover some 20 acres. The Junior School has its own small playing field, and also has access to the facilities of the Upper School. The major College games are Association Football, Hockey and Cricket. Athletics, Badminton, Basketball, Cross-country Running, Fencing, Golf, Rugby Football, Sailing, Shooting, Squash, Swimming and Tennis also flourish. Physical Education forms a regular part of the curriculum for all boys up to the end of Year 11. Some seniors specialise in Outdoor Pursuits (principally canoeing and climbing) as their "sport". This is under the guidance of a fully qualified expert. Despite the size of the Island, plentiful opposition is available. The College competes against other Island schools, has a traditional rivalry with Victoria College in Jersey, makes regular tours to the mainland and hosts return visits from UK schools.

Combined Cadet Force. This is voluntary and optional and is Tri-Service. Cadets travel regularly to the UK and beyond for Proficiency Training, Camps, Courses, Qualifications and Competitions, including Advernturous Training and the Ten Tors Challenge. The BTEC Public Services NVQ is available to all cadets. Competition shooting forms a major part of the CCF and there is a long and distinguished record at Bisley. The CCF has an important role in providing Guards of Honour for Island ceremonial occasions.

Duke of Edinburgh's Award. Boys are encouraged to participate in this scheme. Both Bronze and Gold Awards are offered as extra-curricular activities. The expedition work necessarily takes place on the mainland during the Easter and Summer holidays.

Community Service Unit. This Unit draws boys from Year 10 and above. It serves those in need and those who are handicapped throughout the Island community.

Scouts. There is an active Scout Group, whose headquarters are situated on the College Field. At the Junior School there is a Cub Scout Group.

Clubs and Societies. The College stresses the importance of extra-curricular activity. Among currently active clubs are those which foster Art, Canoeing, Chess, Climbing, Debating, Drama, Fencing, Life Saving, Model Railways, Sailing, Science, Shooting, Squash, Table Tennis and Tai-Chi.

Pastoral Care. In the Upper School each year has a Head of Year assisted by four Tutors. Acorn and Beechwood have a Headmistress. All these staff provide pastoral care and academic guidance for their own sections of the College. They are supported by a full-time Chaplain who conducts services in all three schools as well as preparing boys for Confirmation.

Parental Involvement. Parents are strongly encouraged to take an active part in their child's education. There are regular assessments and reports to which they are invited to respond, either immediately or at annual parents' evenings. Those responsible for pastoral matters are also available on the telephone during out of school hours for discussion about problems or progress.

Admission. The principal ages for admission into the school are 4, 7, 11, 13 and 16, but there are usually vacancies for entry at other ages. Entry is by means of tests and/or interview which are adapted to the age of the applicant. There is a £110 non-refundable registration fee. Applications for entry should be addressed to the Principal.

Scholarships to the College. (*See Scholarship Entries section.*) The Gibson Fleming Fund provides Scholarships for current pupils. The award value depends to some extent upon the needs of the applicant's parents. The Trustees review their Scholars each year and take account of general personal qualities as well as academic performance. Entries should be made by the end of the Lent Term.

Choral and Instrumental Scholarships are also available to current pupils. Details of these may be obtained from the Principal.

Scholarships to the Universities. The College Exhibitions, Scholarships and Prizes include the Queen's Exhibition, the Lord de Sausmarez Exhibition; the Mainguy Scholarship; the Mansell Exhibition and the Mignot Fund. The Gibson Fleming Trust can also provide awards to its Scholars for their future education.

Travel. There are several flights each day from Southampton (half an hour), Gatwick (about three quarters of an hour) and Stansted (about one hour). There are also regular flights to the West Country and to Midlands and northern airports. There are frequent sailings to and from Portsmouth, Poole and Weymouth, which offer vehicle transportation.

Old Boys. The Honorary Secretary of the Old Elizabethan Association is Gresham Barber who may be contacted via www.oea.org.gg.

Fees per term (2011-2012). Acorn (Pre-Prep and Nursery): £2,500; Beechwood (Prep): £2,800; Upper School (11–18): £2,717.

Ellesmere College
A Woodard School

Ellesmere, Shropshire SY12 9AB
Tel: 01691 622321
Fax: 01691 623286
e-mail: hmsecretary@ellesmere.com
website: www.ellesmere.com

Ellesmere College is one of the Schools of the Society of SS Mary and John of Lichfield, part of the Woodard Corporation, and was opened on 8 September 1884.

Motto: '*Pro Patria Dimicans.*'

Founder: The Revd Nathaniel Woodard, DCL, then Dean of Manchester

Visitor: The Rt Revd The Lord Bishop of Lichfield

College Council:
The Provost
Mrs D H Griffith (*Custos*)
G R Wigginton
Mrs F M Christie, MRPhS
Mrs C S Newbold, BA
J A Mathias, FCA
J S Hopkins
A L Morris
C Clutton
Professor S Eisenstein, MB BCh, PhD, FRCS
A Shearer
R A K Hoppins, FCA
Mrs S M Connor, BA Hons
Mr C E Lillis
The Right Reverend M J Rylands, Bishop of Shrewsbury

Headmaster: B J Wignall, BA, MA, MCMI, FRSA

Deputy Head (*Pastoral*): M D T Sampson, BSc
Deputy Head (*Academic*): Mrs S V Pritt-Roberts, BEd, MEd, NPQH
Head of Sixth Form: P A Wood, MA (**General Studies*)
Head of Middle School: Dr R Chatterjee, BSc, MSc, PhD, Cert SpLD (**Biology*)
Head of Lower School: Mrs S Owen, BEd
Director of Activities: Mrs D Joynson-Brooke, BEd
Chaplain: The Revd David Slim, MEd
Director of Finance: N Haworth, ACMA, BA
Director of Operations: M McCarthy, BSc, DMS

Teachers:
* *Head of Department*
† *Housemaster/mistress*

S F W Purcell, BA, FCIEA (**English*)
G Hutchinson, MA
M P Clewlow, BSc
†Mrs J E Purcell, BA
P J Hayes, MA
Mrs H T Scarisbrick, BA
Mrs S E Morgan, BEd
Mrs D Joynson-Brooke, BEd
C R Davies, BA
H B Orr, BD (**Religious Studies and Sociology*)
R P Boswell, BA (**Drama*)
Dr M T Gareh, BSc, MSc, PhD, CSci, CChem, MRSC (**Chemistry*)
T F Bongers, BCom
J H Cowley, BSc, NPQH (**Mathematics*)
†D J Morgan, BSc
Mrs J Evans, BEd, MA, Dip SpLD, AMBDA
Mrs J R Nicolson, MA
Mrs Z J Fisher, BA (**Media Studies*)
Mrs K L Jenkins, BSc, BSc
Mrs L A Paton, BA (**History & Classics*)
†C C Cawcutt, HDE
M Coats, BSc Hons (**Information Technology*)
R J Macintosh, BSc
S B Mullock, BA (**Business Studies and Careers*)
I L Williams, BEd
†Mrs J Heath, CertEd, Dip SpLD, AMBDA
D W Crawford, MA, MSc, MPhil
Mrs P M Fox, BA
Mrs S Phillips, MA (**Art*)
R J Purnell, BSc
R J Townsend, BEd
Mrs V M Howle, BEd, Cert SpLD, Dip RSA
Mrs E Phillips, BSc
Mrs J M Davies, BA
Ms C Allen, BA (**EAL*)

Mrs H L Davenport, BSc (**Physical Education*)
R C Paul, BA, ARCO (**Music*)
Dr J K Collins, BSc PhD
W J Hutchings, BEd
Dr I G Tompkins, MA, BD, DPhil (**IB Coordinator*)
Mrs C Westwood, BA
Ms S M Abbots, MA
†I L Roberts, BA
P E Swainson, BSc
†G Owen, BEd
Mrs V Hart, MA
†J J Baggaley, BA
Miss A C Darrant, BSc (**Physics*)
Mrs J M Hibbott, BA
Mrs M E Hutchings, MA, MA
K J Paul, BSc
Miss L Stewart-Harris, MSc
Mrs E J Baker, BSc Econ, Dip SpLD, AMBDA
Miss M Thomas, MA
Mrs N F Hoy, LTA Club Coach
Dr J B Chatterjee, BSc, MSc, PhD
Miss H Coney, BA
R J Heaton, BSc, MSc
Miss J K Smith, BA
M Mrs H Napal-Gandelin, BA, MA
R J Curtis, BSc (**Design & Technology*)
D M Roberts, BSc, MEd
Mrs S J Bogue, BSc
†L C Bambridge, BA (**Modern Foreign Languages*)
Miss E A Killen, BEd
Mrs R Paul, BA
Mrs G Ansell, CertEd, TESOL, MA
Mrs E Griffiths, BA
Ms D Lensing, BA
Ms M J Tarrega, MA
Miss J M Manion, BA, NPQH (**Support for Learning*)
Miss G Heald, BA
Mr T D Hurst, BEng
Miss R Morris, BSc
A Murphy, BSc
Mrs T Parsons, AA
J Underhill, MA

School Medical Officer: Dr E A M Greville, MBChB

Sanatorium Sisters:
Mrs J Slim, RGN
Mrs M Moore, RGN
Mrs M Haynes, SEN

The College Building. The main school building contains three boys' Boarding and Day Houses, as well as a mixed 10–12 junior Boarding and Day House, bachelor and married accommodation for Housemasters and Housemistresses and/or Assistant Housemasters and Housemistresses, the Chapel and the Dining Hall. St Luke's Boarding House completes the main quadrangle. A 13–16 girls' Boarding and Day house has its own wing in the main building and was opened in response to demand in 1996. The girls' Sixth Form Boarding and Day House which accommodates girls in a combination of shared and single study bedrooms and dayrooms was completed in 1986. A Gymnasium, Big School (Assembly Hall) which houses the Schulze Organ, and three subject Departments are also located in the main building. September 2004 saw the opening of the College's new Sports Hall, which adds to facilities that include two other gymnasia and squash courts.

Additional wings contain the Library and Sixth Form Centre. Other subjects are taught in their own Departmental blocks close to the main building, and include Science Laboratories, a Modern Languages Department with a Language Laboratory, an Art School, a Design & Technology Centre, and a Business Studies Department with its own computer suite. A purpose-built Lower School for Years 3–8 was opened in 1999.

The House System. The Lower School (ages 7–13) has a competitive system based on 3 Houses. The Senior School has a competitive system based on 4 Houses all of which are co-educational and combine boarding and day pupils. Separate from the competitive Houses is the residential House system for living arrangements. There are 2 Girls' Houses, catering for age 13–16 and Sixth Form respectively; there are 4 Boys' Houses: two for age 13–16 and two Sixth Form Houses; there is also a Mixed House catering for boarders of ages 10–12.

Curriculum. In the first year in the Senior School a full range of fourteen subjects is studied, including Art, Design and Technology, Computing and Technical Drawing. This curriculum is designed to give all pupils a comprehensive introduction before reducing to a basic eight subjects for GCSE. At GCSE all pupils take English, Mathematics, and either Dual Award Science or the three Sciences studied separately. Other subjects depend on individual aptitude and choice.

In the Sixth Form over 20 different academic subjects are available for study to A Level or IB Diploma to prepare for University Entrance or entry to the Services and the Professions.

Music. The College has a very strong musical tradition. It possesses two of the finest organs in the country, including the internationally renowned St Mary Tyne Dock Schulze Organ. The Chapel Choir has a wide repertoire of Church Music. There is a Big Band, a Choral Society, a Jazz Group and other ensembles, all of which give regular concerts. There are House Music Competitions every year.

An annual programme of Celebrity Concerts brings distinguished musicians to the College.

The Music School is part of the College Arts Centre which provides first-class facilities, including 8 Practice Rooms, a Recording Studio, Teaching Rooms and a Studio Theatre designed for small concerts and seating 220 people. The department has 2 full-time and 16 part-time teachers.

Arts Centre. This purpose-built complex was opened in 1976 for Drama, Dance, Film, Music and Art Exhibitions. A programme is organised in which international artists in all these fields visit the Centre, which shares its facilities with the local community.

Careers. At all levels pupils are encouraged to seek advice from the College careers masters and mistresses as well as representatives from the Independent Schools Careers Organisation. The ISCO aptitude tests are available for all pupils in their GCSE level year. A Careers' Convention is held each year for pupils in Year 11.

Games and Physical Education. Ellesmere has a long tradition of sporting excellence particularly in rugby and tennis. The sporting excellence is supported by the Rugby Academy programme (3 leavers turned professional in 2008), the Tennis Academy, and the joint College and Community Ellesmere College Titans Swimming Team. The Cricket Academy was launched in 2009 and the Shooting Academy in 2010.

All members of the School are required to participate in a regular programme of games, though particular inclinations and aptitudes are taken fully into consideration. Facilities include a sports hall, a floodlit multi-sports area, a fitness centre, squash courts, a heated indoor swimming pool, indoor and outdoor shooting range, a gymnasium, 6 floodlit all-weather tennis courts, a golf course, rugby pitches, hockey pitches, cricket squares, and an athletics track. Ellesmere has a long tradition of sporting excellence, particularly in rugby and tennis.

Ellesmere is superbly placed for outdoor pursuits. Easily accessible lakes, rivers and hills provide opportunities to develop talents and interests.

Sailing takes place on Whitemere. The School owns six boats and pupils are allowed to bring their own craft. Canoe-ing takes place on the Ellesmere canal and on local rivers such as the Dee and the Severn.

All pupils are expected to join one of the following: Outdoor Training Unit; CCF; Social Service. These activities occur on one full afternoon a week, but, in order to extend their activities, twice a year 3 days are set aside when all members of the School participate in 48-hour expeditions. In the Lent Term a single day is devoted to expeditions.

Admission. Boys and girls are admitted at all points of entry into the school. Entrance examinations are held in February for Lower School entry. Scholarships for Prep School candidates are held in May, while others take the Common Entrance Examination in June.

Scholarships and Exhibitions. (*See Scholarship Entries section.*) A wide range of Scholarships and Exhibitions recognising a range of talents is available. Bursaries are awarded to the sons of Clergy, and Foundation Awards to sons of parents who could not normally afford this type of education. All details may be obtained from the Headmaster. In cases of need these awards may be further supplemented.

Fees per term (2011-2012). Upper School: Boarders £8,679, Weekly Boarders £6,648, Day £5,145. Lower School: Boarders £6,945, Weekly Boarders £6,468, Day £3,141–£3,612. Fees are inclusive of general School charges.

Music lessons are given at a charge of £235 for ten lessons and individual tuition for dyslexic pupils also incurs an extra cost. A scheme of insurance is in force under which the School Fees may be insured for a small termly premium for any number of years and which enables a pupil to remain at Ellesmere to complete his/her education free of all board and tuition fees, if a parent dies before the pupil's School career is ended. There is also a School Fees Remission Scheme for insurance of fees in cases of absence through illness and of surgical and medical expenses. Arrangement can be made for a single advance payment of fees.

'Old Boys and Girls'. Former pupils of the school normally become members of the Old Ellesmerian Club, which in turn enables them to take part in a number of societies and activities. For further information contact: Nick Pettingale, Director of Development, Ellesmere College, Ellesmere, Shropshire, SY12 9AB.

Charitable status. Ellesmere College is a Registered Charity, number 1103049. It exists to provide education for children.

Eltham College

Grove Park Road, London SE9 4QF

Tel:	020 8857 1455
Fax:	020 8857 1913
e-mail:	mail@eltham-college.org.uk
website:	www.eltham-college.org.uk

Eltham College is a school rich in history, variety, vitality and care. Throughout its history, students from Eltham College have been recognized for their scholarship and commitment to serving others; they have gone on to give leadership and service in many areas beyond school life.

The school is set in 60 acres of playing fields and is unique in that it has excellent facilities but with only 641 pupils in the Senior School it is small enough to care and every pupil is known and valued as an individual. It is committed to academic achievement of the highest standards, but its yardstick is always the individual's potential. Students are encouraged to perform at their highest level both academically and in the breadth of school life. In the range of activities here, from sport, through outdoor pursuits, to our justly celebrated music, art and drama, there is scope for everyone to realize that potential.

Governors:
The Governing Body consists of a maximum of 12 elected Trust Governors plus eight Nominated Governors representing the United Reformed Church, the Baptist Missionary Society, the Council for World Mission, the London Boroughs of Bromley and Bexley, two Parent Representatives elected by the parental body and one Staff Common Room representative elected by the staff.

Chairman of the Board: D A Robins, Esq, BSc

Headmaster: P J Henderson, BA, FRSA

Deputy Head – Academic: L Watts, BSc

Deputy Head – Pupils: D J Cooper, BSc, MA

Bursar: D Cooper, ACCA

Development Director: S J McGrahan, MSc

Academic Staff:
P D Agate, BA (*Sculpture and Ceramics*)
J Backhouse, BA (*Head of Mathematics*)
J Baldwin, BSc (*Mathematics*)
K L Barron, MA, FRSA (*Senior Master, English*)
Mrs H Barsham-Rolfe, BSc (*Economics, Business Studies, Head of Careers*)
A D Beattie, MA (*Geography*)
Mrs N Bilsby, BSc (*Mathematics*)
D Boudon, L-ès-L (*French, Head of Community Service*)
Ms E R Brass, BA, MA (*Head of Art*)
V Broncz, BSc (*Mathematics*)
P G Cheshire, MA (*German, RS*)
J Chesterton, BSc (*Head of Geography*)
M E R Chesterton, BA (*History*)
D K Cotterill, BSc (*Registrar, Geography*)
Mrs S M Donaldson, BA (*Physics*)
Ms S Dunne, BA (*Head of Spanish, French*)
Mrs S B Fearn, BA, ALA (*Librarian*)
A Fermor-Dunman, BSc, MA (*Physical Education*)
A Gillespie (*Artist-in-Residence*)
Miss R Gordon, BSc (*Mathematics*)
D R Grinstead, BA (*Head of History*)
M Hamblin, BA (*English*)
A C Hillary, BEd, FRGS (*Design and Technology*)
Mrs C M Hobbs, BSc (*Head of Biology*)
T A Hotham, BA (*Head of Classics*)
P A Howls, BA (*Deputy Head of Sixth Form, French, German, Russian*)
N A Levy, GGSM, Cert Mgmt (*Music*)
M M MacKenzie, BSc (*Head of Physics*)
P J Mander, BA (*History, Head of Politics*)
P C McCartney, BSc, MSc (*Head of Chemistry and Geology, Exams Officer*)
T C Mitchell, BA (*English, Drama, Head of PHSE*)
Dr G S Morgan, MA, PhD (*Chemistry*)
Dr F Morris, BSc (*Chemistry, Biology*)
Dr J Munn, MA, PhD (*Mathematics*)
Mrs L Oldfield, BA (*Music*)
Ms J Perry, BSc (*Biology, Chemistry*)
J B Pollard, MA (*Head of Modern Languages, German and French*)
M S Pollard (*Head of English*)
J P Pringle, BSc (*Head of IT and Computing, Physics*)
K G Roberts, TEng, DipEd (*Head of Design and Technology*)
C K Robinson, BSc (*Biology*)
Ms L Scarantino, BA (*Head of French*)
Revd P Swaffield, BA (*Chaplain, Head of RS*)
A Thomas, BEd (*Head of Physical Education*)
S Thomson, BSc (*Physical Education*)
E Thorogood, BSc (*Physical Education*)
A Tighe, MA (*Director of Music*)
D P Tuck, BA, MA (*Assistant Head of Sixth Form, Head of Liberal Studies, History, Politics*)

J D Walker, BSc (*Head of Sixth Form, Head of Economics and Business Studies*)
O Weatherly, BA (*History*)
J Willatt, BA (*Geography*)
P Wren, TEng, BSc (*Design and Technology*)
E B Wright, MA (*Physics*)
J A C Yarnold, BA (*Head of Drama*)
P Zdarzil, LLM (*Director of Information Technology Services*)

Part-time:
Ms A M Classen (*German*)
Mrs H Clough, BSc (*Biology*)
Mrs M Franklin, BA (*Art*)
Mrs C D Green, DipEd (*English*)
Miss E Hardy, BA (*English*)
Mrs S Horton, BA (*French*)
Mrs S Potter, BA (*Economics and Business Studies*)
Mrs A C E Richards, BA (*Art and Design*)
Ms N Rosado (*Spanish*)
Miss I Sadler (*Spanish*)
Mrs A Senior, L-ès-L (*French*)
Mrs C Shipp, BA, MA, CertSpLD, DipSpLD, AMBDA (*Learning Support*)
M Stickings (*German, Archivist*)
Miss M Su, BA (*Mandarin*)
Mrs C Taylor, BA (*Latin*)
Ms S Wood, BSc (*Mathematics*)
J Zablocki, BSc (*Chemistry*)

Junior School:

Master: E R Cavendish, MA

Deputy Master: P McIntyre, BA, MA, MSc

Mrs N Chamberlain, BA Ed
Ms J Donegan, BA Ed
Mrs A Hallett, BA Ed
R Johnston, BHSc
Mrs L Jones, BA Ed
M O'Dwyer, BEd
J Poole, BA Ed
W Schaper, BA Ed
Mrs J Smith, BSc
Mrs L Wrafter, CertEd

Part-time:
Mrs A McCullough, BA (*Mandarin*)
Mrs K Newham, BEd
Mrs A Pain, CertEd

The aim of the School is to provide a balanced and stimulating education based on Christian principles and practice. Founded originally by Missionaries, it is now a day school for 580 boys and 60 Sixth Form girls in the Senior School, plus 193 boys in the Junior School.

Facilities. The main part of the School is built round a large country mansion, now extended and adapted to include a Library and Sixth Form Reading Room, Dining Hall, Art and Sculpture Studios and other teaching areas. An extensive teaching block includes laboratories devoted to Science, Computing, Technology and Mathematics. The Performing Arts Centre is used for curricular drama, plays and concerts whilst the Sports Centre contains an indoor Swimming Pool, Sports Hall, Fitness Suite and Dance Studio. The School Chapel stands as a separate building. Within the Old Quad, there are classrooms for Modern Languages and a Language Laboratory. A recent development is the creation of the new Music School in 2005 which provides extensive teaching and practice facilities and a new Art Gallery will be completed in Autumn 2011 for school and community use.

Curriculum. In the Lower and Middle School the curriculum is broad based and forms are composed of around 25 boys. There is some setting in languages and mathematics. In the Middle School boys normally take ten subjects for the

GCSE or IGCSE examinations, always including a range of both Arts and Science studies, before entering the Sixth Form in which they specialise in courses leading to the AS and A Level. Subjects available include Art, Biology, Business Studies, Chemistry, Computer Science, Design and Technology, Drama, Economics, English, French, Geography, Geology, German, History, Latin, Mathematics (Pure, Mechanics, Statistics and Further Mathematics), Music, Politics, Physical Education, Physics, Religious Studies and Spanish. 98% of pupils enter Higher Education, with some 12% being accepted to Oxford and Cambridge.

Extra-Curricular. Great emphasis is placed on the non-examined or extra-curricular activities. **Sport** has three major games: rugby, hockey and cricket for boys, but many other sports are offered such as football, cross country, basketball, netball (for girls), swimming, tennis and athletics, as well as fencing and chess. **Music** is particularly strong with over 25 different ensembles and choirs, and high quality visiting music teachers: choral singing is a particular strength, and a music project providing free instrumental lessons to all Junior School pupils has set down excellent foundations for the future. **Drama** is part of the curriculum for all in Years 7–9, and productions at every age range (including musicals) are very popular. **Art** also runs many out-of-hours activities, including study trips abroad. There are many Clubs and Societies linked to subject disciplines. The College's Travel Club oversees a large range of trips in the UK (DEAS expeditions, Geography and Geology field trips) and abroad (language exchanges, sports and music tours, adventure expeditions to Greenland, China, Antarctica and the Galapagos).

A proportion of the Sixth Form timetable is given to non-examined opportunities: Games, Community Service and Liberal Studies.

Admission. Boys are admitted by entrance examination to the Senior School at the age of 11 and a few places may be available at 13 and other ages. Sixth Form places are available by examination for both boys and girls.

Bursaries and Scholarships. (*See Scholarship Entries section.*) As befits a school founded by Missionaries and a former Direct Grant School, many pupils receive financial support to attend. Bursaries and Community Scholarships (for 11+ boys from the immediate neighbourhood) are assessed on financial need (concentrating initially on income and expenditure, assets and liabilities), while Scholarships are awarded on academic performance at 11+, 13+ and 16+. Awards are also made for Sport and Music (11+, 16+), Art and Drama (16+ only).

Term of Entry. The School normally accepts pupils only for the beginning of the academic year in September but, if gaps in particular year groups occur, it is willing to interview and test at any point in the year with a view to immediate or subsequent entry.

Junior School. The Grange, a large house on the school estate has been converted and extended to accommodate about 190 day boys in classes of not more than 25. A major refurbishment and extension was completed in November 2004 providing eight new Form rooms, an Assembly Hall, Science Room, Music Room, and Art, Design and Technology Room. With an emphasis on English and Mathematics, the curriculum, which includes Mandarin as the main Modern Foreign Language along with French in Year 6, provides an excellent foundation. Extra-curricular activities (sport, music, drama, art, and day and residential trips) ensure the boys are buzzing! The school is managed by its own Master who is responsible to the Headmaster. Admission is at the age of 7, though a small number of candidates are admitted at 8, and Junior School boys almost always qualify for admission to the Senior School at 11.

The School thus provides an opportunity for 11 years' uninterrupted education in healthy surroundings.

Junior School applications should be made to the Junior School Secretary.

Fees per term (2011-2012). Senior School £4,260; Junior School £3,675.

Honours. 123 pupils have gained entry to Oxford and Cambridge during the last ten years including 10 choral scholarships in the last 4 years.

Charitable status. Eltham College is a Registered Charity, number 1058438. It exists to provide education for boys and girls.

Emanuel School

Battersea Rise, London SW11 1HS
Tel: 020 8870 4171
Fax: 020 8877 1424
e-mail: enquiries@emanuel.org.uk
website: www.emanuel.org.uk

The School was founded in Westminster by Lady Anne Dacre in 1594, and moved to its present site on the north side of Wandsworth Common in 1883 as one of the three schools of the United Westminster Schools Foundation.

Motto: *Pour bien désirer*

Governing Body:

Chairman: F R Abbott, Esq, BA

B F W Baughan, Esq
Mrs S Chambers
Ms M A D'Mello, BSc, MSc
The Hon Jamie Douglas-Home
P M Kennerley, Esq, RD, FRICS
R Naylor, Esq
Mrs M M Parsons, MA
Professor D B Ricks, FKC King's College London
C Scott, Esq
T Smith, Esq
J Wates, Esq
Dr P Zutshi, University of Cambridge

Clerk and Receiver: R W Blackwell, MA

Headmaster: **M D Hanley-Browne**, MA

Deputy Headmaster: J A Hardy, MA
Director of Studies: W M Rogers, BSc
Head of the Lower School: S J Gregory, MA, ARCO
Head of Middle School: S P Andrews, BA
Head of Sixth Form: Ms K Bainbridge, MA
Assistant Head Pastoral: Mrs S M Williams-Ryan, L-ès-L, MA (*Modern Languages*, *French*)
Assistant Head Co-Curricular: R R Marriott, MA
Chaplain: Revd P M Hunt, MA, MTh
Registrar: J F W Benn, BA, MBA

Teaching staff:
* *Head of Department*

A Ball, BA (*DT*)
R Berlie, MA (*History*)
E Braun, BEng
Dr J C Bruce, MSc, PhD
Ms H Burnett, BA
Miss L Butler, BSc
C Carter, MSc (*Chemistry*)
Ms U S Casais, BA
S R L Clayton, MA Oxon (*History*)
Miss L C Cleveland, BA, MTh (*Religious Studies*)
D Conington, BSc
C Csaky, BASc
Dr M Dancy, BSc, PhD
J Dunley, BA
Ms C Easton, BA (*Classics*)
Ms M Evans, MMath
N Fazaluddin, BSc (*Mathematics*)

Miss L Fitzgibbon, BSc
Miss G Fornari, BA
A P Friell, BEd
Dr M Glendza, MA
D Gundersen, PDip
S J Halliwell, BA
Mrs J Halsey, BA
D C Hand, BA
R Hardy, BA
R B Harker, BA
M Healy, BSc
Miss J L Hendra, BA
Miss J O Henderson, BA
J Holmes, BMus, MA, FRCO, ARCM (*Music*)
Mrs S Holmes, MA, ARCO
H Jackson, BA (*German*)
Miss L L Jones, BA
A F S Keddie, MA, ACIB
P King, BEd
C O Labinjo, BSc
Dr B W Last, BA, MPhil, PhD (*Drama*)
J P Layng, BSc, MNCA
A Leadbetter, BSc
V Le Gac, BA
Mrs R A Lewis, MA
Miss O Lopez, BA (*Geography*)
Miss S E MacMillan, BA (*Art*)
Miss H Malik, BSc
Ms P S Marmion, TCert
Miss K J Martin, BEd, MA
B McKerchar, BSc, MSc
P McMahon, MA
Mrs J Morrison-Bartlett, BSc (*Science, *Physics*)
N M Mullen, MA
Miss R Musson, BA, MA
N Nilsson, BA
Mrs J L Peters, MA
R Price, BSc
Mrs L A Radford, BA
Dr B A Reynolds, PhD (*Biology*)
Miss O Roncero-Refoyo, BA
S Rowley, BA
Mrs S Shaw, DipSpLD
R Skinner, BSc
M Sloan, BA
Mrs L Stansfield, BA
M Swift, BA
R Tong, LLB (*Business Studies*)
L Von Hoff, BASc
Mrs L Whipp, BEd
Mrs G Wright, BSc
J Wright, BA
A Zaratiegui, MA (*Spanish*)

Visiting Music Teachers:
F Baird, Dip TCL, ARCM (*Percussion*)
Mrs Y Burova, PG Dip (*Violin*)
M Christie, BMus GSMD (*Singing*)
M Crowther, Dip GGSM (*Brass*)
Mrs P Crowther, Dip AGSM (*Brass*)
Miss Harwood-White, PG Dip, DAAD Scholar, BMus (*Oboe*)
Ms J Hayter, BMus RAM, LRAM, PG Dip RCM (*Bassoon, Flute, Clarinet*)
Ms K Lauder, BMus RNCM, PPRNCM (*French Horn/Piano*)
M Livingstone, BA (*Percussion*)
J McCredie, MMus, BMus, CertEd
Ms R Middleton, BMus, PGDip RNCM (*Singing*)
J Oldfield MA, PGDip RCM, ArtDipOp RCM (*Singing*)
G Philips, BMus GSMD (*Clarinet, Saxophone*)
Ms L Selwood, MMus (*Cello, Double Bass*)
Ms P Sharda (*Guitar*)
C Stansfield, BMus (*Jazz Piano*)

Mrs H Twoney, BMus, LTCL, PGCE (*Violin, Viola*)
A Watson, BMus LRSM; PG Dip RCM (*Piano, Singing*)
D Watts, BMus RNCM (*Flute*)
Miss V Yannoula, BMus, PG Dipp RCM (*Piano*)

Librarian: T Jones, BA
Director of Finance and Administration: D Taylor, BA
Development Director: Ms S Fisher, BA
Headmaster's Secretary: Mrs J Wood
Admissions Secretary: Ms D Shuttleworth

Emanuel is a fully co-educational day school. We have approximately 710 pupils, with 166 in the Sixth Form.

Admission. Each September about 20 pupils are admitted at age ten, 85 pupils at age eleven and about 15 at age thirteen. There are also about 20 external candidates admitted into the Sixth Form each year.

Entry at age ten and eleven is by competitive examination, held at the school each year in January. Applications to sit these examinations should be made before the middle of November of the preceding year.

Entry at age thirteen is by an Emanuel examination in January.

Entry to the Sixth Form is by interview and tests held in the November before entry. Unconditional or conditional offers may be made.

Full details from the Admissions Secretary.

Fees per term (2011-2012). £4,861 covering tuition, stationery, books and lunch. Extras charged are for individual instrumental tuition and some external visits and trips.

Site and Buildings. Emanuel was founded in 1594. In 1883 it moved from Westminster to the present site in Wandsworth. The original building is the core of the school, with most of its classrooms and a fine library and chapel. The first addition made was the new building of 1896, which now houses our concert hall and music rooms and the science laboratories. These have been completely refurbished in the last few years to a very high standard.

Over the last century many further additions have been made, including a large sixth form centre. The school's playing fields adjoin the school buildings together with a full-sized swimming pool. Our facilities include fives courts and a sports hall. The new library is a superb resource for the whole school. The school has a boathouse on the Thames by Barnes Bridge.

Scholarships, Exhibitions and Bursaries. (*See Scholarship Entries section*.)

Organisation. There is one form for pupils who join at age ten (Year 6). Pupils joining at age eleven (Year 7) are streamed by ability in five forms. Primary responsibility for their care rests with the form teacher and the head of year, under the overall supervision of the Head of the Lower School, who deals with Years 6, 7 and 8. As all pupils move from Year 9 into Year 10 there is a re-grouping along the lines of the subjects chosen for GCSE examinations. In the Sixth Form a tutor system operates.

Pupils are placed in houses when they join the school and they stay in these houses throughout their school career. Although originally intended as a means of fostering competition in games, these houses have developed over many years a strong community spirit.

For fuller details please ask for the school prospectus.

Times. The normal school day runs from 8.30 am to 3.45 pm, but many activities extend into the late afternoon after school. Many school activities, especially games, also take place on Saturday mornings.

Curriculum. Pupils are prepared for the GCSE. There is a wide range of options with most pupils taking nine subjects.

Thereafter, in the Sixth Form, there is a further range of options from which pupils choose four AS Level subjects leading to examination at the end of the Lower Sixth. They can then choose to continue with all four or to take 3 through to A Level. The vast majority of Sixth Form leavers go on to university, art college or other forms of higher education.

Religious Education. The Chaplain works in the school, whose general religious tenor is that of the Church of England. A daily service is held in the school chapel. Pupils in Years 6, 7, 8 and 9 receive one or two periods per week of religious education, which continues into Years 10, 11 and Sixth Forms as a GCSE or A Level option.

The Arts. Emanuel has a long-standing tradition of excellence in these areas and all pupils are encouraged to participate in one or more of these activities. The school has a chapel choir and a chamber choir, an orchestra and ensemble groups and a major musical production is presented each year.

There is a specialist suite of art rooms with facilities for all kinds of creative activity. A great deal of high quality work is displayed around the school and several pupils a year go on to foundation courses at art college.

Drama is taught throughout the school and there is a major school production every year, usually in the autumn term, with many smaller-scale events during the year. The existing Theatre is to be enlarged and updated in 2012.

We have an annual arts festival in July with an art exhibition, summer serenade, performances by pupils and visitors, and a series of talks by visiting speakers.

Games and Activities. At present cricket, rowing, rugby and athletics are the main school games for the boys. For the girls the main activities are netball, tennis, athletics, rowing and swimming. Many other activities become available as a pupil moves up the school. Each pupil will have one games afternoon each week and other opportunities for physical education and swimming. The school has its own playing fields, sports hall, swimming pool, fives courts and boathouse on the Thames.

The Duke of Edinburgh's Award scheme is offered at all levels to pupils from Year 9 upwards. Community service is arranged for senior pupils and can involve hospital visiting or voluntary work in local primary schools, charity shops or our local hospice. More formal work experience is offered as part of an extensive careers and further education advice programme from Year 9 upwards. There is a very strong Young Enterprise programme in the Lower Sixth.

Careers. Careers and further education advice is readily available from an experienced team. There is an annual careers convention for the senior school when many representatives from the professions and commerce visit the school to talk about career options. All pupils become members of the Independent Schools Careers Organisation (included in the fees).

Old Emanuel Association. *Membership Secretary*: Mr R Udall, 43 Howard Road, Coulsdon, Surrey CR5 2EB.

Charitable status. Emanuel School (administered by the United Westminster Schools' Foundation) is a Registered Charity, number 309267. Its aims and objectives are for "the bringing up of children in virtue and good and laudable arts".

Epsom College

Epsom, Surrey KT17 4JQ
Tel: 01372 821004 (Headmaster)
         01372 821234 (Admissions Registrar)
         01372 821130 (Bursar)
Fax: 01372 821237
e-mail: admissions@epsomcollege.org.uk
website: www.epsomcollege.org.uk

Founded in 1855, Epsom College is situated in 80 acres of countryside close to Epsom Downs and 15 miles from central London. Epsom has become one of the most successful co-ed boarding and day schools for able all-round

boys and girls aged 13–18. Almost all leavers go onto degree courses, especially at the research led universities, with historic strengths in Medicine, but now in all subjects. Art, music, drama and sport are strong, with national representatives at Rugby, Netball, Hockey and Target Rifle Shooting. Boarding is central to the College with over 250 boarders living within 25 miles; the House system ensures a strong sense of community and support for others. Academic results are high; 84% of A2 results at A* to B, 75% of all University places secured at Russell and 1994 Group Universities with 15% taking medicine from a stimulating Sixth Form curriculum of A Level and Pre-U.

Motto: '*Deo non Fortuna*'.

Patron: Her Majesty The Queen

President: Professor The Lord McColl, CBE, MS, FRCS, FACS

Visitor: The Right Reverend The Lord Bishop of Guildford

Governing Body:
Chairman: Dr A J Vallance-Owen, MBChB, FRCS Edin, MBA
Vice-Chairman: Dr A J Wells, MB BS, DRCOG, MRCGP
Treasurer: P G Hakim, FCA

G E Andrews, FCA
Dr J Bolton, FRCPsych
Mrs F J Boulton, BSc, MA
Dr H H Bowen-Perkins, LMSSA, MRCS Eng, LRCP Lond, MB BS
K Budge, MA
Mrs B Dolbear
A F Fernandes
J A Hay
D Maunder, MA
G B Pincus, MIPA
Mrs S Piper, BA, MA
Sir John Scarlett, KCMG, OBE, BA, MA
Mrs K Thomas, BM, FRCS

Bursar & Clerk to the Governing Body: Mrs S E Teasdale, BSc, ACA

The Royal Medical Foundation Administrator & Secretary to Council: C Titman

Headmaster: S R Borthwick, BSc, CPhys, FRSA

Deputy Head: P J Williams, BSc
Deputy Head – Academic: Mrs A M Drew, BA, MBA
Assistant Head – Admissions and Communications: P E D Green, BSc, MA, CBiol, MSB
Assistant Head – Senior Master: M C Oliver, BSc
Assistant Head – Teaching Staff: Miss N C Morrow, MA
Director of Extra-Curricular Activities: E A Huxter, MA, PhD, FRGS
Director of Information Technology: C J Davies, BSc, CEng, MBCS, CMath, MIMA
Head of Transition: B G MacDowel, MTheol
Head of Higher Education and Careers Guidance: Mrs R J B Harrop, BA
Sixth Form Coordinator: J M Whatley, BSc

Housemasters/mistresses:
Carr (boys' boarding and day): M Day, BEd
Crawfurd (girls' boarding and day): Mrs H E Keevil, BA (Senior Housemistress)
Fayrer (boys' boarding): S J Head, BSc
Forest (boys' boarding): J F Stephens, BSc
Granville (boys' boarding): R C G Young, BSc
Holman (boys' boarding): C I Holiday, BEd ACP (Senior Housemaster)
Propert (boys' day): A Wolstenholme, BEd
Raven (girls' day): Mrs P S Woolmer, BSc
Robinson (boys' day): M C Conway, MA
Rosebery (girls' day): Miss K D Cloonan, MA

White House (girls' Sixth Form boarding & day): Mrs C C Winmill, MA
Wilson (girls' boarding): Mrs K R Tod, BA

Senior Chaplain: Revd Fr P Thompson, BA
Lay Chaplain: Mrs H H Hynd, BA, MA, FRSA

Teaching Staff:
* *Head of Department*

Art:
*Mrs K H P Lenham, BA
Mrs I Friedler, BA
I D Newman, BA

Biology:
*M D Hobbs, BSc, CBiol, MSB
Dr R L Dowdeswell, BSc, PhD
P E D Green, BSc, MA, CBiol, MSB
Mrs V Patel, BSc, PhD
Mrs R Storey, BSc
S A Wade, BSc, PhD
Mrs P S Woolmer, BSc

Chemistry:
*Mrs T M Muller, MA
L Matthews, BSc
Mrs M Odendaal, MPhil
N S A Payne, BSc
D A Schofield, MChem
Mrs S E Williams, MA

Classics:
*K Siviter, MA, MBA

Design & Technology:
*Miss A M R Wickham, MA
M Day, BEd
P M Shephard, CertEd

Economics & Business Studies:
*P J Gillespie, BA
S J Head, BSc
Mrs E G Irvine, MA, PGDip Tourism
Miss N C Morrow, BA
D N Rice, BSc, DLC
G R Watson, BA
J Whatley, BSc
R C G Young, BSc

English:
*Mrs J Bathard-Smith, BA
Miss K D Cloonan, MA
Mrs A M Drew, BA, MBA
Miss C E Huxter, MA
I M C McClure, MA, PhD
R M Wycherley, BA
M Zacharias, BA

Geography:
*P J Irvine, MA
C J Baverstock, BSc
E A Huxter, MA, MSc, PhD, FRGS
R I Whiteley, MA

History, Government & Politics:
*M A L Tod, MA, PhD, FSA Scot
A J Bustard, BA
Miss K H Butler, BA
M C Conway, MA

T S Cooper, MA
Ms B Gardner, BA
B S H Jerrit, BA
H R Meier, BA, DPhil
Mrs K R Tod, BA
R S Willis, MA

Information Technology:
*T C V Thomas, BSc
C J Davies, BSc, CEng, CITP, MBCS, CMath, MIMA
R A Johnstone, BTheol
I M Winmill, BSc

Learning Support:
*Mrs R Doyle, BEd, BPhil, RSA Dip TEFL, Adv Dip SpEd
Mrs M-A Barnett, BA
Mrs G H Borthwick, BA, Cert Tesol
Mrs A Davies, CertEd, CTEFLA
Mrs B C Day, BA,CTEFLA

Mathematics:
*A J Wilson, BSc, MSc
J Farrelly, BA
Miss S Hassan, MSc
S Hibbitt, BA
M C Oliver, BSc
J F Stephens, BSc
T A Stone, BSc
Mrs K J Symons, BSc, MBA
P J Williams, BSc

Modern Languages:
*R Ellison, MA
Miss H Brabham, MA
Miss C L Creevey, BA
R Gill, MA
Mrs C Guyon, TCert
M P Hynd, MA
Mrs M Jones, TCert
Mrs H E Keevil, BA
Mrs Z Liu, TCert
Mrs D Reisinger, BA
Mrs C C Winmill, MA

Music:
*G A Lodge, MA, BMus, LTCL
M Hampshire, BA, FRSA
C I Holiday, BEd, ACP

Physical Education:
*Mrs F C Drinkall, BSc
Mrs S L Church-Jones, BA
A Wolstenholme, BEd

Physics:
*A W Hughes, BEng, PhD
S R Borthwick, BSc, CPhys, FRSA

R D B Burgess, BSc, ACMA
J M Drinkall, BSc
J R L Hartley, BSc
D R Poore, BSc
D A Wilkinson, BSc

Theatre Studies:
*Miss K Chandley, BA

Visiting Instrumental Tutors for bassoon, cello, clarinet, drum kit, flute, French horn, guitar, harpsicord, oboe, organ, percussion, piano, recorder, saxophone, singing, trumpet, violin.

Librarian: Mrs S Perry, BA, MA
Development Coordinator: Mrs R Holmes
Medical Officer: Dr M Sevenoaks, BSc, MBBS, MRCGP, DRCOG, DFFP
Headmaster's PA: Mrs C Beesley
Admissions Registrar: Mrs C Kent

P A Henson, BA
Theology and Philosophy:
*Mrs H H Hynd, BA, MA, FRSA
B G MacDowel, MTheol
Revd Fr P Thompson, BA

Numbers and Houses. From September 1996 the College became fully co-educational. There are 726 students in the School, 370 boarders, weekly boarders or day boarders and 356 day students, divided among 7 boarding houses and 5 day houses. There are 314 in the Sixth Form. The boy/girl ratio is nearly 2:1.

There are 5 separate houses for girls: two boarding houses, Crawford and Wilson; two day houses, Raven and Rosebery; and a Sixth Form house, White, for both boarding and day girls.

The boys' boarding houses are: Fayrer, Forest, Granville, Holman, with some boarding in Carr. All boarding Sixth and Fifth Formers and Upper Fourth Formers have study-bedrooms in the modernised Houses. In the Michaelmas Term there are two weekend exeats roughly half-way through each half of term, in addition to a two-week half-term holiday. In each of the other two terms there is one exeat in the first half followed by a one-week half-term holiday. Weekly boarders go home every weekend.

The day boy Houses are: Carr, Propert and Robinson. Day boys and girls are full members of the School community and have lunch and tea in College. All members of the School, boarders and day, eat centrally in the Dining Room which makes for efficiency and strengthens the sense of community.

Pupils who are ill are looked after in the School Medical Centre which has 8 beds with a qualified sister always on duty. One of the two (one male, one female) School Doctors visits daily except Sundays.

Academic Work. In the Middle Fourth (Year 9) pupils take English, French, Mathematics, Physics, Chemistry, Biology, Religious Studies, Drama, Geography, History, Art, Music, Information Technology and Design Technology. Latin, Spanish, German, Mandarin and English as an Alternative Language are offered as options. The normal programme is to enter the Middle Fourth at the age of thirteen and take the main block of GCSEs at the end of the Fifth Form (Year 11) but pupils take AS modules in Mathematics, Latin and Critical Thinking at the end of the Fifth Form. Almost everyone then enters the large Sixth Form of approximately 340 pupils. A wide range of A Level subjects is offered with Pre-Us in English and Global Perspectives and Independent Research. At A Level, new options in Business Studies, Politics and Government, Photography and Economics are introduced to complement the broad range of subjects already available at GCSE. In addition to the usual four AS subjects, Sixth Formers may opt to study AS Critical Thinking or join the Young Enterprise scheme and an increasing number of students now choose to undertake an AS Extended Project. There are excellent facilities for work in one's own study, in the main Library or one of the specialist Libraries. The school is fully networked, including all Houses, and has over 500 computers, as well as digital projectors and electronic whiteboards used across the curriculum. There are five fully-equipped Information Technology rooms.

Higher Education. Almost all students go on to university, with the occasional student choosing to follow another path, such as Art Foundation. In recent years, Medicine, Engineering, Economics and Business degrees have proved particularly popular degree options, but Epsom students have been successful in gaining places on a broad variety of competitive courses.

Careers. Careers education is offered from the first term at Epsom and is particularly well developed in the Sixth Form. Epsom has an experienced team of careers tutors with specialists in Medicine, Oxbridge Entrance, Engineering and American University Entrance. There is a well-stocked Careers Room attached to the Library, and much care is taken to assess a pupil's potential and aptitude and to provide proper guidance on careers. All pupils belong to the ISCO Scheme and all Fifth Form pupils take careers aptitude tests through Futurewise. There is a well established work experience programme and a Careers Convention is organised each year for the Fifth Form and Lower Sixth. The College also hosts a GAP Year Fair.

The **Religious Teaching** and the Chapel Services follow the doctrines of the Church of England, but there are always pupils of other denominations and faiths. There are two Resident Chaplains who work together with a visiting Rabbi and a Hindu priest to ensure a multi-faith approach. Muslim pupils attend prayers at the College.

Games and other Activities. Games contribute much to the general physical development of boys and girls at Epsom and the College has a strong tradition of high standards in many sports. The very large number of teams means that almost all pupils are able to represent the School each year. A wide range of sports is available: Rugby, Hockey, Netball, Cricket, Tennis, Athletics and Swimming, Squash (6 courts), Rifle Shooting (with a .22 range), Soccer, Cross-Country, Fencing, Golf, Badminton, Rounders, Basketball, Judo, Sailing and Lacrosse. The Indoor Sports Centre, housing two sports halls, a fencing salle and climbing wall, was opened in 1989 by the Patron of Epsom College, Her Majesty the Queen. In January 2007 a new extensive fitness suite was completed. The Target Rifle Team has been National Champions at Bisley winning the Ashburton Shield 12 times in 19 years between 1990 and 2008.

The CCF has Naval, Army and RAF Sections and pupils over the age of 14 are expected to join for 2 years when much time is spent on camping and expeditions. Older boys and girls may join instead the Duke of Edinburgh's Award Scheme, while others are involved with Social Service work in Epsom.

The College ensures that all pupils take advantage of a wide range of activities from Jazz Dance to Journalism.

Music, Art and Drama. There are three full-time Music teachers and a large staff of visiting music teachers. Over one-third of the pupils learn musical instruments and virtually any instrument can be taught, and many take singing lessons. There are four Choirs, a School Orchestra and seven major instrumental ensembles, including Big Band, Clarinet, Saxophone and Classical Guitar. Visits are arranged each term to concerts in London and elsewhere. The Music School has a Concert Hall and 18 practice rooms. Recent productions have included The Coronation of Poppea and Sweeney Todd.

Art, which includes pottery, printing and sculpture as well as painting and drawing, is housed in a spacious building with 8 studios, a Library, an Exhibition Room and an Exhibition Hall. There are three full-time Art teachers and one part-time, and Art is studied up to GCSE and A Level.

There are several major productions each year, from classical theatre to the modern musical, produced by a range of staff and pupils. These give boys and girls an opportunity to develop their talents and interests in Drama. In 2004 staff

and pupils wrote their own show which was performed at the Royal Albert Hall, with over 1,000 performers, to mark the 150th Anniversary of the College.

Admission. Almost all pupils enter Epsom College in September. Most pupils come at the age of 13 after reaching a satisfactory standard in the Common Entrance or Scholarship Examination or the Epsom College January Entry Test examination set specially for those who are not prepared for Common Entrance. An examination for those who may be deemed borderline may be sat in advance of Common Entrance. Since many girls, and some boys, expect to transfer schools at 11 rather than 13, we offer the opportunity for children to sit an 11+ examination in Year 6. If the required standard is achieved, a pupil will be offered a place for entry at 13+, conditional upon maintaining the same standards at the present school and to a test being taken in the year of entry for setting purposes. Some enter the school later than this and there is always a direct entry into the Sixth Form, both for girls and boys.

A boy or girl may be registered at any age by sending in the registration form and fee. All enquiries should be sent to the Admissions Registrar from whom a prospectus may be obtained.

Fees per term (2011-2012). Boarders £9,730; Weekly Boarders £8,880; Day Pupils £6,650.

The fees are inclusive and cover the normal cost of a pupil's education. The main extras are for examination fees, private tuition and a pupil's personal expenses. Fees for day pupils include lunch and tea.

There is a College Store for the provision of uniform, clothing and other requirements.

Entrance Scholarships and Bursaries. (*See Scholarship Entries section.*) Scholarships are available at both 13+ and 16+ entry in the following areas: Academic, Art, Design/ Technology, Drama/Dance, Music, Sport and the new Headmaster's Award for talented all-rounders at 13+. Over the past six years, Epsom has reduced the value of non means-tested Scholarships and Awards, which can be worth up to 10% per annum. This has enabled us to double the bursary fund which is allocated to families with demonstrable financial need. In turn this has helped us, with Development Trust support, to 'Widen our access' to disadvantaged families which is one of the College's declared aims in line with both Government and HMC guidance. Potential scholarship applicants are encouraged to seek extra financial support, if appropriate, by way of a means-tested Bursary. Application forms are available on request from the Bursar or Admissions Registrar. Candidates must be under 14 on 1st September of the year of entry or entering the Sixth Form.

Old Epsomians. The Old Epsomian Club promotes sporting activities, social gatherings and networking events among its former pupils, with eight international chapters and an online database. On leaving the College, all pupils automatically become life-long members of the OE Club and they are invited back regularly for reunions, the OE Dinner and Founder's Day. They also receive several publications each year, including the OE magazine. Bursaries are available for the sons and daughters of OEs who wish to attend the College.

Charitable status. Epsom College is a Registered Charity, number 312046. It exists for the advancement of education.

Eton College

Windsor, Berkshire SL4 6DW
Tel: 01753 671249 (Admissions)
          01753 671231 (Head Master)
          01753 671213 (Bursar)
Fax: 01753 671248
e-mail: admissions@etoncollege.org.uk

website: www.etoncollege.com

The King's College of our Lady of Eton beside Windsor was founded by Henry VI in 1440. The College Foundation comprises a Provost, 11 Fellows, Head Master, Lower Master, Bursar, Chaplain and 70 Scholars. There are some 1,240 Oppidans, or boys not on the Foundation.
Motto: '*Floreat Etona*'.

Visitor: The Rt Revd The Lord Bishop of Lincoln

Provost and Fellows (Governing Body):
The Lord Waldegrave of North Hill, PC (*Provost*)
Dr Andrew Gailey, CVO, MA, PhD (*Vice-Provost*)
Professor Ross Harrison, MA, PhD
David Verey, CBE, MA
Michael Proudfoot, MA
Professor Christopher Dobson, MA, DPhil, FRS
Sir Michael Peat, KCVO, FCA
Sir Michael Burton, MA
The Marchioness of Douro
David Reid Scott, MA
Professor Kim Nasmyth, PhD
Dr Caroline Moore, MA, PhD

Honorary Fellows:
John Butterwick, TD
Sir David Money-Coutts, KCVO, MA
Sir Simon Robertson
Nicholas Kessler
Sir Eric Anderson, KT, MA, MLitt, DLitt, FRSE
Lady Smith, OBE

Steward of the Courts: The Rt Hon the Lord Carrington, KG, GCMG, CH, MC, PC

Conduct: The Revd Canon K H Wilkinson, MA

Precentor and Director of Music: T J Johnson, MA

Bursar and Clerk to the Provost and Fellows: Miss J S Walker, MA, FCA

Assistant Bursars:
I C Mellor, ARICS, DipProjMan
J G James, MBE, BA
R J Schooley, BSc, FCIPD, ACIS
A Harris, BSc, FRICS

Director of Development: W O'Hearn, AB, JD
College Librarian & Keeper of College Collections: Mrs R Bond, MA
Keeper of Special Collections: M C Meredith, MA
College Archivist: Mrs P Hatfield, MA, DAA

Head Master: A R M Little, MA

Lower Master: R M Stephenson, BSc, PhD

Director of Curriculum: G J D Evans, MA

Director of School Administration & IT: Dr P R Harrison, MA, DPhil

Senior Tutor: J R Clark, MA

Tutor for Admissions: C W Milne, BA, MPhil

School Office Manager: R A Hutton

School Doctor: J J C Holliday, MB BS, MRCS, LRCP, MRCGP, DCH, DRCOG, DFFP

Assistant Masters:
* Head of Department/Subject
† House Master

Art:
I Burke, MA *
A Forsyth, BA
E J V Parker, MA
D Reid, BA

Classics:
A J Chirnside, MA *
I Harris, MA
T E W Hawkins, MA †
M T Holdcroft, BA

S A Lambert, BA
J D Macartney, BA
S K MacLennan, BA
A J Maynard, MA
R D Oliphant-Callum, MA †
J R B Scragg, BA
R E C Shorrock, BA, MPhil, PhD
C J Smart, MA
P B Smith, MA, MSt †

Computing:
D M L Maxwell, MA *

Design:
N W Alston, BA
S E Hearsey, BSc
K R N Ross, BSc *
S G P Tilley, BA

Divinity:
Revd R E R Demery, BTh, MA (*Chaplain*)
W I N Griffith, MA
Revd N G Heap, BA, DPhil (*Roman Catholic Chaplain*)
Revd P A Hess, BA, MTh (*Chaplain*)
Revd C M Jones, MA (*Chaplain*)
E J N Russell, MA, PhD
R Stewart, BA
M L Wilcockson, MA *
Revd Canon K H Wilkinson, MA (*Conduct*)

Economics:
T Allen, MA *
J R Clark, MA (*Senior Tutor*)
D J Fox, BA
D M Gregg, BSSc †
R G G Pratt, MA, MSc †
L J Purshouse, MA, PhD
G B Riley, MA

English:
P Broad, MA
B B Cooper, PhD
L V Court, MA
S H S Dormandy, MA (*Head of Theatre Studies*)
J E Francis, BA
A C D Graham-Campbell, MA
M A Grenier, MA †
M Liviero, Dott Ling, PhD
S M McPherson, BComm, MA †
C W Milne, BA, MPhil
J D Newton, BA †
J M Noakes, MA *
J M O'Brien, MA
H-E Osborne, MA (*Director of Drama*)
N R F Welsh, MA

Geography:
D E Anderson, BA, DPhil *
T F X Eddis, BA
C M M Jenkinson, MA
A S Jennings, MA

P I Macleod, BEd, BA
M G H Mowbray, MA †

History:
V S J Clark, BA
B Cole, MA, DPhil †
J A G Fulton, MA
S L Green, MA
J D Harrison, MA (*History of Art*)
B J C Horan, MA *
N A E Jeffery, MA
G D Mann, MA, MSt
T E J Nolan, MA †
H S J Proctor, MA
A S Robinson, MA, MLitt †
J L Sillery, MA, DPhil †
P E P Walsh, BA

Mathematics:
N Adams, BSc
K J Baker, MA, MSc
J P Barker, BSc
S J Dean, MA
N J Fowkes, BSc
R J Gazet, MA*
D A Griffiths, MA
L J Henderson, BA
B J Holdsworth, MA
S J Lings, BA
P J McKee, MA †
W F Moore, BSc †
J Moston, BSc, PhD
M J Salter, MA
M Strutt, BSc
J E Thorne, BSc
S P Vivian, MA, MSc, CStat
A Warnes, BSc, PhD †
C M B Williams, MA, MSc
P G Williams, MA †

Modern Languages:
T E Beard, BA, PhD
R A A Coward, MA
G J D Evans, MA
R A Fletcher, BA, MPhil
J M Gibbons, BA, MPhil, DPhil †
A D Halksworth, MA, MLitt
N C Hulme, MA
A P Iltchev, BA
J A M Leland, BA
M-L Lin, BA (*Chinese*)
T Masumoto, MA
K S K Pierce, MA (*German*)
M J Polglase, MA †
A Powles, BA (*French*)
P V Reznikov, BA (*Russian*)
N J Roberts, MA †
N C W Sellers, MA †
H A Shirwani, MA (*Arabic*)
D M Stanford-Harris, MA (*Japanese*)
J W F Stanforth, MA

Music:
N D Goetzee, MSc, LRAM
D W Goode, BA, MPhil, FRCO

T J Johnson, MA *
M A O'Donovan, MA, MMus
I M Wallace, BA

Physical Education:
P I Macleod, BEd, BA
P K Manley, BEd, MSc, JP
W E Norton, BA *
G J Pierce, BEd

Science:

Biology:
H W T Adams, BA, BSc
A Z Bridges, MA, MSc *
K Frearson, MA (*Science*)
G D Fussey, BSc
P M Gillam, MA †
K L Hicks, BA
N P T Leathers, BSc
J H Owen, BSc, PhD
R M Stephenson, BSc, PhD
P S T Wright, MA

Jewish Tutor: J M Paull, MA, DIPM, MCIM

Muslim Tutor: Imam M Hussain, BTh

Hindu Tutor: J Lakhani, MSc

Roman Catholic Chaplain: Revd N G Heap, BA, DPhil

Chemistry:
A K Copsey, BSc
R N Edmonds, BA, PhD
S P Hermes, MChem
P K Manley, BEd, MSc, JP
A M Miles, BSc
R R Montgomerie, MA
G R Pooley, BSc, PhD †
A J Saunders, MChem, DPhil *
J A Steadman, MA, PhD

Physics:
W E S Casson, BSc
H G C Clarke, BA
J D Dangerfield, MSc *
M N Fielker, BSc †
R P D Foster, MA †
I R Gray, BSc, PhD
P R Harrison, MA, DPhil
P D A Mann, MSc, PhD
S P Martin, BSc

The **King's Scholars (Collegers)** normally number 70 and are boarded in College, each in his own room, under the care of the Master-in-College. About 14 Scholarships are awarded each year. Candidates need to be registered by the 1st March of the year of entry. For information apply to *The College Examination Secretary, Admissions Office, Eton College, Windsor SL4 6DB. (See also Scholarship Section entries.)*

The Scholarship Examination is held at Eton in May. Candidates must be under 14 (and over 12) on 1st September. Boys normally enter College between the ages of 12.9 and 13.11. All candidates take English, Mathematics A, General I (general questions requiring thought rather than knowledge) and Science. They must also offer three or more of the following: French (written, aural and oral), Latin, Greek, Mathematics B, General II (Literature, the Arts, moral and religious issues, etc), and a paper combining History, Geography and Divinity.

Scholarships are to the value of 10% of the full fee, and all of them will be supplemented up to the value of full fees (subject to means-testing).

A Scholarship is normally tenable for five years.

Term of Entry. With just occasional exceptions, all boys enter in September.

Fees per term (2011–2012). £10,327. Entrance Fee £1,500 (£1,050 refunded when the boy leaves the school with all fees settled).

Oppidans. There are about 1,240 Oppidans (non-Collegers) housed in 24 Boarding Houses, each under the care of a House Master, and every boy has his own room. A boy must normally be aged between 12.11 and 14.01 on 1st September of the year of admission, and must pass the Common Entrance unless granted exemption on his performance in the Scholarship Examination. Details of arrangements for boys entering Eton directly from the maintained sector can be obtained from the Admissions Office.

Parents wishing to send their sons to Eton as Oppidans should apply to *The Tutor for Admissions, Eton College, Windsor SL4 6DB* for a copy of the Prospectus, which gives full details of the registration procedure. Information is also available on the website at www.etoncollege.com. Boys may be registered at any time between birth and the age of ten and a half and take a preliminary assessment at eleven.

Music Scholarships. Up to eight scholarships can be awarded annually, each to the value of 10% of the full fee, and all of them supplemented up to the value of full fees (subject to means-testing). All awards carry remission of instrumental lesson fees up to 135 minutes tuition per week. In addition there are up to six Music Exhibitions, carrying remission of instrumental lesson fees up to 135 minutes tuition per week. One also carries a place in the school, the other five being open only to boys who already have Conditional Places following the assessment at 11. Two Honorary Exhibitions may also be awarded, carrying no financial remission. Special consideration will be given to cathedral choristers who would still be able to sing treble in the College Chapel Choir. Further particulars and entry forms may be obtained from *The Tutor for Admissions, Eton College, Windsor SL4 6DB.*

Bursaries. Eton has substantial financial provision designed to widen access by enabling boys to come to the school who could not otherwise do so, and to allow boys to remain in the event of a change in family circumstances. For boys with scholarships, supplementary bursaries will be awarded up to full fees depending on need. For boys without scholarships, the normal maximum level of assistance is half the school fee, but growing funds are now enabling us to make a number of bursary awards beyond that level and indeed to subsidise the fee entirely in cases of need. No parents with a talented boy should feel that Eton is necessarily beyond their means. Further details are available on the website at www.etoncollege.com.

New Foundation Scholarships. Currently up to four scholarships by examination and interview are awarded to boys who have been educated in the UK maintained (state) sector for at least Years 6, 7 and 8 of their schooling up to age 13. It is aimed at boys who would not be able to attend Eton without very substantial financial assistance (in certain cases full remission may be given), and who are not in a position to prepare easily for the King's Scholarship. The intellectual standard expected will be very high and comparable with the King's Scholarship, but the emphasis in the New Foundation Scholarship is on potential rather than knowledge, and all-round talents and personality will be taken into account.

The closing date for entries is in November of Year 8. Applicants will normally be in that school year. A boy who will become 14 before September 1st is too old to enter. Further information can be obtained from the *Access Adviser: f.moultrie@etoncollege.org.uk.*

Sixth Form Scholarships. Up to 8 Sixth Form Scholarships are offered each year to enable boys to have two years of Sixth Form education at Eton. Each year in February, selected candidates are invited to attend interviews in those subjects which they intend to offer at A Level or Pre-U. All those attending the interviews will sit a written General Paper and verbal and non-verbal reasoning tests. Candidates must register on, or before, a date specified in mid-December. Two of the scholarships may be awarded to boys with exceptional talents in music or drama. The scholarships will cover the whole or part of the fees, and other educational expenses depending on the Scholar's financial need. An Open Afternoon is held in the Michaelmas term for anyone interested in coming to visit the school. For information apply to *The School Office Manager, Eton College, Windsor SL4 6DW.*

Charitable status. Eton College is a Registered Charity, number 1139086.

Exeter School

Victoria Park Road, Exeter, Devon EX2 4NS
Tel: 01392 273679 (Headmaster/Registrar)
        01392 258712 (Bursar/Office)

Fax: 01392 498144
e-mail: admissions@exeterschool.org.uk
website: www.exeterschool.org.uk

Founded in 1633, Exeter School occupies a 25-acre site, located within a mile of the city centre, having moved from its original location in the High Street in 1880. Some of its well-designed buildings date from that time but many new buildings have been added over the past twenty years and the school now enjoys first-rate facilities on a very attractive open site.

The school is fully co-educational and offers education to boys and girls from 7 to 18. It has its own Junior School of around 180 pupils, nearly all of whom transfer to the Senior School at the age of 11. The Senior School has around 660 pupils, including a Sixth Form of 200. (*For further information about Exeter Junior School, see entry in IAPS section.*)

Exeter School is a well run school with high all-round standards and very good academic results. It prides itself on strong cultural, sporting and extra curricular achievement. Its music is outstanding and there is a strong tradition of performance drawn from all age groups in the School. It offers a very wide range of sports and maintains consistently high standards especially in hockey, rugby and cricket. It is well placed for outdoor pursuits (eg Duke of Edinburgh's Award Scheme and Ten Tors on Dartmoor) and has its own very large voluntary CCF unit. The School is closely involved with the life of the City of Exeter and its university and it has a substantial commitment to support the local community.

Motto: ΧΡΥΣΟΣ ΑΡΕΤΗΣ ΟΥΚ ΑΝΤΑΞΙΟΣ

Patrons:
The Lord Lieutenant of the County of Devon
The Right Reverend the Lord Bishop of Exeter
The Right Worshipful the Lord Mayor of Exeter

Governors:
Appointed by the Devon County Council:
Mrs C Channon, MA, ARIC

Appointed by the Exeter City Council:
J A Taghdissian, LLB Exon

Appointed by the Governors of St John's Hospital:
¶A C W King (*Vice-Chairman*)
Mrs M Giles, LLB

Representatives of the Universities of Exeter, Cambridge and Oxford:
Exeter: Dr S C Smart, PhD
Cambridge: ¶Dr T Lewens, MA, MPhil, PhD, FBA
Oxford: Dr M C Grossel, MA, PhD

Co-opted Governors:
¶T E Hawkins (*Vice-Chairman*)
Mrs H Clark
A K Dawson, MA (*Vice-Chairman*)
J D Gaisford, BSc, ACA
Mrs B Meeke, LLB (*Chairman*)
T D Wheare, MA, FRSA
¶A P Burbanks, BA
Dr P R Scott, MA, DPhil
¶Mrs G A Hodgetts, BA, MSc

Headmaster: **R Griffin**, MA

Deputy Headmaster: P M Šljivić, MA
Director of Administration: J W Davidson, MA, MSc
Director of Studies: M J Hughes, MA

Assistant Staff:
* *Head of Department*
† *Housemaster/mistress*
§ *Part-time or Visiting*
¶ *Former pupil*

Art & Design:
*J F Mason, BA
Mrs R A Smith, BA
§Mrs J Mellings, MA

Biology:
*Miss S E Boyns, MA
†P J C Boddington BSc
¶R H S Donne, MA
Mrs J H Metcalf, MA

Chemistry:
*Miss L J Hilton, MSc
C R Birch, BSc
M K Chitnavis BSc, CChem, MRSC (*Careers and Universities Adviser*)
Dr S P Smale, BSc, PhD
§Mrs F J Tamblyn, BSc

Classical Subjects:
*N P L Keyes, MA
Miss S Trica, MA

Computing & Information Systems:
*Mrs R Cull, BSc, MIITT, CMath, MIMA
N F Howard, BA

Design Technology:
*N W Moon, BSc
I R Lowles, BA

Drama:
*Mrs S H Chrupek, BA
§A J Chrupek

Electronics:
*Dr A W Houghton, MA, MSc, PhD
M E Schramm, BSc

English:
*D K Morton, MA
Mrs J H Daybell, MA
Mrs E K J Dunlop, MA, MPhil
Miss E A Hartill, BA, MEd
A S Dobson, MA

Geography:
*Mrs H M Sail, BA
J W Davidson, MA, MSc (*Director of Administration*)
§Miss M J Vaggers, MA
P M Šljivić, MA (*Deputy Headmaster*)
M P Corke, BA

History:
*G N Trelawny, BEd, MA
†J D Poustie, BEd
§Mrs S L Bartholomew, BA
Mrs A-J Culley, BA

Languages:
*M F Latimer MSt
†R C Dawson, MA
†M C Wilcock, BEd
§Mrs J M Fenner, BA
Mrs A M Francis, MA
§Mrs S C Wilson, BA
R Charters, BA

Mathematics:
*A J Reynolds, BSc
§Dr A P Tyrer, MA, DPhil
†G R Willson, BSc
D Beckwith, BA, MSc
†Dr P M Smallwood, BSc, PhD
†W J Daws, BA
M J Hughes, MA (*Director of Studies*)
Dr G J D Chapman, BSc, MSc, PhD (*CCF Contingent Commander*)
Miss E V Marshall, BSc

Music:
*P Tamblyn, MA, MMus (*Director of Music*)
R J Sutton, BA, ARCM, LRAM
§A Gillett, ARCM
§D Bowen, BEd
§P Painter, DipMusEd
§Mrs R Mitchell, BA, Dip Mus, LTCL
§Mrs F McLean, BA, Cert RAM
§B Moore, MA

Physical Education and Games:
*A C F Mason, BA (*Director of Sport*)
Ms C L Gimber, BA
Mrs A J Marsh, BEd (*Head of Sixth Form*)
J W Fawkes, BSc
E P M Jones, BSc
§F L Smith (*CCF SSI*)

Physics:
*G S Bone, BSc, CSci (*Director of Science*)
T J Clark, BSc
M K Chitnavis BSc, CChem, MRSC (*Careers and Universities Adviser*)
Dr A W Houghton, MA, MSc, PhD
Dr J L Wilson, MPhys, DPhil
M E Schramm, BSc

Religious Studies:
*†M H R Porter, BA
†Mrs J M K Murrin, BA
§J A Allan, BA (*Chaplain*)
Mrs A J Marsh, BEd

Social Studies:
*R G Walker, BA (*Economics)
*R J Baker, BA (*Politics)
§I H Chapman, BSc

Learning Support:
§Ms A Southcott, BEd
§J J Marshall, BEd

Junior School

Headmistress: Mrs A J Turner, MA

Assistant Head: J S Wood, BA

Assistant Staff:
R Bland, BEd
§Mrs P L Butler, BA
¶G E L Ashman, BA
Mrs P A Goldsworthy, BA, LTCL
R J Pidwell, BA
§Mrs R Forbes, MA
§Mrs R M Parkin, CertEd
Ms V K Randerson, CertEd
D Cageao, BA
Ms J A Barnes, MSc
Miss R H Bewley, BA

Bursar and Clerk to the Governors: Cdre R C Hawkins RN, BA
Company Accountant and Company Secretary: Mrs G M Robins, BA, ACCA
Registrar: Mrs W M Drake
Headmaster's PA: Mrs A C Goswell
Head of Information Systems: W R T Lines, MSc, CEng
Librarian: Mrs E G Taylor, BSc
School Doctor: Dr A Morris, BM, BS, DRCOG, MRCGP

Buildings, Grounds and General Facilities. The Senior School block includes a large multi-purpose assembly hall, a library, a private study area, dining hall and Sixth Form Centre as well as many well-appointed classrooms. A major refurbishment of the former boarding accommodation to include a new Library and Study Centre was completed for September 2006. There are separate buildings on the site housing the Chapel, the Music School, the Science Centre, Art Studios, Drama Studio, Design and Technology Centre and Exonian Centre. The Science Centre provides 14 laboratories and there are four fully-equipped computer rooms. All departments have access to their own computers and the School has a wide, controlled access to the internet. In 2005 the school opened a new dance studio and a fitness suite to add to the existing sports facilities of a large modern well-equipped Sports Hall with its own squash courts and access to on-site floodlit all-weather sports arena, top-grade all-weather tennis/netball courts and a heated swimming pool. The playing fields, which are immediately adjacent to the School buildings are well kept and provide, in season, rugby, cricket, hockey, football, rounders and athletics areas. The Junior School, which was extended in 2007 to provide two new Mathematics classrooms, has access to all the Senior School facilities but is self-contained on the estate.

Admission. The majority of pupils enter the Junior School at 7 or 8 and the Senior School at 11 or 13. Admission is also possible at other ages where space allows and a significant number of pupils join at the age of 16 for Sixth Form Studies.

Entrance to the Junior School is by assessment in January. This includes a report from the child's previous school, classroom sessions in the company of other prospective pupils, and literacy, numeracy and general intelligence tasks.

Entrance examinations for the Senior School are held in January.

Assessment for entry to the Sixth Form at 16 is by interview and a minimum of 6 B grades at GCSE, including English and Mathematics, with normally an A grade in the subjects chosen for study.

Registration Fee £100.

Fees per annum (2011-2012). Junior School: £9,150 (includes lunch and textbooks). Senior School: £10,140 (includes textbooks).

Sibling discount of 10% for the second child and 20% for the third or subsequent child attending concurrently.

Scholarships and Financial Awards. (*See Scholarship Entries section*.) Academic Scholarships and Exhibitions, in the form of an individual prize, are offered to pupils who excel in the school's entrance tests at 11+ and 13+. Music Scholarships may be offered at 11, 12, 13 and 16. A Sixth Form Art Scholarship may be offered each year.

The School annually makes available a number of means-tested Governors' Awards. These are for external candidates joining the School at 7 and 8, 11 and 13, or in the Sixth Form, who meet the academic entry requirements and whose parents could not afford to send them to Exeter School without financial assistance. As a general guide, gross parental income will need to be below £55,000 per annum to allow consideration for a Governors' award. In addition, there are also a number of special awards made possible by donations from local benefactors for able pupils whose parents require financial assistance. The School is supported by the Ogden Trust and the Rank Foundation.

Curriculum. In the first 3 years in the Senior School all pupils take English, History, Geography, a carousel of French, German and Spanish, Mathematics, IT, Latin, Physics, Chemistry, Biology, Art, Design Technology, Drama, Music and Religious and Physical Education. After this there is a wide choice of subjects at GCSE level, including English, one Modern Foreign Language, Mathematics, dual or triple award Science, Religious Studies and 3 of the following: Latin, French, German, Spanish, Classical Civilisation, History, Geography, Music, Drama, Art, Design and Technology, and Information Technology.

Pupils enter the Sixth Form choosing from 26 different subjects for A Level study and are prepared for university scholarships, university entrance and admission to other forms of further education or vocational training. Over 95% go on annually to Degree Courses.

Houses. There are nine Pupil Houses. Each is under the personal supervision of a Head of House, with whom parents are invited to keep in touch on any matter affecting their child's general development and progress throughout the school.

Religion. All pupils attend Religious Education classes, which include Sixth Form discussion groups. Sunday services are held in the School Chapel once each term. Pupils may be prepared for Confirmation which takes place annually.

Games. Rugby, Hockey, Cricket, Swimming, Athletics, Cross Country, Tennis, Badminton, Squash, Shooting, Basketball, Netball, Fencing, Cycling and Golf. Further activities are available for the Sixth Form.

Community and other Service. All pupils learn to serve the community. Many choose to take part in Social Service, helping old people and the handicapped young. There is a voluntary CCF Contingent with thriving RN, Army and RAF Sections. The CCF offers a large variety of Outdoor Activities, including Adventure Training Camps, Ten Tors Expedition Training as well as specialist courses. Pupils are encouraged to participate in the Duke of Edinburgh's Award Scheme.

Music. Pupils are taught Singing and Musical appreciation and are encouraged to learn to play Musical Instruments. More than one third of all pupils have individual lessons on at least one instrument. There are 4 Orchestras, a Choral Society which annually performs a major work in Exeter Cathedral and 4 Choirs, 3 jazz bands, and numerous smaller groups from string quartets to rock bands. There are over 30 visiting instrumental teachers. Over 20 public concerts are given each year. Different ensembles have performed regularly at the National Festival of Music for Youth at the Festival Hall, and the Schools Prom at the Royal Albert Hall.

Drama. Drama is developed both within and outside the curriculum. The School Hall with its large and well-equipped stage provides for the dual purpose of studio workshop and the regular production of plays, operas and musicals. The recently refurbished Drama Studio is used for smaller productions.

Art and Design. Art lessons are given to junior and senior forms. Apart from the formal disciplines of GCSE and A Level, which can be taken by those who choose, all pupils have opportunity for artistic expression in painting, print-making, photography, pottery, construction in many materials and carving wood and stone. All younger pupils learn to develop craft skills in wood, metal and plastic and to use them creatively in design work. Some then follow GCSE or A Level courses in Design and Technology. There is an annual art exhibition in July.

Expeditions. Throughout the school a large number of residential field trips and expeditions take place each year including a Third Form new pupils' Dartmoor weekend, various departmental excursions, several foreign exchanges and Duke of Edinburgh's Award expeditions. Pupils are also encouraged to compete for external expeditions and, following years of representation on its expeditions, the school has been awarded Star status by the British Schools Exploring Society (BSES). In recent summers, the school has run its own adventure trips to Costa Rica, Argentina, Chile and Namibia and a canoeing trip to Peru.

Societies and Clubs. Pupils are encouraged to pursue their interests by joining one of the School Societies. Groups of enthusiasts can form new Societies or Clubs, but the following are at present available: Art, Badminton, Basketball, Canoeing, Chess, Choral Society, Christian Union, Computing, Dance, Debating, Drama, Electronics, Fencing, Music, Politics, Sailing, Shooting, Soccer and Squash.

Social. Close contact is maintained with the City and the University. Association between members of the School and the wider society outside is fostered wherever opportunity offers.

The staff believe strongly in the value of association with parents, who are invited to meetings annually throughout their sons' or daughters' time at the School. A termly lecture by a visiting speaker is provided for parents. The Exeter School Parents' Association exists to promote closer relations between the School and its parents.

Careers. Careers education begins with group work at the age of 13 and continues on a progressive programme until students leave the school. Careers evenings are held annually when pupils and their parents have the opportunity to consult representatives of the professions, industry and commerce. A work experience programme is organised for Year 11 pupils each summer, and a scheme of mock interviews with career professionals for pupils in the Sixth Form. A major Careers Convention is held at the school each Autumn for pupils from Years 9 to 13.

Honours. Pupils regularly gain admission to Oxford and Cambridge. The School encourages application to the leading universities, including the Russell Group.

Leading musicians have recently gained places at the Royal College of Music and the Royal Academy of Music.

Charitable status. Exeter School is a Registered Charity, number 1093080, and a Company Limited by Guarantee, registered in England, number 4470478. Registered Office: Victoria Park Road, Exeter, Devon EX2 4NS.

Felsted School

Felsted, Essex CM6 3LL
Tel: 01371 822600 (Headmaster)
          01371 822605 (Admissions Registrar)
Fax: 01371 822697 (School)
          01371 822607 (Headmaster)
e-mail: info@felsted.org
website: www.felsted.org

The School, which was founded in 1564 by Richard, Lord Riche, today consists of three sections educating boys and girls from the age of 4 to 18. Close to both London and Cambridge, and within easy reach of Stansted Airport, the School is ideally situated in a picturesque North Essex village.

Felsted is a Church of England foundation but welcomes pupils from all Christian denominations and those from other religious traditions. The Senior School, for 13 to 18 year olds, has around 521 pupils; the majority are boarders and weekend arrangements are flexible.

The School is a newly-appointed World Member of the Round Square. The School's prospectus can be found online at www.felsted.org along with much other information and news, details of forthcoming events and location maps. Each Boarding House has its own web page and a video called 'Boarding at Felsted' can be downloaded. There is also a link to the Independent Schools Inspectorate's report following the inspection in September 2007.

Governing Body:
J H Davies (*Chairman*)

K M R Foster	P J Hutley
The Rt Hon Sir Alan	Mrs M Curtis
Haselhurst, MP	Mrs B Davey
P G Lee	Dr J Nicholson
P J Cooper	C Tongue
S J Ahearne	O Stocken
Mrs J Simpson	J Tibbitts
Professor C Temple	Mrs J Crouch

Bursar & Clerk to the Governors: Mrs M McKenna

Headmaster: **Dr Michael J Walker**, MA, PhD, CertEd, FRSA

Deputy Headmaster (Pastoral): C J Townsend, BA (*Classics*)
Deputy Headmaster (Academic): J Westlake, MA (*Modern Languages*)
Deputy Head (Welfare): Mrs K A Megahey, BSc (*Mathematics*)
Deputy Head (Co-Curricular): T J Vignoles, BA (*English*)

Assistant Head: Dr N R Dennis, MSc (*History*)

Assistant Teachers:
* *Head of Department*
§ *Part-time*
† *Housemaster/mistress*

N L Osborne, MA (*§History, *History of Art*)
A M Homer, MA (*English, *ToK*)
N J Spring, MA (*English; Head of Careers*)
†R L Feldman, MSc (*Mathematics*)
C J Megahey, BA (**Mathematics*)
A D G Widdowson, BSc (*Mathematics Tutor*)
I W Gwyther, BA (*Geography*)
D J Smith, BA (*Arts Coordinator*)
†M J A Sugden, MA (*Modern Languages*)
A G Chamberlain, BA (*Modern Languages*)
Dr C R S Lee MA, PhD (**Drama, English*)
Miss A L F Simpson, BSc (*Biology, Sixth Form Coordinator & Director of Work Education*)
†Mme B J L Chamberlain, L-ès-L (*Modern Languages*)
J D Lowry, BA, ALCM (**Music*)
B Coppel, BA (**Art*)
†Mrs F M Marshall, BSc (*History*)
Mrs J Balchin, BEd (*§SENCO*)
†C S Knightley, BA (*PE, Director of Sport*)
Miss S Hookway, BSc (*Director of Girls' Sport, PE*)
Mrs A L Salmon, BA (*§SEN*)
Miss E Hampson Smith, BA (*Art*)
†P G Bennett, AGSM (**Academic Music*)
W A M Sanderson, MA (*Physics*)
Ms M Valls (*Spanish*)
†Miss N F S O'Brien, MA (*§ESL*)
Snr F Sanchez del Rio, Licenciatura (**Modern Languages, *Spanish*)
Mrs V L Smith, BSc (*§Psychology*)
S J Winter, BA Hons (**Religious Studies, History*)
†Mrs C M Phillips, ALA (*Learning Support*)
T J Hietzker, BSc (**Biology, Deputy Designated Safeguarding Officer*)
Ms J K Mallett, BA (*Modern Languages, *French*)
R Pathak, BA (**History, i/c Oxbridge*)
C L Watkinson, BSc Hons (**Chemistry*)
Mrs A Gregg (*Modern Languages*)
Mrs L T Barrett, BSc (*§Chemistry*)
M J Campbell, MSci (*Mathematics*)
Mrs C A Morgan, BA (*§English*)
Ms E K Rose, BA (*§Geography*)
Mrs R Grant, BA (*§Spanish*)
Mrs J E McArdle, BA Hons (*Business Studies*)
B R Peart, BSc Hons (*Biology*)
Mrs R J P Lagden, BA Hons (**English*)
Ms A Squirrell, BA Hons (*Librarian*)
M A Pitts, BEng Hons (**Design and Technology*)
Mrs C Croydon, BSc Hons (**ICT*)
†Miss A H Sefton, BSc Hons (**Science, Chemistry*)
Miss S R Bushby, MA Hons (**Classics, Junior Scholarships Coordinator*)
G Master-Jewitt, BA (**Geography*)
Ms C Donaldson, BSc Hons (*§ Mathematics*)
Miss B S Downes-Powell, BSc Hons (*Religious Studies, *PACE*)
P J Nash, BEd (*§Design and Technology*)
†F M Barrett, B BS Hons (*Economics and Business Studies*)
Ms L M Muchmore, BA (**Psychology*)
Mrs M Bonnett (*Biology*)

B J Bury, BA (**PE*)
Mrs M E Burns, BA Hons (*English*)
C J Hansen, BA Hons (**Business Studies and Economics*)
B G D Bostock, BSc (*§ICT*)
E Fenning, BA (*Mathematics*)
Miss A M L Farrar, BA (*Geography*)
Dr E Lloyd, BSc (*Chemistry*)
Mrs D K Guerrero, BA (*ESL Coordinator*)
Miss A Thompson, BA Hons (*Music*)
L B P Jones, BA (*Religious Studies*)
Miss R L Speight, BA (*English*)
C L Baldy, BA (*Music*)
A W J Middleton, BA Hons (*Mathematics*)
Miss E M McLaren, BA Hons (*Classics*)
D T Smith, BSc (**Physics*)
R A Shelley, BA Hons (*History*)
Miss K Monk, BA Hons (*Business Studies and Economics*)

Houses and Housemasters/mistresses:

Boys' Houses:
Deacon's: Charlie Knightley
Elwyn's: Michael Sugden
Gepp's: Peter Bennett
Montgomery's: Richard Feldman
Windsor's: Francis Barratt

Girls' Houses:
Follyfield: Nicola O'Brien
Garnetts: Beatrice Chamberlain
Manor: Carolyn Phillips
Stocks's: Frances Marshall
Thorne: Alison Sefton

Head of the Preparatory School: Mrs J M Burrett, BA

Admissions Registrar: Mrs C Clements

Roman Catholic Chaplain to Felsted: Father M Nott

Medical Officer: Dr Bronwen Pitt

The Houses. There are ten Houses at Felsted, a day house for boys, a day house for girls, three boarding houses for boys, three boarding houses for girls, an Upper Sixth House for boys and an Upper Sixth House for girls. Each House is under the direction of a resident Housemaster or Housemistress.

Each Housemaster/Housemistress is supported by a pastoral team comprising a resident Assistant Housemaster/Housemistress, a matron responsible for overseeing the domestic arrangements, and several House tutors.

The Curriculum. All pupils study English, English Literature, Mathematics and Sciences to GCSE and choose a further five subjects from the following: History, Geography, Religious Studies, French, German, Spanish, Latin, Classical Civilisation, Art, Music, Drama, Triple Science, Design & Technology (Resistant Materials or Graphic Design), Physical Education and Computer Studies. One of the options must be a Modern Foreign Language and one must be a Humanities subject.

In the Sixth Form pupils have a choice between A Levels and the International Baccalaureate. Those studying A Levels choose four subjects to study to AS Level and then continue with either three or four subjects to A Level. The following subjects are offered: English Literature, Theatre Studies, History, History of Art, Religious Studies, Psychology, Geography, Business Studies, Economics, French, German, Spanish, Latin, Classical Civilisation, Mathematics, Further Mathematics, Physics, Chemistry, Biology, Sport & Physical Education, Art, Music, Music Technology, Design & Technology.

The IB pupils study six subjects and also have a course on the Theory of Knowledge, write an extended essay and have to be involved in the Creativity Action Service Programme.

Scholarships. (*See Scholarship Entries section*.) Academic, Music, Drama, Art, Design & Technology and Sports

Scholarships are awarded annually up to the value of 20% of the fees for entry at 13+ and to the Sixth Form. Bursaries are available to increase the awards in case of need up to 100% of the fees in certain cases. The examinations for the 13+ Scholarships take place in February and May and for the Sixth Form Scholarships in November and February.

Scholarships are also awarded at 11+ at Felsted Preparatory School and these may be carried through to the Senior School.

Arkwright Foundation Scholarships are also available to talented students in Design at 16+.

All-rounder Awards which recognise all-round ability or specific ability in one area are available on entry at 11, 13 and 16 years old.

Registration and entry. Boys' and girls' names can be registered at any time. All those who pass an examination at the Preparatory School at 11+ and the Felsted School Transfer Exam may enter the Senior School. Before admission to Felsted all pupils at other preparatory schools must pass the Common Entrance or Scholarship Examination. Entry from other schools is by Head Teacher's Report and Verbal Reasoning Test, or, for Sixth Form entry, 6 B Grades at GCSE, Head Teacher's report, Verbal Reasoning Test and interview.

Fees per term (2011-2012). Senior School: £8,645 boarders, £6,470 day pupils.

Preparatory School: £3,720–£4,890; Pre-Preparatory: £2,575; Boarding £6,250.

Registration fee £75.

Felsted Preparatory School, whose Head is in membership of IAPS (The Independent Association of Prep Schools), shares the same governing body as Felsted School. It has its own campus, a teaching centre for 11–13 year-olds and a Pre-Preparatory Department. (*For further information, see entry in IAPS section.*)

Old Felstedian Society organises both social and sporting activities. The Secretary is: P G Norton, Ultima Dimora, 172 Braunston Road, Oakham, Rutland LE15 6RU. The Old Felstedian Liaison Master, Mr N S Hinde, would be pleased to answer queries about the Alumni and further information can be found at www.archives.felsted.essex.sch.uk.

Charitable status. Felsted School is a Registered Charity, number 310870. The charity is based upon the Foundation established by Richard Lord Riche in 1564 with the objective of teaching and instructing children across a broad curriculum as ordained from time to time by its Trustees.

Fettes College

Carrington Road, Edinburgh EH4 1QX
Tel: 0131 332 2281
Fax: 0131 311 6714
e-mail: enquiries@fettes.com
website: www.fettes.com

Founded in 1870 by Sir William Fettes and designed by David Bryce, Fettes College is uniquely situated in extensive grounds and woodland close to the heart of Edinburgh, and enjoys a reputation as one of the pre-eminent co-educational boarding schools in the UK. Fettes College has roughly 655 pupils aged 7–18, boarders and day pupils at a ratio of 70:30. Fettes Students are drawn from all over the British Isles and from abroad and this diverse and healthy mix of backgrounds provides a richness that contributes to the stimulating, warm and energetic community that is Fettes College.

Motto: '*Industria*'.

Governors:
D B McMurray (*Chairman*)
A E H Salvesen, CBE (*Deputy Chairman*)
I G Armstrong, QC

Mrs J A Campbell
Professor I W Campbell, FRCP (*Edinburgh & Glasgow*)
A G H Davidson, FInstD, MCMI
Ms S Davidson
The Hon Lady Dorrian, QC
Mrs H Douglas Miller
Reverend N N Gardner
C Grassie
Mrs E J S McClelland
Mrs L McClure
A A McCreath, MIPD, MIED
C K Oliver, WS
I M Osborne
Dr H W Reid
R Robson (*Convenor of the Executive Committee*)
Professor K Whaler
Councillor I Whyte

Clerk to the Governors: A G Fox, WS

Headmaster: **M C B Spens**, MA Selwyn College, Cambridge

Deputy Head: Mrs H F Harrison, BA
Assistant Head & Director of Studies: A Shackleton, MA
Assistant Head: A F Reeves, MA
Headmaster of the Preparatory School: A A Edwards, BA Hons
Chaplain: The Revd Dr D Campbell, MTheol, CECM, MTheol, DMin
IB Coordinator: A Shackleton, MA
Assistant Director of Studies: Dr L J Whyte, BSc, PhD

Assistant Staff:

A J Armstrong, MA	P F Heuston, BSc
R J Armstrong, BA	Mrs R L Heuston, BA
Miss P Bailey, MA	J M Hobbs, BA, PhD
H Battersby, BSc	Miss A Hope, BA
Mrs H J Battersby, BA	†Mrs P Houston, DipEd
C Boettcher, MA	Mrs J A Hudson-Price, BA
G A Blair, MA	R E Hughes, MA, MPhil
†Mrs S A Bruce, BSc	P M A Jenkins, MA
D Bywater, CertEd	Mrs L Jin
E M J Boulter-Comer, MA	Miss S E Johnston, BSc
Mrs B J Conway, BA	G T Lambert, BA
†Mrs C L Davies, BA	Miss K A Leech, BA
Miss E R Davies, BA	Dr S A Lewis, BSc, PhD
M G Davies, BA, PhD	I J Loudon, MA
†R A Davies, BSc	Miss R MacVicar, BSc
†D Dawson, BSc	Miss J M Maguire, MSc
M Delveaux, MA, PhD	Miss A A F Mair, MA
D Dowey, BSc	Mrs S E Masson, GGSM
C J du Vivier, MA	Miss A F Mitchell, BA
Mrs C Evans, BA	Miss C Montgomery
Dr K J Fairbairn, BSc, PhD	H D McCowan-Hill, BSc
Miss A H F Ferguson, BEd	Miss T J McDonald, BA
S French, BSc, PhD	D B McDowell, MA
Miss S Gausinet, BA	Mrs Y E A Mitchell, BSc
Miss A G Giraud	J J Morris, BA
A B Girdwood, MA, DPhil	A G Morrison, BA
Miss C E Gomm, MA	Mrs R C O Nicol, BA
D A Goodenough, GGSM,	Mrs M J Palfery, MA
FTCL, ARCO, ALCM	D G C Parry, BA
(*Director of Music*)	Miss M A Pawlitza, BA
D M Goude, BSc	Miss L E Pidgeon, MA
Mrs M Goude, BSc	J D Pillinger, BSc
A M Hall, MA, PhD	Miss K L Platt, BSc
†D G Hall, BEd	A B Russell, BA
Mrs M D Hansen, MA	Miss H J Russell, BA
†Mrs C M Harrison, BA	Miss C E E Satow, BMus
D Harrison, BSc	†R F Smith, BA
R H V Harrison, BA	B M Sneddon, BSc
M W Henry, MA	S Sowden, LLB
†S J Herbert, BA	A J Speedy, BA
Mrs T Herries, MA	Mrs D S Spens

Miss L Sutherland, BA, MFA	N C R Ward, BSc
Miss C M Tainsh, BEd, BA	Mrs A Weatherby, BA
Mrs E Thomson, BA, MLitt	†J A Weatherby, BEd
C S Thomson, BA	Mrs S V Weatherly, BSc
Miss M-J Walker, BSc	†B G Welsh, BSc
Dr J Walters, BA, MPhil, PhD	Mrs K Whyte, BSc
	Mrs S J Wightman, BA
	Mrs L Zhang, BA

Bursar: P J F Worlledge, BSc, ACA
Finance Manager: G Burns, MA
Foundation Director: Mrs E H M Anderson, BA
Director of Marketing & PR: Mrs G Gray, MA
Director of Sport: S M Bates, BSc, MBA
Headmaster's PA: Miss J F P Shurmer
Registrar: Mrs H F Marshall
Maintenance Manager: P J Houghton
Medical Officer: Dr S Allan, MB ChB, MRCGP
OFA Secretary: Mrs D A Beaumont
Keeper of the Register: G D C Preston, MA

Situation and Buildings. Fettes stands in a park of 85 acres on a remarkable site between the centre of Edinburgh and the Firth of Forth. Being just 20 minutes' walk to the city centre, means that Fettes students can take full advantage of the wealth of cultural resources on offer in Scotland's Capital city such as galleries, museums and theatres. Students also have every opportunity to enjoy the majestic Scottish outdoors with a full programme of trips and experiences from hill walking to canoeing, camping to white water rafting. Regular national and international school trips further broaden the experience Fettes students are offered.

The main building contains the Chapel, Library, some classrooms including the language laboratory, the Medical Centre and two Boarding Houses. The other five Boarding Houses, the Dining Hall, the Music and Art Schools, the Concert Hall, the Science and Technology Centre, the Sports Centre, Squash and Fives Courts, and the Preparatory School are situated in the grounds.

Transportation links by road, rail and air are excellent.

Organisation. There are approximately 710 pupils aged 7–18, and each member of the School is the responsibility of a Housemaster or Housemistress. There are four Houses for boys, three for girls, an Upper Sixth Form house and a Preparatory School. Our new Upper Sixth Form boarding house provides individual study-bedrooms with en suite facilities for all boarders. There is a strong tutorial system for the encouragement and guidance of each pupil.

Aims. Our mission at Fettes is to develop broadly educated, confident and thoughtful individuals. The hopes and aspirations of each and every one of our students are of central importance to us, and the happy, purposeful environment of the College encourages the boys and girls to flourish and develop fully the skills and interests that they possess.

Curriculum. The academic curriculum in the Preparatory School is based on the Scottish 5–14 Programme, but with a strong element of the English and Welsh national curriculum and Independent School Examination requirements. For GCSE all students take English, Mathematics, Physics, Chemistry, Biology and ICT. Students then choose 4 subjects from: Art & Design, Business Studies, Classical Civilisation, Classical Greek, Drama, French, Geography, German, History, Mandarin, Music, PE and Spanish.

Fettes offers a very broad range of subjects in the Sixth Form with students choosing either A Levels or International Baccalaureate, therefore allowing a choice of curriculum to best suit the needs of the individual student. Over 95% of pupils gain university entry with up to 18 students securing places at Oxford and Cambridge each year.

Careers. The School is a member of the Independent Schools Careers Organisation, and a team of Staff are responsible for providing specialist advice on careers and Higher Education and for developing links with industry and commerce. The Headmaster, Housemasters and Housemis-tresses are also involved in this work, and parents are invited to meet the Staff at termly receptions so that they can discuss pupils' progress, future options and career plans.

Chapel. The College Chapel, situated in the heart of the School, is central to life at Fettes with the daily Chapel service forming the core of the moral and spiritual guidance offered at Fettes. Fettes has a strong Christian tradition but members of other faiths and those with no faith are warmly welcomed, and this is reflected in the tolerant and questioning character of the School.

Games. All students are involved in sports at least 4 afternoons per week. All major sports are offered at Fettes in fact there are very few sports you cannot pursue. Rugby, cricket, hockey, lacrosse, netball athletics, tennis, squash, fives, swimming, badminton, fencing, netball, basketball, volleyball are an example of what is on offer. Fettes College is very proud of the Individual and team success at school and national levels across a range of sports including rugby, fencing and cross-country. Fettes College also has excellent sporting facilities including a purpose-built sports centre, all-weather pitches, indoor Swimming Pool and courts for Fives and Squash and a newly-built shooting range.

Other activities. There is a variety of societies and clubs, and each pupil is encouraged to develop cultural interests. On Saturday evenings, in addition to lectures, plays and concerts, there are regular dances and discos, and committees of pupils, with the assistance of members of Staff, are responsible for planning and organising social events for different age groups.

Music. The College possesses a strong musical tradition, and many pupils receive instrumental tuition. In addition to the orchestras there are ensembles, a swing band, Chapel Choir and Concert Choir. A major concert is held at the end of every term.

Drama. Drama is lively and of a high standard. Each year the School Play and House plays offer great opportunities for large numbers of boys and girls to act and to participate in Lighting and Stage Management.

Art. The Art School is flourishing, and the standards of pupil attainment are very high. Regular House art competitions and gallery display of current work occur.

Combined Cadet Force, Duke of Edinburgh's Award Scheme, Outside Service. Pupils are members of the CCF for two years and may choose to extend their service while they are in the Sixth Form. There are Navy, Army and RAF Sections and a thriving Pipe Band. Training is offered in Shooting, Vehicle Engineering, Canoeing, Rock-Climbing, Skiing, Sub-Aqua and Sailing.

In the Sixth Form many pupils pursue the Gold Standard of the Duke of Edinburgh's Award Scheme, and some 70 members of the School join the Outside Service Unit which provides help for others in difficult circumstances and raises funds for Charities.

Outdoor Activities. The School aims to make full use of its proximity to the sea, the Dry Ski Slope, and the rivers and mountains of Scotland. Outdoor activities are encouraged for the enjoyment that they give and the valuable personal qualities which they help to develop. A number of members of Staff are experts in mountaineering, skiing and water sports, and all pupils have opportunities for receiving instruction in camping, canoeing, sailing, hillwalking and snow and rock climbing. There are regular expeditions abroad.

Preparatory School. The Preparatory School for 150 boys and girls aged 7 to 13 is situated in the School grounds. Boarders stay in the modern purpose-built Houses. Pupils in the Prep School share the facilities of the senior school and participate in the full range of activities enjoyed by the College as a whole. (*For further details see entry in IAPS section*.)

Admission. Personal interviews assess the promise of each individual and determine those who will gain most from a Fettes education. Entrance exams are also required for entry. Pupils may join the Preparatory School at any stage (7–13) with students normally joining the Senior School at 13 and 16. Further details are available from the Registrar.

Scholarships, Foundation Awards and Bursaries. (*See Scholarship Entries section.*) Scholarships to the value of 10% of the fees are available for candidates aged 11+, 13+ and 16+. Any scholarship award can be supplemented by means-tested bursaries that can cover the full cost of the fees.

General Scholarships as well as Music scholarships, Piping Scholarships, Art Scholarships and All-Rounder awards are available.

Children of members of HM Forces qualify for a reduction in fees and Special Bursaries (Todd) are available for descendents of Old Fettesians.

Fees per term (2011-2012). Boarding £9,050, Day £6,745. The fees cover all extras except books and stationery, music lessons and subscriptions to voluntary clubs and activities.

Registration Fee £50.

Old Fettesian Association. *Liaison*: Mrs D A Beaumont, Old Fettesian Association Office, Fettes College (Telephone 0131 311 6741).

Further Details from The Headmaster, Fettes College, Edinburgh EH4 1QX (Telephone 0131 311 6701).

Charitable status. The Fettes Trust is a Registered Charity, number SC017489. Fettes aims to provide a quality education at Junior and Senior level.

Forest School

College Place, Snaresbrook, London E17 3PY

Tel: 020 8520 1744
Fax: 020 8520 3656
e-mail: info@forest.org.uk
website: www.forest.org.uk

Founded in 1834 as 'The Forest Proprietary School' to 'provide a course of Education for youth, comprising classical learning, mathematics and such modern languages and other branches of science and general literature as might from time to time be introduced; combined with religious and moral instruction in accordance with the doctrine of the Church of England'. Incorporated 1947.

Motto: '*In Pectore Robur*'.

Council:
Chairman of the Governors: J W Matthews, FCA

Members of the Council:
Professor J E Banatvala, CBE, MA, MD, MRCP, FRCPath, DCH, DPH
Mrs S R Campion, MA
B M de L Cazenove, TD
G S Green, MA
G Hewitson, MA
Mrs S K Rankin, MA, PhD
G Smallbone, MA
Mrs L Marland, BEd
Mrs G Jenkinson, AGSM, DipEd
B Kotecha, MBBCh, DLO, FRCSEd, MPhil
W Kolade
Mrs P M Oates, BEd
His Honour Judge William Kennedy
The Venerable Elwin Cockett, Archdeacon of West Ham
Dr Elizabeth Sidwell, CBE, BSc, PhD, FRSA, FRGS

Warden: Mrs S J Kerr-Dineen, MA

Deputy Warden and Head of the Boys' School:
M Cliff Hodges, MA

Deputy Warden and Head of the Girls' School:
Mrs P A Goodman, MA

Head of Preparatory School:
Mrs E Garner, BA, MEd

Director of Teaching and Learning:
J W J Mitchell, MA

Director of Co-Curriculum:
J E R Sanderson, BA, BMus

Bursar and Clerk to the Governors: Mrs D Coombs, BSc, MBA

* *Head of Department*
† *Housemaster/mistress*

Boys' School Assistant Staff:
A G van den Broek, MA, PhD (*Senior Master*)
†M Gray, BA (*Senior Housemaster*)
M C V Spencer Ellis, MA (*Director of Sixth Form*)
J D Waller, BA (*Lower School Master*)

†P Henley-Smith, BSc, PhD	P T Baker, BA
I R Honeysett, MA	A V Nagar, BSc
*A R Dainton, BSc	Mrs J Kleiner, BA
S O Jalowiecki, BSc	P Drennan
M J Smith, BSc (*Careers Advisor*)	S M Wiles, MA
†A D Ford, BA	A J Redpath, BMus
†O E Ling, BA	Ms D Holland
T C Hewitt, BA	A C Nicol, BSc
*Mrs A G Gould, MA	Miss A L Feldman, BA
Mrs H P R Miller, BA	Ms S Seehra, BSc
Ms A N Berges	T J Arnold, BSc
†M S Christie, MA	C A Forsdyke, MA
Z H Nazir, BSc, DPhil	D A Bryan, MSc
*J G Holt, BA	E P Watson, MEng
†S F Foulds, BA	Miss D Rathod, MSc
J A C Whitmee, BA	Miss S E Robson, BSc
*S Firek, BSc, PhD	A J Birkhamshaw, MSc
*P T S Aspery, BA	D R Potter, BA
†J Miller, BA	Miss I Symonds, BA
R G Greasley, BEd	Mrs C Saunders, MA, MPhil
A E Foinette, MA	Miss C M Nortier, BSc
B D Adams, BSc	C Bailey, BA
J T Sloan, BA	Mrs R R Keen, MA, MSc
J J Kay, BA	J J Whitton, BSc
*Mrs S Pearce, MSc	L Meaden, BSc
	S Jackson, BA

Girls' School Assistant Staff:
Miss J Benewith, BSc (*Senior Mistress*)
Mrs J K Venditti, BEng (*Senior Housemistress*)
Mrs S M Clarke, BSc (*Assistant Director of Sixth Form*)

*Ms L E Murray, BA	†Mrs L M Surowiec, BA, MA
N V Gray, MA	
A Royall, BSc, MSc, DIC	†Miss J C Baldwin BA
*P M Oliver, MA (*Director of Drama*)	Mrs M L Duraku, BSc
	J F O'Riordan, BA
Mrs S M Harris, BA	*M J Taylor, BA, MA, MSc
*C D Brant, MA	
*Mrs L S Bishop, BA	Miss R H Lang, MA
Mrs J V Taylor	Ms F Anwar, BA
A H Todd, BSc, PhD	Mrs L L Goodey, BA
Mrs S C Keating, BEd	†Mrs J McIsaac, BA
†Mrs T C Christie, BA	*S J Marsh, BSc, PhD
J T McGurran, BA	Mrs K Hersey, BSc
Mrs G Hopkins	Ms V A Kelly, BSc
Mrs D Tubb, BEd	Miss C Risk, BSc
Ms F Pereira, MA	Miss J R Stewart, BA
Ms S M Wood, BA	Mrs F Hoxha, BSc
*S G J Huet Deug, BEd	†Mrs D Graham, LRAM, GRSM
*Miss K Skelding, BA	
*E-W Morris, BA	*Miss C J Spencer Ellis, BA
*†Ms C A Heath, BA	

Miss C Rhead, MSc
Miss M M Duncan, MA
Miss C Mills, BA
S J George, BSc
Z A Munir, BA
J G Brown, BA
Miss D G Holder, BSc
Mrs R J Sym, MA, MEng
M D Bullock, BSc

Miss C R E Pepys, BA
Miss A Meehitiya, BSc
Mrs L Baber, BSc, MSc
Miss K Carmichael, BA
A Cossey, MA
Miss H L Dootson, BA
Ms A Dhanji, BSc
Miss C A Smith, MA

Preparatory School:
Head of Preparatory School: Mrs E Garner, BA, MEd
Deputy Head: Mrs C P A Browne, BEd, MA
Head of Pre-Prep: P McIntosh, PRM, BA

Assistant Staff:
Mrs S A Spanjar, CertEd (*Pastoral Care, Girls*)
Mrs M Healey, CertEd (*Music Subject Leader*)
Mrs L C Dalton, BA (*Pastoral Care, Boys*)
Miss S D Gould, BEd, MA
Mrs C de Jager, BPrimEd
Mrs K L Clark, BEd (*PSHE Subject Leader*)
C de Jager, BPrimEd (*Coordinator of Extra-Curricular Activities*)
Mrs J Chan, BEd (*English Subject Leader*)
Mrs K Cooper, BA (*History Subject Leader*)
Miss J S Pell, BA
Mrs M M Pickwick, BSc (*Learning Support Teacher*)
D Potter, BA
Ms A Moor, Drama Dip
Mrs J Scott, BA (*Mathematics Subject Leader*)
Mrs T L Tyson, BA
Ms L McAllister
Ms E Burgess
Ms S Campbell

Director of Music: J E R Sanderson, BA, BMus
SENCO: Mrs N Coghlan, BA
PA to the Warden : Miss S Woolston

There are currently 1,232 pupils in the School (505 boys in the Boys' School, 504 girls in the Girls' School, 223 boys and girls in the Preparatory School).

The three Schools share the main School campus and facilities such as Chapel, Sports Hall, Theatre and Computer Centre, but each has its own separate teaching block. The Sixth Form is then organised on co-educational lines.

Buildings. The School is situated in an open part of Epping Forest. The original building is Georgian, converted to provide libraries, recreation rooms and offices. 19th century expansion led to the building of the Gothic-style Chapel and Dining Hall. Modern classrooms and changing rooms have been built and the main Laboratory Block extended. The Deaton Theatre, seating 375, a Sports Hall, Music School, Sixth Form Centre and Computer Centre were added between 1967 and 1985. The Preparatory School is a modern block, recently extended. The Girls' School was founded in 1978, its buildings opened and dedicated in 1981. The Jenkin Wing – Art, Drama and Design facilities – was opened in 2001 and the Performing Arts Extension in 2004. The new sports complex, an ambitious project costing £5m, which includes two new swimming pools, opened in September 2006. The surrounding playing fields cover nearly 27 acres.

Organisation. The School is divided into 3 clear sections under the overall direction of the Warden: Preparatory School (ages 4–11); Boys' School (ages 11–18): Girls' School (11–18). There are 8 Houses in the Boys' School and 6 in the Girls' School.

(*See also Forest Preparatory School entry in IAPS section.*)

Curriculum. Courses are designed to give a broad education as far as GCSE, each pupil taking English, Mathematics, either separate Sciences or Balanced Science, one Modern Foreign Language and other subjects depending on the individual's ability. A high priority is given to ICT throughout the School. There is a wide variety of Sixth Form courses designed to prepare pupils to enter University, Business, the Services or the Professions. The full range of AS and A2 levels are offered; all Sixth Formers take General Studies. Private tuition is available in Piano, Organ and Orchestral Instruments, and there are several Orchestras, Bands and Choirs.

Religion. Worship in the School Chapel is in accordance with the faith and practice of the Church of England. All pupils are required to attend the daily services in chapel. Religious Education is broadly based and is taught as an academic subject.

Societies. The School has a thriving Combined Cadet Force, a Voluntary Service Group and a branch of The Duke of Edinburgh's Award Scheme. Other Societies include Chess, Choral, Debating, Film, Music, Natural History, Photography, and Science. There are Badminton, Fencing and Bridge Clubs and a specialised TV studio.

Drama. There are frequent productions and drama competitions. Music, Plays, Concerts and Lectures take place in the Theatre.

Games. The main games are Cricket, Association Football, Hockey, Netball, Athletics, and Swimming. There are Tennis Courts. All pupils are expected to take part in games.

Fees per term (2011-2012). (including lunches) age 11+: £4,650; age 8–10: £3,647; age 7: £3,371; age 4–6 years: £3,145.

Admission. Examinations for pupils at 7+ and 11+ take place in January for entry in the following September. Some places are available at 16+ and occasionally at other ages.

Careers. Almost all pupils go on to Universities to take Degree Courses, including 10-12 each year to Oxford and Cambridge. Careers advice is given to all pupils.

Scholarships and Bursaries. Scholarships and Bursaries are available by competitive process for entry at 11+ and 16+. The maximum non-means tested fee remission awarded in respect of any one pupil is 50% of full fees, whether in one area of excellence or in combination of one or more areas of excellence. Bursaries are means-tested and are awarded in addition to Scholarships, up to and including the total remission of fees.

Up to the equivalent of 14 places may be given annually to pupils at 11+, following Scholarship assessment in January of the year of entry, of which 2 are reserved for excellence in Music.

Up to the equivalent of 2 Forest Exhibitions are awarded at 11+ to those showing all-round promise but who have not been awarded an Academic Scholarship. In the case of Music, Forest Exhibitions meet the cost of lessons in one or more instrument.

Up to the equivalent of 6 places may be given annually to both internal and new entrants to the Sixth Form, of which up to 2 are reserved for Academic excellence and 1 in Music. Scholarships are also awarded for outstanding ability in Art, Drama and Sport.

Up to the equivalent of 2.25 places are generally available to new entrants to the Sixth Form, sponsored by the Ogden Trust, Mulalley and Co, the Old Foresters, and the 175th Anniversary appeal.

Fee reductions are available for children of the Clergy.

For full details visit www.forest.org.uk.

Old Foresters' Club. *Hon Secretary*: Mrs K Hersey, c/o Forest School.

Charitable status. Forest School, Essex is a Registered Charity, number 312677. The objective of the School is Education.

Foyle and Londonderry College

Senior School: Duncreggan Road, Londonderry BT48 0AW, Northern Ireland
Tel: 028 7126 9321
Fax: 028 7126 9425
e-mail: info@foylelondonderry.derry.ni.sch.uk
website: www.foylenet.org

Junior School: Springtown, Londonderry BT48 0LX
Tel: 028 7126 9321
Fax: 028 7137 2216

Foyle and Londonderry College is a Voluntary, Co-educational, Day, Grammar School. The buildings are on two campuses: Junior School (11+ to 14+) on the Springtown site and the Senior School on the Duncreggan site.

Plans are on-going to relocate the College, together with Ebrington Primary School, to a site formerly occupied by the army at Clooney Base in the Waterside area of the city.

Chairman of Governors: Mr R J B Young

Principal: Mr W J Magill, MA Cantab, MA NUU, CertEd Cantab

Vice-Principals:
Mr J H McNee, BA, PGCE, MPhil
Dr P P Carson, BSc, DipCompEd, MSc Ed
Mr P G Gault, BA, PGCE

Senior Management Team:
Mr J S Goodman, BSc, LTCL, MA Ed
Mr W M Lynn, BA, BA
Mr G S Mercer BSc, PGCE
Mrs H Eakin, BEd
Mr R Menown, BA, PGCE
Mrs B McGowan, BA, PGCE

Heads of Departments:

Art & Design:
Mr K F Ward, BA, PGCE

Biology:
Mrs I A Hannaway, BEd

Business Studies:
Mrs H Eakin, BEd

Careers:
Mr K J Thatcher, BA, DASE

Chemistry:
Mr K S Given, BA, PGCE

Classical Civilisation:
Mr J H McNee, BA, PGCE, MPhil

Computing/Information Technology:
Mrs S McLaughlin, BEd

Technology & Design:
Mr A C Moorcroft, BEd, PGCTE

English:
Mrs A B Mercer, BA, PGCE

Geography:
Mrs S Guthrie, BSc, PGCE

Geology:
Mr W M Lynn, BA, BA

History:
Mr S J Heasley, BA, PGCE

Home Economics:
Mrs F Feeney

Mathematics:
Mr G S Mercer, BSc, PGCE

Music:
Mrs B O'Somachain, BMus, PGCE, TTCT

Modern Languages:
Ms L C McAuley, BEd, MA, PGDipLit (*French*)
Mrs P A L Coughlin, BA, PGCE (*German*)
Mrs H Kane-Craig, BA, PGCE (*Spanish*)

Physics:
Mrs S M O'Connell, BSc, PGCE

Physical Education:
Mr G R McCarter, BEd, DLC (*Boys*)
Ms K Eakin, BSc, PGCE (*Girls*)

Religious Studies:
Mrs E Adair, CertEd

Administrative Staff:
Bursar: Mr N Stewart BSc
Principal's Secretary: Mrs M J Deans, BA, DLCC

Age Range. 11–18 Co-educational.

Number of Pupils. The Department of Education specifies the Admission and Enrolment numbers which are: Admission Number 125; Enrolment Number 960.

Fees per annum (2011-2012). Parents pay a Capital Fee of £15 per annum and a Parental Contribution of £120 per annum.

History. Foyle College and Londonderry High School, now Foyle and Londonderry College, have been providing education for young people in the Londonderry area and further afield for 394 years. In 1617 following the Plantation of Ulster, the Free School of Londonderry was founded by Mathias Springham, Master of the Merchant Taylors' Company, to "the honour of God and the spreading of good literature". The school remained on its site within the walls until 1814 when it moved to the fine Georgian building on Lawrence Hill, adopting the name Foyle College shortly afterwards.

The Londonderry Academical Institution, founded in 1868 by a body of influential local merchants, proved to be a vigorous rival for almost thirty years until the amalgamation of the two schools in 1896. The school then had the use of the buildings at Lawrence Hill and Academy Road.

Following the Second World War, and as a consequence of the many changes brought about by the 1947 Education Act, the Governors acquired a site at Springtown on Northland Road, overlooking the school playing fields, to build a new school. This was opened on 2nd May 1968 by His Royal Highness the Duke of Kent.

Londonderry High School also derived its existence from the merging of two independent institutions. The first of these, the Ladies' Collegiate School, was set up in 1877 at 11 Queen Street by Misses MacKillip, pioneers in the movement for the higher education of women in Ireland. The school later moved to Crawford Square and was renamed Victoria High School.

Buildings and Amenities. The Junior and Senior Schools are both well equipped, enabling staff to adopt the most effective teaching methods. In the Senior School there are six Science Laboratories plus several Computer Suites, a Technology Suite, Art and Design Suite, Music Suite, Business Studies Suite including Computer Room, Study Hall, Library, Upper Sixth Social Centre, Lower Sixth Social Centre, Sports Hall and twenty-two General Classrooms. Drama and Musical performances take place in the Assembly Hall.

In the Junior School the Library, two IT Suites and Technology Suite are well established while the Science Laboratories have been completely refurbished and a new Music Suite added. Home Economics and Art rooms have been renovated. There are fourteen General Classrooms, a fully equipped Gymnasium and Assembly Hall.

Serving the 30 acres of school grounds are two pavilions at Springtown where there are rugby pitches, cricket pitches, tennis courts and an all weather hockey and athletics ground. The Senior School has a hockey pitch and tennis courts.

Aims of the School.

1. To create a secure, caring, happy, healthy environment within which pupils can develop both as individuals and as members of a community.
2. To equip each individual with appropriate skills of literacy, numeracy and oracy, and to develop full academic potential through study of a wide but integrated range of subjects.
3. To stimulate an appreciation of aesthetic, literary, scientific, mathematical, technological, environmental, linguistic, physical and spiritual values.
4. To provide a foundation for further study and training by creating opportunities for each pupil to:
   (a) develop a spirit of enquiry;
   (b) practice the skills needed for independent study;
   (c) make realistic career and personal decisions.
5. To help pupils acquire qualifications appropriate to the needs of their future careers.
6. To encourage pupils to cooperate and to appreciate the need for moral values and tolerance of others.
7. To encourage pupils to understand and accept discipline and to develop the power of self-discipline.
8. To provide and encourage participation in a range of recreational and cultural activities.

Framlingham College

Framlingham, Woodbridge, Suffolk IP13 9EY
Tel: 01728 723789
Fax: 01728 724546
e-mail: admissions@framcollege.co.uk
website: www.framlinghamcollege.co.uk

Motto: '*Studio Sapientia Crescit.*'

Chairman of Governors: A W M Fane, MA, FCA

Headmaster: Mr P B Taylor, BA Hons

Senior Deputy Head: Mrs S Webber, NDip, BSc
Deputy Head Academic: C A Norton, MA, PGCE
Deputy Head Co-Curricular: M D Robinson, MA, BEd Hons (*Head of History*)
Deputy Head Pastoral: C E Hobson, BA Hons, PGCE

Heads of Department:
Art: Mrs C E Mallett, BA Hons, AdvDipT
Business Studies & Economics: C Caiger, BA, MSc, PGCE
Careers: R W Skitch, BSc, ACCEG, ACIB, PGCE
Design & Technology: D J Morgan, CertEd CDT
Drama: Ms D Englert, BA Hons, PGCE, Dip Speech & Drama
ESL: Mrs K Cavalcanti, BEd Hons, RSA Dip EFL
English: P R Drummond, MA
Geography: P D Barker, MA, PGCE
Director of ICT: C Rimmer, BA Hons, MSc, PGCE
Languages: B Dyer, BA Hons
Learning Support: Mrs S Wenn, BEd
Mathematics: K R S Hoyle, BSc, PGCE
Director of Music: T Rhodes, BMus Hons
PSHE: D J Boatman, BA Hons, PGCE
Psychology: Mrs J S Hobson, BA Hons, PGCE
Religious Studies: J E Holland, BA, PGCE
Science: Dr D R Higgins, MA, PhD, PGCE
Director of Sport: J Slay, BSc Hons

Finance Director: N J Chaplin, BA Hons, FCCA
Operations Director: A L Payn, Chartered FCIPD

Admissions Registrar: Miss E Rutterford, BA Hons
Headmaster's Personal Assistant: Mrs H Alcoe

Location. The school is situated close to the wonderful Suffolk Coast, in the historic market town of Framlingham, overlooking the Mere and Castle, and is served by good road and rail links to London, Cambridge, Norwich and all the main London airports.

History. The School was founded in 1864 by public subscription as the Suffolk County Memorial to Prince Albert and was incorporated by Royal Charter.

Organisation. Mr Taylor became Headmaster in September 2009; he was formerly Lower Master (Deputy Head) at King's School in Canterbury. He now leads a school that has recently received an excellent ISI Inspection Report, which described the College as highly successful in meeting its stated aims and mission of providing a first-class, holistic education, in a safe and inspiring environment, accessible to a broad range of boys and girls. The Senior School numbers some 425 pupils of whom 251 are boarders. All students are accommodated in seven fully-integrated boarding and day houses: three for girls and four for boys.

Preparatory School. Brandeston Hall, located less than 5 miles away, is a leading preparatory school for boys and girls aged 2½–13. All students are prepared for Common Entrance (*see entry in IAPS section*).

Facilities. An imaginative buildings programme has produced an exciting range of facilities which include the Headmaster Porter Theatre, a state-of-the-art drama and music facility. Science, Technology and Art enjoy purpose-built accommodation, and the Leisure Centre houses an indoor swimming pool and fitness suite, thereby enhancing the superb range of sports facilities. The flourishing Sixth Form is 200 strong and students enjoy their own Centre, which has been recently modernised and overlooks an attractive central concourse, which is used extensively for informal gatherings. There are further plans to improve the warm and friendly boarding houses, with recent completion of Pembroke House, with facilities that include an additional 22 modern study-bedrooms and two Common Rooms.

Curriculum. The College has a fine record in stretching the most able, while the 'value added' rating for those pupils who are not automatically destined to achieve A grades at GCSE and A Level stands among the very best in the country. Department for Education figures covering recent years confirmed this when placing the College among the top 5% in the country at improving pupils' grades between GCSE and A Level, and this is reflected in the ISI Inspection report which describes much of the teaching as *outstanding*.

Extra-Curricular Activities. Our academic success rates are mirrored by outstanding sporting achievements, commitment to the popular and extremely successful Duke of Edinburgh's Award Scheme and the outward-bound work of the voluntary Combined Cadet Force. From the cut and thrust of the debating society there are visiting speakers and musical performances, charity competitions, formal house suppers and many cultural, educational and recreational visits. Whether it is cookery or the choral society, equestrianism or aero-modelling, a round of golf on campus or trekking in Nepal, there is something for everyone.

Games. Framlingham College enjoys an enviable reputation for sport and fields a large number of teams, with students benefiting from an Elite Athlete programme where one student has been selected for the 2012 Olympic K4 Kayaking Development Squad and another for the U16 Great Britain skiing team. The major games are rugby, hockey, cricket, athletics and tennis for boys, and hockey, netball, tennis and athletics for girls. There is a wide range of other sporting opportunities, including squash, football, badminton, basketball, rounders, swimming, archery, shooting, volleyball and table tennis. The immaculately tended grounds include four rugby pitches, an Astroturf with a second Astroturf in development, a golf course and one of the finest cricket squares in the East of England. The facilities also include a sports hall, indoor swimming pool, fitness centre, gym, squash courts, netball courts and tennis courts.

Music and Drama. Framlingham has a very strong choral tradition, and there is a wide range of orchestras and instrumental ensembles. In the past seven years, three pupils have reached the finals of BBC Radio 2 Chorister of the Year. The College's dramatic productions enjoy a very high reputation. The main productions each year generally include one musical, a major drama and a junior play.

Religion. The College has a strong Christian foundation, but students of all backgrounds are welcomed.

Admission. Common Entrance and interview form the normal means of entry to the College at 13+, but special provision is made for students for whom this is not appropriate. Entrance at 16+ is normally on the basis of GCSE results and interview or testing, but special arrangements are made for overseas students who are not following the British Curriculum. Visits from interested parties are welcomed; please contact us to make an appointment.

Scholarships. (*See Scholarship Entries section.*) A wide range of scholarships at 11+, 13+ or 16+ is awarded every year for academic excellence, exceptional ability in art or music or for outstanding talent in another field, such as sport. Successful candidates can be offered further assistance through bursaries in cases of proven financial need.

Fees per term (2011-2012). Boarding £8,274, Day £5,318 (including lunch).

Charitable status. Albert Memorial College (Framlingham College) is a Registered Charity, number 1114383.

Frensham Heights

Rowledge, Farnham, Surrey GU10 4EA

Tel: 01252 792561
Fax: 01252 794335
e-mail: headmaster@frensham-heights.org.uk
website: www.frenshamheights.org

Board of Governors:
President: (*to be appointed*)
Vice-President: Professor T Sherwood, MB, MA, FRCP, FRCR (*Emeritus Professor of Radiology, Cambridge, Fellow of Girton College*)
Vice-President: Mrs J Read, BA, Chartered FCIPD
Chairman: Mr M J Chadwick, ACA, ATTI (*Chartered Accountant*)
Vice-Chairman: Mr M Sant (*formerly General Secretary, Independent Schools' Bursars Association*)
Treasurer: Mr D Smith, FCA (*Management Consultant*)
Mr G Buttle, MA (*formerly Headmaster Churcher's College*)
Mrs M Coltman, BA, LLB (*solicitor*)
Dr J Doulton, MA, MBBS, MSc, MFPHM (*Doctor*)
Mr D Haywood, MA (*formerly Headmaster City of London Freemen's School*)
Mr A Lawman, AFA, FIAB (*Finance Controller for Pitney Bowes International Mail Services*)
Mr R Lowther, CIMA, MSc (*Chartered Management Accountant/Consultant*)
Mr W A Marriott, BA (*solicitor*)
Mrs S V Palfreyman, SRN, SCM, MSc, CertEd (*Lecturer in child development, Open University*)
Mr A J Reid (*Chief Executive, Treloar Trust*)
Mr S Seymour Marsh (*Commercial Property Developer*)
Prof Frank Wibaut, ARCM, Hon RAM (*International concert pianist, worldwide visiting professor, formerly director Australian National Academy of Music*)

Head: Andrew Fisher, BA, MEd, FRSA

Senior Management Team:

* *Head of Department*
† *Housemaster/mistress*
§ *Part-time or Visiting*

Deputy Head: Simon Pettegree, BSc
Deputy Head (*Academic*): Diana Lobban-Small, BSc, PGCE, CChem, MRSC
Bursar and Clerk to the Governors: David Armitage, MBE, MSc
Development Director: Rosellen Mates
Head of Sixth Form: Jonathan Warner, BSc, MSc, PGCE, FRGS
Head of Lower School: †Nic Hoskins, BA
Head of Middle School: Eileen Daw, BEd

Alexander Allan, BA, PGCE
John Atkinson, BSc, PGCE, CertTheol
Jeremy Belas, BSc, GTP
§Hilary Blake, CertEd, BEd
§Anthony Bonello, MMus, BA
*Matthew Burns, BA, PGCE
*Barry Carr, MA, PGCE
Angelos Christofi, CertEd
Heather Clark, BEd, CertEd
§Sophia Colley, MA, PGCE
Russell Crew, BEng, PGCE
§Fiona Cullis, BA, CertEd
Anna Di Gregorio, BSc, PGCE
Andrew Ellison, BSc
Mark Floyer, MA, MPhil, PGCE
Lucy Fox, BSc, PGCE
*Rupert Gardner, BA, CertEd Mus
Rosemary Giraudet, BEd, DipEd
Kate Godeseth, BA
*Lynn Goodburne, BPhil, DipLCDD
*Lisa Graham, BA, PGCE
Shelagh Harris, GGSM, ARCM, PGCE
*Brendan Horsted, BA
§Ashley Howard, MA
§Robert Keane
Charlotte Knight, BSc, PGCE
Deborah Lee, BEd
*Amanda Liddle, BA
†Jeff Loomis, PhD, BSc
§Carol Mallett, BEd, DipRSA
*Hannah Manton, BSc, PGCE
Clare Marsh, BA, PGCE
Karen McBride, BSc, PGCE
Rosemary McMillan, CertEd
Andrew Melbourne, BSc, PGCE
Susan Millerchip, BSc, PGCE
§Nigel Milton, BA, BSc, PGCE
Fiona Morgan-Gibbins, BEd
*Nicola O'Donnell, BA, MEd, PGCE
Nick Oram-Tooley, BA, GTP
Elizabeth Piercey, DipEd
*†Steven Powell, BSc, PGCE
Michele Rickett, BA, PGCE
Hugh Robertson, MBA, BSc, PGCE
§Sylvia Sanguinetti, BSc, PGCE
§Angela Schock-Hurst, MA, BA
*Timothy Seys, BSc, PGCE
Susan Slater, CertEd (*Nursery Supervisor*)
*Andy Spink, BSc, GTP
David Stevenson, BA
*Peter Unitt, BSc, PGCE
§Emma Wyld, BA, DipTESOL

Finance Manager: Wendy Hamilton, FCA
Theatre Manager: Sean Connor, BA
Admissions Registrar: Emily Wood, BA
Domestic Bursar: Kathryn Seaton
Secretary to the Headmaster: Lindsey Boyce

School Nurse: Sarah Burton, RGN, RM
School Counsellor: §Vanessa Edworthy, MBACP
Librarian: Noel Rasmussen
Medical Officers: Dr Jane Elliott, Dr Paul Adams

Founded in 1925 as one of the country's first co-educational boarding and day schools, Frensham Heights has always been characterised by a friendly, informal atmosphere in which the individual child feels secure and happy. As a co-educational community, the school believes in equality of the sexes; it opposes all forms of bigotry, racial, religious or social, and every effort is made to deepen understanding of human nature and behaviour and develop self-esteem.

Pupil numbers. 514 boys and girls aged 3 to 18 years. Average class size: 18.

Entry. Children entering from N–6 have an assessment day. Children entering the school at the age of 11+ sit the Frensham Heights Entrance Examination, held in January. Children entering at the age of 13+ sit the Frensham Heights Entrance Examination in January and may also take the ISEB Common Entrance Examination. Entrance to the Sixth Form is by examination and interview with a minimum of six GCSE passes at Grade C or above (A/B grades in AS/A Level subjects). The school holds Open Days, though, for those who prefer, individual appointments may also be made through the Admissions Registrar.

Curriculum. Most pupils take 9 GCSE subjects of which the compulsory elements are English Language and Literature, mathematics and double award science. The top set take triple award science. Thereafter pupils choose from geography, history, business studies, a second modern language, art, 3D design, dance, design technology, drama, music, ICT or PE. Photography is taught to GCSE outside the curriculum and within at AS and A Level. There are normally 22 subjects from which to chose at AS Level and 19 at A Level. PSME is taught throughout the school. 25 subjects are taught at AS Level and 22 at A Level.

Academic Results. Examination results are very good. There is a strong Sixth Form, most of whom go on to further education, including Oxford and Cambridge Universities. Public examination results: A Level 100% (57% A/B Grades 2010); GCSE Grades A*–C (90% 2010).

Sport. The school has excellent sporting facilities which include an astroturf, playing fields, a swimming pool, tennis courts and an indoor sports centre. Sports include basketball, soccer, rugby, netball, hockey, cross-country running, athletics, volleyball, badminton, rounders and cricket. Annual ski and snowboarding trips take place abroad in the holidays.

Outdoor Education. Outdoor education is part of the curriculum for all pupils in Year 7 and above. Training takes place in the school's extensive adventure centre and leads to weekend and holiday expeditions in camping, climbing, caving, canoeing, scuba-diving and trekking, including World Challenge.

Extra-Curricular Activities. All pupils are expected to take part in extra-curricular activities. An extensive and varied selection of activities includes sports of all sorts, art, music, dance, drama, hobbies and clubs, sailing, and the Duke of Edinburgh's Award Scheme.

Facilities. 100 acres of parkland in beautiful countryside, Performing Arts Centre, new First and Lower Schools, music school, modern science laboratories, art & design centre, ICT centre, junior and senior library, sixth form centre, photographic studio. A new Sixth Form complex opened in September 2006.

Music. Music is held in high esteem at the school and is regarded as an essential part of a person's education. It is studied by all pupils until the end of Year 9. The school has an impressive record for its choral and instrumental music. There are senior and junior choirs, two orchestras, and a large number of instrumental groups. Concerts are put on nationally and locally. An overseas concert tour takes place every year. The Lower School has its own European concert tour.

Boarding. Boarders are housed in small and friendly boarding houses. Each has a resident housemaster or housemistress and house tutor. There is a programme of weekend activities for the boarders, but weekly boarders may leave on Friday afternoon, returning on Sunday evening or Monday morning. The School organises a coach to London at weekends.

Religion. There are no religious services. Pupils are free to attend local churches and several pupils sing in church choirs.

Dress. There is no uniform. There is a dress code.

Welfare and Discipline. The house-staff are supported by a resident school nurse and a part-time counsellor. Every pupil has a personal tutor. The school's discipline is firmly based on good relationships between staff and pupils and reflects the values of the school, which promote a rational and caring approach. Senior pupils act as mentors to younger members of the school. A thriving School Council, consisting of elected representatives from all age groups, meets regularly to discuss matters of mutual interest and concern.

Learning Difficulties. The school is sympathetic to those with dyslexia and other specific learning difficulties and offers limited support.

Overseas Pupils. The school admits a few boarders from overseas each year and provides tuition in English as a Second Language as part of their curriculum.

Frensham Heights **Lower School** is situated in its new purpose-built classrooms. **The First School**, for pupils aged 3–8, is in its own recently enlarged buildings and gardens within the main school grounds. Both schools provide firm foundations in English and Mathematics, supported by a well-balanced curriculum that includes Science, French, Information Technology, Music, Drama and Dance at a level appropriate to the year group. Pupils have access to all the main school's facilities.

Fees per term (2011-2012). Nursery: £19.75 (morning session, lunch £2.90), £19.75 (afternoon session, including lunch); Reception £1,895; Years 1–2 £2,330; Year 3 £2,780; Year 4 £2,845; Years 5–6 £3,510; Years 7–8: £5,055 (day), £7,090 (boarding); Years 9–13: £5,300 (day), £7,990 (boarding); New Sixth Form entrants: £5,575 (day), £8,255 (boarding).

Scholarships and Bursaries. (*See Scholarship Entries section.*) There are scholarships and exhibitions, limited to £750 and £400 respectively, awarded each year for exceptional ability in academic work, music, art and drama. Bursaries are awarded on the basis of a means-tested assessment.

Charitable status. Frensham Heights Educational Trust is a Registered Charity, number 312052. It exists to provide high quality education for boys and girls.

George Heriot's School

Lauriston Place, Edinburgh EH3 9EQ

Tel:	0131 229 7263
Fax:	0131 229 6363
e-mail:	enquiries@george-heriots.com
website:	www.george-heriots.com

Heriot's Hospital was founded in 1628 to care for the fatherless sons of Edinburgh burgesses. Today it is a fully co-educational day school, deeply rooted in the Scottish tradition.

The School is attractively situated in its own grounds close to the city centre and within easy walking distance of bus and rail terminals. A number of bus routes also service the School. Edinburgh Castle forms a magnificent backdrop, and Edinburgh's flourishing financial centre, the University of Edinburgh, the College of Art, the National Library and the Royal Scottish Museum are located close by.

The original building, described as a "bijou of Scottish Renaissance Architecture", has been carefully preserved and, as a historic monument, is open at certain times to the public during school holidays. The Chapel, Council Room and Quadrangle are particularly notable.

Over the years a succession of new buildings has provided the full complement of educational facilities. The most recent additions include the purchase of an adjoining site to extend facilities. Similarly, improvements and additions have been made over the years to provide excellent sports fields and facilities at Goldenacre. The School has sole use of an outdoor centre in the Scottish Highlands.

Motto: '*I distribute chearfullie*'

Governors of George Heriot's Trust:

Chairman: M J Gilbert, CA
Vice-Chairman: A Paton, MCIBS, FRSA
Finance Convener: J D M Hill, CA
Education Convener: Dr P Sangster, MA, PhD
Buildings Convener: N M Irons, CBE, JP, DL
Foundationers' Convener: G Sydserff, BSc
Miss J Armstrong
Ms K Fitzgerald
Revd R Frazer, BD, PhD
Dr P Green, BSc, PhD
F Henderson
Councillor M MacLaren
G Robertson
Dr M W J Strachan
J Thomson

Business Director and Treasurer to George Heriot's Trust:
Mrs J A Alexander

Headmaster: A G Hector, MA

Headmaster's PA: Miss C Macleod

Head of Senior School: C D Wyllie, MA

Depute Headteachers, Senior School:
Mrs C W Binnie, BA
R C Dickson, MA
Mrs M Lannon, BA
K J Ogilvie, MA
Mrs M N Williams, MA, DipRSA

Chaplain: Mrs A G Maclean, BD, DCE

Art:
*Mrs A J E Thomson, BA
Miss J R Crabtree, MA
Mrs C M Fraser, BA
Ms N L Garrioch, BA
Mrs S L Jamieson, BA
Mrs C J McGirr, BA
Mrs S Rasmussen, BA

Biology:
Miss A McKenzie, BSc
Ms D Barnaby, BSc
Miss G E Davidson, BSc
Miss M E Gralewicz, BSc
Mrs G Lippok, DipEd
Mrs A Macleod, BSc
A A N Ramage, BSc
Mrs H Smith, BSc

Business Education:
*Miss K A Macnab, MA
Miss K C Coltart, BA
Mrs A Donaldson, BA
Miss M R Green, BA

Mrs M Lannon, BA
J Payne, BA

Chemistry:
*F I McGonigal, BSc
Mrs J Blaikie, HND
Mrs F Donaldson, BSc
Miss E L Maclean, BSc
J Wilson, BSc

Computing:
*J T Scott, BSc
A Semmler, BA
Ms J McColgan, MA
D A Proudfoot, BEng

Drama:
Mrs J H Douglas, BA
Miss K Henderson, MA

English:
*K Simpson, MA, LLB
R C Dickson, MA
N H Grant, MA
R Gray, MA, MSc

Mrs G K Hay, MA
Mrs D Keohane, MA, CIM Dip
P J Lowe, MA
Mrs M C Massie, BA, MA
Miss K H Morgan, MA
Dr A Neilson, MA
C D Wyllie, MA

Geography:
*Mrs A Hughes, MA
D Armstrong, BSc
Mrs S E A Harris, MA
Mrs A MacCorquodale, BSc
K J Ogilvie, MA
E Watson, BSc

History and Modern Studies:
*M A McCabe, MA, MTh, PhD, BD
Miss M Buchanan, MA
T J Clancey, MA
Ms A Connor, MA
Miss L P Robertson, MA
A Savage, MA
N R Seaton, MA
Miss T Peters, MA

Food, Health & Consumer Studies:
*Mrs J M Mitchell, DipHE

Support for Learning:
*Ms V Higson, BSc, DipSpLD
Mrs H R Fennell, BA
Mrs J Jackson, MA, MSc, PGCE, CPsych
Mrs H A Staines, MA
D Thain, BEd
Mrs M N Williams, MA, DipRSA

Mathematics:
*Miss F Findlay, BSc
G A Dickson, BSc
Mrs J H Dickson, BSc
Miss F Moir, BA
D C Porteous, BSc
P C Walker, BSc
Miss K Weir, BSc

Head of Junior School: D S Adams, BA

Deputy Head of Junior School: Mrs L M Franklin, MA

Depute Headteachers, Junior School:
Mrs H Murphy, BSc, MEd
Mrs K S O'Hagan, BEd
Mr D H Porteous, DipCe

Junior School Teachers (including Nursery):
Miss A Millar, MA
Miss H Bassam, BA, MSc
Mrs C Campbell, BEd
J Caton, MA
Mrs K Duncan, BSc
Mrs V E J Clark, MA
Mrs E S Clarke, DipEd, INSC
G Cockburn, BA
Mrs E S B Couper, DipEd
Miss C L Evans, BA
Mrs L Gilmour, BA
W Hamilton, BSc
Mrs G Happs, BEd

Modern Languages:
*M G Grant, BA
Mrs C W Binnie, BA
Ms C Boscher, MA
Ms E Bottaro, MA
Ms E M Brown, MA
F Hédou, DEUG, MA
Ms E R Mackie, MA
Mrs D M Mullen, BA
Mrs J M Semple, MA
Miss E Sinclair, MA

Music:
*G C W Brownlee, BA, LLCM, ALCM
Mrs J Buttars, BA
Mrs S C Lovell, DRSAMD
G D Maclagan, BMus
Mrs R S J Weir, BMus

PE/Games:
*M Mallinson, BEd
Miss L Blackadder, BSc
G Hills, BEd
Mrs N Kesterton, BEd
Mrs G Mollison, BEd
Mrs K F Rutherford, BEd
R Stevenson, BEd
K M Yuille, DipPE

Physics:
*R M Bush, BSc
Miss R D Connell, BSc
Dr M Crawford, BSc, PhD
Ms W C Morgan, BSc
I Oliphant, BSc

Philosophy, Religious and Classics Education:
*R H Simpson, BD, MTheol
Mrs L Beilby, MA
D Carnegie, BA
Mrs A G Maclean, BD

Design & Technology:
*Mrs E L Watson-Massey, BSc
Miss A Hoban, BA
I Purves, BEd
D W Urquhart, HNDEng, DipTechEd, CertEdComp

Miss E Hay, MA
Miss A Hogg, BA
Mrs B I S Hunt, BEd
Ms A Josiffe, BA
Mrs J Naysmith, BSc
Miss H Oliver, MA
Miss A Pattullo, BEd
G Rand, MA
Mrs L Reid, MA
Miss S L Simpson, BSc
P Swierkot, BA
B Tyler, BSc
Miss L Waddell, MA
R J Waters, MA

I J A S Woolley, DipEd

Enrichment:
Miss J Attenborough, BEd
Mrs E S B Couper, DipEd
Ms S G Gallacher, BA

F N Huda, BSc
Mrs J A Mulholland, BSc
Miss S L Simpson, BSc
Mrs L J Smith, BA
Mrs S Wilken, BEd

Our aim is to introduce all our pupils to the broadest possible spectrum of academic, spiritual, cultural and sporting interests and experiences, which will enable them as articulate, self-reliant adults to play a full part in an ever-changing society.

Heriot's has long enjoyed a reputation for academic excellence, and we strive to help pupils to attain the highest possible level of competence. In the same spirit, every pupil is encouraged to participate in an extensive array of extra-curricular activities. We value sporting achievement, particularly in team games, and we encourage activity in art, music and design. In addition, pupils are introduced to religious, moral and philosophical concepts in the search for the answers to the more abstract questions that life poses.

The Nursery (32 children). The Nursery accommodates children in their pre-school year. It is part of the Early Years Department. Admission to the Nursery is open to all.

The Junior School (615 pupils). The Junior School curriculum enshrines the central aims of Curriculum for Excellence, with a focus on academic rigour and solid subject content, particularly with regard to literacy, numeracy and science, and great is taken over the academic progression of our Junior School pupils into the Senior School. Art, Drama, Modern Languages, Music and all areas of Physical Education are taught by specialists, and Junior School staff liaise closely with their secondary colleagues to provide curricular continuity throughout a pupil's time here.

A very active Junior School extra-curricular programme includes music, drama, adventure weeks and support for charities.

The Senior School (1010 pupils). For the first two years a system of flexible streaming provides a broad curriculum for all. An extensive choice of subjects is available from S3 to S6 in preparation for Scottish Qualifications Agency examinations at every level. Most pupils stay on for a Sixth Year and proceed to university or other forms of tertiary education.

Our vast Senior School extra-curricular programme is designed to suit all interests and abilities, and it provides recreation, enjoyment and excellence. Pupils achieve national and international recognition in their chosen activities, and many Former Pupils have pursued their interests with similar success in adult life.

Music and drama are very strong. Performances are given annually in our two halls, our Chapel, in the adjoining Greyfriars Church, in the Usher Hall and other venues.

The CCF is active and thriving, our Duke of Edinburgh's Award Scheme is one of the largest in Scotland, and an award winning Voluntary Service programme is a key feature of the Sixth Year at Heriot's. The main sports are cricket, cross-country running, hockey, rowing, rugby and tennis but most other sports are available in school or at Goldenacre.

Heriot's enjoys a reputation as a caring community. The greatest importance is given to pastoral care and a sophisticated careers advisory programme is in place. The Support for Learning Department provides invaluable help to all Junior School and Senior School pupils, be it that they have a specific learning difficulty or are outstandingly gifted.

Admission. Admission (other than for Nursery) is by assessment or examination. Application for occasional places is welcome at any time, but for the main stages should normally be submitted by the end of November.

Fees per annum (2011-2012). Junior School: £6,445 (Nursery, P1 & P2), £7,827 (P3 to P7). Senior School: £9,670.

A limited number of Bursaries is available from P1 to S6 and there are Scholarships for entry at S1. Fatherless and motherless children may qualify for free education and other benefits through the Foundation and James Hardie Bursaries. Full information is available from the Treasurer on request.

The Heriot Club. *Secretary*: E Allan, 10 McLaren Road, Edinburgh EH9 2BH.

Charitable status. George Heriot's Trust is a Registered Charity, number SC011463. It exists to provide education for children.

Giggleswick School

Giggleswick, Settle, North Yorkshire BD24 0DE
Tel: 01729 893000 Headmaster's Office
           01729 893012 Bursar's Office
Fax: 01729 893150
e-mail: enquiries@giggleswick.org.uk
website: www.giggleswickschool.co.uk

Giggleswick School, founded by 1512, was granted a charter by Edward VI on 26 May, 1553, at the instance of John Nowell, then Vicar of Giggleswick, and one of the King's Chaplains.

The Governing Body:
Chairman: M H O'Connell Esq, BA, FCA
Vice-Chairman: Miss L M Campbell, OBE, BEd

Dr A M Bowie, MA, DPhil
R A P Brocklehurst Esq, MA, MBA
Mrs S L Capstick
M H Crosby Esq, MA
Dr M Dörrzapf, DPhil
J L Ellacott Esq, MA
Miss S C Fox, BMus, ARCM
Mrs H J Hancock, MA
Mrs G M Harper
The Rt Revd and The Rt Hon Lord Hope of Thornes, KCVO
Miss A L Hudson, MA, MRICS
The Hon W J Kay-Shuttleworth, BA
D S Lowther, Esq, BA
A R Mullins, BSc, MBA, ACA
¶His Honour Judge D A Stockdale Esq, QC, MA
P J S Thompson Esq, LLB, Hon D Laws, MCI Arb

Headmaster: **G P Boult**, BA Hons Dunelm, PGCE

Deputy Head: N A Gemmell, BA
Assistant Head: Ms S L Williamson, BA
Director of Studies: Miss A L Wood, MA

Assistant Staff:
* *Head of Department*
† *Housemaster/mistress*

G Wigfield, CertEd	Mrs A L Coward, MA
S Heap, BEd	*Mrs S C Watts-Wood, BA
*Mrs C Gemmell, BEd	*Mrs M M Davidson, BA
†A J Scholey, BSc	C A Meneses, BA
†Mrs E J Wharton, BA	*A Simpson, BEd
*Mrs J E Farmer, BA	*R M Taylor, BSc
†J P Bellis, BA	Miss E M Rowles, BA
*C D Knight, BA	M D Pugh, BSc
†P C R Andrew, BEng,	*J G Warburton
AMIEE	†A J Pickles, BA
Mrs L M Stott	Miss S J Clarke, BEd
*P K Hucknall, BSc, PhD	*J M Curry, BSc
*J Huxtable, BA	D P Swift, BA
*†W S Robertson, BA	Mrs K R Haynes, MA
P Adams, MBA	*C D Richmond, BSc, MA
*N M Walker, BSc, PhD	*D C Everhart, BA, MA

Revd J E Bavington, BA
S C Griffiths, MSc
Miss J C Landon, BA
Miss H K Lindley, BA
D H Arkell, BA, LRSM
Miss J A Birch, BSc
Mrs D A Taylor, BA
D N Muckalt, BSc
Miss M H Bourne, BSc

J M C Giles, BA
C W D Marsh, BA
D H Morris
C D P Wright, BSc, PhD
A J Ladds, BD
Mrs L J R Ladds, BA
P A Keron, BSc, MSc
Miss K A S Howard, BA

Bursar and Clerk to the Governors: G R Bowring, Esq, MA
Marketing Director: Mrs S Hird
Headmaster's Secretary & Registrar: Mrs D M Lambert

Junior School
Head: M S Brotherton, BEd Hons, NPQH

F D G Ogilvie, BEd
Miss J A Middleton, BA
Ms G C Sismey, BA
Miss S M Butler, ALCM
J R Mundell, LLB
Miss P C Bagot, BA
Miss D A Horsman, BEd

Mrs N L McGoldrick, BA
Mrs H D Brotherton, BA
Mrs P Rees-Jones, BMus
Mrs J R Mahler, BA
Miss H Pritchard, BSc
Mrs L Shepherd
Mrs K Hall

Headmaster's Secretary: Mrs S E Driver

Giggleswick provides boarding and day education for about 400 boys and girls aged from 11–18. It also has its own Junior School for children aged 3–11. The School is situated in beautiful Yorkshire Dales' scenery, close to the borders of Cumbria and Lancashire and is an hour's drive from Leeds, Manchester and The Lakes. It can be reached from the M6 or M1 motorways or by rail via Settle or Giggleswick stations. Overseas students fly to Leeds/Bradford or Manchester Airports.

Senior School. For eleven year olds admission is usually based on performance in Giggleswick's own entrance examination. At thirteen, entrance is based on performance in the Common Entrance Examination for pupils in Preparatory Schools. However, for pupils being educated either abroad or in the maintained sector, other appropriate forms of assessment are used.

Admission direct to the Sixth Form is on the basis of reports and interviews, and is conditional upon the applicant obtaining a minimum of five GCSE passes with Grade B passes in subjects to be taken at AS/A Level. There are approximately 150 pupils in the Sixth Form. Generous Academic, Music, Art, Design & Technology, Drama, Sport and All-Rounder Scholarships are available for entry to Year 7, Year 9 and L6.

Boarding. 65% of Senior School pupils are boarders and the School's routine is entirely geared to boarding education. There are seven Houses, four for boys and two for girls in Years 9–U6, with 50–60 pupils in each, and one for boys and girls in Year 7–8. The Housemaster or Housemistress is responsible for the well-being and progress of pupils in the House and is assisted by House Tutors.

Most Sixth Formers have their own Study Bedroom; other pupils share Study Bedrooms or small Study Dormitories.

Day Pupils. Day pupils are fully integrated with boarders; they arrive before Morning Assembly, share studies and use all School facilities. They have lunch and tea at School and return home after prep. There are bus services from Skipton, Grassington, Colne and Kirkby Lonsdale.

Courses of Study. From Years 7–9 the curriculum comprises English, French, German, Spanish, Mathematics, Sciences, History, Geography, Arts (including Drawing and Ceramics), Music, Drama, Technology (including Home Economics, Graphics and Design), Religious Studies, Physical Education (Gymnastics and Swimming) and PSHE. In Years 10 and 11 a pupil chooses 9 or 10 subjects leading to the GCSE examinations.

In the Sixth Form, a pupil normally studies four subjects leading to GCE AS Level and three to A2 Level examinations. The subjects available are Mathematics, Further Mathematics, Physics, Chemistry, Biology, Business Studies, English, French, German, Classical Civilisation, Spanish, History, Geography, Art, Design, Music, Economics, Theatre Studies, PE and Information Technology.

Pupils are prepared for Oxford and Cambridge University Entrance.

Religion. The religious life of the School is supervised by a full-time resident Anglican Chaplain. At their own wish pupils may be prepared for Confirmation into the Church of England. Catholic pupils are excused certain Chapel services in order to attend Mass. The School respects and allows for other religious convictions.

Health. There is a surgery in the charge of a resident SRN with a Deputy who is also an SRN. The School Doctor visits regularly 4 or 5 days a week and is available in emergencies.

Games. In the Autumn Term the main games are rugby for boys and hockey for girls and in the Spring Term hockey for boys and netball for girls. In the Summer Term the main sports are cricket for boys and tennis for girls, but athletics, swimming, and tennis are available for boys and girls. In addition, there are excellent facilities for soccer, squash, fives, golf, badminton, basketball, netball, cross-country and fell running etc. There are regular overseas tours by the sports teams. Rugby and hockey teams toured Canada in Summer 2008. A netball tour went to Grenada in February 2007 and a cricket tour to Kenya in March 2007 and South Africa in Easter 2010. There is a Quincentenary Sports and Music tour to Australia planned for 2012.

Outdoor Education. This is an important part of the School's extra-curricular life. All pupils have introductory courses in map reading, orienteering and camp craft, and train for the Giggleswick Certificate at the end of Year 9. Many go on to the Silver Award and some each year to the Gold. Trained and qualified members of staff lead these activities.

Music. Tuition, given by four full-time musicians and a number of visiting teachers, is available in all keyboard and orchestral instruments. The Music School has excellent recital, rehearsal, teaching and practice rooms. Concerts are given by the School Orchestra, the Concert Band, Ensembles and the Choral Society. Concert tours have been undertaken in the USA, Holland, Prague and Italy.

Drama. There is a major production each year, as well as public performances of GCSE, AS and A Level work. Drama is a timetabled subject for Year 9 and the subject is offered at GCSE and A Level. The School has an extensive theatre wardrobe of its own. Drama tours are a regular feature of school life, the most recent being a Drama and Music Tour to Italy.

Art. The Art Department is fine-art-based concentrating on drawing, painting, print-making and ceramics. It boasts excellent examination results.

CCF. All pupils follow a structured course in Year 10, divided equally into military and non-military skills. The contingent has Army, RAF and Royal Marine Sections. At the end of the year, pupils may opt to leave or remain in the CCF. Advanced training is given in a variety of skills. The contingent fields strong teams for the District competitions and sends many cadets on further training at camp and on various courses.

Societies. There is a wide variety of societies. Sixth Formers have their own Social Centre.

Recent Developments. More than £13m has been invested in facilities since 1999, including a new dining hall, a Learning and Information centre, a floodlit synthetic hockey pitch, a new Art School, completely refurbished Science laboratories and a Sports Hall. In 2010 the Richard Whiteley Theatre was opened.

Careers Advice and Staff-Parent Conferences. Two experienced Careers Advisors supplement the advice of House Staff and Heads of Academic Departments in guiding academic choices and career decisions. The School is a member of ISCO and uses the ISLO/Morrisby Scheme of Careers Education and guidance. Regular Staff-Parent conferences are held at School to enable discussion of pupils' past, present and future progress and needs. Parents are always welcome at other times, especially at Chapel, sports fixtures, concerts, plays, etc.

Junior School. Giggleswick Junior School stands in its own grounds on a site adjacent to the Senior School. It has its own staff but also has the advantage of specialist teachers and facilities of the Senior School. Recent improvements include a new Library, teaching and IT centre and a new Sports Hall. There is a Nursery for children aged 3 and above.

Admission is possible at any age between 3–11. At eleven, pupils transfer in the Autumn Term to the Senior School, enjoying continuity of environment, curriculum and friendships.

(*For further information see Giggleswick Junior School entry in IAPS section.*)

Entrance. Most pupils enter in the September term, but a few are admitted in January and April. Registration fee £150 (Senior), £50 (Junior).

Entrance Scholarships. (*See Scholarship Entries section.*)

Fees per term (2011-2012). The fees are fully inclusive. Senior School: Boarders £6,395 (Years 7 & 8), £8,980 (Years 9–U6); Day Pupils £4,995 (Years 7 & 8), £6,150 (Years 9–U6). Junior School: Boarders £5,410, Day Pupils £2,115–£4,410.

Further details are available in the Prospectus which may be obtained from the Headmaster, to whom applications for entry should be made.

Charitable status. Giggleswick School is a Registered Charity, number 1109826. It exists to provide education for boys and girls.

The Glasgow Academy

Colebrooke Street, Glasgow G12 8HE
Tel: 0141 334 8558
Fax: 0141 337 3473
e-mail: enquiries@theglasgowacademy.org.uk
website: www.theglasgowacademy.org.uk

Founded in May 1845, The Glasgow Academy is the oldest independent school in the west of Scotland. Its affairs are managed by the Glasgow Academicals' War Memorial Trust, formed to commemorate the 327 former pupils killed in the war of 1914–18.

It has been co-educational since 1991 when it joined forces with Westbourne School for Girls. More recently, its mergers with Atholl Preparatory School in Milngavie and Dairsie House School in Newlands have contributed to its enduring success as a school covering the whole of west central Scotland. Parents now have a choice of three locations for their children in the popular Nursery to Prep 4 age group. Children from Atholl and Dairsie transfer to the main Academy site at Kelvinbridge at Prep 5.

Motto: '*Serva Fidem.*'

Chairman of Governors: JG Jack, MA, CA, CTA

Honorary Governors:
Sir Matthew D Goodwin, CBE, CA
Sir Angus M M Grossart, CBE, LLD, DLitt, FRSE, DL, DBA, MA, LLB, CA, FRSA, FCIBS
A L Howie, CBE, FRAgS
Sir Jeremy Isaacs, MA, DLitt, LLD, FRSA, FRSAMD, FGSM, Com de l'Ordre des Arts et des Lettres France, Mem Ordre pour le Mérite France
The Lord Kerr of Kinlochard, GCMG, MA, LLD St Andrews, LLD Glasgow
Professor Sir Malcolm Macnaughton, MD, LLD, FRCOG, FRCP, FRSE
W M Mann, CA
Professor Sir David Mason, CBE, LLD, BDS, MD, FRCS, FDS, FRCPath, FRSE
C Miller Smith, MA, ACCA, LLD
The Very Revd Dr William J Morris, KCVO, DD, LLD
A D S Rolland, CA, FRCPS Glasgow
Dr Murray Stuart, CBE, MA, LLB, CA, DUniv, FCT, FRSA
Professor Norman Stone, MA
C W Turner, BSc, AKC
The Lord Vallance of Tummel, MSc, DSc, DTech, DBA, DEng

Nominated and Elected Governors:
L M Crawford
B G Duncan, MBA, MRICS
Dr H J Grierson, BSc, BArch, MSc, CABD, DipAAS, ARB, FHEA
G W Henry, CA
J G Jack, MA, CA, CTA
M J Lee, MA
Dr M J McDonald, MBChB, MRCP, FRCPath
Dr G I McLaren, MBChB
R I McNaught, BAcc, CA
Mrs N Mahal, MA, DCG
H A Millar
I G Shankland, CA, MCT
Prof M Siddiqui, BA, MA, PhD, DLitt, DLitt, DCL, FRSE, FRSA (*University of Glasgow*)
W Sinclair, MA, MFB, MIDE, MIOD, MSExpE, MICM, MAPS
I R Spinney, BA Hons, PGDip PR, PG Dip Marketing
Sheriff A E Swanson
I M Veitch, BAcc, CA, FCIBS

Secretary: T W Gemmill, LLB, NP

Rector: **P J Brodie**, MA Oxon, MA Management of Education, Canterbury Christ Church University College

Deputy Rector: Mr G W Horgan, BA Oxon

Assistant Rectors:
Dr J Andrews, BSc Glasgow, PhD London
A L Evans, BSc Strathclyde
B P Farrelly, MA Glasgow

Heads of Department:
English: Mrs A F Watters, MA St Andrews
Mathematics: Mrs L S Moon, BSc Southhampton, CMath, FIMA, CertGuid
Classics: S A A McKellar, MA Glasgow
Modern Languages: Mrs E B Holland, MA Glasgow
History & Modern Studies: S M Wood, MA St Andrews
Biology: J M Shields, BSc Glasgow
Physics: S M Brunton, BSc Glasgow
Chemistry: Mrs F M Macdonald, BSc, MSc Bristol
Geography & Geology: W Robertson, BA Dunelm
Economics & Business Studies: Mrs S McKenzie, MA Glasgow, PGDip BusAdmin Strathclyde
Computing Science: Ms J E McDonald, MA Glasgow
Drama: N J Millar, BA Queen Margaret, Edinburgh
Physical Education:
Mrs S M Crawford, DCE Jordanhill, DipPE Dunfermline, PGDip Guid Glasgow (*Head of Games*)
S W McAslan, BEd Jordanhill (*Head of PE*)
Art/Craft & Design: J M McNaught, BA Glasgow
Music: M B Marshall, BA Southampton, ARCO, DipMus
Outdoor Education: N C Gwynne, BSc Aberdeen

Learning Support: Mrs A A Harvie, BA Strathclyde,
PGDip Ind Admin Glasgow Caledonian
Careers: Mrs E F McCallum, MA Dundee, AccC Stirling,
PGDip Guid Glasgow
PSE: Mrs M T Muirhead, BA East Anglia, Dip Guid &
Pastoral Care Glasgow

Preparatory School:
Head: A M Brooke, BEd Southampton
Deputy Head: R Teall, BA York

Atholl:
Head: Miss J McMorran, DCE, PGDip, DipTEFL

Dairsie:
Head: Mrs S S McKnight, DCE Jordanhill, CPE
Dunfermline

After-School Care:
Childcare Manager: Mrs J Thompson, HNC Childcare &
Education

Chaplains:
Revd D J M Carmichael, MA, BD
Revd A Frater, BA, BD
Revd G Kirkwood, BSc, BD, PGCE
Revd S Matthews BD, MA
Revd J D Whiteford, MA, BD, Dip Soc Wk

Combined Cadet Force:
OC CCF: Lt Col G R M Anderson
SSI: WO2 C J Duff

Administration/Finance:
General Manager: Dr W R Kerr, FCIS, FCIM, FHCIMA,
PhD Strathclyde, MBA Glasgow, MSc Glasgow
Caledonian
Rector's PA: Ms E McGowan, BA Strathclyde
Administration Manager: Miss I Kovacs, BA Strathclyde
School Secretary: Mrs A M Farr
Database Coordinator/Administration Secretary: Mrs D
Hegedus, BA Budapest, MA Pecs

Development:
Director of Admissions and External Relations: M R
McNaught, MA Glasgow
Deputy Director of Development: M G Taylor, MA
Aberdeen

Organisation. The Preparatory School contains some
700 pupils (400 boys, 300 girls) between the ages of 3 and
11 and prepares pupils from the earliest stages for the work
of the Senior School. The Senior School contains 616 pupils
(338 boys, 278 girls). They are prepared for the National
Qualifications at Higher at the end of Fifth or Sixth year.
The Sixth Form provides courses in most subjects leading to
presentation at Advanced Higher. Pupils are prepared for
entrance to Oxford and Cambridge. The Academy has a fine
record both at Oxford and Cambridge and at the Scottish
Universities. The Academy aims to offer a unique combination of academic, musical, dramatic, sporting, extra-curricular, social and outdoor education opportunities, backed up
by a comprehensive pastoral care system.

Buildings. The magnificent main building contains
classrooms for the Senior School. A new purpose-built Preparatory School, open in Spring 2008, provides the most
modern of facilities, and has enabled enhanced accommodation for Nursery, Kindergarten, After School Care and
Senior School pupils. Physics, Chemistry and Biology are
housed in separate spacious buildings. As well as an Assembly Hall, Gymnasium and Sports Hall including miniature
Rifle Range, newer buildings for Music (1994) and Design
(1998) considerably enhance the Academy's facilities. A
comprehensive computer network linking all rooms
throughout the Prep and Senior Schools enables all pupils to
access the Internet, send Email or access facilities from
home. The Library is the centrepiece of the main building.

Music and Drama. Music tuition is offered in a wide
range of instruments. There are Senior, Junior and Theatre
Choirs, a Concert Band, Pipe Band, Brass Group, Percussion
Ensemble, Orchestra and various Prep School groups.
Large-scale drama productions take place regularly and are
supplemented by plays mounted by smaller groups.

Societies and Activities. These range from Public Speaking, Chess and Debating Societies to a Mountaineering
Club. Large numbers of pupils undertake each section of the
Duke of Edinburgh's Award and there is a thriving Young
Enterprise group. Residential education is an integral part of
the curriculum at various stages of both the Prep and Senior
schools. These experiences augment the PSE programme by
promoting team building and personal and social development through outdoor challenges.

Games. All pupils, unless exempted by a medical certificate, take part in Physical Education and Games. Teams represent the school in Rugby, Hockey, Cricket, Swimming,
Golf, Tennis, Athletics, Curling, Shooting and Squash.
Cross-Country running is also offered as an option.

Combined Cadet Force. The Academy has a strong voluntary contingent with RN, Army, Signals and RAF Sections. In addition there is a Pipe Band.

Childcare outside school hours. The Academy provides
care before and after school for its younger pupils. There is
also provision for children between the ages of 3 and 12
throughout the holidays.

Entrance. Pupils may be registered at any age. The main
entry points are (a) in the Preparatory School: age 3, 4 and
10; (b) in the Senior School: age 11 or 12 or for Sixth Form.
Bursaries are available for P7–S6.

Fees per term (2011–2012). Preparatory School: £2,330/
£2,535 (P1–P2), £2,575/£2,765 (P3–P5), £3,295 (P6–P7).
Senior School: £3,095 (S1–S2), £3,360 (S3–S5), £3,360
(Autumn & Spring Terms), £2,735 (Summer Term) (S6).

Charitable status. The Glasgow Academy is a Registered Charity, number SC015638. It exists to provide education for girls and boys.

The High School of Glasgow

637 Crow Road, Glasgow G13 1PL
Tel: 0141 954 9628
Fax: 0141 435 5708
e-mail: rector@hsog.co.uk
website: www.glasgowhigh.com

The new, independent, co-educational High School of
Glasgow came into being at Anniesland in 1976 following a
merger involving the Former Pupil Club of the High School,
a maintained school previously in the State system, and
Drewsteignton School in Bearsden.
Motto: '*Sursum semper*'.

Governing Body:
Honorary President: Lord Macfarlane of Bearsden, KT
Chairman: B C Adair, TD, LLB
Sheriff W Dunlop, LLB
P M A Forgie, MCIBS
Mrs P Galloway, FCA
R J A Hunter, CA
E W Hugh, CA
Mrs L Keith, MA, PGCE, ITQ
S J MacAulay
C M Mackie, BSc, FFA
D J Maclay, BSc, CA
J Y Miller, CA
Professor V A Muscatelli, MA, PhD, FRSE, FRSA
K M Revie, LLB Hons
Dr A C E Short, MBChB, FRCGP, DRCOG
G R White, BEd, MPhil

R M Williamson, MA, LLB, FRSA, FRSAMD

Rector: C D R Mair, MA

Senior Deputy Rector: J O'Neill, MA

Deputy Rectors:
M A M Brown, BEd
Mrs M E R Price, MA

Staff:
* *Head of Department*

English:
*P A Toner, MA
G Baynham, BA
Miss R A Davies, MA
†Mrs G R Fergusson, MA
P D C Ford, MA
T Lyons, MA
Mrs J Muir, MA
Miss K Murphy, BA
(*Drama*)
Mrs M E R Price, MA
Miss M Sabba, BA
(*Drama*)

Mathematics:
*P F Edmond, BSc
Mrs C V M Anderson, BSc
Mrs A A Atherton, BSc
†J G MacCorquodale, BSc
P Moon, BSc
Mrs N Morrison, BSc
Mrs M C Reid, BSc
S Welsh, BEng

Computer Studies:
*D L McCorkindale, BEd
†N R Clarke, BSc
Miss N Fulton, BA
D Semple, BSc, MSc (*ICT Manager*)

Science:
A E Baillie, BSc (*Physics*)
K J A Robertson, BSc
(*Chemistry*)
N M E Dougall, MSc, BSc
(*Biology*)
Mrs L McGuigan, BSc
Mrs A McNeil, BSc, MSc
Dr L A A Nicholl, BSc, PhD
Mrs K S M O'Neil, BSc
Dr N J Penman, BSc, PhD
I J Smith, BSc

Modern Languages:
*M H Bennie, MA
†Mrs J M Horne, MA
N F Campbell, MA, LLB
Mrs V MacCorquodale, MA
Miss K J McAllister, BA
Mrs H O'Driscoll, BA, MA, MPhil
Mrs K Evans, MA
Mrs A M T Drapeau-Magee, L-ès-L, M-ès-L
Ms C Kusian, MA

Classics:
*A H Milligan, MA
Mrs M H S Campbell, MA
C McCay, LLB, MLitt

Economics and Business Studies:
*T J Jensen, MEd, BComm
Mrs E A Milne, BA, MCIBS

Geography and Modern Studies:
*Miss N Cowan, MA
J O'Neill, MA
Mrs L McFarlane, BSc
K F FitzGerald, BSc
Miss J A McAteer, BA
Mrs E M Paton, BSc

History:
*G K Sinclair, MA
R J Broadbent, BA, MEd
(*Careers*)
Miss N Sutherland, MA
Miss G A Clare, MA

Art:
*P J Gilchrist, BA
Mrs C J Bell, BA
Mrs J F MacKechnie, DA

Home Economics:
*Mrs S M K Slatford, DipDomSci
Mrs C Cammidge, DipHE, MBA

Learning Support:
*Mrs R E Hamilton, BA
Mrs N Morrison, BSc

Music:
*P S Douglas, DRSAMD
L D Birch, BA, LRAM, DRSAMD
M Duncan, DRSAMD
D R Fleming, BMus
Ms W MacDougall, MMus, BA, LLCM TD
N G McFarlane, BA
R McKeown, DRSAMD
F Walker, BA, ARCO
Mrs J Tierney, BMus

Religion & Philosophy:
*C F Price, MTheol
Miss G A Clare, MA

Physical Education:
*D N Barrett, BEd
Mrs A Cox, BEd (*Girls' PE*)
M A M Brown, BEd
K F FitzGerald, BSc
Mrs R Owen, BEd
Mrs B A Bell, DPE
Mrs S Dougan, BEd
Mrs M Gillan, DPE
Mrs M Jefferies, DPE
S Leggat, BEd
Mrs C MacKay, BEd

Mrs S Mitchell, BEd
Mrs M Stevenson, DPE
R Dalrymple, BEd
C Muir, BEd

Junior School Staff:
Head Teacher: Mrs K R Waugh, BA, DCE
Mrs A M Gray, DCE (*Deputy Head*)
Mrs A Kiyani, BEd, Masters in TEYL (*Deputy Head, Early Years*)
Mrs C Brown, NNEB
Miss C E Carnall, BMus, MMus (*Music*)
Mrs A J Coutts, BEd
Mrs A M T Drapeau-Magee, L-ès-L, M-ès-L (*French*)
Mrs S A Foster, MA
Mrs E Gibson, BEd
Mrs M J Gillan, DPE, Dip Sfl,ATQ
Mrs W Gray, Dip Ed
Mrs C M Jaberoo, BA, MSc
Mrs J Jackson, Dip Prim Ed
S Leggat, BEd (*Physical Education*)
Mrs E J McConechy, BEd (*Physical Education*)
Mrs E McCormick, DipEd
Mrs S E MacDougall, DCE, ACE
Mrs I McNeill, DA (*Art*)
Mrs L MacRae, BA (*Drama*)
Mrs J Moir, DCE
Mrs M Moreland, Dip Prim Ed
Mrs J O'Neill, NNEB
Mrs C Ritchie, DCE
Miss H M Scott, BEd
Miss I Skinner, MSc (*Principal Teacher*)
G J Walker, BSc
Mrs M Watt, DCE

Bursar: Mrs J M Simpson, BAcc, CA

Rector's Secretary: Miss J Mackay

Buildings. The Senior School occupies modern purpose-built buildings at Anniesland on the western outskirts of the city immediately adjacent to twenty-three acres of playing fields. The Junior School is in the extended and modernised former Drewsteignton School buildings in Bearsden about three miles away. New facilities opened during the last few years include a purpose-built Science extension, a Junior School extension, a Drama Studio, a Refectory, a Fitness Centre, a Grandstand and an Information and Communications Technology building.

Organisation. The School is a day school with about 1,044 boys and girls. The Junior School, which includes a pre-school Kindergarten, has some 367 pupils (ages 3–10). Primary 7 pupils are included in the Senior School which has about 677 pupils (ages 11–18). A general curriculum is followed until the Third Year of the Senior School when, with the Standard Grade and Intermediate 2 examinations of the Scottish Qualifications Authority in view, a measure of choice is introduced. In Fifth Year Higher examinations are taken and in Sixth Year courses for Advanced Highers are offered. Whilst the majority of pupils are aiming for the Scottish universities, places are regularly gained at Oxford, Cambridge and other English universities.

Throughout the School, time is allocated to Art, Music, Personal, Social and Health Education, Physical Education and Religion and Philosophy. All pupils will also take courses in Computing Studies, Drama and Home Economics at various stages in their school careers.

Games. The main sports are hockey, rugby, athletics, cricket, tennis and swimming. Pupils participate in a wide variety of other sports, including badminton, basketball, netball, volleyball, golf, cross-country running and skiing.

Activities. Pupils are encouraged to participate in extra-curricular activities. Clubs and societies include debating, Scripture Union groups, computer, table tennis, chess, art, bridge, chemistry, electronics, drama and film clubs. Pupils take part in the Duke of Edinburgh's Award Scheme and the Young Enterprise Scheme, and parties regularly go on tour.

There are choirs, orchestras, jazz and concert bands and a pipe band and tuition in Instrumental Music is arranged as requested. Each year there are several concerts and dramatic productions.

Admission. Entrance tests and interviews are held in January. The principal points of entry are at Kindergarten (age 4), Junior 1 (age 5), Transitus (age 11) and First Year (age 12) but pupils are taken in at other stages as vacancies occur.

Fees per term (2011-2012). Junior School: £1,076–£2,848; Senior School: £2,885–£2,957.

Bursaries. The School operates a Bursary Fund to give assistance with fees in cases of need.

Former Pupils' Club. The Glasgow High School Club Limited is the former pupils' association of the old and new High Schools. Former pupils all over the world maintain an interest in the life and work of the School. *Secretary*: Murdoch C Beaton, LLB.

Charitable status. The High School of Glasgow Limited is a Registered Charity, number SC014768. It is a recognised educational charity.

Glenalmond College

Glenalmond, Perth PH1 3RY
Tel: 01738 842061
       Admissions Office: 01738 842056
Fax: 01738 842063
e-mail: registrar@glenalmondcollege.co.uk
website: www.glenalmondcollege.co.uk

Glenalmond College, was founded by Mr W E Gladstone and others in 1841 and opened as a School in 1847.
   Motto: '*Floreat Glenalmond*'

Council:
*President of Council: The Primus of the Episcopal Church in Scotland, The Most Reverend David Chillingworth, Bishop of St Andrews, Dunkeld & Dunblane
*Chairman of Council: F E Gerstenberg Esq, BA, MA (*OG*)
*Chairman of Committee of Council: H J Morgan Esq, MA, FSI (*OG*)
The Earl of Home, CVO, CBE
*I R Wilson Esq, CBE
A H Primrose Esq, BA, LLB (*OG*)
Lady Menzies, MBAOT
*D J C MacRobert Esq, LLB (*OG*)
The Right Hon Lord Kingarth, PC, BA, QC (*OG*)
C A Campbell Esq
*D G Sibbald Esq, BArch Hons, RIBA, FRIAS (*OG Club Secretary*)
Prof J G Houston, MA, MD, FRCP, FRCR (*OG*)
Mrs C S C Lorenz, AA Dipl
J M Squire Esq, MBA, MSc
Dr The Hon E C Walker, MA, MBChB, MRCGP
T M Walker Esq, MA, CA (*OG Club Chairman*)
Rt Revd M Strange, The Bishop of Moray, Ross & Caithness
J V Light Esq, MA

* *Committee of Council*
(*OG*) Old Glenalmond

Warden: G C Woods, MA Oxon, PGCE

Sub-Warden: J P Owen, MA, BSc, FRSC, CChem, PGCE
Deputy Head – Academic: Dr S N Kinge, BSc, PhD
Senior Tutor: R D Gower, MA Oxon, FRCO Chm, LRAM, ARCM, FRSA, PGCE
Registrar: J B M Poulter, MA Cantab, PGCE
Chaplain: The Revd G W Dove, MA, MPhil, BD
Director of Finance and Secretary to the Council: Ms L A Kennedy, BA, CA

Director of Development and Alumni Relations: Mrs M Marshall, MBA, MInstF Cert
Head of Marketing: Ms L M Nowell, BA, DipM, Dip DigM, MCIM
Bursar: Lt Col K H Montgomery, BSc, MBA, MCMI, MInstRE, MBIFM
Child Protection Officer: Ms M Trygger, BA, PGCE
Matron: Mrs J Duguid, RGN

Teaching Staff:
* *Head of Department*
† *Housemaster/mistress*

English:
*M Watson, BA, PGCE
J D Byrom, MA Oxon, PhD
Mrs A J Haylock, BEd, MA
J D G Lugton, MA, PGCE
Miss V M Dryden, BA, PGDE

Mathematics:
*Mrs H Yorston, BSc, MSc, PGCE
M T Jeffers, BSc, PGCE (*†Reid's*)
M Allnutt, BSc, CertEd (*Director of Studies*)
S P Erdal, BSc, PGCE
Mrs S Sinclair, BSc, PGCE (*†Lothian*)
M A Orviss, MA Cantab, PGCE
W G R Bain, MA Cantab, PGCE

Classics:
*J D Wright, MA Oxon
G W J Pounder, MA Oxon, PGCE (*†Matheson's*)
Mrs K A Watson, BA

Modern Foreign Languages:
*Mrs J Davey, MA, PGCE
J A Gardner, BA, PGCE
J B M Poulter, MA Cantab, PGCE
P A R Shelley, BA, MPhil Oxon, MIL
I L McDonald, MA, PGCE
Mrs K A Watson, BA Hons (*†Home*)

Geography:
*Miss K Platt, BSc, PGCE
Mrs G Hamilton, BSc, MSc, PhD
C S Swaile, MA, PGCE
Ms M Trygger, BA, PGCE (*†Cairnies*)

History:
*R R Mundill, MA, PhD, PGCE, DipEd, FIHGS
A Norton, BA, BEd
L W R Rattray, MA, MLitt, PGDE

Biology:
*C G Henderson, BSc, PhD
Mrs N Henderson, BSc, PGCE
Dr S Colby, BSc, PhD, PGCE
A C Hughes, BSc, PGCE

Chemistry:
*Dr T S Wilkinson, BSc, PhD, PGCE
J P Owen, MA, BSc, FRSC, CChem, PGCE (*Sub-Warden*)
J Stewart, BSc, PhD, CertEd
Miss T T McLaughlin, BSc, PGCE

Physics:
*R Benson, BSc, PGCE
Mrs N Henderson, BSc, PGCE
Dr S Kinge, BSc, PhD
Mrs Jo Hanson, BSc, PGCE
D M Smith, BSc, MEng, PGCE

Economics and Business Studies:
*J C Robinson, BA, PGCE
S P Erdal, BSc, PGCE, DipAcc
P J Golden, BSocS, EEP Z, PGCE (*†Goodacre's*)

Computing:
*Mrs I Cox, BA, PgD, DipEd

W A S MacAulay, BA, PgD
G Collins HND

Politics:
*A Norton, BA, BEd

Drama:
*C D B Youlten, BA, PGCE (*Head of Academic Theatre Studies*)
*Miss L Kirk, RSAMD, PGCE (*Head of Drama and Performance*)

Music:
*T J W Ridley, GRSM, PhD, LRAM, FRSA
R D Gower, MA Oxon, FRCO Chm, LRAM, ARCM, FRSA, PGCE
B J Elrick, LLB

Art and Design:
*B Wang, BA, MA
Mrs C V Norton, BA
B Whitten, BA, CertEd
Miss N Kitchin, BA, PGCE

History of Art:
*B Whitten, BA, CertEd

Divinity and Religious Studies:
*Revd G W Dove, MA, MPhil, BD

Library and Archives:
Mrs E Mundill, MA, DipLib, MCILIP, Cert TM, TESOL

Design Technology:
*A A Purdie, BSc, BEd
W G R Bain, MA Cantab, PGCE
Miss N Kitchin, BA, PGCE

Physical Education:
*M J Davies, BA, PGCE (*Director of Sport*)
Miss C Bircher, BEd
H G Thomas, BSc (*†Patchell's*)
Miss G Douglas, BPE

Learning Support:
Mrs P Gower, MA Oxon, BSc, DipSpLD, CCET
I Young, BSc, PGCE
Mrs N Henderson, BSc, PGCE
Mrs E Critchley, Montessori Diploma

English as an Additional Language:
J A Gardner, BA Hons, PGCE
Mrs K A Watson, BA
Mrs M Gardner, BA, PGDE

The College is built on the south bank of the River Almond, from the north bank of which rise the Grampian mountains. It is about 50 miles north of Edinburgh and 10 miles from both Perth and Crieff.

The College Buildings, grouped round a cloistered quadrangle, comprise the Chapel, Hall, Library, houserooms and studies, study bedrooms, classrooms and laboratories. A separate block houses additional laboratories and a Theatre. A few metres away are the Art School and the Design and Technology Centre. Next to these are the Music practice rooms and a Concert Hall.

The Sports Complex consists of squash courts, a gymnasium, an indoor sports hall and a heated indoor swimming pool and fitness suite.

The College also has a state-of-the-art Science Block and IT Resources Centre.

Houses. There are 5 houses for boys, and 3 for girls. Each house has married accommodation for resident Housemaster or Housemistress. Senior boys and girls have study-bedrooms of their own.

Religion. The College has an Episcopalian foundation and has a splendid Chapel. However pupils from a wide range of ethnic, religious and cultural backgrounds are welcomed; the needs of other religious groups and recognised faiths will be observed and supported.

Admission. In line with the College's foundation and tradition, entry to Glenalmond is academically selective. Boys and girls may be registered for admission at any time after birth and enter the College between the ages of 13 and 14 via the Common Entrance Examination or Entrance Scholarship papers. Pupils leaving Primary Schools may qualify by tests and examinations for junior entry at age 11 or 12. Girls and boys may also qualify for entry into the Lower Sixth, or at other points during their school career. Boarding and Day pupils are accepted throughout the school.

For those applying from overseas, or whose first language is not English, we expect, as a minimum, an Intermediate standard of written and spoken English (IELTS Grade 4 or equivalent).

Curriculum. In the 2nd and 3rd Form (Years 8 and 9, S1 and S2) all pupils take a vast range of subjects including English, Mathematics, History, Geography, French, Spanish or German, Latin or Ancient Civilisation, Biology, Chemistry, Physics, Technology, Music, PSHCE, Drama, Art and ICT. In the 4th and 5th Form pupils may choose three options, including Greek, along with the core subjects of Mathematics, English Language and Literature, French and the three Sciences. Each pupil is guided by an academic tutor who meets regularly with their tutor group.

The Sixth Form curriculum is designed to allow pupils as wider choice as possible with 24 A Level subjects being offered to AS and A2 Level ranging from Business Studies and Music Technology to Physics and Philosophy. There are weekly lectures from outside speakers on social, economic and cultural subjects which foster academic excellence across the age ranges. The more able pupils are encouraged to join the William Bright Society which promotes cross year group discussion on relevant academic and moral issues.

Careers. Over 97% of pupils qualify for entry to university; some go direct to professional careers, industry, the Services, etc. Great emphasis is placed on careers guidance: careers talks, visits and advice along with a well-stocked careers room assist pupils in their choice. All pupils are encouraged to take psychometric careers aptitude tests at age 16.

The computer network with fibre optic cabling extends to all parts of the campus. ICT is available in libraries and all classrooms, and all pupils have access to e-mail and the internet within their Houses.

Art, Drama and Music. Music plays a central part in the life of the school: there is an Orchestra as well as smaller String, Woodwind and Brass Groups. A large Choir and Choral Society perform at the College, in Perth and in Edinburgh. A new Harrison and Harrison pipe organ supports Glenalmond's central Chapel tradition. The Concert Society arranges recitals and concerts at the College; frequent visits are made to concerts in Perth and elsewhere. There are currently two Pipe Bands.

The Drama and Art departments flourish, in conjunction with the well-established Design and Technology Centre. Both Art and Music as well as Design/Technology form part of the normal curriculum and can be taken at GCSE and A Level.

Sport and Recreation. Rugby (boys) and Hockey (girls) are played in the Michaelmas Term and there is a wide variety of activities to choose from in the Lent Term, including Lacrosse and Netball for girls and Hockey, Football and Cross-Country for boys, with Cricket, Athletics, Shooting, Sailing, Tennis and Golf in Summer. Shooting on the Miniature Ranges takes place during the two winter terms. There is a large indoor heated Swimming Pool and pupils are trained in personal survival and Lifesaving. Instruction in Sub-aqua and Canoeing is given. There are also Squash Courts, Tennis Courts, a nine-hole (James Braid) Golf

Course, and two full-size all-weather pitches for hockey, netball and tennis.

During the Summer, pupils have the opportunity to explore the hills and the neighbouring countryside. There is also a Sailing and Windsurfing Club which uses a neighbouring loch. Weekend camping expeditions are arranged to encourage self-reliance and initiative.

Glenshee is just over an hour away and there are opportunities for skiing in the Lent Term.

Combined Cadet Force. There is a contingent of the Combined Cadet Force which has strong links with the Armed Forces and the Royal Regiment of Scotland (Black Watch Battalion) in particular. The ceremonial dress, as worn by the Pipe Band for example, is the Highland dress with the Murray of Atholl tartan.

Army and Air sections, with a Pre-Service section for Junior Pupils, are organised on the basis of the Duke of Edinburgh's Award. Shooting and Adventure Training figure prominently; pupils may also be engaged on Conservation, Community Service Work or Mountain Awareness Group.

Fees per term (2011-2012). £9,054 Boarders; £6,175 Day Pupils (for whom transport is arranged); £6,788 Junior Boarders; £4,630 Junior Day.

These fees include extras common to all pupils, such as membership of the CCF, Games, Subscriptions, journeys to matches, the use of the Golf Course, etc.

Term of Entry. Entry is normally in September. Entry in January or April can be considered where special circumstances exist.

Entrance Awards. (*See Scholarship Entries section.*) Open Academic and Art Scholarships and Exhibitions are awarded. Music Scholarships worth up to 50% of the fees are also available. All awards can be increased in case of need. The Examination for Scholarships is usually held in March for younger pupils and in November for entrants to the Sixth Form. All-Rounder/Outstanding Talent Awards are available to 13+ applicants and are assessed in March.

'Fil Cler' Bursaries. A number of *Fil Cler* Bursaries are available for sons and daughters of Clergy. The value of these is subject to a means test; they are awarded on the result of the Common Entrance or Scholarship Examination (or special qualifying tests) and an interview.

Services Discount. There is an Award available to the sons and daughters of serving members of the Armed Forces.

Discretionary Awards. These are awarded at the discretion of the College. They are means-tested.

The Old Glenalmond Club. *Hon Secretary*: D Sibbald, 21 Ravelston Park, Edinburgh EH4 3DX.

Charitable status. Glenalmond College is a Registered Charity, number SC006123. It exists for the all-round education of Boys and Girls in the tranquillity of a rural setting.

The Grange School

Bradburns Lane, Hartford, Northwich, Cheshire CW8 1LU

Tel: 01606 74007
Fax: 01606 784581
e-mail: office@grange.org.uk
website: www.grange.org.uk

The Grange was founded in 1933 as a Preparatory School, the Senior School opening in 1978. The School is co-educational, with 1,177 pupils from 4–18 years, and is situated in the village of Hartford, half an hour away from Chester and Manchester and eight miles from the M6 motorway.

Motto: *E Glande Robur*

Governing Body:
Chairman: Mr C Stubbs, CEng, MIMechE, MBA
Mrs A Arthur
Mr S Batey
Mr D M Dunn, BA
Dr W J Forsyth, MBChB, MRCGP, AFOM
Mr J Hobson, MRICS
Mrs S Hudson
Mr C P Jackson, BSc, MIHT
Mrs K Jones, BA, ACA
Mr N Parkinson, BSc
Mr J Stamer, FRCS
Mr A Stothert

Clerk to the Governors: Mr S Dorset, MBE

Head: **Mr C P Jeffery**, BA, FRSA

Deputy Head (*Staff & Pupils*): Mr A Testard, BA
Deputy Head (*Communications & Enrichment*): Mrs P Duke, BA
Deputy Head (*Academic*): Mr G Rands, BSc
Head of Sixth Form Studies: Mr A Reeve, BA York, MCIEA
PA to the Head/Admissions Secretary: Miss S Dickens
Bursar: Mrs J Pointon, ACA
Legal Manager: Mrs R Leaitherland, BA

Assistant staff:
* *Head of Department*

Mr P J Ackerley, BA (*English*)
Mrs N Beardsall, BA (*Art and Technology*)
Mrs J Bloor, BA (*Director of Performing Arts, *Speech & Drama*)
Mr A Boardman, MA (*History*)
Mrs B A Broderick, BSc (*Chemistry, Geography, *Outdoor Pursuits*)
Mrs E Brunsdon, BA (*Art*)
Mr P Buckley, BA (**Classics*)
Mrs V Buckley, BA (**Religious Studies, *Pastoral Support*)
Mrs J Corrigan, BA, CertEd (*PE & Games, English*)
Mrs K Cunningham, BA (*Economics*)
Mr N Cusick, BSc (*PE & Games*)
Ms S Finnegan, BMedSci (*Biology*)
Mr T H Giles, BA (*PE & Games*)
Mr M Goff, BA (*English*)
Mr P Grattage, BSc (*Director of Sport*)
Mr S Gray, BSc (*Mathematics*)
Mrs H Hackett, BA, MSc (*German & French*)
Mr N Hamer, BSc (*Biology*)
Mrs J Hardy-Kinsella, BA (*Drama & English*)
Mr R A Hibbert, BA (**Modern Languages*)
Mrs C Hill, BSc (**Mathematics*)
Mr R A Hough, BA (*Religious Studies, *Philosophy*)
Mr C Howe, BSc (**Chemistry*)
Mr S Howells, BA (**French*)
Mr M Hughes, BSc (*Biology*)
Ms P H Janson, MA (*Mathematics*)
Mr D W Jones, MA (*History & Politics*)
Mr G Jump (**Rowing*)
Mr H Kelly, MA (**English*)
Mr S Kenyon, BSc (*Geography*)
Mr D Kereszteny-Lewis, BA (*Director of Art & Design, *Art*)
Mrs V Kereszteny-Lewis, BA (**German*)
Mrs H Kerr, BA (*History, *Politics*)
Mr M Lambert, BSc (*Mathematics*)
Mrs O Langton, BA (*English*)
Mr R Latham, BA (*Religious Studies*)
Mrs G Lewis, BSc (*Mathematics*)
Miss J Linnell, BA (*Geography*)
Miss H R Lawson, BA (**Girls' Games*)
Mr B Madden, BA (*Music*)
Mr A Masters, BA (**ICT*)

Mr P McAleny, BA (*Graphic Design*)
Miss P Meehan, BA (*Spanish*)
Mr A J Millinchip, MA, FRCO CHM (*Director of Music*)
Mr A Milne, BSc, MSc (*Science, *Biology*)
Mr W Morrison, BA (*Economics & Business Studies*)
Mrs J S Oakes, BSc (*Biology*)
Mrs C J Osborne, BSc (*Mathematics*)
Mrs K Osorio, BA (*Spanish*)
Mr J M Pearson, BA (*Geography*)
Mr S Petts, BA (*Physics*)
Mrs M Plant, MA (*French & German*)
Miss J Popplestone, BSc (*History*)
Mr G Rands, BSc (*Biology*)
Mr A Reeve, BA (*Economics*)
Mr R K Robson, BA (*History*)
Miss C Scott, BA (*English*)
Mr G Sgroi, BA (*Classics*)
Miss S Sharp, BA (*Art*)
Mrs A Stewart (*Food & Nutrition*)
Mrs L Sunners, BA (*Drama*)
Mr B Sutton, BSc (*Mathematics, Physics*)
Mrs J Thayer, BSc (*Mathematics*)
Mrs S Thornes, BSc (*Physics*)
Miss S Thorp, BA (*Philosophy, Graphic Design*)
Mrs P Tideswell, BA (*French*)
Mr T W Tindale, BSc (*Physical Education*)
Mrs K Tomlin, BA (*Drama*)
Dr S Wharton, BSc (*Chemistry*)
Mr R Williams, BSc (*Chemistry*)
Miss H Yates, BSc (*Physics*)

Junior School

Head of Junior School: Mr S D Bennett, MA, BEd
Deputy Head of Junior School: Mrs K J Hill, BEd
Head of Pre-Prep: Miss A Evans, BEd
PA to the Headmaster/Admissions Secretary: Mrs M Shaw

Mrs A Basnett, BA	Mr D Heine, BSc
Mrs J Bradley, BA	Mrs V Houghton, MA, BEd
Mrs L Broster-Jones,	Mr D Jackson, BEng
CertEd	Mrs C Jones, BSc
Mrs D Bull, MEd	Mrs E Jones, CertEd, BEd
Mrs C Carson, CertEd	Mr H Jones, BEd
Mrs A Connolly, BEd	Mrs S Jones, BEd
Mrs A Copping, BA	Mr J P Land, BEd
Miss L Cruddas, BA	Miss J Lloyd, MA
Mrs K Dakin, BA	Mrs S Lucchesi, BA
Mrs R Davies, BA	Mrs Z A Pidcock, BA
Mrs M Dewhurst, BEd	Mrs J Ratcliffe, BEd
Miss H Elleray, BA	Ms T Richardson, BA
Mr G H Evans, BEd	Mrs G L Rosa, BA
Mrs J Haynes, BEd	Miss C Sales, BA
Mrs V Heath, BEd	Mrs A Taunton, MA

Peripatetic Staff:
Ms C Barker, BA, LGSM (*Cello*)
Mrs A Boardman, BMus, LEAM (*Clarinet, Saxophone*)
Mrs G Bolton, GMus RNCM Hons (*Piano*)
Miss J Bruce, BMus Hons, Grad RNCM, LLCM, ALCM
　(*Percussion & Drum Kit*)
Mrs M Bushnell-Wye, ARCM, LGSM, GRSM (*Clarinet,
　Saxophone*)
Mrs N Chapman, Dip RNCM (*Violin*)
Mrs A Duthie, CT ABRSM (*Flute*)
Mr C Gandee, ARCM, LLCM (*TD*), SFLCM (*Brass*)
Mrs B Hammond, BMus, PGCE (*Piano*)
Miss L Hibberd, BMus (*Piano*)
Mrs S Hoffman, BMus (*Flute*)
Mr G Hogan, BA, LRAM, LGSM, LLCM (*Keyboard,
　Piano*)
Mrs C Hughes, GNSM, ARCM (*Piano*)
Mr M Jackson, Grad Dip Jazz & Cont Music (*Guitar*)
Mr B Madden, BA (*Cello, Piano*)
Mrs J Martin, CT ABRSM (*Violin*)

Mrs R Pankhurst, BMus, GRNCM, PPRNCM, LRSM
　(*Oboe, Bassoon*)
Mr S Watkiss, CT ABRSM (*Guitar*)
Miss S Wilks, GMus RNCM (*Singing*)

The Kindergarten and Junior School (449 pupils).
1996 saw the opening of a brand new, purpose-built Kindergarten and Preparatory School for children aged 4–11. In 2010 an additional extension was added incorporating a sports hall, Music Department, Science, Design Technology and Art rooms. These developments have brought together all the children of this age group on to one attractively landscaped eleven acre site which is within walking distance of the Senior School. The main teaching takes place in 21 large, self-contained classrooms on two floors, with the younger children located on the ground floor separated from the older children. The school has its own extensive playing fields and generous play areas while three large halls provide facilities for dining, teaching, sports and school productions. Rooms are provided for specialist teaching in Science, Art, Design Technology and a Music Department with no fewer than 6 individual music practice rooms. As well as a broad curriculum, junior pupils study ICT and a modern language; they have regular swimming lessons and compete in sport with other schools. Close attention is given to each child's progress with two parents' evenings each year. Children learn to use computers from Kindergarten, there is a junior orchestra, and opportunities for private music and drama lessons. Extra-curricular activities are held both at lunchtimes and after school. Before and after school care is available from 7.30 am and until 5.45 pm during term time.

The Senior School (728 pupils). The pupils benefit from excellent extra-curricular and study facilities. There is an ambitious but realistic building programme which saw the opening of a state-of-the-art Science and Information Technology Centre in 2001. This superb facility complements such recent developments as a Modern Languages suite, including Language Laboratory and satellite television and new study and leisure facilities for the Sixth Form. A new teaching centre for the Mathematics Faculty was completed recently and a Library and suite of classrooms opened in May 2003. A 300-seater theatre and classroom facilities for Music and Drama were completed in August 2005.

Curriculum. Years 1, 2 and 3 follow a broad curriculum with all Third Year pupils studying two modern languages. In the Third Year pupils continue to study English, Mathematics, Biology, Chemistry, Physics, History, Geography, Classical Civilisation or Latin, Religious Studies, Information Technology, PE/Games, two Modern Languages, and select three of five practical subjects. At the end of the Third Year pupils opt for nine subjects which must include Mathematics, English, at least one science and at least one modern language. Personal and Social Education is taught in Years 1 to 5.

From the Third Year advice and assistance is available to all pupils on a wide range of career possibilities. The careers team arrange a biannual careers convention supplemented with regular visits and talks when advice is given by consultants from a variety of professions. There is a fully equipped careers room.

Pastoral Care. The School provides a disciplined, caring and secure environment in which pupils may work and play without being subjected to harm or distress, in which they may develop their personalities to the full and enjoy their time at school. The Form Teacher is the key figure in each pupil's academic and pastoral welfare and is the first point of contact with parents. The Form Teacher is supported by Heads of Year and regular meetings are held to ensure that the pastoral needs of all our pupils are met. The system is enhanced by a Peer Support scheme which allows trained senior students to listen to younger pupils' concerns.

House Activities. Each pupil is allocated to one of four Houses on entry to the school; siblings are allocated to the same House. A House Convener arranges meetings with Heads of House to discuss policy, procedure and House activities. These activities range from sporting competitions to an art and a literary competition. Each year the pupils produce their own play for the drama competition and their own repertoire for the music competition. The organisation of such activities is carried out by the pupils themselves with staff providing support and guidance. All pupils are actively encouraged to participate in the full range of activities in order to raise their self-esteem and to allow each to shine; they gain much from the experience. Junior, Intermediate and Senior House Assemblies are held on a weekly basis.

Sixth Form and Higher Education. Students take four or five subjects plus General Studies to AS Level in the Lower Sixth. They continue with three or four of those subjects plus General Studies to A2 Level in the Upper Sixth. The subjects are chosen from an extensive range with 27 presently available. All Sixth Formers participate in Games lessons, where a wide choice of activities is provided. Supplementary courses provided include Information Technology, Application of Number and Communication and ab initio language courses.

Careers guidance is given considerable emphasis in the Grange Sixth. Each student is attached to a member of the careers team and linguists are given the opportunity to undertake their work experience abroad. Almost all the students progress to higher education, with around 15% going on each year to Oxford and Cambridge.

Sixth Formers are expected to play a leading role in school life. They also participate in the extensive programme of House activities as well as in the Duke of Edinburgh's Award Scheme, outward bound courses, Young Enterprise, and the Engineering Council Award Scheme.

All students are required to participate in the execution of duties around school and there is a Sixth Form Council, run by the Head Girl and Head Boy, to coordinate the various aspects of Sixth Form life. Students have the use of their own common rooms.

Reporting to Parents. The School recognises that our pupils are best served when parents and the School work together and to this end we consider it important to report to parents fully and regularly. We encourage full discussion of the pupils' progress and well being. Each pupil receives at least two full reports per year. Each half term brings a progress report with academic grades and a profile of the pupil's extra-curricular involvement and pastoral welfare. There are two parents' evenings each year for all Junior School pupils and Years 1, 4 and Lower Sixth in the Senior School, and one for all other year groups. If parents have any concerns, they are encouraged to discuss these with the relevant staff at the earliest opportunity and the School will always contact parents and invite them to discuss issues should we feel it necessary.

Games. The School has 22 acres of sports fields. The principal games are hockey, netball, rugby, rowing, football, cricket, cross country, athletics and tennis. There are four all-weather tennis courts as well as three badminton courts.

Art, Design, Drama, Music. In addition to timetabled lessons for these subjects there are numerous opportunities to participate in extra-curricular activities.

In the music department no less than 15 peripatetic teachers provide 420 private lessons a week. There are two orchestras, jazz, string, wind and saxophone ensembles, senior choir and choral society. Cantores Roborienses, the School's senior singing group, and the Chamber Orchestra perform at the many informal concerts held during the year and at numerous public events.

Considerable emphasis is placed on Drama in the school with two part-time and two full-time members of staff and pupils participate in a number of drama festivals with a high degree of first and second placings. Over 80 private Speech and Drama lessons take place each week, with all these pupils entering Trinity-Guildhall examinations, from Junior Preliminary to Grade 8. Regular school productions take place each year with frequent theatre trips.

Religion. The School is Christian based but pupils of all faiths and none are accepted as long as they are prepared to take a full part in the life of the School. Full School Assemblies take place twice a week.

Transport. Hartford is served by two main line stations, Manchester to Chester and Crewe to Liverpool. The majority of children travel to and from school by car or by one of the eight private buses.

Admission. Kindergarten by informal assessment at the end of January; Senior School by entrance assessment on the first Saturday in February; Sixth Form by interview and good GCSE results.

Pupils are also admitted at other ages as vacancies occur. Admission is gained by interview and test performance. Enquiries for admission are welcome at any time of the year and a copy of the school prospectus may be obtained by contacting the Admissions Secretary.

Open Morning. The School holds an Open Morning in the Autumn term when prospective parents and pupils are welcome to see the facilities available and to talk to the pupils and staff. Appointments to view the school can be made at other times by contacting the Admissions Secretary.

Fees per term (from January 2011). £2,270 (Kindergarten & Form 1); Junior School £2,455 (Forms 2–6); Senior School £3,040.

Scholarships. Several scholarships are offered for entry to the Senior School for exceptional academic ability and music. A number of Sixth Form Scholarships are awarded for outstanding academic potential after an examination held at the end of spring term preceding Sixth Form entry.

Bursaries worth up to full fees and assessed according to means are available to new entrants to the Senior School.

Charitable status. The Grange School is a Registered Charity, number 525918. It exists to provide high quality education for boys and girls.

Gresham's School

Cromer Road, Holt, Norfolk NR25 6EA

Tel: 01263 714500
Fax: 01263 712028
e-mail: registrar@greshams.com
website: www.greshams.com

The School was founded in 1555 by Sir John Gresham, Kt., and the endowments were placed by him under the management of the Fishmongers' Company.

Motto: '*Al Worship Be To God Only*'.

Governors:
T Boyd (*Prime Warden of the Fishmongers' Company*)
A Martin Smith (*Chairman*)
A Morgan
N Bankes
The Earl of Portsmouth, DL
C Spicer
The Lord Bishop of Lynn
Mrs R Monbiot, OBE
S G G Benson
Dr I M Waterson, FRCP
Mrs A MacNicol, DL
M H Edwards
C I H Mawson, FCA
R Copas
K S Waters
K Martin

Clerk to the Fishmongers' Company: N Cox, Fishmongers' Hall, London Bridge, EC4R 9EL

Headmaster: P D John, BSc, FCMI, MInstD

Deputy Head – Pastoral: N C Flower, BA, PGCE (*English*)
Deputy Head – Academic: D R Miles, MA, PGCE (*Mathematics*)
Head of Boarding: Mrs S Radley, BEd, CertEd (*Biology, PSHE, †Edinburgh*)
Chaplain: The Revd B Roberts, BD, DipTheol
Business & Finance Director: J Stronach, ACA

Assistant Staff:
* *Head of Department*
† *Housemaster/mistress*

Mrs C Alban, BA (*Head of Careers, Business Studies*)
Dr B Aldiss, BSc, PhD, QTS (*Biology*)
D Atkinson, BA, PGCE (**Geography*)
D Bailey, ONC/HND (*Design & Technology*)
Mrs L Barden, BA, PGCE (**French*)
Miss A Barker, BA (*French, Spanish*)
G Bartle, BSc, PGCE (*ICT*)
J Bartlett, BSc, PGCE (*Physics, *Electronics*)
A Bealey, BA, PGCE (*English*)
Mrs L I Betts, Cert Counselling Skills, RGN (*PSHE*)
G J Burnell, BA, MEd, FRGS (**Latin*)
Miss S Buxton, BA (*Drama, English*)
Miss S Charlton, BA, RSACertTEFL, PGCE (*Art*)
Mrs A Colley, BSc, CertEd (*Mathematics*)
N Colley, BEng, DipEM, PGCE (*Physics, Electronics*)
Dr A K Cormack, BA, MA, PhD, PGCE (**English*)
S Curtis, BSc, PGCE (*Mathematics*)
Miss E Delpech, BA, PGCE (*Art*)
P Ellis, BA, PGCE (*Economics*)
Mrs S L Ellis-Retter, BA, PGCE (*ESL*)
S B Gates, BA, MA, PGCE (**Religious Studies*)
Miss F Gathercole, BA (*Biology, †Oakeley*)
M Gillingwater, MSc, BSc, PGCE (*Biology, Chemistry*)
Dr L Gray, MA, DPhil (*Theory of Knowledge Coordinator*)
C Gülzow, MA, DipPädaoge (*IB German*)
C Halsall, BA, MA, DipRSA, DipMS, PGCE (*German, French*)
Dr C Hammond, MPhil, PhD (*French, Spanish*)
P J Hands, BA (**Drama*)
R Hensen, BCom, HDE (*Mathematics*)
N Humphrey, BA, PGCE (**Design Technology*)
A Jenkins, BSc, MA (**ICT, Physical Education*)
M H Jones, GRSM, FRCO, ARCM (**Music*)
Mrs J K Kelsey, BA, MA, LRAM, PGCE (*Music*)
P R Kelsey, BEd (*Design Technology, †Tallis*)
M Kemp, BSc, PGCE (*Chemistry*)
S Kinder, BA, PGCE (**History*)
Miss S King, BSc, PGCE (*Geography*)
P Laidler, BSc, PGCE (**Biology*)
Mrs K Lear, BA (*Japanese*)
S Lowe, BA, QTS (*Mathematics*)
D McKee, BA, MA, ABRSM, PGCE (*Music*)
J P B Martin, BSc (*Chemistry*)
M Matthams, BSc, MA, PGCE (**Physics*)
Mrs J Moore (*Games, †Britten*)
Mrs M Myers, BEd, RSACert TEFL, CertSpLD (*Learning Support*)
C Nichols, BSc, PGCE (*Religious Studies*)
J Norris, BA, MA, MSc, PGCE (**Chemistry*)
Miss B O'Brien, BA, PGCE (*Drama*)
T O'Donnell, BS, QTS (*History*)
C Openshaw, BA, PGCE (**Art*)
Miss V Panea, BA, PGCE (*Spanish*)
Mrs K Patilas, BSc, PGCE (*Economics*)
Mrs A Pitkethly, BA, PGCE (*History*)
P Plummer, BSc, PGCE (*Geography*)
J Quartermain, MA, MPhil, PGCE (*Head of Sixth Form, History*)

Mrs F Read, BSc, PGCE (**Mathematics*)
C Reed, BEng, PGCE (*Physics*)
F J V Retter, BA, PGCE (*Languages, †Woodlands*)
Revd B R Roberts, BD, DipTheol (*Religious Studies*)
Miss L B Roberts, BA, ARCM, AGSM, DipNCOS (*Music*)
Mrs H Robinson, BA, MA (*History of Art*)
Mrs K Robinson, BA (*English, ESL*)
Mrs L Rose, BEd, DipSpLD (**Learning Support*)
D Saker, BSc, MSc, PGCE (*Physics*)
Ms T Sampy, BA (*Art*)
S Satchwell, BA PGCE (*Art*)
M Seldon, BA, MA (*IB Diploma Programme Coordinator, English*)
A Smith, BA, PGCE (*Business Studies*)
A Stromberg, BEng, MSc, AFRIN, PGCE (*Mathematics, †Howson's*)
J Thomson, BEng, PGCE (*Mathematics, †Farfield*)
Dr K C Tsai, MA, PhD, DipEd (*Mandarin*)
Mrs C van Hasselt, BA, PGCE (*English*)
M Walsh, BA, ACIB (**Economics*)
Mrs S Walsh, BA, DipRSA, PGCE (*Learning Support*)
Dr J Ward, BA, PhD (*English*)
P Watson, BA, PGCE (**Spanish*)
M Whitaker, BA, PGCE (*Mathematics*)
Mrs G Wiley, BA, MLitt, Cert TEFL, PGCE (*ESL*)

Prep School:
Headmaster: J H W Quick, BA Hons, PGCE

Assistant Staff:
T J Allison, MRSH (*Laboratory Technician*)
Mrs E Ashcroft, BA, PGCE (*Modern Languages*)
Mrs J Brearley, BA, Dip ELS (*Librarian, English*)
R T N Brearley, CertEd (*Senior Master, *Geography*)
G A Britton, BSc, PGCE (**Mathematics & ICT*)
M Buckingham, BSc ARICS (*Mathematics*)
N P Cornell, BSc, PGCE (*Biology, Science*)
Mrs C Cozens-Hardy (*Design Technology, Art*)
Mrs E Curtis (*Games*)
Mrs K Edwards, BA, MA (*Performing Arts*)
Mrs S Fairbain-Day, BA, PGCE (*Science, Religious Studies*)
Mrs J Fenn, MEd, DipHD (*Learning Support*)
Mrs K Fields, BEd (*†Crossways*)
S Fields, BSc, QTS (*Mathematics, †Crossways*)
Mrs K Gill, BA, PGCE (*Mathematics, English, Science*)
Mrs H Hall (*Sport*)
Mrs V Harvey-Seldon, BA (**English, Drama*)
P A J Hawes, MEd, CertEd, FRGS, FCollT (*Director of Studies, History, Geography*)
A Horsley, BA (*Mathematics*)
Ms J Howard, BA (*Modern Languages, Learning Support*)
Mrs K John BA (*Modern Languages*)
Mrs F Kempton, BEd (**Science*)
Mrs G Kretchetov, MA, RSA CTEFLA (*EAL, French, Learning Support, Cultural Studies*)
Mrs S Laidler, BA, PGCE (*Science*)
P M Laycock, BA, BSc, PGCE (**Design Technology*)
Mrs S Li-Rocchi, BA, MA, PGCE (**Art*)
Miss J Lister (*Games*)
R J G Mansfield, BEd, MA, CertEd (*Deputy Head, *Performing Arts*)
Mrs P Matthams, BSc (*Sport*)
Mrs J Merrick, BSc, PGCE (*Physics, Chemistry*)
Mrs A Nash, BA, PGCE (**Religious Studies, Modern Languages*)
Mrs S O'Leary, BA (**History, English, Drama*)
Miss H E Olby, BA (*ICT, Yr 4 Coordinator*)
Mrs K Quick, BA, PGCE (*History, English, PSHE, Latin*)
Miss L B Roberts, BA, ARCM, AGSM, DipNCOS (*Assistant Director of Music*)
Mrs C Sankey, BA, PDSEN (**Learning Support, English*)
Mrs C Smith, BA, PGCE (*English, Classroom Support*)
M Smith, BA (*Mathematics*)

N Thomas, BA, PGCE (*Modern Languages, English,
†Kenwyn*)
Mrs F Thomas (*†Kenwyn*)
Mrs S Vare, BA (**Classics, PSHE, French*)
Mrs K Walton (*Sport*)
N Waring, BMus, MMus (**Director of Music*)
E Watson, BA (*History, Religious Studies*)
Mrs D West, BA (*English, Head of Girls' PE*)
Mrs L Worrall (*Games*)
S C Worrall, BA, PGCE (*Geography, Head of Boys' PE*)

Pre-Prep School:
Headmistress: Mrs J Davidson, DipEd Scot

Assistant Staff:
Mrs C A Burchell, BEd, MEd (*Deputy Head*)
Mrs K Glennie, BTech
Miss K Hagon, BA, PGCE
Mrs K Kinder, BSc, PGCE
Mrs A King, CertEd
Miss S MacDonald, BEd
Mrs C S Mullis, BA, MPhil, PGCE
Miss J Sandford, BSc, PGCE (*Early Years Coordinator*)
Miss A Scott, BEd
Mrs C Welham, MontDip

Medical Officer: Dr P Roebuck
School Counsellor: Mrs L I Betts
SSI: C C Scoles, MBE

There are 516 pupils in the Senior School, 291 boys and 225 girls, of whom 211 are in the Sixth Form, and 275 are boarders.

The School is situated some 4 miles from the sea near Sheringham and Blakeney, in one of the most beautiful and healthy parts of England. The School has a spacious setting in 150 acres including 50 acres of woodland. Numbered amongst its old boys are W H Auden, Benjamin Britten, Stephen Spender, Lord Reith on the Arts side, Christopher Cockerell, inventor of the hovercraft, Ian Proctor, yacht designer, Leslie Everett Baynes, who first patented swing-wing variable aircraft geometry, Sir Martin Wood of the URI scanner, and Sir James Dyson of more recent fame on the engineering side. It offers excellence in a wide range of fields, from which pupils gain an outstanding, balanced education.

Gresham's is a Church of England foundation but all religious denominations are welcomed. The School has its own Chaplain and a Counsellor who instructs new pupils and present pupils in life skills. Both are available to advise and help pupils throughout their time at Gresham's.

In the Senior School there are four boys' boarding houses and three girls' houses. After the first or second year pupils move into study bedrooms.

There has been a substantial building programme in the last two decades: Sports Hall (1983), Edinburgh Girls House (1987) and Britten Girls House (1996), English department building (1988), Junior and Senior Social Centres (1989), two all-weather Astroturf pitches (1994), the Cairns Centre for Art and Design (1990), and the Auden Theatre (1998).

Curriculum. In their first year (Third Form, year 9) all students follow a broad curriculum covering all the traditional subjects, including separate lessons in the three sciences. There is a comprehensive language tuition programme and pupils can select up to three languages from French, Spanish, German, Latin, Mandarin and Japanese. The curriculum is designed to allow students to experience the full range of subjects prior to making their choices for their two year GCSE programme. For GCSE all students follow a compulsory curriculum of English, Maths, a language and either dual award or all three sciences, together with an option system allowing for a further four subject choices (including further languages) to be made. The flexibility built into our option system allows for virtually all subject combinations to be accommodated.

Entry into the Sixth Form is dependent on students achieving a minimum of six GCSE passes at A* to B grade, to include passes in Maths and English. Students can either follow a traditional A Level course or opt for the International Baccalaureate Diploma Programme.

For those students following a traditional A Level course, four subjects are normally taken in the Lower Sixth year with three of these subjects continued to full A Level in the Upper Sixth year.

For those students entering our IB diploma Programme, six subjects have to be taken, three at higher level and three at standard level. In addition, a Theory of Knowledge (TOK) course is taken, a Creativity, Action and Service (CAS) course followed and an Extended Essay (effectively a 4000-word research project on a subject of the student's choosing) has to be written. This rigorous programme helps pupils become life-long and independent learners and the IB qualification is recognised by universities throughout the world.

Throughout their time with us, all pupils receive appropriate careers advice and computerised aptitude tests are taken by the majority of our Fifth and Lower Sixth Form students. The Junior and Senior Colloquia are academic discussion forums which hold regular meetings and to which our more able pupils are invited to attend. There will typically be approximately 40 students in the Junior Colloquium and 25 students in the Senior Colloquium. A large number of discussion groups are also available for any Sixth Form student to attend and these include The MacLean Society (political and current affairs), The Auden Society (literature appreciation and discussion) and a large number of other societies based around French, Spanish, Economics, Natural History, Philosophy and History.

Since September 2007, we have offered a one year Pre IB course to a small number of students each year. This course is specifically designed to integrate overseas students into life at Gresham's and most students will gain approximately 7 full GCSEs as a result. The course offers the ideal preparation for the IB Diploma Programme and students follow an individually tailored curriculum centred on English Language, Maths, (usually) two sciences and two or three other option subjects.

Recreation, Music and Drama. The School has abundant playing fields. The main games are rugby football, hockey, cricket and athletics for boys, and hockey, netball, rounders, athletics and tennis for girls. Shooting, sailing, swimming, squash, badminton, cross-country running, athletics and golf are also very popular, and national and international success has been consistently achieved in shooting and sailing, and recently in hockey.

There is a flourishing CCF contingent and Duke of Edinburgh's Award section and approximately 25 gold awards are achieved each year. The School has a very strong choir which tours internationally and performs regularly in East Anglia. Six of its members have recently sung in the National Youth Choir. Art and drama are also exceptionally strong, and Drama and Theatre Studies are offered at GCSE and A Level.

Entrance. Those entering at 13+ from Preparatory Schools take the Common Entrance Examination or sit our own Scholarship Examinations. Tests in Maths, English and, where applicable, French are given to those entering from independent schools which do not prepare for Common Entrance, and from the maintained sector. Able foreign pupils are welcomed, especially into the Sixth Form.

Scholarships. (*See Scholarship Entries section.*) There are several Academic Scholarships available for 13+ and Sixth Form entry. Scholarships in Music, Art, Drama and Sport are awarded for 13+ and Sixth Form entry, and All-Rounder Scholarships may also be awarded. The Fishmongers' Company sponsor 3 places annually on Sail Training trips and the Philip Newell Scholarships are available for Gap year activities.

Fees per term (2011-2012). Senior School: £9,100 (boarding), £6,975 (day). Prep School: £6,625 (boarding), £5,050 (day). Pre-Prep School: £2,525–£2,800 (day).

These are inclusive fees; no extra charge is made for laundry, games, medical attention, etc, although some areas, such as individual music tuition and learning support, attract extra charges.

Day pupils' meal charges are included in the fees. Necessary extras are very few.

Honours. In 2010 the A Level pass rate was 99.2% with 73.6% A and B grades, our record best ever results. We consistently send 95% of our Upper Sixth leavers onto higher education, most of these going to their first choice courses. At GCSE in 2010, we achieved 48% A* and A grades, and the average number of GCSE passes per pupil was 9.9.

Gresham's Prep School is a flourishing boarding and day co-educational preparatory school of 238 pupils within half a mile of the Senior School. Its Headmaster is a member of IAPS. (*For further details see entry in IAPS section.*) There is also a Pre-Prep School of 130 pupils.

Scholarships are available at 11+ and enquiries should be directed to the Headmaster at the Preparatory School.

The Old Greshamian Club. The Club is active on behalf of present and former members of the School and it can be contacted through its Coordinator, Mrs J Thomas-Howard, at Gresham's School.

Charitable status. Gresham's School is a Registered Charity, number 1105500. The School is a charitable trust for the purpose of educating children.

Guildford High School
UCST

London Road, Guildford, Surrey GU1 1SJ
Tel: 01483 561440
Fax: 01483 306516
e-mail: guildford-admissions@church-schools.com
website: www.guildfordhigh.surrey.sch.uk

Motto: *As one that serveth*
Established in January 1888.

Governing Body: The Council of the United Church Schools Trust

Patron: The Most Revd and Rt Hon Rowan Williams, Archbishop of Canterbury

Local Governing Body:
Chairman: Mrs L M Keat
Mrs C Cobley
Revd R Cotton
Mrs B Ford
Prof O Hess
Mr D Perrett
Mr J Rigg

Staff:

Headmistress: Mrs F J Boulton, BSc Hons University of Wales, Cardiff, MA London (*Biology*)

Deputy Heads:
Mrs R Cole, BSc Hons Exeter (*Biology*)
Mrs K J Laurie, BA Hons Leeds (*History*)
Mr W H Saunders, BA Hons Bristol, MA St Mary's University College (*History*)

Senior Teacher: Mrs V M Bingham, BA Hons Keble College Oxford (*Classics*)

Head of Junior School: Mrs S J Phillips, BA Hons Reading

* *Head of Department*

Art & Design:
*Mrs K Burrett, BA Hons Staffordshire
Mr I A Charnock, BA Hons Bangor, MA London
Mrs S Kew, BA Hons Kingston
Mrs F Khan-Evans, BA Camberwell College of Arts, The London Institute, MA Wimbledon School of Art, University of Surrey, PCGE London

Classics:
*Miss S N Merali, BA Hons, MA Manchester
Mrs A George, MA St Hugh's College Oxford, PGCE Cambridge
Mrs V Bingham, BA Hons Keble College Oxford
Mrs E Jordan, BA Hons Birmingham

Design & Technology:
*Mrs W A Bengoechea, BEd Hons Bath (*Head of Year 7, Head of Faculty*)
Mrs H P Gowers, BSc Surrey
Miss J Sleigh, BA Hons Sheffield Hallam
Mr T Smith, BA Hons Swansea Institute of Higher Education

Economics:
*Mrs C L Jones, BA Hons Sheffield

English & Theatre Studies:
*Mr J C Baddock, BA Hons UCL
Mrs S L Glyn-Davies, BA Hons East Anglia (*Head of Years 10 & 11*)
Ms A L Fenton, BA Hons University of Wales, Aberystwyth (*Head of Drama*)
Mrs J A Gibson, BA Hons Liverpool
Mr G N Hogg, BA Hons Newcastle upon Tyne
Mrs N J Lewis, BA Hons York
Miss F H S Mackay, BA Hons Ulster
Mrs S Parfitt, MA St Hilda's College Oxford, PCGE LMH Oxford
Miss H A Stephens, MA Hons St Andrews

Geography:
Miss S Agus, BA Hons Belfast
Mrs K N Banks, MA Oxon
*Miss S P B MacDowell, MA Hons St Andrews, DMS Oxford Brookes

History:
*Mrs A Minear, BA Hons Exeter
Mrs K M C Perrin, BA Hons, MPhil Trinity Hall Cambridge
Mr W H Saunders, BA Hons Bristol, MA St Mary's University College
Miss K M Sloan, BA Hons Reading
Miss K J Tromans, BA Hons Leeds

Information Technology:
*Mrs A Taylor, BSc Manchester Polytechnic

Mathematics:
Mrs S E Black, MEng Gonville & Caius College Cambridge (*Curriculum Assistant*)
*Mrs K M Denny, BSc Hons London
Miss C E Halls-Moore, BSc Hons Bristol
Mr M W Holtham, BA St John's College Cambridge (*Examinations Officer*)
Mrs E M Hudson, BSc Hons Warwick
Mrs E Mulgrew, MA Oxford
Mrs K Perryman, BSc Hons York
Mrs G T Rackham, BSc Hons Sheffield
Mrs A S Stevens, BSc Bradford

Modern Languages:
Miss K A Buckley, BA Hons Exeter (*Head of Sixth Form*)
Mrs V A Callaghan, BA Hons Portsmouth (*Head of French*)
Miss C S M Dalet-Puzzanghera, Licence d'Anglais Clermont-Ferrand
Mr J Gonzalez Abia, BA Hons Valladolid Spain

Ms C Igoe, BSc Hons Georgetown Washington DC
Mr A James, BA Hons Worcester College Oxford
*Mrs E L Pattison, BA Hons Leeds (*Head of Modern Languages*)
Miss C H Knight, MA Queens' College Cambridge(*Head of Spanish*)
Miss F Mellor, BA Hons Manchester
Mrs Z N Rowe, BA Hons Exeter
Mrs A B Taylor, BA Hons Rome
Mrs J F Vickerman, BA Hons Southampton (*Head of German*)

Music:
Mrs E M Forrest-Biggs, MA Downing College Cambridge (*Deputy Head of Sixth Form*)
*Mr G T Jones, BMus Hons Birmingham
Mrs J A Shaw, BA Hons Leeds
Miss K T Taylor, BA Hons Trinity College Cambridge

Physical Education:
Miss L J Boyd, BA Hons Leeds Metropolitan
Miss C A Dalon, BA Hons College of William & Mary, Virginia
*Mrs L Fitzroy-Stone, BEd Hons Bedford College
Miss R E Legg, BEd Hons De Montfort
Mrs T J Oxley, BSc Hons Birmingham
Mrs C Wells, BEd Greenwich
Mrs A J Whybro, BA Hons Chichester

Politics:
*Mr D Cleaver, MSc Econ University of Wales, Swansea, MA Econ Manchester

Psychology:
Mrs C Benson, BA Hons Manchester
*Dr J E Boyd, BSc Newcastle, PhD King's College, London

Religious Studies:
Miss S Carr, BA Hons Cardiff
Mrs A E Gillingham, BA Hons Westminster College, Oxford
*Mrs J A Shopland, BA Hons University of Wales, Lampeter

Science:
Mrs R Batchelar, MChem St Hilda's College Oxford, PCGE Trinity College Oxford
*Mrs J Blatchford, BSc Hons Kent, MA Kingston (*Head of Chemistry*)
*Dr J E Boyd, BSc Hons Newcastle, PhD London (*Head of Biology*)
Mrs E Carter, BSc Sheffield
Mrs R Cole, BSc Hons Exeter
Mrs D A Evans, BSc Hons Lancaster
Mrs C Gilmore, BSc Hons Bath
Miss C Henderson, BSc Hons Durham
Mrs C R Kittow, CertEd Homerton College Cambridge (*Head of Years 8 & 9*)
Dr L Lockett, BA Hons Oxford, MSc London, DPhil York
Dr T M Peck, BA Hons, MA, DPhil Oxford
*Mr B J Russell, BEng UCL (*Head of Science, Head of Physics*)
Mrs G A Scott, BSc Hons Surrey
Miss R J Taylor, MChem, MSc Oxford
Dr E L Whitaker, MSc Durham, PhD Edinburgh

Junior School:
Miss S J Bauchop, BEd Hons Leicester
Mrs J A Bottomley, BA Hons Birmingham
Mrs M B Crowley, BSc Hons London
Miss V L Ellis, BSc Cardiff
Mrs J E Flood, BA Hons Reading
Mrs O J Foster, BA Hons Exeter
Mr M Gibb (*Deputy Head of Junior School*)
Mrs W A Gibbs, BEd Hons Winchester
Mrs D Hall, BEd Joint Hons Exeter

Miss G Illsley, BA Hons Birmingham
Mrs J Kinch, BEd Birmingham
Mrs R F Kemp, BSc Hons Exeter
Mrs E A Lloyd, BA Hons Reading
Ms C J Mayhook, BA Hons Exeter
Miss C Middleton, BA Hons Leeds
Mrs K L Nanson, BEd Bedford College
Ms N A Sloane, BEd Hons Kingston
Mrs H M Stamp, BEd Hons East Anglia
Miss L Walker, BA Hons Canterbury
Mrs R J Wardell, BMus Hons Royal Holloway College London
Miss C L Woffenden, BA Hons Homerton College Cambridge
Miss S C Wright, BA Hons UWE

Library:
Mrs Y A Skene
Mrs A Hewson, BA Hons Cilip

Music Administrator:
Mrs D R G Baumann, MA, MusB St Catharine's College Cambridge

Visiting Staff:
Music:
Piano:
Mrs I Bridgmont, BMus, LTCL, ARCM
Mrs D Dawkins, LRSM, LTCL
Miss H Dives, LTCL
Mrs P M Morley, ATCL, ARCM, GRSM
Dr V C Rowe, PhD, MA, GRSM
Mrs G Young, LRAM, ARCM, DipMT Nordoff-Robbins, Grad Dip Mus
Singing:
Mrs S M Hellec-Butcher
Miss K Walker, BMus Hons, LRAM
Head of Strings: Mrs C A Woehrel, Grad Lucerne
Violin and Viola:
Miss L Hill, LTCL, FTCL
Miss C Jackson, GGSM
Mr B Lloyd Wilson, MA, AGSM, ARCM
Mrs S Thomas, ARCM, LRAM
Cello:
Mr R Bridgmont, FTCL, ARCM, LTCL
Miss J Kimber, BMus
Double Bass: Miss N Bailey, ARCM, LRAM
Guitar: Mr P L Howe, ARCM
Harp: Mrs J Carr, BMus
Flute:
Mrs D Ball, LTCL
Miss R E Chappell, AGSM
Mrs F J Howe, ARCM
Oboe: Miss J Lees, ARCM
Clarinet:
Miss C Henry, ARCM, LRAM
Bassoon: Miss R Cow, M Mus, BMus Hons
Brass: Mr L Baker
Saxophone: Mr S D West, GTCL, LTCL
Recorder, Harpsichord & Piano: Miss P Cave, LRAM, GRSM
Percussion: Mr T Henty, BMus Hons, MMus RCM

Director of Marketing and Admissions: Mrs P Crosthwaite, BA Hons Bournemouth
Assistant Registrar: Mrs J Bak
Marketing and Admissions Assistant: Mrs V Young
Bursar: Mrs G A Stead
Accounts Administrator: Mrs V M Livermore
PA to the Headmistress: Mrs J M Waters
HR Administrator: Mrs S M Mooney, BSc Hons Leicester, PG Dip Personnel Mgt Kingston

Number of Girls. 980 Day Girls aged 4–18 years.

Guildford High School is a successful school in which high expectations are set for all pupils, with learning as its key focus. It is a community in which everyone is known, valued and feels secure. Pupils are supported and encouraged to reach their potential.

The school has outstanding pastoral care: it is key to its happy and successful environment. It has a system of Form Tutors, Heads of Year and, of course, a Deputy Head responsible for pastoral matters. When the girls arrive in Year 7, they are assigned a 'buddy' from Year 8 who will steer them through the first term and beyond.

Guildford High School has an extensive extra-curricular and curriculum-enrichment programme, encompassing sport, drama, music, debating and much more besides.

As a result, the girls achieve outstanding success at all levels from SATs to GCSE and A Level. Last year, the A Level pass rate was 100%, with 89% of girls achieving A* or A grades and 44.5% of all grades were the newly introduced A* grade. At GCSE, 91.5% of the results were A or A*. Most importantly, the vast majority of leavers went on to their first-choice university with typically 25% gaining places at Oxford and Cambridge. At Key Stage 2, 96% of girls achieved Level 5 in all three subjects.

Sixth Form. There is a strong Sixth Form and most girls take four AS Level subjects from the wide range offered and continue with 3 of these subjects to A Level. They also follow a non-examined General Studies course. All girls proceed to University or to other areas of Higher Education. The Sixth Form has its own accommodation, which has been extended and refurbished as part of a major development plan.

Music. There is a lively musical tradition and girls are encouraged to play musical instruments and to join one of the orchestras, choirs, chamber groups or the wind bands.

Drama. Drama is taught as part of the curriculum. GCSE Drama is available as well as AS Theatre Studies. There are major productions every term which are actively participated in by girls of all ages taking on acting, directing, producing and backstage roles.

The Duke of Edinburgh's Award Scheme. Around 90% of girls take part in this fun and challenging scheme, which is run jointly by parents and teachers and which offers opportunities for developing character through service, skills and expeditions.

Physical Education. Lacrosse, netball, tennis, rounders, athletics, gymnastics, swimming, badminton and basketball. The girls compete locally, nationally and internationally with excellent results and a 'sport for all' policy provides many opportunities to take part for fun and recreation. Sixth Formers have a wide choice of activities, including yoga, golf and ice-skating, and may use facilities at the University and Sports Centre.

Situation and Facilities. The school is pleasantly situated near the centre of Guildford on a bus route and close to London Road Station; frequent trains to the main station provide links over a wide area. Facilities include libraries, eleven well-equipped laboratories, whiteboards in every classroom, an Information Technology Centre, a Design Technology Centre, Art and Design Studios, a Food Technology Room, Music Rooms, Music Technology Studio, a Careers Room and Dining Hall. The school also opened a new £5 million Sports Hall and indoor swimming pool in October 2006.

The Junior School at Guildford High School combines a warm, caring atmosphere with a stimulating environment, and offers careful preparation for entry to the Senior School. (*See Junior School entry in IAPS section.*)

Normal ages of entry. 4, 7 and 11 years and Sixth Form level.

Admissions. The school sets its own entrance examination. Academic standards are high.

Fees per term (2011-2012). Junior School: Reception £2,681, Years 1 and 2 £2,632, Years 3–6 £3,587. Senior School: £4,434. Fees quoted exclude lunches. Textbooks and stationery are provided.

Extra Subjects. Instruments (orchestral) £175.

Scholarships and Bursaries. (*See Scholarship Entries section.*) Bursaries are available at Sixth Form level.

Charitable status. The United Church Schools Trust (to which Guildford High School belongs) is a Registered Charity, number 1016538. Its aims and objectives are to provide pupils with a sound education based on and inspired by Christian principles.

The Haberdashers' Aske's Boys' School

Butterfly Lane, Elstree, Herts WD6 3AF

Tel:	020 8266 1700
Fax:	020 8266 1800
e-mail:	office@habsboys.org.uk
website:	www.habsboys.org.uk

The School was founded in 1690, endowed by an estate left in trust to the Haberdashers' Company by Robert Aske, Citizen of London and Liveryman of the Haberdashers' Company. In 1898 it was transferred from Hoxton to Hampstead and in 1961 to Aldenham Park, Elstree, Hertfordshire.

Motto: *Serve and Obey*.

Governing Body:
The Governing Body consists of representatives of the Worshipful Company of Haberdashers, the world of education, the catchment area of the school and former pupils.

Chairman: M Powell, BA
Chairman of the Boys' School Committee: D A Hochberg
Chairman of the Girls' School Committee: A Twiston Davies

S Cartmell	M Pereira-Mendoza
Miss D Finkler	N R Scarles
R Gokhale	S Smith
G Parekh	Sir G Torpy

Clerk to the Governors: C M Bremner

Headmaster: P B Hamilton, MA

Second Master: M L S Judd, BA
Deputy Head: Dr A J Craig, PhD
Deputy Head: J Maguire, BSc
Bursar: S B Wilson, MSc, RTR
Director of External Relations: Dr P E Spence, PhD

Director of Staff Development: Mrs M J C Jones, BEd
Assistant Head (Director of ICT): I R Phillips, MA
Registrar: Mrs D L Robertson, BSc
Head of the Sixth Form: P H Parr, MA
Head of the Middle School: M Lloyd-Williams, BA
Head of the Junior School: Mrs D J Bardou, BA
Head of the Preparatory School: Miss Y M Mercer, BEd

Teaching Staff – Main School:
* Head of Department

Art:
*A K Keenleyside, BA
Miss L M Bird, BA
S N Todhunter, BA
Mrs J E Gleeson, CertEd

Classics:
*R C Whiteman, MA
Mrs S Butcher, BA
P H Parr, MA

Design & Technology:
*N P Holmes, BEd

P I Dathan, BEd
T B W Hardman, BEd
P I Roncarati, BA, MSc
G Cox (*Design Technician*)

Drama:
*T J P Norton, BA
Mrs D H Morris-Wolffe, BA
J N Cox, BA
H Silver, BA (*Drama Technician*)

Economics:
*Mrs K Shah, MPhil
A L Campbell, LLB
S Dobin, BA
G J Hall, MBA
Dr S Koestlé-Cate PhD
C G Trinder, MA

English:
*I D Wheeler, BA
C R Bass, BA
Mrs N M Burgess, BA
W D Hall, BA
P P Jolley, MA
T S Li, MPhil
Mrs C B Lyons, MA
Mrs D H Morris-Wolffe,
    BA
T J P Norton, BA
Mrs K R Pollock, MA
A E O'Sullivan, BA

Geography:
*J Maguire, BSc
Mrs M A Carrick, BA
M G Day, BA
M L S Judd, BA
P D Stiff, BSc

History:
*R C Sloan, PhD
Mrs D J Bardou, BA
S P H Clark, BA
Dr A J Craig, PhD
M W S Hale, MPhil
N P Saddington, BA
A P A Simm, BA
Dr I St John, DPhil

*Information Technology &
    Computing*:
*I R Phillips, MA
Miss D F Blyth, BSc
K M Jones, MSc

Music:
*C D Muhley, GRSM, ARCO CHM, ARCM, LRAM,
    FRSA
A J Simm, BA
Miss C Cousens, BA, FRCO
Miss R Gozzard, MA
Mrs H Pritchard, GCLCM, LGSM
Miss R Muhley, BSc (*Music Asst*)

Instrumental Staff:
P Bainbridge, ARCM, DipRCM (*Trumpet*)
B Bantock, BMus, PPRNCM (*Cello*)
D Bentley GGSM (*French Horn*)
J W Beryl (*Percussion*)
S J Byron, BMus (*Trombone and Tuba*)
R A Carter, FRCO CHM, FTCL, ARCM, LRAM
    (*Pianoforte and Organ*)
Miss S L Core, GTCL, LTCL (*Flute*)
Miss K Cox, BMus, PGDip, LRAM (*Viola*)
Miss U Galuszka, MMus (*Guitar*)
L Gee, BA, GBSM, ABSM (*Violin*)
Miss G Harvey, BMus (*Saxophone*)
Mrs R Heathcote, BMus, LGSMD (*Oboe*)
H J Legge, LRAM (*Bassoon*)
S D Lyon, GRSM, MA (*Pianoforte*)
Miss C Maguire, LRAM (*Double Bass*)
Miss I C Mair, GRSM, MMus, LRAM, ARCM
    (*Pianoforte*)
Miss M B Parrington, ARCM (*Violin*)
M P Pritchard, DipRCM (*Clarinet*)
Miss L M Rive (*Violin*)

M C Yu, BSc

Mathematics:
*N P Hamshaw, MMath
J A Barnes, BSc
Mrs A C C Baron, BSc
Dr P A Barry, PhD, ARCS,
    DIC
Mrs J E Beeson, BSc
S D Charlwood, BSc,
    CMath, MIMA
J Hails, BSc
S Haring, BA
Dr I B Jacques, DPhil
G P Kissane, BSc
P C Marx, MPhil
R D Oldfield, BSc
Mrs D L Robertson, BSc
Mrs A Thakar, BSc
A M Ward, BSc
Mrs R M Wright, BA

Modern Languages:
*R J Thompson, BA
Mrs E Childerstone, BA
M J Donaghey, BA
J A Fenn, BA, MA
Mrs E Gomez, BA
H Haldane, BA
P B Hamilton, MA
A B Mansilla, PGBT
Miss A McKenzie, BA
Miss J J Morgan, BA
N B Moss, BA
Mrs J Robson, BA
Mrs J B Swallow, BA
J C Swallow, MA
P A Thackrey, BA

Language Assistants:
J Barloy, BA
Ms M C Griffiths, BA
Mrs E Childerstone, BA

S R Topping, DipRCM, ARCM (*Pianoforte*)
Miss P Worn, LRAM, ABSM, ALCM (*Viola*)

Physical Education:
*R J McIntosh, BA
N Jovanovic, MSc
D H Kerry, BSc
I C Matthews, BSc
A F M Metcalfe, BSc
P D Stiff, BSc

Games:
S D Charlwood (*i/c
    Cricket*)
J N Cox (*i/c Cross
    Country*)
D Cooper (*i/c Hockey*)
T B W Hardman (*i/c
    Sailing*)
J Hails (*i/c Tennis*)
S Lowe (*i/c Athletics*)
I C Matthews (*i/c Water
    Polo*)
S D McKane (*i/c Fencing*)
A F M Metcalfe, BSc (*i/c
    Rugby*)
R D Oldfield (*i/c
    Orienteering*)
P D Stiff, BSc (*i/c
    Swimming*)
A M Ward (*i/c Association
    Football & Golf*)
C K Whalley (*i/c
    Badminton*)

Politics:
Dr A J Craig, PhD
S P H Clark, BA

Science:
*Dr G R Hobbs, PhD
A C Bagguley, BSc, CBiol,
    MIBiol
Dr A Citron, PhD
M Cucknell, MSc
D R Delpech, BSc, CBiol,
    MIBiol (*i/c Biology*)
Mrs L I Dixon, BSc
D S Endlar, MChem
I R Fielder, BSc
C Glanville, BSc, BA
Mrs M J C Jones, BEd
Mrs J Letts, BSc
R O Kerr, BSc (*i/c Physics*)
R J Kingdon, MSc, CPhys,
    MInstP
S D McKane, BSc
E Pauletto, BSc
Dr A D S Perera, PhD
Miss A Pindoria, BSc
Dr S J Pyburn, PhD (*i/c
    Chemistry*)
Mrs D Rhys-Brown, BSc
G C Stead, BA
J B Ward, BSc
C K Whalley, BSc

Theology and Philosophy:
*R J Cawley, MA
R C Garvey, MA
Revd J Goodair, PhD
Dr J S Green, PhD
M Lloyd-Williams, BA
Mrs E J Nelson, MA
A G Stimson, MA

Teaching Staff – Preparatory School:
*M G Brown, BSc (*Deputy Head*)

Mrs S Adat, BA
N Bowley, BSc
Mrs K Bruce-Green, BEd
Miss R Gozzard, MA
Mrs C M Griggs, CertEd,
    DipS&D
Miss C A Grimes, BEd
Mrs S M E Herbert, BEd
M Jenkins, MA

Dr C A Lessons, PhD
S S Lipscomb, BA
S Lowe, BEd
Mrs J I Magnus, BA
Miss S E McLeigh, BA
K Tamura, BA
Mrs J Valente, PGCE
P D Whitby, MA

Teaching Staff – Pre-Preparatory School:
*Mrs A Fielden, CertEd

Mrs J Barber
Mrs D A McKever
Mrs N Patel, BA

Miss V G Peck, BSc
Mrs H M R Pullen, BEd

Chaplain: The Revd Dr J Goodair, BA

Library:
Mrs J B Mulchrone, BSc, Dip LIS, MCLIP
Mrs J P Sutton, BA, MCLIP
Mrs A M Williams

Administrative Staff:
Admissions & Database Officer: Miss C Allison
Bursar's PA: Miss T Phipps
Catering Manager: E Johnson
Development Officer: Miss Z Okpara
Examinations Officer: Dr J A Alvarez, PhD, CPhys, FInstP
Estates Manager: R A Hamzat
Director of External Relations' PA: Mrs S Vithlani
Finance Manager: P Spence
Head Groundsman: D Beckley
Headmaster's PA: Mrs S Lane, BA

HR Officer: Miss R Titley
ICT Support Director: I R Phillips, MA
Payroll: Mrs L Meighan
Preparatory School Secretary: Mrs T A Kennard
Pre-Preparatory School Secretary: Mrs S Muller
School Counsellor: Mrs A Bard
School Nurses: Ms S Carey, RGN; Mrs G McGrath, RGN
School Shop Manager: Miss S Lewis
Transport Manager: Ms R Caterer

The aim of the School is the fullest possible development of the varied talents of every boy within it, and to this end a broad curriculum is provided, together with extensive facilities for the development of each boy's cultural, physical, personal and intellectual gifts. The School sets out to achieve high academic standards and sets equally high standards in cultural and other fields. In matters of behaviour a large degree of self-discipline is expected, and of mutual tolerance between members of the School community.

Organisation. The School, which is a day school, has 70 boys in the Pre-Prep (ages 5–6) and over 200 boys in the Preparatory School (ages 7–11), 300 in the Junior School (ages 11–13), 500 in the Middle School (ages 13–16) and over 300 in the Sixth Form (over 16). There are 6 Houses. The School regards pastoral care as important; all the Housemasters and Deputy Housemasters and Heads of Section have a large responsibility in this field but so also do House Tutors, the Senior Master and the Chaplain, as well as other members of the staff.

Forms. In the Pre-Prep school there are two forms in Years 1 and 2 with approximately 18 boys in each form. In the Preparatory School there are three forms in Years 3, 4, 5 and 6 each with about 18 boys. In the Main School there are 6 forms in Years 7 and 8 with approximately 25 boys in each form. There are 12 forms in Year 9 each with about 14 boys. Years 10 and 11 are divided amongst 18 forms each with 17–18 boys. The usual size of teaching groups in the Sixth Form is about 10–15.

Facilities. The School and its sister Girls' School, the Haberdashers' Aske's School for Girls, enjoy the use of a campus of over 100 acres with extensive woodlands. The playing fields surround the buildings, which in the Boys' School include the following: Assembly Hall, Dining Hall, Sixth Form Common Room, Music Auditorium, Library, special accommodation for Classics, English (including a Drama Room), History, Geography, Mathematics, Information Technology, Modern Languages including 2 Languages Laboratories, Music School, Science and Geography Centre with 19 laboratories and 8 classrooms, a Design Centre for Art, Craft and Technology, Sports Centre, Gymnasium, Indoor Swimming Bath, two Artificial Grass Pitches and Squash Courts.

The Preparatory School is situated on the same campus in a new building of its own. (*For further details, see Preparatory School entry in IAPS section.*) The Pre-Prep is situated on its own nearby campus.

The Curriculum up to the age of 13 is common for all, with no streaming or setting except in Mathematics in Year 8. From the age of 11 in addition to the usual subjects it includes three Sciences and two foreign languages (chosen from French, German, Spanish and Latin). From the age of 13, subjects are taught in sets. GCSE courses start in Year 10, when boys take ten subjects. In the Sixth Form students study four subjects to AS in the Lower Sixth, narrowing to three A2 subjects in the Upper Sixth. The School takes seriously its commitment to General Studies; this non-examined part of the curriculum occupies 10% of the week in both Upper and Lower Sixth. Boys are entered for the GCE examination at A Level at the age of 18 and are prepared for entry to degree courses at Universities. The wide scope of the School's curriculum gives ample opportunity for all its boys whether preparing for University (overwhelmingly their primary interest), for a profession, for the services, or for commerce or industry. The Careers Department has its own modern facilities, and careers advice is readily available to parents and to boys.

Religious Education. The School is by tradition a Church of England school, but there are no religious barriers to entry and no quotas. It is part of the ethos of the School that all its members respect the deeply-held beliefs and faith of other members. The School Chaplain is available to, and holds responsibility for, all boys in the School of whatever faith. She prepares for Confirmation those who wish it, and there are weekly celebrations of Holy Communion and an annual Carol Service in St Albans Abbey. The morning assembly and class teaching, however, are non-denominational in character. Faith assemblies are held on Thursday mornings, and comprise separate meetings for Christians, Jews, Muslims, Hindus, Jains and Sikhs.

Physical Education. A wide variety of sports is available, including Athletics, Badminton, Basketball, Cricket, Cross-country running, Fencing, Golf, Gymnastics, Hockey, Rugby Football, Sailing, Soccer, Squash, Shooting, Swimming, Tennis, Table Tennis and Water Polo. All boys are expected to take part in physical education unless exempt on medical grounds.

Out of School Activities. The extensive range includes a period of 2 hours on Friday afternoon when boys can choose one of a large variety of activities of a service nature. This includes Community Service, both on the School campus and among those who need help in the surrounding district. It also includes the Combined Cadet Force which has Navy, Army and Air Force sections.

Music and Drama. Both have a prominent place in the School. The Music School has a Recital Hall and some 12 other rooms; 21 visiting instrumental teachers between them teach 500 instrumental pupils each week covering all the normal orchestral instruments together with Piano and Organ. There is a Choir of 250, and several orchestras. For Drama the facilities include a generously equipped stage and a separate Drama Room with its own lighting and stage equipment.

School Societies. School Societies and expeditionary activities in term time and holidays include Amnesty, Archery, Art, Badminton, Bridge, Canoeing, Chess, Choral, Classical, Crosstalk, Debating, Duke of Edinburgh's Award, Dramatics, English, Football, History, Jazz, Jewish Society, Life-saving, Life Drawing, Model Railway, Modern Languages, Mountaineering, Philosophical, Photography, Politics, Puzzles and Games, Rifle, Sailing, Science, Squash, Stamp Club, Windsurfing.

Transport. A private bus service is provided from some 130 pick-up points, to enable boys to attend the School from a wide area, and to remain for after-School activities.

Admission. Boys are admitted only at the beginning of the school year in September, except on transfer from a school in another area. They may be admitted at the age of 5 and may remain in the School until the end of the academic year in which the age of 19 is attained, subject to satisfactory progress at each stage of the course and to compliance with the School Rules currently in force. Approximately 36 boys are admitted at age 5 and a further 18 boys are admitted at age 7 each year, approximately 100 at age 11, approximately 25 at age 13 and small numbers at age 16. There are competitive examinations including written and oral tests of intelligence, literacy and numeracy at the ages of 7 and 11, held in January for admission in the following September. Applicants aged 13 also take examinations at the beginning of January and are interviewed later in the month for entry in September. At 16 admission is by GCSE and interview. An Open Day for prospective parents is held each year early in October. Registration Fee: £100.

Scholarships. (*See Scholarship Entries section.*) A number of Scholarships are awarded annually to pupils entering the Main School. Music Scholarships are awarded each year to candidates showing special promise in music. Governors

Bursaries are open to all pupils entering the Main School; they are based upon financial need.

Full details of all these awards are included in the prospectus available from the Registrar at the School who is glad to answer enquiries.

Alternatively you can request a prospectus online from our website which is: http://www.habsboys.org.uk.

Fees per term (2011-2012). Main School £4,889; Preparatory School (Years 3–6) £4,889; Pre-Preparatory (Years 1 & 2) £3,688.

Piano, Organ and Orchestral Instruments (optional) £200; Orchestral classes £127; Aural classes £58.

Honours. In 2011, 36 pupils gained places at Oxford and Cambridge, and approximately 120 gained places at other Universities.

Charitable status. The Haberdashers' Aske's Charity is a Registered Charity, number 313996. It exists to promote education.

Haileybury

Hertford SG13 7NU

Tel:	Reception: 01992 706200; Master: 01992 706222
	Bursar: 01992 706216; Registrar: 01992 706353
Fax:	01992 470663
e-mail:	registrar@haileybury.com
website:	www.haileybury.com

Motto: *Fear God. Honour the King. Sursum Corda*

Visitor: The Most Revd and Rt Hon the Lord Archbishop of Canterbury

President of the Council: The Rt Revd Bishop of St Albans

Council:
R M Abel Smith Esq
The Revd Canon J Cresswell, MA
C S S Drew Esq, MA
M R B Gatenby Esq, FCA
W J Hughes-D'Aeth Esq, TD, BA, PGCE
J C Lowe Esq, JP, MA Oxon
D F Macleod Esq, FCA
D S McMullen Esq, MA, DL
The Venerable Luke Miller Archdeacon of Hampstead
I F R Much Esq, MA
Dr A J Murray, MBiochem, DPhil Oxon
A J T Pilgrim Esq, BSc, FCA
Miss S E Pope, MA, MBA, FCIS
Mrs J G Scott, BSc, PGCE
C N C Sherwood Esq, MA Cantab, MBA
Revd Mrs A J Templeman, MA, DipTh
J D Thornton Esq, BSc Hons, MA, CEng, MICE, MCIOB
J C G Trower Esq, MA
S W Urry Esq, LLB, FCA

Secretary and Bursar: P Watkinson

Master: J S Davies, MA

Second Master: R L Turnbull, MA

Senior Master: P C T Monk, MA, MBE

Head of Lower School: Dr L B Pugsley, MA, PhD
Asst Head of Lower School: Mrs C J Gandon, BA (*Head of Classics*)

Head of Marketing: Mrs T Macpherson-Smith, BHum

Director of Studies: S R Smith, BA

Heads of Departments:
Art: J Marks, BA, LSDC
Biology: Mrs H Woolley, BSc
Careers: E Church, MA

Chemistry: R Dexter, BSc
Classics: Mrs C J Gandon, BA (*Asst Head of Lower School*)
Design Technology: G L D Macpherson-Smith, CertEd
Drama: Mrs R C Beggs, BA
Economics: J Cohen, BSc
English: N Parkin, BA
Geography: Mrs J Burger, BA
Girls' Games: Miss K E Andrew, BA (*Asst Director of Sport*)
History: E R L Bond, BA
ICT: W Irving, BSc, MSc
Learning Support: Mrs S Gates, BA, OCR DipSpLD
Mathematics: Mrs J Howard, BSc
Modern Languages: A N P Searson, BA
Director of Music: Q Thomas, MA, ARCO, MMus
PHSE: Mrs C Cohen, BSc
Physical Education: D J Payne-Cook, BEd
Physics: T Reade, BSc
Politics: M A Perrins, BA
Psychology: B Sandford Smith, BSc
Religious Studies: Mrs A J Baker, MA
Science: A Taylor, MA, BA
Spanish: Miss A Smith, BA
Director of Sport: I K George, DipPE

G Allen, MA	G Mitchell
H Baxendale, BA	Mrs J Mueller-Leighton
R H Bishop, BSc, MA	Miss C Orford, BA
P Blair, MA	Mrs M E Pagliarulo, LAM,
A Box, MA	Equity ISTD
Mrs C Bradley, MA,	A T M Parker, BA
MEng, MIEE	Mrs S Parkin, BA
Mrs M J Brooking, BEd	Mrs A Petrovic, BSc
T Cope, MEng	Mrs J Pilgrim, BSc Hons
J Deveson, BMus Hons,	S C Pinder, BA
MMus	C Pitchford, BA
C Filbey, BA	M Radley, MA
Mrs S Fletcher, BMedSc	Miss J Ross, BA Hons
Mrs B Gerty, MA	Miss G Rowe, BA
J Gillespie-Payne, MA	I E W Sanders, BSc
Dr C Holyoak, PhD, BSc	Miss J Schrader, MA, MEd
W Hopton, BA	Dr S Searson, PhD, BSc
Mrs M Hudson, BSc, MSc	B Shuler, BEng
S Hudson, MA	J N Spavin
R Hunter, BA	Miss S Stokely, BA
C E Igolen-Robinson, BA	Ms A Suarez
L Ilott, BEd	D Taberner, BSc, MSc
Miss A Jeans, BEd	M Tomkins, MMath
P Johns, BEd	Miss C Tomsett, BA
D Johnson, DPhil, MChem	M Tookey, BSc
R Johnson, BA	Mrs K Walsh, BA, OCR
K Kramer, BA	Cert SpLD
G Leman	Miss J Wells, BSc
J Lloyd, BA	J Whitworth, BA
Dr C Loughton, BSc, PhD	R Williams, BSc
K Loughton, BA, MPhil	P R Woodburn, BSc
N McCarthy, BEng	Ms M Wrinch, BA Hons
Dr F Michelli	

plus 15 Visiting Music Staff.

Academic Registrar: N Athey, MA

Senior Chaplain: Revd C R Briggs, BD, AKC

GCSE Examinations Officer: W H Flint Cahan, MA
A Level Examinations Officer: D R A Harvey, MSc, DPhil
IB Coordinator: Miss L Toivo, BA

Development Director: Ms H Tranter

International Students Officer: G Hessing, BSc Hons

Counsellor: Mrs L Othen-Price, MSc, BA, BACP

Librarian: Mrs E Harvey, BA

Instructors:
CCF SSI: WO1 B Eales
Cricket Professional: G Howarth, OBE
Rackets Professional: M Cawdron

Houses and Housemasters/mistresses:
Albans: Mrs E Alexander
Allenby: Mrs T Macpherson-Smith
Bartle Frere: E R L Bond
Batten: A J H Head
Colvin: Dr L Bindley
Edmonstone: S J Dixon
Hailey: Miss C Perri
Kipling: R L Matcham
Lawrence: J S Brammer
Melvill: Mrs A R B Spavin
Thomason: J R Jennings
Trevelyan: J F Alliott
The Russell Dore Lower School: Dr L B Pugsley

Registrar: Mrs E Alexander
Assistant Registrar: Mrs K Howe

Number in School. 749.

Location. Haileybury is situated approximately 20 miles due north of central London, 2 miles east of Hertford and 30 miles south of Cambridge. It is easily accessible by motorway and train to and from London and its airports. The school's 500-acre rural campus, with all its facilities and magnificent grounds on a single site, makes Haileybury unique.

History. Many of its buildings were designed by William Wilkins in the early 1800s for the East India Company's training college. The East India College was closed in 1858 after the Mutiny and re-opened as a school in 1862. During the Second World War the Imperial Service College at Windsor was amalgamated with Haileybury to become Haileybury and ISC, but to all intents and purposes our school is known simply as Haileybury. The old Imperial Service Junior School at Windsor served as Haileybury's junior school until 1997 prior to its amalgamation with Lambrook School in Bracknell to form the now thriving Lambrook Haileybury School.

Co-education. Since 1973 Haileybury has welcomed girls into its Sixth Form. In 1997 the Council took the decision to admit additionally girls aged 11 and 13 with effect from September 1998. There are girls in every year at Haileybury, making up 42% of the school roll.

Student Profile. Pupils can join at three levels: 11 year olds enter the Lower School, which has an annual intake of 48 and is a distinct unit within the Main School. The majority of pupils join the Removes at 13, while a number of girls and boys arrive at 16 to study A Levels and the International Baccalaureate Diploma. Almost 70% of pupils are boarders. Approximately 17% are from overseas.

Campus Life. Pupils joining at 11 enjoy the benefits of self-contained teaching and recreational space within the main site together with access to all the specialist facilities of the senior school. Newly refurbished, small dormitory-style boarding accommodation exists exclusively for under 13 year olds.

All accommodation for 13 to 18 year olds is centred around the Quadrangle and Houses are either recently built, or are newly refurbished older buildings to provide high-quality living and working conditions. In the Fifth Form pupils can expect to share a room, although many benefit from single accommodation, and in their final two Sixth Form years they usually enjoy a single room.

Two of the five girls' Houses have been newly built recently.

Day pupils join members of the boarding community to form houses that total roughly 55 in number. They are expected to remain in school until 6.30 pm each working day, although they are welcome to stay longer if they choose.

By arrangement with their housemaster and housemistress they may stay overnight. This flexibility allows for an easy transition into boarding, an option that increasing numbers of day pupils choose.

Welfare. The provision of a stimulating, caring environment in which all pupils can thrive is at the heart of our school. This is primarily achieved through open communication with children and their parents, vigilance and common sense, underpinned by our responsibilities under The Children Act.

Children in the Lower School have the supervision, support and help of a team of tutors whose pastoral role at Haileybury is dedicated to them. Once they join a House at 13 a pupil's housemaster or housemistress undertakes prime responsibility for his or her care and should be regarded as the first point of contact for pupils and parents alike. Housemasters and housemistresses are supported by teams of tutors, each with an important pastoral role, from the teaching staff.

A full-time doctor is resident at school to attend to all medical and health education matters from the Health Centre. Together with the Chaplains and a School Counsellor, he is available to listen and counsel pupils confidentially as they grow towards maturity.

Tuition and Curriculum. Our students are taught in small groups: 16 during years 7 and 8 in the Lower School, 20 or fewer from Years 9 to 11. A Level and IB classes average about 10–12, and never exceed 15. Pupils' progress is formally monitored by means of three-weekly reports and regular tutorials. Furthermore, teachers are constantly in touch with tutors, housemasters and housemistresses to keep all involved up to date with every pupil's performance.

All pupils have ready access to computers and there is dedicated teaching in their use for younger pupils. A computer leasing scheme exists enabling families to spread costs if they are investing in their own equipment, whilst providing a range of options covering use of equipment at school and home.

In a school that is reasonably selective but not highly selective, the principles of stretching the most able and encouraging those in need of particular support apply. Pupils are 'setted' and 'fast-tracked' on grounds according to ability, where this is deemed appropriate. Years 7 and 8 study English, Mathematics, Biology, Physics, Chemistry, Design Technology, Information Technology, History, Geography, French, Latin and Classical Civilisation, Art, Drama, Religious Studies and PE. Homework is set daily and the day pupils are able to complete it with supervision before going home.

Core elements of the Year 9 programme are Mathematics, the three Sciences, English, History, Geography, French, Art, Music, Religious Studies, Technology and Physical Education. Two options are chosen from: German or Spanish, Latin, Greek, Classical Civilisation, Drama, or EFL (English as a Foreign Language). A programme of PHSE and Information Technology continues throughout the year. Weekly Religious Studies classes are part of the school curriculum.

GCSE courses begin in Year 10. Most pupils will study 10 subjects. The most able will be encouraged to take these examinations early, especially in Mathematics and Modern Languages.

In addition to the AS/A level courses, the IB (International Baccalaureate) Diploma is also offered at Sixth Form.

In the Sixth Form pupils usually choose four AS followed by 3 A Levels in the Upper Sixth from a range of 26 subjects arranged in five groups or follow the increasingly popular IB Programme. Almost all Haileybury leavers proceed to university. A full university and careers advice is continually available and the school is a member of the Independent Schools Careers Organisation.

Out of Class Activities. The principles of a rounded education demand access to rich and varied opportunities. Haileybury provides these in many ways:

Games:

The girls play Lacrosse, Hockey and Netball in the two winter terms and choose between Tennis, Athletics, Rounders and Swimming in the summer. Boys and girls have regular access to our indoor swimming pool enabling swimming to be enjoyed both as a leisure activity and as a competitive sport. The main boys' game in the Christmas term is Rugby. In the winter months there is also provision for Rackets, Squash, Basketball, Cross-Country.

Soccer and Hockey are the main games in the Easter term, and Cricket in the Summer term. In the summer there is also the option of Athletics, Tennis, Swimming, Shooting, Sailing, Rowing and Golf.

The Sports Hall provides excellent facilities for all indoor games, including two indoor tennis courts and gym. The floodlit Astroturf pitch has been resurfaced recently and provides for Tennis (12 courts) in the summer and for Hockey in the winter.

In May 2008 the school will launch a new tennis academy with 8 indoor and outdoor courts, in partnership with the Legends' Tennis Academy, a private company part funded by the Lawn Tennis Association, where free professional coaching will be available to all pupils.

Activities:

School societies and activities flourish, either in the evenings after prep or during set activity times. The Design Technology Centre offers computing, electronics, metalwork, plastics and woodwork, with an emphasis on design and 'hands-on' skills.

Drama at Haileybury has always been strong and there are usually at least 12 productions during the year. There are two venues: the Ayckbourn Theatre providing fully-equipped studio facilities and new seating, and the newly refurbished auditorium in Big School, with a computerised lighting and sound system.

The School's musical life is exceptionally lively. The musicians perform outside Haileybury regularly. The Chapel Choir and Chamber Orchestra perform annually at venues such as St John's Smiths Square, London or West Road Concert Hall, Cambridge and recent tours have included performances in Leipzig and Tuscany. The installation of our new Chapel organ has provided a magnificent focal point for music here. The Chapel Choir has reached the final of the BBC Songs of Praise Schools Choir of the Year competition in two consecutive years and was awarded Schools Choir of the Year 2005.

The Art School is an exciting and creative department producing very high standards. In a separate purpose built area, it has extensive facilities for work in fine art, design and ceramics and it stages regular exhibitions including the annual Speech Day exhibition.

A popular but voluntary CCF exists for pupils who join initially for two years in order to take advantage of the specialist courses, shooting and adventure training. There is an indoor .22 rifle range. Alternatives to the CCF are the Duke of Edinburgh's Award scheme and Community service programmes.

Admission. Pupils can join at 11, 13 and 16. 11 year olds are asked to complete tests in English, Mathematics and Reasoning to supplement references from their current school. Boys and girls joining at 13 are asked to sit Haileybury's own entrance examinations or Common Entrance. Children joining the school at 11 usually gain entry to the Main School at 13 automatically.

Sixth Form entry for girls and boys is by entrance exams and interview. The selection procedure takes place at Haileybury in the November prior to the year of entry.

There is a registration fee of £75, a deposit of £1,000 and an entrance fee of £45 for boarders, £30 for day pupils.

All enquiries and applications for admission should be addressed to the Registry team who are happy to discuss any aspect of the admissions procedure, and from whom details regarding visits and Open Days are available.

Fees per term (2011-2012). Main School: £9,128 Boarders, £6,855 Day. Lower School (11–13 year olds): £5,789 Boarders, £4,556 Day.

The fees are reviewed annually.

Books and stationery are charged as extras and there are extra charges for music lessons, private tuition and for some sports, such as rowing.

Entrance Scholarships. (*See Scholarship Entries section.*) Many scholarships are available upon entrance to Haileybury. Academic and Music awards are available for 11, 13 and 16 year old entrants, All-Rounder Awards at 11 and 13, Art at 13 and 16, and Technology at 13.

Scholarships and All-Rounder Awards can be awarded up to the value of 10% of school fees and are tenable for the whole of the pupil's career at Haileybury. No fee remission is awarded for Art or Technology Scholarships. Successful candidates will be awarded a book token to the value of £100.

Bursaries may be awarded to increase the value of any Scholarship in case of genuine financial need. Application for a bursary entails confidential disclosure of capital and income of the parents, for which purpose a form may be obtained from the Registry or Bursary.

An Additional Information brochure is issued annually in September and this provides all appropriate information regarding dates and application procedure. This can be obtained from The Registrar, Haileybury, Hertford SG13 7NU or e-mail: registrar@haileybury.com. The Registry team will be pleased to discuss with parents any aspects of the scholarship procedure.

Charitable status. Haileybury is a Registered Charity, number 310013. It exists to provide education for boys and girls.

Hampton School

Hanworth Road, Hampton, Middlesex TW12 3HD
Tel: 020 8979 5526
Fax: 020 8783 4035
e-mail: headmaster@hamptonschool.org.uk
          admissions@hamptonschool.org.uk
website: www.hamptonschool.org.uk

Founded in the academic year of 1556/57 by Robert Hammond, a Hampton merchant, and re-established in 1612. From 1910 the School was administered by the local authority, latterly as a voluntary aided school, but in 1975 reverted to independent status.

Motto: *Praestat opes sapientia.*

The Governing Body:

Chairman: A J Roberts, CBE, BA, FRSA, FColl

P Baker, BSc, FRSA
N E Britnor, BSc, FRSA
Mrs M Choueiri, BA, MBA
R Davison, MA, LRPS
Mrs M Ellis, CertEd
His Honour Judge S E Kramer, MA, QC
J A Livingston, MA, DIPL Arch, RIBA
L R Llewellyn, BSc, MBA, FCMA, FRSA
A H Munday, LLB, QC
S C Naidu
J S Perry, BA
Air Vice-Marshal (Retd) G Skinner, CBE, MSc, BSc,
   CEng, FIMechE, FILT, FRAeS
N J Spooner, Cert Arch

M J Turner, FCA
R M Walker, MA
The Revd D N Winterburn, BSc, MA, Vicar of Hampton

Clerk to the Governors and Bursar: M A King, BSc

Headmaster: B R Martin, MA, MBA, FCMI, FRSA

Deputy Heads:
Ms P Z S Message, BSc
K Knibbs, MA
P D Hills, MA, PhD

Assistant Head: Mrs E T Watson, BA

Senior Tutors:
D R Clarke, BHum
A N R McBay, BSc, MSc
J P Orr, MA
S Paraskos, MA
S A Wilkinson, MA

Admissions Manager: Mrs D Jones, BA, Dip Mar
Admissions Assistant: Mrs C Elia, BA

Departmental Staff:
* *Head of Department*

Art:
*Mrs K A Williams, BA
J Baker, BA
A J Bannister, BA, MA
S T Hill, BA, MA

Biology:
*P H Langton, BSc, Dip EnvSci
C J Barnett, MA
R J Davieson, BSc (*Head of Lower Sixth, Safeguarding Designated Person*)
Mrs H Berrow, MA
Miss P A Holmes, BSc (*Head of Fourth Year*)
M I Johnstone, BSc, MSc
Ms K L Martin, MA
Ms P Z S Message, BSc (*Deputy Head, Safeguarding Designated Person*)
G Ryan, BSc
M J Williams, BSc
Mrs L A Holmes, BSc

Careers and UCAS:
*P J Talbot, BA, MA
R D Worrallo, BA

Chemistry:
*S C Clark, BSc, PhD
Mrs H Berrow, BA
P A Coleman, BSc
N J Double, BSc (*Asst Head of Fourth Year*)
Ms C J Gilfillan, MSci
Miss P A Holmes, BSc (*Head of Fourth Year*)
Mrs F Knibbs, BSc
Mrs C Mackey, MSc
J Neville, MChem
W D Partridge, MChem

Classics:
*J W Barber, MA
Miss A H Jacobs, MA
N A Coyle, BA
M D Haswell, BA, MA
P D Hills, MA, PhD (*Deputy Head*)
T J Leary, MLitt, PhD, PGCertARM (*Keeper of the Archives*)

Design & Technology:
*M A Carroll, BSc
R Alvarez
A Goodridge
B Ridley
J Sadler, BSc RDTHSC

J O Sarpong, BSc
Ms D C Woodward, BSc

Drama:
*Miss V K Buse, BA
M J Duda, BA
R K Kothakota, BA (*Asst Head of Fifth Year*)

Economics and Business Studies:
*S Paraskos, MA (*Senior Tutor*)
Z A Higgins, BSc (*Head of Rugby Development and Performance*)
B R Martin, MA, MBA, FCMI, FRSA (*Headmaster*)
N R Newman, BA (*Asst Head of Third Year*)
J D Slater, BA (*Head of Upper Sixth*)
R T Vyvyan, MBA (*Head of Business Studies*)

English:
*Miss C E Goddard, BA
M C Brereton, BA, MA, DPhil
Miss J M Dearden, BA
Mrs C M O'Hanlon, BA, MA
H Hardingham, BA, MA
Mrs C M O'Hanlon, BA, MA
M Payne, BA, MA
P Smith, BA, MA
S Timbs, BA (*Asst Head of Games, Rugby*)
P Thomas, BA
S C A Whitwell, BA, PhD
Ms A C McLusky, BA
Ms H Booker, BA

Geography:
*B S Bett, BA, MA
Ms L J Farrell, BA
J R Partridge, MA (*Head of First Year*)
Miss J A Reid, BSc
P J Talbot, BA, MA (*Director of Careers and UCAS*)
Mrs R Wallace, BA
Mrs A J Boulton, MA

History:
*A J Cook, MA
Miss H E Cheshire, BA (*Asst Head of First Year*)
D R Clarke, BHum (*Senior Tutor*)
Ms J L Glasson, BA (*Assistant Head of First Year*)
D Grossel, BA
H Hardingham, BA, MA
K Knibbs, MA (*Deputy Head, Safeguarding Designated Person*)
A J Lawrence, BA
J Parrish, BA (*Asst Head of Upper Sixth*)
Miss V M Smith, BA
H R Wiggins, MA (*Head of Third Year*)
R D Worrallo, BA (*Asst Director of Careers and UCAS, Talk!*)
M P Cross, BA

Information Technology:
*Ms J L Ah-Sam, BSc
Mrs M W Field, BSc
Mrs J Moran, BA
J Phillips, BA

Learning Support:
*Mrs S Harradine, CertEd, BDA DipSpLD, PG DipEd
Miss T Sainsbury, BSc (*Teaching Assistant*)

Mathematics:
*E B Bowles, MEng
Ms J L Ah-Sam, BSc
D W Anderson, BSc
C G Aubrey, MA
A Banerjee, BSc
J C Clarke, BA (*Assistant Head of First Year*)
A D Gutteridge, MA
A W Kershaw, BSc

J J Lee, MA
A N R McBay, BSc, MSc (*Senior Tutor*)
B C Murphy, MEng (*Head of Junior Football*)
J P Orr, MA (*Senior Tutor*)
D M Perfect, BSc
Miss S C Roberts, BA (*Asst Head of Lower Sixth*)
Miss A Schröder, BA
Mrs A Burke, MA
Mrs H Clarke, BSc
Mrs M W Field, BSc
Mrs H E Marion, MA
Mrs C H Reyner, MA, MSc

Modern Languages:
*A T W Frazer, MA (*Head of French*)
M J Passey, BA (*Head of Spanish*)
D E Peel, BA (*Head of German*)
Mrs J C Owen, BA (*Head of Russian, Head of Second Year*)
Mrs L Barrett, BA, MBA (*Mandarin*)
Ms E Biagioli, BA
C J Blachford, BA
F C Chaveneau, BA
Ms K N Dubova, BA
Ms S Garrido-Soriano, BA
Ms S May, BA
J B Rojas, BA
P Studt, BA, MA
P G Turner, BA
Mrs E T Watson, BA (*Assistant Head*)
Mrs S C D Yoxon, MA
Ms S A Buckley, BA
Mrs M A Chandler, MA

Music:
*I C Donald, BA (*Director of Music*)
C Dawe, MA, MMus, PGDip RNCM, PGCert TCM
Ms C R Jordan, BMus (*Asst Director of Music*)
Miss H-M Lucas, BA
Ms K Ford, BA (*Music Administrator*)

Personal Health and Social Education:
J H Talman, BA
Mrs R J Nicholson, MPhys (*Asst Head of Fifth Year*)

Physical Education and Games:
*P Bolton, BSc (*Head of PE*)
D R Clarke, BHum (*Senior Tutor*)
C Greenaway (*Director of Rowing*)
R Hutterd, BEd (*Outdoor Pursuits*)
C T Mills, BSc (*Head of Games, Football*)
B O Ruse, BA
M K Sims, BSc (*Sports Rehabilitation*)
S Timbs, BA (*Asst Head of Games, Rugby*)
I L MacLean, MA

Physics:
*Ms J Dibden, BSc
Mrs J L Boon, MA
G H Clark, BSc
D J Fendley, BEng (*Head of Fifth Year*)
S Gray, BSc
Ms K E Millar, BEng (*Asst Head of Lower Sixth*)
C D Parr, BSc
W Pope, BEng
L O Rouse, BSc
Mrs R J Nicholson, MPhys (*Asst Head of Fifth Year, Asst Head of PHSE*)
N D Woods, MA, MEng (*Asst Head of Third Year*)

Politics:
*Ms J A Field, BA
Miss H E Cheshire, BA (*Asst Head of Second Year*)
M P Cross, BA
A J Lawrence, BA
Miss V M Smith, BA

H R Wiggins, BA, MA (*Head of Third Year*)
R D Worrallo, BA, MA (*Asst Director of Careers and UCAS*)

Psychology:
*A M MacDonald, BSc
S J Wakefield, BSc

Religious Studies:
*M A J Nicholson, BA (*Asst Head of Second Year*)
M R Grundmann, MA
Miss A Parker, BA
J H Talman, BA
S A Wilkinson, MA (*Senior Tutor*)

Library:
K Hemsley, MA
Mrs J Axton, MA (*Archives Asst*)
Miss J Iredale, BA, DipIM (*Careers Library*)

Examinations Officer: Mrs M Barnes

School Nurse: Mrs R Cash, SRN

Hampton is a day school of around 1,200 boys aged from 11 to 18, including a Sixth Form of about 340. It offers an excellent all-round education, encouraging academic ambition, personal responsibility and independent thinking in an energetic, happy and well-disciplined community.

The most recent ISI inspection (February 2010) found Hampton to be a school where pupils are exceptionally well educated in accordance with the school's holistic educational aims. The school achieves excellence in its pastoral care and moral and spiritual guidance and also in the quality of the pupils' academic and other achievements. The pupils' personal development was deemed outstanding. The teaching at the school, described as dedicated, committed and often inspiring, makes an excellent contribution to pupils' educational progress. It was also noted that the curriculum is enriched by an extensive, varied range of co-curricular activities and links with the community. The inspection report confirmed the School's success in meeting its aim of producing mature, confident yet unpretentious young people who have a helpful, committed attitude both to their school and the wider community.

Hampton is increasingly academically selective and almost all boys go on to leading universities with the vast majority to the Russell Group universities. The Sixth Form has a strong emphasis on deep academic enquiry, breadth of study, critical thinking and independent learning.

An annual exchange programme offers boys the chance to visit Spain, Germany, France, Italy and Russia as well as Asia, Africa and the Far East. Boys visit many other countries through academic and sporting initiatives and there is an extraordinary range of trips available.

Music and drama are central to the character of the school. Concerts, musicals and plays involve all age groups throughout the year. Most boys learn musical instruments and there is a regular orchestral exchange visit to Germany. Singing is also very popular and there are eight different choral groups. A recent theatrical highlight was the joint production of Oklahoma! (with the adjacent The Lady Eleanor Holles Girls' School). A new Performing Arts Centre, The 450 Hall, a centre of excellence for the Performing Arts, was opened in September 2009 to commemorate the School's 450th anniversary.

Hampton has an outstanding reputation for sport and many boys represent their county or country in a wide range of sports. Particular strengths are cricket, football, rowing, rugby, tennis and chess. Hampton has produced many schoolboy internationals in a wide range of sports and also Olympic rowers; the School shares a nearby boathouse on the Thames with The Lady Eleanor Holles School.

Integrity and social conscience are encouraged implicitly through the daily interaction of boys and teachers, as well as explicitly through School Assembly, PSHE lessons, extensive Charity, Environment and Community Service programmes, and a long-standing link with Kiira College in Uganda. The School became the first 'climate neutral' school in the country by offsetting all of its carbon emissions. The School was one of the two founding schools of the 'Mindfulness in Schools Project' promoting pupil wellbeing.

Hampton School and The Lady Eleanor Holles School are served by 24 coach routes across south-west London, Surrey and Berkshire.

Buildings and Grounds. The School has been situated on its present site since 1939. Its buildings include an Assembly Hall, Dining Hall, Sports Hall, Performing Arts Centre, classrooms, and a full set of laboratories for the separate sciences, technology, information technology, and languages.

The School stands within its own grounds of some 25 acres, including four rugby pitches, seven football pitches, six cricket squares and six hard tennis courts.

The Garrick Building is a purpose-built and newly-refurbished music facility, accommodating a large music hall, specialist music technology suite and teaching rooms. The newly opened 450 Hall is an exceptional performing arts facility, doubling as a theatre and concert hall and, equipped with an orchestra pit, also an ideal venue for Music Theatre.

The Technology Department, part of the Teaching Block opened in 2004, includes provision for practical work in metal, plastics, wood and pneumatics, as well as a drawing office, a large project space, a dark room and an applied science laboratory for electronics and control technology. The Mason Library houses a substantial stock of books and journals, supplemented by other information retrieval facilities and online search and information resources. The Library also houses a quiet study area and 20 specially designed IT workstations.

The Steedman Sports Hall, opened by Sir Roger Bannister in December 1987, was designed as a centre for the development of personal fitness as well as for sports training and recreation. A new set of changing rooms, Sixth Form Common Room, Combined Cadet Force rooms and further facilities were completed in February 2003.

The Alexander Centre accommodates the History Department, together with the Careers Centre. The north side of the building houses pavilion and changing room facilities for Cricket. The Shepherd Lecture Theatre, fully equipped for multimedia presentations, seats 150 and adjoins the Alexander Centre. There are six ICT laboratories within the main School building and all members of staff are provided with a wireless-linked laptop computer. Classrooms are equipped with data projectors.

The dining rooms and kitchens were opened in September 1997. The Millennium Boathouse, shared with The Lady Eleanor Holles School, was opened by Sir Steve and Lady Redgrave in 2000. This spectacular riverside facility provides the focal point for a highly successful and popular Boat Club, whose rowing squads regularly achieve both team and individual national and regional success.

A 25-room teaching building was completed in 2000 to provide additional Science laboratories, and to house Art, Geography, Classics, Economics and Business Studies.

A Sports Pavilion/Sixth Form Centre was opened in February 2003 and the 450 Hall, the new Performing Arts Centre, was opened in September 2009.

The latest addition is the Atrium, a three-storey extension, opened in September 2010, comprising 11 teaching spaces, one of which is a state-of-the-art IT based "Classroom of the Future". Connected to the main building, the Atrium also provides additional wash room facilities.

Community. Hampton School enjoys particularly strong links with two neighbouring schools, Hampton Community College (HCC) and The Lady Eleanor Holles School (LEH). These two schools participate in various activities with Hampton pupils, especially Drama and Music, Combined

Cadet Force and the very popular visiting speakers '*Talk!*' programme. A 'United Nations Youth & Student Association' (UNYSA) branch involves pupils meeting to discuss issues of national and international significance. Strong links are maintained with the numerous local state primary schools which provide around 70% of our First Year intake. In conjunction with SHINE (a London-based educational charity), boys from a number of local state primary schools attend on Saturday mornings to take part in teaching sessions that are designed to be *serious*, with a focus on learning but also *fun*.

In addition, Hampton School has a busy Community Service programme and also hosts many events for schools in Richmond Borough. All members of the Lower Sixth undertake a placement in a local primary school as part of the General Studies course, working with young children on literacy, numeracy, computing and sport. Many boys in the Fourth Year and above volunteer their assistance in primary schools, residential homes for the elderly, or the local Barnardos project. Various joint activities are run with LEH, including an annual Christmas Party for the elderly, and a trip to the Science Museum for children with special needs. Several Sixth Formers are involved in holiday schemes for children from more deprived parts of East London each summer.

Curriculum. Boys in the Lower School follow a wide curriculum, including Technology, Physics, Chemistry, Biology, a Modern Language (French, German or Spanish) and Latin. Mandarin has recently been added to the curriculum; Greek, Classical Civilisation and Russian are optional subjects begun in the Third Year. In the Fourth and Fifth Years all boys continue to study, in addition to PE, Games and Religious Studies, the following: English Language, English Literature, a Modern Language, Mathematics and the three sciences for either GCSE or IGCSE. They choose three subjects from the following: Art, Classical Civilisation, Drama, French, Geography, German, Greek, History, Latin, Mandarin, Music, Religious Studies, Russian, Spanish and Technology. Most of these GCSEs/IGCSEs are taken at the end of the Fifth Year. The most able mathematicians take GCSE/IGCSE at the end of the Fourth Year and then move on to AS Level study in the Fifth Year.

The Sixth Form offers a free choice of A and AS Level subjects, in addition to a wide range of courses leading to A Level General Studies, and the option to enter for Critical Thinking. Additional teaching and preparation is provided for boys seeking entrance to Oxford or Cambridge, to which around twenty to twenty-five boys are admitted each year. Many boys also opt to take the Extended Project Qualification.

Games. Games and Physical Education are part of every boy's School week, though other activities are permissible alternatives in the Sixth Form. The majority of boys also take part in voluntary sport on Saturdays; fixtures, at a range of ability levels, are arranged for each age group. Whenever possible boys are able to choose which sport to follow. In winter, the major games are Rugby, Association Football and Rowing; in summer, Cricket, Athletics and Rowing. Other sports include Tennis, Real Tennis, Fencing, Squash, Skiing, Windsurfing, Sailing and Swimming.

Careers. Each boy receives advice from the careers staff at those points when subject choices should be made. The School is a member of ISCO, who provide Morrisby testing as part of the Fifth Year advice programme. A Careers Convention is held annually, there are advice evenings for parents on A Level choice and on university decision-making, and comprehensive work experience is arranged.

Pastoral Care. This is one of the strongest features of the School. A boy's form tutor is responsible in the first instance for his academic and pastoral welfare and progress, and the work of form tutors is coordinated by year heads under the direction of one of the Deputy Heads. Parents are always welcome to discuss their son's work with any of these tutors, and Parents' Evenings provide an opportunity to meet subject teachers. Year group Pastoral Forums provide parents with an opportunity to meet staff responsible for pupil welfare and to discuss a variety of pastoral issues. There is also an active Parents' Association.

Societies. The School's large CCF contingent, run jointly with The Lady Eleanor Holles School, and more recently an intake from Hampton Community College, comprises Army and RAF sections and has a programme which includes adventurous training, orienteering and gliding. Boys may also participate in the Duke of Edinburgh's Award scheme or the activities of the School's Adventure Society, which organises camps and expeditions both in the UK and overseas.

The Music Department fosters solo and ensemble performance as well as composition, and offers pupils an opportunity to perform in the School's orchestras, bands and choirs. The Joint Choral Society, with the neighbouring Lady Eleanor Holles Girls' School, gives a performance of a major choral work annually. There is at least one dramatic production each term, and also an annual musical. In all these activities, as in the Community Service work, the School enjoys close cooperation with The Lady Eleanor Holles Girls' School.

A programme of visiting speakers, '*Talk*!', holds lunchtime and evening meetings and offers boys the opportunity to hear and question distinguished politicians, writers, academics and scientists.

There is also a full range of subject related and hobby societies, among which Chess, Debating, the Technology Club and the Astronomy Society are particularly strong.

Admission. Boys normally join the School in September. We aim for about 120 boys per year to be admitted at 11 by the School's own entrance examination, which is held in the January of Year 6. A further 60–70 enter at 13 through the Common Entrance Examination, following a pre-test in the September of Year 7. Boys are also admitted into the Sixth Form and to fill occasional vacancies at other ages at the Headmaster's discretion. Further details may be obtained from the Admissions Manager (Tel: 020 8979 9273).

Fees per term (2011-2012). £4,870 inclusive of books and stationery.

Scholarships. (*See Scholarship Entries section.*) At present, at 11+ the Governors offer open academic scholarships and one Hammond Scholarship (geographically restricted). At 13+ academic scholarships are offered through the Common Academic Scholarship Examinations. All-rounder and Art awards are available at 11+ and 13+.

Instrumental music scholarships are offered at both 11+ and 13+. A Choral Scholarship is available for boys of 11 with treble voices who are, or will become, choristers of the Chapel Royal at Hampton Court Palace.

The School also has a Bursary Fund, from which awards are made according to parental financial circumstances and the academic or all-round potential which their son may demonstrate. Further details of scholarships may be obtained from the Admissions Manager.

Old Hamptonians' Association. Leavers are entitled to life membership of this association which provides regular communication with members and has active sporting and dramatic sections. The OHA Office is located at School and can be contacted by e-mail: oha@hamptonschool.org.uk.

Charitable status. Hampton School is a Registered Charity, number 1120005. It aims to provide a challenging and demanding education for boys of high academic promise from the widest possible variety of social backgrounds.

Harrow School

Harrow on the Hill, Middlesex HA1 3HP
Tel: 020 8872 8000 (Enquiries)
020 8872 8003 (Head Master)
020 8872 8007 (Admissions)
020 8872 8320 (Bursar)
Fax: 020 8423 3112 (School)
020 8872 8012 (Head Master)
e-mail: harrow@harrowschool.org.uk
website: www.harrowschool.org.uk

Harrow School was founded in 1572 by John Lyon under a Royal Charter from Queen Elizabeth.
Motto: *Stet Fortuna Domus*

Visitors:
The Archbishop of Canterbury
The Bishop of London

Governors:
R C Compton (*Chairman*)
J A Strachan, BSc, FRICS
J F R Hayes, MA, FCA
W G S Massey, QC, MA
Professor D J Womersley, PhD
S J G Doggart, MA
V L Sankey, MA
Mrs J Forman Hardy, LLB
C H St J Hoare, BA
K W B Gilbert, BA, FCA
E J H Gould, MA
R C W Odey, BA
Mrs H S Crawley
J P Batting, MA, FFA
Professor G Furniss, BA, PhD
M K Fosh, BA, MSI
Professor Sir David Wallace, CBE, FRS, FREng
The Hon Robert Orr-Ewing
Mrs S Whiddington, AB
D A Crehan, BSc, MSc, ARCS, CPhys
Rear Admiral G M Zambellas, DSC, BSc
Professor P Binski, MA, PHD, FSA, FRSA
C Stonehill, MA
A P McClaran, BA, FCMI

Clerk to the Governors: The Hon Andrew Millett, MA, 45 Pont Street, London SW1X 0BX

Head Master: J B Hawkins, MA

Deputy Head Master: M L Mrowiec, MA

Senior Master: A S Lee, MA, DMS

Director of Studies: J R Elzinga, BA

Director of Boarding: P G Dunbar, MA

Bursar: N A Shryane, MBE, BA, MPhil

Registrar: A R Taylor, BA

Assistant Staff:
T G Hersey, BSc
A H M Thompson, MA
J P M Baron, MA
C J Deacon, MA
R D Burden, BSc
J E Holland, BA, PhD, MLitt
M E Smith, MA
W Snowden, BA
S J Halliday, BA
M G Tyrrell, MA
P J Bieneman, BA
P J Warfield, BA
S F MacPherson, MA
P D Hunter, MA
S P Berry, MA
A R McGregor, MA
C D Barry, BSc (*Head of Physics*)
M P Stead, MA
The Revd J E Power, BSc, BA (*Chaplain*)

C J Farrar-Bell, MA
Dr P G Davies, BSc, PhD
A D Todd, BA, MPhil (*Head of History*)
M J Tremlett, BA
N J Marchant, BEng (*Head of Academic ICT*)
Mrs L A Moseley, BA
M J M Ridgway, BSc
S N Page, BEd
T J Wickson, BA, MEd, AMBDA
I Hammond, BSc (*Head of Mathematics*)
B J D Shaw, BA (*Head of Classics*)
E R Sie, BSc, PhD
K M Wilding, BA
N Page, BA (*Head of Modern Languages*)
A K Metcalfe, BA
M Roberts, BSc, PhD
E W Higgins, BSc
S M Griffiths, BA (*Head of Design Technology*)
C S Tolman, BA (*Head of Economics*)
N D A Kemp, MSc, DPhil (*Head of Politics*)
C de L Mann, BSc
Miss B R Davies, BA
G H White, BSc
R Murray, BSc (*Head of Statistics*)
J A Hanson
N S Keylock, MSc (*Head of Biology*)
C J A Terry, BSc
R J O'Donoghue, MA (*Head of Geography*)
M G J Walker, BA (*Head of German*)
F E J Wawn, MA
R J Harvey, BA (*Head of Religious Studies*)
S A Harrison, BSc, PhD
J L Roberts, MA
Dr D R Wendelken, PhD
Mrs L Smith, BSc, BEd
C T Buys, BSc
D F Cox, BA
Dr S J Abbott, PhD
C P Bates, BSc
S C Costello, BA
Mrs R L Sharples, BA (*Head of History of Art*)
Miss H Mervis, BA
I A Stroud, BA (*Head of Sculpture*)
Miss S L Mackrory, BA
J S Webb, MA, MSc, MLitt
Dr A F Worrall, MA, MSc, PhD (*Head of Chemistry*)
J Kyte, BA
D R J Bell, BA (*Head of Photography*)
J N James, BA (*Head of English*)
T M Knight, BA
J J Coulson, BA (*Director of Sport*)
R J Try, BA
T M Dalton, BSc
Dr M T Glossop, BSc, MA, PhD
Miss A C Brooking, MA (*Head of French*)
C E Penhale, BSc
R H Potter, BA
S N Taylor, BA (*Head of Art*)
D Llywelyn Hall, BA
W J C Gaisford, BA
S M Sampson, BSc
N G Jones, MEng
J O Thomas, BSc
Fr S P Seaton, MA (*Roman Catholic Chaplain*)
Dr J A P Bedford, BA, PhD
Dr D P Earl, BSc, PhD
Miss J S L Salley, BA
Dr C D O'Mahony, BA, DPhil (*Director of ICT*)
Miss E L Watson, BEng
W Turner, BA
Mrs C J Carroll, BChem
G Allen, BA

Music Staff:
D N Woodcock, MA, FRCO (*Director of Music*)
P J Evans, BA
D N Burov (*Head of Strings*)
G R M Layton, MMus, MSt (*Head of Music Technology*)
S McWilliam, LTCL (*Head of Wind Instruments and Commercial Music*)

and 27 visiting teachers

Librarian: Mrs M Staunton
Careers Master: D F Cox
Officer Commanding CCF: Major N Page
School Medical Officer: The Stanmore Medical Practice

Houses:
Bradbys: Dr D R Wendelken
The Grove: Mr P J Bieneman
Rendalls: Mr K M Wilding
The Park: Mr P D Hunter
West Acre: Mr M E Smith
The Knoll: Dr E R Sie
Druries: Mr M J M Ridgway
The Head Master's: Mr A R McGregor
Elmfield: Mr M J Tremlett
Moretons: Mr P J Evans
Newlands: Mr E W Higgins
Gayton: Mr R Murray
Lyon's: Mr A K Metcalfe

The School. Harrow is distinctive in four ways. First, we aim to achieve very good exam results for all pupils. Second, we are all-boarding. We avoid the difficulties which can arise when some pupils go home at the end of the day and others do not. We are able to put on a range of worthwhile activities at weekends which would not be possible if some pupils had gone home. Thirdly, we place a particular emphasis on a broad approach to education. We believe that some of the most valuable aspects of education can be learnt outside the classroom. Finally, we combine a long history and sense of tradition with a modern approach to the curriculum and education. Harrow is the only full boarding school in London.

Shape of the School Term. For the first two weekends all pupils are in the School and many activities are laid on. If they are able to, parents come and visit. On the third weekend all pupils go home or to friends; the weekend starts at 12 noon on Friday and ends at 9 pm on Sunday. The next two weekends are followed by a nine day half term. This pattern is repeated throughout the term.

Boarding Houses. There are eleven boarding houses, all of a similarly good standard. In all Houses boys have their own bed-sitting rooms, usually shared with one other pupil in the first and second years.

The School estates, on and around the Hill, extend to over 300 acres. They include cricket and football fields, athletics track and sports hall (with indoor swimming pool), golf course and farm.

Admission. Application for admission should be made to the Registrar. Boys are admitted between the age of 12 and 16, but most in the September before their fourteenth birthday. Most candidates take the Common Entrance Examination at their Preparatory Schools usually in the term preceding entrance to Harrow. There are also some vacancies for Sixth Form boys.

Fees per term (2011-2012). £10,310. A small number of optional charges are not covered by the consolidated fee (for private tuition in music, for example).

Entrance Scholarships. (*See Scholarship Entries section.*) 25 Scholarships range in value from £500 per annum to 5% of the fee and are awarded for excellence in academic work, or music, or art, or for some other talent. These Scholarships may be supplemented up to the full fee where financial need is shown although such supplementable Scholarships are awarded only to boys of high academic or musical ability. Full particulars may be obtained from the Admissions Secretary.

Curriculum. Year 1 (aged 13 to 14): English Language, English Literature, Mathematics, Physics, Chemistry, Biology, Computing (Information Technology), Design Technology, History, Geography, Religious Studies, French, German, Spanish, Latin, Greek, Art, Music.

Years 2 and 3 (aged 14 to 16): up to 10 of the above subjects leading to GCSE qualification.

Years 4 and 5 (aged 16 to 18): four of the following subjects leading to AS and A Level qualifications: Mathematics, Physics, Chemistry, Biology, Design Technology, Economics, Business Studies, English, French, German, Mandarin, Spanish, Italian, Latin, Greek, History, Ancient History, Geography, Religious Studies, Art, Photography, History of Art, Music. Japanese and Arabic are also taught to GCSE and A Level.

At this stage students can also be prepared for the SAT tests required by American universities.

At every level students are taught to play a wide variety of sports.

Activities. All pupils take a wide range activities outside the classroom. These include:

* Music. Harrow is one of the UK's leading schools for musical education. Large numbers learn to play an instrument or sing in the School Choirs.
* Drama. The School has one of the best equipped theatres in any UK school and boys perform up to 12 plays each year.
* Sports, including soccer, swimming, rugby, cricket, athletics, cross-country running, riding, polo, fencing, rackets, tennis, fives, archery, basketball, badminton, squash, sailing, climbing. The School has its own golf course.
* Art: drawing, painting and sculpture.
* Clubs designed to foster new interests and develop skills.

Old Boys' Society. Harrow Association. *Director*: C J A Virgin, Harrow School, Harrow on the Hill, Middlesex HA1 3HP.

Charitable status. The Keepers and Governors of the Free Grammar School of John Lyon is a Registered Charity, number 310033. The aims and objectives of the Charity are to provide education for the pupils at the two schools in the Foundation, Harrow School and John Lyon School.

Hereford Cathedral School

Old Deanery, The Cathedral Close, Hereford HR1 2NG
Tel: 01432 363522
Fax: 01432 270834
e-mail: schoolsec@hcsch.org
website: www.herefordcs.com

Founded ante 1384. No record of the School's foundation survives, although its close association with the Cathedral is indicated by Bishop Gilbert's response to the long-standing right of the Chancellor to appoint the Headmaster in a letter of 1384, and it is probable that some educational institution was always associated with the Cathedral, which was founded in 676.

Governing Body:
President: The Very Revd M Tavinor, Dean of Hereford, MA, MMus
Chairman: The Earl of Darnley, MA
R Haydn Jones, BSc, MRICS
C D Hitchiner, LLB, ACIS
Mrs D Bradshaw, BA, MA
C R Potter, FCCA (*OH*)
C M Poole, MBE, LRPS
Prof. E Ellis, MA, PhD
Lady Mynors, BA

Mrs V Oliver-Davies, JP
P A Andrews, MA
A T Teale, BSc

Clerk to the Governors: N J Moon

***Headmaster*: P A Smith**, BSc

Deputy Head: B G Blyth, BA

Deputy Head (*Academic*): J P Stanley, MA, MBA

Head of Sixth Form: J R Terry, BSc

Chaplain: Canon Revd P A Row, MA

Heads of Department:

Art: C A Wilkes, BA
Biology: Mrs E Segalini-Bower, MSc
Chemistry: Mrs A J Burdett, MSc
Classics: Miss E P Sage, BA
Drama: Ms L D A Zammit, BEd
Economics: M R Jackson, BA
English: J B Petrie, BA
Geography: Mrs R M Floyd, BSc
History: P A Wright, BA
Learning Support: Miss L R Stevens, BA
Mathematics: P S Thornley, BA
Modern Languages: T M Lutley, BA
Music: D R Evans, MA, GBSM
PE and Games: R P Skyrme, BA
Physics: Dr S J B Rhodes, BEng, PhD
Religious Studies: Mrs A E D Locke, MA
Technology: C J Howells, BA

Careers Adviser: Mrs M McCumisky, BA
OC CCF: Lt Col A K Eames, RM
Director of Finance and Resources: N J Moon
Headmaster's PA: Mrs S Gurgul
Marketing Director: C J Townend, BA, ACIM
Development Director: Mrs C M Morgan-Jones
Admissions Officer: Mrs S D A Fortey
Tel: 01432 363506, e-mail: admissions@hcsch.org
Examinations Officer: Mrs C J Notley
School Office Administrator: Mrs L G Harding

The Junior School
Headmaster: T C Wheeler, MA, BA
Deputy Headmaster: J M Debenham, BEd
Head of Pre-Prep: Mrs E Lord, BEd

Assistant Staff:
Mrs E A A Ashford, CertEd
Dr I Barber, BSc
Mrs B J Batchelor, BA
T Brown, BA (*History, Geography*)
Mrs M Cadman-Davies, BA, CertEd
Mrs H Copley-May, BA Ed (*Pre-Prep Music*)
Miss K A Davies, BEd (*Girls' Games/Swimming*)
Mrs P Gammage, DipEd
Mrs C Goode, BEd
Mrs K Gummerson (*Art*)
T Hutchinson, BSc, CertEd (*ICT*)
Miss N Jeynes, BEd (*Mathematics*)
Miss C Lambert, BA (*French*)
Mrs S Legge, BA
Mrs K A Matthews, BA
Mrs D J Parry, BA (*English/PSE*)
Mrs S Price, LLB, PGCE
Miss A Sutton, BA (*Drama*)
M Thomas, MA, BMus (*Music*)
S Turpin, BA
Miss H Watkins, BA
M Wilkinson, BEd
Mrs J Windows, BA (*Head of Nursery*)

Secretary: Mrs S Stick
Nurse: Mrs S Warner, RGN

The School is a former Direct Grant and Assisted Places School, which now operates its own Bursary scheme. It is a fully co-educational 11–18 day school of 524 pupils.

Admission. Pupils are normally admitted at the ages of 11, 13 or 16. Admission at age 11 is by sitting the Junior Entrance Examination at the School, or at 13 by sitting the Summer Entrance Examination. Suitably qualified boys and girls may be admitted at Sixth Form level, or at 12+ or 14+, if there are vacancies. The school operates a Deferred Entry scheme at 11 for 13+ entries.

Facilities. The School is situated in the lee of the Cathedral. It occupies many historic buildings and some later ones, all adapted for School use, as well as purpose-built facilities. On the main campus are, in addition to some of the main departments, eight science departments, four which are new, a large music school, an Art, Technology and Computer Centre (that gained Hereford's first RIBA award for architecture), the Gilbert Library and a refurbished Dining Hall. The Zimmerman Building provides 20,000 square feet of robust working space for Classics, Modern Languages, examination/functions hall, Geography and Drama departments and the Sixth Form Centre. A new on-site Sports Hall was opened in April 2009, which has first-class facilities for badminton, five-a-side football, netball, basketball and four sets of cricket nets. Rugby and outdoor cricket is held at the School's Wyeside sports ground, alongside the HCS rowing club.

Curriculum. Pupils are divided on entry at 11 into 4 forms (a maximum of 20 pupils per form) for academic and pastoral purposes. Below the Sixth Form, pupils take a broad range of subjects. Option choices are made at the end of the Third year (Year 9).

In the Sixth Form pupils are prepared for A (AS/A2) Levels, for which there is a wide choice of subjects: Latin, Greek, English Literature/Language (Combined), English Literature, French, Religious Studies, Classical Civilisation, Spanish, Economics, History, Geography, Mathematics, Further Mathematics, Biology, Physics, Chemistry, Design Technology, Art, Textiles, History of Art, Business Studies, Music and Music Technology, Theatre Studies and Physical Education. Almost all students go on to Higher Education degree courses and the vast majority to the university course of their choice.

Religious instruction throughout is in accordance with the doctrines of the Church of England. The School is privileged to have the daily use of the Cathedral for Chapel.

Sports/Activities include Rugby, Cricket, Badminton, Tennis, Hockey, Netball, Athletics, and Rowing. There is a CCF Group and a wide range of societies active within the School. The School is an Operating Authority for the Duke of Edinburgh's Award Scheme. Drama flourishes, with several productions each year. The School has a national reputation in debating.

Music. The School is also particularly strong in Music: over half the pupils receive tuition in the full range of orchestral instruments, piano, organ and classical guitar. There are two orchestras, two concert wind bands, jazz band, chamber choir and two junior choirs, recorder ensembles, and many chamber music groups. There is at least one Musical each year and operas are produced from time to time. The musical tradition is strengthened by the presence of the Cathedral Choristers (and former Cathedral choristers) in the School.

Fees per term (2011-2012). £3,800.

Extras. CCF £15 per term; DoE £35 per level; Instrumental Tuition £29 per hour, plus public examination fees; OH Club £20 per term; PTA £20 per year, per family.

Scholarships. (*See Scholarship Entries section*.). Cathedral choristers are members of the School from entry. They are accepted from the age of 8 as probationers following voice and educational tests held in May each year, and are educated initially at the Junior School. The Governors and the Chapter award choral scholarships jointly annually.

Bursaries. A number of bursaries are awarded competitively to able children from families of limited means.

Old Herefordian Club. *Alumni Coordinator*: Mrs Helen Pearson.

The Junior School. This is situated close by the main school. (*For details, please see Junior School IAPS entry*).

Charitable status. Hereford Cathedral School is a Registered Charity, number 518889. Its aims and objectives are to promote the advancement of education by acquiring, establishing, providing, conducting and carrying on residential and non-residential schools in which boys and girls of all sections of the community may receive a sound general education (including religious instruction in accordance with the doctrines of the Church of England).

Highgate School

North Road, London N6 4AY
Tel: 020 8340 1524 (Office)
          020 8347 3564 (Admissions)
Fax: 020 8340 7674
e-mail: office@highgateschool.org.uk
          admissions@highgateschool.org.uk
website: www.highgateschool.org.uk

Highgate School was founded in 1565 by Sir Roger Cholmeley, Knight, Chief Justice of England, and confirmed by Letters Patent of Queen Elizabeth in the same year.
Motto: *Altiora in votis*.

Visitor: Her Majesty The Queen

Governors:
J F Mills, CBE, MA, BLitt (*Treasurer and Chairman*)
R M Rothenberg, MBE, BA, FCA, CTA, MAE (*Deputy Chairman*)
M Clarke, MA, FCA
J Claughton, MA
B Davidson, MD, FRCS
P E Marshall, BSc, MRICS
Dr K Little, MB, BS, BSc
Miss R Langdale, QC, LLB, MPhil
J D Randall
Professor K J Willis, BSc, PhD
M Danson, MA
A Patel, BA

Bursar and Secretary to the Foundation: J C Pheasant, BSc, LLDip, Barrister

Head Master: A S Pettitt, MA

Deputy Heads of the Foundation:
T J Lindsay, MA (*Principal Deputy Head, Senior School*)
S M James, BA, MA (*Principal of the Junior School, Deputy Head and Director of Admissions*)

Director of Sir Roger Cholmeley's Charity: R C Wilne, MA

Director of Studies: D M Fotheringham, MA

Assistant Heads:
P R Aston, BEd
S N Brunskill, MA
S Evans, BA
J R Lewis, BA, PhD, FRGS
Mrs J F Morelle, BA
Miss L M Shelley, BA

Teachers:
* *Head of Department*
† *Housemaster*

Art and History of Art: Mrs J Horton, BA
J L Allchin, BFA

Miss V Hurr, BA, MA, DipArch
Ms J E W Jammers, MA, PhD
Mrs T A Jay, MA
*Mrs M J Nimmo, BA
Mrs R F Shepherd, BA

Classics:
*G A Waller, BA
Mrs A J Brunner, BA
Miss J Cowen, BA
D M Fotheringham, MA
P D Harrison, MA
Miss D Picton, BA
Mr H Shepherd, MA
Miss V L Smith, BA, MA

Design Technology:
P R Aston, BEd
A B H Sursok, BA
Miss N Schoeneweiss, BEng
*A F Thomson, BSc

Drama and Theatre Studies:
Ms J E Fehr, BA (*Theatre Studies)
T J A Hyam, BA

Economics:
A Golcoldas, BSc
†Miss K P Norris, BA
D Rey, BSc, MA
*J A Stenning, BA

English:
S G Appleton, MA
*G J H Catherwood, BA
R W H Fisher, BA
Mrs C L Heindl, BA
Mrs R J Hyam, BA
W S Knowland, BA
Mrs K L Kramer, BA, MA, DPhil
Miss J E McLoughlin, BA
Miss L J Morton, BA
A J Plaistowe, MA
Miss A K M Saunders, BA
M W M Seymour, BA
Miss L M Shelley, MA

Geography:
†D G Brandt, BA
Miss R S Burridge, BSc
*Mrs H J Broadbent, BA
P J Harrison, MA
Miss R E Joss, BA
J R Lewis, BA, PhD, FRGS

History and Politics:
Ms J R Byrne, MA
B J Dabby, MA, MPhil
*Miss E M Duggan, BA, MA
A E W Grant, BA
A H Henley-Smith, BA
T J Lindsay, MA
R R X Miller, MA (*Politics)
Ms E L Milton, BA, MA
Mr J P R Newton, BA, MSc
Mrs K B Shapiro, MA

Information Technology:
M A O'Connor, BA
*F R Robertson, BA

Learning Support:
Mrs S M Bambrough, BA
*D Jones, BA, MEd

Mathematics:
*D J Abramson, BA
†J P Bennett, MA
A D Bottomley, MMathStat
A G Dales, MA
†Miss H Gardiner, BA
Mrs N S Levin, MA, MBA
B H Newell, BSc
D J Noyce, MMath
J W Partridge, BA
L A Pearce, MA
A B Sainsbury, MA
M P Streuli, MA, MBA
Miss L A Wherity, MMath
J Wright, MMath

Modern Languages:
Mrs N Y Arnold, BA
S N Brunskill, BA
Miss R Church, MA
G D C Creagh, BA (*German)
Miss P A Delatorre, BA (*Spanish)
Dr N Grigorian, BA, MSt, MA, DPhil
Ms Y Jia, BA, MA
*P Le Berre, MA
Ms P-S Lin, BA, MA
Mrs J F Morelle, BA
Miss C Pottier, L-ès-L
I Urreaga Gorostidi, BA
†Mrs C Walker, BA
O P C Williams, BA (*French)

Music:
V J Barr, LRAM
A Cannière, BM, MM
G Hanson, BMus, LRAM
S J King, BMus
†J P Murphy, GRNCM
Miss E C Price, BMus
*L S Steuart Fothringham, MA, FRCO

Physical Education:
*S Evans, BA
C L M Henderson, BEd (Head of Games)
J Humphrey (Head of Football)
Miss S Pride, BSc (Head of PE)
Mrs L Sursok, BA
†A G Tapp, BEd

Religious Education and Philosophy:
*S Bovey, BA
R N Davis, BA
Ms J T Gosney, BA
The Revd P J J Knight, AIB, Dip Theol (Chaplain)
Miss E Shipp, MA

Science:
K Agyei-Owusu, MSci, PhD
W J Atkins, BA
†R C J Atkinson, MA, MSci, PhD, DIC
K S Bains, BSc, ARCS (*Chemistry)
J T M Barr, MEng
†A R Dabrowski, MSci
P D Davey, MChem
†P Doyle, BSc
Miss G V Gulliford, BA
Mrs V C Jauncey, BSc
P Johnston, BSc, PhD

†K M Pullinger, BSc
K E Quinn, BSc, PhD
M J Short, BA
D J Smith, BA, MSc, FInstP (*Physics)
†Ms V E C Stubbs, BSc, PhD
A Z Szydlo, MSc, PhD
Miss S Taylor, BA
Miss M Vranaki, BSc
Mrs J C Y Welch, BSc, MSc, PhD (*Science)
B S Weston, BSc, PhD (*Biology)

Highgate Junior School
Cholmeley House, 3 Bishopwood Road, London N6 4PL
Tel: 020 8340 9193; Fax: 020 8342 8225
e-mail: jsoffice@highgateschool.org.uk

Principal of the Junior School: S M James, BA, MA
(For further details, see entry in IAPS section.)

Highgate Pre-Preparatory School
7 Bishopswood Road, London N6 4PH
Tel: 020 8340 9196; Fax: 020 8340 3442
e-mail: pre-prep@highgateschool.org.uk

Principal: Mrs D Hecht, DCE

There are 970 boys and girls in the Senior School. The Junior School has some 320 boys and girls, aged 7 to 11, and prepares them only for the Senior School. The Pre-Preparatory School has 130 boys and girls aged 3 to 7. The School is fully co-educational and admits girls and boys at each entry point.

Situation and Grounds. The academic centre of the main School is in the heart of old Highgate, which has retained much of its village atmosphere. In addition to the Victorian buildings, such as the Chapel, Big School and Central Hall classrooms, the pupils have the benefit of modern facilities such as Dyne House, with its recently refurbished 200-seat auditorium and dedicated recital space, and the Garner Building for Mathematics and Information Technology. A magnificent Art, Design & Technology Centre opened in 2005. A new classroom building will open in 2012, and a new library will be opened in Big School in 2013.

Highgate underground station, on the Northern line, is a short walk away and there is easy access to the School by car or bus. It is four miles to central London (City or West End).

A few hundred yards along Hampstead Lane in Bishopswood Road lie more than twenty acres of playing-fields together with the Mallinson Sports Centre, indoor swimming pool and other extensive sporting facilities, the dining hall, the Junior School and the Pre-Preparatory School. Hampstead Heath and Kenwood, the largest expanse of open country in London, are adjacent.

Pastoral Care. In the Senior School, pastoral care for Years 7 and 8 is organised by form, with a Head of Year in overall charge. From Year 9, each pupil is a member of a House. There are twelve Houses based on particular areas of North London. A Housemaster, helped by five tutors, is responsible for monitoring the day-to-day progress and welfare of the fifty or so pupils in his or her care and for liaising with their parents.

Academic Curriculum. Pupils enter the Senior School at 11+ (Year 7); there is a further entry at 13+. There are five or six forms in Years 7 and 8 and six or seven forms in Year 9 and the curriculum is broad. At present, in addition to the usual range of subjects in Years 7 to 9, Art, Music and Design Technology are taken by all; the vast majority of pupils take Latin, and two sets study both Latin and Greek in Year 9 as a single timetable option; all pupils take a second modern language option in Year 9. Mandarin was introduced in Year 8 in 2009–10 and will be offered at GCSE from 2011 and A Level from 2013. By the time they start their GCSEs, pupils have developed an appropriate pattern of work, both in the classroom and out of school. Homework is an integral part of each pupil's programme of study.

The two-year GCSE courses begin in Year 10. The core subjects, studied by all, are: English, English Literature, Mathematics, and either double subject Coordinated Sciences (taught by separate teachers of Physics, Chemistry and Biology) or single award separate sciences. A further four subjects (including a modern language) are then chosen from: Art, Classical Civilisation, Design Technology, Geography, French, German, Greek, History, Latin, Music, Religious Studies, Spanish and Russian. In addition to their GCSE subjects, all pupils take Religious Education and Physical Education. All GCSEs are taken at the end of Year 11. The IGCSE qualification is taken in Mathematics, English Language, English Literature, Science, French, German and Spanish.

The teaching staff are experienced and well-qualified subject specialists and the teacher/pupil ratio is about 1:9. Class sizes are generally in the low twenties in Years 7 to 9 and just under twenty in Years 10 and 11, although for some subjects they will be much smaller; in the Sixth Form classes of 6–14 are usual.

Educational resources include an extensive intranet on a large information technology network and parent and pupil portals for remote access. The use of all these is guided by trained professionals and they complement the facilities available in the academic departments, which have their own specialist teaching rooms, equipment and, where appropriate, technicians, computers and libraries. Fieldwork and visits to galleries, museums, exhibitions and lectures are an integral part of the academic programme.

When they enter Year 12, girls and boys choose four subjects from the wide range of AS and A Level courses on offer. Prospective Sixth Formers are assisted in selecting the best programme of study according to their known ability and future plans. A booklet listing the options available and containing details of the courses is published each year and given to Year 11 and their parents before those choices are made.

All Sixth Form pupils follow a Cultural Studies programme which gives them insights of aspects of the arts and the sciences beyond the A Level curriculum; the programme is regularly supplemented by lectures given by visiting speakers. Pupils also follow a critical thinking course, and the Extended Project has been introduced as an additional AS option.

Emphasis is placed on learning to work independently and to develop more advanced study skills. At this stage a pupil will for the first time have a number of private reading periods. Two Sixth Form Common Rooms act as a social and recreational base for senior pupils.

Each Sixth Former has a tutor who, in conjunction with the Housemaster, exercises supervision over general academic progress and who advises on and monitors higher education applications. Highgate is a member of the Independent Schools Careers Organisation.

Religion. Highgate has a Christian tradition but pupils from all faiths and denominations are welcome. Pupils attend Chapel once a week, by houses, and there are occasional voluntary celebrations of Holy Communion; Choral Evensong is sung on some Sundays, at which parents are welcome. Greek Orthodox and Roman Catholic services are also held each term and there are weekly meetings of the Jewish Circle and an assembly for those of other faiths.

Knowledge Curriculum. A structured programme of academic extension is in place in each year group. Particular themes have been identified, to which each department contributes. The curriculum is delivered in lesson time and through a dedicated week once a year which focuses on the relevant theme. The purpose is to expand pupils' cultural and academic knowledge and to develop their critical thinking skills.

Music, Drama and Art. Highgate music has a long and distinguished tradition and many former pupils are now leading composers, conductors or performers. A wide range of musical activities is designed both to encourage the beginner and to stimulate and further the skills of the talented musician. State-of-the-art performance spaces for orchestral and chamber music, complete with computerised recording facilities, are available in Dyne House.

There are five main instrumental ensembles: a symphony orchestra, a chamber orchestra, a symphonic wind band, and string orchestra and a concert band. Two choirs provide music for Choral Evensong on Sundays, with a further three choirs covering a wide range of sacred and secular repertoire. There are four main concerts each year, one taking place in a major central London venue. Numerous chamber groups rehearse weekly and regular concerts are arranged, together with masterclasses, workshops and an annual house music competition.

Individual music lessons are available with specialist visiting teachers in all the main instruments and in singing. Certain orchestral instruments can be hired by beginners who may be offered a free term's trial of lessons.

Every encouragement is given to participate in drama, as actors, in stage management, or by assisting with sound and lighting. Major productions in recent years have included *Sweeney Todd, Les Misérables, Blood Wedding, The Bacchae, Hippolytus, Bugsy Malone, Skellig, Oklahoma, The Merchant of Venice* and *Much Ado about Nothing*. Small-scale plays are staged in most terms, some by younger pupils, and there is annually a play performed in French. A separate drama studio provides additional rehearsal and performance space. Regular visits to the professional theatre are also arranged.

The excellent Art department has facilities for painting, print-making, life drawing, sculpture, pottery, photography, video and computer graphics. Whether taking part in formal classes or working in their free time boys and girls are encouraged to explore their own ways of expressing ideas visually. Their work is regularly exhibited, both in the department and elsewhere in the school.

Games. Highgate is exceptionally fortunate in its sports facilities. The extensive playing fields are complemented by the Mallinson Sports Centre and by courts for squash, tennis and Eton fives, and a new all-weather pitch which opened for use in 2009.

One afternoon each week is devoted to games, in which all who are physically fit take part. Teams are selected in each age group, and they also practise at other times. Matches are played on Saturdays as well as during the week. The main games played by boys are association football, cricket and Eton fives, and netball, hockey and rounders by girls, but there is a competitive fixture list in athletics, swimming and cross-country. A very wide range of other sports is offered at both recreational and competitive level: these include badminton, basketball, canoeing, fencing, golf, gymnastics, hockey, karate, rugby football, sailing, shooting, squash, tennis, volleyball, water polo and weight-training. Countries visited on recent tours by school teams include Holland, Spain and Germany. Many of the magnificent facilities of the fully-staffed Mallinson Sports Centre are also available for family use in the evenings, at weekends and in the holidays.

Activities. We aim to provide as many opportunities as possible in which pupils will develop qualities of self-reliance, endurance and leadership, in which they can serve the community and in which they can develop their own interests and enthusiasms. There are a large number of societies and clubs, usually meeting in the lunch-hour or after school. The School is an operating authority for the Duke of Edinburgh's Award scheme and each year many gain the bronze award and often go on to gain the silver and gold awards. There is also a Community Service scheme and an Urban Survival award scheme.

Admission. Normal entry to the Junior School is at the age of 7. All candidates take an entrance examination in January and a proportion are recalled for interview shortly thereafter, for entry the following September. Application should be made in writing to the Principal of the Junior School, 3 Bishopswood Road, London N6 4PL.

Boys who enter the Senior School at 11+ are mainly from primary schools while girls come from prep and primary schools; those who enter at 13+ are usually from preparatory schools. The remainder enter from Highgate Junior School. Entry for 2012 at 13+ will be by means of tests in January of 2012; thereafter, places will be offered on the basis of pretests in the September of Year 7. 13+ candidates will also sit Common Entrance. 13+ pupils not in preparatory schools should contact the Admissions Office for advice. Girls and boys from other schools are also admitted to the Sixth Form at Highgate following a thinking skills test and interviews. Only occasionally are there vacancies at other levels of the School. All enquiries concerning admission to the Senior School should be addressed to the Director of Admissions, admissions@highgateschool.org.uk.

Fees per term (2011-2012). Senior School: £5,290; Junior School: £4,850; Pre-Preparatory School: £4,580 (Reception–Year 2), £2,290 (Nursery).

Scholarships and Bursaries. *Bursaries*: We offer 10 bursaries per academic year at 11+, 2 at 13+ and 6 at 16+. One bursary is awarded at 11+ for a pupil from St Michael's Primary School, Highgate. Parents who would like to be considered for a bursary are asked to fill in a confidential financial statement. Those children who have reached the required standard in the entrance test are then considered for bursaries worth up to 100% of tuition fees (see the School's website for further details).

Scholarships: Academic and Music Awards are offered at 11, 13 and 16+. The entrance test at each of these points is used to shortlist potential academic awards and final decisions are made through interview. The tests for 11+ and 13+ are held in January and early February, and at 16+ in November and early December. Auditions for music awards take place on or around the same time as the entrance tests. Candidates for 13+ and 16+ music awards additionally sit a short written test. Both forms of award are made for a Key Stage of a child's education. Whilst the award is reviewed at the end of the given Key Stage, it is expected that most will be tenable throughout a pupil's stay at the school. The maximum award that is not means-tested is usually £1,500 of the tuition fees. In addition to these awards made at the time of entry to the school, additional academic awards are made at the end of each year to pupils whose work has been consistently outstanding.

Old Cholmeleian Society. Former pupils are known as Cholmeleians. Enquiries should be addressed to the Foundation Office at the School, oc@highgateschool.org.uk.

Charitable status. Sir Roger Cholmeley's School at Highgate is a Registered Charity, number 312765, committed to meeting its responsibilities to the society that lies beyond the school gates. Two senior teachers lead and develop the charity's activities: the Director of Community Partnerships and the Director of Sir Roger Cholmeley's Charity.

The importance that Sir Roger Cholmeley's School at Highgate attaches to its social responsibilities has become more focused, but is not new; the objects stated in the charity's constitution are:

- the advancement of education by the provision of a school in or near Highgate, the provision of incidental or ancillary educational activities, and the undertaking of associated activities for the benefit of the public;

- in so far as the Governors think fit (and so long as they in their discretion consider that the first object is being properly provided for) the relief of the poor.

The principal ways in which the charity meets these objects are:

- the provision of bursaries and scholarships;
- training teachers;
- running educational summer schools;
- supporting applications to selective universities;
- partnerships with local primary and secondary schools;
- sharing our facilities with community groups;
- an extensive programme of community service;
- events in support of other charities.

More detailed information can be found on the School's website.

Hurstpierpoint College
A Woodard School

Hurstpierpoint, West Sussex BN6 9JS

Tel: 01273 833636
Fax: 01273 835257
e-mail: info@hppc.co.uk
website: www.hppc.co.uk

Founded 1849 by Nathaniel Woodard, Canon of Manchester.
Motto: *Beati mundo corde*

Visitor:
The Rt Revd The Lord Bishop of Chichester

Provost: The Rt Revd Lindsay Urwin, MA, OGS

School Council:
Chairman: Rear-Admiral S Moore, CB

Members:

Professor J P Bacon, MA, MSc, PhD	M S Harrison, FCA
	A Jarvis, BEd, MA, FRSA
Dr J R Brydie, MBBS, MD, MRCGP	The Revd J B A Joyce, BA, DipEd
¶R J Ebdon, BSc, MAPM, MCIOB	¶J P Ruddlesdin, FCA
	G A Rushton
J C Hance, BA, FCA	¶G J Taysom, BSc, FRSA
Mrs B J T Hanson	Mrs M A Zeidler, MEd

Headmaster: **T J Manly**, BA, MSc

* *Head of Department*
† *Housemaster/mistress*
§ *Part-time*
¶ *Former pupil*

Senior Deputy Head & Head of Sixth Form: T Firth, BA
Deputy Head (*Middle School*): R Taylor-West, BA, AKC
Deputy Head (*Academic*): Mrs K J Austin, BSc
Chaplain: Revd Jeremy Sykes, MA
Bursar: S A Holliday, BSc, ACIB
Head of Upper Sixth: T F Q Leeper, BSc (†*St John's House*)

Staff:
R Ashley, MA (*Geography)
¶A C S Battison, BSc (**PE & Sports Science*)
§T J Baxter, BSc, DPhil
N D D Beeby, BA (*Drama, †*Chevron House*)
Dr R M A Bellingham, BSc, PhD
Ms H K Bray, BMus (†*Shield House*)
Miss L J Brinton, BSc (*Mathematics)
Mrs A Browne (†*St John's House*)
Miss V Capelin, BA (*English)
T Church, BA
Miss J C Clarke, BA (*History)

M F Clay, MBA
Miss R L Close, BSc
B Cole, BA (*Classics*)
Ms J Coleman, MA
Ms D B Collins, MA
R J S Cooke, BSc (*IT VIth Form*)
¶N Creed, BA (*Assistant Director of Sport*)
Mrs S Crickmore, MA
S J Crook, BSc (*IT Middle School*)
Ms A De Britt, BEng (*Physics*)
Mrs K V Doehren, BEd (*Learning Support*)
Miss N C Dominy (*Dance*)
§ N J Edey, BSc
C J Eustace, MA (*Years 10 & 11*)
Miss T C I Farrell, BA (*Art*)
Mrs L Gallagher, BSc
Mrs K L Goodard, MA (*ESL*)
P J Goodwin, BSc
M Green, BA, BEd
G J Haines, BComAd (†*Crescent House*)
D M Higgins, BA (†*Woodard House and CCF*)
§Mrs H E Higgins, BA
Mr A J Hopcroft, MEng
Dr G M Hülsmann-Diamond, PhD (*German*)
R G Hurley, BSc (*Director of Information Technology*)
§Mrs A Hurst, BA
§Mrs S Hyman, BA (†*Fleur de Lys House*)
Mrs D C Jackson, BA
D Jameson, MA (*Academic Music*)
R M Johnson, BSc (*Design & Technology*)
R M Kift, BEd (*Director of Sport*)
Miss H Knight, BSc
M Lamb, BSc (*Year 9*)
Mrs K Lea, BSc (†*Martlet House*)
Mrs J Leeper, BA (*Senior Mistress & Careers*)
Miss A Lieutaud, BA, Maître (*French*)
D A Linney, BSc
Miss P Maple, BA (†*Pelican House*)
R S C Martin-Jenkins, BA
N K Matthews, BA (*Director of Music*)
M J May, BEd, MA Ed
Miss S McCrohan, BSc
P J McKerchar, MA, CChem, MRSC (*Science and Chemistry*)
¶N A M Morris, BA
D E Parry, MA
I D Pattison, BSc (†*Red Cross House*)
Ms K Pattison, BA
Mrs M Payeras-Cifre, TFL (*Spanish*)
S P Poole, BEd (*Psychology, *Biology*)
§Mrs S A Read, MA
J R Rowland, BA (*Economics & Business Studies*)
I Sambles, BSc Ed (†*Eagle House*)
B Schofield, BA
Mrs R J Scott, BA (*Head of Girls' Games*)
§Mrs C A Shearman, BA
R L Shearman, MSc, BA (†*Star House*)
Mrs J C Silvey, BA Ed
A Smith, BA
P G Statter, BSc (*Director of Academic Administration & IB Coordinator*)
C B Thomson, BSc
Mrs D Treyer-Evans, BA (*Senior School Registrar*)
Miss K B Ward, BA
Dr S Waugh, BA, MA, PhD
Ms J West, BA
Mrs F Williams, BA
Mrs S Wilson, BA
A P Wood, MA, MSc (*ERS*)

§Mrs C Adams (*Girls' Games Coach*)
M Brigden (*Fencing Coach*)
T Hariki (*Tai Chi Teacher*)
§Miss S F Ivemy (*Girls' Games Coach*)

§Mrs R Jutson (*Girls' Games Coach*)
Ms B S McMullen (*Aerobics Instructor*)
Mrs L J Porter (*Mandarin Teacher*)
F J Simkins (*Director of Outdoor Education*)
R Smith, BA (*Fitness Trainer*)
Mrs A Terry-Salter (*Ballet*)
N Turner (*Tennis Coach*)
E J Waagenaar (*Life Skills*)
C Wilson (*Hockey Coach & Sports Facilities Manager*)

There are 22 visiting Music Teachers.

Preparatory School

Head: Mrs H J Beeby, BH, MA
Deputy Head: N J Oakden, BA
Deputy Head (Academic): Mrs V I Bacon, BEd
Deputy Head (Pastoral/Discipline): Mrs D K Stoneley, BEd (*Games/PE & PSHE*)

Staff:
Mrs C Adams (*Girls' Games*)
Miss A E Albury, MA, MLitt (*History*)
J O Baldwin, BSc
Mrs L M Brunjes, BA
T A Cattaneo, BEd, CertEd (*Mathematics*)
B Cole, BA
Mrs S L Deelman, BSc
C J Eustace, MA
Mrs A J Filkins, BA (*French*)
A A Gardner, BA
L Gasper, MA (*Drama*)
P J Goodwin, BSc (*Science*)
Mrs P Gordon-Stewart, BA (*English*)
Mrs A C Harrap, BEd
§Mrs S Hyman, BA
Ms D Maurice, BA
§Mrs A McQueen, CertEd, RSADipSpLD, AMBDA
Mrs N Mellett, BA (*Art*)
Mrs S H Miles, BEd
§Mrs L A Moakes, BA
Ms L Paul, BSc
Mrs F Pitcher, BEd
M Reay, BA
§Mrs S Sambles, MA
K J Silk CertEd
Mrs Z Taylor-West, BA
A M Travers, MA, GCLCM (*Music*)
Miss H L Turley, BSc
§D Valentine (*Boys' Games*)
T B Williams, BSc (*Geography*)
C Wroth, DipHE (*Information Technology*)

Pre-Prep School:
Head: Mrs K M Finnegan, BEd

Staff:
Miss V Atkinson, BEd
§Mrs B Carter, BEd
§Ms S Jarvis, BA, LGSM
Mrs T Mayfield, BA
§Mrs C P Owen, BEd
Miss A L Rhoades-Walkley, BA
Mrs D A Ross, BEd
Mrs S Sambles, MA
Ms E K Warbey, BSc

Classroom Assistants:
Mrs K Hayles, CACHE Level 3
Miss K Medhurst, NNEB
Mrs D J Murray
Mrs D J Reed, NVQ Level 3
Miss L Taylor, NVQ Level 3, Nursery Nurse

Hurstpierpoint College is a co-educational day and boarding school for boys and girls aged between 4 and 18 years. Pre-Prep, Prep and Senior Schools are linked by common values and a common academic and administrative framework, to provide a complete education. There are currently 364 boys and 268 girls. 55% of the pupils are boarders. The Preparatory School has a further 261 boys and girls and the Pre-Prep currently has 81 pupils.

The school is truly co-educational throughout and offers boarding for boys and girls in the Senior School. Boarding is a particularly popular option at the school with many day pupils and flexi-boarders later opting to become weekly boarders. In their Upper Sixth year at Hurst, pupils join St John's House, a co-educational day and boarding house where, appropriately supervised, they enjoy greater freedoms and are encouraged to further develop their independent learning skills in preparation for university.

Buildings and Facilities. At the heart of the school's large country campus lie the core school buildings and Chapel arranged around three attractive quadrangles built of traditional Sussex knapped flint. Key facilities nearby including the floodlit Astroturf, art school, sports hall, music school, dance and drama studios, 250-seat theatre, indoor swimming pool and Medical Centre. Other facilities include a Learning Resources Centre and Library and fully-equipped IT Centre. The extensive grounds are laid mainly to playing fields and include one of the largest and most attractive school cricket pitches in the Country. In 2011-12 work is in progress on an extension to the Sixth Form accommodation and new Science facilities. A second Astroturf is also proposed with plans well under way.

Chapel. As a Woodard School, Hurstpierpoint is a Christian foundation and underpinned by Christian values, although pupils of other faiths or of no faith are warmly welcomed. Pupils attend up to three assemblies during the week. The main Eucharist, which parents and friends are most welcome to attend, takes place mainly early on Friday evenings, although there are also occasional Sunday services in addition to voluntary celebrations of the Holy Communion. Pupils who wish to do so are prepared in small classes for the annual Confirmation taken by one of the Bishops of the diocese.

Curriculum. The five-day academic week is structured to allow boys and girls to study a variety of subject options that can be adapted to suit their natural ability. The entry year (Shell) gives pupils the chance to experience most of our GCSE subjects before they choose their options. It involves the study of English, History, Geography, French, German, Spanish, Latin, Mathematics, Physics, Chemistry, Biology, Religious Studies, Art, Design & Technology, Music, Drama, Physical Education, IT and Society and Self (a PSHE course). In the second (Remove) and in the third (Fifth) years students study between 8 and 10 GCSE subjects. In addition to the core subjects there are five option blocks offering a choice of 17 subjects, including Ancient Greek, Applied Business and Dance.

From September 2011, Sixth formers have the choice of taking the IB Diploma (selecting from a wide range of subject options). Of those Sixth formers who opt for A Levels, the majority study four AS Levels in the Lower Sixth. The choice is wide, with 28 AS subjects to choose from. Art & Design (Photography), Business Studies, Classical Civilisation, Computing, Dance, Economics, Further Maths, Music Technology, Philosophy and Psychology are introduced in addition to the GCSE options. There is also a General Studies programme. The Upper Sixth can take a varied programme with the most able studying four or five full A Levels, whilst others build a valuable qualifications portfolio by studying a varying number of AS subjects along with at least two full A Levels.

All pupils' work is overseen by academic tutors and we take particular care to ensure that university applications are properly targeted to suit the students' aspirations and talents.

Games. The School operates a "Sport for All" policy that seeks to place pupils in games most suited to their tastes and abilities. During the first two years they are expected to take part in at least some of the major sports but thereafter a greater element of choice occurs. The major sports are Rugby, Hockey, Cricket and Athletics for boys; Hockey, Netball, Athletics and Tennis for girls. Recent tours for major sports include Rugby (Italy), Netball (Barbados), Dubai (Cricket), South Africa (Hockey). In addition there are teams in Basketball, Cross Country, Football, Golf, Polo, Rounders, Shooting, Squash, Swimming, Triathlon, boys' Tennis, girls' Cricket and girls' Rugby. The Sports Hall and indoor Swimming Pool provide opportunities for many other pursuits such as Aerobics, Badminton, Gymnastics, Weight Training and Water Polo, while the Outdoor Pursuits enable pupils to enjoy challenges such as Rock Climbing and Canoeing.

Service Afternoons. On Wednesdays all pupils other than the Shell (Year 9) are expected to take part in The Duke of Edinburgh's Award activities alongside the Combined Cadet Force (Army, RN or RAF sections), Community Service or Environmental Conservation.

Music. There has always been a strong musical tradition at Hurstpierpoint with an orchestra and other more specialised ensembles. A large proportion of the pupils, currently 156, take individual instrumental lessons and give frequent recitals. The Chapel Choir plays a major part in regular worship and there are several other choral groups.

Drama. The Shakespeare Society is the oldest such school society in the country and organises an annual production and an annual musical. Drama covers a wide range and varies from major musicals to more modest House plays and pupil-directed productions. The 250-seat Bury Theatre also gives the more technically minded ample opportunity to develop stage management, lighting and sound skills.

Other Activities. The Thursday afternoon activity programme is for Shell and Remove pupils (Years 9 & 10) and include Art, Climbing, Dance, Fencing, POD Casting, Shooting, Horse Riding, Polo, Karate, Golf Range, Clay Pigeon Shooting, alongside a variety of music clubs and literary clubs. Other activities also take place during the school week.

Hurst Johnian Club. In addition to providing facilities and events for Old Pupils, the Club also assists with careers and supports the current pupils in various ways, eg Gap Year travel fund and tour sponsorship contributions. Contact the Hon Secretary, c/o Hurstpierpoint College.

Fees per term (2011-2012). Senior School: £9,525 Full Boarders (includes ESL); £8,075 Weekly Boarders; £7,615 Flexi-boarding; £6,345 Day Pupils.

Awards. (*See Scholarship Entries section.*) Scholarships and Exhibitions available at 13+ and 16+: Academic, 'Hurst' All-Rounder, Art, Drama, Music, 'Downs' Sports, Design & Technology, and IT.

Admission. For 13+ entry, pupils must be registered on the School's list and pass Common Entrance or Scholarship examinations. Entry from Hurst Prep school is by the College's own examinations. Entrants from maintained schools and from overseas undergo separate tests and interviews.

Places in the Sixth Form are available to students who achieve an A/A* at GCSE in the subjects (or, if a new subject, then in a subject closely related to it) that they intend to study, whether they choose the A Level or the IB Diploma programmes of study. Students should also have a minimum of a C grade at GCSE in Mathematics and English.

Please contact the Senior School & Sixth Forms Admissions Office for further information.

Preparatory School. *See entry in IAPS section.*

Charitable status. Hurstpierpoint College is a Registered Charity, number 1076498. It aims to provide a Christian education to boys and girls between the ages of four and eighteen in the three schools on the campus.

Hutchesons' Grammar School

21 Beaton Road, Glasgow G41 4NW
Tel: 0141 423 2933
Fax: 0141 424 0251
e-mail: rector@hutchesons.org
website: www.hutchesons.org

Founded and endowed by the brothers George and Thomas
Hutcheson (Deed of Mortification 1641). The School is
governed by Hutchesons' Educational Trust.
  Motto: *Veritas*.

Governors:
Not more than 17 in number.
Representatives of the following Bodies:
Glasgow Presbytery of the Church of Scotland (2), Senatus
Academicus of Glasgow University (1), Merchants' House
of Glasgow (1), Trades House of Glasgow (1), Patrons of
Hutchesons' Hospital (2), Glasgow Educational Trust (1),
Senate of the University of Strathclyde (1), FP Club (1),
School Association (1) and not more than 9 persons co-
opted by the Governors.

Chairman: D Dobson, LLB, DipMS, FRICS

Rector: Dr K M Greig, MA Oxon, PhD Edinburgh

Senior Depute Rector: Mr M Martin, BSc Hons

Bursar: I T Keter, BA CA

Depute Rectors (Secondary School):
C Bagnall, BA Hons, MEd
D Campbell, MA Hons, MEd
J McDougall, MA Hons
Mrs L McIntosh, MA

Depute Rectors (Primary School):
Mrs C Haughney, BA Hons, MEd
Miss F Macphail, BA, MBA
Mrs C Hatfield, BEd Hons

Heads of Departments:
Art: Mrs S Breckenridge, BA Hons
Biology: Mrs M J Jheeta, BSc, MS
Chemistry: P H B Uprichard, BSc Hons
Classics: D H Gillies, BA, MSc
Drama: Mrs V Alderson, DipSD
Economics & Business Studies: M Bergin, BSc Hons
English: M J Symington, MA Hons
Geography: C C Clarke, BSc Hons
History: Dr R H Gaffney, MA, PhD
Home Economics: Mrs D Green, DipHEcon
ICT: Ms R Housley, BSc Hons, DipCompEd
Mathematics: Mrs M T Fyfe, BSc Hons
Modern Languages: Mrs E M Bertram, MA Hons
Modern Studies: G F Broadhurst, BA Hons
Music – Curriculum: E W M Trotter, BMus Hons
Music – Performance: K D Walton, BMus Hons
Physical Education:
Director of Sport: S Lang, BEd Hons
Head of Boys' PE: R Dewar, BEd Hons
Head of Girls' PE: Mrs K Robertson, BSc Hons
Director of Hockey: Miss R Simpson, BEd Hons
Physics: Dr S Lonie, BSc Hons, MSc, PhD
Religious Studies: S J Branford, MA Hons
Technology: R W Furness, BEd Hons

Rector's Secretary & Admissions: Mrs M E Norman

Development Director: Ms C Gillen, BA

  The school has just over 1,500 pupils, with 1,000 boys
and girls from 12 to 18 years at the Secondary School in
Beaton Road and 500 aged 5 to 12 at the Primary School in
Kingarth Street. Pupils at the Primary School move automatically to the Secondary School.

  For 118 years Hutchesons' Boys' Grammar School was
situated in Crown Street, but in 1960 moved to new buildings on an open site at Crossmyloof. In 1976 the Boys'
School combined with the Hutchesons' Girls' Grammar
School, founded in 1876, to form one co-educational establishment housed on two sites a mile apart. The Boys' School
in Beaton Road became the Secondary School, with the
Girls' School in Kingarth Street evolving into the Primary
School. The last decade has seen substantial development on
both sites, including a new Infant Block, Science Wing,
Sports Hall, Library, dining room and classrooms. After
acquiring the church adjoining the Beaton Road site, the
School converted and extended it to form a centre for ICT
and music, as well as an auditorium and a multi-purpose stu-
dio/meeting room. The latest addition to the Beaton Road
site is an all-weather floodlit hockey pitch and athletics
track, and a new Drama Building is scheduled for completion Autumn 2011. The nearby Auldhouse Sports Ground
has pitches for rugby, hockey and cricket.

  Admission. Pupils are normally admitted on interview at
age 4/5 and by examination at age 9/10 to the Primary
School or at age 11/12 to the Secondary School, but applications for vacancies at other stages are welcomed.

  New pupils normally start at the beginning of the academic year, but intermediate entries are possible from time
to time where circumstances dictate.

  Fees per term (2011-2012). Primary £2,538–£2,914,
Secondary 1–2 £3,237, Secondary 3–6 £3,153. All fees from
Primary 1 to Secondary 2 include books.

  Financial Assistance. The School offers financially
means-tested bursaries by competitive entry for entry to S1.

  Religion. The School is non-denominational, but assembles most mornings for a broadly Christian service. Muslim
and Jewish assemblies are also held. Religious Studies are
taught in S1 and S2.

  Curriculum. In the Primary School, a strong emphasis
on Mathematics and Language forms the foundation for
confident and successful development across the curriculum, covering Environmental Studies, Religious and Moral
Education, Personal and Social Education and Health.
Pupils benefit from expert teaching by specialists in Art, PE,
Music, Games, ICT, Latin and Modern Languages.

  For the first two years of Secondary School, all pupils
take English, a Modern Language, Latin, History, Geogra-
phy, Mathematics, three sciences, ICT, Technology, Art,
Music, Drama, Physical Education and Religious Studies.
They then follow more specialised courses leading to pre-
sentation for SQA Highers in S5. Most pupils continue into
S6, which offers a wide range of courses, including
Advanced Highers, A Levels and further Highers.

  In general, pupils are prepared for universities and higher
education, including Oxbridge. They are given vocational
and pastoral guidance throughout the Secondary School.

  Games. Rugby, Football, Hockey, Cricket, Rowing, Net-
ball, Tennis, Golf, Badminton, Cross-Country Running and
Curling, with special attention paid to Rugby, Hockey,
Swimming and Athletics.

  Clubs and Societies include the Debating Society, Model
United Nations, Chess, Bridge (the school is the Scottish
Schools' champion), Dramatic Societies, EcoSchools, Art
Club, Computing, Film Club, Photography, Technology,
Choirs, Ensembles, Orchestras, Pipe and Ceilidh Band, and
Scripture Union. More than 500 pupils receive specialist
instrumental and vocal tuition. There is also a very strong
tradition of fundraising for charity, community service,
Young Enterprise and The Duke of Edinburgh's Award.
School pupils publish the School magazine, "The Hutcheso-
nian", every June.

  Charitable status. Hutchesons' Educational Trust is a
Registered Charity, number SC002922.

Hymers College

Hull, East Yorkshire HU3 1LW
Tel: 01482 343555
Fax: 01482 472854
e-mail: enquiries@hymers.org
website: www.hymerscollege.co.uk

Hymers College in Hull was opened as a school for boys in 1893, when the Reverend John Hymers, Fellow of St John's College, Cambridge, and Rector of Brandesburton, left money in his Will, for a school to be built 'for the training of intelligence in whatever social rank of life it may be found among the vast and varied population of the town and port of Hull'.

Although the school has remained true to its Founder's intentions, the catchment area now stretches across East Yorkshire and North Lincolnshire and the school became fully co-educational in 1989.

Governors:
Chairman: M de-V Roberts, FCA
Vice Chairman: District Judge P J E Wildsmith, LLB
S Martin, MA, FCA
J H Robinson, BSc, CEng, FIChemE
J R Wheldon, LLB, MRICS, ACI ArB
Mrs B E Elliott, MSc, BN, RGN, RSCN, RHV, NNDNCert
Mrs G Greendale
Cllr J G Robinson, BA
D J Stone, BA
S G West, BA
M C S Hall, BSc
P A B Beecroft, MA, MBA
Mrs T A Carruthers
D A Gibbons, BSc, MRICS
Dr S A Johnson, BA, MA, PhD
C W I Pistorius, PhD, FIET
N H R Robinson, ACIB
Prof B Winn, BSc, PhD, FAAO, MInstKT, FRSM

Headmaster: **D C Elstone**, MA Ed Mgt

Deputy Head (Academic): A N Holman, MA Cantab
Deputy Head (Pastoral): Mrs C R Gravelle, BA

Bursar and Clerk to the Governors: G D Noble, BA, CDipAF, FIMgt, FInstAM, MInstD

Head of Junior School: P C Doyle, BSc

Teachers:
* *Head of Department*

Mrs S A Atkinson
Ms D Bache, BA (*Art*)
J G Bell, MA (*Science & Physics*)
Mrs J M Brown, BA
Ms A Burgess, BA Hons (*Geography*)
Mrs D Bushby, LRAM
Revd M J Bushby, BSc, MA
Dr V J Byron, MEng, PhD, MBA
A D Cadle, BSc
S Canty, BA
Ms L Catlin, BA (*Drama*)
P Cook, BA (*ICT*)
Mrs C Copeland, BSc
Miss L R Crawley, BA
Dr J Denton, MA
P C Doyle, BSc
Mrs J I Duffield, BA
Mrs R Elstone, MA
Mrs A Exley, BA
N Exley, BA
Miss H L Ferguson, BEd
Mrs P V Ferguson, MA

Mrs J Fillingham
C J Fitzpatrick, BA Ed (*Director of Sport*)
Mrs N Foster, BSc
Dr I Franklin, BSc, PhD
C Gaynor-Smith, BA (*Sixth Form, *RE*)
Mme N Gibson, DEUG Lic Lyon (*Modern Languages*)
Mrs Z L Gillett, BSc
A Gittens, BA
J Gravelle, BSc (*Business Studies & Economics*)
Miss K Halliwell, MChem
D Harrison, MA
Mrs H L Harrison, BA
D Hickman, BSc
R P Huntsman, BEd
Mrs H Jackson, BSc
S Jarman, BA Hons
Dr J M Jarvis, BSc
M Jones, BSc
J R Kennedy, BA
G Lansdell, BEd
Mrs S Lord, BA
Mrs C McDonough-Bradley, BSc
D McPherson, BA (*Latin*)
M McTeare, BA
P Meadway, BSc
Mrs C Mitchell, BA (*Spanish*)
I Nicholls, BA (*German*)
C O'Donnell, BA (*History, *Politics*)
A Penny, GRNCM, ARNCM
Dr M J Pickles, MEng, ACGI, PhD
Mrs A J Powell
R F Poyser
G Prescott, MA (*Chemistry*)
M Pybus, BMus (*Director of Music*)
R Quick, ALCM, ARCM
A Raspin, BSc
A J M Rattenbury, BA
Mrs L Raymond
Mrs L L Roberts, MSc
P J Roberts, MA (*Biology*)
Mrs S E Rogers, BA
C J Ryan, BA, MBA
Mrs S E Sinkler, BPharm
R J Summers, BSc
J Swinney, BSc
E Tame, MMath (*Mathematics*)
Mrs J Tapley, BEd
N A Taylor, BA
Dr S Taylor, BA, MEd (*English*)
D Thompson, BSc
Miss D J Wallis, BA
Mrs L A Walmsley, BA
S J Walmsley, BA
Mrs A Webb, BA
A Whittaker, BA
M Williams, BA
R K Wooldridge, BSc
A G Young, BA (*Design Technology*)
B J Young

Number of Pupils. 968.
The Junior School has 204 pupils aged 8–11. There is a full range of academic, sporting, music and extra-curricular activities.

The Senior School has 540 pupils in Years 7–11 and the Sixth Form has 224 pupils.

Admission is by competitive examination at ages 8, 9 and 11, together with an interview with the Headteacher. Most pupils proceed at age eleven into the Senior School by an examination taken also by pupils from other schools. Almost all pupils qualify for the Sixth Form through GCSE results. Pupils from other schools are admitted to the Sixth Form on the basis of good GCSE results.

Pupils are prepared for the GCSE in a broad curriculum including music, business-related subjects, computer studies, technology and the arts.

There is a full range of courses leading to AS and Advanced Level examinations, and special preparation is given for Oxford and Cambridge entrance.

Facilities. The buildings consist of 35 classrooms, 11 specialist laboratories, a 30-booth language laboratory, extensive ICT facilities, audio-visual room, art rooms, theatre, Design/Technology Centre and a music centre containing teaching, practice and recital rooms, a gymnasium and very large sports hall. A new Junior School building contains 9 classrooms and specialist rooms for music, DT, art, ICT and science, along with a library, hall and changing rooms. The grounds, which extend for over 40 acres, include a newly built all-weather hockey pitch and 12 tennis courts. A swimming pool/sports centre opened in November 2004.

Extra-Curricular Activities. All pupils are strongly encouraged to participate in the very wide range of extra-curricular activities. The main school games are rugby, cricket, hockey, netball, tennis and athletics. There are also school teams in swimming and fencing. The school regularly competes at national level in these sports and provides members of county and national teams. Many pupils take part in the Duke of Edinburgh's Award Scheme and the school has an impressive track record in Young Enterprise. Other clubs include ACF, chess, modelling, debating, photography, community service and Christian Union. Drama is particularly strong, with several productions a year. Music is a major school activity; there are three full orchestras, a large choir, and several chamber and "academy" groups in each part of the school. Individual tuition is available in most instruments.

Fees per term (2011-2012). (including textbooks) Senior School £2,982; Junior School £2,481–£2,622. Hymers Bursaries are awarded at ages 8, 9, 11 and 16.

The Old Hymerians Association, c/o Alumni Manager, Hymers College, Hull HU3 1LW.

Charitable status. Hymers College is a Registered Charity, number 529820-R. Its aims and objectives are education.

Immanuel College

87/91 Elstree Road, Bushey, Hertfordshire WD23 4EB
Tel: 020 8950 0604
Fax: 020 8950 8687
e-mail: enquiries@immanuel.herts.sch.uk
website: www.immanuelcollege.co.uk

Immanuel College is a selective, co-educational day school founded in 1990 by the late Chief Rabbi, Lord Jakobovits to fulfil his vision of an educational establishment that affirms orthodox Jewish values and practice in the context of rigorous secular studies. The College aims at giving its pupils a first-class education that encourages them to connect Jewish and secular wisdom, to think independently and to exercise responsibility. Its ethos is characterised by attentiveness to individual pupils' progress, high academic achievement and the integration of Jewish and secular learning. There are both Jewish and non-Jewish teachers at the school, the common element being enthusiasm for their work and concern for their pupils.

Motto: *Torah im Derech Eretz* (Jewish learning integrated with secular study)

Board of Governors:
Mr Gary Laurence (*Co-Chairman*)
Mr Richard Segal, BA, ACA (*Co-Chairman*)
Mr Michael Dangoor, BSc
Mrs Lynda Dullop, BA
Mr Clive Freedman, QC

Mrs Ruth Hoyland, BSc
Mr Tim Isaacs, BSc, ACA
Mrs Elaine Kornbluth
Mrs Annette Koslover, LLB
Mr Edward Misrahi, BA
Dr David Richardson, BA, PhD
Mr Jeremy Smouha, MA Cantab
Professor Anthony Warrens, MD, PhD, FRCP, FHEA
Mr Richard Werth, BSc, ACA

Rabbinical Adviser: Rabbi Dr Jeffrey Cohen, BA, MPhil, AJC, PhD

Bursar & Clerk to the Governors: Mr Adam Harris, BSc, FCCA

Head Master: Mr Philip Skelker, MA Oxon (*English*)

Deputy Head Master: Dr Millan Sachania, MA Cantab, MPhil, PhD, FRSA (*Music*)

Assistant Masters and Mistresses:

* *Head of Department/Subject*
§ *Part-time*

Mrs Gillian Abrahams, BA (*Teaching and Learning*)
Mr Paul Abrahams, BA (*Modern Languages)
Mrs Naomi Amdurer, BA (*English, French, Spanish*)
Mrs Elisa Angel, BA (*English*)
§Mrs Alison Ardeman, BA (**Art & Design – Fine Art*)
Mr Danny Baigel, BA (*Jewish Studies*)
Mr Mario Brzezinski, BSc (**ICT, Senior Teacher*)
§Mrs Ruth Davis, BA (*Mathematics*)
Mr Nick De Carpentier, BA (*Geography*)
Mr Alexander Coope, MA (*Philosophy and Ethics*)
Mr Paul De Naeyer, BSc (*Geography)
§Ms Laurel Endelman, BA, MA (**PSHE, Drama & Theatre Studies, Head of Middle School*)
Mrs Sue Fishburn, BA, RSADipSpLD (**Teaching & Learning*)
Miss Natasha Fisher, BA, MA (*Head of Preparatory School*)
Mrs Joanna Fleet, BA (**Drama & Theatre Studies*)
Mr Nicholas Garman, BA (*Music)
Mrs Maureen Gatsky, Sp LSA (*Teaching and Learning*)
Mr Mark Gavin, BA, MA (*Economics)
Mr Michael Gillis, BSc, MA (*Biblical Hebrew)
Mrs Shelley Gladstone, BA (*Teaching & Learning*)
Mrs Tami Goldman, BEd (*Jewish Studies*)
§Mrs Yaffit Gordon, BSc (*Mathematics*)
Mrs Judith Graham, BA (*History, Government & Politics*)
§Mr Edwin Hedge, BA (*History of Art)
Mr Robert Hibberd, BSc (*Deputy Head of Science,* *Chemistry)
Mr Frederick Isaac, BA, MA (*Jewish Studies*)
Mrs Ruth Isenberg, BA (*English, Head of Upper School*)
§Mrs Bettina Jacobs, BA (*Art & Design – Fine Art*)
Mrs Susan Jager (*Teaching Assistant, Preparatory School*)
Mrs Naina Kanabar, BSc (*ICT*)
§Mrs Beth Kerr, BSc (*Physical Education, Director of Pastoral Education*)
Miss Sara Levy, BSc (*Mathematics*)
Mr Simon Levy, BA (*Jewish Studies*)
§Mrs Feigy Lieberman (*Jewish Studies*)
Mrs Joyce Mays, BSc (**Psychology, Head of Careers, Assistant Director of Sixth Form*)
Mrs Jaime Minter-Green, BSc (*Physical Education*)
Mr Phil Monaghan, BA (*PE*)
Mrs Mazal Nisner, BEd (*Modern Hebrew)
Ms Kalpana Patel, BA, MBA (*Mathematics*)
Mrs Anne Pattinson, BA (*Deputy Head of Geography*)
Miss Sarah Perlberg, BA (*French*)
§Mrs Emma Phillips, BA (*Sociology)
Mr Felix Posner, BSc (*Biology)
Mr Lee Raby, BA (*Physical Education, Geography*)

Miss Susan Ribeiro, BA (*Deputy Head of Lower School Art*)
Rabbi David Riffkin, BA, MA (**Jewish Studies*)
Mrs Vardit Sadeh-Ginzburg, BA, MA (*Modern Hebrew*)
Mrs Lili Schonberg, BA, BSc Ed (*French*)
Mrs Sharron Shackell, BA (**History*)
Miss Camilla Shifrin, BSc (*Biology*)
§Mrs Claire Shooter, BA (*French, Spanish*)
Mr Philip Silverton, BA (**Design and Technology*)
Mrs Maxine Skeggs, BA (*Teaching and Learning*)
Mrs Ruth Solomons, BSc, MA, MBA (**Science, Senior Teacher i/c Professional Development*)
Mr Gordon Spitz, BA, HDipEd, MA (**English*)
§Mrs Helen Stephenson-Yankuba, BSc (*Psychology*)
Miss Leann Swaine, BA (**Physical Education*)
Mrs Dawn Trober, Sp LSA (*Teaching and Learning*)
Mrs Deborah Unsdorfer, BSc (*Jewish Studies*)
Miss Neha Vadera, BA (**Art & Design – Photography*)
Miss Laura Vogel, BA (*History, Government & Politics*)
Mr Charles Wakely, BSc (**Physics*)
Mrs Annette Weinberg, BSc (*Mathematics*)
Mrs Keffe Wyse, BA (*Modern Hebrew*)

Librarian: Mrs Janet Leifer, MA, MCLIP

Director of the Beit HaMidrash (Jewish Study Centre): Rabbi Eliezer Zobin

School Counsellor: Mrs Nikki Bennett

Visiting Music Staff:
Mr Kenneth Bache, ARCM LGSM (*Brass, Brass Ensemble, Band Method*)
Mrs Samantha Dehaan, BA (*Singing*)
Miss Lindsay Evans, BMus (*Percussion*)
Dr Alexander L Flood, BA Oxon, MMus, PhD ARCO (*Pianoforte*)
Mr Oliver Gledhill, MA, PGCA, ARCM (*Violoncello, Double Bass*)
Mr Richard Herdman, BA (*Guitar & Guitar Ensemble, Bass Guitar, Acoustic/Electric*)
Mrs Rebecca Randall, FTCL (*Violin, Viola and String Quartet*)
Mrs Mandy Sherman, GRSM, ARCM, PGCE (*Clarinet, Saxophone*)
Mrs Hattie Webster, BA, MSc, ABRSM (*Flute*)

Age Range. 11–18. The Preparatory School opens in September 2011 with a Reception class for pupils of 4–5 years of age.

School Roll. There are 454 pupils on roll, of whom 206 are girls and 248 are boys. There are 126 pupils in the Sixth Form.

Buildings and Grounds. The College is situated in a tranquil 11-acre site dominated by Caldcote Towers, a Grade II listed 19th-century mansion, characterised by Pevsner as 'a crazy display … like a hotel in Harrogate'. Facilities include The Joyce King Theatre, a suite of science laboratories, a fitness suite, a large all-weather surface for tennis and netball, cricket and football pitches, and grounds for field events and athletics. Professor the Lord Winston opened a new multi-functional 8-classroom building in September 2010.

Admission (Senior School). Most boys and girls enter in September, though pupils are accepted in all three terms. Admission into the Senior School is on the basis of performance in the College's entrance examination and interview. The principal entry is at 11+, but the school considers pupils for admission into all year groups. A number of boys and girls join the College in the Sixth Form; offers of places are gained by interview and are conditional upon GCSE results.

Admission (Preparatory School). Admission into Reception and Year 1 is on the basis of informal assessment consisting of a play session and a focus activity. During the academic year 2011-12 the College will be considering applications for admission into Reception and Year 1 for the academic year 2012-13.

Fees per term (2011-2012). Senior School: £4,466; Lunch £240. Preparatory School: £2,500; Lunch £200.

Scholarships and Bursaries. Immanuel Jakobovits Scholarships are awarded to the value of 100% of fees on a competitive basis to ten outstanding 11+ entrants. These awards are subject to a yearly review throughout a pupil's time at the College. Exhibitions to the value of £2,000 per annum are awarded to pupils who show exceptional promise in Art or Music. Means-tested bursaries are awarded to a number of boys and girls from less affluent families who are academically and personally suited to the education the College provides.

Curriculum. The articles of the College's faith are that Jewish and secular learning shed light on one another, that the study of each is deepened and appreciated by study of the other, and that the life of the mind and spirit should not be compartmentalised but embraced. As such, the school offers a wide range of secular subjects, including English, Mathematics and the Sciences, as well as Art and Design, Drama, Geography, Modern and Biblical Hebrew, History, ICT, French, Spanish, Music, Personal, Social and Health Education, Photography, Technology and Physical Education. At A Level, additional subjects include Computing, Economics, Further Mathematics, Government & Politics, History of Art, Psychology and Sociology. Sixth-form students also have the opportunity of pursuing Open University undergraduate modules. Throughout a pupil's time at Immanuel, Jewish Studies forms part of her or his core curriculum. Jewish philosophy, history and religion are studied principally by way of close textual learning. All members of the College have informal and formal opportunities to deepen their understanding of Jewish faith and practice with members of the school's Jewish study centre, the Beit HaMidrash.

Pastoral Care. The College prides itself on its attentiveness to the needs of individual pupils. The pastoral team includes form tutors, heads of section and the College counsellor, who in Years 7 to 11 work under the direction of the Director of Pastoral Education. The Director of Sixth Form is in charge of a team of form tutors. Parental consultation evenings take place regularly. The School Council, which meets fortnightly with the Director of Pastoral Education and the Head Master, gives pupils the opportunity to express their views and make suggestions about improving school life.

Religious Life. The College commemorates and celebrates landmarks in the Jewish calendar such as Purim, Chanukah, Succoth and Yom Ha'atzmaut. Each January, on Holocaust Memorial Day, Lower Sixth Form students share the knowledge and insights that they have gained on their trip to Poland with pupils in the first five years of the Senior School. The College also commemorates Yom Hazikaron. Pupils attend morning and afternoon prayers on a daily basis.

The **Teaching and Learning Department** offers courses that enable pupils to become independent and successful learners. In addition to the programme followed by all pupils, the department provides small group teaching to a range of pupils whose learning needs are more specific. Pupils with a variety of learning profiles are thereby helped to develop confidence and do justice to their potential.

Art, Music and Drama. The College enjoys a tradition of excellence in the visual arts (the annual Gottlieb Art Show being the highlight of the artistic year) and drama (the frequent school productions have included *Macbeth, An Inspector Calls, Animal Farm, A Doll's House, Blithe Spirit, The Happiest Days of Your Life* and *Pygmalion*). There is a yearly Music Festival and the calendar includes a number of concerts and recitals involving soloists, ensembles and orchestra.

Games. The PE and Games staff involve pupils in activities that range from aerobics, golf, horse-riding and trampolining to athletics, cricket, football, hockey, netball and tennis. Over twenty sports clubs meet weekly. Physical Education may be studied for GCSE and A Level. Sports facilities include an all-weather surface and a fitness suite.

Enrichment activities. The many co-curricular activities on offer include opportunities for pupils to learn Mandarin and Italian and to participate in public-speaking and debating competitions. There are also clubs in philosophy, chess, art, science and modern European languages.

Educational Journeys. In Year 7 pupils stay in York for five days; in Year 8 they visit Paris; in Year 9 they spend four weeks in Israel; in Year 10 they visit Jewish families in Strasbourg and Madrid; and in the Lower Sixth they spend eight days in Poland. These experiences encourage pupils to bond with one another and help them to understand the forces that have shaped contemporary Jewry. A skiing trip to Colorado is held annually and History of Art and Photography students benefit from trips to Florence and Paris.

Careers. The careers guidance provided by the College enables pupils to research the choices open to them after completing their formal education. Year 11 pupils may undertake testing for the Morrisby Profile, which assists the decision-making process by identifying their innate abilities and strengths, whilst students in the Lower Sixth Form undertake two weeks' work experience. Year 8 pupils participate in the 'Take Your Child to Work' scheme. Language students may undertake work experience in Strasbourg and Madrid.

Charitable status. Immanuel College is a Registered Charity, number 803179. It exists to combine academic excellence and Jewish tradition in a contemporary society.

Ipswich School

Henley Road, Ipswich, Suffolk IP1 3SG
Tel: 01473 408300
Fax: 01473 400058
e-mail: registrar@ipswich.suffolk.sch.uk
website: www.ipswich.suffolk.sch.uk

The School was founded in about 1390 by the Ipswich Merchant Guild of Corpus Christi. Its first Charter was granted by Henry VIII and this was confirmed by Queen Elizabeth I.

Motto: *Semper Eadem.*

Visitor: Her Majesty The Queen

Governing Body:
K Daniels, ACII, FPMI (*Chairman*)
D E Barker, MBE
D E Bertram-Ralph
C D Brown, MA
G Byrne Hill, MA
J A Caudle, LLB
D A Chivers, BA, DipPM
The Revd Dr G M W Cook, MSc, PhD, FIBiol, FRSC
D J Defoe, BSc, PGCE
Professor L A Dobrée, BSc, MSc, RN, RM, CertEd
N C Farthing, LLB
Dr J L H Foster, MA, MSc, PhD
Mrs R E Gravell, BMedSci, BSc
The Bishop of St Edmundsbury and Ipswich (*ex officio*)
J W Poulter, MA
A C Seagers, MA
Ms M J Smith, BA, PGCE, MPhil
N H H Smith, MA, FCA
H E Staunton, BA, FCA
Dr D J Stone, MA, PhD

Professor C M Temple, BSc, MA, DPhil, CPsychol,
   AsFBPS
Dr D Thakerar, MBBS, LRCP, MRCS, DOccMed
Mrs C H Willcox, MSc Econ (*Vice-Chairman*)

Headmaster: **N J Weaver**, BA, MA

Senior Deputy Head (*Academic*): D Ayling, MA
Deputy Head (*Pastoral*): Mrs A Cura, BSc
Assistant Head: Miss J C Limrick, BSc
Head of Sixth Form: W G B Stansbury, MA
Head of Middle School: A R Bradshaw, BA
Head of Lower School: B Cliff, MA
Chaplain: The Revd A C Winter, BSc

Heads of Houses:
J W Orbell, BSc
S J Blunden, BA
D J Beasant, BA
Mrs P M Adcroft, BEng
A K Golding, MA
P R Gray, BA

Heads of Department:
Mrs Z Austin, MA (*Psychology*)
S J Boyle, BA (*Middle School Careers*)
A M Calver, BSc (*Sixth Form Careers*)
Ms J S Clarke, BA (*English*)
R L Clayton, BEd (*Physical Education*)
M J Core, BSc (*Mathematics*)
J R C Cox, MA (*Classics*)
Mrs M O Davis, BEd (*Art and Design*)
S J Duncombe, BA (*Design Technology*)
Mrs K Galbraith, MA (*History, Critical Thinking and
   Academically Gifted*)
Dr R E Tateson, BA (*Biology*)
D J P Halford-Thompson, BSc (*Chemistry & Science*)
J E G Halls (*Games*)
A D Leach, MA, BMus, ARCO, LRAM (*Music*)
J A C Phillips, BEng, MEd (*ICT*)
J A Thompson, MA (*Modern Languages*)
S A Arthur, BEng (*Physics*)
S J Tidball, MA (*Economics & Business Studies*)
Ms T Walker, BA (*Religious Studies*)
Mrs L Ward, BEd (*Drama*)
R G Welbourne, BA, FRGS (*Geography*)

Head of Preparatory School: Mrs A H Childs, BA QTS,
   PGC PSE, DipEd, MA

Bursar: P V Boughton
Registrar: Mrs Y M Morton
Headmaster's Secretary: Mrs R G Connor

Ipswich School occupies an attractive site adjacent to Christchurch Park. The cricket field lies within the perimeter of the school buildings and other playing fields of 30 acres are ten minutes' walk from the school.

There are 811 pupils in the Senior School (11–18), including 38 boarders. Of these, 242 boys and girls are in the Sixth Form. There are 310 pupils in the Preparatory School (3–11).

The Boarding House stands in its own grounds a short distance from the school. There is a choice of full, weekly and occasional boarding for pupils in the Senior School.

All academic subjects have been housed in new or refurbished rooms in the last few years and visitors comment on the quality of the buildings, which are grouped around one of the School's playing fields.

The Preparatory School is housed in purpose-built accommodation on an adjacent campus; it benefits from all the amenities of the Senior School including the Sports Hall, Swimming Pool, Performing Arts Centre and Playing Fields. (*For further details, see entry in IAPS section.*)

Admission. Entry to the Preparatory School after Nursery is by means of an assessment. Pupils must show language and number skill levels that are above their chronological age. The main entry to the Senior School at 11 is by examination in English, Mathematics and a Reasoning test, taken in late January. At 13, more pupils enter the Senior School, taking the Common Entrance Examination in June or the School's own Entrance and Scholarship Examination in March. Admission to the Sixth Form for girls and boys from other schools is by attainment of the required grades at GCSE, a report from the previous Head and an interview in November. Application forms may be obtained from the Registrar. A registration fee of £50 is payable (£25 for brothers or sisters).

Religious Education. There is religious education throughout the age range and weekly chapel services for different sections of the school; pupils normally attend one Sunday service a term at which their parents are also most welcome.

Careers. Computer analyses of interests and aptitudes complement carefully planned advice about GCSE and A Level choices, higher education and professional training.

Curriculum. In the Preparatory School pupils study English, Mathematics, French, ICT, History, Geography, RE, Science, Music, PE, Art and Design Technology and PSHE.

Senior School pupils follow a common curriculum in the first two years with a choice between French and Spanish. An option including Latin, Classical Civilisation, German and Russian is introduced in Year 9. Mathematics and English are taken at IGCSE, one or more Modern Foreign Languages and either separate or coordinated Sciences are taken by all pupils to GCSE level. Apart from these compulsory subjects, pupils are examined in 3 or 4 other subjects chosen from French, Latin, History, Geography, German, Russian, Spanish, Drama, Design and Technology, Classical Civilisation, Art and Design, Religious Studies and Music.

In the Sixth Form AS and A Level subjects are chosen from the following:

Mathematics, Further Mathematics, Physics, Chemistry, Biology, Latin, Classical Civilisation, Economics, Business Studies, Art, Design Technology, Music, History, Geography, English, French, German, Russian, Spanish, Psychology, PE, Philosophy of Religion and Ethics.

In addition to their A Level studies, all Sixth Formers participate in an Enrichment Programme designed to complement and broaden the conventional curriculum. Students are also able to gain qualifications in a range of subjects such as Critical Thinking, ICT, Mandarin, Politics, Photography, Law and Spanish.

Societies and Activities. All are encouraged to participate in a variety of extra-curricular activities which take place in lunchtimes, after school, at weekends and during the holidays. One afternoon a week is devoted to community service, conservation work, CCF (Army and RAF contingents) and a variety of sports and other pursuits. Sixth Formers may participate in the School's International Leadership Programme at this time.

Drama in the school is particularly strong; continuous activity in this sphere maintains a succession of productions throughout the year, in all age groups. Productions in 2010–2011 included: *The History Boys; I Love You, You're Perfect, Now Change; Showstoppers; Pride & Prejudice; A Midsummer Night's Dream*.

Ipswich School aims to give all pupils a rich and satisfying experience of music. There are ample opportunities for music-making, including Choral Society, Chapel Choir, School Choir, Chamber, Symphony and Intermediate Orchestras, Big Band and numerous Chamber Ensembles. Tours have taken the Chapel Choir to Poland and Wells Cathedral. The school has links with the Aldeburgh Young Musicians scheme. There are regular performances at Snape Maltings (Elgar's Gerontius 2009, Duruflé's Requiem 2010). There is an annual Summer Music Course. In 2010 the first Ipswich School Festival of Music was held. Highlights

included a concert by His Majesty's Sagbutts and Cornetts and a master class and recital by Julian Lloyd Webber. Plans for this year include a visit from the internationally acclaimed violinist Chloe Hanslip.

The Duke of Edinburgh's Award Scheme, Young Enterprise and the Sports Leadership Level 1 Award are run within the school.

Games. The main team games for boys are rugby, hockey and cricket and for girls, hockey, netball and athletics. Alternatives for many in the Senior School include rounders, cross-country, golf, tennis, Eton fives, football, squash, polygym, sailing, badminton, swimming and windsurfing. Skiing parties travel overseas each year.

The Mermagen Sports Hall provides facilities for a wide range of indoor sports and is part of a complex which includes a Cricket Gallery, whose indoor nets function as a centre of excellence for the county as well as the School. There is a heated indoor swimming pool, three covered Eton fives courts, two squash courts and a twenty-two station fitness suite.

Fees per term (2011-2012). Day: Senior School £3,895; Lower School £3,553; Preparatory School (Years 3–6) £3,067; Pre-Preparatory School (Reception–Year 2) £2,786.

Boarding (inclusive of tuition fees): Full Boarding: £9,699 (Years 9–13); £8,004 (Years 7 and 8); Weekly Boarding: £7,860 (Years 9–13); £6,720 (Years 7 and 8).

Scholarships. These are available for external candidates at 11, 13 and 16. Academic Scholarships are known as Queen's Scholarships, commemorating the Royal Charter granted to the School by Queen Elizabeth 1 in 1566. Academic Scholarships of up to half fees are awarded on the basis of examinations and interviews at 11 and 13 and for the Sixth Form on the basis of school reports, predicted GCSE grades, interview and scholarship essay. Music and Art Scholarships at 11 and 13 are awarded on the basis of excellence in these areas as demonstrated by audition or portfolio. A Sports Scholarship at 11 is awarded to a pupil who will make a significant contribution to the quality of sport at the school and an All-rounder Scholarship is available at 13. Sixth Form Scholarships are awarded for academic excellence, for exceptional musical talent and for an all-rounder who will do well academically and contribute outstandingly in other areas of school life such as sport or drama. A Sports Scholarship is also available at 16. We also offer Arkwright Scholarships, which focus on Design Technology, and Ogden Trust awards, which are open to pupils from State Schools wishing to study Maths and Physics. The Ogden Trust awards are restricted to those whose parents have a relatively low income.

Bursaries. These are available on a means-tested basis, up to full fee remission, for entry at 11, 13 and 16.

The Old Ipswichian Club. Annual dinners are held in London and Ipswich. There are clubs for cricket, fives and golf. Teams are fielded against the school in several sports and the Club holds many social events each year.

Charitable status. Ipswich School is a Registered Charity, number 310493. It exists for the purpose of educating children.

The John Lyon School

Middle Road, Harrow, Middlesex HA2 0HN
Tel: 020 8872 8400
Fax: 020 8872 8455
e-mail: enquiries@johnlyon.org
website: www.johnlyon.org

The John Lyon School was established as a Day School in 1876 under the Statutes made by the Governors of Harrow School, in pursuance of the Public Schools Act, 1868.

Motto: *Stet Fortuna Domus.*

Foundation Governors: The Governors of Harrow School

Governors:
J F R Hayes (*Chairman*)
D A Crehan
Prof J S Chadha
J R Davies
J H Dunston
A R C Fraser, MBE
K W B Gilbert
P Herman
A P McClaran
Mrs S Symonds

Clerk to the Governors: The Hon Andrew C Millett, 45 Pont Street, London SW1X 0BX

Head: Miss K E Haynes, BA, MEd, NPQH

Bursar: M E Gibson, BA, MSc

Deputy Head: S Miles, BMus, ARCO, ARCM, AMusLCM, NPQH

Assistant Staff:
S J K Andon, BA, MSc
Miss F L Baldwin, BA
Mrs V M L Balavan, Licence LLCE
P D Berry, BA
S Bolderow, BA, MSt (*Head of Sixth Form*)
T Z Brabec, BA, MA
J D Bruce, BSc (*Geography*)
L D Budd, BA, MA
P M Clarke, BA, MSc
Dr A L M Clayton, BSc, PhD (*Biology*)
C J Clews, BA
Miss L F Cooper, BA, MA
P J Cowie, BA (*Classics, Politics*)
Miss N Crathern, BSc
D H Curtis, BA (*Drama*)
O Damree, BSc
T P Dennehy, BA
A K Ferguson, BA
Dr W J Fleming, BSc, PhD
Miss E C Flood, BSc
S G Foster, BA (*Economics*)
R V French, BSc, CBiol, MIBiol
L R Garwood, BA
Miss C Harrison, BA, MA
Ms L Hope (*Art and Design*)
G R Iveson, PGDE, MA
A L Jones, BSc
S J Leach, BSc, MSc (*Physical Education*)
D A Leitch, BA, MA
A S Ling, BSc
C K Longhurst, BA (*History*)
T Mahon, BSc, MA (*Physics*)
Miss J McElroy, BA (*French*)
Mrs E McMillan, BSc, MSc (*Psychology*)
J McNaughton, BSc
J C A Moore, BA, MA
Mrs J Morris, BA, MBA (*Spanish*)
J Orme, BSc
I R Parker, BSc (*Head of Upper School*)
Mrs A L Paul, BA (*English*)
Mrs L S Plummer, BA (*Head of Lower School*)
S Rana, BMedSc
R T Stratton, BVA DipTch
Miss L A Teunissen, BA
Miss L A Twist, BA
M W Vickery, BEng
D P Vosper Singleton, MMath (*Mathematics*)
J F Walker, BSc, MSc
D F Weedon, MA (*Chemistry*)
A S Westlake, BA, BA (*Religious Studies*)
Miss A M Wilby, BA, MMus (*Music*)

A P Wright, BSc (*ICT*)

Part-Time:
Mrs E J Ingham, BSc, MSc

Visiting Music Staff:
C Avison, BMus (*trumpet*)
K Bache, ARCM, LGSM (*trumpet, trombone*)
R Boyle, AGSM (*guitar, guitar ensemble*)
J Clarkson (*voice*)
H Clement-Evans, GRNCM, PPRNCM (*oboe, saxophone*)
V E Davies, BMus (*horn, euphonium, trombone, tuba*)
T Godel, Dip (*bass guitar*)
C Grey, MA, BMus, LRAM (*piano, violin, jazz band, String Ensembles, Grade V Theory*)
Miss G Harvey, BMus Hons (*saxophone, clarinet*)
Ms W Hasegawa (*piano*)
T Hooper, BMus Hons perf, LRAM (*drums & percussion*)
P Huntington, BA (*drums & percussion*)
W Kristiansen, BMus, LRAM (*electric guitar*)
Miss E May, BMus, LRAM (*cello*)
R Marshall, BND (*drums & percussion, electric guitar*)
Mrs N Stokes (*violin, viola*)
Miss S Wilby (*flute*)
Ms V Yannoula, BMus Hons, Dip (*piano*)

PA to the Head: Mrs H S Cade

There are 580 boys in the School, all day boys.

Admission. The School is open to boys residing within reasonable travelling distance.

There are places each September for boys at 11+ for Year 7 and 13+ for Year 9. An entrance examination is set in January. There are also places available in the Sixth Form for boys who have five A grades at GCSE.

Registration Fee: £75.

Fees per term (2011-2012). £4,590, payable in advance, which covers the cost of all textbooks and stationery.

Curriculum. The School Curriculum at present includes Religious Studies, English, History, Geography, Economics, French, German, Spanish, Italian, Latin, Mathematics, Chemistry, Physics, Biology, Art and Design, Music, Drama, Computer Studies, Government and Politics, Psychology and PE. Religious teaching is non-denominational.

Examinations. Boys are prepared for GCSE and IGCSE. In the Sixth Form four subjects are normally chosen to be studied for AS level in the first year leading to three (or four) A2 levels in the second.

Scholarships. Scholarships normally provide for between 5% and 20% of tuition fees.

All boys who sit the 11+ and 13+ entrance examination in January will be considered for Academic and All-Rounder Scholarships; their performance in the examination, current school report and interview will all be taken into consideration. Additional Academic Scholarships are available to Sixth Form entrants on the basis of outstanding performance at GCSE.

Consideration is given to candidates at 11+, 13+ and 16+ of outstanding potential and ability in Art & Design, Drama, Music and Sport. Separate applications need to be made and potential candidates are called for selection interviews and tests as appropriate.

Bursaries. Bursaries up to the value of a full place are available, subject to financial assessment.

Term of Entry. Normal entry date is in the September term.

School Buildings. The School Buildings are on the West side of Harrow Hill and include the usual facilities. Regular additions have been made. In 1973 a wing was built as part of a Development Plan, allowing for the reorganisation and modernisation of existing buildings, which was completed in 1974. In 1981 Oldfield House was built to accommodate the first two years and in 1989 a new assembly hall/theatre/classroom complex called the Lyon Building came into use. A Sports Complex comprising an indoor swimming pool and sports hall was opened by HRH The Duke of Edinburgh in February 1997. Recent developments include a Drama studio, a computerised language laboratory, and a modern library. A new Science block opened in September 2008.

Games. The School playing fields are within 10 minutes' walk on the south side of the Hill. In addition, the School is able to use the Harrow School Athletic Track, Golf Course and Tennis Courts.

The main games are Association Football in the Winter Terms, Cricket and Athletics in the Summer Term, supported by Badminton, Tennis, Basketball, Archery, and other games. PE and Swimming are in the curriculum.

Out of School Activities. Boys are strongly encouraged to play an active part in a wide range of activities. There is a School Orchestra, a Junior Orchestra, a Wind Band, a Jazz Band, large and small choirs. Drama, as well as being taught in the curriculum, is developed through House and School Plays. There is the normal range of School Clubs and Societies.

The School takes an active part in the Duke of Edinburgh's Award Scheme and has a full-time Head of Outdoor Education. The School's CCF operates in conjunction with Harrow School.

Community Service has been developed through various projects which are undertaken in the Harrow Area. Each year the school devotes considerable time to fundraising for a Charity chosen by the boys.

Careers. Advice on Careers is given by the Head of Careers. Specialist advice concerning entrance to Higher Education is given. Morrisby testing is undertaken.

The Old Lyonian Association. The Old Lyonians' Association, which was founded in 1902, has always been a strong support to the School. All boys on leaving the school from the Sixth Form become life members of the Association. The Association has its own ground and pavilion at 74 Pinner View, Harrow, and its President is Mr P R Harrison.

Entries to Universities. The Upper Sixth on average consists of 75 boys who will usually apply for Degree courses at leading Universities and of these the great majority are successful. A steady stream of boys is sent to Oxford, Cambridge and London.

Charitable status. The Keepers and Governors of the free Grammar School of John Lyon is a Registered Charity, number 310033. The purpose of the charity is the education of boys living within reach of Harrow between the ages of 11–18.

Kelly College

Tavistock, Devon PL19 0HZ
Tel: 01822 813100
Fax: 01822 612050
e-mail: headmaster@kellycollege.com
           registrar@kellycollege.com
website: www.kellycollege.com

Kelly College was founded in 1877 by Admiral Benedictus Marwood Kelly.
Motto: *Fortiter occupa portum.*

Governors:

Chairman: D R Milford
Vice-Chairman: Canon Dr W J Rea, DPhil

Professor M S Totterdell	The Baroness Fookes of
Prebendary R Carlton	Plymouth, DBE, DL
Rear Admiral C Snow,	D M Vine
CBE	S J Carder
Mrs E Loosmore	District Judge C J Tromans
Dr H J Ball	K Hollinshead
	D P Jones

Mrs A Childs	Dr C Leeson
J G Taylor	Dr I Luke

Headmaster: **Dr G R W Hawley**, BSc Durham, PhD Durham

* *Head of Department*

Deputy Head (Academic): R McDermott, BEng (*Physics*)
Deputy Head: E H T Noy Scott, BA (*Classics*)

Housemasters/mistresses:
School House: D Tomalin, BSc, MA (*Mathematics, Physics*)
Courtenay House: R J Stanyer, BSc, BEd (**ICT*)
Newton House: Miss R Callard, BSc (*Physical Education*)
Marwood House: D R Bott, BA (*History*)
Russell House: Mrs R Morel, BA (*French*)
Conway House: B G C Donnelly, BSc (*Biology*), Mrs S Donnelly, BSc, MPhil, Mrs T A Bratt, BA (*English*)

Assistant Staff:
Mrs S Baldock, BSc (*Science*)
J Balfour, BA (*Head of Drama*)
Mrs J M Boulton (*Learning Support Assistant*)
Mrs S J Brassil, BSc (*Learning Support Assistant*)
R A Brew, MSc (*Director of Swimming*)
Mrs M Bridger, BA (*English*)
Mrs S J Broughton, BSc (*Mathematics*)
Mrs J Brown, IL (*Coordinator of Spanish*)
Mrs S E Bury, BA (*ESL*)
Mrs D Collard, BEd (*DT*)
G C Collard, BEd (**DT*)
Mrs M J Collier, BA, LGSM (**Modern Languages, French and Spanish*)
Miss K Cuckston, BSc (*Mathematics*)
Mrs M E Duffy, BEd (**Mathematics*)
Mrs F L Dunn, BA (*Head of Girls' Games, *Physical Education*)
A Egford, BSc (*Head of Boys' Games, Physical Education*)
S Fletcher, BEng
Mrs S J Gray, BSc (*Coordinator of Science, *Chemistry, *PSE*)
Mrs A Holwill, BA (*Art*)
Mrs L B Huish, BEd (*History, Religious Studies and English*)
R B J Huish, BEd (**Biology*)
Mrs V J Lanyon Jones, CertEd, AMBDA (*Learning Development Coordinator*)
I Leaman, BSc, (**BTEC National Diploma in Sport, Physical Education*)
C J Limb, BA (**English*)
A Makepeace, BSc (*ICT*)
S Martin, MA, BSc (*Geography*)
Mrs V McCarty, CertEd, ALAM (*Speech and Drama*)
D Page, BA, MA (*History, Head of Careers, General Studies*)
Mrs N Pang (*Industrial Fellow*)
Miss R H Plumptre, BA (**ESLt*)
M Quinlan, BSc Hons
N Rogerson (*Head of Economics & Business*)
T Ryder, BA (*Head of Sixth Form, *Geography*)
Mrs S Speakman (*Netball and Rounders*)
Mrs J Stockman, BA (*Learning Support*)
Mrs A Stokes, BA (**Art, Art Photography*)
R Strain, BSc (*Science, Biology*)
D Sutcliffe (**Religious Studies*)
Mrs S Tranfield, BA (*English*)
D C Turnbull, BA (*Design & Technology*)
J Waymark (*DT Assistant*)
A M Wilson, BMus (*Director of Music*)

Music Department:
R Davies (*Percussion*)
Mrs S Houghton, CertEd, ARCM (*Flute and Recorder*)
P Jones, GRSM, ACI (*Brass*)

R King (*Guitar*)
Mrs O Loewendahl, BMus (*'Cello*)
Ms J Martin, Dip Mus (*Clarinet, Saxophone*)
Mrs M Mazur-Park, BMus, LTCL (*Piano*)
Mrs B Phillips, BMus, PGCE (*Singing*)
T Ryder, BA (*Classical Guitar*)
Mrs E Sturtridge, ABRSM (*Violin*)

Bursar: Mrs M M Sena

Registrar: Mrs K Bailey, BA Hons, MSc
Tel: 01822 813193; Fax: 01822 612050;
e-mail: registrar@kellycollege.com

Marketing Manager: Mrs E Batley
e-mail: batleye@kellycollege.com

Medical Officer: Dr M Eggleton

Headmaster's Secretary: Mrs S C Harding

Kelly College offers a co-educational boarding, weekly boarding and day education for boys and girls aged 11–18. It is a small and friendly school of about 360 pupils of whom half are boarders. The school balances a good academic schooling with a strong commitment to a whole range of extra-curricular activities, be they musical, artistic or sporting. The College plays a significant part in the cultural and intellectual life of the local community. The location of the school next to the Dartmoor National Park naturally enhances the strong 'outdoors' tradition of team games and adventure training.

The school has a happy atmosphere within a disciplined framework, where the care of others, good manners and self-respect are important values. Kelleians typically are contributors and, whilst the school maintains high academic standards throughout, the admission process looks at the whole person and welcomes a range of talents and abilities.

Small class sizes ensure individual attention, and a committed staff seeks to work with parents to achieve the personal goals of each pupil, whether that be a place at Oxford, International sporting representation, or a chosen career path.

All pupils are part of one of the Houses, which is their 'home from home' in the case of the boarders and their working base for day pupils. Boarders and day pupils are integrated throughout the school. Each pupil is cared for by a Housemaster or Housemistress and a tutor who oversees their academic progress and personal development.

Site and Buildings. Kelly College occupies a beautiful site on one bank and hillside of the Tavy valley looking out over the Dartmoor National Park on the edge of Tavistock, Devon. The buildings comprise the School Chapel, Assembly Hall, Performing Arts Centre (opened in 2007), Central Dining Hall, Library and ICT Centre, Art and Design Studios, Technology workshops, Science Laboratories, a heated indoor Swimming Pool, Gymnasium, covered Fives and Squash Courts, Floodlit all-weather surface for Hockey and Tennis, Armoury and Miniature Rifle Range. There is also a residential Adventure Training Centre, including a high-ropes course and trapeze jump. The school has its own Trout and Salmon fishing.

All pupils joining the school at 11 (Year 7) are part of Conway House for two years before progressing on to the senior houses. From 13 (Year 9), there are two Senior Girls' Boarding and Day houses, two Senior Boys' Boarding and Day Houses, and a Senior Mixed Day House (opened in September 2002).

School Structure and Admission Procedures. There are normally two forms in the First and Second form. Admission at age 11 (Year 7) is by school examination in the preceding February. There is an additional form from the Third Form. Admission at age 13 (Year 9) is by the College Entrance or by the Common Entrance Examination. Entrance to the Sixth form is on the basis of GCSE predictions. A report from the present school is required and all

candidates for entry have a formal interview with the Headmaster.

Term of Entry. Pupils may also be accepted in January and April.

Entrance Scholarships, Exhibitions and Awards. (*See Scholarship Entries section.*) All scholarships and exhibitions are competitive on entry to the school. Awards may be awarded at ages 11, 13, and 16 in the following areas: Academic, Art, Drama, Design & Technology, Music, Sport and Swimming. At 11, for entry into the First Form (Year 7), candidates for 'performance' awards are assessed as part of the routine admissions process. At 13, for entry into the Third Form (Year 9), candidates sit the Scholarship papers in February/March, and/or, in the case of 'performance' awards, are assessed on a visit to the school. Sixth form Scholarships are awarded on the basis of GCSE results. Awards of 10% discount off the school fees are available to sons and daughters of Old Kelleians and up to 20% for members of the Forces.

Curriculum. The Lower School curriculum (Years 7–9) introduces pupils to a broad range of subjects in line with the National Curriculum. In Year 9 pupils begin to study a second modern language. All pupils at Kelly study for the International/European Computer Driving Licence, which they may complete as early as the end of the fourth year in the school.

The GCSE curriculum at Kelly is quite flexible and aims to stretch each pupil appropriately. The core subjects are Mathematics, English, Biology, Chemistry, Physics, ICT (ECDL qualification) and a Language. The range of option subjects includes Art, Design & Technology, Drama, French, Geography, German, History, Music, Physical Education, Religious Studies and Spanish.

Pupils entering the Sixth Form need to possess 6 GCSE passes and at least 47–52 GCSE points to study 4 AS Levels, with at least 5 GCSE points in each of English and Mathematics. Most pupils at Kelly study for 4 AS Levels in the Lower Sixth year, but in exceptional circumstances some study five or three subjects. A Level option subjects include Art & Design, Biology, Chemistry, Design & Technology, Drama & Theatre Studies, Economics and Business, English Literature, French, Geography, History, ICT, Mathematics, Further Mathematics, Music, Photography, Physical Education, Physics, Religious Studies and Spanish. Tuition in Latin can be arranged at an additional cost. All pupils in the Lower Sixth year receive tuition in Public Speaking. A Russell University Group class is taught by the Head of Sixth Form for part of the Lower and Upper Sixth years.

Combined Cadet Force. All Fourth Form (Year 10) pupils follow the Duke of Edinburgh's Award Scheme as part of their CCF commitment and can join the Royal Naval, Royal Air Force or the Army Section. The CCF has a strong emphasis on Adventure Training and there are opportunities for sailing, kayaking, sub-aqua diving, orienteering, smallbore shooting and abseiling; many of which are available on site or nearby on Dartmoor. The College, originally founded as it was for the 'sons of Naval Officers and other Gentlemen', enjoys strong links with the Royal Navy at Dartmouth and pupils have the opportunity to visit the affiliated ship, HMS Argyll, when she is in port.

Cultural and Academic Societies and Activities. All boys and girls are encouraged to explore new interests and to make the most of their spare time. Societies and Activities include Literary and Debating, Current Affairs, Drama, Choral, Music, Football, Computing, Photography, Chess, Bridge, Fine Arts, Surfing and Textiles.

Kelly has a strong music department. Kelleians can learn a broad range of musical instruments from the Organ to the Electric Guitar. The school hosts a Concert Society which is open to pupils and members of the local community alike; and the Senior Orchestra and Senior Choir join with the local Choral Society and Orchestra to put on major concerts.

There is also a Junior Choir and Junior Orchestra, plus a number of music ensembles.

There is a strong tradition of Public Speaking and debating and many of the pupils study for LAMDA qualifications. The School Hall is fully equipped for theatrical productions, and there are a number of House and School plays each year. A Performing Arts Centre opened in July 2007.

Sport. Kelly has a strong sporting tradition and has probably produced more Olympians and Internationals than any other school of its size. The major sports for girls are Hockey, Netball, Rounders, Tennis, Athletics and Swimming; and for boys are Rugby, Hockey, Cricket, Tennis, Athletics and Swimming. Many other sports are available in the school: Climbing, Cross Country, Golf, Riding, Rugby and Winchester Fives, Squash, Basketball, Sailing, Surfing, Tennis, Soccer and Yoga.

Dress. The school uniform for girls consists of a school kilt, white blouse and school blazer. Boys wear a blue shirt, grey flannel trousers and school blazer.

Fees per term (2011-2012). Full boarding: £7,175–£8,500; Weekly boarding: £6,450–£7,900; Day Pupils: £3,950–£4,875. Music lessons are among the voluntary extras, which are kept to a minimum.

Application. A prospectus and further details are available from the Registrar, who will be pleased to arrange visits to the school.

Old Kelleian Club: The OK Secretary, The Registry, Kelly College, Tavistock, Devon PL19 0HZ.

Charitable status. Kelly College is a Registered Charity, number 306716. It is a day and boarding school for boys and girls, which also grants maintenance allowances and the provision of assistance for higher education by means of Scholarships, Exhibitions and Means Tested Bursaries.

Kelvinside Academy

33 Kirklee Road, Glasgow G12 0SW
Tel: 0141 357 3376
Fax: 0141 357 5401
e-mail: rector@kelvinsideacademy.org.uk
website: www.kelvinsideacademy.org.uk

The Academy was founded in 1878. Since May 1921, it has been controlled by the Kelvinside Academy War Memorial Trust, which was formed in memory of the Academicals who gave their lives in the War of 1914–18. The affairs of the Trust are managed by a Board of Governors, mainly composed of Academicals and parents.

Motto: ΑΙΕΝ ΑΡΙΣΤΕΥΕΙΝ

The Governing Body:
Chairman: Mr N Fyfe, MA Hons, LLB

Mrs G Buchanan, DBO	Mr D McGillivray, LLB,
Mrs M Eadie, RGN	NP
Mr R Eadie, FRICS	Mr K Cairnduff
Mr W Frame, LLB, FRICS,	Mr C J Mackenzie, LLB,
FCIArb	DIP, LP, NP
Mr N J McNeill, CA	Mr W A Dalziel
Mr C Rutherford, MCIBS,	Mrs E Davis, BA Hons,
MBA	PGCE
Mr C Kerr, BSc	Mr A Brodie (*ex-officio*)
	(*President KAC*)

Secretary to the Governors: Mr D Pocock, FInstAM, MCGI

Rector: Mrs L A Douglas, BEd, CMath, MIMA

Deputy Rector: Mr A J Gilliland, BSc

Director of Studies: Mr N Fischbacher, BEng

Senior School Staff:

Mrs J Cunningham, BMus Hons	Mrs F Whittle, BMus
Mr R W J Moir, BEd	Mrs D Macgregor, BSc
Mr A G Mulholland, BSc	Miss B Davison, BA
Mr D J Wilson, BEd	Mrs J Hardy, MA
Miss S Crichton, BMus	Mrs N Mathews, BA
Mr J Gilius, MA	Mrs J Rynn, BSc Hons
Mrs J B Shields, MA	Miss L Semple, BSc
Mrs G T Ali, MA	Ms E Whatley-Marshall, MA
Mr J I O Cuthbertson, BSc	Miss K Hopkin, MA
Miss A M Dal'Santo, BA	Mr N Reid, BSc
Mrs A Schneeberger, MA	Miss L Bruce, BSc
Mrs H Jephson, MA	Mrs J Clark, BA
Mr I Nicholson, BSc	Mr G Guile, BSc Hons
Mr S Connor, BEng	Mr B Parham, BSc Hons
Ms C Alonso-Bartol, MA	Mr B FitzGerald, MSci
Miss J L Carswell, BA	Mrs M L Prince, MA Hons
Mr S Klimowicz, MA	Miss A Lindsay, BA Hons
Mr C Lawson, BEd	Mrs L Hart, MA Hons
Mrs A Mullan, BA Hons	Mr N Calvert, MSc, PGDE
Miss K Leckie, BSc Hons	Mr J Calder, MA Hons, PG
Mr I Leighton, BSc Hons	Dip, PGCE
Miss F Donald, BA Hons	

Chaplain: Revd Craig Lancaster
Bursar: Mr D Pocock, FInstAM, MCGI
Assistant Bursar: Mrs M Bennett, MA

Head of Junior School: Mr A Dickenson, MA Hons

Junior School Staff:

Mrs M Jeffrey, DPE	Mrs S Paterson, BEd Hons
Mrs G Whittaker, CertEd	Mrs J S Maclean, BEd
Mrs L Woore, DPE	Hons
Mrs P Campbell, BEd	Mrs S Rodger, BEd Hons
Mrs A Stevenson, BEd	Mr I Forrest, MA
Mrs R E Porter, BEd	Mrs F Kennedy, BEd
Mrs L L McColl, BEd	Mr N Armet, BSc
Mrs E Henderson, BEd	Mrs E Laird-Jones, BSc
Mrs B Deutsch, MA	Mrs L Hill, BEd

Nursery School Staff:
Mrs T Nugent, BEd Hons (*Nursery Leader*)
Miss S Garner (*Nursery Nurse*)
Miss K Macfarlane (*Nursery Nurse*)
Mrs J Hartley (*Nursery Nurse*)
Mrs P Argue (*Nursery Nurse*)
Mrs J Park (*Nursey Nurse*)

Registrar: Mrs L Andonovic, MA
SSI: Sgt M McAlister
Development Manager: Mrs E Solman
Marketing Officer: Mrs L Young

Kelvinside Academy is a co-educational day school for some 620 pupils, aged 3 to 18.

The main building is in neo-classical style and Grade A listed but has been extensively modernised within. Further buildings and extensions provide excellent facilities for all subjects and interests, and are symptomatic of the school's progressive approach. Recent additions include state-of-the-art IT and multimedia suites and new sports pavilion.

Curriculum. Junior School pupils (from J1) benefit from specialist input in Art, Music, PE and Modern Languages. The Senior Prep (P7) year is a transitional year with a core curriculum taught by the class teacher but science, languages, art, music and PE are delivered by secondary specialists. Computing is a core compulsory subject up to S4.

Senior 3 and 4 pupils follow 8 Standard Grade/Intermediate courses, followed by Higher and Advanced Higher courses in Senior 5 and 6.

Combined Cadet Force. The hugely popular CCF is compulsory for one year in Senior 3. Pupils embark upon the Duke of Edinburgh's Award Scheme at this stage.

Games. Rugby and hockey are the principal team games in the winter terms with athletics, tennis and cricket in the summer. A range of additional sports and games, from football to basketball and dance, is offered.

Activities. A rich programme of extra-curricular and House activities contributes significantly to the broad educational experience enjoyed by all pupils.

The Expressive Arts. Music, drama, dance and the visual arts have a central role in both the curriculum and the co-curriculum.

Fees per term (2011-2012). Nursery £1,050–£1,900, Junior School £2,110–£3,098, Senior School £2,950–£3,415.

Admission. For Junior Start and P1, children undergo an informal assessment. For P2–Senior 6, children sit an entrance test and informal interview.

Bursaries. Financial support with fees (ranging from 10%–100%) is available to P7 and Senior School pupils.

Charitable status. The Kelvinside Academy War Memorial Trust is a Registered Charity, number SC003962. The purpose of the Trust is to run a combined primary and secondary day school in memory of those former pupils of the school who gave their lives in the war of 1914–18.

Kent College

Canterbury, Kent CT2 9DT
Tel: 01227 763231
Fax: 01227 787450
e-mail: registrar@kentcollege.co.uk
website: www.kentcollege.com

The School was founded in 1885 and occupies an idyllic semi-rural site overlooking the historic City of Canterbury. In 1920 it was acquired by the Board of Management for Methodist Residential Schools. Its Junior School is situated a mile away at Harbledown.

Kent College has been fully co-educational since 1973. The Senior School (11–18 years) has some 460 boys and girls, approximately one-third boarding and two-thirds day, 150 of whom are in the Sixth Form. There are around 200 pupils in total in the Junior School, Infant Department and Nursery section.

The school's Christian heritage continues to inform all its policies and objectives, including its outstanding pastoral tradition, but it happily welcomes pupils of all faiths, or none.

Motto: *Lux tua via mea*

Visitor: The President of the Methodist Conference

Administrative Governors:
Chairman: Dudley Shipton, CertEd Oxon, Dip MathsEd, Mathematical Assoc (*OC*)
Vice-Chairman: Miss J E Neville, JP, BA, SRN, RNT

Secretary to the Governors and Bursar: Mrs A C Hencher, AInstAM

(*OC*) *Old Canterburian*

Head Master: Dr D J Lamper, EdD Hull, BMus, MA London, AKC

Deputy Head Master: J G Waltho, MA Oxon

Director of Studies: G Letley, BA Kent
Senior Master: T J Williams, BEd Loughborough
Senior Teacher: Mrs C A Baker, CertEd London
Senior Teacher: C A Joy, BEd Sheffield Poly
Head of Sixth Form: J Burnage, BSc Loughborough

Head of Middle School: S D Gant, BA Kent
Head of Lower School: Mrs C A Baker, CertEd London
Head of Year 7: Mrs K L McGibney, BA Leeds

Chaplain: Revd Dr P Glass, BA Leeds, MA Cantab, PhD Leeds

Registrar: Mrs J Simpson
Head Master's PA: Mrs D Beaumont

Infant and Junior School:
(*See entry in IAPS section.*)
Head Master: A J Carter, BEd

Facilities. As well as the core buildings where the majority of teaching is carried out, the school has four boarding houses, two for boys and two for girls. The school Chapel has been skilfully adapted to serve additionally as a Theatre.

The school facilities are outstanding with the latest addition being a stunning new music department. Music is thriving at Kent College with our choristers performing at national level twice in the last year. Excellent sporting facilities provide opportunities for all and the school is renowned nationwide for its prowess in this area. The school currently boasts 4 potential Olympians for the 2012 Olympics.

Close to the main campus is the school Farm which is managed by a Farm Manager who runs a Young Farmers' Club and Equine Unit.

The estate at the nearby Junior School is particularly beautiful. The house was owned by Sidney Cooper RA who created the garden there. It is an ideal environment in which young children can flourish.

Curriculum. The curriculum is aligned to the National Curriculum but a greater range of subjects is provided. All pupils are normally expected to take at least one European language at GCSE. It is not the aim to specialise in any one group of subjects but to provide a balanced curriculum which will give full opportunity for students to get a good grounding of general knowledge and later to develop particular talents to a high standard. We pride ourselves on being able to provide a personalised learning experience, where we can organise the curriculum to suit the child.

The International Baccalaureate is offered alongside A Levels in the Sixth Form.

Dyslexia Unit. The school makes provision for a number of dyslexic children of appropriate ability. There is a special unit with very well qualified staff and all staff are trained so that the school offers an understanding approach to children with this difficulty. The objective is to integrate pupils into the mainstream curriculum and activity of the school whilst giving them appropriate support within the Dyslexia Unit.

International Study Centre. A major attraction for overseas students is the school's ISC, which is a department within the Senior School, where specialist tuition in small groups is given to those pupils whose English language skills need enhancement prior to their integration into the mainstream curriculum.

Pastoral Care. All pupils are placed in the care of a Tutor who works closely with the Houseparent and Year Head, liaising with the Head Master on the one hand and parents on the other. Opportunities are arranged several times a year to enable parents to meet staff and in addition the Head Master and all staff are willing to meet parents by arrangement.

Religion. Although the School is controlled by the Board of Management for Methodist Residential Schools, boys and girls of all denominations or none are accepted. During the week all pupils attend Morning Assembly. Confirmation classes are arranged in the Spring Term and a joint Confirmation Service for Methodists and Anglicans is held in the School Chapel early in the Summer Term.

Games and Activities. The school possesses 28 acres of playing fields and a floodlit all-weather hockey pitch. The major games for boys are Rugby, Hockey, Tennis, Cricket and Athletics and for girls Netball, Hockey, Tennis, Athletics and Rounders. Hockey is a particular strength with teams regularly attaining National championship status. Currently the school boasts 3 England Hockey players. The boarding community enjoys full use of the facilities in the evening with regular activities in Basketball, Football and Fitness Training. Senior pupils take part in various forms of community service in the City and the school also has its own Duke of Edinburgh's Award group. There is a full range of optional school activities, including Art, Chess, Pottery, CDT and Photography. The School has its own farm and developing equine unit which provides countless opportunities for outdoor adventure and agricultural experiences.

Music and Drama. Music and drama play an important part in the life of the school.

There are four choirs, two orchestras, a jazz band, rock groups and a variety of other specialist ensembles and singing groups. Many concerts are given each year, including the annual Carol Service in Canterbury Cathedral, and the school is developing the tradition of holding one celebrity recital each year. The last whole-school production was *Annie* which received glowing praise.

Admission. The usual ages of admission to the Senior School are 11, 13 and 16. The Year 7 Entrance Examination takes place in the Spring Term for admission the following September.

Fees per term (2011-2012). Day Pupils £4,793–£5,122; Boarders: £8,987–£9,109 (full), £8,496 (weekly). International Study Centre: £1,250.

Entrance Scholarships. (*See Scholarship Entries section.*) The school awards academic, music, sport, drama and art scholarships to pupils for entry into Years 7, 9 and 12. For Years 7 and 9 academic scholarships are awarded as a result of performance in our Entrance Test, usually held in the Spring Term, for entry the following September. Sixth Form academic scholarships are awarded on the basis of existing performance, a detailed report from the Head of Year or current school, and confirmation of high levels of performance in the final GCSEs. Music, sport, drama and art scholarships are awarded in conjunction with the Entrance Test and appropriate separate performance assessments at Kent College.

Scholarships normally carry a value equivalent to a percentage remission of the tuition fees which would vary according to circumstances but would not exceed a maximum of 50% of tuition fees and would be at the discretion of the Head Master. Full particulars may be obtained from the Registrar.

Bursaries. Means-tested bursaries are available up to 100% of the tuition fee.

Exhibitions. Means-tested awards for academic, music, sport, drama and art achievement and potential are available to children entering Year 4.

Honours. Most school leavers go on to university and a number of pupils secure offers of places at Oxford and Cambridge colleges each year.

Charitable status. Kent College, Canterbury is a Registered Charity, number 307844. The School was founded to provide education within a supportive Christian environment and is a member of the Methodist Independent Schools' Group.

Kimbolton School

Kimbolton, Huntingdon, Cambs PE28 0EA
Tel: 01480 860505
Fax: 01480 860386
e-mail: headmaster@kimbolton.cambs.sch.uk
website: www.kimbolton.cambs.sch.uk

The School was founded in 1600 and was awarded Direct Grant status as a boys' day and boarding school in 1945. Girls were first admitted in 1976. The Preparatory School

(ages 4–11) and the Senior School are fully co-educational with day boys and girls (4–18) and boarding boys and girls (11–18). As a result of the withdrawal of the Direct Grant the School assumed fully independent status in 1978. There are around 300 pupils in the Prep School and 650 pupils in the Senior School (approximately 55 Senior pupils are boarders). There is almost a 50:50 ratio of girls to boys.

Motto: *Spes Durat Avorum.*

Governing Body:
C A Paull (*Chairman*)
J W Bridge, OBE (*Vice-Chairman*)

C R Boyes	Mrs K E S Lancaster
Prof F Broughton Pipkin	S J F Page
Lt Col E Coles	G R K Peace
Mrs J L Doyle	M J Pitt
Mrs S E Duberly	R Repper
J Gray	P Seabrook
Mrs D Hellett	A P Weale
Dr T P Hynes	

Headmaster: J Belbin, BA, FRSA

PA to the Headmaster: Mrs K J Ward

Deputy Headmaster: M J Eddon, BSc

Second Deputy Head: Mrs S Hutchinson, BA

Director of Studies: C J A Bates, MA

Head of Sixth Form: A J Bamford, MA

S C Ball, MA	Mrs S Hart, DipLib
Mrs L D Bamford, MA	S E C Henson, BEd
Mrs A J Bates, BA	C J W Horricks, BA
A J A Beal, BSc, MSc	A B Hutchinson, BEng
Mrs C E Bennett, BSc	A S Jessup, BSc, MA
M Bennett, BA, RAS, PDip	Miss C Kennedy, MA
Dr R Blindt, BSc, PhD	Mrs L V King, BSc
Mrs D C Brough, BA	R E Knell, BA
Miss S J Bull, BSc	A S Lawless, BSc
Mrs K M Chaplin, BA	Mrs E L R Lawless, BSc
D P Conerney, BA	Miss T M Lloyd, BSc
K J Curtis, BSc, CPhys, MInstP	Mrs H L Martin, BSc
Mrs A V Darlow, BA	Miss H M E Morrell, BSc
E C Drysdale, BSc	J C Newsam, MA
Mrs C C Elliott, BA	S K Pollard, MA
Mrs A C Fearing, BA	M Reed, MEng
Mrs C E Firby, MA	Ms D V Robinson, BA
Mrs E F Forbes, RSA DipSpLD	Mrs A M Rushton, BSc
	Mrs C L Sarkies, BA, MA
J R K Garland, BA	J R Saunders, BA
Mrs H F Garland, BSc	Miss J J Shillaw, BA
D C Gibbs, MA	Mrs E Simons, BA
M S Gilbert, BEd	W J Skinner, MA
B I Goakes, BA	K Spencer, BEd
Mrs E R Goakes, BEng, MA	Mrs C A Stokes, BEd
	Mrs L J Stone, BEd
J C Gomez, BA	Mrs C Vincent Bennett
A Gray, BSc	R A Walker, BA
J D Greening, MA	T Webley, BSc
Mrs L A Hadden, BA	T F Webster
O R Hall, BA	S K Whitlock, MA
Mrs J Hart, CertEd	S Wilson, BA
	Dr S P Yallup, MSc, PhD

School Chaplain: Mrs L N Bland, BEd
OC CCF: Squadron Leader L A Hadden, BA, RAFVR(T)
CCF SSI: RSM D V Gridley

Prep School:

Head: R J Wells, BEd, BA

Deputy: O C Stokes, BEd
Director of Studies: Mrs F Y Williams, MA
Lower Prep Coordinator: Mrs P Binham, BSc

Miss L Bainbridge, NNEB
Mrs H K A Belbin, BEd
Mrs M Bettison, BSc
A M Bull, BEd
Mrs H M Cardwell, BEd
Mrs J E Cole, BA
Mrs S L Eddon, LRAM, GRSM
Mrs A K Edwards, BEd
Mrs J F Edwards, BEd
Mrs A M Farrer, NNEB
Mrs T M Garzarolli, BSc
R D Hart, BA

Mrs E J Hartwell, BA
Ms M Kfoury, BA
Mrs A Knell, NNEB
Mrs J M Laino, NNEB
Mrs S J Neal, BEd
Mrs P M Neale, BA
Mrs A M Noakes, BA
Mrs E K Prew, BEd
Mrs Z S Sheffield, BA
Miss K L Umpleby, BSc
P E Wilkinson, BSc
Mrs C Wood, BA
Mrs D A Woodward, BA

Bursar & Clerk to the Governors: E F P Valletta, MBIFM
Finance Bursar: S P Oliver, MA, ACMA
PR & Communications Manager: Mrs A M Ainsworth, MBA, MCIM
Alumni Officer: Mrs H M Hopperton, BA
Registrar: Mrs J Simpson

Mission Statement. Kimbolton School creates a caring, challenging environment in which all pupils are encouraged to fulfil their potential and are given opportunities to flourish in a wide variety of curricular and extra-curricular interests.

It provides a close family environment where young people are educated to be tolerant, socially responsible and independent of mind, equipping them for our changing world. It is a community that challenges pupils to discover their talents, develop socially and excel.

Facilities. The Senior School facilities are situated in and around the main school building, Kimbolton Castle, once the home of Queen Katharine of Aragon and for three centuries the home of the Dukes of Manchester. Now, with its Vanbrugh front and Pellegrini murals, it is a building of considerable beauty and architectural importance. The former Staterooms are study areas for senior pupils and the Castle Chapel is used each day for prayers. Two large classroom blocks house the English, Mathematics, Geography, Biology and Food Technology Departments. The Donaldson Laboratories for Physics and Chemistry contain 8 laboratories. The Design Technology Centre is up-to-date and well-equipped, as is the ICT Centre and the Music School. A state-of-the-art teaching and learning centre, the Queen Katharine Building, complete with a 120-seat multimedia lecture theatre and six new classrooms opened in 2009. The Lewis Hall caters for the performing arts and daily assemblies and provides modern theatre and concert facilities.

A large sports complex, incorporating squash courts, gymnasium, sports hall, multi-gym and changing rooms stands in the Castle's parkland. Closer to the Castle itself, lie a modern Art Centre, new Library and an indoor swimming pool which was opened by the Duke of Gloucester in 2000, as part of the School's quatercentenary celebration. The School has two fine all-weather hockey pitches, one of which is floodlit and was completed in 2009.

One boarding house for girls and one boarding house for boys stand adjacent to the grounds in the picturesque Kimbolton High Street. The boarding community is an important part of the School.

The Prep School is located on its own site. A major rebuilding programme was completed in 2007 providing new classrooms, changing rooms and a hall for music and drama. There is also a gymnasium plus specialist science and information technology rooms. The 4–7 age range is housed in the purpose-built Aragon House.

Admission and Organisation. The Prep School admits children at the age of 4 or 7 (as day pupils) who are expected to complete their education in the Senior School. Entry at other ages is sometimes possible. Tests for entry at the Prep School are held in February. Entry into the Senior School at the age of 11 is open to boarders and day pupils; the Senior School Entrance examinations are also held in February.

There are significant entries at 13+ usually by the Common Entrance Examination in June. Those not preparing for Common Entrance may sit the School's own 13+ examination in February. Entry into the Sixth Form is based on interview and GCSE results.

Arrangements can be made for overseas candidates to take the Entrance Examination at their own schools.

Pupils are accepted in September at the start of the academic year, but a few places may be available for entry in other terms.

The relationship between the Prep and Senior Schools is a close one and contributes to the strong 'family' atmosphere of the whole School. In the Senior School, there are four senior houses and one junior house. It is an important element of our pastoral care that boarding pupils and day pupils are together – there are no day houses. Housemasters/Housemistresses, assisted by Tutors, look after the general well-being and progress of their charges.

Work and Curriculum. For the first two years in the Senior School there are four parallel forms; in each of the third, fourth and fifth years there are five smaller forms with sets for some subjects. Boys and girls entering at 13 join one of the five Third Forms. An option scheme is introduced in the Fourth Form. In the Sixth Form specialisation occurs, and pupils will usually study four AS subjects from the following list: English Language and Literature; English Literature: History; Geography; French; Spanish; Maths; Further Maths; Physics; Chemistry; Biology; Music; Art; Art (Critical and Contextual); Food, Nutrition and Health; Design and Technology; Drama and Theatre Studies; Physical Education; Economics; Business Studies; and Politics. All Sixth Formers follow a 'Preparation for Life' series of lectures, seminars and debates and may opt to take A2 General Studies. In the Upper Sixth pupils usually continue with three subjects to A2 Level.

Almost all leavers go on to University or to Further Education. In 2011, almost 10% of the Upper Sixth received offers from Oxbridge.

Religious Teaching. Pupils attend Chapel once a week and have RS lessons each week in the 1st to 3rd Form. Other services are held in the School Chapel during each term for pupils and parents to attend. Sunday Services are held in the Chapel and occasionally the School worships in the Parish Church.

Sport and Activities. The School owns over 120 acres of land, more than 20 of which are laid out as playing fields. The major sports for boys are Association Football, Hockey and Cricket. For girls the main sports are Hockey, Netball and Tennis. Other sports include Athletics, Gymnastics, Dance, Climbing, Archery, Swimming, Golf, Fitness Training, Rifle Shooting, Clay Pigeon Shooting, Squash, Badminton, Basketball and Rounders. Swimming is popular with before and after school sessions and numerous galas. Extensive use is also made by the Sailing Club of nearby Grafham Water, both for recreational sailing and inter-school matches. Canoeing is popular and each year a team competes in the highly demanding 125-mile Devizes-Westminster challenge. The Equestrian Club competes in around twenty fixtures during the course of the year. The aim is to find a sport that each pupil loves and will continue to enjoy long after leaving Kimbolton.

Music and Drama play an important part in the life of the School and almost half of the pupils take lessons in a great variety of instruments. There is a Choral Society, two orchestras, several bands and many ensemble groups. The School stages plays, musicals or concerts each term

The School contingent of the CCF is a voluntary, keen and efficient body, divided into Navy, Army and RAF Sections with a national reputation for excellence; Community Service is an alternative. There is a successful Duke of Edinburgh's Award scheme with a growing number of participants.

There are many other activities and societies that meet on a regular basis, such as debating, public speaking, Latin, Young Enterprise, forensic science, photography, chess, robotics, bookworms, beekeeping, gardening, modelling, pottery and philosophy.

All pupils are able to participate in the large number of trips in the UK and abroad.

Careers. Advice can be sought at any time by pupils or their parents from the Careers Staff, three of whom specialise in university entrance. There is a well-stocked Careers Room, and the School is a member of the Independent Schools Careers Organisation. Fifth formers take the Morrisby careers tests administered by ISCO. An annual Careers Fair is held for fourth to sixth formers.

Dress. The School colours are purple, black and white. Boys wear blazers and grey flannels (shorts until the final year in the Prep School). The girls' uniform includes a standard skirt, blouse and blazer. Sixth Formers wear a black suit.

Scholarships and Bursaries. A number of scholarships are awarded at 11+ and 13+ to candidates who perform with distinction in the Entrance Examination or in Common Entrance.

The William Ingram Awards are for entrants at 13+ with strengths in music, art, games or leadership.

There are a number of Sixth Form Scholarships and Exhibitions. Two Sir Brian Corby bursaries, available for pupils entering the Sixth Form from state schools, cover up to 100% of fees and may include extras.

There is a bursary scheme for deserving candidates aged 11 or over.

Fees per term (2011-2012). £2,705 (Lower Prep), £3,440 (Upper Prep), £4,215 (Senior Day), £6,975 (Senior Full Boarding), £6,565 (Senior Weekly Boarding).

The fees are inclusive of lunches and there is no charge for laundry, books, stationery and examination entries.

There is a reduction of 2½% in tuition fees when siblings attend at the same time.

Music Tuition Fee: £199–£220 per term for individual lessons. (Half a term's notice must be given in writing before a pupil discontinues music lessons.)

Old Kimboltonians Association. All correspondence to: Mrs H M Hopperton, Alumni Officer, OKA, Kimbolton School, Kimbolton, Huntingdon, Cambridgeshire PE28 0EA; e-mail: alumni@kimbolton.cambs.sch.uk.

Charitable status. Kimbolton School Foundation is a Registered Charity, number 1098586.

King Edward VI School
Southampton

Wilton Road, Southampton SO15 5UQ

Tel: 023 8070 4561
Fax: 023 8070 5937
e-mail: registrar@kes.hants.sch.uk
website: www.kes.hants.sch.uk

King Edward VI School was founded in 1553, under Letters Patent of King Edward VI, by the will of the Revd William Capon, Master of Jesus College, Cambridge, and Rector of St. Mary's, Southampton. The original Royal Charter, bearing the date 4th June 1553, is preserved in the School. The first Head Master was appointed in 1554.

Governors:
B E Gay (*Chairman*)
P W Brazier, BSC, FCIOB (*Vice-Chairman*)
The Lord Lieutenant for the County of Hampshire, Dame M Fagan, DVCO, JP

Rector of Southampton City Centre Team Ministry, Revd J E Davies
Mrs M J Ashleigh, BSc, PhD
Dr Y Binge, MBChB
Dr R B Buchanan, FRCP, FRCR, MBBS
D A Creal, FCA
Councillor T Matthews
M H Mayes, MSc, MA, MBA
A J Morgan, MA Oxon, FCA, ATII
Councillor R Perry, BA
Mrs C Pierce, DCH, DRCOG, MRCGP
M J Rowles, FCA
Councillor A Samuels, BA Cantab
Mrs A Steele-Arnett, CertEd, PGDip, MBA
A L Thomas, MA, PhD
K St J Wiseman, MA

Bursar and Clerk to the Governors: R V Maher, BA Econ, ACA

Head Master: **A J Thould**, MA

Deputy Heads:
Mrs E J Thomas, BSc
R T Courtney, MA

Assistant Heads:
S G Hall, BSc
R J Putt, BSc
Ms H Smith, BSc

Assistant Staff:

J C Allen, BA	P G Kay-Kujawski, BA
R W Allen, BSc	D G Kelly, BA
Ms S L Allen, MA	L J Kelsey, MA
S J B Ayers, BA	Mrs S King, BEd
Mrs E M S Backen, MA	M G Kukla, MA
S H Barker, MA	Miss E M Ladislao, BA
Miss J M Barron, BA	Mrs L M Lander, BSc
Fr K Becker	O J Leaman, BMus
Mlle M Benezech	E T Lewis
M A Bulmer, BA	K N Lindsay, BSc
Mrs P E Burrows, MSc	Miss M Lindebringhs, BA
Mrs S Burt, BA	M W Long, DipAD
Miss C Campbell, BA	Mrs N Lovegrove, BSc
A J Cherry, BA	Miss E K Mackintosh, BA, PhD
Mrs J M Cole, BA	
P D Collins, BSc	P A Mapstone, BSc
Mrs M Cottrell-Ferrat, BA	Mrs E Mayes, MA
K P Coundley, MA	Mrs L S D Millar, BSc
R J Cross, BSc	M G Mixer, BSocSc
N D Culver, MA	Miss J A D Mobbs, BA
Mrs H Dean, BSc, PhD	Mrs N A Moxon, BA
N J Diver, MA	Miss C F Noyes, BSc
C W Eades, BA	Mrs R H K Parkyn, MA
Mrs S Evans, BA	R G Patten, BA
K A Fitzpatrick	M A Paver, BSc, PhD
J M Foyle, BSc	Miss A H Payne, BA
Mrs H Freemantle, MA, LLCM, ALCM	Miss C A Peachment, BSc
	G L Piggott, BA
S D Gamblin, BSc, PhD	Revd J G Poppleton, BA, DipRS
A W Gilbert, BA	
C E Giles, BA	A L Powell, BSc
Dr V A Green, MSc, PhD	D A Price, BA, MIBiol
Ms R M Greenwood, MA	Mrs J Price, BA
Mlle J Guilbaud	G T Purves, MPhys, PhD
J C Halls, BA	P J Robinson, BEng
Mrs J M Hardwick, BA	Mrs S Rugge-Price, MA
G P Havers, BSc	A J Schofield, MA
Mrs L C Henderson, BEd	Mrs E L Sheppard, BSc
L J Herklots, BSc	P Sheppard, BSc
Srta S T Hombria	R S Simm, BSc
S R Hoskins, BSc, PhD	Miss P Sinnett-Jones, BSc, PhD
G S Hunt, BSc	
Mrs J V Jones, BA	J H H Singleton, BSc
P D Jones, BA	Mrs K S Skipwith, BSc

S J Smart, BA, MPhil
Mrs S M Smart, BA
Miss A M L Stone, BSc
P B Tasker, BSc
Mrs E L Thomas, BSc, PhD
Mrs S J I Thould, BA

T H Tofts, MA, DipPhil
A Turner, BSc
M A Walter, BSc, MPhil
B L Watson, BA
R J L Wood, BEd
Miss K J Yerbury, BSc

There are about 960 pupils in the School, of whom over 250 are in the Sixth Form.

Admission. An entrance examination is held in the Spring Term for boys and girls seeking to enter the First Form at age 11 in the following September. Applications from able under-age candidates will also be considered. In addition, admission into the Third Form takes place at age 13. Smaller numbers of entrants are accepted into the other school years if there is space, provided the applicants are of suitable academic ability. Students are also admitted to the Sixth Form.

Registration for entry may be made at any time on a form obtainable from the Registrar, who can supply current information about fees, bursaries and scholarships.

In order to qualify for entrance to the Sixth Form a student will normally be required to have grade B or above in six subjects at GCSE, including English Language and Mathematics, and the subjects to be studied at A Level, but A grades in Modern Languages and Mathematics.

Class sizes average 22; the average size of Sixth Form sets is 11.

Curriculum. All pupils follow a common course in the first two years: this includes French or German or Spanish with Latin, Mathematics, Science and an Extended Studies programme. In years 3, 4 and 5 all pupils study eight 'core' subjects to GCSE: Biology, Chemistry, English Language, English Literature, a Modern Foreign Language, Mathematics, Religious Studies and Physics. In addition there is a range of 'option' subjects: Art, Design and Technology, Economics, Geography, German, Greek, History, Italian, Music, PE, Sports Science, Theatre Studies and Spanish. The syllabus leading to the GCSE Examinations, in which most pupils take eleven subjects, is designed to avoid any premature specialisation. In the Sixth Form, students may either take 3 Advanced Level subjects along with one AS course or four full Advanced Level subjects. In addition, all have an afternoon of games in both years and follow a Foundations Studies programme in both the Lower and Upper Sixth Year.

On entering the First Year pupils join a form of about 22, with a Form Tutor responsible for their general welfare and progress. The other years are organised on a system of pastoral groups of about 16. Each group has its own Year Head. In addition there is a Head of Lower School who has general responsibility for the first three years; a Head of Upper School and a Director of the Sixth Form have similar responsibilities in their respective areas.

Our aim is to provide a congenial atmosphere and a disciplined environment in which able pupils can develop as individuals.

School Activities. 10% of a student's timetable is devoted to physical education. Games are regarded as forming an integral part of life at King Edward's, and none is excused from taking part except on medical grounds. The major sports played in the three terms are rugby, hockey, cricket and tennis for boys; and netball, hockey, tennis and rounders for girls; other sporting activities include athletics, basketball, badminton, fencing, squash, swimming and a number of other games. The School has a large sports hall and a fully equipped fitness studio and an all-weather pitch for Hockey and similar games which provides twelve Tennis Courts in Summer. There are a further 33 acres of off-site sports fields which include a second astro-pitch and floodlit netball and tennis courts.

A considerable range of societies meets during lunchtime, after school, at weekends and in school holidays, catering for pupils of all ages and many differing tastes. All are encouraged to join some of these societies, in order to gain the greatest advantage from their time at the School.

In addition to a large number of sporting teams representing the School, there are such activities as charitable and community work, dance, drama, debating, chess, Duke of Edinburgh's Award Scheme, International Expeditions, sailing, collectors' clubs and music. The School has flourishing choirs, as well as orchestras and a large number of smaller instrumental groups. Art and Design and Technology occupy up-to-date premises. The studios and workshops are usually open during lunchtimes and after school. The science laboratories have been recently refurbished and the Sixth Form Centre has been extended. The School has a 250-seat Theatre.

Fees per term (2011-2012). £3,870. The full fee can be reduced in appropriate cases by the award of Bursaries and Scholarships. Scholarships are available on entry at age 11 and age 13 and further Scholarships may be awarded during a pupil's career in the School. Some Scholarships are awarded for proficiency in the Creative Arts. Foundation Bursaries are available at age 11, 13 and into the Sixth Form.

Charitable status. King Edward VI School Southampton is a Registered Charity, number 1088030. The object of the Charity is the provision and conduct in or near the City of Southampton of a school for boys and girls.

King Edward VII and Queen Mary School
Lytham

Clifton Drive South, Lytham, Lancs FY8 1DT
Tel: 01253 784100
Fax: 01253 784150
e-mail: admin@keqms.co.uk
website: www.keqms.co.uk

The Lytham Schools Foundation was established in 1719. King Edward VII School (for boys) was opened in 1908 and Queen Mary School (for girls) in 1930; both were Direct Grant Grammar Schools and with the withdrawal of the Grant became independent. The two schools merged to form a new school with a co-educational intake in September 1999. In September 2003 the school moved to one site with a multi-million pound development of facilities on its 35-acre campus.

Motto: *Sublimis ab unda.*

The Governing Body includes representatives of the Trust Managers of the Foundation and of the Universities of Lancashire, Liverpool and Manchester, together with co-opted members.

Governing Body:

Chairman: The Revd Canon G I Hirst, BA
Vice-Chairman: Mr D A Webb

Mrs L Beddows, FREC
Revd A Clitheroe, BA, MPhil
Mr W G Cowburn, DipArch
Mr P Cox, MIFirE
Mr P M Gibbons, FCA
Mr M E Gunson, FCA, FRSA, FFA, FIAB, MIMgt
Mr R N Hardy, LLB
Dr S D A Hayes, MBChB
Mrs A Hearne, BSc, CQSW
Miss J E Hilton, MLitt, BA
The Revd D Lyon
Mrs J M Towers, LLB
The Revd D Welch, MA Oxon

Clerk to the Governors and Bursar: (*to be appointed*)

Staff:

Principal: **Mr R J Karling**, MA Edinburgh, MBA Leicester

Deputy Head – Staff & Administration: Mr M G Stephenson, BA Oxford

Deputy Head – Pastoral Care: Mrs J A Cooper, BSc Salford

Art:
*Ms L Heap, BA, UCLan
Miss S Lukasiewiecz, DipAD, ATC Sheffield College

Business Studies/Economics:
*Mr J A Liggett, BSc Cardiff

Design and Technology:
*Mr P F Klenk, BA Loughborough
Mr C K Hill, CertEd Birmingham, BA Loughborough

English & Performing Arts:
*Mr N Walker, MA Oxford
Mrs K E Busby, BA Liverpool
Mrs F M Withers, BA Hull
Mr K Maund, BA Wales
Miss S Roxby, BA UCLAN

Geography:
*Mrs M Ingham, MA UCE
Mrs J A Cooper, BSc Salford

History:
*Mr I D Cowlishaw, BA London
Mrs D Ward, BA Bangor, MA Lancaster
Mrs J Trohear, MA Glasgow

Information Technology:
*Mr B Smith, BSc UMIST

Mathematics:
Mr P Butterworth, BSc Lancaster
Mr K C Dawson, BSc Manchester Polytechnic
Mr P M Rudd, BSc Bangor

Modern Languages:
*Mr J G Finney, BA Nottingham
Miss E S A Hall, MA Oxford
Mr M G Stephenson, BA Oxford
Mrs F M Winterflood, BA Reading
Mrs B MacDougall, MA Open University (*German Conversation*)
Mrs F Boutin, CertEd Central Lancs (*French conversation*)

Music:
*Mr J Pennington, BMus London, ARCM, ARCO, ALCM, DipRCM
Mr L Hills, LLB, LTCL

Physical Education:
Mrs K Hanham, BEd Sussex
Mrs B Storey, CertEdPE Bishop Lonsdale College, Derby
Mrs A Roberts, BA Leeds Metropolitan
Mr S Clarke, BA Liverpool John Moores
Mr A Holmes, BA Lancaster

Psychology:
Mr S Collings, BA Marshall University USA, MSc Chichester (*Head of Sixth Form*)

Sociology:
Mrs D Ward, BA Bangor, MA Lancaster

Religious Studies:
*Mr N J Horan, BA Lancaster
Mrs H House, BA Brunel

Science:
Mrs J M Denver, BEd Nottingham College of Education
Dr J H Lees, BSc Liverpool, PhD Loughborough

*Dr C Jessop, BSc, PhD York
Ms H Walker, BSc University of Western Australia
Mrs G Merrick, BSc York
Mr S Matthews, BSc Liverpool John Moores
*Mr J L Riding, BEng Imperial College London.

Careers: Mrs S M Hampson, BA Leeds, DCG

Librarian: Mrs J Browell

Learning Support Coordinator: Mrs J Klenk, BA London, PGCE SpLD Edinburgh, AMBDA
Learning Support Assistants:
Mrs J Ingle, BA Lancaster
Mrs M Guminski, BSc, PGCE

Registrar: Mrs J Hothersall
PA to the Principal: Mrs E Cope, BA University of Hertfordshire

Facilities. The School stands on an impressive 35 acre site overlooking the Irish Sea. The buildings include a magnificent new Library, eight Science laboratories, Art studio, specialist rooms for Music and Design Technology and a state-of-the-art Multimedia Language Laboratory. The whole campus is networked with broadband internet access and there are three newly equipped Information and Communication Technology suites. A fitness suite, sports hall and international standard artificial sports ground complement the extensive playing fields. A major redevelopment of the School site was completed in the Autumn of 2003, including a purpose-built Preparatory School, a new teaching block for senior pupils, a new dining room and kitchens, and much enhancement and upgrading of the facilities.

Organisation. There are 450 day boys and girls in the Senior School. On site, there is also a co-educational Preparatory School for children from 2 to 11 years.

Curriculum. The broad curriculum, leading to GCSE after five years, comprises the following subjects: Art, Design and Technology, English Language and Literature, Drama, French, German, Geography, History, Mathematics, Music, Physical Education, Religious Studies, Spanish and the Sciences. All pupils take part in Games. A full range of AS and A2 subjects, including General Studies, is available in very varied combinations. There is a choice of over 20 AS/A2 subjects, including the further options beyond GCSE of Business Studies, Further Mathematics, Psychology, Sociology, Sport Studies and Theatre Studies. Students are prepared for university, entry to the professions and careers in industrial and commercial life. The School offers comprehensive careers education and guidance on university choices.

Games and Activities. Cricket, hockey, netball and rugby are the main sports, and considerable choice is available including athletics, badminton, basketball, cross-country, golf and tennis. Extra-curricular activities include The Duke of Edinburgh's Award, mountain biking, canoeing, fell-walking and skiing, aerobics, choir, gymnastics, orchestra and swing band and public speaking. Recent productions have included *Little Shop of Horrors, Pride and Prejudice, A Midsummer Night's Dream* and *Oliver*.

In recent years there have been regular sports tours in the UK and abroad to Holland, Spain and New Zealand, expeditions to India, Namibia and Peru, skiing in the Alps and Canada, trips to the World War One battlefields and student exchanges with Germany and the Czech Republic.

Admission. Admission to the Senior School is by examination for all pupils, aged 11, held each year in January. Pupils may also be admitted at other ages. Application Forms for admission and further details will be sent on request.

Fees per term (2011-2012). Senior School £2,900; Preparatory School £2,040.

Scholarships and Bursaries. A number of open scholarships and means-tested bursaries are offered on the results of the Senior Entrance Examination and include auditions for Music and Sport Scholarships. Means-tested scholarships and bursaries are also available at sixth form level.

Charitable status. The Lytham Schools Foundation is a Registered Charity, number 526315. Its aim is to provide a balanced academic education catering for the talents, needs and interests of each individual pupil.

King Edward's School
Bath

North Road, Bath BA2 6HU
Tel: Senior School: 01225 464313
          Junior School: 01225 463218
          Pre-Prep School: 01225 421681
Fax: Senior School: 01225 481363
          Junior School: 01225 442178
          Pre-Prep School: 01225 428006
e-mail: headmaster@kesbath.com
website: www.kesbath.com

King Edward's School was founded in 1552 by King Edward VI. Originally a Grammar School, the School was fully independent until 1920, when it accepted Direct Grant status, reverting to full independence in 1976. King Edward's is fully co-educational, with girls and boys from age 3–18.

King Edward's School is a busy day school, with a proud record of sustained academic achievement (98% of its pupils regularly proceed to universities and institutions of higher education). It is also committed to providing the broadest possible range of opportunities for all its pupils and a multiplicity of extra-curricular activities, trips and expeditions are on offer. The School has a strong commitment to sport, both recreational and competitive, and the arts flourish, with the Annual Arts Festival providing a showcase for talented pupils in art, music and drama.

There are currently 680 pupils in the Senior School, 180 pupils in the Junior School, and 95 pupils in the Nursery and Pre-Prep.

For over 400 years, the School occupied various premises in the city centre, but in 1961 the Senior School moved to a fine fourteen-acre site on North Road, on the south-eastern slopes of the city. This site has been extensively developed in recent years and now boasts superb facilities. The Junior School moved into outstanding new premises here in 1990.

The Pre-Prep School is situated in an elegant Victorian house on the western side of the city.

Chairman of Governors: Mr A Morsley, BSc, ARCS, FIMA, FRSA

Headmaster: Mr M Boden, MA

Second Master: Mr M J Horrocks-Taylor, BSc, MEd
Deputy Head, Academic: Mr T D Burroughs, BA
Deputy Head, Pastoral: Ms C Losse, MA
Head of Lower School: Mr D J Chapman, BA
Head of Middle School: Mr A M Bougeard, BSc
Head of Sixth Form: Mr P H Simonds, BSc

* *Head of Department*
§ *Part-time*

Mr N P C Barnes, MA
§Mrs W Bedeman, BA
*Mrs P M Bougeard, MA
*Mrs E Brown BA
§Mrs C Bruton BA
§Miss H Burton, MA
§Miss N Canfer BA
§Mrs J Chapman, BA

Mrs S Cooper, MA
Miss T Costanza, BSc
Mrs J Crouch, BSc
Mr C Cunningham, BA
Mr M A Cunliffe, MA
§Mrs M N Davis, MA
*Miss R Davies, BA
Mrs O Doughty, BA

Mr R J S Drury, BA
Mrs H Earle, BSc
Mrs C Faulkner, BA, BSc
Dr A M Fewell, PhD, BSc
Mrs C M Finch, BA
Mr N Folland, MSc
Mrs L Formela-Osborne, BEd
Mr S C Frost, BSc
Mrs E Grainger, BA
*Mrs L Gwilliam, BSc
§Mr S Haan
§Mr D Hall, BA
*Mr M Hawker, BEd
*Mr R Haynes, MA
*Mr J Holdaway, BEng
Miss Z Kayacan, BA
Mr J Kean, MA
*§Dr J Knight, BSc, PhD
*Mr T W L Laney, BSc
Mrs B Lang, BSc
Mrs E Longhurst, BA
Mrs P Lunter, BSc
Mr M Mairis, BA
Mr P J McComish, BSc
*Mr T G Medhurst, BEd
*Mr D Middlebrough, BA
§Mrs T Minty, BA
Mr A Monks, MSc
*Mrs A Munn, BA

*Dr L H Newman, MSc, PhD
Mr M Oehler, BSc
*Mr M R Pell, BA
Mrs A Phillips, MA
Mr N D Purcell, BA, MA
Miss K Rich, MA
Mr M Ruxton, BSc
*Mr W R Satterthwaite, MA
Miss L Scott, MA
*Mrs J Scott-Palmer, BSc
Mrs S Smillie, MA
*Miss V Stevens, BA
Miss H Stewart, BDes
Mr R Thomas, BA, MA
Mr J E G Tidball, BSc
*Mr A W Trim, BA
Mr J Turner, BA
*Mr A I M Vass, MA
Mr N A Vile, BSc
Mr D Viñales, MA
Miss A Ward, BSc
§Mrs A White, BA
§Mrs J Wilcox, BSc
Mrs Willoughby, MSc
§Mr D Willison BA
§Dr M Wood, PhD, MA
§Mr D Wright, BSc
Miss E Young, BEd

Senior School Chaplain: Revd Caroline O'Neill
Acting Director of Music: Mr R J S Drury, BA
Director of Sport: Mrs L Gwilliam
Head of Careers and Pupil Enrichment: Mr J Turner, BA
Head of Operations & Finance: Ms J I Rowell, MBA, BSc
Registrar: Ms A Rashid
Head's Personal Assistant: Mrs A L Plumbridge
School Nurse: Mrs C Morris, RGN
Head of PSHE and School Librarian: Mrs L Bowman, BA, MA, MLS
Finance Manager and School Accountant: Mrs N Rowlands, AAT
HR Officer and Bursar/Second Master's PA: Mrs J Howard
Development Office: Mrs C Davies, BA
Marketing Office: Mrs J Acklam, BSc, CIM Dip

Junior School
Head of Junior School: Mr G Taylor, BA
Deputy Head: Mrs C Lewis, CertEd
Director of Studies: Mr M Innes, BA, PGCE

Mrs R Barrett, MA
Mr S Carr, BEd
Miss L Chapman, MA
Mr J Corp, BSc
Mrs M Edwards, BMus, MA
Mrs R Hardware, BEd
Mr M Howarth
Mr A J MacFarlan, BA

Mrs E MacFarlan, BEd
Mrs A Munn, BA, DipSpLD
Mrs G Oliver CertEd, ASM
Mr D J Orchard, BSc
Mr J Roberts-Wray, BA
Mrs A Sellick, BSc
Mrs S Taylor

Junior School Administrator: Mrs H Lees

Pre-Prep School Staff:
Head of Pre-Prep & Nursery: Mrs J Gilbert, BEd, NPQH
Deputy Head: Mrs D Bright, BA QTS

Mrs L Billington, BA
Mr S Boydell, BA
Mrs C Ford, LTCL
Mrs A Jabarin, BA

Mrs C Alexander-Jupp, CertEd, CTh
Ms K Watson, BSc
Ms L Williams, BSc

Pre-Prep Administrator: Mrs A Fairlie

Buildings. The Senior School is housed in a complex of buildings arranged in four adjoining groups. Nethersole, dating from 1830, has recently been refurbished providing accommodation for Psychology, Economics and Business Studies, History, Classics and Religious Studies and Philosophy. The Main Building comprises a Music block, the Wroughton Theatre, Physics and Chemistry laboratories and classrooms. From September 2009 a new building has been built creating suited departments for the Biology Department with 3 new biology laboratories and preparation room; the Geography Department; a new ICT laboratory; and a Modern Languages suite which will include two dedicated Modern Language Laboratories. The developments include a new IT suite for the Art, Design and Technology Centre. The Willett Hall with adjoining kitchens and servery functions as a dining hall and lecture hall. The Holbeche Centre houses a Sixth Form Centre with adjoining kitchen, an extended and modernised Careers and Higher Education Centre, a new, state-of-the-art Drama Studio and Art Gallery, purpose-built Library and various tutorial rooms. There is also a magnificent Sports Hall, together with an artificial playing surface for hockey and tennis.

The pavilion at Bathampton, completed in March 1998, is surrounded by 17 acres of playing fields and newly added Club House.

Admission. While half the pupils come from the City of Bath or its immediate environs, nearly half are resident in the counties of Gloucestershire, Somerset and Wiltshire – a wide catchment area made possible by excellent public transport services and coaches organised by the parents.

Methods of Entry. *Nursery and Pre-Prep*: From the age of 3, according to the availability of places. There is an informal assessment for entry into Year 1 and Year 2.

Junior School: From our own Pre-Prep by internal assessment and interview.

Pupils from other Primary Schools and Preparatory Schools may be offered places by examination and interview. The main entry is in Year 3 and Year 5 at the age of 7 or 9, but other vacancies may occur at age 8 or 10.

Senior School: From our own Junior School by passing the Senior School Entrance Examination for 11 year-olds.

Pupils from other Primary and Preparatory Schools may be offered places on the results of the same examination held in January of each year.

Older pupils may enter the Senior School, if and where places are available, by sitting an entrance examination appropriate to their age.

Students may also seek direct entry into the Sixth Form. Such students are expected to acquire a sound set of GCSE passes before transfer for advanced study. Applicants are interviewed and a reference is sought from their present schools.

Application forms and further information concerning entry are obtainable from the Registrar, who will arrange prior visits to see the School. Open Days are held in the Autumn Term.

Fees per term (2011-2012). Senior School: £3,730–£3,775; Junior School: £2,950; Pre-Prep School £2,665; Nursery (full-time) £2,190.

Scholarships. Scholarships to a maximum of £500 per annum are awarded at Year 7, either for academic excellence or for an outstanding special talent in art, drama, music and sport. Students who perform outstandingly at GCSE may also receive a Scholarship award. Further details are obtainable from the Registrar.

Bursaries. Income-related entrance Bursaries may be awarded to children entering Years 7 and 12, whose parents are unable to pay the full fee. A general Bursary fund is also available to assist parents during times of unforeseen family circumstances, when they may find themselves unable to fund full school fees. Further details are obtainable from the Bursaries Administrator.

Curriculum. The School is committed to breadth in education. Twenty subjects are taught up to GCSE level. A very flexible choice system is introduced in Year 10. All students study all three sciences to GCSE for the Double or Triple Award.

The AS/A2 subjects on offer are English Literature, English Language, French, German, Spanish, Latin, History, Economics, Business Studies, Geography, Mathematics, Further Mathematics, Physics, Chemistry, Biology, Design and Technology, Religious Studies, Theatre Studies, Classical Civilisation, Greek, ICT, Philosophy, Psychology, Politics, Sport Studies, Art, Photography and Music; and they may be combined in a variety of ways. Pupils are encouraged also to enter for A Level General Studies.

Boys and girls are prepared for all forms of Higher Education, especially for Universities and for entry into the Services. The School has a proud tradition of sending a significant proportion of its students to the best universities in the land.

Music and Drama. There is a healthy and developing musical tradition in the School. Many instrumental and choral groups afford opportunities to explore differing musical styles. There are Senior, Intermediate and Junior orchestras, Early Music Groups, a Baroque Group, a Blues Guitar Group, a Brass Group, a Concert Orchestra, a Choir and a Swing Band. The School is a centre for the examinations of the Associated Board of the Royal Schools of Music and these are held termly. Music is an enjoyable and highly participative activity.

The School has an outstanding dramatic tradition, with two or more major productions a year. The splendid Wroughton Theatre, supported by a full-time technical manager, provides an outstanding facility for productions and concerts of every kind. There is in addition a brand new purpose-built Drama Studio.

Art. Housed in an extended and modernised custom-built suite of studios, the Art Department is a centre of excellence, with a fine tradition within the School and the Bath area. Teaching covers fine art, drawing and painting, ceramics and three-dimensional work, printmaking and photography. Art History and critical studies are taught as an integral part of the course and field trips and visits to galleries along with links to practising artists, are encouraged. Sixth Form Art Tours are planned annually. Every year students are prepared for interview at Art School and related courses.

Games. The main playing fields at Bathampton, comprising 17 acres, are attractively situated at one end of the Limpley Stoke valley, about a mile from the School. An All Weather Synthetic Pitch on the main School site has proved to be invaluable for hockey and tennis, and as an intensively used practice area for all games.

The major games are Rugby Football, Hockey, Cricket and Netball. Minor sports include Aerobics, Athletics, Cross-Country, Tennis, Swimming, Soccer, Shooting, Rounders, Fencing, Judo, Badminton, Squash, Golf, Basketball, Dance, Gymnastics, Table Tennis and Trampolining. Each boy or girl has a full games session per week and has ample opportunities to represent the School or to participate in a wide range of inter-Form activities.

Activities. In Year 9, pupils may opt to join the School CCF, founded in 1896 and the oldest in the West Country. The contingent has a fine record of success in regional and national competitions. The CCF provides many opportunities for adventure training and leadership and there is an Annual Easter and Summer Camp. Each year a number of students win scholarships or cadetships in different branches of the armed services. Students can also participate in the Duke of Edinburgh's Award Scheme.

There is also a strong tradition of mountain walking and adventure training for pupils with trips to Dartmoor, the Welsh mountains and abroad each year. The School enters the Ten Tors Competition each year.

School Societies and Clubs. Pupils are actively encouraged to engage in the many out-of-school activities which supplement their more formal education. A wealth of Societies and Clubs caters for every interest and for every age group. An organised programme of Outdoor Pursuits functions throughout the year. Frequent opportunities for travel abroad, especially during the Easter vacation, are provided by School tours or exchanges conducted by members of Staff. All pupils in Years 7–10 are involved in a residential trip during Activities Week in the Summer Term.

Pastoral Care A newly-appointed Deputy Head (Pastoral) coordinates the pastoral team. Every child has a Form Teacher who is at the centre of their daily life at school. Tutors work in teams managed by Heads of Year or Senior Tutors who are in turn assisted by Heads of Sector (Lower, Middle School and Sixth Form). The pastoral staff are ably supported by a School Nurse and Counsellor. The School prides itself on its family atmosphere and the excellent relationships between pupils of all ages and staff. Advice on Careers and entry to Higher Education is readily available. Parents meet Staff at regular intervals to discuss academic progress, or at social functions. Many of the latter are organised by very active parents' committees.

Dress. Boys in the Main School wear a dark blue blazer and flannels. Younger girls wear a Lindsay tartan kilt, a white open-neck blouse and the school blazer, whilst Middle School girls wear a grey skirt or grey trousers. In the Sixth Form, boys and girls wear suits of their own choosing, appropriate for formal work. Girls may wear trouser suits.

Junior School. The Junior School is an integral part of the foundation and is governed by the same Board. It joins with the Senior School in major events, such as the Founder's Day Service in Bath Abbey, and shares various games facilities and teaching staff. The curriculum is organised in close consultation with the Senior School and the Pre-Prep to ensure that education provided is continuous and progressive from the age of 3 to 18.

Its curriculum comprises English, Mathematics, Science, DT, History, Geography, Art, Music, Religious Education, Physical Education, French, German, Spanish, Drama, ICT taught to all years and Learning Skills, including Philosophy.

All children learn the strings (violin, viola, cello, double bass) in Year 3, recorder in Year 4, whole class orchestra/band and Gamelan in Year 5 and authentic Steel Pans in Year 6. Well over half of the children learn additional instruments under the tutelage of a strong peripatetic music staff. A mixture of French, German and Spanish is taught throughout the School while purpose-built facilities in Art, Science, Technology and IT, coupled with specialist teaching, ensure high standards of achievement in those areas. The Junior School has developed a reputation in the past few years for dramatic productions of the highest quality and a drama club, which runs throughout the year, is always a popular choice. This School is a very busy one renowned for its extra-curricular activities programme. The wide variety of activities on offer include table tennis, gymnastics, fencing, judo, street dance, golf, challenge club, environmental club, computer, chess, art and animation. This is not to mention the various musical and instrumental groups and the many opportunities to play rugby, football, hockey, netball, cricket, basketball, tennis, rounders and athletics. All children throughout the School also go swimming at the pool at Bath University. A large number of competitive fixtures are played against other schools in a wide variety of sports and activities and each year group has their own programme of fixtures. Frequent educational trips are arranged in and around the local area and during the summer Activities Week; residential trips for Years 3–6 include destinations such as France and Devon. Sporting tours also take place; in the last two years there has been a rugby tour to Exeter, a netball tour to Jersey and a joint tour to Oxford.

The House system plays a central role in the life of the School. All children belong to one of four Houses and take part in many events and competitions during the year. These include football, rugby, golf, general knowledge, hockey, unihoc, netball, swimming, tennis, cricket, drama, table tennis, music and a festival of public speaking.

The main entry is at the age of 7 or 9 but other vacancies may occur at 8 or 10. Applications should be made direct to the Junior School Administrator.

Pre-Prep School. The aim of the school is to provide a broad, balanced and creative curriculum that is adapted to individual needs; allowing every child to reach their potential. Children are encouraged to develop academic abilities as well as personal qualities such as enthusiasm, self-motivation, persistence, empathy with other people and social skills which are vital for success in life.

The curriculum is designed to develop well-motivated, independent learners, who develop a joy of learning. Children are encouraged to take pride in their work, strive for high personal achievement and have a confident and positive response to all the new experiences they encounter. A large emphasis is placed on learning from first-hand experiences. School trips and visiting experts are encouraged. The outdoor environment is seen as an extension of the classroom and used continually throughout the day. We develop a child's natural curiosity fostering a real awe and wonder in the natural world.

A wide variety of extra-curricular activities comprising physical education and games skills (PEGS), short tennis, speech and drama, piano, violin and music workshops, judo, dance, football, Mandarin, Spanish, art, environmental learning, cookery, sewing, ICT and recorders, are offered to children during each academic year in addition to the broad and balanced curriculum.

The Pre-Prep caters for children from 3 to 7. The Nursery, which takes girls and boys from 3, has its own self-contained unit and playground to cater specifically for the needs of the very young child. Structured play offers children rich opportunities for controlling and shaping what they do. Children may stay all day or attend separate morning or afternoon sessions. Children in the Nursery and Reception work towards the Early Years Foundation Stage goals and beyond.

Applications should be made to the Admissions Secretary.

Honours. In 2009 pupils performed exceptionally in their A Levels with a 100% pass rate. 91% of all entries were graded A or B with the highest ever A grade rate of 62%. One in three students achieved A grades in all their subjects, with 12 candidates achieving 4 grade As and 2 candidates, gaining the top grade in 5 A Levels. All pupils achieved 5 A*–C passes in their GCSE exams including English, Maths and Science. 74% of pupils were awarded A* or A with over a third of pupils gained nothing less than an A grade in all of their subjects. Five pupils recorded the outstanding achievement of a clean sweep of 10 A* grades.

The Association of Old Edwardians of Bath. c/o The Development Office.

Charitable status. King Edward's School at Bath is a Registered Charity, number 310227. It is a charitable trust for the purpose of educating children.

King Edward's School
Birmingham

Edgbaston Park Road, Birmingham B15 2UA

Tel: 0121 472 1672
Fax: 0121 415 4327
e-mail: admissions@kes.org.uk
website: www.kes.org.uk

King Edward's School, Birmingham, was founded in 1552 and occupied a position in the centre of the city until 1936 when it moved to its present 45 acre site in Edgbaston, surrounded by a golf course, lake and nature reserve and adjacent to the University. It is an independent day school with about 840 boys aged 11 to 18. Approximately 35 boys in each year receive financial assistance with fees from Scholarships and the Assisted Places Scheme. The school belongs to the Foundation of the Schools of King Edward VI in Birmingham (two independent and five grammar schools), and its sister-school, King Edward VI High School for Girls, is on the same campus. Academically one of the leading schools in the country, King Edward's is also renowned for the scale of its provision and its excellence in sport, music, drama, outdoor pursuits and trips and expeditions.

Motto: '*Domine, Salvum fac Regem*'.

Governing Body:
D Holmes (*Chairman*)
S G Campbell (*Vice-Chairman*)

G Andronov	J F X Miller
Mrs G Ball	Professor T Norris
P Burns	M J Price, CBE
P A Christopher	S M Southall
T Clarke	M B Squires
Mrs A East	G P Thomas
S Heer	Mrs A Tonks

Secretary to the Governors: J Collins

Chief Master: J A Claughton, MA

Deputy Head (*Administration and Pupil Discipline*): K D Phillips, BA
Deputy Head (*Pupil Welfare/Health & Safety*): J C Howard, BEd
Deputy Head (*Academic*): J C Fern, MA

Assistant Teachers:

R W Symonds, BSc	I J Connor, BSc
D C Dewar, BSc	R D Davies, BSc
S E Lampard, BSc	Ms S-L Jones, BSc
R T Bridges, MA, PhD	Ms E K Sigston, BA
T F P Hosty, BA, PhD	P W L Golightly, BA
R N Lye, BA	Mrs S Thorpe, BSc, MEd
L W Evans, BA	Miss J L Parkinson, BA,
J P Davies, MA	MSc
J C S Burns, MA	M J Bartlett, BA
L M Roll, BA	Mrs P J R Esnault, MA
T Mason, BSc	Miss S Khan, BA
E J Milton, BA	C A P Johnson, BA
M N A Ostrowicz, BSc	M E Johnson, BSc
B M Spencer, BA	Ms C E Reeve, BA
C D Boardman, BSc	M R Follows, BSc, PhD
S J Tinley, BSc	M A Loveday, BA
Mrs C M L Duncombe, BA	F M Atay, BA
J Porter, BSc	D H Corns, MA, MPhil
T A McMullan, BSc	H M Coverdale, BScEcon
The Revd D H Raynor,	Miss E J Jordan, BA
MA, MLitt	D C Wong, BEng, PhD
M J Monks, GRSM	Ms L C Seamark
R W James, BA	K S Leivers, BA
S L Stacey, MA	T J M Arbuthnott, BA,
T F Cross, BSc	MPhil
R J Deeley, MA	M P Barratt, BA, MA
D J Ash, MA	H A Ferguson, BSc, MSc
M Daniel, BSc, DPhil	C G Irvine, BA
C W Walker, CertEd	Dr L C McDonald, BEng,
Ms R Leaver, MEng	PhD
J P Smith, BA	Ms G J Powell, BA, MA
P B Evans, BMus	C P Stearn, BA, MPhil
R E Turner, BA, MPhil	J A Taylor, BA
Ms D E McMillan, BSc	Dr J L Tsiopani, BSc, PhD
P A Balkham, BA	T Wareing, BA
D M Witcombe, MSc	

Part-time Teachers:

P E Bridle, MBE, GRSM,	LRAM

Mrs J R E Herbert, LLAM,	S Birch, BEd
ALAM	Dr J L Amann, BA, PhD
Mrs A Ostrowicz, BA	Miss J Helm, BA
Dr G Galloway, PhD,	Mrs F Atay, BA
MPhilEd	D C Rigby, BSc, MSc
Mrs G M Gardiner, BSc,	Senora A Estavez
MSc	Fraulein A Havel
Mrs G Hudson, BEd	Miss C R Bubb, BA
Mrs H J Cochrane, BA	S A Willey, BA
Ms H Proops, BA	

Librarian: Ms J Allen, BA

School Medical Officer: Dr M Forrest, MBChB, DRCOG, MRCGP

Admission. The names of candidates must be registered at the School before the closing date as stated in the prospectus. Evidence of date of birth and a recent photograph must be produced when the name of a candidate is registered for the examination.

Term of Entry. Autumn term only.

Admission Examination. Most boys enter the school at 11+, although a small number join at 13+. In addition, applications at 16+ to enter the Sixth Form are encouraged. At both 11+ and 13+ candidates take papers in Mathematics, English and Reasoning at a level appropriate to the National Curriculum. A large number of pupils are also interviewed as part of the admissions process. At 16+ all candidates take an entry paper in four chosen subjects and are interviewed.

Scholarships at 11+ and 13+. (*See Scholarship Entries section*.) Up to twelve academic scholarships of between one-half and one-fifth fees per annum are offered.

Music Scholarships are also available.

Scholarships at 16+. Scholarships to the value of half fees for boys studying either Science or Arts subjects at A Level.

Fees per term (2011-2012). £3,465.

The Assisted Places Scheme offers means-tested support to up to 35 boys a year. The scheme targets primarily 11+ entrants but 16+ entrants will also be eligible to apply.

Academic Success. In 2010 95% of all A Levels were passed at A*–B grade. Almost all leavers go on to University, some after a GAP year. Over 20 pupils a year gain places at Oxford and Cambridge.

Curriculum. *Lower School*: The following subjects are studied by all boys to the end of the third year: English, Mathematics, French, Geography, History, Physics, Chemistry, Biology, (General Science in first year), Latin, Art, Design, Drama, Music, PE and Religious Studies. All boys study one of German, Spanish or Classical Greek in the third year and may take their choice to GCSE or IGCSE and beyond. In addition, boys are required to undertake familiarisation courses in Information Technology. In the Fourth and Fifth year all boys study Mathematics, English, English Literature, French and either Physics, Chemistry, Biology plus 3 other optional subjects, or two Sciences plus 4 other optional subjects, which are taken to GCSE or IGCSE. At present, the school offers IGCSE in Mathematics, Biology, Chemistry, Physics, English, English Literature and modern languages.

Sixth Form: Since September 2010, A Levels have been replaced entirely with the International Baccalaureate Diploma. The school believes that this diploma provides a more challenging and broad Sixth Form education with greater opportunity for independent learning and is a better preparation for university study and life beyond.

However, the school's curriculum goes beyond preparation for examinations. For example, PE and games are compulsory for all, and, above all, for all pupils Friday afternoon is set aside for the pursuit of non-academic activities: Combined Cadet Force, Leadership, service in the community, outdoor pursuits, Art, information technology etc.

Music and Drama. The school has a very rich musical and dramatic life. Many of the musical groups and theatrical productions take place jointly with King Edward VI High School for Girls. There are ten different musical groups and choirs. Each year the school's major concert is performed in Symphony Hall, Birmingham and there is also a large musical production each year.

Games. Rugby, Cricket, Hockey, and Athletics are the major team games in the school. However, many other games prosper including archery, badminton, basketball, chess, cross-country, cycling, fencing, Fives, golf, kayaking, squash, swimming, table tennis, tennis, water polo. The School has extensive playing fields for all these activities plus its own swimming pool, double Astroturf, all-weather athletics track, sports hall, 2 gymnasia and squash courts.

Societies and Clubs. The school has a very wide range of clubs and societies including Christian Union, Islamic Society, Literary Society, Classical and Junior Classical Societies, Historical and Junior Historical Societies, Living History Society, Economics Society, Musical Society, Senior and Junior Dramatic Societies, Shakespeare Society, Art Society, Geographical Society, Debating and Junior Debating Societies, Scientific Society, Biological Society, Mathematical Society, Meteorological Society, Modern Language Society, Chess Club, Photographic Section, School Chronicle, Film Society, Hard Rock Society.

CCF, Outdoor Pursuits and Expeditions. The Royal Naval, RAF and Army Sections of the Combined Cadet Force are very popular amongst pupils. In addition, the Duke of Edinburgh's Award Scheme has grown substantially in recent years, so that the majority of pupils in the third year gain the Bronze Award and about 20 each year gain the Gold Award. All of this forms part of a strong tradition of trips and expeditions, ranging from cycling and caving and walking and skiing trips, to language trips to Europe to major expeditions to Honduras, Venezuela, Peru, Egypt, Morocco. There have also been very successful rugby tours to Australia and South Africa.

Forms and Houses. In the first five years there are five forms in each year, with an average of 24 pupils. In the Sixth Form, forms are on average 12 in number, and often comprise pupils together from the Lower and Upper Sixth. There are 8 houses and the house system continues to provide an important element of pastoral support and competition, not only in sport, but also in music.

Charitable status. The Schools of King Edward VI in Birmingham is a Registered Charity, number 529051. The purpose of the Foundation is to educate children and young persons living in or around the City of Birmingham.

King Edward's School
Witley

Wormley, Nr Godalming, Surrey GU8 5SG
Tel: 01428 686700
Fax: 01428 682850
e-mail: admissions@kesw.org
website: www.kesw.org

The School was founded in 1553 by King Edward VI as Bridewell Royal Hospital. Originally housed at the Bridewell Palace, which was given under Royal Charter to the City of London, the School moved to Witley in 1867, simultaneously changing its name; it became co-educational again in 1952.

The School provides both boarding and day education for 400 pupils aged 11–18 years with equal numbers of boys and girls; approximately a third are day pupils.

There are a substantial number of bursaries, currently over 100, available to help boys and girls whose home circumstances make a boarding style of education a particular need.

Since September 2010 the International Baccalaureate has been the sole Sixth Form curriculum.

Treasurer and Chairman of Governors: P K Estlin, BSc

Headmaster: J Attwater, MA

Senior Deputy Head: S J Pugh, MA

Academic Staff:
* *Head of Department*
† *Housemaster/mistress*

Miss E Bateman, BSc (**Economics & Business Studies*)
Miss S J Brown, BA (*Modern Languages*)
N J Budden, BSc, MA (*Modern Languages)
Mrs C A Cox, BSc (*Mathematics*)
J G Culbert, BSc (*Physics)
B V Doherty, BA (*Art, Photography*)
K B Forster, BA (*Modern Languages, Careers Coordinator*)
Dr E K Foshaugen, BA, MPhil (**Philosophy/Critical Thinking*)
D G Galbraith, BSc (*Science, *Chemistry)
Mrs K M Goundry, BA (*Food & Textiles Technology*)
Mrs J Harris (*Library & Resources*)
P W Head, BSc (*Mathematics)
Ms C D Hedges, BSc (*Modern Languages*)
Mrs A E Hill, BSc (*Biology*, †*Tudor*)
P Humphreys, BSc, MEd (*Geography*, †*Grafton*)
Miss L A Hunter, MA (*Classics*)
A N K Johnson, BSc, MSc (**Design & Technology, ICT*)
Miss A M Kuczaj, BA (*Games*)
Mrs G Lamond, BA (*Art)
J C Langan, BA (*English)
Dr A Lennard, PhD, BSc (*ICT)
Mrs J Lyttle, BA (*English*)
W V Marr, BComm (*Physical Education*, †*Edward*)
Dr R J Meanwell, BSc, PhD (*IB Coordinator, Physics*)
Mrs C J Meharg, BA (*Deputy Head-Director of Studies, Modern Languages*)
Mrs J Millington, BA (*Senior Mistress, Religious Studies*)
Mrs L S Nikolaou, BA (*Learning Support)
T Norton (*Chaplain*)
Miss J A Patton, BSc (*Mathematics*, †*Elizabeth*)
Mrs J H Pearce, BA (**Religious Studies*)
Mrs G A Pedlar, BA (*English*)
S C Pedlar, GRNCM (*Music, Precentor*)
D G K Pennell, BEd (**Physical Education*, †*Wakefield*)
S D Pentreath, BSc (*Head of Lower School, Chemistry*, †*QMH*)
G M Phillips, BA (*Deputy Head-Community Relations,*)
D K Poulter, BSc, FRGS (*Deputy Head-Co-curriculum, Geography*)
S J Pugh, MA (*Senior Deputy Head, Classics*)
Mrs A S Saunders, BA (*Head of Sixth Form, History*)
C R Saunders, BSc (*Biology)
D Slater, BA (*English*)
Miss L E Smith, BSc (*Science*)
Mrs H Stover, BA Ed (*Science*, †*Queens*)
S D Tapp, BA (*English*)
Mrs A J Tinsley, CertEd (**Design & Technology*)
S L Todd, BSc (*Physical Education, Examinations Officer*)
J J Venables, BMus (*Music)
Mrs L M Vitagliano, MA (*History)
J K Webster, BSc (*Mathematics*)
Mrs K A Wilson, DipM, ACIM (*Economics and Business Studies*, †*Copeland*)

Houses and Housemasters/Housemistresses:

Queen Mary House (*Junior Boys*): S D Pentreath
Copeland House (*Junior Girls*): Mrs K A Wilson

Senior Paired Houses:
Wakefield (*Boys*): D G K Pennell and *Elizabeth* (*Girls*): Miss J A Patton
Edward (*Boys*): W V Marr and *Tudor* (*Girls*): Mrs A E Hill
Grafton (*Boys*): Mr P Humphreys and *Queens* (*Girls*): Mrs H Stover

Medical Officer: P R Wilks, MA, MB, BChir

Director of Finance and Administration: A Lewis

Headmaster's Secretary: Ms C Todd

King Edward's School is situated in a well-wooded site of over 100 acres near the Surrey-Sussex-Hampshire border, easily accessible by both road and rail.

The buildings include the School Chapel, Charter Hall (a modern assembly hall with stage and concert platforms), the Warburg Science School with 9 full-sized laboratories, and well-equipped ancillary rooms, a Mathematics and Computing Block, Design Technology, Resistant Materials, Food Technology and Textiles Centres, an Art Centre (equipped for Photography, Pottery and Sculpture), an Exhibition Hall, the Countess of Munster Music School including a Concert Hall and Music Library, the Gerald Coke Library & Information Centre, a Sports Centre, an all-weather playing surface for hockey and tennis, a Dance and Drama Studio, an Indoor Swimming Pool, hardplaying and playing fields provision for Cricket, Football, Hockey (boys and girls) and Athletics, and courts for Tennis, Squash and Netball.

The First and Second Forms constitute the Lower School and are accommodated in a separate boys house (Queen Mary House) and girls house (Copeland). From the Third Form upwards boys and girls live in six modern, purpose-built paired houses where the accommodation and study areas are completely separate but everyone can come together in the shared communal facilities on the ground floor. The unique paired houses allow boys and girls to mix naturally, and are particularly valued by parents whose sons and daughters attend the school and can be placed in adjacent accommodation. The houses are upgraded continually and there are new washroom and shower facilities throughout. Throughout all years of the School, day pupils are fully integrated into boarding houses.

The generous staffing ratio and the exceptional pastoral care provision make possible a wide-ranging curriculum throughout the School. After GCSEs, the great majority of our pupils proceed to the Sixth Form and subsequently to higher education. A Pre-IB course has recently been introduced, targeted at the overseas market or those seeking to relocate to the United Kingdom. It provides a one-year programme to help prepare 15–16 year olds for the IB course itself. The International Baccalaureate Diploma, introduced in 2004, is the sole Sixth Form curriculum.

The School seeks to draw as widely as it can to make up its community, recruiting widely in the top half of the ability range, from over 30 different countries and from all walks of life.

The School was founded as a result of Christian concern, and still aims to provide a full education in a Christian setting, within a caring community. The centre of its spiritual life is the Chapel, where the services are under the direction of the Chaplains, who in turn call on the help of many staff and pupils. Services vary in character although they are based upon the worship of the Church of England. Children who wish to do so can join church membership classes which culminate in a Confirmation Service for those wishing to become members of the Church of England. All pupils attend Chapel Services.

Admission. Children are normally admitted at 11+, 13+ and 16+ but if there is room they may be admitted at other times, and occasionally a child who should clearly be working alongside older children is admitted at 10+. Admission is by the School's own entrance examination and interview taken normally in the January prior to entry.

Fees per term (2011-2012). Boarders: Lower School £6,660, Forms 3–5 £8,325, Pre IB/IB £8,660, including all boarding and tuition fees, books and games equipment, and the provision of school uniform and games clothing.

Day Pupils: Lower School £4,780, Forms 3–5 £5,975, Pre IB/IB £6,060, including meals and uniform. Individual music tuition in piano, organ, singing and all orchestral instruments is available.

Bursaries. Bursaries are available for both boarding and day pupils. The School has an endowment providing support for children whose circumstances make boarding a particular need. Awards are reviewed annually with regard to parental circumstances and to school fees. They may be given in conjunction with Local Education Authority grants or help from a charitable trust. The School has a dedicated Bursaries officer who works with applicants to source the financial support needed to enable worthy candidates to join the School.

Scholarships. Academic, Art, Drama, Music Scholarships and Sports Exhibitions are offered at 11+, 13+ or 16+ for entry to the Sixth Form. These awards will be up to a maximum of 30% of full fees but may be augmented in case of financial need. A discount of 10% of full fees is available to children from service families.

Charitable status. King Edward's School, Witley is a Registered Charity, number 311997. The Foundation exists to provide boarding education for families whose circumstances make boarding a particular need, though the excellent facilities and the high standards of academic achievement and pastoral care make it attractive also to any family looking for a modern and distinctive education.

King Henry VIII School
(Part of the Coventry School Foundation)

Warwick Road, Coventry CV3 6AQ
Tel: 024 7627 1111
Fax: 024 7627 1188
e-mail: info@khviii.net
website: www.khviii.com

"*Success, responsibility and enjoyment – these are our prime aims*" Jason Slack, Headmaster.

There are 474 boys and 352 girls in the Senior School, and 254 boys and 253 girls in the Prep School. The school is entirely a day school.

King Henry VIII School was founded under Letters Patent of King Henry VIII, dated 23 July 1545 by John Hales, Clerk of the Hanaper to the King. Today it is an independent, co-educational day school of a high academic standing. The school is represented on the Headmasters' Conference and on the Association of Governing Bodies of Independent Schools. The governing body is the Coventry School Foundation, on which are represented Sir Thomas White's Charity, the Coventry Church Charities, Coventry General Charities and Birmingham, Coventry, Oxford and Warwick Universities. There are also several co-opted Governors.

Chairman of Governors: Mr Brendan Connor

Senior School

Headmaster: **Mr Jason Slack**, BSc, MA Ed

Deputy Heads:
Mr Simon Bird, MA, DipEd, NPQH, FRGS
Mr Warren Honey, BSc, MEd
Miss Ann Weitzel, MA, NPQH

Teaching Staff:
Dr Simon Ainge, BSc,   MRSC, CChem

Mrs Mary Aldenton, BEd
Mr Tom Andrews, BSc
Mr Conn Anson-
  O'Connell, BA
Miss Emma Barwell, BA
Mr Matthew Blake, MPhys
Mrs Sally Bradley, BA
Mr Ben S Bramley, BSc,
  MSc
Miss Hannah Bredin, BA
Dr Michael Browning, BSc,
  MSc
Dr Helen Buttrick, MA,
  MSCi
Mr James Carlyle, BA
Mr Andrew Carman, BA
Mrs Anna Clegg, BA
Mr John Cooper, MA
Miss Michele Cuthbert,
  BSc, MEd, HDipEd,
  WITS
Mrs Clare Dempsey, BSc
Mr Niall Doherty, BA,
  LTCL
Mr Doug Drane, MEd,
  HNC
Mr Andrew Dutch, BMus
Mr Alan Emberson, BSc,
  MEd, CMath, MIMA
Mrs Tracy Ferguson, BSc
Miss Kate Fisher, BSc
Mr Peter Forse, BA
Mr Colin Foster, MA, PhD,
  CChem, MRSC
Mrs Michele Gawthorpe,
  MA
Mr Peter Geall, BA
Mr John Grundy, BEd
Mr Richard Harrington,
  MA
Dr David Hayton, BSc
Mrs Anna Heathcote, BA
Mr John Henderson, BA
Mrs Julie Holland, BA
Dr Tim Honeywill, MMath
Mrs Linda Horton, MA
Mr Robert Howard, BA
Mr James Hunt, BA
Mrs Karen Hunt, BEd
Mrs Kathryn Hunt, BSc
Mr Peter Huxford, MA
Mr Nicholas Jones, MA

Mrs Victoria Kaczur, BA
Mr Alistair Kennedy, BA,
  BA Mus
Mr Peter Manning, MA
Mrs Rachel Mason, BSc
Mrs Jaynita Mattu, BSc
Mr Antony McAlister, BEd
Dr Mary McKenzie, MA
Mr Nick Meynell, BA
Mrs Pip Milton, BSc
Mr Peter Milton, BA
Mrs Debra Morris, BA
Miss Sarah Mould, BA
Mrs Cindy Neale, MA
Dr Donna Norman, BSc
Mr Francis O'Reilly, BA
Mrs Gill Othen, BA
Mrs Kulwinder Pabla, MSc
Mrs Denise Pandya, BMus
Mr Andrew Parker, BEd
Dr Noel Phillips, BSc
Mrs Dolores Pittaway, BA,
  PG Dip
Mrs Amanda Pontin,
  CertEd
Mrs Annemarie Powell, BA
Dr Michael Reddish, LLM
Ms Sally Ridley, BA, MBA
Dr Tajinder Sanghera, MA
Mrs Helen Savage, BEd,
  CertEd, Dip TEFL
Mr Shaun Schofield, BSc
Mrs Barbara Seagrave,
  CertEd
Mrs Fiona Singer, MA,
  MEd
Mr Toby Smith, MA, PhD
Mrs Chris Spriggs, BSc
Mr Thomas Spillane, BSc
Dr Robert Stephen, BA,
  BD, MTh, FSA Scot
Mr Ian Stickels, BA
Mr Sukhbir Tandy
Mrs Mary Tynan, BSc
Mrs Anne Wade, BSc, MA,
  CBiol, ML
Mr Ieuan Weir, BA
Mrs Lisa Whiteman, Nat
  Dip Perf Arts, Higher
  Nat Dip Dance
Mr Chris Wilde, BA
Mr Steve Wilkes, BEd

Administrative Staff:
Bursar: Mr Vince Iwanek, OBE
School Administrator: Mrs Julie Goodwin, HND
Headmaster's PA/Admissions Secretary: Mrs Amanda
  Skinner
Examinations Officer: Mrs Belinda Leslie, MBA
Careers Advisor: Mrs Sally Pike, BA, Dip Careers
  Guidance
School Nurse: Mrs Cally Lawrie, BSc Nursing
School Network Manager: Mr Tim Lees
Office Manager: Mrs Jacky Matthews
Sports Centre Manager: Mr Rob Phillips, BSc
Librarian: Miss Kirsten Hill, HND Media

King Henry VIII Preparatory School

Headmaster: Mr Nicholas Lovell, BA
Deputy Head (Swallows): Miss Caroline Soan, GMus,
  PGCE
Deputy Head (Hales): Mrs Helen Higginson, BSc, MA

Director of Studies: Mr Steven Dhaliwal, BEd, MSc

Teaching Staff:
Mrs Sian Anson-
  O'Connell, BA, MA Ed
Mrs Rachel Avlonti, BEd
Mr Greg Beaufoy, BSc
Mrs Sarah Brand, BEd
Mrs Claire Brindley, BSc
Mr Julian Brown, BEd
Miss Gill Beck, BEd
Mrs Jenna Booth, BA
Miss Lynn Brown, BSc
Mrs Jane Coles, CertEd,
  BPhil, MSc
Mrs Emma Curran, BEd
Mr Steve Dhaliwal, BEd,
  MSc
Mrs Sarah Emmett, BA
  QTS
Mr Steve Hall, BA
Mrs Julia Halstead, BA
Mrs Helen Harvey, BA
Mr Brian Hewetson, BA
Mrs Barbara Hunt, BEd
Mrs Catherine Jeffcoat, BA
Mr Lau Langkilde
Mrs Jane Lovell, BEd
Mr Philip McGrane, BSc

Mrs Lesley McKenzie, BEd
Mrs Helen Mellor, BEd
Mrs Ruth Morris, BA
Mr Neil Mosedale, BSc
Mrs Elizabeth Ochieng,
  BEd
Mr Ken Pearson, BEd
Mrs Pauline Pepper, BEd,
  MA
Mr Keith Rawlins, BEd
Mr Phil Savage, BA
Mrs Barbara Seagrave, BEd
Mr David Senyk, BA Ed,
  BPhil, STB
Miss Sophia Skarlatos, BA
Miss Tamsin Slack, BSc
Mrs Jill Sutherland, BA,
  QTS
Mrs Sian Westmancoat, BA
  Ed
Mrs Helen Williamson,
  BSc
Miss Nicola Wood, BA
Mrs Karen Wormald, BEd
Miss Kate Wozencroft,
  HND, BEd Hons

Administrative Staff:
Bursar: Mr Vince Iwanek, OBE
School Administrator: Mr Alan Shaw
Headmaster's PA: Mrs Lesley Batson
School Nurse: Mrs Cally Lawrie, BSc Nursing
Librarian: Mrs Joy Schofield, BA

Facilities. The school moved to its present extensive site
in a pleasant part of Coventry in 1885. The Governors have
continually improved, extended and restored the buildings
which are well equipped to cope with the demands of an up-
to-date, relevant and challenging curriculum. The school has
extensive playing fields, some of which are located on the
main site. Other playing fields are five minutes away by
minibus.

The Governors have committed themselves to a major
building programme at the school. A new Prep School, Art
facility, Sixth Form Centre and Sports Hall have recently
been completed. Both Senior and Prep Schools have a first
rate computer network which is available to all pupils. A
new six-lane, 25m swimming pool (and fitness suite)
opened in 2009.

Curriculum. The curriculum is broad and balanced, integrating National Curriculum principles and practices where
appropriate. The Senior School curriculum provides courses
leading to the GCSE examinations and GCE AS and A levels. Subjects available currently are Art, Biology, Business
Studies, Chemistry, Classical Civilisation, Computing,
Technology, Drama and Theatre Studies, Economics,
English, French, Geography, German, Greek, History, Information and Communication Technology, Latin, Law, Mathematics, Music, Psychology, Physics, Religious Studies and
Spanish. Physical Education and Sport are also considered
to be a vital part of the curriculum and are available as an AS
and A2 level option. All students follow a carefully structured PSHE course.

Courses in Key Skills/Complementary Studies and Critical Thinking are offered in the Sixth Form.

Examination results at all levels are excellent.

Games. Rugby, Hockey, Netball, Basketball, Cross-
Country Running, Athletics, Rounders, Tennis, Cricket,
Swimming, Golf, Orienteering and Fencing. Prep School
games include Tag Rugby, Swimming, Soccer, Rounders,
Athletics, Cricket and Cross-Country Running. In 1986 the

Governors took into use the largest artificial turf games area in the country, used mainly for hockey, but providing an additional 24 tennis courts in the summer. This facility is shared with Bablake School.

Extra-Curricular Activities. The School is noted for the excellence of its sport, music, drama, debating, public speaking and outdoor pursuits. All pupils are encouraged to make a contribution to the extra-curricular life of the school. The School has close connections with many universities including Oxford and Cambridge. The Coventry School Foundation owns an extensive property near Fougères in the Normandy region of France, and all pupils will spend at least one week there during the second year in the Senior school.

Admission. Admission is via the School's own Entrance Examination, held annually in January for entrance the following September. The normal age of entry is 11, but there are smaller additional intakes at other ages (12 and 13) and also at Sixth Form level. All enquiries about admission to the school should be addressed to the Headmaster.

Scholarships. The Governors award annually a number (not fixed) of entrance bursaries and scholarships. Full details regarding financial assistance are available from the Headmaster at the school.

Old Coventrians Association. Contact: Mrs Jay Mattu; e-mail: webALUMNUS@khviii.com; website: www.khviii.com.

Fees per term (2011-2012). Senior School £3,056; Prep School £2,313.

Prep School. The Prep School is based on two nearby sites and enjoys excellent facilities which include an Early Years Centre, a Library, ICT rooms with networked PCs, an Art and Design rooms, a Science room, Astroturf and Sports Hall and a Music room. Children are accepted by competitive examination from 7+ to 10+. The emphasis is on a broad education based upon the National Curriculum and children are prepared for the Entrance Examination for entry to the Senior School.

(*For further information about the Prep School, see entry in IAPS section.*)

Charitable status. Coventry School Foundation is a Registered Charity, number 528961. Its aim is to advance the education of boys and girls by the provision of a school or schools in or near the City of Coventry.

King William's College

Castletown, Isle of Man IM9 1TP

Tel:	01624 820400
Fax:	01624 820401
e-mail:	admissions@kwc.sch.im
website:	www.kwc.im

King William's College owes its foundation to Dr Isaac Barrow, Bishop of Sodor and Man from 1663 to 1671, who established an Educational Trust in 1668. The funds of the Trust were augmented by public subscription and the College was opened in 1833 and named after King William IV, 'The Sailor King'.

In 1991, the College merged with the Isle of Man's other independent school, The Buchan School, Castletown, which had been founded by Lady Laura Buchan in 1875 to provide education for young ladies. The Buchan School has been reformed as the junior section of the College for boys and girls up to age 11. (*For further details of The Buchan School, see entry in IAPS section*).

The Isle of Man, being internally self-governing, has a very favourable tax structure and the independence of College would not be affected by changes in UK legislation.

Motto: '*Assiduitate, non desidia.*'

Visitor: The Most Revd and Right Hon Dr J Sentamu, Lord Archbishop of York

Trustees:
Chairman: Vice-Admiral Sir Paul Haddacks, KCB, Lieutenant Governor of the Isle of Man
S G Alder, BA, FCA
T Cullen, MA
M J Hoy, MBE, MA
The Rt Revd Robert Paterson, MA, The Lord Bishop of Sodor and Man

Secretary to the Trustees and Bursar: J V Oatts, BA, MSc, Dip Surv

Governors:
Chairman: N H Wood, ACA, TEP
Mrs J D N Bates, LLB, DipLP
Prof R J Berry, RD, MA, DPhil, MD, FRCP
A C Collister
Miss J M Crookall, BSc, FSI
Mrs E J Higgins, BSc, ACA
Miss S J Leahy, LLB, DipLP
The Ven Brian Smith, MTh, Archdeacon of Man
C P A Vanderpump, BSc, FCA
Sir David Wilson, LittD, FBA

Principal: **M A C Humphreys**, MA

Vice-Principal: Miss R J Corlett, BA

Deputy Head, Academic: J H Buchanan, BA (*Director of Studies, IB Coordinator*)

* *Head of Department*
† *House Parent*

J M Allegro, BA
Mrs M Bailey-Barnes, BA (**Spanish*)
Mrs E J Ballantyne, BSc
Miss S E Bowler, BA
Mrs K E Brew, BEng
Miss C L Broadbent, BA (**PSHE*)
S N Cope, BA (**Geography*)
Miss E R Cowen, BA
M C Crabtree, BSc (**Boys PE & Games*)
Mrs D J Currie, BA (**Religious Studies*)
C Davidson, MA
Miss E F Drane, BA
Mrs B Dunn, BEd (*Director of Sport*)
Mrs I E Ferrier, MA Ed (**German*)
Mrs R J Foxon, BSc
Miss C Ganzo Perez, BA
Miss A L Gelling, BA
Miss A Grigoras, BA
A R Hay, MA (**History*)
M H Hebden, BA
Miss F Heckel, MA (**French, * Modern Languages*)
Miss S Hills, BSc
Mrs A B Holden, MSc (**Junior Science*)
Dr C E Humphreys-Jones, BA, PhD, (**Theory of Knowledge*)
R D Humphreys-Jones, BSc (**Physics, Head of Fifth Form*)
E J Jeffers, BA (*Head of Boarding, †Colbourne House*)
Mrs S A Jeffers, BA
Miss J H Kaye, BA (*Housemistress, School House*)
S P Kelly, BA (**Art*)
Mrs B Kneen, BSc (*Head of Lower Fifth Form*)
Miss C V Ledger, BA (**Drama*)
Mrs N A Litton, CertEd (**Design Technology*)
Mrs Z A McAndry
D McConnell, BSc
D M C Matthews, BSc (**Mathematics*)
G E Moore, BMus
Revd T H Mordecai, MA (*Chaplain*)
Mrs A L Morgans, BA Ed, BSc (*Head of Sixth Form*)

Dr P H Morgans, BSc, PhD (*Science, *Chemistry)
Miss H E Morton, BEd (*Head of Fourth Form*)
Mrs J Munro, BA
R C Parry, BSc
R Riekert, BComm (*Economics*)
Mrs A M Schreiber, MA
A D Ulyett, BSc (*Biology*)
Mrs B Van Rhyn, BA (*English*)
P Verschueren, MSc
W Warwick, BSc
D S Winrow
J Wright (*Director of Music*)

Part-time Staff:
D Cowley, BSc
Miss S Havet
Mrs S A Ross, BEd
Mrs O Stone, BA

Principal's PA: Mrs A Chapple
School Medical Officer: Dr Balakrishnan, MB, BCh, BaO

The College is set in superb countryside on the edge of Castletown Bay and adjacent to Ronaldsway Airport. The Isle of Man is approximately 33 miles long and 13 miles wide and is an area of diverse and beautiful scenery. The Isle of Man is an unusually safe environment with a very low crime rate.

There are approximately 400 pupils at College and a further 200 pupils at the Preparatory School. There is also a Nursery School for 2 to 4 year olds on the Buchan site. Both King William's College and The Buchan School are fully co-educational.

Entry. New pupils are accepted at any time, but most begin at the start of the September Term. Boys and girls are admitted to the Preparatory School up to the age of 11 at which point transfer to King William's College is automatic. Entry to College, including Sixth Form level, is by Head's report and, where possible, by interview.

Further details and a prospectus may be obtained from the Admissions Office to which applications for entry should be made.

Organisation. The school is divided into three sections: Fourth Form (Years 7 & 8), Fifth Form (Years 9, 10 & 11) and Sixth Form (Years 12 & 13). Each section is led by a Head of Year, assisted by a team of tutors who monitor the academic progress and deal with all day-to-day matters relating to the pupils in their charge. In addition, all pupils are placed in one of three co-educational Houses for internal competitive purposes, which provides an important element of continuity throughout a pupil's career at the School.

Boarders. There are two houses: one for boys and the other for girls. The living and sleeping accommodation is arranged principally in study-bedrooms for senior pupils with junior pupils sharing dormitories in small groups. Each House has its own Houseparent who is responsible for the pastoral welfare of the pupils. He or she is assisted by two or three tutors, of whom at least two are resident.

Chapel. The College is a Church of England foundation but pupils of all denominations attend Chapel; the spirit of the services is distinctly ecumenical.

Curriculum. Pupils at both Schools follow the National Curriculum in its essentials.

The curriculum is designed to provide a broad, balanced and challenging form of study for all pupils. At 11–13 pupils take English, Mathematics, French and Spanish or Latin, Science, History, Geography, Design Technology, ICT, Art, Music, Drama, Religious Studies, Physical Education, PSHE. Pupils then go on to study typically 9 subjects at GCSE/IGCSE level from a wide number of options.

In the Sixth Form King William's College offers the **International Baccalaureate**. Students choose 6 subjects, normally 3 at higher level and 3 at standard level, which must include their first language, a second language, a science, a social science and Mathematics. In addition, students write an extended essay (a research piece of 4,000 words), follow a course in the Theory of Knowledge (practical philosophy) and spend the equivalent of one half day a week on some form of creative aesthetic activity or active community service (e.g. Duke of Edinburgh's Award fulfils this requirement).

Music and Drama. There are excellent facilities for drama with House plays and at least one major school production each year, together with regular coaching in Speech and Drama. There are Junior and Senior Bands and Choirs, and a very flourishing Chapel Choir. The House Music competition is one of the many focal points of House activity.

Games. The College has a strong tradition and a fine reputation in the major games of rugby, hockey and cricket. There are regular fixtures with Isle of Man schools and schools in other parts of the British Isles. Netball, athletics, soccer, cross-country and swimming all flourish and there are both House and College competitions. Senior pupils may opt to play golf on the magnificent adjoining Castletown Golf Links or to sail as their major summer sport. There are approximately thirty acres of first class playing fields, an indoor heated swimming pool which is in use throughout the year, a miniature rifle range, a gymnasium for basketball and badminton with an indoor cricket net, hard and grass tennis courts, two squash courts and a sand dressed all-weather pitch.

Other Activities. There is a wide range of societies and activities to complement academic life. The Duke of Edinburgh's Award Scheme flourishes and expeditions are undertaken regularly both on the Island and further afield. There is a thriving Combined Cadet Force and Social Services group. There are strong links with the Armed Services who help regularly with Cadet training. There are regular skiing trips, choir tours and educational trips to the UK and abroad.

Travel. King William's College is easily accessible from the UK and from abroad. Some boarders come by sea from Heysham or Liverpool using the regular service to Douglas but the majority of boarding pupils and parents come by air from the British Isles and much further afield. There are direct flights to London, Belfast, Dublin, Liverpool, Manchester, Bristol and other UK cities. Boarding House staff are fully experienced in arranging international flights and younger pupils are met at the airport.

Health. The health of all pupils is in the care of the School Doctor. There is a sanatorium supervised by a qualified nursing sister and high standards of medical care are available at Noble's Hospital in Douglas.

Fees per term (2011-2012). Day: £4,292 (Years 7 & 8), £5,360 (Years 9–11), £6,103 (Years 12 & 13). Boarding Fee: £2,785 in addition to Day Fee.

A reduction of one-third of the fee for boarders and one half of the fee for day pupils is allowed to children of clergy holding a benefice or Bishop's licence and residing in the Isle of Man. There is a similar arrangement for children of Methodist Ministers. A reduction of 15% is allowed for serving members of the Armed Forces of the Crown.

A reduction of 10% is made for the second child, 30% for the third and 50% for the fourth.

Scholarships. (*See Scholarship Entries section*.) There is a variety of Scholarships and Awards available for pupils entering Year 7 and the Sixth Form.

A bursary fund is available to assist with school fees in cases of need.

Charitable status. King William's College is a Manx Registered Charity, number 615 and is operated as a Company limited by guarantee.

King's College School

Wimbledon Common, London SW19 4TT
Tel: 020 8255 5300
Fax: 020 8255 5309 (Porters' Lodge)
           020 8255 5379 (Senior Common Room)
           020 8255 5359 (Head Master's PA)
e-mail: admissions@kcs.org.uk
           headmaster@kcs.org.uk
website: www.kcs.org.uk

King's College School was founded as the junior department of King's College in 1829. According to the resolutions adopted at the preliminary meeting of founders in 1828, "the system is to comprise religious and moral instruction, classical learning, history, modern languages, mathematics, natural philosophy, etc., and to be so conducted as to provide in the most effectual manner for the two great objects of education the communication of general knowledge, and specific preparation for particular professions". In 1897 it was removed from the Strand to its present site on Wimbledon Common.

Motto: *Sancte et Sapienter.*

Governing Body:

Visitor: The Archbishop of Canterbury

Chairman of the Governing Body:
J M Jarvis, QC, MA

Prof M L Brown, MA, PhD
Mrs F R Cahill, BA
R J Cairns, MA
O L Carlstrand, BSc, CEng, MICE
A J M Chamberlain, MA, FIA
T A Clark, MA, MSc
G Connell, MA, FCA
P Evitt, MA
P Fraser, PhD
B Gidoomal, CBE, CCMI, FRSA
Mrs P L Hughes, BSc, LLB
G W James, MA
Sir Peter Lampl, OBE, MA, MSc
P F G Levelle
R S Luddington, MA, MPhil
Mrs P Reed-Boswell, CertEd
D R J Silver, MA
G C Slimmon, MA, MBA
Mrs C van Tulleken, BA

Head Master: A D Halls, MA, FRSA

Deputy Head (Academic): Miss M Hunnaball, BSc, MA

Deputy Head (Pastoral): R Milne, BA

Senior Master/Mistress:
B J Driver, MA
Miss H L McKissack, MA

Assistant Heads:
M D Allen, MA
W P Brierly, BSc
P Lloyd, BSc, PhD
R J Mitchell, MA
Mrs M-H Collins, MA
M P Stables, MA (*Director of Studies*)

Chaplain: The Revd J W Crossley, BA, MA, PhD

Senior School

R C Clark, BSc, PhD (*Head of Biology*)
Dr J E Blythe, BSc, PhD
N E Edwards, MSc (*Head of Examinations*)
Dr S A Hendry, BSc, PhD (*Head of Major House*)

E H Johnson, MSc
P M Lavender, BSc (*Head of University Entrance, USA admissions*)
Miss A Roper, BA

A M Hayes, BSc, PhD (*Head of Chemistry*)
Miss P Brothwood, BChem
I M Davies, MA
P Lloyd, BSc, PhD
Miss H L McKissack, BSc, MA
R J Mitchell, MA

R W M Hughes, MSc (*Head of Physics*)
G E D Bennett, MA
G Cawley, BSc
Miss M Hunnaball, BSc, MA
Miss N Kersley, BSc
D J Lavender, MA, ALCM

C M Jackson, MA (*Head of Classics*)
G E Bennett, BA
J R Carroll, MA (*Head of Maclear House*)
Miss V R Casemore, BA
Miss M Neckar, MA
Miss C L Tedd, MA (*Head of Sixth Form Girls*)

A G Hepworth, BSc (*Head of Economics & Business Studies*)
W P Brierly, BSc (*Head of Sixth Form*)
Miss S-A Gosher, BCom
Mrs L A High, MA
Mrs C J Shandro, BA

J Cannon, BA, PhD, MPhil
M D Allen, MA
Miss P Alisse, MSt
Miss E Collin, BA
Miss J Connell, BA
A P Cross, BA (*Artistic Director of Collyer Hall Theatre*)
Miss L J Drayton, BA
Miss A V Eilert, MA
W Newhouse, BA, MA
Miss K L Robinson, MA, MPhil
J L B Trapmore, MA (*Head of Curriculum Drama*)

Dr E Laurie, BSc, MA, PhD (*Head of Geography*)
M J Chambers, BSc (*Coordinator of Staff Training and Development*)
J A Galloway, BA (*Head of Alverstone House*)
J Stanley, BSc

A W Thomas, MA (*Head of History*)
Miss R M Davis, BA (*Coordinator of Educational Visits, Exchanges & Development*)
Miss L U Kay, BA
J G Lawrence, MA, MLitt (*Director of Co-curricular Education*)
Miss M-H Collins, MA
J G Ryan, BA
M Stephenson, MA
Mrs J L Woodward

Ms C A Ramgoolam, BEd (*ICT Coordinator*)

S J Nye, BSc (*Head of Mathematics*)
H Bond, BSc
B J Driver, BA, ARCO
T P Howland, BA
G Kennedy, BEng
G C McGinn, CertEd
S Borio, MPhil
M P Stables, BA (*Director of Studies*)
T Squires, MA
Miss S Walker, BEng
Miss A Wilson, BSc

S Tint, MA, FCIL (*Head of Modern Languages*)
B P Andrews, BA

Mrs C R Butler, MA
H Chapman, MA
Miss A J Crook, BA
Miss A V Eilert, MA (*Coordinator of Chinese Studies*)
C C D Fowler, BA (*Head of Kingsley House*)
Mr S C Kent, BA
Dr E Keyes, PhD
S Marshall-Taylor, BA (*Head of Glenesk House*)
Mrs D McBride, Grad Pol Sci Int, Florence Univ
Mrs H M Mulcahy, BA
Miss R C Peel, BA
Mrs J E Purslow, MA
Miss C O Robinson, BA
J M A Ross, BA (*Head of Layton House*)
J-M Saxton, BA
Miss J Turquin, LLCS Anglais

Dr G M Bamford, BSc, PhD (*Head of Psychology*)
S Costello, BSc

J Renwick, BA (*Head of Religious Studies and Philosophy*)
Miss R R Carnighan, MA, MPhil
Miss J J Macdonald, BSc

Mrs E Goodchild, BSc, DipSpLD (*Head of Learning Support*)
Mrs A Tingle, BA

Junior School
Tel: 020 8255 5335; Fax: 020 8255 5339;
e-mail: jsadmissions@kcs.org.uk; HMJSsec@kcs.org.uk

Headmaster: Dr G A Silverlock, BEd Hons, MLitt, PhD

Deputy Head (Pastoral): Mrs H J Morren, MA

Deputy Head (Curriculum): D Jones, BA

Miss V J Attié, BA
N Attwood, BA (*Head of English*)
A Baker, BEd
Mrs S L Beazley, BA
Miss C E Belshaw, BA (*Head of ICT*)
Miss C M Bitaud, BA
Mrs J Blight, BA
P K Brady, BA (*Head of Stuart House*)
R Brambley, BA (*Head of Mathematics; Asst Head – Priory*)
E D Brooks, BA (*Head of PSHE*)
Mrs S V D Howes, BA (*Head of Drama*)
J Chesworth, BEd Hons (*Head of PE & Games*)
M P Culverhouse, BA
Miss L Cunningham, BA (*Head of Norman House*)
Mrs S J de Montfort, BTheol
J Egan, BA (*Academic Administrator*)
Miss E Emmott, BA
Miss L S Gillard, MA, ATC (*Head of Art & Design*)
M J Gould, BA
Mrs O M E Hamilton, MA (*Head of Religious Studies*)
J E A Hipkiss, BSc (*Asst Head – Outreach*)
M J Hortin, BA (*Head of Classics*)
Mrs S V D Howes, BA (*Head of Drama*) (*Maternity leave*)
Mrs A Huckerby, BA
Miss F C Hutchison, BA
Miss T J Leach, BA (*Head of Windsor*)
Mrs J C Lewis, BA
R D Lewis, BA (*Acting Head of Drama*)
Mrs S J Martineau Walker, BA
I D Morris, BA
P Nash, BA (*Head of Tudor House*)
M L Nixon, BMus (*Head of Keyboard*)
Mrs P Saunders, BSc
M A Stevenson, MA (*Head of Music in Junior School*)
J Streatfeild, BA (*Head of Geography*)
R Van Niekerk, BA (*Head of Science*)
Miss J Walters, BTchg (*Head of Rushmere*)
E T Watkins, BA (*Head of History*)

Miss P J Whitwell, MA (*Head of Modern Languages*)

Senior and Junior Schools

D G Phillips, MA (*Director of Music*)
P A Hatch, BMus (*Assistant Director of Music, Head of PSHE*)
R J H Krippner, BMus (*School Organist*)
L Silvera, BMus (*Head of Strings*)
M A Stevenson, MA (*Head of Music in Junior School*)

R A Carswell, MA (*Head of Art*)
Miss E J Emmett, BA
Miss L S Gillard, MA, ATC (*Head of Junior School ADT*)
C A Grimble, BA
N Pollen, MA

Miss D Langenberg, BA (*Head of Design Technology*)
J D Broderick, BA
A R Pleace, BSc
Miss S J Martineau Walker, BA

L B D Kane, BSc (*Director of Sport*)
J Clark (*Deputy Director of Sport*)
J Chesworth
M P Culverhouse, BA
J Gibson, BA
C J Grimble, BA (*Head of Rowing*)
Mrs N Edwards, BA (*Head of Girls' Games*)

Administrative Staff:
Director of Operations: D Armitage
Head Master's PA: Mrs R Ingram, BA
Junior School Headmaster's PA: Mrs S E C Richards
Senior School Admissions Registrar: Ms S Dowling, BA
Junior School Admissions/School Secretary: Mrs J N Worth
Librarian: Miss H J Pugh, BA, ALA
Junior School Librarian: Mrs A Beddoe
Human Resources Officer: Ms L Haydock, BA, FCIPD

Organisation. King's College School is a day school. Boys only are admitted below the Sixth Form. The Sixth Form is co-educational. The School consists of a Senior School, which pupils enter at 13, and a Junior School, which educates pupils aged 7 to 13 in preparation for entry to the Senior School. On entry to the Senior School pupils are placed in one of the six Houses. Every pupil has a Tutor who is responsible for their progress and welfare throughout their school career.

Admission. Entrance to the Senior School is through the Common Entrance Examination for external candidates or the KCS Scholarship Examination. Candidates should normally be registered by their tenth birthday, and will be assessed at 11+ with a view to advising parents on their suitability as candidates for KCS at 13+. Candidates from King's College Junior School sit either the Transfer Examination or the KCS Scholarship Examination. Places for girls and boys are available each year for entry to the Sixth Form. Preliminary enquiries about entry should be made to the Admissions Registrar.

Junior School. Entrance examinations, graded according to the ages of the pupils, are held in the January of the year of entry. Enquiries should be made to the Junior School Secretary. (*For further details of the Junior School refer to entry in IAPS section.*)

Scholarships. (*See Scholarship Entries section.*) In the case of financial need, further contributions to fees may be provided by the bursary fund (see below). Up to fifteen scholarships may be awarded at 13+. One of these may be awarded to a pupil offering Greek who shows particular promise as a classical linguist; two others may be awarded to pupils who show particular promise in modern languages or science. The number of scholarships awarded in any year will vary according to the quality of the candidates. There are separate additional prizes to recognise outstanding ability in the Humanities, Mathematics and English. Up to six Music Scholarships may be awarded to pupils of high musical ability. Two Art and Design and two Sports Scholarships are also awarded. Candidates for all these awards must be under 14 years of age on 1st September of the year in which they sit the examination. Sixth Form Scholarships are available to pupils entering the Sixth Form. In addition to Academic Scholarships, there are Music Scholarships and one Organ Scholarship.

Further information on all scholarships is available from the Admissions Secretary.

Bursaries. The School has its own bursary fund through which it can offer assistance with fees in case of established need. (Pupils already in the School take preference in the award of bursaries.) Awards may be made to pupils entering either the Junior School at 11+ or the Senior School at 13+ or 16+.

Registration. A non-refundable fee of £100 is charged.

Tuition Fees per term (2011-2012). Senior School £5,840. Junior School: £4,660–£5,260. Individual music tuition is charged separately.

Curriculum. In the first year (Fourth Form) pupils follow a common curriculum. In the Lower and Upper Fifths the core (I)GCSE subjects are English, French, Mathematics, Biology, Physics, Chemistry, Religious Studies, PSHE, and PE, with options from Art, Design & Technology, Greek, German, Geography, History, Italian, Latin, Mandarin, Music, Spanish and Russian.

The Sixth Form is housed in College Court, a sixth form centre with teaching and seminar rooms, recreation and study areas. College Court also houses the Careers Department and links with Collyer Hall (the theatre/concert/assembly hall) and the Cotman Art Gallery.

Sixth Form Curriculum. All pupils study the International Baccalaureate and take 6 subjects: literature; a modern language; a science; mathematics; a humanity (eg History, Geography, Psychology, Politics, History of Art or Economics); and either a creative subject, a classical language or another of the first five categories. Three or four of these subjects are taken at Higher Level, the rest at Standard Level. In addition they write an Extended Essay, take a course in the Theory of Knowledge and their contribution to extra-curricular activities through Creativity, Action & Service is also assessed.

Every sixth former also participates in a wider educational programme of classes, lectures and activities, which include spiritual and moral issues, a full programme of games and an afternoon devoted to extra-curricular activities.

Religious Education. King's is an Anglican foundation but welcomes pupils from all churches and faiths. The practice of other faiths is encouraged. The School has a Chaplaincy through which pupils are prepared for confirmation and there is a Chapel for voluntary worship and communion.

Music. There is a purpose-built Music School. Four orchestras, three choirs and two wind bands, as well as various smaller groups and jazz groups, perform a number of major choral and orchestral works each year. There are regular performances at major London venues including Westminster Abbey, Cadogan Hall, St Paul's Cathedral and St John's Smith Square. Also, the choir and orchestra undertake international tours. Some 30% of the pupils have individual music lessons at the School.

Games. After an introduction to a range of games in their first year, pupils have a free choice of termly sports. The major sports are rugby, hockey, soccer and cricket and the games programme also includes athletics, badminton, basketball, cross-country running, fencing, fives, hockey, karate, rowing, sailing, shooting, squash, swimming, tennis and water polo. The School has its own indoor heated swimming pool. The sports hall has a floor area providing 4 badminton courts, as well as volley and basketball, indoor tennis and cricket nets, together with a fitness training room and

four squash courts. There are two all-weather surfaces for hockey and tennis at the West Barnes Lane ground. The School's boathouse is on the Tideway at Putney Bridge.

School societies and activities. Every pupil is encouraged to take part in extra-curricular activities. Societies meet in the two extended lunch breaks and after school. Friday school finishes early to allow pupils to participate in a range of activities such as the CCF and community service. The school runs an impressive outreach programme supporting a number of neighbouring state schools. There are active drama and debating societies, together with a wide range of other societies.

Numbers. In the Senior School 810; in the Junior School 460.

Honours. Places offered at Oxford and Cambridge for 2011: 30.

Charitable status. King's College School is a Registered Charity, number 310024. It exists to provide education for children.

King's College
A Woodard School

South Road, Taunton, Somerset TA1 3LA
Tel: Headmaster: 01823 328210
           Reception: 01823 328200
Fax: 01823 328202
e-mail: admissions@kings-taunton.co.uk
website: www.kings-taunton.co.uk

A Woodard school, Canon Nathaniel Woodard renamed the school King's College in memory of King Alfred, when he bought it in 1879, but its historical links go back to the medieval grammar school which was founded by Bishop Fox of Winchester in 1522.

King's College, Taunton is an independent co-educational boarding and day school for 440 boys and girls aged 13–18 years.

Situated on the outskirts of Taunton, the county town of Somerset, on a splendid 100-acre site, King's College offers high academic standards, a friendly and caring day and boarding community, and has an enviable reputation for music, drama and sport. Kindness, consideration for others, honesty and self-discipline are the values which King's hopes will provide its pupils with the inner resources not just for school, but for life.

Motto: *Fortis et Fidelis*

Senior Provost: The Revd Canon Brendan D Clover, MA, FRSA, LTCL
Provost in the West: The Rt Revd Martin Shaw, AKC

School Council:
R D V Knight, OBE, MA, DipEd (*Custos*)
Dr R A K Mott, BA, PhD (*Vice-Custos*)
The Revd Preb Mrs L M Barley, BA, MSc, PGCE
S J Carder, MA, MBA
C F B Clark, MA, MRICS, FAAV
G P Davis, FCA
Mrs L H Eliot, MA, PGCE, DipRSA
R M Excell, FRSA
Sir Harry Farrington Bt, MRICS
C H Hirst, MA
J E R Houghton, MA
P J LeRoy, MA, DipEd
R D A Lloyd, BSc, MRICS
R I W Marfell, FCA
Mrs R Price

Headmaster: **R R Biggs**, BSc Cape Town, MA Oxon

Chaplain: The Revd M Smith, BA, DipTh St Paul's

Deputy Heads:
R R Currie, BA
Mrs K L McSwiggan, BA

Director of Studies: S B Gray, MA
Administrative Master: C J Albery, BMus
Director of Extra-Curricular Activities: A P McKegney, BA
Director of Finance: M C MacEacharn, BSc, FCA
Director of Operations: A J Prosser, BSc
Director of Marketing: Mrs J M Hake, ACIM
Director of Development: Mrs L M Lavender, MBE
Administration and Exams Officer: Ms F Buchanan, Dip RSA
Admissions Registrar: Mrs B L Lancey

Assistant Teachers:
* *Head of Department*
† *Housemaster/mistress*

C J Albery, BMus (*Administrative Master; Director of Music*)
J Arliss, BA (**Philosophy of Religion and Ethics*)
J Bird, MA (**Geography*)
Mrs F Buchanan (*Exams Officer*)
Mrs A M Butler, BA (*†Taylor*)
O Butterworth, BSc
Miss J W Casely, MA (**Modern languages*)
Mrs L S Cashmore, BA (**Classics*)
Mrs J M Chadwick, BA
D J Cole, BSc (**Induction*)
Mrs K E Cole, BA (**Learning Support; †Carpenter*)
Mrs P Corke, BA
Mrs J M Currie, LLB, Cert TEFL
Miss K M Davies, BA
Mrs K A Dewberry, BA, MA (**Art*)
Miss G Fagan, MA (*†Meynell*)
Miss E Forward, BA
S B Gray, MA (*Director of Studies*)
B M Greedy, MChem, DPhil
Mrs J A Gresswell, BSc (**Physics*)
N S Gresswell (*†King Alfred; Co-Director of Sport*)
J H Griffiths, BTech (*†Tuckwell*)
J W Grindle, BSc (**Design and Technology*)
Miss R L Grove, BSc, MPhys, AMInstP
C S Hamilton, MChem (**Chemistry*)
T J Haynes, BA (*†Woodard*)
Miss I S Hobday, BSc (*Senior Tutor*)
C K Holmes, BA (*†Woodard*)
M M Lang, BSc, MPhil (**ICT*)
J A Lee, BA (*Senior Tutor*)
P D Lewis, BSc
R Llewellyn-Eaton, MA
O H Lloyd, BA (*†Bishop Fox*)
A P McKegney, BA (**Business Education*)
Mrs K M Mulligan, BA, RSA Dip
Mrs K J Paul, BA (*Assistant Director of Music*)
J K Round, MA (**Mathematics*)
P J Scanlan, MA (**History*)
J A Scott, BSc (**Biology*)
Mrs S J Similien, BSc (*Co-Director of Sport*)
T D H Smith, MA (**English*)
Dr D J Snell
A J Wood, BA (**Drama*)
Mrs L D Wrobel, BA
G Wrobel, BSc

CCF:
Lt Col D J Cole (*Officer Commanding*)
Lt P J Belfield, BSc
S Sgt R Mason (*SSI*)

Medical Officers:
Dr Yvonne L Duthie, MB BS, DCH, MRCGP
Dr A F C Fulford, MB, ChB, DRCOG, MRCGP

Dr J Martin, MB BS, MRCPCH, DR, COG, MRCGP
ICT Manager: S J Shaw

King's College, Taunton, delivers success at all ages whilst offering a friendly, happy and safe living and working environment. The school provides an extraordinary breadth of opportunities to pupils and has very high academic standards. As well as the school's academic success, pupils also enjoy the highest levels of achievement in sports, art, drama and music. The school won the 2007 BBC Songs of Praise Senior School Choir of the Year title, as well as the Rosslyn Park 7s Rugby Cup – a taste of the breadth of opportunity available to pupils.

King's College has produced a large number of Oxbridge entrants over the years and is well regarded by the top universities in the UK. Pupils can join the Third Form (Year 9) at 13, going on to take GCSE exams, or in the Sixth Form (Year 12) at 16 or 17 to study for A Levels. The school is blessed with highly-qualified and committed members of staff who see their role as ensuring the happiness and successful development of each individual member of the school community. The word community is very prominent at King's: Boarders and day pupils benefit from a strong Christian ethos: an environment where self-respect and kindness to others are highly-regarded qualities.

Admission. All entries are made through the Headmaster. Pupils normally enter at 13 years in the Michaelmas term and are admitted via Common Entrance or the Scholarship Examination.

The registration fee is £75.

Fees per term (2011-2012). Boarders £8,800, Day Pupils £5,910. The fees are inclusive of all extra charges of general application.

Scholarships. (*See Scholarship Entries section.*).

Old Aluredian's Association. *Secretary*: P J Scanlan, MA, c/o King's College.

Charitable status. Woodard Schools Taunton Ltd is a Registered Charity, number 1103346. King's College exists to provide high quality education for boys and girls aged 13–18.

The King's Hospital

Palmerstown, Dublin 20, Ireland
Tel: 00 353 1 643 6500
Fax: 00 353 1 623 0349
e-mail: admissions@kingshospital.ie
website: www.kingshospital.ie

Voluntary Church of Ireland (Anglican), co-educational, secondary school for boarders and day pupils aged 12–18 with 700 pupils, half of whom are boarders (161 boys, 171 girls) and half are day pupils (202 boys, 161 girls).

The King's Hospital, one of the oldest boarding schools in Ireland, was founded in 1669 as The Hospital and Free School of King Charles II. In 1971 the School moved from the centre of Dublin to its present, modern setting in spacious, scenic grounds of over 100 acres on the banks of the River Liffey in Palmerstown, yet remains only 15 minutes from Dublin International Airport. The King's Hospital attracts pupils from all over Ireland as well as from overseas.

The fundamental values of a Christian conscience, a sense of duty and loyalty and a love of learning are actively promoted.

Chairman of Governors: Mr William Maxwell

Headmaster: **Michael D Hall**, MSc, BEd

Deputy Head: (*to be appointed*)

Assistant Heads:
John Rafter, BA, BSc, HDipEd (*Games & Recreations*)
Siobhán Daly, BA, HDipEd (*Academic Affairs*)
John Aiken, BA, HDipEd (*Pastoral Care*)

Chaplain: The Revd Canon Peter Campion, MPhil, MA, PGCE

Heads of Departments:
Detta Brennan, Dip Fine Arts, Dip ADT (*Art*)
Mark Campion, BA, HDipEd (*Mathematics*)
The Revd Canon Peter Campion, MPhil, MA, PGCE (*Religious Education*)
Norma Clarke, BA, HDipEd (*Business*)
Jane Coburn, BA, HDipEd (*Geography and CSPE*)
Hilda Smith, BA, HDipEd (*English*)
Janet Nelson, MSc, BA, HDipEd, DSEN (*Special Education Needs*)
John Huggard, BA, HDipEd (*History*)
Emma Ryan, BSc QTS (*Physical Education*)
Caroline Brady, BEd (*Home Economics*)
Dymphna Morris, BA, DipComp (*Information Technology*)
Michelle Murray, MEd Mgt, BA Special, HDipEd (*Irish*)
Patrick O'Shea, BTechEd (*Design and Communication Graphics*)
Aileen Polke, BA, HDipEd (*Modern Languages*)
Helen Roycroft, BA, Dip PRII (*Music*)
Susan Tanner, BSc, HDipEd, HDCG (*Career Guidance and SPHE*)
Ciaran Whelan, BSc, HDipEd (*Science*)
Cormac Ua Bruadair, BA, HDipEd (*Transition Year*)

Housemasters/mistresses:
Bluecoat (*Sixth Form boy boarders*): Raymond McIlreavy, MEd, BA, HDipEd
Bluecoat (*Sixth Form girl boarders*): Lorna McGinn, MA, BA, HDSCG
Grace (*Girl boarders*): Rachelle van Zyl, BComm, HDipEd
Mercer (*Girl boarders*): Caroline Brady, BEd
Ormonde (*Boy boarders*): Niall Mahon, BSc, HDipEd
Morgan (*Boy boarders*): Cormac Ua Bruadair, BA, HDipEd
Bluecoat / Blackhall (*Senior School day pupils*): John Huggard, BA, HDipEd
Noel Cunningham, MSc, BSc, HDEnvEng, HDipEd
Desmond (*Middle School day pupils*): Yvonne Duggan, BSc, BComm, HDipEd
Stuart (*Middle School day pupils*): Glenda Ua Bruadair, BA, PGCE
Swift (*Middle School day pupils*): Victoria Malcolm, MA, HDipEd
Ivory (*Junior School day pupils*): David Plummer, BSc, PGCE

Bursar: Ronald Wynne

Secretary to the Headmaster: Lorraine Walker

The King's Hospital believes that every child should achieve his or her true potential intellectually and socially, through personal endeavour and the encouragement and support of our staff, parents and governors. Through our academic, pastoral and extra-curricular programmes, we strive to develop core values of:

- a love of learning which makes all study a discovery and a joy, and which leads to standards of academic excellence appropriate to each child's ability;
- a Christian conscience and awareness which enables our pupils to develop a personal faith in God, to lead fulfilling lives which will enrich the communities in which they live, to uphold truth and show respect for others as well as for themselves, and to accept responsibility for their own actions;
- a sense of duty and loyalty which encourages participation in, and commitment to, every aspect of school life.

Academic. The school has an excellent academic record (98% progression to Higher Education in 2010 – *Irish Times*).

Most pupils pursue a 6 year course on entering the school at the age of 12. The first three years lead to the Junior Certificate Examination, followed by a Transition Year and the final two years are devoted to the Irish Leaving Certificate Examination (equivalent to 4 A Levels) providing access to Universities in the UK and throughout the World. Streaming is not a policy at The King's Hospital and the consistently high level of academic achievement is a reflection of the manner in which the School has always adapted to the ever-evolving education process and the ever-changing needs of its pupils by providing a comprehensive and progressive range of subjects, extensive specialist facilities and a highly qualified teaching staff.

The specialist facilities range from laboratories, workshops and computers to technical equipment and instruments, with Computer/PowerPoint facilities in most classrooms. A highly trained and well-equipped Special Needs department is available for both gifted children and those with learning difficulties. Media technology in the Harden Library provides access to national and international databases for project work as well as a computerised resource centre for information and guidance on careers.

Extra-Curricular. In addition to academic pursuits, The King's Hospital is renowned for its choice of recreational activities and offers a wide variety of sporting, music, drama and academic clubs and societies with unrivalled facilities. Pupils are encouraged to participate and all have the opportunity to represent the School at various levels in the activities of their choice.

An ultra-modern Sports Hall incorporating a fully-equipped fitness centre, a 25-metre indoor heated swimming pool and a floodlit astroturf pitch are among the outstanding facilities providing ample opportunity for Rugby, Hockey, Athletics, Swimming, Canoeing, Rowing, Cricket, Soccer, Basketball, Badminton and Tennis.

The promotion of cultural activities is catered for through Arts and Crafts, Choirs, Orchestras and Drama and Musical productions. A dedicated Performing Arts Centre is a recently built facility with the School's Assembly Hall/Theatre.

A diverse array of recreational activities is covered with clubs and societies, a Student Council, social work and European Studies, theatre and concert trips and trips abroad, both sporting and cultural.

Pastoral. Cooperation and mutual respect between pupils and staff, as well as a specified code of behaviour, are central to the daily life of the School. There are ten houses whose Housemaster or Housemistress has specific responsibility for the general welfare and development of pupils under his or her care. The diverse aspects of health education are included in the School's programme and there is 24 hour nursing care and a counsellor available. Worship, according to the rites of the Church of Ireland and led by the resident Chaplain, is an integral part of daily life and pupils gain an understanding and respect for all religious persuasions.

The Future. A vision for the future of the School is embodied in an ever-evolving School Plan and the Board of Governors is committed to constantly implementing the development strategies within that plan. The School's ambitious development programme is designed to maintain its position as one of Ireland's leading educational institutions. The building of a new Form 6 Bluecoat House was completed in February 2008 – a tremendous addition to the Senior School costing €8 million. The King's Hospital is a school firmly rooted in tradition while continuing to be at the cutting edge of modern education.

Fees per term (2011-2012). Boarders €4,545, Day €1,910.

King's School
Bruton

Bruton, Somerset BA10 0ED
Tel: 01749 814200
Fax: 01749 813426
e-mail: office@kingsbruton.com
website: www.kingsbruton.com

The School was founded in 1519 by Richard Fitzjames, Bishop of London, John Fitzjames, his nephew, Attorney-General, afterwards Chief Justice of the King's Bench, and John Edmonds, DD, Chancellor of St Paul's. It was closed in 1538 on the suppression of the Monasteries, and re-founded by Edward VI in 1550.
   Motto: *Deo Juvante.*

Governors:
E W Thomas, Esq, BA (*Senior Warden*)
K L Lawes, Esq, FCA (*Junior Warden*)
R I Case, Esq, CBE, DL, FREng, FRAeS, MSc (*Chairman of Finance*)
Professor W P H Duffus, BVSc, MA, PhD, MRCVS
R Gallannaugh, Esq, ARIBA
Mrs A L Lee, RGN, RNT, BEd, MA
Mrs E M McLoughlin, CBE
S R Oxenbridge, Esq, MA
P J Phillips, Esq, FIPA
R R Williams, Esq, ACIB
A H Beadles, Esq, MA
Mrs M A Edwards, BA, MA, PGCE, ARCM
Ms H R Sampson, BA, MA, MBA
R A E Davey, Esq, MA
D J Coleman, Esq, MA
E G Hobhouse, Esq, BSc Eng, MBA

Clerk to the Governors: Col S G Adlington

Headmaster: I S Wilmshurst, MA Cantab

Deputy Headmaster: G J Evans, BSc Econ
Second Deputy Head: Mrs A J Grant, BA
Director of Studies: A Kok, BEng, CEng
Head of Teaching and Learning: Mrs M C Startin, BA

Teaching Staff:
* Head of Department
† Housemaster/mistress

M F Parr, MA, DipLit (*Classics, Higher Education Adviser, Gifted & Talented Coordinator*)
N G Watts, MA
R J P Lowry, BA
S W Spilsbury, BEdTech (*Art*)
D R Barns-Graham, MA (*Chemistry*)
C H M Oulton, MA
T Fletcher, BA (*History*)
Revd N H Wilson-Brown, BSc (*Chaplain*)
D Warren, BA (*Geography*)
C A Barrow, BA (*Boys' PE*)
Ms M H King, BA (*Theatre Studies*)
J B Slingo, BSc (*Economics & Business Studies*)
Mrs G de Mora, BSc (*Mathematics*)
Mrs R A Vigers-Belgeonne, BSc (*Food Science*)
Mrs A L Ashworth, BSc (*Physics*)
Mrs L J Bray, BA
G A Tresidder, BA, MA, PhD (*Careers*)
R S Hamilton, BEd (†*Lyon House*)
Dr J C Shepherd, BSc, PhD (†*Priory House,**Biology)
T R N Walker, MA
D J Gorodi, GRSM, LRAM (*Director of Music*)
W R Dawe, BA (†*New House*)
Mrs A Sherrard, BA (**Learning Support Unit*)
D R Cowley, BEd (*Design and Technology*)

Dr S D Osborne, BSc, MSc, PhD
Mrs M C Startin, BA (**English*)
Mrs P G Atkinson, BSc (**Director of Sports*)
J H Eggertsen, BA
Miss J J Hill, BSc
Ms A F Turnbull, BEd
Mrs C Tickner, BA
Mrs S L Wilson-Brown, BEd (**PHSEE*)
Mrs A M Allen, DipSpLD
Mrs A Maistrello, BA (**EAL*)
S M Harkness, BA
N P Bunday, BA, MA (†*Blackford House*)
M K W Jeffrey, BSc (†*Old House*)
Mrs J L Deaney (†*Wellesley House*)
Mrs E Loveless, BA (**Modern Foreign Languages*)
A W Moxon, BSc
Mrs R A Vita
A J Marshfield, BMus
Mrs K Wylie-Carrick, BSc
Mrs B Griffiths, BSc (†*Arion House*)
Ms E H Grasby, BA
B Dudley
Miss C V Smith, MSc, BA
Mrs N Archer, MSc, BA
Dr A M Jeffries, MA, DPhil
S Davies, MSc
Miss K M Flavell, BSc
Miss M J Hill, BSc
Miss S V Liddell-Grainger

Assistant Music Staff:
Mrs S Whitfield, BA, ARCM (*Piano & Theory*)
P Caunce (*Violin/Viola*)
K R Schooley, MISM (*Percussion & Drum Kit*)
P Kelly (*Guitar*)
Mrs J Whitteridge, FTCL, AGSM, ARCM, ALCM, Cert Ed (*Bassoon*)
G Austin, ARCM (*Brass*)
D Bertie, BA, FTCL, DipMus (*Trumpet*)
R Shipley, BSc, MMus, CT ABRSM, LRSM (*Clarinet & Saxophone*)
P Lambton (*Clarinet & Saxophone*)
Mrs B Jenkinson, MA, BMus, GRSM, LRAM, ARCM, PGCE (*Piano*)
Miss M Marton (*Singing*)
D Slater, MA (*Organ*)
Mrs J Brown, BA, AGSM (*Singing*)
T Angel, BA (*Singing*)
Dr J Wood, BMus, PhD, GSMD (*Cello & Double Bass*)

Bursar: Mrs H Feilding, MA, ACA
Finance Bursar: Mrs S L Blundy, BSc, ACCA
Registrar: Mrs C S E Oulton
Headmaster's PA: Mrs S L Carpenter
Bursar's PA: Mrs A M Miles, GLCM
School Administrator: Mrs J L Deaney
School Receptionist: Mrs C A Hunt
Estates Manager: P J Cloney, MBE

Medical Officers:
Dr M H Player, BSc, MB BS, DRCOG, MRCGP
Dr L H Chambers, MB BS, DRCOG
Dr U Naumann, FRG, DRCOG, MRCGP
Dr N Gompertz, BSc, MBChB, MRCP
Dr S Franks, ChB, MB, MRCGP

Hazlegrove (King's Bruton Preparatory School)
Sparkford, Yeovil, Somerset BA22 7JA
Telephone: 01963 440314 (*Headmaster and Secretary*)
Fax: 01963 440569
e-mail: office@hazlegrove.co.uk
website: www.hazlegrove.co.uk

Headmaster: R B Fenwick, MA

Deputy Head: M Davis, BEd Hons

Head of Pre-Prep Department: Miss E Lee, BEd Hons
Assistant Head (Admin): C J Smith, CertEd (*ICT*)
Assistant Head (Pastoral): T Sawrey-Cookson, BA Hons QTS
Headmaster's Secretary: Mrs S Newton
Admissions Secretary: Mrs F O'Neill

Number of Pupils. 322. Boarders: 64 girls, 149 boys. Day: 35 girls, 74 boys. Sixth Form: 136.

Pastoral Care. When pupils first arrive at King's, they are welcomed into a genuinely caring community, where individuals and individuality are valued. At the centre of this community are the boarding houses which are in the care of a Housemaster or Housemistress who has overall responsibility for each pupil and who is that pupil's first and last supporter throughout his or her time at King's. In addition, pupils have their own tutor, who will keep an eye on academic progress, ensure that any problems are resolved, and offer advice and friendship. Housemasters, housemistress, matrons, tutors and senior pupils all work to ensure that each new pupil settles in quickly and successfully.

From the very beginning our pupils lead busy lives, full of work, activities and friends. The size of the School is a particular strength; in a community where everyone is known, pupils cannot remain anonymous.

We believe that close communication between school and parents is very important, and the Housemaster/Housemistress will be the first point of contact for parents, who are kept informed of progress through reports and more informal contacts.

Day pupils are fully integrated into the life of the boarding houses and it is often hard to dislodge them from King's. They will frequently stay late into the evenings and come into school at weekends. For them, and for our many boarders, the friendships they build at King's become of great value to them, both while they are at school and after they have moved on.

Co-education. Girls have been admitted since 1969 to Sixth Form courses subject to GCSE level success, either as boarders or day girls. Junior girls from age 13 have been welcomed since 1997 when two girls' houses were opened and a third was added in 2007.

Buildings. The oldest portion of the buildings date from the early part of the 16th century. This, with numerous additions and alterations, forms Old House. New House was begun in 1872 and has been considerably extended since. Priory House was acquired in 1942. Lyon House was opened in 1954, and extended in 1976 and 1986, and Blackford House in September 1960. Wellesley was opened in 1984 and Arion in 1997. There is a Medical Centre, staffed by a senior nurse. The Memorial Hall, built by Old Brutonians after the First World War, incorporates a classroom wing, a recital and meeting room and the refurbished and extended Music School. A development programme, completed in 1979, included the extension of the Music School, a large Sports Hall with a theatre in the same building, and the self-service Dining Hall, built in 1974, which has classrooms and the Norton Library on the first floor. A classroom block, Chemistry, Maths and Modern Languages, lead to the splendid Design Centre opened in 1989 and incorporating all facilities for Design, Technology, Art and Information Technology. An extension to the Design Centre housing a Physics Department and extended ICT facilities was opened in September 1994. A new Science Centre for Biology, Chemistry and Home Economics was opened in September 1999 and a new Library/Learning Centre built in 2004. 2007 saw the completion of a Sixth Form Social Centre and a third girls' boarding house. The stunning Basil Wright Reception Centre was opened in September 2008. A new synthetic playing surface for hockey was opened in December 2010.

Curriculum. King's is divided into Upper and Lower Sixth, Fifth, Fourth and Third forms. The subjects taught include Art, Biology, Business Studies, Chemistry, Design & Technology, Drama & Theatre Studies, Economics, English Language, English Literature, French, Geography, German, History, Information Technology, Latin, Mathematics, Further Mathematics, Music, Music Technology, Personal, Social, Health and Economic Education, Philosophy & Ethics, Physical Education, Physics, Psychology, Religious Studies, and Spanish. National Curriculum GCSE courses are followed up to the Fifth Form, after which, in the Sixth Form, pupils are able to specialise for subjects at A Level, for entry to Universities, the Services and other Careers. There is a Learning Support department. Gifted & Talented activities include the Extended Project Qualification.

Games. The main school sports are Cricket, Rugby, Hockey and Netball. There is a wide variety of other sports available as options. Boys play Rugby in the Christmas Term, Hockey in the Easter Term; Cross-Country Running for both girls and boys takes place in both. Boys Cricket is played in the Summer, but Athletics and Tennis are also encouraged. Girls play hockey in the Christmas term, Netball in the Easter term, and Tennis in the Summer. There are 2 main playing fields, 17 Tennis Courts, 2 Squash Courts, 2 Fives Courts, and a Sports Hall. A Hard-Play area with 2 All-Weather Hockey Pitches is well used. A new synthetic playing surface for hockey was completed in December 2010. A Physical Education course is provided for all pupils. Judo, Basketball, Badminton, Fencing and Golf are also part of the School sports provision.

There is a Combined Cadet Force which all boys and girls are expected to join for a definite period, after which they can undertake other forms of Service in the community. There is a Rifle Range, and Army ranges are nearby. Pupils are also engaged in the Duke of Edinburgh's Award Scheme.

Music. Vocal and Instrumental Music has for many years been one of the strong features in education at the School, and pupils are strongly encouraged to learn and appreciate music. Frequent concerts are given by Choir, Orchestra, Dance, Jazz and Military bands.

Societies and other activities. There is time every day devoted to a wide range of activities, including Acting, Archery, Art, Chess, Computer Programming, Dance, Debating, Drama, Electronics, Horse Riding, Modelling, Music, Printing, and Photography. Design, Technology, Art and Computing are all provided in the Design Centre. A Community Service activity provides help in the town and the neighbourhood. The Friends' Association provides Travel Scholarships as well as various extra amenities.

Worship. Assembly takes place in the Memorial Hall. A weekly, whole school service takes place in the large parish church of St Mary, Bruton. Pupils are prepared by the Chaplain for Confirmation in the Autumn Term. There is a flourishing Christian fellowship group and many Bible study groups. TGI Friday is a voluntary, weekly chaplaincy activity, hosted by the Chaplain. Around 50/60 attend each week.

Scholarships. (*See Scholarship Entries section.*) Scholarships are awarded annually for competition.

Careers. Careers and Higher Education materials are readily available in the library and via the school intranet. Most of our pupils go on to university so the main thrust of the work of the Careers/Higher Education Department is aimed at university application. Younger pupils are well briefed on the importance of topics such as subject choice, CV writing and work experience. Psychometric testing and consequent advice is available for fifth formers. The King's Bruton Gap Year programme is organised over two years. The first year is spent fundraising, and culminates in an expedition. The teams have previously climbed Mt Toubkal in Morocco and trekked across the Sinai Desert. When they leave school, those involved in the programme will spend time serving in an orphanage in Salam, India.

Admission. No child is admitted to the Senior School before age 13. Entry is via the Common Entrance or Scholarship Examinations.

Fees per term (2011-2012). Boarders £8,782, Day £6,285.

The fees are inclusive of necessary extras, eg Medical Attendance, Games.

The Preparatory School is at Hazlegrove House, Sparkford, 9 miles from Bruton, and takes pupils from age 2½–13. The fullest cooperation and continuity are ensured between the Preparatory and Senior School, boys and girls passing from one to the other having obtained a pass in Common Entrance.

(*For further details, see Hazlegrove's entry in IAPS section.*)

Old Brutonian Association. Contact with the Old Brutonian Association can be made via the school.

Charitable status. King's, Bruton is a Registered Charity, number 1071997. It exists to provide education for boys and girls from 13–18.

The King's School
Canterbury

Canterbury, Kent CT1 2ES
Tel: 01227 595501
        Bursar: 01227 595544
        Admissions: 01227 595579
Fax: 01227 766255
e-mail: headmaster@kings-school.co.uk
website: www.kings-school.co.uk

The origins of King's stand with the arrival of St Augustine in 597 AD. His foundation, centred on monastic life in Canterbury, combined worship, prayer and education, a tradition which has been continuously followed ever since. In 1541, the Foundation was re-formulated under King Henry VIII to become Canterbury Cathedral and the school to become The King's School. Thus it is that the Head Master, Lower Master and King's Scholars are part of the Cathedral Foundation.

Visitor: The Lord Archbishop of Canterbury

Governors:

Chairman: The Very Revd Dr R A Willis, BA, Dip Th, FRSA, Dean of Canterbury Cathedral
Vice-Chairman: Mrs M Berg, MSc Econ, MA
Dr C R Prior, DPhil, PhD
¶P J Stone, MA
¶Prof S J Gurr, BSc, ARCS, DIC, PhD, MA
Dr O Rackham, OBE, MA, PhD
The Ven S Watson, Archdeacon of Canterbury
The Revd Canon E F Condry, BA, BLitt, DPhil, MBA
¶A Stewart
Mrs E McKendrick, BA
The Revd Canon D C Edwards
¶N S L Lyons, MA
R De Haan, CBE, DL
The Revd Canon C P Irvine
J Tennant, MRICS
R C A Bagley, LLB

Clerk to the Governors: M R Taylor

Governors Emeriti:
The Very Revd J A Simpson, OBE, MA, DD
¶The Very Revd D L Edwards, DD
Sir Peter Ramsbotham, GCMG, GCVO
The Lady Kingsdown, OBE, DCL
¶Sir Robert Horton, LLD, BSc, SM, DCL, FIChemE, CMgt

Head Master: P J M Roberts, MA

Head Master's PAs:
Mrs C Finch
Mrs A S Kelly, BA

Lower Master: M J Lascelles, BA

Deputy Head Academic: G R Cocksworth, BA, MA
Deputy Head Pastoral: T Lee, BA

Head of Middle School: Dr H R O Maltby, MA, DPhil
Head of Lower School: R P Cook, BSc

Bursar: M R Taylor
Finance Bursar: Mrs L McKechnie, FCCA
Estates Bursar: G R H Merryweather, BSc

Registrar: R I Reilly, BA, MSc

Senior Tutor: M J Miles, MA
University and Careers Adviser: Ms P D Williams, MA, DipCG

Senior Chaplain: The Revd C F Arvidsson, DipTheol
Assistant Chaplain: The Revd M Robbins, BA, BTh

Librarian: Mrs S A L Gray, BSc Econ, MCLIP

Medical Officers:
Dr W Lloyd Hughes, MB BS
Dr J Fegent, MB BS

* *Head of Department*
† *Housemaster/mistress*

Art:
*D Cameron, BA
M McArdle, BA
Miss G C Oliver, BA
Mrs J Taylor-Goodman, BA, MA
I S Wallace, BA
D K Willis, BA
†N L Phillis, MA
R I Reilly, BA, MSc
*R P Sanderson, BA

Classics:
M W Browning, BA
Mrs H Johnson, BA
R P Mew, MA, ALCM
*Miss J Taylor, BA

Design:
M J Franks, BEd
*G J Swindley, BSc

Drama:
Mrs R J Beattie, BA, FRSA
*G E Sinclair, AGSM

Economics:
*†Mrs B Cocksworth, BSc
†Mrs L A Horn, BSc
R W Ninham, MA
Mrs R J Whitehead, MA

English:
Mrs J M Cook, BA
Miss K J Dover, BCI, BEd
M T Gardner, BA, MA
*A J W Lyons, BA, MA, FRSA
Ms C D Matthews, BA, MA
†Dr C E Pidoux, MA, PhD, ALCM
†Mrs C J Shearer, BA
J Soderholm, BA, MA, PhD
G P Tyndall, BA
Mrs A L Young, MA

Geography:
†S E Anderson, BA
M J Lascelles, BA

History:
Miss C E Anderson, BA, MA
J P Bass, BA
S J Graham, MA
H R O Maltby, MA, DPhil
*D J C Perkins, BA, MA, DipLaw, PhD

History of Art:
*D J Felton, BA, MA
Miss D M Francis, BA, DipEcol, Cert Vis

ICT:
Mrs L M Cousins, BA
*†A J Holland, BSc

Mathematics:
M O Cox, MA, MEng, Dip ITEC
†M P H Dath, L-ès-ScM, M-ès-ScM
J P E Dickson, BSc, MSc, RN
†P W Fox, MSc
Mrs J Gorman, BSc
A McFall, BSc
*S P Ocock, BA
Dr K J Palmer, BSc, PhD
R C Stuart, BSc
†R N Warnick, MA

Learning Support:
*Mme M-D Bradburn, BA
Ms G R Moorcroft, BEd, MA

Modern Languages:
*T J Armstrong, MA, MA Ed
Mrs A Browne, LSc
Miss B Cerda Drago, Lda
Miss R Corp, MA

Miss Z T Crawshaw, MA
J Gallardo Rodrígues, Ldo
Mrs M B Garcés-Ramón, Lda
Mrs N Geoffroy, L-ès-ScEd
T I Jennings, BA
Mrs L Liu, BA, MPhil
M J Miles, MA
†C P Newbury, BA
D P Rowlands, MA
Mrs L J Warnick, MA
Ms C L Wat, MA, BEd
*Miss R E White, BA
Miss F Zanardi, MA

*Mrs C A Cox, BA, MPhil
Miss T Lee, BA
†J W Outram, BA
The Revd M Robbins, BA, BTh
Miss C A Tyndall, BA

Music:
K Abbott, DipRCM
P R Barton Hodges, BMus
*H J P Ionascu, BMus, ARCM
S J R Matthews, MA
A Pollock, MA
N G Todd, MA

Politics:
Mrs D J Ardley, BA
I S MacEwen, MA
*O T Moelwyn-Hughes, BA, LLB, MSt

Physical Education:
Miss K Bradley, BSc
T G Hill, BSpSt
C M Roberts BA
*R A L Singfield, BEd

Religious Studies and Philosophy:
The Revd C F Arvidsson, DipTheol
G R Cocksworth, BA, MA

Science:

Biology:
†J M Hutchings, BA
Miss E J F Mitchell, BA
M J W Smiley, MA
†M J Thornby, BSc
Mrs J A Watson, BA, MSc, MIBiol
*S J Winrow-Campbell, BSc, MIBiol, CBiol

Chemistry:
*D M Arnott, BSc, PhD
R P Cook, BSc
Dr S Samad, BSc, PhD
D A Scott, BSc, MSc, MA Ed, MRSC
A S D Stennett, BSc
A R Stewart, MChem, PhD
E Sykes, BSc

Physics:
Miss C M Astin, MA, LTCL (*Science*)
*Miss L M Comber BSc
J T H Fox, BA
Mrs E S Ladd, BEng
M C Orders, BSc
D M Tanton, MA, MSc, DipD'I, PhD

Geology:
*R Churcher, BSc

Houses and Housemasters/mistresses:

School House: M J Thornby
The Grange: M P H Dath
Walpole: Mrs A L Young
Meister Omers: C P Newbury
Marlowe (*day*): S E Anderson
Luxmoore: Dr C E Pidoux
Galpin's: J M Hutchings
Linacre: J W Outram
Tradescant: N L Phillis
Broughton: Mrs C J Shearer
Mitchinson's (*day*): P W Fox
Jervis: Mrs L A Horn
Harvey: Mrs B Cocksworth
Bailey (*Sixth Form*): R N Warnick
Carlyon (*day*): A J Holland

The Junior King's School
Milner Court, Sturry, Nr Canterbury, CT2 0AY.
Tel: 01227 714000

Headmaster: P M Wells, BEd

(*For further details see King's Junior School entry in IAPS section.*)

Religion. The School's Christian tradition is at its heart and there is a desire to foster Christian virtues of love and justice, faith and courage, hope and perseverance. Of course, pupils and staff comprise individuals of different faiths and beliefs but there is a desire to aspire to Christian values. In the Cathedral, and in other places of worship, school services and prayers regularly take place.
Numbers and Organisation. There are currently 791 pupils on the school roll, 424 boys and 367 girls, 616 of which are boarders (78%). There are 6 boys' boarding houses, 6 girls' boarding houses and 3 day houses. Junior King's, the prep school of King's, occupies a site on the River Stour, in Sturry, 3 miles from Canterbury. There are currently 355 pupils at Junior King's, 198 boys and 157 girls.

The Senior School occupies various sites around the Cathedral and its Precincts. Many teaching departments and the majority of houses are in the beautiful ancient buildings around the Green Court, on the north side of the Cathedral. To the east of the Cathedral, the St Augustine's site is home to 5 boarding houses and the magnificent school library. There are 2 major sites for sport, Birley's and Blore's, each with extensive sports facilities.

Academic Life. The curriculum at King's is based upon strong academic roots. It emphasises and relies upon what is best in traditional independent school education: scholarly excellence supported by a caring pastoral and tutorial system, and a wide-ranging co-curricular programme. However, it is continually adapting and reacting to the changing demands of modern education: new subjects are added, new teaching techniques adopted, and there is an increasing awareness of the need to provide programmes of study that match individual needs and skills.

The curriculum is divided into three units: the Lower School (Shells, Year 9), an introductory year; the Middle School (Removes and Fifths, Years 10 and 11), working to IGCSEs; and the Sixth Form (6b and 6a, Years 12 and 13), taking AS and A Levels.

Music and Drama. The strongest encouragement is given to music and drama, and many entrance awards for music are available. Details are given in the Scholarships Section.

King's Week, the School's own festival of Music and Drama, attracts thousands of visitors each summer.

Sport and Outdoor Education. The major games are Rugby Football, Football, Netball, Tennis, Lacrosse, Fencing, Hockey, Athletics, Cricket, Rowing, Swimming and Sailing. Good facilities exist for all the usual sports. The Recreation Centre includes Swimming Pool, Squash Courts, Fencing Salle and Sports Hall.

Cultural recreation and hobbies are encouraged through some 25 societies managed (with advice) by the boys and girls themselves, and through a programme of "Activities" which occupies one afternoon each week. Many of these "Activities" are linked to the Duke of Edinburgh's Award Scheme and pupils are encouraged to gain the Bronze Award in their second (Remove) year. Lectures and recitals by distinguished visitors take place each term.

CCF, Social Service, Adventure Training and The Duke of Edinburgh's Award. Membership of the Combined Cadet Force is voluntary. The Social Service unit cooperates with kindred bodies in Canterbury. Bronze and Gold awards in The Duke of Edinburgh's Award Scheme may be taken.

Admission. Application should be made to the Assistant Registrar. It is advisable to register pupils at an early age. Admission is normally through the Common Entrance Examination, the King's School entry examination (for non-CE candidates) or, if academically able, through the School's own Scholarship Examination. The age of entry is about 13.

Fees per term (2011–2012). Senior School: £9,990 for boarders and £7,470 for day pupils. Junior School: £6,790 for boarders and £2,950–£5,005 for day pupils.

Entrance Scholarships and other awards. (*See Scholarship Entries section.*) Up to 20 King's Scholarships can be awarded if candidates of sufficient merit present themselves. The examination is held annually in March and is open to boys and girls under the age of 14 on 1st September. The awards may be up to 10% of the annual fee in every year (more in the case of need). Up to 12 Music Scholarships are offered each year in February. Sports Scholarships and

Awards are also offered in February, and Art Scholarships and Exhibitions are offered in March. Pupils entering the Sixth Form may compete for academic scholarships which will be offered as a result of the entrance examination in November. Music and Art scholarships will also be offered for competition in November.

Leaving Gifts and Closed Awards. The School has a number of these.

Some 25 offers of admission to Oxford and Cambridge are received each year.

OKS (Old King's Scholars). *Secretary*: C J R Jackson, c/o OKS & Foundation Office, 25 The Precincts, Canterbury CT1 2ES.

The King's Society exists for all parents, past and present. A termly programme of social and cultural events is open to all members and is published on the school website.

Charitable status. The King's School of the Cathedral Church of Canterbury is a Registered Charity, number 307942. It exists to provide education for boys and girls.

The King's School
Chester

Chester CH4 7QL
Tel: 01244 689500
Fax: 01244 689501
e-mail: info@kingschester.co.uk
website: www.kingschester.co.uk

The School was founded AD 1541 by King Henry VIII, in conjunction with the Cathedral Church of Chester. It was reorganised under the Endowed Schools Act in 1873, and by subsequent schemes of the Ministry of Education. The School is now Independent. The aim of the School is to prepare pupils for admission to Universities and the professions, and at the same time provide a liberal education.

Motto: '*Rex Dedit, Benedicat Deus.*'

Patron: His Grace the Duke of Westminster, KG, OBE, TD, DL

Governors:
D S Hempsall, MA, PhD, FRSA (*Chairman*)
The Rt Revd the Lord Bishop of Chester
The Very Revd the Dean of Chester
The Rt Worshipful the Lord Mayor of Chester
Mrs J L Clague, BA, ACA
M J P Cooke, FCA, MSIDip, AIIMR
J C Davies, MSc, CEng, FICE, MCIOB, MIWM
K Hassett, BA, MSc
K James, FCA
P M H Jessop, BA
Mrs E M Johnson, JP
Mrs K Kerr, MBA, BA
N Kirk, DipM, FCIM, ACIB
Dr D Pawson, BSc, PhD
Mrs R J Phillipson, BA, FCIPD
R A Storrar
Revd I M Thomas, MA
J N C Tweddle, BSc

Clerk to the Governors: S P Cross, LLB
Ex officio: CAOKS President

Headmaster: C D Ramsey, MA, late scholar of Corpus Christi, Cambridge

Deputy Head: Mrs K Crewe-Read, BSc
Deputy Head (*Academic*): J E Millard, BA
Deputy Head (*Pastoral*): M J Harle, BSc
Head of Sixth Form: T R Hughes, MA, MPhil
Head of Academic Administration: S Neal, BA

Head of Learning Support: Mrs S Glass, BA
Head of Co-curricular: R G Wheeler, BA

Assistant staff:
* *Head of Department*

Art and Design:
*S Downey, BA
Miss L Black, BA
Mrs A L Hollingworth, BA

Biology:
*R D J Elmore, BSc, MIBiol, CBS (*Acting Head*)
Ms H M Davies, MSc
Dr H C Faulkner, BSc, DPhil
Mrs P Housden, BEd
Ms J E Meredith, BSc, MIBiol
L A Parkes, BSc, MSc

Chemistry:
*A Cook, BSc, PhD
Dr C A Gleave, BSc, PhD
M J Harle, BSc
B Horne, BSc
Mrs J E Jepson, BSc
Dr J R Macnab, BSc, PhD
Mrs K L Russon, BSc

Classics:
*Mrs E A Shepherd, MA (*Acting Head*)
Mrs S H Gareh, BA, MA
M J P Punnett, MA

Design Technology:
*K M Lloyd, MA
Miss E Hodgson, BA
I Reid, BEd

Economics:
*S D Walton, BA, MSc
Mrs S Glass, BA
Miss E M Rowley, BSocSc
Miss E J Tappin, BA

English:
*R J Aldridge, BA
Miss H Brennan, MA
Ms H F Brown, BA
Mrs D Hearne, BA
Mrs H C Lydon, BA
Dr A M McMahon, MA, DPhil
R G Wheeler, BA

Geography:
*J H King, MA, MSc
Mrs R H Aldridge, BA
J A D Blackham, BA
T R Hughes, BA

History & Politics:
*S Neal, BA
Mrs G K Chadwick, BA
J C Heap, BA
P G Neal, BA

Information Technology:
*D G Lavender, BSc
Miss E J Tappin, BA

Mathematics:
*N A Shepherd, BSc

Junior School:
Head: S A Malone, BEd

Miss H E Bannaghan, MA
S D Bibby, BSc
C J Canty, BSc
Mrs S Cooper, BSc
Mrs K Crewe-Read, BSc
Mrs A Ignata, BSc
Mrs C E Lanceley, BSc
S J Parry, BA
Miss D Roberts, BSc
J M Ward, BSc

Modern Languages:
*P D Shannon, MA
Mrs J M Sabio, BA
M Sabio
Mrs E J Shannon, L-ès-L, Maîtrise
Mrs K L Shapland, MA
Mrs K J Thurlow-Wood, BA
Mme F Vergnaud, MA

Music:
*P F Robinson, BMus, LTCL (*Director of Music*)
Ms K Z Andrews, BMus, MA (*Head of Academic Music*)
Mrs V L S Latifa, BMus
J E Millard, BA
S A Rushforth (*Head of Strings*)
C J Wharton, BA (*Music Technology & Drums*)

Personal & Social Education:
*Ms J E Meredith, BSc, MIBiol

Physical Education:
*R Lunn, BEd
R I D Hornby, BA
B Horne, BSc (*Director of Football*)
Ms J Huck, BA
Mrs K Jones, BA (*Head of Girls' PE*)
C Morris, BEd
Mrs C Sumner, BA

Physics:
*N Heritage, MSc, PhD, MInstP, CPhys
G S Andrews, BEng
S Bosworth, MA, DPhil, FRAS
Ms H M Davies, MSc
N A Grisedale, MPhys
B Horne, BSc
Mrs J E Jepson, BSc

Religious Studies:
*J R Rees, BA
M S Lee, MA
Miss M A Wyatt, BA, MEd

Deputy Head: A Griffiths, BA
Director of Studies: T W Griffin, BA

Assistant Staff:

Miss J M Anderson, BA, CertEd	Mrs M D O'Leary, BA
	D M O'Neil, BSc
Mrs J Benson, BA	Mrs S Parker BEd
Mrs K Dickson, BA	J H Pownall, BEd
H J Duncalf, BEd	Mrs B A Roberts GRNCM
Mrs V M Gibson, BA	Mrs D L Rudd, BA
Mrs M M Griffin, BEd, MEd	Miss K A Savage, BA
K A Hollingworth, BEd	Mrs N M Tomlinson, BA
Mrs N C M Moffatt, BA	Mrs S Tomlinson, BEd

Peripatetic Staff:
Miss C Barker, BA (*Cello*)
Mrs F Cooke, MA, LRAM (*Voice*)
Mrs J Holmes, BA (*Oboe*)
Mrs V L Ierston, LTCL (*Piano & Flute*)
Miss R Jones, GMus, RNCM, LRAM, ARCM, FLCM (*Piano*)
G Macey, ATCL (*Woodwind*)
P D Oliver, BMus, LTCL (*Guitar*)
D Ortiz, BMus (*Brass*)
M Owens, BA (*Double Bass & Bass Guitar*)
A Parker, MA (*Saxophone*)
M Reynolds BA (*Piano*)
Mrs J Riekert, ATCL (*Flute*)
A Stamatakis-Brown, BMus (*Piano and Jazz piano*)
Mrs S E Tyson, MA (*Woodwind, Voice*)
Mrs J Williams, BA (*Bassoon*)
Mr T Wyss, ARCM, LRAM, LTCL (*Brass*)

Extra-Curricular Staff:
Director of Rowing: J A D Blackham, BA
Contingent Commander, CCF: Capt M S Lee, MA
Duke of Edinburgh's Award Coordinator: Miss D Roberts, BSc
Educational Visits Coordinator: R I D Hornby, BA

Bursar: Ms P C Mackay, BSc, ACA, DChA
Director of Marketing: Ms V M Titmuss, BA
Admissions Manager: Mrs E R Sears, BA
Estates Manager: M A Wright, BA
Head Librarian & Archivist: Mrs R Harding, MA
Examinations Officer: R D J Elmore, BSc, CBiol, MIBiol, CBS
School Nurse: Sister S J Catherall, RGN
Care Scheme Supervisor: Mrs L Hornby

Headmaster's PA: Mrs A M E Wilson, BA

Organisation. The School, which at present numbers 990, consists of (i) a Junior School for pupils aged 7 to 11 years, which is housed in a separate building, but is run in collaboration with (ii) the Upper School.

Admission. Boys and girls are admitted to the Upper School aged between 11 and 12, and may remain till the end of the year in which they become 18. Pupils in the Junior School normally move into the Upper School at the age of 11 on the evidence of academic ability tracked during their years at the Junior School. Students are admitted to the Sixth Form on the basis of GCSE results.

The Entrance Examinations for the Junior and Upper Schools are held in the Lent Term. Applications are made on a form obtainable from the School and on the website.

Academic. The subjects offered for study in the Sixth Form are – on the Arts side: Art, Business Studies, Classical Studies, Economics, English, English Language, French, Geography, German, History, Latin, Music, Music Technology, Philosophy, Politics, Religious Studies, Spanish; and on the Science side: Biology, Chemistry, Computing, Further Mathematics, Mathematics, Physics, Sports Science and Technology. It is possible to take most combinations of subjects at AS and A Level. All pupils in the Sixth Form take four subjects at AS Level but may drop to three subjects at A Level if they wish.

Spiritual life. The School is part of the Cathedral Foundation and regularly holds its own services in the Cathedral. Spiritual assemblies are held each week and there are two, pupil-led Christian Unions.

Music. Music is part of the general curriculum for all pupils up to the age of 14. After this music may be taken at GCSE and A Level. Private tuition in orchestral instruments, piano and organ is available. There are many musical ensembles and choral groups including the Schola Cantorum which leads the worship in Cathedral services.

Cadet Corps. There is a CCF contingent which gives pupils opportunities to develop leadership skills and to undertake adventurous training.

Outdoor Education. Opportunities are provided both within and outside the curriculum for outdoor education, and all pupils in each of the first three years of the senior school spend some days away at centres specialising in outdoor activities. In addition many pupils participate in the Duke of Edinburgh's Award Scheme at all levels.

Games. Soccer, Rugby, Hockey, Cricket, Rowing, Swimming, Badminton, Basketball, Athletics, Netball, Tennis, Squash, Golf, Rounders.

Buildings. Formerly situated adjacent to the Cathedral, the school moved into new buildings in 1960 situated in rural surroundings nearly 2 miles from the centre of Chester. Though the Junior and Upper Schools are on the same site of 32 acres, they are housed in separate buildings each having its own playing fields. In 1960 the new school was formally declared open by Her Majesty Queen Elizabeth the Queen Mother. In 1964 a new indoor Swimming Pool and Pavilion were opened.

More new buildings were added in the 1980s. In May 1989 Her Royal Highness the Princess Margaret formally opened a development consisting of ten new classrooms, four new laboratories, a music school, an art room, a Sixth Form centre, sports hall, general purposes room for the Junior School, new kitchen, tutorial rooms and offices. In September 1989 the Senior School went from two to three form entry.

In 1994 an extension to the Junior School buildings was completed and from September 1994 boys were admitted at 7. In 1998 girls were admitted to the Sixth Form. In January 2000 a new Library/IT Centre was opened.

In September 2003 the school became co-educational throughout and the senior school moved to four-form entry. A major building programme has taken place over the last five years. An all-weather playing surface for hockey and football is now in use and the art and technology studios have been considerably enlarged and improved. A new Music School opened in April 2005. The latest development has been the creation of a new performance venue, The Vanbrugh Theatre, which opened in June 2011.

Chester Association of Old King's Scholars. The School has what is believed to be the country's oldest former pupils' association, started in 1866. Hon Secretary: Adrian Ackroyd, 5 St Christopher's Close, Chester CH3 5BP (Tel: 01244 390819; e-mail: adrian.ackroyd@kingsonline. org.uk). This association comes under the umbrella of OAKS, the Organisation for the Alumni of the King's School, whose offices in school administer alumni relations.

Fees per term (2011-2012). Tuition: Upper School £3,544, Junior School £2,716. The School offers a small number of bursaries annually.

Scholarships. *At 11+*: Academic scholarships of £500 are awarded to pupils at the end of their first year in the Senior School. Scholars carry the title 'King's Scholar' throughout their time at the school.

Tenable in the Sixth Form: (1) Alfred McAlpine Scholarship of £1,000; (2) Keith Oates Scholarship of £1,000.

Tenable at Universities: (1) Old King's Scholars Exhibition: £450 over 3 years; (2) Robert Platt Exhibition: £500;

(3) John Churton Exhibition: £500; (4) Haswell Exhibition: £500; (5) Finchett Maddock Exhibition: £500; (6) King's School Parents' Association: two exhibitions of £600 over 3 years.

Charitable status. The King's School, Chester is a Registered Charity, number 525934. The aim of the charity is to provide a sound education to all boys and girls who can benefit from it regardless of their economic and social background.

The King's School
Ely

Ely, Cambs CB7 4DB
Tel: 01353 660701 (Head)
          01353 660700 (Director of Business & Administration)
Fax: 01353 667485 (Head)
          01353 662187 (Director of Business & Administration)
e-mail: enquiries@kings-ely.cambs.sch.uk
website: www.kingsschoolely.co.uk

The school traces its origins back to the 7th century AD and the foundation of the abbey church at Ely. In 1541 Henry VIII reconstituted the school by royal charter; hence its name. Its statutes were confirmed by Elizabeth I and Charles II. Since 1879 the school has been a registered charity.

Henry VIII stipulated that up to twelve senior boys should be King's Scholars, and in 1973 they were joined by twelve girls, at the request of HM Queen Elizabeth II. The King's and Queen's Scholars, together with the Head, are members of the Foundation of Ely Cathedral – an indication of the strong links between school and Cathedral. The magnificent Cathedral is used, in effect, as the school chapel for regular worship, and the school educates the Cathedral choristers.

The King's School Ely has a reputation as an exceptionally warm, friendly and welcoming school. Its pupils represent a wide range of ability and interests, from the highly academic to those with predominantly practical or creative talents. The school turns out young people who are considerate, adaptable and self-confident but free of arrogance – and who are often delighted to acknowledge that they have exceeded their own and their parents' expectations. This is an environment where young people are empowered to achieve beyond expectation.

Visitor: The Rt Revd Stephen Conway, Bishop of Ely

Governors:
Chairman: R P Slogrove
Vice-Chairman: J Hayes
Chairman of Executive and Finance Committee: Mrs J A Swann, LLB, ACA, MABRP
Mrs M Benfield, JP
The Very Revd Dr Michael Chandler, Dean of Ely
B D Fraser, BSc, MBA
Mrs A Kenna, MEd, LRAM
Mrs F Martin-Redman
A J Morbey
C B Morris, FRICS
R Phillips, QC
The Revd Canon David Pritchard, BA, FRCO, LTCL
Prof M Proctor, FRS
Dr N Richardson MA (*Chairman of Academic Committee*)
Dr K Skoyles, LLB, LLM, PhD
Professor A Wyllie, FRS

Head: Mrs S E Freestone, MEd, GRSM, LRAM, ARCM, FRSA

Deputy Head of Senior School: G Parry, BSc, PhD, PGCE
Deputy Head (Academic): I G Young, BSc, PhD, PGCE
Deputy Head (Development): Mrs F A Blake, BA, PGCE

Head of Junior School: R J Whymark, BA Ed
Deputy Head of Junior School: A Marshall, BSc, PGCE

Head of King's Acremont: Dr L Brereton, BSc, PhD, PGCE
Head of Nursery and Deputy Head of King's Acremont: Mrs M Brogan, CertEd

Director of Business and Administration: P A H Coutts, MA, PGCE
Director of Operations: M Hart
Chaplain: The Revd T P Humphry, BA, MA
Medical Officer: A S Douglas, BMedSci, BM, BS, DRCOG, SPCert
PA to the Head: Mr T Kingsnorth
Admissions Coordinator: Mrs D Burton

Assistant Staff, Senior School:

J R Atkinson, MA	I A McWhinney, BSc
Mrs P Blair, MA, BA Hons, PGCE	S Merrell, BA, TCert
Miss C Bond, HBA	M C Nicholas
D Burke, BSc, PGCE	P B North, BA
S G Cavill, BSc, PGCE	Dr W K Pitt, BEd, PhD
Miss A C Charlton, BEd	N J Reckless, MA, PGCE
G Couper-Marsh, BSc, PGCE	Mrs L Reid, MA, FRCO
Miss R Crabtree, MA, PGCE	J Rees, BA, MA, PGCE
F Danes, BA, PGCE	Mrs A J Rhodes, BA, MA
K R Daniel, BA, PGCE	J W Riley, MA, CertEd
Miss M P Day, BA, LRAM, MTC	T Roe
R P Emms, BA, PGCE	Mrs E Salgado, BA Hons, PGCE
M C D Ewan, BEng, PGCE	K Shaw, BSc
Mrs L Goosen, BA, PGCE	Ms C P Skeels, BSc, DPhil, PGCE
G P L Griggs, BMus, MA, GRNCM, FRCO, PGCE	Ms G Smith, MA, MTh, PGCE
O Hancock	L Smith, BA Hons, PGCE
M G Hawes, BA, PGCE	Mr I Sutcliffe, BA Hons
D J Hodgson, BSc, PGCE	Ms P Stevens, BA Hons, PGCE
J Houlston, BMus	Mrs S Stirrup, BEd, MA
B S Jackson, BEng, PGCE	A J Thomas, MEd, BA, PGCE
Miss C Juneau, BA Hons, MA, PGCE	Mrs J R Thomas, MA, PGCE
Ms K Keen, BSc, PGCE	A Thompson, BSc, MSc, PGCE
E W M Kittoe, BSc Hons, PGCE	N A Tooth, BSc, PGCE
D Kittson, HND, CertEd, FETC, ACIS, PACA	T Villalon, QTS
Miss S E Knibb, BA, PGCE	Mrs A Ward, MA, PGCE
P A Lott, BSc, PGCE	T Ward, BA Hons, PGCE
Mrs J P Mackay, BSc	Ms A Whitehead, BSc, MSc, PGCE
Ms R Maguire, BA Hons, MA, PGCE	N Williams, MA Ed, BA Hons, PGCE
Mrs P Maitland, BSc Hons, PGCE	Miss H A Wright, BEd, CertEd
Ms R McLeman, MA Hons, PGCE	F K Young, BA, PGCE

Assistant Staff, Junior School:

D A Boothroyd, BEd	Dr A Duane, BA Hons, MSc, PhD
Mrs R J Chapman, BEd	T Eddy, PGCE
Miss C Collins, PGCE	Mrs P Foulds, BEd
Mrs J Currah, BEd	Miss S Green
E J Davis, BA, BA, PGCE, MA	Mrs E Hammond, BSc, PGCE
Ms M Delaveau, BA, CPLP2, PGCE	H J James
Mrs E Diss, BA, PGCE, DipSpLD	Miss A E Kippax, BSc, HND, DipSpLD

Miss C Kyndt, BA Hons, MSc, PGCE
J A Lowery, BA, PGCE
Mrs C Middleton, BSc, PGCE, MEd
R M Oliver, BSc, PGCE
N M Ovens, BA, CertEd
D M Parratt, BEd
Mrs K Pearce, BA, PGCE
Mrs A R Pearson, CertEd
Mrs B A Pope, CertEd
N Porter-Thaw, LTCL, DipTCL
R F Powell, BA, CertEd

Mrs K Prior, DipSpLD, CertEd
Mrs L H F Roberts, BSc, PGCE
Mrs N Sivier, GMus, LGSM
Miss K Sudbury, BEd, MA
N Tetley, BA, PhD, PGCE
Mrs N Van Wright, BFA
Miss R Watkins, BEd
Ms R Watkins, MEd, BEd
Mrs J Whymark
M A Wilkinson, BA, PGCE
Mrs A J Wilson, BEd

Assistant Staff, King's Acremont:

Mrs C M Burgess, BA, PGCE
Mrs K Furness, BA, PGCE
Ms J H Lyall, BA, PGCE

Miss H Major, BMus, PGCE
Miss T Miller
Mrs K Wylie, BTec Dip
Mrs A G Wynn, BEd

In addition 26 visiting music teachers.

Organisation. The school is fully co-educational from the ages of 3 to 18. The total roll is 1,003 and more than a quarter of pupils over the age of eight are boarders.

The school is divided into four parts: King's Acremont, the Nursery and Pre-Prep for children from age 3 years to Year 2, standing in its own grounds at Acremont House; King's Junior for Years 3–8; King's Senior for Years 9–13 and King's International.

Buildings. The school still uses many of Ely's medieval monastic buildings – as boarding houses, as classrooms and as the dining hall. The 14th century Porta, the great gateway to the monastery, has been converted into a magnificent new Senior School library. Other new buildings show the continuing and substantial investment in modern facilities: the renovated Georgian villa that now houses the Nursery and Pre-Prep section of King's Acremont; a brand new Art School and Performance Studies block, housing the new Dance Studio and 'Black Box' Drama Studio; a Technology Centre; a senior Music School and Recital Hall and a self-contained, two-storey accommodation including seven classrooms and a science laboratory for Years 7 and 8.

The Nursery and Pre-Prep curriculum at King's Acremont introduces children to systematic planned learning. Teaching starts from where each child is, in terms of experience and development, not from a pre-determined idea of where they should be. Children are encouraged to express what they have experienced in their growth and learning – in their own way and at an appropriate pace – to help them absorb and consolidate their experience. Teaching is mainly on a class-teacher basis.

The curriculum in the Nursery and Reception classes is geared towards the Foundation Stage laid down by the Government through the Qualifications & Curriculum Authority. Children in Years 1 and 2 follow – and indeed go beyond – the National Curriculum at Key Stage 1. The areas of learning covered in the Pre-Prep are: Personal, Social and Emotional Development, Communication, Language and Literacy, Mathematical Development, Knowledge and Understanding of the World, Physical Development and Creative Development. French begins in the Reception class.

During Year 2 there is constant liaison with Year 3 staff in the Junior School to ensure that children are fully prepared for the next stage of their education. The move to the Junior School for Year 3 (at age 7+) ensures continuity of teaching of the Key Stage 2 curriculum.

King's Acremont offers working parents the option of an 8 am Breakfast Club, After School Care until 6 pm and Holiday Club.

The Junior School curriculum is planned to give breadth and depth to the pupils' learning experience. Subject

specialists coordinate the work of each department and ensure progression from year to year. Heads of Year supervise the pupils' academic progress and meet weekly with the Director of Studies and Head to review the individual progress. Regular standardised and criteria-referenced assessments ensure that teachers' planning is informed and that pupils' progress in key areas is recorded and reported to parents. QCA Y3–5 interim tests and Key Stage 2 SATs in core subjects allow us to measure pupils against their peer group nationally.

All the foundation subjects are covered in each year but able students commence Latin in Year 7. Modern Foreign Languages begin in Year 3 as do ICT and Technology. Specialised teaching rooms for Science, Art, Design Technology, Drama, Learning Support and a purpose-built Music Suite offer an enhanced learning experience to all pupils. A new building, opened in August 2003, provides excellent Science facilities, eight large modern classrooms, a second ICT suite and an attractive resource and communal area.

Examination results are high and the school prides itself on being at the forefront of developments in the educational world.

During the school day all children are divided among four co-educational Houses for pastoral and competitive purposes; each of these houses is staffed by male and female members of the teaching staff. King's Junior School has one co-educational boarding house and one for the boy choristers of Ely Cathedral who are all pupils of King's Junior School. There is a wide range of extra-curricular opportunities both at lunch times and after school.

The Senior School curriculum. The amount of academic choice that pupils can exercise grows as they move through the Senior School: options in the Sixth Form are very flexible, and the sets are often small. Up to GCSE (Year 11) there is a compulsory core of English, Mathematics, Religious Studies and Sciences. In addition every pupil chooses up to four option subjects from: Art, Business Studies, Classical Civilisation, Design & Technology (Resistant Material Technology, Food and Nutrition), Drama, English as a Foreign Language, French, Geography, German, History, Latin, Music, Physical Education, Spanish.

The entry qualification for the Sixth Form is not less than six C grades with B grades in subjects selected for A Level. Twenty-seven AS/A2 Level subjects are offered in Years 12 and 13.

Extra-Curricular Activities. Music, art, drama, outdoor pursuits, sports, practical hobbies and interests – all are catered for in a large range of lunchtime and after-hours activities.

The Ely Scheme. All pupils in Year 9 are introduced to the school's distinctive outdoor pursuits programme, the Ely Scheme, which provides a training in practical and personal skills and in teamwork, initiative and leadership. For some pupils it leads on to the Duke of Edinburgh's Award Scheme or to specialised activities such as climbing.

Art, Drama and Music. Music is strong, as one would expect in a school that is so closely linked to the Cathedral. There is a full programme of performances for school and public audiences, and regular tours overseas. Nearly half of all pupils have personal tuition in a musical instrument; many learn two or even three. An outstanding new Art School, opened in March 2010, inspires fine art, sculpture, ceramics, photography and textiles. All parts of the school present plays every year in addition to productions by year or ad-hoc groups.

Games. The main sports are rowing, rugby, soccer, netball, hockey and cricket. Athletics, badminton, basketball, tennis, sailing, squash, swimming, golf and horse-riding are also available. All pupils are encouraged to take part in team games, and there is a full programme of fixtures against other schools.

Religious Worship. The Junior and Senior Schools worship regularly in Ely Cathedral. Other services weekly are also in accordance with the principles of the Church of England. The Bishop conducts a confirmation service for pupils in the Lent term. However, all denominations (or none) are warmly welcome.

Exeats. Boarders are granted weekend exeats on the written request of a parent or guardian. Weekly boarding is increasingly popular.

Admission. Application forms can be obtained from the Admissions Department. Admission to King's Acremont is by interview; to King's Junior School by interview and qualifying examination; and to King's Senior School at 13+ by the school's entrance examination or an equivalent. A £65 fee is payable at first registration. Pupils may enter the school at any time, although an Autumn start is recommended; and they may stay at the school until the year in which they become 19.

Scholarships and Exhibitions. (*See Scholarship Entries section.*) Scholarships and Exhibitions up to a cumulative total of 25% (15% in King's Junior School) of fees are awarded for achievement and potential in academic work, music, art, design & technology, drama and sports.

Choristerships are available for both boys and girls. The school supports the music of Ely Cathedral by providing discounts for choristers, ex-choristers and members of Ely Cathedral Girls' Choir. Additional bursary support may be available to new pupils over the age of eleven, whose parents are unable to pay the full tuition fee.

Fees per term (2011-2012). *King's Acremont Nursery and Pre-Prep*: Nursery places are booked by the session (morning or afternoon) and the day of the week; full care for five days a week would be £2,450. The fee for Pre-Prep Reception to Year 2 is £2,636 (no boarding). Pre- and after-school care and holiday club are available at extra charge.

King's Junior: Years 3 and 4: £3,725 (day); £5,939 (boarding); Years 5 to 8: £4,064 (day); £6,268 (boarding). There is no Saturday morning school for Years 3 and 4. There is an optional programme on Saturday mornings for pupils in Years 5 and 6. From Year 7 Saturday morning school is a compulsory part of the school week.

King's Senior: Years 9 to 13: £5,615 (day); £8,128 (boarding).

Flexi-boarding: It may be possible to offer overnight accommodation for day pupils on an occasional basis at a cost of £31.75 per night. The cost of extended flexi-boarding will be quoted in advance upon application to the Bursar.

Concessions: for children of the clergy or of members of the armed services a 10% discount is available. Bursaries may be awarded in cases of financial need.

Old Eleans. Former pupils receive news of the school and of their contemporaries and are invited annually to events.

Charitable status. The King's School, Ely is a Registered Charity, number 802427. Its aims and objectives are to offer excellence in education to day and boarding pupils.

The King's School
Gloucester

Gloucester GL1 2BG
Tel: 01452 337337
Fax: 01452 337314
e-mail: office@thekingsschool.co.uk
website: www.thekingsschool.co.uk

The King's School, Gloucester is one of the seven famous Cathedral Schools established by Henry VIII in 1541. It has grown over the centuries into the leading provider of Independent education in the area, with around 500 pupils, girls and boys aged three to eighteen. King's offers academic excellence, outstanding pastoral care and a unique programme to identify and develop individual talents and personal qualities. The inspiring Cathedral setting is unequalled; giving a special sense of identity and encouraging a moral framework and a powerful sense of community.

In a recent Inspection by the Independent Schools Inspectorate the School was praised for its "outstanding pastoral care" and "special sense of identity" and the pupils were found to have "a positive attitude to study and high standards of behaviour".

Music and Drama play a very important role with regular concerts and performances being staged throughout the year and pupils are actively encouraged to participate in the many extra-curricular activities on offer. King's is also proud of its status within the sporting community particularly with its academy alliances with both Gloucestershire County Cricket Club and Gloucester Rugby Club.

Motto: *Via Crucis via Lucis.*

Governing Body:

Chairman: Mr J H Holroyd, CB, CVO, MA

Canon N Heavisides, MA	Mrs S White, MA
Canon C Thomson, MA	Mr P Markey, BSc
Reverend Canon D Hoyle	Mr C Collier
Mrs A Cadbury, OBE, JP, DL	Mr P Lapping
	Mr A Brett, BSc, PSC, MInst RE
Miss C Holme, JP, LLB	
Mr C Major, LLB	Mr R Slawson, RIBA
Mr J H Smith, BSc, DipEd	Mr P Lachecki, BSc
Mr T Heal, FRICS	

Headmaster: **A K J Macnaughton**, MA

Deputy Head (Academic): Mr D J Evans, MA
Deputy Head (Pastoral): Miss V S Scholes, BEd, MBA

* Head of Department

English & Drama:
*Dr M C Craddock, BA, PhD
Mrs L Harrison, BA
Mr A K J Macnaughton, MA
Miss C J Rowland, BA, PGCE
Mrs S Shousha Ben-Aziza, BA, PGCE
Mrs C Herring

Mathematics:
*Mr P Goldbrum, MSc
Mrs S Rodford, BEd
Mrs S Miskin, BA
Mr J Withers, BA, PGCE
Mr S Cheasley, BSc, PGCE

Modern Languages:
*Mrs S Michell, MIL, PGCE
Mr P Arnison, BA
Miss A F Williams, BA
Mrs H Cleland, MA, MSc

Geography:
*Miss R Lewis, BSc, PGCE
Mr W Joyce, BSc

History:
*Miss Helen Colson, BA
Mr S Munnion, MA
Mr D J Evans, MA

Classics:
*Mr P O'Brien, BA
Mrs P Fayter, BA
Miss J Ruckert, MA

Religious Studies:
*Mr J M Webster, MA, BD (*Chaplain*)
Mr D J Griffiths, BEd, DipRS

Economics & Business Studies:
*Mr D A Lloyd, BSc Econ
Mr D Butler, BA, PGCE, NPQH

Art, Design & Technology:
*Miss C Billingsley, BA
Miss L A Lewis, BDes
Mr J S Collins, BA
Mr R A Gadd, BA, QTS
Mrs J Fowler, BA

Science:
*Mr A G Moore, BSc
Mr S Harrison, MA
Mrs B J Rouan-North, BSc
Miss V Scholes, BSc
Mr G Huband, BSc
Miss A E Talbot, BSc, MPhil
Mr B T Hogg, MSc

ICT:
Mr B Calderwood, BEd

Music:
*Mr D Harris, DipRCM, GRSM
Mrs S Pender, ALCM, BMus, PGCE

Physical Education:
*Mr A J Phillips, BA
Mrs J D Fenn, BEd

Mr L E Robson, BEd
Mrs M J Phillips, BA
Mr A N Bressington, BSc, GTP

Miss L A Pike, BSc

Psychology:
Mrs L Sutton

Junior School:
Head of Junior School: Mr C W Dickie, BEd

Director of Studies: Mrs E I Tuffill, BA

Mrs C J Hadfield, BEd	Miss S M Linton, BA
Mrs C A McKane, MEd, BA	Miss L A Cousins, NNEB
Mrs S E Jelf, NNEB	Mrs N Coates, BEd
Mrs H M McVittie, BA	Mrs K Woodcock, NVQ III
Mrs P Williams, NNEB	Mrs N J Fear, NNEB
Mr S P Williams, BSc	Mrs A Martin, NNEB
Mrs C M Griffiths, BEd	Mr R Cooper, BEd
Mrs R Woodliffe, DipEd, AISTD	Miss J Phillips, BMus, PGCE
Miss J C Johnson, BA	Miss J Bryan, BEd
Miss J Fowler, BA	Mrs A Wyman, BEd

Learning Support:
*Mrs M Connell, CertEd, AGSM, Dip SpLD
Mrs J Rochfort, BEd

Library Support:
Mrs A Youldon, BSc, Dip Inf Sc
Mrs A Houghton, BA, MCLIP

After School Care:
Mrs G Southgate, BEd
Mrs L Hurst

Personal & Social Education: *Mr D J Griffiths, BEd
Careers: Ms A Williams, BA

Music Department (Instrumental and Singing Teachers):
Mrs A Adiri, BMus (*Violin*)
Miss J M Beddoe, LTCL, ATCL (*Clarinet and Saxophone*)
Mrs C Burton, BA (*Piano*)
Mr R A Burton, GBSH, ARCS, ABSM (*Singing*)
Mr S Field, BA
Mrs M Cope (*Piano*)
Mrs H Crown (*Flute*)
Mr R P Goode, ALCM (*Acoustic, Classical, Electric and Bass Guitar*)
Mr I Russell (*Brass*)
Mrs E Platten, BMus (*Singing*)
Ms J Tomlinson, LRAM, RAMProfCert (*Cello*)
Mr J Trim, BMus, MMus, LRAM (*Violin, Viola and Senior Strings*)
Mr G Watson (*Drum Kit*)

Bursar: Mrs N Mosley, BA, ACA
Clerk of Works: Mr A Spencer
Registrar: Mrs S Bird, BA

Medical Centre Staff:
Dr I Jarvis, MB, BCh
Mrs M Johnson

Structure of the School. The school provides a day education for boys and girls aged 3–18 years. The most common ages for entry are at 3, 7, 11, 13 and 16 years, however, children are welcomed across all year groups with provision for entrance at any point during the academic year.

For administrative purposes, the school is divided into the following sections:

Junior School: aged 3–11 (incorporating the Nursery, Wardle House, ages 3–5).

Senior School: aged 11–18.

Junior School (including the Nursery). The Junior School is staffed by class teachers chosen for their expertise in working with young children. There is a close liaison with the specialist teachers in the senior school to ensure continuity in teaching and the curriculum. The Head of the Junior School is responsible to the Headmaster of King's School for the day to day running of the Junior School. The Junior School shares a common site with the Senior School and benefits from use of the Technology Centre, ICT Suite, Gymnasium and Dining Hall, as well as taking part in full school assemblies in the Cathedral. After school care is available and Holiday Club which runs for 50 weeks of the year.

Senior School. The transition from class teaching to subject based set teaching is carried out gradually to enable the pupils to feel secure in their educational environment. Pastoral care is form-based with Tutors and Year Heads monitoring the progress of each pupil and liaising closely with parents.

The Senior School is based round the Cathedral buildings with their attractive gardens. Whilst the classrooms afford a sense of history and excellent learning, as well as having outlooks over the Cathedral Close, the laboratories and Technology suite are housed in modern buildings and are equipped to cope with current curriculum demands. The school playing fields, home to premiership cricket squares and Rugby pitches, are nearby at Archdeacon Meadow. Here, other facilities are available including indoor swimming pool, gym, and tennis courts.

The school is proud of its tradition of personal discipline which is based on mutual respect and self esteem. The relationship between pupils and staff is at the same time friendly and well defined. A coordinator of Personal and Social Education oversees the cross curricular themes essential to the development of the whole person in this challenging world.

The Sixth Form Centre in Dulverton House provides an academic and social focus for senior students.

The Curriculum. The principal foundations on which the curriculum of The King's School rests are The National Curriculum and the distinctive aims of our own school which emphasis individuality and contain a commitment "to stimulate all pupils to the greatest possible academic, creative and extra-curricular achievement".

Through the core curriculum in Junior School and up to the end of the Fifth Form (Y11) a clear emphasis is placed on acquiring skills in speaking and listening, literacy and numeracy. The GCSE core curriculum includes English, Religious Studies, Mathematics and at least one Science subject. The majority of pupils are encouraged to include a foreign language and a second Science subject in addition, but the key focus is on genuine choice based on eprsonal aptitudes and interests.

Although mindful of the national requirements, we also value the freedom to develop our own curriculum in ways that suit the needs of our pupils. With our commitment to small class sizes, we are able to go well beyond the confines of the National Curriculum by offering:

- a flexible and wide choice of subject options, a timetable which is uniquely tailored to individual choices
- a strong moral and spiritual perspective fostered through Chapel, Religious Studies and PSHE
- a commitment to areas of study which are not included in National Curriculum arrangements
- an emphasis on open-ended independent learning and cross-curricular work through special project weeks
- Lessons which are engaging, providing many opportunities for oral participation and encouraging pupils to think for themselves.

Pupil progress is assessed formally through end of unit tests in Junior School and half-termly assessments in Senior School. We also hold examinations in both Junior and Senior School and operate our own internal tracking based on standardised tests. Progress is encouraged through a school ethos which is purposeful without being unduly pressurised or overly competitive.

Junior School is non-selective and caters for a wide range of abilities. Senior School has a more restricted range, since its curriculum is designed for those of high or average academic ability. Within that broad remit, we welcome all those who can access our curriculum and make the most of the opportunities on offer in the school. Treating every pupil as an individual is important to us. We have high expectations of achievement and seek to encourage intellectual curiosity and ambition in our more able pupils through the enrichment programme which operates in both Junior School and Senior School.

Games and Activities. A full range of games is available with the main games being Rugby, Hockey and Cricket for boys and Hockey, Netball, Tennis and Rounders for girls. Senior pupils are able to participate in a whole range of minor games including Squash and Badminton, and Athletics is also available. A well-equipped Gymnasium at The Riverside Centre, at Archdeacon Meadow, provides the focus for Physical Education; Dance and Drama are fully integrated in the curriculum. Swimming lessons are an important part of the curriculum throughout the school, the annual House swimming gala being a very competitive event.

The school's main playing field, Archdeacon Meadow, is an approved county cricket ground. The King's School is a Junior Academy of Gloucestershire County Cricket Club and a Partnership School with the Gloucester and England RFU Junior Academy.

Its proximity to Kingsholm and its special relationship with Gloucester Rugby Football Club has enabled the school to become a centre of excellence in the sport. Overseas sports tours are held regularly for boys and girls.

The school offers the Duke of Edinburgh's Award scheme, a comprehensive outdoor pursuits programme and a wide range of clubs and societies. Annual overseas expeditions go as far afield as Ecuador and Mongolia.

Music and the Performing Arts. There is a strong tradition of musical excellence as befits a Cathedral Choir School, where all pupils are encouraged to appreciate music. A good proportion of the school receives instrumental tuition and the various choirs, orchestras and ensembles play regularly in the Cathedral, and in the local area. Music Technology includes DAT, MIDI, multitrack, synthesis, sequencing and music publishing. The school is a Choir School and as such provides the trebles for the Cathedral choir, and has a number of music scholarships and bursaries endowed for that purpose. As well as providing a succession of Oxbridge organ scholars, the school provides a full range of musical activities.

Dance and Drama are very popular at the school and productions are arranged in the School Hall, the Cathedral, and in local theatres. Both are features of the curriculum throughout the school. The summer Performing Arts Festival has recently become a featured climax to the school year.

Religious Worship. Whilst pupils from all denominations are warmly welcomed, the religious services are in accordance with the principles of the Church of England. Most days start with an Assembly, usually in the Cathedral and of a nature to suit each age group. A strong chaplaincy team, led by the School Chaplain, supports the spiritual development of pupils and staff alike.

Admission. Junior School: a Taster Day and low-key assessment of each child. Senior School: entrance tests are given for each pupil. At key entry points: 11+ or 13+ examinations, Common Entrance Examination or other tests appropriate to a child's previous education. However, applications for entrance are welcomed and accommodated throughout the Academic year.

Fees per term (2011-2012). These are staged according to age. Junior School £1,995–£3,920; Senior School £4,580–£5,320.

Scholarships. (*See Scholarship Entries section.*) Cathedral Choristerships receive a Scholarship worth 75% of tuition fees. Academic Scholarships and Non-Academic Awards for Sport, Music, Art and Drama are available at

ages 11+, 13+ and 16+. Governors' Bursaries are also available.

King's School Society. *Hon Sec*: c/o King's School, Gloucester GL1 2BG.

Charitable status. The King's School of the Cathedral Church of Gloucester is a Registered Charity, number 1080641. It exists to provide for the education of Cathedral Choristers and others, within a co-educational environment.

The King's School
Macclesfield

Macclesfield, Cheshire SK10 1DA
Tel: 01625 260000
Fax: 01625 260022
e-mail: mail@kingsmac.co.uk
website: www.kingsmac.co.uk

Situated in rolling Cheshire countryside on the edge of the Peak District, the School was founded by the Will of Sir John Percyvale in 1502. The school offers an academic education through a unique combination of mixed and single sex education. The school places a high emphasis on high academic standards, its extensive range of extra-curricular activities and prides itself on pastoral care.

Patron: The Rt Hon The Earl of Derby, MC

Chairman of the Governors: A Dicken

Head of Foundation: S Hyde, DPhil

Senior Staff:

Deputy Headmaster: D J Pook, BA, ThM

Principal of Boys: I J Robertson, BSc
Principal of Girls: Mrs S E Spence, BA
Principal of Juniors: Mrs C J Hulme-McKibbin, BEd
Principal of Sixth Form: T H Andrew, BA

Vice-Principal of Sixth Form: Mrs R Roberts, BA
Vice-Principal of Boys: P M Edgerton, MA
Vice-Principal of Girls: Mrs E P Olsen, BA
Vice-Principal of Juniors: Mrs A Lea, BMus
Vice-Principal (Infants): Mrs E L Warburton, BEd
Senior Teacher (Admissions): Mrs C A Harrison, BSc
Senior Teacher (Staff Development): Mrs V B White, BEd, MA
Director of Finance: J M Spencer Pickup

R W Abbotson, BA	Mrs L Booker, MMedSci, BA
Miss M Acharya, BA	Mrs H L Broadley, BSc
Mrs L F Adams, BA	Mrs K Brookes, BA
Mrs R A Agour, BA	Mrs J E Brown, BSc
Mrs A E Alderson, BA	M J Brown, MSc, BSc
Miss Z M Arthur, MEng, BA	Mrs C Buckley, HND
Mrs V F A Atkins, BSc	Mrs M Byrne, BA
Mrs D C Baker, BA	S A Carpenter, BSc
Mrs C M A Bailey, BA	Mrs J Cole, BA
Mrs K L Bailey, BA	P J Colville, BSc, MSc
Mrs A N J Balcombe, BSc	Miss H L Connaughton, BA
Dr G N Banner, BA, MA, PhD	Dr L Craig, BA, PhD
Mrs D M Barker, BEd	Mrs L Cunliffe, BSc
Mrs J T Barratt, GTCL Hons, LTCL Pft	I E Dalgleish, BA
J P Bartle, BSc	Miss E M De Maine, BA
Miss H K Barton, BSc	Miss L C Derby, BA
Mrs J Beesley, BA	Mrs A Eardley, BA
Mrs C H Bingham, BSc	Miss K E Easby, BA, MA
Miss K-J Birch, MEng	C J A Fico, BA
	Dr J A Fitzgerald, BSc, MSc, PhD

D A Forbes, BA
Mrs M A F Gartside, BSc
D Gee, CertEd
Mrs K Griffin, MA
P F Halewood, CertEd
Mrs J Hankinson, TCert
D M Harbord, CertEd, BA
R J Harding, BA, MA
Dr S J Hartnett, DPhil, BSc
Dr A M Hazel, MMath, MSc, PhD
Dr C P Hollis, PhD, BSc Hons, CPhys, MInstP
Mrs M Holmes, BA
Mrs L E Hopper, BSc
M T Houghton, BA
P Illingworth, BSc, CPhys, MInstP
Miss D Inman, BA
R N Jackson, BA
Mrs A M Johnson, BA
Mrs L M Johnston, CertEd
J W Jones, BSc, BEd
Mrs C L Keen, BEd
A Koido, BA
Dr I Lancaster, BSc, MSc, PhD
P P Livingstone, BA
Mrs J Locke, BSc
J MacGregor, MA
Mrs R E Maddocks, BA
D R Marshall, BSc
G A J Mason, BEd
C J Maudsley, BSc
T McIntyre, MEng
Miss M McMaster, BSc, MPhil
S J Mercer, BMus
Mrs N G Morrell, BA
Miss J A I Morris, BA
Ms C A Morton, BA, MEd
Mrs S Moule, BEd

Mrs S I Mounteney, BSc
J Nichols, BEd
C O'Donnell, BSc
Mrs S E Ord, BA
D C Parkes, BA
Miss N Partington, BA, NNEB
M Patey-Ford, BA
Dr J R Pattison, PhD, BSc
Mrs R L C Pegum, BA
P J Percival, BSc
A S Puddephatt, BA
Mrs C L Pyatt, GRSM, LRAM
C A Richards, BSc
Mrs R A Richards, BA
Mrs F Richardson, BEd
M S Robinson, BA
Mrs S J Robinson, BSc
Mrs E Rosenfield, BEd
Miss E Schué, BA
G J Shaw, BA
Miss V H Smalley, BA
Miss E Smith, BA
Miss S L Smith, MA
Mrs N Squares, BMus, MA
R E Stewart, BA
J Street, BSc
Mrs J T Sykes, CertEd
S P C Thomas, MA
Mrs C P Thompson, BA
P A Thompson, BSc
Mrs D A Threlfall, BA
Miss S H Waller, BSc
M K Walton, BEd
M R Ward, BA
Miss L C Watkins, BSc
Mrs K Wells, BA
Miss A-M Whalley, BA
Mrs C Whelpton, BSc
P Williams, BA

Number in School. Infants 3–7: 73 boys, 52 girls. Juniors 7–11: 130 boys, 109 girls. Boys (11–16) 451; Girls (11–16) 339. Sixth Form: 133 boys, 112 girls. Total: 1,397.

Organisation and Curriculum. The Foundation is organised in four Divisions: on one site, a Junior Division (co-educational 3–11) and a Girls' Division (11–16); on the other, a Boys' Division (11–16) and a Sixth Form (co-educational 16–18). Each Division is run by a Principal, who is responsible for day-to-day organisation, and the pupils in the 11–16 divisions of the school are taught separately but undertake a number of joint extra-curricular activities (eg music, drama, trips abroad etc.)

The Foundation has one Board of Governors, one Head and one Deputy Head who manage the school and plan regularly with the Division Principals to carry out the aims and objectives of the school. Girls and boys from 3–18 enjoy the same opportunities.

The curriculum is rich throughout all year groups offering pupils of all ages choice and a breadth of experience.

Pastoral care is a high priority. The divisional structure is key enabling each unit to be small and operate as a community.

Students are assigned to a personal tutor responsible for a group of 10 or so pupils throughout their Sixth Form course. Any justifiable combination of available A and AS Level subjects may be pursued, complemented by General Studies and Recreational Activity. In addition to compulsory core units in General Studies, students choose from a wide range of options designed to extend their breadth of cultural interest and intellectual inquiry, whilst Recreational Activities

are designed to encourage the positive use of leisure time and offers initial experience in sports and activities new to the individual. Pupils are also prepared for University Entrance Examinations where appropriate.

Arts and Craft. Well equipped art rooms and workshops are also available for use by the members of the Art Club and Craft Societies outside the timetable.

Music. Over 400 pupils receive tuition in the full range of orchestral instruments, the Piano, Organ, Classical Guitar and Singing. An introductory tuition scheme enables all new entrants to assess their talent. There are three orchestras, a Concert-band, two Jazz bands, three Choirs and many ensembles, all of which provide regular performing experience. The Foundation Choir was the first BBC, Songs of Praise, Choir of the Year in 2003. Pupils regularly enter music profession in addition to those pursuing academic training.

Drama. Theatre Studies is an important creative option at GCSE and A level and covers all aspects of the theatre. Great importance is attached to the regular school plays and musicals, which involve large numbers of pupils and enjoy a distinguished reputation. Pupils regularly take examinations in performance and public speaking.

Games. All pupils take part in games and athletic activity appropriate to the season. Junior School sports include Soccer, Cricket, Netball, Hockey, Tennis, Athletics and a wide range of individual games. In the Senior School, boys' sports include Rugby, Hockey, Cross-Country, Squash, Badminton, Cricket, Tennis, Athletics, Swimming and Basketball; the girls' sports include Hockey, Netball, Tennis, Football and Athletics. In addition there is a varied programme of sports in the Sixth Form, including Rugby and such activities as Hill Walking, Caving and Rock Climbing which are actively pursued by boys and girls.

Outdoor Pursuits. This is a thriving part of the school. There is a regular programme of activity weekends including canoeing, gorge scrambling, surfing etc. In addition, numerous expeditions are arranged in the many favourable areas near the school and also abroad. Sailing and orienteering are popular and the Duke of Edinburgh's Award scheme attracts 60 pupils each year.

Clubs and Societies. There is a wide range of other clubs catering for most interests and hobbies.

Fees per term (2011-2012). Senior School £3,165, Junior School £2,500, Infants Department £2,195. All fees are payable in advance on or before the first day of term.

Financial Support. (*See Scholarship Entries section.*) Bursaries are available for entry at 11, 13 and 16. In addition seven or more Scholarships are given on performance in the Entrance Examination. Academic, music and organ scholarships are available in the Sixth Form. Funds are available to assist pupils attending courses and field trips and to help in cases of urgent need. Leaving Awards are granted from funds held in trust by the Governors.

Admissions. Admission is normally for September each year through competitive examination for boys and girls aged 7–10, and 11–14 years. Girls and boys are admitted to the Sixth Form subject to academic attainment, interview and course requirement. Admission arrangements are advertised and available on request.

Immediate admission, eg for new arrivals in the area, is possible.

Former Pupils' Association. *Hon Secretary*: c/o The King's School, Macclesfield, SK10 1DA. A gazette and register of names is published regularly.

Visit the Website. The award-winning website is found at www.kingsmac.co.uk.

Charitable status. The King's School, Macclesfield is a Registered Charity, number 1137204. It exists for the education of boys and girls between the ages of 3 and 18.

King's Rochester

Satis House, Boley Hill, Rochester, Kent ME1 1TE
Tel:　01634 888555
Fax:　01634 888505
e-mail:　admissions@kings-rochester.co.uk
website:　www.kings-rochester.co.uk

The School traces its history to 604 AD, when St Justus, the first Bishop of Rochester, formed a school in connection with his Cathedral; it was reconstituted and endowed by Henry VIII as the King's School in 1541. The School has been fully co-educational since 1993.

Patron: The Lord Bishop of Rochester, The Rt Revd James Langstaff

Governing Body:
Chairman: (*to be appointed*)
Vice Chairman: Mr R W Hoile, MS, FRCS
Prof M Andrews, MSc, BSc, PGCE
The Venerable S Burton-Jones, MA, BTh
Mr M J Chesterfield
Mr J K Daffarn, FRICS
Mr E L Darwin, MA, CEng, FICE
Judge L M Grosse, LLB
The Revd Canon Dr P Hesketh, PhD, BD, AKC
The Revd Canon J Kerr, MA, CertEd
Mr J W Lord, FCA, ATII
Mrs R A Rouse, MSc
Mr N A Sampson, MA
Mr C R Shepherd, BSc, CEng, FICE, FRSA
The Revd Canon N Thompson, BEd, MA

Executive Board:

Head Master: Dr I R Walker, KGC St G, BA, PhD, LTh, ThG, ABIA, FCollP, FRSA

Headmaster of the Senior School: Mr K B Jones, MA, MCIL
Headmaster of the Preparatory School: Mr R P Overend, BA, FTCL, ARCM, FRSA
Headmistress of the Pre-Preparatory School: Mrs S E J Skillern, MA, NPQH, BA Hons QTS
Finance Director and Clerk to the Governors: Mr G R Longton, BSc, FCMA
Personnel Director: Mr R V Hubbard
Director of Marketing: Mrs J E Shilling, BA Joint Hons

Senior School:

Headmaster of the Senior School: Mr K B Jones, MA, MCIL
Second Master of the Senior School and Director of Studies: Miss N Steel, BSc
Senior Master: Mr C H Page, BA
Senior Mistress: Miss H L Catlett, BA
Chaplain: The Revd J A Thackray, BSc, ACIB
Head of Boarding: The Revd A M Mitra, MA

Heads of Department:
Art: Mr A J Robson, BA
Biology: Mr B H Aspinall, BSc
Careers: Mr M Lewins, BA
Chemistry: Mr N J McMillan, BSc Hons
Classics: The Revd A M Mitra, MA
Design & Technology: Mr S J Johnson, BEd
English: Mr W E Smith, BA
French: Mrs B M Clarke, Maîtrise
Geography: Miss L Costelloe, BA
German & Russian: Mr B W Richter, BA
History: Mr C M Hoile, BA Hons
ICT: Mr K D S Ranglall, BA, MSc
Mathematics: Mr N C M Abrams, BSc

Music: Mr D B McIlwraith, BA Hons, ARCO, PGCE
Physics: Mr M E Drury, BSc, MA
Physical Education: Mrs A J Richter, BSc
Religious Studies: Mrs L A Rogers, BA
Director of Sport: Mr G J Mitchell, BA

Registrar: Mrs L Davies
PR and Marketing Officer: Mrs J Williams, MCIPR
Librarian: Mrs X Guo, MA
CCF Contingent Commander: Colonel I Rouse

Preparatory School:
Headmaster: Mr R P Overend, BA, FTCL, ARCM, FRSA
Deputy Headmaster: Mr P N Medhurst, BA, MA
Preparatory School Chaplain: Revd A M Mitra, MA

Pre-Preparatory School:
Headmistress: Mrs S E J Skillern, MA, NPQH, BA Hons QTS
Deputy Headmistress: Mrs L A MacDonald, BA, PGCE
Early Years Coordinator: Mrs G A Newman, BA
Honorary Pre-Preparatory School Lay Chaplain: Dr S Hesketh, MB BS, MRCGP, AKC, PRCOG, DCH, DFSRH

Music Department:
Director of Music: Mr D B McIlwraith, BA Hons, ARCO, PGCE
Preparatory School Director of Music & Head of Strings: Mrs J M Hines, BA
Head of Woodwind: Mr G Vinall, BA, LRAM
Cathedral Director of Music: Mr S Farrell, BMus Hons, ARCO, ARCM, PGCE

Medical Officer: Dr M Ojedokun, MB BS, MRCGP

The School is situated close to the Cathedral and Castle in the centre of the city and in a secluded conservation area; it enjoys the open spaces of the Precincts, the Vines and the Paddock, which is one of the School's playing fields. The other playing field, the Alps, is 10 minutes from the School.

The Main School dates from the mid-nineteenth century but the School also has a number of fine listed buildings from the eighteenth century, and considerable extensions of more recent date. Recent additions include a £3 million Conference Centre and dining facility, a girls' boarding house, and a Pre-Prep building with Sports Hall and a modern, self-contained nursery was added in 2010. There is an indoor swimming pool and a well-equipped language laboratory.

The School numbers about 650 pupils, including 60 boarders of which 70% are from overseas. The School is fully co-educational and divided into a Pre-Preparatory School of 130 pupils (4–8 years), + 25 in the nursery, a Preparatory School of 200 pupils (8–13 years) and a Senior School of 300 pupils (13–18 years); this provides 3 units of an intimate size, which are regarded as a single community working closely together. While catering for the whole of a pupil's career from 3 to 18, there is a large entry of pupils at 11 and 13 who bring experience from other backgrounds, and enjoy the advantages of coming into a stable community with a strong family atmosphere.

The boarders, some of whom are weekly, play an important part in the life of the School. Although a minority, they are a large enough part of the School to make a very significant contribution of their own, and enjoy a more intimate atmosphere than is possible in a larger boarding community.

King's is the Cathedral School. The Dean and Chapter are ex officio Governors, the Head Master and King's Scholars are members of the Cathedral Foundation, and the Cathedral Choristers are members of the Preparatory School. The School uses the Cathedral for worship.

Work. In the Pre-Preparatory School, the pupils follow a four year curriculum of Maths, Science, English, Divinity, Geography, History, Information Technology, Art and Craft, Design & Technology, Music, and Physical Education. Daily spoken German lessons taught by native German teachers form part of the curriculum from the age of 4 with German fun and games sessions twice weekly in the nursery.

In the Preparatory School, the syllabus covers Divinity, English, History, Geography, Mathematics, Information Technology, Science (Physics, Chemistry and Biology), Latin, French, Art, Music, Physical Education, General Studies, and Design & Technology.

In the Senior School, all pupils continue with the same range for the first year. In the Fifth Forms, a core of subjects is continued and pupils add a balanced choice of options in preparation for the GCSE and IGCSE examinations at the end of the two-year course.

In the Sixth Form, a wide range of AS and A Level subjects are available. Normally a pupil studies for 4 AS and then 3 A Level subjects, and, in addition, undertakes a programme of General Studies.

All Sixth Formers, who wish to, go on to university or other further education, and are encouraged to think carefully about their ultimate careers. Careers talks are given by outside speakers during the GCSE year, and the advice of specialist careers advisers and the careers teachers is available at all stages.

Activities. The School aims to develop pupils through a wide range of activities, both within the School programme and outside it.

There is a large CCF contingent, with Army, Navy and Air Force sections. Strong Service connections locally give particularly wide scope for CCF activities.

Pupils also undertake a variety of activities in Community Service and participate in the Duke of Edinburgh's Award Scheme.

Out of School there is a range of over 20 school societies in all three parts of the School, and in the holidays there is a strong tradition of annual cultural and outdoor expeditions in this country and abroad for Preparatory and Senior School pupils.

Art, Drama and Music. The School sets great store by the Arts, and uses the comparative proximity to London to take pupils to art exhibitions, concerts and the theatre. The School stages major drama productions each year, recently *Joseph and the Amazing Technicolor Dreamcoat, The Merchant of Venice, Waiting for Godot, Ruckus in the Garden* and *The Dresser* have been the main presentations. There is a strong musical tradition enhanced by visiting music staff, and pupils are encouraged to learn instruments. In addition to concerts in the School and the Cathedral, the Orchestra gives a number of outside performances each year, some by invitation. The choral tradition is strengthened by the presence of the Cathedral choristers in the School who regularly undertake overseas tours. In 2011, the senior choir reached the semi-final of the BBC Songs of Praise Choir of the Year Competition.

Games. The boys' games are Rugby, Hockey, Football (Preparatory School) and Cricket and for girls' Hockey, Netball and Tennis. Other team sport options are Rowing (from our River Medway boathouse), Athletics, Cross Country, Fencing, Tennis and Swimming, and there are opportunities in addition for Squash, Badminton and Sailing. Physical Education is a regular part of the School curriculum and all pupils are required to take part in games. 80% represent the School competitively.

Religious Education and Worship. Although there is no denominational requirement for entry to the School, religious instruction is in accordance with the principles of the Church of England. All three parts of the School begin the day with an assembly or chapel service, some of which are held in the Cathedral.

Admission. Pupils can enter the School at any age from 3 to 18. Entrance to the Senior School is either by Common Entrance at 13 or by the School's own examination for pupils who have not been prepared for Common Entrance.

Sixth Form entry is on the basis of interview and School report, together with satisfactory GCSE results (a minimum of 5 A*–C passes, and grade requirements for A Level courses).

Choristers. Choristerships to Rochester Cathedral (8+/9+) from Cathedral and School are awarded to boys following voice trials and a satisfactory performance in the Preparatory School Entrance Examination. Under normal circumstances, the choristership will continue until a boy transfers to the Senior School or until he leaves the choir.

Scholarships. (*See Scholarship Entries section.*) *Senior School*: Up to five Major King's Scholarships (30%) and five Minor King's Scholarships (15%) may be awarded annually. At least five scholarships are for pupils from the maintained sector.

Up to five Music Scholarships of up to 30% of tuition fees may be awarded annually on the basis of interview and practical test. An Organ Scholarship of up to 30% of tuition fees may be awarded when a vacancy occurs. One Choral Scholarship (£2,500 per annum) and one Music Scholarship (£3,000) are occasionally available.

Governors Exhibitions: these academic awards are available to pupils and may be of value up to 100% of fees; they are means-tested using the same assessment as originally applied to the Government Assisted Places Scheme which they replace.

Preparatory School: Five King's Exhibitions at 11+ of 30% of tuition fees are available. Two are for pupils from a maintained Primary School.

Details of all awards may be obtained from the Head Master. Additional means-tested bursaries may be available.

Remissions. Children of Church of England ministers are given an annually means-tested reduction in tuition fees.

Children of Service Personnel are given a 20% reduction in tuition fees.

Where parents have three or more children at the school a reduction after the second child is given, amounting to 10% of the third child's tuition fees, 20% for the fourth child and 40% for the fifth and subsequent children. This does not apply to the Nursery Class.

Fees per term (2011–2012). Senior School: Boarders £8,550, Day Pupils £5,270. Preparatory School: Boarders £5,950, Day Pupils £3,590–£4,080. Pre-Preparatory School: £2,800–£3,000 (Day only).

Charitable status. King's School, Rochester is a Registered Charity, number 1084266; it is a charitable trust for the purpose of educating children.

The King's School
Tynemouth
A Woodard School

Huntington Place, Tynemouth, Tyne and Wear NE30 4RF
Tel: 0191 258 5995
Fax: 0191 296 3826
e-mail: admissions@kings-tynemouth.co.uk
website: www.kings-tynemouth.org.uk

Motto: *Moribus Civilis*

Governing Body:
The Provost and Fellows of the Society of St Mary and Aidan of York

President:
The Rt Revd Stephen Conway, Bishop of Ely

Visitor:
The Rt Revd Martin Wharton, Bishop of Newcastle

School Council:

His Hon Judge J E Evans, BA (*Chairman*)
D R Bilton, BSc, CEng, MIEE, AMI, MechE
D E T Nicholson, MA
A M Conn, MA, ACA
I A Angus, BSc, ARICS
Dr A E Colver, BSc, MRCGP
D Hodgson, BSc, FIChemE, CEng, MIOSH
Revd G Lowson, BEd, DipTh
Mrs D Parfitt, BSc
E W Mitchell, BA, FRSA
Revd Canon B D Clover, MA, LTCL
Mrs H Buglass, BSc, GradCIPD, Dip S
G T Murray, BSc, ACA
Miss S C Webb, BA

Headmaster: E M Wesson, MA

Deputy Head, Academic: T Spence, BA, PGCE, MEd
Deputy Head, Pastoral: J Davies, BMus, PGCE
Head of Sixth Form: P Angel, MA, BSc, PGCE
Chaplain: Revd C J Clinch, BEd, Bt

Assistant Masters and Mistresses:

W Ryan, CertEd	D E Boardman, BSc, PGCE
C Moore, BA, PGCE	G Bradley, BSc, PGCE
V Gordon, BSc, PGCE	P G Clarke, BA, PGCE
C Johnston, BEd	Mrs C Dunn, CertEd, BA,
Mrs C A Rix, BSc, PGCE	MEd
K Rix, BA, PGCE	Mrs L D Herron, BA,
A C Fowler, BEd	PGCE
P C Hadwin, BSc, PGCE	P Thompson, BA, PGCE
G R Dickson, BA, MA,	Mrs R Watson, BSc, PGCE
PGCE	Miss C M Smith, BA,
A Cutting, BA	PGCE
P A Baxter, BA	Mrs J Johnson, BSc, PGCE
Mrs I M Nicholson, BEd,	Mrs A Ward-Williams,
MA	BSc, PGCE
Miss C E Taylor, BA,	D Fryatt, BSc, PGCE
PGCE	P R S Sanderson, BA, MSc,
P J Nicholson, BA, PGCE	PGCE
R A Marriott, BA, PGCE	S J Chandler, BSc, PGCE
A ul Haq, BSc, PGCE	Mrs C Amsdorf, MEd, BA,
Mrs J N Liddie, BA, PGCE	PGCE
Dr M H Brookes, BSc,	A J J Rhatigan, BA, HDE
PhD, PGCE	S M Sweeney, BA, PGCE
Mrs S E Smith, BA, PGCE	P J Taylor, BSc, DMS,
C Leather, BA, PGCE	PGCE
Miss J Patterson, BEd,	P M Allonby, BSc, PGCE
PGCE	Ms H A Murphy BA,
Mrs D Wallace, BA, BSc	PGCE, MA
Econ, MEd	Mrs F Leather BSc, PGCE
Mrs H Hamilton, BSc,	A Black, BSc, PGCE
PGCE	

Junior School including Kindergarten:

Head of Junior School: Miss K Benson, BEd
A J Russell, BEd
Mrs H C Baines, BSc, PGCE
Mrs J M Large, BSc, PGCE
Mrs C A Spencer, BEd
Mrs S A Porteous, BA, PGCE
Miss J Quinn, BSc, PGCE
Miss H N Boyle, BTec (*Nursery Nurse*)
Mrs J A Ray, BEd
Mrs K M Adams, CertEd

Bursar and Clerk to the Governors: Mrs C Dobson, FCA
Admissions Secretary: Mrs P S Alberici, BA
School Nurse: Mrs J Marsden, RGN
Learning Resource Centre Manager: Mrs J Angel, ACLIP
King's Tynemouth Alumni: Mrs K Bilton
Alumni Development Officer: Mrs E Wotton, BA, PGCE

General. The King's School, founded in 1860, is one of the largest schools of the Woodard Corporation. It is an Independent Day School for boys and girls aged 4–18. There are approximately 700 pupils in the School: 60 pupils in the Kindergarten (4+ to 7); 80 pupils in the Junior School (7 to 10+); and 560 pupils in the Senior School (11+ to 18) with a Sixth Form of 180. All three sections of The King's School work closely together and enjoy many of the same facilities.

King's endeavours to educate 'the whole person' and so the excellence of our classroom teaching and GCSE and A Level results is complemented by a wide range of extra-curricular activities both sporting and cultural. Teaching is in small groups and all pupils are known individually.

As a day school King's aims for a close partnership with parents.

King's is a Christian school and the School Chapel is at its centre, providing a powerful symbol of the School's values and aims.

The School enjoys a remarkably fortunate location: it is situated on the North East coast in the beautiful village of Tynemouth, on direct bus and metro routes from Newcastle and the surrounding areas. There are also private coaches travelling from south of the River Tyne and Northumberland.

Senior School Curriculum. The School aims to give pupils a broad education in general, and in particular to prepare them for public examinations and for entry into Universities (including Oxbridge).

In the first three years all pupils follow a common curriculum consisting of: English, Mathematics, History, Geography, French, Science, Art, Music, Drama, Religious Education, Design Technology, ICT and Physical Education. German and Spanish are introduced in the Year 8.

In Years 10 and 11 pupils are prepared for a wide range of GCSE options. All pupils in Year 11 have a period of work experience immediately after the GCSE examinations.

In the Sixth Form most pupils take four AS Level subjects, followed by three or four A Level subjects in the second year. Practically any combination of subjects is possible and there is no arts-science barrier.

King's maintains excellent links with Industry and is greatly indebted to parents and the thriving King's Tynemouth Alumni for their assistance in this field.

Careers and University Application. Careers education and guidance are provided from Year 9 onwards. The vast majority of Sixth Formers proceed to degree courses and expert advice is given on University applications.

Games and Physical Education. The programme of games and physical education is designed to provide every pupil with an opportunity to gain satisfaction from participation in sport. King's has busy fixture lists and maintains a high standard at Rugby, Cricket, Tennis and Hockey (the major team games) as well as at Athletics, Gymnastics, Cross-Country Running, Netball, Squash, Soccer, Basketball and Badminton. Facilities are also provided for Golf, Sailing, Canoeing, Swimming, Fencing, Archery and Trampolining.

The School has a magnificent new sports centre and also its own playing fields at Priors Park, virtually adjacent to the main campus. King's fosters close links with local Rugby, Cricket and Tennis Clubs.

Many pupils win selection at county and national level.

Activities. Music and Drama are exceptionally strong at King's as are the numerous other clubs and societies which include Art, Bridge, Christian Fellowship, Computers, Chess, Dance, Debating, Orienteering, Table Tennis, Science, Stained Glass, Young Engineers, Young Enterprise.

Many pupils are involved in the Duke of Edinburgh's Award Scheme and in Community Service. The School organises annual skiing, mountaineering, climbing, and adventurous trips; visits to the Inverclyde National Sports Centre and the Outward Bound Mountain Centre at Ullswater; and a Summer Camp. The King's School has a field centre at Alnham in Northumberland, which is used as a base for field study work, for Duke of Edinburgh's Award Scheme activities, and for weekend retreats for choirs and other groups.

Junior School (including Kindergarten). The Junior School (4+ to 11+ years) is staffed by class teachers specially qualified for work with younger children, though there is close liaison with the specialist teachers in the Senior School to ensure continuity in teaching and the curriculum. The Head of the Junior School is responsible to the Headmaster of The King's School for the day-to-day running of the Junior School.

The Junior School shares a common site with the Senior School and although housed in separate accommodation with its own classrooms, Library, Design & Technology room and ICT centre, it makes full use of the school chapel, cafeteria, sports centre, laboratories, workshops, playing fields and field centre.

Admissions. Prospectus and Registration forms can be obtained from the Admissions Office.

All entries are made through the Headmaster. Pupils are admitted to the Kindergarten on the basis of an interview; and to the Junior and Senior Schools on the basis of performance in the School's examinations in English and Mathematics and an interview. The main intakes to the Senior School are at 11+ and 13+. For entry at Sixth Form level a minimum of 14 points at GCSE is normally expected in addition to a satisfactory report from a pupil's current Head.

Fees per term (2011-2012). Senior School £3,330; Junior School £2,642.

Scholarships and Bursaries. Scholarships (including those for Art and Music) are offered for entry to the Senior School at 11+, 13+ and Sixth Form level. Bursaries are available by application to the Headmaster.

Charitable status. The King's School Tynemouth Limited is a Registered Charity, number 269665. It exists to promote education.

The King's School
Worcester

5 College Green, Worcester WR1 2LL
Tel: 01905 721700 (School Office)
        01905 721721 (Bursar)
Fax: 01905 721710
e-mail: info@ksw.org.uk
website: www.ksw.org.uk

A Cathedral School appears to have existed at Worcester virtually continuously since the 7th century. In its present form, however, The King's School dates from its refoundation by King Henry VIII in 1541, after the suppression of the Cathedral Priory and its school. In 1884 the School was reorganised as an Independent School and in 1944 the Cathedral Choir School was amalgamated with The King's School.

Visitor: The Lord Bishop of Worcester

The Governing Body:
H B Carslake, Esq, BA, LLB (*Chairman*)
The Very Revd P G Atkinson
Mrs K L Brookes, MA
Professor M Clarke, CBE, MA, DL
W A Comyn, Esq, FCA
D Dale, Esq, MA, FCA
D L Green, Esq
K D Harmer, Esq
Mrs J H Jarvis, BA, MCIPD
The Hon Lady Morrison
Revd Canon Dr A Petterson

Mrs P Preston, MA Oxon, DipM
Dr H Swift, MA, MSt, DPhil Oxon
Mrs I Taylor, MA Cantab, FCA
Professor J Vickerman, BSc, PhD, DSc
P Walker, Esq, BTech, MPhil, CEng, MIMMM

Clerk to the Governors and Bursar: J G Bartholomew, MBA, AIMBM, PIIA

Headmaster: T H Keyes, MA

Senior Deputy Head: R Chapman, BSc
Second Deputy Head: Miss C Mellor, BA
Director of Studies: R C Baum, MA
Academic Deputy Head: J Ricketts, BSc

Assistant Staff:
* *Head of Department*
§ *Part-time*

Art:
*Mrs E R Hand, BA
C Haywood, BA
Miss J Hewitt, BA
§Mrs C Horacek, BA
Miss G Holden, BA

Biology:
*M Parkin, MA, PhD
§Mrs R Worth, BSc
S M Bain, BSc, MSc
Mrs N Essenhigh, BSc
M J Newby, BEd
J H Chalmers, BAppSc
Miss E Fuller, BSc

Careers:
*S Le Marchand, BA
Mrs L M Brighton, BEd

Chemistry:
*R P Geary, BSc, CChem, MRSC
J T Wheeler, BSc, CChem, MRSC
M C Poole, BSc, PhD
Mrs C E Battrum, MA
R James, BSc, PhD

Classics:
*Mrs S C Bradley, BA (*Acting Head*)
Miss L K Woodruff, BA, MA
Miss J K Wootton, BA
Miss F MacSwiney, BA, MA

Design and Technology:
*C Wilson, BA
Miss H Holden, BA
E Lummas, BA
A G Deichen, BA

Key Skills:
(*to be appointed*)

Drama & Theatre Studies:
*S M Atkins, BA
Mrs S H Le Marchand, BA
S Le Marchand, BA
Mrs T D Marskell, CertEd
Ms J Price-Hutchinson, BA

Economics & Business Studies:
*R P Mason, BA
§G L Williams, BA
§Miss E Gittings, BA

English:
*A J M Maund, MA
S Le Marchand, BA
R J Davis, BA
Mrs S H Le Marchand, BA
D P Iddon, BA (*SEN Coordinator*)
Mrs L L Guy, BA
Mrs E Allen-Back, MA
Mrs L Walmsley, BA
Miss A Briggs, BA

Geography:
*S C Cuthbertson, BA
A W Longley, BA
Miss E Watts, BA
Mrs F L Short, BA
J Eaves, BA
Miss C Lea, BSc
Mrs J D Clark, BEd

History and Politics:
*P T Gwilliam, BA, MPhil
T R Sharp, MA
Miss J Mosley, BA
Miss L Woodruff, BA, MA
A J Ford, BA

Information Technology:
*Mrs J C Vivian, MA

Mathematics:
*Mrs A Hines, BSc
M J Roberts, BSc
Mrs M M Longley, BEd
§Miss A-M Simpson, BSc
§Mrs D Salkeld, BSc
Mrs L M Brighton, BEd
R C Chapman, BSc
A A Kerley, BEng
J Hand, BA
Mrs S Davison, BSc
J N Gardiner, BSc
§Mrs K Beever, BEng

Modern Languages:
*R A Ball, MA
J L Owen, BA
M D Rudge, BA
C A Gallantree-Smith, BA
Miss C Mellor, BA
Mrs R M Rutter, BA
Mrs R Shearburn, BA
Miss C White, BA
Mrs R Stanley, BA
C N Wright, BA

Music:
*D E Brookshaw, BMus, FRCO
Mrs V J Gunter, GTCL, LTCL
G M Gunter, GTCL, LTCL
§C J B Allsop, BA, MA, FRCO
and 30 visiting teachers

PE & Games:
J J Mason, BSc (*Director of Sport*)
A A D Gillgrass, BA (*Boys' Games*)
Mrs F L Short, BA (*Girls' Games*)
Miss O Beveridge, BEd
S M Bain, BSc, MSc
D P Iddon, BA
Mrs T D Marskell, CertEd
Mrs M M Longley, BEd

Headmaster's Secretary: Mrs C Swainston
Registrar: Mrs V Peckston, BA
Medical Officers:
Dr M Smith, MBChB
Dr A Woof, MB,CHB
Sister: Mrs C F Furber, RGN, DipN

The King's Junior Schools

King's St Alban's
Tel: 01905 354906; Fax: 01905 763075;
e-mail: ksa@ksw.org.uk

Head: R Bellfield, BEd
Deputy Head: Mrs R Duke, BA
Head of Pre-Prep: Miss A Roberts, BA

§Mrs L A Jackson, MA
§Mrs C Woodcock, BA, CertEd
§Mrs N Cain, BA
§Mrs K Kear-Wood, BSc
Mrs J Pitts, BEd
§Mrs M A Keyes, MA
D Braithwaite, BEd
J M Bailey, BEd
Mrs F Atkinson, BSc

Mrs H Haggerty, BA
Mrs A Hind, BSc
Mrs L Kilbey, MA, LRSM
Ms L Neeves, MSc
I Fry, MA
Miss E Wyatt, BSc
§Mrs E Lewis, BEd
Mrs J Hadfield, BA
Mrs J Wheeler, BA

Registrar: Mrs A Bellfield
Secretaries: Mrs T Pearman, Ms S Hurley
Matrons: Mrs K Hill, Mrs K Jenkins
Teaching Assistants: §Miss F Hainge, Mrs N Hobson, Mrs E Monkhouse, Mrs N Mountjoy

King's Hawford
Tel: 01905 451292; Fax: 01905 756502;
e-mail: hawford@ksw.org.uk

Head: J M Turner, BEd, DipEd, ACP
Deputy Head: D Peters, BMus
Assistant Head: Mrs C Rawnsley, BA

R B Cook, BSc
Mrs J Bayliss, BSc
Mrs L Baxter, BSc
Mrs L Hyde, BA
Mrs J Redman, BEd
Mrs D Goodayle, BEd

I Percival, BA
R Penn, BSc
Ms K Turk, BA, MA
Mrs A Marshall-Walker, BA

Pre-Prep:
Head: Mrs P M Bradley, BEd
Mrs J N Willis, BA Ed (*Head of Early Years*)

Mrs C A Griffin, BA
Mrs J Farmer, BEd
Miss A Kingston, BA
Mrs C Knight, BEd

Mrs G Riley, BSc
Mrs J Wilson, BEd
§Mrs H Fowler, BA

§Mrs J D Clark, BEd
C Atkinson, BSc
J Chalmers (*Head of Rowing*)

Physics:
*D J Haddock, MA, DPhil Oxon
I C Robinson, BSc
R C Baum, MA
Mrs S K Stone, BEng
Mrs L E Haddock, BSc
§S J Osmond, MA

Religious Studies:
*R Head, BA, PhD
Revd M R Dorsett, BA, MTh, PhD, CertTheol (*Chaplain*)
§Miss A-M Simpson, BSc

PSE:
(*to be appointed*)

Kindergarten:
Mrs A Jeavons, BA
Mrs S A Gwilliam, BA
Mrs S Powell, BA
Mrs R Pearman, BA
Mrs D Field

Mrs N Thomas
Mrs J Simons, NNEB
Mrs S Watts, CertEd
Mrs E Jennings
Mrs D Atkinson, NVQ3

Registrar/Secretary: (*to be appointed*)
Office Secretaries: Mrs J Cartwright, Miss L Greenhill
Hawford Matron: Mrs F Geary, RGN

The School still occupies its original site south of the Cathedral. The buildings are grouped around College Green and the School Gardens. They range in date from the 14th century College Hall and Edgar Tower through the 17th and 18th century buildings surrounding College Green, to a range of modern, purpose-built accommodation, much of which has been constructed in the last twenty years. Recent additions in a continuing development programme include a library located in the heart of the school, the John Moore Theatre, teaching and science provision for the Junior School on site, the refurbishment of the Sports Hall, a covered Swimming Pool and upgraded House accommodation. There are centres for English and Mathematics and a Music School. A Languages Computer Centre with the latest software for the teaching of French, German and Spanish has been established.

There are two Junior Schools. King's St Alban's stands in its own grounds on the edge of the main school site, offering education from age 4–11 with a purpose-built pre-prep department for girls and boys aged 4–7. King's Hawford is in a spacious rural setting just to the north of the city and offers education from age 2–11.

Numbers and Admission. The school is fully co-educational. King's St Alban's has about 212 pupils. King's Hawford has about 330 pupils. The Senior School has about 930 pupils, including 270 in the Sixth Form.

Entrance to the school is by the Junior Entrance Test at 7, 8 or 9, or by the School's Examination at 11, 12 and 13. Boys and girls also join the School at Sixth Form level; this entry is by test, interview and GCSE results.

Term of Entry. Pupils are normally admitted annually in September.

Religion. The School has an historic connection with the Cathedral. Religious education, given in accordance with the Christian faith, is non-denominational. Pupils of all denominations and faiths are welcomed.

Curriculum. Pupils are prepared for the GCSE, and A, AS and Advanced Extension papers, and for Higher Education, the Services, the professions, industry and commerce. The curriculum is designed to give all pupils a general education and to postpone specialisation for as long as possible. Further details will be found in the Prospectus.

Games. The major sports are Rugby, Netball, Hockey, Football, Rowing and Cricket. Other sports include Tennis, Athletics, Cross Country, Badminton, Rounders, Fencing, Squash, Golf, Swimming, Sailing and Canoeing. PE and games are compulsory for all; a wide choice is offered to Sixth Formers. The school has been awarded the Sportsmark Gold award.

Other Activities. The school has a Choral Society and two other Choirs, 3 Orchestras and a Wind Band; there are at least 20 concerts each year. There are more than a dozen dramatic productions each year, including two or three major School plays, one of which is usually a Musical. The School takes part in the Duke of Edinburgh's Award Scheme; there is a CCF and a Welfare and Community Service group. Young Enterprise companies in the Sixth Form are well subscribed and highly successful. A large number of societies and groups cater for a wide variety of other out-of-school activities and interests. The School has an Outdoor Activities Centre in the Black Mountains which is widely used both during the term and in the holidays. The Himalayan

Club takes about 25 pupils on expeditions each year to Nepal or India.

Scholarships. (*See Scholarship Entries section.*) Both Music and Academic Scholarships are available at 11+, 13+ and 16+ in the Senior School, value up to one third of tuition fees. Academic scholarships at 11+ and 13 + are awarded on the basis of the Entrance Test and an interview; at 16+ on the basis of an aptitude test and interview, along with a report from the candidate's school. Full details are available from the Registrar. Scholarships are available at 7+ and 8+, value up to one third of tuition fees (tenable only while in the Junior Schools) and are awarded to candidates of outstanding academic or musical ability. Means-tested Bursaries can be awarded up to 100% of fees and can be combined with scholarship awards. At 11+ and 16+ All-rounder bursaries are available with consideration given to candidates with a broad personal profile which could include strengths in Sports, Art, Music or Drama.

Fees per term (2011-2012). Senior School £3,697. Junior Schools £1,958–£3,452.

Chorister Scholarships. Entry to the Choir is by means of Voice and Academic Tests which are held at various times throughout the year. A high vocal and musical standard is naturally required and boys must also have sufficient intellectual ability to hold their own in the Choir and the School. Boys should be 7–9 years old at the time of entry.

The **Prospectus** and information about Entrance Tests, Awards and Chorister Scholarships can be obtained from the Registrar.

Charitable status. The King's School Worcester is a Registered Charity, number 1098236. It exists to provide high quality education for boys and girls.

Kingston Grammar School

London Road, Kingston-upon-Thames, Surrey KT2 6PY
Tel: 020 8546 5875
Fax: 020 8547 1499
e-mail: head@kgs.org.uk
website: www.kgs.org.uk

A school is believed to have existed in the Lovekyn Chantry Chapel since the fourteenth century. However in 1561, Queen Elizabeth I, in response to a humble petition from the Burghers of Kingston, signed Letters Patent establishing the "Free Grammar School of Queen Elizabeth to endure for ever". In 1944 the School accepted Direct Grant Status and became fully Independent in 1976. Two years later the School went Co-educational, initially with girls in the Sixth Form, but in the following year joining in the First Forms, to progress through the School. There are still close links with the Royal Borough of Kingston upon Thames, but no residential qualification for entry to the School, which now numbers around 450 boys and 350 girls.

Motto: *Bene agere ac laetari.*

Governing Body:
P Marsh, BA, LLD (*Chairman*)
J S Tapp (*Vice Chair*)
Professor F M Brennan, BSc, PhD
R Brown, MA, ACMA
D P D Combe, BA
Mrs S Fowler, CEng, BSc, MCIBSE
I G Galbraith, MA
G P Hughes
E A Kershaw, MA, MPhil
Dr S Ofield-Kerr, BA, MA, PhD
J D Rice, LLB
Mrs H Webster, LLB

Head: **Mrs S K Fletcher**, MA Oxon

Principal Deputy Head: J M Wallace, BA (*Mathematics*)

Deputy Head: Miss V S Pownall, BA (*Geography*)
Assistant Head: G R M Yates, BA, MA (*Geography*)
Assistant Head: N Bond, BA (*English*)
Assistant Head: Miss D M Williams, BSc (*Geography*)

* *Head of Department*

Staff:
Miss A M Adolphus, BSc (*Biology*)
Mrs R Allen, BA (**Director of Drama*)
Miss L S Andrews, BSc (*Mathematics*)
Mrs J Barkey, BA (*Art*)
R L Barker, BA (*Director of Careers and Enterprise*)
Dr R Barrand, BA, PhD (*French & Russian, Head of Sixth Form*)
A J Beard, BA (*History, Head of Fourth Form*)
M Behnoudnia, BSc (*Physics*)
Miss N Bell, BSc (*Assistant Director of Sport, *Girls' Hockey*)
S W Bell, BA (*Drama*)
T G Benson, MSci (*Physics*)
Mrs J Bowen (*Mathematics*)
Miss C A Bradford, BSc (*Mathematics*)
M Britland, BSc (**IT*)
Miss A Bruce, MA (*French & German*)
D G Buttanshaw, BEd (*PE, Mathematics, *Hockey*)
Miss L Collison, BSc (*Second in Mathematics*)
Mrs H B Cook, BSc (*Mathematics*)
P J Cooper, MSc (**Mathematics*)
Mrs S J Corcoran, BEd (**Learning Support*)
Mrs E Coy, BSc (*Mathematics*)
Dr A Crampin, BSc, PhD (**PSHE, Physics*)
Miss P V Crothers BA (*French, German, Head of Second Form*)
J M Davies, MA (**History*)
I Deepchand, BSc (**Physics*)
W G Dunlop, BA (*English, *CCF, Head of First Form*)
J A Dyson, BA (**Art*)
D Farr, BA (**Design Technology*)
J M Fenton, BA (*Religious Studies*)
Mrs P Fine, BA (**Geography*)
N S Forsyth, BSc (*Biology*)
O P Garner, BA (*French, Italian*)
B S Garrard, BA (*Physical Education/Sport*)
Mrs S Garside, BA, MA (**English*)
Miss R L Gladwyn, BA (*English*)
M S Grant, BA, MA (*History, Head of Fifth Form*)
Mrs H Green, BA (**Religious Studies*)
Miss C M Hall, BSc (**Science, *Chemistry*)
J Halls, BA (*Design Technology*)
Miss Z Hamilton, BA (*History*)
Mrs R L Hetherington, BA (*Design Technology*)
Mrs N L Hempstead, L-ès-L (*French, Spanish*)
Mrs E M Hyde, MA (*Assistant Director of Music*)
C A Jackson, MA, FRCO, ARAM (*Master of Music Scholars*)
Mrs N Jackson, BA (*History*)
R King, BA, MA (**Psychology*)
Miss A Lancaster-Thomas, MA (*Religious Studies*)
Dr A M Langdon, BA, PhD (*Mathematics, Head of Academic Monitoring & University Admissions*)
N E MacKay, BA (*French, Spanish, Head of Third Form*)
Miss C Mara, BSc (*PE, *Netball, *Tennis*)
Miss D E McCann, BSc (*Chemistry*)
Miss B A McDonald, BA, MA (*Classics, Deputy Head of Sixth Form*)
Ms H Moriarty, BA (*Economics*)
S R Morris, BSc (*Mathematics*)
L W O'Brien, BA (*Director of Sport*)
Mrs S Osborn, BSc, AIMA (*Mathematics*)
D E Palmer (**PE*)
Mrs K D Pinnock, BA (*French*)
Mrs T C Povey, BA (*Humanities*)

P J Ricketts, MA (*Economics, *Business Studies)
Miss I Ridley, BA (Classics)
S R J Robertson, BA (Geography)
M J C Rodgers, BSc, MSc (*Biology)
Mrs T M Russell, Mag Phil (*Modern Foreign Languages)
J E K Schofield, BSc (Business Studies, *Cricket, *Soccer)
Mrs M E Serjeant, BA, DipLib (*Librarian)
Miss R J Sharp, BA (French and Spanish)
P J Simmons, BSc (*Rowing)
C R Smalman-Smith, BA (Mathematics, Girls' Rowing)
J S Smith, BA, MPhil (Second in English)
D A R Sorley, BA (History, *Politics)
Mrs P W E Stones, MA (English)
Miss E Tuck, BA (*Classics)
Miss R M Twomey, BA (Spanish & French)
Miss E K Varley, BA (Second in English)
M P Von Freyhold, PGDip RCM, DiplomMusiklehrer
    Karlsruhe (*Director of Music)
Mrs R Wakely, BA (Art)
C G Wenham, BA (Chemistry)
P R Williams, BA (Biology, Boys' Rowing)
M P Williamson, BEd (Physical Education, *Boys'
    Hockey)
Dr L H Winning, MChem, DPhil (Second in Chemistry)

Bursar and Clerk to the Governors: E N Lang, BA, ACA
Facilities Manager: J Farmer
Head's PA: Mrs C Pink
Registrar & Marketing Manager: Mrs H Smith

Buildings. Starting with the medieval Lovekyn Chapel, the site of Kingston Grammar School has been developed over 450 years to include modern classroom and laboratories. Recent years have seen the acquisition of land adjacent to the main site and the building of new facilities, most notably The Queen Elizabeth II building, opened by Her Majesty in 2005, with its Performing Arts Centre, Sixth Form Centre and classrooms. There is a rolling programme of refurbishment with new libraries, Art & Design Technology, modernised facilities in MFL, and an extensive state-of-the-art IT network with computer sites across the campus. The school is easily accessible by road and rail links to Kingston. The 22-acre sports ground includes an indoor training area, pavilions, cricket nets, netball courts, two all-weather pitches plus practice area and boat house.

Entry to the School. Admission to the School is by examination: at 11+ candidates sit the School's own examination in January for entry the following September. At the same time we also offer the opportunity for Year 5 candidates to sit a 10+ examination for deferred entry into Year 7. A large number of girls and boys are also admitted in the Sixth Form.

Term of Entry. Apart from occasional vacancies pupils enter in September.

Fees per term (2011-2012). £4,945; this covers all charges except examination fees and lunch.

Scholarships and Bursaries. (See Scholarship Entries section.) The Governors award Scholarships (on academic merit) at 11+ and 16+, and Bursaries (according to parental means) to pupils entering the School at 11+ and 16+. Music, Art and Sports awards are also available.

Curriculum. The academic curriculum through to GCSE emphasises a proper balance between varied disciplines and range of intellectual experience, with all taking Maths, English, the three sciences and at least one modern language as part of 9 or 10 GCSE subjects. Maths GCSE may be taken early by able candidates. Full careers information and counselling are given, though pupils are encouraged to view academic pursuit as a desirable end in itself, using a profiling process to develop their commitment to study. In the Sixth Form, students choose at least 4 AS Level subjects in the Lower Sixth and normally continue with 3 subjects to A2 Level in the Upper Sixth. In addition, students in the Lower Sixth undertake an extended research project, designed to develop the skills necessary to learn independently and to broaden their horizons. All Sixth Form students attend an annual conferences on international themes. Almost 100% of the Sixth Form elect to proceed to higher education, including Oxford and Cambridge Universities.

Care. A pupil's form tutor is responsible for welfare and progress. Heads of Year coordinate the work of form tutors. There is a qualified nurse and a School Counsellor visits one day a week to support any pupils who have concerns in and out of school. Parents' meetings are held annually and pupils receive two written reports per year, in addition to twice termly grade cards. Pastoral evenings are also held, where parents can discuss with each other and staff the difficulties and anxieties faced by young adults.

Games. The school Sports Ground is beautifully situated at Thames Ditton, by the River Thames opposite Hampton Court Palace. Kingston Grammar School prides itself on the large number of pupils who represent Great Britain in Hockey and Rowing.

Hockey (in both winter terms) and Rowing (all the year round) are main games with teams at all levels regularly competing in National Championships, along with cricket and Tennis in the summer. The School also has representative sides in Soccer, Athletics, Cross-Country and Netball, with an emphasis on sport for all and participation as well as on training for performance athletes.

Societies. The School is proud of its extensive co-curricular provision and its programme of House-based activities. A large number of School Societies provides for the interests of pupils of all ages. They range from Chess and Debating, to Natural History and Young Enterprise. The Duke of Edinburgh's Award Scheme is popular and overseas travel is a regular feature of many activities. The Music Department has a vigorous programme of concerts and tours, and a busy and flourishing Drama Department provides a wealth of opportunity for pupils in all aspects of dramatic production.

Combined Cadet Force. The CCF is divided into Army and RAF Sections With a variety of activities ranging from night exercises and flying to Outward Bound and Adventure Training. Camps are held in school holidays and pupils attend courses in a range of subjects. This is an entirely voluntary activity which pupils may take up in the Third Form.

Careers. The Careers Staff assist pupils in their choice of options at all levels, and give advice on possible future careers. They are in close touch with employers in professions, commerce and industry, and all fifth formers undertake a period of work experience after their GCSE examinations. An annual Careers Convention is held at the school. Particular attention is given to advice on entry to the Universities to which the majority of Sixth Form students go. The School is in membership of the Independent School Careers Organisation and pupils are able to take advantage of several computer assessment programs.

Parents' and Staff Association. The Association exists to further the interests of the School in the broadest possible way and does much to strengthen the links between staff, parents and students. The Sherriff Club (rowing), The Ditton Field Society (cricket, soccer, netball, tennis, hockey), Music Society, and Drama & Dance Society also support school activities.

The Old Kingstonian Association likewise does much to foster a spirit of unity and cooperation. All students automatically join the Association on leaving the School.

Honours. An average of 8 or 9 places are gained each year at Oxbridge.

Charitable status. Kingston Grammar School is a Registered Charity, number 1078461, and a Company Limited by Guarantee, registered in England, number 3883748. It exists to enable children to adapt their talents to meet the needs of an ever changing world, whilst holding fast to the principles of self reliance, a sense of responsibility and a determination to seize opportunity.

Kingswood School

Lansdown, Bath, Somerset BA1 5RG
Tel: 01225 734200
Fax: 01225 734305
e-mail: enquiries@kingswood.bath.sch.uk
website: www.kingswood.bath.sch.uk

Kingswood is an independent, co-educational, Christian school represented on HMC. It was founded by John Wesley in 1748 and moved to its present 218 acre site overlooking the World Heritage City of Bath in 1851. Kingswood combines academic excellence with a concern for the development of each individual's talents. Boarders and day pupils are fully integrated within a happy and caring community environment. There are currently 661 pupils (360 boys and 301 girls) at the Senior School and 320 pupils at the Prep School.
Motto: *In via Recta Celeriter*

Chairman of the Governing Body: Wing Cdr C S Burns, RAF Retd

Hon Secretary to the Governors: Mr P Sadler, FCCA

Headmaster: Mr S A Morris, MA

Deputy Head: Mr G D Opie, BEd

Deputy Head (Academic): Mrs S C Dawson, BEd

Deputy Head (Pastoral) & Chaplain: The Revd M L Wilkinson, MA

Bursar: Mr P Sadler, FCCA

Director of Development & Marketing: Mrs A Dudley-Warde

Registrar: Mrs D W Patterson

Full-time Teaching Staff (Senior School):
Mrs A O Bassett, BMus, LRAM
Miss N J Beale, MA
Mrs L J Bradbury, BA, MA
Mrs N E Brett, BSc
Miss S Brooks, BA
Mr B N Brown, BSc
Mr J B Brown, BSc
Mrs M L Brown, BSc
Mr S T Brown, MA, BDes
Mr S J Burgon, BEd, LTCL
Mrs A Y Burt, BSc
Mr R E Burton, BSc
Mr J Chua, MMath
Mr P C Clarke, BA
Mrs J Cook, CertEd
Mrs L J Court, BA
Mrs S Cunliffe, CertEd
Mrs S Dakin, MA
Mr J W Davies, MSc, BA
Miss K M Donovan, BSc
Mr R J Duke, MA
Mr G D Edgell, BA
Mrs C E Edwards, MBA, BSc
Dr M D Fletcher, PhD
Mr S J Forrester, MA, BA
Mrs S C Fountain, MA, BA
Mrs K E Fox, BA
Mr J R Garforth, MA, BSc
Mr D T Harding, BA
Mr J P Hills, BA
Mrs A Hirst, BA
Mr P J Hollywell, BA
Mr D P Hughes, BA
Mrs M Hutchison, MA
Mrs D J Jenner, BA
Mrs A M Knights, BSc Ed
Mr P P G MacDonald, MA
Mr H G L Mackrige, MA
Mrs J L Mainwaring, MA
Mr R Mainwaring, MMus, BA, ALCM
Mr J Matthews, BA
Mr G J Musto, MPhil, CMath, FIMA
Mrs K Nash, BA
Mrs C V Nightingale, BSc
Mrs J R Opie, BA
Mrs M K Patterson, BSc, MSc
Miss U J Paver, BA
Mr I J Prior, Mth, BA
Mr C J Redman, MEng, BA
Mr T P R Reeman, BA
Miss N Robinson, BA
Mr M Sealy, FRCO CHM, GRSM, ARCM
Mrs C M Sergeant, BA
Dr N M H Sheffrin, PhD, BSc
Mr S R Snowden, MSc, MBCS, BA, BSc
Miss M E Telford, MA, BA
Mr D J Walker, BA
Mr M J Westcott, BEd

Mr C B Woodgate, MA
Miss A T Wright, MEd, BEd

Part-time Teaching Staff (Senior School):
Mrs M L Brennan, BEd
Mrs C E Edwards, MBA, BSc
Mrs V Gibson, BSocSc
Mr A E Haines, BA
Mrs S J Marshall, BA
Mrs A K Matthews, BSc
Mrs C D Morris, BA
Mrs J Reeman, BEd
Mr J Richards, BA
Mrs D Westcott, BEd

Kingswood Preparatory School

Headmaster: Mr M R Brearey

Deputy Head: Mr P Dixon, BEd Hons, MA Ed, NPQH

Head of Pre-Prep: Mrs A Parry-Hearn, MA

Head of Foundation Stage: Miss S Caden, CertEd

Housemaster, High Vinnalls: Mr P Titley, BEd Hons, BTec

Full-time Teaching Staff:
Mrs R Briggs, BEd
Miss E Brunt, BA
Mrs S Butcher, MA
Mr M Callahan, BScEcon
Mrs J Cook, CertEd
Mrs J Cross, BA
Miss M Diaz, BA, TESOL
Miss K Elliott, MSc, BA
Mrs K Fox, BA
Mrs C Frey, CertEd
Mrs S Gilmore, BA QTS
Mrs M Gibson, BEd, PGDE
Mrs J Hallett, CertEd, PGDD
Mrs S Higgins, BEd
Mrs A Hirst, BA
Miss R Howe, BEd, PSE
Mrs M McGlynn, BA, LSDE
Miss M Newman
Miss J Rexe, BEd, BASc
Mrs K Simpson, BA Ed, NNEB
Mr I Shrubsole, BA
Mrs H Ward, BA, ATC
Miss A Wright, BA
Mrs P Wynne, BA

Part-time Teaching Staff:
Mr J Chitson, BSc
Mrs J Dix, BA
Mrs R Green, BEd
Mrs J Mason, BEd
Mrs I Turner, BA
Mrs C Ward, BSc

Visiting Music Staff (Senior & Prep):
Mr A Arcoleo (*Acoustic Guitar*)
Mr C Bissex, BA (*Voice*)
Mr A Bull (*Drums*)
Mrs C Burden (*Piano*)
Mrs S Burnett (*Recorder, Clarinet, Saxophone*)
Mr A Cheshire (*French Horn*)
Mrs T Dicker, LWCMD (*Cello*)
Mrs R Faber (*Harp*)
Mr A Foister (*Brass*)
Mrs V Hammond, GRSM, LRAM (*Oboe*)
Mr G Harrup, BA, LGSM (*Electric Guitar*)
Mrs J Hobbs, BMus, LRAM, LTCL (*Piano*)
Mrs C Hollywell (*Flute*)
Mr M James (*Guitar*)
Mr D Kniveton, BA, LTCL (*Flute*)
Mrs S Lane (*Piano*)
Miss N Lemmy (*Voice*)
Mrs V Miche (*Violin*)
Mr J Morgan (*Bass*)
Mr K Morgan (*Saxophone*)
Mrs J Phillips (*Voice*)
Mrs A Salamonsen, MMus (*Violin*)
Mrs L Sealy, BA (*Voice*)
Mr J Scott (*Drums*)
Mrs C Seymour (*Violin*)
Mr D Seymour, ARCM, DipRCM (*Piano*)
Dr D V Shepard, BSc (*Clarinet, Saxophone*)
Mr N Thorne, MA (*Piano*)
Mr G Wells (*Trumpet*)
Mrs P J Wendzina, CertEd (*Piano*)

Mrs A Wilton (*Piano*)

Medical Officer: Dr T J Harris, MD, MCh, MRCOG

Site and Buildings. Kingswood occupies 218 acres of superb parkland overlooking the world heritage City of Bath and within easy reach of the M4 and M5 motorways, as well as rail and air links. In addition to the beautiful main Victorian buildings, there is a state-of-the-art Theatre; a spacious sixth-form centre with facilities for private study and a modern common room; a series of specialist centres for ICT, DT, Drama Studio, Art Studio and a Music School with its own recording studio. A library and resources centre was opened in September 2006 with wi-fi facility. All academic departments also have well-resourced areas including a new modern Language Laboratory. There are seven houses for boarding and day pupils, a beautiful Chapel and excellent sporting facilities, including a Sports Hall, indoor swimming pool, two floodlit astroturfs, and extensive playing fields. In September 2011, a new sports pavilion will also be opened with first-class sports changing facilities and excellent hospitality areas.

The School also has its own Prep School in a Georgian mansion and award-winning modern buildings in a separate section of the parkland.

Curriculum. Kingswood encourages its students to develop lively, enquiring and well-informed minds and the high standard of attainment reached by its pupils has been highly praised. From 11 to 13 pupils follow a broad and balanced curriculum. Each pupil has a tutor to supervise progress and to offer advice and encouragement. At 14 the pupils choose at least eight and up to twelve GCSE subjects to develop their particular talents whilst maintaining a broad range of skills. They are also encouraged to develop independent learning plans which they work on with their tutors. Most sixth formers specialise in at least three or four subjects and all participate in a General Studies programme. Sixteen subjects are offered at GCSE level as well as over twenty at AS/A2 level, including Politics, Business Studies, Sports Studies, Theatre Studies, Psychology and Critical Thinking. The Extended Project Qualification is also offered.

Organisation. *Preparatory*: Pupils are drawn from a wide variety of schools, but Kingswood also has its own prep school for boarders and day pupils. Kingswood Prep School (KPS) caters for c320 boys and girls between the ages of 3 and 11, and offers a variety of activities alongside the academic curriculum. A boarding house for boys and girls aged 7–11 opened in September 1998. This "family-based" unit of 20 boarders is cared for by house-parents who also teach at the school. Children from the prep school are expected to move on to Kingswood, but parents are advised if children are felt to be academically unsuitable for entry to the Senior School at the end of Year 6. (*See Kingswood Preparatory School entry in IAPS section.*)

Westwood: A junior house operates for boys and girls aged 11–13. This is designed to settle new pupils into the school at 11+ or 12+ and provide the special environment that the younger pupils require before going into the senior houses. In effect, it means the pupils enjoy the atmosphere associated with a prep school whilst also enjoying all the facilities of a senior school. Sixth formers are especially selected to act as elder "brothers/sisters" and prefects to the younger pupils. The house is run by four resident house staff, together with house assistants.

Senior Houses: From the age of 13+ pupils are assigned to one of six houses, three for boys and three for girls, each under a resident Housemaster or Housemistress and assisted by other teaching staff. The houses ensure a good and friendly 'home from home' environment and there are also shared social areas in the centre of school. It would be normal to have c200 students in the Sixth Form, which has its own special building.

Houses. The seven houses are all very distinctive and five are set within their own grounds. Emphasis is placed on creating a family atmosphere in each house and the pastoral care provided has been judged at ISI inspection as 'exceptional'. Tutors monitor each pupil's progress and welfare. The school has a number of houses and flats for single and married staff. Half of the staff at the senior school live on the campus which cultivates exceptionally good relationships between teachers and students.

Sports and Games. The sporting and leisure activities programmes have around 90 activities with particular emphasis on sport, drama, music, art and outdoor pursuits. Sporting activities include athletics, badminton, basketball, cricket, cross-country, fencing, golf, hockey, netball, rugby, swimming and tennis. Other activities range from the Duke of Edinburgh's Award Scheme to Computing, from Orienteering to Photography, and Bird Watching to Dance Express. Regular group activities in the instrumental field include orchestra, an award-winning jazz band, string group and wind band. There are also junior and senior choirs and a large-scale choral society and an extensive performance programme. Over 50% of the school are involved in extra music lessons. At least four dramatic productions take place each year.

Health. The well-equipped School Medical Centre is under the supervision of a fully qualified resident Sister and the School Medical Officer.

Religious Activities. Kingswood welcomes pupils from all denominations. In addition to regular morning worship, there is a wide variety of guest speakers and the Christian Fellowship organises its own events. There are regular fund-raising activities for charities and a Community Service programme. Every year a joint Methodist-Anglican Confirmation service is held and there are special services in Bath Abbey for the whole school Carol Service and for Commemoration Day.

Careers. From the earliest stage possible, students are encouraged to participate in all decisions affecting their future. Kingswood subscribes to the Independent Schools Careers Organisation and has links with local career guidance organisations. A programme of work experience is followed by all members of the Lower Sixth and is aimed at providing experience of the entire process of job application, interview and work itself. The School has established close links with local employers to make all this possible. A series of lectures and discussions with visiting employers is also organised and endorsed by the Head of Sixth Form.

Leavers. It is normal for all of our Sixth Form pupils to go on to university courses, around 96% to the place of their first choice.

Fees per term (2011-2012). £3,853 (day), £6,932–£8,303 (full boarding), £6,055–£7,502 (weekly boarding).

EAL teaching is provided for students who do not speak English as their first language – this is invoiced separately as required.

Entry Requirements. Entry is based on Kingswood's entrance examination; a report from the candidate's previous school and, where possible, a personal interview. Candidates at 13+ may also enter by Common Entrance or Scholarship papers. Entry to the Sixth Form is by a minimum of six or more GCSE passes – four at Grade B plus two at Grade C, plus school report and interview. There are some subject specific criteria, details of which are found on the school website. (Most applicants achieve considerably more than the minimum entry grades.) There are normally around 25 places available due to the extended facilities available at Sixth Form level.

Scholarships and Bursaries. (*See Scholarship Entries section.*) Academic and Special Talent scholarships (up to a maximum of 25% of the basic fees) are available annually to pupils entering Years 7, 9 and Lower Sixth. Special Talent scholarships are awarded for excellence in a particular field, e.g. Music, Sport, Drama, Art & DT. A number of means-tested bursaries are also awarded annually at the discretion of the Headmaster and the Governors. Further details of scholarships and bursaries can be obtained from the Registrar or on the school website.

Charitable status. Kingswood School is a Registered Charity, number 309148. Founded by John Wesley, it maintains its Methodist tradition in providing preparatory and secondary education.

Kirkham Grammar School

Ribby Road, Kirkham, Preston, Lancashire PR4 2BH
Tel: 01772 671079
Fax: 01772 672747
e-mail: info@kirkhamgrammar.co.uk
website: www.kirkhamgrammar.co.uk

Kirkham Grammar School, founded in 1549, is a co-educational independent School of 960 pupils aged between 3 and 18. The Senior School of 700 pupils, 65 of whom are boarders, incorporates a Sixth Form of 170, and the Junior School, for day pupils, has 230+ on roll.

Chairman of Governors: Mr R M Dawson

Headmaster: **Mr D R Walker**, MA Cantab, PGCE

Deputy Headmaster: Dr R Luker, BA Hons, MA, PhD, PGCE

Assistant Head (Pastoral): Mrs D C Parkinson, BSc, PGCE, NPQH

Director of Studies & Head of Sixth Form: Mr A R Long, MA Oxon, PGCE

Senior Teacher: Mr R J Watson, BA Hons, PGCE

Director of ICT Systems: Mr M J Hancock, BEd Hons, MA, MBA

Heads of Year:
Sixth Form: Mr A R Long, MA Oxon, PGCE
Assistant Heads of Sixth Form:
Mr M Gaddes, MA, PGCE
Mrs J Stanbury, BA Hons, PGCE
Middle School (Fourth & Fifth Years): Mr M A Whalley, BEd Hons, MEd
Assistant Head of Middle School: Mrs A Walker, BA, PGCE
Third Year: Mr S F Duncan, BA Hons
Second Year: Mr D Gardner, BEng, PGCE
First Year: Mrs K C O'Flaherty, BA Hons, PGCE

Heads of Departments:
Art: Mr S P Gardiner, BA Hons
Biology: Mrs M E Scott, BSc Hons, PGCE
Business Studies: Mrs F M Lang, BA Hons, PGCE
Design & Technology: Mr D Gardner, BEng, PGCE
Drama: Ms J E Barrie, BA Hons, PGCE
English: Mr C J Hawkes, BA Hons, MA, PGCE
Geography: Mr S R Whittle, MA, PGCE
History: Mr T P Miller, BA Hons, PGCE
ICT: Mr R J Browning, BSc Hons, ACCE, PGCE
Latin: Mrs S P Long, BA Hons, PGCE
Learning Support: Mrs P Blackburn, TCert Hons, BA Hons, PG Dip SpLD
Librarian: Mrs C Copland, ALA
Mathematics: Miss S R Howe, BSc, PGCE
Modern Foreign Languages: Miss L E Vicquelin, BA, PGCE
Director of Music: Mr A C Barratt, BA Hons, GRSM, LRAM, MTC
Director of Physical Education & Games: Mr M A Whalley, BEd Hons, MEd

Physics: Mr M Gaddes, MA, PGCE
Politics: Mr M P Melling, BA Hons, MA Ed, PGCE
Psychology: Mrs J Stanbury, BA Hons, PGCE
Religious Studies: Mrs L Bowles, BA Hons, PGCE
Science & Chemistry: Dr A C Hall, PhD, Grad RIC

Houses & Housemistresses/Housemasters:
Kirkham House: Mrs J M Glover, BEd Hons
Fylde House: Mr S R Whittle, MA Cantab, PGCE
School House: Mr M S Marmion, BEd, MA (*Head of Boarding*)
Preston House: Dr A B Rollins, BSc Hons, PhD, PGCE (*Health & Safety Officer*)

Bursar: Mrs C E Brown

Headmaster's PA/Registrar: Mrs C M Seed

Junior School:
Headmistress of Junior School: Mrs A S Roberts, BEd
Deputy Headmaster: Mr B Edgar, BEd
Head of Infant Department: Mrs P Edgar BEd Hons
Pre-School Manager: Mrs T Marsh, BEng Hons, PGCE

Headmistress's PA: Miss J Stewart
School Secretary: Mrs A Giddings

Kirkham Grammar School prides itself on turning out rounded, well-balanced and confident young people, the vast majority of whom continue their education at University. Pupils are encouraged to extend themselves to achieve the best results of which they are capable in order to acquire the necessary qualifications for entry to higher education or the career they wish to follow. As well as excellent academic results and a good Oxbridge entry record, the School introduces pupils to as wide a range as possible of cultural, sporting and creative activities and encourages them to participate in those which appeal to them.

The School has a strong Christian ethos, with an emphasis on care for the individual, traditional family values, good manners and sound discipline. It is a friendly close-knit community where staff and pupils work particularly closely together, fostering leadership and self-discipline, and encouraging cheerful, friendly and supportive relationships within the framework of 'one family'.

Facilities. Occupying 30 acres of its own grounds, Kirkham Grammar School boasts some excellent facilities, which include a large multi-purpose hall, a superb floodlit all-weather pitch, a newly refurbished Sixth Form Centre, an outstanding Technology Centre and Languages Centre, built in partnership with BAE Systems, and a magnificent Dining Complex. Most recently the School has built a new Science Centre alongside a new extended classroom block incorporating interactive facilities and also a new Performing Arts Centre.

Boarding. The School is a member of the Boarding Schools' Association. The recently refurbished Boarding House is pleasant and comfortable and is run under the personal supervision of the Boarding Housemaster and his wife, whose residence is attached to the boarding wing of the School.

Academic Programme. The courses lead to GCSE, A Level and AS Level. In the first three years, the basic subjects studied are English, French, Mathematics, German, Spanish, Geography, History, Physics, Chemistry, Biology, Music, Art, Drama, ICT, Design and Technology, and Religious Studies. The first stage of specialisation takes place on entering the fourth form where the core subjects of English, Mathematics, Physics/Chemistry/Biology and French/German are taught in sets, and there is a further choice of subjects from three option blocks, which include: Art, Design and Technology (Product Design; Graphic Products; Systems), Music, Business Studies, Drama, Geography, History, ICT, Religious Studies, German, Latin and Physical Education.

In the Sixth Form, A and AS Level subjects are chosen from the following: English Language and Literature, Maths, Further Maths, Biology, Chemistry, Physics, French, German, Art, Music, Design Technology, Geography, History, Psychology, ICT, Politics, Theatre Studies, Religious Studies, Business Studies, Physical Education, Electronics (AS only).

In addition all Sixth Formers follow a programme of General Studies and many voluntarily continue in the CCF and/or take up the Duke of Edinburgh's Award, Young Enterprise or Community Service. Extra tuition is provided for Oxbridge candidates. Currently a group of students are following the AQA Baccalaureate.

A comprehensive careers service is available through the Careers Teachers. The School is an active member of ISCO and is also served by Careerlink.

Sport. The School has a long and strong sporting tradition and offers the following sports: Rugby, hockey, cricket, athletics, tennis, netball, cross-country, badminton, squash, swimming, rounders and volleyball.

Music. There is a very active musical life at the School, with regular Concerts both at lunchtime and in the evening, providing a platform for the Orchestra, various ensembles and Soloists.

Extra-Curricular Activities. An impressive range of extra-curricular activities is offered by a School renowned for its sporting prowess, but with strength across the board in music, art, and drama. There is a strong and popular Combined Cadet Force contingent, with Army and RAF sections, and a flourishing House System. A large number of societies cater for a wide range of interests including drama, debating, Duke of Edinburgh's Award, chess, public speaking, gardening, badminton, climbing, magic circle, music and many others.

Admission to Senior School. Four form entry. Pupils are usually admitted at 11 years after passing the entrance examination held in January each year. Admissions to the School in other year groups, especially the Sixth Form, are possible. Day/Boarding applications should be made to the Headmaster who will be glad to provide further details.

Fees per term (2011-2012). Day (excluding lunches): Senior School £3,020; Junior School £2,265; Pre-School: £195 (full week), £40.50 (full day).

These Fees cover tuition, use of class, text and library books, school stationery, scientific equipment, games apparatus.

Senior School Boarding: £2,706 in addition to the Day fee. The boarding fee is discounted by 5% for children resident Monday to Friday (weekly boarders) and for children whose parents are current members of HM Forces.

Scholarships and Bursaries. The School offers an impressive number of Scholarships and Bursaries at 11+ and 16+. A detailed Scholarship Booklet is available from the Registrar.

Junior School (3–11 years). An integral part of the School under the same Board of Governors, the Junior School comprises a Pre-School, an Infant Department and a Junior Department, housed in splendid, purpose-built accommodation. The work is organised in close consultation with the Senior School to ensure that education in its broadest sense is continuous and progressive from the age of 3 to 18.

The curriculum is broadly based and balanced. The core subjects – English, Maths and Science – are given priority as set in the National Curriculum. History, Geography, RE, Music, ICT, Design and Technology, PE and Games are studied as pure subjects and also as they relate to one another in a cross-curricular manner. In the Early Years we offer a fun, stimulating and caring environment, which follows the Early Years Foundation Stage Framework.

Application should be made direct to the Headmistress's PA from whom a separate prospectus may be obtained.

Old Kirkhamians Association. For further details contact the Development Manager.

Charitable status. Kirkham Grammar School is a Registered Charity, number 1123869. The object of the Charity shall be the provision in or near Kirkham of a day and boarding school for boys and girls.

Lancing College
A Woodard School

Lancing, West Sussex BN15 0RW
Tel: 01273 452213
Fax: 01273 464720
e-mail: admissions@lancing.org.uk
website: www.lancingcollege.co.uk

Founded in 1848 by the Revd Nathaniel Woodard, Lancing College is the first of the Schools of the Woodard Foundation.

Motto: *Beati mundo corde.*

Governing Body:
The Provost and the Directors of Lancing College Ltd

Visitor: The Rt Revd The Lord Bishop of Chichester

Governing Body:
Chairman: Dr H O Brünjes, BSc, MBBS, DRCOG, FEWI
Deputy Chair: Lady Conway, BA, MA, PhD, FRGS, FRSA
Provost: The Rt Revd Lindsay Urwin, OGS, MA (*ex officio*)
Chairman of Finance Committee: M Slumbers, BSc, ACA (*OL*)
Chairman of Estates Committee: R H Stapleton, FRICS
S G Alder, BA, FCA
C Baron, MA, LLM
N A O Bennett, MA, ARICS (*OL*)
P Bowden, LLM
Mrs A Edgell, LLB
A C V Evans, MA, MPhil, FICL, FKC
H C R Lawson, MA, MBA (*OL*)
Mrs S Mehta, BA, PG, MA
Major General D Rutherford-Jones, CB (*OL*)
Professor H E Smith, BMedSci, BMBS, MSc, DM, FFPHM, MRCGP

Bursar and Clerk to the Governing Body: Mrs P Bulman, FCA

Head Master: J W J Gillespie, MA

Second Master: J S McCullough, MA
Deputy Head: Mrs H R Dugdale, MA
Assistant Head (Academic): S W Cornford, MA, PhD
Assistant Head (Pastoral): D E Austin, BSc
President of the Common Room: S R Norris, BSc, PhD
Registrar and Director of Marketing: R J Tomlinson, MA
Director of Extra-Curricular Activities: C P Foster, MA
Director of IT: N Allen, MBCS, CITP
Chaplain: The Revd R K Harrison, BA, MA
Director of Development: Catherine Reeve, BA (*OL*)

Assistant Staff:
D E Austin, BSc (*Physics*)
T S Auty, BA (*Photography, Art*)
Mrs A T Barker, BA (*Classics*)
D G Barker, MA, PhD (*Head of Classics*)
A J Betts, BA, PhD, MIL (*French, German*)
A K Black, MA, BLitt (*English*)
N A Brookes, MSc (*Mathematics*)
Mrs E Campbell, MA (*Mathematics*)
A M Chappell, BSc (*Biology, Physics*)
A R Coakes, BA, MSc (*Design & Technology*)

D S Connolly, BA (*Head of Politics, History, Classical Civilisation*)
S W Cornford, MA, PhD (*English*)
D N Cox, MA, FRCO, FTCL, LRAM, ARCM (*Director of Chapel Music*)
Mrs M J Creer, BA (*English*)
C P E Crowe, BEd (*Director of Sport*)
P Dale, BSc, MIBiol (*Head of Psychology, Biology*)
D G Davies, BA, ALCM (*Head of Spanish, French*)
M F Day, BSc, PhD, MIBiol (*Biology*)
Miss N C Dragonetti, BA (*Music*)
G A Drummond, BSc (*Economics*)
Mrs H R Dugdale, MA (*English, PSHE*)
J R J East, BA (*Mathematics*)
Miss K V Edwards, BA (*Head of Girls' Games and DofE*)
Mrs P S Faulkner, BSc (*Head of Biology*)
C P Foster, MA (*Head of Geography*)
J A Grime, BSc (*Geography*)
D J Harman, BA, MA (*English*)
The Revd R K Harrison, BA, MA (*Religious Studies, History*)
Ms J Hayward-Voss, BA (*Head of Business Studies*)
Miss L Jakubikova, BA (*Spanish, French, Italian*)
P D Kennedy, BSc, MSc, DPhil (*Physics*)
D A Kerney, MA, PhD (*Head of History*)
Mrs K Lindfield, HND (*Art*)
D N Mann, BSSc (*Head of PE, Biology*)
Mrs S D Marchant, BA, MCLIP (*Librarian*)
Mrs M A Martindale, MA, MLitt (*English*)
R J Maru (*Director of Cricket*)
Mrs C A McGarry, BSc (*Mathematics*)
Ms A McKane, MA (*English*)
T J Meierdirk, BFA (*Head of Design & Technology*)
J S McCullough, MA (*Mathematics*)
C Metcalf, DLC (*PE, Mathematics*)
Miss M R Mitchell, BA (*French, Spanish*)
C M Mole, BSc (*PE, PSHE*)
Mrs C R Mole, BA (*Economics, Business Studies*)
I Morgan-Williams, GMus, RNCM (*Director of Music*)
S R Norris, BSc, PhD (*Chemistry*)
Mrs C E Palmer, MA (*History*)
M S W Palmer, BA, PhD, MIL (*Head of German and Italian*)
Miss C M Parkinson, BA (*English, History, RS, PSHE*)
R G Pavey, MA (*Head of Modern Languages and French*)
G A Preston, BSc, PhD (*Head of Science and Physics*)
Miss K E Price, BA, MA (*Design & Technology*)
Miss C M Pringle, BA (*Head of Art*)
Mrs K C Rees, BSc (*Design & Technology*)
P C Richardson, MA (*Head of RS, Drama, History*)
O R Ridley, BA (*Head of English*)
Mrs H M Robinson, BSc (*Chemistry*)
Mrs J M Scullion, CertEd (*Learning Support Coordinator*)
J L Sherrell, MA (*Head of Economics*)
M J H Smith, BA (*Head of Drama, Religious Studies*)
Ms H A Stevenson, BLib, MCLIP (*Assistant Librarian*)
Mrs J O Such, BA, MSc (*Head of Mathematics*)
Dr W A Swarbrick, BSc, EdD (*Physics, Chemistry*)
Mrs A W Tritton, BSc, MA, FRGS (*Geography, PSHE*)
Miss K E Vaughan, BA (*Art*)
S J Ward, MMath, MPhil (*Mathematics*)
M W Wilkes, BA (*Biology*)
D J Wilks, MA (*History*)
A P Williamson, MA (*Head of Chemistry*)

Houses & Housemasters/mistresses:

Boys:
Head's: Mr A M Chappell
Second's: Mr D S Connolly
School: Mr C M Mole
Gibbs': Mr M J H Smith
Teme: Dr S R Norris

Girls:
Field's: Mrs M J Creer
Sankey's: Miss N C Dragonetti
Manor: Miss C M Parkinson
Handford (Sixth Form): Ms A McKane

Head Master's Secretary: Mrs H L Betts, BSc
Admissions Officer: Mrs G S Prichard

Medical Officers:
Dr N S Lyons, MBBS
Dr I Cox, MBChB, BSc, DRCOG, MRCGP
Dr H Bentley, MBBS, MRCGP, DA, DRCOG
Dr C Huckstep, MBBS, DRCOG, DCH

There are about 530 pupils in the school, accommodated in nine houses.

Location. The School stands on a spur of the Downs, overlooking the sea to the south and the Weald to the north, in grounds of some 550 acres, which include the College Farm.

By train, Lancing is 10 minutes from Brighton, 30 minutes from Gatwick Airport and 75 minutes from central London.

Buildings and Facilities. The main school buildings, faced with Sussex flint, are grouped around two quadrangles on the lines of an Oxford or Cambridge College.

The great Chapel, open to visitors every day, has the largest rose window built since the Middle Ages.

The College has extensive laboratories, a purpose-built Music School, a Theatre with a full-time technical manager and a modern Design and Technology Centre with computerised design and engineering facilities. Alongside this, a strikingly modern Art School providing vast studio space and a photography suite opened in 2008. Most recently a café has been created in the centre of the school for use by pupils and staff. There are over 330 private studies for boys and girls, many of which are study-bedrooms. There is a sports hall, indoor swimming pool and a miniature shooting range. Sporting facilities also include Squash and Fives courts and an all-weather surface and full-sized astroturf hockey pitch.

Admission. Boys and girls are normally admitted at the beginning of the Autumn Term in their fourteenth year. Admission is made on the result of either the Entrance Scholarship, the Common Entrance Examination or by private testing. A registration fee of £95 is paid when a child's name is entered in the admission register. Entries should be made via the Registrar, who will assign a House, following as far as possible the wishes of the parents. After a pupil has joined the School, parents usually correspond with the Housemaster or Housemistress directly.

Sixth Form Entry. Applications for entry should be made to the Registrar. Testing takes place in November or by private arrangement.

Curriculum. Designed as far as possible to suit every pupil's potential, the curriculum provides the training required for entry to Universities and to a wide range of professions.

In a pupil's first three years the curriculum provides a broad, balanced education without premature specialisation. The total of subjects taken at GCSE is limited to about nine or ten, the object being to promote excellence in whatever is studied and to lay firm foundations for the Sixth Form years.

The following subjects are studied in the Senior School: English Language and Literature, Religious Studies, Mathematics, Physics, Chemistry, Biology, French, Spanish or German, Geography, History, Physical Education, Music, Art, Design and Technology, Latin or Classical Civilisation, Greek and Drama.

In the Sixth Form there is a choice of 23 subjects which can be studied to A or AS Level, together with a General Studies course in the Lower Sixth.

A close connection has been established with schools in Germany and Spain, with which individual and group exchanges are arranged.

Tutorial System. In addition to their Housemaster or Housemistress there are pastoral Tutors attached to each House who act as Academic Tutors to individual pupils. The Tutors' main functions are to supervise academic progress and to encourage general reading and worthwhile spare time activities. A pupil usually keeps the same Tutor until he or she moves into the Sixth Form, where this function is taken over by an Academic Tutor chosen from one of the specialist teachers.

Music and Art form an important part of the education of all pupils. There are orchestras, bands, ensembles and choirs. Organ and Choral awards to Oxford and Cambridge and Colleges of Music are frequently won. There is a full programme of extra-curricular **Drama**. The **Art School** and **Design and Technology Centre**, adjacent to the Science Department, provide for a wide range of technical and creative work.

Other Activities. Boys and girls in their first year are given the opportunity to sample the many activities on offer at the College. A well-organised extra-curricular programme is followed by all pupils, under the supervision of the Director of Extra-Curricular Activities.

Participation in extra-curricular activities is strongly encouraged and there is a vast range on offer. Up to twelve plays are produced each year and pupils are able to write and perform their own plays and to learn stagecraft.

In the Advent term the main sports are Association Football for boys and Hockey for girls; in the Lent term Football and Hockey for boys and Netball for girls. Squash, Fives, Badminton, Basketball, Cross Country and Shooting (the College has an indoor range) take place during both terms for boys and girls. Some Rugby is played in the Lent term. Cricket, Tennis, Sailing, Athletics and Rounders take place in the Summer term, and there is Swimming all year round in the College's indoor heated pool.

The College has a CCF contingent (with Army and RAF sections) and takes part in the Duke of Edinburgh's Award scheme. There is also a flourishing Outreach group, which works in the local community. Pupils help to run a small farm (including sheep, goats, pigs, alpacas and chickens) under the supervision of the Farm Manager.

Links have been established with local industries and pupils are involved in business experience through the Young Enterprise scheme.

Careers and Higher Education. A number of the teaching staff share responsibility for careers advice and there is a well-equipped careers section in the Gwynne Library. Over 98% of pupils go to University with about 10% gaining places at Cambridge or Oxford. All members of the Fifth Form attend the annual Careers Symposium and most enrol in the ISCO Futurewise scheme. ISCO provides a range of Careers lectures and experience days throughout the year.

Scholarships and Exhibitions. Candidates for the following awards must be under 14 years of age on 1st September in the year of the examination. The age of the candidate is taken into account in making awards. A candidate may enter for more than one type of award, and account may be taken of musical or artistic proficiency in a candidate for a non-musical award; but no one may hold more than one type of award, except in an honorary capacity.

A number of Open Scholarships ranging in value from £1,000 per year to half of the annual school fee.

A number of Music Scholarships ranging in value up to half the annual school fee. Scholarships may be offered to pupils from schools where the time for Music is less than in some others, and where a candidate may have less musical experience but greater potential.

One Professor W K Stanton Music Scholarship for a Chorister from Salisbury Cathedral School, or failing that any Cathedral School. A Stanton Exhibition may also be awarded.

A number of scholarships in Art, Drama and Sport, ranging in value up to a quarter of the annual school fee.

A number of Ken Shearwood Awards, ranging in value up to a quarter of the annual school fee, are made to pupils of all-round ability and potential who have made outstanding contributions to their present schools.

Entry Forms for Academic, Art, Music, Drama, Sport and All-Rounder (Ken Shearwood) awards are obtainable from the Admissions Officer.

Sixth Form Awards. Scholarships are available for new entrants to the Sixth Form with special proficiency in Academic subjects, Music or Art. There is also one Organ Scholarship. The candidate's general ability to contribute to the life of a boarding school community will also be taken into account. A small number of Scholarships is also available internally on the strength of GCSE results.

The value of all Entrance Scholarships may be augmented by bursaries, according to parental circumstances.

Fees per term (2011-2012). Boarding £9,615 (£28,845 per annum). Day £6,720 (£20,160 per annum).

Further details about fees, including the scheme for payment in advance of a single composition fee to cover a pupil's education during his/her time in the School, are available from the Bursar.

Charitable status. Lancing College is a Registered Charity, number 1076483. It exists to provide education for boys and girls.

Latymer Upper School

King Street, Hammersmith, London W6 9LR
Tel: 0845 638 5800
Fax: 020 8748 5212
e-mail: registrar@latymer-upper.org
website: www.latymer-upper.org

The Latymer Foundation owes its origin to the will of Edward Latymer, dated 1624. It is a Day School of 1,121 pupils, of whom 340 are in the co-educational Sixth Form. The School moved to full co-education in September 2004, with entry at 11+ for girls as well as boys.

There are also 163 pupils in the co-educational Latymer Prep School which shares the same grounds. (*Please see entry in IAPS section.*)

Chairman of Governors: James Graham, MA, FRSA

Co-opted Governors:
Ruth Caleb, OBE, FRSA, Hon Doc Arts
Ian Elliott, BA
Stephen Hodges, MA
Nicholas Jordan, MA
Rosemary Radcliffe, CBE, MA, MPhil, FIBC
Margaret Salmon, BA, FCIPD
Professor Jim Smith, MA, PhD, FRS, FRSA, FMedSci
Barry Southcott, BSc
Professor Julius Weinberg, BA, BMBCh, DM, MSc, FRCP
Trevor Woolley, CB, MA
Nigel Woolner, Dip Arch, RIBA, FRSA
John Wotton, MA

Ex officio Governor: The Revd Simon Downham, LLB, DipMin, MA

Clerk to the Governors: Simon Porter, MA

***Head*: P J Winter**, MA Wadham College Oxford

Deputy Heads:
A L Hirst, MA Fitzwilliam College Cambridge (*Premises and Resources*)

A R Matthews, MA Sidney Sussex College Cambridge (*Academic*)
Miss A Tomlinson, BSc Cardiff, MA Open University (*Staff Welfare and Development*)

Assistant Heads:
C D Chivers, MA King's College Cambridge (*Sixth Form*)
K Spencer, BSc Hull, MA Cincinnati, USA (*Middle School*)
Mrs N Varma, BSc, MSc Warwick (*Lower School*)
R B Niblett, BA Liverpool (*Co-curricular*)

Heads of Year:
Mrs S J Markowska, BA Westfield College London (*Head of Upper Sixth*)
M G Holmes, BA Bristol (*Head of Lower Sixth*)
Ms D Kendall, BA Leeds (*Head of Year 11*)
P Goldsmith, BA Leeds, MBA Cass Business School (*Head of Year 10*)
Mrs G Snelling, MA St Andrews (*Head of Year 9*)
G Cooper, BSc Port Elizabeth SA (*Head of Year 8*)
Mrs K Temple, BA Durham (*Head of Year 7*)

Assistant Staff:

Art & Design:
D Mumby, BA Wolverhampton (*Head of Art & Design*)
Ms R Bell, BA Bristol
C Blanchard, MA Université Panthéon Sorbonne, MA Westminster
Miss J Clarke, BA Canterbury
D Flynn, BDes Visual Dublin, MA Brighton
Ms J Hillis-Maidment, BA Exeter College of Art, MA London Institute
Miss J Ward, BA, MA Winchester College of Art, Middlesex

Biology:
Mrs M Patterson, BSc Bristol (*Head of Biology*)
G M Hardy, BSc Cardiff, PhD Emmanuel College Cambridge
Ms C Hopley, BSc Cape Town SA
Mrs C Keegan, MA Mansfield College Oxford, MSc Exeter College Oxford
N R Orton, JP, BSc London, CBiol, FLS, MIBiol
K G Paradise, BSc Surrey, MSc Brunel
Ms A Quinn, BA Pembroke College Oxford

Chemistry:
B Chaplin, BSc Portsmouth, PhD Reading (*Head of Science*)
J M Beyers, BSc, BEng Stellenbosch SA, BEd Cape Town
Miss H Davis, MSc University College London
E Forbes, MSc Edinburgh
R Savva, BSc Bedford College London
Mrs A Sellars, BSc University of Wales
M J Teskey, BSc Birmingham

Classics:
M Lewis, BA Durham (*Head of Classics*)
G Cook, MA Queens' College Cambridge
Ms F Ellison, BA Girton College Cambridge
M G Holmes, BA Bristol (*Head of Lower Sixth*)
Mrs S Motz, BA Balliol College Oxford
C Paterson, BA St Anne's College Oxford

Computing/IT:
M D Chandler, MEd Tech Brunel (*Head of Computing & IT*)
B Matthews, BA Manchester Metropolitan, MSc City Univ
Mrs J Price, BA Huddersfield

Design & Technology:
E Charlwood, BSc Aston (*Head of Design & Technology*)
D Baker, BArch Newcastle
Miss S Ip, BA De Montfort
Ms J Selby, BA Sir John Cass School of Art
Miss L Snooks, BA Loughborough

Drama:
J Joseph, BA London (*Director of Drama*)
Miss S Boulton, BA, MA Central School of Speech and Drama
Mrs S Woodham, BA Aberystwyth

Economics & Business Studies:
M Wallace, BSc Birmingham (*Head of Economics & Business Studies*)
C Ben Nathan, BA Exeter, MBA Middlesex
J S Gilbert, MA Wadham College Oxford (*Head of Politics*)
P Goldsmith, BA Leeds, MBA Cass Business School (*Head of Year 10*)
N Sennett, BA Reading
Miss A Tomlinson, BSc Cardiff, MA Open University (*Deputy Head*)

English:
Mrs R Babuta, BA King's College London, MLitt St John's College Oxford (*Head of English*)
Mrs S M T Adams, BA Birmingham, MA Surrey
C D Chivers, MA King's College Cambridge (*Assistant Head Sixth Form*)
Ms H Cross, BA Durham
S P Dorrian, BA Stirling (*Principal of the Prep*)
J Foley, BA, PhD Galway
S Joyce, BA St John's College Oxford
Mrs S J Markowska, BA Westfield College London (*Head of Upper Sixth*)
A Merchant, BA Lady Margaret Hall Oxford
Ms S Muneer, BA Balliol College Oxford
R Riggs, BA, MA King's College London
Ms A Smith, BA Sidney Sussex College Cambridge

Extended Project:
Miss H Davis, MSc University College London
Ms L Cole, BSc, MA Durham
P Drumm, BMus Bangor, MA York, DPhil Sussex
J Foley, BA, PhD Galway
Dr K Hill, BA, MSt, PhD Balliol College Oxford
Mrs M Patterson, BSc Bristol (*Head of Biology*)
J Rogers, BSc, MSc Bristol, PhD Cranfield Institute (*Head of Physics*)
N Sennett, BA Reading
K Spencer, BSc Hull, MA Cincinnati, USA (*Assistant Head Middle School*)

Geography:
M C Ashby, MSc King's College London, FRGS (*Head of Geography*)
Ms L Cole, BSc, MA Durham
A Edwards, BSc Cardiff, MEd Cambridge
A L Hirst, MA Fitzwilliam College Cambridge (*Deputy Head*)
Ms R Monahan, BSc Birmingham
Mrs G Snelling, MA St Andrews (*Head of Year 9*)
K Spencer, BSc Hull, MA Cincinnati, USA (*Assistant Head Middle School*)

History & Political Studies:
J White, MA Selwyn College Cambridge (*Head of History*)
B J Bladon, BA King's College London
J P Foynes, BA, MA King's College London
J S Gilbert, MA Wadham College Oxford (*Head of Politics*)
Ms L Harding-Wyatt, BA Warwick
Dr K Hill, BA, MSt, PhD Balliol College Oxford
R Holder, MA Sussex
S Hole, BA Trinity Hall Cambridge
A R Matthews, BA Sidney Sussex College Cambridge (*Deputy Head*)
R N Orme, MA Gonville & Caius College Cambridge (*Head of History of Art*)

History of Art:
R N Orme, MA Gonville & Caius College Cambridge (*Head of History of Art*)
Ms R Bell, BA Bristol
Ms B Pickles, MA Edinburgh

Learning Support:
Ms J Heywood, BSc LSE, SENCO (*Head of Learning Support*)
Ms C Ellis, BA Sussex, Dip SpLD Hornsey
Ms S Wheldon, BA Wimbledon School of Art, Hornsby Dip SpLD

Mathematics:
P MacMahon, BA Emmanuel College Cambridge, MSc Open University (*Head of Mathematics*)
M Aldham, MMath Nottingham
Mrs N Alishaw, BSc Kent, MSc Imperial College London
Miss T Andrew, BA Mansfield College Oxford
Z Bassman, BA Cornell University
S Cheung, BSc Imperial College London, MSc University College London
G Cooper, BSc Port Elizabeth SA (*Head of Year 8*)
R Fellerman, BA St Edmund Hall Oxford
Mrs M Kazi-Fornari, MA Hertford College Oxford
Dr R Nanayakkara, PhD Imperial College London, MMath Warwick
H Sahota, BA Emmanuel College Cambridge
Mrs N Varma, BSc, MSc Warwick
J Wesolowski, BA, MEng Cambridge

Modern Languages:
A J Rees, BA Swansea (*Head of Modern Languages*)
Mrs C Amodio, BA Lecce
Mrs M Bell, BA Southampton, MA University College London (*Head of Spanish*)
Ms C Desmons, BA Exeter
Mrs G Gauthier, BA Université Paul Valéry, Montpellier
D Gysin, BA King's College London
Mrs C Healy, BA Durham (*Head of German*)
Mrs A-C Hetherington, MA Robinson College Cambridge
Ms D Kendall, BA Leeds (*Head of Year 11*)
Mrs S-A Parra, BA Liverpool, MA Surrey
Ms B Pickles, MA Edinburgh
Srta V Rodriguez de Nova, BA Universidad Autónoma Madrid, MA Birkbeck
Mrs K Temple, BA Durham (*Head of Year 7*)
S N Ware, MA Brasenose College Oxford, MBA South Bank (*Head of Careers*)

Language Assistants:
Mme V Brian, Université de Rouen
Mlle H Butz, MA, Université de Lille, MA Université de Grenoble
Herr R Diesel, Technische Universität Berlin
Mlle A Llorens, MA Université de Picardie Jules Verne
Srta V Rodriguez de Nova, BA Universidad Autónoma Madrid, MA Birkbeck
Snr J Soldevila, BA Universitat Pompeu Fabra Barcelona

Music:
T Henwood, MA Exeter College Oxford, ARCO, FRSA (*Director of Music*)
C Dreamer, BA, MSt St Peter's College Oxford (*Assistant Director of Music*)
P Drumm, BMus Bangor, MA York, DPhil Sussex
R B Niblett, BA Liverpool (*Assistant Head Co-curricular*)

Physical Education & Games:
T Gill, BA Manchester Metropolitan (*Head of PE & Games*)
P Gibson, BA Wolverhampton (*Head of Football*)
Mrs L Foster, BEd University of Pretoria SA
K Paradise, BSc Surrey, MSc Brunel
Mrs L Tanner, BA Leeds Metropolitan

Physics:
J Rogers, BSc, MSc Bristol, PhD Cranfield Institute (*Head of Physics*)
A Birchmore, MSc Nottingham
Miss H Davis, MSc University College London
M Howells, MEng Trinity College Oxford
J Hunt, BSc Manchester
Ms S Gilbert, BSc Imperial College London
Mr J McCarthy, BA Trinity College Dublin
M Twomey, MEng Bristol

Religious Studies & Philosophy:
K Noakes, MA Corpus Christi College Cambridge, MA Theol Manchester (*Head of Religious Studies & Philosophy*)
Ms H Betteridge, MA Edinburgh
A Fleming, BA Nottingham
Ms C Garforth, MA Edinburgh
Ms C Graham, BA Regent's Park College Oxford
P Wizonski, BA King's College London, MA London

Visiting Music Staff:
P Jacobs, ARAM, LRAM, ARCM, ARCO, GRSM (*Head of Keyboard*)
Miss M Sugars, GBSM (*Head of Woodwind and Brass*)
T Marsden, BMus, MMus (*Head of Percussion*)
Ms H Neilson, BSc, PG Dip Adv RCM, MMus (*Head of Strings*)
Ms L Abbott, BMus, LTCL (*Violin & Viola*)
J Arben, BA, BA, MMus, GSMD (*Saxophone*)
Ms R Biggins, BA (*Saxophone*)
A Bottrill, GGSM, Dip GSMD,MA (*Piano*)
Ms E Bradley, GRNCM, MMus (*Double bass*)
G Brooks, MA Oxon, FRCO (*Organ*)
Ms R Buxton, BMus RCM, LGSM (*Clarinet*)
G Caldecott, GRNCM (*Piano*)
S Coleman, MMus (*Electric & Bass Guitar*)
Ms R Coulthard, BMus (*Guitar*)
Ms M Drower, ARCM (*Singing*)
S Evans, BA (*Singing*)
Ms R Fuller, MMus RAM (*Piano*)
S Gibson, BMus, GGSM (*Percussion*)
Ms P Ismay, ARCM (*Clarinet*)
Ms G James, AGSM (*Double Bass*)
Miss F Jellard, BA (*Singing*)
P Jones (*Singing*)
S Kalonaris, GRSM (*Electric & Bass Guitar*)
Ms I Klauke (*Recorder*)
C Lacey, LRAM (*Flute*)
T Lees, RNCM, Dip RCM (*Trombone*)
S O'Regan, DipRCM (*Flute*)
Ms C Philpot, ARCM (*Oboe*)
D Porter-Thomas, Dip RCM, ARCM (*Singing*)
G Proctor, BMus (*Guitar*)
Ms F Purrier, BMus, PG Dip RNCM (*Singing*)
Miss S Rose, GRSM, ARCM, LGSM (*Piano*)
H Rowntree, BMus RCM (*Trumpet*)
Ms J Snell, LRAM (*Violin & Viola*)
Ms O Travers, BA, LRAM (*Piano*)
Ms J Turner, Dip RCM, ARCM (*Bassoon*)
Miss A Whittlesea, BMus, LRAM (*Recorder*)
C Wood, LRAM, ARCM (*Piano*)

Administrative Staff:
Finance Director: J Tyrwhitt, MA, FCA
Facilities Manager: T Fisher
Head's Secretary: Ms E Curlet
Registrar: Mrs C Sutherland-Hawes, MA
Theatre Manager: S Crohill, BA
Office Manager: Mrs C Kava
Network Administrator: D Stanford, BSc
Librarian: Ms T McCargar, MCLIP, MA
School Doctor: M Kaplan, MBBS, MRCGP, DPD, DFFP, LRCP, MRCS
School Nurse: Ms L French, RGN

Co-education. Latymer's Sixth Form has been co-educational since 1996. 11+ entry is open to girls and boys.

Admissions. This is by competitive examination and interview at 11 and 13. Past papers are published and sent to those who register. Details of Open Days and Entry are obtainable from the Registrar. Entry to the Sixth Form is based on interview and conditional offers at GCSE.

Preparatory School. Pupils sit the 11+ Entrance Exam for the Upper School from Latymer Prep School. (*For further details see entry in IAPS section.*)

Fees per term (2011-2012). £4,985.

Scholarships. (*See Scholarship Entries section.*) Some Scholarships are offered in addition to substantial means-tested Scholarships.

Curriculum. A full range of academic subjects is offered at GCSE and A Level. Languages include French, German, Spanish and Italian (European Work Experience and exchanges are run every year), Latin and Greek. Science is taught as separate subjects by subject specialists from Year 7. Form sizes in the Lower School of around 22 and smaller teaching group sizes ensure the personal attention of staff.

Pastoral Care. The School has a strong tradition of excellent pastoral care. There are three Divisions (Lower School, Middle School, Sixth Form) and each Division is led by an Assistant Head. A Head of Year is responsible for the pupils in each year. Teams of Form Tutors deliver a coherent PSHE programme which promotes involvement in the community, charity work, and the personal, social and academic development of the Form.

Sixth Form. The large co-educational Sixth Form offers around thirty-five A Level choices; students opt to take four subjects at A Level. Students have the opportunity to undertake work experience in Paris or Berlin and receive extensive Careers and Higher Education guidance. All students expect to go on to University or Art College; more than 1 in 10 go to Oxbridge each year. The Sixth Form has use of new Common Room facilities as well as a University and Careers Centre.

Music and Drama. These activities play a large part in the life of the School. The Latymer Arts Centre houses music practice rooms and a 300-seat Theatre in addition to increased facilities for Art. In April 2008 a new Performing Arts Centre opened housing a 100-seat recital hall, music classrooms and more practice rooms and a dance/drama studio. There are several orchestras and bands and two major concerts each term. There are five major drama productions each year, and opportunities for all pupils to perform in events.

Science and Library. A state-of-the-art building, housing Science Laboratories, a Library, Sixth Form Study Common Room and Study Centre, opened in September 2010. All year groups have the use of these new facilities.

Sport. There are excellent facilities for sport. The School has a Boat House on site with direct river access, as well as a large sports hall and an indoor swimming pool in the grounds. There are playing fields at Wood Lane near the BBC (recently redeveloped to include a new pavilion and changing rooms and an all-weather, floodlit playing surface). The emphasis is on involvement, participation and choice. School teams enjoy great success in the major sports of rugby, soccer, netball, hockey, rowing, cricket and athletics. Other sports such as karate, swimming and golf cater for individual interests. The School maintains excellent fixture lists for all major sports.

Extra-Curricular Activities. There is a wide range of clubs and societies at lunch time and after school. In addition, every pupil has the opportunity to have residential experience and to take part in outdoor pursuits as part of the annual School Activities Week. A very active Parents' Gild ensures that nobody is excluded from an activity for financial reasons. The Duke of Edinburgh's Award Scheme flourishes with a number of students achieving the Gold Award each year.

Charitable status. The Latymer Foundation is a Registered Charity, number 312714. It exists to provide education for children.

The Grammar School at Leeds

Alwoodley Gates, Harrogate Road, Leeds LS17 8GS
Tel: 0113 229 1552
Fax: 0113 228 5111
e-mail: enquiries@gsal.org.uk
website: www.gsal.org.uk

The Grammar School at Leeds is a selective, independent, day school for girls and boys aged 3 to 18 years. The new school, is the result of a merger in September 2008 between Leeds Grammar School (founded in 1552) and Leeds Girls' High School (founded in 1876).

As individual schools, they have a long-established and proven pedigree in developing well-rounded, mature young men and women ready to embrace further education and to face the world as confident, caring citizens.

The Junior and Senior schools are located in extensive, leafy grounds at Alwoodley Gates in north Leeds. Rose Court Nursery and Pre-Prep is housed in newly expanded premises in Headingley.

Governors:

Mr D P A Gravells, JP, MSc (*Chairman*)
Mr P N Sparling, LLB (*Deputy Chairman*)
Mr N Ahmed
Mrs E E Bailey, BChD, LDS, RCS, DOrthRCS
Mr A Barker, OBE, FCA
Mr C Greenhalgh, CBE, DL, MA
Mr I Jones, MA, MBA
Professor C M Leigh, PhD
Dr H Luscombe, MB BS, DA, DRCOG, MRCGP
Mr K Morton, MRICS
Mr R Obank
Professor D Sugden, PhD
Mr J Woodward
Mr E Ziff

Teaching Staff:

***Principal & Chief Executive*: Michael Gibbons**, BA, AKC

Head of Junior School: Robert Lilley
Head of Rose Court (*Pre-Prep*): Anne Pickering
Deputy Head (*Pastoral Care*): Christine Bamforth
Deputy Head (*Staff Development*): Barry Brindley
Deputy Head (*Activities*): Stephen Field
Deputy Head (*Academic*): Dr Ian Hotchkiss
Director of External Relations: Helen Clapham
Director of Information Systems: Eric R Medway
Director of Finance: David Naylor
Director of Operations: Hayley Richardson

Head of Sixth Form: Christine Jagger
Head of Upper Sixth: Patrick Brotherton
Head of Lower Sixth: Paul Rushworth
Head of Year 11: Sean Corcoran
Head of Year 10: James Veitch
Head of Year 9: Carol Heatley
Head of Year 8: Ruth Rothwell
Head of Year 7: Geoff Thompson

Heads of Department:

Art, Design & Technology: Amanda Tait
Biology: Mark Smith
Chemistry: Ruth Boddy
Classics: David Pritchard
Critical Thinking: Ellis Gregory

Drama: Antoinette Keylock
Economics/Business Studies: Christopher Law
English: Jenny Bolton
Food Technology: Yvonne Wilson
French: Esther Saurel
Geography: Simon Knowles
German: Emma Whittaker
History: Graham Seel
ICT: Andy Longstaff
Instrumental Studies: Andrew Wheeler
Languages: Duncan Moynihan
Mathematics: Orla Fitzsimons
Music: Philippa Bradbury
Physics: Dr Mark Cramoysan
Politics: Andrew Stodolny
Psychology: Alison Wilson
Religious Studies: Helen Stiles
Spanish: Rowan Reed-Purvis
Sport: Paul Morris

Admissions: Angela Boult
Headmaster's Secretary: Judy Watker

Structure. Pupils are taught using the structure that has come to be known as the 'diamond model'. Classes are fully co-educational from age three to eleven and again in the Sixth Form. Between the ages of eleven and sixteen, boys and girls are taught separately, but enjoy mixed extra-curricular and pastoral activities. Pupils therefore have both the social benefits of co-education and the academic benefits of single-sex teaching in the adolescent years.

Junior School pupils progress to Senior School, in most cases automatically. Junior School begins with Year 3, Senior School Year 7 and Sixth Form Year 11.

Pastoral Care. Heads of Section are responsible for the progress of pupils in their part of the school, and give guidance and advice where necessary.

The Form Tutor is directly responsible for the progress of every boy and girl in his or her care.

The School is divided into Houses, four in the Junior School and eight in the Senior School. Each house is under the charge of a Housemaster, assisted by House Tutors. Form Tutors, Housemasters and Heads of Section work closely with the Headmaster and Parents to ensure the well-being of every boy and girl.

Religion. The School has a Chaplain and its own Chaplaincy centre which serves as a focus for worship and pastoral care. Although an Anglican foundation, the School welcomes boys and girls of all faiths and separate meetings are held for Jewish, Muslim, Hindu and Sikh pupils.

Facilities. The Grammar School at Leeds occupies a modern, purpose-built site whose facilities are unrivalled anywhere in the country. They include:

- Specialist suites of teaching rooms for all subjects with the necessary support systems for each faculty.
- Centres for each section of the School, with generous common rooms, locker and cloakroom areas.
- A large assembly hall.
- A newly extended Junior School, having its own identity, specialist resources and operating an independent timetable.
- A library incorporating multimedia facilities.
- IT centre with three inter-locking suites.
- A dedicated art, design and technology unit with computer aided design suite.
- Seventeen specialist science laboratories.
- A fully resourced music school.
- Theatre with fully-equipped lighting gantry.
- A new Food Technology Suite.
- Extensive playing fields with changing facilities and hospitality areas.
- A large indoor sports complex with 2 sports halls, climbing wall, squash courts, conditioning room, a 25m swimming pool of competition standard.
- Extensive grounds with pitches, tennis courts, athletics track.
- Large play and recreation areas for each section of the School.
- Refectory for breakfast, lunch and snacks.
- Provision for a wide variety of indoor and outdoor extra-curricular pursuits.
- Conservation areas.
- A versatile Chaplaincy Centre.
- A new Sixth Form Centre with its own cafeteria, study area and IT and leisure facilities.

Curriculum. Rose Court Nursery and Pre-Prep establishes the foundation for a long and rewarding education – pursuing a broad and balanced curriculum, which builds upon the natural aptitudes, learning skills and interests of each child, whilst enabling each to develop at his/her own pace. We use our own schemes of work, broadly based upon the early years of the National Curriculum, but refined by our own expertise and experience.

In the Junior School pupils concentrate upon the core subjects of English, Mathematics and Science. History, Geography, French/German, Religious Studies, Music, Art and Technology are also taught.

Pupils follow a broad curriculum, including two foreign languages in Years 7–9.

At the end of Year 11 pupils are presented for the GCSE examination.

In the Sixth Form students choose to study up to 5 AS and 3 A2 Level subjects and are encouraged to choose a broad range of subjects.

Games. Rugby, Football, Cricket, Athletics, Swimming, Tennis, Basketball, Badminton, Cross-Country, Volleyball, Hockey, Netball, Rounders, Squash, and Golf. There is a running track, swimming pool and a sports centre, including squash courts.

Other Activities. The School's many clubs and societies offer pupils the opportunity to participate in a wide range of out-of-school activities from Mountaineering and Skiing to Choral Singing, Dancing and Drama. There are regular tours and visits abroad and there are long-established exchanges with French and German schools.

The School has an extensive Arts Programme which covers music, film, drama, debating and creative art and includes visiting groups with national reputation as well as the students' own contributions.

The School provides a contingent of the CCF (Army & RAF sections), and has a Scout Troop, with Cub Pack and Venture Scout Unit. The School participates in the Duke of Edinburgh's Award Scheme and Community Service is compulsory in the Sixth Form.

Admission. The entrance procedure takes place in the Spring term for entry the following September and is based upon an examination, an interview and school report. Very young boys and girls are assessed through a series of observed activities. The usual points of entry are 3+ for Nursery, 4+ for Reception, 7+ for Junior School and 11+ for Senior School, although applications can be made at any time for any age. Entry to the Sixth Form is based upon the attainment of good GCSE grades.

Details of the entrance procedure together with copies of sample papers are available from the Headmaster's Secretary.

Fees per term (2011-2012). £3,585 Senior School, £2,676 Junior School, £2,454 Rose Court Nursery & Pre-Prep.

Scholarships and Bursaries. A number of means-tested bursaries (some full fee) are currently awarded each year to pupils entering the school at 11+ and 16+ (Sixth Form). A limited number of modest scholarships are awarded according to academic merit. In exceptional circumstances, financial support is sometimes available for fee-paying parents who find themselves in difficulty.

GSAL Alumni, Old Leodiensian Association (Leeds Grammar School) and Old Girls (Leeds Girls' High School). Lively and active, c/o Bronwen Ashton, The Development Office, The Grammar School at Leeds, Alwoodley Gates, Harrogate Road, Leeds LS17 8GS.

Charitable status. The Grammar School at Leeds is a Registered Charity, number 1048304. It exists for the advancement of education and training for boys and girls.

Leicester Grammar School

London Road, Great Glen, Leicester LE8 9FL
Tel: 0116 259 1900
Fax: 0116 259 1901
e-mail: admissions@leicestergrammar.org.uk
website: www.leicestergrammar.org.uk

Leicester Grammar School was founded in 1981 as an independent, selective, co-educational day school to offer able children in the city and county a first-class academic education. Its founders sought to create a school which would maintain the standards and traditions of the city's former grammar schools lost through reorganisation and develop them to meet the demands of a rapidly changing environment. The School moved to a new state-of-the-art building on the south-east side of Leicester in September 2008.

Governors:
I D Patterson, LLB (*Chairman*)
C J Castleman (*Vice-Chairman, Finance*)
R W B Atkinson, OBE, MA
G G Bodiwala, MBBS, MS, FICS, FICA
Mrs A Eggleston
S Gasztowicz, QC
P F Goffin
S E Hadley, BM, BS, MRCGP
N P T Hall
M J Holley, MA
K J Julian, MA
Dr D H Khoosal, MB, BCh, LLM RCS, LLM RCP, FRCPsych
Mrs N Lynch
D V M Mitchell
Prof J Saker, BSc, MSc
Dr J J A Scott, BSc, PhD
Prof B H Swanick, BEng, PhD, FIEE, CEng, MInstMC (*Vice-Chairman, Academic*)

Business Director: Mrs A Shakespeare, MA Fitzwilliam, Cantab, ACA, FCA

Headmaster: **C P M King**, MA Dunelm

Deputy Head (*Curriculum*): T R Cawston, BSc Leicester (*Mathematics*)
Deputy Head (*Pastoral*): Mrs A Ewington, MA Nottingham, CBiol, MIBiol (*Biology*)

Assistant staff:
T P Allen, BA Kent (*Head of Sixth Form; History; Politics*)
Mrs G Anthony, MA Hons Cambridge (*Classics*)
Mrs J A P Barrow, BEd Liverpool (*Design & Technology*)
R Berry, MA Cantab (*Geography*)
Miss A Binks, BSc Hons Loughborough (*Physical Education*)
D Bottomley, BSc Hons Leeds (*Mathematics*)
Miss V Brown, BA Hons Warwick (*French & German*)
F W Clayton, BA Wolverhampton (*Religious Studies*)
Dr D M Crawford, BA, DPhil Oxon (*Head of Mathematics*)
Mrs A J Davies, MA De Montfort (*Art*)
N G P Donnelly, BA Leicester (*Geography; DofE Award*)
Mrs K Douglas, BA Hons Liverpool (*French*)

A N Duffield, BSc UCW Cardiff, MIBiol (*Head of Biology*)
Dr S Ewers, BSc Bristol, PhD (*Biology*)
S Faire, BSc Surrey (*Mathematics*)
Dr C W Fearon, BSc Liverpool, PhD Birmingham (*Biology*)
Mrs A Fraser, BA Sussex (*German*)
Dr K Fulton, BSc Durham, PhD (*Biology*)
D W Gee, C&G Tech Cert Nottingham (*Head of Design & Technology*)
M J Gower, BA Leicester (*Head of Geography; Health & Safety Officer*)
Mrs A L Griffin, MA Loughborough (*Head of Drama*)
J M Griffin, MA Cantab (*Deputy Head of English*)
P M Handford, MA Oxon (*Chemistry*)
Mrs B A Harper, BA Warwick (*Head of History*)
S J Harrison, BA Keele (*English*)
A H J Harrop, MA Oxon (*Head of Classics; Examinations Officer*)
Mrs W E Harvey, BA Hons Loughborough College of Art & Design (*Design & Technology*)
S Hayhoe, BA Coventry, MEd (*Head of ICT*)
Ms S Haywood, BEd Worcester College (*Art*)
Mrs M Higginson, MA Toronto (*English*)
Mrs K B Hinshelwood, BA Reading (*Academic Support*)
C W Howe, BEd, CNAA Crewe & Alsager College (*Director of Physical Education*)
Miss N Hughes, BA London (*English*)
G Inchley, BSc Hull, MSc Bristol (*Mathematics*)
C James, MA Cambridge (*Mathematics*)
Mrs C L Jess, BA, MA Cambridge (*French & Spanish*)
R W S Kidd, BA Ulster, MA Ulster (*Head of English*)
Miss C Leney, BSc Hons Durham (*Physics*)
R I Longson, BA UCW Aberystwyth, DipCG, MICG (*Head of Careers; History*)
D M Lupton, BA Exeter (*French and Spanish*)
D W Maddock, BA Bristol Polytechnic, MA Leeds Polytechnic (*Head of Art*)
Mrs H May, BA Hons Wales (*Geography*)
D McCann, BEd Leicester (*Physical Education*)
P Moore-Friis, BA De Montfort (*Economics; Young Enterprise Coordinator*)
Miss J Mould, BEd Bedford College of HE (*Head of Girls' Physical Education; English*)
N Murray, BSc Imperial, MA, MSc Sheffield Hallam (*Mathematics*)
Mrs E C Nisbet, BEd Trent Polytechnic (*Food Technology*)
Mrs H D Painter, CertEd Dunelm, DipEd Leics (*Head of Preparatory Department*)
Mrs B J Panton, MA Edinburgh (*Classics*)
C D Paterson, MA Cantab (*Classics; Master of Choristers; Curriculum Coordinator*)
Miss A M Patterson, BSc Sunderland Polytechnic (*Chemistry; Housemistress of Duke's*)
N C Perry, MA Oxon (*Chemistry*)
Mr D Pilbeam, MChem Hons Nottingham (*Chemistry*)
Mrs K Pollard, BSc Loughborough (*Mathematics*)
L Potter (*Head of Lower School; Physical Education*)
Mrs E Pottinger, MA Edinburgh (*History*)
Mrs A Price, BSc Edinburgh (*Physics; Staff Development Coordinator; SMT Secretary*)
Mrs J Ransone, BSc UWI Cardiff, MSc MMU (*Physical Education*)
P T G Reeves, BSc Manchester (*Head of Physics*)
D E A Roebuck, BSc UCW Swansea, CChem, FRSC, FRSA (*Head of Science; Head of Chemistry*)
Mrs S J Sains, MA Oxon (*Mathematics*)
B H Shaw, GRSM, ARCM, LRAM (*Head of Instrumental Studies; Director of External Relations*)
Ms M Sian, BA Middlesex (*Design & Technology; ICT*)
Mrs S Stout, BSc Combined Hons Aston (*Head of Modern Languages*)

T A Thacker, BEd, CNAA Crewe & Alsager College
(*Head of Boys' Games; Head of Years 10 & 11*)
Dr A Vassiliou-Abson, BA Athens, MPhil Birmingham,
PhD Birmingham (*Classics*)
Mrs B Wallwork, BEd Cantab (*Mathematics*)
M D Wheeler, BSc, PhD Bristol (*Physics*)
Dr D M T Whittle, BMus, PhD Nottingham (*Director of
Music*)
Miss A L Williamson, BSc Loughborough (*Physical
Education; Geography; Head of Year 9*)
D R Willis, BSc, CNAA Portsmouth Polytechnic (*Science;
Housemaster of Vice Chancellor's; Senior Housemaster*)
Dr S G Yeomans, BA QM College, MA Loughborough,
PhD Loughborough (*Politics*)
Mrs C M Young, BA Birmingham (*Head of Religious
Studies; Pastoral Programme Coordinator*)

Visiting music staff:
D Beavan, MA
K L Hall, GRSM, LRAM, LTCL
C Jeans, LRAM (*Brass Coordinator*)
Miss J Kirkland, BMus Hons
Mrs A Mainard, ABSM, ARCM
D McHarg
Miss D Morgan, BMus
Mrs L Nelson, BMus UM KM
P J Nuttall, MA
Miss G E Print, BA (*String Coordinator*)
Mrs C Watkins, BA, CT ABRSM
Mrs P Wood, GMus, LTCL

Headmistress, Junior School: Mrs M Redfearn, BA Hons

There are 779 day pupils in the Senior School (359 girls,
420 boys), of whom 197 are in the Sixth Form. A further 411
pupils, aged 3–11, attend the Junior School.

Admission. An entrance examination is held in the Lent
Term for boys and girls seeking to enter the Preparatory
(10+) and Year 7 (11+) forms in the following September.
Papers are taken in verbal reasoning, English and Mathematics.
In addition admission into Years 9 and 10 takes place at
ages 13 and 14 and there is provision for direct entry into the
Sixth Form, offers of a place being conditional upon the
GCSE grades gained. The normal entry requirement to the
Sixth Form is two A and four B grade passes at GCSE. Visitors
are always welcome to make an appointment to see the
school and meet the Headmaster. All applications are handled
by the School Secretary, from whom all Registration
forms are obtainable. Candidates at all levels may be called
for an interview.

Scholarships. (*See Scholarship Entries section.*) Academic,
music, art and sports scholarships are offered to the
outstanding candidates on examination and the School has
some funds available for bursaries. It has always been the
policy of governors to try to ensure that children capable of
benefiting from education at the School should not be prevented
by financial considerations from entry.

Curriculum. Class sizes are about 20 to 24 in the first
three years; the average size of a GCSE group is 19, of a
Sixth Form group 12.

All pupils in the first three years (and those entering the
preparatory form) follow a balanced curriculum covering
the National Curriculum core and foundation subjects, Religious
Studies and Latin (Classical Studies in the preparatory
form). Classes are split into smaller groups for the creative
and technological subjects, so that all pupils can gain practical
experience, whether in the School's ICT suite or on its
extensive range of musical instruments. From Year 8 the
three science subjects, Biology, Chemistry and Physics, are
taught separately. There is no streaming and setting occurs
only for Mathematics and French. In Year 9 an element of
choice is introduced and pupils must opt from a choice of
third languages and from a list of five creative subjects.

In Years 4 and 5 pupils prepare for GCSE examinations in
ten subjects, as well as doing PE/Games. All study a 'core'
of five subjects: English Language and Literature, Mathematics,
French and Chemistry. The range of 'options'
includes Art, Biology, Chemistry, Classical Civilisation,
Design and Technology, Drama, French, Geography, German,
Greek, Religious Studies, History, Latin, Music, Physics,
Spanish and PE.

Students in the Sixth Form normally study 4 AS levels
leading to 3 or more A levels from a choice of 19 subjects,
including Further Mathematics, Economics, Physical Education,
Politics, Computer Studies and Theatre Studies.
There is no rigid division between arts and science sides. To
ensure that breadth of education does not suffer, a broadly
based cultural general studies course leads on to A level
General Studies. The school has an excellent record of success
at public examinations and university admissions,
including Oxbridge. The Careers Department is very active
in giving help and advice to students.

School activities. A broad range and variety of activities
complements the academic curriculum. Participation rates
are high.

Music, drama and sport form an integral part of life at
LGS. Every pupil in the First Year learns a musical instrument
and a high proportion continue afterwards with private
weekly lessons. The School Orchestra gives two major concerts
a year, whilst a training orchestra, a jazz band, a dance
band, recorder groups and various chamber ensembles
explore other avenues. The School Choir is the resident
choir for the Crown Court Services and tours regularly.
Links are strong with the Leicestershire School of Music
orchestras and several pupils play in national orchestras.
Senior and junior drama clubs function throughout the year,
a major play or musical and a junior play are staged regularly
and house drama extends the opportunity to act to most
pupils.

Games are seen as an important means not only of promoting
health and fitness but also of inspiring self-confidence.
Major winter games are hockey, netball and rugby
and in summer athletics, cricket and tennis. Opportunities
occur for individuals to follow their interest in badminton,
basketball, squash, golf, table tennis, gymnastics, dance,
sailing and cross-country running whilst swimming is an
integral part of the PE programme. The School's own facilities
are extensive and meet all modern standards for sport.
Teams represent the School in the main games at all age
groups and several students achieve recognition at county or
even national level. The school is proud of the fact that it is
one of only eight other schools to have been awarded the
Sportsmark Gold with Distinction, for the quality of the
delivery of sport within the school.

Societies and clubs complement these activities, ranging
from chess to the Duke of Edinburgh's Award scheme, history
and Lit Soc to model aeroplanes, debating to art, design
and technology, for which the workshop and art rooms are
usually open during lunchtimes and after school.

Religion. The school espouses the principles of the
Church of England, teaching the Christian faith, its values
and standards of personal conduct, but also prides itself on
welcoming children of all faiths, who play a full part in the
life of the community. Very strong links exist with Leicester
Cathedral and there is a flourishing Guild of Servers and
cathedral clergy participate in school life and prepare confirmation
candidates.

Pastoral Care. Responsibility for a wide-ranging system
of pastoral care and for the creation of the caring, friendly
and disciplined environment, resides in four Heads of
School, assisted by form teachers, personal tutors and a very
active house system.

Junior School. Entry to the Junior School is by interview
and, where appropriate, assessment at 3+, 4+, 7+ and into
other school years, when places are available. Pupils are prepared
for entry to the Senior School. A balanced curriculum

is followed covering National Curriculum Key Stages 1 and 2 and beyond; French (from 5 years), classical studies and ICT are also taught. A wide range of activities complements the academic curriculum, with a strong stress on music and a rapidly growing games programme. The School is a Christian foundation and lays great emphasis upon the pastoral care of young children. (*See also Junior School entry in IAPS section.*)

Fees per term (from April 2011). Senior School £3,507; Junior School (from Sept 2011): £2,875 (Juniors), £2,756 (Infants).

Old Leicestrians Association. All correspondence to the Secretary, c/o the School.

Charitable status. Leicester Grammar School Trust is a Registered Charity, number 510809. Its aims and objectives are to promote and provide for the advancement of education and in connection therewith to conduct, carry on, acquire and develop in the United Kingdom or elsewhere a School or Schools to be run according to the principles of the Church of England for the education of students and children of either sex or both sexes.

Leighton Park School

Shinfield Road, Reading, Berkshire RG2 7ED
Tel: 0118 987 9600
Fax: 0118 987 9625
e-mail: admissions@leightonpark.com
website: www.leightonpark.com

Governors:
Paul High (*Chairman*)

Liz Banks	Martin Forster
Jeff Beatty	Sarah Freeman
Simon Best	Gill Greenfield
Jonathan Bowen	Valerie McFarlane
Paul Bowers-Isaacson	Andrew Morgan
Glynne Butt	Liza Phipps
Adrian Dixon	Catherine Wilson
John Flynn	Stephen Wright
David Isherwood	

Head: **Alex J McGrath**, BA Durham, PGCE York

Deputy Head: Edward Falshaw, MA

Deputy Head: Nigel Williams, BA Bristol, MA London

Bursar: Marie Gage, FCCA, FMAAT

Teaching Staff:
* *Head of Department*
§ *Part-time*
† *Housemaster*

Irene Bell, MA Cantab (**Physics*)
Julian Berrow, BA (*§Modern Foreign Languages, †Reckitt House*)
Zenon Bowrey, BA (**Economics & Business Studies*)
David Bradford, CertEd, MA Ed (*Design Technology*)
Heike Bruton, MA BA (*German*)
Peter Bulteel, BA (*PE, Head of Middle School*)
§Clive Burns (*Design Technology*)
Simon Cain, BSc (*Biology, Physics, Games; †School House*)
Tom Cartmill, BA (*English as a Second Language*)
Catherine Cheeseman, BSc (*Psychology*)
John Clarke, BSc (*Physics*)
§Deirdre Dyson, BA (*English as a Second Language*)
§Deborah Duggan, BA (**Modern Foreign Languages*)
Jon Emerson, MA Oxon (**Science*)
Bridget Evans, BSc (**Mathematics*)
§Rosemary Few, BEd (*Individual Learning Centre*)
§Kate Findlay, BA (*History*)

Eveline Giblin, Mechanical Engineering (*German Conversation*)
Pablo Gorostidi Perez, MBA (*Spanish*)
Karen Gracie-Langrick, MA (**History, Ancient History, IBDP Coordinator*)
Tim Green, BSc (*Games, History*)
Richard Griffiths, BSc (**History, Games*)
Geoff Harnett, MA Cantab (*Modern Foreign Languages; †Grove House*)
Kathryn Higgins, BSc, PGCE (*Chemistry*)
§Jane Ireland, BA (*Individual Learning Centre, SENCO*)
Joanne Jones, BA, PGCE (*Art and Textiles*)
Elaine King, BA (**Art, Careers, Games*)
§Caroline Kirby, BSc (**Geography*)
Adél Kiss, BSc, BEd (*Mathematics*)
Lan Kuang, MA, BA (*Mandarin Chinese*)
Richard Lade, BSc (**Design Technology, ICT*)
Isabelle Lauzeral-Bataillé, First Degree and Masters (*Modern Languages*)
Sarah Ledger, BA, PGCE, (*Modern Languages*)
Ann Line, BA (*English*)
Jakki Marr, BEd (**PE, Games*)
§Jackie Marsh, BEd (*Individual Learning Centre*)
§Rachael Martin, BEd (*Individual Learning Centre*)
§Rachel Mayne, BSc (*Science*)
Tom McDonnell, MSc, PGCE (*Chemistry*)
§Chris Mitchell, BA (*Assistant Director of Music*)
Jane Mulvihill, BSc (*Mathematics*)
Isabelle Munro, DUEL (*French Conversation*)
§Christine Myers, MSc, PGCE (*Mathematics*)
§Susan Neilson, BSc (*Mathematics*)
§Lynne Parry, BEd (*Individual Learning Centre*)
Judith Parson, BEd (*ILC*)
§Pip Peacock, BSc (*Mathematics*)
Nicola Phillips, BA, PGCE (*English*)
Jonathan Porter-Hughes, BA, PGCE (*English*)
Jeremy Radburn, BA, MA (**English*)
§Claire Reeves, BSc (*Geography*)
§Angela Rigby, BA, BSc, MSc (**ICT*)
Patricia Robson, MA, PGCE (*ILC*)
Premnath Samyrao, MSc, MEd (*Mathematics*)
Rosemary Scales, BA, MA (**Director of Music*)
Howard Shaw, BA (*History, Government and Politics*)
Mark Simmons, BEd (**PE, Games; †Field House*)
Graham Smith, BA (*Games, Geography*)
Ken Sullivan, MA, BSc, PGCE (*Head of Sixth Form*)
Shazia Taj, BA, MA, PGCE (**Beliefs and Values*)
Helen Taylor, BSc (**Biology*)
Geraint Thomas, Graduate Diploma (**Drama*)
Joanna Varnava, MSc, MA, PGCE (*Economics*)
Michael Ward, BEd, MA (**Information Technology, Director of IT*)
§Sherilyn Wass, BSc, PhD (*Chemistry*)
Mitch Whitehead, BA, MA (*Beliefs and Values*)
§Michael Whiteman, BA (*Music*)
Nicola Williams, BEd (*PE, Games, *PSHE, †Fryer House*)
Simon Williams, BA (**Art*)
Françoise Wilson, BA, MA (**Modern Foreign Languages, Latin*)
John Woodings, BA (*English, Activities Coordinator*)
Sue Wright, Dip TEFL (**ESL*)
§Damon Young, BA (*Drama*)

Librarian: Chris Routh, MA, BA
Director of Admissions: Rachael Bolding
Head's PA: (to be appointed)

Leighton Park is a forward-looking, co-educational day and boarding school for 500 pupils aged 11–18, set in sixty acres of attractive parkland, about a mile south of Reading town centre.

Our commitment to academic excellence is balanced by our commitment to the development of every individual, deriving from our Quaker heritage. You will find at Leighton

Park outstanding teaching and excellent academic results. The last ISI inspection stated, "Leighton Park is highly successful in providing an education of good quality in a strongly Quaker ethos. Pupils achieve well academically in relation to their abilities, while experiencing rich opportunities for their personal and social development". The Good Schools Guide remarked "Many schools vaunt their 'special atmosphere' but at LP it's tangible. No room for hypocrites (staff or pupils) here. One of the most distinctive schools we've visited – it gave us a renewed sense of hope for the future. More schools would do well to adopt the LP model, it has integrity and honesty at heart."

For eight successive years, A Level students have achieved a pass rate of 98% or above with an average of three or more passes each. 70% of all passes were Grade A*/B in 2010.

At GCSE, 99% of pupils in 2010 achieved five or more passes at Grade A*–C, 53% A*/A.

Curriculum. In Years 7 and 8 pupils follow a broad curriculum, which extends well beyond the National Curriculum. Mandarin Chinese has been introduced in Year 7 which can be followed through to GCSE and A Level. Year 10 pupils are expected to follow a full GCSE course of nine or ten subjects, comprising both compulsory and optional subjects. In the Sixth Form, a wide range of examination courses is complemented by a broad programme, including Critical Thinking, Film Studies, European Computer Driving License and Dance. A team of qualified specialists works with pupils for whom English is an additional language, and the Individual Learning Centre supports those with identifiable learning needs.

Leighton Park now offers the International Baccalaureate Diploma and is an IB World School.

Facilities. Excellent facilities and resources include a Science and Technology Centre, an ICT Centre, a Drama Studio, a splendid Library and dedicated Individual Learning Centre. Oakview, the dining centre, offers a first-rate choice of meals (breakfast, lunch and tea). A new Sixth Form Centre opened in 2006 and a new Mathematics block in 2007.

Ethos and Pastoral Care. Within Leighton Park's distinctive Quaker ethos, pupils of many faiths and backgrounds flourish in an atmosphere of tolerance, harmony and understanding. They know they will be challenged in their work to achieve the highest standards of excellence.

Boarding and Day Boarding. We offer a highly flexible approach to boarding with full, weekly and day boarding options to suit a family and pupil's needs. The five houses provide a comfortable base in which all pupils, whether day or boarding, genuinely feel at home. Day pupils and boarders both have individual study facilities in the houses. Day pupils are welcome for breakfast and to stay for tea, prep and hobbies, included in the fees. Flexi-boarding is an option, subject to availability of spaces.

Sport. Sport plays an important role in life at Leighton Park with many individual and team performances reaching county and national level. First rate coaching and superb facilities – which include a heated indoor swimming pool, floodlit astroturf pitch, 22 tennis courts and a cricket square – ensure that talented and enthusiastic pupils can develop their sporting abilities to the full. 2007 Hockey and Rugby tour to South Africa.

Music. Music has for a long time been one of Leighton Park's particular strengths with around half the pupils learning instruments and performing a wide range of styles. Our facilities for practice and performance include a suite of ten practice rooms, a digital recording studio, a suite of Apple Macs, recital room and concert hall.

Opportunities to perform include almost weekly concerts and regular foreign tours, in 2006 to France, Switzerland and Italy and in 2008 to Switzerland and Italy and in 2010 to The Netherlands.

Hobbies and other activities. Pupils can participate in an enormous variety of activities both during the week and at weekends, before and after school. The Duke of Edinburgh's Award Scheme is well established and Lower Sixth pupils run their own company in the Young Enterprise programme. In keeping with our Quaker perspective many Leighton Park pupils are involved in Community Service. In August 2008, a group of students went on a trek to India as part of a cultural and charity expedition.

Careers. Pupils have access to the well-resourced Careers Library as well as networked computer software to help them research and evaluate their options. All Year 10 pupils complete a week of work experience and there are many other occasions when career alternatives or gap year possibilities can be explored. Thorough preparation for entry to university is given.

Entry to the school is by exam and interview, with an additional English test where appropriate. Pupils are normally admitted at one of three points: Year 7 (age 11); Year 9 (age 13), and the Sixth Form. Entry to the Sixth Form requires 6 GCSE passes or equivalent at Grade C or above.

Fees per term (2011-2012). Full Boarding £7,783–£9,154; Weekly Boarding £6,844–£8,042; Day £5,095–£5,998.

Scholarships. (*See Scholarship Entries section.*) Several Awards (10% of day fees) are made each year for academic work, music, art and sport. Bursaries may be available on a means-tested basis. Additional awards may be made by the David Lean Foundation.

Old Leightonians. Website: www.leightonpark.com/old-leightonians.

Charitable status. The Leighton Park Trust is a Registered Charity, number 309144. It exists to provide education for young people.

The Leys School

Cambridge CB2 7AD
Tel: 01223 508900
Fax: 01223 505303
e-mail: office@theleys.net
website: www.theleys.net

The Leys is situated less than half a mile from the centre of the university city of Cambridge, close to the River Cam and Grantchester Meadows. The School was founded in 1875 on the initiative of a group of leading Methodists to provide a liberal Christian education, establishing a tradition which has continued unbroken to this day. The School was incorporated as a Charitable Trust in 1878. All the buildings are grouped around the playing field and lie within the estate originally acquired for the purpose; there is a second extensive playing field nearby.

The Leys is a friendly, caring and happy community, large enough to offer many opportunities, but not so large as to lose sight of the individual. The School is fully co-educational; of a total of over 550 pupils, 200 are in the Sixth Form. Girls and boys are accommodated in separate houses. 50% of the pupils are boarders; the remainder, whether home boarders or day pupils, sleep at home but otherwise are able to enjoy all the opportunities of boarding school life.

Motto: '*In Fide Fiducia.*'

Governors:

Chairman: Sir Anthony Brenton, KCMG

N J M Abbott, MA	Mrs H Arthur, CertEd
Mrs J Allison, BA	¶R A Ashby-Johnson, MA
Mrs P Appafram, BA, MCIPD	M D Beazor, BA

¶HH Judge Revd M A
  Bishop, MA
Mrs A Brunner BA
¶R P Cadman
J D Callin, FRICS, FRVA
Mrs C Crawford, MA
Mrs J W Harding, BA
¶R B Haryott, BSc, FREng,
  FICE, FIStructE
C R B Hewitson, LLB
¶C M Kidman, ACIOB, JP
P R Lacey, MA, PGCE,
  FRSA
Mrs M E Mackay, RGN

¶ *Old Leysian*

Headmaster: **Mr M Slater**, MA

Deputy Headmaster: S G Wilson, BSc, LRAM

Assistant Teachers:

A S Erby, BSc
M A Brown, BSc
P White, BEd
E M W George, BEd
R Adamson, BSc, PhD
R A D Hill, BA
D J Nye, BSc
P A Mathieu, MA
Mrs P C A Taylor, BA,
  MEd
Mrs C E Wiedermann, MA
Mrs P J Jessop, BEd,
  DipSpLD
Revd C I A Fraser, BA,
  MA Ed, MCMI, FRSA
Mrs A P Muston, BEd
W J Earl, BSc
G K Howe, BSc, MSc, MA,
  MEd
A R C Batterham, BA
D K Fernandes, BSc
A P Harmsworth, MA,
  FRAS
Mrs C L Howe, BSc, PhD
D R Bell, MA
G J Deudney, BSc, BEd
Revd C J Meharry, BEd,
  PTh
Mrs S Vallance Goode, JP,
  BA
P M Davies, BSc, Med Dip
Miss C E Battison, BA
M A Egan, BSc
Mrs J A Stobbart, BA
Ms L J Clark, BA
Miss C L Brocklehurst,
  BSc
M C Gale, BEd
R A Hall, BA, MA, ARCO
A C R Long, BA
J R Norton, BA
Miss E F Prosser, BSc
Ms E J Fordham, BA,
  DipSpLD, AdvDip, MEd

T L Reed, MA, MSc
Mrs A Lainchbury, BA,
  MCLIP
Mrs E R Culshaw, MA
S A Newlove, BSc, PhD
B A Barton, BA
A J Welby, BA
Mrs J A Samuel, BSc
R S McAlinden, BA
S G Hancock, BA, MA
N R Born, MA
N J Dix-Pincott, BA, MA
S N Leader, BA
A J McGarry, BA, MA,
  Adv DipEd
G F Stentiford, BSc, MSc
Miss J P E Cooke, BA
T P Dunn, BA, MSc, FRSA
Mr J Fawcett, BA, MA
L M Copley, BA, MA,
  MEd
Mrs K J Cox, BSc
C J Foster, BA
Miss R Isdell-Carpenter,
  BA, CELTA
M P J Lindsay, MSc
Mrs L Reyes, MA
W P Unsworth, BSc, PhD
Mrs J George
A J Peploe, BA, HND
P J Crosfield, BA
Miss L Corble, BA
Miss K E Eaves, MA
G C Watson, BA, MPhil
R Francis, BA
Mrs C M Earl, BSc
R Kaufman, BA
D Silk, MSc
Miss A L Carpenter, BSc
A S Phoenix Holland, BA
J Wilson, BSc
Ms C C Howe, BA

Housemasters:
School House: T L Reed
West House: W J Earl
North A House: C I A Fraser
East House: C J Meharry
Barker House: G J Deudney

Housemistresses:
Granta House: Dr C L Howe

Revd Dr Tim Macquiban,
  MA, PhD
Mrs E L Mimpriss, CertEd
G Russell, MA
R C Sadler, FRICS
S H Siddall, MA
¶A V Silverton, BSc, FSI
Revd Canon Graham
  Thompson
¶D C W Unwin, MA, ACA
Dr R D H Walker, MA,
  PhD
R B Webster, FCA

Dale House: Miss C E Battison
Fen House: Dr R Scott-Copley, BA, MA, PhD
Barrett House: Mrs E R Culshaw
Bisseker House: Miss E F Prosser
Moulton House: Miss A Macpherson

Director of Studies: P J Crosfield
Bursar: P D McKeown, BA
Head of Careers: Mrs S Vallance Goode
Marketing and Admissions Manager: J D R Benson, CIM
Higher Education Coordinator: M A Egan
Examinations Officer: Mrs C Maskell
Director of Sport: L M Copley
Head of Outdoor Education: R S McAlinden
Chaplain: Revd C J Meharry
Medical Officer: A J Stewart, MB, BCh
Nursing Staff:
Sister M A Williams, SRN, SCM
Sister G Woolley, RN
Sister V Huffman, RN
Sister J Taylor, RGN
Development Director: S J Williams, MA
Facilities Manager: N Keen
Sports Hall Manager: D Dean
Headmaster's PA: Ms R C Silcock, BA
Bursar's PA: Mrs J C Carruthers
Admissions and Administration Manager: Mrs J A Cooper, BA
Admissions Officer: Ms C A Rudd
Database Officer: Mrs D V Butterworth
Administration Officer: Miss C B Walker

Buildings and Facilities. There is a continuing development programme involving all areas of the School. A state-
of-the-art Music School was opened in 2005. There is an
excellent Humanities Building with first-class facilities for
Geography, History, Classics and Divinity together with a
Museum and Archives Centre, and an award-winning
Design Centre, which contains workshops (metal, plastic
and wood), Art School, Ceramics Studio, Electronics Workshop, Computer Centre, together with facilities for Design,
Photography, Cookery and an Exhibition Centre. A Sports
Hall and all-weather pitch were built in 1995. The Sports
Hall was extended and a second Astroturf pitch was built in
2008. A new climbing wall was constructed in summer
2007. Other major buildings include the Theatre, the Science Building and the Queen's Building, comprising classrooms and a drama studio used for both teaching and
performances. There are 40 acres of playing fields, an
indoor heated swimming pool open all the year, a boat house
on the Cam, and synthetic as well as grass tennis courts. A
radical re-designing and refurbishment of all boarding
houses began in summer 2006, with the aim of providing the
most comfortable and homely of boarding facilities. To date
both Sixth Form Houses and both of the Girls' Houses have
been refurbished. The School Library underwent a major
refurbishment in 2008.

In July 2011, the School commenced the construction of
Great Hall which will include the main assembly hall, theatre, drama studio, dance studio, drama department and
three new science laboratories. The project will take 18
months to complete.

Admission. Admission for girls and boys is mainly at
11+, 13+ and 16+. Registration may be made at any time
beforehand. Entrance tests and Scholarship Examinations
for 11+ and 13+ entry are held in the January prior to entry.
Places in the Sixth Form are available for both girls and boys
who have successfully completed their GCSE or equivalent
courses elsewhere. Application for admission should be
made to the Administration Manager in the first instance.

Scholarships. (*See Scholarship Entries section.*) Academic Scholarships are available for entry at 11+, 13+ and
for entry to the Sixth Form at 16+. Scholarships are also
available for entry at 13+ in Music, Art, Design Technology,

Sport, Drama and All-Rounders, and for entry to the Sixth Form at 16+ in Music, Art, Sport and Drama. The Scholarship Examinations at 11 and 13 take place in the Spring Term and the Sixth Form Scholarship takes place in the November of the year prior to entry. Scholarships up to 5% of the fees are available and these can be supplemented by means-tested bursaries up to a total of 100% in extreme cases. Further particulars may be obtained from the Admissions Officer. The School also participates in the Arkwright Scholarship Scheme, which is an external examination offering Scholarships for those wishing to take Design and Technology in the Sixth Form and who are aiming to read Engineering, Technology or other Design-related subjects in Higher Education.

Curriculum. The academic curriculum broadly conforms to the National Curriculum but is not restricted by it. Each pupil has an Academic tutor who, in conjunction with the Director of Studies and the Housemaster or Housemistress, works to tailor the pupil's programme to suit the needs of the individual wherever possible. Pupils follow a broad programme in the first three years (Years 7, 8 and 9). At the end of Year 9 they choose three from a wide range of GCSE options to add to the basic core of English Language/Literature, Mathematics, separate Sciences, Religious Studies and a Modern Foreign Language. The GCSE examinations are normally taken at the end of Year 11. Religious Education and Physical Education are taught throughout the School.

In the Sixth Form, a similar option scheme operates with pupils choosing from a total of 25 subjects to take normally 4 AS Levels in the LVI and 3 at A2 in the following year.

There is considerable flexibility of combinations possible at both levels, and choices are made after consultation between parents, tutors, careers staff and subject teachers.

About 95% of the A Level candidates proceed to degree courses. A Reading Party for potential Oxford and Cambridge candidates is held during the Summer Term.

Personal and Social Education forms an integral part of the curriculum at all levels. In the Sixth Form this is supplemented by a year-long programme that draws on the cultural resources of Cambridge University and the city as a whole.

The Chapel. The School Chapel is at the heart of the community in every sense. From the time of its Methodist foundation The Leys has been firmly based on non-sectarian Christian principles. It welcomes boys and girls of all denominations and religions, encouraging them to see the relevance of a personal faith of their own. Religious Education forms part of the curriculum. Preparation is also given for Church membership, and a combined confirmation service is held.

Physical Education. The physical education/games programme aims at introducing a wide variety of physical activities. Sports available are Rugby, Hockey, Cricket, Tennis, Athletics, Netball, Badminton, Basketball, Fencing, Gymnastics, Golf, Rowing, Sailing, Dance, Shooting, Climbing, Squash, Swimming, Volleyball, Water Polo. Outdoor activities such as Camping, Orienteering, Canoeing, and Climbing are also encouraged through CCF and the Duke of Edinburgh's Award. PE is offered at GCSE and A level. The School has close links with many Cambridge University Sports Clubs, with the Sixth Form competing in University Leagues.

Careers. In the Lower School, careers guidance forms part of the PSHE programme and is carried out by tutors and members of the Careers Department. Year 9 are supported in their option choices by tutors and Careers staff and are introduced to the Careers Library. Year 11 take the Preview Careers Selection Programme. It matches pupils' interests and abilities to appropriate career fields and is followed up by two individual interviews with career specialists. Year 11 pupils are also encouraged to participate in the Work Experience scheme. Support continues into the Sixth Form with all Lower Sixth being interviewed by Careers staff. An annual Careers Forum is organised in the Lent term, enabling students to investigate various career paths before embarking on their UCAS applications. Work experience is organised throughout the Sixth Form.

Societies. All are encouraged to participate in out-of-school activities of their choice. These range from Literary, Philosophical, Scientific, Mathematical, Languages, Debating, Music and Drama societies to any of the activities available in the Design Centre, which are available after School and at weekends. The life of the School is enriched by its proximity to Cambridge; distinguished visiting speakers are available, and pupils are encouraged to go to plays, concerts and lectures in the town. The programme of visiting speakers is largely run by the pupils themselves, broadly overseen by a member of staff.

Combined Cadet Force. Except in special circumstances, pupils in Year 10 join the CCF (Army or Navy section) and also follow the Duke of Edinburgh's Award scheme. CCF camps take place annually. There is a miniature range, and a Rifle Club exists for small-bore shooting. The School is an authorised centre for the organisation of activities within the Duke of Edinburgh's Award scheme and pupils work towards the Bronze, Silver or Gold awards in the four sections: community service, expeditions, physical recreation and skills or hobbies.

Fees per term (2011-2012). Years 7 and 8: £6,290 Boarders; £4,100 Day Pupils. Years 9 to Sixth Form: £8,640 Boarders; £6,495 Home Boarders; £5,750 Day Pupils.

St Faith's Preparatory School is part of the same Foundation. It was founded in 1884 and acquired by the Governors of The Leys in 1938. There are 520 boys and girls, aged 4–13 years. The buildings, which include the Keynes Building opened in 2006, stand in 10 acres of grounds. Full particulars may be obtained from the Headmaster of St Faith's, Mr N Helliwell, MA. (*For further details, see entry in IAPS section.*)

The Old Leysian Society. *Secretary:* J C Harding, MA, The Leys School, Cambridge CB2 7AD. Handbook and Directory, twenty-second edition, 2010.

Charitable status. The Leys and St Faith's Schools Foundation is a Registered Charity, number 311436. It aims to enable boys and girls to develop fully their individual potential within a School community firmly based on Christian principles.

Lincoln Minster School

UCST

The Prior Building, Upper Lindum Street, Lincoln LN2 5RW

Tel:	01522 551300
Fax:	01522 551310
e-mail:	enquiries.lincoln@church-schools.com
website:	www.lincolnminsterschool.co.uk

Lincoln Minster School is a co-educational day and boarding school for pupils from 2½–18. The Pre-Prep, Preparatory, Senior School and boarding houses are all situated in the heart of historic Lincoln, very close to the Cathedral and Castle.

Chair of Local Governing Body: Mrs A Crowe

Members:
Revd Canon Gavin Kirk, MA, Precentor of Lincoln
    Cathedral

M Lamb	R Childs
P Croft	Mrs H Clarke
R Buttery	Mrs L Heaver
Mrs A Crowe	T Overton
Mrs K McFarlane	

Ex officio:
J Nicholson
C Rickart

Principal & Head of Senior School: Mr Clive Rickart,
BA Hons, PGCE

Acting Head of Preparatory School: Mr M Pickering, BSc
Hons, PGCE

First Deputy Head:
Mr M Jacob, MA, BSc Hons, Cert Immunol, PGCE, NPQH
(*Director of Teaching, Learning and Curriculum*)

Deputy Head – Pastoral: Mrs C McKenzie, MA, BSc
Hons, PGCE

Director of Studies: Mr S Grocott, BSc Hons, PGCE

Head of Sixth Form: Miss T Chappell, BA Hons, QTS

Director of Music: Mr A Prentice, MA, BA Hons, PGCE,
LTCL

Director of E-Learning: Mr L Collins, BSc Hons, PGCE,
CGeog, FRGS

Deputy Head – Pastoral, Preparatory School: Miss J
Matthews-Hall, CertEd

Head of Pre-Preparatory School: Miss J Bunker, BEd

EYFS Coordinator: Mrs S Skinner, BMus, PGCE

Heads of Department:
Mrs E Barclay, BEd Hons, PGCE, Dip RSA SpLD
(*Learning Support*)
Mr N Boot, BA Hons, DipLaw, QTS (*History*)
Mrs A Brown, BA Hons, PGCE (*English*)
Mr J Cochrane, BSc, PGCE
Mr L Collins, BSc Hons, PGCE, CGeog, FRGS
(*Geography & Director of E-Learning*)
Mr C Freckelton, BSc Hons, GTP (*Food Science*)
Mrs A Gilbert, BSc Hons (*Girls' Physical Education*)
Mrs R Gladwin, BA Hons, PGCE (*Religious Studies &
Sociology*)
Mr J Chambers, BSc Hons, PGCE, NPQH (*Business
Studies*)
Mr S King, BEng Hons, PGCE (*ICT*)
Mrs H Mason, BSc Hons, PGCE (*Science*)
Mr A Prentice, BA Hons, MA, PGCE, LTCL (*Director of
Music*)
Mrs C Prentice, BMus Hons, PGCE, LTCL (*Senior School
Music*)
Mrs C Servonat-Blanc, BA Hons, PGCE (*Art &
Photography*)
Mr D Underhill, BA Hons, PGCE (*Psychology*)
Mrs J Wafer, BA Hons, PGCE (*Drama*)
Mr R Wenban, BEd Hons (*Boys' Physical Education*)
Mr J Wynn, BA, PGCE (*Modern Foreign Languages*)

Principal's PA / Office & Communications Manager: Mrs
H Brimblecombe, BA Hons

Registrar: Mrs D Harris

Examinations Officer: Mrs A Pullen, BA Hons, PGCE

Structure and Organisation. Lincoln Minster School
educates pupils from nursery to A Level on several delightful sites situated in the heart of historic Lincoln. In ten years
the school has almost trebled its number on roll without losing the marked friendliness and responsiveness which makes
it so attractive.

In 2010 the £10million Music Centre and Sports Hall
augmented the School's facilities dramatically and is bol-
stering the School's growing reputation for music excellence. With a new strategy to open its doors worldwide, the
School is seeking to build on a growing national reputation
to become a school of international renown. An increased
capacity for boarding is also facilitating this development.

Class sizes, the quality of teaching and discipline are
carefully controlled. There is excellent pastoral care and
award-winning careers provision designed to equip youngsters for life beyond the classroom. The Nursery and Early
Years department recently attained 'outstanding' status from
Ofsted, underlining the quality of provision across all areas.

Lincoln Minster School is a member of the United
Church Schools Trust, which owns and manages independent schools and academies across England. There is no
doubt that membership of a group of this size gives Lincoln
Minster School stability and breadth of contact.

Curriculum. A full range of subjects is offered and the
school is proud of its excellent track record of examination
success.

The curriculum is supported by a wealth of trips, visits
and activities, too numerous to list, plus a comprehensive
sports programme to cater for all tastes.

Pupils of all ages are encouraged to develop intellectual
curiosity, resilience and self-confidence and to begin their
lives within a Christian framework.

Music. As the Choir School for Lincoln Cathedral, Lincoln Minster School provides for the all-round education of
boy and girl choristers. 27 music staff work in the department; approximately 70% of pupils receive individual
instrument lessons. Music is a focal point of school life and
opportunities for public performances abound. The strong
musical and Christian ethic within the school is enhanced by
daily use of the School Chapel and the Cathedral.

Boarding. Weekly and termly boarding is offered. Flexible boarding may be possible, depending on availability. The
large family of boarders is very much at the heart of the
School. In 2010, a further boarding house was acquired and
superbly refurbished and this enabled the school to recruit
more widely. There are 4 boarding houses, all in close proximity to the School and within the beautiful conservation
area of uphill Lincoln.

Admissions. Lincoln Minster School welcomes pupils of
a wide range of ability and all faiths. Admission is by interview and report, and subject to availability of a place.

Chorister Auditions, open to boys and girls 7–10 years,
are held in November and March. These are worth up to
50% of boarding and tuition fees. Other dates by arrangement. For further details apply to The Registrar.

Scholarships. Academic Scholarships are available at
7+, 11+, 13+ and 16+. Music Scholarships are available at
11+, 13+ and 16+. Choral Bursaries are available for members of the Cathedral Choir.

Fees per term (2011-2012). Day (including lunch):
Nursery £2,226 (all day); Early Years £2,558 (all day); Pre-
Prep £2,567; Prep £3,327; Seniors £3,749. Weekly Board-
ing: £5,672 (up to Year 6), £6,565 (Years 7–13). Termly
Boarding: £6,248 (up to Year 6), £7,250 (Years 7–13),
£8,056 (Overseas Boarders).

Charitable status. Lincoln Minster School is part of The
United Church Schools Trust which is a Registered Charity,
number 1016538.

Liverpool College

Queen's Drive, Mossley Hill, Liverpool L18 8BG
Tel: 0151 724 4000; 0151 724 1611 (Admissions)
Fax: 0151 729 0105
e-mail: admin@liverpoolcollege.org.uk
website: www.liverpoolcollege.org.uk

Motto: *Non solum ingenii, verum etiam virtutis.*

Visitor: The Bishop of Liverpool

President: The Rt Hon The Earl of Derby, DL

The Revd Canon Dr D C Gray, CBE, TD, PhD, MPhil, AKC, FRHistS
The Rt Hon The Lord Hunt of Wirral, PC, MBE
The Rt Revd Nigel McCulloch, MA
District Judge R A McCullagh, MA
H M Alty Esq, MBChB, BDS, FDS, RCS
His Honour Judge G M Clifton
B S Clarke Esq
L Holden Esq, DL, LLB
C C Hubbard Esq
I N Lightbody Esq
J D Robertson Esq
R L Sington Esq

Governors:
G N Wood, QC (*Chairman*)
I R Evans (*Deputy Chairman*)
Mrs E J Bramley
Dr H I Eccles
M G Jones
Dr N Kalakonda
J D A Leith
Mrs M L Mason, BSc
N A Rugg
J R Sumner, FCA (*Honorary Treasurer*)
P H Taaffe, FCA, TCA
C E Thompson
B W F Wong, DL, MA, JP

Principal: Hans van Mourik Broekman, MA Hons

Head of Upper School: Dr S P Downes, BSc, PhD, MBA

Bursar: W R E L Thompson

Finance Manager: Mrs A Gemmell

Registrar: Mrs S Loveridge

Chaplain: Revd Dr J N Duff, MA, MSt, DPhil

Staff:

Mrs M Alexander, BA	J G Hutchinson, BA
Dr E J Atkins, BA, PhD	Ms R A Kelly, BA
D J Bishop, BMus	Mrs E Kendall
S I Brady, BA	Mrs M M Lawrenson, MA
P A Cartwright, BEd	C R Leeder, BSc
Mrs K-M Clarke, BSc	Mrs S Lines, BSc
B C Donnelly, BEd	H E Lock, MA
S Doran, BA	B D Martin, BSc
Mrs H E Finch, MA Hons	R McAlea, MA
Miss R M Foster, MSc	B McAuliffe, BCL
A Fox, BSc	Miss K L McCaughey, MA
A D Gammon, BEd	Miss L M Miller, BSc
N W Griffith, BA	Miss E Nixon, MA
P Gunawardena, BSc	Mrs K Reid, BA
D Hall, BSc	E J Richards, BA
Mrs J Hall, BA	B Roberts, BEng
Ms L A Hamilton, BSc	Miss L Townley, BA
Miss N Hannah, BSc	T J Traynor, BEng
T M Harvey, BA	C H Turbitt, MSc
Mrs C A Hunter, BA	G P Wilson, MA

Prep and Pre-Prep

Head: S Buglass, MEd

Deputy Head: W G Kendall, CertEd

Head of Pre-Prep: Mrs G Gannon, BEd

Miss J Anderson, BSc	Mrs R Kerr, NNEB
Mrs H Boyle, NNEB	Mrs E L Lewis, NNEB
Mrs D A Buglass, CertEd	D McClements, BEd
Miss R C Chaffer, BA	Mrs G M McGuinness,
Mrs P A Davey, CertEd	NNEB
Mrs S E Doran, BEd	Mrs E McLennon, BA
Mrs C Hegarty, BA	Mrs S J Nelson, BEd
Miss R J Humphries, BA	Mrs J Poole, NNEB
Mrs B A Jones, MA	

Miss A F Russell-Moore, BSc	J Tegg, BSc
Miss J Saunders, BSc	Mrs K A Ward, BEd
Mrs L Strong, BEd	Mrs N Ward, BA
Mrs K J Taylor, BEd	Miss J L Ware
	Mrs F Wright, BA

Campus and Buildings. The College is situated 4 miles south of the city centre, in 26 acres of wooded grounds and playing fields, adjacent to extensive parkland, and situated in the South Liverpool conservation area. It is easily accessible by public transport or by one of the College buses.

Founded in 1840, the College has expanded and upgraded the buildings and facilities to keep abreast of curricular developments and to create the optimum environment for a modem multi-faith and multi-cultural educational community.

The Preparatory School occupies its own self-contained site within the College grounds (*see entry in IAPS section*) and the Pre-Prep and Nursery has recently been extended and provided with a well-equipped outdoor play area.

A floodlit synthetic pitch has been added to the extensive playing fields, and a Sports Centre with a fully equipped gymnasium, an aerobics/dance studio and facilities for indoor cricket, basketball and tennis was opened by HRH Princess Anne in 1999.

Organisation. There are at present 336 girls and 414 day boys in the school. The College provides a complete and continuous course of education for boys and girls from 3 to 18 years of age in the Preparatory School (3–11) and in Upper School (11–18). Each of the schools has its own Head and staff, but additional specialist teaching is provided in the Prep school in Music, Sport and Modern Languages.

The College introduced a small international boarding programme in September 2010 for pupils aged 16 and over, for Pre-Sixth Form and Sixth Form courses.

Admission. The main points of entry are at ages 3, 5, 7, 11 and 16 by assessment and/or examination, although pupils are admitted at other ages. Tours of the College may be booked through the Registrar.

Scholarships. Academic, Music, Art, Drama and Sport Scholarships are offered, as are Bursaries for children of Clergy of any religion and of members of the Armed Forces. Means-tested Bursaries are also available.

The Curriculum. The curriculum retains an emphasis on a rigorous training in academic subjects while allowing scope for individual preferences. The curriculum to GCSE includes English Language and Literature, French, Spanish, Mathematics, Physics, Chemistry, Biology, Geography, History, Information and Communication Technology, DT, Drama, Art, Music and Physical Education.

Sixth Form. The majority of pupils proceed into the Sixth Form and nearly all go on to Universities or pursue other specialist areas, eg Arts, Drama. While retaining their role as an integral senior part of the community and being required to take some responsibility for the running of the school in a prefectorial capacity, the Sixth Formers enjoy greater independence. They have a separate library. The AQA Baccalaureate was introduced in September 2009. Subjects offered include Art & Design, Biology, Business Studies, Chemistry, Design Technology, Economics, English, English Literature, French, Geography, General Studies, History, ICT, Maths and Further Maths, PE, Physics, Spanish, Theatre Studies, Music and Music Technology.

Careers. The College is a member of ISCO. Careers advice and guidance is provided throughout the school by a Careers and University Advisor as well as a team of staff in liaison with ISCO. There is a full and active Careers programme of both general instruction and individual, specialist counselling, and a well-stocked Careers room. The Head of Choices and the Head of Sixth Form arranges work experience and work shadowing for Year 11 and Year 12 students within their potential career fields. Particular attention is paid to preparation for University entrance.

Religious Education. All faiths are respected and, although the Chapel remains a focus for Christian worship, assemblies are provided for those of other faiths.

Pastoral Care and House System. The Upper School is divided into four Houses, each with its own Head of House and Tutors. Pupils join one of the school Houses on entry and continue in it throughout their school career. Close contact is established and maintained between staff and pupils within the Houses. House activities include music, sport and drama. Tutors and Heads of Houses monitor each pupil's progress and give regular advice on a personal and individual basis.

Medical Care. First aid is provided by a team of fully-qualified first aiders.

Reporting. Regular consultations are held with parents to review each pupil's progress and achievement in terms of both ability and effort and in relation to his or her potential: appointments may be made with the House Tutor or Heads of House if parents have cause for concern about any aspect of their child's progress.

Sport. For boys the main sports are Rugby, Football, Hockey and Cricket. The main sports for girls are Hockey, Netball, Tennis and Rounders. For both boys and girls, cross-country races are held in the Lent term and Athletics in the Summer. There are many other sports and options.

Music. The College has a strong tradition of excellence in Music. All pupils receive tuition in Music as part of the normal curriculum and many learn at least one musical instrument, including the organ. There are bands and other instrumental groups for all ages within the school. Concerts are given regularly on both competitive and informal bases.

Drama. Drama is taught to all pupils up to Year 9. They may then wish to choose a course in Drama for GCSE or A Level Theatre Studies. School plays and other dramatic productions are staged regularly and as many pupils as possible are encouraged to participate.

Activities and Societies. There are more than thirty Societies currently operating: these cover many aspects of pupils' interests from Computing to Tae Kwon Do, from Chess to Debating. Teams from the College regularly participate in Debating competitions. Over 120 pupils take part in The Duke of Edinburgh's Award Scheme.

Activity holidays, Adventure Training and trips abroad which combine recreation and education are organised regularly.

After School Clubs. After School Clubs are provided for children aged 3–11, enabling them to remain on the school premises under qualified supervision until 6.00 pm each day. The Upper School library remains open until 5.30 pm with staff supervision and there is also a large number of after-school clubs and activities.

Combined Cadet Force. The voluntary Combined Cadet Force is one of the largest and oldest in the UK and has RN, Army and RAF sections: pupils spend 2 years in one of these sections after a year of pre-CCF training. About 50% volunteer for a further two years.

Fees per term (2011-2012). Upper School £3,225, Preparatory School £2,585, Pre-Prep and Nursery £1,995. Reductions for brothers and sisters also apply.

Old Lerpoolians. The school fosters and maintains connections with former pupils through the Old Lerpoolian Society and holds regular functions and reunions. Information may be obtained from the College office, Tel: 0151 724 4000.

Charitable status. Liverpool College is a Registered Charity, number 526682. It exists to provide education for boys and girls.

Llandovery College
(Coleg Llanymddyfri)

Queensway, Llandovery, Carmarthenshire SA20 0EE
Tel: Switchboard: 01550 723000
         Bursary: 01550 723044
         Admissions: 01550 723005
Fax: 01550 723002
e-mail: marketing@llandoverycollege.com
         admissions@llandoverycollege.com
website: www.llandoverycollege.com

Llandovery College sits in 50+ acres of grounds in the Towy Valley, Wales. The College, endowed by Thomas Phillips in 1847, remains true to its founding values, providing a well-rounded education in an unspoilt rural setting. Sport, extra-curricular activities and outdoor pursuits are a vital part of College life with excellent academic results and small classes.

Emeritus Trustees:
Sir John Venables Llewelyn, Bart, MA
Mr Owain M R Howell, MA, FCA
Mr Anthony M James, FBIM
Dr T Gerald R Davies, MA, DL, CBE
Mr David E Gravell, MIMI
Mr R Ian H Gollop, MA (*Chairman*)
Mr Paul Hartley-Davies, LLB (*Deputy Chairman*)

Board of Trustees:
Dr Loveday E Gee, BA, MPhil
Mr Jack D Hansen
Sir David John, KCMG
Mr Shaun Parry-Jones, BA Hons, PGDL, PGDLP
Professor Robert E Mansel, MB BS, MS, FRCS, CBE
Mr Derry Nicklin
Mr J Hugh Thomas, MA, FTCL, LRAM, ARCO
Mrs Judith Methuen-Campbell

Warden: Mr I M Hunt, BA, PGCE

Deputy Warden: Mr J G Davies, PGCE, MA Oxon

Bursar and Clerk to the Trustees: Mr T D Williams, BA, FCCA

Senior School Staff:
Mr T J Bayley, BSc (*Biology, Head of Boarding*)
Ms L Burgess, BA (*Head of Modern Languages*)
Mr T J Cannock, MA (*Head of Classics*)
Mrs S E Collins, MA Hons, PGCE (*Head of English*)
Major D Drinkall, BSc (*Head of Outdoor Pursuits, SSI*)
Miss F Earle, BA, PGCE (*Head of Drama*)
Mrs E Edwards, BA, PGCE (*Head of Music*)
Miss N M Evans, BSc, PGCE (*Head of Girls' Games*)
Ms C Flowers (*Director of Sport*)
Mrs T Gong (*Mandarin Teacher*)
Mrs J Hayman, BSc Hons, PGCE (*Mathematics*)
Mr M Hinchcliffe, BA Hons, PGCE (*Head of Art*)
Mr A Hoare, PGCE (*Spanish*)
Mrs V Hope-Bell, BA, MEd, PGCE, AMDA (*Learning Support*)
Mrs H Hunt, BA, PGCE (*Business Studies*)
Major C N H Jennings, BSc, PGCE (*Biology, Chemistry, CCF*)
Mr T Jones, MEd (*Head of Business Studies, Housemaster Ty Cadog*)
Mrs J D Kendrick, JP, CertEd (*ESL*)
Mrs J Livings, BEd Hons (*Head of Learning Support*)
Mr J Mawer, BSc Hons, PGCE (*Head of Geography*)
Mr A W Morgan, MA, PGCE (*Head of Welsh*)
Mr V A Price, BSc, PGCE (*Head of Physics, Examinations Officer*)

Mr S Robertson, BSc, MDA, PGCE (*ICT & Business Studies*)

Mrs D A Rockey, BSc, PGCE (*Head of Biology, Director of Studies*)

Mr N Shaw, BSc, PGCE (*Mathematics, Physics*)

Mrs C Spackman, BA, PGCE (*Mathematics*)

Mr P Spowage, BEd (*Design & Technology*)

Mr L Taylor, BSc (*Maths & ICT*)

Miss M Thomas, BA Hons, PGCE, (*Art and Welsh*)

Mr R Thompson, MSc, BA Hons, PGCE (*International Student Support Officer, Head of EFL*)

Mrs H Wallace, BA, (*English, House Parent Ty Llandingat*)

Mr J Wallace, BSc, PGCE (*Head of Science, Housemaster Ty Llandingat*)

Mr N A Watts, AdDip, CertEd, MEd (*Head of DT, Senior Master*)

Mrs T Webb-Rogers, MA, PGCE (*English*)

Prep School Staff:
Headteacher: Ms S Meadows, BA Hons, PGCE
Mrs P D Bullions, BEd
Miss J Owens, BA, PGCE
Mrs K Pemble, BEd
Mr A Thomas, BSc, PGCE

Classroom Assistants:
Mrs J Dewland
Ms M Davies

School Medical Officers:
Dr J Richards, MB, BCh
Dr R W Salt, MB, BCh
Dr M J M Boulter, MA, MB BS

Medical Staff:
Mrs A Anwyl-Williams, RN
Mrs J Sanger, RGN, RSCN
Mrs A R Jones, RGN, RMN, ONC

Alumni:
Sir David John (*former Chairman, BOC Group*)
Peter Morgan (*former Director General, Institute of Directors*)
Major General P M Davies (*Former Chief Executive, RSPCA*)
James Merriman
Andy Powell
Cerith Rees
Rhydian Roberts
Craig Quinnell
Vivian Jenkins
Alun Wyn Jones
Gwyn Jones
Cliff Jones
A M Rees
Rachel Poolman

Age Range. 5–18.

Number of Pupils. 326.

Progress and Tradition. Since 1848, the College has been dedicated to providing the best all-round education. We respond positively to changes in society while retaining a commitment to honourable standards and values. After 160 years, Llandovery College remains the school of choice for those wanting the widest and most fulfilling of educational experiences.

Location. The College is set amidst the beautiful countryside of mid Wales in the small, safe market town of Llandovery (population c.2500) on the edge of the Brecon Beacons. The area enjoys low levels of pollution, traffic and crime.

Recent Developments. Millions have been invested in new buildings and in refurbishment of teaching and boarding accommodation. Additions include an all-weather pitch, preparatory school, a new ICT department, 9-hole golf course, Welsh language centre, medical centre, small lake, dedicated junior boarding house, Wi-Fi throughout, Costa Coffee franchise, Sixth Form centre and state-of-the-art teaching centre and a new Mandarin centre – the first of its kind in Wales.

Curriculum. Llandovery College provides a well-rounded education. Standards are high with individuals respected and rewarded for their contribution to College life. The College offers more than 20 subjects at GCSE and A Level including Classics and Mandarin. Progress reports issued every half term. Average staff:pupil ratio is 1:13.

School Life. Uniform is mandatory. Houses arranged by age group and sex with a co-educational house for younger boarders, aged 9–13. Head Boy and Girl appointed by the Warden, House Prefects by House Parents, School Prefects voted for by pupils and appointed by Senior Staff. Religion: Church in Wales. Exchange schemes with schools in other countries including Australia, Patagonia and Zimbabwe. High-quality, healthy food is provided by Chartwells, the specialist caterer, in the superb setting of the oak-panelled Great Hall.

Sports. Rugby, hockey, cricket, netball, tennis, squash, rounders, badminton, fencing, swimming, horse-riding, basketball, dance, triathalon, athletics and golf. PE may be taken up to and including A Level. The College has a long, distinguished reputation in sport, particularly Rugby ending most years in the top 5 GB schools. 17 pupils currently represent their country or GB in 24 separate pursuits. More than 40 Full Welsh Internationals are former pupils including Alun Wyn Jones and Andy Powell. There are regular overseas sports tours. The girls' and boys' fixture lists are impressive, competing against the best schools in the UK. The College has its own 9-hole golf course.

Activities. Many pupils undertake The Duke of Edinburgh's Award (30+ Gold Awards pa). The College has the highest completion record for DofE in Wales at 96%. CCF compulsory for 2 years, optional thereafter. CCF field days held throughout the year and annual camps take place in the holidays. Many extra-curricular clubs, eg choir, public speaking, orchestra, music, welsh, art, chess. Young enterprise schemes. Considerable emphasis on outdoor pursuits. Superb countryside around the College lends itself to outward-bound activities such as rock climbing, canoeing, hill walking and fishing. Recent trips include Morocco, Kenya, Russia, Sweden and Patagonia.

Discipline. Discipline and standards are high with pride in our uniform and respect for others. Sanctions of varying degrees are applied to match the level of offence committed. Pastoral and disciplinary policy are operated through a system of individual tutors, house staff and school prefects with reward every bit as important as sanction.

The Arts. Music and Drama are strong and involve most pupils. There is an annual programme of visiting artists and lecturers. LAMDA exams and Ballet available in Prep. School productions each year including, recently, One Flew Over the Cuckoo's Nest, West Side Story, Joseph, Amadeus, Fiddler on the Roof, Les Misérables and The Sound of Music. Art, Design, Pottery and Photography are offered and enjoy high levels of participation. Over 40% of pupils learn a musical instrument or have singing lessons. Instruments can be taught privately or by members of the music department. ABRSM instrumental & singing exams. Musical groups include a school choir, orchestra, swing band, chapel choir, girls choir, senior choir and other ensemble groups. The College enjoys a close partnership with the Royal Welsh College of Music and Drama for master classes and performances.

Boarding. Junior boarding house for pupils to age 13 with roomy dormitories, then separate houses for those of the same age and sex with single study or shared bedrooms. Houseparents are teaching staff and their families. Houses cater for 50 or less. Resident qualified nurse and a new purpose-built medical centre. Laundry services provided. Two

Exeat weekends per term. Visits to local market town allowed. Campus is friendly, mixing across age groups and after-school socialising in boarding life is vibrant. Sixth Formers have their own common room equipped with TV, games, Costa Coffee franchise, Wi-Fi and comfortable seating. ICT Centre and Library opens late every night for study. Lively and varied weekend programme of activities. Lessons on Saturday mornings.

Careers Service. Comprehensive Careers Service support for pupils with regular visits by the Regional Director of the Independent Schools Careers Organisation, the Forces Liaison Officers and the West Wales Careers Service. Well equipped to give advice on higher education.

Admission. Main entry ages are 5, 11, 13, 16 however pupils are welcome in other years when continuity of study is not adversely affected. Entrance Examinations are usually at the College using our own papers or via an approved agent. Exams on request between January and July. Prep school entrants spend a day at the school for assessment. A minimum of 6 GCSEs at grade C or above required for Sixth Form entry.

Scholarships and Bursaries. (*See Scholarship Entries section.*) Thomas Phillips Scholars may receive 100% of boarding or day fees for their entire education through a means-tested scholarship for academically-able Welsh children. Scholarships available for academic, music, drama and sports up to 50% of fees as the maximum. Pupils may apply for more than one scholarship. Exhibitions are awarded on the same grounds but for smaller sums. Scholarships and Exhibitions are contractual agreements and the benefits will be withdrawn if the pupil fails to maintain their enthusiasm for the scholarship activities. In cases of financial hardship a parent may be offered a bursary based on particular circumstances.

Fees per term (2011-2012). Senior School: Day £4,695; Boarding: £6,950 (UK resident), £7,840 (Non UK resident). Preparatory School: Day £2,470; Boarding: £4,725 (UK resident), £5,615 (Non UK resident); Weekly Boarding £3,950.

Charitable status. Llandovery College is a Registered Charity, number 1111878.

Lomond School

10 Stafford Street, Helensburgh, Argyll and Bute G84 9JX
Tel: 01436 672476
Fax: 01436 678320
e-mail: admin@lomond-school.org
website: www.lomond-school.org

Lomond is a co-educational day and boarding school for pupils aged from 3 to 18 years. The original foundations date from 1845 and the current roll is 500 pupils, including 60 boarders who are housed in a new building with en-suite study-bedrooms which was completed in March 2003. A new main building was opened in 1998 which provides excellent purpose-built facilities and a conducive learning environment. Strong examination results are consistently produced leading to high university uptake. New leading-edge sporting facilities, including provision of a multi-purpose Sports Hall, opened in August 2009.

Twenty five miles from Glasgow, a thriving cosmopolitan city which is a centre for art, culture and commerce, Helensburgh is situated on the north bank of the Firth of Clyde in a quiet residential setting and with immediate access to mountain, sea and loch – ideal for outdoor activities.

Board of Governors:
Chair: Mrs C Dobson
Vice Chair:Mr A J D Hope

Mr D Bowman
Professor R Brown
Mr C M Burnet
Captain P Merriman
Dr T Reitano
Mr P Silvey
Mr T Smith
Mrs A Stanley-Whyte
Mr F Thornton
Lt Cdr L Wooller

Staff:

Headmaster: **Mr S J Mills**, MA Cantab

Pastoral Depute: Mr A B H Minnis, MA Hons, PGCE, Cert PP
Academic Depute: Mr I Morrison, BSc, LLB, PGCE
Head of Primary: Mrs S Hart, BEd Hons
Bursar: Mr P McElwee, CA

Subject Teachers – Secondary:

Art & Design:
Mrs B Croft, BA Hons, CertEd
Mrs L Jack, BA Hons, PGCE

Business Studies:
Mrs C McElhill, BA Hons, CertEd

EFL:
Mrs J Pelly, MA Oxon, TEFL

English:
Dr M E Everett, BA Hons, PhD, DipEd
Mrs P Wales, MA Hons, CertEd
Mrs M McKillop, MA Hons, MPhil, PGCE
Mrs E Bruce, MA Hons, PGDE

Geography:
Mr G M Taylor, BSc, MSc, DipEd Comp, CertEd
Mrs N McKenzie, MA Hons, PGCE

Graphic Communication:
Miss A Kelly, BEng Hons, PGDE

History and Modern Studies:
Mrs S Guy, MA Hons, PGCE
Mr A B H Minnis, MA Hons, PGCE, Cert PP
Miss E Trevena, MA Hons, PGCE

ICT:
Mr S J Kilday, DipTechEd, DipComp

Learning Support:
Mr H Hunter, BA Hons, PGDE
Mrs C Greaves, BSc Hons, PGCE
Mrs S Bell, BEd, PGDE

Mathematics:
Mr G Macleod, BSc Hons, MEd, CMath, S Sci FIMA, PGCE, Adv Dip Hist Oxon
Mr A Laceby, BA, Dip Math, PGCE
Mrs E Cameron, BSc Hons, PGCE
Dr A MacBeath, BEng Hons, PhD, PGDE
Mrs E Stewart, BSc Hons, PGCE

Modern Languages:
Mr A Greig, MA Hons, PGCE, PGDip
Miss N Dudley, MA Hons Oxon, PGCE
Mrs J Robertson, BEd
Miss E Clarke, BA Hons, PGDE
Miss I Skowronski, LLCE, PGDE
Mrs E Bruce, MA Hons, PGDE

Music:
Mrs D Philips, Dip MusEd, RSAMD, CertEd
Mr I MacDonald, DipMusEd, RSAMD, CertEd

Physical Education:
Mrs M G Taylor, BEd
Mr D Fitzgerald, BEd Hons

Mr C Dunlop, BEd Hons

RME:
Mr S J Kilday, DipTechEd, DipComp
Mrs L Jack, BA Hons, PGCE

Science:
Physics:
Dr A MacBeath, BEng Hons, PhD, PGDE
Mr C Butler, BSc Hons, CertEd
Chemistry:
Mr D L Dodson, BSc Hons, CertEd
Miss M Ward, BSc Hons, PGCE
Biology:
Mrs E Hunter, BSc Hons, MEd, CertEd, MIBiol, CBiol
Mrs C Normand, BSc Hons, PGCE

Careers Advisor:
Mrs J Barrett-Bunnage, MA Hons, PG Dip CG

School Nurse:
Mrs Lesley Serpell, RGN, MPH

Class Teachers – Primary:
Miss L Boyd, MA, BSc Hons, PGCE
Mrs L Canero, BA, PGDE
Mrs V Cassels, MA Hons, MA, BSc, Dip Env Dev, PGCE
Mrs J Fullarton, BA Hons, PGCE
Mrs C Greig, BA Jt Hons, PGCE, DipEdTech
Mrs J Macleod, BEd Hons, MEd, Dip RSA, Dip APS, DipEd Lead, SQH
Mrs V McLatchie, DCE
Mrs L Robertson, Dip Prim Ed, Dip RE
Miss A Springett, BSc Hons, PGCE

Nursery/Pre-School Group:
Mrs J Reynolds, CertEd, Cert E Ed, Dip E Ed, MSc E Ed
Ms A Goram, SNNEB
Ms L Lovell, SPA Childcare
Mrs J McArthur, SNNEB
Mrs H Windsor, BA

Mrs J Ferguson (*Clarendon Assistant*)
Mrs J Marrison (*Classroom Assistant*)
Mrs F Reid, SNNEB (*Classroom Assistant*)
Mrs G Thomas, HNC Childcare & Education (*Classroom Assistant*)
Mrs L Lloyd (*After School Club and wrap around care*)

Aims of the School. Lomond has a proud academic tradition and nearly all of the Sixth Form will leave to attend University or College. However, it aims to get the best from every pupil regardless of talent and successfully caters for the 'average' youngster as well as those with high ability. It believes strongly in developing the whole person and creating a high achievement environment.

Class sizes are low and there is a close monitoring of all pupils both academically and for extra-curricular input. Pupils sit Scottish Certificate of Education Standard Grade, Intermediate 2 and Higher examinations in Senior 4 and Senior 5 before sitting Advanced Highers or further Highers in the Sixth Form. Maintaining both breadth and depth in senior years enables there to be a flexible approach to individual needs which means that a complete range of ability is successfully catered for.

Extra-curricular. The philosophy of the school looks to involvement in the extensive extra-curricular programme from every pupil. It is expected that pupils will take part in the main sports of rugby, hockey, and athletics and in the Duke of Edinburgh's Award Scheme. There are teams for football, cricket and tennis and a wide variety of activities are strongly represented. Fixtures against other schools take place every weekend and there is a very extensive outdoor education programme. Music and drama are also strong and a plethora of pupils have achieved success at the highest level.

Some distinctive aspects. The extensive Duke of Edinburgh's Award Scheme programme leads to participation in such events as the Lomond Challenge Triathlon (a national event) and the Scottish Islands Peaks Race. A week long Outward Bound programme has been developed for the school which concentrates on leadership and teamwork skills. There are regular canoe and mountaineering expeditions abroad. The international dimension is significant not only with long established exchanges and work experience abroad but also due to special arrangements that have encouraged pupils from abroad to study at Lomond which broadens the outlook of the school's pupils and leads to greater international understanding.

There are state-of-the-art boarding, sporting and teaching facilities, which alongside a very supportive staff bring out the very best in our pupils.

Entry and Scholarships. Means-tested bursaries are available for entry between T2 (P7) and S6 with fee assistance ranging from 10% to 100% depending on circumstances. A means-tested Traditional Music Scholarship is also available. In addition means-tested bursaries are available for services personnel with children who board at Lomond.

Admission is by assessment in Mathematics and English for 11–13 year olds. For younger pupils placement in classes is the main requirement whilst for senior pupils reports and examination results are given due weighting.

Fees per term (2011-2012). Tuition: £1,010 (Nursery), £1,550 (Junior 1), £2,270 (Junior 2), £2,650 (Junior 3–5), £2,895 (Transitus 1), £3,070 (Transitus 2), £3,160 (Senior School).

Boarding (in addition to Tuition Fees): £3,600.

A levy of £50 per pupil per term is payable along with tuition fees.

Charitable status. Lomond School Ltd is a Registered Charity, number SC007957. It exists to provide education for boys and girls.

Lord Wandsworth College

Long Sutton, Hook, Hampshire RG29 1TB
Tel:　01256 862201 (Main Office)
　　　01256 860348 (Headmaster)
　　　01256 860200 (Admissions)
Fax:　01256 860363
e-mail:　info@lordwandsworth.org
website:　www.lordwandsworth.org

Lord Wandsworth College is a co-educational secondary school for 530 pupils between the ages of 11 and 18. There are approximately 215 weekly boarders, 50 full boarders and 265 day pupils.

Motto: '*Vincit Perseverantia.*'

President: Sir Humphrey Prideaux, OBE, DL, MA

Chairman of Governors: R G Janaway

The Governing Body consists of 12 governors.

Headmaster: F Q Livingstone, MA

Deputy Heads:
Dr T Johnson, BSc
S L Badger, MA

Bursar: A C Usborne, BSc

Assistant Staff:

Mrs V Allan, BA	G C Clark-Savage
Mrs S Badger, MA	Miss S J Clinton, BA
Mrs J D Bailey, BSc	M Clinton-Baker, BA
Miss C Bell, BA	E Coetzer, BA
Miss E C Cattle, MA	

Mrs L L Crowther, BMus, MA
Dr M R Eldridge, BSc, PhD
Mrs A-M Englebrecht, BA
Mrs L Faulkner, MA, BSc
P M Gilliam, BSc
A O F Hamilton, MA
J Harris, BEng
C C Hicks, MA
A M Howard, MA
D P Ibbotson, BSc
C Irvine, BSc
Mrs T N Joad, MA
S M Jones, MA
R J Kimber, BEng
A P Lay, BSc
Revd S Leyshon, BTh, MEd
Miss C Liggins, BA
J K Lilley, MA
C Lovelock, BEd
Mrs R P Lovelock, BSc
A E Lumsden, BSc
D O C Machin, BA
Mrs C A Matthews, BA
S P Matthews, BA
G A McKinnon, BA
Mrs J M McKinnon, BA

Miss L McNabb, BA
G J Mobbs, BA
Mrs G R Neighbour
D C Pering, MA
Miss L H Pick, BSc
Mrs L D Power, BA
C H Radmann, BA
Mrs L A Radmann, BA
Mrs N Reeson, BA
Mrs S Richardson, BA
T R Richardson, BA Hons Ed
T J Shedden, BA
Miss M Sinclair-Smith, BA
S Singh, MA
G R Smith, BA
Ms T St Clair Ford, BA
Mrs S Stevens, BA
P R Summers, MA
R J Thorne, BA, MSc
A Turner, BSc
E Walker, BSc
D L Widdowson, BSc
Mrs C J Wisdom, CertEd, RSA DipSpLD
C Wiskin
C Wyndham, BA

Librarian: Mrs S Brown

Director of Admissions & Marketing: Mrs M Hicks

Development Director: Mrs K Chernyshov

Headmaster's Secretary: Mrs N Grossmith

Medical Officers:
Dr R Assadourian, MB BS, BSc Hons, MRCGP, DRCOG, DFFP
Dr C Shand, MB BS, LMSSA, MRCGP, DRCOG, DFFP

Location and accessibility. The school is fortunate in that, although it occupies a magnificent rural setting on the North Hampshire/Surrey border, it has excellent communications, being five miles from Junction 5 of the M3 and under an hour from London. Access to main line trains and all major airports is quick and easy.

Many pupils come from the surrounding towns and villages around Farnham, Alton, Fleet, Basingstoke, Guildford and Reading, and there is a well-established tradition of such children weekly boarding although living relatively close-by.

History. Lord Wandsworth died in 1912 and left a large sum of money for the foundation of a school. The College that bears his name now occupies a 1,200 acre site. The Lord Wandsworth Foundation awards a number of places annually to children who have lost the support of one or both parents through death, divorce or separation with priority to those who have lost a parent through death.

Mission statement. Lord Wandsworth College is a non-denominational foundation which fosters the intellectual, moral and spiritual development of all the young people in its care. It strives to ensure that each pupil realises his or her full potential within a stimulating environment which emphasises concern for others.

The outstanding features of the school are
- that almost all academic staff live on campus allowing them to provide a high level of pastoral care;
- that all pupils, whether day, weekly or full boarding, belong to one of the eight boarding houses and are fully integrated into the social life of the school;
- that the school is purpose-built with an outstanding range of facilities for both academic and extra-curricular activities;
- that the school is an unusually unpretentious, happy and caring community.

Curriculum. The aim of the curriculum is to provide a full and flexible range of subjects to fit the needs of each individual. The school's policy is to follow closely the National Curriculum.

Subjects taught to GCSE are: English (Language and Literature), French, Geography, Mathematics, History, Latin, Classical Civilisation, Drama, Physics, Chemistry, Biology, Spanish, German, Art, Music, Design & Technology and Religious Studies.

Most pupils continue into the Sixth Form where the subjects taught to AS and A2 Level are: English, History, Geography, Economics, Business Studies, Classical Civilisation, Critical Thinking, Music, Latin, French, Spanish, German, Physics, Chemistry, Biology, Mathematics, Further Mathematics, Art, Design, Theatre Studies, PE, Religious Studies and Psychology. We also offer the AQA Baccalaureate and EPQ.

ICT. There has been, and continues to be, significant investment into IT provision. There is a wireless networked system across the whole school.

Games. The school lays great store by its games involvement and has a local and national reputation for many of its pursuits. The main boys' games are rugby, hockey and cricket and for girls hockey, netball and tennis. In addition swimming, athletics, squash, badminton, basketball, golf, cross-country running and canoeing all take place and provide teams which represent the school.

Drama. Drama has a high profile within the school and several shows are staged each year. There is a musical production every other year as well as showcases, reviews and workshops. Pupils are encouraged to participate in all fields of drama either acting, writing, set design, lighting, stage management, prop-making or sound.

Music. There is a large variety of instrumental ensembles, including an orchestra, swing band and many chamber and rock groups. Pupils sing in two choirs. Tuition is available in singing, all orchestral instruments, piano, organ, percussion and guitar. Musicians regularly perform formally and informally both within school and at local venues.

Other activities. There is an extensive extra-curricular programme. Some of the activities on offer are: Cookery, Soccer, Roller Hockey, Chess, Pottery, Drama clubs, Mountain Biking, Horticulture, Archery, Dance, Photography, School newspaper, Life-saving, Self-defence, Scuba-diving, Debating and Climbing.

The Duke of Edinburgh's Award Scheme is thriving and the College has its own licence to run the scheme. There is an active CCF programme for Year 10 pupils and above which has an Army and Air Force Section. All Sixth Form pupils take part in a Community Service programme.

Organisation. There is a two or three form entry at age 11. For the first two years all pupils are in the co-educational Junior House which has its own buildings and sports fields. At 13 there is another entry, mainly from children who have taken Common Entrance. All houses are in the charge of Houseparents assisted by a team of tutors and matrons.

Fees per term (2011-2012). (*See Scholarship Entries section.*) Senior Full Boarders £8,770, Senior Weekly Boarders £8,348, Senior Day Pupils £6,220, Junior Boarders £7,910, Junior Day Pupils £5,906.

Charitable status. Lord Wandsworth College Trust is a Registered Charity, number 272050. It exists to provide education for boys and girls.

Loretto School

Linkfield Road, Musselburgh, East Lothian EH21 7RE
Tel: School: 0131 653 4444
        Headmaster: 0131 653 4441
        Admissions: 0131 653 4455

Fax: School: 0131 653 4445
        Admissions: 0131 653 4401
e-mail: admissions@loretto.com
website: www.loretto.com

Loretto has flourished as a school since its establishment in 1827, 6 miles from Edinburgh, on the banks of the River Esk and surrounded by the beautiful countryside of East Lothian. It is a non-denominational, co-educational boarding and day school and provides for full and flexi boarders, as well as for day pupils, with a distinctive emphasis on the full development of the individual through academic, intellectual, sporting, musical, dramatic and artistic pursuits in a fine, secure environment. Loretto's distinctive ethos fosters in its pupils a quiet confidence in themselves and a spirit of readiness to succeed in the changing world beyond school. Loretto is a small community where staff and pupils know each other personally. Classes are deliberately small so that proper individual attention is possible; recent examination results have been outstanding. Boys and girls take part in a very wide range of activities. Its pupils, from 3 to 18 years, are known and valued for themselves and are expected to respect and support each other. The School makes fullest use of its proximity to Edinburgh, enabling pupils to take advantage of the music, drama, museums and art galleries, as well as giving opportunities for sport and leisure in this capital city. To the east lie the golf courses which provide the fairway for The Golf Academy at Loretto.

Governors:

R L Martin, QC
  (*Chairman*)
P Arthur (*Vice-Chairman*)
M Black
Mrs A Brobbel
K Dobson
D Christie
Mrs S Geddes (*Clerk to the
  Board*)
Lt Col S J M Graham
Dr P Graham

M Hinton
Mrs S Low
Major General P Marriott,
  CBE
Ms R Marshall
J Miller
R J Semple
M Simmers
Mrs A Swanson
W Waterhouse

Headmaster: P A Hogan, BCom, PGCE, MA, FRSA

Headmaster of Junior School: P Meadows, MA

Staff:
* *Head of Department*
† *Housemaster/mistress*

Miss J Addis, BA Hons, PGCE (*English, Drama*)
Dr D J Adamson, MA, PhD (*History and Politics, *Sixth
  Form*)
Dr M J Baker, MA (*Physics, Mathematics*)
N C Bidgood, BSc, MSc, PGCE, FRGS (*Vicegerent;
  Biology*)
Dr J Blair, PhD, MTh (*Mathematics and RE*)
Mrs M Bonner, BA Hons, MA, PGCE, DIS (**Art*)
A J R Brown, BA, MA, PGCE, MEd (**English*)
M T Brown, BMus Hons, MMus (*Music*)
Mrs A Buchanan, MA (*Art*)
J D Burnet, MA (**Modern Languages*)
D A Burton, BEd Hons (*Director of Sport*)
Miss C Cadzow, BDes Hons (*Art, Ceramics*)
Mrs M Campbell (*Modern Languages*)
J S P Child, MA, PGCE (*Classics*)
Miss D Crichton, BSc, MRSC, PGCE (**Science*)
Mrs P Cockburn (*Assistant †Balcarres*)
W E Coleman, MMus ARCO (*Director of Music*)
B A Cooper, MA Hons, MRes (*Director of Studies; History
  and Politics*)
Mrs C A Cursiter, MA (*Modern Languages*)
W D Dickinson, BEd (*†Schoolhouse; Geography*)
Mrs J Dunford, BA, MA (*Head Librarian*)
P S Dunn, BSc, PGCE (*Mathematics*)

Mrs S Feria (*Modern Languages*)
Mrs J Fletcher, BSc Hons, PGCE (**Head of Girls' Games;
  †Balcarres*)
Mrs M Galloway, MA Hons, Dip Trans (*Modern
  Language, †Holm*)
N Guise, CertEd, PGCSE (*Support for Learning*)
M Hambleton, BA, MA, PGCE/FE (*English*)
Ms K Hanson, BSc Hons, MEnvS, PGCE (*Biology*)
G Harbison, BSc Hons, MSc, PGCE (**Business Studies*)
D A Howie, MBE (*Head of Outdoor Pursuits*)
J Karolyi, PGCE (*Modern Languages,Higher Education
  Careers and University Guidance*)
P Sutton, AKC, BD, MTh (*Chaplain*)
Mrs C Lekkas, BSc Hons, DipTEFL/TESOL (**ESL,
  Biology*)
Dr D B Levey, BA, BSc, PhD (*Mathematics*)
S J M Lowe, MA Oxon, Cert Adv Studies GSMD, PGCE
  (*Director of Expressive Arts; Modern Languages*)
S Lucas, BA Hons, MLitt, Dip SpLD, PGCE (**Support for
  Learning*)
Miss K-A McCrum, MA, PGCE (*Geography*)
J McKenzie (*Support for Learning*)
D McLean-Steel, BA Hons (**Drama; English*)
G McSkimming, BSc, PGCE (**Physics, Assistant †Pinkie*)
Mrs E Middlemass, MA, PGCE (*Director of Inspection,
  Compliance and Child Protection; PSE, English and
  Drama*)
J S Mountford, BA Hons, ARCO, ATCL (*Assistant
  Director of Music*)
Miss K O'Brien-Skerry, BA, PGDE (*Mathematics and
  Physics*)
Miss A Peak, BA Hons, PGCE (*Head of Geography*)
D R Pierce, BSc Hons, PGCE (**Mathematics*)
M J Powell (*Director of Cricket; Assistant† Seton*)
Mrs T M Pratt, MTh, DHP, BACP, Accredited Counsellor
  (*PSHE*)
Pipe Major C Pryde (*Piping*)
K Reid, MSci Hons, PGCE (*Mathematics; Assistant†
  Hope*)
D H Rossouw, BSc (*†Hope, PE, Head of Rugby*)
Dr D Tidswell (*Head of History*)
Dr M G Topping, BSc Hons, PhD, PGCE (*Director of
  Academic Progress, *Biology*)
R I Valentine, BSc Hons, PGA (*Director of Golf; †Seton*)
Mrs C Wakeford (*Chemistry*)
Mrs S Ward, BSc Hons, PGCE (**Chemistry, CCF, DofE*)
Mrs S Wauchop, BBS (*Business Studies*)
R P Whait, BSc, C Dip AF (*Head of Activities; Business
  Studies, Mathematics, Head of Personal Finance and
  Examinations Officer*)
Ms J Young BA, Cert TESOL (*ESL*)

Houses and Housemasters/Housemistresses:

Boys Boarding:
Hope House: D H Rossouw
Seton House: R I Valentine

Girls Boarding:
Balcarres House: Mrs J Fletcher
Holm House: Mrs M Galloway

Day (Boys and Girls):
Schoolhouse: W D Dickinson

Junior Boarding:
Newfield House: C Claydon

Bursar: A McGhie, CA
Director of External Affairs: J Hewat
Director of Development: R Baird
Head of Marketing: Mrs B Lamotte

Junior School
Headmaster: P Meadows, MA Hons, PGCE

Staff:

Mrs J Brown, SVQ3 Playwork (*After School Club Coordinator*)
Mrs K Brown (*Classroom Assistant*)
Mrs E Buchanan (*Year 4*)
Mrs E Burgess, BEd Hons
C Claydon BSc Hons, PGCE (*Deputy Head, Houseparent*)
Mrs H Fraser (*After School Club*)
Mrs A Gauld, DCE, ACE (*Year 3*)
K Hutchison, DipTMus (**Music*)
Miss F Innes (*Classroom Assistant*)
J Jackman, BA Hons, PGDE (*Year 2*)
Mrs F Kelly, BA Hons, PGCE (*Learning Support*)
Miss F Kerr, BSc Hons, PGDE (*Year 6*)
Mrs E Karolyi, MA Hons, PGCE (*Assistant Head*)
Miss S A Kettlewell, BA (*Art & Drama*)
P McDouall, MA Hons, PGDE (*Year 5*)
Mrs K McKinnon (*Year 2*)
Mrs J O'Raw (*Nursery Nurse*)
D J Pearce, BSc Hons (*Year 7*)
Mrs V Provan (*Year 7*)
Mrs S Scott, BEd Hons (*Nursery Teacher*)
Miss K Seabra, BEd Hons (*Year 1*)
Mrs J Selley (*Classroom Assistant*)
Mrs J Robertson (*Nursery Nurse*)
Mrs J Robertson, BEd Hons (*Early Years, PE, Drama, IT*)
Ms E Shaw, BA Hons, PGCE (*Year 1*)
Miss R Wallace, SVQ3 Playwork (*After School Club*)
Ms C Ward, MEd, PGCE, BA Hons (*Year 6, French, Assistant †Holm*)
Miss L Watson (*Nursery*)
Mrs K Wells (*Year 4*)

The Senior School consists of 390 boys and girls with almost 70% of pupils boarding.

Academic. An excellent staff/pupil ratio ensures an environment that stimulates, supports and nurtures the potential in everyone. The academic programme aims to challenge pupils and to recognise and reward effort and attainment. A full range of curricular subjects – humanities; drama, music and art; languages and sciences; ICT and business; physical education – is offered. The depth, breadth and quality of a Loretto education encourages each pupil to achieve his or her personal best and to enjoy doing so. Pupils are prepared for success in GCSE, AS and A Level and for a choice of good university careers thereafter. The School is also running the AQA Extension Project Scheme which contributes to UCAS points. In 2010 67% of all A Levels sat were at grade A or B. 91% of GCSEs were at A–C grades. Virtually all pupils go on to higher education.

The facilities keep abreast of changing national academic demands, with modern, well-equipped specialist areas in languages, art and design, music, drama and the sciences. The Communication and Resource Centre provides a traditional library as well as a new Sixth Form Centre and computer network which can be accessed from academic departments and Houses. All pupils become familiar both with modern technology and with books, to facilitate independent learning, essential for success in Higher Education and beyond. The Support for Learning department assists the academically gifted as well as those who have a learning difficulty or those who simply want to improve essential study skills.

Pastoral Care. There are six houses where full and flexi boarders and day pupils can relax "at home", socialise and develop their studies under the experienced supervision of dedicated resident pastoral teams. The House structure is: 4 boarding houses (2 for Sixth Form and 2 for Second, Third, Fourth and Fifth Form), 1 Junior boarding house (boy and girl) and 1 day house (boy and girl). There is excellent pastoral care, nurturing an atmosphere of mutual care and support in which children mature at their own pace and older pupils

are encouraged to take responsibility, not just for themselves, but for their young housemates.

Younger pupils sleep in small dormitories, while sixth formers have double or individual study-bedrooms.

The day pupils at Loretto have access to the same broad and full education provided for boarders, and are able to take full advantage of the facilities of a boarding school, while returning home to sleep.

All academic staff are involved in the boarding houses and so staff are always on hand to guide and encourage. The aim is always to ensure that the well-being and development of every pupil is closely and sympathetically monitored. An excellent programme of personal, social and health education is an integral part of the curriculum.

Health. A medical centre staffed with nurses who are qualified and registered with the NMC. The Doctors surgery is located off site. All health/medical appointments for boarding pupils are made through the Loretto School Medical Centre Staff. There is a school counsellor who visits the school twice a week.

Music, Drama and Art. Loretto is well known for the excellent quality of its Expressive Arts. Pupils are encouraged to enjoy the creative arts and to develop their individual talents. A purpose-built Music School enables a very high proportion to learn individual instruments or to take voice lessons and there is a range of concerts, recitals and performances both in School and in venues in Edinburgh and East Lothian. The choir and orchestra practise weekly. All pupils enjoy whole School choral singing in chapel, while performance music extends from rock, through jazz to classical music. The Loretto Pipe Band competes successfully in national competitions and has a busy schedule of appearances. A theatre is the base for much drama work, with performances – both musical and dramatic – each term involving pupils of all ages. LAMDA exams are also available. The theatre facilities have been refurbished to provide performance areas and technical facilities to the highest specifications. There is also a new campus radio station to complement the modern well-equipped studio theatre and state-of-the-art recording studio. The Art department offers drawing, painting, mixed media, ceramics, sculpture and lino-printing. The School's art gallery allows pupil work to be displayed as well as housing outside exhibitions that encourage experimentation with different techniques and styles.

Games and Activities. Pupils are encouraged to enjoy exercise and to develop their skills. The Golf Academy at Loretto is widely recognised as one of the best independent golfing schools in Britain, with on-site facilities and professional coaching. Cricket is also a major strength with the employment of former England player, Michael Powell, as Director of Cricket. Provision is also made for rugby, hockey, lacrosse, athletics, cricket, tennis, fives, badminton, swimming, shooting, and basketball, to name but a few. A well-equipped fitness centre and an astroturf pitch are also on site. Riding, sailing, skiing and snowboarding are available using excellent local facilities. Team games are important: boys play rugby, hockey and cricket; girls, hockey, lacrosse and netball. There is an extensive range of fixtures for both boys and girls at all levels. Participation in the Duke of Edinburgh's Award scheme is strong and Community Service, the Combined Cadet Force and outward bound programme offer additional experience of a range of skills and challenges. A full programme of activities, from karate to hip hop dance, operates each day and all weekend.

Sixth Form. Preparing its pupils for the world beyond school is something that Loretto takes very seriously. Loretto's Sixth Form is structured to encourage boys and girls to take responsibility for their work and organise their time. Loretto offers a wide range of academic subjects in the Sixth Form and fosters a purposeful work ethic. Academic tutors and pastoral mentors are on hand at every step to provide encouragement and guidance. A comprehensive enrichment programme has been developed which enables students to enjoy concerts, theatre trips, social evenings and outings to Edinburgh.

There is a thriving lecture society which organises visiting speakers from University and industry to enthuse and advise the Sixth Form. Additionally, the Headmaster runs a current affairs seminar by invitation and pupils volunteer to research and deliver lectures to their peers. A dedicated, experienced team of teachers are on hand to guide every pupil through their university applications, gap year choices, career paths and work-experience ventures

Beyond academic matters, Loretto furnishes each pupil with a range of leadership and team-working opportunities. Positions of responsibility and trust are earned. Prefects are selected on the basis of a rigorous application and interview process which mirrors that of the business world. Loretto runs a range of specific leadership and team-working exercises for Sixth Formers in the form of CCF and adventure activities. These are complemented by sessions on interview techniques, organisational skills and "CV loading". After all, in such a competitive job market, Lorettonians need to be well prepared and well informed.

Religion. Services are held in the School Chapel every week. The services are non-denominational and boys and girls are prepared for confirmation in both the Church of England and the Church of Scotland; they are confirmed at a combined service held in the Chapel. Whole School singing is a long-standing tradition at Loretto and continues to be memorable.

Developments. A Loretto Foundation has been established to provide for the mid to long-term future of the School with a particular emphasis on raising money to support scholarships and bursaries. In recent years, a major programme of development has taken place to give six science laboratories, four new classrooms, a further Art room and ICT room, a lecture theatre, and a state-of-the-art recording studio and radio station, all equipped to a very high standard. There is also an ongoing programme of refurbishment in the houses.

Uniform. The uniform is practical and comfortable. Formal dress on Sundays is the kilt for boys and girls. Ordinary School dress is charcoal trousers for boys, navy skirts for girls, with white shirts and the distinctive red jacket.

Entrance. Boys and girls are required to pass either the Common Entrance Examination or the Open Assessment Examination in English, Mathematics and Verbal Reasoning before being admitted, as well as an interview. Entrance to the Lower Sixth is based on interview and a conditional offer subject to satisfactory performance at GCSE/Standard Grade or international equivalent.

Junior School. 'The Nippers' enjoy many of the facilities of the Senior School, such as the playing fields, Theatre, Sports Hall, Music School and Chapel. The boys and girls are under closer adult supervision than in the Senior School but in other respects the system is similar. There are over 200 boys and girls aged between 3 and 12. The majority are day pupils, but occasional, weekly and full boarding are all encouraged. (*For further details, see entry in IAPS Section.*)

Fees per term (2011-2012). Boarding: £5,865–£8,975. These fees include all the expenses of board, lodging, most textbooks (though in the sixth form textbooks may have to be purchased), stationery, games material, medical attendance and medicine, CCF, transport to matches and internal school entertainments.

Day Fees (including meals): £2,085–£6,100.

Optional Expenses. These will be kept to a minimum, but include individual voice and instrumental music lessons; extra-curricular visits and expeditions.

Scholarships. (*See Scholarship Entries section.*) Scholarships are awarded in Academic, Art, Music, Drama, Golf and Sports in recognition of outstanding general, musical, sporting or artistic promise. There are scholarships for Sixth Form entrants from both private and state sectors; these are usually taken in November or January, although, if funds permit, they will be awarded throughout the year.

Leaving Scholarships. A number of awards are given to assist with university education to those who have 'deserved well of Loretto' in recognition of their loyalty and service to the School.

Old Lorettonian Society. *Hon Secretary*: B G Walker, Loretto School, Musselburgh.

Charitable status. Loretto School is a Registered Charity, number SC013978. It exists in order to educate young people in mind, body and spirit.

Loughborough Grammar School

Burton Walks, Loughborough, Leicestershire LE11 2DU
Tel: 01509 233233/233258
Fax: 01509 218436
e-mail: registrar@lesgrammar.org
website: www.lesgrammar.org

Loughborough Grammar School was founded in 1495 by Thomas Burton, Merchant of the Staple of Calais, though it is probable that the Trustees of the Town Charity were managing a free school well before that date. The School is itself part of a larger 'family' known as the Loughborough Endowed Schools. Situated in the spacious and attractive grounds surrounding the Grammar School are Loughborough High School for Girls (*see GSA entry*) and Fairfield School, our co-educational Preparatory School (*see IAPS entry*). Links between all three are very strong.

Motto: *Vires acquirit eundo.*

Governing Body:
Chairman: H M Pearson, DL, DUniv Hon, BA Econ
Vice-Chairman: A D Emson, BPharm, FRPS

Non-Executive Vice-Chairmen:
Mrs M Gershlick, RGN, DipNEd
Dr J E Hammond, BDS
Mrs C Wales

Nominative Governors:
Dr J Clackson, PhD Cambridge
Professor D Robertson, MA, PhD Oxford

Co-optative Governors:
Dr A de Bono, MA, MB, FRCGP, FFOM
Dr P Cannon, MA, BMBch, FRCS, MRCGP
Mrs E Critchley, MA
Professor J Feather, BLitt, MA, PhD, FLA
G P Fothergill, BA, FCIM
Lady Gretton, JP, Lord-Lieutenant of Leicestershire
I A Hawtin, BA, MA
Dr P J B Hubner, MB, FRCP, DCH, FACC, FESC
P M Jackson, FIMI
A M Kershaw
W M Moss
M Mulla, BSc, MSc, MIM
Mrs P O'Neill
Mrs G Richards, BA Hons, MEd

Foundation Secretary & Treasurer: K D Shaw, MBE, MSc, FCIS

Headmaster: P B Fisher, MA Christ Church, Oxford

Deputy Headmaster: J S Weitzel, BSc
Director of Studies & Deputy Headmaster: T G Willmott, BSc, PhD, MBA
Assistant Headmaster: P S Sergeant, BEd, MPhil
Assistant Headmaster: D W Steele, BSc
Head of Main School: J G Hunt, MA
Head of Sixth Form: C G Walker, MA, PhD
Chaplain: Revd D R Owen, BA, HDE, MTh

Registrar/Marketing: Mrs D P Briers
Headmaster's PA: Mrs K Rajput

Assistant Staff:

Miss N Bahl, BSc	Mrs M C Herring, BSc
Mrs H L Baker, BEd	J D Jackson, BSc
R J Ball, BSc, PhD	M M Jackson, BA
A W G Ballentyne, MA,	P P Jackson, BSc
MLitt, AssocRHS	Mrs H E James, BA
Miss E Bancroft, BA	Miss S Jenkins, BA
Dr D C Barrett, BSc, PhD	Miss E Johnson, BA
K Barrett, BSc	Mrs D Kaur, BA
Ms S Bell, BA	G Kerr, BSc
Miss O M Benjamin, MA	R F Kerr, MA
R Bhattacharyya, BA	N B Khan, BSc, MSc
C W Blackman, BA	Mrs E Lax, BA, LTCL
M S E Broadley, BA	E Lewis, BSc
Dr K Buckley, BA, MA,	R L Lightfoot, BA, MA
PhD	N Lipotov, BA, PhD
P D Bunting, MA	A Lloyd, BSc
M D Butcher, BSc, MSc	Mrs N V Lorente
Miss K Cartwright, BEng	C Luke, BSc, PhD
J Clarke	P M Marlow, BSc
Mrs H J Coles, BA	B K McCabe, MA
C V Collington, BA	J M J Mellows, BA, MA
Mrs R L Cooch, BSc	R Michalak, BA
D J Cornell, BA, PhD	D J Miles, BSc
Miss P Cumine, BA, MA	Miss Z Mir, LLB
M I Dawkins, BA, MA	T D Morse, BSc, MSc
Mrs S Daya, BA	A Moreton, BA
A J Dossett, BSc	A L Morris, BA
Mrs E J Eades	T A Moseley, BA
Dr N M A Ebden, BSc,	Mrs D Outwin-Flinders,
PhD	BEd
S G Else, BA, MPhil, PhD	R B Parish, BSc, MSc
D L Evans, BSc	J S Parton, MA
C B Faust, BSc, MEd,	Mrs V M Perino
CChem, FRSC	N Pollock, BA
C J Feakes, BSc, MSc	Mrs A Quigley, BA
Mrs H Fisher, BA, MA	D Reavie, BA
S R Fraczek, BA, MA	J M Rees, MA, PhD
Mrs R French, BEd	P Smith, BEd, MA
P Gacs, MA	D M Starkings, BSc, BA
M I Gidley	R Statham, BSc
Mrs L E Gosling, BA	G I Sutcliffe, BA
M Green, BSc, PhD	Mrs V Thompson, BA
R T Griffiths, BA	H T Tunnicliffe, BEd
A J Haigh, MA	P Viccars, BA
D Happer, BSc	Miss H Walters, MA
S D Hatfield, BEng	A D Waters, BSc, PhD
R C Healey, BEng, PhD	Mrs L Welsby, BA
C S Herbert, BSc	R C Wright, BEd

Music:

A P M Osiatynski, MA, PGCE (*Director of LES Music
    School and Instrumental – Voice*)
Miss N M Bouckley, BA (*Deputy Director of LES Music
    School and Instrumental – Oboe*)
P J Underwood, MA, MMus, PhD, FRCO CHM, FTCL,
    LRAM, ARCM, ADCM (*Head of Senior Curriculum
    Music*)
T H Lax, LRAM, CertEd (*Head of Wind and Brass*)
Mrs A McGee, GTCL Hons, LTCL (*Head of Junior Music*)
Mrs E Foulds, GRSM Hons, LRAM, PGCE (*KS3 and
    Instrumental-Piano*)
Miss C Revell, BMus Hons (*KS3 Coordinator, KS4*)
D Morris, LRAM (*Singing Coordinator and Instrumental –
    Voice*)
Mrs E Jones, MMus, LRAM (*Accompanist*)

Individual Music Teachers:
Dr A Bean, BMus Hons, PGCE, LRAM, AMusD (*Double
    Bass, Piano*)
J Bean, LRAM, CertEd, LGSM MT (*Cello*)
J Boyd, DipMus (*Guitar*)

Mrs K Burns, BA Hons, LLCM, ALCM (*Violin, Viola*)
Mrs A Coady, DipM, ACIM, GLCM (*Clarinet, Saxophone*)
D Cowan, MA FRCO (*Piano, Organ*)
Mrs S Douglas, ARCM, ABSM, CertEd (*Clarinet,
    Saxophone*)
Mrs E Jones, MMus, LRAM (*Piano*)
A Geary, GLCM Hons, LLCM (*Percussion*)
Mrs K Geary, BMus TCM (*Violin, Viola*)
Mrs A Gillies-Loach, GMus, LRSM, LTCL (*Flute*)
C L Groom, PSM (*Brass*)
M Johnson, Cert Mus Ed TCL, LTCL, FVCM Hons, Hon
    VCM CT (*Guitar*)
Miss J Kirkwood, BMus Hons, AdvPGDip Music (*Flute*)
Mrs C Lee, LRAM, ProfCert RAM (*Violin, Viola, Piano*)
G Lumbers, (*Saxophone, Jazz Saxophone*)
Miss V Moore, BA Hons, PGDip (*Saxophone, Clarinet*)
Mrs J Neal, JP, BA (*Voice*)
M Newnham, BA Hons (*Percussion*)
Miss F Orme (*Harp, Flute*)
Mrs A Parker, BA Hons, ABRSM (*Piano, Flute*)
Miss F Richardson, LRAM (*Guitar*)
A Thomas, MMus, BMus (*Guitar*)
C White (*Violin, Viola*)

Head of Careers: R L Lightfoot, BA, MA
Librarian: Mrs V Bunn, ALA
OC CCF: Wing Commander P S Sergeant, BEd, MPhil,
    RAFVR(T)
CCF SSI: WO1 M A Cooper
Estates Manager: T Allardice
Medical Officer: Dr P Cannon
School Nurses: Mrs J Bryan, Mrs N Krarup

There are just over 1,000 boys in the School, including 60
boarders.

The School moved to its present site of some 27 acres in
1852 and is situated away from the centre of the town in
attractive grounds, which contain the beautiful avenues of
trees knows as Burton Walks. At its centre is a handsome
Victorian College quadrangle. There has been an impressive
development programme in recent years – a new Music
School serving the Grammar School, High School and Fairfield opened in September 2006 and in September 2009 the
Grammar School opened a new state-of-the-art Chemistry
building.

Admission. Entry to the School is by examination at 10+,
11+, 13+ and Common Entrance. Sixth Form entry is dependent on interview with the Headmaster and other senior staff
and GCSE results. Entry at other year groups is possible.

Boarding Arrangements. Boys are admitted at the age
of 10 or over to Denton House. Sixth Form boys are in
School House. Termly and Weekly boarding is available.

Fees per term (2011-2012). Day £3,370 (includes books
and stationery). Boarding (includes laundry, board, medical
attendance): £6,182 (full), £5,426 (weekly).

Scholarships. (*See Scholarship Entries section.*) There
are a number of Scholarships at 10+, 11+ and 13+. Choral
and instrumental scholarships are also awarded at 10+, 11+,
13+ and Sixth Form. There are also a number of bursaries,
depending on parental means, as well as School Assisted
Places.

Foundation Bursaries. The Governors have introduced a
replacement to the Government Assisted Places.

Religious Teaching. The School is non-denominational
though there is a strong Christian tradition. The Chaplain
teaches Religion and Philosophy but is available for boys at
any convenient time. On Wednesdays, Boarders attend the
School Chapel, and on request are prepared for Confirmation by the Chaplain.

Curriculum. The aim of the School is to give a broad and
balanced general education to GCSE with greater specialisation afterwards. In Year 6, boys follow a curriculum similar
to that of their last year of junior school; subjects included
are English, Mathematics, Art, Sciences, Drama, Design

and Technology, Geography, IT, History, Music, PE, RE. In Year 7, all boys study English, Mathematics, Sciences, French, History, Geography, Latin, and Music. Additionally, all boys have lessons in RE, PE, PSHE and Games. In Year 8, Design and Technology and Classical Civilisation are introduced and, in addition to French, boys choose a second language from either German or Spanish, and the boys are taught separate sciences. In Year 9 pupils continue with both MFLs, and make some choices from their existing subjects as well as Ancient Greek and Drama.

In Years 10 and 11, for GCSE, boys study English Language and Literature, Mathematics, a modern Foreign Language, and at least two sciences. They also choose three subjects from an extensive options list. Some more able boys study a tenth subject.

The Sixth Form contains 270 boys. In Year 12, boys study 4 subjects to AS Level and in Year 13 they will take 3 or 4 of them to A2 Level. A wide range of subjects and combinations is available, along with General Studies, Critical Thinking, Games and other activities. There are some joint teaching lessons with the Girls' High School.

Games. The school has an excellent First Eleven field and a junior field of over 13 acres within its precinct and within two miles are well equipped playing fields extending to nearly 70 acres.

The school runs teams in Rugby, Soccer, Hockey, Cricket, Athletics, Tennis, Cross Country, Swimming, Badminton, Fencing and Squash. In addition there is a Sailing and Canoe Club and Karting. The School prides itself in an array of mind sports, with teams in Bridge, Chess, Go and Chinese Chess.

Combined Cadet Force. There is an efficient and keen CCF of about 300 boys from Year 10 onwards, run on an optional basis, with 17 Officers, an SSI and a RQMS. Boys have the choice of joining the RAF, Army or Royal Navy Sections. The CCF complex is purpose-built with excellent facilities and many varied and Adventurous Training courses are available to members.

Scouts. There is a flourishing Scout Troop with 1 Scouter and 35 boys.

Duke of Edinburgh's Award Scheme. Over 250 boys and girls from our sister school, Loughborough High, are actively involved in the scheme and each year a large number earn gold, silver and bronze awards.

Music (of which most is joint with the girls' High School): 5 Choirs, 2 Orchestras, 2 Concert Bands, Big Band, Swing Band and over twenty smaller instrumental ensembles take place in an outstanding new Music School, incorporating a recital and recording hall. The Concert Band toured Cornwall in July 2010 and there will be a music tour to Geneva in July 2012. The Burton Chapel Choir (an all boys' choir) sings services regularly at cathedrals around the UK, including Christ Church Oxford in March 2012.

Drama. The School has a fine Studio/Theatre and all boys in Years 6, 7 and 8 participate in a dramatic production. After that, there are productions for other age groups in conjunction with the Girls' High School each term.

Careers. Careers advisors are available to inform boys on options for their futures, with special regard to University or Professional careers. The School is a member of the Independent Schools Careers Organisation.

Academic Successes. An average of 19 boys per year gain admission to Oxford and Cambridge, and over 98% each year begin degree courses at Universities.

Old Loughburians. All pupils of the school become members of the Association. Correspondence should be addressed to Mr N Rowbotham at the School.

Charitable status. Loughborough Endowed Schools is a Registered Charity, number 1081765, and a Company Limited by Guarantee, registered in England, number 4038033. Registered Office: 3 Burton Walks, Loughborough, Leics LE11 2DU.

Magdalen College School
Oxford

Oxford OX4 1DZ
Tel: 01865 242191
Fax: 01865 240379
e-mail: admissions@mcsoxford.org
website: www.mcsoxford.org

Magdalen College School consists of about 750 boys aged 7–18 with girls admitted to the Sixth Form from 2010. Academic standards are amongst the highest in the country and there is a strong emphasis on study beyond the syllabus, most of all in the Waynflete Studies programme, which allows Sixth Formers to develop a personal project which is finally supervised by university academics. Almost all pupils go on to higher education with about a third each year progressing to Oxford or Cambridge. The school seeks to develop the individuality and interests of each pupil. There is a strong emphasis on extra-curricular activity, with particularly proud traditions in sport, music and drama. The school was Sunday Times Independent School of the year in 2004–5 and again in 2008–9.

Motto: *Sicut Lilium.*

Visitor: The Rt Revd The Lord Bishop of Winchester

Governors:
J Palmer (*Chairman*)
Dr C Benson
Dr M Allingham
Sir Jonathan Baker, QC (*Deputy Chairman*)
Ms P Cameron Watt
Mrs C Hall
T M Knowles
J D Martin
Mrs S M McKimm
The Revd Dr M J Piret
N P Record
Dr N P V Richardson
Professor J A C Smith
The Revd Canon K H Wilkinson

Master: **T R Hands**, BA, AKC, DPhil

Usher: J S Hodgson, BA (*Classics*)

Teaching Staff:
* *Head of Department*

M R Baker, MA (*Mathematics*)
C P Anthony, BA, MA (*English*)
A Baker-Munton, MA (**Modern Languages*)
Ms H C Barnard, MA (*Head of Junior School*)
D S Barr, BA, MA (*English*)
D Bebbington, BSc, DPhil (*Chemistry*)
T D Booth, MA (**Head of Geography*)
Miss E J Bowen, BA (*History*)
J A Brown, MA (**Physics*)
M D Bull, BA (**Director of Sport*)
Miss S Cameron, BA (**Art*)
A C Cooper, MSc, BA (*Professional Tutor, Mathematics*)
Dr A K Cotton, BA, MSt, DPhil (*Head of Lower School, Classics*)
K H Cousineau, BSc (*Physics*)
J D Cullen, MA (**Director of Music*)
P A J De Freitas (*Cricket Professional*)
A C W Dixon, BA (**Learning Support, Geography*)
D Dyer, BA (*Head of Junior School Sport*)
Mrs L D Earnshaw, MA (**Mathematics*)
Miss J A Ellis, GRSM, LRAM, MTC (*Head of Junior School Music*)
J N Eve, MA (**English*)

Ms N C C Ferguson, MA (*Modern Languages, Junior School*)
Dr S Floate, BSc (*Chemistry*)
Mr I Forrester, BSc (*Biology*)
N J Fraser, MA (*Academic Deputy, French*)
Mrs M-J Gago, BA (**Spanish*)
Ms L F Giannotti, BA (*English*)
Mrs D Hackett, BEng (*Physics*)
R Hemingway, BA (**History*)
N J Hinze, BA (**Chemistry*)
N Hunter, BA (*Waynflete Intern, Sport*)
Mrs S Hyde, MA (*Classics*)
H Jones, BA (*History, *Politics*)
Mrs M Jones-Christodoulou, BSc (*Assistant Head of Sixth Form, Physics*)
A I Kostyanovsky, BA (*Deputy Head of Sixth Form, *Theology*)
Mrs R E Lambert, BSc (*Biology*)
Revd Dr Tess Kuin-Lawton, BA, MPhil, DPhil (*Chaplain, Theology*)
P S Lemoine, BA (*Geography*)
Mrs C A C Lewis, BA, MEng (*Mathematics*)
Miss E J Liddiard, BA (*Geography*)
P J McDonald, MA (**Classics*)
Dr J Methven, DPhil (*English*)
St J E J Mitchard, BA, MA (*Special Educational Needs*)
Mrs J A Morris (*PSHCE, Junior School*)
J O Morris, MA (*Head of Sixth Form, History*)
C E Newbury, BA (*Junior School Director of Studies*)
Y W Ooi, BA, BMBCh (*Biology*)
S Pahl, BSc (*Physical Conditioning, Games*)
C Pearson, BSc, DPhil (**Biology*)
M Penton, BA (*Surmaster*)
J F Place, BA (*Junior School*)
Mrs F J Pritchard, BA (*Assistant Head of Sixth Form, Art*)
Dr K L Richard, MPhys, DPhil (*Physics*)
A Rush, BA (*Design and Technology*)
D W Short, BA, MA (*Art*)
P A Shrimpton, MA, MEd, PhD (*Mathematics*)
T E Skipwith, BSc (*Head of Middle School, Biology*)
D A Smith, MA, PhD (*Director of Studies, Mathematics, Physics*)
P D Smith, MA, LTCL (*Music*)
S A Spowart, BA (*Classics*)
Mrs E Stapleton, BHum (*Deputy Head of Junior School*)
Mrs M-R Staton, L-ès-L (*French*)
Miss Z Tayler, BA, MSc (*Mathematics*)
A D Thomas, BA (*History*)
J Unwin, BA (**Philosophy*)
T Vaikona, BA (*Head of Sporting Relations*)
A Watts (*Head of Sports Academy and Elite Athlete Development, Head of PE*)
J A Watts, BA (**French*)
B White, BA (*Mathematics*)
T R Williams, BA (*Head of Hockey*)
Mrs C E Winstone, BA (*Junior School*)

Assistant Music Staff:

Miss M Ackrill (*Flute*)	B Giddens (*Piano*)
Ms K Bailey (*Saxophone*)	Ms E Harre (*Double Bass*)
Dr E M Baird (*Violin*)	M R Jones (*Piano*)
Ms A Bendy (*Guitar*)	Mrs S Lynn (*Violin*)
Mr C Britton (*Recorder*)	P Manhood (*Guiltar*)
Ms E H Churcher (*Piano*)	D C McNaughton (*Trumpet*)
A Cole (*Trombone and Tuba*)	Ms V Murby (*Viola*)
R Cutting (*Trumpet*)	J Newell (*Organ*)
T Dawes (*Double Bass, Bass Guitar, Drums*)	Ms H Parker (*Singing*)
Miss J A Ellis (*Violin*)	T Payne (*Clarinet*)
K Fairbairn (*Percussion, Drums*)	Mrs S Perkins (*Piano, Bassoon*)
Dr J Faultless (*Horn*)	M Pickett (*Piano*)
Miss G Fisher (*Piano*)	W Purefoy (*Singing*)
	B P Skipp (*Oboe*)

B Twyford (*Drumkit*)	Dr J P Whitworth (*Guitar*)
	S J Wilson (*Cello*)

Clerk to the Governors and Bursar: Dr N Carter

Master's PA: Mrs L D Beaumont

Registrar: Ms S L Langdale, BA

History. William of Waynflete, born in 1398, rose from unexceptional social origins to become Bishop of Winchester and Lord Chancellor. Having been Headmaster of Winchester, school of the church, and Provost of Eton, school of the court, he determined to use his wealth to repay his debt to the transformative power of education. He determined to found something altogether new, a school of that exciting and rapidly expanding proposition – the university. This school would link primary, secondary and tertiary education in a novel way, and be named after his patron saint, Mary Magdalen.

Magdalen College School opened in 1480, and rapidly acquired an international reputation as a pioneer of new renaissance methods of learning. Early Masters included Thomas Wolsey, early pupils Richard Hooker, John Foxe, Thomas More and William Tyndale. The school, which from an early stage provided choristers for the College choir, was accommodated entirely in college until the late 19th century, when expanding numbers led to the acquisition and erection of buildings on the other side of the Cherwell, opposite the University Botanical Gardens and adjacent to St Hilda's College. Today's school still occupies this picturesque and privileged site.

Buildings. The school buildings include a Chapel and Theatre, Library, Classrooms, Science Laboratories, Music School and Art Department. New Science Laboratories were opened in 1991 and totally refurbished in 2001. The expanded Junior School was opened in 1993, and new changing rooms and English Department in 1996. New classrooms, Lecture Theatre, Careers Centre and a Sixth Form Centre were opened in September 1998. In June 2001, a £2m Sports Complex was opened. In 2002, additional science laboratories were provided as well as a new ICT centre. In 2005, the school opened its new Sir Basil Blackwell library. In Autumn 2008 a new building was opened which houses a modern refectory, Art and Design, senior common room and Reception. In 2010 a redesigned and enlarged Sixth Form Common Room was opened, to accommodate and welcome the first intake of Sixth Form girls.

Pastoral. From 7–11, boys are in form groups. Their form teacher is responsible for day-to-day care, pastoral welfare and academic progress. Boys from age 11 and Sixth Form girls are allocated to one of the six Houses. Houses are divided into four Houserooms. A Housemaster or Tutor in charge of each section is responsible for the pastoral and academic welfare of pupils in his Houseroom. The Heads of Departments, SENCO, Chaplain and Matron also play their part in the pastoral organisation.

Organisation and Curriculum. All boys study a core of subjects to GCSE level, consisting of English, French, Maths and Science. In addition, there is a wide variety of options taken by pupils in their GCSE years including Latin and Greek, Geography, German, Spanish, History, Computing and Art. There is no streaming and very little setting.

Most pupils in the Sixth Form take 4 AS and 3 A2s, but a significant proportion take 4 or even 5 AS and A2 subjects.

Careers. There is a well-equipped Careers Room, and there is a team of Careers Staff. Careers Aptitude Tests are offered to all boys in the Fifth Form, and there is a weekly lecture in the Sixth Form.

Games and Societies. In addition to Physical Education which is taught in the curriculum, games play a major part in the School. Major sports are Rugby in the Michaelmas Term, Hockey and Rowing in Hilary, and Cricket, Rowing and Tennis in the Trinity Term. Other sports include Basketball, Football, Fencing, Cross-Country, Sailing and Athletics. There are Army, Navy and Air Force sections of the CCF and a Community Service Organisation. Many boys participate in the Duke of Edinburgh's Award Scheme. Girls from Oxford High School and Headington School participate in the CCF.

The main playing field, surrounded by the River Cherwell, adjoins the grounds of School House and covers 11 acres. In addition, the school enjoys the daily use of the adjacent Christ Church playing fields, and also uses regularly a number of other university sporting and cultural facilities. An additional field of 13 acres with its own pavilion and changing rooms has been developed at Sandford-on-Thames, three miles from the school. The school also has use of the Magdalen College sports fields one mile from the School.

Music is extremely important in the School and there is a large Choral Society, a Madrigal Group, Senior and Junior Orchestras, a Jazz Band and other ensembles. Many pupils are involved in Drama and there are several productions in the year. There are many other societies and clubs covering cultural and recreational activities. The main school concert is held annually in The Sheldonian Theatre. A Summer Arts Festival began in 2009.

Admission. The main entry points are at 7, 9, 11, 13 and 16. Up to 20 boys are taken at 7, a further 20 or so at 9, and about 70 at the age of 11. Up to 25 boys are taken at 13. Around 30 boys and girls join the School directly into the Sixth Form.

Admission at ages 7, 9 and 11 is by a School Entrance Examination held in January or February each year.

Admission at age 13 is by the Common Entrance Examination for candidates at Preparatory Schools and by a School Entrance Examination held in March each year for candidates at maintained schools.

Offers of Sixth Form places are made after interview, and are conditional on good GCSE grades.

Candidates can be registered at any age. Full particulars can be obtained from the Registrar.

Term of Entry. Pupils enter the School in September. Exceptionally, for example if parents move into the Oxford area, other arrangements can be made.

Fees per term (2011-2012). Day pupils: £4,465 (aged 9–18); £4,303 (7 and 8 year olds). They are payable in advance and are inclusive of textbooks and stationery. The Registration Fee (non-returnable) is currently £50.

Scholarships, Choristerships, Exhibitions and Bursaries. (*See Scholarship Entries section.*) Scholarships, Exhibitions and Governors' Presentation Awards are awarded at all points of entry, and there is a generous bursary scheme.

There are 16 Choristerships. Entry is by Voice Trial and candidates should normally be between the ages of 7 and 9. For a Chorister two-thirds of the tuition fee is remitted. All enquiries about Choristerships should be addressed to the Informator Choristarum, Magdalen College, Oxford. Choristers normally continue at the School after their voices have broken. In deserving cases, further financial help may be available.

Honours. Almost all pupils go on to higher education when they leave. In the five years 2006–2010 inclusive 120 places have been gained at Oxford and Cambridge universities, and 277 places at other universities, from an average Sixth Form year group of 80.

Old Waynfletes. Representative Old Waynfletes of the 20th century include Olympic athlete and soldier, Noel Chavasse, VC and bar; bookseller Sir Basil Blackwell; Nobel Prize winner Sir Tim Hunt; composer Ivor Novello; educationalist Tom Wheare; theatre directors George Caird and Sam Mendes, and sports commentators Nigel Starmer Smith and Jim Rosenthal.

Secretary: D R Dunsmore, 12 Owlington Close, Botley, Oxford OX2 9DP.

Charitable status. Magdalen College School Oxford Limited is a Registered Charity, number 295785. Its aims and objectives are to promote and provide for the education of children.

Malvern College

College Road, Malvern, Worcestershire WR14 3DF
Tel: 01684 581 500
Fax: 01684 581 617
e-mail: enquiries@malcol.org
website: www.malcol.org

Malvern College was founded in 1865 and was incorporated by Royal Charter in 1929. Malvern College is co-educational. The Senior School takes pupils from the age of 13 through to 18. The Downs, Malvern takes pupils from 3 to 13 (*see IAPS entry*).

Motto: '*Sapiens qui prospicit.*' Wise is the one who looks ahead.

Ten members of the Council may be nominated, one each by the Lords-Lieutenant of the Counties of Gloucestershire, Herefordshire and Worcestershire, by the Vice-Chancellors of the Universities of Oxford, Cambridge and Birmingham, by the Service Boards of the Navy, Army and Air Force, and by the Headmaster and Teaching Staff. Ten members are elected by the Governors, and between six and ten are appointed by the Council.

President and Visitor: The Lord Bishop of Worcester

Council:
Lord MacLaurin of Knebworth (*Chairman*)
R K Black (*Treasurer*)

Dr N Bampos	J M J Havard
S P Bennett	S M Hill
P G Brough	Professor P Jackson
W Burke III	G E Jones
P J Cartwright	S R Lister, OBE
Professor K J Davey, OBE	K U Madden
Mrs R Dawes, JP	W H Moore, CBE
Mrs J Edwards-Clark, MVO	D G Robertson
F R R Francis	J D Roseman
Mrs J Grant Peterkin	A G Silcock
R M Green	Dr C W O Stoecker
Mrs L Gullifer	Mrs J Thompstone
Ms J M Hampson	R T H Wilson

Head: A R Clark, MA Cantab

Deputy Head: Dr R A Lister, BA, MTS, PhD
Deputy Head Pastoral: Mrs S G Angus, MA

Director of Studies: J A Gauci, BA

Teaching Staff:
Mrs K Adam, BA	Mrs H E Charman, MA
Mrs M N Adkins	M W Cleal, BA
R E Allen, BSc, MPhil	Mrs C R D Clemit, PGCE
Mrs H R Andrews, BA	Mrs J Cockbill, MA
Mrs S K Angling, MA	A Cook, BA
D J Angus, MA	Dr R H Corrigan, PhD
Mrs L M Atkins, BA	J D Cox, BSc
S F Barakat, MA	M M Cox, BEd
Dr Catherine Baxter, BA, MPhil, PhD	G M Cramp, BSc
Mrs I P M Bijl, BA	S Doidge, BSc
S J Bradley, BEng	D J Eglin, BSc
N Brett, BSc	Mrs J V Ehlers, MA
J P Burns, BA	M C Frayn, BA
Mrs N J Cage, BA	P Godsland, MA (*Senior Master*)
P J Chappell, BA	Mrs S Godsland, BA

P J Gray, MA
Mrs B Gregg, CertEd
A J Grundy, BA
Mrs R Grundy, BMus
C Hall, BSc, CBiol, MIBiol
Mrs L M Hallett, BA
M A Hardinges, BSc
Dr C Hartog, BSc, PhD
M A T Harris, MA
M Henderson, BA
I J Hendy, MA
J C Herod, MA
Miss G Heys, BA
P Hibberd, MSc
Mrs R Hibberd, PGCE
S C Holroyd, BA
Dr S J Holroyd, BA
R A Hookham, BA
R Huguenin, BA
A Hutchinson, MA
A L Hutsby, BA
Mrs C J T James, BA
Miss C M Jones, MA
Mrs N R Lacey BA
R G Lacey, BSc
The Revd A P Law, DipTh
M G Lloyd, BSc
J J W E Major, BA
Mrs M C Maskell, MChem
W Mathews, BA
Mrs D M McCarry, BA
Mr J McCarry, BEd
S P McDade, ARAM
Mrs T McKay
Miss J S Miller, BSc, MRes
M Moss
T P Newman, BSc
T M Newsholme, BA
Mrs F C Packham, BSc
K R C Packham, BA
Mrs T Pain, BA

Miss L Pepper, BSc
M A L Phillips, MA, FRCO, ARCM
Miss E F E Preece, BSc
Miss S S Razavi, BSc
Mrs F Rix, BEd, MA
J Rodriguez, PGCE
J A O Russell, BSc, BA
Mrs S F Schott, BA (*Senior Tutor*)
P N Scurfield, BEng, BEd
Mrs A-I Sharp, BA
Dr D Sibthorpe, BSc, MSc, PhD
I D Sloan, BMus, ARCM
Mrs A Sommi, Deg Rome
S R Spanyol, FTCL, ARCM, LTCL
Dr R P Stafford, BSc, PhD
D A Stokes, MA
Mrs B Swart, BA
C Thomas, BEng
N R Tisdale
Mrs J C A Thomas, BEd, RSASpLD
R G Thurlow, MA (*Careers*)
Mrs H M Varley, Maître
C P J Wastie, MSc
Mrs S J Wastie, BSc
Dr N V Watson, BA, PhD
Mrs P G R Webb
A J Wharton, BTh Hons
R N Whitehead, MA
P Wickes, BSc
R N Willatt, MSc
I C Wilson, BA
Dr R B Winwood, MSc, PhD
Mrs F Wood, BA
Mrs V E Young, BA

Chaplain: The Revd A P Law

Registrar: Mrs S R Jackson, BSc

Medical Officers:
Sarah D Roberts, MBChB, MRCGP
G F J Henry, DRCOG, MRCGP

Boarding Houses:
J A O Russell (*School House*)
A J Wharton (*No.1*)
R G Lacey (*No.2*)
Mrs F C Packham (*No.3*)
Mrs A I Sharp (*No.4*)
T P Newman (*No.5*)
Mrs V E Young (*No.6*)
D J Eglin (*No.7*)
Mrs R Grundy (*No.8*)
P Wickes (*No.9*)
Mrs B A Swart (*Ellerslie House*)

Malvern College is particularly fortunate in its location. Situated on the lower slopes of the Malvern Hills and close to the centre of Great Malvern, the main College campus commands striking views across the Severn Valley towards the Cotswolds.

The College and The Downs, Malvern offer co-education from the age of 3 to 18. Pupils join the senior school at age 13+ where there are five girls' Houses and six boys' Houses, all of which also take day pupils. The school is justly proud of its high academic standards and the high level of pastoral care it provides. The College was rated 'Outstanding' by Ofsted in their 2010-11 report. In the Sixth Form about half

study for the International Baccalaureate and half for A Levels.

Further details of the College are available in the Prospectus which may be obtained by contacting the Registrar or by visiting www.malcol.org.

Curriculum. In the Foundation Year (Year 9), pupils study a wide variety of subjects. Nearly all are introduced to a second modern foreign language. All pupils study debating and creative ICT as well as Physical Education. The object of this year (as in co-curricular activities) is to show pupils as much as possible of what the College has to offer. On entering the Remove (Year 10), pupils choose their GCSE or IGCSE subjects, to be taken at the end of the Hundred (Year 11). In French most or all of the top set take GCSE at the end of the Remove. The compulsory subjects are English, Mathematics and Double Award Science. Most pupils take French (or English as an additional language). The majority of the Remove (Year 10) take a short course GCSE in Religious Studies. Pupils also choose optional subjects from Art and Design, Design Technology, Drama, Geography, German, History, Latin, Music, Physical Education and Spanish. Greek is available for those who began it in the Foundation Year (Year 9). A Separate Sciences option enables pupils to extend the core Double Award Science to the three separate science IGCSEs. Pupils choose either three or four options, according to their academic ability. Pupils decide on their choices in consultation with their Tutors, Housemasters/Housemistresses and parents.

In the Sixth Form, pupils can choose to study either A Levels or the International Baccalaureate. In the IB, combinations of the following subjects are offered: Visual Art, Biology, Chemistry, Economics, English, Environmental Systems and Societies, French, German, Geography, Greek, History, Italian, Latin, Mathematics, Further Mathematics, Music, Physics, Spanish, Technology, Theatre, Philosophy and Sport & Exercise Science. All pupils take the valuable Theory of Knowledge Course. A Levels are available in all of the subjects listed above for the IB (except Environmental Systems and Societies and Italian) and also in Classical Civilisation, Politics and Physical Education. Pupils take four AS subjects in the Lower Sixth and most continue three subjects to A2 Level in the Upper Sixth.

Physical Education. In the FY all students follow core activities from the National Curriculum with the girls being taught games (Hockey, Netball, Lacrosse, Tennis, Cricket & Rounders), Athletics, Swimming and Dance. The boys are taught games (Football, Rugby, Hockey, Cricket, Badminton, Basketball and Tennis) plus Athletics, Health & Fitness and Swimming. During the Remove and Hundred all students select one compulsory water-based unit from Competitive Swimming, Lifesaving or Personal Survival, and a further compulsory unit in Health and Fitness. In addition, there is a wide-ranging option programme including all activities taught at Key Stage 3 plus others which include Rackets, Fives, Squash, and Volleyball. In addition, a large number of pupils opt to study GCSE PE where they follow the AQA GCSE Double Award specification. In the Sixth Form pupils can study the OCR Physical Education specification at A Level or Sport & Exercise Science within the IB Diploma.

A recently opened state-of-the-art Sports Complex includes a 25m swimming pool, an eight-court sports hall, a shooting range, squash courts, studio, climbing wall and fitness suite. The Sports Complex has a Cricket Centre which is also used by Worcester County Cricket Club for its winter training. The College has recently refurbished its two Rackets courts which now offer Rackets facilities at tournament standard. In addition there is an Astroturf pitch, Fives courts, and Tennis courts. The famous Malvern Hills provide marvellously challenging terrain for the College's cross-country runners and mountain bikers.

Co-Curricular Activities. Pupils have the opportunity to take part in a range of additional activities such as sailing, fencing, aerobics, photography, golf, canoeing, Tae kwon do, archery, and scuba diving.

The College has a strong tradition of expedition training and outdoor pursuits, including rock-climbing, kayaking and mountaineering (Summer and Winter, UK and Abroad). Opportunities exist for the use of the College's cottage in the Brecon Beacons. Expeditions go annually to Scotland and have also been to Iceland, the Alps, Kashmir, Scandinavia, Malta and China in the school holidays. Many of these activities are an integral part of the voluntary CCF (which has RM, Army and RAF sections) and The Duke of Edinburgh's Award Scheme. There is also a flourishing Community Service Organisation.

Music. Malvern has a strong musical tradition. Over 35% of pupils learn a musical instrument and there are 8 musical ensembles including orchestras, concert band, jazz band and choirs. The well-equipped Music School (22 practice rooms, 3 large rehearsal rooms) includes a recording studio and a music technology laboratory. Attached to the Music School is St Edmund's Hall, a 150-seat recital hall with a fine Steinway piano. Pupils of all standards are encouraged both instrumentally and vocally, and regular performances (internal, locally and further afield) are given. The Music Department works closely with the Drama Department and musicals are produced regularly, the most recent being *South Pacific* and *The Boy Friend*.

Drama is a thriving creative force within the community of the school. Pupils are encouraged to play a full part in all aspects of theatre, whether as actor, stage manager, costume assistant or technician. This might be through academic study at GCSE, A Level or IB, participation in the Annual House Drama competition or the many co-curricular productions staged each year. Recent productions staged in the College's versatile and well-resourced 300-seat Theatre include *South Pacific, Wyrd Sisters, The Crucible, The Life and Adventures of Nicholas Nickleby, Pride and Prejudice, Les Miserables School Edition, Much Ado About Nothing* and the amateur premiere of *Coram Boy*. Pupils have recently participated in the Shakespeare Schools Festival and are encouraged to audition for the National Youth Theatre in London. Speech and Drama tuition is a popular option for many, with pupils receiving preparation for LAMDA examinations or local public speaking festivals. Regular attendance at the Malvern Theatres in town is complemented by visits to Stratford, London and Bristol.

Art. The modern, purpose-built and spacious Arts Centre has outstanding facilities for Painting, Drawing, Printmaking (including Etching), Ceramics, Photography and 3-Dimensional Design.

Design and Technology. The well-equipped Design & Technology Centre ensures that pupils have the opportunity to develop their knowledge and skills through project work in this exciting subject. Facilities include Textiles Technology, Resistant Materials, Computer Aided Design and Manufacture, Product Design, Architectural Design and Engineering.

Careers. In the GCSE year pupils sit the Futurewise/Morrisby careers guidance tests which assess ability, personality, aptitude and interests. An in-depth interview with an experienced ISCO careers advisor helps pupils to make sensible and informed choices about their future. All pupils in the Lower Sixth are encouraged to spend at least one week in the holidays on work experience. Pupils are given advice on choice of course at University by teachers in the Careers and Higher Education Department, and by their Sixth Form Tutor and Housemaster/Housemistress. Malvern College is a member of the Independent Schools Careers Organisation (ISCO).

Pastoral Care. In addition to their Housemaster/Housemistress and House Tutors, all pupils have a Form Tutor who shares the responsibility for their overall personal development and well-being. Members of the Sixth Form choose their own Tutor. There is also a full-time Chaplain

and two Independent Listeners available by phone or email. In addition, pupils have (free) access to school counsellors.

Health Care. There is a modern and well-equipped Medical Centre staffed 24 hours a day by Registered Nurses.

Coaches. During the school year there are three half-term holidays and about five leave-out weekends. On these occasions, school coaches are run to Exeter, Guildford, London Paddington and Knutsford, according to demand. Coaches to Heathrow and Birmingham airports run at the start of half term and the end of term.

Admission. Most pupils are admitted between their thirteenth and fourteenth birthdays and may qualify for admission to the school by a satisfactory performance in the Common Entrance Examination or the annual Scholarship Examination. Special arrangements are made for pupils who wish to enter from schools which do not prepare pupils for Common Entrance.

Pupils are also admitted to the Sixth Form at 16 on the basis of GCSEs, interviews and tests.

Application for admission should be made to the Registrar.

Scholarships. (*See Scholarship Entries section.*) Malvern College offers a generous number of Scholarships and Exhibitions at 13+ each year, varying in value according to merit and financial circumstances up to 50% of the current fees. These awards are given for pupils with academic ability or special talent in Art, Drama, Music, Sport or Technology.

Candidates for 13+ Scholarships must be under 14 years of age on 1 September in the year of the examination but there is no age limit for Exhibitions.

Fees per term (2011-2012). Senior School: Boarding: £9,910–£10,572; Day £6,566–£6,771.

An acceptance fee is payable 20 months before entry and is refunded as a deduction from the final account.

The Downs, Malvern is situated on the west side of the Malvern Hills and prepares boys and girls primarily for entry to the senior part of the College. Entries are welcomed at all ages. (*For further details, see entry in IAPS section.*)

The Malvernian Society. On leaving, Malvernians retain contact with the College by joining the Malvernian Society. They also become members of the OM Club which organises various teams and a number of social functions. Secretary of the Malvernian Society: Syd Hill (Tel: 01684 581517).

Charitable status. Malvern College is a Registered Charity, number 527578. It is a charity established for the purpose of educating children.

The Manchester Grammar School

Old Hall Lane, Manchester M13 0XT
Tel: 0161 224 7201
Fax: 0161 257 2446
e-mail: general@mgs.org
website: www.mgs.org

The Manchester Grammar School was founded in 1515 to promote 'godliness and good learning' and it has endeavoured throughout its history to remain true to these principles, while adapting to changing times. It is now an independent boys' day school with around 1,500 pupils. Almost all leavers go on to university, about a third of them going to Oxford, Cambridge, London and US Ivy League Institutions. Over 150 qualified teaching staff provide all pupils with a broad traditional curriculum and rich co-curricular opportunities.

The tradition of offering places to clever pupils regardless of their background is maintained by MGS bursaries. Well over 200 pupils in the school are fee-assisted. Our pupils come both from primary and preparatory schools and represent a wide variety of cultural, ethnic and religious backgrounds.

Motto: *sapere aude (dare to be wise)*

Co-optative Governors:

J A Claughton	Mrs J Luca
A M Dean	Dr P Mason (*Deputy*
J B Diggines (*Treasurer*)	*Chairman*)
B Dixon, CBE	J P Wainwright
Professor T A Hinchliffe	E M Watkins (*Chairman*)
Ms J Kingsley	

Ex officio Governors:
The Dean of Manchester
The President of Corpus Christi College, Oxford
The Lord Mayor of Manchester

Representative Governors:
Manchester University: Dr T Westlake
Cambridge University: Professor D A Cardwell
Oxford University: (*vacant*)

Bursar and Clerk to the Governors: Mrs G M Batchelor, BSc

High Master: C Ray, BA, PhD, CPhys, FRSA

Deputy High Master: S V Leeming, BSc, CSci, CChem, MRSC, FRGS
Academic Deputy Head: P A M Thompson, BA, DPhil, MA Ed
Pastoral Deputy Head: Mrs P Squires, BSc, PhD
Surmaster: J W Mangnall, MA
Head of Junior School: Mrs L A Hamilton, BEd
Head of Lower School: Mrs S C James, BA
Head of Middle School: A N Smith, BA
Head of Sixth Form: C P Thom, MA
Director of Development: S P Jones, BA
Senior Master: N A Sheldon, MA, BSc, MPhil, CStat, MBCS, CEng, CITP
Assistant Surmaster: S Foster, BA, MA
Proctor: S J Burch, BSc, PhD, MIBiol
Director of Admissions: R Alderson, MA
Director of Studies: D Jeys, BSc, MA
Assistant Head (*Staff Welfare*): Mrs A P Goddard, BA

Academic Staff:

T Ahmed, BSc	G Clayton, BSc
Miss R E Aldred, BMus, GRNCM	M P A Coffey, MA
Mrs J K Allinson, MA, BA	S G Crawshaw, BSc, MIBiol, PhD
Mrs L J Anderson, BA	M Crewe-Read, BSc
O J Barlow, BA	Miss S M F Cross, BA
P N A Baylis, BA	Mrs A Curry, BSc
G Blackwell, BA	Mrs E R Dalton, L-ès-L
J Blair, BSc	R A H Dean, BA
P L Bowen-Walker, BSc, PhD, CBiol, MIBiol, MCoT, Cert FPA	Mrs J Dobbs, BA
	A P Dobson, BA, MA
R C Bradford, BSc, PhD, MInstP, CPhys	S J Duffy, BSc, MIBiol, CBiol
Miss E Brewer, BA	Miss H L Eckhardt, BA, MA
D J Bristow, MA, MA, MEd	B S Edwards, MA
D Brown, BD, STM, MLitt	M Facchini, BSc, MSc
C Buckley, BSc	D Farr, MA
N T Burin, BSc, AFIMA	Miss F A Forsyth, MA
A P Burrows, BSc, PhD	D E Francis, MusB, GRNCM, ARNCM, LRAM, LTCL, ATCL
Mrs H Butchart, BA, LTCL	
Ms J M Byrne, BA, PhD	P W Freeman, BSc, MSc
Mrs S M Callaghan, BA	J C Gibb, MA
R M Carey, MA	T Glennie, BA
Mrs A E Carolan, BSc	Miss S Graham, MSci, PhD
Mrs E Carter, MA	Miss A Greggs, BA
E C F Cittanova, L-ès-L, L-ès-L, M-ès-L, DEA	T A Gregory, BA, MSc
	B A Hanson, BA

J Hargreaves, BA	T J Pattison, BSc, MIMA, CMath
G W M Harrison, BA	
Mrs K Hellier, BA	Mrs S Paulson, BA
Mrs A V Hemsworth, BA	Miss N M Pickup, BSc
A R T Hern, BA, MPhil	A C Pickwick, BSc, MSc, FRAS, MInstP, MBCS
M S R Hesketh, BSc, MSc	
Miss P J Higgins, BSc	J Potts, BSc
P Holt, BSc, DPhil	D Preston, MA, MSc
Mrs V E Horsfield, BA	W B Pye, BA
Mrs H M Hughes, BSc	Miss F C Roberts, MChem
S J F Hunt, MA	M J Roe, BSc
A C Hunter, BSc, MSc, PhD	Miss K R Sander, BSc
	Miss H D Sayers, BEd, MA
Miss A Jacinto, BA	Miss R L Sharkey, BA
Mrs T C James, BSc	N J Sharples, BA, MA
Miss H L Jones, BA	Mrs J R M Shaw, BA
R N Kelly, BA, MA, MPhil	Ms J Sherratt
Mrs E C Kilheeney, BA	J H Shoard, MA
I Z Khan, BSc	R W Simpson, BA
Mrs M A Koontz, MA	A M Smith, MA
Mrs R Lan, BA, MA	Mrs J L Smith, BA
C Lawrence, BSc	N D Smith, BA
Miss A Lloyd-Hughes, BA	D P Smith, MEng, PhD
Ms E Loh, BSc, MSc, PhD	Mrs L Speed, Mosc Dip
Mrs N A Loughlin, BSc	S P G Spratling, BA
Miss M A S Lowe, BA, MPhil	M G P Strother, BA, MPhil
	D M Taylor, BA
R N Massey, BA	Miss S Taylor, BA
N J Matthews, BSc	Mrs E M Thornber, BA, MPhil
Miss H McNally, BSc	
Mrs L Merlo, BA	G M Tinker, MEng
Mrs C Metcalfe, MA	B Townsend, BA
Mrs K S Michael, BSc	J N Tucker, BA
Mrs D Minguito-Pantoja, BA	M A Walmsley, BSc
	Miss S M Walsh, BBS
S R Molyneux, BA, MBA, MA	Mrs J M Ward, BA
	Mrs Z L Ward, LLB
G J Morris, BSc	N Warrack, MA, MA
D Moss, MA	P J Wheeler, BSc
Mrs L J Murphy, BA	Mrs J A Whittell, BA
Miss L E Nelson, BA, MA	Miss A Wicking, BA
M J Nichols, BSc	N G Williams, BA
D Noble, BA	Miss R G Williams, BA, DPhil
B J North, BA, MA	
Miss S J O'Neill, BSc	Miss C A Worth, BA, MA
Mrs S J van der Ouderaa, MA	Miss V Yonnet, BA
	Miss J T Yuen, BA

Medical Officer: Dr J L Burn, FRCP, FRCPCH
PA to the High Master: Lorraine Coen
Admissions Office Manager: Kath Heathcote
Director of Public Relations: Sally Rogers

Registration and Entry. Boys may be registered at any time prior to the assessment procedure in their year of proposed entry, which is normally at age 7, 8, 9, 10 or 11. Entry to the Sixth Form follows interview and appropriate qualifications. Current details are available from the Admissions Secretary.

Tuition Fees per term (2011-2012). £3,332.

Bursaries. The Governing Body awards means-tested bursaries.

Junior School. The Junior School of 110 boys aged 9–11 opened in September 2008 and will expand to admit an additional 154 boys aged 7–11 in September 2011.

Senior School Organisation and Curriculum. During the first two years the boys will study English, Mathematics, a modern foreign language (French, German, Spanish and Mandarin Chinese are offered), Classics (including Latin) History, Geography, General Science, Religious Studies, PSHE, ICT, Music, Art & Design, Drama, PE, Swimming and Games. Greek, Italian, Russian and Electronics are introduced as options in Year 9 and Classical Civilisation in Year 10. Pupils then proceed to make IGCSE/GCSE choices, typically taking ten subjects, including Mathematics, English, a language and one or more science subjects.

In the Sixth Form boys have a choice of studying either A Levels or the International Baccalaureate; in addition all students participate in the School's own non-examined enrichment programme.

Pastoral Care. Each form in the school is looked after by a Form Tutor, who is responsible, with the appropriate senior members of staff, for the academic and general progress of each pupil. Regular written reports are supplemented by Parents' Evenings and a Form Tutors' Day. The School Medical Room is staffed by a part-time doctor and two full-time Nursing staff. The older pupils selected as prefects are encouraged to help younger pupils in running societies and other co-curricular activities.

Creative Arts. All pupils experience Music, Art & Design and Drama within the curriculum; in addition, each of these areas offers activities to large numbers of pupils during the lunch-hour and after school. There are choirs, orchestras and instrumental tuition; plays, drama workshops and musicals; clubs for art, pottery, and computer design. There are regular exhibitions and public performances both in school and in public venues. A drama development including a new Theatre and studio opened in summer 2010.

Sport. All boys take part in timetabled games and the school produces successful teams in most sports. There is a gymnasium and an indoor swimming pool. A sports hall was opened in March 1997 by Michael Atherton, Captain of Cricket at the School, Cambridge University and England. The choice of sport increases with age to include rowing, climbing and golf in addition to mainstream sports.

Outdoor Pursuits. The school has a long tradition of camping and trekking and there are numerous weekend and holiday excursions as well as the Duke of Edinburgh's Award. Four annual camps cater for the full age range and offer a wide choice of activities. In recent years expeditions have visited the Alps, the Pyrenees, Morocco and Scandinavia. The school has two centres in Cumbria and one in Derbyshire.

Foreign Visits. Many trips abroad are organised each year, providing enjoyable holidays of broad educational value. Destinations include France, Germany, Spain, Russia, Italy, Greece, Mexico, Argentina, Peru, Mexico, Egypt, Tunisia, South Africa, India and China.

Societies and Activities. There are over 50 societies catering for a variety of interests, including Chess and Bridge Clubs, and a school newspaper produced by pupils. The school is active in charitable fundraising and has a very extensive community action programme, including projects in Manchester and Salford as well as in Uganda.

Prizes and Scholarships. In addition to bursaries, funds are provided for grants to help deserving pupils with the expense of a range of co-curricular activities. Prizes are awarded in all subjects in the curriculum.

Old Mancunians' Association and MGS Parents' Society. The Old Boys' Association has many regional sections. There is an annual Old Boys' Dinner in Manchester. The Development Office Secretary is Mrs Jane Graham who can be reached at the School.

The MGS Parents' Society has a membership of parents and friends and exists to support school activities and promote a programme of social events.

Charitable status. The Manchester Grammar School is a Registered Charity which provides Public Benefit. The aim of the School is to prepare able boys from the Manchester area, regardless of their financial background, to proceed to university and make a positive contribution to society in their adult life.

Marlborough College

Marlborough, Wiltshire SN8 1PA

Tel:	Main Switchboard: 01672 892200
	The Master's Office: 01672 892400
	The Bursary: 01672 892390
	Admissions: 01672 892300
Fax:	Main No: 01672 892207
	The Master's Office: 01672 892407
e-mail:	master@marlboroughcollege.org
	admissions@marlboroughcollege.org
website:	www.marlboroughcollege.org

Founded 1843. Incorporated by Royal Charter.

Visitor: The Most Revd The Lord Archbishop of Canterbury

Council:
President: The Rt Revd The Lord Bishop of Salisbury

Sir Hayden Phillips, GCB, DL (*Chairman*)
P A F Figgis (*Chairman of Finance Committee*)
R C H Jeens
Sir Christopher Gent
Major General A S Ritchie, CBE
The Venerable Sheila Watson
I D Coull
J P Hornby
A C V Evans
P J Manser, CBE, DL
Sir Richard Sykes, DSc, FRS, FMedSci
The Right Hon The Lord Malloch Brown, KCMG, PC
The Revd Rachel Weir
The Right Revd T M Butler
Ms S Hamilton-Fairley

Clerk to the Council: W F Wyldbore-Smith, DL

Master: N A Sampson, MA

Second Master: Dr C C Stevens, MA, DPhil
Director of Studies: R T Markham, BA, MA
Director of Co-curricular Activities: Mrs D J Harris, MA
Senior Admissions Tutor: Dr N G Hamilton, BA, PhD
Head of Boarding: Lady Cayley, MA
Head of Upper School: R D A Lamont, BA

Assistant Staff:
* *Head of Department*
† *Housemasters/mistresses*

Ms C C Russell, BA
A J Brown, MA (*Director of Professional Development*)
J N Copp, BEd (*Director of Summer School*)
A S Eales, BMus
A D McKnight, BSc (†*Turner House*)
Revd D J Dales, MA, BD, FRHistSoc
Ms J J McFarlane, BA DPhil
N M Allott, BSc (**Science*)
Dr M J Ponsford, BA, PhD
P G M Ford, MA (**Oxbridge*)
J D C Hicks, BA, ATC
D Allen, BA, MA
N R Cleminson, MA
A B D Harrison, BSc (**Mathematics*)
Mrs P J Harrison, BSc
K J D Richards, MA (**Geography*)
P R Adams, BEd (**Design and Technology*)
I G Crabbe, MA, FRCO, ARCM
J F Lloyd, BA, MPhil (**Classics*)
M W McVeigh, BSc, MA (†*C2*)
C S Smith, BEng, MSc
V J Stokes, BA, ATC
A Gist, BA, MA (*IB Coordinator*)

S J Ellis, BSc
S C Clayton, BA (*Form Coordinator*)
S M D Dempster, BA (*†C3*)
M Conlen, BSc (*†Cotton House*)
A J Arkwright, BA
Mrs L F W Ford, MA (**English*)
P N Keighley, BEng (**Business Studies*)
E G Nobes, MA (**Careers*)
Mrs R L T Bruce, BA
N E Briers, BEd (**Director of Sport*)
Mrs C A Walsh, BSc (*†New Court*)
Revd J G W Dickie, MA, BLitt
T J Gibbon, MA (**Spanish*)
Mrs S L J Greenwood, BSc
N J L Moore, BSc, MA (*†Barton Hill*)
C E Barclay, BSc, FRAS (*Director of the Observatory*)
M A Gow, BA (**Politics*)
N Nelson-Piercy, BA (**Russian*)
W D L Nicholas, BEng (*†Summerfield*)
Dr L J Richards, BSc, PhD (**Biology*)
G B Shearn, BSc (**ICT*)
T G R Marvin, MA (*†Preshute*)
J H Parnham, BA, MA (**Art*)
Miss C Toomer, GGSM
Mrs J Hodgson, BA (*†Morris House*)
M B Blossom, BA (**Medawar Centre*)
J A Hodgson, BSc
Mrs R D Moore, BSc
Miss J Darby, BA, GMus
P J O'Sullivan, BA (**Economics*)
K G A Smith, BA
R Tong (*OA Coordinator*)
T A Kiggell, MA
Mrs H A M Cox, BSc (*†Elmhurst*)
B H Miller, BSc (*†C1*)
R A Sandall, BCom, BA
P A Finn, BA
P V Hampson, BSc
Mrs R F Horton, MA (*†Mill Mead*)
Mrs K J Kiggell, MA
J G Hobby, BA (**German*)
Mrs S A Finn, BA
Dr D G Roberts, MSc, PhD (**Physics*)
Mrs V R Hawthorn, BA, Dip SpLD, AMCollT
Mrs A T Woodford, BA
J P Carroll, BEd (*†B House*)
R A Cockett, MA (**Modern Languages*)
S R Hawthorn, BSc
Mrs J McFarland, BSc
S G Quinn, BSc
Dr G Doyle, BSc, MSc, PhD, DIC, CChem, MRSC
   (**Chemistry*)
C L Harrison, BSc
G D M Lane, BSc
J J Lyon Taylor, BSc (*†Littlefield*)
Miss A C Langdale, BSc
Mrs C E Page, MA, BA (**Learning Support & Study Skills*)
G M Turner, BSc
P T Dukes, FGSM (**Artistic Director*)
Miss D L Goodger, BSc
N O P Gordon, MA
P N Morley-Fletcher, BA
C O Stewart, MA
Mrs R L Collins, BA
D Kenworthy, BA, MFA (**Drama*)
Ms L M Morey, MA
Mrs R Scott, MA
M Baldrey, BA, FTCL
S Taranczuk, MMus, FRCO (*Director of Chapel Music*)
H E B Jones, BA
Dr F S McKeown, BA, PhD (**History of Art*)
T A Birkill, BSc
S J Dennis, MBE, BSc, MSc

Mrs A J Finn, BSc, MSc
E J Hawkins, BSc
G I Macmillan, BA
Miss B S Broughton, BA
D R Armitage, MA
B W Giles, MA
M A Worsley, LLB
Miss A J Palmer, MSc, MEd
T C M Lauze, BA (**French*)
A S Pembleton, BSc
Miss L Smith, BSc
G R Playfair, MA (**Religious Studies*)
D P T Curry, BSc
Mrs S Shearn, MEd
Mrs E Thornburn, BA
Miss S L Green, MA (**History*)
Dr A D Burns, BA, MSc, PhD
M P L Bush, BA
G Mallard, MA
Miss A Willis, BSc
Miss G M Longley, MA, MSt
Dr J P Swift, BSc, PhD

Director of Corporate Resources & Deputy Master: P N
   Bryan, BA, ACA
Deputy Master, International Projects: R B Pick, BSc
Senior Chaplain: (*to be appointed*)
Medical Officers:
Dr R W Hook, MB BS, MRCGP, DRCOG
Dr S Hanson, MB BS, MRCGP, DCH
Director of the Marlborough Association: J P Crawley,
   MA, MBA
Librarian: Mrs L Pilkington, BSc, MSc
Archivist: Dr T E Rogers, BSc, PhD
Master's Secretary: Mrs S Nicholas

There are approximately 880 boys and girls in the 14 houses in the College. The College is fully co-educational, 13 being the normal age of entry for both girls and boys. A limited number of boys and girls are admitted to the Sixth Form.

Registration. For entry to the school at 13+ registrations are accepted no earlier than four years before entry. Registrations for entry at 16+ are accepted at any time.

The College assesses all applicants 20 months ahead of entry and offers places accordingly. After this date a small number of able candidates may still win a place in the school by being accepted onto the Master's List. All applicants to the school must meet our entry criteria and take either the Academic Scholarship or the Common Entrance examination. Please see our website for details of this new policy: www.marlboroughcollege.org. The 13+ Scholarship examination is in February/March of the year of entry and the Sixth Form Scholarship examination is in the November before entry.

Scholarships. (*See Scholarship Entries section.*) There are two levels of award: Major and Minor Scholarships. Awards enable those with a financial need to receive bursarial assistance with the fees. The degree of support given will be subject to a means test. Approximately forty awards (of which 19 are Major) are available at 13+, including Music, Art, Design, Sport and All Rounder; approximately twenty (of which 8 are Major) are awarded at Sixth Form entry. From time to time there are a number of other special categories of scholarship based upon parental occupation and particular abilities. Two means-tested scholarships/bursaries may be worth 100% of full fees; one of these is the College Organ Scholarship and particular consideration will also be given to those applying for a strings award. William Morris All Rounder Bursaries can offer up to 85% reduction of school fees: these awards are based upon strengths in academic work, sport, art or music. A number of Children of Clergy Bursaries are awarded on interview and consultation.

Applications and enquiries about entries and scholarships should be addressed to The Senior Admissions Tutor.

Universities & Careers. Nearly all pupils who come to Marlborough go on into the Sixth Form and virtually all proceed to degree courses. Twenty-five A Level and 2 Pre-U subjects are available in the large Sixth Form, plus additional courses. The International Baccalaureate is offered as an alternative to A Levels. The Careers Department is well-equipped and assists Housemasters and Housemistresses in advising boys and girls and their parents as to careers and university choices, in addition to gap year projects.

Extra-Curricular. Good games facilities are available with a modern Sports Hall, indoor swimming pool, spacious playing fields, two all-weather pitches, an athletics track and numerous tennis courts. The main games are athletics, cricket, football, hockey, lacrosse, netball, rugby and tennis; alternative games include fives, rackets, shooting, squash and swimming. There is a strong Outdoor Activities Department, which offers the Duke of Edinburgh's Award as well as canoeing, climbing, orienteering and sub-aqua; the CCF covers adventure training as part of its basic course, with specialist leadership training to a high standard. School Societies offering activities at different levels enable interests to be nurtured and, for those who enjoy country pursuits, the River Kennet and two trout lakes provide fishing.

Music. The Department is housed in a large and well-equipped centre. Nearly half the boys and girls play a musical instrument. There are three school orchestras, a wind band, a chamber orchestra, a brass band, the Chapel Choir and a choral society; there are numerous small instrumental and choral groups.

Drama. There are over fifteen productions each year, including two school plays, Junior productions and a house drama festival. Many are produced and directed by pupils. The Sixth Form curriculum includes Theatre Studies and Drama is an option at GCSE.

Art and Design. All pupils study Art in their first year and many go on to take the subject at GCSE and A Level or the IB. The new Art Department believes that all pupils can acquire a good standard of visual literacy across a variety of artistic disciplines. There is a purpose-built Design and Technology Centre.

Fees per term (2011-2012). £10,100 Boarding; £8,150 Day Pupils.

The Marlburian Club, Marlborough College. *Hon Secretary*: M C W Evans, Esq.

Charitable status. Marlborough College is a Registered Charity, number 309486 incorporated by Royal Charter to provide education.

Merchant Taylors' Boys' School
Crosby

Liverpool Road, Crosby, Liverpool L23 0QP
Tel: 0151 928 3308 (General Enquiries)
          0151 949 9323 (Headmaster)
          0151 928 5770 (Bursar)
          0151 949 9333 (Admissions Office)
Fax: 0151 949 9300
e-mail: infomtbs@merchanttaylors.com
website: www.merchanttaylors.com

The Boys' School was founded in 1620 by John Harrison, Citizen and Merchant Taylor of London. In 1878 the School was transferred to its present site.
    Motto: *'Concordia parvae res crescunt'*

Governors:
Chairman: Prof P W J Batey, BSc, MCD, PhD, FRTPI, FRSA, AcSS

P J R Evans, Esq, FCS, FCA
D R Jacks, Esq, LLB
Mrs V A P Johnson, BEd
P G Magill, Esq, MSc, FCIPD
R J Walker, Esq, CEng, MIMechE
Miss A Dobie, BA Hons
Mrs B Bell LLB, FCILT, FRSA, FSOE, FIRTE
S Wilkinson, Esq, BA, FCA
D S Evans, Esq, MA
Mrs J L Hawkins, RGN, RM

Bursar and Clerk to the Governors: Mrs A Pope, BA Hons, FCMA, ACIS, MSI

Headmaster: **David Cook**, BA, MA

Deputy Headmasters:
D A C Blower, BA, MA
R A Simpson, MA

Head of Sixth Form: Dr A J Patchett, BSc, PhD
Head of Middle School: Mrs D Knaggs, BSc
Head of Lower School: S G Fletcher, BSc, MSc
Director of Music: D Holroyd, GMus RNCM, PPRNCM, ARCO
Emeritus Chaplain: Revd D A Smith, BA

Teachers:

Miss C L Bailey, MA, MSt	D W King, BA
G Bonfante, BSc	P A Lally, BA
Dr I M Buschmann,	I D McKie, CertEd
DipChem, MSc, PhD	Mrs J R Marshall, BA
Mrs A C Byrne, BSc	W K Miles, BSc
J Carter, BA	D Miller, BSc
Mrs M Casaus, MA	Dr N Myers, BA, PhD
T D Cawthorn, BSc	Dr A J Patchett, BSc, PhD
Dr C M Clay, MChem,	Miss S A Patel, BA
PhD	Mrs E C Peacock, BA
I Crawford, BA, MA	Mrs K E Plummer, BA
K R Connor, MEng	Mrs E Rea, BA, MCLIP
P J Cooper, BSc	F J Rubia Castro, BA
Mrs S A Dunning, BA	B Schober, BSc
J P Farrell, BSc, MA	Mrs D Shepherd, ASA
R M Fawcett, BEd	Level 2
Miss C Ferris, BSc	Mrs K L Siddle, BEd
Ms J Finnegan, BA	R A Simpson, BA, MA
S G Fletcher, BSc, MSc	P R Spears, BA
Mrs A Gaston, BA	M Stanley, BA, MA
Dr J S Gill, BA, MPhil,	G T Stiff, BA
PhD	S P Sutcliffe, BA, MA
J B Green, BA	I Taylor, BEd, MA
Dr S J Hardy, BSc, PhD	Miss J L Thornber, BA
A G Heap, BSc, MSc	M Toney, BSc
P E Howard, BSc	J E Turner, BA, MA
N A Hunt, BA	M Whalley
P A Irvine, BEd	Mrs V A Winrow, BSc,
S J Kay, BSc	HNC
A Kent	Mrs R J Wright, BSc

Junior School:
Head: Mrs J E Thomas, BEd, MEd, NPQH
Deputy Head: D K J Youngson, BA, NPQH

Mrs B P J Ashcroft, BEd,	D I Lyon, MA
PGDE	J O'Shaughnessy, BA Hons
Mrs Y Bonfante, BEd	Mrs L Rogers, BEd
Mrs P Carr	P A Wardle, BEd
Mrs A Davies, CertEd	Mrs H White, BA
Miss R Hargreaves	Mrs A Wynne, BEd
Mrs A Hodson	

Admissions: Mrs P Saffer
PA to the Headmaster: Mrs M Delaney / Mrs S Maitland

The Senior Boys' School consists of about 600 boys, 151 of whom are in the Sixth Form. In addition there is a Junior

Boys' School with 158 boys between the ages of seven and eleven.

The school has a reputation for academic excellence and the majority of our leavers proceed to degree courses at Russell Group universities including Oxford and Cambridge. The emphasis throughout is very much on developing learners who are able to work independently and who have a genuine curiosity in their studies.

Curriculum. In the first three years of the Lower School boys study a wide variety of national curriculum subjects including separate sciences as well as the opportunity to pick up extra modern and ancient languages. They gradually specialise in the Middle School where there is the flexibility to study between 8 and 11 GCSEs including an accelerated IGCSE mathematics course. There is an additional timetabled afternoon (Friday) in Years 7–9 for enrichment activities.

In the Sixth Form the following subjects are available at A Level: Mathematics, Further Mathematics, Physics, Chemistry, Biology, Latin, Greek, Classical Civilisation, English Language, English Literature, History, Geography, Economics, French, German, Spanish, Design and Technology, Art & Design, Music, Theatre Studies and Physical Education. In addition, students in the Sixth Form will have an opportunity to follow a course in General Studies.

Games. A new sports centre was opened in May 2011 incorporating a dance studio, fitness suite and sports hall. Additional facilities include an indoor swimming pool and three tennis courts.

Games played are Rugby, Hockey, Cricket, Athletics, Rowing, Football, Swimming, Tennis and Cross-Country. All boys are expected to participate in one of the many games options available throughout their time at school.

School Societies. A wide range of activities and interests is covered by School Societies.

Music and Drama. About 200 boys receive weekly instrumental tuition and there is a subsidised scheme for beginners on orchestral instruments. There is a School Choral Society, Junior School Choir, Concert Band, Swing Band, a Chamber Orchestra along with various woodwind and brass ensembles and a Samba Band. Boys regularly perform both in and out of School at a variety of events and are given many opportunities to perform publicly.

There are two full time teachers, plus a team of 11 visiting specialist instrument teachers. There are links in Music with our sister school, Merchant Taylors' Girls' School. There are also close links with the Girls' School in Drama, which now forms an integral part of the Senior School curriculum as well as being a major extra-curricular activity.

Combined Cadet Force. The School has a voluntary contingent of the Combined Cadet Force with Royal Navy, Army and Royal Air Force Sections. There are around 270 members of the CCF, many of whom are girls from our sister school.

Admission. Boys are admitted to the Junior School at age 7 and to the Senior School at 11, 13 or at Sixth Form. Some Assisted Places are available at 11.

Fees per term (2011-2012). Tuition: Senior School £3,125; Junior School £2,312.

Old Boys. There is an active Old Boys' Association (The Old Crosbeians) whose Secretary may be contacted via the School and from whom a handbook/register may be obtained.

Charitable status. The Merchant Taylors' Schools Crosby is a Registered Charity, number 1125485, and a Company Limited by Guarantee, registered in England, number 6654276. Registered Office: Liverpool Road, Crosby, Liverpool L23 0QP.

Merchant Taylors' School

Sandy Lodge, Northwood, Middlesex HA6 2HT
Tel: Head Master's PA: 01923 821850
Reception: 01923 820644
Admissions Secretary: 01923 845514
Bursar: 01923 825669
Fax: 01923 845522
e-mail: info@mtsn.org.uk
website: www.mtsn.org.uk

Motto: '*Concordia parvae res crescunt.*'

The Governors of the School:
Chairman: Mr Christopher Peter Hare
R J Brooman
G F Brown
Baroness Elizabeth Butler-Sloss, GBE
M C Clarke, MA Cambridge, FCA
D G M Eggar
Ms L Gadd, MA
R C G Gillott
J A J Price
Miss M Rudland, BSc London
Mr D J Shah
Mrs C Spalton
H W J Stubbs
R-J Temmink
Sir Michael Tomlinson
P H Watkins

Head Master: S N Wright, MA Queens' College Cambridge

Second Master: T R Stubbs, BSc, PhD, CBiol, MIBiol
Development Director: C A Massi, BA
Senior Master: C R Evans-Evans, BA, MEd, NPQH
Director of Studies: J G Taylor, MA
Deputy Head, Communications: C E Roseblade, BA
Registrar: A J Booth, MA
Head of Upper School: M Bond, BA
Chaplain: The Reverend R D E Bolton, MA

Assistant Staff:

Art & Design:
J C P Otley, MA (*Head of Art and Design*)
Miss H C Blowes, BA
S N Leech, BA
J T Ramsay, MA

Biology:
T W Filtness, MA (*Head of Biology*)
C W Gray, BSc
T C H Greenaway, BSc (*Head of Lower School*)
Miss L Lawson-Pratt, MA
N D Light, BA, MSc
T R Stubbs, BSc, PhD, CBiol, MIBiol (*Second Master*)

Chemistry:
D L Brewis, MA (*Head of Chemistry*)
A J W Horrox, MA (*Pastoral and Activities Monitor*)
T J Hingston, MChem
M P Powell, MA
Mrs F A Rashid, BSc (*Head of Science*)

Classics:
M C Husbands, MA (*Head of Classics*)
M F Drury, MA
Mrs C D Fielding, BA (*Staff Tutor*)
Mrs M R Pfeffer, BA (*Head of Andrewes House*)

Computing:
C P Hirst, MA, BSc (*Head of Computing*)
M J Scott, BSc (*Head of White House*)

Design & Technology:
G M Stephenson, BSc (*Head of Design and Technology*)
A S Bannister, BSc (*Head of Walter House*)
J B Coleman, CertEd, MA (*Head of External Relations*)
N J Kyriacou, BEd (*Assistant to Head of Middle School*)

Drama and Theatre Studies:
D Garnett, BA (*Director of Drama*)
Miss S C Blowes, MA, MSc
A R Doyle, MA, DPhil (*Joint Enrichment/Oxbridge Coordinator*)
C E Roseblade, BA (*Deputy Head, Communications*)
S M Simons, BA

Economics & Politics:
A H Ellams, MA (*Head of Economics & Politics*)
Mrs H V Butland, BA
C Chong, MA, MPhil
D Howell, BA, MSc, MSt (*Head of Phab*)
Miss H F Thompson, BA, MSc, MA (*Head of DoE Award Scheme*)

English:
D A Lawrence, MA (*Head of English, Governing Body SCR Representative*)
Miss S C Blowes, MA, MSc
P M Capel, BA (*Learning Support Coordinator*)
A R Doyle, MA, DPhil (*Joint Enrichment/Oxbridge Coordinator*)
Ms H L Freeman, BA
T W Jenkin, MA (*Head of Middle School*)
I J Mitchell, BA, BSc (*Head of Psychology*)
S J Morris, BA
C E Roseblade, BA (*Deputy Head, Communications*)
S M Simons, BA
Ms L V Smith, MA (*Head of Mulcaster House*)

Geography:
Mrs S A Riddleston, BA (*Head of Geography*)
J Bown, BA (*Assistant to Head of Upper School*)
G P Colley, CertEd (*CO CCF*)
C T Tracey, BSc (*Assistant to Head of Lower School*)
S W Turner, BSc (*Head of PSHCE*)

History:
S W Stott, MA (*Head of History*)
Miss K H Balnaves, BA, MA (*Joint Enrichment/Oxbridge Coordinator*)
M Bond, BA (*Head of Upper School*)
A J Booth, MA (*Registrar*)
J G Brown, MA (*School Archivist, Head of General Studies*)
D R D Howell, BA, MSc, MSt (*Head of Phab*)
Miss F E Pace, BA
J G Taylor, MA (*Director of Studies*)
S N Wright, MA (*Head Master*)

Information Systems:
C E Roseblade, BA (*Deputy Head, Communications*)
P Gregory (*Technical Services Manager*)
J Beck (*Senior IT Technician*)
P A J G Gregory (*IT Technician*)
I Rudling (*Webmaster*)
J A Sagnella (*IT Network Supervisor*)

Learning Support:
P M Capel, BA (*Learning Support Coordinator*)
Mrs G M Kantor, BA

Library:
Mrs J Howse, BSc, MA (*Senior Librarian*)
Mrs A South, BSc, DipLib (*Second Librarian*)
Mrs P J Jones, BA, PGDip (*part-time Library Assistant*)

Mathematics:
J D G Slator, MA (*Head of Mathematics*)
Dr F Andrews, BSc, PhD
Mrs N Bigden, MSc (*Head of Clive House*)

C Chong, MA, MPhil
R G Cranston, BA
Miss H L Croft, BSc (*Second in Mathematics*)
M F Illing, MA
A S Miller, BSc
C G P Ralphs, BEng GTP
S L Rowlands, BA (*Head of Manor House*)
Mrs F S Teskey, BSc (*Head of Community Service and Charities Coordinator*)

Modern Languages:
R P Bailey, BA (*Head of Modern Languages*)
Ms M E Broncano, MA (*Head of Spanish*)
Mrs M C R Castro, BA (*Spanish*)
Miss R G Haye, Licence LCE (*French & Spanish*)
Mrs J Li, MA (*Mandarin – part time*)
Mrs V A McCarthy, BA, MA (*French*)
Miss H E McCullough, BA (*Head of German*)
R M McGinlay, MA, MPhil (*Head of French*)
Mrs K Okamura, Dip (*Japanese – part time*)
J M S Rippier, BA (*French, Editor of Concordia & Taylorian*)
T P Rocher, L-ès-L (*French*)
Mrs C E Udell, MA (*German & French*)
F R Vignal, DipHE (*French & Spanish*)

Music:
R N Hobson, MA, ARCO (*Director of Music*)
S J Couldridge, DipTCL
Mrs J H Stubbs, MusB, ARCO, ALCM (*SCR President*)

Physical Education:
J P Cowan, BSc (*Director of Sport, Head of Hockey*)
C M J Lehane, BA (*Head of Academic PE*)
C R Evans-Evans, BA, MEd, NPQH (*Senior Master*)

Physics:
D J Spikings, BA, MEng (*Head of Physics*)
Dr A R H Clarke, MA, DPhil (*Assistant Director of Studies*)
E J Gillett, MSci
N J D Hillier, BA, MSc (*Head of Hilles House*)
N P Migallo, BSc, ARCS, MInstPhys
Ms L A Slator, BSc (*Examinations Officer*)

Psychology:
I J Mitchell, BA, BSc (*Head of Psychology*)

Religion and Philosophy:
Miss K H Balnaves, BA, MA (*Head of Religion and Philosophy, Joint Enrichment/Oxbridge Coordinator*)
The Reverend R D E Bolton, MA, Cert Theol, FRSA (*School Chaplain*)

School Counsellor: A J C Dickinson, BA, MEd, ALCP

Visiting Teachers:
J Atkins, DipRAM, ARCM (*Trumpet*)
G Boyd, DipMus Melbourne (*Double Bass*)
S Byron, BMus Hons RCM (*Trombone*)
Miss S Clark, MA, ARCM, PG Dip RCM, CT ABRSM, LRSM (*Piano*)
Mrs N S Coleman, CertEd (*Flute*)
Miss K Cormican, GTCL, PDOT GSMD (*Violin*)
G Cracknell, LRAM (*Violin*)
A Francis, LRAM (*Clarinet*)
J Francis (*Saxophone & Clarinet*)
Ms N Hawkins, GLCM, FLCM (*Guitar*)
R Halford (*Guitar*)
D Hester, LTCL, DipTCL, PDOT GMSD (*Bassoon*)
C Hooker, BA Hons, LRAM, ARAM (*Oboe*)
J Lawrence, BA (*Percussion*)
D Lewis, LRAM (*French Horn & Brass*)
Mrs N Manington, BMus LGSM (*Piano*)
N Martin (*Drums*)
Ms P O'Sullivan, BA (*Recorder*)
D Saunderson, GGSM (*Singing*)

Mrs M Stone, MA, Dip RAM (*Piano*)
Mrs N Tait, Prof Cert Hons, LRAM Hons (*Cello*)

Sports:
G Davies (*Rugby*)
H C Latchman (*Cricket*)
F Lombard (*Rugby*)
P Loudon (*Hockey*)
J Rayden (*Fencing*)
M Smith (*Judo*)
K Haigh (*Hockey*)
A Wilson (*Hockey*)
D Barrell (*Rugby*)
N Lambert (*Rugby*)
A Mills (*GTP*)
C Ralphs (*Post Graduate Assistant*)
L Foot (*Post Graduate Assistant*)
R Worrell (*Squash*)
M Khalifa (*Squash*)

Bursar: G R H Ralphs
Development Director: C A Massi
Head Master's PA: Mrs C Herbert
Admissions Secretary: Mrs P Wright
Bursar's Secretary: Mrs S Enright

The School has enjoyed a distinguished history since its foundation by the Merchant Taylors' Company in 1561. It was one of the nine original Public Schools as defined by the 1868 Act and its pupils have achieved distinction throughout its history. The School enjoys close links with the Company, which, to this day, constitutes its Governing Body. In 1933 the School moved from central London to its present superb, rural setting of 250 acres at Sandy Lodge, Northwood. We are within easy reach of parents in Buckinghamshire, Hertfordshire, Middlesex and North-West London by car, train or school coach service, as well as a mere half hour by tube from Baker Street.

There are 860 boys in the School.

All pupils have an individual tutor who looks after them throughout their school career in small House tutor groups. They are encouraged to cultivate activities at which they can excel, to have confidence in their abilities and to gain self-knowledge as well as knowledge. The academic achievements of the School are first-rate and are achieved in a humane, civilised and unpressured atmosphere. We place a great emphasis on encouraging boys to organise many activities themselves and to take responsibility for others.

Admission. Entry to the School at 11+, 13+ and 16+ is by the School's own Entrance Examinations, together with an interview.

Scholarships and Bursaries. (*See Scholarship Entries section.*) There are no separate scholarship papers in the examinations. We make awards to boys who perform exceptionally well in the examinations and interview and we take into account information received from the boy's current school.

11+ entry: Up to 10 academic scholarships each to the value of £200 per year. Up to 2 all-rounder scholarships each to the value of £200 per year. Up to 2 sports scholarships.

13+ entry: Up to 20 academic scholarships (some named) each to the value of £200 per year. Up to 2 all-rounder scholarships each to the value of £200 per year. Up to 2 sports scholarships.

For both these age groups bursaries are available depending upon proven financial need. These can also be used to increase the value of the Scholarship.

16+ entry: 1 sports scholarship. One bursary up to the value of the full school fee is available. Lower Sixth Internal Exhibitions: Four Exhibitions may be awarded for boys going into the Lower Sixth.

Music Scholarships: Up to 2 scholarships up to the value of 25% of the school fees, together with 2 Exhibitions up to the value of 10% of the school fees. In addition, Music

Awards are made covering the cost of tuition of up to two instruments per boy. These awards are available to candidates at all the usual ages of entry.

Bursaries: The School welcomes applications from parents whose sons are likely to contribute strongly to the School, and to benefit from it, but who may require financial assistance; a significant sum is set aside each year for this purpose. Awards are made on entry to the School. Applications for bursarial assessment forms should be made in writing to the Admissions Secretary and completed forms must be received by the School by 12th December preceding the year of the boy's entry.

Other Awards: There is a generous variety of awards open to Sixth Formers for travel, Outward Bound and Sail Training, as well as leaving scholarships to assist at University.

Scholarships at Oxford and Cambridge Universities. At the end of their first undergraduate year, Old Boys are eligible for election to a maximum of three Sir Thomas White Scholarships at St John's College, Oxford, a Matthew Hale Scholarship at Queen's College, Oxford and a Parkin & Stuart Scholarship for Science or Mathematics at Pembroke College, Cambridge.

Curriculum and Organisation. The curriculum in years 7, 8 and 9 (Thirds, Upper Thirds and Fourths) is a broad one: Art and Design, Biology, Chemistry, Design and Technology, Drama, English, French, Geography, History, ICT, Latin, Mathematics, Music, Physical Education, Physics, PSHCE and Religious Studies. Greek, German, Spanish or Italian are started when 13+ boys enter the school. All boys take nine or ten GCSEs, chosen from a wide range of subjects, including Music, Drama, PE and Computer Science. Boys are entered for the IGCSE in English, Mathematics and Science. A student entering the Lower Sixth embarks upon a two-year course in which all boys study four subjects to AS Level, followed by three subjects at A2 for most (some continue with four). In addition, all boys do AS General Studies. An extensive choice of options is available and an enriching General Studies programme includes courses in Japanese, Mandarin and Russian.

Music. All orchestral and band instruments, piano, organ, percussion and guitar are taught to boys throughout the School. Choirs, orchestras, bands and chamber groups give frequent concerts throughout the year.

Free tuition for one year is available for selected boys who wish to start learning an orchestral instrument.

Games and Physical Education. Magnificent playing fields over 55 acres are dedicated to the playing of Rugby, Cricket, Soccer, Hockey, Cross-Country and Golf. There are Fives, Squash and Tennis Courts; also, an athletics track and two floodlit, all-weather pitches. The Sports Hall accommodates four badminton courts, a multi-gym, a climbing wall, a fencing piste and indoor cricket nets. The School's lakes provide a marvellous facility for our Sailing Club, canoeing and windsurfing. Physical Education is compulsory for all pupils and all pupils learn to swim. There is an indoor swimming pool and Water Polo is offered. Coaching in Fencing, Basketball, Judo and Karate is excellent and boys enjoy national success in these sports. The School is the UK Centre of Excellence for Handball.

Service Sections. The School has a Contingent of the Combined Cadet Force with RN, Army, and RAF Sections. The CCF includes girls from St Helen's School, Northwood. There is a Rifle Range for the use of the Contingent, and we send a team to Bisley every year. The Duke of Edinburgh's Award Scheme allows boys to achieve Bronze, Silver and Gold Awards, and the Community Service Group which provides an opportunity for a wide range of activities in the local area. All boys in Years 10 and 11 take part in the CCF, The Duke of Edinburgh's Award Scheme or Community Service teams.

The School places great emphasis on charitable endeavour and the boys run a great many societies to support good causes. A special feature of the school's charity work is

Phab, a week-long residential holiday for handicapped children held every Easter and organised by Sixth Form boys together with the girls of St Helen's School.

School Societies. A large number of societies cover a wide field of interests and activities.

Careers. There is a strong Careers Advisory Service, which organises annual Careers and Higher Education Conventions at the School and a range of work experience.

House and Tutorial Systems. The School is divided into eight Houses. Each House is under the care of a Head of House and a team of Tutors, which is responsible for the pastoral care of boys in that House.

Fees per term (2011-2012). £5,340. These cover not only tuition and games but also lunch. There is a registration fee of £100; admission fee deposits will subsequently be charged.

Term of entry. September unless there are very special circumstances.

Charitable status. Merchant Taylors' School Charitable Trust is a Registered Charity, number 1063740. It exists to provide a first-class all-round education for boys, irrespective of their background.

Merchiston Castle School

Colinton, Edinburgh EH13 0PU
Tel: 0131 312 2200
          Headmaster: 0131 312 2203
          Director of Admissions: 0131 312 2201
Fax: 0131 441 6060
e-mail: headmaster@merchiston.co.uk
website: www.merchiston.co.uk

The School was established in 1833 and moved in 1930 from the centre of the city out to its present spacious and attractive site, bordered by the Water of Leith and close to the Pentland Hills.

Motto: *Ready Ay Ready.*

Governors:
Chairman: J M Gourlay, BCom, CA

Members of the Board:
A E Corstorphine
The Hon Lord Hodge
C M A Lugton, MA
W M Biggart, BA
D J Biggar, OBE
H P G Maule, MA
R W L Legget, MBA, CA
G R T Baird
Prof L Waterhouse, BA, MSW
G F Barnet, LLB
P K Young, BSc, MRICS
Mrs S Kuenssberg, CBE, BA, DipAdEd, FRSA
R M Ridley, MA
S P Abram
J L Broadfoot, BA, MEd
B M McCorkell, BA, MA Cantab
I McAteer, LLB
Mrs P Marshall, MA
W A McDonald

Secretary to the Governors and Bursar: D G Smith, BCom, CA

President of the Merchistonian Club: W A McDonald

Headmaster: **A R Hunter**, BA Manchester

Deputy Head: F N Rickard, BA Hull, ACCEG (*English*)

Deputy Head Academic: Mrs M Muetzelfeldt, BSc London (*Mathematics*)

* *Head of Department*
† *Housemaster*

J Rainy Brown, BSc Edinburgh (*Mathematics*)
M C L Gill, MBE, BSc, PhD Edinburgh (*Chemistry*)
J C O Vaughan, BSc Edinburgh (*Mathematics*)
P S Williams, BA Leicester (*English, Classical Civilization*)
P K Hall, MA Oxford (*Head of Merchiston Juniors*)
P K Rossiter, MA Oxford (*Head of Middle Years, Music, †Chalmers West*)
Mrs C A Watson, BA Manchester (*Support for Learning, English*)
Mrs M V Prini-Garcia, L-ès-L Madrid (*Spanish, Careers**)
T J Lawson, BA Sheffield, PhD Edinburgh, FSA Scot (*Geography, Examinations**)
C W Swan, CertEd Loughborough (*PE, History*)
D M Turner, MA Oxford, ARCO (*ICT, Music*)
S J Horrocks, MA Cambridge (*French, Spanish, ESOL*)
P Corbett, MA St Andrews (*French, Latin, ESOL Coordinator*)
Miss F M Blakeman, Dip Des Napier (*Art & Design*)
K J A Anderson, MTh St Andrews (*PSE, Religious Studies, Dean of Sixth Form, †Laidlaw South*)
Revd A S Macpherson, MA Glasgow (*Religious Studies*)
S Campbell, BSc Glasgow (*Mathematics**)
R C Lucas, MEng Aston, MA Sheffield (*Mathematics*)
Mrs J M Williams, BA Leicester (*Librarian*)
N J Mortimer, MA, DPhil Oxford (*English*, Religious Studies*, Classical Civilization*, Assistant Head Academic*)
J M V Cordingley, MA London (*Art & Design*, †Chalmers East*)
F Geisler, LA S11/1 Bochum (*German*)
Mrs F Horrocks, BA Pretoria (*French*)
Mrs M B Watson, BSc Glasgow (*Mathematics, ICT**)
Ms C A Walker, BA Edinburgh (*ESOL*)
R A Charman, BA Canterbury (*Director of Sport, PE*, Mathematics*)
F P J Main, BEd Edinburgh (*Design & Technology**)
R P Nicholls, BSc Durham (*Physics*, Electronics**)
K G Pettigrew, BSc, PhD Edinburgh (*Chemistry**)
Miss S M Twyford, BSc Glasgow, MSc Strathclyde, PhD Glasgow (*Physics*)
N G D Blair, BA, MA Edinburgh (*Religious Studies, English*)
J Palacios, DipEd Buenos Aires (*Spanish, PSHE*)
M J Caves, BSc Belfast (*Mathematics*)
Mrs B G Hunter, BEd Exeter (*Art & Design*)
M S King, BSc Bristol (*Biology**)
Mrs N G Hairs, BA Kent (*J4 Teacher, Head of Pringle Centre*)
G Campbell, MA Aberdeen (*Master in Charge of Pipe Bands*)
J B Bisset, MA, MSc Aberdeen (*Director of ICT Services*)
D D J Cartwright, BSc, PhD Edinburgh (*Junior Science, Chemistry, Pringle Director of Studies*)
R D Heathcote, BSc Nottingham (*Geography, †Laidlaw North*)
Mrs M Hsu-McWilliam, BA Tamkang, MSc Edinburgh (*Mandarin*)
Miss J R Vaughan, BA Newcastle (*Head of Support for Learning in Pringle, Mathematics*)
I H Mitchell, BSc Strathclyde, PhD Imperial (*Physics, †Evans*)
D M George, BSc Edinburgh (*Biology*)
P D R Osborne, BEd Natal (*Director of Pringle Sport*)
W J J Clayton, MA Edinburgh (*History, Economics**)
Mrs A Almeida de Palacios, UCA Buenos Aires (*Spanish*)
A C Dickson, BEd Edinburgh (*Design & Technology*)
J P W Dixon, MA Cambridge (*History**)
M du Coudray (*Tennis Academy Coach*)
Major A D Ewing (*School Staff Instructor*)
Mrs M H Gray, MA Lyon (*Languages*, French*)

Mrs I Stewart, BEd Glasgow (*Faculty of Support for Learning**)
Mrs J A Ghazal (*Pringle Centre Assistant*)
P J Deakin, BSc Durham (*Geography*, Director of Co-curricular Activities*)
Ms F Vian, PhD Parma (*Mathematics*)
Mrs N J Ledingham, BEng Loughborough (*Mathematics*)
Miss J C Kane, MA Edinburgh (*J5 Teacher*)
Mrs M L Osborne, BEd South Africa (*Support for Learning, ESOL*)
S R Thompson, MA Edinburgh (*History*)
Miss K A Tully, BSc, MPhil Edinburgh (*Biology, PSHE**)
N Lundy, BA USA (*Tennis Academy Coach*)
J L Boyd, BA Durham (*History, †Rogerson*)
Ms G Cunningham, BA Stirling (*English*)
S M Dennis, BMus Edinburgh (*Music**)
A M Roache, BSc St Andrews (*Physics*)
E Sharp, BSpLS Waikato (*PE*)
C Harrison, BSc Napier (*PE*)
Mrs A M Horsey, BA, MA Cambridge (*Classics*)
Miss L K Moyes, BSc Robert Gordon's (*Chemistry*)
N J Mylin, BSc, MSc Indiana (*Mathematics, Science, †Pringle*)
R H Allison, MA St Andrews, BPhil Oxford (*Classics*)
J Timms, MA Edinburgh (*English*)
D Yeaman, MChem Edinburgh (*Chemistry*)
Ms J Wyvill, BA Ontario (*Geography*)

Accounts:
D G Smith, BCom, CA (*Bursar*)
Mrs C McIntosh (*Assistant Bursar, Finance*)
C Spittal, MA Heriot Watt, CA (*Finance Manager*)
Miss A C Killin, MA Glasgow (*Accounts Assistant*)

Administration:
Mrs S M Dow (*Headmaster's PA*)
Mrs V C A M Birchmore (*AMT Secretary*)
Ms C L Hall (*Deputy Head's Secretary*)
Mrs G B Gibson (*Receptionist*)
Ms M Linden (*Administration Assistant*)

Development:
Ms J Robertson, BA Strathclyde (*Alumni/Development*)
Miss K Gall, MSc Edinburgh, MA Edinburgh (*Alumni/Development Assistant*)

Admissions:
Mrs C A Rickard, BA London, MSc Napier (*Director of Admissions*)
Mrs K Wilson (*Admissions Assistant*)

Departmental Technical Assistants:
Mrs L Scott (*Chief Laboratory Technician*)
Mrs M Carnie (*Laboratory Technician*)
A R Ross (*Laboratory Technician*)
A C MacNeill (*IT Technician*)
C A Brown, BSc Heriot-Watt (*IT Support Officer*)
N P Burt (*Design & Technology Technician*)

GAP Graduates and Assistants:
Vladimir Snurenco, Dimitrie Cantemir Lyceum, Chisinau
Jan Reyneke, Auckland University of Technology
Amber Grogran, University of Auckland

Marketing:
Mrs T I Gray, BA Napier, ChDipM (*Communications Manager*)
Mrs L Melo da Silva, BA Strathclyde (*Marketing Assistant*)

Medical Staff:
Dr T McMillan, MB, ChB, MRCGP, DRCOG (*Medical Officer*)
Dr D A Reid, BSc, MB, ChB, MRCGP, DipSEM (*Medical Officer*)
Mrs K J Jones, RGN, RM, HV (*Nursing Sister*)
Mrs J N Fisher, RGN (*Nursing Sister*)
Mrs F G McKenzie, DN, DipDHE (*Health Assistant*)

Support Staff:
Mrs F Blair, BA, BSc, MBACP (*School Counsellor*)
Mrs P Wearmouth, Dip PE (*Pringle Housemother*)
Mrs Kupisz (*Pringle Assistant*)
Mrs F Morris (*Chalmers Housemother*)
Mrs M T Cordingley, BA (*Exchange Shop Manager*)
Mrs L Millard (*Bookstore Manager*)
S Capaldi (*Basketball Coach*)
J Hay (*Squash Coach*)
Mrs S Legget (*Swimming Team Assistant*)
T Catlin (*Master in Charge of Transport*)
J Wanstall (*Minibus Driver*)

Visiting Instrumental Music Teachers:
R Baccivius (*Cello*)
Mrs E Beeston (*Violin*)
Ms M C Bell (*Oboe, Clarinet*)
Ms R Cohen (*Music*)
A McGrattan (*Brass*)
A Mitchell (*Guitar, Bass Guitar*)
Mrs K M Nicholls (*Piano*)
C Macgregor (*Percussion*)
J Walker (*Drumming*)
T Speirs (*Piping*)
S Rennard (*Woodwind*)
B Davidson (*Piano*)
B Donaldson (*Piping*)
Ms C Heaney (*Brass*)
Ms S MacLeod (*Singing*)

Visiting Language Teachers:
Mrs J L McKinlay, MA Birmingham (*ESOL Consultant*)
Mrs R Nazipova-Petherick, Omsk (*Russian*)
Ms CA Tsai (*Mandarin*)
Miss M Suzuki (*Japanese*)

Chaplaincy Team:
N G D Blair (*Leader of the Chaplaincy Team*)
K J A Anderson (*Assistant Chaplain*)
P K Rossiter

There are 476 boys in the School, of whom 314 are boarders.

Admission. The normal ages of entry are 8–14 and 16, though from time to time there may be vacancies at other ages. Entry at 8–12 is by entrance assessment, interview and current school report; entry at 13 by the Common Entrance or Merchiston entrance examinations and current school report. Entry at 14 is by Merchiston entrance examinations. Entry to the Sixth Form at 16 depends on a successful showing in the GCSE or Standard Grades as well as on interview and a school report. There are approximately 160 pupils in the Sixth Form. Entry is possible in all three terms where vacancies permit.

A prospectus and further details may be obtained from the Director of Admissions. Prospective parents are encouraged to visit the School. Information is also found on our website: www.merchiston.co.uk.

Courses of study. In the Lower School the curriculum comprises English, English Literature, Mathematics, Biology, Chemistry, Physics, History, Government and Politics, Classical Civilization, French, Latin, German, Spanish, Mandarin, Geography, Religious Studies, Art and Design, Music, PE, Electronics, Design and Technology, and Information Technology.

In the Middle School a 2-year course leading to the GCSE is followed, consisting of a core curriculum: English, English Literature, Mathematics, a foreign language (French, German, Spanish, Mandarin), IGCSE Biology, Chemistry and Physics, and a wide range of option subjects, including History, a second foreign language, Electronics, Information Technology, Geography, Latin, Religious Studies (Philosophy and Ethics), Art and Design, Design and Technology, and Music. Most boys take 10 subjects.

In the Lower Sixth most boys study 4 subjects at AS Level. In the Upper Sixth, boys study generally 3 subjects to A2. The A Levels include English Literature, Mathematics, Further Mathematics, Biology, Chemistry, Physics, French, German, Spanish, History, Geography, Economics, Government and Politics, Classical Civilisation, Religious Studies, PE, Information Technology, Latin, Design and Technology, Electronics (AS only) and Art. Other languages at A Level (including Classical Greek, Italian and Russian) are available on request. In addition to his main subjects, each boy follows a General Studies course offering Modern Language conversation classes, Moral and Social Studies and Careers Guidance. Classes are small throughout the School, and all subjects are set by ability. The School prepares boys for entry to Oxford and Cambridge.

The School makes provision for specialist ESOL teaching for International students including an opportunity to study GCSE English in the Upper Sixth year.

In 2010 the A Level A–B pass rate was 80% with 82% of pupils gaining entry to their first choice and 93% gaining entry to their first or second choice of University. The School was also named The Sunday Times Scottish Independent Secondary School of the Year for 2009.

Learning Support Provision. Able boys with learning difficulties, including dyslexia, enjoy successful careers at Merchiston. Our aim is to enhance self-esteem through genuine praise. We encourage each pupil to find success in his area of strength, whether inside or outside the classroom. The objective is that all pupils have access to a wide and varied curriculum, and that as a result each discovers his own personal strengths and talents, and enjoys the resulting success. All are expected to follow mainstream GCSE courses.

Houses. Each of the boarding houses caters for a particular age group and the atmosphere and activities are tailored accordingly. In January 2009, the new Sixth Form boarding house opened offering 126 en-suite bedrooms, with modern kitchens, a multi-gym and open plan social spaces with stunning views of Edinburgh and Fife. The Housemaster and his House Tutors pay special attention to the care of the individual and to the development of both his studies and interests.

Day boys. The life of day boys is fully integrated with that of the boarders.

Games. The principal games are rugby, played in the Autumn and Lent Terms, and in the Summer Term cricket and athletics. In 2011 Merchiston launched The Golf Academy at Merchiston, which is based both at the School's 100-acre campus and also at nearby Kings Acre Golf Course where coaching, practice and tutorial work take place. Launched in 2007 The Tennis Academy provides specialised coaching and a full training and sports science programme. There is a large indoor heated swimming pool and a sports hall, and there are good facilities for other sports including tennis, football, squash, fives, shooting, sailing, skiing, basketball, fencing, golf, badminton, hockey and curling.

Music. Music plays an important part in the life of the School. Tuition is available in all keyboard and orchestral instruments; currently about fifty per cent of the School are learning a musical instrument, and two choirs flourish. There is also a School orchestra, a close harmony group, a jazz band and two pipe bands. The choir and instrumentalists frequently go on tour, eg to the USA, the Far East, and Europe.

Drama. There is at least one major play production a term jointly staged with our sister school(s), as well as frequent House plays or drama workshop productions in a well-equipped, purpose-built theatre.

Art, Craft, Design and Technology, and Ceramics. The art and design centre offers scope both within the curriculum and in the pupil's free time for painting, pottery, metalwork, woodwork and design work. Courses in Computing and Electronics are also available both within the curriculum or in free time.

Societies. There is a wide variety of clubs including chess, debating and electronics. Visits to theatres, concerts and exhibitions are a frequent part of a boy's life at Merchiston. The Enlightened Curriculum uses Edinburgh as a prime resource for cultural experiences for all age groups.

CCF. All boys join the CCF for a period of three terms, after which point participation is voluntary. This includes outward bound activities such as climbing, hillwalking, canoeing and camping. All senior boys at Merchiston also undertake a Bronze Duke of Edinburgh's Award expedition, with participation at Silver and Gold level on a purely voluntary basis.

The School is also very active in community service work.

Girls. The School does not take girls but has a special relationship as brother/sister school with St George's School for Girls and Kilgraston School in Perthshire. This includes joint expeditions, concerts, tours, seminars, debating, drama, social events and study courses. Merchiston operates a joint fees scheme with St George's School for Girls, Edinburgh; Kilgraston School, Perth and Queen Margaret's School, York.

Careers advice. An expert careers adviser supplements the advice of the Academic Management Team, Housemasters and Academic Tutors. In the LVI year, pupils attend timetabled lessons in Careers as part of the General Studies Programme of the Sixth Form, where they are also encouraged to take a Work Experience placement and to visit local universities in the month of June. When a pupil starts the Fifth Form year they are enrolled in ISCO's Futurewise and sit their Profile Aptitude test. ISCO provides all pupils enrolled with expert Careers advice until the age of 23. There is an annual HE & Careers Fair to which other local schools are invited. A designated careers hub is being developed in the new Laidlaw House.

Links with parents. There are regular parent/staff meetings and parents are fully briefed and consulted with regard to all academic and career decisions. There is also a parents' forum, which holds regular meetings.

Health. There is a medical centre in the charge of the School Nursing Sisters and the School Doctor visits regularly.

Fees per term (2011-2012). Junior School: Boarders £5,495, Day boys £3,875; Forms 2 and 3 Boarders £6,395, Day boys £4,525. Senior School: Forms 4 and above Boarders £8,585, Day boys £6,250.

Sibling, Forces, Clergy and Teaching Profession fee reductions are available.

Scholarships. (*See Scholarship Entries section.*) Ages from 10+ up to 16+, with an emphasis on 13+ entry from Prep Schools. The main categories are Academic, Sport, All-Rounder and Music (including Piping Exhibition). Design & Technology and Art Scholarships are available from 13+. International Scholarships include European, Kenyan and Hong Kong. Merchiston also supports the HMC Projects in Eastern and Central Europe Scholarship scheme. The Community Scholarship (EH postcode only) and Laidlaw Scholarship (for pupils who would otherwise not be able to attend Merchiston) carry a concession in the form of means-tested financial assistance. Other Scholarships bestow honour on the recipient throughout his school career. Other means-tested assistance is available to assist families demonstrating financial need. Further details can be obtained from the Director of Admissions.

Old boys. The Secretary of The Merchistonian Club, c/o the School. Former pupils include: The Rt Hon Lord John MacGregor, MP; Sir Peter Burt, former Chief Executive, Bank of Scotland; John Jeffrey, OBE (ex Scotland XV and British Lions); The Rt Hon Lord Kenneth Osborne PC, longest-serving judge of the current Scottish bench; Air Marshal Sir John Baird, Surgeon General of the British Armed Forces between 1997 and 2000.

Charitable status. Merchiston Castle School is a Registered Charity, number SC016580. It aims to give each boy in his way the capacity and confidence to live in an uncertain world and to make that life as rich as possible; more specifically to encourage him to work hard and to take pride in achievement, to think independently, to face up to challenges, to accept responsibility, to show concern for others and to develop wider skills and interests.

Mill Hill School

The Ridgeway, Mill Hill, London NW7 1QS
Tel: 020 8959 1221 (Admissions)
Fax: 020 8906 2614
e-mail: registrations@millhill.org.uk
website: www.millhill.org.uk

Court of Governors:

Chairman: Prof M R E Proctor, ScD, FRS
Deputy Chairman: Dr R G Chapman, BSc, MB BS, FRCGP

Prof J E Banatvala, CBE, MA, MD, FRCP, FRCPath, FMedSci
A L Brooke, BA, MBA
Dr A P Craig, MBBS, DRCOG
D J Dickinson, DipQS, MRICS
Mrs C G Erskine-Murray, BA
D Harris, BSc, FCA
Miss R E Jackson, LLB Hons, AKC, QC
G Nosworthy
W Skinner, MA
R L Tray, BA Hons, MA Cantab, MBA
A W Welch, BA, MA Oxon
Mrs P H Wilkes, BEd, FRSA
M T Wilson, BSc Hons

Clerk to the Court: Dr R L Axworthy, BA, PhD

Headmaster: Dr D A Luckett, BA, DPhil, FRSA

† *Housemaster/Housemistress*

Deputy Head (Pastoral): Mrs J Sanchez, BSc (*also Geography*)
Deputy Head (Academic): A C Gaylor, BA (*also Mathematics*)
Deputy Head (External Relations): P J P McDonough, MA, ACP (*also History*)

Assistant Head (Pastoral): N J Gregory, BA (*also French & Spanish*)
Assistant Head (Academic): Mrs M Atkins, BSc (*also Biology*)
Director of Boarding: †Miss L J Farrant, BA (*also English*)

Bursar: B D Fraser, BsBA, MBA

Chaplain: Revd Dr R J Warden, BA, MTh, DMin

Assistant Teachers:

Art & Design:
A D Ross, MA (*Head of Art*)
N G Cheeseman, BA
Miss V C Dempster, MA

Business Education:
Miss L H Sharples, BA (*Head of Business Education & Director of Sixth Form*)
S Ali, BA
Mrs V G Miner, MSc
M S Smith, BA

Classics:
A R Homer, BA (*Head of Classics*)
†S T Plummer, BA

Design Technology:
H Barnes, BA (*Head of Design Technology*)
†Ms B D Banks, BEd

English & Drama:
R W Searby, BA (*Head of English*)
D S Proudlock, BA (*Head of Drama*)
Ms E M Coyle, MA (*Head of EAL*)
†D T Bingham, BA
Mrs S Isaacs, BEd
Mrs E Kaplan, BA
J M Lewis, MA (*Director of Academic Administration*)
Mrs S Stagg, LLB
Miss L Sutherland, MA
Miss T T Wijesinghe, BA
Mrs E E Worsdale, BA

Geography:
W R Montgomery, BSc (*Head of Geography*)
†N R Hodgson, MA
D R Woodrow, BA (*also Director of Sport and Activities Coordinator*)

History & Politics:
M Dickinson, MA (*Head of History*)
Mrs R E Bradley, BA
Miss J F Duncan, BA
J D Rees, BA, AKC
Miss A L Roper

Information Technology:
M J Northen, BA (*Head of IT*)
M E Jennings, BSc
Ms P A Newsome, BSc

Mathematics:
K P Bulman, BSc (*Head of Mathematics*)
R P Cross, BSc, CMath, MIMA
G Docherty, BSc
P J Kwok, BEng
A H Slade, BA
Ms E Stewart, BA
T Trhlik, BSc

Modern Languages:
M S V Bardou, BA, (*Head of Modern Languages & Spanish*)
Mrs B K Hazeldine, MA (*Head of German*)
C S Lowe, BA, MEd (*Acting Head of French*)
Miss V S S David, Maîtrise d'Anglais
Miss A C Ellerington, BA
†P R Lawson, MA
Mrs S Schildnecht-Birch, BA
Mr A Mansilla, BA

Music:
N A Williams, MA
M P Kemp, BMus, ARCO, ARCM
K Kyle, BMus Hons, LRAM, PGDipRam (*Head of Vocal Studies*)

Visiting Instrumental Teachers:
J Bradford, BA, BMus, LGSM, LLCM, ALCM, AdvDip KIB, Cert Berklee (*guitars*)
A Cucchiara, GRNCM (*violin*)
J Fleeman, GCLCM, AdvCert GSMD (*percussion*)
O Gledhill, MA Mtpp, ARCM (*violoncello*)
Miss P Goss, BA PGDip (*voice*)
D Grant, LAMI (*guitar*)
P Jaekel, GRSM, LRAM, ARCO (*piano*)
Mrs H Kearns, BA Hons, LTCL (*pianoforte*), LTCL (*flute, piano*)
L Kelly, ALCM, LTCL (*trumpet*)
Mrs H Kyle, BMus Hons, LRAM, PGdipMus/Opera (*voice*)
A Martin, AGSM (*percussion*)
Miss C Overbury, BA Oxon, PGDip (*flute*)

A Poole, BSc (*double bass, guitar*)
Miss J Tate, BA Mus, Grad RNCM (*voice*)

Physical Education:
A T Morton, BSc, MEd (*Head of PE*)
†J D Cuff, BA, MSc
†Miss S H Reynolds, BSc (*Head of Girls Games*)
D M Halford, PGA (*Director of Golf*)
Mrs R M Hyslop, BEd (*also Head of PSHRE*)

Sciences:
J A Barron, BSc, MA (*Head of Chemistry*)
Miss A Bignell, BSc, MA (*Head of Science & Biology*)
J M Murphy, BSc (*Acting Head of Sixth Form Physics*)
L J Stubbles, MSci (*Acting Head of Lower School Physics*)
Dr E J M Evesham, BSc, PhD, CBiol, FIBiol
Mrs K A Gibbon, MSci
†D S Hughes, BSc
Dr S Radojevic, BSc, PhD
G N Saint, BSc
P H Thonemann, MA, MPhil (*also Head of Complementary Studies*)
†G M Turner, BSc
J G W Watson, BSc
C M G Watterson, BEng, MSci

Learning Support:
Miss L N Silverman, BA, Dip SpLD (*Head of Learning Support*)
Miss A Fryatt, BEd, MA
Mrs J R Herbert, BA

Head of Careers:
L J Stubbles, MSci

Officer Commanding CCF: (*to be appointed*)

Medical Officer: Dr S C Hall

Nurse:
Miss A Watford, RGN (*Nurse Manager*)
Ms C Elliott, RGN
Mrs Jane Simpson, RGN

Belmont, Mill Hill Preparatory School
The Ridgeway, Mill Hill, London NW7 4ED
Tel: 020 8906 7270; Fax: 020 8906 3519
e-mail: office@belmontschool.com
website: www.belmontschool.com

Head: Mrs L C Duncan, BSc, PGCE

Deputy Head (Curriculum): Mrs R Alford, BEd
Deputy Head (Pastoral): L Roberts, MA, PGCE
Head of Upper School: J Pym, MA, PGCE
Head of Lower School: Mrs H Hardy, BA (*Acting*)
Director of Activities: J Fleet, BSc, PGCE

Heads of Department:
J McNulty, BA, PGCE (*Art*)
J Clement, BA, PGCE (*Classics*)
Mrs V McSween, BEd (*Design Technology*)
M Russo, BA, DipEd (*English*)
Mrs C McRill, BA, PGCE (*French*)
A Hayward, BSc, PGCE (*Geography*)
R S Pace, MA, MAT (*History*)
Mrs A Gritz, BSc, QTS (*ICT*)
Mrs G Perrin, BA, PGCE (*Music*)
Miss J Harrison, BSc, PGCE (*Mathematics*)
Mr P Symes, BSc, PGCE (*Boys Games*)
Miss J Southam, BSc, PGCE (*Girls Games*)
Mrs H Lawson, BA, PGCE (*RE, PSE*)
Mrs J Fisher, BSc, PGCE (*Science*)
J Buoy, BEd (*Educational Visits Coordinator*)
Miss K Hockley, BA, PGCE

Subject Teachers:
Mrs B Ahmed, BA, MA (*French*)
J Buoy, BEd (*Mathematics, Games*)

A Haigh, BSc, PGCE (*Science/Games*)
J Ince, BA, PGCE (*English*)
J Moon, BA (*Mathematics*)
Miss L Olsson, BA (*English*)
Mrs L Pym, BA (*Girls Games*)
Mrs S Roberts, BA, PGCE (*Mathematics*)
Mrs L Russo, BA (*French*)
A Warden, BA QTS (*DT/Maths/Games*)
A Warren, GTCL (*Music*)

Lower School Tutors:
R Baker, BEd
Mrs N Harris, BSc, PGCE, Dip IT
G Lavelle, BA, PGCE
Miss S Magalo, BA, PGCE
Mrs A Passer, BA, PGCE
Mrs E Pendred, BA, PGCE
Mrs K Pople, BA, PGCE
Miss M Sevani, MA
Mrs M Slade, BEd
Ms R Sutherns, MA SESI
Miss J Swailes, BA, MuEd
A Wright, BEd

Special Needs Coordinator: Mrs B Russo, BA, PGCE

Support Teachers:
Mrs A Caldwell BSc
Mrs S Lewin, RSA Dip SpLD
Mrs M Munro BA, PGCE
Mrs E Shepherd, CertEd, RSA Dip SpLD, AMBDA
Mrs S Sulkin
Mrs S Wiltshire

School Counsellor: S Kohen, BA
Librarian: Mrs L Mason, BA, MCLIP
School Nurse: Mrs R McGinness RGN
ICT Technician: Dr J White, PhD, BSc
Laboratory Technician: Mrs P Daly
Head's PA: Mrs G Ellen
School Secretary and Marketing: Mrs J Armstrong
School Secretary: Mrs N McDavid
Registrar: Mrs I Manfredi

Grimsdell, Mill Hill Pre-Preparatory School
Winterstoke House, Wills Grove, Mill Hill,
London NW7 1QR
Tel: 020 8959 6884; Fax: 020 8959 4626
e-mail: office@grimsdell.org.uk
website: www.grimsdell.org.uk

Head: Mrs P E R Bennett-Mills, CertEd

Deputy Head: K Dobson, BA Hons (*also Pastoral, Health & Safety and Assessment Coordinator*)
Director of Studies: Mrs T Weeks, BA Hons, PGCE (*Year 2 Coordinator; English Coordinator*)

Assistant Staff:
Mrs J Baddick, BSc Hons, PGCE
Mrs J Barnett, BA Hons, PGCE (*RE Coordinator*)
Mrs S Broom, HNC (*Nursery Teacher, Art & Display Coordinator*)
Mrs A Cotsen, BEd (*Learning Support*)
Mrs P Fraser, CertEd (*History Coordinator*)
Mrs M Gold, DCE PrimEd (*SENCO*)
Mrs J Golden, BMus Hons, PGCE (*Year 1 Coordinator, ICT Coordinator*)
Miss C Holliday, BA (*Head of Early Years*)
Mrs B Myburgh, BPrimEd SA (*Science Coordinator*)
Miss H Patel, BA Hons, PGCE (*Geography Coordinator*)
Mrs F Smith, BSc Hons, PGCE (*Maths Coordinator*)
Ms V Suarez-Rivas, BEd Hons, PGCE (*PE Coordinator*)
Miss C Teng, MA Music (*Music Coordinator*)
Mrs J Wallace (*PHSE and Recycling Coordinator*)

School Administrator: Mrs J Clarke
Assistant Administrator: Mrs S Webb

Mill Hill was founded by Samuel Favell (1760–1830) and Revd John Pye Smith (1774–1851) as a grammar school for the sons of Protestant dissenters and opened in 1807. The School's motto, *et virtulem et musas* ('both virtue and learning') continues to characterise the aims of the School. Indeed in September 1997 the School became fully co-educational.

Location. The School is part of Mill Hill village and is situated in a conservation area, on the borders of Hertfordshire and Middlesex, approximately 12 miles from the centre of London. Set in 120 acres of parkland originally formed by the famous botanist Peter Collinson, the grounds provide a spacious setting for the academic buildings, boarding and day houses and offer extensive facilities for sports and activities.

Buildings. Mill Hill combines a rich traditional heritage with modern educational facilities. The present School was designed by Sir William Tite, architect of the Royal Exchange and opened in 1826. Since the late 19th century numerous buildings have been added, including the Chapel, Library, Assembly Hall, Music School and Science Block. Other additions include the Art and Design Technology Centre, a modern Sports Hall, a Sixth Form Centre, the Piper library and learning resources centre, a multimedia language centre, two networked IT suites, a music technology centre including a hard disk recording studio, a theatre, a studio theatre, an indoor swimming pool and 3 Eton Fives Courts.

As well as these facilities, a brand new academic teaching block, The Favell Building, was opened in 2007. This houses 25 new classrooms with libraries, seminar rooms, and departmental offices for the Geography, History, Business Education, Classics, Religious Education and the Modern Foreign Languages departments.

Houses. There are 680 pupils in the School (470 boys, 210 girls in 2011) of whom around 140 are boarders. There are three boarding Houses and seven day Houses. Day pupils take a full part in the activities of the School.

Admission. Application may be made as early as parents wish. The majority of boys and girls enter at the age of 13. Candidates are selected on the basis of interviews, examination (Maths, English, Science, French and Latin as an optional paper) and a Head's confidential reference. Scholarship candidates are identified through the entrance tests and are called back for interviews on the basis of their scores. Single subject awards may be made. Awards are also made for Music, Drama, Sports and Design Technology.

There are two other methods of entry:
(a) A limited number of places are available at 14+. Candidates are selected on the basis of interview, performance in the 14+ Entrance Examination (English, Maths, Science and French) and a Head's confidential reference.
(b) Sixth Form Entry: Admission to the Sixth Form is open to both boys and girls, from the UK and abroad. Entry requirements are 5 GCSE passes, at least 2 at Grade A plus 3 at Grade B, together with at least C grades in Mathematics and English, or equivalent qualifications for overseas pupils. More detailed entry requirements for specific AS courses are given in the School's Sixth Form Curriculum Guide. Candidates unable to offer the number of subjects required (e.g. some overseas candidates) will be considered on their individual academic merit.

Selection is by interview at the School (there are no examinations) and by reference from the candidate's present school. Offers made are conditional on meeting the entry requirements detailed above. International candidates may be asked to complete entry tests in the subjects they wish to study in the Sixth Form. All students with English as a second language will be asked to sit an EAL paper. Scholarships are awarded on the basis of examinations and interviews in January.

Pastoral Care. Pastoral care is organised by House and individual House identities are a significant feature of Mill Hill. All of the Houses (including day houses) have their own designated space including recreational facilities and areas for relaxation and/or study. In the School's most recent full ISI Inspection, the overall quality of pastoral care was rated as *Outstanding* and genuine pride is taken in maintaining and developing this aspect as a real strength of the School as a whole.

A full Ofsted Inspection of boarding provision in Summer 2010 described the school as *good ... with outstanding features* and made mention of how boarding *is central to the school's operations* and of how *facilities are comfortable and welcoming*. One of the areas rated as *Outstanding* was *Helping children achieve well and enjoy what they do*.

One of the principal features of the Mill Hill approach to pastoral care is the continuity of support and involvement offered by Housemasters/mistresses throughout a pupil's five years at Mill Hill, aided by Tutors who work within a House dealing with day-to-day matters for specific year groups.

Another particularly notable element of Mill Hill's pastoral care is the wide range of dynamic and fully involved pupil councils covering areas as diverse as anti-bullying and mentoring, food, boarding, Fourth Form (new Year 9 pupils), charity, spirituality, eco issues and Sixth Form-specific issues. A wide range of pupil councils meet regularly and focus on each of these areas, in addition to a Full School Council.

Curriculum. The School's academic curriculum is broad, flexible and forward-looking and is designed to encourage among pupils intellectual curiosity, sound learning and a spirit of enquiry in the pursuit of academic excellence. It seeks to enable pupils to acquire core knowledge and skills in English, Mathematics, Science and a modern foreign language and, in addition, to develop their own particular academic interests. It also incorporates a full programme of personal, social and health education, appropriate guidance and information for pupils on subject choices, higher education and careers.

Through these aims the School seeks to ensure that each pupil is able to be healthy, stay safe, enjoy and experience achievement, make a positive contribution to the community and achieve economic well-being.

Organisation of the Curriculum. Pupils normally enter the School at 13+ (Year 9). There are normally 6 or 7 sets in each of Years 9, 10 and 11. The Year 9 curriculum aims to consolidate what has been learned in the previous two years, to enable pupils to experience a very wide range of subjects (around 15) and to maintain pace and progression as they prepare for their GCSE courses.

When choosing their GCSE option subjects pupils are encouraged to select a combination of subjects which maintain a sensible breadth of study. This will vary between pupils and is balanced against each pupil's relative strengths in his/her subjects. Greater emphasis is given to each pupil choosing option subjects which they enjoy and in which they are likely to do well, than mere breadth for its own sake. In Years 10 and 11 English, Mathematics, Science and a Modern Foreign Language (either French or Spanish are core examination courses, in addition to PE and Games; pupils also choose three GCSE option subjects from Art and Design, Design Technology, Drama, Geography, German, History, Information and Communication Technology (ICT), Music, Physical Education, Religious Studies and Spanish.

The **Sixth Form Curriculum** offers a wide and flexible choice of A Level courses. It aims to encourage and develop personal skills of study, research and thought and to encourage pupils to consider and discuss issues relevant to them as they move towards adulthood and participation in the full range in rights and responsibilities as citizens.

In the **Lower Sixth** pupils normally take four AS courses. In addition they follow non-examined courses Personal, Social, Health and Religious Education and in Complementary Studies. The most able pupils may take an additional

AS course where the timetable can be arranged to make this possible. For a small number of pupils, a programme of three, rather than, four AS courses is appropriate. Guidance is given to pupils and their parents about making AS subject choices; this includes an external academic/careers guidance test report and interview, discussions with tutors and Housemasters/ mistresses. Detailed information on the Lower Sixth Form curriculum is set out in the guide *Moving Into the Sixth Form*, a copy of which is given to each Fifth Form pupil and their parents/guardian in the Spring Term of the Fifth Form and to parents of all external Sixth Form applicants.

The PSHRE programme covers both years of the Sixth Form and encourages pupils to participate in discussion, to research information, to present short talks, to contribute to a debate and to become involved in various activities across the school curriculum. The programme is modular, and the modules include: sex and relationships, drugs, alcohol and tobacco, presentation skills, personal financial management skills, the environment, and moral values and their relationship with faith and belief. These modules are combined with whole year group presentations and guidance to pupils and parents/guardians on areas such as Higher Education, Gap Year opportunities, and driver education.

In the Complementary Studies Programme pupils have the opportunity to choose from a wide range of short, non-examined, courses which cover aspects of Politics, Science, and the Arts. The purpose of the programme is to encourage independent thought and study which is not related to, or seen as a means to, examination success, and to encourage breadth of study (e.g. those taking predominantly maths/science AS courses will take some arts/social science *units* in Complementary Studies, and *vice versa*).

In the **Upper Sixth** most pupils take three A2 courses plus a weekly timetabled session of Personal, Social, Health and Religious Education. In the Upper Sixth year private study lessons are unsupervised, and pupils may work in House, in the Piper Library or in departmental study areas (which are available in most departments).

Provision for Pupils with Special Educational Needs (SEN) and Learning Difficulties and/or Disabilities (LDD). The School provides those pupils who have a statement of educational need or a learning difficulty or disability support to meet their requirements and a suitably adapted curriculum, where this is appropriate. The Learning Support department plays a key role in this work, seeking to identify, through screening and ongoing monitoring, the particular needs of individual pupils and putting in place strategies (and, where necessary, additional assistance) designed to help them fulfil their potential. Pupils who have a Special Educational Need or Learning Difficulty and/or Disability may have their curriculum modified to take account of their particular needs, as appropriate. Where a pupil has a statement of special educational needs, the requirements of the statement are closely followed in order to ensure that the School provides an effective and accessible educational experience. The progress of all pupils on the School's Learning Support Register is regularly reviewed and support is amended as appropriate.

Academic and Careers Guidance. Through the tutor system, presentations and information evenings, pupils are helped to make the best possible choices of GCSE, AS and A level courses and to make well informed and appropriate higher education choices. In the Sixth Form the School arranges visits to universities as well as presentations, workshops and information evenings. The School has an active Careers Department which provides information and advice on possible future careers paths. Careers Education is included within the School's Personal, Social, Health and Religious Education programme and careers interviews are arranged for pupils in the Fifth Form and in the Lower Sixth, and also on request for other pupils.

Support for pupils with English as an Additional Language. For pupils whose first language is not English, class or individual tuition in EAL is provided as appropriate, to enable them to enjoy all of the social and cultural aspects of life at the School. Some EAL pupils follow a modified curriculum in order to accommodate their needs, where this is appropriate. Extra, individual, EAL tuition in addition to class lessons can be arranged, if required.

Modern Languages. Mill Hill places emphasis on proficiency in the use of Modern Languages in a vocational context. Full use is made of satellite television and other audiovisual and ICT resources including two state-of-the-art digital language laboratories. Irrespective of Sixth Form specialisation, many choose to take AS levels in French, German and Spanish. Thus a good number of pupils, including Mathematicians and Scientists are competent in their use of a foreign language by the time they leave school. All pupils studying French, German or Spanish are encouraged and helped to spend extended study time abroad under the *European Initiative*.

The European Initiative. One of the distinctive features of the Mill Hill School Foundation is that it provides pupils with an education that is firmly set within a contemporary European context. Over the last 40 years the School has pioneered a number of initiatives, such as seminars, exchange visits, work and GAP year placements in Europe. The range of exchange visits is well established: first year pupils have the opportunity to visit France on the Rouen exchange (which has been unbroken for over 40 years), Germany or Spain for a five-day stay in Leipzig and Valencia respectively. In 1997 the European Initiative was recognised by the Central Bureau and Council of Europe by the granting of the European Curriculum Award.

Up to 25 students from the European Continent spend one or two years at Mill Hill. The School also participates in an annual residential seminar week, where pupils and staff from European schools live and learn with Millhillians. Pupils can expect therefore to have first-hand experience of living and working with Europeans together with opportunities to gain qualifications which will enhance a European-based career.

Art, Drama and Music. The Creative Arts have a long and successful tradition at Mill Hill and have increasing become part of the academic curriculum as well as the extracurricular programme. In addition to achieving excellent results in public examinations, there are a substantial and varied programme of extra-curricular activities in these subjects. The Art Department offers facilities and expertise for pupils to develop their interest and skills in painting and drawing, alternative media, film, illustration, multimedia, photography (including digital photography), printmaking, sculpture, textiles, theatre design and video.

In addition to the very extensive range and number of drama performances relating to examination courses there is a biennial inter-House Drama festival, which alternates with the biennial inter-House Music Festival), both of which attract a high level of pupil participation. There is also a biannual programme of non-exam related Drama performances, ranging from Shakespeare to musicals. The School's musical ensembles include an orchestra, wind band, string ensemble, jazz group, full choir, Chapel choir, girls' choir, boys' *a capella* ensemble, and numerous ad hoc pupil bands and chamber ensembles. Individual tuition in most instruments and in singing is available from high quality specialist teachers. There is an extensive programme of concerts and recitals throughout the year, some of which include recitals by professional performers.

Recent tours have included drama performances at the Edinburgh Festival and choir tours to New York and to Paris.

Sport. Every pupil, regardless of physical ability, is encouraged to participate in both individual sports and team games. The major sports for boys are Rugby, Hockey and Cricket and for girls are Hockey, Netball and Tennis. Other opportunities include Athletics, Basketball, Cross-country, Eton Fives, Golf, Horse Riding, Sailing, Skiing, Soccer, Swimming and use of the recently refurbished Fitness Suite. Competition and excellence are valued and the level of professional coaching skills is exceptional. The school has a 25 metre indoor swimming pool, 3 Eton Fives Courts, shooting range, all-weather pitch and Sports Hall, with a range of indoor sports facilities. Mill Hill is the home to the London Golf Academy. In 2011 new golf facilities including a short course facility and new indoor golf coaching facilities were opened. There are strong links with Saracens RFC and special bursaries are available in the Sixth Form for gifted rugby and hockey players. Pupils are given the opportunity of participating in overseas sports tours which have included countries, such as Barbados, Australia, Fiji, New Zealand, Canada, India, South Africa and Spain for Rugby, Netball, Cricket and Hockey. The tennis and cricket teams also run training camps at the renowned La Manga Complex in Southern Spain. Junior sports teams regularly make less ambitious, but equally valuable tours within the UK and Europe.

Extra-Curricular Activities. First year pupils are introduced to the range of minor sports (as above) and aspects of adventure training. All pupils are also offered a range of other activities such as debating, drama, chess, jewellery making and computing. In Year 10 pupils choose between the CCF (Army, Navy and RAF), a Sports Leaders programme, Young Enterprise and Community Service. In addition, many Societies exist to cater for a variety of out-of-school interests.

Fees per term (2011-2012). £8,739 for Boarders and £5,531 for Day Pupils which includes the games fee and the cost of most textbooks and stationery.

Scholarships and Bursaries. Scholarships, which attract a maximum of 10% fee remission, are available to pupils showing exceptional talent in a variety of areas both in the classroom and on the sports field. In addition to major Awards, there are a number of minor Awards or Exhibitions also on offer. The Headmaster, Deputy Headmaster (External Relations) or the Assistant Registrar are happy to advise parents and feeder schools about any of these Awards.

Bursaries are available for those entrants able to demonstrate a financial need. Parents will be asked to complete a detailed statement of their financial circumstances. Applicants for Bursaries will be selected in the normal way. There is provision for the award of full-fee Bursaries for entrants at all levels. It is possible for bursary funds to be used to top up Scholarship Awards. As with scholarship queries, the Headmaster, Deputy Headmaster (External) or the Assistant Registrar are happy to offer advice.

There are also a number of special scholarships and bursaries for the children of Old Millhillians, Christian Ministers, members of the Armed Forces and the Diplomatic Services.

For further information on both scholarships and bursaries please see the school's website www.millhill.org.uk.

Charitable status. The Mill Hill School Foundation is a Registered Charity, number 1064758. It exists for the education of boys and girls.

Millfield

Street, Somerset BA16 0YD
Tel: 01458 442291
Fax: 01458 447276
e-mail: admissions@millfieldschool.com
website: www.millfieldschool.com

The school was founded in 1935 by R J O Meyer with the philanthropic aim of using its resources to generate places for boys who were gifted but not wealthy. The school became co-educational in 1939. In 1945 Edgarley Hall was acquired and the junior pupils were transferred there. This is now Millfield Prep School. The school expanded through the 50s and 60s offering a more orthodox curriculum, although it was never a 'normal' public school. C R M Atkinson became Headmaster in 1971, and carried out a major building programme that established modern purpose-built facilities throughout the academic and recreational areas of the school, including a prize-winning Library and Resources Centre and a large Fine Arts Centre, completed in 1992, a year after his death. Further improvements to the campus include a purpose-built Mathematics Centre, and 500-seat Theatre and Dining Hall. Nine new boarding houses have been opened since 2003. A Design & Technology building with high-tech equipment was completed in 2005 and a Music School complex housing the 350-seat Johnson Concert Hall was completed in September 2006. New Science laboratories and a Science lecture theatre were completed in September 2009. The main part of the school is surrounded by over 100 acres, which includes an equestrian centre, stabling for 50 horses, a 50m Olympic Swimming Pool and an indoor Tennis Centre.

Governors:

Chair of Governors: Sir J G Reith, KCB, CBE

W J Bushell	M W Roulston, MBE
Dr R Clark	Mrs A Sexton
R J R Clark	M A L Simon
Mrs C Cripps	O Tant
Mrs C V Flood	T M Taylor
C H Hirst	R P Thornton
J H Jackson	R S Trafford
A A Patel	D S Williamson

Clerk to the Governors: M K Suddaby

Headmaster: Craig Considine, MEd

Bursar: M Suddaby, MA, ACA

Deputy Headmaster: R Decamp, BSc, MA, FRSA

Second Deputy: F J Clough, BSc, PhD

Tutor for Admissions: C G Coates, BA, DMS

* Head of Department
† Houseparent

Art, Design & Technology:
*P Maxfield, BA
J C M Clements, BA, MA
Mrs E Drake, BA
Miss C Flohr, BA
D Harper, DipAD
D P Holmes, BA
†Ms S G Key, MFA, BFA
Miss A L Kinch, BSc
S A M Lewis-Williams, BA
Miss N C Ritzaki, BA
R W Smith, BEd
†Mrs J Tait-Harris, BEd
Miss J S Wallace-Mason, BA

Biology:
*Mrs J A Frampton, BSc
Miss P Fazal, BSc
†G J Baily, BSc
†Mrs A E Brade, BSc
J M P Hallows, BSc
K F Hawksworth, BSc
Mrs L McEwen, BSc
Miss A T Reebye, BSc
G T Shayler, BEng
G B Smith, MSc, PhD
Z R Watkins, BSc, PhD

Miss J Weal, BSc
S J Whittle, BSc

Business Studies:
*N E Williams, BA, MPhil
Mrs T A Baughan, BA
J J C Brittain, BComm
Miss A Burnett, BA
N A Chamberlain, BSc
B J McEwen, BA
†M P Mills, MSc, LLB
Mrs M A Nash, MA
†R J Owlett, BA
K Shelver, HDipEd

Chemistry:
*J Hill, BSc, PhD
A Angelosanto, BSc
Miss T Bolt, MSc
C A Hedgcock, MA
E T Jones, BSc
†C J Middleton, BSc, MRSC
†C I Page, BSc
M A Perry, BSc, PhD
M S Woodward, BSc, PhD, MRSC

Computing & IT:
*Mrs S A Etherington,
  BEd, MSc
Mrs S J Bishop, MSc
G R Cottell, BSc
Mrs S J Edwards, BSc
S Landry, BA
E E Williams, MEng

Drama:
*M E Cooper, BA
K Barron, BA
Miss A Howell, BA

*English as an Additional
  Language (EAL)*:
*†R L Orton, MA
S J Dye, MA
†Mrs G S Orton, MSc

Economics:
*N R Driver, BSc
J A Brimacombe, BSc
S A Briston, BA
O M Fernie, BA
P N Reed, BA, MA

English and Media:
*S M MacAlpine, BA, MSc
M Brown, BA
R H I Bullock, BEd
Mrs C Byrne, MA, MEd
S B Cole, BA
Mrs A J Gray, BA
Mrs H Heriz-Smith, BA
J M Hill, BA, MTheol
M D J Lewis, BA
M M Milton, MA
J C Shaw, MA
Mrs S A Skinner, MEd
M A Speyers, MA
D J Trevis, BA, MEd

Geography:
*C Lane, MA
Mrs M J Angelosanto, BA
Miss N J A Batchelder, BA,
  MSc
†P R Cookson, MEd
R Decamp, MA
†T J Greenhill, BSc
T B Kingsford, BA
Mrs N S Lewis-Williams,
  BA
A R Woods, BA

History:
*N A T Eatough, BA
D E Askham, BA
D W Burton, MA, DPhil
D W Carr,BA
†Mrs T J Crouch, BA
M N Howard
P A Kelly, BA
C A Mantell, BA
P S Rolf, BA
Mrs C L Trainor, BA
†J N Whiskerd, BA

Languages:
*Ms C Coutand-Moore
D C T Avis
Miss C Barzana, MA
†J A Bishop, BA
Miss C Bowring, BA
S M Coase, MA
Miss L Douglas

Mrs S M Dye, BA
A S Fraser, MA
†N J Gabb, BEd
Miss S McNee, BA
Miss M Mendez Gallego,
  BA
W R Harper-Holdcroft, MA
Mrs M N Harwood, MA
H Kouidri, MA
Mlle P Rouprich, L-ès-L
†C J Skinner, BA, PhD
C W Turner, BA
Mrs B E Wood, BA
Ms R Zhao, MA

Learning Support Centre:
*Mrs J H Clarke
Mrs K S M Butt
Mrs S-L Cella, BA
Mrs S E Coates, BA
M J Cole-Edwardes, BA
Miss E A Dando, BA
Ms K S Lindsell
R J Mylne, BEd
Mrs H J Ryan
Mrs J A Szymkow, BA

Mathematics:
*Dr C C Fiddes, BA, PhD
Ms T A Allen, BSc
†T P Akhurst, BEd
Mrs H J Bevan, CertEd
Mrs N A Bone, BSc Hons
R I Bradshaw, BSc
Mrs J Brimacombe, BSc
B P Brooks, MA, PhD
A P Deamer, MA, MSc
R J Furlong, BSc, MEd
M G Godfrey, MA
Miss V J Harkness, BEd,
  MA
Mrs N A Jones, BSc
Mrs L A Kelly, MA
†J T Knight, BA
I W Payne
Mrs C Pettingell, BSc
J J Rix, MA
Miss D M Scagell, BSc
Mrs M P Speed, BSc
Dr A Steele, BA
G S B S Thomas, BA
Mrs S Woods, BSc

Music:
*J Jensen, BMus Hons,
  PGCE, Dip RAM
A H Dearden, LTCL,
  GTCL
Dr E M Fraser, MPhil, PhD
C J Hughes, AGSM, MA
M A Rhind-Tutt, ARCM,
  GRSM, MA
L G Sheills, ARCM

Physical Education:
*A J Whatling, BA
†B C Boyd
†R M Ellison, BEd
C D Gange, BSc
†D J Hacker, HND
Miss E L Hadfield, BSc
Mrs G A Heavyside, BEd
G N Jennings, BSc
†J A Mallett, BSc
Mrs S Wheeler, BSc

Mrs L-J White, BSc

Physics:
*S P Houghton, BA
Dr C Bull
J B Allen, BSc
F J Clough, BSc, PhD
K Leonard, BSc
M A Lewis, BSc
R L C Lowndes-Northcott,
  BSc

Houses and Houseparents:

Boarding Houses:
Abbey House: Mr and Mrs J N Whiskerd
Acacia House: Mr and Mrs D J Hacker
Butleigh: Mr and Mrs B C Boyd
Etonhurst: Mr and Mrs T P Akhurst
Holmcroft: Dr and Mrs C J Skinner
Joan's Kitchen: Mr and Mrs M P Mills
Keen's Elm: Mr and Mrs C I Page
Kernick: Mr and Mrs D H Landrock
Kingweston: Mr and Mrs T J Greenhill
Martins: Mr and Mrs N J Gabb
Millfield: Mr and Mrs R J Owlett
Orchards: Mr and Mrs R M Ellison
Portway: Ms S G Key and Mr R Bennett
St Anne's: Mr J T Knight and Dr F Radford
Shapwick: Mr and Mrs J A Mallett
Southfield: Mr and Mrs R L Orton
The Grange: Mrs J Tait-Harris
Walton: Mr and Mrs G J Baily
Warner: Mr and Mrs C J Middleton

Day Houses, Boys:
Great: Mr J A Bishop
Mill: Mr P R Cookson

Day Houses, Girls:
Overleigh: Mrs A E S Brade
The Lakes: Mrs T J Crouch

Coaches:

Athletics:
G N Jennings, UKA Level 2
A Lerwill, Senior Coach – Jumps

Badminton:
F J Furlong, BE Level 2
J Elken, BE Level 3

Basketball:
J Knight, Level 2
C Seeley, Level 3

Chess:
M Turner, MA, Grand Master

Cricket:
R Ellison, ECB Level 3
M R Davis, ECB Level 3, EPP & Academy Coach

Dance:
Mrs J Szymkow
Miss J Peach, ARAD, AISTD, Major Teaching Cert Dir
  (*Ballet*)
Mrs D Court, ARAD (*Ballet*)
Miss G Wright, AISTD (*Dance*)
Miss A Ludford
Miss L Stephens

Fencing:
Prof N Golding, BAF Diploma, South West Coach
Prof S Benney, BAF Advanced and County Coach
G Golding, Maitre

Football:
T Akhurst, UEFA A

C J Ridler, MPhys
E J Sanchez, BSc

Religious Studies:
*Miss L F Jackson, BA
M Day, BA
Revd P C A Harbridge, BA,
  LLB (*Chaplain*)
†D H Landrock, BEd
P G Neeve, BA

L Bond, UEFA B
I Rossiter, UEFA B

Golf:
Miss K Nicholls, PGA/LET member
S Wells, PGA
Miss T Woodyer, PGA

Hockey:
D Hacker, EHB Level 2
C Mantell, EHB Level 2
R Keates, HA Coach Level 2
A Park

Martial Arts:
Miss T Bolt
P Hacker, 4th Dan (*Karate*)
M Benney (*Judo*)

Modern Pentathlon:
A Wilsher, National TASS Coordinator & Assistant Youth
    Coach, Pentathlon GB

Netball:
Mrs C Mitchell, UKCC Level 3

Outdoor Activities:
P Bond (*MLA*)
S P Houghton, ML (*summer*), L3 inland kayak, Local Cave
    Leader
J C Shaw
J J C Brittain (*WGL*)

Polo: R Horne, HPA Instructor

Riding:
Director: D O Anholt, BHSI, HT
Assistant Director: Miss K Fontaine, BSHI
Miss R Jonasson, Certified Trainers Degree Danish
    Equestrian Fed

Rugby:
J A Mallett, RFU Level 4
M Baxter, RFU, Level 1

Skiing: R W Smith, BASI Coach Level 1

Squash:
J Barrington, SRA National Coach, Former Men's World
    Professional Champion
I Thomas, Intermediate Level 3 SRA Coach
S P Burrows, SRA Level 2

Swimming:
Director: J Finck, Australia Gold Licence Coach
E G Dale, International Swimmer and Swimming Coach
Mrs C S Blackwell, National All American Swimmer and
    Swimming Coach
R Tweddle, Senior National Swimmer and Strength and
    Conditioning Coach

Tennis:
Director: A A Simcox, Member of Professional Tennis
    Coaches' Association
Miss J Sinkins, PCA Part 3
P R Thomas, PCA Part 3

Trampolining:
Mrs C Mitchell, Level 4

Triathlon:
M J Brown, BCF Level 2
G J Maw, BTF Level 3

The school is fully co-educational with 760 boys and 460
girls; there are 950 boarders.

Housing. There are 19 single-sex, vertically aged boarding houses situated in or near the school; three lie in surrounding villages. All Houses have Resident Assistants. All
Upper Sixth Formers have their own rooms whilst younger
pupils share either in pairs or fours.

Boarding is best described as full time, but exeat weekends can be taken after sporting commitments, three in the
first term, as well as a fixed weekend and three in the second
and third terms.

Day pupils are grouped into five houses, have their own
base on site, are fully assimilated into school life and may
stay in the evenings to do supervised prep.

The Curriculum. The academic programme is consistent with the broad principles laid down in the National Curriculum pre-16. Thus those moving to Millfield from a wide
range of independent preparatory and maintained secondary
schools should find both common academic ground and
unrivalled choice for GCSE, Vocational Courses and AS/A2
Level. A five-year course in Personal and Social Education
is also included within the curriculum.

All pupils entering Year 9 (at age 13), regardless of ability, study English, Mathematics, three Sciences, at least one
language, Design and Technology, ICT, Geography, History,
Religious Studies, Physical Education, Art and Music. The
pupil teacher ratio is 6.5:1. Pupils have a structured co-curricular programme.

In Years 10 and 11 pupils follow courses leading to
GCSEs in the core subjects of English, Mathematics, Science and a Modern Language. In addition, there is a wide
choice of options: Arabic, Art & Design, Business Studies,
Business & Communications Systems, Computer Studies,
Drama, Economics, Food & Nutrition, French, Geography,
German, Greek, Product Design, History, ICT, Italian, Japanese, Latin, Mandarin, Music, Physical Education, Religious Studies and Spanish. The Learning Support Centre
provides individual support for all pupils in need of this.

At Sixth Form level, a wide range of subjects is on offer
leading to AS and A2 qualifications. These include
Accounting, Art & Design, Biology, Business Studies,
Chemistry, Classical Languages, Computing, Drama, Eco-
nomics, English Literature, French, Further Mathematics,
Geography, German, Government & Politics, History, ICT,
Italian, Latin, Mathematics, Media Studies, Music, Music
Technology, Philosophy, Physical Education, Physics, Prod-
uct Design, Psychology, Religious Studies, Spanish, and
World Development. Also on offer are the vocational
courses of BTEC Business Studies (equivalent to a two A
Level course), BTEC National Diploma in Art & Design
(equivalent to a three A Level course), BTEC National Certificate in Sport (equivalent to 2 A Level courses), the Leith
Cookery Course and the British Riding Society Preliminary
Instructor Certificate (BHSPIC). Most students choose four
AS Level subjects in the Lower Sixth and then take three of
these to the full A Level in the Upper Sixth. Wider enrichment opportunities are available to all Sixth Formers. The
curriculum offers breadth, depth and flexibility in course
choice. Pupils are also prepared for STEP papers and Scholastic Aptitude tests for American Universities. EAL and
Learning Support is available at all levels.

Every pupil is guided through his or her school career by
a Group Tutor. Each Tutor cares for between 10 and 14
pupils within a House, taking a close personal interest in
each and maintaining regular contact with parents on academic matters.

Games and Activities. Year 9 pupils are generally
required to play the team game of the term; senior boys and
girls choose from the following games: Archery, Athletics,
Badminton, Basketball, Canoeing, Chess, Climbing,
Cricket, Croquet, Cross Country, Fencing, Fitness Training,
Golf, Hockey, Karate, Modern Pentathlon, Polo, Riding,
Sailing, Shooting, Skiing, Squash, Swimming, Tennis,
Trampolining, Volleyball.

In addition to the above options, boys may choose Rugby
or Football, and girls may opt for Aerobics, Ballet, Dance,
Netball, Rounders or Yoga.

All pupils take part in the school's Activities Programme;
they can choose from more than 80 activities, ranging from
athletics to street dance – encompassing dissection, building

a caterham car, film clubs, photography, scuba diving and growing greens along the way.

Fees per term (2011-2012). Boarding £9,670, Day £6,500.

Scholarships and Bursaries. Scholarships of up to 15% are awarded for exceptional talent in academic work, music, art, sport and chess. Where parental resources are limited, these may be augmented by means-tested bursaries of up to 100%.

Charitable status. Millfield is a Registered Charity, number 310283. Its aim is to provide independent boarding and day education for boys and girls, and to maintain an extensive system of bursary aid to gifted pupils or those in financial need.

Monkton Combe School

Monkton Combe, Bath, Somerset BA2 7HG
Tel: 01225 721102
Fax: 01225 721181
e-mail: admissions@monkton.org.uk
website: www.monktoncombeschool.com

Monkton Combe School was founded in 1868, and today is one of the best known smaller Independent Schools in the country. The School's aim has always been to provide a broad education designed to enable boys and girls to develop all their potential to the full, with an emphasis on high academic standards. The School's tradition is unashamedly Christian, and every effort is made to relate Christian belief and worship to the needs of daily life.

Patrons:
Prof R J Berry, MA, DSc, FIBiol, FRSE
G Coates
The Baroness Cox of Queensbury, SRN, BScSoc, BSc Econ, FRCN, PhD Hon
The Rt Revd T Dudley-Smith, OBE, MA, MLitt
L E Ellis, MA, AFIMA
The Lord Hastings of Scarisbrick, CBE
P W Lee, CBE, MA, DL
The Rt Revd J F Perry, MPhil, LTh Hon
R D Spear, JP, MA
Lady Stanley, BSc, MSW

Governors:
Chairman: S Wilsher, BA Econ
R S Baldock, MA Cantab
Mrs J Brooks, BA, DipSocSi, CQSW
T R Johns, BA, PGCE, FRGS
Rear Admiral C A Johnstone-Burt, OBE, MA, FCIPD, RN
The Ven D S K Kajumba, BA, HND, Dip Theol, Dip IMBM
Prof M R B Keighley, MB BS, MS, FRCS, FEWI
Dr B W Martin, BSc Hon, PhD
J G W Matthews, MB, BAO, MCh, FRCS
J R Myers, BEng Hons
A D Owen, OBE, MA, Hon DSc Aston, D Univ UCE
P C Poulsom
T S Sanderson, MA, MSc Econ
M J Sayer, MA
Mrs M K Townsend, BSc Hons
N Websper
M R A Womersley, MA Cantab

Leadership Team:

Principal: R P Backhouse, MA

Headmaster of Preparatory School: C J Stafford, BA
Head of Pre-Preparatory: Mrs K G Morrell, BEd
Deputy Head (Pastoral): P F Innes-Hill, BA, MEd
Director of Development: Dr A L Kerbey, MA, PhD

Company Secretary, Bursar & Clerk to the Governors: Mrs A C Cracknell, BSc, ACA

Senior School Staff:
† *Houseparent*

Deputy Head (Pastoral): P F Innes-Hill, BA, MEd
Deputy Head (Academic): J B Morley, BA
Director of Welfare: Mrs R H Garrod, BEd
Director of Co-Curricular: Mrs L M Vaughan, BA
Director of Learning: Miss V Armand-Smith, BSc

M C Garrod, BSc (*Senior Master*)
N D Botton, MA
J C Bradby, MA
D M Merricks, BEd, MA
Mrs A Jameson, BA, Dip Dys
Mrs A Mills, BEd (*OC CCF*)
P R Clark
T F Hardisty, BA
A D McPhee, BA, DipTEFL
Miss D W Clark, RGN
P R Wickens, BSc
Mrs C S Morley, BEd
S R Harris, CertEd, MA
Mrs S Vercher, Lic
Miss E M-L L Arnaudet, Lic DEA
D P J Tobias, BA
Mrs F J Davies, BA, Dip Dys
M B Abington, BSc
Mrs R M Glasgow, BA (*†Nutfield House*)
A W R Glasgow (*†Nutfield House*)
Mrs S C Dimond, BSc
G P Reay, BSc, MSc
P Marais, BSc, MEd (*†Clarendon House*)
Mrs L Marais (*†Clarendon House*)
S J Call, BSc (*†Grove Grange House*)
Mrs H Call, BPharm, MRPharmS (*†Grove Grange House*)
Mrs H K Wilkinson, BA (*†Hill House*)
Mrs J A Hildreth, MDes
Ms M C Bensted, BA
R Campbell, MSc
S Chilcott, MEng, MSc
Mrs M Egan, BA
Mrs E Gibson, BA
Mrs J Pring, BA
J D L Shone, BA (*†School House*)
Mrs O Shone (*†School House*)
D Sixsmith, BA
S Wilkinson, BSc (*†Hill House*)
M Parfitt, BA
D H J Bryson, BSc
Mrs A Bryson, MMus
Mrs C L Thomas, BSc
Mrs D R Mucheru, BA
J P C Sertin, BA (*†Eddystone House*)
Mrs C Hudson, BA
Ms S Yuan
G Bevan, MMus, ARCO CHM
P Carter, BA
D Hubbard, BSc
Mrs J A Stuart, BA
S Gent, BSc
Miss L Mawasse, MSc
A Straiton, BA
Revd M Dietz (*Chaplain*)

Visiting Music Staff:
G Bardsley, MA Cantab (*Singing*)
Mrs A Carroll, BA (*Singing*)
Mrs R Gabe, Dip RCM, ARCM Perf (*Violin, Viola*)
Mrs V Hammond (*Oboe*)
Mrs R Kerry, BA, LRSM (*Piano*)
B Lynn, MA (*Guitar, Double Bass*)
Mrs Y Neiuwerf, GMus (*Flute*)

D Pagett, GRNCM, DipRNCM (*Clarinet, Saxophone*)
J Porter, MI (*Drums*)
Mrs S Power, BEd Hons (*Cello*)
J Scott (*Percussion*)
Mrs S Sharp (*Singing*)
P Skelton, BA, LRAM (*Piano*)
S Skews (*Piano*)

Registrar: Mrs P A Neaverson

Medical Officers:
Dr N A Gough, MB BS, MRCP, MRCGP, DRCOG, MRCS
Dr L Paterson, MA, MB BS

Situation. The geographical situation is delightful; the Senior School faces south across the Valley, or Combe, from which the place takes its name, about 200 feet above sea level, while the Preparatory School is at the top of the hill above, some 400 feet higher, with magnificent views over Avon and Wiltshire.

Organisation. The Pre-Prep, Prep and Senior Schools each have their own Heads and the Principal of the Senior School has overall responsibility for the three schools. However, they share the same Board of Governors and there are close links between them. About half of the Senior School pupils come from the Preparatory School; the rest from Preparatory Schools all over the country, State Maintained Schools or from abroad. The Senior School went fully co-educational and merged with Clarendon School, Bedford, in September 1992. The Preparatory School went co-educational in September 1993.

(*For further details see Monkton Preparatory entry in IAPS section.*)

Numbers. *Preparatory School*: There are 363 pupils of whom 50 board and 120 are in the Pre-Prep.

Senior School: There are 384 pupils (249 boys, 135 girls), of whom 234 are boarders. The Sixth Form numbers 132.

Admission. *Preparatory School*. The main entry is at age 7, 8 or 9 but every effort is made to accept boys and girls who wish to join at age 10 or 11. Some scholarships are offered. The majority of pupils from the Pre-Prep go on to the Prep school.

Senior School. There is a one-form entry at 11 by means of report and interview and papers in English, Mathematics and a Reasoning Test. The main entry is at age 13 by means of the Common Entrance or Scholarship Examinations. Candidates from State Schools and schools abroad are admitted on the basis of report and interview and papers in English, Mathematics and a Reasoning Test. Entry direct into the Sixth Form is encouraged. Admission is on the basis of report, interviews and a Reasoning Test, and is conditional on not fewer than 5 subjects at grade C or better in GCSE, normally with an average of B/C across all GCSE subjects taken.

Buildings. The Senior School's buildings are of Bath or Cotswold Dale stone. They have been steadily extended and modernised to meet the changing needs of the School. In recent years two new girls' Houses have been built, the boys' Houses have undergone major upgrading and refurbishing and the Junior Boarding House has moved down into the main school into a newly refurbished property.

A new Information Technology Centre, a Sixth Form Centre, a Sports Centre, a Swimming Centre, and a Drama Studio have recently been opened. The Library has been extensively refurbished to provide a modern Learning Resource Centre and a state-of-the-art Maths & Science centre has just been opened. A new music centre will open in Spring 2012.

The School has extensive playing fields, a newly refurbished Astroturf all-weather playing area for Hockey and Tennis, Boathouses on the River Avon, 3 Netball Courts, 14 Tennis Courts, a covered Rifle Range, a Rowing Tank, a heated outdoor Swimming Pool, 2 Squash Courts, a Sports Centre and a 25m indoor Swimming Centre and Fitness Centre.

The Monkton Campaign was launched during 1995 to assist in the further development of the School over the next few years. To date it has raised £5 million which is part of an exciting £34 million development plan.

Chapel. There is a full-time resident Anglican Chaplain. The Chapel itself stands in the centre of the School and has recently been extended and completely refurbished. A short service or assembly is held every morning and a School Service, at which parents are welcome, each Sunday. There is a Confirmation Service each year. Pupils of other than Anglican tradition are welcomed to Communion Services.

Houses. The four boys' Houses, the two girls' Houses and the Junior House for 11 and 12 year olds are all under the care of Houseparents, who together with their tutorial teams of colleagues are responsible for the boys' and girls' general welfare.

Day Pupils are fully integrated into the boarding houses and the total life of the School and are encouraged but not obliged to stay until the end of evening prep. Senior pupils are given opportunities for responsibility as School or House Prefects during their sixth-form careers.

Tutor System. Each pupil has a Tutor, normally a member of staff of his or her own choice, who keeps in touch with parents and provides guidance and advice over every aspect of School life and over making choices for the future.

Curriculum. Our aim is to provide a broadly based curriculum in the years leading to GCSE. The curriculum reflects the spirit and fundamental goals of the National Curriculum. Those who show particular ability in French and Mathematics may proceed to work more advanced than GCSE before the end of Year 11. Personal, Social and Health Education and Physical Education are included.

In Years 7, 8 and 9 all pupils study English, Mathematics and the Sciences with a foundation course comprising at least one Foreign Language, Art, the Classics, Design Technology, Geography, History, Information Technology, Music, PE and Religious Studies. In Years 10 and 11 all pupils take IGCSE English, Mathematics, and Coordinated Dual Award Science (Biology, Chemistry and Physics). English Literature is taught alongside English to the top three sets. Pupils choose four other subjects from Art, Business Studies with IT, Classical Civilisation, Design Technology, Drama, French, Geography, History, Latin, Music, Religious Studies, Spanish and Sports Studies. Extra English is available as an option for those with particular needs in this subject.

Most pupils stay on for two years in the Sixth Form. The subjects at present offered at AS/A2 Level are: Art, Biology, Business Studies, Chemistry, Critical Thinking, Design Technology, English Literature, English Language, French, Further Mathematics, Geography, History, Mathematics, Music, Photography, Physics, Psychology, Religious Studies, Spanish, Sports Studies and Theatre Studies. Most pupils entering Year 12 study four subjects for one year to AS and continue with three to full A Level. Pupils also attend courses on world religions, the family, personal finance, self-presentation and interview technique. A notable feature of the Sixth Form programme is the wide variety of lectures and presentations delivered by visiting speakers prominent in their field.

Careers Advice and Staff/Parent Meetings. An experienced Careers Teacher works closely with Tutors in advising pupils. There is also a member of staff responsible for advice on higher education. Parents, Old Monktonians and local people are invited to help pupils in their thinking about careers. The School belongs to the Independent Schools Careers Organisation which arranges Aptitude and Interest tests. Annual staff/parent meetings are held at the School to discuss pupils' progress. Parents are of course always welcome at other times.

University Entrance. The great majority of leavers go on to degree courses at Universities and Colleges of Higher Education. Last year 96% of leavers went to their first-choice university.

Games. Those with particular abilities are encouraged to aim for excellence, but we also believe that regular games and exercise are important for all, helping to build a healthy lifestyle for the future and fostering leadership, teamwork and cooperation.

The major sports for boys are: in the Michaelmas Term, Rugby; in the Lent Term, Hockey or Rowing; in the Summer Term, Cricket, Rowing or Tennis. Boys choose either to row or to play Hockey and Cricket, but are allowed to alter their choice during their time at the School. Younger boys are normally required to play the major game of each term but as they become more senior they are allowed a greater degree of choice.

The major sports for girls are: in the Michaelmas Term, Hockey; in the Lent Term, Netball or Rowing; in the Summer Term, Tennis or Rowing. Representative teams are fielded in all these sports. As with the boys, the choice becomes more extended as girls become more senior.

There are also School teams in Athletics, Basketball, Cross-Country, Football, Judo, Squash and Shooting.

CCF and Community Service. There are sections for all three Services, besides various specialist activities such as Venture Section (through which the Duke of Edinburgh's Award scheme is offered) and car maintenance. There is also an active Community Service group.

Leisure Activities. Monkton encourages as many worthwhile leisure pursuits as possible. Between 35 and 40 different activities are offered; up to the age of 15 pupils are expected to be involved in at least one. All the facilities of the School, including the Art and DT Departments, Music Rooms and ICT Centre are available to pupils during their free time. The Choir, Orchestra, Big Band and other less formal music groups play an important part in the School's life and tuition is available in all orchestral instruments. About 45% of the members of the School take music lessons. There is a major School dramatic production in the Michaelmas Term. The School is conveniently close to Bath and Bristol for taking parties to concerts and theatres. Some 30 clubs and societies figure on the School List, ranging from the Bridge Club to the Literary Society and the Christian Union. Bible Study groups meet weekly.

Health. The School Medical Officer visits regularly and all boarders are required to register with him. The Medical Centre is under the care of a fully qualified Sister and Assistant who provide a 24-hour service.

Catering. All pupils take their meals in the Dining Hall, with cafeteria service.

Dress. The Clothes List is kept as simple as possible. All required items can be purchased in the School Shop.

Scholarships. (*See Scholarship Entries section.*) Four Anniversary Awards are offered at the age of 11 for open competition each year. They range in value from 25% to 5% of the appropriate fee.

At least ten Scholarships or Exhibitions, including at least two for Music, at least one for Art, at least one for Drama and at least two for Sport are offered at the age of 13 for open competition each year. These range in value from 35% to 5% of the appropriate fee.

At least four Scholarships are offered at age 16 for open competition to two candidates from other schools and two to candidates from Monkton Combe for entry into Year 12 each year. Academic, artistic, musical or sporting merit will be taken into account in making such awards. They range in value from 25% to 5% of the appropriate fee.

There is a limited number of Bursaries to enable pupils to come to Monkton Combe who would otherwise be unable to do so on financial grounds.

The Governors are prepared to make a remission of up to one-third of the fee to a limited number of children of Clergy and Missionaries, on proof of need.

Fees per term (2011-2012). Senior: £6,732–£9,045 (boarders); £4,722–£5,727 (day pupils). Preparatory: £6,330–£6,732 (boarders); £3,415–£4,722 (day pupils). Pre-Prep: £2,577–£2,762.

Old Monktonian Club. The Monkton Combe School Register has been fully revised and updated. Details from the Development Office at the School.

Charitable status. Monkton Combe School is a Registered Charity, number 1057185, and a Company Limited by Guarantee, registered in England, number 3228456. Its aims and objectives are to provide education for girls and boys combined with sound religious training on Protestant and Evangelical principles in accordance with the doctrines of The Church of England.

Monmouth School

Almshouse Street, Monmouth, Monmouthshire NP25 3XP

Tel: 01600 713143
Fax: 01600 772701
e-mail: enquiries@monmouthschool.org
website: www.habs-monmouth.org

The School was founded in 1614, by William Jones, a merchant of the City of London and a Liveryman of the Worshipful Company of Haberdashers, who was born near Monmouth and bequeathed a large sum of money to found a school and almshouses in the town. The School has derived immense advantage from this unusual association with the City of London.

The School is controlled by a Board of Governors appointed variously by the Haberdashers' Company, the Universities of Oxford, Cambridge and Wales, and local representative bodies.

Motto: *Serve and Obey.*

Chairman of the Governors: J B S Swallow, MA, FCA

Ex officio: The Master of the Worshipful Company of Haberdashers

[1]J A Ackroyd	Mrs L Kelway-Bamber
M H C Anderson	A M Kerr (*Chairman of the*
Dr M G Archer	*Monmouth School*
Dr P E G Baird	*Committee*)
Professor P Blood	Mrs G B Kerton-Johnson
[1]Councillor W A L Crump	[1]Mrs M A Molyneux
[1]Mrs C J Davis	[1]Mrs T Pike
C R S Hardie	[1]R J Stibbs
[1]Canon E J S Hiscocks	[1]Mrs L Stout
[1]D J Hitchcock	Mrs M Wetherell
Miss H Hutton	

[1] *Member of the Monmouth School Committee*

Headmaster: S G Connors, BA, PhD

Second Master: S H Dorman, MA, MPhil
Director of Studies: A J Winter, BSc, PhD
Head of Sixth Form: H F Tatham, MA

Assistant Staff:
* *Head of Department*
† *Housemaster/Housemistress*

D C Adams, MA
Mrs E R Arrand, BA
Mrs S G Atherton, BA
Dr L M Bakker, BTech, PhD
Miss E K Barson, BSc, MSc (**Biology*)
Miss A R Beak, BA

S M F Belfield, BA, MA
J C Bevan, CertEd (†New House)
J Boiling, BA (†Town House)
R C Boyle, BSc (†School House)
M D Clarke, BSc, PhD
J P Danks, BSc, DPhil (*Chemistry, †Dean House)
Miss E R Davies, BSc
Mrs S Davies, L-ès-L
Dr M T Davis, BSc
A J Dawson, BSc, MSc
J Despontin, BSc, MSc
Mrs P G Dollins, BMus
S H Dorman, MA, MPhil
G Dunn, BSc, MSc
S J Edwards, BA
Miss B H Evans, BA
H B Evans, MSc, PhD (*Mathematics)
J D Finn, BA, MSc
A V Francis, BSc, PhD
J F Geraghty, BA
N J R Goodson, BSc
P M Griffin, BA (*Drama)
Mrs C J Hartley, BSc
J M Harrison, BA, PhD (*History)
J J Hartley, MA (*Geography)
A Hawley, BA
Mrs S E Hayter, TEFAL
Miss L G Hockey, BA
D G Hope, BA (†Weirhead House)
Mrs L A Hope (*ICT)
R Howe, BA (†Monmouth House)
P C Hunt, GRNCM, LLCM (†Wye House)
P D Jefferies, BSc
Mrs J Johnston, MA
A J Jones, BA (†Chapel House)
D K Jones, BSc (†Buchanan House)
D F Lawson, BA (Director of Music)
Miss G S Lee, BA, MA (*English)
M Lewis, BA
Mrs L R Livingston, BA
A J S Macdonald, BSc
K J Madsen, BA (*Economics, †Glendower House)
Mrs R J Marsh, BSc
S M F McQuitty, BSc (†Severn House)
K A Moseley, BSc, PhD, FRAS (*Physics)
D Mather, BA (*Spanish)
J A T McEwan, BA
T W H Murgatroyd, BA, MPhil, PhD (*Classics)
Mrs L C Parr, BEng, BSc
Mrs L Parsons, BA (*Modern Languages)
A K R Peace, BSc
M Peake, BA (*Art)
D J Pearson, BSc
Mrs S E Phillips, BEd, MA, Dip SpLD
R D Picken, BA
P Sanders, MA, MSc
A E Shakeshaft, BA
M J Tamplin, BSc (†Hereford House)
H F Tatham, MA (*Religious Education)
K A Tiebosch, BA
P D Vaughan-Smith, BA
D M Vickers, BEd (Director of Physical Education, †Tudor House)
A J White, BA (*Design Technology)
Mrs R Widdicks, BA (*Study Support)
O T R Williams, BSc, MA
Miss S E L Williams, BA, MA
A J Winter, BSc, PhD
Miss R L Wynne, MA

Chaplain: Revd G R Knight, MTh, MTheol, HND

The Grange (Preparatory Department)

Head: Mrs E G Thomas, BA

Deputy Head: Mrs S L Wilderspin, CertEd

D Webb, BEd   D G Murray, MA
P N Morris, BEd   Mrs S M Jones, BEd
Mrs J A Osborne, BEd   D Hayden, MA
D F Gould, BSc   Ms J Morse, BA
K J Shepherd, BA   Mrs K Noel, BSc

Bursar: D A Chowns, BEng, MA

Medical Officer: S H D Shaw, BA, BM

There are approximately 580 boys in the Senior School, of whom 150 are boarders. The Grange, the School's Preparatory Department, caters for over 100 dayboys aged 7 to 11, with boarding available at age 9. (For further details see entry in IAPS section.)

Situation and Buildings. The School was founded in 1614 by William Jones and is one of the schools of the Worshipful Company of Haberdashers. A generous endowment enables the School to provide superb facilities and an excellent academic education whilst keeping fees at a reasonable level. There are many scholarships and bursaries and the Haberdashers' Assisted Places Scheme, which replaced the Government scheme in 1998, ensures that an education at Monmouth School can be available to boys who will benefit from it, irrespective of their parents' income.

The School is enriched by close cooperation with Haberdashers' Monmouth School for Girls in many areas of school life, especially at Sixth Form level.

The School is set in the delightful landscape of the Wye Valley and much use is made of the surrounding countryside for expeditions and other outward-bound activities. There is a strong tradition of music and drama as well as of excellence in sport. A new sports complex was opened in Autumn 1999, a studio theatre in January 2001 and additional outdoor facilities, including an all-weather pitch, in Autumn 2001. The Blake Theatre (500 seats) was completed in Summer 2004. Other recent developments have included greatly expanded ICT facilities and refurbished boarding houses and classroom blocks. The Sixth Form has a dedicated Sixth Form Centre. A superb new Sports Pavilion opened in 2008 and the Prep School, The Grange, moved to an innovatively designed and exciting new building in February 2009.

Boarding. The boarding community forms the core of the School. Junior boarders (9–12 year olds) are accommodated in Chapel House for their first few years and benefit from the care of a dedicated house team who also provide an ambitious and popular programme of extra-curricular activities, tailored to the interests of the age group.

There are three senior boarding houses for boys between 13 and 18. The School has a flexible boarding policy which provides a considerable degree of freedom for families to make boarding arrangements which fit in with their lives, but which encourages boys to take full advantage of the many sporting, cultural and extra-curricular activities for which the School is renowned.

September 2011 will see the opening of Buchanan House, a sixth form boarding house with single study-bedrooms and en-suite facilities.

Admission. The main admission points are 7, 10, 11, 13 and 16, but other stages will be considered if places are available. Candidates aged 7 and 11 sit the School's own entrance tests. At 13, candidates take either the Common Entrance Examination, the School's own Foundation Scholarship Examination or its 13+ examination. Entrants to the Sixth Form are accepted either after sitting the Sixth Form Scholarship Examination or on the basis of GCSE results (or equivalent).

Candidates from overseas are welcome. Those whose first language is not English take a preliminary test of proficiency in English before proceeding to the appropriate entrance test.

The School accepts pupils with Dyslexia or similar specific learning difficulties. They are taught in mainstream lessons and additional study support is available.

Curriculum. The curriculum is designed to provide both flexibility and breadth and to be in step with the National Curriculum without being constrained by it. Those in Forms I and II (Years 7 and 8) study a wide range of subjects including Latin, French and combined Science. In Form III (Year 9) the three Sciences are taught separately and pupils have the option of starting Greek.

Pupils normally take nine or ten GCSE subjects, four of which are of their own choosing. There is a cross-curricular ICT scheme to enable pupils to make full use of the School's extensive facilities.

In the Sixth Form a range of approximately 30 AS subjects is offered along with an enrichment programme which includes the ICT course, Clait Plus. This programme and many of the AS subjects are offered in cooperation with Haberdashers' Monmouth School for Girls.

A particular feature of the curriculum is the extensive range of Modern Languages. French is taught at all levels and Spanish and German are available from Form III. The Welsh Club enables boys to study Welsh for GCSE and Russian is also available at AS/A Level.

The Chapel. The School is an Anglican foundation and the Chapel plays an important part in its life. All pupils attend Chapel at least once each week and there is a weekly service for boarders. A varied programme of preachers is organised, including clergy and lay people of many denominations. The Bishop of Monmouth officiates at the annual Confirmation Service.

Games. The main sports are rugby, rowing, cricket and soccer. Many other sports are also available at a highly competitive level including athletics, cross-country running, golf, sailing, squash and swimming. Several members of staff have international sporting honours and pupils regularly gain places to represent Wales in a variety of sports.

Activities. There is an extensive programme of activities throughout the School. Pupils in Form IV and above may join the CCF (Army and RAF sections) which enjoy excellent links with locally based regular and territorial forces. Community Service is a popular option and many boys participate in the Duke of Edinburgh's Award Scheme. There is a very strong musical tradition with many pupils taking part in choirs, orchestras and bands which achieve high levels of success in competitions, and play to appreciative audiences locally and on the regular overseas tours which take place. Drama is also strong and good opportunities are provided for participation at all levels. A wide range of School clubs and Societies further enriches the life of the School.

Fees per term (2011-2012). Boarding £7,442, Day £4,238; The Grange: Boarding £6,050, Day £2,999.

Entrance Scholarships. (*See Scholarship Entries section*.) Scholarships are available on the basis of performance in the Year 7 Entry Assessments (11+), Foundation Scholarship Examination (13+) and Sixth Form Examination (16+). Bursaries and the Haberdashers' Assisted Places Scheme can also provide up to 100% remission of fees, in certain circumstances.

Old Monmothians. Past members of the School are eligible to join the Old Monmothian Club which enjoys a close relationship with the School. The Membership Secretary is Henry Toulouse, 3 Monkswell Close, Monmouth NP25 3PH.

Charitable status. William Jones's Schools Foundation is a Registered Charity, number 525616. Its aims and objectives are to provide an all-round education for boys and girls at reasonable fees; also to carry out the Founder's intention that local boys qualifying for entry should not be prevented from attending the School by lack of funds.

Morrison's Academy

Ferntower Road, Crieff, Perthshire PH7 3AN
Tel: 01764 653885
Fax: 01764 655411
e-mail: principal@morrisonsacademy.org
website: www.morrisonsacademy.org

Morrison's Academy Boys' School was opened in 1860 with a Girls' Department in 1861, an arrangement which continued until 1889 when a separate school for Girls was opened within the ten acres of the original site. In 1979 these two schools were brought together to become the one Morrison's Academy. The original foundation was possible through the generosity of Thomas Mo(r)rison, a native of Muthill who became a builder in Edinburgh and who in 1813 executed a Trust Deed directing that the fee of the reversion of his estate should be used to found and erect 'an institution calculated to promote the interests of mankind, having particular regard to the Education of Youth and the diffusion of useful knowledge … a new institution which may bear my name and preserve the remembrance of my good intentions for the welfare and happiness of my fellow men'.

Motto: *Ad summa tendendum: Striving for the highest*

Board of Governors:
Chairman: D A Glen, BAcc, CA, CTA

Members:
J C Anderson, MB, MBA, CA
G W Berrie, FCII
P J Brodie, MA, MA Ed, PGCE
H Campbell, BSc Eng, CEng, MICE, MIStructE
Dr M L Clarke, BSc Hons, PhD, MRSC
I Cockbain, ACIS
Mrs E A Gilmour, MA Hons, PGCE
Miss C B Graham, BSc Hons, MBA
Professor W S Hanson, BA, PhD, FSA, FSA Scot
G G Hayton, MA, MEd, DipEd, DPSE
Dr A Jackson, BSc, PhD
L C Johnston
S Logie, BA, DipMan, MBA
G T P O'Donnell, MA
Mrs F R Sharp, MA

Clerk to Governors: J C Andrew, LLB Hons, Dip LP, NP

Staff:

Rector: G S H Pengelley, BA

Deputy Rector: D A L Mackenzie, BSc, PG Dip, MA

Head of Primary: A R Robertson, DipEd

Assistant Rector: A J Law, MA

Head of Pastoral Care: Miss A McCluskey, MA

Bursar: A U Beaton, MSc, FCIPD, MCMI

Admissions Registrar: Mrs A Ross

Teaching Staff:
* Head of Department

Art:
*Miss P M McQue, MA
S Jewell, BDes, MDes

Business Studies:
*H McMillan, DipCom
Mrs E M Fraser, BA, DipCom

Computer Studies:
*D Hamilton, BSc, MSc, CEng, MBCS

Miss K MacDonald, BSc

English:
*P G O'Kane, MA
Mrs T Lafferty, BEd
Mrs N Gregor, BA
Mrs D D Riddell, MA

Geography:
*A Wylie, BA
R S Anderson, MA

History:
*P J Lovegrove, MA
M J Clayton, MA

Home Economics:
Mrs H Neilson, BA

Mathematics:
*I K O Barnett, BSc Hons
D A L Mackenzie, BSc, PG
  Dip, MA
A M Jack, BSc
Mrs M T O'Kane, BSc

Modern Languages:
*E Coffey, MA
A J Law, MA
Miss A McCluskey, MA
R A R Millon, BA
Mrs J C E White, MA

Music:
*Z Fazlic, BA Hons
  (*Director of Music*)
Mrs S Smart, BA

Heads of Year:
Miss E J McCormick, BEd
Mrs E M Fraser, BA, DipCom
L T Howell, BA
Mrs M T O'Kane, BSc
Mrs D D Riddell, MA
Miss D J Nesbit, BEd

Primary School:
Head of Primary: A R Robertson, DipEd
Depute Head, Primary: Mrs L S Anderson, BEd
Ms M M Anderson, BEd
I P Barr, MA
G Chater, BA
Miss N G Dick, BEd Hons
Mrs A Dickinson, LLB
Mrs G M Lauchlan, MA
Mrs J A Longmuir, DipEd
Mrs C Marchbank, BA
Miss K McCain, BDes Hons

Physical Education:
*D N F Pennie, MA
L T Howell, BA
Mrs J Lee, BEd
Miss E J McCormick, BEd
Miss D J Nesbit, BEd

Science:
*J B Beedie, BSc
F Black, BSc Hons
Dr G Noble, BSc, PhD
Miss S MacGregor, BSc
M McKeever, BSc
Mrs A S Taylor, BSc

Design Technology:
R G McDermott, MEd,
BEd

*Learning Support (Primary
and Secondary)*:
Mrs G S Wilkie, MA
Mrs C Jones, BSc

The School. Morrison's Academy is an integral part of the community in Crieff and comprises a 10 acre main campus supplemented by 45 acres of sports fields, main hall, after-school club and nursery housed in a spacious building a short walk from the main campus. The school provides education for 540 boys and girls from 3 to 18 years.

The well-equipped Nursery can accommodate 30 children from 3 to 5 years in an impressive Victorian villa and the dedicated staff stimulate learning in the early years. The Nursery was recently inspected by HMIE and the Care Commission and received an outstanding report, where all areas received 'excellent' or 'very good' indicators. The Nursery and After-School Club together offer care from 8.00 am to 6.00 pm.

The Primary School, housed in a separate building on the main campus, educates 160 pupils in small classes. Transfer between primary and secondary is helped by our Transitional Year (P7), which provides teaching in the primary school by a class teacher supplemented by lessons in the secondary school taught by subject specialists.

The Secondary School has 350 pupils studying towards Scottish Qualifications and entry to universities in Scotland, the rest of the UK and abroad. Academic expectations and achievements are high and small groups encourage individual learning and development. Over ninety-seven percent of our S6 go on to university.

Staff and pupils mix easily and the scale of the school allows for every individual to be known and valued by all.

Situation. Morrison's Academy is situated in the market town of Crieff on the edge of the Scottish Highlands in Perthshire. Strathearn is a beautiful area of mountains, rivers, lochs and rich agricultural land. Pupils attend from the local area and travel from Perth, Pitlochry, Dunkeld, Auchterarder, Stirling and Dunblane.

Curriculum. Pupils in Primary and lower Secondary follow broadly the Scottish 5–14 programme of study, leading in upper Secondary to Intermediate and then to Higher and Advanced Higher National Qualifications. Emphasis is placed upon academic achievement, while the pupils are also always encouraged to develop broad skills and interests outside the classroom. Co-curricular activities are extensive and Morrison's Academy makes good use of its glorious location.

Houses. All pupils are placed in one of the four houses named after local families: Campbells, Drummonds, Grahams and Murrays. There is healthy, competitive rivalry between the houses and senior pupils are encouraged to take charge of teams for sporting, music, debating and other events.

Games and Activities. Morrison's Academy encourages pupils to participate in a wide range of co-curricular activities and sports. All pupils use the playing fields and facilities on the main campus or walk to the 45 acres of playing fields and pavilions at Dallerie. Main sports are rugby, hockey, cricket, tennis and athletics. From upper primary fixtures against other schools take place, generally on Saturday mornings. Other sporting activities include soccer, basketball, netball, swimming, golf, weight training, sailing, short tennis, skiing, climbing, karate and more. To complement the sporting activities, pupils are active in The Duke of Edinburgh's Award Scheme, the Combined Cadet Force, drama, music, debating, chess, Pipe and Drum Band, environment group, Young Enterprise, charity fundraising, Christian groups, highland dancing and more. Pupils are challenged to make the most of their time and all within the wonderful environment of Perthshire.

Fees per term (2011-2012). Day: Primary £2,193–£3,124, Secondary £3,319.

The fees include tuition, textbooks, stationery, external examination fees, sports and curriculum-related travel.

Admission Procedure. Admission to the school is by entrance test and school report and/or exam results and entrance interview. The school's main entrance testing/interview days are at the beginning of February and beginning of May, for entry to the academic year commencing the following August.

For a prospectus pack and any queries please contact the Admissions Registrar.

Scholarships and Bursaries. (*See Scholarship Entries section.*)

Charitable status. Morrison's Academy is a Registered Charity, number SC000458. The school is a recognised charity providing education.

Mount St Mary's College

Spinkhill, Nr Sheffield, Derbyshire S21 3YL
Tel: 01246 433388
Fax: 01246 435511
e-mail: headmaster@msmcollege.com
website: www.msmcollege.com

Mount St Mary's College was founded in 1842 by the Society of Jesus in order to provide an education for the country's growing Catholic population. The manor of Spinkhill in North East Derbyshire was the first home of the College, forming the nucleus of the present school. The Elizabethan manor of Barlborough Hall, 1¼ miles away, is the home of the Preparatory School to the College.

Numbers: College 440; Preparatory School (3–11 years) 240. Boarders, Weekly Boarders and Day Pupils (girls and boys) are accepted at the College.
Motto: *Sine Macula.*

Governing Body:
Chairman: J Kelly, KSG

J Bergin	D Westmoreland
Fr M Beattie SJ	T Wragg
R Gilbert	
Mrs J Kenny	*Members*:
Mrs H Massarella	Fr M Holman SJ
G Montgomery	Revd J Twist SJ
Mrs L Penny	Br A Harrison SJ

Headmaster: **L E McKell**, MA Hons, MEd

Spiritual Father: Fr Michael Beattie SJ
Deputy Head: F Thompson, MA, MPhil
Academic Deputy: Mrs M Smith, BA, MA, FRSA
Bursar: A Bunn, FCA, MBA, Grad Dip CSP

Assistant Staff:
* *Head of Department*
† *Housemaster/mistress*

A Axelby, BA, MA (*History, Games*)
G G Brammer, BEd (*Senior Master, Head of Lower School, Geography*)
R Carey, BA (**EAL, *PHSE*)
Mrs R Carey, BA, MA (*Learning Support, Enhanced Studies*)
H Cartwright, BA (*Mathematics*)
O Cobbe, BA (*UCAS Adviser, Assistant Head of Sixth Form*)
Miss R Craggs, BSc (*Girls' Games*)
Mrs K Dawson, BA (*Mathematics*)
Dr D Dibden BSc, PhD (*Biology*)
A Du Randt, BPrimEd (*Learning Support, Girls' Games*)
W Du Randt, BA, HED (*Head of Boarding, History, Geography, Enhanced Studies*)
Mrs M Forbes-Jones, BTh (*Head of Sixth Form, Religious Studies/Chaplaincy, Enhanced Studies*)
P Forbes-Jones, BTh, MA (*History, Geography, Religious Studies, Enhanced Studies*)
J M Fry, BSc, ARSM (*Physics*)
Ms J Gabbitas (†*Hopkins, Girls Games*)
I Garbett, BA (*EAL*)
M Greene, BA (*English and Drama*)
D Griffiths, BA (**Games and PE*)
Mrs G Kocura-Hackett, BA (*Drama*)
Mrs G Hazlehurst, BSc (*Head of Middle School, *Geography*)
Ms A Hoskin, BSc (*Games, PE, Head of Rudiments*)
S Howes, BA (*English*)
S Jenkins (*Fencing*)
Mrs S Johnson, BA (*Modern Languages*)
Mrs J Kendrick, BSc (**Learning Support*)
G F Kirrane, BA (**History, Boys Games*)
Mrs L Kitchener, BMus, MA (**Director of Music*)
M Krlic, BSc (**Business Studies, Boys Games*)
Mrs L Leadbetter, BA, (*Modern Languages*)
T Leadbetter, MA, BD, AKC, FRSA, FRHistS (*Director of Teaching & Learning*)
Mrs L A Lovatt-Jones, BA, MA, LSDC (*Art & Design Technology*)
Mrs H Madigan, BA (*English, Library, Drama*)
S Madigan, BSc (**Physics*)
Mrs H McKell, BA (*English*)
R McMillan, BTheol (*Religious Studies, Assistant Chaplain*)
M Miller, BSc, MSc (**Mathematics*)
A P Mulkerrins, BSc (*Games*)
J Murphy, BA, FRSA (**English and Drama*)
Dr M B Murray, PhD, ARIC (**Chemistry*)

M Newton, BA (*Librarian*)
D Novosel, MA (*Chaplaincy*)
Dr S Orchard, BEng, PhD (*Chemistry*)
Mrs B D Owers, BA, MIL (*Modern Languages*)
G Powell, BSA Cert Boarding Education (*CCF*)
M Powell, HND (**Loyola*)
Mrs R Powell, BEd (**Girls' Games, Geography*)
S Slater, MA (*Music*)
E Smith, BMus (*Music*)
S Steed, BA (*Mathematics*)
J Stephenson, BTheol (**Religious Studies, Philosophy*)
A Szalai MA Ed (*Religious Studies, English*)
Miss S Unwin (*Sports Coach*)
Miss T Taber, BA (*Religious Studies*)
C White, BA (*DT & Art*)
G Wilks, BSc (*Accounting, Business Studies*)
I M Wilson, BEd (*ICT*)
P Woodhouse, BA (** Art & Design Technology*)
Mrs C Woodward, BSc (*Biology*)

Headmaster's Secretary: Mrs S Badger
Medical Officers: Dr Palmer, Dr Gardner
School Nurse: Mrs A-M Read
CCF: Sqn Ldr J M Fry, Maj G Powell, MISM

Barlborough Hall School:
Headteacher: Mrs W Parkinson, BEd

Mount St Mary's is a co-educational independent boarding and day school and is a member of HMC, BSA, CISC and AGBIS. Entry to the College is at age 11 and to Barlborough Hall at age 3+. Pupils at Mount St Mary's are prepared for GCSEs, AS and A Levels, and University entry. Entry into the Sixth Form is based upon school reports and GCSE results.

Aims. Mount St Mary's College is a Jesuit Catholic school inspired by the ideals of St Ignatius of Loyola. The College seeks to develop the whole person and encourages an appreciation of the needs of others both in the College community and the world at large. Mount St Mary's prepares its pupils for an active life commitment through the development of 'a faith that promotes justice'. The College seeks to produce young men and women for others. Pupils of other religious denominations are welcomed.

Special Features. Mount St Mary's College is well known for its family atmosphere. Pupils benefit from the close interest and encouragement which they receive throughout their time at the College and parental involvement is particularly encouraged. The strong emphasis on extra-curricular activities illustrates the Jesuit commitment to developing each pupil's individual talents in all areas – academic, spiritual, cultural and physical.

Situation. The College lies in an extensive estate of playing fields and parkland and is easily reached from the M1 motorway, junction 30, or from Chesterfield and Sheffield, both of which are about 8 miles away. School minibuses run throughout the region.

Organisation. The Lower, Middle and Upper Schools are each under a Head of School, who is responsible for overseeing academic progress, pastoral care, recreation and discipline, along with Heads of Year. Heads of School work closely with the Deputy Head and Academic Deputy.

Boarders live in the boys' or girls' houses, under the care of a resident boarding housemaster or housemistress, assisted by resident assistant boarding staff. All rooms are en-suite, with either 2-3 sharing or in single rooms.

Curriculum. The curriculum for the first three years (ages 11–13) broadly follows National Curriculum at KS3 with opportunity to pursue a second foreign language and a range of creative arts subjects. The standard GCSE package is 9 GCSEs, although more or less is negotiable according to ability; this includes a core of English, Mathematics, a foreign language and between one and three separate Sciences. Several subjects follow the IGCSE curriculum. Other subjects are chosen from a range of options. In the Sixth Form pupils follow AS Levels (usually four) in the Lower Sixth. The most able pupils will continue with four A Levels in the Upper Sixth, although many pupils will choose to focus on three subjects. The College also runs an "A Level Plus" programme to stretch the more able students. In keeping with the school's Ignatian ethos, all pupils follow a Religious Studies course at every stage in addition to a full programme of Games and Physical Education at every level. Specialist tuition is available in a variety of musical instruments and in speech and drama training. Assessment and monitoring of work is built into the tutorial system and there is a regular timetable of reports, pupil progress interviews and communication with parents. Academic excellence and breadth of knowledge are characteristics of Jesuit education and the curriculum is constantly reviewed to ensure that the widest opportunities are available to each pupil.

Religion. Mount St Mary's College is a distinctively Jesuit school, that welcomes children of all denominations to share its ethos. Ignatian principles inform the College's work in fostering a realistic knowledge, love and acceptance of self and of the world in which we live and this underpins our main objective: the formation of young men and young women for others. There are school masses, year masses and other liturgical celebrations regularly throughout the school year, as well as retreats and pilgrimages. The College enjoys close links with the Hallam Diocese and participates in the diocesan pilgrimage to Lourdes. Religious Education is a part of the curriculum to GCSE and either as an examination or non-examination option in the Sixth Form. The Arrupe programme provides opportunities for Sixth Formers to give service to the local community. The College maintains a strong link with Jesuit missions in different parts of the world, finding ways to further the work of the Society in this area. Pupils have the opportunity to be involved in gap year projects supported by the Jesuits. Pupils and their parents are expected to recognise and endorse the religious commitment of the College.

Sports. The College has extensive playing fields for rugby, hockey, cricket and football. Rugby, for which the College has a strong regional and national reputation, is the major boys' sport. Cricket facilities are excellent with all-weather practice wickets and indoor practice nets. The main girls' sport in the winter term is hockey, for which there is a floodlit all-weather hockey pitch. There is a full-time Level 4 Athletics Coach. Other sports include swimming, tennis, basketball, volleyball, badminton, shooting, netball, fencing, and football. The nearby Rother Valley Country Park and Peak District provide opportunities for sailing, canoeing, windsurfing and hill-walking. There is also a scuba-diving club.

Art, Drama and Music. There are many opportunities to be involved in the Arts within the school, both within the curriculum and as part of the extra-curricular activities. Within the brand new Art and Design department pupils can study fine art, textiles, resistant materials within the workshop, and photography. On Saturday mornings activities are run involving sculpture, textiles, art and photography.

Music is particularly strong, and popular at all levels. Pupils are encouraged to take up a musical instrument, and can participate in a wide number of musical activities, ranging from three choirs and a barber shop group to symphony orchestra, concert band, jazz band and many ensembles. Drama is also strong in the College, and several Senior and Junior productions are put on every year. The music and drama departments collaborate to produce a whole-school musical.

Combined Cadet Force and other Extra-Curricular Activities. All pupils in Year 10 and Year 11 participate in the Combined Cadet Force, in the Army or RAF section. They can continue to be a member, if they choose, in the Sixth Form. The CCF gives opportunities for external leadership courses and adventure training and fulfilling Duke of Edinburgh's Award options. There are extensive opportunities for extra-curricular activities at lunchtime, after school and on Saturday mornings. Pupils can pursue interests in drama, music, sports, the Duke of Edinburgh's Award and many other clubs and societies.

Facilities. Facilities include a new Sixth Form Centre, a Drama Studio, ICT suite of three fully-equipped rooms, Music School with practice rooms, Recital Hall and brand new Music Studio, College Theatre, Library with ICT facilities, various pupil common rooms, Fitness Centre, heated indoor swimming pool, Sports Hall, Rifle Range, Outdoor Pursuits Centre, all-weather tennis courts and 30 acres of games fields. An Olympic standard athletics track was opened in 2007.

Admissions. At 11+ pupils enter via the College's entrance examination, taken early in the Spring term at the College. Pupils at the College's preparatory school, Barlborough Hall, make a seamless transition into the College following sitting a transfer test. At 13+, pupils either sit the College entrance examination or Common Entrance exam through their prep schools. At other ages, pupils are accepted on the basis of school reports, with College entry tests as appropriate and in the Sixth Form, pupils are accepted on the basis of GCSE results, or their equivalent.

Fees per term (2011-2012). Full Boarders: £7,667 (Years 9–13), £5,754 (Years 7 and 8). Weekly Boarders: £6,171 (Years 9–13), £4,794 (Years 7 and 8). Day Pupils: £3,705 (Years 9–13), £3,224 (Years 7 and 8). Barlborough Hall: £2,851 (Day Pupils), £2,140 (Pre-Prep).

Scholarships. Academic scholarships are awarded at 11+, 13+ and Sixth Form on the basis of the College's Scholarship Examination papers. GCSE results also form an aspect of Scholarship awards at Sixth Form. Music and sports scholarships are also available and the College will be happy to provide further information on these. In keeping with the College's ethos, bursaries are awarded in cases of demonstrable need. The Old Mountaineers offer post-graduate scholarships to former pupils of the College and applications are considered annually for these. All scholarships take place early in the Spring Term at the College.

Prospectus. This may be obtained by contacting the Admissions Officer (01246 432872) at the College and parents are always encouraged to visit Mount St Mary's College or its Preparatory School. (*See also Barlborough Hall entry in IAPS section.*)

Charitable status. Mount St Mary's is a Registered Charity, number 1117998. The College was founded in 1842 to provide an education for children.

New Hall School

The Avenue, Boreham, Chelmsford, Essex CM3 3HS
Tel: 01245 467588
Fax: 01245 464348
e-mail: registrar@newhallschool.co.uk
website: www.newhallschool.co.uk

Chairman of Governors: Professor Michael Alder, FRAgS, DL

Principal: **Mrs K Jeffrey**, MA Oxon, PGCE Surrey, BA Div PUM, MA EdMg OU, NPQH

Head of Preparatory School:
Mrs S Conrad, BA, PGCE Dunelm

Vice-Principal:
Mrs J Hopkinson, BSc Hons London, QTS

Bursar: Mrs J Crame, BSc Leeds, ACA, PGCE Mid-Essex

Heads of Academic Departments:

Religious Studies:
Miss K Edwards, BA UEA, PGCE Liverpool

English:
Mrs A Harris, BA Hons Nott, MPhil Nott, PGCE Nott

Mathematics:
Mr C Tye, BSc Hons London, DipMathMan, MA

Information Technology:
Mrs L Fletcher, BSc Surrey

History:
Dr L Shaw, PhD London, GTP, MA Cantab, BA Hons Cantab

Geography:
Mr J Sidwell, BSc Hons Loughborough, PGCE London

Modern Languages:
Mrs N Smart, MA Glasgow, PGCE

Classical Studies:
Mrs S Marshall, Licence-ès-Lettres Grenoble, PGCE

Sciences:
Mr P Thomas, PhD Surrey, BSc Birmingham, PGCE Greenwich (*Head of Science, Head of Physics*)
Dr A Wheadon, BSc Leicester, PhD Leicester, PGCE Aberystwyth, MRSC (*Head of Chemistry*)
Dr K Thacker, BVMS Glasgow, PGCE Greenwich, PhD London, MRCVS (*Head of Biology*)

Music:
Mr A Fardell, BA Kent, LRAM

Drama:
Miss E Nurse, BA Manchester, PGCE Warwick, PGCert Warwick

Art, Design & Technology:
Ms D Colchester, DipAD Kent, ATD Liverpool

Careers:
Mrs S Haddrell

Learning Development:
Mrs J Fawdry, BSc Hull, PGCE London, PGDip SpLD, AMBDA

Physical Education:
Mr S Winsor, BEd Hons Cheltenham & Gloucester (*Director of Sport*)
Mrs M Johnson, BSc, PGCE Loughborough (*Head of Girls' PE*)

Pastoral Care:

Housemasters/Housemistresses:
Hawley House: Mrs E Searle, BA ARU (*Housemistress, OFA Coordinator*)
Dennett House: Mrs E Bennett, BSc Hons Bedfordshire (*Housemistress*)
Earle House: Mr A McMillan, BSc New Zealand, GDTL (*Housemaster*)
Campion House: Mr J Sidwell, BSc Loughborough, PGCE London (*Housemaster*)

Heads of School:
Sixth Form: Mr J Alderson, BA Manchester, PGCE Cantab
Upper School Girls: Mrs N Cooper, BA Oxon, BSc OU, PGCE London
Upper School Boys: Mr G Bickersteth, BA Hons Manchester, PGCE Reading
Middle School Girls: Mrs J McGlynn
Middle School Boys: Mr D Smith, ALLA, BSc Southampton, PGCE OU

Chaplaincy: Mrs J Hopkinson, BSc Hons London, QTS

Medical Department:
Medical Officer: Dr M Edelsten, MBChB
School Nurse: Mrs S Black, Mrs K Felton, Miss M Hennessy
Senior School Health Centre Team Leader: Mrs L Thomson (*Acting*)

New Hall Voluntary Service:
Chairman: Mrs J Hopkinson, BSc Hons London, QTS

Pupil numbers. Senior School (11–18): 691 (Day 468, Boarding 223). Preparatory School (3–11): 359.

New Hall is vibrant and forward thinking. Our aim is to meet the changing needs of young people and their families in the modern technological age. We are proud of our time-honoured values. We have a rich history and a strong tradition of academic excellence, in a community with outstanding pastoral care.

Dedicated, specialist staff work together as a team to enable each student to fulfil his or her potential. We aim to educate the whole person: academically, physically, emotionally, creatively and socially, in a community which also nurtures the spiritual and moral dimensions of human life. This is a place where each individual can be known and affirmed in his or her unique identity. We have high expectations of good conduct and self-discipline.

In a happy and caring environment, students grow in maturity and confidence and make life-long friends.

Location. New Hall benefits from a magnificent campus and stunning heritage setting, with a Grade I listed main building that occupies a former Tudor palace built by King Henry VIII. The school is conveniently situated 35 miles north east of London and close to the town centre of Chelmsford, just off junction 19 of the A12. There is an extensive network of coaches and minibuses for travel to school.

The school is also easily accessible for boarders, being close to London airports; the 19-mile drive to Stansted Airport takes about 40 minutes. There are frequent trains between Chelmsford and central London; the train journey takes 35 minutes. Cambridge is less than an hour's journey by car and the school organises a number of trips to this historic university city.

Our Ethos. "*The Chapel is at the heart of the school.*" (Brentwood Diocese Religious Education Inspection Report)

New Hall has a distinctive Catholic foundation and Christian ethos and welcomes all who support that ethos. Students of many faiths and traditions belong to our community and we believe that everyone benefits from the universal values of love, trust, respect and fellowship that are central to our school life.

The school encourages self-discipline and a sense of responsibility; teamwork and a spirit of service to others are therefore at the heart of New Hall. In particular, a sense of community is fostered through the award-winning and nationally recognised organisation, New Hall Voluntary Service (NHVS). NHVS activities include 8 weekly Action Groups, supporting people in need in the local community through student volunteers and adult volunteer supporters.

Curriculum. An imaginatively taught and well-balanced curriculum is appropriately tailored to the needs of the individual. The staff endeavour to bring out the best in everyone, so that academic potential is realised and individual gifts and talents discovered and nurtured.

The 'diamond model' educational structure provides the optimal combination of co-educational and single-sex teaching. Children progress from the co-educational Preparatory School to the Boys' Division or Girls' Division and then to the co-educational Sixth Form in preparation for university life and future careers. The benefits of single-sex teaching for the first five years of Senior School derive from the ability to tailor pastoral and academic provision more sensitively, gender-specifically and expertly to the needs of young people going through the physical, emotional and social upheaval of adolescence.

Pastoral Care. Our emphasis on pastoral care is a reflection of our core values and ethos and is a real strength of the school. Through the care and attention of class teachers in the Preparatory School and the tutorial and mentoring system in the Senior School, each child is affirmed and encouraged in their personal development. A peer-led group, Willow, provides students with a further support network, run by senior student volunteers, who offer help and guidance.

Building confidence and teaching respect for the self and others is a priority. Through the vertical house system, we foster social integration between boys and girls across the age range, developing team spirit, good humour and creativity.

Boarding. The four boarding houses offer their members a strong sense of identity and opportunities to forge new friendships. The boarders enjoy a relaxed, homely environment and the support and care of a dedicated and enthusiastic staff team. All full boarders may have single study bedrooms from Year 10 onwards. Many younger full or weekly boarders also have single rooms, while some may prefer to share with two or three others. All boarding houses have their own kitchen, well-equipped common rooms, internet access and a selection of books and DVDs.

Music. Music has a long and fine tradition at New Hall. Students may take individual lessons in orchestral instruments, piano, singing, drums and electric guitar. There is a host of performing groups, including: infant, junior and senior choirs; chamber choirs; a chapel choir; a junior and senior orchestra; a strings academy; wind bands; recorder consorts and chamber groups. Students are also encouraged to form jazz and pop bands, for which specialist support facilities are available.

Regular performances are given by students in assemblies, lunchtime recitals and formal concerts. Students take part in regional and national musical festivals and competitions, and groups tour regularly to perform in major venues in Europe.

Performing Arts. The Walkfares Performing Arts Centre is the home of thriving Music, Dance and Drama Departments. Performances, from Shakespeare to modern plays and musicals, give students the opportunity to develop their confidence and creative talents. There is also an annual dance show, with a cast of up to 300 girls and boys aged 4–18.

Students are encouraged to participate in the English Speaking Board (ESB) or London Academy of Music and Dramatic Arts (LAMDA) programmes.

Sport. Team spirit, physical development and good health are promoted through our emphasis on sport throughout the school. New Hall balances elite training for those with particular sporting talent, with an inclusive approach that allows students of all abilities to find at least one sport that they can enjoy. Students compete at county, regional, national and international level in a wide range of sports.

In recent years, there has been a significant investment in the sports facilities on campus. The first-class provision now includes: The Waltham Centre 25m 6-lane indoor swimming pool; a national standard athletics track and floodlit Astroturf; ten floodlit tennis/netball courts; two sports halls; Parsons Hall dance studio; junior and senior cricket wickets and indoor training nets; hockey, rugby and football pitches; and a fitness centre. New Hall also has well-established links with a local riding school and a golf club.

Art, Photography and Design & Technology are popular and successful subjects. Students' work displays a high level of skill and creative imagination. A number of former students have had successful careers in design. The new Technology Centre includes state-of-the-art facilities for Product Design and Cookery.

ICT is an essential part of the curriculum and there are excellent facilities throughout both schools. There is a commitment to a rolling programme of investment, to ensure that students benefit from the latest technology.

Enrichment Activities. Educational opportunities extend far beyond the classroom. The school's educational philosophy is reflected in the variety of challenging activities on offer, which creates a stimulating environment for personal development.

The extra-curricular programme runs during the school day, on weekday evenings and at the weekend. Activities range from debating & public speaking to chess, eco-club, croquet and Air Cadets. Senior School students may participate in the annual pilgrimage to Lourdes and may also undertake expeditions, in particular as part of the Duke of Edinburgh's Award and as members of a World Challenge team.

Careers. New Hall students grow in confidence and learn the communication skills for good relationships with others and for a successful career. From Year 9 onwards, students undertake specialist careers programmes. There are excellent work experience opportunities, with work placements provided by Old Fishes (alumni) and parents, or through contacts made at the New Hall Careers Convention.

Inspection. New Hall School was inspected by ISI inspectors and Ofsted inspectors in October-November 2010. The full reports can be viewed on the school's website.

"The pupils' personal development is outstanding. Pupils are confident, and show mutual respect and a well-developed sense of responsibility."

"Pupils have excellent attitudes to learning that underpin their achievement."

"Pupils are articulate in both formal and informal settings, listen respectfully, question carefully and debate thoughtfully. Pupils make good, and sometimes exceptional progress when compared with others of similar ability."

As a result of the Ofsted Inspection New Hall was rated Outstanding for Boarding: *"The boarding provision is excellent"*.

Fees per term (2011-2012). Senior School: Day £4,768–£5,112; Weekly Boarding £6,324–£7,356; Full Boarding £7,007–£7,901.

Preparatory School: Day £2,512–£3,717; Boarding (from age 8): £5,003 (weekly), £5,539 (full).

Fees shown include Prompt Payment Discount of £100 per term.

Entry requirements. Own entrance papers, plus reports, and if possible interview. Further information on the curriculum and a copy of the prospectus is available from the Registrar.

Scholarships. (*See Scholarship Entries section.*) Details about Scholarships can also be obtained from the School.

Charitable status. New Hall School Trust is a Registered Charity, number 1110286. Its aim is the education of children within a Christian environment.

Newcastle-under-Lyme School

Mount Pleasant, Newcastle-under-Lyme, Staffordshire ST5 1DB
Tel: 01782 631197
Fax: 01782 632582
e-mail: info@nuls.org.uk
website: www.nuls.org.uk

Newcastle-under-Lyme School, which attracts pupils from a large area of North Staffordshire, South Cheshire and North Shropshire, is a co-educational day school for 1,000 pupils aged 3–18. The present School was formed in 1981 through the amalgamation of Newcastle High School and the Orme Girls' School, two schools which were endowed as a single foundation in 1872 under an educational charity scheme for children in Newcastle which has its roots in the 1600s. The two schools enjoyed a reputation for scholarship and for service to the community throughout North Staffordshire, a reputation which has continued with the formation of Newcastle-under-Lyme School. The School is also well known for its high standards in sport, music and drama, which play a major part in the extra-curricular life of the School. The Junior School is adjacent to the Senior School and has some 325 pupils aged 3–11.

Governing Body:

Chair of Governors:
Mrs R E Evans, LLB

Appointed by:

The Council of the University of Keele:
Professor P W Jones, BSc, MSc, PhD, CStat

The Parents' Association – Senior School:
Mrs Lotika Singha, BDS, MDS, MOrth

The Parents' Association – Junior School:
M Segal, BDS

The Committee of the Old Boys' Association of Newcastle High School:
A Curzon

The Committee of the Old Girls' Association of the Orme Girls' School:
Mrs K A Miller, BSc, LLB

Governors:
L J Bassett
I R Cheetham, FRICS
D H Cook, MA
W H P Evans, ACIB
A T Gough
M Lawton, MBA
R E Nadin, FCA
T J O'Neill, CEng, MBA, MSc, MIEE, PhD (*Vice Chairman*)
J S Rushton, BSc, FCA, CISA
D P Wallbank, BA
J P Wenger

Bursar: J Longdon, MInstRE

Headmaster: **N A Rugg**, MA

Deputy Head: G A Cappi, MA

Director of External Relations: I J Cartwright, BEd, MA

Assistant Heads:
Mrs J A Simms, BA, MSc (*Pastoral*)
M S Snell, BSc, MA (*Teaching and Learning*)

Head of Sixth Form: Mrs B A Godridge, BA

English:
*Mrs A A Keay, MA
Mrs J Betts-Nicholson, BA
Mrs B Joughin, BA
R Lench, BA

History:
*D Dunlop, BA, PhD
D A Cawdron, BA
Mrs S J Stockdale, BSc

Mathematics:
*Miss J M Griffiths, BSc
Mrs C M Barber, BSc
D T Buckley, BSc
Mrs J C Cliff, BSc
Mrs J A Cryer, BSc
Mrs S Goodwin, BSc
E J Griffiths, BA

ICT:
*S Luck, BSc

Chemistry:
*Mrs J M Pinkham, BSc, PhD
G Moore, BSc, PhD
P Thomson, BSc, PhD

Physics:
*Mrs S Bremner, BSc, PhD
A Fishburne, MEng
S Rimmington, BSc

Biology:
*N J Simms, BSc
N C Carter, BSc
Miss J Galvin, BSc
Mrs R Moon, BSc

D R Pepper, BSc, PhD (*Assistant Head of Sixth Form*)

Geography:
*T P Jowitt, BSc
D P Sherratt, BA
Mrs F P E Williams, BA

Modern Languages:
*D L Brayford, MA, MEd
C Diaz, BA
Mrs M Isherwood, BA
D G Murtagh, BA
Mrs K H Tan, BA
Mrs D A Woodcock, BA

Religious Studies:
*R W Bridges, BSc

Latin:
*Ms T A Thomas, BA

Economics:
*Miss L Barton, BA
Mrs M L Clutterbuck, BEd

Art and Design:
*Mrs S Parkinson, BA
Mrs J C F Fanthome, BA, MA
Miss L Herian, BA
Mrs B W Jones, CertEd

Design and Technology:
*D Patrick, BA
Mrs A Borrowdale, BA

Home Economics:
*Mrs J Machin
Mrs N G Swindells, BEd

Physical Education:
*G M Chesterman, BSocSc
G M Breen, BSc
P J Butler, FISTC, AIST LS
Mrs D Glenn, BEd
Mrs J Pointon, BEd
S A Robson, BEd
Mrs P Smith, BEd
Miss E A Webb, BEd, MEd

Music:
*T Sagar, MA
D G McGarry, DLM
Mrs C Hughes, BA, MusEd
Mrs M Potter, GGSM, ARCM, PGCE

Careers:
Mrs B Joughin, BA

Learning Support Coordinator:
Mrs J A Cryer, BSc

Librarian: Miss W F Butler, BA, MA, DipLib, MCLIP

Newcastle-under-Lyme Junior School:
Head Teacher: N J Vernon, BSc, MA
Deputy Head: M J Erian, BA, MA
Head of Pre-Prep: Mrs A M Burgess, BA
Nursery Manager: Mrs A Smith, NNEB, NEBS

Mrs C Deakes, BA
Mrs H Eady
Mrs A Farnsworth
Mrs J Grisdale, BEd
G Lewis, BEd
Mrs L Moss, BA
Mrs S Nixon, BEd
Mrs J M Parker, BA

Mrs S Quinn, BEd
Mrs J S Roberts, BEd
Miss F Scott, LLB
Miss C K M Shipton, BA
Miss J Stanton, BEd
Mrs K Tapp, BA
Mrs J Ward, BEd

Buildings and Grounds. Set in 30 acres of grounds, the School is pleasantly situated on high ground in a quiet conservation area close to the centre of Newcastle-under-Lyme. The original buildings still form part of the School and extensions have been added from time to time. A fine dining hall was opened in one of the wings of the original building, part of the continuing programme of development and refurbishment which was begun when the School reverted to full independence in 1981. The Millennium Sixth Form Centre opened in March 2000 affording spacious new accommodation for senior students. In addition to the well equipped classrooms and Science laboratories, the School has language laboratories, workshops, a Music School, an Art and Design Centre, two libraries, a gymnasium, and a Sports Centre which includes a sports hall, a weights room and an indoor swimming pool. Computers are accessible in subject areas and in four modern laboratories, where machines are linked on a network basis. There are also tennis and netball courts and extensive playing fields, providing pitches for cricket, rugby and hockey, adjacent to the School. An all-weather pitch with floodlighting was opened in March 2002.

Organisation. The School is organised in two sections: the Junior School – nursery (2004), pre-preparatory (2004) and preparatory (1982) – which has 300+ pupils in the age range 3 to 11 and the Senior School, with approximately 400 boys and 400 girls. The Sixth Form numbers more than 200 students.

Form Tutors and Heads of Year have particular responsibility for the pastoral welfare of the pupils in their charge.

In Year 7 and Year 8 boys and girls have their own inter-form and inter-house competitions, with separate Lower School assemblies. This structure gives to the Lower School forms a separate identity within the Senior School. The Senior House structure, which extends from Year 9 upwards, consists of four co-educational houses.

Curriculum. A broad curriculum in the first five years has English (Language and Literature), Mathematics, Biology, Chemistry, Physics, and French as core subjects. All pupils also take Latin, History, Geography, Religious Education, Music, Art, Home Economics, Design and Technology, ICT, PE, Swimming and Games; German and Spanish are introduced as option subjects in Year 9. Pupils have the option of taking Biology, Chemistry and Physics as a dual-award GCSE or as three separate GCSEs in Year 10 and Year 11.

Pupils take nine GCSEs and the great majority will proceed to take four AS Levels, in addition to General Studies or Critical Thinking in the Lower Sixth Form. Three or four of these subjects will be continued in the Upper Sixth as A2 qualifications.

Optional choices in the Sixth Form include A Level Business Studies, Economics, British Government and Politics and Physical Education in addition to AS Levels in the subjects available at GCSE. Pupils are also prepared for Oxford and Cambridge Entrance.

Extra-Curricular Activities. The main school games are Rugby, Cricket, Hockey, Athletics, Tennis and Cross-Country for the boys and Hockey, Athletics, Netball, Tennis and Rounders for the girls. Swimming, Waterpolo, Life Saving and Synchronised Swimming, Waterpolo and Life Saving also feature strongly and there are usually opportunities for Shooting, Squash, Aerobics, Basketball, Badminton, Golf and other physical activities in the Sixth Form.

There are also strong traditions in both Music and Drama and standards are very high. More than 300 pupils receive instrumental tuition and there are a number of concerts in each year with major performances being given in local churches and in the Victoria Concert Hall in Hanley. There are several major drama productions each year including one each at Senior and Lower School levels.

The flourishing Combined Cadet Force has naval, army and airforce sections and there is also a large Scout troop, which enrols both boys and girls. Pupils also participate in the Duke of Edinburgh's Award Scheme.

Clubs and Societies meet during the lunch hour and after school.

Careers. The School places much emphasis on the importance of careers guidance, both in the GCSE years and in the preparation for tertiary education. The School is an all-in member of the ISCO Careers Guidance Scheme, through which all pupils in Year 11 receive a careers report based on tests of ability, personality and aptitude. Pupils receive full advice on applications to Universities and other Institutes of Higher Education.

Honours. Between 1987 and 2010 266 of our students gained places at Oxford and Cambridge, while in 2010, some 95% of all Upper Sixth leavers gained entry to degree courses in Higher Education.

Admissions. Entry to the Nursery is on a first-come first-served basis. Entry to the Junior School and Years 7, 8 and 9 of the Senior School is by examination/assessment only, normally at the ages of 7, 11 and 13. A few candidates are also admitted at 8, 9, 10, 12 and 14. The entrance examinations for these age groups are usually held in January and February for entry in the following September but pupils moving into the area may be considered at other times.

Entry at Sixth Form level is by interview and GCSE qualifications.

Registration forms, and copies of the Prospectus, are available on request.

Scholarships and Bursaries. (*See Scholarship Entries section.*) Governors' scholarships are awarded annually on the results of the entrance examination at 11+. Academic and Sports Scholarships are also available for entry at 13+. Scholarships are also awarded in Mathematical Sciences and in Physics for the Sixth Form, on the results of Scholarship Examinations.

The Governors have established a Bursary Scheme to assist parents with school fees.

Further details may be obtained from the Registrar.

Fees per term (2011-2012). Senior School £3,169; Junior School: Preparatory £2,588; Pre-Preparatory £2,306; Nursery £39.50 per day (£21 per session).

Charitable status. Newcastle-under-Lyme School is a Registered Charity, number 1124463. The object of the Charity shall be the provision and conduct in or near Newcastle-under-Lyme of a day or a day and boarding school or schools for boys and girls.

Norwich School

70 The Close, Norwich NR1 4DD
Tel: 01603 728430
Fax: 01603 728490
e-mail: enquiries@norwich-school.org.uk
website: www.norwich-school.org.uk

Norwich School is a co-educational day school for pupils aged seven to eighteen. Set in the Cathedral Close, the School is an historic place. The exact date at which it came into being is unknown, but its origins can be traced back to the foundation of the Cathedral in 1096. In 1547 it was re-founded by Edward VI.

In 2010–11 there were approximately 990 pupils: 825 in the Senior School (age 11–18) and 165 in the Lower School (age 7–11) (*see Norwich School, Lower School IAPS entry*).

Cathedral Choristers are members of the school.

Motto: '*Praemia virtutis honores*'

Council of Management:

Co-optative Governors:
P J E Smith, MA, FIA (*Chairman*)
T J Gould, MA (*Vice-Chairman*)
C H Bradley-Watson, BSc, MRICS
A R Burdon-Cooper, MA, LLB
N J Fischl, MA
Mrs A Fry, MA
E J H Gould, MA
Mrs A J C Green, BSc
C W Hoffman, ACIB
J A E Hustler
A D Jeakings, FCMA
Mrs E McLoughlin, BArch, RIBA
Mrs M C G Phillips, BA
Dr N P V Richardson, MA, PhD
D W Talbot, ACA
Miss T Yates, BA

Representative Governors:
Professor C Andrew, MA, University of Cambridge
J R Chambers, FCA, Worshipful Company of Dyers
The Revd Canon JM Haselock, BA, BPhil, MA, Dean & Chapter
Professor K J Heywood, BSc, PhD, University of East Anglia
R A Leuchars, BSc, Worshipful Company of Dyers
P N Mirfield, BCL, MA, BA, University of Oxford
The Very Revd Graham Smith, BA, Dean of Norwich

Head Master: **S D A Griffiths**, MA Oxon

Principal Deputy Head: Miss L E Péchard, MA

Academic Deputy Head: N M Plater, MA Oxon
M D Barber, BA (*Assistant Head, Co-Curricular*)
P D Goddard, BEd (*Assistant Head, Compliance and Outreach*)
Dr D N Farr, BA, PhD, FRHS (*Assistant Head, Director of Studies*)
Mrs N J Hill, BSc (*Assistant Head, Pastoral*)
C Hooper, BA (*Assistant Head, Head of Sixth Form*)
P A Todd, MA Cantab (*Assistant Head*)
Bursar: B D G Delacave, ACA

Teaching Staff:
Miss K E Adams, BA
R P Allain, BMus, FTCL
Miss E A Allsop BSc
C A Banham, BA, MSc
Mrs C L Barber, BA (*Head of Spanish*)
D P Bateman, BSc (*Head of Politics; Housemaster, Valpy*)
R H Bedford-Payne, BA (*Housemaster, Nelson*)
T D Berwick, BSc
Dr M Bhaduri, BSc, MSc, PhD
Mrs R M Bolton, BSc
Miss A E Boyt, BA
Miss N Bruce, MA
Miss S-A Bunt, BA
R A Bunting (*Head of Boys' Games*)
Miss S V Corthine, BA
W H J Croston, BA (*Head of Careers and Higher Education*)
A P Curtis, BA (*Housemaster*)
Mrs K E Curtis, BA (*part-time*)
G M Downes, BA (*Housemaster, Brooke*)
Mrs F L Ellington, BA Ms R A E Erskine, BEd
Miss L E D Evan, BA
Miss V L Fincham, BA, MA (*Head of German*)
A L Fisher, BA
J C Fisher, BSc (*Housemaster, Repton*)
A Fullwood, MA (*Head of English*)
R C Gardiner, BSc (*Head of Economics*)
Ms J Gautierrez
S J Gibbons (*Director of Sport*)
I M Grisewood, BA (*Housemaster, School House*)
F P A Hanique, BA
G A Hanlon, BSc (*Housemaster, Coke*)
T J Hill, BSc (*Head of ICT*)
Dr A P Hinsley, BSc, PhD
M D Hopgood, BA (*Head of Geography*)
E D Hopkins, BA
Dr J C Hopper, BSc, PhD (*Head of Biology*)
Miss A J Hurrell, BA
Miss A A Ireland, BA
M James, MA (*Head of Drama*)
S A Kettley, MA (*Head of Classics*)
Mme C Le Floch, L-ès-L Maîtrise
Miss M E Ling, BSc
Mrs N B Looker, BA (*part-time*)
B W Mack, BSc
F J Mclvor, MA (*Senior Tutor, Head of Meno*)
Miss T M Mounter, BA (*Head of History*)
M Mulligan, BA, MPhil (*Head of Philosophy & Critical Thinking*)
A Murray, MA
I R Passam, BA (*Head of Art & Design*)
R W Peters, BA (*Head of Mathematics*)
Mrs C M Pywell, BSc (*part-time*)
M Ramshaw, BSc
Ms N J Ravenscroft, MA (*part-time*)
Mrs E Reed, BA (*part-time*)
Dr G Richardson, BSc, PhD
A M Rowlandson, BA
Mrs D Saywack, MA, MA (*Head of Religious Studies*)
Mrs L Slade, BA (*Art Coordinator*)
Mrs P R Staufenberg, MA (*part-time*)
Miss E L Stone, BSc

M W Strickland
Mrs C L Szirtes (*part-time*)
M G Thompson, BSc
The Reverend N Tivey (*Chaplain*)
Mrs J V Turner, BA (*part-time*)
Miss V J Turner, MA
Dr M Venables, MA, PhD (*Head of Science, Head of Physics*)
J E R Waite, CertEd (*Coordinator of Internal Examinations*)
J W Walker, BEd (*part-time*)
Mrs S Ward, MA
T J Watts, LLB
D Whatley (*Head of Chemistry*)
Mrs S Wortley, AGSM, GGSM, CertEd (*part-time*)

Lower School
Master of the Lower School: J K Ingham, BA
Second Master: R A Love, BSc
Director of Studies: C W Parsons, BSc
I K Blaxall, BEd
T J Brook, MSc
C C G Cordy, BA
Mrs N B Dunnett, BA (*Music*)
Mrs S Fisher (*part-time*)
Mrs I R G Grote, 1st & 2nd Staatsexamen (*part-time*)
R E Hambleton, BSc, MA (*part-time*)
Miss E R Porter, BA
J S G Worton, BSc
Mrs G E Wright, BEd (*part-time*)

Head Master's PA: Mrs K E Moore
Registrar: Mrs V A Gaskin, BSc
SMT Administrator: Ms J Algar
Lower School Secretary: Mrs J S Payton
School Secretary: Ms N Hever
Common Room Secretary: Mrs J M Raath
Secretary to Head of Sixth Form: Mrs E Reed, BA
Music School Coordinator: Mrs S Wortley, AGSM, GGSM, CertEd
Chief Examinations Officer: Ms J Powell, BA
Deputy to the Examinations Officer: Mrs S Meader

Medical Officer:
School Nurses:
Mrs C Bennett, RGN, ONC
Miss C Castle, RGN

Archivists: J W Walker, J C Fisher

Learning and scholarship are at the heart of the broad education that Norwich School provides. Christian values – notably love and compassion for one another – underpin our activities and relationships.

Norwich School is committed to:

• producing scholarly, reflective young people who are capable of handling difficult concepts and expressing profound thought;

• providing a rich, varied and broad education that develops the diverse talents of the boys and girls;

• equipping pupils for leadership and service.

Admission. The main points of entry are at ages 7, 11, 13 and 16. There may be small numbers of places available at other ages. Application for admission should be made to the Head Master on the form obtainable from the Registrar.

Fees per term (2011-2012). Senior School £4,058; Lower School £3,696.

Faith and Worship. Members of the Senior School meet in the Cathedral every morning. Services and assemblies provide precious opportunities for corporate gathering and worship. The Christian tradition of the School provides a framework for its spiritual life. Pupils of all faiths are welcomed and it is not the School's intention to proselytize or indoctrinate. It is felt right, however, that all pupils should receive grounding in the liturgy and traditions of Christian worship so that they are acquainted with the faith heritage of the School and the Cathedral that it regularly visits. Familiarity with prayers, hymns and Biblical texts provides pupils with a spiritual vocabulary and a vehicle through which to encounter important ethical and spiritual questions. The School aims to provide pupils with a secure basis from which they can embark upon their own journeys into faith.

Teaching and Learning. Good scholarship is held in high regard at Norwich School. Those pupils who exhibit strong academic ability and the desire to read, learn and express their opinions are at the heart of school activity. Inspirational teaching using imaginative methods and content is fostered throughout the School. Fundamental to all teaching and learning at Norwich School is the shared belief that a well-educated person who loves to learn and is able to think critically and creatively is more likely to lead a fulfilling and positive life. Education is perceived as a worthwhile end in itself.

Pastoral Care and Discipline. The School aims to sustain a friendly atmosphere with genuine trust and respectful camaraderie between pupils and staff. There is firm discipline within that caring environment, enabling pupils to feel secure within clearly defined parameters.

In practical terms, each pupil's welfare is the responsibility of their tutor in whom the parents have a main point of contact for pastoral matters.

The Senior School (age 11–16). There is a distinctive curriculum for the 11 to 14 age group, elements of which are sustained throughout the GCSE years. Alongside the traditional range of subjects is the Meno Programme: approximately six periods per week that incorporate unusual languages – such as Russian, Japanese and Hungarian – as well as the 'philosophy for children methodology', thinking, relaxation skills and practical elements such as engineering and photography. There are practical elements where learning takes place outdoors – to learn, for example, about ecology and food production by experience on school land. Site visits to the North Norfolk coast and other areas of the county are programmed into the year so that different academic subjects such as Art, Biology, Geography and History can combine resources on project work. The aim is to aid learning through varied experiences and stimuli and to excite the pupils about the learning process.

The Sixth Form. Almost all Sixth Form pupils go to university upon leaving Norwich School. There is a long track record of success in large numbers gaining entrance to Oxford, Cambridge and the other top academic institutions. All boys and girls are encouraged to excel in their A Level studies and to be committed to sporting, cultural and extra-curricular activity.

The Advice Team, led by the Head of Sixth Form, tailors a programme of University and career preparation for each pupil and monitors their success from Lower Sixth to A Level results day – and beyond where necessary.

Creative and Performing Arts. The music department is very popular with pupils, welcoming and encouraging boys and girls of all levels of ability to explore their musical creativity. Over 65% of all pupils make music regularly. There are more than twenty-eight specialist teachers and various orchestras, ensembles, bands, choirs and groups. Performances at all levels and ages regularly take place within the School, the Cathedral and in the wider community.

Drama facilities include the purpose-designed Blake Studio. Pupils also have the privilege of performing at some of the finest venues in Norwich: the Senior Play traditionally is performed in the Maddermarket Theatre; other productions take place in the Puppet Theatre, the Lower School and the Cathedral; major musicals are staged at the Playhouse.

Art and Design are well-resourced and, in recent years, several talented artists and designers from the School have gained places at the top Art Colleges.

Sport. Norwich School is unusual among day schools in providing two games sessions each week and fixtures on many Saturdays. Games and sport are perceived as vital aspects of the curriculum.

The major games for boys are rugby, cricket and hockey; and for girls, netball, hockey and rounders. There are strong fixture lists in each of these sports. Boys and girls are able to take up a broad range of other sports including swimming, netball, cross-country running, fencing, lacrosse, rowing, sailing, self-defence, soccer, shooting and badminton – among others.

Activities and Trips. The intellectual life is enhanced by an array of stimulating activities. There is a Debating Society, a Politics Forum and the Thomas Browne Society for the presentation of philosophical papers and intellectual discussion. Many academic departments run clubs to allow pupils to gain a wider experience of their subjects. The School Consultative Committee allows elected pupils to discuss school issues directly with the Head Master.

The variety of clubs and societies is continually changing as new teachers and pupils bring their own particular interests to the School. Debating, creative writing, philosophy, Amnesty International, yoga, the Duke of Edinburgh's Award, conservation, chess, cookery and film clubs are on the list at the time of writing. Music, drama and the practical arts all provide further extra-curricular opportunities.

Overseas visits broaden the experience of many pupils. The Modern Languages Department runs exchanges to France, Germany and Liechtenstein. Recent cultural, sporting or adventurous trips have gone to Austria, Canada, China, Ecuador, Egypt, Greece, Holland, Iceland, India, Israel, Russia and Turkey.

Scholarships and Bursaries. (*See Scholarship Entries section.*) Scholarships are awarded to pupils with outstanding ability and flair, which the school assesses by examination, interview or audition. The financial value of a scholarship will be up to 10% of the annual tuition fee – irrespective of parental means. Scholarships are awarded in five categories: Academic; Music; Sport; Art/Design and Drama.

Academic and Music scholarships are awarded at 11+, 13+ and Sixth Form entry. Sport and Art, Design or Drama scholarships are awarded only at Sixth Form entry. Pupils may apply for more than one scholarship, although the maximum financial benefit that can be cumulated is 20% of the school fees.

We set aside generous bursarial funds to enable boys and girls to come to Norwich School who would not be able to do so without financial help. All bursaries are means-tested and can result in a reduction in fees of up to 100%; there is a sliding scale dependent on family income and finances.

As a general rule, it is unlikely that a bursary will be awarded when family income is greater than four and a half times the school fees. It is possible, indeed not unusual, for a bursary holder to have a scholarship. In such circumstances, up to 10% of the fees would be covered by the scholarship; any bursary funding further to this would, of course, be means-tested.

To supplement the School's bursary provision, the Worshipful Company of Dyers, through its charitable trust, is able to give financial support to a pupil with all-round talent in both L4 and L6. The criteria for the Dyers' Bursary Scheme are similar to those outlined above and potential applicants should simply register interest in bursarial assistance on the application form.

In addition to the above arrangements, the school has an association with the Ogden Trust which is able to give financial support to selected Sixth Form pupils who join us from the state sector with primary academic strengths in mathematics or the applied sciences. The Trust's financial criteria are similar to our own.

Cathedral Choristers hold Chorister Bursaries to the value of 50% of fees. Further assistance in cases of need is possible.

Lower School. *For further details, see entry for Norwich School, The Lower School in the IAPS section.*

Old Norvicensians. All enquiries should be made to Mrs R Lightfoot, Norwich School, 71a The Close, Norwich NR1 4DD.

Charitable status. Norwich School is a Registered Charity, number 311280. It exists solely to provide education.

Nottingham High School

Waverley Mount, Nottingham NG7 4ED
Tel: 0115 978 6056
Fax: 0115 979 2202
e-mail: info@nottinghamhigh.co.uk
website: www.nottinghamhigh.co.uk

Motto: '*Lauda Finem*'
    This School was founded in 1513 by Agnes Mellers, widow of Richard Mellers, sometime Mayor of Nottingham. The first Charter was given by Henry VIII, and supplementary Charters were given by Philip and Mary, and by Queen Elizabeth. The School, which remains independent, is now administered under the terms of a scheme issued by the Charity Commissioners.

Governing Body:
The Lord Lieutenant of Nottinghamshire
The Lord Mayor of Nottingham
Two Representatives of the City Council
One Representative of the Nottinghamshire County Council
Four Representatives of the Universities
Eleven Co-optative Members

Chairman of the Governors: P Balen

Clerk to the Governors: A B Palfreman, MA, 84 Friar Lane, Nottingham

Headmaster: K D Fear, BA Southampton

Deputy Headmaster: P G Sibly, BSc, PhD University College London, ARCM
Deputy Headmaster (*Academic*): D M Williamson, BA Durham, MA York, FRGS
Senior Teacher: I P Spedding, BSc Hull
Director of Finance and Estates: R Dunmore, BA, ACA

Academic Staff:
* *Head of Department*

J F W Knifton, MA (*French*)
Mrs K J Turner, BA Rhodes, HDip (**ICT*)
R G Willan, BA (**Geography*)
R Kilby, BSc (**Mathematics*)
J A Cook, BSc (**Biology*)
G Douglas, LTCL (*Music*)
P G Morris, BA (*Physics*)
A D Holding, BA (**General Studies, Modern Languages*)
W P J Ruff, MA (**English*)
A F Wood, BSc, PhD (*Chemistry, Director of Studies*)
K P Brierley, BSc (*Chemistry*)
M T Cleverley, BSc (*Chemistry*)
A S Winter, BA (*French*)
R J Clarke, BSc (*Mathematics*)
C P Sedgewick, MA (*Geography, Head of Sixth Form*)
J T Swain, MA, PhD, FRHistS (*History*)
Revd S Krzeminski, BTh (**Religious Education and Philosophy*)
S L Williams, BA, MA (*History*)
K C Clayton, BSc (*Biology*)
Dr C Y Fletcher, BSc, PhD (*Biology*)
M D Smith, BEd (**Physical Education*)
A V Martin, BA, DipPsych (**Psychology*)
Mrs M O Mills, BSc (*Mathematics*)

M I Saperia, BSc (*Biology*)
D B Thomas, BEd (*Design Technology*)
R A Gilbert, BA (*Chemistry*)
G Whitehead, MA (*Modern Languages*)
S J Reid, BA, MMus (**Music*)
P J Cramp, BA (**Economics & Politics*)
Mrs A Griffin, BA (*German*)
I F Thorpe, BEd (*Design Technology*)
J G Allen, MA, MSc (*Mathematics*)
P E Hortor, MA (*Physics*)
Mrs K M Costante, MA (*Chemistry*)
D J Poole, BA, MA, FRSA (*Politics, Economics*)
Mrs W Davies, BA (*Geography*)
Mrs B Kruger, BA (*German Assistant*)
P J Dowsett, BA (**History*)
Mrs A R G Lemon, BA (*Geography*)
Mrs C O'Brien, BA, OCR CertSpLD (**Learning Support Coordinator*)
Mrs S D Hills, BA (*Religious Education*)
S A Barr-Smith, BSc (*Mathematics*)
R S C Grant, BA (**Classics*)
Miss M Kirbyshire, BA (*Art*)
Mrs C Howat, BSc (*Mathematics*)
Mrs M Smith, BA (*English*)
S Whitehead, BEd (*Physical Education*)
R M A Batchelor, BSc (*Mathematics*)
D P Brumby, BSc (*Mathematics*)
Mrs S Culshaw-Robinson, CertEd (*ICT Assistant*)
F A Rosas (*Spanish Assistant*)
Ms C Sanford, BA (*English*)
Mrs J Poole, BSc (*Biology*)
K Heath, BSc (**Chemistry*)
Mrs H Wood, MSci (*Chemistry*)
Mrs M Hubbard, BSc (*Psychology*)
Miss L Gritti, MSci (*Physics*)
D J Allerton, BA (*Modern Languages*)
W M A Burn, BA (*English*)
B J Harrison, BA (*Classics*)
A H N Reid, BSc, PhD (**Physics*)
Mrs R E Wheeler, BA (*English*)
Miss E S Yeadon, BA, MA (*Religious Studies*)
Miss K Skidmore, BA (**Art*)
C M Brown, BA (*Modern Languages*)
P B Gray, BSc (**Design Technology*)
Mrs W M Robinson, MA (*Economics*)
Miss R Pearson, BA, MA (*English*)
C S Colman, PhD (*History*)
J L Picardo, BA (**Modern Languages*)
C S Farman, BSc (*Physical Education*)

School Nurse: Ms S Jacob, RGN
Headmaster's PA: Mrs H E Bowen
Librarian: Ms Y Gunther
Development Director: Ms K Scott-Mitchell

Junior School

Headmaster: A R Earnshaw, BA, QTS
Deputy Head: E Jones, BA
Mrs H Whittamore, BA, QTS
Mrs S M Cooke, BA
Miss J Abell, BA
Mrs G K Sethi, BA, MA
Mrs L M Sedgewick, BEd
Mrs K B George, CertEd (*Learning Support*)
A A Simpson, BEd
T Caldwell, BSc, MSc
Miss V Walster, BA
Mrs R Slater, BA
R J Shaw, BA

Lovell House Infant School

Headteacher: Mrs A E Cummings, BEd
Miss A Roberts, BA
Miss C Smith, BA

Mrs A Williams
Mrs E Baker, BEd
Miss A Clarke (*Teaching Assistant*)
Ms J Faulkner (*Teaching Assistant*)
Mrs J Cox (*Teaching Assistant*)

Fees per term (2011-2012). Tuition: Senior School £3,724, Junior School £2,965, Lovell House Infant School £2,550.

Admission. Entrance Examinations and assessments are held in January and February each year. Applicants for the Infant School should be between the ages of 4 and 7 years, for the Junior School between the ages of 7 and 11 years, and for the Senior School between 11 and 12 years on 1 September of the year of entry. Entry is also possible higher up the School, subject to places being available and a successful interview (entry to Sixth Form is also dependent upon satisfactory performance at GCSE).

Organisation and Curriculum. There are 1014 day boys, of whom 185 are in the Infant and Junior Schools and 226 in the Sixth Form. Nearly all Junior School boys go on to complete their education in the Senior School. (*For further details about the Junior School, see entry in IAPS section.*)

The Senior School curriculum leads to examinations at GCSE in the normal range of subjects. Boys in the Sixth Form are prepared for AS and A Levels. The range of subjects is wide – Latin; Classical Civilisation; Modern Languages; English; History; Economics; Politics; Design Technology, Geography; Mathematics; Physics; Chemistry; Biology; Music; Art; Philosophy; Psychology; Classical Greek; Music Technology.

Entrance Scholarships and Bursaries. (*See Scholarship Entries section.*) The Entrance Examination for the Senior School is held in January each year for the award of Entrance Scholarships. An additional school fund provides entrance bursaries for boys who receive grants according to their parents' means. Limited bursary funding is also available for Sixth Form entrants.

Games. The Playing Fields, covering 20 acres, are situated about a mile and a half from the School with excellent pavilion facilities. There are also indoor cricket nets at the school. The School games, in which all boys are expected to take part unless medically exempted, are Rugby Football (together with Association Football in the Junior School) in the winter, and Cricket or Tennis and Athletics in the summer. Other alternatives provided for senior boys include Cross Country, Squash, Hockey, Association Football, Badminton, Golf, Shooting and Basketball. Swimming (the School has its own 25m pool) forms part of the Physical Education programme.

Combined Cadet Force. The School maintains a contingent of the CCF based on voluntary recruitment and consisting of Navy, Army and Air Force sections. There is a small bore range, and the School enters teams for various national competitions.

Societies. Individual interests and hobbies are catered for by a wide range of Societies which meet in the lunch break or at the end of afternoon school. These include Drama, Modern Languages, Mathematics, Chemistry, Biology, English, Politics, Arts, Music and Debating Societies, the Chess Club, the Bridge Club, Christian Union, and the Scout Troop. Over 120 boys a year participate in the Duke of Edinburgh's Award Scheme. The Community Action Group, the Explorer Scouts and other Societies meet jointly with the neighbouring Nottingham Girls' High School.

Music. Apart from elementary instruction in Music in the lower forms, and more advanced studies for GCSE and A Level, tuition is offered by 3 full-time and 18 part-time teachers in the full range of orchestral instruments. There are 2 School orchestras of 50 and 30 players, 2 Choirs, a concert band (wind) of 50, a Training Band and Big Band and choral and orchestral concerts are given each year. Four instrumental bursaries, covering fee tuition on one instrument, are available to boys entering Year 7.

Honours. 11 Places at Oxford and Cambridge.

The Old Nottinghamians Society owns a substantial Social Centre at its sports ground. The Hon Secretary is Mr R J Dunmore, Nottingham High School, Waverley Mount, Nottingham NG7 4ED. (Tel: 0115 845 2210).

Charitable status. Nottingham High School is a Registered Charity, number 1104251. It exists to provide education for boys between the ages of 4 and 18 years.

Oakham School

Chapel Close, Oakham, Rutland LE15 6DT

Tel:	01572 758500
	Admissions: 01572 758758
Fax:	01572 758595
e-mail:	admissions@oakham.rutland.sch.uk
website:	www.oakham.rutland.sch.uk

Motto: '*Quasi Cursores Vitai Lampada Tradunt*'

Trustees:
Chairman: Dr S E Blaza, BSc Hons
Deputy Chairman: P O Lawson, DL, BSc, CITP, MBCS, DipMus

Ex officio:
The Rt Revd The Lord Bishop of Peterborough
The Lord Lieutenant of Rutland, Dr L Howard, OBE, JP
The Very Revd The Dean of Peterborough

Co-optative:
J H Arkell, MA
Mrs K S Blank, LLM, LLB
Dr C Burt, MA Cantab, MPhil Cantab, PhD Cantab
Mrs P A G Corah
P S Douty
R C Gainher, BSc
Mrs G M Harris, MHCIMA
T F Hart, MA
N D G Jones, BSc
A R M Little, MA
S K Mehra
Dr D L Smith, MA, PhD, PGCE, FRHistS
M T D Squires
N Wainwright
M G Wilson

Bursar and Clerk to the Trustees: Mrs A Hedrich-Wiggans, MA Cantab, MSt Oxon, ACA

Headmaster: N M Lashbrook, BA

Deputy Head: B A H Figgis, BA

Second Deputy: Mrs S J Gomm, BSc

Master of the Lower School 'Jerwoods': V J Harvey, BSc

Senior Members of Staff:
Director of Studies: D A Harrow, MA
Head of Upper School: R S Williams, BSc, MBA, MEd
Head of Middle School: Mrs M A Miles, BSc
Director of IB: Mrs S Lorenz-Weir, MA
Registrar: N S Paddock, BSocSc
Marketing Director: Mrs L Penny, BA
Foundation Director: L Lloyd

Heads of Department:
Activities: Dr A G Headley, BSc, PhD
Careers: Dr A J Nicoll, BSc, DPhil, MIBiol, FRSA
Creative Arts: S L Poppy, BA
Business and Economics: P Nutter, BA
English: M M Fairweather, MA
Geography: H A Collison, BSc, MPhil

History: J N J Roberts, MA
ICT: N J F Neve, BSc
Languages: Dr S T Glynn, MA
Mathematics: D A Harrow, MA
Music: P Davis, MA
Religious Education and Philosophy: Dr D J Sheppard, MA
Science: Dr J F Pye, MA
Sport: I Simpson, BSc

Senior Chaplain: The Revd A C V Aldous, BA

Housemasters/mistresses:

Lower School:
Ancaster: Mrs S A Wragg, BSc
Lincoln: Mrs H M Foster, BA, DipLA
Peterborough: S B Foster, GRSM
Sargants: M Durose, BSc

Middle School:
Barrow: A J Williams, BSc
Buchanans: Mrs C L Latham, BEd
Chapmans: C B Dawson, BA
Clipsham: A B Speers, BSc
Gunthorpe: Miss M E Grimley, BEd
Hambleton: Mrs S M Healey, BSc
Haywoods: D M Taylor, BA
Rushebrookes: Mrs T Drummond, GRSM, LRAM
Stevens: Mrs A M Lear, BA, MCLIP
Wharflands: J J Cure, BA

Upper School:
Round House: Mrs L E Asher-Roche, BSc
School House: C J Foster, BSc

History. In 1584 Archdeacon Robert Johnson of Leicester, founded "as many free schools in Rutland as there are market towns therein; one at Oakham, another at Uppingham". With eyes firmly fixed on the demands faced by the young of the 21st century, Oakham both respects traditions and seeks innovative solutions to contemporary challenges.

Today, Oakham School is fully co-educational with 1,080 pupils (553 Boys, 527 Girls) aged 10–18 and a 50:50 ratio of boarders to day pupils. The overall staff: pupil ratio is 1:7. Sixth formers can choose to study either the International Baccalaureate or A Levels.

Facilities. Oakham's facilities include one of the best school libraries in the country, science laboratories, an information and communication technology centre, a new school of design which complements the art and design centre, a theatre and a music school. Sports facilities are extensive with superbly maintained fields, two all-weather pitches and a sports complex with an indoor swimming pool, squash courts, fives courts and fitness centre.

Organisation and Curriculum. There are four Lower School houses (age 10–13) and ten for the Middle/Upper School (age 13–17), whilst separate houses for final year pupils enable them to lead a freer life and to organise their own commitments to a greater degree. All pupils have a Tutor, who is responsible for supervising their work, and a Housemaster or Housemistress.

Lower School pupils study English, Mathematics, French (and in Year 8 a second modern language: Spanish or German), Science, History, Geography, Religious Education and Information & Communication Technology. All pupils also study Creative Arts and Performing Arts courses; most pupils take Latin.

For most Middle School pupils, the established ten subject curriculum will be appropriate: English, English Literature, Mathematics, Double Award Science, History, Geography, French, a second language and a Creative Arts subject, plus a short course in Religious Education. However, there will be some whose particular needs and strengths will be better served by a variation on this pattern and the School offers several options which may include a third language, additional Creative Arts subjects, Computing, Classical Civilisation, Citizenship and PE.

Following GCSE, Upper School pupils may opt either for the AS/A2 course or the International Baccalaureate. AS/A2 students normally take four AS Level subjects following on to at least three A2 Levels. Subjects available are Art and Design, Biology, Business Studies, Chemistry, Classical Civilisation, Critical and Contextual Studies, Design and Technology, Economics, English, Philosophy, French, Geography, German, History, Greek, Latin, Mathematics, Further Mathematics, Music, Physics, Politics, Spanish, PE and Sport Studies, and Theatre Studies. The International Baccalaureate programme has a similar range of subjects.

Music. Over 40% of pupils learn a musical instrument and almost half the school is involved in practical music making through participation in choirs, bands, orchestras, and music theatre productions. Nearly 80 concerts each year present a wide variety of performing opportunities in school, major concert venues and on international tours. Pupils are regularly selected for national youth ensembles and the school Chamber Choir has been acclaimed in major competitions.

Drama plays an important part in the life of the School with several productions each year. A majority of pupils at all levels takes part in at least one dramatic production a year.

Art, Design and Technology. The Richard Bull Centre and the state-of-the-art Jerwood School of Design together offer an extensive array of creative and design technology opportunities, including painting, pottery, sculpture, textiles, print-making, photography, computer aided design and electronics, working in wood, metal and plastics.

Sport and Activities. Our key sports are Rugby football, hockey, cricket, athletics, netball and tennis. Also on offer are some 30 other sports options. Achievements include eleven England schoolboy rugby internationals since 2000. Past pupils represent their country in cricket and rugby, women's cricket, athletics and hockey.

Each week pupils follow both an Activity (or hobby) and, from the Middle School upwards, a Service Option. They can try something new or pursue an existing passion. Our Service Options develop skills and values for life. Pupils may choose from an extensive volunteering programme, the Combined Cadet Force or the Duke of Edinburgh's Award. Oakham is the first institution worldwide to achieve 1,000 Duke of Edinburgh's Award gold medallists.

Entry. (*See Scholarship Entries section.*) Normal entry points are 10+, 11+, 13+ and 16+. Pupils are accepted mainly in September at the start of the academic year. Full admissions information is available from the Registrar.

Fees per term (2011-2012). Lower School (age 10–13): £7,405 (full boarding), £5,840–£6,750 (transitional boarding: 2 to 4 nights), £4,840 (day).

Middle and Upper Schools (age 13+): £9,080 (full boarding), £8,180 (day boarding: 3 nights), £5,450 (day).

Honours. Eight pupils have been offered places this year at Oxford or Cambridge. In 2010, out of a 99% pass rate, 80% of our A Level candidates gained grades A* to B with 57% achieving A*/A grades. All the Oakham International Baccalaureate candidates gained their diploma; 68% achieved the equivalent of A Level A*B passes. The GCSE pass rate was 98.5% with 67% of candidates achieving A or A* grades. 99%+ of leavers go to University or College.

Charitable status. Oakham School is a Registered Charity, number 1131425, and a Company Limited by Guarantee, registered in England and Wales, number 6924216. Registered Office: Chapel Close, Market Place, Oakham, Rutland LE15 6DT. It exists for the purpose of education.

Oldham Hulme Grammar Schools

Chamber Road, Oldham, Lancs OL8 4BX
Tel: 0161 624 4497
         0161 630 6255 (Kindergarten)
e-mail: admin@ohgs.co.uk
website: www.hulme-grammar.oldham.sch.uk

The school, founded in 1611, was reconstituted in the 19th century under the Endowed Schools Act. The main buildings of The Oldham Hulme Grammar Schools were opened in 1895 on a commanding south-west facing site overlooking the city of Manchester.
Motto: *Fide sed cui Vide.*

Patron: The Lord Clitheroe of Downham

The Governing Body:
Chairman: D J Illingworth, BA, FCA (*contactable via the Schools' Bursar/Clerk to the Governors*)
Vice-Chairman: R S Illingworth, BSc
Honorary Treasurer: J E Halliwell

Elected Governors:
Dr K Buckley, MBChB
A Milnes, BA, FCA
Mrs A Richards, BSc
K Sanders
V A J Srivastava, LLB
Mrs V Stocker, LLB
M Taylor, BA, MEd
A P Wild, OBE

Representative Governors, Metropolitan Borough of Oldham:
P M Buckley, BSc, ACG1
Mrs J Capener
Mrs B M Jackson

Principal: Dr P G Neeson, BSc, PhD Brunel

Deputy Principal – Boys: P T Byrne, BSc London
Deputy Principal – Girls: Miss S E Shepherd, BA London
Deputy Principal – Sixth Form: J C Budding, BEd Sheffield Hallam (*Housemaster of Assheton House*)
Deputy Principal – Preps: Mrs C A Wilkinson, BSc Liverpool
Director of Studies: N G H James, MA York
Bursar and Clerk to the Governors: I Martin, BSc, FCA, FCMA
Director of Development: Z Christo, MA Cantab, MSc Imperial College

S P Adamson, MA Manchester (*English, Duke of Edinburgh's Award Scheme*)
Mrs B J Allwood, MA Oxford (*Modern Languages, Teacher i/c German, Head of Year 10*)
W L M Atkins, BSc Keele (*Head of Biology*)
Dr P M Beagon, MA, DPhil Oxford (*Head of Classics*)
Mrs S E Beard, BA York (*Chemistry*)
J M Bibby, BSc Wales (*Chemistry*)
Mrs N Bibi, BSc Manchester (*Mathematics*)
Mrs K Boswell, BA Leeds (*Psychology*)
Dr N Breen, BA Manchester, MA Lancaster, PhD Manchester (*History*)
Miss J C Brown, BA Liverpool (*Physical Education, Head of Year 7*)
Mrs R Chester, BSc Hull (*Biology, Head of Middle School and Year 11*)
N J Chesterton, BA Leeds (*Physical Education and Games*)
Ms J Shepley Clarke, BA Durham, MA Manchester Metropolitan (*English*)
G W Conroy, CertEd Leeds (*Physical Education, Games*)
T M J Cotton, BEd MMU (*Design Technology*)

Miss L J Cowan, MA Dundee (*History, English, RS, Head of Year 8, Duke of Edinburgh's Award Scheme*)
A J Coyle, BEng Brighton (*Physics, Technology*)
C M B Crossley, BA Oxon (*English, Schools' Public Relations Officer, Newsletter Editor*)
D J Dalziel, BSc London, PG Dip Leeds (*Biology, Head of Middle School*)
Miss A Danson, BA Leeds (*Business Studies and Economics, Head of Year 8*)
Mrs C Davies, BA Kent (*Head of Drama, Careers*)
Mrs R Dixon, BA Liverpool, LRAM (*Head of Music*)
M N Dowthwaite, BA Manchester (*Head of History, Schools' Functions Officer*)
Miss C W Duffy, BA Aberystwyth, MPhil Aberystwyth (*History*)
Mrs C A Eliot, BA Heriot-Watt (*Head of Textiles, PSHE Coordinator*)
Miss H A Fitzgerald, BA Manchester (*Art*)
P Galloway, BSc UMIST (*Head of Physics*)
O M Gandolfi, BSc, MSc Bangor (*Biology*)
Mrs H Garside, BA North Wales (*Modern Languages*)
M Goodwin, BA Liverpool (*Modern Languages*)
Miss J V Graystock, BA Liverpool (*Art*)
Mrs K L Gregson, BSc Lancaster (*Head of General Studies, Biology, Psychology, Deputy Head of Sixth Form*)
Mrs R Hall, BA Birmingham, MTh Nottingham (*Religious Studies*)
Mrs E Harris, BA Liverpool (*Physical Education*)
Mrs C Headdock, BA London (*Modern Languages, English, Learning Support*)
J R Hesten, BA Manchester (*Physics, Biology*)
Mrs L Hewitt, CertEd Coventry College of Education (*Mathematics*)
Dr E F Hilditch, BD St Andrews, PhD Nottingham (*Head of Religious Studies and Philosophy*)
Mrs A H Howarth, BEd Manchester Metropolitan, PG Dip, Dip SEN, PG Cert SpLD (*Head of Learning Support*)
Mrs D Howarth, BSc Manchester Metropolitan (*Head of Home Economics*)
G Hulme, ARCO, LTCL (*Head of Music*)
A H B Hurst, BA Manchester Metropolitan (*Head of Physical Education boys*)
Mrs F J Kenney, BSc Manchester (*Home Economics*)
Mrs T A Kershaw, BA Salford (*Head of Modern Languages*)
Miss J P Knighton, BEd Leeds Metropolitan (*Head of Physical Education girls*)
Mrs A J Kremnitzer, BSc Aberdeen (*Chemistry, Website Management*)
Mrs J A Lamb, BSc Liverpool (*Head of Mathematics*)
P Langdon, BEd Manchester Metropolitan (*Head of Information Technology*)
Mrs J Leach, BA Hull (*English*)
D Ledson, BA Humberside (*Information and Communication Technology*)
T A Leng, BA Leeds (*History*)
Mrs D Maders, BSc Leeds (*Chemistry, Physics, Careers*)
C J D Mairs, MA Edinburgh (*Head of English*)
S Manik, BSc Manchester (*Mathematics*)
A H Marshall, BSc Hull (*Geography, Head of Lower School, Master i/c Football*)
Mrs J McCarthy, MA, PG Dip Liverpool (*Art, Design Technology, Head of Year 7*)
Ms E Mills, BA Manchester (*English*)
S McRoyall, BA Sunderland (*Head of Art*)
D C Murray, BA Oxford (*Modern Languages, Teacher i/c Spanish*)
Mrs H J Murray, BA Durham (*Modern Languages, Teacher i/c French*)
Mrs A M Newby, BSc Brunel (*Head of Design Technology*)
Mrs C A Parker, CertEd Manchester Polytechnic (*Biology*)

Mrs B A Parkinson, BSc Liverpool (*Geography, Careers*)
A Peacocke, BA Glamorgan (*Geography, Head of Year 9, Housemaster of Hulme House*)
Miss H R Plews, BA Liverpool, MPhil Cantab (*Classics*)
Mrs P T Ramotowski, BSc London, BA Open (*Biology*)
S G Rawlings, BEng Aston (*Mathematics, Physics*)
D R A Rees, BSc Bradford (*Business Studies, Head of Year 11*)
Mrs A G Robinson, BSc Romania, MSc Manchester (*Physics*)
Mrs A Sheldon, BA Manchester (*Mathematics*)
G R Sims, BA Open (*Information and Communication Technology, Head of Year 10*)
A D Smith, BSc Salford (*Mathematics*)
Mrs S Standring, BA Open, BSc Bolton Institute, MSc Manchester (*Psychology*)
Miss L C Stockton, BSc Loughborough (*Chemistry*)
Mrs J Sullivan, BSc Salford (*Head of Chemistry*)
Dr P J Sutherland, BA Hull, PhD Bradford (*Head of Geography, Induction Coordinator, Housemaster of Lees House*)
C R Sykes, BA Manchester, MA Manchester (*Classics, History*)
Miss N L Taylor, BSc Manchester (*Mathematics*)
Mrs S J Titmuss, BA Manchester (*Head of Government and Politics, History*)
Mrs J Travis, DipM (*Higher Education and Careers, Business Studies, PSHE Coordinator Year 7–11*)
Miss R L Turner, BSc Loughborough (*Mathematics*)
G L Wailes, BA Sheffield (*Head of Business Studies and Economics, Young Enterprise*)
Mrs S A Watt, BA Manchester MA Leeds (*Geography*)
Mrs D Y Wheldrick, BA Preston Polytechnic (*Information Technology, Peer Mentoring Coordinator*)
Mrs J C Wood, BA Leeds (*Religious Studies, Head of Lower School*)
P F Wood, CertEd St John's College, York (*Physical Education*)

Hulme Preparatory Schools:
Deputy Principal: Mrs C A Wilkinson, BSc Liverpool
Head of KS2: Mrs W Maitland, BSc Sheffield
Head of Kindergarten: Mrs J Wood, BEd Manchester
Deputy Head: Ms A L Smith, BSc Bolton Institute
Deputy Head: Miss E A White, BA Durham

Miss C Barnett, BA Edge Hill
Mrs T Bradley, BEd Chester College
Mrs E Brocklehurst, BA Exeter, ABRSM
P S Coulson, BSc Edge Hill College
M G Cowley, BSc Stirling
Miss A A Done, BA Manchester Metropolitan
Mrs Z Fleming, CertEd Edge Hill College
A J Halliwell, BEd Manchester, CertEd Manchester
Mrs B Humphreys, NNEB, HNC
Mrs C Kershaw, BEd Manchester
Mrs Rebecca Knott, BA, Surrey
Mrs M Marland, CertEd Oldham
Miss S E Oates, LTCL, LGSM, CertEd Reading
Mrs A D Pearson, CertEd Chester College
Mrs E M T Schofield, BEd Oxford, CNAA
Miss H A Whitwam, BA Bradford College

Visiting Music Teachers:
A Asquith, GBSM, LTCL (*Clarinet/Bassoon*)
D Browne, GRNCM (*Cello*)
J Dixon, BEng (*Guitar*)
Mrs V Eastham, MA, FTCL, LRSM (*Piano*)
Dr R Gibbon, GMus RNCM, ATCL (*Clarinet & Piano*)
Ms S Gibbon, GRNCM (*Violin*)
Mrs H Greig, GMus RNCM (*Violin & Viola*)
K Heggie, GRNCM (*Guitar*)
Mrs A Holmes, GRNCM Singing
C Holmes, MusB, GRSM, ARMCM (*Piano*)
M Jones, BA, PGDipRNCM, PPRNCM (*Oboe*)

Mrs J Kent, CT ABRSM (*Horn*)
Miss J Lyons, BMus, PPRNCM (*Clarinet & Saxophone*)
Miss P McMillan, BMus (*RNCM*) ALCM (*Percussion*)
Mrs K Ord, BMus, PPRNCM (*Violin*)
Miss J Puckley, BMus (*Clarinet & Saxophone*)
Miss M Rayner, GRNCM, PPRNCM (*Flute*)
Mrs C Strachan (*Singing*)
Mrs E Taylor (*Singing*)
Mrs S Walker, GRSM, PPRCM (*Flute*)
Miss J Wilson, GRSM, PPRCM (*Oboe*)

The Oldham Hulme family of schools is renowned for delivering outstanding levels of education at each stage of a child's development. With unbeatable standards and outstanding achievements, the schools cater for boys and girls aged three to 18 and offer a caring, orderly and academically stimulating environment.

At the age of 3 school life begins in the surroundings of the Kindergarten which has recently moved into new modern premises. Confidence is then built throughout the junior and secondary years and great care is taken in the sixth form to create extremely capable, well-balanced young adults.

The schools' primary aim is to provide a caring, friendly and lively school environment that fosters a desire to learn and at all times, pupils are encouraged to think and work independently. With a reputation for academic excellence and outstanding extra-curricular activities, pupils benefit from the right environment which enables them to achieve their full potential in life so that they go on to become successful, happy and confident young men and women.

The Hulme family of schools value academic achievement and standards are high. Consequently there is an excellent record of examination success at GCSE and A Level. Pupils are taught within small classes by a team of dedicated, well qualified staff.

The schools also offer an excellent pastoral care system which guides and supports pupils, promoting their personal development within the wider school community.

The comprehensive careers education programme on offer widens each pupil's understanding of the opportunities available in the changing world of work, while equipping them with the skills to manage their future career.

A stimulating range of extra-curricular activities provides opportunities for fun, challenge, initiative, leadership and service, while activities within the wider community encourage active involvement and promote a genuine concern for the needs of others.

Fees per term (2011-2012). Hulme Kindergarten £2,150, Preparatory Schools £2,150, Senior Schools £2,940.

A number of bursaries are awarded annually to pupils entering at the ages of 11 and 16. These awards are based on parental income and academic ability and will remain in place for the time in school subject to satisfactory progress by the pupil.

Charitable status. The Oldham Hulme Grammar Schools is a Registered Charity, number 526636. It exists to provide a balanced academic education for pupils aged 3 to 18.

The Oratory School

Woodcote, Reading, Berkshire RG8 0PJ
Tel: 01491 683500
Fax: 01491 680020
e-mail: enquiries@oratory.co.uk
website: www.oratory.co.uk

The Oratory School was founded in 1859, by Blessed John Henry, Cardinal Newman, at the request of a group of eminent Catholic laymen. The Chaplain apart, the School is administered and staffed entirely by laymen.

Motto: '*Cor ad cor loquitur*'

President: The Rt Hon Lord Judge

Vice-Presidents:
His Eminence Cardinal William W Baum
J J Eyston, MA, FRICS, KSG
Archbishop Vincent Nichols, MA, STL, PhL, MEd

Chairman: M H R Hasslacher
Vice-Chairman: C J Sehmer, FCA

The Governors:
B F H Bettesworth, FRICS, ACIArb
The Very Revd R Byrne, BD, AKC, Cong Orat
Mrs M Cochrane
Mrs M Edwards
Professor P W Evans, MA, PhD
F J Fitzherbert-Brockholes, MA
C J French, FRAgS
Dr C B T Hill Williams, DL, MA, FRGS, FRSA
H H Judge K A D Hornby, BA
N F Littlefair, ACII
N R Purnell, MA, QC
The Revd J N Saward, MA, MLitt
M W Stilwell
T A H Tyler, OBE, BA

Clerk to the Governors & Bursar: A F Bradshaw, DMS, MCIM, FInstLM

Head Master: C I Dytor, MC, KHS, MA Cantab, MA Oxon

Second Master: T J Hennessy, BSc

Senior Master: P L Tomlinson, MFA

Lower Master: M H Green, MBE, MEd, FRSA, MRAeS

Chaplain: The Rt Revd Mgr A F M Conlon, STB HEL, PhD

Academic Staff:
* Head of Department
† Housemaster
§ Part-time

Mrs E K Aldington, Dip AD (*§Art*)
J Aldridge, BSc (*Mathematics*)
J Berkley, BA, MA (*French; Italian*)
Mrs M Blaseby, BA Hons, MA (*§Asst Classics*)
S Bosher BSc, DipDes (*Design and Technology; CCF*)
S A Bowles, BSc, PhD (*Chemistry*)
J A Brooke, BA, MA (*English*)
P W Brown, BSc (*Physics*)
I A N Campbell, BSc (*Physics*)
T N Danks, BSc, PhD (***Chemistry*)
J E H G De Bono, BA (*English; Latin*)
D R Dixon, MBA (*Business Studies*)
A P Dulston, BA (*Religious Education*)
P J Easton, BSc (*Biology*)
H Exham, BSc (*Biology*)
D Forster, MA, MSc (*Director of Studies*)
C W Fothergill, BA, MA Ed (**Classical Civilisation; History*)
G W Fox, ACP, CertEd (*§Art*)
Mrs H R Fox, BA (*Art*)
O C Godfrey, BA (**Drama*)
M H Green, MEd, MBE, FRSA, MRAES (**Design and Technology; Lower Master*)
R Guillaud, Licence d'Anglais (*French*)
M P Harrison BA (*Spanish; French*)
I Hart, BSc, PhD (**Physics*)
T J Hennessy, BSc (*Mathematics; Second Master*)
V B A Holden, BSc, PGCE (*Science & Mathematics;†St John*)
N C Jones, BA, ARCO (**Academic Music; Examinations Officer*)

I P Jordan, BEd (*Physical Education & Games; Mathematics; †FitzAlan*)
K Laughton, BA, AIL (**Modern Languages*)
G J Lyke, BSc (**Mathematics*)
K E MacNab, BA, MA (*Religious Education*)
J McNamara, MA, FRCO (**Director of Music*)
Mrs D A Nash, MA (**Religious Education; Head of Sixth Form*)
R A O'Sullivan, BA (*English*)
C N B Pohl, BA (**History; English*)
P E Poynter, BA (*Geography*)
A N Stroker, BA, MA, PhD (*English; †Faber*)
C J Sudding, BEng Hons (*Mathematics*)
M P Syddall, MA (*Classics*)
C W Sykes, MA, MBA, PGCE (*Business Studies & Geography*)
P A Thomas, BA, MA Ed (*Economics; †St Philip House*)
Mrs E S Thomas, BA, MA Ed (*§Curriculum Support*)
P L Tomlinson, MFA (**Director of Art & Design; Senior Master*)
S C B Tomlinson, BSc (**Director of Games*))
N E Topham (*Physical Education; CCF Admin Officer*)
Mrs A D T Tuite-Dalton (*French*)
D O D Watkins, MSc (*Geography*)
Miss S E Wethey, BA (*English*)
A J Wilson, BSc (*Physical Education and Games; †Norris*)
R B Womersley, BEd (*Ancient History; History; Geography*)

Curriculum Support:
Mrs F Harte, DipSpLD, AMBDA
Mrs S Green, BA
Mrs J Kennedy, BA, DipSpLD

Music Staff:
C Caiger (*Guitar*)
A Cary, BA, BMus, FTCL (*Singing*)
J Donnelly (*Drums, Percussion*)
Mrs S L Dytor, ARCM (*Violin*)
S Harper, BA, LRAM (*Oboe & Piano*)
G Howarth, BSc, MA (*Brass*)
R H Herford, MA, GRNCM (*Singing*)
D Horniblow (*Clarinet*)
L Ingram (*Chanter & Bagpipes*)
C C King, FRICS (*Drums & Percussion*)
M Knowles, AGSM (*Brass*)
Miss E V Krivenko, MMus Dip (*Piano*)
Mrs C Lancaster, BMus, MMus, PGDip (*Cello*)
Mrs K E Laughton, BA (*Saxophone, Flute*)
S Nisbett, LTCL (*Guitar*)
Miss J Schloss, BMus, MMus Dip (*Piano and Accompanist*)
J Underwood (*Electric & Bass Guitar*)

School Health Centre:
Mrs P Codner, MSc, RGN, RM (*Health Centre Sister*)
Mrs J E Tomlinson, SEN (*Staff Nurse*)
§Mrs M Gates, RGN

Non-Teaching Staff:
A F Bradshaw, DMS, MCIM, FInstLM (*Bursar*)
A Rajan (*Finance Manager*)
Mrs N Brouard (*§Reception*)
Mrs L Coupland (*Marketing & Public Relations*)
Mrs M Lee (*School Secretary*)
Mrs C Macnab (*Librarian*)
Mrs J Martin (*School Secretary*)
Mrs G Munoz (*§Reception*)
M Sixsmith, BSc, MPhil (**Computer Services*)
§A K Tinkel, MA (*Archivist*)
Mrs S A Waghorn (*Head Master's PA*)
Mrs K Warren (*§Secretary*)

Sports Centre Staff:
Miss R Davies BSc (*Sports Centre Manager*)
A Chinneck (*Professional Real Tennis*)

T Huelin (*Sports Centre Assistant*)
D Rook (*Sports Centre Assistant*)
L Taylor (*Sports Centre Assistant*)

Number in School. There are 420 boys: 220 boarding and 200 day boys.

The School is situated in an area of outstanding natural beauty in grounds of 400 acres, in South Oxfordshire. There are four Senior Houses (13–18) and one Junior House called St Philip House (11–13). Each House is run by a married Housemaster and staffed by a House team, which includes a Housemother. There is at least one other adult in each Boarding House and over three-quarters of the staff live on-site or in the local village.

The Head Master is pursuing a ten-year development programme. Two new boarding Houses have been constructed. There are new Art & Design, DT, English, History, Maths, and Theology Departments.

Organisation. Four Senior Houses and St Philip House offer living facilities for 420 boys, both day and boarding. Particular care is taken to provide an environment which facilitates the assimilation of new boys.

Health. The School Medical Centre is under the supervision of a fully qualified resident Sister and the School Medical Officer visits once a week.

Admission. Boys enter at age 13 through the Scholarship or Common Entrance Examinations, or at 11 by informal interview and exam. A small number of boys are received directly into the Sixth Form.

Religious Education. Catholic spirituality pervades the school in an unobtrusive way. It is at the heart of the school and to be an Oratorian is something special. Respect for the individual within the larger framework of this society is the hallmark of this Oratorian ethos. There is a Resident Chaplain who looks after the needs of both boys and staff. All boys study religions.

Studies. Boys are prepared for A Levels and GCSE. A wide range of subjects is offered in the Sixth Form. There is no rigid division into Arts and Science subjects; almost any combination of subjects can be taken.

Games. In addition to the main games – Rugby Football, Soccer, Cricket and Rowing – boys take part in Cross-Country Running, Shooting, Swimming, Tennis, Badminton, Basketball, Squash, Golf, and Real Tennis. There is a nine-hole golf course on the 400-acre site and a four-lane indoor shooting range. Awarded Independent School of the Year for Sport 2007-8 by The Daily Telegraph & Norwich Union for commitment to sport at all levels and for encouraging boys into national and international teams.

CCF. There is a flourishing contingent of the CCF which, in addition to the Army section, includes the following subsections: RN, RAF, REME, Signals, and Adventure Training. The Duke of Edinburgh's Award Scheme is operated. The school ranks in the top five shooting schools in the country with some team members shooting for Great Britain.

Extra-curricular activities. There are frequent theatre outings, visits to museums and art galleries, careers visits, as well as talks and lectures given in the School by visiting speakers. There is a wide range of clubs and societies, and an Oratory School Enterprise Scheme. Every holiday there is a major trip abroad.

Optional Extras. Instrumental Music, coaching in Real Tennis, Lawn Tennis, Squash and Golf.

Careers Guidance. The Head of Sixth Form provides guidance for boys in their choice of future occupation.

The School is a member of ISCO.

Fees per term (2011-2012). Boarders: £8,980 (Junior House £6,360); Day Boys: £6,485 (Junior House £4,725).

The fees include board, tuition, consolidated extras, and games. An optional insurance scheme is in operation which covers remission of fees in the event of a boy's absence through illness. A full term's notice of withdrawal is required; failing such notice a term's fees are payable. There may be a reduction for younger brothers and sons of old boys.

Scholarships. (*See Scholarship Entries section.*) A number of Academic Scholarships and Exhibitions, and Awards in Music, Art and Sport, are offered.

The Preparatory School is at 'Great Oaks', a property situated in grounds of 45 acres on the same ridge of the Chilterns, about 2 miles from the Main School, between Cray's Pond and Pangbourne. This is co-educational. (*For further details, see entry in IAPS section.*)

The Oratory School Society. *Chairman and Correspondent:* Mr R A Cox, 38 Home Park Road, Wimbledon Park, London SW19 7HN.

Charitable status. The Oratory School Association is a Registered Charity, number 309112. It is a charitable trust dedicated to continuing the aims of its Founder, The Venerable John Henry, Cardinal Newman.

Oundle School

Oundle, Peterborough PE8 4GH

Tel: 01832 277122 (Reception)
         01832 277120 (Headmaster's Office)
         01832 277125 (Admissions Office)
         01832 277116 (Undermaster's Office)
Fax: 01832 277128
e-mail: admissions@oundleschool.org.uk
website: www.oundleschool.org.uk

Oundle School was established by the Grocers' Company with the object of providing a liberal education in accordance with the principles of the Church of England.

The aims of the School are: to promote excellence and allow pupils to reach their full academic and intellectual potential; to develop independence and team players who will contribute to the community; to develop strong values, encourage involvement and an understanding of adult life, and prepare pupils for life beyond Oundle; to provide a full-boarding programme such that its excellence is recognised worldwide.

Motto: '*God Grant Grace*'

Governing Body:
[1]J G Tregoning (*Chairman*)
¶I McAlpine, OBE, DL (*Vice-Chairman*)
[1]P Bostelmann
Mrs F Carey
J Cartwright
The Countess Howe
P R Hutton, OBE
¶D C L Miller
[1]¶R Ringrose (*Master of the Grocers' Company*)
Dr P Rogerson
[1]J Roundell
[1]J Scott
Lady Stringer

Ex-Officio:
[1]T Stubbs (*Master*)
[1]P J Woodhouse (*Second Warden*)
[1]H Colthurst (*Third Warden*)
J H O'Hare, OBE, MBA, BSc (*Bursar and Secretary*)

[1] *Member of the Court of The Grocers' Company*
¶ *Old Oundelian*

Headmaster: C M P Bush, MA

Deputy Head: Mrs D L Watt, MA
Senior Master: P S C King, BSc, MSc
Undermaster: R J Page, BEd
Director of Studies: B J Evans, BSc, FRSC

Senior Mistress: Mrs A M Page, MA
Senior Chaplain: Revd B J Cunningham
Head of Laxton: A B Burrows, MA Ed, BSc
Director of Pastoral Care: Mrs D L Watt, MA

Registrar: G Phillips, BA

Medical Officers:
Dr D Clayton, MBChB, DRCOG, DCH
Dr K Newell, MBChB, MRCGP, DRCOG

* *Head of Department*

Art:
R J Page, BEd (*Undermaster*)
Mrs S J Hipple, BA, BEd
*J D Oddie, BA
M A Case, BA
Miss G C Pontifex, BA, MA

Biology:
J Hunt, BSc, PhD
P S C King, BSc, MSc (*Senior Master*)
W F Holmström, BSc, PhD
Mrs M A Holmström, BSc, MSc (*Child Protection Officer*)
A E Langsdale, BSc, MSc
*Dr P J Rowe, PhD
W W Gough, BSc
Dr K Bier, PhD
Dr C L Pemberton, PhD
Mrs R A Barnes, PhD

Chemistry:
R J McKim, PhD, CChem, MRS, FRAS
R F Hammond, BSc
M A Stephen, BSc, PhD
W E Buckley, BSc (*Proctor*)
M J Bessent, MChem, PhD, AMRSC
*C J Quiddington, MChem, PhD
B J Evans, BSc, FRSC (*Director of Studies*)
A J B Singh, BSc

Classics:
Mrs M P R James, MA
K R Hannis, MA
Mrs D L Watt, MA (*Deputy Head and Director of Pastoral Care*)
N J Aubury, BA
*T J Morrison, BA
Ms C L Westran, BA (*The Academic Assistant*)
D A Burrow, BA
P A Liston, MA

Design and Technology:
*C D Humphreys, BA (*Freeman of the City of London*)
D A Vincent, CAP, BTS, CAPET
R H Lowndes, BSc, MEng
Miss R L Spender, BSc

Drama:
A D Martens, BA
*Ms K A Francis, BA
*A J H Boag, BA (*Director of the Stahl Theatre*)
M Burlington, BA

Economics:
A P Ireson, MA
J Röhrborn, MA
Mrs F L Quiddington, BEcon, MT
*M Tanweer, MA

Educational Support:
*Mrs V C Lacey, BA
Mrs J M T Clay, BA
Mrs C M Redding, BA, MA
Mrs I Chamen, MA
Mrs G T Nacef
Mrs C M Nolan

English:
Mrs M K Smedley, BA (*Publisher*)
N J T Wood, BA
Mrs J T Coles, BA
A D Martens, BA
*T P Hipperson, MA
B Raudnitz, MA (*Child Protection Officer*)
A J Sherwin, MA
Mrs H M Wells, BA
Miss L V Burden, BA
Mrs H K Hopper, BA
R S Harry, BA

Geography:
J R Wake, CertEd
J M Taylor, MA
Mrs M S Turner, BA
G Phillips, BA (*Registrar*)
C W Symes, BSc
J R Hammond-Chambers, BA
*Mrs J L L Banerjee, BSc, MEd

Government and Politics:
*J D C Gillings, BA
M J G King, BSc

History:
*C R Pendrill, MA
P J Pedley, BA
I D Clark, BA
M P H von Habsburg-Lothringen, MA, PLD
A J Brighton, BA
P J Kemp, BA
Mrs T E Harris, BA
M R Parry, BA, MPhil, PhD
J M Allard, BA

Information Technology:
*R J Cunniffe, BSc (*Head of Academic ICT*)
I A Peacock (*Director of Computing*)

Mathematics:
A Butterworth, BSc
D A Turner, BSc
R Atkins, BSc
N D Turnbull, BA
D B Meisner, BA, MSc, PhD (*Assistant Director of Studies*)
D P Raftery, BSc
S G Dale, MEng, MA
*Mrs N S Guise, BSc
J M Devenport, BSc
A G D Furnival, BA
M A Blessett, MA
M A Sanderson, BSc

Modern Languages:
S T Forge, MA
P J Lewins, MA
Mrs N M Mola, BA
M P Bolger, BA
Mrs A M Page, MA (*Senior Mistress*)
Mrs C R Gent, MA (*Head of Careers*)
B Béjoint, L-ès-L
J Röhrborn, MA
Mlle G M Morin-Skinner, L-ès-FLE, L-ès-LCE
Mlle S Fonteneau, L-ès-L
T D Watson, MA
Miss H F P Machin, BA (*Head of Spanish*)
C ben Nacef, BA
*Miss S J Davidson (*Head of Modern Languages; Head of German*)
Mrs L M Brighton, MEd (*Head of Girls' Games*)
S Jessop, BA (*Head of French*)
H Yan, BA (*Head of Chinese*)
Miss C A L Thompson, BA

Physical Education and Games:
*C J Olver, WLIHE (*Head of PE*)
Mrs M Smith, CertEd
Miss R S Goatly, BA
G Terrett, BA (*Head of Boys' Games*)
A J Cowley
G P A Maitre, BSc, MSc (*Head of Rowing*)
Mrs L M Brighton, MEd (*Head of Girls' Games*)

Physics:
*M N Wells, MA
A B Burrows, MA Ed, BSc
P C Clark, BSc, ARCS (*Head of Science*)
Mrs L E Kirk, BSc
Mrs T E Raftery, BSc
M J Meatyard, BSc
H Roberts, BSc
A A Panju, BSc

Psychology:
*S R Heath, BA, MSc
R Banerjee, BSc

Religious Studies:
Mrs V Nunn, BEd
Revd I C Browne, MA
Mrs A E Meisner, BA
R S Ambrose, BA
*B T Deane, BA
Revd B J Cunningham
Mrs C A Deane, BA

Library:
Mrs L Guirlando, BA, MSc, MCLIP
Mrs S Marsden, MCLIP
Ms E Kendall, MA

The Music School:

Director of Music: A P Forbes, BA, LRAM
Organist: J C Arkell, MA, FRCO, FTCL, FLCM, FRSA
Head of Woodwind: D P Milsted, BA, LTCL
Head of Brass: Mrs A S Hudson, GRNCM, PPRNCM
Head of Keyboard: A Hone, BMus, ARCM, ARCO
Head of Strings: A P Gibbon, GRNCM
Academic Music: Mrs S L Ratchford, BA

and 34 peripatetic teachers

Houses and Housemasters/Housemistresses:
Bramston: A J Sherwin
Crosby: H Roberts
Dryden: Mrs V Nunn
Fisher: N J T Wood
Grafton: W W Gough
Kirkeby: Mrs A E Meisner
Laundimer: J R Hammond-Chambers
Laxton: A B Burrows
New House: Mrs M Smith
Sanderson: D A Turner
School House: A E Langsdale
Sidney: C W Symes
St Anthony: I D Clark
Wyatt: Mrs L E Kirk
The Berrystead: N J Aubury

Bursar: J H O'Hare, OBE, MBA, BSc
Finance Bursar: Ms J Jones, BSc, ACA
Estates Bursar: R M C Tremellen, BSc, RICS

Introduction. Oundle School originated from the bequest of Sir William Laxton, a native of Oundle, to the Grocers' Company in 1556 and became fully co-educational in September 1990. It is, perhaps, unique in that the buildings are spread throughout the attractive market town of Oundle and its pupils mix with the town community as they go about their daily business.

Number of pupils (2010–2011). Boarders: 520 boys and 340 girls. Day Pupils: 134 boys and 118 girls.

Admission. Most boarding pupils sit the June Common Entrance Examination or the Oundle Scholarship Examination at thirteen before joining in September. The majority of day pupils, together with candidates for the junior boarding house, The Berrystead, join the School at eleven having taken English, Mathematics, Science and Ability tests. A small number of places are available for entry at other stages, including at Sixth Form level.

Facilities. Academic departments are situated in the Cloisters, the Needham building, the Sir Peter Scott building, the Gascoigne building, Old Dryden and SciTec, Oundle's ambitious and spectacular science building, with its extensive 'green' credentials, opened in June 2007. The teaching areas are very well equipped; the Information Technology Centre includes three fully-equipped computer rooms and there are 'cluster networks' around the School. Thin Client terminals are located for each boarder in the Houses. Electronic whiteboards and computer-driven projectors feature in most teaching rooms and the Modern Languages Department is equipped with two state of the art language laboratories.

Art, Music, Drama and Design Technology are all very strong and are well provided for. The Art Studios are large and airy and well equipped and the department includes the Yarrow Gallery. Facilities in Music include the Frobenius Organ and an electronic Music Studio. The Drama Department is centred on the Rudolph Stahl Theatre, a cleverly converted chapel in the middle of the town, where numerous productions of both the School and visiting companies take place. The long tradition of the Oundle Workshops continues, incorporating courses and projects in Engineering and Industrial Technology with pupils building cars, off-road buggies and boats in the exceptionally spacious Patrick Centre.

The Chapel was built as a memorial shortly after the Great War and its East windows, designed by John Piper, were installed in 1956. Thirty-two stained glass windows by Mark Angus, added in 2005, compliment Piper's original vision. Religious instruction accords with the Church of England, but other faiths are welcomed.

The Sports Centre complex includes two sports halls, a forty three metre long swimming pool, five squash courts, a large and extensively equipped fitness suite, Physical Education classrooms and four new fives courts were added in 2006.

Since 1990, when the renovation of boys' houses, Fisher and Crosby was completed and two new girls' houses, Kirkeby and Wyatt, were built, other girls' houses have been created. Dryden House was renovated and has taken girls since 1993; New House from 1997 and Sanderson from 2001. A continuous cycle of renovation and refurbishment of Houses is in operation; the most recent work has involved extensions to School and Grafton Houses. The fifteen houses are distinct communities defined to some extent by the fact that the pupils dine in separate house dining rooms.

Academic Curriculum. Third Formers (Year 9) take a general course consisting of English, Mathematics, French, Latin, Physics, Chemistry, Biology, History, Geography, Religious Studies, Art, Design and Technology, PE, Music, Drama, ICT, and German or Spanish or Greek. The First and Second Form curriculum is similar.

The traditional importance of Science and Technology in the Oundle Education is still maintained with all pupils being taught the three sciences to GCSE (both Triple Award and Dual Award on offer) and all Third Formers spend time in the Design and Technology Department. Computing and Microelectronics are available at all levels.

Pupils take English, Mathematics, Physics, Chemistry and Biology as the core of their GCSE curriculum and choose a further five subjects from Art, Chinese, Computing, Design Technology, Drama, Electronics, French, Geography, German, Greek, History, Latin, Music, Religious Studies, Spanish and Sports Science. Almost every pupil studies at least one modern foreign language.

In the Sixth Form A Levels are offered in Art, Biology, Chemistry, Classical Civilisation, Design and Technology, Economics, Electronics, English Literature, French, Geography, Greek, Government and Politics, History, Information Technology, Latin, Mathematics, Further Mathematics, Music, Physics, Psychology, Religious Studies, Russian, Spanish, Sports Science and Theatre Studies. The majority of these are assessed as A Levels, though Chemistry, Economics, English Literature, German, History, History of Art, Italian, Physics and Politics, can be assessed by the Cambridge International Examinations Pre-U qualification. Pupils have the option of taking just an AS Level in one of their four subjects. Studies in the Sixth Form are enhanced by pupils opting for one or two of a range of non-examined extension courses, which include Arabic, Critical Thinking, Mandarin Chinese, Music Performance, Russian and Research Projects. In the Upper Sixth they take a General Studies course which is based around invited speakers.

Honours. 99% of Upper Sixth Former pupils go on to higher education at good universities; in 2010–11 twenty-four of the School's pupils were offered places at Oxford and Cambridge.

Sport. The main school sports are Rugby, Hockey, Cricket, Rowing, Netball and Tennis, but others available include Aerobics, Athletics, Badminton, Clay Shooting, Cross-Country, Cycling, Fencing, Fives, Golf, Horse-riding, Sailing, Shooting, Soccer, Squash, Swimming and Volleyball. There are currently two Astroturf hockey pitches, which are also used for tennis in the summer, and more pitches are planned to be built to maintain the School's excellent standard of sporting facilities.

Activities. A full range of activities take place which are an integral part of the wider school curriculum. Events in Drama and Music feature prominently in the School calendar, and Art Exhibitions are held regularly in the Yarrow Gallery. A large number of Societies meet on a regular basis. Links have been established with schools in France, Germany, Spain, Hungary, the Czech Republic, Russia, China, America and Australia, with annual Exchanges taking place. Pupils are able to participate in the very large number of expeditions and trips in the UK and abroad. There is a flourishing CCF comprising Army, Navy, RAF, Fire and Adventure Training sections and a thriving Duke of Edinburgh's Award scheme is in operation. Community Action plays an important part in school life and contributes significantly to the wider community. Much time and energy are devoted to fundraising activities in support of national charities, international aid programmes and holidays run at Oundle for MENCAP and inner-city children.

Entrance Scholarships. (*See Scholarship Entries section.*) An extensive series of entrance Scholarships is offered each year to thirteen year olds, including Art, Academic, Drama, Sport, Technology, General Scholarships and Music awards. In addition, a small number of scholarships are available to eleven year-old boys and girls, and at sixteen to new Lower Sixth entrants. Full details are available from the School.

Fees per term (2011-2012). Boarders: Berrystead Year 1 £7,250; Berrystead Year 2 £8,410; Years 3–7 £9,530.

Day Pupils: Year 1 £4,680; Year 2 £5,430, Years 3–7 £6,160.

Details of extras are given in the School prospectus. The registration fee is £125.

Laxton Junior caters for 4 to 11 year old boys and girls. It moved to a new purpose-built facility in September 2002, increasing in size to have a two-form intake. (*For further details, see entry in IAPS section.*)

Charitable status. Oundle School is a Registered Charity, number 309921.

Pangbourne College

Pangbourne, Reading, Berkshire RG8 8LA
Tel: 0118 984 2101
Fax: 0118 984 1239
e-mail: registrar@pangcoll.co.uk
website: www.pangbournecollege.com

Pangbourne College was founded in 1917 by Sir Thomas Devitt of the Devitt & Moore Company to train boys for a career at sea. It is now a modern, friendly, boarding and day school for about 400 girls and boys aged 11 to 18, offering good academic results, first-class sports coaching and an excellent system of caring for the development of each individual pupil.

Motto: '*Fortiter ac Fideliter*'

Governing Body:
Chairman: M V F Allsop
Chairman Finance Committee: D O Herbert

Headmaster: T J C Garnier, BSc Bristol, PGCE

Deputy Head, Academic: G Pike

Deputy Head, Pastoral: R Bancroft

Bursar: R Obbard

Location and Facilities. Set in fine grounds of 240 acres and a mile from Pangbourne village, neighbouring the town of Reading, the College combines a country environment with easy access to London and Heathrow. The extensive school facilities include the Falkland Islands Memorial Chapel opened March 2000, science laboratories, a recently-refurbished library, a new girls' boarding house, art and music schools and an impressive design and technology centre. The performing arts centre contains a multi-purpose hall/theatre with fly tower. Following a successful fundraising campaign a new music school and ICT centre will open in Spring 2012. The fully-equipped sports hall, Astroturf hockey pitch, spacious playing fields, and boathouses on the River Thames provide excellent sporting facilities. Pupils are accommodated in seven fully-refurbished or new houses. After the first year they share study-bedrooms and have single rooms in the Sixth Form. Meals are taken in a central dining hall although the boarding houses contain kitchens for the making of snacks. Most academic staff live on the campus in College houses and there is an extremely strong community spirit.

Admission. Children normally enter the Junior House (Dunbar) at 11+ through an interview and the College entrance examination. They are joined by more boys and girls at age 13 through the Common Entrance or Scholarship Examinations. Sixth Form entry is based on interview, a satisfactory report from the previous school and good examination results. A Prospectus and Registration Form may be obtained from the Registrar who is always pleased to arrange visits to the College.

Scholarships. (*See Scholarship Entries section.*)

Junior House. The Junior House, Dunbar, offers excellent, purpose-built accommodation and common room areas for 11 and 12 year old pupils in the heart of the College. Fully integrated into the academic, cultural and social life, these pupils enjoy full use of all the Senior School's facilities and its specialist teaching. Pupils transfer automatically to the Senior School without further examination.

Academic Study. The curriculum of the Lower School (11 to 16) is based on the National Curriculum ideal of a broad and balanced education, although we do not enter pupils for the Standard Assessment Tests at 14, using instead our own assessment and reporting system. The majority follow a mainstream curriculum covering all the core and foundation subjects of the National Curriculum: English,

Mathematics, the Sciences, Design Technology, French, German, History, Geography, Art, Drama, Music, Religious Studies, Physical Education, and ICT. A Learning Support Unit, staffed by specialist teachers, is available to help.

At Sixth Form level pupils may choose to follow either the A Level programme or the International Baccalaureate Diploma programme.

The College is proud of the quality of its academic and pastoral support system, and each child is guided by a Tutor, a Housemaster/Housemistress and the Director of Studies.

While the College pursues a deliberate policy of recruiting a broad spectrum of academic ability, it looks for talent of various kinds, believing that its task is to enable each individual to make the very best of his or her potential, no matter where strengths lie.

Careers. The Director of Sixth Form Studies and the Careers Adviser work closely with the individual's Tutor to ensure that wise, informed choices are made in the well-equipped Careers Room. The result is that, while some students will go on to Oxford or Cambridge, the majority will proceed to degree courses at other universities prior to a wide variety of exciting careers.

Games. For a small school Pangbourne has an outstanding reputation for sport, particularly at National levels in several games. The College has won Henley Regatta four times making it one of the top rowing schools in the world. In the recent past it has dominated independent school judo, there is a strong tradition of successful rugby and the girls enjoy county success in hockey. Sports offered include athletics, basketball, cricket, cross-country, golf, hockey, judo, netball, polo (Pangbourne is a first division school), riding, rounders, rowing, rugby, sailing, shooting, soccer, squash, swimming, tennis, orienteering.

Adventure Training. The College has always placed great emphasis on teamwork, leadership and the development of communication skills. There is a full programme of adventure training built into the curriculum from the first form, with weekend and holiday expeditions. Every two years a major expedition abroad is organised. Boys and girls can join the CCF which has Army, Royal Navy and Royal Marine Sections. The College has won the prestigious Pringle Cup on many occasions. A comprehensive high and low Ropes Course is used for leadership training. Third Form pupils are entered for the bronze Duke of Edinburgh's Award.

Music and Drama. Pangbourne has a long tradition of excellence in Music and Drama. The Music School has its own Recital Room, ideal for internal concerts, and also a newly appointed Recording Studio. The College Choirs, Choral Society, Orchestra, Swing Band and Marching Band perform regularly within and outside the College. The Choir undertakes a biennial continental tour and more than a third of the school have individual instrument tuition. Drama has an exciting and flourishing tradition and we have a fine theatre fully equipped with computerised lighting and sound systems. School productions run throughout the year at every level.

Activities. There is a full programme of activities in those afternoons when pupils are not involved in school sport.

Fees per term (2011-2012). At age 11 and 12: Boarders £6,785; Part Boarders £6,045; Day Pupils £4,820. At 13 and above: Boarders £9,330; Part Boarders £8,300; Day Pupils £6,600. These fees are inclusive of medical attendance, games and most textbooks, and there are no obligatory extras.

Charitable status. Pangbourne College Limited is a Registered Charity, number 309096. The objective is to provide an excellent all-round education for boys and girls between the ages of 11 and 18.

The Perse Upper School

Hills Road, Cambridge CB2 8QF
Tel: 01223 403800
Fax: 01223 403810
e-mail: office@perse.co.uk
website: www.perse.co.uk

The Perse School is Cambridge's oldest secondary school, founded in 1615 by Dr Stephen Perse, a Fellow of Gonville and Caius College. The school still maintains close links with both Gonville and Caius and with Cambridge University.

The Perse Upper School is a co-educational independent day school for pupils aged 11–18.

Governing Body:

Representing the University of Cambridge:
R J P Dennis, BSc, MA
Sir David Wright, GCMG, LVO, MA

Representing Gonville & Caius College:
Dr A M Bunyan, BA, PhD
Dr E M Harper, BA, MA Cantab, PhD

Representing Trinity College:
Dr A G Weeds, MA, ScD (*Vice-Chairman*) (*OP*)

Co-opted:
J C Aston, OBE, MA, ACA
L M Capper, MBE, MCIPR
K J Durham, MA
Dr C J Edmonds, BSc, PhD
I G Galbraith, MA
R G Gardiner, MA, FCA (*OP*)
F Harris, BSc
Dr J R Haylock, BSc, LLD (*OP*)
M P H Pooles, QC, LLB (*OP*)
R M Rainey, CertEd
C J Reynolds, BSc
B P Smith, MA, CPFA, FCIHT
C J Stenner, LLB
Dr V J Warren, MA

Bursar & Clerk to the Governors: G A Ellison

Head: E C Elliott

Deputy Head (*Staff*): D R Cross

Deputy Head (*Pupils*): E W Wiseman

Deputy Head (*Curriculum*): C J Pyle

The number of pupils in the Upper School is approximately 940, including over 300 students in the Sixth Form.

Admission. The school welcomes applications at Year 7, Year 9 and Sixth Form. At Year 7 candidates are examined in Maths, English, Verbal Reasoning and Non-Verbal Reasoning. At Year 9 candidates are examined in Maths, English and Non-Verbal Reasoning. Sixth Form candidates are given offers conditional on their GCSE results. All candidates are interviewed and references are sought from their current school.

Facilities. Just over 2 miles from the centre of Cambridge, the Perse Upper School is situated on an attractive 27-acre greenfield site with extensive playing fields and recreational areas. Nearly £20 million has been invested in the last decade to give the school outstanding facilities including a purpose-built sports centre, a music centre, high-specification science labs, a new teaching and learning block incorporating 21 state-of-the-art classrooms and an impressive library and learning resources centre.

Education. Pupils receive an excellent all-round education which, whilst recognising the importance of academic achievement, also emphasises the need for wider social, cultural and sporting development.

Perse pupils achieve some of the best GCSE, A Level and Oxbridge entry results in the country, but also gain the personal qualities, interpersonal skills, character, hobbies and interests needed to make a success of adult life.

The Perse uses its independence and freedom from direct government control to innovate in the best interests of its pupils. As such, in recent years, new exam qualifications have been introduced including International GCSE and the Pre-U. Our foreign language provision has also been extended to include Arabic, Japanese, Mandarin, Russian, Portuguese and Italian alongside French, German and Spanish.

A recent extra-curricular innovation has been the development of the Perse Exploration Society which undertakes ambitious overseas expeditions to Latin America and Asia. These expeditions see Perse students carrying out valuable charity work before completing demanding climbs and hikes.

To ensure balanced intellectual development, a broad based curriculum is offered with equal weighting given to Arts, Humanities and Science subjects. In Years 7–9, all pupils study English Language, English Literature, Philosophy and Religious Studies, Maths, Biology, Chemistry, Physics and a modern foreign language. This compulsory core is supplemented by a number of optional subjects. As they mature, pupils make their own guided subject choices.

To give pupils a head start in an increasingly global world, they have the opportunity to develop their linguistic skills and improve their cultural awareness through our links with schools overseas, pupil exchanges and tours. The Perse has exchange programmes with schools in Australia, Hong Kong and the Middle East, and recent school trips have included visits to Japan, the Caribbean, South Africa, Scandinavia and the USA. The Perse is committed to offering a broad classical education, and pupils can choose to follow courses in Latin, Greek and Classical Civilisation which are supplemented by overseas study trips.

Nearly 30 A Level and Pre-U subjects are on offer in the Sixth Form and pupils can choose to study up to 5. They may either specialise in the Arts or Sciences or create a more diverse programme by mixing disciplines. The Extended Project Qualification provides opportunities for in-depth research, original thought and genuine scholarship.

The success of our approach is reflected in our academic results and in the university offers our pupils receive. In a typical year, over 90 per cent of the Sixth Form will secure an A or B grade at A Level and over 20 per cent will gain places at either Oxford or Cambridge Universities.

There is a full range of sports to cater for most interests. Main sports are rugby, hockey, cricket and netball. Other sports offered are badminton, rowing, aerobics, shooting, basketball, football, squash, fitness training, climbing, tennis and athletics.

At the heart of the extra-curricular life of the school are the many societies that either have strong subject links or arise out of a group of pupils having a common interest. The result is a vibrant range of societies including Scouts, Climbing, Debating, Lego Robotics, Perse Organic Garden and Young Enterprise.

Fees per term (2011-2012). £4,549.

Scholarships. At Year 7 and Year 9 we offer academic and music scholarships. At Sixth Form, we also offer art scholarships and general awards. All scholarships are eligible for bursary supplementation on a means-tested basis.

The Perse has always done its best to ensure that children who would benefit from an education here are not excluded for financial reasons. We offer a number of means-tested bursaries with financial support ranging from 5% to 100% of tuition fees. This financial assistance allows The Perse to be accessible to pupils from a wide range of backgrounds, and the resulting student diversity is a real strength of the

school. For further details please refer to the school's website.

The Perse Preparatory School is a co-educational preparatory school for pupils aged between 7 and 11. Tel: 01223 403920; e-mail: prep@perse.co.uk. (*See The Perse Preparatory School entry in IAPS section.*)

The Perse Pelican Nursery and Pre-Preparatory School is for children aged 3 to 7. Tel: 01223 403940; e-mail: pelican@perse.co.uk. (*See The Perse Pelican Nursery and Pre-Preparatory School entry in IAPS section.*)

Old Persean Society. Alumni Officer, The Old Persean Society, The Perse Upper School, Hills Road, Cambridge CB2 8QF.

Charitable status. The Perse School is a charitable company limited by guarantee (company number 5977683, registered charity number 1120654) registered in England and Wales whose registered office is situated at The Perse School, Hills Road, Cambridge CB2 8QF.

Plymouth College

Ford Park, Plymouth, Devon PL4 6RN
Tel: 01752 203245 (Headmaster and Admissions)
      01752 203300 (School Office)
      01752 203242 (Bursar)
Fax: 01752 203246; 01752 205920 (Headmaster)
e-mail: mail@plymouthcollege.com
website: www.plymouthcollege.com

The School was formed by the amalgamation in 1896 of Mannamead School, Plymouth, founded in 1854, and Plymouth College, founded in 1877. It is now a co-educational school. In 2004 the school merged with St Dunstan's Abbey to form one school, Plymouth College.

Governing Body:
C J Robinson, MA (*Chairman*)
P H Lowson, FCA (*Vice-Chairman*)
The Rt Revd J Ford, The Bishop of Plymouth
Commodore I M Jess
C Lindsay, MA Exeter
Professor M Watkins PhD, MN, RN, RMN, Plymouth
   University
T J Burke
Mrs C Evans
J H Friendship
Miss V Harman
Mrs R Hattersley, BA
Mrs J McKinnel, DipLSN, RGN, RMN, SCM, DipHV
Mrs A Mills ACIS, MCIPD
Mrs J Paull
I Penrose
Miss L P Stevenson, BVetMed, MRCVS
Revd D Waller
B E Walton, MA
D R Woodgate, MBA

Bursar and Clerk to the Governors: D W J Baylis, OBE,
   MA, MSc, MCMI (*Senior & Preparatory School*)

Headmaster: **Dr S J Wormleighton**, BEd Southampton,
   PhD Exeter

Deputy Head: Miss S J Dunn, BSc Exeter

Director of Studies: C R Compton, BA Scholar Exeter
   College Oxford

Assistant Staff:
A J Lewis, BA Open, CertEd Carnegie College (*Director of PE*)
Mrs S Knight, BEd Hons Sheffield (*Senior Teacher*)
M P R Rose, MA Hertford College Oxford

K C Boots, BA Wales, MEd Exeter, AMBDA (*Head of Learning Support*)
J P Gregory, BA Birmingham (*Head of Economics & Business Studies*)
M E Hodges, BA London (*Head of Geography*)
C J Sillitoe, MPhil, MRSC, CChem
J W Hocking, BSc Open, BEd Exeter (*Head of Design Technology*)
R Chapman, BEd College of St Mark & St John
Dr S Jordan, PhD Dundee (*Head of Biology*)
C J Hambly, BSc Manchester (*Head of Chemistry*)
Mrs Z P Thurston, BSc Exeter
Miss A C Blunden, BA Exeter (*Head of Girls' Games*)
Mrs L E S Clark, BA Open (*Senior Teacher*)
G A Ashfield, BA Open (*Head of Psychology*)
M Tippetts, BA Exeter (*Head of Boarding*)
Mrs H J Owen, BA College of St Mark & St John
Miss E D Tremaine, BEd De Montfort
J Shields, BSc Hull (*Head of Sixth Form*)
R J Prichard, MA London (*Head of English*)
A N Longden, BSc Plymouth
Mrs P M Brockbank, CertEd (*Head of EAL Department*)
R P Robinson, MA Queens' College Cambridge (*Head of German*)
Mrs B C Robinson, BA, CNNA
R G Palmer, BA
Dr A Hawker, BSc Plymouth, PhD
A Miller, BSc, PhD Bristol, CChem, MRSC, CPhys, MInstP (*Head of ICT*)
Miss E Williams, BA Greenwich
P J Cragg, BSc Open, AMInstP (*Head of Physics*)
R L Edwards, BA Wales (*Head of Rugby*)
D A Jones, BSc Birmingham (*Head of Mathematics*)
D J Whiteley, BSc Imperial College
P J Randall, BA Oxford Brookes (*Head of French*)
S Vorster, BCom University of Port Elizabeth (*Deputy Head of Sixth Form*)
Miss S Kerr, BEng Brunel
Miss M Labrousse, Licence d'Anglais Bretagne Occidentale
D J Roberts, MA Northumbria, BA Leeds
Miss L M Odendaal, BA Stellenbosch
D J Martin, BA Warwick (*Head of Religious Studies*)
R S Groves, BSc Durham
Miss L M Russo, MSci Imperial College
A R Carr, MA St Andrews
Dr A Norris, BSc Liverpool, PhD
Mrs A-L Chubb, BA Wolverhampton
Mrs A E Hobbs, BA Exeter
R P Wilson, BEng University College London
D Green, BA Dartington College of Arts (*Head of Music & Performing Arts*)
Miss A K Thornton, BA University College Falmouth
Mrs K M Harvey, BA Plymouth, MPhil Southampton (*Head of Learning Support*)
M A T M Tait, BA Cambridge
E J Beavington, BSc Wales, MA Birkbeck College London (*Head of History*)
Miss T Ouhoud, BA Leeds, DELE Barcelona, DUETE St Etienne
Dr C Taylor, BSc Bath, PhD Bath

Part-time Staff:
Miss P J Anderson, MA Emmanuel College Cambridge (*Head of Classics*)
S J A Terry, BA Magdalene College Cambridge
Mrs T K Shields, MSc Leeds
Mrs G C Brown, BA London
Mrs J E Hansford, BEd Reading
Mr C G Nicol, Diploma Duncan of Jordanstone College of Art (*Head of Art*)
Miss A Green, BA Exeter
Mrs V J Wilden, BA Plymouth
C Childs, MSc Imperial College, BSc Sussex

Mrs P R Russell-Copp, BPhil Exeter, BEd TESOL
Mrs J A Pope, BA St Anne's College Oxford
Mrs E Wright, BA UCL
Miss F Venon, Licence d'Anglais Université Saint-Etienne, Maîtrise
Miss S Currie, BA Stirling

Administrative Examinations Officer: Mrs P Taylor

School Nurse: Mrs K Compton, RGN, MEd, CertEd

Headmaster's Secretary & Admissions: Mrs S L Lambie

Preparatory School:
Plymouth College Preparatory School
St Dunstan's Abbey
The Millfields
Plymouth PL1 3JL

Headmaster: C D M Gatherer, BA

Numbers. Currently there are 530 pupils in the school (175 in the Sixth Form) and of these 213 are girls.

Buildings. The Senior School stands on high ground in Plymouth. The buildings include Science Laboratories (extended in 1957 and 1984), Art and Craft rooms including extensive facilities for pottery, photography and print-making, the Dining Hall, an Assembly Hall in which concerts and plays are performed (1974). A well-equipped Design and Technology Block was opened in 1979. The grounds in Ford Park include a Small-bore Rifle Range and a Squash Court. Games are also played on 2 other fields to which the pupils are transported by coach. The Sports Hall was opened in 1986 and a new library was opened in 1996. An astro-surface was built in 1999. A new swimming pool, heated and indoor, was opened in 2001. In 2004 a new hospitality suite and Music School opened. In 2005 a dedicated Sixth Form Centre was opened.

The Preparatory School at The Millfields is approximately half a mile from the Senior School and has its own playing field and sports hall.

Organisation. Below the Sixth Form there is some setting so that pupils may proceed at a pace best suited to their abilities. Pupils are organised in 4 Houses. Each pupil is under the supervision of a Tutor and Head of Year. In Years 7–10 Form Prefects are appointed. There is a Chaplaincy team which also has a pastoral responsibility for all pupils. Every pupil is expected to play a full part in games and other school activities outside the classroom.

English (Language and Literature), French, Mathematics, Physics, Chemistry and Biology are taken by all to GCSE. Normally three more are chosen by the pupils.

Sixth Form. The Sixth Form is based on tutor groups with about twelve in each group. Pupils study usually four AS Levels leading to 3 or 4 A Levels and most prepare for General Studies as well. The tutor keeps a pastoral and academic watch on the pupils' performance. Most standard A Levels are available. The International Baccalaureate Diploma is also offered as an alternative to traditional A Levels.

Sixth Formers are prepared for the Universities, the Services and the Professions; help is given by the Careers Teacher for almost any career, often with the assistance of the Independent Schools' Careers Organisation.

Games. Rugby, Cricket, Hockey, Netball and Swimming are the major sports. There is also Athletics, Badminton, Basketball, Cross-country Running, Sailing, Shooting, Squash and Tennis. Games are compulsory but more senior pupils have a wide range of options available to them.

School Activities. Pupils take part in a very good range of activities. There is a contingent of the CCF with Navy, Army and Air Force Sections. There is also The Duke of Edinburgh's Award Scheme and Adventure Training as well as Ten Tors. Pupils in Year 10 participate in a JSLA scheme with local primary schools. A number of overseas expeditions are also organised each year. School Societies cover a range of activities from Archery to Young Enterprise. A School Yearbook is published annually.

Music & Performing Arts. There is an excellent whole school choir that sings at all major school events, concerts, and church services throughout the school year. The school orchestra, like the choir, provides music at school events and concerts. Both the choir and the orchestra receive invitations to support large-scale events in and around Plymouth. In addition to these groups the school has various small ensembles that are run by the visiting specialist instrumental teachers. The school has a thriving house drama and music competition that attracts whole school support. As well as the formal/organized music making there are innumerable student-led bands that help to ensure that the music department is a vibrant environment. Tuition is provided on all orchestral instruments, including percussion. Voice, piano, organ and all types of guitar lessons are also available. Speech and drama lessons (LAMDA) are offered to all students. The music and drama departments work together on large-scale productions. The drama department offers drama clubs to all year groups. The lower school clubs focus on all aspects of stage technique and improvisation while the upper school groups tie their work in with current productions. A sound and lighting club runs which trains students in all aspects of the technical side of theatre. Both departments work with a number of visiting performers/practitioners throughout the year; these are usually focused on specific year groups or examination groups.

There are annual music and drama scholarships and instrumental exhibitions.

Boarders. In the Senior School there are 5 Boarding Houses. Four of these are situated at Ford Park: one for boys, one for girls (45 in each) and two smaller Sixth Form houses. They are situated close to the school field and are equipped with small dormitories, sickroom, common rooms and games rooms. Meals are taken in the Dining Hall, supplied by a modern, well-equipped kitchen. The fifth house, based at The Millfields site, is a dedicated boarding house for the elite swimmers.

Admission. Admission to the Senior School is normally based on the College Entrance Examination for boys and girls over 10½ and under 12 on 31 August of the year of entry, but it is also possible to enter at 13 via the Common Entrance Examination or a Year 9 Scholarship/Entrance test. Occasional vacancies are available at other ages. Application forms may be obtained from the Headmaster.

Admission to the Preparatory School is from the age of 3+. Application should be made direct to the Secretary to the Headmaster of the Preparatory School.

Scholarships. (*See Scholarship Entries section.*)

Fees per term (2011-2012). Preparatory School: Infant Department: Kindergarten £2,250, Reception £2,350, Years 1 & 2 £2,625. Junior Department: Years 3–4 £2,780, Years 5–6 £2,900.

Senior School: Day: Years 7–8 £3,825, Years 9–11 £4,070, Sixth Form £4,285. Boarding: Years 7–8 £7,650, Years 9–11 £7,970, Sixth Form £8,385.

These fees include books, stationery and games. Music lessons and lunches are extra.

Charitable status. Plymouth College is a Registered Charity, number 1105544. Its aim is to provide private education for boys and girls.

Pocklington School

West Green, Pocklington, York YO42 2NJ
Tel: 01759 321200
Fax: 01759 306366
e-mail: enquiry@pocklingtonschool.com
website: www.pocklingtonschool.com

Inspired for Life

Our ultimate aim is to give our pupils the support and freedom they need to flourish into balanced, fully-rounded and confident adults who are inspired for life.

Pocklington School is a supportive and caring community that has been thriving in the heart of rural Yorkshire for almost 500 years.

Rooted in the values of truth, trust and courage our approach to learning and development is shaped around the spiritual and physical well-being of each child we educate.

We believe that unlocking individual potential means fostering a culture that encourages successful learning and creative thinking while rewarding initiative and independence.

It also means creating an environment in which pursuing personal passions outside lesson time complements the achievements of academic success.

Governors:
C M Oughtred, MA, DL (*Chairman*)
T A Stephenson, MA, FCA (*Vice-Chairman*)
Mrs J Atkinson
Mrs E Bryers
J L Burley, BSc, MRICS
D G Buttery, BA, DL
S C Elliott, BSc
J A Farmer, FCA
The Rt Hon The Earl of Halifax, JP, DL
Canon J Harrison, MA
Revd G Hollingsworth
Mrs N Jennings
Rt Hon G Knight, MP
R C Nolan, MA
Ms D Nott, BA, MA, Dip SocAdmin
Mrs S M Oughtred, BSc
Mrs F C Sweeting, BSc, MSc, MIPD, AKC
Dr A J Warren, MA, DPhil Oxon, FRHS

Life Patrons:
K Appelbee, OBE, MA
Mrs J S Carver, DL
B Fenwick-Smith, MA
R E Haynes, MA
J L Mackinlay, DL, FCA, FCMA
D V Southwell
Major General H G Woods, CB, MBE, MC, DL, MA, DLitt Hon, FRSA, FBIM

Clerk to the Governors and Bursar: P S Bennett, BSc, FLS

Headmaster: M E Ronan, BA

Deputy Head: A M Dawes, BSc
Assistant Head (*Academic*): Miss C L Bracken, MSc
Assistant Head (*Boarding and Pastoral*): Dr D B Dyson, BSc, PhD
Director of Teaching & Learning: J M Webb, MA
Bursar: P S Bennett, BSc, FLS
Bursar's Secretary: Mrs C Haselock
Deputy Bursar: Mrs J L Knott
Premises Manager: M G Partis
Domestic Bursar: A D'Arcy MHCIMA, CertEd
Pocklington 500 Officer: Mrs R J Dare, BA, MBA
Marketing Officer: Mrs M Stefanini, BA, DipM, ACIM
Administration Manager: Mrs J M Whatford
Admissions Secretary: Mrs F A Lambert

* *Head of Department*

English and Drama:
*Miss L J Powell, MA
*A W J Heaven, BHum, MA, CFPS SpLD
Mrs A J Bond, BEd
Mrs E J Cunningham, BA
Mrs E M Girling, BA
Mrs A K V Hallam, BA

Miss L A Lamb, BA
Mrs F B de L Marshall, BA
M P Newhouse, CertEd

Mathematics:
*J F Cullen, BSc
Miss C L Bracken, MSc
Mrs L Deadman, BEd
Miss L J Gray
T M Loten, BA
Miss H M Scott, BSc
Mrs H V Towner, BSc

Modern Languages:
*P M H L Dare, BA, MA, RSA Dip TEFL
Mrs C Baines, BA
D A Galloway, MA
S C Nesom, BA
Mrs M R Peel, BA
Miss C J Postlethwaite, BA
Mrs N C Scott-Somers, BA
Mrs S L Wass, BA

Science:
Biology:
*M J Butcher, BSc
Miss S J Cheadle, BSc
Mrs S A Chiverton, BSc
Dr K J Clow, PhD, BSc
A M Dawes, BSc

Chemistry:
*Mrs S J Pratt, BSc
M R Evans, BSc (*Senior Master*)
Dr D B Dyson, BSc, PhD, GRSC
P R Horne, BEd
Mrs J R McDowell, BSc

Physics:
*G Binks, BSc
D W Hutchings, BSc
S D Ward, BSc

Psychology:
*Dr S McNamee, BSc, PhD (*Head of Sixth Form*)
Mrs R Anderton, BSc, MCIEA
Mrs L L Hutchinson, BSc

Classics:
*I J Andrews, BA
Ms H S McNelly, BA

Art:
*P Edwards, BA, MA
D A Cimmermann
Mrs J T Hall
Mrs S M Green
Mrs C M W Swann, BA (*Head of Middle School*)

Cookery:
Mrs A-M Salmon, BSc

Design:
*J E Playford, BA
S D Ellis, BA

ICT:
*Mrs H T Alexander, BA
S Spruyt, BA
Mrs M S Wilson, BA, MSc

Music:
*M Kettlewell, BA, ATCL
Mrs H J Kneeshaw, MMus
T E W Taylor, MA
M A Currey, BA, ACTL
J Diver, BSc LRSM
D J Hardy
Mrs K E Hart, GRNCM, ARMCM

K Holbrough, GLCM
I F Huntingford, ACLM
Miss C M Jowett, BA
P Judge, MA, PGTC
Mrs J Ledger, MA, PGTC
Miss K Ledger, BA
Mrs K Meinardi, LRSM, DipConsMusic Rome
D Saint John
I C Sharp, BMus, GRSM, ARMCM
M G Smith, BA
M E Stier, LRAM, DipLCM
Mrs D E Wadsworth, GMus

Economics and Business Studies and Politics:
*N A J Tomaszewski, BA
P J Donaldson, BA
D Watton, BA

History:
*G J Hughes, MA
A W Hall
J M Webb, MA (*Director of Teaching and Learning*)
E G Long, MA

Geography:
*I McDougall, MA
R P Bond, BEd
Mrs A L G Cosby, BSc
J Sykes, BSc

PE:
*A E Towner, BA
S A Houltham, BPhEd, BTchg
G M Kilsby, CertEd
Miss S A Metcalfe BSc
Mrs M Newhouse, CertEd (*Head of Lower School*)

Religious Studies:
*M J Davies, BA
Revd J Roberts, BA
Miss H M Young, BA

Sport:
D Byas (*Director of Sport*)
Miss S Barson, BPhEd
Mrs J E Danby, CertEd
G M Kilsby, CertEd
Mrs J S Kilsby
Miss R Spencer, BA

Careers:
Dr R Farrar, PhD, BSc, PG Dip CG

Learning Support:
Mrs L Deadman, BEd, Cert SpLD
Miss J Craggs, BA, Adv Dip AES

Librarian: Mrs A J Edwards, BA
Chaplain: The Revd J Roberts, BA
Director of Teaching and Learning: J M Webb, MA
Director of Activities: M Kettlewell, BA, ACTL

Boarding Houses:
Fenwick-Smith: T M Loten, BA
Dolman: Mr and Mrs I D Wright
Faircote: (*to be appointed*)
Orchard: Mrs J E Midwinter

Day Houses:
Dolman:
Mrs A J Bond, BEd (*Lower School*)
D A Galloway, MA (*Middle School*)
M J Davies, BA (*Sixth Form*)
Gruggen:
Miss C J Postlethwaite, BA (*Lower School*)
Miss S A Metcalfe, BSc (*Middle School*)
Mrs H T Alexander, BA (*Sixth Form*)
Hutton:
J Sykes, BSc (*Lower School*)

Mrs S J Pratt (*Middle School*)
D W Hutchings, BSc (*Sixth Form*)
Wilberforce:
Mrs M S Wilson, BA, MSc (*Lower School*)
G Binks, BSc (*Middle School*)
N A J Tomaszewski, BA (*Sixth Form*)

Number of Pupils (2010–11). There are 659 pupils (386 boys, 273 girls) at Pocklington School (ages 11–18) and 192 pupils (92 boys and 100 girls) at Lyndhurst School (ages 4–11). These numbers include 126 boarders aged 8–18.

Lyndhurst School is on the same site as the Senior School. (*For further details, see entry in IAPS section.*)

Curriculum. Pocklington's curriculum has been developed to motivate and stretch pupils. Following foundations at Lyndhurst and in the Lower School, there are wide-ranging options in Year 9 and GCSE. Sixth Form AS and A2 subjects offer a diverse selection of subjects and combinations. There is excellent careers and university advice. Music, drama and art thrive, as do sport, outdoor education, community service, the CCF and other extra-curricular activities. The main sports are athletics, badminton, basketball, cricket, cross-country, fencing, football, hockey, netball, rounders, rugby, squash, swimming and tennis.

Location, Campus and Development. The school is set in extensive grounds on the edge of Pocklington, a market town 12 miles east of York. Emphasis is given to the importance of personal achievement in an attractive, high-quality learning environment with very good facilities.

Admission is subject to vacancy and to a satisfactory entry exam result and school report. Interviews may also be held. Year 9 applicants sit either a Senior School entry exam or Common Entrance. Sixth Form applicants should have gained at least 4 B grades and 2 C grades at GCSE. Subject to these entry criteria, the school seeks to admit candidates who will benefit from what it has to offer and whom it will be able to support. Children with mild learning difficulties can be supported, as can those who will in due course seek entry to the most demanding university courses.

Scholarships and Exhibitions. (*See Scholarship Entries section.*)

Fees per term (2011-2012). Day £3,855, Boarding £6,898, 5-Day Boarding £6,530, Day Boarding (2–5 nights per week) £274–£658.20.

Charitable status. The Pocklington School Foundation is a Registered Charity, number 529834.

The Portsmouth Grammar School

High Street, Portsmouth, Hants PO1 2LN
Tel: 023 9236 0036
Fax: 023 9236 4256
e-mail: admissions@pgs.org.uk
website: www.pgs.org.uk

The School was founded in 1732 by Dr William Smith, Mayor of Portsmouth and Physician to its Garrison, MD of Leiden, and a member of Christ Church, Oxford, to which he left land in trust for the foundation of Portsmouth's first established school.

Motto: '*Praemia Virtutis Honores*'

Governing Body:
Chairman: B S Larkman, BSc, ACIB
Vice-Chairman: Mrs M Scott, BSc
Mrs F Boulton, BSc, MA
W J B Cha, BA
Mrs J Cockcroft, RGN, FPC, CertEd
M R Coffin, BA Econ, FCA
Mrs J Cockroft, RGN, FPC, CertEd

Rear Admiral N D Latham, CBE, MSc, CEng, FIMarEST, MIMechE
P Parkinson, BA
Professor C B R Pelling, MA, DPhil
M J Pipes, MA, MBA, FInstP
F S K Privett, LLB
Mrs S Quail, BA
Mrs S Resouly, BSc, MRPharmS
Commodore R J Thompson, RN, BSc, CEng, FIMarEST
P F J Tobin, MA, FRSA
The Right Worshipful The Lord Mayor of Portsmouth
The Dean of Portsmouth, The Very Reverend D Brindley, BD, MTh, MPhil, AKC

Governors Emeritus:
D K Bawtree, CB, DL, BScEng, CEng, FIEE, FIMechE
I A Carruthers
C J L Evans, FCA
B N Gauntlett, Dip Surv, FRICS
Air Chief Marshal Sir Richard Johns, GCB, KCVO, CBE, FRAeS, RAF

Clerk to the Governors and Bursar: D J Kent

Headmaster: J E Priory, MA

Second Master: S W Lockyer, BSc
Deputy Head (Co-curricular): B P H Charles, BA, FRSA
Deputy Head (Academic): Mrs L J Wilson, BA
Assistant Head (Head of Sixth Form): N D Gallop, BA, MSc

Upper School Staff:
* *Head of Department/Subject*
† *Head of House*

Art & Design:
*Miss A Dyer, BA
Miss C Bree, BA
S P H Willcocks, BA (*Deputy Head of Smith House*)

Careers:
*A R Hogg, BA

Classics & Modern Languages:
*B P Lister, BA
Mrs N S Alexander-Digby, BA
Mrs G J Charlesworth, BA
Mrs B Clifford, BA Wales, BA London
Miss C L Coward, BA (*German)
W J Crénel, LLCE
Ms J R M Deeks, BA (*General Studies)
D T Doyle, BA (†*Latter House, Languages Coordinator*)
P M Gamble, BA, PGCE (*French)
Mrs C A Gozalbez-Guerola, BA
A R Hogg, BA
Mrs L Nogueira-Pache, LicSc, MA
S Page, BA
Mrs A J Pounds, BA, MPhil (*Spanish)
S C Taylor, MA (*Senior Teacher, Director of IB*)
N G Waters, BA (*Senior Teacher, Head of Years 9–11*)
Mrs D J Willcocks, BA, AKC

Design and Technology:
*L A Ansell, BSc, MA
Mrs L Ashton, BA
Ms S J Green, BSc
M J Kirby, BSc, PGCE
Mrs W Whitaker, CertEd

Drama and Theatre Studies:
*M B Smith, BA, MA
D R Hampshire, JP, BSc, BA, ARCS (*Head of Middle School, Senior Teacher*)
Miss G Meadows, BEd (*Deputy Head of Years 9–11*)
B Sperring, BA, MA (*Director in Residence*)

Economics and Business Studies:
*R P Dolan, BA

S Quinn, BA, PGCE
Miss D A S Tabtab, MSc (†*Hawkey House*)
Mrs A T Wickson, BA, ACA

English:
*Mrs C Jepson, BA (*Senior Teacher*)
Mrs E E Bell, BA
J E Burkinshaw, BA
Mrs S A Burkinshaw, BA
Ms H S Brunner, MA
J Dunne, BA, MA
J J Elphick-Smith, MA, PGCertSpLD (†*Smith House, Senior Teacher*)
Miss B C Hart, BA, MA
Mrs E M Kirby, MA
Mrs M Mitchell, BA (*Senior Teacher, TOK Coordinator*)
M P Richardson, BA, MA, PGCE

Geography & Geology:
*Miss S Stewart, BSc, MEd
J P Baker, TD, BSc, MA Ed, FRGS, FGS (*Head of Outdoor Pursuits*)
Mrs C Giles, BSc (*Senior Teacher*)
Mrs J M Howlett, BSc
Ms F J Nicholson, BSc, MPH
Mrs H Sands, BSc

History & Politics:
*S Lemieux, MA
Miss F E A Bush, BA (†*Whitcombe House*)
Ms A S Cross, BA (*CAS Coordinator*)
Dr P W Galliver, BA, MA, MPhil, EdD (*Senior Teacher, UCAS Coordinator*)
Mrs R J Hammal, BSc

Information Technology:
*A H Harrison, BSc

Learning Support:
*Mrs J M Okell, BSc, DipSpLD, AMBDA
Mrs M G Dray, BA, HDipEd
Mrs S E Palmer, BA, DipSpLD, SpLDAPC
Ms R J McNamara, MA, BA, PCES, ATS

Mathematics:
*Ms M Copin, MA
D P Ager, BSc, MSc
J D Baker, BSc
Dr D J Burridge, BSc, PhD
N L Dawson, BSc, PGCE
S J Dean, BEd (*Deputy Head of Sixth Form [Yr 13]*)
J R C Gillies, BSc (†*Grant House*)
Mrs J Jackson, BSc (*Deputy Head of Middle School*)
Dr M H McCall, MA, PhD
Mrs R L Nash, BSc (*Deputy Head of Years 9–11*)
Miss J J Read, BSc (*Head of Examinations*)
P J Robinson, BSc
Dr L J Ronaldson, MA, PhD

Music:
*A M Cleary, BA (*Director of Music*)
Mrs Y C Hall, MA (*Academic Music*)
Miss S Heath, BMus (†*Summers House*)
Miss K Kingsley, GRSM, LRAM (*Keyboard*)

Physical Education:
*C J Dossett, BSc, MSc (*Senior Teacher, Director of Sport*)
S J Baker, BEd (*Rugby*)
N L Cooper, BPhEd (*Deputy Head of Whitcombe House*)
S J Curwood, BEd (*Cricket, Deputy Head of Latter House*)
Mrs A J Day, BEd (*Athletics*)
M W Earley
Miss S Gardner, BSc, MSc, PGCE (*Netball*)
S D Hawkswell, BA (*Academic PE, †Barton House*)
Miss A C Howarth, BSc

A D Leach, BSc
Miss H V Linnett, BSc (*Deputy Head of Sixth Form [Yr 12], Head of House Sport*)
Mrs H E Prentice, BA, PGCE (*Girls' Tennis*)
D F Rutherford (*Girls' Hockey*)
Dr K Stagno, Msc, PhD (*Hockey*)

Philosophy and Religious Studies:
*Dr R J I Richmond, MA, PhD
Miss T Bennett, BA
Revd A K Burtt, BA, MA, LTh (*Chaplain*)
Mrs A S Carter, BA
Miss J L Kirby, BA

Portsmouth Curriculum:
Mrs E E Bell, BA
Revd A K Burtt, BA, MA, LTh (*Chaplain*)
Miss F E A Bush, BA (†*Whitcombe House*)
Mrs C Giles, BSc (*Senior Teacher*)
Mrs J M Okell, BSc, DipSpLD, AMBDA
Mr J E Priory, MA

Psychology:
*Ms A J Wood, BA, PGCE
Mrs S R Pye, BSc, MSc

Science:
*B C T Goad, BSc (*Physics, Senior Teacher*)
Mrs E-J Akass, MA (*Biology*)
Dr M R Howson, BSc, PhD, CChem, MRSC (*Chemistry*)
Mrs M G Bates, BSc
Miss E J Cox, MSc, CPhys, MInstP
S G Disley, BSc
Miss J C Dunne, BSc, MIBiol (*Deputy Head of Grant House*)
S J Harris, MA (*Surmaster*)
Mrs H Harris, BSc (†*Eastwood House*)
J K Herbert, BSc (*Sixth Form Coordinator*)
P E Nials, BSc, MA Ed, CBiol, MIBiol, CertCouns (*PSHE, Senior Teacher*)
Dr P A O'Neil, BSc, PhD
R V Puchades, BSc
Mrs K L Sparkes, BSc, PGCE
Ms A C Stephenson, BSc
M R Taylor, BSc
J P Thomas, MSc, MInstP
Mrs J M H Tyldesley, BSc
Dr A D Webb, MChem, PhD, PGCE
C M Williamson, BA, MSc

Librarian: Mrs J C J Godfree, MA, PGCE, MCLIP, DipLib
Archivist: Mr J P Sadden, BEd, DipIS, MCLIP

School Medical Officers:
Dr C Foley
Dr A Scott-Brown
Dr M L Saunders

Personal Assistant to Headmaster: Miss J E Moody, BA
Admissions Secretary: Mrs G M Williams

Junior School

Headmaster of Junior School: P Hopkinson, BA, PGCE
Deputy Head: J Ashcroft, BSc, PGCE
Assistant Head: Mrs E R Day, BA, CertEd
Assistant Head: Mrs P Giles, BA, PGCE
Head of Nursery: Mrs L Johnson, BEd, PGDipEd (*Early Years*)

R Ainsworth, BSc, PGCE (*Head of Years 3 & 4, House Coordinator, Senior Teacher*)
Mrs J Albuery, BEd
J Ashcroft, BSc, PGCE (*Head of Reception & KS1*)
Mrs L Budd, BEd
Mrs J Budgen, BAc, PGCE (*Gifted and Talented Coordinator*)
Mrs R J Cooper, BA, PGCE

Mrs J Crossley, CertEd
Mrs R Darlington, BEd
Mrs L Dean, BA, PGCE (*†Privett House*)
Mrs J Dossett, BA, CertEd
Mrs J Ellis, BEd, CertEd, CertEd (*Early Years*)
Mrs A Evans, BEP, MEd (**Girls' Sport*)
G P Evans, BA, PGCE
Mrs R Evans, BA, QTS
W Faulconbridge, BEd
Mrs V Francis, BA, QTS
Mrs P Giles, BA, PGCE (*Head of Years 5 & 6*)
Mrs J Hardy, BA, MA, PGCE
Mrs J E Ingamells, ARCM
Miss D H Jennings, BA, MA, ALCM, LTCL, MusEd, PGCE
M Leclercq
Miss R McGibben, BA, Dip ABRSM, LRSM
Mrs J L Millward, BEd
Mrs C Minall, BA, PGCE
Mrs F Nash, BEd
Mrs K Park, BA, PGCE
G D Payne
Mrs J Pereira, BA, BSc, MA, PGCE
Mrs A Porter, BEd, Cert SpLC (*SEN*)
Mrs A Reader, BA QTS
Mrs C S Sayers, BEd (*†Hudson House*)
E J P Sharkey, BA, PGCE (*†Jerrard House, Senior Teacher, Director of Studies*)
Mrs E G Sharrock, BMus, LRAM
B W Sheldrick, BA (*Senior Teacher*)
Mrs S J Sheldrick, BEd (*†Nicol House*)
Mrs V Shoebridge, BA, PGCE (*Foundation Stage Coordinator*)
Mrs M Smith, BSc, CertEd
Mrs T Squire, BA, PGCE, SpLD (*SENCO*)
Mrs P Stirling, BA, PGCE
Mrs B E Tilling, BSc, PGCE
Mrs N R Townsend, BA, QTS Dance and Education
Mrs S P Tyacke, BEd
M F Warin, BA, PGCE
Miss P A Watkins, BA Primary Ed
I Webber, BA Ed
Miss L Younger, BSc, PGCE

PA to the Junior School Headmaster: Mrs A Stutter
Junior School Admissions Secretary: Mrs K G Bull, BA, PGCE
Junior School Secretary: Mrs P Kaznowski

The School, formerly on the Direct Grant List, assumed full independent status in 1976. It is co-educational throughout. There are 1,109 pupils in the Senior School and 458 pupils in the Junior School. There are no boarders.

The Nursery School opened in 2001 and offers outstanding provision for boys and girls from 2½ years old. Currently there are 53 boys and girls in the Nursery.

The Junior School numbers 455 boys and girls aged 4–11. It is a thriving, dynamic and popular institution, committed to giving Portsmouth pupils the best possible start to their educational lives. The main ages of entry are 4 and 7 by assessment tests held in January. Occasionally there are places available for intermediate entry. (*For further details see entry in IAPS section.*)

Although promotion to the Senior School is not automatic, it is normal for pupils to move there when they are 11.

Senior School. Admission is by the School's Entrance Assessment at 11 and at 13, chiefly by Common Entrance. All entrants at 13+ are pre-tested at 11+ to accommodate demand for places. Pupils are admitted at other ages, should vacancies occur, subject to assessments and satisfactory reports from previous schools. Admission to the Sixth Form, which numbers 298, is subject to satisfactory standard at GCSE and interview.

Curriculum. Pupils are educated for life as well as public examinations, through initiatives such as The Portsmouth Curriculum in Year 7 and the wide-ranging General Studies Programme in the Sixth Form. The curriculum aims to give a general education and to defer specialisation. After GCSE, pupils enter the Sixth Form, which seeks to prepare pupils for the challenges of a rigorous university education and subsequent competitive employment. Pupils have the choice of either studying for the International Baccalaureate Diploma or choosing A Levels, in which case all pupils study 4 A Levels. Subjects available in the Sixth Form include: Art, Biology, Business Studies, Chemistry, Classical Civilisation, Design and Technology, Drama, Economics, Electronics, English Literature, French, Geography, Geology, German, Government and Politics, Greek, History of Art, History, Italian, Latin, Mathematics, Further Mathematics, Music, Physical Education, Psychology, Religious Studies and Spanish. The General Studies Programme is mainly taught by outside professionals and is aimed at widening personal and academic horizons as well as offering some further academic opportunities, such as AS Critical Thinking. The Sixth Form prepares candidates for entry to Higher Education, and the Careers Department provides close relations with various forms of employment.

Religion. The School has always been closely connected with Portsmouth Cathedral. However, Religious Instruction, given in accordance with the principles of the Christian faith, remains, in accordance with a long tradition of latitudinarianism, non-denominational. The School has a Chaplain.

Pastoral Care. Pastoral Care is of paramount importance. Pupils are allocated to one of four Houses on entry. Heads of House and their House Tutors are responsible for the pastoral and academic welfare of all pupils, supported by Heads of Years 7–8, 9–11 and Sixth Form, and provide a focal point for communication between teaching staff and parents. Particular emphasis is placed on the triangular relationship between pupil, parents and teaching staff, including a programme of telephone calls from tutors to new parents in which all senior staff and the Headmaster have a monitoring role.

Games. Rugby football, rugby sevens, netball and hockey are the main games in Winter and Spring, cricket, tennis, athletics and rounders in the Summer Term. Cross-country running, squash, judo, badminton, gymnastics, basketball, aerobics, swimming and sailing are also available. The School has enjoyed national success in recent years in sports such as hockey, netball, athletics, cricket and rounders and was Runner Up in The Daily Telegraph Sports Awards for independent schools in 2007 and again in 2008.

The Co-Curriculum. There are significant opportunities for co-curricular involvement at the school. Music, Sport, Drama, CCF and Outdoor Pursuits including Ten Tors and participation in the Duke of Edinburgh's Award Scheme, play a huge role in the development of our pupils and they provide them with a diverse and popular range of activities. Service to the local community and charity work is also an important feature of the school's ethos. Many clubs and societies cater for a considerable range of co-curricular interests from the Model United Nations to Wildlife Club. Numerous expeditions, holiday activities and trips are actively encouraged and include many foreign tours for sports teams and music ensembles. The School has a flourishing exchange scheme with French, German and Spanish schools. Sports teams have recently gone on tour to South Africa and Australia. Recent expeditions have seen pupils travel to Borneo, Uganda, Cambodia, Argentina and Cuba.

Fees per term (2011-2012). Senior School: £4,186. Junior School: £2,686–£2,978. (Fees quoted include direct debit discount.)

Scholarships and Bursaries. (*See Scholarship Entries section.*) Scholarships are chiefly available for entry at 11 and 13. Full details are available on the website.

Buildings. Nothing remains of the former Schoolroom, destroyed when the present Junior School, now Grade II listed, was erected on the site of the town fortifications. The Lower Junior School and Senior Schools occupy a unique range of former Barrack buildings in an historic location in the High Street: these are now also listed throughout. In the last decade of the twentieth century there was an emphasis on new buildings, including a Music School, Sports Hall and Sports Pavilion and Sixth Form Centre. The acquisition of the Cambridge House Barracks has provided the school with space available for teaching and pastoral care, but also gives the School ownership of a harmonious group of historic buildings. In a major Development Project (2004–2005), the Library has been expanded and refurbished; a new all-weather pitch has been created on the School's playing fields at Hilsea; and a new dining and theatre complex developed. The new Bristow-Clavell Science Centre boasts new laboratories and 21st Century facilities.

Honours. 20 pupils took up places at Oxford and Cambridge in 2010, 23 gained places at medical, veterinary and dental school. Most 6th Formers gain a place at their first-choice University. Sportsmen include England Cricket Captain Wally Hammond and Athletics International Roger Black. Military distinction in abundance, including 3 VCs (one the first VC submariner), several Admirals, Generals and Air Marshals. Medicine is also a continuing theme – from pioneer ophthalmologist James Ware to Viagra researcher Ian Osterloh. Arts are well and diversely represented: dramatist Simon Gray, poet Christopher Logue, novelist James Clavell, cathedral organist Christopher Walsh and pop singer, Paul Jones. Civil Servants and Judges and barristers galore, plus entrepreneur industrialist Alan Bristow.

Old Portmuthian Club. This maintains links with former pupils not least by holding reunions in Portsmouth, London and Oxford, and is enhanced by its relationship with the School's Development Office.

Charitable status. The Portsmouth Grammar School is a Registered Charity, number 1063732. It exists to provide education for boys and girls.

Prior Park College

Bath, Somerset BA2 5AH
Tel: 01225 835353
Fax: 01225 835753
e-mail: info@priorpark.co.uk
website: www.thepriorfoundation.com

Prior Park College is a fully co-educational Catholic Boarding and Day School. Founded in 1830 by Bishop Baines, it was under the control of the Bishops of Clifton until 1924, when it passed to the Congregation of Christian Brothers. Since 1981 Prior Park has been under lay management and has more than doubled in size. Prior Park is a friendly, thriving community of 580 pupils with a strong boarding community, excellent academic standards and a strong devotion to educating the whole person.

The College is housed in magnificent Palladian architecture, built by John Wood for Ralph Allen, with glorious views of the World Heritage City of Bath. The 57-acre site combines an elegant setting for boarding and day education with access to Bath and its numerous cultural attractions. Proximity to the M4 and M5 motorways places the College within easy reach of London, the Midlands, the South-West and Wales. Good rail links and proximity to Bristol, Heathrow and Gatwick international airports allow easy transfer for our international students.

Motto: '*Deo Duce, Deo Luce*'

Patrons:
His Eminence Cardinal Cormac Murphy-O'Connor, PhL, STL
The Rt Revd Declan Lang, BA
The Revd Monsignor Canon R J Twomey, VF
The Rt Hon the Lord Patten of Barnes
Mr F J F Lyons, KSG
Miss J Bisgood, CBE
Sir Cameron Mackintosh
Col R S C Dowden, JP, DL, KCSG
Mr C J B Davy, CB
Mr D R Hayes

Governors:
Commodore Christopher York, KSG Royal Navy (*Chair*)
Mr A M H King (*Vice-Chair*)
Mr Tony Bury, MBA, BSc Hons
Mr Simon Eliot
Sister Andrea Le Guevel, MA, MPhil
Mrs B Huntley, BEd Hons
Ms A Lloyd
Mr D F Lyons, BA, CTA (*Fellow*)
Father W McLoughlin, PhL, BD, MTh, OSM
Mrs N E L Pearson, BA Hons
Mr P S J O'Donoghue, MA, FCA (*Chair of Finance & General Purpose Committee*)
Rear Admiral N J F Raby, OBE
Mrs M M Rae, MSc, PH, DipEd, FFPH, FRIPH
Mr J M Shinkwin, MA Oxon, PGCE
Mr J Webster, BA, BArch, MCD, RIBA

Headmaster: **Mr James Murphy-O'Connor**, MA Oxon

Bursar & Clerk to the Governors: Col M J Vacher, OBE, FCMI
Deputy Headmaster: Mr D G Clarke, BSc (*History*)
Academic Deputy Head: Mr T J Simons, BSc, BA (*Mathematics*)
Director of Communications: Mrs J Kearney, BA (*Classics*)
Assistant Head Co-Curriculum: Mrs L Blake, BA (*Geography*)
Assistant Head Teaching & Learning: Mrs S Forshaw, BSc (*Chemistry*)
Assistant Head Staff Development: Mrs K E McCarey, BA (*Geography*)

Assistant Staff:
Mrs S Andell, BA (*Modern Languages*)
Mrs R Bird, BA, MA (*Modern Languages*)
Mr M Blaikley, BA (*Mathematics*)
Mrs K Bond, BA (*Design & Technology*)
Mr S Burt, BSc (*Head of Geography*)
Mrs C Byron, BSc (*Mathematics; Housemistress, English*)
Mr S Capon, BEd (*Director of PE and Sport*)
Mrs H Cattanach, BA, MBA (*Learning Development Programme*)
Miss R Chambers, BA, MA (*English*)
Mr K Chard, BSc (*Head of Chemistry*)
Miss J Chisholm, BA (*PE & Sport Studies*)
Miss J Clark, BA (*PE & Sports Studies*)
Mr E Clements, BA, MSc (*Economics/Business Studies*)
Mrs L Collison, BA (*Head of History*)
Mrs W Cornish, BEd (*Head of Learning Development Programme*)
Mrs H Cronk, BSc, MSc (*EAL*)
Miss C Cummins, BA (*Theology; Housemistress, St Mary's*)
Miss S Davies, BA (*Drama & Theatre Studies*)
Miss L Dawson, BA (*History*)
Mr S Dorey, BSc (*Physics; OC CCF Royal Navy Section; Gold DofE*)
Mrs J C Eatwell, BSc (*Head of Economics/Business Studies*)
Mrs N Fahey, BA (*Learning Development Programme*)

Mr M Fisher, MA (*Head of Classics*)
Mrs C Ford, BA, Dip CG (*Head of Careers*)
Mrs R Fox BA, MPhil (*Dance*)
Mr R Francis, BA (*Mathematics*)
Mr J C Fry, BA (*Economics/Business Studies; Housemaster, Allen*)
Mr M Glen, BA (*Drama & Theatre Studies; Theatre Technician*)
Mrs H Goodman, BA (*Theology*)
Mr A J R Haines, BA (*ICT Manager; Music*)
Mr A S Hall, BEd (*Head of Boys' Games*)
Miss L Hellberg, BA (*Art*)
Mrs J Jones, BSc (*Head of Mathematics*)
Miss L Justine, BA (*French*)
Mrs H Kershaw, BA (*Library*)
Mrs J Klinpikuln, BEd (*EAL*)
Mr M Knights (*PE & Sport Studies; Housemaster, Roche*)
Mr D Langley, BA (*Director of Drama & Theatre Studies*)
Mrs B Ludlow, BSc (*Design & Technology*)
Mrs A Mallon, MA (*French; Housemistress, Fielding*)
Mr T B C Maxwell, BA (*Head of Theology*)
Dr K McGowran, BA, MA, PhD (*English; History*)
Mr R McGuire, BA, MPhil (*PE & Sports Studies, Head of Rugby*)
Miss E Meehan, BA (*Classics; Deputy Head of Sixth Form*)
Mrs M E Mudie, BSc (*Biology*)
Mrs E Parker, BSc (*Mathematics*)
Miss T Penfold, BA (*Head of ICT; Design & Technology*)
Mrs C M Pepler, BA (*Head of Modern Languages*)
Mr G Pruett, BEd (*Geography; PE & Sports Studies*)
Mrs L Pruett, BSc (*2nd i/c Mathematics*)
Dr C Roberts, BA, PhD (*German*)
Mr R P Robertson, MA, ARCO (*Director of Music*)
Ms C Romero, BEd (*Modern Languages*)
Mr J Rutter, BA (*Head of Design & Technology*)
Mr D M Sackett, BA (*Music; Housemaster, Baines*)
Mr L St John, BA (*PE & Sport Studies*)
Mrs C Saunders-Prouse, BA (*English*)
Mr V Shannon, BSc (*Science; Housemaster, Burton*)
Dr G Smith, BSc, PhD (*Chemistry; Housemaster, Clifford*)
Mrs A Spelman, BA (*English*)
Mr N Tattersfield, MA (*Head of English*)
Mr J Taylor, BA (*Spanish*)
Mr P Thompson, BA (*English; Theology; Acting Head of Sixth Form*)
Dr R Trott, BSc, PhD (*Biology; OC CCF Army Section*)
Mrs K Trott, BSc (*Biology; PE and Sports Studies*)
Mr T Vause, MA (*Library*)
Dr R L Wells, BSc, PhD (*Head of Science; Head of Biology*)
Dr S A Wilcock, BSc, PhD (*Head of Physics*)
Miss C Williams, BSc (*Head of Girls' Games*)
Dr R J Willmott, BA, MA, PhD (*Philosophy*)
Mr D F Wood, BA (*Head of Art*)

Music Staff:
Mr P Badley, PPRNCM (*Voice*)
Miss A Carroll, MA (*Voice*)
Mr T Worley, MMus, BMus (*Piano*)
Mrs J Finch, ALCM, LTCL (*Oboe*)
Miss C Gainford, BMus, GRNCM (*Bassoon, Woodwind*)
Mr A Haines, BA (*Bass Guitar*)
Mr G Harrup, BA Hons, LGSM (*Acoustic/Electric Guitar*)
Mrs A Hickmore (*Voice*)
Mrs J Mason-Smith, BA, ABSM, ALCM (*Flute*)
Mr D Pagett, GRNCM, PG Dip RNCM (*Clarinet, Saxophone*)
Ms S Power, BEd (*Cello*)
Mr S Skews, LTCL (*Piano*)
Ms A Townley, AGSM (*Violin, Viola*)
Mr R Webb, BMus, PGCE (*Trumpet*)
Mrs I Windsor, LRSM, LTCL, BA Hons (*Piano*)

Mr P Woodburn (*Drums, Percussion*)
Mrs J Edgell, BA, MA (*Junior Music, Lower Brass*)
Mrs C Paterson, BMus (*Music Secretary*)

Houses and Housemasters/mistresses:
Baines (*Junior House*): David Sackett
Burton (*Senior day boys*): Vincent Shannon
Clifford (*Senior day boys*): Graham Smith
English (*Senior day girls*): Colette Byron
Fielding (*Senior day girls*): Anne Mallon
St Mary's (*Senior boarding girls*): Charlotte Cummins
Allen (*Senior boarding boys*): Jonathan Fry
Roche (*Senior boarding boys*): Martin Knights

Headmaster's PA: Ms D Miller (*hmsec@priorpark.co.uk*)
Registrar: Mrs A Mundell, BA
Press Officer: Miss L Moss, BA
Chaplain: Father Malcolm Smeaton, BSc
Medical Officer: Dr I Batterham, MB BS, MRCGP, DRCOG
Nursing Staff:
Mrs R Cole, RGN (*Sister i/c Medical Centre*)
Mrs F Whittington, RGN

Structure of the School. Prior Park is a friendly, thriving community of approximately 580 pupils. The annual three-form entry of day pupils aged 11–13 makes up our co-educational Baines Junior House. A further forty enter the school at 13, when we admit both boarders and day pupils. Each boy and girl between 13 and 18 is a member of a boarding or day single-sex Senior House. Year groups also meet regularly for assemblies. Weekly and full boarding is available.

Objects of the College. The College provides an outstanding education, within the framework of a caring Catholic community which warmly welcomes members of other denominations. Our resident Chaplain serves the needs of the whole community and great importance is attached to the commitment of all staff to the ethos of the school. Pastoral care is perceived by the current parent body to be outstanding and great efforts are made to ensure that all pupils are nurtured and supported. A Personal Development Programme aims to equip all our pupils with information and guidance specifically addressing contemporary moral issues and problems. The School makes great efforts to developing the full potential of all its pupils, according to their individual abilities, with particular emphasis being placed on each pupil's academic progress. Through all aspects of College life, through community service, and through shared experiences in sport, music and drama, we engender self-respect and respect for others. We strive to equip our young people with the vitally important communication and other skills which will allow them to leave the College as confident young adults, ready to negotiate successfully the next stage of their lives.

Buildings and Grounds. The Houses, Administration and College Chapel are to be found in the fine 18th century architecture grouped around Ralph Allen's celebrated Palladian Mansion. A major programme of modernisation has enhanced the accommodation for residential staff and their families, and added to the attractive environment for the residential community. Boarding and day accommodation of high quality is provided for all girls in The Priory and All Saints at the eastern end of the estate. A major refurbishment programme of boys' boarding accommodation has provided comfortable study bedrooms, quiet areas and recreational rooms. A rolling programme of refurbishment continues.

Academic teaching is provided in modern classrooms. Eight renovated Science laboratories, an Art Centre, and a well-equipped Design Technology Centre provide a stimulating environment for practical work. ICT provision includes an ICT Centre, several suites of computers in the library, Design Technology Department and the Houses. ICT provision is also made within departments. A Dance studio and purpose-built Theatre are excellent venues for Performing Arts.

An elegant library, with over 11,000 volumes and two part-time librarians enhance private research and independent learning.

Curriculum. The academic curriculum conforms to and goes beyond the requirements of the National Curriculum. Core subjects to GCSE are Mathematics, English, the Sciences, a Modern Language and Religious Studies. The curriculum in Year 7–9 is broad. Great care is taken to ensure that careful guidance is given to pupils in Year 9 and Year 11 when GCSE and AS/A2 choices are being made. The Academic Deputy, his assistant and the House staff work with pupils and their parents to tailor a programme which reflects the strength and interests of the individual. The majority of pupils will study 10 GCSE subjects and 4 AS/A2 subjects in the Lower Sixth, dropping to 3 A2 in the Upper Sixth.

We currently offer 23 AS/A2 courses and there is considerable flexibility of combinations at both GCSE and A Level. The Extended Project Qualification (EPQ) is also offered in the Sixth Form.

Virtually all Sixth Form students proceed to Degree course at Universities, Medical Schools or other Higher Education Institutions, with the majority gaining places at their first-choice university.

A Sixth Form Enrichment programme of visiting lecturers, UCAS and Oxbridge preparation ensures a broad education at Sixth Form level.

Music. The College has a highly deserved reputation for musical excellence. Two chapel choirs provide high quality music for the weekly sung Mass in the glorious surroundings of the Chapel of Our Lady of the Snows. The John Wood Chapel, within Prior Park Mansion, offers a further concert and rehearsal venue for the very many musicians in the school.

The Music Department, also in the Mansion, houses a recording studio and teaching and practice rooms. Around half the pupils learn a musical instrument, and there are several thriving orchestras, chamber groups and bands as well as a large and ambitious Choral Society, annual competitions and festivals. Prior Park musicians go on to Oxbridge and major conservatoires and play in NYO, NCO, NYC etc.

Performing Arts. Drama productions (around 20 a year), Dance, Inter-House Music Competitions, Band Nights and charity events all feature prominently in the life of the school. The Julian Slade Theatre is a wonderful setting for this extensive and diverse performing arts programme. It has been extended to provide a Dance Studio and further teaching and technical support areas. There is also a full-time theatre technician.

Physical Education and Games. Physical Education is included in the curriculum. Games are an important part of school life. Main school games are Rugby, Hockey, Cricket, Tennis for boys; Hockey, Netball, Tennis for girls. Provision is made for Swimming, Badminton, Cross-Country, Soccer, Volleyball, Basketball, Table Tennis, Fencing, Athletics and Rounders.

Sports facilities include a Gymnasium and fitness centre. A new Sports Hall is planned. An Astroturf, refurbished pavilion, netball and tennis courts as well as extensive rugby, hockey and cricket pitches are all on site. An entirely renovated and extended swimming pool and changing room complex opened in 2005.

Activities Programme. The voluntary Combined Cadet Force includes Navy and Army Sections. Adventure training takes place both in the UK and overseas. Cadets are encouraged to participate in the Service and Contingent Camps and Courses.

The Duke of Edinburgh's Award Scheme operates at Silver and Gold Award level. Participants work on the four sections: volunteering, skills, physical, and expeditions; plus a residential project section at Gold Award level.

Boarders and day pupils alike participate in a wide range of activities after school, including arts and crafts, sports, electronics, Radio Club, chess, golf, aerobics, Scrabble, cross-country running, model engineering, dance and a whole host of challenging events. Poetry and literary groups have won national awards. Public speaking and debating thrive. All full-time boarders in Years 9 to 12 take part in Saturday Active, which takes place on a Saturday morning. Courses include Leith Cookery, archery, pony-trekking, climbing, mountain-biking, swimming, tennis and textiles. Some courses are free and in others certificates can be awarded. Over 135 pupils and parents take part in Saturday Active each term, including many day pupils.

The College operates its own Community Service Programme involving extensive work in the local community. Charity work is strongly encouraged, both in the form of fundraising and visits to homes, hospitals and schools. A biennial charity week raises thousands of pounds.

Careers. Our careers guidance programme combines the traditional strength of the House system with the benefits of a specialised central careers department. Every pupil receives individual guidance through the five years from Form 4 (Year 9) to Upper Sixth, with particular support at the three critical stages of choice for GCSE, A Level, and university entrance. At the same time, professional careers advice is available from the Head of Careers, who provides objective information and guidance via a programme of interviews, supported by psychometric testing and on line guidance tools.

The Careers Education input begins as earlier as Years 7/8, as part of the school's PSHCE programme and continues through year 9 with decision making skills and options choices. In Years 10/11, the world of work is explored more fully through Business Dynamics Days and work experience. In the Sixth Form, a comprehensive programme exploring the full range of post 18 options is delivered together with mock interviews, the production of CVs and the transition skills needed for successful university applications. The pastoral and general studies programmes also support the College's aim of "creating an outward looking ethos … enabling our leavers to be confident, capable, compassionate and independent minded".

Our biennial Careers Fair (2011) brings together over 50 different occupations and is attended by pupils and their parents from Year 9 upwards.

Admission and Scholarships. (*See Scholarship Entries section.*) Main points of admission are at 11+, 13+ and 16+ but pupils may transfer into the College at 12 and 14 if places are available. Early registrations are encouraged. Prospective families are encouraged to visit the College on Open Days or on an individual visit.

Entrance and scholarship examinations for 11+ and 13+ take place in January and February prior to entry in September. 16+ scholarship examinations and interviews take place in November. Please contact the Director of Communications for the relevant entrance/scholarship admission booklet.

Academic scholarships are available at 11+, 13+ and 16+. Art, All-Rounder, Drama, Music and Sporting Excellence awards are available at 11+, 13+ and 16+. Dance awards are available at 13+ and 16+. All awards carry with them a fee remission of up to 50% of the appropriate fee.

Fees per term (2011-2012). Boarding: £8,160 (full), £6,466 (weekly); Day 13+ £4,525; Day 11+ £4,061.

Prior Park Preparatory School. The Preparatory School is situated at Cricklade, Wiltshire, 35 miles from Prior Park and within easy reach of Swindon train station and the M4. It has ample boarding and recreational facilities for 180 boys and girls aged 7–13+. In addition, the adjacent nursery and preparatory school offer a wonderful educational environment for day children up to the age of six. In addition, its Pre-Prep Department offers a wonderful educational environment for day children between the ages of 4 and 6. Extra-curricular activity is an important element and the school has excellent standards in Music, Drama and Sport.

Headmaster: Mr Mark Pearce, BA Hons

For further details, see entry in IAPS section.

The Paragon School, Bath – Junior School of Prior Park College. The Paragon School is now part of Prior Park Educational Trust. Housed in an impressive Georgian mansion, the co-educational school for 3–11 years is set in beautiful wooded grounds only a few minutes drive from Prior Park College. A broad and balanced curriculum is delivered within a happy, caring environment.

Headmaster: Mr Titus Mills, BA Hons

For further details, see entry in IAPS section.

Charitable status. Prior Park Educational Trust is a Registered Charity, number 281242.

Queen Elizabeth Grammar School
Wakefield

154 Northgate, Wakefield, West Yorkshire WF1 3QX
Tel: 01924 373943
Fax: 01924 231603
e-mail: office@qegsss.org.uk
website: www.wgsf.org.uk

The 'Free Grammar School of Queen Elizabeth at Wakefield' is supposed to be the descendant of a school existing in Wakefield in the 13th century, and was founded by Royal Charter in 1591, at the 'humble suit made unto us by the inhabitants of the Town and Parish of Wakefield'. The endowment is largely due to the munificence of George Savile, Esquire, of Haselden Hall, and his sons George Savile and Thomas Savile, whose names may still be read on the exterior of the old school.

Motto: *'Turpe nescire'*

Governing Body:
The Governing Body is the Wakefield Grammar School Foundation, consisting of 15 co-opted Governors and 6 nominated Governors (representatives of the Universities of Sheffield, Leeds, Huddersfield and York; Wakefield Cathedral and mid-Yorkshire Chamber of Commerce and Industry).

Spokesman: D Wheatley, BTech, CEng

Clerk to the Governors: L Perry, BA, ACMA

Headmaster: D N Craig, MA, MEd

Deputy Head (Academic): L A Hallwood, BSc
Deputy Head (Staff and Operations): J T Palin, BEng
Assistant Head (Senior Tutor): Mrs L J Firth, BA

Mrs N Allen, ICSA	P L Dryland, BA, ATC
D Andrew, BA, MSc	M C Fascione, BSc
M Archer, BA	Mrs A J Fitzsimons, BA, MA
T Barker, BSc	
A J Barraclough, BSc	M Fitzsimons, BA
D T Benn, BTech	K Fortas, BA
Mrs K Bentham, BMus	T H Gibb, BA
R Bidmead, BA	D N Gratrick, BSc
D A Binney, BA	J Greenwood, BSc
T A Brunt, PhD, MA	C Head, BA
D M Burrows, BSc	R Heery, BSc
Mrs L Burrows, BA	D Higgins, MSc
J P Cholewa, BEd, MA	J Holt, BSc
S Clark, PhD, MChem	Mrs E M Jenkins, BSc
Mrs H L Cowan, BA	J Joy Jones, BA
S E Davies, BA, MA	N Lambert, BSc
J Dinsdale, BA	O K Lambert, BA
D R Dryland, BA	O Leask, BA

Mrs A Lees, BA	Mrs L Ramsden, BA
I Lenihan, BA	A M Rees, BA
Dr J N Lord, PhD, BSc	A N Rhodes, PhD
P Mason, BSc	Mrs S L Roberts, BA
Mrs E Matthews, BA	Mrs J Satari, BSc
Mrs E McGlone, BA	Mrs H M Sheard, BSc
P McWilliam, BSc, MPhil	Miss F E Steer, BA
C Mencatelli, BA	G D Tingle, BA
Mrs S M Monk, BEd, AMBDA	Mrs L van der Schans, BA
M J O'Connor, BA	D Waters, BA
Mrs C L Palin, BA	R Westerdale, BA
M C Parsons, BEd	Mrs P Whiteman, BSc
Mrs E J Peace, BSc	Mrs L Williamson, BA
A T Pesterfield, BSc	C R Winborn, MA
G Pickersgill, BSc	I A Wolfenden, BA
J P Preston, BEd	M I Wood, BA
Mrs S Radcliffe, BEd	Mrs E Young, BA

Headmaster's PA: Mrs H C Smith

Junior School
Head: Mrs L Gray, MA
Deputy Headmaster: I Shuttleworth, BEd

Centenary House:
Mrs L Butler, BEd
Mrs J Dyson, BEd
T Lloyd, BA
Mrs R Mayes, BEd
Miss E Sanders, BA
Miss S White, BEd
Miss G Wigdahl, BA
Miss L Williams, BA

School Secretary: Mrs H Gannon
School Secretary: Miss S Brook

N Brook, BSc
C Cheffins, BEd, MEd
Mrs J S Clayton, ARCM, GRSM
J R Coughlan, BEd
Mrs K E Cousins, BEd, LTCL
N Darnton, BA
A Ferguson, BA
Miss L Kirton, BSc
G Lewis, BSc
Mrs B D Lindley, BEd
Mrs J Middleton, BA
Mrs S Morris, BA
Mrs L Pearson, FISTC
M Pearson, FISTC
Mrs R Pye, BEd
R Ribeiro, BSc
Mrs D J Rogers, BEd
R Thompson, BA

Head's PA: Mrs C Denison
School Secretary: Mrs J Shackleton

Visiting Music Staff:
D Allen, MSc, GCLCM, Grand Dip
C J Bacon, GMus
Mrs S T Bacon, GMus
Mrs C Baker, GMus, RNCH, PPRNCM
Mrs L Berwin, LRAM, GRSM
P Bingham
J Clayton, GRSM, ABSM, ATCL
S Earl
P Francis
J Gibson, GRNCM
Mrs C Goddard, LTCL
Mrs C Hall, DCLCM, LTCL
Mrs E Hambleton, GNSM, LRAM
Mrs M B Hemingway, ALCM
J Hendrickx, BA
Miss A Holmes, BA, LTCL, CertEd

Mrs J Ingham
G Lewis
Mrs J D Maunsell, GBSM, ABSM, LTCL
T Moore, BMus, MA
R O'Connell
M J Roberts, LGSM, DPLM
E Spencer, BA
J Storer
D Taplin
D Waller

Queen Elizabeth Grammar School has a long and proud tradition of achievement and exists to provide an excellent education for your son. There are approximately 950 boys in the school (junior 220 and senior 720).

The Headmaster is responsible to the Governors for the Senior School. The Junior School (for boys of 7–11 years of age) is separately housed and administered by its own Head, who is a member of IAPS. (*For full details, see Junior School entry in IAPS section.*)

Situation and Buildings. The school is situated on Northgate near the centre of Wakefield. It is within walking distance of Wakefield Westgate Station and is convenient for all road links including the M1 and M62 motorways. The main building has been used by the school since 1854. Over the years, the school has expanded greatly, but its core remains the distinguished Early Gothic Revival building, whose architectural merits have been accentuated by extensive stone cleaning and renovation. A gradual programme of building has matched the school's expansion with additions and improvements taking place in all areas. Developments include the Queen's Building named in honour of Her Majesty the Queen who visited the school in 1992 to mark the school's Quatercentenary, a Language Suite and Sports Hall. In 2005 a Theatre, Learning Resources Centre and English Department were opened along with a Sixth Form Centre.

The Junior School is housed in its own building and enjoys its own specialist facilities; Art Room, DT Room, Hall, ICT Room, Library, Music Room and Science Laboratory.

Curriculum. In the Senior School all boys follow a wide ranging common curriculum including various subject options from which they choose their GCSE subjects taken for examination at the end of Year 11. In the Sixth Form boys study subjects in a variety of combinations, following 4 subjects to AS and continuing 3 to A2 level. All in the Sixth Form also follow a General Studies course as an additional subject. An increasing number of subjects in the Sixth Form can be studied with pupils of our sister school, Wakefield Girls' High School.

Religion. The school is a Christian Foundation and maintains close links with Wakefield Cathedral for whom it educates choral scholars, but there is no denominational bias in either teaching or morning assemblies, and those who practise religions other than Christianity are warmly welcomed into the school.

Pastoral Care. A thoughtful programme of induction for new pupils, including a special activities week in the Yorkshire Dales, is administered by the Head of Year 7. Thereafter boys are supervised by individual Heads of Year who coordinate teams of Form Tutors responsible for the progress and development of the boys in their care. A full PSHE programme is delivered and an expert Careers Department offers careful advice on all subject and university choices.

Physical Education and Games. Physical Education is an integral part of the school curriculum throughout the school. The school has some 37 acres of playing fields, with excellent rugby and hockey pitches in the Winter, with four cricket squares, an all-weather athletics track and access to 16 tennis courts in the Summer. The school has a six-badminton-court-size sports hall and fully equipped fitness room. January 2006 saw the addition to the sports facilities of a sand-dressed, all-weather surface, together with three new acrylic show courts for tennis.

The major games for Winter are rugby, hockey and cross-country. In the Summer term cricket, athletics and tennis predominate. All major sports are played to a high level, with boys regularly reaching county and, currently, international level.

Table tennis, basketball, golf, swimming, weight-training, squash and badminton exist at club level, either at lunchtime or after school. Regular competitions take place with other schools.

There is an annual ski trip and the pupils are involved in a wide range of outdoor and extra-curricular activities including mountain biking, climbing and fishing. The Duke of Edinburgh's Award is extremely popular with boys of all ages and there are regular training and assessment expeditions.

Music and Drama. The school has a full programme of musical and dramatic activities, many operating in conjunction with Wakefield Girls' High School. There is a major production each Autumn and Spring. There are in addition other productions and performances throughout the year.

There is at least one concert each term, designed to reflect the range of musical activity, which is wide and varied, ranging from madrigals through orchestral music to jazz and rock. Activities taking place throughout the year include two orchestras, two concert bands, two swing bands, junior and chamber choirs, together with many smaller groups and chamber ensembles. There is a large team of visiting instrumental staff, and close links with Wakefield Cathedral, where some events take place. A music scholarship is available each year on entry to the Sixth Form.

Clubs and Societies. These include Art, Chess, Christian Union, Classics, Debating, Drama, Geography, History, Angling, Bridge, Fell Walking, Film, Table Tennis and Science. The various music groups include brass, woodwind, string ensembles and choirs. The school also participates in the Duke of Edinburgh's Award Scheme, which is extremely popular and undertakes many exciting expeditions. There is also a significant programme of charity collections and related activities.

Entrance. Entry into the Junior School is usually at 7 although places are retained for entry at 8, 9 and 10. Places depend on performance in the entrance tests held in February, and enquiries for entry at this level should be made to the Head of the Junior School (01924 373821).

There is a 5-form entry annually into the Senior School. Entry into the Senior School is possible from any kind of school and is normally:

(a) at 11 after a satisfactory performance in the entrance examinations held early in January or as a result of good academic performance in the Junior School.

(b) at 13 from Preparatory Schools after a satisfactory performance in examinations that are set by the School.

(c) at 16 from any school after a satisfactory performance in the GCSE examinations and interview.

Enquiries about entrance to the Senior School at these or at other ages should be made to the Admissions Secretary (admissions@qegsss.org.uk).

Fees per term (2011-2012). Senior School: £3,332. Junior School: £2,419–£2,641.

Scholarships, Bursaries, etc. The Governors award each year a limited number of scholarships to boys entering the Senior School at 11. Means and asset-tested awards are also available under the Wakefield Grammar Schools' Foundation Awards Scheme. Enquiries about these awards should be made for the Junior School to the Head of the Junior School, and for the Senior School to the Admissions Secretary (admissions@qegsss.org.uk).

Choral Scholarships are provided for boys in the Wakefield Cathedral Choir, and enquiry about these should be made either to the Precentor of Wakefield Cathedral, or to the Head of the Junior School.

The **Old Savilians Society.** President: Mr N Rigby
The **Parents Association.** Chairman: Mrs K Harrison
The **Friends of Queen Elizabeth Grammar School.**
Chairman: Mr W Smith
The **Sports Association.** Chairman: Mr D Sharpe
can all be contacted through the School.
Charitable status. The Wakefield Grammar School
Foundation is a Registered Charity, number 1088415.

Queen Elizabeth's Grammar School
Blackburn

Blackburn, Lancs BB2 6DF
Tel: 01254 686300 (Headmaster)
          01254 686303 (Bursar)
Fax: 01254 692314
e-mail: headmaster@qegs.blackburn.sch.uk
website: www.qegs.blackburn.sch.uk

Blackburn Grammar School was originally a Chantry School founded in 1509 by Thomas, the Second Earl of Derby, and associated with the Parish Church of Blackburn; it was disendowed in the reign of Edward VI, and re-established and constituted a Corporation by Royal Charter in 1567 by Queen Elizabeth. It is now administered by a scheme under the Charitable Trusts Acts dated 1910.

Motto: '*Disce Prodesse*'

Chairman of Governors: M J Gorick, DL

Headmaster: S A Corns, MA, FRSA

Deputy Headmasters:
J Cave, MA
D Hopkinson, BSc

Assistant Staff:
Miss C J Abrey, BA
Mrs A Adam, NNEB
Mrs R Arkwright, DipAD, ATC
Mrs A G Bamber, DipSport Psych
L Barré, BA
Miss A M Berry, BA
T D Birtwistle, BA (*Head of Art*)
Mrs J H Blakemore, BA
P K Broadhurst, BSc, MSc, DMS, TEFL
Dr A M Brown, MA, PhD (*Head of History and Politics*)
A Buckingham, BEd (*Head of Geography*)
M E Butler, BA, PhD (*Director of Physical Education*)
A J Clare, BEd
Mrs R J Cox, BA
Mrs L M Crabtree, MA
Mrs R A Deacon, BA, MA
Miss P J Disley, BSc
Miss N J Eggleston, BA
Mrs M Foxley, CertEd, PGDip (*Director of Complementary Studies*)
Mrs C Y Gammon, BSc (*Head of Mathematics*)
J F Grogan, BA
P T Hargreaves, BSc
J R Hart, BEd (*Head of Design Technology*)
S P Heald, BA
M D Hindle, BSc
Mrs M E Kellock, BA, MA, LCCI
Mrs E J Lashbrook, BMus (*Director of Music*)
Ms K L Lawrence, BA (*Deputy Head of Junior School*)
B Lead, BA, MPhil
M J Lockwood, BA, MA
P J Lowe, BSc (*Head of Psychology and General Studies*)
Mrs K A Marshall, BA (*Head of Early Years*)

Miss S J McCreadie, LLB, BA
J B Morgan, BA
S R Northin, BEd (*Head of Careers*)
Mrs S A Nowell, BA
Mrs A J Nuttall, BEC, NNEB
Mrs K L Perkins, BA, MA
Miss F Pook, BSc, MSc
A F Priory, BA, MA (*Head of Ethics and Philosophy*)
A M Rose, BA (*Head of Modern Languages*)
M W Russell, BSc, MA
A Sagar, BSc (*Head of Chemistry*)
Dr Z M Saunders, BSc, PhD
Mrs G L Simpson, BEd
M A Sirkett, BEd
S A Smith, BSc
Miss J V St Jean, BA, MA (*Head of English and Drama*)
Mrs J E Taberner, BSc
Mrs R M Tattersall, BA
Mrs K Taylor, BEd
P R Taylor, BSc (*Head of Biology*)
S J Taylor, BSc
Mrs A E Trafford, BA
D Westworth, MA (*Head of Classics*)
Miss A C Wharmby, BEd (*Head of Junior School*)
Mrs P Wild, BSc (*Head of Physics*)
Miss R M Wildman, BA
Miss D P Wilkinson, BA
Miss P C Williams, BSocSc
Miss J L Woodcock, BSc
P H Wooldridge, BSc

Bursar: N J Edwards, MA
Director of Marketing and Development: P B Lloyd, BA, MBA, FCIM
Foundation Director: Mrs J H Lavelle, MICFM
Headmaster's Personal Assistant: Mrs D M Tate
Librarian: Mrs V Dewhurst, BA, MCLIP
School Nurse: Miss C Hargreaves, RGN, RSCN, NNEB

There are 626 pupils, of whom 114 are in the Junior Department, aged 3–11, and the Sixth Form numbers about 115. The School has been a fully co-educational day school since 2001. Many pupils are bussed in from a large catchment area.

The Junior School curriculum includes English, Mathematics, Religious Education, Geography, History, Science, ICT, Art, Physical Education, French and Music with optional tuition in most instruments.

Boys and girls join the Main School at the age of 11 with a few places at 13+ CE stage and follow a full range of academic and practical subjects up to GCSE.

Boys and girls who enter the Sixth Form have a wide choice of Advanced courses, including Classics, Modern Languages, English, History, Geography, Economics, Psychology, Music, Art, Design Technology, Mathematics and the Sciences, by means of which pupils are prepared for the universities, the professions and industry.

The School is a non-denominational, Christian school. Religious instruction forms part of the ordinary teaching of all pupils, except those whose parents express a wish in writing to the contrary.

The School was rebuilt on a new site, facing Corporation Park, in 1884. In 1987 Her Majesty The Queen opened the £3.4 million Queen's Wing, which besides providing classrooms also incorporates a library and a language laboratory. A new sports hall was built on the sports fields at Lammack, extended considerably in 2011, and a new 25m swimming pool with sophisticated electronic timing facilities was opened on the school site in October 1990. In 1995 a £1.5 million purpose-built Centre, Singleton House, was completed for the Sixth Form. Since the turn of the century, a new Early Years Department and a state-of-the-art Modern Languages laboratory have come on stream, the Brian Mercer Physics Laboratory has opened, the Biology and Mathematics departments have been completely updated and refurbished in 2008, and there has been a number of major enhancements to the Junior School facilities.

The main School games are Association Football and Cricket, though Tennis, Rugby, Swimming, Netball and Basketball are among the many other physical activities provided. The 13 acres of playing fields are situated at Lammack, a short distance from the School. They have been extensively developed and improved, including new netball and tennis courts in 2005, and a new teaching/catering area and changing rooms in 2011.

Out-of-school activities are provided for by various societies – for example Astronomy, Dance, Debating, Drama, Magic, Squash and Sailing. A School play and a musical are produced publicly each year while the Choral Society and School Orchestra present several concerts. Instruction in the playing of orchestral instruments is provided.

There are educational visits abroad to Europe, America and Africa.

Fees per term (2011-2012). Main School £3,295, Junior School £2,375, Early Years £1,865. The School offers a number of means-tested Bursaries and Scholarships: The John Law Scholarship at 11+; The Ogden Trust Science Scholarship and The Blakey Languages Scholarship at 16+.

Charitable status. Queen Elizabeth's Grammar School is a Registered Charity, number 1041220. It exists to provide quality education for boys and girls.

Miss L Carter, BA	Mrs B Kenchington, BEd
Mrs E Cheetham, BA	P J Kirby, BA
C B Conquest, BEd	H L Kyle, BSc, PhD
S M Cook, MSc	A G Lewis-Barned, BEd
P Davies, BSc	Ms S Maltin, BA
Mrs M Dimes, BSc	J E Martin BA
R Dixon, BSc	R Martineau, MEng
T Dunn, BSc	J R Matthews, BEd
M Dutton, BEd, MA, EdD	Miss B McKean, BA
Miss N Dyer, BA	C Miller, BSc
W R Ellis, BSc	P Moore, BEd
E Gent, BA	Miss N Morgan, BA
C Gamble, BSc	Mrs S Moritz, BSc
Mrs D Guthrie, BSc	P R Murray, BA
M Hale, BSc	W G Plowden, BA
C G Hamlett, BA	R Pandya, BA
M Harris, BA, MPhil	Mrs S Pole, BA
R Harris, BA	Miss J Sharrock, BA
S A Harris, BSc	Miss A Slevin, BA
D Hawkes, BSc	Mrs C E Steen, BA
G Huband, BSc	Mrs R Steven, BA
A Hughes, BA	Mrs L Stotesbury, BA
Mrs N Hunter, BSc	A W H Swithinbank, BA
Dr J Jönsson, MSc, PhD	Mrs F Waite-Taylor, BA
P M Jones, BA	Miss C J Winchester, BA
P E Joslin, BEd	

Junior School:
Headteacher: M J Morris, BA

Visiting Teachers:
Mrs E J Cormack, BA
Mrs D Dickerson, DipLCM, DipABRSM, DipESA
K Figes, LGSM, PG Dip
Miss A Gillies, BMus, MMus, PG Dip
B Groenvelte, BA
Mrs R Hall, BMus, PG Dip
S Hofkes, BMus, Conducting GSMD
Mrs A Howell, BMus, FRCO, LGSM, BA
C Khajavi, BA Mus
C McCann, Dip Mus MoD
T Shevlin, BMus, PG Dip
N Shipman, BMus, LGSMD
A Stewart, BMus
Miss L Tanner, BMus, MMus, PG Dip

Chaplain: The Revd S B Taylor, BA
Headmaster's Secretary: Mrs E Davies
Librarian: Mrs A Robbins

Queen Elizabeth's Hospital (QEH)

Berkeley Place, Clifton, Bristol BS8 1JX
Tel: 0117 930 3040
Fax: 0117 929 3106
e-mail: headmaster@qehbristol.co.uk
          juniors@qehbristol.co.uk (Junior School)
website: www.qehbristol.co.uk

Patron: Her Majesty The Queen

By his Will dated 10 April 1586, John Carr, a Bristol merchant, founded Queen Elizabeth's Hospital, a bluecoat school in Bristol on the lines of Christ's Hospital which was already flourishing in London. The Charter was granted to the School by Queen Elizabeth I in 1590. Originally composed entirely of boarders, the School continued so until 1920 when foundation day boys were admitted. Direct Grant status was accorded in 1945. The School is now independent and day only.

Motto: '*Dum tempus habemus operemur bonum.*'

Governing Body:
N Tyrrell, BA (*Chairman*)
J G Mason (*Vice-Chairman*)

Professor R D Adams	J G Pickard, BSc
G Bird, ACII	H Roberts
H L M Bothamley	Mrs G Rowcliffe, BEd
A J Brackin, BA, FCA	C Russell-Smith, BSc,
P N Gibson	FRICS
N A Mitchell, MSc, FRAeS	Mrs M Shutt, JP
A J Morsley, BSc	D A Smart

Bursar: R N Cook, FCA

Staff:

Headmaster: **S W Holliday**, MA

Deputy Head (*Operations*): S P Ryan, BSocSc
Deputy Head (*Pastoral*): D M Bateson, MA
Director of Studies: J G Sykes, BSc

S Albon, BSc	C Brotherton, BA
Mrs S K Allen, BSc	J F Brown, BSc
P M Amor, BA	Ms P Cawte, BA

Admission. There are 545 boys in the Senior School, ranging in age from 11 to 18. Entrance examinations for both Year 7 and Year 9 applicants are held in January each year.

Term of Entry. Usually September.

Entrance Scholarships. (*See Scholarship Entries section.*) A significant number of scholarships are offered at Year 7, Year 9 and Sixth Form. These are awarded purely on academic merit for outstanding achievement in the entrance procedures and may also carry with them generous assistance for applicants whose parents' means are limited.

Assisted Places. There are many School assisted places available. The School has a substantial foundation income and is able to give generous support to parents whose means are limited.

Music Scholarships. Music scholarships are available at Year 7 and Year 9.

Buildings. The School was originally close by the City Centre but moved to new premises on Brandon Hill in 1847. A major building and improvement programme has included the building of the QEH Theatre (1990), refurbishment of the Art School (2000), new Mathematics rooms and heavy investment in ICT (2004). An 80-strong Junior School opened in 2007 (which expands to 112 from 2011) along with a new Sixth Form Centre. In 2008 a multi-million pound development programme, in conjunction with Bristol City Football Club, saw new football pitches on 23 acres at the Sports Ground at Failand. Science facilities were extensively refurbished in 2009 and the Governors are considering various options for Science long term, building a new gymnasium/swimming pool complex and other ideas connected with the possible expansion of the city site.

Curriculum. Boys are prepared for the GCSE (IGCSE in Mathematics and English) and GCE A Level, and for university entrance. The usual school subjects are offered at GCSE Level, and the AS/A2 Level subjects are: English Literature, English Language, Drama, Economics, Latin, Greek, History, Geography, French, German, Spanish, Art, Music, Mathematics, Further Mathematics, Music Technology, Physics, Chemistry, Biology, PE and Sport, Business Studies, ICT, Ethics and Philosophy, Politics and Psychology.

Music. There is a School Orchestra, Choir, Jazz Band, Brass Group, and Wind Band. Music is included in the timetable for all the junior forms. GCSE and A Level music is part of the School curriculum, and tuition is arranged for a wide range of instruments. The Choir and Instrumentalists perform regularly and also undertake joint ventures with the independent girls' schools in Bristol.

Art. The Department is well equipped and offers ceramics, screen printing, photography and computer imaging.

Religious Studies. The School is a Christian one which welcomes boys of all faiths, or none. Religious Studies is part of the curriculum and boys attend two services a year in Bristol Cathedral.

Games. Rugby, Football, Athletics, Cricket, Swimming, Tennis, Badminton, Sailing, Squash, Fencing, Judo, Climbing and Mountain Biking. A large number of boys also participate in The Duke of Edinburgh's Award and Ten Tors.

Dress. Boys wear either grey trousers and a blazer or a plain dark suit. Traditional bluecoat uniform is worn by some for special occasions.

General. All parents are encouraged to join the Friends of Queen Elizabeth's Hospital, a society whose aim is to promote a close relationship between parents and staff and to further the welfare of the School. There is a flourishing Old Boys' Society (Secretary: Mr N Coombes), which holds regular meetings and circulates a newsletter. A panel of Old Boys, formed from all professions, and working with the Head of Careers, is available to give advice on careers to boys.

The School has long been known in Bristol as The City School and its links with the Lord Mayor and Corporation are strong. Boys read the lessons and sing in the Lord Mayor's Chapel, and groups are in attendance for such occasions as Mayor-making and Council Prayers.

The central position of the School, close to the University, the Art Gallery and Museum, the Central Library, the Bristol Old Vic and the Colston Hall, affords ready access to a wide range of cultural facilities which boys are encouraged to use.

Junior School. 112 Boys aged 7–11. (*For further details see QEH Junior School entry in IAPS section.*)

Fees per term (2011-2012). Senior School £3,753, Junior School £2,453. Fees include educational visits, textbooks and stationery.

Charitable status. Queen Elizabeth's Hospital is a Registered Charity, number 1104871, and a Company Limited by Guarantee, number 5164477. Queen Elizabeth's Hospital has existed since 1590 to provide an education for boys.

Queen's College
Taunton

Trull Road, Taunton, Somerset TA1 4QS
Tel: 01823 272559 School Office
          01823 340830 Admissions
Fax: 01823 338430
e-mail: admissions@queenscollege.org.uk
website: www.queenscollege.org.uk

Queen's College is one of the South West's leading independent day and boarding co-educational schools and has a consistent record of high academic achievement. Queen's' expertise also shows in music, drama and the arts. Please see the school website for further details.

The college has a well-deserved reputation for the quality of its teaching and all pupils are cared for in small tutor groups. The staff works untiringly to encourage students to develop their personal skills and abilities. The class sizes are well below the national average thus helping to develop a friendly, supportive environment.

Queen's operates a very strong co-curricular programme including a wide variety of sports and considerable emphasis is placed on participation in the Duke of Edinburgh's Award Scheme. All students take Bronze, many go on to Silver and to date, over 300 Sixth Form students have achieved their Gold Awards.

The college is controlled by the Board of Management for Methodist Residential Schools and receives pupils of all denominations.

Motto: '*Non scholae sed vitae discimus*' (*We learn not for school but for life*)

Visitor: The President of the Methodist Conference.

Governors:
Chairman: J N Birkett, FCIB, MSI

A J Bloxham	L Oldham, FDSRCS, BDS,
Mrs H J Broderick	LDS, RCS
B M Butt, FCA	Mrs D Perreau
Mrs J A Forsyth, MA, BA,	Revd P Pillinger
FRSA	M F Powell, BSc, FRICS,
Capt P M Gowen, RN	FAAV
Mrs M Hannam	J Rainford, CISSP
N Harvey, BA, MP	G Russell, MA
P Hughes	Mrs A St John Gray, BA
R James, BA	Hons, MA, JP
S A Lawson	Maj Gen M F L Shellard,
P Madhavan, Dip NB Surg,	CBE
FRCS Ed Tr & Orth	G Slocum
I McIntyre	B M Tanner
	Revd B D Thompson

Honorary Governor: The President of the Old Queenians' Association

Headmaster: Christopher J Alcock, BSc Durham, FRGS, FRSA

Chaplain: Revd Robert J Blackhall, BSc, BA

Financial Director & Clerk to Governors: Richard J Abolins, BSc, ACA

* *Head of Department*
† *House Parents*

Senior Leadership Group:
Deputy Headmaster: Marcus K Paul, MA (*English*)
Assistant Head – Pastoral: Mrs Gill Watson, BEd (*Chemistry and Science Education*)
Director of Studies: Graham H Warner, BSc (*Mathematics)

Director of Marketing and Communications: Keith Wheatley, BA (*Law and American Studies*)
Director of Co-Curriculum: Simon Ross, BA (**Geography*)
Head of Sixth Form: David Cooke, BSc, MEd (*Biology*)

Senior School

Teaching Staff:
Miss Donna Ashman, BA (*History, Examinations Office*)
Ralph Bates, BEd (*English*)
Geoffrey Bisson, BA (**History*)
Mrs Kay Bloxham, BEd, MA (*Dance and Physical Education*)
Roger Bowden, BEd (*Mathematics*)
Mrs Jennifer Brierley, BA (*English*)
Miss Laura Burgoyne, BA (*Art*)
Mr Tom Candler, BA (*Economics & Business Studies*)
†Mrs Rebecca Cole, BSc (*Food Technology*)
Paul De Jaeger, BSc (*Geography*)
Mrs Henrietta Drummond, BSc (*Mathematics*)
Mrs Jane Evans (*Performance Studies*)
Stephen Evans, BA (**Theatre Studies*)
Mrs Terri Fisher, BA (*Modern Languages*)
Michael Fletcher, BSc (*Ceramics*)
†Mrs Amanda Free, BA (*Learning Support*)
†Andrew Free, BA, DipSpPsych (**Director of Physical Education and Games*)
Andrew Garton, BA (*Music and ICT*)
Mrs Donna Greenow, BSc (*Modern Languages*)
Mrs Lindsay Hall, BA (**English*)
Angus Hamilton, BA (**Religious Studies*)
†Miss Claire Harrison, BSc (*Biology*)
Miss Julie Harrison, BEd (**Girls' Physical Education and Games*)
David Hedges, BA (*Music*)
Ian Henden, BSc (*Chemistry*)
Mrs Lisa Henden, BSc (*Biology*)
Terri Hicks, BA (*Learning Support*)
Timothy Jolliff, MA (**Chemistry*)
Miss Elizabeth Laycock, BA (*Religious Studies*)
Byron Lewis, BSc (**Design Technology*)
Mrs Caroline Lewis, BH (*Physical Education and Games*)
Ms Kate Littlewood, MA, Cert SpLD (**Learning Support*)
Mrs Grace Mainstone, BA, LRSM, LTCL (**EFL*)
Miss Sarah Male, BA (*Modern Languages*)
Miss Lisa Manley, BA (*Physical Education and Games*)
†Philip Mann, MNASC (**Boys' Physical Education and Games*)
†Damian Marshman, BSc (*Mathematics*)
John Marston, BA (*Theatre Studies*)
†Mrs Carole Mason, BEd (*Mathematics*)
†Christopher Monks, BSc (*Mathematics*)
†Ian Morrell, BEd (*Design Technology, Careers*)
Mrs Virginia Murray, BA (*French*)
Mark Neenan, BEd (*Geography*)
Nicholas O'Donnell, BEng (**Physics*)
Mrs Valerie Orme-Dawson, BA (*EFL*)
Adrian Palmer, BA, Cchem, MRSC (*Science*)
Mrs Pamela Pawley, BA (*Mathematics*)
Mrs Sheila Platt (*Mathematics*)
Miles Quick, BA (**Music*)
Mrs Nicola Ross, BA (*Manager, Learning Resource Centres*)
Mrs Laura Schofield, MA (*Modern Languages*)
Jon Shepherd, BSc (**Biology*)
Miss Melissa Smith, BSc (*History*)
Nigel Smith, BSc (*Physics*)
Leslie Stevens, BSc, BSc (**ICT, Physics*)
Tristan Stone BSc (*Mathematics*)
Mrs Sophie Turpin, BA (*Mandarin*)
Peter Vicary, BSc (**Business Studies*)
Michael Wager BA (**Modern Languages*)
Mrs Sue Wedge-Thomas, BSc (*Biology*)

Mrs Claire Western, BA (**Art*)
Mrs Sharon Wilde, BA (*Physical Education and English*)

PA to the Headmaster: Mrs Cathy Carter
Admissions Secretary: Mrs Anne Slocum
Office Administrator: Miss Judith Poole
School Secretary: Mrs Pam Chapman
Sixth Form Administrator: Mrs Penny Bates

Junior School, Pre-Prep and Nursery

Head: Mrs Tracey Khodabandehloo

Junior School Teaching Staff:
Mrs Linda Alcock, BA
Mrs Sarah Beats, BA
Mrs Patricia Camera, CertEd
Andrew Clark, BA
Philip Dudman, BA
Mrs Gill Harrison, BEd, RSA Dip SpLD
Miss Samantha Horner, BEd
Mrs Belinda Hoskins, BEd
Mrs Sue Marston, BA, LAMDA Gold Medallist
Mrs Annie Mason, DipEd
Mrs Vicky Miller, DipEd
†Christopher Monks, BSc
Mrs Shirley Neale, CertEd, RSA DipSpLD, AMBDA
Mrs Valerie Orme-Dawson, BA
Andrew Owen, BA
Mrs Janet Proud, Dip Teaching Assistant
Miss Sarah Scutt, BA, MA
Mrs Catherine Stirzaker, NNEB
Mrs Anne Wade, BA
Mrs Penny Walker, BSc
Mrs Anthea Watkins, CertEd, RSA Dip SpLD
Miss Margaret Way, LRAM, LGSM, ALAM Gold Medallist AM
Dick Wilde, BEd
Mrs Sharon Wilde, BA

Pre-Prep and Nursery Staff:

Head: Mrs Janet Williams, BEd, CertEd, NNEB

Mrs Charlotte Baker, BEd
Mrs Dawn Coram, NVQ3, DPP, STC
Mrs Jill Fear, BEd
Mrs Kirsty Goss, BTEC Early Yrs, Foundation Degree Childhood Studies
Miss Christina Hardwick, BTEC Early Yrs, Foundation Degree Childhood Studies, BA
Miss Elizabeth Hayes, NNEB, DPQS, NVQ4 (*Head of Nursery*)
Mrs Anne Higgins
Mrs Helen Hitchin, BEd
Mrs Clare Hood, BEd
Mrs Rachel Hoyle, NVQ2
Mrs Rebecca Milby, BSc
Mrs Vanessa Monks, BA
Mrs Sarah Silverwood, NVQ2
Mrs Theresa Underwood, BSc
Mrs Sarah Warner

Secretary to Junior School Head and Head of Pre-Prep & Nursery: Ms Julie Cameron
Assistant Secretary: Mrs Sarah Musgrave

Medical Staff:
Dr David Downs, BSc, MBChB, DRCOG, MRCGP
Dr Gabrielle de Cothi, MBChB, DRCOG, MRCGP
Mrs Lynn Dimery, SRN, SCN
Mrs Susan Parratt, RGN
Mrs Judith Barry, RN, RM, DipHE Health Studies
Miss Rebecca Morgan (*Resident Matron, Junior School*)

Number of Pupils. The Queen's College Pre-Preparatory, Junior and Senior co-educational schools are based on the same site with some facilities shared: continuity of education is assured.

The Senior school (11 to 18 years) has 583 pupils of whom 152 are boarders. The Junior school (7 to 11 years) has 136 pupils, of whom 14 board and the Pre-Prep school has a total of 54 pupils (none of whom are boarders). The full College complement of pupils is therefore 773. Nursery pupils are additional, attendance being a mix of full and part time.

Situation and Buildings. Queen's College was founded in 1843 within Taunton's Castle walls but was relocated to the south western outskirts of Taunton three years later when the present main school buildings were constructed. It is in a good situation with fine views of the Quantock and Blackdown Hills, within easy reach of Exmoor and Dartmoor, just a mile and a half from Taunton town centre, easily accessible by road or rail, junction 25 of M5 is 2 miles away and serviced by Bristol International and Exeter Airports.

The 1846 original Grade II* listed building contained a School House, the School Hall and a Dining Room. Later a Junior School was added, an indoor heated Swimming Pool and a Music Department.

Over the last twenty years there has been an extensive building programme which has included: nine classrooms for the Junior school, applied science, computer and electronics centre, design area, new changing rooms, day girl and day boy accommodation, enlargement and modernisation of girl and boy boarding houses, school hall for the Junior school, new music school, concert/assembly hall for the Senior school and DT block. Latest additions are a new Art & Drama building; Leisure and Performing Arts Centres; a new Science Block and major expansion of Pre-Prep facilities.

Organisation. At Queen's College continuity of education is assured from the Nursery, through Pre-Preparatory, the Junior school, the Senior school and then into the Sixth Form.

There are two day boy houses and two day girl houses and each has a House Master/Mistress and Tutor for each year group. There are two boys' boarding houses and two girls' boarding houses and each is in the care of House Parents, together with a resident assistant House Master/Mistress. Tutors are attached to each house and are responsible for academic progress. They guide each student through GCSE and A Level choices, in conjunction with the Head, Director of Studies and Head of Sixth Form. In the Sixth Form students are able to choose their tutor, who will advise them on university selection and choices of career.

Curriculum. Pupils in the first three years of Senior School follow a broad, common curriculum. This provides them with a sound base in the arts, sciences, humanities and technology based subjects as well as games and PSHME. They are streamed and taught as a form for most subjects and are setted for mathematics, English and French. At GCSE there is a common core of English language and literature, mathematics, three sciences and French. Pupils then choose three option subjects.

In the Lower Sixth pupils choose 4 AS Level subjects and in the Upper Sixth the majority take three subjects to A2 Level. Throughout the Sixth Form some periods of curriculum time are devoted to a general studies course that includes RE, PSHME and key skills.

Co-Curriculum. In addition to games, music and drama, pupils are encouraged to participate in a range of activities including debating, public speaking, general knowledge quizzes, ICT, chess, photography, robotic design, electronics, cookery, bridge and dressmaking. There are also a number of academic societies. Outdoor pursuits such as canoeing, canoe polo and rock climbing are popular and participation in the Duke of Edinburgh's Award Scheme is a particular feature of Queen's. Over 300 Queen's College pupils have now achieved their Gold Award.

Music. The music staff provides teaching cover for keyboard, strings, brass, woodwind, percussion and singing, and give lessons to 25% of Senior School pupils, 50% of Junior School pupils and 40% of Pre-Prep pupils.

The purpose-built Music Department comprises:
• classroom
• 6 large teaching rooms
• 5 practice rooms
• electronic studio for keyboard studies
• audio studio for computer-based composition (GCSE and A Level)
• instrument store with individual lockers of varying sizes

The Music Department also uses the Performing Arts Centre in the main building for rehearsals and small concerts. The Queen's Hall (which adjoins the Music Department) has a 350-seat multi-purpose auditorium with 2-manual pipe organ and Steinway Concert Grand Piano.

Musical organisations:
• Chapel Choir – assemblies and Sunday Services
• First Orchestra – two rehearsals each week
• Middle School Orchestra
• Wind Band
• Chamber Orchestra (Strings)
• Swing Band

Also a wide variety of small ensembles and chamber groups for strings, brass, woodwind with or without piano. A number of concerts are staged each year.

Drama. There is a very active drama programme throughout the college with the Senior school Drama department providing courses from Year 7 to Year 13, the department aims to involve all those wishing to develop their co-curricular and academic interests.

In the Senior school, productions take place once a term. There is a main school production at the end of the Autumn term, Sixth Form and Middle School plays at the end of the Spring term, and a Lower school play at the end of the Summer term. There is also a Dance Show in the Spring term. Major productions and concerts take place in the Queen's Hall and the new Performing Arts Centre stages smaller scale concerts and plays.

Students are offered Performance Studies courses at GCSE, AS and A2 Level and there is an opportunity to study AS Level Dance. Theatre visits are arranged on a regular basis and for those studying the subject at GCSE and A Level the visits form part of their course.

PE/Games. The 30 acre playing fields of Queen's are both extensive and adaptable. In the Autumn term the grass area provides 5 rugby pitches which are also used for sevens in the Spring term.

In the Summer there are 4 cricket squares, a 400 metre athletics track and numerous rounders pitches.

The two Astroturf pitches are used very frequently – daily for hockey in the Autumn and Spring terms – and are of such quality that Queen's has often been called upon to host County hockey tournaments. Both pitches are converted to tennis courts in the Summer, giving a total of 24 tennis courts.

The hard court surface in the middle of the field is used for netball in the Spring term and for tennis in the Autumn and Summer terms. Alongside this area are cricket nets for use in the Summer term.

The Sports Hall is used for the following activities: gymnastics, basketball, badminton, volleyball, indoor hockey and indoor tennis. There is a squash court and a fully-equipped fitness centre adjoining the Sports Hall. Within the complex is an indoor heated pool that is used at various times for swimming from Pre-Prep through to Sixth Form lessons. Team swimming, canoeing, canoe polo and sub aqua are regular activities throughout the year.

Admission. Education at Queen's can start at 3 years on entry to the Nursery. The majority of pupils join the Pre-Preparatory school from the age of 4 years. Junior school pupils start at age 7. Entrance is by examination and those who are successful in gaining places to the Junior school make satisfactory transfer to the Senior school. There are places for boys and girls at the age of 13 from Preparatory schools who take the Common Entrance examination. A number enter the Sixth Form direct on GCSE Level results.

Scholarships. (*See Scholarship Entries section.*) *Academic Scholarships*: Worth up to 50% of fees for students of proven academic ability in one or more subjects. Day and boarding scholarships for students aged 8+, 11+, 13+ and 16+ on 1st September in year of entry.

Music Scholarships: Worth up to 50% of fees for the most gifted scholars. Offers of up to 8 scholarships for talented musicians aged 10+, 11+, 12+ and 13+ at the projected time of entry to the College. Three Sixth Form entry scholarships are also available plus an Organ award.

Performing Arts Scholarships: Worth up to 50% of fees for the students of best ability. Queen's College offers up to 6 scholarships for talented students with proven ability aged 11+ and 13+ at the projected time of entry to the college. Sixth Form scholarships included.

Art Scholarships: Worth up to 50% of fees for the most talented scholars. Scholarships are for talented students with an existing standard and potential for considerable development. Candidates to be aged 11+ or 13+ at projected time of entry to the college. Sixth Form scholarships included. Art scholarships are based on portfolio and interview.

Sport Scholarships: Worth up to 50% of fees for the students of best ability. Queen's College offers up to 6 scholarships for talented students with proven sports ability aged 11+ and 13+ at the projected time of entry to the college. Sixth Form scholarships included.

Awards: Sixth Form November; 10+, 11+ and 12+ January; 13+ February.

Fees per term (2011-2012). Pre-Preparatory School £1,690–£1,750 (day pupils only); Junior Day Pupils £2,080–£3,430; Junior Boarders £3,535–£5,355; Senior Day Pupils £4,150–£4,900; Senior Boarders £6,310–£7,800. These fees include all necessary expenses: books, stationery etc.

Charitable status. Queen's College, Taunton is a Registered Charity, number 310208. The College is a leading Charitable Trust in the field of Junior and Secondary education.

Radley College

Abingdon, Oxfordshire OX14 2HR
Tel: 01235 543127 (Warden)
         01235 543122 (Bursar)
         01235 543174 (Admissions)
         01235 543000 (General Enquiries)
Fax: 01235 543106
e-mail: warden@radley.org.uk
website: www.radley.org.uk

St Peter's College, Radley, was founded by the Rev William Sewell, Fellow of Exeter College, Oxford, to provide an independent school education on the principles of the Church of England. It was opened on 9 June 1847, and incorporated by Royal Charter in 1890. It stands in a park of some 700 acres.

Motto: '*Sicut Serpentes, sicut Columbae*'

Visitor: The Rt Revd The Lord Bishop of Oxford

Council:
Chairman: M E Hodgson, MA, FRICS
Vice-Chairman: S W B Whitworth, MA

I A Balding, LVO   M J W Rushton, MA
D A Peck, MA   Rt Revd Dr A J Russell,
T O Seymour, MA   DPhil

N J Henderson, MA, FRCS   T M Durie, BA, ACA, FSI
D C S Smellie, MA   J C Bridcut, MA
A P G Holmes, MA   R H Warner, MA, ACA
Mrs D J Pluck, FCA   A C Mayfield, MBA
G A Kaye, BSc   Sir John Holmes
Mrs E McKendrick, BA   R N L Huntingford
W S H Laidlaw, MA

Warden: **A W McPhail**, MA

Sub Warden & Director of Studies: A E Reekes, MA

Senior Masters:
M J S Hopkins, BA
H D Hammond, BSc

Teaching Staff:
A C Wallis, BSc, PhD   G H S May, MA
G Wiseman, BA   G R King, BA
J C Nye, MA   D J Pullen, BSc
†B J Holden, MA, BTech   R K McMahon, MA,
  (*D Social*)   MPhil, DPhil
M R Wright, BSc   C J Ellott, BA, LLB
J R Summerly, BA, PhD   J E Gearing, BA
P W Gamble, MA   D S Borthwick, DPhil,
I P Ellis, BA, DipRASchls   MChem
R E Schofield, MA   Mrs G C Porter, MA, MSc
S Barlass, BA   O H Langton, MA
†A J McChesney, BSc (*F   Mrs T Scammell Jackson,
  Social*)   BA, MPhil
C M Bedford, BA, PhD   Mrs N J King, BA
†N Murphy, MA (*K Social*) Ms E E N Danis, BA
I S Yorston, MA   G J A Hughes, BA, MSc,
†R M C Greed, BSc (*B   PhD
  Social*)   D J Palmer, MPhys
†W O C Matthews, BA (*G   S R Giddens, BSc, MSc,
  Social*)   PhD
†T R G Ryder, BA, MFA   T C Lawson, BA
  (*A Social*)   A C Jackson, BA
†D C K Edwards, MA (*H   C J Lee, BA
  Social*)   C E R Scott-Malden, BA,
†R A King, BSc, MRSC,   MA
  CChem (*E Social*)   P R Wallace, BSc, MPhil,
†J M Sparks, BSc (*C   DPhil
  Social*)   Mrs C C A de Bono, BA
S A Hall, BA, MPhil, PhD A D Cunningham, MA,
N L Haggett, MBE, BEd   PhD
Mrs B L M Haggett, ATD,   P J Miron, BSc, DPhil
  DipSLD   M P Hills, MMath
†M K T Hindley, MA, LLB   E J Tolputt, MEng
  (*J Social*)   J C Wheeler, BSc
M R Jewell, BA   E O Holt, BA
R Johnson, BSc   C A San Jose, BA
J R W Beasley, MA   E G Pearson, BA
C R Martin, BA   D J Cresswell, BA
I K Campbell, BA   T G Elphinstone, BA
Mrs M C Hart, BA   Ms N O Hall, BA
B R Knox, BEd   M J Pringle, BA
R D Shaw, MA   J W Schofield, BA, MSc
P M Fernandez, MA   D L Cox, MMath
Ms E D Murtagh, BA   Mrs C F Ellott, BA, MA
D W S Roques, MA   Mrs K C Ison, BA
K A Mosedale, MA, MSc   S Rathbone, BA
Mrs K J Knox, BA   Ms P E Henderson, BA
H Crump, LLB, BA   J M Ambrose, BA, DPhil
S H Dalrymple, BA   Ms L E Nott, BA
S Kerr, BA   A M H Hakimi, BSc,
K Halliday, BSc, PhD   MPhil, DPhil
J F Adams, BA   K J Reid, MSc
R M Lowe, BA   M G Noone, MA
A M Lowe, BSc, PhD   R D Woodling, MChem

Chaplain: The Revd T D Mullins, BA
Assistant Chaplain: The Revd T J E Fernyhough, BA
Librarian: Mrs C D Sargent, MA, MCLIP

Music:
Precentor: S D J Clarke, MA, ARCO
A J A Williams, MMus, DipRAM, GRSM, LRAM
Miss S-L Naylor, MA
T M Morris, MA, DPhil, FRCO

There are 36 peripatetic music staff.

Bursar and Secretary: A Ashton, MA, ACIB
Medical Officer: Dr J N B Moore, BSc, MB BS, DRCOG, MRCGP
Radleian Society Secretariat: Ms R L Davies, BA
Development Director: A L Robinson
Registrar: Mrs V M G Hammond

General Arrangements. There are 680 boys in the school. On admission, boys enter one of the 10 houses known as socials. All are close together within the grounds. All meals are served in Hall on a cafeteria system.

Admission to the School. Boys are admitted between the ages of 13 and 14 in the Michaelmas Term, and qualify by taking either the Common Entrance Examination, our own entrance exam, or the Entrance Scholarship Examination. Registration starts at birth and registration forms can be obtained from the Registrar. All entries are made centrally. A registration fee of £100 is payable when a boy's name is entered. This fee is not returnable and registration does not guarantee a place in the school. Three years before a boy is due to come, a Final Acceptance Form will be sent to parents for whose sons a place can be guaranteed subject to CE. These forms are sent out in date order of registration. An Entrance Fee of £700 (part refundable against the first term's account) is payable on acceptance. A few places are sometimes available for entry to the Sixth Form. Details are available on our website.

Entrance Awards. (*See Scholarship Entries section.*) Up to twelve Academic Scholarships are awarded each year. In addition All-Rounder, Music, Drama and Art Awards are offered. All awards may be supplemented by a means-tested bursary. Details of all awards are available from our website or the Registrar.

Further means-tested bursaries are available for boys who would otherwise be unable to come to Radley.

Work. In the Shells, Removes and Fifth Form a broad curriculum is followed. There is some choice at GCSE with boys generally taking nine or ten subjects.

In the Sixth Form a boy can specialise in a combination of Classics, French, Spanish, German, Theatre Studies, English, History, Religious Studies, Geography, Geology, Biology, Chemistry, Physics, Mathematics, Economics, Politics, Economics and Business, Music, Art or Design, leading to AS/A2 examinations.

Careers. Advice and assistance is available to all boys on a wide range of career possibilities through the Director of Careers. The School is a member of ISCO (The Independent Schools Careers Organisation) and close connections are maintained with the professions, with firms and with the services. Visits and talks by experts in these fields are a special feature.

Games. In the Michaelmas Term rugby football is the major school game. In the other two terms the 'wet-bobs' row; the 'dry-bobs' play hockey (the major game) and soccer in the Lent Term, cricket (the major game), athletics and tennis in the Summer. There are also numerous minor sports which involve boys in competition with other schools.

The playing fields are close to the main buildings.

The College has its own boathouse, and the use of a stretch of the River Thames between Sandford and Abingdon. The VIIIs compete in regattas and Head of the River races.

There are two all-weather hockey pitches, an athletics track, five squash courts, a Real Tennis court, a rackets court, two covered Fives courts, 20 hard tennis courts and a 9-hole golf course. There is a large, well-equipped gymna-

sium and an indoor, heated swimming pool attached to a multi-purpose sports hall.

CCF. All boys, in their fourth term, join the Radley College Contingent, Combined Cadet Force (Army, Navy and Air Sections). They work for the Proficiency examination, which takes three terms. When they have passed Proficiency and done a week's Corps Camp in the holidays they either stay on in a special section for further training or join one of the many Community Action Projects on offer.

Fees per term (2011-2012). £9,875 (inclusive of medical attendance). Lessons in pianoforte and other musical instruments are given at a charge of £27.65 a lesson. There is available a system of insurance against loss of fees caused by illness, accident, or infection. Particulars can be obtained from the Bursar.

Charitable status. St Peter's College, Radley is a Registered Charity, number 309243. It exists for the purpose of the education of youth in general knowledge and literature and particularly and especially in the doctrines and principles of the Church of England.

Ratcliffe College

Fosse Way, Ratcliffe on the Wreake, Leicester, Leicestershire LE7 4SG
Tel: 01509 817000 School Office
01509 817072/817031 Registrar
Fax: 01509 817004
e-mail: registrar@ratcliffe.leics.sch.uk
website: www.ratcliffe-college.co.uk

Ratcliffe College is a co-educational Catholic day and boarding school. The School was founded in 1844 and opened in 1847; the original buildings by A W Pugin were erected with funds provided by Lady Mary Arundel of Wardour, who also bequeathed money for subsequent extensions.

Motto: '*Legis plenitudo charitas*'

Governing Body:
Consists of two members of the Board of Directors of the Company Limited by Guarantee which owns the College (Ratcliffe College Ltd), together with up to 10 additional governors, appointed by the Directors, who hold office for a period.

Present governors:
Mr Richard Gamble (*Chairman*)
Mr Ewan Anderson
Br Nigel Cave (*Director*)
Mrs Mary Espinasse
Mrs Mary Goldstraw
Mr Vincenzo Lallo
Mrs Louise Marsden
Mr Louis Massarella (*Vice Chairman*)
Mr Paul Rudd
Fr Phillip Sainter (*Director*)
Mrs Margaret Smidowicz
Mr Martin Traynor

Headmaster: Mr G P Lloyd, BA Hons, MSc, FMusTCL

Senior Deputy Head: Mrs J P Clayfield, BSc
Second Deputy Head: Mr J Reddin, BSc, MSc
Assistant Head: Mr G J Sharpe, BA, MBA
Director of Finance: Mr D Robson, BCom Accounting, ACA
Head of Junior School: Mrs C Rigby, BA

Father President: Fr D Tobin

Teaching Staff:
* *Head of Department*

Mrs L Arnold, BSc, MPhil (*ICT*)
Mr M Balmbra, BSc (*Physical Education, Geography, OC CCF*)
Mr D Berry, BA Hons (*Art and Design Technology**)
Mrs K Burton, BA (*Food Technology**)
Mr J Cantrill, BA (*History*)
Mrs C Carmichael (*Swimming Coach*)
Miss M Casas-Ojeda, BA, MA (*Spanish*)
Mrs C Caven-Henrys, AISTD (*Drama, Dance*)
Mr A Chorley, MSc (*Head of Year, Physics*)
Dr J Clarke, BSc, PhD (*Chemistry*)
Mrs S Clarke, BA, QTS (*Mathematics*)
Mr E Clayfield, CertEd (*Design and Technology*)
Mr D Cluley, BSc, MSc (*ICT**)
Mrs J Cluley, BEd, CertEd (*SENCO**)
Mrs C Cole, BSc, MA (*Mathematics*)
Mrs K Cooper, BA (*English*)
Mrs A Crebbin, PGCE-MFL (*French, Spanish*)
Mrs S Cushing, BA (*Languages**)
Mr M Darlington, BSc (*Physics*)
Miss D Dempsey, BA (*Junior School*)
Mrs J Dorn, BA (*Languages*)
Mrs A Dungey, BSc (*Science, Food Technology*)
Mr A Dziemianko, BSc (*Head of Year, Geography*)
Mrs L Eccles, BA (*Languages*)
Mrs S Elridge, BA (*English, Drama*)
Mrs A Etty, BSc (*Junior School*)
Mrs C Farrar, CertEd (*Junior School*)
Mrs F Featherstone, NVQ 3 (*Nursery Nurse*)
Miss C Fowler, BA (*Religious Studies*)
Mrs N Gilchrist, BEd (*Junior School*)
Mr P Gilchrist (*Junior School Games Coordinator*)
Fr S Giles, IC (*Chaplain, Rector of the Chapel*)
Mr I Glenn (*Graduate Assistant*)
Miss C Gregory, BA (*Media Studies*, English*)
Mrs G Hadley, BA, DipEd SEN (*Learning Support, Careers Coordinator**)
Mr G Higham, BSc (*Mathematics**)
Mr R Hughes, BA, QTS (*Physical Education, Learning Support*)
Miss C Jeyes, NNEB (*Nursery Nurse*)
Mr M Kaye, BA (*Physical Education*)
Miss J Kearns, BA (*Junior School*)
Mr M Lambert, BSc (*Geography**)
Mrs J Leite, BA (*Senior House Mistress, Junior School, Learning Support*)
Mrs F Lodder, BA, MA (*History**)
Mrs M Markham, BA (*Junior School Music*)
Mr P McCrindell, BA (*Head of Year, Languages*)
Mr P Michel, BA (*Religious Studies, Chaplaincy Assistant*)
Miss L Moore (*Netball Coach*)
Mrs S Neuberg, BA (*Nursery School*)
Miss P Phillipson, BA (*Deputy Head of Junior School*)
Mrs S Rankine, BEd (*Head of Nursery School**)
Mrs J Reddin, BA (*French*)
Mrs S Roberts, BA (*Physical Education*)
Miss M Schlotfeldt, BA (*Head of Year, EAL*)
Miss E Schofield (*Graduate Assistant*)
Mrs J Schofield, BSc (*Science**)
Mr A Seth, BSc (*Design and Technology*)
Mr R Sharpe (*Fencing Coach*)
Mr M Sherwood, BA (*Physical Education*)
Ms L Simpson (*Dance*)
Mr M Sleath, BSc (*Head of Year, Mathematics*)
Mrs H Smith, BSc (*Mathematics*)
Mrs P Smith, BA (*Head of Year, Religious Studies*)
Mr P Spencer, ACIB Banking Dip (*Economics & Business Studies**)
Miss T Spencer, BA (*Economics and Business Studies*)
Miss E Stableforth, BA (*English**)
Dr S Standen, BSc, PhD (*Chemistry*)
Mr P Stone (*Rugby Coach*)
Miss R Streater (*Graduate Assistant*)

Mrs A Taylor, BEd (*Director of Sport**)
Mr N Taylor, BEd (*Senior Housemaster, Physical Education*)
Mrs G Thomas-Atkinson, BA (*Physical Education*)
Mr S Thorpe, BSc (*Science*)
Mrs H Tipper, BSc Hons (*Biology*)
Mr P Trotter (*Science*)
Mr D Turner, BEd (*Junior School*)
Mr G Vickers (*Tae Kwon Do Coach*)
Mr N Walsh, LLB (*Religious Studies**)
Mr S Waterhouse, BMus (*Music*)
Mrs E Waters, BEd (*Junior School, Chaplaincy Assistant*)
Mrs L Whieldon, BA (*English*)
Mr J Wildsmith (*Graduate Assistant*)
Mr D Willcock (*Hockey Coach*)
Mrs M Williams, BA (*Librarian*)
Mr E Woodcock, BA, MSc (*Physical Education*)
Mrs S Worsnop, BSc (*Mathematics*)
Miss A Wright, BA (*Art & Design*)

Medical Officer: Dr T Jennings

Senior Nursing Sisters:
Mrs D Warburton, RGN
Mrs E Weston, RGN

Age Range. 3–18.

Number of Pupils. 682: girls: 291 boys: 391. Sixth Form: 132. Boarders: 95.

Aims. The vision of the College is to educate young people in the spirit of the Gospel and the traditions of the Catholic Church, seeking to nurture the God-given talents and potential of each individual, so that each one may become a confident, responsible and useful member of society. Whilst Ratcliffe is a Catholic school, it welcomes children of other denominations and faiths, whose parents feel they can share in and benefit from the school's ideals and environment.

Location. Ratcliffe College is set in over 400 acres of rolling parkland on the A46, seven miles north of Leicester. It is easily accessible by road and benefits from being free of congestion at peak times. The M1/M6 motorways, main line railway stations and airports of Birmingham and Nottingham-East Midlands are all within easy travelling distance. For day pupils, school buses operate daily from Leicester, Loughborough and Nottingham.

Site and Buildings. The main Senior School buildings surround a quadrangle and contain the Administration offices, Church, Dining Hall, Library, Medical Centre, Computer Rooms and Common Rooms, together with a number of subject departments. In addition, there is a Music Department with Concert Hall; a fully-appointed Theatre; and a Science Centre with additional classrooms for Food Technology. Sporting facilities include extensive playing fields and a floodlit all-weather hockey pitch; the state-of-the-art sports centre comprises sports changing rooms, swimming pool and sports hall with a modern fitness suite. A complex of recently refurbished buildings nearby provides departmental bases for Geography, Modern Languages and Mathematics. Modernised Boys' and Girls' boarding accommodation is situated on the upper floor of the main building, in separate wings, with individual study bedrooms for older pupils.

The Rosmini Sixth Form Centre, named after Blessed Antonio Rosmini, the founder of the Rosminian Order, opened for use by pupils and staff in January 2007. With an upper floor wholly dedicated to independent academic study with full IT accessibility, and ground floor areas providing for social and extra-curricular usage, the Centre provides a flagship modern setting for Sixth Formers.

The Junior School is situated in the Newman Building close to the Senior School. The Nursery School is located nearby in purpose-built accommodation nearby on the campus.

Organisation. The College is divided into 3 sections: Senior School (11–18 year olds), Junior School (5–11 year olds), and Nursery School (3–5 year olds). The sections are closely integrated, allowing continuity of education from 3 to 18. Boarding girls and boys are accommodated in separate wings within the main Senior School building, under the supervision of the resident Senior Housemistress and Housemaster, together with their Assistants. There is a strong emphasis on pastoral care for all pupils. The teacher: pupil ratio in the Senior School is 1 : 10 (The ratio in the Sixth Form is much lower).

Curriculum. In the Nursery School, the emphasis is on early literacy, numeracy and the development of personal and social skills, all of which contribute to a child's knowledge, understanding and skills in other areas of learning. Programmes of study are based on the Department for Education Early Learning Goals, but extend well beyond these guidelines to develop a child's interests, talents, outlook and general knowledge of the world.

The Junior School offers small class sizes, well-resourced classrooms, a clear focus on the National Curriculum, an extended school day and a varied extra-curricular activities programme. Pupils learn French and subjects such as PE, Music, History and Geography are emphasised, whilst pupils use the Senior School facilities for Art, ICT, Drama, Music, Sport and Science.

In the Senior School a broad and balanced curriculum is followed, which aims to identify and provide for individual needs. Most pupils take at least nine GCSEs. All pupils study a core of subjects consisting of English (Language and Literature), Mathematics, Religious Studies, a Modern Foreign Language and Science (Core and Additional or Triple Award). This is augmented by up to three further option subjects. In the Sixth Form, most students choose 4 AS Levels in Year 12 and 3 A2 Levels in Year 13. In addition to A Level work, students take a complementary studies course, which incorporates a general studies programme including preparation for university and careers guidance, study skills and moral and ethical studies.

Games. The playing fields, which surround the College buildings, cover over 400 acres. All pupils participate in Games, including Cricket, Hockey, Rugby, Football, Tennis and Athletics for boys, and Hockey, Netball, Rounders, Tennis and Athletics for girls.

Extra-Curricular Activities. Pupils' talents and interests are developed through an extensive programme of activities on weekdays and at weekends. As well as many sporting opportunities, 25% of pupils learn a musical instrument; there are many musical groups, including brass ensemble, orchestra and choirs. Many pupils are involved in school productions and film-making, and other media activities are popular. The Combined Cadet Force and the Duke of Edinburgh's Award Scheme both flourish. Pupils are encouraged to be caring and to have consideration for others through Chaplaincy groups and Voluntary Service activities.

Admissions. *Nursery School*: Entry is by school report (if applicable) and informal assessment.

Junior School: Entry is by school report and assessment for Years 1–4 or entrance examinations (papers in English, Mathematics, Verbal Reasoning) for entry to Years 5 and 6.

Senior School: Entry is normally at 11+, 12+, 13+ and 14+. Entry is normally by school report and successful performance in the entrance examinations, either Common Entrance or the College's own examinations (papers in English, Mathematics and Verbal Reasoning).

Sixth Form: Entrance examinations may be set, depending on the applicant's educational background and the A Level subjects he/she wishes to study in the Sixth Form. Overseas applicants are usually required to take an English test. In general, applicants will be interviewed and entry will also be based on successful performance in GCSE (or equivalent examinations). Applicants must obtain at least five GCSE passes at C grade or better. For any subject to be studied in the Sixth Form, the student should have at least GCSE grade B in that subject (or, for subjects not taken at GCSE, at least grade B in related GCSE subjects). However, a GCSE grade A is required in order to study Biology, Chemistry, Physics or Mathematics.

Scholarships and Bursaries. (*See Scholarship Entries section.*) A wide range of scholarships to recognise academic, sporting, musical, dramatic and artistic talent amongst applicants for the Senior School are offered on entry to Year 7, Year 9 and the Sixth Form. A limited number of additional awards are available at the Headmaster's discretion. A limited number of Bursaries are available, generally on entry to Year 7. Further details can be obtained from The Registrar.

Fees per term (2011-2012). UK Students: Full Boarding (Years 6–13) £6,954; Weekly Boarding (Years 9–13) £6,195; Weekly Boarding (Years 6–8) £5,528. Boarding fees include the full cost of the programme of boarding weekend trips throughout the year.

EAL Students: Full Boarding £7,654. Boarding fees include the full cost of the programme of boarding weekend trips throughout the year. Boarding fees include the cost of additional teaching of English as a Foreign Language with a minimum of 10 one-hour sessions per term.

Day: £2,464–£2,773 (Nursery aged 3–5); £2,773–£3,262 (Years 1–5); £3,621–£4,548 (Years 6–13).

Fees are subject to such termly increase as may prove necessary. Additional charges are made for: private Music lessons at £195 per term for 10 half-hour sessions (for individual tuition for each instrument); Where additional teaching of Learning Skills is required and agreed with parents, this will be charged at £36 per lesson. There is a registration fee of £75 (£100 overseas) and a deposit of £500 for UK students and £1000 for students from overseas.

Charitable status. Ratcliffe College is a Registered Charity, number 1115975, for the education of children.

Reading Blue Coat School

Holme Park, Sonning, Berks RG4 6SU
Tel: 0118 944 1005
Fax: 0118 944 2690
e-mail: headsec@rbcs.org.uk
website: www.rbcs.org.uk

The School was founded in 1646 by Richard Aldworth, a merchant of London and Reading, and a Governor of Christ's Hospital. There are 676 pupils (aged 11–18) including a co-educational Sixth Form. The School is situated in 46 acres of grounds and riverside woods near the village of Sonning, four miles east of Reading.

Visitors to Trustees:
Vice-Chancellor of the University of Oxford
President of St John's College, Oxford
Warden of All Souls' College, Oxford

Chairman of Governors: B S Walsh

***Headmaster*: M J Windsor**, MA, BA Hons, PGCE
(*German*)

Second Master: A P Colpus, BSc Hons, PGCE
(*Mathematics*)
Deputy Head, Staff Development: Mrs A J Bawden, BA
Hons, PGCE (*Geography*)
Deputy Head, Academic Development: P C K Rowe, MEd,
MA, PGCE (*History, Government & Politics*)
Deputy Head, Pupil Development: R S Slatford, MA,
CertEd, BSc Hons (*Geology*)
Bursar: S A Jackson, BSc, MBA

* *Head of Department*

Mrs S M Adams, BA, PGCE (*Mathematics*)
M J Baker, BA, PGCE (*Geography*)
Mrs K E Bayliss, BA (*Mathematics, Economics*)
Mrs L J Bennett, BEd Hons (*Religious Studies*)
Mrs S E Berry, BA, PGCE, Dip SpLD, AMBDA
  (*Learning Support, French*)
Mrs J M Blair, BA, PGCE (*Mathematics*)
P S Bodinetz, BA, PGCE (*English, Classics*)
J Bowler, BA, PGCE, LTCL, ARCM (*Director of Music,
  Performance Studies/Drama*)
J P Brown, BSc, PGCE (*Chemistry*)
Mrs N E Bruce-Lockhart, BA Hons, PGCE (*English*)
Mrs J A Coates, BSc, PGCE (*Chemistry*)
S J Cook, CertEd, BA (*Physical Education*)
D N Cottrell, CertEd (*Geography, Sport & Physical
  Education*)
Mrs C Dance, BA Ed Hons (*Girls' Games*)
Dr S M Dimmick, BSc, DipEd, MSc, PhD (*Biology*)
Dr A C Dutton, PhD, BA Hons (*Integrated Science,
  Biology*)
R N Ennis, BA, PGCE (*Art*)
Miss N Evans, BA Hons, PGCE (*Classics*)
R J Field, BA, PGCE (*Physics*)
D Gandy, BSc Hons (*Information Technology, *Careers*)
R P Hazle, BA (*English, Music, Performance Studies/
  Drama*)
Mrs S A Head, MA (*Modern Foreign Languages,
  German, French*)
Miss A M Hobbs, BA Hons, PGCE (*French, German,
  Spanish*)
Miss C A Holliday, BA Oxon, PGCE (*German, French*)
E R Hooper, MA, BA, DipEd, GDIESE (*Government &
  Politics, History*)
Miss J Hope, BSc Hons, PGCE (*Geology*)
M J Jerstice, BSc, PGCE (*Chemistry*)
Mrs K S Lambert, BA, PGCE (*English*)
Mrs P J Leonard, BA, PGCE (*Mathematics*)
T J Lewis, MEng, BA (*Mathematics*)
A J Maddocks, BA (*French, German*)
Dr K J Magill, MPhil, BA, PGCE, PhD (*Religious
  Studies*)
Miss M F Maltby, BA, PGCE (*Religious Studies*)
Miss E M Marshall, BA, PGCE (*History, Government &
  Politics*)
N W Martin, BA Hons, PGCE (*History*)
N T P Matenga, BPhysEd, PG Dip Teaching (*Sport &
  Physical Education*)
S McCluskey, BSc Hons, PGCE (*Biology*)
S R McFaul, MEng (*Mathematics, Physics*)
H J McGough, BSc Hons (*Design Technology*)
Mrs I A McGough, BA, PGCE (*Design Technology*)
W E Mitchell, BA, PGCE (*Geography*)
D C Montague, MA, BA Hons, PGCE (*Spanish, French*)
Mrs H J Oliver, BA Hons, PGCE (*French*)
A M Pett, BSc, PGCE (*Economics*)
E A C Rattray, BA Hons, CPGS (*History of Art*)
S R Roberts, BSc, PGCE (*Mathematics*)
Mrs C Ross, BA, PGCE (*Mathematics*)
Mrs C Rule, BA Hons, OCR SpLD Diploma (*Learning
  Support*)
S W Sadler, BA Hons (*English, *Drama*)
D L Salmon, MA, ComputingDip, PGCE (*Physics*)
Dr F B Santos, BSc, MSc, PhD (*Chemistry*)
D H R Selvester, BA, PGCE (*Design Technology*)
R I Shuttleworth, BSc Hons, PGCE (*Mathematics*)
Mrs J P Smith, BSc, PGCE (*Physics*)
W J Statham, BSc Hons, PGCE (*Biology*)
G C Turner, BSc Hons, PGCE (*Sport & Physical
  Education*)
Mrs J M Turton, BSc, PGCE (*Chemistry*)
Miss T van der Werff, MA, PGCE (*History*)
W Voice, BA Hons, PGCE (*Information Technology,
  Sport)

T C Walford, BSc, PGCE (*Information Technology*)
R J Wallis, BA, PGCE (*Art*)
Miss H E Walmsley, BSc Hons, PGCE (*Biology*)
L W G Walters, BA Hons (*English*)
Mrs N Watmough-Starkie, BMus Hons, PGCE (*Assistant
  Director of Music*)
Miss E J Williamson, MA, PGCE (*English, Classics*)
P D Wise, BSc Hons, PGCE (*Geography*)
S Yates, BSc Hons, PGCE (*Information Technology*)
Mrs J F Zambon, BA Hons, PGCE (*Spanish*)

Headmaster's Secretary: Mrs L A Bell
Admissions Secretary: Mrs V M Frost
School Nurse: Mrs G F Montgomery, RGN
Sports Centre Manager: C Bate
Archivist: P J van Went, MA, CertEd

Aims. The School aims to provide a stimulating and
friendly atmosphere in which each pupil can realise his or
her full intellectual, physical and creative potential. Pupils
are encouraged to be self-reliant and adaptable and we hope
that they will learn the basis of good citizenship founded on
honesty, fairness and understanding of the needs of others.

Our School is a Church of England Foundation, and
emphasis is placed on Christian values and standards.

Buildings. The School is set in an attractive 46-acre site
by the banks of the Thames in the village of Sonning. School
House, originally built in the eighteenth century and extensively remodelled in the Victorian era, stands at the heart of
the School. The School's facilities have undergone a continuous programme of improvement over the last decade,
including the construction of a new Science Centre and a
Sports Hall complex, including a dining hall and kitchens.
Recent developments include a new cricket pavilion,
improvements to the swimming pool and a new boathouse
on the banks of the Thames. The School has recently
expanded its facilities for the Sixth Form and is currently
building an ambitious new classroom block.

Curriculum. In Years 7 to 9, pupils study a broad range
of subjects, including Latin, two modern foreign languages
and Religious Studies. In Years 10 and 11, pupils follow
IGCSE courses in English Language and Literature, Mathematics and Science and also opt to complete four further
courses in a wide range of additional subjects, such as History, Geography, Geology and Physical Education, with a
modern foreign language being compulsory. A wide range
of subjects is offered at AS and A2 Level, including subjects
such as Psychology, History of Art and Performance Studies, with nearly every pupil going on to university, including
Oxford and Cambridge.

Sixth Form. The co-educational Sixth Form Centre
accommodates over 200 students. Girls are fully integrated
into all activities. In addition to A Level courses, all Sixth
Formers follow a compulsory enrichment programme which
includes the AQA Baccalaureate.

Games and Activities. A wide range of sports and activities is offered within the curriculum and regular school fixtures for all year groups are arranged. Full advantage is
taken of the River Thames and rowing is a popular sport for
both boys and girls. The main boys' games are Rugby and
Hockey in the Autumn Term, Football and Hockey in the
Spring Term, and Cricket and Athletics in the Summer
Term. Girls play Netball, Rounders and Hockey. Other
sporting activities include Fencing, Squash, Basketball, Tennis, Golf, Table Tennis, Climbing, Swimming, Scuba Diving
and Sailing.

The Cadet Force is voluntary with Army, RAF and RN
Sections. Camping and adventure training activities take
place during holidays and at weekends. There is a wide
range in the Activities Programme which includes the Duke
of Edinburgh's Award, overseas expeditions, community service and sports leadership.

Music and Drama enjoy a high profile in the life of the
School. Well over a third of the pupils receive individual

instrumental lessons and pupils are encouraged to join in activities such as the Choir, Orchestra, Wind Band, Brass Group, Jazz and Swing Bands. Concerts, plays and musicals are presented regularly.

Admissions. The two main points of entry in September are at 11+ and 16+. 11+ entry is by entrance examination taken the previous January. Entry at other levels is by examination and interview and is subject to vacancies. Entry to the Sixth Form for girls and boys is by GCSE results, assessment and interview.

The Foundation makes provision for awards of scholarships and bursaries, including academic, music and art awards, based on merit and need. Foundation Scholarships up to 100% of fees are available according to financial need.

Fees per term (2011-2012). £4,320.

Charitable status. The Reading Blue Coat School is a Registered Charity, number 1087839. Its aim is the provision of secondary education for pupils aged 11 to 18.

Reed's School

Cobham, Surrey KT11 2ES
Tel: 01932 869001
Fax: 01932 869046
e-mail: admissions@reeds.surrey.sch.uk
website: www.reeds.surrey.sch.uk

Reed's is a boarding and day school for boys with girls in the Sixth Form, founded by Andrew Reed in 1813 and incorporated by Act of Parliament in 1845 under the presidency of the Archbishop of Canterbury, the Duke of Wellington and the Marquis of Salisbury. When the School was founded, its facilities were reserved for boys whose fathers had died. In 1958 the School expanded and all boys became eligible for entrance. Sixth Form girls became eligible for entrance in the 1980s. Foundation awards are still granted each year to boys and Sixth Form girls who have lost the support of one or both parents.

Patron: Her Majesty The Queen

Presidents:
Viscount Bridgeman
P B Mitford-Slade, OBE
G M Nissen, CBE

Governors:
I Plenderleith, CBE (*Chairman*)

Mrs I M Barker	Mrs A F Noakes
U D Barnett	T D Page, MA
D R Blomfield, BSc	H M Priestley, MA
D H A C Caddy, FCA	P D Reed
M A Grenier, MA	Miss K Richardson, MA
C R Hawkins	R Stewart, FCIB
Professor J N Hay, PhD, FRSC	P H H Verstage, BCom Hons
A R Merry, FRICS	M Wheeler, BCom, FCA
Mrs L F Napier, FSI	

Secretary to the Governors & Bursar: A D Bott, FCCA

Headmaster: D W Jarrett, MA

Deputy Headmaster: G D Spawforth, MA
Senior Master: P R Kemp, BA
Development Director: R M Garrett, BA
Director of Studies: D J Atkins, BA
Senior Housemaster: †A R W Balls, BEd
Director of Sport & Activities: I A Clapp, BEd
Senior Mistress: Mrs J G Hart, BA (*Psychology*)
Director of Teaching and Learning: Ms C F St Gallay, BA
Chaplain: The Revd A J Clarke, MA

Assistant Staff:
* *Head of Department*
† *Housemaster*

J Allison, BSc
Dr L B Askew, PhD
Mrs S Blackford, MA
†A J Blackman, MA
S M Bramwell, BA (*Modern Languages*, *French*)
Ms J Brewster, BSc (*Chemistry*)
I B Carnegie, MA (*Director of Music*)
C E Cole, BA (*Printing*)
P P Davies, MA
J K Ditchburn, BA
J B Douthwaite, BA
†M R Dunn, HND
†B J Edwards, BA (*Physical Education*)
Mrs P U Espinosa, MA (*Spanish*)
Ms N R Evans, BA
Ms M Fitzgerald, BA (*Librarian*)
Mrs M Francis, BA
W Gatti, BA
B J Goodrich, MSc (*Geography*)
D H Hamilton, BA
R A Harper, BSc
T A Harrison, MSc (*Mathematics*)
G S Hart, HEd
Miss P J Hoskins, BSc
P Jenkins, LRCM
Miss A M Jiménez, BA
Miss A N Johnson, MA, FRSA (*Art*)
A Jolly, BSc
Mrs D Kane, BSc
Mrs C Kemp, BA
M G Kerrison, BA
Mrs K A Lambert, BSc
Mrs J A Lawrence, BA
Mrs S L Leslie, BA (*Learning Support*)
K T Medlycott
†L G Michael, BA
P L Millington, BSc (*Design Technology*)
Mrs T A Millington, BEd (*Religious Studies*)
†T P W Murdoch, BA
J W A Norman, BA
C J Osgood, MA
A R Pascoots
Mrs L Paterson, BSc (*Biology*)
I A Peel, MA
Mrs A L Prior, BSc
†L Pytel, BA
Miss M K Rai, BSc
T Rimmer, BSc
Miss K D Roberts, BSc
C Sandison-Smith, MA (*German*)
Mrs C N Savage, BSc
Mrs S Shoosmith, BSc
T P Silk, BA (*Film Studies*, *Drama*)
Miss F Simpson, BSc
Ms R C Stone, MA
A R Talbot, BEd
D Thompson, BSc (*Physics*, *Science*)
C S Thomson, BA (*Classics*)
Mrs A Trehearn, BA
M C Vernon, BSc
D W R Wakefield, BSc
Mrs V Wakefield, BSc
A J Waller, BA (*History*)
J M Wallis, MEng
T Webb, BA
M P Whitehead, BSc (*ICT*)
S Whiteley, BA (*Economics & Business Studies*)

R Willey, GLCM

Visiting Music Teachers:

J Dalgleish (*Piano*)	E Spevok (*Drums*)
J Dunning (*Guitar*)	J Fryer (*Saxophone*)
S James (*Guitar*)	P Von Wielligh (*Flute*)
K Garrett (*Jazz Piano*)	D Deam (*Voice*)
D Hawkins (*Guitar/Bass*)	N Zoob (*Cello, String*
R Willey (*Trombone*)	*Scheme*)
J Jaggard (*Oboe*)	G Sutton (*Violin, Viola,*
J Calderbank (*Clarinet,*	*String Scheme*)
Saxophone)	A Marshallsay (*Percussion*)
J Shaddock (*Trumpet*)	

Headmaster's Secretary: Mrs A Gregg
Registrar: R M C Gilliat, MA
Admissions Secretary: Mrs P F Gilliat
Medical Officer: R Draper, MBChB, DCH, DRCOG, DA, MRCGP

The School is situated near Esher in 40 acres of heath and woodland. It can be reached in 30 minutes by train from Waterloo and is within half an hour's drive of both Heathrow and Gatwick Airports.

To the original buildings have been added in the last 15 years a Sixth Form House; Chemistry laboratories; three Computer suites; two artificial turf hockey pitches; a swimming pool and sports complex; a new library; a new teaching block for the Physics and Mathematics departments; a Music School; an Indoor Tennis Centre; new Biology, Geography and History departments; extensions to the Day Pupil Centre and an extension to the Sixth Form House which incorporates a lecture theatre; a new Language laboratory and new Language and English classrooms; a new Design and Technology building.

There are 600 pupils, just under 20% of whom are boarders, divided among 5 senior houses, Blathwayt, Bristowe, Capel, Mullens and School House, and one junior house, the Close, for those under 13. There is also a separate Sixth Form House. Admission at the age of 13 is normally by the Common Entrance examination; admission at the age of 11 or 12 is by means of the School's own examination, normally taken at the School. There is admission into the Sixth Form for boys and girls.

Pupils are prepared for GCSE and GCE, AS and A Levels for University entrance, and for entry to the Services, professions and industry. The games are Rugby, Cricket, Hockey, Athletics, Tennis, Swimming, Skiing, Squash, Golf, Netball and Basketball. The School has its own Combined Cadet Force with RAF and Army sections. The Duke of Edinburgh's Award can also be undertaken at Bronze, Silver and Gold levels. Special scholarships may be awarded for tennis, skiing and golf.

Pupils are all involved in a wide-ranging Activities Curriculum. There is also a broad range of Inter-House competitions. There is a School Choral Society, a Chapel Choir, an Orchestra, a Jazz Orchestra and various ensembles.

Religious instruction, which promotes religious tolerance, is in accordance with the principles of the Church of England. An annual Confirmation Service is held in the School Chapel for which pupils are prepared by the Chaplain. Pupils of all denominations are accepted into the School and are expected to attend chapel.

The National Curriculum is broadly followed in Years 7 to 9 and early specialisation is avoided. There is a Careers Team which advises pupils and arranges suitable visits and interviews and gives advice on University degree courses. The main responsibility for each pupil is undertaken by his or her Housemaster, supported by a Tutor. The health of the pupils is in the care of the School Doctor, and a State Registered Nurse is in charge of the Medical Centre.

Fees per term (2011-2012). Day Pupils (including meals): £5,195 (Years 7 & 8), £6,498 (Years 9–13). Boarders: £6,926 (Years 7 & 8), £8,595 (Years 9–13). All boarders may exercise a weekly boarding option. There are no compulsory extras.

Scholarships. (*See Scholarship Entries section.*) All applications should be made to the Registrar, Reed's School (01932 869001).

Charitable status. The London Orphan Asylum (Reed's School) is a Registered Charity, number 312008. Its aims and objectives are to provide an education for pupils who have lost the support of one or both parents.

Reigate Grammar School

Reigate Road, Reigate, Surrey RH2 0QS
Tel: 01737 222231
Fax: 01737 224201
e-mail: info@reigategrammar.org
website: www.reigategrammar.org

Governing Body:

Chairman: Mr A Walker
Vice-Chairmen:
Sir Colin Chandler
Mrs J Langham

Mr D Adams	Mr R Hails
Mr R Bacon	Mr D Hall
Professor F Cotter	Mr P Henderson
Mr K Crombie	Dr K Knapp
Mr W Dunnet	Mrs J Oliphant
Mrs E Fieldhouse	Professor S Sayce
Mrs J Forbat	Mr W Siegle

Headmaster: D S Thomas, MA Oxford

Senior Deputy Head: Mrs M A Collins, BEng Bristol
Deputy Head (Pastoral): Miss S J Arthur, BA Durham
Deputy Head (Staff): G R Sanderson, MA Oxford

Development Director: S Davey, BSc Hons Bristol, MA London

Assistant Head (Assessment): Miss V Godbold, BA Hull

Head of Sixth Form: Mrs J A Richards, MA Oxford
Head of Upper School: P G Stephens, BSc Aberystwyth
Head of Third Form: M S Russell, BEd Bulmershe College
Head of Second Form: Mrs E L Bader, BEd Worcester
Head of First Form: Mrs C H Lawson, BA Liverpool

Chaplain and Head of PSHE: §P J R Chesterton, BA Open, CertEd St Luke's

Assistant Staff:
* *Head of Department*
§ *Part-time*

Art:
*Mrs E J Burns, BA Kent Institute of Art & Design
W H Edwards, BA Staffordshire Polytechnic
N J Fowles, BA Kent
Mrs S J T Genillard, ATC Goldsmiths College London
Miss R L Mansfield, BA Southampton Inst of Art & Design

Biology:
*T S Dare, MA Cambridge
§Dr S L Lawson, BSc, PhD Plymouth
Miss C L Nisbet, BSc Kent
A M Proudfoot, BSc Durham, PhD East Anglia
P G Stephens, BSc Aberystwyth

Chemistry:
*Dr A L Boyes, PhD Southampton
Mrs G Hanlan, BSc Royal Holloway College London
Mrs R E Hood, BA Cambridge
J M Sergeant, BSc King's College London

A J Welch, BA Cambridge

Classics:
M J Buzzacott, BA Durham (**Careers*)
H G Ingham, BA Oxford
Mrs C H Lawson, BA Liverpool
Mrs J A Richards, MA Oxford
*S J M Wakefield, BA, AKC, PhD London

Design and Technology:
M D Hallpike, CertEd Crewe and Alsager College
§Mrs R C Robinson, BA Brighton
*P J Williams, BSc Plymouth

Drama:
*Miss S K Branston, BA Wales
Miss S M Hayes, BA Royal Holloway
D A Jackson, BA Middlesex

Economics and Business Studies:
Ms C E Davies, BA Durham
§Mrs C J Peats, BA Nottingham
*Mrs P A Tucker, BA Brighton

English:
*S T Chevalier, MA Oxford
Miss K Knoesen, BA RAU South Africa
Miss K L Murray, BA Cardiff, MEd Fontys
Miss E J Newton, BA Cambridge
Miss S E Robinson, BA Birmingham
Mrs K J Scaglione, BA Keele
Mrs P S Smithson, BA Exeter

Food Technology:
Mrs E L Bader, BEd Worcester College of HE

Geography:
*M G Cline, BA Southampton
S A Collins, BA Durham (**Outdoor Training*)
Mrs G C Dexter, BA Queen's Belfast
Miss V Godbold, BA Hull
M S Hadley, BSc Edinburgh
P C Klein, BSc Cheltenham & Gloucester
§Mrs V L Ramsden, BA Nottingham

History & Politics:
J M Aiken, BA Liverpool
Miss S J Arthur, BA Durham
Miss C B Green, BA East Anglia
Dr L D Goldsmith, MA, PhD London
*Mrs F A Gunning, MA Oxford
N C Hughan, BA Southampton
G R Sanderson, MA Oxford
C D Thompson, MPhil, PhD Cambridge

ICT:
*N J Stokes, BSc Surrey
A L Lewis, BA Hons Wales

Mathematics:
*D G Bader, BSc Bath
§Mrs F G Buzzacott, BSc Exeter
A R D Davies, BSc Bristol
Mrs F J Grant, BEd Bulmershe College
M H Hetherington, BA Nottingham, GTP
A B Lunberg, BA Otago
P I Rollitt, MSc King's College London
M S Russell, BEd Bulmershe College
§Mrs A E Sharp, BSc Sussex
Mrs L J Stephens, BEd Cambridge
Mrs S M Taylor, BSc Exeter

Modern Languages:
R D Appleton, BA Durham (**Spanish*)
*Mlle F C Chartrain, MA Nantes (**French*)
Miss C R Dumas, BA Durham
Miss L A Mulligan, BA Exeter
Miss M E Sowa, BA Kent (**German*)
Mrs J M Spencer Ellis, BA Hull

Ms B Thomas, BA Bristol
Miss N Veronese, MA Bologna
§Mrs J C Wright, BA Lampeter

Music:
R J Hare, BMus Royal Academy of Music
N J Lobb, BA Bretton Hall
*S J Rushby, BA Surrey

PE & Sport Studies:
§Mrs C L Cline, BSc St Mary's College, Twickenham
D J Cooper, BA Exeter (**PE*)
§Mrs A J Davies, BEd Brighton Polytechnic
Miss L H Eades, BSc Brighton
P R Mann, BSc Loughborough
*Mrs E J Mitchell, BEd Exeter (*Co-Director of Sport*)
*C S Nicholson, BSc Loughborough (*Co-Director of Sport*)
§A K Reid, BEd St Luke's College, Exeter
§Mrs S Sullivan, BEd Exeter
Mrs D S L Trewinnard, BA Chichester
§Mrs R J Wickham, BA Exeter
A J Whiteley, BEd Loughborough College (**Sports Studies; Director of Activities*)

Physics:
Mrs M A Collins, BEng Bristol
Miss G E Cooper, BSc Exeter
§Mrs S M Garcia, BSc Queen's Ontario, BEd Kingston
Mrs D Pricopie, Baccalaureat Diploma Romania
A G Reid, BSc King's College London
*P A Saunders, BEng Southampton

Religion and Philosophy:
*A D Cullen, BA Cambridge
A A Powell, BD, AKC London
Mrs Z E Wood, MA St Andrews
T Wright, BA Durham, MA Cambridge

Learning Support:
*Ms S E Clarke, MA Sussex

Bursar & Clerk to the Board of Governors: J J Jensen-Humphreys, ACA, FCA
Project Manager: D F Aburn, MBIFM, IMBM
Headmaster's Secretary: Mrs B G Eustace
IT Manager: G K Redfern, BSc

Reigate Grammar School is a co-educational day school for pupils aged 11 to 18.

The school was founded in 1675 as a free school for boys. It became an independent Grammar School during the nineteenth century, but after the 1944 Education Act it came under the control of Surrey County Council. On the abolition of the direct grant in 1976, RGS reverted to independent status. At the same time girls were admitted for the first time, initially in the Sixth Form only, but throughout the school from 1993. The school now numbers 890 pupils, of whom 230 are in the Sixth Form. In September 2003, the school merged with Reigate St Mary's Preparatory and Choir School (*see entry in IAPS section*), which provides education to 300 boys and girls aged 3 to 11.

The school is situated in the historic market town of Reigate, just outside the M25 yet with easy transport links into London, Surrey and Sussex. Pupils come from a wide geographical area and from across the social spectrum, thanks to the school's own bursary system, and to the generous support of the Peter Harrison Foundation which provides substantial financial support each year. Around 50% of pupils come from primary schools, the remainder coming from the preparatory sector.

The Governors have invested considerable sums in new buildings in recent years. A new indoor swimming pool opened in January 2009 and new science laboratories and classrooms are due for completion in 2011. In addition to the main school site, the sports ground at Hartswood, two miles from the school, provides some 32 acres of playing fields and a floodlit all-weather astroturf pitch.

Organisation. The school is divided into five sections: First Form, Second Form, Third Form, Upper School (Fourth and Fifth Forms), and Sixth Form. The welfare of pupils is overseen by the Heads of Sections and Heads of Year.

Curriculum. The range of subjects on offer is traditional in the early years, but allowing for a broadening of options in the Sixth Form. Prior to GCSE, all pupils study a core curriculum of Mathematics, English, Science, one or two Modern Languages (French, German or Spanish), Latin, History, Geography, Religious Studies, ICT, Art, Design Technology, Food Technology, Music, Drama, PE and Games. Most pupils take ten GCSEs or IGCSEs, chosen from the above, with the added options of Sports Studies and Greek. Both Dual Award Science and the separate sciences are offered.

Most pupils stay on into the Sixth Form and take four subjects to A2 level. No modules are set in the Lower Sixth. Subjects available include all of the above, with the added options of Business Studies, Economics, Politics and Philosophy and Ethics. Further details are available on the website.

Extra-curricular activities. Reigate Grammar School has a strong tradition of excellence in a wide variety of extra-curricular activities, including an enviable reputation in sport, music and drama; large numbers of pupils participate in the CCF and in the Duke of Edinburgh's Award Scheme and last year the school raised some £20,000 for charities. The main sports are rugby, hockey and cricket for boys, and hockey, netball and rounders for girls, but other sports on offer include athletics, badminton, basketball, gymnastics, football, squash, swimming and tennis. There are several musical groups which rehearse regularly, including two orchestras, a Swing Band and three choirs, and there are frequent concerts both inside and outside the school, including tours overseas. The Drama department presents at least one major production each term, sometimes in collaboration with the music department.

Admissions. Pupils are normally admitted to the School at the ages of 11, 13 or 16, although vacancies may occasionally occur at other ages. There is a registration fee of £60. Except for entry to the Sixth Form, all candidates sit an entrance examination in January or November. All those who perform well in the examination are invited for an interview. All enquiries concerning admission to the school should be addressed to the Headmaster.

Fees per term (2011-2012). Tuition £4,792. Sibling discounts are available.

Scholarships. The school offers a wide range of scholarships and bursaries, aimed at enabling parents who might not normally be able to consider an independent school to send their child to Reigate Grammar School. All scholarships are means-tested, with fee remission of up to 100%. These include Academic scholarships, Music scholarships and a small number of All-Rounder awards (Ragg Scholarships) which are available at age 11 and 13 for pupils who show potential in at least two extra-curricular areas. Sports Scholarships are available for Sixth Form entry.

Bursaries may also be available, dependent on parental income and assets, and candidates living in Reigate and Banstead may be eligible for a Harrison Scholarship, which is also means-tested and made available through the generosity of the Peter Harrison Foundation. Further details are available from the Bursar.

Junior School. Reigate St Mary's Preparatory and Choir School (*see entry in IAPS section*) is the junior and nursery school of RGS. It numbers approximately 300 pupils aged 3 to 11 and is one of the few choir schools in the country not attached to a cathedral or college.

Charitable status. Reigate Grammar School is a Registered Charity, number 1081898. Its aim is to provide high-quality education for boys and girls.

Repton School

Repton, Derbyshire DE65 6FH
Tel: 01283 559221(Headmaster)
         01283 559200 (School)
Fax: 01283 559223 (Headmaster)
e-mail: registrar@repton.org.uk
website: www.repton.org.uk

Situated in the heart of England, Repton School has been home to a spiritual community for over 800 years and the inspiring buildings of the 12th century Priory remain at the centre of our life together today.

Over its 450 years Repton has established a strong tradition of distinguished alumni in public life, sport and the arts including Roald Dahl, Archbishop Michael Ramsey, C B Fry, Graeme Garden and Jeremy Clarkson.

The 21st century Repton is a fully co-educational school with a strong boarding ethos and is home to 650 pupils. Individuality flourishes within the context of a real community and every Reptonian is encouraged to discover those areas in which he or she can excel, and to prepare for the world of possibilities that lie beyond the Arch.

Chairman of Governors: J M Fry

Headmaster: R A Holroyd, MA late Scholar of Christ Church Oxford

Deputy Head (Pastoral): Mrs S A B Tennant, MA late Scholar of Somerville College Oxford
Deputy Head (Academic): T C Owen, MA late Exhibitioner of St Edmund Hall Oxford
Chaplain: The Revd A J Watkinson, MA Keble College Oxford

Heads of Department:
Classics: R G Embery, BA Durham
Modern Languages: Mrs S L Checketts, BA Cardiff
English: (to be appointed)
Director of Drama: J C Sentance, MA Goldsmiths College London
History and Politics: Dr N F Pitts, BA, PhD Leeds
Geography: Miss A H McKenzie, MA London
Economics: C M Keep, MA Queen's College Cambridge
Mathematics: P V Goodhead, MA late Scholar of Pembroke College Oxford
Ethical & Religious Studies: D T Clark, MTheol St Andrews
Physics: J S Mitchell, BSc Sunderland
Biology: Dr S M Ingleston, BSc, PhD Nottingham
Chemistry: D Morris, BSc Manchester
Director of Music: A J R Bowley, MA King's College Cambridge, ARCM
Director of Art: J H Bournon, BA Wimbledon School of Art
Academic ICT: A C Cooke, BA Leeds Metropolitan
Design and Technology: I Setterington, BEd Loughborough
Physical Education: S J Clague, BSc Crewe and Alsager College of HE

Boys' Boarding Houses:
School House: T H Naylor
The Priory: J G Golding
The Orchard: A J Smith
Latham House: J E L Dahl
The Cross: S Earwicker
New House: W G Odell

Girls' Boarding Houses:
The Abbey: Mrs L E Wilbraham
The Garden: Mrs J P Mitchell
Field House: P J Griffiths & Mrs J Griffiths
The Mitre: Mrs A F Parish

Bursar: C P Bilson, MA, MBA Jesus College Cambridge
Registrar: Mrs C Hanneford-Smith
Headmaster's Secretary: Miss J J Taylor

Admission. Pupils are admitted at 13+ (Year 9) and 16+ (Year 12) but exceptions may be made in other years. Application for admission should be made to the Headmaster. There is a registration fee of £80. Candidates will normally have passed Common Entrance at their preparatory schools, but there is also an entrance examination for candidates not being prepared for CE.

Fees per term (2011-2012). Boarders £9,407; Day pupils £6,980. Some additional expenses (for books, stationery, pocket money, etc) will be incurred.

There is a Bursary Fund from which grants in the form of remissions from full fees may in certain circumstances be made. No remission of fees can be made on account of absence.

Scholarships. (*See Scholarship Entries section.*) Academic Scholarships and Exhibitions are awarded annually after a competitive examination: senior in November, junior in May, though in exceptional cases candidates may be considered for awards at other entry points. The value of any award may be increased where need is shown.

C B Fry Awards: A number of awards are made annually to candidates exhibiting outstanding all-round leadership potential.

Art, Design Technology, Drama, Information Technology, Music and Sport scholarships are also offered to candidates showing outstanding potential.

In addition, there are nominated Foundation Scholarships and Endowment Fund Bursaries.

Curriculum. The curriculum in Year 9 is broad to enable pupils to make an informed choice of GCSE subjects at the beginning of Year 10.

In Years 10 and 11, pupils study a combination of core and optional subjects. All pupils study English, Mathematics, Biology, Chemistry and Physics (leading either to two GCSEs in Science and Additional Science or three GCSEs in separate sciences for the more able students). The vast majority of pupils also take English Literature and French as core GCSEs. Pupils choose three subjects as optional GCSE subjects from: Art, Business Studies, Classical Civilisation, Classical Greek with Latin ("Gratin"), Design and Technology, Drama, Geography, German, History, Latin, Music, Physical Education, Religious Studies, Spanish and Three Dimensional Studies. Art and Music may also be taken "off the timetable" to provide pupils with the choice of a fourth optional subject. In Year 10, all pupils also receive one lesson in ICT and one lesson in PSHCE per week.

Most pupils study four subjects in the Lower Sixth at AS Level, though Further Mathematics can be taken as a fifth option. In the Upper Sixth many pupils choose to take three of these subjects to the full A Level; some opt to continue with all four or indeed five. The following are available as full A Levels over two years or as AS Levels over one year: Art, Biology, Business Studies, Chemistry, Classical Civilisation, Classical Greek, Design and Technology, Drama and Theatre Studies, Economics, English, French, Geography, German, Government and Politics, History, Latin, Mathematics, Further Mathematics, Music, Physical Education, Physics, Religious Studies, Spanish and Textiles. In the Lower Sixth, most pupils take "Civics", a course designed by the School to consolidate and extend their AS Level studies. In the Upper Sixth, there is a timetabled lecture programme where pupils have the opportunity to hear distinguished speakers talk on a wide variety of subjects.

Potential Oxbridge candidates are identified by the end of their second term in the Sixth Form and prepared for interview.

Chapel services are those of the Church of England and boarders are expected to attend a service every Sunday unless specially excused. A Confirmation is held each year.

Other activities. Every opportunity and encouragement is given to pupils to develop their creative interests in Art, Music, Drama and Design Technology. Facilities include dedicated Art, Drama and Music Schools, newly renovated Theatre, Studio Theatre and Textiles Studio. There are numerous School societies, covering a wide variety of interests.

Games and sports. Football, hockey (three astroturf pitches – 2 water-based, 1 sand), cricket, netball, rugby, fives, squash, tennis (2 indoor courts and 14 hard courts), cross-country, athletics, sailing, climbing, canoeing, swimming, fencing, golf and horse riding. Superb facilities are provided for physical education including a sports hall, fitness suite, gymnasium and indoor swimming pool.

Combined Cadet Force. The School maintains a contingent of the Combined Cadet Force and every pupil is a member in Year 10. Subsequently pupils may remain in the CCF to take part in The Duke of Edinburgh's Award scheme or specialise as instructors. Sixth Formers have the additional choice of Community Service.

Houses. All pupils belong to a House, which is their home in the School, where they eat all meals, and is at the heart of their life at Repton. The Housemaster or Housemistress, who has overall responsibility for an individual pupil's work and development, lives in the House with his/her own family and is supported by a resident Matron and team of Tutors.

Repton Preparatory School and Pre-Preparatory School at Foremarke Hall are approximately 1½ miles from the main school and house 63 boarders, 273 day boys and girls and 110 pre-prep day boys and girls. Pupils are taken from age 3 and prepared for entrance to Repton and other schools. Academic Scholarship examinations take place in January.

Further information may be obtained from The Headmaster, Foremarke Hall, Milton, Derbyshire DE65 6EJ. (*See Foremarke Hall's entry in IAPS section.*)

Charitable status. Repton School is a Registered Charity, number 1093166. It exists to provide high quality education for boys and girls.

Robert Gordon's College

Schoolhill, Aberdeen AB10 1FE
Tel: 01224 646346
Fax: 01224 630301
e-mail: enquiries@rgc.aberdeen.sch.uk
website: www.rgc.aberdeen.sch.uk

Motto: '*Omni nunc arte magistra*'

The College was founded as a residential establishment in 1729 by Robert Gordon, a member of a well-known Aberdeenshire family, who made his fortune as a merchant in the Baltic ports. In 1881 it was converted into a Day School, but a boarding facility was re-established for a very small number of pupils from 1937 to 1995. Formerly a grant-aided school in receipt of a Direct Grant from the Scottish Education Department, the College became a fully independent school on 1st August, 1985, though retaining its statutory link with The Aberdeen Educational Endowments Scheme 1958 (amended 1985). It has been fully co-educational since 1992.

Governors:
Convener of Aberdeen City Council (ex officio) and representative of the following bodies:

Aberdeen City Council (2), University of Aberdeen (1), Aberdeen Presbytery of the Church of Scotland (2), Aberdeen Endowments Trust (2), Gordonian Association (2), Seven Incorporated Trades of Aberdeen, Trades Unions,

Chamber of Commerce, and not less than 4 nor more than 6 co-opted members.

Chairman of Governors: Colin A B Crosby, OBE, LLB, CA

Head of College: **Hugh Ouston**, MA, DipEd

Deputy Head of College: Jennifer M S Montgomery, MA, DipEd

College Secretary: Robert M Leggate, MA, CA

Deputy Heads (Secondary):
Michael S Elder, MA
Carol Oliver, BA
Phyllis Thomson, MA
Willem Smit, BSc, BTh
Michael S Elder, MA

Departments:
* *Head of Department*
‡ *Principal Teacher (Learning)*

Art:
*Andrew L Hopps, BA
Fraser Beaton, DA
Susan Blue, BA
Louise Charlton, BA
Fiona Michie, DA

Biology:
*David Strang, BSc
‡Wendy MacGregor, BSc
Gail Clark, BSc
Alexandra Hendry, BSc, MSc
Jessica Power, BSc, BEd
Tracy Reid, BSc
Matthew Richardson, BA
Peter Shand, BSc, PhD

Business Studies:
*Caroline Boyd, BA
Tracey Christie, BA, ACCA
Jackie Farquhar, BA
Valerie Ingram, BA
Scott McKenzie, BA, DipM

Chemistry:
*Jane Kennedy, BSc, PhD
‡Kevin S Cowie, BSc
Sarah Coates, MSc
Kanola David, BSc, PhD
John Duncan, BSc
Michelle Molyneux, BSc
Stephanie Rigby, BSc, PhD
Neil Montgomery

Classics:
*Allan M Bicket MA, MLitt
Patricia Ashenford, MA
Craig Galbraith, MA, MLitt, PhD
Veronique Oldham, Licence en Philologie Classique

Computing Studies:
*Fiona M Currie, BSc
Lorna Hawthorn, BSc
Sarah Johnson, BSc

Drama:
*Andrew Milarvie, BA, DipDA
Laura Fyvie, BA
Scott Neish, BA

English:
*Claire Cowie, MA, MLitt
‡Amy MacBrayne, MA
Shona M Bruce, MA, MEd
Miles Carter, MA
Michael S Elder, MA
Arlene Knudson, MA
Marie Mancellon, MA
Kathryn McLeod, MA
Helen Rees, BA
Cheryl Saunders, MA
Natalie Walker, MA

Geography:
*Jennifer Gray, MA, PhD
Louisa Maddox, MA
Anna Nicoll, BSc
Keith Paul, BSc
Fiona Stone, BSc, MSc
Kate Templeton, MA

History and Modern Studies:
*Robin Fish, MA Oxon
Anna Cordey, MA Oxon, MSc, FRSA
Anne Gilks, MA, PhD, BA, MLitt
Stewart Hardie, MA
Margaret Hogg, BA
Noel Shearer, MA

Mathematics:
*Victoria Fletcher, BSc, MA Ed
‡Donna Ellis, BSc
‡Andrew Prentice, BSc
‡Lorna Taylor, MA
‡Roy Wakeford, BSc
John Gibb, MA
Arthur Jamieson, BSc
Rebecca Lynch, MA
Shirley MacKenzie, MA
Elaine Pascoe, BEd
Eileen Smith, MA
Gemma West, BSc

Modern Languages:
*Thomas C Cumming, MA, DipEd
‡Pamela McGregor, MA, DipEd
Linda Berg
Graeme Campbell, MA
Gregor Duncan, MA

Derek A Harley, MA, DipEd
Nathalie Mills
Daniel Montgomery, MA, DipEd
Judit Moscoso, MA
Carol Oliver, BA
Ulrike Plasberg, BA, DipEd
Simonetta Quarta
Phyllis Thomson, MA
Elizabeth Webster
Anne Watson, BA

Music:
*Kevin Haggart, BMus, MMus
Christopher Pearson, BMusEd
Calum Massie, BMusEd
Kevin Cormack
P Louise A Counsell, AGSM
Rachel Mackison, GRSM
Lydia Thom, LTCL

Physical Education:
*Andrew G Dougall, DPE
*Stacey Lamont, BEd
‡Richard Anderson, BA
‡Colin B Filer, BEd
‡James Lamont, BEd
Carolyn Armstrong, BEd
Shirley Blake, BEd
Louise Macklin, BEd
Jocelyn Roberts, BEd

Guidance (Principal Teachers):
Gail Clark, BSc
Sarah Coates, MSc
Kevin Cowie, BSc
Colin Filer, BEd
Arthur Jamieson, BSc
Scott McKenzie, BA, DipM
Noel Shearer, MA
John Thomson, BSc

Principal Teacher Guidance/Careers: Fraser Beaton, DA
Principal Teacher Guidance/Universities: Daniel Montgomery, MA, DipEd
Development Director: Frances Loughrey, MA
Data & Research Coordinator: Isabel Mitchell
Alumni Relations: Laura Pike
Network Manager: Gordon Crosher
Admin Systems Supervisor: Gina Rathbone
Administration/Exams: Shona M Bruce, MA, MEd (*Principal Teacher*)
Health & Safety Coordinator: Stuart W Robertson, MA (*Principal Teacher*)
Support for Learning: Sheila Sanderson, BA
Press and Communications Officer: Shelley Foreman
Graphic Designer: Fiona Reid, BA
School Nurse: Janet Murdoch, RGN
School Librarian: Elaine Brazendale, MA, MCLIP
Assistant Librarian: Jennifer Strang, MSc
Archivist: Penny Hartley, BA
Duke of Edinburgh's Award Manager: Craig McEwan, BEng
House Competition Coordinator: Walter Craig, MA, DipEd
Personal Assistant to Head of College: Ann Gannon
General Office: Lynda Cunningham
Senior School Receptionist: Fiona McKay
Human Resources Manager: Frances Winter, MA

Junior School:
Head of Junior School: Mollie Mennie, DPE, MBS, DipEd
Deputy Heads:
Sally-Ann Johnson, BEd, MEd
Varie Macleod, BEd

Class Teachers:

Wendy Smith, BEd
Nicola Stephen, BEd
Sandra Inglis, DPE
Sarah Baxter
Dave Swanson, DPE
Stuart Scorgie
George Watson

Physics:
*Stuart Farmer, BSc, MBA
‡Graham P Sangster, BSc
‡Dawn Pirie, BSc
Tim Browett, BSc
Craig McEwan, BEng
Sheila B Sanderson, BA
John Thomson, BSc
Lara Woods, BSc

Psychology:
Carmen Fyfe, BSc, PhD

Religious Education:
Paul McIntyre, BD
Dawn Nolan
Lesley Ross, MA
Willem Smit, BSc, BTh

Technology:
*David McLaren, DipTechEd
‡Roy Wakeford, BSc
Colin J Lavery, BSc, DipTechEd
Joseph Leiper, BEng
Lyndsey MacLean, BA

Anne McDonald, DipEd

Karen Miller, BEd
Laura Mackay, BEd
Sophie Main, BEd
Kirsten McLachlan, BEd
Fiona Keating, BA
Michelle Irvine, MA
Vivien Scott, BEd
Lorraine Wright, MA
Helen Crichton, BEd
Maureen Drummond, BEd
Patrick Robertson, BEd
Susan Jamieson, MA
Sally Kinsey, BA
Ashleigh Cameron, LLB
Heather Crowther, BEd
Claire Rae, BSc
Katherine Harris, BEd

Samara McIntyre, MA
Susan Rust, MA
Scott Anderson, BEd
Ingrid Stanyer, BA
Robert Cowie, BA
Norma Murray, BSc
Catriona Graham, MA

Class Assistants:
Fiona McCracken
Moira Murray, BA
Diane Legg
Elisabeth MacDougall
Moira Craig, Dip DomSc
Lesley Dougall, DipEd
Fiona Coull, BSc, RGN
Fiona Montgomery

Support for Learning: Hilary Esson, BEd
Art: Giles Rencontre, BA
Drama: Elizabeth Hawkey, BA
French: Evelyn Johnstone, MA; Morag Ryan, BA
ICT: Caireen McDonald, BA
Music: Amanda Watt, BEd; Yvonne Ouston, DipMusEd
PE/Games: Carolyn Armstrong, BEd; Shirley Blake, BEd
George Watson
Swimming: Sandra Inglis, Sarah Baxter
Science: Tracy J Geddes, MA; Matthew Northcroft, BEd
Librarian: Alison Lloyd-Wiggins, BA, CILIP

Nursery Teacher: Ailsa Reid, BEd

Nursery Nurses:
Deborah Browne, SSNB
Fiona McRae, BA
Michelle Duguid, HNC

Nursery Assistants:
Pauline Greenhalgh, PDA
Elizabeth Wilson

After School Club Supervisor: Sarah Baxter

Junior School Secretary: Dorothy Hardie, BA
Junior School Receptionists: Julie Adams, Coleen Manson
Head's PA: Lesley Cameron, MA

Admission. The College is divided into two sections: the Junior School (Primary, Classes 1–7) 490 pupils and the Senior School (Secondary, Forms 1–6) 1,091 pupils. The normal stages of entry are to Primary 1, Primary 6 and Secondary 1.

Entry to Primary 1 (age 4½–5½ years) is by interview held in February, and to Primary 6 (age 9½–10½ years) by Entrance Test held in February.

Entry to Secondary 1 is by an Entrance Examination held in January.

Entry at other stages depends upon vacancies arising, and the offer of a place is subject to satisfactory performance in an Entrance Test and interview.

There is also a **Nursery** for some 35 children (age 3–5).

Fees per annum (2011-2012). Nursery: £3,735 (half day exc lunch), £7,855 (full day inc lunch). Junior School (exc lunch): £6,560 (P1–2), £8,915 (P3–7). Senior School (exc lunch): £10,215. These fees are inclusive and cover Games. Pupils provide their own books.

Bursaries. A significant number of bursaries are awarded to pupils entering S1 on the basis of performance in the Entrance Examination and of financial need. In addition, some bursaries are awarded to pupils entering the Sixth Year. In total around 20% of pupils in the secondary department receive financial help.

Buildings. The centre block was erected in 1732, but there have been many modern additions. The College is fully equipped with Assembly Hall, Library, Laboratories, Art Rooms, Computing areas and Workshops. There are two Gymnasia and a Swimming Pool at the School. A new playing field was opened in 1992 on a 40-acre site 3m from the school incorporating first-class accommodation and facilities, including a water-based hockey pitch and an astroturf

all-weather sports surface. A five-storey teaching block, incorporating a Dining Hall, was opened in 1994, and a new Library and Information Centre in 2000. A new Junior School building opened in Spring 2009, with newly located and renovated Senior classrooms following in Summer 2009. Further expansion is planned into buildings to be purchased from The Robert Gordon University, including new Music and Drama facilities.

Curriculum. In the Junior School the usual subjects of the primary curriculum are covered, with specialist teachers in Art, Drama, French, Computing, Music, Science and Physical Education. The first 2 years of the Senior School have a general curriculum; in Third and Fourth Year some specialisation is permitted; and in Fifth and/or Sixth Year SQA Higher and Advanced Higher Grade, or Cambridge Pre-U courses are provided in Classics (Latin, Greek and Classical Studies), Electronics, English, Mathematics, Physics, Chemistry, Biology, Human Biology, Modern Languages (French, German, Italian, Spanish), History, Geography, Modern Studies, Music, Art, Photography, Drama, Physical Education, Psychology, Philosophy, Religious Moral and Philosophical Studies, Computer Studies, Information Systems, Technical Subjects (Technological Studies, Graphic Communication), Economics, Accounting and Finance, and Business Management. Pupils are prepared for the Scottish Qualifications Authority examinations in the majority of subjects which lead directly to university entrance. All pupils have classes in Personal and Social Education, Religious Moral and Philosophical Studies, Games and Physical Education, with ICT being delivered in the first 2 years and Fourth Year. Special courses are run for Sixth Year on entrepreneurship, sports leadership, psychology, sociology, ceramics, photography, electronic publishing, cooking for students, Japanese, Chinese (Mandarin), First Year Scots Law (at Aberdeen University) and European Computer Driving Licence (ECDL).

Examination results are among the best in Scotland, with 96% annually going on to University.

Games. Rugby, Hockey (boys and girls), Cricket, Netball, Tennis, Athletics, Cross-Country Running. A wide range of other sports is offered, including Badminton, Basketball, Volleyball, Golf, Squash, Skiing, Swimming, Orienteering, Hill-Walking, Kayaking and Football.

Extra-Curricular Activities. There is a Contingent of the Combined Cadet Force (Army and RAF sections) and a Pipe Band. The Choirs, Concert Band and Orchestras play a prominent part in the life of the School, as do Literary and Debating Societies, which meet weekly, and dramatic societies, which present a variety of performances. Many other clubs and societies flourish, making over 60 in all. A very large proportion of pupils undertake The Duke of Edinburgh's Award.

Charitable status. Robert Gordon's College is a Registered Charity, number SC000123. It exists to provide education for boys and girls.

Rossall School

Fleetwood, Lancs FY7 8JW
Tel: 01253 774201
Fax: 01253 772052
e-mail: enquiries@rossall.org.uk
website: www.rossallschool.org.uk

Motto: '*Mens agitat molem*'
Rossall School was founded in 1844 on the coast of Lancashire. It is incorporated by Royal Charter, granted in 1890, and is under the management of a Council.

Life Governors:
The Earl of Derby, President of Corporation

Mrs H N Trapnell
Mr M E L Melluish

Governors:
¶Mr S J B James, MA (*Chair*)
Colonel S Davies, MBE
¶Mr A N Stephenson, MA (*Vice Chair*)
Mrs A E Bott, JP
¶Mr CC Fayle, BSc, CEng, MIMechE
¶Mr M J Reece, MA
The Rt Revd Robert Ladds, SSC, BEd, The Bishop of
    Whitby
¶Mr J Parr
Mrs C Preston, BSc, ARICS
Mr M Craven, MA
Dr R W F Oakley
¶Mr J A R Prestwich, FCA
The Revd Cannon P Warren, MA
¶Dr H O Fajemirokun
Mr D O Winterbottom, MA, BPhil
Mr H H Aird, MA
Mr M R Mosley, MA
¶Mr C Littler, FCA
Mr B E Clark, MBE
Prof J Davies, BSc, CEng, FIMechE, FIoD
¶Mr S J Fisher, MA

¶ *Old Pupil*

Secretary to the Corporation and Council: Mr B E Clark,
    MBE

Headmaster: Dr Stephen C Winkley, MA, DPhil

* *Head of Department*
† *Housemaster/mistress*
§ *Part-time*

Deputy Head: Mr A Maree, BA, HED (*History*)
Director of Studies: Mrs G Pryor, BSc Hons, PGCE
    (*Mathematics*)

Assistant Staff:
* *Head of Department*
† *Houseparent*

Mr M E Bradley, BSc, PGCE (*Head of Sixth Form,
    Geography*)
†Mrs A Jurczak, CertEd, DipRE (*SENCO*)
Mr M G Roberts, BSc, PGCE (*Science*)
†Miss J Mercer, BSc, PGCE (*Science*)
†Mr S L Corrie, BMus (*Assistant Director of Music*)
Mrs S J Cross, BA, PGCE (*English*)
Dr D Dohmen, DPhil, PGCE (*Modern Languages, IB
    Coordinator*)
Mrs E L Williams, BSc, PGCE (*Physical Education*)
Mrs S Holder-Williams, MA, RSADipPA (**Art*)
Mr J McCafferty, BSc, PGCE (*Mathematics*)
Mrs K Griffiths, BSc, PGCE (*Chemistry*)
Mr D Wright, BA, PGCE (*Economics & Business Studies*)
Mr A Fairhurst, BA, PGCE (**Geography*)
Mrs S Alonso, UGDFL, AIOL, CertEd (*Spanish*)
§Dr R W F Oakley, PhD, BSc (*Physics*)
Mrs L Furniss, BSc Hons, QTS (*Mathematics*)
Mr S P Hoffman, BA (**Economics & Business Studies*)
Mr P Jurczak, BA, MTh (**Religious Studies, Philosophy
    and Ethics inc Psychology*)
Mrs S Byrne, BSc, PGCE (*Mathematics*)
Mr D Hall, BA Hons, PGCE (*History*)
Mr L Hodgetts, BA Hons (**Design & Technology*)
†Mr M Metcalfe, BSc, PGCE (*Biology*)
Mr I Moore, BA, PGCE, TESOL (*English, ICT, Art*)
Mrs R Barker, BA, CertTEFL (*English*)
Miss I H Riley, BA, CertTEFL (*English*)
Mr A Carter, BA, PGCE (*Business Studies*)
§Mrs N Sinclair, MSc (*Mathematics*)
Mr T McNab, BA, PGCE (*English*)

§Miss M Welch (*Independent Listener*)
Mr T Birchall, BA Hons, PGCE (*Mathematics*)
Mrs C Wolstencroft, BA, MEd, Cert TEFL (**ISC*)
Miss M Young, BA Hons, LTCL, LRSM (*Director of
    Music*)
†Mr G Emmett, MA, PGCE (**History*)
Mr A Butcher, MA, PGCE (*Modern Foreign Languages*)
Mrs A Forster (*Science*)
†Ms S Hayes (*Science, Mathematics*)
Mrs J Evans, BEd, Dip RSA TEFL (*English*)
Ms C Sharp, BA Hons, BTEC Dip, FA (*Art*)
Miss K N Allen, BSc Hons, BA Hons, Cert TEFL, LTCL
    Psychol, Dip TESOL (*English, ICT, Modern Languages
    and Psychology*)
Mrs J C Pritchard (*English*)
†Miss H A Lockyear, BA, HED (*English*)
Ms M Hodgson, BA Hons, BLing, PGCE (*EFL*)
Mrs E Simmons, BA Hons (*Librarian*)
Mr M A Pryor, BSc Hons, PGCE (**Mathematics*)
†Mr H M A Winkley, MA Oxon, Cert TEFL (**EFL*)
Mrs H Ayling, BSc, PGCE, ARCS (*Mathematics*)
Mrs E Almond, BA, MA, PGCE (*Economics*)
Mr D P Hobbs, BA Hons (*Design & Technology*)
Mrs R Taylor, BSc Hons, PGCE (*Mathematics*)
Ms I Marsters, MA, Dip TEFL (*English*)
Ms J M Merris, BSc Hons, MSc, PGCE (*Mathematics*)
Miss L Norton, BA Hons (*Physical Education*)
Miss J Park, BSc Hons, MSc (*Physical Education*)
Ms V Reynolds, BSc Hons, PGCE (*Mathematics*)
Mr M Gray, BA Hons (*EFL*)
Miss A C Houghton, BA Hons, PGCE (*Art*)
Mrs H Park, BA Hons, PGCE (*Art*)
Mrs S Jackson, BSc, MSc (*Mandarin*)
Mr W R McDowell, BA Hons, PGCE (*MFL*)
Mr C P Willman, BA Hons, PGCE (*Business Studies/
    Economics*)
Mrs H McCormack, BSc Hons, PGCE (*Geography*)
Mr B Rund,MA, PGCE (*SEN*)
Mrs J Mindham-Walker, BA Hons, PGCE (**Modern
    Foreign Languages*)
Mr P Harrison, BA (**English*)
Mr R Castle, BSc Hons, PGCE (*Business Studies and
    Economics*)
Mr G De Beer, PGCE (*Mathematics*)
Mr S Taj, BSc Hons, MSc, PGCE (*Physics*)
Miss S Gomersall, HND, BA Hons, PGCE (*Physical
    Education*)
Mr D Jones, BSc Hons, PGCE (*Chemistry*)
Mr M Vauvilliers (*Foreign Language Assistant*)

Head of Junior School: Mrs K M Lee, MA, CPP, CertEd

Houses/Houseparents:
Anchor House: Mr & Mrs M Metcalfe
Dolphin House: Mrs A Jurczak
Lugard Boys House: Mr H M A Winkley
Lugard Girls House: Miss J Mercer
Mitre & Fleur de Lys House: Mr S L Corrie
Pelican House: Mr G Emmett
Rose House: Ms S Hayes
Spread Eagle House: Mr & Mrs I McCleary
Wren House: Miss H A Lockyear
Maltese Cross House: Mr R Castle

Instrumental Music:
Mr G Banks (*Brass*)
Dr A G Keeling (*Flute, Guitar, Composition*)
Mrs R Hall
Mr S L Corrie (*Organ*)
Mr G Lister (*Percussion*)
Mr S Lea (*Clarinet, Saxophone*)
Mrs J Jackson (*Violin*)
Mrs B Miller (*Piano*)

Registrar: Mrs M Metcalfe

Examinations Officer: Mr R Asher, BSc, PGCE
Head, International Study Centre: Mrs C Wolstencroft, BA, MEd, Cert TEFL
Medical Officer: Dr P G Carpenter, MBChB, MRCGP, DRCOG, FPA

Academic Curriculum. All entrants are expected to take a broad based curriculum prior to GCSE. At this stage pupils study English Language, English Literature, Maths, Sciences and a Modern Foreign Language (French, German and Spanish: SEN students possibly excepted); there is then a choice of three options taken from History, Geography, Religious Studies, Art, DT, PE, Music and ICT.

In the Sixth Form the International Baccalaureate and A Levels are offered. At AS/A2 all the subjects at GCSE are on the curriculum, with separate sciences, Economics, Psychology, Law and Philosophy also on offer. There is a similar wide range of subjects offered within the IB, where Psychology and Business Studies are also taught. Much emphasis in the IB is also placed upon the 'Core', the teaching of the Theory of Knowledge, the Extended Essay and the Creativity, Action, Service component.

Some 95% of the Upper Sixth follow on into Higher Education both at home and abroad. Special arrangements are made for those seeking entry to Oxbridge and specialist institutions abroad.

The Arts, Science and Technology. The Music Department, housed in the Thomas Beecham Music School, provides the basis for individual instrumental tuition. The Chapel Choir sings choral services in the magnificent Chapel of St John the Baptist. There are other choral groups, a junior and senior orchestra, a jazz band, etc.

The Art and Design Technology departments offer extensive art and design facilities within purpose-built art and design workshops containing state-of-the-art tooling image making machinery.

The School's Astronomy and Space Science Centre incorporates an observatory, permanent planetarium, lecture theatre and classroom suite. This is not only used within the school for curriculum teaching but is also available for outside use. The Science Department is well used with some 50%+ of students following science at 16+. Within the school grounds there are 3 Sites of Scientific Interest, which are maintained by staff and students. The sea, beach and dunes in front of the school are similar sources for study.

The IT provision is also housed primarily within the Science area with 300+ state-of-the-art machines available through the working day and beyond both in the IT suite and in departments around the campus. The machines are part of a secure cabled network. The Junior School and International Study Centre have their own provision.

The House System. All pupils are members of a House. At age 13 there are three boys' day and boarding houses, two girls' day and boarding houses and one girls' day house. All boarding boys and girls entering at 7+ are in Anchor House, which has its own residential unit. (The International Study Centre also has a boys' and girls' house.) Houseparents have responsibility for each pupil's welfare and are supported by deputies, tutors, medical, careers staff, etc.

Religious Instruction. Rossall was founded as 'the Northern Church of England School' and Chapel remains central to the well-being of the community. Pupils of all faiths are encouraged to share in this community.

Games. 45 acres of playing field and a gymnasium, floodlit Astroturf and indoor 25 metre swimming pool, along with squash, tennis, and fives courts allow all pupils to pursue a sporting interest. The boys mainly play rugby, hockey, cricket, football and basketball, with the girls playing hockey, netball, cricket, rounders and tennis. All pupils are taught to play the unique game of RosHockey on the sandy beach owned by the School. There are full programmes of competitive fixtures against other schools and clubs. House matches occur in all major games, including

football, cross-country in the Lent Term. Archery, athletics, shooting, golf, horse-riding and many other activities are offered.

The CCF. Rossall proudly lays claim to having the oldest CCF in the country and last year celebrated its 150th anniversary. Currently most of Years 9–11 are in either the Army, Navy or Air Force contingents. In Year 9 all cadets will follow the Bronze Duke of Edinburgh's Award, progress to Silver and Gold is optional. All cadets also have the chance to follow the BTEC Service award within the corps, the equivalent to 4 GCSEs this is completed entirely within CCF time. The school has a shooting range, keeps boats on the Wyre and there is opportunity to fly at RAF Woodvale.

Activities and Clubs. Time is set aside after school 4 days a week and at weekends for activities and clubs which operate over the 3 terms. Clubs and activities include but are not limited to: The Literary Society, Choir, Sports, and bi-half termly excursions.

Admission. Any term in the year for boys and girls aged 11+ and 13+, September preferably at 16+ or 17+. All applications for entrance should be made to the Registrar. On registration a fee of £50 will be charged to day applicants and £175 to boarding applicants. Applicants will be put in touch with a Housemaster or Housemistress as soon as appropriate.

Fees per term (2011-2012). Day £2,330–£3,900; Full Boarding £5,900–£9,960; Weekly Boarding £3,960–£6,450.

Scholarships and Bursaries. (*See Scholarship Entries section.*) All enquiries about Scholarships and Bursaries and other awards should be addressed to the Registrar.

Substantial bursaries continue to be awarded to children of the clergy and those in the armed forces.

Rossall Junior School. Rossall has its own Junior School for children aged 7–11 situated within the same grounds. There is also a Nursery and Infants School for day boys and girls aged 2–7.

Access. Motorway: 15 minutes from M55 (spur off M6). Railway: Blackpool North (6 miles). Air: Manchester International Airport (55 miles by road).

The Rossallian Club. Secretary: Jen Booth c/o Rossall School. This Former Pupils Club keeps a record of more than 5,000 members and coordinates the activities of eight Branches. A Newsletter is published twice each year.

Charitable Status. The Corporation of Rossall School is a Registered Charity, number 526685. It aims to provide a sound Christian education for boys and girls.

Rougemont School

Llantarnam Hall, Malpas Road, Newport, South Wales NP20 6QB
Tel: 01633 820800
Fax: 01633 855598
e-mail: registrar@rsch.co.uk
website: www.rougemontschool.co.uk

President: Mr I S Burge

Governors:
Chairman: Mr I G Short
Vice-Chairman: Mr D Blayney, LLB
Mrs J Clark, BA, PGCE
Mr R Pugsley, MSc, FCCA
Dr R M Reynolds, BSc, DipEd
Mr T Rose, CBE, BSc, CEng, FIChemE
Mrs S Routledge, BPharm, MRPharmS
Miss J Sollis, BA, AKC
Mr M Tebbutt
Mrs A C Thomas, JP, SRN, SCM
Prof D Fone, MB BS, MD, FFPH, FRGS, MRCGP, DCH, DRCOG

Headmaster: **Dr Jonathan Tribbick**, BA, LLB, PGCE, FCMI, JP

* *Head of Department*
§ *Part-time*

Head of Preparatory School: Mrs L Turner, BEd
Deputy Head (Academic): Mr R Carnevale, MA Ed, BSc, PGCE *(Physics)*
Deputy Head (Pastoral): Mrs E Ferrand, BEd (*Extra Mural Progamme, Mathematics*)
Academic Registrar: Mr M James, MA Ed, BEd, BA, BSc, CBiol, MIBiol, CertMaths Open *(Biology)*
Finance Manager: Mrs H Perry, FCCA
Operations Manager: Mr C Whitney

Senior School:
Miss S Ashton, BA, PGCE *(Spanish)*
Mr K Bell, BA, PGCE (*Physical Education*)
Mrs K Benson-Dugdale, BMus, MA, QTS, PGEM *(Higher Education Advisor, *Music)*
Mr M Bowman, BSc, PGCE *(Mathematics)*
Mr D Cobb, BSc, PGCE (*Biology*)
Miss C Dugdale, BA, PGCE (*§Games, History, Religious Studies*)
Mrs S Eley, BA, PGCE (*§Dyslexia Dept*)
Mrs S Elson, LLB (*§Latin, Religious Studies*)
Mrs R Garrod, BA, PGCE (*§History*)
Mr L Godfrey, BSc, PGCE *(Mathematics, House Tutor)*
Mrs J Goodwin, BSc (*Physics, Pupil Performance Coordinator*)
Mr J Hardwick, BSc, PGCE *(Biology, Chemistry)*
Mrs J Harris, CertEd, Dip Theol (*Religious Studies, PSE*)
Miss R Hayes, BA, PGCE *(Design & Technology, ICT)*
Miss C Heirene, BSc, PGCE *(Chemistry)*
Mrs F Heirene, BA *(Librarian)*
Mr M Jenkins, MA Cantab, PGCE (*History*)
Mr I Kelly, BA, PGCE (*§German*)
Mrs J Lloyd, BA, PGCE (*English*)
Miss L Meredith, BSc, PGCE *(Physical Education)*
Miss A Mintowt-Czyz, BA, PGCE *(English)*
Mr L Mintowt-Czyz, BA, BTec, PGCE (*Art*)
Mrs D Moore, BA, PGCE (*Drama*)
Mrs D Morgan, BA, PGCE (*Modern Languages*)
Mrs S Morgan, MSc, BSc, PGCE, Cert Lit/Dyslexia *(Dyslexia Dept)*
Mrs S Munro, DEUG, Licence, PGCE *(French)*
Mrs A Page, BSc Econ, PGCE *(Economics & Business Studies)*
Miss K Page, BSc, PGCE *(Physical Education)*
Miss L Parr, BA, PGCE *(Art)*
Mr F Pearce, BSc, PGCE, DipComp (*ICT*)
Mr A Rees, BA, PGCE *(Senior Tutor Y10, Y11, Physical Education, DofE Award Scheme)*
Mr A Richards, BSc, PGCE *(Mathematics, ICT, House Tutor)*
Mrs S Roberts, BSc, PGCE (*Mathematics*)
Miss A Robst, BA, PGCE *(English, Media Studies)*
Mrs P Rogers, MA Ed, BSc, PGCE (*Geography*)
Mr A Scarfi, BA, PGCE *(English)*
Mrs C Sims, BA, PGCE, AMBDA, CCET *(Dyslexia Dept)*
Mr H Singer, BA, PGCE *(Senior Tutor Y8-9, *Design & Technology)*
Mr A Short, BSc, PGCE *(Geography)*
Mrs L Thickins, BA, PGCE *(Senior Tutor Sixth Form, English, Media Studies)*
Mrs T van der Linde, BSc, PGCE *(Senior Tutor Y7, *Chemistry, Pupil Performance Coordinator)*
Mrs R Taylor, BA, PGCE, AMBDA *(English, Dyslexia Dept)*

Preparatory School, Junior Department:
Mrs J Bolwell, CertEd *(Deputy Head)*
Mrs R Carroll, BA, PGCE *(Class Teacher)*
Mr C Dobbins, BMus, DipMus, LRSM, PGCE *(Music)*

Mrs K Galloway, KS2 *(Classroom Assistant)*
Mrs J Greenaway, CertEd *(Class Teacher)*
Miss L Hallas, BA, PGCE *(English)*
Mrs A Jenkins, BSc (*§Science*)
Mr P McMahon, BSc, MSc, QTS *(Mathematics)*
Mrs C Poore, BEd *(Science, Mathematics, Geography, KS2 Coordinator)*
Mrs K Williams, BEd *(Class Teacher)*
Mr S Rowlands, BA, QTS *(Class Teacher)*

Preparatory School, Infant Department:
Mrs H Ashill, NNEB *(Nursery Nurse)*
Mrs A Burridge, BSc, PGCE *(Class Helper)*
Mrs A Exley *(Class Helper)*
Mrs J Farouzan, NNEB *(Nursery Supervisor)*
Mrs S Hotchkiss, BA, QTS *(Deputy Head, Class Teacher)*
Mrs L McLoughlin *(Class Helper)*
Mrs T Mountford, BEd *(Class Teacher)*
Mrs N Noor, BA, PGCE *(Class Teacher, KS1 Coordinator)*
Mrs R Payne, NNEB *(Nursery Nurse)*
Miss Z Rees, NNEB *(Nursery Nurse)*
Mrs C Richards, BA, QTS *(Class Teacher)*
Mrs C Townsend, NVQ *(Nursery Supervisor)*

Registrar: Mrs D Lunt

Rougemont was founded in a house of that name immediately after the First World War as a co-educational day school taking children through to grammar school entrance at 11. It moved to Nant Coch House just after the Second World War and grew to about 200 pupils.

In 1974 the school was re-founded as a Charitable Trust. Since then it has bought extensive new buildings and has 656 pupils on roll in the Preparatory School (Infant Department – Nursery to Year 2 and Junior Department – Years 3–8) and Senior School (Years 9–13).

The Preparatory Junior Department and Senior School moved to a new site at Llantarnam Hall, a large Victorian mansion set in 50 acres of grounds, between 1992 and 1995, with the Infant Department joining them in April 2004. The grounds have been landscaped to provide playing fields and an extensive building programme has taken place on the site. During 1998 a Liberal Arts area including Sports Hall, Music suite and Drama Studio was completed. In 1999 a new classroom block and library was completed and in 2000 additional classrooms together with Art studio were built.

Admission to the Preparatory and Senior Schools is by interview and examination. Entry to the Sixth Form is dependent on GCSE results.

The following paragraphs refer to the Senior School although peripatetic specialists work in both and there is some interchange of teachers.

Curriculum. Pupils follow a wide syllabus to age 14. For the two years to GCSE pupils study nine subjects of which English Language and Literature, Mathematics, a language, science and a humanities subject are normally compulsory. 18 subjects are available.

Sixth Form. 17 AS/A2 levels are available. Sixth Form pupils have their own common room and study area. Sixth Form pupils can also study AS level Critical Thinking and take part in a range of extra-curricular activities and games.

Religion. Rougemont School has no direct affiliation to a Christian Church or denomination. However, the religious instruction, corporate worship and moral value system of the School is based on that of the broad tradition of the mainstream Christian Churches.

Careers. The School belongs to the Independent Schools Careers Organisation. The Senior teachers advise on all aspects of further education and careers.

Music. In addition to specialist teachers of music a large number of peripatetic teachers cover the range of orchestral instruments. There are choirs and instrumental ensembles for all ages.

Drama. In addition to the Infant Department's Spring Festival and the Senior School Eisteddfod, two major plays and two musical events take place each year.

Elocution and Dance. Visiting staff hold weekly classes for LADA courses, ballet and modern dance.

Sport. The School has developed a high standard of performance in most major sports. There is a wide fixtures programme for both boys and girls, as well as the opportunity to participate in numerous coaching courses.

Clubs. A wide variety of extra-curricular activities and clubs is available at lunch time and after school, as is supervised prep.

Duke of Edinburgh's Award Scheme. This is a very successful activity within the school and over 60 pupils have gained the Gold Award in the last twenty years.

Fees per term (2011-2012). Preparatory School: Infant Department £2,240–£2,360, Junior Department £2,700; Senior School £3,080–£3,500.

Scholarships. An annual scholarship examination is held for entry to Year 7. A limited number of means-tested bursaries is offered from Year 7 upwards, with a separate scheme for Sixth Form entry.

Further information. A prospectus and other details are available from the Registrar (Tel: 01633 820800, e-mail: debra.lunt@rsch.co.uk).

Charitable status. Rougemont School is a Registered Charity, number 532341. It exists to provide education for boys and girls.

The Royal Grammar School
Guildford

High Street, Guildford, Surrey GU1 3BB
Tel: Headmaster: 01483 880608
       School Office: 01483 880600
Fax: 01483 306127
e-mail: office@rgs-guildford.co.uk
website: www.rgs-guildford.co.uk

The Royal Grammar School has occupied its fine Tudor buildings in Guildford's High Street for five centuries. It was founded by Robert Beckingham in 1509 and established by King Edward VI's Charter of 1552, which decreed that there should be '... one Grammar School in Guildford ... for the Education, Institution and Instruction of Boys and Youths in Grammar at all future times for ever to endure'. Among the first in the country to be purpose-built, the original buildings contain a remarkable Chained Library, which is now the Headmaster's Study.

Governing Body:
Chairman: H J Pearson, OBE, MA, PhD, CMath, FIMA
Vice-Chairman: J McCann, BMus, ACIB
C D Barnett, MA
M Brett-Warburton, MA RCA, MA URB, RIBA
Mrs C Cobley, MIPD
The Reverend R L Cotton, MA, DipTh
¶D J Counsell, FCA
Mrs S K Creedy, MA
B Creese, BA, MA
H H J Critchlow, LLB, DL
B Hartop, BSc
Dr L S K Linton, MA, MB, ChB, MRCP
The Mayor of Guildford
The Earl of Onslow, High Steward of Guildford
P G Peel, FCA
Professor S Price, MSc, PhD, FBTS, ERT, FHEA
Mrs C Rimmer
C T Shorter, CEng, MIStructE, FConsE, FFB
J A Smith, CEng, FCIBSE

¶N E J Vineall, QC, MA
Mrs M P Waghorn, MA, FRSA

¶ *Old Guildfordian*

Bursar and Deputy Clerk to the Governors: S N White, BA

Headmaster: J M Cox, BSc, PhD

Deputy Heads:
M W Hoskins, BA, MA
G T Williams, MA

Director of Studies: Miss H Pike, MA, MA

Assistant Staff:
S W Armstrong, MA
E J Badham, ARCS, BSc, CBiol, MIBiol
A H S Barras, BA, MA, PhD
Mrs S Barrass, BSc
E T Batchelar, MChem, DPhil
B M Baulf, BA, MA
S G Black, MMath
Mrs J Bodmer, BSc, PhD, MBA
Mrs M C Booth, BEd
E J P Bradnock, BA
J S Braithwaite, BSc, PhD
P J Bridges, BSc
M A Burbidge, BSc
E K D Bush, MA
J A Casale, BSc, MBA
D H Chambers, BMus, PCASS
W D Cowx, BSc, MSc
A M J Curtis, MA
Mrs H Curtis, BA
G T Davies, MPhys, PhD
A C Dodd, BA, MA
A H Dubois, BSc
P J Dunscombe, BSc
C J Eldridge, BA, MPhil
J Gent, BSc
Mrs M R Goodman, BA
N W Gough, BSc, MSc
Miss N S Goul-Wheeker, BA
C J Grace, BA, MA, LTCL, AMusLCM
Mrs K Handley, BSc
L M Holland, BSc
J P Hood, BA, MSci
P J Hosier, BA, MEd
D M Hoyle, BEng
E J Hudson, MA, MSc, PhD
Mrs S F Hudson, BSc, MSc
M R Jenkins, BSc
M J Jennings, BA
J B Kelly, BA, MA, MA RCA

G M Knight, BA
K J Knight, BSc, MSc
W S Lau, MChem
Mrs C L Laver, MA
O C Lawson, BSc
P M Leamon, BA
Miss M E L Linden, BA
A R Lowe, BA
A J Mackowski, BA
I G Maynard, BSc
Ms N C McClean, BA, MA
Mrs E D McIntyre, MA
R B Meadowcroft, BA, MA
Miss C J S Moorehead, MA, FRGS
P G Nathan, BA
S J Orchard, BMus, MMus
D Patel, BSc, PhD
Mrs S J Perrett, BA
N C Pinhey, BSc
J W Pressley, MA
M R F Royds, BEng
A N Rozier, BA
Miss A Sánchez, BA
J R Saxton, MA
J-M Saxton, BA
R E J Seymour, BEd, FRGS
T W Shimell, MChem
S B R Shore, BEd
A F Smith BA, MA, MA
Mrs C E Smith, BA
R Stark, BEd, MSc
Mrs H L Suenson-Taylor, BA
S G Thornhill, MA, DPhil
O M Torri, BA
Miss A V E Tournier, Lic
Revd J P Whitaker, MA
P H White, MA
Mrs D Whitehead, BTech
N E Wild, BA
I Wilkes, BEd
M P Wood, BA
A U Woodman, BSc, MA
D J Woolcott, BA
S J H Yetman, BSc

Admissions Registrar: Mrs K L Sweet, BA

The Royal Grammar School of the 21st century is a day school for around 900 boys, some 250 of whom are in the Sixth Form. The age range is 11 to 18.

Buildings and Facilities. The School occupies a large site in the centre of Guildford. As well as the Chained Library, the Old Buildings contain the Sixth Form Common Room and the Music and Art departments. The New Building, opened in 1965, contains Great Hall, the Careers Centre, the Library, the Dining Hall and kitchens, a fully refurbished Language Laboratory and a large number of classrooms and laboratories. A continuous programme of building development has recently provided a Drama Studio, excellent facilities for Science and Technology, a Sculpture Studio and a large Resources Centre and Study Area. A new Sports and Outdoor Activity Centre with an all-weather outdoor training area, an Auditorium, a new Art block, new music facilities and a Sixth Form Centre have all opened recently.

Curriculum. The Royal Grammar School has an established reputation for academic excellence. Virtually all its Sixth Formers comfortably pass at least three A Levels and gain entry to higher education. About a quarter of them go on to Oxford and Cambridge.

The School's day is from 8.45 am to 4.00 pm. There are no lessons on Saturdays.

In the first three years (Years 7, 8 and 9 nationally), all boys follow a common curriculum embodying the programmes of study for Key Stage 3 of the National Curriculum. The subjects studied are English, French or Spanish, Geography, History, Latin, Maths, Information Technology, RE, PE, Art, Music and Science with Technology, which includes aspects of Astronomy, Earth Science, and Biotechnology. In the third year (Year 9) all boys choose between Spanish, German and Greek and study the separate sciences and Technology.

In the fourth and fifth years (Years 10 and 11) all boys follow a broad and balanced curriculum and take at least nine GCSEs which include English, Maths, French and Science. In addition, all boys take RE, PE and Games. A course in Study Skills, Problem Solving and Personal, Social and Health Education is taught through a timetabled tutorial programme. After the GCSE examinations, all boys participate in the work experience programme.

In the Sixth Form, in addition to the subjects already mentioned, boys may take Classical Civilisation, Further Mathematics, Electronic Systems, Economics, Politics, Drama and Theatre Studies and PE through to A Level. Although many boys prefer a predominantly Maths/Science or Arts choice of subjects, there is no Arts/Science barrier, and more or less any combination is possible. There is an enterprising programme of Sixth Form General Studies organised in conjunction with two local girls' schools.

Religion. The Royal Grammar School is not a specifically religious foundation, but Religious Education (non-denominational) is naturally an integral part of the School's curriculum. RE periods are compulsory at all levels in the School, although parents with conscientious objections may ask the Headmaster for alternative arrangements to be made. The school day normally begins with an Assembly at which every boy is required to be present. The short Act of Worship which features twice a week within Assembly is a Christian one. The School also holds annually its own Carol Service, Commemoration Service and Remembrance Service. The School is closely linked with Holy Trinity Church, a few yards down the High Street.

Pastoral Care. Each boy's progress through the School is monitored with care. Below the Sixth Form a boy is looked after mainly by his Form Tutor; in the Sixth Form there is a system of tutor groups. Boys in the Fourth Form upwards are also encouraged to choose a personal tutor. All boys belong to one of the six Houses, which exist mainly to provide a framework for competitive sport, but which also give further pastoral care opportunities.

Extra-Curricular Activities. Clubs and Societies flourish. Activities include Chess, Computing, Debating, Electronics, Model Railway, History, Geography and Philosophy Societies. There is an Explorer Scout Group, a Combined Cadet Force contingent of Army, Navy and RAF sections, the Duke of Edinburgh's Award Scheme and Outdoor Pursuits. Many boys play musical instruments and there is a School Orchestra, a Big Band, a variety of instrumental groups and a strong Choral Society. There are frequent opportunities for boys throughout the school to participate in dramatic productions.

Games. The School's principal games are rugby, hockey and cricket, although as boys move up the School their sporting options widen considerably. Sports available include tennis, swimming, cross-country running, shooting, sailing, athletics, golf, squash, basketball, football, fencing and badminton.

Admission. Boys may be considered for entry to the Royal Grammar School at any age between 11 and 18. The usual ages of entry, however, are at 11, 13 and 16 into the Sixth Form. Applicants at 11 take the School's entrance examination early in the year of entry; those for 13+ entry take the Common Entrance examination or Scholarship papers after 11+ assessment.

New boys are admitted in September of each year.

The Headmaster is pleased to meet parents, arrange for them to see the School, and discuss the possibility of their son's entry to the School. Appointments may be made through the Registrar, who will supply the School's prospectus on request.

Fees per term (2011-2012). Years 7–8: £4,635 (including lunch); Years 9–13: £4,540 (plus £220 lunch) inclusive of all tuition, stationery and loan of necessary books.

Scholarships. (*See Scholarship Entries section.*) Details of Scholarships and Bursaries are also available from the Registrar.

Preparatory Department. Lanesborough (*see entry in IAPS section*) is the preparatory department of the RGS.

Old Boys. The Membership Secretary of the Old Guildfordians' Association is D H B Jones, BSc, who can be contacted at the School.

Charitable status. The King Edward VI Royal Grammar School, Guildford is a Registered Charity, number 312028. It exists to provide education for boys from 11 to 18.

Royal Grammar School
Newcastle upon Tyne

Eskdale Terrace, Newcastle-upon-Tyne NE2 4DX
Tel: 0191 281 5711
Fax: 0191 212 0392
e-mail: admissions@rgs.newcastle.sch.uk
website: www.rgs.newcastle.sch.uk

The Royal Grammar School was founded and endowed in 1545 by Thomas Horsley, and by virtue of a Charter granted in 1600 by Queen Elizabeth it became 'the Free Grammar School of Queen Elizabeth in Newcastle upon Tyne'. For over 450 years and on six different sites the School has been of major educational importance in Newcastle and in the North East as a whole. It has valued its close links with the city and region, and its Governing Body consists largely of representatives of Local Authorities and Universities.

The School benefits from its central position, being within easy walking distance of the Civic and City Centres and of Newcastle's two Universities, and linked with the whole region by easily accessible rail, bus and metro services.

The School is a Day School and moved towards full co-education in 2006 with places being allocated to boys and girls at all entry points (7+, 9+, 11+, 16+). There are about 1,240 students, including 1,000 in the Senior School (age 11–18) and 240 in the Junior School (age 7–11).

Governing Body:

Co-opted Governors:
Chairman: P A Walker, BA
Vice-Chairman: Professor A C Hurlbert, BA, MA, PhD, MD

A J Applegarth, BA
Mrs L R Bird
P A Campbell, MA
N A H Fenwick, MA
J C Fitzpatrick, BA, FCA, ACI Arb
P A Kramer, LLB, FCIArb
D Marshall, BSc, MSc, PGCE
I Evbuomwan, MD, MRCOG
P Harrison, BA, ACA

Nominated Governors:
R D Armstrong, PhD, DSc
Dr D W Wheeler, MA, DM, PhD, MRCP, FRCA
Professor E W N Glover, MA, PhD, CPhys, FInstP, ILTM
A Hobson, MA
Councillor G Holland
Councillor I Tompkins, BSc
Dr S Ali, PhD
Professor N G Wright

Clerk to the Governors and Bursar: R J Metcalfe, MA, FBIFM

Headmaster: B St J Trafford, MA, MEd, PhD, FRSA

Deputy Head: A A Bird, BMus, MEd, LRAM

Assistant Staff:

* *Head of Department*

Art:
*K Egan-Fowler, BA
Mrs C Egan-Fowler, BEd
G P Mason, BA
P Edwards, BA
Mrs M Wood, PhD

Biology:
*P J Heath, BSc
Dr M H Bell, BSc, PhD
Mrs J A Malpas, BSc
  (*Assistant Head of Lower
  School*)
L Shepherd, BA
C J H Wancke, BSc
Dr C J Murgatroyd, BSc, D
  Phil
§Mrs S F Hutchinson, BSc

Chemistry:
Dr A J Pulham, BA, DPhil
  (**Science*)
*R W Wiggins, BSc
T Kelso, BSc
Miss N Brennan, BSc
Dr J Henshaw, BSc, PhD
Miss S L Richardson, MSc
Dr E A Sconce, BSc, PhD

Classics:
S P Broadbent, BA
T C Clark, BA (*Head of
  Lower School*)
Mrs P Coningham, BA,
  MA
S Robertson, MA
*Miss V C Coyle, BA

Economics/Politics:
*P Shelley, BA, MSc
R C M Loxley, BSc, MEd
  (*Director of Studies*)
*J D Neil, MPhil (*Politics*)
M J Smalley, BA, QTS
Y Moreno-Lopez, MEcon

English:
*Dr S J Barker, BA, PhD

Miss S G Davison, BA
A R D King, BA, MA
Dr C Goulding, BA, MLitt,
  PhD
S C Masters, BA, MA
Mrs K J Keown, BA
L J Gilbert, BA

Geography:
*D A Wilson, BSc
Miss S J Longville, BA
  (*Head of Year 11*)
M G Downie, BA (*Head of
  Careers*)
Miss K E Jarvis, BA
§Mrs R J L Laws, MA
  (*Assistant Head of
  Careers*)

History:
*S E Tilbrook, BA
D C Greenhalgh, BA, MA
O L Edwards, BA
S P Wright, BA, MA
A S W Davies, BA, MSt
Mrs S J Baillie, BA
  (*Pastoral Director*)

Mathematics:
*J A Smith, BSc
T E Keenan, BSc, MSc
A Delvin, BSc, MSc
Dr J Argyle, BSc, MSc,
  PhD
P M Heptinstall, BSc, PhD
H Rashid, BSc, MSc
Mrs E Temple, BSc
W Gibson, MA
S D Watkins, BSc (*Head of
  Middle School*)
G D Dunn, BSc
A Snedden, BSc
D A Jardine, BSc

Modern Languages:
*Miss K E Sykes, BA
Miss S Demoulin, DEUG
  (**French*)

Mrs C L Diaz-Crossley, BA
  (**German*)
Mrs L M Boucaud, BA
M S Bailie, BA, MA
Miss J Budd, BA
M Metcalf, BA, MPhil
Miss E L Hayes, BA
§Mrs C Dixon, BA
§Mrs C A M O'Hanlon,
  BA
§P T Gaffney, BA

Music & Performing Arts:
*N T Parker, BA (*Director*)
T W S Rhodes, BMus,
  RCM (*Assistant Head of
  Music*)
Mrs G M Blazey, BMus,
  MA (*Head of Junior
  School Music*)
D M Key, MMus, BA
T Walters, BA
§Mrs R A Shaw-Kew, BA

Philosophy:
*H H H Baker, MA (*Third
  Master; Head of Upper
  School*)

Physical Education:
*Mrs A J Ponton, BSc
F Dickinson, BEd
D W Smith, BEd (*Senior
  Master*)
P D Taylor, CertEd, DipPE
A G Brown, BSc
A E Watt, BA
Miss S E Davidson, BEd

Miss P Stead, BSc
§R V MacKay, BSc

Physics:
*E T Rispin, BSc
J L Camm, BSc
P Wilson, BSc, MSc
Dr M B A Read, MA,
  MPhil, PhD
Mrs N C McGough, MSci

Psychology:
*D J Merritt, MA
  (*Counsellor*)
Mrs A Robinson, BA

Design & Technology:
*I Goldsborough, BEd,
  MSc
Mrs C A Pipes, BA
P M Warne, MEng

Junior School:
R J Craig, BEd
  (*Headmaster*)
J K Wilkinson, BEd
  (*Deputy Head*)
Mrs C Biggins, BA
J A Pollock, CertEd
Dr A J Spencer, BSc, PhD
Mrs K Wall, BA
Mrs R M Breslin, BA
Mrs L M Stairmand, BA
J N Miller, BA
Ms A J Whitney, BA
Miss E Frost, BA
Miss A S Dargan, BEd
§G Scrafton, BA

School Medical Officer: Dr C J Dias, MB BS, MRCGP
Admissions Secretary: Mrs J M Glendon

Curriculum. The aim of the curriculum up to Year 11 is to offer a general education, culminating in GCSE in a wide range of subjects. All students study English (Language and Literature), a Modern Language, Mathematics, Biology, Physics and Chemistry to this level and three further examination subjects are taken at GCSE level from Art, Classical Studies, Economics, Geography, German, Greek, History, Latin, Music, Spanish, Design & Technology and Drama. Additionally there is a programme of Art, Drama, Music and Technology for all in Years 7 to 9.

Sixth Formers will normally choose 4 subjects for study to AS Level in the Lower Sixth, and in the Upper Sixth 3 subjects to A Level, most combinations from the following list being possible: Art, Biology, Chemistry, Classical Civilisation, Economics, English, French, Geography, German, Greek, History, Latin, Mathematics, Further Mathematics, Music, Physics, Politics, Psychology, Spanish, Technology, Philosophy, Theatre Studies and Film Studies. There is a substantial course of General Studies available.

Almost all sixth-formers go on to University, and success in gaining entry at Oxford and Cambridge, and medical schools, has been an outstanding feature of the school's record.

Physical Education. All students are required to take part in a Physical Education programme which, up to Year 10, includes Rugby, Football, Cross-Country, Cricket, Athletics, Gymnastics, Hockey, Netball, Tennis, Rounders, Swimming. At the upper end of the School a wider range of activities is offered: in addition to the above students may opt for Badminton, Basketball, Climbing, Fencing, Fitness training, Karate, Orienteering, Squash, Tennis, Table Tennis, Volleyball and Dance. A wide range of activities is available to all through voluntary membership of various Sports Clubs.

Activities. Art, Drama and Music are strong features in the life of the School, all of them overflowing from scheduled lessons into spare-time activity. There are some 30 music groups and ensembles ranging from choirs and orchestras to bands, jazz ensembles, rock groups and an early music consort. There are a number of productions in the theatre each term. Numerous societies meet in the lunchbreak or after school, some linked with school work but many developing from private enthusiasms. There is a thriving Duke of Edinburgh's Award scheme. There is an entirely voluntary Combined Cadet Force Contingent. Annual overseas visits include ski-parties, sporting tours, Classics trips, visits to art galleries and to the battlefields of World War I.

Supervision and Pastoral Care. Each student is within the care of (a) Form Supervisor and (b) Tutor. The latter will normally be associated with the student throughout their school career, and the aim is to forge a personal link with students and their families.

The Careers programme begins in Year 9; in Year 11 and the Sixth Form every possible care is taken to advise each student individually about Careers and Higher Education.

The School's Medical Officers are available regularly for consultation; there is also a School Counsellor.

Buildings. Some of the School's buildings date from 1907 and are described by Pevsner as "friendly neo-Early-Georgian". Recent years have seen many developments and improvements, including the rebuilding of the indoor swimming pool in 1990, the opening in February 1996 of a new Sports Centre, a new Science and Technology Centre which opened in 1997, and new Maths and ICT departments in 1998. A new Junior School extension opened in 2005 and a Performing Arts Centre opened in September 2006.

Junior School. Years 3 and 4 of the Junior School are separately housed in Lambton Road opposite the Senior School playing fields. Years 5 and 6 are housed in a new extension on the main school site. Junior School students use the Sports Centre, Swimming Pool, games fields and dining hall. English and Mathematics are taught by Form Teachers, while Environmental Studies, French, Science, Religious Education, Music, Art and Physical Activities are taken by specialists.

Entrance. Entry is by examination. Application forms are available from the Admissions Secretary.

Junior School at 7+ and 9+. Prospective students attend Assessment Days held in November (7+) and January (9+) when they take part in a number of activities and sit a number of short tests. A reference is sought from previous/current school.

Senior School at 11+. The Senior School examination is held each January for prospective students who will be 11 on 1 September of the year in which entry is desired. Applications by 15 December (later application at School's discretion). A reference is sought from previous/current school.

Sixth Form at 16+. Applicants are considered for direct entry to the Sixth Form if their GCSE results are likely to form an adequate basis. All external candidates are interviewed and a reference is sought from the previous/current school.

Each year a small number of places may be available at entry points other than the main ones listed. Please contact the Admissions Secretary for details.

Term of Entry. Autumn, although a small number of places may become available throughout the year.

Fees per term (2011-2012). Senior School £3,332, Junior School £2,808.

Bursaries. Some bursaries, awarded on the basis of parental income, are offered. They include those awarded by the Ogden Trust, which may cover all fees and expenses depending on parental income. Details are available from the Bursar.

Charitable status. The Newcastle upon Tyne Royal Grammar School is a Registered Charity, number 1114424.

RGS Worcester

Upper Tything, Worcester WR1 1HP
Tel: 01905 613391
Fax: 01905 726892
e-mail: office@rgsw.org.uk
website: www.rgsw.org.uk

The Royal Grammar School Worcester was founded ante 1291, received its Elizabethan Charter in 1561 and was granted its 'Royal' title by Queen Victoria in 1869. The Alice Ottley School was founded in 1883 as Worcester High School for Girls. The two schools merged to form RGS Worcester & The Alice Ottley School in September 2007 and was re-named RGS Worcester in September 2009.

Board of Governors:
Chairman: R A Ingles
Vice-Chairman: R F Ham

F H Briggs	C W Parr
I L Carmichael	J Q S Poole
R G Fry	J Preedy
H Kimberley	S J Shaw
K Meredith	T G Walker

Bursar & Clerk to the Governors: I T Roberts, OBE, MA

Headmaster: A R Rattue, MA

Second Master: P J Lee, BA

Senior Master: N W Lowson, BA

Assistant Heads:
P J Ehlers, MA, PhD (*Sixth Form*)
H Sykes, BSc (*Middle School*)
Mrs A M Fitch (*Lower School*)
S J Richards, BSc (*Academic*)
M J Ridout, BA, MSc (*Academic*)

Teaching Staff:

M Adlington, BA	R T Gibson, MA
S N Alexander, BA	Mrs D M Greenwood,
A J Barr, BSc	CertEd, FPLD
D B Bayliss	H Groves, MA
S M Bee, BA	T J B Hallett, BA, MPhil
D Beer, PhD	M Hamilton, BA
R N Berry, BSc	Mrs D Harkness, BA
S Blincoe-Deval, BSc, MSc	E B Hayton, BSc
Miss R S Briggs, BSc	Mrs S Hobby, BA
P J Carter, BSc	R J Houchin, BA
Mrs G Cartwright, BSc	M A Howard, B.Tech
P Chesworth, BA	S D Howells, BA
A E Clemit, MA	Mrs C A Hunter, BA
Mrs S C Coggins, BSc	Mrs V C James, MA
Mrs S Cooper, BD	Mrs E V Jordan, MA
D J Cotterill, BEd	Mrs L Kettle, MA,
Mrs P Cunnington, BA	MSocSci, BEd
T S Curtis, BA	Mrs E Kilburn, BA
Miss K M Dale, BEd	Mr J G Lyons, MA
S C Davis, BSc	Mrs V McKee Pearson,
Mrs A Dimond, MA (SEN)	MA
Miss E Dovey, MA	Miss J E Marsh, BA
Mrs D Drew, BA	Mrs S A Mather, BA
Miss C Duckworth, BSc	M Matthews, BA
Miss E Dukes, BA	R J Michael, BA
Miss J Dutfield, BA	J D Moffatt, BA
P Evans, BSc	P H Mullins, BSc, PhD
Mrs A J Freeman, BA	P J Newport, BA
J C Friend, BSc	G Nicholas, BEng
Miss L Gallagher, BSc	Mrs S Nicholls, BA

P J O'Sullivan, BSc
Mrs A Park, BA
Miss S E Partridge, BSc
N Phillips, MA
M D Ralfe, MA
J M Shorrocks, BSc, BA
H S Smith, PhD
B D Taylor, BSc
Mrs L F Taylor, BSc
M H Vetch, MA

Mrs E L Walker, BA
J N Waller, MA
Mrs D Warman, BA
J G Wilderspin, BSc, ARCO
M D Wilkinson, BSc
M P Williams, BEd CPhys, MInstP
A N Wood, BSc

Preparatory School: RGS The Grange

Headmaster: G W Hughes, BEd Hons

Deputy Head: S Howkins, BA

Head of Pre-Prep: Mrs S Atkinson, BEd

Teaching Staff:

Mrs J Allen, NNEB (*Nursery*)
Mrs B Ashby, Cert Ed
T C Barnes, MSc
D Bousfield, BA
Mrs V Bradley, BA, SpLD
Miss E M Bussey, BEd
Mrs S Coleman, BA
Mrs M J Corrie, GTCL, LTCL, ALCM
Mrs J Davies, BSc
Mrs M C Egginton, BSc
Miss N Evans, BA

J Hodgkins, BSc
Mrs A E Parish, BEd
Mrs C Roberts, BA
Mrs J Sach, BEd
R Scase, PhD
Miss G Taylor, BSc
Mrs T A Turner, BA
Mrs L Walsh, BSc
Mrs E Walker, BA
Mrs P White, BEd
Mrs M Yarnold, BEd
Mrs R Young, BA

Preparatory School: RGS Springfield

Headmistress: Mrs M Lloyd, BEd CNAA

Teaching Staff:

Mrs P M Arr, CertEd
Mrs D Bennett, NVQ3
Mrs C Carr, CertEd
Mrs E McCabe, BA
Mrs A Myers, BSc
Mrs S Salisbury, BEd
A Powell, BA

Miss N Perrins, BA
Mrs E Walker, BA
Mrs J Walker, BEd
Mrs A Webster, BEd
Mrs G Williams, BEd
Mrs E Williams, BSc

Situation and Buildings. The Senior School is situated a few minutes' walk from the centre of the City and is convenient for rail and bus stations. The Headmaster's office is housed in the Grade II* listed Britannia House, and there are several other historic buildings on the site, including the RGS Main Block, dating from 1868. Educational facilities are outstanding: there are two Sports Halls, specialist Art, ICT, Technology and Textiles rooms, a theatre, library, Science Block, music technology room, and a lecture theatre, as well as several assembly halls. The playing fields and boathouse are close by and the School has good use of the local swimming pool. A full-size, floodlit all-weather pitch was opened in 2007 and a state-of-the-art fitness centre in 2008. A new Dance Studio plus changing facilities, two new Science Laboratories and a Digital Language Laboratory were also completed in 2008.

There are two co-educational Preparatory Schools. RGS The Grange (*see IAPS entry*) is set in 48 acres of grounds to the north of the city and has recently opened a 16 classroom, £4.5 million extension to complement the original Victorian building that houses the Pre-Prep. RGS Springfield (*see IAPS entry*) is housed in a beautiful Georgian building in the centre of the nearby Britannia Square, close to the city centre. It is secluded and secure, and benefits from its close proximity to the Senior School.

Organisation. The Senior School population is c900 (400 girls and 500 boys). The Senior School is divided into three sections – Lower (Years 7 and 8), Middle (Years 9, 10 and 11) and Sixth Form – with an Assistant Head responsible for each. The basic unit is the form, and the form tutor,

under the Head of Year, is responsible for all day to day matters relating to the pupils in their charge. In addition all pupils are placed in Houses which exist mainly for internal competitive purposes, but which do provide an important element of continuity throughout a pupil's career at the School. Both Preparatory Schools admit pupils from the age of two and a half, and most proceed to the Senior School at the age of eleven, into Year 7. RGS The Grange and RGS Springfield are both well known for the high standard of their pastoral care and for stretching the brightest children. Learning Support is particularly well organized.

Aims. A high level of academic achievement is sought within a caring and civilised society. By placing emphasis on a wide range of sporting, artistic and extra-curricular activities, we aim to extend our pupils in as many ways as possible. Overall, we offer a balanced and challenging education which will stand our pupils in good stead for their future careers and within the community at large.

Curriculum. Pupils follow a common curriculum for the first three years in the Senior School which includes the usual academic subjects, plus IT, Design Technology, Music, Drama and PE. The GCSE option arrangements (Years 10 and 11) allow a wide choice, subject to final selection, giving a balanced curriculum which does not prejudice subsequent career decisions. Normally 9–10 subjects are studied: English, Mathematics, a Modern Foreign Language and Sciences being setted and compulsory, plus three from French, German, Latin, Spanish, Geography, History, RE, Drama, Art, Music, Textiles, Design Technology. Most members of the Sixth Form study four subjects to AS Level and at least three to A2 Level. In addition to those subjects studied at GCSE Level, PE, ICT, Classical Civilisation, Business Studies, Economics and Politics may be taken up.

Careers. The School is a member of ISCO; the well-equipped Careers Rooms are readily available and the Head of Careers is responsible for ensuring that all pupils receive basic careers education, and subsequently, access to all the necessary information and experience on which a sound decision may be made regarding future career and Further or Higher Education.

Physical Activities. The School aims to satisfy a wide range of sporting interests and abilities. For boys, Rugby Football, Association Football, Cricket and Athletics are the main activities. Girls take Netball, Hockey and Lacrosse in the winter and spring, and Athletics, Tennis and Rounders during the summer Term. Cross-Country Running and Rowing have a full programme of fixtures. Gymnastics, Trampolining, Basketball and Badminton share priority in the Sports Halls throughout the year, and high quality cricket coaching is given throughout the winter months.

Outdoor Pursuits. Combined Cadet Force and The Duke of Edinburgh's Award Scheme: all pupils may choose to join one or the other at the end of Year 9. The strong CCF comprises Royal Navy, Army and Air Force sections. Good opportunities exist for attachments to regular units in UK and abroad, for flying training, for leadership training and for Adventure Training. Those who choose The Duke of Edinburgh's Award Scheme may work for the Bronze, Silver and Gold Awards, and undertake adventure training and community service.

Other Activities. There is a wide range of clubs and societies. All Lower School pupils receive drama lessons as part of the curriculum and school productions take place each term. School music is also strong: in particular, there is a fine organ, a Big Band, several brass ensembles, two choirs, several smaller vocal ensembles and a very popular Jazz Band. The School fosters a range of international links including regular exchanges with schools in France, Germany, Spain, China and the USA. The School has strong links with schools in the developing world via the World Challenge Organisation, and the school community raises large sums for a range of local, national and international charities every year.

September Admission. This is by our own examination held in February, mainly at 11+ but also at 12+ and 13+. Pupils are also admitted into the Sixth Form on the basis of a test, interview and GCSE results. Exceptionally, pupils may also be examined and admitted at any time of the year. Admission to the Preparatory Schools is by assessment from age 6+ and by classroom visit before this age.

Fees per term (2011-2012). £1,780–£3,244.

Scholarships and Bursaries. Scholarships are offered for academic achievement as well as for music and art of up to 33% remission of fees. Bursaries of up to 100% are also available according to parental means and academic potential. Further details can be obtained from the Registrars at the schools.

Charitable status. RGS Worcester is a Registered Charity, number 1120644. The aim of the charity is the education of boys and girls.

The Royal Hospital School

Holbrook, Ipswich, Suffolk IP9 2RX
Tel: 01473 326200
Fax: 01473 326213
e-mail: admissions@royalhospitalschool.org
website: www.royalhospitalschool.org

The Royal Hospital School is a co-educational full boarding and day school with 700 pupils aged 11 to 18. Founded in Greenwich in 1712 by the Crown Charity, Greenwich Hospital, it moved to its present 200-acre estate overlooking the River Stour in 1933. The School is magnificently situated and well equipped with a recent multi-million pound development programme. The School's ethos is based on a values-driven education where pupils are taught the importance of self-discipline, service to others, commitment and learning skills for later life.

Official Visitor: HRH The Duke of York

Director of Greenwich Hospital: Mr M Sands

Chairman of Governors: Mr H Strutt

Headmaster: Mr H W Blackett, MA Oxon

Deputy Headmaster: Mr J A Lockwood, BEd, MA
Bursar: D Charlton, MBA
Director of Studies and ICT: Dr J Allday, MA Cantab, ALCM, PhD
Director of Teaching and Learning: Mr M R Christmas, MA Oxon
Director of Professional Development: Mrs H Anthony, BA
Director of Pastoral Care: Mrs S E M Godfrey, BA
Director of Co-Curricular: Mr C A Rennison, BSc

Head of Lower School: Mrs J Hewitt, BA
Head of Middle School: Mr C M Graham, BSc
Head of Sixth Form: Mr C J White, MA, PGDL

Head of Ceremonial: Mr J Snoddon, MBE, MSM
Chaplain: Reverend Philip McConnell, MA, BEd, BD, DASE

Teaching Staff:

Art:
Mr G D Ravenhall, BA, PGCE, ATD (*Head of Art*)
Mr D W Hawkley, BA, CertEd
Mrs D K Hitchen, BA
Mrs S L Tansley, BA
Ms R Van Zee, BA

Business Studies:
Mr I V Simmons, BA (*Head of Business Studies*)
Mr T Wood, LLB

Mr J Cullen, BSc
Mr L Thompson, BEd

Careers Office:
Mr D W Hawkley, BA, CertEd (*Head of Careers*)
Mr L Menday, Dip Psych Sport, AIST

Classics:
Mr D J Cousins, BA (*Head of Classics*)
Mr S R Warr, MA, ACP

Design Technology:
Mr P Hall, MA, Adv DipEd, AMIMechE (*Head of Design Technology*)
Mr J R Dugdale, BEd
Mrs S J M Du Toit, BSc
Mr D P Simmons, BEd
Mr A J Wilding, BEd

Drama and Theatre Studies:
Mrs M Bloor-Black, BA (*Head of Drama and Theatre Studies*)
Mr S R Warr, MA, ACP (*Head of School Drama Productions*)
Mr W Bowry, BA, MFA
Mr S Turner, BA, LAMDA

English:
Mr C F Morgan, BA (*Head of English*)
Mr W Bowry, BA, MFA
Mr C Gould, BA
Mrs J Hewitt, BA
Mr T H Hodson, BA Oxon
Mr P Madge, BA
Mrs A Pearson, BEd
Mr L Thompson, BEd

Geography:
Mr L G Frost, BEd, BSc, MA (*Head of Geography*)
Mr H W Blackett, MA Oxon
Miss S J Bourhill, CertEd, LRPS
Mr R J Mann, BA, FCII, FIRM
Miss S L Smith, BA

History:
Ms S L Nicholls, BA (*Head of History*)
Mr M J Barraclough, BA
Mr C D Barker, MA Cantab
Mr J C Herbert, BSc Econ, MA
Mr M R Warren, BA
Miss J M Smith, BA Cantab

Information Technology:
Mr P C Du Toit, BComm, HDE, FDE (*Head of Computing*)
Mr T Wood, LLB

Mathematics:
Mr R Trowern, BSc (*Head of Mathematics*)
Mr P A Cuddihy, BSc
Mrs N J Christison, BSc
Mr C M Graham, BSc
Mr A J Loveland, BSc, ACGI, MA
Mr B Hocking, BEd, MCollP
Mr C A Rennison, BSc
Ms J Wilby, BA
Mr A P Wynn, BA

Media Studies:
Mr S E Maunder, BA (*Head of Media Studies*)

Modern Foreign Languages:
Mr N J Hele, BA (*Head of Modern Foreign Languages*)

French:
Mr N J Hele, BA (*Head of French*)
Miss M C Bigot, MA
Mrs S E M Godfrey, BA
Mr S R Warr, MA, ACP
Miss A Marbaix

German:
Mrs N Mann, MA (*Head of German*)
Mrs H Anthony, BA
Ms S Dannhauer, BA

Spanish:
Mr R G Encinas, BA (*Head of Spanish*)
Ms E Muniz

PSHE:
Mr D W Hawkley, BA, CertEd (*Head of PSHE*)
Mr L R Menday, Dip Psych Sport, AIST
Mrs S L Tansley, BA

PE and Games:
Mr D P Hardman, BA (*Director of Sport*)
Mr T D Topley (*Head of Sporting Development and Master
i/c Cricket*)
Mrs C J Herbert, BSc (*Head of Girls Sport*)
Mrs S J Williams, MA, BEd (*Head of Academic Physical
Education*)
Miss S J Bourhill, CertEd, LRPS
Miss C R Anderson, BA

Politics:
Mr M H Godfrey, BSc (*Head of Politics*)
Mr J C Herbert, BSc, MA

Psychology:
Ms M Brennan, BA (*Head of Psychology*)
Mr J A Lockwood, BEd, MA

Religious Studies:
Mr C J White, MA, PGDL (*Head of Religious Studies*)
Miss C R Anderson, BA
Revd Philip McConnell, MA, BEd, BD, DASE

Sailing:
Mr A Nutton (*Director of Sailing*)
Mr C D Boughton

Science:

Biology:
Mr M A Callow, BSc, MA, CBiol, MIBiol (*Head of
Biology*)
Mr J F Pooley, BEd
Mr A D Quentin, BSc
Mrs C A Stevens, BSc
Miss G Tachauer, BSc

Chemistry:
Mr P G Mussett, BSc (*Head of Chemistry*)
Mrs R M M Gladwell, BSc, MA
Mrs P G Noble, BSc
Mrs A E Skitch, BSc

Physics:
Mr P A Surzyn, BSc (*Head of Physics*)
Dr. J Allday, MA Cantab, PhD, ALCM
Ms N Rouse, BEng
Mrs M Z H Warren, BSc
Miss G Tachauer, BSc

Curriculum Support:
Mrs H Evans, BA, AMBDA (*Head of Curriculum Support*)
Mrs C Allday

Overseas Centre:
Mr D Coleman, BA, DELTA (*Head of English as a Second
Language*)
Mr J Shirley, BA

Music School:
Mr P H Crompton, GRNCM (*Director of Music and Organ
Teacher*)
Mr P McCaffery, BMus Hons, LRAM, ARCM, LTCL
(*Assistant Director of Music*)
Mr R B Jones, ARCM (*Bandmaster*)
Mrs C J T Peacock, MA Cantab (*Head of Vocal Studies*)

Mrs A Mann (*Music School Secretary*)
Miss K Bicknell, BMus, PGDip (*Flute*)
Mr D Bolton, GMus (*Brass*)
Mr T Brown (*Jazz Piano*)
Mr R Caird (*Bagpipes*)
Mrs L Cherry, GMus (*Piano*)
Mr C Cocker (*Clarinet and Saxophone*)
Mrs L Creasey, BA (*Harp*)
Mr G Gillings (*Percussion*)
Ms K Holmes, MMus (*Oboe*)
Miss M K Ingram, BMus RCM (*Violin and Viola*)
Mr S Lock (*Bassoon*)
Miss S Maxwell (*Guitar*)
Mrs M Pells, MA, LRAM (*Cello and Piano*)
Mr D Storer, GTCL, LTCL (*Strings and Bass*)
Miss K Smith (*Singing*)
Miss M J Tricker, Dip RCM (*Oboe*)

House System. With 75% of pupils boarding full time there is a strong House System and the recently completed £18 million programme of refurbishment and development provides superb facilities and accommodation.

Pupils joining the School at 11+ are accommodated in either the boys' or girls' Junior House. These purpose-built Houses accommodate 11 to 13 year olds in 4/6-bedded rooms, with facilities, routines and pastoral care that assists the transition between junior and senior school. Weekly boarding and the opportunity to stay overnight on an ad hoc basis are available for Junior pupils.

At Year 9 (13+) all pupils, whether joining the School at this stage or moving up from the Junior Houses, join a Senior House. One is a new co-educational Day House with both a Housemaster and Housemistress, created specifically for pupils who routinely go home at 6.00pm and, in many cases, use the daily school transport services. There are 4 boys' and 3 girls' Senior Boarding Houses which are each home to approximately 58 boarders and 10 day boarders. Day boarders can choose to go home at around 9pm, after completing their prep and any evening activities, and they may stay overnight in the house on an ad hoc basis. Boarders in Years 9 and 10 share rooms with up to four other pupils and older pupils have double or single studies, often with en-suite facilities.

In the Upper Sixth both boarding and day boys and girls join Nelson House, where they learn to live more independently in preparation for university.

Curriculum and Academic Development. The School's curriculum shadows the National Curriculum Key Stages 3 and 4. On joining the School, pupils are placed in forms on the basis of assessed ability from entrance testing or at 13+ the results of Common Entrance examinations. The School subscribes to the Durham University Value Added Measuring Scheme at all levels, allowing tutors to map pupil progress. In core subjects setting takes place from the outset and at GCSE level setting occurs in all core curriculum subjects. The working week consists of up to 38 x 55min periods over a two weekly timetable.

Lower School (Years 7–9): The subjects studies are English, mathematics, science (biology, physics and chemistry), modern foreign languages (core French with additional options of Spanish and German), Latin, geography, history, design technology, art, drama, IT (Information Technology), music, religious studies, PHSE (Personal, Social and Health Education) and PE. There are usually four forms in Years 7 and 8, rising to five in Year 9. The average class size varies from about 16 to 20 pupils. Homework is set daily and both boarders and day pupils in Years 7 and 8 complete it with supervision during the working day. In Year 9 homework is done by boarders and day boarders during the evening in the boarding houses or by day pupils at home.

Middle School (Years 10 and 11): GCSE courses start in Year 10 and most pupils will study 10 subjects including English language and literature, mathematics, a modern foreign language, physics, chemistry, biology (either as three separate sciences or as the dual award) as the core subjects and three options from history, geography, PE (Physical Education and Sports Science), French, German, Spanish, media studies, religious studies, art, music, theatre studies, design technology and business studies.

Sixth Form (Years 12 and 13): Pupils choose four AS followed by three or four A2 options from 26 subjects. Subject choice depends upon average point scores at GCSE and grades gained in specific subjects. All pupils are encouraged to follow the Sixth Form Enrichment and Activities Programmes which may include GCSE Russian or Greek, AS Law, Community Action, music and culture, community sports leadership, Young Enterprise Scheme and other activities and interest useful for University applications and personal statements. Almost all pupils go to the University of their choice, and approximately 50% to Russell Group and other top-class universities.

Pupils' progress is formally monitored by means of at least two assessments or reports per term which grade the academic performance and effort of the pupil. Every pupil has a personal tutor and weekly tutorial meetings are an opportunity to deal with any problems and check on progress.

All pupils have access to computers in their boarding or day house as well as in the IT department and computer suites around the school. Every pupil has his or her own email address and electronic communication is regularly used by teaching staff. There is dedicated teaching in the use of computers for younger pupils.

Through high quality, enthusiastic teaching, excellent resources and dedicated tutorial support, every pupil is encouraged to aim high and achieve his or her personal best. The most able pupils' potential is realised through the mentoring of scholars, a gifted and talented scheme and Oxbridge preparation.

Sport and Leisure. The facilities include ninety-six acres of playing fields, golf course, shooting range, assault course, sports hall, large heated indoor swimming pool, squash courts, tennis and netball courts and an all-weather sports surface. The School has a strong sailing tradition and all pupils joining in Year 7 receive sailing instruction to RYA Level 2. For those who wish to continue with their sailing, the School keeps a fleet of 40 dinghies on the adjacent Alton Water Reservoir, as well as traditional Cornish Shrimpers on the River Stour. The main sports are rugby, hockey, netball, cricket, athletics, cross-country, rounders, football, tennis, riding and swimming. The swimming pool also offers opportunities for canoeing and sub-aqua.

Music and Drama. The School has a particularly strong musical tradition and has recently opened a state-of-the-art £3.6m Music School with recital hall, specialist rooms, technical suite and "rock room". Almost half the pupils are involved in music on a regular basis. The Chapel is of cathedral proportions and has one of the finest organs in Europe, much used by pupils as well as professional performers. Peripatetic teachers offer tuition in a wide range of instruments and the choir and chamber choir perform both nationally and internationally. As well as drama in the curriculum, productions are often combined with the music department for whole school performances and there is a full programme of plays, competitions and festivals each year.

CCF and Community Service. All pupils participate in the Combined Cadet Force in Years 9 and 10 and are able to choose between Army, Naval, RAF and Royal Marine Sections. The emphasis is on adventure training and personal development. More that 300 pupils take part in The Duke of Edinburgh's Award Scheme and 100 of these to Gold Award. The Community Action Team promotes the School's social responsibility and is actively involved in a wide range of charitable activities and involves the School in the local community. Pupils are encouraged to give something back to the community in which they live.

Religion. The core values of the School are based on the Christian faith but pupils from a variety of religions and cultural backgrounds attend the School and all beliefs are respected, The magnificent Chapel, that holds over 1,000 people, is the spiritual hub of school life and the whole community gathers there most mornings for worship.

Admission. Entry to the School is normally at 11, 13 and 16 years. Pupils are asked to sit an entrance examination, comprising papers in English, mathematics and verbal reasoning, in the January prior to the September of the year of entry unless following Common Entrance for entry in Year 9. Entry into the Sixth Form is subject to an average GCSE point score of at least 5.5 (A=7, B=6, C=5) and specific grades in chosen AS subjects. Entry is also subject to an interview with the Headmaster and a satisfactory reference from the pupil's current school.

Fees per term (2011-2012). Boarding: £6,655 (Years 7 and 8), £7,663 (Years 9–13). Day: £3,959 (Years 7 and 8), £4,153 (Years 9–13). Day Boarders: £4,999 (Years 9–13). Discounts are available for services families eligible for the MOD Continuity of Education Allowance (CEA) and siblings where three or more children are in the School at any time.

Scholarships. (*See Scholarship Entries section.*) Scholarships are awarded annually, at the Headmaster discretion, for academic excellence, musical talent, sport and for sailing to pupils entering at 11+, 13+ or 16+.

Bursaries. The parent charity, Greenwich Hospital, awards generous means-tested bursaries and discounts to the children and grandchildren of seafarers. Children of serving or retired Naval personnel are actively encouraged to apply.

Charitable status. The Royal Hospital School is owned by Greenwich Hospital which is a Crown Charity. The School exists to provide education for boys and girls aged from 11 to 18.

Royal Russell School

Coombe Lane, Croydon, Surrey CR9 5BX

Tel: 020 8657 4433
Fax: 020 8657 0207
e-mail: headmaster@royalrussell.co.uk
website: www.royalrussell.co.uk

Royal Russell School is a co-educational, boarding and day school, founded in 1853 by members of the textile trade. Set in 100 acres of woodland, it enjoys very easy access to London, the South, and the airports at Gatwick and Heathrow. There are nearly 900 pupils of whom 162 are in the Sixth Form and 286 in the Junior School.

Motto: *Non Sibi Sed Omnibus*

Patron: Her Majesty The Queen

President: R P Green

Vice-Presidents:
J P B Hecks
P E Reynolds
B J Welch
R N Martin

Board of Governors and Trustees:

Chairman: K Young
Deputy Chairman: P J McCombie

Mrs A D Greenwood	A Merriman
C T Shorter	Dr A Fernandes
Mrs P Hornby	Mrs E Brown
Dr D J Begley	J Penny
Mrs S M Loughlin	Mrs A Martin
S Kolesar	P Moor

Senior School

Headmaster: **C J Hutchinson**, BMet Sheffield, PGCE

Deputy Head – Pastoral: Mrs S Thomas-Webb, BA Leeds, MA OU

Deputy Head – Administration: D J Selby, BA Durham

Director of Studies: G R Moseley, BEd, MA

Assistant Staff:
* *Head of Department*
† *Housemaster/Housemistress*
§ *Part-time*

†J Piggin, BA (*History*)
†M J Tanner, BSc, MA (**Geology, Marketing Director*)
N A Marshall, BEd (**Biology*)
Mrs A R Roseweir, BSc
K W Owens, DipAD (**Art & Design, Child Protection Officer*)
†J Davies, BSc (**PE*)
†Miss K J Palenski, BA MA
Miss M P Latessa, DLing, RSA Cert TEFLA (**EFL*)
Mrs M J Clower, BA, ALA (*Librarian*)
H R Sutton, BA, ARCM, MEd (**Director of Music*)
†S J Keable-Elliott, BA (**Politics*)
†S J Greaves, BSc (**Examinations Officer*)
†Miss M J Davenport, BA
Mrs S Lower, BA, MSc (**Learning Support*)
P J Endersby, BSc (**Science*)
P C Cook, BSc
†Mrs J Kirby-Jones, CertEd, DipEd (**Food Technology*)
A W Moore, BA
Mrs S M Culbert, MA, MA EdMan, DipM (**Careers and PHSE, Head of Sixth Form*)
M L Stanley, BA, MBA EdMan (**Mathematics*)
Mrs D I Pepperdine, BA
Miss F S Cassim, BA
G Parmar, Cert/Dip CDT & IT
Mrs A Mawer, BA (**Modern Languages*)
Mrs G Missan, BSc, BA (**Spanish*)
†Mrs S M Strutt, BSc
Miss C A Roe, BSc
J S Baron, BSc (**Chemistry*)
C P Dear, BA (**Media Studies*)
M C Finch, BEd (**Design Technology*)
Miss L T Hicks, BA (**Girls' Physical Education*)
N P Rocca, BA (**Business Studies*)
J I Bueno, Basque University
E S Hutchinson, BA (**History*)
§Mrs S Milton-Thompson, BSc
§Mrs M Womack, GMus
Revd S J Padfield, MA, BA
Ms D Baldwin, BA
Ms E Cripps, CertEd (**Drama*)
Miss S Calvet, FLE
Miss L Faulkner, BA
D Jewiss, BEd
Mrs L Smith, BSc, MA
Ms C Allison, BEd, MA, MA (**English*)
Mrs F Taylor, GIBiol
M Callow, MA
§Mrs V Corcoran, CertEd, MA
Mrs H Hadjam, BCom
Mrs J Jordan, BEd
A R Moore, BEd, CertEd, CLT, FCoT
Mrs K Hanna, BSc
§Mrs B Johnsson, BA
Miss K El-Asmar, BA
Ms R Demuynck-Grove, BTec, HND
Mrs M Wade, BA
Miss A Conde del Rio, PhD
Miss Hiroko Kato
§M Muchall, BA, MA

A Tansley, BSc
C Donegan, BSc
M Dunton, BSc, MEd (**Geography*)
A Karagiannis, BA (**ICT*)
S Culliford, BSc
Ms L Green, BA
R Khuman BSc
J Muir, BA

Houses and Housestaff:

Boarding:
Cambridge: J Piggin
Oxford: S Greaves
Queen's: Miss M Davenport

Day:
Buchanan: Mrs J Kirby-Jones
Keable: E Hutchinson
Madden: M J Tanner
Reade: Miss K J Palenski
St Andrews: S Keable-Elliott
Hollenden: Mrs S Strutt

Junior School
Headmaster: J Thompson, BA QTS Surrey
Deputy Head – Head of Upper Juniors: Miss H Hughes, BSc, PGCE, MA EdMgt

Mrs R Coker, BEd	Mrs L Soyvural, BAGA
D Naidoo, HrDipEd	Mrs J Quinn, BEd Hons
Mrs S Macpherson, BA	F Appleby (*Head of Music*)
R Hoyle, BEd, MA, PhD	J Hughes, BA, MSc, PGCE
P Venier, BEd	Mrs L Woolfe, BEd
Mrs J Bennett, BA, PGCE	Mrs M Lindsay
Mrs F Rizvi, BA, MA, PGCE	Mrs L Lloyd, BA

Lower Juniors & Early Years Department
Deputy Head – Head of Lower Juniors: Mrs A Flynn, BA QTS, MA Ed

Mrs C Trim, CertEd	Mrs A Netherway, BSc, PGCE
Mrs S Fladgate, BEd	
Miss J Lingley, BA, PGCE	Ms S Wilson, MA, BEd
Mrs A King, BEd	Mrs J Moseley, CertEd
Mrs H Walsh, CertEd	Mrs J Wragg, BA, PGCE

Learning Support:
Mrs S Lower, BA, MSc
Mrs F Blount, CertEd

Bursar: P Barlow

Admissions Registrar: Mrs M King

Medical Officer: Dr S A Shaikh, MB BS, DRCOG, MRCGP
Medical Centre Sister-in-Charge: Mrs S Smith, RSCN
Boys' Assistant Housemistress: Mrs P Jeffree
Girls' Assistant Housemistress: Miss D Cripps

Number in School. In the Senior School there are 608 pupils: 123 boarders, 485 day pupils. Of these, 325 are boys, 283 girls. In the Junior School there are 285 pupils: 152 boys and 133 girls.

Admission. Most pupils enter the school in the Autumn term at the age of 3+, 11 or 13. Space permitting pupils may be considered and admitted at other ages and there is a direct entry into the Sixth Form.

Religion. The school's religious affiliation is to the Church of England but pupils of all persuasions are welcome. Our approach to daily life is founded on Christian principles and we try to maintain an atmosphere of mutual respect, affection and understanding.

The resident Chaplain is responsible for the conduct of all services and the teaching of Religious Education throughout the school. Weekly Chapel assemblies allow a brief act of worship and an opportunity to share ideas and concerns. The

Sunday service is compulsory for those boarders at school, and the voluntary Eucharist is specifically for those with a Christian commitment. Enquiries regarding Confirmation to the Church of England are encouraged.

Curriculum. The keynote of curriculum organisation is flexibility and there is close alignment with the requirements of the National Curriculum. In the early years everyone follows a curriculum designed to give a sound foundation across a broad range of subjects. Equipped with this experience pupils are helped in selecting their GCSE examination subjects from a wide range including Information Technology and Drama. Great care is taken to achieve balance in each pupil's timetable and to ensure that an appropriate number of subjects is studied.

A high proportion of pupils continue to the Sixth Form where, typically, four subjects are studied in Year 12 with three continuing into Year 13. At present A Level courses available are Mathematics, Further Mathematics, Information Technology, History, Geography, Geology, Physics, Chemistry, Biology, English, Business Studies, Economics, Politics, French, Spanish, Drama and Theatre Arts, Media Studies, Art and Design, Design and Technology, Music, Food Technology and Physical Education.

It is our expectation that all pupils will leave the Sixth Form to go on to higher education and we regularly secure places at Oxford and Cambridge for our strongest students.

Facilities. The School lies in 100 acres of grounds providing excellent academic and sporting facilities for all age groups.

Recent new-build and refurbishment programmes have transformed the boarding houses and provided a purpose-built School Library and Sixth Form Study Centre.

In summer 2004, the extension to our Sports Hall was opened to provide a Sports Centre with an additional Gymnasium and changing facilities.

Other recent improvements have included a new Swimming Pool, six Computer Laboratories, a Food Technology room, a CDT Centre and a Language Laboratory.

A detached Science building contains six modern and very well equipped laboratories.

An outstanding purpose-built Music and Performing Arts building was opened in December 2010 along with a new kitchen, servery and Sixth Form Café facility.

Careers. The Head of Careers coordinates Careers advice, giving individual counselling and helping with all University applications. The School is a member of the Independent Schools Careers Organisation whose services are available to all pupils. Towards the end of the Summer Term work experience placements are organised for those who have completed GCSE examinations, and members of the Lower Sixth participate in organised visits to Universities and Colleges.

Organisation. The Senior School is divided into nine Houses each of approximately 60 pupils, 2 boarding and 3 day for boys, 1 boarding and 3 day for girls. Each House has its own premises, Housemaster or Housemistress and assistant House Tutors. All Sixth Formers are accommodated in single or double study bedrooms, fully carpeted and newly furnished. The members of the school fall into three categories: full boarders, weekly boarders and day pupils. It is expected that all pupils should be able and encouraged to participate as fully as possible in the extra-curricular life of the school, becoming involved in evening and weekend activities, irrespective of their status. Supervised homework sessions are provided for day pupils participating in evening activities and they attend supper with the boarders. Tutors play a vital pastoral and academic role, monitoring overall progress and development.

Games. The main games are hockey, cricket, soccer, netball, tennis and athletics. There are four hard tennis courts, a gymnasium, a Sports Hall, a heated indoor swimming pool and a small bore rifle range. Badminton, basketball, volleyball and judo are popular. It is possible to go riding.

Music, Drama and Art. Music in the Senior School is in the hands of the Director of Music whilst the Assistant Director of Music concentrates on the Junior School. They are assisted by a large number of visiting teachers. There is a Senior School Orchestra and smaller wind, brass and string ensembles. Choral Society, Chapel Choir and Junior School Choir and Orchestra meet and perform regularly. A new Junior School Music Centre has recently opened.

Drama is taught as part of the Creative Studies programme in the lower school and is available at GCSE and A Level where pupils make use of our Drama Studio.

Instruction is offered in a wide range of Artistic techniques using a variety of materials – paint, ink, screen printing, ceramics and pottery.

Clubs and Activities. Computer, Young Engineers, Art, Drama, Dance, Pottery and Chess Clubs are very popular and meet regularly.

There is a flourishing voluntary CCF unit. There are regular camps and weekend activities and The Duke of Edinburgh's Award Scheme operates. The school's involvement in Model United Nations programmes is unique in this country. The annual October conference attracts 400 student delegates from all over the world.

Junior School. The aim in the Junior School is to prepare pupils as thoroughly as possible for entry to the Senior School. The Junior and Early Years Section provides a happy, secure and purposeful environment for those just starting school and during the early years of schooling. (*For full details please see our entry in the IAPS section.*)

Scholarships. A number of scholarships are available each year to pupils aged 11+ to 13+ who show particular academic promise. Sixth Form scholarships are also awarded annually. Special awards are available to members of the Armed Forces.

For further details or an appointment to visit the school apply to the Headmaster.

Fees per term (2011-2012). Senior School: Boarders £9,370 (Years 9–13), £6,930 (Years 7 & 8); Day £4,740 (inclusive of lunch and supper). Junior School: Years 3–6 £3,500 (inclusive of lunch and supper), Reception–Year 2 £2,865 (inclusive of lunch), Kindergarten £1,265–£2,865 (full day inclusive of lunch).

Charitable status. Russell School Trust is a Registered Charity, number 271907. It exists solely for the education of boys and girls.

Rugby School

Rugby, Warwickshire CV22 5EH
Tel: 01788 556216 (Head Master)
      01788 556260 (Bursar)
      01788 556274 (Registrar)
Fax: 01788 556219 (Head Master)
      01788 556267 (Bursar)
      01788 556277 (Registrar)
e-mail: head@rugbyschool.net (Head Master)
         bursar@rugbyschool.net (Bursar)
         registry@rugbyschool.net (Registrar)
website: www.rugbyschool.net

Motto: '*Orando Laborando*'

Rugby School was founded in the year 1567 by Lawrence Sheriff, native of Rugby, one of the Gentlemen of the Princess Elizabeth, a Grocer and Second Warden of the Grocers' Company. The School was endowed with estates in the neighbourhood of Rugby and in London. In 1750 the School moved to its present site on the edge of Rugby town. Between 1809 and 1814 the Head Master's House, School House and the Old Quad were built. Under Dr Arnold and subsequent Head Masters, including two later Archbishops of Canterbury, Rugby was influential in establishing the pattern of independent education throughout the country.

There are currently 790–810 pupils in the School (45% girls : 55% boys) of whom around 20% are day pupils.

Rugby values scholarship, team work in games, music and drama, and qualities of leadership and self-reliance in the pupils. Rugby prides itself on a sharp edge of academic excellence but its aim, as a fully co-educational school, is to encourage cooperation, seeing a wide range of enterprises through to their conclusion, an awareness of the wider world and a lively approach to a very broad range of opportunity. The boys and girls who come to Rugby are expected to have a go at a variety of things. As they leave they should feel ready for (almost) anything; that they have stretched themselves and have been asked to do a great deal; and finally that along the way life at Rugby has been fun.

Governing Body:
R W A Swannell, Esq, FCA (*Chairman*)
Mrs P A Williams, BA, ACA (*Deputy Chairman*)
C H E Imray, Esq, FRCS
The Lord Lieutenant of Warwickshire, M Dunne, Esq, JP
The Rt Revd the Lord Bishop of Birmingham, D A
  Urquhart
Sir R H Friend, FRS
M J Mansell, Esq, LLB Hons
Lady S McFarlane, MCSP
T R Cookson, Esq, MA
R W B Williams, Esq, MA
Mrs L Holmes, BA
R Hingley, Esq, MA
E Wood, OBE, DL, MSc, EdD, Hon LLD
M Ruffell, Esq
P Bennett-Jones, Esq, MA
D Bennet, Esq, MA
Mrs F Hughes-D'Aeth, MA
C Howe, Esq

Bursar and Clerk to the Governing Body: G Lydiatt, BSc,
  FCCA

Medical Officer: Dr P J Kilvert, BSc, MB BS, DRCOG,
  DCH

Head Master: P S J Derham, MA

Deputy Head: Mrs S A Rosser, BEd

Assistant Heads:
Dr N G Hampton, MA, PhD
K J McLaughlin, MA
M Semmence, BA

Registrar: H G Steele-Bodger, MA

Assistant Teaching Staff:

Chaplaincy:
The Revd R M Horner, BSc (*Chaplain*)
Miss L Greatwood, BSc

Classics:
Miss C Le Hur, MA (*Head of Department*)
A Christie, MA
Miss R Coombs, BA
T J Day, BA
Miss E J R Nicoll, BA
H W F Price, MA

Design:
C P John, BA, FRSA (*Director of the Design Centre*)
A D Bradbury, BA, AIIP (*Head of Photography &
  Graphics*)
P A Byrne, BA (*Head of D & T*)
R B Drennan, DSD, CDS (*Director of Theatre
  Productions, Head of Media*)
M Howard, DipAD (*Head of Art*)

Mrs S Murenu, BA Hons (*Head of Drama & Theatre
  Studies*)
Miss A K Hardy, BSc
Mrs S E Phillips, BA (*Ceramics*)
Miss J Rayner, BA
P Shelley, BA
M R Williams, BA

Economics and Business Studies:
P J Shipley, MA (*Head of Department*)
A J Darby, BA
P J Rosser, BA
M Semmence, BA
H G Steele-Bodger, MA

English:
A Fletcher, MA (*Head of Department*)
R J Smith, MA (*Second in Department*)
Mrs B C Almond (*Head of Learning Support*)
Mrs E M Barlow, BA
Mrs E M Beesley, MA
J B Cunningham-Batt, BA
A J Naylor, BA
Mrs J Scanlon, MA
A T Shaw, PhD, MA
J A Sutcliffe, PhD

Geography:
J C Evans, BA (*Head of Department*)
Mrs A J V Moreland, BEd
Mrs S A Rosser, BEd
A E Smith, BSc, MPhil, PhD, FRMetS, FRGS
Mrs A D Tooke, BSc

History:
G Spreng, MA (*Head of Department*)
T Beaumont, MA
E A Beesley, BA, PhD
P S J Derham, MA
P W Dewey, BA
F J Hemming-Allen, BEd, MEd
Miss K Hollings, BA
J D Muston, MA, MPhil, DPhil
Mrs A Naylor, BA

Information Technology:
Miss L Dixon, BSc (*Head of Department*)
T E Rennoldson, BSc
A M Waples

Mathematics:
P Jewell, BSc (*Head of Department*)
M A Hennings, BA (*Second in Department*)
P K Bell, MA
Miss G L Dixon, BA
C J Edwards, MA
Miss H Grant, BSc
J E Ingram, MMath
A J Siggers, BSc
R Higson, MA
B Rigg, MA

Modern Languages:
D Gillett, BA (*Head of Department*)
Mrs J M Jordan, BA, (*Second in Department*)
Mrs W J Corvi, Bed
R M Horner, BSc
N D Jarvis, BA, MA
Mrs R Kayada, BA
Dr A C Leamon, BA, MA, PhD
A M Maguire, BA
Mrs C A M O'Mahoney, BA
Miss S Perkins, BA
J C Smith, MA, DPhil

Music:
R Dunster-Sigtermans, MA, BMus, FRCO, ARCM
(*Director of Music*)
T W Bentham, BA (*Head of Brass*)
Mrs A Brogaard (*Head of Strings*)
R F Colley, MA, DipRAM, LRAM, ARCM (*Head of Piano*)
D Eno, BMus (*Head of Woodwind*)
M C Martin, BMus, LTCL (*Cello & Music Technology*)
J A Williams, MA

Philosopher in Residence:
Miss E L Williams, MA

Physical Education:
F J Hemming-Allen, BEd, MEd (*Head of PE*)
S J Brown, BSc (*Director of Boys' Games*)
Mrs L Hampton, MSc, BEd (*Director of Girls' Games*)
Miss H E Grant, BSc

Politics:
P Teeton, BA (*Head of Department*)
E Trelinski, MA

Science:
M A Thompson, BSc (*Head of Science*)
M A Monteith, BSc (*Head of Biology*)
A G Davies, BSc (*Head of Physics*)
T M White, BSc (*Head of Chemistry*)
Mrs N Cannock, BSc
R Dhanda, BSc
C Douglas, BEd
Miss H E Grant, BSc
Miss L J Greatwood, BSc
Mrs G Harris, BSc
Mrs L M Hampton, BEd, BSc
N Hampton, MA, PhD
J H G Jarvis, BSc, MSc
K J McLaughlin, MA
R B McGuirk, BSc
N J Morse, BSc, PhD, CChem, MRSC
P D Richard BSc
Mrs C Shelley, BEd
E G Taylor, PhD
J L Taylor, BA, BPhil, DPhil
E A Tilley, BSc

Careers and Higher Education: Mrs D J Horner, BA
Rackets Professional: P J Rosser, BA
Sports Centre: H D P Bennett (*Manager*)

Houses and Housemasters/mistresses:

Boarding Houses (boys):
Cotton: Mr Matt Williams
Kilbracken: Dr Justin Muston
Michell: Mr Tim Day
School Field: Dr Ed Beesley
School House: Dr Nick Morse
Sheriff: Mr Henry Price
Whitelaw: Dr Andrew Smith

Day Boy House:
Town: Mr Tony Darby

Boarding Houses (girls):
Bradley: Mrs Monica Barlow
Dean: Miss Amy Hardy
Griffin: Mrs Anne Naylor
Rupert Brooke: Mrs Colette O'Mahoney
Stanley (Sixth Form only): Mrs Carlien Shelley
Tudor: Mrs Debbie Horner

Day Girl House:
Southfield: Mrs Lizzie Beesley

Junior Day House (boys and girls):
Marshall: Mr Barrie Cunningham-Batt

Director of Development: Mrs K Wilson

Situation. Rugby is situated near the junction of the M1 and M6 motorways and is not far from the M40. It is just one hour by hourly rail service from London (Euston) and is close to Birmingham International Airport as well as being within easy reach of Heathrow. Though the School is close to the countryside and has a 150-acre campus with a full range of facilities and games fields, it is essentially a town school and has the practical advantages of links with industry and opportunities for experience and service in the wider world.

Facilities. The main classroom block, the Macready Theatre, the Chapel, the Temple Reading Room and Gymnasium were designed by William Butterfield and to these have been added further buildings of architectural distinction, among them the Temple Speech Room and the Science Schools.

Since then there have followed a Multimedia Language Laboratory, IT Centre, a state-of-the-art Design Centre, housing Art, Design and Technology, History of Art, Photography and a professional standard TV studio for Media.

Other developments include a Sports Centre, opened by HRH The Duchess of Kent in 1990, and recently extended to include a new cafeteria, seminar room and fitness suite. There are extensive floodlit astroturf pitches and hard courts for hockey, tennis and netball. The Lewis Gallery, a new art and design exhibition space was opened in 2006 and is proving very popular with professional artists. In October 2008 HRH the Earl of Wessex opened the refurbished Science School and in April 2009 Lord Coe unveiled a plaque celebrating the link between Thomas Arnold, Pierre de Coubertin and the Modern Olympic Movement.

The School is fully networked. All pupils have a laptop computer for use in the classroom and all classrooms are equipped with Promethean Boards.

Boarding Houses. All boarding houses undergo a continuous programme of improvement. Houses provide small dormitories of 4 to 6 in the first one or two years and study-bedrooms thereafter. Meals are eaten in House Dining Halls.

GCSE. All the usual subjects are offered as well as German, Spanish, Latin, Greek, Design, Art and Music.

AS/A2. A2 Level is offered in all the GCSE subjects as well as in Economics, Business Studies, English Language, PE, Media, Theatre Studies, History of Art and Politics. AS Level is offered in Graphics, Music Technology, Italian and Religious Studies. Increasingly popular are the newly accredited Extended Projects which include Perspectives on Science, Culture and Identity. Other EPs include Culture and Identity, Digital Innovation, The Global Environment, Performance, Engineering Technology, Chemistry Investigation and People, Power and Wealth. All boys and girls go on to Higher Education and about 10% receive Oxbridge offers.

There are several learned societies and each academic department invites distinguished speakers to the School. Recent speakers include Lord Hurd, Lord Falconer, Anthony Seldon, Lord Carey and Giles Clarke.

Spiritual life. The experience of holiness, an understanding of right and wrong, and respect for the worth of each human being are the bonds of community. These values are learned in every part of our lives, but the School Chapel and the activities connected with it are a particular focus.

There are two full-time chaplains, one male and one female, who involve themselves with all the School's activities. On Mondays, Wednesdays and Fridays the School day begins with a ten-minute service in Chapel. On Sundays there is usually a morning service for the majority of the pupils, often with a guest preacher.

There is an active Christian Union, and a weekly service of meditation with Holy Communion, both of which are optional for the pupils. Members of faiths other than Christian are encouraged to attend worship and instruction within their own faith.

Sport. Sports include Athletics, Badminton, Basketball, Cricket, Cross-country, Fencing, Football, Golf, Gymnastics, Hockey, Judo, Netball, Polo, Rackets, Riding, Rugby, Sailing, Squash, Sub Aqua, Swimming and Tennis.

Activities. All boys and girls are encouraged to undertake a full programme of extra-curricular activities. The School aims to ensure that music touches the lives of all pupils as well as catering for outstanding musicians. With School, House and visiting productions and a very well-equipped theatre, drama is well to the fore. Other activities include Ballet, Canoeing, Camping, CCF, Choirs, Climbing, Duke of Edinburgh's Award, First Aid, Orienteering, Pottery, Sculpture, Target and Clay-pigeon shooting, Silver-smithing, Social Service, Television Production and School Journalism. The aim is to give all boys and girls a wide variety of experience so that they can excel in a few things but understand and develop some appreciation of most areas.

Entry. Entry for boys and girls is at 13+ by Common Entrance, Scholarship, or – for those from schools which do not prepare for Common Entrance – by interview, report and specially designed tests. All 13+ boarding applicants attend a pre-assessment interview five terms before they join the School, following which conditional places are offered subject to passing Common Entrance with an average of at least 55%. Day pupil places are offered two years before entry, following an interview and a computerised test, and are also subject to success at Common Entrance.

Boys and girls also enter the Sixth Form on the basis of written examinations in their proposed A level subjects, interviews and a report from the current school, or by scholarship.

The Junior Department. At age 11 boys and girls enter Marshall House as day pupils by taking a computerised test. Foundation Scholarships and Music Scholarships are available at this stage. There is one class of 11-year-olds and one of 12-year-olds. Classes run from 8.45 am to 4.00 pm. A full programme of extra-curricular activities is offered, most of it based on the Senior School's extensive facilities. All of the teaching is done by staff from the Senior School but Marshall House has its own Head.

Scholarships. (*See Scholarship Entries section*.)

Fees per term (2011-2012). The consolidated termly fee for boys and girls: £9,725 (boarding), £6,060 (day). Junior Department: £3,570 (Marshall House).

Optional charge for instrumental or singing tuition: £265.

Further Information. Full information about the School's aims, its academic curriculum, facilities and activities will be found in the School's prospectus (available on the School website: www.rugbyschool.net). Enquiries and applications should be made in the first instance to the Registrar who will be pleased to arrange for parents to visit the School and to meet members of the staff and the Head Master.

'**The freedom, sophistication and civilisation of Rugby struck me as absolutely miraculous. I just loved my time there.**' (Robert Hardy, actor).

Charitable status. The Governing Body of Rugby School is a Registered Charity, number 528752. It exists to provide education for young people.

Rydal Penrhos School

Pwllycrochan Avenue, Colwyn Bay, North Wales LL29 7BT
Tel: 01492 530155
Fax: 01492 531872
e-mail: info@rydal-penrhos.com
website: www.rydal-penrhos.com

Penrhos College was founded by Thomas Payne in 1880 as a Methodist girls' school; its neighbour, Rydal School, was founded five years later by Thomas Osborn, also as a Methodist boarding school. In 1999, after just over a century of co-existence, the Schools merged under the name of Rydal Penrhos; now Rydal Penrhos School. A second merger took place in 2003 when Rydal Penrhos Preparatory School merged with another local prep school, Lyndon School. The school is fully co-educational from 3 to 18, with a total roll of 620 pupils.

The Governors:
Chairman: The Revd Philip Barnett
Vice-Chairman: Mr J I Morris

Mr N Bickerton	Mr J Payne
Mr M P Bream	Mr D J S Rae
Mr J P Burgess	Mr G Russell
Mr P V Dixon	Mr P D S Slater
Mr R W Dransfield	Mrs B A M Watson
Mrs D A Draper	Dr S Wigley
Dr G J Green	Mr J M A Wilford
Mr D C Lewis	
Revd M J A Long	*Honorary Governor:*
Mrs P E Morris	Mrs E P Jones

Headmaster: P A Lee-Browne, MA

Head of Preparatory School: R McDuff, BEd Hons, MA
Chaplain: The Revd N Sissons, MA
Director of Finance: Miss K Baines
Deputy Head: T Cashell, BEd
Deputy Head (Academic): J P Noad, BSc
Head of Sixth Form: J Matthews, BA
Head of Lower School: Mrs I M Proudlove, CertEd
Director of Studies: Mrs S Harding, BA

Assistant staff:
* *Head of Department*
† *Houseparent*

A Akram, BSc (*Chemistry)
Miss S Ashworth, BA (*Learning Support*)
A P Bathie, BSc (*Registrar*)
P Baxter, BEd
Dr M F Brown, BSc, PhD (†*Walshaw*)
Mrs S Brown, BA, MSc
Mrs S M Brummitt, BA (**Religious Studies*)
Mrs A Cashell, BEd (*Learning Support)
Mrs N J Cosgrove, BA (**Girls' Games*)
Ms L Cunnah, BA (*Drama)
Dr D G Edwards, BA, DPhil (*English)
M J Farnell, BA (*ICT)
Mrs P P Healy, BEd
Miss R Hearn, BMus (*Music)
Miss R Hughes, BA
B Jones, BEd
Miss P Jones, BSc
M T Leach, BSc (*Games)
Ms A Margerison, BSc (*Biology)
P J Mather, BEd (**Boys' Games and Activities;* †*Hathaway*)
Mrs J Mottershead, BSc
Mrs G Murphy, BA
J B Murphy, BA (†*Netherton*)
E M Parri BA
G V Price, BSc (*Physics)
B J Proudlove, BA
I Richardson, BSc, MSc (†*Beecholme*)
Mrs M Richardson, BA
Dr G Roberts, BSc, PhD
D Robson, BSc, BEng (*Science)
Dr P Rowlands, BSc, PhD (*Mathematics)
P W Russell, BA
Miss J K Simpkins, BA (*EFL)
P D Stevenson, BA

Mrs B Taylor, BA (*†Edwards*)
Mrs K Teal-Shaw, BA, MEd (**Art & Technology*)
R Tickner, BA, MA (**MFL*)
Ms C Vallée Licence, LLCE
S C Wales, BA (**History*)
Mrs S Walsh, BA
Dr A Warrington, BSc, MSc, PhD
Ms N Wynne-Jones, BA

Admissions Officer: Mrs J Marsden

Situation and Buildings. Rydal Penrhos School is within 45 minutes drive of Chester, and only 1 hour away from Manchester and Liverpool and the large airports that have easy access to Europe and beyond. There are also excellent rail links to London and the Midlands. The school is located in Colwyn Bay and is close to the Snowdonia National Park. It is therefore ideally placed to combine a broad academic curriculum with a rich variety of outdoor activities that make the most of the sea and the mountains. The Preparatory School (Rydal Penrhos Preparatory School), which takes pupils from 3 years, is on the former Pwllycrochan estate owned by the Erskine family, overlooking Colwyn Bay and adjacent to Rydal Penrhos School.

Teaching facilities include nine science laboratories, dedicated study areas for senior pupils, specialist art, music and design technology centres, a lecture theatre and a drama studio. There are also a library and information technology suites, and a recently created Sixth Form centre. A sports hall, swimming pool, fitness suite, dance studio and astroturf pitch complement the outdoor sporting facilities.

Many of the boarding houses started their existence as large Victorian or Edwardian residences in the fashionable seaside resort of Colwyn Bay. As a result, each has a very distinctive character, and a strong sense of being a 'home-from-home'. There are four boys' houses and one girls' house. Each boarding house is supervised by resident houseparents, with the assistance of a team of tutors and matrons.

Numbers and Organisation. There are currently 399 pupils in the senior school (236 boys and 163 girls) of which 120 are boarders. There are 214 pupils in Rydal Penrhos Preparatory School, comprising 113 boys and 101 girls.

The Prep School is divided into Early Years (age 3–4) Pre-prep (Reception to Year 2) and Prep (Year 3 to Year 6) departments, with separate and distinct curriculum and routines. The senior school is arranged into the Lower School (Years 7–11), Middle School (GCSE / pre-Sixth) and Sixth Form (IB and A Levels), each with its own Head of School. Pupils in the Prep and senior schools are also allocated to competitive Houses for academic, sporting and cultural events. The well-being and academic life of the school is being driven by a tutorial structure that creates a strong framework bringing pupils, teaching staff and parents together in an effective partnership.

Religious aims. Rydal Penrhos School is a Christian school in the Methodist tradition, but welcomes pupils from all faiths or none. Prayers are held daily in St John's Church, ownership of which has now been transferred to the school. Special services are held to mark key festivals and occasions in the Church year, and there is an annual confirmation service for members of the School community.

Curriculum. The National Curriculum is shadowed and supplemented to afford the best opportunities and choices for the pupils.

At KS3, pupils study English, Mathematics, the three sciences, Religious Studies, French, German, Geography, History, Drama, Art & Design, Home Economics, Design & Technology, Music, ICT, Physical Education, and PSHE. Pupils have a choice for languages options into Years 8 and 9.

In Year 10, the core GCSE subjects are English and English Literature, Mathematics, Science (either separate sciences or Dual Award), a modern foreign language and Religious Studies. Pupils will choose two further subjects to complete their GCSE options, and all pupils participate fully in both Physical Education and the PSHE programme. GCSEs in other languages (notably Welsh and Latin) are also available by request. EFL and Learning Support are provided to support pupils at the appropriate level and allow them to take full advantage of the academic programme.

The School welcomes new entrants into the Sixth Form, which offers both the International Baccalaureate Diploma programme and A Levels in a full range of subjects. Pupils are expected to have Grade C or above in at least 5 subjects at GCSE before entering the Sixth Form. With a wide range of options available, pupils are able to choose courses that reflect their own particular strengths and interests.

Sports and Activities. All pupils undertake a balanced programme of extra-curricular activities, with the aim of acquiring a range of physical and social skills, and developing the pupils' innate talent. The importance of competitive sport is recognised, and the School has a strong fixture list in rugby (it is a partner and host of the WRU North Wales Rugby Academy), cricket, netball, hockey (its teams are regular National champions at various age levels), athletics and tennis. The skiing and swimming teams also enjoy considerable success, and in the full range of sports available at Rydal Penrhos the School teams compete and win at regional and national level.

The school's coastal location within a few miles of the Snowdonia National Park offers unrivalled opportunities for a full programme of adventurous activities including mountaineering, climbing, hill-walking and kayaking. The Duke of Edinburgh's Award is very well supported by pupils. The school runs its own RYA sailing training centre and hosts the annual Rydal Penrhos School Laser Pico Challenge; sailing is an integral part of the core activities programme.

The Arts. The school has a fine tradition in both music and drama, and pupils are actively encouraged to develop an enthusiasm for the performing arts. The Music department presents two full school concerts at Christmas and Easter, and pupils perform regularly in chapel and at other whole-school occasions. The Drama department has enjoyed real academic success for many years, and this is reflected in the high standard of performance in school plays and other performances throughout the year.

Careers. The school prides itself on the quality of its advice on careers and higher education, and the library has a well-equipped careers centre to support this function. All pupils in Year 11 are expected to arrange work experience in collaboration with the Careers department, and the School holds an annual careers convention and industrial conference. In the Spring term of Year 11, pupils are given an individual interview to discuss their Sixth Form programme to ensure that they are fully informed about their options. In preparation for university mock interviews are arranged with local businesses and the professional community. Sixth Form pupils are expected to move on to university, and the vast majority do so.

Admission. Pupils can be admitted at the beginning of any term after their 11th birthday; the largest entry is in September. Entry is normally via the school's entrance examination, held in January, or equivalent tests.

Awards and Bursaries. (*See Scholarship Entries section.*) Awards and bursaries are available to the most able pupils and are awarded annually by examination for excellence in academic studies, art, drama, music and sport. These are available for entry into Year 7, Year 9 and the Sixth Form. The scholarship examination will take place on Saturday 4 February 2012.

Children of Methodist and Anglican ministers are admitted at substantially reduced fees, and Forces bursaries are also available. Forces families may also be eligible for the North Wales Day Allowance.

Fees per term (2011-2012). Boarding £7,400–£9,905, Weekly Boarding £6,555–£8,090, Day £3,745–£4,500.

Rydal Penrhos Preparatory School. Co-educational Boarding and Day. Ages 3–11. (*For further details see entry in IAPS section.*)

Charitable status. Rydal Penrhos is a Registered Charity, number 525752, and a Company Limited by Guarantee. The object of the charity is the advancement of education in accordance with Christian principles.

Ryde School with Upper Chine

Queen's Road, Ryde, Isle of Wight PO33 3BE
Tel: 01983 562229
Fax: 01983 564714
e-mail: school.office@rydeschool.org.uk
website: www.rydeschool.org.uk

Ryde School was founded in 1921 by William Laxon McIsaac and moved to its present site in 1928. In 1994, it was joined by Upper Chine School.

The School is fully co-educational at all levels. There are some 520 pupils between the ages of 11 and 18 in the Senior School, and some 260 aged 3 to 11 in the Junior School which shares part of the same site. (*See Junior School entry in IAPS section.*) There are full and weekly boarders who board on the Bembridge site (see below). The remainder are day pupils from the Island, with a small handful commuting on a daily basis from the Portsmouth area.

Motto: '*Ut Prosim*'

Governors:
Chairman: R J Fox, MA, CMath, FIMA
Vice-Chairman: I J Rawlinson, OBE
Hereditary Governor: A McIsaac, MA, DPhil

Mrs N Beckett	Mrs E Millett
R W Bradbury, MA	Mrs J V Minchin
Ms C R Clark MA	E Poku, BEng, MBA
Dr M Legg	D M T Rhodes, FRICS
C J Martin, BSc, MBA, DPhil, FIChemE	N J Wakefield, MA

Clerk to the Governors: P C Taylor, JP, FCA

Headmaster: Dr N J England, MA, DPhil

Deputy Head: A Shaw, BA

Senior Teachers:
K J Dubbins, BEd (*Head of Year 9; OC CCF*)
Mrs S E Evans, BA (*Director of Drama*)
B W Penn, BSc, CBiol, PGCE (*Director of Studies*)

Senior School:
Miss C L Amstutz, BA, PGCE
Mrs M Armstrong, BA, PGCE (*Head of Year 8*)
Mrs J Barclay, BA, PGCE
S R Baxter, BA, PGCE (*Head of Sixth Form*)
Ms K Bishop, BSc, PGCE (*Head of Psychology*)
N Brady, BA, PGCE (*Head of Economics & Business Studies*)
K G Bridgeman, MA (*Head of Science*)
Miss S Broyé, BA, MA, PGCE
Mrs J M Bryant, BEd
T Bull, BA
Mrs M E Burgess, BSc, PGCE (*Head of Geography*)
J C Comben, BA, PGCE
Miss A Drinkwater, BEd, MA (*Head of Girls' Games & PE*)
Miss J A Dyer, BA, PGCE
Mrs K Gavin, BA, PGCE
M J Glasbey, BSc, PGCE (*Head of Year 11; Head of CDT*)
A Graham, BA, HNTD (*Director of Studies, Sixth Form*)
A Grubb, BMus, PGCE (*Director of Music*)
Mrs T A Hall, BA, PGCE (*Head of Modern Languages*)

Mrs R A Hamar, BA (*Librarian*)
R Hoare, BA, QTS
K J Hothersall, CChem, MRSC
Mrs K E Ireland, BSc, MSc, PGCE. DipSpLD (*Head of Learning Support*)
P A Johnson, BSc, BA, PGCE (*Head of Mathematics*)
A Johnston, BA (*Head of ICT*)
S H Jones, MSc, PGCE
Revd J Leggett (*Chaplain*)
K Long, BEd (*Director of Sport*)
Ms H McComb, BA, PGCE (*Head of RE*)
S M Mead, BEd (*Head of Year 10*)
J H Mitchell, BHum, PGCE (*Head of Academic PE*)
A P Munn, MA, CertEd
C M Ody, BA, PGCE (*Head of Year 7, Head of PSHE*)
Mrs L E O'Sullivan, BSc Ed
Mrs S Patel, BSc, MSc, HNC, FIMLS, PGCE, MA
M Postelnyak, MA, DPhil
Mrs S R Prewer, BEd (*Examinations Officer*)
Mrs J Ratcliff, BA, PGCE
Ms C Smyth, BSc, MSc
P J Stott, BA, PGCE (*Head of History and Politics*)
Miss A Sutton (*Head of Boarding*)
Mrs B Sutton, CertEd (*Head of Art*)
C Sutton, BA, PGCE
G Taylor, MA, PGCE (*Head of English*)
C G S Trevallion, BSc, PGCE (*Head of Biology and Environmental Science*)
Mrs R Tweddle, GTCL, LTCL (*Choral Director*)
Mrs C Vince, BA, PGCE
Mrs K Vowell, BSc, PGCE (*Head of Chemistry*)
Miss K J Wagg, BA, PGCE
Mrs L L Waldron, BA, PGCE
H Wilkie, BA, CertEd
M J Windsor, BSc, PGCE
Mrs M A Woodhams, MA, PGCE

Junior School
Head: H Edwards, BSc, PGCE
Director of Studies: R A Hutchins, BEd, CertEd
Senior Teacher: Miss D J Meadows, BEd, CertEd

M Bowes, BEd	Mrs G Gallerwood, BA
Mrs A Bull	Ms J McKay, BEd
Mrs S Burgess, BA	Mrs A Selby
Mrs L J Dickinson, BEd	Mrs D Shepherd, CertEd
P Dickinson, BEd	Mrs H Vann, BA
Mrs J Edwards, BSc, PGCE	Mrs K Woodward, BA
A Gallerwood, BA	

'FIVEWAYS' Nursery and Pre-Prep:
Head: Mrs S A Davies, BEd

Miss K Clarke, NNEB	Mrs S Hawker, BA, CertEd
Miss S Crocker, BTech	Mrs K King, NNEB
Mrs F Curtis, BA, PGCE	Mrs S Lea, NTD
Mrs G Elsom, BEd	Miss V Lovell, BEd
Miss D Gillam, BEd	Miss N Noott, BA
Miss S Glover, NNEB	Mrs P Ong, DipPP
Mrs D Grubb, BA, PGCE	Miss A Townson, NVQ3

Situation and Buildings. The School stands in its own grounds of 17 acres in Ryde overlooking the Solent, and is easily accessible from all parts of the Island and the near mainland. It is within walking distance of the terminals which link Ryde to Portsmouth by hovercraft (10 minutes) or catamaran (15 minutes). In recent years there have been many additions to the School buildings. The School now enjoys up-to-date and extensive facilities. New Art and CDT departments will open in 2011, alongside a new dining hall.

Organisation and Curriculum. The School aims to provide a good all-round education based upon Christian principles, and enjoys an enviable reputation on the Island for high standards both inside and outside the classroom.

In the Junior School strong emphasis is laid on basic skills and on proficiency in reading, writing and number work. Pupils are prepared in this way for entry into the Senior School, and, following a recommendation from the Head of the Junior School, they are offered places in the Senior School at the age of 11.

The programme of work in the Senior School is designed to provide as broad an education as possible up to the end of Year 11. The subjects taught to GCSE level are English, English Literature, Mathematics, Physics, Chemistry, Biology, French, Spanish, Geography, History, Religious Education, Business Studies, ICT, Art, Music, Physical Education, Drama and Craft, Design and Technology. All pupils also follow a programme of Religious Education, Health Education and Games.

In the Sixth Form pupils are normally required to select three or four subjects at AS/A2 level from a wide choice. In addition, pupils may follow a General Studies course, designed to add breadth to their academic studies. The School is an IB World School and offers the Diploma Programme. Courses lead to entrance to universities, the Services, industry and the professions. The Careers Department provides advice and guidance to all pupils.

Tutorial System. Each pupil has a tutor who is responsible for his or her academic and personal progress and general pastoral welfare. The tutorial system encourages close contact with parents, which is further reinforced by parents' meetings which are held at regular intervals. The School aims to maintain sound discipline and good manners within a traditionally friendly atmosphere.

Games. The main games in the Senior School are rugby football, hockey, cricket and athletics for the boys, and netball, hockey and athletics for the girls. In the Junior School, Association football is also played. Other games include basketball, squash, golf, swimming and tennis. Regular matches are arranged at all levels against teams both on the Island and the mainland.

Music and Drama. The Music School incorporates practice and teaching facilities and a well-equipped recording studio. The School has a flourishing choral tradition, with opportunities for participation in a variety of choirs and instrumental groups. Concerts and musical plays are performed in both Senior and Junior Schools, and concert tours abroad have taken place in recent years. Full-length plays are produced each year by both Senior and Junior Schools, and special attention is given in the English lessons of the younger forms to speaking, lecturing and acting. Public speaking is a particular strength. The School has its own theatre and studio theatre.

Activities. There are many societies which cater for a wide range of individual interests. The School has a contingent of the Combined Cadet Force with Royal Navy and Royal Air Force sections. Sailing, canoeing, gliding, and other forms of venture training are strongly encouraged. There is a flourishing Duke of Edinburgh's Award scheme. Holiday visits and expeditions are regularly arranged, and there are opportunities for exchange visits with schools on the continent.

Boarding. Boarding for both boys and girls is available for pupils on the Bembridge campus which offers approximately one hundred acres of playing fields and woodland overlooking Whitecliff Bay and Culver Cliff, some six miles from Ryde. Transport is provided to and from Ryde for the school day.

Fees per term (from January 2011). Tuition: Foundation Stage: £1,620 (full day), £895 (half day); Pre-Prep £1,810–£2,570; Junior School £3,110; Senior School £3,405.

Boarding (excluding tuition): Senior School: £3,595 (full), £3,150 (weekly).

Scholarships and Bursaries. (*See Scholarship Entries section.*) The School offers a number of Ryde Assisted Places. These are awarded to suitable candidates from outside the school. These places are means tested. Some scholarships are also awarded on merit.

Charitable status. Ryde School is a Registered Charity, number 307409. The aims and objectives of the Charity are the education of boys and girls.

St Albans School

Abbey Gateway, St Albans, Herts AL3 4HB
Tel: 01727 855521
Fax: 01727 843447
e-mail: hm@st-albans-school.org.uk
website: www.st-albans.herts.sch.uk

The origins of the School date back, according to tradition, to the monastic foundation of 948, and there is firm evidence of an established and flourishing school soon after the Conquest. Following the Dissolution, the last abbot, Richard Boreman, sought a private Act of Parliament to establish a Free School. Charters, granted to the Town Corporation by Edward VI and Elizabeth I, together with endowments by Sir Nicholas Bacon from the sale of wine licences, secured the School's continuance.

Visitor: The Rt Revd The Lord Bishop of St Albans

Governors:
Chairman: S P Eames
Vice Chairman: Prof R J C Munton, BA, PhD, ACSS
J Barber, MA, PhD
A S Barnes, BSc, BPharm
R B Blossom, BSc, CertEd
Prof M J Collins, MA, DPhil
A L Dalwood, BSc, BA Cantab, UKSIP
B S Kent, BA
A R M Little, MA
Mrs J M Mark, BA
C McIntyre, BA
Dr M Pegg, MB BS, BSc
Mrs R Phillips, BSc
A Woodgate, BA, Dip Land Admin, MRICS

Advisory Council:
The Mayor of St Albans
The Dean of St Albans
The President of the Old Albanian Club
D S C Bevan, BA
P G Brown
G R Dale, MA, MCIPD, FRSA
Mrs A Fletcher, MA
Cllr D E Lloyd, BA, FRSA
D S Mercer, BSc, FCSI
Cllr G Myland
P M Rattle, BA
Mrs J F Tasker, FCCA

Bursar and Clerk to the Governors: D Todd, MA, FCA

Headmaster: **A R Grant**, MA, FRSA

Second Master: R D W Laithwaite, BA
Director of Studies: M E Davies, MA
Heads of Sixth Form:
Mrs R K Hardy, MA
Mr G J Walker, MA, FRSA
Head of Middle School: P R Byrom, MSc
Head of Lower School: D Swanson, RADA
Senior Master: P W Taylor, BEd

Assistant staff:

Miss L H Andrews, BSc	I J Black, MA
T D Asch, BA	Mrs C C Bolton, BA
Mrs K M Bailey, BSc, PhD	A J Brien, HNC, BEd, MSc
B S Balden, MA	Miss M L Bruton, BA
A J Bateman, BA	G J Calvert, BEd
Miss R J Baxter, BA	Mrs J J M Carman, BSc

N J Cassidy, BA
I Charlesworth, MA
B T Clark, BA
Miss E M Clarke, BSc
N S Cragg, BSc
P F G Craig, BA
Mrs J C Crouch, BSc
R D Daurge, BSc
Mrs E W Davies, BA
R Dear, MA
J P Dray, MA, DPhil
T O Eames-Jones, BA
A W G Ford, BA
Mrs V L Ginsburg, BA
C P A Gould, BSc
Mrs T J Gott, ARCS, BSc
Mrs V H Graveson, BA
Miss J M Grieveson, MA
M J Guy, MSc, PhD
G C Higby, MA, PhD
Mrs J Higgins, BA, ARCM
Mrs S J Hopkin, BSc, MSc
C C Hudson, BSc
C J Humphreys, BSc
T N Jenkins, BA, MFA
A K Jolly, BA
Miss K Kaur-Lillian, MA
M J Langston, BSc
R J Lockhart, BA
T J Martin, BA
Mrs V C McClafferty, BA
D K McCord, BMus, ARCM
P M McGrath, BA
Miss G Mendes da Costa, BA
Mrs P M Mills, MA

D K Murphy, MA, LRAM, Dip Perf RAM
I Murray, BA
G D Nichols, BA
Mrs S J Offord, BSc
C J A Palmer, BA
V Pappert, MA
Mrs H R-M Pavan, CertEd
D M L Payne, MA
M A Pedroz, MA
Ms T M Peek, BA
Mrs D S Percival, MA, MIL
Miss D Porovic, MSci
Mrs G Renz, MA, MPhil
D C Richards, BCom, MBA
C A Roberts, BEng
Mrs H J Robertson, BEng
T N Ross, BSc
D M Rowland, MA
J R Russ, BA
D S Russell, MSc
Dr J H Saunders, BA, PhD
B C Scott, BSc
I M Shillcock, BSc, PhD
G L Smithson, BSc
M J Smyth, BSc
D J Stone, BA
M R Stout, BMus
Mrs M O Stratton, MSc
Mrs J H Swain, MA
R E Tanner, DPhil, BSc
A C R Thompson, BA
B D Wall, BA
D Whitehead, BA
P G Yates, ACertEd
Mrs H Zaver, BSc

Chaplain: The Revd Dr C D Pines, MB BS, MA
Medical Officers:
Dr M Bevis, BSc, MRCGP, DCH, DRCOG
Dr A Sudarshan, MB BS, MD, DRCOG, MRCGP
OC CCF: Major K J Everitt
CCF SSI: WO1 W J Wilson

Visiting Staff:

Poet-in-Residence: J D Mole, MA

Music:
P A Bainbridge, DipRCM, ARCM
D Bentley, GGSM
Miss L Hayter, BMus
Miss M Laffy
Mrs V Parker, GRSM, ARCM
Lady R Runcie, LRAM, ARCM
Miss J E Simmons, BMus, GGSM
Ms J Trentham, GLCM, LLCM, TD
N Woodhouse, FLCM, LTCL, LLCM, ALCM
M Woodward, BMus

St Albans is a day school of about 780 pupils which, after being for many years part of the Direct Grant System, reverted to full independence. Girls were admitted into the Sixth Form in September 1991. Its atmosphere and ethos derive from its long tradition and its geographical position near the city centre of St Albans in close proximity to the Abbey and overlooking the site of the Roman City of Verulamium. Whilst maintaining a high standard of academic achievement, it offers wide opportunities for development in other fields, and a strong emphasis is laid upon the responsible use of individual talents in the service of the community.

Buildings. For more than 3 centuries the School was in the Lady Chapel of the Abbey. It moved in 1871 into the Monastery Gatehouse, a building of considerable historic and architectural interest where teaching still continues. Since 1900, extensive additions include the award-winning Hall, the Library, the Design Technology Centre, new Science laboratories and a well-equipped fitness centre. A nearby building has been converted for use as a fully-equipped Drama School and a sports hall and swimming pool are under construction.

The School has close historical and musical ties with the Cathedral and Abbey Church of St Alban. By permission of the Dean, morning prayers take place twice weekly in the nave, where the School Choir sings regularly and an annual oratorio is performed in collaboration with St Albans High School for Girls.

Admission. The majority of boys enter at the age of 11 or 13 but there are also entries at 16, when girls are also admitted; candidates are accepted occasionally at other ages. For the main entry at 11 an examination in basic subjects is held at the School each year, normally in January, and parents of interested candidates should write to the School for a prospectus and application form. Candidates at 13 enter through the Common Entrance examination, and conditional offers of places are normally made about one year before entry, following a preliminary assessment. Ideally parents should apply to the School at least 2 years in advance for entry at 13.

Pupils are admitted only at the start of the Autumn Term unless there are exceptional circumstances.

Enquiries about entry should be addressed to the Admissions Officer.

Fees per term (2011-2012). £4,598.

Bursaries and Scholarships. (*See Scholarship Entries section*.) Some assistance with tuition fees may be available in cases of proven need from the School's own endowments. Such Bursaries are conditional upon an annual means test and will be awarded according to a balance of merit and need. Numerous scholarships are awarded on academic merit at each age of entry. Choral Scholarships are offered at 11+ and Scholarships in Art and Music are offered to existing pupils or new entrants at 13+ who show exceptional talent.

Curriculum. The curriculum for the first three years is largely a common one and covers a wide range. All boys study three sciences and two languages, and devote some part of their timetable to Art, Drama, Music, ICT and CDT. Mathematics IGCSE is taken at the end of the fourth form (Y10), and in the fourth and fifth forms a system of compulsory subjects and options leads in most cases to the taking of at least a further nine GCSEs or IGCSEs. In the Sixth Form most pupils study four subjects at AS Level in the Lower Sixth Form and three or four A2s in the Upper Sixth. In addition, all pupils take General Studies either as an AS or a full A Level and are prepared for an AS in Critical Thinking. The choice is wide, and the flexibility of the timetable makes it possible for almost any combination of available subjects to be offered.

Virtually all Sixth Form leavers go on to universities or other forms of higher education, a good proportion to Oxford or Cambridge.

Out-of-school activities cover a wide range, and there are clubs and societies to cater for most interests. Several of these are run in conjunction with other schools. Musical activities are many and varied and include regular concerts and recitals by the School Choir, Choral Society and ensembles and by professional artists. Plays are produced 3 or 4 times a year either in the New Hall, the Drama Centre Studio, the English Centre Studio Theatre or in the Open-air Theatre, and there is ample opportunity for creative work in the Art school and the Design Technology Centre. There is a strong contingent of the CCF with sections representing the Army and RAF. Other groups train under the Duke of Edinburgh's Award Scheme and do various forms of social service and conservation work in and around the city of St

Albans. The School owns a Field Centre in Wales which is used for research and recreation in holidays, as part of the Lower School curriculum and as a base for field studies and reading parties. The School also owns a working 400-acre farm within 3 miles of the school where the Woollam Playing Fields, extending to 45 acres, were opened in 2002 by HRH The Duke of Gloucester. The grounds include an Astroturf all-weather pitch and a superb state-of-the-art pavilion. There are good links with Saracens RUFC, whose training is based at the Woollam Grounds.

Games. The School competes at a high level in Rugby Football, Hockey, Cross-country, Cricket, Tennis and Athletics in addition to a range of other sports including Association Football, Squash, Shooting, Sailing, Swimming, Orienteering, Basketball, Golf and Table Tennis. The playing fields are within easy reach of the School, and the spacious and pleasant lawns on the School site, stretching down to the River Ver, give access to the open-air theatre, Tennis Courts and Shooting Range.

Old Albanian Club and the St Albans School Foundation. Information may be obtained from the Development Manager: Ms Kate Le Sueur at the School address or at: development@st-albans.herts.sch.uk.

Charitable status. St Albans School is Registered Charity, number 1092932, and a Company Limited by Guarantee, number 4400125. The aims and objectives are to provide an excellent education whereby pupils can achieve the highest standard of academic success, according to ability, and develop their character and personality so as to become caring and self-disciplined adults.

St Aloysius' College

45 Hill Street, Glasgow G3 6RJ
Tel: 0141 332 3190
Fax: 0141 353 0426
e-mail: mail@staloysius.org
website: www.staloysius.org

Motto: *ad majora natus sum* (I am born for greater things).

Board of Governors:
President: Rev Michael Holman, SJ (Jesuit Provincial)
Chairman: Dr Francis Dunn
Mr David Boyce
Mrs Maureen Brogan
Dr Harry Burns
Fr Michael Smith, SJ
Mr Greg Hannah
Ms Ruth Holgate
Mr John Hylands
Mrs Margaret McGarry
Prof Eileen A Millar
Mr Matthew Reilly

Bursar and Clerk to the Board: Mrs Kathleen Sweeney, FCCA

Head Master: Mr John Stoer, BA

Depute Head Master: Mr Frank Reilly, BSc

Assistant Headmaster: Mr J Phillip Crampsey BEd

Administrative Officer: Mrs Margaret Wright

Head of Junior School: Dr Aileen Brady, BSc Hons

Head of Early Years: Mrs Marie Forbes, DipEd

PA to the Head Master: Mrs Monica Harper

St Aloysius' College, founded in 1859 and sited in Glasgow city centre, is a Roman Catholic independent school under the Trusteeship of the Society of Jesus.

The school is fully co-educational at all stages (Kindergarten to S6) with a total roll of over 1,300, drawn from a wide catchment area including Strathclyde and beyond.

Jesuit education is inspired by the vision of St Ignatius Loyola (1491–1556) in which God reveals his love for us in all things. As a Jesuit school, the aim of St Aloysius' College is the formation of men and women for others, people of competence, conscience and compassion.

Entrance. Entrance to the school is by open examination at S1 and P7 and by interview and assessment at P1 and Kindergarten. There may be places in intermediate years from time to time.

Buildings. The Senior School occupies buildings from 1840, 1866, 1908 and 1926. A new £3.7m maths, science and technology building was opened in 2002. The Junior School is accommodated in an award-winning building opened in 1998. Playing fields are located four miles away.

Curriculum. The Junior School and lower years of the Senior School follow internally devised courses which are suitable for academically able children. All Junior School pupils study French and science from Kindergarten and P1. Intermediate II is taken at the end of S4 and pupils take five Highers in S5. A wide range of Advanced Highers and other courses are available in S6.

Co-Curricular Activities. The main sports are Rugby, Hockey, Athletics and Cross Country. Pupils are extensively involved in community service and charity work. There is a wide range of co-curricular activities.

Fees per annum (2011-2012). £6,804–£9,009.

Bursaries are available on consideration of parents' income.

Charitable status. St Aloysius' College is part of the wider work of the British Jesuit Province which is a Registered Charity, number 230165.

St Bede's College

Alexandra Park, Manchester M16 8HX
Tel: 0161 226 3323 (Senior School)
          0161 226 7156 (Preparatory School)
Fax: 0161 226 3813 (Senior School)
          0161 227 0487 (Preparatory School)
e-mail: head@stbedescollege.co.uk
          enquiries@stbedescollege.co.uk
          prep@stbedescollege.co.uk
website: www.stbedescollege.co.uk

Motto: '*Nunquam otio torpebat*'

St Bede's was founded in 1876 by Bishop Herbert Vaughan, who later, as Cardinal Archbishop of Westminster, went on to found Westminster Cathedral. From small beginnings the College has grown and changed whilst remaining faithful to Bishop Vaughan's ideals. Over 500 priests have received their early training at the College; although the number of priests on the staff has been reduced in recent years our religious faith remains central to the life of the College.

Throughout the many changes that have taken place since its formation the College has remained true to its founder's intention: to provide a thorough academic education for Catholic children, in an atmosphere of stability, care and concern.

We therefore seek the highest standards of performance so that pupils are stretched to, but never beyond, their personal limit. The provision of this education within a Catholic environment remains one of the chief characteristics of the College. High expectations of personal behaviour and discipline are rooted in our faith.

The College was one of the first Catholic schools in the country to enter the Direct Grant system. St Bede's was the only school which opted to retain that independence when the Catholic secondary schools in Manchester were re-organised in 1976.

The Governors introduced co-education in 1984, so that they could offer girls from Greater Manchester and beyond the benefits of a Catholic Grammar School education.

Governors:
Chairman: Rt Revd Mgr M R Quinlan, DCL
Vice-Chairman: H B Ellwood, PhL, BA, RIBA

Rt Revd Mgr J Allen, STL, PhL
Rt Revd T J Brain, Bishop of Salford
A Carr, LLB
Mrs L Edwards
Mrs C Finnigan, LLB
M Gillespie, BA
Revd T Hopkins, MA
A J Keegan, BA
G Lanigan, FCA
Revd P McMahon
Dr S O'Driscoll, BSc, MB BS
K O'Flynn, MB, BCh, BAO, FRCS, FRCS Urol
M Quinn, BA
J Walsh

Clerk to Governors: Mrs A Webb

Senior Management Team:

Headmaster: **D Kearney**, BA

Deputy Heads:
Mrs R A Meehan, GRSM
Mrs S Pike, BSc

Deputy Head & Head of Sixth Form: D Grierson, MA

Assistant Heads:
J Bowden, BA
Dr A Dando, BSc, PhD

Examinations Secretary: I Service, MA

Assistant Staff:
* *Head of Department*

Art:
*Mrs J Hudson, BA
Mrs S Dittman, BA
H Peers, BA
H Weiss, BEd (*Head of Lower School*)

Business Studies/Economics:
D Grierson, MA (*Deputy Head & Head of Sixth Form*)
*P Glancy, MSc
Miss M Delaney, BA (*Assistant Head of Upper Fifth*)
M Gallagher, BEd

Classics:
*J Gibson, MA
J Dumbill, BA (*Deputy Head of Sixth Form*)
P Wilcock, MA

Drama:
*Mrs N Alderson, BA

English:
*Mrs M Hazell, BA
Mrs N Alderson, BA (*Head of Drama*)
Miss F Cochran, BA
B Peden, MA (*Head of Upper School*)
Miss C Berry, BA
Miss J Holland, BA

Geography:
*Miss J C Tomkinson, BA
Mrs M Vidouris, BA (*Assistant Head of Lower School*)
H Weiss, BEd (*Head of Lower School*)
K Rafferty, BEd
P J C Loader, BSc

Geology:
*P J C Loader, BSc (*Head of Middle School*)

History:
*P G Griffin, BA
J Bowden, BA (*Assistant Head*)
Mrs M Harter, BA (*Head of Lower Fifth*)
T Fisher, CertEd
P Wilcock, MA

ICT:
*P McDaid, BSc
S Fallon, BEd
Mrs C Earles (*Network Manager*)

Mathematics:
*Dr A Dando, BSc, PhD
D McCotter, BSc
S Bargery, BSc
M Cahill, MSc (*Assistant Examinations Secretary*)
I Service, MA (*Examinations Secretary*)
C Wright, BSc (*Teacher in Charge of Assessments*)
Mrs C Brewer, BA
Dr R Bennett, PhD

Modern Languages:
*P Lee, MA
French:
Mrs S de Castro, BA (*Teacher in charge of French*)
P Lee, MA
Mrs M B Girolami, BA (*Head of Upper Fourth*)
Miss R Evans, BA
Spanish:
*Mrs J Wallwork, BA
Miss M Barry, MA
German:
*P Lee, MA
Miss R Evans, BA

Music:
Mrs R Meehan, GRSM (*Deputy Head*)
*Miss R Darby, BMus

PE:
*K Rafferty, BEd (*Head of Boys' PE*)
*T Fisher, CertEd (*Cricket*)
*S Fallon, BEd (*Football*)
Mrs N McCormick, BEd (*Head of Girls' PE*)
Mrs E O'Neal, BEd
Mrs N Lavorini, BEd

Politics:
*Mrs R Lockett, BA (*Teacher in Charge of Careers*)

Religion:
*Mrs E Meakin, BA
Mrs M Andrews, CertEd
Miss M Curry, BSc (*Assistant Head of Sixth Form*)
Mrs K Griffin, MA (*Head of Lower Fourth*)

Science:
*Mrs S Pike, BSc (*Deputy Head*)
Physics:
*Mrs C Aspinall, BSc
N O'Hagan, BSc
M Byrne, BEng
Chemistry:
Mrs S Pike, BSc (*Deputy Head*)
*Mrs S Quirk, MSc (*Head of Lower School Science*)
Miss P Brammer, BSc
P Gill, BSc
Biology:
*Miss C Hennity, BSc
M Nally, BSc
Dr S Powell, BSc, PhD
J Hodson, BA

Technology:
*A Hennigan, BEd
J Lalley, BSc
Mrs M Collins, BEd
S Fallon, BEd

EAL:
Mrs S Alexopoulou

Preparatory School:
Headmaster: P Hales, BA, DASE

Medical Officer: Dr M Cunningham

Headmaster's PA: Mrs B McGoff

Admission. The rapid growth of recent years enables us to offer 830 senior school places (250 of them in the Sixth Form).

Most pupils enter St Bede's at 11+ by taking the College Entrance Examination. There are occasional vacancies in other age groups, and there is an additional intake of students from outside the College into the Sixth Form each year.

The College Entrance Examination takes place in January and is open to Catholic boys and girls who will not have reached the age of 12 by 31st August in the year of the examination. Christians of other denominations are also welcomed. Details of the examination and copies of past papers may be obtained from the College Administrator. Occasional vacancies occur in other years. There is also direct entry to the Sixth Form for boys and girls who expect to obtain good GCSE results. Interviews are held from the beginning of the Easter Term.

Sixth Form Bursaries. Each year the Governors provide a number of bursaries for Catholic boys or girls from other schools, who would like to enter the Sixth Form at St Bede's. The bursaries are awarded both on the basis of interview and performance in an examination which is held in January and according to financial need. Further details may be obtained from the Head of Sixth Form.

Music Scholarships. The Governors award Music Scholarships; details of the award may be obtained from the College Administrator.

St Bede's Educational Trust. St Bede's College Educational Trust awards bursaries to Catholic pupils of good academic ability who can demonstrate financial need. At present one third of pupils are in receipt of means-tested bursaries.

Curriculum. Curriculum provision is constantly being refined to improve the education offered to all pupils. It is supported by the most modern facilities, including recently built technology rooms, a new 17,000 volume library and four ICT suites.

A common Lower School curriculum offers all expected subjects together with Latin, ICT, Technology, ample PE/Games and pastoral time. In the Middle School four subjects are chosen from French, German, Greek, Spanish, Latin, Economics, Business Studies, ICT, Design & Technology, Art and Music for a one year course to further enhance GCSE options.

At GCSE, 9 or 10 subjects are taken from a choice of 21 which are available in any combination.

Students must usually achieve 7 GCSE passes (grades A*–C) to be admitted to the Sixth Form where they usually take four subjects to AS Level in the Lower Sixth and three A2 subjects in the Upper Sixth. The 30 subjects available can be combined in any way and no group exceeds 12 students for A Level.

All Sixth Form students in addition have pastoral time, General Religion lessons and preparation for General Studies.

Music. In the early years there is curricular music time to provide a thorough theoretical introduction to the subject as well as much practical experience. The pupils thus learn to read music fluently and study the lives and music of the major composers.

Music is an option at both GCSE and A Level.

Instrumental tuition is available in string, woodwind, brass instruments and voice. In addition, specialist tuition in electric guitar and drum kit is offered. There is a full programme of evening concerts.

Art. Art is a flourishing area of cultural expression. Textiles and photography are particular areas of expertise along with fine art. A specialist sixth form art studio housed separately gives these students a better opportunity to study the subject at a more mature level. In 2003 full computer-aided provision was added to the art suites. All pupils take Art in the Lower School and the subject is a very popular GCSE and A Level choice.

Drama. There are two productions each year in late November and March. There are also one act plays for younger pupils and occasionally some open-air productions. Every two years we stage a drama festival, which is particularly successful in encouraging participants from all levels at the College.

Games. The Physical Education curriculum includes Badminton, Basketball, Netball, Volleyball, Cross Country, Gymnastics, Rounders, Cricket, Tennis, Athletics, Rugby, Soccer and Aerobics. We have extensive facilities which include a modern Sports Hall, 13 acres of playing fields and tennis and netball courts. On any Saturday there may be over three hundred pupils representing the College and 20 members of staff on duty, supported by large numbers of parents. A floodlit, all-weather surface for soccer, hockey and tennis was opened in October 2003.

ICT. There are 163 networked computers, both in departments and in four dedicated air-conditioned computer suites. Broadband internet access, an intranet allowing students to access the school network from home and all-day access to ICT are all available. Digital projectors are to be found in all departments and there is access to interactive whiteboards. All students receive teaching in ICT skills in their first year. Thereafter, the subject is delivered in a cross-curricular manner. A state-of-the-art language laboratory was completed in January 2005.

Other Activities. A wide range of expeditions and excursions are organised each year as part of our programme of activities.

There are regular trips and exchanges (including France, Spain, Cuba, Czech Republic, Poland, Russia, Italy, Germany and the USA). Other extra-curricular activities include: The Duke of Edinburgh's Award Scheme, Debating and Public Speaking, Drama, Theatre Visits, Orchestra and Choir, Chess, Photography, Community Service, Geological Society, Computing Group, Scientific Societies, Orienteering, United Nations Group, Politics Group, Quizzes, Art Club and Literary & Philosophical Society.

Fees per term (2011-2012). Senior School £2,966, Preparatory School £1,995.

Careers Education. The Careers Room with its library contains an extensive range of literature on Careers and higher education opportunities and is open every day and manned by two members of staff with responsibility for careers guidance. We make extensive use of computer based information sources and in particular the Prestel Database.

Every two years, a Careers Convention is organised for pupils from Upper Fourth to Sixth Form and for senior pupils a higher education conference is organised every February.

Honours. 40 Oxford and Cambridge offers in the last 5 years. One student to Harvard.

Preparatory School. St Bede's College Preparatory School, a co-educational day school for pupils aged 4–11, was founded in 1985. The school has the same Governing Body as the College and the Prep School is situated within the main College campus and has full use of College facilities.

Charitable status. St Bede's College Limited is a Registered Charity, number 700808. Its aims and objectives are the advancement and provision of education on behalf of St Bede's College.

St Bede's Senior School

Upper Dicker, East Sussex BN27 3QH
Tel: 01323 843252
Fax: 01323 442628
e-mail: school.office@stbedesschool.org
website: www.stbedesschool.org

Founded in 1978 St Bede's discovers the talents of each student through breadth of academic curriculum and co-curricular. It is academically ambitious for all and is proud of its ethos of inclusiveness. The pastoral care, delivered through the House and Tutor systems, is inspiring and nurturing and ensures St Bede's sends its young people into the outside world self-aware, happy and confident in what they can achieve and looking forward to the challenges they will meet.

The Senior School owes its existence in part to the success and vitality of St Bede's Preparatory School in Eastbourne, one of the first boys' Preparatory Schools to become fully co-educational and now one of the largest co-educational Preparatory Schools in the country. The Senior School has 900 students. Of these 350 are boarders (full and weekly boarders), 550 are day students, 400 are Sixth Formers, 60 per cent are boys and 40 per cent are girls. St Bede's enjoys an enviable reputation internationally. Currently 18% of our students are from over 40 countries.

The School takes great pride in the variety of its students and the outstanding range of opportunities available to them. The breadth of choice means every student can find what they naturally excel at. St Bede's is primarily a boarding school and is, therefore, organised with the aim of providing a happy and challenging atmosphere for those who are resident seven days a week. Thus a positive programme of weekend activities is always provided.

Governors:
Major-General Anthony Meier, CB, OBE (*Chairman*)
Christopher Bean, LLB Hons
Adrian Bull, MD (*Deputy Chairman*)
Jeremy Courtney, FRAgS, MBIAC
Christopher Doidge
John East ACII
Sally-Anne Huang, MA, PGCE
Tom MacGibbon, FCA
Timothy Martin-Jenkins, MA, MBA
Lady Rosemary Newton, MA
Patrick Tobin, MA, FRSA
Clive Ward
Lucy Whistler, BSc Hons
Lorna Almonds Windmill, BA Hons

Senior Management:

Headmaster: Dr R J Maloney, MTheol Hons St Andrews, MA, PhD King's College London, PGCE

Principal Deputy Head: Mr J Lewis, BA Hons, MA, PGCE (*Economics and Business Studies*)
Deputy Head Academic: Mr J Tuson, MA (*English*)
Deputy Head Staff: Mr R Frame, BA Hons, HDE (*History*)
Deputy Head Co-Curricular: Ms R Woollett, BA Hons, PGCE (*Religious Studies*)
Senior Housemaster: Mrs L M Belrhiti, BEd, Dip TEFL (*EFL*)
Business Manager: Mr D Neely, FCCA
Director of Marketing: Mrs S P Wellings, NCTJ (*Media Studies*)

Director of Admissions: Mrs C Rattray, BA Hons
Facilities Manager: Mr S Pantrey
Director of Digital Resources: Mr G Cleverley
Director of Summer School: Mr S Wood

Housemasters:
Bloomsbury House (*Day*): Mrs M Leggett, BA Hons, MA, PGCE (*Home Economics*)
Camberlot House (*Boarding*): Mr R Jones, BA Hons (*History & Film Studies*)
Charleston House (*Day*): Miss S Muxworthy, BA Hons, MA, PGCE, Dip Sport Psych (*Physical Education*)
Crossways House (*Boarding*): Mrs J Lambeth, BSc Hons, PGCE (*Physical Education*)
Deis House (*Day*): Mr E Dickie, BA Hons, MA Hons, PGCE (*Politics & History*)
Dicker House (*Day*): Mr R Mills, BA Hons, PGCE (*Economics & Business Studies*)
Dorms House (*Boarding*): Mr S Gough, BA Hons, Dip Sport Psych (*Physical Education*)
Dorter House (*Boarding*): Mr D Leggett, BA QTS (*Physical Education*)
Knights House (*Day*): Dr A Carroll, BSc, PhD (*Mathematics*)
Stud House (*Boarding*): Mr A Walker, BA Hons, PGCE (*Modern Languages*)

Teaching Staff:
Miss T Algar, BA Hons, QTS (*Physical Education*)
Dr P Allison, BSc, MSc, PhD, PGCE (*Head of Biology*)
Miss R Armitage, BA Hons (*Art & Ceramics*)
Mr K Ayers (*Director of Swimming*)
Mr L Backler, BA Hons, PGCE, Cert Professional Studies (*Head of Year 9, Learning Support*)
Mrs C Ballard, BEd Hons (*Head of Home Economics*)
Mr A Barclay, Dip Mus, CertEd (*Director of Music*)
Mr I Barr, BSc Hons, PGCE (*Head of ICT*)
Mr S Beale, BSc Hons, PGCE (*Business Studies*)
Ms R Beech, BA Hons, PGCE (*French, Italian*)
Mrs I Berryman, MPhys, PGCE (*Mathematics*)
Mr J Berryman, JP, BA, MSc, ACP, FCollP, FRGS (*English, Religious Studies, History*)
Mrs C Bilham, BA Hons, PGCE, Hornsby Dip SpLD (*Dyslexia*) (*Learning Support*)
Mr D Bioletti, BEng Hons, PGCE (*Mathematics*)
Ms K Blok, BA Hons, CPE, LPC, Solicitor (*English*)
Ms S Brooks, BSc Hons, PGCE (*Mathematics*)
Mr N Brown, MA, LGSM, ALAM-LAMDA (*Head of Academic Drama*)
Mrs S Bunyard, BSc Hons, PGCE, DMS, Adv Dip (*Director of Learning Support, SENCO*)
Ms S Cakebread, BA Hons, PGCE (*Head of Drama*)
Mr D Caryer, BA Hons, QTS (*Physical Education*)
Mr S Chambers, BSc Hons, (*Business Studies*)
Mr D Cheshire, BA Hons, MA, GTP (*English*)
Ms K Chinn, BA, PGCE (*Acting Head of History*)
Mr S Clark, BEd (*Mathematics*)
Mr J Cook, RSA, TEFLA (*Head of EAL*)
Mr M Costley, BSc, MSc, PGCE (*Head of Science Faculty, Chemistry, Biology, Science*)
Dr L Dart, BEd Hons, MA, DPhil (*Head of Curriculum Enhancement, English*)
Mr J David, BA, PGCE (*Head of Classics, Latin, Greek, English*)
Dr S Dawson, MPhys, PhD (*Physics*)
Mr C Dixon, MA, Dip RAM, NOS (*Music*)
Mr D Dozgic, BSc (*English as an Additional Language*)
Mr N Driver, BCom, PGCE (*Mathematics*)
Mr P Edwards, BSc Hons (*Head of Design Technology*)
Mr T Elwell, BA Hons, PGCE (*Geography*)
Miss E Excell, BA Hons (*Art & Photography*)
Mrs A Fernandez, BA, CAP (*Spanish & Latin*)
Ms J French, BSc, PGCE (*Head of Year 10, Biology & Science*)

Ms V Ganivet, BA Hons, PGCE (*Head of Lower Fifth, French & German*)

Mrs J Garred, BA Hons, GTP, PGCert SpLD (*Learning Support*)

Mr P Gibbs, BA Hons, PGCE (*Head of English*)

Mr N Gill, BEd, MA (*Head of Languages Faculty, English*)

Miss C Girardot, BA Hons, PGCE (*Physical Education*)

Mrs K Goldring, BA Hons, PGCE (*Drama*)

Mr S Gough, BA Ed Hons, QTS, Dip Sport Psych (*Physical Education*)

Miss F Goulden, BA Hons, MA, PGCE, Dip Educational Therapy, DipSpLD (*Head of Psychology*)

Mr D Graham, BA, ATD, (*Head of Art*)

Mr M Grover, CertEd, Dip Cat (*Home Economics*)

Mr A Hallford, BA Hons, MA, PGCE (*Media & Film Studies, English*)

Mr A Hammond, BA Hons, MA (*Head of Ceramics, Art*)

Miss S Harris, BA Hons, MA, PGCE (*Art*)

r R Hart, BA Hons, PGCE (*Head of Geography*)

Mr A Hayes, BSc, PGCE (*Director of Curriculum Management and Data Analysis*)

Mr J Henham, BSc Hons, PGCE (*Head of Year 13, Mathematics*)

Mr R Hickman BA Hons (*Media Studies, Film Studies*)

Mr C Hiscox, BSc Hons, PGCE (*Head of Physics*)

Mr S Hodges, BSc, PGCE (*Biology, Environmental & Land Based Science, Science*)

Mr S Hopkins, BA Hons (*Music Production*)

Ms K Hughes, BSc, PGCE (*Science*)

Mr B Jackson, BSc, PGCE (*Business Studies, Politics*)

Mr P Jones, BSc Hons, MSc, PGCE (*Science*)

Mrs J Jones, BA Hons (*English*)

Mr S Jordan, BA, PGDFA Royal Academy Schools, ATC (*Art*)

Mr P Juniper, BSc Hons, PGCE, CBiol, MSB (*Head of Environmental Science, Science and Animal Management, Science*)

Mr W Kemp, BEng Hons (*Physics, Science*)

Mr D King, BSc Hons, PGCE (*Acting Head of Geography*)

Mr M Krause, BEd (*Mathematics and E-Safety Coordinator*)

Ms C Laws, BA Hons, PGCE (*Design Technology, ICT*)

Mrs R de Mallet Morgan, BA Hons, BA, DipSpLD, CELTA (*Asst SENCO*)

Mrs C Mander, BEd, Adv Dip (*Learning Support*)

Mr J Martinez Garcia, BA Hons, MA, PGCE (*Spanish*)

Mr F McKeefry, BA Hons, PGCE (*Business Studies*)

Miss M McKenna, BA Hons, MBA, Dip TEFL (*EAL & Spanish*)

Mr A McPhail, BSc, PGCE (*Mathematics*)

Mrs K Merchant, BSc, PGCE (*Head of Physical Education*)

Miss L Morris, BMus Hons, PGCE (*Head of Academic Music*)

Mr R Morrison, CBiol, MSB (*Environmental Science & Science*)

Mr T Mpandawana, BSc, DipEd, QTS (*Chemistry, Science*)

Mr R Mutimba, BScEd (*Computer Science, ICT, Citizenship*)

Mr T van Noort (*Assistant Director of Cricket*)

Mr M Oliver, BA Hons, PGCE (*English*)

Mr G Parfitt, MBA (*Head of Economics & Business Studies*)

Mr G Parker, BA Hons, MA, PGCE (*English & History*)

Ms J Parker, BA Hons, MA, PGCE (*History & Politics*)

Mrs E Parkes, Cert Ed (*Home Economics*)

Ms C Parris, BA Hons, PGCE (*Art & Textiles*)

Mrs W Parry, BA Hons (*Computer Science, ICT*)

Mrs J Pendry, BA Hons, MMus (*English, Music*)

Mr M Peattie, MPhys Hons, GTP (*Mathematics*)

Mr N Potter, BSc Hons, PGCE (*Design Technology*)

Mr M Rattray, BA, MA, PGCE (*Religious Studies*)

Mrs S von Riebech, BMus, PGCE (*Music*)

Mr W Richards, BSc, GTP (*Activities Manager, Mathematics, Computer Science*)

Mr M Rimmington, BSc Hons, Dip Ind St, GTP (*Director of Academic Performance*)

Mr H Rohmer, MA Hons, 1 Staatsexamen Hons, GTP (*Head of Modern Languages, German*)

Mr G Rudnick, BSc, PGCE (*Head of Psychology*)

Miss J Salmon, Senior Performance Coach (*Director of Tennis*)

Mrs J Savage, BA Hons, PGCE (*English & History*)

Mr R Scamardella, BMus Hons, MMus, MMP(*Pianist in residence, Music*)

Mrs L Sparkes, BEd Hons, CAPS Special Needs (*Learning Support*)

Mr P Trenaman, BA Hons, PGCE (*English*)

Mr J Turner, BA Hons, PGCE (*Head of Photography*)

Ms A Turton, BSc Hons, PGCE (*Design Technology & ICT*)

Miss G Wainwright, BA Hons, PGCE (*Business Studies*)

Mrs R Walpole, BA Hons (*Art*)

Mr R Waring, BSc Hons, PGCE (*Head of General Studies, Drama, Psychology, PSHE*)

Ms J Warren (*Director of Riding*)

Mrs M Warren, CertEd (*Home Economics*)

Mr A Waterhouse, HDE Secondary (*Director of Sport, Business Studies*)

Mrs M Waterhouse, HDip, FDE (*Accounting & Business Studies*)

Mr A Webb, BTech Hons, BA, MA (*Head of Chemistry*)

Mrs P Webb, CertEd, Sp Ed Needs (*Science*)

Mr A Wells (*Director of Cricket*)

Mr C White, BSc Hons (*Geography*)

Mr P Wilkinson, BSc, PGCE (*Head of Mathematics*)

Mr R Williams, BA Hons, Dip Media Ed (*Head of Film & Media Studies*)

Mr M Wood, BSc, PGCE (*Mathematics*)

Legat School of Dance:

Ms E Holland, BPhil, LRAD, ARAD, AISTD (*Director of Dance*)

Professor P Melis (*Artistic Advisor*)

Miss C Blewer, PGDip, DMT

Miss E Harris, BA Hons LCDS

Mrs Louise Mizon, Dip RBS TTC

Miss N Skilton, Dip DD LSC

Miss D Curry, AI CHOR

Mrs R Egerton-Stein, ARAD, Dip PDTD

Aims. St Bede's discovers the talents of each student through breadth of academic curriculum and co-curricular. Academically ambitious for all, the School is proud of its ethos of inclusiveness. Students grow in confidence by being constantly encouraged to expect more: more of themselves, more of their teachers, more of the opportunities on offer. St Bede's pastoral care, delivered throught the House and Tutor system, is inspiring and nurturing and adds to developing the confidence with which St Bede's students move into the outside world, looking forward to the challenges they will meet.

Facilities. In 2007 the School opened two innovative and award-winning boarding houses and two more will open in the Autumn of 2011. The Multi-Purpose Hall, also opened in 2007, is used for School Assemblies, examinations and many sports, including basketball, badminton, cricket, football, netball and tennis. The Performing Arts Centre, in a beautiful setting next to the lake, provides studio space for both drama and dance and 2008 saw the opening of a new Music Centre. In addition, new tennis courts have been built and a new cricket pitch and pavilion and additional football pitches will be ready for use in the next academic year. St Bede's buildings are friendly, in enviable settings and a far cry from the overbearing, institutional character of much school architecture.

Curriculum. During the first year in the School students follow a very wide introductory course which includes the following subjects: Art and Design, Classics, Dance, Design & Technology, Drama, English, Geography, History, Home Economics, ICT, Mathematics, Modern Languages, Music, Physical Education, Science.

In the Fifth Form (Year 10) most students begin 2-year courses leading to the GCSE (Key Stage 4) examinations. Students usually follow 9 subjects at GCSE; Mathematics and English are compulsory subjects. Potential optional courses include: Art and Design, Business Studies, Dance, Design & Technology, Drama, Geography, History, Home Economics, Environmental Science, Information Technology, Latin and Greek, Media Studies, Modern Languages (French, Spanish, German), Music, Performing Arts (Dance), Physical Education, Religious Studies, Environmental and Land-Based Science, Science (Triple Award), Science (Double Award), Science (Single Award). Some IGCSEs are also offered along with some short-course GCSEs. A Pre-Sixth course is offered for those who need a year of intensive English before embarking on an A Level course.

During the first three years those with particular needs, such as those with any form of Dyslexia and those who are non-native speakers of English, can follow organised programmes within the timetable taught by suitably qualified teachers.

In the Sixth Form students can follow the traditional three or four A Level courses or a combined programme of A and AS Levels which can provide a broader education. Most GCSE subjects are offered at AS and A2 Level plus Accounting, Economics, Film Studies, Government & Politics, History of Art, Certificate in Professional Cookery, Performing Arts, Statistics and Theatre Studies. St Bede's also offers Cambridge Pre-U in a number of subjects. Equine Studies NVQ Level 1 and 2, Creative Skills – Fashion Certificate are also offered outside the curriculum. All Sixth Formers take part in a wide-ranging and challenging General Studies programme offering cultural and religious studies, current affairs, career advice and an innovative programme of guest speakers.

Vocational provision: BTEC National Certificate in Sport, National Award in Music Performance, National Award in Animal Management, National Award in Business Studies.

St Bede's also runs the Legat Professional Dance Course which is fully integrated with the academic programme.

Current class sizes average 16 up to GCSE level and 12 at A and AS Level.

Co-Curricular Programme including Games. The extensive programme includes the many sporting and games playing opportunities open to students, The Army Cadet Force, The Duke of Edinburgh's Award Scheme, numerous outdoor pursuits and a daily programme of activities within the fields of Art, Drama, Music, Journalism, Science, Technology, Engineering and Social Service. There are currently over 140 Club Activities running each week and an average daily choice from 40 options. Games and Sports include Aerobics, Archery, Athletics, Badminton, Basketball, Canoeing, Climbing, Cricket, Cross-Country, Dry-Skiing, Fishing, Football, Golf (the School has its own practice course), Hockey, Judo, Dance, Netball, Orienteering, Photography, Riding (the School has its own stables), Rounders, Rugby, Scrabble, Squash, Swimming, Table Tennis, Target Rifle Shooting, Tennis and Volleyball.

Pastoral Care. There are three boys' boarding houses and two girls' houses, the numbers in each house varying between 40 and 70, with three resident staff in each. An appropriately selected tutor provides a mentor for each student during their time at the School. These tutors are responsible for ensuring that each student's academic and social well-being is carefully looked after. Tutors act in liaison with Housemasters and Housemistresses and are readily available

for discussions with parents. All parents have several formal opportunities each year to meet those who teach or otherwise look after their sons or daughters.

Religion. The School shares the Village Church with the local community. Confirmation classes are available, if requested. All students attend weekly meetings in the church which are appropriate to boys and girls of all religions and are of outstanding variety. We do not wish to impose any singular religious observance on our students but would rather either that their existing faith is further strengthened by their being full members of the congregation of local churches or that they grow to appreciate and value the importance of a strong spiritual life through the thoughtful and varied programme of 'School Meetings'. There is a choice of four types of observance on Sundays: the Multi-Religious School Meeting, Church of England, Roman Catholic and Free Church.

Admission. The normal age of entry to the School is between 12½ and 14 years. The Common Entrance Examination, our own Scholarship Examination and Entry Tests are primarily used to determine a student's placing within sets and streams. Places are open each year to those wishing to join the School as Sixth Formers and at other levels in the School.

Scholarships and Bursaries. St Bede's invests in excess of 10% of its annual income in scholarships and means-tested fee remission. Academic, Art, Dance, Drama, Music and Sport scholarships are available. Parents of children applying for scholarships have three options: (a) to accept the scholarship without fee remission and as a recognition of excellence; (b) apply for means-tested fee remission up to a fully-funded place; and (c) apply for a small non means-tested award which will not exceed 25% of the full day fee. Prospective students who wish to join outside of the scholarship process are able to apply for means-tested fee remission. Sixth Form scholarship interviews and examinations are held in November and 13+ scholarships in January and February.

Further details regarding scholarships and bursaries are available from the Director of Admissions, e-mail: admissions@stbedesschool.org.

Fees per term (2011-2012). Full and Weekly Boarders £9,115 Day Pupils £5,475.

Charitable status. St Bede's School Trust Sussex is a Registered Charity, number 278950. It exists to provide quality education.

St Bees School

St Bees, Cumbria CA27 0DS
Tel: 01946 828000
Fax: 01946 823657
e-mail: mailbox@st-bees-school.co.uk
website: www.st-bees-school.org

Motto: '*Expecta Dominum*'
Founded by Edmund Grindal, Archbishop of Canterbury, in 1583. Now conducted as a co-educational independent school under a scheme approved by The Charity Commission.

Governors:

Chairman: W Lowther, Esq, CBE, OBE, DL, JP
Chairman of Executive Committee: W M Roberts, Esq, BSc, FCA

J A Cropper, Esq, BA, FCA, The Lord Lieutenant of Cumbria
N A Halfpenny, Esq, BSc, MSc, MIMgt
M P T Hart, Esq, FRICS, DipQS
G R Smith, Esq, BSc, DL

Mrs C T McKay
D G Beeby, Esq, FCA
A J Wills, Esq
M G Rigby, Esq
Sir D Hart
Dr K M Illsley, MBChB, MRCGP
S D Holmes, Esq
Dr A L N Creed, MA, MB, Bchir, DRCOG, DIH, AFOM
P Ireland, Esq, MA, MEd
The Rt Revd J W S Newcome, Bishop of Carlisle

Head: Mr P J Capes, BSc, MA

Deputy Head: D J Evans, BSc, MRSC, MBA
Senior Teacher: Miss J L Dyer, BSc
Senior Housemistress: Mrs J C Malan, BA (†*Lonsdale House*)

Teaching Staff:

† *Housemaster/mistress*

H M Turpin, GNSM	T H Bell, BSc
H L Lewis, Cert Ed	M J George, BA
Mrs G F Hudson, MA	Miss R C Richards, BSc
J M Mellor, BA	Mrs S G A Ollis, BA
J D Evans, MA	B R Allen, BA (†*School House*)
Mrs J A Bell, LLCM	
Mrs S L Bromiley, BA	Mrs V Smart, BSc, PhD
Mrs J A Carnegie, BA	R A Young, BSc, MSc, PhD (†*Grindal House*)
Mrs W Mellor, BA	
M A Williams, BA	Mrs V E Rowe, BA (†*Abbots House*)
Mrs S J Williams, BA (†*Abbots & Bega Houses*)	D A Rowe, BEd (†*Abbots House*)
M K Midwood, BA	Mrs M France, BSc
Mrs J Skeen, BSc	R B Bardsley, BA
S McNee, BA	Miss B Lavin Campo, BA
Mrs C M Dearden, CertEd	Ms A F Considine, BA
M Ollis, BA	Mrs C M Mauger, BEd
Mrs S J Evans, BEd	S W Taylor, BSc
Mrs C O Reed, BSc	J Lynch, MA

Prep School:
S S Sewill, BSc
Mrs P Lynch, BA
Mrs H Capes, BA

Medical Officers:
G J Ironside, MBChB, MRCGP, DRCOG
S E Megan, BMedSci, BM BS, MRCCP, DRCOG, DCH

Bursar: G Stokes
Director of Marketing and Admissions: Mrs H Gascoyne, BSc
Registrar: Mrs J Hawley
Head's Secretary: Mrs E Graham

Situation and Buildings. The School stands in 150 acres of the attractive Valley of St. Bees, half a mile from a fine sandy beach and on the western edge of the Lake District National Park.

The principal older buildings, including the Chapel, Library, Art & Design Department, Gymnasium and Swimming Pool are of St. Bees sandstone and are situated on a raised terrace overlooking the main playing fields. The original school-room, which dates from 1587, now forms one side of a quadrangle and is used as the dining hall.

More recent developments include a self-contained Music School with extensive teaching and practice facilities, plus a basement studio which houses a 24-track digital recording studio, a new Sixth Form Centre, a totally refurbished indoor swimming pool and changing rooms, establishment of a Golf Academy.

Organisation. There are approximately 300 pupils aged 4–18, divided into a Senior School and a Preparatory Department. In the Senior School each pupil is the responsi-

bility of a Housemaster or Housemistress and a personal tutor. There are three Houses for boys and two for girls. All Sixth Form boarders have study bedrooms while junior boarders share a room with up to four occupants. Boys and girls who live within commuting distance of the School are accepted as day pupils and the School also admits weekly boarders. The School operates an extensive bus service.

Religion. The Chapel stands at the centre of the School buildings and there are short services on certain weekdays before morning school. The Vicar of the Parish is the Chaplain and on Thursdays the whole School attends a short service in the Parish Church, The Priory.

Aims. The purpose of the School is to provide an education based on Christian principles, which will enable each pupil to develop his or her individual talents to the full. Particular emphasis is placed on academic excellence, good personal relationships and strong pastoral care. Thriving artistic, dramatic and musical traditions coupled with a wide range of sporting facilities help to avoid any narrow specialisation.

Curriculum. In the Preparatory Department, the curriculum is carefully planned to meet the needs of each individual child. Literacy and Numeracy objectives follow the National Framework guidelines, but look to challenge and extend the pupil as appropriate. Science covers the main programmes of study from the National Curriculum and promotes the understanding of Science through 'hands on' investigative work whenever possible. The majority of the work is topic based and during this time cross-curricular links are forged. Pupils are also given the opportunity to experience learning a foreign language such as French or Spanish under the guidance of one of the Language Assistants employed by the School.

In the Senior School, the curriculum provides GCSE courses in English, Latin, French, Spanish, History, Geography, Mathematics, Physics, Chemistry, Biology, Information Technology, Home Economics, Art, Physical Education and Music; option systems permit pupils to select the combination of subjects best suited to their abilities. Most members of the Sixth Form will study four subjects at AS Level and three at A2 Level together with a Key Skills and General Studies programme. Virtually all proceed to higher education. There is a highly successful Dyslexia and Learning Support Unit and Specialist EFL tuition is also provided.

Careers. The Senior School has developed good links with the locally-based Careers Offices. Members of the Staff are responsible for providing specialist advice on careers and higher education and for developing links with industry and commerce. The Head, Housemasters and Housemistresses are also involved in this work and there is regular contact between parents and staff so that progress, future options and career plans can be discussed.

Games. The major sports for boys are Rugby Football, Cricket and Athletics. The girls play Hockey and Rugby 7s and are given a wide choice of games, including Tennis and Athletics, during the Summer Term. The School provides many County and Regional Representatives in all major sports. A large number of other sports flourish; the School has its own Golf Course, indoor heated Swimming Pool, large multi-purpose Sports Hall, and courts for Eton Fives, Squash Rackets, Tennis and Badminton.

Other Activities. There is a wide variety of societies and clubs, for example Young Enterprise, Debating and Public Speaking, and each pupil is encouraged to develop cultural interests. The School offers an extensive and varied weekend programme for boarders. Recently these have included theatre excursions to Stratford, days out to York, Glasgow, Edinburgh and Newcastle, beside the usual cinema, ten-pin bowling etc. activities.

Music. The School possesses a strong musical tradition and a large proportion of the pupils receive tuition in an instrument. In addition to the Orchestra and Choir there are strings, brass and woodwind ensembles. Keyboard players have access to a Willis organ. The Choir and instrumentalists perform regularly at the School and in the locality. There are close links with drama.

Drama. Drama is part of the Lower School curriculum and each year there are several productions involving all age groups.

Combined Cadet Force. Pupils are members of the CCF in the Third and Fourth Forms (Years 9 and 10) and may choose to extend their service while they are in the Fifth (Year 11) or Sixth Form. There are Army and RAF Sections and all cadets receive instruction in Shooting. The Duke of Edinburgh's Award scheme can be taken through to Gold whilst pupils are cadets. Advanced courses are available in Leadership Training. Courses in flying and pilot training are also arranged.

Outdoor Activities. The School makes full use of its unique location between the Lakeland Fells and the sea and outdoor activities are encouraged for the enjoyment that they give and the valuable personal qualities which they help to develop. Adventure Training is part of the curriculum for Lower School pupils. Experts in mountaineering and water sports are employed by the School and all pupils have opportunities to receive instruction in camping, canoeing, hill walking, orienteering and rock climbing. There are annual skiing parties to Europe.

Admission. Candidates for entry between 7 and 10 is by individual interview and submission of previous school reports. Candidates for entry at age 11 or 13 sit the Scholarship and Entrance Examination in early March. Boys and girls from Preparatory Schools take the Common Entrance Examination for entry to the School at age 11 or 13. Entry to the Sixth Form is dependent on interview, school report and the gaining of a minimum of five GCSE passes. The Head is prepared to give individual consideration to candidates entering at other ages.

A fee of £40 is payable at the time of registration.

Further particulars from The Registrar; Tel: 01946 828010; Fax: 01946 828011; e-mail: jane.hawley@st-bees-school.co.uk.

Scholarships and Bursaries. (*See Scholarship Entries section.*) Scholarships are available to pupils who are entering the First Form and are under the age of 12 on 1st September and to pupils entering the Third Form who are under the age of 14 on 1st September. Music Scholarships are available at the ages of 11, 13 and 16. Academic Scholarships with Art and Sports Awards are available to pupils entering the Sixth Form.

The School also offers a limited number of means-tested Bursaries.

Fees per term (2011-2012). Senior: £8,421 (full boarding), £7,116 (weekly boarding), £4,998 (day). Junior: £6,108 (full boarding), £4,964 (weekly boarding), £3,872 (day).

Former Pupils. The St Beghian Society Secretary: c/o St Bees School, St Bees, Cumbria. Tel: 01946 828000. Handbook and Register of Members. Latest Edition 2000.

Charitable status. St Bees School is a Registered Charity, number 526858. It exists to provide high quality education for boys and girls.

St Benedict's School

---

54 Eaton Rise, Ealing, London W5 2ES

Tel: 020 8862 2000 (School Office)
020 8862 2010 (Headmaster's Office)
020 8862 2254 (Admissions)
020 8862 2183 (Bursar)
Fax: 020 8862 2199
e-mail: headmaster@stbenedicts.org.uk
enquiries@stbenedicts.org.uk (Admissions)
website: www.stbenedicts.org.uk

Motto: '*A minimis incipe*'

St Benedict's was founded in 1902 by Abbot Hugh Edmund Ford to provide a Catholic education in London incorporating the Benedictine ethos. In the tradition of St Benedict the School's mission is to '*teach a way of living*'. The School occupies a lovely site in West London, with outstanding sports facilities a mile away. The total number of pupils on roll is 1035 of which 731 are in the Senior School (202 in Sixth Form), 285 in the Junior School and 19 in the Nursery. Boarders are not accepted. The School is fully co-educational from 3 years through to 18.

Governing Body: The Abbot & Community of Ealing Abbey, assisted by a lay Advisory Body.

Headmaster: Mr C J Cleugh, BSc, MSc

Deputy Headmasters:
S Oliver, BA, MLitt
Dom Thomas Stapleford, BA
Mrs P Lightfoot, BSc

Bursar: Mrs C de Cintra, BA, ACA

Headmaster's PA: Mrs D Simmons

Registrar: Mrs M Moore

Old Priorian Association: P Fagan, President, c/o The School

Admission to the School is in September at the age of 11, by interview and special examination. Admission to the Sixth Form is subject to good GCSE results. Application for admission should be made to the Headmaster. Registration Fee: £75.

Religion. A specifically Christian and Catholic atmosphere is fostered through contact with the Monastery. There are regular periods for liturgy, both formal in the Abbey Church and informal in small groups. However the School welcomes pupils of other denominations and faiths.

Curriculum. In the Senior School, for the first year all pupils follow a common curriculum including ADT, French and Music. In the second year additional languages are offered: German or Spanish. Religious Studies is undertaken by all in every year. Pupils normally take between 9 and 11 GCSE subjects. A wide choice of subjects is available at AS and A Level. The Sixth Form is large, nearly 200, and almost all proceed to University or further education. Pupils are also prepared for Oxford and Cambridge entrance, where there is an impressive record.

Physical Education and Games are part of the curriculum throughout the School. Rugby and cricket are the principal games for boys and netball, hockey and rounders for girls. Fencing is available for both boys and girls. Other sports are also promoted, including tennis, swimming, athletics, karate, volleyball and table tennis. The School has 15 acres of playing fields nearby at Perivale, with a state-of-the-art Pavilion and changing rooms. The School has a national reputation for rugby. A full-size Astroturf pitch was completed in February 2011.

In the nature of a wholly day school, contact with parents is frequent and regular.

Facilities. In the past five years there has been huge investment in computer technology, science lab refurbishment and the building of an extension to the Junior School. On top of this comes the £6.2 million Cloisters complex, which opened in October 2008. It connects the School across three levels and provides excellent facilities for music and modern languages, a central multi-purpose hall, a chapel, 14 extra classrooms and a new School reception and medical facility.

Activities. School activities are too many to mention but include Combined Cadet Force, The Duke of Edinburgh's Award Scheme, and over 70 lunchtime or after-school clubs and societies. Drama is strong with annual major productions. The Musical provision is expanding; almost any instrument can be learnt and activities include choirs, wind band, samba band and two orchestras. Public concerts are held several times each term. Art is outstanding, with a large number of pupils passing from the Sixth Form to Art Colleges each year. Considerable use is made of opportunities available in London for visits to concerts, theatres, museums and art galleries.

Careers. There is a Careers Centre with experienced careers staff and some work experience in appropriate fields is organised. Close contact is enjoyed with the Services.

Fees per term (2011-2012). Tuition fees: Senior School £4,120, Junior School £3,620.

Charitable status. St Benedict's is a Registered Charity, number 242715. Its aim is to promote the Christian and Catholic education of young people.

St Columba's College

Whitechurch, Dublin 16, Ireland
Tel: 00 353 1 490 6791 (Warden's Office)
           00 353 1 493 2860 (Bursar's Office)
Fax: 00 353 1 493 6655
e-mail: admin@stcolumbas.ie
website: www.stcolumbas.ie

Motto: *'Prudentes Sicut Serpentes et Simplices Sicut Columbae'*
St Columba's College was founded in 1843 by the Revd William Sewell, the Lord Primate, the Earl of Dunraven and others. The College was incorporated by Royal Charter in 1913.

Visitor: The Right Revd A E T Harper, OBE, BA, Archbishop of Armagh and Primate of All Ireland

Fellows:
The Most Revd J Neill, MA, LLD, Archbishop of Dublin
H D Thompson, MA, BAgricSc
Mrs A C Kennedy
Mrs A Budd, MA, HDipEd
J N White, FIAVI
C D S Shiell, BSc, FCIS
R H Simpson, BBS, FCA
Mrs K M Erwin, MA
Dr M O'Moore, MA, PhD, FTCD
P Myerscough
G D Crampton, MA, BBS
J Bailey, MA
I Roberts, BA, BAI, CEng, FIEI, FIStructE, FICE (*Chairman*)
R M Ridley, MA
G Caldwell, BBS
M Greene

Warden: Dr L J Haslett, BA, DPhil, PGCE

Sub-Warden: J M Girdham, BA, HDipEd

Bursar: Mrs S Gibbs, MA, MSc, HDipEd

Assistant Staff:
* *Head of Department*
† *Housemaster/mistress*

F H Morris, BA, HDipEd (*Senior Master*)
P J Jackson, BSc, HDipEd (*Science, Director of Boys' Boarding*)
J R Brett, MA, MSt, HDipEd (*Classics, Senior Tutor, Librarian*)
P R Watts, DipArt, HDipADE (*Art*)
Mrs A Morris, BA, HDipEd (*Director of Girls' Boarding*)
D C Sherwood, MA, HDipEd (*Geography, Master i/c Sport and Extra-Curricular Activities*)

B A Redmond, BTech, DipID (*Technology*)
G R Bannister, MA, PhD, HDipEd (*Irish*)
L Canning, BA, HDipEd (†*Stackallan*)
Miss A Maybury, BA, HDipEd (*SPHE*)
J J Stone, BSc, PhD, HDipEd (*Drama, Transition Year Coordinator*)
Dr M Singleton, MSc, PhD, HDipEd (*Registrar, Director of Studies, *Physics*)
P G McCarthy, MA, HDipEd (*Business Studies, Classical Studies*)
Mrs D Sherwood (†*Iona*)
Ms S McEneaney, BA, PGCE
Mrs F G Heffernan, PGCert (*SLD*), CertEd, ACLD, ILSA, AMBDA (*Learning Support*)
Mrs A Stone, BA, HDipEd (†*Hollypark*)
Miss D Cullen, BEd (†*Beresford*)
D Higgins, MA, HDipEd (†*Glen*)
Mrs G Malone-Brady, MA, LRAM, ARCM, LRSM (*Director of Music*)
P Cron, MA, NDip (*Boys' Games, †Gwynn*)
Mrs M D Haslett, BA, MPhil, PGCE (*History*)
Mrs S-J Johnson, BEd (*Girls' Games*)
Ms K Hennessey, BSc
R Swift, BA, HDipEd (*CSPE*)
N Coldrick, BSc
S Crombie, BSc (*Director of ICT*)
Ms R Howell, BA, HDipEd (*Economics*)
H Jones, BScEd, PGDipGC (*Guidance and Careers*)
Ms A Kilfeather, BA, HDipEd
M Patterson, MSc, PGCE (*Mathematics, †Tibradden*)
M O'Shaughnessy, MA (*Modern Languages*)
B Finn, MA, HDipEd
E Jameson, MA, HDipEd
Ms J Robinson, BA, HDipEd
Ms K Smith, BA, PGDipEd
T Clarke, BA, PGDipEd
The Revd N Crossey, MA, MTh, PDipTheol, Chaplain (*Religious Education*)

A Grundy, MA Mus, HonVCM, FTCL, LRSM, ALCM (*Guitar*)
Ms S Taylor, MBA, BA, LTCL (*Piano & Theory*)
L McGuinness, LRAM (*Voice*)
Ms K Snowe, BA, LRSM, ALCM (*Piano*)
Ms A Murnaghan, BA Mus, LRAM (*Cello, Piano, Theory*)
Ms T Lawlor, ALCM, LLCM (*Guitar*)
Ms A Ennis (*Harp*)
Ms M Comiskey, MA Mus (*Flute*)
Ms L Morris (*Clarinet/Saxophone*)
B Reilly (*Percussion*)
Ms C Meehan, LRAM (*Violin, Viola*)
R Molloy (*Piano*)
Ms S Campbell, BMus (*Singing*)
D Kelly, MA Mus (*Harp*)

Accountant: N Grannell, FCA
Admissions Secretary: Ms N Crisp
Warden's Secretary: Ms E Bainton
Medical Officer: Dr A Khourie
Infirmary Sister: Mrs L Hanna, RGN

The College is a co-educational boarding school, with a number of day pupils, of about 300 pupils. It is situated on the slopes of the Dublin Mountains about 7 miles south of the city overlooking Dublin Bay in an estate of 138 acres. Much of this comprises playing fields, a 9-hole golf course and a deer park.

Having occupied its present site for over 160 years, the College combines the best of architecture old and new. Recent additions include a new Library and Reading Room, a Sports Hall, a Computer Centre, a Careers Library and an Arts Centre. Two completely new boarding houses and four classrooms opened in 2004. A new Music School was opened in 2008. A second astroturf hockey pitch and an additional dining hall were also added in recent years.

Admission. Application for admission should be made to the Warden. There is a registration fee of €100. There are two junior Houses for entrants between the ages of 11 and 13 years. An assessment day is held for 11/12 year old entrants in October prior to the year of entry. Entry is determined by a number of factors, including family association, geographical spread (including Northern Ireland, the UK and overseas), date of registration and an understanding of the values which underpin the College. Entrants from Preparatory Schools take the Common Entrance Examination.

Curriculum. In the Upper School, a wide choice of subjects and a large number of courses are available for the Irish Leaving Certificate. This examination keeps many options open for third-level colleges. It is the qualifying examination for entry to Irish universities and is acceptable (with requisite grades) to the faculties of all British universities. The Irish Junior Certificate is taken in the third form. A compulsory Transition Year programme follows the Junior Certificate.

Religious Teaching. Chapel services and religious instruction are based upon the liturgy and doctrine of the Church of Ireland. Boys and girls of other denominations and faiths are included.

Other Activities. Music, Art, Pottery and Technical Graphics (which are part of the curriculum in the Lower School) and Drama, Debating, Photography, Computers and various other clubs and societies function at all levels.

Games and Pursuits. Rugby Football, Hockey, Cricket, Athletics, Cross-country Running, Tennis, Badminton, Basketball, Golf, Swimming, Hill-walking, Horse-riding, Polocrosse, Sailing, Archery and Aerobics.

Fees per term (2011-2012). Day Pupils €3,355–€4,025, Day Boarding €4,010–€4,805, Full Boarding €5,920–€7,105.

The above fees are expressed in Euros. Fees may be paid in the Sterling equivalent.

Entrance Scholarships. Junior and senior awards are made at age 12 (entry to Form I), 14 (entry to Form IV) and 16 (entry to Form V). Entrance exhibitions are often awarded to candidates for entry to Form II through the Common Entrance Examination. Generous discounts are available for the sons and daughters of the Clergy of the Church of Ireland. Old Columban and sibling discounts are also available. Details on request.

Leaving Scholarship. Norman Scholarships, for three years or more at all university colleges in Britain and Ireland, are open to the sons and daughters of Clergy of the Church of Ireland.

St Columba's Former Pupils' Society. Old Columban Society. *Hon Secretary*: J M Girdham, St Columba's College.

Charitable status. St Columba's College is a Registered Charity, number 4024. Its aims and objectives are the provision of Secondary Education facilities.

St Columba's College

King Harry Lane, St Albans, Hertfordshire AL3 4AW
Tel: 01727 855185
Fax: 01727 892024
e-mail: admissions@st-columbas.herts.sch.uk
website: www.stcolumbascollege.org

St Columba's College has been a school in the tradition of the Brothers of the Sacred Heart (New England Province) since 1955 and is a Catholic, selective boys' school, but with about half of its pupils coming from other denominations and faiths. Brothers and lay teachers (now in the majority) work together with pupils and parents to provide a Christian education based on traditional values, balancing a friendly community with sound discipline and academic rigour.

St Columba's College stands in its own grounds overlooking the picturesque vale of St Albans and the Roman settlement of Verulamium. In the last few years extensive improvements have been made to Science, English and Drama, Sixth Form and Preparatory facilities.

Motto: '*cor ad cor loquitur*'

Trustee and Dean: Br Raymond Hetu, SC, MA

Governors:
Chairman: Mrs G Cummings, JP
Vice-Chairman: K Rudd
Professor J Cilliers, MBA, PhD, CEng, CSci, FIChemE, FIMMM
Mrs D Garfield, BSc, PGCE
Mrs J Harrison, BEd
Mrs A P M Hartnett, LLB
The Revd Canon Stephen Lake, BTh
Br Ivy Leblanc, SC
Br Joseph Rocco, SC
C Thorpe, MBA, BA, FCIM, FRSA
P Lane, BA, ACA
C Savvides, MA Oxon, AMCT
C Cleugh, MSc Chem, JP
Mrs J Carolan, BSc, MRICS
C Cook, LLB

Bursar & Clerk to the Governors: Neville De Lord, BSc

Headmaster: David Buxton, BA, MTh, MA

Deputy Headmaster: D Shannon-Little, CertEd, BA
Academic Deputy Head: I T Nash, BSc
Head of Sixth Form: S Robins, BSc
Head of Preparatory School: Mrs R Loveman, BSc
Prep Pastoral Deputy: M Ioannou, BEd
Prep Academic Deputy: Mrs M Shannon-Little, BEd
Senior Master & Director of Admissions: A K Smith, CertEd, DLC

Chaplain: Fr T Edgar, BD, AKC, STD

Heads of House:
Charles: S D'Souza BSc
Guertin: R McCann, BA
Joseph: J Tatham, BA
McClancy: P J Baker, BSc
Stanislaus: R J Byrne, BSc
Vandebilt: A Colville, BA

* *Head of Department*

Art:	Mrs C Gwynn, BEd
*(to be appointed)	D Shannon-Little, BA
J Tatham, BA	P Smith, MA
Miss H Bromfield (*Art Technician*)	Mrs G Sorrell, BA
	Geography:
Careers:	*D Hughes, BSc
*Mrs K Skinner, BSc	Mrs S Hassall, BSc
	M D Lyons, BSc
Classics:	
*S Graves, BA	*History*:
Ms C Jackson, BA	*K Roberts, MA
	R J Byrne, BSc
Design Technology:	Miss R Finn, MA
*Miss V Risianova, BA	Mrs M James, MA
L Correya, BA	R McCann, BA
	Mrs C Powesland, BA
Economics:	
*Mrs K Healer, MA Cantab, LLB	*Information & Communications Technology*:
J Turner, BA	
Mrs J Greaves, BSc	*S M Leadbetter, MA
	Br P Vaillancourt, SC, MA
English & Drama:	J Twyman (*Head of IT Services*)
*E Waters, BA	
Miss K Constantinou, BA	

J Lagrue, BSc (*ICT Systems Manager*)
Mrs M Cooper (*ICT Training & Administration Coordinator*)

Learning Support:
A L G Nevard, BSc, OCR Dip SpLD

Library/Media:
Mrs S Mathieson, Dip Lib (*Head Librarian*)
Mrs J Foster, BA
Mrs C Hart

Mathematics:
*I Devereux, BEd
Mrs K Parsons, BSc
K Blyth, BA
Mrs M Dattani, CertEd
C Jewell, MPhil
Mrs N Rowlands, BSc
A Wilkins, BA
I T Nash, BSc

Modern Foreign Languages:
Ms S Jasieczek, BA (*French*)
Mrs I Yates, BA (*Spanish*)
D Gaze, MA
Mrs W Koning, BA
R Kopel, BA
Miss M Manrique, BA
Mrs L McCann, BA

Music:
J Woodhall, MA Oxon, ALCM, LTCL

The Music Department is assisted by visiting instrumental teachers.

Preparatory School:
Mrs P Almond, BA (*Modern Foreign Languages*)
Mrs L Bills, BA LGSM (*Music*)
M Bridge, BSc (*Social Studies*)
Miss D Harvey, MA (*Science*)
Mrs S Burgon, BA (*Art and Design*)
Mrs U Kelly, BSc (*Mathematics*)
E Lowe, BSc (*PE and Games*)
Mrs H McLeod, MA, ALA (*Librarian*)
N Smart, BSocSci, DipT
Mrs D Sumpter, BA (*Learning Support*)
Mrs M Turner (*ADT Technician*)
R Webster, BEd (*History*)
Mrs M Willcock, BEd (*English*)

Miss C Harding, BEd (*Pre-Prep 1 Derry*)
Mrs A Alexander-Fishwick, BA (*Pre-Prep 1 Kells, *RE*)
Mrs L Brown, BEd (*Pre-Prep 2 Derry*)
Mrs L Latham, BEd (*Pre-Prep 2 Kells*)
Miss K Leahy, BA (*Pre-Prep 3 Derry*)
Mrs G Lewis, BEd (*Pre-Prep 3 Kells*)
Mrs P Knox, DipEd (*Music*)

Teaching Assistants:
Mrs D Brown
Mrs L Cartman
Mrs M Scott
Mrs K Walker
Mrs A Wynn-Owen

Administration:
College Accounts: Mrs W Gerrard, BSc, ACMA
Marketing Coordinator: Mrs C Tominey
Headmaster's PA: Mrs R Crowley

Physical Education:
M P Swales, BA (*Director of Sport*)
B Alway, BSc
K Boland, BA
A Lowles, Bed
S Murphy, BSc
S Robins, BSc

Politics:
*R McKenzie, BA

Religious Education:
*Ms L Cronin, BA
Mrs M Adair, MA Oxon
E Castle, BA
S Jones, BA, CTS
Miss C Treacy, BA
Ms J Hudson, BA

Science:
*Dr K Bridge, BSc, PhD
Mrs M Mester, BSc (*Biology*)
J G Sapsford, BSc (*Chemistry*)
Mrs O Chizhova (*Physics*)
S D'Souza, BSc
P J Baker, BSc
Dr R Baker-Glenn, MA Cantab, PhD
Mrs S H Payne, BSc
Mrs H Camm, MSc

Science Technicians:
Mrs J Dewar, BSc
Mrs E Green, BSc
Dr V Sullivan, BSc, PhD
Dr E Walls, BSc, PhD
Mrs E Webb, BSc
Mrs R Wright, BSc

Sociology:
N Hogan, BA (*Department Coordinator*)

Senior School Secretaries: Mrs C Wood & Mrs S Bradley
Head of Prep's PA: Mrs C Tominey
Prep School Secretaries: Miss L Cancelliere & Mrs O Cumine
Registrar: Br D Bessette, SC, BA
Examinations Officer: Mrs T Bovington
College Nurse Manager: Mrs G O'Sullivan, RGN
College Nurse: Mrs C Newton, RGN
OC CCF: Ft Lt S D Leadbetter, MA
Alumni Coordinator: J Lewis, BEd

Entry. St Columba's College admits boys from 4–18. Currently there are 255 boys in the Preparatory School, aged 4–11, and 625 boys in the Senior School, aged 11–18. The main entry for the Senior School is at 11, by Entrance Test and interview, with a significantly smaller group being offered deferred entry at 13+.

Scholarships. Academic Scholarships are awarded at 11, 13 and for the Sixth Form. Additionally, the College offers two Music Scholarships each year and means-tested Coindre Bursaries.

The Curriculum. This is kept as broad as possible up to GCSE, pupils usually taking 9/11 subjects from the traditional range of Arts and Science options. There are 21 A Level (A2) subjects for pupils to choose from, all of which are also available as a fourth option up to AS. Sixth Form education is complemented by an enrichment course which prepares students for extra qualifications including the Extended Project, ICT and Personal Finance. Almost all of the Sixth Form go on to universities, including Oxford and Cambridge.

Careers. A full-time Head of Careers and Higher Education works from a fully-equipped Careers Centre to ensure that all students receive high-quality guidance in order to make informed decisions about subject choices and university courses with subsequent career options in mind.

Pastoral Care. St Columba's is a Catholic foundation welcoming students from all traditions. The spiritual and moral well-being of our pupils is a matter of primary importance for all of our staff, the majority being tutors. The six Housemasters and their teams are supported by a Ministry Team. Relations between the College and parents are open – a strength of the Foundation – and they are in regular contact with each other in monitoring the progress of the boys. The College seeks to nurture the academic and personal talents of each individual.

Sport. All boys participate, and the College has a strong sporting reputation. A rich variety of sports is available, including Rugby, Basketball, Football, Tennis, Cricket, Athletics, Swimming and Cross Country. For Sixth Form boys, not selected for the major sports, an even wider range of activities is available. Facilities include a large gymnasium and sports field on site. The Sports Department makes extensive use of soccer and rugby pitches, an athletics track, swimming pool and a golf course which are all immediately adjacent to the College site.

Extended and Extra-Curricular Activities. The College offers a mix of activities both at lunch-time and after school. These include sports clubs, such as archery and lacrosse, drama, art, chess, computing, Young Enterprise and many others, as well as a variety of academic and social clubs. There is a number of music ensembles, including a choir, orchestra and jazz band and four choirs of hand-bell ringers.

CCF. The Combined Cadet Force includes an Army and an RAF section. A full-time SSI (School Staff Instructor) is employed and the sections now include girls from The Princess Helena College, Hitchin and Loreto College, St Albans. The Duke of Edinburgh's Award Scheme comes under the same management.

Preparatory School. The Preparatory School is on the same site as the Senior School and shares many of its facilities. The College has a strong family atmosphere, providing a secure and purposeful environment in which expectations are high. It admits boys only, by assessment, into the Lower Prep and Upper Prep phases. In their final year, most Preparatory School pupils are offered unconditional places at St Columba's College Senior School, following recommendations by Prep School staff.

(*See also St Columba's College Preparatory School entry in IAPS section.*)

Fees per term (2011-2012). Senior School £3,770; Prep 4–6 £3,360, Prep 3 £3,065, Reception–Prep 2 £2,898.

Charitable status. St Columba's College is a Registered Charity, number 1088480. It exists to provide a well-rounded Catholic education for pupils from 4–18 years of age.

St Columba's School

Duchal Road, Kilmacolm, Inverclyde PA13 4AU
Tel: 01505 872238
Fax: 01505 873995
e-mail: secretary@st-columbas.org
website: www.st-columbas.org

Junior School:
Knockbuckle Road, Kilmacolm, Inverclyde PA13 4EQ
Tel: 01505 872768
e-mail: juniorsecretary@st-columbas.org

Founded in 1897, St Columba's School is a non-denominational, co-educational day school for pupils aged 3–18. The School currently has just under 730 pupils with around 346 at Senior School. It is situated in the small rural community of Kilmacolm, surrounded by delightful countryside and located only 7 miles from Glasgow Airport.

Motto: *Orare Laborare Literisque Studere*

Governing Body:

Honorary President: Mr Guy Clark, Lord Lieutenant of Renfrewshire

Honorary Vice-Presidents:
Geoffrey C C Duncan, BL, NP
John C Ritchie
Dr Helen M Laird, OBE, MA, PhD, DL
Ron M Kennedy, TD, FCCII, FLIA

Board of Directors:
David Ward, MA, DUniv (*Chairman*)
Hugh M Currie, BSc, CEng, MICE (*Deputy Chairman*)
Nicola Anderson, MCSP
Thomas Anderson, LLB
Sara Bishop
Graham Cunning, BAcc, CA
Dr Aileen Findlay, BSc, MBChB Ed, MRCGP
Helen M MacConnacher
James McAlpine
Colin McClatchie
George Morris, LLB, MBA
Paul Yacoubian, BAcc, CA

Rector: Mr D G Girdwood, DL, BSc St Andrews, MEd Stirling, SQH

Business Manager & Senior Depute Rector: Mrs J Wallace, DipPE Dunfermline, DipSEN

Head of Junior School: Mrs D L Cook, DCE Jordanhill, ITQ, DipAdPrStudies, DipEdMan Strathclyde

Depute Rector: Mrs J E Stevens, BEd Aberdeen

Depute Rector: Mr M J McLaughlin, MA Greenwich, BA Thames

Depute Head of Junior School: (*to be appointed*)

Senior Master: Mr C S Clark, BEd Glasgow

Company Secretary: Mr A D Gallacher, CA

Registrar: Mr B A Manson, DipPE Jordanhill

Rector's PA: Mrs Dorothy Motherwell

Heads of House:
Strathgryffe: Mrs N Smith, MA Glasgow
Killallan: Mr G Robertson, MA Glasgow
Craigmarloch: Mrs J Scott, BA Edinburgh, DipSL
Duchal: Mrs V Reilly, MA Edinburgh

Senior School Teaching Staff:
* *Head of Faculty*
‡ *Chartered Teacher*

Ancient & Modern Languages:
*Ms L Rodger, MA Edinburgh
Mrs E A Hunter, MA Glasgow
Mrs V Reilly, MA Edinburgh
Mrs N Smith, MA Glasgow
Mrs A Holt, MA St Andrews
Mrs P Kennedy, MA Glasgow
Ms K A Sturt, MA St Andrews

Design:
*Mrs H Beall, BA Reading
Mrs M R Robinson, BA Glasgow School of Art
Mrs H Macdonald, DipDomSc Glasgow West of Scotland Coll, DipSecEd Jordanhill
Mr A Morrison, BEd Strathclyde
Mr T Boag, DipTechEd Jordanhill

English:
*Mr G McNicol, BA Hertfordshire
Mrs K Brash, MPhil Queensland
Mrs V Kennedy, BA Stirling
Mrs J E Stevens, BEd Aberdeen
Mrs A Moran, MA Glasgow
‡Mr G Smith, MA Glasgow, MEd West of Scotland
Mr M J McLaughlin, MA Greenwich, BA Thames

Humanities:
*Mrs L T Eadie, BEd Aberdeen
Mrs M McCaffer, BSc Glasgow, DRLP, DIRM
Mr G Robertson, MA Glasgow
Mrs J Scott, BA Edinburgh, DipSL
Dr C Gilmour, BA, PhD Stirling
Ms A Elkin, MA Glasgow
Mrs T Carlysle, BA Dundee
Mrs R Kerr, MA Glasgow
Ms Shaw, BA Glasgow Caledonian

Mathematics & ICT:
*Mrs F I Bruce, BSc Glasgow
Mr C S Clark, BEd Glasgow
Mrs J Judd, BSc Paisley
Mr A Walkey, BSc, MSc Glasgow
Mrs N Gardner, BA, MPA Indiana
Mr A Sutherland, BEng, PGED Glasgow

Music:
*Ms Y Carey, DipMusEd Glasgow
Mrs A G Sutherland, DipEd, LTCL Piano, LTCL Voice

Physical Education:
*Mr E Milligan, BEd Edinburgh
*Mrs C Marr, MBE, DipPE I M Marsh College of PE
Mr B A Manson, DipPE Jordanhill
Mrs J Bellew, BEd Dunfermline
Mrs L Urie, BEd Dunfermline
Mrs G Green, BEd Heriot-Watt (*maternity leave*)
Mr A Tait, BA Stirling, BEd Edinburgh

Science:

Biology:
*Mrs P Nicoll, BEd St Andrews Coll

Mrs E Wilson, BSc Paisley
Chemistry:
*Mrs T Munro, BSc Paisley, PGDipComp Jordanhill, SQH
Ms L Robertson, BSc Strathclyde, PgDip IT Paisley
Physics:
*Mr I Weir, BSc Paisley, MBA Strathclyde
Dr I Spencer, BSc, PhD Glasgow

Junior School Teaching Staff:
*Mr A MacKay, BEd Strathclyde
Mrs J Andrews, BA King Alfred's, MA Ed Open
Miss G Beggs, BEd Dundee
Mrs E M Black, DCE Jordanhill
Mrs M Blackie, DCE Jordanhill
Mrs M S Campbell DCE Jordanhill
Mrs E Corbett, BEd Jordanhill
Mrs I Evans, DCE Jordanhill, ALCM
Mrs G Henderson, BA Paisley
Miss S MacLean, MA Glasgow
Mrs H Manceau, MA Glasgow, PGCE Strathclyde
Mrs F MacFarlane, BEd Strathclyde
Mrs A Moore, DCE Craigie
Mrs S Robertson, DipEd Jordanhill
Mrs S Swinnerton, DCE Craigie
Mrs L Melville, BEd Strathclyde
Mrs G Hall, BA Cambridge

With a roll of just under 730 across both the Junior and Senior Schools, teachers know each child by name. Considerable effort is made to create an environment which encourages each pupil to realise their potential, and nurtures polite, articulate and informed young people. The School consistently achieves excellent academic results, regularly placing it as one of the highest-achieving schools nationally. St Columba's was awarded Investor in People status in 2007.

Facilities. The School buildings and sports facilities are located within a quarter of a mile radius of each other. A major extension to the Senior School is planned for the immediate future.

Sports facilities include: gym area for gymnastics and dance, large purpose-built sports hall including fitness suite, all-weather floodlit hockey/tennis ground, access to three rugby pitches and a large playing field used for athletics and cross-country running.

The School has a dedicated transport service and an after-school care facility.

Curriculum. St Columba's School follows the Scottish Curriculum at all stages. Junior School pupils are taught French, music and PE by specialist staff. Transitus (P7) is a transitional year with core curriculum taught by the class teacher and science, languages, art, music and PE delivered by specialist secondary teachers. Pupils in SIV are presented for Standard Grade/Intermediate 2 examinations followed by Higher Grade and Advanced Higher Grade examinations in SV and SVI.

Games. Rugby, hockey, tennis, athletics, badminton, gymnastics, swimming, volleyball, basketball, soccer, dance (girls), orienteering. Optional: netball, squash, cricket, golf, skiing/snowboarding, curling, street dance, weight-training.

Extra-Curricular. The importance of extra-curricular activities is emphasised at both Junior and Senior School level. The School offers over 20 clubs including The Duke of Edinburgh's Award, debating, sport, chess, drama and music (choirs, orchestras, ensembles, pipe band, jazz band). Individual tuition in a wide range of instruments and in Diction is available. Public performances and school shows are arranged on a regular basis.

From SIII upwards, The Duke of Edinburgh's Award Scheme attracts very large numbers with its emphasis on skills, service, sport and the expedition section at bronze, silver and gold level.

There is a very strong tradition of fundraising for charity and community service within the School.

St Columba's has strong links with schools in Australia and Canada and has annual exchanges between students for periods of time.

Organisation. The school is organised into four Houses for both pastoral and competitive purposes. Each house has a Head of House as well as pupil Captain and Vice-Captain. Career guidance is supported by ISCO.

Admission. Entry to St Columba's is by a combination of entry test, interview and, where applicable, a report from the applicant's previous school. An open week is held in November and entrance tests are held in January. The main entry points are Junior 1 and Transitus however pupils are taken in at other stages as places become available.

Fees per annum (2011-2012). Nursery £2,420, Prep £3,230, J1 & J2 £6,950, J3 £7,610, J4 £8,070, J5 & J6 £8,480, Trans & SI £9,440, SII £9,750, SIII–SV £9,440, SVI £9,500.

A number of bursary places, ranging from 10–100% of fees, are available for new applicants entering Transitus (P7), SV to study Highers and SVI to study Advanced Highers.

Charitable status. St Columba's School is a Registered Charity, number SC012598. It exists to provide education for pupils.

St Dunstan's College

Stanstead Road, London SE6 4TY
Tel: 020 8516 7200
Fax: 020 8516 7300
e-mail: info@sdmail.org.uk
          admissions@sdmail.org.uk
website: www.stdunstans.org.uk
          intranet: www.sdonline.org.uk

Motto: '*Albam Exorna*'
The College was founded in the 15th Century in the Parish of St Dunstan-in-the-East, part of the Tower Ward of the City of London. In 1888 the school was re-founded in Catford, South East London. It became co-educational in 1994.

Governors:
Chairman of the Governors: ¶Sir Paul Judge, MA, MBA, LLD Hon

Deputy Chairman: P L Coling, Esq, FRICS

Miss S Ahmed, BSc
Mrs V Alexander
C R Berry, Esq, CR
Mrs J Davies, MA, FRSA
¶P W France, Esq
¶The Very Revd Dr John Hall, Dean of Westminster
Mrs L Kiernan, MA, DipEd
K L Marshall, Esq, RD, FICS, ACII
Ms S Mayne
Revd B Olivier
Mrs K Price, MA, FRSA
Miss D Robertshaw, BSc
¶F A Robinson, Esq, BSc, MPhil, Dip TS, FRTPI, CMILT
¶C L Watts, Esq

¶ *Old Dunstonian*

Clerk to the Governors and Bursar: Colonel N Wallace

Senior School Academic Staff:

Headmistress: Mrs J D Davies, BSc

Deputy Head: T Kirk, MA
Head of Key Stage 5: P A Glavin, BA
Head of Key Stage 4: N M Adriano, BA
Head of Key Stage 3: B Harrild, BA

* Head of Faculty

Mrs S E Algeo, BA, MA
Mrs J Atkinson, GRSM, NCOS
R Austin, BSc
G Bailey, BSc
Mrs H S Baptiste, BSc
Miss G L Barlow, BSc
*J W Bennie, BSc
Miss D A Berthoud, BSc
Miss L Boquet, BA
*R R D Bodenham, BSc
Miss C L Brady, BA
Miss C M Buchanan, MA
Ms M M Callaghan, BA
Mrs A E Chandler, BA, MA
R W Davies, BA
Ms M Diaz Blanco, MA
J P H Elmes, MA
P A Glavin, BA
P Glyne-Thomas, BA
Miss R Halfacree, BA
Mrs L Hartwell, BSc
Mrs S Hearn, BSc
R Hill, BSc
W J Holroyd, BA
Miss S Hussein, BSc

Miss M-L Inglebert, BA
*A W Johnston, MA
A J C Kinnear, BEd
R W Lea, BA, BEd
*Ms S Lee, BA
Mrs D S Malpart, BSc
Ms D K Mitchell, MA
Mrs E C Mitchell, MSc
*Ms K Molteni, BA
T Neal, BA
J M Newman, BA
Miss T Pearson, BA
G S Phillips, BSc, MSc
Mrs K A Plummer, BA
Mrs S E Besly-Quick, BA
D Read, BSc
R Sharkey, BSc
Miss C Sivvery, BA
Mr P J Stobart, BA
Miss E Vile, MA
*Miss D M Warren, BEng
D J Webb, BA
Mrs J V Williams, BEd
Miss R J Wilson, BSc
M Wood, BA
Miss L E Zatloukal, BA

Headmistress's Personal Assistant: Mrs P Phillips
Marketing & Admissions Officer: (*to be appointed*)
Assistant Admissions Officer:Mrs A Adriano
Junior School Secretary/Registrar: Mrs R Scard
College Doctor: (*to be appointed*)

Buildings. The College is located in mainly Victorian buildings on a 15-acre site three minutes' walk from Catford and Catford Bridge railway stations. Facilities include an imposing Great Hall, a well-equipped Learning Resource Centre, a drama studio, three state-of-the-art ICT suites and refurbished chemistry laboratories. To complement extensive playing fields on site, St Dunstan's has a sports hall, fully-equipped fitness rooms, floodlit netball/tennis courts, rugby fives courts and an indoor swimming pool, recently modernised to a very high standard.

Organisation and Curriculum. The College educates boys and girls from the ages of 3 to 18. The Junior School comprises a nursery class for 20 children (3+), a Pre-Prep Department for 100 children aged 4–7 and a Prep Department of 120 children aged 7–11.

In the Junior School great emphasis is placed on letting children learn in a friendly, caring and stimulating environment. Pupils study a broad curriculum and participate in a wide variety of extra-curricular activities. The Head of the Junior School is a member of IAPS (*see entry in IAPS section*).

The Senior School, with a total of 722 pupils, comprises Key Stage 3 (Years 7–9), Key Stage 4 (Years 10 and 11) and Key Stage 5 (Years 12 and 13). A considerable choice of subjects is on offer – English, Drama, French, German, Spanish, Italian, Latin, Classical Civilisation, History, Geography, Religious Studies, Economics, Business Studies, Mathematics, Physics, Chemistry, Biology, Environmental Systems & Societies, Psychology, Design & Technology, ICT, Physical Education, Music, Art & Design, and Personal, Social and Health Education (PHSE).

In the Sixth Form students can choose whether to study for the International Baccalaureate (IB) Diploma, or for AS/A2 Levels. The College received accreditation from the IBO in 2004. Virtually all students proceed to Higher Education.

The College is a vibrant, academic community with a friendly atmosphere. It values cultural diversity and has a reputation for high academic standards and excellent pastoral care.

Pupils have the opportunity to join a wide range of extra-curricular activities to develop their special interests and personal strengths, for example:
- A thriving Combined Cadet Force
- The Duke of Edinburgh's Award Scheme – among London schools, the College has very strong numbers of pupils involved at all Award levels
- Community service – every year the College supports a range of British and overseas charities and local organisations
- The Armstrong Society (Science)
- Modern Languages Society
- The Stanford Tuck (History) Society
- Debating Society
- Christian Forum
- Literary Society
- Puzzle Club
- Drama Club
- Chess Club
- Electronic Workshop
- Visual Arts Society

Music. Pupils from all parts of the school participate in a variety of choirs, orchestras and instrumental ensembles. There is an annual Choral & Orchestral Concert for the whole College at St John's Smith Square.

Sport. The chief sports are cricket, hockey, netball, rounders, rugby, soccer and swimming. Students also have opportunities to take part in cross-country running, fives, tennis, basketball, badminton, sailing, golf and fitness training.

Entrance. The main entrance points are at the age of 3, 4, 7, 11, 13 or 16. Admission to the College is competitive in all years with the exception of the Nursery, and depends on academic ability and the demonstration of potential. At 11+ and 13+ an Entrance Examination is held annually in January.

Entrance Scholarships. Scholarships are offered for academic merit and also for excellence in Music, Sport, Art and Design and Drama. Means-tested bursaries are available.

Fees per term (2011-2012). The consolidated fees (including lunch) are: Nursery £2,561; Junior School £3,261–£4,263; Senior School £4,507.

Old Dunstonian Association. The ODA has 4,000 members. All pupils subscribe to the ODA while at school and automatically become life members when they leave.

St Dunstan's College Family Society. This parent-run fundraising body works to support the educational, social and extra-curricular activities of the school for the benefit of all pupils. All parents are automatically members of the Family Society.

Charitable status. St Dunstan's Educational Foundation is a Registered Charity, number 312747.

St Edmund's College & Prep School

Old Hall Green, Ware, Herts SG11 1DS
Tel: 01920 821504
Fax: 01920 823011
e-mail: admissions@stedmundscollege.org
website: www.stedmundscollege.org

Motto: '*Avita pro Fide*'

Located on a beautiful 400 acre site in the East Hertfordshire countryside, St Edmund's College & Prep School is an Independent, fully co-educational, day and boarding school for pupils aged 3 to 18 (boarding from 11 years). As

England's oldest Catholic School, founded in 1568, St Edmund's welcomes not only Catholics, but students from all faiths and denominations, who appreciate the values of a Catholic education.

Situated between London and Cambridge, the College is easily accessible by road and rail and is conveniently located near to London's Stansted Airport. There is an extensive bus service for students with routes spanning North London, Enfield, Essex and Hertfordshire.

The College's wonderful Catholic heritage continues to provide inspiration to its 800 pupils today, as it delivers its main objective, unchanged for over 400 years; to foster the spiritual, intellectual, physical and emotional development of every person in its community.

Patron and President: Most Reverend Vincent Nichols, Archbishop of Westminster

Governors:
Chairman: J Gillham, BA
Deputy Chairman: P J Mitton, MSc
The Very Revd Canon M Brockie, JCL
The Revd Monsignor J P Curry, STB
M Hutchison, FCA
Mrs M Lynch, BSc, ARCS, NPQH
Dr F MacIntosh, MA, MRCP, MFPM
M McEvoy
N Ransley, MA, MEd
Sister J Sinclair, BSc, SHCJ
Revd Dr J Sweeney, CP, BD, BA, Mth, PhD, MA

Director of Finance & Administration and Clerk to the Governors: B A Tomlinson, BA, ACMA

Headmaster: C P Long, BA

Head of St Edmund's Prep School: L Blom, BEd, BA, NPQH
Deputy Head & Registrar: P Durán, BA, MA (*Languages*)
Assistant Head (*Pastoral*): A D Petty, BA, FRSA (*History*)
Assistant Head (*Director of Studies*): A Celano, BSc, MEd (*Geography*)
Chaplain: The Revd M P A Pinot de Moira
Head of Sixth Form: Mrs M McCann, BA (*English*)

* *Head of Department*
† *Housemaster/Head of House*

P Bahia, BSc (*Mathematics*)
Mrs J Ball, CertEd (†*Pole, Director of Sport*)
C Benham, BA (*Music*)
Miss P Bissett, BA (*Drama*)
Mrs A Brady (*Examinations Officer*)
C R J Breese BA, MPhil (*Media Studies, English*)
D Brett, MA (*History*)
Mrs G A Burrows, BA (*Mathematics*)
Mrs R Carter, BA, MA (*Languages*)
N Cattermole, BEd (*Physical Education*)
Miss E Cobb, BSc (*Physical Education, Director of Activities, Educational Visits Coordinator*)
A Cunnah, BA (*Physical Education*)
Mrs J Daly, BSc, MFC (*DT, Careers Adviser*)
D R Davies, BSc (**Business Studies & Economics*)
Mrs P Davies, CertEd (†*Poynter*)
D D'Cruz, BA (*Religious Studies, Gifted & Talented Coordinator*)
G Devine, BEd (*Religious Studies*)
Miss A Dunning, BA (†*Talbot, Languages*)
H Evans, BSc (**Science, *Biology*)
Mrs E Franco, MA (*Languages*)
K Fry, BSc, MSc (**ICT*)
D A Gallie, KM, BEd (**Religious Studies, Head of Boarding, College Archivist*)
Mrs J Gentle, BA (*SEN Assistant*)
Mrs A Goring, CertEd (*English*)
Mrs S Gribbin, BA (*Librarian*)

Miss A M Healy, BA (**DT*)
Dr R G Hacksley, BA, PhD (*English, Careers, UCAS Coordinator*)
J Hayes, MA (*English*)
J Hounsell, BSc, BCA (†*Challoner, Mathematics*)
Miss C Humphries, BA (*International Department*)
Miss C Hugo, CertEd, Dip RSA (*Director, International Department*)
Mrs M Inglessis, BA, MA (*Psychology*)
Mrs V L Jefferies, BA, MA, MA (**Languages*)
K D Jones, BA (*Head of Boys' PE*)
Miss K Jordan, BA (*Physical Education*)
Miss S Kobylec, MSc, Dip EM MInstP (*Physics*)
B Kovacevic, BSc Middlesex, BSc (*ICT*)
R M Lewis, BEd (*Geography*)
B Liddle, BSc (*Biology*)
Miss D Madden, BSc (*Science*)
C McCauley, BEd (*Business Studies & Economics*)
Miss C McShane, BEd (*Business Studies & Economics*)
Mrs S Miller, CertEd, DipSpLD (*Mathematics, SEN Coordinator*)
S Mohana, MSc, BEd (*Mathematics*)
R Moore, MA (**English*)
Mrs J Morley, BA, HHD (**Art & Design*)
J W Morley, BA (**Geography*)
A L Moss, BEd, CertEd (†*Douglass, Chemistry*)
Mrs P M Peirce, BD, AKC (*Religious Studies, Chaplaincy Coordinator, Charities Coordinator*)
Mrs N Pitman, BA (*Geography*) (*maternity leave*)
Miss T Rankin, BA (*Art & Design, PSHE Coordinator*)
Miss H Rees, BSc QTS (*Chemistry*)
Mr A J D Robinson, BEd (*Religious Studies, Head of Boys' Boarding*)
Mrs K Salter-Kay, GTCL, LTCL, ALCM (*Director of Music*)
Mrs M Sargent, NVQ3 (*SEN Assistant*)
Mrs J Sharpe (*SEN Assistant*)
A Simmonds, BA, MA (*English*)
Miss M C Simon (*Languages*)
S Smith, MA (*Geography*)
J R Stypinski, BA (**History*)
Mrs C Taylor, BSc (*Chemistry, Head of Girls' Boarding*)
Mrs S Theroulde-O'Neill, MA (*Modern Foreign Languages*)
Miss M Towns, BSc (*Biology*)
D Webster, BEng (*Science*)
G West, BSc (*Head of Elements, Mathematics*)
Mrs R A K West, BEd (**Mathematics*)
Mrs A White, CertEd (*English*)
Mrs C Wilkin, BSc (*Mathematics*)

St Edmund's Prep School:
Head: L Blom, BEd, BA, NPQH
Deputy Head: S Cartwright, BSc
Assistant Head (*Director of Studies*): Mrs S Mills, BEd
Director of Music: Dr F J F McLauchlan, MA, PhD

Mrs G Boulter, Diplome	G Goodfellow, BA
Miss A R Boyes, BEd	Mrs R Hunt, BA
Miss R Butterworth, BA	Mrs C Mitton, BEd
Mrs A Cutler, BA	Mrs E Roper, BA
G Duddy, BEd	Miss K Simpson, BA
Mrs Y Elliott, BA	Miss J Warnes, BA
Miss K Fordham, BA	

Admission. Pupils are mainly admitted at the ages of 3, 11, and 16, although entry may be considered at other ages if there are spaces available.

Scholarships and Bursaries. (*See Scholarship Entries section.*) The College offers Academic, Art, Sport, Music and All-Rounder Scholarships to the value of a maximum of 50% of the fees. Applications should be made to the Headmaster. Means-tested Bursaries are also available at 11+, of up to 100% of fees.

Fees per term (2011-2012). Day Pupils: £3,035–£4,860; Weekly Boarders: £6,335–£7,235; Full Boarders: £7,005–£8,010; all depending on age of the pupil. There are reductions for families of HM Forces and for siblings.

Curriculum. All pupils follow the National Curriculum. At the end of NC Year 11, pupils take GCSE examinations in all courses that they have followed, usually more than is required by the National Curriculum.

In Rhetoric (Sixth Form) students will study four AS Levels in the Lower Sixth and 3 or 4 A2s in the Upper Sixth. Tuition is provided for entry to Oxford, Cambridge and other Universities.

Religious Instruction. St Edmund's is a College for all those who appreciate the values of a Catholic Education. All students receive instruction in Christian doctrine and practice from lay teachers. Importance is attached to the liturgical life of the College and the practical expression of faith. All faiths and denominations are welcomed.

Sport and Extra-Curricular Activities. Great importance is attached to sport and physical education throughout the College. All pupils are required to participate in a variety of sports on two afternoons a week. The major sports for boys are rugby, football, cricket and athletics, while for girls they are hockey, netball, rounders and athletics. The other sports available are cross-country, tennis, swimming, basketball, badminton, volleyball and squash. A floodlit artificial pitch, large sports hall, indoor swimming pool, tennis and squash courts, fitness room, together with 400 acres of grounds provide excellent facilities.

There are many extra-curricular activities including regular concerts and drama productions. The CCF (RAF and Army sections), Community Service and The Duke of Edinburgh's Award Scheme play a prominent part in developing a self-reliant and confident individual.

Careers. There is a Careers teacher and Careers Library. Careers advice is available to pupils from the age of 13. There are regular careers lectures and visits to industry and Universities.

The Prep School is situated on the same estate. It consists of a Nursery, Infants and Junior School for pupils from age 3 to 11, which feeds into the Senior School at 11. The pupils are able to make use of many of the amenities of the Senior School such as the Refectory, Chapel, Swimming Pool and Sports Hall. There is no boarding at the Prep School.

Charitable status. St Edmund's College, Ware is a Registered Charity, number 311073. It aims to provide a Catholic Education for students of all faiths between the ages of 3 and 18.

St Edmund's School
Canterbury

Canterbury, Kent CT2 8HU
Tel: 01227 475600
Fax: 01227 471083
e-mail: info@stedmunds.org.uk
website: www.stedmunds.org.uk

Motto: '*Fungar Vice Cotis*'

St Edmund's is an independent, co-educational day and boarding school for pupils aged between 3 and 18 years, comprising the Pre-Prep, Junior and Senior Schools. Its aim is to provide varied opportunities for academic, sporting, artistic, musical and dramatic achievement. The Schools have excellent teaching facilities, well-resourced libraries, access to information technology and numerous options for extra-curricular activities.

First established in 1749 as the Clergy Orphan School in Yorkshire, the School later moved to London and settled in its present location in 1855. The School's commitment to its origins endures, as does its Christian ethos. However, the School welcomes pupils from all backgrounds and places a particularly strong emphasis on pastoral care.

St Edmund's is situated on a beautiful site at the top of St Thomas Hill, adjacent to the University of Kent and overlooking the historic city of Canterbury. It is within easy reach of the towns of East Kent, and is just over an hour from London. The proximity to London's airports, the Channel ports and Eurostar stations at Ashford and Ebbsfleet gives international pupils convenient access to the School.

The school is owned by St Edmund's School Canterbury, a charitable company limited by guarantee, registered in England and Wales.

Patron: The Lord Archbishop of Canterbury

Governors:
Chairman: M C W Terry, Esq, FCA
P F Atkins, Esq, ACIB
J P W Coleman, Esq, LLB
Dr P Eichorn, MD
Mrs M P Gibson
Dr M Griffin, FRSA, PhD
C Harbridge, Esq, FRICS, FCIA, ISVA
The Revd Canon Christopher Irvine, MA, BTh
Mrs M L Lacamp, CertEd London, DipRSA
Mrs N Leatherbarrow, BSc, MBA
Dr L Naylor, BSc, PhD
Councillor P A Todd
Col P R M Whittington, FCMI

Head: Mrs L J Moelwyn-Hughes, BA Hons Cantab, MA, MEd

Master of the Junior School: Mr R G Bacon, BA Dunelm, PGCE

Head of Pre-Prep School: Mrs J Frampton-Fell, BA Hons Kent

Chaplain: The Revd M-A B Tisdale, BA, CTM

Bursar: Mr R S Smith

Deputy Head & Director of Studies: Mrs J E Mander, BSc Hons Nottingham, FEDA

Assistant Deputy Head (*Pastoral*): Mr L A Millard, BSc Hons Loughborough

Assistant Director of Studies: Mrs J J Mitchard, BSc Hons London

Assistant Staff:

[1] *Department serving both Senior & Junior Schools*
* *Head of Department*
† *Housemaster/Houseparent*

[1]*Art*:
*Mrs A A Slater-Williams, BA Hons Glasgow School of Art, PGCE
Miss Z J Fountain, BA Hons Staffs
Mr N J Hodge, BTec National Diploma Blackburn College, BA Hons Sheffield Hallam, PGCE
Miss S C Passmore, MA Birmingham

Business Studies:
*Mr R N Comfort, BSc Hons Wales (†*Owen*)

Curriculum Support:
Mrs S Williams, BA Hons Nottingham, RSA DipSpLD, DipTEFL
Mrs N A M King, CertEd
Ms J R Moorcroft, BEd Hons Lancaster, MA Kent, QUECO

Drama and Theatre Studies:
*Mr M Sell, NCDT Acc Diploma ALRA, PGCE (*Director*)

Miss E Sears, BA Hons Central School, PGCE (*Head of GCSE, †Warneford*)

¹*English*:
*Mr J P Dagley, MA Oxon, MA Kent
Mr M J Brewer, BA Hons Christ Church, PGCE
Dr M G Caiazza, BA MSMC, MA Kent, PhD Kent, PGCE
Mr P G Quince, BEd
Miss E Sears, BA Hons Central School, PGCE
Mr M J Whitmam, BA Hons Nottingham Trent, MA Nottingham, PGCE
Mrs J C Wilkinson, MEd Bristol

EAL:
Mrs H E Copland, TESOL Trinity College
Mrs J O'Sullivan, BA Southampton, PGCE, CELTA Cambridge

Film Studies:
*Dr M G Caiazza, BA MSMC, MA Kent, PhD Kent, PGCE

Geography:
*Miss D T Burren, BSc Hons Middlesex, PGCE
Mrs V Burton, BSc Hons Newcastle, PGCE

History:
*Mr N Johnson, BA Hons Surrey, PGCE
Mrs V A Gunn, BA OU, BA Kent, MA Kent
Ms F Martin, BA Hons Oxon, PGCE

¹*ICT Coordinator*:
Mrs J J Mitchard, BSc Hons London

Latin:
Mrs A I Heavens, MA Hons St Andrews, PGCE

¹*Mathematics*:
*Dr E Jones, BSc Wales, MSc Liverpool, PhD Wales
Mrs J E Mander, BSc Hons Nottingham, FEDA
Mr L A Millard, BSc Hons Loughborough
Mrs J J Mitchard, BSc Hons London
Mrs A J Potter, BA Hons York, PGCE

Modern Languages and European Studies:
*Mrs D F Micheloud, LL Fribourg, DipMG
Mrs S C Newton, BA Hons Nottingham, PGCE (*†Baker*)
Ms S Thelliez, FLE Littoral, PGCE
Miss M Judi, BA Hons Kent, Cert TEFL

¹*Music*:
*Mr W Bersey, BMus, Hons London LTCL
Mr S J Payne, BA Hons, MA, ARCM, LTCL, ARCO (*Head of Academic Music*)
Mr I G Swatman BA Hons, Dip Orch Studies NCOS (*Head of Instrumental Studies*)
Mr R Underwood, BA Hons Middlesex (*Head of Percussion & Music Technology, †Wagner*)

Visiting Music Staff:
Mr K Abbott, Dip RCM (*French Horn*)
Miss D Bailey, GGSM Hons (*Clarinet/Saxophone*)
Mrs J Chapman, BA Hons, PGCE, ATCL (*Recorder*)
Mrs H Cleobury, ARCM (*Piano*)
Ms R Davies (*Violin*)
Dr A de la Cour, PhD, BMus Hons (*Bass Guitar*)
Miss E de la Porte, ARCM, LRSM (*Piano*)
Dr D A Flood, MA, FRCOChM, Hon FGCM (*Piano*)
Ms S Geering, BMus Hons, Dip ABRSM, LLB Hons, (*Piano*)
Mr M Gove (*Trumpet*)
Mr R Hall, MAMus (*Piano*)
Mr J Hazelby (*Bass & Electric Guitar*)
Mrs J Jaggard, AGSM, Dip NCOS (*Oboe*)
Mrs K Lewis, BA, ARCM (*Voice*)
Mr G Mann, BA Hons (*Percussion*)
Miss P Martin-Smith, BMus, LGSM (*Voice*)
Miss S Meikle, BA Hons (*Percussion*)
Miss M Morley, BA Hons, DipOrchStudies (*Harp*)

Miss R A Rathbone, BA Hons, LRAM (*Flute*)
Mr C Reid, BA, Cert AdvSt RAM (*Trombone*)
Mrs K Shave, ARAM, LRAM (*Violin*)
Miss J Vohralik, MA, ARCM (*Cello*)
Mrs R Waltham, DRSAM (*Cello*)
Ms H Ward, BA Hons, LTCL (*Piano*)
Mrs D Wassell, GRSM, ARCM, CertEd, PGCE (*Violin*)
Mr S J Wassell, ARCM, LTCL, CertEd (*Low Brass*)
Ms F Whiteley, LRAM (*Violin*)
Miss K Willison (*Bassoon*)
Mr N Wright, GMus Hons, RNCM, FRCO (*Piano*)

Personal, Social and Health Education:
*Mrs D F Micheloud, LL Fribourg, DipMG
Miss M Judi, BA Hons Kent

¹*Physical Education*:
*Mrs J C Wilkinson, MEd Bristol
Mr H Alleyne
Miss T M Cliff, CertEd Sussex (*†Watson*)
Mr A R Jones, BSc Sheffield
Mr J C Maylam
Mr L Millard, BSc Hons Loughborough

Psychology:
*Dr C F Sotillo, MA, PhD Edinburgh

¹*Religious Studies*:
Mr M J Brewer, BA Hons Christ Church, PGCE (†Owen*)
Mrs V A Gunn, BA OU, BA Kent, MA Kent

¹*Science*:
*Dr L J Ashby, BSc, PhD London

Biology:
*Mr C J Mount, BA Hons, MSc Cantab, PGCE
Mr J M Clapp, BSc Hons, MA Reading
Dr G Jones, BM BS Warwick, PGCE Birmingham

Chemistry:
*Dr L J Ashby, BSc, PhD London
Dr S McGuire, BSc Hons, MSc, PhD Manchester
Mr P I O'Connor, BSc Kent, MA York

Physics:
Dr J C Horn, BSc, PhD Leeds (†Wagner*)
Miss R E Hummerstone, BSc Hons Surrey
Mr D G Whitehouse, BSc Hons Nottingham

¹*Technology (Design, Graphics, Food)*:
*Ms K Lloyd, MSc Christ Church
Ms M Florence, BTec, BA Hons
Mr P Gadenne, MCSD

Additional Responsibilities:
Careers Adviser: Ms K Lloyd, MSc Christ Church
Public Examinations Officer: Mr D G Whitehouse, BSc Nottingham
Hall Manager: Mr M G S Hawkins, MA, MSc Cantab
Hall Technical Director: Mr G N Hawkins, BSc London, ARCS
Higher Education Adviser: Mr J P Dagley, MA Oxon, MA Kent
Contingent Commander CCF: Capt M G S Hawkins, MA, MSc Cantab
President of Common Room: Mr D G Whitehouse, BSc Hons Nottingham

Junior School

Second Master: Mr R A Austen, BEd Hons Bulmershe (*Mathematics*)
Senior Master: Mr T Hooley, MA Cantab (**Latin, English, Mathematics*)
Director of Studies: Mrs E A Swallow, MA, BEd Dunelm (*Form 7*)
Head of Lower School: Mrs M Yearsley, BA Hons (*Form 3*)

Preparatory:
Mrs L Bradley, BA Ed Hons Kent (*Form 4*)
Mr S Buckingham, BEd Natal (*Games*)
Mrs J A Burden, BA Ed Christ Church (*Form 6, Science*)
Mrs C V George, BSc Christ Church (*Girls' Games*)
Mrs J Haworth, CertEd Leeds (*Lower School Curriculum Support*)
Mrs J Heywood, BSc OU, PGCE (*Form 5*)
Mrs R H Kroiter, BA Hons Liverpool, DipTEFL (*EFL, French, Mathematics*)
Mrs C D James, BSc Hons Dundee, MSc, PGCE
Mr J Lambert, BA Hons Liverpool, PGCE, ATCL (**Junior School Music*)
Mrs K Lambert, BA London, PGCE (*Religious Studies*)
Mrs C M Lawrence, BA Christ Church (**English*)
Mrs C McCabe, BA Bedford (*PE*)
Mr A J McKean, BA, BSc Christchurch (*Geography*)
Mr C Penn (*Head of Boys' Games, PE, Mathematics, †School House*)
Mrs L Relf, BA Ed Hons Exeter (**PE and Girls' Games*)
Mrs L V Richardson, BA QTS Hons (*Form 5*)
Mr E J Southey, CertEd Dartford (**History*)
Mrs H R Surridge, BA Hons Kent, PGCE (*Form 5*)
Mrs J Vafidis, BEd Christ Church, CETHIC (*Curriculum Support*)
Mr M G B Walters, BA Hons London (**French*)
Mr P A Yearsley, BA Hons, PGCE (*Form 5*)

Master of Choristers:
Dr D A Flood, MA Oxon, FRCO ChM (*Cathedral Organist*)

Pre-Prep School

Abingdon House:
Mrs C Atkinson, BA Hons Christchurch, MA Christchurch (*Curriculum Support*)
Mrs R George, NNEB (*Ladybirds*)
Mrs A J Johnson, BEd Leeds (*Honey Bees*)
Mrs H M Millard, BSc Hons Loughborough (*Performing Arts, French*)
Mrs A Purnell, BEd Hons OU (*Dragonflies*)
Mrs E A Sherwin, BA Hons, PGCE Reading (*Crickets*)

Teaching Assistants:
Miss E Day (*Crickets*)
Mrs C Lawlor (*Honey Bees*)
Mrs M Stanley (*Ladybirds*)
Mrs V Wisker (*Dragonflies*)

Support Staff:
Librarian: Miss J Pierce
Medical Officer: Dr G. Manson
Head's PA: Ms E Ottaway
Junior School Master's Secretary: Mrs Y King
Admissions Secretary: Mrs A Selmon

St Edmund's is proud of its reputation as a place where pupils enjoy their school years. Within a caring and disciplined community, it provides a broad education, which seeks to ensure that girls and boys are happy and successful. As well as nurturing individual interests and talents, the School emphasises the crucial importance of developing compassionate relationships.

It offers rich academic and cultural experiences which encourage children to achieve their potential, wherever their talents and interests lie. As a result, St Edmund's is the academic choice of school for the rounded child and pupils leave well-educated, balanced and confident young people.

Organisation. The Pre-Prep, Junior and Senior Schools are on the same site and are closely integrated, using the same Chapel, music and art facilities, theatre, dining hall, science laboratories, sports hall, and so on. However, for practical day-to-day purposes the Junior School is under the control of the Master of the Junior School and the Pre-Prep under the Head of Pre-Prep. St Edmund's derives much of its strength and its capacity to work efficiently and economically from its close-knit structure.

The Senior School is divided into four Houses: Baker, Wagner, Warneford and Watson, the respective Housemasters each being assisted by a team of Deputies and Tutors.

The Chapel. All pupils attend at least two of the morning services a week. Confirmation is conducted annually by the Archbishop of Canterbury (as Patron of the School) or by the Bishop of Dover acting on his behalf; the candidates are prepared by the School Chaplain. The School Carol Service is held in Canterbury Cathedral, by kind permission of the Dean and Chapter.

Buildings and Facilities. Over the past twenty years there have been extensive additions to and modernisation of the school's buildings and facilities: a new Junior School building, a new Sixth Form Centre, the main hall with tiered auditorium and exhibition area, the sports hall, the technology department, additional classrooms and major extensions to the science, art, information technology, and the Pre-Prep School, as well as the conversion of all Senior School boarding accommodation to study-bedrooms and refurbishment of Junior boarding premises. A new music school opened in 2005 and new recreational facilities for Senior School boarders and a refurbished library in 2008. An Astroturf pitch is being built shortly and the school has plans for an extensive classroom building programme.

Academic Organisation. At St Edmund's, the academic expectations are high. The breadth and balance of the academic programme exceeds the requirements of the National Curriculum and pupils begin to be grouped by ability while they are in Junior School. This approach encourages children to apply their talents and aptitudes with diligence and perseverance. Comprehensive reports are sent regularly throughout the school year. A system of interim reports, as well as regular parents' meetings, ensures close communication with parents.

Pre-Prep School: The Pre-Prep School has its own classroom buildings and playground, creating a warm, secure and friendly learning environment in which pupils can develop to the full. The happy and purposeful atmosphere helps pupils develop their confidence.

The School has a wide range of excellent activities and teaches a broad-based curriculum that emphasises academic development as well as art, music, drama and sport. The teachers have many years' experience of working with Early Years' children and the small classes allow staff to focus on the needs of every pupil.

Junior School: The aim of the Junior School is to produce independent learners who are confident and motivated. In Forms 3 to 5, the National Curriculum is broadly followed and, while placing particular emphasis on English, Maths and Science, there is also focus on subjects such as Art, French, Geography, History, Information Technology, Latin and Music. Subject specialists teach Forms 6 to 8, helping to prepare pupils for Senior School. Music (from Form 3), Technology and Art (from Form 6) and Science (from Form 7) is taught in specialist facilities.

The House system gives older pupils the opportunity to experience the skills of organisation, cooperation and leadership, by helping and encouraging younger members of their Houses and assisting with the organisation of House teams and events. Taking on more responsibility and developing greater initiative is valuable in smoothing their passage to Senior School.

Choristers: The 26 choristers of Canterbury Cathedral are all members of the Junior School. They board in the Choir House (in the Cathedral Precincts) in the care of Houseparents appointed by the school. All their choral training is undertaken in the Cathedral by the Master of Choristers and Cathedral Organist; the remainder of their education takes place at St Edmund's.

Senior School: In the first year of the Senior School (Year 9) pupils follow a core curriculum in English, Mathematics,

French, Physics, Chemistry, Biology, History, Geography, Art, Music, Information Technology, Religious Education, PSHE, Physical Education, and Technology. Drama, Spanish and Latin are options.

GCSE core subjects are: English, English Literature, French, Mathematics and the three (separate) Sciences. Options include Latin, Spanish, History, Geography, Art (Ceramics), Art (Drawing and Painting), Technology: Resistant Materials, Food Technology, Graphic Products, ICT, Music, Drama and Religious Studies.

The following subjects are offered for AS/A2 Level examinations: Art, Biology, Business Studies, Ceramics, Chemistry, Design and Technology, English Literature, Film Studies, French, Geography, History, Mathematics and Further Mathematics, Music, Music Technology, PE, Photography, Physics, Psychology and Theatre Studies.

The Sixth Form Curriculum additionally offers the AQA Baccalaureate, a qualification that will run alongside the A Level programme. The course takes A Levels as its central academic core, but then adds both breadth and depth in ways totally compatible with the educational ethos St Edmund's has promoted consistently. This includes the study of AS Critical Thinking and all AQA Bacc pupils take the Extended Project Qualification.

Pupils in the Lower Sixth are expected to study four AS Levels, most then proceeding to three A2 subjects in the Upper Sixth. In addition to their A Level choices, Lower Sixth pupils also attend Study Skills and General Studies classes.

Careers and Higher Education. The School is affiliated to the Independent Schools Careers Organisation and the Careers Research and Advisory Centre. Pupils have the opportunity to undergo careers aptitude testing in the GCSE year, and all pupils are assisted in finding a placement for a week or more of work experience in the GCSE year. The careers and higher education staff give all possible help in the finding of suitable careers and in selecting appropriate universities and colleges of further education. Most A Level candidates go on to degree courses after leaving school; others join Art or Music conservatoires.

Music. Music is woven into the fabric of school life at St Edmund's, reinforced by the presence of the Canterbury Cathedral Choristers. In the purpose-built Music School, specialist teachers give lessons to pupils from Form 1 through to the Sixth Form. Pupils of all ages participate in numerous musical ensembles which cater for a range of vocal and instrumental abilities. As a result, there is an exceptional practical examination record, with more than 80% of entrants achieving Distinction or Merit. Over twenty-five concerts and performances take place each year, from the Pre-Prep's 'Little Voices' festival and small lunchtime recitals in the Recital Hall to large gala concerts in Canterbury Cathedral. The school acts as a focus for musical excellence for children throughout East Kent and works closely with the English Chamber Orchestra.

Performing Arts. Dramatic performance is included in the curriculum from the earliest years. Every term, the Pre-Prep School holds thematic drama workshops. Pupils in Junior and Senior Schools participate in school plays and other performances with vitality and enthusiasm, as an outlet for expressing their talents in acting, dancing, singing, music, choreography and technical production. The consistently outstanding GCSE and A Level results are testament to the emphasis placed on drama within the curriculum and school life in general.

Art. The emphasis St Edmund's places on creative subjects means that art is embedded in the curriculum across the three Schools. Pupils studying Art and Design enjoy excellent facilities and teaching. Drawing, painting, print-making, photography (traditional and digital), sculpture and ceramics are offered to pupils in the Junior and Senior Schools.

Sport. Association football, hockey, cricket, athletics, tennis, squash and (for girls) netball and rounders are the principal sports but there are opportunities for many other forms of exercise, including cross-country running, golf, badminton, basketball, volleyball, swimming and gym-based fitness training. The large playing fields adjoin the school buildings. There is an open-air heated swimming pool. The sports hall is well-equipped. There are eight tennis courts (both hard and grass), a compact golf course and a rifle range. The School has access to the climbing wall, gym and astroturf pitches at the University of Kent.

Activities. For those in the first four years of Senior School one afternoon a week is given over specifically to a broad range of activities. A number involve helping the local community, while other pupils learn new skills, eg archaeology, broadcasting, Eco-Schools, Japanese language and culture, kite making, literary and debating societies, photography, Rotary Interact and yoga.

In the second year all Senior School pupils join the Combined Cadet Force, a highly successful unit commanded by a member of the teaching staff and administered by an ex-soldier. There is an annual camp in the summer and an adventurous training camp at Easter, attendance at which is voluntary. Cadets may remain in the CCF for the duration of their school career if they wish, and are encouraged to do so if contemplating a career in the armed forces.

Pupils may also participate in The Duke of Edinburgh's Award Scheme and the British Association of Young Scientists. There are regular ski and field trips, choir and music tours, sports tours and many other one-off trips.

In Junior School, too, there is a diverse range of extracurricular activities, many of which draw on the school's excellent facilities for sport, music and drama. As part of the adventurous training programme there is an annual adventure course in the Hebrides and a Year 8 outdoor activities week in the South of France.

Health. The School Medical Centre is staffed by state registered nurses at all times. The health of the pupils is supervised by a senior local general practitioner under the NHS. A counselling service is available.

Admission to Pre-Prep School. Entry at any age from 3–7. Once registered, children are invited to visit the School for informal assessment. For further details please contact the Head of Pre-Prep School.

Admission to Junior School. Entry at any age from 7–12. Candidates will sit entrance tests and all prospective pupils will be interviewed or attend an assessment day. For further details please contact The Master of the Junior School or the Master's Secretary.

Chorister Admission. St Edmund's is the school of the Canterbury Cathedral choristers. For details of the voice trials please contact the Master's Secretary.

Admission to Senior School. Entry at 13 from preparatory schools is through the Common Entrance Examination. Candidates from other schools will be tested appropriately or sit the School's own entrance tests. There is also a large entry of pupils into the Sixth Form, usually on the basis of interview and GCSE grade estimates from their present school. For further details please contact the Head or the Admissions Secretary.

Fees per term (2011-2012). Senior School: Boarders £8,849; Day pupils £5,686.

Junior School: Boarders £6,185, Weekly Boarders £5,636, Choristers £6,084, Day pupils £4,333. Pre-Prep: £2,656–£3,070, Nursery £2,163 (mornings only £1,215).

Music fees: £220 per term. Extras have been kept to the minimum.

Entrance Scholarships. (*See Scholarship Entries section.*) The School offers various awards at 11+, 13+ and 16+ each year. Academic, Music, Art, Drama and Sport scholarships of up to half fees are offered. Full details are available from the School Secretary.

Bursaries and Fee Concessions. Originally founded to provide a free education for the fatherless sons of the clergy of the Church of England and the Church of Wales, St

Edmund's now accepts applications from boys and girls for Foundationer status. Bursaries to provide a temporary (no more than 12 months) cushion are granted on a means-tested basis to existing pupils. Fee concessions, also means-tested, can be provided to the children of the clergy, members of the armed forces, diplomatic personnel and to the third and subsequent children of the same family in the school at the same time.

Applications should be made to the Head.

The St Edmund's Society (for former pupils). President: Professor T James.

Charitable status. St Edmund's School Canterbury is a Registered Charity, number 1056382. It exists to educate the children in its care.

St Edward's, Oxford

Oxford OX2 7NN

Tel: Warden: 01865 319323
          Bursar: 01865 319321
          Registrar: 01865 319200
Fax: 01865 319242
e-mail: wardensec@stedwards.oxon.sch.uk
website: www.stedwards.oxon.sch.uk

St Edward's, Oxford was founded in 1863 by the Revd Thomas Chamberlain. Originally the School buildings were in New Inn Hall Street, Oxford. In 1873 it was removed to Summertown, and the present School was built by the Revd A B Simeon.

Motto: '*Pietas Parentum*'

Visitor:
The Rt Revd The Lord Bishop of Oxford

Governing Body:
M P Stanfield, Esq (*Chairman*)
H W Bolland, Esq, BA
J R Burchfield, Esq, MA
Dr L Fawcett-Posada
G Fenton, Esq
E J H Gould, Esq, MA
The Revd R G Griffith-Jones, MA
M G Hay, Esq, BA, PhD, MBA
Dr A Holloway, BM, MRCGP
D J Jackson, Esq
C I M Jones, Esq, MA, FRSA
K MacRitchie, Esq, MA, BD, LLB
P M Oppenheimer, Esq, MA
Mrs J M Peach, BSc, MA, DPhil
R G P Pillai, MB BS, FRCS
Sir Bob Reid
Prof D A Roe, Esq, MA, PhD, DLitt
Mrs K A Ross, MA
M Roulston, Esq

Warden: Stephen C I Jones, BA, MSc, MLitt, FRSA

Sub-Warden: Thomas A James, BSc, MSc

Academic Director: Ian R M Rowley, MA, ALCM

Chaplain: Revd E Charles Kerr, MA, MTh

Director of Sports and Activities: Keith J Shindler, MA, MSc

Director of Cultural Activities: Neville C Creed, MA

Assistant Teachers:
Vaughan Abigail, BA
Laura K Allen, BSc
Lucy R D Baddeley, MA
Julian V Baker, BSc
Charles F Baggs, BSc
Naveed Barakzai, BSc
Dominic Barker, MMath
Philip N Barras, MA
Oliver J Barstow, BA
O Stuart Bartholomew, MA
Rebecca M Bates, BSc
Elizabeth A Boast, BA
Kathrine K Booth, BA, MA, PhD
Phoebe Brookes, BA, MA
Susan F Buchan, BA, MEng
Anthony Bullard, BSc, PhD
Stephen J Chambers, BA
Henry Chitsenga, BSc
Jason E Clapham, MA, MSc
Edward J Clark, BA
Rebecca E Clark, BA
Debra Clayphan, BA, MSc
Florence M C Corran, BA, MPhil
Sarah Cox, BA
Rosa Crespo-Sergio, BA
Andrew J Dalgleish, BSc, MSc
Gabriele Damiani, BMus, ARCO
Andrew J Davis, BSc, PhD, FRGS
Edward A Dingwall, BA, MA
Rebecca E Drury, BSc
Katrina J Eden, BA, MA
Lewis Faulkner, MA
Anna Fielding, BA
David Finamore, BSc
Robert E Fletcher, BA, MA, MLitt
Sarah Gee, BSc
Rachel E Grange, MA
Michael Gray, BA, MA
Andrew J Grounds, BA
Adam R Hahn, BA
Mark J Hanslip, BEd
Tova Holmes, BFA
Richard W J Howitt, BSc
Edmund T Hunt, BA, MA
Nicola F Hunter, BA
Philip A Jolley, BA, BEd
Huw J Jones, MSc
Jonathan T Lambe, BA
Simon Larter, BA
Margaret Lloyd, BSc
Peter Lloyd-Jones, DipFA
Philip H H Mallaband, BA, MA, PhD

Jeremy E Mather, BA
Lucy Maycock, BA, DipRADA
Helen R McCabe, BA, DPhil
David S Moore, BSc, PhD, AKC, CChem, MRSC
Marta Morales Nevado, BA
Garrett E Nagle, MA, DPhil
Jonathan Nelmes, BA
Einar M Olive, BSc
Matthew Parker, MA, MSc
Nicola J S Perkins, BSc
Catherine I Phillips, BA, MA
Sophie J Pollard, BA
Christopher T Pollitt, BA
J Richard Powell, GRSM, LRAM, ARCM
Ben J Pyper, DipAD
Michaella Prince, MA
Simon Roche, BA
Peter J B Rudge, BA, BA
Jonathan Saunders, BA
Charlotte S Schofield, MA
Mark I Sellen, BA, MMus, ARCM
Joanna M Sephton, BA
Joanna L Shindler, BSc, MSc
Nicoletta M Simborowski, MA
John R McK Simpson, BEng
Bethany A Steer, BA
Alastair M Summers, BSc
Mark J Taylor, BA
Alex C W Tester, MA
Jonathan Thomson, BA
Mary R Trotman, MA
Lorraine R Turley, BA
Philip R Waghorn, BSc, MSc
Kerry F Walsh, BA
A John Wiggins, MA
Kendall A Williams, BSc, PhD
M Alice Wishart, BA
Mark S Woodward, BSc, PhD

Houses and Housemasters/Housemistresses:

Cowell's: Nicholas H Coram-Wright, MA
Sing's: David P Corran, BA
Field House: J Richard Murray, BA, MA
Macnamara's: Sarah L Sephton, BEng
Apsley: Oliver L Richards, MA
Tilly's: Lewis Faulkner, MA
Segar's: David R Gibbon, BSc, BSc
Kendall: James E B Cope, BA, MA
Oakthorpe: Judy Young, BSc
Corfe: Eve Singfield
Avenue: Rachel Bellamy, BA, MA

Administrative Officers:
Bursar: Stephen Withers Green, MA, ACA
Registrar: Sarah K Munden, BEd
Examinations Officer: Dr David Moore, BSc, PhD, AKC, CChem, MRSC
Librarian: Marian O Oyedoh, MSc, BSc
Head of Careers: Emma Whalen

Medical Officers:
Dr Roisin McCloskey, MBChB, MRCGP
Dr Matthew Cheetham, MB, MS
Dr Bridget Geer, MBChB, MRCGP, DRCOG

Ethos. The education offered at St Edward's is designed to promote the all-round development of the children in its care. It is our objective that each pupil will leave the school with the qualities, skills and qualifications necessary for a fulfilling life. To that end, St Edward's offers a genuinely broad education to a wide range of pupils of varying talents within a boarding context which allows time for pupils and teachers to benefit from the impressive resources in and out of the classroom.

History and Development. Founded in 1863, St Edward's moved to its present site of over 100 acres in North Oxford in 1873. The School roll is c660 boys and girls, of whom about eighty percent are full-time boarders. Pupils live in one of the 11 houses (4 for girls, 7 for boys), and in addition to having the run of extensive playing fields, they benefit from the use of our facilities, including the Chapel, Library, Common Rooms, Sports Hall and Sports complex (including two pools and 4 indoor tennis courts), a Performing Arts Centre, astroturfs, golf course and boathouses on the Thames. A new Life Sciences building opened in September 2008, and in July 2009 a new Sports pavilion was completed. The School is currently developing a new music building.

Pastoral Care. Our network of pastoral care lies at the heart of what we try to achieve. Each pupil is in the direct care of a Housemaster or Housemistress who communicates regularly with a team of tutors, some of whom are resident in the House. Pupils' academic progress is carefully and systematically monitored by academic tutors who meet their charges in tutor periods, as well as in house. A great deal of pastoral work is done by subject teachers, music, drama and games coaches, and we lay emphasis on good communication. We aim that pupils learn to take responsibility for their actions and to note their consequences: this is the basis of our attitude to discipline.

Academic Work. We aim that all pupils may proceed to University, if that is their choice. This implies a wide curriculum and St Edward's offers most subjects. We lay emphasis on independent learning and this is achieved through good practice in teaching and learning and through the comprehensive tutorial system, with its important aspects of self-assessment. In 2010 73% of our A Level presentations resulted in an A or B pass, and 55 A* and A grades at GCSE. We also offer the International Baccalaureate Diploma Programme in the Sixth Form and in 2010 our average point total was well over 35 points, with many pupils achieving more than 40 points. A good number of the Sixth Form gain offers from Oxford and Cambridge Universities and, recently, Harvard. Shells (Year 9) follow a wide common course, with a choice to be made from Spanish, German, Ancient Greek or French, and two of these for the ablest linguists. The Fourth and Fifth Forms follow courses leading to 9 or 10 GCSEs. In the Sixth Form pupils are expected to take 4 or 5 A Levels or to follow the IB Diploma Programme in place of A Levels. We provide learning support for pupils who are mildly dyslexic or dyscalculic.

Higher Education and Careers. The Department is staffed by two teachers, and draws on the expertise of ISCO for Careers advice and psychometric testing. It runs sessions on the University application procedure and interviews, as well as a highly participative 'Team Challenge' conference. There is a programme of work experience for Fifth form pupils, and Lower Sixth pupils take part in the Young Enterprise Scheme. Younger pupils take part in whole-day careers activities.

Music, Drama and the Arts. The Arts are highly valued at St Edward's. The Music Department delivers about 500 lessons every week, taught by a team of 40 visiting specialists. The main school groups include the Orchestra, Chamber Orchestra, Chapel Choir, Chamber Choir, St Edward's Singers, Concert Band, Big Band, Jazz Band and various Chamber Music groups. There are around 60 concerts a year, with regular foreign tours. The Drama department is flourishing: main school productions, including musicals, are complemented by devised pieces, House plays, Shell plays and a Speech and Drama programme. The Art Department is strong and vibrant, benefiting from recently enhanced facilities and the stream of visiting exhibitions to The North Wall. The Dance programme is extensive, with over 30 classes every week – covering styles from ballet to cheerleading – generating a range of material for the dance shows. In addition, the cutting-edge programming of the award-winning North Wall Performing Arts Centre enriches the cultural life of both the school and the wider community, placing St Edward's right at the forefront of development in Arts education.

Sport, Games and Activities. A very wide variety of sports, games and activities is on offer. We compete at the highest level in several sports and can boast of county and national representatives. We also encourage all our pupils to participate and to enjoy playing at more modest levels. We have fielded as many as 27 teams on one day – over 400 children representing the School. These sports, games and activities include Rugby, Football, Hockey, Cricket, Rowing, Athletics, Netball, Squash, Swimming, Tennis, Cross-Country running, Sailing, Clay Pigeon Shooting, Golf, Soccer, Judo, Basketball, Canoeing, Rock-climbing, Chess, Bridge, Debating, and Community Service. We operate a Combined Cadet Force with Navy, Army and RAF sections, and offer all levels of the Duke of Edinburgh's Award Scheme.

Admission to the School. Registration forms can be obtained from the Registrar. There is a registration fee of £75. Places in the School, conditional upon performance in the entrance exam, are offered 18 months before entry at 13+. Boys and girls are expected to take the Common Entrance Examination or Scholarship in their last Summer term at their Preparatory School. Separate assessment arrangements can be made for applicants from schools not preparing candidates for the Common Entrance Examination. Lower Sixth scholarship and entrance examinations are held in November prior to entry; offers of places in the sixth form are subject to good performance at GCSE (at least six B grades and above) and a satisfactory report from the previous school.

Scholarships. (*See Scholarship Entries section.*) Open Scholarships and Exhibitions are assessed by examination and interview. Academic, Music, Art, Dance & Drama and Sports Scholarships are available at both 13+ and 16+ entry. In addition All-Rounder Awards are available at 13+.

Bursaries. There are three Widening Access bursaries available each year: two at 13+ and one at 16+. There is also one bursary for the children of serving RAF personnel and the School may offer bursaries of up to 30% of current fees for children of clergy and university dons at the Warden's discretion.

Fees per term (2011-2012). Boarding £9,935; Day Pupils £7,948.

Charitable status. St Edward's, Oxford is a Registered Charity, number 309681. The aims and objectives of the School are to provide education for pupils between the ages of 13 and 18.

St George's College

Weybridge, Surrey KT15 2QS
Tel: 01932 839300
Fax: 01932 839301
e-mail: contact@st-georges-college.co.uk
website: www.st-georges-college.co.uk

Founded by the Josephite Community in 1869 in Croydon, the College moved in 1884 to its present attractive grounds of 100 acres on Woburn Hill, Weybridge. Within its particular family orientated ethos, the College seeks to encourage a wide, balanced Christian education in the Catholic tradition encouraging excellence and achievement across a broad spectrum of academic, sporting and extra-curricular activities. Almost all pupils move on to higher education, gaining places at a wide range of institutions including Oxford and Cambridge. The College is co-educational throughout the school.

Motto: '*Amore et Labore*'

Governing Body:
Chairman: Mrs K Quint

Governors:

Mr K Alexander	Mrs M Hackett
Mrs S Bell	Mr P Morgan
Mr D Bicarregui	Revd W M Muir, CJ
Mrs L Burell	Mrs J Ranson
Fr A Cadwallader, CJ	Mr J F Rourke
Mr M Davie	Mrs S Wood

Clerk to the Governors and Bursar: Mr G Cole

Headmaster: Mr J A Peake, MA Oxon, PGCE

Deputy Headmaster: Mr M A Saxon, BA, MA, PGCE (*History*)
Director of Studies: Ms F M May, MA, BA, PGCE (*English*)
Curriculum Coordinator: Mr A M Gunning, BA, PGCE (*Geography*)

Mrs J A Andrew, MA Oxon, PGCE (*Physics*)
Miss V M Athony, PGCE (*Economics & Business Studies*)
Ms S Arif, BSc, PGCE (*Mathematics*)
Fr Martin Ashcroft (*Josephite Chaplain*)
Mr M J Barham, BA Hons, PGCE (*History, Senior Tutor*)
Mrs A L Barnett, BSc, PGCE (*Chemistry, Head of 5th Year*)
Mr A A Barton, BA, PGCE (*Music*)
Miss R E Baylis, MA 1st class (*Mathematics*)
Mrs M Bigwood, BSc, HDE (*Mathematics*)
Mr A M Blyth, MSc, BA, PGCE (*Mathematics*)
Mr D J Bradford, BHum, PGCE (*Mathematics, i/c Examinations*)
Ms C A Butler, BA, PGCE (*Art*)
Ms A Byrne, BSc, PGCE (*Physical Education, Girls' Games*)
Mrs T Castledine, BA Oxon, RAM, MA, ARCO (*Director of Music*)
Miss T A Cooke, BSc, MSc, PGCE (*Physical Education, Games, Head of Middle Section*)
Mr M J Crean, BA, PGCE (*Physical Education, Games, Head of Rugby, Head of Kilmorey*)
Mr J M Cunningham, BA, PGCE (*Religious Studies, PSE Coordinator, i/c D of E*)
Mrs J Davies, CertEd, PGCE (*Academic Support*)
Mr J E Davies, BA, PGCE (*Head of Geography,*)
Mr T Deive, BA, PGCE (*Acting Head of Languages, i/c Spanish*)
Dr J V Drayton, BSc, PhD (*Head of Chemistry*)
Miss E Drysdale, BA Hons, PGCE (*Art, Careers Coordinator*)
Ms E Duke-Gill, BA Hons, PGCE (*Languages*)
Mr P S Ellwood, BA, PGCE (*History, Careers Coordinator, Head of 3rd Year*)
Mrs V G Emad, BA Hons, PGCE (*Head of Art*)
Mr I C Facey, BSc (*Technology*)
Miss A Fincher-Jones, BA (*Girls' Games, Physical Education*)
Mr A Z Fonfe, BA (*Tennis*)
Miss S Frawley, MA, MPhil (*English, i/c Oxbridge Entrance*)

Mr R A Frisk, BSc, PGCE (*Physics*)
Mr J R Garbett, BA, PGCE (*Drama*)
Ms P L George, BEd, BA, MA (*Religious Studies & Philosophy*)
Mr W Glover, BA, MEd, PGCE (*Head of Economics & Business Studies, Assistant Director of Studies*)
Mr S H Graham, BSc (*Chemistry, Head of Stirling House*)
Mr P J Graves, BSc, PGCE (*Languages, Co-Curriculum Coordinator*)
Miss E Grigsby, BSc Hons, PGCE (*Mathematics*)
Mr R P Grimmer, BSc, PGCE (*Physics*)
Mrs G Hale, Deug LL France (*Classics*)
Miss S L Hall, BSc, PGCE (*Geography, Head of Lower Section*)
Mrs T A Hall, BSc, Msc, PGCE (*Physical Education, Games, Head of Middle Section*)
Mr M T Harrison, BSc Hons, GTP, QTS (*Physical Education, Games, i/c Cricket, Head of 1st Year*)
Mr G B Hobern, BA, PGCE (*Languages*)
Ms C Hulf, BA Hons (*Rowing Coach*)
Miss V B King, BA, PGCE (*Mathematics*)
Miss H L Knight, BSC Hons (*Physical Education, Games, i/c Netball*)
Mrs S M Knights, BSc, PGCE (*Geography, Head of Careers*)
Mrs T M Lambie, BA, PGCE (*Business Studies, Economics*)
Mr R J Lawrence, BS Hons, PGCE (*English*)
Ms L C Lever, BA, PGCE (*Languages*)
Mrs K Maguire, BSc Hons, PGCE (*Biology*)
Miss S J Marlow, BA, PGCE (*Geography, Head of 4th Year*)
Mr E S Mason, BA, Teach First (*English*)
Mr T A McIlwaine, BA, BTEC, PGCE (*Art*)
Mrs A M Morison, BA Hons, PGCE (*Drama*)
Ms S L Morris, BSc (*ICT Assistant Director of Studies*)
Mr J G Oliver, MA Hons, PGCE, MEng (*Head of Mathematics*)
Mr M Parnham, BSc, BA (*Head of Technology, PGCE*)
Mr J O Parsons, BA, MA, PGCE (*English*)
Mr A J Reynolds, BA, PGCE (*Director of Sport*)
Mrs S Rowlatt, BA Hons, MA, PGCE, DipLE (*Head of English*)
Mr M A Schofield, MA (*Director of Drama*)
Mrs J M Sciortino Nowlan, BA Hons, PGCE, MPhil (*Head of Religious Studies*)
Mrs I A Seymour, BSc, MSc, GTP (*Mathematics*)
Dr H A Shaw, PhD, BSc, PGCE (*Chemistry, Senior Tutor*)
Mrs D A Skitch, MA, PGCE (*Languages*)
Mrs M D Smith, BA, PGCE (*Head of Sixth Form, English*)
Mr M T Stather, BSc Hons, PGCE (*Biology, Assistant Examinations Officer*)
Miss K A Stevens, BA, PGCE (*English*)
Mr D N Strange, BMus Hons, PGCE (*Music*)
Mr K Taggart, BEng, PGCE (*Head of Physics*)
Mr C Tapscott, BA, PGCE (*History*)
Dr C A Taylor, PhD, MSc, BSc, PGCE (*Science, Mathematics*)
Miss E Thomson, HSc, HDE (*Mathematics, Head of 2nd Year*)
Mrs C S Thorne, BSc, CertEd (*Biology*)
Mr M P Tiley, MA (*Head of History*)
Mrs S H Turner, MA, BA, PGCE (*Religious Studies*)
Mr N Waight, BA, PGCE (*English, Head of Southcote House*)
Mr G P Walters, BSc (*Biology, i/c Rowing, Head of Petre House*)
Miss L E Watson, BA, PGCE (*Languages*)
Mr A B Watters, BA, Dip BA, PGCE (*Politics*)
Mrs J B Weaver, BA Hons, PGCE (*Food Technology*)
Mrs S E Wedgwood, BA, PGCE (*History*)
Mrs K Wilkinson, BSc, PGCE (*Physics*)
Mr J Williams, BA, BSc, PGCE (*English, i/c Hockey*)

Mr A O Wingfield Digby, BA, MA, PGCE (*Geography*)
Mr N J Wingrove, BA, PGCE (*Languages*)
Mr O Yanez Vila, BA, PGCE (*Religious Studies*)
Mrs K York, BSc, PGCE (*Head of Biology*)

Librarian: Mrs I Monem
Library Assistant: Mrs B Wing
Library Assistant: Mrs L Batten
Marketing Executive: Mrs B Roberts
Headmaster's P.A: Miss P Bell
Admissions Secretary: Ms F Pink
Matron: Mrs A Sweeney, BSc School Nursing, RGN

There are approximately 891 boys and girls in the school.

Admission. Entry is normally at age 11 (First Year), 13 (Third Year) or 16 (Sixth Form). Students are accepted in September each year. Entry is also possible during an academic year if a place is available.

Admissions details may be obtained from Ms Freda Pink, Admissions Secretary.

Entrance Scholarships. (*See Scholarship Entries section.*) Academic Scholarships are awarded at 11, 13 and for the Sixth Form. Additionally, the College offers Music, Drama, Sport and Art Scholarships.

Bursaries. The College provides short-term financial assistance for existing families who find themselves in difficult financial circumstances. Further information is available from the Bursar.

Assisted Places Scheme. St George's offers financial assistance of up to 100% relief on fees via its means-tested Assisted Places Scheme. The scheme allows families, who would not normally be able to consider the independent sector, to seek a St George's education for their academically able son or daughter. Places are awarded from the age of seven at the Junior School and eleven at the College. As with all applications, children will need to reach the academic entry standards required at both schools. Further information is available from the Admissions Secretary.

Facilities. The Henderson Centre was opened in September 2010. Our new state-of-the-art building provides Sixth Form group and silent study rooms, social space, five History and five Geography classrooms, staff offices and meeting areas. Refurbishment over the past three years has provided modern facilities for Music, Languages, English, Mathematics, Theatre and Technology. There is an extensive Arts Centre, an impressive Library and a large indoor Sports Hall with an adjacent fitness training room. The College has 19 tennis courts, including three international standard grass courts, clay courts and an impressive four-court Indoor Tennis Centre. In addition there are floodlit netball courts, an all-weather athletics track and two astroturf hockey pitches. The College Boat Club is situated nearby on the Thames.

The Curriculum. This is kept as broad as possible up to GCSE, with a balance between Arts and Science subjects. Students usually take a maximum of 10 GCSEs, A level candidates may choose from over 20 subjects. The vast majority of the Sixth Form go on to Russell Group universities including Oxford and Cambridge.

Careers. Guidance is given throughout a student's career but particularly in making GCSE, A level and university choices. The Careers Coordinator has a modern well stocked Careers Room and makes effective use of COA testing, portfolios, work experience, trial interviews, Challenge of Industry days and computer software.

Art. The Art Department attracts large numbers of students at GCSE and A level who achieve consistently high results in public examinations. A large proportion of A level candidates successfully apply to Art Colleges, often each receiving several offers in this highly competitive field.

Music. Music plays a vital part in school life. There is a wide range of music-making encompassing early music, madrigal groups, jazz, rock, African Drumming as well as more traditional ensembles, orchestras and wind bands. The choir and orchestra give regular performances (including radio broadcasts), and tour Europe annually. Tuition is available on all orchestral instruments from a team of 36 visiting specialists who teach over 400 students each week. Students play in youth orchestras including the NYO and have gained scholarships to the major conservatoires.

Responsibility and Service. Many boys and girls are engaged in the care for the elderly at home or in old people's homes, as well as the mentally and physically handicapped. Each Easter and Summer groups of Sixth Formers accompany handicapped people on visits to Lourdes. Students find these activities a rewarding exercise in Christian service. The Prefect system and the mentor system offer positions of responsibility to the oldest students. The Duke of Edinburgh's Award Scheme is encouraged and there is a flourishing College Council.

Pastoral Care. The spiritual, moral and academic wellbeing of the students is the concern of every member of staff at the College. Nearly all staff act as Group Tutors with particular responsibility for the daily care of their students and for forging links with parents. Each Year Group is led by a Head of Year, and the Chaplain has a general pastoral role. All groups have a day of retreat away each year. The College also has four Houses to which the students are affiliated and all students have one period per week as part of their PSE programme.

Extra Curricular Activities. There is a very wide range of clubs and societies taking place both at lunchtime and after school. In addition to music and sport, a broad range of interests is catered for such as the Science Club, Cookery, Young Enterprise, Philosophy and Model Clubs.

Sport. All students participate and there is a variety of sports: rugby, hockey, netball, cricket, tennis, rowing, and rounders, plus a wide range of other activities such as golf, athletics, badminton, basketball and cross-country. Each student has the opportunity to develop his or her own talents in small coaching groups. The College has its own boat house on the Thames, nineteen tennis courts (including four indoor), two floodlit artificial pitches with viewing stand, floodlit netball courts, six artificial cricket nets, one main pavilion and two smaller cricket pavilions, eight rugby pitches. The College has access to the Junior School heated swimming pool. All facilities are of a very high standard in an attractive setting. Overseas tours to Holland and Malta have been completed recently by hockey and cricket teams. Attendance at national hockey finals is an annual event and the College hosts a very popular U18 Hockey Sixes every year. International honours have recently been gained in hockey, cricket, rowing and tennis.

Junior School. St George's College Junior School is located nearby in Thames Street, Weybridge, and is co-educational, catering for boys and girls from 3 to 11.

(*For further details, please see Junior School entry in IAPS section.*)

Fees per term (2011-2012). First and Second Forms £4,300; Third–Sixth Forms £4,900. Lunches £240.

Charitable status. St George's College Weybridge is a Registered Charity, number 1017853, and a Company Limited by Guarantee. The aims and objectives of the Charity are the Christian education of young people.

St John's School

Leatherhead, Surrey KT22 8SP
Tel: 01372 373000 Switchboard
      01372 385441 Headmaster
      01372 385446 Bursar
Fax: 01372 386606
e-mail: school@stjohns.surrey.sch.uk
website: www.stjohnsleatherhead.co.uk

Founded 1851. Royal Charter, 1922.

St John's School was founded in North London in 1851 for the education of the sons of Anglican clergy. The move to Leatherhead was made in 1872 and a Royal Charter was granted in 1922. St John's is a Day and Boarding School for boys and girls aged 13–18 and has grown to some 550 pupils, including Foundationers (the sons and daughters of clergy).

Motto: '*Quae sursum sunt quaerite*' "Seek those things which are above."

Patron: HRH The Duchess of Gloucester, GCVO

Visitor: The Archbishop of Canterbury

The Council:

Chairman: P C F Hickson, MA, FCA

A M Airey, LLB (*OJ*)	Mrs J Harris, BA
T Beckh, MA	H J Malins, CBE (*OJ*)
P A Crossley, BA, BArch, RIBA (*OJ*)	Mrs S Meikle, BA
The Rt Revd The Bishop of Dorking	A J L Peake, FCA (*OJ*)
	B Shaw, BSc, MRICS
P G Gardner, FRICS (*OJ*)	L F Speller, FCA
R M Gordon Clark, LLB (*OJ*)	Mrs C Swabey, MA, MSc
	P H Thorne, MA (*OJ*)
Mrs J Grant Peterkin, BA	S A Westley, MA, MIMgt
The Rt Revd The Bishop of Guildford	D J Woodhead, BA, FRSA
	J Willis, BA Oxon

Bursar and Secretary to the Council: Mrs J V Maynard, BA, DMS

Headmaster: Martin A R Collier, MA Oxon

Deputy Headmaster: M D Mortimer, BA
Deputy Head (Academic): M W Clarke, BSc
Director of Studies: J Nuttall, BSc, MSc, PhD, BPhil
Senior Housemaster: R W L Allan, BA
Senior Mistress: Mrs D J Burgess, BSc

Assistant Staff:
* *Head of Department*
† *Housemaster/mistress*

P C Noble, BSc	Miss P J Whittingham, BSc
A B Gale, BSc, CPhys, MInstP	D C Atkinson, BSc, MSc
A J Phillips, BA	*J H Davies, BSc, MSc
*A P King, BA, FSA	G D Hicks, BA
*Mrs D J Burgess, BSc	Miss A M Littlejohns, BA, MSc
*Mrs L S Culm, BEd, DipRSA SpLD, AMBDA	Miss T G King, MA Cantab
	*M Probert, BA
Miss J A Belfrage, BA, MA	*A C M Vargas, BA
*M Rogers, BSc	S Y Eales, HDE
†R W L Allan, BA	I Sheffield, BEd
†A Bass, BEd	*Miss J Day, BSc
*P Reilly, BSc, MA, PhD	S H Blatch, BSc
*N T Whitmore, BA, MA	Ms L Pedret, BA
*J Ward, BSc	Miss C E Hughes, BA, MA
*†N Smith, BA, Dip RSAMD	Miss S L Gush, BSc
	*R J Bristow, BA
Mrs B I Davies, BSc, MA, AMBDA	R G Jones, BA
	Ms C L Byfield, BA
Mrs J H Moriya, BA	Mrs L J Parker, BA
†Q Wiseman, BA, FRGS	*Miss A D Rawlings, BSc
*R L Davidson, BA	M D Lotsu, BSc
Ms J Fowler, BSc	*Mrs G White, BA
R J Gregory, BSc	G V Solomon, BA, BSc, MPhil
†J A Passam, BA, FRSA	T Ashton, BA
*N Johnston-Jones, BA	M W Bawden, MA Cantab
*J Kidd, BA, MA	Dr M J Slade, BSc
*N S Platt, BA Ed	M W Bawden, MA
M A Sartorius, BA	G Wade, MA
S G Briggs, CertEd	The Revd S Bryant, BA, MTheol
J P Sutcliffe, BMus	
†P Thomas, BSc	Mrs J R Kirk, BSc

J K M Fulton-Peebles, BSc	Miss S D Dixon, BA
*L D Bastin, BA	Miss C S Finnegan, BSc
Miss K H Hughes, BA	Mrs J H Chaddock, BA
Miss J C Michael, BA	Miss H Halford, BA
*A Mooney, BEd	S Hughes, BSc

Houses & Housemasters/mistresses:

Boarding Houses (Boys):
West: Q Wiseman
East: J A Passam
Churchill: N Smith

Day Houses (Boys):
North: R W L Allan
Surrey: P Thomas
Montgomery: A Bass

Day & Boarding (Girls):
South: Miss P J Whittingham
Haslewood: Miss T G King

Marketing Director: R J Heptonstall, BA
Admissions Registrar: Mrs S Stuart
HR Manager: Mrs C J Robinson, Chartered MCIPD
Librarian & Archivist: Mrs S Todd, BA, MA Ed, MCLIP
Medical Officer: Dr W S R Barr, MBBS, FRCS, MRCGP

Boarding. Full and weekly boarding places are available.

Houses. Currently there are three boarding houses (West, East and Churchill) and three day houses (North, Surrey and Montgomery) for boys. There are two day and boarding houses (South and Haslewood) for girls.

Buildings. The School occupies a 50-acre site in Leatherhead within easy reach of the M25. The original 19th Century buildings form an open cloistered quadrangle, comprising the boarding and day houses, the oak-panelled dining hall, and the Chapel. The School has a Multimedia Studio, a Sixth Form Study Centre, a Performing Arts Centre, a Sixth Form Social Centre. The Henry Dawes Centre, a new Classroom block opened in September 2010, accommodates purpose-built Design & Technology workshops, Library, Art Studios, IT suites as well as classrooms.

Religion. As a Church of England Foundation, St John's has always had a special place for worship in the life of the School and benefits from a modern Chapel on site.

Curriculum. On entry into the Fourth Form, all pupils study English, Mathematics, Religious Education, French, Spanish, Physics, Chemistry, Biology, Geography, History, Information and Communication Technology, Art, Design and Technology, Music, Physical Education (including Health Education) and either Latin or Classical Civilisation.

In the second year, pupils will study English (including Literature), Mathematics, a Modern Foreign Language (French or Spanish), Science (Physics, Chemistry and Biology) and three other subjects to GCSE. In addition, all pupils will continue with Information and Communication Technology and a non-examined Religious Education course. The other subjects studied to GCSE include a second Modern Language, History, Geography, Religious Studies, Latin, Information and Communication Technology, Physical Education, Design and Technology, Drama, Art, Graphic Communication and Music.

In the first year of the Sixth Form, pupils will begin their Advanced Subsidiary course, generally choosing four subjects. A wide range of choices is possible from the following subjects: Art, Biology, Business Studies, Chemistry, Design and Technology, Drama and Theatre Studies, Economics, English Literature, French, Geography, Government and Politics, History, Information and Communication Technology, Latin, Mathematics, Further Mathematics, Music, Music Technology, Physics, Psychology, Religious Studies, Spanish and Sport and Physical Education.

In the second year of the Sixth Form, pupils will generally continue three of their subjects to Advanced Level.

Over the first four terms of the Sixth Form, pupils will follow a General Studies programme. This includes a range of talks from outside speakers, aimed at encouraging an interest in different aspects of culture and society, and a course on entry to Higher Education.

Music. There is a strong musical tradition. The Chapel Choir effectively complements worship in Chapel. Many boys and girls study musical instruments and are encouraged to participate in the School orchestra, wind band, string quartets, choral society, chamber choir, jazz band and rock groups. There are regular informal concerts to encourage informal performance.

Art and Design and Technology. As well as providing the facilities for pursuing the academic curriculum, the Art and Design facilities and the Technology workshops are used extensively in co-curricular activities.

Drama. Drama plays an important part in the life of the School, with most boys and girls taking to the stage at some point, in both House Drama competitions and a variety of School productions during the year.

Information and Communication Technology. There is a school-wide network of computers and other ICT resources that support many activities and areas of school life. Interactive Whiteboards in every classroom provide an invaluable resource for curricular and co-curricular activities of all descriptions. Computers are available for use throughout the School both during and outside the School day. Pupils and staff have widespread access to the internet for research and preparation.

Debating. The School competes in national and regional competitions and other inter-school events. There are inter-House competitions at junior and senior level each year.

Careers. All boys and girls are advised on their Advanced Level and Higher Education courses. ISCO careers aptitude tests are offered, as are regular careers evenings and visits. There is a work experience programme, business enterprise opportunities and regular careers events for pupils.

Sport. Cricket, Rugby and Football are the major sports for boys, with Hockey, Netball, Cricket and Rounders for girls. Many other sports flourish, including Tennis, Fives, Squash, Swimming, Sailing, Badminton, Athletics, Volleyball, Basketball, Cross-Country and Shooting.

Combined Cadet Force. The contingent comprises RN, Army and RAF sections. Cadets train for the Services Proficiency Certificates and the various stages of the Duke of Edinburgh's Award Scheme. Field Days, Adventure Training expeditions, annual camps and courses are an integral feature of CCF training.

Admission. For entry at Year 9, each boy and girl applying to St John's will be required to register, following which candidates will have a pre-assessment in the January of Year 6 and a report and recommendation from the respective feeder school will be requested. Based on this information a conditional offer may be made. The offer of a confirmed place is subject to achieving 55% at Common Entrance (or the equivalent) and a continued positive recommendation from the respective feeder school.

There are also a number of Day and Boarding places available for boys and girls who wish to enter the School in the Lower Sixth (Year 12). Boys and girls will have an academic assessment and are interviewed in the November before their entry into the Sixth Form to determine whether a conditional place is offered. They will be required to satisfy the School's minimum academic entry requirement of six B grades at GCSE, which must include B grades or above in the subjects they wish to study at AS Level.

Term of Entry. The only term for entry, except in special circumstances, is the Autumn term.

Foundationers. In accordance with the Foundation of St John's, places are available for sons and daughters of Anglican clergy who are resident in any Diocese of the Church of England or the Church in Wales and who are engaged in the Ministry of the Church. A Foundation place is awarded on the result of the Common Entrance or Scholarship Examination, or Sixth Form entry tests.

Scholarships and Bursaries. A number of scholarship awards are made to candidates who demonstrate excellence in their particular discipline at 13+ and 16+ as follows:

Academic: 13+ Common Academic Scholarship Examination Papers. 16+ is assessed on predicted GCSE results, interview and references.

All-Rounder: Assessed by general character, academic ability, leadership qualities and a level of excellence in one or more areas of Art, Drama, Music or Sport.

Art, Music and Sport: Assessed by audition/assessment and interview together with supporting references.

Scholarship assessments take place in January/February prior to entry for 13+ and November for 16+.

Means-tested Bursaries are available. The value of a scholarship may be supplemented by a means-tested Bursary.

Two Albany Awards are available each year. These are free places for disadvantaged boys or girls funded by The St John's Foundation.

For further details, please contact the Admissions Registrar, St John's School, Epsom Road, Leatherhead, Surrey KT22 8SP. Tel: 01372 373000; Fax: 01372 386606; e-mail: admissions@stjohns.surrey.sch.uk.

Fees per term (2011-2012). Full boarding £8,865, Weekly boarding £8,175, Day £6,465.

Charitable status. St John's School is a Registered Charity, number 312064.

St Lawrence College

Ramsgate, Kent CT11 7AE
Tel: 01843 572900 (Headmaster)
         01843 572912 (Junior School)
         01843 587666 (Bursar and General Office)
         01843 572931 (Registrar)
Fax: 01843 572901 (Headmaster)
         01843 572913 (Junior School)
         01843 572915 (Bursar and General Office)
         01843 572901 (Registrar)
e-mail: hm@slcuk.com (Headmaster)
         hjs@slcuk.com (Junior School)
         bursar@slcuk.com (Bursar and General Office)
         ah@slcuk.com (Registrar)
website: www.slcuk.com

Co-educational, Day: age 3–18 years, Boarding: age 7–18 years.

The Council:

President: C Laing

Vice-Presidents:
The Baroness Cox, BSc, MSc, FRCN
¶Sir Martin Laing, CBE, MA, FRICS
G H Mungeam, MA, DPhil
S Webley, MA
The Revd Canon Nigel M Walker
A T Emby, FCA
¶B J W Isaac
M G Macdonald, MA, LLM

Chairman: D W Taylor, MA Oxon, PGCE, FRSA

Members:
¶M Iliff, MSc
Mrs G E Page
J Furmanek
J B Guyatt, MA
Mrs A G Burgess, TCNFF, ACP

J H Tapp, BSc
¶N G Marchant
Revd H V Thomas, LLB, Dip Th
Dr C H R Niven
¶T L Townsend, LLB

¶ *Old Lawrentian*

Clerk to the Governors and Bursar: J A Connelly, Esq

Headmaster: Revd M Aitken, BA Hons Durham, Cert
   Theol Fitzwilliam College, Cambridge, FRSA

Deputy Head: Dr E B Gill, BSc, PhD London, CSci,
   CChem, FRSC (*Chemistry*)
Director of Studies: I D Dawbarn, BA York, MSc Oxon
   (*Mathematics, Head of Careers*)
Chaplain: Revd Peter R Russell, BA, Dip Theo Mins, PG
   Dip OM, CCCU
Registrar: Miss A Hall, CertEd Cambridge Inst of Ed,
   NPQH

Heads of Department:
I M Anderson, MA St Andrews (*Economics, Mathematics,
   GPR, Head of Social Sciences*)
Mrs A E Bailey, MA Sussex, BEd London (*Games, PE,
   English, Head of PSHE*)
Miss E Barrs, BA Hons, PGCE (*Head of Drama*)
R A Bendall, BA (*Modern Languages, Classical
   Civilisation, PSHE, Head of Religious Studies*)
G A Bryant, MA London, BEd Manchester (*Enterprise
   Coordinator, Business Studies*)
Dr T A Clarke, BSc Durham, DIC, MSc London, PhD
   Liverpool, MIBiol, CBiol, FRGS (*Head of Biology*)
I D Dawbarn, BA York, MSc Oxon (*Mathematics, Head of
   Careers*)
Mrs A J Fletcher, BEd, CertEd, Dip TEFLA (*Head of EAL*)
Mrs S J Glynn-Brooks, BSc CCUC, PGCE (*Head of
   Academic PE*)
J Good, BA Hons Manchester (*Head of Design &
   Technology*)
P W Graham, BA Exeter (*Head of Modern Languages,
   French, Spanish*)
Mrs J A Green, PGCE Bath (*Head of Home Economics*)
A Izzard, BA Chichester (*Head of Games and PE*)
D P Lewis, BA KIAD (*Head of Art & Design*)
Mrs J Löcsei-Campbell, BSc, BA, BEd (*German, Head of
   Psychology*)
Miss A E Monk, BSc Cardiff (*Head of Chemistry*)
T Moulton, BA Leeds (*Head of History, Classics*)
Dr C J Ransom, BSc, PhD, MA, AKC, PGCE (*Head of
   Physics and Science*)
J M Rawbone, BA Hons Leeds, PGCE Manchester, PgDip
   Sheffield, MA (*Head of Learning Support*)
P M Stubbings, BMus Manchester, Prix d'Excellence-Cum
   Laude Amsterdam (*Director of Music*)
Mr C J Taylor, BA Hons, MA, PGCE (*Head of English*)
Mr N Watts, BA Hons Brighton, QTS (*Head of
   Geography*)
R B Wilkening, BA London, MA Kent (*Head of ICT*)
Mrs W J Wilkening, BSc York (*Head of Mathematics*)

Houses and Housemasters/mistresses:
Lodge: N O S Jones, BA OU (*Geography; Games and PE*)
Tower: G Davies, BSc Hons Cheltenham, PGCE
   (*Geography*)
Newlands: P W Graham, BA Exeter (*Head of Modern
   Languages, French, Spanish*)
Bellerby: Mrs A Izzard
Laing: Miss A E Coe, BA Hons Hull, PGCE (*History,
   English, PSHE*)
Kirby House (*Middle School*): R E Muncey, BEd Soton
   (*English, Religious Studies*)
Kirby House Boarding (*Middle School*): D D Spencer, BSc
   Hons Southampton, PGCE (*PE Coordinator Junior
   School*)

Junior School
Head: S J E Whittle, BA Hons, PGCE
Deputy Head: S C Bithel-Vaughan, BA (*English, ICT,
   History*)

   Number of Pupils. Senior School: 328: 207 boys (124
boarders, 83 day), 121 girls (62 boarders, 59 day).
   Junior School: 16 boarders, 170 day pupils (of whom 28
attend the Nursery).
   Who we are. Walk through the historic arch at St
Lawrence College in Kent and you will immediately feel at
home. The school welcomes students from all over the world
and is a happy and caring community. Recently modernised
rooms and dormitories provide some of the best boarding
accommodation in the country.
   Outstanding results are achieved by the most academic
students who progress to top universities. The school is also
regarded as a centre of excellence for 'value added'; students who need additional support perform well beyond
expectation.
   The school has beautiful surroundings and outstanding
sports facilities. These include a magnificent new Sports
Centre opened this year with a Fitness Suite, Squash Courts,
Climbing Wall, Dance Studio and a large area for badminton, basketball and other sports. The buildings reflect the
nature of the school: steeped in history and tradition, yet
modern, creative and forward-thinking. Kirby House,
opened in January 2007, accommodates our 11–13 year olds
in modern 5-bedded dormitories with en-suite facilities. It is
an imaginative design, architecturally striking, with a glass
atrium and a virtual library at its centre. Throughout the
school the lively, professional approach to education and an
innovative curriculum provide a challenging and stimulating
framework for teaching and learning, but most of all, the
school really takes care of its pupils.
   Our aim is to encourage in our students a real intellectual
curiosity about life so they understand that there is more to
life than the facts of the matter. This approach, growing out
of deep Christian roots, produces a particular atmosphere
within our school. It is enhanced by the size of the community which allows every pupil to be known personally by the
staff.
   The school is close to the Channel Tunnel and the port of
Dover, has excellent transport links to London and Europe
and within an hour and a half of Heathrow and Gatwick airports.
   Selecting a school can be one of the most important decisions we have to make and we therefore encourage parents
and prospective pupils to visit the school if at all possible
and to ask the following question. Are these pupils the kind
of role models, companions and possibly life-long friends
that I would like for my child? I am confident that you will
say 'yes'. The school is justifiably proud that St Lawrence
students leave as confident, compassionate and capable
adults.
   Exam Results. In 2010 92% of GCSE candidates
achieved grade C or above in 5 or more subjects and the total
pass rate at A/AS Level was 94.8%.
   Admissions. *Junior School*: An initial parental tour with
the Headmaster will be followed by a pupil visit. A taster
morning as a follow up allows the prospective pupil to be
assessed in numeracy, literacy and reasoning, as well as getting to know the school from the inside.
   Senior School: At 11+ admissions are based on an Interview with the Headmaster. A copy of a recent school report
will also be required. Testing will be carried out where
appropriate.
   At 13+ the offer of a place will be dependent on the Common Entrance Examination, GCSE predications and/or an
assessment of a recent school report.
   At 16+ the offer of a place will be dependent on a minimum of 5 GCSEs passes.

EU and Overseas Students will be admitted on the basis of current performance, references and a short language test as interviews are not always possible. Our special EFL centre will assess and integrate overseas pupils into the curriculum by offering a range of English teaching options, including an intensive English course, which is charged as an extra at £340 per term.

Fees per term (2011-2012). Boarders £8,835, Day £5,090. Fees are due and payable before the commencement of the relevant school term.

Individual Private Tuition: £44.70 per hour. Individual Instrumental Music: £223.50 per term (10 half-hour sessions).

Siblings. St Lawrence College offers generous sibling allowances. For the academic year 2011/12 these rates will be 10% of the fee rate for the second child, 35% for the third child and 50% for the fourth and subsequent children, providing no other financial benefit in respect of fees is received by the parent in respect of children at the College (excluding Scholarships) above or in addition to the foregoing sibling allowance – the foregoing arrangement for siblings does not apply to the Nursery or Junior School.

Bursaries. In accordance with tradition children of Clergy and Missionaries and of serving members of HM Forces will be considered for bursaries. Parents in HM Forces pay the MOD CEA (Continuity of Education Allowance) plus 10% of our main boarding and tuition fees.

Bursaries may be awarded to new or existing pupils of the College and pupils who have been awarded a scholarship which requires supplementing. Parents may apply to the Governors' Bursary Committee for assistance and will be required to complete a confidential grant application form.

Scholarships. (*See Scholarship Entries section.*) The value of Academic Scholarships will range from 10% to 50% of the fees. Music Scholarships can be awarded in the Senior School and range in value from 10% to 50%. They can be awarded in conjunction with the academic scholarships. Sports Scholarships are also available in the Junior and Senior Schools and range from 10% to 30%. Scholarship exams are held in November and January although late applicants will be considered.

Charitable status. The Corporation of St Lawrence College is a Registered Charity, number 307921. It exists to provide education for children.

St Leonards School

St Andrews, Fife KY16 9QJ
Tel: 01334 472126
Fax: 01334 476152
e-mail: info@stleonards-fife.org
website: www.stleonards-fife.org

Situated in the heart of idyllic St Andrews, St Leonards offers day and boarding education for 5–18 year old boys and girls, combining academic achievement and opportunity with an inspirational atmosphere.
Motto: *Ad Vitam*

Members of Council:
Chairman: Mr James Murray, MA, LLB, DL
Mr Ian Adam, CA
Mr Hamish Alldridge, MA, DipEd, CertEd
Lord Balniel
Mrs Victoria Collison-Owen
Mr Alan Constable, BSc
Mr Roy de C Chapman, MA
Lady Fraser of Carmyllie, MSc
Col Martin Passmore, MA, GCGI, FRSA
Dr Louise Richardson, BA, MA, MA, MA, PhD
Mr Aubyn Stewart-Wilson, BSc

Mrs Clare Wade

Academic Staff:

Headmaster: **Michael Carslaw**, BSc Hons Newcastle, MBA Nottingham, PhD London

Deputy Headmaster & Deputy Head Pastoral: Geoffrey Jackson-Hutt, BSc Hons, PhD Southampton
Deputy Head Academic: Dawn Pemberton-Hislop, BA Hons Sheffield, MBA Keele
Head of Sixth Form: Karen Wowk, MA Hons St Andrews
Head of Senior School: Andrew Lang, MA Hons St Andrews

Art & Design:
Donna Rae, MA Glasgow, BFA Chicago
Susan Welsh, BA Hons Dundee
Lisa Ann Donald, BEd Manchester
Willliam Clark, MA Winchester, BA Hons Dundee

Classics:
Roseanna Bochenek, MA Hons St Andrews

Economics:
John Lambert, MA Hons Dundee
Peter Haselhurst, MA Hons St Andrews

English:
Rupert Crisswell, BA York, MEd Cantab
John Taylor, MA Hons St Andrews
Denise Johnston, BA Hons Cardiff
Mick Kitson, BA Hons Newcastle
Vanessa Samuel, BA Hons Cantab

Geography:
Samantha Watson, MA Hons Aberdeen
Elaine Boyd, BA Hons Abertay, MRes Strathclyde

History & Politics:
Mark Dunkerley, BA Oxon
Lorna Greenwood, MA Hons Edinburgh

ICT:
Marcia Julius, BA Maryland, BSc Maryland, MAS Johns Hopkins

Learning Support:
Rona Wishart, MA Hons Edinburgh
Jim Boyle, BA Hons OU, BSc Paisley, MA OU
Gillian Greenwood, MA Hons Cantab

Mathematics:
Graeme Baxter, BSc Hons Aberdeen
Jonathan Edwards, BEd Hons Wales
Paul McDonald, BSc OU
David Pearce, BSc St Andrews
Kristina Struck, State Exam MA Berlin

Modern Languages:
Joyce Duncan, MA Hons St Andrews
Susana Aranzana-Gonzalez, BA, MA, CAP Valladolid
Dan Barlow, MA Hons St Andrews
Anna Beck, BA Columbia MBA Cornell
Oriana Kelly, BA Hons Dunelm
Irene Kretschmann, Diplom BA Bonn
Elizabeth Semper, MA Hons St Andrews
Christina Steele, MA Hons St Andrews
Haiyan Wang, BA, MA Sichuan, Chengdu, MSc Dundee
Mario Prisco, MA Hons Napoli

Music:
Glynn Jenkins, BA Hons, PhD Mus Exeter
Fraser Burke, BA RSAMD
Marjorie Cleghorn, LGSM
Sheila Cochrane, DRSAM, CertEd Edinburgh
Jane Colvin, GRSM Hons, LRAM
Martin Dibbs, MA, MLitt St Andrews, DMS
Marie Downes, BA Hons Sussex
Winston Emmerson, BSc Hons Rhodes, MSc, PhD UPE

Stuart Foggo
Janice Gibson, ALCM, Dip ABRSM
Kenneth Irons, SADJ
Anne Marie Ives, Dip MusEd, LLCM TD, LTCL, LTCL CMT
Fiona Love, BMus Hons Glasgow
Claire Luxford, MMus, PGCE Mus, MPhil Cantab
Dorothy McCabe, GRSM, ARCM, ATCL, CertEd London
Susan McCathie, BMus Hons Aberdeen
Rosemary Mair, LTCL
Louise Major, BMus, BSc Hons Victoria, PhD Otago
Ashley Malcolm, BA Mus Stud RSAMD
Simon Milton, BSc Reading, MMus Sheffield
Jennifer Prestana, GRSM Hons, LRAM
Lynne Ruark, DRSAM, LRAM Glasgow, CertEd Edinburgh
Toni Russell, BA Hons Applied Music Strathclyde

Physical Education:
Iain Watson, BEd Hons Edinburgh
Nicola Davidson, BEd Hons Edinburgh
Rosie Dawson, BA Hons Bangor
Elizabeth Dunsmuir, Dip PE
Andrew Durward, BEd Hons Edinburgh
Sarah Hall, BEd Hons Edinburgh
Isabel Myles, BEd Edinburgh

Science:
Aileen Rees, MA Hons Cantab
Catherine Dunn, BSc Hons, PhD St Andrews
Carla Grilli, BSc Hons St Andrews
Charlotte Kirby, BSc Hons St Andrews
Diane Lindsay, BSc Hons Aberdeen
Marlene Lloyd-Evans, MSc, BSc Hons Rhodes SA
Anna Radons-Harris, BSc Hons Lancaster
Hailey Howorth, MChem Heriot-Watt
Alison Hill, MSc Glasgow BSc Hons Aberdeen PhD Belfast
Keith Hall, HNC Electrical Engineering

Speech and Drama:
Nichola Ledger, BEd Hons London
Claudia Daventry, BA/MA Hons Oxon, MLitt St Andrews

St Leonards-New Park
The Preparatory School of St Leonards

Headmaster: Andrew Donald, BSc Aberdeen

Deputy Heads:
Dianne Cormack, BSc Hons St Andrews
Derek McFadden, BEd Glasgow

Head of Early Years: Alison Turnbull, BEd Jordanhill

Lisa Adair-Brown, BA Hons Stirling
Claire Boissiere, MA Hons Dundee
Valerie Donald, MA Hons St Andrews
Anna Fisher, MA Hons Dundee
Linda Gault, Dip PrimEd Callander Park, Falkirk
Irena Harris, LLAM, ATCL
Beatrice Hood, MA St Andrews
Gordon MacDonald, DipEd ECA
Kenny McDonald, BEd Dundee
Kathleen McKimmon, BCom Edinburgh
Karen Napier, BSc Abertay
Nicola Nejman, MA Hons St Andrews
Jenny Nicoll, Dip Sp Ed Natal

Bursar: Wg Cdr Johnston Calder
Registrar: Caroline Routledge, BSc, PhD

There are approximately 520 pupils in the School with an equal number of boys and girls and more than 120 boarders.

Ethos. Founded in 1877, St Leonards aims to prepare young people for the challenges of life ahead and to provide them with the skills and abilities that will enable them to step into the world with confidence and integrity. We offer a broad, rigorous education and exceptional opportunities, while instilling confidence, responsibility and independence.

Location and Campus. St Leonards combines a beautiful, historic campus with the inspirational buzz that comes from being in the heart of the university town of St Andrews.

The School is situated in a beautiful and secure, self contained campus within the medieval walls of the former St Andrews Abbey. Our campus has served as a place of learning since the 16th century and contains several buildings of historical significance, including our library, a building once used by Mary Queen of Scots as lodgings.

On their doorstep our pupils have golden sandy beaches, historic landmarks, world famous golf courses and the friendly town of St Andrews itself, in which our pupils are made to feel very much part of the community.

St Andrews is only 45 minutes from the cultural highlights and international airport of Edinburgh and just 20 minutes from Dundee (a one-hour flight from London).

Curriculum. The Sixth Form at St Leonards prepares pupils for the International Baccalaureate Diploma and the School is the only in Scotland to have an all IB Diploma Sixth Form.

The Senior School (Years 8–11) prepares boys and girls for GCSEs – typically around ten.

The Preparatory School (Years 1–7) follows the Curriculum for Excellence 'plus', delivering a seamless and coherent transition into the Senior School.

University Link. The School has close links with the University of St Andrews and each year appoints an Associate Researcher, a postgraduate student who provides a link for the pupils to the research community at the University. St Leonards students also have access to the University Library and regularly attend special lectures.

Sport, Drama, Art and Music. Opportunities in sport, music, drama and art abound. Our pupils regularly enjoy success on the sports field, earning team success and individual recognition in sports including rugby, lacrosse, hockey, tennis and football. They are also encouraged to make the most of living just a few hundred yards from the most famous golf links in the world. The School has close links with SALJGA (St Andrews Links Junior Golf Association).

A large number of pupils learn a wide variety of musical instruments, leading to ABRSM recognition.

Drama students have the chance to take part in a number of professional quality productions staged at the nearby Byre Theatre, a leading regional theatrical venue. Our Art students show off their inspiring work every year in an exhibition that is open to the public.

Co-Curricular. There is a wide range of activities in which pupils can take part, including Duke of Edinburgh's Award expeditions, falconry classes, rock climbing, skiing and debating. Foreign trips are also regularly organised with recent destinations including New York, Rome, the Italian Alps and Dresden. Community awareness is important at St Leonards and in the past few years our pupils have raised over £30,000 for charity.

Boarding. The School excels in its boarding provision, our boarding houses offering friendly and welcoming 'home from homes'. According to the latest Care Commission inspection report, St Leonards offers its boarding pupils, "an outstanding, Scottish, boarding experience", with the quality of care and support and the quality of the environment rated as "excellent". Both weekly and full boarding options are available.

Fees per term (2011-2012). Preparatory School: £2,647 (Years 1–5), £2,967 (Years 6–7). Senior School and Sixth Form: Day £3,650; Boarding £8,690.

Admission. The main ages for intake are Years 1, 4, 7, 8 and 9 and the Sixth Form though applications can be considered at any time during the School year. Bursary support may be given, based on need. Full details are available from the Registrar.

Charitable status. St Leonards School is a Registered Charity, number SC010904.

St Mary's College

Crosby, Merseyside L23 5TW
Tel: 0151 924 3926
Fax: 0151 932 0363
e-mail: principalsmc@stmarys.lpool.sch.uk
website: www.stmarys.ac

St Mary's College is an Independent Catholic School for boys and girls of all faiths aged 0–18. We are a thriving community which places a high value on outstanding academic achievement and all-round personal development. Our school is built on strong values which emphasise the importance of caring for others and striving for excellence in all we do. Boys and girls can start at our Bright Sparks & Early Years department (0–4 years) soon after birth and progress to our Preparatory School The Mount (4–11 years) before moving on to the College (11–18 years), where typically they achieve up to 99% pass rates at both GCSE and A Level. Our rich programme of extra-curricular activities equips our pupils with the skills and values which will guide and support them throughout their lives. Scholarships and bursaries are available.

Motto: '*Fidem Vita Fateri*'

Governors:
Chairman: C J Cleugh, BSc, MSc

P Burns, LLB Hons, PG	Mrs P Old, LLB
Dip Law, Barrister	M McKenna, LLB
Mrs L Byrne	M Mansour, BSc Pharm
Councillor S Dorgan	Mrs S Ward, FCMA, BSc
Mr M Guerin, BSc	K Williams
Councillor A Hill, Solicitor	C Wright, BSc
Mrs G Mackay	

Principal: M Kennedy, BSc, MA, NPQH, CChem, MRSC

Deputy Head: F Connolly, BSc

Bursar & Company Secretary: H Ewins, BA Hons

Senior Teachers:
T Lane, BSc, PhD, MRSC
Mrs C Killen, BEd (*Head of Sixth Form*)
Mrs K Lane, BEd (*Head of Lower School*)
N Rothnie, MA
Mrs J Thomas, BSc (*Assistant Principal & Head of Middle School*)

Assistant Teachers:
* *Head of Department*

Miss N Addy, BSc
J Armstrong, BA
Mrs B Baden, BA
Mrs D Barbosa, MPhil
Mrs S Bartolo, BEd
Mr C Buckley, MA
A Byers, BA
Mrs C Cahill, BSc
Mrs E Connolly, BA (**English*)
Mrs L Clark, BSc (**Chemistry*)
L Doherty, BEd
P Duffy, MPhil (**Religious Studies*)
Miss S Foster, BSc (**Girls' PE & Games*)
Mrs E Ford, BA
J J Hayes, BA
Mrs C Hearty, BEd
Mrs C Hyland, BA

M Ireland, BEng, MSc (**Design & Technology*)
R S Johnston, BSc (**Biology*)
Mrs M C Jones, BA, PhD
Mrs A Jordan, BSc
Mrs C Killen, BEd
Dr M Leach, BA (**Physics*)
Mr D Linley, MA
P E McColgan, MA (**Careers*)
Mrs M McKean, BA (**Modern Foreign Languages*)
Mrs N Moore (**Classics & Latin*)
Mrs M A Murphy, BA
P Nagington, BEd, MDes
Miss H Orrett, BA
D Phillips, BA
H Piotr, BSc (**Geography*)
I Rhead, BSc
N C Rothnie, BA (**History*)
H Sage, BSc
Miss L Shevlin, BA
Miss J Simpson, BA (**Business Studies & General Studies*)
A Stagogiannis, BA (**French*)
Mrs J Thomas, BSc (**Mathematics*)
N Vagianos, BSc, MBA (**Information Technology*)
Mrs A Whelan, MA (**Art*)
D Williams, BA (**Boys' PE & Games*)

Preparatory Department:
Head: M Collins, CertEd, DipMgt
Deputy Head: J Webster, BA Hons QTS
Head of Early Years: Mrs A Haigh, BEd

Assistant Teachers:

N Antrobus, BA Hons QTS	J B Mitchell, BEd
Miss J Batisti, BSc Hons QTS	J Moran, BEd
G Bates, BA, PGCE	*Claremont House*:
Mrs L Gallagher, CertEd	Mrs A Haigh, BEd
M Hewlett, CertEd	Mrs A Fielding, NNEB
Mrs V Mason, BA Hons QTS	Mrs S Alldritt
	Mrs S Seiffert

Numbers. There are 477 pupils in the Senior School and 148 in the Preparatory Department. There are no boarders.

Preparatory Department. Open to boys and girls up to the age of 11. There is an Early Years Unit (0–4) comprising baby unit and kindergarten. Pupils are admitted to the Preparatory Department after an interview at 4, 5 and 6 years of age and by informal assessment during a day visit.

The Mount has a strong family atmosphere, providing a secure and lively environment in which expectations are high. The school takes what is best from the National Curriculum and follows an enhanced programme with greater emphasis on the 3 Rs and fostering self-discipline.

Sciences play an important part in the curriculum. Sport and Music are particularly strong. Tutoring in a wide range of musical instruments is provided. French and Spanish are taught in small groups from Reception.

The Head of the Preparatory Department, Mr M Collins, will be pleased to meet you and show you round.

Senior School. Fully co-educational, the Senior School admits pupils at 11 both from The Mount and from primary schools over a wide area. An Entrance Examination is held in January each year. Generally speaking, pupils must be between the ages of 10½ and 12 on 1 September of the year in which they wish to enter the School. There is also a 13+ entry. A Registration Fee of £40 is payable with the form of application for admission.

The **Curriculum in the Senior School** includes English Language and Literature, French, German, Spanish, History, Geography, Classical Studies, Latin, Physics, Chemistry, Biology, Mathematics, Information Technology, Art, Music, Drama, Design and Technology and Physical Education. A broad curriculum of 14 subjects is followed for the first 3 years. In the Fourth and Fifth Years, pupils normally take 10 subjects at GCSE, including either single Sciences or Core plus Additional Science, and all pupils study for GCSE Religious Studies and an OCR National qualification in Information Technology. In the Sixth Form there are Advanced courses in all the subjects mentioned above. Psychology, Business Studies, Theology and Drama may also be taken to A Level and all Sixth Formers take A Level General Studies. The Sixth Form options system is flexible allowing combinations of 3 or 4 A Levels.

St Mary's is a pioneer school on Merseyside in the inclusion of **orchestral music** as a normal feature of the School curriculum. All pupils are given the opportunity to play an orchestral instrument. The School Band and Orchestra give an annual Concert in the Liverpool Philharmonic Hall, win regional contests and undertake tours abroad.

Religious Education. Religious Education is a core subject through to GCSE. In the Sixth Form there is the option of Christian Theology A Level. General Religious Education in the Sixth Form is integrated with social work for the handicapped and deprived.

Careers. The College works in partnership with the Independent Schools Careers Organisation. Arrangements are made each year for interviews for Fifth Formers to which parents are invited. Sixth Formers are interviewed several times to help them choose appropriate courses at University or in Higher Education. Advice is given to Third Year pupils in choosing options.

Games. Games periods provide opportunities for Rugby, Cricket, Football, Hockey, Netball, Squash, Golf, Cross-Country, Tennis and Basketball. The main games for girls are Netball and Hockey. There is an adjacent modern Sports Centre.

Activities. Some 40 extra-curricular activities and societies are available, including the Duke of Edinburgh's Award Scheme.

Combined Cadet Force. There is a very active Combined Cadet Force which contains Army and Air Force sections. Membership of the Combined Cadet Force is voluntary.

Fees per term (2011-2012). Senior School £2,997; Preparatory Department £2,027–£2,060.

Open Academic Scholarships. There are up to six Open Scholarships based on performance in the College Entrance Examination, worth up to half fees. The awards are based on academic merit alone and are currently irrespective of income. There is also a small number of Art, Music and Sports Scholarships.

There are also School Assisted Places, known as Edmund Rice Junior Scholarships, at 11+. These are income-related and are open to pupils whose parents' joint income would have brought them within the Government scheme.

Sixth Form Scholarships. Edmund Rice Scholarships (worth approximately 10% of fees) are available on merit, and are awarded on the basis of a Scholarship Examination in January.

Charitable status. St Mary's College Crosby Trust Limited is a Registered Charity, number 1110311. The aims and objectives of the Charity are to advance religious and other charitable works.

St Paul's School

Lonsdale Road, Barnes, London SW13 9JT
Tel: 020 8748 9162
Fax: 020 8746 5353
e-mail: hmsec@stpaulsschool.org.uk
website: www.stpaulsschool.org.uk

St Paul's School was founded in AD 1509, by John Colet, DD, Dean of St Paul's. An ancient Grammar School had previously existed for many centuries in connection with St Paul's Cathedral, and was probably absorbed by Colet into his new foundation. Colet laid down in the original statutes, still preserved at Mercers' Hall, that there should be 'taught in the scole children of all Nacions and Countres indifferently to the Noumber of a CLIII', the number of the Miraculous Draught of Fishes. There are still 153 Foundation Scholars, in a school of 850 pupils, in addition to about 440 pupils in the Preparatory School. Colet appointed 'the most honest and faithfull fellowshipp of the Mercers of London' as Governors of his School. The Governing Body has been extended to include University Governors and other nominees. The School was moved from its original site adjoining the Cathedral to West Kensington in 1884 and to its present position on the River Thames at Barnes in 1968. A history of the school entitled 'A miraculous draught of fishes' by A H Mead was published in 1990.

Motto: '*Fide et literis*'

Governors:
Chairman: Dr F C G Hohler, MA, DPhil
Deputy Chairman: Ms J Rickard

Appointed by the Mercers' Company:
L Dorfman, CBE
N A H Fenwick, MA
Ms A Macleod
Professor C P Mayer, MA, MPhil, DPhil (*in consultation with the University of Oxford*)
J M Robertson, BSc
The Earl St Aldwyn, MA
A Summers, BSc, MSc
¶Sir Nigel Thompson, KCMG, CBE

Clerk to the Governors: Mrs G Begbey, BSc, MA, ACIS

High Master: M Bailey, PhD, FRHistS

Surmaster: R G Jaine, MA, FRGS

Director of Studies: P Woodruff, MA, MSc

Undermasters:
T A Peters, BSc (*Senior Tutor*)
E A du Toit, BPE
P J King, MA
A J Mayfield, BSc, MSc, DPhil
A G Wilson, BA

Assistant Director of Studies: I Poots, BSc, PhD, CChem, MRSC

Housemaster: S J Clarke, MChem

St Paul's School Academic Staff:

Art:
§T P M E Flint, MA
Mrs P C Holmes, BA, UED
*N W Hunter, BA Hons, MEd
§Mrs S E W Hunter, MEd
§Miss E Stravoravdi, MA
I J Tiley, MA, ATC

Classics:
D J Cairns, MA
J T Harrison, BA (**PSHE/Citizenship*)
P J King, MA
*S A May, MA
Ms L R Nicholas, MA
M O McCullagh, BA, MPhil, PhD
A G Wilson, BA

Drama:
T Y Benyon, MA (*also English*)
W A le Fleming, BA (*also English*)
*E J T Williams, MA

Economics and Politics:
P R K Bird, BA
G L Boss, BA

E A du Toit, BPE
M Homayounnejad, BSc
Miss A R M O'Dwyer, BA (*Politics)
*S P Schmitt, BSc
A J Sykes, MSc, MA

English:
A J Broughton, MA
P R J Hudson, MA, PhD
Miss J McLaren, MA
B J O'Keeffe, MA
A C Shouler, BA
*J C Venning, MA

Geography:
A J Boardman, BA
A P D Isaac, BSc, MSc
P S Littlewood, BSc, MSc, FRGS (*General Studies)
V J Light, BA
*J R Williams, MA

History:
*M G Howat, BA
Dr H M Larkin, BA, MA, PhD
Mrs S Mackenzie, BSc, MA
N J Sanderson, MA
N G D Watkins, BA

Learning Support Coordinator:
Miss J A Isnardi-Bruno, BA

Mathematics:
R J Baxter, BA, PhD
D P Eves, MEng, PhD
B R Girvan, BA, MEng
M L Harvey, BSc
A J Mayfield, BSc, MSc, DPhil
T C I Morland, MA, CMath, MIMA
T A Peters, BSc
P Robson, BSc
D Rowland, BA, MMath
M Sheehan, MMath, PhD
M J R Slay, BA, MSc
J M Stone, BA
K Tadinada, MEng, DPhil
*O L C Toller, MA
P Woodruff, MA, MSc

Modern Languages:
†P A Collinson, MA
P J C Davies, MA (*Spanish)
D J M Hempstead, BA, MPhil (*French)
*S N Hollands, BA, MA
Miss C M von Loeper, BA, MSc
Miss E J James, BA (*German)
Miss L Lapaire, BA
G C Larlham, BA
Ms J M Newitt, BA
D E B Perrin, BA
S J Wood, BA (*Italian)

Music:
*P W Gritton, MA, LRAM
R A Hepburn, BA, MA
T Evans, BA, MPhil, PhD

Physical Education:
S Bill
J R Blurton, BSc
A G J Fraser
W T D Hanson, BA
*R G Harrison, BSc
M Jurco, MA
J B H Reed, BA, MSc, DPhil
S Tulley

Religious Studies:
*Revd P L F Allsop, MA

R A Duits, BA, MPhil, PhD

Sciences:
J R Bennett, DPhil (*Biology)
Dr F M Burke, BA, PhD
S J Clarke, MChem
M O Fitzpatrick, BSc, PhD
S Holmes, MPhys, DPhil (*Physics)
Mrs A Jeffery, BSc (*Chemistry)
N A Lamb, BSc, PhD
T Lowes, MChem
G S Miller, BSc, MA, MInstP, CPhys
D E B Perkins, MPhys, PhD
I Poots, BSc, PhD, CChem, MRSC
S J Roberts, MA
C A P Sammut, BSc, MSc
M J P Smith, MChem
M Thain, BA, MSc
T N Thomas, BSc, PhD
T E Weller, MSci, PhD
J T Wong, BSc
K P Zetie, MA, DPhil, MSc, MInstP, CPhys (*Science)

Engineering & Technology:
O V Avni, BSc, ARCS (*Electronics)
R A Barker, BA, MA (*Computing)
Miss K N R Douglass, BA
*A Gardam, MSc, PhD, CEng, FIMechE
C T Malik, BA, MEng
O J Rokison, MEng
D R Smith, MA (*Director of ICT)

Chaplain: Revd P L F Allsop
Finance Director: I E S May, FCMA, BSc, FPC
Operations Director: D J Imrie, MA
Medical Officer: Dr O G Evans, BSc, MBBS, MRCP
Counsellor: Dr R Bor, CPsychol, AFBPsS, UKCP
Librarian and Archivist: Mrs A M Aslett, BA, ALA

Colet Court
The Preparatory School adjoins St Paul's School.
(*For further details see Colet Court entry in IAPS section.*)

Colet Court Academic Staff:

Headmaster: T A Meunier, MA, CChem, FRSC

Deputy Headmaster: C G Howes, MA
Senior Tutor: J Barlow, BSc
Director of Studies: Miss A J Gordon, BA
Director of Administration: A P C Fuggle, MA
Head of Juniors: A K Lee, DPhil, BA, CGeog, FRGS

Miss S Amaslidis, BA, MA
Mrs A L Baker, BA
Mrs J R Baldock, CertEd
P J Berg, ARCM, FRCO
Miss E Cleasby, BA, MA
Miss J J M Clough, BA
Miss A L Cuthbertson, BA, MSc
D M Edwards, BEd
T W Foster, BA DipActing
I P Gamble, BSc
Miss C H Gill, BA
N W Groom, BFA, DipT
T M Hall, BSc
T J Harbord, CertEd
Mrs S E J Harrison, BSc, MPhil
Mrs E L Howe, BA
N E L Howe, BEd
R L Humphrey, BA
Mrs A James, BEd

M D Jelf, BA
I St J Maynard, BEd
Miss C McCabe, BSc
M McRill, BTech, PhD, CBiol, MIBiol, NPQH
Mrs I E Mitchell, BSc, MA
Mme V C M Nolk, L-ès-L (*Archivist*)
Mrs J S Olney, BEd
C A Porter, BA, MA
J A J Renshaw, MA
P H Reutenauer, L-ès-L
A E R Roberts, BSc
Miss S L Sammons, BSc
G C Tsaknakis, BSc
Mrs C A B Waterworth, BA
M J Weeks, BSc
M J C Young, BA
T S Young, BA

Admission. Application for Admission to St Paul's is to be made via an Application form to be obtained via the

School's website. Candidates at 13+ take the Common Entrance Examination in June prior to entry in September. For 16+ applications should be made one year in advance. Further details can be found on the School's website.

There is a registration fee of £175.

A Deposit of one third of the termly day fee is required when a parent accepts the offer of a place for his son after interview. The Deposit will be returnable if the boy fails to reach the necessary standard in the entrance examination or when the final account has been cleared after the boy leaves St Paul's.

Fees per term (2011-2012). The Basic Fee for St Paul's is £6,275. This covers Tuition, Games, Loan Books, Stationery, Libraries, Medical Inspection, a careers aptitude test in the GCSE year, certain School publications and Lunch, which all boys are required to attend. Charges are made for the purchase of some books (which become the personal property of boys) and Public Examination Fees.

There are facilities for up to 50 boarders (ages 13 to 18) and boarding is flexible allowing boys to go home at weekends as they wish. The Boarding Fee is £9,297 per term.

Bursaries. A number of bursaries are available whereby the school maintains the spirit of the former Government Assisted Places scheme. The bursaries are means-tested and boys joining Colet Court at 10+ or 11+, or St Paul's at 13+ or 16+ are eligible.

Foundation Scholarships. (*See Scholarship Entries section.*)

Other Scholarships. Music: A number of Foundation Music Scholarships are available at St Paul's each year. Candidates are expected to have attained at least grade VI on their principal instrument. A Dennis Brain Memorial Scholarship is available from time to time and a Sharp scholarship for entry to St Paul's at 16+. South Square Choral Awards are offered each year in conjunction with Colet Court for treble voices of age 8, 9 or 10.

South Square Art Scholarships: One or more scholarships are available each year to boys who have taken GCSE to assist them in following a career in practical art. These scholarships can be awarded for the candidate's A Level course at St Paul's.

Arkwright Scholarships: The School is a member of the Arkwright Scholarship Scheme which offers financial assistance to sixth-formers who intend to pursue a career in Engineering, Technology, or other Design-related subjects.

Leaving Scholarships or Awards. A number of Prize Grants and Exhibitions (including the Lord Campden's exhibitions, founded in 1625 by Baptist Hicks, Viscount Campden) are given by the Governors every year to boys proceeding to Oxford or Cambridge or to any other place of further education.

Curriculum. All boys follow a broadly based course up to GCSE. Thereafter in the Eighth Form, AS and A Level subjects are so arranged that boys can combine a wide range of Arts and Science subjects if they so wish. Boys take four or five AS Level subjects, including the possibility of an Extended Project, followed by three or four A Level subjects.

Games. Games offered include: Athletics, Cricket, Fencing, Fives, Golf, Judo, Rackets, Rowing, Rugby, Sailing, Soccer, Squash, Swimming and Tennis (hard and grass).

The School has its own Swimming Pool, Fencing Salle, Tennis, Squash, Fives and Rackets Courts, and its own Boat House. The Games Centre also comprises a Sports Hall and Gymnasium. The Sports Hall is equipped for Tennis, Badminton, Basketball and indoor Cricket nets. There are Cricket and Rackets Professionals.

Music. Tuition is available in piano, organ, harpsichord, all the standard orchestral instruments, jazz, bagpipes and the Alexander Technique. There are three choirs, two orchestras, several jazz bands and a wealth of small ensembles. There is a purpose-built Music School and Recital Hall.

School Societies. There is a wide choice of more than 30 Societies, including Musical, Artistic and Dramatic activities, Debating, Historical and Scientific Societies, Politics and Economics, Bridge, Chess, Natural History, Photography, European Society, a Christian Union and Social Service.

Colet Court, the Preparatory School to St Paul's adjoins the School. (*For details see entry in IAPS section.*)

Charitable status. St Paul's School is a Registered Charity, number 1119619. The object of the charity is to promote the education of boys in Greater London.

St Peter's School York

Clifton, York YO30 6AB
Tel: 01904 527300
Fax: 01904 527302
e-mail: enquiries@st-peters.york.sch.uk
website: www.st-peters.york.sch.uk

Founded in 627AD, St Peter's is one of Europe's oldest schools. It provides both outstanding boarding and day education for boys and girls from 13 to 18. St Peter's School has an unrivalled record of academic achievement in the North of England. Its adjacent Prep School, St Olave's, admits boarding and day boys and girls from 8 to 13 and Clifton Pre-prep School admits day girls and boys from 3 to 8.

Motto: '*Super antiquas vias*'

Governors:
Visitor: The Right Honorable the Lord Archbishop of York

Chairman: Mr P N Shepherd

Vice Chairs:
Mrs M Loffill
Mr J C Moris

Members of the Board:

Mr G J Binns	Professor P V Lamarque
Mr J Burdass	Ms S Palmer
Mr J Coles	Mr L Richardson
Mr D Dickson	Mrs V M Rose
Mrs D M Hayward	Mr D Salter
Mr M Hepworth	Mr G J Thompson
Mrs D N Jagger	Miss C E Wesley

Head: **L Winkley**, MA Oxon, MEd OU

Deputy Head: Mrs M C Wike, BSc, PGCE

Director of Teaching & Learning: M C Lawrence, MA

Director of Studies: D J Watkinson, BSc

Heads of Departments:
Art: J Darmody, BA
Biology: M C Lawrence, MA
Careers: Mrs P Bollands, BA, PGDip LSE, MBA, CertEd, MCIPD
Chemistry: P D Northfield, BSc, CChem, FRSC
Classics: M Adams, MA
Drama: Dr T Coker, BA
Economics/Business Studies: B White
English: Mrs E K G Mallard, BA
Geography: Miss E C Ullstein, BSc
Government & Politics: B Fuller, BA, PGCE
History: R J Trevett, MA
Information Technology: Miss L McCarten, BSc
Mathematics: D J Spencer, BSc
Modern Languages: M Duffy, BA
Director of Music: P Miles-Kingston, MA, LRAM, QTS
Physical Education & Games: S J Williams, BEd
Physics: D K Morris, BSc

Religious Studies: Revd D Jones
Technology: J Whitehouse, BEd

All other St Peter's academic staff are listed on the school website.

Administrative Staff:
Bursar: Miss P J Lacy, ACA
Head Master's Secretary: Mrs S Emson

The Prep School (St Olave's)
Master: A Falconer, BA, MBA

Deputy Head: D S Newman, MA
Senior Master: C W R Lawrence, BSc
Director of Studies: Ms C McGregor, BEd Hons
Head of Boarding: Mrs S L Bennett, BSc

All other St Olave's academic staff are listed on the school website.

Clifton Pre-prep School
Headteacher: P C Hardy, BA, PGCE

Assistant Heads:
Mrs G D Spaven, CertEd
C Tidswell, BEd

Nursery:
Mrs F Bonas, BA, NNEB

All other Clifton Pre-prep academic staff are listed on the school website.

St Peter's is a co-educational boarding and day school with 540 boys and girls. There are 300 girls and boys in the Junior Prep School, St Olave's, and a further 150 boys and girls in Clifton Pre-prep School. There are 170 boarders housed in five boarding houses and all St Peter's day pupils belong to a day house, all of which are on the campus. St Olave's offers full, weekly and flexi boarding.

Buildings & Facilities. The School occupies an impressive 47-acre site close to the centre of York with playing fields stretching down to the River Ouse as well as 3 large sports centres. There is a new multi-surface pitch and a 25m 6-lane swimming pool opened by Tom Daley.

Recent developments have provided the most up-to-date conditions for the teaching of science and design & technology with CAD/CAM software. There are also three performance spaces, a music school, an outstanding art school with its own exhibition gallery and a superb library.

Entrance. Pupils are admitted through the School's entrance examinations held at the end of January for both 13+ and 16+. St Olave's entrance examinations are held in January (8+) and February (10+ and 11+) and pupils can enter in any of the years. Clifton Pre-prep school entrance is by assessment in March.

Means-tested Bursaries from age 11 for those who will qualify for more than 50% of the fees are also available.

Scholarships. (*See Scholarship Entries section.*) Honorary academic scholarships and music awards for instrumental tuition are available.

Curriculum. A very broad middle school curriculum including Music, PE, Art, Design & Technology, Community Action and courses in personal and social education.

Nearly all pupils proceed into the Sixth Form, and A Level courses in all subjects studied for GCSE and in Economics, Politics, Business Studies, Further Mathematics and PE are available. Global Perspectives is an extension course for Upper Sixth and a similar programme, called Horizons, is in place for younger pupils.

Academic and pastoral care. A comprehensive house and tutorial system with interim assessments and reports during the term ensure the close scrutiny by all the teaching staff of pupils' academic and general development.

Religious education and worship. Religious Studies are part of the curriculum, and Chapel is seen as an opportunity for pupils to be made aware of the School's Christian heritage.

Careers and university entrance. The School is an 'all-in' member of the Independent Schools Careers Organisation. Careers staff are available for consultation, maintaining an extensive library relating to careers and higher education and organising a full programme of events for the Sixth Form.

Games and Physical Education. Physical education is a significant part of the curriculum. There is an extensive games programme and excellent sports facilities. Rugby football, netball, hockey, cricket and rowing are major sports, and many other options including swimming, athletics, cross-country, basketball, climbing, squash, badminton, tennis, fencing, golf, mountain biking, trampoline, fitness and weight-training.

Combined Cadet Force. A flourishing and voluntary CCF contingent of over 120, with army and air sections, allows the pursuit of many activities including a full programme of camps, expeditions and courses.

The Duke of Edinburgh's Award is also on offer with expedition training for all levels as part of the activities programme and 150 pupils are currently participating.

Music. Musical ability is encouraged throughout the School. There is an orchestra, bands, choirs, choral society and over 10 smaller groups, with concerts a regular feature of the school year as well as tours abroad. Tuition in all instruments is provided, and GCSE and A Level music courses.

Art. Drawing, painting, print-making, ceramics and sculpture may all be taken up both in and out of school hours in an outstanding department.

Drama. The School has three performance spaces: the main school hall, the newly refurbished Shepherd Hall and the smaller, more flexible Drama Centre. There are various productions through the year giving opportunities both for acting and back-stage skills.

Clubs and societies. Many societies flourish including chess, debating, discussion groups, etc. The Community Action programme has over 100 regular participants. Use outside school hours of such facilities as workshops, library, computer department and art studio is encouraged.

Travel and expeditions. Recent holiday opportunities, which are regularly available, have included skiing trips, Classics trips to Greece, trekking in Morocco, hill-walking in Scotland and sports tours abroad.

The Friends of St Peter's. Parents are encouraged to join the Friends, a society whose aim is to promote a close relationship between parents and staff.

The Old Peterites. Honorary Secretary of the Old Peterites' Club: W Hudson, contact via the school's website.

Fees per term (2011-2012). Full Boarding £7,791, Day £4,839. These fees cover all costs (including books and stationery) except individual music lessons and external examination fees.

Further information. Prospectuses for St Olave's, Clifton Pre-prep and St Peter's, containing full details of the three schools' entry requirements, are available on request: tel: 01904 527300, e-mail: enquiries@st-peters.york.sch.uk, or via the website: www.st-peters.york.sch.uk.

(*See also entries for St Olave's School and Clifton Preparatory School in IAPS section.*)

Charitable status. St Peter's School York is a Registered Charity, number 529740. Its aims are to promote education.

Seaford College

Lavington Park, Petworth, West Sussex GU28 0NB
Tel: 01798 867392
Fax: 01798 867606
e-mail: jmackay@seaford.org

website: www.seaford.org

The College was founded in 1884 at Seaford in East Sussex and moved to Lavington Park at the foot of the South Downs in 1946. The grounds cover some 400 acres and include extensive sports facilities and scope for future developments. The campus includes a newly-opened Prep School for pupils aged 7–13 (*see IAPS entry*), a superb Art and Design department, a Sixth Form Centre, purpose-built boarding houses, a state-of-the-art Maths and Science block, and a Music School, with its own performance arena, rehearsal rooms and recording suite.

Seaford College is controlled by an independent non-profit making Charitable Trust approved by the Department for Education and the Charity Commissioners and is administered by the College Board of Governors.

Motto: *Ad Alta – To The Heights*

Governing Body:
G Sinclair (*Chairman*)
S Kyd
J H Crosland
Mrs P Hadley
N Lacey
A G Mason, MBE
R Venables Kyrke
Dr S Gilroy
Mrs S Sayer, OBE
Mrs E Lawrence

Headmaster: T J Mullins, MBA, BA

Deputy Head: J P Green, BA Hons, PGCE
Academic Deputy Head: Mrs B Jinks, BA Jt Hons, MA, NPQH

Teaching Staff:
* *Head of Department*

Art & Design:
*A G Grantham-Smith, BA, PG Dip ArtEd
Mrs K Grantham-Smith, BA (*Photography*)
B Murphy, BA (*Ceramics*)
A Kirkton, BA Hons

Business Studies:
T Clark, BEd
M Pitteway, BComm Hons

Design Technology:
*D Shaw, BEd
W Etherington, BSc
Miss A Prince-Iles, BA Hons, PGCE

Drama:
*Dr J Askew, BA Hons

EFL:
Ms Y Clarke, CELTA, BA Hons

English:
*Mrs J Kean, MA, JT Hons
P R Jennings, MA Oxon
Miss J Brown, BA Hons, PGCE
Mrs S Roberts, BA Hons, PGCE
Mrs P White, BA, PG DipSpLD
Mrs J Gargon, BA Hons
D Pilgrim, PGCE, BA (*Media Studies*)

Geography:
*N Q Angier, BSc, MA
J Hart, BA, PGCE

History:
*T D Phillips, BA
P Griffin, BA, PGCE
R Stather, BA (*Head of Prep School*)

Information Technology:
*D Crook, BA
P Bain, BA

LAMDA:
*Mrs S Arnold, LLAM
T Darrington, LLAM
Miss J Walton, LLAM

Learning Support:
*N Foster, BA, Hornsby Dip
Mrs M Gilbert
Ms A Jensen, DipSpLD
Miss J Lorimer-Green, DipSpLD
Mrs E Barden, BA, PGCE
Mrs P A Angier, BA, Dip CG, DipSpLD
Mrs S Dallyn, BEd
Mrs L Ferris
Mrs I Hopkins, CertEd

Mathematics:
*S Kettlewell, BA
Mrs B Jinks, MA, BA, NPQH
Mrs K Miliam, BSc, PGCE
M Hawes, PGCE
C Arlott, BSc Hons, MBA, PGCE
Miss S Coxon, BEd, MA

Modern Languages:
*N Kyte (*Spanish*)
Mrs S Weekes, BA Hons, PGCE
Ms H Martin, PGCE (*French*)
Miss H Arundel, PGCE
C Thorpe, PGCE, BEd, MA

Music:
*S Buckman, BA Hons, PGCE (*Director of Music & Performing Arts*)
Mrs J Hawkins, PGCE, BMus (*Asst Dir of Music*)
Mrs S Reynolds, BA Hons (*Choirmaster*)

Physical Education:
*J Thompson, BA Hons, PGCE
Miss E Teague, BA Hons QTS
T W Gregory, BEd
W Cuthbertson (*Coach*)
Mrs D Strange (*Coach, Head of Year 9*)
A Cook, BA, PGCE
C Sayell (*Adventure Training Coordinator*)
N McFarlane (*Golf Professional*)
J Smedley, PGCE
D Barnes, BA, PGCE
Miss G Sims, BA Ed, PGCE

Religious Studies:
*R Bailey, BA, MPhil

Science:
*J Rollinson, BSc, PGCE, RSA CTEFLA
D Coulson, BEng Hons, MEng, CEng, PGCE (**Chemistry, Head of Sixth Form*)
Mrs G Pasteiner, BSc (**Biology, Head of Year 10*)
C Kulin, BSc Hons, PGCE
Miss C Haestier, BSc, PGCE
Miss S Clapton, BSc, QTS

KS2 Teachers:
Mrs A Hobbs, BA
Mrs S Lewis, BEd Hons
Mrs H Stevens, BA Hons
Mrs F Jones, CertEd

Careers/Exams:
D C Garrard, BA

CCF:
WO2 S Gerrard

Chaplain: Revd S Gray

Finance Manager: A Golding
Facilities Manager: G Burt
Headmaster's Secretary: Mrs C Mullins
Admissions Secretary: Mrs J Mackay-Smith

Pupils. Seaford College offers options of Full Boarding, Weekly, 4-Day and Day facilities to girls and boys aged 7 to 18. There are 600 pupils at the College with over 100 in the Sixth Form. There are two boys houses and two girls houses and a junior house for both girls and boys aged 10–13.

Aims. Seaford College's aim is to provide an all-round education that equips students with the skills needed to function in the commercial world after leaving their academic studies. The College takes students with a range of abilities and aims to provide the greatest possible 'value-added' for their given abilities. Streaming children in core subjects allows them to work at their own speed and makes them aware of others skills and shortcomings.

Academic. The new Preparatory School (incorporating Years 3–8) offers a wide ranging curriculum which includes core subjects of English, Mathematics, Science, a language, Information Technology and extra English, as well as all the usual topics of Geography, History, Art and DT etc.

Years 10 and 11 lead up to the GCSE examinations. Students study the core subjects of English Literature, English Language, Mathematics and Double Science and then choose four other syllabuses to follow from a comprehensive list of subjects which include: Art, Business Studies, Ceramics, Drama, Design and Technology, Geography, French, History, Music, Physical Education, Spanish.

All students in these forms also study Information Technology and Religious Studies and take part in the College sports.

The A Level subject list is comprehensive with new subjects, such as Textiles and Graphics. In the Lower Sixth students follow a College set curriculum and choose four subjects to study for the first year at the end of which pupils sit AS examinations. They usually then choose to continue with three subjects through to A Level. Over and above this in their first year students will undertake to achieve the Duke of Edinburgh's Silver Award. In the Upper Sixth year students will concentrate on their three A Level subjects. The school has also been piloting the Cambridge Pre-U.

Music is an important part of Seaford's life and the new Music School offers the latest in recording and performing facilities. The College boasts an internationally renowned College Chapel Choir who have been requested to visit countries such as Ecuador, America and Russia to sing at Ambassadors' Christmas parties or raise money for underprivileged children; they have recorded several CDs. The College also has an orchestra and offers lessons for all instruments. Music can be studied at GCSE and AS Level.

Sports. With superb facilities available in the grounds, and staff that have coached and played at international level, the College has a reputation for sporting excellence. Facilities include: six rugby pitches, eight tennis courts, squash courts, pool, a water based all-weather hockey pitch, a large indoor sports hall that allows tennis and hockey to be played all year round, and a 9-hole golf course and driving range.

Art. The College has an excellent Art department which allows students to exercise their talents to the fullest extent in every aspect of art and design, whether it is ceramics, textiles, fine art or any other medium they wish to use. Many pupils from Seaford go on to study at design school and work for design and fashion houses or advertising companies. Students are encouraged to display their work throughout the year in the department's gallery.

Combined Cadet Force. The College has strong ties with the Military and has a very well supported Combined Cadet Force, with each wing of the armed forces well represented. Weekend exercises and training are a regular feature in the College calendar and include adventure training, canoeing, climbing, sailing and camping.

Admission. Entry at age 7 consists of a trial day only. Entry at age 10, 11 and 13 is determined on cognitive ability testing and a trial day at the school. 13+ pupils will still be expected to take the Common Entrance Examination. Sixth Form entry is dependent upon GCSE results and interview. Pupils are required to have at least 45 points at GCSE (=9 C grades) and these should include English and Mathematics. Pupils may enter the school without one of these subjects on condition they retake. Overseas students are required to take an oral and written examination to determine level of comprehension in English.

Scholarships and Bursaries. (*See Scholarship Entries section.*) Scholarships offered: Academic, Art, Design and Technology, Music (Choral and Orchestral) and Sport (13+ only). At 11+: Music/Choral only. Scholarship examinations are taken in February of the year of entry and are worth £500. Where a potential recipient of a scholarship is also in need of discounted fees, they must make an application through the bursary system and 'means testing'. Bursaries are offered to children of serving members of Her Majesty's Forces and siblings of existing pupils.

Fees per term (2011-2012). Years 9–13: £8,300 (Full/Weekly Boarding), £7,050 (4-day Boarding), £5,355 (Day). Years 7 & 8: £5,480 (4-day Boarding), £4,325 (Day). Years 3–6: £5,275 (Year 6 4-day Boarding), £2,455–£4,125 (Day).

Extras. Drama, Clay Pigeon Shooting, Fencing, Duke of Edinburgh's Award, Golf, Kayaking, Museum & Theatre trips, Creative Writing, Model Railway, Debating Club, Rock Climbing, etc.

Charitable status. Seaford College is a Registered Charity, number 277439. It exists to provide education for children.

Sedbergh School

Sedbergh, Cumbria LA10 5HG
Tel: 015396 20535 (Headmaster)
          015396 20303 (Bursar)
Fax: 015396 21301
e-mail: enquiries@sedberghschool.org
website: www.sedberghschool.org

Sedbergh School was founded in 1525 by Dr Roger Lupton, Provost of Eton, and endowed by him with lands connected with a chantry. Sedbergh School offers a blend of academic learning and all-round development of the individual through a strong and caring House system and a wide range of exciting and challenging extra-curricular activities. It is known for its excellence in sport, art and music, magnificent location and happy atmosphere. The £4.5 million Robertson Trust provides for Academic, Music and All-Rounder Scholarships and there are further awards in other disciplines, such as Sport.

Motto: '*Dura Virum Nutrix*'

The Governing Body:
H M Blair (*Chairman*)
The Most Revd and Rt Hon The Lord Archbishop of York, represented by The Venerable N J W Barker, Archdeacon of Auckland
Her Majesty's Lord Lieutenant of Cumbria, Sir James Cropper, BA, FCA
The Master of St John's College, Cambridge, represented by Dr P T Wood, ScD
Mrs S E Bagot
Miss K Bruce Lockhart
M J Cuthbertson
F J Hilton
I K MacAskill, BEd
The Hon Sir Richard McCombe, QC, MA
S A M Rayner

W M Richardson
J S Rink, LLB
R G T Stenhouse
D M Strachan, MA

Clerk to the Governors and Bursar: P S Marshall, BSc, ACIB, AISMM

Foundation Director: R W Witt, BSc, CertEd, MIF

Headmaster: A A P Fleck, BSc, MA

Second Master: P M Wallace-Woodroffe, BA

Senior Mistress: Mrs S J Wallace-Woodroffe, BSc

Senior Master (Pastoral): G T Ayling, MA

Senior Master (Co-curricular): D J Harrison, MA

Senior Tutor: M P Ripley, MA

Director of Studies: J M Sykes, BSc, MSc

School Chaplain: The Revd P L Sweeting, BSc, BA

Assistant Staff:

Miss A P Astin, BA
*S R Arnold, BA
Mrs H L Ayling, BA, MA (*Admissions*)
N H Brown, BSc
†Mrs H J Christy, BEd
P K S Collins, BA
*S J Cooling, BSc
J Cooper-Colliander, MA
J Cruz Gonzalez Mendia, BA
H R Davies, BSc
Mrs S A Doherty, GRNCM
S J Elmore, DipCeramicDes, SDC, SIAD
Miss K Farrand, BA
*J E Fisher, BSc
†*The Revd C D Griffin, BA
Mrs S A Griffin, BA, AdvDipEd SEN
†*C D Gunning, BEd
Mrs C S Hall, BSc
†*S E Hall, BA, MA
*R C J Hartley, MA
†C Hattam, BA
Miss D Hirst, BSc
P R Hoskin, BSc, DPhil
Mrs R C Hubbard, BSc
Miss K L Iliff, MA, MSc (*Archivist*)
R J Kellett, BA

A R Lewis, BPhil, NABBC, LTCL (*Bandmaster*)
J Lidiard, MA
Mrs N Lidiard, MA, LLb
M L McVoy (*Careers*)
†C P Mahon, BSc
S R D Milner, BEng, MSc
*Mrs C M Morgan, BSc
C R I Morgan, BA
J R D Morgan, BA
D Newell, MA (*Head of Drama*)
S W Oliver, BA (*Head of Boys' Games*)
†Mrs G E Parry, BA
Mrs P J F Prall, BA
Mrs J M Priestley, MA
*M A F Raw, MA
J D W Richardson, BA
Miss F E Robinson, BA
T G Sands, BA
*J H Seymour, BA, LTCL (*Director of Music*)
Miss LM Sdao, BEd (*Head of Girls' Games*)
*S M Smith, MA
C W Swanson, BA, MFA
Mrs D K Thomas, MA
J Tiffany, BA (*Director of Rugby*)
*M J O Valentine, BA
†*C P Webster, BSc

Houses & Housemasters/mistresses:
Evans: C D Gunning
Hart: The Revd C D Griffin
Lupton: Mrs G E Parry
Powell: C P Webster
Robertson: Mrs H J Christy
School: C Hattam
Sedgwick: S E Hall
Winder: C P Mahon

Medical Officer: Dr P D Batty, MBChB, FP Cert, DRCOG, MRCGP, Dip SEM Bath, FFSEM UK

Headmaster's PA: Miss A J Bird, BA

There are 430 pupils in the Senior School, of whom 97% are boarders, distributed among eight boarding Houses where pupils live, eat all meals and have their studies/bedsitting rooms.

Pupils are looked after in their Houses by a Housemaster or Housemistress, the House Matron and a House Tutor, who keep in close touch with pupils' parents. If the pupils are ill, they are treated in the School Medical Centre, which is managed by fully qualified staff. The School has its own GP.

The Junior School (120 pupils) is sited in the grounds of the Senior School and offers day, flexi, weekly and full boarding for pupils aged 4–13. (*See Sedbergh Junior School entry in IAPS section.*)

Both schools are fully co-educational.

The academic curriculum is designed to give pupils a thorough grounding in essential subjects and to delay as long as possible the need to specialise. Greek and Latin remain popular.In the Sixth Form, a flexible system makes possible a large number of combinations of A and AS Level subjects. A new career development programme starts in Year 8 (Sedbergh Junior School) and encompasses emerging economies and industries supported by a comprehensive programme of visiting speakers from a very wide range of industries. A programme of work experience and GAP year opportunities (exclusive to the School) extends the career development programme beyond school and university. Sports medicine is a speciality and pupils who aspire to this career have opportunities to work with consultants in this field.

There are also various academic societies (eg Art, History, Music and Science), and a programme of Civic Lectures throughout the year. The School has excellent computing facilities.

The School welcomes pupils of all denominations. It is usual for pupils to attend a Service in Chapel on Sundays and Confirmation services are held each year for both the Church of England and Church of Scotland.

Sedbergh tries to develop as many as possible of the pupils' individual skills and talents and to introduce them to a wide range of interests and activities.

Art and Design Centre. The Art School includes Studios for Painting, Pottery and Sculpture, Photographic Darkrooms and an Exhibition Gallery. The Design Centre provides multimedia workshops and Design Studios with CAD/CAM, and digital editing facilities. All pupils work in the studios and workshops as part of the curriculum, and have opportunities to do so in their spare time. Also in the Centre is a Lecture Theatre with facilities for video, films and drama.

Music. Music is encouraged at all levels and the School has strong Cathedral associations. There is a Chapel Choir and a Choral Society which performs two major works each year. Instrumentalists may join the Orchestra, String Orchestra, Junior or Senior Bands and Jazz Orchestra, and there is a considerable amount of music-making in small ensembles. There are two Music Schools, one dedicated to Brass. Music lessons, given by full-time music staff and visiting teachers, are offered for more than 40 orchestral and keyboard instruments. The School has two fine organs.

Many pupils study Music at GCSE, AS and A Level. Sedbergh is also probably the only school regularly producing degree-level graduates in orchestral and brass band instruments: in recent years, 12 Sedbergh pupils have achieved ATCL and LTCL (degree-level) diplomas while still at the School, with many others achieving Grade VIII diplomas with distinction.

An annual Concert Series brings distinguished artists to the School and there are regular School concerts throughout the year. Music Scholarships are available.

Drama. As well as visits to theatres there are usually two major School plays a year and one Junior production; there are also House plays and year-group productions. Houses also organise entertainment for their own parents and pupils, usually plays, songs and revue sketches. Past pupils have been accepted at RADA.

The Setting. The School capitalises on its beautiful situation in the Yorkshire Dales National Park and has a very active Natural History Society, which manages three conservation sites in the area. The School also runs numerous expeditions on the fells and in the Lake District. The programme includes Geography and Biology Field Courses, Adventure Training, Duke of Edinburgh's Award and CCF camps, Climbing, Caving, Canoeing, Horse Riding and Sailing trips. It also includes major expeditions abroad: musical, geographical, historical, philanthropic, sporting and pure adventure. Pupils are encouraged to enter for the Duke of Edinburgh's Award Scheme and various Volunteer schemes.

CCF. The School CCF has Army, Navy and Air Force Sections, and as well as undertaking Basic Training it gives boys and girls an experience of camping and preliminary instruction in Shooting in its indoor range. Rifle Shooting is encouraged and a high standard is achieved both on the indoor and open ranges. The School is a regular winner of major trophies at Bisley. There is a flourishing CCF Band with pipers and Corps of Drums which regularly tours the country and overseas.

Games. There is an extensive programme of games, almost all of which are open for boys and girls. The School has produced international level pupils in Shooting, Sailing, Rugby, Lacrosse, Hockey and Cricket. The main games are Athletics, Cricket, Cross-Country Running, Fives, Hockey, Lacrosse, Netball, Rugby Football, Sailing, Shooting, Soccer, Squash, Swimming and Tennis. There is a fitness suite, sports hall, indoor swimming pool and astroturf pitch. There are opportunities for Game Keeping, Stalking, Rough/Clay shooting and Fishing, and School societies make provision for many other activities including Debating, Natural History, Archaeology, Geology, Photography and Art.

Fees per term (2011-2012). Senior School: Boarding £9,060, Day £6,675. Junior School: Boarding £5,565–£6,300, Weekly Boarding £5,150–£5,980, Day £2,175–£4,190. In addition there are voluntary fees (eg for Instrumental Music, CCF, EFL).

Scholarships and Bursaries. (*See Scholarship Entries section.*) Scholarships and Exhibitions are awarded annually to those demonstrating Academic excellence, or talent in Music, Art, Drama, Design Technology and Sport, as well as all-round ability. All such awards can be supplemented by a further Bursary award, based upon the financial circumstances of the candidate's parents. All Scholarship examinations are held annually at the School in the Lent Term. Full details available from The Headmaster's Secretary.

Admission. A registration fee of £75 is payable at the time of registration.

Senior School: Application for admission at any age should be made to the Headmaster. At the age of 13 it is usual that a pupil would sit Common Entrance or Scholarship. Pupils are also accepted into the Sixth Form on the basis of GCSE results.

Junior School: Entry to the Junior School is either by Entrance examination, interview or assessment – according to age. Junior Bursaries are available to those parents who would encounter considerable hardship in the payment of fees.

The Old Sedberghian Club (c/o Malim Lodge, Sedbergh School, Sedbergh) flourishes and has branches all over the world.

Charitable status. Sedbergh School is a Registered Charity, number 1080672. It exists to provide boarding education and pastoral welfare to pupils from the ages of 4 to 18.

Sevenoaks School

Sevenoaks, Kent TN13 1HU
Tel: 01732 455133
Fax: 01732 456143
e-mail: regist@sevenoaksschool.org (Admissions)
        hm@sevenoaksschool.org (Head)
website: www.sevenoaksschool.org

Founded in 1432, Sevenoaks School is a co-educational, day and boarding school for pupils aged 11–18.
    Motto: '*Servire Deo Regnari Est*'

Governing Body:
Chairman: A C V Evans, MA, MPhil, FIL
Vice-Chairman: Ms C Pimlott, BA

Governors:
The Rt Revd Dr B Castle, PhD
I Doherty, MA
Mrs S Dunnett, BA
Mrs E Ecclestone, LLb, Dip LP
A N Golding, MA
R N H Gould, BA
D Griffiths, MA, FCA
M Hughes, MA
Ms E Johnson, MBE, MA
A R M Little, MA
D M Phillips, BA, ACA
P Shirke, MBA
D R Walker, MA
J Warde, DL, MA
Prof M J Waring, ScD, FRSC
M Whittow, PhD

Bursar and Clerk to the Governors: Air Vice-Marshal A J Burton, OBE, BSc Econ, FCIS, Chartered FCIPD

Academic Staff:

Head: Mrs C L Ricks, MA

Undermaster: M J Bolton, BA
Deputy Head (Pastoral): Miss T M Homewood, MA, BSc
Deputy Head (Academic): C D Greenhalgh, BA, PhD
Deputy Head (Co-curriculum): N P Tetley, MA
Director of Admissions and Communications: Mrs A M Stuart, BSc
Director of Information Systems: Mrs S J Williamson, BA, MSc
Director of International Baccalaureate: J T Sprague, BA, MA
Director of Administration: Miss A A Franks, MA
Chaplain: The Revd N N Henshaw, BA
Sixth Form Registrar: A D Waldron, BA

Assistant Teachers:
* *Head of Department*
† *Housemaster/mistress*

Miss N L Atkinson, BSc (*Design Technology*)
†Mrs E M Bassett, BA (*Chemistry*)
P R Bassett, MA (*Mathematics*)
M P Beverley, BA, MA (*English*)
Miss E Boulton, BA (*History*)
Miss M T Boyd, BSc, MA (*Mathematics*)
Mrs R L Brown, BA (*Design Technology*)
J N Burger, MA (*Mathematics*)
S Burley, BA, MPhil, PhD (*English*)
I C Campbell, BSc (**Psychology*)
Mrs R Campbell, BA (*English*)
M R Capelo, BSc (**Spanish*)
T J Carden, BA, MA (**Instrumental and Vocal Studies*)
Miss T H Cardon, BA (*Biology*)
S Carr, MA (**Classics*)
C R Cockerill, BSc (*Mathematics*)
†N K Connell, BEd (*French*)
Miss M T Connolly, BSc (*Physics*)
S A J Coquelin, MA (*French*)
T L Corcoran, BA (*Classics*)
J P Cox, BA (*Computing*)

A G Day, MA (*Economics & Business Studies*)
Miss M-L Delvallée, MA (*French*)
G R Dinsdale, BA (**Physical Education*)
J Drury, MA (**Russian*)
A J Dunn, MA, DPhil (**History*)
Miss A M Durnford, BA (*English, Drama*)
C H J Dyer, BA (**Music*)
M T Edwards, BA, MPhil, PhD (*Biology*)
J C Emmitt, BA (*Physical Education*)
Mrs J R Estop, MA (*English*)
P L Eversfield, MA (**Economics & Business Studies*)
Miss N M Fayaud, MA (**French*)
T J K Findley, MSc, PhD (*Chemistry*)
I A Fletcher, BSc (*Chemistry*)
P Ford, BSc (**Computing*)
T B Fugard, PhD (*Mathematics*)
Miss C E Gilliat-Smith, BA (*Design Technology, Physical Education*)
Mrs J L Gladstone, BA, MSc (*Biology*)
S J Gladstone, BA (*Music*)
Mrs C E Glanville, BA, MA (*English*)
J W Grant, BA (*Drama*)
Mrs R A Greenhalgh, BA (*Spanish, French*)
Mrs P O Hargreaves, BA (**Drama*)
P Harrison, MA (*English*)
†Mrs N J Haworth, MA (*Physics*)
N T Haworth, BA (*IB Diploma Coordinator, History*)
G E Henry, BA, MA (*Director of Drama*)
Mrs C J Henshaw, BA (**English*)
Mrs W J Heydorn, MA (*Religious Studies*)
P T Hill, BEd (*Physical Education, Geography*)
Mrs B R Hobbs, BA (*Art*)
S Holden, BEd (*Physical Education*)
G Howden, BSc, MA (*Mathematics*)
J D Hughes, BA (*English*)
P J Hulston, BSc (*Economics & Business Studies*)
Miss L N Jones, BA (*English*)
T R Jones, BA, MA (**Mathematics*)
Mrs E A Joseph, BA (*Physical Education*)
†L C Kiggell, MBA (*Economics & Business Studies*)
P I Kino, BA (*German*)
N Kunaratnam, BA (*French*)
P M La Rondie, BA (*Mathematics*)
G A Lawrie, BSc (**Science, *Design Technology*)
†Mrs K Lewis, BSc
Miss V L Longhurst, MA (*Geography*)
C R Martin, MA, PhD (*Biology, Chemistry*)
P G de May, BA (*Classics*)
Mrs A J Maynard, BA (**Head of Learning Support, French*)
Miss R L McQuillin, MA (*History*)
D W Mott, BA (**Modern Languages*)
Mrs K A Mylod, BSc (*Biology*)
Miss A E Nairn, BHPE (*Physical Education*)
M Ogretme, BSc, MSc (*Physics*)
Mrs D Orme, BSc, MSc, PhD (*Mathematics*)
S M Owen, MA, PhD (**Chemistry*)
G P Parker-Jones, BA, MA (**History*)
A T Patton, BA, MA (*Geography*)
Mrs K L Pitcher, BSc (**Biology*)
S Reid, BA, MA (*History*)
Mrs A E Rochdi, BA (*French, Spanish*)
Mrs H E Roff, BSc, DPhil (*Physics*)
Miss A K Russell, MA (*French*)
Miss J L Sassen, BA, MA (**German*)
Ms L U Seetharaman, BA, MA (*English*)
S J Sharp, BSc, PhD (**Physics*)
A C Smith, BComm (*Economics & Business Studies*)
T D Stuart, BA (**Philosophy, Biology*)
J L Tate, BSc (*Physics*)
C J Tavaré, MA (*Biology, Physical Education*)
Miss H Tebay, MA (*Mathematics*)
C M Thomas, BA (**Art*)

P R Thompson, BA, MA (**Geography*)
R M Thompson, BSc (*Design Technology*)
Miss A E Tully, BSc (*Biology*)
D J Vaccaro, BA (*Mathematics*)
W R Vincent, BSc, MSc (*Biology*)
Miss C S Watson, BA (*Classics*)
D R Whiffin, BSc (*Mathematics*)
Mrs G P Williams, BSc, PhD (*Mathematics*)
†G J Willis, BA (*Geography*)
A G Wilson, MA (*English*)
R C Woodward, BSc, MA, ARCS (*Chemistry*)
†J D Wyld, BA (*French*)
Miss S R Yu, BA, PhD (*Chemistry*)

Part-time Staff:
Mrs K Agarwal (*Hindi*)
O C Barratt, BA (*Art*)
Mrs M Bedford, BA, MA (*Classics*)
A J Cornah, LLB, MSc (**Sailing*)
Ms F L Cramoisan, MA (*French*)
Mrs J Douglas (*Careers*)
Mrs C Draper, BA, MSc (*Mandarin*)
Mrs C Duran-Oreiro (*Spanish*)
Mrs C E Dyer, BA (*French, German*)
Ms S M Gale, BA (*Classics*)
Mrs M Gower (*Japanese*)
Miss L A Gray, BSc (*Geography*)
Mrs J Hendry (*Music*)
Mrs A M Hulston, BA (*English as an Additional Language*)
Mrs K S Jay (*Swedish*)
Mrs E Kelly (*Russian*)
Mrs J L Kiggell, MA, ARCM, AMus, TCL (*Music*)
Mrs Y Knott (*Japanese*)
Mrs H de May, BA (*Classics*)
Mrs A Mack, BA, MA (*History*)
Mrs S J MacLeay (*Geography*)
D Merewether (*Photography*)
A C Mitchell, BA (*Film, Video*)
Miss P A Morecroft (*Physical Education*)
Miss S Rahman, BA (*English*)
B A Richards (*Drama*)
Mrs H Smith (*Learning Support*)
Mrs A Symons, MSc (*Italian*)
Mrs E E Taylor (*Swedish*)
T T Wey (**Keyboard*)
Mrs A Williams-Walker, BSc (*Mathematics*)
C M Yelf (*Design Technology*)

Head of Library: Mrs P Kino, BA
Head's PA: Mrs M Thomas

Sevenoaks School is situated on an attractive 100-acre campus adjoining Knole Park and on the edge of the town. Sevenoaks is in Kent, just 30 minutes from central London, and is conveniently close to Gatwick and Heathrow airports, the Channel Tunnel and continental Europe. The school, while set firmly in its local community, has a strong international dimension – not only in its student body, but also in its ethos, its culture and its curriculum.

Sevenoaks was certified as the top UK co-educational IB school in 2010 in the league tables published on www.best-schools.co.uk and www.baccalaureate.eu.com. The school was named as *The Sunday Times* Independent School of the Year 2007–8 and was described as 'outstanding' in the Ofsted Boarding Inspection 2009.

There are seven boarding houses: a co-educational junior house (11–13), two boys' houses (13–18), two girls' houses (13–18) and two single-sex Sixth Form houses (16–18). All of these welcome students from the UK and from around the world. Accommodation ranges from a charming Queen Anne house to modern, purpose-built facilities. There are lessons and sport for all pupils on Saturdays and a full programme of activities for boarders on Sundays.

A wide range of subjects is offered at GCSE and IGCSE, with setting in core subjects. In the Sixth Form all pupils study the International Baccalaureate – a rigorous two-year diploma designed to provide a broad and balanced education. It is a well respected qualification for UK, US and other leading universities worldwide. Academic results in the school are excellent, with an average IB Diploma score of 39.5 points in 2010 (world average around 30 points) – and 50 pupils were offered places at Oxford and Cambridge in 2010, in both the arts and sciences. An increasing number of students choose to go to Ivy League and other top American universities.

There is also a strong emphasis on the co-curriculum, from sport to music, drama and art. Pupils regularly achieve representative honours at rugby, cricket, netball, hockey, sailing, basketball, shooting and tennis and there is a wide range of concerts, plays and exhibitions for pupils of all ages. A variety of clubs and societies provide opportunities for all pupils to find and develop their interests. The school has a voluntary Combined Cadet Force and is also proud of its strong tradition of community service and involvement in The Duke of Edinburgh's Award scheme.

The facilities are first class: The Space, a performing arts centre with a world-class concert hall, opened in April 2010. The Sennocke Centre, a major new sports centre, was completed in 2005, and a dining hall, Sixth Form centre, language centre and athletics track have been built in recent years.

Admission. The main points of entry to the school are at 11, 13 and 16 years and a small number are admitted at other levels. At 11+, pupils are admitted on the basis of a competitive examination held in January, an interview and Head's report. At 13+, a pre-assessment day in October is followed by those in prep schools taking the ISEB Common Entrance Examination in June or, for others, the school's own Year 9 Entrance Examination in February. Alternatively, pupils can take the Year 9 Scholarship examinations in March. At 16+ students are admitted into the Sixth Form based on their performance in interview and academic entrance tests, and on the strength of their current school reports. There are boarding and day places for boys and girls at all ages. All applications for entry should be addressed to the Director of Admissions (regist@sevenoaksschool.org).

Fees per term (2011-2012). Boarders £9,537; Day Pupils £5,946 (including lunch). Fees for pupils entering directly into the Sixth Form are £10,346 (boarding) and £6,755 (day).

Scholarships and Bursaries. (*See Scholarship Entries section.*) Up to 50 scholarships are awarded annually at 11+, 13+ and 16+. A number of means-tested bursaries are available for pupils who could not otherwise afford the fees.

Charitable status. Sevenoaks School is a Registered Charity, number 1101358. Its aims and objectives are the education of school children.

Sherborne School

Sherborne, Dorset DT9 3AP
Tel: 01935 812249
Fax: 01935 810422
e-mail: registrar@sherborne.org
website: www.sherborne.org

The origins of Sherborne School date back to the eighth century, when a tradition of education at Sherborne was begun by St Aldhelm. The School was linked with the Benedictine Abbey, the earliest known Master was Thomas Copeland in 1437. Edward VI refounded the School in 1550. The present School stands on land which once belonged to the Monastery. The Library, Chapel, and Headmaster's offices which adjoin the Abbey Church, are modifications of the original buildings of the Abbey.

Royal Arms of Edward VI: *Dieu et mon droit*.

Governors of the School:

Chairman: Professor R Hodder-Williams, MA, FRSA
Vice-Chairman: Major General P A J Cordingley, DSO

Ex officio:
The Representative of Her Majesty's Lord Lieutenant for the County of Dorset
The Representative of the Lord Bishop of Salisbury
The Vicar of Sherborne, the Revd Canon E J Woods, MA, FRSA

Co-optative:

M R Beaumont, Esq	M L French, Esq, BSc,
D R Burgess, Esq, ACA	FCA
Ms F H Maddocks	R S Fidgen, Esq, FRICS
R M Morgan, Esq, MA	Dr S Ball, BM, MRCPsych
Mrs H Greenstock, MA	R Robson, Esq
S H J Macdonald, Esq, BA	N Bowles, Esq, MA
	G Marsh, Esq, MA, CertEd

Staff Representative: R A L Leach, MA

Bursar and Clerk to the Governors: Mrs L Robins, BSc, MRCIS

Headmaster: C J Davis, MA

Second Master: W A M Burn, MA
Deputy Head (Pastoral): M A Weston, MA
Deputy Head (Academic): D M Smith, MPhil, PhD

Housemasters:
Abbey House: M J McGinty, AKC, BA, MSc (Tel: 01935 812087)
Abbeylands: S J Clayton, CertEd & Mrs VA Clayton, BA, MCLIP (Tel: 01935 812082)
The Digby: M J Brooke, MA (Tel: 01935 810170)
The Green: A M Hatch, BA (Tel: 01935 810440)
Harper House: J J B Wadham, BSc, PhD (Tel: 01935 812128)
Lyon House: G Brière-Edney, BSc (Tel: 01935 812079)
School House: K Jackson, BA (Tel: 01935 813248)
Wallace House: G T W Robinson, BA (Tel: 01935 813334)

Staff:
R D Ambrose, MA, AFIMA (*Mathematics*)
B D Bates, BSc (*Geography*)
Mrs E J Bonnell, BEd (*Head of Learning Support*)
G Brière-Edney, BSc (*Geography*)
M J Brooke, MA (*Classics*)
D C Bryson, BA (*Modern Languages*)
W A M Burn, MA (*Director of IB and Modern Languages*)
D B Cameron, MA (*Modern Languages*)
R J Carpenter, BSc (*Physics*)
P R Chillingworth, BA (*Head of Design Technology*)
S J Clayton, CertEd (*Physical Education*)
Revd L Collins, BD (*Chaplain*)
S Correia, BA (*Modern Languages*)
J Crouch, BA (*History and Politics*)
R A Cuerdon, MA (*Art*)
Miss S L Cummings, BA (*Chemistry*)
B J Davey, GRSM (*Music*)
T A J Dawson, BSc (*Head of Mathematics*)
Mrs R de Pelet, MA (*Head of English*)
Miss S Drury, GRSM Hons, GRSM, ARCM (*Music*)
W M Duggan, BA, MA (*Head of Classics*)
D J Dunning, BA (*Theology*)
P S Francis, MA (*History*)
Mrs C E Greenrod, BA (*English*)
S P H Haigh, MA (*English*)
C G B Hamon, PhD, CChem, MRSC (*Chemistry*)
R T B Harris, BA, MBA (*Head of Business Studies*)
G R Harwood, BSc (*Biology*)

A M Hatch, BA (*Geography*)
D Hedison, BSc (*Head of Economics*)
J E C Henderson, MA (*Director of Music*)
R W Hill (*Assistant Director of Sport and Personal Development*)
J J Kimber, BSc (*Physics*)
Mrs C Le Sueur, BA, CertTEFL
S D Lilley, MSc (*Physical Education*)
M McGinty, BA (*Economics & Politics*)
Mrs L J McMillan, BSc (*Mathematics*)
P R Miles, BEd (*Physical Education & Director of Sport*)
Miss K L Millar, BA (*Geography*)
A C Morgan, BSc, MSc, FRSA (*Mathematics*)
A D Nurton, BA (*Modern Languages*)
A R Oates, BA, MLitt (*Modern Languages*)
M P O'Connor, BA (*English*)
Mrs V O'Gorman, BA (*Economics*)
J-M Pascal, DEA, PhD (*Modern Languages & Theology*)
T R Patterson, MA (*Theology*)
T W Payne, BA (*English*)
Miss C Pemberton, BSc, PhD (*Biology*)
J R Preston, BSc (*Head of Geography*)
G D Reynolds, MA (*Head of History*)
D J Ridgway, BSc (*Head of Biology*)
Mrs E L Robinson (*Head of Drama*)
G T W Robinson, BA (*English*)
P Rogerson, MA (*Classics, Head of Careers*)
Miss C E Rule, BSc (*Geography*)
B A Ryder, BEng (*Physics*)
J Salisbury, BEd (*Technology*)
Mrs S Salmon, MA (*Business Studies*)
N C Scorer, MChem (*Chemistry*)
T J Scott, BA (*Modern Languages*)
Mrs J M Slade, BA (*Modern Languages*)
I C Smith, BA, MSci (*Head of Chemistry*)
Miss C M Standen, MA (*Mathematics*)
A J Stooke, BA (*Head of Art*)
J R Storey, BA (*Classics*)
B P Sunderland, BEng (*Mathematics*)
J A Thompson, BA (*Mathematics*)
Mrs J R Thurman, BA (*Head of Modern Languages*)
M D Thurman, BSc (*Head of Physics*)
S Tremewan, BA, PhD (*Classics*)
J J B Wadham, BSc, PhD (*Biology*)
R M Warren, BA (*History*)
D A Watson, BSc (*Chemistry*)
P J Watts, BSc (*Physics*)
M A Weston, MA (*Modern Languages*)
B A Wild, BA, PhD (*Geography*)
J G Willetts, BA, CPhys, MInstP (*Head of ICT, Physics*)
J L Winter, MA (*English*)
Miss P Wood, BSc (*Biology*)

Medical Officers:
C P Cleaver, MB, ChB, MRCGP
K Dixon, MB BS, MRCGP, DFFP
I A Latham, MB BS, MRCP, DFFP

Sister: Mrs C Ellwood, RGN
Headmaster's Secretary: Mrs L Moubray (Tel: 01935 812249)
Sports and Uniform Shop: Mrs S Eldor (Tel: 01935 810506)
Registrar: M J Cleaver, BA (Tel: 01935 810402; Fax: 01935 810422; e-mail: registrar@sherborne.org)

Situation. The School lies in the attractive Abbey town of Sherborne. By train, Salisbury is forty minutes away, London and Heathrow two hours.

Organisation. There are about 525 boarders and 45 day boys accommodated in eight houses, all of which are within easy walking distance of the main school.

Admission. Entry is either at 13+ through the Common Entrance, Scholarship examinations, or special entrance papers or at 16+ after GCSE.

Parents, who would like to enter their sons for the School, or have any queries, should contact the Registrar.

Boys can be entered either for a particular House or placed on the general list.

Visits. Visits can be arranged at any time of the year by ringing the Headmaster's Secretary on 01935 812249.

Scholarships/Exhibitions. (*See Scholarship Entries section*.) Sherborne offers a wide range of scholarships and exhibitions, Academic (March), Music (February), and Sport, Art, Design & Technology (March). Candidates should be under 14 on 1 September in the year of entry. Further details of all these awards are available from the Registrar.

Sixth Form Entry. Places are available for boys who wish to join the Sixth Form to study A Levels or the IB for two years. Both the entrance and scholarship examinations take place in November. There are up to two full fees worth of scholarships offered annually. Also available, for good A Level candidates, is the Arkwright Scholarship for Technology.

Curriculum. All pupils follow a broadly based curriculum for their first three years to GCSE. In the Sixth Form boys study at least three A Levels and one AS Level drawn from 27 A Level and 30 AS courses, as well as some non-specialist courses designed to broaden the scope of their studies. From 2007 the International Baccalaureate will be available as an alternative. Some of the courses for IB and A Level are run jointly with Sherborne School for Girls.

Careers and Universities. The Careers Department has an enviable reputation. Boys experience work shadowing programmes in the fifth and lower sixth forms – these are followed by careers conventions, university visits, parents' forums and lessons in interview techniques. There is an encyclopaedic, fully computerised Careers' Room with regularly updated contacts with those at university and at work. The department has visited all universities and places of higher education. Virtually all leavers go on to university.

Pastoral Care. The boys in each house are in the care of a Housemaster and his wife, resident tutors, and a resident matron. The School Chaplain also plays a major rôle and will talk with a boy whenever required. A School Counsellor is available.

Tutor. Each boy has a personal Tutor who not only monitors his academic progress but provides a useful contact point. Specialist Sixth Form tutors are available.

Religion. Theology courses are designed for each academic year. There is a wide variety of weekday and weekend services, which are held in the School Chapel or in Sherborne Abbey. Holy Communion is celebrated every Sunday and on some weekdays, including a Friday night candlelit Eucharist service. Boys are prepared for confirmation by the School Chaplain.

Community Service. Boys take part in a busy programme aimed at encouraging a sense of responsibility towards the local community. Entertainment, fundraising and assistance are organised for the young, elderly and handicapped in and around Sherborne.

Art. The Art School is well known and highly regarded. The core disciplines are based around the study of fine art and architecture. Alongside these, there are extensive printmaking facilities, photographic dark rooms and the opportunity for boys to work in computer-aided design, film and media studies, history of design and museum and heritage studies. The annual study tour to Europe or America allows all boys to appreciate culture in an international context.

Design and Technology. The Design and Technology Department has recently been completed refurbished. The subject is taught to advanced level and pupils go on to higher education courses in Product and Aeronautical Design, Architecture and Engineering. The department has developed links with local industries where pupils can see CAD/CAM production, commercial furniture design and precision casting in process. The department runs afternoon activities on all weekdays and at weekends.

Music. There is a strong music tradition in the School – over 400 music lessons take place every week. There are two full orchestras, various chamber music groups, many different types of jazz band, a brass group, a swing band, Chapel choir and a choral society, not to mention rock bands. Many of these groups tour both home and abroad. Numerous concerts, recitals and musical productions are held throughout the year. Lunch time concerts take place every Friday. Regular subscription concerts are given by visiting professional musicians.

Drama. Drama productions of all kinds are a major feature of school life, from large scale musicals to classical drama, substantial modern works and fringe performances, many staged with Sherborne Girls. The sophisticated technical resources of the Powell Theatre attract programmes from professional touring companies.

Information Technology. The main network links all academic departments, boarding houses, Library and the Careers Room. The School has a sophisticated Intranet system.

Sports. There are over fifty acres of sports fields, where, at any one time, seventeen various games or matches can take place. Other facilities include two astroturf pitches, twenty tennis courts, rugby fives courts and a shooting range. Within the School's sports centre there is a sports hall, a twenty-five metre swimming pool, a fitness suite and squash courts. A wide variety of sports and activities are offered including athletics, badminton, basketball, canoeing, cricket, cross-country, fencing, rugby fives, golf, hockey, polo, riding, rugby, sailing, shooting, soccer, sub-aqua, swimming and tennis.

Societies and Activities. Numerous academic societies meet regularly throughout the term. Other activities and clubs take place on Wednesday afternoons and whenever time allows. They include: bridge, chess, computing, debating, fishing, instrument making, modelling, model railways, photography, and woodland management.

The Duke of Edinburgh's Award Scheme is well supported. Expeditions are organised to Scotland, the Lake District, Wales, Exmoor and Dartmoor. Boys also take part in the annual 'Ten Tors Challenge'.

Membership of the Combined Cadet Force is voluntary – however the Army, Navy and Royal Marine sections usually attract about 150 boys each year. A large number of trips and camps are arranged during the term time and the holidays.

Old Shirburnian Society. Secretary: Old Shirburnian Office, Sherborne School, Dorset DT9 3AP. Tel: 01935 810557. Fax: 01935 810551. e-mail: OSS@sherborne.org

Girls' Schools. There is close liaison with the neighbouring girls' schools, which allows us to offer many of the real benefits of co-education with all the advantages of a single-sex secondary education. As well as the Joint Sixth Form academic courses with Sherborne Girls, drama, music and social activities are arranged throughout the year.

Fees per term (2011-2012). Boarders: £9,725; Day Boys: £7,875.

Charitable status. Sherborne School is a Registered Charity, number 1081228, and a Company Limited by Guarantee, registered in England and Wales, number 4002575. Its aim and objectives are to supply a liberal education in accordance with the principles of the Church of England.

Shiplake College

Henley-on-Thames, Oxon RG9 4BW
Tel:　0118 940 2455
Fax:　0118 940 5204

e-mail:　info@shiplake.org.uk
website:　www.shiplake.org.uk

Founded by Alexander Everett in 1959, Shiplake College is an Independent School for day boys aged 11–18 and boarding boys from 13–18. Day and boarding girls join the Sixth Form.

Motto: '*Exemplum docet*' (Example teaches)

Governing Body:
Chairman: The Rt Hon T J C Eggar, LLB
S J A Cromack
D T Dalzell, BSc, PhD
J Dunston, MA
J S Gordon, LLB
J R B Hobbs, BA
R C Lester
The Hon Sir William McAlpine, Bart
Lady Phillimore
Mrs S J Ryan, BSc
D W Tanner, CBE, BA, FRSA
J P Turner, BSc, FCA
D S Williamson, BA

Headmaster: A G S Davies, BSc St Andrews, Cert Mgmt

Bursar and Clerk to the Governors: J N Walne, BSc Loughborough, MBA Cranfield

* *Head of Department*

Senior Staff:
Deputy Headmaster: R Jones, BA Swansea, PGCE Worcester
Director of Studies: D Mackey, BSc Oxford Brookes, PGCE Reading
Senior Housemaster: N J Brown, BA, PGCE East Anglia
Senior Master: R T Mannix, BSc London, PGCE Bath
Head of Sixth Form: B D P Pavey, BSc Durham, PGCE London, MA London
Head of Lower School: *S D Cane-Hardy, BA Cardiff, PGCE Sussex
Chaplain: The Revd S Cousins

Housemasters:
*R Curtis, BEd Brighton (*Orchard*)
N J Brown, BA, PGCE East Anglia (*Senior Housemaster and College*)
A D Dix, BSc, PGCE Loughborough (*Skipwith*)
Miss S G Andrew, BSc Heriot-Watt, PGCE St Martin's (*Gilson Housemistress*)
A F J Hunt, BEd S Australia (*Welsh*)
*G S Lawson, BSc Swansea, MSc, MPhil Southampton, PGCE OU (*Everett*)
C A M Lowndes, MA Oxon, BA, PGCE, MEd OU (*Burr*)
D D Seymour, BA South Africa, PGCE Natal (*Orchard Assistant*)

Teaching Staff:
C E Alcock, BA, PGCE Reading
T Armstrong, BA Exeter, Bachelor of Teaching UoT Sydney
*Miss E Arnold, Dip Design Farnham
*Mrs M A Baker, BA Oxon, PGCE
*S Balderson, BA London, QTS
Mrs A M Bingham, BMus London, MMus London, PGCE Roehampton
*R T Bradley, BA, PGCE, MEd Cantab
D J Brenton, BSc Aberdeen, PGCE Aberystwyth
J Brownley, BA Reading, PCGE Chester
Miss J Condon, BA Oxon
*L Cottrell, BSc Reading, PGCE Sussex
T E Crisford, BSc Southampton, GTP Brunel
*M Daniel, BA Essex, PGCE Worcester
*K Dolan, BSc Brunel, PGCE Birmingham

M Edwards, BA Southampton, PGCE E Anglia, MBA
    Reading
*Miss J C Erasmus, BSc Potchefstroom
T Fitton, MEng Durham, PGCE Chester
*Mrs H Gillings, BA Leeds, PGCE Liverpool John Moores
P C J Gould, BEd Reading
Miss N Handyside, BA Exeter, PGCE Reading
*Miss K A Harper, BMus Surrey, PGCE Cantab, LRSM
    Teaching
*Mrs A Higgins, BEd Reading, MSc Brunel, Dip Law
    Kingston
J Howorth, BSc Birmingham, PGCE
W H Mackworth-Praed, BSc Durham, PGCE Cantab
*M Milburn, BA Glamorgan, PGCE Reading
*S Le Paih, L-ès-Lettres Nantes, PGCE London
E Pugh, BSc Swansea, PCGE UWI
*Miss C Saker, BA London, AGSMD
*G Seccombe, BA Leeds, PGCE
Miss V Sedgwick, BA York, PGCE Reading
K F Settle, BSc York, PGCE London
*R C Snellgrove, BSc, PhD CNAA
R P Starr, BA Bradford, PGCE Reading
*D T Swan, BA Brunel

Part Time Teaching Staff:
Mrs L Bell, BA Liverpool, PGCE Leeds
Mrs D J Clark, BA Cardiff, PGCE Exeter
Mrs S A Clark, BA Liverpool, PGCE Manchester
J A Cooksey, BEd Leeds, MEd Nottingham
Mrs N Cox, BSc Cardiff, PGCE Cambridge
Mrs A M E Davies, JP, BA Edinburgh, PGCE Leeds
Dr J E Hart, BSc, PhD Bristol, PGCE Oxford Brookes
Mrs E C Hallam, BA Wales, PGCE Cantab
Mrs S Krause, BA Buckinghamshire Chiltern
Mrs A Morgan, HND Bristol
Mrs S Satch
W Smith, BA Manchester Polytechnic, PCGE Bristol
Mrs P Wallace, BA Dublin, PGCE London
G Vick, BSc Hons Nottingham, MSc Reading

SEN Administrator/TA: Mrs A C White, HLTA

Medical Staff:
School Doctor: Dr Philip Unwin, MB BS, DRCOG
Senior Nurse: Ms S Wallace, SRN, RSCN, ENB
Sister: Mrs J Fitzgerald, RGN, RM
Resident Healthcare Assistant: Ms D Gow

Administrative Staff:
Registrar: Mrs J Jarrett
Admissions Assistant: Mrs J Thomas
School Accountant: Mrs K Burrell, MAAT
Bursary Assistant: Mrs C Fry
Finance Assistant: Mrs L Reynolds
School Secretary: Ms S Bond
Office Administrator: Ms A Cooper
Marketing Manager: Mrs S Kilgour, BA Hons Cardiff
Data Manager: Miss H Edimoh, BA Bucharest
Catering and Events Manager: Mr S Beaumont, MIH
Careers Assistant & Music Assistant: Ms L E Rapple, BA
    Hons Reading
Estate Manager: D Greer, Dip SM, MIIRSM
Head Groundsman: R Evans
Examination Administrator: Mrs J Brenton, BA Open,
    TCert Cambs

Matrons:
Burr: Mrs L Lowndes
Everett: Ms K Strickland
Orchard & Domestic Bursar: Mrs J Burtt
Skipwith: Mrs J Miles-Thomas
Welsh & Senior Matron: Mrs J Knight
College: Mrs F Bensaad
Lower School & Gilson: Mrs L Kirkup

Technical Support Staff:
Mrs M A Cousins
Mrs G M Findlay
Mr A Reford
Mrs F J Varnals, CertEd Bristol

Ethos. Whilst Shiplake College has evolved and moved forward since its founding in 1959, many principles remain the same. We aim to admit a well-balanced intake of pupils with a variety of skills and talents, be they in the classroom, on the sports field, in the theatre or the Chapel. We look for young men and women who will take the opportunities that they are given and grasp them with both hands. We challenge the pupils in our care to help them move on to bigger and better things.

We firmly believe that in addition to a solid academic grounding, sporting, social and cultural achievement is vital to a pupil's long-term development. Shiplake offers a wide range of challenging enrichment activities to ensure an all-round education.

Academic. Although Shiplake does not select pupils solely according to academic ability this does not mean that we are not selective. Rather, we assess each pupil on his or her potential to make the most of the opportunities that Shiplake can offer and the value we can add to their education. We are proud of our superb value-added results. At Shiplake, teaching and learning concentrates on delivering excellent teaching through small classes and individual attention with a supportive but stimulating environment. Pupils have time to understand and explore their subjects thoroughly and the opportunity to ask questions and discuss interesting issues.

Pastoral Care. Boys joining at 11+ enter the Lower School which houses Year 7 and 8. From Year 9 all pupils become a member of one of the five houses: Burr, Skipwith, Welsh, Everett or Orchard. Both day and boarding girls join Gilson House, the purpose-built girls' house, but are attached to one of the boys' houses for social purposes, duties and inter-house competitions. The Upper Sixth boys enjoy the separate facilities of College House which helps establish independence before the move to University or a career. There is a strong house spirit in evidence with competitions organised for arts, games and academic progress.

The houses provide excellent support for the pupils in addition to ensuring a comfortable, homely environment for pupils to study or relax.

Each house is run by a Housemaster who is supported by a strong team of staff including the House Matron, House Tutor, Visiting Tutors, the Medical Staff and the Chaplain. The Pastoral Committee meets regularly to ensure liaison between teaching and house staff in order that pupils' successes and challenges can be monitored closely.

As a Christian School there is an extensive programme of worship, very often provided in the neighbouring Parish Church. The Chaplain, whose role is purely pastoral, is always available to any member of the College community. Shiplake also welcomes pupils of other faiths.

Location. The College enjoys a beautiful riverside site of 45 acres including an island in the River Thames. It sits high above the river, just over two miles upstream of Henley-on-Thames.

Although pupils love the acres of sports pitches and the country trails, parents appreciate the fact that Shiplake is conveniently placed for access to the M4 and M40 and the railway stations at Henley and Reading. This idyllic countryside location is just an hour from London and within easy reach of Heathrow and Gatwick airports.

Facilities. Shiplake House, built in 1889 as a family home, is at the heart of the school. Pupils and staff take their main meals in the wood-panelled Great Hall beneath the Minstrels' Gallery. The College is fortunate to have the use of the twelfth-century Parish Church, where the poet Lord Tennyson was married, for assemblies and worship.

In addition to the main school buildings, Shiplake boasts a range of facilities including the Tithe Barn Theatre, Music Rooms, Sports Hall and Fitness Suite. The boathouses are a short walk from the main buildings, allowing direct access to the Thames; all pupils are encouraged to try rowing.

The College has state-of-the-art ICT and computing facilities available to all pupils.

Developments. A new day and boarding house for girls opened in September 2009 as did the new Lower School. The Governors are currently planning for future developments.

Academic Structure. Boys entering the College in Year 7 follow the specially designed curriculum for Years 7 and 8 before moving on to the Upper School. In the Upper School they will enjoy the broad and balanced Year 9 curriculum which provides a strong foundation for GCSE. In the Sixth Form, pupils select up to four subjects from a choice of twenty-two.

Learning Development. Shiplake has a dedicated Learning Development Department to provide additional help for those pupils who need it. As we are a school with small class sizes our teaching staff is committed to providing individual attention for all abilities. Pupils are able to approach their subject teachers for additional support whenever necessary. For those who require ongoing help the Learning Development Department provides either a structured programme to support the curriculum or help on an ad hoc basis both for the academically gifted and those who find certain subject areas difficult to access.

The aim of the Learning Development Department is to improve all pupils' confidence and self-esteem as well as equipping them with the skills they need to access the curriculum and demonstrate the knowledge they have acquired.

Sport. Our extensive site on the banks of the River Thames makes Shiplake an ideal location for pupils who love sport. The College has excellent sporting facilities and most pupils take part in a sporting activity every day. The College enjoys direct access to the river and boathouses, hockey, cricket and rugby pitches, tennis courts, squash courts and an outdoor swimming pool. The sports hall offers a variety of indoor sports, a weight-training gym and a fitness room.

Almost all boys play rugby football in the autumn term. In the spring term boys play hockey or row, and in the summer term there is the choice of cricket, tennis or rowing. The girls enjoy a mixed programme of sports and activities using the sporting facilities available.

Soccer, basketball, badminton, squash, judo, cross-country running and athletics provide additional activities to develop skills and fitness.

For a small school, Shiplake has a remarkable number of crews and teams taking part in events and competitions with national success. There have been a number of overseas tours involving the rugby, cricket, hockey and rowing clubs.

Music, Art and Drama. The College has a thriving mixture of Arts activities and performances and all pupils are encouraged to enjoy the Arts. The annual House Music Competition ensures that every pupil in the school is involved in preparing for a performance and every term there is at least one concert for pupils to demonstrate the progress they have made. The Mad Dogs Theatre Company provides opportunities for the theatrically inclined and the Headmaster's Hymn Practice furthers the growing reputation for community singing at the College.

Activities. Pupils choose from a wide range of activities including art, ballroom dancing, cookery, debating, football, golf, log-chopping and canoeing. The College has a thriving Combined Cadet Force with Air Force, Army and Navy sections. Pupils who are not members of the CCF take part in regular community service activities and the school has links to a Kenyan School for which fundraising activities are regularly undertaken. The College also runs a Duke of Edinburgh's Award Scheme with a number of pupils each year collecting Gold Awards. In addition there are drama productions, debates and music recitals.

Careers. There is an experienced Careers Adviser and particular attention is paid to the choice of University and career from Year 11 onwards. The School is a member of ISCO.

Admission. The Registrar is the first point of contact for all admissions and admissions enquiries. Boys are admitted at 11+ into Year 7 and at 13+ into Year 9. There is an intake into the Sixth Form for boys and girls. Places are offered for Years 7 and 9 following an assessment day. Please contact the Registrar for further details. Occasional places arise in other years and there is a waiting list held by the Registrar.

Scholarships. Means-tested scholarships and bursaries are offered to outstanding sportsmen, artists or musicians at Year 9 level and in the Sixth Form for all academic subjects.

Fees per term (2011-2012). Boarders £8,510, Day Pupils: Years 7 & 8, £4,600, Years 9–13 £5,740.

Alumni. The Old Viking Society has an annual programme of events including sports fixtures and a formal dinner. The Society produces an annual newsletter for Old Vikings.

Charitable status. Shiplake College is a Registered Charity, number 309651. It exists to provide education for children.

Shrewsbury School

Shrewsbury, Shropshire SY3 7BA
Tel: 01743 280500 (Switchboard)
          01743 280525 (Headmaster)
          01743 280820 (Bursar)
          01743 280552 (Registrar)
Fax: 01743 340048 (Headmaster)
          01743 243107 (Reception)
          01743 280559 (Registrar)
e-mail: registrar@shrewsbury.org.uk
website: www.shrewsbury.org.uk

Shrewsbury School was founded by King Edward VI in 1552 and augmented by Queen Elizabeth in 1571. In 1882 it moved from the centre of the town to its present site overlooking the town and the River Severn.

Motto: '*Intus si recte, ne labora*'

Governing Body:

Chairman: R Burbidge, OBE, DL, BA
Dr Rosalind P Blakesley, MA, DPhil
Lt Col S S Caney, MBE, BA
M H Collins
Prof C Dobson, FRS
A Haining, MA
Dr Fiona Hay, MA, BM, BCh, DRCOG, MRCGP, DFFP
T H P Haynes, MA
A E H Heber-Percy
A G A Hillman, ACA
W R O Hunter, QC
Prof E W Jones, OBE, BSc Hons, PhD, FRAgS
Ms Lyndsey Pollard, LLB
Prof D A Ritchie, CBE, FRSE, DL
Alderman D W L Roberts
The Rt Hon Sir Stephen Tomlinson
H P Trevor-Jones, DL, BSc

Headmaster: **M Turner**, MA

Bursar and Clerk to the Governors: M J Ware, MA, ACA
Senior Master: P A Fanning, MA
Second Master: M J Tonks, BA
Director of Studies: M J Cropper, MA
Head of Careers and Staff Training: C W Conway, MA
Registrar: R E D Case, BA

Assistant Masters/Mistresses:
* *Head of Faculty*
† *Housemaster/Housemistress*

Mrs R W Adams, BEc, BEd
S F Adams, MA, MSc (**Science*)
A J Allott, MA (**Biology*)
J C Armstrong, BA (**Mathematics*)
J Balcombe, BSc
A S Barnard, BA (*†Port Hill – day boys*)
M W D Barrett, BSc
G St J F Bell, BA (*†School House*)
S J Biggins (*Master i/c Football*)
Mrs N J Bradburne, BA
A D Briggs, BSc, PhD (**Chemistry*)
Dr J A Brydon, MA, DPhil
Miss J M M Burge, BSc
J R Burke, BSc
Dr R A J Case, BSc, PhD
R F Charters, MA
M D H Clark, BA
Mrs A J Clemson, BA
C E Cook, MA
S K P Cooley, MEng
S H Cowper, MA (**Spanish*)
A Dalton, BA (**Religious Studies*)
N P David, BSc
The Revd G W Dobbie, MA (*Chaplain*)
Mrs L J Drew, BA
M S Elliot, MA, PhD
P G Fitzgerald, MA
T R Foulger, BSc, PhD (**Geography*)
S A A Fox, BA
J Gabbitas, MA
J Godwin, MA, PhD (**Classics*)
P Greetham, BA (*Director of Sport*)
Mrs S L Hankin, BA (*†Mary Sidney Hall – Sixth Form girls*)
D M Hann, MA (*†Radbrook – day boys*)
M H Hansen, BSc
M J Harding, BA
S Hellier, BA
R T Hudson, MA (*†Churchill's Hall*)
W A Hughes, BA (*†Ridgemount*)
R N R Jenkins, OBE, MA
M D B Johnson, BSc, BA (*†Oldham's Hall*)
D M Joyce, DipRCM, ARCM
P A Kaye, BEng (**Educational ICT*)
C W Kealy, BComm (**Business Studies*)
M A Kirk, BSc (**Physics*)
Mrs V L Kirk, BSc
D Kirkby, BSc
P H Lapage, BA
Mrs K Leslie, BA (**English*)
J V Lucas, LLB
A E Mason, BA, MMus
P A Merricks-Murgatroyd, BA (**Economics*)
P J Middleton, BA (*†Rigg's Hall*)
C J Minns, MA, PhD (**German*)
J F Moore, BA, LRAM (**Music*)
T S Morgan, BSc, PhD
R H Morris, BEd
M M Morrogh, BA, PhD
M A J Mostyn, BA, MA
D A G Nicholas, BA (*†The Grove*)
D Nickolaus, CertEd (**CDT*)
Mrs D B Nightingale, MTD, LTCL
C W Oakley, MMath, DPhil
J L Pattenden, MA, DPhil
P Pattenden, MA, DPhil, CPhys, MInstP (*†Moser's Hall*)
H R W Peach, BA
T P Percival, MA
Miss R E Pile, BSc
D Portier, BA, MA

A P Pridgeon
F O L Reid, MA
Miss C E Rule, BSc
C M Samworth, BSc, PhD
M Schofield, BSc
M A Schutzer-Weissmann, MA
J A Sheppe, MPhil
W M Simper, BSc
M Twells, MA (**IT*)
P R Vicars, MA (*†Severn Hill*)
M F Wade, MA, PhD
T D J Warburg, MA
Mrs K M Weston, MSc (*†Emma Darwin Hall – Sixth Form Girls*)
T C Whitehead, BA (**French*)
Miss L J Whittle, BA (**History*)
R M Wilson, MEng Hons
Miss G Y Y Woo, MSc
P N Woolley, BA, MFA (**Art*)
M P J Wright, BA (*†Ingram's Hall*)

Visiting American Fellow: N E Sceery, AB Harvard

Visiting French Fellow: D Ithurbisque, MA University of Bordeaux

School Doctors:
The General Practitioner Team, Mytton Oak Surgery, Racecourse Lane, Shrewsbury

Dental Adviser: R J Gatenby, BDS, DGDP, RCS

Headmaster's Secretary: Mrs J Gibbs

Number in School. There are 722 pupils in the School (601 boarding and 121 day).

Admission to the School. Most admissions are in September. Boys are admitted at 13 or (direct to the Sixth Form) at 16. Girls are admitted to the Sixth Form. Entrance forms and other information can be obtained from the Registrar. The registration fee, which is non-returnable, is £30.

Entry at 13. Boys usually take the Common Entrance Examination or the Scholarship Examination in the term preceding that in which they wish to come. The School has its own entrance test for boys who have not followed the Common Entrance syllabus. A Secured Places Scheme operates whereby boys aged 11 can take an examination set by the School and may receive an offer of a place, subject to a satisfactory school report in the final year of preparatory school at 13.

Scholarships. (*See Scholarship Entries section*.) The Scholarships are inflation-linked. In 2011 the Governors expect to offer 4 Academic Scholarships up to the value of 50% of fees, 6 up to the value of 25% of fees and 7 worth at least £2,000 per annum, but this is currently subject to revision.

In addition, they offer 10 House Foundation Awards worth up to the value of 50% of fees, 2 Music Scholarships up to the value of 50% of fees, 2 Music Scholarships up to the value of 20% of fees, 2 Art Scholarships up to the value of 20% of fees, 2 Sports Scholarships up to the value of 20% of fees and 2 All-Rounder Scholarships worth up to the value of 20% of fees.

Sixth Form Entry. Direct entry into the co-educational Sixth Form depends on an interview, examination at Shrewsbury and a favourable report from the applicant's present school. There are 8 Academic Scholarships: 2 up to the value of 25% of the fees and 6 up to the value of 15% of fees. In addition there are 6 Specialist Scholarships (for Art, Drama, Music or Sport), 2 worth up to 25% of fees, and 4 worth up to 15% of fees. There is also 1 Cassidy Sports Scholarship worth up to 100% of fees, subject to means testing.

Buildings. The school operates a rolling programme of refurbishment for all boarding houses. Similarly, large-scale refurbishment of the teaching accommodation is currently under way. All classrooms are professionally equipped to a very high standard. A Music School, including an auditorium and a large ensemble room, was opened in February 2001, a cricket academy and a new boarding house (now accommodating sixth form girls) opened in 2006, a new swimming pool opened in 2007, a new sixth form centre was completed in 2008, and a second boarding house for sixth form girls will be opened in September 2011.

The Moser Library houses The School Library, the Moser collection of water-colours, and the Ancient Library, which contains medieval manuscripts and early printed books.

Courses of Study. All boys follow a general course as far as the GCSE Level Examinations. In the Sixth Form it is usual to study 4 subjects to AS Level and 3 to A2 Level. The number of combinations of subjects for which it is possible to opt is very large. Recent additions are PE and Theatre Studies AS and A2, and Cambridge Pre-U courses in French and Physics.

Games. Rowing, Cricket, Association Football, Swimming, Hockey, Netball, Cross-Country, Eton Fives and Rugby. The School has its own indoor Swimming Pool, Gymnasium, Multigym, Miniature Rifle Range, all-weather playing surface, Tennis Courts, Squash Courts and Fives Courts. The River Severn flows just below the Main School Building and the Boat House is within the School grounds.

Activities. Pupils are offered a considerable range of outdoor activities via the Combined Cadet Force, leadership courses and the Duke of Edinburgh's Award Scheme. The programme of activities and opportunities continues to broaden as a pupil moves up the School.

Art and Design. Art and Design are taught to all boys in their first year. For those not doing GCSE or A Level courses they subsequently become activities followed mainly, but not exclusively, out of school hours. The Art and CDT centres are available 7 days a week. The CDT department offers the chance of advanced design work and of creative work in a variety of materials. AS and A2 and GCSE Level design are also offered, as are AS and A2 ceramics and photography.

Societies. These range from Literary, Political, Debating, Drama and Language societies to those catering for practical skills. Hill-walkers and Mountaineers make use of the unspoilt country on the doorstep and of the Welsh hills.

Music. Teaching is available in any orchestral instrument, as well as the Piano and Organ. The charge for this is £21.61 per 40 minute lesson for all instruments. Regular Choral, Orchestral and Chamber Concerts both at the school and elsewhere (St John's, Smith Square; CBSO Birmingham) are given by the pupils. In addition concerts are given during the winter months by distinguished visiting artists.

Drama. Drama is a major feature of school life, with two school plays and up to nine house plays per year, together with regular accolades at the Edinburgh Fringe.

Field Study Centre. Shrewsbury owns a farmhouse in Snowdonia, which is used at weekends throughout the year as a base for expeditions.

Careers. There is a full time Careers Master. Pupils are offered the Morrisby Aptitude Tests and the services of the Independent Schools Careers Organization.

Community Service. In association with other schools in the town, pupils play an active part in caring for the old and needy in the Shrewsbury area.

Shrewsbury House. Founded in Liverpool as a Club for boys in 1903, it was re-built as a Community Centre in association with the Local Authority and the Diocese in 1974. There is residential accommodation in the Centre and groups of pupils from the School have the opportunity to go there on study courses.

Shrewsbury International School. The school has close links with Shrewsbury International School in Bangkok. Teaching and pupil exchanges take place between the two schools, and Governors of Shrewsbury School serve on the board of management of the International School.

Fees per term (2011-2012). Boarders: £9,420, including tuition, board and ordinary School expenses. There are no other obligatory extras, apart from stationery. Day Pupils: £6,595.

Application for reduced fees may be made to the Governors through the Headmaster.

Old Pupils' Society. Most pupils leaving the school join the Old Salopian Club, The Schools, Shrewsbury SY3 7BA; e-mail: oldsalopian@shrewsbury.org.uk.

Charitable status. Shrewsbury School is a Registered Charity, number 528413. It exists to provide secondary education.

Silcoates School

Wrenthorpe, Wakefield, West Yorkshire WF2 0PD
Tel: 01924 291614
Fax: 01924 368693
e-mail: head@silcoates.org.uk
website: www.silcoates.org.uk

Silcoates was founded in 1820 on its present site, two miles north-west of Wakefield. While retaining its links with the United Reformed Church, the school aims to provide a broad, first-class education for boys and girls of all denominations and faiths. The Silcoates School Foundation comprises three schools: Silcoates School (Senior and Junior sections), Sunny Hill House School and St Hilda's School.

Motto: '*Clarior ex ignibus*'

Board of Governors:

Chairman: Mrs M C Chippendale, BSc
Vice-Chairman: J R Lane, LLB, AKC, TEP

Mrs T W Barker
Professor J C G Binfield, OBE, MA, PhD, FSA
G A Briggs, FCA
J H Bryan, LLB
Dr P H Clarke
Mrs R M Copley
Dr M Gallagher, MBE
Mrs J M Healey, ATCL
J D Hendry, BEng, CEng, MICE, MIGEM
Mrs V Jenkins, MEd, BPhil, ADB, ALAM, CertEd
Mrs A M Johnson, MA
Revd S R Knapton, MA
Revd Dr J A Lees, MPhil, MTh, MRCSLT
T J Mulryne, MA, BEd, DipPE
D E Payling, MA, ACA
J E Payling, MA, FCA
Mrs D S Procter, BA
C N Shannon, MA, MBA

Clerk to the Governors: D Dinmore, MBE, DL, MCIPD, MCMI

Staff:

Headmaster: D S Wideman, MA

Deputy Heads:
D A Curran, BSc
S Fox, MA
Miss H M Wren, BA, MA

Head of Junior School: A P Boyer, BEd

Chaplain (Temporary): Dr Janet Lees, MPhil, MTh, MRCSLT

Assistant Staff:
M Affleck, BA
Mrs L Burdekin, CertEd
Mrs N Chambers, BA
Mrs A Clewarth
J C Clewarth, BEd, MEd
D Coll, BEd

Mrs S Coll, BEd
J Cooling, BSc, MMedSci, PhD
D B Coulson, BSc
Mrs H Crompton, BMus, MMus, LTCL
Mrs R L Dews, BEng
Miss H Drayson, CertEd
Mrs A Eckersley, MA, BSc
R Elliston, BA
Miss L Featherstone, BA
R J Fenn, BEd
P Franks, BA
Mrs M Hayes, DipAD, SIAD
Mrs L Hoyland, BA
C Hugill, BSc
N Jackson, BSc
M D Jeanes, BSc
W F Jepson, BSc, MSc
Miss A Knowles, BA
J M Lee, BA
Miss S Loren, BA
Mrs K March, BEd
Ms C A Marsh, BEd
Miss J Masters, BA, MA
Miss L McLoughlin, BSc
Mrs J L McManus, BA
T J Mills, BEd
A Mistry, BA
J M Newell, BSc, CPhys, MInstP
Mrs J M Newell, BA
Miss E L Nuttall, BA
S Ogden, BSc
N Owen, BA

A W Paling, BSc
Miss H M Peach, BA
J R L Piggott, BSc
Mrs R Platt, BA, DipABRSM
A Potter, BEd
Miss C Powell, BA
B G Pye, BEd
D J Raggett, BSc
P A Richards, BSc
G Roberts, BEd
T J Roberts, BA
S J Rodgers, BSc
C Rowe, BA
S C Scholfield, BA
Mrs J Senadhira, BSc
Mrs B W Shaw, BA
T P Sprott, BSc
Ms H Stalker, BA
Mrs L Sugden, BSc, MSc, PGCert
Mrs D J Townsend, BSc
T Verinder, BA
Miss G Walker, BSc
Mrs M Ward, CertEd, Cert Dyslexia & Literacy
S W Wardle, BA
P V Watkin, BSc
Miss T Watson, BA
G Wetherop, BA
G S Wickstead, BSc
Mrs F J Wideman, MA
Miss N Widnall, BA
Miss A J Wray, BA
P A Wright, MSci, PhD

Bursar: J A J Dickson, MA, MA
Finance Manager: A Gracie
Headmaster's PA: Mrs C Woodhead
PA to the Deputies: Mrs L Druce
School Secretaries: Mrs L M Nutbrown & Mrs C Wade
Junior School Secretary: Mrs A Dix
Bursar's PA: Mrs F Reed
Sixth Form Supervisor: Mrs T Watkin
Development Assistant: Miss L Leach

Admission. There are 750 pupils at Silcoates. Boys and girls are admitted to the Junior School from the age of 5 and to the Senior School from the age of 11. Places are available for girls and boys wishing to study for A Level in the Sixth Form.

Entrance Examinations take place in January for admission the following September.

The Foundation also provides a pre-preparatory education for boys and girls from 2 to 5 years at Sunny Hill House School and at St Hilda's School, Horbury, for boys and girls from 0 to 7.

(*See also entries for Silcoates Junior School and St Hilda's School in IAPS section, and Sunny Hill House School's entry in ISA section.*)

Curriculum. Recent inspection reports have been highly complimentary about the school's academic performance. Nearly all pupils sit a minimum of 9 GCSEs, 4 AS and 3 A2 Levels, and the vast majority go on to degree courses. There is great flexibility of subject choice at GCSE and A Level. Small class sizes and good facilities create a positive atmosphere for learning. Value added scores are very strong.

Games and Activities. Drama, art, music and sport all flourish at Silcoates. The school has an excellent record of individual and collective achievement in all of its extra-curricular activities. The outstanding sports facilities include an indoor pool and extensive sports pitches. There is a well-equipped Music School. Our very successful Duke of Edin-burgh's Award programme makes extensive use of various venues in the north of England and abroad.

Pastoral Care and Careers Guidance. With a generous pupil:personal tutor ratio, the quality of pastoral care is of a very high order. We provide a full programme of careers advice and guidance for university entrance.

Fees per term (2011-2012). Senior School: £3,876; Junior School: £1,970–£3,020.

Entrance Scholarships. (*See Scholarship Entries section.*) Academic Scholarships are offered at 11+ and above; Sixth Form entrants are eligible for these awards.

Bursaries are available for the sons and daughters of Ministers and Missionaries of the United Reformed Church or of the Congregational Church, and of other recognised Christian denominations and to other parents subject to a financial assessment.

Charitable status. The Silcoates School Foundation is a Registered Charity, number 529281. It aims to provide a first-class all-round education for boys and girls, with an academic edge.

Solihull School

Warwick Road, Solihull, West Midlands B91 3DJ
Tel: 0121 705 0958 (Headmaster)
          0121 705 4273 (Admissions)
          0121 705 0883 (Bursar)
Fax: 0121 711 4439
e-mail: admin@solsch.org.uk
website: www.solsch.org.uk

Motto: '*Perseverantia*'

Chairman of the Governors: M T Hopton, FCA

Bursar and Clerk to the Governors: C Warren

Headmaster: D E J J Lloyd, BSc, PGCE

Senior Deputy Headmaster: S A Morgan, BA
Deputy Headmaster (*Academic*): D G Morgan, BA, MA Cantab

Senior Teacher (*Pastoral Care*): Mrs L A Fair, BA, MA
Senior Teacher (*Co-Curricular*): M J Garner, BSc
Senior Teacher (*Director of Studies*): Ms D Harford, BA

Head of Sixth Form: Mrs L A Fair, BA, MA
Head of the Middle School: Mrs R Lancaster, BSc
Head of the Lower School: D Reardon, BSc
Head of the Junior School: Mrs L J Brough, BA, LTCL
Director of Studies (*Junior School*): Mrs J Humphreys, BEd

Assistant Staff:
* *Head of Department*

G Affleck, BA (*History)
O Anderton, BSc
Mrs N J Atkins, BEd
Dr R A Atkinson, BA, DPhil Oxon
M P Babb, BSc
S Baddeley
Mrs M A Barrett, BA, MEd (*Modern Languages)
O W H Bate, BSc
L A Benge, BA, BEd
M R Bishop, MSc (*Mathematics)
Mrs C Black, BA
P D Brattle, BSc
D Brough
Mrs J S Brown, BA, MA
Miss T J Bryan, BA
Mrs D L Buckle, BSc
A Bussey, BA (**Economics & Business Studies*)
Miss E Campbell, BA

Mrs E Cassano
Mrs C Checketts, BA
Mrs N A Cheetham, BA
Revd Canon Dr N Cluley, JP, BA, BSc, MA, DD
Miss S Compton, BSc
N Corbett, BA
M J Covill, BSc
Mrs P Cramb, BA
Miss S Crowther, BEd
G J Cureton, BSc
Mrs C D L Davies
Miss P J Davies, GBSM
Ms H Dolby, AGSM, ATC
T Emmet, BSc (*Psychology*)
D A Farrington BSc
Miss E Ford, BSc
J Geldard, MA
Miss V Gill, MEd
J Grandrieux, Dip UEL
Miss C M Greswold, GLCM, AMus LCM, ALCM
P G Gunning, BA
Miss J Guy, BA, MPhil (*Classics*)
E Hadley, BA Cantab
Mrs R R Hadley-Leonard, BEd (*Director of Learning
   Support*)
S A Hart, BA (*English*)
D Hemp, MBA
S Hifle, QTS
P M Higley, BA, CertEd (*Design & Technology*)
P T Holt, MA Oxon
Mrs J Humphreys, BEd Cantab
Mrs Eleanor Hurst, BA, Cert SpLD
Revd Canon A C Hutchinson, BA, MEd
P J Irving, BA, ARCM, FRCO (*ICT*)
P R Jackson, BSc
D Jenkinson, MEd
A Jones, BSc (*Science*)
N W S Leonard, BEd
Miss R Lowe, BA
Miss L J Lynch, BSc
Miss S L Mackie, BA
P May, BSc
C I Mayer
Mrs H Middleton, BEng, BCom
S Mitchell, BSc
P Morgan, BA
Mrs U Mynette, MA
J J Nickson, MA (*Art*)
Dr M Partridge, BA Oxon, MA, PhD
Mrs D E Penney, BSc
M Penney, BA
S J Perrins, MA Cantab, FRCO (*Director of Music*)
Mrs S J Phillips, BSc
Miss H E Pike, MA, BA
Dr K A Powell, PhD, MBA
Miss G J Powell, BA, MA
R D Pugh, BSc, MSc
D Reardon, BSc (*Director of ICT*)
Mrs A C Roll, BA (*Geography*)
Mrs B M E Rossay-Gilson
Miss H M Smith, BA
M K Smith, BSc (*Physics*)
Mrs H Smith
Miss S Smith, BSc
P F Spratley, BA, MA
Mrs C Steele, BEd
Mrs K Sykes, BA
Mrs V Taylor, CertEd
H J Thomas
Mrs S Thomas, BSc
S J Thompson, BSc (*Director of Sport*)
Miss C Townsend, BSc
Miss D L Trim, BA

J Troth, PhD, BSc (*Chemistry*)
O M Walker, BA Oxon
Mrs D H Wild, BSc (*Biology*)
Mrs J Wilde, BA (*Director of Drama*)
Mrs L C Wolsey, BA
M Worrall, MA
R C Wright, BA (*Religious Studies*)

Careers: Revd Canon Dr N A Cluley, JP, BA, BSc, MA,
   DD

OC CCF: Major N W S Leonard
SSI: WO2 P G Dean, MBE

Medical Officer: Dr S Kotecha, MBChB, FRCGP, MSc
School Matron: Mrs E Haynes, RGN
Assistant to Matron: Mrs M M Thorne, RGN, RSCN

Headmaster's PA: (*to be appointed*)
Admissions Secretary: Mrs J Edwards
Bursar's PA: Ms S K Baldwin
Librarian: Mrs A M Vaughan

Solihull School was founded in 1560 with the income
from the chantry chapels of the parish of Solihull. The
School is particularly proud of the richness and diversity of
the education that it provides. The School has always been
closely involved with the community, making its sporting
and theatrical facilities available, forming links with local
schools.

Organisation. The School now provides education for
nearly 1,000 day pupils aged between 7 and 18. The Junior
School, which occupies its own separate building on the site
and has its own Head, has 170 pupils aged from 7 to 11. In
the Senior School there are 559 pupils from Year 7 to Year
11 and 263 pupils in the Sixth Form. In 1973 girls were
accepted into the Sixth Form and there are now over 100
Sixth Form girls in the School. From September 2005 the
School became fully co-educational, with girls being admitted at 7+, 8+, 9+, 10+ and 11+. In total there are currently
365 girls in the School.

Site and Facilities. The School moved to its present site
in 1882 and the original school building, School House, survives. The site now comprises over 50 acres of buildings and
playing fields, which enable all teaching, games and activities to take place on the one site. In the last decade there has
been a very substantial building programme. This programme originally involved the extension of the Science
Department and Design and Technology Centre, the laying
of an Astroturf pitch and three squash courts, the substantial
redevelopment of School House. In 2002 a new hall/theatre,
the Bushell Hall, was built. This hall can accommodate a
theatre audience of 500 and an assembly for 800. At the
same time the old hall was transformed into a library and IT
rooms. In 2003, a new pavilion, the Alan Lee Pavilion, was
completed. In September 2005 a new teaching area, the
George Hill Building, was unveiled to provide 16 new classrooms and extensive social space. The Junior School has
been extended and entirely refurbished. A new music school
was unveiled in September 2009 – The David Turnbull
Music School. Throughout the School there are excellent IT
facilities for staff and pupils, including 51 interactive whiteboards.

Curriculum. In the Junior School particular emphasis is
placed on establishing good standards in core subjects. The
Junior School also has specialist areas for Art, Design and
Technology and Music and benefits from the facilities of the
Senior School.

At the beginning of the Senior School, all pupils have at
least one year of Latin and in the second year Spanish and
German are option subjects. English Language and Literature, Maths, French, Physics, Chemistry and Biology remain
compulsory subjects to GCSE. Three other subjects are chosen from a wide range of options.

The size of the Sixth Form enables the school to offer a very wide range of subjects and combinations. These subjects are Art & Design, Biology, Business Studies, Chemistry, Classical Civilisation, Design & Technology, Drama & Theatre Studies, English Literature, Economics, French, Geography, German, History, Latin, Maths (and Further Maths), Music, PE, Photography, Psychology, Physics, Religious Studies, Spanish. There is also a substantial programme of Enrichment for all pupils in the Sixth Form, ranging from Mandarin Chinese to Skiing.

Academic Success. For the last four years, on average, 7 pupils have received offers from Oxford and Cambridge each year. In 2010 more than 85% of A Levels were passed at A*, A or B grade.

Games. Games are an integral part of the school curriculum and all pupils in the School are involved. PE is compulsory until Year 11 and all pupils in the School have a games afternoon. The School has a very strong tradition in the major team games for both boys and girls, but also offers a very wide range of other options. The principal team games are rugby, cricket, hockey (for both boys and girls), netball and rounders. The Junior School pupils play football in addition to these sports. The School also has school teams in tennis, where the School has had national success, athletics, swimming, clay-pigeon shooting, cross-country, badminton, basketball and fencing. In recent years the School has organised very extensive tours for pupils of differing ages: in the Summer of 2008, a rugby tour of New Zealand, a boys hockey tour of South Africa, and girls netball and hockey teams in Barbados. Summer 2010 witnessed our senior rugby players in South Africa, and our girls hockey teams in Singapore and Malaysia.

Music and Drama. The School has a very strong tradition in music and drama, which has been enhanced since the building of the Bushell Hall. Over one third of all pupils learn a musical instrument and there are over 20 different musical groups in the Senior School, ranging from a school orchestra to a samba band. Several of these groups are very successful in competition in local festivals. There are many opportunities for pupils to perform at concerts, both formal and informal, throughout the year. There is also an excellent chapel choir that performs during the school week but also at the voluntary chapel services which take place on each Sunday in term. The David Turnbull Music School was opened in September 2009.

There are two major dramatic performances each year: a school musical (*The Scarlet Pimpernel* 2008; *My Fair Lady* 2009; *South Pacific* 2010; *Grease* 2011) and a school play (*Romeo and Juliet* 2007; *Tom Jones* 2008; *Oh What a Lovely War* 2009; *Blood Brothers* 2010). In addition, there are several smaller productions in the course of the year.

Outdoor Pursuits. Outdoor pursuits play a major part in the School's life. In Year 7 pupils take part in an outdoor activities programme called Terriers. In Year 8 every pupil spends a week at the School's mountain cottage in Snowdonia. From Year 9 pupils are able to participate in the CCF, which has an Army and an RAF section, and/or the Duke of Edinburgh's Award Scheme. There are some 150 pupils, including a number of girls, in the CCF and a similar number are involved at different stages of the Duke of Edinburgh's Award scheme. The School has a popular Mountain Club and organises biennial major expeditions: Tibet/Nepal in 2005, Chile in 2007, Ladakh India 2009. Alaska is the proposed destination for 2011.

Admissions. Pupils are accepted into the Junior School through examination at 7+, 8+, 9+ and 10+, although the majority of pupils enter at 7+. Almost all Junior School pupils pass from the Junior School into the Senior School. The major point of entry is at 11+ (Year 7). Places and scholarships are awarded on the basis of written exams in English and Maths and, in many cases, an interview. Some pupils are also accepted to enter the School at 12+ and 13+. A substantial number of pupils, about 60 on average, enter the School

at Sixth Form level. Admission to the Sixth Form, for both internal and external candidates, requires a minimum of 6 B grades at GCSE.

Fees per term (2011-2012). Tuition: £3,320 (£2,724 for pupils aged 7–10). Lunch charges per day: £2.75 Junior School, £3.10 Main School. There are few obligatory extras.

Scholarships and Assisted Places. (*See Scholarship Entries section.*) The School offers approximately 25 academic scholarship awards at 11+ and around 30 at 16+. The number of awards and their value is at the discretion of the Headmaster. There are also music scholarships at 11+, 13+ and 16+. In addition to academic scholarships, means-tested Assisted Places are available to allow able children the opportunity of an education at Solihull School. Applicants for such awards are considered for entry at age 11+ and into the Sixth Form.

Old Silhillians Association. *Secretary*: Mr P Davies, Memorial Clubhouse, Warwick Road, Knowle, Solihull. The aim of the Old Silhillians is to support and maintain links with the School. They also have their own clubhouse and extensive sports facilities.

Charitable status. Solihull School is a Registered Charity, number 1120597. It exists to provide high-quality education for pupils between 7 and 18 years old.

Stamford School

Southfields House, St Paul's Street, Stamford, Lincolnshire PE9 2BQ
Tel: 01780 750300
Fax: 01780 750336
e-mail: headss@ses.lincs.sch.uk
website: www.ses.lincs.sch.uk

Founded by William Radcliffe, of Stamford, 1532.
Motto: '*Christe me spede*'

Chairman of the Governing Body: Malcolm Desforges, Esq

***Principal of the Stamford Endowed Schools*: S C Roberts**, MA

Vice-Principal, Head: W Phelan, MBA

Director of Staff & Student Development: W C Chadwick, MA
Director of Studies: Mrs T E Griffiths
Director of Teaching and Learning: H P Hewlett, BSc
Head of Sixth Form: G P Brown, MA
Head of Middle School: K J Mills, BA
Head of Lower School: K J Chapman, BEd
SES Chaplain: The Revd M Goodman, BA, BTh, MTh
Director of ICT: N A Faux, MA

Assistant Staff:
† *Boarding Housemaster*

Miss S Angove, MA	N S Davies, BA
B D Bates, BSc	J W Dawson, MA
Mrs L Blissett, BA	R G A Dexter, BA
M J Blissett, BA	Dr R Fielden, MA, DPhil
E J Board, BA	C D Fox, BA
C W Brace, BSc, MSc	Mrs J C Fox, BA
P Braud, Baccalaureate	B Gantry, BSc
R A Brewster, BSc	G Grainger, BA
Miss E L Calvert, BSc	Dr R Gosling, BSc, PhD
M C Caseley, MA	Ms F Harrison, BA
Mrs A Chauvaux,	Mrs F L Haunch, BSc
Staatsexamen	Miss K M Hawkswell, BSc
Ms H M Chew, BA, MPhil	R J B Henry, BEd
Mrs S L Child, BA	D Hodder, BSc
Mrs N A Cliffe, BSc	J P Hodgson, BSc
D Colley, BEd	M V Holdsworth, BA
Ms A Davies, BA	Mrs A J M Holland, MA

Miss P Ingle, BSc
D N Jackson, BSc
Mrs K Jones
T P Jones, BEd
S M Jordan, MBA, BEng
C V Killgren, BA
D J Laventure, BA
G S Lee, CertEd
Mrs K Leetch, MA
D Lennie, BA
J M Livingstone, BA
Mrs S Manning, BSc
Mrs F I McClarty, BA
M K Milner, BSc
G Mitchell, BSc
K G Nally, BEng, MBA
J A Peckett, BSc
A N Pike, BA (*†Byard House*)

Mrs C Pike, BA
N J Porteus, BSc
A Ramsey, BSc
Mrs M Rigg, BSc
B J Russell
P J Scargill, MSc
M P Scriven, BA
Miss C Scott, BA
Miss A L Spong, MA
D L R Stamp, BA
Mrs A Steven, BSc
Miss R L Tomlinson, BA
Mrs C A Walklin, DipEd
L H Ware, BSc (*†Browne House*)
C West-Sadler, MA
G J Whitehouse, BEd
D F Williams, CertEd
Mrs C A Wray, BA

SES Music Department:
G E Turner, BA (*Director of Music*)
D McIlrae, BMus, HED (*Assistant Director of Music*)
S Chandley, CT ABRSM (*Head of Brass*)
D Leetch, MA, GRSM, LRAM (*Head of Strings*)
Mrs J E Roberts, GRSM, LRM, ARCM
N S Taylor, BA

Visiting Music Staff:
S Andrews (*Kit Drum/Percussion*)
F Applewhite (*Violin, Viola*)
J Aughton (*Flute*)
S Barber (*Organ*)
C Bell, BSc, LRAM, ARCM (*Guitar*)
Mrs M Bennett, LRAM, LTCL (*Singing*)
Mrs S Bond, GLCM, LLCM TD, FLCM (*Singing*)
Mrs K Bentley, GTCL, LTCL (*Cello, Double Bass*)
F Black (*Singing*)
G Brown, BMus (*Oboe, Pianoforte*)
Mrs H Brown, BA (*Clarinet*)
P J Casson (*Saxophone, Clarinet*)
Revd Mrs J Dumat, ARCM (*Clarinet*)
Mrs J Dustan (*Flute*)
J Furrow (*Classical Guitar*)
M Duthie, BSc, ARCO (*Organ*)
N Gray (*Electric Guitar*)
Mrs E Hanlon, ARMCM (*Pianoforte*)
Mrs J Lamb (*Pianoforte, Accordion/Keyboards*)
Mrs S Latham (*Violin, Viola*)
Mrs C Lee, LRAM (*Violin*)
Miss F Maclennan (*Pianoforte*)
Mrs M Maclennan, LRAM, ARCM (*Pianoforte*)
Mrs A McCrae (*Bassoon, Pianoforte*)
Mrs E Murphy, GTCL, LTLL, PGCE (*Violin, Pianoforte*)
D Price, LRAM (*Brass*)
Mrs G Spencer, CertEd, ACRM (*Pianoforte*)
Mrs A Sumner, CertEd, ARCM (*Pianoforte*)
Mrs E A Taylor, BA (*Violin, Viola*)
Mrs L Williamson, LTCC (*Pianoforte*)

Medical Officer: C S Mann, MBChB, BSc

Introduction. Stamford School is one of three schools within the overall Stamford Endowed Schools Educational Charity, along with Stamford High School (girls) and Stamford Junior School, the co-educational junior school.

Buildings and Grounds. Stamford School dates its foundation to 1532. The grounds include the site of the Hall occupied by secessionists from Brasenose Hall, Oxford, in the early 14th century. The oldest surviving building is the School Chapel, which was formerly part of St Paul's Church, but which from 1548 until restoration in 1929 was used as a schoolroom. Extensive additions to the School continued to be made throughout the nineteenth and twentieth centuries. In 1956 the Old Stamfordians gave the School a swimming

pool as a war memorial. The science school was built in 1957 and extended in 1973 when a new dining hall and kitchens also came into use. These were subsequently completely redesigned and upgraded in 2003. A music school was built in 1977 and extended in 1984. A further extensive development programme was begun in 1980 and included the building of one new senior boarding house (Browne), opened in 1981, and extensive and comparable provision in the other (Byard). Development works in 2009 saw the creation of a new Research and Learning Centre in the School House building, providing a library, study space and additional IT facilities. The Sixth Form Common Room is now located in a newly-renovated section of Brazenose House, containing quiet study areas, IT and recreation facilities. A glass atrium linking School House and the Hall has been erected, providing a new focal point for the School in a unique architectural style. The Science rooms were also upgraded. Work has begun on a new Sports Centre, including a 25m indoor swimming pool, which will be completed in late 2011. The old gymnasium will then be renovated to become the Performing Arts Centre.

School Structure and Curriculum. The school consists of around 680 boys divided into Lower School (11–14), Middle School (14–16) and Sixth Form. The Heads of each section, with their assistants and Form Tutors monitor the academic progress of each boy and manage the pastoral arrangements.

The National Curriculum is broadly followed but much more is added to the curriculum to make it stimulating and rewarding. Information Technology, Art & Design and Design Technology form an integral part of the curriculum and from Year 8 boys may begin German, Spanish or Russian. All boys are prepared for a complete range of GCSE examination; the great majority of them continue into the Sixth Form and then onto higher education.

In the Sixth Form of about 190 boys (and 190 girls) the timetable is so arranged that a wide range of combinations of subjects is possible. In partnership with Stamford High School all Sixth Form students can choose from the full range of 27 subjects available across the two schools.

Activities. Art, Music, Drama, Games and Physical Education form part of the normal curriculum. There is a choral society, an orchestra, a band and a jazz band, and a chapel choir. The musical activities of the school are combined with those of the High School under the overall responsibility of the Director of Music for the Endowed Schools. The school maintains RN, Army and RAF sections of the CCF and there is a rifle club. A large number of boys are engaged at all levels of the Duke of Edinburgh's Award Scheme.

The school plays rugby, football, hockey, cricket, tennis, golf. The athletics and swimming sports and matches are held in the summer term. In winter there is also badminton, cross-country running and basketball. Four squash courts were built in 1973. A full-sized astroturf hockey pitch suitable for most sports was opened in 1983 to which floodlights were added in 2006 and a new sports hall in 1985. There are many school clubs and societies and a thriving weekend activity programme.

Close links are maintained with the local community. The school welcomes performances in the hall by the music societies of the town and uses the excellent local theatre in Stamford Arts Centre for some of its plays.

Careers. The school is a member of ISCO and has a team of careers staff. There is an extensive new careers library, computer room and interview rooms.

House Structure. Boarding: Byard House (11–15) Mr A N Pike; Browne House (15–18) Mr L H Ware.

Weekly and three-night boarding are available, as well as full boarding.

Competition in games, music and other activities are organised within a house system. Housemasters with their assistants monitor boys' commitments to the wider curriculum and act as counsellors when boys need to turn to someone outside the formal pastoral and disciplinary system.

Admission. Registration Fee £50; Acceptance Fee £250.

The main point of entry is at age 11, but boys are considered at any age. A number join at age 13 or directly into the sixth form. Application forms for admission may be obtained from the school office. The school's entrance examinations take place in late January, but arrangements may be made to test applicants at other times. Entry into the sixth form is considered at any time. Boys who enter through the Stamford Junior School progress automatically on to Stamford School at age 11 without having to take further entrance tests.

Fees per term (2011-2012). Day £4,084; Full Boarding £7,452; Weekly Boarding £6,496; 3 Night Boarding £5,644.

These fees include stationery, textbooks and games. School lunches for day boys are at additional charge.

Scholarships. (*See Scholarship Entries section.*) Governors' Scholarships at 11+ and for the Sixth Form. Awards are given for musical ability and art. Bursaries up to full fees are available.

Charitable status. As part of the Stamford Endowed Schools, Stamford School is a Registered Charity, number 527618. It exists to provide education for boys.

Stewart's Melville College

Queensferry Road, Edinburgh EH4 3EZ
Tel: 0131 311 1000
Fax: 0131 311 1099
e-mail: secretary@esmgc.com
website: www.esms.edin.sch.uk

Governing Council:
Chairman: Mrs Judy Wagner

Clerk to the Governors: Mr D Wright, LLB

Principal: Mr J N D Gray, BA

Bursar: Mr J B Molloy, MA Hons

Deputy Headmaster: Mr N G Clark, MA
Director of Studies: Mr G Johnston, MPhys
Head of Upper School: Mr M R Kane, MA
Director of Sixth Form: Dr I Scott, MA, PhD, FRSA
Assistant Head Teacher, Regent: Mrs M Elswood, BA, Dip TESL
Assistant Head Teacher, Guidance: Mr G J Brown, BEd
Registrar: Mr P G Waine, CertEd, BEd
Director of Administration: Mr H I McKerrow, BSc
Director of Technology: Dr K Hussain

* *Head of Department*
† *Head of House*

Art:
*Mr M Crichton, BA
Mr C A Nasmyth, BA

Biology:
*Mr D Lloyd, BSc, MEd
Mrs L A Lim, BSc
Mr R D Miller, BSc, CBiol, MIBiol
Mr S W Primrose, BSc

Chemistry:
*Mr P Johnson, BSc
Mr C P Kerr, BSc
Mr G Mitchell, BSc

Classics:
*Mr I Crosbie, MA
Mr M T Garden, BA

Computer Studies:
*Mr A Thomson, BA

Design & Technology:
*Mrs L Burt, BSc, FRSA
Mr S Longair, BEd Des Tech
Mr A Scott, BEng (*†Kintyre*)

Drama:
*Miss A Marshall, BA

Economics:
*Ms S Burns, MA
Mr R Alexander, BA

English:
*Mr David Higgins, BA, MA

Mr J C Allan, BA (*†Appin*)
Mrs G Bakewell, MA
Mrs M Bryce, MA
Mr N G Clark, MA
Mrs S Frost, BA, MPhil
Mr S Hart, MA
Mr M R Kane, MA
Mr I A Major, BA

Geography:
*Mr K Turnbull, MA
Mr D Foulds, BSc, LLB
Mr J Hunter, MA
Mr M S Kemp, MA (*†Torridon*)

History:
*Mr M Longmuir, BA, CAM
Mrs J D Bennett, MA (*†Ettrick*)
Mr C D Currie, MA
Mrs A J Ferguson, MA
Mrs L McDiarmid, BA

Mathematics:
*Mr A J T Dunsmore, BEng, MSc
Mr S Ashforth, MA, DipCT
Mr R I Canter, BSc, HDE
Dr G Henderson, BA, BSc
Mr G Johnston, MPhys
Mr S Love, BA, MA, CEng, MBCS
Mr J J Robertson, BSc (*†Galloway*)
Mr G Smith, BSc

Media Studies:
*Mr D A Orem, MA, MPhil, Cert Media Ed, DipEd

Modern Languages:
*Mr M Z Hamid, MA
*Mrs C R Siljehag, MA
Miss N Bellington, MA
Mrs V Chittleburgh, BA, MA
Mr N A C Connet, MA
Mr M Constable, BA
Mrs M Elswood, BA, Dip TESL
Mr A J Hyslop, MA

Mrs V Longbottom
Mr J F Marsh, BA
Mrs I Richardson, MA

Music:
*Mr J Orringe, BA Hons, MA
Mr A J Samson, Dip RSAMD
Mr J Skuse, BA Hons, PGCE

Physical Education:
*Mr C S Spence, BEd
Mr G J Brown, BEd
Mr M R Burgess, BA Ed
Mr R Deans, BSc
Mr J Hunter, MA
Mr H Lingard, BSpLS
Mr B G Lockie, BEd
Mr J Moran, BA, BEd
Mr P G M Waine, CertEd, BEd

Physics:
*Miss J Macdonald, BSc
Mr J Balfour, BSc
Mr B W J Dunlop, BSc
Mr S D Jackson, MSc, BSc, BEd

Product Design:
*Mrs L Burt, BSc, FRSA
Mr S Longair, BEd Des Tech
Mr A Scott, BEng (*†Kintyre*)

Religious, Moral and Philosophical Studies:
*Mr G F W Park, BD
Miss L E Foster, MA
Mr G Innes, BD (*†Lochaber*)

Support for Learning:
*Mrs C G C Maxwell, BA
Miss R Meredith, BSc, PGDip
Mrs M Nimmo, BEd

Educational Psychologist:
Mrs M Brown, MA, DipEdPsyc

Junior School:
Head Master: Mr B D Lewis, BA Hons, H DipEd Hons
Deputy Head (*Primary 4–7*): Mrs G Lyon, DCE, DipRSA
Deputy Head (*Early Education*): Mrs M Rycroft, DipCE
Assistant Head (*Primary 4–7*): Mr D McLeish, DCE
Assistant Head (*Primary 4–7*): Miss S Mackay, ALCM, LLCM, BMus Hons, PGCE
Assistant Head (*Early Education*): Ms C Macpherson, BEd

'Daniel Stewart's Hospital' was founded (1855) by Daniel Stewart and has been administered since its inception by the Company of Merchants of the City of Edinburgh. Melville College, formerly The Edinburgh Institution, was founded in 1832 by the Reverend Robert Cunningham. The two schools combined in 1972 to form Daniel Stewart's and Melville College (now Stewart's Melville College). Since 1989 management of the School has been delegated by the Merchant Company Education Board to the Erskine Stewart's Melville Governing Council.

The School enjoys a commanding position on Queensferry Road, a mile from the City Centre. The original College building is occupied by the Senior School while the Junior School is in a modern building. There are a number of excellent facilities including a Sixth Form Centre, Games Hall, Swimming Pool and The Tom Fleming Centre for Performing Arts.

Since 1978 the school has been twinned with The Mary Erskine School (*see entry in GSA section*). This includes a fully co-educational Junior School for children between the ages of 3 and 11, single-sex but very closely twinned secondary schools between the ages of 12 and 17 and a fully co-educational pre-university Sixth Form which provides the ideal bridge between school and university. Boys and Girls from Stewart's Melville College and The Mary Erskine School come together in the Combined Cadet Force, in orchestras, choirs, drama and musicals and in numerous outdoor education projects.

The Senior School (744 boys). S1 and S2 follow a broad curriculum, whereby boys are equipped to pursue all routes to Intermediate 2. In S3 boys commence eight courses, including English, mathematics, at least one modern language, at least one science, and a social or creative subject. In S5 boys are expected to take 5 subjects at Higher level. A majority will continue their studies for a Sixth Year, usually three Advanced Highers to provide a firm foundation for degree courses in Scotland and England. Most boys proceed to such courses.

The School has a sophisticated system of guidance. Boys in the first year are with a Form Tutor, under the overall direction of an Assistant Head Teacher. The next four years are spent in Houses of approximately 90 boys, each with its own Head of House and House Tutors. The Sixth Form is a co-educational year, as the girls from The Mary Erskine School join with the boys of Stewart's Melville College in a completely 'twinned' Sixth Form. There is a well-established Careers department. The Support for Learning Department helps boys with specific learning difficulties.

Games. Rugby and Cricket are played on the school playing fields at Inverleith, while Hockey and Tennis are played at Ravelston. There are also opportunities for Athletics, Curling, Golf, Swimming, Squash, Sailing and Shooting as well as the many sports played in the Games Hall. Boys from the school are frequently selected for national teams in many sports.

Music is much-valued and flourishes within the school. Approximately 500 instrumental lessons are given each week by an enthusiastic staff of 25 visiting teachers. Most orchestral activity is combined with The Mary Erskine School, including junior and senior orchestras, two concert bands, a jazz band and numerous chamber groups. Choral singing is also very strong, from large junior choirs to more specialised groups for madrigals and close harmony. A full programme of public performances includes two major musicals every year and large choral and orchestral concerts in which our musicians combine with an active parents' choir.

Activities. The School encourages boys to take part in The Combined Cadet Force which comprises Army and RAF sections or in The Duke of Edinburgh's Award Scheme. Each week the School offers approximately 70 clubs and societies to suit the appetites of all boys. In sport the school has particular strengths in rugby, swimming, sailing, basketball, hockey, athletics and skiing with representation at district or national level.

Boarding. Dean Park House, adjoining the school grounds, serves as the Boarding House for up to 25 boys. They share dining and recreational facilities with The Mary Erskine boarders next door in Erskine House.

Fees per term (2011-2012). Day: Primary Start to Primary 7 £2,141–£2,578 (lunches included for Primary 2–7); Secondary £3,032 (plus £154 for optional lunches). Boarding (including tuition and laundry): Primary 4–7 £5,410–£5,475; Secondary £6,083.

Scholarships and Bursaries. Means-tested Bursaries worth up to 100% of the tuition fee may be available to parents of children entering any year group in the Senior Schools and at P7 in the Junior School. Academic scholarships worth £250 annually are offered to boys applying to enter S1, following a competitive selection process. These are known as Merchant Company Scholarships. The top scholarship holder at Stewart's Melville College receives the Cunningham Scholarship, worth £1,000 annually. Scholarships are paid to the pupil and are held in trust by the school until completion of their Sixth Form year. Music Scholarships of £250 per annum are offered from S3.

Junior School. In The Mary Erskine and Stewart's Melville Junior School (1,226 pupils), girls and boys are educated together from age 3 to 11. Children in Primary Start to Primary 3 are based on the Mary Erskine School site at Ravelston, while boys and girls in Primary 4–7 are taught on the Stewart's Melville College site. Normal entry points are Primary Start (age 3 or 4), Primary 1, Primary 4, Primary 6 and Primary 7. The school is remarkable for the breadth of its educational programme and the quality of its sporting and cultural activities, in particular the professional standards attained in Music and Drama.

Daniel Stewart's & Melville College Former Pupils' Club. *Sec:* Bobby Clark, Tel: 0131 552 2331.

Charitable status. The Merchant Company Education Board is a Registered Charity, number SC009747. It is a leading charitable School in the field of Junior and Secondary education.

Stockport Grammar School

Buxton Road, Stockport, Cheshire SK2 7AF
Tel: 0161 456 9000 Senior School
          0161 419 2405 Junior School
Fax: 0161 419 2407
e-mail: sgs@stockportgrammar.co.uk
website: www.stockportgrammar.co.uk

Founded in 1487, Stockport Grammar School is one of England's oldest schools. The founder, Sir Edmond Shaa, was a goldsmith, 200th Lord Mayor of London and Court Jeweller to three Kings of England. The School's rich history and traditions are celebrated in the annual Founder's Day Service in Stockport.

A co-educational day school, Stockport Grammar School is non-denominational and welcomes pupils from all faiths and cultures. Almost all leavers go on into Higher Education, including many to Oxbridge. Although academic performance is formidable, it is not the be-all and end-all of life at Stockport Grammar School.

Motto: '*Vincit qui patitur*'

Patron: The Prime Warden of the Worshipful Company of Goldsmiths

Governing Body:

R L E Rimmington, BA, FCA (*Chairman*)
R H Astles (*Vice-Chairman*)
P A Cuddy, BA (*Vice-Chairman*)
Lady Beatson, MA
F A Booth, FCA
Miss S E Carroll, BA
Professor J Dainton, MA, DPhil
P H Davies, LLB (*Ephraim Hallam Educational Foundation*)
P L Giblin, MA, MEd (*Teaching Staff*)
K Lansdale, MRICS
P H Locke, BVSc, MRCVS
Dr E M Morris, MBChB, DCH
J J Mott (*Old Stopfordians' Association*)

S Nuttall, BSc, PhD, FRSA
Dr R Shah, MBE, DL, JP, BSc, PhD
R P Yates, FIMI

Clerk to the Governors and Bursar: C J Watson, MA

Headmaster: A H Chicken, BA, MEd, FRSA

Deputy Headmaster/Proctor: J P Ashcroft, BSc, MA
Deputy Headmistress/Director of Studies: Miss V L
  Barrett, MA
Head of Lower School: R W Wallington, BSc
Head of Middle School: Mrs H K Bridges, BSc, MIBiol
Head of Sixth Form: Mrs J White, BA
Senior Tutor: D W Howson, MA

Assistant Masters and Mistresses:
* *Head of Department*

Art:
Mrs C A Beckett, Dip AD
*R A Davies, BA, MA
Miss R J Upton, BA

Biology:
Mrs H K Bridges, BSc
Miss J Gilbert, BA, PhD
*P J Grant, BSc
J R Metivier, BSc, PhD
Miss L J Service, BSc
Mrs J White, BA
Mrs M Whitton, BSc
Mrs L J Withers, BA

Chemistry:
*Ms A L Abbott, MChem,
  PhD
K Airey, BSc, PhD
R D Heyes, BSc
Miss R F Hindley, MChem
W Krywonos, BSc, MSc,
  PhD
Mrs L Pitts, BSc, PhD

Classics:
J P Ashcroft, BSc, MA
J P Bird, BA
*A C Thorley, BA
P A Urwin, BA
Mrs E Zanda, BA, PhD

Drama:
Mrs A K Moffatt, BA

Economics:
*R Parker, MA
R Young, BEd

English:
Miss V L Barrett, BA
*Mrs G A Cope, BA
Miss S L Ginty, BA
D W Howson, MA
Mrs R G Johnson, BA, MA
Mrs H J Jones, BA
Ms H R Lawson, MA
B J Masters, BA, MA
Miss E E Spence, BA

French:
Mrs S L Belshaw, BA
Mrs B Garnier, MSc
*Miss S M Gibson, BA
D Lorentz, BA, MA, DEA
J D Wilson, BA

Geography:
Miss S Banning, BA
Mrs A C Hicks, BA, FRGS
*R Howarth, BA

D S Martin, MA, FRGS
Mrs K Palfreyman, BA

German:
Mrs T Kampelmann, MA,
  PhD
Mrs L M Morgan, BA
*Mrs C S Muscutt, BA

History:
Mrs H R Ashton, BA
Mrs K J Chesterton, BA,
  MA
S A Moore, BA
J P Russell, BA, MA
*S J D Smith, BA, PhD
Mrs A M Wilson, DipEd

Information Technology:
N S Clarke, BA
*M J Flaherty, BSc
Mrs P W Hodkinson, BSc

Life Studies:
Mrs C M Bartlett, MBA
*A G Ehegartner

Mathematics:
A B Cheslett, BSc, MSc
Miss R Darch, BSc
Mrs M Evans, BA
M Hamilton, MSc, PhD
*Mrs D L Harris, BSc
Miss M E Higgins, BSc
Mrs L Lammas, BA
Mrs A S Larkin, BSc
Mrs C L Marshall, BSc,
  MSc
R W Wallington, BSc

Music:
*M G Dow, MA, ALCM
Mrs E N Short, MA, LLCM
Mrs E Taylor, BMus

Philosophy/RS:
P P Elliott, BA
*Mrs K E Farrington, BA

Physics:
Mrs Z Dawson, MSc
M Ellis, BSc, DPhil
*Mrs H M Fenton, BSc
Mrs C M Hird, BSc
I Killey, BSc, BEng
Mrs G M Lockwood, MA

Physical Education:
R Bowden, BA
E H Corbett, BA
Mrs A Jones, BEd

A S Hanson, BEd
Mrs J Maskery, BEd
Mrs K Wilkinson, BA
Miss S Withington, BEd
*C J Wright, BA

Psychology:
*Mrs S J Braude, BA
N I Browne, MA

Spanish:
Miss K A M Psaila, BA
Mrs K Christmann, MA

Technology:
Mrs R E Groves, BA
Mrs T H Samways, BSc
Mrs H Tadman, BEng
Mrs Z A Vernon, BEd
G M Whitby, BSc
*N Young, MA

Learning Support:
Mrs J M Farmer, BSc
Mrs D H Meers, BA, MEd

School Chaplain: Revd L E Leaver, MA, BTh
Director of Music: M G Dow, BA, MA
Director of External Relations: Mrs R M Horsford, BA
Librarian: Ms J Pazos Galindo, BA, MA
Headmaster's Secretary and Admissions: Mrs J E Baker
School Nurse: Mrs P Ward, RGN, DipHE

Junior School

Headmaster: L Fairclough, BA
Deputy Head: S P Milnes, BA
Director of Studies: Mrs K Horrocks

Assistant Masters and Mistresses:
Mrs H Carroll, BEd
Mrs R Cole, BA
Mrs S Coombes, BSc
Mrs C Hampson, BA
Mrs L Hardy, BEd
Miss J Haslam, BEd
Mrs N Hurst, BEd
Mr M Johnson, BSc
D Makinson
Mrs J Mercer, BA
Mrs C M Nichols, BEd

Miss R Penhale, BA
Mrs K Roberts, BEd, MA
Mrs R Scott, BA
Mrs H Shanks
Mrs C Smith, BA
Mrs A Sullivan, BEd
Mrs J Swales, BA
A Taylor, BSc
Mrs H Tunney, BEd
Mrs L Turner, BEd

Headmaster's Secretary: Mrs B Cheyne

Stockport Grammar School aims to provide the best all round education to enable pupils to fulfil their potential in a friendly and supportive atmosphere. The backbone of the school is academic excellence, with a clear framework of discipline within which every activity is pursued to the highest level. Entry is at 3, 4, 7, 11 and 16, but vacancies may occur at other stages. There are over 1,400 pupils aged 3–18 years, with 350+ in the Junior School and over 250 in the Sixth Form.

The Senior School. Admission at age 11 is by competitive entrance examination. This is held in late January or early February, for admission in the following September. There are several open events: see website for details. Occasional vacancies are considered on an individual basis and a few places are available in the Sixth Form each year. Visitors are always welcome to make an appointment to see the school.

Curriculum. The emphasis is on how to learn. The GCSE philosophies are introduced in the first three years as part of a broad general education. The sciences are taught as separate subjects and all pupils study Latin, French and German.

On entering the fourth year, at the age of 14, pupils retain a core of subjects but also make choices, so that individual aptitudes can be fully developed. GCSE examinations are taken in the fifth year; the percentage pass rate has not been less than 97%. In 2009, 67.7% of entries gained an A* or A. On entering the Sixth Form, pupils take four AS Level courses. The pass rate at Advanced Level was 100% in 2009, with 82% of all entries gaining the top two grades.

Art. A high standard is set and achieved. There are facilities for all aspects of two-dimensional work and textiles, plus a fully equipped ceramics area and a sculpture court. There are regular exhibitions in the School's Brooke Gallery.

Music. The curriculum provides a well-structured musical education for all pupils for the first three years. GCSE and Advanced Level are offered for those who aspire to a musical career as well as for proficient amateurs. Three main areas of musical ensemble – choirs, orchestras and wind bands – are at the centre of activities with opportunities open from First Year to Sixth Form. Emphasis is on determination, commitment and a sense of team work. All ensembles are encouraged to reach the highest standards.

Drama. A particularly strong tradition has been fostered over many years and regular productions involve all year groups. Drama is part of the English curriculum in the first three years and there are drama clubs, trips to local theatre groups and workshops in school.

Physical Education. The Physical Education curriculum is diverse, with activities including aerobics, ball skills, badminton, basketball, dance, gymnastics, health-related fitness, squash, swimming and volleyball. The main winter games for boys are rugby and football, and for the girls hockey and netball. In the summer, boys concentrate on cricket and athletics, whilst the girls focus their attention on tennis, athletics and rounders. Up to 400 pupils represent the school at Saturday fixtures and the teams have an excellent reputation, gaining success in regional and national competitions. Almost fifty pupils have represented their country, region or county in the last year.

Information Technology. Three dedicated Computer Suites accommodate full classes, each pupil having access to a Pentium PC on the school's site-wide network. All pupils have their own password and email address, and are able to use the Internet for research. The rooms are available to everyone as a computer resource at lunchtimes and after school. Information Technology skills are taught as part of the curriculum and academic departments incorporate the use of computers and interactive whiteboards into their everyday lessons. The subject is not currently studied for public examination.

Houses. Every pupil is a member of one of the four Houses, each led by two Heads of House staff assisted by a team of senior pupils. The Houses organise and compete in a wide range of sporting and non-sporting activities.

Clubs and Societies. The School has many active clubs and societies covering a wide variety of extra-curricular interests, for example, debating, where Fifth and Sixth Formers have the opportunity to participate in up to four Model United Nations Assemblies around the world each year.

Development. The new Library and Learning Resource Centre and Physics Department were completed in summer 2005. A Nursery for children aged 3+ opened in September 2006.

Visits. Well-established language exchange visits are made every year to France and Germany, in addition to hill walking, camping, mountaineering, skiing, sailing and cultural trips.

Assembly. Formal morning assemblies are held daily for all pupils; there are separate Jewish and Muslim assemblies. House assemblies, which include Junior School pupils, are on Wednesdays; the Sixth Form have an additional fortnightly assembly.

Pastoral Care. Form teachers get to know each pupil in the form individually, and are supported by Year Heads and by the Head of Lower School (years 1 to 3), the Head of Middle School (years 4 and 5) and the Head of Sixth Form.

Discipline. This is positive and enabling. Much importance is attached to appearance and to uniform, which is worn throughout the school.

Fees per term (2011-2012). Senior School £3,090; Junior School £2,382.

Bursary Scheme. The School's own Bursary Scheme aims to provide financial assistance on a means-tested basis to families who have chosen a Stockport Grammar School education for their children. Details available from the Bursar.

Stockport Grammar Junior School. (*See also entry in IAPS section.*) With its own Headmaster and Staff it has separate buildings and a playing field on the same site. The Junior School has boys and girls between the ages of 3 and 11 years.

Boys and girls join the Nursery when they are three. In its own building and with a designated play area, the Nursery is very well resourced. The children are looked after by qualified and experienced staff.

Entrance is by observed play at the age of 4 years into two Reception forms, and by assessment in February for an additional form at the age of 7. All pupils are prepared for the Entrance Examination to the Senior School at the age of 11.

The Junior School buildings provide special facilities for Art, Technology, Music and Computing. The winter games are soccer, hockey and netball, with cricket and rounders being played in the summer. There are swimming lessons every week; other activities include the gym club, life saving, athletics and chess. There are clubs running each lunchtime and after school for both infants and juniors. Matches are played every Saturday against other schools in the major sports. Many pupils have instrumental music lessons and there is an orchestra, band, recorder group and a choir. The musical, held in May each year, is a very popular event in which all pupils participate. Visits are made annually to Paris at Easter and to the Lake District in May. Short annual residential visits, are introduced from age 7.

Charitable status. Stockport Grammar School is a Registered Charity, number 1120199. It exists to advance education by the provision and conduct, in or near Stockport, of a school for boys and girls.

Stonyhurst College

Stonyhurst, Clitheroe, Lancashire BB7 9PZ
Tel: 01254 826345; 01254 827093 (Admissions)
Fax: 01254 827135 (Admissions)
e-mail: admissions@stonyhurst.ac.uk
website: www.stonyhurst.ac.uk

Stonyhurst College is a co-educational Catholic boarding and day school. We are a Jesuit school, which means that we attach particular importance to emotional and spiritual development as well as academic excellence. Founded in 1593, it stands in its own estate of 2,500 acres in the beautiful Ribble Valley on the slope of Longridge Fell, ten miles from the M6 motorway, and just over 1 hour by car from Manchester International Airport. We are 2 hours away from London by train.

The College houses a remarkable collection of items relating to the history of the Church in England. These are used as a learning resource. The College has a full-time curator.

Motto: '*Quant je puis*'

Governors:
President: Very Revd M Holman, SJ

Chairman: Mr J Cowdall
Deputy Chairman: Mr M J Prior, JP, FCA

Miss B Banks	Mr T O Mayhew
Mr M J Belderbos	Mr G J Lagerberg
Mr M I Davis	Fr K McMillan, SJ
Mr W P Boylan	Mrs K Mills
Fr A Howell, SJ	Fr M Power, SJ
Sr M Walmsley, CJ	Mr R Brumby
Mr A C F Verity	Lord D Alton

Headmaster: **Mr A R Johnson**, BA

Father Superior: Fr A Howell, SJ

College Chaplain: Fr J Twist, SJ

Deputy Headmaster: Mr A S Gordon-Brown, BCom Hons, MSc

Deputy Head Pastoral: Mr J D Hopkins, BA

Director of Studies: Mrs H Harris, BSc, MA

Head of Higher Line: Mrs L North, BA

Assistant Staff:
Mr E Allanson, BA (*Religious Studies*)
Mr S Andrews, BSc, MA (*Chemistry*)
Mr P R Ansell, BA (*Head of Modern Languages*)
Ms D Atherton, BSc (*Graduate Assistant*)
Major A Barber (*OC CCF*)
Mr A J Callinicos, BA, MA (*Poetry-Year 12-Playroom Master; Classics*)
Dr A Chadwick, BSc, PhD (*Chemistry; Science*)
Mr S J Charles, MSc, BA (*Head of Games & PE*)
Mrs R Crossley, BA (*Head of Geography*)
Mr I Cunliffe, BSc, MBA (*Biology; Chemistry*)
Mrs H C Davies, BEd (*Head of Special Educational Needs*)
Mrs A Deane, BA (*Lower Line Girls' Housemistress; Spanish*)
Mr D A Eachus, BTech (*Grammar-Year 10-Playroom Master; Head of Design & Technology*)
Mrs J Eachus (*Non-Teaching Assistant, Registration*)
Miss J R Egar, BA (*Head of Drama and Theatre Studies*)
Mrs E Ellis, MA (*English*)
Miss L Ellis (*Graduate Assistant*)
Dr P Ellis, MA, Phd (*Head of English*)
Mrs L Fisher, BSc (*Head of Science; Head of Physics*)
Mrs H L Flatley, BSc, MSc (*Biology*)
Miss M Gadsden, BA (*Assistant Director of Music*)
Mrs A Goodall, BA (*Higher Line Girls' Housemistress; Head of PSHE*)
Mrs J Graffius, MA (*Curator*)
Dr D Hallam, BDS, BSc, DMS (*Biology; Chemistry*)
Mrs H Harris, BSc, MA (*Head of Geography*)
Mr M Heaven (*Design & Technology*)
Mrs M de Hickford (*Spanish*)
Mr B Hodgson (*Syntax-Year 11 Playroom Master, Chemistry*)
Mr P E Hodkinson, BSc, MSc (*Mathematics*)
Mr G Hunter, BSc (*Physics and Lower Grammar-Year 9 Playroom Master*)
Mrs N Jones, BA, RAD, TCert, AISTD, MB, NB, BB, NBS dip (*Dance*)
Mrs A Jackson (*French, Italian*)
Mr H M Kaaber, BSc (*Head of Physical Education*)
Ms E Kay (*Head of Girls' Games*)
Mr J Ketchell, MA (*Mathematics*)
Mrs D J Kirkby, BSc (*Economics; Business Studies; Head of Enterprise*)
Mr D N Knight, BA (*Archivist*)
Miss M Lane, BA (*Religious Studies*)
Mr P Lea, BA, MSc (*Director of ICT*)
Mrs Y Luker, BEd (*Physical Education*)
Mr D G Mann, BA (*Director of Music*)
Mrs C M Markarian, BSc, MSc (*Senior Teacher; Mathematics*)
Mrs K Marshall, BA (*Head of Art*)
Mrs P Massey, BA (*English Literature; Latin*)
Miss H Mercer, BA (*Hispanic Studies*)
Mr S McGinnis, BSc (*Graduate Assistant, Boarding Activities Coordinator*)
Miss K Mitchell, BA (*English as an Additional Language*)
Mr J Middlebrook, BA, MSc (*Head of Chemistry*)
Dr K Morgan, BA, FRCO, LRAM, LTCL (*College Organist, Head of Keyboard and Master in charge of Music Scholars*)
Mr D Morley, BA (*German*)

Mrs L Morris, BSocSc (*Learning Mentor*)
Mr B J P O'Connor, BSc (*Physics*)
Mr F J O'Reilly, MA, CertObsAst (*Classics; Astronomy*)
Mrs G P Parkinson, BA (*Modern Languages*)
Miss J M Parkinson, MPhil, MA, BA (*Head of Classics*)
Mr D N Rawkins, BSc (*Head of Mathematics; Prefect of Studies*)
Mr D C Ridout, BA (*Head of Politics*)
Mr A Roberts, BA (*Modern Languages*)
Mrs J Robinson, BEd (*Art*)
Mr G Shaw, BSc(*Biology; Science*)
Mr D J Soars, MA (*Theology; Religious Studies*)
Mr J M B Sharples, BA (*Modern Languages*)
Mr J Smith, BA (*English*)
Mr T Strain, BEd (*Rhetoric-Year 13-Playroom Master; Economics & Business Studies*)
Mr G Thomas (*Games*)
Mrs L W Timmins, BA (*Head of Economics*)
Mr M J Turner, MA (*Head of History; Religious Studies*)
Mr T J Warner, BSc, PhD (*Head of Biology*)
Mr P A Warrilow, BD (*Head of Religious Studies*)
Mr S Waterhouse, BSc (*ICT*)
Mrs V Watson, BEd (*Girls'Games*)
Mrs E Whalley, BSc (*Geography*)
Mrs I M Williams, BEd (*Geography*)
Mrs J Wood, BA (*Higher Line Boarding Mistress*)
Mrs K Wright, BA (*Head of Business Studies*)
Mr R Youlten, MSc, MEng (*Mathematics*)
Miss S Young, BA, MA (*Lay Chaplain*)

Visiting Music Staff:
Mrs K Riddle (*Piano*)
Mr G Banks, BA (*Brass*)
Mrs J Barlow (*Clarinet*)
Mr D Hessian (*Saxophone*)
Miss A Cooper (*Oboe, Bassoon*)
Mr P Greenhalgh, BMus, ARCM, ALCM (*Piano*)
Mrs J Howarth (*Singing*)
Mrs E Hudson (*Harp*)
Mr J Lamburn (*Cello*)
Mr D Lewis (*Percussion*)
Mr G Lister (*Drum Kit*)
Mrs C Lorriman (*Flute*)
Mr C Marks (*Guitar*)
Mrs J Moon, BA, ALCM (*Singing*)
Miss M Molin-Rose (*Harp*)
Mr K Parry (*Guitar*)
Ms F Prince (*Singing*)
Mrs M Rigby, GRSM, ARMCM (*Violin*)
Ms L Shaw, BEd (*Violin/Viola*)
Miss S Wagner (*Singing*)
Mr R Waldock, GMus (*Double Bass*)
Mrs S White (*Head of Strings*)
Mrs S Buttler (*Piano*)

Bursar: Mr J Ridley, BA, MA, FCMA
Development Director: Mrs R Hindle
Director of Marketing and Communications: Mrs K Walker, BSc, MA
Registrar: Mrs L Carr
Careers Coordinator: Mrs C Anderton
Domestic Bursar: Miss F V Ahearne
Headmaster's PA: Mrs R Taylor

College Doctors:
Dr J Saunders, MBChB, MRCGP, DRCOG, DSM SA
Dr S Owen, MBChB, BA Hons, MRCGP, DRCOG, DFFP

Senior Nurse: Mrs N Fogden, RGN
Assistant Nurses:
Mrs A Bell, RGN, RSCN, DipFN, DN
Mr N Riley, RGN
Mrs J Warburton, RGN

Stonyhurst St Mary's Hall
Stonyhurst Preparatory School (Boys and Girls 3–13)

(see entry in IAPS section)

Headmaster: Mr L A Crouch, BA, MA, PGCE
Chaplain: Revd Fr A Howell, SJ

Aims. The School curriculum is intended to reflect the ideals of the founder of the Jesuits, St Ignatius Loyola: the importance of trying to find God in all things; the development to the full of each individual's talents whatever his or her gifts; the need for thoroughness and breadth in learning, helping pupils to think for themselves and to communicate well; above all an awareness of the needs of others. We aspire for our pupils to be men and women of competence, conscience and compassion.

Religion. The College is Roman Catholic and strives to educate its pupils in the principles and practice of their Faith. Christians of other denominations are welcomed and encouraged to be active in the school's worship and spiritual life.

Organisation. There are 470 pupils in the College, with 280 in the adjacent preparatory school, Stonyhurst St Mary's Hall, which admits boys and girls from 3 to 13 *(see Stonyhurst St Mary's Hall entry in IAPS section)*. There are 170 day pupils. The school is fully co-educational from 13 to 18. The pastoral care is based on 5 year groups called 'Playrooms' each of which is in the care of married Playroom staff assisted by others including a Jesuit priest acting as Chaplain and a Lay Chaplain. The younger girls are in the care of a resident Housemistress, and occupy their own designated area of the College. A resident Housemistress takes particular responsibility for the boarding and day girls in the Sixth Form. The Health Centre is self contained but within the main building; medical care is available on a 24 hour basis.

Academic organisation. A broad curriculum is offered up to GCSE in an attempt to avoid undue specialisation at an early age. There are 26 AS/A2 Level subjects available and all Sixth Formers must follow a course in Morals and Ethics. Academic progress at all ages is monitored on a regular basis by Tutors and progress reports are sent to parents throughout the term. There are five central ICT resource centres with Video Conferencing facilities. Sixth Formers have their own ICT resource centre and networked computers in their rooms with e-mail and controlled internet facilities. Recent developments have created the highest quality teaching areas across the whole curriculum, with a particularly impressive Science Department and provision for the Performing Arts. A splendid Library/Learning and Resource Centre has also opened recently. Staff from the Special Needs Department are available to give help and support where required and EAL classes are held on either an individual or group basis without extra charge.

Music, Art, Design and Technology. These subjects form an integral part of the curriculum. The opportunities for both formal and informal music are extensive: there are several orchestras, a Concert Band, small string ensembles, several Choirs and other groups. Design and Technology is taught to all first year pupils along with Art, prior to the choice of GCSE subjects; the facilities for both these subjects are outstanding thanks to recent developments. Drama is strong and there are opportunities for taking part in a wide range of dramatic productions throughout the year either in our own Theatre or in the nearby Centenaries Theatre at Stonyhurst St Mary's Hall.

Games. The main games are Rugby Football, Cricket, Hockey, Netball and Athletics, but it is our aim to offer the widest possible range of sporting and recreational opportunity to all pupils. In addition to playing on our own golf course, pupils can take part in Soccer, Tennis, Badminton, Squash, Fencing, Basketball, Netball, Clay Pigeon Shooting, Sub Aqua and Cross Country. Our indoor six-lane swimming pool offers first-class opportunities for both competitive and recreational swimming, and the Sports Hall provides the usual range of indoor activities. An aqueous-based all-weather pitch is available for Hockey and other sports.

Cadet Corps and Other Extra-Curricular Activities. In Year 10 all pupils are members of the Cadet Corps, which introduces pupils to a number of activities such as canoeing, orienteering, climbing, trekking and shooting, in addition to an extensive programme of Army-based training. After the second year, membership of the Cadet Corps is by selection; it is invariably over-subscribed. An active Outdoor Pursuits Department offers opportunities for climbing, sailing, fell-walking and caving; the Duke of Edinburgh's Award Scheme is very popular with boys and girls at all ages.

Voluntary Service. Active work in the Community is a hallmark of Stonyhurst's commitment to others. Weekly programmes of community work are arranged and thousands of pounds a year are raised for charitable causes, in particular the College's own annual holiday for children with disabilities.

Higher Education and Careers. Up to 98% of our leavers go on to higher education either in the UK or abroad, with 10% to Oxbridge. We also send a number of students to medical schools each year. An average of 50% of our leavers have entered The Russell Group of Universities in the last few years. Our Careers department, based in a well-stocked Careers library with extensive research facilities, enables pupils to be fully informed about university choices and Tutors are actively involved at all stages in the decision making. Careers conferences are regularly organised.

Fees per term (2011-2012). Boarding £9,010, Weekly Boarding £7,606, Day £5,151.

Bursaries and Scholarships. *(See Scholarship Entries section.)* A large number of bursaries and scholarships are awarded each year at all age levels including the Sixth Form and 13+. Bursaries are intended for pupils likely to benefit from a Stonyhurst education and to contribute to it, and whose parents are unable to pay the full fees. Scholarships are awarded on the basis of academic achievement or potential after competitive examinations in May. Scholarships are also available each year for Music and Art. Details of all these awards can be gained by application to the Headmaster.

Admission. Enquiries about admission should be addressed to the Registrar, Tel: 01254 827073 or 827093. Candidates entering at 13+ are normally required to pass the Common Entrance Examination, but alternative Tests are available for candidates from maintained schools or from abroad. Applications for Sixth Form boarding and day places for girls and boys are particularly encouraged.

Charitable status. Stonyhurst College is a Registered Charity, number 230165. The Charity for RC Purposes exists to provide a quality boarding and day education for boys and girls.

Stowe School

Stowe, Buckingham, Bucks MK18 5EH
Tel: 01280 818000
Fax: 01280 818181
e-mail: enquiries@stowe.co.uk
website: www.stowe.co.uk

Stowe aims to provide an all-round education of the highest standard, supporting Stoics in their passage to adulthood by developing individual talents, intellectual curiosity and a lasting sense of moral, social and spiritual responsibility. Confidence and tolerance of others flourish in a close community. The School provides a caring environment which promotes academic excellence, sporting prowess and artistic and musical creativity. Through teaching of the highest calibre, Stoics are encouraged to think for themselves, challenge conventional orthodoxies and pursue their own enthusiasms. Stoics acquire skills that enable them to live happily, work successfully and thrive in their future lives.

Motto: '*Persto et Praesto*'

Visitor: The Rt Revd The Lord Bishop of Oxford

Governing Body:
C Honeyman Brown, FCA (*Chairman*)
J R C Arkwright, FRICS
N W Berry
J M A Bewes, BA, ACA
Admiral Sir James Burnell-Nugent, KCB, CBE, MA
D W Cheyne
S C Creedy Smith, BA, ACA
Ms Juliet Colman, BA, Dip Arch, RIBA
The Revd J J M Fletcher, MA
Professor Sarah Gurr, BSc, ARCS, DIC, PhD, MA
Mrs J E Hastie-Smith
D Hudson, MA Cantab
R A Lankester, MA
Lord Magan of Castletown, FCA
Lady Stringer
C J Tate, BA, MIMC
Air Vice-Marshal M van der Veen, MA, RAF Retd (*Vice Chairman*)
Mrs S M van der Veen, MA Oxon, MA Warwick, DipEd
C P J Wightman, BA, ACA
Ex officio: M I H B Forde (*Chairman of Old Stoic Committee*)

Secretary to the Governors: M B M Porter, BA, MSc

Headmaster: **A K Wallersteiner**, MA, PhD

Deputy Head (*Pastoral*): M J L Bashaarat, MA
Deputy Head (*Academic*): C C Robinson, MA, MPhil
Registrar: D Fletcher, BEd

Assistant Staff:
* *Head of Department*

Art:
*B L Johnson, MA
G A Irvine, BA

Biology:
*R R Akam, BSc, MEd
Dr E Chare, BA, DPhil
Miss P Gleave, BSc
Mrs J M Gracie, BSc
A D D Murphy, BSc
M A Righton, MA

Business Studies:
*P John, BSc
M B Blew, BCom

Chemistry:
*D S Jeffreys, BSc
R G Johnson, BSc, MA
Mrs K M McMahon, BSc
J Peverley, MChem
J M Tearle, BA

Classics:
*M J Bevington, MA, MEd

Design & Technology:
*M C Nash, BA
S Grimble, CertEd
C Peratopoullos, BEd
M D G Wellington, BSc

Drama & Theatre Studies:
*N D Bayley, Dip Acting & Theatre
C D Walters, BEd

EAL:
*Mrs J Y Johnson, BA, MA
A P Longworth, BA

Economics and Politics:
*K K Ryce, BA, MSc
C Barker, BA
M B Blew, BCom
Mrs J L Hamblett-Jahn, LLB
H J L Swayne, BA

English:
*J W H Peppiatt, MA
Miss L S Ashe, BA
M J L Bashaarat, MA
T K J Chan, BA, LLB
Miss V L Kinmond, BA, MA
P S Miller, MA, PhD
D A Roberts, MA

Games Coaching:
*I Michael, BEd
S A Cowie, FIST (*Swimming*)
N Crossley (*Athletics, Football*)
Mrs J M Duckett, BEd (*Lacrosse*)
J Fair, BSc (*Hockey*)
A Hughes (*Rugby*)
J A Knott (*Cricket*)

Geography:
*Mrs Z Cass, BSc

Mrs S L Akam, BA
Mrs A J Dawson, BA
B G Durrant, BA
P A Last, BA, Adv DipEd
A K Murray, BSc

History:
*J W Hayden, BA
A Lewis, BD, MA
J R H Sayers, BA
A K Wallersteiner, MA, PhD
M J Way, BSc

History of Art:
*I O Young, MA
C C Robinson, MA, MPhil

ICT:
*S Gabbatiss, BSc
T D Higham, BSc
N J Mellor, BA, MSc, LPC

Library:
*Mrs C M Miller, BA, Dip Lib Stud

Mathematics:
*D P C Blewitt, BSc
Mrs P A Bennett, BSc, MS
M P Dawson, BA, CertEd
Ms V A Green, BSc, CertEd
R D Knight, BSc
A McDaid, BEd
M B Moller, BA
Mrs R E Trace, BA, Dip Spec Ed

Modern Languages:
*Mrs T L Jones, BA
Mrs H Browne, BA
Mrs C Dickson, MA, Dip ETI
S G Dobson, MA
G D Jones, BA
Mrs C A Lawrance-Thorne, BA
G R Moffat, BA
K P Staples, BA

Mrs A R G Tearle, MA

Music:
*S P Dearsley, MA, MMus (*Director of Music*)
Ms D J Arscott, ABSM, GBSM
H R Jones, MA, FRCO
Mrs J L Nelson, LRAM, DipRAM
J T J Young, RAM, RNCM

PE & Sports Science:
*P R Arnold, BSc
Mrs J M Duckett, BEd
R S Pickersgill, BA
R C Sutton, BA
Mrs S E Sutton, BA

Physics:
*S H Malling, MSc, CPhys, MInstP
I Findlay-Palmer, BSc
B Hart, BEng
J L Ing, MSc, CPhys, MInstP
T O'Toole, BSc

PSHE:
*Miss K J McKlintock, BA, MA

Skills Development:
*Mrs S Carter, BA, MA, MEd
Mrs F E Atherton, BA, AMBDA
Mrs S Rawlins, HLTA
Ms E A Sheard, BA, Cert SpLD
Mrs R E Trace, BA, Dip Spec Ed
Mrs H Milne, BSS

Religious Studies:
*D C C Mochan, BA, MA
Miss E Donaldson, BA
A A Macpherson, BA, MA
M P Rickner, BA

Houses and Housemasters/mistresses:

Boys' Houses:
Bruce House: R C Sutton
Temple House: A A Macpherson
Grenville House: A D D Murphy
Chandos House: B G Durrant
Cobham House: M J Way
Chatham House: J L Ing
Grafton House: G R Moffat
Walpole House: P A Last

Girls' Houses:
Nugent House: Mrs J M Duckett
Lyttelton House: Mrs J M Gracie
Queen's House: Mrs J L Hamblett-Jahn
Stanhope House: Mrs J L Nelson

Medical Officer: Dr R D Pryse, MB BS, DCH, DRCOG, DFSRH

Director of Finance: Mrs J L Hill, MA, FCA
Director of Operations: N Morris, BA, MSc, FRSA, FCILT, MIL

Stowe is a country boarding school with boys and girls from 13 to 18. The School roll is 750, comprising 630 boarders and 120 day pupils. Pupils are also accepted each year for 2-year A Level courses.

Houses. There are eight Boys' and four Girls' Houses, six of which are within the main building or attached to it and six at a short distance from it.

The Curriculum allows pupils to enjoy a wide variety of subjects before they settle down to work for their GCSEs (nine or ten) taken in the Fifth Form. A flexible Options system operates at this stage. Most boys and girls will go on to take 4 AS and 3 A Levels. Throughout the School, boys and girls have a Tutor to look after their academic welfare and advise them on higher education. A course in Visual Education was introduced in 1996 for boys and girls in their first year at Stowe. It promotes an understanding of Stowe's architecture and landscape gardens in particular and the built environment in general.

Art, Design and Information Technology. All pupils are introduced to these in their first year at Stowe. Art and Design are popular both for those pursuing hobbies and for those studying for formal examinations. Traditional skills are covered alongside more modern techniques such as computer-aided design and desktop publishing.

Music and Drama flourish as important and integral parts of the School's activities both within and outside the formal curriculum. There is plenty of scope to get involved in the School Orchestras, Jazz Band, Clarinet Quartet, Choirs, School plays, House plays and House entertainments. The timetable is sufficiently flexible to allow special arrangements to be made for outstanding musicians to study outside school. Drama Clubs and Theatre Studies groups have two fully-equipped theatres at their disposal.

Careers Guidance. Pupils are provided with a variety of opportunities which allows them to make sound career decisions. Seminars, Gap Year advice and an interview training programme are all offered. The Careers Centre is extremely well resourced, with a suite of computers and appropriate software, video facilities and a wealth of literature. Every encouragement is given to pupils to make regular visits to the Centre at Stowe and parents are always welcome to attend Careers events and to spend time using the available resources.

Religion. The School's foundation is to provide education in accordance with the principles of the Church of England and this is reflected in its chapel services on Sundays. Pupils of other faiths and other Christian Churches are welcomed and in some cases separate arrangements are made for them on Sundays. Every pupil attends the chapel services on weekdays.

Games. The key sports for boys are rugby, hockey and cricket, and for girls, hockey, lacrosse and tennis. The other main sports range from badminton, basketball, cross country, football, Eton Fives, fencing, golf, netball, squash, swimming and water polo in the winter to athletics, golf, polo, rowing, sailing and swimming in the summer; there are inter-school fixtures in most of these sports.

The School enters national competitions in many sports and encourages pupils to challenge for representative honours. The School has a heated 6-lane 25m indoor swimming pool with electronic timing system, a sports hall, squash courts, Eton Fives courts, a weight training/fitness room and two floodlit Astroturf pitches which also provide 24 tennis courts in the summer. There are also hard tennis courts available all the year round, plus outdoor netball and basketball facilities, an 8-lane sandwich surface athletics track, an indoor shooting range, a clay-pigeon shooting tower, a nine-hole golf course where the National Prep Schools (IAPS) annual tournament is played, and extensive playing fields for rugby, hockey, football, cricket and lacrosse. Sculling, canoeing, sailing and fishing take place on a lake within the Landscape Gardens as well as at Northampton Rowing Club and Glebe Lake, Calvert. Horse riding is growing in popularity and the school enters local and regional competitions.

Other Activities. Pupils complement their games programme with a large variety of extra-curricular activities, including clubs and societies. There is a full weekend programme of events and activities. Stowe's grounds lend themselves to outdoor pursuits such as fishing and clay pigeon shooting, and the School has its own pack of Beagles. On Mondays a special activities programme is based on Service at Stowe and at the heart of this is the Combined Cadet Force with all three service arms, the Duke of Edinburgh's Award Scheme, Community Service (in the neighbourhood) and Leadership skills.

Fees per term (2011-2012). Boarders £9,655, Day Pupils £7,005 payable before the commencement of the School term to which they relate. A deposit is payable when Parents accept the offer of a place. This deposit is repaid by means of a credit to the final payment of fees or other sums due to the school on leaving.

Scholarships. (*See Scholarship Entries section.*)

Admissions. Boys and girls can be registered at any age. Full details can be obtained from the Admissions Department, who will supply entry forms. The School is always prepared to consider applications from pupils to enter the School at 14 if they have been educated overseas or in the maintained sector. The date of birth should be stated and it should be noted that boys and girls are normally admitted between their 13th and 14th birthdays.

The Old Stoic Society. The OS Society Manager is Tim Scarff, The Old Stoic Society, Stowe, Buckingham MK18 5EH

Charitable status. Stowe School Limited is a Registered Charity, number 310639. The primary objects of the charity, as set out in its Memorandum and Articles of Association, are to acquire Stowe House, which was achieved in 1923, and to provide education in accordance with the principles of the Church of England.

Strathallan School

Forgandenny, Perth, Perthshire PH2 9EG
Tel: 01738 812546
Fax: 01738 812549
e-mail: secretary@strathallan.co.uk
website: www.strathallan.co.uk

Strathallan School was founded by Harry Riley in 1913 and moved to its present site in Forgandenny, Perthshire in 1920. The School is fully co-educational and numbers 544 pupils, of whom 194 are day pupils and 350 are boarders.

Motto: '*Labor Omnia Vincit*'

Governors:

Chairman: D L Young, BArch, DipArch
A Brown, BSc
Professor J S Cachia, BSc, MBChB, MD, FRCGP, DRCOG, FRCPE
S J Cannon, MA
J A R Coleman, DipEstMan, MRICS
K C Dinsmore, BA, LLB, DipLP
Mrs K J Dunn, LLB
R G A Hall, BArch, DipArch, RIAS, RIBA
S J Hay, BA, MSc
N Houston, MA, DipMusEd, PGDipEdTech CNAA, PGDipCouns, MScR Mus, FHEA
Dr J W Huggett, BA, PhD
Professor R E Leake, MA, DPhil
J A Leiper, CA, BA
R K Linton, LLB, NP
Mrs E Lister, BSc, DipEd
J G Maguire, DipBS, MRICS
Mrs P A Milne, MA, MBA, MCIPD
P J McKee, MA, PGCE

B Raine, BA, PGCE
Sheriff D O Sutherland, MA, LLB, MSI, NP
A M D Wilkinson, MBA, MA, FSI
Mrs G M Wilson, MA, PGCE

Headmaster: B K Thompson, MA Oxon

Assistant Staff:
Mrs T Ailinger, Staatsexamen, Cert TESOL
D J Barnes, BSc, PGCE, PGCG, FRGS (*Second Master*)
G J Batterham, BSc, PGCE (*Simpson House*)
D E Billing, MA, PGCE (*Nicol House*)
Mrs D Billing, MA, PGCE
Dr K E M Blackie, PhD, PGDE, BSc
G A Bolton, BA, MSc
J S Burgess, BSc
P W W Bush, DipIAPS (*Riley House*)
Miss L Carroll, BEd
Miss E de Celis Lucas, BA, CAP
Dr A N Collins, BSc, BA, PhD
Dr B Cooper, BSc, PhD, PGCE
S Cowper, BA, PGCE
Mrs M-L Crane, BA, PGCE
Dr S B Downhill, BA, MSc, PhD, PGCE, FRGS
C R Drummond, BA, RSAMD
N T H Du Boulay, BA
Mrs E C Duncan, MA, PGCE
A L M Dunn, MA, PGCE
Dr S Ferguson, MA, PhD, MSc, PGCE
R H Fitzsimmons, MA
Ms C Flannery, MA, PGCE
Dr C Flanagan, MA, PhD
J R Fleming, BEd
Mrs S E Fleming, BEd
N P Gallier, MBE, MA, MSc, PGCE
G Gardiner, BSc, PGCE
D R Giles, BA QTS, CertPP
J Goddard, BSc, PGCE
N Hamilton, BMus
B A Heaney, BSc, DipEd (*Freeland House*)
A Henderson, UKCC
D M Higginbottom, MA, PGCE
Mrs J Higginbottom, MA, PGCE
Mrs C G Howett, BA, DipEd
Mrs D S Hunter, DA, DipEd
Mrs A Ingram-Forde, BA
P J S Keir, BEd, CertSpLD
E G Kennedy, BA, PGCE
G Kitson, BSc, PGCE
Mrs E Lalani, BEd, DipMan
Miss C Laurie, BSc, PGCE
Mrs F MacBain, BA, MA (*Glenbrae House*)
Miss M J Mackie, BSc, PGDE
J A MacLean, MA, PGDE
Mrs I I M McFarlane, MA, CertSpLD, LLAM
Miss V S M McKay, BEd, DipLibInf, CertSpLD
Miss G McLean, BA, PGDE
A E C McMorrine, DA
Mrs C Menzies, BSc, PGCE
Miss J L Morrison, BTechEd
Miss U Nastashchuk, BA
M R Price, BEng, PGCE
Mrs D L Raeside, BSc, HDE PG
G S R Robertson, BA DMS
Miss S E Robertson, BSc, PGDE
Mrs M C Robertson-Barnett, MA, PGCE
G R M Ross, BSc, MSc, FSA
Dr J D Salisbury, MA, PhD, PGCE
Mrs L Salisbury, BA, DipEd, PGCE, ALCM
Mrs C Sim Sayce, BMus, PGCE
Miss A Sime, BEd (*Director of Sport*)
N Smith, BSc, BA, PGCE
A C W Streatfeild-James, MA, PGCE (*Director of Studies*)
Mrs K Streatfeild-James, BA, PGCE, Dip SpLD

Mrs R C W Stuart, BA, MA, PGDE (*Thornbank House*)
Mrs J A Summersgill, BSc, PGCE
P R Summersgill, MA, PGCE
A Thomson, BA, MPhil, ACP
Mrs A J Tod, MA, PGCE (*Woodlands House*)
M R A B Tod, BSc (*Woodlands House*)
Ms L Toye, BSc, PGCE
P M Vallot, BSc
R C A Walmsley, BA, MA (*Director of Music*)
A Watt, BComm, HDE (*Ruthven House*)
Miss K E Wilkinson, BSc, PGCE
T Zhou, MSc, PhD

Bursar and Clerk to the Governors: A C Glasgow, MBE, BEng, MSc, CEng

Director of Marketing & Development: Mrs T C Howard-Vyse
Marketing Executive: Mrs L Leslie
Alumni Coordinator: Mrs A Wilson

Medical Officers:
Dr A M Lewis, MBChB
Dr L D Burnett, MBChB, BSc, DRCOG, MRCGP

Situation. Strathallan School is located 6 miles south of Perth in the village of Forgandenny. It occupies a glorious rural location, situated in 150 acres of richly wooded estate on the northern slopes of the Ochils and overlooks the Earn valley. At the same time, Strathallan is within easy reach of the international airports – Edinburgh (35 minutes) and Glasgow (1 hour) – and Perth (10 minutes).

At the centre of the School is the main building which dates from the 18th century and was formerly a country house and home of the Ruthven family. The School continues to invest in outstanding facilities. Recent additions include modern laboratories, a Theatre, Computer Centre, Library, Design Technology Centre, Sports Hall, Fitness and Weight Training Room, 2 Floodlit Synthetic Hockey pitches, Medical Centre, Art School and new Girls' Boarding House. All boarding houses have been built within the last thirty years with modern facilities and a single study-bedroom for every boarder in the last four years.

Aims. At the heart of the School's philosophy is the commitment to provide opportunities for all to excel, to help pupils to make the most of their abilities within the framework of a caring environment.

Organisation. The School is primarily a boarding school yet also takes day pupils who are integrated into the boarding houses. There are four Senior Boys' houses (Ruthven, Nicol, Freeland and Simpson). There are three Girls' houses (Woodlands, Thornbank and Glenbrae). All boarding houses have their own resident Housemaster or Housemistress, assisted by House Tutors and a Matron. Boys have single study-bedrooms from the Fourth Form and Girls have single study-bedrooms from the Third Form.

The Junior House, Riley, is designed to cater for boys and girls wishing to enter the School at 9+. Riley is run by a resident Housemaster and his wife, assisted by tutors, two of whom are resident, and a resident Matron. After Riley, pupils move directly to one of the Senior houses. Riley is situated within its own campus, yet also enjoys the facilities of the main School. It has its own Common Room, Library, dormitories and music practice rooms.

The whole School dines centrally and there is a wide choice of hot and cold meals as well as vegetarian options. All boarding houses have "brew rooms" for the preparation of light snacks.

Religion. Strathallan has a Chapel and a resident Chaplain who is responsible for religious studies throughout the School.

Curriculum. Pupils entering the School before the age of 13 are placed in Forms IJJ, 1J, I, or II, while those who join at 13 are placed in the Third Form where they are setted by ability for their core subjects. Up until the Fourth Form, all follow the same broad curriculum which comprises English, Mathematics, French, German/Spanish, Latin, Physics, Chemistry and Biology, History, Geography, Computing, Art, Design Technology, together with Divinity, Personal and Social Education, Music and Physical Education. Instruction in French and Latin begins in Form 1.

In the Fourth and Fifth Forms, pupils take nine subjects for GCSE and Computing at Standard Grade. All the above subjects (plus Business Studies) are available at this level.

A satisfactory performance at GCSE (a minimum of five passes at C grade or equivalent) qualifies a pupil for entry to the Sixth Form where he/she prepares for AS and A2 examinations or Scottish Higher. Scottish Higher examinations are generally taken at the end of the Upper Sixth year. AS and A2 examinations are taken in the Lower and Upper Sixth.

In the Sixth Form, there is greater flexibility in the range of courses available and full details of these are issued to parents in advance. Potential Oxbridge candidates are identified in the Lower Sixth Form and additional tuition is provided. On average, more than 95% of senior pupils go on to University.

Each pupil is allocated a tutor who is a member of the academic staff and one of the duty staff of the boarding house. The tutor monitors pupils' academic and social progress and is responsible for discussing their regular reports with them. Teacher : Pupil ratio 1 : 7.

Games. The main School games are rugby, cricket, hockey, netball, athletics and tennis, and standards are high. Other sports include skiing, squash, rounders, football, fencing, judo, badminton, table tennis, basketball, swimming, golf, horse riding and cross-country running in all of which national and regional success have been achieved in recent years.

Strathallan has 2 squash courts, 15 hard tennis courts, 3 netball courts, 2 floodlit synthetic pitches, a heated indoor swimming pool, sports hall, gymnasium and a fitness and weight training room. The sports hall comprises a basketball court, three badminton courts, a rock climbing wall as well as facilities for six-a-side hockey and indoor cricket coaching. Sailing, canoeing and skiing are recognised pastimes, and pupils participate in School ski days in the Spring term. Strathallan also has its own nine-hole golf course.

Activities. All pupils are encouraged to take part in a range of activities for which time is set aside each day. There are over 50 weekly activities to choose from including dance, drama, pottery, chess, photography, first aid, lifeguarding, judo, horse riding, shooting (both clay pigeon and small bore) and fishing. There are also many societies and a programme of external speakers who visit the School. Pupils also work towards awards under The Duke of Edinburgh's Award scheme. They are also encouraged to take part in Community Service.

Music. The Music department has its own concert room, keyboard room and classrooms, together with a number of individual practice rooms. Music may be taken at GCSE, Higher and AS/A2 Level. There are choirs, traditional music ensembles, jazz band, wind band, an orchestra, folk bands and rock bands. A house music competition takes place annually and there are regular concerts throughout the term. Individual tuition is available for virtually all instruments. Recitals and visits to concerts in Edinburgh, Perth and the environs are arranged. The School has a Pipe Band and a full-time Piping Instructor. There is also a specialist Choral Scholarship programme.

Art. Art is recognised as an important part of the School's activities and there are opportunities to study the subject at GCSE and AS/A2 Level. Pupils benefit from regular art trips abroad and have the opportunity to exhibit their work both locally and further afield. A purpose-built Art School features facilities for ceramics, sculpture and print-making. National awards reflect pupils' achievements in this area.

Drama. Drama thrives throughout the School and the department makes full use of the theatre. There are junior and senior performances each year and pupils are encouraged to become involved in all aspects of production. The School also provides tuition in public and verse speaking and pupils regularly win trophies at the local festivals. There is also an annual Musical and pupils enter musical theatre exams.

Combined Cadet Force. There is a large voluntary contingent of the Combined Cadet Force with Navy, Army and Marines Sections.

Careers. Careers guidance begins in the Third Form. The Careers Adviser maintains close links with universities and colleges and regularly visits industrial firms. We have exchange programmes with schools in Australia, New Zealand and South Africa. There is a dedicated Careers Library, well-stocked with prospectuses, reference books and in-house magazines. Strathallan is a member of the Independent Schools Careers Organisation, a representative of which visits regularly and of the Scottish Council for Development and Industry.

All pupils have the opportunities to gain work experience in the Fifth Form, after their GCSEs. There is also a GAP year programme which provides placements for pupils to work overseas prior to going to university. Strathallan is developing particular links with Charities in Kenya and India.

Pastoral Care. There is a strong emphasis on pastoral care. The School has drawn up its own welfare guidelines in consultation with parents, governors and Perth and Kinross Social Work Department.

Medical Centre. Strathallan has its own purpose-built Medical Centre with consulting and treatment rooms. There are nursing staff at the Centre and the School's Medical Officers visit four times a week. Physiotherapy, chiropody, and relaxation also take place in the Centre during term time.

Entrance. Junior Entrance – Boys and girls are admitted to the Junior School (Riley House) at either age 9, 10, 11 or 12. An Entrance Day (including those sitting scholarship examinations) is held in early Spring each year. Entry is based on a satisfactory school report.

Entry to the Senior School – Candidates for entry into the Senior School at 13 may enter via the Open Scholarship examination, Common Entrance or a satisfactory school report.

Sixth Form – Boys and girls may also enter at Sixth Form level, either via the Sixth Form scholarship examination (which takes place in November) or on the basis of a satisfactory school report and GCSE/Standard Grade results.

Scholarships. (*See Scholarship Entries section.*) Awards are made on the basis of competitive examination/assessment. Bursary help is available to supplement awards for outstanding candidates on a financial need basis.

Further information is available on the School's website: www.strathallan.co.uk. All enquiries about scholarships to: The Admissions Office, Strathallan School, Forgandenny, Perthshire PH2 9EG. Tel: 01738 815003, email admissions @strathallan.co.uk.

Bursaries. Bursaries are awarded dependent on financial circumstances and are available to pupils who have qualified for entry through exam or school report or both. It is not necessary for successful candidates for bursaries to have achieved scholarship standard but it may be possible to add a bursary award to a scholarship to enable a pupil to come to Strathallan.

Fees per term (2011-2012). Junior School (Riley House): £6,260 (boarding), £3,907 (day). Senior School: £8,776 (boarding), £5,955 (day).

Prospectus. Up to date information is included in the prospectus which can be obtained by contacting the Admissions Office or via the School's website.

Charitable status. Strathallan School is a Registered Charity, number SC008903, dedicated to Education.

Surbiton High School

UCST

Surbiton High Senior School:
Surbiton Crescent, Kingston-upon-Thames KT1 2JT
Tel: 020 8546 5245
Fax: 020 8547 0026
e-mail: surbiton.high@surbitonhigh.ucst.co.uk
website: www.surbitonhigh.com

Surbiton High Boys' Preparatory School:
3 Avenue Elmers, Surbiton KT6 4SP
Tel: 020 8390 6640
Fax: 020 8255 3049
e-mail: surbiton.prep@surbitonhigh.ucst.co.uk

Surbiton High Junior Girls' School:
95–97 Surbiton Road, Kingston-upon-Thames
KT1 2HW
Tel: 020 8546 9756
Fax: 020 8974 6293
e-mail: surbiton.juniorgirls@surbitonhigh.ucst.co.uk

Governing Body: The Council of the United Church
   Schools Trust

Local Governing Body:
Mrs Eileen Carroll
Revd Val Cory
Mr David Cunningham
Mr Martin Donnelly
Mr Gordon Faultless
Ms Ann Haydon
Mr Ruairidh Hogg (*Acting Chair*)
Ms Christina McComb
Mrs Gillian Norton
Mr Nick Pickles
Mr Stuart White

Staff:

Principal: Ms E A Haydon, BSc Hons London

Deputy Heads:
Mr S Edmonds, BA Keele
Mr I Smith, BA, MA
Mrs H Morgan, BA Wales

Head of Junior Girls' and Boys' Preparatory Schools: Miss
   C Bufton, BA Wales

Assistant Staff:
Mrs J Aldous, CertEd Bedford
Mr S Bachelor, BA Oxford
Mrs M Bailey, BSc
Mrs S Beere, BSc Brunel
Mrs J Bennett, BA Sheffield
Miss R Bezant, BA Cardiff
Ms H Brazier, MA OU
Miss H Brennan, BSc Manchester Metropolitan
Miss C Broadway, BSc Surrey
Miss C Bufton, BA Hons Wales
Mrs E Carr, CertEd London
Mrs A Carter, MA Sheffield
Mrs C Catlin, BEd Bristol
Mrs E Clark, BA City of London Poly
Ms H Cowie, BA Kent
Mrs I Coyle, CertEd London
Ms A Crump, BA Camberwell
Mr B Dallaway, BSc Birmingham
Mrs A Dara, BSc Kingston

Mr G Davidson, BA Leics, MPhil St Andrews
Miss C Davis, BA King's College
Mrs A Deighton, BEd Brighton
Ms C Demetz, BA Exeter
Mrs B Doe, BA Warwick
Mr S Edmonds, BA Hons Keele
Mr G Ekins, BSc
Miss Helen Feeney, BSc Liverpool
Mr T Ferguson, BSc Staffordshire
Miss M Fernandez, BSc Surrey
Miss Helen Fisher, BA QTS Brunel
Miss S Forrester, BA Dunelm
Mrs V Foster, BA Exeter
Mrs R Francis, BA Nottingham
Mrs D Frisk, BSc Salford
Mrs C Furlong, BEd
Mrs C Geard, BA CNAA
Mrs A George, BA OU PGCE
Mr M Gibbons, BA Oxford
Mrs A Godbold, BA Manchester
Mrs A Hamilton, MA Warwick
Mrs A Hammill, BSc Leeds
Miss K Hansell, BA Reading
Dr L Hansen, PhD London
Mr L Hardie, BA York
Mrs E Harris, BSc Durham
Ms D Haroon, BA Hons Kings' College
Mrs H Hart, BSc Birmingham
Ms J Hawkins, MA Hons Edinburgh
Ms A Haydon, BSc London
Mrs E Hewitt, BEd Oxford Brookes
Miss K Hockey, BA Cambridge
Mrs C Holmes, BA Bangor
Mrs H Horwood, BSc Leeds
Ms V Howard, BA Portsmouth
Ms B Huntley, BA Lancaster
Mrs S Jarman, MSc Oxford
Mrs A Jackson, BA London
Mrs S Johnston, BA Hons
Mrs N Jones, BA, Dip Central School of Art & Design
Mrs A Keeling, BSc London
Miss L Keers, BA Wales
Mrs S Kendall, BA Canterbury NZ
Ms S Kettlewell, BSc Hons Loughborough
Mrs A King, BSc Manchester
Mrs M King, BA OU
Miss T Kruger, BSc Cape Town
Ms G Kumar, BSc Swansea
Ms B Lee, BA Central School of Speech and Drama
Mrs L Leggo, Cape Town
Mrs R Le Prevost, BA North London
Ms A Lewis, BEd Perth
Ms A Limbuwala, BA Thames Valley
Mrs L Luke, BEd Kingston
Mrs R MacKenzie, BA Kingston
Mrs K Mair, MA Brunel
Mrs R Marshall-Taylor, BA Camberwell College of Arts
Miss T McIntyre, BA Sheffield Hallam
Mr J Montgomery, BSc Bradford
Ms N Lockwood, BA Exeter
Mrs E Magennis, BA Queen's Belfast
Mr E Marsh, BA Exeter
Mr J Martin, BA Victorian College of Arts
Mrs R McDermott, BSc Hons Leeds, PhD London
Mrs H Mehra, BSc Sussex
Mrs B Middleton, BSc Hons Surrey
Ms M Milsom, BA Hons Bradford, Dip Law College of
   Law, BVC ICSL
Mr D Morgan, BSc Wales
Mrs D Morito, BA Kingston
Mrs A Nayler, CertEd, DipMaths Roehampton
Mrs G Newton, BSc CNAA
Ms L Newton, BEng Hons Bath

Mrs M North, CertEd Dartford College
Mrs M O'Connor, BA London
Mrs A Orlovac, BSc Birmingham
Mr J Owen, BSc Nottingham
Ms H Parker, BA Hons Leeds Metropolitan
Mrs J Partridge, MA Cambridge, MA Surrey
Ms G Paul, MA Hons Glasgow
Mrs J Paynter, BSc Leeds
Miss R Pedder-Smith, MA, BA
Mme V Pegnall, CertEd Greenwich
Miss S Pett, BA Cambridge
Ms K Pink, BSc Hons Exeter
Dr S Pinniger, PhD Southampton
Ms E Puchois, BA Lille
Mrs S Ralph, BEd Bath
Mrs S Rawlinson, BSc Bristol, ACA
Miss A Reckermann, MA Dortmund
Mr M Read, BA
Mrs S Regel, BSc Aberystwyth
Mr I Richardson BSc Greenwich
Ms J Richardson, MA Edinburgh, PGCE Kingston
Ms L Roberts, BSc Exeter, MA Brunel
Miss T Rockall, BA Kingston
Mrs K Ross, BA Kingston, Diploma RA
Mrs J Rosser, BA Sheffield
Mrs G Russ, BA St Mary's College
Ms J Russell, BA Leeds
Mr J Russell, MA London
Mr T Ryan, BEd St Mark's & St John
Miss B Sacher, BA Roehampton
Mr K Salisbury, BSc, Bangor
Mrs J Scholes, BA Bristol
Mrs S Sikka, BSc UCL
Ms L Skinner, BA Durham
Mr R Skinner, BA Bournemouth
Mr I Smith, BA Lancaster
Mrs J Smith, QTS, MA Berlin
Mrs M Spooner, BA, PGCE
Mrs D Stanley, BA Warwick
Mrs S Stead, BA Surrey
Mrs C Stewart, BA UEA
Miss S Strachan, BA Kingston
Ms F Sullivan, BA Hons Kingston
Miss D Sunda, BA Oxford
Ms K Sutherland, BSc Hons East Anglia
Mrs L Syred, BA Wolverhampton
Mrs P L Thomas, BEng Liverpool, MEd Wolverhampton
Ms L Tupper, BA Hons UEA
Mrs A Vaughan, BA
Mrs M Vazquez, BA Portsmouth
Ms C Veitch, PGCE London
Mrs G Walker, BA Wales
Mrs V Wiklund, BA UCL
Mr T Wiggall, BA Hons Cantab
Mrs J Wilkey, CertEd Dartford College
Miss L Williams, BSc Birmingham
Mr B Wilshere, PhD Goldsmiths College
Miss H Windsor, BA Cardiff
Miss N Yellop, BA Brunel

Extra Subject Staff:

Flute:
Caroline Li, BA London
Clarinet:
Sarah Douglas, BA Royal College of Music
Oboe:
Lorna John, BA Birmingham
Woodwind:
Cheryl Taylor, BMus, Dip ABRSM LRSM
Brass:
David Shead, Associateship Dip Royal College of Music
Violin:
Sara Wolstenholme, BA Manchester

Cello:
Paul Brunner, Cert Adv Studies Royal Academy of Music
Piano:
Lorna John, BA Birmingham
Eleni Mavromoustaki, BA Royal College of Music
Daniel Tong, GCE Music
Vicky Yannoula, BA Royal College of Music
Guitar:
Camilo Salazar, BA University of Texas
Singing:
Jillian Arthur, LTCL Performer Singing Trinity College of Music
Alice Hyde, MUS North Texas State University
Emily Rowley Jones, BA Southampton

Speech and Drama:
Miss C De Brett
Mrs C Jones, FTCL, LGSM, LNEA
Mr N Ware, ATCL

Skiing: Mr M Telling
Aerobics: Mrs Z Bennett
Tennis: Mr M Codling
Rowing Coordinator: Mr S Walker
Hockey: Mrs F Benzies
Netball: Mrs E Neilson; Mrs T Gregg
Trampoline: Mr M Douglas; Mrs K Nash
Gymnastics: Miss N Watson

Medical Officer: Dr J Setchell, MA, BS London
School Nurse: Mrs A McCool
School Registrar: Mrs M Try, BA London
School Librarian: (*to be appointed*)

A Day School, founded in 1884 and accommodating 1,300 pupils between the ages of 4 and 18. There are 192 pupils in the Sixth Form. The main age of entry to the Boys' Preparatory School and Junior Girls' School is at age 4 and 7, and to the Senior School for girls at 11 by the School's own examination, however the school does admit pupils at other age groups dependent on the availability of places. Entry to the Sixth Form is by interview and qualifications.

The School is situated in the Kingston upon Thames postal area near the river and close to Surbiton Station. It is well served by public transport and draws its pupils both from the immediate neighbourhood and further adjacent districts. A school bus system operates over ten different routes.

The extensive school site consists of a Sixth Form, two junior schools, Surbiton Assembly Rooms, a Science and Technology block, as well as the redeveloped main school site, including modern classrooms, an open-plan Art School and a landscaped recreation area. There are specialist facilities for Information Technology, Modern Languages, Music, Drama and Sport, as well as spacious dining facilities and a well-equipped stage and performing area.

The School's sports ground includes an astroturf multipurpose pitch with floodlighting, tennis courts and grassed areas. All three schools are generously resourced with interactive whiteboards, linked to the School's computer network.

The School Curriculum includes English Language, English Literature, History, Geography, Religious Studies, French, German, Spanish, Latin, Mathematics, Biology, Chemistry, Physics, Design Technology, Theatre Studies, Information Technology, Economics, Business Studies, Government & Politics, Music, Art, Ceramics, Photography, Psychology, Critical Thinking, Physical Education and Sports Studies.

Extra Subjects: Piano, Cello, Flute, Violin, Voice, Dance, Percussion, Clarinet, Saxophone, Oboe, Bass, Bassoon, Guitar, Speech and Drama, Ballet.

Sixth Form. A wide variety of courses is offered in the Sixth Form so that the girls may choose a suitable group of AS and A2 level subjects to prepare them for University

Headmasters' and Headmistresses' Conference

courses, Schools of Medicine, Art School, Colleges of Education and other professional training. Information and Communications Technology is an integral part of Sixth Form study with a dedicated ICT room in the Sixth Form. There is also a Library and Resources room for individual study. A £1.9 million development was completed in 2003.

Games. Hockey, tennis, rounders, netball, rowing and athletics. Seniors, from Year 10 upwards, have a choice of activities on their games afternoons including aerobics, basketball, football, netball, squash, trampolining, youth leadership, martial arts, self-defence and weight-training. The School has skiing teams in all age groups and regularly holds several national titles. Girls have also won national competitions and represented Great Britain in rowing. The School has nine GB gymnasts who have also represented the School in national competitions.

Religious Services. There is a daily assembly and all pupils are expected to attend.

Fees per term (2011-2012). Junior Girls and Boys' Preparatory: £2,626 (Reception); £2,578 (Years 1–2); £3,510 (Years 3–6). Senior School: £4,305.

When two or more children of the same family attend the School, a reduction in fees will be given. Reductions are also made for daughters of members of the Clergy.

Scholarships and Bursaries. (*See Scholarship Entries section.*) Bursaries are available in the Sixth Form, along with Academic, Music, Art, Drama and Sport Scholarships. Academic, Art, Music and Sport Scholarships are available at 11+.

For further particulars apply to the Admissions Registrar.

Assisted Places. The United Church Schools Trust offers a limited number of Assisted Places at 11+.

Surbiton High Boys' Preparatory School. Day school for boys aged 4–11.

The main age of entry is at 4 and 7 by assessment and examination, with occasional places in other year groups.

Surbiton Preparatory School follows an enhanced National Curriculum combining traditional values with the best of modern methods. French, music and physical education are taught by specialist teachers throughout the school and information technology is a particular strength. The School has contact with some 20 senior schools in south-west London and north Surrey. Regularly the children's success in entrance examinations allows the opportunity to choose between three or more senior schools and many pupils gain scholarship awards.

(*For further details, see entry in IAPS section.*)

Surbiton High Junior Girls' School. The Junior Girls' School opened in January 1994 and provides a caring, happy and secure education for girls aged 4 to 11. The main age of entry is at 4 and 7 by assessment and examination, with occasional places in other year groups.

The School is housed in its own purpose-built, modern accommodation with bright modern classrooms, extensive computer facilities, a well-stocked library and performance areas. Specialist teaching is offered in French, music, physical education and a wealth of extra-curricular activities broaden and enliven the pupils' learning experience. At 11 almost all girls continue their education in the Senior School. Girls are not required to sit the entrance examination to the senior school unless they are applying for a scholarship.

(*For further details, see entry in IAPS section.*)

Charitable status. The United Church Schools Trust is a Registered Charity, number 1016538. It exists to provide high quality education in keeping with the teaching of the Church of England.

Sutton Valence School

Sutton Valence, Maidstone, Kent ME17 3HL
Tel: 01622 845200
Fax: 01622 844103
e-mail: enquiries@svs.org.uk
website: www.svs.org.uk

Sutton Valence School has over 425 years of proud history, founded in 1576 by William Lambe. Today the School is co-educational with 520 boys and girls on roll and occupies an area of about 100 acres on the slopes of a high ridge with unequalled views over the Weald of Kent in the historic, beautiful and safe village of Sutton Valence.

We believe that education does not finish at the classroom door. The School provides a "total curriculum", whilst never forgetting the primacy of the classroom, allowing pupils to learn through diverse and various activities that engage and encourage them both to develop new skills and to delight in the effort and achievement of all within our community.

Bruce Grindlay, Headmaster, is a great believer in a bespoke education – an education that tailors its teaching and available opportunities to engage and enthuse all students, helping them to achieve more than they could have believed, and pushing them to realise their potential.

Motto: '*My Trust is in God alone.*'

Visitor: The Lord Archbishop of Canterbury

Foundation: United Westminster Schools
Director/Clerk: R W Blackwell, MA

Governing Body:
B F W Baughan, FSI (*Chairman*)
Major General David Burden, CB, CVO, CBE
The Venerable Philip Down, MTh, MA
M S Hall, BSc
The Revd Canon D H Hutt, MA, AKC
T D Page
Mrs D Perry, MA, DMS, FRSA
Mrs Z Reader
C J Saunders, MA
D W Taylor, MA, FRSA
C H Tongue, MA
Lady Vallance, JP, MA, MSc, PhD, FRSA, FCGI
E Watts, OBE, BA, FRSA

Headmaster: **B C W Grindlay**, MA Cantab, MusB, FRCO CHM

Deputy Head: J J Farrell, MA Cantab
Director of Studies: D E Clarke, BSc Bristol, CBiol, MIBiol
Asst Deputy Head and Director of Co-Curricular Activities: Mrs M T Hall, BEd Southampton

Academic Staff:
† *Boarding Staff*

†G N Alderman, BEd Avery Hill College (*Director of Sport, Housemaster*)
Mrs K L Andersen, CertEd Elizabeth Gaskell College (*Head of Home Economics, Head of Sixth Form Section, Director of Professional Development*)
Miss J M Beaton, BEng Nottingham (*Mathematics*)
A R Bee, BSc Manchester (*Head of Geography*)
F-Y Belver, MA, BA (*Modern Languages*)
A Brook, BA (*Head of Drama*)
M Brown, BSc, PhD (*Physics, House Tutor*)
W D Buck, CertEd St Luke's, Exeter (*Modern Languages, RS, Games*)
Miss L J Burden, BA Anglia, BSc Open (*Head of Second Year, Psychology, Community Service*)

†R H Carr, BA St John's College, Durham (*History, Games, Head of Boarding*)
D E Clarke, BSc Bristol, CBiol, MIBiol (*Biology*)
C M Davenport, BA Keele (*Head of English*)
Ms A Derricott, BA Sheffield (*Head of History, CCF*)
Miss T Draude, BA Stirling (*Head of Media Studies, Higher Education Coordinator*)
Ms S V Easter, BA Exeter (*Art, Editor of 'The Suttonian' magazine*)
Mrs J P A Fletcher, BSc Greenwich (*Head of Sixth Form Section, Chemistry*)
L Fuentes Olea, BA Granada (*Head of MFL*)
†P N Gorman, BA Edinburgh (*Head of Art, House Tutor, Games*)
B Gipps, Royal College of Music
Mrs F M Gosden, BA Rhodes (*Head of First Form, English, CCF*)
Mrs L Grindlay, MA Cantab (*English*)
Mrs M T Hall, BEd Southampton (*Geography*)
Mrs N S Hall, BMus Manchester (*Assistant Director of Music*)
Miss P L Hallett, BA Brighton (*Head of Academic PE and Girls' Games*)
A P Hammersley, BSc York (*Biology*)
P J Harcourt, MA Cantab (*German*)
G Harris, BA King's College (*Head of Fifth Form, Mathematics*)
Ms M E Harrison, Dip Int Des Glasgow College of Building (*Design and Technology*)
Mrs J Harvey, BSc Sussex (*SEN*)
D W Heath, BA, MPhil London (*Religious Studies*)
Ms S E Herold, BA New York University, Hornsby Dip (*SEN teacher*)
Mrs H Heurtevent-Robin, BA Caen, Normandy, DEUG I and II Université Catholique, Angers (*Head of French*)
S P Hiscocks, BSc Essex, PhD, CChem, MRSC (*Head of Science, Chemistry*)
†D W Holmes, LRAM (*Head of Strings, Assistant Housemaster, Games*)
†Miss K E Horgan, BA Coventry (*Head of Economics and Business Studies, Assistant Housemistress*)
P J Horley, BA, ARCO, ALCM, College of Ripon and York St John (*Director of Music, CCF*)
Mrs A M Kane, BA Canterbury Christ Church (*SEN*)
D J J Keep, MA Greenwich, BEd Avery Hill College (*Head of Design and Technology, Head of Third Form, CCF*)
D R Kennedy, BSc Leeds, CBiol, MIBiol (*Head of Biology, Games*)
Rev P A Kish, BD London, AKC, MA, DipSpPsych, MTh (*Chaplain*)
Mrs C J Kitchen, BEng Bradford, MSc Birmingham, BSc Open (*Head of Sixth Form Section, Head of Mathematics*)
R J Lindley, BEng Leeds and De Montfort, PhD Leicester (*Head of Physics*)
J C Llanes-Thays, Maîtrise Bordeaux (*Modern Foreign Languages*)
Mrs K W J Luxford, BA Hull (*Head of Second Form, English*)
D R Mathews, BSc Brunel (*Sports Studies, Games, i/c Hockey*)
R Lyle, BA (*English, German, i/c Fives*)
G J Millbery, BA Lampeter (*Director of ICT, Duke of Edinburgh's Scheme, CCF*)
Miss K J McConnachie (*ICT, PE, i/c Netball*)
Miss L A Mitchell, BA (*Mathematics*)
I V Overton, BA Loughborough (*Geography, Games*)
A Penfold, BA Surrey (*Head of Religious Studies*)
R W J E Plowden, MA Wales, BA Newcastle (*History*)
Mrs F H Porter, BA Leeds (*English, CCF*)
Miss S Pritchard, BA (*Business Studies, i/c Social Enterprise Group*)

Mrs S Rose, BEd Bishops Otter College (*English, Games*)
†D R L Sansom, BSc Swansea (*Geography, Assistant Housemaster*)
†Mrs J Stanford, CertEd Lady Mabel College (*Science, Housemistress*)
Mrs E Taylor, CertEd St Mary's College (*SEN*)
J Walsh, MSc Imperial, BSc Liverpool, CBiol, MIBiol (*Biology*)
Mrs S Watson, BA Heriot-Watt (*DT Textiles*)
†K R Webster, MEd Crewe & Alsager College (*Mathematics, Housemaster*)
P Webster, MA Oxon (*Modern Foreign Languages*)
†C D Wesselink, BA South Africa (*Mathematics, Head of Third Form, Games*)
C J Westlake, BSc (*Mathematics*)
Mrs A F F Wilkinson, Cert Ed Calder College, Liverpool (*Home Economics, OC CCF, Head of Fourth Form*)
A Wyles, BSc London, MEd Open University, FRGS (*Geography, Director of Sixth Form*)
Miss C Yoxall, BA (*English*)

Bursar: S Fowle
Assistant Bursar: Mrs D van Leeuwen

Headmaster's PA: Mrs S O'Connell
Admissions Officer: Mrs K Webster
Development Manager: Mrs H Knott, BSc

Sports Hall Manager: J van Vuuren (*House Tutor*)

Curriculum Organisation. The academic curriculum is innovative and aims to achieve a balance between the needs of the individual and demands of society, industry, the universities and the professions. Classes are small and the ratio of graduate teaching staff is 1:9.

In 1st and 2nd Form (Years 7 and 8) the National Curriculum is broadly followed, covering English, Mathematics, Chemistry, Physics, Biology, French, Spanish, History, Geography, Religious Studies, Design Technology, Home Economics, ICT, Art, Music, Physical Education and Drama.

The National Curriculum is again broadly followed in 3rd Form (Year 9) where subjects offered are the same as in 1st and 2nd Form. However, the syllabi are designed to cater for not only those who enter 3rd Form via 1st and 2nd Form, but also the large number of pupils who join the school at 13+.

In 4th and 5th Form (Years 10 and 11) pupils usually study nine or ten subjects to GCSE level. These are divided between the core – English and English Literature, Mathematics, a Modern Language (French, Spanish, German), Science, Religious Studies, PSHE and ICT – and option groups. Each group contains a number of subjects, offering a choice which allows every pupil to achieve a balanced education whilst, at the same time, providing the opportunity to concentrate on his or her strengths. Subjects on offer are History, Geography, Drama, Business Studies, a second Language, DT, Home Economics, Art, Music, i-media and PE.

In the two years covered by the Lower and Upper Sixth (Years 12 and 13) pupils usually study four subjects at AS Level. Pupils continue with three, or occasionally, four subjects in their final year to A Level and are well positioned to meet the entrance requirements of the universities and professions. Psychology, Media Studies and Theatre Studies are included in this programme.

Potential Oxbridge candidates are identified in the Lower Sixth year and suitable tuition is arranged.

Choice of Subjects: Separate booklets on GCSE and A Level options are available.

Setting, Promotion, Reporting. In 1st to 5th Form Mathematics and French are setted. In 1st to 3rd Form a top group is selected.

The minimum qualification for entry into the Sixth Form is normally considered to be five B grade passes at GCSE Level. Academic progress is monitored by tutors and at regular intervals throughout the term every pupil is graded for achievement and effort in every subject. Parents are invited to a 'monitoring morning' at every half term to discuss their child's progress and to set targets for improvement next half term, if required. At the end of term full subject reports are written on all pupils. Promotion between sets is always possible.

ICT (iMedia). In addition to well-equipped computer suites the School has developed a sophisticated campus-wide network with its own intranet and online systems of communication with parents.

The school network serves the whole site providing open access for pupils in the computer rooms and throughout the school via a Microsoft Windows-based system working on industry-standard software. The library stocks many CD ROMs and there is a CAD system in Design and Technology. Access to the network is available to pupils in their own rooms in boarding houses.

Higher Education and Careers. Sutton Valence has a modern and well-equipped Sixth Form Centre which incorporates a careers library and the latest technologies to help in degree and career selection.

Every pupil sits a series of aptitude and ability tests during the two years prior to GCSE. This is followed by a thorough interview with trained members of staff in conjunction with the Kent Careers Service, when suggestions are made for Sixth Form academic courses and possible degrees or careers are explored.

In the Sixth Form further interviews are conducted, the Higher Education Coordinator gives advice on university and college applications and a range of career lectures and visits are laid on, including trips to Oxford and Cambridge universities.

Music. Music plays a very important part in the life of the school, and we have a deservedly fine reputation for the quality and range of our music-making. The music school contains a concert hall, five teaching rooms, ten practice rooms and an ensemble room.

One third of the pupils learn a musical instrument; there are four choirs, an orchestra, wind band, string group, jazz band, and a very full programme of concerts. Music tours to Europe have been arranged, and the Music Society organises a programme of distinguished visiting performers every year.

Drama. As with Music, Drama is central to the life of the school and the creative expression of our students. Every year there will be a number of productions, in addition to theatre workshops and reviews. Drama scholars and others also receive one-to-one drama coaching lessons in preparation for LAMDA exams. The Baughan Theatre provides an adaptable venue seating up to 250 for drama, music and lectures, along with rehearsal rooms, technical gantry and scene dock.

Sport and Physical Education. Sutton Valence has a deserved reputation as a strong sporting school, competing in seventeen sports. On average forty pupils will have representative honours at County, Regional and National levels in the main sports as well as in other disciplines.

Our 100-acre site has one of the best cricket squares in Kent, two floodlit Astroturf pitches for hockey, a six-lane indoor swimming pool, tennis, netball and squash courts, a sports hall encompassing a full-size indoor hockey pitch, sprung-floor cricket nets and fitness suite, six golf practice holes and a floodlit all-weather running track. In all, there is a tremendous range of choice for both boys and girls, all of whom will have timetabled sport on at least two days every week and could be involved in a sporting activity every day, if they wished. Additional sports, such as football, judo, dance, horse-riding, badminton, basketball, fives and fencing are offered through our activities programme.

Pastoral System. The School is arranged in Year Groups – from First to Upper Sixth. Each year group has a Head of Year and within each year group, pupils are divided into

Tutor Groups. The Sixth Form is led by the Director of Sixth Form, supported by two Heads of Section. Pupils meet with their Tutor every day and this allows their progress to be monitored as well as giving pupils an opportunity to seek guidance. In addition to monitoring academic progress, tutors help pupils develop their potential through the Personal, Social and Health Education (PSHE) programme.

The School is a Christian foundation, however, our values are very much based on openness, tolerance and inclusivity. As such, we welcome students from all faith backgrounds, as well as those families who have no faith commitment.

Community Service, CCF and Duke of Edinburgh's Award Scheme. All pupils are expected to join one or more of the service schemes offered by the School. The CCF, with Army, RAF and Royal Navy sections, is exemplary and very successful. It offers a wide variety of activities through regular camps, adventure training, field weekends and range days which feed personal development and leadership skills. The Duke of Edinburgh's Award Scheme is, similarly, well supported. Others participate in Community Service activities whereby pupils visit local primary schools, old people's homes, hospitals, undertake charity work and help out with local conservation projects.

Clubs and Activities. Time is specifically set aside each week for clubs and activities. Every pupil spends time pursuing his or her own special interests, and with up to forty clubs or activities from which to choose, the range and scope is very wide. In addition, various school societies and some other activities take place out of school hours, for example the Kingdon Society for Academic Scholars.

Entrance Scholarships. (*See Scholarship Entries section.*) Scholarships and Exhibitions are available in Drama, Music, Art, Design Technology and Sport. Junior and Senior Academic Scholarships are available. Further discretionary support is available through the Bursary Committee.

Fees per term (2011-2012). Full Boarders £6,960–£8,840; Day pupils £4,430–£5,800 (Lunch £230).

Instrumental Music: £220 per term (10 lessons).

Extras: Books, stationery and clothing are charged for as supplied. A small charge is also made for entry at each stage to The Duke of Edinburgh's Award Scheme. Any other extras are those expenses personal to the individual. We have a series of bus routes available to families from areas across Kent costing up to £300 per term. Further details of routes can be obtained on request.

Charitable status. United Westminster Schools Foundation is a Registered Charity, number 309267. Its aims are to promote education through its two independent schools and one state comprehensive school.

Taunton School

Taunton, Somerset TA2 6AD
Tel: 01823 703703
         01823 703603 Headmaster
         01823 703700 Admissions
Fax: 01823 703704
e-mail: enquiries@tauntonschool.co.uk
website: www.tauntonschool.co.uk

Motto: '*Ora et Labora*'

Taunton School is a friendly, purposeful co-educational boarding and day community with high academic standards and a full extra-curricular programme. Pupils are expected to develop their talents to the full and to learn habits of self-discipline that will stand them in good stead in Higher Education and professional training. The School is exceptionally well-equipped and attractively situated with extensive grounds. It has four parts: the Senior School (13–18) of about 563 pupils (with a Sixth Form of around 268), the

Preparatory School (7–13) of about 300, the Pre-Preparatory and Nursery (2–7) of about 140, and an International School with 83 pupils. Each section has a distinct persona within the whole family, but the School has the advantage of offering a coordinated curriculum.

Governors:

President & Chairman: Mrs Jane E Barrie, OBE, BSc, ARCS, FSI, DL
Deputy Chairman: Miss Alannah E Hunt, FCIPD
Treasurer: Mr Christopher C Butters, FCA

Mr Charles N C Abram, CertEd
Mr Clive N G Arding, FRICS
Vice Admiral Sir Tom Blackburn, KCVO, CB
Revd David Grosch-Miller BA
Major General Jonathan Hall, CB, OBE, FCMI, DL
Mr John R Hine, LLB
Mr Mark Hobbs, MA
Mrs Gillian Hylson-Smith, BA Hons
Mr Richard Kennedy, LLB, FCA
Mr Alan M Large, LLB
Mr Geoffrey A Matthews, BA, LLD Hons
Mrs Elaine Waymouth

Honorary Life Vice-Presidents:
Mr Brian P Bissell, MBE, MA, BD
Air Vice Marshal Peter J Harding, CB, CVO, CBE, AFC, FRAeS
Major General Barry M Lane, CB, OBE
Mr David T Watson, MA, FCA
Mrs Joan M R Williams, LLB, AKC

Bursar & Clerk to the Governors: Mr David J A Taylor, GradICSA

Headmaster: Dr John H Newton, MA, FCollP, DipMS Ed

Deputy Head: Mr Lee C Glaser, MA
Director of Studies: Mr Neil Mason, BSc
Director of Recreation: Mr Hugh K C Todd, CertEd (*†Wills East*)
Head of Sixth Form: Mr Simon N J Smith, BEng
Head of Middle School: Mrs Carol Manley (*†Jenkin*)
Head of Boarding: Mr Alistair J Hallows, BSc (*†Weirfield*)
Staff Development Coordinator: Mrs Mary Mason, MRSC

Assistant Staff:
* *Head of Department*
† *House Staff*

Mr Rob Abell, BSc (**Business Studies; †Evans*)
Mrs Christabel Ager, BA, ALA (*Librarian*)
Mrs Fiona Baker, BMus (*Assistant Director of Music*)
Mr Jonathan Baker, BA (**Design & Technology*)
Miss Barbara Battaglino (*Modern Languages*)
Mr David Bearman, BSc (*Physics*)
Mrs Annegret K Beere (*Modern Languages*)
Miss Lizzie Birkett, BA (*English*)
Mrs Jane Bluemel, MA (*Physics*)
Mr Martin Bluemel, MA, CChem, MRSC (**Chemistry; IB Coordinator*)
Mrs Louise Bolland, BA (*Modern Languages*)
Miss Laura Brayley, BA (*History*)
Mr David Bridges, GRSM, ARCM, ARCO (*Chapel Organist; Choirmaster*)
Mr Jonathan Brooker, BSc (*Design & Technology*)
Mr A John Brown, MA (*Modern Languages; Examinations Officer*)
Mr T Mark Chatterton, BA (**History*)
Mrs Tracey Coleman, MSc (*Physics*)
Miss Susannah L Commings, MA, MPhil (*English*)
Mr Mike Cook, BSc (*Biology; †Marshall*)
Mrs Laura A Cooke, MPhil, MSc (*Science*)
Mrs Ruth Coomber, BSc, MTeg (*Geography*)

Mr Mark Cracknell, BA (*Director of Music*)
Mrs Alexandra Cutts, BA (*English*)
Mr Philip Cutts, MA (*Mathematics*)
Mrs Lisa Davey, BA (*Economics*)
Mrs Loreto Diaz, BA, Lic en Derecho (*Spanish*)
M Greg R Fabre, Maître, LLCE (*Modern Languages*)
Mrs Susan Falkingham, MA, BEd (**Spanish; *Psychology*)
Mr Peter Finan, BA (*Biology*)
Mrs Gill Foster, BA (*English*)
Dr Alison S Franklin, BSc (*Chemistry*)
Miss Lin Gao, MA, BEd (*Modern Languages*)
Mrs Audrey Gaskell (*Head of Modern Languages*)
Mr Paul Gibson, BSc (*Mathematics*)
Mr Robert Goodhand, BSc (*Mathematics*)
Mr Thomas E Grant, BA (*Art*)
Mr Neil Gush, BA (*Design & Technology*)
Mrs Sally Hale, BA (*Academic Development & Mathematics*)
Mrs Tracy Hallows, BSc (*†Weirfield*)
Dr Lotte Hammer, BA (**Art*)
Miss Geraldine Harris, BA (*Art and Photography*)
Mr Alastair Harrison, BA, FDA (*English*)
Ms Claire Harvie, BSc (**Physical Education i/c Girls' Hockey*)
Mr David R O Hawkins, BA (*History*)
Mrs Sarah J Hearn, BA (**Classics*)
Mr Simon Hogg (*Mathematics; Master i/c Cricket*)
Mrs Fiona Holford, BA (**EFL*)
Mr Andrew Hopwood, BSc (*Mathematics*)
Miss Judy Iredale, BA, Dip St Couns (*Modern Languages; *German*)
Mr Richard Judd, BTh, BEd (*Religious Studies*)
Mr Cyril Kelly, BA (*†Goodland; i/c Rugby*)
Mr Andrew D Kemp, MSc (**Mathematics*)
Mrs Ruth Kemp, MA (*Mathematics & Academic Development*)
Mr Alastair Kirby (*Drama*)
Mr Clive Large, BA, MA, MBA (*Mathematics*)
Mrs Jeanne Leader, BSc (**Geography*)
Mrs Carrie Marsden, BA (*Religious Studies & Critical Thinking*)
Mrs Charlotte H Marshall, BA (*Classics*)
Mr Neil McPherson, BA (**English*)
Miss H Mortimer, BA (*Head of PE i/c Netball*)
Mr Christopher A F Moule, MA (*History*)
Mrs Catherine Newton, BEd (*Asst Exams Officer & PSHE*)
Mr David H Parvin, MA (**ICT*)
Dr James H J Penny, BSc (**Science*)
Mrs Sally Phillips, BA (*English & EFL*)
Mr Ian Piper, BSc (*Chemistry*)
Mr Roger Priest, BA (*Classics*)
Mr Stephen Pugh, BSc (*†Wills West; Business Studies*)
Mrs Lynda Rixon, BSc (*Economics and Business Studies*)
Mr Adrian Roberts, BSc (*Geography*)
Mr Declan Rogers, MA (*†Fairwater; English; Registrar*)
Miss Sue V Roper, BEd (*Art*)
Miss Emma H Slade, BSc (*Biology*)
Miss Meryl Smart, BEd (**Theatre Studies and Drama*)
Miss Joanna Southcott, BCom (*Business Studies*)
Mrs Kate M Stent, BA (*Modern Languages*)
Mr David Tarr, BSc (*Head of Boys' Games; Master i/c Hockey & Tennis*)
Mrs Susan Treseder, MEd (*English; EFL*)
Mrs Lucy Turner, BA (**Leisure and Recreation*)
Mrs Caroline Vaughan, BSc (*Academic Development*)
Mr Luke Waller, BSc (*Physics*)
Mr Tim Waller, BM, MA (*Music*)
Mrs Kate Walters (**Learning Support*)
Mrs Annabel White, BA (*Theology*)
Mr James Wood, BA (*Classics*)
Mr Tony Workman, BSc (*Mathematics*)

Headmaster's Secretary: Mrs Carol Cotton, BA
Registrar: Mr Declan Rogers, MA

Assistant to the Registrar: Mrs Sue Goodall
Bursar's Secretary: Mrs Jean Eales
School Secretary: Mrs Susanna Sinclair
Medical Officers:
Dr Tim Howes
Dr Hilda Gormley
Foundation Director: Mr Neil Longstreet, BA

Situation. The School stands in its own grounds of over 50 acres on the Northern outskirts of Taunton, within easy reach of some of the most attractive countryside in England. Taunton is exceptionally well placed on the M5 and the Paddington to Penzance main line with easy access to all parts of the British Isles and Bristol and Heathrow airports.

Facilities. The School moved to its present site in 1870 to a fine range of buildings, purpose built in the Gothic style. The original house, Fairwater, dating from 18th century is a boys' boarding house. The Wills family, notably Lord Winterstoke, made a series of munificent gifts including the Chapel (completed in 1907), a Library, and two boys' boarding houses, Wills East and Wills West.

A separate Science Building was added as a War Memorial after the Great War, and subsequently extended. Building has proceeded continually as a result of good housekeeping and appeals, adding specialist teaching facilities, including a Drama Studio, and a purpose-built girls' boarding house. A policy of continuous modernisation has seen additions to the Houses, and in 1998 further accommodation for boarding girls. There have also been improvements to the Science laboratories and other teaching facilities. The Preparatory School (*see separate entry in IAPS section*) was rebuilt in 1994/95. A new Arts Centre was built in 1995. A new Astroturf was opened in 2007 and an extension to the Music School will open in Sept 2008. DT and Art facilities have seen significant recent investment.

Worship. The Chapel plays a central role in the life of the community. The School is no longer denominational and welcomes members of all Christian beliefs, or other faiths. There is a daily service and a service on Sundays for all boarders in residence. The Chapel Choir plays a major role in the enhancement of worship on special occasions. There are also instrumental music items, as part of chapel services, each week. The present Chaplain prepares candidates for confirmation and membership of all Protestant denominations and celebrates Holy Communion for all who are in good standing with their church. Preparation for Roman Catholic First Communion and Confirmation can be arranged.

Curriculum. In the first year of the Senior School the timetable sets out to give a wide experience of subjects, including the separate sciences.

At 16 pupils may study up to 11 GCSEs. These include English (Language and Literature), Mathematics, a Modern Foreign Language and Science as a core, and a choice from Art, Business Studies, Classical Civilisation, Design & Technology, Drama, Geography, German, Greek, History, Latin, Music, PE, Religious Studies and Spanish. All Year 10 pupils take a Religious Studies short course.

Twenty-three subjects are offered at AS & A2 Level, the latest additions being Theatre Studies, Physical Education and Psychology, with the majority of Sixth Formers aiming at university or college entry.

The School has recently added the International Baccalaureate to the courses available to Sixth Form students. Subjects available include English, German, French, Spanish, Mandarin, History, Geography, Economics, Philosophy, Biology, Chemistry, Physics, Maths, Further Maths and Visual Arts.

Careers. Careers advice is an important part of school life with work experience for all in the Lower Sixth. The Head of Careers and Director of Studies advise on applications for Higher Education.

Music. Music plays a vital part in the life of the School: about one third of the pupils take lessons in a great variety of instruments, and there are choral groups, orchestra, windband, ensembles, and a jazz band.

School Societies. Everyone is encouraged to participate in extra-curricular activities and a wide range is offered including debating, drama, the Duke of Edinburgh's Award Scheme, Combined Cadet Forces, community service and astronomy. The School has a distinguished international debating record.

Games. The School has an outstanding record in games and has strong fixture lists. The principal games are rugby, hockey, netball, cricket and tennis, with excellent facilities also for squash, badminton and basketball. The School has a shale and an artificial turf hockey pitch which was replaced in Summer 2007. The latter provides twelve tennis courts in the Summer. There are outdoor and indoor heated swimming pools. The Sports Hall is equipped with an up-to-date Fitness Suite, climbing wall and a wide range of indoor games. Pupils also take part in athletics, cross-country, canoeing, sailing, riding and golf. There is also a miniature rifle range. The School's philosophy is to encourage athletic excellence giving opportunities for all to enjoy physical activity.

Medical. The School Medical Centre provides the medical service for the whole School community, and is staffed by qualified nurses under the supervision of the School Medical Officer who visits daily.

Admission. The main ages of admission to the Senior School are 13 (Year 9) and 16 (Year 12), but entry into other year groups is also possible. Prospectuses and registration forms are available from the Registrar, who will also be pleased to arrange visits (01823 349223; registrar@tauntonschool.co.uk).

The Admissions Secretary at the Preparatory School (01823 349209) will be pleased to assist with enquiries for children up to the age of 13 (Nursery, Pre-Prep and Preparatory).

Entry at 13: The admission process usually requires the pupil to attend for interview and to submit recent school reports and a school reference. In some cases, the candidate may be required to sit assessment tests. Candidates attending Preparatory Schools may apply by sitting Common Entrance Examinations in June. Taunton Preparatory School pupils proceed to the Senior School on the basis of a Record of Progress.

Entry to the Sixth Form: Entry to the A Level course and the International Baccalaureate Diploma will normally be conditional on a minimum of 5 GCSE passes at grade A* to C, but interview and report play an important part in determining the offer of places. Candidates not taking GCSE examinations may be required to sit assessment tests.

Scholarships and Bursaries. A number of Scholarships (normally up to 50% of full fees) are awarded at the ages of 13 and 16.

13+ Scholarships: 13+ Open Scholarships take place in the Spring term and are open to all candidates, entering Year 9, who are under the age of 14 on 1st September in the year of entry. Academic and All-Rounder Scholarships are available with examinations taking place in February/March. Scholarships and Awards in Sport, Art, Music (including an Organ Scholarship), ICT and Drama are also available. Candidates for these awards are not required to sit the Open Scholarship examinations but will be required to attend for interview and audition or assessment in January/February.

The Open Scholarship examinations (for Academic and All-Rounder candidates) are held at Taunton School in the Spring term. (In special circumstances, papers may be taken at a candidate's Preparatory School.) Compulsory subjects are English, Mathematics, a Modern Language (French, German or Spanish), Science, History, Geography, Religious Studies and a General Paper, with optional papers in Latin, French, Spanish, German and Design & Technology.

Sixth Form Scholarships: These are awarded annually in November preceding the year of entry to the Sixth Form. Awards are made to outstanding boys or girls who will be taking GCSE examinations, or equivalent, in the current year and who are regarded as strong University candidates. Academic and All-Rounder examinations are taken in November. Applicants for Sport, Music, Art or Drama Scholarships are not required to sit these examinations, but will be asked to attend for interview and audition or assessment during November.

For further information and details on 13+ and 16+ scholarships please contact the Registrar on 01823 349223 or e-mail: registrar@tauntonschool.co.uk.

11+ Scholarships: A number of Scholarships are awarded to boys and girls, entering Year 7, who are under the age of 12 on 1st September in the year of entry. The examinations are held at Taunton Preparatory School in January and awards continue into the Senior School. Please call the Admissions Secretary on 01823 349209 for more information.

Bursaries: Ministerial Bursaries may be offered to the sons and daughters of Ministers of all recognised denominations, from the age of 11, on condition that the candidates satisfy the academic requirements of the School. Service Bursaries are available for the children of Service families.

Fees per term (2011-2012). Senior School: Boarders £8,535; Day £5,150.

Taunton Preparatory School: Boarders £3,705–£6,715; Day £2,225–£4,185. Pre-Preparatory & Nursery (full-time) £1,925.

Charitable status. Taunton School is a Registered Charity, number 1081420. It exists to provide education for boys and girls.

Tonbridge School

Tonbridge, Kent TN9 1JP
Tel: 01732 365555
Fax: 01732 363424
e-mail: hmsec@tonbridge-school.org
website: www.tonbridge-school.co.uk

Tonbridge School was founded in 1553 by Sir Andrew Judde, under Letters Patent of King Edward VI.

Tonbridge is an all-boys, 13–18, boarding and day school. 780 boys from a variety of backgrounds are offered an education remarkable both for its breadth of opportunity and the exceptional standards routinely achieved in all areas of school life.

The school aims to provide a caring and enlightened environment in which the talents of each individual flourish. We encourage boys to be creative, tolerant and to strive for academic, sporting and cultural excellence. Respect for tradition and an openness to innovation are equally valued. A well-established house system at the heart of the school fosters a strong sense of belonging. We want boys to enjoy their time here, but also to be made aware of their social and moral responsibilities. Tonbridgians should enter into the adult world with the knowledge and self-belief to fulfil their own potential and, in many cases to become leaders in their chosen field. Equally, we hope to foster a life-long empathy for the needs and views of others.

Tonbridge boys are extremely successful at obtaining places at leading universities (almost a quarter of leavers go to Oxford or Cambridge).

Visitors to Tonbridge are always welcome and full information about the school is available on our website: www.tonbridge-school.co.uk.

Motto: '*Deus dat incrementum*'

Governors:
J L Cohen, QC (*Chairman*)

J Aisher	D J Flint
C Brodie	G H Lucas
R D Brown	A Mayer
Mrs A Buggé	C Rudge
J Coldman	Professor S Stallebrass
D P Devitt	C A Stuart-Clark
R J Elliott	Mrs S Tozzi
C J D Emms	The Earl of Woolton

Clerk to the Governors: B Plummer, CBE

Headmaster: T H P Haynes, BA

Second Master: C W Jones, MA
Director of Studies: J C Pearson, MA
Director of Teaching and Learning: R M Brookes, MChem, DPhil
Director of Admissions: A J Leale, BA
Bursar: A C Moore, MA, MBA, INSEAD
Upper Master: A J Edwards, MA
Foundation Director: J R Underhill, ARICS

Assistant Staff:
* *Head of Department/Subject*

Art:
*Mrs C H Chisholm, BA
Mrs J de Pear, MA
T W Duncan, BA
Mrs E R Glass, MA
Mrs B L Waugh, BA
   (*maternity leave*)
Art Librarian: Mrs M P Dennington
Art Technician: Mrs J M Brent
Designer & Art Gallery Tech: B Stenning

A J Edwards, MA
R H Evans, MA
Mrs D M Hulse, MA, DipModDrama
J Johnson, BA, MPhil
N J Waywell, BA

Geography:
*C M Battarbee, BA
C M Henshall, BA
G P Gales, BEd
J E Perriss, BA
M G Rowan, MA, FRGS
D H Tennant, BSc

Classics:
*J S Taylor, MA, DPhil
H B Cullen, BA
J D Gibbs, MA, LLB
J A Nicholls, MA
P W G Parker, MA
A P Schweitzer, MA

History:
*L W B Ramsden, BA, MSt
D Cooper, MA
Mrs F C Dix Perkin, MA
J C Harber, MA
C W Jones, MA
R W G Oliver, MA
Miss M L Robinson, MA

Design Technology:
*D Dixon, BA
W D F Biddle, BSc
J M Woodrow, BA
D L Faithfull, BTech, MSc, CEng
Technology Technician: A Perry
Teaching Assistant: C Martin

Mathematics:
*I R H Jackson, MA, PhD
S Burns, BSc
M J Clugston, MA, DPhil
T G Fewster, BSc
R J Freeman, MA
K A Froggatt, MA
J D King, MA, PhD
M J Lawson, BA
N J Lord, MA
V Myslov, BA
A P Schweitzer, MA
S J Seldon, MA, MEng
A R Whittall, MA

Divinity:
*J C F Dobson, MA
R Burnett, MA
J C Carter, BA
The Revd D A Peters, MA
H Swales, BA

Drama:
*G D Bruce, MA
M I Morrison, BA, MEd
L Thornbury, DipDrama

Modern Languages:
*L S McDonald, MA (*French)
C E Wright, BA (*German)
J R S McIntosh, MA (*Spanish)
A L Austin, MA
Mrs B H P Austin, M-ès-M
A E Bissill, MA
R Burnett, MA
Mrs T Coomber, L-ès-L

English:
*R B Malpass, BA, PhD
J P Arscott, MA
J R Bleakley, BA
P S D Carpenter, MA
D Cooper, MA

Mrs C Cordero, Lda en Fil
R D Hoare, MA
  (*International
  Coordinator*)
Miss D M McDermot, MA
J A Nicholls, MA

P W G Parker, MA
T W Richards, BA
S M Wainde, MA
X J Wu, MA (*Mandarin
  Chinese*)
Mrs X Y Wu, BA

Music:
*M A Forkgen, MA, ARCO (*Director of Music*)
D J Clack, ARCM (*Brass*)
J R P Thomas, MA, FRCO (*Head of Academic Music &
  Choirmaster*)
A E L Pearson, BMus, ARCM, LRAM (*Strings*)
D L Williams, GRSM, ARCM, LRAM (*Piano*)
S J Hargreaves, BA, ATCL
Miss E M Jones, BA

Physical Education:
Director of Sport: A R Whittall, MA
Head of PE: C D Morgan, BSc

Science:
*W J Burnett, BSc, PhD
R L Fleming, MA, MInstP (**Physics*)
T S Banyard, BA
G M Barnes, BSc
S Chalk, BSc, PhD
D L Faithfull, BTech, MSc, CEng
D S Knox, MPhys
A G McGilchrist, MA
D S Pinker, PhD, MSci
J A Fisher, BSc (**Chemistry*)
R M Brookes, MChem, DPhil
M J Clugston, MA, DPhil
D A Cruse, MA, PhD, CChem, MRSC, MRI
C R Lawrence, MA
J C Pearson, MA
Miss K E Wood, MChem
P M Ridd, MA (**Biology*)
P J Belbin, BSc, MEd
W J Burnett, BSc, PhD
A T Sampson, BSc
C J C Swainson, MA
D H Tennant, BSc

Social Science:
J D W Richards, MA, PhD (**Economics*)
N R V Rendall (**Politics*)
J Blake, BA, MSc (**Business Studies*)
Ms H M Harris, BA, MSc
A J Leale, BA
J H Maynard, BA
Miss K E Moxon, MA
T G Settle, BSc, MSc

Director of ICT Services:
I N Lucas BSc

University Entrance and Careers:
Mrs A Rogers, BA

Learning Support:
Mrs P Brandling-Harris, BA, DipSpLD, AMBDA
Mrs C Clugston, MA
Mrs G Firmston, CertEd, DipSpLD, AMBDA
Mrs R Thomson, BA, DipHE, TESOL

Houses & Housemasters:

Boarding:
School House: R Burnett
Judde House: G P Gales
Park House: A E Bissill
Hill Side: J Johnson
Parkside: J E Perriss
Ferox Hall: A R Whittall
Manor House: C J C Swainson

Day:
Welldon House: R H Evans
Smythe House: C M Henshall
Whitworth House: W D F Biddle
Cowdrey House: R W G Oliver
Oakeshott House: J R Bleakley

Administration:
Librarian: Mrs B Matthews, MCLIP
Headmaster's PA: Mrs L R O'Neill
Admissions Secretaries:
Miss I C Beeson (*LoVIth Admissions*)
Miss R Hearnden
Mrs S L Maynard (*pre-selection testing*)
School Administrator: Miss E J Day

Location. Tonbridge School is just off the M25, on the edge of the Kent / Surrey / Sussex borders and attracts families from all over southern England and beyond. It lies in about 150 acres of land on the edge of the town of Tonbridge, and thus provides a good balance between town and country living.

Admissions and Scholarships. (*See Scholarship Entries section*.) The majority of boys join the school at the age of 13, having gained admission through the Common Entrance Examination or the school's own Scholarship Examination (held in early May). About 140 boys are admitted at the age of 13 each year. An additional 20 places are available for entry to the Sixth Form at the age of 16. We also have up to 6 places for boys aged 14 (Year 10).

About 45 scholarships are offered each year, including 21 academic scholarships and awards for Music, Art, Drama, Technology and Sport. Sixth Form scholarships (academic/music) are also awarded. All scholarships entitle the award holder to a minimum 10% fee reduction and the value of any scholarship may be increased, by any amount up to the full school fee, if assessment of the parents' means indicates a need.

Registration of a boy for 13+ entry should be made as early as possible, and preferably not later than three years before the date of intended entry. Boys will then be asked to come to Tonbridge to sit a short computer-based cognitive test. The results of this test, in conjuction with the current school Head's report, will determine whether the offer of a place may be made, conditional upon either Common Entrance or Scholarship entry at 13 years old. Applications for 14+ and Sixth Form entry are best made by September a year before entry, but may be considered later. Admission at 14+ (and at 13+ from schools who do not prepare boys for common entrance) is gained via our own Maths and English exams. Boys sitting for entry at 16+ will take papers in the 4 subjects they wish to study for A Level.

Parents wishing to send their sons to Tonbridge should apply to the Director of Admissions for a copy of the Prospectus, which gives full details of the registration procedure. Information is also available on the website: www.tonbridge-school.co.uk.

Fees per term (2011-2012). Boarders £10,421; Day Boys £7,780.

Charitable status. Tonbridge School is a Registered Charity, number 1097977. It exists solely to provide education for boys.

Trent College

Derby Road, Long Eaton, Nottingham NG10 4AD
Tel: 0115 849 4949
         0115 849 4920 Bursar
         0115 849 4950 Admissions
Fax: 0115 849 4997
e-mail: enquiry@trentcollege.net
website: www.trentcollege.net

The Foundation Stone of Trent College was laid by the seventh Duke of Devonshire in 1866 and the School opened two years later. The School was founded by Francis Wright.
  Motto: '*Sapientia Fons Vitae*'

President: His Grace, The Duke of Devonshire, CBE

Chairman of Governors: Mr C M McDowell, FCIB

Senior Management Team:

Head: Mrs G Dixon, BSc Warwick, MBA Leicester

Bursar: Mr H Nelson, FCMA, ACIS
Deputy Head, Academic: Dr P D Kelly, BSc, PhD Loughborough
Deputy Head, Pastoral: Mr M A Cowie, BSc Glasgow, MEd Manchester
Head of Sixth Form: Ms L Matthews, BA Hull
Head of Main School: Mr G A Wright, BA Liverpool
Head of Lower School: Mr W A Webster, BA Rhodes, SA
Head of Curriculum: Mr D J Tidy, BEd Nottingham Trent, MA Loughborough

Head of The Elms: Mr K B Morrow, BA Hull, NPQH

Director of Admissions: Miss R Appleton, BA Nottingham Trent
Admissions Manager: Mrs S Christie

Chaplain: Revd Father Timothy Whitwell, BTh Oxford, PhD Durham, MA Leeds

Boarding Houses & Housemasters/mistresses:
Bates: Mrs M Daykin
Martin: Mrs C Rayfield
Blake: Mr K P Taylor
Shuker: Mr P J Millward

Heads of Department:

Art:
Mrs K O'Hare, BA Chester

Biology:
Dr S Wastie, BSc PhD Nottingham

Business:
Mrs D Mansell, BA UMIST

Chemistry:
Dr C Wakerley, BSc Nottingham Trent, PhD Loughborough

Design & Technology:
Mr J Prince, BSc Loughborough

English:
Mrs E D Dunford, BA York

Geography:
Miss V G Bletsoe-Brown, BSc Reading

History:
Mr P S Mayfield, BA Nottingham

Latin:
Mrs C Applegate, BA Liverpool, MA Nottingham

Learning Support:
Mrs P Pemberton, BA Birmingham, Dip SpLD, AMDBA

Mathematics:
Mr J W Bratton, BA York, MEd Nottingham, MBA Nottingham

Modern Languages:
Mr K D Price, BA Cardiff

Music:
Mr J Rayfield, BMus Birmingham (*Director of Music*)

Physical Education/Games:
Mr A M Benstead, BA QTS, MA Warwick (*Director of Sport*)

Miss C C Salisbury, BSc Loughborough, MSc Loughborough

Politics:
Mr M Stevens, MSc Nottingham Trent, BSc Salford

Psychology:
Mr L Taylor, BSc Brunel, MIfL

Physics:
Dr J E Morley, BSc, PhD Leicester (*Director of ICT*)

Religious Studies:
Mrs A Bruzon, BA Surrey

Theatre Studies:
Mr D Brown, BA WCMD (*Director of Drama*)
Mrs A L Bolton, BA Nottingham

School Sports Coaches:
Mr D Barnes (*Tennis*)
Mrs J Malinski (*Netball*)
Mr C Gray (*Rugby*)
Mr M Taylor (*Cricket*)

Head of Library Services: Ms A Dase, MA Nottingham Trent, MA Loughborough
School Counsellor: Mrs M Braine, BA Hull, MA Birmingham
School Matron: Mrs M Douglas
CCF SSI and Health & Safety Advisor: Mr A J McIntyre, WO1

Junior School – The Elms:
Head: Mr K B Morrow, BA Hons, NPQH
Deputy Head: Mrs L Deller, BA Hons University of Wales

Location. Trent College is situated in 45 acres of beautiful grounds, midway between Nottingham and Derby, near the town of Long Eaton.
  Pupils. The Nursery and Junior School, The Elms, caters for 350 children from the age of 3 to 11. (*See IAPS entry.*)
  The Senior School is divided into three key areas: the Lower School (11–13) with around 200 pupils, the Main School (13–16) with about 350 pupils and the Sixth Form of around 220. Pupils may choose to board from the age of 11 and there are currently 120 boarders.
  Ethos and Aims. Though we value our unique and distinguished past, at Trent College we have our eyes firmly set on the demands being made on young people in the 21st century and a spirit of energy, creativity and innovation shapes our school life.
  Academic study is important and we expect our students to achieve high standards. We are, however, committed to offering a broadly-based education, which celebrates all; the academic, creative, physical, emotional and spiritual, and which allows our young people to discover all of their strengths and make the most of their talents. Our aspiration is for each individual here to achieve their absolute personal best, in whatever they do.
  Trent College has a boarding school ethos: day pupils may stay in school until 5.40 pm on each weekday; three lessons are taught on Saturday mornings (except for those in the Lower School) and there are games for the vast majority on Saturday afternoon. We appreciate the changing needs of parents and we offer flexible boarding, where pupils can go home after their commitment on Saturday or stay and join in the weekend activities.
  Buildings. As well as the fully functioning 145 year old original School building and Chapel, there has been an impressive development programme over the last 20 years with the addition of an Art, Design & Technology Centre; Sixth Form Boarding Houses; a Biology Centre; teaching facilities for Modern Languages and History; a Business Centre and a refurbished Sixth Form Centre. The Obolensky Dining Hall and the Lee Conference Room were opened in 2009 and provide a venue for whole-school community din-

ing and events. The School also boasts an excellent library facility in the newly created Devonshire building which also houses a separate Learning Support Suite.

Academic. Whilst taking full note of the implications of the National Curriculum, Trent has its own curriculum to GCSE. All pupils take Maths, English Language and English Literature at GCSE. Six additional GCSEs are taken from a wide range of options. The School also offers IGC-SEs in Physics and Mathematics. In the Sixth Form every student takes four Advanced GCE AS subjects; the more able may take further courses selecting from a wide range of options. The AQA Baccalaureate is also available for students who wish to follow this broader course. The School offers the very successful EPQ Programme which encourages the independent exploration and knowledge development of a subject of a student's choosing to enhance their university applications alongside their A Level portfolios. The vast majority of the pupils leaving the school proceed to degree courses at university, including places at Oxford or Cambridge.

Physical Education. The major sports, played on three afternoons a week, are rugby, hockey and cricket for boys and hockey, netball and tennis for girls. There are also extensive facilities for a vast array of other sports. The School places great emphasis on all pupils being given the chance to develop their sporting talent, whatever their level, and the School, with its large number of teams, tries to provide as many as possible with the opportunity of representing the School. The very well-established PE department has run playing tours to Canada, Italy and Belgium and regularly organises master classes involving prominent athletes and team players.

Music and Drama. Many pupils learn musical instruments and many play to a very high standard. With a First, an Intermediate and a Junior Orchestra, together with several other bands and ensembles, all musicians, no matter what their standard or age, are given every opportunity to perform with others. An early experience of public performance helps maintain the overall high standard of musicianship.

There is a whole range of excellent dramatic productions each year, performed in either the May Hall or the Melton Studio Theatre, so that as many as young thespians as possible are given the chance of developing their dramatic talent.

Societies. Tutors encourage their tutees to make good use of the many and varied societies and activities which are on offer either at lunchtime, late afternoon or early evening. This area of the school is flourishing and helps pupils develop broad interests. The enrichment opportunities at the School are very broad and students are encouraged in many ways such as visits, charity work and participation in clubs and competitions to broaden their horizons and empathise with other ways of life. The Whole School Programme is the central vision and format for academic lectures, societies and activities. The programme sees exciting speakers from all possible walks of life address the students to offer inspiration, stimulation and encouragement.

Service Activities. On one afternoon each week, every pupil in Year 10 and above opts for one 'Service' activity. These choices include: CCF (Army or RAF section), Community Service, Duke of Edinburgh's Award, Adventure Training and Life Saving. Many of the Service Activities, particularly CCF, Duke of Edinburgh's Award and Scouts, organise exciting holiday activities.

Expeditions. Over the last few years, Trent has established an impressive record of organising overseas mountaineering/trekking expeditions. An extremely diverse range of countries have been visited including: Mongolia, Iceland, Turkey, India and Greenland. Skiing trips are also a regular feature of School life.

Art, Design, Technology and Computing. Art, Design, Technology and Computing flourish at Trent, both as academic subjects and interests. Extra-curricular involvement is strongly encouraged and, in recent years, Trent has established a most successful record in regional, national and international competitions.

Fees per term (2011-2012). Junior School: £2,500 (Foundation Stage), £2,500 (KS1), £2,625 (KS2). Lower School (Years 7 and 8): £3,735 (day). Main School: Year 9: £4,235 (day), £5,650 (weekly boarding), £7,290 (full boarding); Years 10–Sixth Form: £4,665 (day), £6,125 (weekly boarding), £7,905 (full boarding).

As far as possible we aim to make fees all-inclusive and only charge for genuine extras.

Admission. Entry to the Junior School is mainly at Nursery, Reception or Year 3. All pupils are assessed, and entry can be assured at any time during the year. Most pupils enter the Senior School in September, although it is entirely possible for entry to take place at other times in the year.

Lower School (11+ entry): Approximately 110 day places are available each year. Entry is dependent on the result of a competitive examination held in late January, an interview and a confidential report from the child's current school.

Main School (13+ entry): 14 places are available, predominantly boarding entry. Entry is decided as a result of a competitive examination held in late January, an interview and a confidential report from the child's current school.

Sixth Form Entry: there are approximately 20 places available each year for girls and boys. Places are awarded following an interview and the receipt of a confidential report from the applicant's present school, but are ultimately conditional on a satisfactory performance at GCSE (3 B grades and 2 C grades).

Scholarships. A large range of Scholarships is available and Trent College Assisted Places are also available to those in need of extra financial support.

Awards are made for excellence in Music, Drama, Art, Sport and Academic ability at 11+ 13+ and Sixth Form. The 'Devonshire Scholarships', for the attainment of academic, sport, music, drama and art excellence are means-tested scholarships that may account for up to 75 per cent of fees for successful applicants. It is open to students of any age not currently studying at Trent College.

The value of an award depends on the age of the child, their ability and whether they are a day pupil or a boarder.

Full details of all scholarships, examinations and entrance procedures are available from the Admissions Manager, Tel 0115 849 4950.

School Prospectus. A prospectus and registration details may also be obtained from the Admissions Manager. Parents are warmly encouraged to visit the School for a personal tour.

Charitable status. Trent College Limited is a Registered Charity, number 527180. Its aims are to provide education for boys and girls between the ages of 3 and 18.

Trinity School
Croydon

Shirley Park, Croydon CR9 7AT
Tel: 020 8656 9541
Fax: 020 8655 0522
e-mail: admissions@trinity.croydon.sch.uk
website: www.trinity-school.org

The School was founded by Archbishop John Whitgift in 1596. The full title of the school is Trinity School of John Whitgift.

Motto: '*Vincit qui Patitur*'

Visitor: His Grace The Archbishop of Canterbury

Governing Body:
Chairman: I Harley, MA, FCA, FCIB

His Honour William Barnett, QC, MA Oxon
The Revd Canon C J L Boswell, The Vicar of Croydon
C J Houlding
Mrs R A Jones, MA
Cllr T Letts, OBE
P J Squire, MA
G H Wright, TD, DL, FCIOB
G Barwell, MP
Cllr D Mead, FCCA, FCMA, FCIS
Ms N Clarke, MA
D C Hudson, MA
Miss P Davies, BSc, MEd

Clerk to the Governors: M Corney

Headmaster: M J Bishop, MA Oxford, MBA

Deputy Headmaster: J P McKee, BA Cambridge
Head of Upper School: Miss S L Ward, BSc Birmingham
Head of Lower School: R Brookman, BSc London
Director of Studies: N H Denman, MA Oxford
Estates Manager: R M McKinlay

Assistant Staff:
* Head of Department
§ part-time

Miss A M Abad, BA Murcia, MA London (*Spanish**)
P G Abbott, BSc Cardiff (*Economics & Business Studies*)
M I Aldridge, BEd Lon (*Design Technology, Deputy Head of Sixth Form*)
E M Alexander, BEd St Luke's, Exeter (*Geography, General Studies**)
Mrs J L Anderson, BSc Bath (*Biology*)
M Asbury, BSc Bath (*Mathematics, Internal Exams**)
M S Asquith, BA, MA, PhD London (*English*)
D Bastyan, BSc Warwick (*Mathematics*)
Ms N M Beaumont, BSc Oxford (*Mathematics*)
Miss H A Benzinski, BSc London (*Mathematics*)
G C Beresford-Miller, BA Rhodes (*PE*)
J Bird, BSc Kent (*Biology*)
Mrs N Blamire-Marin, BA Granada (*Lektora*)
N A Bowling, BA Oxford (*Classics*)
C R Burke Port Elizabeth (*Physical Education, English*)
T W Chesters, BSc Strathclyde (*Design Technology*)
S W Christian, BA Liverpool (*French, Spanish, Language Awareness*)
A J Codling, BA Portsmouth (*Director of Sport**)
A Cornick, BA Southampton Institute (*Physical Education*)
§Miss E Couling, BMus RAM, LRAM (*Music*)
R L Day, BSc Loughborough (*Design Technology**)
Mrs S E Dickens, BA Cambridge (*History*)
S J Dickens, BA Oxford (*English*)
A B Doyle, MA, MA Glasgow, Open (*English**)
G du Toit, BA, BEd Pretoria (*Religious Studies*)
R G Evans, BSc Aston (*Electronics, Design Technology*)
§Mrs J E Farnfield, BA Swansea (*Economics and Business Studies, Marketing Manager*)
L M Flanagan, BSc Cambridge (*Physics*)
Mrs M Fletcher-Hale, BA Wales, DipLib, ALA (*Librarian*)
W J Foulger, MA St Andrews (*Religious Studies*)
Mrs A A Fulker, BA Oxford Brookes (*Art, French, Deputy Head of Junior School*)
A M Godfrey, BA Bretton Hall College (*Drama Productions**)
M E Holiday, BA Oxford (*Head of Academic Music, Assistant Director of Music*)
§J Janda, BA, ATC London (*Artist in Residence*)
§Mrs C S Jennings, BSc London (*Biology, ICT*)
M V Johnson, BSc London (*Biology, Careers*)
Ms R Kanji, BSc, MEd Auckland (*Chemistry*)
D G Klempner, MA Cambridge (*Physics*)
D A Lawson, BEd Exeter (*Geography, Physical Education*)
B S Laundon, BA Warwick (*English, ICT*)
Mrs J M Layden, MA Edinburgh (*English*)
R E Lee, MA Oxford (*Religious Studies*, CCF**)

Mrs Z Liu, Shenyang Education College, China (*Chinese Language Assistant*)
P March, BA Oxford (*French, Latin*)
Mrs D R M March, L-ès-L Strasbourg (*Lectrice, Language Awareness*)
M Mariani, BSc Kent, PhD UCL (*Physics*)
§Mrs A E Martin, BA Leeds (*Chinese*)
C Marvin, BSc London (*Electronics*, Director of ICT**)
P Mazur, BA Wales, MA London (*Classroom Drama*, English, PSE Coordinator*)
Mrs S J McDonald, MA St Andrews (*English*)
S A McIntosh, MA Oxford (*German**)
§Mrs R E McKee, BA Oxford (*French*)
Mrs S Million, MIL, CertEd, DipRSA (*German, Latin*)
Miss A L Moffatt, MA Edinburgh (*Spanish*)
R H Moralee, BSc Johannesburg (*Biology*)
D Moran, BSc, MA Dublin (*Chemistry, Biology*)
Mrs C Morgan, BA Exeter (*Economics and Business Studies*)
Mrs L C Murphy, MA Cambridge (*English*)
P D Murphy, BA Cambridge (*History*)
Dr J E Older, BSc, PhD East Anglia (*Chemistry, Head of Sixth Form*)
R J Paler, BA Kent (*History*)
B J Patel, MA Cambridge (*Mathematics*)
B Patel, MSc UCL (*Mathematics*)
C P Persinaru, DipRAM, LRAM London (*Music*)
Mrs R J Petty, MA Oxford (*English*)
J E Pietersen, BA Cambridge (*History*)
Miss G C Plummer, BA Durham (*Music*)
S Powell, BSc Durham (*Geography*)
D J Preece, BSc Oxford, PhD UCL (*Geography*)
D K Price, 3D Design Wimbledon College of Art (*Design Technology*)
G V Pritchard, BSc Durham (*Chemistry*)
M D Richbell, BSc Liverpool (*PE**)
Miss F A Ring, BA Cambridge (*History*)
R J Risebro, BSc Manchester Met (*PE*)
N W Rivers, BSc Leicester (*Science*, Chemistry**)
A J Rogers, BA Plymouth (*Art and Photography*)
K R Rogers, BSc Cardiff, PhD London (*Chemistry*)
P H Rule, BSc Leicester CBiol, MIBiol (*Biology**)
Mrs V G Salin, MA Northumbria (*French**)
J J Samuel, BSc Leeds (*Mathematics*)
Mrs M Sanders, BEd London (*Drama, English*)
J A Short, BA UCL (*History*)
A C Smith, MA Kingston (*Art**)
§A E Smith, BA York, MA London (*Religious Studies*)
J J Snelling, BSc Swansea (*Geography**)
J E Stone, BA Cambridge (*Classics**)
Ms T Stevens-Lewis, BA Goldsmiths (*Art*)
D J Swinson, MA, FRCO, ARCM, LRAM Cambridge (*Music**)
J G Timm, BA Cambridge (*History*)
W S Tucker, BSc Exeter (*Physics**)
D G Urmston, BA Wales, MSc Surrey (*Economics and Business Studies**)
A J Webster, BA Oxford (*English*)
Miss H C Whiteford, BSc Durham (*Religious Studies*)
R J Wickes, BSc Warwick (*Mathematics**)
S H Wilberforce, MA Oxford (*Physics*)
Ms J C Wiskow, MA Berlin (*German*)
J A Young, MA Cambridge (*Mathematics*)

Admissions Registrar: Mrs P S Meyer
Sixth Form Admissions: Ms S Redican
Headmaster's Secretary: Mrs S E Rimell

The School, one of the three governed by the Whitgift Foundation, is an Independent Day School for boys aged 10–18 with a co-educational Sixth Form from September 2011. The School aims to give a wide education to students of academic promise, irrespective of their parents' income.

Buildings and Grounds. Trinity School has been in its present position since 1965, when it moved out from the middle of Croydon (its old site is now the Whitgift Centre) to a completely new complex of buildings and playing fields on the site of the Shirley Park Hotel. The grounds are some 27 acres in extent, and a feeling of openness is increased by the surrounding Shirley Park Golf Club and the extensive views to the south up to the Addington Hills. There are additional playing fields in Sandilands, ten minutes' walk from the School.

The resources of the Whitgift Foundation enable the School to provide outstanding facilities. All departments have excellent and fully equipped teaching areas.

Admission. The main ages of admission are at 10, 11 and 13. Entry is by competitive examination and interview. A reference from the feeder school will also be required. The School attracts applications from over 150 schools, with approximately 60% entering from state primaries. Entries of boys and girls into the Sixth Form are also welcomed.

Fees per term (2011-2012). £4,154 covering tuition, books, stationery and games.

Bursaries. From September 2008 the revised Bursary Scheme substantially increased the level of support to families on low incomes, and a raised income threshold benefits a wider range of middle-income families.

Scholarships. (*See Scholarship Entries section.*) Academic, music (instrumental), sports, drama, art and design technology scholarships are awarded to pupils who show outstanding promise. They are awarded without regard to parental income, and are worth a percentage (maximum one-half) of the school fee throughout a pupil's career.

Organisation and Counselling. The School is divided into the Lower School (National Curriculum Years 6–9) and the Upper School (Years 10–13). The Pastoral Leader in charge of each section works with the team of Form Tutors to encourage the academic and personal development of each boy. There is frequent formal and informal contact with parents.

There is a structured and thorough Careers service, which advises boys at all levels of the School and arranges work experience and work shadowing.

While the academic curriculum is taught from Monday to Friday, there is a very active programme of sports fixtures and other activities at the weekend, and all boys are expected to put their commitment to the School before other activities.

Curriculum and Staffing. The School is generously staffed with well qualified specialists. The organisation of the teaching programme is traditionally departmental based. The syllabus is designed to reflect the general spirit of the National Curriculum while allowing a suitable degree of specialisation in the Upper School.

The normal pattern is for pupils to take 9 or 10 GCSE subjects, and to proceed to the Sixth Form to study an appropriate mixture of AS and A2 level subjects, complemented by a wide-ranging General Studies programme, before proceeding to university.

Games and Activities. The main school games are Rugby, Football, Hockey, Cricket and Athletics, with the addition of netball for girls in the Sixth Form. Many other sports become options as a boy progresses up the school. Games are timetabled, each boy having one games afternoon a week.

At the appropriate stage, most boys take part in one or more of the following activities: Community Service, CCF, Duke of Edinburgh's Award Scheme, Outdoor Activities. There are many organised expeditions during the holidays.

Music. Music at Trinity has an international reputation, and every year Trinity Boys Choir is involved in a varied programme of demanding professional work. The Choir has performed at the BBC Proms for the past five years and sings at the Royal Opera House 3–4 times each year. Recently the choristers have travelled to Vienna, Brussels,

Venice and Hiroshima where they were invited to sing at the anniversary commemoration of the bombing. They also appear regularly on radio and television. Trinity Choristers, who specialise in religious music, hold an annual residential Easter Course at a British cathedral. Choral Scholarships are awarded annually and enable boys to receive additional professional voice training without charge.

Many boys learn at least one musical instrument, and a large visiting music staff teach all orchestral instruments, piano, organ and classical guitar. There are numerous orchestras, bands and other instrumental groups for which boys are selected according to their ability. Musicians recently travelled to Dubai and instrumentalists are regular finalists in the Pro Corda National Chamber Music competition.

Drama. There are two excellently equipped stages in the school and a lively and developing programme of formal and informal productions directed by pupils, staff and members of the Old Boys Theatre Company. Drama forms part of the formal curriculum in Years 6–9 and can be studied for GCSE and A Level.

Art and Design Technology. As well as the formal curriculum, which has led to 70% of the School taking a GCSE in art or design technology, pupils are encouraged to make use of the excellent facilities to develop their own interests.

Charitable status. The Whitgift Foundation is a Registered Charity, number 312612. The Foundation now comprises the Whitgift Almshouse Charity for the care of the elderly and the Education Charity which administers three schools.

Truro School

Trennick Lane, Truro, Cornwall TR1 1TH

Tel:	01872 272763
Fax:	01872 223431
e-mail:	enquiries@truroschool.com
website:	www.truroschool.com

Truro School was founded in 1880 by Cornish Methodists. In 1904 it came under the control of the Board of Management for Methodist Residential Schools and is now administered by a Board of Governors appointed by the Methodist Conference. Although pupils come from all parts of the country and abroad, the roots of the school are firmly in Cornwall and it is the only HMC school in the county.

The religious instruction and worship are undenominational though the school is conscious of its Methodist origins.

There are over 850 pupils in the senior school (11+ and above), of whom 60 are boarders. There are another 250 pupils in the Preparatory School, where boys and girls may start in the pre-prep section at the age of 3.

The school is fully co-educational throughout and there is a strong Sixth Form of some 220 pupils.

Motto: '*Esse quam videri*'

Visitor: The President of the Methodist Conference

Administrative Governors:
Chairman: G Rumbles
G Best, MA
R R Cowie, FCA
Revd M Dunn-Wilson
Dr S Evans, BSc, MBChB, PhD, FRCP
Mrs C Fortey, BEd
R S Funnell, MA
C N Harding, BSc
J Hay
Mrs C Hogg, BSc, MBA
P Kerkin, BSc, FCIB
Mrs I Livingstone, BA, MA

R Oliver, FCIB
M Pearse, BA, LLM
G Russell, MA
C S F Smith, DipArch, RIBA, FFB
Mrs S Stokes
Revd S Wild, MA

Headmaster: P K Smith, MA, MEd

Deputy Heads:
N A Fisher, BSc, MSc, MA (*Academic*)
Mrs A L Firth, BA (*Pastoral*)

Head of Sixth Form: P N Brewer, BA

Chaplain: A de Gruchy, MTheol

Boarding House Staff:
Mrs C Murphy, BA (*Malvern*)
J K Austin, BA (*Trennick*)
Mrs T Fisher, BA, BEd (*Pentreve*)

Heads of Year:
J C Cornish, BA (*Lower Sixth*)
G D Hooper, PGCE (*Fifth Form*)
Mrs R Vaughan, BA (*Fourth Form*)
S J Latarche, BEd, ARCM (*Third Form*)
D J Hunt, BA (*Second Form*)
S A Collinge, BSc (*First Form*)

Heads of Department:
D Meads, BA (*Art*)
G Baines, BA (*Biology*)
C Shaw (*Chemistry*)
I C MacDonald, MA, DipEd (*Drama*)
T R Tall, BEd (*Design and Technology*)
J C Cornish, BA (*Economics, Business Studies and Politics*)
Mrs S Spence, MA (*English*)
Mrs J Wormald (*Geography*)
I G Kenyon (*Geology*)
Dr M H Spring, MA, PhD (*History*)
S J McCabe, MA (*Mathematics*)
Mrs I Quaife, BA (*Modern Languages*)
M D Palmer, BMus, FRCO, LRAM (*Music*)
G C Whitmore, BEd (*PE and Games*)
A L Laity, BSc (*Physics*)
M Huckle, BA, MA, CertRE (*Religious Education*)

Truro School Preparatory School
(*see entry in IAPS section*)

Headmaster: M Lovett, BA Ed
Deputy Headmistress: Mrs J P Grassby, MEd, CertEd, CAP
Head of Pre-Prep Unit: Mrs A Allen, CertEd

Bursar and Clerk to the Governors: R G Burdell

Number in School. Main School: 854 pupils (534 boys, 320 girls; 799 day, 55 boarders). Preparatory School: 145 pupils (80 boys, 65 girls). Pre-Prep: 109 pupils (67 boys, 42 girls).

Boarding. At the Senior School girl boarders (3rd–U6th) live in Malvern supervised by a married couple and a single member of staff. Boy boarders (3rd–U6th) live in Trennick House, again supervised by resident married couples. 1st and 2nd year boarders (girls and boys) live in the newly refurbished Pentreve House supervised by a married couple and single resident member of staff. Pupils eat in the central dining room with a cafeteria system. There is a School Medical Centre on site.

Campus and Buildings. The Prep School's campus is built around a country house acquired by the school in the 30s. It has an indoor heated swimming pool, a large assembly hall and extensive areas for science, modern languages, computing, art and crafts, as well as a modern sports hall. The purpose-built Pre-Prep unit opened in September 1991 and a new extension opened in September 2009.

The Senior School occupies an outstanding site overlooking the Cathedral city and the Fal Estuary; it is only five minutes from the centre of the city but the playing fields reach into the open countryside. The school is excellently equipped. There is a first-class Library, extended and refurbished for October 2010, extensive science laboratories, excellent Technology and Art facilities, a computer centre, music school, Sixth Form centre, a Sixth Form cafeteria and a range of classroom blocks. Sports are well served by a covered swimming pool, two large sports halls, an astroturf, squash and tennis courts and 30 acres of playing fields. September 2001 saw the opening of a fine new block, containing six classrooms, a drama centre and the Burrell theatre, which has been extended to provide a Modern Languages Centre in The Wilkes Building (opened September 2004). An attractive and newly refurbished chapel provides a focus for the life of the school. A new Dining Hall and social area opened in November 2009.

Organisation and Curriculum. Pupils are unstreamed in the first three years except for Mathematics (from Year 1) and French and German (from Year 2). The academic programme is conventional and the school follows the National Curriculum. All pupils take the basic subjects including the three sciences, design and technology and at least one foreign language until the end of the third year when the students adopt their own balanced GCSE programme. All pupils take IT GCSE at the end of the 3rd year and a half GCSE in RE at the end of the 4th year. GCSE subjects taken include English Language, English Literature, French, German, Spanish, Geography, Drama, Geology, History, Religious Education, Music, Art, Design and Technology, PE, Physics, Chemistry, Biology and Mathematics. All pupils take Music, Religious Education and Physical Education at most stages and games appear in the timetable for the first five years.

Sixth Formers usually study for four AS levels in the Lower Sixth and these include English, History, Geography, Geology, Mathematics, Further Mathematics, Design and Technology, Art, Critical Thinking, Music, Religious Education, Physics, Chemistry, Biology, Economics, French, German, Spanish, Business Studies, PE and Theatre Studies. General Studies include modules on Careers, Religious Education, ECDL (European Community Driving Licence) and Creative Studies. Since September 2010 students have had the opportunity to follow the Extended Project Qualification. It is likely three subjects will be most commonly continued into the Upper Sixth at A2 level. The vast majority of Sixth Formers go on to further education when they leave.

Out-of-School Activities. Extra-curricular life is rich and varied. There is a choir, school orchestra, a jazz group, a brass band and many other ensembles. Facilities such as the ceramics room, the art room and the technical block are available to pupils in their spare time. A huge variety of activities includes fencing, climbing (2 indoor walls), squash, sailing, golf, basketball, debating, surfing, and many others. Many boys and girls take part in the Ten Tors Expedition, an exceptional number are engaged in the Duke of Edinburgh's Award Scheme, as well as local Community Service, and the Young Enterprise Scheme. Computing and electronics are very well catered for. The School has an outdoor activities centre on Bodmin Moor and pupils have a chance to spend time there during the course of their education at the school.

Games. All the major team games are played. Badminton, cross-country, hockey, netball, squash and tennis are available throughout most of the year. Rugby and Girls Hockey are played in the Winter Term and Soccer and Netball in the Spring Term. In the summer, cricket, athletics and tennis are the major sports. The covered pool is heated.

Scholarships. Truro School was once a Direct Grant Grammar School and most pupils join at the age of 11. There are vacancies for entry at other ages, particularly at 13 and 16. Scholarships are available and also a limited number of places under the School's own successor scheme to Government Assisted Places.

Fees per term (2011-2012). Main School: Boarders £7,120; Weekly Boarders £6,300; Day Pupils: £3,835 (1st and 2nd Year including lunch), £3,720 (3rd Year–U6). Prep (including lunch): £3,515 (Years 5–6), £3,450 (Years 3–4). Pre-Prep (including lunch): £2,650 (Years 1 and 2), £2,600 (Nursery and Reception).

Academic results. A number of pupils proceed to Oxbridge every year (8 received offers for September 2011) and 97% of the Sixth Form to other degree courses. The 2010 A Level pass rate was 99.3%, with 75.6% at A* to B grades. At GCSE the 2010 pass rate was 95% with over 56% at grades A* and A.

Former Pupils' Association. There is a strong Former Pupils' Association with centres locally and in London and it has its own webalumnus. The Truro Schools Society involves parents, staff, old pupils and friends of the school in social events and fundraising.

Charitable status. Truro School is a Registered Charity, number 306576. It is a charitable foundation established for the purpose of education.

University College School

Frognal, Hampstead, London NW3 6XH
Tel: 020 7435 2215
Fax: 020 7433 2111
e-mail: seniorschool@ucs.org.uk
website: www.ucs.org.uk

University College School is a day school providing places for 500 boys aged 11–16, with a co-educational Sixth Form of 300 places. UCS admitted its first cohort of girls into the Sixth Form in September 2008. 30 girls will join UCS each year.

Established in 1830 as part of University College, London, the School moved to its present site in Hampstead in 1907. Though now independently governed, UCS has sustained by continuous reinterpretation many of the ideals of its founders. Its basis remains the provision of the widest opportunities for learning and development without the imposition of tests of doctrinal conformity, but within a balanced and coherent view of educational needs and obligations. This in turn rests on the recognition that care for a pupil's social, moral and spiritual upbringing is a shared responsibility between home and school, an understanding fostered by mutual trust and regular communication. Thirdly, the distinctive ethos of the School stems from the conviction that a positive, lively and humane community, both within and beyond the School, can only be created by the liberal encouragement and disciplined fulfilment of the diversity of gifts among its individual members.

It is in this spirit that the School day begins with a short Assembly.

Council:

Chairman: The Rt Hon Sir Brian Leveson, MA, LLD Hon

Honorary Treasurer: L D Bard, MA, FCA, CTA

Professor P Bayvel, PhD, FREng, FIEE, FInstP, SMIEE	A Halls, MA
	R I Harrington, MA
	A G Hillier, BA, MBA
C W Eccleshare, MA, FIPA	C Holloway, MA, FRSA
E Fordham, BA	A S Jacobs, MA
W H Frankel, OBE, BA, FRSSAf	Sir Brian Leveson, MA
	S D Lewis, MA
Professor S Goldhill	D Maclean-Watt, MA,
Sir Alan Greengross, MA	FRICS, FNAEA
J Hall, OBE, MA	Professor P Sands, QC

Senior School

Headmaster: **K J Durham**, MA

Vice Master: C M Reynolds, BSc, MSc, FSS
Deputy Head (Academic): S R J Marshall, MA, MA, MPhil
Deputy Head (Pastoral): D J Colwell, BA, PhD

Teaching Staff:

T J Allen, BA	W M McAteer, BSc
Mrs K J Anthony, BA	Mrs R McCann, BA
E A Barnish, BA, MA	Ms C C McCormack, BA
I A Barr, MA	Dr M McSherry, BSc, MSc,
B J Bateman, BEd	DPhil, DSc
O Bienias, BA	A M Mee, MA
Miss L C Birchenough, BA	Miss K A Merricks, BA
S M Bloomfield, BA	P S Miller, BSc
C Bowes-Jones, BEd	M B Murphy, BA
J M Bradbury, MA, GBSM,	Miss K E Murray, BA
ABSM, FRSA	Ms T O'Neill, BEd
Miss P J Bradford, BA	J R L Orchard, BA
A H Brammer, BSc	G P J Parker-Jones, BA,
S J Button, BA	MA
R H Chapman, BSc	N R Peace, BSc, MA
Mrs L R Cheng, BA	[2]Dr G A Plow, MA, MA,
J A Clifford, BSc	PhD
M P Collins, BA	Miss T B Postalian, BA,
J P Cooke, BA	MA
A Davis, MSc	Mrs F Pusey, BSc, MSc,
Miss C E Davies, BA	CPsychol, AFBPsS
Dr P Dawson, PhD	Dr A M Quirke, BSc, PhD
J O Enemuwe, BSc	Ms G R Rabie, BA
R J Finch, BA	D P Rance, CertEd
Ms E M Fitts, BA	Ms S Reddy, BSc
[2]S A P FitzGerald, BA	A B Richards, BA, BSc,
I C Gibson, MA	MA
A H Gray, BA	Dr D A Robb, BSc, PhD
Miss R J Gudger, BSc	E D Roberts, MSci
D G Hall, BA	S J Rynkowski, CertEd
T A B Hardy, BA	Mrs A Sánchez-Blanco, BA
J L Hartley, BA, MA	A R M Sandford, BSc
R A K Hawkins, BTech,	E P Sawtell, BA
AMIMechE	Mrs S L Slater, BA
[2]S Hawley, BSc	Mrs P R Spencer, MA
Ms J L Heaton, BA, MA	A J Steven, BA
Miss R Hemming, BA,	Miss A Stewart, BSc
MusB Hons, MSc	Mrs C E Taylor, MSc, BSc
M J Hind, BA	R F J Tear, BSc
M J Hitchcock, BA, MA	J Thomson, MA, DipLaw
A H Hon, MA	T P Underwood, BA
J H Houghton, BA	A G Vaughan, BA
Miss M Hudson, BSc	S C Walton, MusB
R Hyde, MA, MA	Dr A R Welch, BEd, MSc,
Mrs A H Isaac, BA, MA	PhD, CBiol
T W Jenkin, BA	Dr B T Wells, BA, MA,
[2]Mrs L M Jenkins, MA	PhD
[2]Ms J Kung, BA, BA	[2]A R Wilkes, BA
Miss E Lodato, BA	D J Woodhead, BA
Ms S F Mackie, BA	Mrs G J Woodhead, L ès L
M J Matuszak, BSc	T F Youlden, BA, MSc
A R M McAra, MA	

[2] *Deme Warden*

Director of Finance & Administration: J J Witts, DSO, MSc, FRAeS
PA to the Headmaster: Mrs J A Scott
Consulting Physician: Dr A Stuart

Junior Branch
11 Holly Hill, NW3 6QN. Tel: 020 7435 3068;
Fax: 020 7435 7332; e-mail: juniorbranch@ucs.org.uk

Headmaster: K J Douglas, BA, BSc
Deputy Head (Pastoral): Mrs S E Martin, BSc

Deputy Head (*Curriculum*): M A Albini, MA, BSc

Teaching Staff:

N Arnold, BA	S Lanigan-O'Keeffe, BMus
Miss N Banihashem, BEd, BA, MA	Mrs S Miller, BEd, RSA Cert SpLD
M de Caires, RCA, MDes	Miss G K Scott, BA
Mrs M Carnegie, BEd	Mrs L Strange, BEd
M Cassell, BSc	J R Thomas, BA
Miss E Couture, BA, MA	Mrs T Thomas, BA
D Edwards, BA	Miss L Trinnaman, BSc
Mrs J Eggleton-Rance, BEd	A G Walliker, BHum, BA
S D B Hall, BA	D R Warwick, BEd
W G Jones	Miss E Waterhouse, BA
M Lall-Chopra, BA	

Headmaster's Secretary: Miss D Campbell
Consulting Physician: Dr M McCollum

Entry. Entry is in September only.

Admission. Boys are normally admitted to the Senior School at either 11+ or 13+. Admission at 11+ is either by promotion from the Junior Branch or by examination held in January of the year of entry. Admission at 13+ is by the Common Entrance following the UCS Preliminary Assessment, and interviews. These are held two years prior to entry.

Applications for entry should be made to the School Admissions Secretary at any time up to mid-September two years prior to admission (13+), or by the end of November preceding the proposed year of entry (11+). There is a registration fee of £50. A substantial deposit is required when a place is accepted which will be credited against the first term's account. Fee assistance is available through a means-tested application process. Applicants of sufficient academic standing who lack financial resources are encouraged to apply to the Foundation's generous bursary programme.

Applications for 16+ entry for boys and girls should be made to the School Administrator by October one year prior to admission. Assessment for Sixth Form is by examination and interview.

The Lower and Middle Schools. The Curriculum is designed to provide a broad range of knowledge and experience for all boys over 5 years from ages 11 to 16. In the first 2 years boys take English, French, Geography, History, Mathematics, Biology, Physics, Chemistry, Latin, Art, Design Technology, Drama, Music, Information Technology and Personal and Social Education. At 13+ they add a further subject choosing two from Latin, Greek, German and Spanish. Some modifications are made one year later according to aptitude and ability and most boys offer 10 subjects at GCSE.

The Sixth Form. All boys and girls take 4 subjects to AS Level in the Lower Sixth, with the option of narrowing to 3 in the following year.

AS Level subjects may be chosen from: Art, Biology, Chemistry, Design & Technology, Economics, English, French, Further Mathematics, Geography, German, Greek History (Early Modern or Late Modern), Information Technology, Latin, Mathematics, Music, Philosophy, Physics, Politics, Spanish, Theatre Arts, and History of Art.

Boys and girls in the Sixth Form have their own spacious study and social areas in the Sixth Form Centre, opened in 1974 and remodelled in 2008, and have the major responsibility for its use and upkeep. Senior Tutors, in collaboration with the Careers Teacher, provide detailed advice for each pupil about the selection of courses at Universities and other further education opportunities as well as ensuring that a student's course in the Sixth Form meets the entrance requirements of his/her intended future course and professional career. The enormous majority of leavers go on to degree courses.

Students are prepared for entrance to Oxford and Cambridge. Tuition is on a seminar basis.

Pastoral Care. In the Lower School (11–12) boys are cared for by form teachers and Lower School Wardens (Heads of Year). The Middle and Senior Schools are divided into 6 Demes, each under the supervision of a Deme Warden. Many activities outside the classroom are organised by Demes, but the primary responsibility of the Deme Warden is to maintain a personal relationship with each member of his/her Deme, constant throughout a student's school career. Consequently, in all important pastoral and disciplinary matters he/she deals directly with the student in consultation with parents and other teachers and is answerable to the Headmaster for the general welfare of his/her Deme.

In addition to parents' evenings, parents are encouraged to consult informally with teachers about any issues that arise with their child. A Parents' Guild exists to promote the general welfare of the School.

Careers. Pupils are guided by means of interviews and tests towards careers appropriate to their gifts and personalities. Pupils are given opportunities to attend holiday courses directed towards specific careers. Also, visiting speakers are invited to the School and there are frequent Careers Conventions. There is a full Careers Library and a comprehensive programme of Work Experience. The Parents' Guild and Old Gowers' Club (alumni organisation) also provide advice and support.

Physical Education and Games. The State-of-the-Art Sir Roger Bannister sports complex opened in December 2006. The pupils have periods of Physical Education within their normal timetable in the sports complex.

The School playing fields cover 27 acres and are situated a mile away in West Hampstead. In addition to grass surfaces, there is a large all-weather pitch and two fully refurbished pavilions. The major sports for Lower and Middle school boys are Rugby in the Autumn Term. In the Spring there is an open choice between Soccer, Hockey and Cross-Country Running and cricket and tennis in the Summer Term. The School has its own Tennis and Fives courts at Frognal, together with an indoor heated Swimming Pool. Other sports include Fencing, Athletics, Squash, Badminton, Basketball, Fives and outdoor pursuits. For sixth form boys and girls there is a wide choice of indoor and outdoor sports.

Music and Drama. There is a strong musical tradition at UCS and many pupils play in the Orchestras, Wind Band and a great variety of groups and ensembles. Choral music is equally strong and Jazz is a particular feature. Instrumental tuition is given in the Music School, opened in 1995, and this and Ensemble Groups are arranged by the Director of Music.

The School's Lund Theatre, opened in 1974, is the venue for a range of Drama from major productions to experimental plays, mime and revue. An open-air theatre was completed in 1994. A regular programme of evening events is arranged for the Autumn and Spring terms.

In both Music and Drama, there are many opportunities for collaboration with South Hampstead High School.

Other School Societies. These cover a wide range of academic interests and leisure pursuits, including the Duke of Edinburgh's Award Scheme. There is a very active Community Action Programme, which works in the local community and there are regular fundraising initiatives for both local and national charities.

Development Programme. The Foundation completed the final phase of an ambitious programme of redevelopment in 2008. A state-of-the-art Indoor Sports Centre opened in late 2006, comprising Sports Hall, Swimming Pool, Fitness Centre and Health Club. The new Jeremy Bentham Building houses Modern Languages and Art & Design Technology and opened in October 2007. There was extensive refurbishment and reorganisation of classrooms, indoor and outdoor play spaces, administrative areas of the School and Sixth Form Centre. A fundraising appeal helped to achieve these improvements and enabled the School to double the provision of fee assistance.

At the same time, three educational initiatives are under way: a learning strategy initiative is focusing on the learning experience of the pupils and the teaching styles that best promote good learning and work habits; an intellectual enrichment programme to complement the academic curriculum; and the development of an extranet site to enable efficient communication and e-learning opportunities.

Fees per term (2011-2012). Senior School: £5,335; Junior Branch: £4,930. Excludes fees payable in respect of music and other private lessons, and books.

Entrance Scholarships. (*See Scholarship Entries section*.) A number of Scholarships may be awarded at 11+ to boys whose performance in the UCS Entrance Examination is outstanding. Music Awards are awarded through competitive audition. Additional means-tested fee assistance is available for pupils with sufficient need.

The Junior Branch. (*See entry in IAPS section.*) The Junior Branch is housed in separate buildings at Holly Hill, a few minutes' walk from Frognal. Like the Senior School, its main purpose is to provide full scope for the steady maturing of a boy's personality and capacity and for the preparation of boys for the Senior School in order to ensure a continuity of care, stimulation and reasoned discipline. It has its own Library, Computer Room and Laboratory and shares with the main School the playing fields and sports complex. A specialist building accommodates Art, Craft and Technology.

Boys are admitted at the ages of 7+ and 8+. Admission is by preliminary examination and interview. Applications should be made to the Headmaster's Secretary, The Junior Branch, 11 Holly Hill, Hampstead, at least a year in advance. There is a registration fee of £50.

History. A new History of the School was published in June 2007.

Old Pupils' Society (Old Gowers). The School maintains an active register of former pupils and plans events throughout the year.

Charitable status. University College School, Hampstead is a Registered Charity, number 312748. Its aims and objectives are the provision of the widest opportunities for learning and development of students without the imposition of tests and doctrinal conformity but within a balanced and coherent view of educational needs and obligations.

Uppingham School

Uppingham, Rutland LE15 9QE
Tel: 01572 822216
Fax: 01572 822332 (Headmaster)
          01572 821872 (Bursar)
e-mail: admissions@uppingham.co.uk
website: www.uppingham.co.uk

Uppingham School was founded in 1584 by Robert Johnson who obtained a grant by Letters Patent from Queen Elizabeth I. The transition to one of the foremost public schools of its time from an unremarkable local Grammar School took place with the arrival of the great educationalist and headmaster, Edward Thring, in 1853. His pioneering beliefs in the values of an all-round education still mark the School strongly today and have determined many of its distinguishing characteristics: that Houses should be small and family-like; that boys (and now girls) should have privacy; that an all-round education should be offered to a broad range of pupils and that children are happier and learn better in inspiring surroundings.

The Governing Body:

Chairman: ¶The Rt Hon Stephen J Dorrell, MP
Vice-Chairmen:
Mrs J Richardson, MA

W J A Timpson, Esq, CBE

The Rt Revd Lord Bishop of Peterborough, The Rt Revd D Allister
The Very Revd C Taylor, The Dean of Peterborough
Dr L Howard, OBE, JP, BSc, The Lord Lieutenant of Rutland
W F B Johnson, Esq
¶A J Trace, Esq, MA, QC
Professor J Holloway, OBE
¶M C Allen, Esq
¶M L Glatman, Esq, LLB
Group Captain A R Thompson, MBE, MA, MPhil
¶Mrs F K Walter
J C Hanson-Smith, Esq
A G Hancock, Esq, MA
Professor J A Pickett, CBE, DSc, FRS
R Peel, Esq, BSc, FRSA
¶D P J Ross, Esq
Dr P Chadwick, MA, MA, FRSA
The Rt Revd P F Hullah
Mrs R J N Morris
A J D Locke, Esq, MA

¶ *Old Uppinghamian*

Bursar/Finance Director, Clerk to the Trustees: S C Taylor, MA, ACA

Headmaster: Mr Richard S Harman, MA

Deputy Head: Mrs P J Rowell, BA, MSc
Director of Studies: B Cooper, MA
Senior Mistress: Mrs W F McLachlan, BSc, CBiol
Registrar: C S Bostock, MA, MSc
Chaplain: The Revd Dr J Saunders, BA, PhD

Assistant Staff:
* *Head of Department*
† *Housemaster/mistress*

Art, Design & Technology:
*S A Sharp, BA
*A Wilson, BA, FRPS
J A Davison, BA, MEd
S T Hudson, BA
Miss C F M Krone, BA
§Mrs J D Miller, BA
C Simmons, BSc

D Beggs, BSc
D P Lovering, BSc
T G MacCarthy, BA
§T J Montagnon, BA

English:
*Mrs C A Miller, BA
§Mrs J S Broughton, MA, Dip RSA SpLD
R S Harman, MA
Mrs M N L Hunting, MA
D A McLachlan, MA
C R O'Hanrahan, BA
Mrs N L Reihill, MA
I M Rolison, BA
Dr J N Waddell, BA, PhD

Biology:
*P L Bodily, BSc, MEd, CBiol, MIBiol, AIB
†N K de Wet, BSc, CBiol
Mrs W F McLachlan, BSc, CBiol
†Dr S J Müller, MSc, PhD
Miss A S Roebuck, BSc

Geography:
*J Barker, BA
T P Davies, BSc
†Mrs N L Hunter, BA
Mrs S J Kowhan, BA
†N S Merrett, BEd, FRGS

Chemistry:
*L G Bartlett, BA (*Science)
C L Howe, HDE
A Kowhan, BSc
Dr C Owens, BSc, PhD
Miss N Waring, BSc

History:
*T P Prior, BA, MA
J S Birch, MA
M R J Burton, MA
T Makhzangi, BA
Miss K E Price, BA
†J A Reddy, BA
Mrs P J Rowell, BA, MSc
Revd Dr J B J Saunders, BA, PhD

Classics:
*Mrs K J Gaine, MA
P J Canning, BA
†W A M Chuter, BA
Miss A J Cook, MA
†S G Dewhurst, BA
†G S Tetlow, MA

Economics & Business Studies:
*A C Hunting, DMS

History of Art:
*D S R Kirk, BA

Information Technology:
*Miss S E L Webster, BSc
†Mrs L J Allen, BSc,
MBCS

Learning Support:
*Mrs N C Halliday-Pegg,
BEd, NDT
§Mrs J S Broughton, MA,
DipRSA SpLD
Mrs M Cuccio, DipSLD
§Mrs L Howe, BA
†§Mrs A M Merrett, BA
§Mrs K L Tetlow, BA

Library:
§H H S Spry-Leverton,
BLib

Life Skills:
*Mrs M N L Hunting, MA

Mathematics:
*P G Logan, BSc
†Mrs L J Allen, BSc,
MBCS
§A R W Dawe, BSc
§Mrs M A Eales, BSc
P Gomm, BSc
Mrs R A Kelly, HDE
B Lane, BSc
†J C E Lee, MA
O W Packer, BSc
Q H Sayed, MPhys

Modern Languages:
*M R Fries, BA (*French*)
†D J Jackson, BA (*Italian*)
§P Stocker, BEd, FIL
(*German*)
Miss M A Barefoot, BA
(*Spanish*)
Miss V C Allan, BA
M R Broughton, MA
†Ms F C Buckley, BA, MA
†Mrs H M Draper, BA
Mrs J E Newcombe, BEd
Mrs E M A Nicholls, BA

Visiting Music Staff:
Miss I Adams, GRSM (*Viola*)
S Andrews (*Drums*)
Mrs J Burgess, BMus, LGSM (*Oboe*)
Dr J T Byron, BA, MA, PhD (*Piano*)
Mrs L Clements, BA (*Flute*)
T P Crooks (*Violin*)
Miss R A Cullis (*Singing*)
Mrs J A Dawson, GRSM, LRAM (*Piano*)
Miss A D Douglas, ARCM (*Harp*)
M Fatichenti, MMus, DipRAM (*Piano*)
Mrs L H Ffrench, GRSM, LRAM (*Piano*)
N M France, GMus (*Drums*)
Mrs N J Gibbons, MMus, MPhil, LRAM, LRSM (*Piano*)
Mrs C J Gunningham, BA, MSTAT (*Alexander Technique*)
I Hildreth (*Bagpipes*)
Miss E J Hosford (*Double Bass*)
R O Hutchinson (*Jazz Bass*)
K Learmouth, ALCM, FRSA (*Classic Guitar*)
Ms R R E Leyton (*Cello*)
Mrs C Li, BMus, LRAM(*Flute*)
T Locke, (*French Horn*)
G K Lumbers, BMus (*Saxophone*)
Miss J A Moffat, DipRCM (*Singing*)
S P Morris, BMus (*Clarinet, Saxophone*)
Mrs V F Morris, AGSM, LRAM (*Clarinet & Saxophone*)
Ms S Organ, MA (*Bassoon*)

P A Westgate, BA, MA
†R M B Wilkinson, MA
T R Worthington, BA

Music:
*S J Williams, BA
*P M Clements, BA, FRCO
S K Drummond, DRSAM,
ARCM
A A Ffrench, MA, AGSM,
PGDip GSMD
A Laing, BA, DipPSMP
§O N Parker, MMus,
BMus, FGMS, FASC
§P A Siepmann, BSc,
LRSM, ARCO
S A Smith, BA, PPRNCM
Miss J Stevens, GGSM,
MA

Physical Education:
*Mrs S M Singlehurst,
BEd, MSc
Miss K L Smith, BSc
K G Johnstone, BEd

Physics:
*J D Hoult, BSc
W S Allen, BEd
B J Fell, MA
C L Howe, HDE
G S Wright, BSc

Political Studies:
*T Makhzangi, BA
Mrs P J Rowell, BA, MSc
†K M Seecharan, BSocSci

Religious Studies:
*R C Hegarty, BA
B Cooper, MA
Revd Dr J B J Saunders,
BA, PhD
Miss S Staziker, MA

Theatre Studies:
*A K Chessell, BA
D A McLachlan, MA

L Parés, BMus, MMus (*Piano*)
E Pell (*Accordian*)
D N Price, LRAM (*Trumpet*)
Ms M Reinhard, ARCT, LPRCM (*Piano*)
Mrs A M Reynolds, MusB, GRNCM (*Piano*)
Miss H Ross (*Violin*)
Mrs Y S Sandison, PPRNCM (*Singing*)
N Scott-Burt, BA, MMus, LRAM, ARCO (*Piano, Organ & Composition*)
K Slade, BMus (*Clarinet & Saxophone*)
Miss S E Stuart (*Percussion*)
Miss C M Tignor (*Creative Music Production*)
J P Turville, MA, MMus, LLCM (*Piano*)
Ms P Waterfield, ARCM, MSTAT (*Alexander Technique*)
B Weakliam (*Singing*)
B J Weston, BA (*Creative Music Production*)
T J Williams, MA (*Singing*)
Mrs V D Williamson, GMus, RNCM, LRAM (*Singing*)

Houses and Housemasters/mistresses:
Brooklands: Nick de Wet
Constables (*Girls*): Nic and Anna Merrett
Fairfield (*Girls*): Nicola Hunter
Farleigh: David Jackson
Fircroft: Jim Reddy
Highfield: Richard Wilkinson
Johnson's (*Girls*): Lesley Allen
The Lodge (*Girls*): Stephan and Kyi Müller
Lorne House: Kurt Seecharan
Meadhurst: Sam Dewhurst
New House (*Girls*): Fiona Buckley
Samworths' (*Girls*): Helen Draper
School House: Simon Tetlow
West Bank: Jonathan Lee
West Deyne: Will Chuter

General Information. Uppingham School is a fully boarding school for boys and girls aged 13–18.

There are around 780 pupils in the School, of which some 380 are in the Sixth Form. More than 98% of the School's pupils are full boarders. Girls have been accepted into the Sixth Form since 1975 and make up 47% of the Sixth Form numbers. Girls were first admitted at 13+ in September 2001 and 40% of all pupils are girls. Around 6% of the School's pupils are foreign nationals, mainly from the European Union, Eastern Europe and South East Asia.

Uppingham is a Christian Foundation. That was the intention of the School's Founder, Archdeacon Robert Johnson in 1584, and it remains the policy of the School today. Some Uppinghamians are members of other faiths and every consideration is given to their needs. A monthly Roman Catholic Mass is celebrated in the School Chapel. The whole School meets in the Chapel five days a week; on Sunday there is a morning service usually with a visiting speaker. Pupils are prepared for Confirmation every year.

Situation and Facilities. Uppingham is a small market town set in beautiful countryside in Rutland. It is about 100 miles north of London and midway between Leicester and Peterborough on the A47. It is roughly equidistant from the M1 and A1/M11, and the A14 link road makes connections with the Midlands and East Anglia easier and faster. It is served by Kettering, Oakham, Peterborough and Leicester train stations, and by Stansted, Luton, Birmingham and East Midlands airports.

At the heart of the School is a traditional campus with innovative and award-winning recent additions: the developments of a new sports centre (with a 6-lane swimming pool, fitness studio, dance studios, sports hall and gymnasium), third music school (state-of-the-art facilities, a 120-seat recital room, recording studios), drama studio and workshops, sports pavilions and two Astroturf pitches reflect the importance of the all-round education on offer.

The facilities within the central area of the School include the Victorian School Room and Chapel (designed by George

Edmund Street, who designed the Law Courts in the Strand), the Memorial Hall, a well-stocked Library (housed in a building dating back to 1592), Music Schools, Language Centre and classrooms. The western campus comprises the Science School, Sports Centre, Leonardo Centre (purpose built for Art and DT), Theatre, Drama Studios and Workshops, and Maths and IT Centre. Ranged around these facilities, like a university campus, are the fifteen boarding houses each with its own garden, recreational facilities and dining room.

There is a dedicated sixth form social centre, which also houses the Higher Education, Careers and Gap Year Departments.

Academic Matters. Whilst the School is noted for its strong commitment to all-round education, its superb pastoral care and magnificent facilities, the pupils' academic studies are the priority. In 2010, 61.3% of all A Levels were A*/A grades; 90.5% A*–B. More than one in three A Level candidates achieved straight A*/A grades. At GCSE the A*–C pass rate was 97.6% and 28% of all entries gained A*; 62.4% A* or A. The average UCAS score for 2010 was 393. In 2011 half of all Oxbridge applicants received offers.

With a staff: pupil ratio of almost 1 : 7 all subjects enjoy the benefits of small class sizes and a wide range may be taught. 27 different A Level subjects and 22 GCSE subjects are offered.

Until GCSE, specialisation is minimal and pupils are taught in sets for most subjects. Most take a minimum of nine GCSE subjects. All members of the Sixth Form study four or five AS Levels in the Lower Sixth and three or four A Levels in the Upper Sixth which are complemented by a lecture programme and a wide variety of extra-curricular activities. Extended Projects are offered in addition to the A Level subjects.

The progress of all pupils is monitored by an assigned Tutor and their Housemaster or Housemistress, as well as by a system of regular reviews and reports from subject teachers. Parents and pupils may also call on the School's Higher Education and Careers advisers; visiting speakers from universities and careers are featured throughout the year. The School uses the professional careers services of Cambridge Occupational Analysts. At all stages of a pupil's career, the Housemaster/Housemistress keeps in touch with parents regularly. Parent-teacher meetings take place annually for all year groups and additional meetings are held to discuss options and higher education.

Nearly all pupils go on to further education. The School offers advice on planning GAP years. Pupils have access to a beautiful, well-stocked central Library, as well as extensive, more specialist libraries for most subject departments.

For those with learning difficulties the School has trained staff to help with special education needs and any pupil may use the services of a professional psychologist or the School's trained counsellor.

Extra-Curricular Activities. Around 40 clubs and societies flourish within the School with a further 30 areas of activity on offer. Pupils can take bronze, silver and gold Duke of Edinburgh's Award. After the first year pupils can opt to join CCF for 2–3 years or community service (visiting the elderly, assisting in primary schools, Riding for the Disabled etc).

Boarding. There are fifteen boarding houses, which are dotted around the town and School estate: nine for boys, one for Sixth Form girls and five for 13-18 year old girls. Houses are kept small and are usually home to around 50-60 children, 45 in the case of the Sixth Form girls' house. All pupils eat their meals in their own house dining room and are joined at lunch by teaching and non-teaching staff.

Almost all boys have their own private study upon arrival and, by the time they reach the Sixth Form have their own study-bedroom. All girls entering at 13 share a room with up to 3 other girls and also have their own study area. This arrangement changes in the Lower Fifth and Upper Fifth

when girls have bed-sit rooms, usually shared with one other. Sixth Form girls almost all have their own single study-bedrooms.

Much of the non-teaching life of the School is organised around the houses and they engender strong loyalties. In addition to excursions and social events, there exists a long-standing tradition of house drama productions, music concerts, artistic displays, as well as inter-house debating and sports competitions.

The resident Housemasters and Housemistresses are helped by a team of at least five tutors who are assigned to particular pupils. They assist with monitoring academic progress and social development.

Music. Uppingham has always had a very distinguished reputation for music since being the first school to put music on its curriculum for all pupils. In 2006 the School opened its third music school. This inspirational music facility offers a unique environment in which to rehearse, cutting-edge music technology, and a 120-seat recital room. The School has an outstanding Chapel Choir, numerous orchestras and chamber groups, wind bands, a professional concert series as well as many thriving musical societies and rock groups. A busy programme of weekly recitals, house and year-group concerts, and larger public performances in the UK and abroad offer pupils of all abilities regular chances to perform. More than 50% of pupils learn an instrument. 43 visiting staff and 9 full-time staff enable pupils to receive conservatoire-style tuition at the school.

The School has produced several Oxbridge organ scholars and numerous choral scholars in recent years and the distinguished results also extend to Conservatoires.

Further enquiries may be made directly to the Director of Music (01572 820696).

Sports and Games. Uppingham has a strong tradition of sporting excellence and often has pupils gaining international honours in a variety of sports. All students participate in sports or games three times a week. The major sports are Rugby, Hockey, Cricket, Tennis, Cross-Country and Athletics for boys, and Hockey, Netball, Tennis, Cross-Country and Athletics for girls. Many other sports are available from Aerobics through to Sailing.

There is a full programme of formal house matches across all sports, providing an opportunity for all pupils to contribute within a team environment. The able are stretched and the very able are offered a high level of coaching from experienced coaches/professionals in all major sports, often going on to represent club, academy, county, regional or national teams. Success at first team level against rival schools is an expectation.

A fabulous new Sports Centre opened in September 2010. The building includes a sports hall, six-lane 25m swimming pool, fitness studio, gym, squash courts and dance studios. The new centre houses the School's PE department and has a hospitality suite for match-day entertaining. In addition, there are more than 60 acres of playing fields including the Upper (dedicated to First XI cricket), three Astroturf surfaces (one is floodlit), Tennis, Netball and Fives courts, and a shooting range.

All these facilities are open seven days a week under the guidance of the Sports Centre manager and appointed staff.

The Leonardo Centre. The award-winning Art, Design and Technology Centre was designed by Old Uppinghamian, Piers Gough, CBE. The glass-fronted structure allows a broad range of creative activities to take place in a single open-plan space and thereby stimulate each other. The Leonardo Centre houses a Fine Art and Printing space (which has the facility for 3D printing), studios for Design (including CAD design), Ceramics, Sculpture, Photography, Sound and Video Engineering, workshops primarily for wood, metal and plastic, and teaching rooms dedicated to History of Art. The Sunley Gallery is used to display the work of pupils, staff and other visiting artists. The Centre is manned and open seven days a week, and is open to all pupils, whatever their public examination options.

Drama. Theatre and Drama flourish at the School and the subject is taught at GCSE and A Level. There is a well-established 300-seat theatre and in 2006 the facilities were extended to include a new foyer, two drama classrooms, a workshop space and a state-of-the-art drama studio. Major school productions are staged annually and range from big musicals, such as *Guys and Dolls*, to more classic productions, like Shakespeare's *A Midsummer Night's Dream*. The theatre also hosts a wide variety of visiting professional companies and as such it plays a significant role in the cultural life of both the school and the wider community.

Technological Environment. Uppingham is proud of the breadth and depth of its ICT provision. More than 1800 outlets exist around the School through which pupils can access an enormous variety of networked educational resources. Every single pupil is provided with a computer in his or her study or bedsit, and is also provided with an individual email account.

There is a School-wide intranet that assists in the delivery of the teaching and learning process, and there is a 20Mb high-speed broadband connection to the internet, suitably filtered by the School's IT Department. Dedicated ICT suites exist throughout the School, offering rich access to resources across all curriculum areas. In addition, a high proportion of classrooms are fitted with data projectors and digital smartboards.

The School recognises that proficiency in ICT is important in the marketplace of the 21st century, so all pupils take a course in ICT skills in their first two years to develop their skills. As technology continues to move forward, every endeavour is made to ensure that all pupils get to use the latest tools and software.

Admission. A prospective pupil may be registered for admission at any time after birth.

For 13+ entry, most prospective pupils and their parents visit the School at least three years before the final stages of the Admissions process. Prospective pupils should register at this time, if not already.

Two years before entry, at 11+, all registered pupils are invited to tests and interview at Uppingham. All applications must be supported by a satisfactory reference from the present school. The Headmaster offers places to the successful candidates after this process has concluded. Parents then complete and return an Acceptance Form together with an entrance deposit. Receipt of the entrance deposit guarantees a place in the School subject to the prospective pupil qualifying for admission. In completing the Acceptance Form parents also confirm that Uppingham is their first choice of school.

An offer of a place in the School is conditional upon the pupil qualifying academically (see below), and on his or her record of conduct.

There are three possible ways of qualifying academically:
i. via the Common Entrance Examination (for which the qualifying standard is an average of 55% in the compulsory papers).
ii. via the Common Academic Scholarship Examination.
iii. in the case of pupils who have not been prepared for the Common Entrance Examination, by means of a report from the Head Teacher of their present school and tests and interviews at Uppingham.

To continue into the Sixth Form all Uppingham pupils are required to achieve six passes of grade B or above in academic subjects at GCSE, excluding short course GCSEs.

Most pupils are admitted in the September following their thirteenth birthday. If places are available, a few pupils may be admitted into the second year (Year 10).

Places for girls, and a limited number of places for boys, are available in the Sixth Form. Girls may register an interest in Sixth Form entry to Uppingham at any time, but the final interview, testing and offer procedures take place in November in the year prior to admission. Admission at this level is dependent on tests and interviews at Uppingham, and achieving six passes of grade B or above in academic subjects at GCSE (or equivalent), excluding short course GCSEs.

Enquiries and requests for information about admissions should be addressed to the Assistant Registrar (01572 820611).

Scholarships. (*See Scholarship Entries section.*) A large number of scholarships are awarded annually.

At 13, boys and girls may apply for Academic (ISEB Common Scholarship), Art/Design & Technology, Music, Sport and Thring All-Rounder Scholarships (usually two disciplines of Sport, Music, Art/Design & Technology and Drama are assessed).

At 16, Academic, Art/Design & Technology, and Music Scholarships are awarded. All scholarships are worth up to 50% of the school fees.

Means-Tested Bursaries are available up to 100% of the full fee in cases of real financial need, to assist children whose parents might not otherwise be able to afford an Uppingham education to take up such an opportunity.

For details of scholarships please contact the Admissions Office (01572 820611).

Fees per term (2011-2012). Boarding £9,800; Day £6,860. There is a scheme for paying fees in advance; further details may be obtained from the Deputy Bursar (01572 820627).

Former Pupils. The Uppingham Association was founded in 1911 to maintain the link between OUs and the School. All pupils may become life members when they leave and a database of their names, addresses, school and career details is maintained at the School by the OU Administrator. In addition to a range of OU events that are organised each year for members, a magazine is published annually, which contains news about OUs and activities at the School, and all members are encouraged to make full use of the OU Website. Enquiries may be made directly to the Secretary to the Uppingham Association (01572 820616).

Charitable status. The Trustees of Uppingham School is a Registered Charity, number 527951. It exists to provide education for boys and girls.

Victoria College
Jersey

Jersey, Channel Islands JE1 4HT
Tel: 01534 638200
Fax: 01534 727448
e-mail: admin@vcj.sch.je
website: www.victoriacollege.je

The College was founded in commemoration of a visit of Her Majesty Queen Victoria to the Island and opened in 1852. It bears the Arms of Jersey.

Motto: '*Amat Victoria Curam*'

Visitor: Her Majesty The Queen

Governing Body:

Chairman: C Barton
Vice Chairman: J Giles

Headmaster: **Alun D Watkins**, BEd Hons, MEd Oxon

Assistant Staff:

Miss H Bell, BSc Hons	C McCready, BSc Hons
G C Bloor, BD, MA	Miss H R Medhurst, BA
Miss J Bryan, BA Hons	Hons
G Burton, BEd Hons	Ms D B Montgomery, BA
B F Carolan, BA Hons	Hons
D Clark, MMath Hons	A J Murfin, BSc Hons
S Coe, BSc Hons	Mrs E L O'Prey, BEd Hons
S Cooke, PhD, BEng	Ms M Perestrelo, BA Hons
J S Craik, BSc Hons, MA	Miss R O Pett, BA Hons
J Crill, BSc Hons	A G Pickup, BSc Hons, Dip
P J Davis, GWCMD,	Mus, MIBiol
CertEd	A J Picot, BA Hons
Miss L Douglas, BA Hons,	R J Picot, BSc
LTCC	J Randles, BA Hons
D Dowson, BA Hons, MA	S Roberts, BA Hons, MA,
M P Evans, BEd Hons, Dip	PhD
Sport Psych	D J Rotherham, BEd,
A Gilson, BA, MPhil	FRGS
W Gorman, BA Hons	Mrs J A Roussel, BA Hons,
M Gosling, BA Hons	M-ès-Lettres
P J Gray, BSc Hons	Ms H Ryan, BSc Hons, BA
J Hale, MPharmacol	Hons
A R Hamel, MA	I Simpson, BSc Hons
Mrs C Herrera-Martin, BA	M D Smith, BA
Hons	T Smith, BEng Hons
I A Hickling, BSc, MSc	R L Stockton, BA Hons,
Miss S Humphries, BMus	BSc Hons, Dip Geog
Hons	M R Taylor, CertEd
Mrs G Johnson, BA Hons	Mrs M Taylor, BSc, MSc
Oxon	P Toal, BEd Hons
C Kemble, BA Hons	Ms V G Videt, Lic-ès-
Miss R J Linder, BSc	Lettres
Miss A Matthews, BSc	M C Widdop, MChem
Hons	Oxon, MRSC

Preparatory School
Headmaster: Russell Price, BSc, MPhil

There are currently 730 boys in College, 276 in the Preparatory School and 90 in the Pre-Prep.

The fine building of 1852 with its Great Hall, libraries and administrative areas is set at the centre of new teaching accommodation including classrooms, a music centre, an extensive Science suite opened by Her Royal Highness The Princess Royal, a Sixth Form centre, Art and Design Technology suite, five computer suites and the Howard Davis Theatre refurbished in 1996. The College is situated in extensive grounds above St Helier and looks south over the Bay of St Malo.

College Field is adjacent to the main buildings and includes an all-weather hockey pitch. In the grounds are located a 25-yard shooting range, Squash courts and CCF Headquarters. A multi-million pound sports complex with swimming pool opened in 2003.

Education. There is an emphasis on academic success; nearly all boys go on to University in the UK. The curriculum conforms to the requirements of the National Curriculum. In the Junior School boys study Religious Education, English, Mathematics, French, Spanish, History, Drama, Geography, Biology, Chemistry, Physics, Music, Art and ICT.

Thereafter the basic curriculum includes Religious Education, English, Mathematics, a language, Sciences and ICT. In addition, boys select from optional subjects those which best suit their natural talents, the choice being guided by teaching staff in consultation with students and parents.

Boys may study four or five A Level subjects suited to their objectives and abilities. Enrichment skills are developed through the CCF, Duke of Edinburgh's Award and wide-ranging co-curricular programmes.

At all Key Stages there is opportunity for voluntary work, Music and the Arts, and these, with other subjects, are also encouraged by numerous School Societies.

Prizes. Her Majesty The Queen gives three Gold Medals annually for Science, Modern Languages and Mathematics as well as two Prizes for English History. The States of Jersey offers a Gold Medal and a Silver Medal annually for French. There is an award given to the boy achieving the top score in Year 7 Entrance Examination called the St Mannelier et St Anastase Gold Medal.

Physical Education and Games. The College places strong emphasis on sport and each year there are sports tours to different countries, and to the United Kingdom.

Winter games include Association Football, Rugby, Hockey, Squash; and in the summer Cricket, Swimming, Shooting, Tennis and Athletics.

Matches are played against Elizabeth College, Guernsey and College sides visit the mainland for matches against English Independent Senior Schools.

The College has an excellent CCF Contingent with an authorised establishment of 105 in the Army Section, 75 in the RAF Section and 75 in the RN Section. It is commanded by Wing Commander David Rotherham.

Admission. The age of admission is 11 years though boys are considered for entry at all ages. Entrants must pass the College Entrance Examination.

Fees per term (2011-2012). £1,482. A grant is payable by the States of Jersey to supplement fees.

Preparatory School. The College has its own Preparatory School which stands in the College grounds. Boys, on passing the Entrance procedure, progress to the College at the age of 11. (*For further details see entry in IAPS section.*)

Leaving Scholarships. There are a number of Scholarships (of varying amount). The Queen's Exhibition is tenable for three years at University; the Wimble Scholarship, the Sayers Scholarships and the Baron Dr Ver Heyden de Lancey Scholarship each of up to £750 a year, tenable at British Universities and the Rayner Exhibitions are recent additions to the rich endowment of Scholarships enjoyed by the College for its students.

Warminster School

Church Street, Warminster, Wiltshire BA12 8PJ
Tel: 01985 210100 (Senior School)
          01985 224800 (Preparatory School)
Fax: 01985 214129
e-mail: admin@warminsterschool.org.uk
website: www.warminsterschool.org.uk

The original boys' school was founded in 1707 by the first Viscount Weymouth, an ancestor of the present Marquess of Bath. It became an Independent Educational Trust in 1973 formed by the amalgamation of the Lord Weymouth School with the long-established local girls' school, St Monica's, founded in 1874. The School is a Limited Company whose Directors are Trustees elected by and from within the Board of Governors which is in membership of the Association of Governing Bodies of Independent Schools. The Headmaster is a member of both the Headmasters' and Headmistresses' Conference (HMC) and the Society of Heads of Independent Schools (SHMIS).

Patrons:
The Most Honourable the Marquess of Bath
R C Southwell, QC
Canon E J Townroe

Chairman of Governors: R A Payn, MA Oxon

Staff:

Headmaster: **M J Priestley**, MA Oxon

Deputy Head (Academic): Mrs O Bourne, BEd
Director of Studies: G Collins, MA, PGCE
Head of Pastoral Care: Mrs T Wilcox, CertEd
Head of Sixth Form: G McQueen, MA, PGCE
Head of Middle School: Ms N W Davies, BSc Hons, PGCE
Head of Lower School: Mrs N Curtis, BA, PGCE

Examinations Officer: Dr M Martin BSc Hons, PhD,
   PGCE, MIBIOL

Heads of Department:
Mrs S Barns-Graham, BA, LLB Hons, Dip LP (*Modern
   Languages*)
Mrs F Beck, BSc Hons, PGCE (*Psychology*)
Mrs M Caron-Courtney, MA SEN, BA Hons, RSA
   DipSpLD, CertEd (*Learning Support*)
J Mace, BA (*Business Studies & Economics*)
Mrs L Clayton, MA, PGCE (*Art*)
Mrs S Shanks, BA Hons, PGCE, RSA Dip TEFL (*EFL*)
Dr D Hankey, BSc, PhD, MRSC (*Science*)
C Knight, BEd Hons (*Director of Sports*)
R Lincoln, BA, CertEd (*Mathematics*)
Mrs J Walker, BA, QTS (*History*)
B Martineau, BA Hons, PGCE (*Director of Music*)
Miss S Matthews, BA, PGCE (*Geography*)
Mrs C Morgan, BEd Hons (*D&T*)
Mrs R Mace, MPhil, MTheol (*RS*)
M Thompson, BA Hons, PGCE (*English*)
D Todres, BA Hons, PGCE (*Drama*)

There are 30 other full-time and part-time staff.

House Staff:
Mr and Mrs J Bonnell (*St Boniface*)
Mr and Mrs G Knapman (*Stratton House*)
Mr and Mrs J Mace (*St Denys*)
Mr and Mrs C Knight (*Old Vicarage*)
Mr and Mrs D Crinion (*Northdown*)
Mrs H Arter, RGN (*School Nursing Sister*)

Bursar & Clerk to the Governors: Mrs A C Martin, MBA,
   FMAAT
Admissions Registrar: Mrs G Webb

General. Founded in 1707, the School is a co-educational boarding and day school numbering some 620 pupils (150 in the Sixth Form) from 3 to 18, of whom around 200 are boarders. The Preparatory School of 160 pupils works in close cooperation with the Senior School and enjoys many of the same facilities. (*For further details see Warminster Preparatory School entry in IAPS section.*)

The School is situated along the western periphery of the town, looking out over open countryside, while its buildings are linked by extensive gardens and playing fields.

It is easily accessible by rail (via Warminster or Westbury) from London, Heathrow, the South Coast and the West, and by road (via the M3, M4 and M5).

Aims and Philosophy. The School aims to provide a stimulating and caring environment in which all pupils develop as individuals and achieve their potential in as many areas as possible. We encourage our pupils to have respect for the rights and beliefs of other people, and wish to provide for them the opportunity to acquire social, academic and personal qualities which will enable them to live happy and productive lives, both within the School and as part of local, national and global communities. The School is proud of its reputation for friendliness and the close working relationship between staff and pupils.

The School is a Church of England foundation, but welcomes pupils of all denominations and faiths or of none, and hopes that, whatever their religious background, they will learn tolerance and concern for other people.

Buildings. As befits a school with a long history, there is a wide variety of historic buildings. The History department, for example, teaches in the School's oldest building, School House, which was founded by Viscount Weymouth in 1707.

The school boasts one of the oldest working Fives courts in England.

A multi-million pound development programme has taken place in recent years and has included a new state-of-the-art science centre, a new library, design technology centre as well as additional boarding facilities. Existing boarding accommodation has been extensively refurbished.

Boarders are cared for by Housemasters or Housemistresses, Resident Tutors and Matrons. Pupils typically enjoy single study-bedrooms in the Sixth Form.

Curriculum. In the first three years of the Senior School, all pupils follow a broad curriculum and GCSE pupils study a full and varied range of subjects. All pupils are involved in PE and Games, and Health and Social Education, as well as a comprehensive programme of Careers advice.

In the Sixth Form greater individual freedom and responsibility are encouraged. Sixth Formers are offered a choice between studying A Levels (more than twenty different subjects are offered) and the International Baccalaureate Diploma, which is an increasingly popular choice for many of our pupils with others joining the Sixth Form from elsewhere to follow our successful IB programme. The first school in the South-West to offer the IB Diploma, our IB results have placed us each year within the top thirty UK IB schools. Overall Sixth Form results (UCAS points per pupil) rose by over 21% in the last two years. Although the vast majority of pupils will be aiming for University, with over 95% winning places at leading institutions including Oxford and Cambridge, some will pursue gap years or enter business or the Armed Services directly. The overall pupil/staff ratio is under 10:1. Pupils receive an exceptional amount of individual attention and are encouraged to realise their full potential in as many areas as possible. There is an extensive tutorial system and a strong sense of the importance of the individual within the community. The school is at the forefront of developing 'personal, learning and thinking skills' both through the tutorial system but also via its academic and its rich co-curricular programme. A small learning support unit is staffed by expert and dedicated specialists.

Activities. A very wide range of activities is on offer, and pupils are encouraged to involve themselves fully. The School has a strong tradition of drama, and the musical activities, including choir, orchestra and jazz band, are a real strength. There are currently over 40 hobby activities available.

The School enjoys close links with the Armed Services, and the CCF, though voluntary, is traditionally strong. There is also a large involvement in the Duke of Edinburgh's Award Scheme, whilst a number of pupils are actively engaged in Community Service in Warminster and the local area.

Games. Sports offered include Rugby, Hockey, Cricket, Tennis, Athletics, Netball, Rounders, Swimming, Cross-Country running, Basketball, Squash, Badminton, and Volleyball.

There is a spacious Sports Hall with recently renovated squash courts, hard tennis courts, heated swimming pool, a new Astroturf all-weather pitch and an indoor shooting range. Pupils have access to the local Golf Club and Riding stables.

Admission. Pupils are admitted to the Preparatory School from the age of 3. Boarders are admitted from the age of 7. Pupils who enter after the age of 8 will be required to sit the Warminster School entrance examinations relative to the proposed year of entry. A report from the Head of a pupil's present school will always be requested. Older pupils who qualify by good GCSE results and school report may be admitted directly to the Sixth Form. Scholarships are available for entry at 7+, 9+, 11+, 13+ and 16+. Examinations for Scholarships are held in May and November. Details may be obtained from the Headmaster.

Progress throughout the School, including the transfer from the Preparatory to the Senior School, is not automatic but will be based on the School's assessment at key points of each student's ability and will always be dependent on the student's continued commitment and progress in all areas of activity.

Great care is taken to consider individual needs and circumstances. The School provides a Special Support Facility for pupils who are mildly dyslexic, or who have other similar needs. Parents of such pupils should ask to meet Mrs Caron-Courtney, who is the SENCO.

Please telephone the School (01985 210160) to arrange a visit, and to meet the Headmaster and the Head of the Preparatory School.

A Registration Fee of £50 is payable and, upon the acceptance of a place, a guarantee fee of £500 for UK based parents and £1,000 for overseas based parents, credited to the final account, will be payable.

Fees per term (2011–2012). Day: Preparatory School £2,165–£3,465; Year 7 to Sixth Form £4,340. Boarding: Preparatory School £5,855; Years 7 to Sixth Form £7,810.

Fees are as inclusive as possible, covering meals, stationery and textbooks. The Bursar welcomes consultation with parents over fees, insurance and capital payment schemes. As the School is an Independent Educational Trust, any financial surplus is used exclusively for the further improvement of the School. Fees are kept to the minimum required to run the School effectively, employ first-rate staff and keep the facilities and resources up to the level expected by parents.

Charitable status. Warminster School is a Registered Charity, number 1042204. It exists to promote the education of boys and girls.

Warwick School

Myton Road, Warwick CV34 6PP
Tel: 01926 776400
e-mail: enquiries@warwickschool.org
website: www.warwickschool.org

Warwick School is the oldest boys' school in the country and can produce documentary evidence that suggests its existence in the days of King Edward the Confessor; it probably dates from 914. In 1123 the School was granted to the Church of St Mary of Warwick. In 1545 King Henry VIII increased and re-organised the endowments. The School subsequently moved to the Lord Leycester Hospital. In 1571 it moved to another site within the boundaries of Warwick, and in 1879 to its present site south of the town on the banks of the Avon.

Motto: '*Altiora Peto*'

Governing Body:
R M Dancey, MA (*Chairman of Warwick School Committee*)
A C Firth (*Vice-Chairman of Warwick School Committee*)
J P Cavanagh
Mrs P A Goddard
D E Hanson
Mrs S M Rhodes
C Gibbons
I Thorpe
Prof R H Trigg, MA, DPhil
Mrs C A I Sawdon
Mrs S Swan
T P Jackson
D B Stevens, BA (*Chairman – Warwick Independent Schools Foundation*)
Mrs V M Phillips (*Chair – Warwick Preparatory School*)
Mrs J Marshall, BA (*Chair – King's High School*)

Clerk to the Governors: R D James

Head Master: **E B Halse**, BSc, FRSA

Deputy Head Master: W M Phelan, BA, MBA

Deputy Head, Pastoral: T Hoyle, BA
Deputy Head, Staff: C G McNee, BA
Deputy Head, Academic: P J O'Grady, MA

Director of Studies: S R Chapman, BA, PhD

Head of Sixth Form: J N Jefferies, MA
Head of Upper School: C M Bond, MA
Head of Middle School: Mrs M Yates, BSc
Head of Lower School: T G Barr, BA

* *Head of Department*

Art:
*R Flintoff, BA
Mrs G K Odling, BA
D Snatt, BA

W S Macro, MSc, BSc
N A Martlew, BSc
P J O'Grady, MA
D J Shield, CertEd

Classics:
*D A Stephenson, MA, BA
M G L Cooley, MA, MSt
R Hudson, MA, MA
Mrs R E Morgan, MA, BA
Mrs A Morris, BA

Design and Technology:
*B V N Schalch, BA
M E Browning, BSc Hons
C Riman, BA
J D Stone, BSc

Drama:
*M C Perry, MA
Miss J E Gurnett

Economics:
*D A Williams, MA, BA, MBA, EdD
A F J Coe, BA, MPhil
P J Shipley, MA

English:
*Mrs K J Wyatt, MA, BA
C M Bond, MA, MA
Mrs L M Haines, BA
Mrs L Hodge, BA
Miss C E Larvin, MA
G I R Ogdon, MA
Mrs A S Quinn, BA

Geography:
*Dr A Hodskinson, BSc, PhD
Miss H J Bowie, BSc
Dr S R Chapman, BA, PhD
Mrs E Thornton, BA

History and Politics:
C G J Gibbs, BA (*History)
J N Jefferies, MA (*Politics)
O R O'Brien, BA
A J Scott, BA Hons
S J Wood, BA

ICT:
*M J Colliver, BSc, MA
P Nield, MBA, BSc
D Seal, BSc

Mathematics:
*W K Hamflett, BSc
K F Hayward-Bradley, MA
J W Clift, MA, MPhil
K C Davenport, BEng
B L Davies, BSc
G Giudici, MA

Modern Languages:
*E J Hadley, MA
Mrs A E Dickinson, BA (*French)
Miss J A Wiltsher, BA (*Spanish)
Mrs A Coe
R Hue, Lic d'Anglais
Mrs A C Hadley, BA
Mrs E Heissler, Diplom Kommunikations
Mrs K Ingram, BA
Miss A M Latzke, Diplom/ Vordiplom, MA
C G McNee, BA
Mrs C Morel-Bedford, BA
Mrs A E Paley
Mrs O P Thomas, Lic d'Anglais

Music:
*T G Barr, BA, LTCL
*S Hogg, GRSM
R G Appleyard, GBSM
K D Johnson, BMus
Mrs N G Parsons, BA
J J Sampson, BMus

Physical Education:
*G A Tedstone, BEd
S R G Francis, BA
T Hoyle, BA
M Nasey, BEd, Masters Sph (*Director of Rugby*)
T D Pierce, BSc
N M K Smith
G M F Wade

Religious Education:
*Revd A W Gough, BA
Revd M D Hewitt, BSc, BA
L D Eaton, MA, BA

Science:
I S Dee, BSc (*Biology)
Mrs C L Dowding, BSc (*Chemistry)
A D Millington, BSc (*Physics)
S J Cook, MSc, BSc
G J Field, MA
G N Frykman, MA
Dr C H Hurst, PhD, MA, BA
D L Jones, BSc Hons
G C E Joyce, BSc Hons
M E Lucas, MSc, BEng

Dr C M L Nuttall, BSc, PhD
Mrs S E Rose, BSc
P A Snell, BSc
Dr B M Twohig-Howell, BSc, MSc, PhD
Mrs M Yates, BSc

Curriculum Support:
*Mrs C McNee, BA, MA
Mrs J Downes, BA Hons
Mrs C M Fellows, MEd, BA
Mrs P J Kitchen, BSc
Mrs C Oates, BA
(*Careers*)

Junior School

Head Master: G R G Canning, BA

Deputy Head Master: J L Elston, BEd

Mrs A J Appleyard, MA
Mrs C J Asquith, BA, MA
Mrs K Bull, BEd
Miss R J Fuller, BEd
Mrs E J Gemmell, BEd
T W Hancock, BSc
O R Herringshaw, BA Hons
Mrs O Hartwell, BA
Miss J E Hirons, MA

Mrs H J Jackson, BEd
B M Kruze, BA Hons
T C Lewis, CertEd
K Marshall, BEd
Dr S E Marshall, BSc, PhD
Miss H Mellor, BA
Miss J Needham, BSc
Mrs A C A Williams, BMus, LRAM, ATCL
Miss E Williams

Librarian: Ms A Best
Medical Officer: Dr H Mulder
Headmaster's PA: Mrs C Dixon
Admissions Registrar: Mrs P Norton
Marketing Manager: Mrs A Hartin
Alumni Relations Officer: Mrs A Douglas

Warwick School is an independent day and boarding school for boys. There is a Senior School (approx 900 boys), age range 11 to 18 years, and a Junior School (approx 240 boys), age range 7 to 11 (*see also Junior School entry in IAPS section*). There is boarding accommodation for about 50 boys.

The School Buildings and Grounds. The school is situated on the outskirts of Warwick town with fine views over the River Avon and Warwick Castle. In 1879 the school moved into its present buildings designed in a rococo Tudor style with 50 acres of playing fields attached to the school. Many buildings have been built over the years. There is a programme of continuous development. In the last few years this has improved and extended the boarding, indoor sports facilities, music, drama and teaching facilities, an ICT and Library Building, a Performing Arts Centre, Music Department and a state-of-the-art Science Centre. A new classroom block was completed in September 2008.

Admission is by entrance examination set by the School. Entry to Junior School is at the ages of 7, 8, 9 and 10. Entry to Senior School is at 11, 12, 13 and 16. The assessment at 11+ includes Non-Verbal Reasoning, English and Mathematics. The assessment at 13+ is based on the syllabus for the ISEB Common Entrance and includes English, Maths, MFL, Science and NVR. Sixth Form entry requires a minimum of 5 B grades at GCSE.

Curriculum. The aim of the school is to provide a broadly based education which allows pupils to achieve academic excellence. All pupils are encouraged to develop their individual talents to the full and to accept responsibility for themselves and others.

In the Junior School the curriculum aims to give a firm grounding in the National Curriculum foundation subjects English, Mathematics and Science. A range of other subjects including History, Geography, Technology, French, IT and Religious Education are taught throughout the school by specialist subject teachers. French is taught throughout as is Art, Music and Physical Education.

In the Senior School the curriculum offers a range of options but there is a core curriculum of English, Mathematics, French and Science (including Physics, Chemistry and Biology as separate subjects) up to GCSE which all boys take in their fifth year. Virtually all boys continue into the

Sixth Form where AS Levels are taken after one year and full A Levels after a further year. There is a wide range and programme of General Studies. The curriculum is designed to give all boys a broad general education and to postpone any specialisation for as long as possible.

Games and other activities. Active interest in out of school activities is much encouraged. Winter games are rugby, hockey, cross-country running and swimming. These are played in the Michaelmas and Lent Terms and our national reputation is strong throughout. Summer games are cricket, tennis and athletics. Badminton, basketball, clay pigeon shooting, golf, squash and volleyball are played throughout the year. There are fine sporting facilities in the indoor Sports Complex, including a 25m 6-lane Pool, squash courts, state-of-the-art rock climbing wall, fitness suite and Sports Hall.

There are usually some 80 different clubs and societies active in school life. There is a CCF contingent (with Army and RAF sections) an outdoor activities group and a Voluntary Service Group linked with the local community. Other activities include drama, music, debating, and fencing.

Religious teaching. The Chapel Services and teaching are according to the Church of England, but there are always pupils of other denominations and race and for these other arrangements may be made. Pupils attend services during the week, and boarders and some day pupils the service on Sunday. The Chaplain prepares members of the school for Confirmation each year, the Confirmation Service taking place in the Lent Term.

Boarding. Senior School boys may be weekly or full boarders. Boarding can sometimes be arranged for day boys to accommodate short term parental requirements. There is also an opportunity for an extended day facility.

Fees per term (2011-2012). Senior School Tuition: £3,453; Boarding (in addition to Tuition): £3,916 (full); £3,453 (weekly). Junior School Tuition: £2,686–£3,415.

Scholarships. (*See Scholarship Entries section.*)

Charitable status. Warwick Independent Schools Foundation is a Registered Charity, number 1088057. It exists to provide quality education for boys.

Wellingborough School

Wellingborough, Northamptonshire NN8 2BX
Tel: 01933 222427
Fax: 01933 271986
e-mail: headmaster@wellingboroughschool.org
website: www.wellingboroughschool.org

The endowment of this School was first set aside for charitable purposes in the year 1478. Further land, purchased from the Crown, was granted by Letters Patent in the reigns of Edward VI and Elizabeth I. The endowment was confirmed as being for educational purposes by an Order of the Lord Keeper of the Great Seal in 1595. The School moved to its present site in 1881 upon which new and improved buildings have from time to time been added.

The School offers day co-education for boys and girls from the age of 3 to 18. The School is firmly wedded to Christian principles, to equality of opportunity and the enrichment of individuals in the community. The School is divided into a Pre-Preparatory School (age 3–8: 169 pupils), the Preparatory School (age 8–13: 322 pupils) (*see also entry in IAPS section*), and the Senior School (age 13–18: 408 pupils).

Motto: '*Salus in Arduis*'

Governors:
J J H Higgins (*Chairman*)
C A Odell (*Vice-Chairman*)
A W Bailey

Mrs A Coles
Dr J K Cox
D K Exham, MA
Mrs E Higgins
Mrs D Line
S M Marriott (*Representative of the Old Wellingburian Club*)
J H Morris
Reverend Christine Ostler
Mrs P Perkins, OBE
P S Phillips
A H Robbs
C A Westley
Mrs Clare Colacicchi (*School Solicitor*)
T Baldry (*School Accountant*)
M P Skidmore (*Bursar & Clerk to the Governors*)

Headmaster: G R Bowe, BA Kent

Senior Deputy Headmaster: D C Williams, BA, Kingston, MSc Reading

Second Deputy Head (Academic): Mrs S M Barnhurst, BSc Salford, MA Northampton

Assistant Head (Co-Curricular): D A Ramsden, BA Fitzwilliam College Cambridge (*Head of History & Politics*)

Assistant Head (Target Tracking): A P McGinnes, BSc Exeter (*Head of Mathematics*)

Assistant Staff:
S M Adams, BEd Exeter (*Director of Sport*)
Mrs S J Baxby, BA Northampton (*Head of Business Studies*)
Miss L Belford, BSc Lincoln
Dr J A Bialacki, PhD Loughborough (*Head of Chemistry*)
Mrs F J Burgess, BEd Exeter
Mrs R E Cowley, BA Manchester Metropolitan
J A Dutfield, DipAD, CertEd UCW (*Head of Art*)
S L Egan, BEng Leicester (*Head of Design Technology*)
Mrs C Y Elwyn, Dip LIC
P J Farley, MA Liverpool
Mrs S E Fellows, BA Birmingham
A R Gamble, BA St Edmund Hall Oxford (*Head of English*)
Miss C L Gavin, BSc Loughborough
Mrs S E Gibson-Foy, BA Sheffield
Mrs A J Gillam, BA Exeter
J R Gray, BSc Bangor
Dr A Higginson, PhD UMIST (*Head of Science & Physics*)
Mrs H L Hodgson, BEng Liverpool
Mrs A S Holley, BA Birmingham (*Head of Classics*)
Miss C E M Horry, BA Kent
G E Houghton, BA Durham
Mrs F Kirk, BA Sheffield
P A Knox, BEd Durham
Dr K M Loak-Crisp, PhD Aston
P J Lowe, BA Southampton (*Head of Geography*)
P R Marshall, BA Wales, LRAM (*Director of Music*)
C Martin-Sims, BSc Sussex, MSc Reading, BA Open (*Head of Drama/Psychology*)
Ms J A Mason, BA Teesside
Mrs L J McAuley, BSc Glasgow
G B Moss, CertEd Madeley College of FE, Cert CEG Leicester (*Head of Careers*)
M A Nugent, BA Leicester (*Head of Modern Languages*)
Mrs S Pyke, BSc Bradford
Mrs G M Rodgers, MA Newnham College Cambridge
I Runnells, BA Northampton
Mrs R Russell, BEd Reading
C Scott, BSc Durham, MA Christ's College Cambridge
Mrs K A Shutt, BSc LSE (*Head of Business Studies and Economics*)
M E Thompson, MA The Queen's College Oxford

Revd M J Walker, BA Lincoln College Oxford, DipES St John's College, Durham (*Chaplain*)
P B Waugh, BEd Manchester Metropolitan (*IT Manager*)
R J Wilson, B Metallurgy Sheffield
Mrs C L Woodward, BA Surrey Inst of A&D

Housemasters/Housemistresses:
M H Askham, BEd Loughborough (*Garne's House*)
R Campbell, BA Auckland NZ (*Fryer's House*)
T J Fourie, MSc Port Elizabeth SA (*Platt's House*)
K C M Hargreaves, Rose Bruford College of Speech & Drama (*Cripps' House*)
T H J Hurdman, BSc Southampton (*Parker Steyne's*)
Miss C S Irvin, BSc Loughborough (*Marsh House*)
Miss J M Livingstone, BA Queen's Belfast (*Nevill House*)
Mrs H M Pattison, BSc King's College London (*Weymouth House; Head of Biology*)

Registrar: Mrs Yvonne Pullen

Officer Commanding CCF: Major S Garfirth

School Nurses:
Mrs L R Wood, RGN, Cert DN
Mrs D Barclay, RGN
Mrs L Bate, RN

Director of Music: P R Marshall, BA Hons, PGCE, LRAM
Assistant Director of Music: I Runnells, BA Hons, PGCE, ARCO
Pre-Prep Music Coordinator: S Garfirth, DipRCM, ALCM
Music Department Administrator: Mrs E A Burleigh

Instrumental Music Teachers:
John Bowman, GLCK, LLCM, PGCE (*Piano, Jazz Piano*)
Peter Collins, BA Hons, PGDipRCM (*Brass*)
Martin Gill, LTCL, GTCL (*Violin*)
Mrs Karen Goss, BLIB, LTCL, FTCL (*Clarinet, Bassoon*)
Steve Hamper (*Percussion*)
Mrs Susan Healey, MA, GRSM Hons, CertEd, ATCL, ARCM, LTCL, LRSM (*Piano, Keyboard, Aural, Theory*)
Miss Janice Hooper-Roe, ARCM, GBSM, ABSM (*Singing*)
Tim Jones (*Percussion*)
Wyn Jones, BMus Hons II2, PGCE (*Cello, Bass*)
Keith Learmouth, CertEd, ALCM, FRSA (*Guitar*)
Ms Bridget Marshall, BA Hons, FLCM, ARCM, LRAM, PGCE (*Piano, Organ, Theory*)
Mark Pescott, FTCL, LRAM, ARCM (*Piano, Organ, Theory*)
Philip Slane, AGSM, DipEd ARCM (*Singing*)
Edward Swindell, BMus Hons, MMus
Mrs Karen A Whitelaw, BA Hons, LRAM, LGSM, ALCM (*Piano*)

Preparatory School:

Headmaster: R J Mitchell, BEd College of St Paul's & St Mary's
(prep-head@wellingboroughschool.org)

Deputy Headmaster: R W H Smith, BEd De Montfort
Assistant Head – Pastoral Care: Mrs L Leakey, MA Open
Assistant Head – Curriculum and Teaching: T J Gray, BEd London
Assistant Head – Pupils' Academic Development: Mrs K Owen, BSc Exeter
Assistant Head – Extra-Curricular Activities: Mr S Wintle, BEd De Montfort

Club Presidents:
R Batley, CertEd Borough Road College, London (*Jaguars*)
D A Coombes, BA Liverpool John Moores (*Panthers*)
Miss C L Gavin, BSc Loughborough (*Tigers*)
J Knight, M Teach Kingston (*Bears*)
L Williams, MSc Brunel (*Lions*)
Mrs A J Staughton, BA Leeds Polytechnic (*Wolves*)

Teaching Staff:
Miss S C Allan, MA Cardiff
Mrs C Allen, SpLD Cert
Mrs A Ashton, BA Sheffield
Mrs P Butler, BEd Westminster College Oxford
Mrs J Burns, BSc Greenwich
L J Davies, BSc Open University
Mrs F J Drye, BA Wales
O W Figgis, BA Leeds
N R Grove, MA Liverpool
Mrs C Handford, CertEd Trent Park College
Mrs J C Hennessy, BA Leicester Polytechnic
Mrs C J Hughes, BA Durham, SpLD Cert
Miss A S Kingstone, BA University College Northampton
Mrs E Mestraud, Middlesex
C W Picket, BSC Auckland
P P Ricca, MFLE LSL LA Montpellier & Toulouse
Mrs R Russell, BEd Reading
Miss R J Sanders, MA Durham
Mrs A M Simmons, BA Stirling
Mrs C L Whitaker, BA Brighton

Senior School colleagues who teach in the Preparatory School:
S M Adams, BEd Exeter
Mrs F J Burgess, BEd Exeter
S L Egan, BEng Leicester
Mrs S E Fellows, BA Birmingham
Miss C L Gavin, BSc Loughborough
Mrs A J Gillam, BA Exeter
Mrs A S Holley, BA Birmingham
G E Houghton, BA Durham
Miss C S Irvin, BSc Loughborough
P R Marshall, BA Wales, LRAM
Ms J A Mason, BA Teesside
M A Nugent, BA Northampton
I Runnells, BA University College Northampton
Revd M J Walker, BA Lincoln College Oxford, DipES St John's College, Durham
H K Williams, CertEd London

School Nurses:
Mrs L R Wood, RGN, Cert DN
Mrs D Barclay, RGN
Mrs L Bate RN

Librarian: Mrs K Cooper, BA Aberystwyth

Registrar: Mrs J Wilson

Pre-Preparatory School:
Headmistress: Miss J M Everett, BEd Froebel Institute, MA Heriot-Watt
Assistant Head (Curriculum): D C Popplewell, BA Warwick
Assistant Head (Pastoral): Mrs R M Girling, BEd Cambridge

Teaching Staff:
Mrs J C Bradford, BEd St John's College, York
Mrs J E M Espin, BA New Hall Cambridge
S Garfirth, DipRCM, ALCM
Mrs L Gillard, BA QTS Northampton
Mrs S A Jamieson, BA University College Northampton
Mrs J Mellor, BEd Kingston
Mrs L C Potter, BA Leeds
Miss C M Sullivan, BSc Nottingham
Mrs C H Waite, BEd Ripon and York St John
Mrs E Jakeman, BEd Worcester College

Nursery:
Mrs S M Sandall Dip Early Years Ed & NNEB Solihull Technical College
Mrs M Gutteridge, NNEB Southfields College
Mrs H Cockbill, West Bridgford College of FE
Miss S Pacan, NNEB Triangle Training

Teaching Assistants:
Mrs M E Campbell, BTEC Art Diploma Tresham College
Mrs K Harris, NNEB Tresham Institute
Mrs A Martin, NNEB Stoke on Trent College
Mrs C Ward, NNEB Northampton College
Miss A M Ystenes, NNEB Nene College
Miss B Gosling, NNEB Northampton College
Mrs Z Shah, NNEB Northampton College
Mrs K Robson, NNEB CACHE

Sports Coach: Miss S Peters
IT Coordinator: Ms M Mannion

Wellingborough is situated 63 miles from London, 10 miles east of Northampton. Close to the main railway line from St Pancras to Leicester and Sheffield, it is served by an excellent network of motorways and dual carriageways connecting the A1, A14 and the M1.

Buildings and Organisation. The School occupies a fine site on the south of the town, and stands in its own grounds of 45 acres. In the Senior School there are five boys' houses and three girls' houses, organised on boarding house lines. Each house has about 45 pupils. The Sixth Form numbers around 140 pupils, 90% of whom go directly to higher education.

Admission at 13+ for boys and girls is by means of entry tests and interview or the Common Entrance Examination from preparatory schools. Direct entry into the Sixth Form is on the basis of an interview, school report and likely GCSE results confirmed before entry. Please note that A Level courses begin in June after GCSE examinations.

The Preparatory School, while sharing some of the facilities of the Senior School, has its own buildings and classrooms on the east side of the campus. In recent years work has been completed on a large new library, incorporating a computer research, fiction and non-fiction working areas, classroom and science laboratory, with up-to-date facilities and IT throughout. The Pre-Preparatory School occupies its own modern purpose-built buildings which have been substantially refurbished and extended.

The main school buildings include an ICT study centre, a library, assembly hall, careers room, chapel, and three classroom blocks including seven newly refurbished science laboratories and the information technology department. There is a design technology centre, music school, modern languages centre, sports hall, 2 art buildings and central dining hall.

Religion. Religious teaching is according to the Church of England. Pupils attend a mixture of morning prayers and longer services on weekdays, and a morning service on some Sundays during term. The Chaplain prepares members of the School for confirmation each year, the confirmation service taking place in the Lent Term.

Curriculum. In the Pre-Preparatory School and the Preparatory School the curriculum is an enriched version of the National Curriculum. French, Latin and Spanish are also taught in the Preparatory School.

In the first year of the Senior School, pupils follow a core curriculum in English, Mathematics, French, Physics, Chemistry, Biology, History, Geography, Design Technology, Art, Music, RE, Information Technology and PE. German and Latin are both options in this year. GCSE courses are offered in English, English Literature, French, Mathematics and dual award sciences. Options include separate Sciences, Latin, German, History, Geography, Art, Design Technology, Music, Drama, PE and Religious Studies.

The following subjects are offered for A Level examination: Art and Design, Biology, Business Studies, Chemistry, Design Technology, Economics, English Literature, French, German, Geography, History, Mathematics and Further Mathematics, Music, PE, Physics, Politics and Psychology. Information Technology, Drama, English Language and Religious Studies are offered as freestanding AS Levels.

Music, Drama, Art, Design. The Music School contains a new central teaching hall, a second newly refurbished teaching room and several practice rooms. Professional tuition is given on all instruments and there are chapel and concert choirs, junior and senior bands and a school orchestra.

Concerts, school and house drama productions and lectures are held in the School Hall, which has well-equipped stage facilities. The Richard Gent Design Centre offers workshops and studies for design technology and ceramics. The highly successful Two-Dimensional Art Department has its own dedicated building. Pupils are encouraged to make full use of these facilities in their spare time.

Sport. The playing fields, over 40 acres in extent, are used for the main boys' sports of rugby, soccer and cricket and hockey and netball for girls; cross country, athletics, and tennis are also highly popular. The school site also boasts a nine-hole golf course, astroturf pitch, five all-weather tennis courts, two squash courts, shooting range, gymnasium and sports hall. The latter has four badminton courts, indoor cricket nets and facilities for fencing, table tennis, basketball and dedicated fitness suite.

Other Activities. After their first term in the Senior School pupils join the Combined Cadet Force (RN, Army, Commando or RAF Section) until the end of Year 10 at least. Training is given in first aid, map reading and orienteering, and camping expeditions take place at weekends. There is an annual CCF camp and there are opportunities for band training, open range shooting, REME work, canoeing and sailing. The Duke of Edinburgh's Award Scheme is also a very popular option for older pupils.

A wide range of extra-curricular interests is available through various societies and clubs. Pupils may also take part in local community service work.

Careers. Guidance is available to all pupils on further education and careers prospects through the Head of Careers and other members of staff. The School is a member of the Independent Schools Careers Organisation.

Scholarships. (*See Scholarship Entries section.*) Foundation scholarships are offered to external candidates for entry to the Preparatory School at 11+. At 13+ entrance scholarships are offered to pupils entering the Senior School. At 16+ Sixth Form academic scholarships are offered. Performing Arts (Music and Drama) scholarships and awards are available at 13+ and 16+ for candidates of outstanding ability and potential. Art scholarships and awards are offered at 13+ and at 16+. Sports scholarships and awards are awarded at 13+ and at 16+.

Bursaries. Some bursaries are available for candidates who can make an outstanding/special contribution to the School where there is a proven case of financial need. All awards are means-tested and subject to satisfactory performance both academically and in other respects.

Further details and application forms for all the above awards may be obtained from the Registrar.

Fees per term (2011-2012). Senior School: £4,202 (Years 9–11), £4,086 (Years 12–13); Preparatory School £3,923, Pre-Preparatory School £2,422–£2,534 (reduced rates are offered for children in Nursery Class not attending all sessions and children from age 3–5 are eligible for the Government's Early Years Funding). Fees include most extras apart from instrumental lessons (termly payment), public examination fees and books.

Admission. Applications should be made to the Registrar for entry of boys and girls at 13+ and for direct entry into the Sixth Form. Enquiries concerning entries between the ages of 3 and 7 should be addressed to the Headmistress of the Pre-Preparatory School and entries between the ages of 8 and 12 to the Registrar of the Preparatory School.

Term of Entry. New pupils are accepted at the beginning of any term. The largest entry is in September each year.

Old Wellingburian Club. All former pupils who have spent at least one year in the School are eligible for membership. Correspondence should be addressed to the OW Club Secretary at the School.

Charitable status. Wellingborough School is a Registered Charity, number 1101485. It exists to provide education for boys and girls from the age of 3 to 18.

Wellington College

Duke's Ride, Crowthorne, Berkshire RG45 7PU
Tel: The Master: 01344 444101
          Director of Admissions: 01344 444013
          Bursar: 01344 444020
          Reception: 01344 444000
Fax: 01344 444002
e-mail: info@wellingtoncollege.org.uk
website: www.wellingtoncollege.org.uk

The College was founded by public subscription as a memorial to the Great Duke. It was granted its Royal Charter in 1853 and took its first pupils in 1859. The school is set in a woodland estate of 400 acres.

Visitor: Her Majesty The Queen

President: HRH The Duke of Kent, KG, GCMG, GCVO, ADC, DL

Vice-President & Chairman of Governors: Sir Michael Rake

Ex officio Governors:
The Archbishop of Canterbury, FBA, DD, DPhil, MA
The Duke of Wellington, KG, LVO, OBE, MC, DL

Governors:
P G C Mallinson, BA, MBA
Mrs O Deighton
Rear Admiral H A H G Edleston, RN
Dr R Groves, BA, PhD
Dr P J A Frankopan, MA, DPhil, FRSA
Mrs A E T Dean, BSc
Dr E M Sidwell, BSc, PhD, FRSA, FRGS
T B Bunting, MA
R Perrins, BSc Hons, ACA
C G C H Baker, MA
H W Veary, BA, FCA
Mrs M Chaundler, OBE
Rt Hon The Lord Strathclyde
Sir Ron Dennis, CBE
J Turnbull
T Cookson
E Chaplin, CMG, OBE

Legal Adviser: Mrs Y Gallagher

Master: A F Seldon, MA, PhD, MBA, FRSA, FRHistS

Second Master: R I H B Dyer, BA
Deputy Head: Mrs J T Lunnon, BA
Director of Admissions: R J W Walker, MA
Deputy (Organisation): Mrs E A Worthington, MA
Deputy (Performance): R C Auger, MA
Deputy (Academic): Dr M J Milner, MA, DPhil
Deputy (Pastoral): Mrs D A Draper, BSc

Assistant Staff:
* *Head of Department/Year*
† *Housemaster/mistress*

C M St G Potter, BSc	A R Dewes, MA
J D Oakes, ARCM	M Farrington, BSc, MSc,
R A Peter, BA	PhD
*Mrs L P Walker, MA	M N Halpin, MSc
J J Breen, MA, BA	J L Price, BA
I C E Mitchell, BSc	Dr E M Hood, BSc, PhD
T J Head, BA	P Hucklesby, MA

†J C Rawlinson, BSc
†C M Oliphant-Callum, MA
I M Henderson, BA
Mrs C J Henderson, BA
B N Roth, BSc, BA, AFIMA
†N C Lunnon, BSc
†M T Boobbyer, BA
P G S Boscher, BA, PhD
*S R J Williamson, MA, FRCO
Ms S A Lang, BA
J A F Jeffrey, BA
S D Laverack, BSc, PhD
*Mrs C J Blunden-Lee, BA
*M J Oakman, BA
Mrs D E Cook, BA
*M J D Ellwood, BEd
Mrs B F Boscher, BA
†J S White, BA
B A Bayman, BA
I Frayne, BSc
G I Woodrow, MA
†Mrs L Raabe-Marjot, BA
J M Gale, BA
B Wielenga, BCom
*S C D Gutteridge
C B Ewart, MA
*D Wilson, MA
*M P Ford, BSc
*I R Morris, BA
Mrs K J Hamilton, BA
*Miss S L Spencer, BA
*S J Allcock, BA
Miss B C Thomas, BA
Miss M Churchill, MA
†D Walker, BSc
Mrs Y Tang, MA
*L W Hedges, MA
*N J Amy, MA
W Heathcote, MPhys
*Dr D A James, MA, PhD
G J Williams, MA
Mrs K E Granville-Chapman, BA
*Mrs E-J Haining, BA
Mrs S J Henwood, GRSM Hons
*Miss K Jack, MA
S A S Owen, BA
*Mrs J M Grillo, BEd
†Mrs J M Waugh, BEd
*M J Albrighton, MA
Dr R S Kirkham, MA, PhD
Dr J L Chapman, PhD, BSc
J W Higham, BA
Miss K Murphy, BSc
†Ms M J Chodak, BA
†G D Pearson, BEng
Mrs S Y N Jobson, Lic d'Anglais, Dip d'Étude IFI

*S Shortland, BEd, MSc
*M Goves, BA
†Mrs R E Loaring, BSc
*Dr R J Cromarty, MA, PhD
*E B R Venables, BA
†J Giannikas, BA
B P Lewsley, BA
Miss C L Edwards, BA
K J Brennan, BA
†G D Franklin, BA
X Iles, BA
Ms R G Shawe-Taylor, MA
Miss F K Smith, BSc
Dr J Seldon, MA
D Quinlivan-Brewer, BMus Hons, PGDip RCM
Miss F C MacLean, BEng
S J Kirkham, BA
†T C Hicks, BA
Mrs L Wielenga
H Macgregor, PG Dip
Mrs R C Jarrett, BA
*J R Heal, BA
B T Attenborough, BA
Mrs R L Cunliffe, BA
Mrs P P Gutteridge
T C H Norton, BA
*Miss D A Stansfield, BSc
*J O'Loughlin, MSci, PhD
*A J Sproat, BA
M E Denhart, BA
D M Townley, MChem
I J Sutcliffe, MA, MBA
P W Thistlethwaite, BA, MSt
Miss V E M Woods, MA
A Edwards, BSc, MEd
Miss A E Brown, BEd
S A Farrell, BA
†Miss E Prescott, MA
Miss G E Devlin, BA
A M Wilkinson, BA
Mrs C I Goldsmith, MSc
*R H Atherton, BSc, MPhil
Mrs M V Ogilvie, Lic d'Anglais
Mrs A J E Campion, MA
C R Mitchell, BEng
†Miss J C Baldwin, BA
Mrs E J Bidston, BA
G A Bough, BSc
R Drummond, BA
*M T Finn, PhD, MPhil
*R J A Macpherson, MSc
Miss K E Manns, BA
*Miss H-J Stubbings, BA
Miss R R Trafford, MA
*T F C Wayman, MPhil
Mrs J C Wayman, BA
A Williams, BSc
Mrs N Ma, MA

plus 45 visiting instrumental teachers

Senior Chaplain: The Revd T W G Novis, BA, MDiv

Houses and Housemasters/mistresses:
Anglesey: Mrs R E Loaring
Apsley: Ms M J Chodak
Benson: T C Hicks
Beresford: G D Franklin
Blücher: M T Boobbyer
Combermere: Miss E Prescott

Hardinge: C M Oliphant-Callum
Hill: J Giannikas
Hopetoun: Mrs J M Waugh
Lynedoch: G D Pearson
Murray: J C Rawlinson
Orange: Mrs L Raabe-Marjot
Picton: R I Clarke
Raglan: D Walker
Stanley: N C Lunnon
Talbot: J S White
Wellesley: Miss J C Baldwin

OC CCF: Major T C H Norton
Librarian: Ms J L Shepherd, BA, ALA
Group Finance Director & Bursar: S J Crouch, BA Oxon, ACA
Director of Finance: P F Thompson, MA, ACMA
Works Bursar: G Burbidge, FCIOB, MCIOSH
Operations Bursar: S J Blosse
Medical Officer: A Sachdev, MB ChB, CFP, D Pall Med
Medical Centre Sister: Mrs B J Gilbert
Registrar: Mrs L Peate, BSc
Master's PA: Mrs A Reed
College Secretary: Mrs E L Browne
Bursar's Secretary: Mrs L J Thompson

Wellington College is the place where a fusion of originality, innovation and 150 years of tradition and history produces an education unlike any other. Our unique Eight Aptitudes approach to education and our emphasis on promoting well-being develop the whole child.

The school life of every pupil is organised around these aptitudes: linguistic, logical, cultural, physical, spiritual, moral, personal and social. Our curriculum is challenging, ambitious and global. We offer the IB Diploma and the IB Middle Years Programme alongside A Level and GCSE.

Organisation. There are approximately 1,020 pupils, with 628 boys and 392 girls, the latter spread across all age groups.

Pupils belong to one of the 17 Houses (seven in the main College buildings and ten in the grounds). Boarders (and some day pupils) at 13+ join one of nine Houses taking boys and four Houses taking girls. There are two (16+) Sixth Form Houses, one each for girl and for boy boarders (and a small number of day pupils), and two day Houses, one each for girls and for boys. 13+ boarders share rooms in their first year, and may do so in a second or third year, but then move on to their own room. Some day pupils, with day rooms, a longer school day and some facility for very occasional stay overnight, are spread amongst the boarding Houses. Day pupils share common rooms. There is a central dining hall with modern kitchens and serveries. Meals are taken here on a cafeteria basis by most of the pupils although some Houses outside the main buildings have their own dining facilities. The newly-opened Victoria and Albert social centre is also open during school hours for drinks and snacks. The school has its own Medical Officer and an 8-bed Medical Centre constantly staffed by fully qualified nurses. All Houses have their own House Matrons and domestic staff.

Academic Work. Academic standards are very high. GCSE and A Level pass rates are in the 98–100% range and nearly all pupils go on to university. There is a good rate of entry to Oxford, Cambridge, Durham, Edinburgh and many other good universities.

The school is divided for teaching purposes into the Lower School (Third and Fourth Forms), the Middle School (Fifth Form) and the Sixth Form (Lower Sixth and Upper Sixth). Wellington's curriculum is firmly grounded in the school's commitment to developing the full range of every pupil's inherent aptitudes. The academic curriculum is designed to give pupils a broad and rounded education while allowing them maximum opportunity to develop their individual interests and strengths through their chosen fields of specialist study.

All pupils entering the Third Form undertake the International Baccalaureate Middle Years Programme (IB MYP). The curriculum, tailored by Wellington College's staff to meet the aspirations of an increasingly academically gifted intake, is varied and stimulating, offering rich breadth and depth. It provides an excellent transition between prep schools and the middle years at Wellington, whilst developing strong cross-curricular links and study skills. When entering the Fourth Form, pupils may choose to continue the IB MYP or to take GCSEs.

In the Sixth Form, pupils have the option to study the International Baccalaureate Diploma Programme, an increasingly popular choice, or a wide range of AS and A2 Level choices is available. These include all the usual combinations but at least one-third of our pupils do a combined Arts/Science grouping.

Facilities. Most work takes place in modern specialist blocks near to the main buildings. The Queen's Court building also contains a theatre. The Science laboratories are numerous and the Kent Building houses well-equipped Design & Technology and Information Technology centres. A new Art School and Physics laboratories have been built. A new Modern Languages block is now open. The old Art School in the main buildings has been converted into a new lecture room and conference room. New IT suites have been built in Queen's Court and near the Science laboratories.

Enrichment Activities. Personal enrichment is an imperative at Wellington and each student takes part in a range of activities that broaden and refine their education. Such Enrichment is structured within the eight aptitudes of learning with dedicated time on a Monday, Wednesday and Friday. There are some fifty-two clubs, societies and other Enrichment activities which include Archery, Ancient Hebrew, Mandarin, Meditation, Mountain Biking, Real Ale, Noble Rot (wine-tasting), Photography, Model United Nations, Petrol Heads, Food for Thought, Bush Craft, Law Society, Dance Classes, Bardophile, Film Society, Creative Writing and Understanding Disability. All pupils on arrival join the Junior Society which introduces them to a wide variety of activities. A Creative Writing Group meets regularly, and two literary magazines are produced by pupils: The Wellingtonian and South Front.

Art, Music and Drama are outstanding. There are regular visiting lecturers on a variety of topics, an Artist in Residence, and master-classes in Art, Music/Drama and Literature.

The school has built upon its historic legacy of leadership, that dates back to the First Duke of Wellington, and has established programmes to offer each pupil training and opportunities in leadership throughout their time at the College. The College runs annual inter-schools conferences on leadership; one for head pupils and the other, a combined conference for staff and pupils to share ideas on leadership. Wellington introduced pioneering well-being classes in September 2006.

Wellington has been a Round Square school since 1995; membership of the Round Square organisation is a fundamental part of Wellington's holistic approach to education. Partnership with over seventy schools worldwide allows us to pursue our aim to produce compassionate global citizens of the future.

Sport. Wellington's sporting reputation continues to thrive. Excellence, participation for all and a lifetime investment in sport and recreational activities is the adopted culture within the school. This sporting ethos is linked to the College's inspirational well-being programme. The school also has a national reputation for prowess in a number of sports, particularly in rugby, hockey, cricket, netball, shooting, swimming, athletics, rackets, squash, golf and polo.

There are numerous opportunities for pupils to represent the College in teams across a wide range of competitive sports as well as recreational activities, all of which are supported by the outstanding College facilities. These include over 80 acres of playing fields, two all-weather pitches for hockey and all-weather tennis courts. There is a sports complex which incorporates a rackets court, five squash courts, an indoor pool and a large sports hall. This has a main hall in which a wide variety of indoor games may be played as well as specialist weight training and rock climbing areas. A spectacular nine-hole golf course was opened in September 2001 and is enjoyed by many in the community. Successful links have also evolved with the Duke of York's Scholarship Scheme. The traditional pattern of boys' sport is rugby (we regularly field up to 20 XVs) in the Michaelmas Term, hockey, football and cross country in the Lent Term and cricket, athletics and swimming in the Summer. For the girls, hockey has been the main sport in the Michaelmas Term, with netball in the Lent and cricket, rounders, athletics and swimming in the Summer. There is also the opportunity for girls to play lacrosse competitively. Recently sporting options throughout the school have been expanded and many other sports have been made available as a first or second choice option for pupils which include squash, basketball, tennis, sailing, football, rugby 7s, triathlon, fencing, karate, badminton, canoeing, cross country and a variety of fitness and health-related activities. All are aimed at promoting active participation, enjoyment, excellence and a healthy lifestyle.

Admission to the School. Most pupils enter the school in September when they are between 13 and 14 years of age. There are occasionally places available for pupils at 14+. Two Sixth Form Houses (one for girls and one for boys) mean that there are places for entry at 16+. Applications for registration should be addressed to the Director of Admissions, or in the case of Foundationers, to the Bursar. On registration, a fee of £200 is charged which entitles a child's name to remain on the register until two years or so before entry is due. Those registered for 13+ entry (by 30th June of Year 6) are invited for Pre-testing (usually in the first term of Year 7). Those successful in Pre-testing are either invited onto the 'Places List' and asked to confirm their intention to take up a place (with payment of a Confirmation of Entry fee), or invited to accept a 'Waiting List' place. Confirmed places are guaranteed, subject to satisfactory results in the Scholarship, Common Entrance or other entry exams. An Acceptance Deposit is payable (as is, where appropriate, an overseas deposit).

Scholarships. There is a wide range of 13+ Scholarships and Exhibitions offered – Academic, Music, Art, DT, Drama, Dance and Sports. Details are shown on the website and in a separate booklet available from Admissions. Candidates for non-academic awards must satisfy our general entry requirements. Scholarships of all values may be augmented by a bursary where the financial situation of the parents makes this appropriate. Candidates must be under 14 on 1st September in the calendar year in which they sit the examination.

For pupils entering at 16+ there is a similar range of awards across the disciplines.

Fees per term (2011-2012). Boarders £10,025, Day Boarding £8,515, Day £7,515. For pupils in the Sixth Form, there is an additional charge of £86.50 per term. Separate charges totalling £239.50 per instrument are made for musical tuition (10 lessons). The school runs an attractive fees in advance scheme for parents with capital sums available.

Old Wellingtonian Society. The OW Society has branches in ten countries, clubs representing ten different sports, around 7,000 members (including 500 girls) and a Secretary based at College (Tel: 01344 444069; Fax: 01344 444007).

Charitable status. Wellington College is a Registered Charity, number 309093. It exists to provide education for boys and girls aged 13–18.

Wellington School

Wellington, Somerset TA21 8NT
Tel: 01823 668800
Fax: 01823 668844
e-mail: admin@wellington-school.org.uk
website: www.wellington-school.org.uk

Founded in 1837, Wellington School is a co-educational, academically selective school providing a friendly, disciplined environment and a wide range of co-curricular opportunities.

Motto: '*Nisi dominus frustra*'

Governing Body:

Chairman: D R Wheeler, BSc, FCA
Vice-Chairman: P H Nunnerley, BA, FCIB
Miss S Adams
J Clark
J P Elder
L Dodds
Mrs A Govey
Mrs T Humphreys
Dr D Lungley
B McDowell
S P Meredith
K B Phillips, BSc
H Richards
T M Taylor, MA Oxon, FRSA
Mrs S E Watts, ACIS, MBIM, JP
Mrs A Weekes, BA
E G Whall, BSc

Clerk to the Governors: T Pangraz

Headmaster: M S Reader, MA Oxon, MPhil, MBA

Senior Deputy Head: R S Page, MA
Deputy Head (Academic): Dr A J Daniel, BSc, PhD

Academic Staff:

A Anderson, BA
G J W Arnold, BSc
C A Askew, BA
Mrs A E Bazley, BEd
Ms A J Beaumont, MA
Mrs J C Bernard, BA
J F Bird, BA
P J Buckingham, BA, MA
Mrs L Burton, BA
A R Carson, BSc
D A Colclough, BSc
Miss M Collins, BA, MA
Miss J A Copley, BA
Mrs S A Dean, BA
A N Denham, BA, ATC
M E Downes, BSc
W Duggan, BA, MA
H D H Elkington, BA, MA
Mrs J Elliott
Dr I J Everton, MA, PhD
G Felletar, DipEd
Dr P T Galley, BSc, PhD
A Garcia, CertEd
Miss A Gunga, BA
Mrs H C Hawkins,
    MBioCh
J F Helliar, BSc
The Revd J P Hellier, BD,
    AKC, DipRE, CF
T J Hill, BA
Miss F E Hobday, MA
Dr K A Hodson, BA, MA

S W James, BA
Dr A R Jolliffe, BA, MA,
    DPhil
C G D Jones, BSc, CChem,
    MRCS
P Jones, BA, FRGS
S Jones, BSc
Mrs T Kaya, BA, TESOL
J Leonard, BA
Mrs L E Leonard, BA
Miss R L Marsden, BA
R Marsh, BA
Miss S Middleton, BA
Miss S Miller, BA
N McGuff, BSc
Mrs M H McIlveen, BEd,
    Dip TEFL
D Millington, BA, MSc
Mrs A D Musgrove, MA,
    MBA
Mrs S Page, MA
Mrs V Parsons, BSc
G Paterson, MA
A Phillips, BSc
I Reade, BA
M H Richards, BEd
Mrs V K Richardson, BSc
N Ridgway, BSc
Miss L A Rowe, BSc
Mrs H J Salter, BA
C J Sampson, BMus
A C Shaw, BA, MSc

J P W Shepherd, MA
Mrs K Simon, MA
N S Smith, BSc
R E Stevens, BSocSci
A W Stevenson, MA
Mrs P Sweet, MA
Mrs L Tabb, BSc
Miss S F L Toase, BSc,
    MIBiol

A J Trewhella, BA, ARCO
Dr W Vacani, BA, PhD
N H Vyse, MA
Mrs F Vyse, BSc
Mr C Waddilove, Dip
    Drama
I G Webb-Taylor, MA
Mrs F N Wreford, BA

Bursar: T D Williams, BA, FCCA
Registrar: Mrs C Loftus Owen, BA
Medical Officer: Dr J G Scott, MB BS, DRCOG

Situation. Located on the southern edge of Wellington, at the foot of the Blackdown Hills, this fully co-educational School is equidistant from Tiverton Parkway and Taunton Railway Stations. The M5 approach road (Junction 26) is within a mile. Currently there are 700 pupils in the Lower and Senior Schools (11–18 years), of whom 20% board.

Buildings. The School has witnessed an extensive building programme over the last twenty years, the new buildings having been carefully and tastefully blended in with existing architecture.

Most recent buildings include the John Kendall-Carpenter Science Centre with its state-of-the-art laboratories and lecture theatre, a multi-million pound sports complex which opened in 2002, a purpose-built Junior School and a new classroom block and examination hall. Major improvements to Performing Arts facilities, including a new foyer and theatre space, were completed in 2010.

Grounds. There are 29 acres of playing fields as well as a floodlit all-weather hockey pitch, squash courts, an indoor swimming pool and a climbing wall.

Houses. There are separate Houses for boys and girls, and for Seniors and Lowers. All Houses have their own changing, work and recreational facilities.

There is a central Dining Hall and all meals are served on a cafeteria basis. The School also has its own well equipped laundry.

There is a fully equipped Medical Centre, with a trained staff under the direction of the School Medical Officer.

Academic Organisation. The School is divided into the Upper School (Year 9–Sixth Form) and the Lower School (Years 7 and 8). The Junior School (Nursery–Year 6) is on a separate, adjoining campus.

Most pupils enter the School at Year 7 or 9. The curriculum in Years 7, 8 and 9 is designed to allow pupils to develop the skills needed to succeed at GCSE and features a good range of practical and more academic subjects including Latin. At GCSE all pupils study English, English Literature, Mathematics and a Short Course in Religious Education as well as a Modern Foreign Language and a further five or six subjects. Pupils have a free choice of studying three sciences separately or as Dual Award Science. The Mathematics and Science courses lead to IGCSE qualifications. The most able mathematicians take IGCSE at the end of Year 10 before taking Additional Mathematics in Year 11. Students have a free choice from a wide range of subjects in the Sixth Form: most start on 4 AS Levels before reducing to 3 A2 courses. A system of grades every four weeks and tutor groups ensure that academic monitoring of pupils is supportive and effective.

Religious Education is part of the curriculum throughout the School. The School is Christian in tradition and there is a short Act of Worship in the School Chapel on each weekday with a longer Sunday service. The content and form of these services are based on contemporary Anglican procedures. Attendance is expected although sensitivity is shown towards pupils of other faiths for whom alternative provision can be made.

Music. Tuition is available on all orchestral instruments, as well as piano, organ, drum kit and percussion, classical and electric guitars and voice. The department consists of 3 full-time, 2 part-time and 25 specialist instrumental staff. Facilities include a fine Steinway model D Concert Grand Piano and there is a large Rodgers Digital Organ in the Chapel. Some 30 ensembles rehearse each week, giving plentiful opportunities to performers of all ages and all instruments. The department currently runs 7 choirs of various kinds and styles from the renowned Chapel Choir to the lighter sounds of Girlforce9. Concerts of all kinds take place throughout each term and the Wellington Professional Concerts Series bring world class musicians to the School to give recitals and masterclasses. The 'Full Circle' series invites former pupils who have pursued Music to return and perform at the School. Pupils are entered for ABRSM, Trinity Guildhall and Rockschool exams each term.

Physical Education and Games. All pupils play games regularly, unless exempt for medical reasons. Physical Education, which is also part of the curriculum for Years 7 to 11, takes place in the Sports Complex. All pupils learn to swim and are given the opportunity to take part in as many sports as possible. In the winter term, rugby and hockey are the main sports; in the spring term hockey, netball and cross-country running; in the summer term athletics, cricket, tennis, swimming and rounders. Team practices take place throughout the week with matches on Saturday afternoons. The school has a specialist fencing teacher and the Sports Complex houses a purpose-built fencing salle.

Out of School and CCF Activities. All pupils from the Year 10 upwards either join the large CCF contingent, with army, naval and RAF sections, or are engaged in other activities on a weekly basis, ranging from community services and conservation, to gardening and stage crew. Outward Bound Activities, both within the CCF and as part of the flourishing Duke of Edinburgh's Award Scheme, are very popular, with many trips organised. The CCF also has a highly respected Corps of Drums, which frequently features in local ceremonial events. Societies, in addition to the above, include art, chess and drama at various levels, cookery, computing and others.

Careers. A complete careers guidance service is offered in a well-equipped suite of Careers Rooms.

Admission. Entrance exam for Year 7. Interviews for Year 8 and above. There is a registration fee of £50 for all pupils and a refundable deposit of £500.

Scholarships and Bursaries. A significant number of academic and all-rounder scholarships are offered each year for entry at 11+ and 13+. Music scholarships are awarded for entry at 11+, 13+ and above. Most awards are means-tested and may be increased by an income-related bursary. A small number of awards are offered for the Sixth Form.

Academic Grants. A number of reduced-fee places are given annually to those academically able pupils whose parents would not otherwise be able to meet the fees.

Fees per term (2011-2012). Boarders £7,220 which includes tuition, board, laundry, medical attention and Medical Centre, stationery and games. Day pupils: £4,010.

Extras. Apart from purely personal expenses, the termly extras are private music lessons from £190 to £240; EAL lessons at various rates depending on need.

Charitable status. Wellington School is a Registered Charity, number 310268. It aims to provide a happy, caring co-educational day and boarding community, where pupils are provided with the opportunity of making best use of their academic experience and the School enrichment activities, in order to enhance their overall preparation for life after the age of eighteen.

Wells Cathedral School

Wells, Somerset BA5 2ST
Tel: 01749 834200
Fax: 01749 834201

e-mail: admissions@wellscs.somerset.sch.uk
website: www.wells-cathedral-school.com

In 909AD there was a Cathedral School in Wells providing education for choir boys. Today, Wells Cathedral School is fully co-educational. Its spirit is a passion for learning and life; its dream an inspiring education set in a musically alive and beautiful environment as a brilliant foundation for life; and its focus, inspiring success.

Patron: HRH The Prince of Wales

Governors:
Chairman: The Very Revd John Clarke, MA, BD (*Dean of Wells*)
The Revd Canon Andrew Featherstone, MA
The Revd Canon Patrick Woodhouse, MA
Prebendary Barbara Bates, BA, MA, FRSA
Peter McIlwraith, FCA
Prebendary Helen Ball, OBE
Robert Sommers, BA
Prebendary Elsa van der Zee, BA, ALAMDA
Martin Smout, BSc, CEng, MICE
Mrs Jo Ballan-Whitfield, BSc, ACA
Patrick Cook, MA

Consultant to the Governing Body:
Prof David Strange, FRAM
Prof Colin Lawson, MA, PhD, DMus, FRCM, FLCM
Jonathan Vaughan, Dip RCM Perf, Dip RCM Teach

Music Consultant:
Christopher Adey, FRCM, FRAM

Head: Elizabeth Cairncross, BA

Deputy Head: C W L Cain, BA
Deputy Head (*Curriculum and International*): N D Walkey, MSc, FSS
Director of Music: Mrs D Nancekievill, BA, BMus, PGCE, Hon ARAM

Senior School

Teaching Staff:
Mrs A M Armstrong, BMus, LRAM, PGCE
M J Ashton, BA, PGCE
Ms C Barker, BSc
J Barnard, BSc Hons, PGCE
P Baron, MA, MLitt, Cert Theo, CertEd
Mrs H Bennett, BA Hons
Prof J Berry, BSc, PhD, FIMA, CMath
J Boot, BA, FRGS
N Bowen, BA, PGCE
Ms H Brown, BA, TEFL
J Byrne, Dip Moscow Cons, GRNCM
A Clements, CertEd, PGCE
Mrs N A M Connock, BSc, PGCE
Mrs S Cowell, BA Hons, CTEFLA
A Davies, BA, PGCE
C S Day, BA, PGCE
Mrs S Deans, MA
P Denegri, FTCL, LTCL, Hon ARAM
Ms C Downs, BA, PhD, PGCE
Mrs R Edwards, BSc, PGCE
Ms J El-Labany, BSc, PGCE
Mrs M C Fielding, BSc, PGCE, Cert SEN, Dip SpLD
C Finch, MA, BMus Hons, LRSM, Dip ABRSM
Mrs K Finch, BA
Mrs A Friend, BA, PGCE
Mrs P J Garty, BSc, PGCE
Ms J Gearon, BA, MA, PGCE
D Gowen, BA, PGCE
M Grogan, MA, DipTEFL
J Grogono-Thomas, BSc, PGCE, Cert SpLD, NPQM
D C Hansom, BMus, LRSM, ARCM
Mrs F Hockey, Diploma Dance

Revd J Hulme, BEd Hons, Cert Theo & Min, Dip Christian
  Spirituality
K H Humphreys, BSc, PGCE
Mrs M Humphreys, BA, PGCE, AMBDA
Ms S Jameson, BSc, PGCE, CSci, FIMA, FCIEA
Mrs T Jarman, BA, QTS
B Jones, BSc
D Jones, BSc, QTS
Miss C Kelly, MPhil, BA Hons, PGCE
R Ladley, MSc, BEng Hons
M A Laing, MA, PGCE
Miss C Lord, ARCM, Juilliard Diploma
Mrs C Meade, BA Hons, RWCMD
M Meally, MA, BA, BEng, PGCE, Dip HSWW
R Murdock, BA, MA, PGCE
Dr H Murphy, MA, BMus, LRAM, PhD, PGCE
Dr K Murphy, BA, MMus, PhD
Mrs E Nelson, BA Hons, QTS, CertEd
R Newman, BA, PGCE
Mrs C Newman, MA, PGCE
Mrs J Obradovic, LTCL
K Orchard, BSc
K Padgett, BSc
Mrs C Pattemore
Mrs E Paul, BA, PGCE
L Plum, BA Hons, AKC, PGCE
Ms G Pritchard, BSc, PGCE
R Robbetts (*Examinations Officer*)
D Rowley, BSc, PGCE
Mrs S G Rowley, BA Hons, PGCE
S Smyth, BSc, PGCE
M Souter, AGSM, Hon ARAM
Mrs L J Stockdale-Bridson, BA, PGCS
M Swarfield, BA, PGCE, PGC
Mrs J S Tapner, BA, ADT, PGCE
S Tapner, BSc, CertEd
B Taylor, MA, PGCE
Mrs L E Walkey, CertEd
Ms K Wells, BSc, QTS, MEd
L Whitehead, BA, MA, GGSMD, PGCE
J Williams, BA Hons, PGCE

Junior School

The Head of Junior School: Mrs K Schofield, BA Hons,
  NPQH
Deputy Head: Mrs J Barrow, BEd
Head of Early Years and Foundation Stage: Mrs J Bennett,
  BA
Director of Studies: Miss A Clark, BEd

Mrs R Ashton-Butler, BEd, Hornsby Dip SpLD
Mrs C Bolton
Mrs J Burns, TDip CSSD, LUD Drama
Miss P Daniels, BSc, QTS
Mrs K Dennis, BEd
Mrs J Edmonds, BSc, ALCM
Mrs K Fairey, BEd
K Gibson, Dip Teach, BEd
Miss A Maidment, BEd
Mrs E Morley, BEd
Mrs M Thomas
Mrs J Tucker, DipEd
J Ward, BSc, PGCE
Ms R Warner, BA, QTS

Bursar and Clerk to the Governors: S Webber, MA,
  FCMA, FCIS
Assistant Clerk to the Governors: D Shortland-Ball
Admissions Registrar: A Deacon, BSc, ACIB, FRSA
Head's PA: Mrs C Edwards
Communications Technology Director: J Pearce
Development Director: M Coote, BA, MA Ed
Publicity Manager: Mrs K Chantrey, BSc Hons

School Doctor: Dr C Bridson, MB BS, MRCGP, DipOCC,
  MED
School Sister: Mrs L Wiscombe, RGN

There is a Senior and Junior School with 719 boys and
girls aged from 3 to 18. Boarders number 230, whilst the
remainder are day pupils. Once accepted, a child normally
remains in the School without further Entrance Examination
until the age of 18+.

Fees per term (2011-2012). Senior School (Years
10–13): Boarders £8,218, Day £4,893. Lower School (Years
7–9): Boarders £7,910, Day £4,728. Junior School (Years
3–6): Boarders £6,745, Day £3,868. Pre-Prep (Reception–Year 2): Day £2,079. Nursery: £19.14 per 2 hour, 35
minute session.

Scholarships and Entrance. (*See Scholarship Entries
section.*) Scholarships and Academic Awards are awarded as
a result of Entrance and Scholarship Tests taken in January
at the School. These consist of tests and interviews, whilst
also considering any specialist gifts or aptitudes.

Sixth Form Scholarships and Academic Awards are
awarded on the basis of rigorous interview, predicted GCSE
results and a confidential reference from the applicant's current school.

Cathedral Choristerships and Bursaries are awarded as
the result of a Choral Trial. Applicants should be between 8
and 11 at the time of the Trial. Entrance Tests can be
arranged in any term and special arrangements can be made
for children overseas.

Situations and Buildings. The mediaeval city of Wells,
with its famous Cathedral and a population of only 10,500,
is the smallest city in England. It is just over 20 miles from
Bath and Bristol where there is a good rail service, and easily accessed from the M4 and M5 motorways. Bristol International Airport is a 40-minute drive away. The School
occupies all but one of the canonical houses in The Liberty.
This fine group is planned to keep its mediaeval and 18th
Century atmosphere while providing for the needs of modern boarding education. There are modern classrooms and
science laboratories built amongst walled gardens. A Sports
Hall provides indoor facilities for Tennis, Badminton,
Cricket, Basketball, Volleyball, Hockey, Five-a-Side Football, Climbing and Multi-Gym. There are Theatrical and
Concert facilities, a Music Technology Centre, a Computer
Studies Centre, Art, Design and Technology Department,
Drama Studio, Library, Sixth Form Centre, 25-metre covered Swimming Pool, Tennis and Netball courts, three sports
fields and an all-weather hard play area.

There are two Boarding Houses in the Junior and Lower
School and a further six in the Senior School, three for boys
and three for girls, the most senior pupils having study-bedrooms. The aim is to give security to the younger and to
develop a sense of responsibility in the older.

Organisation and Curriculum. Despite its national and
international reputation, the School has retained close links
with the local community, and its fundamental aim is to provide all its pupils with an education consistent with the
broad principles of Christianity. More specifically, the
School aims to be a well-regulated community in which
pupils may learn to live in harmony and mutual respect with
each other and with the adults who care for them. The curriculum has been designed to enable all children who gain
entry to the School to develop fully all their abilities, and to
take their place in due course in tertiary education and the
adult community of work and leisure. Forms are limited to a
maximum of 25; average class sizes are typically less than
this. Two years before GCSE a tutorial system is introduced
whereby some ten boys and girls are the responsibility of
one member of Staff for academic progress to GCSE. Pupils
then choose a subject faculty for sixth form tutoring in similar groups.

The emphasis is on setting by ability in particular subjects rather than streaming. There is every attempt to avoid

early specialisation. All take the International Mathematics GCSE, English, double Science, and a foreign language to GCSE. There is a Sixth Form of some 200 taking A Level courses in all major academic subjects.

Many places have been gained at Oxford and Cambridge in recent years and most Sixth Formers leave for some form of higher education.

Societies. There is a wide range of indoor and outdoor activities in which pupils must participate, although the choice is theirs. Outdoor education is an important part of the curriculum. Besides a Combined Cadet Force with Army and RAF sections and a Duke of Edinburgh's Award scheme, activities as diverse as chess and kite making, photography, sailing and golf are also on offer. Ballet and riding lessons are also arranged.

Music. The School is one of five in the UK designated and grant-aided by the Department for Education (DfE) to provide special education for gifted young musicians, who are given substantial financial assistance. Wells is unique in that both specialist and non-specialist musicians are able to develop their aptitudes within a normal school environment. These talents are widely acknowledged by audiences at concerts given by pupils from Wells throughout the world.

There are over 215 talented pupils following specially devised timetables which combine advanced instrumental tuition and ensemble work with academic opportunity. More than half of the School learns at least one musical instrument. Violin and cello is taught to all children in the Pre-prep as part of the curriculum. Pupils receive the highest quality teaching, often leading to music conservatoires and a career in Music. Central to specialist music training are the opportunities to perform in public and there is a full concert diary. There are also regular concerts by the many ensembles in the School.

For further details contact: The Registrar, Wells Cathedral School, Wells, Somerset BA5 2ST. Tel: 01749 834200, e-mail: admissions@wellscs.somerset.sch.uk.

The Wellensian Association. Old Wellensians, Wells Cathedral School, Wells, Somerset BA5 2ST.

Charitable status. Wells Cathedral School Limited is a Registered Charity, number 310212. It is a charitable trust for the purpose of promoting the cause of education in accordance with the doctrine of the Church of England.

West Buckland School

Barnstaple, Devon EX32 0SX
Tel: 01598 760281
Fax: 01598 760546
e-mail: headmaster@westbuckland.devon.sch.uk
website: www.westbuckland.devon.sch.uk

West Buckland School was founded in 1858 "to provide a first class education at reasonable cost". It has always stressed the importance of all-round character development alongside good academic achievement. Our size allows pupils to receive plenty of individual care and attention to their needs and talents.

West Buckland Preparatory School educates children between the ages of three and eleven. There is strong cooperation and support between the schools which share the same grounds, so making the transition as easy as possible.

West Buckland is fully co-educational.

Motto: *'Read and Reap'*

President: Mr Paul Orchard-Lisle, CBE, TD, LLD(hc), DSc(hc), MA, FRICS

The Governing Body:

Chairman: A C Parker, CBE

Vice-Chairmen:
The Countess of Arran, MBE, DL
S D Fox, BA

Governors:

C Fletcher-Wood, OBE, BA	C D Phillips, BSc, FRICS, ACI, Arb, MEWI
The Venerable David Gunn-Johnson, MA, STH	M R Popplewell, BSc Hons J K Singh, JP
G G Harrison, BSc, FRICS	Mrs R M Thomas, CBE, DL, BA, DSc(hc)
Mrs S Husband	D Walker
Mr A Jackson	Mrs K Watson
J G L Nichols, MA, FRSA, FCollP	Mrs C M Williams, BA

Headmaster: **J F Vick**, MA St John's College Cambridge

Deputy Head: D M Hymer, BSc University College London

Director of Studies: C J Burrows, MA Exeter College Oxford

Pastoral Deputy: Mrs R C Tibble, BA Open University

Headmaster, Preparatory School: A D Moore, BEd

Chaplain: The Revd A M Kettle, MA

Houses & Housemasters/mistresses:
Brereton House: Mrs R H Berry, MA Bristol
Courtenay House: C J Allin, BA Leicester
Fortescue House: Miss E Rushe, BSc University College Dublin
Grenville House: J A Ralph, BA Aberystwyth

Teaching Staff:

M J Adams, BSc Hons	Mrs T Hill, MSc
C J Allin, BA	A P Hooper, BSc
Mme M LeBarth	Mrs E M Kent, BMus
Mrs J Beech	Revd A M Kettle, MA
Mrs B Joly-Bloodworth	A M Kimberley, BSc Hons
C J Block, BA	Mrs A Klemz
P J Brand, BSc Hons	Miss H Lane, BEd
M T Brimson, BA	Miss E MacKay, CertEd
Mrs J E Brock, MEd	Miss K P MacBride, MA
Mrs J F Bunclark, MA	N Minard, BA
Miss A Callow, BSc	W D Minns, BEng
Mrs J M Carter, BSc	J R Moor, MA
R D Clarke, BA, BEd	Mrs L Napier, BEd
Mrs H C Clements, BA Hons	T O'Brien, BSc
	P J C Ponder, BEd
P H Davies, BSc	Miss A-S Prian
C H Dawson, BSc	D Price, Ed Ord
J W R Dougall, BSc Hons	S J Prior, BSc
A D Evans, BEd	Mrs A L Pugsley, BA
D R Ford, BA Hons	Miss D J Sharman, BSc
Mrs S G Fowles, BSc	N T Shawcross, BSc
J E Freeman, BEng	M G Stuart, BA
J M Goode	Mrs R L Thompson, BEd Hons
M J Greer, BA	
Dr E N D Grew, PhD	M J Tucker, CertEd
Miss A Griffiths, BA Hons	Miss K Venner, BSc Hons
Mrs S P Hartnoll, BEd	Mrs K Wicks, BA Hons
Mrs Y Helicon, BA	Mrs A J Willmott, BEd

Visiting Music Staff:
Mrs P Adie (*Singing*)
M Bosworth (*Organ and Piano*)
Ms J Buckingham (*Clarinet*)
C Bundy (*Saxophone*)
Ms E Collingham (*Cello*)
Mrs L Cooper (*Piano and Flute*)
Mrs A Hammond (*Violin and Keyboard*)
Mrs J Norris (*Violin, Viola, Oboe*)
R Norris (*Jazz Piano*)
T Parker (*Guitar*)

A Parton (*Brass*)
Mrs A Prior (*Piano and theory*)
Ms R Priscott (*Piano*)
Ms S Sherratt (*Harp and Recorder*)
Mrs S Steele (*Flute, Piano*)
B Waring (*Percussion*)

Bursar: Cdr A R Jackson, MILT, MInstAM
Assistant Bursar: I R Worledge
Finance Officer: Mrs J Ramsey
Domestic Bursar: Mrs T Widlake
Bursar's Secretary: A Meakin
Fees Secretary: D Foster
Headmaster's Secretary: Mrs S Harris
Registrar: Mrs L A Millar
Receptionist/Admin Assistant: Mrs L Lancaster
Registration Secretary/Admin Assistant: Mrs A Swinton/
  Mrs C Smalley
Medical Officer: Dr C A Gibb, BMed, BM, DA, MRCGP,
  DRCOG, DPD
School Sisters: Mrs C E Pouncey, RGN; Mrs G M Davies,
  RGN

Houseparents:
Mr M J Tucker
Mr P C P Ponder
Mrs M Goode
Mr J Goode
Mrs N Stuart
Mrs A Booker
Mrs J Hemus
Mrs V Ford
Mrs A Melchior

Development Office:
Mrs S Pollard (*Director*)
Miss A Rutter-Jerome (*Assistant to Development Director*)

Librarian: Miss L Warrillow
Uniform Shop: Mrs C Cawsey
School Staff Instructor: D J Morgan

Situation. The School stands in its own grounds of 100 acres on the southern edge of Exmoor. Barnstaple is 10 miles away and the M5 motorway can be reached in 40 minutes. Boarders arriving by train at Exeter station are met by coaches.

Buildings and Grounds. The central range of buildings, dating from 1861, still forms the focus of the school, and now includes a performing arts centre. Other developments include a Sixth Form Centre, Mathematics and Physics Centre, boarding houses for boys and girls, a Preparatory School classroom block and the ICT Centre. The campus offers extensive sports facilities, including a 9-hole golf course, an indoor heated 25-metre swimming pool, and an Astroturf hockey pitch. The Jonathan Edwards Sports Centre opened in 2008 and the outstanding 150 Building for Art and Design, Design Technology and a Theatre opened in April 2010.

Admission. Boys and girls are admitted as boarders or day pupils. The present number of pupils is: 80 boarding, 609 day.

Entrance to the Preparatory School is by interview and assessment. Entry to the Senior School is by examination at 11+ and 13+, or to the Sixth Form upon interview and school report. Entry at other ages is usually possible, and arrangements are made to suit individual circumstances.

Fees per term (2011-2012). Senior: Boarding £6,400–£7,510; Day £3,975. Preparatory: Boarding £6,400; Day £2,130–£3,235. Nursery: £3.62 per hour (first 15 hours), £4.00 per hour (each additional hour).

Scholarships and Bursaries. (*See Scholarship Entries section.*) Several scholarships are offered at 7+, 11+, 13+ and 16+ (up to a value of 10% of the tuition fees). Candi-

dates must be under 8, 12, under 14, or under 17 years of age on 1st September.

With the support of the West Buckland School Foundation, means-tested bursaries are available for boarders and day students at all ages.

Curriculum. In the Preparatory School the main emphasis is upon well-founded confidence in English and Mathematics, within a broad balance of subjects that adds modern languages to the national curriculum. Particular attention is given to the development of sporting, artistic and musical talents.

In the Senior School breadth is complemented by specialisation. All students study the three separate sciences from Year 7, while French and Spanish are the principal languages offered. Our flexible options arrangements at GCSE respond to students' individual strengths and preferences. A wide range of A Level subjects is offered to sixth formers whose results uphold the high academic standards of the School.

Careers. The Careers Staff advise all pupils upon the openings and requirements for different careers. They make full use of the facilities offered by Connexions.

Games, The Performing Arts and other activities. One of the most impressive features of life at West Buckland is the quality and range of extra curricular activities. The level of involvement by pupils and staff is very high indeed.

The school has a strong sporting tradition. Rugby, hockey, cricket, netball, tennis, athletics, swimming, cross-country, squash, golf, shooting and many other sports offer opportunities for inter-school and inter-house competition and for recreation.

About a third of all pupils receive instrumental and singing tuition from specialist teachers. The wide range of choirs and instrumental groups give concerts at least once a week throughout the year. Drama is a strength of the school with productions of many kinds throughout the year.

Music. Over 120 members of the school receive instrumental tuition on all instruments. They are encouraged to perform in concerts, in choirs and instrumental groups. Music Technology is a strong feature of the department's work.

Outdoor Education. Much use is made of the proximity of Exmoor and the coast for climbing, kayaking, mountain biking, surfing and other adventurous activities. All pupils receive instruction in camp craft, first aid and map reading. The Combined Cadet Force has Army and Royal Air Force sections, and offers a range of challenging pursuits. Our students succeed at all levels in the Duke of Edinburgh's Award Scheme each year, and there is a regular programme of expeditions in this country and overseas.

Religion. The tradition is Anglican but all denominations and religions are welcome. Services of worship are held throughout the week including many Sundays. A number of services are held at East Buckland Church. The Chaplain prepares boys and girls for confirmation every year.

Attitudes and values. The School sets out to be a friendly and purposeful community in which happiness and a sense of security are the foundation on which young lives are built. At all levels members of the school are asked to lead a disciplined way of life, to show consideration for others, to be willing to be challenged and to recognise that the success of the individual and the success of the group are inextricably linked.

Charitable status. West Buckland School is a Registered Charity, number 306710. Its purpose is the education of boys and girls from 3 to 18.

Westminster School

17 Dean's Yard, Westminster, London SW1P 3PB
Tel: 020 7963 1042 (Head Master)
        020 7963 1003 (Registrar)

020 7963 1000 (Other enquiries)
020 7821 5788 (Westminster Under School)
Fax: 020 7963 1002
e-mail: registrar@westminster.org.uk
website: www.westminster.org.uk

Westminster School is a Boarding and Day School which is co-educational in the Sixth Form. The present number of boys and girls is about 740.

The School traces its origins to the grammar school that was attached to the Benedictine Abbey at Westminster. Queen Elizabeth I re-founded the School in 1560 as part of the College of St Peter at Westminster.

Motto: '*Dat Deus Incrementum*'

Visitor: Her Majesty The Queen

Governing Body:
Chairman: The Very Reverend Dr John Hall, The Dean of Westminster
The Dean of Christ Church, The Very Reverend Dr Christopher Lewis
The Master of Trinity, Lord Rees of Ludlow, OM, FRS
The Reverend Canon Andrew Tremlett
The Reverend Canon Robert Reiss
Professor Judith Pallot
Professor Stephen Elliott
Lord Hunt of Chesterton, CB, FRS (*OW*)
M C Baughan, Esq (*OW*)
C N Foster, Esq, FCA (*OW*)
Dr Priscilla Chadwick, MA, FRSA
Professor Sir Christopher Edwards, MD, FRCP, FRCPEd, FRSE, FMedSci, HonDSc
Dr A C N Borg, CBE, FSA (*OW*)
B A Segal, Esq
A J T Willoughby, Esq (*OW*)
Sir Peter Ogden
T M S Young Esq MA
E R Neville-Rolfe Esq MA (*OW*)
Dame Judith Mayhew Jonas, DBE
I W Harrison Esq

Secretary to the Governing Body and Bursar: C A J Silcock

Head Master: M S Spurr, MA, DPhil

Under Master: M A Boulton, BEng, PhD

Master of The Queen's Scholars: M H Feltham, MA

Director of Studies: R R Harris, MA

Senior Master: J R G Beavon, PhD

Senior Tutor: J J Kemball, BSc

Registrar: J M Curtis, MA

Assistant Staff:

R Agyare-Kwabi, BEng, MPhil, PhD
E Alaluusua, MA
H A Aplin, BA, PhD
K Y Au, MMath
S Baldock, BA
Mrs S M Barry, ARCM, LRAM
C J Barton, BA
J B Baughan, MA, MLitt, PhD
S G Blache, MA
S J Berg, BA
P A Botton, BSc
G P A Brown, MA, DPhil
Ms C M Buchanan, BA, MA
Mrs A E Cave-Bigley, MA
Mrs E Chappell, BA, MA

P J Chequer, DipPA
Miss J L Chidgey, BA, MA
P Choffrut, BA, MA, PhD
Miss B Choraria, MPhys
Mrs J L Cockburn, MA, PhD
E T Coward, BA, MSci
S Craft, MA
A M L Crole, BA, MA
S Crow, BA
S N Curran, BA
M C Davies, MA
D East, MA, PhD
T P Edlin, MA
D L Edwards, MA
Miss R J Evans, PhD
N A Fair, MA
Miss G M French, MSc, MRSC, LTCL, FRSA

T D Garrard, BA
G Griffiths, BA
Miss V Guichard, BA, MA, PhD
P D Hargreaves, MA
P A Hartley, BSc, PhD
S C Hawken, MA
G D Hayter, MMath
D R Hemsley-Brown, BSc, MIEE
U Hennig, BA
R J Hindley, MA, CMath
J N Hooper, BA
R M Huscroft, MA, PhD
J A Ireland, MA
A Johnson, BA
G K Jones, MA
Mrs A J Jørgensen, MA
N G Kalivas, BSc, DPhil
J D Kershen, BA, MA
C M C Kingcombe, BSc
R A Kowenicki, MA, MSci, PhD
A J Law, BA
N Lebrasseur, BSc, MSc, PhD
Miss C M Leech, MA
Mrs A E Leonard, MA
Miss S E Leonard, BSc
Mrs F Lofts
C R L Low, MA
Mrs L D MacMahon, BA
G D Mann, BA, MSt, DPhil
Ms A Marquez, BA
S McGregor, DipRCM, ARCO, ARCM
Mrs H L J Monro, BA
J Moore, BA
A E A Mylne, MA
K Olding, MMath, LlB
B D M Omrani, BA

Mrs L J Newton, BSc
Miss S Page, BA, MSc
T D Page, MA
B W Parker-Wright, BA
Miss H J Prentice, MSci, MA, PhD
R J Pyatt, MA
Miss K E Radice, BA
Ms S A Ragaz, PhD
C D Riches, BEd, MSc
M N Robinson, BA
Miss G V Rutherford, BA
H R R Salimbeni, MPhil
S C Savaskan, BA, MMus, DPhil
K Shah, BA
Mrs F G Sharp, MA
P Sharp, MA, MSc
N J Simons, MMath
G J A Simpson, BSc
B J Smith, MA
E A Smith, MSc
Mrs C Stevens, BSc
A Theodosiou
A C Tolley, BA
K D Tompkins, BA
C J R Ullathorne, MA, MSci
Ms M-S von Halasz, L-ès-L
K A P Walsh, BSc, PhD
B D Walton, BA
Miss G D Ward-Smith, MA, PhD
Miss E D Wethered, BA
Revd G J Williams, MA
P H Williams, BSc, PhD
J C Witney, MA, MIL
J G Woodman, BA
T D W Woodrooffe, BA, BTh, MA
S D Wurr, BA

Houses and Housemasters:

Boarding House for Queen's Scholars:
College: M H Feltham

Boarding and Day Houses:

Boys:
Grant's, 2 Little Dean's Yard: P D Hargreaves
Rigaud's, 1 Little Dean's Yard: Dr P H Williams

Mixed:
Liddell's, 19 Dean's Yard: T D Page
Busby's, 26 Great College Street: P A Botton

Girls' Boarding House:
Purcell's, 5 Barton Street: Dr G D Ward-Smith

Day Houses:
Ashburnham, 6 Dean's Yard: A Johnson
Dryden's, 4 Little Dean's Yard: D R Hemsley-Brown
Hakluyt's, 19 Deans' Yard: G StJ Hopkins
Milne's, 5A Dean's Yard: Dr P A Hartley
Wren's, 4 Little Dean's Yard: S D Wurr

Chaplain: Revd G J Williams
Director of Music: T D Garrard, BA
Librarian: Mrs C Goetzee
Archivist: Miss E Wells
Head of Girls: Miss S E Leonard

Westminster Under School

Master: Mrs E A Hill, MA

Deputy Head: D S C Bratt, BA

Assistant Staff:

Miss E-L Allison, BA, MA	C H W Hill, MA
A J P Busk, Dip Fine Art	Ms F M Illingworth, BA
O Campbell-Smith, MA	S R H James, BA
C R Candy, MA	E Jolliffe, BA, MMus
Miss S E K Corps, BSc	D Kendall, BA
R Dilks, BSc	Mrs N C Nicoll, BSc
Miss A C Dixon, MA	P A Rosenthal, BA
A J Downey, BA, MA	S Spurvey, MA
Miss M Ellis, BEd	S Thebaud, BSc
P J E V Evans, MA	Mrs R Thorn, BMus,
Miss N Fivaz, BA	MMus
Miss H Gifford, BSc	J S Walker, BEd, LRAM
G Gougay	(*Director of Music*)
I D Hepburn, BA	M J Woodside, BSc

The Queen's Scholars, who normally number 40, board in College, one of our 6 boarding houses. 8 Queen's Scholarships worth 50% of the boarding fee are awarded annually following a competitive examination called The Challenge. Boys, who must be under 14 on 1 September of their year of entry, sit The Challenge at Westminster School in early May. Application forms and past papers may be obtained from The Registrar's Secretary (tel: 020 7963 1003, email: registrar@westminster.org.uk). The Challenge consists of papers in Mathematics, English, French, Science, Latin, History and Geography. There is also an optional Greek paper. A scholarship, which is not means-tested, is normally tenable for 5 years.

Music Scholarships. Up to 6 Music Scholarships worth 25% of the boarding or day fee and free tuition for 3 instruments are awarded annually. There are also several Music Exhibitions which provide for free music tuition on two instruments. Candidates must be under 14 on the 1 September of their year of entry. Applications close in early January and the auditions take place in early February. It is recommended that parents contact the Director of Music, Tim Johnson, to arrange an informal audition before submitting an application. (Please telephone the Music Secretary on 020 7963 1017) Music Scholarships are also available at Westminster Under School at 11+.

Bursaries. Westminster School has, since its first foundation, made it possible for academically able pupils to attend the School who would not otherwise have been able to do so without financial support. Bursaries (remission of fees) up to a maximum of 100% are available and are awarded to pupils who gain a place on academic merit and according to individual need following a full financial assessment, which may include a home visit. Bursaries are awarded at 13 + and 16+ entry to Westminster School and at 11+ entry to Westminster Under School. All bursaries continue until a pupil leaves the School at 18, although they may be adjusted up or down if financial circumstances change. Parents who wish to apply for financial assistance should request a Bursary Application Form from the Registrar at Westminster School (tel: 020 7963 1003) or Westminster Under School (tel: 020 7821 5788) as appropriate.

Admission. The two main points of admission are 13+ (boys only) and 16+ (girls and boys). Parents are advised to register their sons for 13+ entry by the start of Year 6 – the academic year of a child's 11th birthday – although registration does not close until towards the end of Year 6. While he is in Year 6 the boy will come to Westminster School to sit tests in Mathematics, English and Verbal Reasoning and he will also be invited for interview on a separate day. On the basis of the candidate's test results, the interview and a report from his present school a decision will be made whether to offer a conditional place. Boys with conditional places must still qualify for entry to the School by sitting the Common Entrance examinations or The Challenge (scholarship examinations) when they are 13, but failure at this stage is rare. Candidates who are not offered a conditional place

may be placed on a waiting list and they may sometimes be invited to sit further tests at the start of Year 8. Registration for 16+ entry opens in the summer a year before entry. Entry is by competitive examination and interview at the School in November. Candidates choose four entry examination subjects, usually the four subjects they plan to take for A Level. For further information about entry at 13+ or 16+ or to arrange a visit to the School please telephone 020 7963 1003.

Fees per term (2011-2012). Boarding: £10,146, £5,073 (Queen's Scholars). Day Pupils (inclusive of lunch): £7,026, £7,618 (entry at Sixth Form). Under School: £4,892.

Preparatory Department (Day Boys only). The Under School has 260 pupils; entry is at 7, 8 and 11. All enquiries should be addressed to the Master (Mrs E A Hill), Westminster Under School, Adrian House, 27 Vincent Square, London SW1P 2NN (tel: 020 7821 5788).

(*For further details, see entry in IAPS section.*)

Charitable status. St Peter's College (otherwise known as Westminster School) is a Registered Charity, number 312728. The school was established under Royal Charter for the provision of education.

Whitgift School

Haling Park, South Croydon CR2 6YT

Tel:	020 8688 9222
Fax:	School Office: 020 8760 0682
	Headmaster: 020 8649 7594
e-mail:	office@whitgift.co.uk
website:	www.whitgift.co.uk

Foundation: The Whitgift Foundation originated in 1596 and the School was opened by Archbishop Whitgift in 1600. It is an Independent Day School for boys aged between 10–18.

Motto: '*Vincit qui patitur*'

The Whitgift Foundation:
Visitor: His Grace The Lord Archbishop of Canterbury

Five members are appointed by the Archbishop of Canterbury, 2 by the London Borough of Croydon and 4 by co-optation. The Bishop of Croydon and the Vicar of Croydon are appointed ex officio.

Chairman of the Court of The Whitgift Foundation: I Harley, MA, FCA, FCIB

Whitgift School:
Patron: HRH The Duke of York, KG
Chairman of the Whitgift School Governors: G H Wright, TD, DL, FCIOB

Whitgift School Governors:
The Headmaster
His Honour W Barnett, MA
The Revd Canon C J Luke Boswell, Vicar of Croydon
P J Squire, MA
D C Hudson, MA
Cllr D S Mead, FCCA, FCMA, FCIS
R J A I Catto, MA, DPhil
N L Platts, MA, FCA
M Johnson, MBBS, DRCOG, DFFP
M J Irwin (*OWA Representative*)
Chair of the Whitgift School Association
The Second Master
The Deputy Headmaster
The President of the Common Room
The Bursar
The Clerk to the Foundation

Headmaster: **C A Barnett**, MA, DPhil Oriel College, Oxford

Second Master: J D C Pitt, MA
Deputy Headmaster: P J Yeo, BA
Assistant Head (Proctor): D E C Elvin, BSc, MSc
Assistant Head (Pastoral) & Head of IB: S D Cook, BA, MPhil
Assistant Head (Academic): D W Munks, MA, MSc, LRAM, ARCO
Head of Upper School: M J Brown, BA
Head of Lower School: A C Kingsbury, BA

Assistant Teaching Staff:
J T Barber, MA (*Housemaster Andrews*)
J Barfield, BA
S A Beck, BEd (*Registrar*)
L S Beecham, BA (*Director of Drama*)
T A Biddle, MA (*Head of English*)
D Binacchi, BA
M J Bradley, BA
C Carolan, HDE (*Head of Third Form*)
J Carroll, BSc
F E Carter, BA
D Chan, BSc
K J Coffin, BA
W E Collinson, BA
N J Croker, MSc
M L Croston, MMus
J C K Cumberlege, MA
L G d'Arcy, MChem (*Head of First Form*)
L M Deliss, BA
R J Dinnage, BA
P Dinnen, MA
S E E Donwa, MMath
D J Edwards, BA (*Housemaster Mason's*)
P W Elliott, BSc (*Head of Science*)
P J Ellis, BSc (*Head of Mathematics*)
V R Ellwood, BA
F L Exley, BSc
F J Fannon, BA
L Faux-Newman, BSc, PhD
O M Fernie, BA
P C Fladgate, BEd
A J Gaster, BA
E A Gell, MA
B Gouttenoire, BA
B Graoui, BSc
J B Green, BSc (*Housemaster Brodie's*)
C B Griffin, BA (*Director of Art*)
K Gross, MA (*Head of Bilingual Studies & Housemaster Ellis's*)
I P Hanley, BSc
D F Hares, BSc (*Head of Biology*)
N P Harries, MPhys, DPhil
D R Harkin, BA
C J Harwood, BSc (*Head of ICT*)
S E Herring, BSc
T Hibberd, BA (*Head of Theology & Philosophy*)
S M Hooker, MA (*Head of Careers & Guidance*)
M K Hughes, BA
J S E Humphrey, BA
A J Hunt, MPhil (*Head of Modern Languages*)
M J Ibáñez, MA
R B Johnstone, BEd (*Head of Design Technology*)
N M Kendrick (*Head of Golf & Cricket Coach*)
C J Kibble, BEd (*Director of Sports Facilities & Development*)
E G Lance, BSc (*Head of Fifth Form*)
A Landi, BA
S E Lane, BA
B Lewis, BA (*Head of ICT Coordination*)
P Liberti, U de Studi di Udine (*Head of Italian*)
S W Litchfield, BEd (*Head of PE*)
J F Lowson, MA
L Ma, BA
A J Marlow, BSc

N A Martin, BSc
R F Martin, MA (*Senior Housemaster; Housemaster Tate's*)
R M C McGrath, BA (*Head of Classics*)
I A McGregor, BA (*Head of Academic Music*)
S Merlin, BA
S F Michael, BA
N P Morgan, BA
B R H Morris, BA (*Housemaster Cross's*)
P J Morrison, BSc
C A Mulley, BSc
K G Mund, BA
P Munoz-Pardo, BA
R I Munro, BSc
S L Mynott, BA
L Nieddu, BA
A Norris, BA (*Head of Sixth Form*)
M Ofner, PhD, (*Head of Spanish*)
A G Osborne, BA (*Director of Sport*)
J A Owen, BSc, PhD
C Pates
S B Payne, BA
A J Pearson, BSc
A T Peck, BA
E A Poole, MA
H M Poullain, MA
B Prestney, BA
S C B Ratnayake, BSc
R D Ravenscroft, HDE (*Head of Games and PE*)
J W Rhatigan, BSc
D J Richards, BA (*Housemaster Dodd's*)
A-M C Rigard-Asquith, L-ès-L, M-ès-L
P Rynes, MA
A D Seal, BEng
C D Shaw, BA
M L Shepherd, BSc
A J Sims, MA
K A Smith, BA (*OC CCF*)
K M Stagno, BSc, PhD (*Head of Hockey*)
D J Stanley, BSc (*Head of Geography*)
A H Starmer, BSc
N J R Stebbings, BEng
F M Stedman, MA
L F Temple, LRAM, ARCM
M C Thompson, BA
T A Thompson, BSc (*Head of Chemistry*)
V A Tidswell, BSc
D Tredger, BSc (*Head of Economics & Business Studies*)
P M Trewin, BA (*Head of Learning Support*)
P C Tsai, MA
B C M Turner, MA
K S Walker, MChem
W R Walker, BA
S E Wall, MA
H L Wallis, BSc, PhD
D Ward (*Head of Cricket*)
N Watts, BA
A E Weakley, MA
D C Webb, BEd (*Housemaster Smith's*)
R C Whitfield, DipRCM
C J Wilkins (*Director of Rugby*)
D R Williams, BTech (*Exams Officer*)
P S Wilson, MA (*Director of Music*)
P Winter, GBSM, DipNCOS (*Director of Orchestral Music*)
S J Woodward, BSc
R P Yates, BA

Bursar: J T Stremes, BA
School Medical Officer: Dr C J Wilcock, MBBS
Headmaster's PA & Marketing Manager: Mrs C McCormack, DipM, ACIM

Numbers. There are 1,272 boys on roll, 639 in the Upper School and 633 in the Lower School.

Buildings and Grounds. The School has buildings of great character, opened in 1931 and situated in some 45 acres of attractive parkland with extensive playing fields. The original park, sited around a fine quadrangle, includes Big School, classrooms for most Arts subjects and Mathematics. 1990 saw the completion of a very substantial and superbly equipped extension which links Science, Computing, Design Technology and Art and also incorporates a large Library. In February 2005, a major new Sports and Conference Centre was opened, comprising state-of-the-art facilities, such as a range of indoor halls, squash courts, fitness centre, swimming pool, classrooms and a conference suite.

Other separate buildings include the Lower School and the Music School. Sports facilities include courts for fives, squash, tennis, and all-weather hockey. North Field cricket ground stages first-class cricket for Surrey CCC.

Aims. The School offers a challenging and balanced education. It aims to combine high academic achievement with the all-round development of the individual through games and co-curricular activities, and a strong encouragement of the pursuit of excellence.

Admission. Entry for boys aged 10, 11, 12 or 13 is by competitive examination and interview. Admission is on the basis of performance in the School's entrance tests and on an assessment of a boy's potential to contribute to, and benefit from, the co-curricular programme and the wider life of the School. The majority of boys enter at 10 or 11. Application forms may be obtained from the School Office.

Fees per term (2011-2012). £4,808 covering tuition, books, stationery, and games. A substantial number of Bursaries is awarded each year according to need.

Scholarships. (*See Scholarship Entries section.*) For entry at the age of 10 or 11, approximately 70 awards carrying partial remission of fees are offered to candidates of outstanding merit in the Selection Tests. At all ages, boys may be considered for all-rounder awards or for scholarships in particular subject areas as well as for academic scholarships. Awards carrying free instrumental tuition are available to musically talented pupils, either on admission or subsequently. Music, drama, art and other particular scholarships are also awarded.

Curriculum. In the first three year groups a general preparation is given. With a few exceptions, boys take all of their GCSE examinations in the Upper Fifth Form. There is no early specialisation but various options are available, with a particularly wide range of languages, including Japanese and Chinese, available. There are bilingual sections in French, German and Spanish and a Section Française for native speakers of French. PSHE is taught to all boys throughout the School. A Learning Support department assists boys with specific learning difficulties.

In the Sixth Form, A and AS level subjects can be taken in a wide range of combinations. The International Baccalaureate is also offered in the Sixth Form; in additon there are vocational BTec courses for Sports Science, Music Technology and Business Studies. Pupils are also prepared for the Oxford and Cambridge entrance process.

Organisation. The academic progress of boys in the First and Third forms is under the supervision of the Head of the Lower School and that of the Fifth and Sixth Forms under the supervision of the Head of the Upper School. Pastoral matters are dealt with by the respective Heads of Year and their assistants. Boys are allocated to one of eight Houses, which have Upper and Lower School sections, and Housemasters have general responsibility for supervising pupils' development in co-curricular activities. Boys in the Upper Fifth and Sixth Forms have a personal tutor to whom they can turn for help and advice if required.

Religious Education. Every attempt is made to stress the relevance of religious thought to modern living. Although the School has a close link with the Anglican Church, teaching is given in an ecumenical spirit.

Physical Education. All boys, unless excused on medical grounds, take Physical Education, swimming and organised games: rugby, hockey, football, cricket, athletics and many options are available. Facilities are provided for modern pentathlon, badminton, basketball, fencing, fives, soccer, squash, tennis, shooting and a range of other sports. Up to 30 sports in total are available.

Music. All 10 and 11 year old entrants have the opportunity to learn a musical instrument for the first term free of charge.

Boys perform in various choral and instrumental ensembles. Concerts are regularly held and operas and musicals are performed each year.

Other activities. There are a Combined Cadet Force, with specialist Royal Navy, Army and RAF sections and a Duke of Edinburgh's Award group. There is a large number of play productions (more than ten a year) and boys are encouraged to join some of the many School societies. Field courses and foreign exchange visits are regularly arranged in the holidays, and there is a very large number of link schools in many parts of the world.

Careers Advice. There is a well-equipped Careers Room and a very full service of guidance is offered over choice of career and courses in higher education. The vast majority of pupils go on to universities and colleges after leaving school.

Charitable status. The Whitgift Foundation is a Registered Charity, number 312612. It exists to provide education for boys and girls.

Winchester College

College Street, Winchester, Hampshire SO23 9NA
Tel: 01962 621100 (Headmaster and Office)
             01962 621200 (Bursar)
             01962 621247 (Admissions)
Fax: 01962 621106
e-mail: admissions@wincoll.ac.uk
website: www.winchestercollege.org

Winchester College – 'the College of the Blessed Virgin Mary of Winchester near Winchester' – was founded in 1382 by William of Wykeham, Bishop of Winchester. Wykeham planned and created a double foundation consisting of two Colleges, one at Winchester and the other (New College) at Oxford. The two Colleges are still closely associated.

Motto: '*Manners Makyth Man*'

Visitor: The Bishop of Winchester

Warden: Sir David Clementi, MA, MBA

Fellows:
J B W Nightingale, MA, DPhil
R H Sutton, BA
The Rt Hon Sir Andrew Longmore, PC, MA
M St John Parker, MA
R B Woods, CBE, MA
M A Loveday, MA
Ms J H Ritchie, QC, LLM
Professor Sir Curtis Price, KBE, AM, PhD, Hon RAM, FKC, FRNCM, Hon FASC
Professor C T C Sachrajda, FRS, PhD, FInstP, CPhys
C J F Sinclair, CBE, BA
P Frith, MD, FRCP, FRCOphth

Bursar and Secretary: J E Hynam, BEd, MPhil, ACP

Headmaster: **R D Townsend**, MA, DPhil

Second Master: R J Wyke, MA

Director of Studies: J G Webster, MA, DPhil (*Acting Head of History*)

Undermaster: Ms E A Stone, BA, LLB, MLitt, AMusA

Registrar: K M Pusey, MusB, GRSM, ARMCM

Deputy Registrar: Mrs K A Richards

Assistant Masters:
P J Krakenberger, MA
M R S Nevin, BA
N Fennell, MA, PhD
G Eyre, MA
J D Falconer, MA, ARCM
T P J Cawse, BSc, PG Dip Dyslexia (*Head of Learning Support*)
C J Tolley, MA, DPhil, FRCO
S P Anderson, MA (*Senior Tutor*)
R S Shorter, BSc, ARCS, DIC, PhD, MInstP, CPhys (*Head of Science*)
A P Wolters, BSc, PhD, CChem, MRSC
L C Wolff, MA, FRSA (*Head of History of Art*)
C H J Hill, MA (*Head of Mathematics*)
P A Nash, BA, ARCM, LTCL
M D Wallis, MA
A S Leigh, MA
Dr B L H MacKinnon, BA, PhD (*Head of Modern Languages*)
N I P MacKinnon, BA
W E Billington, MA, MICE
P G Cornish, BA, MMus, FTCL, ARCM, PhD
D J Ceiriog-Hughes, MA, PhD, FRSA
Miss C J Ovenden, MA
A P McMaster, BSc
P S A Taylor, BA
I E Fraser, BSc (*Head of Biology*)
L N Taylor, BA Ed
S K Woolley, MA
M D Hebron, BA, DPhil
P J M Cramer, MA, PhD
C Cai, BA, MA, PhD
C J Good, BEd
J E Hodgins, BSc, PhD
G J Watson, BA (*Head of Economics*)
C G Yates, BA (*Head of Careers and Higher Education*)
J P Cullerne, BSc, DPhil
C S McCaw, BSc, DPhil, DES, CChem, MRSC
T N M Lawson, MA
A D Adlam, Dip Mus
A P Dakin, BA (*Acting Head of English*)
M Romans, BA, MA, PhD
Mrs L J Quinault, BA
J McManus, MChem, PhD
Mrs K A Mendelsohn, MA
N A Salwey, MA, MSc, DPhil, ARCM, LGSM (*Deputy Master of Music*)
R W Chee-A-Tow, MA
P M Herring, MA
J R Hunt, MA
D E Pounds, BSc (*Head of Geography*)
W M A Land, MA (*Master in College*)
R Price, BA, PhD (*Director of Drama*)
Mrs A M Lombardo, MA, BA (*Head of French*)
J J L Douglas, BA, MSc (*Head of Physics*)
Mrs G Dowell, BA, MA
D I Follows, MChem, MSc, DPhil (*Head of Chemistry*)
N P Wilks, MA, ARAM (*Master of Music*)
D E Yeomans, BA
M G Crossland, MPhys
M J Winter, MA
The Revd Dr P A Burt, BA, MA (*Senior Chaplain*)
G E Munn, MSci (*Head of PSHE*)
The Revd J M White, BA, MEng, MA (*Head of Theology & Philosophy*)

M D Archer, MA, FRCO, FGCM, FNMSM, ARCM (*Director of Chapel Music*)
J R Fox, BSc, ARCS
M L Broughton, BA (*Head of PE*)
S E Hart, MEng (*Head of Sport*)
S A Tarrant, MEng (*Head of Design Technology*)
Ms E A Stone, BA, LLB, MLitt, AMusA
J P Spencer, MA (*Head of Classics*)
P E Hepworth, BSc, PhD
S D Rich, BA
Mrs C L Talks, MA
Mrs E C Macey, BA, BDes (*Head of Art*)
T E Giddings, BA, MSt
A P Savory, BSc, PhD
C N Berry, PhD
A P Jaffe, BSc
Miss S Atwill, BA
Mrs C Crowther, MA (*Head of Spanish*)
Dr A French, MA, MPhil, MSc, PhD
M Rogers, BSc

In Junior Part (Year 9) all boys study Biology, Chemistry, English, French, Geography, History, Latin, Mathematics, Physics and PE. A third foreign language is chosen from Chinese, German, Ancient Greek and Spanish. A further choice is made between Art & Design, Russian and Music. In the final term of Junior Part, boys may opt to continue with these subjects or choose from Art, Design Technology and Religious Studies. Geography is also available as an option against a third foreign language from the end of Junior Part. The core curriculum and the two option blocks continue throughout Middle Part (Year 10) and Vth Book (Year 11). In VI Book (Years 12 and 13), almost any combination of arts and sciences can be studied. The School teaches the Cambridge Pre-U syllabus in all VI Book subjects. Division – a daily lesson encompassing many aspects of culture and civilisation – plays a central role throughout the curriculum at all levels.

Scholarships and Exhibitions. The election of Scholars and Exhibitioners takes place in May each year. Full particulars of the examination can be obtained from the Master in College.

About 14 scholarships and 6 exhibitions are awarded each year. Exhibitions ensure places in Commoner Houses; the 70 Scholars live together in College. All scholarships are means-tested. Bursaries are available in cases of financial need.

Music Awards. An unspecified number of music Scholarships and Exhibitions are given each year. *For full information see entry in Music Scholarships section.*

Sixth Book entry. A number of places are offered each year to boys joining Sixth Book from other schools. Examinations and interviews take place in Winchester in late January each year. Enquiries should be sent to the Deputy Registrar.

Fees per term (2011-2012). Boarders £10,450 (£31,350 pa). There is an entrance fee of £500.

Commoners. There are about 60 Commoners in each House. The Housemasters are:
Chernocke House (A): T N M Lawson
Moberly's (B): P M Herring
Du Boulay's (C): L N Taylor
Fearon's (D): M J Winter
Morshead's (E): Dr J McManus
Hawkins' (F): Dr J E Hodgins
Sergeant's (G): D E Yeomans
Bramston's (H): Dr J P Cullerne
Turner's (I): C J Good
Kingsgate House (K): Dr M Romans
Initial visits and registration for a particular House should take place during Year 5. Places are offered after tests and an interview in Year 6. The Registrar holds a Reserve List, which includes the names of late applicants, but it is essen-

tial to have a place at another school unless and until a firm place at Winchester has been confirmed. The usual age of entry to the school is between 13 and 14, but exceptions may be considered in special circumstances.

The entrance examination covers the normal subjects; particulars and copies of recent papers may be obtained from the Registrar.

Term of entry. Usually September.

Old Boys' Society, Wykehamist Society. *Secretary*: D L Fellowes, 17 College Street, Winchester SO23 9LX.

Charitable status. Winchester College is a Registered Charity, number 1139000. The objects of the charity are the advancement of education and activities connected therewith.

Wisbech Grammar School

North Brink, Wisbech, Cambs PE13 1JX
Tel: 01945 583631 Senior School
          01945 586780 Magdalene House
Fax: 01945 476746 Senior School
          01945 586781 Magdalene House
e-mail: hmsecretary@wisbechgs.demon.co.uk
website: www.wgs.cambs.sch.uk

Founded during the turbulent reign of Richard II in 1379, Wisbech Grammar School was established by a society of local merchants, the Guild of the Holy Trinity, to provide education for poor boys of the town. Now a fully co-educational day school, it draws its 650 pupils aged four to 18 from the three counties of Cambridgeshire, Norfolk and Lincolnshire.

Occupying a prime site on North Brink, one of England's most handsome Georgian streets and a magnet for film makers, the school – the finest in Fenland – is set in 26 acres of magnificent grounds in a conservation area. Open, friendly and welcoming, the school is small enough for staff to know all the pupils individually, but large enough to provide an impressive range of opportunities. The traditional emphasis on the pursuit of academic success is complemented by a sensitive and effective pastoral care system. All members of the senior school and the preparatory school, Magdalene House, are encouraged to develop their confidence and unlock their true potential, both inside and outside the classroom, as well as engaging with the wider community.

In recent years the expansion of the teaching staff has helped to reduce class size and foster more individual learning. The ongoing development programme has included a performing arts centre and a floodlit, all-weather Astroturf pitch. A new hall and two more classrooms have been constructed for the rapidly expanding preparatory school, which takes its name from Magdalene College. The Cambridge college has enjoyed a close connection with the Grammar School for over 350 years and the master and fellows appoint two of their number to the governing body. Junior pupils also enjoy the extensive benefits of the senior school facilities and teaching expertise. The latest addition to the campus, a new sixth form centre, opened in 2010.

Governing Body:

Chairman: Dr D Barter, MB, BS, FRCP, FRCPCH, DCH
Vice Chairman: J E Warren
C Goad, ACA
F A N Grounds, MA Cantab, ARICS, MRAC
The Venerable Hugh McCurdy, Archdeacon of Huntingdon and Wisbech
Mrs S Meekins
Mrs E Morris, LLB
M J Potter, BEd Hons
M Rayner

Dr F Sconce, MBChB, DFFP
Dr F P Treasure, MA, MSc, PhD, CStat

Nominated by the Master of Magdalene College, Cambridge:
R L Skelton, MA, CEng, FIChemE, MIMechE, FINucE
Revd P Hobday, Chaplain of Magdalene College

Bursar and Clerk to the Governors: S Halls, DMS, ACMA, MCMI

Teaching Staff:
* *Head of Department*
† *Head of House*
§ *Part-time*
¶ *Old Pupil*

Headmaster: N J G Hammond, MA Cantab (*History, RE*)

Deputy Headmistress: Miss C M Noxon, BA (*German*)
Senior Tutor: A W Ayres, BA (*Chemistry, Higher Education Adviser*)
Director of Studies: M L Forrest, MA (*Chemistry, *General Studies*)
Head of Sixth Form: D Williams, BSc (*Biology*)

§Miss M P Barrington, BSc (*Duke of Edinburgh's Award*)
§Mrs A Beck, BA (*History, Geography*)
Mrs Z R Booth, BSc (*Mathematics, IT, Lower Sixth Form Lead Tutor*)
Mrs J Braybrook, BA (**Spanish*)
§Mrs M Calton, BSc (*Biology*)
Mrs J Challinger, BA (**German*)
T D Chapman, MA (*History, †Peckover*)
§T W Claydon, BSc (*PE and Games*)
Miss A M Clayton, BA (*English*)
¶Miss D C Cook, BSc (*Girls' PE and Games*)
Mrs S D Cooper, BA (**Textiles, Art & Design, Deputy Head of Lower School*)
§Mrs J Emsley, BA (*IT*)
Mrs E M Farr, BA (*English*)
§Mrs C A Fear, BA (*English*)
¶Mrs L Feaviour, BA (*Textiles, Art & Design*)
J G Fitzsimmons, BMus (*Director of Music*)
Miss K M Flanagan, BA (**Economics, Business Studies*)
Miss K Forbes, MA (*French*)
Mrs S C Fox, BA (**Lower School Science*)
R D Frost, BEd (**Design Technology*)
¶D S Garfoot, BSc (*PE & Games, Geography, †Sparks*)
Mrs S M Goodier, BSc (*Girls' PE and Games*)
¶Miss J M Gomm, BSc (*Psychology, Girls' PE and Games*)
Miss S E Harris, BEd (**Girls' PE and Games*)
P J Harrison, BA (*Art, †Clarkson*)
G E Howes, BSc (**Mathematics*)
¶B J Hoyles, BSc (*Boys' PE and Games*)
H J Hutchings, BA (*Design Technology*)
A P Jarvis, MA, MEd, PhD (**English*)
R D Killick, BSc (**Geography, Upper Sixth Form Lead Tutor*)
P J King, MA (*English, Marketing Director*)
K J Mann, BA, PhD (**History; Head of Lower School*)
S J Miller, BSc, PhD (**Science, *Biology*)
Mrs J M Missin, BA (*Assistant Director of Music*)
R W Morgan, BSc (**Chemistry*)
Mrs N Neighbour MA (**French*)
G H Nunnerley, BSc (**Careers, Geography*)
Mrs A Ogston, BSc (*Mathematics*)
§Mrs J T Reavell, BEd (*Girls' PE and Games*)
I P Ross, BSc, MA, CPhys, MInstP (**Physics*)
§Mrs M Skinner, BA (*German*)
¶Mrs A L Sloan, BSc, MA (**Food & Nutrition*)
M P Stump, BA (**Art & Design, Deputy Head of Middle School*)
Miss K Taylor, BA (*Geography*)
C Thursby, BA, MA (*Mathematics*)

A Tomlins, BSc (*Boys' PE and Games*)

¶Mrs M Tooke, BSc (*Food and Nutrition*)

¶Miss E Wagstaffe, BA (*German*)

P J A Webb, BA (**Boys' PE and Games, History*)

B P Wiles, BSc, MInstP, CPhys (*Physics, Learning Skills Coordinator*)

¶J D Williams (*Boys' PE and Games*)

K L Wood-Smith, BSc (*Mathematics*)

Chaplain: Father P West

Headmaster's Secretary: Mrs K Massen

Admissions Secretary: Mrs S Davies

Magdalene House Preparatory School

Headmaster: C E Moxon, BA

Deputy Head: Mrs G D Reinbold, MA

Senior school admission. The main entry is at age 11 by a competitive examination which is designed to discover potential. Pupils can also enter at second, third and fourth form levels. Offers of sixth form places are made on the basis of interview and a report from a student's current school.

Fees per term (2011-2012). Fees are substantially below the national average: senior school £3,530 per term; Magdalene House preparatory school £2,430 per term. Means-tested bursaries are available at Key Stages 3, 4 and 5. These are known as governors' assisted places and are reviewed annually. Currently, 205 pupils receive support from the scheme. Application forms for governors' assisted places are available from the bursar.

Travel to school. The school's catchment area embraces King's Lynn, Peterborough, Whittlesey, March, Hunstanton and Long Sutton. School buses run from a number of these places, visiting villages en route, and there are late buses to most destinations for pupils involved in after-school activities.

Teaching and learning. The school aims to foster a love of learning and to provide an environment which nurtures talent and breeds success. There is a high regard for the traditional disciplines, but the school is also ready to open up exciting new fields of study. An extensive academic curriculum in the first three years of the senior school includes opportunities to sample a number of technology subjects, and Spanish is offered from the third form. The option system at GCSE ensures a broad-based curriculum as well as allowing pupils to play to their strengths. At A Level 25 subjects are provided and students have their first chance to take business studies, economics, government and politics, music technology, computing, graphics and drama and theatre studies. The school also provides support which allows bright children with learning difficulties and disabilities to rise to the challenge of a rigorous academic education. Two thirds of the student body enter the Maths Challenge competition and technology enjoys a high profile: sixth form food and nutrition students have recently worked with Gordon Ramsay at the BBC Good Food Show and members of the Twin Cambs teams have reached the national finals of the Greenpower competition to design and build an electric racing car for the last four years in a row.

The sixth form experience. The school has a first-class track record in enabling students to realise their university and career aspirations. Entrusted with a greater degree of independence, sixth form members are encouraged to make their mark and develop leadership qualities, both within the house system and at a wider level. Their new uniform, a stylish business suit with a discreet lapel badge, was adopted following meetings of the student council. The recently opened sixth form centre provides a fine facility for the school's most senior students.

Creative and performing arts. The flourishing music department provides practical opportunities for pupils to develop their creative talents. Ten visiting instrumental and vocal tutors give individual tuition to a sixth of the students, and there are numerous opportunities to join in choirs, wind and steel bands and perform in the annual concerts and community charity events.

A dynamic tradition of drama allows pupils to build their confidence and hone their acting skills, both in major productions on the main stage and in more intimate performances in the studio. Audiences have sampled everything from Renaissance drama to experimental twentieth century works, as well as popular musicals, and ambitious recent productions have included *She stoops to conquer*, *My fair lady*, *Amadeus* and *The Duchess of Malfi*.

The art and design department is a highly visible presence in the school, mounting exhibitions on-site and at the Reed Barn at the neighbouring National Trust property, Peckover House, and talented artists and designers regularly win places at the top art colleges. Girls taking A Level textiles were branded the best in the country in the 2009 Good Schools Guide.

A competitive spirit. The sports department arranges a competitive fixture list against schools across the eastern counties and in the midlands, and Wisbech Grammar School takes pride in punching above its weight. An extensive interhouse programme also allows pupils of all abilities to develop their competitive spirit. The main games for boys are rugby in the autumn term and hockey and rugby sevens in the spring, together with cricket and athletics in the summer. Girls play hockey and netball in the first two terms and rounders and athletics in the summer. There is also tennis for boys and girls. For pupils above the third form who are not involved in a major team game, the options range from squash and basketball to archery and spinning. The facilities include a recently refurbished, full-size sports hall and the extensive on-site Astroturf pitch, together with generous playing field provision. Pupils also enjoy access to a covered swimming pool, a sports hall, a dance studio and a fitness centre at a neighbouring leisure centre.

Beyond the classroom. Wisbech Grammar School believes in learning on location. Geography students have recently investigated tectonic activity in Iceland and explored the breath-taking Amalfi coastline. Spanish students head to Salamanca for a week of intensive language tuition and cultural activities, and there are frequent art trips to New York. There is a flourishing exchange with the Willibrord Gymnasium in Emmerich in north Germany, as well as a chateau trip and a study visit to France. Students also criss-cross the country for hands-on learning, and excursions such as the third form trip to Shakespeare's Globe run regularly. A sports tour to Barbados provides a chance to compete in the Caribbean sun, while over 70 students participate in the Duke of Edinburgh's Award, with those at the highest level mounting expeditions to the Lake District, Snowdonia and the Yorkshire Dales. The senior school adventure begins with an outdoor activity week for the first form in rural Shropshire.

Closer to home, sixth formers sharpen up their business skills in the Young Enterprise scheme, regularly reaching the regional finals. Clubs such as astronomy, philosophy, wake up walk and grow, cook, eat help to stretch the mind and develop life skills. Members of Caritas, the charity and community service team, reach out to those in need in the town as well as hosting a party for pensioners.

Magdalene House Preparatory School caters for boys and girls from reception to year six. (*For further details see entry in IAPS section.*)

Old Wisbechians Society. Further information about the society can be obtained from the Admissions Secretary at the school, to whom requests for the school magazine, *Riverline*, should be sent. News of past pupils is published on the school website, www.wgs.cambs.sch.uk.

Charitable status. The Wisbech Grammar School Foundation is a Registered Charity, number 1087799. It exists to promote the education of boys and girls.

Wolverhampton Grammar School

Compton Road, Wolverhampton WV3 9RB
Tel: 01902 421326
Fax: 01902 421819
e-mail: wgs@wgs.org.uk
website: www.wgs.org.uk

Wolverhampton Grammar School was founded in 1512 by Sir Stephen Jenyns – a Wolverhampton man who achieved success as a wool merchant, became a member of The Merchant Taylors' Company then Lord Mayor of London. He decided to benefit his home town by founding a school "for the instruction of youth in good manners and learning". The school retains close links with the Company.

Wolverhampton Grammar School is now an independent, selective day school for girls and boys aged 11–18 from a wide catchment area throughout the West Midlands, Staffordshire and Shropshire.

From September 2011 WGS will also offer a junior school (Wolverhampton Grammar Junior School) for students aged 7–11.

Its philosophy places scholarship at the heart of a challenging education which promotes achievement through active involvement. It seeks to develop self-awareness and a sense of responsibility, values both individuality and altruism, and fosters the spirit of community traditional to the school.

The school was inspected in January 2007. The report can be read on the ISI website: www.isi.net.

Governors:

Chairman: Dr S Walford, MA, MD, FRCP
Vice Chairman: E A Sergeant, BSc, BTh (*OW*)
The Mayor of Wolverhampton (*ex-officio*)
M Anderson, BA, ACA
Mrs A Brennan
Mrs T Crisp
D J Hughes, MA (*OW*)
Professor K Madelin, OBE, MSc, CEng, FICE, FIHT
Mrs J Mills, BA
J M Mumford, BSc, FIPD
Dr M Nicholls, BA, MA, PhD
R Purshouse, LLB (*OW*)
S Sanghera, MA (*OW*)
P Sims, ACIB
A J Smith, FCIS, FCT, FCMI, FRSA
C Tatton, BA, ACMA
His Honour M B Ward, MA, LLM (*OW*)
Dr E Westlake
P E J White, FInstMgt (*OW*)
Mrs C Wood, JP, LLB, SRCh, MChS

Head: J V Darby, BA Lancaster, NPQH

Deputy Heads:
P A Hills, BA Nottingham
N J C Anderson, BSc Leeds

Assistant Staff:
Mrs K E Baker, BA Swansea
T Baker, BSc Edinburgh
B M Benfield, BA Leeds, GCD Birmingham
A J Bennett, BSc Birmingham, MA Manchester
    Metropolitan
N J Bradley, BSc, PhD Nottingham
R J Brandon, MA Trinity Hall Cambridge
Mrs S F Brentnall, BA Birmingham
T J Browning, BSc London
J-P Camm, BSc, PhD Sheffield
A P Carey, BSc London
R B Charlesworth, BA Lady Margaret Hall Oxford
N H Crust, BA Bangor

Mrs H S Dalzell, BA Birmingham
J G David, BA Newcastle-upon-Tyne
O P Davies, BSc Birmingham
Mrs J R Dovey, BA East Anglia
J D Edlin, BSc, PhD Manchester
Mrs K L Finn, BA Manchester
Dr K J Flavell, BSc, PhD Wolverhampton
Mrs V E Fogarty, BSc Salford
Mrs V N Gilchrist, BA Open University, ARIAM, ARCM
Mrs P D Grigat-Bradley, Erstes und Zweites Staatsexamen
    Ruhr-Universität Bochum
T D Guard, MA St Andrews, MSt, DPhil Hertford College
    Oxford
Ms N T Guidotti, BA Anglia Polytechnic University
Mr J Hall, BA Newcastle upon Tyne
Mrs S K Hannah, BA Reading
Mrs E S N Harris, BA Southampton
Miss L M Harris, BA Wales
Mrs H Hills, BSc Nottingham
S Hinchliffe, BA Durham, PhD St Andrews
A M Hopkins, BA St Peter's College Oxford
Mrs M I Howard, BA Leicester
J M Johnson, BSc Aston
P Johnstone, BA Hull
Miss C Jones, BA Nottingham Trent
D Jones, BA UCE, MA Wolverhampton, DMS
L J Judson, BSc Leeds
T King, ICC, Senior Coach
Mrs A J Kingshott, BA Royal Holloway College London,
    MA Bedford New College London
Mrs R M Laurino-Ryan, CertEd London
Mrs P K Mahey, BA UCE
Mrs P Manzai, BA Turin
C W Martin, MA Jesus College Cambridge, PhD
    Birmingham
Miss A M McAllister, BSc Birmingham, MA
    Wolverhampton
J J Millichamp, BA Wolverhampton
R Morris, BEd Wolverhampton
Mrs R E Mosley, MA Oriel College Oxford
Mrs M J Moss, BA London
Miss K A Munden, BA Gloucester
N P Munson, BSc Birmingham
Mrs R E Munson, BA Leeds
C O'Brien, BSc, PhD Imperial College London
S L J O'Malley, BA Wolverhampton
T D Page, BA Middlesex Polytechnic
R A Pawluk, GRAM, LRAM, LTCL, ALCM
J W Perkins, BA Manchester Polytechnic
Mrs C A Preston, BSc Sheffield
A A Proverbs, BA Huddersfield Polytechnic School of
    Music, ALCM
V P Raymond-Barker, BA Kent
J P Ryan, BEd Crewe & Alsager College, MEd, Adv Dip
    SNE Open University, AMBDA
Mrs L E Stanley, BSc Manchester
J A Sutherland, BA Oxford
Mrs O Trafford, ATD Birmingham
R J Tuck, UWE Bristol
I H M Tyler, BA Saskatchewan, MEd Birmingham, Dip
    DA RADA
K Uppal, BA Wadham College Oxford, MPhil Birmingham
Mrs D M Ward, BA, MA Birmingham
Miss K I Ward, BA, MSc Birmingham
Miss H V Whittaker, MChem York
J R Wood, BA Royal Holloway College London

Bursar: S T Jones, FCMA
Head's PA: Mrs J E Boss

Buildings. The school has a purpose-built music block, a magnificent Sixth Form Centre and a £3.8 million Arts Centre, opened in April 2007. A Sports Centre and floodlit Astroturf pitches provide some of the best facilities in the area, while the early 20th century Merridale and Caldicott buildings house laboratories that have been refurbished to the highest modern standards. State-of-the-art ICT facilities provide broadband internet access to all parts of the school.

Admission. Boys and girls usually enter the school in September. The school's own entrance tests are held in the preceding January. The main intake is at age 11 with small numbers admitted at age 12 and 13. A significant number of boys and girls join the school in the Sixth Form: offers of places are made subject to GCSE results and interview. Transfers at other ages can be made by arrangement.

Fees per term (2011-2012). Junior School £2,968, Senior School £3,775.

Entrance Scholarships. (*See Scholarship Entries section.*) Following the January entrance tests, eight Governors' Academic Scholarships (equivalent to 25% fees) are awarded to the highest-placed candidates at 11+ and one Scholarship (25% of fees) is offered at 13+. Music Scholarships are available remitting 25% of fees, one at either 11+ or 13+ and one at 16+, with free music tuition within the school on the instrument of the student's choice. Two Governors' Academic Scholarships are awarded at 16 to students entering the Sixth Form. Applicants are expected to achieve high academic standards and be able to make a significant contribution to extra-curricular activities.

Assistance with Fees. The Governors offer a number of means-tested Bursaries to children from less affluent families who can demonstrate academically and personally that they will benefit from the opportunity of a WGS education.

Curriculum. In the first three years students study a broad curriculum of English, Mathematics, three Sciences, History, Geography, Art, Information Communication Technology, Design Technology, Theology & Philosophy, PE & Games and Music, in addition to French, German and Latin. In the fourth form students pursue a core of English Language and Literature, three separate Sciences, Mathematics, at least one Modern Language, and an IAM (Institute of Administrative Management) qualification. There is a wide range of additional optional subjects, and most students take ten GCSEs. 90% of students proceed to the Sixth Form to take three or four subjects at AS/A2 Level and some 98% continue in Higher Education, including a number of students who go to Oxford or Cambridge.

Games and Outdoor Activities. A 'sport for all' attitude exists in games and PE, where the staff endeavour to match the student to a sport or activity in which they can succeed. There is a commitment to the highest standards of skill and sportsmanship but the emphasis is also placed on enjoyment. The school participates in The Duke of Edinburgh's Award Scheme which is flourishing and students find that there are opportunities to undertake field trips and foreign exchanges. There is a vigorous outdoor education programme.

Special Needs (Dyslexia). The WGS OpAL (Opportunities through Assisted Learning) programme, which started in September 1998, is designed to allow bright children with Specific Learning Difficulties (Dyslexia) to enjoy the challenge of a first-rate academic education. In the last six years OpAL students have consistently achieved 100% A*–C grades at GCSE, and all A Level students have been offered university places.

Arts and Other Activities. The Music Department runs several choirs, bands and orchestras which practise and perform regularly to popular acclaim. Theatre is an integral part of the vibrant arts policy at the school which mounts three full-scale drama productions yearly involving students of all ages as actors, technicians, set and costume makers, stage managers and directors. The Art Department exhibits regularly and has an artist-in-residence. There is a wide variety of extra-curricular clubs and activities giving students the opportunity to discover and cultivate new interests, both inside and outside the classroom. A Community Service programme and an active student Charity Fundraising Com-

mittee ensure that all students are involved in working for the good of others.

Pastoral Care. The school is proud of the pastoral care and support it offers to its students. In the Lower and Middle Schools care is provided by a form tutor under the overall responsibility of the appropriate Heads of Schools. Regular consultations are held with parents supported by full and frequent reports. An important forum is the Student Parliament which consists of elected representatives from all year groups who are encouraged to voice concerns and suggest improvements to the running and organisation of the school. The weekly meetings, with the Head plus one other member of staff in attendance, are run by an elected Chair and Secretary.

Charitable status. Wolverhampton Grammar School is a Registered Charity, number 529006.

Woodbridge School

Woodbridge, Suffolk IP12 4JH
Tel: 01394 615000
Fax: 01394 380944
e-mail: admissions@woodbridge.suffolk.sch.uk
website: www.woodbridge.suffolk.sch.uk

Motto: '*Pro Deo Rege Patria*'

Governing Body: The Trustees of The Seckford Foundation

Chairman: R Finbow, MA Oxon

Headmaster*: S H Cole, MA Oxon, MA Ed Mgt, CPhys, MInstP, PGCE

Deputy Head: M R Streat, MA, PGCE
Director of Studies: G B Bruce, MA, CertEd
Senior Master: R F Broaderwick, BA, PhD
Senior Mistress: Miss H V Richardson, BA, PGCE
Chaplain: The Revd I A Wilson, BTh

Assistant Staff:

J R Penny, MA, CertEd	Mrs E Mitchels, BA, CertEd
I T Saunders, BTech	
S J Ashworth, BSc, PGCE	Mrs W E McNally, BSc, CertEd
Miss S Theasby, BA, CertEd	J A Wharam, BSc, PhD, PGCE, CBiol, MIBiol
M R Ringer, BEd, CertEd	J M Percival, BA
S E Cottrell, BEd, CSci, CPhys, MInstP	Mrs T H Knowles, BEd
R E Fernley, BA, PGCE	A G Lubbock, BSc, CertEd
A P Jackson, BSc, PGCE	Mrs C E Brown, CSci, CPhys, MInstP
Miss J A Gill, BEd, MA Ed	R J H Thorley, BA, PGCE
Mrs N J Ingold, CertEd	Mrs A Hillman, BSc, CertEd
J A Hillman, BSc, CertEd	Miss S E Norman, BA, PGCE
J H Stafford, ARCM	
Mrs A McGlennon, BA, PGCE	C Eager, BA, CertEd
Mrs A P Willett, CertEd, AdDipEd SEN	P M Lawrence, BA, MA, CertEd
R A Carr, BA, ATC	D J Neuhoff, BA, UED
B T Edwards, BA	Mrs J A Hill, BSc, CertEd
P A Trett, BSc, CertEd	A C Hunt, BSc (*Sabbatical*)
Mrs C V E Johnson, BA, PGCE	Mrs C F Neuhoff, DipEd
N E Smith, BA, CertEd	Mrs M M Barclay, CertEd, TEFL
Mrs C Odedra, MA	D A Brous, BSc, CertEd, MA Ed
Mrs L R Chandler, MA, PGCSE	S D Richardson, BA, CertEd, CertTEFL
K J Stollery	I W Elder, MA, CertEd, CertTEFL
L V Rickard, BSc, PhD, CertEd	
M Davis, MA, BA	Mrs E R Green, BA, PGCE

H J Tebbutt, BA
J P Chandler, MA
Mrs C R Parker, BSc, CertEd
J M C Allen, BSc, MSt, PGCE
Mrs M G V Pilkington, BA, CertEd
Mrs H Guan, BA, CertEd
Mrs I Brown, BMedSci, MEd
Dr A E Renshaw, BA, MA, PhD, CertEd
J R Hill, BSc, PhD, QTS
Miss N L Sanders, BA
R N Bradshaw, BA, CertEd
Mrs J M Wright, BA, QTS
R S Willis, MA, CertEd
Mrs R Oldfield, BSc
M R Fernley, BA
Mrs D J Jachertz, BA

B Wiltshire, MSc, PhD, QTS, Eur Ing, CSci, CEng, MIMechE, MIET, MIMMM
Mrs M L Verona, BA, MSc, QTS
Ms N S Carter, BA, QTS
A C Garvie
Ms G L Mayes, BA, QTS
Mrs C F Davis, BA, CertEd
Mrs M K Carlson, DipRAM
Mrs M Wynn-Higgins
Miss C Weston, BA
J Williams, BA, QTS
Miss A Bealings
Mr R N Bradshaw, BA, PGCE
Miss S L Cousins, BSc, PGCE
Miss L K Doggett, BSc
Dr G Gilbert, MA, PhD

Bursar: G E Watson, ACIS
School Medical Officer: Dr J P W Lynch, MBChB, MRCGP, FPCert
Headmaster's Secretary: Miss C Shaw, BA

The Abbey (Woodbridge Junior School)
Tel: 01394 382673

Master: N J Garrett, BA, PGCE
Second Master: Mrs C M T Clubb, BEd
Head of Pre-Prep: Mrs J King, BEd

Assistant Staff:

A H A Clarke, GRSM, ARCM, CertEd
C J S French, BA, CertEd
Mrs S J Booth, ARCM, ATCL
M D Staziker, BEd
D A Graham, BEd
R D O Earl, BA, CertEd
Mrs L B Ford, DipEd
Mrs S J E Woolstencroft, MA, CertEd
Mrs S K Cox-Olliff, BA
Mrs R C Walker, BEd
Mrs M-L Simpson, CertEd, SEN
Mrs G R Baylis, BEd

Mrs H Norman, BEd
C C Smith, BSc, CertEd
Mrs J Chamberlain, MA
Mrs J Lawrence, BSc, CertEd
Mrs R M Copestake, CertEd
Miss K C Theobald, BEd
Ms S Campbell, BA
Miss A J Kininmonth, MA, PGCE
Mrs D P Warwick, CertEd
Mrs C R Parker, BSc, CertEd
Miss H C King, BA

Situation. Woodbridge is an attractive market town on the River Deben, opposite the site of the famous royal Saxon ship burial at Sutton Hoo. Timber-framed buildings dating from the Middle Ages, and Georgian facades draw many visitors to the town throughout the year as does the Aldeburgh Festival at the nearby international Snape Maltings Concert Hall. Excellent sailing facilities are available on the River Deben. Woodbridge is seven miles from the Suffolk coast and close to the continental ports of Felixstowe and Harwich. The rail journey to London takes a little over an hour.

History and Buildings. Woodbridge School was originally founded in 1662. The scholars were to be taught "both Latin and Greek until thereby they be made fit for the University (if it be desired), but in case of any of them be unapt to learn those languages … they should be taught only Arithmetic, and to Write, to be fitted for Trades or to go to Sea". They were also to be "instructed in the principles of the Christian Religion according to the Doctrine of the Church of England".

For 200 years, the School existed in cramped quarters in the town until its incorporation with the Seckford Trust.

Endowment income then enabled it to move to its present undulating site overlooking the town and the River Deben and to begin the steady expansion and development which have accelerated over the last 25 years. The School has been fully co-educational for nearly four decades. The latest additions are the new state-of-the-art 350-seat Seckford Theatre and refurbished Britten-Pears Music School.

Woodbridge has had close links with the local community and, through its outstanding Music and Science, with Finland, France, Spain, The Netherlands, Hungary and Germany. Woodbridge has a British Council International School Award for its international links, pupils are able to go on cultural exchange to countries as diverse as Australia, Oman, South Africa, India and China.

The Abbey prep school is centred in a beautiful house dating from the 16th Century in the town, adjacent to which two large new buildings have been added. Taking pupils from 7–11, it has full use of the Senior School swimming pool, sports hall, tennis courts, etc. (*For further details, see entry in IAPS section.*)

Queen's House, the pre-prep department for 100 pupils aged 4–6, opened in 1993 in its own building on the Woodbridge School site.

Organisation. There are 950 pupils. The Senior School (11–18) numbers 340 boys and 277 girls, with a Sixth Form of 200. There is a co-educational Boarding House for pupils aged 13+. A Day House system exists with a Junior House for 11 year old entrants and four other Day Houses for those aged 12–16. All Sixth Form day pupils are based in the Sixth Form Centre.

Music, Games and Activities. Music is at the heart of much of the life of the School. Over 60 concerts every year, large and small, offer pupils opportunities to perform at all levels. Some 45% of pupils study at least one instrument. In recent years Woodbridge School has had more members of the National Youth Choirs of Great Britain than any other school in the UK.

Woodbridge is a chess centre of excellence, representing England at the world chess championships.

Sailing, riding, shooting and hockey are real strengths. Other main games are rugby and netball in the winter; cricket, also tennis, athletics, swimming and rounders in the summer. The Sports Hall has facilities for most indoor sports.

The first-class Combined Cadet Force embraces Army, RAF, and Royal Navy Sections. The large variety of clubs and societies includes the Duke of Edinburgh's Award Scheme. All 11 and 12 year olds follow the Seckford Scheme which paves the way for these, and many other, activities.

Careers. The School offers comprehensive careers advice and there are close links with county and university careers departments.

Chapel and Religious Education. The School has a strong Christian ethos and pupils attend Chapel every week. There is an annual Confirmation Service.

Admission. The majority enter the Senior School at 11 through the School's own examination, interview and report. At age 13, entry is through the School's own or the Common Entrance examination. Entry to the Sixth Form is based on interview and GCSE results. Admission to The Abbey is at any stage from the age of four.

Registration Fee £50. Acceptance Fee £300 (Overseas Boarders £500).

Fees per term (2011-2012). Day: Pre-Prep (Queen's House) £2,412; Prep (The Abbey) £3,721; Senior School: Years 7–9 £4,278; Years 10–13 £4,508. Boarding: £8,050.

Remission of Fees. Due to its generous endowment, the School is able to offer remission of up to 100% of fees to pupils whose parents have incomes in the lower and middle ranges through Awards and/or Means-Tested Bursaries.

Scholarships. (*See Scholarship Entries section.*) These are awarded on the results of the annual entrance examinations at 11+ and 13+. At 16+, Scholarships are awarded on the basis of interview. There are many Music scholarships, Drama, Art, All-Rounder and Sports scholarships and one Chess scholarship each year.

Charitable status. The Seckford Foundation is a Registered Charity, number 1110964. Its aims are to give education for "poor children" by the provision of scholarships and fee remissions out of charity funds, and to maintain "the elderly poor" by providing a subsidy out of the charity for the Almshouses and Jubilee House.

Woodhouse Grove School

Apperley Bridge, West Yorkshire BD10 0NR
Tel: 0113 250 2477
Fax: 0113 250 5290
e-mail: enquiries@woodhousegrove.co.uk
website: www.woodhousegrove.co.uk

Woodhouse Grove is situated in spacious, well-kept grounds on the slopes of the Aire Valley and within easy reach of Bradford and Leeds. The moors are within view and the Dales National Park is not far away.

The School was founded in 1812 for the education of the sons of Wesleyan ministers but now welcomes members of all denominations and none, both as pupils and as staff. It is fully co-educational, taking pupils from the age of 3–18.

Motto: '*Bone et fidelis*'

Visitor: The President of the Methodist Conference

Administrative Governors of the School:

A Wintersgill, FCA (*Chairman*)
S Burnhill, BSc
Mrs P Burton, CertEd
Mrs E E Cleland
P Crewes, BA
R Davy, JP
A Ekoku, BA
Mrs P M Essler, BSc
G B Greenwood, JP
His Honour Judge Stephen Gullick, LLB
Dr G H Haslam, MBChB
A S P Kassapian
M D Leigh, BA, MA, DipEd
P Robertshaw
J H Robinson, FREng, BSc, CEng, FIChemE
G Russell, BA
I M Small, BA, DipEd
Dr J N Tunnicliffe, BA, DPhil
J Weaving, BA, ACA
Revd P Whittaker, BA

Secretary, Methodist Residential Schools: G Russell, BA

Staff:

Headmaster: D C Humphreys, BA

Deputy Headmaster: D N Wood, BA
Second Master: J K Jones, CertEd
Deputy Second Master: J C Cockshott, CertEd
Director of Studies: Dr J A Wilson, BSc, PhD
Head of Year 7: Miss E Farley, BA
Head of Year 8: Miss E R Landy, BSc
Head of Year 9: P Maud, BA
Head of Year 10: P Moffat, BA
Head of Year 11: K D Eaglestone, BSc
Assistant Head & Head of Sixth Form: Mrs E Enthoven, BSc
Chaplain: Revd D H Bonny, BA, BD
Clerk to the Governors: R Hemsley, MA, FCA
Operations Manager: R G Morton, BA

Finance Manager: D Ainsworth, BA, ACA

* *Head of Department*
† *Head of House*

Mrs E Ainscoe, MA (**Biology*)
J Allison, BA (*Design Technology*)
S Archdale (*Speech and Drama*)
J A Baker, CertEd (**Design Technology*)
Miss A Barron, BA (*German, †Southerns*)
E Bean, BSc (*Physics,†Vinter*)
A Cadman, BA (*PE*)
J Carter, BA (*History & Politics, RE, †Findlay*)
Mrs P N Charlton, MA (*Art & Design*)
J C Cockshott, CertEd (*Design Technology*)
A J Copping, MA (**Languages, English and Media Studies*)
Mrs C J Couzens, BA (**PE and Games*)
A N Crawford, BA, ARCO (*Music*)
Miss C Couper, BA (**Drama and Theatre Studies*)
Mrs K Curtis, BSc (*PE and Games, †Towlson*)
Miss H Dale, BA (**Dance, English & Media Studies*)
T Davis, BA (*Chemistry*)
M Dewhirst, BSc (*Physics, Mathematics*)
S Dillon, BA (*Mathematics*)
K Eaglestone, BSc (*Mathematics*)
Mrs E Enthovan, BSc (*Mathematics*)
Mrs J L Edger, BSc (**Physics*)
Mrs E Farley, BA (*English & Media Studies*)
R I Frost, BEd (**PE and Games*)
Miss L Gale, MA (*English, †Vinter*)
Mrs C Gibson, BA (*Business Studies and Economics*)
Mrs K L Goodwin-Bates, MA (*English & Media Studies*)
J Gowon, BA (*PE and Games*)
C K Henderson, BSc (*Chemistry, Biology*)
D Hole, BSc (**Chemistry*)
Mrs A Howard, BA (**PSE, Physics*)
E R Howard, BA, BEd (**PE & History*)
Mrs F L Hughes, BEd (*French*)
A Jarvis, BA (*Modern Languages*)
Miss C D Jemmett, BA (*English*)
A Jennings, BA (**Religious Studies*)
Mrs K Jennings, BEd (*PE*)
R Johnson, BA (*English, †Atkinson*)
J K Jones, CertEd (*PE and Games*)
P Lambert, BA (*Modern Foreign Languages*)
Miss E Landy, BSc (*Chemistry, Biology*)
P W Lodge, BA (**Modern Foreign Languages*)
O Mantle, BA (*IT, Business Studies and Economics*)
P Maud, BA (**Learning Support, PSE, Religious Studies*)
J M McCabe, BSc (*Chemistry*)
Mrs H Mitchell, BA (*Modern Foreign Languages*)
P J Moffat, BA (*Geography*)
Miss B Monk, BA (*ESOL*)
M F Munday, BA (**Geography*)
Miss L Oakley, BA (**English, Theatre Studies*)
Miss C Pearce, BA (*PE and Games, Geography*)
A J Pickles, BA (**Art & Design*)
J B Robb, BA (*Religious Studies, †Stephenson*)
Miss J Russell, BA (*IT*)
C J Shepherd, BSc (*Mathematics, Physics*)
Mrs D L Shoesmith-Evans, BA (**History & Politics*)
D Sugden, BSc (*Mathematics*)
A Sweeney, BA (**History*)
J P A Tedd, MA (**Music*)
Miss R V Thompson, BA (*Geography*)
Mrs R Ward, BA (*English*)
Mrs R Warner, BA (*Politics*)
Mrs P L Watson, MA (**Business Studies, IT*)
G Williams, BSc (**Science*)
J Wilson, PhD (*Biology*)
R Wincer, BA (*Mathematics*)
D N Wood, BA (*English and Media Studies*)
E Wright, BSc (**Mathematics*)

Headmaster's Secretary & Registrar: Mrs T Gilks

Brontë House
Headmaster: S Dunn, BEd
Deputy Head: J Peacock, BEd
Director of Studies: Mrs N Woodman, MPhil
KS1 Coordinator: Mrs H J Simpson, BA
Foundation Stage Coordinator: Mrs A Hinchliffe, BA

Numbers. There are 755 pupils in the Senior School including 97 boarders and 199 students in the Sixth Form. Brontë House (3–11) has 319 pupils including 10 boarders.

Buildings. Our buildings include a new sports centre with a multi-functional sports hall, a fitness suite, a swimming pool, squash courts, floodlit outdoor courts and a state-of-the-art Performing Arts Centre. We have good science laboratories, well-equipped DT and Art centres, a spacious new Music and Drama block, language suite, fully-equipped IT rooms. Our facilities have been enhanced with the refurbishment of the Sixth Form Centre and the completion of a new Senior Boys Boarding house which has en-suite rooms, recreational areas and staff quarters. A new music and drama facility was opened in February 2009 and developments continue, with work on a new ADT centre starting in 2010 and a new swimming pool and sports hall planned for 2012.

Sport and Music. Playing fields adjoining the School cover about 40 acres. Cricket, Netball, Rugby, Squash, Basketball, Athletics, Swimming, Tennis and Rounders are the main games, and there are several all-weather Tennis Courts and a floodlit outdoor court for netball and tennis. The Sports Centre includes a large multi-functional hall, a fitness suite and an aerobics studio.

There are 3 Orchestras, many ensembles, several Choirs and a Concert Band. Many pupils take extra instrumental lessons.

Curriculum. Boys and girls enter the Senior School at the age of 11, 13 or 16 and the curriculum is arranged to provide a continuous course through Brontë House and upwards through the Sixth Form to University entrance. Special support is available for dyslexic pupils. For GCSE, all pupils take the following core subjects, (English, French, Maths, Science–Dual Award, IT), together with three others chosen from German, Geography, RS, History, Art, CDT, PE, Spanish, Drama, Music. In the Sixth Form each pupil selects 4 subjects from 23 possible options for study at AS and A2 level. In addition, all Sixth formers can take a two-year course in General Studies or other broadening options, such as Italian.

A school-wide IT network, full-time IT Manager and IT Technician, state of the art PCs ensure that all pupils enjoy access to excellent IT facilities.

Sixth Form Entry. Places are available for students who want to come into the School at the Sixth Form stage.

Entrance Awards. (*See Scholarship Entries section.*) Academic scholarships are available at 11+ and 13+ and several Music and Art awards are made each year. Means-tested bursaries are available and special allowances for children of Methodist Ministers and Service Personnel. Sports scholarships are awarded in the Sixth Form.

Term of Entry. Pupils are normally accepted in September, though special arrangements may be made for entry in other terms. This applies to Woodhouse Grove and Brontë House, but admission to Ashdown Lodge can take place throughout the year.

Brontë House (named after Charlotte Brontë who was a governess at a house on the same site, and after her parents who were married from the Main School) is a Preparatory School and takes boys and girls, both boarding and day. The Pre-Prep department, Ashdown Lodge, takes boys and girls on a day or part-day basis, all year round. (*See Brontë House entry in IAPS section.*)

Ashdown Lodge opened in September 1993 to extend the family of Woodhouse Grove to the pre-preparatory age range of 2½ to 7, and takes boys and girls on a day or part-day basis, all year round.

Fees per term (2011-2012). Main School: £7,090–£7,140 (boarders), £6,570–£6,670 (weekly boarders), £3,435–£3,520 (day). Brontë House: £6,300 (boarders), £5,775 (weekly boarders), £2,760–£3,100 (day). Ashdown Lodge: Nursery and Reception £2,300 (full day), £1,420 (half day), Years 1 & 2 £2,550. Fees include meals, books, stationery, examination fees and careers tests.

Extra Subjects. Piano, Violin, Viola, Violoncello, Organ, Flute, Clarinet, Oboe, Trumpet, Trombone, Horn, Saxophone, Bassoon, Guitar, Percussion, Singing, Speech and Drama Training, Dancing, Judo, extra sports coaching.

Old Grovians Association. *Secretary*: Mrs Heather Garner.

Charitable status. Woodhouse Grove School is a Registered Charity, number 529205. It exists to provide education for children.

Worksop College
A Woodard School

Worksop, Nottinghamshire S8O 3AP
Tel: 01909 537100
          Headmaster: 01909 537127
Fax: 01909 537102
e-mail: headmaster@worksopcollege.notts.sch.uk
website: www.worksopcollege.notts.sch.uk

Foundation. Worksop College is the last of the Woodard (Church of England) Schools to be founded personally by the 19th Century educationist Canon Nathaniel Woodard, who died between the School's foundation in 1890 and its opening in 1895.

Motto: '*Semper ad Coelestia*'

Governing Body:
The Board of Woodard Schools (Nottinghamshire) Limited

Visitor: The Rt Revd The Bishop of Chichester

Board Members:
The Revd Canon B Clover, MA, LTCL (*Provost*)
C J D Anderson, MA (*Custos*)
T D Fremantle, MBA, DL
R P H McFerran, FRICS, CAAV
His Honour Judge J V Machin, LLB
Mrs J C Richardson, MBE, BA, JP (*Vice-Custos*)
M A Chapman, MLIA Dip
M E Hartley, BSc, FCA
Mrs P A Rouse (*Vice-Custos*)
Mrs M F T Critchley, BA
K S Jones, BSc, FRICS, FAAV
Ms J H Smith
Mrs E Lee
R R Steel, BSc
G A R Cormack, BA
P Spillane, BA
D Wilson, FCA, CTA
J Palmer, BA
J S Browning, MA, MBA

Headmaster: **R A Collard**, JP, MA Sidney Sussex College, Cambridge

Deputy Head: J Anderson, BA (*Geography*)

Director of Studies: T S Purser, PhD, BA (*History*)

Assistant Deputy Heads:
Mrs E A Warner, CertEd (*Physical Education*)
T J Halsall, MEd, BA (*English and Theatre Studies*)

Chaplain: Revd P Finlinson, MA, BA (*Head of Spiritual and Moral Studies*)

Teaching Staff:
Mrs W H Bain, BA (*English, Head of Drama and Theatre Studies*)
Mrs C M Beckett, BA (*Learning Support*)
M P Boler, BSc (*Head of Physics*)
Mrs G Burton, CertEd (*Food & Nutrition*)
E A Carr, BSc (*Physics*)
Mrs M J Christodoulou, BEd (*Head of Food and Nutrition*)
C D Cook, BA (*Design Technology*)
J A S Driver, BSc (*Biology*)
G R Duckering, BEd (*Head of Design Technology*)
M Fagan, BEd (*Mathematics*)
N R Forbes, BA (*Latin*)
T J Franse, BA (*Chemistry and Physical Education*)
Mrs C Futter, BA (*Modern Languages*)
M K Gillard, BSc (*Head of Chemistry*)
Mrs S J Gillard, BA (*Head of English*)
Mrs A A Gray, BEd (*Learning Support*)
Miss K J Grice, BA (*Modern Languages*)
C J Hamlet, BSc (*Physical Education*)
Mrs J E Ireland, BSc (*Head of Business Studies and Economics*)
J R Johnson, BA (*English*)
Miss G J Johnston, BSc (*Head of Geography*)
P C Jones, BSc (*Business Studies and Economics*)
A B B Kenrick, MA, BA (*Head of Art and Design*)
N A K Kitchen, MA (*Head of History, Head of Sixth Form*)
S N Koon, PhD, MA (*Classics and Ancient History*)
T P Larkman, BSc (*Geography*)
R J M Leach, BA, ARCO (*Assistant Director of Music*)
R J Marks, BEd, BPhil (*Learning Support*)
J R Mather, BSc (*Head of Physical Education*)
I C Parkin, BSc (*Director of Games*)
Mrs K M Parkin, BSc (*History*)
Mrs P S Parkinson, BA (*Head of Modern Languages*)
C G Paton, BA (*Modern Languages*)
Mrs H Platt-Hawkins, MA (*Art*)
Mrs S Powell, BSc (*Games*)
P N Richardson, BA (*English, History*)
W G Robinson, BSc (*Mathematics*)
Mrs G J Robson-Bayley, BA (*English*)
J W Sampson, BA (*Business Studies & Economics, Head of Careers*)
Mrs E Sutton, L-ès-L (*Modern Languages*)
G R Tattersall, BSc (*Mathematics*)
Mrs C E Tilley, BEd (*Physical Education*)
K D Topham, MSc, BSc (*Biology*)
J D Turner, BSc (*Head of Mathematics*)
T Uglow, MA, ARCO (*Director of Music*)
Mrs S R White, BA (*Geography, Head of General Studies*)
Mrs A Wright, BSc (*Head of Science and Biology*)

Houses and Housemasters/mistresses:

Boys:
Mason: W G Robinson
Pelham: T P Larkman
Portland: T J Franse
Shirley: C J Hamlet
Talbot: P N Richardson

Girls:
Derry: Mrs S Powell
Gibbs: Mrs C E Tilley
School House: Mrs P S Parkinson

School Doctor: Dr K Fairholme
Bursar: J K Wheeler, OBE, BA
Admissions Registrar: Mrs D Murray
Old Worksopian Society Secretary: Mrs W Marks

Ranby House Preparatory School
Headmaster: D Sibson, BA Ed

There are 404 pupils in the College of whom about 39% are girls.

Situation. The College is situated in its own estate of 300 acres with extensive playing fields and an 18-hole golf course. It is on the edge of Sherwood Forest, a mile or so south of Worksop in North Nottinghamshire, overlooking the Clumber and Welbeck Estates. Lying close to the M1 and A1 and only 7 miles from Retford on the main East Coast Inter-City route from London to the North, the College is easily accessible by road, rail and air from most parts of the country. It is also well placed for contact with the universities, museums, theatres and cultural life of Nottingham, Sheffield, Leeds, York and other cities in the region.

Buildings. Earlier buildings include the Chapel and the Great Hall, a swimming pool, the Churchill Hall, the main quadrangle of classrooms and boarding houses, a well-equipped Theatre and an Art School. Recent modernisation has taken place of all facilities, most particularly the boarding houses and classrooms, including extensive ICT and electronic whiteboard provision. In recent years a Computer Centre, a Music School, a Drama Studio and a Learning Support Unit have been added. A Sports Hall was opened in January 2003, a new girls' Boarding House and a new girls' Day House opened in 2007, and a new Modern Languages Department language laboratory opened in September 2008.

Houses. There are 8 Houses. The 4 boys' Boarding Houses, the boys' Day House and a girls' House are all in the main College. The girls' Boarding House and Day House are in separate buildings. The housemaster or housemistress, assisted by the house tutors, associate tutors and academic tutors, has the principal responsibility for the individual welfare and programme of the boys or girls in the house, with whom they are in constant contact. At the same time the compactness of the buildings makes it easy for boys or girls to seek advice from other members of staff, in particular the Chaplain, and to make friendships with boys or girls in other houses as well as their own.

Religion. The Anglican religion is at the centre of the School's life, in Chapel services and throughout the school routine. A genuine effort is made to show that Christianity remains a vital response to the challenges of the 21st Century. While the great majority of pupils are Anglican, pupils of other creeds and faiths are also welcome, not least for the distinctive vision of God which they contribute to the School's experience.

Curriculum. Because the College enjoys the ratio of 1 teacher to fewer than 10 pupils, close attention can be given to individual needs at every level. The Curriculum is designed to give pupils as wide an education as possible in the first three years, leading to the GCSE examinations. In the Sixth Form, a broad range of A and AS Level examinations is available including English, History, Geography, French, Spanish, Latin, Classical Civilisation, Mathematics, Physics, Chemistry, Biology, Further Mathematics, Economics & Business Studies, Music, Art, Design Technology, Theatre Studies, Physical Education and General Studies. Additionally, Applied Business, City & Guilds Culinary Skills and AS Home Economics are offered. About 97% of Sixth Form leavers go on to Higher Education.

Music. A large Music School containing a recital and rehearsal room with a capacity of 150, 10 teaching and practice rooms with pianos and a Music Library is the focal point for the Director of Music and a large visiting staff.

Art. The Director of Art has at his disposal 2 large studios for painting and drawing, a room for graphics and digital photography, textiles and sculpture areas and a library and teaching room.

Design and Technology. A purpose-built Technology Centre has facilities for design, the use of computers and areas for work in metal, wood and plastic, as well as CAD-CAM facilities.

Drama. There is a fully-equipped theatre as well as a Drama Studio, and plays involving boys and girls are put on

3 or 4 times a year. Theatre Studies is offered as a Sixth Form option.

Physical Education and Games. Physical Education is an integral part of the curriculum for a pupil's 5 years. The major games for boys are Rugby (Michaelmas Term), Hockey and Cross-Country (Lent Term), and Cricket, Athletics, and Swimming (Summer Term). For girls, they are Hockey (Michaelmas Term), Netball (Lent Term) and Tennis, Athletics and Swimming (Summer Term). Pupils are also encouraged to play other sports (Badminton, Basketball, Golf, Sailing, Soccer, Squash, Sub-Aqua, Tennis, Trampolining, Volleyball, Water Polo, Weight Lifting) and, as they become more senior, are permitted to specialise in them rather than in the main games if they choose. The Sports Hall has facilities for many sports and additional features for cricket as well as a fully-equipped fitness suite.

Activities. In their first year all pupils are taught life-saving, first-aid and other basic skills. There is then the choice of joining a section of the CCF and later to do voluntary community service. There is training in camping, orienteering, climbing, canoeing, motor engineering, shooting (the school has its own 25-yard range), signalling, and survival swimming. Boys and girls have all these options as well as the chance to take part in the Duke of Edinburgh's Award Scheme.

One afternoon a week is also set apart for Societies and Hobbies. These have included Archery, Art, Badminton, Boat Maintenance, Car Maintenance, Chess, Canoeing/Kayaking, Climbing, Cookery, Dance, Drama, Duke of Edinburgh's Award, Fencing, Golf Coaching, Judo, Kick-Boxing, Mountain Bikes, Music, Pop Lacrosse, Soccer, Sub-Aqua, Squash, Table Tennis, Trampolining, Weight Training/Fitness Suite and Yoga.

Ranby House. Over a third of the boys and girls in the School come from Ranby House, the preparatory school for Worksop, which is about 4 miles from the College and offers boarding and day education to boys and girls from 7–13. It also has a Pre-Prep Department.

See Ranby House entry in IAPS section.

Fees per term (2011-2012). Boarders £7,840; Day Pupils £5,115. Flexi Boarding £6,090.

Scholarships. (*See Scholarship Entries section.*) Scholarships and Exhibitions may be awarded annually, examination in February. (Candidates must be over 12 and under 14 on 1 May in the year of entry.) Sixth Form Scholarships are held in February each year.

Music Scholarships, Art Scholarships, Sports Awards and Golf Awards are also available.

The value of an award may, in special cases, be increased if the financial circumstances of the parents make this necessary.

A number of Bursaries are awarded to the children of Clergy and to children of members of Her Majesty's Armed Services (up to 15%) on the basis of financial need.

Admission. The main intake is in September each year, but pupils do join at other times. Pupils for September from preparatory schools will join through either the Entrance Scholarship or the Common Entrance Examination. Other Entry Tests are held at the College in March and May for 13+ applicants from the maintained sector. Increasingly boys and girls are joining the College after GCSE to study in the Sixth Form.

Charitable status. Woodard Schools (Nottinghamshire) Limited is a Registered Charity, number 1103326. It exists for the purpose of educating children.

Worth School

Turners Hill, West Sussex RH10 4SD
Tel: 01342 710200
Fax: 01342 710230

e-mail: registry@worth.org.uk
website: www.worthschool.co.uk

Worth is a Catholic Benedictine boarding and day school for boys and girls aged 11–18. It is a truly distinctive school, known for its strong community values, friendly atmosphere and the excellence of its all-round education.

Our magnificent school is in the heart of the Sussex countryside, about halfway between London and Brighton, and only 15 minutes from Gatwick airport. We are ideally placed to allow students to sample some of the cultural highlights that Britain has to offer, while providing a safe and beautiful environment in which to learn.

In January 2010 we had a full Ofsted inspection on provision for Boarders at Worth. The school was found to be 'Outstanding' and no recommendations were made. In the words of one pupil quoted by Ofsted, "This school grows happy pupils, organically."

The school offers a broad curriculum, where students can opt for the International Baccalaureate Diploma or A Levels. The School has offered the IB since 2002 so has a proven track record in this area. Examination results are high and improving (Worth rose some 248 places in the *Financial Times* list of Top 1,000 Schools published in February 2011) and pupils enter the best universities in the UK and abroad, including Oxford and Cambridge.

The wider curriculum is rich and varied with a huge range of activities, societies, lectures and trips from which to choose. There is also a lively sporting programme which has produced students of national and county standard, and the school's reputation for performing arts is outstanding.

The Abbot's Board of Governors, comprising both monks and laity.

President: Abbot Kevin Taggart, MA

Chairman: Mrs A Andreotti, FCILT

Dom Mark Barrett, MA
Sir David Bell
Mr N Deeming, BA, MBA
Mrs C Fitzsimons, BSc
Mr J Guyatt, BA
Dom Luke Jolly, BA
Mr G Moore, BA Econ, CA
Dom Aidan Murray, BSc, BA, PhD, PGCE
Mrs F Newton, BA, PGCE
Mr J Scherer, MA

Head Master: Mr Gino Carminati, BA, MA

Second Master: Dr James Whitehead, MA, MPhil, PhD
Deputy Head Academic: Mrs Anne Lynch, BA
Deputy Head Pastoral: Mr Patrick Doyle, BA, MA
Assistant Head: Mr Alan Mitchell, BSc

Teaching Staff:
* *Head of Department*

Miss Elizabeth Abbott, BA (*Religious Studies*)
Miss Siobhan Aherne, BA (*Girls' Games*)
Mr Paul Ambridge, BA (*Physics*)
Dr Sheena Bartlett, BSc, PhD (*Sciences*)
Mr Jonathan Bindloss, BA (*Religious Studies*, Theory of Knowledge*)
Mr Stuart Blackhurst, HND (*Network Manager, IT*)
Mr Matthew Boughton, MA (*Drama **)
Miss Anouck Brenot, BA, PGCE (*French**)
Mrs Judith Bridge, BSc (*Learning Support*)
Ms Amanda Brookfield, BA (*Head of Sixth Form & IB Coordinator*)
Mrs Caroline Brown, PDLS (*St Mary's Housemistress*)
Mrs Caroline Brown, MA (*Religious Studies*)
Mr Nathan Brown, BA, Dip EFL (*English, St Bede's Housemaster*)
Mrs Lucinda Button, BA (*Art*)

Mrs Anne Carminati, BA (*Learning Support*)
Mr Darren Carrick, BSc (*Director of Sport*)
Ms Louise Chamberlain, BSc (*Biology**)
Mr Raj Chaudhuri, BCom (*Cricket Coach*)
Mrs Minakshi Chaudhuri, BA (*Learning Support*)
Mr Philip Chorley, MA (*English**)
Mrs Julia Cook, BEd, OCR Dip SpLD (*St Anne's Housemistress, Learning Support**)
Mr Damian Cummins, BA (*Rutherford Housemaster, Physical Education*)
Mr Paul Curtis, BSc (*ICT**)
Mrs Jayne Dempster, BSc (*Mathematics**)
Mr Stephen Doerr, BA, CertEd (*Learning Support*)
Dr Brian Doggett, BSc, PhD (*Sciences**)
Mr Sebastien Donjon, Deg Math (*Mathematics*)
Mr Jeremy Dowling, BEd (*Mathematics*)
Dr Elizabeth Fielder, BEng, PhD, PGCE (*Chemistry*)
Ms Joanne Geraghty, BA, MA, DELE (*Spanish**)
Mr Kevan Goddard, BA (*Mathematics*)
Mrs Joanna Gray, BA (*Assistant Director of Music*)
Mrs Sheila Gupta, BA, Dip ELICS (*EAL*)
Miss Sarah Hardman BA, (*English, Drama*)
Ms Juley Hudson, BA (*Art**)
Mrs Kate Huxley, MA (*Mathematics*)
Dr Daniel Koch, BA, DPhil (*History**)
Mr Andrew Lavis, BA (*Geography*)
Mrs Daniele Lloyd, L-ès-L, TEFL (*Modern Languages*)
Mr Mark Macdonald, BSc (*Geography*)
Dom Martin McGee, BA, MA (*School Chaplain*)
Mr Al Matthews, BA, MA (*Media Studies*, English*)
Mr Mike Matthews, BA (*Music, Austin Housemaster*)
Mr Bruce Morrison, BEd (*Physical Education, Core PE**)
Mrs Mousavi-Zadeh, BA, MA (*Senior Librarian*)
Mrs Karen Murphy, BA (*Art & Design*)
Miss Eimear Neeson, BSc (*Mathematics*)
Mr Michael Oakley, BA, MMus (*Director of Music*)
Miss Elizabeth Ockford, BA, MA (*Design*)
Mr Robert Outen, GNVQ (*Rugby Development Officer*)
Mr Andrew Oxley, BSc (*Sciences*)
Mrs Joanna Phillippo Nevill, BA (*Girls' Physical Education**)
Mr Tom Phillips, BA, MA (*History*)
Ms Alessandra Pittoni, Laurea in Lingue (*Italian*)
Dr Duncan Pring, MA, PhD (*Economics and Business Studies, Careers*, Farwell Housemaster*)
Mr Christopher Quayle, BA (*Geography*)
Mr Philip Robinson, MA (*Classics**)
Dr Peter Scott, MA, PhD (*Biology*)
Mr Stephen Shields, BA (*Economics & Business Studies*)
Mr Christopher Smith, MPhys (*Sciences*)
Mr Stefan Steinebach, Staatsexamen (*Modern Languages*, Latin*)
Mrs Rebecca Steinebach, BA (*Modern Languages, Latin*)
Mr Andrew Taylor, MA (*History, Gervase Housemaster*)
Mrs Louise Taylor, BA (*English*)
Mrs Tricia Taylor, BA (*French*)
Mr Guy Teasdale, BEd (*Economics and Business Studies**)
Miss Marta Viruete, MA (*Spanish*)
Mr Giles Watson, BA (*History*)
Mrs Sarah Watson-Saunders, BA, MA-Lit (*English, Debating**)
Mrs Susan Wilkinson, BA (*Learning Support Assistant*)
Mr James Williams, BSc (*Sciences, Physics*, Chapman Housemaster*)
Mr Julian Williams, BSc, MA, BSocSc, PG Dip LTCL, TESOL (*History, Butler Housemaster*)
Mrs Naomi Williams, BA (*Psychology**)
Mrs Suki Wilson, BSc (*Biology*)

Bursar: Mrs Angela Higgs, BSc, ACA
Registrar: Ms Yvonne Lorraine
Head Master's Secretary: Mrs Diane Coulson

Medical Officers: Dr A Cooper, Dr B Bartman

Senior Nursing Sister: Cheryl Cheeseman, SRN, Paediatric Dipl
Nursing Sisters:
J Doyle, RN
L Lindo, SRN
N Whiting, SRN

History. Worth School is situated in the midst of the beautiful Worth Abbey estate where a monastery was founded in 1933 by a group of monks from the Benedictine community at Downside in Somerset. The monks bought a large country house called Paddockhurst and its 500-acre estate situated on a ridge of the Sussex Weald which had formerly been the property of the first Lord Cowdray and opened a prep school for boys. In 1957, the monastery became independent and Worth admitted the first boys to its own senior school in 1959.

Worth welcomed girls into Years 7 and 9 in September 2010. They joined other girls in an already thriving co-educational Sixth Form, and by 2012 the School will be fully co-educational.

Courses of study. At GCSE level, students usually take between nine and eleven subjects at GCSE. The compulsory core is: English, Mathematics, Religious Studies, Sciences, French or Spanish or German, and ICT (plus PE and PSME). Two or three options are chosen from: Art, Drama, Economics & Business Studies, English Literature, French or Spanish as a second language, Geography, History, Latin, Music and Physical Education. Tuition is available (for an additional fee) in Greek, Italian and Chinese to GCSE and A Level.

There is a wide choice of subjects at A Level: Art, Biology, Business Studies, Chemistry, Drama, Economics, English, Film Studies, French, Geography, German, History, ICT, Maths and Further Maths, Music, Music Technology, Physics, Physical Education, Psychology and Spanish. There is also the opportunity to take the Extended Project Qualification (EPQ).

Alternatively, Sixth Form students may study the International Baccalaureate. This involves the study of six subjects, three at higher level and three at standard level. Students study one subject from each of the following groups:

Group 1: English, German

Group 2: English, French, German, Greek, Italian (also ab initio), Latin, Spanish (also ab initio)

Group 3: Economics, Geography, History, Philosophy

Group 4: Biology, Physics

Group 5: Mathematics (HL), Mathematics (SL), Mathematical Studies (SL)

Group 6: Music, Theatre Arts, Visual Arts, Chemistry, French, History, Greek

Virtually all students go on to university. Sixth Form students may also choose to study for Oxbridge entrance and a significant number gain places at either Oxford or Cambridge.

A Benedictine school. Worth believes that each person is on a spiritual journey and that the school should support them wherever they are on that journey, and try to encourage a faith which will sustain pupils in later life. Over half of the 530 students at Worth are from Roman Catholic families, and there are a significant number of Christians from other denominations. Equal members of the community in every way, non-Catholic pupils have no difficulty integrating in the school and bring a different perspective which is most welcome. The School Chaplaincy team includes an Anglican Chaplain, as well as Catholic Chaplains and lay members. Everyone is expected to subscribe to the School's Benedictine values which include Hospitality, Service, Worship and Community amongst others.

There are prayers each day in Houses, whole school worship each Thursday and Mass every Sunday for those boarding over the weekend and for local families.

Pastoral Care. Care of each student is of central importance throughout the School, as evidenced by our 'Outstanding' Ofsted grading for Boarder provision. Each pupil is a member of a House and has a personal tutor who monitors work progress and assists the Housemaster/Housemistress with overall care. The House support structure also includes a chaplain and, for boarding houses, a matron. There is a counsellor who is available should pupils need him. The Benedictine tradition of community life underpins everything. Many staff families live on-site and parents are welcomed as integral to the school. There are regular points of contact, with parent-teacher consultations, meetings, social events and active support from the Friends of Worth (the parents' association).

Sport. Worth loves its sports. The main sports are: rugby, football, hockey, netball, cricket, tennis and athletics. Other sports played at competitive level include fencing, squash, golf and basketball and sports are also available through school clubs and activities (see below). There is an eight-hole golf course, squash courts, tennis courts, fencing salle, dance studio and fitness suite. The school also makes use of the excellent athletics facility and 50m swimming pool at the new multi-sports centre nearby.

Music is important at Worth. There is a flourishing choir that is involved in tours and recordings as well as regular appearances in the Abbey Church. Parents, local friends and students join the Choral Society for at least two concerts each year (performing such works as Requiems by Faure and Durufle). The School orchestra performs regularly, as does the Jazz Band. The annual House Music, Battle of the Bands and Worth Unplugged competitions provide all pupils with an opportunity to perform and encourage an interest in music.

Drama also flourishes with regular productions at all levels and the standard of performance is exceptional. Major productions in 2010–11 were a very challenging *Don Quixote Part 1* by the senior school and a fantastic version of *Joseph and the Amazing Techicolor Dreamcoat* by Worth juniors. Performances take place in our purpose-built Performing Arts Centre which comprises a 250-seater theatre, box office, drama office and workshop, dressing rooms, recording studio, a sound-proofed 'rock room', rehearsal rooms, a recital room and music classrooms.

Extra-curricular activity. On Wednesday afternoons every pupil participates in one or more activity, ranging from Age Concern, photography and circus skills to sailing, clay pigeon shooting, horse riding and polo. Worth is also a centre of excellence for The Duke of Edinburgh's Award Scheme.

Continuous investment. Worth has invested in its facilities and will continue to do so. The last decade has seen the opening of Gervase House (2002) for Upper Sixth Form boys, St Mary's boarding house for girls (2008) and St Anne's house for day girls (2010). The new social centre – The Pitstop – opened in 2010. We are currently investing to provide 2 new laboratories and additional classrooms, an astroturf pitch and an entirely new building for boarding house St Bede's which will open in autumn 2012.

The most striking and important 'new' building since 1933 is the modern Abbey Church which has undergone an extensive refurbishment during 2010–11. It continues to be an inspiring place of prayer and retreat as well as an iconic building in its own right.

Admissions Policy. *Entry at 11+:* Entrance tests in English, Maths and Non-Verbal Reasoning are held in January each year. Offers are based on test results, a report from the student's current school and an interview with the Head Master.

Entry at 13+: Entrance tests in English, Maths and Non-Verbal Reasoning are held in January each year. Worth now also offers the entrance process one year earlier for those seeking entry into Year 9; the entrance tests for Year 9 entrants for September 2012 will be held in January 2011.

Offers are based on test results, a report from the student's current school and an interview with the Head Master. Common Entrance examination results will be used for setting purposes only.

Entry at 16+: Entrance into the Sixth Form depends on the student's GCSE results or equivalent, an interview with the Head Master and a satisfactory reference from their current school. The normal requirement for students entering the Sixth Form at Worth is six GCSE passes at grades A to C, with at least three at grade B or above.

For further information on Admissions please contact the Registrar on 01342 710231.

Scholarships. (*See Scholarship Entries section*.) Academic, Music, Sport and All-Rounder scholarships are awarded annually, varying in value up to 40% of the annual fees. The Academic and All-Rounder examination for Year 9 entrants is held in the Lent Term, others in the Summer Term and candidates must be under 14 years of age on 1 September of the year in which they take the examination. Scholarships are also available for entry at 11+ through the entrance examination. Sixth Form Scholarships are awarded to students aged 16, based on scholarship examinations in November, good GCSE results and an interview. Music and All-Rounder Scholarships are available for entry at 11+, 13+ and 16+.

St Benedict's Scholarships enable local Catholic children of real ability, whose parents' financial circumstances would normally preclude attendance at Worth, to benefit from the opportunities offered by the school. One day place is available for Year 7 and two day places for Year 12 are available each year.

Fees per term (2011-2012). Senior: Boarding £8,883, Day £6,517; Junior: Boarding £7,462, Day £5,694.

Friends of Worth. The parents of children at Worth run their own programme of social events to which all parents are invited. Typical events are coffee mornings, drinks receptions and a bi-annual ball.

Worth Society. All Worthians are entitled to join the alumni society. Contact Olivia Henley at Worth School.

Charitable status. Worth School is a Registered Charity, number 1093914. Its aims and objectives are to promote religion and education. If Worth had a motto it would be: *The glory of God is a person fully alive.*

Wrekin College

Wellington, Shropshire TF1 3BH
Tel: 01952 265600
            Headmaster: 01952 265602
Fax: 01952 415068
e-mail: info@wrekincollege.com
website: www.wrekincollege.com

Wrekin College was founded in 1880 by Sir John Bayley and in 1923 became one of the Allied Schools, a group of six independent schools including Canford, Harrogate, Stowe and Westonbirt.
Motto: *'Aut vincere aut mori'*

Visitor: The Rt Revd The Lord Bishop of Lichfield

Governors:
¶H W Campion, ACA, ATII (*Chairman*)
Rt Hon The Viscount Boyne, MRICS
R D Bubbers
D P Crow
¶J A Grant
A F Lock
Mrs E Moore, LLB
P Nutley, MA
J T S Peacock
R J Pearson

D B Sankey, MA
A J Stilton, MA
Capt I P Somervaille, CBE, RN
N A Wilkie
M P Willcock

¶ *Old Wrekinian*

Headmaster: Richard Pleming, MA Pembroke College
  Cambridge

Deputy Head (Academic): H P Griffiths, BSc, PhD

Deputy Head (Pastoral): Mrs S E Clarke, BA, FRGS

Assistant Head: I Williamson, BA

Chaplain: Revd M Horton, MA, MA CertTh, DipTh

Assistant Staff:
† *Housemaster/mistress*

J Ballard, BSc	Mrs J D Kotas, BA
P J Berry, BA	K B Livingstone, BA
A J I Brennan, BA	D McLagan, BA
H S R Brown, BA	Miss A May, MA, PhD
S Cale, BSc	F Murton, BMus, LRAM,
†Mrs J Cliffe, BSc	LTCL, ARCO
Mrs F Coffey, BSc	Mrs M Pattinson, MA
J M Coffin, BEng	Mrs E Perry, BSc
Mrs G Cordingly, BSc	†J G Phillips, BA
†Mrs M Crone, BA	E Roberts, BA
Mrs L J Drew, BA	†G N Roberts, BSc, PhD
A Francis-Jones, BSc	T A Southall, BSc
J C Frodsham, CertEd,	Mrs C Thust, BSc
AdvDipEd	C J Tolley, BSc
H R Gray, BSc	A J Ware, BSc
Miss J Harris, BA	Mrs A E Wedge, BSc
S J Hield, BSc	Mrs M N J Warner, BSc
†J M Holliday, MA	Mrs P M Willmott, BA
A R Hurd, BSc	M de Weymarn, BA
†Mrs A John, BA	Ms G T Whitehead, BA
E John, CertEd, MEd	†D J Winterton, BA

Learning Support:
Mrs B Harbron, BA, CFPS
Mrs A H Livingstone, MA, RSA CELTA
A Savage, BSc, DLC
Miss S Schroer

Visiting Music Staff:
Miss S Croxon, BMus (*Brass*)
M M Davy, FRCO, LRAM, ARCM (*Organ*)
N Gregoire (*Organ*)
M I W Hall, BMus, MMus (*Piano & Saxophone*)
D Heywood, ABSM (*Trombone*)
Mrs J Horton, ARCM (*Piano*)
C J Jones, BMus (*Piano*)
M Kam, BMus (*Piano*)
B Lam, BMus (*Singing*)
G Lamplough, BMus (*Trumpet*)
Mrs S Lamplough, BMus, MA (*Singing*)
Miss S A Lane, ARCM (*Flute*)
D Leeke, MA (*Organ*)
Ms J Magee, MA, GRSM, LRAM, ARCM, ABSM (*Cello*)
P Parker (*Guitar*)
G Santry (*Drums*)
Mrs F Stubbs, MA, GCLM (*Bassoon*)
M Svensson, BMus (*Head of Strings*)
Ms R Theobald (*Piano, Oboe & Singing*)

Games:
J M L Mostyn (*Head of Games*)
Mrs C A Ritchie-Morgan (*Head of Girls' Games*)

Sports Coaches:
S Aston (*Cricket*)
Mrs K Bennett (*Girls' Games*)
D Clarke (*Swimming*)

J Field (*Basketball, Cricket & Squash*)
S Floyd (*Hockey*)
K Holding (*Fencing*)
K F Hughes (*Cricket – Umpire*)
Mrs M Jenkins (*Girls' Games*)
R Oliver (*Cricket*)
R J Pinder (*Rugby*)
Mrs R Reilly (*Swimming*)
A K Reynolds (*Rugby*)
A C Sammons (*Rugby*)
C t J Sheperd (*Cricket*)
Mrs C Still (*Gymnastics*)
M de Weymarn (*Cricket*)

Medical Officers: Dr J Middleton & Dr E Williams

CCF:
SSI & Outward Bound Instructor: RQMS, E J Fanneran,
  late RA
Secretary OWA: M Joyner, BSc

Bursar: Mrs Y K Thomas, MBA, FCA

Deputy Bursars:
Facilities: B C Crone
Operations: D N Broomfield

Foundation Manager: Mrs S Kyle
Marketing Manager: Mrs A Nicoll
Admissions Officer: Mrs C Williams
Headmaster's Personal Assistant: Mrs C L Barefoot

    The College is situated in an estate of 100 acres on the outskirts of the market town of Wellington. We pride ourselves on the excellent quality of our people, as well as the excellent quality of our facilities, and we measure our achievements not only by our outstanding examination results, but also by the whole development of individuals within the school. Being a relatively small school, about 470 pupils, the quality of relationships is good and enables a purposeful atmosphere to prevail in which students can achieve their potential, both in academic and extra-curricular activities. We are splendidly equipped with many modern facilities including a purpose-built Theatre, a double Sports Hall, Astroturf and 25m indoor swimming pool, together with all the expected classrooms, ICT facilities and a new Sixth Form Centre. Teaching is expert and disciplined. Co-educational since 1975, there are 7 Houses, which cater for both Day and Boarding pupils, and these include dedicated Junior Houses for the 11 to 13 intake. Everyone eats together in a central Dining Room and there is a Medical Centre available to all pupils. The Chapel is central to the school both geographically and in the impact it makes on the ethos of the school.

    Admission. Boarders and day pupils are admitted at 11+ or 13+ after passing the Entry Examination or Common Entrance. There is also a Sixth Form entry based on GCSE achievement.

    Term of entry. The normal term of entry is the Autumn Term but pupils may be accepted at other times of the academic year in special circumstances.

    Fees per term (2011-2012). Full Boarding: £7,190 (Years 7–8); £8,325 (Years 9–Sixth Form). Weekly Boarding: £5,885 (Years 7–8); £6,865 (Years 9–Sixth Form). Day: £4,175 (Years 7–8); £5,044 (Years 9–Sixth Form). Private tuition may be arranged at an extra charge.

    Music Fees are £20 per lesson. Registration Fee £100.

    The School Curriculum is framed to meet the needs of the GCSE Examination, AS and A levels. In the Upper School boys and girls are prepared for entrance to Oxbridge and other Universities. Every pupil has an academic tutor. Expert careers advice is given and all members of the Fifth Form take an aptitude and assessment test before selecting their A levels. The school's careers staff organise work experience for Sixth Form pupils. Regular careers lectures take place in the two winter terms. Special courses in study skills and interview techniques are conducted in the Sixth Form. All pupils undergo a counselling course on important moral and social issues and Sixth Form pupils take part in a Leadership Course.

Games and Activities. We are particularly strong in Netball and Cricket, and the main games for girls are hockey, netball, tennis, athletics and rounders; for boys, rugby, soccer, hockey, cricket, tennis and athletics. Many other sports are available, including squash, basket-ball, volley-ball, cross country, fencing, shooting, climbing, badminton, sailing, canoeing and swimming for both boys and girls. On Tuesdays or Fridays, pupils select from a large range of other activities. Over one hundred pupils are involved with the Duke of Edinburgh's Award Scheme and there is a strong tradition of Community Service. There is also a Combined Cadet Force.

Art, Crafts, Music and Drama. There is a flourishing tradition of all these at Wrekin. Art, Pottery, Multimedia Design Technology and Music are all taught in the junior forms and it is hoped that everyone will continue with one of these creative activities throughout his or her time at the school. All can be taken at GCSE and A level. There is a large Choir and Orchestra and other instrumental and Jazz Bands. Many plays are performed by Houses, year groups and at school level.

Scholarships, Exhibitions and Prizes. (*See Scholarship Entries section.*) Academic Scholarships and Exhibitions, open to boys and girls, are offered annually. Sixth Form scholarships are awarded to candidates entering Wrekin after GCSE. These are awarded in advance, based on GCSE predictions of at least six A grades and following an interview at the school. Valuable Music Scholarships, and Exhibitions are awarded annually. Bursaries are awarded to candidates who offer outstanding ability in games. Music and Art examinations and assessments take place in the Lent Term and are open to pupils for entry at all levels of the school. There is an important link with the Services and bursaries are available to support the sons and daughters of service personnel. Particulars of all scholarships and awards may be obtained from the Headmaster.

Old Wrekinian Association. A flourishing Wrekinian Association of over 3,500 members exists to make possible continuous contact between the School and its Old Pupils, for the benefit of both and to support the ideals and aims of the school. It is expected that boys and girls will become members of the Old Wrekinian Association when they leave Wrekin.

Charitable status. Wrekin Old Hall Trust Limited is a Registered Charity, number 528417. It exists to provide independent boarding and day co-education in accordance with the Articles of Association of Wrekin College.

Wycliffe College

Stonehouse, Gloucestershire GL10 2JQ

Tel: 01453 822432
Fax: 01453 827634
e-mail: senior@wycliffe.co.uk
website: www.wycliffe.co.uk

The School was founded in 1882 by G W Sibly and placed on a permanent foundation under a Council of Governors in 1931.

President: S P Etheridge, MBE, TD, JP, MBA, FIFP, CFP, FCII, ACIArb

Chair of Governors: Mrs G E Camm, BSc

Vice Presidents:
Major General G B Fawcus CB, MA, MInstRE

Air Chief Marshal Sir Michael Graydon, GCB, CBE, FRAeS

Vice Chairman: Brigadier R J Bacon, MBA, Chartered FCIPD, FCMI, CMILT

Mrs K R Fife, BA, BSc
S J Fisher, LLB
T G Hale
Mrs S J Lacey, MEng, BA
I Paling, BMet, MMet
J H Powell-Tuck, FRICS
J C H Pritchard, DipM, FIMC, MCIM, MIMI
Group Captain G Reid, MB ChB, FRCPsych, RAF
J Slater, FRICS
J R E Williams, FCA

Financial Director and Company Secretary: A C Golding, ACA

Head: Mrs M E Burnet Ward, MA Hons, PGCE

Deputy Head: P Woolley, BA (*Politics*)
Assistant Head and Director of Studies: S V Dunne, BA (*Media*)
Assistant Head and Director of Pastoral Care: Mrs E A Buckley, BSc (*Physical Education*)
Head of Sixth Form/Head of Higher Education and Careers: J M Hardaker, BA (*Economics & Business Studies*)
Head of Lower School: S Knighton-Callister, BA, MA (*Head of Art*)
Director of ICT: B Ittyavirah, BSc, MSc
Chaplain: Mrs C Welham, MA (*Head of Religious Studies*)
Visiting Chaplain: The Reverend N Tucker, BSc

House Staff:
Haywardsfield: J R Welham BSc (*Mathematics*)
Ward's House: A M Golightly, BA, MA (*Head of Drama*)
Ivy Grove: Mrs L M Morris, CertEd, PG DipSpLD (*SEN*)
Haywardsend: Mrs S Trainor, H DipEd (*Biology*)
Loosley Halls: G P Buckley, BA, M Inst SRM Dip, MILAM (*Head of Physical Education*)
Robinson House: J S Mace, BSc (*Head of Biology*)
Lampeter House: Mrs L Knighton-Callister, BSc (*Head of Applied Science*)
Collingwood House: Mrs L A Nicholls, BA (*Geography*)

Teaching Staff:
G J Wheeler, BEd (*Head of Design & Technology*)
Miss A James, BA (*Design & Technology*)
Mrs C V Collins, MA, DIDipSpLD (*Head of SEN*)
Mrs J Cottrell, BA (*SEN*)
Mrs L Longthorn, BA (*Head of Business Studies, Economics & Accounting*)
Ms S Collinson, BA (*Business Studies*)
J O'Sullivan (*Economics & Business Studies*)
Ms J Schulte im Hof (*Economics*)
M J Archer, BSc (*Curriculum Leader Science*)
Ms S Knight, MChem (*Chemistry*)
Dr R Rose, MA, MSc, PhD (*Chemistry*)
J Clements, BEng (*Head of Physics*)
Ms C Brasher, BSc, MSc (*Physics*)
B D Cadenhead, BSc (*Physics, Careers Advisor*)
Mrs A M Creed, BSc, CertEd (*Biology*)
I Williams, BSc (*Biology*)
Mrs V Ralph, BSc (*Science*)
Miss K F Elliott, BA (*Head of ESOL*)
W H Helsby, BA, RSADipTEFL (*ESOL*)
Mrs J A White, BSc, RSADipTEFLA (*ESOL*)
Mrs L A Wong, BSc, PGCE, RSADipTEFLA (*ESOL*)
W H Day-Lewis, BA DiELTA (*Head of Development Year*)
Mrs N J Halford Scott, BA (*Head of History*)
K Patrick, BA (*History*)
R Pender, BSc (*Head of Geography*)
T R Brown, BA (*Head of Media Studies*)

R Beamish, BA (*English & Media*)
E O Jenkins, BA (*Director of Music*)
Miss G Leach, BA (*Music*)
Mrs S Matthews, BSc (*Head of Psychology*)
Mrs H S Phelps, BA, BSc, MSc (*Psychology*)
A C Naish, BSc (*Director of Sport*)
M J Kimber, New Zealand Coaching Cert, ECB Level 1, RFU Levels I & II (*Head of Boys' Games*)
Miss S M Pearce, BSc (*Head of Girls' Games*)
J Garrow, Level 2 Rowing Coaching (*Rowing Coach*)
S R Garley, BAF (*Fencing Coach*)
Miss J Howard, BA (*Games Teacher*)
Major P N Rothwell (*OC CCF; Physical Education*)
Miss A Dibbs, BA (*Head of Mathematics*)
Miss N Borovac, BEng (*Mathematics*)
P Burford, BSc (*Mathematics*)
Miss E Martin, BSc I (*Mathematics*)
I Russell, BSc (*Mathematics*)
P D Scott, MBioChem (*Mathematics*)
Mrs B Cooke, BA (*ICT*)
Mrs E J Hughes, BSc (*ICT*)
Mrs H P Williams, BA (*Head of English*)
Miss E Brown, BA (*English*)
Ms E Lambert, BA (*English*)
J J Pyle, BA (*English*)
Miss A M Williams, BA (*English*)
Miss J Wilson, BA (*English*)
Mrs N Golightly, BEd (*Drama*)
Miss S Rosser, MA (*Drama*)
Mrs J Smith, BA (*Curriculum Leader Modern Languages, French & Spanish*)
Dr T Bailey, BA, MA, PhD (*Head of German*)
Ms S Revie, BA (*Head of Japanese*)
Miss L Gomez, BA (*Head of Spanish*)
Miss C Green, BA (*Japanese & French*)
Mrs M Hardwick, MA (*French & Spanish*)
M Martinez, PGCE (*Spanish*)
Ms M Sartore-Wallace, BA, MA (*French & Spanish*)
Mrs S Suzui (*Japanese*)
Miss N Green, BA (*Art*)
S J Hubbard, BA (*Art*)
Mrs R Wordsworth, BA (*Artist in Residence, Ceramics & Photography*)
Mrs P M Rhymes, BSc (*Careers Education Manager*)

Teaching Support Staff:
T Dyer, BSc Eng (*Engineering Projects*)
Mrs S A Hodgkins (*Librarian*)
Mrs M Bray (*Teaching Assistant*)
R Feather, BA (*Data & Exams Manager*)

Visiting Music Staff:
M Bucher, DipPerc (*Percussion*)
I Dollins, BMus, ARCM (*Voice & Piano*)
G Rees, Dip Trpt (*Trumpet*)
Mrs V Green, GRSM, ARCM, LRAM (*Piano & Double Bass*)
Mrs M Cope, GMus, LTCL, CT ABRSM (*Piano*)
Mrs S Blewett, FTCL, LTCL, LWCMD (*Flute*)
N Nash (*Saxophone*)
Miss J Orsman, GBSM (*Violin*)
P Reynolds, BA (*Guitar*)
Mrs R Howgego, MA, LRAM, DipRAM (*Violoncello*)
Mrs D Denton (*Keyboard*)
Mrs T Pemberton (*Oboe*)
J Harris (*Harp*)

Medical Officers and Staff:
Dr J Sivyer, MBChB, DRCOG, & Partners
Mrs J Lewis (*School Nurse*)
Mrs P Norman (*School Nurse*)

Administration:
Director of Operations: Mrs A Bromley
Director of Marketing: Mrs M Gray

HR Manager: Mrs C Rimell MCIPD
Alumni Relations Manager: Mrs C Roberts
School Secretary: Mrs C Glynn
Registrar: Miss C Phillips
Head's PA: Mrs D McCarthy

Preparatory School
(*see also entry in IAPS section*)

Headmaster: A Palmer, MA, BEd
Headmaster's Wife: Mrs J Palmer, CertEd
Deputy Head: Mrs V Jackson, BA
Director of Pastoral Care: Mrs L Askew, LAMDA (*Head of Drama*)

Teaching Staff:
S J Arman, BEd (*Head of Shaftesbury; Head of Humanities*)
Mrs J Baylis, Clait, NVQ3
D Broadhead, BA
Mrs C Brown, BA (*Head of Lincoln; Head of Modern Foreign Languages*)
Mrs A Cleere, BEd
P Duffy, BMus (*Director of Music*)
Miss C Flowers, BSc
Mrs S Fynn, BA (*Middle Prep Manager*)
R Gaunt, BA QTS (*Head of Mathematics*)
Mrs N Gaunt, BEd
Mrs L Gillard, BSc (*Head of Geography*)
Mrs C Graham, BSc
C Guest, BSc (*Head of Scott; Head of SEN*)
W A Humphreys, BEd (*Able Pupils Coordinator*)
R Irwin, BSc
Mrs Y Martin, BEd
Mrs E Muszasty, Dip HE
J D Newns, CertEd (*Head of Grenfell; Head of Games*)
Mrs A Oliver, BEd (*Head of Lower Prep*)
H Parsons, BSc (*Head of Science*)
Miss M Potts, BA (*Head of ICT*)
Mme N Robinson, BA
Ms S Sabin, BEd
Mrs E Shearer, BEd
Mrs L Sherwood, SENAC
A Sinclair, BA
Mrs C Stanley, BA
M Stopforth, BA (*Head of Art & DT*)
G Stotesbury, BA
Miss E Upadhyay, BEd
Mrs N C Warden, BEd (*Head of Girls' Games*)
Mrs S Warren, BEd
Ms R White, BEd (*Head of English*)
Mrs C Young, BEd (*Upper Prep Manager*)

Boarding House Staff:
Mrs C Williams
Mrs L Field
Mrs A Chappell
Mrs J Bloodworth

Matrons:
Mrs S Phillips
Mrs A Seymour

Administration Staff:
School Secretary: Mrs J Fisk
Registrar: Mrs W Robertson
Head's PA: Mrs S Rogers

Nursery:
Mrs C Marsh (*Nursery Manager*)
Mrs A Hawes (*Assistant Nursery Manager*)
Miss C Holmes
Mrs B Overs
Mrs C Taylor
Miss S Tyndall
Mrs S Weaving
Miss C Woollard

Mrs C Young

Out of School Care:
Mrs R Sampson
Mrs L Summers

Location. Wycliffe is in a semi-rural setting of 60 acres, blending the best of traditional and modern. The School has excellent transport links: M5 (J13) 2 miles; Stonehouse Railway Station 200 metres; London Paddington under 2 hours; Bristol, Birmingham and Heathrow Airports 50-90 minutes. A flexi-boarding Day House opened in January 2003, a new Sports Centre in January 2004, and an Advanced Learning Centre in September 2004. The Preparatory School (under its own Headmaster) is on a separate, adjacent campus with extensive facilities including a new Performing Arts Centre, Dining Hall and refurbished swimming pool.

Organisation. Senior School 13–18: 259 Boys, 153 Girls, 323 Boarders, Sixth Form c 176. Class sizes vary from 3–17 pupils. Preparatory School 2–13: 200 Boys, 163 Girls.

Admission. Pupils are admitted at key entry points following interview and assessment, via Common Entrance or Scholarship examinations at 13+ and via GCSE or Scholarship examinations into the Sixth Form. Application should be made to the Head who is whole-hearted in her desire for all pupils to achieve their full potential in every sphere of education and undertakes to be readily available to parents.

Religion. Christian interdenominational, all faiths welcome. Confirmation classes, Christian Fellowship group and daily worship in keeping with this generation are an integral part of College life.

Houses. Wycliffe's House system promotes a strong sense of community, building staunch friendships and promoting healthy competition, and ensuring high levels of personal and pastoral care. There are eight Houses with dedicated study areas for day pupils and three Sixth Form Halls of Residence, each with study-bedrooms and en-suite facilities. All boarding houses are refurbished on a rolling programme. Main meals are taken in the award-winning Wycliffe Hall.

Tutors. Each pupil has a House-based tutor in the Lower School and a specialist tutor in the Sixth Form. Supported by a Housemaster/Housemistress, Tutor, Chaplain and Head of Year, each pupil gains maximum advantage towards personal fulfilment in a community noted for its friendly and caring support.

Medical Centre. 24-hour attendance is provided by qualified staff in a state-of-the-art Centre. The Health Centre is nearby. Special dietary requirements for health or faith are met by first-class catering facilities.

Development Year. The Development Year (DY) is for international pupils who wish to study at A Level but who may not yet be ready for its challenges. DY aims to develop not just their English but also to improve their study skills and subject knowledge to a level adequate for studying alongside British pupils. Pupils are fully integrated into all aspects of school life, yet their lessons are targeted to their needs rather than purely exam focussed. Development Year (DY) pupils must study a broad range of subjects including English, Maths and the Sciences; they also receive an introduction to a large proportion of subjects offered at A Level. This might include a second foreign language, such as Japanese or Spanish, media studies, psychology, business studies, geography, art or drama.

A Levels. As a general rule students choose four, or occasionally five, AS subjects to study in the Lower Sixth or one of two available BTEC courses. Most students then continue to study three subjects in the second year to A2 Level. Apart from the traditional subjects, the following are also on offer to A2 Level: Art and Design, Design and Technology, Japanese, Psychology, Business Studies, Media Studies, Government and Politics, Theatre Studies, Music Technology and Physical Education.

GCSEs are usually taken three years after 13+ entry. The School offers a wide range of subjects supported by outstanding tutorial practices. Four modern languages and four sciences are among those on offer to students who may make a free choice at age 14.

Scholarships and Awards. (*See Scholarship Entries section.*) Thanks to the generosity of Trustees, Old Wycliffians and Friends of Wycliffe, awards are available offering a reduction of up to 40% of the fees. These may be supplemented in cases of financial need up to a maximum of 90%.

For 13+ entry a candidate must be under 14 on 1 September of year of entry and sit the examination in the Spring Term.

For 16+ entry, examinations are held in the Autumn prior to arrival or by arrangement.

At other ages, applications to be made to the Head.

Awards are made to candidates with academic talent or potential and also specifically in music, art, design technology, IT, drama and sport including pupils highly talented in cricket, rugby, girls' hockey, netball, squash, rowing and fencing.

Special awards are also available to (a) those with all round merit, (b) children of serving members of the Services (up to 25% Forces Bursaries), (c) vegetarians.

Physical Education. Our sports and physical education programme gives opportunities to develop talents and skills and to enjoy sport as a team member, individual or for recreation. We recognise and support gifted sports players and have the facilities to offer a wide range of sports such as rowing, rugby, hockey, soccer, netball, squash, badminton, basketball, swimming, cricket, tennis, athletics, health and fitness, shooting, and cross country.

Training for Service is available via the Combined Cadet Force, Duke of Edinburgh's Award Scheme, Leadership Courses, and the Wycliffe Charitable Organisation.

International Travel is regularly organised for varied groups; trips can enhance academic study, provide exchanges with our sister schools in Chicago and Osaka, be part of the Comenius partnership with schools in Europe or specific sporting or musical tours. Pupil trips and exchanges are arranged for those studying foreign languages.

School Societies. Among 90 available are Drama Workshops, Stage Management, Philosophy, Language, Debating, Archaeology, Pottery, Craft, Computing, Electronics, Astronomy, Shooting, Choral, Instrumental Music, First Aid, Cookery, Dance and a Sixth Form Club.

Sunday Specials. Brunch is a highlight of Sunday morning and a variety of activities, both at the College and locally, are organised for boarders.

Music. A purpose-built music school including a dedicated Music Technology suite with enthusiastic staff enables high standards to be achieved. Music is taken at GCSE and A Level with Music Technology also offered at A Level; several pupils each year continue their music studies at the Conservatoires and universities. There are two choirs, numerous large ensembles and bespoke chamber ensembles developing a high level of performance in all styles of music. Associated Board Examinations are taken every term as well as Trinity and Rock school exams. The School hosts professional concerts and dramatic productions annually as well as the School's own artistic output.

Careers Guidance forms a vital department which is recognised as a centre of excellence. The College has its own experienced Careers Manager who is available to advise and support students throughout the school day. The Careers Library is well-equipped with information on careers and entrance to Higher Education.

Teacher Training. Wycliffe has been selected as a training centre for teachers, reflecting the high esteem in which the College is held.

Fees per term (2011-2012). Senior School: Boarders £8,570–£8,670, new Sixth Form entrants £9,240, Development Year £9,995; Day pupils £5,120–£5,600, Development

Year £7,815. Preparatory School: Boarders £4,925–£6,270, Foundation Year £7,250, Residential Short English Course £625 per week; Day pupils: £1,870–£3,865.

Extras are kept to a minimum but may include expeditions and certain Society subscriptions.

Alumni. The Old Wycliffian Society supports OWs through its website, mailings, reunions, OW Carol Service, and a termly issue of the Wycliffe magazine. Visit the OWS website: www.wycliffe.co.uk or contact the OW Registrar tel: 01453 820439, e-mail: ow@wycliffe.co.uk for further details.

Charitable status. Wycliffe College Incorporated is a Registered Charity, number 311714. It exists to provide education for boys and girls.

Yarm School

The Friarage, Yarm, Stockton-on-Tees TS15 9EJ
Tel: 01642 786023
Fax: 01642 789216
e-mail: dmd@yarmschool.org
website: www.yarmschool.org

Yarm School, a co-educational day school, was established in its present form in 1978. It has its own co-educational Preparatory School for pupils from 4 to 11 years of age and a nursery for 3 year olds.

Governing Body:
Chair: Ms C Evans, MA, MBA, ARCM
Vice-Chairman: A W Wright, BSc

Mrs S Anderson, FCA, BSc
Dr A Bonavia, MBChB, MRCGP
Mrs S E Cardew, MSc
His Honour Judge J de Guise Walford
C G Edmundson, MA, FRCO CHM, ADCM, ARCM, FRSA
J M James, BA, FCA, CTA
Dr R S Sagoo, MBChB
M Thompson, BA, ACMA
A Thomson, LLB, FCCA, FIDM

Headmaster: D M Dunn, BA

Deputy Headmaster: D G Woodward, BSc, CBiol, MIBiol
Director of Studies: J Ferstenberg, BA, JD
Head of Sixth Form: Dr A M Goodall, MA, PhD
Head of Middle School: Mrs K A Gratton, BEd

Senior Master: §Dr P M Chapman, MA, PhD

Headmaster's PA: Mrs J L Herbert, BSc, MIL

* *Head of Department*
† *Housemaster/mistress*
§ *Part-time*

G Addison, BSc
Mrs J C Ankers, BA
J E Armitage, BSc (*Head of Fifth Year*)
Ms H Blakemore, BA
G C Booth, MA
Ms R L Bownas, BSc
*K R Brown, BMus, ALCM, FGMS, FRSA
*I H Burns, BSc
*I T Chamberlain, MA, MA
§Mrs P Clarke, BSc
*P J Connery, MA, BA
Miss S Cottrell, BEd
S H A Crabtree, BSc (*Head of Careers*)

*E M Craig, BA
§P E Crookes, MA
§Mrs R M Crookes, BA
T J Day, CertEd
Mrs F C Dunn, BEd (*Deputy Head of Sixth Form*)
*D V G Dunn, MA, BA
W P Eastwood, BSc
S Edwards, BA, MPhil
G Emerson, BA (*Head of Fourth Year*)
T L Foggett, MSc, BA, BSc
*A I Guest, BEd
§Mrs J L Guest, BEd (*Head of Second Year*)
Mr J S Hall, BA

*Mrs E L Harrison, BA
S P Hardy, BEd
§Mrs S M Heavers, BA
*Frau J Heinen, MA
§J G Hulme, BSc
§Mrs A Jackson, BSc (*†Oswald*)
*§H A Killick, BA, MPhil, ARCM
§ Mrs L Kneale, BA
*A D Law, MA
Mrs G A Leary, BA (*Head of Third Year*)
§Mrs J R Menzies, BA
A J Morrison, BA
C P Mulligan, BSc (*Head of First Year*)
*A O Newman, BA
*Mrs J H Nickson, BA, CPE Law
*§ Mrs J Nixon, BA
*Ms M J Pallister, BSc
T J Parker, BA
*T D J Pender, BA
*Dr K W Perry, BSc, PhD
Dr P D Prideaux, BSc, PhD (*†Bede*)

§Mrs S J Pyke, MA (*†Aidan*)
*S R Ravenhall, BA, MPhil
Mrs S M Rea, BA, MEd
Miss N E Redhead, BEd
Miss C E Rhodes, BSc
Miss E C Robinson, BA (*†Cuthbert*)
§Mrs D E Ruston, BA
M C Rye, BA
§Mrs H C Salvage, BSc, MBA
§Miss K F Serdecka, BA, BSc, CertSocSci
P C Skerratt, BA
§Mrs S Snape, BA, PGDip
*Ms E Stebbings, BA
I Stewart, BSc
P N Telfer, BA
C Thomas, BEd
Mrs G Thompson, CertEd
S M Thompson, BSc
§A A D Tulloch, MChem, PhD
C A C Webb, BA
§Mrs H L Walton, BSc
Miss K E Woodhead, MSci

School Manager: Mrs N L Brown, LLM

Preparatory School

Headmaster: W J Toleman, BA

Deputy Headmaster: G N Stone, BEd, MA
Director of Studies: S G Pearce, BA, BEd, ADEE
Early School Coordinator: Mrs J Speight, BEd, QTS
Head of Yarm at Raventhorpe: D Boddy, BA, MCIEA, FCollT

Mrs A Arrol, BA, PGCE
Mrs J J Catterall, CertEd
§Mrs F A Cook, LGSM, ALCM
Mrs P Covell, BEd
C R Davis, BEd
§Mrs B Desmond, BEd
Mrs A J Gray, BEd
J Grundmann, BSc
Miss R Hall, BEd
K Harandon, BA, MA
Dr R G Harrison, BMus, PhD
Mrs V Harrison, BPhil, PGCE
§Mrs S Heavers, BA
Mrs H N Jones, BEd
Mrs K Mavin, BSc, QTS
Mrs H J McCormack, BA, PGCE
Miss K Moran, BA

Mrs C A Pearce, BA, Cert TESOL
§Mrs J Pratt
Miss F E H Rogers, BA, PGCE
Miss L H Rowlands, BMus, QTS
M Sellers, BSc
§Mrs S Snape, BA, PGDip
Mrs A White, BEd
Mrs C Williams, BEd, MA

Teaching Assistants:
Miss R Clarke, BTEC Nat Dip
Mrs J Jones, NNEB
Miss K L Phillips
Mrs G Selby, PPA Cert
§Mrs D M Symington
§Mrs S Thomas, NCFE St2

There are about 1,000 pupils in the School including 330 pupils aged 3 to 11 years who are in a separate Preparatory School (*see entry in IAPS section*). There are about 200 in the Sixth Form. The school is fully co-educational. The School also owns and runs a satellite Preparatory School in Darlington for pupils aged 3–11. Known as Yarm at Raventhorpe, it can accommodate 100 pupils.

Situation and Buildings. Yarm School is situated in the attractive and historic town of Yarm on a beautiful site with the River Tees running through it.

The Senior School is set around The Friarage (an impressive eighteenth century mansion). There are outstanding facilities, including a first-rate science and design technology building, Sixth Form Centre, sports hall, fitness suite and two all-weather, floodlit pitches. A performing arts centre for music, dance and drama is under construction and will be ready in late 2011.

The Preparatory School, opened in 1991 in response to public demand for traditional preparatory school education, occupies an adjacent site and also has a range of first-class facilities.

Admission. Pupils are admitted to the Senior School at 11 and 16 by means of the School's own Entrance Examination. The Preparatory School has its own entrance procedures.

Curriculum. The School's academic reputation in the area is high and virtually all leavers go on to take university degrees. In 2010 over 12% of the leavers went to Medical School and a further 8% to Oxbridge.

In the Preparatory School the curriculum is both wide ranging and demanding. Whilst the basics in English and Mathematics are given great emphasis, the Sciences, Technology and Modern Languages also form an important part of the timetable.

In Year 7 all pupils study the following subjects: English, Mathematics, Physics, Chemistry, Biology, Technology, French, German, Latin, History, Geography, Information Technology, Art, RS and Music. Setting by ability takes place in Mathematics, English and Modern Languages. In Year 8 there is also setting in the Sciences. GCSE is taken as a two-year course comprising seven compulsory core subjects (English, English Literature, Mathematics, German or French, Physics, Chemistry and Biology) and 3 or more options. Options can usually be selected from French, German, Spanish, Latin, Classical Studies, Greek, History, Geography, Information Technology, Technology, Design and Realisation, Art, PE, Music and Religious Studies. The more able pupils (perhaps a third or more of a year group) will take IGCSE Mathematics and Classics a year early enabling them to take these subjects to levels beyond GCSE whilst still in Year 11.

In the Sixth Form A Levels are selected from about twenty options. All Lower Sixth students take 4 AS Levels and 3 or 4 A2s in the Upper Sixth. General Studies is also taught in the Upper Sixth.

Modern languages are enhanced by means of regular exchanges with twin schools in France, Germany and Spain. Teams entered for nationwide Mathematics and Science/ Technology competitions have won several awards in the last three or four years.

Organisation. Pastoral care is based on both a year group and a House system. Every pupil belongs to one of four Houses for his/her whole school career. Houses exist to promote competitions, sports events, charity fundraising etc. Each pupil also has a personal Tutor and Head of Year whose task it is to look after all the pupils within a given year group. Sixth-formers have the opportunity to serve as House Monitors and School Prefects.

Games and Activities. The school believes firmly in "education for life" and has more sport and activities within its timetable than is offered in most schools. Its sporting reputation is enviable, with success being achieved right up to national level and the wide range of sports offered caters for most tastes and both genders.

Rugby, hockey, rowing, football and netball are the School's main winter games and there are representative teams in these sports for all age levels. In the summer, rowing, cricket, tennis and athletics become the major sports. In addition canoeing, squash, orienteering and cross-country are also pursued at inter-school level throughout the year. Several other games are available as options.

There are many school societies. A great deal of extra-curricular activity is centred on the Duke of Edinburgh's Award Scheme. Rock climbing, canoeing and other aspects of outdoor education are given some prominence and residential weekends at an outdoor pursuits centre are a fixed part of the curriculum. There is a flourishing CCF contin-

gent (membership, though popular, is entirely voluntary). School excursions are frequent and very varied. Expeditions in recent years have travelled as far as India, America and Guyana. Drama (at least three major productions a year) and Music (several choir and orchestral concerts are given each year) are given every encouragement and have a strong following. Activities which are an extension of Art or Technology or Biology also flourish particularly well.

Religion. The School is an inter-denominational community comprising pupils of both Christian and non-Christian backgrounds. There are regular assemblies and occasional services held in the local Parish Church.

Fees per term (2011-2012). Senior School £3,539; Preparatory School £2,669–£2,953; Early School/Nursery £2,096–£2,132; Early School/Nursery (for children qualifying for Nursery Grant) £1,436. Lunches are extra.

Scholarships and Bursaries. (*See Scholarship Entries section.*) A range of scholarships and bursaries is available. Please contact the School for further details.

Former Pupils. Past members of the School are eligible to join the Former Pupils' Society whose Hon Secretary may be contacted via the School Office.

Charitable status. Yarm School is a Registered Charity, number 1093434. It exists to provide quality education for boys and girls.

Entrance Scholarships

Abingdon School (see p 7)

The majority of awards are made at 13+ entry and are open to external and internal candidates. Some additional awards are available on entry to Sixth Form and to the Lower School. All scholarships and bursaries are means-tested. Scholarships carry an entitlement to a nominal fee remission of £300 per year plus remission of up to 100% of the tuition fee on a means-tested bursary basis. Music Scholarships also carry an entitlement to remission on instrument tuition fees. Many of our awards carry names of benefactors who have given funds or supported the school, such as the Duxbury Scholarship and the Mercers' Company Scholarship.

Academic Awards:

A number of awards are available at 11+.

Between 15 and 18 scholarships available at 13+.

A flexible number of scholarships is awarded on entry to the Sixth Form.

Ackworth School (see p 8)

Academic Scholarships are awarded annually. At ages 11+, 12+ and 13+ the awards are made on the basis of performance at the Entrance Tests and a subsequent interview.

At Sixth Form level an offer of a Scholarship is made following a scholarship examination and interview in February.

Bursaries are also available for Members or Attenders of the Society of Friends and in other cases where need can be shown.

Aldenham School (see p 10)

Available at each point of entry, Scholarships and Exhibitions are awarded to boys and girls who have demonstrated outstanding achievement and who have the potential to make a special contribution to the School. In addition to Academic there are also opportunities for Music, Art, Sport and Design Technology scholarships and exhibitions.

Alleyn's School (see p 11)

At 11+ and 13+ Academic scholarships of up to £3,000 pa, plus Art, Music and Sports scholarships. Means-tested bursaries available for academically able candidates of up to 100% fees.

At 16+: Academic and Music scholarships, plus means-tested bursaries available for academically able candidates of up to 100% fees.

Ampleforth College (see p 13)

Scholarships are awarded annually on the results of examinations held at Ampleforth. They are honorary and carry no remission of fees. However, the award of a scholarship will support a bursary application.

Academic Scholarships at 13+. ISEB Common Academic Scholarship examinations are sat in February.

Sixth Form Entry. Academic Scholarship examinations are held in November.

Further details can be obtained from The Admissions Office, Ampleforth College, York, YO62 4ER. Tel: 01439 766863; e-mail: admissions@ampleforth.org.uk.

Arnold School (see p 17)

Several scholarships (including those for Music, Art & Design, and Sport) are available for entry at 11+. Music, Sport, Art & Design and Drama scholarships are available in the Sixth Form. United Church Schools Foundation Assisted Places are also available. Further particulars from the Admissions Secretary (01253 346391).

Ashford School (see p 18)

Academic, sport and music scholarships are available at Year 5. Academic, art & design, sport and music scholarships are available in Years 7, 9 and 12 with theatre arts additionally in Year 12. Further details may be obtained from the Head.

Bancroft's School (see p 22)

The School awards up to 15 Scholarships at 11+ entry; these are typically worth one half, one third or one quarter of school fees and are awarded on the basis of performance in the school's 11+ Entrance Examination. Two of the Scholarships may be Music Scholarships; these are worth up to 50% of fees plus extra music tuition. Up to five Francis Bancroft Scholarships, which are means tested and which can cover the full fees, are awarded at age 11 as a result of the school's Entrance Examination in January. Two means-tested Francis Bancroft Scholarships are available for entrants to the Prep School at age 7; these only cover Prep School fees. There are five Scholarships worth up to 50% of the fees for Sixth Form entrants which may include Music awards. Means-tested Scholarships may also be available for entrants at 13+ and into the Sixth Form.

Barnard Castle School (see p 25)

Scholarships are awarded to entrants to the Senior School at any level including the Sixth Form, on the basis of the School's own examinations held in February. As well as academic scholarships, awards may be made for Music, Art, Sport or all-round ability. The School also has a small number of means-tested Assisted Places. Particulars from the *Headmaster's Secretary*.

Bedales School (see p 27)

Academic scholarships are available for entry at 13+ and 16+; Music scholarships for entry to Dunhurst (10+ and older; exceptionally, 8+) and to Bedales (13+ and 16+); Art scholarships for entry at 13+ and 16+.

The basic award for scholarships is £750, which can be increased through means-testing.

Means-tested bursaries are also available to those of proven need.

For full details of the scholarships and timing of assessment, please apply to the Registrar.

Bedford School (see p 31)

Awards are available for boys joining the School at our 11+, 13+ and 16+ entry points.

For more information about Bedford's Access Awards & Scholarships, please visit our website www.bedfordschool.org.uk.

Berkhamsted School (see p 35)

Academic Scholarships are awarded on the basis of academic merit alone on entrance to the School.

Who can apply? Applications are welcome from pupils who qualify from their performance in the Entrance Examination and sit Scholarship Examinations in English, Mathematics and other appropriate subjects. These are usually only at 11+, 13+ and 16+.

Incent Awards are made to talented pupils from financially or socially disadvantaged backgrounds.

They are awarded to enable pupils who would not otherwise be able to attend Berkhamsted, to afford to do so.

Candidates must demonstrate academic potential or have a particular talent(s) or skill(s) so that they will make a significant contribution to some other area of School life.

The Award shall be up to 100% of the school fees, and, where appropriate, will also include financial assistance for School uniform and sports kit, travel to and from school, school trips and expeditions, extra lessons e.g. Music, Drama etc if applicable.

Whilst most applications for Incent Awards will be received from candidates who are presently in maintained sector schools, Berkhamsted does work with a number of feeder schools in the independent sector who offer awards on a similar basis and thus will entertain applications from pupils who are presently in receipt of means-tested awards of this nature.

Bursaries are awarded for academic or other merit, taking into account parental income and pupils' needs.

Music, Drama, Art and Sports Scholarships are also offered.

More information about all Scholarships and Bursaries may be obtained on application to The Director of External Relations.

Birkdale School (see p 37)

11+ Scholarships: One Open Scholarship is offered, and up to three Foundation Awards are available only to candidates attending maintained junior Schools. The value of each Scholarship is up to 25% of tuition fees, but bursaries are available to increase the award to 100% of fees in case of proven financial need. Candidates should be under the age of twelve on 1 September and must excel in the School's 11+ Entrance Tests and subsequent Scholarship Examinations. Assessments take place early in the Easter Term.

16+ Scholarships: One Open Scholarship is offered, and up to four Foundation Scholarships are available only to new entrants to the co-educational Sixth Form. The value of each Scholarship is up to 25% of tuition fees, but bursaries are available to increase the awards to 100% in case of proven financial need. Additionally an Odgen Science Scholarship is available to a candidate from a maintained school. Assessments take place early in the Easter Term.

16+ Bursaries: A limited amount of Bursary funding is available for allocation to Sixth Form candidates for whom a Birkdale education would be beneficial but for whom there is a proven case of financial need. Assessments normally take place early in the Easter Term, but may be arranged at other times at the discretion of the Head Master.

Music Scholarships: Candidates must satisfy the school's general admission standards. One award is available at 11+ and one at 16+ of up to 25% of tuition fees plus free tuition by Birkdale staff on one instrument. Candidates should be of good Grade 3 (11+) or Grade 5/6 (16+) standard in their first instrument and show general musicianship commensurate with technical skill. A Music Scholar is expected to enter fully into the school's musical life. Assessments take place during the Easter Term.

Further details of the above awards are available from The Registrar.

Bishop's Stortford College (see p 41)

Scholarships are awarded at three levels: Sixth Form and under 14 in the Senior School, under 12 in the Junior School. There are Academic, Music and Art Awards available.

Bloxham School (see p 43)

Scholarships and Exhibitions are awarded on the basis of a competitive examination. The value of these awards is up to 20% of fees according to academic merit.

Among the awards offered are Roger Raymond Scholarships and John Schuster Scholarships (reserved in the first instance for Sons of Clergy or of members of the teaching profession). Boarding exhibitions may be awarded to sons of members of the HM Forces on the grounds of academic and/or all-round merit and promise.

Awards are made for all-round academic performance but subject Scholarships may be awarded for promising performances in a particular subject area. There are Art and Design Awards, Music Awards with free instrumental tuition, and Sports Awards (not at 11+). The auditions for the latter are held in February/March each year.

Day-boarders are eligible for all awards at equivalent value related to day-boarder fees. Candidates should preferably be under 14 on 1st September. An age allowance is made to young candidates.

Sir Lawrence Robson Scholarships or Exhibitions are awarded each year to Sixth Form entrants. The value of these will be up to 20% of fees. Candidates must be under 17 on 1st September. The examination is held in October.

Blundell's School (see p 45)

Open Scholarships and Exhibitions: Up to half of the chosen designation fee (ie boarding, weekly, flexi, day) are offered on the basis of our own examinations held in March (13+) and November (Sixth Form). Awards for Art, Music, Sport and All-round ability are also made. At 11+ Exhibitions only are awarded (January examination) and are deducted from the basic tuition fees.

Foundation Awards: Up to full day fees based on completion of a Statement of Financial Means. Candidates should be resident in the County of Devon and preference will be given to those living in the Borough of Tiverton.

Services Package available to the sons and daughters of serving members of the Armed Forces and Diplomatic Corps.

Awards may occasionally be supplemented by bursaries at the discretion of the Head Master.

Full details may be obtained from *The Registrars, Blundell's School, Tiverton, Devon EX16 4DN. Tel: 01884 252543.*

Bootham School (see p 48)

Academic Scholarships (Honorary and without fee reduction) are awarded on the basis of academic performance, for entry at 11+ and 13+ (Years 7 and 9). All candidates taking the entrance examination at the main sitting (usually held at the end of January in the year of entry) will be considered.

Sixth Form: We collaborate with the Ogden Trust to provide a means-tested Bursary to candidates who intend to study Physics at university.

Bradfield College (see p 50)

At 13+ awards are made on the results of a competitive examination held at the College in the Lent Term: up to five Stevens Academic Scholarships annually. Candidates must be under the age of 14 on 1 September. Further Honorary Awards conferring the status and privileges of a scholar are awarded at the end of the Year 11 (post GCSE).

At 16+ Scholarships, Exhibitions and Awards are awarded annually after competitive examinations in the Michaelmas Term.

All awards are augmentable according to financial need. Further information and entrance forms can be obtained on application to the Admissions Office.

Brentwood School (see p 54)

At 11+ and for entry to the Sixth Form Music, Drama, Art, Sport and Choral scholarships are awarded in addition to Academic scholarships. These may be supplemented by means-tested Bursaries.

The school offers a considerable number of Bursaries in addition to the awards described above. Over a fifth of pupils receive such assistance.

Further details are available from the Headmaster.

Brighton College (see p 56)

The following awards are offered annually:

Academic Scholarships to pupils entering the College at age 11 or 13 (for 13+ entry candidates should be under 14 on September 1st of the year of entry and for 11+, they should be under 12). Entries must be in by 1st April for 13+ and early January for 11+.

One or two *Gill Memorial Scholarships* for the children of Regular Army Officers (serving or retired) up to a maximum of £1,000 pa.

A number of *Art, Music, Drama and Dance Scholarships* are available for entry at 13+.

All-Rounder Scholarships are available for entry at 11+ and 13+.

Lloyd's Cuthbert Heath Memorial Bursary worth up to £1,000 pa awarded to a pupil wishing to enter the College at 13 who has a positive contribution to make to the life of the College, and whose parents would otherwise be unable to afford the fees.

A *Cooper Rawson Bursary* for children of Clergy. An award of up to £500 pa can be considered by the Committee which meets in June each year.

Sixth Form entry Scholarships: Candidates take papers in two A Level subjects plus general paper, or three A Level subjects. Entries by November 1st.

Further particulars can be obtained from the *Director of Admissions, Brighton College, Brighton BN2 0AL*.

Bristol Grammar School (see p 58)

The School offers fifteen scholarship awards to students joining BGS in Year 7 (each worth 25% remission of fees). Thirteen (Pople) Scholarships are awarded for academic excellence and a further two awards recognise specific talent in sport or the creative and performing arts. In addition to this the School offers four scholarship awards to students joining BGS in Year 9 (each worth 25% remission in fees). Two Scholarships are awarded for academic excellence and a further two awards recognise specific talent in sport or the performing and creative arts.

The School runs an Honours Programme designed to meet the educational needs of its most gifted students. This programme offers extended individual learning opportunities, group activities and mentoring in and out of School by the Leader of the Honours Students. At 16+ students may apply to become Subject Scholars and work more closely with Heads of Subject.

Bromsgrove School (see p 61)

Awards are made on the results of open examinations held at the school in January. A significant number of scholarships, means-tested bursaries and Foundation bursaries for pupils of academic, artistic, musical, sporting and all-round ability are awarded at 11+, 13+ and 16+. Any award may be augmented by means-tested bursaries in case of financial need. Further details are available from the Admissions Department.

Bryanston School (see p 64)

Academic, Art, ICT, DT, Music, Sport and Richard Hunter All-Rounder Scholarships are available annually for entry at 13+.

Academic and Music Scholarships and Udall Awards for Sport are available annually for entry to the Sixth Form.

Scholarships range in value and may be supplemented by means-tested bursaries.

Further details may be obtained from the Admissions Registrar.

Canford School (see p 70)

Scholarships. It is Canford's policy to encourage excellence and to enable pupils to come to the school who, without the assistance of a scholarship, would not be able to do so. In accordance with the agreement of the majority of HMC schools, Canford limits the value of any one scholarship to 50% of the fees. All Canford's scholarships are indexed as a percentage of the fees so that their relative value remains constant throughout the scholar's school career.

13+ Scholarships: Scholarship examinations are held in February and March for the following awards: Academic, Music and Sport scholarships worth from 10% to 50% of the fees; Art, Drama and Design Technology scholarships worth from 10% to 20% of the fees; an academic Royal Naval scholarship worth 20% of the fees to the son/daughter of a serving Naval Officer. Candidates must be in Year 8 at the time of the examination. All scholarships are tenable with effect from the September of the year in which they are awarded. Candidates may enter for more than one scholarship.

16+ Scholarships: Entrants to the school at Sixth Form level may apply for any combination of the following scholarships: Academic, Music, Assyrian (for extra-curricular excellence, including Sport). The examinations are held in the November prior to entry. Assyrian awards are offered for an extra-curricular contribution of excellent quality to school life and are worth from 10% to 40% of the fees;

Academic and Music scholarships are worth from 10% to 50% of the fees.

Further details about any awards can be obtained from The Registrar.

Caterham School (see p 73)

Academic scholarships are available at 11+, 13+ and 16+. They are awarded on the basis of examinations and interview. At 11+ and 13+ the awards are made on the basis of the entrance examinations and interviews; there is no separate scholarship examination and all candidates are automatically considered.

All-Rounder scholarships (for pupils entering at the age of 13), Music, Art and Sport scholarships at 11+, 13+ and 16+, Boarding scholarships and Sixth Form Science scholarships are also available.

Charterhouse (see p 75)

For entry at 13+. Up to 10 Foundation Scholarships and 5 Exhibitions are offered annually. The examination is held in May.

In addition a Benn Scholarship is offered for proficiency in Classics.

Five Peter Attenborough Awards are made annually to candidates who demonstrate all-round distinction.

2 Park House Awards are made annually to exceptional sportsmen.

The Blackstone Award, for sons of lawyers, is offered annually to boys when aged 11 for entry to Charterhouse at the age of 13.

For entry into the Sixth Form. The following awards are offered annually:

6 Sir Robert Birley Academic Scholarships and 7 Academic Exhibitions. In addition Music and Art Scholarships are offered (*see relevant sections*).

The Surrey Scholarship, sponsored by the University of Surrey, is awarded each year to a pupil entering the Sixth Form from a maintained school within the county.

All Awards (except Exhibitions) may be increased to the value of the full school fee in cases of proven financial need.

For full details apply to the Admissions Secretary, Charterhouse, Godalming, Surrey GU7 2DX.

Cheltenham College (see p 78)

Academic scholarships and exhibitions are available at 13+ and 16+ entry. Awards are also made for Music, Drama, Art, Sport, Design Technology and All-round.

Chigwell School (see p 83)

Academic scholarships are awarded at age 11 and 16. Art and Drama scholarships are awarded awarded at 16. Music scholarships are awarded at 11, 13 and 16.

Further details can be obtained from the Admissions Registrar; email: admissions@chigwell-school.org.

Christ College (see p 85)

Up to 10 Academic scholarships and exhibitions, tenable at 11+, 13+ and 16+ and ranging in value from 10 to 50% of the fees, are offered annually. Also available at 11+, 13+ and 16+ are Sports and Music scholarships and are of similar value. Available at 13+ and 16+ are Science scholarships also ranging from 10 to 50% of the fees. A partnership with a leading pharmaceutical company has resulted in a 50% science award for a 16+ pupil. In addition three scholarships are awarded each year to those entering the Sixth Form each worth £1500 a year: a Lord Brecon, Roydon Griffiths and a G John Herdman Scholarship. W G Fryer All-Rounder Scholarships are available at 13+ and 16+ each year.

Bursaries are available for sons and daughters of personnel serving in the Armed Forces. There is a remission of 25% of the fees for the sons and daughters of Clergy. The value of any award may be augmented in case of need.

Scholarship examinations are held at Christ College in early February (11+ and 13+). Age limits: seniors under 14 and juniors under 12 on 1st September in the year of examination.

Further details from The Head, Christ College, Brecon, Powys LD3 8AG.

City of London Freemen's School (see p 90)
City of London Scholarships are awarded as follows:

At 11+ up to 3 Scholarships of not more than 50% of the tuition fee, tenable for seven years. These Scholarships are awarded on the basis of performance in the School's Entrance Examination, school reports and an interview.

At 13+ up to 5 Scholarships of not more than 50% of the tuition fee, tenable for five years. These Scholarships are awarded on the basis of performance in the 13+ Scholarship examinations, school reports and an interview.

At 16+ (Sixth Form entry) up to 10 Scholarships are awarded of not more than 50% of the tuition fee tenable for two years. These Scholarships are awarded on the basis of performance in the Sixth Form Scholarship papers, school reports and an interview.

City of London School (see p 92)
The School offers at least 30 Academic Scholarships each year to the value of up to half the cost of school fees. These Scholarships are available at any of the normal entry points. For ages 10+, 11+ and 13+ a Scholarship interview is awarded on the strength of a candidate's performance in the School's normal entrance examinations, which take place in January. At 16+ an Academic Scholarship may be awarded on the strength of a candidate's GCSE results.

The School offers a number of means-tested Sponsored Awards at 11+ and 16+ entry to very bright candidates whose parents could not otherwise contemplate private education.

Clifton College (see p 96)
Entrance Scholarships: Candidates must be under 14 on 1 September. Boys and girls who are already in the School may compete. At least ten awards are made. The maximum value of scholarships will not exceed 25% of the fees, although awards will be augmented by a Bursary if need is shown.

There are special awards available for the sons and daughters of Old Cliftonians.

Scholarships are also awarded to boys and girls for entry to the Sixth Form.

Particulars of the conditions of examination from The Director of Admissions, Clifton College, Bristol BS8 3JH.

Cranleigh School (see p 103)
At 13+: Academic, Music and Art Awards are available, along with Eric Abbott Awards for candidates with at least one other clearly established area of excellence and the potential to have a positive impact on life at Cranleigh. In addition, Head's Awards are made, at his discretion, in recognition of attributes of a true Cranleighan – leadership, commitment and service. Music Awards include free musical tuition. In certain circumstances, additional consideration may be given to sons or daughters of public servants, members of the armed forces and clergy of the Church of England.

At Sixth Form: Academic, Music, Art and Eric Abbott Awards (for candidates of good academic ability with at least one other clearly established area of excellence) are offered.

All Awards are fees-linked and may be augmented in cases of proven financial need. Awards can be made to boys and girls already at the School if their progress merits it.

Full details of Awards can be obtained by telephoning 01483 276377.

Culford School (see p 105)
Scholarships and Exhibitions are awarded according to merit in the following categories:

At 7+: Academic Exhibitions

At 11+: Academic, Music, Tennis and Sport

At 13+: Academic, Art, Drama, Music, Tennis, Rugby, Sport and Design Technology

At 16+: Academic, Art, Drama, Music, Tennis, Rugby and Sport

At 11+ and 13+: Jubilee Scholarships for all-rounders who board are worth 25% of boarding fees.

At 16+: The William Miller Scholarship for a pupil studying sciences is worth up to 25% of tuition fees. The Arkwright Scholarship for a pupil studying design technology allows an amount over two years to be shared between the pupil and the School.

Tennis Scholarships and Exhibitions may be available at any age from 10+.

Bursaries are available to those in genuine financial need and for children from a Methodist background.

A generous Forces Allowance is available to parents who are serving members of the Armed Forces and are in receipt of the MOD CEA.

For further details apply to The Registrar, Culford School, Bury St. Edmunds, Suffolk IP28 6TX. Tel: 01284 385308, Fax: 01284 729146 e-mail: admissions@culford.co.uk.

Dauntsey's School (see p 108)
Scholarships and Exhibitions are awarded on examinations held in November (Sixth Form), January (First Form) and February (Third Form) for the following September.

There is a wide range of Scholarships available for entry into the Third form (Year 9) including: academic, music, art, drama, sport, DT, science and the Jolie Brise "All Rounder" scholarships.

Full particulars are available from the Registrar, Mrs Jo Sagers.

Dean Close School (see p 110)
A competitive examination is held annually at the school in February/March. All awards are open to both boys and girls. Candidates must be under 14 on 1 September in the year of the examination.

Academic Scholarship: ISEB Common Scholarship Examination, for which specimen papers are available from the ISEB. (Direct entry candidates should contact the Admissions Tutor.)

Awards are also offered at 11+ and 16+.

Denstone College (see p 112)
Scholarships and Exhibitions are available in the following categories – All-Rounder, Academic, Design and Technology, Art, Music, Drama, and Sport – and are at the discretion of the Headmaster. They are mainly awarded at the ages of 11, 13 and for Sixth Form entry. Scholarships carry a remission of up to 40% of the fees. Recently launched awards, which are usually made annually, are the Alastair Hignell Scholarship and the Governors' Award.

For further details please visit www.denstonecollege.org or contact the Admissions Secretary, Denstone College, Uttoxeter, Staffordshire ST14 5HN.

Dulwich College (see p 115)
Academic Scholarships are available for entry to the Junior School (Year 3), Lower School (Year 7) and Middle School (Year 9).

Specialist Scholarships: Music, Art and Sports Scholarships are available. Applicants are required to meet the academic requirements of the College at all points of entry.

Scholarships range in value from 10% to one-third of tuition fees and can be enhanced by Bursaries in cases of financial need. Scholarships may be held by day boys and boarders.

For further information please contact the Registrar, Mrs Sarah Betts, on 020 8299 9263 or by email: the.registrar@dulwich.org.uk.

Durham School (see p 118)
A generous range of Academic, Drama, Music, Art, Design and Technology and Sports Scholarships is available. These are means-tested awards.

Eastbourne College (see p 120)

Academic, Art, Design & Technology, Drama, Music and Sports Scholarships are offered up to 50% of the fees if candidates of sufficient merit present themselves. Candidates must be under 14 on 1st September.

Academic, Science and Music Scholarships are offered up to 50% of fees at 16 to pupils entering the College at Sixth Form level.

Entry forms for scholarships can be obtained from The Registrar.

The Edinburgh Academy (see p 122)

A number of Scholarships are offered for award to candidates of very high ability either academically or for Art, Music or Sport. Scholarships have a maximum value of £500 and are awarded on an annual basis. This is held by the School until the pupils leave at the end of the formal schooling or until their 17th birthday, whichever comes first. The examination is held in January. Means-tested Bursaries are also available, which can increase the award as required. Further details from the Admissions Secretary.

Ellesmere College (see p 126)

A wide range of Scholarships and Exhibitions recognising a range of talents is available. In cases of need, all these awards may be supplemented further. Regional and Foundation Awards are also available. Application forms are obtainable from the Headmaster.

Eltham College (see p 128)

Up to 20 Academic Scholarships awarded at 11+ entry, a couple at 13+ entry and up to 15 at 16+ entry. Annual value up to 50% of tuition fee for full time spent at the school, subject to academic review.

Further details from the Admissions Secretary.

Emanuel School (see p 130)

Scholarships, Exhibitions and Bursaries

There are three types of scholarship at Emanuel: Foundation Scholarships (50% reduction in fees), Dacre Scholarships (25%) and Normal scholarships (10%).

All types of scholarship can be topped up using school bursaries to a maximum of 100% of the school fee, depending on financial need. It is also possible for a pupil to apply for and be awarded a scholarship in more than one category. Categories can be added together.

Academic scholarships are awarded at 10+, 11+ and 13+ on the basis of outstanding performance in the school entrance examinations held in January. At 16+ Academic scholarships are awarded to internal candidates on the basis of internal tests and to external candidates on the basis of their performance in the interviews and assessment tests.

Candidates applying for Music, Art, Drama and Sports scholarships must meet the general criteria for admission to Emanuel (eg reach the required standard in the academic entrance examinations) before a scholarship can be awarded. Thereafter each department has specific criteria for their scholarship requirements.

Exhibitions are awards of up to £500 on the basis of a pupil's high attainment in the entrance exams.

Bursaries are intended to help parents of pupils who can demonstrate financial need. Most bursaries are used to top up scholarships.

Full details of Scholarships, Exhibitions and Bursaries can be found on the School Website or by contacting the Admissions Secretary.

Epsom College (see p 132)

Candidates may compete for one or more of the following types of Award: Academic, Music, Drama/Dance, Art, Design Technology, Sports, and Headmaster's Award (All-Rounder).

Eton College (see p 134)

The Examination for King's Scholarships is held at Eton in May in the year of entry. Candidates need to be registered by 1st March. Candidates must be under 14 (and over 12) on 1st September.

Subjects of Examination: All candidates take the following four papers: English, Mathematics A, General I (general questions requiring thought rather than knowledge) and Science. Each must also offer *THREE or more* of the following: French (written, aural, oral), Latin, Greek, Mathematics B, General II (Literature, the Arts, moral and religious issues, etc) and a paper combining History, Geography and Divinity.

A King's Scholarship is normally tenable for five years.

Full particulars and entry forms may be obtained from *The College Examination Secretary, Admissions Office, Eton College, Windsor SL4 6DB*.

Exeter School (see p 136)

Academic Scholarships and Exhibitions, in the form of an individual prize, are offered annually to pupils who excel in the School's entrance tests at 11+ and 13+. Music and Art Scholarships are awarded annually following audition/assessment and are conditional on applicants achieving the School's academic requirements for entry. A number of means-tested Governors' Awards may be available to external candidates whose parents could not afford to send them to Exeter School without financial assistance.

At age 7: Junior Academic Scholarships and Exhibitions, in the form of an individual prize.

At age 11: Senior Academic Scholarships and Exhibitions, in the form of an individual prize.

At age 13: Academic Scholarships, in the form of an individual prize.

At age 16: one Ogden Science Scholarship, means-tested, offering up to 100% discount off tuition fees.

Felsted School (see p 139)

Academic, Music, Drama, Art, Design & Technology and Sports Scholarships are awarded annually up to the value of 20% of the fees for entry at 13+ and to the Sixth Form. Bursaries are available to increase the awards in case of need up to 100% of the fees in certain cases. The examinations for the 13+ Scholarships take place in February and May and for the Sixth Form Scholarships in November and February.

Scholarships are also awarded at 11+ at Felsted Preparatory School and these may be carried through to the Senior School.

Arkwright Foundation Scholarships are also available to talented students in Design at 16+.

All-rounder Awards which recognise all-round ability or specific ability in one area are available on entry at 11, 13 and 16 years old.

Full particulars from the *The Admissions Registrar, Felsted School, Dunmow, Essex CM6 3LL*.

Fettes College (see p 141)

Scholarships to the value of 10% of the fees are available for candidates aged 11+, 13+ and 16+. Any scholarship award can be supplemented by means-tested bursaries that can cover the full cost of the fees.

General Scholarships as well as Music scholarships, Piping Scholarships, Art Scholarships and All-Rounder awards are available.

Children of members of HM Forces qualify for a reduction in fees and Special Bursaries (Todd) are available for descendents of Old Fettesians.

Full details of all awards are available from The Headmaster, Fettes College, Edinburgh EH4 1QX (Telephone: 0131 311 6701).

Forest School (see p 143)

Academic and Music Scholarships are available annually to pupils at 11+ and 16+. Drama, Sports and Art Awards are available at 16+, as well as awards sponsored by the Ogden Trust, Mulalley and Co, the Old Foresters, and the 175th Anniversary appeal.

Framlingham College (see p 146)
Scholarships are available at the following points of entry:
13+ and 16+: Academic, Art, Design & Technology, Music, Drama, and All-Rounder (including Sport).
Porter Science Scholarship (13+) is for excellence in Science.
Sixth Form Stapleton (Academic) Scholarships (16+) are available to students who are attaining academic excellence and have the potential to achieve 3 Grade As at A Level.

Frensham Heights (see p 147)
Scholarships and Exhibitions, limited to £750 and £400 respectively, are awarded for Academic distinction or exceptional promise in Music or the other Performing and Creative Arts at 11+, 13+ and for Sixth Form entry.
Candidates for the Music or the other Performing and Creative Arts awards need to satisfy the school's entrance requirements.
Candidates for Music awards are expected to have reached at least Grade 5 in one or more instruments or voice.
Bursaries are awarded on the basis of a means-tested assessment.

Giggleswick School (see p 150)
Generous academic scholarships and exhibitions are offered for boys and girls as boarding or day pupils. The examinations are held in February and may be taken at age 10/11 or at age 12/13 and for Sixth Form entry to Senior School. The following categories are available: Academic, All-Rounder, Music, Sports, Art (13+ and Sixth Form only), Drama and Design and Technology (Sixth Form entrants only). A leaflet containing full details of the awards and examinations can be obtained from the Registrar.

Glenalmond College (see p 155)
Up to 10 Scholarships and Exhibitions worth up to 10% of the fees are offered for competition each year; all awards can be increased in case of need. Also available annually are Music Scholarships worth up to 50% of the fees. Awards are also made for Art.
The Entrance Scholarship Examinations are usually held in March for younger pupils and in November for entrants to the Sixth Form. Candidates may be considered for an All-Rounder/Outstanding Talent Award.
Junior Scholarship candidates must be under 14 on 31 May of the year of entry. A short statement showing the scope of the examination will be forwarded on application, and copies of last year's papers may be obtained. Scholarship candidates will be examined at Glenalmond.
For further particulars application should be made to the *Warden, Glenalmond College, Perth PH1 3RY.*

Gresham's School (see p 159)
The School is extremely grateful to benefactors, in particular the Fishmongers' Company, for financing many of the awards below.
An Open Scholarship examination is held each year at Gresham's in late February or early March. Candidates are usually under 14 on 1st September in the year of entry.
As many as 15 Academic Scholarships are available to entrants each year and, though these generally represent a reduction of fees of up to 25%, in certain cases such scholarships may be increased, by way of a bursary, to 100%.
Some awards are restricted to pupils who are from state schools or pupils resident in Africa.
In addition to the above, awards may be made in Art, Drama, Music and Sport to promote these areas and to recognise excellence in them. These awards generally represent a fee reduction of between 25% and 33%, but for exceptional candidates can be increased to 50%.
Sixth Form Scholarships: Deserving candidates are assessed in November each year for acceptance into the Sixth Form in the following September and Academic Scholarships, as well as scholarships for those who are exceptional in Music, Art, Drama or Sport may be awarded. These generally represent a fee reduction of up to 25%,

though, in rare cases, such scholarships may be increased, by way of a bursary to 100%.

Guildford High School (see p 162)
Academic Scholarships are offered at 11+ and 16+. Academic Exhibitions (lesser award) are also available at 7+, 11+ and 16+.

Haileybury (see p 167)
Many scholarships are available upon entrance to Haileybury. Academic and Music awards are available for 11, 13 and 16 year old entrants, All-Rounder Awards at 11 and 13, Art at 13 and 16, and Technology at 13.
Scholarships and All-Rounder Awards can be awarded up to the value of 10% of school fees and are tenable for the whole of the pupil's career at Haileybury. No fee remission is awarded for Art or Technology Scholarships. Successful candidates will be awarded a book token to the value of £100.
Bursaries are available to increase awards, in cases of financial need, and can supplement up to 100% of the fees in some cases.
An Additional Information brochure is issued annually in September and this provides all appropriate information regarding dates and application procedure. This can be obtained from The Registrar, Haileybury, Hertford SG13 7NU or e-mail: registrar@haileybury.com. The Registry team will be pleased to discuss with parents any aspects of the scholarship procedure.

Hampton School (see p 169)
Scholarships (remitting up to 25%) are awarded for academic, musical, artistic and all-round merit on entry at 11+ and 13+.

Harrow School (see p 173)
The examination takes place annually in March at Harrow. About 12 Academic Scholarships of up to 5% of the fees. Up to 6 Scholarships each year can be supplemented to the full amount of the school fees in cases of proved financial need. These supplementable Scholarships are awarded only to boys of good academic ability. In addition fifteen awards are made for excellence in Music, Sport, Design Technology or Art, some of which can be supplemented with means-tested bursaries. Full particulars and forms of application can be obtained from The Admissions Secretary.

Hereford Cathedral School (see p 175)
Up to 8 Dean's Scholarships are awarded as a result of the Junior Entrance and 11+ Scholarship Examination. Up to 3 Dean's Scholarships are also awarded at 13+. Up to 8 Dean's Scholarships are competed for entry to the Sixth Form. Sports Scholarships and Music Scholarships are also available. All Scholars are admitted to the Foundation by the Dean of Hereford each Autumn term.

Highgate School (see p 176)
Academic Awards are offered at 11+, 13+ and 16+. See website for details.

Hurstpierpoint College (see p 179)
Scholarship examinations are held annually in May for candidates aged under 14 on 1st June of the year of entry and awards are offered for Academic Scholarships. All-Rounder, Art, Drama, IT, Design & Technology, and Sports Scholarships are held in March. Awards for Music Scholarships are offered in February for entrance into the Prep School or Senior School the following September.
Sixth Form awards are offered to external candidates for Academic, All-Rounder, Art, Drama, IT, Design & Technology, Music and Sports.
Supplementary means-tested bursaries may be available for scholarship entrants.

Ipswich School (see p 186)
Academic Scholarships, known as Queen's Scholarships commemorating the Royal Charter granted to the School by Queen Elizabeth 1 in 1566, are available for external candi-

dates at 11, 13 and 16. Academic Scholarships of up to half fees are awarded on the basis of examinations and interviews at 11 and 13, and for the Sixth Form on the basis of school reports, predicted GCSE grades, interview and scholarship essay.

Ogden Trust awards are also available to pupils from State Schools wishing to study Maths and Physics in the Sixth Form. The Ogden Trust awards are restricted to those whose parents have a relatively low income.

The John Lyon School (see p 187)
Scholarships normally provide for between 5% and 20% of tuition fees.

Academic and All-Rounder Scholarships will be awarded to outstanding boys entering through the School Entrance Examinations at 11+ and 13+. Additional Academic Scholarships are available to Sixth Form entrants on the basis of outstanding performance at GCSE.

Art & Design, Drama, Music and Sports Scholarships are also available at 11+, 13+ and 16+.

Kelly College (see p 189)
Entrance Scholarships are available ranging from 10% to 40%. Our Entrance Scholarships are awarded annually in February (via our own 11+ entrance examination), and in March for candidates at under 14 on 1st September. Entries must be received by end-December for 11+ and end-January for 13+ candidates. All scholarships and exhibitions are competitive on entry to the school. Awards may be made at 11+, 13+ and 16+ in the following areas: Academic, Art, Drama, Design and Technology, Music, Sport (Swimming, Cricket, Rugby, Hockey etc).

Sons and daughters of Old Kelleians are eligible for 10% reduction in fees.

Further particulars can be obtained from The Registrar, Kelly College, Tavistock, Devon PL19 0HZ.

Kent College (see p 192)
The school awards academic, music, sport, drama and art scholarships to pupils for entry into Years 7, 9 and 12. For Years 7 and 9 academic scholarships are awarded as a result of performance in our Entrance Test, usually held in the Spring Term, for entry the following September. Sixth Form academic scholarships are awarded on the basis of existing performance, a detailed report from the Head of Year or current school, and confirmation of high levels of performance in the final GCSEs. Music, sport and art scholarships are awarded in conjunction with the Entrance Test and appropriate separate performance assessments at Kent College.

Scholarships normally carry a value equivalent to a percentage remission of the tuition fees which would vary according to circumstances but would not exceed a maximum of 50% of tuition fees and would be at the discretion of the Head Master. Full particulars may be obtained from the Registrar.

Kimbolton School (see p 193)
A number of Scholarships are awarded at 11+ and 13+ to candidates who perform with distinction in the Entrance Examination or in Common Entrance.

Further Scholarships, known as William Ingram Awards, may be awarded at 13+ to external candidates with strengths in music, art, games or leadership.

Sixth Form Scholarships and Exhibitions are awarded to those who achieve outstanding results in GCSE. Two Sir Brian Corby bursaries, available for pupils entering the Sixth Form from state schools, cover up to 100% of fees and may include extras.

King Edward's School, Birmingham (see p 200)
Scholarships at 11+ and 13+: Up to twelve major scholarships of between half fees and one-fifth fees are offered. These scholarships may be increased to full fees in cases of financial need.

Music Scholarships are also available.

All scholarships are indexed to increase with increases in fees.

At 16+: Scholarships to the value of half fees for boys studying either Science or Arts subjects at A Level.

King William's College (see p 205)
Year 7 Academic Scholarships are offered up to the value of 20% of the current tuition fee and examinations take place in late January. There are papers in English and Mathematics and an interview.

Sixth Form Academic Scholarships are offered up to the value of 20% of the current tuition fee and examinations are normally held in November of the year prior to entry. There are papers in Mathematics, English, one other subject chosen by the candidate and an interview.

Music Scholarships, Drama and Sports Awards to the value of 20% of the tuition fee are available to candidates entering either the Lower Fourth or the Lower Sixth Form who demonstrate exceptional talent or potential. Examinations and auditions take place by arrangement.

There is also a Bursary fund to support students if the financial circumstances of parents make this necessary.

There is a separate bursary scheme for pupils in their last year in Manx Primary Schools run in conjunction with the Isle of Man Department of Education.

Further details of all scholarships may be obtained from the Admissions Office and on the website.

King's College School, London (see p 207)
Academic Scholarship examination in early May, Art & Design Scholarship, Sports Scholarships and Music Scholarship in February. Candidates must be under 14 years of age on 1st September of the year of entry. 12–15 academic awards, up to 2 art and design awards, up to 2 Sports Scholarships, and up to 6 music awards are made. From 2010, the maximum award for major scholarships will be £1500. Smaller awards – minor scholarships, exhibitions etc – will be fixed sums of £1000, £750 or £500, which will not be revised in line with inflation. If a pupil is awarded two scholarships, the maximum fee remission will be £2000. All additional financial benefits will be means tested, so that any award could be supplemented by fee remissions of up to 100% inclusive of the scholarship. Scholarships and bursaries are also available on a similar basis for pupils for entry into the Sixth Form. Notice of intention of applying for bursarial assistance must be given at the time of application but, if financial need occurs later, the School will always consider cases on their merits. Full details of all awards are available from the Admissions Secretary.

King's College, Taunton (see p 209)
Scholarships are available to boys and girls going into the third form (13+) and sixth form. Major Academic scholarships are awarded, as well as scholarships for Music, Drama, Art, DT and Sport.

King's School, Bruton (see p 212)
The maximum financial value of any award or combination of awards is 20% of fees. The number and value of awards are at the Headmaster's discretion. Further details of specific entry requirements can be obtained from the Registrar on 01749 814220.

13+ Entry:

All applications require the support of the candidate's current school. Candidates for awards other than Academic Scholarships should be of good Common Entrance standard. All candidates for all awards sit a Verbal Reasoning Test and have one or more interviews.

Academic Scholarship examinations take place in February. Candidates must be under 14 on 1 September the year they join King's. Candidates take papers in English, Mathematics, French (including an oral examination), History, Geography and Science. They may also offer optional papers in Latin and RS.

An Old Brutonian Scholarship, worth not more than £3,000 per annum, may be awarded at the discretion of the OBA.

All-Rounder Awards: March. Candidates must demonstrate ability or potential in two areas outside the classroom. If sport is offered, 1st team experience is expected.

Sports Scholarships: March. Candidates must demonstrate ability in two team games to at least 1st team level. Reports are required from county/representative coaches.

Art and/or Technology Scholarships: March. Candidates undertake a practical test and provide a portfolio of recent work.

Sixth Form Entry:

All applications require the support of the candidate's current school in the form of a report. Candidates for awards other than Academic Scholarships need to reach the school's minimum requirement for entry to Sixth Form in order to take up their place at King's. All candidates for all awards take a Verbal Reasoning Test and have one or more interviews. All Sixth Form scholarships and awards are held in November.

Academic Scholarships: Candidates sit an English paper, a General paper and an academic paper in a subject of their choice (which is offered by King's at AS level, other than English).

Art Scholarships: Candidates undertake a practical assessment on the day of examination and provide a portfolio of recent work.

Sports Scholarships: Candidates must show exceptional ability in one or more major team sports. Candidates must demonstrate their ability on the assessment day. Reports will be expected from candidates' county/representative coaches.

The King's School, Canterbury (see p 214)

Up to 20 King's Scholarships and Exhibitions are offered annually for competition in March to pupils under 14 on 1st September in year of entry. The awards will be up to 10% of the annual fee in every year and will be 'inflation proof'. Further assistance above 10% is available but would depend on parental income.

For details of Music Scholarships see that section.

A scholarship leaflet is issued annually in the Autumn, and may be obtained from the Assistant Registrar.

The King's School, Ely (see p 218)

Entrance Scholarships and Exhibitions (i.e. scholarships of lesser value) recognise exceptional promise in academic work, Art, Design & Technology, Drama, Music or Sports.

The total value of scholarships will not exceed 25% of day fees (up to 15% in King's Junior School at Year 7).

King's Junior School Academic Awards are for the two final years (Years 7 and 8). A competitive examination is held in January each year and successful candidates enter Year 7 the following Michaelmas term. These Scholarships will be continued until the end of Year 11, subject to satisfactory progress, after which an application for a Sixth Form Scholarship may be made.

King's Senior School Academic Scholarships are for the three years leading to the GCSE examinations and are made on the basis of a competitive examination set by the school in February. Candidates may also sit the Common Entrance Scholarship paper, should they prefer. Successful candidates enter Year 9 the following September.

Sixth Form Scholarships are for the two years of the AS/A2 course and are made following an examination in November and an interview. Candidates should be on course for at least six A* or A passes at GCSE.

Music Scholarships are available for choral and/or instrumental excellence, including organ-playing and may include free weekly tuition on two musical instruments. Candidates for entry into Year 7 and Year 9 are invited to the school for auditions in February and in November for entry into Year 12 the following September.

All boy Choristers of Ely Cathedral are full boarders of King's Junior School and receive a choristership worth 50% of fees while they remain in the choir and a bursary worth 33% of fees on transfer to King's Senior School. Members of the Cathedral Girls' Choir are all boarders in King's Senior School and receive a bursary worth 33% of boarding fees.

Sports Awards, for entry into Years 7, 9 and 12, are open to boys and girls with potential for major county, regional or national representation or with all-round sporting excellence. Reports will be sought from the candidates' coach(es) and practical tests, if required, will be held at the school in February.

Art and Drama Exhibitions are also available for Years 7 and 9 and a Design and Technology Exhibition is available for Year 9. Interviews are held in late January or early February.

Full particulars of all awards are available from The Admissions Coordinator, The King's School, Ely, Cambridgeshire CB7 4DB. Tel: 01353 660702; e-mail: admissions@kings-ely.cambs.sch.uk.

The King's School, Gloucester (see p 220)

Academic Scholarships at this Cathedral School may be awarded to outstanding boys and girls at age 11, 13 and 16. A number of lesser Exhibitions are also available at this age. Scholarship examinations are held annually in November for 11+, March for 13+ and February for 16+. Awards will also be considered for candidates on the results of the Common Entrance Examination at age 13. Awards in Sport, Music, Art, and Drama are available at age 11, 13 and in the Sixth Form.

Choral Scholarships for Cathedral Choristers are available for boys aged between 7 and 9½.

Full particulars from the Headmaster.

King's Rochester (see p 224)

Up to five Major King's Scholarships of 30% of tuition fees and five Minor King's Scholarships of 15% of tuition fees may be awarded annually – at least five will be for pupils from the maintained sector. King's Scholars become members of the Cathedral Foundation.

Candidates are normally expected to be under 14 years old on 1st September of the year in which they sit the examination. Allowance is made for age.

Candidates will be expected to sit the Common Entrance Scholarship Examination in June or, if not prepared for this, may take the King's Senior School Entrance Examination.

Governors' Exhibitions, all means-tested, are available up to 100% of tuition fees.

Up to five King's Exhibitions of 30% tuition fees are available for pupils aged 11+. Two are reserved for pupils from a maintained school.

Details of Music Scholarships are given elsewhere. A Bursaries brochure, and further information, may be obtained from The Registrar.

The King's School, Worcester (see p 227)

Scholarships are available at 11+, 13+ and 16+ in the Senior School, value up to one third of tuition fees. At 11+ and 13+ awards are made on the basis of the Entrance Test and an interview; at 16+ on the basis of an aptitude test, interview and a report from the candidate's school. Full details are available from the Registrar. Scholarships are available at 7+ and 8+, value up to one third of tuition fees (tenable only while in the Junior Schools) and are awarded to candidates of outstanding academic or musical ability.

Kingston Grammar School (see p 229)

At age 11 there are Academic Scholarships attracting 10% fee remission awarded on the results of the Entrance Examination in early January.

Academic Scholarships (valued at 20%) are also awarded to entrants to the Sixth Form, following a written examination, interview and successful GCSE results.

Kingswood School (see p 231)
Academic Scholarships (maximum value up to 25% off the basic fees) are available annually to pupils entering Year 7, Year 9 or Lower Sixth. John Wesley All-Rounder awards are available for boarders in Years 7, 9 and Lower Sixth.

Special Talent Scholarships (maximum value up to 25% off the basic fees) are also available annually to pupils entering Year 7, Year 9 or Lower Sixth in Art, Design Technology, Drama, Music or Sport.

John Wesley All-Rounder Awards: A special All-Rounder Scholarship is available for those pupils who can demonstrate a high level of academic ability in addition to extra talents in either Art, DT, Music, Drama or Sport. This award is available at entry to Year 9 (new boarders only) and to the Lower Sixth (boarders only). A report from the pupil's current school outlining contribution to school life will also be required.

Lancing College (see p 234)
Candidates for the following awards must be under 14 years of age on 1st September in the year of the examination. The age of the candidate is taken into account in making awards. A candidate may enter for more than one type of award, and account may be taken of musical or artistic proficiency in a candidate for a non-musical award; but no one may hold more than one type of award, except in an honorary capacity.

A number of Open Scholarships ranging in value from £1,000 per year to half of the annual school fee.

A number of Music Scholarships ranging in value up to half the annual school fee. Scholarships may be offered to pupils from schools where the time for Music is less than in some others, and where a candidate may have less musical experience but greater potential.

One Professor W K Stanton Music Scholarship for a Chorister from Salisbury Cathedral School, or failing that any Cathedral School. A Stanton Exhibition may also be awarded.

A number of scholarships in Art, Drama and Sport, ranging in value up to a quarter of the annual school fee.

A number of Ken Shearwood Awards, ranging in value up to a quarter of the annual school fee, are made to pupils of all-round ability and potential who have made outstanding contributions to their present schools.

Entry Forms for Academic, Art, Music, Drama, Sport and All-Rounder (Ken Shearwood) awards are obtainable from the Admissions Officer.

Sixth Form Awards: Scholarships are available for new entrants to the Sixth Form with special proficiency in Academic subjects, Music or Art. There is also one Organ Scholarship. The candidate's general ability to contribute to the life of a boarding school community will also be taken into account. A small number of Scholarships is also available internally on the strength of GCSE results.

The value of all Entrance Scholarships may be augmented by bursaries, according to parental circumstances.

Latymer Upper School (see p 236)
A number of means-tested scholarships are awarded every year. These range from 25% of fees to full fees and are available at 11+ and 16+.

Academic Scholarships (£1000 at time of entry) can be offered as a result of performance in the 11+ entrance examinations and at interview. The examinations are held every year in January followed by interviews in late January/early February.

A small number of pupils are admitted at 13+, following entrance examinations in the February of the year of entry. Academic Scholarships (£1000 at time of entry) are also offered at 13+.

At 11+ and 13+ Entry: Music Scholarships of varying amounts are offered, together with music awards of free tuition on two instruments.

At 16+ Entry: Academic Scholarships are offered, together with scholarships for Art, Drama and Sport. Candidates who have satisfied the academic requirements will be invited to an interview and assessment in January.

Further details are available from the Registrar (0845 638 5978; registrar@latymer-upper.org).

Leicester Grammar School (see p 241)
Academic scholarships (maximum 25%) are available at all ages from 11+ upwards and are given on the results of the Entrance Examination (or, at Sixth Form entrance, GCSE results). Music scholarships are also available, awarded following audition, as are a small number of art scholarships, awarded on examination and portfolio.

Leighton Park School (see p 243)
Candidates can apply for any combination of academic, art, music and sport scholarships. Pupils may be awarded more than one scholarship but will only receive the financial benefits of one. The financial benefit will be in the region of 10% of Day Boarder Fees.

The Leys School (see p 244)
Scholarships are available for entry at 11+, 13+ and for the Sixth Form. The value is expressed as a percentage of the fees, the maximum value being 5%, but this can be supplemented by a means-tested bursary up to a total concession of 100% in extreme cases.

At 11+ two scholarships are available with the emphasis being on academic performance.

At 13+ and at Sixth Form the categories are Academic, Art, Music, Sport, Drama and Design Technology (Arkwright Award Scheme at Sixth Form level). There is also an All-Rounder Award at 13+. The number and value of awards is dependent on the calibre of the candidates in a particular year.

Full particulars are available by application to the Admissions Office for a prospectus.

Llandovery College (see p 249)
Thomas Philips Scholarships are for academically-able pupils from Wales or Welsh families. This means-tested scholarship is for a child's entire education whether boarding or day and may be as much as 100% of fees. Up to three Thomas Phillips Scholarships are awarded each year for entry at 11 (Year 7) on the basis of candidates' performance in demanding tests of English, Maths and Non-Verbal Reasoning skills. Exams held in January.

Lord Wandsworth College (see p 252)
Scholarships and Awards:
First Form (Year 7): Academic, Music and Sport;
Third Form (Year 9): Academic, Drama, Music, Art, Sport and All-Rounder;
Sixth Form: Academic, Drama, Music, Art, Sport and All-Rounder.
Further details may be obtained from the Admissions Office.

Loretto School (see p 253)
Junior School: Academic and All-Rounder scholarships are available to pupils joining the Junior School at Year 6 and Year 7 and are for the duration of the Junior and Senior School.

Senior School (Second–Lower Sixth Form): Means-tested Academic, Art, Drama, Golf, Music and Sports Scholarships are available. Almond Academic Scholarships (means-tested up to 100%) are also available for pupils currently at a State School.

Please contact the Admissions Department on 0131 653 4455 for further details.

Loughborough Grammar School (see p 256)
A number of Scholarships are offered at 10+, 11+ and 13+/Common Entrance, based on performance in the Entrance Examination. Sixth Form scholarships are based on GCSE results. Choral and instrumental scholarships are also awarded at 10+, 11+, 13+/Common Entrance and Sixth Form. There are also a number of bursaries, dependent on parental income.

Magdalen College School (see p 258)

A limited number of bursaries is available to boys of 7, 9, 11 and 13, awarded on a combination of academic merit and financial need. Ogden Trust Sixth Form Scholarships are available to candidates of sufficient merit from state schools.

At age 13, up to 16 Scholarships of up to £300, but capable of increase up to half fees in case of need, are awarded each year on the results of a two-day scholarship examination in March. Candidates should be under 14 on the subsequent 1 September. Closing date for entries: 1 February.

Music, Art and Sports Scholarships are awarded each year on the results of assessments held in February (Music) or March (Art and Sports). Music award holders also receive free tuition in one instrument.

Further information can be obtained from the *Registrar, Magdalen College School, Oxford OX4 1DZ.*

For details of Choristerships (for boys aged 7–9) application should be made to the *Informator Choristarum, Magdalen College, Oxford OX1 4AU.*

Malvern College (see p 260)

13+ Scholarships and Exhibitions are offered for competition in our Scholarship Examination which is held at the school. Candidates for all 13+ Scholarships must be under 14 years of age on 1st September in the year of the examination but there is no age limit for Exhibitions. Entries for practical scholarships must be received three weeks before the examination. Entry forms are available from the Preparatory School or the Registrar at Malvern College. For academic scholarships Malvern College offers the Common Academic Scholarship. Details and entry dates are available from the ISEB or the prep school.

Up to twenty Academic awards are offered. They range from Scholarships of up to 50% of the fees to Exhibitions of a lesser value. Scholarships and Exhibitions are also offered for Art, Drama, Music, Sport and Technology, as well as the The Malvernian Society All-Rounder Award.

Further particulars may be obtained from The Registrar, Tel: +44 (0)1684 581515, or e-mail: registrar@malcol.org.

Marlborough College (see p 264)

The College offers Open, Foundation (Clergy) and Armed Services closed scholarships. Candidates must be under 14 on 1st September.

At least 15 Major and 15 Minor academic scholarships will be available at 13+. Awards enable those with a financial need to receive bursarial assistance with the fees. The degree of support given will be subject to a means test.

The closing date for entries is late January.

There are also scholarships available for Sixth Form Entry.

A Scholarship Prospectus and copies of past papers may be obtained from The Senior Admissions Tutor; tel: 01672 892300; e-mail: admissions@marlboroughcollege.org.

Merchant Taylors' School, Northwood (see p 267)

11+ entry: Up to 10 academic scholarships each to the value of £200 per year.

13+ entry: Up to 20 academic scholarships (some named) each to the value of £200 per year.

Scholarships can be supplemented by means-tested bursaries where there is a proven need.

Details from the Admissions Secretary, Tel: 01923 845514.

Merchiston Castle School (see p 270)

Scholarships (Academic, Sport, All-Rounder and Music) are offered for competition from 10+ up to 16, with an emphasis on 13+ entry from Prep Schools. Junior Scholarship assessments (Academic, Sport and All-Rounder) for boys aged 10+ to 12 are held mid-January (as are Junior entrance assessments). Senior School Scholarship assessments are held late January (Sport /All-Rounder) or in March (Academic). Senior non-scholarship assessments: late January. Music Scholarship (including Piping Exhibition),

Design & Technology / Art held late January. Sixth Form Scholarship (Academic, Sport, All-Rounder) assessments held early March. Laidlaw and Community Scholarships assessed at any of the above times. Further details can be obtained from the Director of Admissions.

Mill Hill School (see p 273)

Academic, Music, Drama, Art and Design, and Sports Awards are available at 13+.

Sixth Form Academic Scholarships and Exhibitions are available.

For further information please visit the school's website www.millhill.org.uk.

Monkton Combe School (see p 280)

Four Anniversary Awards are offered at the age of 11 for open competition each year. They range in value from 25% to 5% of the appropriate fee.

At least ten Open Scholarships are offered at age 13 (including at least two for Music, at least one for Drama, at least one for Art and at least two for Sport) of value ranging from 35% to 5% of the appropriate fee.

Additional bursaries are available to supplement Scholarships in case of need. Candidates must be under 14 years of age on 1st September. Further particulars and copies of specimen papers can be obtained from the Registrar.

At least four Sixth Form Scholarships are also offered each year, ranging in value from 25% to 5% of the appropriate fee.

Details of all awards can be obtained from the Registrar.

Monmouth School (see p 282)

A generous number of Entrance Scholarships are awarded on the School's Year 7 Entry Assessments (held in February) for boys entering at the age of eleven, on the Foundation Scholarship Examination (held in February/March) for boys entering at the age of thirteen, and the Sixth Form Scholarship Examination (in February). In cases of need, Scholarships may be augmented by a Bursary.

At eleven: 1. Open Scholarships for dayboys or boarders.

2. Further Scholarships and Bursaries, including those from the Old Monmothian Scholarship Fund, will be awarded, their value being determined and annually adjusted according to parental need.

At thirteen: Foundation Scholarships are for day boys or boarders who are not currently pupils of Monmouth School. Candidates must be between the ages of 12 and 14 on the first day of September following the examination.

Sixth Form Scholarship awards for day boys or boarders. Candidates to be under the age of 17 on the first day of September following the Scholarship Examinations. The E F Bulmer Award is available to suitable Sixth Form candidates living in Herefordshire; awards range in value from 50% to 100% of the fees.

Morrison's Academy (see p 284)

Sixth Form Scholarships: A number of Scholarships are awarded after examination and interview in May. The awards, which carry a nominal financial value, recognise both achievement and potential. Full details from The Rector, Morrison's Academy, Crieff PH7 3AN.

New Hall School (see p 287)

At 13+: One or two of 50% of fees awarded on academic merit. Any Scholarships that are not awarded to the prospective Year 7 intake in a particular year will be transferred to external candidates for 13+ entry who would be joining that particular intake 2 years later.

At 11+:

One of 50% of fees – awarded on academic merit.

One of 50% of fees – candidate must be a Catholic who is currently attending an Independent Catholic School.

One of 50% of fees – candidate must be a Catholic who is currently attending a voluntary-aided Catholic Primary School.

Three of 20% of fees – awarded on academic merit.

At 16+ (Sixth Form):

2 at 16+ in the range 30-75% each (50+ part subject to means test) open to external applicants.

3 at 16+ following the results of the mock GCSE examinations. Total combined value will not exceed 75% of fees.

Various subject Awards are made to internal candidates in the following subject areas: Art, Drama, English, Geography, History, Languages, Latin, Mathematics, Music, Religious Studies, Science, Sport.

There is an award for the best GCSE results open to internal and external candidates worth 20% of day fees.

There is an internal award, "The Thomas More Award", for the greatest all-round contribution.

Newcastle-under-Lyme School (see p 289)

The following Scholarships and Bursaries are available:

Governors' Scholarships: One Scholarship of value up to £1,000 per annum for one year following entry and Scholarships of up to £1,000 per annum for one year following entry to be awarded on the results of the 11+ and 13+ Entrance Examinations.

Sports Scholarships: A number of Sports Scholarships may be awarded to candidates at 13+ entry offering particular sporting prowess. These will be of value up to £1,000 per annum for one year following entry.

The Robert S Woodward Scholarships: One or Two Scholarships, of value up to £1,000 per annum, to be awarded annually to pupils entering or in the Sixth Form, for outstanding performance in the field of Mathematical Sciences.

The JCB Sixth Form Scholarship: One Scholarship, of value up to £1,000 per annum, to be awarded annually to pupils entering, or in the Sixth Form, for outstanding performance in Physics.

Music Scholarships: To cover the cost of music tuition throughout the student's school career.

Bursaries: The Governors have established a Bursary Scheme to assist parents with school fees.

Further details may be obtained from the *Headmaster, Newcastle-under-Lyme School, Mount Pleasant, Newcastle, Staffordshire ST5 1DB*.

Norwich School (see p 291)

Scholarships are awarded to pupils with outstanding ability and flair, which the school assesses by examination, interview or audition. The financial value of a scholarship will be up to 10% of the annual tuition fee – irrespective of parental means. Scholarships are awarded in five categories: Academic; Music; Sport; Art/Design and Drama.

Academic and Music scholarships are awarded at 11+, 13+ and Sixth Form entry. Sport and Art, Design or Drama scholarships are awarded only at Sixth Form entry. Pupils may apply for more than one scholarship, although the maximum financial benefit that can be cumulated is 20% of the school fees.

Nottingham High School (see p 294)

Part-Scholarships of a fixed sum may be awarded. They are not linked to parental finances and will normally continue throughout a boy's school career. Application does not have to be made for part-scholarships as these are awarded at the discretion of the Headmaster, subject to entrance examination performance and interview. Following the ending of the Government Assisted Places Scheme, Nottingham High School has introduced its own Bursaries to be awarded to boys entering the Senior School at either age eleven or sixteen. Odgen Trust Bursaries are available for Sixth Form entry for students studying Science and Mathematics. All Bursaries will be awarded at the Headmaster's discretion and will normally continue until a pupil leaves the School.

Oakham School (see p 295)

The following scholarships are available: Academic (11+, 13+ and 16+), All-rounder (13+), Art (13+ and 16+), Design and Technology (13+ and 16+), Drama (16+), ICT and Computing (16+), Music (11+, 13+, 16+), Science and

Engineering (16+), Sport (13+ and 16+). The value of these awards is advised at the time the Scholarship is awarded and top-up means-tested support may be available. Means-tested financial support (bursary) is also available. For further information see www.oakham.rutland.sch.uk or request an information booklet from the Registrar, Tel: 01572 758758.

The Oratory School (see p 298)

A number of Scholarships and Exhibitions of varying values, not exceeding half fees. Academic, Music, Art and Sports Awards. Particulars from The Head Master.

Oundle School (see p 300)

11+ Academic Scholarships: 13-14 January 2012

13+ Academic Scholarships: 9-12 May 2012

16+ Academic Scholarships: 11-13 November 2011

11+: Four Junior Academic Scholarships for entry to The Berrystead or Laxton, at 10% of the fees. Pupils transfer directly into the Senior School at 13+. Closing date: 1 December 2011.

13+: Fifteen Academic Scholarships at 10% of the fees. Candidates must be below the age of 14 on 1st September 2011. A qualifying examination will take place during w/c Monday 30 January 2012. The Grocers' Scholar is elected annually after completion of one year in the School.

13+: Twelve General Scholarships at 10% of the fees (4-5 March 2012).

16+: Two Sixth Form Academic Scholarships at 10% of the fees.

These Scholarships are tenable during the whole of the pupil's time at the School, provided progress is satisfactory.

Further details may be obtained from Helen Vincent, The Undermaster's Assistant, Oundle School, Oundle, Peterborough, PE8 4GH. Tel: 01832 277116. Fax: 01832 277119. e-mail: hev@oundleschool.org.uk.

Pangbourne College (see p 303)

Scholarships and Awards of up to 20% of fees are mainly offered at 13, when entering Form III, and at 16, when entering the Sixth Form, but some are occasionally offered at the age of 11, when entering Form I. Means-tested bursaries are available.

Academic Scholarship papers for entry at 13+ are set and held at the College.

The College is an Arkwright Technology Scholarship Centre and also offers one Design Technology scholarship every year.

Music, Art, Drama and Sport Scholarships, All-rounder Awards and Sixth Form Scholarships and means-tested Bursaries are available. Please see the relevant section for details or contact our Registrar for more information (registrar@pangcoll.co.uk).

Plymouth College (see p 305)

For pupils entering at 11 there are 2 Major Scholarships (50% of fees pa) and 3 Ordinary Scholarships (one-third of the fees pa). Two of these awards are restricted to pupils coming from Plymouth College Preparatory School. There are also smaller awards for Art, Music, Performing Arts, Drama and Sport and on occasion All-Round awards are given. Awards are made on the basis of the Entrance Examination.

At 13+ there is one Major and one Ordinary Scholarship and these are awarded on a Scholarship Examination.

For those entering the Sixth Form two further awards are made based on interview and GCSE results.

There are 8 Scholarships and Awards for Art, Music, Drama and Sport. Four of these are awarded at 13 and four to Sixth Form entrants. The value of these are up to one-third of the fees.

Further information from the Headmaster's Secretary.

Pocklington School (see p 307)

Eight academic scholarships up to the value of £1,000 and eight exhibitions up to the value of £500 are offered to entrants to the First Year, Third Year and Sixth Form.

Means-tested Sixth Form bursaries providing up to 100% of day fees are also available.

Awards are available to internal and external candidates. Tenure of all awards is for the duration of the pupil's time at Pocklington School subject to satisfactory performance and behaviour.

Portsmouth Grammar School (see p 309)
A small number of Scholarships, each amounting to no more than 10% of full fees, are awarded to outstanding candidates in the 11+ Entrance Assessments. All candidates are automatically considered for Scholarships. No application is required.

Peter Ogden Scholarships, worth up to full fees, are offered at 11+ to outstanding candidates with parents of limited income from state primary schools. Additional assistance up to 100% of fees is available through the award of means-tested Foundation Bursaries.

Scholarships from the A D Nock Trust are offered at 13+ to both Common Entrance candidates and existing pupils.

Academic Scholarships and Bursaries are awarded for entry to the Sixth Form. Full details of all scholarships and bursaries are available on the School's website.

Prior Park College (see p 312)
Scholarships at 11+ are awarded following results of the general entrance examination. No further scholarship examinations are set at 11+.

Scholarships are awarded annually to external candidates for 13+ entry and the examination is held in January/February. Sixth Form Scholarships are held in November.

All Scholarships are up to a maximum of 50% fee remission.

Candidates must be under 14 years of age on September 1st following for the March Scholarship and under 12 years of age on September 1st following for the January Scholarship entrance exam.

Queen's College, Taunton (see p 319)
Queen's College Scholarships: 11+ scholarships are awarded in January, 13+ in February and Sixth Form in November.

Academic Scholarships by examination: up to 50% of fees for students of proven academic ability in one or more subjects. Up to 8 academic scholarships for students aged 11+ and 13+ on 1 September in year of entry. Eight Sixth Form scholarships are also on offer.

Music, Performing Arts, Art, Sports and All-Rounder Scholarships are also available (*see relevant section*).

For further information apply to the Headmaster.

Radley College (see p 322)
Up to 12 Academic Scholarships and Exhibitions are awarded annually. Awards may be supplemented by a means-tested bursary where necessary. Further details from our website or the Registrar.

Ratcliffe College (see p 323)
Ratcliffe College offers a wide range of scholarships to recognise academic, sporting, musical, dramatic and artistic talent amongst applicants for the Senior School.

Each scholarship is worth £1000. Points at which scholarships are offered are Years 7, 9 and 12.

Year 7: available to internal and external Year 6 pupils, with auditions and tests associated with sport, music and art & design scholarships held in the January prior to the year of entry (and therefore just after the academic entrance examinations) and conditional upon meeting our academic expectations for entry into the School.
- Three academic scholarships
- One boy's Sports Scholarship
- One girl's Sports Scholarship
- One Music Scholarship (The Henry Goldstraw / Gerald Yell Scholarship)
- One Art & Design Scholarship

Year 9: available to internal and external Year 8 pupils, with auditions and tests associated with sport, music and all-rounder scholarships held in the January prior to the year of entry (and therefore just after the academic entrance examinations) and conditional upon meeting our academic expectations for entry into the School.
- Three academic scholarships
- One boy's Sports Scholarship
- One girl's Sports Scholarship
- One Music Scholarship (The Henry Goldstraw / Gerald Yell Scholarship)
- One Drama Scholarship

Year 12: available to internal and external Year 11 pupils, with auditions and tests associated with the sports and music scholarships held in the January prior to the year of entry, and conditional upon meeting our academic threshold for entry into the Sixth Form.
- A range of academic scholarships (worth up to £1000) linked to strong performance at GCSE – for separate details, please contact the Registrar, Miss Kelly Smith, on 01509 817072
- One boy's Sports Scholarship
- One girl's Sports Scholarship

A small number of additional awards are available at the Headmaster's discretion.

Scholarships are reviewed annually and, provided that good scholarly and discipline standards are maintained, remain with the pupil throughout his or her school career.

For further details and how to apply, please contact the Registrar.

Reed's School (see p 327)
Academic Scholarships are offered each year at age 11, 13 and 16. The maximum value of any award given for exceptional performance is half fees per annum. All enquiries should be addressed to the Registrar.

Repton School (see p 330)
A number of scholarships and exhibitions are offered annually, generally at 13+ and 16+, though in exceptional circumstances candidates may be considered for awards at other entry points. The value of any award may be increased where need is shown.

Entrance Scholarships at 13+: The examination for non academic awards is held at Repton in January for entry the following September, and the examination for academic awards is held at Repton in May for entry the following September. In exceptional circumstances candidates may be considered at other entry points in the year. Candidates must be under 14 on 1 September in the year of the examination.

16+ Scholarships: The examination for both academic and non academic awards takes place in November for entry the following September. Candidates may, in exceptional circumstances, be considered at other entry points in the year. A number of awards are available for pupils joining Repton from both the maintained and independent sectors.

The value of an award may be increased through bursarial assistance when need is shown.

Further information on all awards, including the closing date for entries, can be obtained from The Registrar, Repton School, Repton, Derby DE65 6FH. Tel: 01283 559222. Fax: 01283 559228. e-mail: registrar@repton.org.uk.

Rossall School (see p 333)
Scholarships are offered in academic, music, sport and all-round achievement. Scholarships are awarded up to 100% of the fees.

Apply to *The Registrar, Rossall School, Fleetwood FY7 8JW*.

Royal Grammar School, Guildford (see p 337)
Scholarships of up to 20% fee remission are awarded in recognition of outstanding academic merit. For boys entering the First Form at 11 there is a competitive examination in English and Mathematics, held in mid-February. For boys entering the Third Form at 13 there is a two-day exam-

ination covering all Common Entrance subjects, held in February or March. The top scholar of a year group is designated the King's Scholar.

For full details of these and of arrangements for boys entering the School at 11, 13 and 16, write to the Registrar.

The Royal Hospital School (see p 342)

Scholarships are awarded annually, at the Headmaster discretion, for academic excellence, musical talent, sport and for sailing to pupils entering the school at any age but normally Year 7 (11+), Year 9 (13+) and Year 12 (16+). All scholarship candidates are required to sit the school entrance examination (unless taking Common Entrance or GCSE examinations), have an interview with the Headmaster and take the scholarship examination in the case of academic scholarships or undergo an assessment in their relevant field for music, sport and sailing scholarships. Full details from the Admissions Office, Tel: 01473 326210 or email: admissions@royalhospitalschool.org.

Rugby School (see p 346)

Approximately 10% of the School's annual income is currently expended in Scholarships, Foundationerships, Bursaries and other awards. Scholarships are intended to open access to talented boys and girls irrespective of parental means. All scholarships therefore carry a nominal reduction of 10% of the fee; all may be augmented to 100% of the fees subject to means testing.

Academic Scholarships at 13+: Boys and girls who are 12 or over and under 14 at midnight on August 31st in the year the examination is taken may sit. Candidates who were previously registered for entry and who do not obtain awards are normally admitted to the school on the result of the Scholarship examination. The examination is held at Rugby in early May for entry in September of the same year. A generous number of scholarships are usually awarded.

Academic Scholarships at 16+: Boys and girls aiming to enter the School after GCSE may compete for a number of 16+ Scholarships. The Scholarship interviews are held at Rugby in mid-November in the year preceding the pupil's entry to the School. Candidates must first take the Sixth Form Entrance Examination and those showing scholarship potential will be called for Scholarship interviews with the relevant Heads of Department.

Music Scholarships: Several Scholarships are awarded each year at 11+, 13+ and 16+. At 16+ the examination audition is held at Rugby in November, at 11+ in early January, and at 13+ in late January or early February of the year of entry.

Art Scholarships: At 16+ potential Art Scholarship candidates are interviewed and present their portfolios as part of the 16+ Academic Scholarship in November and at 13+ in the May of the year of entry.

Design and Technology Bursary/Scholarship: Awards are offered at 13+ and 16+. The examinations are held in conjunction with the Academic Scholarships. At 13+, candidates can, but need not, take the Academic Scholarship as well.

Sports Scholarships: A number of Scholarships are awarded each year at 13+ and 16+ to candidates with outstanding ability in team games. At 13+ applicants should be nominated by their Head Teacher to attend an initial assessment at Rugby. Short-listed candidates will then be observed at match conditions. At 16+ candidates will be interviewed as part of the sixth form entrance examination in November and will be observed in match conditions or be invited to participate in a training session at Rugby. Short-listed candidates will subsequently be observed in match conditions.

The Arnold Foundation: The Arnold Foundation aims to raise funds through charitable donations to support the education of talented boys and girls whose families would not be able to fund boarding school fees. Funds are available for several awards for entry to the sixth form and at 13+. Pupils offered a place through this scheme may be awarded up to 100% of the full boarding fee plus extras. The final selection is through interviews. Candidates are expected to pass the School's normal entrance requirements. Initial enquiries should be made via the Registry.

Foundationerships: In 1567 Lawrence Sheriff in his Will bequeathed money to establish a school in perpetuity in Rugby 'to serve chiefly for the children of Rugby and Brownsover'. It is in the execution of the terms of this Will that Foundation Scholarships are offered. Several awards are made each year to day boy and day girl candidates of 11+ and 13+. Awards are 10% of the fees but may be augmented up to 100% (subject to means testing) of the day pupil fee. All candidates for Foundation Scholarships must reside within a radius of 10 miles from the Rugby Clock Tower.

For further information and details of all scholarships please contact the Registrar, School House, Rugby School, Rugby, Warwickshire CV22 5EH; e-mail: registry @rugbyschool.net.

Rydal Penrhos School (see p 349)

Academic, Art, Drama, Music and Sport Awards worth up to 50% of school fees are available by examination in January for Year 7, Year 9 and Sixth Form entry. An award may be increased through a means-tested bursary up to 75% of the school fees.

For full details of all these awards, please apply to Mrs Jenny Marsden, Admissions.

Ryde School with Upper Chine (see p 351)

Some Scholarships worth 10% of fees may be awarded on merit to external or internal candidates for entry at 11+ and 13+. Scholarships are also awarded to our best GCSE candidates. Scholarships may be supplemented by bursaries, which are means tested. Further details from the Headmaster.

St Albans School (see p 352)

There are numerous scholarships awarded on academic merit at each age of entry.

St Bede's School (see p 357)

Academic, Art, Dance, Drama, Music and Sport scholarships are available for entry at 13+ and 16+ (Sixth Form). Parents of children applying for scholarships have three options: (a) to accept the scholarship without fee remission and as a recognition of excellence; (b) apply for means-tested fee remission up to a fully-funded place; and (c) apply for a non means-tested award.

St Bees School (see p 359)

Scholarships and Exhibitions are awarded to candidates under the age of 12 on 1 September. All candidates must take papers in English, Mathematics and Verbal Reasoning.

The School offers a limited number of means-tested bursaries.

St Edmund's College (see p 367)

At 11+, the *Douay Academic Scholarships* are decided by the mark in the entrance exam, the school report, the confidential school report and the interview with the Headmaster.

At 16+, the *Cardinal Allen Academic Scholarships* are decided by open competition using the results of specially set scholarship examinations, interview and previous school reports. Candidates for these scholarships would be expected to achieve all A/A* grades in their GCSEs. Music, Sport and Art scholarships may also be offered at 16+ through competitive test.

St Edmund's School (see p 369)

Competitive scholarships of up to 50% of fees are offered in academic achievement, music, drama and sport at 11+, 13+ and 16+. In addition, art scholarships are available at 13+ and 16+. At the discretion of the Head and the Master, an All-Rounder scholarship may be made to a candidate whose combination of talents merits an award. Such a candidate will have sat the academic scholarship paper and been assessed for a scholarship in at least one other discipline.

St Edward's, Oxford (see p 373)
All scholarships carry a maximum value of 10% of current boarding fees with the opportunity of a means-tested supplement up to a value of 100% fee reduction.

Up to fifteen Academic scholarships and exhibitions are available each year. 16+ academic scholarships take place in the November prior to entry in the September, 13+ academic scholarships take place in the May prior to entry.

St George's College (see p 374)
Up to three Scholarships (5%–25% of the basic school fee) will be awarded at 11+, one of which must be awarded to a boy or girl at St George's College Junior School and at least one should be awarded to an applicant not at the Junior School.

Up to three Scholarships will be awarded at 13+ for entry to the Third Form of St George's College.

Details may be obtained from the Admissions Secretary.

St Lawrence College (see p 378)
Academic and Sports Scholarships are offered to candidates at 8+.

Academic, Music, Sport, Art and All-Rounder Scholarships are offered to candidates at 11+, 13+ and 16+ for entry into Years 7, 9, and 12.

St Paul's School (see p 383)
A few Foundation Scholarships may be awarded to 11 year old boys at Colet Court on the basis of examinations. The Scholarship Examination for St Paul's is held in May. Candidates must be under 14 on 1 September. There are 153 Scholars at any given time and about 30 vacancies arise each year. All new Academic Scholarships are honorary, and carry an award of £60 per annum. Bursary assistance may be available for families whose circumstances do not allow them to meet the cost of fees, subject to interview, means-testing and available funds.

Further particulars from the Finance Director.

St Peter's School (see p 385)
Honorary Academic Scholarships at age 13 and 16 are available for those doing very well in the entrance tests, who are then invited to compete for honorary subject scholarships.

Seaford College (see p 386)
Academic, Choral Music, Instrumental Music, Art, Design Technology and Sports scholarships may be awarded to boys and girls entering the senior school at 13+. Music/Choral scholarships may be awarded to boys and girls entering The Prep School at ten or eleven. These scholarships are worth a fixed value of £500 per annum.

Special consideration will be given to pupils entering from maintained schools who have not studied the Common entrance syllabus.

Bursaries are available to pupils whose parents are in the Forces and siblings.

For further information please apply to the Admissions Secretary.

Sedbergh School (see p 388)
Major and Minor Scholarships and Exhibitions may be awarded annually as a result of examinations held in February.

Scholarships are usually offered for entry to the Senior School at 13+ and 16+ (Sixth Form). Scholarships are offered for entry to the Junior School at 11+. In exceptional circumstances other years of entry may be considered.

In addition to Scholarships for Academic excellence, Art, Drama, Design Technology, Music and Sport awards are also available for all-round potential.

All awards may be supplemented by means of a Bursary according to parental need.

Further particulars and specimen papers are available from *The Headmaster, Sedbergh School, Sedbergh, Cumbria LA10 5HG*.

Sevenoaks School (see p 390)
Up to 50 awards available at: 11+ (Junior School), 13+ (Middle School), 16+ (Sixth Form), for:
- outstanding academic ability or promise;
- outstanding ability in music;
- outstanding ability in sport;
- outstanding ability in art (at 13+ and 16+ only);
- outstanding ability in drama (at 16+ only);

Scholarships are awarded to the value of 20% or 10% of the day fee. These may be augmented by bursaries in cases of financial need. Priority is given to local candidates.

Applicants are invited to apply for 11+ scholarships on the basis of performance in entrance tests and interviews, and for music scholarships when confirming their application. For 13+ awards, application should be made to the Director of Admissions by 1 January in the year of entry.

Sixth Form academic scholarships are offered on the basis of performance in entrance tests and interviews. Applications for Sixth Form Art, Music, Drama and Sport scholarships should be made by expressing an interest during the application procedure.

Sherborne School (see p 392)
The following awards are offered:

Open Scholarships: up to six Scholarships of up to 20% of fees (the top scholarship being the Alexander Ross Wallace Scholarship) and up to eight Exhibitions of up to 10% of fees may be awarded. In awarding one of these Exhibitions regard will be paid to special proficiency in a particular subject.

In addition Awards are available to those who are able to demonstrate outstanding ability in one of the following areas: Art, Design & Technology, Sport.

Closed Awards: Raban Exhibition of 10% of fees for the sons of serving or ex-service officers, a Nutting Exhibition of 10% of fees for sons of RN Officers.

All candidates should be under 14 on 1st September.

Music Awards: A number of Awards are available at 13+. In addition one Marion Packer Scholarship of £600 pa for an outstanding performance on the piano may be offered. Those given Awards receive free instrumental tuition.

Sixth Form Scholarships and Exhibitions are offered annually.

In common with most other HMC Schools the maximum value of any award is 25% of the fees but this may be supplemented in cases of financial need.

Further particulars and copies of specimen papers can be obtained from the *Registrar, Sherborne School, Dorset DT9 3AP. Tel: 01935 810402. Fax: 01935 810422.*

Shrewsbury School (see p 396)
The Academic Scholarship examination is held during the Summer term. Seventeen Scholarships are open to competition. Four are to the maximum value 50% of fees, six up to the value of 25% of fees and seven worth at least £2,000 per annum. However, these are currently subject to revision.

There are also two Music Scholarships up to the value of 50% of fees, two Music Scholarships up to the value of 20% of fees, two Art Scholarships up to the value of 20% of fees. Candidates must be under 14 on 1 September, following the examination.

In addition, there are two Sports Scholarships up to the value of 20% of fees, two All-Rounder Scholarships worth a maximum value of 20% of fees and ten House Foundation Awards, worth up to the value of 50% of fees, which are available for exceptional all-rounders and tied to particular day and boarding houses.

There are eight Sixth Form Scholarships: two up to the value of 25% of the fees and six up to the value of 15% of fees.

Silcoates School (see p 398)
Academic Scholarships are offered at 11+ and above; Sixth Form entrants are eligible for these awards.

Solihull School (see p 399)

The School offers approximately 25 academic scholarship awards at 11+ and around 30 at 16+. The number of awards and their value is at the discretion of the Headmaster. There are also music scholarships at 11+, 13+ and 16+. Sixth Form scholarships are awarded on the basis of examination in a variety of subjects.

The dates for 11+ entrance examinations and Sixth Form scholarship examinations are shown on the school website.

Stamford School (see p 401)

There are Scholarships and Bursaries available on entry. These are for Academic, Music, Art, Sporting and All-Round ability.

For further particulars apply to the Head.

Stonyhurst College (see p 406)

Open Major and Minor Scholarships are awarded annually at 13+ on the result of an examination held at Stonyhurst in May. These vary in value up to a maximum of half fees. Open Major and Minor Music scholarships are also awarded in February. Sixth-form academic scholarships, scholarships for Art and Design and Technology and All-rounder awards are also made.

For further details please apply to the Headmaster.

Stowe School (see p 408)

Academic Scholarships up to the value of 25% of the School fees are available for pupils at aged 13+ entering Stowe's Third Form, and are awarded to gifted children already following the ISEB Common Academic Scholarship syllabus at their Preparatory School.

Stephan Scholarships are awarded to academically bright pupils from independent or state schools which do not follow the ISEB Common Academic Scholarship syllabus.

Academic Scholarships are also available to pupils wishing to join the School in the Lower Sixth Form after GCSE at 16+. Competitive Entry Examinations are held in the November of the candidate's GCSE year. Successful Scholarship candidates would normally be expected to gain A* and A grades in all their subjects at GCSE.

Full details may be obtained from The Registrar.

Strathallan School (see p 410)

Awards are made on the basis of competitive examination/ assessment. Bursary help is available to supplement awards for outstanding candidates on a financial need basis.

Awards are available in the following categories to candidates entering the school at three levels:

Junior School: Academic and Music/Choral/Performing Arts/Piping/Drumming. Candidates should be under 13 on 1 September in the year of entry. Scholarship Examination: January.

Third Form: Academic, Music/Choral/Piping/Drumming, Art, Design Technology, Sports, and All-Rounder. Candidates should be under 14 on 1 September in the year of entry. Scholarship Examination: March.

Sixth Form: Academic, Music/Choral/Piping/Drumming, Art, Design Technology, Sports, and All-Rounder. Candidates should be under 17 on 1 September in the year of entry. Scholarship Examination: November.

Further information is available on the school's website: www.strathallan.co.uk. All enquiries about scholarships to: The Admissions Office, Strathallan School, Forgandenny, Perthshire PH2 9EG. Tel: 01738 815003, email admissions @strathallan.co.uk.

Surbiton High School (see p 413)

Scholarships are offered at 11+ and 16+. There are several Academic Scholarships offering up to 50% reduction in the standard fees. The School also offers Scholarships in Music, Art, Sport and Drama of up to 33% reduction on standard fees.

Sutton Valence School (see p 415)

Academic Scholarships and Exhibitions are awarded at 11+, 13+ and for Sixth Form entry and can be in addition to scholarships in other disciplines.

The Westminster Scholarship supports well-motivated and able pupils who enter Sutton Valence School at Sixth Form level and who are expected to achieve 5 A grade passes at GCSE.

Further details may be obtained from the Admissions Officer.

Tonbridge School (see p 420)

Up to 21 Academic Scholarships (awarded by examination in early May); 10 or more Music Scholarships (examination in early February); up to 10 Art, Drama or Technology Scholarships (examination in early February); up to 4 Cowdrey Scholarships, for sporting ability and sportsmanship (assessment in early February) and; Choral Boarding Awards, for Choristers of Cathedral or other Choir Schools. 3 or 4 Sixth Form Academic or Music Scholarships are also awarded.

The value of a Scholarship may be increased, by any amount up to the full school fee, if assessment of the parents' means indicates a need.

For boys over 10 and under 11 on 1st September, two Junior Foundation Scholarships are awarded, tenable at a preparatory school. Candidates must be attending a State Primary School. Junior academic and music awards may also be made to 10 or 11 year old sons of needy parents in fee-paying Prep Schools. They are awarded as 'advance' Scholarships by competitive examination in November 2¾ years before entry to Tonbridge.

Entry forms and full particulars of all Scholarships and Foundation Awards may be obtained from the Admissions Secretary, Tonbridge School, Tonbridge, Kent TN9 1JP. Tel: 01732 304297; email: admissions@tonbridge-school.org.

Trent College (see p 421)

Awards are made for excellence in Music, Art, Sport, Drama and Academic ability at 11+, 13+ and 16+. Means-tested 'Devonshire Scholarships', for the attainment of academic, sport, music, drama and art excellence, are available to students of any age not currently studying at Trent College and may account for up to 75 per cent of fees.

Trinity School (see p 423)

Up to thirty Entrance Scholarships are awarded annually to boys applying at 10+, 11+ or 13+. Boys must be of the relevant age on 1 September of year of entry. Awards are based on the results of an entrance examination and interview. Scholarships are also available for entry to the Sixth Form, based on GCSE results. The value of the Scholarship is up to half of the school fee and this may be supplemented up to the value of the full fee if there is financial need. Academic, Art, Design Technology, Drama, Music and Sport Scholarships are offered.

University College School (see p 427)

Fee assistance is available through a means-tested application process. Applicants of sufficient academic standing who lack financial resources are encouraged to apply to the Foundation's generous bursary programme.

UCS is keen to also recognise the ability and achievement of the candidates who sit our admissions tests. UCS is proud to offer prizes to those candidates whose performance is exemplary. These prizes take the form of generous book tokens, with book plates inscribed to commemorate the candidate's achievement. The books will be presented at a private occasion for the pupil and his/her family, when he/ she joins the school.

Uppingham School (see p 429)

Approximately 30–40 scholarships worth between one-tenth and one-half of the fees are awarded annually, if suitable candidates present themselves. The scholarships awarded are academic, Thring (All-Rounder), music and art/design and technology. A number of music exhibitions (granting free tuition on all instruments) are also awarded. Scholarship exams for 13+ entry are held in the February/March prior to the September pupils hope to enter the School. Academic, music and art/design and technology scholarships for Sixth Form entry are awarded in November in the year preceding entry to the School.

Details of all scholarships, examinations and procedures may be obtained from the Admissions Office (01572 820611).

Warwick School (see p 435)
Governors Scholarships (11+, 12+, 13+, 16+) are available to reward academic excellence and talent. Scholarships are awarded up to the value of 20% of fees based on the results of the entrance examination and interview. For existing Sixth Formers, the scholarships are awarded based on GCSE results and school reports.

Sixth Form Science Scholarship: The Ogden Trust sponsors pupils of outstanding scientific ability to attend Warwick School in the Sixth Form. Awarded up to 100% of fees, funded jointly by Ogden Trust and Warwick School. For pupils educated entirely in state sector achieving a minimum of 5 GCSEs at Grade A, including Mathematics. The successful candidate must study Mathematics and Physics at A Level and intend to read a science-related degree at university. Joint parental income should be less than £50K.

Further details from the Admissions Registrar, Warwick School, Warwick, CV34 6PP. Tel: 01926 776400; e-mail: enquiries@warwickschool.org.

Wellingborough School (see p 436)
Scholarships and Exhibitions are offered annually. Awards are based on the Common Entrance Examination held in June for candidates under 14 on 1 September following. Candidates who have not been prepared for the Common Entrance examination may be allowed to sit a restricted range of papers. Entries are required by the end of April. Foundation Scholarships are offered annually. The examination is held in January for candidates over 10 on 1 March. Entries are required by the end of December.

Music, Drama, Art and Sports Scholarships are also available at 13+ and 16+.

Further details and application forms may be obtained from the Headmaster, Wellingborough School, Wellingborough, Northants NN8 2BX.

Wellington College (see p 439)
There is a wide range of 13+ Scholarships and Exhibitions offered – Academic, Music, Art, Design & Technology, Drama, Dance and Sports. Details are shown on the website and in a separate booklet available from Admissions. Candidates for non-academic awards must satisfy our general entry requirements. Scholarships of all values may be augmented by a bursary where the financial situation of the parents makes this necessary. Candidates must be under 14 on 1st September in the calendar year in which they sit the examination.

For pupils entering at 16+ there is a similar range of awards across the disciplines.

For further information apply to The Director of Admissions.

Wells Cathedral School (see p 443)
Scholarships and Academic Awards are offered to those who show outstanding ability on the Entrance Scholarship Tests held in late January/early February at the School. The value of the awards will depend on individual financial circumstances. Auditions are held over the same weekend for those seeking places as specialist musicians.

Further details may be obtained from The Registrar, Wells Cathedral School, Wells, Somerset BA5 2ST. Tel: 01749 834200, Fax: 01749 834201, e-mail: admissions@ wellscs.somerset.sch.uk.

West Buckland School (see p 445)
A number of scholarships are awarded for entry at 7+,11+, 13+ or 16+ (up to a value of 10% of the tuition fees). Candidates must be under 8, 12, under 14, or under 17 years of age on 1st September following the examination, which will take place in late January or early February.

Westminster School (see p 446)
An examination (The Challenge) will be held in May to elect The Queen's Scholars. There are 40 Queen's Scholars in College and the average number of Scholarships awarded annually is 8. The value of a Scholarship is 50% of the current boarding fee. All Queen's Scholars board in College. Boys who do not wish to board may be candidates for the title of Honorary Scholar. Up to 5 exhibitions may be awarded each year to those who narrowly miss being offered a scholarship. The Challenge consists of papers in Mathematics, English, French, Science, Latin, History, Geography and an optional Greek paper.

The value of a scholarship may be supplemented by a bursary (remission of the fees) up to a maximum of 100% if there is proven financial need. Parents who wish to apply for financial assistance should request a Bursary Application Form from the Registrar (tel: 020 7963 1003; email: registrar@westminster.org.uk).

Whitgift School (see p 448)
Up to 27 scholarships are awarded at age 10 with up to 45 being available at age 11. Further scholarships are also available at age 13 and at Lower Sixth level. Awards for sport, music, drama, art and design, design technology and all-round ability are also available.

Winchester College (see p 450)
The Scholarship examination (Election) is held in May each year, and about 14 scholarships are awarded. All scholarships are means-tested. Bursaries are available. Scholars live together in College.

As a result of the Scholarship Examination about six Exhibitions may also be awarded which ensure a place in a Commoner House. Applications for bursaries are encouraged. There are also Music Scholarships (means-tested) and Music Exhibitions, which offer free tuition in one or more specified instruments. Enquiries about these awards should be directed to the Master of Music. Music Award candidates who are not taking the Scholarship Examination will be required to take the Entrance Examination.

Candidates must be over 12 and under 14 on 1st September following the examination.

Further particulars and copies of specimen papers can be obtained from *The Master in College, Winchester College, College Street, Winchester, Hampshire SO23 9NA.*

Wolverhampton Grammar School (see p 454)
Up to eight Governors' Academic Scholarships (25% fees) will be awarded to the highest placed candidates in the January 11+ entrance examination and subsequent interview. One scholarship will be offered at 13+ (25% fees), also awarded on the basis of the January examination and interview. Two Music Scholarships (25% of fees) will be offered to outstanding performers, one at 11+ or 13+ and another at 16+.

Sixth Form Scholarships: Two Governors' Academic Scholarships will be offered to candidates entering the Sixth Form.

For further particulars apply to the Head.

Woodbridge School (see p 455)
Academic Scholarships are available for entry at 11, 13 and 16. Art, Drama, Music, Chess, Sports and All-Rounder awards are also available.

Woodhouse Grove School (see p 457)
Academic scholarships are available at 11 and 13 on the basis of examination performance, interview and school report. In addition, parents may apply for financial assistance via our Bursary Scheme for which a means test is

applied. Further details can be obtained from the Headmaster.

Worksop College (see p 458)

Scholarships (up to 25% of fees pa) and Exhibitions may be awarded annually by Examination in February.

Bursaries may be given in addition to Awards if the financial circumstances of the parents make this necessary. Application for such an increase in the event of an award being made should be sent to the Headmaster at the time of entry.

Sixth Form Scholarships: Several Sixth Form Scholarships are available each year, for which there is an examination for external candidates in February.

For further information, please contact the Admissions Registrar.

Worth School (see p 460)

At 11+: Awards of up to 40% of annual fees, based on tests in English, Maths and Non-Verbal Reasoning, held at Worth in the Lent Term.

At 13+: Awards of up to 40% of annual fees. Worth is part of the Common Scholarship Scheme and exams take place at Worth in February.

At 16+: Sixth Form scholarships of a value up to 40% of annual fees. These awards are based on examinations in the Autumn Term, a good school report, good GCSE grades and an interview.

St Benedict's Scholarships at 11+ and 16+: Assisted places, with scholarships up to a value of 100%, for one day place at 11+ and two day places at 16+ to allow local Catholic children of real ability to benefit from the opportunities available at Worth.

Wrekin College (see p 462)

Examinations for Academic Entrance Scholarships are held annually in March. All candidates must be under 12, under 14 or under 16 on 1st September in the year in which the examinations are held.

Wycliffe College (see p 464)

Scholarships and Exhibitions are available up to a maximum of 40% of school fees. In addition, the Wycliffe College Foundation provides funding which includes a Sibly Scholarship (for vegetarians), a Wilson Scholarship for Art or Music and Pearson Bursaries which may be awarded to pupils of all-round merit whose parents cannot afford full fees. Fees may also be supplemented up to a maximum of 90% where there is a clear case of financial need. The Wards Scholarship is awarded to a Wycliffian to assist with university fees.

Yarm School (see p 467)

Several (usually six each year) Academic Scholarships, up to the value of 20% of the full fee, are awarded as a result of performance in the 11+ Entrance Examination (held late January).

Ogden Trust Sixth Form Science Scholarships are available and awarded on academic merit (subject to other criteria being met) based on the January scholarship examination.

The school also offers Music Scholarships which provide for a reduction of up to 20%. Candidates for major awards are normally expected to offer a minimum of two instruments or one instrument plus voice. Music Scholarships can be awarded at any stage in the pupil's school career and modest awards can be upgraded in the light of further outstanding progress.

Music and/or Performing Arts Scholarships

Abingdon School (see p 7)

Music Awards:

Up to two Music Exhibitions at 11+.

A flexible number of scholarships and exhibitions is available at 13+ and to the Sixth Form.

The scholarships include free tuition on up to three instruments, and when appropriate the Duxbury Scholarship. Exhibitions are also available which offer free tuition on one or two instruments.

Drama:

A drama award can be given on entry at 13+ or to the Sixth Form.

Ackworth School (see p 8)

Music Scholarships are usually awarded at age 11, 13 or 16+. The awards are made on the strength of a half-hour audition and recognise achievement and potential, preferably on two instruments. Free tuition on one or two instruments may be offered to promising musicians who do not gain a scholarship.

Aldenham School (see p 10)

Scholarships and Exhibitions are available at 11+, 13+ and 16+ for Music under the same terms as for academic awards. Free Tuition is given to Music Scholars. Any combination of choral and instrumental ability may be offered for the audition.

Alleyn's School (see p 11)

Foundation Music Scholarships available at 11+ and 13+, worth up to £3,000 pa plus free tuition on principal instrument. Alleyn's Music Scholarships also available (free tuition on principal instrument). At 16+ Hans Keller Music Scholarship is worth up to £1,500 pa.

Ampleforth College (see p 13)

Music Scholarships are available for entry to the College at ages 13 and 16. All scholarships carry free music tuition.

Further details can be obtained from The Admissions Office, Ampleforth College, York, YO62 4ER. Tel: 01439 766863; e-mail: admissions@ampleforth.org.uk.

Bancroft's School (see p 22)

Two Music Scholarships at 11+ for children with outstanding musical talent which cover half fees and extra music tuition, plus up to two music awards at Sixth Form level.

Bedales School (see p 27)

Music scholarships are awarded each year to outstanding musicians for entry to Dunhurst (10+ and older; exceptionally, 8+) and to Bedales (13+ and 16+).

Full details from the Registrar.

Birkdale School (see p 37)

Candidates must satisfy the school's general admission standards. One award is available at 11+ and one at 16+ of up to 25% of tuition fees plus free tuition by Birkdale staff on one instrument. Candidates should be of good Grade 3 (11+) or Grade 5/6 (16+) standard in their first instrument and show general musicianship commensurate with technical skill. A Music Scholar is expected to enter fully into the school's musical life. Assessments take place during the Easter Term.

Bishop's Stortford College (see p 41)

Music candidates can compete for all major awards at Sixth Form level, under 14 and under 12.

Bloxham School (see p 43)

Music Scholarships and Exhibitions of up to 20% of fees with free tuition and music. Musical ability taken into account in Open Scholarship and Common Entrance Examinations.

Bootham School (see p 48)

Music Scholarships: Awards of up to 50% fee remission are available for candidates of good all-round musical and academic ability or potential. These are available for entry at 11+ and 13+ (Years 7 and 9) and are awarded on the basis of performance in the entrance examination, and in tests and an audition with the Director of Music.

Bradfield College (see p 50)

At 13+ up to five, at 16+ up to three, Music Scholarships up to 50% of full fees plus free tuition on up to three instruments. In addition, two Music Exhibitions may be awarded annually.

At 13+ one Drama Award annually. At 16+ one Performing Arts Award annually.

Brighton College (see p 56)

A number of scholarships and exhibitions will be offered each year to candidates showing outstanding ability in Music, Drama and Dance. Examinations and interviews will be held at the College in February (Music), April (Drama) and May (Dance) for candidates intending to enter at 13+ in the following September. The value and number of the awards will depend on the calibre of the candidates.

Bromsgrove School (see p 61)

A number of Music scholarships and exhibitions are awarded each year at ages 11, 13 and 16, offering fee remission and free tuition on up to two instruments. Means-tested bursaries may be used to supplement scholarships. Full details are available from the Admissions Department.

Bryanston School (see p 64)

Junior and Sixth Form Music Scholarships, which carry free music tuition and may be supplemented by means-tested bursaries.

Further details may be obtained from the Admissions Registrar.

Canford School (see p 70)

A number of Music scholarships ranging from 50% to 10% of the fees, with free tuition on two instruments, are awarded at 13+ and 16+. One or two Drama scholarships worth a total of 20% of the fees are offered annually at 13+.

Caterham School (see p 73)

Music scholarships are available to pupils joining the school at 11+, 13+ and 16+ who have exceptional musical promise on at least one instrument. In addition to a music audition, a candidate must have achieved the required standard in the entrance examination.

Charterhouse (see p 75)

At 13+ entry. Up to 5 Music Scholarships and 2 Exhibitions are offered. The examinations are held at the school in February.

Sixth Form entry. Three Music Scholarships are offered annually. These are normally awarded in December. In addition, there is the John Pilling Organ Scholarship.

Music tuition on two instruments is free for Music Scholars and Exhibitioners.

All Awards (except Exhibitions) may be increased to the value of the full school fee in cases of proven financial need.

For details write to the Admissions Secretary, Charterhouse, Godalming, Surrey GU7 2DX.

Cheadle Hulme School (see p 77)

Some Music Scholarships are available for entry at 11+ and Sixth Form.

Cheltenham College (see p 78)

Various awards for Drama and Music, including Choral and Organ are made annually at 13+ and 16+ entry.

Chetham's School of Music (see p 81)

Entry is by audition only; all who are selected (at any age between 8 and 16) qualify for grants from the DfE under the Aided Pupil Music and Dance Scheme. Parental contributions are calculated according to means, and parents on low incomes qualify automatically for full fee remission. The Bursar will be glad to advise about the scales.

Chigwell School (see p 83)
Music scholarships are offered each year at 11+ and sometimes at 13+ and 16+ and these make a substantial contribution to school fees. In return, scholars are expected to play a full role in the performing life of the department. Currently, two scholars attend the Junior Guildhall School of Music on Saturdays.

Drama scholarships are awarded at 16.

Christ College, Brecon (see p 85)
Up to 8 Music scholarships in total are available each year, for award at 11+, 13+ or 16+ ranging in value from 10 to 50% of the fees, together with free tuition on one instrument. The value of any award may be augmented in case of need.

City of London Freemen's School (see p 90)
Music Scholarships are awarded as follows:

At 11+ up to 2 awards of not more than 25% of the tuition fee. Applicants must have reached Grade 3 in one instrument and be able to offer a second study. Auditions and interviews are held with the Director of Music.

At 13+ up to 2 awards of not more than 50% of the tuition fee. Applicants must have reached Grade 5 in one instrument and be able to offer a second study. Auditions and interviews are held with the Director of Music.

At 16+ (Sixth Form) up to 2 awards of not more than 50% of the tuition fee. Applicants must have reached Grade 7 in one instrument and be able to offer a second study. Auditions and interviews are held with the Director of Music.

In all cases, music scholarships include free tuition in one instrument provided by teachers at the School.

City of London School (see p 92)
Several Music Scholarships, up to half fees, are available each year to candidates at any of the normal entry points. They are awarded after audition and interview, and candidates must also satisfy the School's academic entrance criteria.

In addition, choristers of the Temple Church and the Chapel Royal are members of the School and receive substantial bursaries from the Choirs while they remain choristers.

Clifton College (see p 96)
Awards for Music of up to 25% of fees, with free tuition in two instruments. Music awards are also available for entry to the Sixth Form.

Dauntsey's School (see p 108)
Musical ability or potential is considered for Awards at all ages. Music and Drama Scholarships are awarded at 13+. Details from the Registrar, Mrs Jo Sagers.

Dean Close School (see p 110)
Scholarships in Music (including Choral and Organ) and Drama, based on audition, interviews and exam (Drama). Individual specialist tuition is free to all scholars and exhibitioners.

Carducci Strings Scholarship: linked to the Carducci Quartet.

Denstone College (see p 112)
Instrumental and Choral Scholarships of up to not more than 40% of the fees are available. In cases of need these Awards may be supplemented with Bursaries.

Durham School (see p 118)
Music Scholarships are available at 11, 13 and 16. At least one scholarship is available at each age group in each of the following categories: strings, brass, woodwind, piano. A Sixth Form organ scholarship is available annually. All holders of Music Awards receive some free music tuition.

Drama Scholarships are available at 11, 13 and 16.

Eastbourne College (see p 120)
Instrumental or Choral Scholarships and Drama Scholarships are offered.

The Edinburgh Academy (see p 122)
One or more Music Scholarships annually to the value of free tuition in two instruments (with means-tested Bursary assistance as required).

Ellesmere College (see p 126)
Music Scholarships of not more than 50% fees, several choral Exhibitions of up to 25% of fees. In cases of need, all these awards may be supplemented further. Tenable while candidate remains at school, subject to progress.

Eltham College (see p 128)
Music Scholarships of not more than 50% of fees at 11+, 13+ and 16+.

Drama Scholarships of not more than 50% of fees at 16+.

Candidates are auditioned and also need to sit the entrance papers.

Emanuel School (see p 130)
Music scholarships may be awarded at 10+, 11+, 13+ and 16+. Free tuition in two instruments is included as part of a music scholarship.

Drama scholarships are also available at 10+, 11+, 13+ and 16+.

Full details can be found on the School Website or by contacting the Admissions Secretary.

Epsom College (see p 132)
Music candidates compete for all Open Scholarships. Music can be offered at a lower level as part of a candidature for an All-Rounder Award.

Drama/Dance awards are based upon a performance audition, interview and authorised record of achievement.

Candidates must be under 14 on 1st September of the year of entry or entering the Sixth Form.

Eton College (see p 134)
Up to eight Music scholarships may be awarded annually, each to the value of 10% of the full fee, and all of them supplemented up to the value of full fees (subject to means-testing).

In addition there are several Music Exhibitions carrying remission of the fees for instrumental lessons. Last year 26 awards in all were made.

Special consideration will be given to cathedral choristers who would still be able to sing treble in the College Chapel choir.

Further particulars and entry forms from *The Tutor for Admissions, Eton College, Windsor SL4 6DB*.

Exeter School (see p 136)
Music Scholarships are offered annually following auditions early in the spring term and are conditional on applicants achieving the School's academic requirements for entry.

The *Sammy Sargent Music Scholarship*, the top scholarship award made to an outstanding Music scholar, may be awarded at age 11, 12, 13 or 16 and has a value of 25–50% discount off tuition fees, according to ability and means-testing.

At ages 11, 12, 13 and 16 – One Music Scholarship offering a discount of £720 per annum off tuition fees. At 16, there are two additional music scholarships each offering a discount of £720 per annum off tuition fees. Music Exhibitions offering smaller discounts and/or a contribution to music lessons may also be awarded. Contributions to music lessons may be offered in addition to a Music Scholarship, Music Exhibition or other award.

Felsted School (see p 139)
Music and Drama Scholarships of up to 20% of fees are available at 13+ and for entry into the Sixth Form.

Fettes College (see p 141)
Music Scholarships to the value of 10% of the fees are available to instrumentalists at any age between 10 and 16; high

musical potential is sought. The standard required at age 13 is normally at least Grade 5 in the main instrument. Preference will be given to orchestra players and singers. Ex-choristers and brass players are particularly welcome.

These awards can be supplemented by means-tested bursaries in the case of financial need.

Forest School (see p 143)
Music Scholarships and Exhibitions are available at 11+.
Music and Drama Scholarships are available 16+.

Framlingham College (see p 146)
Music and Drama Scholarships are offered at 13+ and 16+.

Giggleswick School (see p 150)
A number of Music awards are available at 11+, 13+ and Sixth Form. Award holders receive free musical tuition.
Drama Scholarships are available at Sixth Form level.

Glenalmond College (see p 155)
Music scholarships worth up to half fees per annum (which may be increased in the case of need) may be available to boys or girls at 12+, 13+ or Sixth Form. Candidates will usually offer two instruments at least to Grade V. Promising string players and singers will be considered with great interest. Award holders receive free musical tuition.

Guildford High School (see p 162)
Music Scholarships are offered at 11+ and 16+.

Haileybury (see p 167)
Music Scholarships are available on entry at 11, 13 and 16.

Hampton School (see p 169)
Instrumental Scholarships (remitting up to 25%) may be awarded on entry at 11+ and 13+. At 11+ Choral awards are available in conjunction with the Chapel Royal, Hampton Court Palace.

Hereford Cathedral School (see p 175)
Two-thirds reductions in tuition fees are available for Cathedral Choristers (*see Scholarships section in main entry*). Up to four Music Exhibitions are awarded each year as a result of auditions held in the first half of the Spring Term. 11+, 13+ and Sixth Form Music Scholarships are also available. Details are available from the Director of Music.

Highgate School (see p 176)
Music Awards are offered at 11+, 13+ and 16+.

Hurstpierpoint College (see p 179)
Awards are offered with free musical tuition in two instruments. Informal auditions are encouraged and may be held at any time by arrangement with the Director of Music. The Awards are given subject to satisfactory Scholarship or Common Entrance results or the College's own entry tests.
Drama Awards are available at 13+ and 16+.

Ipswich School (see p 186)
Music auditions for promising instrumentalists entering Years 7 and 9 are held in January/February. Sixth Form Music Scholarships are also available and auditions are held in November. Awards may be supplemented by bursaries in cases of proven need.

Kent College (see p 192)
Music/Drama scholarships of up to half the tuition fee are offered in conjunction with the Entrance Test to candidates for entry into Years 7, 9 and 12. Free tuition on two instruments is offered to Music Scholars. Full particulars may be obtained from the Registrar.

King's College School, London (see p 207)
Up to 6 Music Scholarships or Exhibitions may be awarded to pupils of high musical ability. Candidates must be under 14 years of age on 1 September of the year in which they sit the examination.

A Music Scholar/Exhibitioner will be expected to play an active part in the musical life of the School throughout his career at KCS.

Music Scholarships are available for pupils in the Sixth Form. One award is specifically reserved for an organist. Further information is available from the Music Secretary or the Admissions Secretary.

King's College, Taunton (see p 209)
Auditions for Music and Drama Scholarships and awards are held in February (13+), and in November for Sixth Form.

King's School, Bruton (see p 212)
All Music Scholarships offer free tuition in two instruments in addition to any other financial benefit.

Candidates should offer two instruments, one at Grade 5 or above (for 13+ entry) or at Grade 7 or above (for Sixth Form entry). They will be tested on both instruments at the assessment which is in February. The closing date is in January.

Fitzjames (Drama) Scholarships are available at Sixth Form entry only. Candidates need to show extraordinary aptitude in either acting or theatre production skills. They will undertake a practical assessment in their field of choice.

The King's School, Canterbury (see p 214)
Up to 12 Music Scholarships are offered annually for competition in January or February to pupils under 14 on 1 September in year of entry. They vary in value, but all carry free tuition in 2 instruments. Further awards are available, sometimes tenable in conjunction with the regular Music Scholarships: the system is flexible, and enquiries should be addressed to the Director of Music.

Those with exceptional ability in Drama may apply for a special Award two years after entry.

A Scholarship leaflet is issued annually in the Autumn, and may be obtained from the Assistant Registrar.

The King's School, Ely (see p 218)
The boy Choristers of Ely Cathedral are all full boarders in the Junior School. Choristers receive a 50% choristership while they remain in the choir. Bursaries worth 33% of the appropriate fees are available if a boy continues into the Senior School. A bursary of 33% of boarding fees is available to all members of Ely Cathedral Girls' Choir, aged 13–18, who are King's Senior School pupils in Years 9-13. Additional means-tested additional funding may be available. Chorister auditions are held in February for boys who will be aged 8 and for girls who will be 13 by the following September.

In addition, a very limited number of Music Scholarships are available by competitive audition to a maximum value of 25% of the tuition fee.

Music Scholarships and Exhibitions (ie scholarships of lesser value) are awarded during the Lent Term to candidates showing exceptional promise in music. Awards are available for choral and/or instrumental excellence, including organ-playing and may represent up to 25% of fees and may include free weekly tuition on two musical instruments. Candidates for entry into Year 7 and Year 9 are invited to the school for auditions in February and in November for entry the following September into Year 12.

Drama Exhibitions of up to 10% of fees are awarded for entry into Years 7 and 9. Auditions are held in January.

Full details are available from The Admissions Coordinator, The King's School, Ely, Cambridgeshire CB7 4DB. Tel: 01353 660702; e-mail: admissions@kings-ely. cambs.sch.uk.

The King's School, Macclesfield (see p 222)
Two Senior School Music Scholarships are available for instrument or singing.

King's Rochester (see p 224)
Up to five Music Scholarships and an Organ Scholarship may be awarded annually with a value of up to 30% of tuition fees.

Free tuition on all instruments studied in School is given to holders of major and minor awards.

The Scholarships, available from 11+, will be awarded after an examination, usually in February, consisting of aural, sight reading and practical tests, and a viva voce. In addition, candidates at 13+ will be expected to be of Grade 5–6 standard and capable of passing Common Entrance, or a genuine A Level candidate if 15+. 11+ candidates should be at about Grade 4 level.

The Peter Rogers Scholarship of £3,000 per annum is awarded from time to time to assist an exceptionally talented musician, and a Dame Susan Morden Choral Scholarship of £2,500 is occasionally available to a Cathedral Chorister.

Boy Choristerships to Rochester Cathedral (8+/9+) from Cathedral and School.

Details of Academic Scholarships are given elsewhere. A Bursaries brochure, and further information, may be obtained from The Registrar.

The King's School, Worcester (see p 227)
Music Scholarships and awards are available at 11+, 13+ and 16+.

Kingston Grammar School (see p 229)
Instrumental Scholarships, valued at 10% plus free tuition on one instrument, are available. Auditions are in early February for candidates who are applying for entry at either 11+ or 16+.

Lancing College (see p 234)
A number of Music Scholarships ranging in value up to half the annual school fee. Scholarships may be offered to pupils from schools where the time for Music is less than in some others, and where a candidate may have less musical experience but greater potential.

One Professor W K Stanton Music Scholarship for a Chorister from Salisbury Cathedral School, or failing that any Cathedral School. A Stanton Exhibition may also be awarded.

Drama Scholarships, ranging in value up to a quarter of the annual school fee, are available at 13+ entry.

Leicester Grammar School (see p 241)
Up to four scholarships are offered at any age. The scholarships are given on audition in recognition of achievement and potential in musical ability and are confirmed by a pass in the Entrance Examination. All awards can be supplemented by bursaries when appropriate.

Llandovery College (see p 249)
Music and Drama Scholarships available. Performance at audition and interview as well as exam results are assessed.

Lord Wandsworth College (see p 252)
Music Awards are made annually at all stages of entry to the College. Further details may be obtained from the Admissions Office.

Malvern College (see p 260)
Music: Awards are made by audition and interview.
Drama: The award will be decided by an audition and interview.

Marlborough College (see p 264)
Up to eight instrumental/choral scholarships are offered for competition each year in February to boys and girls at 13+. Four of these are Major awards. Up to seven instrumental/choral equivalent awards are available for pupils entering the Sixth Form each September. Awards enable those with a financial need to receive bursarial assistance. The degree of support given will be subject to a means test. One College Organ Scholarship/bursary is offered, which may be worth 100% of school fees, and particular consideration will be given to those applying for a strings award. Major Scholars will receive free tuition on up to three instruments. At least grade 5 Merit or Distinction will be expected on the principal instrument of 13+ candidates: grade 7 to 8 Merit or Distinction for Sixth Form candidates; ability on a second instrument will be helpful but not essential. The examination will include two contrasting pieces on the main instru-

ment and supporting skills will be tested. There will be a viva voce but no written test. Special consideration is always given to cathedral choristers and their potential for the Chapel Choir, even if their instrumental attainment has not reached the appropriate grade level.

All scholarship candidates must be under 14 on 1st September. Boys and girls should apply direct to the Director of Music for a preliminary audition (01672 892481). General information and registration forms are obtainable from the Senior Admissions Tutor, Marlborough College, Marlborough, Wiltshire SN8 1PA (01672 892300).

Merchant Taylors' School, Northwood (see p 267)
Up to 2 Scholarships up to the value of 25% of the school fees are available, together with two Exhibitions up to the value of 10% of the school fees. In addition, Music Awards are made covering the cost of tuition of up to two instruments per boy. These awards are available to candidates at all the usual ages of entry.

Details from the Admissions Secretary, Tel: 01923 845514.

Merchiston Castle School (see p 270)
Music Scholarships (including a Piping Exhibition) may be awarded to suitably qualified candidates. Means-tested financial assistance (which may include free music tuition) is also available where families demonstrate financial need. Assessments: late January each year.

Mill Hill School (see p 273)
Music and Drama Scholarships and Exhibitions are available at 13+.

For further information please visit the school's website www.millhill.org.uk.

Monkton Combe School (see p 280)
Of the ten Open Scholarships offered at age 13 at least one may be for Drama and at least two may be instrumental Scholarships (see details under Entrance Scholarships). Free tuition in one or two instruments.

Monmouth School (see p 282)
Music Scholarships and Exhibitions may be awarded at 11, 13 and 16 up to the value of half of the fees and carrying free instrumental tuition. Sixth Form organ or instrumental scholarships also available.

New Hall School (see p 287)
1 at 11+: One Music of one-third fees and tuition in up to two instruments open to any applicant.

1 at 13+: One Music of one-third fees open to any applicant.

1 at 16+: One Music and one Drama Award open to internal or external candidates.

Norwich School (see p 291)
Music Scholarships are awarded at 11+, 13+ and Sixth Form entry to pupils with outstanding ability and flair, which the school assesses by examination, interview or audition. The financial value of a scholarship will be up to 10% of the annual tuition fee – irrespective of parental means. Assistance is also given for instrumental tuition.

Drama Scholarships are awarded at Sixth Form entry only.

Cathedral Choristers hold Chorister Bursaries to the value of 50% of fees. Further assistance in cases of need is possible.

Oakham School (see p 295)
Music Scholarships may be awarded to candidates for 11+, 13+ or Sixth Form entry. Music Scholars also receive free music tuition.

A number of Drama Scholarships are available to Sixth Form entrants wishing to follow either an AS/A2 level or IB course in Theatre Studies.

The normal academic entry requirements must be satisfied. A scholarships and bursaries information booklet is available from the Registrar, Tel: 01572 758758.

The Oratory School (see p 298)
All annual scholarships are open to music candidates. Awards include free music tuition in two disciplines.

Oundle School (see p 300)
Music.
11+: Two Junior Music Scholarships to the value of up to 20% of the fees (Saturday 14 January 2012; closing date 1 December 2011).

13+: Ten Music Scholarships to a value of up to 30% of the fees, including One Junior Organ Scholarship (w/c Monday 30 January 2012; closing date 2 January 2012).

16+: One Sixth Form Music Scholarship at 10% of the fees (11 November 2011; closing date 22 October 2011).
Drama.
13+: One Drama Scholarship at 10% of the fees (4 March 2012).

Further details may be obtained from Helen Vincent, The Undermaster's Assistant, Oundle School, Oundle, Peterborough, PE8 4GH. Tel: 01832 277116. Fax 01832 277119. e-mail: hev@oundleschool.org.uk.

Pangbourne College (see p 303)
Several Music Scholarships of up to the value of 20% of College fees are offered annually. All awards carry free tuition on two instruments.

Candidates should be approximately Grade V standard or above on their main instrument. A second instrument, or experience as a chorister is an advantage. String players will be given special consideration for an award even if the standard is below Grade V provided that sufficient potential is shown.

Candidates should be under fourteen on September 1 in the year of entry. The exact date of the Scholarship Examination, which is in early March, may be obtained on application. Music Scholarships are also available for entrance to the Junior School at the age of eleven.

Drama awards are available at 11+, 13+ and 16+. Candidates are invited to attend an audition in the Lent term with the Director of Drama.

Plymouth College (see p 305)
One Open Music Scholarship (age 13+) of up to one-third of the fees.

One Open Music Scholarship (age 16+) of up to one-third of the fees.

One Open Drama Scholarship (age 13+) of up to one-third of the fees.

One Open Drama Scholarship (age 16+) of up to one-third of the fees.

One Open Performing Arts Scholarship (age 13+) of up to one-third of the fees.

One Open Performing Arts Scholarship (age 16+) of up to one-third of the fees.

Portsmouth Grammar School (see p 309)
A variable number of Music Scholarships are available at 13+ and 16+, depending upon the quality of applicants. A Sixth Form Choral Scholarship is available up to 50% of fees. Candidates are obliged to attend for tests, interview and audition on two musical instruments.

Prior Park College (see p 312)
Music awards are available at three levels of entry: a Junior Exhibition or Scholarship (for entry at age 11), a Scholarship (for entry at age of 13), and Sixth Form Scholarships. Drama scholarships are available at 11+, 13+ and 16+. All awards are worth up to 50% of fee remission. Dance scholarships are available at 13+ and 16+.

Queen's College, Taunton (see p 319)
Music Scholarships: up to 50% of fees for the most gifted scholars including free tuition in one or two instruments. Up to 8 scholarships for talented musicians aged 10+, 11+, 12+ and 13+ at the projected time of entry to the college. Three Sixth Form entry scholarships are also available plus an Organ award.

Performing Arts Scholarships: Worth up to 50% of fees for the students of best ability. Queen's College offers up to 6 scholarships for talented students with proven ability aged 11+ and 13+ at the projected time of entry to the college. Sixth Form scholarships included.

Radley College (see p 322)
Music: On average five Instrumental Scholarships and several Exhibitions are offered annually. Free tuition.

Drama: A maximum of two awards will be offered annually.

Awards may be supplemented by a means-tested bursary. Further details from our website or the Registrar.

Reed's School (see p 327)
Scholarships may be awarded for Music or Drama at age 11, 13 or 16.

Repton School (see p 330)
Music Scholarships and Exhibitions are awarded, usually at 13+ and 16+. Examinations take place in November (16+) and January (13+). An open day for potential music scholars is held in October.

Drama Scholarships are also offered, usually at 13+ with auditions and interviews taking place in January.

Rossall School (see p 333)
Instrumental or vocal Music Scholarships are offered. Awards can include free tuition in two instruments.

Royal Grammar School, Guildford (see p 337)
Music scholarships of up to 20% fee remission are available at 11 and 13. It is hoped that a King's Scholarship can be awarded each year to a boy of outstanding musical potential.

St Albans School (see p 352)
Choral scholarships are available only to candidates entering at 11+.

A variable number of Music awards is offered for internal candidates or for pupils entering at 13+.

St Bees School (see p 359)
Music Scholarships are awarded to candidates under 12 or under 14 on 1st September or to candidates for entry into the Sixth Form.

St Edmund's College (see p 367)
Music Scholarships are available at 11+ and are decided by audition and include the provision of free tuition in two instruments. Scholars will normally be required to play two instruments with at least one to a high standard (voice can be counted as one instrument). Exhibitions may also be awarded which give free tuition in either one or two instruments.

St Edmund's School (see p 369)
Music scholarships and exhibitions of up to one half of the boarding or day fees (which may be supplemented by means-tested bursaries at the Head's discretion) are available for applicants aged 11–16. The Scholarship also covers the cost of occasional lessons with London teachers for pupils reaching a sufficiently high standard. Music Scholars are expected to take a full part in the School's instrumental and choral ensembles, and attend concerts specified by the Director of Music, either locally or in London (the cost being covered by the Scholarship).

Examination requirements: Candidates should be at least Grade 5 standard at age 13. Two contrasting pieces on first instrument, one on second. Scales, sight-reading, aural tests. Melody repetition, clapping rhythms, viva voce and musical tests covering basic rudiments and their application.

Drama scholarships and exhibitions of up to one half of the boarding or day fees are available for applicants aged 11+, 13+ and 16+.

St Edward's, Oxford (see p 373)
Music scholarships are available at 13+ and 16+ entry. Normally candidates will be expected to perform on two instruments and all are encouraged to offer singing. Candidates are also encouraged to offer original compositions.

Dance and Drama scholarships are available at 13+ and 16+ entry. Candidates for both these awards will be expected to demonstrate considerable natural ability and also confirm that they have begun to reach high standards on the stage.

13+ scholarships take place in the January/February prior to entry, 16+ in the November prior to entry.

St Paul's School (see p 383)

Several Foundation Scholarships and other scholarships and exhibitions are offered for Music. The value depends on parental circumstances and may, in the case of Foundation awards, amount to full fee remission. One Sharp Scholarship is awarded at 16+. One Dennis Brain Scholarship is available on an irregular basis. Up to three South Square Scholarships may be awarded annually, in conjunction with Colet Court, for boys aged 8, 9 or 10 to sing with St Paul's Chamber Choir. Instrumental awards at Colet Court for boys aged 10 or 11 may be converted to Foundation awards at St Paul's after a further audition. Free tuition for Foundation Scholars in two instruments.

Candidates for Scholarship entry at age 13+ must be aged under 14 on 1st September.

Full particulars available from the Director of Music.

St Peter's School (see p 385)

Various music awards up to half music tuition fees are available for entrants at 13+ or Sixth Form. Additionally, up to five pupils in each Senior School year may hold an award which carries with it free tuition in a musical instrument. Interviews and auditions for these awards are held in February or early March.

Full particulars from the Head Master's Secretary, Mrs Sarah Emson, Tel: 01904 527408.

Sedbergh School (see p 388)

Music and Drama Scholarships are offered for competition. Music Scholars are usually offered free tuition in two instruments, and Scholarships up to the value of half fees may be awarded.

The Director of Music will be happy to meet prospective candidates at any time.

Further details may be obtained from The Headmaster.

Sherborne School (see p 392)

A number of Awards are available for entry at 13+. In addition one Marion Packer Scholarship of £600 pa for an outstanding performance on the piano may be offered. Those given Awards receive free instrumental tuition. The examination takes place in February.

Shrewsbury School (see p 396)

Two Music Scholarships up to the value of 50% of fees and two Music Scholarships up to the value of 20% of fees.

Sixth Form Music and Drama Scholarships are available up to the value of 25% of fees.

Solihull School (see p 399)

There are several music scholarships which are awarded at 11+, 12+, 13+ and 16+. These are based on musical ability and potential with a satisfactory level of achievement in the entrance examination. There is also an organ scholarship.

Stonyhurst College (see p 406)

Music Scholarships are offered annually on a generous scale related to parents' income and pupils' talent.

Stowe School (see p 408)

As an approximate guide, in order to win a Music Scholarship (the maximum for which is 25% fees remission at age 13), the candidate should be at least Grade Five standard on at least one instrument. An Exhibitioner may be around Grade Four standard. A good Pass standard for those sitting Common Entrance or Stowe's own Entry Papers will also be expected.

In order to win a Major Scholarship of 25% fees remission at age 16, candidates should be at least approaching Grade Six on one of their instruments. A candidate gaining a

Minor Scholarship of up to 10% or an Exhibition may be around Grade Five standard.

Full details may be obtained from The Registrar.

Strathallan School (see p 410)

Music/Choral/Performing Arts/Piping/Drumming Awards are available for entry to the Junior School (at age 9, 10, 11 and 12) and to the Senior School at 13+ and 16+.

Sutton Valence School (see p 415)

Awards are available at 11+, 13+ and Sixth Form entry. Free tuition in two instruments is given.

Tonbridge School (see p 420)

Music Scholarships: About 10 are awarded each year. In addition, a number of Music Exhibitions, giving free instrumental tuition, are awarded.

Choral Boarding Awards: Offered to Choristers at Cathedral or other Choir Schools.

Drama Scholarships: Up to 3 may be awarded annually.

The value of any Scholarship awarded may be increased, by any amount up to the full school fee, if assessment of the parents' means indicates a need.

Full particulars of all Scholarships may be obtained from the Admissions Secretary, Tonbridge School, Tonbridge, Kent TN9 1JP. Tel: 01732 304297; email: admissions@tonbridge-school.org.

Trent College (see p 421)

There are several awards for Music and Drama available at 11+, 13+ and 16+.

Trinity School (see p 423)

Music Scholarships are available of up to 50% of full fee, with free tuition in one or two instruments. Applicants are required to play two pieces on principal instrument and show academic potential in the Entrance Examination. Awards are available for all instruments and singing ability can be taken into consideration. Further details from the *Director of Music*.

University College School (see p 427)

A Standard Music Award at UCS will entitle the holder to a reduction in the annual school tuition fee of between 10% and 25%. In cases of need, Supplementary awards may be awarded up to 100% of annual tuition. Details of these special awards and their values are available from the Director of Music or www.ucs.org.

Music Awards involve competitive auditions. Applicants will be required to play two contrasting pieces of their own choice on a main instrument or voice. Competition is often quite strong. We expect a minimum of Grade V at 11+, Grade VI at age 12–13 years, and Grade VIII at 16+. The age of younger candidates will be taken into consideration. There will be ear tests, sight reading and an interview. Demonstration of ability on a second instrument, or as a singer, will be welcomed.

Uppingham School (see p 429)

A number of Music scholarships worth between one-tenth and one-half of the fees are awarded annually, if suitable candidates present themselves. An indefinite number of music exhibitions may also be awarded, granting free tuition on instruments. Music scholarships and exhibitions for 13+ entry are awarded in February/March of the year of entry and for Sixth Form entry in November in the year preceding entry to the School.

Details may be obtained from the Admissions Office (01572 820611).

Warwick School (see p 435)

Senior School: Governors Music Scholarships at 11+ and 13+ are awarded up to the value of 20% of fees based on musical ability and potential with a high level of achievement in the entrance examination.

Junior School: Two J M A Marshall Music Scholarships are available to be awarded to boys entering Year 5 in the

Junior School – 50% of the music tuition fees for two years for one instrument.

Two Choral Scholarships, each to the value of £1350 per annum, may be awarded each year to boys aged between 7 and 11 years on 1st September, who are either entering or who are in attendance at Warwick Junior School and the Choir of St Mary's Church, Warwick.

Further details from the Admissions Registrar, Warwick School, Warwick, CV34 6PP. Tel: 01926 776400; e-mail: enquiries@warwickschool.org.

Wellingborough School (see p 436)
Performing Arts (Music and Drama) Scholarships are available at 13+ and Sixth Form.

Wells Cathedral School (see p 443)
A number of Music Awards are available depending upon the standard and quality of applicants and individual financial circumstances.

In addition, the School is one of only four in England designated by the DfE providing specialist musical education. The DfE therefore provides generous assistance with tuition, boarding and music fees for up to 74 gifted musicians, grants being linked to parental income, under the DfE Music & Dance Scheme.

Cathedral Choristerships are awarded annually for boys between the ages of 8 and 11, which can provide up to 25% of boarding and tuition fees. School bursaries to the value of 10% of tuition fees are available for girl choristers.

Ex-Chorister Bursaries: On ceasing to be a Chorister, boys and girls are eligible for an ex-Chorister Bursary to the value of 8% of tuition or boarding fees.

Further details may be obtained from The Registrar, Wells Cathedral School, Wells, Somerset BA5 2ST. Tel: 01749 834200, Fax: 01749 834201, e-mail: admissions@wellscs.somerset.sch.uk.

West Buckland School (see p 445)
Music scholarships for entry at the age of thirteen.

Westminster School (see p 446)
Up to six Music Scholarships up to the value of 25% of the boarding or day fee, including free music tuition for 3 instruments, are offered annually. These may be supplemented by additional means-tested bursaries to a maximum of the full fees. In addition, several Exhibitions may be awarded covering music tuition for two instruments. The closing date for entries is early January. Candidates, who must be under 14 years of age on the following 1st September, must subsequently take either the Common Entrance or gain admission through the Scholarship Examination, The Challenge.

The Director of Music is happy to give informal advice to possible applicants (Tel: 020 7963 1017).

For further information on all Scholarships, write to the Registrar, Westminster School, Little Dean's Yard, London SW1P 3PF (tel: 020 7963 1003; email: registrar@westminster.org.uk).

Whitgift School (see p 448)
A number of Music scholarships and awards (for free instrumental tuition) is available up to the value of half the school fees to young musicians with outstanding potential. The closing date is mid-January with auditions shortly after that date. Further details are available from the Music Administrator.

Winchester College (see p 450)
Music scholarships are available annually; they are subject to means-testing and carry free instrumental tuition on two instruments and singing. In cases of financial need additional bursary grants will be awarded. One or more awards may be reserved for Winchester College Quiristers and for Sixth Form entrants. Successful candidates are generally at the level of Grade VI-VIII distinction. Music award tests take place in late January/early February each year. Music can also be offered as an option in the academic scholarship examinations in May.

The award of all Music Scholarships is conditional upon candidates satisfying the academic requirements for entry into the School. For 13+ entry, candidates must be under 14 on 1 September of the year they come into the School.

The Master of Music is pleased to answer queries and to see prospective candidates at any time. Full details available from *The Secretary, Winchester College Music School, Culver Road, Winchester, Hampshire SO23 9JF.*

Wolverhampton Grammar School (see p 454)
Two Music Scholarships (25% of fees) will be offered to outstanding performers, one at 11+ or 13+ and another at 16+. For further particulars apply to the Head.

Woodbridge School (see p 455)
Music Scholarships and Bursaries are available, ranging from 50% of fees plus free music tuition to free music tuition.

Drama Scholarships are available to the value of 25% of fees.

Woodhouse Grove School (see p 457)
Music scholarships are awarded to promising musicians. Awards generally contribute to or cover tuition fees on one or two instruments.

Worksop College (see p 458)
Music Scholarships and Exhibitions up to 25% fees. Entry forms and further details about the Scholarships are available from the Admissions Registrar.

Worth School (see p 460)
At 11+, 13+ and 16+: Awards of up to 40% of annual fees. Exhibitions are also offered giving free instrumental/vocal tuition. Auditions are held in the Lent Term.

Wrekin College (see p 462)
Music Awards will not exceed 50% of the fees and offer free instrumental/voice tuition up to a maximum in the year of thirty lessons in two instruments.

Wycliffe College (see p 464)
Instrumental Scholarships and Exhibitions up to a maximum value of 20% of fees plus free tuition in music.

Yarm School (see p 467)
Several music scholarships are awarded each year up to a maximum value of a 20% fee reduction. Free instrumental tuition is usually included. Music scholarships can be applied for at any age.

Art and/or Design & Technology Scholarships

Abingdon School (see p 7)
Up to two Art and Design Scholarships at 13+.
 Scholarships also available at Sixth Form.

Ackworth School (see p 8)
Art Scholarships are awarded at age 11 or 12. The awards are made on the strength of a 3-hour Art Scholarship examination and the submission and discussion of a portfolio of work, all of which must be supported by competent performance in the Entrance Tests.

Aldenham School (see p 10)
A small number of awards at 11+, 13+ and 16+ is available each year. These are based on the candidate's portfolio and a short exercise at the school on a mutually convenient date.

Alleyn's School (see p 11)
11+ Art scholarship, up to the value of £1,000 pa.

Bedales School (see p 27)
Art scholarships are awarded for entry at 13+ and 16+. These scholarships attract an automatic award of £750, which can be increased through means-tested bursaries.
 Full details from the Registrar.

Bishop's Stortford College (see p 41)
Art candidates can compete for all major awards at Sixth Form level, under 14 and under 12.

Bloxham School (see p 43)
Art and Design Scholarships and Exhibitions of up to 20% of fees. Artistic ability taken into account in Open Scholarship and Common Entrance Examinations.

Bradfield College (see p 50)
At 13+ up to four Art and up to two Design Awards annually. At 16+ up to three Art Awards annually.

Brighton College (see p 56)
A number of scholarships and exhibitions will be offered each year to candidates showing outstanding ability in either Art or Design & Technology. Examinations and interviews will be held at the College in January (Art), May (DT) for candidates intending to enter at 13+ in the following September. The value and number of the awards will depend on the calibre of the candidates.

Bryanston School (see p 64)
Art, ICT and DT Scholarships, for 13+ entry, which may be supplemented by means-tested bursaries.
 Further details may be obtained from the Admissions Registrar.

Canford School (see p 70)
One Art scholarship worth 20%, or two of 10%, of the fees is offered annually and one Design Technology scholarship worth 20%, or two of 10%, of the fees is offered annually at 13+.

Caterham School (see p 73)
Art scholarships are available at 11+, 13+ and 16+.

Charterhouse (see p 75)
Two Art Scholarships are offered for entry at 13+ as a result of an examination held at the school in February. In addition two Art Scholarships are offered for Sixth Form entry; the examinations for these awards will normally be held in November. All Awards (except Exhibitions) may be increased to the value of the full school fee in cases of financial need. For details write to the Admissions Secretary, Charterhouse, Godalming, Surrey GU7 2DX.

Cheltenham College (see p 78)
Awards for Art and Design Technology are made annually at 13+ and 16+ entry.

Chigwell School (see p 83)
Art scholarships are awarded at 16.

Christ College (see p 85)
One Art scholarship may be awarded each year at 13+, up to the value of 20% of the fees.

Clifton College (see p 96)
A number of Art awards are made annually, including the Roger Fry Scholarship.

Dean Close School (see p 110)
Art and Design Technology Scholarships may be awarded, based on portfolio, drawing / technical test and interview.

Durham School (see p 118)
Art Scholarships are available at 13 and 16; DT scholarships are available at 13.

Eastbourne College (see p 120)
Art or Design & Technology (including Textiles) Scholarships are offered.

Ellesmere College (see p 126)
One or two Art Exhibitions awarded each year in May on the basis of an exam and a portfolio of pupil's work.

Eltham College (see p 128)
Art Scholarships of not more than 50% of fees at 16+.

Emanuel School (see p 130)
Art scholarships may be awarded at 10+, 11+, 13+ and 16+.
 Full details can be found on the School Website or by contacting the Admissions Secretary.

Epsom College (see p 132)
Art candidates compete for all Open Scholarships. They should submit a varied portfolio of about 15 pieces of work and they will then be invited to Epsom to discuss their work at interview and, at 13+, to do a timed drawing test.
 Design Technology awards are based upon a portfolio presentation composing several contrasting items and, at 13+, a timed design test.
 Candidates must be under 14 on 1st September of the year of entry or entering the Sixth Form.

Exeter School (see p 136)
One Art Scholarship is offered annually to a sixth form pupil following an assessment and interview. This scholarship offers a discount of £720 per annum off tuition fees. Art Exhibitions offering smaller discounts may also be awarded.

Felsted School (see p 139)
Art and Design & Technology Scholarships of up to 20% of the fees are available at 13+ and for entry into the Sixth Form. The School is a participant in the Arkwright Foundation Scholarship Scheme for Talented Students in Design at 16+.

Forest School (see p 143)
Art Scholarships are available at 16+.

Framlingham College (see p 146)
Art and Design & Technology Scholarships are offered at 13+ and 16+.

Giggleswick School (see p 150)
Art Scholarships and Exhibitions are available at either 13+ or Sixth Form level. Design Scholarships are available at Sixth Form level.

Glenalmond College (see p 155)
Candidates are invited to apply at 12+, 13+ or Sixth Form for Art Awards of up to 50% of fees.

Haileybury (see p 167)
Art Scholarships are available at entry to those joining at 13 and 16.
 Technology Scholarships are available on entry at 13.
 No fee remission is awarded for Art or Technology scholarships. Successful candidates will be awarded a book token to the value of £100.

Hampton School (see p 169)
Art Scholarships (remitting up to 25%) may be awarded on entry at 11+ and 13+.

Hurstpierpoint College (see p 179)
Awards are available for Art and Design & Technology Scholarships at 13+ and 16+ for external candidates. A folio of work is presented and there is an objective test as well as an interview. Academic assessment will be on the basis of a sound pass at Common Entrance or by the College's own entry tests.

Ipswich School (see p 186)
Art Scholarships are available for entry at 11 and 13. Pupils submit a portfolio of their work prior to their entrance examination. Awards may be supplemented by bursaries in case of proven need.

Arkwright Design Technology Scholarships are available for entry to the Sixth Form.

King's College School, London (see p 207)
One or two Art and Design Scholarships or Exhibitions may be awarded annually to pupils of high artistic ability and potential. Candidates must be under 14 years of age on 1 September of the year in which they sit the examination.

Selection will be by folio inspection, and by invitation to a half-day of practical work in an informal and friendly atmosphere in the KCS studios. Candidates will be offered a number of objects or groups of objects from which to work in their chosen medium.

An Art Scholar will be expected to take Art as an examined subject throughout the pupil's career in the School.

Further information is available from the Director of Art or the Admissions Secretary.

King's College, Taunton (see p 209)
Applicants for Art and Design & Technology Scholarships are invited to visit the school during the Lent term with a portfolio of work.

King's School, Bruton (see p 212)
Art and/or Technology Scholarships are available at 13+ entry.

Art Scholarships are available at Sixth Form entry.

The King's School, Canterbury (see p 214)
Art Scholarships are available to candidates of outstanding ability. Candidates must be under 14 on 1 September in year of entry. Further details from the Assistant Registrar.

The King's School, Ely (see p 218)
Art Exhibitions of up to 10% of tuition fees are awarded during the Lent term to candidates showing exceptional promise for entry into Years 7 and 9.

A Design and Technology Exhibition of up to 10% of tuition fees is available for entry into Year 9.

Candidates will be invited to the school in February for interview with the appropriate Head of Department.

Full details are available from The Admissions Coordinator, The King's School, Ely, Cambridgeshire CB7 4DB. Tel: 01353 660702; e-mail: admissions@kings-ely.cambs.sch.uk.

Kingston Grammar School (see p 229)
Art Scholarships (valued at 10%) may be awarded at 11+ and 16+ following practical test, interview and submission of portfolio.

Lancing College (see p 234)
Art Scholarships, ranging in value up to a quarter of the annual school fee, are available.

Lord Wandsworth College (see p 252)
Art Awards are offered to entrants to the Third Form and Sixth Form. Further details may be obtained from the Admissions Office.

Malvern College (see p 260)
Art: A special examination is set and candidates will be required to bring a portfolio of their work.

Technology: The award will be decided by work carried out prior to the examination, a practical examination and an interview.

Marlborough College (see p 264)
Four scholarships are offered annually for Art and two for Design at 13+. Awards enable those with a financial need to receive bursarial assistance with the fees. The degree of the support given will be subject to a means test.

Candidates will be required to submit their portfolio for short listing. It should contain a range of studies, colour work, objective drawing, imaginative work and indeed anything found to be visually interesting. Promise as well as achievement will be taken into account.

Award winners must satisfy entrance criteria and they will be judged for the art and design scholarships entirely on the strength of their promise as artists/designers. They must be under 14 on 1st September. Details of these scholarships can be obtained from The Senior Admissions Tutor, Marlborough College, Marlborough, Wiltshire SN8 1PA (01672 892300).

Merchiston Castle School (see p 270)
An Art (Art & Design) or Design & Technology Scholarship is available to a suitably qualified candidate (aged 13 years or more). Candidates are required to provide a portfolio of work; undertake a practical assessment and interview, and achieve a sound academic standard. The Colin Paton Technology Award is open to boys aged 13+ to 16 who can demonstrate a particular aptitude in Electronics. Assessments: late January each year.

Mill Hill School (see p 273)
Art and Design Awards are available at 13+.

For further information please visit the school's website www.millhill.org.uk.

Monkton Combe School (see p 280)
Of the ten Open Scholarships offered at age 13 at least one may be for Art.

New Hall School (see p 287)
1 at 16+: Award open to internal and external candidates.

Norwich School (see p 291)
Art and Design Scholarships are awarded at Sixth Form entry only.

Oakham School (see p 295)
Art and Design and Technology Scholarships and Exhibitions may be awarded to candidates for 13+ and Sixth Form entry. The normal academic entry requirements must be satisfied. Awards made to Sixth Form candidates are intended for those who wish to follow an A Level course in Art or Design and Technology, with the aim of taking up a career in these fields.

A scholarships and bursaries information booklet is available from the Registrar, Tel: 01572 758758.

The Oratory School (see p 298)
Any of the existing Scholarships and Exhibitions may be awarded for Art.

Oundle School (see p 300)
13+: Two Art Scholarships at 10% of the fees (9 May 2012).

13+: Two Technology Scholarships at 10% of the fees (9 May 2012).

16+: One Art Scholarship at 10% of the fees (11 November 2011; closing date 22 October 2011).

16+: One Technology Scholarship at 10% of the fees (11 November 2011; closing date 22 October 2011).

Further details may be obtained from Helen Vincent, The Undermaster's Assistant, Oundle School, Oundle, Peterborough, PE8 4GH. Tel: 01832 277116. Fax: 01832 277119. e-mail: hev@oundleschool.org.uk.

Pangbourne College (see p 303)
Art scholarships of up to 20% of fees are available at 13+ and 16+. Candidates must present a folio of work completed over the previous two years and attend an interview in the

Lent term. Successful candidates are likely to be those who have worked in a variety of media and can show depth of thought on individual pieces.

As an Arkwright Technology Scholarship centre, Pangbourne may nominate outstanding students at 16+ for this prestigious award. Further details of the application procedure are available from the College Registrar.

Plymouth College (see p 305)
One Open Art Scholarship (age 13+) of up to one-third of the fees.

One Open Art Scholarship (age 16+) of up to one-third of the fees.

Portsmouth Grammar School (see p 309)
Art Scholarships are available at Sixth Form level.

Prior Park College (see p 312)
Art Scholarships are available to exceptionally able applicants at ages 13+ and 16+. An Art Exhibition (minor Scholarship) is available to exceptionally able applicants at age 11+, who may then become eligible for the 13+ Scholarship when they reach the appropriate age.

Queen's College, Taunton (see p 319)
Art Scholarships: Worth up to 50% of fees for the most talented scholars. Scholarships are for talented students with an existing standard and potential for considerable development. Candidates to be aged 11+ or 13+ at projected time of entry to the college. Sixth Form scholarships included. Art scholarships are based on portfolio and interview.

Radley College (see p 322)
Up to two Art Scholarships and an Exhibition will be offered annually. Awards may be supplemented by a means-tested bursary. Further details from our website or the Registrar.

Reed's School (see p 327)
Scholarships may be awarded for Art at age 11, 13 or 16. Design & Technology scholarships are available at age 13 or 16.

Repton School (see p 330)
Art Scholarships and Exhibitions are offered, usually at 13+ and 16+. Examinations take place in November (16+) and January (13+). Candidates will be assessed by examination, interview and an assessment of their portfolio.

Design and Technology (DT) and Information and Communication Technology (ICT) Scholarships and Exhibitions are offered, usually at 13+. Examinations take place in January. Candidates will be asked to complete a practical session and interview and to provide a folder of work for assessment.

Royal Grammar School, Guildford (see p 337)
One Art Scholarship at 13+ is available annually.

St Albans School (see p 352)
At least one Art Scholarship is offered for internal candidates or for pupils entering at 13+.

St Edmund's College (see p 367)
Art Scholarships are available at 11+ and are decided by examination of a portfolio and a test. Scholars are required to make a significant contribution to the artistic life of the College and to contribute work to an annual Art Scholars' Exhibition.

St Edmund's School (see p 369)
Art Awards of up to one half of the boarding or day fees (which may be supplemented by bursaries at the Head's discretion) are available for pupils entering at 13 or into the Sixth Form. The departments teach drawing, painting, sculpture, ceramics, photography, printmaking, textiles, and design technology. Art may also be taken as part of the academic scholarship examination. A candidate offering Art will be expected to produce a folio of recent work.

St Edward's, Oxford (see p 373)
Art scholarships are available at 13+ and 16+ entry. Candidates must submit a portfolio of work prior to the assessment. On the day of the award they will be asked to draw from observation and take a simple test to assess colour sense. 13+ scholarships take place in the January/February prior to entry, 16+ in the November prior to entry.

Sedbergh School (see p 388)
Art and Design Technology Scholarships are offered for competition.

Sherborne School (see p 392)
Art and Design & Technology Awards are available.

Shrewsbury School (see p 396)
Two Art Scholarships up to the value of 20% of fees.

Sixth Form Art Scholarships are available up to the value of 25% of fees.

Stonyhurst College (see p 406)
Stonyhurst offers Scholarships in Art. Applicants are invited to submit portfolios of their work, personal as well as set pieces, which demonstrate a lively interest in and enthusiasm for the subject(s). There should also be evidence of proven ability through a variety of media and approaches. Portfolios should be sent or brought by the applicant early in May.

Stowe School (see p 408)
Some Art and Design & Technology Scholarships are available for pupils entering Stowe at age 13 or 16, and are offered to candidates who submit evidence of outstanding ability and a strong interest in these areas.

13+: Art candidates will be required to sit an examination in Art in the course of one day. They should bring a portfolio of recent work. This portfolio should contain a broad selection of work in whichever field of Art the candidate has studied. Two-dimensional work need not be mounted. Photographs of three-dimensional work are preferred. In general, particular attention will be paid to good objective drawing.

13+: Design candidates will sit a written paper and interview based on theory of materials/process; graphic work and a solution of a design problem. They should bring a portfolio of their recent work, providing evidence of research and influence, drawing skills and graphical communication ability, on a selection of Design Briefs to showcase their creativity and imagination. Candidates will be assessed through photographs or examples of recent practical work on their practical ability and we are interested in those who express themselves clearly about the world of Design and Technology and demonstrate a passion for its related fields.

A good Pass standard for those sitting Common Entrance or taking Stowe's own Entry Papers will also be expected.

16+: Art candidates will be required to provide a portfolio of recent work for assessment. This should contain a broad selection of work in whichever field of Art has been studied. Two-dimensional work need not be mounted. Photographs or slides of three-dimensional work are preferred. Particular attention will be paid to good objective drawing.

16+: Design candidates would usually have studied the subject at GCSE (either Product Design, Resistant Materials or Graphic Products), achieving an exceptional quality of design work and a clear ability to produce high quality, well resolved artefacts that demonstrate the true essence of client led Product Design. Candidates would be expected to show outstanding graphical skills when designing, and this evidence would usually be supported by GCSE practical coursework and additional evidence from extra-curricular work that may include three dimensional artefacts or photographs of them.

Design Sixth Form Arkwright Scholarships: Stowe is one of over 600 schools affiliated to the Arkwright Scholarship Trust, which will provide a number of scholarships in 2012 in conjunction with member schools. The awards will be of £950 over two years: the student receives £250 per year and the Design and Technology Department £225 per year per scholar, as well as the support of an external sponsor and the offer of work placements throughout the scholarship period. Arkwright Scholarships are available to students, both internal and external, completing their GCSEs in 2012 and who will be studying Maths and Design and Technology in the Sixth Form, preferably to A2 Level, and intend to read Engineering, Technology or another Design-related subject at university. The application process which is managed by the school in the Lent term of the Fifth Form involves an externally assessed examination and interview.

All 16+ candidates are also required to pass Stowe's Entry Examinations, held in the November of their GCSE year, in two subject papers (related to their AS Level choices), a Verbal Reasoning paper and an interview.

Full details may be obtained from The Registrar.

Strathallan School (see p 410)
Art and Design Technology scholarships are available for entry to the Senior School at 13+ and 16+.

Sutton Valence School (see p 415)
Available at 11+, 13+ and 16+ entry.

Tonbridge School (see p 420)
Up to 8 Art or Design Technology Scholarships may be awarded annually.

The value of any award may be increased, by any amount up to the full school fee, if assessment of the parents' means indicates a need.

Full particulars of all Scholarships may be obtained from the Admissions Secretary, Tonbridge School, Tonbridge, Kent TN9 1JP. Tel: 01732 304297; email: admissions@ tonbridge-school.org.

Trent College (see p 421)
Awards are available for Art at 11+, 13+ and 16+.

Uppingham School (see p 429)
Scholarships between one-tenth and one-half of the fees may be awarded for Art/Design and Technology annually to pupils entering the School at 13+ and 16+.

Details may be obtained from the Admissions Office (01572 820611).

Wellingborough School (see p 436)
Art Scholarships are available at 13+ and 16+.

Whitgift School (see p 448)
A small number of Art and Design Technology awards is available to promising pupils. Please apply to the Admissions Secretary for further information.

Woodbridge School (see p 455)
An Art Scholarship to the value of 10% of fees at 11+ and 25% of fees at 13+ and 16+ is available annually.

Woodhouse Grove School (see p 457)
Art scholarships are available each year.

Worksop College (see p 458)
Art Scholarships up to 25% of fees. Folios should be sent to the Director of Art by the beginning of February. Candidates will be called to the school in February. They will be required to take a practical examination and, in some cases, a written examination in English comprehension and composition.

Entry forms, available from the Admissions Registrar, should reach the school by mid-January.

Wrekin College (see p 462)
Art Scholarships worth a maximum of half fees are available.

Sports and/or All-Rounder Scholarships

Abingdon School (see p 7)
Up to two Sports Awards at 13+.
Sports Scholarships also available at Sixth Form.

Alleyn's School (see p 11)
At 11+ and 13+ Foundation Sports scholarships up to the value of £3,000 pa, and Alleyn's Sports Scholarships (£250 pa) are available.

Ampleforth College (see p 13)
All-Rounder Scholarships at 13+ – The Basil Hume Scholarships. For candidates who have a strong commitment to extra-curricular activities. The scholarships are honorary and carry no remission of fees. However, the award of a scholarship will support a bursary application.

Further details can be obtained from The Admissions Office, Ampleforth College, York, YO62 4ER. Tel: 01439 766863; e-mail: admissions@ampleforth.org.uk.

Bloxham School (see p 43)
Sports Awards of up to 20% of fees are available at 13+ and 16+ entry.

Bradfield College (see p 50)
At 13+ up to eight, at 16+ up to three, Dr Gray Bradfield Exhibitions are awarded annually for a combination of academic merit and distinction in music, drama or sport (or any combination of these).

Up to ten Sports Awards (up to five each at 13+ and 16+) are awarded annually to pupils who are outstanding in one or more sports and who would make a significant contribution to this area of College life.

Brighton College (see p 56)
All-Rounder Scholarships are available for entry at 11+ and 13+. Examinations and interviews will be held at the College in February for candidates intending to enter the College the following September. The value and number of the awards will depend on the calibre of the candidates.

Bryanston School (see p 64)
Sport and Richard Hunter All-Rounder scholarships are available annually for 13+ entry and Udall Awards for Sport for entry to the Sixth Form, which may be supplemented by means-tested bursaries.

Further details may be obtained from the Admissions Registrar.

Canford School (see p 70)
At 13+ a number of Sports scholarships ranging from 50% to 10% of the fees are offered annually. At 16+ a number of Assyrian scholarships for excellence in non-academic areas ranging from 40% to 10% of the fees are offered annually.

Caterham School (see p 73)
Sport scholarships are available at 11+, 13+ and 16+. All-Rounder scholarships are available for pupils entering at age 13+.

Cheadle Hulme School (see p 77)
Sports Scholarships are available for entry at 11+.

Cheltenham College (see p 78)
Awards for Sport and All-round are made annually at 13+ and 16+ entry.

Christ College (see p 85)
Sports scholarships are available annually at 11+, 13+ and 16+ to candidates showing outstanding talent ranging in value from 10% to 50% of the fees.

One or more All-Rounder awards are available at 13+ and 16+.

Clifton College (see p 96)
Sport awards are available at 13+ entry and for entry to the Sixth Form.

Dean Close School (see p 110)
Sports Scholarships are awarded to reflect all-round sporting ability and commitment. Assessment by conditioning tests, skills tests in two or more sports and interviews.

Worcester Warriors Rugby Scholarship: linked to Worcester RFC.

Colin Cocks and All-Rounder Scholarships: assessed by exams, activities and candidates' description of service or roles of responsibility.

Durham School (see p 118)
Sports Scholarships are available at 11, 13 and 16 for suitably talented pupils.

Eastbourne College (see p 120)
Sports Awards are offered.

Eltham College (see p 128)
Sports Scholarships of not more than 50% of fees at 11+ and 16+.

Emanuel School (see p 130)
Sports scholarships may be awarded at 10+, 11+, 13+ and 16+.

Full details can be found on the School Website or by contacting the Admissions Secretary.

Epsom College (see p 132)
Sport awards are based upon a combination of skills' tests and authorised records of achievement.

Headmaster's Awards (All-Rounder) require applicants to offer an academic element plus two or more elements to be selected from Art, Design Technology, Drama/Dance, Music and Sport. The latter are assessed through tests and interviews.

Candidates must be under 14 on 1st September of the year of entry or entering the Sixth Form.

Felsted School (see p 139)
Sports Scholarships and All-Rounder Awards which recognise all-round ability or specific ability in one area are available on entry at 11, 13 and 16 years old.

Forest School (see p 143)
2 Forest Exhibitions are awarded at 11+ to those showing all-round promise but who have not been awarded an Academic Scholarship.

Sport Scholarships are available at 16+.

Framlingham College (see p 146)
Albert Memorial Scholarships are available at either 13+ or 16+.

Haileybury (see p 167)
All-Rounder Awards, up to the value of 10% of the fees, are available to those entering at 11 and 13.

Hampton School (see p 169)
All-Rounder Scholarships (remitting up to 25%) may be awarded on entry at 11+ and 13+.

Hurstpierpoint College (see p 179)
Sport and All-Rounder Scholarships are available at 13+ and 16+.

Ipswich School (see p 186)
Sports Scholarships are awarded at 11+ and 16+ and All-Rounder Scholarships at 13+ and 16+.

Kent College (see p 192)
Sports Scholarships of up to half the tuition fee are awarded to pupils for entry into Years 7, 9 and 12. For Years 7 and 9 these will be awarded in the Spring Term in conjunction with the Entrance Test and on the basis of assessment at Kent College. For Year 12, Sports scholarships will be based on current performance and other assessment methods during the year. Full particulars may be obtained from the Registrar.

King's College School, London (see p 207)
One or two Sports Scholarships are awarded annually to pupils with exceptional sporting talent and potential. Assessment takes place in February. Candidates must be under 14 years of age on 1 September of the year in which they sit the examination.

Further information is available from the Director of Sport or the Admissions Secretary.

King's College, Taunton (see p 209)
Haywood Scholarships (for Sport) and Barrow Scholarships (for all-round contribution to the life of the school) are available for competition each January. Sports scholarships are also available in November for entry into the Sixth Form. The Somerset Scholarship, for academic achievers from the maintained sector, is for entry into the Sixth Form, again available in November.

King's School, Bruton (see p 212)
Sport Scholarships and All-Rounder Awards are available at 13+ entry.

Sports Scholarships are available at Sixth Form entry.

The King's School, Canterbury (see p 214)
Gower Sports Scholarships (up to 10% of fees) and Awards (a set annual financial award) are available for boys and girls of character and integrity who display both excellent sporting ability and sportsmanship in at least one of the main school team games.

The awards will be determined by recommendation and assessment. Candidates must be proposed and recommended by the Head of their current school, though this may be accompanied by references/testimonials from other sources (club/county/national coaches etc). Selected candidates will then be invited to the school for an Assessment Day in February, when they will be examined in their chosen sports and in generic sports aptitude and teamwork exercises.

The King's School, Ely (see p 218)
Sports Awards, for entry into Years 7, 9 and 12, are open to boys and girls with potential for major county, regional or national representation or with all-round sporting excellence. Reports will be sought from the candidates' coach(es) and practical tests, if required, will be held at the school in February.

Full details are available from The Admissions Coordinator, The King's School, Ely, Cambridgeshire CB7 4DB. Tel: 01353 660702; e-mail: admissions@kings-ely.cambs.sch.uk.

Kingston Grammar School (see p 229)
Awards (valued at 10%) for candidates demonstrating outstanding sporting potential are available at 11+ and 16+. Further details are available from the Registrar.

Lancing College (see p 234)
Sports Scholarships, ranging in value up to a quarter of the annual school fee, are available annually at 13+ entry.

Ken Shearwood Awards, ranging in value up to a quarter of the annual school fee, may be made at 13+ entry to pupils of all-round ability and potential who have made outstanding contributions to their present schools.

Llandovery College (see p 249)
Scholarships are offered for sporting excellence and all-round ability and potential. Sixth Form rugby scholarships available. Assessment days held December to April.

Lord Wandsworth College (see p 252)
Sport and All-Rounder Awards are offered to entrants to the First Form, Third Form and Sixth Form. Further details may be obtained from the Admissions Office.

Malvern College (see p 260)
Sport: Proven record of performance, or evidence of potential, at County, Regional or National level.

The Malvernian Society All-Rounder Award: This award is for candidates who meet the following criteria:

Satisfactory marks in the Common Entrance or Scholarship Examination;

Strong interests outside the classroom and a proven record of performance in them;

An exceptional report from the Head of his/her present school;

Good performance at interview.

Marlborough College (see p 264)
Sports scholarships, 8 for entry at 13+ and 4 at 16+, are available, as well as a number of All Rounder awards.

Merchant Taylors' School, Northwood (see p 267)
11+ entry: Up to 2 all-rounder scholarships each to the value of £200 per year. Up to 2 sports scholarships.

13+ entry: Up to 2 all-rounder scholarships each to the value of £200 per year. Up to 2 sports scholarships.

16+ entry: 1 sports scholarship.

Details from the Admissions Secretary, Tel: 01923 845514.

Merchiston Castle School (see p 270)
Junior Sports and All-Rounder Scholarship available for boys aged 10+ to 12. Junior assessments: mid-January each year in conjunction with academic entrance tests. Junior All-Rounder candidates must offer two or more specialisms drawn from sport, music, drama, art. Senior Sports and All-Rounder assessments (13+ and 14+) held in late January and Sixth Form in early March. Senior and Sixth Form All-Rounder candidates may choose from sport, music, drama, art and design & technology specialisms. Sixth Form, Senior and Junior Sports candidates must offer at least two sports, of which one must be rugby, cricket or athletics.

Mill Hill School (see p 273)
Sports Awards are available at 13+.

For further information please visit the school's website www.millhill.org.uk.

Monkton Combe School (see p 280)
Of the ten Open Scholarships offered at age 13 at least two may be for Sport.

Monmouth School (see p 282)
Sports Awards are available to suitable candidates at 11, 13 and Sixth Form entry.

Old Monmothian and Mountjoy Award: Good all-round candidates are encouraged to apply for awards that are made at the Headmaster's discretion.

New Hall School (see p 287)
At 11+: One Sports Scholarship of 25% of fees open to any applicant.

At 13+: Two Sports Scholarships of 25% of fees open to any applicant.

At 16+: One Sports Award open to internal and external candidates.

Norwich School (see p 291)
Sports Scholarships are awarded at Sixth Form entry only.

The Oratory School (see p 298)
Awards are made to sportsmen of outstanding ability. All-round boys are recommended by the Head of their Prep School.

Oundle School (see p 300)
13+: Twelve General Scholarships at 10% of the school fees (4-5 March 2012).

13+: Five Sports Scholarships at 10% of the School fees (21 November 2011)

Further details may be obtained from Helen Vincent, The Undermaster's Assistant, Oundle School, Oundle, Peterborough, PE8 4GH. Tel: 01832 277116. Fax 01832 277119. e-mail: hev@oundleschool.org.uk.

Pangbourne College (see p 303)
All-Rounder Awards are given to pupils of outstanding all-round talent, in academic work and a number of other areas of College life, such as sport, music and drama.

Candidates come to Pangbourne on the first Monday of the scholarship week in May and undertake a variety of academic and practical tasks relevant to their talents. Their current Headteacher's report carries considerable weight.

The College offers a small number of Sports Scholarships to candidates who are gifted in one or more sports. Candidates will be asked to demonstrate academic potential to achieve at least B grades at GCSE or C grade at A Level and sporting potential to be a significant member of our first teams in one or more major games, and the ability to compete at county or higher representative level.

Plymouth College (see p 305)
One Open Sport Award (age 13+) of up to one-third of the fees.

One Open Sport Award (age 16+) of up to one-third of the fees.

Prior Park College (see p 312)
Sporting exhibitions are available at 11+. These can be converted to full scholarships at 13+ following further assessments in the major team sports. Sporting Excellence scholarships are available at 11+, 13+ and 16+ for suitable candidates who have already achieved national recognition in their sports, which may not be one of our major team sports.

Queen's College, Taunton (see p 319)
Sport Scholarships: Worth up to 50% of fees for the students of best ability. Queen's College offers up to 6 scholarships for talented students with proven sports ability aged 11+ and 13+ at the projected time of entry to the college. Sixth Form scholarships included.

Radley College (see p 322)
On average six to eight All-Rounder Scholarships will be awarded annually. Awards may be supplemented by a means-tested bursary. Further details from our website or the Registrar.

Reed's School (see p 327)
Scholarships may be awarded for Sport at age 11, 13 or 16.

All-Rounder Scholarships are available to applicants who offer a high performance in more than one area.

Repton School (see p 330)
Sports Scholarships are offered, usually at 13+ and 16+, to pupils of exceptional talent. Assessments are held by arrangement with the Director of Sport, during the Lent Term.

C B Fry All Rounder Award: awards worth up to 20% of the Repton boarding fee may be offered at 13+ to candidates exhibiting outstanding all-round leadership potential. Assessments take place in March or April when candidates are in Year 7.

Royal Grammar School, Guildford (see p 337)
One Sports Scholarship is available for boys joining at 11+ and one at 13+ annually.

St Edmund's College (see p 367)
Sport Scholarships are available at 11+. They are decided by open competition and references from sport clubs or teachers where the child is already involved in sport at a very high level. Scholars will be expected to play a full and sustained role in the sporting life of the College.

All-Rounder Scholarships are available at 11+ and are decided by interview, school report, confidential report and mark in the entrance exam. For this award, the child will be competent academically and also be able to make a substantial contribution to other areas of life at the College such as drama, technology, the religious life, specialised sports or outdoor pursuits.

St Edmund's School (see p 369)
Sport scholarship awards of up to one half of the boarding or day fees are available for applicants aged 11–16. It is expected that candidates will be playing sport outside school

and have the potential to play at county or national level in at least one of the principal sports played at St Edmund's.

St Edward's, Oxford (see p 373)
Sport scholarships are available at 13+ and 16+ entry. Candidates will show considerable natural ability in at least one sport. We are particularly looking for players of rugby, cricket, hockey, netball, tennis and rowing.

All-Rounder awards are available at 13+ only. Candidates must be academically sound, expecting to obtain over 65% at Common Entrance, show strong leadership qualities and be able to demonstrate considerable talent in two of the following areas: art, design technology, music, dance, sport and drama.

13+ scholarships take place in the January/February prior to entry, 16+ in the November prior to entry.

Shrewsbury School (see p 396)
Two Sports Scholarships up to the value of 20% of fees, two All-Rounder Scholarships worth a maximum value of 20% of fees and ten House Foundation Awards, worth up to the value of 50% of fees, which are available for exceptional all-rounders and tied to particular day and boarding houses.

Sixth Form Sports Scholarships are available up to the value of 25% of fees.

Additionally, one Sixth Form Cassidy Sports Scholarship worth up to 100% of fees, subject to means testing.

Stowe School (see p 408)
Sports Scholarships may be awarded for exceptional candidates showing outstanding potential in at least one of Stowe's key sports: hockey, lacrosse, netball or tennis for girls and rugby, hockey or cricket for boys.

Candidates at 13+ must be able to demonstrate significant potential for sporting achievements at a high level in one of Stowe's key sports. Assessment will take the form of a full day at Stowe. Candidates will sit Stowe's own Entry Examinations in Maths and English, followed by a fitness test and a sports assessment. A good Pass standard for those sitting Common Entrance will also be expected. Candidates must also submit a portfolio for assessment which should show clear evidence of their sporting achievements and two references from people who have coached them.

Candidates at 16+ must be playing at County or Divisional level in one of Stowe's key sports. Assessment will take the form of a full day at Stowe, sitting Entry Examinations followed by a fitness test and a sports assessment. The Entry Examinations are held in the November of the candidate's GCSE year and will be two subject papers, related to their AS Level choices, a Verbal Reasoning paper and an interview. Candidates must also submit a portfolio for assessment which should show clear evidence of their sporting achievements and two references from people who have coached them.

Roxburgh (All-Rounder) Scholarships at 13+ and 16+ are intended to enable any boy or girl of outstanding all-round ability and leadership potential to benefit from Stowe's unrivalled environment to develop fully his or her talents. In addition to the strongest academic potential, which will be demonstrated in Stowe's Entry Examinations, candidates would be expected to demonstrate a high level of achievement in at least one of the following: sport, music, art and drama. Nominations for this Scholarship at 13+ will normally be made by the candidate's Headmaster or Headmistress, supported by a full school report.

Full details may be obtained from The Registrar.

Strathallan School (see p 410)
Sports and All-Rounder scholarships are available for entry to the Senior School at 13+ and 16+.

Tonbridge School (see p 420)
Up to 4 Cowdrey Scholarships may be awarded annually on the basis of sporting excellence and sportsmanship in one or more of the main team games: rugby, hockey and cricket.

The value of any award may be increased, by any amount up to the full school fee, if assessment of the parents' means indicates a need.

Full particulars of all Scholarships may be obtained from the Admissions Secretary, Tonbridge School, Tonbridge, Kent TN9 1JP. Tel: 01732 304297; email: admissions@ tonbridge-school.org.

Trent College (see p 421)
Sports Awards are available at 11+, 13+ and 16+.

Uppingham School (see p 429)
A number of All-Rounder, known as Thring, scholarships worth between one-tenth and one-half of the fees are awarded annually to pupils entering the School at 13+. Pupils are usually assessed in two disciplines of Sport, Music, Art/Design & Technology and Drama.

Sports Scholarships will also be available for the cohort joining the School in 2012. Talented pupils can be assessed in one or two sports and should be at least county standard. School major sports preferred.

Details may be obtained from the Admissions Office (01572 820611).

Wellingborough School (see p 436)
Sports Scholarships and awards are available at 13+ and at 16+.

West Buckland School (see p 445)
Sports scholarships at 11+, 13+ and 16+.

Whitgift School (see p 448)
A significant number of awards for Sport and All-Round ability is available.

Woodbridge School (see p 455)
Sports and All-Rounder awards are available for entry at 11, 13 and 16.

Woodhouse Grove School (see p 457)
Sports scholarships are awarded in the Sixth Form.

Worksop College (see p 458)
Sports Awards, to the value of up to 25% fees pa, available for entrants at 13+ and at Sixth Form. Examinations in March and May. For further details contact the Admissions Registrar.

Wrekin College (see p 462)
Scholarship and bursaries may be given for outstanding ability in games. Applications for Sports Awards should be made directly to the Headmaster during the academic year before entry to the school.

Bursaries/Educational Awards

Aldenham School (see p 10)
Bursaries are also available to help boys and girls who will benefit from education at Aldenham but whose parents would not otherwise be able to afford the full fees or to help in cases where parents' financial circumstances have changed during their son's or daughter's time at the School. These Bursaries include generous awards made available by the Brewers' Company and awards made by the OA War Memorial Fund.

Alleyn's School (see p 11)
At 11+, 13+ and 16+ means-tested bursaries of up to 100% of the fees are available to academically able candidates whose parents could not afford full fees.

Bishop's Stortford College (see p 41)
Means-tested bursaries are awarded based on individual need. This may be up to 100% in some cases.

Bloxham School (see p 43)
Generous support is available to children of Armed Forces parents, Clergy and Teachers. Bursaries based on financial need are also considered on an individual basis.

The Roger Raymond Trust Fund sponsors the boarding education of outstanding pupils who would not otherwise be able to attend the school.

Bootham School (see p 48)
Means-tested Bursaries (supported by the Bootham Trust) are available:

To assist Friend (Quaker) children, or the children of Friend (Quaker) parents, to attend the School

To assist children, whose families would not be able to afford an independent school education, to attend the School. Applicants will be assessed by academic performance in the entrance examination at 11+ and 13+ and in addition, for Music Scholars, their performance at the Music Scholarship tests and audition.

Brighton College (see p 56)
One or two Gill Memorial Scholarships offered in the Senior School and one in the Junior School for children of regular Army officers (serving or retired). Fee concessions may also be made to children of clergy of the Church of England where there is financial hardship. Cuthbert Heath Memorial Bursary available 3 years out of 5 for pupils who have a positive contribution to make to the life of the College.

Canford School (see p 70)
Means-tested bursaries worth up to 100% of the fees are available from the school where the financial need of prospective or current parents has been established. Further details about any awards can be obtained from the Admissions Office.

Caterham School (see p 73)
We wish to ensure that Caterham School is accessible to talented students, irrespective of parental income. Therefore, any prospective pupil from a low-income family is eligible to apply for a Caterham Bursary to obtain means-tested financial support in respect of day fees. A fully-funded day place for a Sixth Form student is provided by a Wilberforce Bursary. Bursaries do not preclude pupils from holding a scholarship award. Bursaries are also available for the sons and daughters of URC Clergy, Regular Forces and FCO personnel.

Charterhouse (see p 75)
For sons of lawyers the Blackstone Award is offered annually to boys when aged 11 for entry to Charterhouse at the age of 13.

A limited number of Bursaries is available for pupils who would benefit from a Charterhouse education, but whose parents are unable to afford the fees. These may be awarded at age 13 or 16.

For details write to the Admissions Secretary, Charterhouse, Godalming, Surrey GU7 2DX.

Cheadle Hulme School (see p 77)
Bursaries are offered at 11+ based on academic merit and financial eligibility. A number of other Bursaries are available for entry to the Sixth Form on the same basis.

Cheltenham College (see p 78)
Discounts for Services Families and bursaries are available.

Chigwell School (see p 83)
A number of means-tested bursaries are offered.

Christ College (see p 85)
There is a 25% fee remission for sons and daughters of the Clergy, and 10% bursaries are available each year for the children of serving members of the Armed Forces.

City of London Freemen's School (see p 90)
A significant number of Bursaries from Livery Companies are also available.

City of London School (see p 92)
The School offers a number of means-tested Sponsored Awards at 11+ and 16+ entry to very bright candidates whose parents could not otherwise contemplate private education.

Clifton College, Bristol (see p 96)
Special awards are available for the sons and daughters of old Cliftonians.

The Birdwood Award, for sons and daughters of serving members of HM Forces, is awarded on the results of the Entrance Scholarship exam.

Dean Close School (see p 110)
Means-tested bursaries for sons and daughters of clergy and missionaries. Automatic discounts, known as Thierry Awards, are offered to parents serving in HM Armed Forces on a scale according to rank. Foundation Bursaries for families in the locality unable otherwise to benefit from a Dean Close education.

Denstone College (see p 112)
Bursaries are available for the sons and daughters of the Armed Forces and Clergy.

Dulwich College (see p 115)
Entry Bursaries: A substantial number of Bursaries are awarded annually to new boys entering Year 3, Year 7 or Year 9 where parents are unable to pay the full tuition fee.

Applicants will be considered on the basis of their performance in the entrance examination and interview. Bursaries are means-tested and reviewed annually.

Durham School (see p 118)
Bursaries are available at all ages in cases where appropriate. There are generous concessions for brothers and sisters, children of clergy and of members of the Armed Forces.

Eastbourne College (see p 120)
Bursaries are awarded in appropriate circumstances. All are means tested according to the Charity Commission criteria.

A 10% boarding discount is available to HM Forces and Diplomatic Service families.

Ellesmere College (see p 126)
Reduction in fees for children of the clergy. Foundation and Regional awards for children of parents of limited means.

Eltham College (see p 128)
Bursaries are available up to 100% of fees subject to ISBA confidential means test. Community Bursaries with positive assessment for living in the locality are also available.

Please contact the Admissions Secretary for further details.

Epsom College (see p 132)
Scholarships and bursaries for children of the medical profession.

Eton College (see p 134)
Apart from the King's Scholarships, Music Scholarships, Sixth Form and New Foundation Scholarships described in the main entry, Eton offers a number of Bursaries. Application should be initiated immediately after a Conditional Place is offered at age 11. Further particulars and application forms from *The School Bursar, Eton College, Windsor SL4 6DJ.*

Felsted School (see p 139)
Special Bursaries for children of Clergy in the County of Essex and Diocese of Chelmsford, and children of those in the Armed Services. Up to two Open Bursaries for those who might otherwise be unable to consider Felsted due to financial circumstances.

Forest School (see p 143)
Bursaries are means-tested and are awarded in addition to Scholarships, up to and including the total remission of fees.
Fee reductions are available for children of the Clergy.

Framlingham College (see p 146)
Special bursaries are available for the children of serving members of HM Forces.

Giggleswick School (see p 150)
Discount available for children of HM Forces.

Glenalmond College (see p 155)
A number of means-tested bursaries are available each year for up to 100% of fees. Applications should reach the Director of Finance no later than 15th March in the year of entry. Bursaries are also available for the sons and daughters of Clergy and the children of serving Armed Forces families.

Guildford High School (see p 162)
Bursaries are available at Sixth Form level. Bursaries are available throughout the School for daughters of Clergy.

Haberdashers' Aske's Boys' School (see p 164)
A significant number of Governors' Bursaries are awarded at age 11+, valued from a few hundred pounds to full fees, depending upon financial need. Open equally to boys already in the School and to those applying from other Schools. One Bursary is reserved for Music.

Haileybury (see p 167)
Bursaries are available to increase awards, in cases of financial need, and can supplement up to 100% of the fees in some cases.

Harrow School (see p 173)
A number of means-tested Bursaries up to full fees are available for boys who do very well in the Academic, Outstanding Talent and Music Scholarship examinations.

Highgate School (see p 176)
We offer up to 10 bursaries per academic year at 11+, 2 at 13+ and 6 at 16+.

Ipswich School (see p 186)
Bursaries are available on a means-tested basis, up to full fee remission, for entry at 11, 13 and 16.

Kelly College (see p 189)
A generous reduction in fees for sons and daughters of Forces families is available (10% in Year 7 and 8, 20% in Years 9 to 13).

Kent College (see p 192)
Bursaries will be awarded in accordance with, and after consideration of, the financial circumstances of parents. Parents will be invited to complete a financial assessment form and the scale of bursary awarded will be based on the information provided and the financial criteria which the school applies to all bursary awards. All bursaries are reviewed annually.

In addition, the school operates an awards system for the children of HM Forces, NATO and War Graves Commission personnel, whereby the parents pay a set figure, normally 10% of the inclusive fee, plus the amount of Boarding School Allowance which they receive. The balance is treated as a Bursary Award. Full particulars may be obtained from the Registrar.
Exhibitions: Means-tested awards for academic, music, sport, drama and art achievement and potential are available to children entering Year 4. Full particulars may be obtained from the Bursar.

King's School, Bruton (see p 212)
The School offers a 20% remission of fees to all boarding students with one or both parents serving in the Armed Forces. The maximum combined value of Forces remission plus other awards is 25%. Other awards may be subsumed within the Forces remission. Both Forces remission and other awards may be augmented by means-tested bursaries.

The King's School, Ely (see p 218)
A 10% discount in fees is available from age 4 upwards for children of clergy serving the Christian faith and boarders who are children of service personnel in receipt of BSA. Bursaries may be awarded in cases of financial need. Parents should contact the Bursar for details of these and any sibling discounts that may be available.

King's Rochester (see p 224)
Children of Church of England ministers are given an annually means-tested reduction in tuition fees.
Children of Service Personnel are given a 20% reduction in tuition fees.
Parents with three or more children at the School are given a reduction after the second child of 10% of the third child's fees, 20% for the fourth child and 40% for the fifth and subsequent children.
Governors' Exhibitions is a means-tested scheme for the purpose of assisting financially the parents of academically gifted children who, in the opinion of the Governors, qualify to take up a place at the School.

The King's School, Worcester (see p 227)
Means-tested bursaries of up to 100% tuition fees may be available.

Kingswood School (see p 231)
Very special provisions are made for the children of Methodist Ministers (up to 100% bursary assistance) and consideration may also be given to assist the sons and daughters of clergymen of other denominations, with a reduction in fees according to circumstances. Means-tested bursaries, worth up to 100% of fees, are available in Years 7, 9 and Lower Sixth.
HM Forces families receive a reduction in boarding fees of up to 20% for each child, although the scheme is limited depending on demand for places within any particular year group at this rate.

Leighton Park School (see p 243)
Bursaries may be available, in cases of financial hardship, to existing and prospective pupils. Bursaries are always means-tested and subject to annual review.

The Leys School (see p 244)
Special awards for children of Methodist Ministers and members of HM Forces are available. Special consideration is given to the sons and daughters of Old Leysians. Bursary awards are made on a means-tested basis, and applications for bursaries must be made before entry tests are taken.

Llandovery College (see p 249)
Forces bursaries are available for the children of serving members who are guaranteed to pay no more than 10% of fees.
Sons or Daughters of the Clergy from the Province of Wales are eligible for a discount.
Means-tested bursaries are available in some cases.

Lord Wandsworth College (see p 252)
Foundation places are available to pupils who have lost one or both parents through death, divorce or separation. Apply to the Foundation Office for full details.

Loretto School (see p 253)
Bursaries are available to support scholarship and non-scholarship award candidates who pass Loretto's entrance criteria and who the School feels would benefit from a Loretto education. Bursaries can be used to supplement a scholarship award if the financial amount of a scholarship is insufficient to allow a pupil to attend Loretto. Bursaries are means-tested and are available for prospective pupils as well as existing pupils who experience unforeseen financial difficulty. Bursary funds are limited.

Loughborough Grammar School (see p 256)
The School offers a 25% boarding fee remission to sons of HM Forces and sons of Clergy.

Marlborough College (see p 264)
Bursaries are available each year for children of Clergy, and other endowed scholarships and bursaries for children of Armed Forces personnel are available from time to time when vacant.

Merchant Taylors' School, Northwood (see p 267)
Bursaries are available depending upon proven financial need. These can also be used to increase the value of a scholarship.
Details from the Admissions Secretary, Tel: 01923 845514.

Merchiston Castle School (see p 270)
Community Scholarship: One Scholarship per year carrying a means-tested concession (up to 75%) for a candidate (from EH postcode area only and who is 12+ years or older). Candidates must show above-average academic ability and talent in one or more of the following areas: art, drama, music, technology or sport.
Means-tested financial assistance: May be available to families whose sons would otherwise not be able to attend Merchiston. Further information is available from the Director of Admissions or on the School website under Admissions/Scholarships & Bursaries.
Forces: 10% (means-tested) fee remission is available to the sons of serving members of HM Forces.
Trust Applications: The School can apply to charities on behalf of prospective candidates who can demonstrate financial need.

Mill Hill School (see p 273)
Means-tested Bursaries may be awarded to pupils entering at 13+,14+ and 16+.
There are also a number of special scholarships and bursaries for the children of Old Millhillians, Christian Ministers, members of the Armed Forces and the Diplomatic Services.
For further information please visit the school's website www.millhill.org.uk.

Monkton Combe School (see p 280)
Some Bursaries to supplement Scholarships on proof of need. Remission of up to one-third of the composite fee to a limited number of children of Clergy and Missionaries on proof of need.

Monmouth School (see p 282)
Service Bursaries are available for the sons of serving members of HM Armed Forces, thus guaranteeing no more than the minimum 10% of fees is payable by parents.
Boarding Bursaries are available, depending on parental circumstances.

Morrison's Academy (see p 284)
Means-tested assistance with tuition fees is available to both existing pupils and new applicants, the main awards being made at entry to From 1 in the Secondary School.

A limited number of awards are granted at other stages of the Secondary School but these are determined by the availability of funds at the time. Many of these awards are intended to assist existing pupils where there has been a significant change in financial circumstances, such as loss of income, which threatens the pupil's continued attendance at Morrison's Academy. Further details are available from The Rector, Morrison's Academy, Crieff PH7 3AN.

Norwich School (see p 291)
In addition to the School's bursary provision:
The Worshipful Company of Dyers, through its charitable trust, is able to give financial support to a pupil with all-round talent in both L4 and L6.
The school has an association with the Ogden Trust which is able to give financial support to selected Sixth Form pupils who join us from the state sector with primary academic strengths in mathematics or the applied sciences. The Trust's financial criteria are similar to our own.

Oundle School (see p 300)
Financial help towards the payment of fees in cases of proven need is available in some instances. This assistance is available in the form of bursaries which vary in size according to circumstance; some may be as high as 100%. Bursaries are not dependent on scholastic merit but are awarded to pupils who are likely to gain most from an Oundle education and who will contribute fully to the life of the School. The pupils in question must satisfy the School's academic entry requirements and continue to work to capacity as they progress through the School. Parents who feel that they may need the support of a bursary are encouraged to discuss the matter with the School well in advance of the child's due date of entry. Decisions regarding bursary assistance are made approximately two years ahead of entry. Judgements are dependent on a supporting reference from a candidate's previous school, an informal interview and on scrutiny of the family's financial circumstances.
Further details may be obtained from Helen Vincent, The Undermaster's Assistant, Oundle School, Oundle, Peterborough, PE8 4GH. Tel: 01832 277116. Fax: 01832 277119. e-mail: hev@oundleschool.org.uk.

Plymouth College (see p 305)
Bursaries of up to half fees, together with various similar Scholarships.
Forces and sibling discounts are also available.

Prior Park College (see p 312)
Bursaries are available, including HM Forces Bursaries of up to 20% of fees. The Bursar is pleased to discuss individual cases. Sibling discounts apply.

Ratcliffe College (see p 323)
A limited number of Bursaries are available, generally on entry to Year 7.

Reed's School (see p 327)
A large number of Foundation awards are made each year to boys and girls who have lost one or both parents, or whose parents are divorced or separated or whose home life is for some special reason either unhappy or unsatisfactory. The awards, which are means tested, vary according to circumstances. Enquiries should be addressed to the Registrar.

Repton School (see p 330)
Bursaries may be available to those who would not otherwise be able to attend an independent school. These may, in appropriate circumstances, be used to supplement Academic or non Academic awards. Means-tested bursaries are also available to Forces families.

Rossall School (see p 333)
A number of clerical bursaries, awarded on a means test to sons of Clergy who can sustain a proportion of the Fees themselves but who need extra help. Bursaries are also available to families from the British military forces.
The bursaries rise to meet increases in the Fees.

Rydal Penrhos School (see p 349)
There are 2 fully-funded (means-tested) day places for Year 7 entry reserved for candidates residing in North Wales.

Reductions are available for children of Ministers of the Methodist and Anglican Churches and bursaries for children of serving members of the Armed Forces are also available.

Ryde School with Upper Chine (see p 351)
Bursaries are awarded to suitably qualified candidates who are already attending the school or pupils who apply from outside. Bursaries are means tested. Further details from the Headmaster.

St Albans School (see p 352)
Means-tested Bursaries are available, awarded according to a balance of merit and need.

St Bede's School (see p 357)
Prospective students who wish to join outside of the scholarship process are able to apply for means-tested fee remission.

St Bees School (see p 359)
The School offers a limited number of means-tested bursaries.

St Edmund's College (see p 367)
Reductions are offered for siblings and for sons and daughters of serving members of the Armed Forces. Means-tested Bursaries are available at 11+, of up to 100% of fees.

St Edmund's School (see p 369)
Originally founded to provide a free education for the fatherless sons of the clergy of the Church of England and the Church of Wales, St Edmund's now accepts applications from boys and girls for Foundationer status. Bursaries to provide a temporary (no more than 12 months) cushion are granted on a means-tested basis to existing pupils. Fee concessions, also means-tested, can be provided to the children of the clergy, members of the armed forces, diplomatic personnel and to the third and subsequent children of the same family in the school at the same time.

Applications should be made to the Head.

St Edward's, Oxford (see p 373)
There are three Widening Access bursaries available each year: two at 13+ and one at 16+. There is also one bursary for the children of serving RAF personnel and the school may offer bursaries of up to 30% of current boarding fees for children of clergy and university dons at the Warden's discretion.

St Lawrence College (see p 378)
Bursaries are awarded annually to pupils in need of financial assistance and who are likely to make a positive contribution to the life of the school. Sibling discounts are also available in the Senior School.

St Peter's School (see p 385)
Means-tested Bursaries from age 11 are available for those who qualify for more than 50% fees assistance. Those eligible are likely to have a gross household income below £45,000.

Sedbergh School (see p 388)
Grants are made from the Sedbergh School Education Fund to sons and daughters of Old Sedberghians. The Headmaster has at his disposal other funds to help with the expenses of educating pupils at Sedbergh.

Sherborne School (see p 392)
Exhibitions are available for the sons of serving or ex-service officers, for the sons of RN officers and bursaries for the sons of Church of England clergy.

Silcoates School (see p 398)
Bursaries are available for the sons and daughters of Ministers and Missionaries of the United Reformed Church or of the Congregational Church, and of other recognised Christian denominations and to other parents subject to a financial assessment.

Solihull School (see p 399)
The school runs its own means-tested Assisted Places Scheme to offer opportunities to able pupils with financial needs.

Sons and daughters of the clergy are offered a 50% fee remission.

Stonyhurst College (see p 406)
A number of Bursaries up to half fees are awarded annually to pupils in need of financial assistance and who are likely to make a positive contribution to the life of the school.

Stowe School (see p 408)
Scholarships may be supplemented by means-tested bursaries, with a limited number of fully-funded places, where there is proven financial need.

Full details may be obtained from The Registrar.

Strathallan School (see p 410)
Bursaries may be awarded dependent on financial circumstances and are also available to pupils who have qualified for entry through exam or school report or both. It is not necessary for successful candidates for bursaries to have achieved scholarship standard, but it may be possible to add a bursary award to a scholarship to enable a pupil to come to Strathallan. We very much wish to encourage high-calibre candidates. We do not show particular preference to one scholarship area, but value all aspects of the academic programme and the extra-curricular provision which is available in the School. All Bursary applications are dealt with on an individual basis; for more information please refer to our website.

Tonbridge School (see p 420)
Foundation Awards provide means-tested support (up to 100% of the full school fee) for a Tonbridge education to boys who can clearly and substantially benefit from what the school has to offer. Awards may be made at three ages: in Year 6 (for entry to Tonbridge in Year 9), in Year 8 (for entry to Tonbridge in Year 9) and in Year 11 (for entry to Tonbridge in Year 12). Boys from the State sector who earn an Award in Year 6 will receive means-tested support through preparatory school (for Years 7 and 8); this should put them in a position to sit the Tonbridge School Scholarship Examination in Year 8 (although the place at Tonbridge is guaranteed from Year 6).

Forces bursaries are available for children of serving members of the armed forces.

Trent College (see p 421)
Trent College Assisted Places are available to those in need of extra financial support.

Trinity School (see p 423)
Whitgift Foundation Bursaries (means-tested) are available providing exceptionally generous help with fees.

Uppingham School (see p 429)
Means-Tested Bursaries are available up to 100% of the full fee in cases of real financial need, to assist children whose parents might not otherwise be able to afford an Uppingham education to take up such an opportunity.

Wellington College (see p 439)
Foundation places are available to applicants who are sons or daughters of deceased military servicemen and service-women and of others who have died in acts of selfless bravery.

Whitgift School (see p 448)
A large number of bursaries is available each year courtesy of the Whitgift Foundation.

Winchester College (see p 450)
Particulars of bursaries may be obtained from the Bursar. In cases of financial hardship bursaries are available to support boys entering the school. All bursaries are awarded on a means-tested basis.

Wisbech Grammar School (see p 452)
Means-tested bursaries are awarded each year with fee remission according to circumstances.

Woodhouse Grove School (see p 457)
Means-tested bursaries are available.

Special assistance is given to the children of Methodist ministers (to boarders and day pupils) and to boarders who are sons and daughters of serving members of HM Forces.

Worksop College (see p 458)
A wide range of bursaries is offered to enable talented pupils to attend the school who would not otherwise be able to do so.

Wrekin College (see p 462)
We offer a 10% discount to serving members of the Armed Forces; to children of Old Wrekinians; and for a second boarder from the same family. When three siblings are enrolled in Wrekin College/The Old Hall School each child attracts a 20% remission in fees.

Bursaries may be awarded on entry and can be awarded in addition to a scholarship. All bursaries are means tested and could in some circumstances cover the whole school fee.

Yarm School (see p 467)
Means-tested bursaries are available to allow children who satisfy the entry criteria to be educated at Yarm School.

Headmasters' and Headmistresses' Conference
International Members

Schools in Europe

The British School of Brussels

Leuvensesteenweg 19, 3080 Tervuren, Belgium
Tel: 00 32 2 766 04 30
Fax: 00 32 2 767 80 70
e-mail: principal@britishschool.be
          admissions@britishschool.be
website: www.britishschool.be

Patron:
Her Excellency the British Ambassador to the King of the
Belgians

Chairman of the Board: Mr Ian Backhouse

***Principal*: Mrs Sue Woodroofe**, BA Hons, NPQH

Creation. The British School of Brussels (BSB) was
founded in 1969 as a non-profit making organisation in Belgium and was opened in 1970 by HRH The Duke of Edinburgh. It is run by a Board of Governors, comprising
distinguished British and Belgian citizens from both the professional and business worlds, together with parent and staff
representatives.

Site. The School occupies a beautiful site of ten hectares,
surrounded by woodlands and lakes near the Royal Museum
of Central Africa in Tervuren, which is 20–25 minutes by car
from the centre of Brussels. The site belongs to the Donation
Royale, the Foundation which manages the estates left to the
Belgian people at the beginning of the 20th century by King
Leopold II.

Facilities. The School has excellent modern facilities,
including a science and maths centre, networked IT suites,
all with internet access, an Apple Mac suite, dance and
drama studios as well as eight science laboratories, four art
studies and three technology workshops, including a state-
of-the-art design & technology workshop opened in 2010,
comprehensive modern languages and humanities suites and
a self-service cafeteria. "Kindercrib", the BSB's own nursery, is situated in a separate Villa next to the School.

Organisation. The British School of Brussels is an independent, fee-paying, non profit-making international school.
English is the language of tuition. In 2011 the school opens
bilingual classes in the Primary School, teaching 50% of the
curriculum in English and 50% of the curriculum in French
to complement its existing English-medium teaching. The
School is a co-educational non-selective day school for students from 3 to 18 years of age, with 1,150 currently on roll.
49% of the students are British and there are 70 other nationalities represented in the School. Our curriculum, both in the
Primary and Secondary Schools, is based on the National
Curriculum for England, adapted to suit the needs of our
international students. In the Secondary School, students sit
GCSE/IGCSE examinations at the end of Year 11 (aged 16).
Senior students then study either the International Baccalaureate (IB) Diploma (with English/French or English/Dutch
bilingual options) or the GCE A Level course prior to moving on to Higher Education in the UK, Belgium or beyond.
Provision is also made for Oxbridge tuition. Our examination results are impressive.

We introduce the teaching of French to Reception Year
children and Spanish, German or Dutch as optional additional languages in the Secondary School. We have developed programmes to help students with learning differences
and to help students who join us with little or no English
skills. There is an Educational Psychologist and a Learning
Support Department as well as two counsellors.

Sports and Extra-Curricular Activities. Use of the
extensive sports facilities (two gymnasia, all-weather artificial pitches, grass pitches, floodlit training area, four outdoor tennis courts, squash courts, indoor sports hall and the

240-seat Brel Theatre), together with programmes for children over the summer), make the School a focal point for the
local and international community. In addition to curricular
sport, a wide range of competitive sports is offered: athletics, cricket, cross-country, gymnastics, hockey, rugby, football, swimming and tennis, as well as recreational activities
such as basketball and golf. The School participates very
successfully in the International Schools Sports Tournaments.

Music and Drama. The Music Department houses a
well-equipped music technology studio, a recording studio
and a rehearsal studio for the School's orchestras, concert
bands and instrumental ensembles. Individual instrument
lessons are available from visiting specialist teachers, and
take place in the suite of music practice rooms. The School
is the largest Associated Board centre in Europe. Each year
up to fifteen drama productions – including student-directed
performances – are presented across the full student age-
range. The Theatre has its own workshop and Green Room,
as well as a more intimate studio space that seats 80.

Careers. The School has the highest expectations of its
student population and advice on careers, as well as higher
and further education opportunities, is of vital importance to
the further development of the students. The School takes
part in many careers conventions as well as hosting its own
annual Careers Week each spring.

Fees per annum (2011-2012). From €13,200 (Reception
class) to €27,450. Some assistance with tuition fees may be
available.

Past Students' Association. The School has a growing
association of Alumni with its own WebAlumnus. Visit the
Alumni section of the School website: www.britishschool
.be.

The British School in The Netherlands
website: **www.britishschool.nl**
e-mail: **admissions@britishschool.nl**

BSN Junior School Leidschenveen (3–11 years)
Vrouw Avenweg 640, 2493 WZ, The Hague
Tel: 00 31 (0)70 315 4040
Fax: 00 31 (0)70 315 4054

BSN Junior School Diamanthorst (3–11 years)
Diamanthorst 16, 2592 GH, The Hague
Tel: 00 31 (0)70 315 7620
Fax: 00 31 (0)70 315 7621

BSN Junior School Vlaskamp (3–11 years)
Vlaskamp 19, 2592 AA, The Hague
Tel: 00 31 (0)70 333 8111
Fax: 00 31 (0)70 333 8100

BSN Senior School (11–18 years)
Jan van Hooflaan 3, 2252 BG, Voorschoten
Tel: 00 31 (0)71 560 2222
Fax: 00 31 (0)71 560 2200

Principal: **Mr Martin Coles**
Principal's Office: **Boerderij Rosenburgh,**
Rosenburgherlaan 2, 2252 BA, Voorschoten
Tel: 00 31 (0)71 560 2251
Fax: 00 31 (0)71 560 2290

The British School in The Netherlands (BSN) was
founded in 1931 as an independent, non-denominational
school. Since then, it has grown into a school of around

2,000 pupils from Foundation 1 (age 3) to Year 13 (age 18). Although around 40% of the pupils are of British origin, the school truly serves the international community, with children on roll from over 80 nations. The BSN has four sites in The Hague.

Aims. The School aims to develop the potential of its pupils by providing a caring environment, in which they are offered the greatest possible educational opportunities. Pupils are helped to develop their powers of reasoning, increase their knowledge and become aware of the importance of their individual contribution and responsibility to society. All are encouraged to aim for excellence and to respect one another. These aims are achieved in a happy school whose pupils join with high expectations and where they are encouraged in the belief of their fulfilment.

Junior School Leidschenveen. JSL opened in 2010 and can provide around 570 places for children. Within its landscaped grounds, the campus includes dedicated facilities for Out of School Care, a Day Care Centre for 0 to 3 year olds and a Sports and Community Centre.

Junior School Diamanthorst. JSD opened in September 2003 and was recently further extended. The school now offers accommodation for around 380 children. The site boasts excellent resources including a new dance and drama studio.

Junior School Vlaskamp. JSV can provide accommodation for approximately 760 children. This award-winning building was opened in 1997 and provides a range of excellent resources, including notably extensive outside play and environmental areas.

Senior School. The Senior School is located in Voorschoten (a small town just north of The Hague). A huge building project was completed in 2003 offering enviable state-of-the-art facilities, including new science laboratories, information technology stations, library resources, gymnasium and much more. This investment represents a commitment to providing a modern and stimulating learning environment, to support the comprehensive educational programme.

Staff. Each school has a Headteacher, supported by Deputies. The Principal has overall responsibility for all schools in the BSN group. All teachers (192 full-time, 97 part-time) are fully qualified and are mostly recruited from the United Kingdom.

Transport. An independent school bus service links the schools and covers most of The Hague, Voorburg, Leidschendam, Wassenaar, Voorschoten, as well as parts of Rotterdam, Rijswijk, Leiden, Amsterdam and Zoetermeer.

Curriculum. Pupils follow challenging programmes of study based on the National Curriculum for England and Wales but with an added international dimension. All pupils study English, mathematics, science, technology, history, geography, music, art and physical education from the age of five years. Dutch is taught from the age of five and French from the age of ten. In the Senior School, Spanish, German, French and Dutch are taught from Year 7. Pupils prepare for the GCSE (at 16+) and IB Diploma Programme or AS/A2 Level examinations at 17/18 years. The School has a long and proud record of success with the majority of pupils entering universities and other higher education establishments all over the world.

The School was inspected by HMI in November 2003 using the inspection criteria for Independent Schools. The report stated that GCSE results were "well above those of comparable schools [...] close to that of selective (grammar) schools" and that "overall performance at A Level is very good".

Sport. Facilities are available for indoor and outdoor games, including rugby, hockey, aerobics, tennis, athletics, judo, football, basketball, volleyball and gymnastics. At Senior School level, fixtures are arranged with local clubs and other schools, including annual tours and tournaments in the United Kingdom and elsewhere in Europe.

Activities and Trips. The School takes pride in its regular participation in the annual Model United Nations Conference in The Hague. It also operates a full programme of field and activity trips in The Netherlands, the United Kingdom, France, Switzerland, Spain and Germany, capitalising on its central location in Europe.

Pastoral System. To ensure that each pupil is known individually, and cared for, there is a pastoral system which begins with the form teacher, who is responsible to a year group leader. Together they work to care, support and guide the individual in all aspects of school life. Success is achieved only through close cooperation between home and school, a positive learning environment and high standards of discipline.

Special Needs & EAL. Special provision is made for pupils with learning difficulties. Any child with Special Needs will be considered according to the School's policy on Special Needs Provision, which is available on request. Specialist help is provided throughout the School for pupils requiring individual tuition in English as an Additional Language.

Admission. Admission is granted at any time in the school year, depending on availability and the School's ability to meet the academic needs of the child. Great care is taken to ensure the academic and social integration of each child.

Fees per annum (2011-2012). Foundation Stage €12,510, Years 1–2 €12,630, Years 3–6 €12,750, Years 7–9 €16,740, Years 10–11 €17,160, Years 12–13 €17,430.

Charitable status. Vereniging The British School in The Netherlands is a Registered Charity, number V409055. It aims to offer a British education to international children living temporarily or permanently in The Netherlands.

The British School of Paris

38 quai de l'Ecluse, 78290 Croissy sur Seine, France
Tel: 00 33 1 34 80 45 90
Fax: 00 33 1 39 76 12 69
e-mail: enquiries@britishschool.fr
website: www.britishschool.fr

Chairman of Governors: Mr P Kett

Headmaster: **Dr Steffen Sommer**

Deputy Head – Academic: Dr J Batters

Deputy Head – Pastoral: Mr K Pearey

Head of Junior School: Mr J Hornshaw

Registrar: Mrs V Joynes

Age Range. 3–18.
Number of Pupils. 810 (Boys and Girls)
Fees per annum (2011-2012). Senior School €20,999–€23,080; Junior School €12,000–€18,936.

The BSP provides, in a caring environment, a high-quality British-style education for international students, to enable them to become caring citizens and to lead fulfilling lives.

Located just 15 kilometres from Paris, the School caters for English-speaking children of over 50 nationalities (about 30% are British) from ages 3–18. It is a not-for-profit association in France and is presided over by a governing body under the patronage of His Excellency the British Ambassador to France.

The **Junior School** provides education for primary aged children from 3–11 years. The purpose-built Junior School is located very close to the Senior School along the leafy banks of the river Seine. There are 35 classrooms accommodating up to 550 pupils, as well as 4 bespoke classrooms and 2 activity areas that are dedicated to our foundation stage/

nursery section. Studies are based on the English National Curriculum with emphasis on English, Maths and Science, and of course, the French language. Being a holistic educator the BSP has a strong extra-curricular base with a special focus on music and drama as well as a large variety of sports. (*For further information about the Junior School, see entry in IAPS section*).

The **Senior School**, which caters for pupils aged from 11–18 years, is situated beside a beautiful stretch of the Seine in Croissy sur Seine. The buildings, with the exception of two nineteenth century houses, have been built since 1990. The Science and Technology block provides excellent facilities for Science, Information Technology, Electronics and Design. There are six large, well equipped science laboratories. The other classroom blocks house Humanities, Art, Business Studies, Modern Languages, Music, English and Mathematics. Other facilities include a generously staffed and resourced student career guidance programme, a library, IT labs, a refectory, a large sports hall and fitness centre. Students enter at the age of 11 and for the first three years, a broad general education is maintained in line with the National Curriculum. Pupils are prepared for the GCSE and AS/A Level examinations in a comprehensive range of subjects.

Music and drama are an integral part of school life; the music centre includes teaching and practice facilities as well as a well-equipped electronic studio. Specialist teachers visit the School to provide individual lessons in a wide range of instruments. Children take the Associated Board exams at regular intervals.

The School has had considerable sporting success over the years, winning the International Schools' Sports Tournament competition in girls' field hockey, and boys' rugby. Our international fixture lists provide an incentive to gain a place in school teams. As well as local matches our teams travel regularly to Belgium, Holland and the UK.

Small overall numbers, modest class sizes and a supportive pastoral system all help new pupils integrate quickly. Our examination results are outstanding. At A Level 55% of all grades were A* and A and more than 60% of all grades at GCSE were A* and A in 2010. 100% Pass Rate at A Levels consecutively since 2002. These results compare extremely favourably with high-calibre schools in the UK. Most students continue their education at prestigious universities in the UK, USA, France and worldwide. BSP students have been successfully admitted to the Universities of Cambridge and Oxford, London School of Economics, University of Pennsylvania, Stanford University, McGill University, University of Australia, Universidad de Madrid, Seoul National University, L'Université de la Sorbonne, to mention but a few.

King's College
The British School of Madrid

Paseo de los Andes 35, 28761 Soto de Viñuelas, Madrid, Spain

Tel: 00 34 918 034 800
Fax: 00 34 918 036 557
e-mail: info@kingscollege.es
website: www.kingscollege.es

King's College is a British co-educational day and boarding school founded in 1969. It is the largest British curriculum school in Spain and the first school to have had full UK accreditation through the Independent Schools Inspectorate. The Headmaster is an international member of HMC, while the school is a member of COBIS, NABSS and BSA.

The school is governed by the Board of Directors and School Council which is composed of distinguished members from the business and academic communities.

Head: **Elaine Blaus**, BA Hons, PGCE

Deputy Headmaster: Joseph Swash, BA Hons Kent, PGCE Oxon
Head of Spanish Studies: Fernando Lage, Lic Filosofía UAM
Head of Residence: (*to be appointed*)
Director of Admissions: Helen Williams, BA Hons Sheffield

There are three separate schools in Madrid which cater for children of approximately 48 nationalities between the ages of 2 and 18 years. Pupil enrolment is 1,989 (977 boys and 1,012 girls), including 20 boarders. There are over 140 fully qualified staff, most of whom are British.

The aim of King's College, under the key phrase of its Charter "A British Education in Spain for Europe and the World", is to provide students with an excellent all-round education while fostering tolerance and understanding between young people of different nationalities and backgrounds.

King's College, Soto de Viñuelas caters for 1,350 pupils between the ages of 2 and 18 years and stands on a 12-acre site in a residential area about 25 km from the centre of Madrid near the Guadarrama mountains and surrounded by open countryside. It is well connected to the city centre by motorway and rail. There is an optional comprehensive bus service to the city of Madrid and its outlying residential areas and all routes are supervised by a bus monitor.

Facilities. There are extensive, purpose-built facilities which include 7 science laboratories, 2 libraries, art studio, 3 computer centres with multimedia stations, and 2 music rooms. All classrooms are fitted with interactive whiteboards and there are computers in all Primary classrooms. The school offers a purpose-built Early Learning Centre, an Auditorium with seating for over 350 people and a Music School with 6 rooms for individual or small group tuition. The sports facilities include a 25-metre indoor heated swimming pool, a floodlit multi-purpose sports area, football pitches, basketball and tennis courts, a gymnasium with fitness centre and a horse riding school. Future development includes plans for a covered sports hall.

The Residence (boarding) is currently located on two floors of the school's west wing and has a capacity for approximately 40 Secondary age pupils. A brand new purpose-built Residence will open in the school grounds in September 2011 offering pupils a breakfast room, kitchen, laundry, work room, lounge, TV room, storage and easy access to the new astroturf pitch and sports facilities.

King's College School, La Moraleja. The school caters for approximately 500 pupils aged 3 to 14 (Nursery to Year 9) and is located in a residential area just 16 kilometres from the centre of the city. The modern on-site facilities include a library, ICT centre, laboratory, music room, multi-purpose sports surface and gymnasium.

At the age of fourteen, at the end of National Curriculum Year 9, pupils transfer to King's College, Soto de Viñuelas to complete their final four years of study.

King's Infant School, Chamartín. Conveniently located in the Chamartín area of central Madrid, the school offers purpose-built facilities for boys and girls between the ages of 3 and 6 (Nursery to Year 2) and has a capacity of 200 pupils. There are spacious, well-equipped classrooms, complete with independent bathrooms for the Nursery pupils, a library and computer room and a playground area. At the age of seven, at the end of National Curriculum Year 2, pupils from King's Infant School automatically transfer either to King's College, Soto de Viñuelas or King's College School, La Moraleja.

Curriculum. Pupils at all three King's College schools in Madrid follow the English National Curriculum leading to (I)GCSE, GCE AS and A Level examinations. A wide range of subjects is available. All pupils learn Spanish. There is also a Spanish section at King's College, Soto de Viñuelas for pupils wishing to follow the Spanish Baccalaureate from the age of 16 (Y12). The school has a reputation for high academic standards and excellent examination results with students going on to top universities in Britain, USA and Spain amongst others. An Oxbridge preparatory group works with the most able students to prepare university applications. There is a very experienced Careers and University Entrance Advisory Department for all students.

Activities. King's College has choirs, musical ensembles and drama groups, which participate in numerous events throughout the year. Pupils are encouraged to explore their capabilities in the areas of music and the arts from a very early age.

Sports play an important role at the school and pupils are encouraged to take part in tournaments and local competitive events, in addition to their normal PE classes. King's College currently has football, basketball and swimming teams participating in local leagues, and also takes part in inter-school championships in athletics and cross-country.

There is a programme of optional classes which includes horse riding, ballet, judo, Spanish dancing, swimming, tennis, tuition in various musical instruments, performing arts and craft workshops.

Admission. Pupils entering the school at the age of 7 or above are required to sit entrance tests in English and Mathematics and possibly other subjects, while younger candidates are screened by our Educational Psychologist. For those applying to the Sixth Form, admission depends on the results of the (I)GCSE examinations, or equivalent.

Fees per term (2011-2012). €1,871–€3,593 excluding lunch and transport. Boarding fees are an additional €2,703 per term.

Scholarships. The school offers a small number of scholarships to Sixth Formers selected on academic merit.

Further information may be obtained from The Director of Admissions at the School.

St George's British International School

Senior & Junior Schools:
Via Cassia, La Storta, 00123 Rome, Italy
Tel: 00 39 06 3086001
Fax: 00 39 06 30892490
e-mail: secretary@stgeorge.school.it
website: www.stgeorge.school.it

Junior School:
Via Spallanzani 12–14, Via Nomentana, 00161 Rome
Tel: 00 39 06 44230486
Fax: 00 39 06 4402609
e-mail: sarah.mattei@stgeorge.school.it
website: www.stgeorge.school.it

Visitor: HM Ambassador to Italy

Principal: **Martyn J Hales**, BSc

Assistant Staff. 82 full-time and 4 part-time teachers, all fully qualified (95% British with degrees from British universities, including Oxford or Cambridge).

Enrolment. Around 830 pupils, ages 3 to 18, evenly balanced boys and girls; approximately 40 in each Primary and 60 in each Secondary year-group, 120 in the Sixth Form.

Founded in 1958, St George's is a fully independent school owned by a non-profit-making Association and run as a limited company. Its purpose is to provide the international community of Rome with a British-system education, with a full academic programme, enriched by extra-curricular activities, good pastoral care and encouragement of self-discipline and independence. Children come from over 60 nationalities, the majority having had all their education in English; most would expect to stay at St George's until completion of their school years.

The school owns a 14-acre site on the north-west side of Rome, with 17 school buses serving all principal residential areas of the city. Facilities include a full range of standard and specialised classrooms, gymnasium, a library with first-class internet facilities, 7 science laboratories, 4 ICT/technology rooms and 3 art/design studios. The music and drama departments are very active and sports facilities are considerable, with an athletics track, rugby, cricket and football pitches and all-weather courts for tennis, volleyball and basketball.

It has also leased a large villa, set in its own garden off the Via Nomentana, to provide an additional city-centre Junior School for children aged 3 to 11.

The 15 years of schooling provided at the St George's schools incorporate the work of British primary and secondary schools, leading to GCSE and International Baccalaureate in all standard subjects. Maximum class size is 25, with key subjects divided into smaller 'sets' in the secondary age-group, according to ability. Special care is taken over the teaching of English, whether mother-tongue or English-as-an-Additional-Language. The school organises many educational trips, to take advantage of its splendid location, as well as many activities in breaks and after school.

Most children go on to university or other further education, the majority to the UK with an average of 8% to Oxbridge.

2010 GCSE results. 89% pass rate grades A, B or C with 47% grade A or A*.

2010 International Baccalaureate. 96.7% awarded diploma. 28.3% gained 38 points or more (pass 24 points). Average diploma score: 34 points.

Admission is dependent on interview, reports from previous school and a screening test. Entrance is possible at any time of the year. The school year runs from early September to late June, Mondays to Fridays. Fees are set in Euros and adjusted each year in the light of inflation.

Fees per annum (2011-2012). Junior Schools: €11,380–€15,300. Senior School: €16,360–€18,030.

Other International Schools

Africa

South Africa

Bishops Diocesan College
Bishops Camp Ground Road, Rondebosch, Cape Town 7700, South Africa
e-mail: principal@bishops.org.za
website: www.bishops.org.za

Principal: Grant R B Nupen

Michaelhouse
Balgowan 3275, Kwazulu-Natal, South Africa
e-mail: guypea@michaelhouse.org
website: www.michaelhouse.org

Rector: Guy N Pearson

Zimbabwe

Peterhouse
Private Bag 3741, Marondera, Zimbabwe
e-mail: rector@peterhouse.co.zw
website: www.peterhouse.org

Rector: Jon B Calderwood

St George's College
Private Bag 7727, Causeway, Harare, Zimbabwe
e-mail: btiernan@stgeorges.co.zw
website: www.stgeorges.co.zw

Head: Brendan T Tiernan

Asia

Brunei Darussalam

Jerudong International School
PO Box 1408, Bandar Seri Begawan BS8672, Negara Brunei Darussalam
e-mail: office@jis.edu.bn
website: www.jis.edu.bn

Principal and CEO: Andrew J Fowler-Watt, MA Cantab

India

Bishop Cotton School
Shimla 171 002, Himachal Pradesh, India
e-mail: headmaster@bishopcotton.com
website: www.bishopcottonshimla.com

Head Master: Roy C Robinson

The Cathedral & John Connon School
6 Purshottamdas Thakurdas Marg, Fort Mumbai 400 001, India
e-mail: cajcs@mtnl.net.in
website: www.cathedral-school.com

Principal: Mrs Meera Isaacs

The Doon School
The Mall, Dehradun 248001, Uttaranchal, India
e-mail: hm@doonschool.com
website: www.doonschool.com

Headmaster: Dr Peter McLaughlin

The International School Bangalore
NAFL Valley, Whitefield-Sarajapur Road, Near Dommasandra Circle, Bangalore – 562 125, Karnataka State, India
e-mail: head@tisb.ac.in
website: www.tisb.org

Principal: Dr Matthew Sullivan

The Lawrence School
Sanawar 173202, District Solan, Himachal Pradesh, India
e-mail: contact@sanawar.edu.in
website: www.sanawar.edu.in

Headmaster: Praveen Vasisht

Indonesia

The British International School
Bintaro Jaya Sector 9, Jl Raya Jombang – Cileduk, Pondok Aren, Tangerang 15227, Indonesia
e-mail: principal@bis.or.id
website: www.bis.or.id

Principal: Dr Christian Barkei

Singapore

ACS (International)
The Anglo-Chinese School
61 Jalan Hitam Manis, Singapore 278475
e-mail: admission@acsinternational.com.sg
website: www.acsinternational.com.sg

Principal: P Kerr Fulton-Peebles

Tanglin Trust School
95 Portsdown Road, Singapore 139299
e-mail: admissions@tts.edu.sg
website: www.tts.edu.sg

Chief Executive Officer: Peter J Derby-Crook

Thailand

Harrow International School
45 Soi Kosumruamchai 14, Kosumruamchai Road, Kwaeng Sikun, Don Muang, Bangkok, Thailand
e-mail: his@harrowschool.ac.th
website: www.harrowschool.ac.th

Headmaster: Kevin Riley

Shrewsbury International School
1922 Charoen Krung Road, Wat Prayakrai, Bang Kholame, Bangkok 10120, Thailand
e-mail: enquiries@shrewsbury.ac.th
website: www.shrewsbury.ac.th

Principal: Stephen Holroyd

Australia and New Zealand

Australia

All Saints' College
PO Box 165, Ewing Avenue, Bull Creek, Willetton, WA 6149, Australia
e-mail: info@allsaints.wa.edu.au
website: www.allsaints.wa.edu.au

Principal: Dr Geoffrey Shaw

Barker College
91 Pacific Highway, Hornsby, NSW 2077, Australia
e-mail: hm@barker.nsw.edu.au
website: www.barker.nsw.edu.au

Headmaster: Dr Roderic E Kefford

Brighton Grammar School
90 Outer Crescent, Brighton, VIC 3186, Australia
e-mail: msurwin@brightongrammar.vic.edu.au
website: www.brightongrammar.vic.edu.au

Head: Michael S Urwin

Camberwell Grammar School
PO Box 151, Balwyn, VIC 3103, Australia
e-mail: pgh@cgs.vic.edu.au
website: www.cgs.vic.edu.au

Headmaster: Dr Paul Hicks

Christ Church Grammar School
Queenslea Drive, Claremont, WA 6010, Australia
e-mail: gwynne@ccgs.wa.edu.au
website: www.ccgs.wa.edu.au

Headmaster: Garth E Wynne

Cranbrook School
5 Victoria Road, Bellevue Hill, NSW 2023, Australia
e-mail: head@cranbrook.nsw.edu.au
website: www.cranbrook.nsw.edu.au

Headmaster: Jeremy J S Madin

The Geelong College
PO Box 5, Talbot Street, Newtown, VIC 3220, Australia
e-mail: turner@geelongcollege.vic.edu.au
website: www.geelongcollege.vic.edu.au

Principal: Dr Pauline C Turner

Geelong Grammar School
50 Biddlecombe Avenue, Corio, VIC 3214, Australia
e-mail: principal@ggs.vic.edu.au
website: www.ggs.vic.edu.au

Principal: Stephen Meek

Haileybury College
855 Springvale Road, Keysborough, VIC 3173, Australia
e-mail: registrar@haileybury.vic.edu.au
website: www.haileybury.vic.edu.au

Principal: Derek Scott

The King's School
PO Box 1, Parramatta, NSW 2124, Australia
e-mail: headmaster@kings.edu.au
website: www.kings.edu.au

Headmaster: Dr Tim F Hawkes

Knox Grammar School
7 Woodville Avenue, Wahroonga, NSW 2076, Australia
e-mail: weeksj@knox.nsw.edu.au
website: www.knox.nsw.edu.au

Headmaster: John Weeks

Melbourne Grammar School
Domain Road, South Yarra, Melbourne, VIC 3004, Australia
e-mail: mgs@mgs.vic.edu.au
website: www.mgs.vic.edu.au

Headmaster: Roy Kelley

Mentone Grammar School
63 Venice Street, Mentone, VIC 3194, Australia
e-mail: enquiry@mentonegrammar.net
website: www.mentonegrammar.net

Principal: Malcolm Cater

Scotch College
1 Morrison Street, Hawthorn, VIC 3122, Australia
e-mail: scotch@scotch.vic.edu.au
website: www.scotch.vic.edu.au

Principal: I Tom Batty

The Scots College
Victoria Road, Bellevue Hill, NSW 2023, Australia
e-mail: reception@tsc.nsw.edu.au
website: www.tsc.nsw.edu.au

Principal: Dr Ian P M Lambert

Shore School
PO Box 1221, Blue Street, North Sydney, NSW 2059, Australia
e-mail: headmaster@shore.nsw.edu.au
website: www.shore.nsw.edu.au

Head: Dr Timothy Wright

Sydney Grammar School
College Street, Darlinghurst, NSW 2010, Australia
e-mail: kmr@sydgram.nsw.edu.au
website: www.sydgram.nsw.edu.au

Head: Dr John T Vallance

Trinity Grammar School
PO Box 174, 119 Prospect Road, Summer Hill, NSW 2130, Australia
e-mail: mcujes@trinity.nsw.edu.au
website: www.trinity.nsw.edu.au

Head: G Milton Cujes

Wesley College
577 St Kilda Road, Melbourne, VIC 3004, Australia
e-mail: principal@wesleycollege.net
website: www.wesleycollege.net

Principal: Dr Helen Drennan

New Zealand

Christ's College
Rolleston Avenue, Private Bag 4900, Christchurch, New Zealand
e-mail: headmaster@christscollege.com
website: www.christscollege.com

Headmaster: Simon Leese

King's College
PO Box 22012, Otahuhu, Auckland 1640, New Zealand
e-mail: b.fenner@kingscollege.school.nz
website: www.kingscollege.school.nz

Headmaster: Bradley Fenner

Wanganui Collegiate School
Private Bag 3002, Wanganui Mail Centre, Wanganui 4540, New Zealand
e-mail: wcs@collegiate.school.nz
website: www.collegiate.school.nz

Headmaster: Tim J Wilbur

Central and South America

Argentina

St Andrew's Scots School
Roque Saenz Peña 654, 1636 Olivos, Buenos Aires, Argentina
e-mail: gabriel.rshaid@sanandres.esc.edu.ar
website: www.sanandres.esc.edu.ar

Head: Gabriel Rshaid

St George's College North
C Rivadavia y Don Bosco, Los Polvorines 1613, Buenos Aires, Argentina
e-mail: informes@stgeorge.com.ar
website: www.stgeorge.com.ar

Headmaster: Ian D Tate

St George's College Quilmes
Guido 800, CC2 (1878), Quilmes, Buenos Aires, Argentina
e-mail: info@stgeorge.com.ar
website: www.stgeorge.com.ar

Headmaster: Derek Pringle

Brazil

St Paul's School
Rua Juquiá 166, Jardim Paulistano, CEP 01440–903, São Paulo, Brazil
e-mail: spshead@stpauls.br
website: www.stpauls.br

Headmaster: Crispin Rowe

Chile

The Grange School
Av Principe de Gales 6154, La Reina, 687067, Santiago, Chile
e-mail: rectoria@grange.cl
website: www.grange.cl

Rector: Rachid R Benammar

El Salvador

Academia Británica Cuscatleca
Apartado Postal 121, Santa Tecla, El Salvador
e-mail: headmaster@abc.edu.sv
website: www.abc.edu.sv

Head: J George Hobson

Europe

Cyprus

The English School
PO Box 23575, 1684 Nicosia, Cyprus
e-mail: head@englishschool.ac.cy
website: www.englishschool.ac.cy

Head: Mrs Deborah Duncan

Czech Republic

The English College in Prague
Sokolovska 320, 190-00 Praha 9, Czech Republic
e-mail: headmaster@englishcollege.cz
website: www.englishcollege.cz

Headmaster: Mark Waldron

Greece

Campion School
PO Box 67484, Pallini, Athens 153 02, Greece
e-mail: satherton@campion.edu.gr
website: www.campion.edu.gr

Headmaster: Stephen W Atherton

St Catherine's British School
PO Box 51019, Kifissia GR 145 10, Greece
e-mail: info@stcatherines.gr
website: www.stcatherines.gr

Headmaster: Peter Armstrong, MA

Italy

Sir James Henderson School
Via Pisani Dossi 16, 20134 Milan, Italy
e-mail: info@ @sjhschool.com
website: www.sjhschool.com

Principal: Dr Carlo Ferrario

Portugal

Oporto British School
Rua da Cerca 326/350, 4150-201 Porto, Portugal
e-mail: school@obs.edu.pt
website: www.obs.edu.pt

Headmaster: David Butcher

St Julian's School
Quinta Nova, 2776–601 Carcavelos Codex, Portugal
e-mail: mail@stjulians.com
website: www.stjulians.com

Headmaster: David Smith

Middle East

Qatar

Doha College
PO Box 7506, Doha, State of Qatar
e-mail: execassistant@dohacollege.com
website: www.dohacollege.com

Principal: Mark Leppard

United Arab Emirates

The British School – Al Khubairat
P O Box 4001, Abu Dhabi, United Arab Emirates
e-mail: principal@britishschool.sch.ae
website: www.britishschool.sch.ae

Principal: Paul Coackley

Dubai College
PO Box 837, Dubai, United Arab Emirates
e-mail: dubcoll@emirates.net.ae
website: www.dubaicollege.org

Headmaster: Mr Peter Hill

Jumeirah English Speaking School
PO Box 24942, Dubai, United Arab Emirates
e-mail: jess@jess.sch.ae
website: www.jess.sch.ae

Director: Mr R D Stokoe

North America

Canada

Ridley College
PO Box 3013, 2 Ridley Road, St Catharine's, Ontario L2R 7C3, Canada
e-mail: headmaster@ridleycollege.com
website: www.ridleycollege.com

Headmaster: Jonathan Leigh

Shawnigan Lake School
1975 Renfrew Road, Postal Bag 2000, Shawnigan Lake, BC V0R 2W1, Canada
e-mail: dbr@sls.bc.ca
website: www.sls.bc.ca

Head: David Robertson

Upper Canada College
200 Lonsdale Road, Toronto, Ontario M4V 1W6, Canada
e-mail: admin@ucc.on.ca
website: www.ucc.on.ca

Principal: Dr James Power

Headmasters' and Headmistresses' Conference

Additional Members

The Constitution of the Headmasters' and Headmistresses' Conference provides that the membership shall consist of Heads of Independent Schools. At the same time, it is held to be a strength of the Conference that its membership includes heads of schools of other status. There is provision, therefore, for the election of a small number of heads of maintained schools when it is felt that their contribution to education makes their membership appropriate.

Heads elected in this category are in every way full and equal members of the Headmasters' and Headmistresses' Conference, but profiles of their schools are not included in the Independent Schools Yearbook which gives details of the Independent Schools.

The following is a list of Heads in this special category of membership:

BRIDGET TULLIE
Batley Grammar School, Batley, West Yorkshire
Tel: 01924 474980
website: www.batleygrammar.co.uk

DR STUART D SMALLWOOD
Bishop Wordsworth's Grammar School, Salisbury, Wiltshire
Tel: 01722 333851
website: www.bws.wilts.sch.uk

DR MARK FENTON
Dr Challoner's Grammar School, Amersham, Bucks
Tel: 01494 787500
website: www.challoners.com

ROBERT J MASTERS
The Judd School, Tonbridge, Kent
Tel: 01732 770880
website: www.judd.kent.sch.uk

ANDREW M JARMAN
Lancaster Royal Grammar School, Lancaster
Tel: 01524 580600
website: www.lrgs.org.uk

TRACY LUKE
The Marsh Academy, New Romney, Kent
Tel: 01797 364593
website: www.marshacademy.org.uk

RT REVD PETER HULLAH
Northampton Academy, Northampton
Tel: 01604 402811
website: www.northampton-academy.org

SHAUN FENTON
Pate's Grammar School, Cheltenham, Glos
Tel: 01242 523169
website: www.pates.gloucs.sch.uk

IAN C CARTER
Poole Grammar School, Poole, Dorset
Tel: 01202 692132
website: www.poolegrammar.com

PAUL D SPENCER ELLIS
Royal Alexandra and Albert School, Reigate, Surrey
Tel: 01737 649000
website: www.raa-school.co.uk

MICHAEL THOMPSON
St Ambrose College, Altrincham, Cheshire
Tel: 0161 980 2711
website: www.st-ambrosecollege.org.uk

SIMON DUGGAN
St Anselm's College, Birkenhead, Merseyside
Tel: 0151 652 1408
website: www.st-anselms.com

JOHN E WASZEK
St Edward's College, Liverpool
Tel: 0151 281 1999
website: www.st-edwards.co.uk

DR ALAN C MCMURDO
Thomas Deacon Academy, Peterborough, Cambs
Tel: 01733 426051
website: www.thomasdeaconacademy.com

TONY HALLIWELL
Welbeck – The Defence Sixth Form College,
Loughborough, Leics
Tel: 01509 891700
website: www.dsfc.ac.uk

ANDREW J BAKER
Westcliff High School for Boys, Westcliff-on-Sea, Essex
Tel: 01792 475443
website: www.whsb.essex.sch.uk

PART II
Schools whose Heads are members of the Girls' Schools Association

ALPHABETICAL LIST OF SCHOOLS

The following schools, whose Heads are members of both GSA and HMC, can be found in the HMC section:

Berkhamsted School
New Hall School

GEOGRAPHICAL LIST OF GSA SCHOOLS

Individual School Entries

The Abbey School

Kendrick Road, Reading RG1 5DZ
Tel: 0118 987 2256
Fax: 0118 987 1478
e-mail: schooloffice@theabbey.co.uk
website: www.theabbey.co.uk

Founded 1887. Incorporated 1914. Church of England Foundation.

Board of Governors:
Chairman: Mr P Smith, MA
Mrs M Blackburn, OBE
Mrs J Burrell, MBS Part 1 Open, AMA
Mrs J Cornell, BA
Mrs M Cottingham, BA
Mr S Dimmick, LLB
Mrs M Edwards
Mr M Emmanuel
Mrs L Garthside, BA Hons
Prof A Jones, BA Hons, PGCE, DipSoc, FRSA, FCP, FCMI, FInstCPD, FQMW
Mrs C Lane, DPSE SEN
Dr I Kemp, MB BS, FRCP, MRCGP, DCH, DRCOG
Mrs B McDiarmid, CertEd, DipSEN, DipSpLD
Mr G O'Brien, BBS, FCCA, CTA
Revd Béatrice Pearson, BTh, PGCE, MA, BA France
Dr C F Print, DBA, ACMA, ADipC
Mrs H Rennie, ACA
Prof D Reynolds, PhD, CB
Mr S Smith, BSc Est Man, FRICS, FCIArb, FBEng

Head: Mrs Barbara Stanley, BA Queen's Belfast, PGCE, FRGS

Vice Principal: Mrs S Jones, NPQH, MA Ed Open, BSc Reading, PGCE Oxon

Deputy Head – Senior School: Mrs R S Dent, BA Southampton, QTS Reading

Deputy Head – Operations and Communications: Mrs K Macaulay, BEd Newcastle

Director of Sixth Form: Mr B Fanning, BA, MSc, PGCE Oxon

Head of Junior School: Mrs C J Ryninks, MA Warwick, BA Cape Town SA

Deputy Head of Junior School: Mrs L Glithro, BSc St Andrews, MA Ed Open, PGCE

Heads of Department:
Art: Mrs E Harvey, BA Reading, PGCE
Biology: Dr M Spencer, BSc, MSc, PhD Cairo, PGCE
Business Studies: Mrs S Watt, FCA
Chemistry: Mrs J Harrison, BSc Warwick, PGCE
Classics: Mrs L Lyle, BA QUB, MLitt Newcastle PGCE
Drama: Miss C V Sutton, MA Oxon, PGCE
Economics: Mrs V Whistance, BScEcon Aberystwyth, PGCE
English: Mrs J Turkington, BA Lancs, BA Open, MA Lancaster
Food Technology: Mrs S Parsons, CertEd Bath
French: Mrs I Berrow, Lic-ès-Lettres, PGCE
Geography: Mrs J Gray, BSc, PGCE
German: Mr C Hammond, BA Reading, PGCE
History: Miss A Cole, BA Newcastle upon Tyne, PGCE

ICT: Mrs K Macaulay, BEd Newcastle
Mathematics: Miss E Cook, BA, MA Oxford, PGCE
Modern Foreign Languages: Mrs U Byrne, IPTS Kiel, QTS
Music: Mr S Willis, BA, MA Cambridge, PGCE
Instrumental Music: Mrs B Salisbury, ARCM, LRAM (*also Assistant Head – Pastoral Support*)
Physics: Mrs M Robinson, BSc Liverpool, PGCE (*also Head of Careers*)
Physical Education: Miss V Clark, BA Chichester, QTS
Psychology: Miss A Davies, BA Sussex, PGCE
Religious Studies: Mrs V J Gibson, BA, MA Exeter, PGCE
Science: Mrs R Johnson, BSc, ARCS London
Spanish: Mrs I Fanning, MA London
Textiles: Mrs J Lesbirel, BEd Cardiff

Junior School:
Science: Mrs L Glithro, BSc St Andrews, MA Ed Open, PGCE
IT: Mrs N Kaura, BDS London, BSc Surrey, DMS, PMP, PMI
Music: Mrs R Adams, BA Ed Music Exeter
PE: Mrs N Orr, BA Birmingham

There are 20 Visiting Music Staff, 1 Teacher of Speech & Drama, and a School Nurse.

Bursar: Mrs L Maunder
Development Director: Mrs F M Rutland, MA
Registrar: Mrs J Miles

Number of Girls. 1,055 aged 3–18.

School Ethos. The Abbey School has a reputation for academic excellence that is achieved through strong pastoral care and the particularly broad curricular and extra-curricular programme. A Church of England School that warmly welcomes girls of all faiths and of none.

Facilities. Major new Jane Austen Wing opened in 2008 with state-of-the-art classrooms for Years 8 and 9, Art Studios and an additional ICT Suite. A 12-lab science block, a separate sixth form centre, six computer rooms, an extensive modern library, a music centre with rooms for class teaching and individual instrumental teaching, and two large assembly halls. There is a language laboratory, indoor heated swimming pool, gym, dance studio and sports field.

The Junior School has its own buildings, including science lab, music facilities (for group and peripatetic lessons), computer room and a fine assembly hall. 2006 saw the opening of a superb new building for Years 5 and 6 and an expanded library. The Early Years Centre (Nursery and Reception) is housed in a self-contained house with a secluded garden, so that outdoor education is incorporated into the curriculum.

Education. The Abbey School provides an enriched education from Nursery to Sixth Form. Younger girls thrive in the happy, stimulating environment of the Early Years and Junior Schools, where academic, physical and social skills are developed. They easily make the transition to the Senior School, where girls enjoy an excellent education. A very broad range and flexible timetabling enables girls to choose from a wide range of academic subjects. The International Baccalaureate is now offered as an alternative to A Levels in the Sixth Form and results in both are excellent. Many girls go on to top universities including Oxbridge.

Standards of Music, Sport and Art are very high and Inspectors described extra-curricular provision as outstanding, with many varied clubs and trips on offer. Level of participation in Duke of Edinburgh's Award at Silver and Gold Level is impressive.

Optional Extra Subjects. Music and Speech and Drama lessons are available to children from the age of 7. Tuition is available in a wide variety of musical instruments and singing.

Admission is by assessment for the youngest girls and examination and interviews from Key Stage 1 upwards.

Fees per term (2011-2012). Early Years Centre: Nursery (3+ years) £2,650, Reception (4+ years) £3,050. Junior School (Years 1–6): £3,250–£3,680. Senior School (Years 7–13): £4,200.

Scholarships and Bursaries. (*See Scholarship Entries section.*) Academic Scholarships are available at point of entry to Senior School. Music, Drama, Sport, ICT and Art Scholarships are also offered.

A means-tested bursary scheme (up to 100%) is in place to enable families who could not otherwise afford the fees to send their daughters to The Abbey School.

Charitable status. The Abbey School is a Registered Charity, number 309115. The School exists to educate academically able girls.

Abbots Bromley School for Girls and Roch House Preparatory School
A Woodard School

Abbots Bromley, Staffordshire WS15 3BW
Tel: 01283 840232 (24 hrs)
Fax: 01283 840988
e-mail: head@abbotsbromley.net
website: www.abbotsbromley.staffs.sch.uk

Founded in 1874, the school is part of the Woodard Schools Corporation (Midland Division).

Visitor: The Rt Revd The Bishop of Lichfield

Council:
Chairman: Prebendary H Ball, OBE
Vice-Chairman: Mr R Mansell, ACIB
Mr J Bridgeland, MA
Mr M Copestake
Revd S Davis
Mrs S Fisher
Mrs P Norvall
Mrs J Morgan
Dr P Stoate
Major R Wilson
Revd Canon B Clover (*ex officio*)

Clerk to the Council and Bursar: Mr R Beresford, BSc, MSc, ACMA

Head: **Mrs J Dowling**, MA Cantab, PGCE, NPQH

Deputy Head: Mr M A Fisher, BEd Hons
Head of Roch House Preparatory School: Mrs A Johnson, CertEd, Cert Prof St Ed
Chaplain: The Revd Dr P Green, PhD, MA, PGCE, PGDip
Medical Sister: Sister B Terry, RGN, NEBSM
Relief Sister: Sister J Fox, RGN Dip

Boarding Staff:
Head of Boarding: Miss R Francis, BA Hons, Dip RE
Deputy Housemistress: Miss B Aston
Resident Boarding Tutors: Miss S Fenton; Miss R Hesford; Mrs J Rashid, BA Hons
Day Matron: Mrs L Woolley

Senior School Academic Staff:

Art:
*Mrs D Crispin, CertEd
Mrs A Moore, BA Hons, PGCE
Miss N Gandy, BA Hons

Business Studies:
*Mr M A Fisher, BEd Hons
Mr M Warrilow, BSc Hons, PGCE

English:
*Mrs M Steer, BA Hons, PGCE, DipSEN
Miss E Godwin, BA Hons, PGCE, MA

Geography:
*Mr M Warrilow, BSc Hons, PGCE
Mrs A Copley, BA Hons, PGCE

History:
*Mrs S Towell, BA Hons, PGCE
Mrs F Kersley, BA Hons, PGCE

Information Technology:
*Miss J Hill, BEd Hons
Mr R Ellis (*Technician*)

Learning Enrichment & Support/Gifted & Talented Coordinator:
Mrs U Griffiths, BA Hons, DipT SpLD
Mrs J Turnbull
EFL: Mrs E Lampard, BA Hons, PGCE, CELTA, OU Dip
Miss R Hesford

Mathematics:
*Mr K Wardell, BSc Hons, PGCE
Mrs S Booth, BSc Hons, PGCE
Mrs M A Clapham, BSc Hons, PGCE
Mr G Johnson, BA, NPQH, PGCE
Mr M Fisher, BEd Hons

Modern Languages:
*Mrs K Rowlands, BA Hons, PGCE (*German/French*)
Mrs B Coulthard, BA Hons, PGCE (*Spanish/French*)

Music:
Director of Music: Mr C Walker, MMus, ARCM, AMusTCL, LTCL, LRAM
Assistant Director of Music: Miss E Barter, MA Cantab, PGCE, FRCO

Physical Education:
*Mrs Y Menneer, BEd Hons
Miss J D Hill, BEd Hons
Miss N Lewis, BSc, PGCE
Miss S Fenton

Religious Studies:
The Revd Dr P Green, PhD, MA, PGCE, PGDip
Miss R Francis, BA Hons, Dip RE

Sciences:
*Dr Walker-Taylor, PhD, PGCE (*Biology*)
Miss C Tipper, BSc Hons, PGCE (*Chemistry*)
Mr L Grant, BA, PGCE(*Physics*)
Mrs E Ellis, BSc Hons, PGCE (*Biology*)
Mr S Nandi, BSc, PGCE (*Chemistry*)
Technician: Miss L Smith

Sociology & Politics:
Mrs V Hawley, BA Hons

Pastoral Coordinator (*Senior School*) and Designated Safeguarding Officer: Mrs K Rowlands, BA Hons, PGCE
Senior House Coordinator: Mrs B Coulthard, BA Hons, PGCE

Head of Sixth Form: Mrs A Copley, BA Hons, PGCE
Key Stage 4 Coordinator: Mr M Warrilow, BSc Hons, PGCE

Key Stage 3 Coordinator: Miss J Hill, BEd Hons
Careers Coordinator: Miss E Godwin, BA Hons, PGCE, MA
Curriculum Coordinator: Mr K Wardell, BSc Hons, PGCE
Curriculum Enrichment Coordinator: Mrs D Crispin, CertEd
Educational Visits Coordinator: Mrs S Slater
Internal Events Coordinator: Mrs V Hawley, BA Hons
PSHE Coordinator: Mrs D Crispin, CertEd

Roch House Preparatory School:
Head: Mrs A Johnson, CertEd, Cert Prof St Ed
Deputy Head & Curriculum Coordinator: Mrs W Gordon, BEd Hons
Mrs S Crout, DipEd
Mrs L S Pickering, CertEd
Mrs C A Spratt, BA Hons, PGCE
Mrs L Evans, CertEd
Mrs M Swinnerton, BA Hons, PGCE, Cert SpLD

Kindergarten: Mrs A Dunmore, NVQ3
Pastoral Coordinator & LES Coordinator: Mrs M Swinnerton, BA Hons, PGCE, Cert SpLD
Pastoral Assistant: Miss S Barrow, BA Hons
Early Years Apprentice: Miss M Blacker
Administration: Ms S Harris

Dance & Musical Theatre:
Artistic Directors:
Mr Russell Alkins, RAD Cert
Mrs Marianne Alkins, RAD Cert
Guest Choreographers and Specialist Teachers

Riding (Abbots Bromley Equestrian Centre):
Director of Equitation:
Miss S Vickers, BHSI, CertEd, Senior Assessor, First Aid at Work
Instructors:
Mrs S Hemingfield, BHS IntSM, BHSIT, First Aid at Work
Mrs D Atkin, BHS PTT, BHS Stage 3 HK & C, First Aid at Work
Trainees:
Miss D Jones, BHS 2, First Aid at Work
Miss C Latham, BHS 2, First Aid at Work

Duke of Edinburgh's Award Scheme:
Mrs S Slater
Mr P Gardner
Mr W Dowling
Mr M Warrilow, BSc Hons, PGCE
Dr A Walker-Taylor, PhD, PGCE

Speech & Drama:
Mrs A-M Morrell, LLAM, FRSA, HND Theatre Design, Dip Fashion & Design

Administration:
Bursar: Mr R Beresford, BSc, MSc, ACMA
Assistant Bursar: Mrs M Cochrane
Finance Assistant: Mrs J Bara
Examinations Officer: Dr A Walker-Taylor, PhD, PGCE
Assistant Examinations Officer: Mrs J Simon
Personnel Secretary: Mrs H Meadows

Headmistress's Office:
Mrs S Slater
Mrs J Dale
Mrs K Addy

AB Connects Coordinator: Mr R Alkins, RAD Cert
Marketing Assistants: Ms J Turner, Mrs S Russell

"*Abbots Bromley Cares*" is the resounding message that greets you whenever you visit Abbots Bromley School for Girls. The Christian ethos, 'family' community, natural surroundings and boarding tradition help to make for a secure and happy environment. Unique traditions blend comfortably with the needs of the 21st century pupil.

Alongside the importance of excelling academically, key life skills can also be gained from the myriad of extra-curricular programmes that are on offer.

A Vocational Dance Course is available on-site and is carefully constructed to include Classical Ballet, Repertoire, Jazz, Modern Dance, Performance Skills, Drama and Musical Theatre alongside core academic subjects.

The purpose-built Equestrian Centre set within the school grounds boasts superb facilities for beginners and experienced riders alike.

Abbots Bromley School for Girls is today very much a flourishing local day and boarding school for girls aged 11–18.

Roch House Preparatory School is situated on the same site and offers a vibrant co-educational environment for boys and girls aged 3–11.

Fees per term (2011-2012). Boarding: £5,300–£7,995; Day: £1,405–£4,775.

Charitable status. Abbots Bromley School for Girls is a Registered Charity, number 1103321.

Abbot's Hill School

Bunkers Lane, Hemel Hempstead, Herts HP3 8RP
Tel: 01442 240333 (both Junior & Senior Depts)
Fax: 01442 269981
e-mail: registrar@abbotshill.herts.sch.uk
website: www.abbotshill.herts.sch.uk

Founded 1912.
Motto: *Vi et Virtute*

Chairman of the Governing Body: Mrs J Mark, BA Hons, QTS

Headmistress: Mrs K Lewis, MA, BSc, PGCE

Head of Junior Department: Miss K Twinn, BA Hons QTS

Head of Senior Department: Miss P Maynard, BEd Hons, MA, JP

Bursar: Mr Mark Stephens, BA Hons, FCMA

Registrar: Ms A Cooper

Abbot's Hill School is an Independent Day School for girls aged 3–16 years and boys aged 3–5 years. There is a total of 440 pupils in the School from Nursery through to Year 11.

A great emphasis is placed on providing a complete and balanced education. Class sizes are deliberately kept small, which helps to ensure that pupils are well motivated and eager to learn, and allows individual attention from staff members. Each pupil is actively encouraged to achieve their potential, and parent-teacher relationships are excellent in this warm and enabling environment. Excellent results are achieved that are at least commensurate with pupil ability, and the outstanding Key Stage results in particular can be seen as a reflection of the School's success.

With small classes and a high teacher-pupil ratio, the school aims to develop the academic and creative talents, social skills and confidence of each pupil. Every pupil benefits from being known personally by the Headmistress and teaching staff who seek to create a happy and caring environment.

Premises. The School is situated in 76 acres of parkland on the edge of Hemel Hempstead. The main building is a spacious and comfortable 19th Century house, which, combined with purpose built teaching blocks, Science, Sport, Performing Arts and ICT suites, provides our pupils with first class facilities.

Curriculum. During the first three years, a broad programme based on the National Curriculum is followed, encompassing both academic and creative subjects. Each girl's potential and progress is carefully monitored by both teaching staff and a personal tutor. Subjects studied include English, Maths, Science, French, Spanish, Geography, History, Media Studies, Information and Communication Technology, Religious Studies, Music, Personal, Social and Health Education, Art and Design, Food Studies and Home Economics, Physical Education and Child Development.

In Years 10 and 11 a core GCSE curriculum of 6 subjects is followed with girls choosing up to three further subjects.

Music. The School has a very strong Music Department with excellent facilities. The Performing Arts building includes studios for dance, drama and music. The School Choirs and Orchestra perform regularly in concerts, recitals, plays, musicals and various functions throughout the year.

Sports. The School has a strong sporting tradition. There is a well-equipped Sports Hall, lacrosse pitches, grass and hard tennis courts, and a heated outdoor swimming pool. The main sports played are Lacrosse, Netball, Athletics, Tennis, Rounders and Swimming. All girls are encouraged to participate in the sporting opportunities at Abbot's Hill and currently there are a number of girls who have reached County and National standard in selected sports.

Extra-Curricular Activities. Many activities and clubs are held outside of School and these vary in range from Dance, Art, Duke of Edinburgh's Award Scheme, Music, Speech and Drama and all sports.

Sixth Form and Beyond. Baird House girls are encouraged to consider their future prospects and are very well prepared to choose from a wide range of A level and GNVQ courses offered to them when they leave. There is a comprehensive careers programme available to further enhance their decisions including an annual Sixth Form Forum where many schools exhibit their Sixth Form Courses.

Religion. Abbot's Hill is a Church of England foundation. Children of all faiths are welcome at the School and all religious observations are respected.

Admission. (*See Scholarship Entries section.*) Admission to Abbot's Hill is by Entrance Examination, interview, and a report from the previous school. Girls are admitted to the Senior Department at 11. There may be occasional vacancies at 12 and 13. Bursaries and scholarships are available.

Fees per term (2011-2012). Baird House: £4,880 (Years 7–11); St Nicholas House: £2,735–£3,405 (Reception to Year 6); Nursery: £275 (per morning session), £185 (per afternoon session).

Junior Department. The Junior Department of Abbot's Hill, St Nicholas House, is situated in the same grounds as Baird House. St Nicholas House provides nursery, pre-prep and preparatory education for girls aged 3–11 and boys aged 3–5. St Nicholas House mixes the formal setting of the classroom with the wealth of opportunity provided by our physical surroundings. Children are given the freedom in which to grow, learn and play. Classrooms and corridors are bright and well decorated with children's work reflecting the diversity of the curriculum.

The Junior School plays a very important role within our school community and is an integral part of the school as a whole. It is our aim at Abbot's Hill to nurture the whole child, thus enabling our pupils to develop their talents whether they be academic, artisitic or sporting. Specialist teaching is introduced from a child's earliest days; French, Music and PE are introduced in the pre-school year. This is added to as a child progresses to include Drama, Games, ICT and Geography. By the time a girl reaches Year 5 she is being subject taught and is able to adapt to moving around whilst being supported by a class teacher.

The small class size at St Nicholas House enables those needs to be recognised and met early with the minimum disruption. For those who need extra support this is offered within the classroom setting or one-to-one as appropriate. Gifts or talents for a particular area of learning can be extended and developed to their potential.

The wider curriculum plays a key role. Educational visits are an integral part of the teaching programme and children are regularly taken on visits to galleries and museums to enhance their learning experience. Outside visitors lead workshops at school for year groups or the whole school as appropriate. The extra-curricular programme is wide ranging and ever changing. It currently includes such wide-ranging pursuits as knitting, trampolining and board games as well as a wealth of musical and sports clubs.

Further information. Abbot's Hill welcomes visits from prospective parents and pupils. If you would like to visit the School. please contact the Registrar for an appointment on 01442 240333 or e-mail registrar@abbotshill.herts.sch.uk.

Charitable status. Abbot's Hill Charitable Trust is a Registered Charity, number 311053, which exists to provide high quality education for children.

Alderley Edge School for Girls

Wilmslow Road, Alderley Edge, Cheshire SK9 7QE

Tel: 01625 583028
Fax: 01625 590271
e-mail: admissions@aesg.co.uk
website: www.aesg.info

Chair of Governors: Mrs S Herring

Headmistress: Mrs Sue Goff, BA Hons Durham, PGCE Oxford

Deputy Headmistresses:
Mrs T Pollard, BEd Hons Secondary
Mrs C Wood, BA Hons, PGCE Leicester

Director of Studies: Mrs J Hodson, MA, PGCE Nottingham

Head of Junior School: Mr L Groves
Head of Lower School (Years 7-9): Mrs A Baker
Head of Upper School (Years 10-11): Mrs J Waterhouse
Head of Sixth Form: Mr D Parkes
Director of Studies: Mrs J Hodson
Bursar: Mrs P McGill
Registrar: Mrs J Bedigan

Heads of Department:

Art: Mrs J Jamieson
Business Studies: Mr D Blair
Chemistry: Mrs C Broady
Classics: Mrs C Kilshaw Walster
Design Technology: Mrs B Milner
Drama: Miss C Bonham
English: Ms L Telford
Food Technology: Mrs C Leigh
Geography: Miss N Johal
History: Mrs J Nicholson
ICT: Mr J Chadwick
Mathematics: Mrs K Birch
Modern Foreign Languages: Mrs S Jones
Music: Dr S Oxley
Physical Education: Mrs S Waite
Physics: Mrs K Torr
Psychology: Mrs A Raval
Religious Education: Mrs A Laing
Science: Mrs C Broady

Age Range. 3–18.
Number in School. Nursery 32; Junior School 148; Senior School 325, Sixth Form 75.
Fees per term (2011-2012). Nursery £1,690; Key Stage 1 £2,032; Key Stage 2 £2,441; Senior £3,067.
Background. For many years the village of Alderley Edge was the location for two of the finest Independent

Girls' Schools in the North West of England. In September 1999 the two schools became one. An independent, all girls, ecumenical school is unique in England and the merger of the two schools was welcomed and supported by the Anglican and Roman Catholic clergy and the founders of both schools.

The Sisters of St Joseph, a Roman Catholic Order, founded Mount Carmel School in 1945. St Hilary's was founded in 1817 and became part of the Woodard Corporation, a Church of England foundation, in 1955. Alderley Edge School for Girls is linked to the Woodard Corporation, the largest group of schools in England. Among them are independent and maintained schools in England, the United States and Australia.

General. This forward-looking girls' school offers a high level of personal attention. Respect for hard work, the development of the whole person and good discipline are the traditional principles on which our creative and innovative educational philosophy is based. We aim to provide a well-balanced education which celebrates achievement in all aspects of school life from Nursery to Sixth Form.

Location. The school is situated in a semi-rural area of Alderley Edge in Cheshire, 15 miles south of Manchester, with easy access to the motorway network and only minutes from Manchester Airport and two Intercity main line stations. Transport is readily available throughout the area.

Admissions. The Nursery School caters for girls from 3 years. Admission for girls to the Junior School is at 4/5 years old. Admission to the Senior School is at 11 years by Entrance Examination and interview.

Curriculum. *Senior School*: Students follow a broad and balanced curriculum based on the National Curriculum but with many additions. Subjects include: Mathematics, English Language, English Literature, IT, Biology, Chemistry, Physics, French, German, Spanish, Latin, History, Geography, Music, Drama, Religious Studies, Food Technology, Art, Design Technology, Business Studies, PPE (Philosophy, Politics, Economics), PSHE (Personal, Social, Health Education) and Physical Education. At A Level the following subjects are offered in addition those listed above: Further Mathematics, Philosophy & Ethics, Psychology and Theatre Studies.

In addition to their normal academic studies, all Lower Sixth pupils study AS General Studies.

Academic excellence is the school's main aim and attention is paid to meeting the individual needs and abilities of the students. Small classes and continuous assessment ensure high levels of pupil achievement.

Junior School: Creative learning is at the heart of the Junior School. The work is based on the National Curriculum with English, Mathematics and Science providing the foundations for learning with History, Geography, RE, Art, Design, ICT, Music, PE and French completing the curriculum. Latin is also taught from Year 5.

Examination Results 2010. Junior school pupils undertake InCAS (Interactive Computerised Assessment System) assessments.

GCSE results: Overall pass rate (A*–C) 97%.

A Level results: Overall pass rate 100%.

The Arts. *Music*: A very large percentage of pupils learn a musical instrument and examinations may be taken. The school runs 4 choirs, 2 orchestras, a jazz band and numerous smaller instrumental ensembles including string groups, a brass group and 5 different woodwind groups. Many cups have been won in local festivals and pupils perform in local youth orchestras.

Drama and Dance: Both are offered. The majority of pupils are involved in school productions and all pupils participate in House and other productions.

Sports and Clubs. *Sports*: tennis, rounders, hockey, athletics, netball, gymnastics, football, swimming, dance, cross-country, badminton, volleyball, squash, fitness, self-defence. In the Sixth Form a huge variety of options are available for the girls including golf and aerobics.

Senior Clubs: language club, Biology/Chemistry workshop, Physics workshop, French club, book club, DT club, magazine committee, dance, drama, poetry, public speaking, hockey, netball, tennis, rounders, athletics, Duke of Edinburgh's Award, Games, Comenius European Educational Project, Model United Nations, Young Enterprise, Youth Speaks and Mock Trial.

Junior Clubs: Contemporary Dance, Drama, Judo, Short Tennis, Brownies, Fencing, Gardening, Fit 'n' Funky, French, Netball, Spanish, Library, Beacon Prayer Group, Cycling Proficiency and many more.

Facilities. In building a new school we have achieved our objective to remain small enough to care for every child's needs and yet the school enjoys all the benefits and resources of a much larger school. A multi-million pound investment programme has provided a new Senior School, and a completely refurbished Junior School. Facilities include six superbly equipped science laboratories, four ICT suites with online facilities throughout the school, Language Suite with language laboratory, Humanities block with Business Studies centre, competition-size Sports Hall, Gymnasium, Performing Arts Centre, Chapel and a Library with breathtaking views over the Cheshire Plain.

Scholarships and Bursaries. Several Academic scholarships and scholarships for Music are awarded at 11+, 13+ and 16+. Art and Sport scholarships are available at 11+. Bursaries are also available (income linked).

Charitable status. Alderley Edge School for Girls is a Registered Charity, number 1006726. It exists to provide education for children.

Amberfield School
Ipswich

Nacton, Ipswich, Suffolk IP10 0HL
Tel: 01473 659265
Fax: 01473 659843
e-mail: office@amberfield.suffolk.sch.uk
website: www.amberfield.suffolk.sch.uk

Chairman: Mr A Lang, MA, MBA, MCIBS

Governors:
Revd Canon G Grant
Mr G Hall
Mrs J Hall
Mr G Thomas
Mrs C Whight
Miss P Kelleher

***Headmistress*: Mrs L Ingram**

Head of Junior School: Mrs C Dungey

Bursar: Mr T Llewellyn

Leadership Team:
Mrs L Ingram
Mrs M Wilkins
Mrs A Holmes
Mrs C Dungey
Mr T Llewellyn

Registrar: Mrs S Stanfield

Amberfield School is an independent day school for girls aged 2–16 and boys aged 2–7 years that nestles in pleasant woodland on the edge of Nacton village, near Ipswich. Benefiting from its peaceful, out-of-town location it is nonetheless well placed for major routes including the A12 and A14. In addition to the original buildings there are modern, purpose-built classrooms, laboratories, ICT suites and a Drama Studio: all rooms are light, airy and well equipped. Within the grounds there are plenty of opportunities for outdoor learning including a full range of outdoor sports facilities.

We have a wonderfully supportive and friendly environment with talented, enthusiastic and expert teachers who will really get to know your child. Our small classes mean that we can nurture our pupils' individual talents. Personalised education is not a new concept at Amberfield. We create an environment that is safe and happy in which we all have fun learning together.

We are justly proud of the achievements of our pupils; our value added scores are high. A full set of GCSE A grades, outstanding musical and sporting achievements and highly-developed leadership skills are not unusual. In our care, all our pupils grow in confidence.

Our ethos is to 'have a go and believe in yourself'. There is a wealth of opportunity for involvement in a wide range of sporting and cultural activities. Our robot team has been world champions for three consecutive years and younger pupils have enjoyed regional and national success at Lego League. Teamwork and leadership skills are important; these are developed as the girls go through the senior school. In Year 9 they can opt for the Duke of Edinburgh's Award Scheme and by Year 11 the girls are at the top of the school so they have many opportunities to gain posts of responsibility.

The School Day. For all children the school day begins at 8.40 am. We have provision for supervised care beyond the school day from 8.00 am to 5.30 pm. Nursery children attend on a full-time or session basis and the Nursery is open from 7.30 am to 6.30 pm.

Entry to the School. There is an 11+ test in January for girls entering the Senior school. Juniors are tested informally in a classroom situation. Nursery children must be 2 years of age before entry. We encourage prospective pupils to spend a day with us to experience the unique Amberfield atmosphere for themselves.

Curriculum. A broad range of subjects is offered at GCSE (including Astronomy).

ICT plays an important part in delivering the curriculum throughout the school from a basic introduction in Reception to GCSE in the senior school. The school is fully networked and well equipped with computers and interactive whiteboards.

The careers staff are supported by Suffolk Connexions and advice is provided to help pupils select the most appropriate subjects for their planned career path. Amberfield students continue their studies in a variety of local sixth forms, both in the independent and maintained sector.

Pastoral Care. Maintaining the highest standards of pastoral care is at the heart of Amberfield School's philosophy. This is crucial to each pupil's self-confidence and success. Every effort is made to ensure pupils are happy and at ease with school life.

Form teachers are the mainstay of the pastoral care system. By developing an open and trusting relationship with their pupils, form teachers can provide a receptive ear and the essential support that may be required. There is excellent communication with parents so that school and family can work in partnership.

Creative Life. Artistic talent and practical skills are encouraged at all ages. Original and exciting work is produced in art, textiles and home economics. There are junior and senior choirs, specialist singing and ensemble groups and orchestras. The Drama Studio with its sound and lighting box provides many opportunities for dance and theatre studies.

Sport. Sport is an integral part of life at Amberfield. Physical fitness is essential to our well-being and pupils benefit greatly from the experience of working as a team. There are regular matches against other schools in netball, hockey, cross-country, athletics and tennis. Amberfield pupils have played at county and national level in all these sports and also in sailing and table tennis. Tennis is particularly strong with LTA coaching and we have huge success in tournaments across the full age range. The wide range of sports on offer, from aerobics and trampolining to volleyball, enables every pupil to find their forte.

Fees per term (2011-2012). Senior School: £3,505; Junior School: £2,685; Nursery (full time) and Reception: £2,380.

Scholarships and Bursaries. Academic, Art, Music, Sport and Tennis Scholarships are awarded annually to pupils at 11+.

Bursaries are awarded at the discretion of the Headmistress on completion of a financial statement form.

Badminton School

Westbury-on-Trym, Bristol BS9 3BA
Tel: 0117 905 5271
Fax: 0117 962 8963
e-mail: admissions@badminton.bristol.sch.uk
website: www.badminton.bristol.sch.uk

Motto: *Nurture. Inspire. Empower*
    Founded 1858. Non denominational.

Board of Governors:

Chairman: Mrs Alison Bernays

Vice-Chairman: Mr P Ashmead

Clerk to the Governors, Secretary and Bursar: Mr T Synge

Vice-Presidents:
Professor Sir Mark Richardson
Mr R Hodder Williams

Headmistress: Mrs J A Scarrow, BA Manchester

Deputy Head: Mrs V Drew, BA Wales
Head of Sixth Form: Mrs K Dodd, MA Essex
Head of Junior School: Mrs E Davies, BA Cardiff

Heads of Department:

English: Miss L Griffith, BA Oxon
Theatre Studies: Mr S Gentry, BA Leicester

Mathematics: Dr D Cook, BA Oxon

Science:
Chemistry: Mr B Wharton, BA Hons Bristol
Physics: Mr P Foster, BSc London
Biology: Mrs N Warden, BSc Exeter, BA Oxon
Home Economics: Mrs F Williamson, BEd Wales
ICT: Dr C Enos, PhD Swansea

Languages:
French: Mrs N Walton, BA Durham
German: Miss S J Whyatt, BA London
Spanish: Mrs K Dunn, BA Hull
Classics: Mrs C Hamlett BA Classics Bristol

Humanities:
History and Politics: Ms M Stimpson, MA Edinburgh
Geography: Mrs T Yates. BA Exeter
Economics: Mrs D Betterton, BA Exeter
Religious Education: Miss H John, MA Exeter

Music: Mr M Bale, GRSM, LRAM, LGSM

Creative Arts: Miss F Creber, BA Wales

Physical Education: Miss G Richards, CertEd Bedford

Houses and Housemistresses:
Head of Boarding: Mrs S Mitchell, OU

Housemistresses:
Miss L Van Os, BA Leeds
Mrs S Joyner, BA Reading
Mrs S Carr, NNEB Eastbourne
Mrs L Clubbe, BTEC Weybridge

Assistant Housemistresses:
Miss A Dowling, MA St Andrews
Miss L Hunter, BA Cardiff
Miss B Li, BA Hons Cambridge
Miss H Owen-Frawley, BA Bristol
Miss C Guennink, Lehramt Frankfurt
Miss S McCarty, Lehramt Frankfurt

School Doctor: Dr D Kershaw, MBChB, MRCGP

Marketing and Admissions Director: Mrs H Lightwood,
   BA Leicester, PG Dip Marketing
Admissions Officer: Miss K Balmforth
Headmistress's P.A: Mrs P Thompson

Badminton is an independent girls' boarding, weekly
boarding and day school situated in a 20-acre site on the
edge of Durdham Downs on the outskirts of the university
city of Bristol.

Age Range of Pupils. 3 to 18.

Number of Pupils. 434 in total including Junior School:
Boarding 197; Day: Senior 127, Junior 110.

Number of Staff. Full-time teaching 45, Part-time teaching 12. Teacher Pupil ratio is currently 1:7.

Educational Philosophy. At Badminton a broad curriculum, the study of national and international affairs, adequate
leisure and self-disciplined freedom give opportunity for the
fullest development of personality and individual talent.
Girls at Badminton regularly achieve outstanding academic
results. However the School is certainly not a production
line for bright girls destined for top university honours. Girls
leave Badminton not only having gained first-rate results but
having developed into thinking and independent young
women. Constant encouragement is the key to the success of
girls in a relaxed yet purposeful environment, in which they
are well taught, challenged and enabled to achieve.

Staff/pupil relations are mature and friendly, based on the
principles of courtesy and mutual respect; high standards are
expected for both work and behaviour, and an honest and
open response is particularly valued. The ethos of the School
has traditionally encouraged caring moral attitudes, individuality and challenge.

Boarding. Boarders need security, affection and lots to
do at weekends, and life is geared towards keeping them
busy and fully occupied. Full-time, weekly or flexi boarding
are offered, allowing girls to easily combine their academic
schedules with the many activities that are on offer after
school and at weekends. Junior boarders have their own
house adjacent to gardens and play area and within easy
access of the swimming pool and other facilities. Sanderson
House, a state-of-the-art new boarding house with outstanding facilities opened recently to accommodate boarders in
Years 9, 10 and 11. Bartlett House is the new Junior Boarding house which opened in 2009 and offers cosy bedrooms
for boarders in Years 5–8. The Sixth Form are accommodated in the Sixth Form Centre where they have single or
double study-bedrooms. In each House boarders have the
support of a resident Housemistress, an Assistant Housemistress and House Tutor and there are a range of clubs and
activities on offer every day and a full weekend programme.

Curriculum. The School Curriculum reflects the career-
minded aspirations of both parents and pupils and there is an
outstanding record of academic achievement and entry to
higher education. The emphasis at Badminton is on all-
round education, not narrowly academic, and both the curriculum and the timetable are constructed to create a balance
between academic achievement, personal development, life
skills and other enterprising activity.

The school currently offers 18 subjects at GCSE and A
Level: most of the girls take 9 GCSE Levels and go on to
take 4 or 5 AS and 3 or 4 A Levels in the Sixth Form. Mathematics and Science are particularly strong. Class size averages 16 in the main school, and about 12 in the Sixth Form.

There is a full general studies course in the Sixth Form
which includes Health Education, Politics, Model United
Nations, European Youth Parliament, First Aid, Computing,
Information Technology and additional languages. The
Careers section is particularly strong.

Academic Record. Badminton has a fine academic
record at GCSE, AS and A Levels and believes in the pursuit
of academic excellence without cramming. The school is
currently No 4 in the national league tables. Girls are
expected to produce results according to their ability and to
develop their individual talents. The GCSE and A Level pass
rate is 100% and 100% of the Sixth Form go on to degree
courses, including Oxford and Cambridge (15%).

Facilities. The School is well equipped with classrooms,
including a large modern block containing 8 science laboratories, a Creative Arts Centre, several re-equipped computer
rooms, a languages listening room, new humanities suite,
theatre, gymnasium, fitness suite, 7 tennis courts, playing
fields, heated indoor swimming pool, all-weather sports
facility, Casson Library, fiction, careers, music and art
libraries, eight common rooms, an extended and refurbished
Sixth Form Centre and two Music Schools.

Music and Creative Arts. It is the policy that all girls are
involved in the Creative Arts, both within the curriculum
and as extra-curricular activities, and the School attaches
great importance to the development of musical and artistic
talent.

Music is extremely popular at Badminton with over 85%
of all pupils studying at least one musical instrument. There
is a wide range of choral and instrumental groups available
to choose from at the school including Junior and Senior
Choir, Schola (choral group), Barbarella (female barber
shop), orchestra, swing band, rock groups, string ensembles,
woodwind ensembles and other mixed musical groups. With
nearly 30 visiting peripatetic teachers, all of whom are professional musicians, the students can study any instrument
of their choice. There are a wide variety of performance
opportunities including informal concerts, concerts for the
local community, music festivals, two major concerts a year
plus a rock concert. Badminton musicians have also toured
internationally to Ireland, Hungary and Italy.

There is a wide choice of Creative Arts – Art, Drama,
Pottery, Light Crafts, Textiles, Printmaking, Design, Jewel-
lery-making and Photography. There are seven dramatic
productions every year where the girls have the chance to
produce, direct and stage-manage house plays: there are also
joint music and drama productions with boys' schools.

Clubs and Societies. Science, Politics, Young Enterprise,
Languages Vivantes, Geographical, Mathematical, Debating, Public Speaking, Social Service, Drama, Art, Librarians, Historical, Young Engineers, Model United Nations,
European Youth Parliament, Christian Union, Chess.

Games and Activities. The School offers hockey, tennis,
netball, swimming, athletics, rounders, squash, gymnastics,
badminton, volleyball, trampolining and enters girls for
county trials where appropriate. There are international
sports tours every year.

Optional extras include self-defence, fencing, riding,
driving, golf, judo and skating. All girls participate in activities which include the full choice of games and creative arts
as above and boarders have the opportunity of additional
activities at the weekend. The Duke of Edinburgh's Award is
taken by over half the pupils with many gaining bronze, silver and gold awards. There are regular trips abroad to European countries, especially for art, history, music, geography,
skiing and exchanges with trusted schools in France, Germany and Spain.

Badminton is fortunate in being in a university city; regular visits are arranged to concerts, lectures and theatres, including municipal and civic activities, and there is considerable contact with the University and outside visits to industry and universities; girls attend short courses on Industry. There is a flourishing Social Services Group, where girls help in primary schools, day nurseries, and with elderly people, gardening and cooking.

Admission. Entry to the Junior School is by personal interview, English, Mathematics and non-verbal reasoning tests; to the Senior School it is by a Badminton entrance examination for girls aged 11–14. The Headmistress likes to see all girls and their parents before entry where possible. Entry to the Sixth Form requires girls to sit entrance exams in two subjects they would like to study for A Level plus a general paper.

Prospective parents are encouraged to visit the school individually. To obtain a prospectus and arrange a visit, please contact the Admissions and Marketing Department.

Scholarships and Bursaries. (*See Scholarship Entries section.*) Scholarships of up to 20% of fees are offered both for entrance to the Senior School and the Sixth Form for academic excellence, music, art and all-round ability. In addition, parents are encouraged to apply for means-tested bursaries (up to 100% of fees) in addition to a scholarship.

Fees per term (2011-2012). Day: Seniors £4,970–£5,270, Juniors £2,350–£3,470. Boarders: Seniors £9,470–£9,880, Juniors £6,280–£6,550.

Charitable status. Badminton School Limited is a Registered Charity, number 311738. It exists for the purpose of educating children.

Bedford Girls' School

Cardington Road, Bedford MK42 0BX

Tel:	01234 361900
Fax:	01234 344125
e-mail:	admissions@bedfordgirlsschool.co.uk
website:	www.bedfordgirlsschool.co.uk

Foundation – The Harpur Trust.

"Let me keep an open mind so I understand as much as I can in my lifetime and not reach the limits of my imagination."

Chair of Governors: Mrs R Wallace, FRCS

Clerk to the Governors and School Bursar: Mr J-M Hodgkin, BSc, FCA, FSI, ACIS

Head: Miss J MacKenzie, MSc, BSc

Deputy Head: Mrs F McGill, BEd

Assistant Head: Mrs K Jones, BSc
Assistant Head: Mrs N Keeler, BSc
Assistant Head: Mrs S Mason-Patel, BA
Assistant Head: Mrs S Willis, BLib

Head of Bedford Girls' School Junior School: Mrs C Royden, MA

Director of IB and Thinking Skills: Mr C Canning, BA, BD, HDipEd

Senior School Pastoral Team:
Head of Sixth Form: Mrs A Goodman, BEd
Head of Years 10 and 11: Mrs J Wilkins, BA
Head of Years 8 and 9: Mrs S Hardy, BA
Head of Transition: Mrs F Clements, BSc

Heads of Department/Subject:
Art and Technology: Mrs C Lugsden, MA Ed
Biology: Mrs V Lockren, BSc

Careers: Dr L Penney, BSc, PhD
Chemistry: Dr N Holmes, MRCS
Classics: Mrs D Day, BA
DT: Mr D Jackson, CertEd
Food Technology: Mrs G Sayce, CertEd
Textiles: Mrs C Randall, BEd (*Teacher in charge*)
Dance and Drama: Mrs S Perren, CertEd
Dance: Mrs S Winter, BEd (*Teacher in charge*)
Economics and Business Studies: Miss L Birch, BA, CertEd
English: Mrs C Hopkins, BEd
French: Mrs C Fourey-Jones, L-ès-L
Geography: Mrs D Whiteley, BSc
German: Mrs C Lessig, GTP, MA
History and Politics: Ms V Sanders, MA
ICT Director: Mr J Potter, BA, MA
Languages: Mrs M Gomez-Alonso, Lic en Fil
Mathematics: Mrs G Hubbard, BSc
Music: Mrs S Aylen, MA, BMus, ALCM, ARCM
Physical Education: Mrs J Axford, BA Ed
Physics: Mr O Bowden, BEng, PGCE
PSHE: Mrs P Milton, BEd
Psychology: Mrs P Harrold, BA, MA (*Teacher in charge*)
Religious Studies: Mrs E Pagliaro, BEd
Science: Mrs V Lockren, BSc
Spanish: Mrs M Gomez-Alonso

Admissions Manager: Mrs V Hicks

A new beginning: a rich heritage. Bedford Girls' School is a new independent day school for girls aged 7–18. Formed by the merger of two distinct and respected schools, Dame Alice Harpur School and Bedford High School for Girls, its new beginnings build firmly upon the long and rich heritage of the two schools that first opened their doors in 1882. Today it is our ambition that Bedford Girls' School will be an exceptional girls' school – continuing this long tradition of commitment to the education of young women.

Expanding horizons: raising expectations. Our philosophy is to be innovative, outward looking and open minded. We have unashamedly high standards and expectations across our school community. We look to each individual to act as an inspiring role model and bring a can do approach to their day. We foster connections within our local and international community, learning from the lives of those around us and developing sensitivity to culture and difference.

Learning for fun: learning for life. Our approach to learning is forward thinking, dynamic and vibrant. You can feel the energy and enthusiasm of the teaching and learning in the classroom and beyond. From Year 3 to Sixth Form it is our belief that learning should be exciting and spark a lifelong desire to engage in the wonder of the world around us.

An holistic approach: the right tools for the job. We are lucky to be part of the Harpur Trust Charity, one of the 200 largest charities in the UK. The Charity is committed to inspiring and supporting the people of Bedford and has been enriching lives by providing education, breaking down barriers and creating opportunities for over 400 years. This solid and stable backing ensures our future and means we are blessed with the funds to continue to innovate in our practice and invest in our resources.

Discover BGS: share in our vision. We invite you to get to know us better. Explore our website, or better still come and visit us – we hope your experience of Bedford Girls' School will inspire you to join us.

Admissions. Entry to the Junior School is on the basis of informal assessment and written tests. Entry to the Senior School is on the basis of interview, written tests, school report and reference. Sixth Form entry is on the basis of interviews, GCSE results, school report and reference.

Registration and Entrance Examination Fee: £100.

Fees per term (2011-2012). Junior School (7–10 years) £2,534; Senior School & Sixth Form (11–18 years) £3,561.

Bursaries. Bedford Girls' School welcomes bursary applications for the Senior School from families who require financial assistance. Each year a finite sum is available to award and many factors are taken into account before deciding on the level of award to be made. All awards are means tested and subject to annual reassessment. Bursaries can be awarded from a value of 25% of fees up to a full bursary place at the discretion of the School.

Charitable status. Bedford Girls' School is part of The Bedford Charity (The Harpur Trust) which is a Registered Charity, number 204817.

Benenden School

Cranbrook, Kent TN17 4AA
Tel: 01580 240592
Fax: 01580 240280
e-mail: registry@benenden.kent.sch.uk
website: www.benenden.kent.sch.uk

Council:
Mr C A A Covell, MA (*Chairman*)
Mrs R J Johnston (*Vice Chairman*)
Mr G S Cherry (*Chairman of the Building Committee*)
Mrs F H Crewdson, BSc Hons
Mr O R Darbishire, MA, MSc, PhD
Mr D P Ereira, LLB, BSc, MSc
Mr M C C Goolden, MA (*Chairman of the Finance
    Committee*)
Mr S Green (*Chairman of the Benenden School Trust*)
Mrs S J Hayes, BA
Mr T H P Haynes, BA
Mr H Salmon, BA (*GBGSA Representative*)
Mr S Smart, BSc, FCA
Mr W E H Trelawny-Vernon, BSc
Mr M K H Leung, BA, Dip Soc (*Honorary Representative
    for the Hong Kong Trust*)
Mr N Allen (*Secretary to the Council and School Bursar*)

Headmistress: Mrs C M Oulton, MA Oxon (*History*)

Deputy Head: Dr H M D Petzsch, MA Edinburgh, BD, PhD
    Edinburgh FSA Scot (*History*)

Assistant Head/Director of Studies: Mrs L A Tyler, MA,
    BD, PhD Edin, FSA Scot

Assistant Head/Head of Boarding: Miss A Steven, BA
    Bristol (*English*)

Housemistresses/masters:
Echyngham: Miss R Ross, BSc Exeter (*Physical
    Education*)
Guldeford: Mrs N Hart, Licence Caen (*Physical Education*)
Hemsted: Mrs M Cass, CertEd (*Information Technology*)
Marshall: C W Humphery, MA St Andrews (*English*)
Medway: Mrs E Custodio, BA Aberystwyth (*History*)
Norris: Mr S Mansfield, BA Staffs (*History of Art*)
Founders:
Beeches: A Nicol, BA Canterbury (*Religious Studies*)
Elms: (*to be appointed*)
Limes: Mrs S J Perry, BSc Liverpool (*Biology*)
Oaks: Mrs B Scopes, BA Kent (*History*)

School Chaplain: Mrs J Ashton, MA London

Administrative Staff:
Bursar: N J Allen
Finance Bursar: N Hollamby
Estates Bursar: S Brophy
Domestic Bursar: Mrs S E Franklin, HCIMA
HR & Compliance Officer: Mrs J Card

Development Office:
Mrs D Price (*Development Director*)

G E Smith (*Deputy Development Director*)
Mrs E A Ward (*Admissions Secretary*)
Mrs S K Davies (*Admissions Assistant*)
Mrs K H Barradell (*Seniors' Officer*)
S Thorneycroft (*Marketing Assistant – Publications*)
Mrs D Bradford (*Marketing Assistant – Events*)
Mrs S B Leathart (*Web Assistant*)

Secretariat:
Mrs J A Sullivan (*Headmistress's Personal Assistant*)
Mrs D M Benson, LTCL, FTCL (*Music Administrator*)
Miss E Carrington-Moore (*Head of Boarding's Secretary*)
Miss A Chittenden (*Deputy Head's Personal Assistant*)
Mrs R Judd (*Academic Administrator*)
Mrs J McColl (*Development Director's Personal Assistant*)
Mrs A G Pissarro (*School Secretary – termtime*)
Mrs A Molloy (*Secretary to the Housemistresses/masters*)
Mrs H Doherty (*Bursar's Personal Assistant*)
Mrs N K Wood, BA Cornell (*Director of Studies's
    Secretary*)
§Mrs C Andrews (*Common Room*)
§Mrs S Cramp (*PE Administrator*)
§Mrs M E Murphy (*Careers Administrator*)

Medical:
Dr A M Wood, MBChB, MRC Psych (*Medical Officer*)
Sister J L Mallion, RGN
Mrs E O'Dell, BSc Manchester, RSCN, RGN
Mrs K Perry, RGN

Academic Staff:
§ *Part-time/Visiting*

English:
N van der Vliet, BA UCW Aberystwyth
Ms F Brown, BA Cantab
C W Humphery, MA St Andrews
A Schagen, BA York
Mrs R Smith, BA, MPhil Oxon
Miss A Steven, BA Bristol
§Mrs S Carroll, BA Oxford
§ Dr H Goodwin, BA Dunelm, MA King's College
    London, PhD Middlesex

Mathematics:
Mrs D G Swaine, BSc Wales
Mrs V A Burgess, BSc Dunelm
M Gossage, BSc Liverpool
L Ramoutar, BSc LSE
Mrs G Thomson, BA Cape Town Technical
Mrs J Tremble, BA Open
§Mrs J Mills, BSc Reading
§Mrs E Peacock, BSc Oxford Brookes

Science:
Mrs J Hall, BSc London
Dr N J Dowrick, BA Oxon, DPhil Oxon
O N Hunter, BSc Durham, MA Open
Ms N Marshall, MA Oxon, MIBiol
S C Heron, BSc London
Dr M Mahon, BSc London, PhD London
N Moxham, BSc London
Mrs S J Perry, BSc Liverpool
G Piper, BSc Newcastle
§Mrs A Linney, BSc Birmingham
§Ms S Stevens, BSc Birmingham
§Miss K Gouldstone, BA Brighton
§Mrs W Grosvenor
§Mrs F Hadfield
§Mrs S Harris

Modern Languages:
Miss C L Lesieur, BA, MA Amiens
J D Crouzet, L-ès-L, M-ès-L St Étienne
Mrs M S Curran, BA Oxon
Miss V Fleitas Diaz, DTAS BA Madrid
Mrs M S Griffith, BA Brighton

Mrs A Jarman, MA Oxon
Dr C L J Tsai, MA, PhD Kent
Mrs R van der Vliet, BA UCW Aberystwyth
§Miss C Cintas (*Assistante*)
§Dr S Fra, MA Milan
§Mrs A Fuentes-Mansfield, MA Caen
§Mrs M Gower, BA (*Japanese*)
§Miss P Lavasseur (*Assistante*)
§Mrs N Maslova-Wale, MEd Kazakhstan (*Russian*)
§Miss A Navarro-Silla, LLB Valencia
§Mrs C Rennick (*French Conversation*)
§Mrs C White (*Dutch*)
§Mrs D Wyles, BA Bath, MCIL
§Ms X Yu, BA Fuden
§Miss T Zhang

Classics:
A D Matthews, BA, MLitt Newcastle
Miss L Boyce, MA Oxon
Mrs J Chapman, BA Bristol, TESOL
Miss L Holloway, BA Oxon

Drama:
J McCarthy, BA, MA Cantab, PGCE Bristol
Ms D Caron, BA Loughborough, LGSM, AIMENTS
M S Kemp, HND Stage Mgt/Tech Theatre Bristol Old Vic
    Theatre School
Mrs L Perry, BA York
A D Sargeant, BEng Kent, DipStgMan UWE
§G R Lee, CertEd Roehampton
§Ms N Thorndike, Dip LAMDA
§Mrs E Vernon, Dip Drama Studio Acting
§Miss A L Wickens, LLAM, LAMDA

Economics:
Mrs S J Northridge, BHum London, MBA Reading
C E Williams, BSc Southampton

Geography:
Mrs S Bosher, BHum London
Miss P A Hubbard, BSc Leicester

History and Politics:
J Watts, MA Oxon, BPhil York
Mrs E C Custodio, BA Aberystwyth
Miss K M Dobson, BA Newcastle
M Loy, BA Durham, PGCE Durham
Mrs C M Oulton, MA Oxon
Dr H M D Petzsch, MA Edinburgh, BD, PhD Edinburgh,
    FSA Scot
Mrs B Scopes, BA Kent
J S Wilson, BA Oxon

Religious Studies:
A Nicol, BA Canterbury
Mrs J Ashton, MA London
Dr B Harding, BA Kent, PhD Essex
P Sage, BA Leeds
§C Huxley, BA Canterbury

Art & Design:
R S Leighton, BA Stourbridge
Mrs P J Futrell, BA Middlesex Polytechnic
Dr B Harding, BA Kent, PhD Essex
Miss J S Large, BA Loughborough, BTEC Diploma
S H Mansfield, BA Staffs (*History of Art*)
Mrs J L Taylor, BA Nottingham Trent (*Textiles*)

Design and Technology:
A Vincent, BA Manchester
Mrs L F Palmer, BA Camberwell
C Fahy

Information Technology:
A D Sanderson, BSc Warwick, MSc Bath
Mrs M E Cass, CertEd

Critical Thinking:
P J Sage, BA Leeds
A Nicol, BA Canterbury
Mrs S J Northridge, BHum London, MBA Reading
Mrs D Price
Mrs L Tyler, MA London

Music:
E S Beer, MA Oxon, LRAM
J Fitzgerald, BA Bristol
Mrs S Lamberton, BA Wales
Mrs V Lewis, ARCM, DipRCM (*Piano, Cello*)
§Mr S Chapman, ALCM, LLCMTO (*Guitar*)
§Mrs J M Colman, LTCL (*Piano*) (*Double Bass*)
§Ms C Considine, MMus Perf, PGDip, MMus Hons
§A Ellingworth, Military School of Music, Knellerhall
    (*Clarinet, Saxophone*)
§Mrs K Fish, LTCL, Dip TCL (*Clarinet, Saxophone*)
§Ms S Graham, GRSM, LRAM, DipRAM (*Singing*)
§A W Haigh, ARCM, LRAM (*Piano*)
§Miss R J Hanson-Laurent, BMus BMUS (*Hons*)
§M D Hines, AGSM (*Bassoon*)
§Ms M Lowbury, BA Bristol, ARCM (*Cello*)
§D M Manente, BMus, PGDip (*Strings*)
§Mrs H Manente, BMus, MMus RCM (*Flute*)
§Miss G A Mendes, GDipM Huddersfield, LTCL
    (*Recorder*)
§Ms L Pont, LTCL (*Singing*)
§Mrs S Purton, LRAM (*Oboe, Piano*)
§Ms H Ramsay, BMus Glasgow (*Piano*)
§J Raper, BMus Trinity (*Percussion*)
§Miss E J Roberts, GRNCM, PPRNCM, PDOTGSMD
    (*Horn*)
§Mrs I Sellschop, LRAM (*HFYO Strings Tutor*)
§Mrs J M Tilt, GGSM LRAM (*Singing*)
§Mrs R Waltham, PGDip RAM (*Strings*)
§M Williams, BMus Dunelm, GRSM, Hon LCM, FRCO
    (*Piano, Organ*)
§Ms A Wynne, BA Birmingham, MMus Leeds (*Harp*)

Physical Education:
Miss V A Sawyer, MBA Keele, LLB Hons Open, BEd
    Hons Reading
Mrs J E Fahy (*Sports Centre Supervisor*)
Mrs N Hart, BA Caen
Miss S Kenny (*Fitness Instructor*)
Miss L Lynch, BSc, PGCE Loughborough (*Head Lacrosse
    Coach*)
Ms J Marlowe, BEd Leeds
J Mitchell, BA Hons Bedford
Mrs Y Reynolds, CertEd Dartford College
Miss R Ross, BSc Exeter
Miss K Vincent, BA Brighton
Mrs H Vesma (*Fitness Instructor*)
D Weighton, DipPhysEd Strathclyde
§N J Allen (*Rugby Coach*)
§C Bowles (*Judo & Self Defence Coach*)
§J Chorley (*Fencing*)
§Mrs R M Elliott, RAD, ISTD, LAMDA (*Modern & Tap
    Dance*)
§M D Geer (*Swimming Coach*)
§Mrs V Mitchell, BEd Hons Bedford
§J Morris (*Lifeguard*)
§Mrs J Morris (*Lifeguard*)
§M Morris (*Lifeguard*)
§T Sayer (*Squash Coach*)
§Mrs K M Steel, BEd Hons Bedford
§Miss J Wilson, ISTD, Dip LCDD (*Ballet*)

Careers & College Guidance:
Miss K M Dobson, BA Newcastle
§Mrs M Murphy (*Administrator*)
§Mrs C Saint, BA Dublin

Personal, Social, Health and Economic Education:
Mrs S Bosher, BHum London

Academic Support:
Mrs A P Simpson, BSc London, Cert ADS Greenwich,
   ATC C&G
Mrs J H Edwards, BEd London, MEd UCNW, TCert,
   DipPsych
Mrs J Chapman, BA Bristol, DipMSE Greenwich,
   DipTESOL Trinity
Mrs D Mackinnon, LL.B, Dip LA, QTS, AMBDA/ATS
§Mrs M Lamplugh de Smith, BA London, CCK Modern
   Greek
§Mrs A Martin-Clark, CertSpLD, Cert CLANSA OCR
§Mrs C M Pearson, BEd SEN CNAA
§Dr F Westcott, BSc, PhD Liverpool

Professional Tutor:
§Mrs D E Wyles, BA Bath

Librarian:
Miss A Morley, BA Brighton, MA Sussex, MCLIP,
   DipTEFL, DipPub

Assistant Librarians:
Ms A Rae, BA Sussex
§Mrs L J G Traill
§Mrs A M Taylor

Benenden School aims to give each pupil the chance to develop her potential to the full within a happy and caring environment. We want her to feel ready to take on whatever challenges lie ahead and able to make a positive difference to the world, whether that is at work or at home or both. Whilst we aim to help each girl to achieve her best possible results in public exams, we also emphasise the importance of spiritual growth and of developing as a person, most particularly in confidence, compassion and courage. We want to encourage each pupil to develop as an individual as well as a responsible and caring member of a community.

We aim to do this by providing
- a full and balanced curriculum and a very wide range of extra-curricular and co-curricular activities, designed to promote academic, cultural, creative, physical, spiritual and social development;
- well-taught lessons within facilities designed to encourage the best teaching and the best learning;
- supportive individual academic and pastoral care;
- group and individual higher education and careers guidance designed to help every student to make wise personal choices;
- a wide range of opportunities for leadership within the school;
- a culture of praise, encouragement and support within a framework designed to develop self-reliance and self-esteem;
- the experience of learning to understand other people which a full boarding school can provide;
- opportunities for a close partnership with parents so that school and home can work together to help every pupil.

General Information. The School is an independent girls' boarding school standing in its own parkland of 240 acres. In the heart of the Kentish Weald, it is easily reached by road, or by rail to the neighbouring main line station at Staplehurst, and is well placed for the air terminals of Gatwick and Heathrow, the continental ferry ports of the South East coast and the Channel Tunnel (Ashford International).

The School provides education for girls between the ages of 11 and 18 years. There are 530 students at Benenden; all are boarders and they come from a wide range of backgrounds.

Girls are taught by highly qualified full-time staff of over 80 men and women, together with some 40 part-time specialists, many of whom are leaders in their particular fields.

Each student belongs to a House in which she sleeps and spends much of her private study and leisure time: it is, in effect, her home from home. There are six Houses for 11 to 16 year olds, while Sixth Form students live in the Founders' Sixth Form Centre in one of four Sixth Form Houses.

Each House has a resident Housemistress or Housemaster, who is also a member of the teaching staff and responsible for the academic and pastoral well-being of each student in the House. Much of the day-to-day work is shared with Deputies and Day and Resident Matrons, while other non-resident members of the teaching staff are Personal Academic Tutors.

The School's facilities have been greatly improved in recent years. A new £9 million Science Centre is currently under construction, opening in Autumn 2012. A new eco-classroom was constructed and opened in October 2009. The classroom is completely self sustaining, with solar power and rainwater harvesting. The School was awarded Eco School Green Flag status in 2009. The Benenden School Theatre and Drama teaching complex was officially opened in October 2007. The Clarke Centre, a £3.5 million Study Centre, providing state-of-the-art classrooms equipped with the latest computer technology, library and IT Centre. Since 2001, a programme of extensive refurbishment has taken place in boarding houses, including a new suite of classrooms and floor of study bedrooms which opened in 2003. Extensions to the Sixth Form centre have taken place in 2006 and 2007. For physical recreation there are nine lacrosse pitches, 11 all-weather tennis courts, sports hall containing a further full-sized tennis court, an indoor heated swimming pool, a second sports hall (also used for badminton, volleyball, netball and fencing), a fitness centre and gym, two squash courts and a grass running track.

The School is a Christian community, based on Anglican practice, and the ethos of the School reflects Christian principles. Members of other communions and beliefs are welcomed to the School and every effort is made to help them in the practice of their own faith, in an atmosphere of respect and toleration for the views of others.

Entrance to the School is after internal assessment at Preview Weekend, but dependent upon candidates meeting the School's standard at 11+ and 13+ Common Entrance or in entrance papers. There is also a small intake at Sixth Form level, with competitive entry by the School's own examination. All of the School's students are expected to qualify for degree courses, leaving School with at least three A Levels and at least eight subjects at GCSE. A full careers programme is a key component of the Personal Development Programme, aimed to foster the widest range of skills.

The core subjects up to GCSE are English, English literature, mathematics, science and a modern language. The compulsory balanced science course ensures that all three sciences are studied (either for single sciences at GCSE or the option of Core Science plus Additional Science)), and every student studies in Key Stage 3 at least two of the three modern languages offered in addition to Latin. Cross-curricular skills and the balancing of theoretical concepts with practical applications are actively encouraged. The ability to work independently is critical to enjoyment and success, and students are given every opportunity to acquire appropriate study habits. The curriculum is under constant review and development, reflecting national initiatives and the aspirations of staff and students.

Benenden believes in close cooperation between School and parents and there is regular contact with them, including a weekly email newsletter. Formal reports are sent at the end of every term. Parents are encouraged to visit the School for concerts, plays and other events, as well as to take their daughters out for meals or weekend exeats. There is a flourishing programme of social events for parents.

Curriculum. *Lower School*: English, mathematics, biology, chemistry, physics, French, German or Spanish or Classical Greek, Latin, geography, history, religious studies, art

& design including textiles, design technology, information technology, drama, music, physical education.

GCSE Core: English, English literature, mathematics, biology, chemistry, physics, a modern foreign language.

GCSE Options: German, Spanish, Classical Greek, Latin, Mandarin, geography, history, religious studies, art, textiles, design & technology, music, drama & theatre arts.

A Level Options: English language and literature, English literature, mathematics, further mathematics, biology, chemistry, physics, French, German, Spanish, Greek, Latin, classical civilisation, economics, geography, history, politics, religious studies, art & design, history of art, music, theatre studies, design and technology. All Sixth Form students take Critical Thinking.

(All students' programmes also include academic extension programmes, careers education, information technology, physical education, religious education, personal, social and health education.)

Sport. Lacrosse, tennis, swimming, netball, rounders, badminton, athletics, volleyball, squash, basketball, gym, dance, fencing, trampolining, aerobics, hockey, riding.

Opportunities in Music. Tuition is available in all orchestral and keyboard instruments as well as singing. Numerous opportunities exist for instrumental and choral performance. The School is home to a full youth symphony orchestra, and in which students from other schools also play. Benenden also enjoys a strong choral tradition and hosts recitals by musicians of international calibre.

Opportunities in Speech and Drama. Students are able to pursue drama as an extra-curricular activity throughout their School career by participating in drama workshops, House and Lower and Upper School plays. Speech and drama lessons are available and students are prepared for both English Speaking Board and LAMDA examinations. There are several debating societies and students compete at the Oxford and Cambridge Union debating competitions. Sixth Formers are encouraged to run drama and debating clubs. Many pupils are involved in MUN clubs and represent the school at MUN conferences in the UK and abroad.

Optional Extras. Speech and drama, ballet, tap, modern dance, brass, guitar, percussion, piano, string, voice, woodwind, squash, tennis, fencing, judo, self-defence, yoga, riding, clay pigeon shooting, Duke of Edinburgh's Award Scheme, foreign languages.

Fees per term (2011-2012). £9,980 payable before the start of term, or by the School's Advance Payment of Fees Scheme.

Scholarships. (*See Scholarship Entries section.*)

Admission. Prospective parents are encouraged to visit the School, either individually or with others at a Prospective Parents Morning. Prospectuses and full details of entry and scholarship requirements may be obtained from the Admissions Secretary.

Charitable status. Benenden School (Kent) Limited is a Registered Charity, number 307854. It is a charitable foundation for the education of girls.

Blackheath High School
GDST

Vanbrugh Park, London SE3 7AG
Tel: 020 8853 2929
Fax: 020 8853 3663
e-mail: info@bla.gdst.net
website: www.blackheathhighschool.gdst.net

Junior Department: Wemyss Road, London SE3 0TF
Tel: 020 8852 1537
Fax: 020 8463 0040
e-mail: info@blj.gdst.net

Founded 1880.

Blackheath High School is part of the GDST (Girls' Day School Trust). The GDST is the leading network of independent girls' schools in the UK. As a charity that owns and runs 24 schools and two academies, it reinvests all its income in its schools. For further information about the Trust, see p. xxi or visit www.gdst.net.

Additional information about the school may be found on the school's website and a detailed prospectus is available from the school.

Chairman of Local Governors: Mr C Young, MB BS, FRCOG, MSc

Headteacher: Mrs E A Laws, BA Liverpool, PGCE

Deputy Head: Mrs S Clements, BSc Southampton, PGCE

Assistant Head: Mrs C Maddison, BA Staffordshire, MSc Leicester, PGCE

Head of Junior Department: Miss A Cordingley, Licentiate, Trinity, PGCE

Head of Sixth Form: Mrs K Elliott, BSc Cardiff, PGCE

Admissions Secretary: Mrs F Nichols, BA London

School Business Manager: Mr A W L Sutherland, MBE

Blackheath High School is a good-sized school – small enough for all girls to be valued as individuals but large enough to offer stimulating competition. With support from well-qualified and enthusiastic teachers, our girls work hard and attain excellent results (100% GCSE and A Level). The vast majority of our sixth formers go on to Higher Education, gaining places at top universities.

Rated 'outstanding' in our last ISI and Ofsted inspections (Feb and June 2008), academic success is at the heart of what we offer, but good exam results are only part of the package. The school's happy, caring environment and impressive range of extra-curricular activities including free instrument tuition for all Year 2 and Year 7 pupils, help girls to develop well-rounded personalities and the skills and understanding they will need to be happy and successful in their adult lives.

The school was recently awarded Artsmark Gold by The Arts Council in recognition of its commitment to, and excellence in, arts education and belief in the power of creativity.

Good communication skills are encouraged through activities such as Drama, debating, event management and public speaking, plus an emphasis on modern languages. Pupils study French throughout the school from Nursery and Year 7 students are also offered Spanish, German, Mandarin and Latin. As information communication technology (ICT) is increasingly important, the school's forward-thinking approach to ICT, officially recognised by the prestigious Becta ICT Mark, has led to a range of developments including: laptops for every Sixth Former; a student-run digital radio station; audio podcasting in lessons for everything from debating to poetry. Video conferencing, and two multimedia resource centres help girls develop the necessary ICT skills and qualifications needed for the modern workplace.

The school aims to ensure that every girl achieves the very best that she can through a holistic approach to learning. The learning environment is enhanced to include a daily programme of 'wellbeing' form-time activities such as relaxing visualisation video clips to a philosophical "Thought for the day". In recognition that the teenage years can be a stressful time for young people, activities such as tai chi are on offer, together with a peer mentor group and outstanding pastoral care. The key to success for girls is confidence, and the confidence developed through taking on challenges spills over into all areas of their life, including the academic. All students are encouraged to participate in activities that challenge them physically, emotionally and socially, such as sport, performing arts, debating, outward bound courses and the Duke of Edinburgh's Award Scheme.

The Junior School is housed in the original 19th Century premises in Blackheath Village and includes a purpose-built nursery with its own entrance, playground and forest area. The Senior School is just across the Heath, near to Greenwich Park, and combines historic buildings with modern purpose-built facilities, including a state-of-the-art Theatre and a language laboratory. The school's five-acre sports field includes a sports pavilion, an all-weather pitch and 13 tennis courts.

Many of our students live in the local area whilst others travel from further afield. The area is well served by public transport but we also provide school transport to East London, Docklands & Surrey Quays, destinations in South East London and Chislehurst.

Admission to the school is by examination and interview; scholarships and bursaries are available. Regular Open Days are held in the autumn and spring terms, but visitors are always welcome and the Headteacher likes to discuss each girl's particular needs individually with pupils and parents. Please telephone our Admissions Secretary on 020 8557 8409 for a prospectus and to arrange a visit.

Curriculum. We offer a broad choice of subjects at GCSE and an even wider choice at AS and A Level. We offer all the traditional A Level subjects plus other newer but popular ones, such as Psychology, Business Studies, Mandarin, Photography, Music Technology and Theatre Studies.

Fees per term (2011-2012). Senior School £4,171, Junior Department £3,303, Nursery £2,548.

The fees cover the regular curriculum, school books, stationery and other materials, choral music, games and swimming, but not optional extra subjects or school meals.

Bursaries. The GDST makes available to the school a number of scholarships and bursaries. The bursaries are means tested and are intended to ensure that the school remains accessible to bright girls who would profit from our education but who would be unable to enter the school without financial assistance.

Scholarships. (*See Scholarship Entries section.*) A number of Scholarships are available to internal or external candidates for entry at 11+ or to the Sixth Form.

Charitable status. Blackheath High School is part of The Girls' Day School Trust, which is a Registered Charity, number 306983.

Bolton School Girls' Division

Chorley New Road, Bolton, Lancs BL1 4PB
Tel: 01204 840201
Fax: 01204 434710
e-mail: seniorgirls@boltonschool.org
website: www.boltonschool.org/seniorgirls

Bolton School Girls' Division seeks to realise the potential of each pupil. We provide challenge, encourage initiative, promote teamwork and develop leadership capabilities. It is our aim that students leave the School as self-confident young people equipped with the knowledge, skills and attributes that will allow them to lead happy and fulfilled lives and to make a difference for good in the wider community.

We do this through offering a rich and stimulating educational experience which encompasses academic, extra-curricular and social activities. We provide a supportive and industrious learning environment for pupils selected on academic potential, irrespective of means and background.

Chairman of Governors: M T Griffiths, BA, FCA

***Headmistress*: Miss S E Hincks, MA**

Deputy Heads:
A J Green-Howard, BSc
Mrs L D Kyle, BSc

Head of Sixth Form: Mr S King, MA
Head of Upper School: Mrs P B Keenan, BA
Head of Middle School: Mrs C A Greenhalgh, BEd

Senior School:

Heads of Departments:

Art: Miss J A Fazackerley, BA
Careers and Higher Education: Mrs E Lowe, BA
Classics: Mrs J Hone, BA
Design Technology: P J Linfitt, BSc, MEng
Economics & Business Studies: Miss L Jones, BA
English: Mrs J T M Sowerby, BA
Food Technology: Mrs I M H Smalley, BSc
Geography: Ms S Noot, BA
History: Mrs S A Heap, BA
ICT: Mrs S Brace, MSc
Learning Support Coordinator: Mrs J A Derbyshire, BSc, MSc
Mathematics: G Heppleston, BSc
Modern Languages: Mrs A Shafiq, BA
French: Miss C Slatter, BA
German: Mrs P Sheaff, BA
Spanish: Mrs A Shafiq, BA
Music: A MacKenzie, GRNCM
Physical Education: Mrs K A Heatherington, BA
Religion and Philosophy: Mrs K E Porter, BA
Science: Mrs S M O'Kelly, BSc
Biology: Mrs A D Furey, BSc
Chemistry: Mrs K B Blagden, BSc
Physics: Mr R Ball, BSc
Psychology: Mrs J Sanders, BSc
Textile Technology: Miss R Stafford, BEd

Instrumental Music Staff:
Brass, Cello, Clarinet, Flute, Guitar, Oboe, Organ, Percussion, Piano, Saxophone, Singing, Violin.

Librarian: Mrs L M Frew, BA, ALA
Headmistress's Secretary: Mrs L Graham

Lower Schools:

Junior Department (Age 7–11):
Head: Mrs R Brierley, CertEd
Deputy Head: Mrs H Holt, BEd

Beech House (Age 4–7):
Head: Mrs D Northin, BEd
Deputy Head: Mrs L Procter, BEd

Bolton School Girls' Division was founded in 1877 as the High School for Girls and quickly gained a reputation for excellence. In 1913 the first Viscount Leverhulme gave a generous endowment to the High School for Girls and the Bolton Grammar School for Boys on condition that the two schools should be equal partners known as Bolton School (Girls' and Boys' Divisions).

The School occupies a superb 32-acre site and the Girls' Division contains 1,200 day pupils. The co-educational infants' school, Beech House, offers an education for 225 pupils aged 4–7 and a further 200 girls are educated in the Junior Girls' School (age 7–11). In the Senior School of 800 girls, 220 are in the Sixth Form. The School also has its own nursery.

Facilities. The Girls' Division has a Great Hall to seat 900 people, two fully computerised libraries, staffed by a chartered librarian and her assistant, a drama theatre, seven laboratories, three ICT suites, a language laboratory, a Design Technology Suite and many well-appointed specialist teaching rooms. Our computer network allows pupils access to software, CD-ROMS and the Internet in the Libraries, Careers Room, the Computer Suite, several departmental areas and the Sixth Form Common Room, where there is wireless access. The Sixth Form Suite includes a kitchen and study area with networked computers. The Careers Department is staffed by two experienced assistants and has a resource centre giving access to all the latest information. Besides having its own fully-equipped gym, the Girls' Division shares the modern sports hall, swimming pool and sports pavilion with the Boys' Division. In addition to these excellent facilities for Physical Education, the school has an outdoor pursuits centre at Patterdale in the Lake District which is used regularly by girls from the Junior and Senior schools. Pupils also have the option of spending a week undertaking sailing lessons in the Irish Sea on the School's own boat, Tenacity of Bolton.

Beech House Infants' School. The curriculum, though based on the National Curriculum, extends far beyond it. Specialist teaching is provided for older pupils in Physical Education and Music and all children are taught French. The school has recently moved to purpose-built state-of-the-art premises and in addition to its own resources, Beech House benefits from the use of Senior School facilities such as the swimming pool, playing fields and Arts Centre.

The Girls' Junior School. There are 2 classes in each of Years 3–6. In September 2010, the junior girls moved into their new £5m school which has its own hall, laboratory, art and design facility, IT suite and library, as well as large classrooms. Besides following the National Curriculum with Senior School specialists teaching PE, Music and French, pupils have additional opportunities. The many clubs and wide range of extra-curricular activities ensure a full and well-balanced programme.

The Senior School. The curriculum encompasses all the National Curriculum but also offers the study of two modern languages, the classics and a wide range of modules in Technology. At age 11 all girls follow a similar weekly timetable. The twelve subjects offered are: Art, English, French, Geography, History, Classical Studies, Mathematics, Music, PE, Religion and Philosophy, Science and Technology. All pupils in Year 9 begin to study GCSE Biology, Chemistry and Physics. The above list does not fully show the great variety of opportunities available which also include: Athletics, Biology, Chemistry, Computer Graphics, Dance, Drama, Earth Science, Electronics, Food Technology, Gymnastics, Information Technology, Lacrosse, Netball, Physics, PSHE, Resistant Materials Technology, Rounders, Swimming, Tennis and Textiles Technology. This breadth is maintained to GCSE with a second language, German, Latin or Spanish, being offered in Year 8. In Years 10 and 11 we also offer Badminton, Basketball, Football, Unihoc and Volleyball.

GCSE. There is extensive choice at GCSE. All follow a common curriculum of English, English Literature, Mathematics, Biology, Chemistry and Physics (with an option to consolidate down to Dual Award Science at the end of Year 10) together with non-examined courses in Information Technology, PE, and Religion and Philosophy. Personal aptitude and inclination are fostered by allowing a maximum of 11 GCSEs: the core subjects plus options chosen from Art, Biology, Business and Communication Systems, Chemistry, Food Technology, French, Geography, German, Greek, History, Information Technology, Latin, Music, Physics, Religious Studies, Resistant Materials Technology, Spanish and Textile Technology. Essential balance is maintained by requiring all to include one Humanity and one Modern Language, but the choice is otherwise entirely free.

The Sixth Form. Flexibility is a key feature of the Sixth Form. Students choose from a list of approximately 30 AS courses. Breadth is promoted further by our complementary Curriculum Enrichment Programme. All students have the opportunity to follow a range of non-examined courses as well as Physical Education (sports include golf, football, life-saving, rugby, self-defence, tennis and yoga). Links beyond school include the Community Action Programme and Young Enterprise scheme, as well as opportunities with

Business Awareness and Work Experience.

Teaching in the Sixth Form is in smaller groups. Students have greater freedom which includes wearing their own clothes, exeat periods and having a common room and private study facilities. Joint social events are organised with the Boys' Division and girls and boys have access to each other's common room facilities. There are opportunities for students to assume a variety of responsibilities both within the school and in the wider community. Increasing personal freedom within a highly supportive environment helps students to make the transition to the independence of the adult world. Some students stretch themselves by taking the AQA Baccalaureate qualification.

Almost all students (95%) go on to Higher Education (10% to Oxford and Cambridge).

Music and Drama are popular and students achieve the highest standards in informal and public performances. The wide variety of concerts and productions may take place in the Arts Centre, the Great Hall or the fully-equipped Theatre, all of which make excellent venues for joint and Girls' Division performances. The School regularly performs at Manchester's Bridgewater Hall.

Personal, Social and Health Education, and Citizenship. PSHE and Citizenship are targeted in a variety of ways and coordinated centrally. Some issues may be covered within departmental schemes of work while others will be discussed in the informal atmosphere of form groups led by the form tutor. Those areas which require specialist input are fitted into longer sessions run by experts from outside school.

Careers. The Careers Department helps prepare students for adult life. The extensive programme starts at age 11 and includes communication skills, work sampling, and support in making choices at all stages of schooling. In addition, girls prepare their CVs and applications to Higher Education with the individual help of a trained tutor.

Extra-Curricular Activities. Patterdale Hall, our outdoor pursuits centre in the Lake District, offers many activities including abseiling, gorge walking, orienteering and sailing, both on Lake Ullswater and in the Irish Sea on the School's boat. Awards are regularly made to enable individuals to undertake a variety of challenging activities both at home and abroad while every year over 50 pupils embark on the Duke of Edinburgh's Award Scheme. In addition to the annual exchanges for Modern Languages students, we also offer a wide range of educational and recreational trips both at home and abroad. All have the opportunity to follow a wide range of non-examined courses of their choice, including Physical Education.

Admission. Entrance to the school is by Headteacher's report, written examination and interview in the Spring term for girls aged 7 and 11. New girls are also welcomed into the Sixth Form.

One in six Senior School pupils receives assistance with their fees through the School's own bursaries.

Fees per term (2011-2012). Senior School £3,290; Junior and Infant Schools £2,514. Fees include lunches.

Charitable status. The Bolton School is a Registered Charity, number 1110703. Under the terms of the Charity it is administered as two separate Divisions providing for boys and girls under a separate Headmaster and Headmistress.

Bradford Girls' Grammar School & Lady Royd Preparatory School

Squire Lane, Bradford, Yorkshire BD9 6RB
Tel: 01274 545395
Fax: 01274 482595
e-mail: headsec@bggs.com
website: www.bggs.com

The Charter of Incorporation was granted by Charles II to invite girls to the Grammar School, Bradford in 1662. Established under a Scheme of the Endowed Schools' Commissioners on 5 August 1875, Incorporated 4 November 1879, under the Charitable Trusts Act, 1872. Now administered under a Scheme of the Charity Commission of 13 April 1983.

Motto: *Aspire. Succeed. Lead.*

Governors:
J M Holmes, Esq (*Chairman*)
N J Shaw, Esq, LLB (*Vice-Chairman*)
Miss N. Bashir, MBA, Dip MS
Mrs R J Hicks, MA Oxon, MCIM, LRSM
Ms L-D Morris, MA
Mrs S Sedgwick, FCA

Headmistress: **Mrs K T M Matthews**, BSc Leeds, MA Leeds

Assistant Head (*Strategic ICT*): Mrs I Bostrom, BSc Leeds, MSc Leeds
Assistant Head (*Pupil Welfare*): Mrs J Cockroft, BA Swansea, MEd Leeds
Assistant Head (*Teaching & Learning*): Mrs L Atkinson, BA Kent

Heads of Faculty:
Humanities: Mrs L Atkinson, BA Kent
Languages: Mrs J Cockroft, BA Swansea, MEd Leeds
Creative Arts: Mr D Ham, BA Manchester
Science & Mathematics: Mr W Steel, BSc Leeds, DipEd University West Indies, MEd Open University

Head of Sixth Form: Mrs J Cockroft, BA Swansea, MEd Leeds
Head of Upper School: Mrs L Stead, BSc Manchester
Head of Lower School: Mrs J Hemsley, BA Liverpool

Head of Preparatory School: Mrs J Jenkinson, BA Leicester

School Business Manager: Mrs M Taylor
Headmistress's P.A, Head of Secretariat & Clerk to the Governors: Mrs J Fearnley
Admissions Secretary: Mrs J Fearnley

Founded in 1875 Bradford Girls' Grammar School is an independent day school for girls aged 2–18 with a co-educational Preparatory School for boys and girls aged 2–11 years. The School motto is *Aspire, Succeed, Lead* in school, at university and on into the world of work. Described as a centre of excellence in the development of women leaders, Bradford Girls' Grammar School encourages girls to excel in male-dominated subjects such as Mathematics, Engineering and The Sciences.

Small classes mean that the school is able to focus on the development of the 'whole child'. Every teacher knows each child and children grow in both confidence and academic ability as they progress through the school.

Location and Buildings. Bradford Girls' Grammar School is situated in a very pleasant 17-acre green site, approximately a mile from the centre of Bradford, perfectly situated for pupils travelling from Baildon, Bingley, Crossflatts, Ilkley, Skipton, Leeds, Huddersfield, Dewsbury and Halifax.

Facilities available to both senior and junior schools include a well-equipped sports hall and heated swimming pool, all-weather hockey pitch, netball and tennis courts intertwined with gardens and trees to create a very pleasant and peaceful environment.

Art Rooms support the extensive fine art program, and 11 Science Laboratories support excellence in the sciences. Language Laboratories, Craft, DT Technology Centre, Information Technology Centre, libraries and a specialist sixth form centre are all provided.

There is a continuous programme of renewal and extension to buildings and facilities.

Junior School Curriculum. Art, English, Mathematics, Geography, History, Combined Science and IT. Children also benefit from specialist teaching in music, physical education, Design & Technology, and languages.

Senior School Curriculum. Subjects studied include but are not limited to: Business & Communication studies, Design Technology, The Classics, English Language, English Literature, Mathematics, Modern Foreign Languages, Religious Studies, Science, Art & Design, Geography, History, Home Economics, Physical Education and Drama.

Sixth Form Curriculum. Subjects studied include Art & Design, Biology, Business Studies, Chemistry, Economics, English, French, Geography, General Studies, German, Government & Politics, Greek, History, Home Economics, Latin, Mathematics, Further Mathematics, Physical Education, Physics, Product Design, Psychology, Religious Studies, and Spanish. The Extended Project Qualification (EPQ) will be introduced from September 2011. This presents the unique opportunity for students to develop research and independent learning skills essential for higher education whilst gaining valuable additional UCAS points.

Each curriculum is supported by an extensive programme of extra-curricular activity which can be accessed during lunchtimes and after school. These include art clubs, drama, debating, dance, and volunteer groups, World Challenge, Global Young Leaders, Young Enterprise and Sport.

Pastoral. Our pastoral care is both extensive and effective. Small-group tutoring builds confidence and ensures that students are developing the personal and social skills that they will need in the future.

Dedicated teachers are committed to bringing out the best in each individual. The school works hard at promoting a child's self-esteem alongside their academic ability. Staff make time to talk, share interests and encourage children to fulfil their potential. Good manners, consideration for others and individual success are nurtured and rewarded.

Hours of attendance. Monday to Thursday (inclusive) 8.35 am–12.30 pm, and 1.45 pm–3.50 pm. Friday 8.35 am–12.30 pm, and 1.20 pm–3.30 pm.

Examinations. Public examinations are taken in the Upper Fifth and Sixth Forms at GCSE, Advanced, and Scholarship standards, according to the requirements of individual pupils.

Fees per term (2011-2012). Senior School £3,722; Preparatory School (age 3-11) £2,697; Kindergarten (age 3) and Nursery (age 2) £2,276 (full-time).

The fees include all subjects of tuition and stationery. Music fees are calculated according to instrument.

Bursaries have been given by the Governors in the Senior School each year since September 1976. These are of varying amounts and include one entirely free place per year and an additional free place in the Sixth Form.

Charitable status. Bradford Girls' Grammar School is a Registered Charity, number 528674. It exists to provide high quality education for girls.

Brighton and Hove High School
GDST

The Temple, Montpelier Road, Brighton, East Sussex BN1 3AT
Tel: 01273 734112
Fax: 01273 737120
e-mail: enquiries@bhhs.gdst.net

website: www.bhhs.gdst.net

Junior School:
Radinden Manor Road, Hove, East Sussex BN3 6NH
Tel: 01273 505004

Founded 1876.

Brighton and Hove High School is part of the GDST (Girls' Day School Trust). The GDST is the leading network of independent girls' schools in the UK. As a charity that owns and runs 24 schools and two academies, it reinvests all its income in its schools. For further information about the Trust, see p. xxi or visit www.gdst.net.

Additional information about the school may be found on the school's website and a detailed prospectus is available from the school.

Chair of Local Governors: Mrs J Smith

Head: **Mrs L Duggleby**, BA York, MSc Leeds M, PGCE

Deputy Head: Mrs S Mashford, BSc Manchester

Head of Junior School: **Mrs S Cattaneo**

Head of Sixth Form: Miss W Fox, BA Durham

(*Full staff list available in prospectus.*)

Number of Pupils. 417 Girls in the Senior School (age 11–18), including 73 in the Sixth Form; 245 in the Junior School (age 3–11).

Location. The school stands in its own grounds in the centre of the city of Brighton and Hove. It is about half-a-mile from Brighton Railway Station and pupils come in from Lewes, Haywards Heath and Lancing by train. It is easily reached by bus from all parts of Brighton and Hove.

The Junior School is housed in premises in Radinden Manor Road. The Senior School is in the Temple, a gentleman's residence built by Thomas Kemp in 1819 which has been considerably altered and enlarged to offer all modern amenities, most recent of which is a Sports Hall and Dance Studio. There is a self contained Sixth Form Centre and the school owns a Field Centre on the River Wye in mid-Wales.

Curriculum. The school course is planned to provide a wide general education. Girls are prepared for the General Certificate of Secondary Education and in the Sixth Form a wide choice of subjects is offered in preparation for universities and other forms of professional training. In addition to their Advanced Level subjects girls take Key Skills courses and can choose work experience as an option.

The school has an all-weather hockey pitch at the Junior School site with facilities for hockey, rounders, netball and tennis. Gymnastics and dance are also taught with swimming for junior forms, and senior forms choose from activities including badminton, squash, swimming, aerobics and self-defence.

Fees per term (2011-2012). Senior School £3,426–£3,459, Junior School £2,292–£2,430, Nursery £1,894.

The tuition fees cover the regular curriculum, school books, stationery and other materials, choral music, games and swimming, but not optional subjects or school meals.

The fees for extra subjects (instrumental music and speech and drama) are shown in the prospectus.

Admission at all ages is by interview and test/entrance examination, except at 16+ where GCSE qualifications are essential. The main entry points are 3+, 4+, 11+ and 16+, though occasional vacancies occur at all ages.

Scholarships and Bursaries. The GDST has made available to the school a number of scholarships and bursaries. The bursaries are means tested and are intended to ensure that the school remains accessible to bright girls who would profit from our education but who would be unable to enter the school without financial assistance.

A few Trust Scholarships are available on merit, irrespective of income, to internal or external candidates for entry at 11+ or to the Sixth Form.

Charitable status. Brighton and Hove High School is part of The Girls' Day School Trust, which is a Registered Charity, number 306983.

Brigidine School Windsor

Queensmead, King's Road, Windsor, Berkshire SL4 2AX
Tel: 01753 863779
Fax: 01753 850278
e-mail: registrar@brigidine.org.uk
website: www.brigidine.org.uk

Governors:
Chairman: M Fleming, Esq
Miss R Bailey
Mrs A Bradberry
Mrs V Dhariwal
P Lock, Esq
Dr H Miller
Sister Patricia Mulhall
Cllr E Quick
M Wyld, Esq

Headmistress: **Mrs E Robinson**, MA, BSc Hons, PGCE, FRGS, NPQH

Assistant Head (*Head of Juniors*): Mrs T Milton, CertEd Cambs

Senior Department Teaching Staff:
Mrs A Bersier, BEd Hons, CertEd
Mrs C Cahillane, BA Hons, PGCE
Mrs M Davy, BA Hons, PGCE
Mrs I Deo, BEd Hons, CertEd
Mrs A Finlay, BSc Hons, PGCE
Mrs A Gittins, BEd Hons
Miss R Graham, BA Hons, PGCE
Mrs J Johnson, BSc Hons, PGCE
Mrs G Lilley, BSc Hons, PGCE
Mrs D Mallinson, MA, TCert, BEd
Mrs M Morris, BA Hons
Mrs R O'Hara, BSc Hons, PGCE
Mrs A Pallister, BA Hons, PGCE
Miss C Parker, BSc Hons, PGCE
Mrs F Pelly, BA Hons, PGCE
Mrs J Pratt, BSc Hons, PGCE
Ms G Reilly, BSc, MEd
Miss T Robertson, BA, Grad DipEd
Mr J Samson, BSc, PGCE
Mrs J Shapley, BA Hons, PGCE
Mrs N Simmonds, MA Oxon Joint Hons, PGCE
Mrs G Slater, BSc Hons, PGCE
Miss K Smith, BA Hons, PGCE
Mr P Thompson, BA Hons, BEd
Miss J Walker, BSc Hons, PGCE
Mrs L Williams, BA Hons, PGCE, DipM, MInstM, ACBSI

Junior Department Teaching Staff:
Mrs B Baguley, DipEd Dist
Mrs Z Gallagher, DipEd
Mrs T Lega, CertEd
Mrs C Lever, BA Hons, PGCE
Mrs J Perrett, BA Hons
Miss S Rippington, BA
Mrs S Whittaker, BEd Hons

Classroom Assistants:
Miss C Abbott
Miss J Coutts, BA Hons
Mrs W Dodds

Mrs S Furby
Mrs B Guise, Dipl Soc Pedagogue
Miss P Osinski
Mrs H Rouse

After School Assistant: Miss W Stevens

Administrative Staff:
Mrs D Bates (*Head's PA/Registrar*)
Mrs S Clark, BSc Hons (*Lab Technician*)
Mrs K Daniels (*Finance*)
Mr I Folwell (*Catering Manager*)
Mrs K Grewal (*Reception*)
Mr T Guise (*Site Manager*)
Mr M Chidzey (*ICT Technician*)
Ms P King, BLS, MCLIP (*Librarian*)
Mrs J Manzo (*Administrator*)
Mrs C Rowland (*Examinations Officer*)
Mr M Studd, FCA (*Accountant*)
Mrs N Walsh (*Marketing & Communications*)

Age Range. Girls: 2–18 years; Boys: 2–7 years.
Number of Pupils. 260 day pupils.
School Hours. 2–11 years: 8.30 am – 3.30 pm. 11+–18 years: 8.30 am – 4.10 pm.

Brigidine is a small and flourishing community based upon the values and ethos of the Brigidine Sisters who founded this Roman Catholic school in 1948. Today, it continues its Roman Catholic foundation whilst welcoming children of other faiths and those of none.

It offers a broad and balanced education in a friendly, caring atmosphere and caters for children with a wide range of abilities and talents. It provides support and opportunities for each girl to develop her full potential as a unique individual so enabling her to become a confident, compassionate and accomplished young adult.

The full curriculum is available to all pupils with girls studying, on average, ten GCSE subjects in Years 10 and 11. Our Sixth Form offers a very good range of subjects at Advanced Level.

There is a wide range of extra activities and children are encouraged to participate in these: tuition in ballet, street dance, speech and drama and musical instruments being available. Sporting extras on offer include tennis coaching, rowing, self-defence, aerobics, fitness training, swimming and The Duke of Edinburgh's Award schemes. The school also offers opportunities to experience a variety of overseas trips including World Challenge.

Admission. The usual ages for entry are 2, 3, 9, 11 and 16, but entry can be at any stage. From Year 7 upwards, the pupils are interviewed and assessed prior to entry.

Registration fee (non-returnable): £25.

Fees per term (2011-2012). Senior School: £4,270–£4,585, Sixth Form £4,350. Junior School: £3,125–£3,710. Early Years: Reception £2,495, Nursery: £2,890 (full day), £1,455 (mornings only). Fees include Lunch for full day Nursery and Reception to Year 11.

Charitable status. Brigidine School Windsor is a Registered Charity, number 1104042. It exists to provide quality education for girls.

Bromley High School
GDST

Blackbrook Lane, Bickley, Bromley, Kent BR1 2TW
Tel: 020 8781 7000
Fax: 020 8781 7002
e-mail: bhs@bro.gdst.net
website: www.bromleyhigh.gdst.net

Founded 1883.

Bromley High School is part of the GDST (Girls' Day School Trust). The GDST is the leading network of independent girls' schools in the UK. As a charity that owns and runs 24 schools and two academies, it reinvests all its income in its schools. For further information about the Trust, see p. xxi or visit www.gdst.net.

Additional information about the school may be found on the school's website and a detailed prospectus is available from the school.

Chairman of the Local Governors: Mr A Michael, BA, MBA, JP

Head: Louise Simpson, BSc UCW

Head of Junior School Mrs E Hill, BEd Sussex
From January 2012: Mrs P Jones

Senior Deputy Head: Miss J A Butler, BEd Sussex

Deputy Head Academic: Mrs P Anderson, MBA Leicester, BSc Manchester (*Senior Deputy Head from January 2012*)

Deputy Head Pastoral: Mrs H Elkins (*from January 2012*)

School Business Manager: Mrs A Shepherd

Assistant Head (Head of Sixth Form): P Isted, BA Bristol

Assistant Head (Co-curricular): A Morter-Laing, BSc Swansea

Admissions and Marketing Manager: Mrs D Woodfield, MCIM

Founded in 1883 by the Girls' Day School Trust, Bromley High School was originally situated in the centre of Bromley. In 1981 it moved to Bickley to occupy new buildings set in 24 acres of beautiful grounds.

Pupil Numbers. Senior School (ages 11–18): 600 (including the Sixth Form).

Junior School (ages 4–11): 312.

Sharing the same site, the buildings of both departments provide excellent facilities.

The Junior School. Our two-form entry Junior School is housed in separate purpose-built accommodation on the same site as the Senior School. We provide a stimulating and happy environment in which our pupils are encouraged to strive for excellence in all they do and to derive satisfaction from their achievements both great and small. From the earliest years we offer a broad curriculum which encourages, challenges and excites the young mind. Our aim is to foster a love of learning, develop independent thinking and promote a spirit of enquiry. In our approach to teaching and learning we blend the traditional with progressive insights into learning styles and the particular needs of young girls as learners in a modern world. We teach the full range of the National Curriculum, including French, Spanish, German, and Mandarin, and accord sports and the creative arts a significant place in the timetable whilst ensuring that the foundations of the core subjects are well established. Class lessons are differentiated and we offer extension and support where appropriate and specialist teaching, sometimes from Senior School staff, in a number of subjects. Our girls achieve high standards and we are proud of our excellent results in public examinations. We have an extensive extra-curricular programme. From 2010 the school will be adopting the Creative Curriculum for the youngest pupils.

In the delivery of our curriculum we are well served by outstanding facilities which, in addition to comprehensively equipped classrooms, include a music wing, a library, and ICT suite, a science room, and an art and technology room. We share many other facilities with the Senior School including a swimming pool, gymnasium, sports hall, tennis courts and an all weather pitch. Our pupils have their lunch in the main school dining room where a wide variety of hot dishes or sandwiches are served.

The Senior School. The school provides an environment in which girls of all ages work hard to develop their abilities. Academic studies are of paramount importance and standards are high with a curriculum making equal provisions for arts, sciences, practical and creative subjects The school also provides for a wide range of extra-curricular activities and has a reputation for excellent pastoral care, delivered by teams of tutors overseen by year heads and the pastoral deputy. The school community focuses on the individual and strives to encourage girls to believe that anything is possible. An environment of supportive encouragement and a staff of teachers who are experienced in teaching girls allows our young women to develop skills and interests in all curriculum areas.

The senior school building is a purpose-built, largely refurbished building built in the 1980s. New science facilities, library, sixth form centre drama studio and specialist teaching rooms for the creative arts enable departments to have their own dedicated spaces for teaching and extra-curricular activities. The visual and creative arts are well supported and their work is very present throughout the school. Every year girls go on post A Levels to study dance, drama, music and art at the highest level. In Key Stage 3 girls study a wide and well-balanced curriculum which includes Latin and two modern languages (3 are offered), the humanities, creative arts, ICT GCSE and sport (including cricket and dance) as well as the core subjects. Most teaching rooms are equipped with Smart Boards and all have wifi and digital projector facilities which allow pupils to use their own mobile computer devices. Teachers are encouraged to teach lively, challenging lessons and the annual enrichment activities in the summer are a key part of the curriculum provision to support and extend girls' learning in preparation for GCSE study. Myriad trips and activities, including music tours abroad for Year 7, residential field work for Y8 geographers and Y9 art trips to European cities mean that girls are confident and independent learners by the time GCSE choices are made in Y9. All KS3 girls study ICT GCSE, leading to the public examination qualification in June of Y9.

At KS4 girls study 9 or 10 GCSE subjects. Beyond the core subjects, modern languages, including a thriving German department, are very strong, Theatre Studies GCSE is a popular option subject and the vast majority of girls opt to study history or geography. In 2010 82% of pupils qualified for the English Baccalaureate, despite a free choice option system which builds the timetable around the girls own selections (both at GCSE and A Level). Alongside the other option subjects Latin is available at GCSE as is economics.

Sport. Sports facilities include a large, well-equipped Sports Hall, a gymnasium, a 400-metre athletics track, two grass hockey pitches, netball and tennis courts, a fine indoor heated swimming pool, and an Astroturf pitch, which was opened in 2000. Sport is both integral to the curriculum and an important part of the extra-curricular life of the school. Individuals and teams compete regularly at county and regional level in sports ranging from swimming to skiing, gymnastics and netball.

Sixth Form. The large Sixth Form enjoys a wide A Level and AS Level curriculum, with sciences and modern languages retaining a high profile alongside the arts and humanities. Recent additions to the A Level programme include photography, textiles and classical civilisation. There is a broad provision for minority studies, opportunities for taking responsibility and for work experience and travel to Europe and beyond. An International Dimension Programme offers Year 12 girls the opportunity to visit Mumbai and is of particular appeal to those who study mathematics, economics and/or business studies or who are contemplating a career in management. Additionally girls have the opportunity to visit China as part of this International Programme. In addition to the many sports available in the Senior School, Sixth Formers are able to participate in a range of sports including rowing. Almost all students go on to higher education and each year girls maintain the school's "Oxbridge" tradition. Applications for Sixth Form entry are welcome. Careers education has a high profile throughout all key stages and the school is a member of ISCO. In the Sixth Form the benefits of GDST-wide initiatives, such as leadership conferences and Oxbridge preparation residential visits, are especially relevant and beneficial to both staff and pupils.

Extra-Curricular Activities. A great emphasis is put on an enthusiastic involvement in music, art, sport, drama and community activities. The school has a high local reputation for its annual dance production and holds several sports championships. Major school concerts are organised at venues such as Westminster Abbey and Southwark Cathedral. To celebrate the School's 125th anniversary, an extravaganza 'Flying High', a bespoke expression of Music, Drama and Dance, was held at the Royal Albert Hall.

All extra-curricular activities flourish in this lively community where Young Enterprise, work experience, work shadowing, Neighbourhood Engineer and Challenge to Industry schemes have considerable support. The Bromley High Parents' Association supports the school most generously. Girls enjoy contributing to local, national and international charities and to community service. They are prepared for the Duke of Edinburgh's Award Scheme and there is a keen interest in environmental issues. There are many clubs in which girls of all ages take a share of responsibility, including a recently-formed guide and brownie unit. There are regular exchanges to France, Germany and Spain as well as annual Geography and Biology field trips. World challenge expeditions have visited Laos, Malaysia, Ecuador, Thailand, Guyana, Namibia and Vietnam, Zambia, Guatemala, Belize and Mexico. The Annual Music Tours have travelled to Australia, Venice, Malta, South Africa, Malawi, Slovenia, Catalonia, the United States, China and Estonia. The Year 6 and 7 Music Tours have visited Paris, Brussels, Normandy and Bruges.

Fees per term (2011-2012). Senior School £4,202, Junior School £3,332.

Fees cover tuition, stationery, textbooks and scientific and games materials as well as entry fees for GCSE and GCE Advanced Level examinations. Extra tuition in Music and Speech and Drama is available at recognised rates.

Bursaries. The newly-introduced scheme of Founders' Awards is seeking to actively increase levels of fees assistance to pupils who would otherwise not have access to independent education. These are means-tested awards which provide, for successful applicants, a minimum of 50% of fees and may also include uniform and trips allowances for those on very high awards.

Scholarships. There are Academic scholarships for the most successful candidates in the 11+ examinations and for entry into the Sixth Form. There are also Music and Sports scholarships at 11+ and Music, Arts, Sports and Drama scholarships are awarded in the Sixth Form.

Admission and Entrance Examination. Admission into the school is at 4+ (Reception) and 7+ (Year 3) by assessment and testing. Pupils from the Junior School progress automatically to the Senior School but external applicants, or those wishing to be considered for scholarship or bursary are assessed at 11+. This covers verbal and quantitative assessments as well as creative writing. Entry into the Sixth Form is dependent on at least six GCSE subjects at A/B grade. Common Entrance (Year 9) and entry for GCSE (Year 10) may be available on occasion.

Charitable status. Bromley High School is part of The Girls' Day School Trust, which is a Registered Charity, number 306983.

Bruton School for Girls

Sunny Hill, Bruton, Somerset BA10 0NT
Tel: 01749 814400
Fax: 01749 812537
e-mail: info@brutonschool.co.uk
website: www.brutonschool.co.uk

Founded in 1900.
Day places for Girls and Boys aged 2–7
Day and Boarding places for Girls aged 8–18
Full, weekly and flexi-boarding options

Governors:
Chairman: Mr D H C Batten

Headmaster: **Mr John Burrough**, BA, PGCE

Deputy Heads:
Mrs Rachel Robbins, BA, PGCE
Mrs Linda Smallwood, BSc, PGCE

Head of Preparatory School: Mrs Helen Snow, BEd

Bursar: Mr A H D Harvey-Kelly

Director of Admissions: Mrs Emma Campbell

A preparatory, senior school and sixth form of approximately 320 pupils, of whom roughly 100 board. The teaching week is Monday-Friday with no Saturday lessons.

Ethos. Bruton School for Girls aims to create a structured but challenging environment where students develop a lively intellect and enjoy success. In a community based on mutual respect, students are encouraged to think of others and they gain self-confidence without arrogance. When they leave, girls are well-prepared to make good decisions and to succeed in life.

Academic and Personal Expectations. Academically, the school has high expectations and many girls gain places at prestigious universities. The girls are encouraged to have self-belief, to set challenging goals, display independence of thought and enjoy learning for its own sake.

There are many opportunities for leadership and the development of personal and social skills, particularly in the Sixth Form, where students may take up the role of prefect or hall captain.

Location. Set on a 40-acre campus in beautiful countryside, the school is close to the Somerset, Wiltshire and Dorset borders, and has easy access to the M3/A303 corridor between London and the South West. Bristol, Bath, Salisbury and the south coast are all within approximately one hour's travel. Castle Cary station, served by London Paddington-Exeter express trains, is 4 miles away and Templecombe on the line to London Waterloo is 10 miles; the school offers minibus connections. Students are collected from London Heathrow, Bristol International and other airports. A network of daily buses serves the school from surrounding areas.

Sunny Hill Preparatory School has its own separate accommodation for the nursery, pre-prep and prep departments. A low pupil-teacher ratio and good relationships enable creative and dedicated teachers to make the most of the inquisitive childhood years. Pupils develop strong learning habits. In a broad curriculum, they explore the exciting world of science, information technology, humanities, French, music, design technology and creative arts. Mathematics and English programmes build firm foundations for purposeful learning. (*See also entry in IAPS section.*)

Bruton Senior School is a thriving community of girls aged 11–16 years. Girls joining the Senior School come from a wide variety of local, national and international schools, as well as from Sunny Hill, the school's own Prep School. At GCSE, 18 subjects are offered with an A* to C pass rate well above the national average, most girls taking 9 or 10 subjects. Pupils are set for Mathematics, English, Modern Languages and Sciences to maximise individual achievement. The curriculum offers three separate sciences and three foreign languages. Additional learning support is available from specialist Skills Development teachers where appropriate.

Bruton Sixth Form offers excellent preparation for university, with tutorial support and individual study programmes. The school has a considerable reputation for academic achievement, "Oxbridge" and university entrance. Cultural and social skills are developed to enhance independence and career ambitions. An extensive range of A levels is complemented by cultural activities, extension studies and extra-curricular activities which include public speaking and the Leiths Certificate in Food and Wine. Career and Higher Education advice feature prominently at this stage. Many girls entering the Sixth Form transfer from the Senior School but are joined by students from other schools which may be local, national or international.

Boarding. Three boarding houses provide comfortable and well-appointed accommodation appropriate to the different age ranges of pupils. Facilities include common rooms, games rooms, kitchens and dining areas as well as access to computer facilities and telephones. Younger girls share dormitories while Fourth, Fifth and Sixth Form students have their own study bedrooms or, in Form 4, may share with one other girl. Sixth formers enjoy an increased degree of independence that aims to bridge school and university. The boarding houses are situated on the school campus and girls are cared for by experienced Housemistresses and assistant house staff. A variety of activities is offered each weekend.

The school has its own medical centre with a qualified nursing Sister on duty every weekday during term time and comprehensive medical care available at Bruton Surgery.

A high standard of catering is provided, with a wide variety of choice. Specific dietary needs are catered for.

Extra-Curricular Activities. Art, Drama, Music and Sport feature strongly. The outstanding success of the Art department is reflected in work displayed around the school. The Hobhouse Studio Theatre provides a professional-standard performance space for productions and 'speech and drama' presentations. There is a wide range of opportunities for both instrumental and choral performance, with four choirs performing music across a range of styles and numerous instrumental groups, including two school orchestras and a wind band. The sports department offers a wide range of activities in which every girl can participate either competitively or for her own enjoyment. There is a full fixture list of competitive matches in the traditional sports of hockey, netball, rounders, swimming, athletics and tennis. Tennis coaching, horse-riding, judo, trampolining, modern and classical dance, yoga and individual exercise regimes are available. There is also the popular Duke of Edinburgh's Award programme. Having been awarded the Eco Schools "Green Flag", many girls participate in the Eco Club and assist with the schools recycling programme. In the Preparatory School, all pupils from Reception to Prep 6 participate in Forest School.

Entry. There is open entry into the pre-prep and preparatory school from which pupils normally progress seamlessly into the senior school. The senior school entry process includes the school's own diagnostic assessments or Common Entrance. Entry into the Sixth Form is by interview and GCSE or equivalent qualifications.

Fees per term (2011-2012). Day: Day: £4,325 (Senior School and Sixth Form), £3,100–£3,200 (Preparatory School), £1,550–£2,065 (Pre-Preparatory School), £18.75 per session (Nursery).

Boarding: £5,635–£7,820 (full), £5,110–£6,810 (weekly boarding), £47 per day (casual boarding).

Scholarships. (*See Scholarship Entries section.*) Bruton School for Girls has a range of scholarships and awards, which are offered on the basis of aptitude and achievement in particular areas, including academic studies, music, art, sport and drama. Means-tested exhibitions and bursaries are available.

Charitable status. Bruton School for Girls is a Registered Charity, number 1085577, and a Company Limited by Guarantee. It exists to provide education.

Burgess Hill School for Girls

Keymer Road, Burgess Hill, West Sussex RH15 0EG
Tel: 01444 241050
Fax: 01444 870314
e-mail: registrar@burgesshill-school.com
website: www.burgesshill-school.com

This independent day and boarding School was founded in 1906.

Chairman of Governors: Mr C Bedwin, FCA

Headmistress: Mrs A Aughwane, BSc Hons, PGCE, NPQH

Deputy Headmistress: Mrs E Laybourn, BEd Hons

Senior Teacher: Mr R Tapping, BSc Hons, PGCE, NPQH, CGeog, FRGS

Head of Sixth Form: Ms H Beaman, BA Hons, PGCE, MA

Head of Junior School: Miss F Fulleylove, BEd

Deputy Head of Junior School: Mrs T Pearson-Rujas, BSc Hons, PGCE, QTS, Cert Mgmt

Head of Upper School: Mr T Clarke, BA Hons, PGCE

Head of Lower School: Miss M Bramley, BSc Hons, PGCE

Heads of Faculty:
English: Ms S Triviĕre, BA Hons, MA, PGCE
French: Mrs I Martin, Licence Maîtrise, DDT
German: Mrs J Edey, MA Hons, PGCE
Spanish: Mrs S West, BA Hons, PGCSE
Classics & Latin: Mrs B Johns, BA Hons, PGCE
Mathematics: Mrs L Woroniecki, MA, BSc, Adv DipEd
Biology: Miss V Hulme, BSc Hons, PGCE
Chemistry: Mrs S Lympany, BSc Hons, MSc, PGCE
Physics: Mrs S Marsh, BSc Hons, MSc, PGCE
Business Studies & Economics: Mrs J King, BEd
Information Technology: Mrs N Williams, BSc Hons, MBA, PGCE
Geography: Mr T Lucas, MA, PGCE
History: Mr T Clarke, BA Hons, PGCE
Psychology: Mrs C Humprey, BSc Hons, PGCE, GMBPS
Art: Mrs M Carruthers, Dip AD, ATC, PGCPD
Music: Nr R Haslam, BEd Hons, ARCM
Drama: Miss E Tarratt, BA Hons, PGCE
Physical Education: Mrs C Tagg, BA Hons, PGCE
Technology: Mrs S Bradley, BEd City & Guilds Embroidery & Fashion, C & G
Religious Studies: Mr T Lucas, MA, PGCE

Bursar: (to be appointed)
Registrar/Marketing Executive: Miss Y Lowe, DipM ACIM
Senior Housemistress: Mrs L Bussell, Cert PPB
Housemistress: Miss M Buckley
School Nurse: Sheila Ramanan, RGN
Careers Advisor: Mrs J Edey, MA Hons, PGCE

General. The ethos of the School is to provide a happy, challenging and supportive atmosphere which encourages young people to use their initiative, be inquisitive and creative and develop responsibility and independence. Boys are welcome in the Nursery. Ours is a school in which girls flourish; from age 4 the focus is firmly on girls and the way they learn. They develop self-esteem and confidence and go on to make a positive contribution in their chosen professions. We have small classes with fully qualified, professional staff dedicated to catering for the needs of the individual child. The School has established a reputation for excellence in Music, Sport, Art, Textiles and Drama and achieves impressive academic results. We are consistently highly ranked nationally and regularly lead the field in Sussex. We believe that education for life involves much more than academic success alone. Girls can, and do, strive for excellence wherever their talents lie.

School Facilities. In September 2006 the School completed the extension to the Sixth Form Centre providing a spacious new Upper Sixth Common Room, new teaching rooms and an exciting, large and flexible space for lectures, events and activities. Also opened in September 2006, enhanced outdoor PE facilities provide new tennis courts and an Astroturf training area. The Senior School also benefits from an excellent Learning Resource Centre, a Design and Technology laboratory and specialist Textiles room. The Sports Pavilion houses a well resourced Drama studio. In the Junior School, an enlarged computer suite and upgraded music room add to the excellent facilities available to support the curriculum. In November 2008, the new Nursery and Infant block was opened and a new art studio for the Senior School opened in the Spring Term 2009. In March 2010, two new Chemistry Laboratories were opened in the Senior School. There are 3 boarding houses, two adjoining the school grounds. The rooms and common rooms are spacious, light and pleasantly furnished and the atmosphere is informal and friendly.

Curriculum. The curriculum is broad and challenging and relevant to the needs of young people. There is a wide choice of subjects both at GCSE and A Level with many extra-curricular activities.

ISI Inspection. The 2009 inspection reports clearly confirm that the School has a great many strengths in nearly all aspects of its provision. The Early Years provision was judged to be outstanding. Moving through into the Junior School the inspectors commented that, "The highly effective teaching and excellence of the whole educational experience inspire a love of learning and exceptional motivation to achieve the highest possible standards in academic work, sport, drama and music".

The Junior School was also delighted to note that the inspectors picked up on the happy atmosphere of the School commenting that, "The quality of relations between staff and pupils is excellent. Respect and courtesy are evident and so is humour; relations are clearly warm and relaxed and there is an air of happiness and purpose".

The Senior School report concludes that, "The educational experience enables pupils of all abilities and interests to find success and personal achievement. The quality of pastoral care is outstanding. The support for and nurturing of individuals are key elements in shaping the outstanding personal development of pupils".

The full report can be viewed on www.isi.net.

Entrance Procedures. Entrance to either the Junior or Senior school is by examination and school reference. Senior girls are also interviewed by the Headmistress. Scholarships are awarded each year for academic and/or musical excellence into Years 3, 4, 7, 8, 9 and the Lower Sixth. Creative scholarships are available for students entering Year 9 and the Lower Sixth.

Fees per term (2011-2012). Senior School: £4,520 (day girls); £7,970 (boarding). Junior School: £2,155–£3,780 (day girls).

Old Girls' Association. The Old Girls' Association is an association run by Girls. It helps to keep them in touch with each other and what is happening at the School. Chairman: Mrs S Arnold. Secretary: Mrs K Ruff (katharineruff@yahoo.com).

Charitable status. Burgess Hill School for Girls is a Registered Charity, number 307001. It exists to promote the education of any age.

Bury Grammar School Girls

Bridge Road, Bury, Lancs BL9 0HH
Tel: 0161 797 2808
Fax: 0161 763 4658
e-mail: info@bgsg.bury.sch.uk
website: www.bgsg.bury.sch.uk

Motto: *Sanctas Clavis Fores Aperit*

Chairman of Governors: Revd Dr J C Findon

Bursar and Clerk to the Governors: Mr D A Harrison, BSc Econ, FCA

Headmistress: **Mrs R Georghiou**, BA Manchester, MEd Liverpool

Deputy Headmistresses:
Mrs L D Billinge, BSc Leicester
Mrs J A Buttery, BA Lancaster

Senior Teacher: Mrs S Fielden

Heads of Departments:
Mr D Ashworth, BA Manchester Metropolitan (*ICT*)
Mrs C Bevis, BA Bolton (*History*)
Miss R Britton, BMus Manchester (*Music*)
Miss J D Cebertowicz, BA Bath (*Art and Design*)
Mrs J E Coulthard, BA Cambridge (*Classics*)
Mrs S Fielden, BSc London (*Science and Biology*)
Mrs H Hammond, BA Liverpool (*Theatre Studies*)
Mrs Y G Hanham, BSc Salford (*Mathematics*)
Mrs L C A Kerr, BA Manchester (*RS*)
Mrs V Leaver, BSc Hull (*Geography*)
Mr D Lehan, BEng Liverpool, BA Oxon (*Physics*)
(*to be appointed*) (*English*)
Mrs V Livsey, BA Liverpool (*Modern Languages*)
Ms C McDermott, BA Sheffield (*Psychology*)
Mrs J Slade, BSc Loughborough (*PE*)
Mrs S Taylor, BSc Manchester (*Careers*)
Mrs S Thorpe, BA Salford (*Politics*)
Mrs M Whitlow, BA York (*Economics and Business Studies*)
Mr J Wilkinson, CertEd Loughborough (*Design and Technology*)
Dr J Yates, BSc Durham, PhD Bristol (*Chemistry*)

Head of Sixth Form: Mrs H Ward, BA Leicester
Head of Upper School: Mrs I Petela, BA Nottingham
Head of Middle School: Mrs J Haworth, BA Keele
Head of Year 7: Mrs S C Banfield, BA Bangor

Kindergarten and Junior School:
Mrs H Hutton, BA Open University (*Kindergarten*)
Mrs V Hall, BSc Cardiff (*Junior School*)

The Girls' School was founded in 1884 as the Bury High School for Girls and amalgamated, a few years later, with the Bury Grammar School (Boys). The school maintains high academic standards and traditional grammar school values whilst encouraging each girl to develop her individual talents and abilities as far as she can in a lively environment which responds to the challenge of change.

The numbers at present are 37 in the Pre-School, 190 in the Kindergarten Department, 138 in the Junior School and 612 in the Senior School.

The **Senior School** is housed in a distinctive Edwardian building which dates from 1906. The school is conveniently situated near the centre of the town and the bus-tram interchange. Facilities are regularly improved and updated; the school is currently at the beginning of a major building project which will lead to new and refurbished accommodation for Modern Foreign Languages, Art, Design and Technology, Textiles and Food Technology. ICT facilities will be re-housed in a new specialist teaching area and the final stage of the project will be the creation of a dedicated sixth form pre-university centre which will be used jointly by girls and boys. This will contain a multi-purpose Lecture Theatre and Drama Studio, seminar rooms with full access to interactive learning, private study areas which will allow students to complement their lessons with independent learning and access to the library and internet and a Cafetorium with a central sixth form entrance and landscaped gardens.

The curriculum is broad and balanced in the first five years of the Senior School. At Key Stage Three all girls follow a core curriculum of Mathematics, English, the three Sciences, PE, RS, History and Geography which is enhanced by courses in Art, ICT, Design Technology, Food and Nutrition, Latin, Classical Civilisation, Business Studies and two Modern Languages from a choice of French, German and Spanish. Traditional teaching methods are combined with pupil-centred learning work, group work, investigative work and a problem-solving approach. In a variety of cross curricular projects, pupils seek solutions to problems and take an ever-increasing responsibility for their own learning.

PE and Music are well established; in recent years the School has been represented in National Netball, Tennis and Swimming Championships and on County Netball, Hockey, Cross-Country, Swimming, Tennis, Athletics and Badminton teams. Each year the Festival Choir gives concerts internationally and in the UK. There are also two orchestras, string quartets, a flute choir and a jazz band.

The School works closely with Bury Grammar School (Boys) for dramatic and musical productions, and other extra-curricular activities. The Sixth Form common rooms are open to both boys and girls.

Public examinations are taken in Years 10, 11, 12 and 13, according to the requirements of individual pupils. There is a wide choice of subjects in the Sixth Form and each year all or virtually all students proceed to degree courses at prestigious universities, including Oxford and Cambridge. The School achieves high pass rates in public examinations.

These successes and initiatives, along with PSE, careers advice and extra-curricular activities, clubs, visits, holidays in England and abroad, charity work and school productions, offer wide educational opportunities and encourage links to be forged with industry and commerce and with the community in Bury and beyond.

The **Junior School** has its own purpose-built premises on the Senior School site, has shared use of the Roger Kay Hall, Gymnasium, Sports Hall, and Swimming Pool. The eight large and attractive classrooms, Music Room and large Library/Computer suite provide a comfortable and very pleasant environment in which the girls aged 7–11 learn and work.

The Junior School curriculum is based on the National Curriculum but with enhancements. The curriculum includes the three core subjects and Design/Technology, ICT, History, Geography, Religious Education, Art and Craft, Music and Physical Education. Particular emphasis is placed on the teaching of skills in reading, writing and mathematics. The aim is to provide a broad and balanced education and to give each girl the opportunity to develop her full potential. The combination of a dedicated staff and excellent facilities allows girls to maintain the high academic standard enriched by many extra-curricular activities with particular strengths in music and sport.

The School has a purpose-built **Pre-School and Kindergarten** for boys and girls aged 3–7 situated on the school campus. In lively and stimulating surroundings the children progress rapidly in all six areas of learning. They make use of the Senior School pool and have specialist PE instruction, their own dedicated gymnasium and tuition in music in a specially designed music room. The focal point of the new building is the central octagonal hall used for assemblies and performances. Pupils also have access to a unique and exciting rooftop play area and a Learning Resource Area with supervised computer access. There is a Breakfast Club before school and an After-School Club.

Bursaries. At 11+ the Governors offer a number of means-tested bursaries.

Fees per term (2011-2012). Pre-School, Kindergarten and Junior School £2,164; Senior School £2,912.

Charitable status. Bury Grammar Schools Charity is a Registered Charity, number 526622.

Casterton School

Kirkby Lonsdale, via Carnforth, Lancashire LA6 2SG
Tel: 015242 79200
Fax: 015242 79208
e-mail: admissions@castertonschool.co.uk
website: www.castertonschool.co.uk

The School was founded at Cowan Bridge in 1823 by the Reverend W Carus Wilson for the education of daughters of the clergy and was moved to Casterton in 1833. Famous alumnae include the Brontë sisters.

Casterton is now a boarding and day school for girls aged 11–18. A separate Preparatory School caters for day boys and girls aged 3–11 and for boarders (girls only) between the ages of 8 and 11.

Governing Body:
Mr C Tomlinson (*Chairman*)
Mr M Baucher
Mr R Bulman
Mr M Darch
Mrs A L Denney
Mr S Fairclough
Mr P Hoyle
Miss J Panton
Mr P Ridsdale
Mrs G Robson-Bayley
Dr C Story

Visiting Governor: The Right Revd The Lord Bishop of Carlisle

Staff:

Head: Mrs M Lucas, BA Hons Lancaster, MA Bristol, PGCE Bristol

Deputy Head Academic: Mr P Fairclough, BA Hons York, PGCE York
Deputy Head Patoral: Miss J Helm, BSc Hons Durham, PGCE York
Bursar: Mrs J Thistlethwaite, BA Hons UCLan, MAAT
Medical Officer: Dr P J I Hall, MBChB, MRCGP

Senior School

* *Head of Department*

Art:
*Mrs V Eden, CertEd, Dip Ceramics
Mr D Norman, BA Hons Manchester Polytechnic
Miss R Twist, BA Hons UCLan, PGCE St Martin's Lancaster
Mr B Yeoman, BA Open, MA Hons Aberdeen, PGCE Middlesex (*History of Art*)

Business Studies & Economics:
*Mrs C Compton, BA Hons Leeds Met, PGCE Manchester

Drama:
*Mrs N Marriott, BA Hons Birmingham, PGCE Leeds
Mrs L Blackwell, BEd Coll of Ripon & York St John

English:
*Mr D Rose, BA Hons Kent, MA Kent, PGCE Cambridge
Mrs C Allen, BA Bretton Hall College, PGCE UCLan (*English/EFL*)
Mrs F Norman, BA Hons Manchester
Ms M Scott, BEd Nottingham, TCert

Geography:
*Mr D Elphick, BSc Hons East Anglia, PGCE St Martin's Lancaster
Miss H L Rowland, BA Hons Nottingham, PGCE Nottingham

History:
*Miss K Haigh, BA Hons UCW, PGCE Hull
Mrs L Wareing, BA Hons Durham, PGCE Durham

Home Economics:
*Mrs V Parkinson, BEd Manchester

Information & Communication Technology:
*Mr A Mellor, BSc Hons Northumbria, PGCE Bradford College
Mrs T Gunning, BA Hons Southampton, PGCE Southampton

Languages:
*Mrs M Emptage, BA Hons Leeds, MA Lancaster, PGCE St Martin's Lancaster
Mrs E Goodman, BA Hons Bradford, MA Salford, PGCE Manchester
Miss L Legeard, English Studies Degree, University of Rennes
Mrs C A Ortega Del Blanco, MA University of Valencia, MSc Lancaster
Mr J Renton, BA Hons Bangor, PGCE Newcastle
Mr G Service, BA Manchester, PGCE Newcastle

Learning Success:
*Mrs D Airey, BEd Cambridge

Mathematics:
*Mr D Kelly, BSc Hons Bolton, PGCE Manchester
Mrs A Cox, BEd Liverpool, CertEd Chester
Miss T Ferrandiz, BSc University of Valencia
Mrs J Fielden, BSc Hons Nottingham, PGCE Bristol
Mrs J Larton, BSc Hons Manchester, PGCE Manchester

Music:
*Mr D C Chapman, MA Oxon, LRAM Accompaniment, LRAM TDip (*Director of Music*)
Mr R Fudge, BMus Hons Birmingham, ARCM
Mrs K Guidici, GMus RNCM Hons, PPRNCM

Physical Education:
*Miss A Thomas, BEd Hons Leeds (*Director of Sport*)
Mrs G Barton, BEd Hons Sussex
Miss F Davison, BA Hons Birmingham, PGCE Leeds
Miss C Farris, BA Hons Liverpool John Moores
Mr J Griffin, Tennis Coach, CCA Performance
Mrs P Sneddon, BEd Neville's Cross, RYASI

Religious Studies:
*Mr K Walton, MA Sheffield, PGCE Cumbria

Riding:
*Miss S Nelson, BSHII Regd
Mrs A Gardner, Senior Riding Instructor, BHSAI Regd
Miss C Bellamy, Riding Assistant
Mr C Hall, Riding Assistant (*School holiday only*)
Mrs E O'Hagan, Riding Assistant
Miss F Porter-Shaw, Riding Assistant
Miss Taylor, Riding Assistant, BSHAI

Science:
*Mr R J Sanders, BSc Liverpool, PGCE Chester
Mr M Appleton, BEng Hons Exeter, PDip Eng Liverpool,
  PGCE Edge Hill
Mr A Bell, BSc Hons St Andrews
Dr A McMeechan, MSc Glasgow, PhD Bristol, PGCE
  Bristol
Dr A Worgan, BSc Hons Bangor, MSc Bangor, PhD
  Liverpool John Moores, PGCE Cumbria
Mrs N Edmondson, BA Open (*Lab Technician*)
Dr N Hetherington, MSc Bristol, PhD Bristol (*Lab
  Technician*)

Sociology and Psychology:
*Mrs J Clarke, BSocSci Birmingham, PGCE Avery Hill

Careers:
*Mrs L Wareing, BA Hons Durham, PGCE Durham
Miss H L Rowland, BA Hons Nottingham, PGCE
  Nottingham

Outdoor Pursuits:
Mrs A Cox, BEd Liverpool, CertEd Chester
Mr D Elphick, BSc Hons East Anglia, PGCE St Martin's
  Lancaster
Mr R J Sanders, BSc Liverpool, PGCE Chester

House Staff:
Miss J Anderson
Miss C Clancy
Miss J Howe
Mrs S Lehmann
Miss K Poole
Mrs P Sneddon
Miss S Tamplin
Miss K Tily

Administration:
Bursar's PA: Miss S Booth
Finance Assistant: Mrs J Knowles
Finance & Facilities Coordinator: Miss E Clark, BA
  UCLan
Head's PA: Mrs J Hartley, BA Hons Manchester
Admissions Registrar: Ms A Clowes
Travel Secretary: Mrs C Coggins

Preparatory School:
Head: Mrs S Tatham, BEd Chester, MA
Deputy Head: Mrs H Dootson, BSc London, PGCE St
  Martin's Lancaster, MRICS
Mrs L Hoskin, BSc Hons Durham, PGCE Homerton Coll
  Cambridge
Mrs A Mason, BEd Lancaster
Ms V May, CertEd Madeley College of Education

PE:
Miss F Davison, BA Hons, PGCE Birmingham
Mr M Harris, Nat Dip Sports Science, BTEC
Mrs P Sneddon, BEd Hons, RYASI

Nursery:
Head: Mrs D Baines, BA Hons UCLan
Miss J Brown, Cache Level 2
Mrs J M Slater, BA Hons QTS Lancaster

Drama:
Miss J Howe, BA British Columbia

Number of Pupils. There are 238 pupils in the Senior
School and 57 girls and boys in the Preparatory Department.

Situation. The School is situated where three counties
meet: North Yorkshire, Cumbria and Lancashire. Casterton
is one mile from the town of Kirkby Lonsdale and only 7
miles from the M6. Harrogate and Ilkley are only an hour
away, on good road links. International links are via
Manchester, Liverpool and Leeds Bradford airports.

Facilities and Development. Casterton is a boarding
school and a strong House system prevails. All current

boarding Houses are light and airy. Day girls are fully integrated in to the House system. Casterton has an outstanding
purpose-built Art and Design Centre as well as a very spacious purpose-built Science and Maths Centre, large Gymnasium Hall, Library, Classrooms, Home Economics
Centre, Music Wing, ICT Centre, Language Laboratory,
Theatre and Sixth Form study area. A new Sports Pavilion
with full changing facilities and a full-size, floodlit, all-
weather pitch for hockey and tennis are also supplemented
by lacrosse pitches, athletics track and indoor pool.

Education. The curriculum includes; RE, English Lan-
guage, English Literature, History, Geography, French, Ger-
man, Spanish, Latin, Mathematics, Physics, Chemistry,
Biology, Computer Studies, Economics, Business Studies,
Politics, Psychology, Sociology, Music, Art, History of Art,
Physical Education, Home Economics and Drama.

Examinations. Pupils are prepared for GCSE, AS Level
and A Level examinations, the Universities (Entrance and
Scholarships) and the examinations of the Associated Board
of the Royal Schools of Music, LAMDA, Royal Academy of
Dance, Duke of Edinburgh's Award and equestrian examinations.

PE and Games. These form part of the normal curriculum and include Hockey, Lacrosse, Tennis, Rounders, Athletics, Cross-Country and Swimming. Riding is available at
the school's own stables. Sailing and training for the Duke of
Edinburgh's Award scheme are also offered.

Age of Admission. Entrance can be considered at any age
– there is an Entrance Examination for applicants from the
age of 8 upwards.

Fees per term (2011-2012). Boarding: £8,520 (Year 9
and above), £7,778 (Year 8), £6,664 (Years 6–7 full and
weekly), £6,216 (Years 3–5 full and weekly).

Day: £5,082 (Year 8 and above), £4,243 (Years 5–7),
£3,330 (Years 3–4), £2,527 (Years 1–2), £2,275 (Reception).

Extras, which are optional, include instruction in a wide
range of musical instruments, singing, speech and drama,
riding, tennis coaching, ballet and jazz dance classes. Termly rates for these are available on request from Emma
Clark, e-mail: emma@castertonschool.co.uk.

Scholarships and Bursaries. (*See Scholarship Entries
section.*) There are Bursaries available for the daughters of
Clergy and Armed Forces. There are also means-tested bursaries available; for details please contact the Bursar, e-mail:
finance@castertonschool.co.uk.

Casterton School Old Girls Association. *Secretary*:
Sarah-Jane Dunhill, e-mail: cogasecretary@hotmail.co.uk
or via the school.

Charitable status. Casterton School is a Registered
Charity, number 1076380.

Central Newcastle High School
GDST

Eskdale Terrace, Newcastle-upon-Tyne NE2 4DS
Tel: 0191 281 1768
Fax: 0191 281 6192
e-mail: cnhs@cnh.gdst.net
website: www.newcastlehigh.gdst.net

Junior School:
West Avenue, Gosforth, Newcastle-upon-Tyne NE3 4ES
**Chapman House, Sandyford, Newcastle-upon-Tyne NE2
1NN**
Tel: 0191 285 1956
Fax: 0191 213 2598

Founded 1895.

Central Newcastle High School is part of the GDST
(Girls' Day School Trust). The GDST is the leading network
of independent girls' schools in the UK. As a charity that

owns and runs 24 schools and two academies, it reinvests all its income in its schools. For further information about the Trust, see p. xxi or visit www.gdst.net.

Additional information about the school may be found on the school's website and a detailed prospectus is available from the school.

Chair of Local Governors: Mrs M Martin, BA Hons

Headmistress: Mrs H J French, MA Oxon, MEd, PGCE Durham, NPQH

Deputy Head: Mr M Tippett, MA Oxon, PGCE Cantab, NPQH

Head of Junior School: Miss A Charlton, BA Hons, PGCE Newcastle, NPQH

Head of Sixth Form: Mrs C Robertson, MA PhD Newcastle, PGCE Westminster College

Pupil Numbers. 900: Senior School 600 (aged 11–18 years) of whom 180 are in the Sixth Form; Junior School 300 (aged 3–10 years).

As one of the leading schools in the country, Central Newcastle High School takes its cue from the city; it is a lively, exciting and challenging place where each girl can be herself and give her best. It offers an excellent education built on strong traditions but also values innovation and forward thinking. Following the School's recent inspection in May 2011 by the Independent Schools Inspectorate, Central High was judged to be *outstanding, excellent* and *exceptional* in all areas.

The School's ethos encourages curiosity, independence and enthusiasm as well as a lifelong love of learning. It offers girls aged 3–18 the opportunity to develop and mature in an environment that focuses on their needs as individuals. Central Newcastle High School is a centre of academic excellence. Creativity flourishes across the whole curriculum and the pupils at the school are motivated and full of energy. There is outstanding provision for Sport, Music, Art, Dance and Drama and the girls have the opportunity to develop many new interests and skills through the varied extra-curricular programme on offer from Debating to Go Green, Medical Society to creative writing. The School also has one of the largest Duke of Edinburgh's Award Schemes in the region.

The School strongly believes that one of the main reasons why girls succeed is its impressive pastoral care system underpinned by strong pupil teacher relationships and a supportive and caring school community.

The facilities across the whole School are excellent and all girls are able to take full advantage of them. The Junior School includes Nursery and Infants based at West Avenue, Gosforth. During Key Stage Two girls move to Chapman House, Sandyford. Both locations offer spacious surroundings in which to grow and develop. The Senior School is based at Eskdale Terrace, Jesmond. Extensive redevelopment of the site in recent years has created a school with an uplifting atmosphere and excellent facilities. Attractive classrooms, up to the minute laboratories, modern Library, generous ICT provision and specialist centres for Art, Music, Modern Languages, Sport and the Sixth Form all provide the perfect learning environment.

Central High consistently achieves outstanding GCSE and A Level Results and in 2010 was one of the top 100 schools in the country.

Curriculum. While the Junior School follows the national curriculum, it is also able to offer a rich and varied programme which far exceeds these recommendations. Music Art, Drama and Dance are all part of the enhanced curriculum and girls have ample opportunity to explore and express their creativity. Exercise and sport is an integral part of Junior School life and French is taught from a very early age.

The Senior School's curriculum combines the best of traditional, modern, scientific, creative and practical subjects to produce a broad and inspiring education. In Year 9 discussion of career opportunities begins and girls make their GCSE subject choices. Most girls take ten subjects. In the Sixth Form 30 subjects are offered at AS Level. Most can be continued to A Level. There is a high take-up of all three Sciences and Mathematics.

Admissions. Junior School: by assessment and interview. Senior School: by entrance examination, interview and school report.

Sixth Form: by GCSE results, interview and school report.

Fees per term (2011-2012). Senior School £3,370, Junior School £2,443, Nursery £2,016.

The fees cover the regular curriculum, school books, games and swimming but not optional extra subjects or school meals.

Bursaries. The GDST Bursaries Fund provides financial assistance in the Senior School to suitably qualified girls whose parents could not otherwise afford the fees to enter or remain in the School.

Charitable status. Central Newcastle High School is part of The Girls' Day School Trust, which is a Registered Charity, number 306983.

Channing School

Highgate, London N6 5HF
Tel: 020 8340 2328 (School Office)
        020 8340 2719 (Bursar)
Fax: 020 8341 5698
e-mail: info@channing.co.uk
website: www.channing.co.uk

Governors:
Mr M Steiner, MA Oxon (*Chairman*)
Mrs M R Banks, MBE, MEd
Mr S Barber, BSc, FCA (*Vice-Chair*)
Ms C E A Budgett-Meakin, BA Kent
Mr J M Burns, MA Oxon
Baroness C Coussins, MA Cantab
Miss J A M Davidson, BSc London
Mr R Katz
Mrs V A Schilling, MCSP
Mrs C Stephenson, CertEd
Dr A G White, MBChB, FRCP, DPhysMed
Dr D J Williams, MB, BCh

Bursar & Clerk to the Governors: Mr R Hill

Headmistress: Mrs B M Elliott, MA Cantab (*Modern & Medieval Languages*)

Deputy Head: (*to be appointed*)

Assistant Heads (Senior School):
Mr A Atkinson, MA Dundee (*Teaching and Learning*)
Mrs W Devine, BA Reading (*Outreach*)

* *Head of Department*
§ *part-time*

Miss S Ablewhite, BA Bath (*French, Assistant Head of Middle School*)
Mr A Atkinson, MA Dundee (**Geography, Assistant Head Teaching and Learning*)
Mrs V Atkinson, MA Cantab (**Classics, Head of Upper School*)
Ms G Best, MA Cambridge (**History*)
Mrs G Bhamra-Burgess, BA, MSc London (*Economics*)
Ms J Bramhall, BA Oxon (*Geography*)
Mrs J Brown, BA Oxon (**English*)
Mr P Boxall, GRSM, ARCO (*Director of Music*)

§Dr M Bremser, DPhil Oxon (*English, *Critical Thinking*)
Ms A Gill-Carey, BA Kent (**Drama & Theatre Studies*)
Mr D Coram, BA Durham, MA London (*Classics*)
Ms A Cornacchia, BA Hamilton, Canada, BEd London
  (*Mathematics, PE*)
Ms A Derbyshire, BA Central School of Art & Design (*Art*)
Mrs W Devine, BA Reading (*History, *Politics, Assistant
  Head Outreach*)
§Dr N Devlin, DPhil Oxon (*Classics*)
§Ms L Feilden, BA Brighton (*Art*)
Mr S Frank, BSc Birmingham (**Biology*)
Miss S-L Fung, BSc Coventry (*Physics*)
Ms E Gale, BA, Leeds Met (**PE*)
Mr P Gittins, BA Wolverhampton (*Art, *PSHE*)
Mrs J Glasser, BA UEA (**Additional Learning*)
Mrs R Harper, BA Kent, ALAM (*English, Head of Middle
  School*)
Mr M Holmes, BSc City of London Polytechnic (**ICT*)
Ms S Ikram, BSc Alberta (*Chemistry*)
Mr R Jacobs, BA Oxon (**Science*)
Miss E Johnson, BSc Birmingham (*PE*)
Mrs H Kanmwaa, BA Oxon (*English*)
§Mrs T MacCarthy, BSc Edinburgh (*Mathematics*)
Mrs S Mahmood, MSc, BEd Alberta (*Chemistry*)
Ms M Mort, BSc Sydney (*PE*)
Mrs E Morton, BA Sheffield (**Modern Languages*)
Ms J Newman, BA Leicester (**Economics, Head of Sixth
  Form*)
§Ms H Nissinen-Lee, MA London (*Geography*)
Mrs J Ogidan, BSc Liverpool (*Biology, Careers
  Coordinator*)
Mr H Rees, BMus Wales (*Music*)
Mr H Ross, BA Hull (*French, *Spanish*)
Ms S Saig, BA Ontario, Canada (*French, Spanish*)
Mrs M Sharma-Yun, BSc London (*Mathematics*)
Ms D Shoham, MSc London (*Biology*)
Ms A Stöckmann, MA Westfälische Wilhelms (**German*)
§Mrs L Thomas, BA Hons Exeter (*PE*)
§Mr P Thompson, MA Oxon (*History*)
Mrs K Thonemann, MA Oxon (*Director of Studies*)
§Revd S M Tinker, BA Birmingham (**RE*)
§Mrs R Williams, BSc London (**Mathematics*)
Miss M Wharmby, BA Loughborough, ALA (*Librarian*)

Junior School:
Head Teacher: Ms L Tarr, BA Port Elizabeth, SA (*Primary
  Education*)
Deputy Head: Mrs H Reznek, BEd Herts (*Form Teacher,
  Year 6*)

Miss J Cameron, MA Edinburgh
Miss B Gayton, BEd Reading
Miss D Green, BA Manchester (*ICT Curriculum
  Coordinator – Both Schools*)
§Mrs I Hawkins, BEd London
Mrs N Morgan, BA Sheffield
§Miss M Pepper, LTCL
Ms A Phipps, BEd Middx Polytechnic
Mrs L Robson, MA Cambridge
Miss S Snowdowne, BEd Plymouth
Miss J Tunnicliffe, BEd New Zealand

Learning Support Assistants:
Ms S Ahmed
Ms S Ibrekic
Ms B Tadros

Visiting Staff:
Mr S Allen, ARCM (*Clarinet*)
Miss Y Behar, BA, LRAM, ARCM (*Piano*)
Miss S Bircumshaw, GRSM (*Violin*)
Mr A Brown, DpTCL (*Percussion*)
Mrs P Capone, AGSM (*Piano*)
Ms V Curran, GSMD, RAM PG Dip (*Trumpet*)
Miss L Forbes, LRAM, LTCL, DipNCOS (*Cello*)

Ms J Herbert, BA York (*Double Bass*)
Miss R Kerr, BA Hons (*Voice*)
Mr A Khan, LTCL (*Guitar*)
Mr R Martyn, AGSM, LRAM (*Brass*)
Mrs C H Mendelssohn, LRAM (*Violin*)
Miss N Myerscough, ARAM (*Violin*)
Miss C Philpot, LRAM (*Oboe*)
Ms S Riches, BMus RAM (*Double Bass*)
Miss H Shimizu, BMus (*Piano*)
Ms A Szreter, BA Oxon (*Voice*)
Mr T Travis, BMus (*Saxophone*)
Miss S Vivian, LTCL (*Voice*)
Miss J Watts, FRCO, GRSM, LRAM (*Piano*)
Ms H Webster, GRSM (*Flute*)

Assistant to the Clerk to the Governors: Miss E Lismore-
  Burns
Headmistress's Secretary: Ms L Carreras, BA London
Registrar: Mrs M McHarg
Senior School Secretary: Mrs E Ingram
Assistant Senior School Secretary: Ms S Glazier
Junior School Secretary: Mrs L McInerney
Development Secretary: Mrs N Sharman
Nurses: Mrs C Cooper & Mrs T Franklin

Founded in 1885, Channing is a day school for girls aged
4 to 18, approximately 550 in the Senior School (Sixth Form
100 girls) and 200 in Fairseat, the Junior School. It is situated in Highgate Village, in attractive grounds, and offers a
balanced education combining a traditional academic curriculum with modern educational developments. The complex
of old and new buildings has been constantly adapted to provide up-to-date facilities, and there are strong links with the
local community and local schools.

Teaching groups are small in size, which allows a friendly
relationship between girls and staff. Girls usually take nine
or ten subjects to GCSE and there is a wide range of A and
AS Level choices, including Ancient Greek, Further Maths,
Government and Politics and Theatre Studies. Option blocks
are re-drawn each year to suit the needs of the current year
groups. The Junior School has its own building – the elegant
and gracious family home of Sir Sydney Waterlow, one-time
Lord Mayor of London – set in spacious gardens, and is
notable for its happy and secure atmosphere.

Art, Drama, Music and Sport are all strong. Most girls
learn at least one instrument and there are frequent concerts
and theatrical productions. The school is fortunate in its gardens and open space (there are seven tennis courts on site)
and in its facilities. There is a new Sixth Form Centre and
fully-equipped performing arts studio.

Entry is by test and interview at 4, 11 and 16, and is subject to a satisfactory report from the entrant's current school.
There are occasional chance vacancies.

Further information can be obtained from the School
Prospectus, the Sixth Form Handbook, available from
the School Office and from the school website
(www.channing.co.uk).

Scholarships and Bursaries. (*See Scholarship Entries
section.*)

Fees per term (2011-2012). Junior School (Reception to
Year 6): £4,320; Senior School (Years 7–13): £4,680.

Charitable status. Channing House Incorporated is a
Registered Charity, number 312766. It aims to provide full-
time education for girls aged between 4 and 18 years.

The Cheltenham Ladies' College

Bayshill Road, Cheltenham, Glos GL50 3EP
Tel: 01242 520691
Fax: 01242 227882
e-mail: enquiries@cheltladiescollege.org
website: www.cheltladiescollege.org

The Cheltenham Ladies' College has been at the forefront of girls' education for over 155 years. With a reputation for academic excellence, College encourages a real love of learning and nurtures the personal development of every girl and member of staff. We seek to develop the talents of each girl and provide an environment in which girls can achieve the very highest standards in whatever they choose to do. There is a friendly openness about College which makes it a very happy place to live and learn.

Chairman of the Council: Mrs C Kirby, LLB

Principal: Miss Eve Jardine-Young, MA

Finance Director: Mr Jeffrey Speke, BSc, MPhil, ACA

Vice-Principal (Academic): Miss J R Adams, BSc

Vice-Principal (Pastoral): Ms E Stone, BA, LLB, MLitt, GradDipEd, AMusA

Admissions Tutor: Mrs F J Weldin, BA, MA

Heads of Division:
Sixth Form College: Mr J Hole, BA, MA
Upper College: Mrs D J Vass, BA
Lower College: Mrs C M Pellereau, BSc, MA

Director of Extra-Curricular Studies: Dr Joanna Bratten, BA, MLitt, PhD

Marketing and Communications Director: Mrs A Naylor, BSc

Chaplain: The Revd T Merry, BA, AKC

The pattern of day-to-day life revolves around two centres which complement each other – the College teaching buildings and the Boarding and Day Girl Houses. College is divided into three divisions: Lower College for girls in years 7–9, Upper College for girls in years 10 and 11, and Sixth Form College. The latter normally comprises about 300 girls and nearly all go on to university in the UK and the US. In the Sixth Form girls can choose between the International Baccalaureate Diploma or A Levels.

Numbers. Day 220, Boarding 650.

Fees per term (2011-2012). Day £6,455, Boarding £9,615. Some extras are charged, eg music, riding.

Admission. Entry at 11+, 12+ and 13+ via the College's own examinations or Common Entrance. Sixth Form entry is via the College's own entrance papers.

Pastoral Care. The systems of pastoral care are exceptionally good. Each girl is looked after by her Housemistress, the House Staff and a Tutor. All Tutors are full-time academic members of staff and advise girls on matters relating to their academic work and progress, including university advice and applications.

Buildings. The main building is built in a Gothic revival style and its interior decorations owe a great deal to the Arts and Crafts Movement. There are three Libraries, 17 laboratories, 5 networked computer rooms, state-of-the-art language laboratories, an Art and Technology Wing (including etching studio) and a professional guidance centre. In September 2009 the brand new Parabola Arts Centre opened. All the resources available to pupils are constantly kept up-to-date.

Houses. There are six Junior Boarding Houses and three Day Houses. All girls move House at Sixth Form which is an excellent stepping stone to university life. Day girls are fully integrated into all College activities, regularly joining boarders on weekend trips and expeditions.

Music, Drama and Dance. Over 900 individual music lessons take place each week, and there are generally five choirs and five orchestras running at any time. 450 girls have individual drama lessons in addition to the large number of productions put on each year. Dance and gymnastics are also available and very popular.

Sport and Extra-Curricular. College's aim is to encourage all girls to enjoy physical exercise and to take up an interest which will last throughout their lives. The main sports are hockey, lacrosse, netball, swimming, athletics and tennis but the College provides what girls enjoy and about 40 different sports are offered, including rowing, cricket, football, squash and golf. There is a large and superbly equipped sports centre, including a fitness suite, indoor swimming pool and two synthetic astroturf pitches (one floodlit). Over 80 clubs and activities are on offer including art and design, cheerleading, chess, computer programming, dance, debating, drama, fencing, golf, journalists, keep fit and martial arts, model UN, music, natural science, philosophy, street dance, young engineers, young enterprise, environmental clubs and international clubs.

Scholarships and Bursaries. (*See Scholarship Entries section*.)

Former Pupils, known as The Guild. There are 7,700 former pupils throughout the world, and they are a valued source of help to current girls, particularly in providing work-shadowing and careers advice.

Charitable status. The Cheltenham Ladies' College is a Registered Charity, number 311722. It exists to provide a high standard of education for girls.

City of London School for Girls

St Giles' Terrace, Barbican, London EC2Y 8BB
Tel: 020 7847 5500
Fax: 020 7638 3212
e-mail: info@clsg.org.uk
website: www.clsg.org.uk

Motto: *Domine Dirige Nos*

Staff:
Headmistress: Miss D Vernon, BA Hons Dunelm

Deputy Head: Mr W A Douglas, BA Hons Oxon
Director of Studies: Mrs E Harrop, BA Salamanca, MA Ludwig-Maximilians-Universität, MPhil Cantab
Head of Sixth Form Years 12 & 13: Ms J Henderson, BA Hons Dunelm
Assistant Head of Sixth Form: Miss R Lockyear, BA Hons Cantab
Head of Senior School Years 9, 10, 11: Mrs C Tao, BSc Surrey, MSc LSE
Assistant Heads of Senior School:
Mme N Signeux, English-Orléans, MFL-Lancaster, FLE
Mr J Murray, MA Oxon
Head of Lower School Years 7 & 8: Mrs K N Brice, MA Cantab
Assistant Head of Lower School: Miss J Norman, BEd De Montfort
Head of Prep Department: Miss J Rogers, MPhil, BA Hons London
Bursar: Colonel E L Yorke

Heads of Department:

Art:
Miss J Curtis, BA Hons London, St Martin's School of Art, ATC London

Classics:
Mr D Themistocleous, BA Hons Oxon

Design Technology:
Miss S McCarthy, BSc Hons Brunel

Drama:
Mr S Morley, DipCCSD Acting, Full Equity Member

Economics:
Mr N Codd, BA Hons Oxon

Politics:
Miss R Lockyear, BA Hons Cantab

English:
Mr B Ward, BA Hons Ulster

Geography:
Ms E A Moore, BA Hons Liverpool, FRGS

History:
Mrs K N Brice, MA Cantab

History of Art:
Mrs D M B B Southern, MA Edinburgh

ICT:
Mr D Libby, BSc Hons Bristol

Mathematics:
Mr K Latham, BSc Hons Liverpool

Modern Languages:
French: Mr G Tyrrell, BA Oxford Brookes, MA
Spanish: Miss M Leturia, Granada, MA London
German: Mrs V W Potter, Mag Phil Innsbruck
Italian: Ms J Henderson, BA Hons Dunelm
Mandarin: Mr A Stark, BA Hons Leeds, MA Westminster

Music:
Mrs M Donnelly, BEd Hons London

Physical Education:
Mrs E A McLean, CertEd Dartford

Psychology:
Mr C Taylor, BBusSc Cape Town

Religious Education:
Mrs K Bullard, MA Cantab

Science:
Biology: Ms N Brown, BSc Hons Edinburgh, MRes
   Edinburgh
Chemistry: Miss S Clements, BSc Hons Southampton
Physics: Mr M Wilkinson, BSc Nottingham

Careers:
Mrs C E Lipman, BA Hons Manchester

Assistant Bursar: Mrs C Bright, MIMgt
Admissions Officer: Mrs T Clifton-Brown, BA Hons
   Greenwich
PA to Headmistress: Mrs R Smith, BA Hons Leicester
Marketing & Development Officer: Miss L Hollaway

Health and Support Network:
School Doctor: Dr D Soldi, MBChB, DCH
School Sister: Mrs D Patel, RSCN
School Counsellor: Ms D Marcus, BA Hons (UK CP
   Registered)
Learning Support Teacher & Special Needs Coordinator:
   Mrs A Shilsler, CertEd, RSA DipSpLD, CAPS
   (Communication Difficulties)

City of London School for Girls is an academically selective, non-denominational, independent day school for girls from 7–18 years old. There is an infectious vibrancy and energy at "City". Its distinctive location in the Barbican Centre provides immediate access to the wealth of London's educational and cultural opportunities, while the teaching staff and girls imbue the place with a sense of happiness, purpose, enthusiasm and fulfilment.

The School Course includes English Language and Literature, History, Geography, Religion, Philosophy and Ethics, Latin, Greek, French, German, Spanish, Mathematics, Biology, Chemistry, Physics, Economics and Politics, Art, Music, Physical Education, Classical Civilisation, Design and Technology, History of Art, Theatre Studies, Psychology and Mandarin.

Pupils are prepared for the General Certificate of Secondary Education and for Advanced Supplementary and A2 Level Examinations offered by EDEXCEL, OCR and AQA. They are also prepared for Entrance to Oxford, Cambridge and other Universities. The Sixth Form courses are designed to meet the needs of girls wishing to proceed to other forms of specialised training.

Facilities are provided for outdoor and indoor games and the school has its own indoor swimming pool and an all-weather sports pitch. Extra-curricular activities before school, in the lunch hour or at the end of afternoon school include Debating, Football, Drama, Science, Technology, Fencing, Cheerleading, Netball, Gymnastics, Swimming, Tennis, Climbing and classes in Mandarin. Guest speakers are frequently invited to meetings of societies. There are also Junior and Senior Choirs, a Madrigal group, a Barbershop group, Junior and Senior Orchestras, a Wind Ensemble, a Chamber Orchestra and a Swing Band. Lunch hour music recitals, with visiting professional players, are encouraged. Many girls take the Duke of Edinburgh's Award Scheme at bronze, silver and gold level.

Admission. Main entry points to the school are at 7 and 11 and 16 years of age. For girls over 11 years old, vacancies are only occasional. The entrance examinations for age 11 admission in September will usually be held in the previous November and January. For age 7 the entrance exam is held in the Autumn Term. Admission to the Sixth Form is also by written examination and interview during the Autumn Term.

Applications for 11+ and 16+ should reach the Admissions Officer by the start of the previous October. Specific deadlines can be found on the website.

Scholarships and Bursaries. The School has a variety of academic, art, music and drama scholarships and means-tested bursaries for entry at 11+ and 16+.

Further details may be obtained from the Admissions Officer.

Fees per term (2011-2012). Preparatory Department: £4,377 (including lunch); Main School: £4,377 (excluding lunch).

Senior School lunches are paid for with a cashless system based on credited payment cards. Pupils in the Preparatory Department are expected to take school lunch for which there is no extra charge. After-school supervision is also available at £156 per term.

Extra Subjects: Pianoforte, Violin, Cello, Flute, Clarinet, Organ, Guitar and a wide variety of other instruments, including Singing: £219 per term (fees are all payable in advance).

Cobham Hall

Cobham, Kent DA12 3BL
Tel: 01474 823371
Fax: 01474 825906
e-mail: enquiries@cobhamhall.com
website: www.cobhamhall.com

Founded 1962.

Governing Body:
Mr C Sykes (*Chairman*)

The Earl of Darnley	Mrs L Ellis
Mr A Tuckwell	Dr M Griffin
Mr C Balch	Mr W Trelawny-Vernon
Mr M Frost	Mr J Dick
Ms P Cook	Mr M Pennell

Staff:

Headmaster: Mr P Mitchell, BSc Newcastle

Deputy Headmistress, Director of Studies: Dr S Coates-
   Smith, BSc, PhD London
Bursar: Mr D Standen, BSc Bradford

Assistant Head: Mrs W Barrett, BSc London
Senior Tutor for Middle School: Mr R Allen, BA Christ
  Church College, Canterbury
Senior Tutor for Lower School: Mrs E Wilkinson, BA
  London
Head of Boarding: Dr E Smalova, MSc Bariska Bystrica,
  PaedDr Nitra, CELTA

* *Head of Faculty*

English:
*Miss J Stevens, BA Hull
Mr R Allen, BA Christ Church College, Canterbury
Miss J West, BA Oxford, MA Oxford

Mathematics:
*Mr P Gilchrist, BSc Leeds
Mrs W Barrett, BSc London
Mrs M Martin, BSc Loughborough

Science:
*Mr J Fryer, BSc Leicester, MA Kent (*Biology*)
Dr S Coates-Smith, BSc, PhD London (*Physics*)
Mr I Geldard, BSc Durham (*Chemistry*)
Dr E Smalova, MSc Bariska Bystrica, PaedDr Nitra,
  CELTA
Dr N Hann, BSc Warwick, PhD Liverpool
Mr P Hosford, BSc Thames Polytehnic

Art:
*Mrs K Walsh, BA Kent Institute of Art & Design
Mrs A Lockheart, BA Illinois State University, PGCE
  London

Classics:
Miss A L Quinn, BA Hons Durham, PGCE King's College
  London
Mrs S-A Edmonds, BA Kent, MA Bristol, MA UCL, MiFL

Drama:
Miss K Martin, BEd Queensland, MA RADA and King's
  College London

Economics:
(*to be appointed*)

Film Studies:
Mr R Allen, BA Christ Church College, Canterbury

Geography:
Mr N Draper, MA Leicester

History:
*Miss A Howard-Williams, BA Brasenose College Oxford
Dr E Smalova, MSc Bariska Bystrica, PaedDr Nitra,
  CELTA

ICT/IB Coordinator: Mr A Owen, BA Wales

Modern Foreign Languages:
*Mrs E Barry, BA, MA London (*German, French*)
Mrs H Lazenby, BA Lima (*Spanish*)
Mrs E Wilkinson, BA London (*French, German*)
Miss J Caro Quintana, Licenciada en Filologica Inglesa,
  Valencia, Spain
Mrs X-W McArthur, BA China, PGCE Canterbury

Music:
Ms P Clements, BA London

Psychology:
Mrs K-A Beharry, BSc Middlesex

Physical Education:
Mrs K Hooper, BA Greenwich
Mrs S Carney, BEd Exeter
Miss K Lambert, BSc Gloucestershire
Mrs M Martin, BSc Loughborough

Religious Studies:
Mrs A Howard-Williams, BA Brasenose College Oxford

EFL:
Mrs C M von Bredow, BA Hons Birmingham, MA Exeter,
  PGCE Open University, RSA Dip TEFL
Miss M Aird, BA St Thomas University, Canada, CELTA

Student Support Department:
*Mrs D Rabot, BA Lancaster, OCR Dip SpLD
Mrs J Balson, BTEC Level 3 (*Teaching Assistant*)

Careers:
Sixth Form: Mrs W Barrett, BSc London
Middle School: Mr R Allen, BA Christ Church College,
  Canterbury
Lower School: Mrs E Wilkinson, BA London

Librarian:
Mrs K Smith

Laboratory Technicians:
Mrs B Reed
Mrs D Weaver

Art Technician:
Mrs L Hunt

Computer Support:
Mr D Wright

Boarding Staff:
Dr E Smalova, MSc B Bystrica, PaedDr Nitra, CELTA
  (*Head of Boarding*)
Miss M Aird, BA St Thomas Univ, Canada, CELTA, TESL
  Birmingham (*Housemistress*)
Mrs D Didzinskiene, BA Šiauliai Univ Lithuania, MS
  Vytautas Magnus Univ Lithuania (*Day Housemistress*)
Mrs E Fong (*Housemistress*)
Mrs M Gardner, RGN/RSCN (*Resident Nurse/
  Housemistress*)
Miss K Lambert, BSc Gloucestershire (*Housemistress*)
Miss B Largier, BComm RMIT Univ, Melbourne, Australia
  (*Housemistress*)

Visiting Staff:
There are visiting staff for Cello, Clarinet, Double Bass,
Drums, Flute, French Horn, Guitar, Keyboard, Oboe, Per-
cussion, Piano, Recorder, Saxophone, Trombone, Trumpet,
Tuba, Viola, Violin, Drama, Voice and Communication,
Ballet, Self Defence and Tennis.

Administration:
Registrar: Mrs S Ferrers
Marketing Assistant: Mrs J Booth
Receptionist: Mrs S Hammock
Headmaster's PA: Mrs C Blackwell
School Secretary: Mrs W Friend, Dip Couns
Bursar's Secretary: Mrs J Brace
Accountant: Mr B Jelley, CPFA
Accounts Administrator: Mrs K Pinder, MAAT
Accounts Assistant: Mrs P Gambell
Estates Manager: Mr T Curran, ARICS
Grounds Foreman: Mr T Gilbert

Cobham Hall is an international boarding and day
school for 200 girls aged between 11 and 18. It is an IBO
World School and offers the International Baccalaureate
Diploma Programme in the Sixth Form.

Situation. The school is set in 150 acres of parkland. Situated in North Kent, close to the M25 and adjacent to the
M2/A2. Thirty minutes from London, 60 minutes Heathrow,
45 minutes Gatwick and Stansted, 60 minutes Dover and
Channel Tunnel, 10 minutes Ebbsfleet International Eurostar Railway Station.

School Buildings. This beautiful 16th century historic
house was the former home of the Earls of Darnley. There
are many modern buildings providing comfortable accommodation for study and relaxation. Brooke and Bligh
Houses are separate buildings within the school grounds
offering Sixth Form accommodation in single or twin study-

bedrooms, many with en-suite facilities. Both Houses have common rooms with a kitchen and computer room.

Curriculum. An IBO World School, Cobham Hall offers the IB Diploma Programme in the Sixth Form with a wide range of subjects across Languages, Social and Experimental Sciences, Mathematics and the Arts.

Sixth Form. The Sixth Form numbers 60–70 students. Academic tutorial groups are spread across the two years and facilitate interaction between students. There are exceptional leadership opportunities, including election to the Student Leadership Team which plays a significant part in the management of the school. University destinations include University College London, Warwick, Leeds and Manchester, as well as Oxford and Cambridge.

Sporting and other activities. The school's main sports are Tennis, Swimming, Hockey, Athletics and Netball. There are seven hard tennis courts, six netball courts, a large, indoor multi-sports complex, including fitness centre, dance studio and a heated indoor swimming pool, which is in use throughout the year. Horse-riding and golf may be taken as 'extras'. A wide variety of extra-curricular activities is available.

Careers. High-quality Careers Guidance and personal support is offered across Lower and Middle School and in the Sixth Form by school staff. Activities in partnership with external providers include Futurewise Profiling, Interview Training and an annual "Dragons Den" Day.

Round Square. The school is a member of this international group of schools, which subscribes to the philosophy of educationalist Dr Kurt Hahn. Annual conferences are attended by a school delegation including Sixth Formers. In recent years these have been held in Australia, America, India, South Africa and Germany. Younger students attend Round Square conferences in the UK and Europe. Students have the opportunity to visit other member schools on an exchange programme as well as visit other countries by taking part in service projects and relief work organised by the Round Square.

Health. Residential trained nursing staff providing 24-hour medical care.

All Terms. Girls have two Exeat Weekends and a Half Term holiday.

Admission. Admission is by the School's own entrance examination which can be taken on Entrance Assessment Days in October (Lower/Middle School) and November (Sixth Form) or at a girl's own school. Girls normally enter the school between the ages of 11+ and 13+ and follow a course leading to GCSE level at the end of the fifth year and to the International Baccalaureate Diploma at the end of the seventh. Girls wishing to enter the Sixth Form should achieve at least five GCSE or equivalent examination passes at Grade C or above.

Scholarships. (*See Scholarship Entries section.*) Scholarships are available for 11+, 13+ and Sixth Form entry.

Bursaries. Special bursaries are available for boarders from British Services families, diplomats and those families working for UK Charitable Trusts overseas and charitable bursaries for very able children from certain areas. (For further information, contact The Registrar.)

Fees per term (2011-2012). Day girls: £4,700–£5,950. Boarders: £7,100–£8,950.

Old Girls' Association. Known as Elders. There is a representative committee which meets regularly in London or at the School. The Chairman is Mrs Tracey Balch, e-mail: tracey.balch@virgin.net.

Charitable status. Cobham Hall is a Registered Charity, number 313650. It exists to provide high quality education for girls aged 11–18 years.

Combe Bank School

Combe Bank Drive, Sundridge, Kent TN14 6AE
Tel: Senior School 01959 563720 or 01959 569011
          Preparatory School 01959 564320
Fax: Senior School 01959 561997
          Preparatory School 01959 560456
e-mail: enquiries@combebank.kent.sch.uk
website: www.combebank.kent.sch.uk

Council of Management:

Chairman: Mr P Dickinson
Mrs J Branson
Mr D Earl
Mrs A Gilbert
Father R Harvey
Mr P McGregor
Mrs L Stringer
Mr I Whitlock

Bursar: Mr D Rossi, MAAT

Headmistress: Mrs E J Abbotts, BA Hons, MEd, PGCE, NPQH

Senior School Staff:

Deputy Head (Academic): Mr M Broderick, MSc, PGCE
Deputy Head (Pastoral): Mrs J Tricks, BA Hons, MSc, PGCE

Mrs D Arrowsmith, BSc Hons, PGCE
Mrs L Baker, BEd Hons (*Director of Sport*)
Mrs K Burns, BSc Hons, PGCE
Miss E Caffrey, BA Hons, PGCE (*Head of Drama*)
Mrs J Cazaly, CertEd PE
Mrs P Chandler, BA Hons, CertEd, Adv Cert CEG (*Head of Geography, Head of Careers*)
Mr C Clarke, BSc, PGCE
Mr J Davis, BSc Tech Hons
Mrs K Downer, BEd, PGCE (*Head of Learning Support*)
Miss E Francis, BA Hons Dunelm, PGCE Cantab
Mrs H Gibb, BA Hons (*Coordinator, Gifted and Talented*)
Mrs J Goldsmith, BA Hons, PGCE
Mrs B Graham, BSc Hons, PGCE
Mrs E Griffiths, BA Hons, PGCE (*Head of English*)
Mrs D Halls, Erstes Staatesexamen, PGCE
Mrs G Hibbs, CertEd (*Head of Home Economics*)
Miss D Hopper, BSc
Mrs M Howard, BA Hons (*Head of Science*)
Mrs S Hubble, BEd Hons
Mr G Hughes, BA (*Head of Sixth Form*)
Mr P Hutchin, BA, PGCE (*Head of History*)
Dr H Isom, PhD, BA Hons, DipRSA, HonGCM (*Director of Music*)
Mr P Isom, BA Hons, LRSM, DipABRSM, DipRSCM, ACertCM
Mrs J Jenkins, BEd Hons (*Head of Mathematics*)
Ms M Keefe, BA Hons, MA, PGCE
Ms G Leake, BSc Hons, MEd
Mrs S Leaver, BSc Hons, PGCE (*Head of ICT*)
Mrs H Lorigan, BA Hons, PGCE (*Head of Art & Design*)
Mrs J Pettitt, MA Cantab (*Head of Modern Languages*)
Mrs J Redpath-Johns, BA Hons, PGCE
Miss S Rye, BA Hons, PGCE
Mrs M Southgate, BA Hons, PGCE (*Head of Religious Education*)
Mrs H Welch, CertEd, AMBDA
Mrs D Westwater, BA, PGCE
Mrs J Wiltshire, BEd, MA (*Head of Business Studies, Deputy Head of Sixth Form*)

Preparatory School Staff:
Head of the Preparatory School: Mrs S Walker, BA Hons, CertEd Cantab
Deputy Head: Mrs E Dale, CertEd

Mrs S Adkins, BA Hons, PGCE
Mrs S Allford, BA Hons, PGCE
Mrs J Barnes, BA, TCert, LTCL, LRSM (*Head of Science*)
Miss P Beacom, BA Hons, PGCE (*Director of Music*)
Mrs E Black, CertEd
Mrs S Burge, BA Hons, PGCE, TEFL
Miss J Conlin, BA, PGCE
Miss A Cooper, BEd, BA (*Head of Mathematics*)
Mrs T Dolman, BA Hons Ed
Mrs S Fenor-Lloyd, BSc Hons, PGCE
Mrs C Mackrell, CertEd
Mrs J Keeble, RSA CLANSA
Miss R Miles (*Speech and Drama*)
Mrs R Mortlock, BA, DipSpLD
Mrs Z Sargent, BA Hons, PGCE
Mrs D Spencer, MSc, BA Hons, PGCE
Mrs A Tarrant, BSc Hons, PGCE (*PE*)
Ms J Turnbull, CertEd (*Head of Humanities*)
Mrs A Vowles, BA Hons (*Head of English*)
Mrs L Wales, BEd
Miss E Wright, MA Hons, PGCE

School Chaplain: Father Behruz Raf'at
Registrar: Miss S Daley

Combe Bank is an independent day school for girls with entry from the term that pupils are 3 up to the age of 18. Founded in 1924 by the Roman Catholic Society of the Holy Child Jesus, it is now an ecumenical school welcoming girls of all faiths. (*See also Preparatory School entry in IAPS section.*)

Aims and Ethos. The school aims to provide a modern and challenging education for all girls so that they become discerning and resourceful young women well prepared for today's world. The purposeful ethos and commitment to very good quality pastoral care are a distinctive feature of school life. High academic standards are expected.

Location. Situated in a Palladian Mansion built for the Campbell family, Dukes of Argyll, and set in superb grounds with 27 acres of parkland just outside Sevenoaks, the school has excellent facilities. The Preparatory School and Senior School and Sixth Form are on the same site and there are many positive links between them so that girls are well prepared for each stage of their education.

Curriculum. A modern and broad range of subjects is taught at all age levels. English, Mathematics, Sciences, a modern language and RE are compulsory at GCSE. In addition girls choose from History, Geography, IT, PE, Business Studies, Drama, Music, Food and Nutrition, Art and Design, Textiles. History of Art, Photography and Government and Politics are additional options for AS/A2. The school boasts strong Art and Music Departments with regular exhibitions and musical performances in which wide participation is encouraged. Combe Bank has a well earned reputation for competitive success in PE and also provides a very wide range of sports and activities to interest all girls. Swimming in the 25-metre covered pool is a particularly popular activity at Prep and Senior level.

Admission. Entrance to the Preparatory School is from the term that pupils are aged 3 and takes the form of an interview and assessment in school. For the Senior School, girls take the School's entrance examination at 11+. Good passes at GCSE are also expected for the AS/A2 subjects of choice in order to join the Sixth Form.

Transport. Coach transport is organized for 4 significant routes, to be paid for on a termly basis.

Fees per term (2011-2012). £2,710–£4,870.

Charitable status. Combe Bank School Educational Trust Limited is a Registered Charity, number 1007871. It exists to provide a good education for girls aged 3 to 18.

Cranford House School

Moulsford, Wallingford, Oxfordshire OX10 9HT
Tel: 01491 651218
Fax: 01491 652557
e-mail: office@cranfordhouse.oxon.sch.uk
website: www.cranford-house.org

Members of the Board of Governors:
R Bray, Esq (*Chairman*)
S J W McArthur, Esq, BSc, MA
Miss E A Scoates, BSc, MPhil
B Howell Pryce, Esq
G Cole, Esq
A Harper, Esq
Mrs G Walsh
S J McNaught

Headmistress: Mrs Claire Hamilton, MA Cantab

Head of Senior School: Mrs P Hawson, CertEd Bristol
Head of Junior School: Mrs L Lawson, BA Hons, PGCE
Head of Lower School: Mrs G Smeeton, BSc, QTS Ripon & York St John

Senior School Teaching Staff:
Mr R Barker, BSc, PGCE Edinburgh
Mrs M Bradley, BA Reading, PGCE
Mrs N Butler, BA, CAPES
Mrs D Carter, BA, PGCE
Miss C Chaplin, BEd Hons Bedford College of HE
Miss M Clark, BSc Hons London, PGCE Open
Mr C Cooper, BSc Hons London, PGCE East Anglia, MA Warwick
Mr C Corr, BSc Cambridge, PGCE Reading
Mrs S Dixon, BEd
Mrs S Eccles, BA UNISA
Mrs S Elston, BSc Manchester
Mrs P Hawson, CertEd Bristol
Mrs K Heard, BA Hons, PGCE
Mrs S Kirkwood, Higher DipEd South Africa
Mrs J McCallum, MA Hons Edinburgh, PGCE Cambridge
Mrs J Powell, BA Hons, Dip Adv Studies RAM
Mrs M Powell, CertEd Bath
Mme C Robichez, BA Sorbonne
Mrs M Sardeson, BSc Hons Nottingham, PGCE Reading
Mrs C Shaikh, CertEd Oxford
Mrs C Smythe, BA Hons, DipEd

Junior School Teaching Staff:
Mrs A J Cheeseman, BEd London
Mrs L Lawson, BA, PGCE
Mrs J Morris, BA
Miss C Oliver, BA
Mrs J Powell, BA Hons, Dip Adv Studies RCM
Mrs V Stretch, BA
Mrs F Weikert, CertEd London

Lower School Teaching Staff:
Mrs E Day, BSc Hons, PGCE
Mrs E Drury, BEd Herts
Mrs A Greedy, BEd, TEFL
Mrs A Howell, BEd
Mrs J Lake, BA Hons London, PGCE Oxford
Mr P Meakin
Mrs G Smeeton, BSc, QTS Ripon & York St John

Nursery Staff:
Mrs N J Pearce, NNEB North Tyneside (*Head of Nursery*)
Mrs K Knight, BEd Early Years Education
Mrs J Ireland
Mrs E Davies
Mrs A McIver

Centre for Individual Development:
Mrs G Mabbett, BEd, RSADipSpLD (*Head of Learning Support*)
Mrs V Little, BEd, RSADipSpLD
Mrs J Redly, BA Hons, PGCE
Mrs R Townsend, BEd, RSA DipSpLD

Visiting Music Staff:
Mr C Bache (*Clarinet/Saxophone*)
Mr J Boughton, BA Hons Bath, ALCM (*Piano & Recorder*)
Mrs C Bromley (*Violin*)
Miss L Gifford-Guy, BMus Hons (*Singing*)
Mrs S Murrell (*Piano*)
Miss A Pickering, LLCM TD, ALCM (*Flute*)
Mrs R Powell (*Brass*)
Mrs M Thorns, BMus Hons, CertEd, LRAM (*Cello and Piano*)

Other Visiting Staff:
Mr H Batten, MSc, 5th Dan, Renshi (*Judo*)
Mrs H Griffiths, BA Hons (*Dance*)
Mrs N Lawson (*Self-Defence*)
Mr P Worroll, LTA Level 1 Licence

Support Staff:

Mrs S Sulley	Mrs W Rant
Mrs R Mannell	Mrs J Sangan
Mrs J Goddard	Miss H Stanley
Mr M Howard	Mrs S Steggeman
Mrs J Plant	Mrs M Stoker

Administrative Staff:
Mrs S Crowe (*Matron*)
Mrs J Cuffe (*Receptionist/Administrator*)
Mr M Patrick (*ICT Manager*)
Mrs E Hayward (*Bursar's Assistant, Staff Development Officer*)
Mrs E Taylor (*Bursar*)
Miss S Treadwell (*Receptionist/Administrator*)
Mrs S Jubb (*Bursar's Assistant*)
Mrs J Simmons (*Registrar*)
Mrs J White-Zamler (*Assistant Head*)
Mrs S Colton (*School Secretary*)

Cranford House is an independent day school for around 360 pupils, girls aged 3–16 years and boys 3–7 years.

The Lower School (pre-preparatory) caters for boys and girls aged 3–7 years and includes a purpose built Nursery. Pupils work towards the Foundation stage in Nursery and Reception and on to Key Stage 1 in Forms 1 and 2.

The Junior School (preparatory) comprises Forms 3 to 6 where a balance is struck between the traditional reading, writing and numeracy skills and the enquiry based approach of modern science, design technology and information and communication technology. The Juniors benefit from Senior School facilities. Specialist subject teachers are increasingly used in French, Mathematics, Science, Religious Studies and Physical Education. Lesson content is based on the National Curriculum Key Stage 2 programmes of study, and results are consistently very good.

For the first three years in the Senior School girls follow a common core curriculum of English, Mathematics, Science, History, Geography, French, Spanish, German, Art, Music, Drama, ICT, Textiles and Food Technology. In Forms 10 and 11 they study their chosen GCSE subjects, with the majority of girls sitting between nine and eleven subjects. Physical Education, Religious Studies and Personal, Health and Social Education are studied throughout the Senior School. Girls belong to a House system and, on reaching Form 11, enjoy positions of responsibility and privilege. The school has extensive recreational and games fields. In winter, hockey and netball are played, and in summer, tennis and athletics. Swimming takes place in the school's heated out-door swimming pool. Dramatic, musical and dance productions are an important aspect of school life.

In addition to the many clubs and activities offered throughout the school, all pupils have the opportunity to join educational trips and excursions. For Senior pupils, the Duke of Edinburgh's Award Scheme and the Fox Award can be undertaken. There are opportunities for travel with the Senior Choir and the Modern Languages department who have visited France, Germany, Holland, Italy and Belgium. Ski trips are offered bi-annually. School transport operates over a wide area.

Scholarships are offered for entry into the Senior School: Academic, Sport, Drama, Music and All-Round.

Our aim is to encourage pupils not only to achieve the best possible academic results, but to become responsible and useful citizens; happy, and with a high degree of self esteem – adaptable and equipped for life.

Fees per term (2011-2012). £1,500–£4,475.

Charitable status. Cranford House School Trust Limited is a Registered Charity, number 280883.

Croydon High School
GDST

Old Farleigh Road, Selsdon, South Croydon CR2 8YB
Tel: 020 8260 7500
Fax: 020 8657 5413
e-mail: info2@cry.gdst.net
website: www.croydonhigh.gdst.net

Founded 1874.

Croydon High School is part of the GDST (Girls' Day School Trust). The GDST is the leading network of independent girls' schools in the UK. As a charity that owns and runs 24 schools and two academies, it reinvests all its income in its schools. For further information about the Trust, see p. xxi or visit www.gdst.net.

Additional information about the school may be found on the school's website and a detailed prospectus is available from the school.

Chairman of Local Governors: Mr R Crail

Head: Mrs D Leonard, BEd, MEd Birmingham

Deputy Head: Mrs P Clark, MA London

Assistant Head, Enrichment: Mrs I Bennett, BEd Leeds Met

Assistant Head, Sixth Form: Mrs H Mester, BA Nottingham

Assistant Head, Curriculum: Mr M Pickering, BA, MSc Manchester

Acting Head of Junior School: Mrs E Wilson, BEd South Bank

Head of Junior School (from Jan 2012): Miss A Cordingley, LTCL Trinity College of Music

School Business Manager: Mr D Gibson, BA Heriot-Watt

For more than a century, Croydon High School has provided a superb all-round education for girls, around the Croydon area and further afield. The school was founded in 1874 and combines tradition with a forward-looking, supportive and nurturing atmosphere where every girl is encouraged and supported to achieve her personal best. The school welcomes girls from a wide range of backgrounds; excellent pastoral care ensures that each girl is known as an individual.

Croydon High offers girls a wide range of extra-curricular opportunities ensuring that each can find something she enjoys. The school regularly achieves local, regional and national success in Sport; its Arts are also outstanding, with a vibrant Music department offering opportunities to musicians at varying ability levels to develop their talents in all musical genres. Termly productions involve students across all year groups and young artists are motivated and inspired to develop their creative talents in different media.

The school aims to develop confident young women with wide ranging interests and abilities who have also achieved excellent academic results. Emphasis is placed on ensuring that girls are happy and fulfilled in whatever career path they choose for the future, be this as a business high flyer or a contented homemaker.

Number of Pupils. Senior School (aged 11–18): 409 girls (including 85 in the Sixth Form). Junior School (aged 3–11): 248 girls (including 16 in the Nursery).

Facilities. The purpose-built school has outstanding facilities; including specialist music rooms, a drama studio, a language laboratory, 5 computer suites, 10 science laboratories, design technology room and a recently refurbished sports block incorporating sports hall, gym, indoor swimming pool, fitness room and dance studio. The school is surrounded by spacious playing fields with netball/tennis courts, athletics track and an all-weather hockey pitch.

The Junior School, which has its own Nursery, is in an adjacent building on the same site.

The Sixth Form have their own suite of rooms, including a common room and quiet study area, adjacent to the school library.

Curriculum. Most girls take 10 GCSE subjects with the aim of providing a broad and balanced core curriculum which keeps career choices open. Over 23 subjects are offered at AS and A Level including Government & Politics, Economics, Latin and Physical Education. Most girls take four AS Levels and then three A Levels. Almost all girls proceed to University, and, each year, a number are offered places at Oxbridge.

Admission. A whole school Open Day is held annually in October. An Open Evening is held in the Summer Term.

The school admits girls to the Junior School on the basis of either individual assessment (younger girls) or written tests (girls of 7+ and above). Selection procedures are held early in January for Juniors and assessments for Infants are held during the Autumn and Spring Terms for entry in the following September.

For entrance to the Senior School in Year 7, the school holds Entrance Tests in November for entry in the following September. All applicants are interviewed by the Headmistress and references are taken up.

For the Sixth Form, the school interviews applicants and requests reports from the present school. A Sixth Form Open Evening is held in October.

Fees per term (2011-2012). Senior School £4,203, Junior Department £3,270, Nursery £2,526.

Scholarships and Bursaries. Following the ending of the Government Assisted Places Scheme, the GDST has made available to the school a number of scholarships and bursaries.

Academic scholarships are available for entry at 11+ or to the Sixth Form. Music, art & design and sports scholarships are also available at 11+ and 16+.

Bursaries are means tested and are intended to ensure that the school remains accessible to bright girls who could not otherwise benefit from the education we offer. These are available to Senior School girls.

Charitable status. Croydon High School is part of The Girls' Day School Trust, which is a Registered Charity, number 306983.

Dame Allan's Girls' School

Fenham, Newcastle-upon-Tyne NE4 9YJ
Tel: 0191 275 0708 (School); 0191 274 5910 (Bursar)
Fax: 0191 275 1502 (School); 0191 275 1501 (Bursar)
e-mail: enquiries@dameallans.co.uk
website: www.dameallans.co.uk

The School was founded in 1705 by Dame Eleanor Allan and in 1935 was moved to Fenham on a site of 13 acres.

Governors:
Chairman: Mr E Ward
Vice-Chairman: Mr B W Adcock
Mrs S Banerjee
Mrs K Bruce
Mrs O Grant, OBE
Mr J Hargrove
Dr J A Hellen, MA, PhD
Prof P D Manning
Mrs M E Slater, MBE, JP
Mrs J Slesenger
Mr A M Stanley
Mr D Tait Walker
Mr T St A Warde-Aldam
Miss J Weatherall
Revd N Wilson

Ex officio:
The Lord Mayor of Newcastle upon Tyne
The Dean of Newcastle
The Vicar of the Parish of St John

Clerk to the Governors and Bursar: J Fleck, ACMA

Principal: J R Hind, MA Downing College Cambridge, MEd Newcastle, PhD Durham

Vice-Principal: M J Middlebrook, BA Leeds
Assistant Head: E C Fiddaman, BA Hertford College Oxford
Director of Studies: A Hopper, BA Merton College Oxford
Head of Sixth Form: D C Henry, BSc Heriot-Watt, FIMLS

Z Allonby, BA Glasgow School of Art
A Brown, BA Newcastle
C Cedeyn, CertEd
C Charlton, BA Newcastle
L Clough, CertEd IM Marsh College of PEd
V Cooke, BA Durham, MA Durham
J Donald, BEd Durham CNNA
H Dresser, BA Liverpool
S Dutton, CertEd Leeds
K Fraser, BSc, PhD Newcastle
A H Gillis, BSc, MSc, PhD Durham
D Gillott, BSc Hull
J Golding, BA Northumbria
B Green, LLB Warwick
P Halliwell, BEd Liverpool
K F Heatherington, BA Newcastle
K Henderson, BA Glasgow
M Hill, BSc Leicester
H Leahy, BA Leicester
A Lill, BSc Northumbria
P Lincoln, BA Newcastle
S McDougall, BSc Sheffield Hallam
C McFall, BSc Hull
G M Maughan, BEd Homerton College Cambridge
P Moir, BEd Northumbria
G S Mundy, MA Newnham College Cambridge
I Le Moallic-Parker, DEUG Nantes, BAEd Sunderland
J Murray, BA London
R Ogg, BA Durham
C Parker, MBA Sunderland

M Pyburn, BSc Manchester
S Rickaby, CertEd Lady Mabel College of PE
F Ripley, BSc Newcastle
J Strong, MA Queens' College Cambridge
K Tew, BSc Northumbria
S Whewell, MSc Sunderland
A Wiegand BA Sunderland
S A Winton de Lezcano, BSc Nottingham, MSc Imperial
College London

Junior Department:
Head: A J Edge, MA St Andrews

A Brown, BSc Northumbria
L P Cruickshank, BA Newcastle
D M Farren, BA Warwick
J Loraine, BEd Newcastle
B Metcalf, BSc York
R Watson, BA Leeds

There are approximately 400 girls in the School which has a three-form entry at 11+. With the Boys' School, which is in the same building, it shares a mixed Sixth Form and a mixed Junior Department (8+ to 10+).

The Main School follows the normal range of subjects, leading to examination at GCSE. German is introduced in Year 8 and Spanish is offered in Year 9.

Most girls stay on into the Sixth Form and from there normally go on to Higher Education.

Buildings. In recent years, developments have included additional classrooms, a new Library, Computer Resource Centre, Technology Centre, ICT network, a new Sixth Form Centre, and a Drama and Dance Studio.

School Societies. The current list includes: outdoor pursuits (including Duke of Edinburgh's Award scheme), choirs, orchestra, drama, computing, art, Christian Fellowship, Amnesty International, history, science, electronics, mathematics, dance, public speaking and debating.

Pastoral. Each girl is placed in the care of a Form teacher who oversees her progress and development. In the Sixth Form she has a Tutor who is responsible for both academic and pastoral care.

Careers. There is a structured programme, beginning in Year 9, with a significant contribution from Connexions.

Sixth Form. In 1989 the Sixth Form was merged with that of our brother School, giving both Schools the rare constitution of single-sex education (11–16) with a co-educational Sixth Form. The Head of Sixth Form is Mr D C Henry who will welcome enquiries concerning admission.

Physical Education. Hockey, Netball, Tennis, Gymnastics, Athletics, Fencing, Badminton, Squash, Swimming. The playing fields adjoin the school. Instruction in swimming is given at a local pool. Dance is particularly popular.

Admission. Governors' Entrance Scholarships are awarded on the results of the Entrance Examinations held annually in the Spring Term at all ages from 8+ to 13+. A limited number of Bursaries are available to pupils aged 11+ and over on entry.

Fees per term (2011-2012). Senior School £3,291; Junior Department £2,586.

Dame Allan's Allanians Association. President: Mr B Sanderson, c/o Dame Allan's Schools.

Charitable status. Dame Allan's Schools is a Registered Charity, number 1084965. It exists to provide education for children.

Derby High School

Hillsway, Littleover, Derby DE23 3DT
Tel: 01332 514267
Fax: 01332 516085
e-mail: headsecretary@derbyhigh.derby.sch.uk

website: www.derbyhigh.derby.sch.uk

Founded in January 1892; taken over from the Church Schools Company in 1910 by a local Governing Body. In 1959 the school became associated with the Woodard Corporation.

Governors and Foundation Governors:
Chairman: Dr R Faleiro
Mr B Bailey
Miss H Barton
Revd Canon B Clover, MA, FRSA, LTCL
Mr D Eade
[1]Mr M R Hall, DL, Hon D Univ, FCA, FCMA, FCT
Mrs R Hughes, BA, ACIB
[1]Mr H M L Jenkins, DM, FRCOG
Mrs F Lazenby
[1]Mrs M Moore
Mr T Ousley
Mrs C Owen, BDS
Canon D Perkins
[1]Mr J G R Rudd, DL, FCA, FCMI
Mrs H Smart
Mrs R Williams

[1] *Foundation Governor*

Headmaster: Mr C T Callaghan, BA Comb Hons Exeter, MA OU

Deputy Head: Mrs A K Penny, BA Comb Hons Birmingham, PGCE Loughborough, MEd Nottingham

Director of Studies: Mrs J Sample, BSc Hons Durham, PGCE Cambridge

Head of Sixth Form: Dr N Brown, BSc Leeds, PhD Leeds, PGCE Leicester

Chaplain: Revd R Barrett, MA Exeter, BA Hons Exeter, PGCE Exeter (*PSHE, Religious Education*)

Bursar: Mrs S Marson

* *Head of Department*

Mrs A Arthey, BA Comb Hons Birmingham, PGCE Nottingham (*French, *Careers*)
Mrs M Aspinall, BA Hons Durham, PGCE Durham (*Modern Languages*)
Mrs J Bennion, BA Sheffield Hallam (*Art*)
Mrs A Brown, BA NSW, BEd Adelaide, DipEd Adelaide, CGeog (*Geography*)
Mrs T Bullas, BEd Hons London (*Physical Education*)
Mrs S Bussey, BSc Econ Hons Aberystwyth (*Information Resources and Marketing Manager*)
Mrs J Charlton, BA Hons Leeds, PGCE Leeds, MA Derby (*Economics and Business Studies*)
Mrs C M Cleave, BSc Hons Exeter, PGCE Cambridge (*Physics and SENCO*)
Mr D Connell, MBA Derby, PGCE Staffordshire, ACIB (*Economics and Business Studies, *ICT*)
Mrs N Driver, BEd Hons Lancaster (*Religious Education, PSHE, Head of Years 7-9*)
Mrs C Eales, CertEd Birmingham (*Mathematics*)
Mrs J Fraser, BSc Hons Derby, PGCE Nottingham Trent (*Psychology*)
Miss A Jordan, BA Hons Wolverhampton, PGCE Newcastle (*History*)
Mr P Gould, GRSM, FRCO, ARAM, LRAM, ARCM, DipEd, Hon M Music (*Music*)
Mrs L Hamblett, BSc London, PGCE Derby (*Mathematics and DofE Award*)
Mrs J Hancock, BEd Hons Manchester Metropolitan (*Physical Education*)
Mrs K Hewitt, BA Hons Birmingham (*Biology*)
Mrs L Hough, BSc Hons Brunel, CertEd (*Design Technology, Young Enterprise*)

Mrs S Jukes, BA Hons, PGCE (*Drama*)
Miss S Kelliher, BA Hons Dublin, PGCE Birmingham
(*German*)
Mrs M Martinez Hernandez, BA Salamanca, PGCE Madrid
(*Spanish*)
Mrs S Martin-Smith, HND Swansea, BA Hons Swansea,
PGCE Swansea (**Art*)
Dr S Mathews, BA Hons Sheffield Hallam, MSc
Manchester, PhD Manchester (*History*)
Mrs C McDonald, BSc Hons Manchester, PGCE
Manchester (**Home Economics*)
Dr J Myers, BSc York, PGCE Leics, PhD Edinburgh
(*Chemistry*)
Dr J A Nelmes, BSc Hons London, PGCE Nottingham,
PhD Loughborough (*Physics and Chemistry*)
Mrs G Rumford-Warr, BSc Birmingham, PGCE Keele
(**Mathematics*)
Mrs J A Priestnall, BSc Hons Hatfield, PGCE Leicester
(*Biology*)
Mrs C E Read, BA Hons Reading, PGCE London
(*English, *General Studies*)
Miss M Render, BA Hons Hull, PGCE Hull (*English*)
Miss C V Riley, BSc Hons Leeds, PGCE Leeds
(**Chemistry, Head of Years 10 & 11, DofE Award*)
Mr N Robinson, BA Hons (*Director of Music*)
Mrs M Roe, BA Hons Nottingham (**Geography, DofE
Award*)
Mrs L Seymour, BA Hons, PGCE Notts (*German*)
Miss K Southall, BSc Aberdeen, PGCE Bath (*Biology**)
Mrs D G Stringer, BEd Hons Cardiff, DipEdMan
Nottingham (*Home Economics*)
Mrs F Supran, BA Hons Manchester, PGCE Oxford, Cert
TEFLA Oxford Brookes (*English and *Drama*)
Miss S Walton, BSc Hons Sheffield, PGCE Sheffield
(*Physical Education, Deputy Head Sixth Form*)
Mrs J Webster, MA Hons Cambridge (**English &
Psychology*)
Mr S Williams, BSc Hons Birmingham, PGCE Nottingham
(*Mathematics*)

Music:
Mr R Abraham (*Drums and Percussion*)
Mrs C A Barker, TCert Manchester, CT ABRSM (*Flute
and Fife*)
Mrs V Cunningham, BA Hons (*Oboe and Clarinet*)
Mrs D Gould, CertEd (*Violin, Viola*)
Mrs M Marubbi, MA, BA Hons, ALCMTD (*Flute and
Piano*)
Mrs S Robinson, BMus London, ARCM (*Piano*)
Mr A Rutter (*Brass*)
Miss S Watts, BMus Hons, LRAM (*Clarinet and
Saxophone*)

Primary School:
Head of Primary: Mrs M Hannaford, BEd Hons Derby,
MA Ed OU, NPQH
Deputy Head of Primary: Mrs K M E Carey, BEd
Liverpool Chester College
Deputy Head of Junior School: Mr S Bullas, BEd Exeter
Mrs C A Alvis, BEd Notts, MA
Miss L Baker, BA Hons Derby, PGCE Derby
Miss S Evans, BA Hons, QTS PrimEd Bishop Grosseteste
College, Lincs
Mrs K Hopkinson, BEd Hons Derby
Mrs L Soutar, BA Hons Nottingham, PGCE Leeds
Miss S Stocker, BA Hons Warwick, PGCE Central
England
Mrs J Swainston, BEd Hons Sheffield
Mrs A Trindell, BSc Hons London, QTS
Mrs L Brebner, DipEd Jordan Hill College, Glasgow, ITC
Notre Dame College, Glasgow
Mrs M Blount, BEd Hons Derby
Mrs J Bowden, BA Ed Primary Reading
Mrs P R Charge, CertEd Poulton-le-Fylde

Mrs A Dowell, BSc Hons, QTS Newman Coll of HE
Mrs E Sanderson, BEd Hons Derby
Miss L Pitt, BA PrimEd Birmingham

Headmaster's PA: Miss S Callaghan, BA Hons Warwick

There are 580 pupils in school of whom 320 are in the
Senior School, which is for girls only, and 260 are in the
Juniors and Kindergarten which are both co-educational.

The Primary Department follows an enhanced national
curriculum course. KS1 and KS2 take internal assessments.
ASPECTS are used for nursery and INCAS for Year 1, Year
3 and Year 5. There is considerable enrichment in the curriculum with a wide variety of sports, music, drama and other
activities available both within the curriculum and at club
time.

The Senior School offers courses in Art and Design, Biology, Chemistry, Design Technology, Drama, Economics &
Business Studies, English Language and Literature, French,
General Studies, Geography, German, History, Home Economics, ICT, Mathematics, Further Maths, Music, Physical
Education, Psychology, Physics, Religious Studies, Spanish
and Theatre Studies. The curriculum is enhanced by activities such as Young Enterprise, The Duke of Edinburgh's
Award Scheme, World Challenge and the charitable work
undertaken in Ethiopia and Thailand. Sports, drama and
music are also strengths, with pupils gaining recognition at
county and national level.

The main points of entrance are at 11+ and 16+ where
Scholarships and Assisted Places are available. Entrance is
by examination and interview. Entrance at other ages is by
assessment and takes place by arrangement.

The school has an active Christian ethos and broadly follows the teaching of the Church of England, but pupils of all
faiths are welcomed and valued.

Examinations. Pupils are entered for ASPECTS,
INCAS, GCSE and GCE AS and A Level examinations,
some Sixth Form pupils take the EPQ. The school takes part
in INCAS and MIDYIS testing. Short course GCSE ICT is
taken by all pupils. Many pupils have individual music lessons and take music examinations through the Associated
Board of the RCM. LAMDA is offered in the Junior School,
leading to examinations. The Young Enterprise examination
may be taken by Company members.

Games. Hockey, Netball, Rounders, Tennis, Swimming,
Athletics, Short Tennis, Tag Rugby, Football and Trampolining are major sports.

Fees per term (2011-2012). £2,370–£3,360.

Charitable status. Derby High School Trust Limited is a
Registered Charity, number 1007348. It exists to provide
education for children.

Dodderhill School

Droitwich Spa, Worcestershire WR9 0BE
Tel: 01905 778290
Fax: 01905 790623
e-mail: enquiries@dodderhill.co.uk
website: www.dodderhill.co.uk

Founded in 1945, Dodderhill School is an independent day
school for girls from 3–16 years and boys from 3–7 years.

Governors:

Revd D Chaplin	Mr P Martin
Mrs L Cliff	Judge M D Mott
Mr N Goodman	Mrs R J Shearburn
Mrs L Grimer	Mrs G E Warman
Mrs K Hill	Mr D Watson
Mrs J E Lowe	Mr J Wheatley (*Chairman*)

Headmistress: Mrs C Mawston, BA Hons

Deputy Headmistresses:
Miss G Betteridge, CertEd
Mrs A Clancy, BEd Hons, DipRSA

Director of Studies: Mrs A Benigno-Thomas, BA Hons

Academic Staff:

Mrs J Allen Griffiths, BA Hons	Mrs S C Johnson, MEng Hons
Mrs S J Amos, BA Hons	Mrs S G R Loveday-Fuller, BEd Hons
Mrs E R Barnett, BA Hons	
Miss S Berwick, BA Hons	Mrs A L MacRae, BA Hons
Mrs R Bradley, BA Hons	
Mrs A Cartwright, BSc Hons	Mrs S Maciej, CertEd
	Mrs T Palmeri, BEd Hons
Mr P D Cross, BSc	Mrs C E Radcliffe, BSc Hons
Mrs J Feltham, CertEd	
Mrs H R Forecast, BEd Hons	Mrs J Randell, BA Hons
	Mrs C A Salter, BSc Hons
Mrs C German, BA Hons	Mrs C E Shepherd, BA Hons, MA
Mrs E J Hadley, BA Hons	Mrs C Vinson, BMus Hons
Mrs R Hatfield, BA Hons	Mrs S Young, BEd Hons

Administrative Staff:
Bursar: Mrs P A Lewis
Domestic Bursar: Mrs A Beaven
Headmistress's PA: Mrs Y Wood
School Secretary: Mrs A Lane
Matron: Mrs J Cameron-Price
ICT Technician: Mr C A Payne
Administrative Assistant: Mrs M Paget
Marketing Consultant: Ms R Key, BA Hons

Introduction. Dodderhill School is a non-denominational day school administered by a Board of Governors. The school provides a seamless education for girls aged 3 to 16 years and welcomes boys from 3 to 7 years. Small classes and experienced, motivated staff mean that pupils can achieve their academic and personal potential. Excellent pastoral care and a friendly, family atmosphere help pupils to build the confidence, self-esteem and maturity that will help them to continue to achieve in the world of post-16 and higher education.

Location. The school is set in its own grounds on the outskirts of Droitwich Spa and only minutes from the M5/M42 interchange. It serves families from Droitwich Spa, Bromsgrove and a wide area of North Worcestershire. Minibus transport is provided between school and Droitwich Spa station and many pupils take advantage of the excellent local rail network.

Facilities. A superbly designed foundation stage and junior block incorporating a spacious multi-purpose school hall complements the newly refurbished original Georgian buildings. An ongoing development programme instituted by the governors in 1998, included in March 2004 an exciting new Nursery providing babies and toddlers (6 weeks to 3 years) with the same warm, happy, caring and family friendly atmosphere enjoyed throughout the school. In 2008 a new building was opened providing further classroom accommodation and a new food technology room. During 2009 a second ICT room for use by teaching staff was completed and in October the redesigned and enlarged outside area for the Early Years Foundation Stage was opened. In 2009 and 2010 science laboratories were refurbished to provide the latest up-to-date facilities for girls in Years 4–11.

Curriculum and Teaching. From the Early Years until Year 3 emphasis is on literacy and numeracy and children are class taught with specialist input in ICT, French, Music, PE and, from Year 3, DT. From Year 4 all subjects are specialist taught and in Years 5 and 6 increasing use is made of senior facilities to ease transition and enhance learning opportunities. In Years 7, 8 and 9 in addition to the core subjects of English, mathematics, science, RE and PE, all girls learn French, German, geography, history, art, catering, ICT,

music and textiles. For GCSE all girls take English, mathematics, science, RE, a modern foreign language, history or geography and two additional subjects from a choice of a second foreign language, a second humanity and the creative subjects. Class sizes are small, expectations are high, teachers are well qualified and experienced and the individual is paramount. Results are excellent. Dodderhill is regularly at or near the top of the Government GCSE performance tables for Worcestershire. In 2010 the School topped the tables for the second successive year.

Extra-Curricular Activities. The school offers a stimulating and diverse range of extra-curricular opportunities. Creative arts, music, outdoor activities, including the Duke of Edinburgh's Award and sport are all catered for. Pre-school care is available at no charge from 8.00 am. There is an after-school club until 6 pm and a Holiday Club in the long holidays – a charge is made for these services.

Admissions and Scholarships. Formal entrance examinations are held in February each year for entry at 9+, 11+ and 13+. Two 11+ academic scholarships and an 11+ music scholarship are available at this time. Children may transfer from other schools at any time during the year and admission is then by taster day, examination and school reference. Entrance for younger children is by taster day and individual assessment.

Bursaries. The Board of Governors has set up a Bursarial Fund to widen access to Dodderhill by providing assistance to girls entering the school at Year 5 or later.

Fees per term (2011-2012). Tuition fees are from £1,820 in Kindergarten to £3,125 in the senior school, inclusive of lunches and textbooks. There is a 5% reduction for siblings.

Charitable status. Dodderhill School is a Registered Charity, number 527599. It exists to provide education for girls and boys.

Downe House

Cold Ash, Thatcham, Berks RG18 9JJ
Tel: 01635 200286
Fax: 01635 202026
e-mail: correspondence@downehouse.net
website: www.downehouse.net

Founded 1907.

Governors:
Chairman: Mr R Parry, BA
Dr C Alsop, MA, MB BS, MRCGP
Mr S Creedy-Smith, BA, ACA
Mr R C Farquhar
Mrs D R Flint, BA
Mr N Gold, FCA
Mrs J M Grant Peterkin
Ms F Hazlitt
Mr D S Jenkins, FCA
Mr C D Keogh
Mr M J Kirk
Mr A L Robinson
Mr S J Robinson, BA, FRSA
Mr J Stephen, BSc, FRICS
Mrs B N Wheeler

Headmistress: Mrs E McKendrick, BA Liverpool

Deputy Head: Mrs N Huggett, MA Oxon
Assistant Headmaster: Mr M Hill, BA Hull, MA Reading, MEd Open
Assistant Headmistress: Mrs T MacColl, MA Hons Aberdeen
Head of Sixth Form: Mrs L Elphinstone, MA Cantab
Head of Upper School: Mrs G Ford, BA Bristol

Head of Lower School: Mrs J Gilpin-Jones, LWCMD
   Royal Welsh College of Music and Drama
Director of Admissions: Mr K Simpson, BSc Leeds
Director of Co-Curricular Activities: Mr M Scott, BSc
   Brunel, BA Open, MA Open
Director of Information Systems: Mr S Finch
Director of External Relations: Mrs M Scott, BEd Brisbane

Housemistresses/Housemaster:
Hermitage House: Mrs S Haughey, MA London, MPhil
   Cantab
Hill House: Mrs F V Capps, CertEd Bedford College
Darwin: Mrs S Moore, BSc Newcastle
Veyrines (France): Mrs A Gwatkin, MA London
Aisholt: Mrs R Wilson, MA Cantab
Ancren Gate North: Mrs S Dixon, BA Leeds
Ancren Gate South: Mrs C Jones, BA Plymouth
Holcombe: Miss A Hamilton
Tedworth: Mrs W D Nurser, BA Birmingham
Willis House East: Mr J Long, BA Natal
Willis House West: Mrs V Ryan, BA Bangor
York House North: Mrs J Fletcher-Dyer, BA, BEd
   Queensland
York House South: Mrs K Simpson, MA Oxon

Heads of Department:
English: Mr L McBratney, MA Manchester
History: Mr A J Hobbs, MA Cantab
Classics: Miss L Hippisley, MA Camb
Religious Studies: Mr P Evans, BD London, MA London
Modern Languages: Mrs J Basnett, BA Westminster
Geography: Mr R Barnes, BSc Bristol
Social Sciences: Dr A R Mickleburgh, BA ANU, MPhil
   Sussex, PhD Cantab
Science: Mrs Y J Charlesworth, BSc Reading
Biology: Miss C M Pugsley, BSc Warwick
Chemistry: Mr A Reynolds, BSc Loughborough
Physics: Mrs V Owen, BSc York, PGCE Open
Mathematics: Mr R S Barnes, BSc East Anglia
ICT Coordinator: Mrs D Evans, BSc Oxford Brookes
Technology: (*to be appointed*)
Music: Mr A B Cain, ARAM, FTCL, FLCM, LRAM,
   ARCM
Art: Mrs S J Scott, BA Central England
Drama & Theatre Studies (Acting): Mrs D L Fallon, BA
   Cardiff, MA RADA/KCL
Physical Education: Mrs L J M Rayne, BEd Brighton

Photography: Miss N Bloor, MA Wales
Personal & Social Education: Mrs N Riddle, B PhysEd
   Dunedin NZ
Learning Support: Mrs T Evans, BA, DipSpLD, RSA
   TEFL
Careers: Ms M Akhtar, BA, MA Lucknow, India

Chaplain: Revd Dr Simon Thorn
Medical Department: Mrs R Nicklin, RN

Numbers on roll. 531 Boarding girls, 28 Day girls.
Age Range. 11–18.
   Downe House is situated in 110 acres of wooded grounds,
five miles from Newbury and within easy reach of Heathrow
Airport. The school's proximity to the Universities of
Oxford and Reading allows the girls to take part in a rich
variety of activities outside the school.
   Buildings. There are Junior Houses for girls aged 11+
and 12+, and five recently refurbished mixed-age Houses
for those between 13 and 16. When girls enter the Sixth
Form they move into one of two Sixth Form Houses where
they have twin-shared or single study-bedrooms and facilities appropriate to their needs. All the Housemistresses are
members of the teaching staff and are responsible for the
coordination of the academic, pastoral, social and moral
development of the girls in their care.

The school buildings include up-to-date Science Laboratories, an Art School, Design and Technology suite, a Music
School, an indoor Swimming Pool and Squash Courts and a
Library. The games facilities are excellent; a Sports Centre
and new all-weather pitch. The school also has a Performing
Arts Centre and a Concert Room which are used for lectures, concerts and plays, and a new recording studio.
   Religion. Downe House is a Church of England school
having its own chapel, which girls attend for daily prayers
and for a service of either Matins or Evensong on Sunday.
Holy Communion is celebrated once a week and girls are
prepared for confirmation if they wish. Other denominations
are welcome. Girls can go to mass on Sundays and are prepared for Roman Catholic Confirmation.
   Curriculum and Activities. The curriculum includes the
study of English, History, Geography, Religious Studies,
French, German, Spanish, Italian, Latin, Greek, Mathematics, Physics, Chemistry, Biology, Design and Technology,
Information & Communication Technology, Music, Art,
Drama and Theatre Studies, Food and Nutrition and Textiles. In addition, Classical Civilisation, Business Studies,
Sports Science, Politics, Economics, Photography and History of Art are offered at A Level or Pre-U, as well as Global
Perspectives and writing a 5000-word Independent Research
Report. Leiths Food & Wine Certificate is also offered to
girls in the Sixth Form. Girls are prepared for GCSE,
IGCSE, AS, A Level and Pre-U examinations, with all girls
going on to University or some other form of Higher Education.
   ICT skills are developed across the years with all girls
following a general ICT course. All girls have an e-mail
address.
   All girls in the Lower Fourth, aged 12, spend a term at the
School's House in France in the Dordogne, to study French
and increase European awareness.
   Careers Specialists give help to the girls in selecting their
careers and a Careers Resource Centre is available to all
ages.
   There are many extra-curricular activities, including a
variety of musical instruments, Fencing, Drama, Sub Aqua,
Pottery, Photography, Art, Craft, Singing, Speech & Drama
Training, Cookery, Dance (Tap, Modern, Ballet, Hip Hop,
Street) and Self-Defence. There is a regular programme of
varied weekend activities, including the Duke of Edinburgh's Award Scheme. Expeditions abroad such as World
Challenge, which develops leadership qualities, are offered
alongside Young Enterprise which offers an insight into
business practice in the UK.
   Fees per term (2011-2012). £10,010 for Boarders and
£7,245 for Day Girls.
   Admissions. Girls may enter the school at 11+, 12+ or
13+ after assessment, interview and Common Entrance. A
few girls annually are given places in the Sixth Form after
interview and entrance test.
   Application for entry should be made well in advance.
Prospective parents are asked to make an appointment to see
the Headmistress, at which time they are offered a comprehensive tour of the school.
   Scholarships. (*See Scholarship Entries section.*) The
School offers a number of Academic Scholarships at 11+,
12+, 13+ and for entry into the Sixth Form. Scholarships are
also awarded in Music, Art and Drama (13+ and 16+ only)
and there are Head's Scholarships awarded to outstanding
all-round performers.
   Alumnae Bursaries are available for the daughters of
alumnae if their parents are in need of financial assistance.
   Full Bursaries. The School is able to award a small number of full means-tested Bursaries for girls to join the School
at 11+, 12+ or 13+. Girls should be able to meet the entry
requirements and benefit from a busy boarding environment.
   Charitable status. Downe House School is a Registered
Charity, number 1015059. Its aim is the provision of a sound

and broadly based education for girls, which will fit them for University Entrance and subsequently for a successful career in whatever field they choose.

Dunottar School

High Trees Road, Reigate, Surrey RH2 7EL
Tel: 01737 761945
Fax: 01737 779450
e-mail: info@dunottarschool.com
website: www.dunottarschool.com

Day School for Girls.

Trustees:
Chairman: Miss J Buchan
Mrs A Gabb
Mrs D-A Hammond
Mr D Martin
Miss S Pattenden
Mr N Pinks
Mr T Seckel
Mr R Wilman
Mrs M Young

Headmistress: Mrs N Matthews, BSc Hons Sheffield, PGCE Liverpool

Senior Management:
Assistant Head – Pastoral Care & Welfare: Mrs L Hale, BA Hons Lampeter, PGCE
Assistant Head – Teaching & Learning: Mr J N Walker, MA Manchester, BSc Hons St Andrews, PGCE
Head of Junior Department: Miss C Macleod, MSc Leicester, BA Glasgow, PGCE, DipM Strathclyde
Director of Sixth Form: Mrs M Gannon, BEd Hons London, CertEd
Director of Academic Support: Mrs M Kennedy, BA Hons Newcastle, PGCE, CFPS Bristol, ACCEG Kent
Bursar: Mr S Heald, FCA

* *Head of Department*

English Department:
*Mr A Simmons, MA Greenwich, BA Hons London, PGCE
Mrs L Hale, BA Hons Lampeter, PGCE
Miss T Katesmark, BA Hons Surrey, PGCE (**Theatre Studies*)
Ms K Lewis, MBA De Montfort, BEd Hons Sunderland
Mrs T Munro, BEd Hons Leeds, PGCE
Mrs C Turner, BA Hons London, PGCE

Mathematics Department:
*Mrs L Smith, BSc Hons Oxford, PGCE
Mrs M Gannon, BEd Hons London, CertEd
Miss S Gough, BA Rhodes, S Africa, GRSM Hons, MMus Performance, LRSM, ARCM, FTCL, HDE Cape Town QTS
Mrs J Pardoe, MA Cantab, PGCE

Science Department:
*Mr H Loughlin, BSc Hons Durham, PGCE, CChem, MRSC, MCoT (*Senior Chemist*)
Miss P Wood, CBiol, MSB, CertEd (*Senior Biologist*)
Mr C Dew, BSc Hons Reading, PGCE
Mrs L Klein, BSc Hons, South Queensland Australia, Grad DipEd (*Senior Physicist*)
Mrs J O'Dwyer, BSc Hons Durham, PGCE
Mrs J Prothero, BSc Hons Leeds, PGCE (*PSE Coordinator, Biology*)
Mr J N Walker, MA Manchester, BSc Hons St Andrews, PGCE
Mr P Hazell, BSc Hons Imperial, MSc NELP, PGCE

Foreign Languages Department:
*Mrs B Collett, Maîtrise-ès-Lettres Aix-en-Provence
Miss S Gough, BA Rhodes, S Africa, GRSM Hons, MMus Perf, LRSM, ARCM, FTCL, HDE Cape Town (*Latin*)
Mrs B Jackson, BA Hons Loughborough, DipIL, PGCE
Ms S Saward, BA Hons London, LTCL, QTS, CELTA
Miss A-M Vaughan, BA Hons Durham, PGCE

Information and Communications Technology Department:
Mr J Lyne, HND Surrey, PGCE

Design and Technology Department:
Miss H Tekeste, BA Hons Chelsea College of Art, PGCE

Geography Department:
*Mr D Lock, BA Hons London, PGCE
Mrs S Thorne, BA Hons Leicester, PGCE

Economics and Business Studies Department:
Mrs N Wintle, MA Oxon, PGCE

History Department:
*Mrs J Boden, MA St Andrews, PGCE
Mrs M Kennedy, BA Hons Newcastle, PGCE, CFPS Bristol, ACCEG Kent

Sociology Department:
*Mrs J Boden, MA St Andrews, PGCE
Mrs N Wintle, MA, BA Hons Oxon, PGCE

Art and Design Department:
*Mrs S Emblem, BA Hons Wimbledon, PGCE
Mrs M Baker, BA Hons Bath Academy, PGCE

Music Department:
*Mr D Black, MMus Newcastle, BA Hons Berkley, BEd Hons, FTCL, LTCL, LGSM, LRSM, QTS (*Director of Music*)

Peripatetic Staff:
Miss N André, MMus Hons RNCM (*Piano*)
Miss R Calaminus, BA Hons Cantab, LRAM, DipPG Perf RAM (*Violin*)
Miss K Eves, MMus, BMus Hons Manchester, GRNCM, PPRNCM (*Piano*)
Mr M Hobson (*Percussion*)
Mr R LeServe, ALCM, LLCM (*Clarinet, Saxophone*)
Mr E Maxwell, BA Hons, DipRCM, TCL (*Brass*)
Mr G Morrison, GGSM, Dip Adv Studies Perf (*Flute*)
Mrs A Morse-Glover (*Recorder*)
Miss L Nagioff, DipNCOS (*Violoncello*)
Mr B Rest, MMus London, GCLCM (*Guitar*)
Mr C Thompson, BA Hons East Anglia, MTC (*Voice, Piano*)
Miss C Walford, AISTD Dip (*Dance*)

Physical Education Department:
*Mrs T Lock, BEd Hons De Montfort
Mrs E Pieters, BA Hons Brighton, QTS
Miss L Upchurch, BEd Hons Brighton, QTS

Religious Studies Department:
*Mrs A Runcorn, BA Hons Southampton, PGCE

Home Economics Department – Food Technology:
Mrs J Prothero, BSc Hons Leeds, PGCE (*PSE Coordinator*)

Careers & Work Experience:
Mrs M Gannon, BEd Hons London, CertEd (*Sixth Form*)

Junior Department:
*Miss C Macleod, MSc Leicester, BA Glasgow PGCE, DipM Strathclyde
Miss N Callaghan, BA Hons Maynooth, Ireland, PGCE
Mrs A Dempster (*Teaching Assistant*)
Mrs E Denny, BA Hons Leicester (*Music*)
Mrs L Doughty (*Teaching Assistant*)
Mrs N Dryburgh (*Teaching Assistant*)
Mrs J Embury, BEd Hons West Sussex Inst HE, CNAA

Mrs L Caley, NAMCW Diploma
Miss A Lawrence (*Teaching Assistant*)
Mrs M McIntyre, BEd Hons Cheltenham, CNAA
Mrs L Nicholson, BEd Hons Avery Hill, CertEd
Mrs D Read, BSc Hons Reading, PGCE
Miss J Stokes, BA Hons Bristol, PGCE

Support Staff:
Headmistress's PA, Admissions Secretary: Mrs S Edwards
Special Needs Coordinator: Mrs A Aylwin, RSA Dip
  SpLD
Marketing Officer: Mr M Robinson, BTech Brunel, PGCE
Assistant Bursar: Mr S Carey
Bursar's Secretary: Mrs P Kerven, BA Hons University
  College London
Financial Controller: Mrs S Fribbance
School Secretary: Mrs J Jones
School Matron: Mrs L Kelly
Laboratory Technician: Mrs S Evans
Laboratory/Art & DT Technician: Mrs S Machacek
After-School Care Supervisor: Miss A Lawrence
IT Systems Manager: Mrs S Ameen, BSc Hons
  Southampton, AIEE

Dunottar is a day school for girls between the ages of 3
and 18. The School was founded in 1926 and became an
Educational Trust in 1961. It is situated in 15 acres of gardens and playing fields on the outskirts of Reigate, convenient to mainline stations and bus routes. Development over
the years has provided additional classrooms, art and design
& technology studios, careers room, Assembly hall, music
rooms, Sixth Form common room and 25-metre heated
indoor swimming pool. The school is fully networked and
has three dedicated computer suites. A Science Block
opened in the early 1990s, followed by a block of eight
classrooms in 1997. A major development programme has
also provided a sports hall, sixth form facilities, library and
art studios.

Aim. The School's aim is to ensure that we provide an
inspiring, happy and fulfilling place of learning for every
girl. She will be taught and encouraged to work hard, to discipline herself, to make the most of her opportunities, while
recognising and responding to the needs of others. In June
2008 the School received an outstanding Ofsted inspection
for every aspect of education in the Nursery and Reception
class. High standards of behaviour are maintained. Parents
receive detailed reports twice yearly and have regular opportunities to discuss progress with teachers. Appointments can
be made at any time to see the Head. There is a flourishing
Friends' organisation.

Religion. The School holds the Christian ethos paramount and welcomes children from any denomination or
none.

Curriculum. Eighteen GCSE and nineteen A Level subjects are on the curriculum, which is planned to provide a
broad education and to preserve a balance between arts and
science subjects. Early specialisation is avoided, though
some subject options become necessary from the beginning
of the GCSE year. Subjects include Religious Studies,
English Language and Literature, French, German, Spanish,
Latin (Years 7 to 9), History, Geography, Mathematics, Biology, Physics and Chemistry taught for Science and Additional Science examinations and also as separate subjects,
Business and Economics, Design & Technology, Information and Communications Technology, Physical Education,
Theatre Studies, Home Economics, Music, Art & Design
and Sociology. The School has strong sporting and music
traditions. Teaching is given in a wide range of musical
instruments and girls are encouraged to join the School
orchestras and music groups. There are a number of School
choirs. Instruction is available in Speech & Drama, in
Dance, and in a wide variety of musical instruments. Drama
and music performances are given frequently. There are
excellent on-site games facilities including a large indoor

heated swimming pool and playing fields. A great number
of extra-curricular activities are provided and the School
participates most successfully in The Duke of Edinburgh's
Award Scheme at Bronze, Silver and Gold levels.

Careers. Advice is provided at each key stage of education. Girls are encouraged to research and discuss career
plans and opportunities with staff and work experience is
offered in a variety of careers.

Physical Education. Sports and games are an important
part of School life, and there are excellent facilities for tennis, badminton, rounders, lacrosse, netball, volleyball, croquet, gymnastics, athletics and swimming.

Examinations taken. GCSE and A Levels, Associated
Board of the Royal School of Music, London Academy of
Music and Dramatic Art, Imperial School of Dancing, Royal
Society of Arts.

Admissions. 11+ entrance examinations are held in January prior to entry the following September. Early application
is advised. Girls are accepted directly into the Sixth Form.

Fees per term (2011-2012). Range from £2,400 (Nursery) to £4,200 (Year 7 to Upper Sixth).

Scholarships. Academic Scholarships are awarded annually at 11+ and 13+ to those girls who reach the highest standard in the entrance tests, effective for five and three years
respectively. 16+ scholarships will be awarded to those girls
who reach a high standard in the scholarship papers. The
16+ scholarship examinations take place in November.

Music Scholarships at 11+, 13+ and 16+ are offered to
pupils who show exceptional promise and talent in Music,
effective for seven, five and two years respectively to the end
of the Upper Sixth.

The School offers Sports Scholarships to girls who show
exceptional talent and promise in at least two sports. The
awards are offered at 11+, 13+ and at 16+, effective for
seven, five and two years respectively to the end of the
Upper Sixth.

Art and Design Scholarships are offered at 13+ and 16+
to pupils who show exceptional talent and promise in either
Art, or Design & Technology, or both, effective for five and
two years respectively to the end of the Upper Sixth. Assessments take place in November.

All scholarships are offered to both new and current
pupils except for the prestigious John Zinn Scholarship,
which is awarded annually to a current prospective Sixth
Form student on the basis of academic performance and
contribution to the life of the school.

Further particulars may be obtained from the Headmistress's PA who will also arrange an appointment to visit the
school and meet the Head.

Charitable status. Dunottar School Foundation Limited
is a Registered Charity, number 312068. It exists to provide
high quality education for girls.

Durham High School for Girls

Farewell Hall, Durham DH1 3TB
Tel: 0191 384 3226
Fax: 0191 386 7381
e-mail: enquiries@dhsfg.org.uk
website: www.dhsfg.org.uk

Governors:
Mr W Hurworth (*Chairman*)
Professor J Barclay
The Rt Revd Mark Bryant, The Bishop of Jarrow
Mr S Cheffings
Mrs A M Chapman, BA
Mrs M Cummings, BA
Mr K Delanoy, FCCA
Mrs D Dunsford
Mrs V Hamilton, MA, MEd

Mrs D Hedley, MB BS, MRCP, MRCGP, DCH
Captain M Hill
Revd Canon Kennedy
Mrs G Prescott, BVM&S, MRCVS

***Acting Head*: Mr A Whelpdale**, BA Wales, NPQH

Assistant Heads:
Mrs L Ibbott, BA Cardiff (*English*)
Mrs I Woodland, MA Cantab (*Geography*)

Head of Junior House: Mrs G Settle, BEd Leeds

Bursar: Mrs S Ruskin, FCA

Director of Marketing and Development: Mrs K Anderson, BEd Nevilles Cross

Senior House:
Mrs C Ackerley, BA Dunelm (*Psychology*)
Dr N Alvey, MPhys, PhD Kent (*Physics*)
Mrs S Baker, MA Cambridge (*Music*)
Mrs T S Bickerdike, BSc Dunelm (*Mathematics*)
Mrs K Breckon, BEd Hons Bedford (*Physical Education*)
Dr R A Brinham, BSc Hons Dundee, PhD Bristol (*Chemistry*)
Mrs M I Brown, BA Hull, MSc LSE (*History*)
Mrs R Bruce, BA Oxon (*French, German*)
Mrs C Cardy, BDes Ulster (*Textiles*)
Mrs P G Clarke, BSc Cork (*Physics, PSHE, Citizenship*)
Miss G Colon, BA Hons London (*Modern Languages*)
Mrs J Coxon, BEd Liverpool (*Physical Education*)
Mrs C I Creasey, BA Dunelm (*Geography*)
Mrs V M Dyson, BA Dunelm (*LTCL, Music*)
Mrs S A Egglestone, BEd Dunelm (*ICT*)
Mrs D L Elliott, BSc Dunelm (*Biology*)
Mr C Everett, BA Leicester (*Business Studies*)
Mrs J Flavell, MA Cambridge (*Chemistry*)
Mrs C Gamble, BA, MA Cambridge (*Mathematics*)
Mrs E Gentry, BSc St Andrews (*Science*)
Dr S Grant, BSc Newcastle (*Chemistry*)
Mrs S Harrison, BA Hons Dunelm (*Geography*)
Mrs A Hawkins, BA London (*English, Sociology*)
Mr P Hitchcock, BA Sunderland (*Art*)
Mrs J Huish, BA, MA Dunelm (*Classics*)
Mrs J M Hush, BSc Open University (*Mathematics*)
Miss K Jackson, BA Manchester (*History & Economics*)
Mrs M Kenyon, BSc York (*Chemistry*)
Mrs A Lee, BA Manchester (*Learning Support*)
Mrs J Lonsdale, BA, MA Leeds (*Drama*)
Mr T Lonsdale, BA Leicester (*French, German*)
Mrs S May, BEd Cheltenham and Gloucester (*Physical Education*)
Mrs L Middleton, BA Dunelm (*Religious Studies*)
Mr J Neeson, MA Manchester (*Art*)
Mrs J Newby, BSc Warwick (*Biology*)
Mr J Priest, MSc Bath (*Mathematics*)
Mrs D Rabot, MA Ed Sunderland (*ICT*)
Mrs K Rochester, BA Hons Northumbria (*Physical Education*)
Mrs J V Slane, BSc Surrey (*Physical Education*)
Mr D Smith, MA Oxon, CertTh York (*History*)
Mrs M Thomas, MA St Andrews (*French, German*)
Ms D Todd, BA Hons Sunderland (*English*)
Mrs J Tomlinson, BSc Newcastle (*Biology*)
Revd B Vallis
Mr A Woodward (*Multi Sports Coach*)
Mrs D Woodman, BA Newcastle (*Classics*)
Miss R Wright, BA Newcastle (*English*)

Junior House:
Mr P Allaker, BA Hons Dunelm
Mrs K A Anderson, BEd Nevilles Cross
Mrs E Brothers, BSc Sheffield (*Deputy Head*)
Mr R Dellar, MSc Birmingham
Mrs J Dilley, CertEd Sussex
Mrs P Everett, BEd Hons Cambridge

Mrs K A Hall, BA Central Lancashire
Mrs S Hart, BA Dunelm, MA Sunderland
Mrs C M Hopper, BA Nottingham
Mrs G H Hudson, BEd Bristol
Mrs L Mock, BA Dunelm
Miss L Pickering, BA Dunelm
Miss S Rose, BSc Wales, MSc London, MA Durham
Mrs L C Tallentire, CertEd Nottingham
Mr G Wright, BA Hons Sunderland

Junior House Support Staff:
Mrs A Maddison, NNEB Durham
Mrs C Gorman
Mrs M Marsden

Visiting Staff:
Miss V Bojkova, Diplomas in Conducting & Piano Performance (*Singing and Piano*)
Miss S Innes, BMus, LRAM (*Violin & Viola*)
Mr P Judson (*Bassoon*)
Mrs R Barton-Gray (*Cello*)
Dr L Hardy (*Flute*)
Mrs T MacLellan, CELTA, EAL
Mrs J Orchard (*Drum kit and Percussion*)
Mrs J Rousseau (*Oboe*)
Mr G Ritson, GRNCM, PPRNCM (*Brass*)
Miss R J Shuttler, BA, MMus, LTCL (*Piano*)
Miss C Smith, BA, FRSA (*Clarinet & Saxophone*)
Mrs B Fox (*Violin*)
Mrs J D Wakefield, Gold Medal LAM (*Speech & Drama*)

Administrative Staff:
Head's PA: Mrs A Thompson
SMT Secretary: Ms S Dawson
Marketing/Publicity Secretary: Mrs A Wright
Admissions Secretary: Ms L Brown
Librarian: Mrs J Durcan, ALA
Assistant Bursar: Mr B Craig
Accountant: Mrs K Atkinson
ICT Systems Manager: Mr J Kerton
ICT Technician: Mr P Cass
Receptionist: Mrs J Lathan
Catering Manager: Mrs A Hibbart
Laboratory Manager: Mrs M A Bartley, BSc Open University
Laboratory Technician: Mrs Gemski, BA Robert Gordon
Laboratory Assistants: Miss J Cummings, Mrs L Deveaux-Robinson
Reprographics Technician: Mrs C Gillham
Caretaker: Mr K Riding
Assistant Caretakers: Mr D Wilson, Mr P Tennant, Mr P Davis

Durham High School for Girls aims to create, within the context of a Christian ethos, a secure, happy and friendly environment within which pupils can develop personal and social skills, strive for excellence in academic work and achieve their full potential in all aspects of school life.
- Highly qualified, specialist staff.
- Excellent examination results.
- Continuity of education from 3 to 18 years.
- Entry at 3, 4, 7, 10, 11 and 16.
- Superb modern facilities include state-of-the-art Science/ICT/Library Block and Performing Arts Suite.
- Academic, Music, Performing Arts, Art, Drama and Sports Scholarships.
- Academy for Girls' Sport.
- Financial assistance available at all stages.
Number on roll. 591 day pupils.
Age range. Seniors 11–18; Juniors 7–11; Infants 4–7; Nursery from age 3.
Entry requirements. Assessment, formal testing and interview if age is applicable. Sixth form entry is dependent on the level of achievement at GCSE.

Junior House (age range 3–11). A purpose-built Nursery provides a stimulating environment for children aged 3–4 years. Children may start the day after their 3rd birthday. Early Years Funding available. Superb Outdoor Learning environment.

Junior House follows a topic-based curriculum linked to the National Curriculum which enables girls to enjoy every aspect of learning and discovery. Form teachers encourage and support a high standard of achievement in all areas of the curriculum and promote a feeling of warmth and security.

Extra-curricular activities include: Choirs, Instrumental Tuition, Young Textiles Group, Drama, Gymnastics, Hockey, Rounders, Netball, Tennis, Ballet, Chess, Karate, Dance and Drama. A range of sports fixtures are made with other schools.

The immediate environment plays an important role in stimulating learning and regular visits are made to the theatre, museums and places of educational interest.

Senior House Curriculum. The curriculum is designed to be enjoyable, stimulating and exciting, providing breadth and depth in learning.

* Wide choice of options at GCSE and Advanced Levels.
* Languages: French, German, Latin and Classical Greek.
* Separate Sciences.
* Personal and Social Awareness programme.
* Careers Education and Guidance.

Extra-curricular activities include regular visits abroad, foreign exchanges, visits to the theatre, art galleries, museums and concerts. There is also a thriving programme of Music, Drama and Sport, as well as a flourishing Duke of Edinburgh's Award scheme. Sixth Form students have the opportunity to spend one month's service in Lesotho.

The Sixth Form. The Sixth Form of 106 girls takes a full and responsible part in the life and organisation of the school. A wide range of A and AS Level subjects is available. Girls take 4 or 5 subjects in L6, 3 or 4 in U6.

Fees per term (2011-2012). Nursery £2,090, Infants (Reception–Year 2) £2,240, Juniors (Years 3–6) £2,475, Seniors (Years 7–13) £3,315.

Extra subjects. Speech and Drama and Music (piano, strings, brass, woodwind, singing).

Scholarships and Bursaries. Means-tested Scholarships are available at 7–9+.

At 11+ a number of academic Open Scholarships are offered and bursaries are available in cases of financial need. There is also the Barbara Priestman award of £600 per annum for daughters of practising Christians. Scholarships (Academic, Performing Arts, Sport and Music) are awarded at 11+ and financial help is available at all stages from age 11.

At 12–14+ Academic, Music, Performing Arts and Sport Scholarships are available.

At 16 there are a number of academic scholarships available to external and internal candidates. Music scholarships are also available at 16+, as well as Performing Arts, Sports and an Art Scholarship.

Transport. Transport is available from most local areas and the school is also accessible by public transport.

After School Care. After School Care is available until 5.30 pm and is free of charge.

Further information. The Headmistress is always pleased to welcome parents who wish to visit the school. For further information and a full prospectus please contact the School on: tel: 0191 384 3226; fax: 0191 386 7381; website: www.dhsfg.org.uk; e-mail: enquiries@dhsfg.org.uk.

Charitable status. Durham High School for Girls is a Registered Charity, number 1119995. Its aim is to create a friendly, caring community based on Christian values and to encourage academic excellence.

Edgbaston High School

Westbourne Road, Birmingham B15 3TS
Tel: 0121 454 5831
Fax: 0121 454 2363
e-mail: admissions@edgbastonhigh.co.uk
website: www.edgbastonhigh.co.uk

President: The Rt Hon Sir Stephen Brown, GBE, Hon LLD

Vice-Presidents:
Sir Dominic Cadbury, BA, MBA
Her Honour Judge Sybil Thomas, LLB

Council:
Chairman: Mr G H Tonks, BSc, FCA
Deputy Chairman: Mr J D Payne ARICS

Ms H J Arnold, BSc
Lord Bhattacharyya, KB, CBE
Mrs S A England Kerr
Mrs C Fatah, RGN
Mrs V J Fuller
Mr S Hampton
Mrs A E Howarth, CertEd, DipEd
Mrs D K Johnson, BCom Acc, FCA
Dr J Leadbetter, PhD, PGCE, BSc Hons, MEd Ed Psych, AFBPsS, CPsychol
Mrs V Nicholls, MCIPD
Mr I Marshall, BA
Dr J F C Olliff, FRCR
Mr G I Scott, MA

Representing the Old Girls' Association:
Mrs C Bell

Clerk to the Governors: Mrs M Osborn

School Staff:

Headmistress: Dr Ruth A Weeks, BSc, PhD Birmingham

Deputy Head Academic: Dr H M Gay, BSc, PhD London
Deputy Head Pastoral: Mrs J Coley, BA Reading

§ *Part-time*

Ms G Ajmal, BA Wolverhampton (*English*)
Miss H Barlow, BA Birmingham (*PE*)
Mrs L Batchelor, BSc Birmingham (*PE*)
Mr G Bateman, BA Sunderland (*Music*)
Mr D Berman, MA Oxford (*Chemistry*)
Miss A G Bosc, BSc Birmingham (*§Biology*)
Ms L Browning Goss, BSc Exeter, MA Leicester (*§Classics*)
Mr P M Brassington, BA Leeds, MSc Cranfield, MA Exeter (*§Business Studies*)
Mrs A M Brooks, BSc Brunel (*§Chemistry*)
Dr C Brown, BA London, MEd Birmingham, PhD (*Classics*)
Mrs C Cardollino, BA Leicester (*German*)
Mrs J Chalmers, BA York (*Mathematics*)
Mrs A Cirillo-Campbell, BA UCE Birmingham (*§ICT*)
Mr M Cleland, BEd Goldsmiths College London (*Drama & Theatre Studies*)
Dr F Cook, MA Cambridge, PhD Warwick (*Physics*)
Mrs M-P Dalal, BA Open University (*French/German*)
Mr M L Dukes, BA Wolverhampton Polytechnic (*Art*)
Mr S Durrant, BA, MA Durham (*English*)
Miss S Easton, MA Oxford (*Classics*)
Mrs C A Evans, CertEd Anstey (*§PE*)
Mrs S Flitter, BA Oxford, MA Oxon (*§Classics*)
Mr A Flox-Nievo, BA Castilla, Spain (*Spanish*)
Mrs J Forrest, BSc Open University (*§Biology*)
Mrs A E Gunning, BA, ACE Birmingham (*§§Spanish*)
Miss M Harper, GRNCM, ARMCM (*Music*)

Miss J P Harrison, BA Southampton, MA Birmingham
(*English*)
Mrs J Hayward, BSc Newcastle upon Tyne (*§Mathematics*)
Mrs G Hennesey, CertEd Bath College of FE (*HE, Textiles*)
Mrs S Hewison, BA Ed Exeter (*§PE*)
Mrs H Howell, GBSM, ABSM (*§Music*)
Mrs J K Hundal, BSc Birmingham (*§Chemistry*)
Mrs R Jackson-Royal, BA King's College London, MA
School of Oriental & African Studies, London
(*§Religious Studies*)
Mrs J Johnson, BA Aberystwyth (*§French/Spanish*)
Miss N Jones-Owen, BA Manchester Metropolitan
(*English*)
Miss N Khodabukus, MBiochem Oxford (*Chemistry/
Physics*)
Ms M Khuttan, BSc Keele (*Mathematics*)
Mrs A Lacey, BSc University of East Anglia (*Biology*)
Mrs P M Lampard, CertEd Bath College of HE (*HE,
Textiles*)
Mrs A Lee, BSc Birmingham (*ICT*)
Mrs C Lund, BD Wales, MA Cheltenham & Gloucester
College of HE (*Religious Studies*)
Mrs L Maile, BA Cambridgeshire College of Arts &
Technology (*§History*)
Mrs R J Matthews, BSc Aberystwyth (*Biology*)
Miss K Moffat, BA Liverpool (*Geography*)
Mrs L Mooney, BA Wolverhampton (*§Design Technology*)
Miss S Mullett, BA Nottingham (*Art*)
Mrs K E Newling, Birmingham (*Mathematics*)
Mrs R Norman, BSc Liverpool (*Mathematics*)
Mrs S Park, BA Cardiff, MPhil Cardiff (*§English*)
Mrs M S Petchey, BEd Leeds, MEd Birmingham (*French,
Spanish*)
Mr C J Proctor, BA Swansea (*English*)
Miss J Rance, BSc Birmingham (*PE*)
Miss F Richards, BSc Bristol, BA Birmingham Polytechnic
(*§Art*)
Miss R Richardson, BA Reading (*History*)
Miss R Richardson, LLAM, ALAM, Dip BSSD (*Drama*)
Mrs J Rodgers, BEd Worcester College of HE (*§ICT, Art*)
Mrs J Ruisi, BEd Sussex (*§PE, Psychology*)
Mrs J Shutt, BA Keele (*§ICT*)
Mr P Smith, BA Staffordshire (*Religious Studies*)
Mrs K J Stocks, BMus Birmingham, ARCM (*Music*)
Miss G Suter, BSc Cardiff (*PE*)
Miss A Taylor, BA Oxford, MSc Aston (*History*)
Miss R Thomas, BSc Bristol (*Physics*)
Mr M Tomaszewicz, BSc Birmingham (*Chemistry*)
Miss S E Vann, BEd De Montfort (*PE*)
Dr C Watts, BA, PhD Birmingham (*History*)

Librarian: Mrs S E Sansom, BA Bangor, MCLIP
Library Assistant/Examinations Officer: Mrs J Hall, BSc
Surrey

Language Assistants:
French: Ms M Romero
Mandarin: Mrs Y Shang
Spanish: Mrs C Nickson

Technicians:
Mrs C Harris
Mrs A Jan Mughal, BTEC HND
Mrs A Duvnjak, BSc Coventry, MSc Birmingham
Miss V Gutzmore, HND
Mrs S Griffiths

Network Manager: Mrs S Srinivas, MSc

Preparatory School:
Head: Mrs S Hartley, BEd Bristol
Deputy Heads:
Mrs S Alderson, CertEd City of Birmingham College of
Education
Ms K Gater, BA Manchester Metropolitan

Mrs A Aston, BSc, PGCE Birmingham
Mrs C Barrick, CertEd Bedford
Mrs A M Collins, BEd Birmingham, TCert Dudley College
of Education
Miss R Crawford, BSc Birmingham
Mrs S Draper, BSc Swansea
§Mrs S Dudley, CertEd Northumberland College of
Education
Mrs A L Gelderd, BSc Leeds
Miss L Hannabuss, BSc Birmingham
Miss A Hornsby, CertEd West London Institute
Mrs L Jervis, BSc Bangor
Mrs H Jones, BA Surrey
Miss L Jones, BA Swansea
Mrs J Knott, BA, PGCE Birmingham
Mrs M Macartney, BEd Worcester
Ms K McKee, BA Sussex, PGCE Warwick
Mrs C Paton, BA Exeter, PGCE UCE Birmingham
Miss C Robinson, BA Exeter
Mrs F Scott Dickins, BA London
Mrs A Stanley, BA Bath College of HE
Miss C Thiele, BMus Adelaide
Mrs F Watson, BA Leeds, PGCE Worcester
Mrs V Woodfield, BEd Birmingham

Classroom Assistants:
Mrs D Audley
Mrs C Mills
Mrs J Russon
Mrs M Bracey
Mrs H Coulson

Technician: Mr R Sejic
Secretary: Mrs L Barton

After-School Supervisors:
Mrs J Eyres
Mrs K Hancox
Mrs M Henry
Mrs M Rees
Mrs C Mills
Ms S Hunt

Pre-Preparatory Department:
Miss H Ashworth, BA, PGCE Carmarthen
Mrs L Bowler, BA Leicester
Miss R Deacon, BSc QTS Newman College Birmingham
Mrs A Hartland, BEd Birmingham, CertEd Dudley
Mrs D A Kennedy, BEd West Midlands College of HE
Miss V Walker, BA Warwick

Classroom Assistants:
Mrs R Aulak
Mrs E Barnsley
Mrs J Corbett
Miss E Cornelius
Mrs D Deakin
Mrs F Green
Mrs A Knight
Mrs A de Salis
Mrs K Thomas
Mrs P Varma

Visiting Staff:
Ballet: Miss D Todd

After School Supervisors:
Mrs D Audley
Mrs C Osborne

Special Subjects:

Head of Music Department: Miss M Harper, GRNCM,
ARMCM
Pianoforte:
Mrs J Gopsill, LRAM
Mrs H Howell, GBSM, ABSM
Mrs L Kitto, GBSM, ABSM, LTCL

Miss M Mugnaini, MA, LGSM, LRSM
Mrs C J Purkis, GBSM, ABSM, LRAM
Flute:
Mrs A Humphreys, ARCM
Miss H Jones, BA
Mrs S Wilson, BA
Oboe/Recorder:
Mrs K J Stocks, BMus, ARCM
Clarinet/Saxophone:
Miss C Pountney, LTCL
Bassoon:
Mr P Brookes, GBSM, ARCM, DipOrchStudies
Violin/Viola:
Miss A Chippendale, BMus
Mrs S Gough, BA, ARCM
Cello:
Miss J Carey, GRSM, ARCM
Double Bass:
Mrs N Rolinson, GBSM
Guitar:
Miss F Griffin, LGSM, LTCL
Miss L Larner BMus
Miss D Saxon Reeves, BMus
Singing:
Mrs S Allsop, ARCM, ABRSM
Miss S Purkis, BMus
Miss R Skinner, BA
Brass:
Mrs M Brookes, DRSAMD
Percussion:
Mr J Huxtable, BMus

Fencing: Professor P Northam, BAF

Facilities Manager: Mr S Watson, MHCIMA
Nurse: Mrs J Irving, RGN, SCM
Headmistress's PA: Ms G Franchi
Registrar: Miss A Scott

This independent day school, founded in 1876, attracts girls both from the immediate neighbourhood and all over the West Midlands. They come for the academic curriculum, the lively programme of sporting, creative and cultural activities, and for the individual attention and flexibility of approach.

Personal relationships at EHS are of paramount importance. Parents, both individually and through their association, give generously of their time to support our activities; while staff, through their hard work and good relationship with the girls, create an atmosphere at once orderly and friendly.

Organisation and Curriculum. There are three departments working together on one site which caters for over 950 day girls aged two and a half to eighteen. One of the features of EHS is the continuity of education it offers. However girls can be admitted at most stages. Staff take special care to help girls settle quickly and easily. Pupils enjoy a broadly based programme which substantially fulfils the requirements of the National Curriculum and much more.

The Pre-Preparatory Department, known as Westbourne, offers facilities for about 100 girls aged two and a half to five in a spacious, purpose-built, detached house. The staff aim to create an environment in which they can promote every aspect of a girl's development. A brand new Nursery (part of the new £4 million Octagon building) was opened in February 2005.

The Preparatory School accommodates over 350 girls from 5+ to 11 in up-to-date facilities, among them a new IT suite, Science Laboratory, Library and Design Technology Centre. A full curriculum, including English, Mathematics, Science and Technology, is taught throughout the department.

The Senior School caters for about 500 girls aged 11+ to 18. Girls follow a well-balanced curriculum which prepares them for a wide range of subjects at GCSE and Advanced Level.

Examination results are very good with high grades distributed across both Arts and Science subjects. All the girls in the Sixth Form of over 100 proceed to Higher Education. Every year girls obtain places at Oxford and Cambridge.

Extra Curricular Activities. Girls can take part in a broad range of activities including art, ceramics, dance, drama, Duke of Edinburgh's Award, music, sport and Young Enterprise. There are clubs during the lunch hour and after school. Instrumental music lessons are available. There is a strong music tradition in the school. Girls go on visits, expeditions and work experience in this country and abroad. We encourage girls to think of the needs of others.

Accommodation. There is a regular programme of improvements to the buildings. The Pre-Preparatory and Preparatory Departments have recently been refurbished and the Music Department doubled in size. In 2005 the Sixth Form Centre was completely refurbished. An exciting new multi-purpose hall, The Octagon, was opened in February 2005. A floodlit all-weather surface was opened in Summer 2006. The school has its own indoor swimming pool, 12 tennis courts and 8 acres of playing fields. Work on extended Sixth Form accommodation, a new library and fitness suite, at a cost of £3.5m, was completed in January 2011.

Location. The school is pleasantly situated next to the Botanical Gardens in a residential area, 1½ miles south-west of the city centre. It is easily accessible by public transport and also has its own privately run coaches.

Fees per term (2011-2012). Pre-Prep: £1,305 (mornings to 11.45 am), £1,413 (mornings to 1.00 pm), £2,064 (5 days); Prep £2,136–£3,000; Senior £3,176.

Scholarships and Bursaries. (*See Scholarship Entries section*.). Scholarships are available at 11+ and 16+, including two for Music (see relevant section). Sport and Art Scholarships are also offered in the Sixth Form. A bursary fund exists to help girls enter at 11+ and the Sixth Form and to assist those whose financial circumstances have changed since they entered the Senior School.

Further information. Full details may be obtained from the school. Parents and girls are welcome to visit the school by appointment.

Charitable status. Edgbaston High School for Girls is a Registered Charity, number 504011. Founded in 1876, it exists to provide an education for girls.

Farlington School

Strood Park, Broadbridge Heath, Horsham, West Sussex RH12 3PN
Tel: 01403 254967
Fax: 01403 272258
e-mail: office@farlingtonschool.net
website: www.farlingtonschool.net

Founded 1896.
    Motto: *Vive ut Vivas*

Governing Body:
Council of twelve members
Chairman: M Simpkin, OBE

Headmistress: Mrs J Goyer, MA, PGCE

Deputy Head: Miss L Higson, BSc, PGCE

Assistant Head (Academic): Mrs A Binns, BA, PGCE

Assistant Head (Pastoral): Mrs A Higgs, BEd

Head of Prep School: Mrs J Baggs, BEd, CertEd

Deputy Head of Prep School: Mrs S E Povey, BEd, CertEd

Bursar: Mr R Bosshardt, MCIPD, BSc, MSc

Registrar: Mrs E Healy

Boarding Staff:
Mrs K McKinney, BA
Mrs V Kelly, BA
Mrs Y Crook
Mrs J Humphreys

Nurses:
Mrs C Parsons, RGN
Mrs C Agranoff, RGN, BA, PGCE

The School. The official foundation of Farlington School (then Farlington House) was in 1896 at Haywards Heath. The School moved to its present site in 1955. It is situated in 33 acres of beautiful parkland on the Sussex-Surrey border. It has two lakes, sports and recreational facilities.

Farlington has approximately 400 girls aged from 3 to 18. Girls can board from the age of 8, on a full, weekly or occasional basis, or attend as day girls. All are equally important members of the School community. In September 2008 our new Courtyard Building opened, designed to complement the existing Prep School building which opened in 1997. This offers facilities for our new co-educational Nursery Class for children aged 3–4 years. The new building also includes further classrooms, a multi-purpose hall, a kitchen, a library and administration offices. Girls at Farlington also enjoy a purpose-built Science Building, a Sports Hall with facilities for badminton, volleyball, netball and basketball, a floodlit all-weather hockey pitch, and a modern Sixth Form Centre.

Farlington received an Independent Schools Inspectorate report in January 2011. Farlington was rated excellent/outstanding in every standard. The report includes the following two quotes: "An overall excellent curriculum and outstanding teaching enable preparatory and senior school pupils to achieve excellent all-round standards." "As a result of excellent guidance pupils exhibit outstanding personal development. The school is successful in fostering individuality, pupils are happy, succeed and flourish, and relationships are very positive. It is a very friendly, welcoming school."

Curriculum. We aim to provide a broad and balanced curriculum for all age groups. Our academic standards are high, and we encourage girls to raise their own expectations of achievement. Our approach involves good teaching practice coupled with clearly set targets and positive encouragement throughout every girl's school life. The rewards are excellent examination results: in 2010 a 100% pass rate at A Level with 80% at grades A*–B, and 95% overall pass rate at grades A*–C at GCSE. Over 95% of our sixth formers go on to the university of their first choice.

Important though academic standards are, Farlington is about more than examination results: we aim to educate the whole child. We are concerned to encourage spiritual, physical and personal development, as well as academic achievement.

Spiritual awareness, care for others, tolerance and compassion are the basis of our religious education. We are a Church of England foundation, but we welcome all faiths. There is an assembly most weekday mornings, and boarders are given the opportunity to attend a service at a church of their choice on Sundays. Work for charity and service to the community are part of the ethos at Farlington.

Farlington's emphasis on care and guidance in personal development is underlined in our tutorial system. Each girl is placed in a tutor group where she is given individual attention. Tutors liaise with other members of the teaching staff, boarding staff (where appropriate) and parents. They monitor academic progress and extra-curricular activities. Each week a tutor period is devoted to the discussion of a wide range of topics within our Life Skills programme, including moral issues, personal relationships, health education and study skills.

Extra-Curricular Activities. Opportunities for pursuing activities of all sorts exist after school and during lunch hours. Some are physical activities, such as The Duke of Edinburgh's Award Scheme, trampolining, fencing; others are more creative like Art or Drama club. Musical activities are popular with numerous choirs, ensembles, orchestras and bands on offer. There is a strong drama and music tradition within the School, and three major productions are staged each year. A wide range of sporting activities is available and the School enjoys considerable success at county and national level in many sports. Other activities include Debating, Chess Club and Ballet. All girls are encouraged to take at least one activity, and there is also supervised prep until 5.45pm.

Admission. Admission is by the School's own entrance examination and interview.

Scholarships and Bursaries. (*See Scholarship Entries section*.) A variety of Scholarships is available at 11+, 13+ and Sixth Form entry.

The School offers means-tested bursaries for all prospective and current pupils from Year 5 upwards.

Fees per term (2011-2012). Tuition: Prep School £2,269–£4,054, Senior School £4,831. Boarding (in addition to Tuition fees): £2,728 (weekly), £3,054 (full).

Charitable status. Farlington School is a Registered Charity, number 307048. It exists to provide education for girls.

Farnborough Hill

Farnborough, Hampshire GU14 8AT
Tel: 01252 545197/529811
Fax: 01252 529812
e-mail: admissions@farnborough-hill.org.uk
website: www.farnborough-hill.org.uk

Founded 1889.
   Motto: *In Domino Labor Vester Non Est Inanis*

Board of Governors:
Sister E McCormack, RCE (*Chairman*)
Mr J Hull (*Deputy Chairman*)
Mrs S Bell
Mr T J Flesher
Mrs C E Hamilton
Mr M D Hoad
Miss M Holt
Mr J D MacMahon
Mrs D O'Leary
Mr S Nelson
Mrs G Rivers

Headmistress: **Mrs S Buckle**, BSc Exeter, MA, PGCE Reading, NPQH

Deputy Head: Mrs A Griffiths, BEd Roehampton, MA Surrey, NPQH

Assistant Head Teachers:
Mrs C Dales, BA Sussex, PGCE Reading
Mr B Waymark, BA, MA, PGCE Soton

Teaching Staff:
Miss G Adams, BSc Brunel, PGCE Reading (*Physical Education*)
Miss D Andrews, BSc Cardiff, PGCE Homerton (*Biology, Chemistry*)
Dr M Baker, MSc, PhD Reading (*Psychology*)
Mrs S Bond, BA Soton, CertEd Sheffield Hallam (*Art and Design*)
Dr M Bright, BSc Sierra Leone, MSc PhD Birmingham (*Chemistry*)

Mrs G Brocklehurst, BSc UWIST, PGCE OU
(*Mathematics*)

Mrs O Brophy, BSc LSE, PGCE Inst Ed (*English*)

Mr F Budge, BA OU, CertEd London, Dip BusEd
(*Information Technology*)

Mrs S Burtsell, CertEd Battersea (*Design and Technology*)

Mr P Butler, BA, PGCE Reading (*French, Classics*)

Mrs R Byrne, BA South Glamorgan Inst, Art TCert
Goldsmiths College (*Art and Design*)

Mrs S Camprubi-Reches, BA Barcelona, MEd Cardiff,
PGCE Barcelona (*Spanish*)

Mrs C Cantor, BA Bath, PGCE Oxon (*German*)

Mr N Cartledge, BMus, DipRCM London (*Music
Technology*)

Mrs R Cartledge, BMus Surrey (*Music*)

Miss E Casey, BA Exeter, PGCE Roehampton (*French,
Spanish*)

Mrs G Chapman, BSc, DipEd Reading (*Physics*)

Miss K Clarke, MA Cardiff, PGCE Bath Spa (*English*)

Mrs L Craven, BA Berkeley, MA Kent, PGCE Oxon
(*English*)

Mrs K Davis, BSc London, PGCE Surrey (*Mathematics*)

Mrs A de Winter, BA Liverpool, PGCE Lancaster
(*Careers*)

Mrs J Eckermann, BA Luton, PGCE Manchester Met
(*Spanish, German and French*)

Mr P Forrest-Biggs, MA London, QTS CfBT (*Classics*)

Miss K Gibson, BA QTS St Mary's (*Physical Education*)

Mrs L Glover, BEd, CertEd Manchester (*Religious
Education, English*)

Mrs C Goldsmith, BA W Surrey College of Art and Design
(*Art and Design*)

Mrs M Gosney, BA Hull (*French*)

Mrs S Gregory, MA Cantab, PGCE Moray House (*French,
Spanish, Italian*)

Mrs E-J Harrison, BA QTS Brighton (*Physical Education*)

Mrs F Hatton BEd London (*Biology and Chemistry*)

Mrs S Hayes, BSc Leicester, PGCE Ripon and York St
John (*Biology*)

Mrs S Haynes, BSc Imperial College, PGCE Reading
(*Chemistry, Physics*)

Mr J Hoar, BA Hull, PGCE Southampton (*History*)

Miss S Hunt, BA Reading (*Drama*)

Mrs L Hooper, BSc Liverpool, GTP Reading
(*Mathematics*)

Mr K Johnson, MA Cantab, DipEd Oxon (*Greek*)

Miss F Kelsey, BA QTS St Mary's (*Physical Education*)

Mrs S Macey, BSc UMIST, PGCE Cantab (*Chemistry*)

Mr S McSweeney, BA Liverpool, PGCE Liverpool Hope
(*Music*)

Mrs E Matthews, BA QTS Brunel (*Design and
Technology*)

Miss L Miller, BA Reading, PGCE UWE (*Economics*)

Mrs E Nelson, BSc St Andrews, CertEd Dundee
(*Mathematics*)

Mrs J Nix, BEd Winchester (*Design & Technology,
Information Technology*)

Miss D O'Laoire, MA Nottingham, PGCE King's College
(*Classics*)

Mrs A Payne, BSc Bath, PGCE Bristol (*Geography*)

Mrs V Peters, BA, PGCE Leicester (*Economics, Business
Studies, Geography*)

Mrs K Phillips, BA Reading, ALCM (*Music*)

Miss K Price, BA Bristol, PGCE Southampton (*History*)

Mr J Quinnell, BA Winchester, MA Durham, PGCE
Lancaster (*English*)

Dr S Rawle, MA, DPhil Oxon (*Physics*)

Mr A J Richardson, BA Cardiff, MA Southampton, PGCE
Leeds, CAES SEN Winchester (*Religious Education,
History and Maths*)

Mrs H Rix, BATh Maynooth, HDipEd Trinity College
Dublin (*Religious Education*)

Mrs D Robinson, BEd Central School of Speech & Drama
(*Drama*)

Mrs A Smith, MA Cantab, PGCE Cantab (*Mathematics
and ICT*)

Miss B Stevenson, BSc Wales, PGCE Plymouth
(*Geography*)

Mrs L Storrie, BSc Salford, PGCE Manchester (*Biology*)

Mr R Thain, BA UCA (*Design and Technology*)

Miss B Weeks, BA Birmingham, PGCE Southampton
(*Geography*)

Mr R Wellington, BA Exeter, PGCE Birmingham
(*Theology*)

Mrs M Williams, BSc LSE, PGCE Institute of Education
(*Mathematics*)

Mrs L Winch-Johnson, BA Hertfordshire, MSc, PGCE
Surrey, CCRS Dip Perf Coach Newcastle (*English,
Drama, Learning Support Coordinator*)

Librarian and Website Manager: Mrs J Wood, MA Cantab,
DipLIS London

Matron: Mrs C Wilding, RGN

Bursar: Cmdr A Woolston, CDipAF

Director of Admissions: Mrs C Duffin, BA Hons, FCIM
Chartered Marketer

Chaplain: Miss S Farmer, BA Hons, DipCounselling UEA,
MBACP

ICT Coordinator: Mr A Labuschagné

Examinations Officer: Mrs S Cahalane, BSc Hons

Farnborough Hill is a leading independent Roman Catholic day school for 525 girls aged 11 to 18. The school was established in Farnborough in 1889 by The Religious of Christian Education and is now an educational trust. It welcomes girls of all Christian denominations, other faiths or no faith, who are supportive of the ethos. Farnborough Hill is committed to the education of the whole person in a happy, caring Christian community in which each individual is valued.

Academic standards are high with students usually taking ten GCSE subjects. In the Sixth Form most students take four AS subjects in the Lower Sixth and three A Levels in the Upper Sixth. The vast majority then go on to Higher Education. The school is a member of ISCO and there is a well-equipped Careers department and a specialist Careers teacher.

Farnborough Hill offers a wide range of extra-curricular activities and is especially renowned for its reputation in music, sport, drama and art.

The school's impressive main house, once the home of Empress Eugenie, has had modern purpose-built facilities added. These include a sports hall, indoor swimming pool, newly refurbished laboratories, IT suites, art and design technology centre, a chapel and extensive playing fields.

Although within a few minutes' walk of both Farnborough Main and Farnborough North railway stations, the school is situated in 68 acres of parkland and woodland with magnificent views over the Hampshire countryside. Girls come from Hampshire, Surrey and Berkshire with many travelling by train or by school coach.

Admission and Scholarships. (*See Scholarship Entries section*.) Entry is by examination taken in January for the following September. The school offers academic, music and sports scholarships and also bursaries for parents who are in need of financial assistance.

Fees per term (2011-2012). Tuition: £3,725.

Further information. The prospectus is available from the Director of Admissions. The Headmistress is pleased to meet prospective parents by appointment.

Charitable status. The Farnborough Hill Trust is a Registered Charity, number 1039443.

Francis Holland School
Regent's Park

Clarence Gate, Ivor Place, London NW1 6XR
Tel: 020 7723 0176
Fax: 020 7706 1522
e-mail: admin@fhs-nw1.org.uk
website: www.francisholland.org.uk

Founded 1878.

Patron: The Right Revd and Right Hon The Lord Bishop of London

Council:
Chairman: Professor K Hoggart, BSc, MSc, PhD
Vice-Chairman: Mrs A Edelshain, BA, MBA, MCIPD
Professor C Carpenter, MA, PhD
The Revd J Cave Bergquist, BA
Miss E Buchanan, CVO, LLD, ARAgS
Mrs C Elliott, MA, MBA
Miss G Gourgey, BA
Mrs S Graham-Campbell
Dr B Hohnen, BSc, PhD, DClinPsy
Mr B Lenon, MA
Mr R Lewis, MA
Ms S Mahaffy, BA
Mrs B Mathews, BA, FCA
Miss S Ross, BSc, FInstP
Mr C Sheridan, FCIB, MSI
Professor J Yeomans, MA, DPhil

Bursar and Secretary to the Council:
Mr C W Martinson, BSc, MRICS
The Bursary, Francis Holland Schools Trust,
35 Bourne Street, London SW1W 8JA.
Tel: 020 7730 8359, e-mail: bursary@fhst.org.uk

Headmistress: Mrs V M Durham, MA Oxon

Senior Deputy Headmistress : Miss J B Addinall, MA Cantab

Deputy Headmistress (Pastoral): Mrs F J Forde, CertEd Dartford College

Director of Studies: Miss J Green, MA Cantab, MSc London

Head of Sixth Form: Mrs H L Forbes, BA Oxon, MA

Head of Year 7: Mr M Chiverton, BA, MA
Head of Year 8: Mrs S Bexon, BA Kings London
Head of Year 9: Miss V Bacon, BA Dunelm
Head of Year 10: Miss M Gustave, BA Montpellier, MA Montpellier
Head of Year 11: Miss C Mahieu, BEd Sydney

Teaching Staff:

Art:
Mrs Rosie North, BA Byam Shaw School of Art
Miss H Gardner, BA Hons Nottingham
Miss J Orr, BA NkU, MA Sussex
Miss A O'Toole, BA NSW
Miss V Taylor (*Pottery*)

Careers/Librarian:
Mrs J M McGinlay, BA Wales

Classics:
Mr S F Jenkin, MA Oxon
Miss J B Addinall, MA Cantab
Mrs J Cohen, MA Oxon
Miss H Baig, BA Cantab
Mrs A Hillier, MA Cantab

Economics:
Miss A M Conway, MA St Andrews
Miss J Green, MA Cantab, MSc London

English:
Miss E Williams, BA Leeds
Mrs N Foy, MA London
Mrs M Bachle-Morris, BA
Mrs K F Oakley, BA London
Mr A Smith, BA York
Miss L Wilkinson, BA East Anglia, MA City

Geography:
Miss S Hack, BA Portsmouth
Mrs F Forde, CertEd Dartford
Miss A Sainty, BA Queen Mary College

History:
Mr H Clayton, BA Liverpool
Mr M Chiverton, BA, MA
Miss V Bacon, BA Durham
Mrs H Forbes, BA Oxon, MA

History of Art:
Miss A O'Toole, BA NSW

Information Technology:
Mr P Phillips, BSc, CertEd Leeds
Miss V Rusu, BEd Alberta Canada

Mathematics:
Mrs A Martin, BSc UCL
Mrs J Merry, BA Reading
Miss N Murugan, BSc Heriot-Watt
Miss R Le Roux, BSc Nottingham Trent, MSc Essex
Miss R Francis, BSc Sheffield

Modern Languages:
Mrs B Edwards, BA
Mr N Gridelli, BA Bologna Italy
Miss A Senegas, MA Académie de Marseille
Herr R Diesel, Technische Universitat Berlin (*German*)
Miss M Gustave, BA Montpellier, MA Montpellier
Mrs R Pithouse, BA Lyon France
Mrs M Salvatierra Romero, BA Seville
Miss E Mazzon, BA Trieste
Miss M Sierra Fernandez, Deg Ed FFL Barcelona
Mrs F Boschi, AVCE

Music:
Mrs E Rolfe Johnson, BMus
Mr P Thorne, BA Oxon, MMus UEA
Miss K Taylor, BMus/BEd NSW Australia
Mr A Smith, BA York

Visiting:
Mr K Abbs, FTCL (*Clarinet/Saxophone*)
Ms F Firth, LTCL (*Voice*)
Ms L Friend, ARCM (*Flute*)
Mr E Hackett, LRAM (*Percussian & Drum*)
Mrs C Hall, LRAM (*Voice*)
Miss K Hodges, BMus, PG Dip
Mr O Lallemont, MA (*Accompanist*)
Miss R Lindop, LLCM, ARCM (*Voice*)
Ms J McLeod, ARCM (*Theory*)
Mr D Parsons, ARCM (*Guitar*)
Mr M Radford, ARCM (*Cello*)
Mr P Robinson, MA Camb (*Voice*)
Miss E Rolfe Johnson, MA, (*Violin & Viola*)
Ms J Schloss, BMus Qld (*Piano*)
Ms A Thwaite, BMus Guildhall (*Piano*)

Also visiting teachers for:
musical instruments, aerobics, kick boxing, ju jitsu, pottery, cookery, fencing, yoga and Alexander Technique, according to demand.

Physical Education:
Miss J Tucker, BEd Queensland University, Australia

Mrs S Drummond, CertEd Nevilles Cross Durham
Miss K Gallagher, BEd Canterbury
Miss C Mahieu, BEd Sydney, Australia
Miss J Laytham, BEd Newcastle, Australia
Miss C Barras, BSc Loughborough

Psychology:
Mrs T Chaimowitz, BA RAU South Africa

Religious Education:
Miss J Farthing, BA Bristol
Mrs Z Curtis, BA Durham
Mrs S Bexon, BA King's College

Speech and Drama:
Ms K Mount, BA Rose Bruford College

Science:
Mr F Murphy, BSc Cantab
Mr D Ward, BSc Nottingham Trent, MA Open University
    (*Physics*)
Mr J Peters, BSc Swinburne
Mr P Davy, BSc Bath, PGCE London, MA King's College
Miss R Francis, BSc Sheffield (*Biology/Chemistry*)
Dr A Welch, MChem Kent, PhD London (*Chemistry*)
Mrs K Wright, BSc Kingston

Art Technician: Miss N Stowell, BA Goldsmiths College
    London
ICT Technician: Mr S Andrews
Laboratory Technicians:
Mrs G Unwin, BSc Greenwich
Mrs N Kazemi, BSc North London
Mrs M Shah, BA Tribhuwan University Nepal
Examination and Database Administration Officer: Mrs S
    Gurini
Admissions Registrar: Mrs S Bailey
School Secretary: Mrs K Stevenson
PA to the Headmistress: Mrs D Fahy, BA Dublin City,
    MSc UCD
Caretakers:
Mr J Saguiguit
Mr C Alarcon Mejia
Mr P Kulatungage
Catering Manager: Mr S King
Learning Support: Mrs J Denniston, BA Edinburgh
School Counsellor: Mrs D Webb

There are about 450 day girls and entry by examination
and interview is normally at 11+, with a number joining at
16+ for the Sixth Form. The school was founded in 1878 and
is affiliated to the Church of England, but girls of all Christian denominations and other faiths are accepted.

Curriculum. Girls are prepared for GCSE, A and AS
Levels, and for admission to Universities, and Colleges of
Art, Education and Music. Games are played in Regent's
Park and full use is made of the museums, theatres and galleries in central London. Extra lessons are available in fencing, music, pottery, Speech and Drama, Alexander
Technique, kick boxing, ju jitsu, and cookery. For the first
five years, to GCSE, girls follow a broad curriculum and
normally take 10 GCSE subjects. Careers advice is given
from the third year, and all pupils receive individual guidance through to the Sixth Form. In the Sixth Form a wide
choice of Advanced Level subjects is combined with a general course of study. All girls are expected to stay until the
end of the Advanced Level course.

Scholarships and Bursaries. (*See Scholarship Entries
section.*) These competitive awards are given each year:

At 11+ entry: One Academic Scholarship and one Music
Scholarship, each of value up to 25% of the current school
fee for seven years.

Sixth Form: Two Academic Scholarships of value up to
50% of the current school fee for two years and one Music
Scholarship of value up to 25% of the current school fee for
two years.

The school is able to offer a limited number of bursaries
at entry to the school at 11+, of value of up to 100% of the
current school fee. These bursaries are means tested and
reviewed annually. Further information is available from the
Bursar.

Fees per term (2011-2012). £4,800.

Situation. The school is situated just outside Regent's
Park and is three minutes from Baker Street and Marylebone
stations. Victoria and Hampstead buses pass the school.

Charitable status. The Francis Holland (Church of
England) Schools Trust Limited is a Registered Charity,
number 312745. It exists to provide high quality education
for girls.

Francis Holland School
Sloane Square

39 Graham Terrace, London SW1W 8JF
Tel: 020 7730 2971
Fax: 020 7823 4066
e-mail: office@fhs-sw1.org.uk
website: www.francisholland.org.uk

Founded 1881.

Patron: The Right Revd and Right Hon The Lord Bishop of
    London

Council:
Chairman: Professor K Hoggart, BSc, MSc, PhD
Vice-Chairman: Mrs A Edelshain, BA, MBA, MCIPD
Professor C Carpenter, MA, PhD
The Revd J Cave Bergquist, BA
Miss E Buchanan, CVO, LLD, ARAgS
Mrs C Elliott, MA, MBA
Miss G Gourgey, BA
Mrs S Graham-Campbell
Dr B Hohnen, BSc, PhD, DClinPsy
Mr B Lenon, MA
Mr R Lewis, MA
Ms S Mahaffy, BA
Mrs B Mathews, BA, FCA
Miss S Ross, BSc, FInstP
Mr C Sheridan, FCIB, MSI
Professor J Yeomans, MA, DPhil

Bursar and Secretary to the Council:
Mr C W Martinson, BSc, MRICS
The Bursary, Francis Holland Schools Trust,
35 Bourne Street, London SW1W 8JA.
Tel: 020 7730 8359, e-mail: bursary@fhst.org.uk

Headmistress: Miss S J Pattenden, BSc Durham

Deputy Headmistress: Mrs A Hems, MA Oxon

Director of Studies: Mr P H Williams, BA Oxon

Senior School:

Full-time Staff:
Miss D Adams, BA Wellesley College USA (*History/
    English*)
Mr C Bartram, BSc Portsmouth (*Biology, Science*)
Mr P Bennett, BSc, MA Durham (*Natural Science/Maths/
    Philosophy*)
Ms M Bonnaud, Licence Montpellier (*French & Spanish*)
Miss E Boon, BA Oxon (*History*)
Miss P Broadhurst, BSc Durham, PGCE King's College
    (*Physics*)
Mr C Chisnall, BSc UCW Aberystwyth (*Computer
    Science*)
Mrs K Cronan, BA York (*English*)
Miss S Deadman, BEd Bedford (*Physical Education*)

Mr D Edes, BA Exeter (*Art*)
Mrs G Hammond, BA Sheffield (*Psychology*)
Mr M Hill, BA Durham, MSc London (*Geography*)
Miss D Kaleja, I and II Staatsexamen (*German*)
Mr M Kenny, BA Leeds (*Religious Studies*)
Ms H Lambert, BA London (*Classics*)
Miss M McLaren, BSc Glasgow (*Chemistry/Science*)
Mrs A Margetson, PECert, Australian CPE (*Physical Education*)
Miss D Powell, BA York (*Biology*)
Mrs C Remy-Miller, BSc, MSc France (*French*)
Ms A Sidwell, BA Liverpool (*Geography*)
Mrs K Sinnett, BA Cantab (*Mathematics*)
Miss A Stevenson, BA Durham (*French & Spanish*)
Dr N Upcott, BSc, PhD Leeds (*Physics, Science*)
Mrs K von Malaisé, MA Cantab (*English*)

Part-time Staff:
Dr G Allen, BA, DPhil Oxon (*Chemistrym, Science*)
Mrs J Banks, BA Durham (*English*)
Miss C Barras, BA Loughborough (*Physical Education*)
Miss S Bryant, BA Camberwell (*Art*)
Mrs L Carr, BA Leeds (*French & Spanish*)
Ms S Carr-Gomm, BA UEA, MA London (*History of Art*)
Ms J de Rome, BEd London, CertEd Homerton (*Art*)
Mrs M Gepfert, BA Essex, MSc (*Computing, Mathematics*)
Mrs P Homer-Norman, BA Exeter, MA (*English*)
Ms M Leaf, BA London (*Drama*)
Mme A Lenec'h, Licence Rouen, MA Connecticut USA (*French*)
Mrs S McGarr, BA, PGCE King's College (*Classics*)
Mrs V Mrowiec, BEd Liverpool (*Physical Education*)
Mrs E Nash, BA London (*Spanish*)
Ms D Ortega, MA London (*Spanish*)
Miss M Pryce, BA, MA Sydney Australia (*English*)
Dr B Snook, BA, PhD Cantab (*History*)
Ms M Tetzlaff, BA, MTheol London (*Religious Studies*)
Mr C Thomas, MA Edinburgh (*Religious Studies*)
Miss H Varty, BMus Birmingham, PGCSE Roehampton (*Music*)
Miss H Vickery, MA Cantab, DipRAM, LRAM (*Music*)
Mr K Wadsworth, BSc London (*Economics*)

Junior School:
Head of Junior School: Miss S Styles, BA Surrey, MA London

Full-time Staff:
Mrs V Adamson, BA OU, CertEd
Miss R Darr, BEd Queensland Australia, Cert Gifted Ed, NSW Australia
Mrs L Fairley, CertEd Lancashire
Miss E Gallagher, BEd, CertEd London
Miss M Gallagher, CertEd London, BA London, DipMathEd
Ms J Jeevanjee, Montessori Dip
Mrs N Mikac
Miss S Rideout, BA King Alfred's
Mrs S Roberts, CertEd London
Miss E Scatchard, BA London
Miss G Tabony, BA Roehampton
Miss C Wheeler, BA Nottingham, MA Courtauld Institute (*History of Art*)

Part-time:
Miss S Pope, BSc City
Miss K Taylor, BMus/BEd NSW Australia

Visiting Staff:
Ms G Bailey-Smith (*Jazz Dance*)
Mr Y Bouvy, CertAdvStudies, RAM, Diplôme d'État de Professeur de Musique Traversier (*Flute*)
Miss C Constable, MMus London, BMus, ABSM (*Cello, Piano*)
Miss B Corsi, FTCL (*Clarinet, Recorder, Piano*)
Miss A Cviic, BA, PGDipRCM (*Singing*)

Mr J Godfrey, BMus, PGDipRCM (*Percussion*)
Mrs V Hitchen, RBS, TTCDip, Children's Examiner, RAD (*Ballet*)
Miss M Leaf, BA London (*Speech & Drama*)
Mr S Mantas (*Chess*)
Mr M Mason (*Cricket*)
Ms A Moore, ARCM, DipRCM (*Harp*)
Mr P Moore, BMus, LRAM, LGSMD, DipRAM, PPRAM (*Piano*)
Mrs S Pratschke, MMus (*Singing*)
Mrs S Shaub, LRAM, GRSM (*Piano*)
Miss V Smith, BMus RCM (*Violin*)
Mr J Sparks, BA, MA, FCCM (*Guitar*)
Ms S Stewart, BMus, LRSM, PGDipRCM (*Singing*)
Miss V Taylor (*Pottery*)
Miss E Tingey, BMus (*Oboe*)
Mr R Turner, BMus (*Trumpet*)
Mr C Weale, BMus, PGDipRCM (*Piano*)
Mrs S Wykeham, BA Music (*Violin*)

Librarian: Mrs E Curran, BA, Dip Lib, MCLIP
Lab Technicians:
Mrs C Bradshaw
Mr P Bannister, BSc New South Wales
Computer Technician: Mr P da Costa, BSc
Registrar: Mrs J Ruthven, BA
School Secretary: Miss V Phillips

Numbers and age of entry. There are 450 Day Girls in the School and entry by the School's own examination is at 4+ for the Junior School (ages 4–11), 11+ for the Senior School (ages 11–18) (member of London Schools consortium) and 16+ for Sixth Form.

Curriculum and Aims. The school aims to provide a strong academic education and girls are prepared for GCSE, AS and A Level and admission to Universities and Colleges of Art and Music. Full advantage is taken of the school's proximity to museums and art galleries.

Junior School. There is a Junior Department attached to the school.

Religious Education. The school's foundation is Anglican but girls of other faiths are welcomed.

Physical Education. Hockey, Netball, Volleyball, Gymnastics, Athletics, Tennis and Swimming are taken. Senior girls have a choice of other activities as well including Squash, Step Aerobics, Jazz and Rowing. Optional activities open to girls are Kick Boxing, Fencing, Rowing and Jazz.

Fees per term (2011-2012). £4,210–£4,880.

Scholarships and Bursaries. (*See Scholarship Entries section.*) There are the following competitive awards each year:

At 11+: 1 Academic and 1 Music scholarship, both up to the value of 25% of fees.

Sixth Form: 4 Academic scholarships (3 internal, 1 external) up to the value of 50% of fees and 1 Music scholarship up to the value of 25% of fees for the two years leading to A Level.

3 up to full fees Bursaries are available at 11+ and one at 14+.

For daughters of Clergy there is a remission of one-third of the School Fee.

Charitable status. The Francis Holland (Church of England) Schools Trust Limited is a Registered Charity, number 312745. It exists to provide high quality education for girls.

Gateways School

Harewood, Leeds LS17 9LE
Tel: 0113 288 6345
Fax: 0113 288 6148
e-mail: gateways@gatewayschool.co.uk

website: www.gatewayschool.co.uk

Governing Body:
Chairman: Mr M Shaw
Revd Canon A F Bundock, Rector of Leeds
Mrs L Croston, BSc Hons, PGCE, ALCM
Professor D Hogg, BSc Hons, MSc Hons, DPhil
Dr S Lee
Mr R Marsh, BSc, FCA
Professor D Shorrocks-Taylor
Dr R H Taylor, BEd, MA, PhD
Ms R Thornton
Dr C Wilson, BSc Hons, MBBS, MD, FRCP
Mr R Webster, BSc

Staff:

Headmistress: **Mrs Y Wilkinson**, BA Hons, PGCE, NPQH

Deputy Headmistress: Mrs R Burton, BSc Hons, PGCE (*Chemistry*)

Head of Preparatory School: Mrs S A Wilcox, BEd Hons

Miss J Ansbro-Westmoreland, BA Hons, NNEB (*Nursery Nurse*)
Miss K Ashurst, BSc Hons, PGCE (*Physics*)
Mrs C Bartle, NNEB (*Head of Early Years*)
Mrs S Blackwell (*Foundation Stage*)
Mr N Box, BEd Hons (*Physical Education*)
Mrs G A Brennan, BA Hons, PGCE (*French and Spanish*)
Mrs K Brown, BEd Hons (*Prep School*)
Mrs M Burns, BA Hons, PGCE (*English*)
Mr P Chatterton, BSc Hons, MBA, PGCE (*Biology*)
Mr M Dalrymple, MA Hons, PGCE (*English*)
Mr M Davison, BA Hons, PGCE (*Head of Sixth Form, English, Media Studies*)
Mrs S Derrig, BEd Hons (*Business Studies and Economics*)
Mr P Dutton, MA, LTCL, PGCE (*Head of Creative Arts Faculty, Music*)
Miss S Ellison, BTEC, FdA in Early Years (*Foundation Stage*)
Mrs J Emerick, BA Hons, Dip Dramatic Art (*English and Drama*)
Miss F Feeney, BA Hons, PGCE (*Prep School*)
Mrs S M Finan, BEd Hons (*History*)
Mrs N Forrest, NVQIII (*Nursery Nurse*)
Miss C Fox, BA Hons, QTS (*Physical Education*)
Mrs M Gilliver, BA Hons, PGCE (*Prep School*)
Miss E M Green, CertEd, DPSE (*Learning Support*)
Mrs E Hayward, BSc Hons, PGCE (*Geography, Psychology*)
Mrs B Hetmanski, BEd Hons (*Religious Studies*)
Mrs S Holmes, BA Hons, QTS (*Head of Upper School, Technology*)
Miss M James, BSc Hons, PGCE (*Mathematics*)
Miss A Jeffords, BA Hons, QTS (*Prep School*)
Mr C Keeton, BA Hons, PGCE (*Art and Design Technology*)
Mrs D Kennedy, BSc, PGCE (*Head of Mathematics & Science Faculty, Mathematics*)
Mr S Llewellyn, BA Hons, PGCE (*Classics*)
Mrs C McDermott, MEd, BA, PGCE (*Geography*)
Mrs A McKeefry, BA Hons, PGCE (*English*)
Dr S Newton, BSc, PhD, PGCE (*Physics, Biology*)
Mrs J Ralph, MA, BA Hons, PGCE (*Head of Classical & Modern Language Faculty, German and French*)
Mrs T Richmond, BSc Hons, PGCE (*Mathematics and ICT*)
Mrs J Rooney, FdA in Early Years, NNEB (*Foundation Stage*)
Mrs S Roth, NVQIII (*Nursery Nurse*)
Mr Q Sands, BEd Hons (*Drama and Theatre Studies*)
Mrs R Schofield, BSc Hons, PGCE (*Prep School*)
Mrs H Sharpe, BA Hons, PGCE (*Modern Languages*)

Miss H Shipton, BA Hons, QTS (*Reception*)
Mrs K Titman, BEng, PGCE (*Director of Studies, ICT*)
Mrs A Tunley, MPhil, BA Hons, CertEd (*Religious Studies*)
Mr P Walker, BA Hons, PGCE (*Business Studies*)
Mrs H Wallis, BA Hons QTS (*Prep School*)
Mrs F Wilson, BA Hons, PGCE (*Spanish*)
Mrs K Wood (*Nursery Nurse*)
Mrs L Wood, BSc Hons, PGCE (*Head of Middle School, Chemistry*)

Associate Staff:
Mr J Halliday (*Interim Business Manager*)
Mr S Bartle (*Maintenance Supervisor*)
Miss K Bland (*Teaching Assistant*)
Miss S Britton (*Assistant Chef*)
Mrs L Brydon (*After School Supervisor*)
Mrs J Chennells, BA Hons, MHSM, DipHS (*Extra-curricular Coordinator*)
Mr S Clark (*Laboratory Technician*)
Mrs D Dixon (*Registrar*)
Mrs S Drake (*Nursery Assistant*)
Mrs S Forbes (*Catering Assistant*)
Mrs J Foster, BA Hons (*Study Supervisor*)
Mrs K Franklin (*Catering Assistant*)
Mrs N Harris (*PA to the Headmistress*)
Mrs A Hill, BEd, CertEd (*Homework Club Supervisor*)
Mrs B Leeming (*Learning Support Assistant*)
Mrs S Logan (*Learning Support Assistant*)
Mrs G MacHugh (*School Secretary*)
Miss V Marais (*IT and Theatre Technician*)
Mrs N Marathoo, LLB Hons (*Learning Support Assistant*)
Mrs S Nelson, HND Business & Finance (*Head of Admissions & Marketing*)
Mr K Robinson (*Operations Manager*)
Miss J Smith (*After School Assistant*)
Mr T Smith (*Maintenance Supervisor*)
Mr P Walker, BA Hons, PGCE (*Business Studies*)
Mr B Wallace (*Catering Manager*)
Mrs D White, RGN (*School Nurse*)
Mrs S Wood (*Finance Assistant*)
Mrs S Wright (*School Secretary*)

Visiting Teachers:
Miss W Crawford, LTCL (*Classical Guitar*)
Mr D Darling, BA Hons, QTC (*Voice and Piano*)
Mr I Davies (*Brass*)
Mrs H Fitton (*Oboe*)
Mrs D Lee, CT ABRSM (*Woodwind*)
Mr N McGill (*Woodwind*)
Mr D Roberts (*Brass*)
Mrs S Robertson, DipMusEd, LTCL (*Piano*)
Mr C Shaw (*Guitar*)

Gateways School is an independent school, founded in 1941, located in a delightful rural area on a 20-acre site in Harewood village between Leeds and Harrogate. It currently welcomes girls from age two to 18 and boys aged two to seven. The school is delighted to announce that from September 2011, boys will be able to continue their education at the school up to the age of 11.

The school was recently awarded international status in recognition of its work in promoting multiculturalism, global issues and internationalism. The school has an active Community Outreach programme which organises several events throughout the year to raise funds for charities supported by the school, while the proactive Environment club, and its commitment to green issues, has contributed to Gateways' ongoing status as a Green Flag school.

The ethos and objectives of Gateways School are to provide, within a structured framework, the opportunities and encouragement for every pupil to achieve his or her personal best. The environment is safe and caring, with outstanding pastoral care. Pupils develop self-confidence, self-discipline and a breadth of interests.

Teaching and Learning. Gateways consistently achieves excellent academic results – GSCE and A Level grade results continue to rise year on year – while encouraging students to make the most of the wide range of extra-curricular and enrichment activities on offer. Smaller class sizes allow pupils to develop academically through high-quality teaching from dedicated staff in a supportive environment.

The curriculum at Gateways is broad and challenging and pupils are always encouraged to think for themselves, and to become inquiring and independent learners. French and Latin are taught in the Prep School and all girls entering the High School study three modern languages – French, German and Spanish – as well as Latin. There is also the opportunity to study Mandarin and Greek. A wide range of subjects is offered at AS and A2 Level, including Critical Thinking.

The Stella programme ensures that the most able girls are challenged and support is available to help individuals with specific learning needs.

Pupils participate in a variety of extra-curricular activities including Drama, Music, Sport, the Duke of Edinburgh's Award Scheme, Leeds Young Enterprise and Community Outreach.

Facilities. The school has an ongoing programme of development to renew and enhance its facilities. Recent projects have included a brand new reception area and new sixth form study area and ICT suite. There is a state-of-the-art Performing Arts Centre, extensive playing fields, well-equipped Sports Hall and Fitness Suite, the Cox-Simpson Library and specialist facilities for Science, Mathematics, Languages and Business Studies.

The Gateways Community. The Friends of Gateways (PTA) and The Old Gatewegians Association both play an active role within the school community.

Location and Transport. Gateways School is set in beautiful parkland in the village of Harewood, just north of Leeds. The former Dower House of the Harewood Estate forms the heart of the School. Gateways is within easy reach of Harrogate, Wetherby, Leeds, Ilkley, Otley and the surrounding villages. A comprehensive school transport service is available. The also school has its own mini-bus.

Scholarships and Bursaries. (*See Scholarship Entries section.*)

Fees per term (2011-2012). Sixth Form £3,390 (ex lunch); High School £3,582 (Upper 3–Upper 5); Prep School: £2,817 (Upper 1–Lower 3), £2,329 (Lower 1, Transition and Reception); Pre-Reception: £2,472 (extended day), £1,942 (school day) – excludes lunch at £3.00 per day; Nursery: £38.48 (full extended day), £30.36 (school day).

Charitable status. Gateways Educational Trust Limited is a Registered Charity, number 529206. It exists to offer a broad education to girls aged 2–18 and boys aged 2–11, where they are encouraged to strive for excellence to the best of their ability.

The Godolphin and Latymer School

Iffley Road, Hammersmith, London W6 0PG
Tel: 020 8741 1936; 020 8563 7649 (Bursar)
Fax: 020 8735 9520
e-mail: office@godolphinandlatymer.com
website: www.godolphinandlatymer.com

Motto: *Francha Leale Toge*

Foundation: Godolphin and Latymer, originally a boys' school, became a girls' day school in 1905. It was aided by the London County Council from 1920 onwards and by the Inner London Education Authority when it received Voluntary Aided status after the 1944 Education Act. Rather than become part of a split-site Comprehensive school it reverted to Independent status in 1977.

Governors:
Chairman: Mr C S H Hampton, BA, FCA
Miss J Barfield, MBE, AA, Dip RIBA
Mr J B Boyer, BA, MSc
Mr C R Cowpe, MA
Mrs C Davies, BA, ATD
Mr A Fry, BA
Mr J R Gabitass, MA
Mr T D Gardam, MA
Ms S J D Illingworth
Mrs A J S Paines, BA
Mr D R W Potter, MA, FKC
Mr R D Sidery, BSc Econ, FCA, FCMA, MIMC
Mrs P Stout-Hammar, BA
Miss J M Taylor, BSc

Clerk to the Governors: Mr A F B Harvey, FCA, JDip MA, AGI Arb

Staff:

Head Mistress: Mrs R Mercer, BA London, PGCE Oxford

Deputy Head Mistress: (*to be appointed*)

Senior Teachers:
Mr W Cooper, MPhil Cantab, BA Cantab
Mr P M Culling, MA Cantab, LRSM
Miss C E Drennan, MA Oxon, MA UEA
Miss J A Hodgkins, MA Brunel, BEd CNAA
Mrs S Kinross, BA Exeter
Mrs C M Trimming, BA London, BA Open

Teaching Staff:
Ms S Adams, BEd Melbourne
Miss S Adey, BEd Brighton
Mrs S Andreyeva, BA Leningrad
Dr P Arnold, DPhil, MA Oxon
Miss A J Arthurton, BSc Bristol
Mrs S Banks, L-ès-L Paris
Miss K Barac, BSc, BEd British Columbia
Mr J M Barot, MSc Open, MSc Durham, MA Cantab
Mr P Barnes, BSc London
Mr A Belfrage, CertEd Leeds, Dip Computer Ed WLIHE
Mr J F Bell, BA Cantab, MA Sussex
Dr P Bickley, PhD London, BA London
Miss N H H Bishop, BA Durham
Ms D Blease, MA Oxon, BA Open
Miss L Boone, MA London, BA Oxon
Mrs S Briffa, MA Kingston, BA Central St Martins
Dr A C Bunting, PhD Soton, MA Soton, BA Soton
Miss A M Clark, BA Oxon
Mrs M Cockbain, MA Oxon
Miss L Cooper, MA Wimbledon School of Art, BA Staffordshire
Mrs N Cooper, BSc Leicester
Mr P Cosgrove, BA Bristol College of Art & Design
Dr M M Creagh, PhD Exeter, MA Nottingham, BA Exeter
Mrs G Cuming, MA Sorbonne
Mr A Davies, BA Cardiff Institute
Mr Q J Davies, MA Keele
Miss T Dean, BSc Edinburgh
Mrs A Devadoss, BSc London
Mr G C de Villiers, BA RAM, LRAM
Miss E C Elfick, BEd Exeter
Mrs U D Fenton, Diploma PH Freiburg
Miss H Ford, BA Cantab
Miss E S Fox, MA Oxon, MSc LSE
Miss S V R Fryer, BA Bristol
Mrs J Garcia, BMus Surrey

Mrs C E C Gatward, BA Oxon
Mrs L Grigson, BA Oxford Brookes
Mrs V A Halls, BA Sorbonne
Miss N J Hanger, BA Oxon
Mrs J H Hardie, BA Oxon
Mrs K Harrison, MA Oxon
Ms R E Hart, BA Oxon
Miss F L Hasteley, BA Falmouth
Miss K Healy, BA Leicester
Mrs R J Hollis, PhD Birmingham, BSc Portsmouth
Miss I Jacobson, BA Bristol
Miss S Johnston, BPhEd Otago
Dr I W Jones, PhD CNAA, MSc Cardiff, BSc Liverpool
Miss V Juckes, MA Oxon
Mr M Laflin, MA Oxon, ARCO, ATCL
Mrs C Lee, MA London, BEd Exeter
Mr A Leithes, BSc London
Miss E M Lorys, BA Exeter
Miss F Mabley, BSc Bath
Mrs J M Mackenzie, BA Southampton
Mrs S Main, BEd Middlesex
Mr P D Martin, BA Cantab
Mrs H Mason, MA London, BA Durham
Miss H J Matthews, BA Cantab
Mr C J McCarthy, MSc Aberystwyth, BA Keele
Miss N S McDonald, BA Bristol
Mr J McGrath, MSc Cranfield, BSc Wales
Mr P McGuigan, BA Open, CertEd St Mary's,
	Twickenham
Mrs F Meyers, BA Kent
Miss A A Newton
Miss S J Nicholas, BA Loughborough
Mrs L G Norrie, BSc Newcastle
Miss L Ockenden, MA RCA, BA Central St Martins
Mrs D O'Connor, MSc London, BSc Galway
Mrs C Osborne, MA Sussex
Miss L R Padalino, BA Bologna
Mrs C M Preston, BSc Bath
Miss A Prodhomme, BA Sorbonne
Mr S Raleigh, BA Cantab
Mrs S H Rendall, BA Manchester
Mr S J Ridgwell, BA, MPhil Swansea
Mrs V L Robinson, BA Durham
Miss A F Romero-Wiltshire, BA Nottingham
Mrs E A Rooke, BSc London
Miss M Row, MSc Brunel, BSc Brunel
Miss A M Salmon, BA London
Mrs A R Sellars, BSc Cardiff
Mr T Seth, MA Cantab
Miss L H Shackleton, BA Cantab
Miss P M Shadlock, MA Sheffield, BA London
Mr A Shah, MEd Sheffield, BA City
Dr B Snook, PhD Cantab, MPhil Cantab, BA Cantab
Miss I C Squire, BA Cantab, LPC Guildford College of
	Law
Dr J M Stevens, PhD London, MA London
Mrs S V Sutherland, BA Aberystwyth
Miss J J Taylor, BA Durham
Mrs M T Troya, BA Santa Cruz de Tenerife
Mr A J Vettese, BA Oxon
Miss C E Vickers, BA Oxon
Miss S von Haniel, MA Edinburgh
Miss L Wallace, BA Reading
Ms J A Waltham, BSc Manchester
Miss A Weldon, BSc Durham
Dr A R Werker, PhD Cantab, BSc Bangor
Mr D White, MEd Warwick, BSc Leeds
Mr N S White, BSc London
Mrs J Wright, BA Bristol, BEd Bath College

Visiting teachers in Music and Speech Training:
Ms E Bradley, MMus London
Miss R Buxton, BMus RCM, LGSM Guildhall
Miss D Clarke, BMus Manchester

Mrs J Clark-Maxwell, BMus London, LTCL
Mrs H Davey, BMus Guildhall
Miss E Doroszkowska, BMus Manchester, RNCM
Miss M Drower, ARCM
Miss C J Egan, BMus London, PgDip Birmingham
Mrs K Feltrin, MA Cracow, PGDip Guildhall
Miss V L Galer, BA York
Mrs K Hempsall, BA Warwick
Miss R A Latham, BMus, ARCM
Mr M Lewington, DipRCM
Miss C-C Lim, MMus RCM, LRSM, FRCL, LTCL
Miss A J Lower, MMus, BMus, BA, Queensland
Mr A Mitchell, GMus RNCM, PPRNCM
Miss C Morphett, BMus Sydney
Ms V L Munday, BMus Sydney
Mr D Neville, BA RCM
Miss C Pay, BMus RAM, LRAM
Mrs R Richardson, MMus Guildhall
Ms C Riley MMus Auckland NZ, LRSM
Mrs K Ryder, MMus London, DSCM NSW
	Conservatorium
Miss C Sampson, BA Cantab
Miss J A Staniforth, Virtuosité DipRAM, GRSM,
	DipALCM
Miss E Tingey, LWCMD, ACC WCMD, TCM
Miss L Tricker, BEd CSSD
Mrs P Whinnett, GMus, RNCM
Mr R K J Williams, M Mus Guildhall, BMus Exeter
Miss E Zakrzewska, BMus RAM, RSAMD, DipRAM,
	LRAM

Bursar: Mrs D Lynch, BSc Kingston, FCCA
Registrar: Mrs F R Beckwith
Head Mistress's Secretary: Mrs V S Cox, BA
School Doctor: Dr L B Miller, MA Cantab, MB, BChir,
	DRCOG, MRCGP
School Nurse: Mrs C A Owen, SRN, Mrs V Dickins, RCN

Godolphin and Latymer is an independent day school for 730 girls, aged 11 to 18. The school stands in a four acre site in Hammersmith, near Hammersmith Broadway and excellent public transport. The original Victorian building has been extended to include a gymnasium, pottery room, computer studies room, language laboratory, science and technology laboratories, art studios, a dark room and an ecology garden. The girls benefit from an all-weather surface for hockey and tennis, as well as netball courts and a Sixth Form Centre. Since September 2006, the school has leased St John's Church and its Vicarage, both adjacent to the existing site. The Vicarage, renamed the Margaret Gray Building, provides additional classrooms. The new Rudland Music School opened in the Autumn Term 2008 and the renovated church, The Bishop Centre, for the performing arts was completed in early Spring 2009. These state-of-the-art developments provide a range of teaching and performance spaces, recording studios and a music technology suite. The Bishop Centre provides an auditorium to seat over 800.

The Godolphin and Latymer School aims to provide a stimulating, enjoyable environment and to foster intellectual curiosity and independence. We strive for a love of learning and academic excellence, emphasising the development of the individual, within a happy, supportive community.

While girls are expected to show a strong commitment to their studies they are encouraged to participate in a range of extra-curricular activities. We aim to develop the girls' self-respect and self-confidence, together with consideration and care for others so that they feel a sense of responsibility and are able to take on leadership roles within the school and the wider community.

Pastoral Care. The school has a close relationship with parents, and every member of the staff takes an interest in the girls' academic and social welfare. Each girl has a form teacher and a deputy form teacher and there is a Head of

Lower School, Head of Middle School and a Head of Sixth Form, each with at least one deputy.

Curriculum. We offer a broad, balanced curriculum including appropriate education concerning personal, health, ethical and social issues. During the first three years Philosophy and Religion, English, French, Latin, History, Geography, Mathematics, Physics, Chemistry, Biology, Food Technology, Design Technology, Art, Music, and Physical Education are studied. In Year 8 there is a choice between Spanish and German and in Year 10 Italian, Russian, Greek, Classical Civilisation and PE become available. Girls take ten or eleven subjects to GCSE. Drama is studied in Years 7, 8, 9 and 10.

In the Sixth Form there is a choice of curriculum between the Advanced Level (AS and A2) and the International Baccalaureate Diploma. All subjects offered to GCSE can be continued into the Sixth Form with the addition of Ancient History, Drama and Theatre Studies, Economics, Government and Politics and History of Art. Sixth Formers also follow a General Studies programme (AL) or Theory of Knowledge (IB), including lectures given by outside speakers.

The Sixth Form. The Sixth Form facilities include a Common Room, Work Room and Terrace. The 200 girls in the Sixth Form play a leading role in the school, taking responsibility for many extra-curricular activities, producing form plays and organising clubs. They undertake voluntary work and lead our social service programme.

Higher Education and Careers Advice. A strong careers team offers advice to girls and parents. Our specialist room is well stocked with up-to-date literature and course information, and lectures and work shadowing are arranged. Almost all girls proceed to Higher Education degree courses (including an average of 15 a year to Oxford and Cambridge).

The Creative Arts. Music and Drama flourish throughout the school. The Rudland Music School has outstanding facilities for music: 20 soundproofed rooms for individual or group work, a recording studio, ICT suite and two classrooms which open out into a very large rehearsal space for choirs and orchestras. There are four choirs, two orchestras and several small ensembles, and a joint orchestra and choral society with Latymer Upper School. Individual music lessons are offered in many different instruments. Each year there is a pantomime, Year 10 and Sixth Form plays as well as the school productions. The refurbished church, known as The Bishop Centre, offers a superb performing arts space for music, drama and dance. Venues out of school have included the Cochrane Theatre, Lyric Theatre, Riverside Studios and the Edinburgh Festival.

Physical Education is a vital part of a girl's development as an individual and as a team member. Younger girls play netball, hockey, tennis and rounders and have gymnastic and dance lessons. In the senior years there is a wider range of activities offered, including rowing and squash off-site. There is a gymnasium and fitness room.

Extra-Curricular Activities. The many opportunities for extra-curricular activities include the British Association of Young Scientists, Computing, Chess, the Young Enterprise Scheme, Debating, Creative Writing, Classics Club and the Duke of Edinburgh's Award Scheme, as well as a wide range of sporting activities such as karate, fencing, rowing and canoeing.

Activities outside the School. We organise language exchanges to Hamburg, Nantes and Moscow, a musical exchange to Hamburg and Sixth Form work experience in Versailles and Berlin. There is also an exchange with a school in New York. Each year, Year 9 girls ski in the USA and there are study visits to Spain and History of Art visits to Paris, Bruges, Venice and Florence and, for the Upper Sixth, a visit to the Sinai Desert.

We take advantage of our London location by arranging visits to conferences, theatres, exhibitions and galleries.

Field courses are an integral part of study in Biology and Geography.

Admission. Girls are normally admitted into Year 7 (First Year Entrance) or into our Sixth Form. Examinations for First Year entrance are held in January and for the Sixth Form in November. There are occasional vacancies in other years. Entry is on a competitive basis.

Fees per term (from January 2011). £5,175. Fees may be raised after a term's notice. Private tuition in music and speech and drama are extra. Most girls have school lunch, but it is an option from Year 8.

Scholarships. (*See Scholarship Entries section.*) There are music scholarships available on entry to Year 7 and, in the Sixth Form, music and art scholarships. All scholarships are worth up to 30% of fees and may be topped up by means-tested bursaries in cases of need.

Bursaries. A number of school bursaries are available annually.

Uniform. Uniform is worn by girls up to and including Year 11.

Charitable status. The Godolphin and Latymer School is a Registered Charity, number 312699. It exists to provide education to girls aged 11 to 18.

The Godolphin School

Milford Hill, Salisbury SP1 2RA
Tel: 01722 430500
           Preparatory School: 01722 430652
Fax: 01722 430501
e-mail: admissions@godolphin.wilts.sch.uk
website: www.godolphin.org

Motto: *Franc Ha Leal Eto Ge* (Frankness and Loyalty be Yours)

Founded by Elizabeth Godolphin in 1707; date of the will of the Foundress, 24 June 1726; a new scheme made by the Charity Commissioners and approved by HM, 1886, and re-issued by the Charity Commissioners in February 1986. The Godolphin School is an independent boarding and day school for girls aged 11–18, with its own purpose-built preparatory day school for girls from the age of 3. Of the 412 girls in the senior school, over 130 are in the Sixth Form.

Governing Body:
G Fletcher, Esq (*Chairman*)
M R T Bryer Ash, Esq
Mrs A George
Lady Ruth Hawley
Mrs S Herd
G W Green, Esq
S Hill Esq
J S Lipa, Esq, LLB, MJur, FINZ, ICFM
M J Nicholson, Esq
The Revd C Mitchell-Innes
Mrs Susan Thomson
Mrs T Watkins, BA
Dr B Whitworth

Bursar and Clerk to the Governors: K G M Flynn, Esq, BSc, FCMA

Headmistress: **Mrs S A Price**, MA Edinburgh

Deputy Head: R T W Dain, Esq, MA Oxon
Director of Studies: Mrs H Portas, BA Wales
Admissions Secretary: Mrs V Power, BSc Hons London

Staff:
* *Head of Department/Subject*

Religious Studies:
*F R Spencer, Esq, BA Essex, BTh Southampton

P Sharkey, Esq, BA London
Mrs M Drummond, MA Winchester

English:
*Mrs J Carlisle, BA London
Mrs M Johns, BA Wales
Mrs L Hodgson, TCert Bromley, AMBDA
Mrs T Nicholls, MA Keele, BEd Cambridge
Mrs R Carville, BA Hons Birmingham
Ms S Jones, BA Hons Wales
R T W Dain, Esq, MA Oxon

History:
*Miss J Miller, BA Belfast, MEd Open
Dr A Dougall, Esq, LLB London, MA, PhD Southampton
Mrs S Eggleton, MA Aberdeen
Mrs H Portas, BA Wales

Psychology:
Miss A Bowler, BA Manchester, BA Wimbledon
Mrs N Archer, BA Wolverhampton, MSc Chichester

Business Studies and Economics:
*D J Miller, Esq, BA Nottingham
Mrs S Lamont, BA Hons Cheltenham and Gloucester, PGCE

Geography:
*Miss S L Collishaw, BSc Swansea
Mrs J Morris, MA Bath
Mrs C Vaughan, BA Manchester
Mrs L Cotterell, MA Oxford

Classics:
*A Mackay, Esq, MA Cantab
C De Vido, Esq, BA London
Mrs S Radice, BA Reading
Mrs M Highcock, MA Cantab

Modern Languages:
*Mrs S Smith, MA Cantab
Mrs J Campling, BA Cape Town
Ms M A Cibis, BA, MA Sheffield
M Dunning, Esq, MSc Southampton, DSE Madrid
Dr L Rojas-Hindmarsh, DPhil Leeds
Miss M Reyes Avila Cabrera, Lda Alicante
Miss S Naranjo Uroz Almeria
Mrs S Dawson (*Assistentin*)
Mlle M Beillet (*Assistentin*)

Mathematics:
*Mrs K Healey, BSc Bristol
*Mrs J L Robson, BSc Bristol
Mrs R C Stratton, BSc Exeter
Mrs N Owers, BA Hons Nottingham, PGCE
Mrs A Bacon, BSc Hons Southampton PGCE
Mrs A Strong, BA Keele, BSc Open

Science:
*Dr C Thrower, PhD, MSc, BSc Manchester (*Chemistry*)
A J Brown, Esq, BSc Dunelm
Dr B Medany, BSc London, PhD Nottingham (*Biology*)
Mr J Eyre, BSc Hons, MSc Southampton (*Physics*)
Miss H Broughton, BSc Edinburgh
P Hill, Esq, BSc London
Miss R Gillingham, BSc Hons London
J McNulty, Esq, MSc Leicester

Design and Food Technology:
*M Berry, Esq, BEd Leeds, MA Open
Mrs P Parry-Jones, BSc Bath College of Higher Education
Mrs C Complin, BSc Bath College of Higher Education

Information and Communication Technology:
*Miss J A Thomas, BEd Worcester
Mrs W Laptain, BEd Manchester
D J Miller, Esq, BA Nottingham
Mrs S Eggleton, MA Aberdeen

Art and Design:
*N Eggleton, Esq, BA London, ATC
Miss A Bowler, BA Manchester, BA Wimbledon
Mrs S Duggan, BA Winchester
Miss E Findley, BA Leeds Metropolitan
C Wright, Esq, BA Napier
Mrs J G Whiteley, BA Camberwell
Mrs J Josey, C&G TCert Basingstoke
Mrs A-M Fieber, BA Middlesex
Mrs C Spender, BA Manchester Met

History of Art:
*Mrs S Radice, BA Reading

Music:
*R A Highcock, Esq, BMus London
Mrs O Sparkhall, BA Dunelm
T Young, MA Royal College of Music

Drama:
*D Hallen, Esq, BA Hons Middlesex, PGCE
Mrs L Hodgson, TCert Bromley, AMBDA
Miss N Strode, BA Cardiff
Mrs M Ferris, LGSM, LTCL (*Speech and Drama Coach*)

Instrumental Staff and Ensemble Coaches:
Miss S Cox, BA
Mrs G Cullingford
N Ellis, Esq
C Hobkirk, Esq, BA MusEd, ARCO
R Leighton Boyce, Esq
Mrs J Littlemore, BMus, LRAM
Mrs C Long, GTCL, LTCL
Ms S McKenzie-Park
Miss S Stocks, LRAM, LGSM
M Wilkinson, Esq, CertEd
C Holmes, Esq, ARCM
Ms S Bevis
Mrs F Brockhurst, ARCM
Mrs M Brookes, CertEd Birmingham
Miss M Chelu, MusB Manchester
J Gilbert, Esq
H Hetherington, Esq, MA Cantab
Mrs E Huntriss, GNSM, LRAM
C Hurn, Esq, LGSM, BA
Ms E Innes, GGSM, AGSM
R Priestley, Esq

Physical Education:
*Mrs S Pokai, BA Brighton
Mrs W Laptain, BEd Manchester
Mrs L Norris, BSc Hons Loughborough
Mrs S Ramsdale, BEd Liverpool
Mrs A J Venn, BA Manchester, PGSC Physical Education
Miss S Trentham, BSc Hons Cardiff
D J Miller, Esq, BA Nottingham
Mrs S C Harvey, BEd Exeter

Chaplain: The Revd J Ball, BEd Lancaster
Librarian: Mrs H Clarkson, BSc Bristol, ALA
Senior Sixth Form Tutor and Higher Education Adviser: Dr A Dougall, LLB London, MA, PhD Southampton
Upper School Tutor: Dr C Thrower, BSc Plymouth, MSc Exeter, PhD Manchester
Middle School Tutor: Mrs S Eggleton, MA Aberdeen
Lower School Tutor: Miss J Miller, BA Belfast
Careers Adviser: Mrs B Ferguson, BA Hons Newcastle upon Tyne

Further Learning:
Mrs D Bentley, BA Exeter, SpLD
EFL Coach: Mrs M Dance

Sixth Form Centre:
Ms S Jones, BA Wales (*Housemistress*)
Mrs L Hodgson, QTS Stockwell College (*Deputy Housemistress*)

Jerred House:
Miss E Findley, BA Leeds Metropolitan (*Housemistress*)
Mrs L Cotterell, MA Oxford (*Deputy Housemistress*)

Houses:
Cooper:
Mrs P Loxton, CertEd Sussex (*Housemistress*)
Ms C J Dougherty, LLB Hons Lancaster, PGCE (*Deputy Housmistress*)
Walters:
Mrs W Laptain, BEd Manchester (*Housemistress*)
Mrs M Reyes Avila Cabrera, Lda Alicante (*Deputy Housemistress*)
Sayers:
Mrs S Ramsdale, BEd Liverpool (*Housemistress*)
Miss J Tatem, BEd Southampton (*Deputy Housemistress*)

Sanatorium:
Mrs G Davey, RGN
Mrs V Block, RGN
Mrs R Nicholls, RGN
Mrs V Coupe, RGN
Mrs J Palk

The Godolphin School stands in 16 acres of landscaped grounds on the edge of the historic cathedral city of Salisbury, overlooking open countryside.

A strong academic life combines with thriving art, drama, music and sport. A five-studio art centre provides excellent art and design facilities, while the Blackledge Theatre provides a professional environment for drama and music performance. Other notable developments include the Baxter Pool and Fitness Centre, a new boarding house and a dedicated Sixth Form Centre, the latter providing a focus for careers and higher education advice, and the Sixth Form social programme, as well as study-bedrooms, work space and recreational areas. Sciences are taught within the well-equipped laboratories and have a strong tradition of Oxbridge success. The whole site is served by a wireless network.

Religious Instruction. Godolphin has strong affiliations with the Church of England, but religious instruction covers all the major world faiths.

Curriculum. High academic standards (96% A* to C grades at A Level and 98.9% A* to C grades at GCSE and IGCSE in 2010) are combined with a wide range of clubs, societies and weekend activities; also an outstanding programme of trips and expeditions. Activities include: cookery, photography, Duke of Edinburgh's Award, Combined Cadet Force, community service, debating, creative writing, academic societies and wide ranging opportunities in art, drama, music and sport. 24 subjects are available at A Level, and virtually all students continue to higher education, most to universities, including Oxbridge; some to art colleges, drama schools and music conservatoires. There is considerable emphasis on Careers guidance, including an excellent work shadowing scheme.

Physical Education. Strong sporting record with pupils regularly selected for county and regional teams; also at national level. 22 sporting options include lacrosse, hockey, netball, tennis, athletics, swimming, gymnastics, dance, rounders and cross-country. Each girl is encouraged to find at least one sport she really enjoys during her time at Godolphin.

Entrance Examination. Generally through Common Entrance Examination for Girls' Schools Ltd at 11+, 12+ and 13+. Godolphin's own examination and interview at other levels, including Sixth Form candidates.

Scholarships and Bursaries. (*See Scholarship Entries section*.) 11+ and 13+ Academic, Art (13+ only), Music and Sports Scholarships are awarded for outstanding merit and promise. It is likely that a music award would only be made to a candidate who has attained at least Grade 4 at 11+ (Grade 6 at 13+) on one instrument.

Sixth Form Academic, Art, Drama, Music and Sports scholarships are also available.

Six means-tested Foundation Bursaries, each worth 70% of the fees, are available from time to time to boarding candidates from single parent, divorced or separated families who have been brought up as members of the Church of England.

The Old Godolphin Bursary, a means-tested bursary worth up to 50% of the boarding fees, is awarded from time to time by the Old Godolphin Association to the daughter of an Old Godolphin.

Fees per term (2011-2012). Full Boarding £8,273, 5-Day boarding £8,031, 3-Day Boarding £7,742, Day Girls £5,754. Prep School: Full Boarding £6,064, 5-Day Boarding £5,164, 3-Day Boarding £4,464, Day Girls £1,845–£3,564. Fees include tuition, textbooks, stationery, sanatorium, laundry, and most weekday and weekend clubs and activities.

Extra Subjects. Individual tuition in music, speech and drama, Italian, tennis, fencing, judo, EFL and learning support.

Old Godolphin Association. *Secretary*: Miss H Duder, Keith Cottage, Cold Ash, Thatcham, Berkshire RG18 9PT, or via Development Office, Tel: 01722 430570.

Charitable status. The Godolphin School is a Registered Charity, number 309488. Its object is to provide and conduct in or near Salisbury a boarding and day school for girls.

Greenacre School for Girls

Sutton Lane, Banstead, Surrey SM7 3RA
Tel: 01737 352114
Fax: 01737 373485
e-mail: admin@greenacre.surrey.sch.uk
website: www.greenacre.surrey.sch.uk

Motto: *Fides et opera*

Council:
Chair: Mr J P Staddon

Mrs S Gilbert	Mrs J Triffitt
Mr P Owens	Mr P Watts
Miss G Smith	Mr G Wildig
Mr R J Steward	

Bursar and Clerk to the Council: Mrs K A Maltby, AIAM Dip

Headmistress: Mrs L E Redding, BSc Hons

Deputy Head: Ms L Clancy, BEd Nottingham

Teaching Staff:
* Head of Department

Mrs D Atkinson, BSc Hons (*Mathematics*)
Mr D Ayling, BA Hons (*Juniors, Learning Support – Juniors*)
Miss C Black, BA Hons (*Head of Year 10, PE*)
Mrs B Bradley, BEd (**Business Studies*)
Mrs K Bramley, BTEC Dip, BA Hons (*Textiles, Art*)
Mrs S Burge, BSc (*Geography*)
Mrs C Carter (*Learning Support*)
Mrs L Chessell, BSc Hons (**Mathematics*)
Mrs P Clarke, CertEd, DipT (*Juniors*)
Mrs L Collins (*Learning Support*)
Ms L Cooper, BA (*Biology, House Coordinator*)
Mrs N Durward, BA Hons (*Performing Arts*)
Mrs M Y Emery, BA Hons (**Spanish, Head of Sixth Form*)
Miss L Entwistle, BSc Hons (*i/c Biology*)
Mrs D Fewtrell, BA, M-ès-L (*Head of Year 8 and Year 9, French*)
Mr T Finch, MA (**Humanities, *RS*)
Mrs C Garrod, C&G Catering (*Food Technology*)

Mrs M George (*Learning Support*)
Mr P Griffiths, BA Hons, MA (*Latin*)
Mrs P Hanham, BSc Hons (*Psychology*)
Mrs R Hart, BA Hons (*Head of Infants*)
Miss G Hipp, BSc Hons, MA (*Dance*)
Mr S Hume, BEd, MA (**ICT*)
Mr M Huxley, BSc Hons (*Photography*)
Mrs J Ince, CertEd (*Juniors*)
Mrs M-J Jeanes, MA (*Science, *Chemistry*)
Mr J Laver, BA Hons, MSc (*Media Studies*)
Mr C Lester, BSc Hons, PG Dip (*Teacher i/c Physics*)
Mrs J Long, BSc Hons (*Biology*)
Mrs S Maundrell, DEUG (*French*)
Mrs T Milbourn, BA Hons (*Junior PE*)
Mrs R Murphy, CertEd (*Juniors*)
Mr A Newman, BMus Hons (*Music*)
Mrs E Nissan, BA Hons, PhD (*Juniors*)
Mr M Norris, BA Hons (*English*)
Mrs C Paine, BEd
Mrs R M Pedrick, BA Hons (**Modern Foreign Languages*)
Mrs D Perry, BA Hons (*English*)
Mrs S Potter (*Learning Support*)
Mrs L Richards (*Learning Support*)
Mrs S Sevier (*Learning Support Coordinator, Exams
    Officer, Duke of Edinburgh's Award Coordinator*)
Mrs S Sheehan BSc, HDipEd (*Mathematics*)
Mrs Jill Skidmore, BSc Hons (*Junior Mathematics*)
Mrs A Smith, BEd Hons (**Physical Education*)
Mrs H Smith, BA Hons (*Nursery Teacher*)
Mrs I Smith, BA, MA (**English*)
Mr S Stuart, BA Hons (**Geography*)
Mrs A Tharp, BA Hons (**PE*)
Mr J Tizzard, BMus (**Performing Arts, Director of Music*)
Mr I Tunnell, BA Hons (*Juniors, Junior Music*)
Dr R Waller, DPhil Oxford (**History & Politics*)
Mrs J Windett, BEd Hons (*Head of Juniors*)
Mrs M Wraith, CertEd (**Creative Arts*)

Head's PA: Miss C Berger
Assistant to the Bursar: Mrs S Ball
Admissions Registrar: Mrs L Armstrong
Careers and Sixth Form Secretary: Mrs J Rawlins

A local school at the heart of the community.

Greenacre School was established in 1933 by two exceptional young women: Miss Sabine Pasley and fellow teacher, Mrs Patricia Wagstaffe. Both had a deep flair for teaching and a vision for a school that would provide not only excellent academic standards, but also an education tailored specifically to the needs of girls and young women. That vision is still central to the school today.

Greenacre is a medium-sized school, large enough to offer variety, challenge and opportunities for all talents and interests, but small enough for each girl to be known as a unique individual, enabling her to realise her full potential. Staff are highly qualified and committed to instilling the very best work habits in the girls and preparing them for an active role in the world. Academic standards are high and the school offers a very broad curriculum at all levels and class sizes allow teachers to respond to individual girls and their preferred learning styles. This results in the girls reaching the very best of their academic ability, as our exam results demonstrate.

Greenacre is also a human and sociable school in which girls of all ages, from 3 to 18, have the opportunity to develop fully, with all its resulting freedom and happiness. Pastoral care is exceptional and all girls are known and treated as individuals. Staff and parents work in partnership to support and develop each girl. There is a discernible atmosphere of consideration, friendliness and compassion throughout the school.

It is a very happy community that values its links with the wider world, both locally and globally. Girls are encouraged to develop as responsible citizens and rounded individuals through many varied activities. Many girls are involved in sport, music, drama and the Duke of Edinburgh Award scheme; fundraising events for nominated charities are imaginative and well supported; varied and exciting overseas trips are on offer as well as opportunities to develop skills in public speaking, leadership and team work.

The original ethos of the school is still in place today and is shared by the Headmistress, Mrs Redding. She says "I am delighted that Greenacre School continues to uphold and further these principals. Greenacre girls flourish in the school's wonderful environment and atmosphere where an innovative and outward looking approach is aligned with a respect for traditional values. They emerge as articulate, confident and inquisitive, accomplished, yet considerate young women of whom we are rightly proud."

Fees per term (2011-2012). £2,400 (Nursery full day) – £4,200 (Year 11), including lunch. Sixth Form: £4,100, excluding lunch.

Scholarships. (*See Scholarship Entries section.*)

Charitable status. Greenacre School for Girls Ltd is a Registered Charity, number 312034. It exists to provide education for girls.

Haberdashers' Aske's School for Girls

Aldenham Road, Elstree, Herts WD6 3BT
Tel: 020 8266 2300
Fax: 020 8266 2303
e-mail: theschool@habsgirls.org.uk
website: www.habsgirls.org.uk

Motto: *Serve and Obey*

This School forms part of the ancient foundation of Robert Aske and is governed by members of the Worshipful Company of Haberdashers, together with certain representatives of other bodies.

Clerk to the School Governors: Mr C M Bremner

Headmistress: Miss B A O'Connor, MA Oxon

Personal Assistant to the Headmistress: Mrs B Cohen

Deputy Head: Mr R James-Robbins, BA London
Deputy Head: Dr S Lindfield, BSc Reading
Deputy Head: Miss G Mellor, BA Exeter

Bursar: Mr D Thompson, BA Manchester, ACIB

Teaching Staff:
* *Head of Department*

Art:
*Mrs P White, BA Sheffield School of Art & Design
Mrs S Deamer, BA Manchester
Mrs D Hobbs, BA Lancaster
Miss S Wiseman, MA London

Careers:
*Mrs R Davies, BA Cardiff

Classics:
*Mr A Doe, BA Oxon
Miss A Dugdale, BA Oxon
Miss C Jessop, MA Cantab
Miss D Spain, MA Oxon

Design and Technology:
*Mr M Squire, BSc South Bank
Mrs S Deamer, BA Manchester
Mr J Oliver, BA Warwick
Mr S Turner, BSc Brunel

Economics:
*Mr M Catley, BSc LSE
Mrs S Kaur Hender, BA Leeds
Mrs K Sobczyk, BSc London (*Deputy Head of Sixth Form*)

English and Drama:
*Mrs A Leifer, BA Birmingham (*Acting Head of Department*)
Mr R James-Robbins, BA London
Dr F Miles, BA Cantab (*Head of Upper School*)
Mrs K Nash, MA Cantab
Mr D Thakerar, BA London
Ms E Tyerman, MA Cantab
Mr D Walker, BA Dunelm
Mrs L Winton, BA Manchester (*Head of Middle School*)

Geography:
*Mrs S Ashton, BSc Keele
Mrs A Bowen, BSc Manchester, MSc London
Mrs C Gilbert, BA Nottingham
Miss A McCrea, BSc Bristol

History:
*Mrs A Pearson, BA Dunelm
Mr K Davies, MA London
Mrs R Davies, BA Cardiff
Mrs E Devane, BA Cantab
Mr B Greatorex, BA Oxon
Mr P Harper, BA Oxon
Mrs C Wilding, BA Bristol (*Government and Politics*)

Individual Educational Needs:
Mrs A Baker, BA Oxford Brookes (*Senior School*)
Mrs S Stringer, BEd Exeter (*Junior School*)

Information Technology:
Mrs N Verma, BSc Westminster

Library:
Mrs A Fynes-Clinton, BA Canterbury, New Zealand

Mathematics:
*Mrs C Godfrey, BSc Leicester
Miss L Chelliah, BSc Kent
Mrs N Gohil, BEng Aston
Miss R Haycox, BSc Leeds
Mr C Howlett, BSc Dunelm
Mr J Kinoulty, MSc Dublin
Mrs S Lee, BSc Manchester
Miss L Marx, BSc Edinburgh
Mrs R Patel, BSc LSE
Mrs K Roantree, BA York

Modern Languages:
*Sr J Carbonell, MA London (*Spanish*)
Miss J Bouchard, Licence Lyon
Mrs D Clayden, BA Leeds
Mrs E Green, BA Oxon
Miss R Maldonado, BA Anglia
Miss G Mellor, BA Exeter
Miss E Meloni, MA London
Miss A Millet, MA Le Mans, France
Mrs K Osmond, BA Bristol
Mrs F Ray, L-ès-L Maîtrise, CAPES (*French*)
Miss H Robinson, BA Cantab
Mrs M Tamura, BA Yokohama, Japan
Miss A Tebb, BA Oxon (*German*)
Ms K Ting, BA Soo Chow University, Taiwan
and 5 visiting oral teachers

Music:
*Mr A Phillips, MMus London
Mrs R Bardou, BA Mus Cardiff
Mr D Davies, BA Keele
Mr T Scott, BA Cantab (*Assistant Director of Music*)
Miss A Turnbull, LRAM
and 25 visiting teachers

Physical Education:
*Miss C Hill, BSc Birmingham
Miss L Crane, BSc Bedfordshire
Mrs M Franklin, BA Brighton
Mrs C Prendergast, BA Brighton
Miss K Roberts, BSc Loughborough
Miss A Williams, BSc Manchester Metropolitan

Religion and Philosophy:
*Mrs M Wax, MA Essex
Ms L Childs, BA Manchester
Mrs A Saunders, BA Cantab
Ms C Shannon, BA Oxon

Science:
*Mrs V Leigh, BSc London (*Biology*)
Miss C Badger, MA Cantab (*Chemistry*)
Dr H Burgess, BSc Cantab
Dr R Catchpole, BSc London
Mrs J Dabby-Joory, BSc Southampton
Miss E Dinsey, BSc London
Mrs N Ghinn, BSc Nottingham
Dr S Harnett, BA Oxon (*Head of Sixth Form*)
Mr G Jervis, MA London
Miss R Lane, BA Cantab
Dr S Lindfield, BSc Reading
Mrs C Linton, BSc Edinburgh
Mrs Z Makepeace-Welsh, MA Oxon
Mrs J McNally, BSc Hatfield
Dr S Mirza, BSc Greenwich
Mrs D Moynihan, BSc Birmingham
Miss N Percy, BSc Leeds (*Physics*)
Mr E Stock, MPhys Oxon

Junior School:
Head: Mrs J Charlesworth, BSc Nottingham
Deputy Head: Mrs A Latimer, BA Hull
Head of Infants: Mrs B Mayho, DipEd Auckland, New Zealand
Miss R Brant, BSc London
Miss E Burman, BA Surrey
Mrs P Dear, BSc Aberystwyth
Mrs M Demetriou, BEd Hertfordshire
Miss E Galvin, BA Warwick
Mrs C Gibson, BSc Worcester
Ms M Hirsch, BMus London
Mr N Hobley, BSc Oxford Brookes
Dr J Hogg, BSc Bangor (*Curriculum Coordinator*)
Mrs E Miller, BA Hertfordshire
Mrs J Millman, BEd Leeds
Mrs J Nicholas, BA Newcastle
Miss C Sawkins, BA Surrey
Mr I Stroud, BSc North East London Polytechnic
Mrs M Tatman, BA Hertfordshire
Ms S Tersigni, BA Middlesex
Mr R Verrill, BA Manchester
Mrs T Wilkin, BSc Loughborough
Ms Y Yokozawa, BA Kyorin, Japan

Haberdashers' Aske's School for Girls is situated on a site of over 50 acres, and has an excellent reputation for academic, sporting and musical achievements. Entry to the Junior School is at 4+, 5+ or at 7+; at the Senior School, it is at 11+ and Sixth Form. The academic results are outstanding, the reflection of able pupils who enjoy learning and thrive on a full and challenging curriculum.

First-class facilities, including a new swimming pool in 2008, and a very wide range of extra-curricular activities, are provided within the school. Sport, music, drama, art and debating thrive and there are many other opportunities for leadership within the school community including the Duke of Edinburgh's Award Scheme, the Community Sports Leadership Award and a very active community service programme. Life at Habs is busy and challenging, embracing new technology, for example, digital language labs, touch-screen interactive whiteboards and remote access to all electronic work areas via the intranet, alongside old traditions, which include the celebration of St Catherine's Day as patron of the Haberdashers' Company.

Over 110 coach routes, shared with the Haberdashers' Aske's Boys' School next door, bring pupils to school from a thirty-mile radius covering north London, Hertfordshire and Middlesex. The provision of a late coach service ensures that pupils can take part safely in the wide range of the many clubs and societies organised after school. The St Catherine Parents' Guild, the school's parents' association, provides enormous support to the school through fundraising and social events.

Junior School. There are approximately 300 day girls aged 4–11 in the Junior School, with one reception class and two parallel classes of equal ability from Years 1–6.

Pastoral Care: Class teachers and teaching assistants maintain close contact with girls and their parents. It is very important that the girls feel happy and comfortable. Every adult has a responsibility for the girls' welfare and security and there are many layers of care in place. From the outset, through the behaviour code, girls are encouraged to be friendly and polite to everyone else in the community, adults and children. There are two nurses, a counsellor and an individual needs specialist as well as the teaching and assistant staff available for pastoral care. Where appropriate, older girls have responsibility for younger ones and Senior School sixth formers regularly help juniors in the classroom. A programme of PSHCE (personal, social, health & citizenship education lessons) covers important issues of self-development. Many parents are involved in the classroom, clubs and outings.

Spiritual and Moral Education: Haberdashers' is a school with a Christian tradition which welcomes the rich diversity of faiths within the community. Assemblies are held for the whole school twice a week and on other days are separate for Infants and Juniors. Themes, stories and prayers are drawn from a range of cultures and faiths. Once a year, each class performs an assembly to which their parents are invited. Parents are also invited to attend Harvest Festival, the St Catherine's Day service and the Carol Service.

Enrichment: There is a wide range of over 30 clubs covering the girls' interests in sport, music, arts and crafts, languages, science, maths, creative writing, reading, games and puzzles, cookery and gardening. Termly visits linked to the curriculum are arranged for every class and there are regular visitors to school such as theatre companies, historical re-creations, authors, illustrators, musicians and scientists.

The curriculum provides a core of gymnastics, dance, swimming, netball, tennis, athletics and rounders. Teams in netball, cricket, football, gymnastics, rounders and pop lacrosse compete against other schools. There are two major drama productions annually: an Infant production for all girls in Reception and Key Stage One, and a musical production with the whole of Years 5 and 6. The annual Spring Concert showcases the orchestra, wind band, string group, brass and recorder ensembles and two choirs as well as a massed choir of all Key Stage Two girls. The summer Chamber Concert features ensembles of girls who learn a musical instrument. Informal lunchtime concerts occur at least once a term for Year 4 to 6 soloists or duets. Art and design work is displayed around the school.

Curriculum: There is a broad and challenging curriculum with the provision of opportunities for active and independent learning, with plenty of practical tasks and problem solving, to enable girls to develop their bright young minds. Fun is a vital ingredient. There are curriculum evenings for parents to learn about our approach to particular subject areas and how they can best support the girls at home and work in true partnership with the school.

The Early Learning Goals of the Foundation Stage are met through a balance of child-initiated opportunities and teacher-led activities. There is a daily range of stimulating, play-based activities which prompts girls to ask questions, to discover, to wonder and to learn new skills. No homework is set in Reception or Year 1 so that girls can enjoy the precious childhood pleasures of imaginative play and being read to by a parent when they get home. Music and daily PE lessons are taught by specialist teachers. Phonics teaching enables girls to make rapid progress with reading and to gain an easy independence in their writing while the foundations of mathematical thinking are laid through carefully selected practical tasks. Girls spend time in the ICT suite mastering computing skills. Creativity is fostered in music and dance, in art, design technology, literacy activities, drama and role play. The school grounds provide a rich environment for building knowledge about the world of nature as well as space to develop physical skills.

At Key Stage One, curriculum subjects are English, mathematics, science, history, geography, religious studies, Japanese, ICT, art, design technology, music, PSHCE and physical education, including swimming. Fostering a love of reading is paramount. A little homework is introduced in Year 2.

As girls progress through Key Stage Two they encounter more subject specialists. Science lessons, which are taught in the well equipped laboratory, strongly feature practical and investigative work. The Art Room is a magnificent space for the creation of stunning works of art while girls can feel transported to another culture as soon as they step into the Japanese Room. In Year 6, girls also start to learn French.

Senior School. There are approximately 870 day girls aged 11–18 in the Senior School.

Pastoral Care: In such a big and busy school, care for each individual girl is deeply important so that all girls flourish and fulfil themselves in every way. Looking after them is a pastoral team consisting of the Deputy Head, Heads of Section, Form Tutors, two nurses, a counsellor and an individual needs specialist. The provision of pastoral care is designed to help girls make decisions and to care about others within the framework of a very diverse community. There is an outstanding range of opportunities for the girls' personal development and to help them consolidate a system of spiritual beliefs and a moral code. The welfare of the girls is of paramount importance and it is the responsibility of all members of staff, teaching and support staff, to safeguard and promote it. From the moment a girl joins the school, emphasis is placed on the partnership with parents so that, hand-in-hand, school and parents can support each girl, operating on a basis of trust and with people she knows from the start.

Spiritual and Moral Education: Haberdashers' is a school with a Christian tradition which welcomes the rich diversity of faiths within the community. Every day begins with a whole school or Section assembly, often led by the girls themselves. Once a week there are separate Christian, Hindu, Jain and Sikh, Humanist, Jewish and Muslim assemblies. Girls can choose which one they attend. Holy Communion takes place monthly. Roman Catholic Mass is celebrated each half term, either in the Girls' or the Boys' School. Muslim girls may pray at lunchtime in a room set aside for them to do so. Girls organize and run many charitable events throughout the year. This enhances their awareness of the wider world as well as raising funds for charities small and large, at home and abroad.

Enrichment: There is a wide range of clubs on offer in the Senior School, including art, creative writing, cricket, dance, debating, design technology, drama, football, Japanese, maths, philosophy, science, and swimming; there are also campaigning groups such as Amnesty International and the Animal Welfare Society. Trips and visits include a Year 7 adventure holiday and various trips abroad, with language exchanges, work experience, and study visits. Subject specific trips in the UK and abroad include field trips, theatre visits, trips to sites of historical importance, museums and art galleries, music and sports tours.

The core curriculum includes gymnastics, dance, swimming, lacrosse, netball, tennis, athletics and rounders. For older girls, there are additional options in self defence, basketball, volleyball, football, step-aerobics, trampolining, badminton, weight-training, judo, life-saving, synchronised swimming, water polo, golf and squash. There are clubs in a range of sports for recreational enjoyment as well as for the teams. There are major drama productions in all sections of the school and symphonic concerts showcasing a variety of ensembles including three orchestras, wind and jazz bands, percussion groups, flute choirs, and rock bands as well as recitals and chamber concerts. There are annual Drama and Music Festivals; occasionally, there are joint productions and orchestral concerts with the Boys' School. Girls' painting, sculpture and design installations are displayed around the school.

Opportunities for leadership and challenge are valued and encouraged. Activities include: The Duke of Edinburgh's Award; Tall Ships; Community Service; Community Sports Leader's Award; European Youth Parliament; Model United Nations; English Speaking Union; and the Oxford Union.

Curriculum: The school follows its own wide-ranging academic curriculum tailored to the needs of its very able pupils. It preserves the best of a traditional education whilst responding positively to curricular developments. Much emphasis is placed on developing the girls' ability to think and learn independently, nurturing an intellectual resilience and self confidence which will prepare them for the world beyond school. In all subjects, the curriculum aims to be something that inspires the girls and stimulates discussion and ideas. A high value is placed upon creativity, imagination and the opportunity to pursue topics beyond the confines of the exam specifications. The school is not required to follow the National Curriculum but draws upon the best practice of what is happening nationally and in other schools. In the first three years of the Senior School, girls follow a set curriculum, choosing either Spanish or German as their second modern language. As they progress through the school they are given greater choice and the opportunity to personalise their curriculum to suit their needs and interests. Thus the GCSE curriculum has space for up to four optional subjects. In the Sixth Form the girls have a free choice of subjects from the 21 subjects we offer. At each level, the curriculum is designed to prepare them for the opportunities, responsibilities and experiences of the next stage of their education and their lives.

Fees per term (2011-2012). Senior School £3,983; Junior School £3,282. A number of scholarships are awarded annually and means-tested financial assistance (up to full fees) is also available.

Charitable status. The Haberdashers' Aske's Charity is a Registered Charity, number 313996. It exists to promote education.

Haberdashers' Monmouth School for Girls

Hereford Road, Monmouth NP25 5XT
Tel: 01600 711100
Fax: 01600 711233
e-mail: admissions@hmsg.co.uk
website: www.habs-monmouth.org

Motto: *Serve and Obey*

Trustees: The Worshipful Company of Haberdashers

Governing Body:
Chairman: Mr J B S Swallow, MA, FCA

The Master of the Worshipful Company of Haberdashers (*ex officio*)

Mr J A Ackroyd	Miss H Hutton
Mr M H C Anderson	Mrs L Kelway-Bamber
Dr M G Archer	Mr A M Kerr
Dr P E G Baird	Mrs G B Kerton-Johnson
Professor P Blood	Mrs M A Molyneux
Cllr W A L Crump	Mrs T Pike
Mrs C J Davis	Mr R Stibbs
Mr C R S Hardie	Mrs L Stout
Canon E J S Hiscocks	Mrs M Wetherell
Mr D J Hitchcock	

Clerk to the Governors: Mrs F Creasey, BCom, ACMA

Bursar: Mrs Tessa Norgrove

Headmistress: Mrs Helen Davy, MA Oxon, PGCE London

Deputy Head: Mr T Arrand, MA Oxon, PGCE Cantab

Director of Studies: Mrs J Treasure, BA Hons Bristol, MA Wales, PGCE London

Director of Teaching and Learning: Mrs O E Davis, BSc Joint Hons Salford, PGCE York, MA Ed Wales

Director of Sixth Form: Mrs K J MacDonald, BA Manchester, PGCE Wales, MSc Econ Wales

Head of Boarding: Mrs P J Mills, BA Hons Sheffield, PGCE Cambridge

Chaplain: Dr S G Barnden, BA Hons Waterloo, Canada, MA Victoria, Canada, PhD Indiana, USA, PGCE Oxon

* *Head of Department*

Art:
*Mrs V E Reynolds, BA Hons Oxford Brookes, MA Brighton, PGCE Wales
Mr C Beer, BA Hons, PGCE UWIC
Mr G Nicklin, CertEd Wales
Miss L Porritt, BA Hons Wales, PGCE Wales

Biology:
*Miss L Woodburn, BSc Hons Glasgow, PGCE Glasgow
Mrs L Cartwright, CertEd Birmingham
Miss R J Higgins, BSc Hons Cardiff
Mr L J Ison, BSc, PGCE
Mrs V Lyons, BSc Hons Cardiff, PGCE
Mrs C Natt, BSc Hons Swansea, MA Open, PGCE Worcester

Business Studies:
*Mr D R Evans, BA Hons Coventry, PGCE Wales
Ms M C Attrill, BTEC Dip Bus Studies, CertEd UWCN
Mrs C Jones, BSc Hons, PGCE Wales

Careers:
*Mrs A Jervis, BSc Hons Wales, MA UWCN, PGCE Wales

Chemistry:
*Mrs M M Newcomb, BSc Hons London, PGCE Bristol
Mrs D E Clarke, BSc Hons Newcastle, PGCE Durham
Mrs S P Marks, BSc Hons Open, PGCE Wales
Dr I Wallace, BSc Newcastle, PGCE, PhD

Classics:
*Mrs L Beech, BA Hons Birmingham, PGCE Cambridge
Mrs B Bell, BA Hons London, PGCE Bristol
Mrs J Treasure, BA Hons Bristol, MA Wales, PGCE London
Mrs L Reynolds, BA Hons Liverpool, PGCE CNAA

Design Technology:
*Mrs N Clayton, BA Hons Central England, PGCE UWCN
Mr S McCluskey, BSc Hons Wales, PGCE Wales

Drama & Theatre Arts:
*Mr T Clegg, BA Hons West Yorkshire, PGCE Canterbury Christchurch, Prof Acting Dip Webber Douglas Academy
Ms H Wragg, BA Hons Leeds

Economics:
*Mr D R Evans, BA Hons Coventry, PGCE Wales

English:
*Mrs Z Harvey, BA Hons Wales, PGCE London
Dr S G Barnden, BA Hons Waterloo,Canada, MA Victoria, Canada, PhD Indiana, USA, PGCE Oxon
Mr J A Edwards, BA Hons, MA Warwick, PGCE Wales
Mrs D M Hardman, BA Hons Kent, PGCE Oxon
Mrs J Read, BA Hons Wales, CertEd
Mrs R Wallis, BA Oxford, PGCE London

Geography:
*Mr N Meek, BA Hons Middlesex, MA Leicester, PGCE Wales, MEd Birmingham

History:
*Mr D Griffiths, BA Hons Wales, PGCE Wales
Mrs K J MacDonald, BA Manchester, PGCE Wales, MSc Econ Wales
Mrs R Griffiths, BA Hons Wales, MA Wales, PGCE Wales
Mr M Seaton, BA Hons, PGCE Swansea

Home Economics:
*Mrs P Curtis, CertEd Leicester
Mrs J Vickers, CertEd Wales
Mrs C M Ward, CertEd Bristol
Mrs P A Ward, CertEd Leicester

ICT:
*Mrs C Jones, BSc Hons, PGCE Wales
Mrs E Martin, BA Hons Wolverhampton, PGCE London
Miss S Guha Roy, BEng Hons Liverpool

Mathematics:
*Mrs C L McGladdery, BSc Hons, PGCE Manchester
Mrs D J Crawshaw, BSc Hons, PGCE Bristol
Mrs B M Keyton, BSc Hons, PGCE Wales
Dr S Lawlor, BSc Hons UCD, PhD
Mrs J E Morris, BSc Hons, PGCE Wales
Mrs J A Poyner, BSc Hons Exeter, PGCE Wales
Mrs V R Price, BSc Ed UWCN

Modern Languages:
Ms A P Thiry, BA Hons Lille, PGCE Sheffield (*French*)
Mrs H K Smail, BA Hons Wolverhampton, MA Reading, PGCE Birmingham (*German*)
Mrs K Wellings, BA Hons Hull, PGCE London (*French,*Spanish*)
Mrs O E Davis, BSc Jt Hons Salford, MA, PGCE York (*Spanish*)
Mrs C A Griffiths, BA Hons London, PGCE Reading (*German, French*)
Mrs R Rees, BA Hons Manchester, PGCE Bristol (*French*)
Ms M R Mertes (*Foreign Language Assistant*)

Music:
*Mr M Conway, BMus Hons, MA, PGCE Wales, LTCL, ARCM
Mrs R Friend, LRAM
Miss A Edwards, BA Hons Bristol, MA Cardiff, PGCE UWIC

Personal and Social Education:
Mrs C A Griffiths, BA Hons London, PGCE Reading

Physical Education:
*Mrs C F Crawford, BA Hons UWIC, PGCE UWIC (*Head of Physical Education*)
*Miss E Poole, BA Hons Theatre Arts Manchester, MA Bedford (*Head of Games*)
*Mrs K Callaghan, BA Joint Hons (*Head of Rowing*)
Mr J C Cheesman, BSc Hons (*Senior Rowing Coach*)

Miss R Halliday, BSc Hons UWIC, PGCE Exeter
Mrs C E Jones, BSc Hons Wolverhampton, MSc Wales, PGCE
Mrs S J Rossiter, BSc Hons South Bank, PGCE Wales
Miss C Rose-Hinam, BSc Hons UWIC, PGCE Wales
Ms S Wiseman, BSc Swansea

Dance:
*Ms R V Parry, BA Hons Bedford, PGCE Bedford
Mrs R Pavey, IDTA, BA Hons Rotterdam, Dip Vocational Training, Rotterdam Dance Academy Netherlands, Teaching Certificate Israel
Ms Z Pritchard

Physics:
*Mrs A B Kavanagh, BEd Hons Cheltenham
Mrs D L Davies, BSc Hons Wales, PGCE
Miss C Soler-Avila, BA Wales, PGCE Wales
Miss S Guha Roy, BEng Hons Liverpool

Psychology:
*Mrs A E Jervis, BSc, Hons Wales MA UWCN, PGCE Wales
Miss J Johnson, BSc Open, PGCE Carmarthen
Mrs J McQuitty, BSc Hons Nottingham

Religious Studies:
*Mr J M Lewis, BDiv MTh, PGCE Wales, MPhil
Mr T Arrand, MA Oxon PGCE Cantab
Dr S G Barnden, BA Hons Waterloo, Canada, MA Victoria, Canada, PhD Indiana, USA, PGCE Oxon
Miss J Johnson, BSc Open, PGCE Carmarthen

Learning Support:
*Mrs J Jefferies, BEd Liverpool, PGCE Gloucestershire
Mrs J Johnston, MA Hons St Andrews, TESOL London
Mrs C Llewelyn Somers, Learning Support Diploma RFDC

Inglefield House (Preparatory Department):
*Mrs S Riley, BSc Hons Swansea, PGCE Bristol
Mrs P M Champion, Dip Primary Education, Moray House
Mrs A Copley, BHEd Kingston Polytechnic
Mrs M E Dummett, BSc Open
Mrs H D Edmunds, BEd Liverpool
Mr T Evans, BA Hons Aberystwyth, PGCE Cardiff
Mrs A Griffiths, BA Hons Bristol
Mrs R J Hallett, BEd Hons Bristol
Mrs J A Jones, BA Hons Surrey, PGCE Kingston
Miss I L Kershaw-Naylor, BA Hons Cardiff, PGCE UWCN
Mrs H Rees, BA Joint Hons Cardiff, PGCE Wales
Mrs L C Reynolds, BA Hons Liverpool, PGCE CNAA

Librarian:
(*to be appointed*)

Speech and Drama:
Mrs M Hill, BA Belfast, Cert Ed, LGSM

Duke of Edinburgh's Award:
Mr A W Hunt, BSc, RMN, WGL

Haberdashers' Monmouth School for Girls is one of the three schools of the Jones's Monmouth Foundation, arising from a bequest of William Jones, Merchant, in 1615, and administered by the Worshipful Company of Haberdashers. The School stands high on the outskirts of the town of Monmouth, in the beautiful countryside of the Wye Valley.

There are 501 girls in the Main School including a Sixth Form of 156. Pupils aged from 7 to 11 years have their own preparatory school, Inglefield House, of 106 girls on site. A thriving Boarding Community with accommodation on the school site, includes a Junior House and modern Senior House with study-bedrooms. A Sixth Form Boarding House will open in September 2012 incorporating 45 en-suite bedrooms.

Classrooms and laboratories are extensive, with special Sixth Form provision. Specialist workshops are provided for

DT and Drama. Full use is made of the ample sports facilities: spacious playing fields, all-weather pitch, tennis courts, sports hall, indoor swimming pool and gymnasium. All are adjacent to the School. A new classroom extension, including 4 new ICT suites, opened in September 2006 and an updated Sixth Form block and Library in 2010.

The School has its own Chaplain and is a Christian foundation. Girls are encouraged to attend the places of worship of their own denomination.

A large and fully qualified staff of graduates teaches a modern curriculum, which aims to achieve high academic results within a broader education, acknowledging our cultural inheritance and technological and social needs.

Classics is taught throughout the School. At examination level, Latin GCSE, Latin AS/A Level, and Classical Civilisation AS/A Level are offered. Classical Greek is offered by request as an extra-curricular activity.

Almost all pupils progress to Higher Education. With excellent careers advice, girls are aware of the scope of degree subjects. A number annually enter Oxford and Cambridge.

Every encouragement is given to creative and practical work, especially Music and Drama. Girls frequently attend concerts, plays and exhibitions, and an active interest is taken in industry and management. Local businesses lend support to the School's Young Enterprise schemes.

Girls participate in the Duke of Edinburgh's Award scheme, CCF at Monmouth School, help in the community and many also belong to local voluntary organisations.

Main sporting activities include lacrosse, netball, tennis, rowing, fencing, hockey and dance, many played at County, National and International level.

Fees per term (2011-2012). (*See Scholarship Entries section*.) Day £3,142–£3,929, Boarding £6,593–£7,381.

Entry is usually at 7, 11, 13 (Common Entrance) or post GCSE, although occasionally other vacancies occur. Entrance to the first year of the Senior School is by examination, report from the current school and interview in January; scholarships and bursaries are awarded at this age, 13+ and for the Sixth Form.

Tests for entry to Inglefield House for girls of 7 years are held in the Lent Term.

Prospectus etc on application to the Admissions Registrar, e-mail: admissions@hmsg.co.uk.

Old Girls' Association. *Secretary*: Mrs S Rossiter, c/o Haberdashers' Monmouth School for Girls, Monmouth. The OGA Annual General Meeting is held at the school on the second Saturday in November.

Charitable status. William Jones's Schools Foundation is a Registered Charity, number 525616. The object of the Foundation shall be the provision and conduct in or near Monmouth of a day and boarding school for boys and a day and boarding school for girls.

Harrogate Ladies' College

Clarence Drive, Harrogate, North Yorkshire HG1 2QG
Tel: 01423 504543
Fax: 01423 568893
e-mail: enquire@hlc.org.uk
website: www.hlc.org.uk

Board of Governors:
Mrs R Bradby
Mrs L Byrne
Mr R Court
Mr C Davies
Mrs V Davies
Dr A Fahy
Mrs S Gosling
Mrs P Jones

Mr J Poskitt
Mrs S Pullan (*Chairman*)
Mr A Taylor
Mr A Thompson
Mrs R Tunnicliffe

Secretary to the Governors and General Manager of Allied Schools: Mr M Porter, BA, MSc

Headmistress: Mrs Rhiannon Wilkinson, MA Oxon, PGCE, MEd, DipSpLD

Deputy Head: Mrs N Dangerfield, BA Brighton
Director of Studies: Miss C Preece, BSc Manchester, MA OU, PGCE
Assistant Head (External Communications): (*to be appointed*)
Assistant Head (Pastoral & Boarding): Mrs H Stansfield, BEd Bedford
Director of Admissions: Mrs J Benammar, BA Leeds, M-ès-L Lille

Academic Staff:
Dr R Ashcroft, BA, PhD Huddersfield (*Head of History & Government and Politics*)
Mrs B Beckett, BA Leicester, PGCE (*English*)
Miss C Blake, BA UCL, PGCE (*Head of Classics*)
Mrs J Burnell, BA OU, Teaching Cert (*Mathematics*)
Miss N Butters, BA Leeds, PGCE, MMedSci Sheffield (*Head of Physical Education*)
Mrs A Chestnutt, BSc Bristol, PGCE (*Biology*)
Miss H Clothier, BA Salford, PGCE (*Head of Geography*)
Mr M Cook, Dip NCDT, MA King's College, PGCE (*Head of Drama*)
Miss J Cuthbert, BEd Coventry, MA Leeds (*Head of Support for Learning*)
Mrs J Davison, BA Leeds, PGCE (*Head of Lower School, German, French*)
Mrs R Donegan-Cross, BA Durham (*Chaplain*)
Mrs C Faber, MA Cantab, PGCE (*French, Spanish*)
Mr P C Gill, BA Leeds, MA Leeds, PGCE (*Head of Religious Studies*)
Mrs J Grazier, BEd Warwick, ACA (*Director of Business School*)
Miss P D Harrison, BA Sheffield, PGCE (*English*)
Mrs F Irvine, BEd Bedford (*Head of Middle School, Physical Education*)
Mr J Johnson, BA York St John, PGCE (*Head of Design Technology, Product Design*)
Miss J Kilburn, BA Liverpool (*Physical Education*)
Mr S Langford, BSc Heriot-Watt, PGCE (*Mathematics*)
Mrs J List, BA York, PGCE (*Biology, Head of Science*)
Mrs E Livesey, BA Central Lancashire, PGCE (*Head of Food & Nutrition, Head of Textiles*)
Mrs B Lumber, BSc Manchester, PGCE (*Head of Mathematics*)
Mr K Malone, BEng Bristol, CEng (*Mathematics*)
Mrs C M Martin, BA Leeds Polytechnic, AIL, PGCE (*French, Head of Modern Languages*)
Miss A Mitchell, BA Kent, PGCE, CELTA (*English, D of E*)
Mrs K Morgan, BMus, MusM Manc, PG Dip Music Therapy, PGCE (*Director of Music*)
Mr L Moya-Morallón, LLB Jaen, Spain, Diploma, PGCE (*Spanish, French*)
Mrs D M Murray, BA Cardiff, MA Bretton Hall PGCE (*Head of English*)
Miss C Preece, BSc Manchester, MA OU, PGCE (*Director of Studies, Head of Physics*)
Mr P Pritchard, BSc Exeter, PGCE (*Head of Chemistry*)
Miss C Reed, BSc UW, Bangor (*Psychology, Religious Studies*)
Mr A Riddell, BA Sheffield (*Economics*)
Mr S Rouse, BSc Imperial, PGCE (*Head of Physics*)

Mrs A J Saunders, BSc York, PGCE (*Chemistry, Examinations Officer*)
Mrs J Scarfe, BA SecEd QTS (*French*)
Mrs H Stansfield, BEd Bedford (*Assistant Head – Pastoral & Boarding, Physical Education*)
Mr R Tillett, MA Cantab (*Head of Sixth Form, History, Government & Politics*)
Mrs H Wakefield, BSc Aberystwyth, PGCE (*Science*)
Miss K Williams, BEd Leeds (*Head of Art*)

Academic Support Staff:
Mrs C S Alp, GRSM, LRAM, LGSM (*Pianoforte, Flute*)
Mrs M Bovino, BA Mus Hons (*Singing*)
Mrs F Brady, BSc Leeds Polytechnic, MCLIP (*Librarian*)
Mrs M Bushby, BA Leeds, LTCL, PGCE (*Piano, Violin*)
Mrs P M Coghlan, ALCM, LAM Gold Medal Speech and Drama (*Speech and Drama*)
Mrs J Frazer, LRAM, ARCM (*Piano, Flute*)
Mr R Horton, BSc Dunelm, PGCE (*Director of IT Systems*)
Mrs J Jackson, BA Hons OU, LRAM, PGCE (*Piano*)
Miss S Laverick, BA Mus (*Cello*)
Mrs D Martoglio, Montessori Teaching Diploma, CELTAA, CELTYL (*TEFL*)
Mr I Peak, BEd, LGSM (*Clarinet, Saxophone*)
Mr A P Selway, FRCO, GRSM, ARMCM P, ARMCM T (*Organ, Pianoforte, Choir Accompanist*)
Mr M Sidwell, BA, LRSM (*Trombone*)
Mrs L A Taylor-Parker, LRAM Speech and Drama (*Speech and Drama*)
Mr D Webster, BA Mus (*Guitar, Brass, Percussion, Music Technology*)
Miss N Woods, BA Mus (*Cello*)
Mrs R Yarborough, BA (*Singing*)

Support Staff:
Mr C Robinson (*Dining Room Manager*)
Mr J Brown (*Laboratory Technician*)
Mrs P O'Dowd (*Laboratory Technician*)
Mrs J Constance, RGN (*Health Centre Nurse*)
Mrs P Hall, RGN (*Health Centre Nurse*)
Mrs L Lenehan, RGN (*Health Centre Nurse*)
Dr S O'Neill, MB Bchir, MA, DRCOG, MRCGP, FPCert (*School Medical Officer*)
Mrs J Power (*PA to Headmistress*)
Mrs M Laverack, BEd Reading (*Data Manager*)
Mrs L O'Neill (*Office Secretary*)
Mrs J Childs (*Admissions Secretary*)
Mr D Sadler (*Clerk of Works*)
Mrs M Hamblin (*Property Lets*)
Mrs S Haider (*Pupils Accounts*)
Mrs J Holroyd (*Reception / Administrator*)
Mrs K Cave (*Reception / Administrator*)
Mrs J Horner (*Assistant Bursar*)
Mrs S Mitchell (*Purchase Ledger*)
Miss J Kilburn (*Housemistress*)
Mrs J Scarfe (*Housemistress*)
Mrs V Hutton (*Housemistress*)
Mrs A Thompson (*Housemistress*)
Miss C Cantwell (*Assistant Housemistress*)
Miss F Pattinson (*Assistant Housemistress*)
Miss P Jones (*Assistant Housemistress*)
Miss C Crowley (*Assistant Housemistress*)
Miss L Herd (*Assistant Housemistress*)

Numbers and Location. Harrogate Ladies' College is a Boarding and Day school for 315 girls aged 11–18. Situated within the College campus, Highfield Prep School, which opened in 1999, is a Day prep school for over 214 boys and girls between the ages of 4–11. The College is situated in a quiet residential area on the Duchy Estate about 10 minutes walk from the town centre and is easily accessible by road and rail networks. Leeds/Bradford airport is 20 minutes' drive away. Harrogate itself is surrounded by areas of natural interest and beauty.

Accommodation. Approximately half of the pupils are full or weekly boarders. Houses are arranged vertically from Upper Three (Year 7) to Lower Sixth. Upper Sixth Formers enjoy a greater sense of freedom in their own accommodation called 'Tower House'. This contains a large, modern kitchen, comfortable lounges and relaxation areas and girls have individual study bedrooms. Each house has a Housemistress and Assistant Housemistress who are responsible for the well-being of the girls.

Curriculum and Examinations. The College aims to provide a broad-based curriculum for the first three years in line with National Curriculum requirements. This leads to a choice of over 28 subjects at GCSE, IGCSE, Applied, AS and A Level mainly using syllabuses of the Northern Examination and Assessment Board (AQA). Each girl has a form tutor who continuously monitors and assesses her development.

Facilities. The central building contains the principal classrooms, hall, library, and dining rooms, and a VI Form Centre with studies, seminar rooms, kitchens and leisure facilities. The College Chapel is nearby. An extension provides 8 laboratories for Physics, Chemistry, Biology and Computer Studies. Three dedicated computer suites, provision in the boarding houses and throughout the school, form a computer network of 235 computers running Windows XP. Sixth formers have network access using their own laptops from studies and bedrooms. Additional facilities for specialised teaching include studies for Art, Pottery, Design and Technology, Drama and also for Home Economics and Textiles. A major innovation is the opening of our HLC Business School in the Autumn Term 2010, where Business, Accounting, Economics and Psychology are taught by specialist teachers. There is a well-equipped Health Centre with qualified nurses.

Sport. The College has its own sports hall, a full size indoor swimming pool, gymnasium, fitness centre, playing field, 9 tennis courts and 2 squash courts. Girls are taught a wide range of sports and may participate in sporting activities outside the school day. Lacrosse and netball are played in winter, and tennis, swimming and athletics are the main summer physical activities. Extra-curricular sports include badminton, sub-aqua, skiing, self-defence, judo, sailing and canoeing.

Sixth Form. The College has a thriving Sixth Form Community of 120 pupils. Girls have a choice of 26 courses at AS/A Level. There is a broad range of general cultural study. In preparation for adult life, Sixth Formers are expected to make a mature contribution to the running of the school and many hold formal positions of responsibility. Personal guidance is given to each girl with regard to her future plans and most pupils choose to continue their education at University.

Religious Affiliation. The College is Christian Evangelical although pupils of other religious denominations are welcomed. Religious teaching is in accordance with Christian principles and all girls attend Chapel services. A school confirmation is held each year in the chapel and girls may be prepared for acceptance into membership of churches of other denominations.

Music. A special feature is the interest given to music and choral work both in concerts and in the College Chapel, and the girls attend frequent concerts and dramatic performances in Harrogate. There are Junior and Senior choirs, orchestra, string, wind and brass groups.

Scholarships. Scholarships for music, art, drama and sport as well as some bursaries are awarded annually on the results of an examination held each Spring term and there are also several awards to girls already in the School.

Fees per term (2011-2012). Full and Weekly Boarding £7,825; International Boarders £9,417; Day £4,481. There is a reduction for a girl joining her sister in the School. The fees cover most normal school charges. Individual tuition in a musical instrument, Dance (Ballet/Tap/Modern), Riding or Diction is an extra charge.

Entry. Entry is usually at age 11, 13 or at Sixth Form level. Entry is based on the College's own entrance examination and a school report. Sixth Form entry is conditional upon GCSE achievement and an interview with the Headmistress.

Charitable status. Harrogate Ladies' College Limited is a Registered Charity, number 529579. It exists to provide high-quality education for girls.

Headington School

Oxford OX3 7TD
Tel: 01865 759100
           Admissions: 01865 759113
Fax: 01865 760268
e-mail: admissions@headington.org
website: www.headington.org

School Council:
Chairman: Mrs H Batchelor, BSc
Dr A Banning, MB BS, FRCP, MD, FESC
Mrs C Bevan, BSc, ACA, CTA
Mrs D Dance, MSc, MRICS
Dr K Drummond, MA Oxon, PhD
Mr C Harris
Mr S Harris
Lady N Kenny
Mr G Paine, JP, FCA
Miss M Rudland, BSc

Company Secretary: Mr J Clarke, BA
Clerk to the Council: Mr M Clarkson, MSc, CEng, MIMechE, MAPM, FCMI

Staff:
* *Head of Department*

Headmistress: Mrs C L Jordan, MA Oxon, PGCE

Senior Management Team:
Deputy Headmistress: Dr J Jefferies, BSc Hons, PhD Exeter, QTS
Deputy Headmistress: Mrs C Knight, BSc Strathclyde, PGCE Westminster College
Assistant Head/Director of Sport: Mr R Dodds, BSc Hons Exeter, PGCE Oxford
Assistant Head: Mr R Smith, MA Hons Aberdeen, PGCE Cantab
Bursar: Mr M Clarkson, MSc, CEng, MIMechE, MAPM, FCMI

Heads of Section:
Head of Boarding: Mrs V Ludwick, BA Hons Durham, PGCE Exeter
Celia Marsh Housemistress: Mrs A Bold, BA Hons, Maîtrise et License Marc Bloch University
Davenport Housemistress: Mrs S Gauntlett, BA Hons Plymouth, MA Exeter, PGCE Worcester College
Hillstow Housemistress: Mme C Sillah, Licence Orléans, PGCE Westminster College
Napier Housemistress: Miss R Challenor, BA Hons Christ Church Canterbury, PGCE Cambridge, MA Ed Bishop Grosseteste University College Lincoln

Head of Sixth Form: Mrs R Kitto, MA Open University, PGCE
Head of U6: Mrs J Perrin, BSc Hons UCW, MSc Open University (**Biology*)
Head of L6: Mrs S Wilkinson, BA Hons Newcastle, PGCE Oxford (**History*)

Head of Middle School: Ms B Dyer, BEd Hons Central School of Speech & Drama, ATCL Performing Trinity Guildhall

Head of U5: Mrs S Scott-Malden, BA Hons London, PGCE Oxford
Head of L5: Mrs M Clarke, BSc Portsmouth Polytechnic, PGCE Homerton

Head of Lower School: Mrs E Bedford, BA Hons Dunelm, MA Oxford Brookes, PGCE Oxford, FRGS
Head of U4: Miss R Ermgassen, BSc Bath
Head of L4: Mrs S Lowe, BMus, Grdip Tch & Lrn
Head of U3: Mrs S Young, BSc Bristol, MA Cantab, PGCE London

IB Team:
IB Coordinator: Mr J Stephenson, BSc Hons Nottingham, PGCE Oxford
Theory of Knowledge Coordinator: Mr M Wilson, MusB Manchester, PGCE Christ Church Canterbury
Creativity Action Service Coordinator: Mrs V Sinclair, CertEd Froebel Inst, CELTA Oxford Brookes

Art and Design and Art History:
*Mr M Taylor, BA Hons Coventry, PGCE Birmingham
Mr N James, BA Hons Cheltenham & Gloucester College, PGCE Surrey
Dr D Morrish, BA Hons York, MA Kent, DPhil York
Mrs M Taylor, DipArt Edinburgh, PGCE Birmingham
Ms K Turnbull, BA Hons, MA Central St Martins School of Art and Design

Business Studies:
*Mrs R Kitto, MA Open University

Classics:
*Mr D Hodgkinson, MA Oxon, MLitt Dublin, MCIEA
Mr R Batters, MA Hons Cantab, PGCE
Mrs L Workman, BA Hons Dunelm, PGCE Queens' College Cambridge (*part time*)

Drama and Theatre Studies:
*Mrs C Rigby, BA Hons, MA, Rose Bruford College of Speech and Drama
Miss F Curtis, MA Mountview Drama School (*visiting Trinity Guildhall coach*)
Ms B Dyer, BEd Hons Central School of Music & Drama, ATCL Performing Trinity Guildhall
Miss A Enticknap, BA Hons Roehampton Institute, PG Dip Oxford School of Drama (*visiting Trinity Guildhall coach*)
Theatre Staff:
Mr D Ferrier, BA Hons Rose Bruford College of Speech and Drama (*Theatre Manager*)
Mr J Welton (*Technician*)

Economics:
*Mrs M James, BA Hons London, PGCE London (*part time*)
Mrs C Buchanan, North Carolina State License
Mr P Kitovitz, BA Hons UCL

English:
*Mrs N Archer, BA Hons, PGCE London
Mr H Cumming, BA Hons UCL, PGCE Aberystwyth
Mrs J Hamilton, BA Hons, PGCE Leicester, MPhil Sheffield, Cert Adv Prof Practice Oxford Brookes
Mrs K Hegarty, BA Hons, DipEd Queen's Belfast
Dr D Morrish, BA Hons York, MA Kent, DPhil York
Mrs W Rooney, BA Hons Loughborough, PGCE Oxon (*part time*)
Mrs V Sinclair, CertEd Froebel Inst, CELTA Oxford Brookes
Mr R Smith, MA Hons Aberdeen, PGCE Cantab
Mr P Waddleton, BA Hons, MA Oxford Brookes, PGCE Westminster College, CTEFL

English as an Additional Language:
*Mrs V Sinclair, CertEd Froebel Inst, CELTA Oxford Brookes

Miss H Archer, BA Hons Oxon, MSt Oxon, CELTA (*part time*)
Mrs C Friedli, CELTA
Mrs S Hawkins (*part time*)
Miss A Pearson

Environmental Science:
*Mrs J Quirk, BSc Hons Birmingham, PGCE Oxford Brookes
Miss N Stanton, BA Oxford Brooks, PGCE Oxford

Examination Officers:
Mrs K Hegarty, BA Hons, DipEd Queen's Belfast

Geography:
*Mr D Cunningham, BSc Hons, PGCE Glasgow
Mr C Allen, BEd Bristol, MSc London, CertEd Bristol
Mrs E Bedford, BA Hons Dunelm, MA Oxford Brookes, PGCE Oxford, FRGS
Mrs L Gregory, BA Hons, PGCE Exeter
Dr J Jefferies, BSc Hons, PhD Exeter, QTS
Miss N Stanton, BA Oxford Brooks, PGCE Oxford

History:
*Mrs S Wilkinson, BA Hons Newcastle, PGCE Oxford
Mrs S Allerby, BA Hons Oxon, PGCE Oxford (*part time*)
Ms J Fitch, BA Hons UCW, MA Oxford Brookes, PGCE Bristol
Mrs S Scott-Malden, BA Hons London, PGCE Oxford
Mrs R Edsall, BA Hons Oxford, PGCE Cambridge

Law:
*Mrs C Shepherd, LLB Solicitor Birmingham (*part time*)
Politics:
*Mrs J Ormston, BA Hons UCL, PGCE London (*part time*)

Home Economics:
*Mrs M Colquhoun, BEd Hons Bath
Mrs Dianne Bates-Brownsword, BEd South Australian College of Advanced Education
Mrs J Peacock, CertEd Birmingham

Information & Communication Technology:
*Mr M Howe, BA Hons, PGCE East Anglia
Mr R Demaine, BA PGCE Rhodes University
Mr M Wilson, MusB Manchester, PGCE Christ Church Canterbury

Learning Development:
*Dr J Leadbeater, BA Hons, PhD Durham, Cert SpLD, CCET, CPT3A, SpLD APC
Mrs S Colman, PHN, Oxford Cert SpLD Masters Level, BDA Accredited (*part time, Specialist Teacher*)

Mathematics:
*Mrs R Bowen, MA Oxon, PGCE Oxon
Mrs M Clarke, BSc Portsmouth Polytechnic, PGCE Homerton
Mrs J Fouweather, BSc Hons, PGCE Hull (*part time*)
Miss R Hudson, BA Hons Oxon, PGCE Oxon
Mrs S Keen, BSc Hons Portsmouth, PGCE Cardiff
Mrs C Knight, BSc Strathclyde, PGCE Westminster College
Mr M Longson, BA Hons
Mrs J Moulds, BEd Middlesex
Mrs J Sephton, BA Hons Oxon, PGCE Sheffield (*learning development*)
Mrs S Young, BSc Bristol, MA Cantab, PGCE London
Mr T Duncan Ross, BA Hons Oxford, PGCE Oxford (*part time*)

Modern Languages:
*Mrs R Pike, BA Hons Exeter, PGCE Birmingham (*Spanish*)
Mrs C Casasbuenas, Graduada en Ciencias Bogotá (*Spanish Teacher and Assistant*)
Mme V Crépeau, Licence Caen, PGCE Oxford Brookes (*French, German*)

Mrs C D Cruz, MCIL, PGCE London (*French, Spanish*)
Mrs B Hamdy, BA University of Alexandria; PGCE Sheffield (*German*)
Mrs L Léchelle, BA, PGCE Oxford Brookes (*French*)
Mrs C Lau, MA Ed Oxford Brookes
Mme C Sillah, Licence Orléans, PGCE Westminster College (*French*)
Ms E Soar, BA Hons MSt Oxon, PGCE Brunel (**French*)
Mme M St Germain, DEUG, City & Guilds Cert (*French Assistant*)
Mrs G Thomas, Business Admin & Auditing Bogotá, MA, PGCE Oxford Brookes (*Spanish*)
Mrs E Whiteley, BA Hons, PGCE London (**German, French*)

Visiting teachers of Modern Languages:
Mrs S Hallas, BA, PGCE Leicester (*French, German, part time*)
Miss E Gernez, MA Diptrans (*French*)

Music:
*Mr M Paine, BA Hons, ARCM, PGCE Reading
Miss H Gillespie (*Graduate Assistant*)
Miss R Challenor, BA Hons Christ Church Canterbury, PGCE Cambridge, MA Ed Bishop Grosseteste University College, Lincs
Mr C Humphries, MA Huddersfield (*Technician*)
Mrs S Lowe, BMus, Grdip Tch & Lrn
Mr J Penman, BMus, MMus King's College, PGCE London

Visiting Instrumental Music Teachers:
Mr O Bonnici, ARCM, Gold Medal ENM (*Head of Strings; Violin, Viola, Quartets*)
Mrs J Cairns, GLCM, ALCM (*Clarinet, Clarinet Ensemble, Music Orders*)
Mrs M Cooper, GRSM, ARCM, PGCE (*Head of Piano, Piano, Accompaniments*)
Mr S Cooper, GRSM, MSTAT (*Bassoon*) Mrs J Dallosso MA, LGSM (*Cello*)
Mr T Dawes, BA, MSc (*Double bass, Percussion, Bass Guitar, Jazz*)
Mr S Dunstone, MA, CertEd (*Harp*)
Mrs E Emberson, AGSM, CT ABRSM (*Singing, Third and Fourth Form Choir*)
Ms G Fisher, ARCM, ALCM, CPPed (*Piano*)
Ms J Froomes, Grad Dip Mus (*Violin, Viola*)
Miss C Goble, BMus (*Head of Woodwind and Brass; Flute, Fl Group*)
Miss F Hedges, MA, ARCM, PGCE (*Piano, Double Bass*)
Mr G Howe, BA, FLCM, FNMSM, LTCL (*Sibelius Technician*)
Ms J Johnson, BMus (*Cello*)
Ms E Kreager, BA, DPhil, CT ABRSM (*Piano*)
Ms K Lawrie (*Piano*)
Mr M Leigh, BA, MA, PhD (*Piano*)
Mr R Leigh-Harris, MMus, GRSM, PGCE (*Harpsichord, Piano*)
Mr M Longson, BA (*Piano, Double Bass*)
Mr P Manhood, ATCL (*Classical Guitar, Guitar Group*)
Mr D McNaughton, BA (*Brass, Brass Ensemble*)
Mr T Perkins, LTCL (*Rock and Pop Guitar, Folk Group*)
Mrs E Reed, BA, MA (*Violin, Viola*)
Mr P Richardson, BA, MMus, LRAM (*Piano, Accompaniments*)
Mr P Riordan, BMus, LRAM (*Oboe*)
Mrs A Rogers, GRSM, LRAM (*Singing, Small vocal ensemble*)
Mrs L Stott, CT ABRSM (*Saxophone, Flute, Piano, Saxophone ensemble*)
Miss C Sweeney, BMus, PGCE (*Piano, Junior School Class Music*)
Mrs P Terry, DipEd, Dip ABRSM (*Recorder, Flute*)
Mr B Twyford (*Drum Kit*)

Physical Education:
*Miss P Thomas, BEd Hons De Montfort
Miss C Trenaman, BA Hons Durham, PGCE Exeter
Miss A Charania, BSc Hons Luton, PGCE Cheltenham
Miss L Cockshott, BEd PhyEd Bedford
Mrs J Collinson, BA Open University, CertEd Dartford
Mr R Demaine, BA, PGCE Rhodes University (*Director of Rowing*)
Miss F Ermgassen, BSc Hons Bath, PGCE Exeter
Miss A Groves, BEd Hons College of St Martin and St John, Plymouth
Mrs J Wareham, BEd Hons Reading
Graduate Assistant: Miss A Kyrke-Smith

Psychology:
*Mrs K Piggott, BA Cape Town, MA Oxford Brookes, PGCE Cape Town
Miss H Loughran, BSc Hons Dunelm
Miss S Patterson, BSc Hons Edinburgh, PGCE Oxford
Dr J Collett, BA Hons Middlesex, DPhil Oxford (*Part time*)

Religious Studies:
*Mr C Fox, BA Hons Sheffield, MA Warwick
Mrs S Lowe, BMus, Grdip Tch & Lrn
Mrs K Pringle, BA Hons Durham, MPhil Cambridge, PGCE Cambridge
Miss C Hegarty, BA Hons Durham, PGCE Oxford Brookes, NQT

Science:
*Mrs C Al-Sabouni, BA Hons Open University, PGCE Oxford (*Chemistry*)
Dr H Brooks, BSc Hons, PhD, PGCE London (*part time*)
Mrs A Coutts, BSc Hons, PGCE, MEd Warwick
Mrs A Curtis, MA Hons Cantab PGCE Homerton
Mr R Dodds, BSc Hons Exeter, PGCE Oxford
Mr J Kelly, MChem Oxon, PGCE Oxford
Miss E Krebs, BSc Hons Bristol, PGCE Oxford (*maternity leave*)
Ms H Mason, BA Hons Cambridge (*maternity cover*)
Mrs J Perrin, BSc Hons UCW, MSc Open University (*Biology*)
Mrs H Perry, BSc Hons, PGCE Cambridge (*part time*)
Mrs J Quirk, BSc Hons Birmingham, PGCE Oxford Brookes
Mrs M Rogers, BSc Hons Exeter, PGCE Oxford Brookes
Dr P Smaldon, BSc University College of Swansea, PhD Heriot-Watt University, CertEd Moray House Edinburgh
Mr J Stephenson, BSc Hons Nottingham, PGCE Oxford
Dr T Waite, BSc Hons, PHD Oxford Brookes
Miss R Warner, BSc Hons Nottingham, PGCE Loughborough
Miss C Wilkinson, BA Hons Oxon, PGCE Oxford
Miss S Patterson, BSc Hons Edinburgh, PGCE Oxford
Mrs A Waite, BSc Hons Rutgers University, USA, PGCE Delaware

Science Technicians:
Mrs K Oxley (*Senior Technician*)
Mrs I Kupce
Mrs N Rickets
Mrs M Smith
Mrs S O'Sullivan
Mrs H Woods

Administration and Maintenance:
PA to the Headmistress: Mrs L Hughes
PA to the Deputy Heads: Mrs C Escreet
PA to the Assistant Heads and IB Coordinator/School Secretary: Mrs J Martin
School Secretaries: Mrs E Puddefoot, Mrs F O'Neill
Sixth Form Administrator: Mrs C Lee
School Administrator/Napier Assistant: Mrs K Williams
Reprographics Technician: Ms A Clark

Bursary:
Bursar: Mr M Clarkson, MSc, CEng, MIMechE, MAPM, FCMI
Deputy Bursar: Mr A Rolfe, MDA Cranfield, BSc City of London, Dip Mgmt, FCMI, CMILT
Assistant Bursar: Mrs K Hoy, BSc, ACA
Estates Manager: Mr P Mulvany
Personnel Manager: Mrs J Seetaram
PAs to the Bursar: Mrs L Painter, BSc, Mrs A Miell
Bursary Assistants: Mrs K Jones, Mrs J Miller
Swimming Pool and Sports Hall Manager: Mr G Arman
School Staff Instructor: Mr P Dooley
Head of Grounds and Gardens: Mr D Hedger
Catering Manager: Mrs E J Giddy, MIH
Head Chef: Mr A Lawrence
Housekeeping Manager: Miss K Buxton, BSc Hons
Housekeeper: Mrs E Graham

Admissions, Development and Marketing:
Admissions Registrar: Mrs S Sowden, BSc, AKC, PGCE King's College London, Adv Dip Ed Man Open
Marketing Manager: Ms N O'Shea
Communications Officer: Ms J Nijssen
Deputy Admissions Registrar: Mrs T Wright
Admissions Assistant: Mrs B Coombes
Development & Alumnae Relations Officer: Mrs R Fraser
Administrative Assistant: Mrs M Velk

Boarding:
Head of Boarding: Mrs V Ludwick, BA Hons Durham, PGCE Exeter
Celia Marsh:
Housemistress: Mrs A Bold, BA Hons, Maîtrise et License Marc Bloch University
Residential Matron: Mrs Lyn Davies, LTCL
Matron Nurse: Mrs J Talkington, BA Hons PCET, RGN, CertEd
Graduate House Assistant: Miss E Hennah
Davenport:
Housemistress: Mrs S Gauntlett, BA Hons Plymouth, MA Exeter, PGCE Worcester College
Matron Nurse: Mrs Y Peacock, SEN, SRN
Graduate House Assistant: Miss J Wasilewska
Hillstow:
Housemistress: Mme C Sillah, Licence Orléans, PGCE Westminster College
Matron Nurse: Mrs C Heyns
Graduate House Assistant: Miss L Nixon
Napier:
Housemistress: Miss R Challenor, BA Hons Christ Church Canterbury, PGCE Cambridge, MA Ed Bishop Grossteste University College Lincoln
Matron Nurse: Mrs F Graham, RSCN, RGN
Graduate House Assistant: Miss R Beharell, BA Hons Oxford Brookes

Information Centre:
Mrs L Winkworth, MCLIP, Chartered Librarian
Ms C Friedli, CELTA
Miss L Shlugman, BA Hons

IT Support:
IT Manager: Mr J Carver, MCSE, MCP+I, FETC, AIITT
Network Manager: Mr M Levett, Dip Eng Oxford Brookes
Information Manager: Ms E Kalinina, MCSE, MA Moscow, Power Engineering Inst
Support Engineer: Mr P Branson MCP
Support Engineer: Mr N Salter MCDST, MCP, COMPTIA A+, COMPTIA N+
Support Engineer/Music Tech: Mr C Humphries, MA Huddersfield

Medical Staff:
School Doctors from the Manor Surgery, Headington
Dr G Sacks, MB
Dr H Merriman, MB BS, FFARCS, MRCGP, DRCOG

Health Centre Nurse: Ms C Gordon, RGN

School Counsellor:
Miss S Tucker, BSc Hons Surrey, MA Southern Illinois

Visiting Coaches:
Badminton: Mr I Grierson, BBA
Basketball: Mr S Cruz, BBA
Dance: Miss E Hardy
Fencing: Mrs J Douglas
Gymnastics: Mrs K Hogan
Judo: Mrs L Scarlett, BJA
Rowing:
Mr P Barnett, J14
Miss A Briegle, J13
Mr R Demaine, Director
Mr C Hermes, Boatman and Senior Support
Miss H Loughran, J16
Miss C Murphy, J15
Mrs K Solesbury (née Greves)
Mr S Wells, J15 Support
Miss C Van Besouw, J13 Support
Swimming: Dr R Porter, RLSS
Tennis: Mr J Baker, BTCA
Trampolining: Miss S Costigan, BTF

Headington School Oxford is a boarding and day school for 750 girls aged 11–18. Despite our position in the academic first division, our true strength lies in our commitment to meeting the needs of each individual pupil. Whether your daughter's strengths are academic, musical, sporting, creative or even entrepreneurial, we can provide the facilities and expertise that will enable her to develop her natural talents and to succeed.

A separate Preparatory School for 280 girls aged 3–11 occupies its own site just across the road. (*See Headington Preparatory School entry in IAPS section.*)

The school was founded in 1915 and moved to its current buildings in 1930, set amidst 23 acres of grounds just one mile from the centre of Oxford and under 60 miles from London. It is a Church of England Foundation but girls of all denominations are actively welcomed.

Facilities. A steady programme of building and upgrading has ensured excellent facilities for living and working. Our state-of-the-art new Music School, complete with electronics studio, recording studio and performance spaces both indoors and out, opened its doors in 2009. The Theatre at Headington – a 240-seat professional theatre – is the focus for a broad programme of school events and touring shows, ranging from music, theatre and comedy to monologues, fashion shows and a Sixth Form lecture series. Other recent developments cover a broad spectrum of school life, and include a new purpose-built boarding house for 45 girls, an art and design centre, an additional science laboratory, a sports hall, a fitness centre and a new dining hall.

Curriculum. The National Curriculum is broadly followed up to GCSE level. In addition all girls take a three year course in Latin, from 12–14, and take either German or Spanish for one year before choosing GCSE subjects. All girls take GCSEs in English, French, Mathematics and Science and half or full GCSEs in Religious Studies and Information Technology. Up to five other subjects are chosen from Geography, History, Spanish, German, Greek, Latin, Classical Studies, Music, Drama, Art and Design, Food, Textiles, Physical Education. Personal and Social Education and Physical Education are also compulsory.

90% stay at Headington for their Sixth Form education, and are joined by a number of new girls, some of whom come from overseas. The International Baccalaureate is offered as an alternative to A Levels, providing a challenging curriculum for independent learners keen to continue to study a wide range of subjects. A Level students choose from a range of 30 subject options, typically studying four or five to AS Level, and reducing to three for A Level.

Parents are kept closely informed of their daughter's progress, and regular parent meetings are held.

Physical Education. There is a very high standard of Physical Education and the school has an inclusive approach to sport for all. Our sports facilities include 23 acres of playing fields and grounds, a 25m swimming pool, a modern gym complex including multi gym facilities, netball, hockey and tennis courts, a dedicated rowing building, a new fitness trail and a shared boat house in Oxford. The school "match" sports are hockey, netball, tennis, athletics, fencing, swimming with teams regularly named County Champions, and with girls playing in County and regional teams. Our Equestrian Team is active, and Headington runs an annual Showjumping Competition. Headington is amongst the leading girls' schools for rowing in the UK, with alumnae and current pupils frequently representing England and Great Britain at international and Olympic levels. Physical Education is also available as a GCSE and A Level subject.

Music. The completion of the new Music School in 2009 reflects the school's commitment to musical excellence in all areas. Over 400 individual music lessons take place every week, and all musicians are encouraged to join our orchestras, choirs and ensembles. The Chamber Choir regularly tours Europe, and the Show Band supports our school productions.

Drama. The Theatre is home to a thriving drama department. There are numerous major and minor productions each year and girls of all ages become involved in all aspects of theatre, from writing and producing their own plays, to lighting, costume and make-up. They may study for GCSE Drama and Theatre Studies at AS and A2 Levels, and many girls take Guildhall Speech and Drama courses. There are regular professional productions, as well as English and drama workshops.

Extra-Curricular Activities. Extra-curricular activities and clubs are an integral part of school life and take place at lunch time as well as after school. Over 50 clubs are on offer, including a Dragon's Den-style 'Running Your Own Company' scheme, an active CCF contingent and a thriving Duke of Edinburgh's Award programme. Recent World Challenge expeditions have headed for India, Nepal, Botswana and Zambia. There is a strong tradition of community service, with numerous charity events as well as the opportunity to help in local hospitals, schools for the handicapped and charity shops. Much use is made of Headington's proximity to London, Stratford and particularly Oxford. There are regular trips for all age groups to theatres, concerts, lectures, museums and galleries, while Oxford draws many visiting speakers, who often include Headington in their itinerary.

Higher Education and Careers. All girls continue to higher education, heading to leading universities in the UK and abroad. A significant number of girls choose Oxbridge each year; some head for medical or veterinary college and others take up Art Foundation courses. Girls graduate from a wide range of arts and science degrees in subjects as diverse as civil engineering, architecture and textiles. Detailed assistance on choice of universities is given in the Sixth Form through specialist computer programmes and careers tutors. A careers programme is in place throughout the school, with plenty of individual help as girls reach their GCSE years.

Boarding. Boarding at Headington is designed to offer maximum flexibility to families and there are a number of different options available. Full boarding follows the traditional format, with a full programme of weekend activities on offer, ranging from trips to London for the ballet, theatre, exhibitions or shopping to ice skating, horse riding or indoor skiing. Weekly boarding is popular choice, with girls going home on Friday or Saturday and returning to school on Sunday or Monday. Flexi-boarding sees girls board a regular one or two nights a week, whilst occasional boarding is for the one-off night, either to accommodate parental commitments or to allow girls to try the boarding experience.

There are four boarding houses, each with its own distinct character, run by a dedicated team of house staff. The Sixth Form houses offer a secure link between school and university, with a number of girls opting to board for the first time at this stage.

Uniform. The blue-checked skirt, pale blue shirt, jumper and blazer are smart, comfortable and easy to care for. Girls in the Sixth Form wear their own smart-casual clothes.

Entrance. Contact Sue Sowden, Admissions Registrar, to request an application form and prospectus. Places in the Preparatory School are offered in order of application for those aged 3–6 and, for pupils aged 7+ upwards, is subject to an interview and a short test. Entrance to the Senior School is by examination: Common Entrance Examination for 13+, and school's examination for 11+, 12+, 14+ and 16+ ages. Early application is advised and applications should usually be made at least a year before the proposed date of entry.

Registration Fee: £95 (UK) and £150 (Overseas). Overseas Examination Fee: £100. Deposit: UK: £2,000 (day), £3,000 (boarding); Overseas: £4,000 plus £10,000 fee advance.

Fees per term (2011-2012). Full Boarders: £8,018–£8,606; Weekly Boarders: £7,368–£7,760; Day Girls £4,360–£4,445.

Scholarships and Bursaries. (*See Scholarship Entries section.*) Means-tested bursaries of up to 100% of fees are available at age 9, 11, 13 and 16. Academic, Music, Drama, Art and Sport awards are also available; these carry a fixed value of £300 (with the exception of music awards, which comprise free tuition on one or two instruments). Scholarships may be augmented with means-tested bursaries, should families wish it. The school may be prepared to waive registration, scholarship and examination fees where the payment of these will cause undue hardship – please contact the Registrar for details. Bursaries are also available to girls whose families are in the armed forces or clergy.

Charitable status. Headington School Oxford Limited is a Registered Charity, number 309678. It exists to provide quality education for girls.

Heathfield School
Ascot

London Road, Ascot, Berkshire SL5 8BQ
Tel: 01344 898343
Fax: 01344 890689
e-mail: registrar@heathfieldschool.net
website: www.heathfieldschool.net

Board of Governors:
Chairman: Mr Tom Cross Brown, MA Oxon, MBA Insead
The Revd Jonathan Baker, MA Oxon, MPhil, Dip Theology
Mrs Sally-Anne Barrett
Mr Stephen Bishop
Mrs Penny Bristow
Mr Jonathan Davie, FCA
Mr Guy Egerton-Smith
Mr Robert Gregory, BSc Hons
Miss Caroline Slettengren, BSc Hons
Mrs Sally Tulk-Hart
The Revd Canon Dr Philip Ursell, BA Wales, MA Oxon
Dr Meg Weir, MBBS, FRCP

Headmistress: Mrs J Heywood, BSc Hons Kingston, PGCE Kingston

Deputy Headmistress: Miss B Kelly, BA Hons Dunelm, PGCE Exeter

Bursar: Mr J Bueno, FAIA, MCMI

+ *Head of Faculty*
* *Teacher in Charge/Subject Leader/Coordinator*

Head of Mathematics & Sciences Faculty: Miss C Wells, BSc Hons Bath, PGCE Exeter

Business Studies & Economics:
*Miss J Dawson, BA Hons Exeter, PGCE St Mary's
Mrs G Kendall, BA Reading, PGCE London

Mathematics:
Miss T Cole, MSc Reading, PGCE Reading
Mr J Doyle, BA Canberra, DipEd Canberra
Miss E Fagin, BSc Hons Galway, DipEd Galway
*Mr A Mughal, BA Hons Kingston, PGCE Brunel
Mrs K Sawers, BEd Glasgow, ACCA

Science:
*Miss T Cole, MSc Reading, PGCE Reading
Miss E Fagin, BSc Hons Galway, Dip. Ed Galway
Mrs J Kemp, BSc London
+Miss C Wells, BSc Hons Bath, PGCE Exeter
Mrs C Hobden, BSc Jnt Hons Birmingham (*Senior Lab Technician*)
Mrs A Milner, HND Ulster, BSc Ulster (*Lab Technician*)

Head of Creative Arts Faculty: Mrs C Smith, Cert HE & Ed London

Art:
*Mrs J Leibovici, BA Southampton, PGCE Reading, RSA Royal Society of Arts
Mrs A Rutili, BA Hons Fine Arts Academy Italy, PGCE Greenwich
Mrs M Blackburn, BEd Cardiff

Cookery:
+*Mrs C Smith, Cert HE & Ed London
Mrs M Blackburn, BEd Cardiff

Dance:
Mrs N Shaw, BA West Sussex, ALAM, RAD TC, AISTD

Drama:
*Mrs H Bamford, BA Hons Surrey, PGCE Reading
Mr S Brant, BA Hons Loughborough, MA London (*Actor in Residence*)
Mrs N Shaw, BA West Sussex, ALAM, RAD TC, AISTD

Music:
*Mrs J Dance, BA Hons Birmingham, PGCE Birmingham
Mr N Sayers, BA Hons Cantab (*Musician in Residence*)
(*plus visiting peripatetic staff*)

Photography:
*Miss K White, BA Hons Oxford Brookes, ABIPP

Head of Humanities & Languages Faculty: Mrs B Mason, BA Hons Nottingham, PGCE London, Cert SpLD

English:
Mrs R Fotheringham, MA Natal, BA Hons Natal, BEd Natal
*Mr A Grey, MA Oxon, PGCE Lancaster
Miss M Harris, MA, MSc Edinburgh

EFL:
*Mrs E O'Kelly, Cert TESOL Trinity
Mrs R Fotheringham, MA Natal, BA Hons Natal, BEd Natal

Geography:
+*Mrs B Mason, BA Hons Nottingham, PGCE London, Cert SpLD
Mrs S Ingram, BEd Hons London

Librarian & Head of Careers:
Mrs K Bramley, MA Wales, Dip Lib

History & Politics:
*Miss N Holsgrove-Jones, BA Hons, PGCE East Anglia
Miss E Murray, BA Hons St Andrews, PGCE Cumbria

History of Art:
Ms J Meeson, BA Hons East Anglia

Modern Foreign Languages:
*Mrs F Rayner, MA Strasbourg, PGCE Oxford Brookes (*French & Spanish*)
Mrs R Lankshear, M-ès-L Pau, L-ès-L Pau (*French & Spanish*)
Mrs A Pullen, BA Hons Madrid (*Spanish*)
Mrs A Diaz, BA Hons Open University (*French and Spanish*)
Miss J Vara (*French Assistant*)

Religious Studies & Classics:
Mrs R Reeves, MA Div Edinburgh, PGCE Roehampton
*Miss K Sass, BA Hons Middlesex, PGCE Exeter
Mr A Valner, MA Nottingham, PGCE London

Spectrum Learning Development:
Mrs A Jones, Diplome de Langues Paris (*Teaching Assistant*)
*Mrs J Marin, BEd Hons Manchester
Mrs B Mason, BA Hons Nottingham, PGCE London, Cert SpLD
Mrs S Butler, BA Hons Oxon

Physical Education:
Miss S Kay, BA Hons Manchester Metropolitan
Miss A Rubin, BA Hons Wooster, Ohio
Miss J Talbot, BPhysEd Otago, NZ
*Miss S Windle, BSc, PGCE De Montfort
Mrs S Bettison, DipEd London (*PE Technician*)
(*plus visiting Lacrosse, Tennis and Fencing coaches*)

Equestrian Coordinator:
Mrs G Glimmerveen

Duke of Edinburgh's Award Coordinator:
Ms D Hunt

PSHE:
*Mrs A Diaz, BA Hons Open University

Pastoral:
Head of Boarding: Miss E Pointon
Head of Sixth Form: Mrs S Ingram, BEd Hons London
Head of House, Austen: Mrs R Lankshear, M-ès-L Pau, L-ès-L Pau
Deputy Head of Austen: Miss J Dawson, BA Hons Exeter, PGCE St Mary's
Head of House, De Valois: Ms J Talbot, BPhysEd Otago, NZ
Deputy Head of House, De Valois: Mrs R Reeves, MA Div Edinburgh, PGCE Roehampton
Head of House, Seacole: Mrs J Kemp, BSc London
Deputy Head of House: Miss S Kay, BA Hons Manchester Metropolitan
Head of Somerville: Mr J Doyle, BA Canberra, DipEd Canberra
Deputy Head of House, Somerville: *Miss K White, BA Hons Oxford Brookes, ABIPP

Head of Lower School: Mrs J Kemp, BSc London
Housemistress, Form I: Mrs C Beresford
Housemistress, Form II: Ms S Crafer
Housemistress, Form III: Ms A Brooks
Housemistress, Form IV: Mrs V Leathart
Housemistress, Form V: Mrs J Liepa, BA Hons London, PGCE Middlesex
Housemistress, UVI Form: Mrs P Munro and Mrs P Kerley
Housemistress, LVI Form: Miss S Broomfield
Housemistress, Forms III & IV: Mrs A Diaz

Senior Nursing Sister: Sister E Hill, SRN, DN Cert
Nursing Sister: Sister M Couzens, RGN
Nursing Sister: Sister L Brazel, BSc Hons London, RGN

Administration:
Director of IT: Mr M Taylor, BSc Eng London, PGCE Greenwich, FIDM, MBCS, MCIM
Headmistress's PA & Administrative Coordinator: Ms P Lavender, BA Hons Open University
Registrar: Mrs R Farha
Deputy Bursar: Mrs L Farrin

Introduction. Heathfield is a leading boarding school for girls aged between 11 and 18 years. The school is set in thirty-five acres of stunning grounds with outstanding facilities, just twenty-five miles from London and within easy reach of major airports, motorways and rail networks.

Heathfield is unashamedly comfortable but also competitive and academically rigorous. The day does not finish at 4 pm, or the week on Friday! We offer unrivalled opportunities for personal growth and development, seven days a week.

Being part of our community is a real joy. We believe the time spent outside the classroom is just as important as the time spent in it. Evenings and weekends are filled with a diverse range of activities, from clubs and sports to the Duke of Edinburgh's Award and foreign trips.

Atmosphere and Ethos. At the heart of our school runs a guiding and enlightening Christian ethos. We also embrace technology and use contemporary teaching methods to achieve academic goals. Our aim is to help every student get the most out of life by providing the very best intellectual stimulation, physical challenges and pastoral care.

Pastoral Care. Heathfield is a true home from home. Every girl is supported by a team of academic staff, Housemistress, Head of House and Sixth Form prefects. They work together to provide the highest level of pastoral care, which is one of the school's hallmarks. We believe in individual attention for every girl and teachers will meet with your daughter regularly to discuss her particular needs and to ensure she is achieving her maximum potential.

Curriculum. While the more traditional subject combinations remain most popular, there is also excellence in the creative subjects. Twenty-four subjects are offered at AS and A Level, along with the Leith's Basic Certificate in Food and Wine. Academic results are consistently impressive and all girls go on to higher education including Oxbridge.

Activities. The St Mary's Theatre and the Sports Hall are always hives of activity and there are many other extra-curricular activities: frequent museum and theatre trips, field trips and overseas visits.

Sport. We have a large multi-purpose gym, two squash courts, dance studio, five lacrosse pitches, tennis courts and an indoor swimming pool. The school competes in lacrosse, netball, polo, skiing and swimming.

Boarding Accommodation. Our boarding accommodation is excellent. From Form IV onwards all girls have single rooms, offering all-important privacy. For more freedom and independence, the Upper Sixth live in a modern Sixth Form House with comfortable lounges and kitchen facilities.

Medical Welfare. We are not just focused on a healthy mind. Two full-time nursing sisters and the school doctor are in charge of the girls' medical welfare supported by Heads of Houses, Housemistresses and Tutors. If you have any concerns please call your daughter's Head of House or Housemistress who is available at all times.

New Facilities. An extended and refurbished library was opened in 2007 and the new St Mary's Theatre was completed in spring 2009. Further development will be undertaken over the course of the next few years in line with the growing demand for places.

Admission. Entry for the majority of pupils is at eleven; a few girls join at twelve or thirteen or come into the Lower Sixth Form for A Level studies. Junior entrants are assessed at the school on 'invitation days' which involve examinations, workshops and interviews and to which girls are invited to bring work that they are proud of. Common

Entrance examinations are also used as a guide to setting if they are taken.

Entry into the Lower Sixth Form is via predicted GCSE grades and interview.

Scholarships and Bursaries. A number of "All Rounder" scholarships for entry to the Junior School and both Academic and Creative scholarships for the Sixth Form are awarded each year. The school also offers a number of means-tested bursaries each year amounting to almost £200,000.

Fees per term (2011-2012). £9,150 for Forms I and II and £9,650 for Forms III and above.

Charitable status. Heathfield School is a Registered Charity, number 309086. It exists to provide a caring boarding education leading to higher education for girls aged between 11 and 18.

Heathfield School
GDST

Beaulieu Drive, Pinner, Middlesex HA5 1NB
Tel: 020 8868 2346
Fax: 020 8868 4405
e-mail: enquiries@hea.gdst.net
website: www.heathfield.gdst.net

Founded 1900.

Heathfield School is part of the GDST (Girls' Day School Trust). The GDST is the leading network of independent girls' schools in the UK. As a charity that owns and runs 24 schools and two academies, it reinvests all its income in its schools. For further information about the Trust, see p. xxi or visit www.gdst.net.

Additional information about the school may be found on the school's website and a detailed prospectus is available from the school.

Governing Body:
Sir Michael Partridge, KCB (*Chairman*)

Headmistress: Mrs A Stevens, BA Hons, PGCE, NPQH

Deputy Headmistress: Ms K Hollingdale, BA East Anglia

Head of Sixth Form: Ms L Smith, MA, BSc Open University

Head of Junior Department: Mrs C McCulloch, BA Leeds

Head of Careers: Mrs K Walley, BA Oxon

Examinations Officer: Mr R J Pimlott, BA Middlesex

Admissions Secretary: Mrs J Smith

Number of Pupils. 530 (Juniors 157; Seniors 373 including 83 in the Sixth Form).

Heathfield School was founded in Harrow and it moved to its present location in September 1982, and became a member of the Girls' Day School Trust in September 1987. The School is situated on a nine-acre site, including 6 tennis courts and playing fields, and is well served by trains and buses, the nearest stations being Eastcote and Rayners Lane.

We aim to provide a broad and balanced education which will enable girls to achieve their academic personal and social potential within an intellectually stimulating, caring and secure environment, and to prepare them to take responsibility for themselves and others.

The accommodation includes seven Science Laboratories, four Computer Rooms, Art Rooms, Textiles Room, and a large Learning Resources Centre. The Junior Department is housed in new purpose-built separate accommodation where there are 11 classrooms, a Hall, Library and specialist rooms for Music, Science and Technology. A new indoor

Swimming Pool, Sports Hall and Senior Library were opened in January 2000. These have been followed by a new Music Suite, ICT Rooms, Careers Room and Science laboratories. A new dining room and Drama Studio followed in 2004. A new Sixth Form Centre was completed in September 2008.

In the Nursery, children learn through the teaching of specific skills and structured play. All the National Curriculum subjects are then taught up to Year 6. ICT is an integral part of the curriculum for all girls and the Juniors have their own computer room, library, science lab and art room. A second nursery class opened in January 2011.

The Senior School then provides a general education up to GCSE and AS/A2 Level, and also offers a wide range of trips, visits and extra-curricular activities. All Sixth Form leavers continue to Universities, including Oxford and Cambridge. All the National Curriculum subjects are offered, plus Textiles, Drama, Latin and Classics. Mandarin, Spanish and French are taught. A particular emphasis is placed on the use of ICT across the curriculum. The girls take nine or 10 GCSEs and non-examined courses in PE and Personal, Social and Health Education. Twenty-four subjects are taught at A Level including Government and Politics, Economics, Business Studies, Psychology, History of Art, and Philosophy and Ethics. Sixth Form classes are small and the students are encouraged to take greater responsibility for their own learning. Careers education begins in Year 8 and continues right through the Sixth Form. Emphasis is placed on the development of enterprise and leadership skills at all ages.

A special feature of the school is its happy, caring and friendly ethos and its family atmosphere. Pastoral care is accorded a high priority throughout the School and we believe strongly in a triangular partnership between parents, girls and staff. Sport, Music and Drama have a high profile as does Public Speaking and The Duke of Edinburgh's Award. The International School Award was given in 2008, The Artsmark Silver in 2008, the Career Mark in 2009 and the ICT Mark in 2010. A wide range of clubs and societies are on offer covering activities as varied as Young Enterprise, Speech and Drama, Chess and dance. Girls are also encouraged to take their share of responsibility for school affairs by serving as form captains and participating in the School Council, as well as serving the local community through social service work.

Admission. Girls enter the School in the Junior Department at 3+, 4+ and 7+, or the Senior School at 11+ and 16+.

An Entrance Examination is held each January for girls wishing to enter the Senior School at 11+ in the following September. Sixth Form places are available for girls who have reached a certain standard at GCSE.

A number of scholarships and bursaries are available. The bursaries are means-tested and are intended to ensure that the school remains accessible to bright girls who would profit from our education but who would be unable to enter the school without financial assistance.

Fees per term (2011-2012). Senior School £4,223; Junior Department (for age 4+ to 10) £3,286 (including lunches); Nursery (for age 3+) £2,538 (excluding lunches).

Prospectus and registration forms may be obtained from the Admissions Secretary at the school; e-mail: admissions @hea.gdst.net.

Charitable status. Heathfield School, Pinner is part of The Girls' Day School Trust, which is a Registered Charity, number 306983.

Hethersett Old Hall School

Norwich Road, Hethersett, Norwich, Norfolk NR9 3DW
Tel: 01603 810390
Fax: 01603 812094

e-mail: enquiries@hohs.co.uk
website: www.hohs.co.uk

Chairman of Governors: Mrs Miranda Richards

Head: Mr S G Crump, MA

Deputy Headmistress: Mrs J Davies, MA

Senior Housemistress: Mrs C Swallow

Financial Administrator: Mrs L Findlay

Head's Secretary: Mrs S Cheshem-Panam

Registrar: Mrs K Borrer

Hethersett Old Hall School, founded in 1938, is located in 16 acres of beautiful Norfolk countryside in the heart of East Anglia, just minutes from Norwich city centre.

The school is a charitable trust administered by a Board of Governors, which is in membership of AGBIS. The Head is a member of GSA and the school is also in membership of BSA.

The school provides full, weekly and flexi- boarding and day education for 205 pupils aged between 4 and 18 years old. The school welcomes international students and accepts girl boarders from Year 5 or age 9. The Pre-Prep and Junior Departments are co-educational and the Senior Department and Sixth Form are for girls.

Younger boarders live in the historic main house and sixth formers have their own separate building. All girls are cared for by resident house staff that organise an exciting programme of evening and weekend activities.

Aims. Hethersett offers a friendly, supportive community in which each child is encouraged to develop their academic, creative and practical skills and to become self-reliant, tolerant and concerned for others.

Curriculum. Classes are small and teaching staff are well qualified, well informed and enthusiastic.

The Pre-Prep Department is situated in modern, purpose-built accommodation with a dedicated play area. The key skills of reading, writing and numeracy are developed in a stimulating atmosphere that builds on children's natural inquisitiveness and enthusiasm for learning.

The Junior Department provides a thorough grounding in the core curriculum. Sport, drama and music feature strongly in each year's programme of study. There are many opportunities for pupils to compete against other schools in swimming galas and games fixtures.

Pupils in the Senior School are offered a broad range of academic, technological and creative subjects. Their achievements at GCSE are consistently high. In 2010, 85% of pupils gained 5+ GCSEs A*–C, 80% of pupils gained 5+ GCSEs A*–C including Maths and English, making HOHS one of the Top 5 schools in Norfolk. Support, advice and individual care throughout the senior school enables pupils to be confident in planning their future education and careers.

Sixth Form. A wide range of AS and A Level subjects are offered, from the unusually creative combination of art, photography and art textiles to the traditional three sciences. Most sixth formers go on to university after benefiting from personal guidance in choosing courses, completing their UCAS form and composing their personal statement. In 2007–2010, 100% of applicants gained entry to their chosen university, including Oxford and St Andrews to study medicine.

Buildings and Facilities. The school has excellent teaching facilities with bright, modern, purpose-built Pre-Prep and Junior Departments. The main teaching blocks feature an ICT suite, science laboratories, library and an art and technology suite with photography dark room. Pupils also benefit from the dedicated music rooms, 'The Barn' for drama, indoor heated swimming pool, tennis courts and sports fields. Sixth formers have their own common room,

kitchen and study rooms. The boarding facilities include bright, attractive accommodation for younger girls with en-suite bathrooms. Older girls move onto single study-rooms and sixth formers are housed in their own separate building.

Recreational Activities. The school offers a wide range of recreational activities and optional extras which includes drama, singing and music tuition, sport fixtures and galas, The Duke of Edinburgh's Award scheme, Young Enterprise Award Scheme and the Schools' Challenge Quiz.

Entrance. Entry is by the school's own assessment designed to give staff an indication of the child's stage of development, so that an appropriate programme of study can be arranged. The assessment focuses on Maths, English and a Reasoning Test. Entry to the Sixth Form is by interview, school record and assessment. For further information or to obtain a prospectus please contact the Admissions Secretary.

Fees per term (2011-2012). Pre-Prep Department £2,525; Junior Department (age 7–11): £2,975 (day), £4,275 (weekly boarding); £4,975 (full boarding); Senior School: £3,975 (day), £5,700 (weekly boarding); £7,400 (full boarding).

Scholarships. (*See Scholarship Entries section.*) Year 7: there are 3 types of scholarship; academic, creative (drama, music or art) and sporting. Years 7–10: two boarding scholarships worth 20% of the boarding fee. Sixth Form: two types of scholarship; academic and citizenship. A Sixth Form Boarding Scholarship can also be awarded on the criteria of either of the above.

Charitable status. Hethersett Old Hall School is a Registered Charity, number 311273. It exists to provide a high quality education.

Hollygirt School

Elm Avenue, Nottingham NG3 4GF
Tel: 0115 958 0596
Fax: 0115 989 7929
e-mail: info@hollygirt.co.uk
website: www.hollygirt.co.uk

Trustees:
Mr R A Heason, FCA (*Chairman*)
Mr D Ackroyd
Mrs S Allan
The Revd S Hippisley-Cox
Mr A Jamieson
Mr W S Phillips, FCA
Mrs B Rimmer, CertEd

Headmistress: **Mrs P S Hutley**, BA Hons Worcester, PGCE Wales, MSc Huddersfield

Deputy Head: Mrs S Brooksby, BA Hons Leeds, PGCE Bristol (*Head of History*)

Senior School:
Mrs C Anstey, BEd Alberta, Canada (*Joint Head of Design & Technology*)
Mrs S W Atherton, MA Oxon, PGCE Oxford (*Head of Science, Biology*)
Mrs C Barker, BSc Hons, PGCE Bristol (*Examinations Officer*)
Mr R A C Bill, BEng Hons Liverpool, PGCE Oxford, MIT (*Director of ICT*)
Mr D Briggs (*Head of Geography*)
Mrs C Ebbage, BA Open University, PGCE Liverpool (*Physical Education*)
Mrs D Forrest, BEd Leicester College of Education (*Mathematics*)
Mrs D Griffiths, BA Hons Leicester, PGCE Nottingham (*Head of Religious Studies*)
Miss L Howd, BSc Hons East Anglia, PGCE Nottingham (*Head of Mathematics, Senior Teacher – Curriculum*)

Miss M Ifould, BEd Ilkley, Dip Careers Education (*Head of Physical Education & Outdoor Pursuits, Head of Careers*)

Mrs B McEwen, BA Hons CNAA, Cheltenham, PGCE Leeds (*Art & Design, Design & Technology*)

Dr D McKitterick, BSc Hons, PhD Nottingham (*Physics*)

Miss J C Melia, BEd Hons Leeds (*Head of English*)

Mrs S C Price, BSc Hons York (*Chemistry, Special Educational Needs*)

Mrs J Purchase, BA Hons, CertEd Keele (*Joint Head of Music*)

Mrs C Searle, BEd Cardiff (*Joint Head of Design & Technology*)

Mrs A R Standing, BA Hons Newcastle, PGCE Leeds, MA Northumbria (*Head of Art & Design*)

Dr L Stannard, BA Hons, MA, PhD, PGCE NTU (*English*)

Mrs J E Storey, GRSM Music, ARCM Saxophone (*Joint Head of Music*)

Mrs F Twomey, BA Hons Nottingham, PGCE Leicester (*French and German*)

Mrs A M Whitaker, BA Hons Coventry, PGCE Huddersfield (*Head of Modern Languages*)

Mrs C Wood, BEd Hons Nottingham

Junior School:
Head: Mrs S Payne, BA Hons Sheffield, PGCE Warwick
Deputy Head: Mrs E Pietrantonio, BA Hons Hull, PGCE Nottingham, MEd Sheffield

Assistant Staff:
Mrs S Allen, BA Hons, PGCE Leicester
Miss V Carlin, BSc Hons Warwick, PGCE Kingston
Mrs J Fitzgerald, CertEd London, DipSpLD Nottingham (*Learning Support*)
Mrs C Keyworth, BA Hons NTU
Mrs D Plumb, BA Hons, PGCE
Mrs G Wand, BEd Hons Exeter
Mrs H Nicholson, NNEB Nottingham
Mrs K Hewitt (*325 Club Assistant*)
Mrs P Upton, NVQ3 (*325 Club Assistant*)
Mrs J Woodfield, ASA (*Swimming*)

Classroom Assistants:
Mrs L Swift, NNEB (*Healthcare Coordinator*)
Mrs S Mahl (*325 Club Supervisor*)
Mrs P Mason, BTEC

Bursar: Mrs D M Zinsaz, BA London
Marketing Manager: Mrs W Nuttall, BSc Hons Coventry, Dip Mktg NTU
Registrar & Headmistress's Secretary: Mrs L E Wilkins, BA Hons NTU
School Secretary: Mrs L Costall
Receptionists: Mrs L Clark, Mrs J Kells
Science and Technology Technician: Mr R Arnold, BA Hons, BTEC Nat Science
Senior ICT Technician: Mr J Beaumont

Visiting Staff:
Mrs S Bellamy, BMus Hons Birmingham Conservatoire, ALCM, LLCM (*Singing*)
Mr C Bowen (*Drums*)
Mrs J Ibbett, ALCM, LRAM, LLCM, DPSE (*Piano*)
Mr M Johnson, Cert Mus Ed TCL, LTCL Dip Mus Ed Hons (*Guitar*)
Mrs M A Land, Gold Medal LAM, MSTSD (*Speech and Drama*)
Mrs J McDouall, ARCM London (*Singing*)
Miss A Nicholson, ABRSM, NVQ Dip (*Clarinet & Saxophone*)
Mrs C A Seedhouse, BMus Sheffield, CertEd Nottingham (*Violin*)
Mrs M Wright, LRAM, LLCM (*Piano*)

Located in a tree-lined walkway, just North of the city centre, Hollygirt School occupies several large Victorian houses, which are designed to create a 'family feel'.

Founded in 1877, Hollygirt is a day school and administered as a non-profit making educational trust. There are about 240 girls in the School between the ages of 3 and 16 of whom about 70 are in the Junior School. The school has the use of Nottingham University's sports facilities, including a swimming pool, as well as Harvey Haddon Athletics Stadium. Recently the school purchased a new garden to provide recreational facilities for the Senior School and extended facilities for 3–5 year olds.

The school aims to provide a well-balanced education in a caring environment with emphasis on the needs and abilities of individual girls. In addition to academic success, the school is concerned with the spiritual, moral, cultural and physical development of each girl as she is prepared for the opportunities, responsibilities and experience of adult life. All girls are encouraged to take a positive and enthusiastic approach to whatever they undertake, whether in form, games or leisure activities. Extra help in Mathematics and English is given on an individual or small group basis.

After leaving Hollygirt, nearly all girls proceed to A Level courses in the sixth forms of local sixth form colleges and schools or other independent day and boarding schools.

Curriculum. The curriculum includes English, Mathematics, Science, French, German, Design and Technology, Art, History, Geography, Religious Studies, ICT, Music, Drama, Vocational Studies and Physical Education.

Games. Hockey, netball, athletics, tennis, basket and volleyball, unihoc, rounders, football, softball, badminton and swimming.

Careers. A programme of careers advice begins in Year 9. The School is a member of the Independent Schools Careers Organisation, which offers careers guidance to parents, staff and girls in member schools.

Extra-Curricular Activities. These are wide and varied and include Orchestra, Choir, Duke of Edinburgh's Award, Netball Club, Fencing, Public Speaking, trips to the theatre, ice skating, a programme of sports matches, drama productions and AS Level Critical Thinking. Lunchtime clubs include Art, French, Gardening, Choir and Table Tennis. School travel opportunities have included visits to France, Germany and skiing in various parts of Europe.

Admission. Admission to the Junior School (age 3–11) can be at any age, providing there is an available space. Girls are invited to spend a whole day in school so that their general standard can be assessed. Entry to the Senior School is at age 11 (Year 7), although some places become available in other years.

Fees per term (2011-2012). £2,328 (Nursery and Reception), £2,339 (Years 1 and 2), £2,495 (Years 3–6), £3,061 (Years 7–9), £3,120 (Years 10 and 11).

Charitable status. The Rhoda Jessop Educational Charity is a Registered Charity, number 508617. The aim is to provide an all round education which will prepare a girl for today's competitive, uncertain and rapidly changing world.

Howell's School
Denbigh

Denbigh, North Wales LL16 3EN
Tel: 01745 813631
Fax: 01745 814443
e-mail: enquiries@howells.org
website: www.howells.org

Trustees: Howell's 2000 Limited

Governors:
Chairman of Governors: Mr J Gardner, Trustee

Principal: Mr Bernard Routledge, MA Hons, PGCE

Senior School Staff:
Miss Julie Anglesea (*Careers, Examinations Officer*)
Mr Oliver Hall, BA Hons, PGCE (*ICT*)
Mrs Frances Bagnall, BSc, PGCE (*Physics*)
Mrs Jane Fellows, BSc, PGCE (*Business Studies*)
Mrs Lorraine McCale, BA Ed (*Head of History & RE,
    Associate Head – Academic*)
Miss Carys Hughes, BSc Hons, PGCE (*Chemistry*)
Mrs Patricia Jones, MEd, BS Ed, BA (*PHSE, Psychology*)
Miss Emma Jones, BSc Hons, PGCE (*Head of
    Mathematics*)
Miss Noura Benzerfa, MA, PGCE (*Head of Languages*)
Mrs Donna MacLennan, BEd (*Geography, Head of Sixth
    Form*)
Mme Benedicte Gillet, MEd, BA (*French*)
Dr Daniela Molinari, PhD
Mrs Chris Morris, BSc, PGCE (*Biology*)
Mrs Morwen Murray, BA, AGSM (*Music*)
Miss Helen Price, BA, PGCE (*PE, Associate Head –
    Pastoral*)
Mr Matthew Jones, BSc PGCE (*Mathematics*)
Mrs Rebbeca Raven, BA, PGCE (*Art*)
Mrs Anne Wales, BA, PGCE (*Drama, English & German*)
Dr Michelle Wilton, BSc, PhD, PGCE (*Biology*)
Mrs Trudie Tough, BA Hons, PhD, PGCE (*English
    Language*)
Miss Fflur Roach, BSc Hons Sport Development, PGCE
Mr James Ryan, BA Hons, PGCE (*Drama*)
Mrs Elizabeth Bennett, BA, PGCE (*English*)

Preparatory School Staff:
Mrs B Glover, BPhil Ed
Mrs Anne Lowe, BA, MA, PGCE (*Year 1 Teacher, PE
    Coordinator*)
Mrs Diana Stafford, BEd (*Technology, Art*)
Mrs Valerie Sydenham, BSc, PGCE (*KS1*)
Mrs Sioned Terry, BMus, DipTech (*Music, Club & Music
    Productions*)
Miss Rachael Jones (*Nursery*)
Miss Emma Birkett-Evans, BA Hons, PGCE

Principal's Assistant: Mrs Patricia Pearson
School Officer: Mrs Cathy Hughes
Bursar: Mrs Metta Smith
Prep School Secretary: Mrs Sue Salt

Peripatetic staff:
Music:
Mr Martin Hamilton
Mr Terry Dando
Mr Geoff Coward
Mrs Lorna Todd
Mrs Nia Roberts
Mr David Hopkins
Mrs Mary Hopkins
Speech and Drama:
Mrs P Evers-Swindell, LAM, LSRB

Nursing Staff:
Ms Debbie Hughes

Technical Staff:
Mrs Beryl Lamb (*Science*)
Mr Mark Hill (*IT*)

Boarding Staff:
Stanley House (5th and 6th): Mrs Marion Lockwood, Miss
    Amy Choen
St George's (Prep, 1st–4th): Miss Pebbles Owen, Mrs
    Kerry Evans

Equine Staff:
Ms Sian Davies
Miss Kelsey Rees

Estates Staff:
Caretaker/Porter: Mr Paul Gibson
Catering Manager: Mr Phil Watson
On-site Catering Manager: Mrs Gwenfyl Wynne
Housekeeping Manager: Mrs Carol Jones

Howell's is a flourishing Boarding and Day School for some 250 girls and boys. The Senior School is all girls, the Preparatory School and Nursery co-educational. Academic performance is strong and 95% of the Sixth Form go on to Higher Education at Universities. Pupils gain places at Oxford and Cambridge.

The School is situated in delightful surroundings on the edge of the market-town of Denbigh and is easily accessible via the motorway network from the North and the Midlands. Chester is 40 minutes distant and Liverpool and Manchester one hour away. Centres in Shropshire are up to two hours driving time away. British Rail operates frequent services to Rhyl and to Chester.

The Principal will be happy to send a prospectus, DVD, fact sheet and examination results on request and to meet parents, sons and daughters at any time, to provide full information and to show them round the School.

Fees per term (2011-2012). Boarders: £4,850–£6,900 (age 7–18); Day Pupils: £2,100–£3,900 (age 3–18).

Entrance requirements. The main 11+ examinations take place in January. Assessments for other age groups (3 to 16) occur throughout the year and scholarships/awards are available. A limited number of Scholarship awards are also reserved for those who exhibit special talents such as in Art, Music, Speech and Drama or Sport. Service Bursaries and reductions for siblings are also offered.

Buildings. The original school was built in 1859, and has been enlarged and improved on numerous occasions since that time. The School contains all the normal facilities including six science laboratories, a large library, twenty-five individual music practice rooms, Art and Design complex, a drama studio, a theatre workshop area and recording studio, IT teaching floor consisting of a teaching classroom and 12 individual computer suites.

Grounds. There are completed laytex courts, 4 grass tennis courts and grounds of a quality to have been used for international matches, a heated swimming pool, a magnificent sports complex and aerobics suite. The equestrian centre provides riding as well as equine qualifications. The School also has lakeside facilities at Brenig Lake.

Curriculum. The School presently has an overall staff student ratio of 1:9. The school subjects include Religious Studies, English, English Literature, Media Studies, History, Geography, French, Performing Arts, German, Spanish, Welsh, Mathematics, Information Technology, Business Studies, Physics, Chemistry, Biology, Physical Education, Art, Music, Spoken English, Gymnastics and Games, Drama, Sports Leadership and Duke of Edinburgh's Award. Additionally, at Sixth Form level: Photography, Psychology, Equine Studies and Young Enterprise, CSLA.

Examinations. Girls are prepared for GCSE, AS and A Level examinations; University Entrance and Scholarship Examinations; Schools for Music and Speech and Drama, the Poetry Society and Guildhall School of Music and Drama and London Academy of Music and Dramatic Art examinations.

Charitable status. The Foundation of Howell's School, Denbigh is a Registered Charity, number 1061485. The income derived from the charity is to be awarded to pupils or former pupils in the form of prizes, scholarships, allowances or grants. The school functions within a framework of Christian beliefs and values.

Howell's School Llandaff
GDST

Cardiff Road, Llandaff, Cardiff CF5 2YD
Tel: 029 2056 2019
Fax: 029 2057 8879
e-mail: admissions@how.gdst.net
website: www.howells-cardiff.gdst.net

Founded in 1860 as a school for girls, the school was built by the Drapers' Company from the endowment left in 1537 by Thomas Howell, son of a Welshman, merchant of London, Bristol and Seville and a Draper.

Howell's School Llandaff is part of the GDST (Girls' Day School Trust). The GDST is the leading network of independent girls' schools in the UK. As a charity that owns and runs 24 schools and two academies, it reinvests all its income in its schools. For further information about the Trust, see p. xxi or visit www.gdst.net.

Additional information about the school may be found on the school's website and a detailed prospectus is available from the school.

Chairman of Governors: Mrs A Campbell, JP, DL

Principal: **Mrs S Davis**, BSc London

Deputy Principal: Mrs M Gosney, BSc Bristol, MA EdMgt London, NPQH

Head of Sixth Form College: Mrs N Chyba, BA London

Head of Senior School: Dr S Southern, BSc PhD Durham

Head of Junior School: Mrs J Ashill, BEd Swansea

School Business Manager: Mr J S Williams, BSc Wales

Student numbers. 772: Nursery 13; Junior School 246; Senior School 513 (193 in Sixth Form College).

Howell's School is regarded as the leading academic school in Wales, with consistently outstanding results. In November 2008 it achieved the highest grade (1) in each of the seven key areas assessed by the Welsh Schools' Inspectorate, Estyn. All students are encouraged to fulfil their potential by becoming confident, independent learners, a process which begins in the Nursery and Junior School and continues throughout the Senior School and College. There is a strong commitment to pastoral care, and a wide range of talents and essential life skills are fostered through the academic curriculum and the extensive extra-curricular programme. Links with overseas schools, great environmental awareness (the school has recently gained Fair Trade status) and a wide variety of language provision all aim to prepare the students to be tomorrow's global citizens. With its first-class facilities for music, sports, drama and art, the school provides an all-round education for girls between the ages of 3 and 16 and for male and female students between the ages of 16 and 18.

The school is situated within easy reach of the Cardiff city centre and set in 18 acres of grounds. The splendid grey stone building, designed by Decimus Burton, which has been expanded and modernised, is still the focal point of the school. In addition there are four large Victorian houses and new purpose-built accommodation which house the Junior School, the Nursery, Music School and the Sixth Form College.

A co-educational Sixth Form College opened in September 2005. It is located in the newly refurbished Sixth Form houses and offers students a distinctive programme of education designed to prepare students for higher education and equip them with the necessary life skills for the workplace and their future careers. The Careers Department has gained the Careers Wales Award for the quality of its guidance.

There are six ICT suites and interactive whiteboards or projectors in all teaching rooms; all students achieve a recognised ICT qualification. Outstanding art work and subject displays enhance all areas of the school. The renowned Senior Girls' Choir recently performed at the Forbidden City Concert Hall in Beijing, where it received a standing ovation. In recent years the school has achieved major successes in the areas of public speaking and debating.

Curriculum. All National Curriculum subjects including Welsh are taught at Key Stages 1, 2 and 3. In addition, girls in the Junior School have a taster of Spanish, German and French. Latin is started in Year 7 and girls choose three of French, German, Spanish and Welsh. A broad range of AS and A2 subjects is available in the College. Examinations in all AS subjects are taken at the end of Year 12. Active learning styles are seen as an essential part of the classroom experience. The curriculum is made more diverse by:

* educational visits, locally and abroad;
* visiting authors, poets, musicians, artists and lecturers;
* Book Week and other weeks with special activities focusing on particular areas of the curriculum.

Extra-curricular activities. Howell's is proud of its aim to fulfil the potential of all the students, which it achieves through a rich extra-curricular programme of activities:

* orchestras, choirs, chamber and jazz groups;
* reading and reviewing, green, science, maths, history, geography, language and religious and cultural clubs;
* concerts, plays, drama festival and eistedfoddau;
* tennis, hockey, rounders, lacrosse, swimming, athletics, cross-country, netball, rugby and football teams;
* The Duke of Edinburgh's Award, First Challenge, World Challenge, Envision and Interact;
* quiz, public speaking and debating teams;
* community service and fundraising for charities.

The school seeks to support the widest range of students' needs through specialist dyslexia teaching at our on-site Dyslexia Institute satellite, and through an extensive and comprehensive careers programme.

Admission. A selection process operates for all points of entry. Contact Admissions for further details.

Fees per term (2011-2012). Sixth Form College £3,535; Senior School: £3,562 (Year 7), £3,404 (Years 8–11); Junior School: £2,665 (Rec–Year 2), £2,689 (Years 3–6); Nursery £2,110.

Scholarships and Bursaries. Bursaries, which are means-tested, are available in the Senior School and in the Sixth Form College; these are intended to ensure that the school remains accessible to bright girls (and in the College, to able students of both sexes) who would profit from our education, but who would be unable to enter the school without financial assistance.

Details of scholarships, bursaries and music exhibitions are available, on request, from the school.

Charitable status. Howell's School Llandaff is part of The Girls' Day School Trust, which is a Registered Charity, number 306983.

Ipswich High School
GDST

Woolverstone, Ipswich IP9 1AZ
Tel: 01473 780201
Fax: 01473 780985
e-mail: admissions@ihs.gdst.net
website: www.ipswichhighschool.co.uk

Founded in 1878.

Ipswich High School is part of the GDST (Girls' Day School Trust). The GDST is the leading network of independent girls' schools in the UK. As a charity that owns and runs 24 schools and two academies, it reinvests all its income in its schools. For further information about the Trust, see p. xxi or visit www.gdst.net.

Additional information about the school may be found on the school's website and a detailed prospectus is available from the school.

Chairman of Local Governors: Annie Reid

Headmistress: Ms Elaine Purves, BA Hons Hull

Head of Junior School: Mrs Eileen Fisher, BEd

Registrar: Mrs Bernadette Ross-Smith

A pioneering heritage
Ipswich High School's early pupils were among the first women to obtain university degrees and to enter professional work. Today, although the school has grown and changed immeasurably, the pioneering spirit and commitment to education for young women remain.

An inspiring choice
Our philosophy is to create an environment in which our girls – be they in our Nursery School, Junior School, Senior School or Sixth Form – are inspired to reach new heights.

Outstanding results
We provide an extraordinary breadth of education and as a single-sex school there is no gender stereotyping in the choice and enjoyment of subjects. It is not considered unusual to excel in Maths, Science or Design & Technology any more than in Languages, Arts or Humanities. We have high standards and expectations of all our pupils in every subject and that is reflected in our outstanding exam results at all age ranges.

Developing the whole girl
We spend time with our pupils in extra-curricular activities such as sport, music and drama to enhance their personal development. This helps them develop not just academic skills, but social skills as well – preparing them for their life ahead.

An enriching environment
We are privileged to have the magnificent Woolverstone Hall as our home with 80 acres of beautiful parkland, splendid buildings and an incredible array of facilities – a huge sports hall, theatre, spacious labs, design technology workshop, language laboratory, IT suites, a 25m indoor swimming pool and most recently an all-weather pitch for hockey and tennis – providing us with a stimulating and inspiring environment in which our girls can learn, play and grow.

The support of the GDST
As part of the GDST, Ipswich High School has a strong and secure future. The GDST gives each of the schools autonomy to identify its own needs and determine its own development, but then gives guidance, helps planning and supports financially to realise projects.

Prepared for the future
Above all, at Ipswich High School no girl is silent. Even those who lack confidence when they join us soon find the space and encouragement to discover their voice. Our girls act as inspirational role models for each other. They are ambitious, enthusiastic and have a real zest for learning and life. When the time comes for them to leave us, all our girls go forward with the confidence and courage not to be held back by social stereotypes, but to take themselves to new levels of success.

Ipswich High School has a proven track record and a bright future ahead – we hope you will choose to be part of it.

Admissions. Admission to the Nursery School is on the basis of informal assessment in a play situation. Entry to the Junior School is on the basis of informal assessment or written test. Entry to the Senior School is on the basis of interviews, written tests and school report. Sixth Form entry is on the basis of interviews, GCSE results and school report.

Fees per term (2011-2012). Senior School: Years 12 & 13 £3,402, Years 9–11 £3,450, Year 7 & 8 £3,402; Junior School: Years 3–6 £2,466, Years 1 & 2 £2,326, Woodland Pre-Prep £1,920.

Scholarships. Our Scholarships are highly sought after and are reserved for those candidates we believe to be of an exceptional standard. We look to our Scholars to continuously raise the standard in their chosen field and to provide inspiration to others. For entry at 11+ (Senior School) and 16+ (Sixth Form) we offer Academic, Art, Drama, Music and Sports Scholarships.

Bursaries. The GDST provides the school with a number of bursaries for entry at 11+ and Sixth Form. These are means tested and ensure that the school remains accessible to bright girls who would profit from the education provided but who would be unable to enter the school without financial assistance.

Charitable status. Ipswich High School is part of The Girls' Day School Trust, which is a Registered Charity, number 306983.

James Allen's Girls' School (JAGS)

East Dulwich Grove, London SE22 8TE
Tel: 020 8693 1181
Fax: 020 8693 7842
e-mail: enquiries@jags.org.uk
website: www.jags.org.uk

Governing Body:
Mrs Mary Francis, CBE, LVO, MA (*Chair*)
Mr Michael Brooke, BA Hons
Mrs Nicola Meredith, BA Hons, FCCA
Professor John Moxham, MD, FRCP
Mrs Jane Onslow, MA
Miss Erica Pienaar, BA Hons, MBA, FRSA
Mrs Frances Read, MA Cantab, FCA, MSI
Mr David Smellie, MA
Dr Geraldine Strathdee, OBE, MB, BCh, BAO, MRCPsych
    London
Sir Hugh Taylor, BA Hons, KCB
Ms Sarah Tunstall, BA Hons
Mr Thomas Van Oss, MA

Clerk to the Governors and Bursar: Miss Sarah Buxton, MA Hons, ACA

Headmistress: Mrs Marion Gibbs, BA Hons, MLitt, PGCE Bristol, FRSA

Deputy Head: Mrs Deborah Bicknell, BSc Hons Durham (*Biology*)

Teaching Staff:
* Head of Department

Miss Helen Adie, BA Hons London (*Drama and English*)
Miss Alice Allgrove, BA Hons Bristol (*Religious Studies &
    PSHCE)
Mrs Luisa Alonso, BA Hons Durham (*Spanish*)
Mr Arvind Arora, Staatsexamen Germany (*German*)
Mrs Vikki Askew, MA Hons Edinburgh (*History, Head of
    Sixth Form*)
Mrs Hélène Bardell, Licence-Maitrîse Poitiers (*French*)
Mrs Wendy Barratt, BSc Hons Kent (*Biology & Careers*)
Mrs Corrine Barton, BA Hons Sheffield (*History and
    Politics*)
Mrs Christine Berrill, BA Hons Reading (*History of Art*)
Mrs Joanna Billington, BA Hons Middlesex (*Drama*)
Mr Timothy Billington, BA Hons London (*German,
    Critical Thinking, ICT*)
Ms Katherine Bishop, BA Hons Cambridge (*English*)
Ms Aude Boulanger, BA Sorbonne (*French*)
Mrs Fabienne Branson, BA Provence (*French*)

Miss Antonia Buccheri, BSc Hons Manchester
(*Mathematics*)

Mrs Monica Buckley, BA Hons Oxford (*History*)

Dr David Burns, BSc Hons London (*Economics*)

Mr Stuart Byfield, BSc Hons London (*Biology*)

Mrs Anita Carpenter, BEd Liverpool John Moores
(*Physical Education*)

Mr Andrew Carter, BA Hons Central St Martin's (*Art*)

Miss Louise Cook, BA Hons Wolverhampton
(**Technology*)

Miss Elinor Corp, BA Hons Bristol (*Music*)

Mr Paul Davies, BSc Hons Newcastle (*Physics*)

Mrs Margaret Davis, BA Hons Newcastle (*Geography*)

Ms Kay Dickson, GRSM, Dip RCM London (*Music*)

Ms Melanie Duignan, MA Manchester (*English*)

Dr Matthew Edwards, BA Hons, PhD Bristol (**English*)

Mrs Rachel Edwards, BA Hons Cambridge (*English*)

Mrs Catherine Ferrar, MA Hons Cambridge (*English*)

Mrs Katharine Firth, BA Hons CNAA (*Art*)

Mr Martial Fouilleul, BA Hons (**French*)

Mrs Sally George, BA Hons London, MA London
(**Russian*)

Miss Chantal Gillingham, BA Hons Norwich School of Art
(*Art*)

Ms Sara Glover, BSc London (**Mathematics*)

Mrs Clare Grant, BSc Hons Sussex (*Chemistry*)

Mr Michael Grant, MA Royal College of Art (**Art*)

Mr Peter Gravell, BA Hons Oxford (*Physics*)

Mr Thomas Hamilton-Jones, BA Hons Oxford
(**Economics*)

Mrs Marilyn Harper, MA Cambridge, FRCO, GRSM,
ARMCM (*Music*)

Ms Claudia Harrison, BA Hons Oxford (*Geography*)

Mrs Elizabeth Head, BA Hons Brighton (**Physical
Education*)

Mrs Catharine Henley, BA Hons Bristol, MA Canada
(*Classics*)

Mr Andrew Hicklenton, BSc Hons Southampton (**Physics*)

Mrs Alexandra Hutchinson, BSc Hons Oxford (*Chemistry*)

Miss Julia Johnson, BA Hons Oxford (*English & SENCO*)

Miss Wendy Johnson, BEd Hons London (*Physical
Education*)

Mrs Anna Jones, BA Hons Nottingham (*English*)

Mrs Ruth Jones, BA Hons Durham, MA Southampton
(*Classics*)

Mr Alex Kerr, MA Hons Edinburgh (*Drama*)

Dr Sarah Knight, BSc Hons, PhD London (**Chemistry*)

Ms Georgina Legg, BA Hons Sussex (*French*)

Mrs Deborah Lewis, BA Hons Sheffield (**Religious
Studies*)

Miss Alice Little, BA Hons, MA Oxon (*Chemistry*)

Dr Mary Lloyd, BSc Hons Birmingham, DPhil Oxford
(*Biology*)

Ms Lorna Macleod, BA Hons Bristol, MBA Warwick
(*French*)

Ms Sarah Macpherson, MA Hons Edinburgh (*History &
Politics*)

Mrs Giulia Marchini, Dottoressa Bari (**Italian*)

Mrs Ann Massey, BA Hons Oxford (*History*)

Mrs Emma Mayo, MA Cambridge (*History, Head of Years
7-9*)

Mrs Catherine McCleave, BD Hons KCL (*Religious
Studies & Dance*)

Ms Paula McCormick, BA Hons London (*Design
Technology*)

Mrs Lara Meeran, BEng Hons London (*Design
Technology*)

Mrs Cherie Millsom, BA Hons Sheffield (*Classics*)

Mrs Alice Mollison, MA Hons Edinburgh (**Geography*)

Mr Daniel Monks, BA Hons Keele (*Music*)

Miss Fiona Murray, BEd Hons London (*Physical
Education*)

Mr Roger Nicholls, BSc London, MSc London
(*Mathematics*)

Mrs Kathryn Norton-Smith, BA Hons Birmingham
(*Drama*)

Mr Leigh O'Hara, BA Hons York, MMus London
(*Director of Music*)

Mr Hiroshi Okura, BA Waseda, Tokyo (*Japanese*)

Mrs Gillian Oxbrow, BSc Hons Exeter (*Mathematics,
Assistant Head*)

Miss Nicola Paine, BSc Hons UCL (*Biology*)

Mr John Pattison, BSc Hons Newcastle, MA Lancaster
(*Mathematics*)

Miss Samantha Payne, BA Hons Central St Martins (*Art,
Head of Years 10 & 11*)

Dr Howard Peacock, BA Hons Oxon, MPhil London
(*Classics & Philosophy*)

Mrs Clare Phillips, BA Hons Oxford (*Spanish*)

Mrs Natalie Plant, BSc Hons Bristol (*Mathematics*)

Mr John Putley, BSc Hons Nottingham (*Science*)

Miss Jane Quarmby, BA Hons Bristol (*English*)

Ms Irene Riddell, BA Hons Glasgow (*Art*)

Mrs Sally Ann Rosier, BSc Hons Durham (*Physics*)

Miss Natalia Rukazenkova, MPhil Cambridge, BA
Cambridge (*Mathematics*)

Miss Cristina Sanchez-Satoca, BA Hons Barcelona, MA
London (**Spanish*)

Mr Peter Sanders, BSc, MSc London (**Computer Studies,
Information Systems Coordinator*)

Mrs Frances Shaw, MA Oxford (**Classics & Philosophy*)

Miss Pauline Simpson, MA Cambridge (*Mathematics*)

Miss Gina Thomson, BA Hons Brighton (*Physical
Education*)

Mrs Marta Totten, BA Hons Bergamo (*Italian*)

Ms Karen Trinder, BSc Hons York (*Biology*)

Miss Stella Turner, BSc Hons Nottingham (*Mathematics*)

Ms Anne-Marie von Lieres, BA Hons Paris (*French*)

Mr Robert Wallace, MA Birmingham, MBA Nottingham
(*Design Technology, Asst Head*)

Mrs Alexandra Ward, MA KCL (*Religious Studies*)

Miss Heather Webb, MA Oxford (*Chemistry*)

Mr Laurence Wesson, BSc Hons London (**Biology*)

Librarians:

Mrs Cynthia Pullin, BA Hons York, DipLib

Mrs Susan Stacey, BA Hons Manchester (*Library
Assistant*)

Mrs Susan Stevens, BA Hons London (*Library Assistant*)

Deputy Bursar: Mr Kevin Barry, ACA

Registrar: Mrs Julie Ellis

PA to Headmistress: Mrs Elaine Kingsley-Perkins

Communications Director: Mrs Alison Venn, BEd Hons
Cambridge

School Nurses:

Mrs Karen Cattanach, RGN

Ms Jacqui Martin, RGN

Mrs Helen Mandefield-Chang, RGN

The school was founded in 1741 as part of the Foundation
of Alleyn's College of God's Gift and is the oldest independent girls' school in London.

JAGS is set in 22 acres of grounds in the heart of Dulwich, with extensive playing fields and long-established
Botany gardens. The school buildings include a well-
equipped modern library, 13 science laboratories, a purpose-
built suite of language laboratories, 6 art rooms, 4 computer
rooms, design technology workshops, new indoor swimming
pool, floodlit artificial turf pitch, dance studio, sports hall
with squash courts and fitness room, a professionally-man-
aged theatre and a music school. The Sixth Form Centre has
its own tutorial rooms, common rooms and lecture theatre.
A new two-storey dining hall and teaching block opened in
2008.

There is a four-form entry at 11 and JAGS senior school has about 770 pupils with 200 in the Sixth Form. About a third of girls come up from our junior department, James Allen's Preparatory School (qv) with about two-thirds entering from other preparatory and state primary schools.

Girls follow a broad curriculum with a wide choice of GCSE options, structured to ensure a balanced programme. Advanced Level courses are available in all the usual subjects as well as Classical Civilisation, Greek, Latin, Russian, Spanish, Italian, Japanese, Economics, Philosophy, Physical Education, Politics, Music and Theatre Studies. Art is a particular strength throughout the school.

The extra-curricular programme is a key part of the JAGS education. The excellent Prissian Theatre enables first class, full scale drama productions, while the active music department plays a central role, offering some 30 ensembles including 6 choirs, 4 orchestras, brass ensembles, wind ensembles plus jazz and big bands. A great variety of other interests is encouraged, from The Duke of Edinburgh's Award, debating, photography, and the Literary Society, to Politics and Amnesty International. Study visits to Russia, France, Germany, Italy, and Spain are regularly organised. The choirs, orchestras and sports teams also visit overseas. Community Action plays an important part in school life, and there are extensive partnership activities with other local schools and community groups.

Sports: Hockey, netball, football, aerobics, basketball, gymnastics, dance, tennis, rounders, swimming, athletics and self-defence are taught in the curriculum, with opportunities for fencing, rugby, badminton, sailing, ice-skating and golf.

Individual lessons in Instrumental Music and Speech and Drama are available (fees on application).

Fees per term (2011-2012). £4,520.

Admission. Girls are mainly admitted at 11+ and also into the Sixth Form. Casual vacancies at other ages. Registration fee: £50.

Entrance Examination. Every candidate for admission will be required to pass an examination, graduated according to age. For details and method of admission apply to The Registrar, Mrs J Ellis.

Scholarships. (*See Scholarship Entries section*.) Up to twenty Foundation Scholarships are awarded every year to girls of 11 years of age on entry to the School. Sixth Form scholarships are also available. Scholarships are awarded for academic ability and for Music and Art; there is also a Sports Exhibition.

All Scholarships are augmented by a means-tested element in cases of need.

Following the demise of the Government Assisted Places Scheme, the School has introduced James Allen's Bursaries to continue to enable talented girls from families of limited means to enter JAGS. Fee support up to 100% is available.

Charitable status. James Allen's Girls' School is a Registered Charity, number 1124853 and exists for the purpose of educating girls.

Kent College Pembury

Old Church Road, Pembury, Tunbridge Wells, Kent TN2 4AX

Tel: 01892 822006
Fax: 01892 820221
e-mail: admissions@kentcollege.kent.sch.uk
website: www.kent-college.co.uk

Kent College Pembury is a day and boarding school for girls aged 3 to 18. A happy thriving school with high academic standards and an ethos of providing opportunities to build confidence. The school provides for the educational and cultural needs of day students and boarders from all over the world. Set in beautiful countryside, just 35 miles from London, students benefit from high teaching standards in a superbly equipped environment, within a caring Christian community. All girls participate in the imaginative programme of music, drama, sports, clubs and other activities. The school has strong EAL and learning support provision and accepts girls with a wide academic background. ICT and drama are major strengths of the school and the provision of Design and Technology is wide. Art, Sport and Music have a growing profile in the school and local area.

Board of Governors:

Chairman: Mr E Waterhouse
Vice-Chair: Mrs V Knight

Mrs H Alleyne	Revd S Mann
Mr R J Bamford	Mr J Morgan
Mrs V Burch	Mr I Pattenden
Mrs P J Darbyshire, MBE	Mrs M Richards
Mr J Harrison	Mr D Robins
Revd J Hellyer	Mr G Russell
Mr J Ingram	Mrs J Stevens
Mrs G Langstaff	Mr T Sturgess
Mr I Leroni	Mrs C Veall
Mr G Mackichan	

Headmistress: Mrs S A Huang, MA Oxon, PGCE

Head of Finance: Mrs A Jenkins, BA Hons Aberystwyth, ACA

Head of Administration & Clerk to the Governors: Mrs J A Bearne

Senior Deputy Head: Mr A Kirk-Burgess, BSc Bath, PGCE Oxford

Senior School Staff:

** *Head of Subject Group*
* *Head of Department*
§ *Part-time*

Mr B Allberry, HND University College Chichester (*PE*)
§Mrs A Barton, BA Hons Warwick (*English Support*)
§Mr C Armour (*Drama*)
§Mr N Ashton, BA Hons Worcester College, PGCE London (**Drama*)
§Mr T Bailey, BSc Hons Plymouth, MSc London, PGCE Canterbury (*Mathematics, Science*)
Ms E A Benfield, BA Birmingham, MA London (*EAL*)
Miss H Bruce, BMus Hons Edinburgh, MMus GSM, PGCE London (*Music*)
Miss J Burisky, BSc Hons Staffordshire, PGCE Brighton (*Science*)
Mrs S Caird, BA Hons Stirling, PGCE Cambridge (**History*)
Mr A Chan, MEng Hons UCL, PGCE Greenwich (**Physics*)
§Miss A M C Church, BA Oxford, PGCE Birmingham (*Second in Dept, English*)
Mrs E Cliff, MBiol Bath, PGCE Wales (**Biology, Science, Assistant Housemistress Hawkwell & Hargreaves*)
§Mrs J Cuthbert, BA OU, MA Canterbury, CertEd Chichester (*Maths and Science support*)
Mrs C Davidson, BA Hons QTS Kent, AEP Dib Brighton (*PSHE, Head of Pastoral & Outdoor Education*)
Ms N Davies (*Gym & Aerobics Coach*)
§Mrs J Denman, BA Hons, PGCE Durham, PG Dip Courtauld Inst (**MFL, *German, French*)
§Mrs L Denning, BA QTS Roehampton (*Art*)
§Mrs N Denton, BSc Hons Loughborough QTS (**PE*)
Mr A Dixon, BA Hons Kingston, PGCE Canterbury (*Art & Photography*)
§Mrs M Doe, BA Hons Christ Church, PGCE Greenwich (**Economics & Business Studies*)

§Mrs J Dooley, BA Hons Kent, MA Nottingham, PGCE Chichester (*Film Studies, English*)

§Mrs C Evans, BA Hons QTS Brighton (**PE*) (*Maternity Cover*)

§Mr K Fitzell, BEd Hons Reading (*English*)

Miss H Gibbs, BA ITT St Mary's College, Twickenham (*Second in Dept, PE, Dance Coordinator, Weekday Activities Coordinator, PE*)

§Mrs Angela Goff, BSc Leicester QTS (*Geography*)

§Mrs M Gower, BA Aichi, TCert Japan (*Japanese*)

Mrs L Hallam, BA Hons Southampton (*Spanish, French, Head of Lower School*)

Mrs M Hambleton, BA Hons Reading, PGCE London (**Geography*)

Miss R Hannam, BSc Plymouth, PGCE Exeter (*Mathematics*)

§Mrs C Harrison, BA Hons, PGCE Keele (*History, Politics*)

§Mrs M Haslett, CertEd London (*Food Technology*)

Mrs R A Havard, BSc Hons Roehampton (*Dyslexia Specialist*)

Miss E Hayes, MA King's College, BA Hons Manchester (*Classics, Latin*)

§Mr C Hayward, PGCE Leigh City, MIBiol Bromley College (*Science*)

Mrs F Hedgeland, BA, MA Cambridge, PGCE Cambridge, DipM CIM (*Head of Sixth Form, English*)

Mrs J Hill, BSc Hons, PGCE Hertfordshire (*Second in Dept, Mathematics*)

Mrs A Hobrow, BScEcon Bristol, PGCE Sussex (*Mathematics, Economics, Head of Middle School*)

§Mr K Hoffmann, Dip Speech & Drama Scottish Academy of Music, PGCE Glasgow (**Film Studies, Media Studies, English*)

§Mrs A Hutchinson, BA, MA, PGCE Oxon (*Classics Latin, Greek*)

Mrs L Jeal, BSc Hons Exeter, PGCE Reading (*Mathematics, Head of Ecology & Sustainability Issues*)

§Mrs M Keech, BA Hons Bristol, ATC London (***Performance & Creative Arts, *Art and Art Critical & Contextual, HSBC Coordinator*)

Mr M Kent-Davies, BMus Hons Sheffield, PGCE Manchester Polytechnic (**Director of Music, Boarders Band & Services*)

§Mr A Knowles, BSc, MSc (*IT, Geography*)

§Mr R Langridge, BSc, DipEd lNZQA, Cert TESOL (*Science*)

§Mr D Lee, BSc London Guildhall, QTS (***Humanities and Social Sciences, *Psychology*)

Mrs L Lewis, BSc Hons Leeds, GDL London, PGCE Greenwich (*Science*)

§Mrs S Mahillon-Goddard, Licence de Langues Poitiers, PGCE Hertfordshire (*French, German*)

Mr J Marshall, BA Oxon, PGCE (*French, German, DofE Assistant Unit Leader*)

Mrs L Maule, BSc Hons Greenwich (*ICT*)

§Mrs B Mitchell, BA Hons Durham, MA London, PGCE London (*RS, PHSCE*)

Miss C Mortlock (**ICT and Business Studies*)

§Mr J Mossman, BA Hons, MA, PGCE King's College London (***Linguistics, *Classics*)

Mr R F G Nash, MA Cantab, DipEd East Africa (***Mathematics and Sciences, *Chemistry, *Acting Head of Science*)

§Mrs A Nieto, BA Madrid, PGCE London (**Spanish*)

§Miss C Noyek, BA Hons Surrey (*Dance*)

Mrs L J Oliver-Murphy, BEd Bedford College (*Weekend Boarders' Activities Director; PE; Senior Housemistress James & Osborn*)

§Mrs J Packer, BA South Africa, (*Drama*)

Mrs K Pusey, GGSM, PGCE Middx (*Second in Dept, Music*)

§Mrs A Quiqley, MA Oxon, MA London (*Physics*)

§Ms K Russell, BA Hons Guildhall (*Geography*)

Mrs J Sambrook, BA Hons Oxon, PGCE Sussex (**Mathematics*)

§Mrs E Sharnock-Smith, BA (*Drama, Head of Prep School Peri Speech & Drama*)

Mrs C Skinner, BA Hons Kent, PGCE Lancaster (**English*)

§Mrs C Snowball, BA Hons Leeds (*Drama, Houseparent Hawkwell & Hargreaves*)

Mr O Snowball, BA Hons Nottingham, MA Goldsmiths, PGCE London (*English, Senior Housemaster Hawkwell & Hargreaves*)

§Mr R Starkey, BA Hons Cambridge QTS (*Mathematics*)

§Mrs D Stein, BA Hons, PGCE (*Spanish, French*)

Mrs A Stone, BEd I M Marsh (**Prep School PE to Y8*)

§Mrs R Su, BEd China (*Chinese tutor*)

§ Mrs C Sutton, BA Ed Hons Exeter (*PE*)

§Ms S Tidey (*Trampoline Tutor*)

Miss G Thorpe, BA Hons Lancaster, QTS (*Second in Dept Drama, Theatre Manager, Assistant Head of Lower School*)

Mrs J Tobin, BA Hons, PGCE Canterbury Christ Church (**Religious Studies, DofE Assistant Unit Leader*)

Mrs H Tomlin, Cert Ed Bristol (**Food Technology, Leith's Food and Wine*)

Miss K Wall, BA Hons Oxon, PGCE Southampton (*Assistant Head of Sixth Form, English*)

§Ms C Waller, Acting Dip Mountview Theatre School (*Drama*)

Mr B Wallis, BA Hons West Surrey, MA Hons Textile Institute, PGCE Exeter (*Art and Textiles Technology*)

Mr J Watson, BSc Canterbury QTS (*Assistant Head of Middle School, Science, Psychology, Housemaster James & Osborn*)

Mrs W Young Min, BA Hons London, PGCE Nottingham (**French*)

plus 12 Visiting Instrumental Staff.

Chaplain:
§Revd H Matthews, BSc Leeds, BA Hons Cambridge, PGCE London

Head of Careers:
§Mrs G E Shukla, BEd Bradford College, PGCE Reading

Library & ICT:
Mrs S Waller, BA Hons Anglia Ruskin, MCLIP (***Learning & Life Skills, Librarian*)
Mrs J Manning, BA Hons (*Library & ICT Assistant*)
Mrs C Songhurst (*Library and IT Assistant*)

Duke of Edinburgh's Award Scheme:
Mrs Carol Davidson, BA Hons QTS Kent, AEP Dib Brighton

House Staff:
Mr O Snowball, BA Hons Nottingham, MA Goldsmiths, PGCE London (*Senior Housemaster, Hawkwell & Hargreaves*)
Mrs L J Oliver-Murphy, BEd Bedford College (*Senior Housemistress, James & Osborn*)
Mrs C Tarr (*Housemistress, Hawkwell & Hargreaves*)
Mr J Watson, BSc Canterbury QTS (*Housemaster, James & Osborn*)
Mrs C Snowball, BA Hons Leeds (*Houseparent, Hawkwell & Hargreaves*)
Mrs J Parker, BA South Africa, BSA Cert Prof Boarding Practice, Speech TDip Rose Bruford College (*House Tutor*)
Miss I Stafford (*Assistant Housemistress, James & Osborn*)
§Mrs E Cliff, MBiol Bath, PGCE Wales (*Assistant Housemistress, Hawkwell & Hargreaves*)
§Mrs V Cowan (*Relief Housemistress*)

Medical Staff:
Medical Officer: Dr P Lautch, MB BS, MA, MRCGP
Nursing Sister: Mrs J M Devine, RGN

Medical Assistant: Mrs S Greenhalgh

Administrative Staff:
Head of Administration: Mrs J Bearne
Head of External Relations: Mrs E Chandler, BA Hons Surrey Institute
Director of Admissions: Mrs D Sainsbury
Development Officer: §Mrs M Roper, BSc Hons OU
School Secretary: Mrs A Masters
Assistant School Secretary: §Mrs V England
Admissions Officer: §Mrs N Sneddon, BEd Hons Cheltenham
Marketing & Admissions Assistant: Miss L Rushman
Receptionist: §Mrs J Gowen-Smith
Afternoon Receptionist: §Mrs L Bone
Examinations Officer & Cover Supervisor: Ms A Linford
HR Administrator & Database Manager: Miss M Gow
Secretary to the Senior Leadership Team: Mrs L Roberts

Bursar's Office:
Head of Finance: Mrs A Jenkins, BA Hons Aberystwyth, ACA
Operations Manager: Miss A Mehta, MBIFM
Estates Bursar: Mr D Darbyshire
Finance Manager: Mrs I Scinteie, BA Bucharest
Bursar's PA: §Mrs A West
Finance Assistant: Mrs V Carter

Technical Support Staff:
Ms J Hinton (*Senior Laboratory Technician*)
Mr C Hayward (*Laboratory Technician*)
Mr G Hougham HND Northbrook College (*Theatre Technician*)
Mrs S Coggins (*Design & Technology Technician*)
Mrs L Bright, BTec, Dip Design (*Design Technology Technician*)
Mrs L Denning BA Hons, QTS (*Art Technician*)

Catering Manager: Mrs S Stone

Kent College Preparatory School:

Headmistress: Mrs A Lawson, BEd Hons Exeter

Miss V Armstrong, BA Hons Warwick, PGCE London (*Year 3*)
Mrs S Beazleigh, BA Hons Brighton (*PE*)
§Mrs L Bon, BEd Cert Hons Brighton (*Learning Support*)
§Miss L Budden, National Diploma in Counselling, NNEB Croydon College (*Play Therapist*)
Mrs H Chapman, BEd Brighton, London College of Music (*KS1 Music Coordinator, Year 6*)
Mrs C Corp, BEd Derbyshire (*Year 2, KS1 History & Drama Coordinator*)
Mrs P Dabin, CertEd London, BSc Hons OU (*Early Years Coordinator, Reception Class*)
Miss R Dalby, BA Hons Wales, BA Hons OU, PGCE (*Senior Teacher, KS2 Mathematics Coordinator, Year 6*)
Mrs J Dearlove, BEd Hons Montreal, CertEd Canterbury (*KS2 English Coordinator, Year 4*)
Mrs C Goodrum, CertEd Nottingham (*Year 2*)
Mrs C Gregory, CertEd Nottingham (*Year 3*)
Mrs S Hall, BSc Hons Wales, PGCE Canterbury (*Senior Teacher, Year 5*)
§Ms R Hood, BSc Durham, PGCE London (*Learning Support Teacher*)
§Mrs R Hunton, BSc, PGCE Goldsmiths (*KS1 Maths Coordinator, Mathematics, Year 4*)
§Miss P Lamb, BA Hons Staffordshire, CertEd Keele (*KS2 Science Coordinator, Year 5*)
Mrs A Lees, CertEd London (*Art Coordinator, Year 1*)
§Mrs C Marnane BA Ed Goldsmiths (*Geography Coordinator, Year 3*)
Ms K Munro, BA Hons London College of Fashion, PGCE Southbank (*Reception Teacher, KS1 Science Coordinator*)

§Dr C Parr, MBChB, PGCE Leeds (*Technology Coordinator, Year 2*)
Miss K Soutter, Dip Montessori (*Nursery*)
§Mrs S Vincent, BSc Hons Surrey, PGCE Roehampton (*Senior Teacher, KS1 English Coordinator, Year 4*)
Mrs C Wilson, BEd Hons London (*French*)
Mrs T Youdale, CertEd Brighton, BA Hons Manchester (*Senior Teacher, PSHE Coordinator, Year 5*)
§Mrs E Andrews (*KS1 ICT Coordinator, Teaching Assistant, After School Care*)
Mrs M Cuttill, ASA Cert (*Swimming*)
Mrs A Cyster (*Teaching & Admin Assistant*)
Mrs S Morris (*Classroom Assistant, Swimming, After School Care*)
Mrs J Rhoades, NVQ Level 3 (*Reception Classroom Assistant*)
Mrs K Wicks (*Nursery Classroom Assistant, Admin Support, Second Hand Uniform Coordinator*)
Mrs J Wolton (*After School Care, Teaching Assistant*)

Administrative Staff:
Headmistress's PA: Mrs D Shepherd
School Secretary: §Mrs S Williams
Assistant School Secretary: §Mrs A Knapp

Ethos and Aims. The Prep School (ages 3–11) and the Senior School (ages 11–18) are part of a group of Methodist Schools, which have an ethos of being caring, Christian environments, and welcoming pupils from all faiths or none. Kent College is a happy school with high academic standards and pupils achieve excellent results in public examinations. With 200 girls in the Prep School and 410 in the Senior School there is a real community feel and teaching staff know each girl as an individual. Building self-esteem is at the heart of our ethos. All girls get a chance to shine, try something different, feel good about themselves and develop new and existing talents. Exciting opportunities to develop confidence are an integral part of school life: overseas music, drama and sports tours, an Australian exchange, 65 extra-curricular activities, and Leith's Food & Wine Course to name a few. Our aim is to equip students with the confidence, skills and positive attitude to succeed in their examinations, at university, in their chosen career and in life ahead.

Location and Facilities. The Prep School and the Senior School share the site which is set in 75 acres of beautiful green countryside in Pembury, three miles from Royal Tunbridge Wells. It is just forty minutes to London by train and within easy reach of Gatwick, Heathrow and Luton airports, channel ports and the Channel Tunnel. The Senior School campus comprises an elegant Victorian manor house, used for offices and boarding, and purpose-built facilities include language laboratories, a music school, Sixth Form Centre, science laboratories, dance studio and onsite outdoor adventure confidence course. The two schools benefit from an excellent range of shared facilities including a large sports hall, state-of-the-art theatre, an indoor heated swimming pool and dining hall; excellent ICT facilities include Apple Mac suite, wireless laptops and smartboards in the majority of the teaching rooms. The boarding house Hawkwell and Hargreaves is home to all boarders in Year 9 and below while James and Osborn is home to all boarders in Year 10 and above. The Prep School is based in its own modern, purpose-built building with spacious playgrounds. The Preparatory School has its own range of after school clubs and also offers supervised prep, late after prep care facility including supper and an early morning breakfast club.

(*See also Prep School entry in IAPS section.*)

Curriculum. In the first years of the Senior School all girls follow a wide curriculum which includes academic as well as creative and practical subjects. They learn keyboard skills and develop confidence in the use of computers and technology. At GCSE level, all girls take English language, English literature, mathematics, science, and select other

GCSE option subjects. At 16+, girls take the two-year Advanced Level course in four subjects and all follow a structured Curriculum Enrichment programme. In addition to A Levels, students can take the prestigious Leith School's Basic Certificate in Food and Wine. All students are given extensive careers and higher education advice and academically able students are prepared for admission to Oxford and Cambridge. The majority of students proceed directly to universities and colleges of higher education.

Sport. Sporting activities include hockey, netball, rounders, basketball, athletics, cross-country, water sports, horse riding, swimming, tennis, trampolining, dance and gymnastics. The school has a reputation for achievement in inter-school matches and talented athletes can enter county and national competitions. The superb facilities include an indoor heated swimming pool, sports hall, dance studio and spacious grounds with a variety of courts and pitches. The school also runs its own Gymnast Academy.

Extra-Curricular Activities, Music and Drama. The school prides itself on offering an extensive programme of extra-curricular activities at lunchtimes, after school and at weekends which are open to day girls and boarders. Senior School pupils are expected to take part in at least two activities from a list which includes sports, pottery, horse riding, choirs, orchestra, first aid, Duke of Edinburgh's Award, archery and drama. There are frequent visits to London theatres and overseas trips in the holidays. The school has a reputation for high standards in music and drama. There are opportunities for girls of all ages to take part in drama productions.

Christian Community. Kent College was founded by the Wesleyan Methodist Schools' Association in 1886. The school continues to benefit from having its own resident Chaplain. There are Christian assemblies on some weekdays and a school service each Sunday.

Entrance. (*See Scholarship Entries section.*) Main intakes to the Prep School are to the Nursery (aged 3) and Reception (aged 4) classes. The school will take girls into other year groups subject to places being available. Entrance is based on a place being available; however entrance into Years 3–6 pupils is based on the school's own entrance tests.

The main entries to the Senior School are at 11+, 13+ and 16+. Entrance is by the school's own Entrance Examinations, interview and a report from the previous school. Academic, Drama, Music, Art and Sport Scholarships are awarded to outstanding entrants at 11+, 13+ and 16+. Girls wishing to study A Levels are required to gain at least six GCSE passes at grade C or above. Boarders are welcomed from age 10.

Fees per term (2011-2012). Senior: Day £5,364, Boarders £8,648. Prep: Day £2,443–£3,678, Boarders £6,650. 20% discount for Forces' personnel. Discounts for sisters.

Charitable status. Kent College Pembury is a Registered Charity, number 307920. It exists for the education of children.

Kilgraston

Bridge of Earn, Perthshire PH2 9BQ
Tel: 01738 812257
Fax: 01738 813410
e-mail: headoffice@kilgraston.com
website: www.kilgraston.com

Chairman of Board of Governors: Mr Timothy Hall

Principal: Mr Michael Farmer, BA Hons, PGCE

Bursar and Secretary to the Board: Mr B Farrell, BCom, FIDE, ACIS

Deputy Head (Academic): Mrs C A Lund, BA Hons, MA, MA Ed Man, PGCE

Deputy Head (Pastoral & Boarding): Mrs J Watson, MA Hons, PGCE

Head of the Preparatory School: Mrs K Ebrahim, BSc Hons, PGCE

Chaplain: Father Andrew Clark

Academic & Pastoral Staff:
Mr A Allan, PGDE (*Business Education*)
Mrs J Baird (*Classroom Asst/Playground Supervisor*)
Mrs L Baxter, BEd (*Head of Curriculum Physical Education*)
Miss C Beveridge (*Geography, Mater Asst Boarding Mistress*)
Mrs A Bluett, BA Hons, PGCE (*French, Latin*)
Miss S Bookless (*Swimming Pool Manager*)
Mr B Campbell, DipEd (*Geography, PE & Weekend Activities, Duke of Edinburgh's Award*)
Mr C Campbell, MA, PGDE (*History, Modern Studies & Religious Studies, Form Teacher*)
Mrs J Carmichael, LLB, PGCE (*Form Teacher, Prep Coordinator*)
Miss A Christie (*Equestrian Assistant*)
Mrs C Clarke, BSc (*Home Economics*)
Mrs P Corral, HNC (*Early Years Practitioner & Classroom Assistant*)
Miss V Curry, MA Hons, PGCE (*Religious Studies, Sacred Heart Coordinator, ICT Coordinator*)
Mlle I Dépreux, BA Hons, Maitrise, PGCE (*French, Form Teacher*)
Mrs M A Farmer (*Mater Asst. Residential Mistress*)
Mrs C Farrell, DipEd (*Butterstone Asst Residential Mistress*)
Mrs P Ferguson, MA Hons, PGCE (*Form Teacher, Early Years Coordinator*)
Miss D Finnegan, MA Hons (*English for Speakers of Other Languages, Asst to the Head of Sixth Form*)
Mr A Fynn, MA Hons, PGDE (*German, French*)
Mrs J Gordon (*Barat/Swinton Asst. Boarding Mistress*)
Miss K Greig, BHSAI (*Equestrian Manager*)
Mrs D Hally, HNC, PDA Child Care & Education (*Nursery Manager*)
Mrs M Halmarack, BA Hons, MSc, PGCE (*Biology, Form Teacher*)
Mrs S Hewett, MSc, BSc, PGCE (*Physics*)
Mr D Hewitt, BSc (*ICT Manager*)
Miss R Humphreys (*Musician in Residence, Barat/Swinton Asst Boarding Mistress*)
Miss A King, BA (*Boarding Assistant/Support for Learning*)
Mrs S Lockett, MA Hons, PGCE (*Form Teacher*)
Miss A M Losty, BSc, PGCE (*Chemistry, Arran Housemistress*)
Mrs M McCabe, MA, PGCE (*Spanish, RE, Inchcolm Housemistress*)
Mrs D McCormick, BSc Hons (*Science Teacher, Kinnoull Housemistress*)
Dr D McDonald, PhD, BSc Hons (*Biology*)
Mrs G McFadden (*Moncreiffe Housemistress, Mater Boarding Mistress, Physical Education*)
Mr A McGarva, BA, PGCE (*Director of Music*)
Mrs J McGregor (*LAMDA*)
Mr K McKinney, BEd (*Mathematics*)
Miss G McMaster, BA Hons, PGCE (*Art*)
Miss C McShane, BA Hons (*English*)
Mrs M Malloch (*Prep Classroom Assistant*)
Miss K Morrison (*Groom/Assistant Instructor*)
Mrs L A Murray, RGN, SCM (*Matron*)
Mrs P Murray (*Barat/Swinton Asst Boarding Mistress*)
Ms A Neilson, Dip Art, DipEd (*Art & Design*)
Mrs A Ness (*LAMDA*)
Mrs A O'Hear, BSc Hons, PGCE (*Biology, Teaching & Learning Coordinator, Form Tutor*)

Mrs L Oswald, BEd Hons (*History, Form Teacher & Senior Prep Coordinator*)
Mrs E Prentice, BSc, PGCE (*Head of Sixth Form and Geography*)
Mr D Reed (*Tennis Academy Coach*)
Mrs R Reid, MA, BEd (*Learning Support & ESOL*)
Mrs E Rodger, BEd Hons (*Physical Education, Form Teacher*)
Mrs L Sale (*Butterstone Residential Mistress, Nursery Teacher*)
Mrs M Saunders, BA Hons (*English*)
Mrs I Scott (*Barat/Swinton Boarding Mistress*)
Miss L Scott, BA (*Drama*)
Mrs E Shand (*Equestrian Deputy Manager*)
Mrs S Speed, BSc Hons, PGCE (*Mathematics*)
Miss B Spurgin, MA Hons (*Librarian*)
Mr A Stewart, DipEd (*Form Teacher*)
Mrs E Stewart, DipEd (*Form Teacher*)
Mrs P Stott (*Director of Sport*)
Miss A Taylor, BSc Hons, PGDE (*Mathematics, Asst to the Head of Sixth Form*)

Director of Development: Mr R Baird, MInstF Cert
Head of Marketing: Mr L Plaster, BA Hons

Administration Staff:
Mrs L-A Drane (*Principal's PA & Admissions Coordinator, Administration Manager*)
Mrs J Gordon (*Development Assistant*)
Mrs S Harrison (*School Secretary*)
Mrs J MacMillan (*Receptionist*)
Mrs B McGarva (*Receptionist*)
Mrs A Marnoch (*Asst Secretary/Receptionis*)
Mrs P Murray (*Asst Secretary/Receptionist*)
Miss T Stack (*School Secretary*)

The School was founded in 1920 by the Society of Sacred Heart and moved from its original site in Edinburgh to Kilgraston in 1930. Today Kilgraston is an independent Catholic charitable trust but is still a member of the International Network of Sacred Heart Schools which provides invaluable worldwide contacts for the school and pupils. Kilgraston warmly welcomes girls of all denominations and faiths who make up a large proportion of the pupil population.

Kilgraston is a Georgian mansion house and the campus is set in 54 acres of stunning parkland three miles from the centre of Perth with Edinburgh and Glasgow less than an hour's drive by car. An exciting long-term capital development programme has seen recent significant investment in ICT and boarding facilities and in April 2008 the completion of the new state-of-the-art 25m indoor Swimming Pool Complex. There has also been an exciting upgrade of the school's equestrian centre which now incorporates a 60m x 40m floodlit arena with show jumps. Most recently Kilgraston invested £0.5 million in a new floodlit international-sized all-weather hockey pitch along with the refurbishment of 8 floodlit all-weather tennis courts.

The Curriculum. Generally Kilgraston follows the Scottish educational system with all the girls following a broad curriculum before selecting subjects to continue at Standard Grade (GCSE equivalent). Over 18 subjects are offered at Higher/Advanced Higher (A Level equivalent). Kilgraston has a record of high academic achievement and the girls gain entrance to top universities including Oxford and Cambridge. Kilgraston has been in the top three schools for Advanced Highers in Scotland for the last four years.

Classrooms are well equipped and modern IT facilities with wireless internet access are spread throughout the school.

Music, Art and Drama play an important part of life at Kilgraston. The Music Department alone has 14 individual teaching rooms, a new recording studio and two large music rooms designed to suit all needs. There are also many opportunities for pupils to perform throughout the year by participating in orchestra, string orchestra, fiddle, woodwind and brass groups, samba band, rock group or one of several choirs.

The Art Department is housed in the top of the mansion with superb views across the Ochil Hills and the school boasts an impressive number of past pupils who are practicing artists.

Sports and recreation are catered for within a superb sports hall including a climbing wall and fitness gym. The extensive grounds incorporate the indoor 25m swimming pool, nine floodlit all-weather courts, playing fields and athletics track. Whilst the main sports are hockey, netball, tennis, rounders, swimming and athletics other sports include football, touch rugby, skiing, cricket, badminton, yoga, karate, aerobics, ballet, modern dance and highland dancing. Fixtures and competitions are also arranged against other schools throughout the year. Kilgraston is the only school in Scotland to have an Equestrian Centre on campus and the school hosts the Scottish Schools' Equestrian Championships every Spring.

Kilgraston is divided into houses which compete against each other in games, music and debating. The girls can also take part in the Duke of Edinburgh's Award Scheme and are encouraged to use all the facilities not only for curriculum lessons but also for leisure activities.

Kilgraston Preparatory School and Nursery is co-educational up to the age of nine. The boarders live in the newly refurbished Butterstone House. Girls in the Prep School are prepared for Common Entrance to Kilgraston and other leading schools. Until the age of nine the girls are with class teachers at which stage they begin to be taught by specialist teachers in the Senior School. All of the pupils benefit from the many facilities of the Senior School. (*See separate entry in IAPS section.*)

Admission is normally interview and school report. Entry to the Prep School is by interview and assessment.

Means-tested bursaries are available on application. Scholarship Examinations are held in early February and awards are also offered each year as a result of outstanding performance in the Academic Scholarship Examinations. Scholarships are also offered in Art, Music, Drama and Sport.

Fees per term (2011–2012). Senior: Day £4,690, Boarding £7,995. Prep: Day £2,675–£4,350, Full Boarding £6,350.

Charitable status. Kilgraston School Trust is a Registered Charity, number SC029664.

King Edward VI High School for Girls
Birmingham

Edgbaston Park Road, Birmingham B15 2UB
Tel: 0121 472 1834
Fax: 0121 471 3808
e-mail: admissions@kehs.co.uk
website: www.kehs.org.uk

Independent, formerly Direct Grant.

Governing Body: The Governors of the Schools of King Edward VI in Birmingham

Principal: **Miss S H Evans**, BA Sussex, MA Leicester, PGCE

Vice Principal: Miss A C Warne, BA Birmingham, PGCE

Teaching Staff:
Mrs R M Arnold, MA Cambridge, PGCE

Dr B Ashfield, BA Oxon, PhD Birmingham, PGCE
Mrs M Atkins, MA Reading
Mrs N Azmat, BA London, ACCA, PGCE
Mrs J L Bagnall, BSc Sheffield, PGCE
Mr R P Barrett, BA Leeds Polytechnic, PGCE
Mrs S Bhagi, BSc Birmingham, PGCE
Mrs L D Birchall, LLCE France, PGCE
Miss S A Blanks, BA Birmingham, GTP
Mrs M C Britton, BA London, PGCE
Miss C A Brown, MA Cambridge, PGCE
Miss A L Buckley, BA Oxon, GTP
Mrs L J Burnett, BA London QTS
Ms H Chambers, MA Cambridge, PGCE
Mrs G K Chapman, BEd Brighton
Mrs R M Coetzee, MA Cambridge, PGCE
Mrs C E Coleman, BA Warwick QTS
Dr S Collisson, MusB Manchester, PhD London
Mr T O Cooper, BA Bristol, PGCE
Mrs K Cowan, BSc Glasgow, PGCE
Mrs E B Cummings, BA Nottingham, PGCE
Mrs R D'Aquila, BA Italy
Mr R Devey, BSc Derby, PGCE
Mr A E Duncombe, MA Cambridge, PGCE
Miss E M Edwards, BEd Bristol
Dr C E Gruzelier, MA Auckland, DPhil Oxon, PGCE
Mrs F Hall, MA Oxon, PGCE
Mr C Hammel, AB Princeton, MLitt St Andrews
Mrs L Harniess, BA Essex, CertEd
Dr S Hayton, BSc, PhD Newcastle, PGCE
Mrs J Herbert, ALAM, LLAM
Mr C Hope, BA Hull, PGCE
Mr R M Hopkinson, BSc Hull, MSc London, PGCE
Mrs C M Hosty, BA York, PGCE
Mrs S A Huxley, BEd Bradford
Mr H J Kavanagh, BA Cantab, PGCE
Mrs H D Kavanagh, BA Bristol, PGCE
Miss V Krutin, BA Bath, PGCE
Miss R Laurent, Diplome Haute Alsace, PGCE
Mr F Mackinnon, BA Strathclyde, PGCE
Mrs J K Mahon, BSc London, PGCE
Mrs A Marquette, BA, MA France, PGCE
Mrs S M May, BSocSci Birmingham, PGCE
Mrs S J Merrall, BA Oxon, PGCE
Mrs J E Moule, BA Durham, PGCE
Miss J Oldfield, BSc Durham, PGCE
Ms S Pallister, MA Birmingham, PGCE
Miss S Platt, BSc Manchester, PGCE
Mrs C M Pollard, BSc Nottingham, PGCE
Dr M Popat-Szabries, BSc London, MA Warwick, PhD Warwick, PGCE
Miss H Proops, BA Central School of Speech & Drama, GTP
Mrs P J Rutter, BSc Birmingham, ACE
Mrs K Sangha, BA De Montfort, MBA, PGCE Warwick
Ms L C Seamark, BA Birmingham, PGCE
Mr R T Sheppard, BEng Manchester, PGCE
Mrs S K E Shore-Nye, BA Swansea, PGCE
Dr M Simpson, BSc Birmingham, PhD Birmingham, PGCE
Mrs J C Smith, CertEd Bedford College of PE
Mr R W Symonds, BSc Nottingham, PGCE
Dr B L Tedd, BSc London, PhD Leicester, PGCE
Miss O N Terry, BA Cardiff, PGCE
Mrs B Thompson, BSc Sheffield Hallam, PGCE
Mrs J Whitehead, BSc Birmingham, PGCE
Mrs A Young, BA Birmingham, PGCE

Librarian: Mrs A Z Moloney, BA, MA, PGCE

Principal's PA and Registrar: Mrs C L Tovey

Matron: Mrs E Mathers

Founded in 1883, the School moved in 1940 to its present buildings and extensive grounds adjacent to King Edward's School for Boys. There are 540 girls from 11 to 18 years of age, all day pupils.

Curriculum. The curriculum is distinctive in its strong academic emphasis and aims to inspire a love of learning. The purpose of the curriculum is to help girls realise their full potential. Excellence is sought in aesthetic, practical and physical activities as well as in academic study. Our aim is to achieve a balance of breadth and depth, with dropping of subjects postponed as long as possible so that girls may make informed choices and have access to a wide range of possible careers.

In **Year One** all girls take English, Mathematics, separate Sciences, Religious Studies, French, History, Geography, Music, Art and Design, Drama, Information Technology, Games, Swimming, Dance and Creative Skills.

In **Years Two and Three** all girls take English, Mathematics, separate Sciences, Religious Studies, French, Latin, History, Geography, Music, Art and Design, Information Technology, Physical Education, Creative Skills.

Core subjects in **Years Four and Five** are English Language, English Literature, Mathematics, Biology, Chemistry, Physics, Latin, French. Girls then choose from 3 option blocks their other GCSE subjects. Another modern language can be taken as a two-year GCSE course.

In the **Sixth Form** girls choose for AS and A2 from a wide range of subjects, all Arts, or all Sciences or a mixture of the two. Some subjects are taken jointly with King Edward's School. Stress is placed on breadth at this level. All girls take General Studies at A Level (normally as their fifth subject) with courses for all in Critical Thinking. Various philosophical, scientific and practical topics are explored in short courses.

All girls follow a course in personal decision-making in which they explore and discuss a wide range of issues which call for personal choice and which helps develop life skills.

Religious and moral education are considered important. Academic study of them is designed to enable girls to be informed and questioning. In the last two years, courses (apart from the choice of Religious Studies at A Level) are designed as part of the General Studies programme. There is no denominational teaching in the school in lessons or morning assembly. Girls of all faiths or of none are equally welcome.

Girls take part in Physical Education, until the Upper 6th Form where it is voluntary, with increasing choice from gymnastics, hockey, netball, tennis, rounders, dance, fencing, badminton, squash, fives, swimming, athletics, basketball, volleyball, self-defence, aerobics, archery, health related fitness. We have our own swimming pool, sports hall and extensive pitches, including two artificial hockey areas.

In addition to the music in the curriculum, there are choirs and orchestras which reach a high standard. These are mostly joint with King Edward's School. Individual (or shared) instrumental lessons, at an extra fee, are arranged in school in a great variety of instruments. Some instruments can be hired. Individual singing lessons can also be arranged.

A large number of clubs (many joint with King Edward's School) are run by pupils themselves with help and encouragement from staff. Others (eg Drama, Music, Sport) are directed by staff. Help is given with activities relating to the Duke of Edinburgh's Award scheme. Some activities take place in lunch hours, others after school and at weekends.

As part of the school's commitment to developing an awareness of the needs of society and a sense of duty towards meeting those needs, girls are encouraged to plan and take part in various community service projects as well as organising activities in school to raise money to support causes of their choice.

A spacious careers room is well-stocked with up to date information. Individual advice and aptitude testing is given at stages where choices have to be made. One member of staff has overall responsibility but many others are involved with various aspects. Girls are encouraged to attend conferences, gain work experience, make personal visits and enquiries. Old Edwardians and others visit school to talk about their careers. There is good liaison with universities and colleges of all kinds. Virtually all girls go on to higher education. A wide range of courses is being taken by Old Edwardians.

Admission of Pupils. Entry is normally for girls of 11 into the first year of the school in September. Applications must be made by January for entry in September. Girls should have reached the age of 11 years by 31st August following the examination. Girls up to 1 year younger than this can be considered in some circumstances; parents of such girls should communicate with the Principal in the previous autumn term. Girls are examined at the school in English, Mathematics and Reasoning. The syllabus is such as would be normally covered by girls of good ability and no special preparation is advised.

Girls from 12 to 15 are normally considered only if they move from another part of the country, or in some special circumstances. Applications should be made to the Principal in writing as soon as the move is planned. Such girls can be admitted at any time if there is a vacancy.

There is an entry into the Sixth Form for girls wishing to study four main A Level subjects and General Studies. Application should be made to the Principal as early as possible in the preceding academic year.

Fees per term (2011-2012). £3,405.

Scholarships and Assisted places. (*See Scholarship Entries section.*) The equivalent of up to a total of two full-fee scholarships may be awarded on the results of the Governors' Admission Examination to girls entering the first year, with a maximum of 50% for any individual scholarship. These are independent of parental income and are normally tenable for 7 years.

Governors' Assisted Places are available for girls entering the first year and additional places are available for girls entering at 16+. These are means tested.

The Principal will be pleased to provide further information.

Charitable status. The Schools of King Edward VI in Birmingham is a Registered Charity, number 529051. The purpose of the Foundation is to educate children and young persons living in or around the city of Birmingham mainly by provision of, or assistance to its schools.

King's High School

Smith Street, Warwick CV34 4HJ
Tel: 01926 494485
Fax: 01926 403089
e-mail: enquiries@kingshighwarwick.co.uk
website: www.kingshighwarwick.co.uk

Chairman of Governors of Warwick Independent Schools Foundation:
Mr D B Stevens, BA

Chairman of King's High School Committee:
Mrs J Marshall, BA

Ex-Officio:
The Lord Lieutenant of Warwickshire
The Mayor of Warwick

Members of the King's High School Committee:
Mr R V Cadbury, MA Cantab
Mr A J L Cockburn
Mrs J Edwards, BA, MBA
Professor D Grammatopoulos, PhD, FRCPath
Mr D E Hanson
Mr N Keegan
Mrs S Lampitt, BA, DipEd (*Vice-Chairman*)

Mrs E Moloney
Mrs P Snape
Professor R H Trigg, MA, DPhil Oxon

Foundation Secretary: Mr S Jones

Staff:
Head Mistress: Mrs E Surber, BA, MA Exeter

Deputy Head (*Academic*): Mr S Bethel, BSc Birmingham
Deputy Head (*Pastoral*): Mrs C Renton, BSc Leicester, MSc London

Head of Sixth Form: Mr J W Wood, BA Nottingham, MSc Leicester
Head of Key Stage 4: Mrs K Hewitt, BA Bristol
Head of Key Stage 3: Dr R Cheetham, BSc London, PhD
Head of Careers: Miss J A Dormer, BA Durham
Head of Science: Mrs R Chapman, MA Oxon
Examinations Secretary: Mrs L Y Sherren, BSc Sheffield

* *Head of Department*
§ *Part-time*

Art, Design and Food Technology:
*Miss S J Lewis, MA Wales
Mrs E Ashby, BA Kent
§Mrs S Didlick, BEd, CNAA (*Teacher in Charge of Food Technology & Voluntary Service Coordinator*)
§Miss L Sinden, BA, MA Nottingham Trent
Mr N C Walker, BSc Brunel (*Teacher in Charge of Design Technology & DofE Award Coordinator*)

Business Studies:
§Mrs E A Thornton, BA Nottingham (*Teacher in Charge*)
§Mrs A E Browning, BA London

Careers:
*Miss J A Dormer, BA Durham
§Mrs A E Browning, BA London (*Work Experience Coordinator*)
Mrs M E Forde, BA Oxon, MA Birmingham (*Careers Advisor*)
Dr R Lidgett, BA, PhD Birmingham (*Careers Advisor*)
Miss R Bradbury, BA York, MA Leeds (*Oxbridge Coordinator*)

Classics:
*Ms I Peace BA Durham
Miss J A Dormer, BA Durham

Drama:
*Ms J Whitehouse, MA Sussex
§Mr P Atkins, MA Leeds
Mrs S Marshall, BA Guildhall

English:
*Miss R Bradbury, BA York, MA Leeds
§Mrs A Baker, BA Nottingham
§Mrs R Barton, BA University College London
§Mrs K Greaves, BA East Anglia
Miss L Marvin, BA Birmingham
Miss R Wareing, BA Northumbria

Economics:
§Mrs J Roberts, BA Leeds (*Teacher in Charge*)
Mr J W Wood, BA Nottingham, MSc Leicester

Geography:
*Mrs S Watson, MA Oxon
§Mrs A E Browning, BA London
Mrs C Renton, BSc Leicester, MSc London
§Mrs E A Thornton, BA Nottingham

History & Politics:
*Miss E Carney, BA Manchester
Dr G Gifford, PhD, MSc MA Edinburgh
Ms I Peace, BA Durham
§Mrs J Roberts, BA Leeds

Mrs C Wellman, BA Warwick (*Teacher in Charge of Politics*)

Mr J W Wood, BA Nottingham, MSc Leicester

Information Technology:
*Mrs P Prance, BSc Warwick
§Mrs N Russell, BSc Loughborough
Miss S Kaur, BSc Coventry, MSc Brunel

Mathematics:
*Mr A Wild, BSc Wales
Mr H Ashby, BEng CNAA
Mr S Bethel, BSc Birmingham
Miss U Birbeck, BA Warwick
Miss R M Court, BSc London
Mr R Sharpe, BEd Bristol Polytechnic, Dip DA New College of Speech and Drama
Mrs L Y Sherren, BSc Sheffield

Modern Languages:
*Mrs M E Forde, BA Oxon, MA Birmingham (*Teacher in Charge of Spanish*)
§Mrs C Esposito Faraone, MA Naples
§Ms K Gibson, BA Salford
§Mrs M Hedley, Dip Inst of Linguists, MBA Leicester (*Teacher in Charge of German*)
Mrs L King, BA Warwick (*Teacher in Charge of French*)
Mrs C Murphy, BA Royal Holloway
Miss E Montiel Bonsignore, Licenciatura en Educación
§Mrs M Esteban-Stephenson (*Spanish Assistant*)
§Mrs E Heissler (*German Assistant*)
§Mrs M H Quinney, DEUG Nantes & Chartres (*French Assistant*)

Music:
*Mr M Smallwood, BA Mus Anglia Polytechnic University
Mrs D Wallace, BMus, LRAM, LTCL, LTCL

Physical Education:
*Miss C E A Gilbert, BA Liverpool John Moores
Mrs K J Bryce, BSc Brunel
Miss L McFarlane, BSc Sheffield Hallam
§Mrs C Walker, BEd Chelsea School of Movement

Psychology:
§Mr N Orrock, BA Leicester (*Teacher in Charge*)

Religious Education:
*Dr R Lidgett, BA, PhD Birmingham
§Mrs J Day, BA, MA Oxon (*Voluntary Service Coordinator*)
Dr G Gifford, PhD, MSc, MA Edinburgh
Mrs K Hewitt, BA Bristol

Science:
*Mrs R Chapman, MA Oxon
Biology:
*Mrs A Sims, MA Cantab
Dr P M Boulton, BSc London, PhD Birmingham
Mrs S Burgham, BSc London
§Mrs J M Grant, BSc Durham
§Dr C M Pickup, BSc Manchester, DPhil Oxon, AMBDA
§Mrs K Pitchford, BSc Southampton
Chemistry:
Dr A Grist, BSc, PhD Leicester (*Teacher in Charge*)
Mrs S Burgham, BSc London
Mrs R Chapman, MA Oxon
Dr R Cheetham, BSc, PhD London
§Mrs E Mottram, BA Oxon
§Mrs K Pitchford, BSc Southampton
Physics:
Dr A Chamberlain, BSc, PhD Warwick (*Teacher in Charge*)
Mrs J M Grant, BSc Durham
Miss J Kneeland, MPhys Durham
§Mrs E Mottram, BA Oxon
Mrs B Stewart, BSc Manchester

Special Educational Needs Coordinator:
§Mrs P Cronin, BA Cardiff, OCR DipSpLD, AMBDA

Gifted & Talented Coordinator:
Dr A Chamberlain, BSc, PhD Warwick

Visiting Music Staff:
Mr C Allison, BMus (*Saxophone*)
Mrs L Braithwaite, BMus LTCL, PGRNCM (*Oboe*)
Mr C Druce, FRCO, GBSM, ARCM (*Piano*)
Mrs S M Irving, BEd Cantab, MMus (*Piano/Violin*)
Mr N Jones (*Drum Kit*)
Mr P Luckhurst, ATCL, TDip (*Guitar*)
Miss D Mason, BA, LTCL, ABRSM (*Flute*)
Mrs J J Matthews, LRAM (*Flute*)
Mr R B Meteyard, AGSM (*Violin*)
Mrs S Meteyard, GBSM, ABSM (*Violin/Viola*)
Miss B Morley, BA Coll (*Bass/Singing*)
Mrs M Stringer, BA, MA, BMus (*Singing*)
Mrs M Todd, Diploma Lucerne Conservatoire (*'Cello*)
Miss A H Whelan, DRSAMD (*Brass*)
Mrs A Williams, LRAM, ARCM (*Singing*)

Visiting Coaches/Teachers for Activities:
Mr D Abini (*Lacrosse*)
Mrs E Barkans (*Yoga*)
Mr D Bryce (*Hockey*)
Mrs L England (*Dance*)
Mr P Helps (*Clay Pigeon Shooting*)
Mr G Henderson (*Tennis*)
Miss S Higgins, Teacher of Dance, BTDA (*Ballet*)
Mrs C Masterson (*Pilates*)
Mr A Millington, Warwick School (*Climbing Club*)
Mrs D Monnington (*Badminton & Gym*)
Mr C Osborne (*Badminton*)
Mr T Perkins (*Dance*)
Mrs E Slater (*Badminton*)
Mrs M Yeates, Warwick School (*Lifesaving*)

Marketing/Communications Manager: Mrs M K Bray
Marketing Assistant: Mrs H Cartwright
Registrar: Mrs G Worrall
Head's Secretary: Mrs D Ralphs
Administration Manager: Miss H Shawcross
Staff Secretary: Mrs G Brown
Data Administrator: Mr A Sherren
Finance & Resources Manager: Mrs S Jasinska
Receptionist: Mrs R Short
Matron: Mrs S Ward
Network Manager: Mr T Rushton
Assistant Network Manager: Mr J Wiltshire
Administrative Assistant, Music Dept: Mrs A Williams
Librarian: Mrs A Falconer Hall
Alumnae Relations Officer: Mr R Gellert-Binnie
Database and Administration Assistant: Mrs E Guest
Domestic Services Manager: Mr A Pepper
Secretary of Old Girls' Association: Mrs P Beidas

King's High School is an independent day school for girls aged 11 to 18. From its beginning in 1879 it has been a forward looking, friendly school which is proud of its reputation for both academic success and the personal development of its girls. The school is part of the Warwick Independent Schools Foundation, alongside Warwick School and Warwick Preparatory School.

Located in the heart of Warwick, the school has remained on the same town site for 131 years. The 18th century Landor House is complemented by superb ultra-modern additions: the Sixth Form Centre and St Mary's Building opened by Dame Judi Dench in 2006, and the Creative Arts Centre opened in December 2009 by Miss Catherine Bott.

The curriculum aims to give pupils as broad an education as possible. All students study two modern languages and Latin, and ICT is widely used across the curriculum. There is a wide choice of A level subjects.

Our winning formula of hard work and lots of fun has produced consistently good performances for King's High which has appeared within the top 100 schools for the past five years.

The school also recognises the importance of the creative arts: it has numerous music and drama groups. Yoga, ballet and creative textiles are some of the activities on offer outside of the curriculum, most of which take place at lunchtimes. All girls are encouraged to enjoy some form of exercise or sport and some perform at the highest levels in individual events or school and county teams. There are strong links with our brother school in the Foundation, Warwick School.

The school organises many day, evening and residential trips to complement the curriculum. Recent visits abroad include trips to India, Iceland and the USA, with exchange trips to France, Germany and Spain.

Admission. Girls are required to take an entrance examination and attend an interview.

Fees per term (2011-2012). Tuition £3,252. Music: Brass, Pianoforte, Strings, Woodwind, Guitar, Drums, Singing £199 for 10 lessons.

Financial Assistance. Scholarships are available on entry at age 11 and for internal and external candidates to Sixth Form. Warwick Foundation Awards, up to the value of full fees, are also available on entry at 11+ and at Sixth Form.

Charitable status. King's High School is a part of the Warwick Independent Schools Foundation which is a Registered Charity, number 1088057. The aim of the charity is "to provide for children (3–18) of parents of all financial means – a high proportion of whom shall come from Warwick and its immediate surroundings, but subject to satisfying academic standards where required – education of academic, cultural and sporting standards which are the highest within their peer groups".

The Kingsley School

Beauchamp Hall, Beauchamp Avenue, Leamington Spa, Warwickshire CV32 5RD
Tel: 01926 425127
Fax: 01926 831691
e-mail: schooloffice@kingsleyschool.co.uk
website: www.thekingsleyschool.com

Independent Day School for Girls aged 3 to 18, and boys up to 7 years, founded in 1884.

Council:
President: Mr A Noble

Joint Chairs:
Mrs A Darling
Mrs J White, BSc Eng, FCA

Vice-Chair: Mrs R Skilbeck, BDS

Governors:
Mrs L Bartlett
Mr T Baumfield
Mrs J Burns
Mr R N Button
Mr A Bye
Mr D Cleary
Mr N Evans, BSc, FRICS
Mrs M P Hicks, CertEd
Dr L Long, MA, PhD
Professor R Naguib
Mrs E Smith

Head: **Ms H Owens**, BA, PGCE, NPQH

Deputy Head (*Pastoral*): Mrs C Robbins, BA, MPhil, PGCE

Assistant Headteacher (*Curriculum & Administration*): Ms R Dyson, BA, PGCE

Head of Preparatory School: Miss A Hornsby, MSc, CertEd

Head of Sixth Form: Mrs J Bailey, BA, CertEd

Staff:

* *Head of Department*

Art:
*Mr E Lax, BA Hons Fine Art, PGCE

Classics:
*Dr M Palmer, BA, DPhil

Design & Technology:
*Mrs C Dempsey, BEd
Mrs K Hughes O'Sullivan, MA, BEd

Economics & Business Studies:
*Mrs M Bennett, BEd, MA

English:
*Mrs A Hamilton, BA, PGCE
Mrs D Morgan, BA, PGCE
Mrs C Robbins, BA, MPhil, PGCE
Mrs K Todman, BA, PGCE

Geography:
*Mrs R Rogers, BSc, PGCE
Mrs J Bailey, BA, CertEd
Mrs D Frydman, BSc, CertEd

History:
*Mrs S Waterson, BA, PGCE
Miss R Dyson, BA, PGCE

Home Economics:
*Mrs L Le Poidevin, BEd
Mrs K Hughes-O'Sullivan, MA, BEd

Information Technology:
Mrs C Dempsey, BEd
Mrs J Hilton, BSc, PGCE, CPhys, MInstP

Mathematics:
*Miss K Davis, BSc, PGCE
Mrs L Laubscher, HE Dip SA, QTS
Mrs S Morris, BSc, CertEd

Modern Languages:
*Mrs S Jessett, BA, PGCE
Mrs F Harris, BA, MA, PGCE
Mrs C Cocksworth, BA PGCE
Mrs J Smith, MA, BA, PGCE

Performing Arts:
*Mrs J Walton, BEd
Mr J Smith, BMus, PGCE
Mrs A Vallance, BA QTS

Physical Education:
*Mrs S Bates, BA, CertEd
Miss S Windsor, BEd
Mrs K Close (*Badminton and Swimming coach*)

Psychology:
Mrs K MacLeod, BSc
Miss S Rooke, BA Hons

Religious Studies:
*Mrs E Mackenzie, BPhil, MEd, CertEd

Science:
*Mrs J Hilton, BSc, PGCE, CPhys, MInstP
*Dr C Robertson, BSc, PhD, PGCE
Mrs C Duke, BSc, PGCE
Mr A Edwards, BA, PGCE

Mrs G Hermitage, BSc, PGCE

Preparatory School:
Head: Miss A Hornsby, MSc, CertEd
Mrs G Adair, BN, PGCE
Mrs J Bunce, General TCert (*Music*)
Mrs C Hall, BEd
Mrs Y Hargreaves, NNEB
Mrs R Harrold, PGCE
Mrs S Holmes BA, PGCE
Mrs C Machin, BA, PGCE
Mrs K Parker
Mrs J Pendred, BEd
Miss L Tilley, BA, PGCE

Careers:
Mrs R Rogers, BSc, PGCE

Learning Support:
*Mrs L Stevenson, LLB, AKC, Dip SpLD
Ms J Harper, BA
Mrs Y Raja, Cert Learning Support

Learning Resources Centre:
Miss K Hilder, BA, PGCE
Mrs C Apparu

Finance Office:
Mr B Cheney, ACMA (*Senior Finance Manager*)
Mrs S Punj (*Finance Assistant*)
Miss M Franks

Administration:
Mrs J Bostock (*PA to Headteacher*)
Mrs A Griffiths (*School Secretary*)
Mr A Savage (*Premises Manager*)
Mrs M Wright (*Attendance Registrar/Receptionist*)

Marketing:
Mrs E Hickman, BA (*Marketing Manager*)
Mrs C Watson (*School Registrar*)
Mrs A Radley (*Public Relations*)

Duke of Edinburgh's Award Scheme:
Mrs K Hughes-O'Sullivan, MA, BEd

After School Care:
Mrs J Clinton
Mrs C Apparu

Speech and Drama:
Mrs J Parkinson, LAMDA

Dance:
Ms N Shurvinton (*Modern Dance Tutor*)

School Nurse: Mrs T Ball, SRN, BSc
Assistant School Nurse: Mrs K Parker

The Kingsley School has a long history of success in every area of the curriculum and its traditions and ethos combine to make it a happy and secure environment for its pupils. The school is a Christian foundation but welcomes pupils of different faiths. Since 1884, Kingsley has upheld traditional values in a happy, purposeful and well-disciplined environment. It enjoys an enviable teacher: pupil ratio of 1:9 and the talents of each individual are recognised and nurtured academically and socially.

Kingsley **Preparatory School** offers a rich, vibrant and extensive curriculum which goes way beyond the National Curriculum, with pupils achieving excellent results. There are specialist teachers in the key areas of French, music, drama, PE, games and swimming.

Throughout their junior years, children thrive in a caring, homely and academically stimulating setting that prepares them well for entry to the Senior School.

The **Senior School** provides a wide range of GCSE subjects including 3 separate sciences, astronomy, 2 modern languages, Latin, business and communication studies,

physical education, drama, dance and music. Academic standards are high, with the 2010 GCSE results showing a 98% pass rate at grades A*–C in at least 5 subjects, of which 53% of passes were at grade A or A*. In addition, 18 Year 10 pupils took early entry Maths GCSE and all attained A or A*.

The Sixth Form at Kingsley combines the desire for academic success with the creation of confident, self-motivated and independent young women. Curriculum provision and choice is broad as the School offers traditional A Level subjects as well as economics, politics, psychology and business studies. Last year's A Level results showed a 100% pass rate, of which 80% were at grades A–C, with 27% A or A*. Most girls go on to the university of their first choice, including Oxbridge.

Extra-curricular Activities. The diverse selection of clubs and activities on offer include: astronomy, art, badminton, Bookworm Club, child development, Chinese, cross stitch, classics, Food Club, hockey, Kung Fu, orchestra, public speaking, swimming, swing band, tennis, quiz club and the Kingsley Riding Squad.

From a young age, pupils are encouraged to explore their creative abilities through a rich programme of expressive arts including speech and drama, singing, dance and music. A high proportion of girls take LAMDA and ABRSM exams as well as work towards the Arts Award.

Older girls can take part in Young Enterprise, World Challenge and a thriving Duke of Edinburgh's Award scheme; last year 23 sixth form girls achieved their gold award.

Many cultural and sporting trips are organised every year to enrich the taught curriculum and learning: recent examples include visits to local businesses, museums and theatres as well as destinations further afield such as Barbados, India, Pompeii and Ypres.

Fees per term (2011-2012). Preparatory School: £2,785 (Reception to Year 2), £3,250 (Years 3–6). Senior School: £3,495.

Scholarships and Bursaries. Academic, art, music, drama and performing arts scholarships are available at 7+, 11+, 13+ and 16+.

Up to 100% bursaries are available.

Private transport serves a wide area and before and after-school care is available.

Charitable status. The Kingsley School is a Registered Charity, number 528774. It exists to provide high quality education for girls aged 3 to 18 and boys up to 7 years.

The Lady Eleanor Holles School

Hanworth Road, Hampton, Middlesex TW12 3HF
Tel: 020 8979 1601
Fax: 020 8941 8291
e-mail: office@lehs.org.uk
website: www.lehs.org.uk

This Independent Girls' School derives its endowment from a Trust established in 1710 under the will of Lady Eleanor Holles. The Cripplegate Schools Foundation administered the Trust from 1711, when the original school for girls was founded in Cripplegate in the City of London, until 1 November 2009 when a new charitable company limited by guarantee (named 'The Lady Eleanor Holles School' with company registration number 06871042 and registered charity number 1130254) became active, and the Memorandum and Articles of Association of the company now form the constitution of the School. The School is therefore now established as a new legal entity with a distinct and separate legal personality from that of the Foundation. The Foundation continues to exist as an unincorporated charity and to own the buildings and land in which the School operates. The Governors are now the directors and charity trustees of the incorporated School. The present school in Hampton accommodates about 870 girls, aged from 7 to 18 years.

The Cripplegate Schools Foundation

Chairman of the Foundation: Mrs J Ross, BSc, CPFA

Governors:
Mr G Cox, ACE, CA SA
Mr P Gray, ACA, CA SA
Mrs M Lomax
Dr S McCormick, MA Oxon, PhD, CBiol, FIBiol
Ms A Meyric Hughes, BA, PGCE, MA
Mrs M I Nagli
Dr V J Newman, MB BS, FRCA
Mr C S Stokes
Mr R T Welch, FCA
Mr R Young, BSc Hons, DipArch Hons

Clerk to the Governors: Mr A Pitchers, BEd Hons, MCIPD

Head Mistress: Mrs G Low, MA Somerville College Oxford

Deputy Headmistress: Mrs L C Hazel, BA Hull

Assistant Headmistress: Miss M E Beardwood, CertEd Dartford College of Physical Education, BA Open, MA Reading

Assistant Head: Mr R J J Nicholson, BA Pembroke College Oxford, ARCO, PG Cert Ed Man

Assistant Staff:

Senior School

Art and Craft:
Miss S Pauffley, BA Goldsmiths College London
Mrs M Barclay, DipAD Hons, ATC Hornsey College of Art
Mr L Curtis, BA Slade School of Art, MA Royal College of Art
Ms K Jeffery, BA Leicester (*History of Art*)
Mrs E Knight, BA Wimbledon School of Art
Miss H Peat, BA Loughborough College of Art and Design
Ms A E Seaborn, BA Winchester School of Art

Classics:
Mr D Piper, BA King's College London
Mrs R Brown, BA Durham
Miss H Carmichael, BA Newnham College Cambridge, MA SOAS London
Miss K C Eltis, BA Balliol College Oxford
Miss M Hart, BA Exeter
Mrs L C Hazel, BA Hull
Miss M Yan, BA Bristol (*Head of Middle School*)

Design Technology including Home Economics:
Miss A M Travers, BEd Surrey
Mrs A M Angliss, BEd Trinity College Dublin
Mr S G Bicknell, BSc Brunel, PG Dip

Drama:
Dr B J Tait, BA CSSD, PhD Royal Holloway College London
Miss S Fanning, BA Surrey, MA Open

Economics:
Miss A J Matthews, BA Leicester
Miss D A Self, BSc Brunel

English:
Mrs H M Ndongong, BA St Edmund Hall Oxford
Ms A Crompton, BA Salford
Mrs C L Gilroy Scott, BA Birmingham
Mrs V Griffin, BA Homerton College Cambridge
Mr S Halse, BA London, MA London
Miss R S Levick, BA Trinity College Cambridge

Mrs J Morris, BA King's College London
Mrs C Richardson, BA Reading
Miss A-M Wright, MA Aberdeen

Geography:
Mrs S E Coggin, BA Swansea, FRGS
Mrs A R Lloyds, BSc Exeter
Mrs J M Mackay, BSc Southampton, MA London
Mr L M Tresserras, BA Southampton

History:
Mrs A M Bradshaw, MA St Andrews
Mr G M D Falconer, MA Jesus College Cambridge, MA Lancaster
Miss R Hillsdon, BA Sidney Sussex College Cambridge (*Acting Head of History*)
Miss S E Stowe, BA Warwick

Information Technology:
Mrs F M Wimblett, BSc Royal Holloway College London
Miss M E Beardwood, CertEd Dartford College of Physical Education, BA Open, MA Reading
Mrs C Hutterd, BA Auckland University of Technology
Mrs P M Stewart, BSc Bath

Mathematics:
Mrs M Read, BSc Durham
Mrs N Banerjee, BA Delhi
Mrs S Leigh, BSc Edinburgh
Mr S Maloney, BA York
Mrs P A Sharp, BSc Sheffield (*Acting Head of Mathematics*)
Mr G M Stevens, BA Manchester
Miss C Swainston, BSc Surrey
Mr S J Waters, BA Gonville and Caius College Cambridge
Mr M J Williams, BA City of London Polytechnic (*Head of Upper School*)
Mrs F M Wimblett, BSc Royal Holloway College London

Modern Languages:
Miss Y Steinruck, BA Staatsexamen Universität Würzburg (*Head of Modern Languages and German*)
Mrs A Buck, Licenciada en Filología Anglogermanica Universidad de Valencia (*Spanish and German*)
Mrs S M Clarke, MA Merton College Oxford (*French*)
Mrs I M Colclough, BA Royal Holloway College London (*German*)
Mrs R A M Johnson, BA Cologne (*German*)
Mrs V M Kean, BA Leeds (*Head of French*)
Mrs K M Munday, BA Manchester (*German; Director of Studies*)
Ms N Murray, MA Leeds
Miss U Peña-Lekue, BA Deusto, Bilbao (*Head of Spanish*)
Mrs N J Rees, MA New Hall Cambridge (*Spanish*)
Miss D L Robbins, MA St Andrews (*French*)
Mrs A Rowe, BA Nottingham
Mr M Tompsett, MA Selwyn College Cambridge (*German; Head of Sixth Form*)

Music:
Director of Music: Mrs M Ashe, MA St Catherine's College Oxford
Mrs N C Rook, BA Southampton, LTCL, PGCE (*Head of Curriculum Music*)
Dr B L Hughes, MA St Catherine's College Oxford, MMus Goldsmiths College London, PhD London, QTS (*Composer-in-Residence*)
Mr R J J Nicholson, BA Pembroke College Oxford, ARCO, PG Cert Ed Man
Miss N G Redman, BA Manchester
Mr J Akers, BMus RCM, MMus, PGADip RCM (*Classical Guitar*)
Mr B G Ashe, BA York, PGCE, LRAM (*Piano*)
Miss F Chesterman, BMus, Dip Perf (*Violin*)
Ms A Cohen, DRASM, ARCM, LRAM (*Piano*)
Mr F D'Albert (*Electric Guitar, Rock Bands*)

Ms J Dossor, BMus, PGDip, LRAM (*Double Bass*)
Miss E Drury, BMus Hons (*Voice and Saxophone*)
Mr J Fichert, MMus RCM, PG Dip Adv RCM Dist, Dip-Musiklehrerprüfung Karlsruhe (*Piano*)
Miss L H Goddard, MA Girton College Cambridge (*Violin*)
Mr G Hobbs, BMus, PGDipMus (*Bassoon*)
Mrs D L Hume, DSCM (*Violin*)
Miss S James, BMus, LRAM, DipRAM (*Saxophone*)
Miss I Jones, BMus, Dip RCM, Advanced RCM (*Oboe*)
Ms D Kemp, BA, MA, ARCM PG, Dip RCM (*Viola*)
Mrs P A Kent, GRSM, LRAM (*Piano*)
Miss L Knight, BA, MA (*Voice, Music Theatre*)
Mr R Millett, Dip RCM (*Percussion, Percussion Group*)
Ms A Moore, Dip RCM, ARCM (*Harp*)
Miss S Morfee, ARCM, LTCL (*Flute*)
Miss A Prowse, BA Girton College Cambridge (*Voice*)
Mrs H Roberts, MMus, GTCL, LTCL, FTCL (*Voice*)
Mr T Sharp BSc, MSc, LGSM (*Piano, Jazz Piano*)
Miss E Sheridan, BMus Hons, RCM, PG Dip RCM (*Clarinet*)
Ms L Singh-Levett, BMus, AdvPGDip RCM (*Piano*)
Mr N Stringfellow, BA Mus, Grad RNCM, ARCMPG (*Cello*)
Mr D Ward, AGSM Grad GSMD (*Brass*)

Mrs V Gibbens, BA (*Administrator*)

Natural Sciences:
Mrs H Beedham, BSc Hull, MSc Kingston (*Chemistry, Head of Science*)
Mrs L J Anstey, MA New Hall Cambridge (*Psychology and Biology*)
Miss A Ballard, BSc Exeter, MSc Aberdeen (*Biology*)
Mrs J Barwise, BSc Manchester, MA London (*Head of Physics*)
Mr J R Bossé, BSc, BEd Université de Moncton, Canada (*Head of Biology*)
Mrs N C Camilleri, BSc Manchester (*Physics*)
Mrs J Crook, BSc Nottingham (*Chemistry*)
Mrs P Earl, BSc Swansea (*Biology*)
Mrs K M Ellis, BSc Durham (*Physics*)
Mr A Hayter, BSc Durham (*Head of Chemistry*)
Ms H Humbles, BSc University College London (*Biology*)
Mr R Ives, BSc Sheffield Hallam (*Physics*)
Mrs S Jansz, BSc Bangor (*Chemistry*)
Mrs J Monteil, BSc Swansea, MSc London (*Head of Psychology, Biology*)
Mrs C R Nicholls, BSc Cardiff (*Biology*)
Miss S S Ostrander, BSc Bristol (*Psychology and Biology*)
Ms C Packer, BSc University College London (*Chemistry*)
Miss R Parker, BSc Manchester (*Chemistry*)
Miss K Whitehouse, BSc Manchester (*Biology*)

Physical Education:
Director of Sport: Mrs V E Sumner, BA Brighton
Mrs L J Brennan, BEd University of Sydney, Australia
Mrs N Budd, BSc Brighton
Ms K Hoffman, BA University of North Carolina
Miss G A Lindsay (*Rowing*)
Miss M J Waters, BEd Bedford College of HE (*Head of Lower School*)

Religious Education:
Dr P Gibbons, BA Surrey, MA Surrey, DPhil Regent's Park College Oxford
Mrs L Kennedy, BA St Mary's, University of Surrey
Mrs J A B Perkins, BA, MPhil Exeter, MA Heythrop College, London
Miss L Prothero, BA Harvest Bible College, Melbourne, Australia, MA University College London

Careers Advice:
Miss A J Matthews, BA Leicester Polytechnic (*Economics*)
Mrs H Beedham, BSc Hull, MSc Kingston (*Chemistry*)
Miss M Hart, BA Exeter (*Classics*)
Mr A Hayter, BSc Durham (*Chemistry*)

Ms H Humbles, BSc University College London (*Biology*)
Mrs R A M Johnson, BA Cologne (*German*)
Mrs H M Ndongong, BA St Edmund Hall Oxford (*English*)
Mrs C R Nicholls, BSc Cardiff (*Biology*)
Miss S S Ostrander, BSc Bristol (*Psychology and Biology*)
Miss R E Parker, BSc Manchester (*Chemistry*)
Mr M Tompsett, MA Selwyn College Cambridge (*German; Head of Sixth Form*)
Miss K Whitehouse, BSc Manchester (*Biology*)

Manager LRC: Mrs L Payne, MA San Francisco

Junior Department

Head of Department: Mrs F Robinson, BA Cardiff, MA King's College London

Assistant Staff:
Mrs J E Allden, BSc London, MSc Kingston
Miss V M Barnes, BA Kingston
Mrs M M Bass, BEd Natal
Mrs R Bhadeshia, BEd De Montfort
Miss E Brannon, BA Leeds Metropolitan
Mrs M Crowley, BA Exeter
Mrs J Deverson, BEd Oxford Brookes
Mrs J Dilworth, BSc UCL, MPhil Cambridge
Mrs J Gazetas, BSc Newcastle
Mrs S Grant-Sturgis, BA Exeter
Mrs S Harding, BEd De Montfort
Mrs K Hide, BEd La Sainte Union College of Education
Miss M Jenkins, BA Canterbury Christchurch
Mrs C Lyne, Dartford College of PE, BA OU
Mrs V M Moran, BA Durham
Mr P J Ward, BEd London, MEd USA
Mrs V Wood, BEd College of St Mark & St John, Plymouth

Administration:
Bursar: Mr A Pitchers, BEd Hons, MCIPD
Estates Manager: Mr M Walburn, BSc
Marketing & Development Coordinator: Ms S Newton
Head Mistress's Personal Assistant: Mrs C E Grieveson
School Secretary: Mrs R Filby
Registrar: Mrs R D'Albert
Medical Adviser: (*to be appointed*)
School Nurse: Sister S Brew, RGN
School Secretary (*Junior Department*): Mrs J Rees

The school dates from 1711 and is named after its benefactress The Lady Eleanor Holles who directed that the surplus from her Will should be used to establish a school for young girls. Originally in the Cripplegate Ward of the City of London, it moved in the nineteenth century to Hackney and then in 1937 to Hampton. The present, purpose-built, school was opened by Princess Alice, Duchess of Gloucester and accommodated 350 pupils. Numerous additions to the building and the acquisition of more land have enabled the school to increase in size to some 720 girls who enjoy a wealth of specialist facilities and the use of 30 acres of playing fields and gardens. Nine science laboratories, new Learning Resources Centre and Sixth Library, an Art Block, a Design and Technology suite, a Music and Drama wing, extensive IT and multimedia language facilities and a dedicated Careers area are complemented by grass and hard tennis courts, netball courts, 5 lacrosse pitches, track and field areas and a full-sized, indoor heated swimming pool. A Boat House, shared with Hampton School, was opened in October 2000 and a large Sports Hall, adjacent to the swimming pool, in September 2001.

Both the Junior and Senior Departments are equipped with a lift for the disabled.

The School's Statement of Purpose embodies the original aim, to encourage every girl to develop her personality to the full so that she may become a woman of integrity and a responsible member of society. It also emphasises the value of a broad, balanced education which gives due importance to sport, music and the creative arts in general whilst providing the opportunities for girls to achieve high academic standards within a framework of disciplined, independent study.

The Curriculum. In Years 7–9 girls experience two modern, foreign languages, two years of Latin, the separate sciences, dedicated ICT lessons and a PSHE programme which continues throughout the school. Selection rather than specialisation for GCSE allows girls to respond to individual abilities and attributes whilst the School's scheme ensures that every girl continues to experience a broad education in which as few doors as possible are closed. A large sixth form of about 190–200 girls enables a wide choice of Advanced and Advanced Subsidiary subjects to be offered by the School. Most girls will study four or five subjects at Advanced Subsidiary Level, proceeding to A Level with three or four and most are entered for the A Level General Studies examination. The girls have the option of entering for the AQA Baccalaureate, which embraces their A Levels, General Studies AS, an Extended Project and extra-curricular activities. Girls will also have the opportunity of studying for the European Computer Driving Licence (ECDL) Advanced Award. All sixth form students move on to further training, the majority to universities, and there is a sizeable Oxbridge contingent annually. The formal Careers programme which begins in Year 9, before GCSE choices are made, continues throughout the school and uses external specialists, parents and past pupils, ECCTIS and other computer programmes as well as the School's own, trained staff.

Extra-Curricular Activity. A key strength of the school is the range and diversity of its flourishing extra-curricular provision. Some 120 clubs run each week ranging from Music, Drama and PE to Outward Bound and subject clubs, all aiming to further stimulate and inculcate a love of learning outside the classroom: 'The Other Half'. Sixth Formers lead a number of groups which focus on various political, environmental and ethical issues, including 'Model United Nations', 'Amnesty' and 'Make Poverty History'. Girls are encouraged to take the initiative to form their own clubs with a Medic Group, Law Society and Book Club formed in the recent past. The school is very much at the heart of the educational community and has developed a wide range of activities to ensure that students are aware of their social responsibilities, including Service Volunteers which works with disadvantaged students and the elderly, and running numerous activities in local primary schools, including language and drama clubs. Pupils are strongly encouraged to participate in extra-curricular activities.

The Junior Department (188 pupils aged 7–11) is accommodated in a separate building in the grounds, which was very extensively renovated and refurbished in 2003. It is an integral part of the whole school community and uses some specialist facilities.

(*See entry in the IAPS section for more details.*)

Entrance. (*See Scholarship Entries section.*) The majority of girls in the Junior Department are offered guaranteed places in the Senior Department in Year 5, based on an assessment of their performance and attitude. Those that are not may sit the Senior Department entrance examinations if they wish. All external applicants must sit the School's competitive entrance examinations, which are held in November (Sixth Form) and January (7+ and 11+) each year for admission in the following year. Pupils may enter the Junior Department from the age of 7, and the Senior School at 11 years. Girls with good academic ability may apply for direct entry to the Sixth Form.

Registration and Entrance Examination Fee: £100.

Scholarships and Bursaries. (*See Scholarship Entries section.*) Some Academic and Music Scholarships are available for both internal and external candidates at 11+ and Sixth Form entry stages and the Governors of the Cripplegate Schools Foundation offer a small number of Foundation Entrance Bursaries which are available to girls of suitable

academic standards. The amount of assistance is calculated on a sliding scale which is related to family income.

Fees per term (2011-2012). £3,820 in the Junior Department; £4,900 in the Senior School, inclusive of Books, Stationery, Games and Public Examination fees.

Former Pupils' Association. The Holly Club address for communications: Alumnae Administrator c/o The Lady Eleanor Holles School; email: avogel@lehs.org.uk.

Lavant House

West Lavant, Chichester, West Sussex PO18 9AB
Tel: 01243 527211
Fax: 01243 530490
e-mail: office@lavanthouse.org.uk
website: www.lavanthouse.org.uk

Governors:
Mrs P E Senior (*Chair*)
J Bartlett
Mrs J Buckley, BA, PGCE
Mrs A Hancock, BA, ACP, FRSA
Mrs H Herson, CertEd Bedford
R Hoare, OBE, MA Oxon
Mrs R Kamaryc, BA, MSc, PGCE
A MacFarlane, LLB Buckingham
R H Malcolm-Green, CEng, BSc London
Mrs R M Moriarty, MA Oxon, MTh London
M J Pressdee, FCA
B Richardson

Clerk to the Governors: Mrs M Lowe

Headmistress: Mrs K Bartholomew, MA London, PGCE

Senior Staff:

Deputy Head: Mrs E Houghton-Connell, BA Hons, PGCE London
Director of Studies: Mrs J Martin, BEd Hons Chichester
Head of Lower School: Mrs D van Beek, BEd Exeter, DipEd Southampton
Head of Junior Department: Mrs Z Woolley, BA Hons Birmingham

Teaching Staff:

Sciences:
Biology: Mrs E J Marks, BSc Hons Warwick, SRN, RM, PGCE Leicester, MSc Open University
Chemistry: Dr D Cook, BSc Hons, PhD St Andrews
Mrs S Watson, MA, BA, PGCE Cambridge
Physics: Mrs J Dowle, BSc Hons Exeter, PGCE Southampton
Mathematics: Mrs D van Beek, BEd Exeter, DipEd Southampton
Mrs J Martin, BEd Hons Chichester
Mrs S Watson, MA, BA, PGCE Cambridge
Computer Studies: Mrs H Williams, BSc Hons Plymouth, PGCE Southampton

Humanities:
English: Ms M Mack, BA Hons Durham, PGCE London
History & Head of Sixth Form: Mrs L Ayling, BA Hons Chichester, PGCE Chichester
Geography & RE: Mrs J Adams, BA Hons Hull, PGCE King's College
French: Mrs H Rice, BA Hons University of Wales, PGCE Exeter
Spanish: Mrs G Rosado, BA Cuidad Real, PGCE Granada University
Classics & Latin: Dr N Sturt, BA Hons, PhD, PGCE London
Drama: Miss C Boyd-Wallis, BA Hons, PGCE Chichester

Art & Textiles: Mrs E Houghton-Connell, BA Hons West Surrey College of Art & Design, PGCE London

Mrs S Stone, BA Hons Ravensbourne College, MA Hons Royal College of Art, PGCE Dist Greenwich

PE: Miss C Cawte, BSc Hons Gloucestershire, PGCE Southampton

Mrs H J Kyffin, CertEd Avery Hill College

Business Studies: Mrs P Furmidge, BEd Hons, MA Sussex, BA Open University

Media Studies: Mr P Crew

Communication Studies & Psychology: Mrs C Howard, MA, BA, CertEd, MInstM

Director of Music: Mrs S Howell Evans, GTCL Trinity College, London, ARCM, LTCL, PGCE London, ARSCM, FGMS

SENCo: Mrs S Jones, BA Hons Open University, CertEd Gloucester, DipSpLD Kingston

Learning Support: Mrs C Skewis, BA Hons, PGCE Roehampton, Dip SpLD

Mrs L Kyffin, BA Hons Chichester

EAL: Mrs B Harrison, BA London, PGCE Cantab

Speech & Drama: Mrs J Pressdee, LGSM, ANEA Stage Technique

Tennis: Mrs E Ellicott, LTA registered

Junior Lavant House:

Mrs Z Woolley, BA Hons Birmingham

iss G Baker, BEd Cambridge, CertEd

Mrs E Hall, BA Hons, PGCE Chichester

Mrs L Eldred, CertEd London

Miss H Frampton, BA Hons Canterbury

Mrs L Taylor, CertEd Southampton

Mrs E Taws

Mrs A Parker

Boarding:

Mrs H J Kyffin, CertEd Avery Hill College (*Senior Housemistress*)

Mrs C Costello (*Deputy Housemistress*)

School Nurses:

Mrs F Campbell, RGN, SN

Mrs J Dawes, RGN

Counsellor: Mrs L Kyffin

Administration:

Bursar: Mrs M Lowe

Assistant Bursar: Mrs S Greenwood

Registrar & Head's PA: Mrs L Cranfield

Secretary: Mrs J Shrubb

Librarian: Ms J Thurston, BA Hons Reading

Domestic Bursar: Mrs L Darvill

Catering:

Mr A Nelson

Mrs K Staples

Lavant House is a forward-looking independent school. It aims to provide girls with a challenging and positive academic education within a caring community, to enable each individual to develop her abilities to the full whilst acquiring a strong set of personal values. The school is small with about 165 pupils throughout the age range from 5 to 18. The intimate size of its classes creates an opportunity for personalised learning within an atmosphere of trust and cooperation, bringing out the best in every pupil and resulting in confident, happy, sociable and successful young women ready to meet the challenges of the future.

Boarding. The school has a mix of day and boarding pupils, with both full and flexible boarding arrangements. There is an informal family atmosphere in the House, and Sixth form boarders have a considerable degree of independence in their own adjacent accommodation, "The Cottage".

Situation and Facilities. The school is situated between the South Downs and the sea, just north of the historic cathedral city of Chichester, in the heart of glorious Sussex countryside. The lovely eighteenth century flint buildings and well tended gardens and grounds contribute to a secure and tranquil environment, which nevertheless has modern facilities for Science, ICT, Drama and Sport. A new Art Studio opened in September 2006. All main teaching rooms have computers with Internet access, in addition to the main Computer Suite which contains 20 networked PCs. The Junior Department is housed separately on site with its own safe play area.

Curriculum. A traditionally broad academic curriculum is taught through to GCSE and a full range of subjects is offered at AS and A Level in the small, lively Sixth Form. The school boasts strong Art and Drama departments which regularly run exhibitions and major productions, and there is an accomplished Senior Choir, Strings and Flutes groups and Chamber Orchestra. Regular Chamber Concerts give young musicians a chance to perform.

Specialist help for dyslexic pupils is available, and English as an Additional Language for overseas students is offered.

Sport. Games provision includes a large playing field, three superbly surfaced netball and tennis courts, and an outdoor heated swimming pool, as well as the gymnasium The main curriculum sports are netball and hockey in winter, and rounders, tennis, athletics and swimming in the summer, but girls also do badminton, volleyball, aerobics, dance, gymnastics and table tennis. Many matches are organised for girls of all age groups, and the teams are very successful in area competitions. The senior netball team has been West Sussex West Area and League Champions for the last four years.

Lavant House Stables are next to the school and many girls ride. There are two floodlit all-weather arenas in addition to fifty acres of pasture and woodland.

There is an active Duke of Edinburgh's Award scheme, with expeditions organised during the summer.

Transport. The school operates four minibus routes over a twenty mile radius for daygirls. From Chichester there are rail links along the South Coast and up to London; Heathrow and Gatwick airports are about one and a half hour's drive away.

Admission. Admission is by interview and informal testing. There is an assessment day in the Spring Term for entry at 11+. Academic scholarships are available for the Senior School and the Sixth Form.

Fees per term (2011–2012). Junior Day: £2,750 (Years 1 and 2), £3,575, (Years 3 and 4), £3,735 (Years 5 and 6) Senior Day: £4,470. Boarding: £5,865 (Junior), £7,035 (Senior). A returnable deposit of one term's boarding fees is charged for overseas pupils.

Charitable status. Lavant House School Educational Trust Limited is a Registered Charity, number 307372.

Leicester High School for Girls

454 London Road, Leicester LE2 2PP

Tel: 0116 270 5338

Fax: 0116 244 8823

e-mail: enquiries@leicesterhigh.co.uk

website: www.leicesterhigh.co.uk

The school is a Trust with a Board of Governors in membership of AGBIS and the Headmistress belongs to the GSA.

Board of Governors:

Chairman: Mr P S Bonnett

Mrs M R Banks, MBE, MEd

Ms D Bolland, BA, MSc

Mrs M Bowler, JP
Mr A Jarvis, FCA
Mr J Jethwa, BSc
Mrs M Neilson, B Ed
Mr G Norris, JP, MEd, FCMI
Mr A Rodgers, Dip Arch, RIBA Chartered
Mrs M Sheldon, LLB
The Revd Canon Peter Taylor, MEd, MA
Mrs H Warren-McCaughey, BA
Mr A Williams

Clerk to the Governors: Mrs A Morris, ACMA, BA
   Manchester

Headmistress: Mrs J Burns, BA Southampton

Deputy Head: Miss D E J Wassell, BA Leeds

Assistant Head: Mrs S M Dobson, BA London

Senior School:

* *Head of Department*
§ *Part-time*

Assistant Staff:
Miss R Amin, BSc Lancaster
Mr A Chappell, BSc Leicester (**Science*)
Mrs J Davison, BEd Cheltenham & Gloucester Coll HE
   (**Physical Education*)
Mrs C Dwyer, BA Exeter
Mrs P Formoy, BA Manchester (**Modern Languages*)
§Mrs P Gascoigne, BA Wolverhampton
§Mrs R Hall, BSc Aberystwyth
Mrs K Haresign, BA Leicester (**Geography*)
Mrs E Heap, BA Leicester (**English*)
Dr S Hills, BSc York, MSc Leicester, PhD Nottingham
   (**Mathematics*)
Mr P Hoyle, BSc Rhodes, South Africa
Miss S Jackson BA London (**History*)
§Mr M Joannou, BSc Salford, MEd Leicester
Miss S Khachik, BA Durham
§Mrs B L Krokosz, BA Coventry
§Mrs E Martin, BEd Bedford
Mrs L C Martin, BA London, DipPsy (**Social Sciences*)
Mrs D A Morgan, BSc Warwick (**PSHCE*)
§Mrs W Noble, CertEd Keele
Mr S Norbury, BSc Liverpool (**Information Technology*)
Miss A Paul, BA Leicester
Ms L P Pearson, BA Leicester
§Mrs N Pulham, BA Southampton
§Mrs H Rai, BSc Birmingham, MSc Bradford
Mrs H Rees, BA Birmingham
Mrs J M Robbins, Dip Art & Design Edinburgh (**Art*)
§Mrs J L Scherrer, Ecole Supérieure de Commerce de
   Chambery
Dr N Singleton, BSc Birmingham, PhD De Montfort
Miss E Stell, BA Liverpool
Mr A Stewart, BSc Leicester
Mrs A Sykes, CertEd Leicester (**Careers*)
Miss C Teal, B Theol Oxford (**Religious Studies*)
Miss E Tyler, BSc Leicester
Mrs S Varnam, BA CSSD (**Performing Arts*)
Miss K Ward, BA Hull
§Mrs J Whalley, BSc Leicester

Bursar: Mrs A Morris, ACMA, BA Manchester
Accounts Assistant: §Mrs E J Mackay, AAT
Payroll: §Mrs J T Greasley, FCCA
Headmistress's PA and Registrar: Mrs B Brand
SIMS Coordinator: Mrs K Lock
Examinations Officer: §Mr B Holness
Secretary: Mrs K Clark
Librarian: Miss A Adams, MA Liverpool
Assistant Librarian: Mrs L M Humrich, BA Lancaster,
   DipLib
IT Systems Manager: Mr A Collins

Laboratory Technicians: Mrs M Cupac, Ms L A J Ritchie
School Nurse: Mrs A Cox, HE RN Leicester

Visiting Staff:
Mr N Bott, BA Leicester (*Drums*)
Mrs J Bound, GBSM Exeter (*Piano*)
Ms A Donnelly, BA York (*Piano*)
Mr T Gascoigne, BA Middlesex (*Tennis*)
Mrs K Loomes, FIDTA (*Ballet*)
Mrs A Mitchell, LTCL (*Clarinet, Flute, Saxophone*)
Mrs R Pells, GSMD, LAMDA, EMPA, IDTA (*Speech and
   Drama*)
Mrs W M Philpott, BA Newcastle, PGCE, LTCL ('*Cello,
   Piano*)
Miss C Sullivan, BA Coventry (*Speech & Drama*)
Mrs S Cotterill (*Singing*)
Mr C Beadling (*Fencing*)
Mr T Ashby, BMus Guildhall School of Music & Drama
   (*Brass*)
Mr P Phillips, MA Warwick, PPhil Birmingham (*Drama*)
Mrs C Lee, LRAM (*Violin*)

Junior Department:

Head of Department: Mrs L Fowler, BA Ed Brunel
Assistant Head: Mrs S J Davies, BA Ed Exeter
Foundation Stage Coordinator: Miss C Pow, BA
   Southampton
Administrator: Mrs M Singh
Mrs S Adams, NNEB
Mrs P Jackson, NNEB
Mrs K Jarvis, BA QTS Nene
Mrs R Gardner, NNEB
Mrs J Hunter, NNEB
Mrs J Preston, BA Canterbury
Mrs J Vick, BA Leicester
Mrs S Wayman, BEd Manchester
§Mrs V Williams BEd Nene
Miss S Biant, BA Manchester Metropolitan
Mrs J Woodcock, BEd Birmingham

Ancillary Staff:

Mrs L Dunn	Mrs N Sturmey, NNEB
Mrs R Graham	Mrs J Jethwa
Miss S Gray, NNEB	Miss J McBride
Mrs S Lonergan	Miss S Goodhart
Miss L Newton	Mrs A Cobley

Leicester High School is a well established day school for
girls situated in pleasant grounds on the south side of the
city. Founded in 1906 as Portland House School, it now
comprises a Junior Department of 110 girls (3–9 years) and
a Senior School of 325 girls (10–18) sited on the same campus.

The school offers an academic education of a high standard, and the Sixth Formers almost invariably go on to
Higher Education. It is a friendly community where an
emphasis is placed on honesty, integrity and respect for the
views of others. Class size is kept small so that there is every
opportunity for each girl to achieve her full potential whilst
developing the self-confidence and self-discipline to help in
her future.

The Headmistress is responsible for both the Junior
Department and Senior School. The staff are well qualified
specialists and the school is renowned for both its academic
excellence and extra-curricular programme. At present 19
subjects are offered at GCSE Level and 24 subjects at A
Level.

Facilities. The premises are a combination of modern
purpose built units and the original Victorian house, skilfully adapted to its present purpose. The facilities of the
school have been systematically improved. A purpose-built
library and resource centre was opened, followed by a new
sixth form centre in September 2001. The junior department
has also benefited from new buildings which opened in Jan-

uary 2002. The extension and improvement includes a computer suite and new library, enlarged hall, dining facilities and new classrooms. The EYFU has been extensively redesigned in 2009. The school has just completed an exciting building programme for Science, Art & Design and Modern Foreign Languages that opened in September 2010.

Religion. The school has a Christian foundation but welcomes those of other faiths or of none.

Admission. All candidates over the age of 7 are required to pass an entrance examination for admission into the Junior and Senior sections. Entry into the Senior School would normally be at Year 6 or Year 7, but entry at other ages is considered. There is also direct entry into the Sixth Form dependent on GCSE results. Entrance into the Foundation Unit is by assessment. A registration fee of £50 is payable for all applicants.

Fees per term (2011-2012). £2,350–£3,175.

Extras. Individual Music lessons, Speech and Drama, and Ballet are offered.

Scholarships. (*See Scholarship Entries section.*) These are awarded annually to girls completing entry to Year 7 in the Senior School through the Entrance Examination. Music scholarships are also available throughout the school, including the Sixth Form, and bursaries are available from Year 3 onwards.

The Headmistress is always pleased to meet parents of prospective pupils and to show them the school. All communications should be addressed to the Headmistress from whom prospectuses, application forms and details of fees may be obtained.

Charitable status. Leicester High School Charitable Trust Limited is a Registered Charity, number 503982. The Trust exists to promote and provide for the advancement of education based on Christian principles according to the doctrines of the Church of England.

Leweston School

Sherborne, Dorset DT9 6EN
Tel: 01963 210691
Fax: 01963 210786
e-mail: admin@leweston.dorset.sch.uk
website: www.leweston.co.uk

Independent Boarding (full, weekly and flexi) and Day School for Girls aged 11–18 with a separate, purpose-built, co-educational Prep School for girls and boys aged 2–11 on the same campus. Roman Catholic foundation but all denominations welcome. Excellent academic reputation and strong Sixth Form.

Governing Body:
Mr A May (*Chairman*)

Mr N Bathurst	Sir K Lindblom
Mr I Crowther	Mrs A Littlewood
Mr N Durkin	Mr E Newton
Mrs H Harper	Mrs T Skepelhorn
Mrs M Head	Mrs E Treichl
Mr M J F Hudson	Mrs A Wedge
Fr Peter Knott SJ	Mrs B Wingfield Digby

Head: **Mr A J F Aylward**, MA Oxon

Deputy Head, Head of Sixth Form: Mrs J Miles, MA Oxon, PGCE (*Modern Foreign Languages*)

Director of Studies, Head of Careers: Mr G Smith, BSc Hons Open University, PGCE (*Mathematics*)

Director of Boarding: Miss L Fielding, BA Hons Newcastle, PGCE Lancaster (*Art*)

Bursar: Mrs P Graham, BA Hons Durham

Visiting Chaplain: Fr Rodney Schofield, MA Cantab, MA Oxon, DMin Wales, PGCE Bristol

Teaching Staff:

Classics:
Dr R Chiappiniello, MA Naples, PhD Manchester, DEFL Naples/Paris French (*Head of Classics*)
Miss O Rothbury, BA Hons King's College Cambridge (*Classics, Assistant Housemistress*)
Miss L Flannery, BA Hons Warwick (*Classics, PE, Assistant Housemistress*)

English and Drama:
Miss S Evans, BA Hons Sheffield, PGCE London (*Head of English*)
Mrs C Nash, BA Hons Southampton, PGCE Southampton, MEd Gloucestershire (*English*)
Mrs K Reynolds, LLB Bristol, PGCE Bath (*English*)
Mr A Irvine, MA Oxon, PGCE, Adv Cert Royal Welsh College of Music & Drama (*Head of Drama*)
Mrs C Dempsey, Gold Medal Verse & Prose LAMDA, BA Hons Graphic Design (*Drama*)
Mrs L Provera, MN, BA, BGS, BN, Dip Teach (*Speech & Drama*)
Mrs J A Miller, MEd Bristol, BA Hons Southampton, PGCE Keele, DipSpLD Hornsby Int (*Head of Individual Needs, Head of Year 7*)
Mrs J Ogilvie, PG Dip Dyslexia & Literacy York (*Individual Needs Literacy*)

Modern Languages:
Mrs L Bryson, BSc Hons Bournemouth, CertEd Exeter (*Head of Modern Languages, Spanish*)
Mrs S O'Connor, BEd Hons London (*German, French, Head of Years 10 and 11*)
Mrs C Cot, MA Aberdeen, PGCE Edinburgh (*French*)
Mrs L Maynard, MA Hons University of Liberec (*French*)
Mrs J Miles, MA Oxon, PGCE (*Spanish, French, Deputy Head, Head of Sixth Form*)

Geography:
Mr D Barlow, BSc Hons Nottingham, MSc London, PGCE Birmingham (*Head of Geography, Physical Education*)
Mrs E Massey, BSc Hons Oxford Brookes, PGCE Chichester (*Geography, Maths, Coordinator of Global Perspectives*)

Mathematics:
Mr M Crozier, BSc Hons, PGCE Dunelm, CMath, MIMA, CSci (*Head of Mathematics*)
Mr J Cross, BSc Hons London (*Mathematics, Careers*)
Mr G Smith, BSc Hons Open University, PGCE (*Mathematics, Director of Studies*)
Mrs H Claxton, BSc Hons Napier (*Mathematics, Outdoor Pursuits*)

Religious Studies:
Miss J Kelly, BEd Hons Leeds, MA, Catholic TCert Leeds (*Head of Religious Studies*)
Ms C O'Toole, BA Hons London, PGCE, Catholic TCert Liverpool (*Religious Studies, PSHE Coordinator, Head of Years 8 & 9*)

Psychology:
Mrs S Hunt, BA Hons Bournemouth, PGCE Exeter

Science:
Mrs F M Crossman, BSc Hons, MEd Manchester, PGCE (*Head of Science, Physics*)
Mrs A Harwood, BSc Hons London, PGCE Oxon (*Head of Biology*)
Mr J Ralph, BSc Hons Liverpool, PGCE King's College London (*Biology, Chemistry, Physics, Sports Studies*)
Mr J Sherwood Taylor, BA Open University, MSc York, CertEd (*Chemistry*)
Dr O Kemal, BSc Hons, PhD London, PGCE Surrey, MRSC (*Head of Chemistry*)

Mrs A Valentine, BSc Hons Swansea, PGCE London (*Physics*)

Economics and Business Studies:
Mrs S Antill, BA Hons Kingston-upon-Thames, PGCE Brighton (*Economics & Business*)
Mrs L Rondeau-Robinson, MBA Rivier College, Nashua, NH, USA, BA Cum Laude University of Lowell, MA, USA, C&G TCert Yeovil College (*IT Coordinator, UCAS Administrator, Business and Communication Systems*)

History:
Mr M Hayward, BA Hons Oxon (*Head of History, History of Art*)
Mrs G Gregory, BA Hons Worcester, MA Hons Exeter, PGCE (*Government and Politics, History*)

Art, Design and Technology:
Mrs E C Williams, BA Hons London, PGCE Manchester (*Head of Art & Design*)
Mr F Bush, BTEC Nat Dip Plymouth, BA Hons St Martins (*Art*)
Miss J Lacey, BA Hons Winchester School of Art (*Art Textiles*)

English as a Foreign Language:
Mrs A Kennedy, BEd Oxford Inst of Ed, MA TESOL, RSA DTEFLA
Mrs K M Walker, MA Birmingham, BA Hons Bristol, Dip TEFSL

Physical Education:
Miss K Mullen, BEd Hons Sussex, CertEd Chelsea (*Head of Physical Education, Head of Sports Studies*)
Miss K Persey, BSc Hons UWIC, PGCE Exeter (*Physical Education*)
Miss G Phipps, CertEd Chelsea (*Physical Education, Housemistress – Yrs 9, 10 and 11*)
Mr M Long, LTA Coach (*Tennis*)
Mr S Wilson, DCA, BTCA (*Tennis*)

Music:
Mrs C Hawkes, BMus Hons Royal College of Music, ATCL, FSRCM (*Director of Music*)
Mr P Bray, BMus, DSCM, ARCO, LTCL (*Organist/ Organ, Piano*)
Mrs W Bednall, BA Hons Southampton, ALCM (*Pianoforte*)
Miss C Bentley, GTCL, ARCM, LTCL (*Flute*)
Mrs J Fenton, ARCM (*Singing*)
Miss A Garrett, BA Hons Cambridge (*Music*)
Mrs A Heaton, BMus, MMus (*Singing*)
Mr M Hewitt, BA Hons, LGSM (*French Horn*)
Mr P Huddleston, BTech (*Percussion*)
Miss M Nightingale, LGSM (*Recorder*)
Ms S Page (*Oboe*)
Mr D Price, LRAM (*Violin, Viola*)
Mrs N Price, GRSM Hons, ARCM, LRAM (*Pianoforte, Bassoon*)
Mrs J Robotham, BA Hons, PGCE (*Music*)
Ms K Sheriff, BA Hons (*Violoncello*)
Mrs A Slogrove, BA Hons, LRSM, PGCE (*Piano*)
Miss J Smith, Graduate of Durham University (*Music, Assistant Housemistress*)
Miss M Verity (*Harp*)

Marketing & Admissions Manager: Miss L Cox, BSc Hons
Registrar: Mrs C Damant
Librarian: Mrs A King
Headmaster's Secretary: Mrs S Chant
Domestic Bursar: Mrs J Wareham

Leweston School welcomes girls aged 11–18 as full, weekly and flexi boarders or as day pupils. Admission is usually at eleven, but girls are also admitted at twelve, thirteen and sixteen.

Situated in 46 acres of beautiful Dorset parkland, 3 miles south of Sherborne, the school offers all the advantages of both the traditional and modern in education with excellent facilities, particularly in the Sciences, Design & Technology and Sport.

Founded by the Sisters of Christian Instruction in 1891, the school is a Catholic School but has a large percentage of pupils from other denominations. There are approximately 250 girls in the School of whom around 100 are boarders. The ethos of the school is based on a wide social mix with a spread of talents, firm but friendly discipline and a keen sense of Christian and moral values. The Head is forward looking with a strong sense of leadership and vision. The school has a Visiting Chaplain and girls are expected to attend Chapel once a week. Preparation for confirmation is available for both Catholic and Anglican pupils.

The academic standard of the school is high. At both GCSE and A Level pass rates are consistently over 95% and the school's reputation for excellence in Music and Drama runs parallel with academic achievement in Sciences and The Arts. The real success of the school, however, is achieved by realising the full potential of each individual girl, whether they are high fliers or not. Each year girls gain places at leading universities and go on to read a wide range of degrees.

Teachers are dedicated and imaginative, including specialist teachers for Dyslexia and EFL. The school's special quality is its ability to encourage in each pupil a sense of her own worth and ability. Girls are outgoing, well-mannered and unstuffy. While Leweston has a high proportion of day girls, the school is fully committed to boarding offering a wide programme of activities in the evenings and at the weekends. Riding is especially popular.

The school has close links with Sherborne School and there are many combined social, recreational, musical and cultural activities between the schools. Milton Abbey join in with many of our music activities and in recent years the Sixth Form has visited Italy with Winchester School. Sherborne is an attractive historic abbey town with few of the distractions of a large city but at the same time is served by regular Network Express trains to and from London and good road links to Salisbury, Exeter and Bath. The school's facilities are among the best in the West Country. There is a fine floodlit all-weather sports pitch, Design and Technology Centre, modern Senior Science Centre, arts studio, health centre, heated swimming pool, sports hall, multi-gym, squash courts, tennis courts and extensive well-maintained grounds and playing fields. Recently opened are the new dining hall and library.

Leweston Preparatory School (IAPS) for girls and boys aged 2–11, with boarding provision for girls from age 7, is situated on the same campus, thus offering continuity of education for girls to age 18. Excellent early years provision including French from 3 years, beautifully equipped Nursery and weekly Parent and Toddler Group. Head Teacher: Mrs M Allen, Tel: 01963 210790. (*For further details, see entry in IAPS section.*)

Scholarships. (*See Scholarship Entries section.*) Scholarship provision for Academic, Music, Sport, Art, Drama, Science and a limited number of All-Rounder awards are also available.

Further particulars may be obtained on application to the Head or Registrar.

Fees per term (2011-2012). Full Boarding £6,695-£8,195; Weekly Boarding £5,995-£6,950, Day £5,080-£5,295. Flexi Boarding (including supper) £41 per night.

Charitable status. Leweston School Trust is a Registered Charity, number 295175. It is a charitable foundation set up for educational purposes.

Loughborough High School

Burton Walks, Loughborough, Leicestershire LE11 2DU
Tel: 01509 212348
Fax: 01509 215720
e-mail: admin@leshigh.org
website: www.leshigh.org

Loughborough High School is part of Loughborough Endowed Schools. Loughborough Grammar School (*see HMC entry*) is the brother school and the co-educational junior school is known as Fairfield (*see IAPS entry*). We enjoy a very old foundation, established in 1850 as one of the earliest girls' grammar schools in England. The High School is located on a delightful 46 acre site close to the town centre with many first rate facilities, which are being added to and improved continuously.

Loughborough High School is an 11 to 18 school of approximately 600 day girls with a large Sixth Form numbering above 170. At the High School we aim to provide an excellent academic education in a caring atmosphere. Since we are a comparatively small school, we are able to know our pupils as individuals and this leads to a strong community spirit. In providing a strong academic education in a disciplined atmosphere we hope to enable each girl ultimately to enter the career of her choice. The school offers a wide range of cultural, recreational and sporting activities and there are clubs and societies for virtually all tastes and interest (many in the senior school are run jointly with Loughborough Grammar School). We believe that our academic curriculum and extra-curricular activities nurture our pupils and encourage them to become active citizens of a modern world.

Further details about the school can be obtained by contacting the school's Registrar.

Governing Body:

President: Professor R J Mair, The Master, Jesus College, Cambridge
Chairman: H M Pearson, BA Econ, LLB, ACIS
Vice-Chairman: A D Emson, BPharm, MRPharmS

Non-Executive Vice-Chairmen:
Mrs M Gershlick, RGN, DipNEd
Dr J E Hammond, BDS
Dr P J B Hubner, MB, FRCP, DCH, FACC, FESC

Nominative Governors:
University of Oxford: Professor D Robertson, MA, PhD
University of Cambridge: Dr J Clackson

Co-optative Governors:
Dr A de Bono, MA, MB, BChir, MFOM
Dr P Cannon, MA Cantab, BMBch Oxon, FRCS, MRCGP
Mrs E K Critchley, MA
Professor J Feather, BLitt, MA, PhD, FLA
G P Fothergill, BA, FCIM
The Lady Gretton, JP, Lord-Lieutenant of Leicestershire
I A Hawtin
P M Jackson, FIMI
A M Kershaw
W M Moss
M Mulla, BSc, MSc, MIM
Mrs P O'Neill
Mrs G Richards, BA Hons, MEd
Mrs C Wales

Foundation Secretary & Treasurer: K D Shaw, MBE, MSc, FCIS

Headmistress: **Mrs G Byrom**, BSc Manchester (*Science*)

Deputy Head: (*to be appointed*)

Assistant Head, Curriculum: Dr S Jackson, BSc, PhD UMIST (*Head of Science Building*)
Assistant Head, Staff: Mrs P J Kent, BA Bristol (*Classics*)

Assistant Staff:
Mrs L Beasley, BA Reading (*Economics*)
Mrs S Bell, BSc Nottingham, PGCE Nottingham (*Physics*)
Ms S E Boon, BA Plymouth (*Head of Drama*)
Miss S Budzik, MA Surrey (*Art*)
Mrs R Burn, MA Cantab (*Head of Classics*)
Miss A E Chambers, MA Nottingham (*History*)
Miss E Claricoates, BA Leicester (*English*)
Mrs J Conway, MA Ulster (*Head of PSHCE*)
Mr A Cooper, BSc Loughborough (*Head of Geography*)
Mrs I F E Dance, BA Wales (*Geography*)
Mrs J Day, BSc Manchester (*Geography*)
Mrs A Denyer, BA Oxon (*Biology*)
Dr J Downing, BSc Bristol (*Head of Chemistry*)
Dr E C Eadie, BA Birmingham, PhD Cantab (*History*)
Mrs M Ghaly, BSc Teesside (*Chemistry*)
Mr D Gough, BA Sheffield (*Modern Languages*)
Mrs J Harlock, CertEd Wales (*SENCO*)
Mrs L Harrison, BA Leeds Metropolitan (*English*)
Mrs S R O Henson, BA Loughborough (*Head of Fine Art*)
Ms C Hitchen, MEng Newcastle-upon-Tyne (*Head of Mathematics*)
Miss S Jogee, BSc Leicester (*Biology*)
Mrs K Kroon, BSc Nottingham (*Head of Physics*)
Miss A Levy (*Modern Languages*)
Mrs J A Lewis, BA Nottingham (*Head of Religious Studies*)
Ms R Lewis, BSc Leeds (*Mathematics*)
Mrs B Lott, BA Sussex (*Modern Languages*)
Mrs C Mackie, MA Cantab (*Modern Languages*)
Mrs J Mayfield, BSc Loughborough (*Head of Physical Education*)
Miss G McAndrew, BA Manchester Metropolitan (*Physical Education*)
Mr P Melanaphy, BEd Manchester Metropolitan, MA Loughborough (*English*)
Mrs F Moore, BEd De Montfort Bedford (*Physical Education*)
Mr R J L Needs, BA Nottingham, IMS Cert, ACCA, Dip EdMgt (*Head of Economics*)
Miss C E Nelson, BSc Manchester (*Chemistry*)
Ms J M Partridge, BA UCE Birmingham (*Textile Design*)
Mrs M A Reilly, BSc Surrey (*Head of Home Economics*)
Mrs E Raouf, BA Salford (*French*)
Dr A Robinson, BSc Edinburgh (*Biology*)
Miss C Shawcross, BSc Loughborough (*Mathematics*)
Mr J Singh, BA Coventry (*Director of Academic ICT*)
Miss A Smith, BA Oxford (*Mathematics*)
Mrs J Squire, CertEd Nottingham (*Home Economics*)
Miss V Standring, BSc Chester (*Physical Education*)
Dr M Starbuck, BA Kent, MSc Leicester and Oxford, DPhil Oxford (*Head of Psychology and Sociology*)
Mrs M Starkings, BSc Nottingham, BA Open (*Physics*)
Mr G C Stevens, BA Liverpool (*Classics & Religious Studies*)
Dr R Strong, MPhys Bath, PhD Cantab (*Mathematics*)
Mrs J E Stubbs, BSc Nottingham (*Head of Biology*)
Miss C E Todd, BSc Manchester (*Biology*)
Mr L Toone, BSc Edinburgh, PGCE Loughborough, MSc Warwick (*Biology*)
Mr R W Tomblin, MA Oxford (*Head of Modern Languages*)
Mrs C Urwin, BSc Warwick (*Mathematics*)
Mrs L Webster, BA Leeds Metropolitan (*Physical Education*)
Dr A Williamson, BSc Imperial College London (*Chemistry*)
Mrs C Winship, BSc Reading (*ICT*)
Mrs A Woollard, BA Huddersfield (*History*)
Mrs N J Young, BA East Anglia (*Head of English*)

Accountant: Mr R Harker, BA Coventry, FCAA
Estates Manager: Mr T Allardice
Librarian: Mrs G Burton, BLS
Examinations Officer: Mrs S English
Matrons:
Mrs S Chad-Smith, RGN
Mrs A Cannon, RGN
PA to the Headmistress: Ms L Shipman
School Secretary: Miss B McKay
Receptionist: Mrs R Westran
Data Manager & Registrar: Mrs A Brackstone, BSc Aston
Laboratory Technicians:
Mrs J F Owens, BA Hons Keele, MPhil Loughborough
Mrs S Savidis, BSc, MSc Loughborough
Miss N Walker
Art/Food Technician: Mrs B Armstead
Modern Languages/Humanities Technician: Mrs T Hicks
Reprographics Technician: Miss J Calow

LES Music School:
Mr A P M Osiatynski, MA Oxon (*Director*)
Miss N Bouckley, BA Durham (*Deputy Director*)
Mr T H Lax, LRAM, DipMus, CertEd Huddersfield (*Head of Performance Studies*)
Dr P J Underwood, MA Cantab, MMus Lond, PhD Birm (*Head of Senior Curriculum Music*)
Mrs E Foulds, GRSM, LRAM (*KS3 Music*)
Miss C E Revell, BMus Huddersfield (*KS3/4 Music*)
Dr A P Bean, BMus, LRAM, AMusD Sheffield (*KS4/5 Composition*)
Miss J Marshall, BA Nottingham (*Music Manager*)

A list of Visiting Music Teachers is available separately.

School Curriculum. Art and Textile Design, Biology, Chemistry, Classical Civilisation, Drama, Economics, English, French, Games (hockey, netball, tennis, rounders, swimming and athletics), Geography, German, Greek, Gymnastics, History, Latin, Mathematics, Modern Dance, Music, Physics, Politics, Religious Studies, Spanish, Food, Nutrition and Health, ICT, Sociology, Psychology and Theatre Studies. Careful note is taken of the National Curriculum with additional subjects included within the curriculum to provide breadth and depth.

Fees per term (2011-2012). £3,139. Additional Fees: Music (individual instrumental lessons) £205.50.

Entrance Awards and Music Scholarships. (*See Scholarship Entries section*.) Foundation Bursaries replace the Government Assisted Places.

Charitable status. Loughborough Endowed Schools is a Registered Charity, number 1081765, and a Company Limited by Guarantee, registered in England, number 4038033. Registered Office: 3 Burton Walks, Loughborough, Leics LE11 2DU.

Luckley-Oakfield School

Wokingham, Berks RG40 3EU
Tel: 0118 978 4175
Fax: 0118 977 0305
e-mail: registrar@luckley.wokingham.sch.uk
website: www.luckley.wokingham.sch.uk

Governing Body:
Mrs P Adomakoh (*Chair*)
Mr B Brouwer
Reverend G Curry
Mrs J Farmer
Mr B Gardiner
Ms L Moor
Dr J Ledger
Mrs E Percival

Mr G Sanderson
Mrs S Sayer
Mr M Walker
Dr K Weir
Mr G Williams
Mrs S Wingfield Digby
Mr M F Browning, ACIB, MIMgt, MIITT, MRIPHH
Miss V A Davis, BSc Hons London, ARCS

Head: Miss V A Davis, BSc Hons London, ARCS (*Chemistry*)

Deputy Head: Mrs J Tudor MA Ed OU, BSc Hons London
Assistant Head: Mrs K McGonnell, BEd Hons Exeter
Head of Sixth Form: Mrs M E Matthews, BA Hons London (*History*)

Staff:
* *Head of Department/Subject*

English:
Mrs G Powell, MA Reading, BA Hons Reading
Mrs M Kempton, MA, BA Hons Reading, BEd Hons London, Cert TESOL, Dip RSA (*also EAL*)
Mrs M Pearce, BA Hons Reading (*also SEN*)
Mrs N Lamb, BA Hons Liverpool

Mathematics:
Mrs J A Eifler, BSc Hons Leicester
Mrs A Bell, BEng Hons Cardiff
Miss R Duncan, BSc Hons Surrey
Mrs M Parker, BA Hons Oxford
Mrs M Sherwood MA Canterbury

Science:
Mr R Everatt, BSc Hons York (**Chemistry, *Science*)
Mr S Bond, MA Oxon (**Physics*)
Mrs H Chaddock, BSc Hons Reading
Mrs J Collett, BSc Hons Manchester
Dr R Jones, PhD Aberdeen (**Biology*)
Mrs J Tudor, BSc Hons UCL, MA Ed Open University
Mr W Sluman, MIBiol

Modern Languages:
Mrs J H Goodall, BA Hons Liverpool
Mrs S Berns, BA Hons Reading
Mrs K McGonnell, BEd Hons Exeter
Mrs E Samnée-O'Brien, BA Cologne University, Germany

Business Studies:
Ms L Stephens, BA Hons York

Classics:
Mrs D Gummery, BA Hons Southampton

Geography:
Mr G Cromb, BSc Hons London
Miss A Caldwell, BSc Hons Hull, MSc London (*also Religious Studies & Careers*)

History:
Mrs M E Matthews, BA Hons London
Miss S Torry, BA Hons London

Politics:
Mr P Smith, MA Warwick

Psychology:
Mrs E Kermode, BA Hons University of South Africa

Religious Studies:
Mrs B Gathercole, BA Hons Nottingham

Information Technology:
Mrs G Edwards, BA Hons Chester
Mr D Kirkup, BSc Surrey

Design & Technology (Food Technology & Textiles Technology):
Mrs S Gibson, BSc Home Economics
Mrs C McCafferty, HND CertEd MlfL QTLS

Mrs A O'Sullivan, BA Hons Central Lancashire

Art:
Miss J Simmonds, BA Hons London
Mrs S Dixon, City & Guilds Fashion and Design

Drama & Theatre Studies:
Mrs J Cordery, Dip Musical Theatre
Mrs E Clay, BA Hons Winchester

Music:
Mrs M E Vogel, BEd Hons East Anglia, LGSM
Mr N Efthimou, GRSM Hons Royal Academy of Music

Physical Education:
Miss C Edgerley. BA Brighton
Mrs C Bennett, BEd Hons Plymouth (*also ICT*)

Outdoor Education:
Ms A Moore, BA Hons St Martins Lancaster

SEN:
Mrs S Hills, MSc London, BEd Hons Leeds Polytechnic
   (*also Outdoor Education*)

Bursar: Mr M Browning, ACIB, MIMgt, MIITT, MRIPHH
Registrar: Mrs M Cope
School Secretaries: Mrs J Leatherby, Mrs L Laing
Headmistress's PA: Mrs N Hall
School Nursing Sister: Mrs J Craven
Marketing and Development Manager: Mrs D Ennis,
   MCIPR
ICT Manager: Mr B Clarke

Luckley-Oakfield has high expectations for all its students, achieves excellent academic results and is proud of its exceptional added-value record. Luckley was founded on its present site in 1918. In 1959 it amalgamated with Oakfield School, established in 1895 in the Lake District. Initially the school was administered by the Church Society but in 1969 it became an independent educational trust. A gracious Grade II listed Edwardian country house forms the centre of the school, which is on a 14-acre site with views of the countryside and woodlands. More recent buildings provide accommodation for classrooms, laboratories and the Sixth Form. There is also a sports hall, covered swimming pool, a new state-of-the-art Music Centre and a superb library and English faculty complex.

The school numbers approximately 300 girls aged 11 to 18. The majority are day pupils, but approximately 30–40 girls are either full or weekly boarders. Pupils are selected on the basis of an entrance examination and interview. The main age of entry is at 11, 13 and into the Sixth Form. A number of coach routes are available.

Curriculum. The curriculum is broad and challenging with girls taking 9.5 subjects for GCSE. A wide variety of AS and A2 courses is offered and almost every girl goes on to higher education as a preparation for careers in, for example, languages, medicine, engineering, law, business and design.

The school has a well deserved reputation for Art, Drama, Music and Sport and offers a range of other activities including computing, debating, riding, polo, The Duke of Edinburgh's Award Scheme, CCF and Young Enterprise. Boarders and Day girls are encouraged to join in this extensive programme of extra curricular activities during the extended day slot from 4.30–5.30 pm. Instrumental lessons, Singing, Speech and Drama, and Latin are offered as additional subjects.

Boarding. Weekly and flexi boarding offer the opportunity to experience the fun of boarding while keeping close links with home and avoiding long daily journeys. Full boarding, with an extensive weekend activity programme, can provide a stable and secure education for girls whose schooling would otherwise be interrupted. Year 7–11 boarders live in the Main House, while sixth form boarders have their own study-bedroom accommodation within the Sixth Form Centre.

Ethos. Luckley-Oakfield encourages high aspirations, independent thinking and community spirit. Each student experiences a truly holistic education, developing her academic, cultural, creative, physical and ethical dimensions. At Luckley-Oakfield pastoral care is considered paramount because every girl is important. The school has an evangelical Church of England Foundation, but girls of all faiths and none are welcomed. Christian values shape the ethos of the school and there is a regular Sunday service for boarders.

Fees per term (2011-2012). Boarders £7,862; Weekly Boarders £7,286; Day Girls £4,492.

Scholarships and Bursaries. Scholarships are awarded at 11+ on the results of the Entrance Examination and on entry to the Sixth Form. Music, Drama, Art and Sports scholarships are also available.

Means-tested Bursaries of 100% and 50% of fees are offered at Year 7 and Sixth Form entry. Forces Bursaries are also available.

Charitable status. Luckley-Oakfield is a Registered Charity, number 309099. It offers day and boarding education for girls on the basis of Christian values.

Malvern St James

Avenue Road, Great Malvern, Worcestershire WR14 3BA
Tel: 01684 584624
Fax: 01684 566204
e-mail: registrar@malvernstjames.co.uk
website: www.malvernstjames.co.uk

Malvern St James, at the forefront of girls' education.

Governors:
Mrs S M E Adeney, BEd, BLit
The Revd Prebendary Carl Attwood, BA, MA (*Vice-Chair*)
Mr W Ballard, BSc, FCA
Mrs A Borrowdale, LLB (*Chair*)
Mr R Capper, LLB Hons, LLM
Mr S Dawson, BSc, MRICS
Mrs V J Dukes, BA
Mr C S Galliers, FCA
Mrs H Kingham, BSc, PGCE
Mrs A Lloyd, MA Ed, CertEd Oxon, LGSM
Mrs G M Lumsdon, BPharm, MEd
Miss E Mullenger, BA, CertEd, FRSA

Leadership Team:

Headmistress: **Mrs P Woodhouse**, BMus Hons

Deputy Headmistress: Mrs S Musgrave, BSc Hons Bristol,
   PGCE

Director of Teaching and Learning: Mrs A Hewitt, MA
   Oxon, PGCE

Assistant Head responsible for Boarding: Mrs E Drake, BA
   Hons Southampton, MA Sussex, PGCE, MA Ed, Man
   AIL

Assistant Head responsible for Sixth Form: Miss R Webb,
   BSc Hons Newcastle, PGCE Oxford

Assistant Head responsible for Years 10 and 11: Mrs J
   Newby, BA Hons Worcester, PGCE

Assistant Head responsible for Years 7, 8 and 9: Miss G
   Owen, BA Hons Open, CertEd

Registrar: Ms J Bailey

Malvern St James Girls School is a leading boarding and day school for approximately 400 girls between the ages of 4 and 18. The school is located in the heart of Malvern, and has excellent transport links, with Great Malvern train station situated opposite the main school and a daily mini-bus service in operation. Following an Ofsted boarding inspection in November 2009, the School was awarded an 'Outstanding' result. The system in place to promote the safety and welfare of boarders was described as 'outstanding' with girls living in a 'positive and nurturing environment where their welfare is paramount'.

Aim. Malvern St James presents an imaginative vision of education for girls from the age of 4 through to 18, taught within a positive, purposeful atmosphere. MSJ fosters creativity and bold thinking; we challenge and encourage every girl to extend her personal horizons and realise her full potential. The School is home to a warm and welcoming community with a buoyant atmosphere of shared celebration, extolling success in every field of endeavour.

Curriculum. Our teaching and learning strategies develop the competence and confidence of all our girls by actively challenging and stretching them. Experienced and inspirational staff have high expectations to ensure each girl makes maximum progress and realises her full potential. Recognition of individual learning styles enhances the classroom experience.

A full range of academic subjects is offered in the Arts and Humanities, Languages, Science and Technology up to Advanced Level.

Learning Support. Critical Thinking is offered throughout the School to provide an exciting challenge for the most able pupils whilst the Learning Support Department is recognised for the excellent level of support it provides for girls.

Boarding. MSJ offers a range of boarding options with excellent flexibility, including full and weekly, whilst flexiboarding is available to day girls wishing to stay overnight. House staff work with the girls to organise a busy weekend programme of social and weekend activities, creating a happy atmosphere in each boarding house.

Extra-Curricular Activities. Girls take full advantage of the enviable setting and superb facilities, which inspire a wonderfully rich and imaginative extra-curricular life.

Sport. The school offers a wide range of sporting options, including lacrosse, netball, golf, hockey, tennis and athletics with excellent facilities including a state-of-the art Sports Centre and Fitness Suite.

Admission. *Junior Department*: There are no formal examinations for the entrance into the Junior Department, girls are invited to enjoy a School Taster Day, during which they are assessed within the classroom environment.

Senior School Entry (aged 11+): Girls are invited to take Entrance Examinations at Malvern St James. The examinations take the form of Cognitive Ability Tests (CAT3) and a comprehension examination.

Alternatively, girls may apply via the Common Entrance Examination. We are also happy to send entrance papers to schools overseas to administer on our behalf for those girls applying from outside of the UK.

Sixth Form Entry: Girls will study four subjects during their time in the Sixth Form; four to AS Level and continue three to A Level.

As part of the application procedure UK girls are required to take a written paper in one of the subjects the student intends to study at Advanced Level and a general essay paper.

Girls applying from overseas are required to take a written paper in one of the subjects the student intends to study at Advanced Level and an English as a Second Language (EAL) paper.

For details please contact the Registrar, Ms Jennifer Bailey, e-mail: registrar@malvernstjames.co.uk.

Fees per term (2011-2012). Full Boarding: £7,415–£9,645 (Years 7–13); £10,650 (new Sixth Form entrants); £5,320–£5,645 (Years 3–6). Weekly Boarding: £7,045–£8,680 (Years 7–13); £9,585 (new Sixth Form entrants); £4,785–£5,365 (Years 3–6). Day: £2,235–£4,930.

Scholarships and Bursaries. Academic, Music, Art, and Sport Scholarships are available for Senior School entry; Academic, Music, Art, Drama and Sport Scholarships for Sixth Form entry. A Scholarship is worth up to a maximum of 20% of annual fees and an Exhibition is worth up to a maximum of 10%. Means-tested top-up bursaries can be awarded.

Charitable status. Malvern St James Limited is a Registered Charity, number 527513, which exists to support excellent education for girls.

Manchester High School for Girls

Grangethorpe Road, Manchester M14 6HS
Tel: 0161 224 0447
Fax: 0161 224 6192
e-mail: administration@mhsg.manchester.sch.uk
website: www.manchesterhigh.co.uk

Board of Governors:
Chairman: Mrs C Walker, BA
Mrs S Beales, MA
Mr A Clarke, FCA
Professor R Cooper, PhD
Dr J Dwek, BSc, BA, DSc, CBE
Mrs M Grant, CertEd
Mrs S Klass, MA Oxon
Mrs D Kloss, LLB, LLM, Hon FFOM, MBE
Her Honour Judge L Kushner, LLB, QC
Professor R W Munn, DSc
Mr S Ruia, BSc
Mrs C V F Sargent, BSc
Mr C J Saunders, OBE, MA, FSI
Mr F R Shackleton, MA, LLM
Mrs S E Spence, BA
Professor A K Webb, FRCP
Mr P Wood, LLB
Mr K S Yeung, MBE

Hon Treasurer: Mr A Clarke, FCA

Head Mistress: Mrs A C Hewitt, BSc, NPQH

Deputy Head Mistresses:
Ms H Huber, BA Manchester, Dip Management of Education Manchester Metropolitan (*Geography*)
Mrs S M Smith, BSc Leeds, MEd Bristol, NPQH (*Mathematics*)

Assistant Head Mistresses:
Mrs M G Hobson, BSc, MA Salford (*Modern Languages*)
Mrs P L Roberts, BA Durham (*French*)

Staff:
* *Head of Department*
§ *Part-time*

§Mrs R C Abson, BA Chester (*Drama*)
Mrs B M Alvarez Taylor, Lic en Filología Zaragoza (*Modern Languages*)
Mrs D Austin, BSc Bolton Institute, MSc (*Psychology*)
Miss J Axford, BA Manchester (*Philosophy & Literary Studies*)
Mrs J Bailey, BA York (*Mathematics*)
§Mrs P Bell, BA Leeds Polytechnic (*Art & Design Technology*)
Mrs C Bennett, BSc Staffordshire (*Physics*)
Mrs A G T Chambers, BA West Surrey College of Art & Design, ATC (**Art & Design Technology*)
Mr J Clarke, BA, MPhil Manchester (**History*)
Miss L Cooke, BSc Wales (**Careers*)
§Mrs D Crichton, BA London (*Modern Languages*)

Dr S Crook, BSc, PhD Dundee (*Biology*)

§Mrs R E Crowley, BSc Manchester (*Mathematics*)

Miss S A L Davies, BA Cardiff (*Modern Languages*)

Mrs E A Diamond, BA Birmingham (*Religion & Philosophy*)

§Miss L Farnandez-Barba, BA Madrid, MA Madrid (*Spanish*)

Mrs J L Fordham, CertEd Manchester (*Art & Design Technology*)

Ms S C Gaskell, BA, MA Oxon (*English*)

Mr K Gilkes, BSc Bolton (*ICT*)

Dr D Haggerston, BSc, PhD Southampton (*Physics*)

Miss C Hannan, MA Cantab (*Classics*)

§Mrs J Haves, BA De Montfort Leicester, PGCE (*Drama*)

Mrs J R Heydecker, BA Leicester (*History*)

§Mr C Hilton, BA, MA Cambridge, Dip TEO QTS Manchester (*Mandarin*)

Dr R E Hoban, BSc, PhD Newcastle (*Chemistry*)

Mr S P Holmes, BSc Nottingham (*Mathematics*)

Mrs P Inglis, BSc Manchester (*Chemistry*)

Mrs H F Jeys, BA Durham (*Religion & Philosophy*)

Mr D L Jones, BSc Manchester (*Mathematics*)

Ms H Keegan, BA Durham, MA Durham (*English*)

Miss E S King, BA Leeds, MSc Birmingham (*French, German*)

Miss K Large, BSc Leeds (*Chemistry*)

Miss K Martin, BA Birmingham, MPhil Birmingham (*History*)

Dr F Menon, MSc Padova, PhD Manchester (*Biology*)

Mrs J Miles, BA Liverpool (*History*)

Mrs C Mills, MChem Oxford, PGCE (*Chemistry*)

Dr L Moore, BSc Lebanon, MSc UMIST, PhD (*Chemistry*)

Mrs N Morgan, BMus Lancaster (*Music*)

Miss I Murphy, BSc Hull (*Mathematics*)

Mrs S Newman, BEd Leeds Metropolitan (*Physical Education*)

Mr R Nisar, BSc King's College, London (*Physics*)

Mr P J O'Brien, BA Hull (*German,*Modern Foreign Languages*)

§Mrs C J Ousey, BA Southampton (*English*)

Mrs C Pattison, BSc Newcastle (*Mathematics*)

Miss K Player, BA Liverpool (*PE*)

Dr C M Poucher, BSc, PhD Leeds (*Biology*)

Mrs M Price, BA Manchester (*English*)

Ms A N Protheroe, BSc Swansea (*Mathematics*)

§Mrs C Purvis, BA Lancaster (*Religious Studies*)

Mr M Randall, BA CNAA, MA Leicester (*Business Economics IT*)

§Mrs S Reynolds, BA UCL, MSc Kingston (*Geography*)

Miss S C Rowley, BA Staffordshire (*Physical Education*)

Mrs P Scott, BA Duncan of Jordanstone College of Art (*Art & Design Technology*)

Mrs T Slack, BA Manchester (*Modern Languages*)

Dr R Smither, BSc Bath, MPhil, PhD Cambridge (*Biology*)

Mr N M Tattersall, MPhys Oxford (*Mathematics*)

Dr I K Tranter, BSc, PhD Birmingham (*Chemistry*)

§Mrs D E Troth, BA Exeter (*History*)

§Mrs C M Tynan, BA York (*Physics*)

Mr S R F Vance, BA Manchester (*Art & Design Technology*)

Mr P R Warburton, BA Portsmouth Polytechnic, MPhil Leicester (*Geography*)

Miss L Warwick, BSc Manchester Metropolitan (*Physical Education*)

§Mrs D M Watkins, BEd Liverpool (*Physical Education*)

§Mrs A T Wells, BA Essex (*English*)

Miss J Welsby, BA Manchester (*Classics*)

Mrs K A Whelan, BSc Bradford (*Business Economics and IT*)

Mrs C Wickes, BA Sorbonne, MA Rennes (*Modern Languages*)

Preparatory Department Staff:

Head Mistress: Mrs R H Edwards, BEd

Mrs A Allman, Teacher's Dip Sedgely Park

Mrs R A Anderson, BEd Glasgow

Mrs C Callanan, BA MMU

Miss S Diamond, BEd Cantab

Miss J H Floyd, BA Charlotte Mason College

Mrs M R Heggie, BMus, BEd New South Wales

Mrs J C Philip, BA Manchester

Mrs K Robinson, BA London

Mrs C I J Steiner, BA Econ Manchester

Miss S Stent, BA Derby

Mrs C Westall, BA Huddersfield

Miss V Wilson, BSc Lancaster

Bursar: Mr J P Moran, FCCA

Registrar: Mrs L Hughes

PA to Head Mistress: Mrs S Bowker

Librarian: Miss Z Hawker, BA Liverpool, MSc Northumbria

Archivist: Dr C Joy, BA, PhD Leeds

School Medical Officer: Dr J Herd, BM BS, DFFP, DRCOG, MRCGP

Manchester High School for Girls (MHSG) offers students a vibrant atmosphere and a strong sense of community. In such a supportive environment, each girl feels happy, cared for and valued as an individual. Its academic record is outstanding, in both GCSE and A Level, and girls are taught not just how to achieve excellent examination results, but how to enjoy learning.

MHSG was founded in 1874 and has a long and successful history. The School offers a seamless education from age 4 to 18 and has extensive experience of helping girls to achieve their best. All members of the school community have a strong sense of the School's traditions, but MHSG is forward looking and keen to embrace new educational developments. Since September 2010, girls entering the Sixth Form have been able to choose to study the International Baccalaureate (IB) Diploma.

At MHSG, artistic and sporting talents are nurtured and students enjoy a diverse range of extra-curricular activities. These are complemented by superb modern facilities which include a state-of-the-art sports complex, a fitness suite, a dance studio, all-weather sports pitches, a multi-purpose auditorium and a purpose-built Music House. Instrumental and Speech & Drama lessons are optional extras.

Students at Manchester High come from a wide range of backgrounds and this rich social and cultural mix gives the School a warm and friendly feel. The girls learn about the importance of social responsibility with charity, voluntary and community work encouraged.

Highly skilled and committed staff ensure that every MHSG student leaves the School a well-educated young woman, with highly-developed interpersonal skills and a broad range of interests. Our girls are confident in their own worth, prepared for an independent life and capable of making a positive contribution to society. It is from this cornerstone that they go on to pursue varied and fulfilling careers.

MHSG is committed to providing education to academically gifted girls regardless of circumstance. In the Senior School financial assistance is offered through a limited number of part or full means-tested bursaries. A scholarship may also be awarded to a student who has shown exceptional performance in academic work and/or music, sport or dance (*see Scholarship Entries section*).

Entry to the Reception class is by assessment while an entrance examination is set for the Juniors and Year 7. From time to time vacancies in other year groups can become available, but the main entry levels are at ages 4, 7, 11 and 16. Sixth Form assessment is by interview and GCSE qualifications.

Further details and a prospectus are available from the School Registrar.

The Report of the ISI Inspection in October 2010 can be viewed on the School's website.

Fees per term (2011-2012). Seniors £3,214, Juniors £2,338, Infants £2,290.

Charitable status. Manchester High School for Girls Foundation is a Registered Charity, number 532295. The aim of the charity is the provision and conduct in Manchester of a day school for girls.

Manor House School

Manor House Lane, Little Bookham, Surrey KT23 4EN
Tel: 01372 458538
Fax: 01372 450514
e-mail: admin@manorhouseschool.org
website: www.manorhouseschool.org

Motto: *To Love is to Live*

Governors:
Chairman: Mr P Barlow, FIA
Treasurer: Mr H von Bergen
Miss Z Axton, BSc Hons, PGCE
Mr J Compton
Mrs F Culshaw (*Parent Governor*)
Mr M Parkhouse, BA Hons, MA, MSc
Mr M Ruscoe
Mrs C Turnbull, BA Hons
Mr D Wright

Headmistress: Miss Z Axton, BA Hons, PGCE

Deputy Head: Mr M Gates, BMedSc Hons, MEd

Senior Department:
Mrs G Arnold, BSc Hons, PGCE (*Science*)
Mrs T Banfield, BEd Hons (*Physical Education*)
Mrs S Beasley (*Learning Support*)
Mr K Boyd, MA Hons, PGCE (*English*)
Mrs S Buck, BSc Hons, PGCE (*Physical Education*)
Mr G Chester, BA Hons, PGCE (*Mathematics*)
Mr J Conway, BSc Hons, PGCE (*ICT*)
Mrs K Dabill, PGCE (*Mathematics*)
Mr A Delin, MA, PGCE (*French*)
Mrs V Diprose, BA Hons, PGCE (*French*)
Mrs G Gibson, BEd Hons, CertEd (*Chemistry*)
Miss C Grindrod, BSc Hons, PGCE (*Geography*)
Mrs E Hunter, MA, BEd Hons (*History*)
Mrs S Hutton, MA Oxon, PGCE (*Religious Studies*)
Mrs H Jewell, CertEd OU Dip (*Spanish*)
Mrs L McCartney, LLB (*Learning Support*)
Mrs C Parish, CertEd (*English*)
Mrs J Perkin, BSc Hons, PGCE (*Science*)
Miss C Poultney, BEd Hons (*Physical Education*)
Mrs S Parsons, BA Hons, PGCE (*Art*)
Mrs C Peel, MA, PGCE (*German*)
Mrs E Pillar, BEd Hons (*Religious Studies*)
Mrs V Robinson, BA Hons, PGCE (*Science*)
Mrs K Slaughter, BA Hons, PGCE, CCET, AAC, Dip RSA (*Learning Support*)
Mrs S Smith, BCom (*Mathematics*)
Mrs L Stephens, BA Hons, PGCE (*Latin*)
Mrs K Tercan, BEd Hons (*Home Economics*)
Miss J Ward, BA Hons, PGCE (*Music*)
Mrs T Williams, BA Hons, PGCE (*Art and Drama*)

and 14 Peripatetic staff

Junior Department Staff:
Head: Mrs T Hilleard, MA, BEd Hons
Mrs J Baker, BA Hons, PGCE
Mrs A Coleman, CertEd

Mrs D Horrocks, HDip PrimEd
Mrs I Rodwell, BEd Hons
Mrs J Lewis, BA Hons, PGCE

Prep Department Staff:
Head: Mrs V Kyte, DipEd
Mrs V Burden, CertEd, NVQ3
Mrs V Cannon, BA Hons, PGCE
Mrs C Drage, DipEd

Nursery Department:
Head: Mrs J Roy, Montessori Dip Dist
Miss R Beirne, BA Hons, NVQ3
Miss C Brazil, Cache Level 2
Mrs A Harvey, NNEB
Mrs J Morrison, BA Hons, NVQ3
Mrs S Viscione, NNEB

Bursar, Finance: Mrs C Miller, MBA
Bursar, Admin: Mrs V Allcott
Admissions Secretary: Mrs J Clifford

Manor House is an independent day school for girls between the ages of 2 and 16 years. Founded in 1920, the school is a charitable trust situated in a Georgian building and set in seventeen acres of parkland within easy distance of London. Our own minibuses meet the trains at Effingham Junction station and collect pupils from other points before school each day. Manor House is a day school with a day boarding system (8 am to 6 pm).

The recent building programme has provided a new Early Years Department block, new Art, Drama, Music and Home Economics rooms and extended and refurbished Science Laboratories. The School has excellent sports facilities which include an open-air heated swimming pool, five tennis and netball courts, two of which are floodlit, with all-weather surfaces, hockey and rounders pitches, and an athletics track.

The girls follow a wide curriculum throughout their school career and generally take 9 or 10 GCSE subjects which must include English, Mathematics, Science and usually a modern language. Girls are expected to partake fully in the life of the school and develop their individual talents in Drama, Music and Sport. Tuition is available for a wide range of musical instruments including piano, flute, brass, saxophone, violin, cello, guitar, clarinet, drums and harp. The school has flourishing choirs and instrumental groups.

The aim of the school is to create a happy, secure and disciplined environment where each girl can achieve her individual academic potential. Pastoral care is a particular strength of the school. Senior girls are caring role models for younger pupils and there is a flourishing peer support group. Manor House is a Christian non-denominational school but has close links with the Church of England. A Manor House girl is confident and outgoing with a strong sense of values and the ability to succeed in her chosen career. Girls are encouraged to be independent and to take responsibility for themselves and others.

Admission. (*See Scholarship Entries section.*) Admission to the Senior Department is by Entrance Examination at 11+. Senior Department Scholarships may be awarded as a result of these examinations. Entry at other ages is subject to availability of places and is determined by assessment and interview. Means-tested bursaries up to 100% may also be applied for.

Fees per term (2011-2012). Tuition: £1,060–£4,420.

Charitable status. Manor House School is a Registered Charity, number 312063. It exists for the promotion of children's education according to their academic, social, sporting and musical abilities.

The Marist Senior School

Kings Road, Sunninghill, Ascot, Berkshire SL5 7PS
Tel: 01344 624291
Fax: 01344 874963
e-mail: officesenior@themaristschools.com
website: www.themaristschools.com

Independent Catholic Day School for Girls aged 11–18 founded in 1870 by the Marist Sisters. The school has been at the current site since 1947 and is set in 60 acres of attractive woodland in the village of Sunninghill near Ascot.

Chair of Governors: Mrs M Cairns

Headteacher: Mr K McCloskey, BA Hons, PGCE, MA

Deputy Headteacher: Mrs C Trelfa, BA Hons, PGCE, NPQH

Assistant Headteacher: Miss W Grantham, BA Hons, PGCE

Heads of Department:
Art: Mrs S Maynard, CertEd
Classics: Mrs A Osmond, BA Hons
Drama: Miss J May, BA, PGCE
Economics/Business Studies: Mrs P Elstone, BA Hons, PGCE
English: Mrs L Lutton, MA Hons, PGCE
Food Science: Mrs G White, CertEd
Geography: Mrs E Guinney, BA Hons, PGCE
History: Mrs D Bishop, BA Hons, PGCE
ICT: Mrs J Shill, CertEd, CertSpLD, DipWp
Mathematics: Mrs A Hynds, BSc Hons, PGCE
Modern Foreign Languages: Mrs M Halksworth, L-ès-L, PGCE
Music: Miss J Slocombe, BA Hons, MMus, ARCM, PGCE
Psychology: Mrs J Cope, BA, HDipEd
Physical Education: Mrs J Bishopp, BA Ed Hons
Religious Education: Miss L Vaughan Neil, LLB, BA, PGCE
Science: Mrs A Royston, BSc Hons, PGCE
Textiles: Miss M Tooman, BSc, PGDipEd

Number of Pupils. 337 girls.
Mission Statement. The Marist is a community where Christian values inspire all aspects of learning and where the potential of each individual is recognised, valued and affirmed.
Strengths.
* Strong reputation for academic excellence as well as sport, drama, music and creative arts.
* Able to offer a wide range of both academic and extra-curricular activities.
* Strong emphasis on pastoral care, spiritual and personal development; care and consideration for others.
* Small class sizes to enhance individual progression and recognition.
* The school is renowned for its high standards regarding moral values, community spirit, respect and care. This is in line with the overall ethos of the Marist order which has a worldwide presence, providing a truly international dimension to a girl's education.
Facilities. Indoor swimming pool, dedicated Sixth Form suite, comprehensive ICT suite, new music and drama building, language laboratory and library.
Academic Curriculum. Art, Biology, Business Studies, Classical Civilisation, Chemistry, Drama/Theatre Studies, Economics, English, French, Geography, German, History, ICT, Italian, Latin, Mathematics (also Pure & Mechanics, Pure, Statistics, Pure & Statistics), Music, Personal, Social & Health Education, PE, RE, Religious Studies: Philosophy & Ethics, Science, Spanish, Sports Studies, Textiles, Food Science, Psychology.
Sixth Form. The school offers a total of 26 subjects at AS/A2 Level. Year 12 students will study 4 four subjects at AS Level in their first year (in certain circumstances some students can take 5). After AS Levels, girls will decide which 3/4 subjects they wish to continue on to A2 Level.
Extra-Curricular Activities. Art, Athletics, Cheerleading, Choir, Clarinet & Saxophone Ensemble, Drama Club, Duke of Edinburgh's Award, Flute Group, French Films, Greek (Ancient), Guitar Group, History Films, Hockey, Human Rights, ICT, Latin, Library Club, Literacy, Netball, Orchestra, Prayer Group, Public Speaking/Debating, Recorder Club, Rock Band, Science, Strategy/Numeracy, Swimming, Swing Band, Textiles, Tennis, Young Enterprise.
Results. 2010: 100% of A Level students passed with 75% achieving A and B grades. GCSE students achieved 85% A*, A and B grades, and also enjoyed a 100% pass rate.
Admission. Entrance examination tests in (1) English, (2) Mathematics and (3) cognitive abilities, (4) Portfolio, (5) Compulsory Interview with the Headteacher and (6) Reference from Primary/Preparatory Headteacher.
Sixth Form Entry. General requirements for 3 or 4 AS subjects: a minimum of 5 GCSEs at C grade or above, preferably B grade in subjects to be studied.
General requirements for 5 AS subjects: most grades at GCSE should be A*.
Note: there are recommended subjects and grades at GCSE for each AS subject available in the Sixth Form Prospectus and on the school's website.
Fees per term (2011-2012). £3,565. Extra benefits: Generous sibling discount scheme (4th and any subsequent children free), after school care provided.
Scholarships. Year 7 and Sixth Form Academic, Art, Drama, Music and Sport scholarships are available.
Preparatory School. We also have a Preparatory school on the same campus which is for girls aged 2½–11. This allows girls to continue their education with their friends in the happy and secure environment they are used to. (*For further details, see the Marist Preparatory School entry in the IAPS section.*)
Affiliations. Girls' Schools Association (GSA), Catholic Independent Schools Conference (CISC), Silver Artsmark, Eco Schools award and Healthy School.
Charitable status. The Marist Schools is a Registered Charity, number 225485. The principal aims and activities of the Marist Schools are religious and charitable and specifically to provide education by way of an independent day school for girls between the ages of 3 and 18.

The Mary Erskine School

Ravelston, Edinburgh EH4 3NT
Tel: 0131 347 5700
Fax: 0131 347 5799
e-mail: schoolsecretary@esmgc.com
website: www.esms.edin.sch.uk

Governing Council:
Chairman: Mrs Judy Wagner

Clerk to the Governors: Mr D Wright, LLB

Principal: Mr J N D Gray, BA

Bursar: Mr J B Molloy, MA Hons

Deputy Head: Mrs L A Moule, BA Hons, PGCE
Director of Studies: Mrs A Y Angus, BSc, PGCE
Staff Development Coordinator: Mr N Dawson, MA Hons, MEd
Head of Upper School: Dr E A Murray, BSc Hons, MEd, PhD, PGCE

Head of S1/Admissions: Ms K S S Nicholson, MA Hons, PGCE

Director of Sixth Form: Dr I R Scott, MA Hons, PhD, FRSA, CertEd

* *Head of Department*
† *Head of House*

*Mrs F J MacGregor, BDes Hons, PGCE
Mrs C Burns, BA Hons, PGCE

Biology:
*Dr S Corbet, BSc Hons, MSc, PhD, PGCE
Miss K Davies, BSc Hons, DipEd
Mrs L J McCreath, BSc Hons, PGCE
Miss S Newman, BSc, PGCE
Dr C Turnbull, BSc, MSc, PhD

Business Studies:
*Mrs F K McCrudden, BA Hons, PGCE
Mr A Kuryluk, BA Hons, PGCE

Careers:
*Mrs P McInally, BA Hons, PGCE

Chemistry:
*Dr C J Spracklin, BSc Hons, PhD, PGCE
Mrs S Ferrington, BSc Hons, PGDE (†*Appin*)
Mrs C Murdie, BSc Hons, PGCE
Dr E A Murray, BSc Hons, MEd, PhD, PGCE (*Head of Upper School*)

Classics:
*Miss A E Cowperthwaite, MA Hons, PGCE
Mrs C D'Arcy, BA, PGCE

Computing:
Mr J D Hamilton, MSc

Drama:
*Miss G Henderson, BA Hons, LLCM Hons, LAMDA
Mrs L Howarth, MA Hons, PGCE

English:
*Ms D Esland, BA Hons, PGCE
Miss N Anderson, MA Hons, PGCE (†*Ettrick*)
Mrs R Connet, BA Hons, PGCE
Mr N Dawson, MA Hons, MEd (*Staff Development Coordinator*)
Mrs A Holt, BA Hons, PGCE, ALCM (†*Lochaber*)
Mrs C S Park, MA Hons, PGCE (†*Torridon*)
Mrs M Tetley, BA Hons, MSc, QTS
Mrs K A J Yip, BA Hons, MA, PGCE

Geography:
*Mrs J A Wright, MA Hons, DipEd
Ms K S S Nicholson, MA Hons, PGCE (*Head of S1/ Admissions*)
Miss J F Pollitt, MA Hons, PGCE
Mrs C Wallace, MA Hons, PGCE
Miss M Tucker, MA Hons, PGDE

History:
*Mr A P McDiarmid, BA Hons, PGCE
Mrs L F Alexander, MA Hons, PGDE
Mrs L J Allan, MA Hons, PGCE (†*Kintyre*)
Mr R Robertson, MA Hons, PGCE

Home Economics:
*Mrs J Hetherington, Dip DomSc, LSSN
Mrs N L Murray, BA, PGCE, PGC

Mathematics:
*Dr B Duncan, MPhys, PhD, PGCE
Mrs A Angus, BSc, PGCE (*Director of Studies*)
Mr J D Hamilton, MSc
Mrs F J Houbert, BEd Hons
Mrs E King, MMath Hons, MSc, PGCE
Miss C A Leslie, BSc, DipEd (†*Galloway*)
Mrs J Smart, BSc Hons, FFA, PGDE

Modern Languages:
*Mr M G Chittleburgh, MA Hons, DipEd, PGCE
*Mrs S Old, MA Hons, DipEd
Dr S M Benn, MA, PhD, PGCE
Ms J H Bremner, MA Hons, PGCE
Mrs J Fitzgerald, MA Hons, PGCE
Mrs E R Hyslop, MA Hons, DipEd (*Deputy Head, Sixth Form*)
Miss L McGuinness, MA, PGCE
Mrs P McInally, BA Hons, PGCE
Mrs M L Thornton, MA, DipEd
Miss C Watson, MA Hons, PGDE

Modern Studies:
*Mrs J A Wright, MA Hons, DipEd
Mrs C Wallace, MA Hons, PGCE

Music:
*Mrs S Headden, DRSAM, DipEd
Mr J Matthews, BMus, PGDE
Mrs J Wilson, BA, PGCE

Philosophy:
*Dr I R Scott, MA Hons, PhD, FRSA, CertEd (*Director of Sixth Form*)

Physical Education:
*Mrs V G Thomson, BEd Hons, BSc
Mr G Blackhall, BEd Hons
Miss M Cooper, BEd Hons
Miss C Lampard, BEd Hons
Mrs G Longmuir, BEd Hons
Miss K Mackay, BEd Hons
Mrs J L Miller, BEd Hons
Mrs K A Mundell, BEd Hons

Physics:
*Dr T Hely, MSc, PhD, PGCE
Miss J Collings, MEng Hons, PGDE
Mrs M E T Sutherland, BSc Hons

Product Design:
*Mr D K Bowen, BA Hons, ATC, DipSIAD
Mrs C A Hemmati, BSc Hons, PGCE, MSc

Religious Moral and Philosophical Studies:
*Mr D Kemp, MTheol, PGCE
Mr M Hughes, BA, PGDE
Mrs L A Moule, BA Hons, PGCE (*Deputy Head*)
Miss O Williams, MA Hons, PGDE

Support for Learning:
*Mrs C Maxwell, BA, DipEd
Mr S Hollins, BA Hons, PGCE
Miss R Meredith, BSc, PGCE, PGDip

Educational Psychologist:
Mrs M Brown, MA, DipEdPsyc

Junior School:
Head Master: Mr B D Lewis, BA Hons, H DipEd Hons
Deputy Head (Primary 4–7): Mrs G Lyon, DCE, DipRSA
Deputy Head (Early Education): Mrs M Rycroft, DipCE
Assistant Head (Primary 4–7): Mr D McLeish, DCE
Assistant Head (Primary 4–7): Miss S Mackay, ALCM, LLCM, BMus Hons, DCE
Assistant Head (Early Education): Ms C Macpherson, BEd

The Mary Erskine School was founded by Mary Erskine and the Company of Merchants of the City of Edinburgh in 1694. It is therefore one of the oldest schools in the UK endowed specifically for girls. Known in its early years as 'The Merchant Maiden Hospital', its aims were to educate and care for the daughters of City Burgesses who found themselves in reduced circumstances. Throughout its history, the school has been administered by the Edinburgh Merchant Company. In November 1989 this authority was devolved to the Erskine Stewart's Melville Governing Council.

The school, named The Mary Erskine School in 1944 to mark the 250th anniversary of its foundation, has been housed on various sites in the city – the Cowgate, Bristo, Lauriston and Queen Street – and the buildings are depicted on the engraved glass panels in the Sports Centre and on murals in the Assembly Hall. The current school buildings, at Ravelston, command splendid views of the nearby city and castle.

Since 1978 the school has been twinned with Stewart's Melville College (*see entry in HMC section*). This includes a fully co-educational Junior School for children between the ages of 3 and 12, single-sex but very closely twinned secondary schools between the ages of 12 and 17 and a fully co-educational pre-university Sixth Form which provides the ideal bridge between school and university. The girls and boys from The Mary Erskine School and Stewart's Melville College come together in the Combined Cadet Force, in orchestras, choirs, drama and musicals and in numerous outdoor education projects.

The Senior School (759 Girls). The school curriculum corresponds predominantly with practice in Scotland. Girls generally sit the public examinations prescribed by the Scottish Qualifications Authority.

SI and S2 follow a broad curriculum, whereby girls are equipped to pursue all routes to Intermediate 2 or Standard Grade. In S3 girls commence eight courses, including English, Mathematics, at least one modern language, at least one science, and a "humanities" subject. In S5 the majority of girls take five subjects at Higher level. Girls are expected to achieve their full potential. The majority will continue their studies for a Sixth Year, usually at Advanced Higher level, to provide a firm foundation for degree courses in Scotland and England. Most girls proceed to such courses.

The playing fields at Ravelston underpin a fine tradition in hockey and tennis. Physical Education facilities include grass hockey pitches, two floodlit astroturf hockey pitches, a running track and twelve tennis courts. A Games Hall and Fitness Suite complement the other sporting facilities. The Pavilion, which provides the Sixth Form girls and boys with a Common Room and Study area during the week, is available to parents and friends as a coffee area on Saturday mornings and other times when sports events take place.

Staff from the well-equipped Technology Centre work closely with those in the bright, modern Home Economics Department. The attractive Library is next to one of the computer rooms, forming a combined resource centre which is accessed by all departments.

In the Art Department the girls enjoy first class facilities which help them develop diverse artistic talents. There is a specially designated area for Sixth Form girls, many of whom proceed to Art colleges, as well as darkroom facilities for keen photographers.

The Music Department possesses fine facilities in Ravelston House and the school enjoys a notable reputation for the quality and range of its musical activities. The attractive School Hall and designated Studio offer good facilities for drama and there are frequent productions involving girls and boys of all ages.

The Combined Cadet Force comprises Army and RAF sections. The combined Pipe Band has an international reputation and girls in the Highland Dancing team also achieve frequent success in competition. Many girls participate in the Duke of Edinburgh's Award Scheme, as well as in hill-walking and other forms of outdoor recreation. Each week the school offers to girls a wide variety of extra-curricular clubs and societies ranging from curling to drama.

The school has a sophisticated system of Guidance. SI tutors, led by the Head of S1, help girls to make the transition from Junior School to Senior School a smooth and happy experience. During the next four years girls belong to one of six houses. The Heads of House, led by the Head of

Upper School, liaise closely with colleagues on each girl's academic progress, teach the personal and social education programme in house groups and encourage each girl to derive maximum benefit from the school's extra-curricular programme.

The Sixth Form is co-educational with the Sixth Formers of Stewart's Melville College. While girls sustain their loyalty and commitment to The Mary Erskine School, they are equally at home in the Sixth Form Centre of the boys' school. We see the Sixth Form as a preparation for university, when girls and boys assume greater responsibility for their academic programme and their career aspirations. All girls in the school receive guidance and help from the staff of a well-established careers department based in the Library Resource Centre.

Boarding. There is a boarding house (Erskine House) with accommodation for approximately 28 girls in brightly decorated study-bedrooms. The girls share dining and recreational facilities with the Stewart's Melville boarders in Dean Park House. Both Houses have a friendly, family atmosphere and provide an ideal "home from home" for brothers and sisters.

Fees per term (2011-2012). Day: Primary Start to Primary 7 £2,141–£2,578 (lunches included for Primary 2–7); Secondary £3,032 (plus £154 for optional lunches). Boarding (including tuition and laundry): Primary 4–7 £5,410–£5,475; Secondary £6,083.

Scholarships and Bursaries. Means-tested Bursaries worth up to 100% of the tuition fee may be available to parents of children entering any year group in the Senior Schools and at P7 in the Junior School. Academic scholarships worth £250 annually are offered to girls applying to enter S1, following a competitive selection process. These are known as Merchant Company Scholarships. The top scholarship holder at The Mary Erskine School receives the Mackay Scholarship, worth £1,000 annually. Scholarships are paid to the pupil and are held in trust by the school until completion of their Sixth Form year. Music Scholarships of £250 per annum are offered from S3.

Junior School. In The Mary Erskine and Stewart's Melville Junior School (1,226 pupils), girls and boys are educated together from age 3 to 12. Children in Primary Start to Primary 3 are based on the Mary Erskine School site at Ravelston, while boys and girls in Primary 4–7 are taught on the Stewart's Melville College site. Normal entry points are Primary Start (age 3 or 4), Primary 1, Primary 4, Primary 6 and Primary 7. The school is remarkable for the breadth of its educational programme and the quality of its sporting and cultural activities, in particular the professional standards attained in Music and Drama.

The Mary Erskine School Former Pupils' Guild. Contact: MES Guild Office, The Mary Erskine School, Ravelston, Edinburgh, EH4 3NT. Tel: 0131 347 5722.

Charitable status. The Merchant Company Education Board is a Registered Charity, number SC009747. It is a leading charitable school in the field of Junior and Secondary education.

Marymount International School

George Road, Kingston-upon-Thames, Surrey KT2 7PE
Tel: 020 8949 0571
Fax: 020 8336 2485
e-mail: admissions@marymountlondon.com
website: www.marymountlondon.com

An Independent boarding and day school for girls aged 11–18. A member of GSA, ECIS and MSA (USA).

Headmistress: Ms S P Gallagher, BA, HDipEd, MA Classics, ABD Classics USA

Number of Pupils. 248, including 90 boarders.

Established in 1955 by the Sisters of the Sacred Heart of Mary, Marymount International School is an independent day and boarding school for girls, aged 11–18 (grades 6–12), representing approximately forty different nationalities. The school is within a half-hour's drive of Heathrow Airport and conveniently located for M25/A3 road links.

The school aims to provide an intellectually stimulating and emotionally secure environment in which the academic, social and personal needs of each individual student may be met. Education is seen as a continuous process of growth in awareness and development towards maturity in preparation for participation in the world community. Small classes enable students to attain their full personal and academic potential. Each student's schedule is individually tailored to the subjects she wishes to follow. The overall student:teacher ratio is 12:1 and the average class size numbers 14 students.

Entry requirements and procedures. Previous reports, teachers' recommendations, placement testing and interview.

Facilities in the beautiful seven-acre campus include Library, Computer Centre and classrooms, as well as a Sports Hall, Auditorium, Art Studio, Language Laboratory, Science Centre, Music Centre, Design Technology Centre and tennis courts. A new boarding wing was recently completed incorporating additional facilities for day and boarding students alike.

An integral part of the school programme each year is the option to visit a variety of foreign locations to learn about the history and culture of the area. For 2009 the choice was Switzerland and a Costa Rica Tour.

Examinations. Students are prepared for the International Baccalaureate Diploma (ages 17/18, grades 11–12) by the IB Middle Years Programme (ages 11–16, grades 6–10). Marymount was the first British school to be accepted to teach the MYP, and now offers students an IB curriculum from ages 11–18 (grades 6–12).

The IB diploma syllabus leads to UK university admission and US college credit. On average, ninety-eight percent of graduates go on to third level education in the UK and abroad. Two students in 2007 and another in 2008 received perfect scores of 45, the equivalent of 5 A grades for A level.

Fees per annum (2011-2012). Tuition: £16,590 (Grades 6–8); £18,960 (Grades 9–12). Boarding Supplement: Grades 6–12: £11,520 (5-day), £12,870 (7-day).

Charitable status. Marymount International School is a Registered Charity, number 1117786. It exists for the promotion of education.

The Maynard School
(Sir John Maynard's Foundation)

Denmark Road, Exeter, Devon EX1 1SJ
Tel: 01392 273417
Fax: 01392 355999
e-mail: office@maynard.co.uk
website: www.maynard.co.uk

Endowed 1658.

The Governors:
Appointed by the Governing Body of St John's Hospital:
Mrs L Kingdon
Mr S Gregory
Mr S Marsh
Lady J Stanhope

Co-opted by the Governors:
Mrs J Jones
Mr G Myers (*Chairman*)

Mrs S Pritchard
Mr N Shiel
Ms M Pearse

Appointed by the Exeter City Council:
Mrs Y Henson

Appointed by Devon County Council:
Mr P Bowden

Appointed by the University of Exeter:
Mr I C Powell

Parent Governors:
Mr P Morrish
Mr N Bruce-Jones

Staff Governors:
Dr P Le Gallez
Mrs H Reynolds

The Right Worshipful, The Lord Mayor of Exeter (*ex officio*)

Secretary to the Governors: Mr T A Hughes-Parry

Headmistress: Ms B Hughes, BEd Hons, MBA, NPQH

Deputy Head: Mrs P Wilks, MA Oxford (*History*)

Director of Studies: Dr P Rudling, MA Cambridge, MSc, PhD Exeter (*Psychology*)

Head of Sixth Form: Miss K James, BA University of Wales (*English Literature*)

Head of Junior School: Mr S Smerdon, BEd Exeter (*History*)

Senior Academic Administrator: Miss M Ellis, MA Cambridge (*Physics*)

Staff:
Ms J Bellamy, BA Manchester (*Drama*)
Mrs A Cox, MA Bristol (*Classics*)
Mrs W Dersley, BSc Open University (*Mathematics*)
Mrs J Elson, BSc, MPhil London (*Geography*)
Mrs S Fanous, BEd Keele (*Food & Nutrition, Textiles*)
Mrs C Finnegan, BA Central Saint Martins (*Food & Nutrition/Textiles*)
Mr I Flower, BSc Sussex (*Chemistry, Physics*)
Miss K Gwynne, MTheol St Andrews, ThM Princeton (*Religious Studies*)
Mrs R Halse, BA University of Arizona (*Spanish*)
Mrs A J Horton, BSc Exeter (*Mathematics*)
Mrs S Kerrane, BSc Swansea (*Biology*)
Dr P Le Gallez, BA Bristol, MA, PhD Exeter (*English*)
Mr W Lodge, BSc Sussex, MEd Open (*Chemistry*)
Mrs V Martin, BA Hull (*English*)
Mrs L Masson, BSc Pietermaritzberg (*Junior School*)
Dr P Merisi, MPhil, PhD Exeter (*Mathematics*)
Miss L Millar, BEd Belfast (*Physical Education*)
Miss R Miller, BSc Cardiff (*Physical Education*)
Mr D O'Neill, BA York (*German*)
Dr E Ouldridge, BSc Birmingham, PhD Leeds (*Biology, Physics, Chemistry*)
Mrs I Powell, BSc, MSc Rennes (*French*)
Mrs H Reynolds, BSc Open University (*Junior School*)
Mrs C Rowe, DipEd Edinburgh (*Junior School*)
Dr P Rudling, MA Cambridge, MSc, PhD Exeter (*Psychology*)
Mr S Ryder, BSc Hons Birmingham, MSc London (*Information & Communications Technology*)
Mrs S Thorne, BSc Nottingham (*Chemistry, Biology*)
Mrs S Wood, BA Ed Exeter (*Physical Education*)
Mrs S Woolley, MA Oxford (*Study Skills & Learning Support*)
Mrs V Woulfe, BSc Keele (*Mathematics*)
Mrs Z Vingoe, BA Manchester Metropolitan (*Art*)

Part-time Staff:
Mrs C L Austin, GRSM, LRAM (*Music*)
Mrs E Burrow, BA Plymouth (*Art*)
Mrs G Cameron, BEd Cheltenham (*Physical Education*)
Mrs J Dalton, BSc Open University, (*Maths*)
Mrs K Fry, BEd Exeter (*Junior School*)
Mrs C M Gabbitass, BSc Loughborough (*Physical Education*)
Mr A Ganley, BA Nottingham (*Drama*)
Mr N V Horton, BA Bristol, ARCM (*Music*)
Dr S Kennedy, MA Exeter, PhD Exeter (*Classics*)
Mrs E Kilkelly, BA Exeter (*Religious Studies*)
Mrs R Khreisheh, BA Oxford (*Junior School*)
Mrs D Lewis, BA Cheltenham (*Geography*)
Miss T Lothingland, BA Plymouth (*EFL*)
Mr P Pienkowski, BSc London (*Economics, ICT*)
Mrs A Rowley, BA Liverpool (*English*)
Mrs R Simmons, BSc Cardiff (*Junior School*)
Mrs C Smith, MA Tours (*French, Spanish*)
Mrs A Weeks, BSc Loughborough (*Physics*)

In addition there are 17 Visiting Music Staff and 4 Visiting Coaches for extra-curricular activities.

Headmistress's PA: Mrs T Taylor
Assistant Secretary: Mrs J Crowley
Estate Manager: Ms J Beever
Marketing & Development Manager: Mrs J Conway
Admissions Manager: Mrs M Linnen-Jones
School Nurse: Mrs S Ayres
School Counsellor: Mrs B Ripper

Ethos. A dynamic and supportive community, the Maynard is committed to excellence in providing learning opportunities that inspire and challenge. Students will demonstrate creativity, be socially responsible and through their shared experience, become independent and reflective learners. A wide-ranging extra-curricular programme enables students to achieve in all aspects of school life. Pastoral care is a vital component to ensure every student is valued. Students achieve highly in all public examinations.

Numbers. There are approximately 380 day girls in the School, of whom 80 are in the Junior School and 90 in the Sixth Form.

School Buildings. The School is situated in an attractive conservation area five minutes from the centre of the city. The extensive buildings include a separate Sixth Form Centre; a purpose-built block for Science, Mathematics, and ICT; well-equipped Food & Nutrition and Textiles Rooms; Music and Art Rooms, a large Gymnasium, and an impressive Sports Hall which provides full-scale indoor facilities. The Junior School is situated in a detached building within the grounds, and is fully equipped for the education of girls aged 7–10 years.

Curriculum. The curriculum is academically rigorous and maintains a good balance between Arts and Science subjects. English, Mathematics, the Sciences and Sport are particular strengths; full scope is given to creative and practical activities, as well as ICT skills. The School prepares all girls for University, including Oxford and Cambridge. A carefully developed programme of careers advice, begun at 11+ and continuing through to the Sixth Form, ensures that all pupils are individually guided in subject options etc with their long-term career interests at heart.

Examinations. Candidates normally take 10 subjects at GCSE and 3 at A Level. The AQA Baccalaureate is offered in the Sixth Form. Students are fully prepared for Oxford and Cambridge University Entrance.

Physical Education. Hockey (outdoor and indoor), Netball, Badminton, Basketball, Volleyball, Fencing, Dance and Gymnastics are offered in the winter terms; Tennis and Rounders are played in the Summer Term. Training is given in Athletics and regular instruction in Swimming as part of the normal timetable for all girls during the Summer Term.

Besides its excellent indoor facilities and the three hard courts in its own grounds, the School is close to three heated swimming pools and an Astroturf playing area. The school has an extensive fixture programme in Netball, Hockey, Indoor Hockey, Badminton, Basketball, Tennis, Swimming, Athletics and Rounders. Teams have regularly reached national standard.

Admission. All admissions are subject to an Entrance Assessment graduated according to age and are held in January each year for entry in the following September.

Fees per term (2011-2012). Junior School £2,852, Senior School £3,566.

Scholarships and Bursaries. (*See Scholarship Entries section.*) Academic and Music scholarships are available for senior school entry. There are Sixth Form scholarships available in Art, Music, Science and Sport, plus Academic Scholarships. Up to four Governors' Leaving Exhibitions are awarded in the Upper Sixth year.

A number of means-tested Governors' Bursaries are awarded annually.

Further Information. The Prospectus and Governors' Bursaries information are available from the Admissions Office. Visitors are very welcome by appointment, and tours and taster days can be arranged for girls considering the school.

Old Maynardians' Society. *Secretary*: Mrs Jane Jones, 5 Matford Avenue, Exeter, Devon.

Charitable status. The Maynard School is a Registered Charity, number 1099027. It exists to provide quality education for girls.

Merchant Taylors' Girls' School
Crosby

Liverpool Road, Crosby, Liverpool L23 5SP
Tel: 0151 924 3140
Fax: 0151 932 1461
e-mail: admissionsmtgs@merchanttaylors.com
website: www.merchanttaylors.com

Motto: *Concordia Parvae Res Crescunt*

Governors:
Chairman: Prof P W J Batey, BSc, MCD, PhD, FRTPI, FRSA, AcSS
P J R Evans, Esq, FCS, FCA
D R Jacks, Esq, LLB
Mrs V A P Johnson, BEd
P G Magill, Esq, MSc, FCIPD
R J Walker, Esq, CEng, MIMechE
Miss A Dobie, BA Hons
Mrs B Bell, LLB, FCILT, FRSA, FSOE, FIRTE
S Wilkinson, Esq, BA, FCA
D S Evans Esq, MA Oxon
Mrs J L Hawkins, RGN, RM

Bursar & Clerk to the Governors: Mrs A Pope, BA Hons, FCMA, ACIS, MSI

Headmistress: **Mrs L A Robinson**, BA Hons York, PGCE, NPQH, MEd Liverpool

First Deputy Headmistress: Miss J Tyndall, BD Hons/AKC King's College London

Deputy Headmistress: Mrs M L Bush, MA Liverpool, BMus Hons Wales, FRSA, NPQH

School Staff:
§ *part-time*

Art & Craft:
Mr M Gill, BA Hons Newcastle upon Tyne, MA Royal
  Academy
§Miss L McWatt, BA Hons Bristol

Biology:
Mrs J Johnson, MA Oxon, BSc OU
Mrs N Houghton, BSc Hons Liverpool John Moores
§Mrs L Dickinson IM Marsh College of PE, CertEd
Mr J S Jones, BSc Hons Liverpool
Dr M McWatt, PhD Birmingham, BSc Hons Birmingham

Business Studies:
Mrs A H Irwin, BA Hons Preston

Careers Coordinator:
Miss S Burke

Chemistry:
Mrs B Miller, BSc Hons Bristol
Mrs H Heaton, BSc Hons Durham
Dr M McWatt, PhD Birmingham, BSc Hons Birmingham
Mrs L Syms, BSc Hons Central Lancashire
Mrs V Copley, MChem Hons Manchester

Classics:
Mr D Lamb, MA Liverpool, BA Hons Liverpool
Mr M Routledge, BA Joint Hons Nottingham
Mr D Donnan, MA Cantab
Mrs A Wadsworth, BA Hons Durham

Drama & Theatre Studies:
Ms S Tickle, BA Manchester

English:
Mrs J Cecil, BA Joint Hons Aberystwyth, DipEd Liverpool
Mr D Donnan, MA Cantab
Mrs M Myring, MPhil Bangor, BA Hons UCNW, MA
  SDUC
§Mrs E Neophytou, BA Birmingham
Mrs A O'Connor, BA Joint Hons Lancaster
Mrs D Butler, BA Hons, Exeter

Geography:
Mrs C Mason, BSc Hons Manchester
Mrs H M Peppin, BSc Hons Leeds
Mrs R Hames, BSc Hons Leeds

Gifted and Talented:
Mrs M Hart, MA Liverpool, BA Hons Liverpool

History & Politics:
Mrs C Grindley, BA Hons Leeds
Mr G Evans, BA Hons Hull
Mrs S Heywood, MA Oxon

Home Economics:
Mrs M Hutchins, BA Hons Newcastle-Upon-Tyne
Mrs B Jones, BEd Liverpool

Information Technology:
Mr J Power, BEd Hons

Librarian:
Mrs A Barry, BLib Aberystwyth, MCLIP, Dip Arc

LDD Coordinator:
Miss L Rimmer

Mathematics:
Dr S R Barge, DPhil Oxon, BA Hons Oxon
§Mrs P M Carter, BSc Hons Liverpool
Mrs H F Hurst, BSc Joint Hons Keele
Mrs A Bradshaw, BSc Joint Hons Nottingham
Mr M Wood, BSc Hons Aberystwyth, MSc Dundee

Modern Languages:
Mrs C Y Whalley, BA Hons Leeds
Mrs J Doyle, BA Hons Nottingham
Mr R Griffiths, MA Manchester
Mrs F Menzies, CLA d'Abidjan

Mrs P Mistry, Licence University of Metz
Mr F Rubia
§Mrs C Southworth, BA Hons Bristol
Mrs S M Thomson, BEd Hons Liverpool

Music:
Director of Music: Mrs J Thompson, MA, BMus Hons
  Wales, ALCM
Mrs M L Bush, MA Liverpool, BMus Hons Wales, FRSA,
  NPQH

Visiting and Part-time Music Staff:
Miss J A Carr (*Voice*)
Miss S Hayes (*Voice*)
Mr S Lock (*Clarinet, Saxophone*)
Mr B Johnson (*Flute, Oboe*)
Mr D Bridge (*Guitar*)
Miss L Gregg (*Percussion*)
Mr D Byles (*Percussion*)
Miss D O'Hara (*Piano*)
Mrs J Richards ('*Cello, Double Bass*)
Mrs L Mycock (*Violin, Viola, Flute*)
Mr C Jones (*Clarinet, Saxophone*)
Mr M Palmer (*Brass*)

Physical Education:
Miss E Jones, BEd Hons Liverpool
§Mrs L Dickinson IM Marsh College of PE, CertEd
Mrs A P Stenson IM Marsh College of PE, CertEd

Physics:
Mr N Dalton, BSc Hons Manchester
Mrs H Heaton, BSc Hons Durham
Mr P Price, BSc Hons Leeds

PSHE Coordinator:
Mrs N Houghton, BSc Hons Liverpool John Moores

Psychology:
Miss S Ladbrook, BSc Hons Central Lancashire

Religious Studies:
Mrs G Vaughan, BA Hons Manchester
Mr B Wilson, BA Hons St David's Lampeter
Miss J Tyndall, BD Hons, AKC London

Marketing and Admissions:
Marketing & Development Director: Miss M J Riches, BA
  Hons
Marketing and Administrative Assistant: Miss L E Karban,
  BA Hons Liverpool
Admissions Officer: Mrs S Barrington

Administration:
PA to Headmistress: Mrs J Baccino
School Secretary: Mrs A Regan
Receptionists: Mrs A Cave, BA Hons Liverpool, Mrs J
  Kirkwood, Dip Counselling
Examinations: Mrs J E Custard, BSc Hons Coventry
Examinations Secretary: Mrs G Hurst
Computer Network Manager: Mr S Coughlan, BSc Hons
New Media and ICT Technician: Mr A Heighway-Sephton
Central Reprographics Manager: Mrs S Nield
Central Reprographics Assistants:
Mrs A Bramhall, Mr S Dixon, Mr A Best
Lab Technicians:
Mrs J Heckford, Mrs S Childs, Mrs S Cheetham, Miss L
  Harrison
School Nurse: Miss A Dalton, RGN, RSCN, Dip Child
  Health

Junior School 'Stanfield':
Head of Junior School: Miss J E Yardley, BA Hons
  Liverpool, PGCE, NPQH
Deputy Head: Mrs J Roberts, BEd Hons Lancaster

Miss V Beckerleg, BA Hons Leeds
Mrs J Birtwistle, BA Hons Loughborough
Mrs K Bonner, BA Hons London, MA Brighton

Mrs S Curwen, BEd Hons Lancaster
Mrs C Darbyshire, BTech Child Ed (*Nursery Nurse*)
Mrs A Dunne BSc Hons Coventry, MBA Open University
   (*Teaching Assistant*)
Mrs C Evans (*Netball Coach*)
Mrs S Garforth, BEd Hons Lancaster
Mrs L Gaskell, BA Hons Huddersfield
§Mrs J Hill, BEd Hons Coventry
Mrs A-L Hodkinson (*Swimming Coach*)
Mrs J Howard (*Infant PE*)
§Mrs R Loan, BA Hons Nottingham
Mrs L Lymath, NNEB (*Nursery Nurse*)
Mrs K MacKenzie, CertEd Bristol
Mrs S McEvoy, BA Hons Liverpool
§Mrs A Nagy, BEd Liverpool
Mrs C Oakes, BA Hons Manchester
Mrs J O'Mahony, BA, CertEd Lancaster
Mrs B Richardson, BEd London
Mr T Roberts, BA Hons Dunelm, ATCL
§Mrs S Ryan, NNEB (*Nursery Nurse*)
Mrs A Saunders (*Nursery Nurse*)
Mrs M Silverman, BA Hons Liverpool
Mrs S Taylor, BEd Leeds
Miss C Watkins, BA Hons Lancaster
Miss K Wilson, BA Hons
Mrs L Ramsdale, BA Hons

PA to Head: Mrs M Langham

ICT Coordinator: Ms A Crichton

Visiting Music Staff:
Miss H Burgoyne (*Piano*)
Ms L Gregg (*Percussion*)
Mr S Lock (*Flute, Clarinet, Saxophone, Oboe*)
Mrs L Mycock (*Violin*)
Mrs J Richards ('*Cello and Double Bass*)
Mrs S Rookyard (*Singing*)
Mr D Elliott (*Guitar*)

The Senior Girls' School was opened in 1888 on the site which had been occupied by the Boys' School for over 350 years; the original grey stone building, erected in 1620, is still in daily use as the Library. Extensions have been made from time to time including a Fitness Suite, Science Laboratories and Sixth Form Centre in 2007. The Centenary Hall provides exciting accommodation for concerts, plays and as a Sports Hall. The School is beautifully situated approximately 8 miles from Liverpool and within 10 minutes' walk of the Sefton coastline. There are Netball and Tennis Courts on the premises and a playing field a short distance away.

In 2009 the school took pleasure in opening its new Vitreum entrance which incorporates a reception and art gallery space. The Vitreum gallery has been used to showcase pupils work as well as exhibitions from local, national and international artists.

The Schools have recently completed a state-of-the-art Sports Centre built on the site of the Boys' School for use by all the Schools. The Centre incorporates a Sports Hall suitable for a variety of indoor sports, dance and fitness studios, a refreshment area and classrooms.

There is a separate Mixed Infants and Junior Girls' School situated in self-contained buildings near to the Main School with Girls aged 4–11, and Boys aged 4–7. The Senior Girls' School age range is 11–18. There are at present 900 pupils in the School.

The girls receive a broad academic education. Subjects included in the curriculum are the AQA Baccalaureate, Art, Astronomy, Biology, Chemistry, Classics, Drama and Theatre Studies, Economics, English Language and English Literature, French, Geography, German, Government and Politics, History, Home Economics, Information Technology, Latin, Mathematics, Music, Physical Education, Physics, Psychology, Religious Studies, and Spanish.

Fees per term (2011-2012). Senior School £3,125; Junior School £2,312.

Examinations. Pupils are prepared for the GCSE and A Level examinations.

The Music Examinations taken are those of the Associated Board of the Royal Schools of Music, The London College of Music, Trinity Guildhall.

Parent Teachers' Association. *Hon Sec*: Lynne Grimmant; *Chairperson*: Andy Oakes, c/o The School.

Old Girls' Association. *Hon Secretary*: Mrs S Duncan, 'Fairhaven', The Serpentine South, Liverpool L23 6UQ.

Charitable status. The Merchant Taylors' Schools Crosby is a Registered Charity, number 1125485, and a Company Limited by Guarantee, registered in England, number 6654276. Registered Office: Liverpool Road, Crosby, Liverpool L23 0QP.

Moira House Girls School

Upper Carlisle Road, Eastbourne, East Sussex BN20 7TE
Tel: 01323 644144
Fax: 01323 649720
e-mail: info@moirahouse.co.uk
website: www.moirahouse.co.uk

Established 1875.
   Motto: *Nemo A Me Alienus*

The Council:
Chairman: Ms J A Jackson-Hill, BA Hons, FRSA
   (*Company Director and former pupil*)
Dr P Frost, PhD, MSc, BA Hons (*University lecturer, parent of pupil*)
Mr P Hawley, FHCIMA (*Hotelier, parent of former pupil*)
Mrs J Henshaw, BSc Hons, ARICS, MAPS (*former pupil*)
Mrs J Herold, BSD, FDSRCPS, MSc, MOrth, RCS
   (*Consultant Orthodontist, parent*)
Mr Simon Dodds (*Solicitor and parent of former pupil*)
Mr Michael Ogilvie, FCA, CPC

The Common Room:
* *Head of Department*

Senior Management Team:

Principal: Mrs Lesley Watson, MA Ed, MInstD

Bursar: Mr David E Ingham, BSc, ACA (*Clerk to the Council*)
Head of Junior School: Mrs Linda Young, CertEd, NPQH
Deputy Principal: Mr Kevin D Ashby, MA, BA Hons, QTS
Director of Pastoral, Boarding and Sixth Form: Mrs Carol J Richards, BA, PGCE (*Business Studies, Economics and Careers*)
Director of Human Resources, CIPD: Mrs Patricia Gates
Director of Admissions: Mr James Harding
Staff Development Coordinator: Miss Aileen M Rickard, BSc, PGCE, NPQH (*Mathematics)

Senior School Staff:
Miss Gillian Aitken, MA, PGCE, RSA DipTEFL, Dip Psych, AMBDA (**EAL, English, Special Needs*)
Mrs Barbara E Ashby, GGSM, PGCE (*Music, Music Coordinator KS4 & 5*)
Miss Georgina Bates, BA Hons, BIPP (*Photography*)
Mrs Veronica Berry (*SENCO*)
Mrs Cheryl Burchett, BEd Hons (*Science Technician*)
Mrs Alison Burge, TDip RSA, BA (*EAL*)
Mr Peter Burge, BMus Hons, PGCE, ALCM (*Director of Music*)
Miss Dawn Cook, BEd (*Physical Education*)
Ms Nathalie Couture, BA Hons, MBA, PGCE (*French, Junior and Senior*)

Mr Stephen D Crum, BA Hons, PGCE (*Mathematics, KS3 Pastoral Coordinator*)

Miss Katharine M Fermor, BA Hons, PGCE (**History*)

Mrs Alison Gamester, BA Hons, PGCE (*Religious Education, History*)

Mrs Ruth Harris-Moss, BAHons, PGCE (**German, Deputy Head of Sixth Form*)

Mr Alan Hodge, BSc Hons, PGCE (*Examinations Officer*)

Miss Katherine A James, BA Hons, QTS (**PE*)

Mrs Natasha Jordan, Dip Prof Acting Hons (*Director of Drama*)

Mrs Jane Lambert, BA Hons (*KS5 Mathematics Coordinator*)

Mrs Ella Lewis, BA Hons (*Assistant Librarian*)

Mrs Jillian Lindley, FSRSB, AISTD (*Dance*)

Dr Fiona Mansfield, BSc, PhD (*Subject Leader Biology*)

Mr Duncan Martin, BA Hons, PGCE, CELTA (*EAL*)

Mrs Bernardine M Mcnamara, BA Hons, PGCE (*French*)

Mr Christopher M O'Reilly, BA Hons, PGCE, TEFL (*Spanish*)

Mrs Barbara Power, PG Dip, CertEd (**ICT*)

Mrs Lesley A Pyle, BEd Hons (*Physical Education*)

Miss Katie Reid, BEd Hons (*Physical Education, Mathematics*)

Mrs Moira Reid, BA Hons, PGCE (*Art*)

Mrs Claire Richard (*Languages; School Fundraiser*)

Mr Patrick Richard, BSc Hons, PGCE, AM Inst P (**Science, Physics*)

Mrs Sylvia Robinson, MIScT (*Laboratory Technician*)

Ms Linda Rosson, BA Hons, PGCE, MA (*English*)

Miss Hannah Savage (*Subject Leader Psychology*)

Mr Stephen M Simpson, BSc Hons, PGCE (*Science*)

Mrs Alison J Standen, BA Hons (*Senior Librarian*)

Ms Tamara Stevens, BSc Ed (**English*)

Mrs Sandra Twaites, BA Hons QTS (*Science*)

Mrs Alison Upton, BA Hons, PGCE (*Subject Leader Religious Education, PSHE*)

Mrs Siân Waite, MA, BA Hons (*English*)

Mrs Lucinda Westwood, BA Hons, PGCE, CTEFLA

Mrs Pamela J Wigmore, CertEd, CTEFLA (*Food Technology*)

Mrs Karen Williames, BA Hons, PGCE (*Subject Leader Art*)

Mrs Jacqueline Wood, BSc Hons, PGCE (*Geography, Science*)

Mr Stephen Wood, MA Ed, BA Hons, PGCE (**Business Studies & Economics*)

Administration:

Mrs Linda Burnett (*School Receptionist*)

Mrs Jayne Hollister-Sheppard (*School Accountant*)

Mrs Anna Ingham (*Old Girls Liaison*)

Mr Kevin R Ives, BSc Hons (*IT Manager*)

Mr Graham James, MIH (*Operations Manager*)

Miss Rhiannon Jones (*School Office Administrator*)

Mrs Nicola Langford (*Principal's PA*)

Mrs Laurie Marsden (*Admissions and Marketing Administrator*)

Mrs Jane K Mole (*Database Administrator*)

Mrs Elizabeth Powell (*Bursar's Secretary*)

Mr Eric Reynolds (*Marketing*)

Mrs Jayne Ring (*Accountant's Assistant*)

Mr Jonathan Whale (*IT Support Administrator*)

Junior School Staff:

Mrs Linda Young, CertEd, NPQH (*Head of Junior School*)

Mrs Theresa Bees, BSc, QTS (*Year 2 Teacher*)

Mrs Jane Fisher, BEd (*Year 4 Teacher, Head of KS2*)

Mrs Lisa J Gough, BA Ed Hons (*Year 3 Teacher*)

Mrs Annette Hacker, NVQ3 (*Teaching Assistant*)

Mr Christopher Kerswell, BA Hons (*Year 5 Teacher*)

Mrs Wendy Lambert, BA Hons, PGCE (*Physical Education*)

Mrs Fiona D Martirossian, BA Hons, PGCE (*Year 1 Teacher*)

Mr Martin Neill, Dip Mus, BMus Hons, PGCE (*Head of Junior School Music*)

Mrs Karon F Pont (*Teaching Assistant*)

Mrs Ruth M Sibson, BEd (*SEN, Year 6 Teacher and Deputy Head of Junior School*)

Mrs Linda Whicker (*Lunchtime Supervision, After School Club Supervisor*)

Junior School Administration:

Mrs Jennifer Hafernik (*Junior School Secretary*)

Mrs Anne Head (*School Administrator*)

Nursery:

Mrs Sarah Hughes, BTEC Nat Dip Childcare (*Head of Nursery*)

Miss Carly Brooks, Dip Childcare & Education (*Deputy Nursery Manager*)

Mrs Judith H Partridge, Dip Childcare & Education (*Nursery Nurse*)

Miss Helen Wallis, NVQ2 Childcare (*Nursery Nurse*)

Miss Carly Winter (*Nursery Nurse*)

Residential House Staff:

Mrs Christine Armstrong, BA Hons, CertEd, Dep TEFL (*Senior Residential Housemistress, Boston House, Activities Coordinator*)

Mrs Jenny Shuman (*Residential Housemistress, School House*)

Mrs Samia Slim (*Residential Housemistress, School House*)

Medical Centre:

Dr K Leeson, MBBS, DCH, DRCOG, FPA Cert (*School Doctor*)

Mrs Irene Hatton, RGN (*Sister*)

Mrs Audrey Bushnell, RGN (*Sister*)

Mrs Tracy Martin, RGN (*Bank Sister*)

Swimming Pool:

Mrs Claire L Bryant, FIST, IOS ISTC (*Pool Manager*)

Mr Paul Standen-Payne (*Swimming Teacher*)

Ms Wendy Pritchard, ISTC (*Swimming Teacher*)

Visiting Staff:

Miss Clare Adams, CertEd, LRSM Dip, ABRSM, ALCM, Dip LCM (*Brass*)

Mr Mark Ashworth (*Youth Worker, All Saints Church*)

Mr Jonathan Chappell (*Percussion*)

Mrs Maeve Cooper, Dip RCM Perf, Dip RCM Ten (*Violin*)

Miss Valerie Dent (*LAMDA*)

Miss Eileen Godier, GLSM, LLCM TD, ALCM, PGCE (*Piano, Wind*)

Ms Susan Gregg, BA, ABRSM (*Flute*)

Mrs Maki Hallinon, Cert FET (*Japanese*)

Mr Michael Hatchard (*Piano*)

Mrs Franciska Laursen, DRS (*Piano*)

Revd Robert Lovatt (*School Chaplain, All Saints Church*)

Miss Vieda Mercer, BMus Hons (*Violin*)

Mr Kevin Pallister (*LAMDA*)

Mrs Elaine Patience, BA Dip, NCOS (*Violin, Viola*)

Mrs Rebecca Swingle Putland (*Singing Teacher*)

Ms Angelika Schlussel, MA (*Languages Teacher*)

Ms Helen Sheppard (*Voice Coach*)

Mr Michael B Shirley, BA (*Guitar*)

Ms Esther Ward-Caddle, BA Hons (*Cello*)

Mr Wancai Zhong, BA Eng (*Mandarin*)

Foundation. Moira House was founded in 1875 in Surrey. The School moved to its present site in 1887. The founders, Mr and Mrs Charles Ingham, were regarded in their time as gifted pioneers in the field of female education. In 1947 the School was converted into an Educational Trust. The Principal is in membership of the Girls' Schools Association, the Boarding Schools' Association and the British Council and is an associate member of SHMIS.

Situation and Facilities. Situated on high ground in Eastbourne with views over the sea, the grounds open directly onto the Downs which provide magnificent walking country and offer opportunities for expedition work and field studies. There are extensive playing fields with facilities for Tennis, Cricket, Soccer, Hockey, Netball and Athletics, a 25-metre indoor heated swimming pool and an excellent all-weather sports hall. Each subject has its own resource base. Eastbourne is a thriving cultural centre containing 3 theatres, an art gallery and a concert hall.

Faith. The School is inter-denominational.

Organisation. *Junior School* (IAPS): The Junior School has provision for 120 day girls starting at age 2 and junior boarders starting from the age of 9. (*See Junior School entry in IAPS section.*)

Senior School: The Senior School has provision for 120 boarders and 150 day girls.

Boarding Houses: There are two boarding houses, one of which is dedicated to Sixth Form students with single and twin study-bedrooms. Each house has a team combining resident staff and house mothers. Emphasis is placed upon a full range of extra-curricular activities, both in the evenings and at weekends.

Curriculum. *Junior School:* We offer a wide curriculum, whilst preparing for transfer to the Senior School.

Senior School: The formal academic courses follow a broad curriculum offering 22 subjects leading to GCSE, AS and A Level and University Entrance. At GCSE we offer English, English Literature, Mathematics, Additional Mathematics, Biology, Chemistry, Physics, Science, French, German, Spanish, Latin, History, Geography, Religious Studies, Music, Economics, Photography, Drama, Art and Design, Design/Technology, ICT, Physical Education and Statistics.

Sixth Form: A Levels are offered in Art, Craft and Design, Biology, Business Studies, Chemistry, Drama and Theatre Studies, Economics, English Literature, Further Mathematics, Geography, History, ICT, French, German, Spanish, Mathematics, Music, Photography, Physical Education, Physics, Psychology and Religious Studies.

Careers Counselling. We have a strong programme of Careers Counselling, led by our Careers Counsellor.

Drama and Music. Drama and Music have always been strengths of Moira House. We are aware of the part Speech and Drama play in the development of clear communication and creative expression. There are a number of School productions and concerts each year, and school choirs take part in performances throughout Sussex. We also enter the local festival of Music and Drama and proximity to Glyndebourne gives girls a chance to have their first taste of opera at an early age. As well as regular class music lessons, there is every opportunity to learn a musical instrument, and the exams of the various musical examining bodies are taken. There is also a state-of-the-art recording studio. Overseas tours to Europe, America, Australia, Dubai and Hong Kong also take place bi-annually.

Physical Education and Sport. We provide excellent new facilities. The main sports are Swimming, Netball, Tennis, Athletics and Hockey, and teams represent the School in these and in cricket and football. In addition, coaching is given in Sailing, Riding, Squash, Dance, Golf and Badminton.

Activities. Activities are considered an essential part of the curriculum. Many activities are offered, including: Drama, Music, Trampolining, Pottery, Chess, Local History, Sailing, Down-walking, Environmental Studies, Poetry/Play Reading, Table Tennis, Duke of Edinburgh's Award, Mandarin, Japanese, and Debating. Girls are also encouraged to be aware of the needs of others. Old people and disabled people are visited on a regular basis and senior girls work with local charities. There are annual expeditions both within this country and to Europe and the School has links with French, German and international schools of a similar nature to ours.

Health. The school doctor holds regular surgeries at the School and there are Sisters in charge of the health centre.

Entry. Entry is by interview and review of previous school reports and references. Admission to the Junior School at any age; to the Senior School usually at 11–13+ and 16+.

Scholarships and Bursaries. (*See Scholarship Entries section.*)

Fees per term (2011-2012). Senior School: £4,140–£4,765 (Day Pupils); £6,535–£7,710 (Weekly Boarders); £7,340–£8,510 (Boarders).

Junior School: £2,050–£3,740 (Day Pupils); £6,170 (Weekly Boarders); £6,640 (Boarders).

Charitable status. Moira House Girls School is a Registered Charity, number 307072. It exists to provide quality education for young women.

More House School

22–24 Pont Street, London SW1X 0AA
Tel: 020 7235 2855; Bursar: 020 7235 4162
Fax: 020 7259 6782
e-mail: office@morehouse.org.uk
website: www.morehouse.org.uk

Governing Body:
Chairman: Mr J Davidson, BA, OBE
Mr P I Ewings, BA Belfast, Solicitor of the Supreme Court in England and Wales
Fr K J Fox, SJ, MA Oxon
Mr J Fyfe, BA Birmingham
Mr J C McIntosh, OBE, MA Sussex, FRSA, HonFASC, HonFCP
Ms N Patel, BA Nottingham Trent, MCIPD, CQSW
Mrs S Shale, BA Birmingham, FCA (*Vice-Chairman*)
Mrs S Sturrock, BMus London, ARCM
Mr J W Wates, MA Oxon, BSc, FRICS

Clerk to the Governors: Mr D D A Leslie, BA London, MA London

Headmaster: Mr R M Carlysle, BA Hons, MBA, AKC, PGCE, Cert Dysl & Lit, MCollP

Deputy Head: Mrs A Leach, BSc Liverpool

Senior Teachers:
Mrs A Blenkinsop, BA Newcastle
Mrs G Clapham, BSc Reading
Mr M R Keeley, BMus London, MSc Manchester
Mrs A Maudsley, BA London

Bursar: Ms J Milligan

Chaplain: Father Peter Burrows, PhD, MTh, BFS, Lic MFCC

PA to the Headmaster and Registrar: Ms A McCarthy
Admissions: Ms M George-McFarlane, BA London

Staff:
* *Head of Department*

Ms L Beatty, BA London (**Art*)
Mr R Benson, BA London (*Geography*)
Mrs A Blenkinsop, JP, BA Newcastle (*Mathematics, Latin*)
Miss S Brown, BA Bristol (*French*)
Mrs G Clapham, BSc Reading (*Biology, Chemistry*)
Ms G Collins, BA Birmingham (**History*)
Ms J P Crowe, BSc Aberdeen, MA London (*Chemistry, Physics*)
Miss E Crozier, BA Cambridge, MA Cambridge (*English and Drama*)
Miss K Devine, BA Bristol (*Art*)

Miss K Eccles, BA Cambridge (*History of Art*)
Mr M C A Ginever, BSc Exeter (*Mathematics)
Ms C Gremillet, BA Leeds, MA London (*French, Spanish*)
Mrs M Haig, MA Glasgow (*History, Geography*)
Mr P Hegarty, BA London (*English*)
Miss F Ho, BA Southampton (*Music*)
Miss C Hungerford, BA Edinburgh (*Biology*)
Mr M R Keeley, BMus London (*Music)
Mrs A Leach, BSc Liverpool (*Biology*)
Mr A Lloyd, BSc Birmingham (*Physics)
Miss A Maher, BSc Bangor (*PE*)
Mrs P A Maudsley, BA London (**German, French*)
Ms J North, BA London (*English)
Mrs V Parrott, BA London (*French*)
Miss S Reimer, BEd Manitoba (*Learning Support*)
Ms P Revell, BA Wellington, NZ, TIC, DipT NZ
  (*Economics*)
Ms D Rigby, MA Chelsea (*Art*)
Mrs R Smith, BA Durham (**Religious Studies*)
Mrs J Taylor, BA Bristol (*Drama*)
Miss C Vardon, MMath Oxon (*Mathematics*)
Mrs A Williams, MA Cantab (*Learning Support*)
Miss J Zloof, BA Birmingham, MA London (*Classics*)

Mr S Keeley (*Network Manager*)
Miss M Barratt (*Science Technician*)

Peripatetic staff:
Mrs T Henderson, ISTD (*Dancing*)
Ms D Matthews Forth, RAD TC, BBO TD, IDTA T, IDTA
  M
(*plus various instrumental teachers*)

More House is an Independent Day School of up to 220 girls between the ages of eleven and eighteen. It occupies two adjoining houses, conveniently situated in Knightsbridge, retaining many of the original architectural features, but modernised to include four laboratories, two computer rooms, common rooms, study room and computer room for the sixth form, a chapel, a library and a newly refurbished drama and dance studio. More House is a small and happy community in which a generous teacher: pupil ratio allows the talents of each girl to flourish with all the stimulus and encouragement that she needs. The maximum class size is normally fifteen, streamed where necessary in mathematics, science and languages. All girls leaving the Sixth Form proceed to Higher Education, including Oxbridge, and then to careers in every field. Girls are given full advice about careers and Higher Education.

A Catholic Foundation, More House was opened in 1953 by the Canonesses of St Augustine; since 1969 it has been under lay management as a charitable trust and with a Board of Governors which has always included parents of present pupils. More House celebrated its Golden Jubilee in the academic year 2003–2004. The School attracts pupils from a wide area of London. More House warmly welcomes girls of all faiths.

Places at the school are usually awarded on the basis of an interview, a report from the candidate's previous school, and an examination held in January each year. Girls who join us in the Sixth Form are required to have achieved grades A–C in at least five subjects at GCSE Level.

Our level of pastoral care is very high indeed, supporting the girls in all aspects of their lives.

Instrumental tuition is available in school and in recent years the School Choir has given performances in Portugal, Spain, Paris, Rome, Malta and the USA. The most recent school choral concert featured our five choirs performing Carmina Burana. Full advantage is taken of the school's position in Central London and regular visits to lectures, galleries and exhibitions are organised. In 2008, six Year 11 Art pupils had their GCSE performance placed in the top 10 nationally.

Extra-curricular activities include Music, Drama, Sport, Dance, Art, Fencing, Photography and the Duke of Edinburgh's Award Scheme and World Challenge Expeditions. The latest school drama production was 'The Mikado' performed at the POSK Theatre in Hammersmith.

The Curriculum. The school curriculum offers a wide range of subjects at all levels. In the first two years all girls study Mathematics, Science, English, French, German, Latin, History, Geography, Religious Studies, Information Technology, Drama, Art, Physical Education and Music. Spanish is added in Year 9, giving the possibility of taking two modern languages at GCSE, where the core curriculum of Mathematics, Science, English Language and Literature and Religious Studies is supplemented by four further options.

The Advanced Level courses offered are structured around each girl's choice of subjects, new options available at this stage being History of Art, Business Studies, Classical Civilisation, Economics, Physical Education, Textiles and Theatre Studies; further breadth of study is achieved through a General Studies programme. Each subject has its own specialist rooms and for Physical Education the excellent sport and leisure facilities available in the neighbourhood are used.

Fees per term (from January 2011). £4,685 including lunch, stationery and some educational visits. Academic and Music Scholarships are available on merit.

Charitable status. More House Trust is a Registered Charity, number 312737. It exists to provide an academic education for girls aged 11 to 18 within the framework of a Catholic Day School.

Moreton Hall

Weston Rhyn, Oswestry, Shropshire SY11 3EW
Tel: 01691 773671
Fax: 01691 778552
e-mail: forsterj@moretonhall.com
website: www.moretonhall.org

Moreton Hall was founded in 1913 by Ellen Lloyd-Williams (Aunt Lil) in Oswestry and moved to its present location in 1920. In 1964, the school became an educational trust. Although the school is predominantly boarding, a number of day pupils are admitted each year.

Member of GSA, AGBIS, ISCO.

Governing Body:

Chairman: N Bevan, MA

L A C Ashby, BA
R Auger, MA
Christine, Lady Bibby
Dr L V Boon, MBBS, LLCPMRS
D Edwards (*Chairman of Finance Committee*)
Mrs J France-Hayhurst, LLB Hons
R Graham-Wood, MA, FRICS
M Heath
Mrs K Neilson
Mrs D Rylands
Mrs S Tunstall
C Waters, BA

Principal: **J Forster**, MA, FRSA

Vice Principal: Mrs C Tilley, GRNCM, PPRNCM
Head of Moreton First: Mrs S Mostyn, BSc, MA
Assistant Head/Registrar: Miss S Hughes, MTheol
Director of Studies: J Peat, BA

Teaching Staff:
* *Head of Department*
† *Housemaster/mistress*

Mrs C Ashworth, BEd (*Business Studies*)
Mrs J Barlow, BA (*Special Needs Coordinator*)
Miss C Barnardo (*Physical Education, Games*)
Mrs S Bayton, DipEd (*Food Technology*)
Miss J Blanchard, BA (**Religious Studies*)
Mrs K Booth, HND (*Business Studies*)
Miss K Bromley, BA (*Geography, History*)
Mrs J Cantrill, BSc (*Biology*)
Miss L Challiner, ELS (*Moreton First*)
Mrs S Champion, MSc (*Science, ICT*)
T Corbett, BSc (*Chemistry*)
T Davidson, MA (**English*)
Miss A Davies, BA (*Music*)
Miss M Davies, BA (*Moreton First*)
Mrs C Dilks (*Lacrosse Coach*)
Mrs V Eastman, MA, (**EFL*)
M Edmunds, BA, MA, PhD (*German*)
I Edwards, BA, MA (**Art*)
Ms S Evans, BA (*Spanish*)
Mrs L Eyre, BA (**French*)
Mrs J Field, BEd (**Food Technology*)
I Fitton, BSc (**Mathematics*)
Mrs C Ford, MA, BSc (*Deputy Head Moreton First*)
Mrs P M Forster, BA, DipLib (*Assistant Librarian*)
Mrs A Greaney, BA, MA (*French*)
Miss P Greenhalgh, BSc (*Physics*)
Miss I Grisdale, BA (*Religious Studies*)
Miss K Groves, BCom, MSc (**Physical Education;
†Pilkington House*)
Miss M Halsall-Williams, BA, LGSM, ALAM, FESB
(*Spoken English*)
Mrs K Hatcher, BA (*EFL*)
P Hillier, BSc, PhD (*ICT Coordinator; Biology*)
Mrs K Howells, BA (*Drama*)
Miss S Hughes (*Assistant Head, Registrar, Religious
Education, †Lloyd-Williams House*)
Mrs H Ingoldby, BA (*German, EFL*)
Mrs J Knight, CertEd (*Drama*)
Mr D Kynes, BSc (*Chemistry*)
Mrs C Lang, BA, MA (*English*)
Mrs E Langford, BA (*Art*)
Mrs C Lapage, BMus,MA, ARCO (*Music*)
Miss S Lee, BA (*Chinese*)
Mrs L Lewin, BEd (*Lacrosse*)
Mrs V Lewis, BA (*English*)
A Macdonald-Brown, MA (*English & Drama*)
Mrs A J Matthews, BSc, MSc (*Economics*)
Mrs R McKechnie, MA (*Careers*)
Miss J Milner, BA (*Moreton First*)
Mrs J Morton, MA (**Classics*)
J Nanson, BA, MA (**Geography*)
Miss A Neal, BA (*Geography*)
Mrs E Nolan, BA (*Librarian*)
T Nolan, BEd (**ICT*)
Mrs H Paul, MA (*English*)
J Peat, BA (*Director of Studies, Mathematics, Physics*)
Mrs S Peat, BSc (*Mathematics; †Charlesworth House*)
Mrs H Peel, MA, MSc (*Biology and Chemistry*)
Mrs N Perry, BEd (*Moreton First*)
Mrs H Rayner, BMus (**Director of Music*)
D Reffell, BA (**History*)
Mrs A Rincon, RSA CELTA (*EFL, †Rylands House*)
Miss S Roberts, BA, MA (*Latin*)
Mrs J Sanderson, BEd (**Lacrosse*)
Mrs A Simpson, BA, MA (*Careers Advisor*)
R Singleton, BSc (**Science*)
B Sutcliffe, BA (*Moreton First*)
Mrs B Taylor, BA (*Mathematics*)
Mrs S Thomas, BSc (*Mathematics*)
Mrs C Tilley, GRNCM, PPRNCM (*Vice Principal, Music,
†Gem House*)
Ms J Yu (*Chinese*)

School Doctors:
Dr J Roberts, BA, MA, BMBCH, MRCP, DRCOG,
MRCGP, DFFP
Dr E Thompson, MBChB
School Sister:
Sister A Davies, RGN

Admission. Moreton First takes girls and boys from Reception to Year 6.

Girls are admitted to Moreton Hall, normally in September at the age of 11 and 13, either by Common Entrance or by the School's entrance examination which is held at the end of January each year. This examination requires no knowledge of foreign languages and is designed to test potential ability rather than factual recall. This examination can be taken by pupils at 10+, and with supplementary papers at 12 and 13. Candidates from preparatory schools may enter through Common Entrance if they so choose at 11, 12 and 13. Sixth Form entrance is by current school report and interview, and numbers are limited. All applications should be addressed to the Principal.

Though predominantly boarding, day girls are welcomed.

Scholarships. (*See Scholarship Entries section.*) A number of scholarships worth up to 10% of fees will be made to pupils at 11+, 12+, 13+ and 16+. Students may apply for more than one scholarship. Awards for Music, Drama, Art and for outstanding sporting talent are made at 11+, 12+, 13+ and 16+. Means-tested bursaries may be awarded up to the value of 100% of fees.

Fees per term (2011-2012). Boarders: £5,910 (Moreton First), £8,640 (Years 7 and 8), £9,115 (Years 9–13). Day Girls: £2,570–£3,620 (Moreton First), £6,900 (Years 7 and 8), £7,465 (Years 9–13).

Curriculum. Going well beyond the National Curriculum, some 20 subjects are available at GCSE, varying from traditional academic subjects such as Latin and the Sciences, to practical subjects such as Drama, Dance and Physical Education. Modern Languages available include French, German, Spanish, Mandarin Chinese and Russian. A Levels in History of Art, Social Biology, Business Studies and Theatre Studies extend the range of the curriculum. Information Technology is a compulsory subject up to Sixth Form, optional thereafter.

Examinations offered. GCSE (MEG, SEG, NEAB, London), A Level (Oxford, JMB, London). ABRSM (English Speaking Board). Over three quarters of second year Sixth Form go on to University.

Religious activities. Non-denominational. Weekday service, longer service on Sunday, visiting preacher.

Academic, Sporting and Extra-Curricular facilities. Moreton Hall is engaged in an ambitious development programme and has facilities of the highest quality designed to provide the right environment for the education of girls in the twenty-first century.

Younger girls are housed in the Stables building under the supervision of resident houseparents, assistants and matrons. The building is designed to create a family atmosphere with dormitories split into smaller units, close to common rooms, washrooms and staff accommodation.

As pupils progress up the school, the dormitories are gradually replaced by double and finally single study bedrooms, as girls move from middle school houses to the new Sixth Form Houses which provide single and double ensuite facilities. Here, within the structure of a boarding school, senior girls are given the necessary freedom to prepare for the next stage in their careers.

The laboratories, Information Technology rooms and Art and Design Centre are housed within a short distance of the central classroom, careers and library complex.

In 1999 a new ICT development plan was implemented to network classrooms, libraries and laboratories linked to a new ICT Centre. All classrooms, libraries and boarding houses are networked and all Sixth Formers have internet access from their study-bedrooms.

An exceptionally well-equipped Sports Centre comprising a sports hall and floodlit tennis courts along with a heated indoor swimming pool, tennis courts, nine-hole golf course, a new all-weather surface, and playing fields are set in one hundred acres of beautiful parkland at the foot of the Berwyn hills. The school offers a wide range of sporting options, including Lacrosse, Netball, Hockey, Cricket, Tennis and Athletics. Sailing and Riding are also popular.

The Musgrave Theatre, Outdoor Theatre and Music School stimulate theatrical and musical activities ranging from house plays, lunchtime shows and jazz evenings through to ambitious school plays and orchestral concerts. A full digital sound studio was completed in 2000. Great emphasis is placed on girls taking part in as wide a range of extra-curricular interests as possible.

The nationally acclaimed Moreton Enterprises offers the girls real business experience. Supervised by professional advisers but all run by the girls themselves, Moreton Enterprises consists of 5 retail businesses on site with a turnover of £35,000.

Old Moretonian Association. Katy Tanner, c/o Moreton Hall.

Charitable status. Moreton Hall Educational Trust Limited is a Registered Charity, number 528409. It exists to provide a high quality education for girls.

The Mount School

Milespit Hill, Mill Hill, London NW7 2RX
Tel: 020 8959 3403
Fax: 020 8959 1503
e-mail: admin@mountschool.com
website: www.mountschool.com

School motto: *Esse quam videre – to be rather than to seem to be.*

Chair of Governors: Mrs S Williamson

Headteacher: Ms C Cozens, BSc Exeter, PGCE, NPQH

Assistant Headteacher (Curriculum): Mrs A Lalova, MA Blagoevgrad Bulgaria
Assistant Headteacher (Pastoral): Mrs S Mitchell, BA John Moores, PGCE
Co-opted Member SMT: Mrs J Smith, BSc Hons Edinburgh, PGCE Manchester
Head of Juniors: Miss J Sweeney, BSc Hons London, BA Hons Open, LLAM

Head of Art: Mr J Sumray, BA Brighton
Head of Classics: Ms R Wiley, MA Cambridge
Head of Design & Technology: Mr C McKay, BA Hons, BTEC, GTP
Head of Drama: Mrs N Stimler, BA Hons, PGCE
Head of Economics: Mrs C Collins, BA North London, CertEd
Head of English: Mrs C Hughes, MA Newcastle upon Tyne, PGCE
Head of ESOL: Miss K Ferson, BA Hons Sussex, Dip TEFLA, MA
Head of Geography: Ms A Perez, BA Oviedo, Spain, CAP
Head of History: Mr Havardi, MA, MPhil, BA Hons, PGCE
Head of ICT: Mrs C Mrozek, HND
Head of Mathematics: Mr B Broadhurst, MA Cantab, PGCE
Head of Modern Languages: Mrs G Hutcheon, BA Hons, MA, PGCE
Director of Music: Mrs N Hirsch, BMus RCM, ARCM, PGCE

Head of PE: Mrs J Rafter, BA Hons QTS Surrey
Head of PHSEE and Exams: Miss K Lingwood, BEd Liverpool
Head of Science: Mr A Ward, BA Canberra, PGCE

Bursar: Mr N Webb, MA Oxon, ACA
Registrar: Mrs P Lewis
PA to Headteacher: Miss L Hutchings, CSBM Anglia

The Mount School is a GSA Independent day school for girls aged 4 to 16. It was founded in 1925 to provide a school where the personalities of the children could develop along wide and individual lines and where a true love of learning for its own sake could be fostered. This caring and nurturing environment continues to this day.

Curriculum. We offer a well-rounded academic environment where girls are given the opportunity to develop their full potential, balancing intellectual growth with physical, emotional, cultural, spiritual, creative and moral growth enabling them to make positive contributions as good citizens in all realms of their future lives.

Early Years: The Early Years Foundation Stage goals form the basis on which later learning will grow. These include: personal, social and emotional development; communication, language and literacy; problem solving, reasoning and numeracy; knowledge and understanding of the world; physical development and creative development. A profile of development is established forming a clear picture of the needs and abilities of each girl.

Infants: The education provided builds on their existing knowledge and skills. We offer a structure for learning with a range of starting points, content that matches each girls' needs and activities that provide opportunities for learning in a variety of ways. This provides a rich and stimulating environment.

Juniors: We give our girls appropriate work to challenge and consolidate their knowledge to provide the best opportunity for progression in their learning. We use assessment throughout the department to assist planning and teaching. From Year 6 we provide a smooth transition into the Senior School.

Girls take part in whole school productions and have use of both Junior and Senior School facilities. Girls have specialist teachers for PE, Drama, French, Japanese, Design Technology and Music. Swimming, ballet and jazz dance are popular junior lessons. We organise a wide range of visits, trips and activities to enrich our curriculum and to allow girls to experience learning in a wider environment.

Seniors: In the Senior School the girls experience a broad and balanced curriculum; a mixture of Mathematics and Music, Science and Drama, English and Physical Education, Religious Education and Modern Languages, Classical Civilisation, Design Technology and Art, amongst others. Above all, we aim to enable each girl to develop both academically and holistically, encouraging new skills, providing new opportunities, and developing a sense of responsibility – all within a caring family ethos. The class sizes are small, giving the girls the opportunity to grow in confidence, participate in their learning and fulfil their potential.

A rich and varied extra-curricular programme enhances the girls' academic work. Senior girls have the opportunity to become School Parliament, House and Sports captains, working with girls across the school as leaders and role models.

ESOL: Our ESOL (English for Speakers of Other Languages) Department serves girls from overseas who join us speaking little or no English. Girls are assessed when they enter the School and a personalised programme of study with trained specialists, is created.

Method of Entry. Open Events are held each half term. Dates are published on the website. The Registrar oversees the admissions process and can be contacted by telephone on 020 8238 8108 or by e-mail to registrar@mountschool.com.

Junior School: We have a 4+ entry into reception class each September. Those registered are invited to attend an assessment day in the January prior to entry. At the assessment we judge whether or not a new girl will fit happily into the class and will be able to keep up academically.

Senior School: We have an 11+ entry into Year 7 each September. Those registered sit an entrance examination in the January prior to entry. This examination is also sat by girls in our own Junior School. The examination consists of papers in Mathematics and English and is based on the Key Stage 2 syllabus. Places are allocated to those who pass the examination and are considered most able to make a positive contribution to school life.

Occasional vacancies across all years may occur. Applicants for mid year or non 4+ and 11+ places are asked to spend a half or whole day in school, carry out an assessment and spend time in class with our pupils.

Overseas pupils: It is possible for girls from overseas to sit the entrance papers at their own school, under the supervision of the British Embassy or a nominated educational representative.

Fees per term (2011-2012). £2,915–£3,775.

Scholarships. The Mount School awards scholarships at two stages:

Year 7: Academic Scholarships are awarded to girls who achieve the highest scores in our entrance exam papers. These scholarships apply until the end of Year 9 and will be up to a maximum of 20% of fees, to be distributed at the Headteacher's discretion.

Music Scholarships are awarded by the Director of Music. Applicants must have a minimum of grade 4 in an instrument of their choice. Candidates for these scholarships attend a music assessment. Two scholarships will be awarded and will apply until the end of Year 9. Music Scholars will be expected to join the school Orchestra.

Year 10: Academic scholarships are awarded to the top scorers in the end of Year 9 exams. These scholarships are valid until the end of Year 11 and will be up to a maximum of 20% of fees, to be distributed at the Headteacher's discretion.

Music Scholarships are awarded to two girls at the discretion of the Director of Music. Applicants must have a minimum of grade 6 in an instrument of their choice. These scholarships are valid until the end of Year 11.

Bursaries. The Governors of The Mount School are committed to broadening access to the school by offering to eligible parents/guardians means-tested financial support with the payment of school fees.

Bursary awards are subject to repeat testing of parental means each year and may be varied upwards or downwards, depending on parental circumstances.

Charitable status. The Mount School is a Registered Charity, number 312593.

The Mount School
York

Dalton Terrace, York YO24 4DD
Tel: 01904 667500
          01904 667529 (Registrar)
Fax: 01904 667524
e-mail: registrar@mountschoolyork.co.uk
website: www.mountschoolyork.co.uk

Motto: *Fidelis in Parvo*

Founded in 1785, it moved to its present site in 1857 – a beautiful 16-acre campus with splendid gardens, mature trees and playing fields. The facilities are excellent; subjects are taught in specialist rooms with full access to modern technology. There is a drama suite, multi-purpose sports hall and fitness suite, a 25m indoor swimming pool, grass tennis courts and a sixth-form centre. The Junior School uses many of the senior school's facilities.

A Quaker school, its ethos is to encourage and develop the individual within a small, caring community. It prides itself on a welcoming atmosphere but aims, also, for academic excellence. It has all the advantages of a small school, with a good staff:pupil ratio. Examination results are excellent. Very strong in Mathematics, Science, music, drama and art. Also offers the AQA Baccalaureate including the Extended Project Qualification. Much involvement in local cultural activities and full use is made of the city's amenities, plus expeditions further afield. There is a wide range of sport and games (many regional and national representatives) and extra-curricular activities. Also a big commitment to local community services, Prince's Trust, Independent and State Schools Partnership, AEGIS and an outstanding record in the Duke of Edinburgh's Award Scheme.

Committee of Management:
Clerk: Elisabeth Wilson
Secretary: Julie Davis

Christopher Moore	Roger Pierce
Denise Stimson	Aileen McLeish
Sarah Woods	Trina Mawer
Philip Green	Stephanie Bilton
Adam Sinclair	

Staff:

Principal: **Julie Lodrick**, BA Hons University College, Chichester, West Sussex, NPQH National College for School Leadership, Cert Professional Practice in Boarding Mgt BSA and Roehampton, MA Ed Mgt Open University, PGCE Kingston

Deputy Head: Victoria Sherwood, BEd Manchester

Director of Studies: Michael Lingard, MA Oxon, PGCE Bristol

Head of Sixth Form: Joanne Hayward, MA Cambridge, PGCE Leeds

Heads of Departments/Subjects:
English: Louise Williams, BA Hons Lancaster, PGCE Eltham College
Mathematics: Helen Mumby, BSc London, PGCE Durham
Modern Languages: Cherry Bailey, BA Hons Cantab, PGCE Sheffield
Latin, Greek and Classical Studies: A Rosemary McEvoy, BA Hons Lancaster, PGCE Nottingham
Science: Anthony Welbrock, BSc Hons Edinburgh
Religious Education: Linda Moore, BEd Hons Sussex, MA College of Ripon & York St John
History: Helen Snelson, BA Hons Oxon, MSc Hull, PGCE York
Geography: Carol Cook, BA Hons London, PGCE Newcastle upon Tyne
Art & Design: Sian Gabraitis, BA Hons Bristol, PGCE Cardiff
Design Technology: Rachel Milton, BA Hons, PGCE Coll of Ripon & York St John, MSc Huddersfield
Business Studies and IT: David Blamires, BA Hons Humberside, PGCE Leeds
Music: Derek Chivers, BA Hons York, DPhil Keele, PGCE Open University
Special Needs Coordinator: Juliet Bleasdale, BA Hons Sheffield, PGCE Bath
Sociology: Gerry Hallom, BA Hons York, PGCE Huddersfield
Psychology: (*to be appointed*)
Physical Education: Rachel Blatchford, BSc Hons, PGCE Loughborough

Careers: Wendy A Thompson, CertEd Edge Hill College, Lancaster, CFPS Cambridge

English as an Additional Language: Jo Soden, MA York, BA Hons Bristol, PGCE York

Learning Support (Dyslexia): Juliet Bleasdale, BA Hons Sheffield, PGCE Bath

Librarian: (*to be appointed*)

Housemistresses:

School House: Nicola Pentalow, BA Hons Queen's Belfast, PGCE Durham

College House: Elizabeth Pywell, BA Hons York, PGCE York, MA Open University

Health Centre:
Angela Wardale, SRN, SCM
Alison Oliver, SRN, SCM

Medical Officer: Dr Hazel Brown, BM, DRCOG

Administrative Staff:
Bursar: Julie Davis
Finance Officer: Jayne Copeland
Registrar: Julia Hampshire
Principal's PA: Sarah McLaughlin
Bursar's PA: Jane Wright

Numbers on roll. 58 Boarding, including Weekly boarding, 168 Day, 151 Junior School.

Age range. 11–18 (Senior), 3–11 (Junior).

Statement of Values. The Mount School encourages everyone to:

* respect and value every individual
* have the freedom to flourish in a calm and caring community
* strive for personal excellence
* think and live adventurously
* make a positive contribution to our changing world.

Curriculum. GCSE, AS and A Levels plus AQA BACC, incorporating Extended Project Qualification (EPQ). 20 AS/A Level subjects. Sixth Form: Most sixth formers take 4 or 5 subjects at AS Level (mix of arts and sciences), 3 at A Level; in addition, some take AS and A Level general studies. Vocational: Work experience available and encouraged in Year 11. Special provision: Specialist learning support teacher. Qualified EAL provision. Languages: French, German and Latin offered to GCSE, AS and A Level (French or German compulsory to GCSE); also GCSE Spanish in Sixth Form and clubs in other languages eg Russian and Japanese. Regular visits to Europe; classical trips to Italy biennially. ICT: computers with internet access (access at all times) in computer rooms and all departments; pupils have email addresses; wireless networked throughout school; OCR Nationals in ICT offered.

Extra subjects (in addition to a wide curriculum). *Crafts*: eg ceramics, textiles, photography. *Dancing*: as required. *Languages*: eg Spanish. *Music*: piano, brass, strings, wind (Associated Board examinations). *Speech and Drama*: LAMDA examinations. *Sports*: eg fencing, riding and judo.

Entrance. Girls must be registered before taking part in the entrance procedure. The registration form is included with the prospectus and can also be obtained from Julia Hampshire, Registrar, Tel: 01904 667529.

The Mount School Entrance Examination takes place on 17 January 2012. The School can also arrange for the Entrance Examination to be taken at other times of the year; however, Scholarships cannot be awarded unless candidates sit the examination in January 2012.

Entry at age 11 and above (into Years 7–10): Girls sit our entrance exam and take papers in English, Mathematics and Verbal Reasoning (for entry to Years 7–9 only). The English paper comprises a reading comprehension exercise and a piece of writing; the Mathematics paper (one part to be completed with the use of a calculator and one without) includes a wide variety of questions. Year 10 candidates take papers in English and Mathematics only. In addition, the girls attend the school for a taster day when they are interviewed by the Principal. School references and the interview are given weight alongside exam performance.

Entry at 16+ (A Level study): Prospective entrants are invited for interview. There is no examination if the entrants are studying for GCSE or IGCSE. The offer of a place will usually be conditional upon gaining at least 6 GCSEs at Grade C or above and at least Grade B in the subjects the student wishes to pursue at A Level. School references and the interview are given weight alongside exam performance. Prospective pupils who are not studying for GCSE or IGCSE will be expected to take papers in English and Mathematics.

Scholarships. Academic and Music scholarships are available for Year 7 entry; also Academic, Music, Drama, Art, and Sport scholarships in Year 9 and College (Sixth Form). A Scholarship is awarded for the duration of a girl's school career at The Mount up to and including College (Sixth Form). The value of awards is 5% of the current day fee (to which a means-tested bursary may be added which can be worth up to 100% of fees).

Means-tested bursaries for other candidates are also available.

Fees per term (2011–2012). Senior School (Years 7–13): Boarders £7,625; Weekly Boarders (Years 9–13) £6,775, Junior Boarders (all Boarding Options Year 7 and Year 8) £5,300; Day £4,900.

Additional charges are made for private lessons, craft materials, external examination fees, outside lectures and concerts. Parents not expected to buy textbooks. Further details about registration, offers of places and Awards may be obtained from the Registrar, Julia Hampshire.

Junior School: £2,950 Juniors (7 to 11 years); £2,220 Infants (4 to 7 years); £1,950 Nursery class. Government Nursery Vouchers are accepted in part payment.

Composition Fees Scheme. Parents are encouraged to consider paying School Fees by lump sum in advance. This can generate considerable reductions in the overall cost. The acceptance of a Composition Fee Payment is not a guarantee that a place can be offered at the appropriate time, but such payments are normally transferable between schools. Composition Fees may be accepted at any time prior to the probable date of entry and may be supplemented by additional payments either prior to or during the child's schooling. Further particulars are available from the Bursar.

The Junior School, for day children aged 3 to 11 years, shares the ethos of the Senior School, to encourage and develop the potential of the individual. There is a creative and stimulating learning environment which promotes the exploration of skills and the development of confidence. Academic standards are high and progress is carefully observed.

See The Mount Junior School entry in IAPS section.

Mount Old Scholars' Association. *Hon Secretary*: Elizabeth Morgan, via The Mount School, York.

Charitable status. The Mount School (York) is a Registered Charity, number 513646. It exists to provide education for girls from 3 to 18 and junior boys.

The Newcastle upon Tyne Church High School

Tankerville Terrace, Jesmond, Newcastle-upon-Tyne
NE2 3BA

Tel: 0191 281 4306
Fax: 0191 281 0806
e-mail: info@churchhigh.com
website: www.churchhigh.com

Motto: *Vincit Omnia Veritas*
Founded in 1885.

School Governors & Staff:

President: The Lord Bishop of Newcastle

Governors:
Chairman: Mr P Buchan
Mr C Beer
Mrs E I Ferguson
Canon R E Gage
Prof N Girdler
The Reverend D R J Holloway
Mrs S Jacques
Prof K McCourt
Mrs J L McShane
Mrs E S Stobart
Dr B Tasker
Mr M R Thompson

Executive Group:
Headmistress: Mrs J Gatenby, BA Dunelm, PGCE
Deputy Headmistress: Mrs A Roe, BA Hons Newcastle, PGCE
Head of Junior School: Miss J A Cunningham, BPhil Newcastle, TCert
Bursar: Mr P J Keen, FCCA

Senior Management Team (Senior School):
Headmistress: Mrs J Gatenby, BA Hons Dunelm, PGCE
Deputy Headmistress: Mrs A Roe, BA Hons Newcastle, PGCE
Head of Pastoral Care: Mrs LF Crawford, BSc Hons Edinburgh, PGCE
Senior Teacher: Mr J L Fleck, BA Hons Oxon, PGCE
Director of Studies: Mrs A Hardie, BA Hons Oxford, PGCE
Head of Sixth Form: Mrs H Harrison, BA Hons Huddersfield, PGCE

Senior Management Team (Junior School):
Head of Junior School: Miss J A Cunningham, BPhil Newcastle, TCert
Deputy Head of Junior School: Mrs J Brown, BEd Hons Leeds Metropolitan
Key Stage 2 Coordinator: Mrs D Colwell, BEd Hons Sheffield Hallam
Key Stage 1 Coordinator: Mrs J Kirkham, BEd Bath

Teaching Staff – Junior School:
Mrs K Aarvold, BSc Hons Edgehill, PGCE
Miss J Atkin, BSc Hons Manchester, PGCE
Mrs E Barnett, BEd Hons Northumbria
Mrs PA Breakey, BEd Roehampton Institute of Higher Education
Mrs J Brown, BEd Hons Leeds Metropolitan
Miss SE Carolan, MA Glasgow, PGCE
Mrs D Colwell, BEd Hons Sheffield Hallam
Mrs R Fairless, TCert Bangor
Mrs J Gordon, TCert
Mrs V Henderson, BA Hons Nottingham Trent, PGCE
Mrs J Kirkham, BEd Bath
Mrs L Riley, QTS Leeds
Mrs J Rollings, TCert Birmingham
Mrs S Scott, BEd Hons Northumbria
Mrs J Wrighton, BSc Hons UCL, PGCE, AdvDipEd Special Ed, MEd OU
Mrs K Younger, BA Hons Leeds, PGCE

Junior School Support Staff:
Mrs S Fenton (*Nursery Nurse*)
Mrs S Glover, BA Hons Durham (*Teaching Assistant*)
Mrs J Goodwill, NNEB (*Teaching Assistant*)
Mrs C Reed, NNEB (*Teaching Assistant*)
Mrs K Salkeld, BTEC National Diploma (*Nursery Nurse*)

Teaching Staff – Senior School:
* *Head of Department*

Art:
*Mr J G Wells, BA Hons Trent Polytechnic, Slade UCL, PGCE
Ms Z Robinson, MA Hons Northumbria, PGCE

Biology:
*Mrs L F Crawford, BSc Hons Edinburgh, PGCE
Ms H Hall, BSc Hons Leicester, PGCE
Dr H Parry, BSc Hons Imperial College London, PGCE

Business Studies:
*Mrs K Thomas, CertEd Birmingham, BA Northumbria

Careers:
*Mr P Dicks, BA Hons Newcastle, MSc UWIC

Chemistry:
*Dr DP Raymond, BSc Hons, PhD Cardiff, PGCE
Mr T Gaughan, BSc Hons Manchester, PGCE

Dance:
*Mrs K Brett, BA Hons RAD Durham, LRAD; AISTD
Miss M Wade, BA Hons Bath, GTP

English:
*Mr J L Fleck, BA Hons Oxon, PGCE
Miss C Chapman, MA Hons Aberdeen, PGCE, DTP, NCFE
Miss P Hutson, BPhil Newcastle, DipEd
Mrs J K Thew, BA Hons Durham, PGCE

Film Studies:
*Ms R Everton, BA Hons Newcastle, MA, PGCE

Geography:
*Miss K Bailey, BA Hons Durham, PGCE
Miss C Chambers, BA Hons Gloucester, PGCE

History:
*Mr D Hyde, BA Hons Durham, PGCE
Mr C Doyle, BA Hons Sunderland, PGCE
Mrs Z Elder, BA Hons Manchester Met, PGCE

Home Economics:
*Mrs L Kitto, BA Hons Manchester
Mrs L Batchelor, BEd Bath
Mrs H Hodgkiss, BA Hons Northumbria, PGCE

ICT:
*Mrs H Harrison, BA Hons Huddersfield, PGCE
Miss J MacKenzie, BA Hons Lancaster, PGCE

Mathematics:
*Mr K Jones, BSc Hons Newcastle, PGCE
Mrs SM Harris, BSc Hons Newcastle, PGCE
Miss D Rowbotham, BSc Hons Cardiff, PGCE

Modern Foreign Languages:
Mrs C Oliver, BA Hons London Institute of Linguists, PGCE (*French)
Mrs L Parry, BA Hons Birmingham, PGCE (*German)
Mrs B Mayhew, BA Hons Newcastle, PGCE (*Spanish)
Mrs G Montague, BA Hons Sheffield, PGCE
Mrs H Temperley, BA Hons Newcastle Polytechnic
Mrs R Gee, BA Hons London, CertEd

Music:
*Mr P J Noble, BMus Huddersfield, PGCE
Mrs F Merrick, BA Hons Durham, PGCE

Physical Education:
*Miss C Fitzgerald, BSc Hons Northumbria, PGCE
Miss D Hefford, BA Hons Northumbria, PGCE
Miss L Thompson, BA Hons Leeds Met, PGCE

Physics:
*Mr R Simpson, CertEd Durham
Mrs C Packham, BSc Hons Birmingham, PGCE

Politics:
*Mr D Hyde, BA Hons Durham, PGCE
Mr C Doyle, BA Hons Sunderland, PGCE

Psychology:
*Mrs M Michie, BA Hons Leeds, PGCE

Religious Studies:
*Mrs A Hardie, BA Hons Oxford, PGCE
Mrs L Dodd, BA Hons Lancaster, PGCE
Mrs J Evans, BA Hons Leicester, PGCE

SEN Coordinator:
Mrs P Roberts, BA Hons Durham, Dip Dyslexia, Language
  & Literacy York

Textiles:
*Mrs J Kinnersley, BA Hons Teeside
Mrs M Pattullo, BA Hons Cleveland, PGCE

Theatre Studies:
*Ms R Everton, BA Hons Newcastle, MA, PGCE

Alumnae & Events Coordinator; Staff Induction:
Mrs S Timney, BEd Hons Newcastle, FRSA

Marketing Manager:
Miss N Redhead, BA Hons Sunderland

Sports and Activities Manager, Health and Safety Officer:
Mrs D Chipchase, PGD, BAF Master Coach

School Nurse:
Mrs S Leighton

Administrative Staff:
Mrs B Cavanagh (*Bursar's Assistant*)
Mrs M Cowell (*School Secretary & Admissions Secretary*)
Mrs L Ferguson (*Secretary*)
Mrs K Murdoch, BA Hons Warwick (*Junior School
  Secretary*)
Mrs L Watson (*Secretary*)

Systems Management:
Mr S Farrell (*IT Systems Manager*)
Mr D Cocallis (*IT Technician and Systems Administrator*)

Site Management:
Mr G Qeku (*Site Manager*)
Mr W Ewing (*Assistant Site Manager*)
Mr C Melrose (*Assistant Site Manager*)

Technicians:
Mrs L Lant, (*Senior Laboratory Technician*)
Miss S Beadle (*Laboratory Technician*)
Mrs J Kirkup (*Reprographics Technician*)

Church High School is a caring, challenging and inspiring girls' school, committed to "giving every girl a voice". Our ethos recognises the individual in every girl and provides them with a unique and secure learning environment, allowing them to flourish and reach their full potential both academically and personally.

Our Christian ethos provides a solid foundation for developing the strong moral values that create confident and considerate young women who have respect for others.

The Church High experience from Day Nursery to Sixth Form is, quite simply, exceptional. Church High girls enjoy happy, rewarding years; make great and lasting friendships; develop a diverse range of talents and interests and achieve levels of academic success that could not be surpassed elsewhere.

Church High incorporates all stages of education for girls, from Nursery through to Sixth Form. Established in 1885, many of the values adopted by the school back then are still prevalent today. There has always been a great emphasis placed on developing the individual and ensuring that each child achieves their full potential in every sense. You only have to meet one of Church High's Sixth Formers to realise that the school continues to be very successful in producing its end product – articulate, mature young women who are quietly confident and understand how to achieve their personal objectives. The school remains true to its strong ethos of developing strong moral values and equipping girls to deal with the modern world.

The excellent pastoral care at Church High is widely recognised and girls know that they are going to get that individual support and the attention that they need to develop academically and personally. Parents, too, are secure in this knowledge.

The school is large enough to offer a really challenging learning environment and strong sense of community throughout each year group, but small enough to ensure every girl is known to staff as an individual. It means all their needs really can be met and that produces something quite special.

In the classroom, our academic results at all levels and for all abilities are outstanding. Church High continues to achieve some of the best academic results in the region. Our school is a mixed-ability community, where the individual really does matter.

The success of this support and encouragement is reflected in the grades attained by the pupils, which surpass external benchmark predictions. The school has many strengths and in recent years has achieved top marks in the country at GCSE for Religious Studies, English Literature, and Home Economics. Art, Music, Drama and Sport are also highly valued here and the wide range of subjects available in the Sixth Form reflects changing demand. Subjects such as Theatre Studies, Psychology, Dance and Sports Studies are offered alongside the more traditional A Level subjects.

The school is very forward looking and is open to change. Our aim is to send out into the world young girls with the attributes that are necessary for them to lead successful lives.

A Church High education, then, is about more than just academic excellence. We care for, nurture and develop students' whole potential in a challenging and stimulating learning environment. A Church High girl is prepared for all aspects of life and supported to realise her personal ambitions.

Fees per term (2011-2012). Infant Department and Junior School £2,745, Senior School £3,625.

Allowance for daughters of the Clergy: 25% of basic tuition fees.

Wrap-around care is also available with our Day Nursery, Zone4Kids after-school club and Holiday club.

Awards and Bursaries. Governors' Awards are offered at 11+ and for girls already in school at 16+. Bursaries may be made available to parents/guardians of children in Junior 1 (Year 3) onwards.

Details of these may be obtained from the School Secretary.

Charitable status. The Newcastle upon Tyne Church High School is a Registered Charity, number 528151.

North London Collegiate School

Canons, Canons Drive, Edgware, Middlesex HA8 7RJ
Tel: Senior School: 020 8952 0912
          Junior School: 020 8952 1276
Fax: 020 8951 1391
e-mail: office@nlcs.org.uk
website: www.nlcs.org.uk

North London Collegiate School has provided an outstanding education for girls since its foundation in 1850 by Frances Mary Buss.

Named "Independent School of the Year" by *The Sunday Times* in 1999 and again in 2006, this unique school is distinctive in several ways: it is a large London day school set in 30 acres of beautiful country estate; it has a stunning academic record offering a choice of A Levels or the International Baccalaureate in the Sixth Form; and it runs a comprehensive extra-curricular programme, now enhanced by the opening of its state-of-the-art, 350-seat Performing Arts Centre.

The Governing Body:
Ms H Stone, OBE, BSc, CEng, FICE, FRSA (*Chairman*)

Mr J Allen, FRICS
Mr K M Breslauer, BSc, MBA
Mr N Carrington, MA, CGDHA
Mrs S Carter, BSc Hons, Associate CFA
Professor J Drew, BSc, PhD, FRSA, FRAS (*Imperial College London nominee*)
Mrs C Froomberg, MA, FCMA
Dr L Goldman, BA, MA, PhD (*University of Oxford nominee*)
Ms L Hill, BSc, MBA
Mr S Jaffe, BSc Hons
Mrs S James, BA, JD
Dr D Popplewell, MA, MB, BChir Cantab, MRCP
Ms J Quinn, LLB Hons, BCL
Mr L Rabinowitz, QC
Mrs E A Raperport, BA, FCT
Mr D Shah, BSc, ACA
Ms R Sector, BA, MBA (*University of London nominee*)
Dr S Stoddart, PhD, FSA, MIFA (*University of Cambridge nominee*)

Bursar and Clerk to the Governors: Mr Graham Partington

Headmistress: **Mrs Bernice McCabe**, BA, MBA, FRSA

Deputy Head – Pastoral:
Mrs B J Pomeroy, BSc Nottingham

Deputy Head – Curriculum:
Mr M Shoults, MA Oxon, PGCE Cantab

Director of Studies and Administration (IB Coordinator):
Mr M Burke, BA Newcastle, MA Durham

Development Director:
(*to be appointed*)

Head of Sixth Form:
Mrs H A Turner, MA Cantab

Head of Upper School:
Mrs M A Fotheringham, MA Oxon

Head of Junior School:
Mrs J M Newman, BEd Cantab

Head of Middle School:
Mrs C Wagner, BA Bristol

Director of University Admissions:
Mrs K Hedges, MA Cantab

Careers Advisor:
Miss E Lane, BA Birmingham, MEd Birmingham

Heads of Academic Departments:
Religious Studies: Mrs A Wilson, MA London
English: Mr D James-Williams, MA London
Drama: Miss D Gibbs, BA Surrey
History and Government & Politics: Mrs C Chandler-Thompson, BA Exeter
Geography: Miss M Wheatley, BSc London
Economics: Mrs G Hurl, BSc Liverpool, MSc London
Classics: Mrs D O'Sullivan, BA Cantab
Modern Languages: Mr M English, BA Oxon, MA Liverpool
Italian: Mr P Langdale, MA Oxon
Spanish: Mrs G Robinson, BA Durham
French: Ms H Murphy, MA Newcastle
Russian: Mrs T Kinsey, BA Tver
Mathematics: Miss J Zugg, BSc Cape Town
Science: Mr E Nicol, BSc Strathclyde
Biology: Miss S Bentley, BSc Bangor
Chemistry: Dr P McKeating, MChem Oxon, DPhil Oxon
Physics: Mrs N Timoshina, MSc Moscow
Information Technology: Dr A P Cripps, PhD London
Art and Design: Mr T Hardy, BA Middlesex
Music: Mr L D Haigh, BMus Edin
Physical Education: Mrs A Ansell, BSc Birmingham

Assistant to the Headmistress: Miss N Carter, BA Surrey

The pupil teacher ratio is 11:1

North London Collegiate School combines the beauty and space of a rural setting with the convenience of being only a short distance from the heart of London. The school provides an ambitious education for girls from a wide range of social backgrounds. The very best of academic teaching is coupled with the widest range of extra-curricular activities to help the pupils fulfil their potential.

There are 1,082 girls at North London Collegiate School: approximately 120 in the First School, aged from 4+ to 7, 190 juniors, aged from 7–11, and 769 in the Senior School, 11–18, of whom 236 are in the Sixth Form.

North London Collegiate School draws on a rich tradition. It was founded by Miss Frances Mary Buss in 1850 to provide an education for girls that would equal that of boys and produced many of the first women graduates.

The school's academic record is outstanding. It has been named as *The Sunday Times* "Independent School of the Year 2006" and *The Daily Telegraph* has described it as the most consistently successful academic girls' school in the country. Results in 2010 were again consistent with the school's academic profile. 98% of A Levels were A* and B grades, with 80% of pupils gaining straight A*/A grades in all subjects taken.

For the fifth year the school has maintained its top position as the leading International Baccalaureate school in the UK, with 100% of IB Diploma results graded 7,6 (equivalent to A grade) or 5 (equivalent to B grade), with an average score of 41. Three students achieved a "perfect score" of 45 points – only achieved by approximately 65 students out of over 30,000 worldwide each year.

Over a third of the year group (34) went to Oxbridge.

The GCSE results were equally outstanding, with 96% of grades at A*/A.

The facilities at the school are first class, designed to offer the girls every opportunity to develop themselves both academically and socially. These facilities include lacrosse pitches, all-weather tennis courts and a Sports Centre with indoor swimming pool and fitness centre.

A new Performing Arts Centre opened in Autumn 2007, with a 350-seat auditorium, orchestra pit, galleries and rehearsal rooms. Music and Drama are strong, with opportunity for all to take part in productions, choirs and orchestras. The music programme includes challenging pieces for the most able, with such events as the National Chamber Group competition where the school has won the Founder's Trophy as the most successful competing school on several occasions. On the campus are a Music School, Drawing School and Design Technology Block, all situated around the lake, where waterlilies in the summer make it the ideal place to relax during the long lunch interval. Alternatively, girls may visit the beautifully light and spacious four-floor library.

There is an extensive school coach scheme.

Full details of Open Days and "Taster Afternoons" are on the school's website. Midweek visits can be arranged by appointment. Please contact 020 8952 0912 to arrange a visit.

Bursaries. Enabling bright girls from all backgrounds is central to the ethos of the school. Many bursaries are offered to girls who do well in the 11+ test and those entering the Sixth Form, whose parents can demonstrate financial need.

Scholarships. (*See Scholarship Entries section.*)

Fees per term (2011-2012). Senior School: £4,841; Junior School: £4,092.

Charitable status. The North London Collegiate School is a Registered Charity, number 1115843. It exists to provide an academic education for girls.

Northampton High School
GDST

Newport Pagnell Road, Hardingstone, Northampton NN4 6UU

Tel: 01604 765765
          01604 667979 Junior School
Fax: 01604 709418
e-mail: nhsadmin@nhs.gdst.net
website: www.gdst.net/northamptonhigh

Northampton High School is part of the GDST (Girls' Day School Trust). The GDST is the leading network of independent girls' schools in the UK. As a charity that owns and runs 24 schools and two academies, it reinvests all its income in its schools. For further information about the Trust, see p. xxi or visit www.gdst.net.

Local Governing Body:
Dr S D Gregory (*Chairman*)
Mr C Oliver (*Vice Chairman*)
Mrs J Howell Williams (*Vice Chairman*)
Mrs M Adams
Dr M Blake
Mrs R Eden, MBE
Mrs A Rowe
Mrs D Runchman
Mrs D Newham

Staff:
* *Head of Department*
‡ *Holder of Teacher's Certificate or Diploma*
§ *Part-Time*

Senior Management Team:

Head Mistress: ‡Mrs S A Dixon, BA Hons Warwick (*English*)

Deputy Head – Pastoral: ‡Mrs L Davies, BA Sheffield (*German, French*)

Director of Studies: Mr J Rickman, MBA Leicester, BA Kent (*French*)

Head of Junior School: Mr A Noakes, BA Hons De Montfort, MA Ed Open University

Business Manager: Mrs K L Willis, MA Oxon, FCA, GradICSA

Senior School Teaching Staff:
Miss J Ainsworth, MA Cambridge (*Classics*)
‡Mr W Asbury, BSc Sheffield (**Science, *Physics*)
‡Mr R Attwood, BSc Leeds (**Biology*)
§Mr D Balazik, CertEd Manchester (*Design Technology*)
‡Mr D Balfe, BA Ed Hons Wales (*Psychology*)
‡Mrs S Barker, BA Open University (**Chemistry*)
§Mrs S Battams, BSc Nottingham (*Physics*)
‡Mrs M Beacroft, BA Northumbria (**Art*)
‡Mrs J Bell, BA Leeds (*French, Spanish*)
‡Miss J Bentley, BEd De Montfort (**Physical Education*)
‡Mrs R Boyce, BA Lancaster (*German, French*)
‡Miss A Buxton, BA Wolverhampton, PG Dip Lib Northumbria (*Librarian*)

‡Miss C Cadwallader, BA Liverpool (*English*)
‡Mrs J Cantwell, BSc Hons Durham (*Science*)
‡Dr N Carr, BSc, PhD Hull (*Chemistry*)
‡Mr G Chamberlain, BSc Hull (*Geography*)
‡Mrs K Corbett, MA Glasgow (*Classics*)
‡Mrs C Courtheoux-Allison, L-ès-L Rouen (*French*)
‡Mrs K Cowell, BEd Birmingham (**Mathematics*)
‡Miss L Cramp, BA Bangor (**English*)
‡Miss C Davies, MA Hons Edinburgh (*Modern Languages*)
‡Mrs J Davis, CertEd Ilkley College (*Food, Textiles & Design Technology*)
‡Mr A Donaldson, BA Hons Warwick (**History*)
‡Mrs A Down, BSc London (*Mathematics*)
‡Mrs J Drew, BA Cardiff (**Music*)
‡Mr J Earp, BA Hons Nottingham (**Geography*)
‡Mrs J Edge, BA, DipEd Cardiff (*English*)
‡Mrs C Fieldhouse, BA, PGDip, CertEd Northampton College/Hertfordshire Theatre School (**Drama*)
‡Mrs E Ford, Business Studies Dip Northampton (*Physical Education*)
‡Miss S Fraser, BA De Montfort (*Physical Education*)
‡Mr J Glover, BA London (**Religious Studies*)
§Mrs G M Gray, BA, MA London (*History*)
‡Mrs A Halstead, BA London (*English*)
‡§Mrs K Harrison, BA Lancaster (*Mathematics*)
‡Mrs D Hill, BA Leeds (**Modern Languages, French*)
‡Mr T Hoddle, BA London (**Information Technology*)
‡Mr J Holland, BA Leicester, MA Hertford, MSc Cambridge (**Classics*)
‡Mrs S L Holland, MA Oxon (**Classics*)
‡Miss C Hurst, BA Brighton, QTS (*Physical Education*)
‡Mrs R Hymers, BSc Bradford (**Business Studies & Economics*)
‡Mrs C Jacobs, BSc Birmingham (*Chemistry*)
‡Mrs J Jennings, BEd De Montfort (*Physical Education*)
‡Mrs S Lamb, MA (*Religious Studies*)
‡Mrs M Langhorn, BSc Coventry (**Business Studies & Economics*)
‡Mr D Laubscher, BA South Africa (*Art*)
Mrs R Laubscher, BSc South Africa (*Mathematics*)
‡Mrs J Leech, BA, MA Oxford (*French*)
‡Mrs R Littlewood, BEd Liverpool (*Physical Education*)
‡Mrs K Loughney, BSc Portsmouth (*Mathematics*)
‡Mrs D MacArthur, CertEd Bath College of HE (*Design Technology*)
‡Ms S Margareto, BA, DipEd Macquarie, Sydney (*Special Education Needs*)
‡Mrs S Moss, BEd Keele (**Design Technology*)
‡Mrs J Ogilvie, MEng Leeds and Pennsylvania State (*Mathematics*)
‡§Mrs E Pearson, MSc Birmingham (*Biology*)
‡Miss F Smith, BSc Hons Brunel (*Government & Politics, Director of Sixth Form*)
‡Mr M Watson, BA Liverpool (*French and Spanish*)
‡Ms A Workman, BA Hons Open University (*Art*)

Junior School:
Deputy Head: ‡Mrs K Allport, BA Kent
Assistant Deputy Head: Mrs J Purvey-Tyrer, BEd Leeds

‡Mrs J Arrowsmith, BEd Sheffield
‡Mrs C Bleech, BSc Bristol
Miss N Brandon-Jones, BA Hons Wales
‡Mrs J Cumming, BEd Hons Northampton
‡Mrs S Dadge, BA Warwick
‡Mrs S Dale, BA, QTS Bedfordshire
§Mrs A Davis, OGCE Ripon and York St John
‡Mrs K Farrar, BEd Hons Northampton
‡Mr M Francis-Scott, BA Hons College of St Mark & St John, MA Surrey
‡Mrs L Green, BA Manchester Polytechnic
‡Mrs H Greenbank, BEd Plymouth

‡Mrs A Love, BEd Southampton and Salisbury College of Education
Miss S Mayes, BA Surrey
‡Mrs C Miller, GTCL Trinity College of Music, London
‡§Miss G Moss, BA Hons Worcester
‡Mrs J Purvey-Tyrer, BEd Hons Leeds
‡Mrs E Shaw, BEd Newman College, Birmingham
‡Mrs J Stock, BEd Newland Park College
‡Miss N Taylor, BSc Bristol
‡Mrs S Waters, BA Northampton

Headmistress's Secretary: Mrs D Brown

Peripatetic Instrumental Staff:
Miss F Brannon, BMus (*Flute, Recorder*)
Mrs D Couling, LRSM, DipABRSM, CTABRSM (*Piano*)
Mrs A Cowley, BEd (*Clarinet, Flute*)
Mr P Cunningham, LLCM, GLCM, LTCL, AMUSLCM (*Piano, Jazz Piano, Theory*)
Mr B Duncan, LGSM (*Classical Guitar*)
Doctor B Gates, BA, LGSM (*Clarinet, Saxophone, Theory*)
Miss T Holderness, BMus,CTABRSM
Miss J Hooper-Roe, ARCM, GBSM, ABSM (*Singing*)
Mrs C Jones, BMus MTC (*Cello, Double bass*)
Miss C Leech, BMus, PGDip RCM, DPS (*Violin/Viola*)
Mr D Lloyd (*Oboe*)
Mrs N Roberts, Dip RCM (*Violin*)
Ms R Sherry, BA Comb Hons, MA, LRAM (*Singing*)
Mr P Slane (*Singing*)
Ms A Sparks (*Singing*)
Ms K Tompkins (*Piano*)
Mr R Truman, ARCM, Dip RCM (*Brass*)
Mr A Turner (*Violin/Viola*)
Mr M Wild (*Drum Kit*)

Our school, which opened in 1878, is an independent day school for girls. We encourage our pupils to develop values which will provide them with a constant base in an ever-changing world and aim to respond to the individual needs of every girl. In 1992 we moved to a 27-acre site on the southern edge of town. Our extensive purpose-built accommodation includes 8 well-equipped laboratories, Art, Textiles, Information Technology, Music, Design Technology, Home Economics, Modern Languages and other specialist rooms for all curriculum areas. A large library with computer facilities for independent study is also provided.

The Junior School, which takes girls from the age of three, adjoins the main buildings and has its own hall, dining facilities, library, practical room and IT suite. At the age of 11 the majority of girls transfer to the Senior School.

There are splendid sports facilities on the site. These include a 25m swimming pool, all-weather pitch, badminton, squash, netball and tennis courts and hockey pitches.

Girls are prepared for GCSE and Advanced Level examinations and go on to universities and other institutions of higher education.

Scholarships are offered at 11+, 13+ and in the Sixth Form. Means-tested bursaries are available in the Senior School.

Fees per term (2011-2012). Senior School: £3,731 (Yrs 7–9, inc lunch), £3,573 (Yrs 10–11, exc lunch), £3,731 (Yrs 12–13 inc lunch). Junior School: £2,819 (Rec–Yr 2, inc lunch), £2,730 (Yrs 3–6, exc lunch).

Old Girls and Associates. *Secretary*: Mrs C White, Northampton High School, Newport Pagnell Road, Hardingstone, Northampton NN4 6UU.

Charitable status. Northampton High School is part of The Girls' Day School Trust, which is a Registered Charity, number 306983.

Northwood College

Maxwell Road, Northwood, Middlesex HA6 2YE
Tel: 01923 825446
Fax: 01923 836526
e-mail: admissions@northwoodcollege.co.uk
website: www.northwoodcollege.co.uk

An independent day school for girls.
   Motto: *Discover, Learn, Succeed*

Governing Council:
Chairman: Mr G Hudson

Mr S Brown	Mrs C Pain
Mrs D Dalton	Mr A Patteson
Mrs S Dunkerley	Mr J Soughton
Mr A Mansell	Mr D Tidmarsh
Mrs S Marris	Mr K Wild

Head Mistress: Miss Jacqualyn Pain, MA, MA, MBA, NPQH

Deputy Head Mistress, Teaching and Learning: Miss J Jackman, BA Hons Manchester, PGCE Southampton, MBA Nottingham

Deputy Head Mistress, Pupil Wellbeing and Development: Mrs E Skelton, MA St Andrews, DipEd Edinburgh, NPQH

Head Mistress Junior School: Mrs H Thaker, BA Hons East London, PGCE North London

* *Head of Department/Faculty*
§ *Part-time*

Miss L Armitage, MEd, BA Queensland (*Drama*) (*maternity cover*)
Mrs N Asquith, BSc Hons Birmingham, PGCE Bristol (**Biology*)
Mr A Bailey, BMus Hons London College of Music & Media, PGCE Inst Ed London (*Music*)
Miss S Ballantyne, BA Hons Bristol Polytechnic, MA Chelsea College of Art (**Art*)
§Mrs J Barraclough, BEd Hons College of St Mary & St Paul, RSACertSpLD (*Junior School*)
Dr K Baskerville, BSc Hons Melbourne, PhD Cambridge (**Mathematics*)
Miss M Bennett-Goodman, AGSM, PGCE (*Assistant Director of Music*)
Mrs G Bhatia, BSc Hons Kingston, PGCE London (*Mathematics*)
Mrs C Brant, BSc Hons Exeter, PGCE OU (*Science*)
Mr S Brant, MA Oxon, PGCE London, FCSM, FGMS, FFCM (*Director of Studies, Chemistry*)
Miss L Brodie, BA Hons Nottingham Trent, PGCE London South Bank (*Junior School*)
Mr D Brown, BA Hons Hull (**English*)
Mrs L Brown, BSc Hons UCL, PGCE Inst Ed London (*Psychology, Head of Year 9*)
§Mrs E Buckler, BA Hons York, PGCE Newcastle (*Junior School*)
§Ms T Bush, BA Hons Kingston, MA Camberwell College of Arts, PGCE London (*Art*)
Mr L Casey, BA Hons Polytechnic of Wales, MA Middx Polytechnic, PGCE Sheffield Polytechnic (*Economics and Business Studies*)
Mrs E Chandler-Thompson, MA Birkbeck, BSc Hons Loughborough (**History & Politics*)
Mr L Coleman, BEng Bath, PGCE Inst Ed London (*Physics*)
Mr V Connolly, MEd New Zealand (*Head of E-Learning*)
§Mrs M Cooper, BEd Hons West London Inst (*Religious Studies*)

§Mrs M Coulson, AGSM (*Junior School, Speech and Drama*)

Ms E Cullen, BEd Wollongong, Australia (*Physical Education*)

Mrs K Delaney, MA London, PGCE Cambridge (*Junior School*)

Ms E D'Souza, BSc Hons Aston, PGCE Herts (*Junior School*)

Miss J Dabski-Nerlich, BA Hons, PGCE Inst Ed London (*Infant School*)

Miss A Direkze, BSc Hons UMIST, MA London, PGCE Middlesex (*Infant School*)

§Mrs P Douglas, BEd Hons Brighton Polytechnic (*Mathematics, Latin*)

Miss B Eagles, BEd Hons Cheltenham (*Junior School*)

Mr R A Elliott, BA Hons Southampton (*Assistant Head, Head of Sixth Form, History and Politics*)

Mrs A S Evans-Evans, BSc Hons, PGCE Manchester (*Physics, Examinations Officer*)

Mr D A Ezekiel, BA Joint Hons Manchester, PGCE Cambridge, MA London (*French, *German*)

Mrs K Fellas, BSc Hons London, PGCE Inst Ed London (*Mathematics*)

Miss H Freeman, BA Hons Exeter, PGCE Hertfordshire (*English*)

Mrs R Gaynor, BSc Hons Brunel, PGCE St Mary's Twickenham (*Infant School*)

§ Mrs S Gladstone, BSc Hons Open University, PGCE Herts (*German*)

§Mrs S Gray, BEd Univ of Wuppertal (*German*)

Miss C Guthrie, BA Hons Toronto, PGDE Edinburgh (*English/History*)

§Mrs M Hamilton, BSc Hons, PGCE Primary Swansea (*Infant School*)

Ms A Harne, BA Hons Winchester School of Art, PGCE Brighton (*Art*)

Miss C Hinchliffe, MA East Anglia, PGCE (*Head of Science*)

Miss G Hughes, BA Swansea, PGCE Wales (*Infant School*)

Miss L Johannes, BSc Hons Southampton Inst, PGCE Inst Ed London (**Humanities & Social Sciences, *Psychology*)

Mrs C Jones, CertEd Twickenham (*Infant School*)

Mrs E LeRoux-Baker, HDipEd Boland College of Education, SA (*Physical Education*)

Ms N Lindsay, BA Hons London, PGCE Inst Ed London (*English*)

Mrs H Levy, BSc Witwatersrand, PGCE London (*Chemistry, Head of Year 10*)

Ms J Maloney, MA Hons St Andrews, PGCE Inst Ed London (*Deputy Head Mistress Junior School*)

Ms F McConnon, MSc Beijing, MSc OU, BA Hons UCL, PGCE (*Head of Languages*)

Miss C McCoy, BA Hons, PGCE, MA Central School of Speech & Drama (**Drama*)

§Mrs J McDermott, BSc Hons, PGCE Birmingham (*Chemistry*)

Mrs C McMahon, CertEd College of St Mary & St John (*Junior School*)

§Mrs G Mead, BA Hons Kent, PGCE Canterbury (*Religious Studies*)

§Miss K Millen, BSc Hons, PGCE Newcastle (*Geography*)

Mr A Miller, BSc Hons York (*Mathematics*)

Mrs D Miller-Smith, BSc Hons Thames Valley, PGCE OU (*Assistant Director of Studies, French, Spanish*)

§Miss J Monk, BMus Hons London College Music, PGCE Trinity College (*Music*)

Miss S Morrish, BSc Hons, PGCE Roehampton Inst (*Technology*)

Mrs S Norris, BSc Hons London, PGCE London, MSc Cambridge (*Chemistry, DofE Coordinator*)

Mrs J Onslow, BEd Bath, Cert Sec Maths Chelmer Inst (*Technology Coordinator, Textiles, Head of Year 11*)

Mrs K Opie, BA Hons, MA, PGCE London (**Religious Studies*)

Miss S Parnaby, BA Hons Dunelm, PGCE Dunelm (**Classics*)

Mrs A Pearson, BA Hons Reading, PGCE Southampton (*Junior School*)

Miss R Pink, BEd Hons W London Inst Ed, CertEd (*Junior School*)

Mrs C Pritchard, Dip Home Econ Queens College, CertEd Jordanhill Coll of Ed (*Food Technology*)

Miss C Quirk, MA Liverpool, PGCE Durham (**Spanish, French*)

Mrs E Rees, BA Hons W Sussex Inst HE, PGCE Brunel (*Physical Education, Head of Year 7*)

Dr I Roche, BA OU, MMus, DMus London, CertEd London (**Director of Music*)

§Mrs S Roche, BA Hons OU, CertEd London (*History*)

Mr J Rogoff, BA Hons Oxon, PGCE Oxon (**Geography*)

§Mrs V Rowntree, BSc Hons Bristol, PhD London, PGCE Chelsea College (*Biology*)

Miss S Shirman, BA Hons Brunel, PGCE Herts (*Head of English*)

Miss L Silverstone, BA Hons Middlesex, PGCE Inst Ed London (*Drama, English*)

Mrs J Simister, MA Hons Cambridge, PGCE Roehampton (*Director of The Advanced Cognitive Development Programme*)

Miss J Simpson, BA Hons Exeter, (**Physical Education*)

Mrs T Smith, BA Hons Leeds, MA London, PGCE London (*Asst Director of The Advanced Cognitive Development Programme, Head of Year 8*)

§Mrs A Spicer, BSc Hons LSE, PGCE London (*Geography*)

§Mrs L Spicer, BEd Hons Westminster College, Oxford (*English, Asst Exams Officer*)

Mrs P Spikings, BSc Hons Nottingham (*Mathematics*)

Mrs M Sullivan, BSc USA (*Biology*)

§Mrs F Sykes, BSc Hons Leicester (*Coordinator of Learning Support*)

Mrs J Talbot, BEd Hons Bretton Hall (*Junior School*)

Mrs E Taylor, BA Hons Nottingham, PGCE Cambridge (*Classics*)

Miss V Taylor, BA Hons, PGCE St Mary's College Twickenham (*Physical Education*)

Mrs C Thompson, BEd (*Nursery Teacher*)

§Mrs M Thomas, CertEd Bristol, AdvDip Children's Language & Literature Cambridge, RSADipSpLD (*Junior School, Learning Support*)

Ms R Thompson, BA Hons, PGCE Sheffield (**Careers*)

Mrs C Weeks, MA Oxon, PGCE Oxon (*French, Spanish, Drama*)

Mrs M Wong, BSc Hons Edinburgh, PGCE Hertfordshire (*Biology, Chemistry*)

Mr A Wright, BSc Hons Westminster, PGCE Bath (*ICT*)

Mrs H Yarde-Martin, BSc Hons Southampton, PGCE Bath (*Physics, Chemistry*)

Mrs L Annetts (*Librarian*)

§Mrs P Pandit (*Assistant to Librarian*)

Visiting Staff:

Mrs C Anderson (*French Conversation*)

Mrs C Gauci (*Spanish Conversation*)

Miss S Price (*Ballet*)

Mr J Hodgson (*Chess*)

Mr J Bridge (*Brass*)

Mrs A Chancellor (*Strings*)

Mr R Cole (*Acoustic/Electric Guitar*)

Mrs R Ferguson (*Violin*)

Mrs J Gallagher (*Strings*)

Miss O Hinman (*Singing, Piano*)

Mrs R Hinman (*Singing, Piano*)

Miss H Lambert (*Clarinet, Saxophone*)

Mrs J Maclean (*Cello, Piano*)
Miss L Peacock (*Clarinet, Saxophone*)
Mr E Puddick (*Drums*)
Mrs J Rippon (*Piano*)

Admin Staff:
Bursar and Clerk to the Governors: Mr J Boal
PA to the Head Mistress: Mrs W Staff
PA to the Bursar: Mrs K Forbes-Mitten
Registrar: Mrs J Davidson

Foundation. Northwood College was founded in 1878 as one of the first girls' schools in London, and now educates 800 girls aged 3 to 18 years.

Ethos. Our aim is to raise young women who know their own minds and are creative and flexible thinkers, as well as being able to achieve outstanding exam results.

We are academically selective, but not narrowly exclusive. We value girls for more than simple academic performance, because our unique approach to advanced thinking skills means that we can develop, stretch and challenge every single one of them. We think that makes for an interesting and vibrant school community – and it's what makes Northwood College special.

Thinking Skills. Our approach to thinking skills is another one of our defining characteristics. It sets Northwood College apart, and gives our girls an edge in the way they approach any task or challenge. Our Thinking Skills Programme is led by C J Simister, who has taught at Northwood College for many years and is a renowned expert, author and consultant on cognitive development. Through the programme, we ensure our girls start to understand and develop the way they think from the day they join Nursery through to the end of the Sixth Form. Over the years, they build up their reasoning skills, improve their creativity and acquire strategies for tackling complex problems and decisions. It gives them a life skill that will be as useful at university and in the workplace as it is at school.

Location. The school is 14 miles from Central London and a 5 minute walk from Northwood tube station on the Metropolitan Line. There are several good local bus services and five different supervised school bus routes. These bring girls from Edgware, Canons Corner, Stanmore, Hatch End, Queensbury, Kingsbury, Kenton, Harrow, Pinner, Borehamwood, Elstree, Radlett, Bushey, Chalfont St Peter, Chorleywood, Rickmansworth, Beaconsfield, Gerrards Cross, Denham, Uxbridge, Hillingdon, Ruislip, Ealing, Greenford and Ickenham.

Single Site. All parts of the school share a single site, divided into distinct areas. The Junior School occupies its own self-contained buildings and our youngest girls have a brand new, purpose-built Early Years Centre. (*See also Junior School entry in IAPS section.*)

Facilities. We have enviable facilities for all subject areas in both the Junior and Senior Schools. Highlights include three art rooms, nine science laboratories, four newly-equipped computer rooms and specialist centres for Technology and Modern Languages. We also have a fabulous Performing Arts Centre, with sophisticated sound-recording and music technology suites.

Sports facilities include a sports hall and 25-metre six-lane indoor swimming pool, as well as three hard tennis/netball courts, a hockey/rounders pitch and an all-weather pitch.

Examinations. Pupils are prepared for the General Certificate of Secondary Education (GCSEs), for AS and A2 Levels and for University Entrance.

Curriculum. The College offers all National Curriculum subjects. In addition, French is taught from Year 3. Spanish and German are taught from Year 6, Latin from Year 4. Drama is taught throughout the school. A very wide range of A Level subjects is available in the Sixth Form, including Psychology, Economics, Politics, and Music Technology.

Music and Drama are real strengths at Northwood College with a fantastic range of opportunities for young musicians and budding thespians. The school has a wide range of orchestras, bands and choirs and we hold concerts each term, as well as music competitions and fully staged musical productions. Instrumental tuition is extensive and girls are prepared for the Associated Board examinations.

There is one major school play or musical every year in both Junior and Senior Schools that is always a highlight in the school calendar and often elicits rave reviews in the local paper. A number of smaller productions take place year round and girls may take individual drama lessons with visiting teachers.

Physical Education. We recognise the importance of encouraging girls to stay physically fit and active. Trained staff teach a wide variety of sports such as Hockey, Netball and Gymnastics during the winter months and Tennis, Rounders, and Athletics in the summer. Swimming is taken all year round and senior girls are able to explore other sports such as Golf, Self-Defence and Fitness Training.

Entry Requirements. Entry to the College is by examination and interview, except for Nursery, which uses a play-based assessment. At 11+ we use the North London Girls' Schools Consortium exam. Entry to the Sixth Form is by GCSE results and interview.

Scholarships and Bursaries. Academic scholarships are available for girls joining Northwood College Senior School in Year 7 (11+) and the Sixth Form. At Year 7 the College uses the North London Independent Girls' School Consortium examination as part of its assessment. Interview and a school reference are also part of the assessment. At Sixth Form entry (16+), girls are required to sit an examination prior to entry into the Sixth Form. A number of scholarships in other subjects including Art and Design, Sport and Music are also available for girls with particular talent in these areas. In addition, a number of means-tested bursaries are offered to the value of full fees.

Fees per term (2011-2012). Senior School and Sixth Form £4,350, Junior School £3,675, Pre-Prep £3,000, Nursery £2,750.

Charitable status. Northwood College Educational Foundation Limited is a Registered Charity, number 312646. It exists to provide education for girls between the ages of 3 and 18 years.

Norwich High School
GDST

95 Newmarket Road, Norwich NR2 2HU
Tel: 01603 453265
Fax: 01603 259891
e-mail: admissions@nor.gdst.net
website: www.norwichhigh.gdst.net

Founded 1875.

Norwich High School is part of the GDST (Girls' Day School Trust). The GDST is the leading network of independent girls' schools in the UK. As a charity that owns and runs 24 schools and two academies, it reinvests all its income in its schools. For further information about the Trust, see p. xxi or visit www.gdst.net.

Additional information about the school may be found on the school's website and a detailed prospectus is available from the school.

School Governors:
Chairman: Mr S Thompson, BSc, MBA

***Headmaster*: Mr J J Morrow**, MA Oxon, MA Wake Forest, North Carolina

Deputy Head: Mr S D Kavanagh, BA Leicester, NPQH

Deputy Head Academic: Mr A P Walker, MA Oxon, NPQH

Assistant Head (Learning & Teaching): Miss P J Dunn, MA Oxon, MA Essex

Assistant Head (Co-curriculum): Mrs H Dolding, BEd De Montfort

Head of Junior School: Mrs J A Green, BSocSc Cape Town, NPQH

Senior Master: Mr S Orton, MA Cantab

Director of Sixth Form: Mrs A E McCourt, BA Keele, MSc East Anglia, PGCE

School Business Manager: Mr P O'Connor, BA East London, CertEd Greenwich, DipM

Registrar: Miss A Ready

Number of pupils. Senior School: about 600, aged 11–18 years, of whom about 160 are in the sixth form. Junior School: about 250, aged 3–10 years.

Norwich High School draws its pupils in almost equal numbers from the city of Norwich and the county of Norfolk. It stands in 13 acres of grounds on the main Newmarket Road, a mile-and-a-half from the city centre. The main buildings are attached to a distinguished Regency house, built in 1820. In addition, there is a junior school with many specialist rooms, a recently extended sixth form centre, music school, spacious sports hall, 25m indoor heated pool and a performing arts centre. All the playing fields are around the school and a wide range of indoor and outdoor physical activities is offered, including netball, hockey, lacrosse, athletics, tennis, rounders, badminton, gymnastics and dance. The school holds the International Schools' Award, the Sportsmark Gold Award for its sporting achievements, Artsmark for creative subjects and Investors in People.

The school is a caring community and parent-friendly. We are open early for breakfast and late for tea. Girls may use the ICT and library facilities after school in the senior school; the junior school has its own after-school club. There is a minibus service from Norwich Railway Station before and after school.

Admission. All girls are assessed prior to entry. The normal ages of admission are 3, 7, 11 and 16. Occasional vacancies may occur at other ages.

Curriculum. The school has always been proud to provide a broad and rich education, preparing girls for admission to universities, professions, commerce and industry. A wide range of subjects is available, currently 25 at A Level and 22 at GCSE.

Information systems. A computer network is shared by all departments, including the laboratories, library, all teaching rooms, two computerised language laboratories, the sixth form IT suite as well as the two senior and two junior IT suites. All girls take the Short Course ICT GCSE in Year 9 and work towards the European Computer Driving Licence qualification in the sixth form. Computers and interactive whiteboards are widely used for teaching, along with extensive digital and Intranet based learning resources.

Careers education and advice. A carefully planned Careers Information Education and Guidance programme commences in Year 7. Virtually all sixth formers continue on to higher education and the school ensures that they have received comprehensive guidance and preparation from their tutors, the Head of Sixth Form, the careers department and outside speakers and experts from a higher education background and the world of work. The well-stocked careers room keeps up-to-date information through a variety of resources. Girls attend regular careers talks and events, both in and out of school. They also undertake work experience and job shadowing.

Co-curricular Activities. These are extensive, for infants through to seniors. Music, sport and drama are all strong features of the school. Girls also participate in both the Duke of Edinburgh's Award and Young Enterprise schemes, rowing, equestrian, debating and chess clubs, Amnesty International, Christian Union, fencing and life saving.

Many excellent residential and day trips are arranged each year, by various departments. These are finely tuned to the curriculum and cover a full range of activities.

Fees per term (2011-2012). Senior School £3,420, Junior School £2,575, Nursery £2,140.

The fees cover the regular curriculum, school books, stationery and other materials, games fixtures and swimming lessons, but not optional extra subjects or school meals. The fees for extra subjects, including individual music tuition, are shown in the prospectus.

Financial Assistance. The GDST has made available to the school a substantial number of scholarships and bursaries.

Bursaries are available on or after entry to the senior school and applications should be made to the Head in cases of financial need. All requests are considered in confidence. Bursaries are means tested and are intended to ensure the school remains accessible to bright girls who would profit from a GDST education, but who would be unable to enter the school without financial assistance.

Various **Scholarships**, including music scholarships, are available to internal or external candidates for entry at 11+ or to the sixth form.

Charitable status. Norwich High School is part of The Girls' Day School Trust, which is a Registered Charity, number 306983.

Notre Dame Senior School

Burwood House, Cobham, Surrey KT11 1HA
Tel: 01932 869990
Fax: 01932 589481
e-mail: headmistress@notredame.co.uk
website: www.notredame.co.uk

Notre Dame is a Catholic Day School for Girls established in Cobham in 1937 and is a foundation of the Order of the Company of Mary our Lady.

Governors:
Chairman: Mr Glen Travers
Deputy Chairman: Mrs Suzanne Ware, LLB

Mr Stephen Arthur
Sister Anne Gill, ODN
Mrs Veronica Heffernan
Sister Patricia Kelly, ODN
Sister Catherine McLenaghan, ODN
Mr Brian Mepham, FCA
Sister Maria Nieves, ODN
Mr Gerald Russell
Sr Ernestine Velarde, ODN
Father Mervyn Williams, SDB

Financial Controller: Mrs Tracy Jones, ACA

Headmistress: Mrs Bridget Williams, MA, NPQH, BEd

Deputy Headmistress – Curriculum: Mrs A King
Pastoral Deputy: Mrs V Cochrane, BEd, Cert in Counselling
Head of Sixth Form: Mr G Thomas, BA Hons, MA, PGCE
Chaplaincy: Sister Catherine McLenaghan, ODN

Staff:
Mrs S Avizius BA Hons, PGCE (*Art*)
Miss K Adams, BA Hons, PGCE (*Food Technology*)

Ms S Badger, BSc SpHons, PGCE (*Mathematics*)
Mrs S Barney, ASA FIST, TCert (*Swimming Coach*)
Mrs C Chislett, BA, HDE (*English*)
Mr M Coackley, BA Hons, PGCE (*History*)
Mrs V Cochrane, BEd, Cert Counselling (*English*)
Miss Z Davison, BA Hons, PGCE (*Art*)
Miss H Dean, BA Hons (*History*)
Mrs S Duckworth, BA Hons, TESOL, DipSpLD (*Learning Support*)
Miss S Dudgeon, BEd Hons (*Physical Education*)
Dr R Fenton, BMus, MMus Hons, PGCE, PhD (*Music*)
Mrs I Gallon, BA Hons (*Classics*)
Sr Patricia Grady, ODN (*Theology*)
Miss C Graham, BA Hons, PGCE (*Drama*)
Mr C Griffin, BA Hons, PGCE (*Drama*)
Mrs A Griffiths, BA Hons (*Geography*)
Miss M Grzesik, BA Hons, PGCE (*French and Spanish*)
Mme G Guibert, MA, PGCE (*French*)
Miss C Claveau
Mrs A Ingram, BSc (*Mathematics*)
Mrs I James, Odessa State University (*Science*)
Mrs C Johnson, BA Hons (*English*)
Miss J Judd, BA, BTEC (*Textiles*)
Mrs M Lewis, BA Hons, PGCE (*English*)
Mr K McClenaghan, BA Hons, MA (*English*)
Mr D Marshall, BA Hons, PGCE (*Theology*)
Mrs A McVay, BA Hons, PGCE (*French, Spanish*)
Mrs H Marsh, BA Hons, PGCE (*Physical Education*)
Mrs J Newton, BA Hons, PGCE (*Head of Learning Support*)
Ms C O'Keeffe, BSc (*Science*)
Mrs L Plummer (*Information Technology*)
Miss A Ponniah, BSc Hons, PGCE (*Science*)
Ms R Sahota, BA Hons, PGCE (*Business Studies*)
Mrs L Shore, BSc, MSc (*Mathematics*)
Miss C Shipley, MA Oxon, BA Hons, PGDip Law Bar Vocational (*Music*)
Ms S Siddiq, BSc (*Biology*)
Mrs J Slade, BA, PGCE (*Science*)
Mr M Smith, MA Cantab, PGCE (*Maths*)
Mrs K. St. John, BA Hons (*Learning Support*)
Mrs M Turner, BA Hons, PGCE (*English, French*)
Mr P Walsh, BEd Ord (*Acting Head of Geography*)
Miss K Wills, Joint Hons BSc (*PE*)

Associate Staff:
Headmistress's PA: Miss C Wright
Receptionist/Administrator: Mrs L Harper
Administrator: Mrs J Russell
Registration enquiries: Mrs J Clay
Librarian: Mrs P Thomas
IT Manager: Mr D Coplus
Computer Technicians: Mr L Hepworth, Mr D Barnett
Laboratory Technicians:
Mrs V Catalano
Mrs J Matkin
Art/Technology Technician: Mrs G Goldfarb
School Nurses:
Ms N DeVizia, DipRN, BSc
Mrs K Utchanah, RN, BA Hons

Foundation. Notre Dame School was established in 1937 by the Sisters of the Company of Mary, Our Lady who have a four hundred year old tradition of excellence in education worldwide. The Sisters of the Company of Mary continue to play a very important role in the pastoral life of the school ensuring that the ethos is maintained. Through the Company of Mary the school has well-established links with schools in France, Spain and the USA.

Notre Dame is a Catholic school which welcomes families from all religious denominations. Whilst helping our Catholic children to deepen their understanding of our faith we teach universal tolerance and understanding of all religious beliefs. The school provides a friendly and caring

environment in which every girl is encouraged to fulfil her potential. There are approximately 383 girls aged from 11 to 18 in the Senior School. Notre Dame Preparatory School occupies the same site and has approximately 316 girls from 2¾ to 11. (*See IAPS entry*)

General information. Located in tranquil rural surroundings, easily accessible by road and served by an extensive network of school coaches, Notre Dame boasts comprehensive facilities for the pursuit of academic work, drama, music, art, sports and other activities. Facilities include a heated indoor swimming pool and fitness studio, sports hall, state-of-the-art, well-equipped science laboratories, opened in Autumn 2007, following the opening of the new Lestonnac Resource Centre containing extensive computer network suites. A beautiful Chapel is located in the heart of the school. A 375-seat Performing Arts Centre is currently being built and is scheduled to open in Autumn 2011.

Curriculum. All pupils follow a broad curriculum leading to the achievement of up to 10 GCSEs. In addition to the core subjects of English (literature and language), Mathematics, Science and Religious Studies, girls may choose to take French, German, Spanish, Latin, History, IT, Geography, Drama, Music, Art, Food and Textiles Technology and Physical Education. In the Sixth Form most girls will take four AS Level and three A Level subjects chosen from a large range of options. All girls are prepared for university entrance (including Oxbridge).

Extra-Curricular Activities. Notre Dame excels in swimming and netball and offers a wide range of other sporting activities including tennis, athletics, gymnastics, badminton, lacrosse and rounders. The school boasts thriving Drama and Music Departments with all girls having the opportunity to participate in productions, various choirs and musical ensembles ranging from the chamber orchestra to jazz groups. All girls take part in a weekly activities programme. Other ongoing extra-curricular activities include The Duke of Edinburgh's Award Scheme, Young Enterprise and community service within the local parish.

Admission. Admission is normally at 11+, although girls may be admitted at other ages subject to an entrance examination and the availability of places. Academic scholarships are awarded at 11+ based on the entrance examination. Scholarships are also awarded to girls entering the Sixth Form. A number of means-tested assisted places are available on entry to the school. Short-term bursaries may be made available to assist parents in times of personal financial hardship. Approximately half our intake at 11+ comes from Notre Dame Preparatory School.

Fees per term (2011-2012). £4,300.

Charitable status. Notre Dame School Cobham is a Registered Charity, number 1081875. It exists to advance the Roman Catholic religion through the operation of a School or schools.

Notting Hill and Ealing High School
GDST

---

2 Cleveland Road, Ealing, London W13 8AX
Tel: 020 8799 8400
Fax: 020 8810 6891
e-mail: enquiries@nhehs.gdst.net
website: www.nhehs.gdst.net

Founded 1873.

Notting Hill and Ealing High School is part of the GDST (Girls' Day School Trust). The GDST is the leading network of independent girls' schools in the UK. As a charity that owns and runs 24 schools and two academies, it reinvests all its income in its schools. For further information about the Trust, see p. xxi or visit www.gdst.net.

An academically selective, independent day school for girls aged 4 to 18. Separately housed and run Junior Department (ages 4+–11) and Senior Department (ages 11+–18) on the same site.

Chairman of Local Governing Board: Mr Julian Simmonds BA Hons

Head: **Ms Lucinda Hunt**, BSc Hons London, ARCS

Deputy Head – Pastoral: Mrs Katie Swift, MA, BA Hons, PGCE

Deputy Head – Academic: Mrs Olivera Raraty, BA Hons, PGCE

Head of Junior Department: Mrs Gabrielle Solti, BA Hons Oxford, PGCE London

History and Ethos. This is a school with a long tradition of academic excellence and creativity within an exceptionally warm and supportive environment. Notting Hill and Ealing girls are well grounded, confident and independent. They are proud of their school and value kindness and laughter, fun and friendship. This is a place where tolerance and mutual respect are nurtured; where you can be yourself. With a wide variety of activities and opportunities, and a strong emphasis on charitable giving, everyone can enjoy being part of a vibrant community and express their passion for learning, and for life.

Pupils and Location. Approximately 880 pupils. 570 in the Senior School (140 in the Sixth Form) and 310 in the Junior Department. Transport links are excellent (Ealing Broadway station is nearby and several buses stop outside the school). Girls come from Ealing and all over west London.

Pastoral Care. The system of pastoral care is overseen by the Deputy Head – Pastoral working through the Heads of Year and Form Tutors. The Head also takes a personal interest in all pupils. The result is a well structured system that is sufficiently flexible to support every girl and to ensure that she is treated as a whole person with individual strengths and needs. In the Sixth Form the tutor team is led by the Head of Sixth Form and her deputy.

Curriculum. Throughout the Junior and Senior Schools our curriculum is broad and balanced and encourages independence of learning and thought. In Years 7–9 everyone follows courses in English, History, Geography, Mathematics, Physics, Chemistry, Biology, Design Technology, ICT, Religious Studies, Art, Music, and Drama. In Year 7 all girls study Mandarin plus a second modern language (French or Spanish). In Year 8 German and Latin also become available. Girls usually take ten subjects at GCSE, including a compulsory core of English Language and Literature, Mathematics, 3 Sciences (IGCSE) and a Modern Language. 22 subjects are offered at AS and A2 Level and those who wish may also take the Extended Project Qualification which is highly regarded by university admissions tutors. Most girls take 4 or 5 subjects at AS Level and 3 or 4 at A2 level. There is help for those preparing for additional entrance tests such as UKCAT, BMAT, LNAT or STEP and lessons in personal health, ethical and social issues appropriate to each age and stage. Physical Education is taught throughout the school.

The Sixth Form. Our sixth formers play an important role in the school. They enjoy the independence of their own new Sixth Form Centre with common rooms, outdoor space for relaxing, café and fitness centre. They take responsibility for many extra-curricular activities such as organising clubs and act as mentors for girls in the lower years. Additional leadership opportunities are offered by the House system, and voluntary and charity work. All go on to Higher Education and, with excellent results (98% achieving grades A*, A or B in 2010, with 30% of grades being A*), successfully

secure places at their choice of university (including Oxford and Cambridge).

Extra-Curricular Activities. As well as covering a wide variety of sports and activities connected with art, drama and music these range from computer animation to Amnesty International, from Chinese to competing in the London-wide Hans Woyda Maths competition and from debating to the Duke of Edinburgh's Award Scheme.

We take full advantage of everything London offers, with visits to theatres, museums, galleries, performances, and conferences incorporated into the curriculum. Trips abroad are arranged for modern languages, history, art and art history, politics and economics. There is an annual ski trip and sixth form expedition.

Careers Advice. All girls are offered the Morrisby test free of charge in Year 10 and the school is a member of ISCO (the Independent Schools Careers Organisation) which entitles all students to careers help and advice until the age of 23. Sixth formers receive extensive support with university applications, including mock interviews. The GDST Alumnae Network, the unique resource from the GDST, offers each student access to a database of former GDST students, who will give advice and support on careers (including helping with work experience) and universities. An annual Careers Evening typically featuring senior representatives from almost 70 different professions and occupations is organised by the Parent's Guild.

Creative Arts. There are three orchestras, three choirs, and many chamber and ensemble groups. School productions offer opportunities either to perform or to work with production, lighting, sound, costume and staging. Art thrives within the curriculum and through various art clubs. It also contributes to work in design technology and various aspects of ICT, such as web design and animation projects.

Sport. Sport is taken seriously with success in local fixtures and championships, and we encourage participation and enjoyment at all standards. There is specialist teaching throughout the school, and the Senior school makes use of the facilities at a local club. Gymnastics and dance are particularly popular, and there is an excellent gym squad. Lifeguard training is available for sixth formers, as well as swimming in our own indoor pool. Fencing, aerobics, self-defence, and football are among the extra-curricular sports clubs currently available.

Fees per term (2011-2012). Senior School £4,343, Junior Department £3,380.

The fees cover the regular curriculum, necessary school books, normal examination fees, membership of the FUTUREWISE scheme including the Morrisby careers aptitude test, stationery and other materials, but not optional extra subjects or school meals. Fees for extra subjects including instrumental music, speech and drama, are shown in the prospectus. Certain off-site sports are charged for separately, as are school trips.

Scholarships and Bursaries. Academic and music scholarships are available at 11+. At 16+ there are academic awards as well as awards for Physical Education, Drama, Art, and an All-Rounder scholarship.

Means tested bursaries are available in the Senior Department only. Application should be made via the school.

Admission. Usually at 4+, 7+, 11+ and 16+, by appropriate test and/or interview.

Occasionally, vacancies may become available in other year groups.

Charitable status. Notting Hill and Ealing High School is part of The Girls' Day School Trust, which is a Registered Charity, number 306983.

Nottingham Girls' High School
GDST

9 Arboretum Street, Nottingham NG1 4JB
Tel: 0115 941 7663
Fax: 0115 924 0757
e-mail: enquiries@not.gdst.net
website: www.nottinghamgirlshigh.gdst.net

Founded 1875.

Nottingham Girls' High School is part of the GDST (Girls' Day School Trust). The GDST is the leading network of independent girls' schools in the UK. As a charity that owns and runs 24 schools and two academies, it reinvests all its income in its schools. For further information about the Trust, see p. xxi or visit www.gdst.net.

Additional information about the school may be found on the school's website and a detailed information pack may be obtained from Central Admissions at the school.

Chairman of Local Governors: Professor Jenny Saint, OBE

Headmistress: **Mrs S M Gorham**, BA, MA Ed Mgt

Joint Deputy Heads:
Miss J Keller, BA
Miss S C Peacock, BSc

Head of Junior School: Mrs F Potter, BA

School Business Manager: Mr J C Dunn, ACA

Central Admissions:
Mrs S Webb-Bowen
Mrs C L Haddow

Number of Pupils. Senior School 775 (including 200 in the Sixth Form); Junior School 300.

A selective day school, NGHS is on a single site adjacent to a park in the middle of Nottingham. The original Victorian houses have been modernised and there have been extensive additions to create a well-resourced school. The junior school is housed in separate buildings on the same campus as the senior school, and has recently been extended to include a new library and ICT learning resources centre as well as four new classrooms. A major programme of refurbishment in the senior school includes refitting eight of the science laboratories.

There is a self-contained Sixth Form Centre (opened in 2009) providing a large coffee shop-style common room and recreational area. The tutorial rooms are spacious and light, all fully equipped with the latest technology.

The school grounds include a large all-weather pitch, gymnasium, sports hall and fitness suite. There is also a sizeable sports field close to the school. The modern dining hall has excellent facilities for providing a wide choice of snacks and meals throughout the day. The school is immediately adjacent to Nottingham High School and some extra-curricular activities are organised with their boys.

Although examination results are among the best in the country, the school believes that education for life involves much more. Leadership, confidence, teamwork, flexibility and reliability are among the qualities increasingly demanded in today's ever changing society. Everyone is encouraged to take the opportunity to participate fully in a wide range of extra-curricular activities to develop skills and qualities that will lead to a happy, successful and fulfilling life.

At all ages, it is hoped that the girls will enjoy their studies. The school provides a lively, stimulating learning environment to encourage girls to discover the excitement and satisfaction of high academic achievement coupled with growing knowledge and understanding.

Curriculum. The curriculum is designed to give a broad academic education and due regard is taken of the National Curriculum. In the Junior School as well as following a pattern of work designed to help develop a confident grasp of core skills, the girls benefit from the highly-praised theme weeks which stimulate creativity. Girls take government Key Stage 2 SAT tests in Year 6 which form part of internal assessment procedures and results are consistently very high. There is liaison with the Senior School staff, helping to ensure continuity for pupils at 11+. In the Senior School girls are prepared for GCSE, AS and A2 Levels, with almost all girls proceeding to university.

Girls at all ages follow a comprehensive programme of personal and social development including aspects of careers, citizenship, health and sex education, current affairs and environmental issues.

Throughout the school girls are encouraged to develop their physical skills and the school has an excellent sports record; teams regularly win trophies at City and County level with many being selected to compete at regional or national level.

Admissions. At 4+ entry is by an informal test and assessment of group play activities. Entry at 7+ and 11+ is by interview and a written test which includes English and mathematics and is designed to determine potential and understanding. Most of the existing students stay on at 16+ and a number of students are admitted into the Sixth Form from other schools. The entry requirement is 8 GCSE subjects at an average of grade B, with grades A or B in any subject to be studied in the Sixth Form as specified by the department. This is supported by individual interviews and a report from the current school. The school will consider applications for admission into most year groups if there are available places.

Fees per term (2011-2012). Seniors £3,370 excluding lunch, Juniors £2,443 plus £150 for lunch.

The fees cover the regular curriculum, school books, stationery and other materials, class music, games and swimming, but not optional extra subjects.

Scholarships and Bursaries. The GDST makes available a substantial number of bursaries. These are means tested and intended to ensure that the school remains accessible to bright girls who would profit from our education but who would be unable to enter the school without financial assistance. Up to 100% of the tuition fee may be awarded. Bursary application forms are available through Central Admissions at the school.

A limited number of scholarships are available each year for entry to the Senior School at both 11+ and direct into the Sixth Form. The value of a scholarship is to a maximum of 5% of the current tuition fee. Scholarships are awarded solely on the basis of academic merit and no financial means test is involved.

Charitable status. Nottingham Girls' High School is part of The Girls' Day School Trust, which is a Registered Charity, number 306983.

Ockbrook School
Derby

The Settlement, Ockbrook, Derbyshire DE72 3RJ
Tel: 01332 673532
Fax: 01332 665184
e-mail: jfowkes@admin.ockbrook.derby.sch.uk
website: www.ockbrook.derby.sch.uk

Founded in 1799.

Independent Day and Boarding School for boys aged 2–11 and girls aged 2–18. Member of GSA and AGBIS.

Motto: *In Christo Omnia Possum*

Governing Body:
Chairman of Governors: Revd Robert Hopcroft
Dr G D Lamming
Mr J Luke
Mrs J Newbold
Mrs V Poultney
Mr C Purcell
Mrs M Ralph
Mrs G Redgate
Revd K Woolford

Clerk to the Governors: Mrs J Buckley

Staff:

Head Teacher: Mrs A M Steele, BSc Leeds

Deputy Head: Mrs J Gwatkin, CertEd Birmingham

Director of Studies: Mrs R West, BA Hons London
  (*Economics*)

Manager with Responsibility for Finance & HR: Mr S
  Malkin

Examinations Officer: Ms V Lee, BA Leeds (*French*)

Teaching Staff:
Mrs L Archibald, BA Leeds (*Food Technology*)
Miss J Biss, BA Warwick (*Mathematics*)
Mrs S Breedon, BEd Nottingham (*Primary*)
Dr E Burguin, BSc Sheffield (*Languages*)
Miss K Cleland, BA Hull (*English, SEN Coordinator*)
Mrs F Faulkner, BSc Newcastle, MA Nottingham
  (*Technology/ICT*)
Mrs C Fletcher-Eaton, BSc Loughborough (*Religious
  Studies*)
Mr N Gupta, BSc, MAPSE Leicester (*Physics/
  Mathematics*)
Mr D Hannigan, MA London (*Drama*)
Ms S Humberston, BA Hull (*German, French, Spanish*)
Mrs L Ireland, BEd Derby (*Primary*)
Mrs H Killip, BEd Sheffield (*Food Tech/Technology*)
Mrs M Lamell, BA Newcastle (*Primary*)
Mrs G Lloyd, BEd Derby (*Primary*)
Mrs A Logie, BA Hull (*Geography*)
Mrs H Marsden, BEd Northampton (*Primary*)
Mrs E Marsh, BSc Leeds (*Physics/Sciences*)
Mr G Maskalick, MA Carnegie USA, CT ABRSM (*Music*)
Mrs C McBeth, MEd Loughborough (*Primary*)
Mrs S McCool, BEd Manchester (*Primary*)
Mrs J McGahey, BA Birmingham (*Art and Design*)
Mrs S Mitchell, BA Hull (*English*)
Mrs K Moorhouse, BSc Loughborough (*PE*)
Mrs K Morris, BA Norwich School of Art and Design
  (*Primary*)
Mrs J Mullineux, BEd Bedford College (*PE*)
Mrs A Newton, BSc (*Mathematics*)
Mrs C Reader, BA Hons Leeds (*Dramatic Arts*)
Mrs R O'Reilly, BA Liverpool (*PE and Dance*)
Miss A Renow, BA, MEd Nottingham (*History*)
Mrs C Saunders, BA London (*Religious Studies*)
Mrs S Taylor, BA Scarborough (*Primary*)
Mrs B Thornton, BEd Derby (*Primary*)
Miss D Throup, BA Hons Nottingham (*Psychology*)
Mr A Walsh, BA Hull (*Economics, Business Studies*)
Mrs P Ward, CertEd Esteven (*Primary*)
Mrs M Watkins, BA Leeds (*French/Spanish*)
Mrs J Whitaker, MSc Leicester (*Biology*)
Mr D Williams, BEd Wales (*Primary*)
Mrs W Wilton, MEd, BPhil Nottingham (*Mathematics*)
Mrs S Worthington, BA Exeter (*Head of Primary*)

Head's PA & Admissions: Mrs J Fowkes
Marketing Manager: Mrs J Fowkes
*Manager with Responsibility for Operations and Health &
  Safety*: Mrs J Buckley
Finance Manager: Mrs E Green

Website & Data Manager: Mrs C Derbyshire
School Administration: Mrs N Brierley & Mrs M Lawrence

Boarding House Staff:
Mrs S Adamji (*Assistant Housemother*)
Mrs S Ainsworth (*Assistant Housemother*)
Mrs S Cooper (*Assistant Housemother*)
Mrs J Cresswell (*Assistant Housemother*)
Mrs K Fisher (*Assistant Housemother*)
Nurse W Holmes, EN (*Assistant Housemother*)
Mrs C Horspool (*Assistant Housemother*)
Mrs M Smith (*Assistant Housemother*)
Mrs P Parker (*Assistant Housemother*)

Medical:
Nurse: Mrs L Tanser, EN

Classroom Assistants:

Mrs C Bower	Mrs L Holmes
Mrs S Cooper	Mrs A Kenyon
Mrs J Federici	Mrs J Leighton
Miss K Fisher	Mrs E Nason
Miss N Gajic	Mrs C Newby
Mrs J Harvey	Mrs M Oliver
Mrs A-M Heaps	Mrs S Ritchie

Technicians:
Mr S Garbett
Mrs L Kendall
Mrs S Miller

Catering Manager: Mr Z Goodwin
Grounds & Maintenance Manager: Mr D Bailey

Visiting Music Teachers:
Mrs K Burton, LRAM Perf Cert (*Violin/Viola*)
Mrs J Ford, LGSM, BA Hons Birmingham (*Piano & Harp*)
Mrs D Hensler, MA Hons Music, BA Hons Music
  Manchester (*Piano*)
Mr P Marshall, ABRSM (*Voice*)
Mrs A Negus, University of Performing Arts, Stuttgart
  (*Woodwind*)
Mr J Rippingale, BPA Leeds (*Guitar*)
Mr M Thorpe (*Woodwind*)

Situation. Situated in the heart of the Midlands, Ockbrook School lies equidistant between the historic towns of Derby and Nottingham and is easily accessible from the motorway network, rail and air transport. The School is set in a superb rural position overlooking the Trent Valley and it is surrounded by its own estate including landscaped gardens, grounds, playing fields and farmland. This setting and the high standard of facilities within it provide an excellent environment for learning … free from urban noise and distractions.

Pupils. There are c400 pupils, girls aged 2–18 and boys aged 2–11, who are divided between the Primary (2–10) and Senior (11–18) Departments. Female only boarders are accepted from the age of 11 years for entry into Year 7.

Ethos. We aim to develop individual potential and self worth through stimulating and positive relationships and through an understanding of Christian values so that our pupils are prepared for the changes they will face in their future lives. We believe that education should be a partnership between School, pupils and parents. To this end we provide comprehensive feedback on progress in the classroom and welcome family and friends at our extra-curricular drama productions, concerts, sports events, open door days and acts of worship.

Curriculum.
Primary Department:
Early Years (Ages 2–5). A dynamic programme of language, numeracy and scientific activities provide a secure foundation for later conceptual development.

Key Stage 1 (Years 1 & 2). The core subjects of Mathematics, Science and English are covered in addition to nine other subject areas including French and Information Communications Technology.

Key Stage 2 (Years 3–6). Study for the core of subjects continues with additional experience in nine other subjects including Dance, Drama and Gymnastics.

Teachers' assessments are carried out throughout both Key Stages and form the basis of internal assessment procedures for progression through to the Senior Department at 11+.

Senior Department:

Lower School (Years 7–9). Pupils study the core subjects and a broad range of additional subjects including ICT, French, Drama and PSHCE (Personal, Social, Health & Citizenship Education). In Year 9 from September 2010 students can study German and Spanish in addition to French and the school will introduce IGCSE courses in Mathematics and the three sciences.

Upper School (Years 10–11). At GCSE level all pupils study Mathematics, English Language and English Literature, plus additional subjects; there is a wide range of options.

Sixth Form. Students usually study for 4 AS Levels in the Lower Sixth and proceed to 3 A2 subjects in the Upper Sixth. A wide range of subjects is available. Great emphasis is placed on the development of Life Skills which help to develop the competencies so necessary for adult life, whilst adding to the breadth of study. The vast majority of pupils leaving the Sixth Form proceed to higher education, including Oxbridge.

Sport. As well as the core PE subjects the school has a strong tradition in sport, ie athletics, cross-country, netball, swimming and rounders etc. A rapidly expanding programme of outdoor pursuits is also available for pupils which include sailing, waterskiing and golf. Teams of various ages, in most sports, have full fixture lists with neighbouring schools and the School is proud of its County and National representatives. We are also a member of the Sports Leaders Award Scheme.

Activities. The Duke of Edinburgh's Award Scheme is available to pupils over the age of 14, together with a wide range of trips and outdoor holidays, walking, canoeing and skiing. Other activities include Young Enterprise, Wilderness Expertise, Community service, chess, debating, and numerous other clubs or societies. A School Holiday Club also operates from the School.

Music and Drama. Many pupils learn musical instruments and a large number play to a high standard. Opportunities are provided by the Primary and Senior choirs, orchestras, chamber choir, strings group, and windband. Performance venues include Westminster Abbey, Manchester, Derby and Barcelona Cathedrals, Ojab-Haus Aigen, Salzburg, Saltzburg Cathedral, Pfarrkirche Bad Ischl Saltzburg and Chatsworth House, Derbyshire. There is a wide range of dramatic productions each year providing as many pupils as possible with the chance of developing their dramatic talents.

Art and Design & Technology. Great emphasis is given to the development of creative talent both as academic subjects and interests. Out of class involvement is strongly encouraged.

Fees per term (2011-2012). Tuition: £2,230–£3,275. Boarding (in addition to tuition fees): Weekly £1,895, Full £2,945.

Admission. *Primary Department.* Entry is decided as a result of a combination of interview, assessment day and school report (if applicable).

Senior Department. Entry is decided as a result of a combination of interview, assessment, school report and entrance examination held throughout the year and in January for Year 7.

Sixth Form. Entry is decided as a result of a combination of interview, school report, and ultimately a good performance in the GCSE examinations.

Scholarships and Bursaries. Scholarships are available for Academia, Sport, Art, Drama and Music (including voice) for Year 7 and Sixth Form entry. Bursary applications are considered by way of a full means test which may also include a home visit assessment. Full details are available from the Admissions Secretary, Mrs J Fowkes.

School Prospectus. A prospectus and registration details may be obtained from the Admissions Secretary (Tel: 01332 673532; Fax: 01332 665184; e-mail: jfowkes@ admin.ockbrook.derby.sch.uk; website: www.ockbrook. derby.sch.uk). Parents are encouraged to visit the School and appointments may be made by contacting the Admissions Secretary.

Charitable status. Ockbrook School is a Registered Charity, number 251211. Its aims are to provide an education for boys aged 2–11 and girls aged 2–18.

Oxford High School
GDST

Belbroughton Road, Oxford OX2 6XA

Tel: 01865 559888
Fax: 01865 552343
e-mail: oxfordhigh@oxf.gdst.net
website: www.oxfordhigh.gdst.net

Founded 1875.

Oxford High School is part of the GDST (Girls' Day School Trust). The GDST is the leading network of independent girls' schools in the UK. As a charity that owns and runs 24 schools and two academies, it reinvests all its income in its schools. For further information about the Trust, see p. xxi or visit www.gdst.net.

Motto: *Ad Lucem.*

Chairman of School Governing Board: Mrs M Shannon

Head: Mrs J Carlisle

Deputy Head: Mrs O B Curry

Deputy Head – Academic: Dr P Secker

Head of Junior School: Mrs E Stacey

Business Manager: Mrs C Charlton

Head of Sixth Form: Miss R Pallas-Brown

Director of Admissions: Mrs J Brown

Pupil numbers. 921: Junior School 331, Senior School 590.

The school is on three sites in North Oxford. Opened in September 2011, new buildings at the Senior School include the School Hall, Lecture Theatre, Dining Hall, Library, Drama Studio and Language Suite. Already extremely well resourced the Senior School has a sports hall, indoor swimming pool, The Mary Warnock School of Music, and separate purpose-built centres for all other subjects and the Sixth Form. The school is networked with well-equipped ICT areas.

Curriculum. The broad curriculum offers a full range of subjects, incorporating ICT throughout the curriculum. Girls are prepared for GCSE and AS/A Level. Sixth-formers choose from 27 subjects. Mandarin is a compulsory language for Year 7 along with French. The school offers 8 languages including Latin and Ancient Greek. Approximately 30% proceed to Oxbridge annually. Many girls take examinations in Music, and Speech and Drama, as well as belonging to the Duke of Edinburgh's Award Scheme, Young Enterprise and the Combined Cadet Force.

A strong extra-curricular programme offers about 100 clubs at any one time, with everything from rock band to gardening.

Admission. The main points of entry are at Nursery, Reception, Years 7, 10 and 12. Contact Mrs Jenny Brown, Director of Admissions, for details.

Fees per term (2011-2012). Senior School £3,567, Junior School £2,585, Nursery (mornings only) £1,068.

The fees cover the regular curriculum textbooks, stationery and other materials, choral music, games and swimming, but not optional extra subjects or school meals. Lunch (currently £210 per term) is compulsory for girls from Year 2 to Year 11. Children in Reception and Year 1 bring a packed lunch.

Bursaries. The GDST provides the school with a number of bursaries. These are means tested and ensure that the school remains accessible to bright girls who would profit from the education provided but who would be unable to enter the school without financial assistance. Bursaries are available before or after entry throughout the Senior School and confidential application can be made to the GDST.

Scholarships. Academic and Music scholarships are available for Year 7. Academic, Music, All-Rounder, Art and Sport scholarships are available in the Sixth Form.

Charitable status. Oxford High School is part of The Girls' Day School Trust, which is a Registered Charity, number 306983.

Palmers Green High School

Hoppers Road, London N21 3LJ
Tel: 020 8886 1135
Fax: 020 8882 9473
e-mail: office@palmersgreen.enfield.sch.uk
website: www.pghs.co.uk

Founded 1905.
  Motto: *By Love Serve One Another*

School Council
Chairman: Dermot Lewis FCIB IAC
John Atkinson, FRICS
Anna Averkiou, International Media Consultant
Anne Coyne, GRSM, LRAM, ARCM, PGCE
Melanie Curtis, Solicitor
Dr Anita Goraya, BSc Hons, MBBS, MRCGP
Gay Kettle MBE
Joyce Mayhew, Retired Teacher
David G Orfeur, JP, FRICS
Brian Smith, FRIBA
Jeffrey Zinkin, FEA

Headmistress: Mrs Christine Edmundson, BMus London, MBA Exeter, PGCE, LRAM, ARCM

Bursar: Mrs Deborah Ivory-Webb, CSBM
Deputy Headmistress: Ms Laura Morrison, BA Strathclyde, MA Middlesex, PGCE
Assistant Head KS4 and Head of Careers: Dr Mark Caddy BSc, PhD Warwick PRI
Assistant Head KS2 and Head of ICT: Mrs Karen Thompson, BA Denver, Colorado

Mrs A Atkinson, BEd (*Nursery Manager*)
Mrs H Bhundia, Dip Playgroup Practice (*Lower School Teaching Assistant*)
Mrs J Billingham, BA Nottingham (*Art*)
Miss K Brandon, CACHE Level 3 (*Nursery Assistant*)
Mrs I Brittain, RSA 1 & 2 (*Teaching Assistant*)
Mrs B Broad, BEd Leeds (*Head of Physical Education*)
Mrs E Christodoulou, BA Middlesex, PGCE (*Class Teacher Reception*)
Mrs K Conlon, MSc London, BSc London (*Librarian*)

Mrs L Corbett, BA Leeds (*French*) (*Maternity Cover*)
Mrs V Davies, BEd Cambridge, BA Kent (*Class Teacher Year 3*)
Ms A Davey, BA Leeds, PGCE (*English*)
Mr A Desai, BEng, BEd India, OTTP, PGCE (*Mathematics*)
Mrs P de Hénaut, GGSM Guildhall, Post Grad TC Bath (*Music*)
Mrs C Doe, BA East Anglia, MA Ed Open, PGCE (*Head of English*)
Mrs L Dufton, BA Middlesex (*Class Teacher Year 6*)
Mrs H Eve, BA Bristol, PGCE (*Head of Drama*)
Miss N George, BA Liverpool, PGCE (*Head of History*)
Mrs M Torres-Giron, Licenciado en Ciencias de la Educación Spain (*Spanish*) (*Maternity Cover*)
Mrs S Hagi-Savva (*Assistant School Secretary/Classroom Assistant*)
Ms S Harding, BSc Kingston, PGCE (*Head of Science*)
Mrs E Hassan (*Lower School Teaching Assistant*)
Mr D Healey, MA London, CertEd, DipAD, DipCDT London (*Head of Design and Technology*)
Mrs E Kariolis, BSc Guildhall, Dip Higher Education (*Teaching Assistant*)
Miss M Laratonda, MA London, BEd Buenos Aires, PGCE (*Spanish*)
Mrs A Lee, BEd Birmingham (*Class Teacher Year 4*)
Miss H Lucas, BSc Sussex, MSc, PGCE (*Prep Coordinator, Class Teacher Year 2*)
Mrs S Mandal, BSc, MSc Visva Bharati, India, PGCE (*Science Teacher*)
Miss L Martin BA Manchester, MSc London (*Individual Needs Coordinator*)
Mr J Matthews, BMus Cardiff, LTCL (*Head of Music*)
Mrs M Mehran, BSc North London (*Science Technician*)
Mrs E McNally, BSc Gloucester, MEd Exeter, PGCE (*Physical Education*)
Mrs A Michael, NNEB (*Nursery Assistant*)
Mrs G Moris, MA Oxford, PGCE (*Class Teacher Year 1*)
Miss J Newman, BA London, PGCE (*French*)
Ms L O'Leary, BA Liverpool, MCD, PGCE (*Head of Geography*)
Mrs K Parry-Garnaud, Licence Anglais Tours France, BA Sunderland (*Head of Modern Foreign Languages*)
Mrs J Pauk, BA Aberystwyth, PGCE (*Class Teacher Year 5*)
Mrs A Rollé, BA Bristol, GTT, (*Drama*)
Mrs C Shaw, BSc Warwick, PGCE (*Head of Mathematics*)
Mrs M Suleyman, NVQ3, Childcare (*Reception Teaching Assistant*)
Mrs S Turanli, BSc London, PGCE (*Physical Education*)
Mrs J Weinstock, BA Newcastle, MA, PGCE (*Head of Art*)
Mrs S Worringham (*ICT Systems Manager*)

Visiting Staff – Instrumental Tuition:
Cello: Miss L Seddon, BMus, Dip ABRSM
Clarinet /Saxophone: Mr J Matthews BMus, LTCL
Flute: Miss G Browne, MA, BMus
Piano: Miss S Pope, LRAM
Voice: Miss M Armstrong, DRSAM, GSMD
Violin/Viola: Miss V David AGSM
Violin/Viola: Miss M Pound FTCL, LTCL

Administrative Staff:
Bursar: Mrs D Ivory-Webb, CSBM
Assistant Bursar: Mrs A Monty
Assistant to the Bursary Department: Mrs M Soudah
Headmistress's P.A. and Office Manager: Mrs M Harding
Assistant School Secretaries: Miss V Bennett, Mrs A Dudley and Mrs S Hagi-Savva
Marketing Officer: Mrs D Simmons, BA Bournemouth, Dip Marketing
School Caretaker: Mr D Spurling
Assistant Caretaker: Mr G Stevens

Palmers Green High School is an independent day school for approximately 320 girls aged 3–16. Located in the pleasant suburb of the London Borough of Enfield, the school has good transport links by car, bus rail and tube. It is close to British Rail Stations in Winchmore Hill and Palmers Green. Southgate on the Piccadilly Line is the nearest Tube Station.

The school has a reputation for excellence and the girls flourish in its friendly and challenging environment. At secondary level average teaching group sizes are 12–14, helping the girls to achieve the very best results at GCSE. In 2008 seven girls were placed in the top ten nationally in at least one subject. Primary age pupils enjoy subject specialists teaching them in Art, DT, Drama, Music and PE – frequently in half class groups.

A broad range of extra-curricular activities enriches the multi-cultural school community and educational visits feature regularly in the school calendar with excursions to local, national and international places of interest. These include educational visits to the nearby London museums, art galleries and theatres as well as field trips to Dorset and the Isle of Wight, outdoor pursuits and the Duke of Edinburgh's Award scheme for senior pupils. There are also optional winter ski courses and watersports activity weeks.

The School was founded by the late Alice N Hum in buildings in Green Lanes, Palmers Green and transferred to Avondale Hall on its present site in Hoppers Road, Winchmore Hill in 1918. The School's motto 'By Love Serve One Another' was carefully selected by Miss Hum to reflect her deep Christian convictions derived from her membership of the Society of Friends (Quakers). The motto epitomises the school's special ethos, where individual talent is fostered, celebrated and appreciated, and where contribution to the community is greatly valued.

Palmers Green High School continues to provide the warm and supportive environment of a small school in which both sound academic and personal development go hand in hand. The School aims to foster and maximise the individual talents of each girl while encouraging her to think independently, act in a responsible way and acquire self-discipline.

The compact site has been developed in recent years to extend the school's facilities. The games facilities used are among the best in the area, covering a wide range of sport. Outward bound courses are organised on a regular basis and this wide range of sporting activities forms the basis for the study of a GCSE in Physical Education at the age of 14.

In 2008 the school opened a new nursery for 3–4 year olds – The Alice Nursery – in Bush Hill Park which can accommodate up to 24 children. The Alice Nursery is situated approximately 10 minutes' drive from the main school and is open from 8.45 am until 3.45 pm. The day is divided into morning and afternoon sessions with a break in the middle of the day for lunch. Girls may attend Nursery for the whole day or morning with lunch only. Being an academic nursery, pupils follow a stimulating but demanding curriculum in preparation for Reception at the main school.

The curriculum, embracing the National Curriculum, is designed to give a broad education in which the active acquisition of skills, as well as knowledge is encouraged. Children are familiarised with computers from the Preparatory Department upwards. The performing arts are encouraged in the school and each term sees a large number of pupils taking part in plays, musicals and concerts. Careers education is an integral part of the timetabled curriculum from 11–16 and all pupils participate in careers lectures, exhibitions and work experience placements. Pupils are prepared for up to 10 GCSE subjects, with a view to continuing their studies to A Level and beyond.

Fees per term (2011-2012). Nursery: £2,225 (Full time), £1,275 (Part time); Reception–Year 2 £2,685; Years 3–6 £3,065; Years 7–11 £3,945.

Scholarships. Academic scholarships and bursaries of up to 100% of fees and Music awards are available to candidates aged 11+ for entry in September.

Entrance. Admission to all forms is by test and interview, the main intakes being at 3+, 4+ and 11+.

Charitable status. Palmers Green High School Limited is a Registered Charity, number 312629. It exists for the education of girls.

Pipers Corner School
High Wycombe

Great Kingshill, High Wycombe, Bucks HP15 6LP
Tel: 01494 718255
Fax: 01494 719806
e-mail: theschool@piperscorner.co.uk
website: www.piperscorner.co.uk

Visitor: The Rt Revd The Lord Bishop of Buckingham

Board of Governors:
Chairman of Governors: R Corner, Esq, LLB Hons
Lady Allison (*Vice-Chairman*)
M F T Harborne, Esq (*Vice-Chairman*)
Mrs B Y Boyton-Corbett, CertEd, DipEd
The Countess of Buckinghamshire
B Callaghan, Esq, FCA
S Egan
D B Jones, Esq
Professor P B Mogford
J H Phimester, Esq
H Roberts, Esq

Headmistress: **Mrs H J Ness-Gifford**, BA Hons Exeter, PGCE

Deputy Head: Mrs H Murphy, MA Oxon, PGCE

Bursar and Clerk to the Governors: Mr P R Forrester, MA, FCA

Director of Studies: Mrs D Walmsley, MPhil, MSc, BSc Hons

Pipers Corner is an independent boarding and day school for girls aged 3–18. From Pre-Prep through to Sixth Form there is a focus on academic excellence as girls are supported and challenged to achieve their full potential. Academically successful, our girls progress to further study at Oxbridge and other top universities or specialist dance, drama and music colleges.

Set in 36 acres of beautiful Chiltern countryside, the school is less than one hour from central London and Heathrow airport, 4 miles north of High Wycombe and 2 miles from Great Missenden (40 minute rail links to Marylebone Station in London).

The standard and extent of our excellent facilities along with our commitment to a programme of continual improvement means that our girls have all the space and equipment they need to enable them to excel. Sport is popular at Pipers and from the 25 metre indoor swimming pool, to the sports hall and outdoor pitches we can accommodate a wide range of activities. Similarly those with creative interests benefit from the use of dance, drama and art studios within our Performing Arts and Technology Centre.

In addition to providing a stimulating learning environment we also encourage the girls to cultivate any sporting or creative talents they have through a wide range of lunchtime and after school clubs and activities. Girls are able to develop their own interests in areas including: sport, music, dance, drama, technology, languages and outdoor pursuits. Team spirit is developed through a regular programme of sports fixtures.

Our friendly boarding community offers flexibility, freedom and peace of mind to both girls and their parents. Our range of boarding options means that we can provide practical solutions to the often demanding needs of modern family life. Excellent staff/student ratios, regular group activities and a home-from-home environment means that fun and friendships are allowed to flourish.

The Pipers Corner environment allows girls to thrive. Whatever their strengths, the girls are challenged and supported as they pursue their own unique learning journeys. This approach enables them to fulfil their academic and personal potential and emerge as mature, confident and independent young women.

Fees per term (2011-2012). Day Girls £2,315–£4,490; Weekly Boarders £6,010–£7,320; Full Boarders £6,090–£7,400.

Scholarships and Bursaries. Pipers Corner girls are extremely successful in many areas of achievement. In recognition of this success, the Governors are keen to encourage girls with talent and potential and to widen access to ensure that as many talented girls as possible are able to take advantage of the excellent education that Pipers Corner can provide.

Girls from any primary school, as well as girls from Pipers Corner Prep Department may apply for an 11+ Scholarship for entry into the Senior School in any one of the following areas: Academic, Art, Drama, Music and PE.

Means-tested Bursaries are also available up to a maximum of 100% of day or boarding fees (including any Scholarship award).

The Jessie Cross Bursary – an award for an all-rounder at 11+ – is a means-tested bursary of up to 100% of fees, available to a deserving student currently educated in a maintained primary school and who shows promise in a number of areas. Students applying for the award would need the recommendation of their Headteacher and would also need to provide supporting evidence of their achievements and involvement in their school, church or community. Girls applying for the Jessie Cross Bursary may not also apply for a scholarship.

Applications for Scholarships and Bursaries must be received by the end of November of the year preceding the intended entry to the School. Pipers Entrance Examinations are held early in January and potential scholars will be invited back shortly afterwards for further interview and assessment.

A limited number of Sixth Form Scholarships are also available at 16+. Examinations are held annually in January for student entry into the Sixth Form the following September. Short-listed candidates will be interviewed by members of the governing body, the Headmistress and the Deputy Head. Please contact the school for further details.

Charitable status. Pipers Corner School is a Registered Charity, number 310635. It exists to provide high quality education for girls.

Polam Hall School

Grange Road, Darlington, Co Durham DL1 5PA
Tel: 01325 463383
Fax: 01325 383539
e-mail: information@polamhall.com
website: www.polamhall.com

Motto: '*Concordia Crescimus*' – *We Grow in Harmony*

Governors:
Mrs S Pelham (*Chair*)
¶Mrs D M Bateman
Dr M M Carr
Mrs B Atkinson

Mrs Angela Elliott
Mr K Gordon
Mr N Millar
Miss C Nichols
Mr C D W Pratt
Dr N J G Wright

Headmaster: **Mr John Moreland**, MA Oxon, NPQH

Acting Deputy Headmistress: Mrs S J Hardy, BA Hons, PGCE

Bursar and Clerk to the Governors: Mr M N Carr, ACIB

Polam Hall School was founded in 1848 and admits boys and girls aged 2 to 18 of all religious denominations. Boys and girls join us at 2 where they are taught together until the age of 9 (Year 4). Between Year 5 and Year 11 the boys and girls are taught separately where appropriate. Classes are co-educational at Sixth Form. Boarding is for boys and girls.

Polam Hall stands in 20 acres of parkland within 5 minutes' walking distance of Darlington town centre. The school is ideally placed, being close to the main east coast rail line, the A1(M) and Durham Tees Valley Airport, providing excellent access for both local and overseas students.

Numbers on roll. There are over 350 pupils, including 45 boarders, 50 Sixth Form students and 140 Juniors.

Age and method of entry. From age 7 upwards: Assessment/examination and interview with Headmaster where applicable.

Scholarships and Awards. (*See Scholarship Entries section.*) Scholarships and Bursaries available at 7+, 11+, 14+ and 16+, Music Awards at 11+, 14+ and 16+, Sports Scholarship at 16+.

Fees per term (2011-2012). Early Steps: £575–£1,075 (mornings or afternoons), £1,650–£2,150 (full day with lunch). Junior School: £2,150–£2,980 (Day), £6,050 (Boarding). Senior School: £3,890 (Day), £7,475 (Boarding). Fees for weekly boarders are reduced by £200 per term. Lunch for Day Pupils £185 per term.

Academic. From Early Steps Nursery to Sixth Form students are encouraged and supported so that they achieve to their full potential. Small classes and dedicated teachers provide students with an excellent education – both in and out of the classroom.

Early Steps and our Reception Class provide Foundation Stage education for girls and boys aged two upwards and the children link with the main school for various activities, joining the Junior School for lunch. These year groups are staffed by specialists in Foundation Stage education. When the children progress to Year 1 and 2, they have a dedicated teacher for all subjects. Moving on to Year 3 they embark on a very varied curriculum with a more structured timetabled day and are taught by specialist staff in all subjects.

Students entering the Senior School take a diagnostic examination, which helps to identify their educational needs. A broad curriculum in Years 7 to 9 leads to students taking a wide range of GCSE subjects. A choice of 20 subjects is currently available, including the three separate sciences, and flexible timetabling allows for individual needs to be addressed. Educational visits are arranged to various points of interest around the area and further afield.

The Sixth Form is co-educational and over 22 A Level subjects are available. The students are allocated a Personal Tutor to guide them through Career and University choices. A Careers room is available to them and a UCAS advisor and a Careers Convention assist in making choices. Almost all pupils go on to higher education. The School has an outstanding record in helping students secure places at their chosen university. In 2010 35% of subjects achieved the new gold-standard A* grade at A Level and all students were awarded places at the University of their choice. At GCSE over half of the papers taken gained A*/A grades.

Our Study Centre has specialists trained in helping pupils with learning difficulties, such as dyslexia or dyspraxia.

There is also specialist teaching for those for whom English is a second language.

Extra-Curricular Activities. A tremendous range of activities is available throughout the school. There are regular sports fixtures in athletics, cricket, football, hockey, lacrosse, netball, rounders, rugby, tennis, Pupils also do basketball, gymnastics, modern dance, orienteering, swimming, trampolining, and volleyball. There is a Brownie Pack for the Junior girls and the Duke of Edinburgh's Award is widely taken up by the Seniors.

Boarding is available for boys and girls from age 8. There are 3 boarding houses and the students are looked after by 7 Housemistresses who take a sensitive interest in each pupil's personal welfare. A full programme of evening and weekend activities is arranged.

Facilities. The school boasts a fully-equipped Science block containing 5 laboratories, a Domestic Science lab, 3 Computer Suites, a school Library containing fully-networked flat-screen computers, and a fully-equipped Theatre seating over 200 people. The Sixth Form has its own Centre for both study and leisure.

A Resource Centre complements teaching in the Junior School and is equipped with computers, interactive whiteboard and library.

PHOSA Polam Hall Old Scholars' Association. *Secretary*: Mrs V Price, c/o Polam Hall School, Grange Road, Darlington, DL1 5PA.

Charitable status. Polam Hall School is a Registered Charity, number 527369. Its aim is to provide, maintain, and carry on a school for the education of children.

Portsmouth High School
GDST

---

25 Kent Road, Southsea, Hampshire PO5 3EQ
Tel: 023 9282 6714
Fax: 023 9281 4814
e-mail: headsec@por.gdst.net
website: www.portsmouthhigh.co.uk

Founded 1882.

Portsmouth High School is part of the GDST (Girls' Day School Trust). The GDST is the leading network of independent girls' schools in the UK. As a charity that owns and runs 24 schools and two academies, it reinvests all its income in its schools. For further information about the Trust, see p. xxi or visit www.gdst.net.

Additional information about the school may be found on the school's website and a prospectus pack is available from the Admissions Officer at the school.

Chair of the School Governing Board: Mrs S Pulvertaft, BSc, MBA, MCIM

Headmistress: Mrs J Prescott, BSc Cardiff, PGCE, NPQH

Deputy Head: Mr C J Campbell, BSc Aston, MSc Surrey

Assistant Head (*Sixth Form*): Mrs J Cresswell, BA Dunelm

Assistant Head (*Pastoral*): Mrs H Trim, MSc Leicester, BSc Southampton

Head of the Junior School: Mrs P Harris-Burland, MA, BA Hons Southampton, Mont Dip

Deputy Head of Junior School: Mr P Marshallsay, BA Exeter

Marketing Manager: Mrs E Blunt, BA Portsmouth

Number of Pupils. 370 are in the Senior School (11–18), 120 in the Junior School (rising 3–11).

Portsmouth High School is a community of learning committed to academic excellence and preparing girls to be the leaders of tomorrow. Each girl is encouraged to develop her own voice and her own views and to understand and build on her strengths. This aim was confirmed in the last ISI Inspection report (October 2009). A broad based education encourages each girl's talents and potential to the full in an atmosphere of achievement and excellence. Characteristic of the GDST philosophy, Portsmouth High School has a profile of sustained academic achievement, strong relationships with the local community and outstanding pastoral care. Situated close to the sea, the school draws pupils from an extensive area of Hampshire, West Sussex and the Isle of Wight. All major transport providers serve the area.

The Senior School is accommodated in the original building, and a recent capital investment programme has seen the development of a Sport, Design Technology and Geography building on the senior school site. The most recent addition is a new café for senior pupils.

A partnership with the University of Portsmouth means the school has joint use of the Langstone sports ground facilities, including a floodlit synthetic turf pitch and a new multi-use games area; the site is just 2 miles from the school. In addition, the school site facilities include a Sport England standard sports hall, 4 hard tennis courts and 6 netball courts. Sixth Form students do not wear uniform, but have a 'Dress for Work' code. Sixth Formers have a Sixth Form Centre with a large common room, kitchen, study rooms and IT room.

The Junior School is located 2 minutes' walk away in a wonderful period house with extensive gardens including 4 netball courts, and a range of indoor and outdoor facilities. Major investment in the Junior School saw the completion of an award-winning Pre-Prep building. With the addition of a nursery class, which along with reception, was judged 'Outstanding' in all categories in recent Ofsted and ISI inspections, the school is able to offer continuity of education throughout the Foundation Stage.

The Curriculum. The aim at Portsmouth High School is to foster in each girl the confidence to take risks and tackle new challenges within an atmosphere of ambition and enterprise, by providing appropriate teaching, advice and support. A balanced programme of study delays the need to make subject choices as long as possible and in this way, the widest career options are maintained. There is the highest level of achievement in a wide variety of academic subjects, sport, music and drama. The is a generous provision for ICT with both Junior and Senior pupils making the most of a Virtual Learning Environment (VLE) to access school work at home.

Extra-Curricular Activities. There is an extensive programme of extra-curricular activities in both the Junior and Senior schools. The lunchtime and after-school clubs range from street dance to public speaking. There is an enthusiastic involvement in music, art, sport and drama with many performances and fixtures throughout the School calendar for Junior and Senior girls. Senior Girls have the opportunity to become involved in World Challenge and the Duke of Edinburgh's Award Scheme as well as a Sixth Form Seminar Group and Enrichment Programme. There are regular exchange trips, overseas tours, music tours and opportunities for pupils to undertake work experience.

Admission Procedures/Entrance Examinations. At 11+ and 13+ entry the examinations in Mathematics and English are designed to test potential rather than knowledge. Prior to the 11+ examinations all girls take part in a series of team activities in school. At 13+ girls take part in a Shadowing Day and are interviewed by the Headmistress. Sixth Form entry is based on having at least 7 GCSEs at grade B or above. Most subjects will require at least grade A as a prerequisite for A Level study and applicants are invited for interview. Entry into the Junior School is based on assessments and examinations dependent on age.

Fees per term (2011-2012). Senior School £3,467, Junior School £2,513, Nursery £2,076.

The fees cover the regular curriculum, school books, stationery and other materials, public examinations, choral music, games and swimming. The fees for extra subjects, including individual lessons in instrumental music and speech training, are shown in the Admissions Handbook.

Scholarships and Bursaries. The GDST makes available to the school a number of scholarships and bursaries. Bursaries are means tested and are intended to ensure that the school remains accessible to bright girls who would be unable to enter the school without financial assistance.

Academic and Music Scholarships are available for 11+, 13+ and Sixth Form, with Art, Drama and Sport Scholarships available in the Sixth Form.

Charitable status. Portsmouth High School is part of The Girls' Day School Trust, which is a Registered Charity, number 306983.

Princess Helena College

Preston, Hitchin, Hertfordshire SG4 7RT
Tel: 01462 432100
Fax: 01462 443871
e-mail: head@princesshelenacollege.co.uk
website: www.princesshelenacollege.co.uk

Motto: *Fortis qui se vincit*

Patron: Her Majesty the Queen

President: HRH The Duchess of Gloucester

Vice-President: Miss Mary Beattie, MBE, JP, DL

Governing Body:
Chairman: Dr Mary Buchanan, MA, MIMMM, CEng, PhD
Vice-Chairman: Major Gen Andrew Ritchie, CBE
Treasurer: Mr David Prosser, BSc, FCA

Clerk to the Governors and Bursar: Dr James Bentall, MA, MBA, PhD, ACII, ACMI

Headmistress: Mrs Jo-Anne Duncan, MA

Deputy Head: Mrs Camilla Wilson, BEd

Assistant Head – Learning and Communication: Mr Keith Miller, MA, BEd

Assistant Head – Academic: Ms Rachel Poston, BSc, PGCE

Head's PA & Registrar: Mrs Heather Baim

Old Girls' Association Secretary: Mrs Susannah Goodbody

Princess Helena College is a dynamic school, where you will find happy, successful and confident day girls and boarders aged 11–18. We provide a vibrant, modern and challenging education whilst respecting and encouraging traditional values.

History. Founded in 1820 we are one of England's oldest academic girls' schools. We are extremely proud of our heritage and aim to maintain high academic standards and respect for traditional values. The school was founded for daughters of officers who had served in the Napoleonic Wars and daughters of Anglican priests. We now encourage this tradition by offering bursaries to daughters from families that are in the forces and the clergy.

Ethos. At Princess Helena College, we believe every girl is an individual and aim to inspire her to achieve both her academic and personal goals. We choose to remain a small school because we strongly believe this unique approach provides many benefits in academic, extra-curricular and pastoral areas. The educational benefits include a flexible curriculum and small classes. Both result in individual atten-

tion and excellent value-added attainment. A smaller school allows teachers to understand girls' individual learning styles, to recognise their particular strengths and weaknesses and to set individual learning targets. Pastoral care is strengthened by excellent relations between pupils and staff, which result in a strong family atmosphere. Knowing our girls well allows us to encourage them to take risks safe in the knowledge that we will support them. This allows every girl to be challenged, to achieve and to grow. Within a small school your daughter's chances of being selected for a team, a place in the orchestra, a part in a play or a position of responsibility are far higher. Having the opportunity to take part or perform in these activities will increase her confidence and self-belief. The value of this should not be underestimated.

Facilities. As well as an idyllic and safe learning environment, Princess Helena College has excellent educational facilities. The main building is a beautiful Queen Anne mansion that lies in fine Gertrude Jekyll gardens and 183 acres of parkland. Over the past 5 years the school has invested heavily in developing the facilities for all girls: a new fitness suite has been added, the Sixth Form boarding facilities have been improved and the school dining room has been refurbished. Other developments include a new science centre, art and design studios, a Sixth Form study and recreational area in the main school, and a refurbished learning resources centre.

Curriculum. We offer every girl the opportunity to excel within a varied and stimulating curriculum. Taught in small classes by highly qualified and enthusiastic teachers who are dedicated to supporting each girl's talents and interests, our girls attain high levels of academic excellence and confidence. Girls are taught in sets that rarely exceed 18 and their potential and progress is carefully monitored.

The lower school curriculum (Years 7–9) consists of English, French, Spanish, Latin, German, Mathematics, Information Communications Technology, Biology, Physics, Chemistry, History, Geography, Religious Education, Music, Drama, Physical Education, Art, Design and Technology. There are also programmes in PCC (PSHE, Citizenship and Careers), touch typing and information resource skills.

In Years 10–11, girls follow their chosen GCSE subjects, following much consultation with staff and parents. On average, girls study between 8 and 10 GCSE subjects. The pass rate A*–C is 98% with nearly 60% of the GCSEs being passed at A* or A grade.

In the Sixth Form, A Level courses are available in all the traditional academic subjects, as well as Economics & Business Studies, Dance, Government & Politics, Health & Social Care, Media Studies, Psychology and Theatre Studies. Extensive career and Higher Education support and advice is provided.

A flexible approach to boarding. Princess Helena College is a vibrant community made up of boarders and day girls. We offer a very flexible approach to boarding and full, weekly, and flexible boarding are well established. Day girls can choose to stay into the early evening to make full use of the optional extended school day, participating in supervised prep or one of the numerous after school activities.

The Arts. Princess Helena College is particularly strong in Art & Design, Dance, Drama, Music and Speech & Drama. Girls may enter examinations in all these areas. Dance is a hugely popular activity, with girls learning jazz, modern, ballet, Irish and tap. Most of the College is involved in some form of musical activity, with many girls choosing to take part in one of the many different music groups or ensembles. Plays are staged throughout the year and there are regular joint productions with neighbouring boys' and co-educational schools.

Sport. In addition to timetabled lessons, there are sports activities on weekdays after school and on some Saturdays. Girls participate in a wide range of sports including lacrosse, netball, tennis, athletics, badminton, cross-country, rounders and swimming. Girls are given the opportunity to participate in competitive sport, recreational sport and fitness – we aim to encourage all girls to find an activity they will enjoy at school and in the future.

Extra-curricular activities. Life is busy at Princess Helena College – there is an exciting array of extra-curricular activities and clubs. Girls can choose to join in with these activities either during their extended lunch break or in the early evening. From photography to public speaking, from language club to life saving and from touch typing to trampolining, there is an activity for everyone. The Duke of Edinburgh's Award Scheme is also a popular activity, with girls attaining Gold, Silver and Bronze awards each year, as is CCF, held with St Columba's College.

Lifeskills Programme. We recognise the importance of developing young women who demonstrate a range of abilities above and beyond their academic achievements. Our lifeskills programme provides all girls with the enrichment experiences required to prepare them for their future lives. These include independence of thought, self-confidence, teamwork, effective communication and problem-solving. There is a regular schedule of events including seminar suppers, lectures and activities specifically designed to encourage all students to cultivate these valuable skills.

Religion. Girls attend the nearby village church of St Martin's in Preston, which is also used for the school's Confirmation Services. Although the school's affiliation is to the Church of England, girls of other denominations and religions are welcomed.

Location. Set in 183 acres of rural parkland the College offers an easily accessible location within a safe and beautiful environment. The College is situated 30 minutes north of London between the A1 and the M1, just 5 minutes from the market town of Hitchin. Our excellent transport links include rail access (35 minutes to King's Cross) and proximity to several airports (Luton 15 mins, Stansted 45 mins and Heathrow 60 mins). There is an extensive network of school bus routes to Brookmans Park, Buntingford, Cottered, Cuffley, Digswell, Enfield, Gustard Wood, Hadley Wood, Harpenden, Hertford, Kimpton, Little Wymondley, London Colney, Luton, Potters Bar, St Albans, Stevenage, Welwyn and Wheathampstead. Possible future routes may include Elstree, Knebworth and Radlett.

Admission. We welcome girls aged 11–18. Most girls join the school at age 11 (Year 7), but there are also entrants at age 13 (Year 9) and the Sixth Form (Year 12). Please contact Heather Baim, Registrar (01462 443888) for a prospectus or to find out the date of our next Open Day. All girls must sit either the College's own Entrance Exam or the Common Entrance Exam. Sixth Form places are conditional on GCSE results.

Fees per term (2011-2012). Day Girls: Years 7 and 8 £4,500; Years 9–Sixth Form £5,680. Weekly Boarding or Full Boarding: Years 7 and 8 £6,425; Years 9–Sixth Form £8,205. Fees include lunch and supervised prep but exclude some books. Flexible boarding costs between £43 and £51 per night.

Scholarships and Bursaries. Scholarships (worth up to 15% of annual fees) are available for academically able pupils. Art, Drama, Music and Sport scholarships are also available. Bursaries of 10% of fees are available for daughters of the clergy and of members of the armed forces. Sibling bursaries are 5% of fees.

Charitable status. Princess Helena College is a Registered Charity, number 311064. It was founded in 1820 for the purposes of education.

Prior's Field

Godalming, Surrey GU7 2RH
Tel: 01483 810551
Fax: 01483 810180
e-mail: office@priorsfieldschool.com
website: www.priorsfieldschool.com

Founded in 1902.
    Motto: *We live by admiration, hope and love.*

Board of Governors:
Chairman: Mr R P Green, FCA
Mr N A Andrews, LLB
Mr B G Burton-Brown, BSc
Mr A K B Cater, ACCA, MA
Mrs D C C Colvin
Nr I N H Davis, BA, BArch, RIBA
Dr L Elghali, MSc, EngD, AIEMA
Mr G J Haig, OBE
Mr I Hinckley, ACA, CTA
Mrs C W J Formstone, HDCR
Mr R W J Long, FRICS
Mr J R MacLeod
Mrs A Morris, BSc, PGCE
Mrs E A S Prescott-Decie, MA

Headmistress: Mrs Julie A Roseblade, MA (*English, Drama*)

Deputy Head (Pastoral): Mrs Ruth Saunders, BSc, PGCE (*ICT*)
Deputy Head (Academic): Dr Richard Hoskins, MA, PhD, QTS (*Religious Studies*)
Bursar and Clerk to the Governors: Mrs Leonie Ranson, BA, DipEurHum, MBIFM

Academic Staff:
Ms Nadia Ali, BSc, PGCE, PGDip (*Biology*)
Miss Jane Allen, BSc Hons, PGCE (*Head of Biology*)
Mrs Ann Barnes, BA, PGCE (*Textiles*)
Mrs Rachel Bartlett, BSc, PGCE (*Mathematics*)
Miss Antonia Berry, BA, QTS (*Head of English*)
Mrs Jillian Buckley, MEd, DMS, CertEd, MCMI (*Head of Careers*)
Mr Marc Carter, BA, PGCE (*Head of History*)
Mr Nigel Cassidy, BMus Hons, GSMD, LTCL, PGCE (*Music, Singing*)
Mrs Ros Cocks, BA, PGCE (*French*)
Miss Cendrine Conchon, Maîtrise LCE, PGCE, QTS (*French and Spanish*)
Mrs Mary Claire Cook, BEd, CertEd (*Geography, Charities, Head of Lower School*)
Mr Bruno Di Mario, MA, QTS (*Photography*)
Miss Georgina Doyle, BSc, QTS (*Physical Education*)
Mrs Pamela Edworthy, BSc, PGCE, DipSpLD (*Head of Learning Support*)
Ms Andrea Fairbairn, MA (*Mathematics*)
Mrs Sarah Farnell, BSc, QTS (*Physical Education*)
Miss Alison Finch, BA, QTS (*Physical Education, Head of Frank House*)
Miss Joanne Gellard, BA, PGCE (*Art, Textiles, Photography*)
Mrs Charlotte Gomez, BA, PGCE (*Spanish, French, Head of Modern Foreign Languages*)
Miss Louise Gordon, BSc, PGCE (*Head of Physical Education*)
Mr Gary Hayes, BA, PGCE (*Head of Religious Studies*)
Mr Jeremy Hepworth, BA, MIA (*Head of ICT, Coordinator of Adventure Training*)
Mrs Susan Holmes, BA, CertEd (*History of Art*)
Mrs Penny Horton, BA, PGCE (*Drama*)
Mrs Catherine Humphreys, BSc, PGCE (*Science*)

Mrs Jillian Jan, BA, PGCE (*Pscyhology*)
Mr Geoffrey Jones, BSc, MSc, PGCE (*Head of Sciences*)
Ms Marie Kervin, BA Hons, PGCE (*English*)
Mr Stephen Kinder, BA, PGCE (*Head of Creative Arts*)
Ms Valerie Klein, BA, PGCE (*French, Spanish*)
Mrs Anna Lenton, BA, MBA, QTS (*Spanish and French*)
Mr Stuart Lodge, BA, PGCE, BELA (*Head of Drama*)
Mrs Desi Lyon, MA, QTS (*English, Head of Upper Sixth Form*)
Mrs Natasha Macdonald, BSc, GTP (*Sciences*)
Mrs Anne Morrison-Lyon, MA, QTS (*English*)
Mrs Amanda Morwood, MA (*Head of History, Head of Lower Sixth Form*)
Mrs Sarah Onions, MA, FEC (*Media Studies*)
Mrs Valerie Page, BA, PGCE (*English as an Additional Language*)
Miss Emma Petch, BA, QTS (*Physical Education*)
Mr Jonathan Pledger, BA, PGCE (*Business Studies, Economics*)
Mr Trevor Pratt, BA Hons, ARCO, LTCL (*Director of Music*)
Miss Hester Pretorius, BSc, MEd, QTS (*Design Technology, Science, Head of Pankhurst House*)
Mrs Joanna Prudence, BA, TESOL (*Religious Studies, Learning Support & Oxbridge*)
Mrs Jose Purkiss, BA (*Head of Boarding, PSHE*)
Miss Neus Rayner, MA, QTS (*Spanish, French*)
Mrs Amanda Rusholme, BSc Hons, PGCE (*Head of Mathematics*)
Mrs Kerry Sapseid, BA, DipEd (*English, Head of Upper School*)
Mr Peter Sapseid, BA, HDE (*English, Debating, History*)
Dr McDonald Smith, BSc, PhD, PGCE (*Chemistry*)
Mrs Wendy Spencer, BSc CertEd (*Mathematics, Duke of Edinburgh's Award*)
Miss Tiffany Teasdale, BSc, PGCE (*Food Technology*)
Ms Catrin Treanor, BSc, PGCE (*Head of Geography, Exceptionally Able Coordinator, EPQ Coordinator*)
Ms Rachel Troup, BSc Ed (*Mathematics, Assistant Head of Lower School*)
Miss Emma Watts, BA, PGCE, HQT (*Art, Photography*)
Mrs Gillian Westerman, MSc, PGCE (*Geography, Mathematics*)
Mrs Karen Wilcock, BSc, PGCE (*Mathematics, Director of Studies*)

Visiting Staff:
Mrs Barbara Awbery (*Tennis Coaching*)
Mrs Rachel Bowen-Perkins, BMus Hons (*Classical Singing Vocal Tutor*)
Miss Amie Jane Brown (*Rock Singing Vocal Tutor*)
Mrs Fiona Burton, BA Hons, DipSpLD (*Learning Support*)
Mr Nigel Cassidy, BMus Hons, PGCert, GSMD, LTCL (*Singing*)
Mr Vic Cox, BA Hons, PGCE (*Bass Guitar*)
Miss Anne Marie Curran, BMus, LRAM (*Violin*)
The Revd John Fellows, MA (*Chaplain*)
Mrs Nicola Fournel, BAMus Hons (*Piano, Theory*)
Mrs Ruth Harrower, BA (*Speech Therapist*)
Mrs Rebecca Hersham, CertEd (*Learning Support*)
Mr Nicholas Higgins, BMus, PGCE (*Flute, Clarinet, Saxophone*)
Ms Jan Kobzik, ISTD, LLAM (*Speech and Drama*)
Mr Darren Lucas (*Guitar, Head of Rock and Pop*)
Ms Emilia O'Connor, GRSM, BMus (*Singing*)
Mrs Karen Porter, BSc, PGCE (*Mathematics*)
Mr Bob Price (*Trumpet, Trombone*)
Mr Hamish Robertson (*Bagpipes*)
Mrs Anna Rogers, LLAM (*Speech and Drama*)
Mr Ian Skelton-Smith, MA, PGCE (*Economics*)
Miss Jayne Spencer, AGSM, LGSM, ALCM (*Cello, Theory*)
Mrs Jean Stevens, ATCL, MISM (*Piano, Theory, Associated Board Accompanist*)

Dr M Helena Tostevin, PhD, QTS (*Portuguese*)
Mr Adam Turner (*Tennis Coaching*)
Mr Jonathan Wills (*Drums*)

Administration:
PA to Head: Mrs Anne Robinson
PA to Deputy Heads: Miss Nicola Bartlett
Registrar: Miss Penelope Harris, BSc Hons, MSc
Admissions Manager: Miss Amanda Lay
Registry / Marketing Assistant: Mrs Celia Toms
Alumnae Coordinator: Mrs Samantha Bushell, BSc
School Accountant: Mrs Juanita Percival, FCCA
Assistant Accountant: Mrs Diane Cant
Bursary Assistant: Mrs Allyson White
Bursary Clerk: Mrs Charlotte Smith
PA to Bursar: Mrs Liz Harker
Examinations Officer: Mrs Anne Sheldrake, CertEd
Facilities Manager: Mr Richard Hughes, MBIFM
IT Systems Manager: Mr Mark Roberts-Barter
Network Support Technician: Mr Richard Hibbert
Trainee Network Support Technician: Mr Tom Hughes
Digital Media Coordinator: Mrs Angela Barker-Lewis, BA
Management Information Coordinator: Mrs Christine Milton
Development Consultant: Ms Louise Hunter
School Secretary and Office Manager: Mrs Sophie Irving, BA
School Receptionist/Secretary: Mrs Caroline Cook
Medical Centre:
Mrs Miin Worsdell, RGN, BSc
Mrs Helen Whiffen, SRN, DN
Mrs Tina Trafford, RN
School Counsellor: Kim Bradshaw
Laboratory Technician: Mrs Joanne Slaytor, Mrs Hazel Kimber, MEng
DT Technician: Mr Nic Quick
Art Technician: Mrs Clare Benzikie, BA
Food Technician/Technician Assistant: Mrs Marilyn Lambert
Senior Librarian: Mrs Wendy Hilliam
Librarian: Mrs Braith Harris, MA, MCLIP
Stationery Shop Manager: Mrs Sheila Steele

Boarding:
Head of Boarding: Mrs Jose Purkiss, BA
Junior Housemistress: Mrs Deborah Roberts-Barter
Sixth Form Housemistress: Mrs Emma Picken (*Head of Austen House*)
Sixth Form House Tutors:
Miss Tiffany Teasdale, BSc, PGCE
Miss Hester Pretorius, BSc, MEd, QTS
Boarding House Tutor (1st-5th Forms):
Ms Val Klein, BA
Ms Louise Hunter

Age Range. 11–18.
Numbers. Boarders 35, Weekly Boarders 76, Day Girls 295.

The School was founded by Julia Huxley, mother of Aldous and Julian, to provide a progressive and exciting education that also broadened the girls' outlook. This legacy lives on today as Prior's Field provides an excellent all-round education which recognises achievement in all its forms.

Visitors to Prior's Field frequently tell us that it has a unique and distinctive 'feel'. We are fortunate in our size – small enough to provide tailored, individual care and large enough to offer a wide and exciting curriculum. Girls choose from over 20 subjects at A Level and from a range of over 40 clubs and activities.

Relationships are key to our success and pupils of all abilities do exceptionally well in an environment that builds confidence and encourages everyone to aim high. At Prior's Field each individual can find something at which to shine and we are proud of our track record of 'adding value' (within the top 1% nationally). This is achieved without unnecessary stress and pressure, through small classes, excellent teaching and a careful balance of challenge and support. We know our girls well and encourage them to be themselves, think independently and engage fully in the life of the school and wider community. Opportunities for leadership, initiative and responsibility mean that girls are well equipped for the world ahead. The Sixth Form leave, for the Universities of their choice, as self-assured, well-qualified and interesting young women of integrity.

The *Good Schools Guide* 15th Edition, published in 2010, concludes that *"For parents who ... seek a more balanced approach to life and learning for their daughter, Prior's Field provides a refreshing option".*

Buildings. The original buildings were designed by Charles Voysey and the garden by Gertrude Jekyll. Additions in recent years have been two new ICT rooms, a new Sports Hall, an extension to the Sixth Form House, a new Hall/Theatre, dining room, superb Science Centre, a brand new Library and outdoor heated swimming pool. In addition to the classrooms, the main building includes a Drama studio, technology area and new multimedia digital language laboratory. A project to build new classrooms for the teaching of creative arts is currently under way and, from September 2011, the school plans to have an all-weather sports pitch.

Boarding. From September 2011, girls in Years 7 and 8 will have the chance to flexi-board for the first time, alongside our very popular weekly and full boarding options. Staying for a maximum of 2 fixed nights per week, flexi-boarders will share bedrooms of 2–4 girls under the care of the Housemistress. Year 7 boarders have a dedicated area within the house, including study, kitchen and sitting area. All other year groups have a separate pantry and common room and senior girls (Years 9–11) have single study-bedrooms. Sixth Form boarders reside in a separate sixth form house, which incorporates 20 en-suite study-bedrooms. Here they lead more independent lives under the supervision of the resident Sixth Form Housemistress. Throughout the boarding houses the emphasis is on working together and the creation of a warm, supportive, environment which enables the girls to achieve highly and mature into young women who think for themselves.

Curriculum. Girls at KS3 follow a broad curriculum including Art, Music, ICT, Design and Technology (including digital photography), as well as all the 'core' subjects. Languages include French, Spanish and Latin. Girls in the First and Second Form follow a course in Thinking and Learning which involves philosophy, touch-typing, debating, library/research and study skills.

GCSE and A Level courses are offered at KS4 and in the Sixth Form. Girls are prepared for Oxbridge and other competitive universities by a dedicated tutor. Others typically go on to study at a wide range of universities and art colleges. Careers is taught across the school as part of the PSHE programme. In addition, visits are arranged to university open days and the school also arranges talks by visitors from a wide range of professions. Fifth formers are encouraged to join a work experience scheme. Those studying languages at A Level are encouraged to take up work placements in Europe. The school has excellent IT provision to support teaching and learning; a well-established programme for its most able students and a programme specifically for scholarship girls.

Music. Music flourishes throughout the school. A wide range of instruments is taught and 70% of the girls take individual lessons. Extra-curricular activities include 3 main choirs, an orchestra, jazz group, rock groups and many instrumental and vocal ensembles. Professional engagements include the RPO at Wembley, local festivals, the Royal Albert Hall and churches in London. Music Technology is taught in Years 9 to 11 and offered alongside Music at A Level.

Extra-Curricular Activities. Girls may join over 46 clubs ranging from Drama and Young Engineers to Photography, Golf, Climbing and Art. Older girls can join the Duke of Edinburgh's Award Scheme, Young Enterprise and Model United Nations. Outings and social events with a range of boys' schools, including Eton, Harrow and Charterhouse, are arranged for boarders at the weekends, whilst throughout the year there are numerous educational visits to theatres, adventure and field centres and venues for debating and public-speaking competitions. Each year trips go off to Europe and beyond. In 2009 the Gold Duke of Edinburgh's Award girls went to Norway and another group went to South Africa. The World Challenge girls will go to South India in 2012.

Sport. Hockey, netball, tennis, athletics and rounders are the main games, but opportunities exist for many other sports and dance through the after-school clubs and activities. Games take place in the 23-acre site. Tennis coaching is available throughout the year and, in Spring 2011, the school launched an Elite Tennis Academy in conjunction with Orbit Tennis for girls with exceptional tennis potential. Coaching in golf, fencing, self-defence and aerobic training is also available. Ice skating, bowling and swimming take place at the Guildford Spectrum for all pupils who are interested and the equestrian team practises locally and competes in 'eventing'. A number of girls are regular horse-riders at local stables.

Access. The school is situated between Godalming and Guildford and is less than a mile from the A3. Godalming and Guildford are the nearest railway stations, and we are conveniently placed (via the A3 and M25) for both Heathrow and Gatwick Airports. At the start and finish of term, girls may be escorted to, or met from, either airport or railway station. There is a weekly minibus to and from London and girls are collected from and returned to Godalming station each day.

Admission. Admission is by the School's entrance examination. Open days are held every term and individual visits are arranged at parents' convenience by the Registrar.

Scholarships and Bursaries. (*See Scholarship Entries section.*) Academic Scholarships of up to 20% of school fees and Exhibitions for Academic promise of up to 10% are offered at 11+ along with scholarships for Art, Music, Drama and Sport worth up to 20% of fees. There is also a 10% reduction in fees for the daughters of Old Girls and for siblings. Pupils who have a parent serving in the Armed Forces are eligible for a 10% discount on the fees, plus the MOD's CEA. Scholarships are also available at 13+ and again in the Sixth Form; a number of 95% Academic Bursaries are available for Sixth Form day places, for those who would not otherwise be able to access an independent school education.

Fees per term (2011-2012). Boarders £7,995; Day Girls £4,995.

Charitable status. The Prior's Field School Trust Limited is a Registered Charity, number 312038. It exists to promote education and to offer and provide Scholarships, Exhibitions, Prizes and Awards at any school carried on by the Trust.

Putney High School
GDST

---

35 Putney Hill, London SW15 6BH
Tel: 020 8788 4886
Fax: 020 8789 8068
e-mail: putneyhigh@put.gdst.net
website: www.putneyhigh.gdst.net

Founded 1893.

Putney High School is part of the GDST (Girls' Day School Trust). The GDST is the leading network of independent girls' schools in the UK. As a charity that owns and runs 24 schools and two academies, it reinvests all its income in its schools. For further information about the Trust, see p. xxi or visit www.gdst.net.

A more detailed prospectus may be obtained from the school or via the school's website.

There are about 870 pupils, of whom 555, including a Sixth Form of 150, are in the Senior School (ages 11–18) and 315 in the Junior School (ages 4–11).

Local Governing Body:
Mr P Wake, MSc (*Chairman*)
Mrs C Boardman, MA, MBA
Prof J Broadbent, BA, MA, PhD
Mr J David, BA
Prof C Kinnon, BSc, PhD
Mrs J Railton, BA
Ms A Scott-Bayfield, MA, Solicitor of the Supreme Court
Mr M Wright
Mr T Wheare, MA, DipEd, FRSA (*GDST Council*)

Headmistress: Dr Denise V Lodge, BSc, MSc, PhD London, PGCE

Senior Leadership Team:
Deputy Head (Academic): Ms O Carlin, BSc Imperial
Deputy Head (Pastoral): Mrs K von Malaisé, MA Cambridge, PGCE
Head of Junior School: Mrs J Wallace, BMus, MA Bath, PGCE
Head of Sixth Form: Mrs S Longstaff, BA Durham
Director of Assessment: Mrs G John, BSc Exeter, MSc London, MSc Sheffield Hallam
School Business Manager: Mrs A Hinkson, BA Sussex, MBA Kingston

Senior School:

Art:
Mr A J Bacci-Andreoli, BA Goldsmiths, MA London
Mr N Murray, BA Camberwell
Mrs I Vickers, BFA Oxford

Business Studies and Economics:
Mrs S Butt, BA London

Classics:
Miss A Ferris, MA Oxford
Mrs G Witty, BA Liverpool
Mrs C Christie, BA London, MPhil Cambridge

Design Technology:
Ms M Mescall, BEd Surrey
Ms D Burton, BA Goldsmiths
Miss S Norman, BA Brunel

Drama:
Mrs R Pugh, BA London, PGDip Central School of Speech and Drama
Ms E Burford, BA London

English:
Miss J Sharp, BA, MLit Newcastle
Mr E Artro-Morris, MA Oxford
Mrs C Child, BA Birmingham
Ms J Wyer, BA London, MA Camberwell
Ms K Fereday, BA Cardiff

Geography:
Mrs E Lang, BSc Liverpool
Mrs M Beaumont, BA Newcastle
Mrs E Matthews, BA Exeter

History:
Miss B Britten, BA Sheffield
Miss A Simmons, BA Bristol
Ms S Knowles, BA London

Mrs S Meakins, MA Cambridge

History of Art:
Mrs I Vickers, BFA Oxford

ICT:
Ms S Longstaff, BA Durham

Learning Enrichment:
Mrs M Lewis, BA Lancaster, MA London
Mrs D Tizzano, BA Cambridge

Mathematics:
Mr M Finnemore, BSc Imperial, ARCS
Ms S Longstaff, BA Durham
Mrs S Fairlamb, BSc Birmingham
Miss C Halls-Moore, BSc Bristol
Mrs B Hawkins, BSc Hull
Mrs I Heycock, BSc Leicester
Mrs G John, BSc Exeter, MSc London, MSc Sheffield Hallam

Modern Languages:
Mrs J Seth, BA Manchester, MA London
Mrs E Cleary, BA London
Ms J Holl, BA Reading
Miss P Coate, MA Oxford
Mlle C Pamart, Maîtrise Orléans, MA Southampton
Mrs J Patton, MA Oxford
Miss H Zhang, MA Brunel

Music:
Mr D Hansell, MA Durham, ARCO CHM
Ms J Nicholls, BA Bristol

Physical Education:
Mrs E Fraser, BA Brighton
Ms L Rigon, BSc Australia
Miss L Westcott, BSc Manchester
Miss L Nordan, BSc Roehampton

Psychology:
Miss E Keeble, BSc Cardiff

Religious Studies:
Miss J Heap, BEd Cambridge
Mrs M Lewis, BA Manchester, MA London

Science:
Mr H Gunasekara, BSc Sussex (*Head of Science*)
Biology:
Mr M O'Brien, BA Cambridge
Mr J Bright, MA Cambridge
Mr H Gunasekara, BSc Sussex
Chemistry:
Mr A Stylianou, BSc London
Ms O Carlin, BSc Imperial
Ms V Filsell, BSc London
Mr J Walia, BSc London
Physics:
Mr M Rivers, MA Oxford
Mr S Farrow, BSc London
Mrs M Baines, MSc London

Junior School:
Head of Junior School: Mrs J Wallace, BMus, MA, PGCE
Deputy Head of Junior School (Academic): Mrs A Musgrove, BA Warwick
Deputy Head of Junior School (Pastoral): Mrs W Archibald, BA OU, LTCM
Miss T Bryce, BA Middlesex
Mrs L Bennett, BA Dublin
Miss A Brennan, BA Surrey
Ms A Cross, BSc Wales
Mrs A Davies, MA Oxford
Miss A Grimwood, BA University of the West of England
Miss G Hardaker, MA, MEd, BA Hons Cantab
Miss S Hathaway, BSc Wales
Mrs A Hudson, BA Durham

Miss T Kemp, BSc Hons Birmingham
Mrs R McNamara, BA Sussex
Mrs P Proctor, CertEd London
Miss A Williams, BEd Cheltenham & Gloucester
Mrs R Wyatt, BSc London

Visiting Staff – Instrumental Music:
Ms H Ashenden, BMus (*Cello*)
Ms J Edwards, ARCM, RCM (*Violin*)
Miss A Gledhill, BMus (*Clarinet, Saxophone*)
Ms K Halsall, Dip RCM, ARCM (*Performer*)
Ms J Holland, LRAM (*Clarinet*)
Ms E Hosker, ARCM, GRSM (*Violin*)
Ms G James, AGSM (*Double Bass, Flute*)
Ms A Kendall, BMus London (*Voice*)
Mr S Keogh, GGSM, ARCM (*Trumpet*)
Mrs M McGhee, BEd Cambridge, ABRSM (*Flute*)
Ms R Munro, BA London (*Voice*)
Mr T Murray, MMus (*Piano*)
Mr L O'Donnell (*Bassoon*)
Ms C Philpot, ARCM (*Oboe*)
Mrs J Raeburn, BA Durham, ARCM (*Recorder*)
Mr I Stott (*Horn*)
Mr P Taggart, ARCM (*Flute*)
Mr M Wheeler, ACM (*Percussion*)
Mr G Williams, RCM (*Saxophone*)

PA to the Headmistress: (*to be appointed*)

School Doctor: Dr G Provost

Putney High School is an independent selective girls' day school located on a green and leafy site close to the heart of Putney in London.

Putney offers a stimulating, nurturing environment where girls are supported and encouraged to make the most of their individual gifts and talents.

We are a school with a caring ethos where each girl encounters stimulating personal and intellectual challenges within a warm, supportive environment. This nurtures success.

Girls take pleasure in discovery and work together to engage in discussion, to debate and challenge the opinions of each other and those from outside.

We anticipate that each girl will contribute to our school, through her studies and many other activities including art and design, drama, music, sport and through charity and working with the local community.

Students leave here conscious of their own worth, prepared for an independent life and capable of making a positive contribution to society. It is from this basis that they go on to pursue a variety of fulfilling careers.

Established in 1893, we are well known for providing the challenge of a rich and broad education to bright girls from 4–18.

With the expertise of dedicated staff, girls develop the self-confidence they need to take intellectual risks and to think independently.

We are proud of the high academic achievements of our girls, with many accepting places at popular universities such as Oxford and Cambridge.

Indeed, we have an extensive World Class Universities programme in place to support girls in making the right choice for them, and in helping to secure places at the best universities both in the UK and abroad.

However, we place equal importance on ensuring that ours is a friendly school and recognise all girls are individuals, each making a positive and valuable contribution.

A strong network of parents and friends share our values, building upon the school's integrity and sense of community spirit.

Facilities. Our state-of-the-art new Sixth Form Centre, opening in early 2012, aims to set a new benchmark for sixth form development, with outstanding facilities such as a rooftop terrace, internet cafe and fitness suite, as well as latest ICT and inspiring study areas.

In the Senior School facilities include a new library with state-of-the-art audio-visual equipment, a mezzanine level with laptops and private study space. There is a newly-developed language lab and a music ICT composition room as well as purpose-built classroom blocks, an impressive Music Centre, seven well-equipped Science laboratories, excellent Art studios, a Design and Technology centre, a superb Sports Hall, newly-opened drama studio and extensive ICT provision.

Our on-site Junior School houses a well-equipped Hall, specialist Science facilities, an Art Studio, a large ICT suite and a well-stocked, comfortable Library.

Sport. Putney High School has earned a reputation for excellence in sport. Each term has a full extra-curricular fixture list and squads regularly compete and achieve success in regional and national level competitions. The school also promotes a 'sport for all' policy which encourages participation of all pupils for enjoyment and fun.

The school's facilities – as well as use of additional off site grounds – enables a wide range of sports to be played and has allowed further extension of both the curricular and extra-curricular activities on offer.

All girls have lessons in netball, lacrosse, gymnastics, tennis and athletics. Additional extra-curricular clubs include dance, badminton, trampolining, cross-country, fencing and rowing. Tennis, lacrosse, netball, cross country, gymnastics, athletics and sports acrobatics teams compete successfully nationally. Girls are regularly selected to join county, South of England and national and international lacrosse teams.

Curriculum. Well-qualified, specialist staff provide continuity of education from Reception through to A Levels at 18. Girls are welcome to enter the school at 4+, 11+ and 16+ or in other years if an occasional vacancy arises.

In the Senior School, the girls follow a broad and balanced curriculum, which includes Latin, French, Chinese (Mandarin), German, Spanish and Design Technology. On entering the GCSE years, all girls study the core subjects plus Biology, Physics and Chemistry and at least one modern language. They are also able to choose from a wide list including Statistics, Textiles, ICT, Design Technology, Art, Drama, Latin, Classics, PE, Music, and Humanities. At AS and A Level these subjects may be supplemented by others such as Business Studies, Economics, Government & Politics, History of Art, Further Mathematics, Psychology and Critical Thinking. In addition to their A Level studies, students can also complete an Extended Project on a topic of their choice. A carefully structured Life Skills programme broadens their interests and skills and helps prepare them for life beyond school. Indeed, in the Sixth Form, students enjoy increased academic freedom as well as a wealth of extra-curricular opportunities.

Sixth Form. Sixth Formers play an important part in school life, acting as role models for younger children. The Head Girl, Deputies, House Officials and Prefects are essential to the smooth running of the school and there is ample scope for all to become involved in School Council, the organisation of House events, debating, charity work, lunchtime clubs, drama, music and sport.

The **Junior School** provides a secure and encouraging environment where the girls grow in skills and confidence. A warm relationship is established with each family so parents and staff work together throughout the girls' years with us.

A cross-curricular approach to learning is adopted and many visits to places of interest, concerts, museums, art galleries and theatres are included. Wide opportunities capture the girls' unlimited enthusiasm and enable them to explore and extend their natural talents.

The Junior School has earned a reputation for success in music, netball, tennis, gymnastics, chess, and writing skills in local, county and national events in recent years. The choirs have been invited to perform for the BBC – and at the Royal Festival Hall and the Royal Albert Hall several times.

Music. Putney is renowned for its musical excellence throughout both Junior and Senior schools. A high percentage of girls learn a musical instrument; many are accomplished musicians, studying at the junior conservatoires and/ or are members of nationally auditioned choirs and orchestras.

Homefield, the Music suite, provides spacious and well-equipped facilities for class teaching, private tuition and practice rooms. Private tuition is available in all instruments and voice. Girls have many opportunities to participate in music – three orchestras; four Senior Choirs and a Junior Choir and many smaller ensembles. There are two annual composition competitions and an Inter-House Music Festival attracting hundreds of entries.

The school has achieved success in prestigious national competitions and there have been choir tours to New Zealand, Barcelona, Venice and Lisbon.

Fees per term (2011-2012). Senior School £4,388, Junior School £3,496.

The fees cover the regular curriculum, school books, stationery and other materials, choral music, games and swimming, but not optional extra subjects or special sports. All pupils below the Sixth Form take school meals for which the charge is £160 per term. The fees for instrumental tuition are shown in the Prospectus.

Financial Assistance. We are committed to offering opportunities to bright girls whose parents would not be able to afford the fees. The GDST has its own Bursary Scheme that is means-tested.

Scholarships. At present there are available to internal or external candidates, a number of academic and music scholarships (up to 50% of fees) for entry at 11+. At 16+ we provide academic, art, drama, music, modern languages, science and sport scholarships.

Charitable status. Putney High School is part of The Girls' Day School Trust, which is a Registered Charity, number 306983.

Queen Anne's School

Henley Road, Caversham, Berkshire RG4 6DX
Tel: 0118 918 7300
e-mail: office@qas.org.uk
website: www.qas.org.uk

Queen Anne's is an independent boarding and day school for girls with just under 400 pupils aged 11 to 18 years. Renowned for academic success, the school is committed to connecting with and understanding the individuals in its care.

Governing Body: The Grey Coat Hospital Foundation

Chairman of School Council: Vice-Admiral P Dunt
Vice-Chairman: Mr J Noakes, MA

Governors:
The Revd Canon Jane Hedges, BA
Mrs M S K Elliott, BSc
Mrs C Gray, BA
Lady Laws, BLitt, MA
Mrs J M Timlett
Mr R Gill, FCCA
Mr R Penfold
Miss A Wiscarson, BSc
Mr M Sealey BA, MSc

Clerk: Mr R W Blackwell, MA

Headmistress: **Mrs J Harrington**, BA Exeter, PGCE, NPQH, Dip Counselling

Deputy Head (Pastoral): Miss N Coombs, BEd, Safer Recruitment in Education Certificate
Deputy Head (Academic): Mr M Richards, BMus, MMus, Research Fellowship
Director of Sixth Form: Dr V Vincent, BSc, DPhil, CertEd

Set in a beautiful and inspiring setting just north of the River Thames Queen Anne's has occupied its current 35-acre site near Henley-on-Thames since 1894. The grounds combine traditional Victorian architecture with new and contemporary buildings to provide cutting-edge facilities. The school is located just 40 minutes from London.

All girls are taught in small classes where each individual can explore the learning culture in a supportive environment while being challenged and stimulated by group discussions and debate. The pupils are encouraged to discover their passions and achieve in all areas including sport, music, drama and the arts, whilst developing their interpersonal skills and confidence.

Pastoral organisation. Queen Anne's has an excellent reputation for pastoral care. Girls can attend Queen Anne's daily or on a full, weekly, flexi- or occasional boarding basis according to individual family needs. Each girl, whether day or boarding, belongs to a House and the House system is integral to our academic and pastoral care.

The staff believe that students perform best when they are happy and secure, and Queen Anne's has effective pastoral systems in place to ensure this. The support network includes Housemistresses and the House Pastoral Team, Academic Staff and Tutors, Heads of Year and a resident Chaplain.

Curriculum. All girls follow a broad and varied curriculum up to GCSE. Separate subject sciences are taught, as well as Dual Award; mathematics and music follow IGCSE; Spanish or German may be taken from Year 9; Latin is studied from Year 7. Music, art and drama form part of the girls' timetable until the end of Year 9. Information technology is taught throughout the school. A wide range of A Level subjects is offered. A programme of personal, social and health education is followed by all girls.

Careers. All girls go on to Higher Education, many to top universities in the UK and overseas.

Extra-curricular activities. Queen Anne's is reputed for many of its achievements. It offers a full extra-curricular programme and excellent opportunities for sport, including tennis, lacrosse (National Champions on many occasions), 'rock' climbing and rowing on the nearby Thames. Music, drama and art are very strong. The Duke of Edinburgh's Award, Young Enterprise, public speaking and debating (National and International finalists), photography, dance, riding, socials and many more activities are available. A full programme of optional activities is available on Saturday mornings.

Admission. Girls are admitted at 11+, 13+ and at Sixth Form by Queen Anne's Entrance Examination or by Common Entrance. Sixth Form places are offered on the basis of GCSE results. For further information please contact the Registrar.

Scholarships. Scholarships are offered for entry at 11+, 13+ and 16+ and are awarded for excellence in one or more fields of the life of the school. Awards may be made in respect of Academic Excellence, All-Round Contribution, Art, Drama, Music or Sport.

Fees per term (2011-2012). Full Boarding £8,975; Flexi Boarding £8,090–£8,535. Day girls £6,090.

Charitable status. Queen Anne's School is part of The Grey Coat Hospital Foundation, which is a Registered Charity, number 312700.

Queen Margaret's School

Escrick Park, York YO19 6EU
Tel: 01904 728261
Fax: 01904 728150
e-mail: enquiries@queenmargarets.com
website: www.queenmargarets.com

Motto: *Filia Regis*

Board of Governors:

Chairman: Mrs Emma Carnegie-Brown

C D Forbes Adam, Esq
Mrs E Bell
Mrs C M Gooder
T S Kettlewell, Esq
The Hon Mrs Justice Eleanor King, DBE
N Lambert, Esq
Miss E Pearson
The Duchess of Rutland
F A Scott, Esq
D T Sheppard, Esq
I M Small, Esq
D Ward, Esq

Company Secretary & Clerk to the Governors: M D
  Oakley, Esq

School Solicitors: Messrs Addleshaw Goddard, Messrs
  Crombie Wilkinson
School Auditor: PricewaterhouseCoopers LLP

Headmaster: Dr P R Silverwood, MA Cantab, MSc, PhD
  Manchester, QTS, CChem, MRSC

Deputy Head: Mrs C Cameron, MA Open, BA Hons
  Reading, PGCE, NPQH, FRGS
Bursar: S P Bentley, LLB Hons Hull, ACA
Senior Master: C S Nettleship, MMus, BMus Hons Wales
Director of Studies: Dr A S Buchan, PhD Leeds, BSc Hull,
  PGCE
Director of Pastoral Care: Miss A Proctor, BA Hons
  Oxon, MSc Dunelm, PGCE
Director of Marketing & Admissions: Mrs R Hicks, MA
  Oxon, MCIM, LRSM
Chaplain: The Revd R L Owen, BD Wales, PGCE
Doctor: Dr S J Butlin, MBChB, DRCOG, DCH

Art:
*G J Alcock, BA Bristol Polytechnic, PGCE
Miss H L Colman, MA Newcastle, BA Hons Leeds, PGCE
Mrs L J Heaton, MA Leeds, BA Hons Trent Polytechnic
Mrs D Stewart, MA Leeds, BA Hons Wolverhampton,
  PGCE (*Design and Technology*)

Careers and Higher Education:
Senior Tutor: Mrs C P Bennett, MA Cantab, PGCE
UCAS Coordinator: Ms J C Millhouse, MA Cantab, PGCE

Classics:
*W M Grant, MA Hons St Andrews, MSt Oxon, PGCE
Mrs R Waugh, BA Hons York, MA Hull, PGCE

Dance:
*Miss A E Leadley, RAD, AISTD, UABPA Dip, BA
  Surrey, MA Leeds Met
Mrs S Bolsher, AISTD
Miss R Firth, AISTD
Miss R Goodall, AISTD
Miss A Pithers, AISTD

Drama:
*Mrs D Whitcombe, BEd Hons London
Q Sands, BEd Hons Central School of Speech & Drama

Economics and Business Studies:
*Mrs S M P McDougall, BA Oxford Polytechnic, PGCE

English:
*Ms J C Millhouse, MA Cantab, PGCE
I Giles, BA Hons Sussex
Mrs R M Doyle, MA York, BA Hons York, PGCE
Dr N J L Onyett, BA Hons, DPhil York, PGCE
M G Payton, MA Oxon, PGCE

Food Technology:
*Miss G M Rickard, BEd Manchester
Mrs G Milnes, CertEd Newcastle, BA OU

Geography:
*Mrs L Seeney, BSc Hons Leicester, PGCE
Miss F J Whittle, BEd Hons Bedford CPE
Miss A Proctor, BA Hons Oxon, MSc Dunelm, PGCE

History and Politics:
*Mrs C E S Batten, MA Michigan, BA Hons Queen's
  Belfast, PGCE, DASE
Mrs C P Bennett, MA Cantab, PGCE
Mrs G F Hobson, BA Hons Nottingham, PGCE
Miss H S Peacock, BA Hons Lancaster, PGCE

History of Art:
*Ms H Moore, MA UCL, BA Hons Bristol, MA Leeds Met

ICT:
Network Manager: G Mark, BScEE, MCSE
Systems Engineer: G M Howe

Mathematics:
*A Taylor, MA Cantab, PGCE
Mrs C I Herbert, BSc Hons Leeds, PGCE
D Lamb, BSc Edinburgh, MA OU, PGCE
Mrs C Sutcliffe, BA Hons Birmingham, PGCE
Mrs A Viant, BSc Hull, PGCE

Modern Languages:
*Miss E Leclerc, BA Hons Leeds, PGCE (*Spanish, French*)
Miss A Botti, BA, BA, MA Paris (*Arabic, French, Spanish*)
Mrs A J Debenham, BA Hons Newcastle, PGCE (*French,
  Spanish*)
Mrs B Kirkham BA Hons Halle, Germany (*German*)
Mrs I L Leaf, BA Lyon, France, PGCE (*French*)

Music:
Director of Music: J D Bowyer, MusB Manchester,
  FRCO, GRNCM, PGCE
C S Nettleship, MMus, BMus Hons Wales
Mrs D Pomfret, LGSM, DipEd

Part-time staff:
N A Bellamy, BA Hons Dartington, Exeter, RCO (*Piano*)
Mrs J Brewer, BA Hons York, PGCE (*Cello*)
Mrs D Clough, BA York (*Flute*)
Mrs K Cooper, BA Hons York, PGDipMus (*Singing*)
Mrs C Ferguson, DRSAM, ARCM (*Oboe, Piano*)
Mrs G Goodier, DipTCL (*Harp*)
Mrs C Griffiths, GMus RNCM, PGCE, PDVT, GSMD
  (*Singing*)
J Le Grand, AGSM (*Clarinet, Saxophone*)
J Mackenzie, BEng Hons, FTCL, FLCM, LGSM, LRAM,
  MIFireE (*Guitar*)
V Parsonage, BSc OU, PGDipMus, LTCL, CertExMus,
  DipABRSM (*Viola, Violin*)
A Passmore (*Organist, Accompanist, Piano*)
B Robinson, BEd Sunderland (*Scottish Bagpipes, Snare
  Drumming*)
J Sage BA York, MA York (*Clarinet, Saxophone &
  Bassoon*)
P Selwesiuk, MA Wroclaw (*Brass*)
D Smyth, BA, York (*Percussion*)
Mrs J Sturmheit, GGSM MTC (*Singing*)
P Titcombe, BA Hons York (*Piano*)
Music Assistant: Mrs M Nettleship

Physical Education:
Director of Sport and Games: Miss A Davies, MEd
University College Swansea, CertEd, PGCE
Asst Director of Sport and Games: Ms C Shaw, BEd Hons
Liverpool
Miss C O'Brien, BSc Loughborough, QTS
Mrs L O'Grady, BEd Hons Bangor
Miss E Kelly, BA QTS Leeds Met
Miss J Rastall, BSc Hons UWIC, QTS
Mrs L Trumper, BEd Hons Liverpool
Miss J L Whay, BEd Hons IM Marsh, Liverpool
Miss F J Whittle, BEd Hons Bedford CPE
Sports & Swimming Pool Technician: N S Allison, BA
Hons Ripon & York St John
Riding: Miss G Sanders, BHSAI, CertEd
Tennis: Mrs C Place, LTA Coach, CertEd Bedford CPE

Religious Studies:
*The Revd R L Owen, BD Wales, PGCE (*Chaplain*)
S Ottewell, BA Hons Leeds

Science:
*J Hazlewood, MA OU, BSc Aston, PGCE (*Head of
Science*)
*R Lightfoot, MSci Nottingham, PGCE (*Physics*)
*Mrs E A Morton, BSc Hons London, PGCE (*Chemistry*)
Dr A S Buchan, PhD Leeds, BSc Hull, PGCE (*Chemistry*)
Mrs S Gorton, BSc Hons Leeds, PGCE (*Chemistry*)
D Lamb, BSc Edinburgh, MA OU, PGCE (*Physics*)
Miss A Lawrence, BA Hons York, PGCE (*Biology*)
Mrs S Thomas, BSc Hons York, PGCE (*Physics*)
Technicians: N Jackson, Mrs G Labonté-Hazlewood, Mrs E
Rust

Pupil Support:
*Mrs M Tate, CertEd Leeds, MA OU
Mrs J Edwards, BSc Hons Dunelm, MA Leeds, PGDip
Psych OU, PGCE
Mrs D Hill, BA Hons, PGCE

Librarian: Mrs S Hall, MA Teesside, BA OU, BLib Hons
UCW, PGCE, MCLIP

Head of Upper School Boarding: Mrs N Hart, BA Caen
Head of Lower School Boarding: Mrs J Skarratt BA Open

Resident House Staff:

Ms P Alpine	Mrs S Pickering
Mrs J Clark	Ms M Richardson
Miss C Goddard	Miss E Roper
Mr J Hart	Mrs J Simpson
Miss R Hart	Miss C Thackray
Miss G Kelly	Mrs L Thackray
Miss A Kirkham	Miss J L Whay
Miss H Macrae Simpson	Ms L Wright
Dr A Ottewell	

Medical Centre:
*Mrs G M Swinglehurst, RGN (*Senior Sister*)
Mrs J Crowther, RGN
Ms H Coyne, RGN

Marketing & Admissions:
Director of Marketing & Admissions: Mrs R Hicks, MA
Oxon, MCIM, LRSM
Admissions Officer: Mrs J Hallewell
Marketing Assistant: Miss E Pike
Events & Communications Officer: Miss J Warner

Administrative Staff:
Headmaster's Secretary: Miss N Craig
Deputy Head's Secretary: Mrs J Pringle
Examinations Officer: Mrs M Randall
Receptionists: Mrs K Hargreaves, Mrs S MacGregor
Bursar's Assistants: Mrs E Ryan, Mrs H Brown, Mrs L
Walton
Administration Assistant: Mrs F McHale

Buildings & Services Manager: Q Cardy
Maintenance Supervisor: S Bramley
Maintenance Department Assistant: Mrs J Jackson
School Housekeeper: Ms P Bridges

Foundation. Queen Margaret's was founded in Scarborough in 1901 by the Woodard Foundation and named in honour of Scotland's only female saint. Following eventful years which included evacuation to Pitlochry during the First World War, and Castle Howard during the Second, the school came to its current home in 1949.

In 1986, following an initiative by the parents and governors, the school was re-established under a new company, limited by guarantee and registered with the Charities Commission. At the same time the school became independent of the Woodard Foundation and began a period of dramatic expansion, investing almost £10 million in new and improved facilities to create the superb learning environment enjoyed by pupils today.

Situation. Escrick Park is an idyllic location in which to study and relax. The beautiful grounds provide a serene backdrop to the busy and purposeful life of the school. Yet the ancient city of York is just 6 miles away; home to two universities, world-class museums and the renowned Minster as well as theatres and cinemas. Our proximity to York station with its direct train services to all major cities and a number of airports makes travelling to Queen Margaret's very straightforward. London is just 2 hours away, Edinburgh 2½ and Manchester even closer.

Numbers. Boarding 265; Day 55.

Admission is by Entrance Examination at 11+, 12+ and 13+. There is also entry at 16+.

Fees per term (2011–2012). Boarding £8,700; Day £5,513.

Curriculum. QM offers a wide academic curriculum. Girls usually complete 9 or 10 GCSEs and have a free choice of A Level subjects, taught by specialist graduate teachers. Class sizes are small and, from the classroom to the laboratory and from the studio to the study, we encourage girls to think for themselves.

The Sixth Form at QM offers the best possible preparation for life at University and beyond. Students have increasing independence and take on greater responsibility for their own learning. Comprehensive and highly personalised guidance on Higher Education and possible careers helps each girl to understand and realise her individual ambitions by evaluating the available options and making wise choices for the future. Over 20 subjects are offered for A and AS Level in a wide variety of Arts and Science subjects. Candidates are prepared for all University entrance including Oxbridge. High academic standards are achieved at all levels.

Classrooms are modern and well equipped and ICT provision is widespread and up-to-date. There are seven science laboratories. Art, Design and Food Technology are located in a purpose-built centre. Pottery, sculpture, textile and fabric design, printing, as well as drawing and painting, are on the curriculum. Recent additions include the spectacular theatre and dance complex, competition-sized indoor swimming pool, superbly equipped Medical Centre and Languages suite as well as purpose-built senior boarding accommodation in Winifred Holtby House.

Drama is important in the curriculum and school productions are mounted regularly. In addition girls can take classes in modern, tap and ballet dancing and individual tuition is available. Music plays a major role in school life at Queen Margaret's and there are three full time and twenty specialist music teachers on the staff. There are two orchestras and two bands, smaller ensembles, rock bands, chapel choir and junior choir. The school's choir provides the music for services in Chapel as well as the Parish Church and local concerts and regularly sings in York Minster and occasionally abroad.

Sport. The school has first-class sports facilities including astroturf, sports hall and competition swimming pool.

All-weather courts ensure year-round tennis of a high standard, and there are two squash courts and a nine-hole golf course. Main activities are lacrosse, hockey, netball, tennis, rounders, swimming and athletics with fixtures at all ages against schools and clubs of all types. Other clubs and societies cater for fencing, badminton, rowing, canoeing, martial arts and skiing.

The Riding School is situated within the grounds adjacent to the main school campus and offers riding to girls of all standards from beginners to Pony Club B Test level.

The School is divided into six Houses which compete in Games, Music, Drama, and other activities. Girls take part in the Duke of Edinburgh's Award Scheme at Bronze and Gold level.

Scholarships. (*See Scholarship Entries section.*) Awards can be made at any age. Academic, Art, Dance, Drama, Music and Sport awards are available. For further details apply to the Admissions Office or consult the school's website.

Charitable status. Queen Margaret's School, York is a Registered Charity, number 517523, which aims to provide high quality education for girls.

Queen Mary's School
A Woodard School

**Baldersby Park, Topcliffe, Thirsk, North Yorkshire
YO7 3BZ**
Tel: 01845 575000
Fax: 01845 575001
e-mail: admin@queenmarys.org
website: www.queenmarys.org

Queen Mary's is an all-girls boarding and day school for pupils aged 7 to 16. It has a co-educational Early Years and Pre-Prep department for day pupils aged 2 to 7. The total school roll is currently 247.

Queen Mary's has a unique family atmosphere with friendliness and concern for others being an important part of the school's ethos. The country setting provides a safe haven for girls to thrive and develop self-confidence.

Chairman of Governors: Dr M Denyer, MB BS, FRCP

Head: Mrs S Lewis-Beckett, BSc Cardiff, PGDip Cardiff

Deputy Head: Mrs D Hannam Walpole, BEd Hons

Miss E Abrahams, Mont Dip (*Year 1*)
Mr P Bailey, BA Hons, PGCE (*Head of Mathematics*)
Miss H Benson, BA Hons QTS (*Year 3*)
Miss V Charmer, BA Hons (*Outdoor Education*)
Mr N Carter, GRSM, ARCM, LRAM, LGSM, PGCE (*Director of Music*)
Mrs J Coles, BEd Hons (*Year 5, KS2 Science*)
Mrs D Coull, BA Hons, PGCE (*English*)
Mr A Cowey, BEd Hons (*Year 2, KS1 Coordinator*)
Mrs T Devenish, BEd, BA Hons (*Head of Design Technology*)
Mrs C Donaldson, BA Hons, PGCE (*Head of Art and Design*)
Mrs R Foster, BSc Hons, PGCE (*Year 4*)
Mrs V Foulser, BA Hons, MA, PGCE (*Head of Religious Studies*)
Mrs M Grant, MA, PGCE (*Learning Support*)
Mrs S Grimshaw, BEd Hons (*Physical Education/Dance*)
Mr I Hamilton MA, PGCE (*Head of English*)
Mrs D Hannam Walpole, BEd Hons (*Deputy Head, PE, Maths*)
Mrs E Hopkins, CertEd (*Head of Modular Science, Learning Support Coordinator*)

Mrs E Lindsley, BSc Hons, PGCE (*Head of Physical Education*)
Mrs J Nuttall, BEd Hons (*Year 6 KS2 English*)
Mrs L Nuttall, BSc Hons, PGCE (*Mathematics*)
Mr P Nuttall, BSc Hons, PGCE (*Director of Studies, Head of Science*)
Mr J Payne, BA Hons, QTS (*Head of Classics*)
Miss A Pearson, BA Hons, PGCE (*Head of History*)
Mrs A Petty, CertEd (*Special Needs*)
Mrs V Potter (*Phyical Education*)
Mrs C Punshon, BA Hons, PGCE (*French*)
Mrs D Sheppard (*Teaching Assistant*)
Miss A Shepherdson, GRSM, PGCE (*Assistant Director of Music*)
Mrs M Smerdon, BA Hons, QTS (*Religious Studies*)
Mrs C Sommerville, BSc, DipEd (*Head of Chemistry*)
Miss K Vaughan, BEd Hons, ALAM, UCPD (*Drama*)
Mr D Walker, BA Hons QTS, MEd (*KS2 Mathematics*)
Mrs C Wiggins, BSc Hons, PGCE (*Head of Geography*)
Miss L Wood, BA Hons, PGCE (*German/Spanish*)

Early Years Department:
Head of Early Years: Mrs M-J Foster, BA, PGCE
Reception Assistant: Mrs J Tindall
Nursery Supervisor: Mrs L Welburn

Careers and Work Experience: Mrs D Williams, BA Hons

Head of Boarding: Mrs A Hickling
School Nurse: Mrs S Beaumont

School Chaplain: (*to be appointed*)
Roman Catholic Chaplain: Fr Leo Chamberlain, OSB

Drama: Mrs P M Coghlan, ALCM, LAM, Gold Medal (*Speech & Drama*)
Riding: Mr R Blane

School Secretary: Mrs C Collin
Finance and Estate Manager: Mrs J Wright
Admissions: Mrs V Robeson

Location. Queen Mary's is situated at Baldersby Park in a beautiful Grade 1 Palladian mansion, with 50 acres of grounds, including formal gardens, playing fields, and riding stables. Despite its idyllic surroundings, it is only 2 miles from Junction 49 of the A1 and within ten minutes of Thirsk railway station. York and Harrogate are within easy reach and so are Leeds/Bradford and Teesside airports. Six minibuses, each covering a twenty-five mile radius, transport girls to and from home on a daily basis.

The Curriculum. The National Curriculum forms the basis of what is taught, and all pupils sit Key Stage tests at the appropriate age. However, pupils are offered much more in terms of breadth and depth of learning. Generous time is given to core subjects, English, mathematics, science and modern languages, but strong emphasis is also placed on the supporting subjects – geography, history, religious education, classics, ICT, design technology, music, art and a varied programme of physical education. Classes are kept deliberately small, which means that every girl can receive plenty of support from her teachers. The school has an excellent learning support department for those pupils who have specific learning difficulties. The two years leading up to GCSE are full and focused, with most girls taking nine or ten subjects at GCSE. The public examination results are outstandingly good and the school is one of the highest achieving non-selective schools in the country.

Pastoral care. All girls in school have personal tutors who oversee the academic, social and emotional development of each of their tutees. Building self-confidence and developing the individual talents of each pupil is seen as a vital aspect of the education offered. Each girl is encouraged to be self-reliant from an early age and pupils are taught a real concern for the needs of others. Girls in their final year at Queen Mary's undertake a number of important responsibilities to help the school community function smoothly.

Boarding. Queen Mary's offers a number of boarding options to suit the needs of parents and their daughters. Those who choose to board may be weekly or full boarders. The experience of boarding is considered to be valuable for all girls and, when space permits, day girls may board on a nightly basis to fit in with extra-curricular commitments or parental need. The boarding accommodation is all within the main building and the girls find their dormitories cheerful and comfortable. The full boarders, who stay at weekends, enjoy lots of varied activities and trips, often much to the envy of those who go home. The Housemistress, together with her colleagues, looks after the general health of the girls, while the school nurse and the school doctor oversee all medical care.

Extra-Curricular Activities. An impressive range of extra-curricular activities is available to all members of the school community. Choral and orchestral music are both huge strengths of the school; sport is good too with hockey, lacrosse and netball being played in the winter terms and tennis, rounders and athletics in the summer. Facilities include a modern indoor swimming pool and astroturf pitch. Drama, debating and The Duke of Edinburgh's Award at bronze level are highly popular choices and the new, all-weather outdoor riding manège allows more than 90 girls to ride each week. All children also enjoy the weekly Adventure Club, which gives them the opportunity to climb the newly installed Climbing Wall and canoe on the adjacent River Swale.

Religious Affiliation. The school is part of the Woodard Corporation, an Anglican foundation which promotes Christian education and high academic and pastoral standards within all its schools. The school has its own Church of England chapel. The school Chaplain prepares girls for confirmation. Girls of other denominations are welcome.

What happens after GCSE? Queen Mary's has no Sixth Form and this is seen as a real strength of the school. Specialist careers advice is offered throughout the senior school and well informed staff support the girls as they seek to make application to their new schools and colleges. Each senior girl is able to choose a school or Sixth Form college which can offer her exactly the courses and educational environment she requires for her Sixth Form studies. A healthy proportion of the girls join their new schools as scholars. A few girls will embark on GNVQs or vocational training. Queen Mary's girls can be found in the Sixth Forms of over 30 different schools and colleges.

Scholarships. Scholarships are offered at 11+, 12+ and 13+ to those candidates who show particular academic flair or have special talent in Music or Art. Examinations are held early in the Spring term.

Entrance. By interview with the Head. Entry can be at most stages, subject to availability. An up-to-date prospectus will be dispatched immediately on request. The school's website also provides useful information.

Fees per term (2011-2012). Day: Nursery £17.50 per half-day session; Reception £1,940; Years 1–2 £2,320; Year 3 £3,635, Years 4–6: £3,835, Years 7–8: £4,135, Years 9–11 £4,640. Boarding: Years 4–6 £5,180, Years 7–8 £5,500, Years 9–11 £6,120.

Extra subjects per term. Music £179, Speech and Drama £70, Riding £16.50 per lesson.

Charitable status. Queen Mary's School (Baldersby) Ltd is a Registered Charity, number 1098410. It exists to educate children in a Christian environment.

Queen's College, London

43–49 Harley Street, London W1G 8BT
Tel: 020 7291 7070
Fax: 020 7291 7090
e-mail: queens@qcl.org.uk
website: www.qcl.org.uk

The College was the first institution to provide higher education and proper qualifications for young women. It was founded in 1848 by F D Maurice, Professor of Modern History at King's College, and in 1853 received the first-ever Royal Charter for Women's Education.

Today it is a thriving school of 360 girls aged from 11–18, of whom 90 are in the Sixth Form. Queen's College Preparatory School (020 7291 0660), which opened in 2002 at 61 Portland Place, takes girls from age 4–11.

Patron: Her Majesty The Queen

Visitor: The Rt Revd and Rt Hon the Lord Bishop of London

Council:
Chairman: Bernard Clow, FCA
Vice-Chairman: Ms Jessica Pulay, MA Oxon, MCIL
Miss Gillian Adams, BSc, MBchB, FRCS Ed, FRCOphth
Ms Sally Cass
The Revd Dr James Hawkey, MA, MPhil, PhD Cantab
Lady Hopkins, AADip, Hon FAIA, Hon FRIAS
James Hutchinson, BA MA London, MSc Kingston
Nicholas Inge, BA Oxon
Miss Imogen Lloyd Webber, MA Cantab
The Revd Dr Emma Loveridge, MA Cantab
Mrs Gillian Low, MA Oxon
Daniel Peltz, BA MA London
Mrs Danielle Salem, BA Farnham
Michael Sharman, BSc Southampton
Sir Tom Shebbeare, KCVO, BA Exeter
Tim Streatfeild, MA Oxon, FCA

Bursar and Secretary to the Council: S N Turner

Principal: Dr F M R Ramsey, MA DPhil Oxon

Headmistress of Queen's College Preparatory School: Mrs A-M Dempsey, BA London

Senior Tutor: T W A Lello, BA Newcastle, MA London, NPQH

Senior Mistress: Mrs K C Woodcock, BA Bristol

Admissions Secretary: Miss R M Bostock

Queen's College is situated in Harley Street, combining the beauty of four eighteenth century houses with modern facilities for science, languages, art, drama and ICT, as a well as a Hall and gymnasium. Two libraries, in the care of a graduate librarian, offer the students some 17,000 books, with frequent new acquisitions, and we also preserve a unique archive recording the history of the College.

Curriculum. Class sizes rarely exceed twenty and the normal size of a year group is 50–55, the three forms being grouped geographically in the first year. The year-group is streamed for mathematics and French during the first year and at a later stage for English, Latin and science.

The curriculum is wide, including five modern languages at GCSE and A Level, as well as Latin, Greek and classical civilisation. Girls usually take nine or ten subjects at GCSE, and the three sciences are offered separately for more able girls. At A Level it is possible to study history of art, economics, government and politics, or psychology as well as the subjects already taken at GCSE.

Regent's Park and the University of Westminster offer further opportunities for physical education, netball, lacrosse, rounders, tennis and swimming being supplemented by self-defence, yoga, badminton and other leisure pursuits. Dance and PE are offered at GCSE. Regular sports fixtures are arranged against local schools. The Duke of Edinburgh's Award is organised at bronze and silver levels. Individual music lessons are offered in all instruments including voice, and the musical or dramatic productions and jazz concert are highlights of each year.

The location of the College means that theatre and other educational visits in London are an integral part of the curriculum, complemented by opportunities to travel abroad or to other parts of the country. Every summer Year 7 visit Northumberland for a week and in recent years groups of girls have visited France, Greece, Germany, Italy and Russia, joining parties from Queen's College Preparatory School for skiing holidays in France or Switzerland.

Almost all girls leaving Queen's proceed to university, including Oxford or Cambridge; and several students each year choose to take an Art Foundation course at one of the London colleges. Former students are prominent in medicine, education, writing and the media; they retain contact with each other and the college through the Old Queen's Society, which also gives bursaries to families in financial need.

Pastoral Care. Queen's College prides itself on its friendly and informal atmosphere, highly valued by girls, parents and staff. Pastoral care is strong and we have a full-time nurse to support the work of form tutors and pastoral staff. A specialist in various special educational needs works individually with pupils once the need has been identified. We send reports to parents every half-term and hold regular Parents' Evenings; contact with parents benefits from the use of e-mail by all members of staff. Parents also support the College through membership of the Parents' Association, giving practical and some financial assistance to College functions.

Admission. The College is a member of the North London Independent Girls' Schools' Consortium for entry at 11+ and all candidates are interviewed individually. As well as high academic standards we value enthusiasm and creativity, and academic, music and art awards are available to 11+ entrants.

If vacancies arise we also welcome applicants at other ages, particularly after GCSE, where there is a long-standing tradition of accepting students to complete their school education at Queen's. Some scholarships are available on entry at this stage. Means-tested bursaries are available at all points of entry.

Fees per term (2011-2012). £4,950.

Charitable status. Queen's College, London is a Registered Charity, number 312726. It exists to provide education for girls. It is an Anglican foundation, open to those of all faiths or none who are prepared to subscribe to its ethos.

Queen's Gate School

133 Queen's Gate, London SW7 5LE
Tel: 020 7589 3587
Fax: 020 7584 7691
e-mail: registrar@queensgate.org.uk
website: www.queensgate.org.uk

Governors:
Mr Michael Cumming (*Chairman*)
Mrs Laura Marani (*Deputy Chairman*)
Mr Angus Cameron
Mr William Gillen
Mr Gary Li
Dr Shirley A Radcliffe
Ms Izzy Reeves
Mr Peter Trueman

Mrs Manina Weldon
Mr Geoffrey Wilmot

Staff:

Principal: Mrs R M Kamaryc, BA Hons, MSc, PGCE Queen's Belfast

Director of Teaching and Learning: Mr M Alter, BSc, PGCE
Director of Pastoral Care: Mrs P Bleazard, BA Hons, PGCE
Senior Tutor: Mrs I Jones, BA Hons, PGCE
Assessment & Learning Coordinator: Mr M Crundwell, BSc, MPhil
Head of Sixth Form: Ms C A Yates, MA, BEd
Upper School Section Head: Mr M Crundwell, BSc, MPhil
Lower School Section Head: Mr C Seletto, BSc, Grad DipEd
Head of Remove: (*to be appointed*)

Art and Design:
Mr S Mataja, BA, PGCE
Miss K Clackson, BA Hons, PGCE

Art, History of:
Mrs A Bridges, MA Cantab, MA

Biology:
Miss N Mia, BSc Hons, MSc, PGCE
Mr C Seletto, BSc, Grad DipEd

Careers Education & Guidance:
Mrs A Gallagher, MA, PGCE

Chemistry:
Mrs C Mayne, BSc, PGCE

Classics:
Dr T Bell, MA
Miss C Fox, BA Hons, PGCE
Mr R Moss, BA Hons, PGCE

Design and Technology:
Miss C Murtagh, BA Hons, PGCE
Mrs B Polanski, BA, ATC, PGCE
Mr J Francis, BA Hons, PGCE

Drama and Speech Training:
Ms L Arthur, MA Hons, MA RADA/London, Dip Teaching NZ
Ms R Reeves, MA
Ms J Doolan, MA

English:
Mr J Denchfield, BA Hons, PGCE
Ms C A Yates, MA, BEd
Mrs P Bleazard, BA Hons, PGCE
Miss R Wade, BA Hons, PGCE
Miss V Quinn, BEd Hons

Learning Support:
(*to be appointed*)

French:
Mme T Burrows-Delbarry, L-ès-L Moderne
Mlle A Merin, Maîtrise de Littérature Afro-Américaine, PGCE
Dr M Cadei, Mod Lang Milan
M A Pierrejean, BA

Geography:
Mr M Crundwell BSc, MPhil
Miss S Scott, BSc Hons, PGCE, PCET, MEd

German:
Mrs I B Atufe-Kreuth, MA, Mag Phil, CertEd

History:
Mrs J S Ditchfield, MA Hons, PGCE
Miss N Townsend, MA, PGCE
Mrs S Carter-Esdale, BA Hons, PGCE

ICT:
Mrs I Jones, BA Hons, PGCE

Italian:
Dr M Cadei, Mod Lang Milan

Mathematics:
Miss M Newland, BSc Hons, GTP
Mrs T McCann, BA, HDE
Miss P Howe, BA Hons
Mr M Alter, BSc, PGCE
Mrs R M Kamaryc, BA, MSc, PGCE

Music:
Mrs K Casper, MA, BS, QTS
Miss S Horcsog, BA Hons

Physical Education:
Miss B Ward, BEd Hons
Miss C Hurlbatt, BA Hons, PGCE
Miss N Chamelo, BA Hons, QTS
Mrs G McHenry, BA, QTS

Physics:
Dr J Mercer, PhD, BSc, PGCE
Mr C Pollock, BSc Hons, ARCS, PGCE

Psychology:
Mrs B Tincknell, MSc, PGCE

Religious Studies:
Mrs N Clear, BA Hons, PGCE
Mrs M White-da Cruz, BA Hons

Sociology:
Mrs S E de Rougemont, BA Hons, PGCE

Spanish:
Miss S Gomez, Licenciada en Filología

Laboratory Technicians:
Mr D I Swan, BSc
Mr M Sell, BSc

Librarian:
Mrs E Scott, BA, MSc

ICT Technicians:
Mr P Manning
Mr S Marshall

Junior School:
Headmistress: Mrs N Webb, BA Hons, PGCE
Senior Tutor and Director of Studies: Mrs S Neale, BEd,
   ARCM, LTCL
Secretary: Mrs C Stevens

Form Tutors:
Mrs S Neale, BEd, ARCM, LTCL
Miss E Allan, BA, BEd, PGCE
Mrs C Makhlouf, BEd
Miss J Hasler, BSc Hons, PGCE
Miss G Davies, BA Hons, MEd
Mrs H Ellis, BA Hons, MA, PGCE
Mrs L Lamb, BSc, PGCE

Part Time Tutors:
Mrs V Feeny, CertEd
Mrs C Wilson, BEd

Learning Support:
(to be appointed)

Assistant Teachers:
Mrs L Menez
Mrs A Crawford
Miss L Skabickaite

French: Mrs J Tweedie, L-ès-L Moderne, PGCE

Music Staff:
Mrs G Haynes, Mus USSR, DipAcc (*Piano*)
Mrs A Chua, MA, FLCM, LLCM (*Piano*)

Miss N Jackman, BMus (*Violin*)
Mr L Sollory, ALCM (*Guitar*)
Miss S Moore, BMus, DipARCM (*Flute*)
Mr R Russell (*Clarinet*)
Miss R Garland (*Oboe*)
Mrs S Mailey-Smith, BMus Hons (*Singing*)
Miss O Chaney, BMus, LRAM (*Singing*)
Miss R Nolan, BA Mus, BSc, LRAM (*Singing*)

Fencing: Mr V Meshkov

Bursar: Mr L Green
Financial Assistant to the Bursar: Mrs M Spasova
Bursar's Assistant: Lady Wilkinson
Registrar: Miss J Micklewright
Principal's Assistant: Miss I Brotherton-Ratcliffe, MVO
School Secretary: Miss E Mockeviciute, BA
School Archivist: Miss E de Leeuw

Queen's Gate School is an independent school for girls between the ages of 4 and 18 years. Established in 1891, the school is an Educational Trust situated in five large Victorian Houses within easy walking distance of Kensington Gardens, Hyde Park, Stanhope Gardens, the Natural History and Science Museums.

The aim of the school is to create a secure and happy environment in which the girls can realise their academic potential and make full use of individual interests and talents. We encourage the development of self-discipline and create an atmosphere where freedom of thought and ideas can flourish.

Close cooperation with parents is welcomed at every stage.

There is no school uniform except for games and gymnastics, but the girls are expected to wear clothing and footwear suitable for attending school and taking part in school activities.

Curriculum. Girls follow as wide a curriculum as possible and generally take GCSE in ten subjects which must include English, Mathematics, Science and a modern language.

An extensive range of AS/A Level subjects is offered. Four or five AS Levels are studied in the first year and three (or four) of these are taken at A2 Level.

Games. Netball, Hockey, Tennis, Swimming, Athletics, Basketball and Volleyball.

Admission. By test and interview in the Junior School, The London Day Schools' Consortium Entrance examination at 11+, and the School's own Entrance examinations for second, third or fourth year entry. Applicants for the Sixth Form are expected to have passed a minimum of six GCSEs at A Grade with A grades in those subjects they wish to pursue to A Level.

There is no entrance fee. Registration fee: £60.
Fees per term (2011-2012). £4,250–£5,100.

The Queen's School
Chester

City Walls Road, Chester, Cheshire CH1 2NN
Tel: 01244 312078
Fax: 01244 321507
e-mail: secretary@queens.cheshire.sch.uk
website: www.queens.cheshire.sch.uk

Founded 1878.
   Motto: '*Honour Wisdom*'

Governing Body:
Chairman: Dr C H Laine, MSc, FRCR

Deputy Chairmen:
Mr S Denton, BSc, CEng, FIMMM
Mr E A Elliott, BSc, MRICS

Revd Canon Professor L C A Alexander, MA, DPhil
Mrs M E Ardron, BA Hons Oxon
Mr N Canning, BA
Father D N Chesters, OBE, FRSA, FSA Scot, BA Hons
Mr M A H Fearnall, FNAEA, FICBA
The Lord Bishop of Chester, The Rt Revd Dr P R Forster, MA, BD, PhD
Mrs E J Lunn, BA, CPFA
Dr M McDonald, BSc, PhD
Mr D G Mason, LLB
Mrs C M E Mosley, MA, LLB, BA Hons, DipM
Ms S C Shepheard-Walwyn, BA Hons, MSc
Mrs A L Unett, MA Cantab, TEP
Cllr A P Walmsley
Mrs M Yorke, MEd

Clerk to the Governors: Mr B Dutton, FCA

Headmistress: Mrs E S Clark, MA Cambridge, PGCE

Deputy Head: Mrs I Jones, BA Hons Leeds, PGCE

Headmistress's PA: Mrs T Brooks
Secretaries: Mrs K Swinnock, Mrs L Amey, Mrs A Wallace, Miss A Concannon
Admissions Officer: Mrs F J Taylor
Bursar: Mrs M E Kelly
Bursar's Assistants: Mrs K Brown, Mrs L Jones
Administrator: Mrs L Rushforth
Public Examinations Officer: Mrs F Lennon, BA Lancaster
Development Director: Mr P G Virgo, BSc Hons Bristol, MBA
General Services Manager: Mrs L Aspden
Director of ICT: Mr P Foster
Network Manager: Mr G Blackwell, BA Teeside
Librarians: Ms G Mayes, Mrs C Roberts

Teachers:
* *Head of Department*

Art:
*Mr A Tucker, BA Bristol
Miss L Boyd, BA Manchester

Biology:
*Mrs C Dillamore, MA Cambridge
Dr J Threadgold, BSc Leeds, PhD
Miss S Bayliss, BA Hons Edinburgh, PGCE
Mrs L Povey, BSc Birmingham, PGCE

Careers:
Mrs V Carpenter, BA Nottingham
Mrs S Bright, BA Leicester

Chemistry:
*Mrs F Costigan, BSc UMIST
Mr D Cripps, MSc Huddersfield
Mr I Abell, BSc Teesside

Classics:
*Dr E Fernandes, PhD Cambridge, BA Hons Liverpool
Mrs P Tolley, BA Hons London, PGCE
Mrs E S Clark, MA Cambridge, PGCE (*Headmistress*)

Graphic Products:
*Mrs S Bright, BA Leicester

Economics & Business Studies:
*Mrs B Edwards, BEd Wales

English:
*Miss J Stockton, BA Lancaster, PGCE
Mr R Ainsworth, BA Durham, BPhil Newcastle, ACP
Mrs S Chafer, BA Wales, ALCM
Mrs J Dunham, BA Hons Cardiff, PGCE
Mr S O'Meara, BA Hons UCD, MA Liverpool, PGCE

Geography:
*Mr T Palfreyman, BA Hons, MA Liverpool, PGCE
Mrs R Morrison, BA Hons, PGCE

History:
*Miss N Jarvis, BA Hons Cardiff, MA Manchester
Miss L McCale, BA Hons Liverpool, PGCE

Food and Nutrition:
*Mrs G Hoyle, CertEd Madeley, BA OU
Mrs M Leigh, CertEd F L Calder, Liverpool

Information and Communications Technology:
*Mr D McKeown, BEng Liverpool John Moores
Mrs J McKeirnan, BA Hons London, PGCE

Mathematics:
*Mr I Armstrong, BSc Durham
Mrs S Osborne, BSc London
Mrs J O'Donnell, BA Lancaster, MSc Sheffield Hallam, PGCE
Mrs K Whitwell, BSc UMIST
Mr C Godfrey, MA Hons Sheffield, PGCE

Modern Languages:
*Miss L Ketchell, BA Durham
Mrs J Coupland, MA Oxford, PGCE
Mrs V Carpenter, BA Nottingham
Miss I Ruiz, BA Seville, PGCE
Miss S Laloyer, Licence Arras, PGCE
Mrs L Whittam, BA Beijing

Language Assistants:
Mrs A Bosch, Hons Spain
Mrs M Hutchinson, BA Nantes
Ms C Koch-Bradshaw

Music:
*Mrs R Broome, BMus Hons RWCMD, PGCE
Mrs J Healey, BA Hons Salford, PGCE
Mrs I Jones, BA Hons Leeds (*Deputy Head*)

Cello, Piano & Double Bass:
Miss C E Barker, BA Glasgow, LGSM
Piano:
Miss R Jones, GMus, RNCM, LRAM, ARCM, FLCM
Violin & Viola:
Mrs J Van Ingen, ATCL, ORAM
Ms A Whittaker, BMus, MA Music Perf
Woodwind:
Mrs J Williams, BA Hons Newcastle, PGCE
Mr G C Macey, ATGL
Mrs J Riekert, ATCL, CTA, BRSM
Brass:
Mr A Harper, BMus Manchester
Voice:
Mrs L Clayton, BA Hons Huddersfield
Percussion:
Mr M Whiteman, BA Hons Birmingham
Guitar:
Mr T Moore, BA Hons Liverpool
Mr A Jones
Music Theory:
Mr C Pilsbury, MA, MEd Liverpool, FTCL, ARMCM

Physical Education:
*Mrs C Moore, CertEd Coventry College
Miss S Littler, BEd, CertEd Astey College

Physics:
*Mrs P Steventon, BSc Exeter
Mrs E Robinson, BSc Hons Warwick, PGCE

Psychology:
*Dr J Russell, BA Keele, PhD UCL

Religious Studies:
*Mrs H Daniels, BA Durham
Dr J Scherer, MA Bangor

Drama:
*Mrs K Larder, BA Hons Huddersfield, PGCE

Speech and Drama:
Mrs A Mistry, LGSM, ALAM

Specific Learning Difficulties Adviser (senior and lower school):
Mrs S Hazzledine, MA Cambridge, PGCE, PGDipEd, AMBDA

Lower School, 55-57 Liverpool Road, Chester, CH2 1AW:
Mrs F Taylor, BA Hons OU, CertEd Dunelm (*Head of Lower School*)
Mrs S Lindop, BEd Cambridge
Mrs C Tottey, BEd IM Marsh College of Physical Education
Mrs M Ainsworth, LLB Hons Leeds, PGCE (*Deputy Head*)
Mrs K Morris-Yousaf, BA Warwick, PGCE
Mr J Wheldon, BSc Ripon Carlisle, PGCE
Mrs M Corlett, BA Hons Royal Holloway College, London, PGCE
Miss R R Morgan, BA Hons Wales, PGCE
Mrs J Podmore-Childe (*Speech and Drama*)
Mrs J Callaghan, BEd Hons Manchester Poly (*Head of Key Stage 1*)
Mrs F Carder, BEd Hons Exeter
Mrs D Thomas, BEd Hons Sussex
Mrs D G Heron, BEd St Katherine's College, Liverpool
Mrs H Stockley, BSc Hons Derby, PGCIT Bangor
Mrs R Evans, BEd Hons St Katherine's College, Liverpool
Mrs A Worsfold, BA Chichester
Mrs Y Pearson, BEd Hons, Lancaster
Mrs M Green, BEd Hons Liverpool
Miss G Platt, BA Hons Sheffield, PGCE

Teaching Assistants:
Mrs S Talbot, NVQ2 & 3
Mrs S Howell
Mrs A Morris, BA Leeds
Mrs H Singh, BEd India
Mrs H Long ASA Level 1
Mrs K Davies, BA Bath, NVQ2 & 3
Mrs J Maughan, Early Years

Childcare Supervisor (after school): Mrs S Smith

Childcare Assistants (after school): Mrs S Talbot, Miss E Dillamore, Miss R Bell

Senior Administrative Officer: Mrs F Ralph

Secretaries:
Mrs E Thomas
Mrs C Hardy

The Queen's School is an independent day school for girls aged 4–18.

Senior School. Number of pupils: 382.

Situated within the city walls of Chester, the Victorian gothic building was built on land donated by the first Duke of Westminster. Throughout the last century, the school acquired neighbouring properties, building classrooms, a science block and sports facilities. In 1998 MacLean House was named after a former headmistress and transformed into a sixth form centre, providing excellent facilities for both relaxation and work. It comprises lower and upper sixth common rooms, library, study and ICT facilities, with a modern languages study room.

The school's gardens, playing field, tennis courts and astroturf are set against the stunning backdrop of the city walls.

Curriculum: A very broad curriculum, aimed at keeping options open, is taught throughout the school. Girls take 10 subjects at GCSE and 4 or 5 subjects at AS Level, including Critical Thinking in Year 13. They take 3 or 4 subjects to A2 Level in Year 13 and may opt to take the EPQ. As well as the core subjects, English, mathematics, the three sciences,

PSE, PE and religious studies, girls may study a range of modern languages: Spanish, Mandarin, French and German. The school offers Latin, classical civilisation, geography, history and the practical subjects art, drama, food & nutrition, graphic products, ICT and music. A Level subjects also include business studies, economics and psychology.

Sports: Hockey, lacrosse, tennis and athletics are major sports, played at county and in some cases national and international level. Also gymnastics, netball, running, cross country, swimming, rounders, dance, skiing, badminton, volleyball, basketball, table tennis and football; either as part of the curriculum or the extra-curricular timetable.

Extra-Curricular Activities: Pupils undertake The Duke of Edinburgh's Award from Year 9 and involvement in Young Enterprise is a strong tradition in the Sixth Form.

There are over 70 active clubs to participate in: Debating Society, Equine Club, Christian Union, Psych Soc, Eco-Club, Craft Club, Composition Club, Languages, Drama and Sports clubs. Music is an important part of life at Queen's and there are many opportunities for all girls of varying musical abilities to make music together.

Lower School. Number of pupils: 203.

The Lower School is set in beautiful landscaped grounds, with a large playing field, tennis courts and outdoor play areas, within easy walking distance of Chester city centre. The school has been significantly extended in recent years with the building of a library and teaching wing, as well as the award-winning swimming pool built in 2009. The Lower School has its own ICT suite. Before and after school supervision is available.

Curriculum: In the Lower School we deliver a broad and balanced curriculum which is designed to excite and develop learning. Lessons are differentiated to enable every child to progress and achieve. The most able pupils are able to strive ahead and be stretched and challenged academically. We teach in a cross curricular way in KS1 and parts of KS2. In KS1 we are keen to embrace investigative play and discovery learning wherever it is appropriate. The 'outdoor' classroom is fast developing and offers a superb range of equipment for all areas of the curriculum. Gradually girls are introduced to more specialist teachers in preparation for Key Stage Two. Here we have specialist staff for modern foreign languages, PE, Swimming, Music, Art and Ceramics. Staff are able to demonstrate appropriate subject knowledge and an approach to teaching which motivates, encourages and promotes learning. They are encouraged to be multi sensory in their approach to assist different learning styles and interact with pupils. Girls are usually set by ability in Maths and English in Upper Key Stage 2.

Sports: We provide a well-balanced programme which includes challenge, competition, aesthetic movement, teamwork and physical fitness. Specialist staff teach the girls for three hours of physical activity lessons per week; swimming and a variety of other traditional sports. Pupils take part very successfully in inter-school matches against other prominent independent schools.

Extra-Curricular Activities: We offer a wide range of sporting clubs from fencing to hockey and also give girls a wide range of foreign language opportunities. Girls also enjoy cookery, science and chess clubs. They run the school newspaper by writing articles and taking their own photographs. Drama and music are well supported too, giving all pupils the chance to develop their talents outside the classroom.

Admission. Girls are admitted into the Lower School at the start of the academic year (1st September–31st August) in which they will be five years of age. Each girl is invited for interview in the previous spring term, and her assessment takes into account maturity, conversational skills, dexterity, concentration and memory. In addition, there is entry into Year 3, the start of Key Stage Two (7–8 year olds) for which assessments also take place in the spring term. Vacancies in other year groups are sometimes available.

Girls wishing to enter the senior school in Year 7 take papers in English, mathematics and verbal reasoning in the spring term of Year 6. Candidates for entry at this stage should be under the age of 12 on 1st September in the year of admission.

Girls are also warmly welcomed into the Sixth Form from other schools, subject to obtaining satisfactory grades at GCSE, reference from current school and interview.

Bursaries. The school has a number of means-tested bursaries which are awarded on a combination of academic merit and financial need. Further details may be obtained from the Clerk to the Governors, e-mail: bdutton@ queens.cheshire.sch.uk.

Fees per term (2011-2012). Senior School: £3,550; Lower School: £2,485.

Additional Music and Speech & Drama lessons are available and charged per term.

Visiting. Annual Open Days are held in the autumn term for Senior School and Lower School. Two evenings for prospective Sixth Formers are held in October and November. Taster days arranged to suit pupils of all ages. Contact Mrs Jane Taylor, Admissions Officer, e-mail: jtaylor@ queens.cheshire.sch.uk.

Alumni. There is a vibrant and active community of former pupils. Reunions and events are held at regular intervals throughout the year. Contact The Queen's School Alumni Office on 01244 356015 or e-mail: alumni@queens.cheshire.sch.uk.

Charitable status. The Queen's School is a Registered Charity, number 525935, for the advancement and provision of education for girls aged 4 to 18.

Queenswood

Hatfield, Hertfordshire AL9 6NS
Tel: 01707 602500
Fax: 01707 602597
e-mail: go@queenswood.org
website: www.queenswood.org

Founded 1894.

Governors:

Chairman: Mrs M C A King, BA, FCA
Vice-Chairman: W J Sykes

D A J Baldry, BSc
Revd A E Brown, BSc
J de Sausmarez, BA Hons
D J Harvey
A M Love, FCA
Professor Q McKellar, CBE, BVMS, PhD
Mrs A S Moores (*Fellowship Representative*)
Mrs V R Neale (*Old Queenswoodian Representative*)
Miss A M Rawlinson, BA, MA Hons, NPQH
R H Reid, FCA
Mrs L A Robinson, BSc, MRICS
G Russell, MA (*Methodist Representative*)
E M Sautter, MA
Ms S J Thomas, BA, PGCE
Dr A J Vallance-Owen, MBA, FRCS Ed
Mrs P M Wrinch

Principal: **Mrs P C Edgar**, BA Hons London, PGCE

Director of Business Development: Mr P J Walker, CBE, FCMI

Deputy Principal (*Pastoral*): Mrs J Wright, BA Hons Warwick, PGCE

Deputy Principal (*Academic*): Mrs V Renaudon-Smith, BA Hons Keele, PGCE

Chaplain: Revd G J A Wright, Dip Th, Dip Min

Bursar and Clerk to the Governors: Mr S Lee

Heads of Departments:
Art and Design: Mr J Hills, BA Hons Reading, MA London, PGCE
Design & Technology: Ms M Archer, BSc Hons UCL, PGCE
Drama: Mrs A Kelley, BA Hons Wales, MA Portsmouth (*Director of Drama*)
English: Mr P Merrell, BA Hons UCL, MPhil Birmingham, PGCE
Geography: Mrs S Sanders, BA Hons Royal Holloway, PGCE
History: Dr S Murray, BA Hons Warwick, MA Warwick, DPhil Oxon
History of Art: Dr W Bird, BA Hons Leicester, PGCE, PhD Reading
ICT Life Skills: Mrs S Goodwin, RSA Teaching Cert
Languages: Mrs L Law, BA Hons Middx, PGCE
Mathematics: Mr P Vincent, BA Hons East Anglia, PGCE
Music: Mr J Dobson, Prof Cert Hons RAM, LRAM (*Director of Music*)
Physical Education: Mrs J Wakeley, BEd Hons London (*Director of Sport*)
Practical Cookery: Mrs J Lee
Religious Studies: Miss H Last, BA Hons, PGCE
Science: Mrs M F T Davidson, BSc Hons Leicester, PGCE

Head of Sixth Form: Dr A Seele, MA Konstanz, Germany, PhD
Head of Middle School: Miss P Sex, BA Hons Swansea, MA Ed Hertfordshire, PGCE
Head of Lower School: Mrs M Gourd, BA Hons Nottingham, MA London, PGCE
Head of Lower School Boarding: Miss S Hardie, CertEd, TESOL
Head of Pupil Enrichment: Mrs A Wakefield, BMus Hons Sheffield

Head of Admissions: Mrs A Steiger, BSc Hons

Queenswood is a progressive boarding and day school for about 400 girls, aged between 11 and 18, where boarders make up more than half of the School. An all-round education focuses on equipping the girls with all the life skills required of women in the 21st century. Within a caring and supportive framework, the girls enjoy a dynamic academic curriculum, supported by a diverse and exciting extra-curricular programme.

It is a warm and friendly community where everybody knows each other. Girls thrive within a nurturing house structure tailored to meet the needs of the girls as they progress from the Junior School, through the Middle School, and on into the Sixth Form. Day girls are fully integrated within the houses, are able to enjoy all the facilities and opportunities available to the boarders, but choose to go home at night after a packed school day. There is a flexible approach to boarding to meet the varying needs of individual families; girls may choose to be full boarders or just to remain in School for four or five nights a week.

Queenswood is proud to be an international community with an outward-looking approach; overseas girls make up around 20% of the pupils. We welcome girls of all faiths and none, recognise and support an individual's adherence to her own faith, but expect all girls to embrace the School's broad spiritual ethos.

The girls are ambitious high achievers, winning places at the top universities both at home and abroad prior to embarking upon a range of exciting careers. The School is, however, resolutely neither an academic hothouse nor overly selective. Individual talent also flourishes in sport and the creative and performing arts. As important as individual achievement is the development of a sense of responsibility for each other and the world in which they live. Queenswood girls are thoughtful young people with a secure set of values and self-confidence.

The beautiful Queenswood estate provides the perfect educational environment. Being just 25 minutes from central London, it also has the advantage of easy access to the cultural richness of the capital. At the same time, its proximity to major international airports provides ease of travel for both our overseas girls and for those participating in the School's foreign exchange and visit programmes.

Entry. Entrance to Queenswood is by examination (CEE or Queenswood's papers), interview and a report from the pupil's current Headteacher.

Scholarships. Scholarships (honorary) are available at 11+, 13+, Sixth Form and for: tennis, sports, drama and music. Bursaries are means tested and reviewed annually.

Fees per term (2011-2012). Boarders: Sixth Form £9,555; Years 9–11 £9,165; Years 7–8 £8,765. Day: Sixth Form £7,275; Years 9–11 £6,965; Years 7–8 £6,495.

Old Queenswoodians' Association (OQA) with 3,000+ members, organised in regional branches throughout the UK and the world, contactable through the school and website.

Charitable status. Queenswood School Limited is a Registered Charity, number 311060, which exists to provide high-quality education for girls.

The Red Maids' School

Westbury-on-Trym, Bristol BS9 3AW
Tel: 0117 962 2641
Fax: 0117 962 1687
e-mail: admin@redmaids.bristol.sch.uk
website: www.redmaids.co.uk

We are the country's oldest girls' school, founded in 1634 due to the inspiration and vision of Mayor and MP of Bristol, John Whitson. Today we continue the vision and spirit of our founder, to empower and equip our young women to make their mark in the world.

Governing Body:
Chairman: Mrs J MacFarlane, BSc, MA
There are 13 members of The Governing Body.

Head Mistress: Mrs I Tobias, BA New Hall Cambridge
(*English*)

Senior Deputy Head: Miss K Welham, BSc Bristol
(*Mathematics*)
Deputy Head (Academic): Mr R Cameron, BA
Southampton (*History*)

Assistant Teaching Staff:
Miss B Abbott, BA London (*Design Technology*)
Mr H Besterman, MA Cambridge (*Biology*)
Mr H Briggs, MA Bristol (*Theology*)
Mr S Browne, GRSM, LRAM, ARCM (*Music*)
Miss E Buckland, BA Cambridge (*Theology & Religious Studies*)
Miss L Bullion, BA Liverpool John Moores (*Home Economics*)
Mr J Cooper, MA St Andrews (*Modern History*)
Miss J Dalley, MA Bath Spa (*Technology*)
Mrs L Davies, BA Kent (*English*)
Mr M Fielding, BSc Exeter (*Mathematics & French*)
Mr N Folland, BA Leeds (*Economics*)
Mrs J Gupta, BA Manchester (*Italian, Latin*)
Dr N Hanbury, BSc PhD Reading (*Physics*)
Miss S Hannah, BA UEA (*English*)
Mrs S Higgins, BSc Hull (*Chemistry*)
Miss S Hunter, BA Birmingham (*Sport & PE*)
Mrs E Jackson, MA Cambridge (*Classics*)
Mr T Johnston, BA Bath College of HE (*Design Ceramics*)

Mrs R Killick, BA Liverpool Hope (*Music*)
Miss J Lowe, BSc Birmingham (*French, German*)
Miss K Markwell, BA Bristol (*English*)
Ms Z Matthews, BSc Durham (*Mathematics*)
Miss V Michell, BSc Bristol (*Psychology*)
Mr A Newman, BA Bradford (*German, French*)
Mrs C North, BA Exeter (*French, Spanish*)
Mr J Owen, MA Cambridge (*English Literature*)
Miss K Rolfe, BA Bath (*Physical Education*)
Miss L Savage, BSc Bristol (*Mathematics*)
Mr D Seamark, BSc Imperial College, London
(*Mathematics*)
Miss C Shearn, BSc Bath Spa (*Geography*)
Mr C Stainthorp, BSc Warwick (*Mathematics*)
Miss C Stephens, BSc UWIC (*History*)
Miss N Stubbs, MSc Warwick (*Mathematics*)
Miss M Tomaszewski, BA Oxford (*French, Russian*)
Mrs V Turner, BSc Bristol (*Biology*)
Mr C Watson, BSc Leeds (*Chemistry*)
Mrs P West, BSc Bristol (*Geography*)
Mrs C Woodman, GBSM, ABSM, LLCM, ALCM (*Music*)
Mrs P Wooff, BSc Sheffield (*Biology*)

Part-time Staff:
Mrs M Appleton, BSc UWIST (*Economics*)
Mrs R Beaney, BA St Mary's University College
(*Religious Studies*)
Mrs C Besterman, MA Cambridge (*Classics*)
Mrs C Barratt (*Piano*)
Mrs L Begbie (*Bassoon*)
Mrs J Browne, LRAM (*Flute*)
Ms J Bryant, BSc Birmingham (*Physical Education*)
Miss L Coulton, MSc Edinburgh (*Biology*)
Mrs J Evans, BMus, ARCM (*Flute*)
Mrs J Francis, GRSM, ARCM (*Cello*)
Mrs H Goodman, GRSM, ARCM (*Violin and Piano*)
Mr B Gruenevelt (*Double Bass*)
Mrs J Hammersley (*Harp*)
Miss J Hart, BA Cardiff (*Spanish*)
Mrs E Hinkins, BEd Cheltenham & Gloucester (*Physical Education*)
Mrs C Joyce, BA Warwick (*English & Drama*)
Miss C Knight, MA Bath Spa (*Fine Art*)
Mrs K Lewis-Barned, MEd Bristol (*English*)
Ms A Lister, BEd Bristol College of St Matthias (*French*)
Mrs V MacDonald, BSc Open University (*Psychology*)
Miss R MacKay, BSc Glasgow (*Biology*)
Mr P Mahon (*Electric Guitar*)
Mr M Martin, BA Malaga, Spain (*Spanish*)
Mr C McCann (*Percussion*)
Dr J Moe, PhD Bristol
Mrs F Palmer, BA London (*Drama and English*)
Mrs Y Penn, BEd Wales (*ICT, Mathematics*)
Miss L Porter (*Clarinet, Saxophone*)
Miss C Quainton, MSc Bristol (*Spanish*)
Mrs A Ransom, BA Durham (*Modern Languages*)
Miss J Ratcliffe, BA Bristol Polytechnic (*Art and Ceramics*)
Miss M Rhind, BSc London (*Biology*)
Mr P Riley, BA, ARCM (*Piano*)
Miss S Russe, BSc Bath Spa (*Physical Education*)
Mr P Slade, BSc Oxford (*Physics*)
Mrs R Saunders (*Singing*)
Mr T Shevlin (*Trumpet*)
Ms F Trezevant (*Singing*)
Mrs I Trinner (*Oboe, Recorder*)
Mrs A Tyler, BA Cardiff (*Classics*)
Mrs N Weir BEd Trent Polytechnic (*Information Technology*)
Mrs T White, ARCM (*Brass*)
Miss S Woods, BA Belfast (*History*)

Head of Junior School:
Mrs G Rowcliffe, BEd Bristol

Teaching Staff:
Mrs L Bennett, BA Reading
Mrs L Brown, BSc Leicester
Miss S Browning, BA Manchester Metro
Mrs M Edbrooke, BEd King Alfred's College, Winchester
Ms B Fenton, BEd Bristol Polytechnic
Mrs S Hiley, BSc Lancashire
Mrs L Joslin, BEd Dunfermline College of Physical
    Education
Dr J Moe, PhD Bristol
Mrs E Noad, BA Swansea
Ms J Ratcliffe, BA Bristol Polytechnic (*Art and Ceramics*)
Mrs L Woodward, BSc Birmingham
Mrs A Purdy, MA York

Bursar: Mr P Taylor
Headmistress's PA: Mrs J Bell
Registrar: Mrs E Bamber

Character. Red Maids' is a friendly, purposeful school; intellectual curiosity, energy and enthusiasm are characteristic of students and teachers alike. Red Maids are encouraged to discover and develop their own abilities, to think for themselves and to strive for success whether this is academic, on the sports field, in the creative arts or in the practical technologies.

Facilities. Set in 12 acres of peaceful parkland, sports facilities are all on site including an international standard astroturf and two new competition standard grade 1 netball courts. The award-winning Junior School expansion opened in November 2007 as part of ongoing investment that has also included refurbishment of the school's science laboratories and the re-development of the Sixth Form Centre.

Extended Day. We offer an extended day at no extra charge. Girls may purchase breakfast from 7.45 am and can stay at school until 6.00 pm, taking part in the free After School Club, making use of supervised prep and participating in the numerous extra-curricular activities. These include: Young Enterprise, choirs, orchestras, The Duke of Edinburgh's Award, Public Speaking and a wide range of sports clubs, teams and societies.

School Life. The School Council and Sixth Form leadership positions encourage students to take responsibility for others. Peer support systems, clubs run by older students and staff and charitable fundraising of all sorts demonstrate the pupils' energetic involvement in their community.

Assemblies celebrate pupils' achievements in every sphere, examine current affairs and topical issues and offer opportunities for thought, reflection and spiritual exploration.

Curriculum. Subjects taught include Religious Education, English, History, Geography, French, German, Italian, Latin, Russian, Spanish, Economics, Mathematics, Philosophy & Ethics, Psychology, Sciences (Physics, Chemistry, Biology), Design Technology, Food Technology, Textiles Technology, Art, Music, Drama, Sports Studies, Physical Education, Business Studies, Information Technology, Classical Civilisation, and Theatre Studies. Girls are well prepared for GCSEs, and at Sixth Form they can opt for the International Baccalaureate Diploma Programme or the A Level Programme. Mandarin is the modern foreign language taught in the Junior School.

Sixth Form. Sixth Form students enjoy both the continuity of excellent teacher relationships and the independence of the new Sixth Form Centre which includes dedicated teaching rooms, seminar rooms, common rooms, café, an ICT suite and a dedicated careers library. Students achieve their full academic potential through challenging teaching and the encouragement to develop habits of independent study and academic rigour. Almost all students go on to study at University, including Oxbridge.

Sixth Formers have many opportunities both for new experiences of leadership within the school and for a broader understanding of the wider world through the varied community service programme and the general studies course.

Fees per term (2011-2012). Senior School £3,480, Junior School £2,305. Curricular school trips are included in this fee. The only extras are Music lessons (piano, clarinet, flute, viola, French horn, oboe, bassoon, violin, cello, saxophone, singing, trumpet, guitar), Speech and Drama lessons and optional non-academic trips.

Admission to Junior School. The main points of entry to the Junior School are in Year 3 and Year 5. Girls are assessed during a day visit when they also spend time with their peer group.

Admission to Senior School. Entrance to the Senior School for girls aged 11 depends on the results of an examination and interview during Year 6. These are held at the end of January for admission the following September. There are also entries in other years, subject to availability, and to the Sixth Form. For full particulars about fees, scholarships and admission procedures, application should be made to the Registrar.

Scholarships. (*See Scholarship Entries section.*) Academic, Music and Sport Scholarships are awarded for Year 7 entry with additional Headmistress's Scholarships available. A further discretionary scholarship may be awarded to those applying to the school for Year 9 entry.

Sixth Form Scholarships are available for both the two-year A Level Course and the International Baccalaureate Diploma. Applications are made in the Spring Term and are open to those already in the school and those intending to join in the following September.

Charitable status. The Red Maids' School is a Registered Charity, number 1105017. It has existed since 1634 to provide an education for girls.

Redland High School for Girls

Redland Court, Bristol BS6 7EF
Tel: 0117 924 5796
Fax: 0117 924 1127
e-mail: admissions@redlandhigh.com
website: www.redlandhigh.com

Motto: *So hateth she derknesse*

The School was founded in the year 1882, and established at Redland Court in 1884. The aim for which the School was instituted was to provide for the girls of Redland and its neighbourhood a non-denominational public school education of the highest class, fitting pupils for home life, for professional life, and for the Universities.

We hope to provide a broad and balanced education which will enable each girl to reach her potential, help her to form secure relationships and provide her with the skills and qualifications for a career and for creative leisure.

Governors:

School Council:
President: Mrs C Lear, BA
Chairman: Mr P J F Breach, BA, FCA, ATII, ACT, IIMR
Deputy Chairman: Mrs P Pyper, BA
Mrs A M Ebery, BA
Mrs C Y Fleming, MA
Dr J S Littler, BA, BSc, MA, DPhil
Sir Alexander Macara, FRCP, FRCGP, FFPHM, DSc
Mrs C Melvin, BA, MA, MCIPR
Mrs S Perry
Mrs E J Robb, BEd
Dr J Shemilt, MBBS, BSc
Mr M Whife, BSc, MRICS, MAPM, ACIArb
Miss J Yerbury, CertEd
Mr P Cheek, FCCA
Ms S M Dore, MA

Bursar and Clerk to Governors: Mr B W Blackwood, MSc Warwick

Headmistress: Mrs Caroline P Bateson, BA UCL, PGCE London, MA UWE

Senior School Staff:

Deputy Headmistress: Mrs P Davidson, BA, PGCE Bristol
Director of Studies: Mrs S E Barnes, BA, Dip HE Bloemfontein
Head of Sixth Form: Ms D Heywood, BSc Bristol, PGCE Cambridge
Head of Lower School: Miss H A Drew, BA Leeds, PGCE Cambridge
Head of Year 10: Mrs L McLaughlin, BSc, GradDipEd Charles Sturt University
Head of Year 11: Ms R Nelson, BSc Montreal, PGCE Bristol

Heads of Houses:
Rowan: Miss C Wedgwood, BSc Manchester, PGCE Bristol
Maple: Mrs A Stean, BSc Leicester, PGCE Bristol Polytechnic
Willow: Mr M A K Sloan, BSc Bristol, PGCE Edinburgh
Chestnut: Mrs A Brake, BA, PGCE Nottingham

* *Head of Department*

Art including Ceramics, Print Making and History of Art:
*Mr J E Icke, BEd Goldsmiths
Ms R V Clapp, BA Middlesex
Ms L Dickson, BTEC BA Staffordshire
Mrs C Smith, BA Essex

Biology:
*Dr M Quick, BSc Liverpool, PhD, PGCE Bristol
Ms D Heywood, BSc Bristol, PGCE Cambridge
Miss C Wedgwood, BSc Manchester

Careers:
Mrs A Brake, BA, PGCE Nottingham

Chemistry:
*Mrs L D Fletcher, BEd London, MRSC (*also Head of Science*)
Miss A McAxup, BSc, PGCE Southampton

Classics including Latin, Greek and Classical Civilisation:
*Ms S Knights, BA, PGCE Bristol
Mr W G Horstead, BA Bristol

Critical Thinking:
*Mrs A Brake, BA, PGCE Nottingham

Drama and Theatre Studies:
*Ms S McCormack, BA Manchester, PGCE Cambridge
Ms J Owens-Powell, BA Bristol, PGCE UWE
Mrs L J Sharman, BA Glamorgan

Economics & Business Studies:
*Mrs K M Buff, BA, PGCE UWE

English:
*Mrs C Rodliffe, BA, PGCE Bristol
Mrs A J I Adams, MA St Andrews, PGCE Christ Church
Mrs P Davidson, BA, PGCE Bristol
Ms C Kitcatt, BA, MEd East Anglia, PGCE Southampton
Ms S McCormack, BA Manchester, PGCE Cambridge, MA Bristol
Mrs J Nield, CertEd
Dr L White, BA Oxford, MA UWE, PhD Birmingham

French:
*Miss C M Douglas, BA Keele, PGCE Cardiff
Mrs P M Hamilton, BA Belfast, PGCE Oxford
Mrs K M McMahon, BA, PGCE Birmingham
Miss S Saberi, BA Bordeaux 111 (*French Assistant*)
Ms E Sefer, Maîtrise, LLCE Provence, PGCE Wales

Geography:
*Mrs J Neil, BSc, MSc Lancaster, PGCE Edinburgh
Mrs S M Argent, BA Worcester College, PGCE Exeter
Mrs A Brake, BA, PGCE Nottingham

German:
*Mrs K M McMahon, BA, PGCE Birmingham
Mrs P M Hamilton, BA Belfast, PGCE Oxford
Mrs K Roberts, BA Bern (*German Assistant*)

Government & Politics:
*Mrs D L Alderson, BA Reading, PGCE Leicester, TTCIT
Mrs S Knight, MA St Andrews, PGCE London

History:
*Ms A L Earle, BA Brunel, PGCE Exeter
*Mrs S Knight, MA St Andrews, PGCE London
Mrs C P Bateson, BA University College London, PGCE University of London Institute
Mrs M Bishop, First Degree University of Venice, MLitt Cambridge, PGCE Bath

ICT:
*Ms J Gale (*Director of ICT*)
*Mrs J Marsden, BA OU, PGCE UWE (*Head of ICT – Academic*)
Mr A Chappell (*IT Support Technician*)
Miss Z L Leach, BSc, PGCE Exeter
Ms M R Viney, BA, PGCE University of Wales, MEd Bristol

Library:
Mrs C J Spalding, BA Hull, ALA

Mathematics including Mechanics and Statistics and Further Mathematics:
*Mrs S E Barnes, BA, DipHE Bloemfontein
Mr M P Ehrlich, BA Cambridge, MBA London Business School, PGCE Bristol
Mrs S Locke, BEd UWE
Mrs A Stean, BSc Leicester, PGCE UWE

Music:
*Mr S M Daykin, PgDip, BMus Royal Welsh College of Music & Drama
Mrs N Cooper, BMus Cardiff, PGCE Bristol
Miss S Rowlands, BA, PGCE Bristol

Visiting Music Staff Junior & Senior Schools:
Ms E Adams, ALCM (*Voice*)
Ms V Bremner, BA, ATCL, ALCM (*Voice*)
Mrs N Cooper, BMus Cardiff, PGCE Bristol (*Piano*)
Mr M Davies, BMus, Dip ABRSM, Dip RWCMD (*Piano*)
Mr B Fitzpatrick (*Percussion*)
Miss C Hiles, MA, Dip TCM (*Piano*)
Miss V Hodges, BA, ALCM (*Clarinet, Saxophone*)
Mr A King, GBSM, ABSM, LTCL (*Oboe*)
Ms M Krawiec, BA (*Flute*)
Ms J McCarthy, GGSM ('*Cello*)
Mr G Smith, LRAM (*Violin, Viola*)
Mr P Tedbury (*Guitar*)
Mr R Webb, BMus (*Brass*)
Ms E Whitfield, BA Nottingham (*Bassoon*)
Mrs R Whitworth, BSc Bristol (*Violin*)

Physical Education:
*Mrs L McLaughlin, BSc, Grad DipEd Charles Sturt University
Miss E R Harrington, BSc, PGCE Gloucestershire
Miss Z L Leach, BSc, PGCE Exeter
Ms J Wood, BEd Sussex, MSc Leicester
Mrs S Thomas (*Tennis Coach, Junior & Senior School*)

Physics:
*Mr M A K Sloan, BSc Bristol, PGCE Edinburgh
Miss R L Nelson, BSc Montreal, PGCE Bristol
Mrs A Stean, BSc Leicester, PGCE UWE

Psychology:
*Ms L Jephcote, BA Reading, PGCE Wales

Religious Studies:
*Miss H A Drew, BA Leeds, PGCE Cambridge
Mrs C Barker, BA, MA, PGCE Oxford
Mrs L Gillion, CertEd

Science Curriculum Support Staff:
Mrs J Boynton
Mrs L Michie
Mr J Icke

Spanish:
*Miss T Asiain-Escobar, MA Eastern Michigan University
Ms M E Rodriguez Dominguez, BSc Valladolid (*Spanish Assistant*)

Special Educational Needs:
Mrs A E Cartwright, BEd Oxon
Mrs J R Anstee, BEd Sheffield, Prim Ed CAPSE Special Needs

Technology including Design, Food & Textiles:
*Mrs L M Hunt, BA Nottingham Trent, PGCE Gloucestershire
Mrs J E Madden, CertEd Worcester College
Ms M R Viney, BA, PGCE University of Wales, MEd Bristol

Junior School:

Head Teacher: Mr J P Eyles, BEd Bath Spa

Deputy Head Teacher: Mrs A E Cartwright, BEd Oxon

Lower Foundation: Mrs J Nash
Upper Foundation: Mrs K Vaughan, BSc, PGCE UWE
Early Years Assistant: Miss A Tippett, NNEB Bristol
Year 1 Teachers:
Miss K Carpenter, BSc Portsmouth, PGCE UWE
Mrs J Lear, BA UWE, QTS
Year 2 Teacher: Mrs E Scott, BA, PGCE Durham
Year 3 Teacher: Ms A Mackenzie, BA TVU Brunel
Year 4 Teacher: Mrs R Hayward, CertEd Bristol
Year 5 Teachers:
Miss S F Rendall, BA Bristol, PGCE Bath Spa
Mrs S Falconer, BA Sussex, PGCE London
Year 6 Teacher: Mrs K Lashley, BA, PGCE Carmarthen
After School Care: Ms R J Acreman, Cache Diploma
Ballet: Miss D Sims, ARAD, Adv TDip, LISTD, Dip RBS TTC
French: Ms E Sefer, Maîtrise, LLCE Provence, PGCE Wales
German: Mrs P M Hamilton, BA Belfast, PGCE Oxford
Director of ICT: Ms J Gale
IT Assistant: Mrs J Trump, Cache Diploma, CTA3
Latin: Ms S Knights, BA, PGCE Bristol
Special Educational Needs: Mrs A E Cartwright, BEd Oxon
Classroom Assistants:
Miss R Acreman, Cache Diploma
Mrs C Cheek, Cache Diploma
Mrs A Doherty
Mrs J Smith, Cache Diploma
Mrs J Trump, Cache Diploma, CTA3
Library: Mrs C J Spalding, BA Hull, ALA
Music:
Miss S F Rendall, BA Bristol, PGCE Bath Spa
Miss S Rowlands, BA, PGCE Bristol
(*Visiting Music Teachers as for Senior School*)
Physical Education:
Mr J P Eyles, BEd Bath Spa
Miss E Harrington, BSc, PGCE Gloucestershire
Miss Z L Leach, BSc, PGCE Exeter
Mrs L McLaughlin, BSc, Grad DipEd Charles Sturt University
Ms J Wood, BEd Sussex, MSc Leicester

PSHE: Mrs A E Cartwright, BEd Oxon
Redland Rascals Holiday Club: Mrs F C O'Brien
Science: Mrs K Lashley, BA, PGCE Carmarthen
Speech & Drama: Mr J Butler, BA UWE

Administration:
Bursar: Mr B W Blackwood, MSc Warwick
Bursar's Secretary: Miss F Atkin, BEd Exeter
Payroll Officer: Miss A Brice, BA Portsmouth
Fees Officer: Mrs K L Gardner, FCCA
PA to Headmistress and Office Manager: Mrs A O'Callaghan
Admissions Secretary: Ms C Jenner
School Secretary: Mrs D L Waine
Junior School Secretaries:
Mrs L Stannard
Mrs J Trump, Cache Diploma, CTA3
Receptionist: Mrs H Kent
Director of Marketing & Development: Mrs J F Butterworth, BSc London
Alumni Officer: Mrs L Spencer-Small, BSc Bristol
Marketing Officer: Ms M Oakley, BA Sheffield
Resources Technician: Mrs J Walker
Head of Maintenance: Mr D Edwards
Maintenance Staff: Mr M Cox, Mr K Harris, Mr R Hutton, Mr S Pope
Catering and Cleaning: Ms H Tovey, Manager, Chartwells
Golden Hill Sports Ground: Mr and Mrs Cato

Redland High is an Independent School for girls between the ages of 3 and 18, with approximately 150 Juniors and 500 Seniors. All girls are given a broadly based education aimed at developing the ability and potential of each individual. The school is a friendly, purposeful, disciplined and caring community.

The Junior School is housed in Victorian houses close to the Senior School. We place due emphasis on ensuring that the Junior girls acquire excellent core skills but also devote time to many extras that are not part of the National Curriculum. Our extra-curricular activities programme (which includes judo, orienteering and chess club) ensures that girls throughout our age range can choose something to suit their interests whether sporting, musical, artistic, scientific or literary. We strongly encourage our pupils to try at least one activity to ensure she receives the benefit of a rounded education. Many educational trips are run through the year to enhance classroom learning. Class sizes are small to ensure each girl gets optimum attention and to enable the girls to express their individuality and know that they are special members of our close-knit community. In 2008 we opened a new Activity Hall which gives additional space for Year 5 and 6 pupils, in response to the demand for places. We also offer after-school care and our Redland Rascals Holiday club in support of working families. Visitors notice straight away that there is a buzz about this school that is to do with purposeful and innovative approaches to enhancing the girls' learning experiences. Because we are determined to 'reach' each and every pupil, we try lots of different methods so that each one of them will have the opportunity to find and develop her own learning style with enthusiasm and success. The Junior and Senior schools work very closely together enabling Junior pupils to benefit from specialist teachers for Music, Latin and Modern Languages and to use the Senior School facilities for Art, PE and Technology.

The Senior School is situated in a beautiful eighteenth-century mansion to which additional classrooms and excellently equipped laboratories have been added. There is a very impressive Art department housed in an Arts Centre, an ICT Suite, a Technology Workshop a well-equipped Home Economics unit and a gymnasium with a climbing wall and a large stage, well designed for dramatic productions. Music, which is a particular strength of the school, is housed in a dedicated Music School close by. Redland High has a fine tradition of very high examination results, effective and supportive pastoral care and a wide range of extra-curricular activities. The school's undoubted proficiency in encouraging all its pupils comes from outstanding teaching and having a school of optimum size: sufficient students to make a considerable subject choice viable but a low enough pupil to staff ratio for each individual pupil to be appreciated.

The school curriculum consists of Religious Studies, English Language and Literature, Drama, French, German, Spanish, Greek, Latin, Classical Civilisation, History, Geography, Mathematics, IT, Design Technology, Biology, Chemistry, Physics, Textiles, Art, Home Economics, Craft, Music and Physical Education which includes Gymnastics and Dancing, Hockey, Netball, Athletics, Tennis, Badminton, Squash, Cricket and Swimming. The recent introduction of Mandarin has proved extremely popular and is available to GCSE level. Additional subjects available in the Sixth Form are Business Studies, Critical Thinking, History of Art, Government & Politics, Psychology and Theatre Studies.

Students who enter the Sixth Form have the exclusive use of the Mary Crook Study Centre which provides excellent facilities and spacious accommodation for teaching and study; there is also a large common room available where the girls can relax. Sixth Formers do not wear uniform and are encouraged to develop their independence by sharing responsibility in the running of the school. The Senior School has a well-established link with a school in Marburg, Germany and pupils take part in the annual Bristol/Bordeaux exchange. Other educational trips are organised and girls may take part in the Duke of Edinburgh's Award and the Young Enterprise Scheme.

Girls throughout the school can learn a broad variety of musical instruments and there are Junior and Senior choirs and orchestras. Wide reading and individual work is strongly encouraged supported by generous library and computer provision in both schools.

Fees per term (2011-2012). Senior School: £3,400 (which includes stationery and books). Junior School: £2,100–£2,400. Nursery fees: £19.00 per half day session.

Scholarships. (*See Scholarship Entries section.*) Particulars of Scholarships including School Bursaries and Music Scholarships in the school will be given on application.

Charitable status. The Redland High School for Girls is a Registered Charity, number 311734.

Roedean School

Brighton BN2 5RQ
Tel: 01273 667500; Admissions: 01273 667626
Fax: 01273 680791
e-mail: info@roedean.co.uk
website: www.roedean.co.uk

Founded 1885.
Incorporated by Royal Charter 1938.

President: Lady Patten of Barnes, BA (*OR*)

Vice-Presidents:
The Rt Hon Baroness Chalker of Wallasey, PC, FSS (*OR*)
Mrs S M Fowler-Watt, RGN (*OR*)
Dr J M Peacey, MB BS, MRCGP (*OR*)

Chairman of Council: Mr C W Jonas, CBE, FRICS

Vice-Chairman of Council: Mrs M S Chaundler, OBE, BA (*OR*)

Council:
Ms J M Briggs, BA, MA, PGCE, Adv Dip BFM CIPFA
Mr M R Buchanan, BSc, NPQH
Mr H Fajemirokun, PhD
Ms S Glynn
Mr R S H Illingworth, BA

Mr M F Lyne, FCA
Ms D Patman, FRICS
Dr J M Peach, BSc, MA, DPhil
Mrs M Winckler, MA

Clerk: Mr S J Launchbury, MA

ORA President: Ms S Glynn

Staff:

Headmistress: **Mrs F King**, MA Oxon, MA London, MBA Hull

Deputy Head: Mrs S Brett, BA Durham, MA London

Bursar: Mr S J Launchbury, MA London

Assistant Head Teaching and Learning: Mr P Tarbet, BSc Durham, DipEd London, FRAS

Assistant Head for Holistic Care: Mr G Rainey, BA Durham, MA Reading

Director of Admissions & Communications: Miss Z Marlow, BA Lancaster

Head of Sixth Form: Miss C Carragher, BSc Southampton, PGCE

Head of Middle School: Mrs H Heron, BA London, PGCE Reading

Head of Lower School: Mrs A Wilkinson, BEd Leeds

Heads of Department:
Mathematics: Mr J Atkins, MA Oxon, PGCE
English: Mr M Back, BA Sussex, PGCE
Science: Mr A England, MA Cantab, PGCE
Biology: Miss A Fraser, BSc London
Chemistry: Mr A England, MA Cantab, PGCE
Physics: Dr D Fisher, BSc, PhD London, MInstP, CPhys, FRAS
Modern Languages: Ms A Fafalios, BA London
Geography: Ms A Rae, MA St Andrews, PGCE
Economics, Government & Politics: Mr K Thomson, BA Sheffield, PGCE
Classics: Ms J Jones, BA London, PG Dip
History/History of Art: Mr J M Davis, BA Lancaster, MA, MSc London, ARHistS, PGCE
Design Technology: Mrs P McNeill, BA Manchester
Art: Mrs S Stanway, Chelsea School of Art, DipAD, ATC London
ICT & Business Studies: Ms S Bakhtiari, BA, MA Brighton
Dance: Miss S Stidston, LISTD Dip, RAD Teaching Dip
Music: Miss V Fewkes, BA Bath, PGCE
Speech & Drama: Mrs K P Armes, BEd CSSD, MA Ed Southampton
Physical Education: Mrs J Chandler, BEd Sussex, CertEd

Admissions Manager: Mrs D Banham

Introduction. Roedean is primarily a boarding school with 400 girls aged 11–18, including approximately 120 day girls.

The three Lawrence sisters founded Roedean in Brighton in 1885. Their original aims were to give due emphasis to physical and outdoor education, to encourage independence and self-reliance, 'to give as much liberty as can be granted with safety' and to supply a sound intellectual training.

Today the school community is made up of 40 different nationalities and remains committed to the founders' emphasis on independent learning and the development of self-confidence in readiness for professional life. The school buildings are set on a spacious, yet safe, 45-acre site surrounded by a further 70 acres of farmland. The campus commands enchanting views of the English Channel.

Philosophy. The Roedean philosophy is for pupils to be self-reliant, to explore their talents, to strive for excellence, to develop their intellectual curiosity, to lead as well as to be part of a team and to appreciate cultural diversity. A girl educated at Roedean will have respect for herself and others, be qualified to enjoy a fulfilling career and feel confident she has the skills to balance her personal and professional life.

The boarding approach is ideally suited to the school's 'whole life' philosophy as it provides a rich and balanced programme of learning and activities in a structured yet informal environment. Day girls benefit from this ethos as they are well integrated into the House system. The single-sex environment has particular advantages for girls: it prevents stereotyping, raises expectations and develops self-confidence by offering many opportunities for leadership and responsibility.

Curriculum. Girls are given a structured grounding in basic skills and offered a very broad programme of knowledge and experience. Subject specialists work together in a coordinated approach to achieve maximum reinforcement and continuity across 30 subjects. The benefits of traditional subjects, including Latin, are balanced by Psychology, Design and Technology and Critical Thinking.

Each girl's GCSE programme is individually tailored to provide a broad, balanced education and to ensure that requirements for higher education are met.

The strong sixth form offers an extensive range and combination of A and AS Levels covering 25 subjects. Over time, the school has developed a strong link with the University of Sussex, enabling the most able sixth form mathematicians to study undergraduate geometry alongside their AS and A Level courses.

Co-curricular Activities and Physical Education. The range of music, art and design, speech, debating, drama and dance opportunities within the curriculum are further supported by optional private tuition and club activities. The school is particularly strong in the performing arts: music (choirs and orchestras), drama and dance.

The school has an excellent record in the Duke of Edinburgh's Award and Young Enterprise Business Scheme which offer girls opportunities to develop a spirit of discovery and independence and encourage links with the wider community.

Netball, hockey, tennis, swimming, athletics, cricket and rounders are the principal sports with sailing, lacrosse, badminton, basketball, volleyball, squash, trampoline, gymnastics, fencing, golf, scuba diving and karate also available. Inter-school fixtures are part of all the major sport programmes and girls are encouraged to enter local, county and national tournaments.

Boarding. The House system provides the supportive and caring environment necessary for each girl, boarder or day, to flourish as an individual and a member of the community.

The four main Houses (for girls 11 to 17) and the separate sixth form House, Keswick, each have a dedicated team of staff in close contact with parents. Facilities range from bedrooms shared by 3 or 4 younger girls to university-style study-bedrooms for sixth formers.

Continuity of individual guidance and care is ensured by the school's tutorial system. Tutors monitor each girl's academic progress and involvement in extra-curricular activities and liaise with House staff on a regular basis to maintain a balanced, realistic timetable which meets each individual's needs and abilities.

Health. The School Health Centre is run by a Registered General Nurse who is assisted by a team of similarly qualified nurses. Two doctors visit the School and hold clinics regularly each week. They are "on call" in case of an emergency. There is also a Counsellor who runs sessions in school each week.

Religion. The School welcomes students of all faiths, or none. Arrangements are made for Anglicans to be prepared for Confirmation, for Roman Catholics to attend Sunday Mass locally and for Jewish girls to receive instruction.

Facilities. All subjects are taught in specialist rooms. The campus is wireless and has over 250 computers for pupil use. There is a main library and resources centre to support individual study. There are two art studios adjacent to a Design & Technology Centre, a multimedia Language Centre, a Performing Arts complex (theatre and studio, dance studios, music suite) and a Science wing with nine laboratories for biology, chemistry and physics. A multi-purpose sports hall with gym, heated indoor pool, 13 newly-refurbished hard tennis and netball courts, squash courts, ample playing fields and the use of two astroturf pitches close by support the PE/Sports programme.

School Year and Leave Out. There are three terms, beginning in September, January and April. The summer holidays last eight weeks and Christmas/Easter up to four weeks each. Girls go home for half term and there are two weekend exeats each term. All boarders are free to go home at weekends – although the majority of girls choose to stay. The school provides a full boarding programme, but there is considerable flexibility to accommodate the individual needs of families.

Admission. Entry at 11+, 12+, 13+ and 16+ is through the Common Entrance Examination or Roedean Entrance Examination which can be taken at any time up to two terms before entry. A number of suitably qualified girls are admitted each year to the Sixth Form.

Scholarships and Bursaries. (*See Scholarship Entries section.*) Junior scholarship papers are taken in January for 11+, 12+ and 13+ entry. Roedean Sixth Form scholarship papers are taken in November.

Fees per term (2011-2012). Boarders £9,045–£10,050; Day Girls £5,050–£5,820. For girls entering the Sixth Form from other schools, there is an additional supplement of £1,100 per term (boarding). Parents who wish to pay a single composition fee should apply to the Bursar.

Extra fees are charged for individual tuition in musical instruments, speech training, ballet and some athletic activities.

For further details please contact the Admissions Manager.

Charitable status. Roedean School is a Registered Charity, number 307063. It exists to provide quality education for girls.

The Royal High School, Bath

GDST

Lansdown Road, Bath BA1 5SZ
Tel: 01225 313877
Fax: 01225 465446
e-mail: royalhigh@bat.gdst.net
website: www.royalhighbath.gdst.net

The Royal High School is part of the GDST (Girls' Day School Trust). The GDST is the leading network of independent girls' schools in the UK. As a charity that owns and runs 24 schools and two academies, it reinvests all its income in its schools. For further information about the Trust, see p. xxi or visit www.gdst.net.

We are a Day and Boarding School for Girls aged 3–18 with a Sixth Form College.

Chairman of Governors: Mrs Carol Lear, BA Hons

Head: **Mrs Rebecca Dougall**, BA Hons, MA

Senior Deputy Head – Curriculum: Mrs Emma Ellison, BSc Hons

Deputy Head – Pastoral: Mrs Debbie Dellar, BEd Hons

Director of Sixth Form College: Mr Andy Melton, BEd Hons

Head of Junior School: Mrs H Fathers, BEd

Senior Resident Housemistress: Mrs S Walworth, CertEd

Registrar: Miss Lynda Bevan, BA Hons

Number of Pupils. 760, including 180 in our Junior School and 190 in the Sixth Form.

Boarding. The Royal High School is unique among Trust schools in offering the enriching experience of boarding in the Junior School (from Year 5), Senior School and Sixth Form College. This gives parents the flexibility to choose the type of education best suited to their daughter's needs. If family circumstances change, so too can school arrangements. Our boarding accommodation is comfortable, spacious and well-equipped. The school enjoys a splendid location in beautiful grounds in the World Heritage City of Bath.

The Junior School includes an 'outstanding' Ofsted rated Nursery School in its own grounds. In addition to the core requirements of the National Curriculum, our juniors have the opportunity to learn French, Spanish and Mandarin. The Royal High Junior School was the top performing independent junior school in the area in a recent Sunday Times 'Parent Power' guide. The school recently gained the Arts Council's Artsmark Gold award for its extensive provision in the expressive and performing arts. Many girls have individual drama or music lessons. Extra-curricular activities include judo, theatre club and pottery. We have an after-school care programme which enables pupils to stay in school until 6.00 pm. The junior school also offers holidays clubs, which prove very popular.

The Senior School is a dynamic, caring and inspirational learning community, which has seen substantial investment in recent years. We have recently opened a superb new art school, a fitness suite, a second performing arts centre and an updated outdoor pool. In common with all GDST schools, academic standards are excellent. The broad curriculum includes a choice of four modern European languages plus Mandarin. Most students study three sciences separately at GCSE. Girls can also take Latin or Classical Greek.

Sixth Form College. The Royal High Sixth Form College offers the International Baccalaureate Diploma Programme as an alternative to our extensive choice of A Level courses. We are one of a growing number of approved IB World Schools, which share a commitment to high-quality, challenging, internationally-focused education. In addition to a choice of academic pathways, the college offers a real alternative to the traditional sixth form experience, with a greater measure of responsibility and a clear understanding that these two years are the preface to the next step of Higher Education and employment. All students are provided with a laptop to enhance learning. Results are excellent and the majority of students move on to Russell Group Universities and leading international institutions. Support for the UCAS process is superlative with tailored programmes to support applicants to particular disciplines, eg Medicine.

Extra-Curricular Activities. Students are encouraged to participate in our rich extra-curricular programme, including weekend activities. We have a strong tradition in music and drama; we stage a number of major performances each year, in addition to informal lunchtime concerts. Our students regularly win prizes in the local annual performing arts festivals. We currently have record numbers of students participating in The Duke of Edinburgh's Award scheme.

Sport. We believe in nurturing all sporting talent, both in individual and team sports and in recent years a number of our students have represented their country in a range of sports including swimming, diving, gymnastics, rowing, fencing and badminton. A large number of teams is fielded for weekend and evening fixtures.

Students who prefer non-competitive sport are encouraged to join in other fitness activities, such as one of our dance classes. Opportunities for sport and exercise are available every day at lunch times and after school and, as we are a boarding school, at weekends too. The school holds the prestigious Sportsmark awarded by the Sport England Foundation for its extensive provision and commitment to sport. Our elite sportswomen also benefit from using the wonderful facilities at Bath University nearby.

Entry Procedures. In the Junior School, admission is by informal assessment. In the Senior School, entry at Year 7 is by examination and personal interview in January. For pupils currently in our Junior School, transfer to the Senior School is automatic, unless parents have been informed in writing (by the end of Year 5) that the transfer cannot be guaranteed. We have students who join later, subject to availability of places. Admission in these years is by entrance examination. While Y11 students automatically transfer to the college, a substantial number of students also join us for the Sixth Form. All students entering the Sixth Form College are expected to have passes in at least 6 subjects at grades A*–B, with grade A/A* in any subject they intend to study, together with a minimum of a C in maths and English.

Fees per term (2011-2012). Full Boarding £5,910–£6,827; Day £2,454–£3,419. 10% discount on full boarding fees for serving members of the Armed Forces. Weekly and flexi-boarding available.

Scholarships and Bursaries. Scholarships are awarded at both 11+ and for entry into the Sixth Form College for all-round academic excellence or for outstanding promise in specialist areas such as art, music, sport and drama. A Scholars' Programme ensures additional enrichment opportunities for the most able students.

Our bursary scheme ensures that the school is accessible to bright and talented students from families who require financial assistance towards the fees. Bursaries up to 100% (means-tested) are awarded at 11+ and into the Sixth Form to students who demonstrate outstanding all-round academic excellence or exceptional promise in a specialist area. A leaflet about our bursary scheme is available from the school.

Charitable status. The Royal High School is part of The Girls' Day School Trust, which is a Registered Charity, number 306983.

The Royal Masonic School for Girls

Rickmansworth Park, Rickmansworth, Herts WD3 4HF
Tel: 01923 773168
Fax: 01923 896729
e-mail: enquiries@royalmasonic.herts.sch.uk
website: www.royalmasonic.herts.sch.uk

Governing Body: Royal Masonic School for Girls

Chairman of Governors: Mr J Gould

Dr S J Tucker

Bursar: Mrs D Robinson

Headmistress: Mrs D Rose, MA Cantab

Director of Studies: Mrs E Couldridge, MA London

Assistant Heads:
Mr D Cox, BEng Brunel
Mrs K Young, BSc Notts

Head of Sixth Form:
Mrs N Wade, BSc Newcastle, PGCE Durham

Senior Teachers:
Mrs R L C Bloomfield-Proud, MA London, BA Leeds,
   PGCE
Mrs C Bomford, MA Greenwich, BA Manchester, PGCE
Ms V Gunn, MA York, BA Hons Cape Town, HDE Cape
   Town, PGCE

Chaplain:
Mr A Harper, MA Oak Hill, BA Oak Hill, BA Brunel,
   PGCE

Housemistresses:
Connaught: Miss K Batty (*Head of Boarding*)
Harris House: Mrs W Benjamin
Weybridge House: Mrs N Harrison
Zetland House: Miss K J Lord
Alexandra House: Miss K Davies

Heads of Year:
Miss H S Stanley, BEd Liverpool (*Year 7*)
Miss S Hards, BA Durham, PGCE (*Years 8 & 9*)
Mrs DE Heaffey, BA Middlesex, PGCE (*Year 10*)
Mrs C E Freeman, BSc Durham,PGCE (*Year 11*)

Heads of Departments:
Mr M Bannister, MSc London, MBA London, PGCE
   London (*Economics*)
Mrs V Bannister, BCom Dublin, MBA (*Business Studies*)
Mrs R Bloomfield-Proud, MA London, BA Leeds
   (*Textiles*)
Mrs E Boast, MA, BA, Licence d'Anglais (*Modern
   Languages*)
Mr D Buddie, BSc Dundee (*ICT Coordinator*)
Miss K Cook, BSc Reading, PGCE London (*PSHCE*)
Mr D Cox, BEng Brunel (*Mathematics*)
Miss M Dines, BA Bucks (*Design Technology*)
Mrs C E Freeman, BSc Durham (*Geography*)
Mr F Grogan, BA York (*History*)
Ms V C Gunn, BA Cape Town, South Africa (*English*)
Miss S Hards, BA Durham (*Religious Studies*)
Mr D Hyde, BMus Birmingham, ALCM (*Director of
   Performing Arts*)
Mrs P Kenyon, BA Keele, PGCE (*Science and Biology*)
Mr A Martin, MEng London (*Chemistry*)
Mrs A Ralph, BSc Lancaster (*Head of Learning Support*)
Mr D Spain (*Photography*)
Mrs L Spendiff, BSc Staffordshire (*Physical Education*)
Mrs S Reeve, MSc London (*Psychology*)
Mrs D Ronaldson, BEd Newcastle (*Home Economics*)
Mr T J Ward, BA London (*Art*)
Mrs J Whitbread, MA Trinity, LRAM, CertRAM (*Music*)
Mr N M Young, MA Oxon, MCIBS (*Latin & Classical
   Civilisation*)

Preparatory Department:
Head: Miss L E Beckett, BEd Bucks
Deputy Head: Mrs A Brown, BA Reading

Pre-School:
Head: Mrs K Woodhead

Visiting Music Teachers for bassoon, brass, cello, clarinet, drum kit, flute, guitar, oboe, organ, percussion, piano, saxophone, singing, steel pans, viola, violin.

Peripatetic Staff for Dance, Learning Support, Speech and Drama, EAL.

Administration & Services Officer: Mrs J Heaven
School Doctor: Dr T Downes
Personal Assistant to the Headmistress: Mrs J Beal
Admissions Secretary: Mrs G Braiden

There are 822 pupils in school, of whom 179 are in the Preparatory Department and 52 are in our new mixed Pre-School, which opened in January 2010. There are 178 girls in the Sixth Form. 150 of the current school population are boarders and integration of day girls and boarders is achieved through the Houses.

Premises and Facilities. Founded in 1788, the School came to Rickmansworth in 1934. It stands in 300 acres of parkland on an attractive site overlooking the valley of the River Chess. The buildings are spacious and well-appointed. They include excellent ICT facilities, a well-equipped Science building, a Chapel and Library of exceptional beauty.

The Sports Hall is equipped to the highest international standards. There is a heated indoor swimming pool, 12 tennis courts, 4 squash courts and superb playing fields. The School has been awarded Sportsmark status.

Location. Central London is 15 miles to the south and Amersham is just north of the town. The M25 is 1 mile from the school and links it to London (Heathrow) – 30 minutes, London (Gatwick) – 50 minutes, and Luton Airport – 30 minutes. London Underground services (Metropolitan Line) and British Rail from Marylebone enable Central London to be reached by train in 30 minutes.

General Curriculum and Aims. The first three years of Senior School provide a broad general education which fulfils the requirements of the National Curriculum and reaches beyond it. As well as the traditional academic subjects of English, Mathematics, Science, History, Geography and Religious Studies, girls study Design Technology, Information Technology, Home Economics, Art & Textiles, Performing Arts, Physical Education and PSHCE. Language Studies begin with French or Spanish and Latin. In Year 8 German and Mandarin are also offered.

GCSE options are chosen from among all the subjects taught in Years 7 to 9 and new possibilities, such as Child Development, Expressive Arts, Drama and Business are introduced at this stage. Most pupils take nine or ten GCSE subjects and girls are guided in their choices by subject teachers, in full consultation with parents. Triple Science is available.

The Sixth Form. The School offers a wide range of A and AS Level subjects in flexible combinations. Politics, Economics, Performance Studies, Classical Civilisation, Photography, Music Technology and Psychology are all new additions to the curriculum at this stage. There are also practical and vocational courses leading to qualifications in Business and Health and Social Care. Virtually all sixth formers go on to higher education.

Religion. Girls of all faiths and none are welcome. School assemblies are traditional and inclusive in nature and Chapel Services for boarders are held according to the rites of the Church of England.

Health. The School Doctor attends the Medical Centre regularly. There are three Nursing Sisters and a Medical Assistant.

Admission. Applications should be made to the Admissions Secretary. The School sets its own entrance examinations at all levels. New boarding and day pupils are accepted into the Sixth Form where there are wide-ranging opportunities for girls of all abilities.

Scholarships. (*See Scholarship Entries section*.) A number of scholarships are available at 7+, 11+ and 16+, and some means-tested bursaries. The former are for open competition; the latter are restricted to certain categories of pupils in need. There are a number of Foundation Scholarships available at 11+ for the daughters of Freemasons. These are based on academic ability and are means tested.

Fees per term (2011-2012). Senior School: Boarders £7,480 (Sixth Form new students £7,730); Weekly Boarders £7,295 (Sixth Form new students £7,540); Day Pupils £4,485 (Sixth Form new students £4,730).

Preparatory Department: Boarders: £4,750 (Years 3–6); Weekly Boarders: £4,670 (Years 3–6); Day Pupils: £2,670 (Reception, Years 1 and 2), £3,100 (Years 3–6). Pre-School (boys and girls aged 2–4): please visit our website for range of fees.

Free places may be available for daughters of Freemasons in need of assistance.

Charitable status. The Royal Masonic School Limited is a Registered Charity, number 276784. Its aims are the advancement of education.

Royal School Hampstead

65 Rosslyn Hill, Hampstead, London NW3 5UD
Tel: 020 7794 7708
Fax: 020 7431 6741
e-mail: enquiries@royalschoolhampstead.net
website: www.royalschoolhampstead.net

Founded in 1855. Independent day and boarding school celebrating 155 years of educating and caring for girls.

Board of Trustees:
Chairman: Mr R Field-Smith, MBE
Vice Chairman: Mr M Greene
Major General J Milne, CB
Mr J Smouha, QC
Mrs A Parvizi-Wayne
Mr J Milton
Mr P Hatt
Parent Representative: Mr T Colman & Ms C Harper

Headmistress: Ms Joanna Ebner, BEd Cantab, MA London, PGDip Couns, Cert FT, NPQH

Head of Junior School: Dr Zoë Dunn, BEd Cantab, PhD, NPQH
Head of Senior School: Mrs Jennifer Bailey, MA, PGCE, Dip SpLD (*SENCO*)
Head of Senior School: Mr Jonathan Bach, NPQH, MI, PGCE, BSc

Curriculum Directors:
Mrs Mary Anastasi, BSc (*Technology – Whole School*)
Miss Sarah Campbell, BA, PGCE (*Early Years Coordinator*)
Miss Courtney Clelland, PGCE (*English – Senior School*)
Mrs Helen Dowling, MA, PGCE (*Literacy – Junior School*)
Dr Zoë Dunn, BEd Cantab, PhD, NPQH (*Acting Humanities – Junior School*)
Miss Emma Golden, BA, PGCE (*Humanities – Senior School*)
Mrs Victoria Levy, BA, PGCE (*Performing Arts – Whole School*)
Mr Florian Luddecke, BA, PGCE (*Languages – Whole School*)
Heads of Senior & Junior Schools (*PSHE – Whole School*)
Mr Richard Shopland, MSc, PGCE (*Maths & Science – Senior School*)
Mr Paul Woodrow (*Curriculum Coordinator – Junior School*)

Teaching Staff:
Miss Clare Bateman, BHSc, PGCE (*Science*)
Mrs Louise Blair, BA, MA (*Textiles*)
Miss Abigail Buckland, BSc (*Year 3 Class Teacher*)
Miss Sarah Campbell, BA, PGCE (*Nursery Class Teacher*)

Miss Courtney Clelland, PGCE (*English*)
Mrs Hrisoula Dowie (*KS1 Class Assistant*)
Mrs Helen Dowling, MA, PGCE (*Year 5 Class Teacher*)
Miss Carol Eby, BEd
Miss Erika Eisele, BMus, PGDip, LRAM (*Year 2 Class Teacher*)
Miss Emma Golden, BA, PGCE (*History*)
Miss Helen Greenham (*Music*)
Miss Marie-Claire Guttery (*French – Junior School*)
Miss Maike Hallenga, BA Hons, PGCE (*Reception Teacher*)
Mrs Victoria Levy, BA, PGCE (*Drama*)
Miss Jennifer Martin, PGCE, PG Dip, BSc (*Art*)
Ms Sarah Moody, BEd (*Food Technology*)
Mrs Wendy Munoz, BSc, BA, PGCE (*Early Years Teaching Assistant*)
Miss Victoria Newland, BA, PGCE (*Year 4 Class Teacher, KS2 French Specialist*)
Mrs Lada Pospisilova, MA (*PE*)
Miss Deborah Pretty (*PHSE*)
Ms Caroline Quist (*Trampoline*)
Mrs Laila Rabi (*Early Years Class Assistant*)
Dr Ioannis Raptis, BSc, PGCE, PhD (*Science & Maths*)
Dr Jessica Scaife, PhD, BSc Hons, PGCE (*Science*)
Miss Rachel Sutton (*English*)
Mrs Gill Steiner, BSc, BA, PGCE (*Maths/Art*)
Miss Heather Williams, BA (*Reception Class Teacher, EY & KS1 French Specialist*)
Mr Paul Woodrow, BA, PGCE (*Year 6 Class Teacher*)

Child Protection Officer:
Dr Zoë Dunn, BEd Cantab, PhD, NPQH (*Whole School & Junior School*)
Miss Sarah Campbell, BA, PGCE (*Early Years*)

Residential Staff:
Director of Boarding : Miss Deborah Pretty
Housemistress & School Nurse: Ms Maureen McGillicuddy, SEN
GAP Housemistresses:
Miss Lucy Fisher
Miss Sarah Cusworth

Administration:
Bursar: Mr Peter Luard
Finance Officer: Mr Paul Vivek
Executive Assistant to Headmistress: Mrs Bonnie Hughes
Admissions Secretary and Registrar: Mrs Maria Schlatter, BSc, MITI, MIL
Bursar's Assistant: Mrs Carrie Andrews
Receptionist: Miss Yolanda William
Catering Manager: Mrs Christine Ardener
Maintenance Supervisor: Mr Simon Day
School Doctor: Keats Group Practice

Visiting Teachers:
Mrs Caroline Dodsworth, BA, CTEFLA, RSA Dip SpLD (*EAL*)
Ms Ronit Bird, BA, PGCE, RSA Dip SpLD (*Learning Support*)
Mrs Carol Sachs, BA, BSc, MRCSLT, HPC (*Learning Support*)
Mrs Gabby JacobyOwen, BEd, BSc, RSA Dip SpLD (*Learning Support*)
Miss Louise Keller, MA (*Counsellor*)
Miss Marie-Claire Gutttery (*Learning Support*)
Ms Portia Mishcon (*Speech & Language Therapist*)
Miss Julia Craig, BMus, Adv PGDip (*Singing*)
Miss Camilla George, BA, Music Dip (*Woodwind*)
Ms Jane Griffiths, BA (*Piano & Strings*)
Mrs Erna Kuenen, PGCE Performing Arts PC, BPhil, LRAD, LISTD, ARAD (*Ballet, Creative Movement*)
Mr Jason Ridgway, ARCM, BMus, GSMD, LRCM (*Piano*)
Miss Rebecca Wood, BMus, PDot (*Piano*)
Ms Naomi Tsega, BA Mus, MA (*Piano*)

Mr Nicholas Durcan (*Piano*)

Support Staff:
IT Technican: Mr Reza Nourouzi
School Counsellor: Mrs Gail Phillips, BA, MSc
School Counsellor: Ms Louise Keller, Dip SpLD, Dip
TEAA
Librarian: Ms Maria Schlatter, BSc, MITI, MIL
Science Technician: Miss Karina Rechidi
Cleaner: Ms Asta Stankaitiene
Cleaner: Miss Valerija Brinkeviciute
Cleaner: Mrs Janet O'Brennan

The Royal School is the school with the heart in the heart of Hampstead.

The Royal School, Hampstead was founded in 1855 with the original aims to "nurse, board, clothe and educate the female children, orphans or not of soldiers in Her Majesty's Army who had served or were serving in the Crimean War". Today it is open to all girls.

Age Range and Number of Pupils. The Royal School is now a day and boarding school for over 200 girls from 3–16 years, with boarders from 11 years.

Educational Philosophy. The school's aim is to provide an excellent education based on individual attention, in a happy, positive and secure environment, to allow each girl to develop her full potential and to become a self-confident, responsible young adult with a clear sense of duty towards others.

The Royal School is known for tailoring its education to each child as well as its work in the community and its caring ethos. Our aim is to ensure our girls are happy, well educated, confident and polite and able to make their mark in society.

Location and Facilities. The school is situated in pleasant surroundings in the heart of Hampstead Village. It is a well resourced school, with spacious, light classrooms and comfortable modern boarding accommodation with panoramic views over London. The Royal School has a strong provision in the visual and performing arts, a phenomenal new textiles/food technology centre, a wide range of extra-curricular activities and provides individual EFL teaching as part of our SEN department. There is also an Early Years Unit.

Curriculum. The Early Years Programme seeks to provide three to five year olds with a firm foundation upon which to build. This is developed and extended throughout the Junior School, where girls are offered a diverse curriculum within a positive and caring community. Pupils are encouraged to become confident independent thinkers who behave responsibly and courteously. Senior School girls follow a balanced curriculum, including 3 modern languages and 3 Sciences, leading to GCSE. The performing and visual arts are a particular strength of the school, for which the school holds an Artsmark, and charity work and life enrichment programmes are important aspects of the school's ethos, which feature strongly throughout the school. The school is consistently placed amongst the highest positions in the Value Added Key Stage 3 to GCSE Performance Tables.

All the girls are taught in small classes enabling them to develop a variety of skills to the best of their ability. There is an extremely high teacher/pupil ratio and girls are offered an excellent level of individual attention and positive help.

Extra-curricular activities feature widely in the school's daily routine, and include The Duke of Edinburgh's Award scheme, drama, art, music, ballet, dance and a wide range of games and sports.

Boarding. The school offers a homely and friendly boarding environment where girls thrive. Each new boarder is assigned a 'buddy' who acts as a companion and helper. Communication between parents and staff is excellent. Weekly boarding is a popular option; 'flexi-boarding' and 'sleep-overs' can be arranged when required.

Fees per term (2011-2012). Day £3,375–£3,950; Weekly Boarding £6,550; Boarding £7,850; Flexi-Boarding £32.50 per night.

Admission. Girls are admitted throughout the age range although the majority are admitted at 3 and 11.

Entry Requirements. Girls applying to the Junior School are invited to attend school for a session of informal assessments. Admission to the Senior School at 11+ is through the Consortium of North London Independent Girls' Schools as the school is a member of the Girls' Schools Association, and also by an interview. Previous school reports are required for all pupils.

Bursaries and Scholarships. Bursaries may be awarded throughout all year groups including boarding – priority is given to British Armed Forces personnel. Scholarships are awarded at Year 7.

Religious Affiliation. All religions are welcome. The school is designated as Church of England.

Charitable status. The Royal School, Hampstead is a Registered Charity, number 312286, and exists for the purpose of educating girls.

Rye St Antony

Pullen's Lane, Oxford OX3 0BY
Tel: 01865 762802
Fax: 01865 763611
e-mail: info@ryestantony.co.uk
website: www.ryestantony.co.uk

Rye St Antony is an independent Catholic Boarding and Day School, founded in 1930.
Motto: *Vocatus Obedivi*

Governing Body:

Chairman: Mrs H Stafford Northcote, BA
Vice-Chairman: Mr T J Morton
Mr I Callaghan
Mr S Calnan
Miss J Clarke, FRCS
Dr T M M Czepiel
Revd Dr J F Jackson
Dr E Lowe, BA, PhD
Mr D Parke
Mrs T Sanderson
Mrs M Shinkwin, BA, MEd, NPQH
Ms F Smith, BA

Clerk to the Governors: Mrs T Hudson

Headmistress: Miss A M Jones, BA York, PGCE Oxon

Deputy Headmistress: Mrs A Neil, BA Southampton
(*History and Politics*)

Director of Studies: Mr C Cooper, BSc Imperial College
London, MA, PGCE UEA, MA Warwick

Senior School Staff:
Mr P Atkey, BA Portsmouth, PGCE Pemboke College
Cambridge, MSc Stirling (*Spanish, French, Business Studies*)
Mr J Bass, BA Leeds, MA King's College London, PGCE
Bath (*History*)
Miss S Brookes, BA East London, PGCE Cantab (*Art and Design*)
Miss L Burgoine, BSc Sheffield Hallam, PGCE Sheffield
Hallam (*Home Economics, Food Technology*)
Miss E Calver, BA Oxon, PGCE Oxon (*Music*)
Mrs S Campbell, BA Cantab, CertEd London (*Economics, Business Studies*)
Mrs E Caprotti, Italian Teaching Degree (*Italian*)
Mrs G Chang, MSc, CPhys, MInstP (*Physics*)

Mrs H Clapham-Burns, BA Queensland, MA Queensland (*Psychology, Careers*)
Miss J Croft, Maîtrise Strasbourg, BA QTS Westminster (*French*)
Miss S Defoe, BA Loughborough (*Art and Design*)
Miss N DeRushie, MA Waterloo, PGDE Edinburgh (*English*)
Mrs P D'Souza-Eva, BA Essex, PGCE London (*Mathematics*)
Mrs A Evans, BA Nene University College, QTS Reading (*Drama*)
Mr M Evans, BA Durham, PGCE London, MEd Oxon (*Mathematics*)
Mrs P Evans, BA, MA Open, CertEd Leeds (*Religious Studies*)
Miss A Gate, BA Oxon (*Latin and Classics*)
Mrs J Ganly, BA Leeds, PGCE Bath (*French*)
Mrs K Harman, BSc Cardiff, RSADipTEFLA Bournemouth (*EAL*)
Miss A Hartnell, BA Oxon (*Chemistry*)
Miss P Horlock, BA Stellenbosch, PCGE Stellenbosch (*Physical Education*)
Miss L Howard, BA Oxon, PGCE London, MPhil Cantab (*Classics*)
Mrs M Jones, BA Cardiff, PGCE Oxon (*Music*)
Mrs C Lau, BA Hong Kong, MA Oxford Brookes (*Chinese*)
Mr S H Lau, BA Hong Kong, MPhil Hong Kong (*Chinese*)
Mrs A Newsome, BSc, MSc London, PGCE Reading (*Geography*)
Dr T Newsome, BSc Reading, PhD Stirling, PGCE Reading (*Biology*)
Mrs J Owens, BSc Aberystwyth, CBiol, MIBiol, PGCE Lancaster (*Biology*)
Mrs B Pillman, BA Brighton College of Art (*Learning Support*)
Miss F Pujos, Licence La Sorbonne Nouvelle, Paris, PGCE Oxford Brookes, Maîtrise Angers (*French*)
Mrs E Roberts, BA York, PGCE Cantab (*English*)
Dr F Ross, MA Glasgow, PhD Glasgow, PGCE Strathclyde (*English*)
Mr B Sharland, BEd Cape Town (*ICT*)
Miss T Simpson, BA Cambridge, MA Cambridge, PGCE (*Geography*)
Miss J Smail, BA Lancaster, MA Lancaster, PGCE Southampton (*History*)
Mrs C Steinke, BA Ulm, MSc New York (*German and Mathematics*)
Mrs F Stuart, MA, PGCE Oxon, ARCM (*Music*)
Ms E Thompson, BSc Queensland, DipT Christchurch College of Education (*Mathematics*)
Miss H Tomlinson, BEd Brighton (*Physical Education*)
Miss C Trenaman, BA Durham (*Physical Education*)
Mr A Vesty, BSc Manchester (*Chemistry and Physics*)
Mr D Willcock, BA Oxon (*Religious Education*)

Junior School Staff:
Head of Junior School: Ms J Reed, BEd Cambridge

Mrs S Blandy, BA Manchester
Mrs A Dyar, MontDip Dublin
Miss C Eadle, BEd Oxford
Mrs J Haigh, BSc London, QTS Reading
Mrs H Holland, BA Oxford Brookes, CertEd Warwick
Mrs M-E Judges, MA New York, BEd Oxford Brookes, PGCE Oxford Brookes
Ms C Kamenski, MA Boston, BA Milwaukee
Miss C Kelly, BMus Queen's University, PGCE Oxford Brookes
Dr C Kirtley, BSc Durham
Miss S Lee, HLTA British School in Tokyo
Miss K Northcote, BA Birmingham
Mrs A Saunders, BEd Lancaster

Nursery Department Staff:
Mrs C Annells, NVQ3
Mrs B Crowther, BEd Toronto, BA Toronto
Miss K Repikova, NVQ3
Miss B Sandy, DipEd Primary Graaff-Reinet Teachers' College
Mrs A Utechin, MontDip Oxford

Visiting Music Staff:
Ms A M Ackrill, BA Music (*Flute*)
Miss Claire Bradshaw, GRNCM (*Singing*)
Mr S Dunstone, BA Cantab, PGCE Durham (*Harp*)
Miss B Evans, BA Bath (*Singing*)
Mr P Foster, LTCL (*Saxophone*)
Mr R Foster, BA Oxford Brookes (*Drumkit*)
Mrs C Goodall, MA Oxford (*Clarinet and Piano*)
Miss E Hodson, MA, DPhil, PGDip (*Violin and Viola*)
Mr P Manhood, ATCL (*Guitar*)
Miss F McIntosh, BMus RNCM, PGDip (*Singing*)
Mrs P Miller, BA, LTCL (*Clarinet*)
Mrs S Palys, LTCL Trinity College of Music (*Singing*)
Mrs C Rees, BMusEd, SRAsT (*Oboe, Piano*)
Mrs F Stuart, MA, PGCE, ARCM (*Piano, Cello*)

Librarian: Mrs E Kirby, BA Manchester
Assistant Librarian: Mrs A Goodall, BA Oxford Brookes

Medical Adviser: Dr K Johnson
School Nurses:
Mrs S McIlvenna, RGN
Mrs J Dawson, RGN

Administrative Staff:
Bursar: Mrs T Hudson
Finance Officer: Mrs N Sanhotra
Bursary Assistant: Mrs J Curl
Human Resources Manager: Miss E Phelips, BA
Headmistress's Personal Assistant: Mrs E Cheeseman
School Secretary: Mrs Fern Saxton
Staff Secretary: Miss I Ripper

Rye St Antony was founded in 1930 by Elizabeth Rendall and Ivy King, two school teachers who reached the decision to start a school of their own during a visit to Sussex and the Church of St Antony in Rye, in commemoration of which the School was named. In 1939 the School moved to its present site, twelve acres of exceptionally beautiful grounds a mile to the north east of the centre of Oxford on Pullen's Lane, overlooking the city.

A steady programme of building and development has provided excellent teaching and residential facilities, all new buildings being carefully harmonised with the architecture of the original handsome Victorian houses. King House was opened in 1986, the Art, Design and Technology centre in 1989, the Information and Communications Technology unit in 1991, the new wing of the Rendall Building in 1993 and the Sumpter Building with its Science laboratories in 1995. In recent years the computer network has been extended into all teaching and boarding areas, the Performing Arts centre was opened in February 2005 and the new Sports Centre was completed in July 2008. The Chapel was extensively refurbished in 2009, and the extensions to the Sixth Form Centre will be completed in 2010.

The School is highly regarded for its happy and purposeful atmosphere, its strong sense of community and its emphasis on the value of each member of the community as an individual. Pupils are helped to understand their strengths and weaknesses and the reasons for their successes and failures; they are encouraged to accept challenges and learn initiative and independence. They also have many opportunities to contribute to decision-making for the School, thereby learning how to play an active part in the school community and in future communities to which they will belong.

The School offers boarding and day places for girls aged 5–18, some day places for boys aged 5–8, and in Beech Tree Nursery School whole-day and half-day places for boys and girls aged 3–5. Short-stay and occasional boarding arrangements, varying in length from a single night to a whole term or more, can be made according to need.

Religious Life. The School's sacramental life is of fundamental importance, the Eucharist in particular uniting the School with Christ and his Church and giving a focus to prayer, both liturgical and private. Several Oxford priests regularly celebrate Mass for the whole School on special feast days and at the beginning and end of each term; they also celebrate the Sunday Masses, form Masses and weekday Masses. Religious Education is an integral part of the curriculum throughout the School, and all pupils are involved in the Christian life of the school community, not least its liturgical celebrations.

Senior School Curriculum. Academic standards and expectations are high, girls are offered many opportunities in music, art, drama and sport, and there is a busy programme of evening and weekend activities.

In the Senior School all girls follow a broad and balanced common course for the first three years, comprising English, Mathematics, Physics, Chemistry, Biology, Religious Education, French, History, Geography, Technology, Information and Communications Technology, Art, Music, Drama and Physical Education. Latin and Spanish are optional subjects. There is a cross-curricular Health Education programme.

Twenty plus subjects are offered as GCSE subjects. For the two-year GCSE course girls usually study 10 subjects, a mixture of options and core subjects (including Coordinated Science, a double award subject).

In the Sixth Form girls typically study four AS subjects in the first year of Sixth Form and continue with three of these subjects as A2 subjects in the second year, thus completing Sixth Form with certification in 3 A Level subjects and an additional AS subject.

Careers Guidance. The School's careers advisory service provides help and guidance for all girls, and there is a formal programme of careers advice throughout Years 9, 10 and 11 and Sixth Form. All girls go on to university and are helped to investigate thoroughly the Higher Education and careers options open to them, careful guidance being given concerning their applications and interviews. The support of the Headmistress, the Deputy Headmistress and other senior staff is available at all stages. Work experience placements are organised, and girls are encouraged to make particular use of this option at the end of their GCSE courses. The School belongs to the Independent Schools Careers Organisation and benefits from its many services. Visiting speakers give lectures on various higher education and careers topics; visits to appropriate conferences and exhibitions are arranged; and the School organises and hosts a biennial Careers Convention. The school has two well-resourced careers libraries of printed, video and computer-accessed information.

Junior School Curriculum. The Junior School and Senior School are closely linked, and Junior School pupils are steadily introduced to the specialist teaching and facilities of the Senior School. In the early years the teaching of most subjects is undertaken by the class teachers. In Years 5 and 6 girls are taught by subject teachers, some of whom also teach in the Senior School, and this arrangement gives girls the benefit of specialist teaching and encourages them to develop a feeling of confidence and continuity when the time comes for them to move into the Senior School. Use of the Senior School facilities is particularly valuable in Science, Art, Music, Physical Education and Drama. There is a Junior Library in Langley Lodge, and older Juniors may also use the King Library in the Senior School.

Performing Arts. The School has a strong tradition of debating and public speaking, and girls have many successes to their credit in city, county and regional competitions. A major drama production each year, and various smaller presentations give girls the opportunity to develop their skills in performing, directing, lighting, sound, stage design, costume design and make-up. There are frequent visits to Stratford, London and regional theatres including the Oxford Playhouse and some girls perform at the Playhouse in the annual schools' gala. The majority of girls learn one musical instrument and some learn two or more; there are two choirs, one orchestra and several smaller ensembles, and some girls are members of the Oxford Girls' Choir, the Oxford Youth Chamber Choir, the Oxford Schools' Symphony Orchestra, the Oxfordshire Youth Orchestra and the Thames Vale Orchestra. Instruments learnt include piano, violin, viola, 'cello, flute, oboe, clarinet, trumpet, bassoon, saxophone, French horn, guitar and percussion. Through musical productions, concerts and the liturgy there are many opportunities for girls to contribute to the musical life of the School. In both Drama and Music, pupils take the Guildhall School of Music and Drama examinations.

Sport. The School has a new Sports Centre, good playing fields, all-weather hard courts and an outdoor heated swimming pool. The principal winter sports are netball and hockey; the principal summer sports are tennis, swimming, athletics and rounders. Girls compete regularly in local, county and regional tournaments.

Duke of Edinburgh's Award. The School has an outstanding record in the Duke of Edinburgh's Award, each year about 35 girls achieving the Bronze Award, 20 girls or so achieving the Silver Award and 20 or more girls achieving the Gold Award. The purpose of the Award is to give challenge, responsibility and adventure to young people, thus encouraging them to develop initiative and team skills.

Visits. Fieldwork, conferences, lectures, art exhibitions, plays and concerts give girls an interesting programme of visits within the UK. Visits abroad include study courses, exchanges, sports tours and skiing holidays, and the School regularly hosts visiting groups from schools overseas.

Health. The School Nurse works closely with the School Doctor who sees girls at her nearby Health Centre. Dental and orthodontic treatment can be arranged locally, and the John Radcliffe Hospital is five minutes away.

Admissions. Admission to the Junior School is by interview and the School's own entrance tests. Admission to the Senior School is by interview and entrance examination (Common Entrance at 11+). Admission to the Sixth Form is by interview, school report and GCSE results.

Scholarships. Scholarships are available at 11+, 13+ and 16+.

Fees per term (2011-2012). Full Boarders £6,650; Weekly Boarders £6,350; Day Pupils £4,100.

Charitable status. Rye St Antony School Limited is a Registered Charity, number 309685. Its purpose is the furtherance of Christian education.

St Albans High School for Girls

3 Townsend Avenue, St Albans, Hertfordshire AL1 3SJ
Tel: 01727 853800
Fax: 01727 792516
e-mail: admissions@stalbans-high.herts.sch.uk
website: www.stahs.org.uk

Motto: *The fear of the Lord is the beginning of wisdom*

Visitor: The Right Reverend The Lord Bishop of St Albans

Council:
The Dean of St Albans
D Alterman, MA
R Allnutt, Esq, LLB
Dr P Barrison, MBBS

Mrs J F Boulton, MRICS (*Chairman*)
Mrs C Callegari, BA, CertEd
Mrs E Curtis
Mrs H Greatrex, BA, ACA
Mrs D Henderson, BA
Mrs J Jennings-Mares
B Kettle, Esq
Miss R Musgrave, MA, MA, FRSA
Dr D Porcelli
Mrs J Stroud, MA
Mrs S Williams, FCA
Mrs J Woolley

‡ *Holder of Teacher's Diploma or Certificate*

Head Mistress: **Mrs Rosemary Martin**, MEd, NPQH, FRSA

Bursar: Mr F Campbell, BSc Glasgow, FCMA

Head of Wheathampstead House: Miss G M Bradnam, BEd WSIHE, MA Ed Mgmt De Montfort, NPQH

Academic Deputy: ‡Mrs J Taylor, MA Cantab

Deputy Head Pastoral: ‡Mrs H Monighan, BA Durham

Assistant Head: ‡Ms J Healy, BA Oxon, MPhil Trinity College Dublin

Chaplain: The Revd Diane Fitzgerald Clark, BA Rhode Island, MDiv GTS, NYC

* *Head of Department*
§ *Part-time*

Senior School:
‡Dr G Alderton, PhD Leeds
Miss M Bacon, BEd Exeter (**Physical Education*)
‡Mr R Bailey, BSc Bath
‡Miss C Bannon, BSc Edinburgh
‡Miss N Best, BA Melbourne
‡Mr D Bowker, MA Cantab
‡Miss J Broman, BA Birmingham
‡Mrs S Brown, MA Manchester
‡Mrs A Bullen, BA Aberystwyth
‡Miss A Burgess, MA Cantab
‡Mr D Carr, BA Southampton
‡Mrs A Chapman, BA Exeter (**Classics*)
‡Miss N Collins, BSc Brunel
‡Mrs S Cooper, BA Exeter
‡Mrs S Cubbon, MSc London, MA Oxon
‡Mrs G Davies, MSc Wales (**Design Technology*)
‡Mrs J Douglas, BA Durham (*Senior Housemistress*)
‡Mrs E A Draper, BA Oxon
‡Mr P Duddles, BEng Warwick
‡Mrs W Emes, BA Bath, MSc Reading
‡Miss C Foster, BA Manchester
Miss A Fox, BA Oxon
‡Mrs R Frost, BA Open, BEd Dundee, MA Ed Open (*Senior Teacher*)
‡Mrs F Gee, BSc Cardiff
‡Mrs S Gillman, BSc Exeter
‡Mrs K Gorman, BA Birmingham (**English*)
‡Mrs K Guille, MA Bath, BA Birmingham (**Modern Languages*)
‡Mrs M Harcourt BEd Cantab
‡Mr A Hattam BSc Southampton
Miss A Hedley, BEd Edinburgh
‡Mr R Hillebrand, BA Oxon
‡Mr A Jackson, MA, MPhil, King's College London
‡Mrs A Jallport, BSc Hertfordshire
§§Mrs C Johns, BA Wales, MA Open
§§Mr E Kay, Cert Ed Lancaster, RSA SpLD
‡Dr S Legg, BSc Birmingham, DPhil Oxon (**Science*)
§Mrs D Lewis, MA Oxon, MPhil Cantab
‡Miss R Marsh, BA Southampton
‡Miss S MacCarron, BSc Leeds

§‡Mrs R L McDermott, MSc Bristol
‡Mr S McGuinness, BA Manchester Polytechnic (**Art*)
§‡Miss A McGuirk, BA Oxon
‡Mrs H McSherry, BSc Plymouth
‡Mr S R Mew, MA Essex, BA Essex (**History*)
§‡Mrs B Mitchell, BSc Sheffield
‡Mr S D Moore, CEng, MIMechE, MEng Cantab, MA Cantab
‡Miss H O'Neill, BA Leeds
Mrs K Osborne, BEd London
‡Miss J Pascoe, BA, Brunel
‡Mrs M Patel, BA Wales (**Religious Studies*)
‡Mrs J A Powell, BA Durham
‡Miss E Pritchard, BA York
‡Mr S Ramsbottom, BSc Reading (**Geography*)
‡Mrs P Ray, BA Leeds
§‡Mrs L Ryan, MA Cantab
‡Dr N Springthorpe, PhD BMus, Surrey, FLCM, PG CertRCM Surrey (**Music*)
‡Mr J Stanford, BA York (**Economics*)
‡Mrs S Stewart, BSc Leicester
‡Miss K Sumner, BSc Warwick (**Mathematics*)
Miss N Taylor-Imrie, BSc Hertfordshire, Dip SpLD Hornsby
‡Mr I Thomson, BA London, AKC (**Sixth Form*)
‡Mrs K Thomson, BSc London
‡Mrs K Trenor, BA Sheffield
§‡Mrs D Tubb, BEd Liverpool Polytechnic
Mrs C Turkington, BMusEd Cape Town
‡Miss L Turner, BA Oxon
§‡Miss E Wadey, BA Winchester
‡Mr C White, BSc London (*Examinations Officer*)
§‡Mrs D Whiting, BSc De Montfort
‡Miss H Whymark, BA Hull (**Drama*)
‡Miss P I Willmott, BA London
‡Mrs C A Wright, BA Ulster (*ICT Coordinator*)

Librarian, Senior School:
Mrs R Borgeat, BA Open

Wheathampstead House (Preparatory School):
Head: Miss G M Bradnam, BEd WSIHE, MA Ed Mgmt De Montfort, NPQH
Deputy Head: ‡Mr J Wadge, BA Durham
Director of Studies: Mrs J Jeavons, BA QTS Leeds
Head of Infants: Mrs R Darvill, BEd Cambridge

§‡Miss C M Allin, Licence LLCE Poitiers, France
§Mrs J Bowskill, BSc Loughborough
‡Mrs N Davies, BA London
‡Mrs A Fletcher, BSc Bath
‡Mrs S Edwards, GRSM, ARCM
‡Mrs M Hartley, BA Dublin City/Tokyo
Mrs C Hilton, BEd Hertfordshire
‡Mrs L Hughes, BA Canterbury Christ Church
§Mrs J Julians, MSc Loughborough
Mrs M McClean, BEd Hertfordshire
‡Miss M Pope, BA Surrey
‡Mrs S E Rose, BA Leeds
‡Miss T Skuse, BSc Manchester
Mrs L Still, BA Ed Exeter
‡Mrs R Such, BSc Cardiff
Miss G Thomas, BA Portsmouth
‡Mrs E Whiteford, BA Durham

Classroom Assistants, Wheathampstead House:
Mrs P Bate, BA St Martins
Mrs A di-Lieto, BA Hull
Mrs A Gibbs, CertEd Sussex
Mrs S Holmwood, BA Manchester Polytechnic
Mrs J McMullen
Mrs S Millac, BSc University College
Mrs S Smith
Mrs C Strang
Mrs L Davies

Librarian, Wheathampstead House:
§Mrs J Miles, LLB Hong Kong

School Medical Officer: Dr A E Margereson, MMBS
London

Visiting Staff:
Music:
Mrs J Blinko, GRSM, DipRCM, PGCert RCM (*Flute*)
Mrs K Bradley, LRAM (*Violin*)
Ms C Charlesworth, BMus (*Flute*)
Miss S Dumbrill, BMus, PGDip RNCM (*Flute*)
Mrs L Hayter, BMus, PGDip (*Oboe*)
Mrs C Heller-Jones, BMus, PGCE, PGCert GSM (*Singing*)
Mr J Holling, DipTCL, LTCL (*Percussion*)
Miss P Jeppesen, PGDip GSM (*Violin*)
Mr S Jones, GTCL, LTCL, MTC (*Singing*)
Miss E Lane, GRSM, ARCM (*Singing*)
Ms A Le Hair, BMus, DipRCM (*Piano*)
Mrs M Miller, LLB, CT ABRSM, LRSM, FRSM, ATCL
(*Piano*)
Mr K Milton, AMusA AMB, DipT&P Sydney, Kunstl Dip
Luebeck, MSc (*Violin*)
Miss C Morris Jones, AGSM, LRAM (*Harp*)
Mr I Muncey, AGSM (*Trumpet*)
Miss F Nisbett (*Cello, Piano, Double Bass*)
Mr M Onissi, LTCL (*Saxophone and Clarinet*)
Miss G Pevy, LTCL, FTCL (*Recorder*)
Lady R Runcie, Hon ARAM, LRAM, ARCM (*Piano*)
Mrs H Shabetai, BMus (*Piano*)
Miss M Tsuji, BMus, LRAM, PGDip RAM (*Piano*)
Miss A Tysall, BMus (*Piano*)
Mrs B Valdar, AGSM (*Clarinet*)
Mrs L Watson, LRAM, PGDip RCM (*Bassoon*)

Physical Education:
Ms B Amos (*Tennis – WH*)
§Mrs E Davies, BA Warwick (*Games*)
Miss G Fitzjohn (*Yoga*)
Mr D Lawlor (*Tennis – WH*)
Mrs P Moxham (*Trampolining*)
Miss S Oakley (*Yoga*)
Mr W Rayden (*Fencing – WH*)
Mr H Shah (*Badminton*)

Marketing and Admissions Office:
Communications Officer i/c ICT: Miss J Evans, BA
Leicester, PGCE
Marketing Manager: Mrs A Gavin
Registrar: Miss S Nicholls, BEd Cantab

Technicians:
Mr P Abbott (*IT*)
§Mrs C Ametrano (*IT*)
§Mrs K Burchmore (*Physics*)
Mrs A Hodsden (*CDT*)
§Mrs A Kellard, BA Hertfordshire (*Art*)
§Mr A Morris (*CDT*)
§Mrs N Phillips, BA Surrey (*Art*)
§Miss R Randall (*Biology*)
§Mr C Veasey (*Chemistry*)

Administration:
Network Manager: Mr L Miles, BSc Glamorgan
Assistant Network Manager/VLE Technical Coordinator:
Mr J Shackley, BA Gloucestershire
Account Manager: Mr M Langley
Fees Administrator: Mrs C Anderson
Domestic Bursar: Mrs H Stopps, MIH
Headmistress's PA: Mrs E Roberts
School Secretary: Mrs E Bullivant
School Secretary, Wheathampstead House: Mrs D Pope

St Albans High School for Girls is a day school for 950
girls aged 4 to 18. Since its foundation in 1889, it has been
closely linked with the Cathedral and Abbey Church of St
Alban and the Christian ethos is very important in the life of
the School. Services are held regularly in School or at the
Abbey. The Senior School is only a few minutes' walk from
the town centre.

The Preparatory School, Wheathampstead House, is a
very popular, academically selective school with a welcoming family atmosphere, offering outstanding pastoral care. It
is set in 18 acres of grounds, within the village of
Wheathampstead. The extensive site includes play areas, an
adventure playground, woods and an outdoor learning classroom. (*See entry in IAPS section.*)

St Albans High School is uniquely placed in being able to
offer all the advantages of a continuous education in two
very different settings. From the ages of 4 to 11, the girls
have the freedom to grow and develop in an attractive rural
environment, before moving on to the more urban setting of
the Senior School, close to the heart of the City of St Albans.

The Senior School has facilities for the teaching of a wide
range of subjects. There are nine modern science laboratories, a Design and Technology Centre, a Drama Studio, an
Assembly Hall with a fully equipped stage, specialist rooms
for IT, Art, Music, Textiles, Food Technology, Geography
and Modern Languages, as well as excellent provision for all
the usual academic subjects. The curriculum, which is kept
under review, includes all the subjects of the national curriculum plus Latin, a Modern Language and Drama. There are
two well stocked libraries and a Sixth Form Centre to
accommodate some 170 girls undertaking their A Level
studies.

Girls are encouraged to participate in a wide range of
extra-curricular activities, among which Sport and Music
feature strongly, as well as the Duke of Edinburgh's Award
Scheme, Young Enterprise and Community Service. Pastoral care is important at all levels of the School and girls are
encouraged to feel that they are valued for their contributions to the life of the School community.

In the grounds of the Senior School there is a modern
Sports Hall with adjoining leisure complex comprising
indoor pool, fitness suite and dance studio. The main games
field is ten minutes' walk from the School and there are
eight hard tennis courts, two lacrosse pitches and a new
sports pavilion.

Pupils are prepared for GCSE and IGCSE examinations
at the age of 16, for A Level examinations, for Oxford and
Cambridge entrance and for the examinations of the Associated Board of the Royal Schools of Music.

Fees per term (2011-2012). Reception (age 4) £3,220,
Years 1 and 2 (age 5–6) £3,395 (inc Lunch); Years 3–6 (age
7–11) £3,395 (exc Lunch); Senior School (age 11–18)
£4,095.

Private music lessons, special tennis coaching, School
lunch and daily School coaches are all optional extras.

Scholarships. (*See Scholarship Entries section.*) Music
Scholarships are awarded annually at age 11+ and Academic
Scholarships at ages 11+ and 16+. There are fees assistance
awards available for cases of hardship.

Admission. Pupils are normally admitted in September at
the age of 4, 5 and 7 for entry to the Preparatory School, 11
for the Senior School and 16 for the Sixth Form. Offers of
places in the Sixth Form are provisional until the results of
the GCSE examinations are known: girls are required to
have a minimum of 5 subjects at grade A, including A
grades in the subjects to be taken at A Level. Entrance
examinations are held in the Lent Term for admission in the
following September.

Charitable status. St Albans High School for Girls is a
Registered Charity, number 311065. It exists to provide an
education for girls "in accordance with the principles of the
Church of England".

St Andrew's School
Bedford

Kimbolton Road, Bedford MK40 2PA
Tel: 01234 267272
Fax: 01234 355105
e-mail: standrews@standrewsschoolbedford.com
website: www.standrewsschoolbedford.com

Founded 1897.
Motto: *Non Sibi Sed Deo et Alteria*

Governing Body:
Chairman: Mr K Sanders

Clerk to the Governors and Company Secretary: Mrs S Heaney

Staff:

Headteacher: Mr S P Skehan, BA, MA, NPQH

Deputy Head: Dr D J Pacini, BSc, PhD, MIEA, Adv Cert EdMgt

Mrs L Backhurst (*Music*)
Mrs J Bassett-Gilham (*PE*)
Mrs L Chaplin (*Art*)
Mr S Clarson
Mrs J Curzon (*Speech and Drama*)
Mr B Heathcote (*History; Careers*)
Ms G Jackson (*Science and Maths*)
Mr C Jones (*Mathematics; ICT*)
Mrs C Long (*German*)
Miss J Pearce (*Physical Education*)
Mrs J Randall (*Geography*)
Mrs H Ryan (*Science; Head of Senior School*)
Miss A Scorer (*Technology*)
Mrs S Shepherd (*Mathematics*)
Mrs A Sprake (*English*)
Mr M Stellman (*Maths*)
Mrs S Stott (*Drama*)
Mrs S Tribe (*Modern Language*)
Mrs F Turner (*Physical Education*)
Mrs F Williams (*English*)
Mrs H Wittering (*Food Technology*)

Junior School:
Head: Mr N Hearn

Mrs K Joiner   Mrs H Moody
Mrs L Wayles   Mrs J Russell
Mrs G Ayres   Mrs N van der Sande
Mr J Farnsworth   Mrs M Watt
Mrs M Frame   Mrs K Young
Mrs A Howe

Nursery Department:
Ms L Dempsey   Ms E Niro
                       Miss S McFarlane

Learning Support Department:
Mrs A Hepher   Mrs J Prentice
                       Mrs E Elliott

Librarian: Mrs C Grimes
Secretary to the Head/Admissions: Mrs S Heaney

There are a number of visiting Music staff and Speech and Drama staff, offering a wide range of individual tuition.

St Andrew's is a small day school for girls from the ages of 6 weeks to sixteen and boys from 6 weeks to nine who are taught in small classes.

A 19th Century house is at the heart of the School, which has expanded to provide modern facilities to meet the demands of the National Curriculum and beyond. The Jun-

ior School occupies separate accommodation. The Nursery/Junior School buildings cater for boys as well as girls.

The School prepares girls for the GCSE examinations and further education in the Sixth Form of local Independent Schools, Upper Schools or Colleges. There is an extremely wide range of extra-curricular activities, which includes sport, music, drama and The Duke of Edinburgh's Award Scheme.

For further details contact the School Office: Tel: 01234 267272; Fax: 01234 355105; e-mail: standrews@standrews schoolbedford.com.

Fees per term (2011-2012). Nursery £2,075; Junior School: £2,075 (Reception to Year 2), £2,690 (Years 3–6); Senior School: £3,492 (Years 7–11).

Charitable status. St Andrew's School (Bedford) Limited is a Registered Charity, number 307531. It offers a broad based education to pupils of all abilities, who are encouraged to strive for excellence in all they do.

St Catherine's School
Bramley

Bramley, Guildford, Surrey GU5 0DF
Tel: 01483 893363
Fax: 01483 899608
e-mail: schooloffice@stcatherines.info
website: www.stcatherines.info

Founded as a Church of England School for Girls in 1885.

Governing Body:
Chairman: Mr Peter J Martin, BA, FRGS, FCCA
Vice-Chairman: Dr Janet F McGowan, MB BS, FCA
Mr C Murray R Campbell, MA
Dr Fiona Green
Mrs Miranda Greenway
Dr Janet E Johnson, MA, DPhil
Mr Mark Ommanney
Mrs Sue Shipway
Mrs Gloria Stuart
Mr Jonathan C M Tippett, BSc, FCA, TEP
Mr B Mark Way, DipArch, RIBA

Headmistress: Mrs Alice Phillips, MA Cantab

Business Manager: Mrs Christine Silver, BSc Durham, PGCE
Head of Boarding: Mrs Lorinda Munro-Faure, MA Oxon, PGCE
Director of Studies: Dr Stephen Pumphrey, PhD Imperial College, BSc, PGCE
Senior Housemistress: Mrs Kirsty Meredith, BA Hons London, AKC, PGCE
Director of Staff: Mrs Caroline Rose, BA Nottingham, PGCE
Head of Sixth Form: Mrs Claire Wyllie, MA Durham, PGCE
School Administrator: Mrs Heather Bryn-Thomas, BSc Kent, PGCE
Head of Prep School: Mrs Kathleen Jefferies, BSc Bridgewater, Massachusetts, PGCE
Deputy Head – Curriculum: Mrs Fiona Thomas, BA Victoria, New Zealand, Dip Tchg, TTC
Deputy Head – Pre-Prep: Mrs Jill Cochrane, BEd, CertEd Leicester, PGCPSE Open
Deputy Head – Staff : Miss Naomi Bartholomew, MA London, BEd Cantab

Marketing: Mrs Gill David, BA Manchester, PGCE
Development Director: Mrs Joanne Dowling
Association Director: Mrs Katherine Stocks

Chaplain: (*to be appointed*)

School Housemistresses:
Ashcombe: Mrs Chris Peskett
Merriman: Mrs Rosa McQuade
Midleton: Mrs Kirsty Meredith
Musgrave: Mrs Penny Harris
Russell-Baker: Mrs Susan Hall
Stoner: Mrs Simone Berry

Boarding Housemistresses:
Bronte: Miss Laura White
Keller: Miss Katrina Bayley
Sixth Form: Mrs Jane Leitner

Heads of Departments:
Careers: Miss Rhiannon Morgan, BA Hons London, Teachers' Certificate, DCG
Classics: Mrs Sophia Ridley, BA Hons Durham, PGCE
Drama: Ms Madeleine Lewis
Design Technology: Mr Alastair White, BA Hons Winchester
Economics/Business Studies: Mr Nigel Watson, BA Hons Ealing College of Higher Education, PGCE
English: Mr Jonathan Worthen, MA Oxon, PGCE
Examinations Coordinator: Mr Philip Friend, BSc Lancaster, PGCE
Fine Art/History of Art: Miss Verity Vinen
French: Mrs Lucy Strong, BA Hons Bristol, PGCE
Food and Nutrition: Mrs Nicola Genzel, BA Hons Roehampton, PGCE
Geography: Mrs Sophie Mackness, BSc Hons London, PGCE
German: Miss Elodie Nevin, MA Oxon, QTS
History: Mrs Gill David, BA Hons Manchester, PGCE
ICT: Mrs Catherine Lamb, BA and DipE Central Queensland University, QTS
Librarian: Mrs Sue Lawrence, ALA
Learning Support Coordinator: Miss Caroline Cross, BA Hons Lancaster, PGCE
Mathematics: Mrs Sheila Kelsall, MA Open, BSc Hons Brighton, PGCE
Director of Music: Mr Geoffrey Field, GRSM Hons, DipRAM, ARCO, LRAM
Physical Education: Mrs Vic Alexander, BEd Hons Brighton
Politics: Mr Carl Gladwell, BA Hons London, PGCE
Psychology: Mrs Jean Arrick, BSc Hons Liverpool, PGCE
PSHE: Mrs Chris Peskett, BEd Hons Wales
Religious Studies: Mr Alistair McNally, BA Hons Belfast, PGCE
Sciences:
Biology: Mrs Lorinda Munro-Faure, MA Oxon, PGCE
Chemistry: Miss Nicola Hindley, MChem Oxon, QTS
Physics: Mr Matthew Greenfield, MEng Oxon, QTS
Sixth Form General Studies: Mr Carl Gladwell, BA Hons London, PGCE
Spanish: Mrs Rebecca Rathmell, BA Hons Exeter, PGCE
Textiles: Mrs Lorna Crispin, BA Hons Manchester
Timetable:
Mrs Heather Bryn-Thomas, BSc Kent, PGCE
Mr Matthew Greenfield, MEng Oxon, QTS

Administration:
Senior School Registrar: Mrs Judy Corben
Prep School Registrar: Mrs Annie Daniell
PA to the Business Manager: Mrs Diane Haeffele
PA to the Headmistress: Miss Toppy Wharton
Office Manager: Miss Sally Marshall

This has been a particularly exciting year at St Catherine's, Bramley as we not only celebrated the School's 125th anniversary in Guildford Cathedral but also saw the opening of an impressive new sports complex and a performance hall, known collectively as The Anniversary Halls.

The outstanding results gained in public examinations by girls at St Catherine's secure them places at the top universities, in competitive disciplines like medicine and veterinary science, law and languages. The School has had a record number of Oxbridge offers this year in a wide range of disciplines. This success comes not only as a result of the fine quality of the teaching, but is also due to the individual attention received by every girl. St Catherine's places great emphasis on creating a happy environment where every girl is encouraged to work hard to maximise her talents. The atmosphere is friendly and one in which children can develop and grow in a very stimulating environment.

Pivotal to the life of St Catherine's are the six school Houses. The girls' loyalty and affection for their Houses is impressive with memories of inter-house plays, competitions and matches enduring long after School days have ended.

A broad and varied curriculum allows all pupils to participate in many challenging and rewarding extra-curricular activities. As a Church of England School girls are encouraged to think of others and impressive sums of money are raised for charity each year. The School has its own beautiful chapel which is used by the girls on a daily basis.

The School's flexible approach to boarding is making it increasingly attractive to busy, professional families; the ISI team picked out boarding as one of the outstanding features of St Catherine's. The School welcomes both weekly and full boarders who enjoy a busy and exciting programme.

Activities Week is held each year in the Summer Term when every girl in the School participates in a variety of programmes organised to both support the curriculum and offer challenges not normally met in the classroom. Pupils participate in outward bound ventures, an industrial heritage tour to the north and midlands, modern language courses in France, Germany and Spain, whilst Sixth Formers focus on university choices. Activities Week costs are included in the fees.

International links are also very important. St Catherine's has an exchange programme with St Catherine's Melbourne, Australia and there are also links with schools in Kenya, South Africa and Afghanistan.

St Catherine's has an unrivalled reputation in art, music, sport and drama; photography and textiles are popular options amongst the Sixth Form, and younger girls are encouraged by an enthusiastic Art and Design department to take advantage of the superb facilities, and join many after-school clubs.

Music is an important feature of school life, with numerous choirs, orchestras and concert bands rehearsing each week and performing regularly. There are in excess of 500 individual music lessons taking place each week where over half the girls learn to play a musical instrument. There are flute choirs, string quartets, recorder groups and ensembles to cater for all levels of ability. Concerts and recitals are held regularly. An exciting venture has been the Organ Academy and the Jennifer Bate Organ Scholarship in conjunction with Guildford Cathedral. The Senior School Summer Concert was held, this year, in St John's, Smith Square, London.

Many girls go on to represent their county in netball, lacrosse, swimming, squash and athletics. Every girl is encouraged to take part in sport at school, whatever her level of expertise. The PE Department regularly fields four or five teams for lacrosse and netball, allowing every girl who wishes to play competitively the opportunity to do so.

Drama and Theatre Studies are extremely popular options and all girls are encouraged to audition for the annual middle and senior school plays. As well as acting opportunities, pupils are also offered the opportunity to help backstage and front of house and learn many valuable skills as a result. LAMDA classes are offered to all year groups. With the opening of the impressive new performance halls including state-of-the-art lighting and acoustics, facilities for Theatre are second to none.

The Preparatory School offers a full academic and games curriculum; most girls join at 4 with a limited number of places available in other years. It aims to support families in helping younger pupils develop a strong sense of values, high standards of behaviour and consideration to others, as well as achieving excellent academic success. The girls benefit from specialist teaching, combining the best of traditional methods with modern technology to prepare them for the Entrance Examinations to all Senior Schools at 11+, including St Catherine's.

St Catherine's is situated in extensive grounds, in the heart of the attractive Surrey village of Bramley, three miles south of Guildford which has a main line station (Waterloo 35 minutes). There is easy access to Heathrow and Gatwick and travel arrangements are made for overseas boarders. Close proximity to London allows frequent visits to theatres and galleries and the miles of countryside on our doorstep is an asset to the many girls who take part in the Duke of Edinburgh's Award Scheme.

Fees per term (from January 2011). Day Girls (including lunch): Pre-Prep 1 £2,350, Pre-Prep 2 £2,845, Pre-Prep 3 £3,355; Prep School £3,965; Middle and Senior School £4,780.

Boarders: Middle and Senior Boarding and Tuition £7,865.

Fees include the Activities Week programme for Senior School girls.

Entry. This is by Entrance Examination held in January. The Preparatory School also holds its entrance tests in January.

Scholarships and Bursaries. (*See Scholarship Entries section.*) Entrance Scholarships are offered at 11+, together with a number of Sixth Form scholarships of 20% of fees. A number of music exhibitions, providing music tuition, music and instrument hire are also offered. A Sixth Form Art Scholarship is available.

Prospectus and School Visits. Please apply to the Registrar. The Headmistress will be pleased to see parents by appointment.

Charitable status. St Catherine's School Bramley is a Registered Charity, number 1070858. It exists to provide education for girls in accordance with the principles of the Church of England.

St Catherine's School
Twickenham

Cross Deep, Twickenham, Middlesex TW1 4QJ
Tel: 020 8891 2898
Fax: 020 8744 9629
e-mail: admissions@stcatherineschool.co.uk
website: www.stcatherineschool.co.uk

Motto: '*Not Words But Deeds*'

Chair of Governors: Mr Edward Sparrow

Headmistress: **Sister Paula Thomas**, BEd, MA

Deputy Head: Ms M Fisher, BA

Bursar & Clerk to the Governors: Mr I G Stewart, BAcc, CA

Admissions Secretary: Mrs A Faulkner

Age Range. Girls 3–18 years.
Number in School. 390 Day Girls.

Founded in 1914 by the Sisters of Mercy, St Catherine's moved from its original site to its current location in 1919. Today the school is under lay management. St Catherine's is a Catholic School in the ecumenical tradition, and pupils of all denominations are welcome.

Aims. Our aim is to provide an excellent all-round education so that every pupil can achieve her personal academic best. We strive to provide a broad and balanced education within a stimulating and supportive environment which encourages learning. Success is achieved through personal responsibility, high expectations and a close partnership between parents and school. Emphasis is placed on self-discipline, responsibility and the importance of respect for others. Since we are a relatively small school with small class sizes the staff are able to know the pupils as individuals and there is a strong sense of community which promotes academic success.

Situation. The School enjoys an enviable position being located next to the River Thames. It is a short distance from the centre of Twickenham and approximately 10-15 minutes' walk from Strawberry Hill and Twickenham Stations. Both have regular services to London (Waterloo), Surrey, Berkshire and Middlesex. There are also a number of local bus routes.

Entrance. Main points of entry are at 3, 7, 11 and 16 but girls are accepted at any stage subject to space. Places at the school are usually awarded on the basis of an interview, a report from the candidate's previous school and an assessment (examination in the senior school).

Scholarships and Bursaries. Academic Scholarships, up to the value of 50% of the fees, are awarded annually at 11+ on the basis of the entrance examination and interview. Music, Sports and Art Awards are also awarded annually following an audition/assessment and are conditional on the applicant achieving the School's academic requirement for entry.

A limited number of Bursaries are offered depending on need and funds available.

Curriculum. In the Senior School pupils follow courses in English, Mathematics, Science, Religious Studies, History, Geography, Drama, Music, Art, PSHE and Physical Education. All pupils in Years 7 to 9 study French, Spanish and German. Spanish is offered at GCSE as are the three Separate Sciences. Emphasis is also placed on the development of ICT skills and the school has two ICT Suites that can accommodate whole classes. Most pupils study ten subjects to GCSE level. A wide range of A Level subjects are available at sixth form level.

There is a strong commitment to sports, music, drama and extra-curricular activities. The school has its own hockey pitch and indoor swimming pool as well as tennis and netball courts. Sports include swimming, netball, athletics, hockey, tennis, gymnastics and rounders and our pupils achieve considerable success at county, regional and national level.

Music plays an important part in the life of the school; all pupils are encouraged to participate in choirs, orchestras and ensembles, and the varied programme of concerts and informal performances. Drama is popular and regular theatre visits take place during the year.

Buildings. The Preparatory and Senior departments are on one site. The buildings include a large multi-purpose hall as well as a smaller assembly hall, a well-stocked Library, two ICT Suites, a spacious Art room with a Pottery and Photography room, and a Food Technology Room. The Music Centre has class and individual practice rooms. There are fully-equipped laboratories for Physics, Chemistry and Biology. A large programme of new building has recently added new teaching blocks, a sixth form centre, drama studio and fitness suite.

Extra-Curricular Activities. These play a significant role in the school. Activities include the Duke of Edinburgh's Award scheme, Spanish, Badminton, Science Club, Football, Rugby, Chess and Photography. Trips, both locally and abroad, add to the extensive range of activities on offer.

Pupils also take part in community service and fundraising activities.

Fees per term (2011-2012). Nursery £2,650, Reception £2,830, Year 1 to Year 2 £2,905, Year 3 to Year 6 £3,055, Year 7 to Year 12 £3,705 (excluding examination fees).

Charitable status. St Catherine's School, Twickenham is a Registered Charity, number 1014651. It aims to provide for children seeking education in a Christian environment.

St Dominic's High School for Girls

Bargate Street, Brewood, Staffordshire ST19 9BA
Tel: 01902 850248
Fax: 01902 851154
e-mail: enquiries@stdominicsschool.co.uk
website: www.stdominicsschool.co.uk

St Dominic's HSG is a leading independent girls' school in Staffordshire, providing education for 300+ girls from rising 3 to 18 and boys from rising 3 to 7. Development of the 'whole person' is at the heart of our school. We believe each child has special talents and we act to develop those gifts so that they may achieve their full potential within a caring environment. Our aim is to develop the pupils academically, socially, creatively and spiritually. Our School has an excellent record of GCSE and A Level results and we have consistently topped the Staffordshire League Tables over the last 10 years for GCSE results and all of our girls who have applied to University have taken places at their chosen University. In the recent ISI report, the school was rated *excellent/outstanding* in every aspect – *The pupils' achievements are well supported by the quality of the teaching, throughout the school, which is excellent and often inspirational.*

Chairman of the Board of Governors: Mr R Turton

Headteacher: **Mrs S White**, BSc Hons, PGCE, Dip Comp, NPQH, ACIEA

Deputy Head (*Curriculum*): Ms J Marshall, MA, PGCE, BA Hons

Deputy Head (*Pastoral*): Mrs L Read, BA Hons

Heads of Faculty:
Mathematics: Mrs R Cowley, BA, CertEd
Expressive Arts: Ms L Hovland, BEd Hons
Science and Technology: Dr G Probert, PhD, MPhys, PGCE
Communications: Miss R Mason, BA, PGCE
Humanities: Ms C Morris, BSc Hons, PGCE

Head of Foundation Years and Pre-Preparatory: Mrs K Grevett, BEd Hons, NCertEd, CertEd

Head of Preparatory: Mrs S Kirwan, BA, QTS

Bursar: Mr R Wallis, ACCA, ONC, HNC

Admissions Officer: Ms F Allen

School Secretaries:
Mrs J Marson
Mrs S Molloy

Teaching and Learning. Small class sizes facilitate individual attention and enable teachers to build a profile of each pupil: strengths and weaknesses are diagnosed and all work is tailored to match individual needs.

Teachers and pupils work closely together to make learning challenging, interesting and fun. We believe in close partnership with parents, keeping you informed about your daughter's progress.

Work is differentiated to challenge and support individual pupils and progress is closely tracked and monitored to ensure optimum learning opportunities.

As girls enter Year 7 they are taught by dedicated specialist subject teachers in small classes. The enhanced curriculum delivered allows some students to be fast tracked at GCSE level and gives excellent Value Added, with pupils exceeding expectations based on their initial entrance assessment. We are in the top 5% of schools nationally achieving value added based on the Yellis system.

Curriculum. We offer a broad and balanced curriculum with enhancement and enrichment. The National Curriculum is taught throughout the school and this is further enhanced with additional subjects such as dance, drama and singing, which are integrated into the weekly timetable. A full range of 24 subjects is currently on offer at AS and A Level.

Expressive Arts. St Dominic's HSG is renowned for its musical and dramatic excellence and is frequently approached by companies for our girls to audition in local productions. Our contemporary Performing Arts Centre houses a Drama and Dance Studio, a Music Suite and a Recording Studio.

Girls are encouraged to join the choirs, play an instrument, take up dance or singing or tread the boards. Throughout the year there are a variety of performances ranging from the Pre-Preparatory Christmas play, to the all-singing and all-dancing productions such as Oklahoma and Annie.

The girls participate in many competitions, local, regional and national. They regularly take part in local festivals and public speaking events. Many girls do LAMDA examinations and all Year 7 girls take English Speaking Board examinations.

Sports. We offer a broad and interesting curriculum which includes netball, hockey, dance, gymnastics, aerobics, football, volleyball, basketball, badminton, rounders, tennis, athletics and cross-country and some children have even represented the Country in their sport.

Our all inclusive extra-curricular programmes provide further sporting variety and include kung fu, gymnastics, trampolining, modern dance and ballet, with all abilities encouraged to attend.

There is a comprehensive fixtures programme, as well as our competitive inter-house events including Annual Junior and Senior Sports Days. We take part in ISA sporting events at local, regional and national level.

The facilities used to deliver this popular subject include newly resurfaced and extended netball and tennis courts and our playing fields which include a hockey pitch, athletics track, football pitch and rounders pitches. We also have an excellent fully-equipped sports hall.

Extra Curricular Activities. Four days a week there is an all-inclusive after-school programme where the girls can undertake a variety of activities ranging from The Duke of Edinburgh's Award Scheme to Street Dancing, Debating and Gardening.

Throughout the year, girls are encouraged to become involved in fundraising for local and national charities. These activities help each girl develop a good community spirit with respect and consideration for others.

Pastoral Care. Our outstanding pastoral care system and Christian ethos create an atmosphere which fosters trust and mutual respect between pupils and teachers. Pupils feel relaxed and secure and develop their self-respect, self-confidence, personal discipline and consideration for others.

Examination Results. Our pupils achieve outstanding examination results, with most years being 100% pass rate in 5 or more A*–C grades over the last 10 years. In 2009 we were placed in the top 5% of schools nationally on Value Added. Girls also achieve exceptionally well at A Level and all girls have been accepted at their chosen Universities. This year we have 100% pass rate at A/S with 72% at grade

A and B, with predictions of 60% A and B grades at A Level.

Our students who take external examinations for dance, drama and music also achieve very high marks.

Facilities. We have a whole school state-of-the-art ICT system and a purpose-built Kindergarten and junior building, which encompasses a junior hall, IT room, DT and Art room, Home Economics room and a library. The Senior building has fully-equipped science laboratories, IT room and a library. All classrooms have networked computers and interactive whiteboards. Plasma information screens are installed in the foyers. The Sixth Form and Performing Arts Centre is a modern, state-of-the art facility housing the latest technology in music, IT and the Performing Arts.

The new Sixth Form Centre has a common room with terraces and a well-equipped Library with wi-fi laptop technology.

Admissions. Although selective, we draw our pupils from a wide ability range, which makes our record of results outstanding. Interview is followed by time spent in school (1 or 2 days) when assessment of potential can be made. Entry into the Senior department is through entrance exams and a place in the Sixth Form is conditional upon GCSE results.

Fees per term (2011-2012). Pre-Prep (inc lunch): £1,045 (Transition, 5 mornings), £1,955 (Reception), £2,357 (Year 1), £2,565 (Year 2). Prep (exc lunch): £2,976 (Years 3–6). Senior (exc lunch): £3,611 (Years 7–9), £3,780 (Years 10–13).

Scholarships and Bursaries. Scholarships are available for Preparatory (Y3–6) and Academic and Performing Arts scholarships are awarded for entry into Year 7. Sports and Art scholarships are awarded for entry into Year 8 with a full range of scholarships awarded in Year 12. Bursaries are available across all years and application forms can be obtained from the Bursar.

For further information view our website which also contains a copy of our ISI Inspection report March 2011.

St Dominic's Priory School

21 Station Road, Stone, Staffordshire ST15 8EN
Tel: 01785 814181/814411
Fax: 01785 819361
e-mail: info@stdominicspriory.co.uk
website: www.stdominicspriory.co.uk

Founded 1836 by the Dominican Congregation of Catherine of Sienna.

Governors:
Chairperson: Dr E M Court
Father Duncan Campbell OP
Mrs A Foxall
Dr T Gillow
Mr E D T Leadbeater
Mrs E Moran
Mrs H Phillips
Mr N Kingston
Mr P Bowyer
Sister Mary Pauline OP
Sister Angela Mary OP
Sister Mary Jadwiga OP

Headteacher: **Mrs M P Adamson**, BA Hons, PGCE, CTC, NPQH

Senior Department:

Full-time Staff:
Mrs M P Adamson, BA Hons, PGCE, CTC, NPQH (*History*)
Miss B Capper, BEd Hons (*PE*)
Mrs J Deakin, BA, CertEd (*Sociology/Psychology*)

Mrs J Dunk, MBA, BA Hons, PGCE (*IT/Business Studies*)
Mrs A Hughes (*Learning Support*)
Mrs J Kirkland, BSc, CertEd (*Mathematics*)
Miss K Lynch, BA Hons, ABSM, GBSM, PGCE (*Music*)
Mrs C Phillips, BA, PGCE (*Italian/French*)
Mrs P Porter, BEd, CertEd (*Mathematics*)
Mr N Soar, BA, PGCE, Post DipEd (*Deputy Head, English*)
Miss L Underhill (*Learning Support*)
Mrs A Wright, BA Hons, MA, PGCE (*Art*)

Part-time Staff:
Mr S Booth (*History*)
Mrs V Burge, BSc, PGCE (*Chemistry*)
Mrs R Chatburn, BA, PGCE (*English/General Studies*)
Mrs J Cook, BA, PGCE (*RE*)
Mrs L de Cruz, BA Hons, PGCE, CCRS (*English*)
Mrs M Hignett, BSc, PGCE (*Biology*)
Mrs H Johnston, BEd (*French*)
Mrs M Kitchener, BA, PGCE (*French*)
Mr B Lewis (*Geography*)
Miss S Sahota (*Physics*)
Mrs S Whitehouse, BSc Joint Hons, PGCE (*Biology*)

Preparatory Department:

Full-time Staff:
Mrs S Brunt, NNEB, BEd
Mrs J Carey, BA Hons, PGCE, DipHEd
Mrs J Coombs, BSc Hons, PGCE, CCRS
Mrs S Dickson, LRAM
Mrs J Holland (*Nursery*)
Mrs J Lake (*Learning Support*)
Mrs K Lanyon, NNEB
Miss F McDermid (*Nursery*)
Mrs G Turner, CertEd

Part-time Staff:
Miss K Davies, BA, PGCE
Mrs A Whitfield, BEd Hons, CTC

Visiting Staff:
Mr M Davies (*Percussion*)
Miss J Hames (*Keyboard*)
Mr P Nevins (*Brass*)
Mr P Rogers (*Guitar*)
Mr D Watson (*Flute /Saxophone*)
Mr T Mvula (*Singing*)

Mrs B Abbots (*Dance*)
Mrs A Alston (*Aerobics*)
Mrs A Miller (*Dyslexia Support*)
Miss E Sawyer (*Speech & Drama*)
Mr J Trickey (*LTA Coach*)

St Dominic's Priory School is a highly successful Catholic Independent Day School for girls aged 2 to 18 and boys aged 2 to 11. We provide a friendly place of learning where imagination grows and minds sharpen.

We are proud of our reputation for academic excellence and proud that our ethos and vision value the worth of each individual. High quality teaching and small class sizes create an environment in which true potential can be maximised at all times.

Location. Centrally located within North Staffordshire, the school is situated in the picturesque canal town of Stone, Staffordshire, within easy reach of Newcastle Under Lyme, Stoke-On-Trent, Stafford, Uttoxeter, Cheadle and the surrounding villages.

Aims and Ethos. Life is a journey, and every journey has a beginning. We aim to give each child the best possible start, to give them the tools to navigate their chosen path and the confidence to believe in themselves. Teachers and pupils work together with energy and imagination; they motivate and inspire each other in order to achieve their very best.

We promote a strong sense of personal responsibility based on the Gospel values of truth, justice, compassion, partnership and community. A spirit of collaboration is fostered between pupils, staff and parents.

Children of all faiths and ethnic backgrounds are welcomed at St. Dominic's Priory School. The Dominican motto, Laudare, Benedicere, Praedicare – to praise, bless and preach the Word of God, is embraced while ensuring that diversity is recognised and respected.

Curriculum. Boys and girls are co-educated from the age of 2 within the purpose-built Nursery. The beginnings of reading, writing and number work are introduced at an early age.

The curriculum within the Preparatory Department encompasses all aspects of the National Curriculum with specialist teaching in many subjects including French, Drama and Music. Great emphasis is placed on high standards of presentation and regular homework reinforces the work undertaken at School.

Girls join the Senior Department for a specialist girls-only education. Here the School aims to develop the capacity for independent thought through a rigorous and stimulating academic education. One of St Dominic's great strengths is taking a broad ability range of pupils and achieving outstanding A Level and GCSE results. With the benefit of small classes, teaching is geared to the needs of individual girls who are supported throughout by a strong pastoral care system. The School provides regular opportunities for all girls to take on positions of leadership and to develop a sense of their own worth and a determination to realise all their talents.

Religion. St Dominic's Priory is a Catholic School where children of all faiths are welcomed.

The Arts. The School is particularly strong in the Visual and Performing Arts. Pupils regularly take part in public speaking competitions, plays, festivals, concerts, recitals and exhibitions both within and outside the School.

Sport. The School has a strong sporting tradition. The main sports played are tennis, badminton, unihoc, netball, volleyball, gymnastics, athletics, football, tennis and cross-country running.

Extra-Curricular Activities. Numerous clubs and activities are held after school and during lunchtimes for both the Prep and Senior Schools.

Sixth Form and Beyond. The School has an extensive and well-resourced careers programme which includes work experience, work shadowing, a Careers Library, help from school careers staff and advice from Connexions.

Admission. Please contact the school directly for information on admissions or visit the website.

Scholarships. Academic, Art and Performing Arts scholarships are available, along with Bursaries throughout the School. Details can be obtained from the Admissions Office.

Fees per term (2011-2012). Nursery £2,076, Reception–Primary 6 £2,859, Seniors £3,135, Sixth Form £3,256.

Further Information. The School welcomes visits from prospective parents and pupils. If you would like to visit or attend one of our Open Mornings, please telephone the School Office on 01785 814181.

Charitable status. St Dominic's Priory is a Registered Charity, number 271922, providing quality education for children aged 2 to 18 years.

St Francis' College
Letchworth Garden City

The Broadway, Letchworth Garden City, Herts SG6 3PJ
Tel: 01462 670511
Fax: 01462 682361

e-mail: enquiries@st-francis.herts.sch.uk
website: www.st-francis.herts.sch.uk

Governors:
Mr J Procter (*Chairman*)
Mrs P J Barlow
Mrs S Boardman
Mr A W Goodwin
Miss E Ismay
Mr P J McKay
Dr V McNicholas
Mr C G Nott
Mrs R Rainey
Mrs M Rochester

Headmistress: **Mrs D MacGinty**, BEd, NPQH

Deputy Headmistress: Mrs P Wilkinson, BA, PGCE, NPQH (*Religious Studies*)

Acting Head of Preparatory Department: Mrs H Stone, MEd, AdvDipEd, CertEd

Bursar: Mr M Collis, BSc

Senior Teacher: Mrs S Pope, BEd, AdvDipIT, NPQH (*IT Coordinator, Technology Coordinator*)

Sixth Form Coordinator: Mrs M Fenton, MA, BA, PGCE (*Head of History*)

School Chaplain: Revd P Bennett, BTh, SSC

Teaching staff:
Mrs N Ashbrook, BA, TEFL, Cert TESOL (*EFL*)
Mr A Bond, BSc, PGCE (*Mathematics*)
Mrs E Carroll, BA, PGCE (*Director of Music*)
Dr R Clarke, BSc, DPhil, PGCE (*Chemistry, Science*)
Mrs H Coley, BA, PGCE (*English – Maternity Cover*)
Mrs C Cowley, BA, PGCE (*Art*)
Miss K Dickinson, BA, PGCE (*Latin – Maternity Cover*)
Mrs L Drake, BA, Cert TESOL (*EFL*)
Mr B J Eaton, MA, BEd (*Head of Religious Studies*)
Mrs H Eaton, MA, BA, PGCE (*Head of English*)
Mrs K Elliott, BA, PGCE (*Religious Studies*)
Dr I Fengler, Ph D, BSc, QTS (*Head of Chemistry, Science*)
Mrs M Fenton, MA, BA, PGCE (*Head of History, Sixth Form Coordinator*)
Ms C Gaviria-Velez, MA, DEA, BA, PGCE (*French, German, Spanish*)
Mrs A Gillan, BSc, PGCE (*Head of Geography, Examinations Officer*)
Mrs J Glanville, BSc, PGCE (*Biology, Science*)
Mrs J Grant, BSc, BA, DipEd (*Mathematics*)
Mrs D Hammond, CertEd (*PE, Games and Swimming*)
Mr R Hayes, BA, PGCE (*Creative Textiles*)
Mr A Hetherington, MA, PGCE (*History, Careers Coordinator, PHSE Coordinator*)
Mrs L Hetherington, BA, PGCE (*English*)
Mrs A Hinnells, BA, PGCE (*Head of Mathematics*)
Mr J Hobbs, MA, BA, PGCE (*English*)
Mr M Ketcher, MSc, BSc, PGCE (*Physics*)
Miss R Leek, BA (*Latin*)
Mrs C McDermott, BA, PGCE (*Head of Drama*)
Mrs A Middleton, CertEd, CertCC (*Home Economics*)
Mrs C Moore, BA, PGCE, TEFL, TESL (*Head of EFL*)
Mrs P Moore, BEd (*Physical Education*)
Mrs S Pope, BEd, AdvDipIT, NPQH (*Senior Teacher, IT Coordinator, Technology Coordinator*)
Mrs C Rahim, BSc (*Mathematics*)
Miss S Roberts, CertEd (*Head of Physical Education*)
Mrs S Sanders, BA, PGCE (*Geography*)
Miss V Semmens, BBS, DipBusAdmin, TTC (*Head of Economics, Head of Business Studies*)
Mrs S Simpkin, BSc, PGCE (*Head of Biology*)

Mr R Tabraham, BA, PGCE (*Director of Art, Photography*)
Mrs A Taylor, BSc, PGCE (*Mathematics*)
Mr P Taylor, BA, PGCE, DPSE (*Head of German*)
Mrs R Thompson, BA, PGCE (*French*)
Mrs J Thomson, BA (*Mathematics*)
Mrs K Tipping, BSc, PGCE, MBA (*Head of Science, Head of Physics*)
Mrs S Twigg, RSA Dip (*Individual Needs*)
Mrs N Wait, BA, PGCE (*German, German Assistant*)
Mrs E Walden, BA, ATCL, MusEd, PGCE (*Music*)
Mrs J Whyte, BA, PGCE (*Head of Foreign Languages*)
Mrs S York, MA, BSc, BA, MSTAT (*Psychology, Flute, Alexander Technique*)

Librarian: Mrs K Purchon, MA, BA
IT Technician: Mr P Monaghan, BEng

Preparatory Department Staff:
Mrs H Stone, MEd, AdvDipEd, CertEd (*Acting Head of Prep Department*)
Mrs Mrs N Parsons, BA (*Kindergarten*)
Mrs J Day, BA (*Reception*)
Mrs V King, MEd, BEd, CertEd, CCRS (*Prep I*)
Mrs A Balcombe, BA, PGCE (*Prep IIB*)
Mrs M Mitchell, CertEd (*Prep IIM*)
Mrs R de Wolf, BA, GTP (*Prep IIID*)
Mrs J White, CertEd (*Prep IIIW*)
Miss S Naughton, BA, PGCE (*Prep IVN*)
Mrs L Thayer, BA, QTS (*Prep IVT*)
Mrs W Bailey, CertEd (*Prep VB*)
Mrs M Elliot, BEd (*Prep VIE*)
Mrs A Glew, BA, PGCE (*Prep VIG*)
Mrs D Bassnett, BA, PGCE (*Speech and Drama*)
Mrs R Baldwin, BA, LTCL, TD Violin, LTCL, TD Voice (*Music*)
Mrs A Greenhalgh, BA (*French*)
Miss S Roberts, CertEd (*PE, Games and Swimming*)
Mrs M Drew, CertEd (*PE, Games and Swimming*)
Mrs A Blomfield, BEd (*PE, Games and Swimming*)
Mrs P Moore, BEd (*PE, Games and Swimming*)
Mrs D Hammond, CertEd (*PE, Games and Swimming*)

Preparatory Department Classroom Assistants:
Mrs N Ahern
Mrs J Eversden
Mrs S Lockhart
Miss K Potts
Mrs J Roseblade
Mrs S Thomas
Mrs J Watts

Mrs K Kandola (*After School Club Supervisor*)
Ms P Keane (*After School Club*)

Residential Staff:
Mrs S Reed, FET Cert, TEFL, BPhil, CPP Hons (*Head of Boarding*)
Mrs D Heard (*Housemistress*)
Mrs L Everitt (*Assistant Housemistress*)
Mrs C Rogers (*Assistant Housemistress*)

Visiting Staff:
Mr R Atkinson, BA (*Electric Guitar*)
Mrs M Beecroft, BA, PGCE (*French Assistant*)
Mrs A Borner, BSc, CertABRSM (*Piano*)
Mrs S Card, LTCL (*Piano*)
Miss V Cheesman, LTCL, FTCL (*Clarinet*)
Mrs F Dearman, BA, CertEd (*Guitar*)
Mrs A Guill, BA, LRAM, DipRAM, PGDip (*Voice*)
Miss D Jellis, FISTD CB, Dip ICDD, Enrico Cecchetti Dip, RAD, ISTD (*Ballet, Tap, Modern*)
Mrs A Kelly, ARCM (*Violin*)
Mrs C Lee, BA (*German Club*)
Mr P Marriott (*Drums*)
Mr P Maundrell, FTCL, GTCL, LTCL, CertEd (*Piano*)

Mr A Robinson, ALCM, LLCM TD, PGCMT (*Brass*)
Miss M Roche, ARCM, CertEd (*Singing*)
Mr O Sirinathsingh, DipMusPerf (*Saxophone, Clarinet*)
Mrs R Thompson, BMus, LRAM, ARCM (*Violin*)
Mrs L-M Yuen-Brooker, LRAM, CertEd (*Piano*)
Mrs D Wakeling, LAMDA (*Speech & Drama*)
Mrs S York, MA, BSc, BA, MSTAT (*Flute, Alexander Technique*)

Secretarial/Support Staff:
Mrs R Atkinson (*HR Coordinator, Payroll*)
Mr K Bray (*Site Manager*)
Mr K Buckland (*Caretaker*)
Mrs C Cartwright (*Events Organiser, Office Assistant*)
Mrs S Circuit (*Bursar's Assistant – Accounts*)
Mrs Y Deards (*Reprographics*)
Mrs T Dickerson (*Bursar's Assistant – Fees*)
Mrs D Gilbert, BSc (*Laboratory Technician*)
Mr G Haycroft (*Catering Manager*)
Mrs T Jesson (*Health Centre Administrator, Office Assistant*)
Mrs M Kerr, BSc (*Laboratory Technician*)
Mrs C Lee, BA (*Lower Prep Secretary*)
Mrs H Lomax (*Personal Assistant to the Headmistress*)
Mrs J Luggeri (*Reprographics*)
Mrs W Roskilly, BA (*Upper Prep Secretary, Prep Admissions Secretary*)
Mrs L Shaw (*Receptionist*)
Mrs G Wrigley (*Receptionist*)

The College was founded on its present site in 1933 by Sister Elizabeth of the Trinity, one of the Sisters of Charity of Jesus and Mary, an order of Roman Catholic Sisters based in Belgium. It grew steadily and flourished for the next fifth years until 1983 when the Belgian Order decided to reduce its educational commitment in the United Kingdom. The College was taken over by a newly-formed Educational Charity, The St Francis' College Educational Trust, and is administered by a Board of Governors, which is in membership of AGBIS. The Headmistress is a member of The Girls' Schools Association.

Within the ethos of the College the aim is to provide a modern education based on Christian principles. Pupils receive close individual care promoting spiritual, moral, intellectual and physical development. The College recognises the unique qualities of each pupil and encourages social responsibility and respect for others. With its Roman Catholic foundation and heritage, St Francis' is a Christian community, ecumenical in outlook, which has always welcomed pupils from other faiths. Religious Education plays a vital part of life in the College and remains part of the curriculum for all girls in the College. Organised community service is an important feature of the extra-curricular life of the College for pupils from Year 10 and 11 and girls in the Sixth Form.

Education is about encouraging talent and developing new interests. Small classes ensure that each girl is given individual attention and a professional and dedicated staff enable pupils to achieve success in a wide range of areas both academic and extra-curricular. St Francis' is committed to the provision of an all-round education where each girl is valued and each can contribute towards enriching the life of the community. There are 505 pupils on roll of whom about 40 are boarders.

Girls are prepared for GCSE and Advanced Level examinations as well as for Oxford and Cambridge entrance. The majority of girls take 10 GCSE subjects and stay on into the Sixth Form from where they proceed to University and Higher Education. The Sixth Form is housed in a newly-created Sixth Form centre, with common rooms, quiet study areas and tutorial offices.

Admission. (*See Scholarship Entries section.*) Entrance to the College is by examination but due importance is also attached to school reports and interviews. Scholarships are available for entry at 7, 11, 13 and 16+.

Fees per term (2011-2012). Senior School: £3,925 (day), £7,720 (full boarding), £6,490 (weekly boarding 4 nights). Preparatory School: Kindergarten from £1,120 (morning) to £2,015 (full day including lunch); Infants (including lunch) £2,435; Prep III–VI: £2,915 (day), £6,665 (full boarding), £5,420 (weekly boarding 4 nights).

Charitable status. The St Francis' College Trust is a Registered Charity, number 287694. It has charitable status on three counts: it advances education, it provides an education founded on strong Christian ethos and it also helps many of its pupils financially by means of Scholarships and Bursaries.

St Gabriel's School

Sandleford Priory, Newbury, Berkshire RG20 9BD
Tel: 01635 555680
Fax: 01635 555698
e-mail: info@stgabriels.co.uk
website: www.stgabriels.co.uk

Church of England Independent Day School for Girls, in membership of GSA, AGBIS and IAPS.

Governing Body:
Mr S Barrett
Mrs S Bowen
Mr N Garland, BSc Hons (*Chairman*)
Mr A Hills
Dr L Hobby
Revd Mrs J Ramsbottom
Mrs A Rowse
Mr S Ryan
Mr M Scholl
Mrs M Steel

Principal: **Mr A Jones**, LTCL, LWCMD

Vice-Principal: Mrs C Sams, CertEd London (*Mathematics*)
Bursar & Clerk to Governors: Mr N Erskine, MCIM, CDipAF
Director of Studies: Mrs W Rumbol, BA Hons, PGCE, DMS (*French & Spanish*)
Head of Junior Department: Mr P Dove, BA Hons, PGCE
Head of Pre-Prep Department: Mrs J Bindloss Gibb, MA, DipSEN, DipSpLD
Pastoral Head, Years 7 & 8: Miss K Rayner, BSc Hons, QTS (*Biology*)
Pastoral Head, Years 9, 10, 11: Mrs R Wright, BSc Hons, PGCE (*Physical Education*)
Head of Sixth Form: Mrs C Reseigh, BA Hons, PGCE (*French*)

Senior School Teaching Staff:
* *Head of Department*

Mrs L Aikman, BA Hons, PGCE (*English & Drama*)
Mrs S Baxter, BEd, ACSD (**Drama*)
Mrs A Beake (*Science Technician*)
Mr P Berry, BEng Hons, PGCE (*Design Technology*)
Mrs S Brooks, BSc Hons (*Science Technician*)
Mrs J Cameron, BSc, PGCE (**Science & Challenge & Extension*)
Mrs C Causer, MA, BA Hons (*Latin & Classics*)
Mrs A Chicken, BA Hons, PGCE (*Mathematics & Academic Data Manager*)
Mrs K Cook (*Art Technician*)
Mr B Drew, BA Hons, QTS (**Art & Design Technology*)
Miss S Ferretti, BA Hons, PGCE (**Modern Foreign Languages, Italian & French*)

Mrs M Forsgren, BA Hons (*French & German*)
Mr J Franey, BSc, PGCE (*Physics*)
Mrs E Fraser, BA Hons Cantab, PGCE (*Politics*)
Mrs M Goodhead, Cert SpLD (*Individual Needs*)
Mrs A Greenwood, MSc, BSc Hons, PGCE (*Chemistry*)
Mr R Hall, BA Hons, FE Cert (**ICT Curriculum, Graphics & Photography*)
Ms S Hall, BA Hons, PGCE (*English*)
Mrs P Highton, BA Hons, PGCE (*Drama*)
Mrs R Horner, BEd Hons, DipSpLD (**Individual Needs*)
Mrs H Humphreys, BA Hons (*Dance*)
Ms M Hunter, BA Hons (*Art*)
Mr M Ives, MA, PGCE (**Latin & Classics*)
Mrs C James, BA Hons (*Mathematics*)
Mrs A Jennings, MSc, PGCE (**Food Technology*)
Mrs P Joseph, MEd (*Physical Education*)
Ms A Kazem, MA Cantab, PGCE (*French & Spanish*)
Miss A Keenleyside, BEd Hons (*Photography*)
Miss L Kelleher, BA Hons (**Dance*)
Mr B Lewis, MA Cantab, PGCE (**History & *Politics*)
Mrs S Lumley Kreysa, BA, CertEd (*Physical Education*)
Mrs P Lyons, BA Hons, PGCE (**Business Studies*)
Miss P Mannarelli, BA Hons, PGCE (*Italian & Spanish*)
Mr J Mannion, BA Hons, PGCE (**ICT in Teaching & Learning & History*)
Miss T Matthews, CertEd (*Religious Studies*)
Miss C McQuitty, MA Cantab, BA Hons, QTS (*Music*)
Mrs H Porter, BSc Hons, PGCE (*KS3 Science Coordinator*)
Miss R Quinn, BA Hons, QTS (*English*)
Ms H Rayner, BA Hons, PGCE (*Physics*)
Mrs J Ribeiro, BSc Hons, PGCE (**Psychology & *Sociology*)
Mrs R Robinson, BEd (*English*)
Mr A Ross, BA Hons, DPhil Oxon (*Latin & Classics*)
Miss C Searle, BEd (**Physical Education*)
Mrs S Sim, BSc Hons, PGCE (**Mathematics*)
Mrs S Syddall, BA, CertEd (*Mandarin*)
Dr P Tebbs, DPhil Oxon (**Music*)
Mrs A Thayer, MA Cantab (*English*)
Miss H Tomlinson, BSc, QTS (*Geography*)
Miss A Tweedie, BA Hons (**Religious Studies*)
Ms V Vaughan, BSc (*Mathematics*)
Mrs S Vines, BEd Hons (*Textiles Technology*)
Mrs A Walters, CertEd (*Food Technology*)
Mrs R Wildsmith (*Science Technician*)
Mrs P Willetts, BA Hons, PGCE (**Geography & *Economics*)
Mrs S Yeoman (*Technology Technician*)

Junior Department Teaching Staff:
Mrs S Cherrington, BA Hons, PGCE (*Modern Foreign Languages*)
Mrs A Cope, CertEd (*Form Tutor Year 4*)
Mrs M Davidson, BEd Hons (*Form Tutor Year 4*)
Miss V Fowler, BSc Hons, PGCE (*Form Tutor Year 4*)
Mrs C Harding, BSc Hons, PGCE (*Form Tutor Year 6*)
Mrs P Highton, BA Hons, PGCE (*Drama*)
Ms G Mead, BA Hons Ed, QTS (*Form Tutor Year 3*)
Mrs C Moriarty, BEd Hons, CertEd (*Form Tutor Year 5*)
Mrs A Pasternakiewicz, BEd Hons (*Form Tutor Year 6*)
Mrs R Robinson, BEd (*Form Tutor Year 5*)
Miss A J Smith, BEd Hons (*Lead Teacher – Challenge & Extension & Form Tutor Year 3*)

Pre-Prep Department Teaching Staff:
Mrs S Bloxsom, BA Hons (*Form Tutor Year 2*)
Mrs J Greenfield, CertEd (*Form Tutor Nursery*)
Mrs C Lawrence, BA Ed, PGCE (*Form Tutor Reception*)
Mrs S Webb, BSc Hons, PGCE (*Form Tutor Year 1*)

Teaching Assistants:
Ms C Adams
Mrs D Atkinson
Mrs J Garry
Mrs C O'Brien, NNEB

Miss M Russell

Examinations Officer: Mrs A Purnell, DipHE, PGCE
Librarian: Mrs A Borzoni, BA Hons, PG Dip
Medical Officer: Mrs M Bullock (*Matron*)

Visiting Music Staff:
Mrs E Begley, RGKNCM, CertEd (*Singing*)
Mr T Bott, BMus Hons, PG Dip (*Violin*)
Mr T Bryanton (*Guitar*)
Mr N Burrage, BA Hons (*Guitar, Drums*)
Mrs S Chappell, MA, BA Hons (*Piano*)
Mr N Cope (*Piano & Singing*)
Mrs J Frith, CT ABRSM (*Flute*)
Mr M Lijinsky, CT ABRSM (*Piano*)
Mrs C Millar, BA (*Bassoon*)
Mr S Parker, ALCM, LLCM, CT ABRSM (*Clarinet &
   Saxophone*)
Mrs H Rawstron, BA, LTCL (*Oboe*)
Mrs S Riddex, BA Hons, PECE, LTCHM, LESMD (*Cello*)
Mr N Streeter, CertEd (*Percussion*)
Mr P Tarrant, ARCM, CertEd (*Brass*)
Mrs V Toll, LRAM, CertEd (*Piano*)
Mr D Wirdnam, BA Hons, LRSM (*Flute*)

Administrative Staff:
Mrs J Benney (*Registrar*)
Mr G Eagles (*Assistant Bursar – Operations*)
Mrs J Goodman-Mills (*Transport Coordinator*)
Miss C Jackson (*Executive Secretary*)
Mrs P Jones (*Payroll Administrator*)
Mrs A Kail (*Data Manager*)
Mrs T Robinson (*School Secretary*)
Miss N Smith (*Marketing Assistant*)
Mrs S Thomas (*Bursar's Office Assistant*)
Mrs S Willson (*Assistant Bursar – Finance*)
Mrs J Wood (*HR Advisor*)

Number of Pupils. 489.

Visitors to St Gabriel's quickly recognise that this is no
ordinary school. From Nursery to Sixth Form they are struck
by the enthusiasm and sense of purpose of both staff and
pupils. Some parents choose St Gabriel's because of its reputation for achieving exceptional academic standards; others
welcome the individual attention which is given to all pupils.

Curriculum. The formal curriculum is broad and well-
balanced, providing an education that is both traditional and
forward-thinking. A choice of 26 subjects is offered at
GCSE of which English, English Literature, Mathematics,
all three sciences, a Modern Foreign Language and Religious Studies are compulsory. The majority of students take
10 subjects.

At Sixth Form, students choose four subjects to study to
AS Level from the 29 offered, with at least three being pur-
sued through to A Level. Students may also study for the
Extended Project Qualification.

Extra-Curricular Activities. As well as offering a thorough academic education, the school provides a wide range
of opportunities outside of the classroom. Numerous activities and visits extend and enrich the girls' learning experience throughout the school. The performing and creative
arts, sport and a wide range of clubs and societies ensure
that the girls progress to the next stage of their education
with confidence. Whether it is through The Duke of Edinburgh's Award or World Challenge, the girls constantly rise
to meet new challenges.

Music. There are two orchestras, four choirs a wide range
of ensembles including two string quartets, jazz and rock
bands and several woodwind ensembles. Any orchestral
instrument may be learned.

Sport. Netball, Hockey, Swimming, Rounders, Athletics,
Cross-Country, Dance, Gym and Tennis.

Facilities. State-of-the-art ICT and MFL block, multi-
disciplinary sports hall, digital theatre and dance studio.

Christian Community & Ethos. St Gabriel's has a
Church of England foundation but girls of other faiths are
welcome. A strong moral code and Christian values ensure
the girls leave the school as well-balanced, unpretentious,
spirited individuals with the confidence to be assertive and
decisive with warmth and without arrogance. The girls are
always encouraged and supported to resist pressures and to
have the confidence to make the right choices.

Supervised Prep. This is provided on a daily basis
between 4 pm and 6 pm.

Scholarships & Bursaries. Academic, Sport, Art,
Dance, Drama and Music scholarships are awarded at 11+
and 13+. Sixth Form scholarships are also awarded at 16+.
Full bursaries are available through the Montagu Award
scheme, which aims to ensure that St Gabriel's is accessible
to girls who would otherwise not be able to enjoy the unique
education the school offers.

Admission. Entry to the Junior School for girls aged
6–10 years is by assessment. An entrance exam is held in
January for entry at 11+ and 13+ and girls are accepted in to
the Sixth Form on the basis of their GCSE results and an
interview.

Fees per term (2011-2012). £4,260–£4,410.

Junior Department. (*See entry in IAPS section*).

Charitable status. The St Gabriel Schools Foundation is
a Registered Charity, number 1062748. It exists to provide
education for girls.

St George's School
Ascot

Ascot, Berks SL5 7DZ
Tel: 01344 629900
Fax: 01344 629901
e-mail: office@stgeorges-ascot.org.uk
website: www.stgeorges-ascot.org.uk

Member of GSA, AGBIS, BSA.

Governors:
Mr E Luker (*Chairman*)
Mr G W P Barber, MA Oxon, LVO
Mr P James
Mrs A Laurie-Walker, BSc, MSc
Mr J M G Markham, FCA
Mr A Miles, BSc, PGCE
Mrs H Pheysey
Revd K Ramsay
Mr C Tongue, MA Cantab

Headmistress: Mrs R Owens, MA Oxon, PGCE (*History*)

Bursar: Mrs J Wood, BA Hons Exeter, ACCA

Deputy Head: Miss S Moody, BSc Hons East Anglia,
   PGCE (*Mathematics*)

Assistant Head (Pastoral): Ms C Masters, TEFL, Dip Child
   Psych (*Head of Boarding*)

Assistant Head (Sixth Form): Miss J Mann, BSc Hons
   Southampton, PGCE (*Geography*)

Staff:
Miss K Alman, BA Hons Farnham UCA (*Resident Tutor*)
Mrs M Bruce, BSc Hons Bristol, TEFL Cert RSA/UCLES
   (*TEFL Coordinator*)
Mrs F Burrows, Maîtrise Toulouse, GTP (*French and
   Spanish*)
Mrs A Bushill, BSc Hons Southampton, PGCE (*Biology,
   Psychology*)
Mr A Carroll, BA Hons St Mary's University College,
   PGCE (*Drama*)

Mr I Charnock, BA Hons Wales, MA London, PGCE
(*History of Art, Film Studies*)
Mrs K Collingwood, BSc Hons Loughborough, PGCE
(*Physical Education*)
Miss R Cooper, BA Hons Reading (*Resident Tutor*)
Mrs S Cope, Licence d'histoire Orléans, PGCE (*French*)
Mr N Cudjoe-Calvocoressi, BA Hons Leicester, PGCE
(*Politics*)
Mrs S Davies, Cert TESOL Trinity (*EAL*)
Miss S Doodson, BSc Hons Leeds (*Resident Sports Coach*)
Mrs A Dourountakis-Coultan, BA Hons Durban, PG
Higher DipEd, ESL Diploma (*Religious Studies, History*)
Mrs L Errington, BEd Hons Durham (*English*)
Mrs C A Fidler, BA Hons Wolverhampton, PGCE (*Art*)
Miss L Fontes, BA Hons Leeds, PGCE (*Classical
Civilisation, Latin, French*)
Ms K Gilbert, BA Hons Chichester, PGCE (*Textiles*)
Mr P Goldsbrough, BSc Hons Nottingham, PGCE
(*Science*)
Miss C Graham, BA Hons Durham (*Resident Tutor*)
Mrs E Gregan, BA Hons Liverpool, PGCE (*Drama*)
Mrs S Hetherington, BSc OU (*Science, Markham
Housemistress*)
Mr I G Hillier, GLCM, FLCM, FCSM, FGMS, PGCE
(*Director of Music*)
Mr M Hodges, BSC London, PGCE (*Mathematics*)
Miss L Jackson, BA Hons University of Wales, PGCE
(*History*)
Mrs S Johnson, BSc Hons Exeter, PGCE (*Geography, RS,
PSEC*)
Mr T Lange, BEng Hons Coventry (*ICT*)
Mr N Lee, BD Hons London, BA Hons London, MA
London, PGCE (*English*)
Mrs C Lilley, BSc Hons London, PGCE (*Mathematics*)
Miss K Lofthouse, PT1 Cert Army (*Physical Education*)
Mrs A Mason (*Upper Sixth Housemistress*)
Miss P May, BMus Hons Edinburgh, PGDipAdv TCM
(*Music*)
Mr N Mohammad, HDipE Dublin, MA Punjab, BSc Punjab
(*Mathematics, ICT*)
Mr D Moran, BA Hons, PG Dip Info Mang (*Librarian,
Careers*)
Mrs A Morgan, BA Hons Dundee, PGCE (*Art, Textiles*)
Mrs W Moyles, BEd Hons London, CertEd (*English,
Learning Skills*)
Miss C Phipps, BA Hons Nottingham, PGCE (*Classics*)
Mrs V J Potter, BA Hons Lancaster, PGCE (*French,
History*)
Mrs D Ractliffe, CertEd, CTEFLA, DipTESOL Trinity
Miss D Schmidt, MSc Pretoria, BEd South Africa (*Physics*)
Mr T Sharkey, BA Hons Exeter, PGCE (*History*)
Mrs J Smith, BEd Hons Reading (*Chemistry*)
Mrs J Spooner, BSc Hons Birmingham, PGCE (*Science,
Psychology*)
Miss E Townsend, BA Hons East Anglia, PGCE (*Art,
Photography, Textiles*)
Miss A van Ravenstein, BEd Canterbury, NZ (*History,
Knatchbull Housemistress*)
Mr A Verma, PhD Nottingham, BA Hons Oxford, MBA
Nottingham (*Economics*)
Miss L Wilcockson, BA Hons University of the Arts
London (*Artist in Residence*)

Visiting Staff:
Mrs K Baldwin, FETC Reading (*Chinese*)
Mrs R Baxter, BA Hons, PGCE, DipSpLD (*Learning
Support*)
Mr N Beckett (*Golf Coach*)
Mrs N Bolt, Dip SEN (*Learning Support*)
Ms S Bullock, BA Hons University of Wales (*Harp*)
Mrs D Burt, LTCL, FTCL (*Flute*)
Mr T Carleston (*Singing*)
Mr J B Clark, BA (*Guitar*)
Mrs M Fitzgerald, DipS&D (*Speech & Drama*)

Mrs K Forrester (*Japanese*)
Ms R Frankland (*Squash Coach*)
Mrs D Head, LLCM (*Clarinet and Saxophone*)
Ms L Heath, BMus Hons, PGDip (*Double Bass*)
Mrs J Hooper, BComm Hons, DipSpLD (*Learning
Support*)
Mrs S Huggins (*German*)
Mr N Ingham (*Tennis Coach*)
Mrs E Lee, MMus Moscow Conservatoire (*Piano*)
Ms P Leybourne (*Aerobics*)
Miss L Mogford (*Netball Coach*)
Mr S Perkins, BMus (*Violin*)
Ms H Rawaf (*Arabic*)
Mrs E Roberts (*Italian*)
Mr R S Smith (*Percussion*)
Mrs F Smyth, MSc Reading (*Turkish*)
Mrs K Stanley, BMus Hons (*Piano*)
Mr M Stanley, BMus, ARCM (*Piano*)
Mrs M Strain (*Russian*)
Mrs T Velazquez (*Spanish*)
Mrs A P Watson, BA Hons (*Singing*)

Support Staff:
Deputy Bursar: Mr M Heather, ACIB
Bursar's Assistant: Mrs K Beddell, CA, BAcc
Bursar's Assistant: Mrs T Barber
PA to the Headmistress: Mrs J Witt
School Secretaries: Mrs S Alexander, Mrs D Macro
School Administrator: Mrs C Reader
Senior Administrator: Mrs A Revell
Registrar: Mrs R Lloyd, BA Hons London
Examinations Secretary: Mrs A Shevills
General Services Manager: Mrs S Hemchaoui
School Doctor: Dr L Gardner, MB BS
School Nurse: Mrs S Horth, RNG General & Paediatric
School Matron: Mrs J Pittard, RGN
School Chaplain: Revd J Sistig, MTh Kwa-Zulu Natal
Theatre Technician: Mr R Pearn, BA Hons Leeds
Art & Design Technician: Mr C Esling, HND Portsmouth
College of Art & Design
Science Technicians: Miss S Bale, Mrs C Grater
IT Manager: Mr S Kerwood
Cover Supervisor: Mrs V Foss

St George's is a School with approximately 300 girls, half
boarders and half day girls. There are 80 in the Sixth Form.
The boarders are arranged in house groups, dependent upon
their age. The small size enables all the staff to take a personal interest in each pupil and each pupil is assigned a personal tutor. The school work is planned to give a good
general education for girls in classes of 12–18. A high academic standard is maintained without subjecting the girls to
undue pressure and there is a happy and friendly atmosphere. Both day girls and boarders benefit from a full programme of activities into the evenings.

The School stands on high ground with lovely views in a
beautiful estate. There are 8 floodlit hard tennis courts, a
heated swimming pool, an extensive sports field for lacrosse
and athletics and a magnificent Sports Hall. Other sports
played include netball, rounders and football. There are four
science laboratories, music school and computer rooms.
There is a computer network which provides each girl with
her own e-mail address, computer/network access from
every classroom, common room and senior bedroom. A
multi-purpose Hall opened in September 2002 for Drama,
Music performances and teaching. It is an extremely versatile space allowing a huge range of events to take place, such
as Prize Giving, Parents Evenings and other school occasions.

The health of the girls is under the supervision of a registered nurse and the school doctor attends at least twice a
week.

Curriculum. The curriculum includes English Language, English Literature, Drama and Theatre Studies,

Mathematics, Information Technology, Combined Science, Biology, Chemistry, Physics, Latin/Classics, French, German, Spanish, Geography, History, Economics, Politics, Religious Studies, Psychology, Critical Thinking, Art, History of Art, Textiles, Music, PE. Girls are prepared for GCSE, and, in the Sixth Form, for AS and A2 examinations, as well as for Oxbridge entrance. Girls may also study for the AQA Baccalaureate in addition to A Levels. Girls throughout the school work towards the examinations of the Associated Board of the Royal School of Music, LAMDA in Acting and Verse and Prose, and Computer Literacy and Information Technology. Girls are given full advice about careers and Higher Education.

At weekends girls take part in a wide variety of recreational activities including drama, art, music, cooking, photography, sport, Duke of Edinburgh's Award Scheme, first aid courses, school matches and visits to theatres and concerts, art galleries, etc, in London. Girls are encouraged to follow some form of social service.

Entrance. Applicants take the Common Entrance examination for Girls' Independent Schools. The normal age range is 11+ and 13+. Sixth Form entry requires at least 6 GCSEs at A* to C, with preferably a B grade in subjects to be studied at A Level.

Fees per term (2011-2012). £9,460 Boarding, £6,150 Day.

Scholarships. Scholarships are available at 11+ and 13+ for outstanding potential, as evidenced by examination results. Art and Music scholarships and instrumental awards are available at 11+ and Art, Music, Drama and PE scholarships at 13+.

Extra Subjects. Other languages (including Mandarin), Music (most instruments), Speech and Drama, Ballet, Modern Stage and Tap Dancing, Individual Tennis, Dry Skiing, Polo, Riding and Yoga.

Charitable status. St George's School Ascot Trust Limited is a Registered Charity, number 309088. It exists to provide independent secondary girls' education.

St Helen & St Katharine

Faringdon Road, Abingdon, Oxon OX14 1BE
Tel: 01235 520173
Fax: 01235 532934
e-mail: info@shsk.org.uk
website: www.shsk.org.uk

The School was founded in 1903 and is a Church of England Independent Day School for girls. There are around 660 girls of whom 160 are in the Sixth Form.

Governors:
Miss J E Cranston (*Chairman*)

Ms A J Allden
Professor K M Burk
Mrs P E Cakebread
His Hon Judge H W P Eccles
Mr J Gabitass
Revd J Herapath
Mrs R M Kashti
Mrs H Knight
Mr D J Lea

Mr I Mason
Mrs D M May
Miss B O'Connor
Dr M Oppenheimer
Mrs P A Penney
Mr G Steinsberg
Mrs S Tinson
Mr I Todd
Mr J J H Wormell

Clerk to the Governors: Mrs K E J Wait

Headmistress: Miss R Edbrooke, BEd Hons Bedford

Bursar: Mr D Eley, BSc, ACA
Deputy Headmistress: Mrs B Stubley, MA Greenwich, PGCE

Assistant Head, Director of Students: Mrs L Hughes, BA Warwick, PGCE
Assistant Head, Director of Staff (from January 2012): Mr J Hunt, MA St Andrews, QTS
Chaplain: Revd J Taft, BA Sheffield, Dip Biblical & Theological Studies OU, PGCE
Head of Upper School: Mrs J Armstrong, BSc Leeds, PGCE
Head of Middle School: Mrs C Douglas, BA London, PGCE
Head of Lower School: Mrs K Taylor, BA Wales, PGCE

Head of Year 13: Mr O Hogben, BA Warwick, PGCE
Head of Year 12: Mrs A Mobbs, BSc Cardiff, MSc OU, PGCE
Head of Year 11: Mrs C Russell, BSc London, PGCE
Head of Year 10: Mr P Moylan, BA Oxon, PGCE
Head of Year 9: Ms K Meuleman, BEd Eeklo, Belgium, PG Worcester
Head of Year 8: (*to be appointed*)
Head of Year 7: Mrs H Nash, BA Southampton, PGCE
Head of Juniors (Year 5 & 6): Mrs C Sánchez, BMus London, PGCE

Art, Design and Technology:
Mrs J McDonald, MA RCA, ATC London
Mr B Drew, BA London, QTS
Mrs C Langston, BA Middlesex, PGCE
Mr K Stiles, BA Falmouth, PGCE
Miss H McCague, BA UWE, PGCE

Business Studies & Economics:
Mrs C McKenna, BSc Manchester, PGCE

Higher Education and Careers:
Mrs J Armstrong, BSc Leeds, PGCE, Adv Cert CEG
Mrs D Croft, Tech IOSH, MInstLM
Mr O Hogben, BA Warwick, PGCE
Mrs D Laidlaw, BA London
Mrs J Bridge, BA Liverpool, Grad CIPD

Classics:
Mrs E Poole, MA Cantab, CertEd
Mrs J Shearan, MA Oxon, PGCE
Mrs J Twaits, MA Cantab, PGCE
Mrs S Butcher, BA Reading, PGCE

Drama and Theatre Studies:
Ms J Watt, BA Durham, PGCE
Mr O Hogben, BA Warwick, PGCE
Mrs M Mason, BA Dublin, PGCE
Mr A Verjee, BA UEA
Miss R Pearmain, BA London

English:
Mrs C Nash, MA Oxon, PGCE
Mrs S Hughes-Morgan, BA Exeter, PGCE
Mrs E Haines, BA Oxon, PGCE
Dr F Macdonald, BA, MSc, DPhil Oxon, PGCE
Mrs M Mason, BA Dublin, PGCE
Mrs H Nash, BA Southampton, PGCE

Examinations Officer:
Mrs C Cooper, BSc Salford, PGCE

Food & Nutrition:
Mrs G Grant-Ross, BEd Liverpool, CertEd

General Studies:
Ms S Hayward, BA Durham, PGCE

Geography:
Mr R Delacour, MSc Liverpool, BSc Surrey, PGCE
Ms L Snowdon, BA London, PGCE
Mrs C Douglas, BA London, PGCE

Government and Politics:
Mrs E Poole, MA Cantab, CertEd
Dr L Gribble, MA Münster, DPhil Oxon, PGCE

Mrs B Stubley, MA Greenwich, PGCE

History:
Miss D Smith, BA Durham, PGCE
Dr L Gribble, MA Münster, DPhil Oxon, PGCE
Mrs L Hughes, BA Warwick, PGCE
Mrs B Stubley, MA Greenwich, PGCE

History of Art:
Ms E Cobb, MA Manchester Met, BA OU, BEd Bristol,
    CertEd

Information Technology:
Mr P Burnett, BSc Manchester, PGCE
Mrs F Fisher, BA Oxon, PGCE

Junior Department:
Mrs C Sánchez, BMus London, PGCE
Miss J Wright, BA Napier, PGCE

Library:
Mrs D Pocock Bell, BA Wales, MA London
Mrs K Gray, BSc Manchester, Dip IPM
Mrs E Dickens, BA Birmingham

Mathematics:
Mr C Morris, MA Oxon, PGCE
Mrs J Campbell, BSc Bristol, PGCE
Miss N Copeman, BSc Coventry, PGCE
Mrs P Hall, BSc Exeter, PGCE
Miss S Kennedy, MA Cantab, PGCE
Mrs M Moore, BSc Lancaster, PGCE
Mr P Moylan, BA Oxon, PGCE
Mrs C Russell, BSc London, PGCE

Medical:
Dr H Hodgson, MBBS
Mrs F Campbell, BEd Durham
Nurse A Dexter, RGN
Nurse C Swales, RGN

Modern Languages:
Miss L Hillier, BA Exeter, PGCE
Mrs M Delvaux-Abbott, CFS Liège, Dip French Alliance
    Française, Brussels
Mrs L Astbury, BA Birmingham, PGCE
Miss J Attia, MA Nice, QTS
Dr G Clark, MA Cantab, DPhil Oxon, PGCE
Mrs C Fisher, Milan, BA Milan, PGCE
Mrs L Fuller, MA Oxon, PGCE
Mrs K Taylor, BA Wales, PGCE
Mr J Earnshaw-Crofts, MA London, BA Reading, PGCE
Mrs L Littlejohn, MA Cantab, PGCE

Music:
Ms H Rakowski, BA, MA Oxon, PGCE
Mr A Knowles, MA Oxon, FRCO, PGCE
Miss H Birt, BA Oxon, PG Dip Viola, PG Dip Baroque
    Violin (*Head of Strings*)
Mr P Foster, LTCL (*Head of Wind and Brass*)
Miss P Grant, BA Oxon (*Head of Singing*)
Miss F Parker, BA, LLCM (*Band Master, French Horn*)
Miss J Thomas, BMus Birmingham, PGCE (*Singing*)
Miss J Broome, MA Cantab (*Harp*)
Miss A Brunton, MA, BMus, LRAM, LGSM, PGCE
    (*Oboe*)
Mr R Burley, ALCM, LLCM (*Guitar*)
Mr R E Cutting, RMSM Kneller Hall (*Brass*)
Miss R Gladstone, BA, MA Cantab (*Cello*)
Miss E Harré, LRAM, GRSM, Dip Ex Sc (*Double Bass*)
Mrs H S Haskell, ARCM (*Violin and Viola*)
Miss E Hayes, Dip RCM, CTABRSM (*Head of Keyboard*)
Dr R Manasse, BSc London, DPhil Cantab (*Flute*)
Mr D McNaughton, BA Oxon (*Brass*)
Mrs S E Mears, MA Oxon, LRAM, PGCE, DipHSWOU
    (*Piano*)
Mr W Dutta, BMus, LTCL (*Piano*)
Miss O Newbold, BMus, PG Dip, MMus (*Piano*)

Mrs A Phillips, BMus RCM, ARCMPg, ARCM (*Singing*)
Mr M Parkin, BMus (*Percussion*)
Miss H Morgan, MMus Perf, BMus (*Clarinet*)
Miss C Scott, BA Oxon, MMus Perf, PPRNCM (*Clarinet*)
Mr N Somerville, BA, ARCM, LTCL, ABSM (*Brass*)
Miss A Strevens, MA, BSc, SRAST M, BSCH (*Flute*)
Mr R Thorne, BA Mus, A Mus A (*Flute*)
Mr R Thompson, PG Dip, BMus, ATCL, ALCM (*Piano*)
Mr G Williams, LRAM, ARCM, FTCL, FLCM, MSTAT,
    PGCE (*Bassoon, Clarinet & Saxophone*)
Mr S Wilson, BA Oxon (*Cello*)

Personal Social & Health Education:
Mrs F Fisher, BA Oxon, PGCE

Physical Education:
Mrs S Wilson, MA OU, BSc Brunel, QTS
Mrs J Chilvers, FTI
Mrs S Evans, IM Marsh CPE, CertEd
Miss S Furneaux, BSc Exeter
Miss D James, BEd Exeter
Mrs S Keogh, BSc Birmingham, QTS
Mrs A Wilson, BEd Brunel
Dr M Leigh, BSc, MSc, PhD Newcastle
Mrs M Moore, BSc Lancaster, PGCE
Mrs C Russell, BSc London, PGCE

Psychology:
Mrs C Canlan-Shaw, BSc Loughborough, PGCE
Mrs K Collett, BSc Worcester, PGCE

Religious Studies:
Ms S Hayward, BA Durham, PGCE
Ms K Meuleman, BEd Eeklo, Belgium, PG Worcester
Mr J Williams, MTheol St Andrews, PGCE

Science:
Mrs G Lydford, BSc UEA, QTS
Miss C Bulmer, MSc Oxon, MSc Roehampton, PGCE
Mrs J Edwards, BSc Nottingham, PGCE
Mrs J Armstrong, BSc Leeds, PGCE
Dr T Bainbridge, BSc Leeds, PhD London, PGCE
Mrs D Jackson, MSc OU, BSc Keele, PGCE
Dr C Holyoak, BSc Manchester, DPhil Manchester
    Metropolitan
Mrs K Homann, MA Cantab, PGCE
Mrs R Kingcombe, BSc Bristol, MSc Oxon, PGCE
Dr M Leigh, BSc, MSc, PhD Newcastle
Mr T Marjot, BSc London, PGCE
Mrs A Mobbs, MSc OU, PGCE

Special Educational Needs Coordinator:
Mrs S Lindsay, Cert SpLD, Dip SpLD

Admissions Officer: Mrs J Wilmore
Headmistress's PA: Mrs J Pointer

St Helen and St Katharine is located on the outskirts of
Abingdon within easy reach of Oxford and surrounding villages. An extensive network of school buses, shared with
Abingdon School and the Manor Preparatory School facilitates access from as far afield as Newbury, Faringdon, Witney, Woodstock, Thame, Henley and Reading. The school is
situated in extensive grounds which include netball and tennis courts, lacrosse pitches and an athletics track.

Buildings. The original school building dates from 1906.
In recent years an extensive building programme has been
undertaken. Most recent developments include a Performing
Arts Centre with studio theatre, dance studio and extensive
music rooms, a refurbished refectory and new Sports Centre
with fitness suite. An exceptional library facility which
includes ICT Suites, lecture theatre, careers library and a
sixth form study area was opened in 2010.

Curriculum. The school encourages girls to maintain a
broad and balanced curriculum which includes the following
subjects: Art, Biology, Business Studies, Ceramics, Chemistry, Classics, Design Technology, Drama and Theatre Stud-

ies, Economics, English Language, English Literature, Food Studies, French, Geography, German, Government and Politics, Greek, History, History of Art, ICT, Italian, Latin, Mathematics, Further Mathematics, Music, Physical Education, Physics, Pottery, Psychology, Religious Studies, and Spanish. A programme of citizenship and personal, social and health education encourages girls to be responsible for themselves and take care of others. The school has its own Chapel in which a weekly Eucharist is offered to staff and girls.

Music and Drama. The school has a very strong musical tradition with many girls learning at least one instrument. Tuition is provided in all major instruments including the harp and organ. There are numerous orchestras, choirs and ensembles that cater for all abilities and achieve significant recognition and success in festivals and competitions. The drama department, based in the Performing Arts Centre, delivers a busy schedule of productions of the highest quality making it a popular and rewarding part of the extra-curricular programme as well as supporting significant success and GCSE and A Level.

Sports. Sport is a key part of school life. Competitive teams at all age groups are involved in lacrosse, netball, hockey, athletics, tennis and rounders. There is also a wide range of recreational sports clubs available including dance, tai chi, sailing, swimming, fencing, trampoline, basketball, gym and football.

Societies. All pupils are encouraged to take part in the wide range of extra-curricular activities available. Of particular note are The Duke of Edinburgh's Award Scheme and Young Enterprise Programme which enjoy a strong tradition in the school.

St Helen's has strong links with Abingdon School and in the Sixth Form selected subjects are taught jointly. The close relationship between the two schools also enables music, drama and debating as well as many social events to take place together.

Admission, Scholarships and Bursaries. Admissions at ages 9+, 10+, 11+, 13+ and 16+. An entrance examination is held in January for 9+, 10+ and 11+ and in November for 13+ for admission in the following September. Girls are accepted into the Sixth Form on the basis of their GCSE results and an interview. There may be occasional vacancies in other years of the school.

Academic scholarships up to 1/8th of the school fee are awarded on merit following the entry assessments into Years 7 and 9, at ages 11+ and 13+. Governors Scholarships for the Sixth Form are awarded after exams and interviews for current and new pupils. Music scholarships covering the cost of tuition in one or two instruments may be awarded on merit in all years from 11+. There are also exhibitions for Art and Music recognising special ability, for which an award of £100 is made.

Bursaries up to 100% of the fees are available to pupils from Year 7 and are based on a means-tested assessment of financial circumstances.

Fees per term (2011-2012). £3,945.

Charitable status. The School of St Helen and St Katharine Trust is a Registered Charity, number 286892. The Trust was established to promote and provide for the advancement of education of children in the United Kingdom and elsewhere; such education to be designed to give a sound Christian and moral basis to all pupils.

St Helen's School

Eastbury Road, Northwood, Middlesex HA6 3AS
Tel: 01923 843210
Fax: 01923 843211
e-mail: enquiries@sthn.co.uk
website: www.sthn.co.uk

Founded 1899.
   Independent Day School for Girls.
   Member of GSA and IBO.

Council of Governors:
Chairman: Ms R Faunch, MSc Manchester
Dr D J Chivers, MA, PhD, ScD
Mr M Clark, MSc London
Professor V Isham, PhD, DLC, BSc, ARCS
Mrs J Kirchheimer, BVetMed, MRCVS
Mrs J Lewis, BSc, FCIPD
Mrs A Little, BA Cantab
Mr T R Roydon, BSc London, MBA Pittsburgh
Mrs M Weerasekera, Mont Dip
Ms S Woolfson, BSc, FCA

Staff:

Head: **Dr M Short**, BA London

Deputy Head: Mr P Tiley, BSc Bristol
Deputy Head: Mrs J Parker, BA Liverpool

Head of Sixth Form: Mr H Dymock, BA Durham, MA London
Head of Upper School: Mrs D Sinclair, MA London
Head of Middle School: Mrs C Hill, BA Newcastle
Head of Junior School: Mrs K Serinturk, BEd London
Head of Little St Helen's: Miss J Chaventré, BEd West Sussex
Professional Development Manager: Mrs A Weaver, MA St Andrews
Resources Director and Clerk to the Council: Mr R Ukiah, MA Oxon

IB Coordinator: Mrs M Bowman, BEd Leeds
Deputy Head of Sixth Form: Miss E McKinley, BA Heriot-Watt; Dr A Berriman, PhD Nottingham Trent, BA Bristol
Deputy Head of Upper School: Mrs K Newby, BA Loughborough; Miss K Baker, BSc Southampton
Deputy Head of Middle School: Mrs J Barton, BA Oxford Brookes; Mrs E Serrano, Gilologia Inglesa Degree Madrid; Mrs L Kingston, BA De Montfort
Deputy Head of Junior School: Mrs K Head, BEd London; Mrs E Sami, BEd Herts
Acting Deputy Head of Junior School: Mrs M Pratt, BA Griffith, PDipEd Queensland
Deputy Head of Little St Helen's: Mrs S Begley, MPhil Pontypridd, BSc Bangor; Mrs D Smith, BEd Warwick

* *Head of Department*

Art:
*Mrs V Wichel, BA Bristol
Mrs L Kingston, BA De Montfort
Mr P Wiciel, CertEd
Mrs J Restick, BA London Guildhall (*Technician*)

Careers:
*Miss E McKinley, BA Heriot-Watt
Mr H Dymock, BA Durham, MA London

Classics:
*Mr K Buck, BA Johannesburg
Dr A Berriman, PhD Nottingham Trent, BA Bristol

Design and Technology:
*Mr B Gee, MA OU
Mrs K Gibbons, BSc Nottingham Trent
Mrs L Hallam, BA Middlesex
Mr R Shaikh, BA Brighton
Mr C Falco, BSc South Bank (*Technician*)

Drama:
*Mrs M Connell, BA Manchester
Mrs K Newby, BA Loughborough
Mrs D Sinclair, MA London

Economics & Business Studies:
*Mrs M Bowman, BEd Leeds
Mrs F Britten, BEd UWE, BSc OU
Mr J Firestone, MA Brighton
Mr M Hoffman, BA S Africa

English:
*Mr R Johnston, BA Liverpool
Miss H Boobis, MA Cantab
Mrs J Cox, BA Durham
Mr T Gerig, BA Illinois
Miss L Kennedy, BA Liverpool
Mrs V Lumley, MA Manchester
Mrs J Threlfall, BA Leicester

Geography:
*Miss E Rynne, MA London
Mrs C Beake, BA London
Mr D Froggatt, BSc Cardiff

Government & Politics:
*Mr B Nemko, BA Birmingham, MSc City, MA London
Mr P Whalley, BA Portsmouth

History:
*Mr B Nemko, BA Birmingham, MSc City, MA London
Miss H Anderson, MA St Andrews
Miss L Hamilton, MA Manchester, MA St Andrews
Mrs C Hill, BA Newcastle
Mrs R Reidel-Fry, MA Courtauld, MA, MPhil Columbia
   (*History of Art*)
Mrs A Weaver, MA St Andrews

Information and Communications Technology:
*Mr M Hoffman, BA S Africa
Mr J Firestone, MA Brighton
Mrs K Palamarchuk, MA Crakow
Mr R Shaikh, BA Brighton
Mrs S Standen (*Technician*)

Mathematics:
*Miss C Kerry, BEng London
Miss H Blazewicz, BSc Bristol
Dr J Donovan, PhD, MEd, MSc London
Mrs S King, BEng Bristol
Mrs S Michaels, BSc Manchester
Mr C Norris, BSc Royal Holloway
Mrs T Onac, BSc London
Mrs A Pateli, CertEd St Mary's College
Mrs A Stiff, BA Liverpool

Modern Languages:
*Mr E Terris, BA London

French:
*Mr E Terris, BA London
Miss J Birkett, BA London
Miss L Louiset, BA, MA Antilles
Mrs J Orme, BA Durham
Mrs S de Vaux-Balbirnie, BA Reading (*EAL*)

German:
Mrs J Parker, BA Liverpool
Mr D Weinmann, BSc Kent
Mrs N Wright, BA Manchester

Italian:
Mrs N O'Hagan, CertEd

Japanese:
Mrs M Ishikawa, MA London

Mandarin:
*Mrs N Wright, BA Manchester
Mrs G Shen, BA Tainan, MA Bath
Mrs B Lee, BEng China

Spanish:
*Mrs E Serrano, Filología Inglesa Degree Madrid
Mrs R Chaperlin, BA Birmingham

Miss E McKinley, BA Heriot-Watt
Mrs J Orme, BA Durham
Mr D Weinmann, BSc Kent
Mrs C Gauci (*Language Assistant*)

Music:
Director of Music: Mr R Crowley, BMus London, MSc
   Herts, ARAM, DipRAM
Mrs R Yates, GRSM, LRAM, ARCM

Visiting Music:
Ms C Barry, BA Dublin, LTCL
Miss J Chen, BSc London, DipRAM
Miss E Coleman, BMus, MA Chichester
Mr A Francis, Prof Cert LRAM
Mrs S Furzey, ATCL, ALCM
Mr A Gathercole, GGSM, ALCM
Mrs S Gregory, LRAM, LTCL
Mr C Hooker, ARAM, DipRAM
Mr P Judge, LTCL
Miss D Kemp, MA Oxon, DipRCM, ARCM
Miss R Krbilkova, DiS Pardubice Conservatory Czech
   Republic
Mrs S Lawman, ARCM, GRSM
Mr J Little, BA Central St Martins, DipTCM
Mr I Marcus
Mrs D Martin, BMus, PGDip, LRAM
Mr N Martin
Mr A McAfee, BA Nottingham Trent, PG Cert
Mrs N Tait, Prof Cert LRAM
Mr K Tomita, MMus, BMus
Mr M Vishnick, MSc, LLCM TD, ALCM

Physical Education:
*Mrs R Jackman, CertEd Bedford
Mrs A Arnot, BEd Bedford
Mrs J Ball, BEd Manchester Metropolitan
Mrs J Barton, BA Oxford Brookes
Mr K Dunne, BSc Sydney
Miss E Harris, BA Beds
Miss S Heath, MA Brunel
Miss K Hudson, NVQ3 (*Dance Coach*)
Miss J Huggett, BA Sydney
Miss C Lusted, BSc Brunel

Psychology:
*Dr S Brown, BA Reading, MA Lancaster, MA Brunel,
   MEd East Anglia, PhD Exeter
Mr G Marshall, BSc Cantab, MSc London

Religious Studies & Philosophy:
*Miss V Chamberlain, MA Cantab, MA Oxon
Mr H Dymock, BA Durham, MA London
Mr A Giblin, BA Lancaster
Mr E McCartney, BSc London
Miss H Williams, MA Edinburgh

Science:
Head of Science: Mr S Inger, BSc East Anglia

Biology:
*Dr J Mynett, PhD, BSc Leeds
Miss K Baker, BSc Southampton
Mrs K Barnes, BSc Leeds
Mr J Salmon, MA Cantab
Mrs V Wickens, BSc London
Mrs Z Alidina (*Technician*)

Chemistry:
*Mr M Reynish, BSc York
Mrs J Arthur, BSc Reading
Dr G Bates, PhD Southampton
Dr C Jones, PhD London, BSc Nottingham Trent
Mr P Tiley, BSc Bristol
Mrs S Wardley, BSc Southampton
Mrs Y O'Connor (*Technician*)
Mrs B Lee (*Technician*)

Physics:
*Mrs A Adlam, BSc Southampton, MSc London
Mr C Le Bas, BSc Edinburgh
Mr S Inger, BSc East Anglia
Mrs S Williams, BSc Exeter
Mrs E Jacob (*Technician*)
Mr C Watters (*Technician*)

Library:
*Ms E Howard, BA, ALA Chartered Librarian
Mrs F Ayache
Mrs S Gleave
Mrs G Hill, BA, DipLib (*Archivist*)

Junior Department:
Head: Mrs K Serinturk, BEd London
Deputy Head: Mrs K Head, BEd London
Acting Deputy Head: Mrs M Pratt, BA Griffith, PDipEd
   Queensland
Deputy Head: Mrs E Sami, BEd Herts
Mrs L Bain, NNEB Uxbridge
Mrs D Brooks, DipSW, BSc London
Mrs A Cawthorne, BSc Surrey, MA Middlesex
Mrs J Cheetham
Mrs L Crawford
Mrs A Dewhurst, BEd Melbourne
Mrs J Edward, CACHE 3
Miss S English, BA Portsmouth
Miss L Fox, BEd Birmingham
Miss G Furphy, BEd London
Mr D Gaffney, BA John Moores, MA St Mary's
Mrs A Gourley, BA Waikato New Zealand
Mrs A Groves, BA Brunel
Mrs T Hopkins, NVQ3
Mrs J Hunt, BEd Herts
Miss J Van Krinks
Mrs N Lawson, BA Bath
Mrs C Lax, BEd Manchester Metropolitan
Mrs K Palamarchuk, MA Crakow
Mrs P Prosser, BEd Durham
Mrs S Sharma, BA Surrey
Miss L Steerwood, BA St Mary's
Mrs M Tanna, NVQ2
Mrs R Tukia, BEd Massey University New Zealand

Pre-Preparatory Department (Little St Helen's):
Head: Miss J Chaventré, BEd West Sussex
Deputy Head: Mrs S Begley, MPhil Pontypridd, MSc
   Bangor
Deputy Head: Mrs D Smith, BEd Warwick
Mrs D Allsopp, Mont Dip London
Miss H Corbett, BA Manchester Metropolitan
Mrs L Crawford
Miss L Crocker, BEd Cambridge
Mrs N Johar, BA Brunel
Miss R Kansagra, BA Leeds
Mrs A Lam, BA Essex
Miss H Manber, BA Birmingham
Miss D Masters, BEd Oxon
Mrs K Palamarchuk, MA Crakow
Mrs D Roberts, BA Surrey
Mrs R Sirera, BA MA Manchester
Mrs C Smithers, HEd Junior Primary South Africa
Mrs T Wood, BA Surrey
Mrs M Da Rocha (*Teaching Assistant*)
Mrs G Davis, NVQ3 Early Years (*Teaching Assistant*)
Mrs P Edwards (*Teaching Assistant*)
Mrs F Gallagher, NNEB Uxbridge (*Teaching Assistant*)
Mrs A Player, NNEB London (*Teaching Assistant*)
Mrs D Ransom, BA Herts (*Teaching Assistant*)
Mrs S Sharman, Mont Dip (*Teaching Assistant*)
Mrs T Shearwood, NVQ3 Early Years (*Teaching Assistant*)
Mrs E Speed, CLANSA (*Teaching Assistant*)
Mrs P Spokes, NVQ3 Early Years (*Teaching Assistant*)
Mrs D Thakrar, NVQ3 Early Years (*Teaching Assistant*)

Mrs A Miah, NNEB Chiltern (*Welfare Assistant*)
Miss N Coburn, CACHE Dip (*Gap Student*)
Miss G Knox, CACHE Dip (*Gap Student*)

Administration:
Accountant: Mr D Dhrona, FCCA
Accounts Assistants: Mrs C Jay, MAAT; Miss E Simpson,
   BSc Oxford Brookes, ACCA; Mr A Shah
Admissions and Marketing Manager: Miss K Ogden, BA
   Birmingham
Admissions Secretary: Mrs L Hailey
Registrar: Miss S Heath, MA Brunel
Marketing Assistant: Miss H Palmer, BA Kingston
Domestic Bursar: Mrs L Toms
Estates Manager: Ms A Steele, BA Manchester
Examinations Officer: Miss C Murphy
Human Resources Manager: Mrs S Hart, BSc, MIPD
IT Systems & Projects Manager: Mr D Nanton
Senior IT Technician: Mr I Bremner, BEng Southampton
IT Technicians: Mr S Bhambra, BSc Herts; Miss L
   Tsikkos, BSc Bucks Chilterns
AV Technician: Mrs J Dean
Office Coordinator: Mrs S Page
Front Office Assistant: Mrs S Welsh
PA to the Head: Mr D McLaren
Head's Secretary: Mrs J Phillips
PA to Head of Junior School: Mrs J Botten
PA to Head of Little St Helen's: Mrs L Jones, Mrs L
   Quilley
Resources Assistant: Dr E Green, PhD St Thomas's
Secretaries: Mrs K Campbell, Mrs F Kahan, Mrs A Nunes,
   Mrs L Quilley, Mrs V Sharwood-Smith, Mrs L Sheerin
Junior School Technician: Mrs J Webb
CCF Coordinator: Mrs P Cullen, BSc, MSc London
Breakfast Club Supervisor: Mrs D Ransom, Foundation
   Degree Early Years
Breakfast Club Assistant: Mrs S Hamirani
After School Club Coordinator: Rev A Jacobs, NVQ3
After School Club Assistants: Mrs H Collen-Jones; Mrs D
   Brooks, DipSW, BSc London; Mrs D Bowles; Mrs M
   Tanna
School Nurses: Sister S Shackman, RGN; Mrs J
   Godecharle, SRN/RSCN
School Counsellor/Independent Listener: Mrs M Abedian

St Helen's School has a commitment to academic excellence that has given us an enviable reputation for over 100 years. We provide an excellent academic education for able girls, developing personal integrity alongside intellectual, creative and sporting talents. The staff are highly qualified and enthusiastic, the facilities are excellent, discipline is good and we know and care for every individual pupil.

Above all we encourage all the girls at St Helen's to chase their dreams and achieve a successful and fulfilling life.

The school is divided into three departments: Little St Helen's (3+ to 7), Junior School (7+ to 11) and Senior School (11+ to 18), enabling continuity and progression in the education of every pupil. Main entries are at 3+, 4+, 7+, 11+ and 16+.

St Helen's has an excellent academic record and girls achieve outstanding results in public examinations at all levels. In our flourishing Sixth Form there are approximately 160 girls. The International Baccalaureate Diploma and A Levels are offered in the Sixth Form, with girls able to choose from over 20 subjects and going on to prestigious universities, including Oxford and Cambridge.

The curriculum is designed to enable every girl to achieve intellectual and personal fulfilment and to develop her talents to the full. We support the aims of the National Curriculum, but offer a wider range of subjects and teach to greater depth, so enabling the girls to explore their interests and talents. The staff are subject specialists whose aim is to inspire a love of their subjects. They help the girls to learn how to study independently and develop good study habits, through stimulating and rigorous teaching. All girls in Senior School study two modern foreign languages together with Latin. Science is taught throughout the Senior School as three separate subjects. We expect the girls to study with commitment and we attach particular importance to the diligent and prompt completion of homework assignments. Music, Art, Drama and Sport are all an integral part of the life of the school and involve every girl. Many also take extra Music, Ballet, Speech and Drama lessons and Games coaching.

Girls take a full part in the broader life of the school and, through extra-curricular activities, discover interests to complement their academic achievements. Clubs and societies abound and we have a flourishing programme of optional outdoor and adventurous activities. A vertical House system also thrives which girls help to run, and all participate in inter-House competitions.

St Helen's is easily accessible using the Metropolitan Line. Northwood Station is less than five minutes from the school. The School also runs extensive and flexible coach services from the surrounding areas.

Our popular breakfast club and after-school care programme allow girls to extend their day in the safety of the school environment. Our highly qualified staff involve the girls in many activities, such as baking, games and paper craft, and enable them to complete their homework before they go home. Breakfast club and after-school care are housed in Longworthe House in familiar surroundings and tea and supper are provided.

Fees per term (2011-2012). Senior School: £4,443. Junior School (including Speech & Drama): £3,491. Little St Helen's (including Lunch, Ballet, Speech & Drama) Reception, Year 1 and Year 2: £3,335; Nursery (including Lunch, Ballet, Speech & Drama): £3,057.

Registration Fee: UK £50; Overseas £75.

Scholarships. Academic Scholarships are awarded to girls entering the Sixth Form and at 11+. Music Scholarships and Exhibitions, and Art and Sport Scholarships at 11+ and 16+. Also Sixth Form Drama Scholarship. Leader-Baker Scholarship awarded every four years at 14+. Bursaries are available.

St Helen's Old Girls' Club. *Secretary*: Mrs Sally Fleming, 2 Moneyhill Road, Rickmansworth, Herts WD3 2EQ.

Charitable status. St Helen's School for Girls is a Registered Charity, number 312762. It exists to provide quality education for girls.

St James Senior Girls' School

Earsby Street, London W14 8SH

Tel:	020 7348 1777; Admissions: 020 7348 1748
Fax:	020 7348 1717; Admissions: 020 7348 1749
e-mail:	admissions@sjsg.org.uk
website:	www.stjamesgirls.co.uk

Motto: *Speak the truth. Live generously. Aim for the best.*

Governors:
Mr Jeremy Sinclair (*Chairman*)
Mr Michael Cranny, FCII, Chartered Insurer
Mr George Cselko, BA Hons
Mr Aatif Hassan, BSc Hons, CA (*Joint Deputy Chairman*)
Mrs Elinor Line, Lic Français Lille, Dip M
Mr Jon Pickles BA, ACMA
Major Ben Roberts, BA
Mr John Story, FRICS (*Joint Deputy Chairman*)
Mr Hugh Venables, BSc, MBA
Mr Jerome Webb, MA, MRICS
Dr Fenella Willis, BSc, MBBS, MRCP, MRCPath

Headmistress: Mrs Laura Hyde, CertEd, MEd

Deputy Headmistress (Academic): Mrs S Labram, BA

Deputy Headmistress (Pastoral): Mrs J Andrews, RSA, Dip TLABE (*SENCO*)
Director of Studies: Dr J MAcRae, BSc, MSc, PhD, QTS
Head of Sixth Form: Mrs K Bayes, BA, PGCE
Head of Humanities: Mrs A Lubikowski, BA, MPhil, PGCE
Bursar: Mr William Wyatt

Teaching Staff:
Mrs G Addison, MA, TESOL, PGCE
Mr S Allen, MA Cantab, MSci, PGCE
Mr N Burrows, BSc, PGCE
Ms M Chaudagne, Licence MA, PGCE
Mrs E Clarke, BSc
Mrs H Cleaves, BA
Mrs L Consiglio, BA, QTS
Mrs S Cooper, BA, Assoc RSA
Dr J Craven, BA, MPhil, PhD
Mrs H de Mattos, BA, PGCE
Mr N de Mattos, BA, PGCE
Mr D Derham, BSc, PGCE
Mrs D Downs, MA, DipRS, AMI, PGCE
Mrs S Forrester, BA
Miss S Galal, BA, PGCE
Miss J Gillick, MA Cantab, QTS
Dr J Gogarty, BSc, MSc, PhD, PGCE
Mrs C Hilsdon, BSc, PGCE
Miss A Holliss, BA, QTS
Mr P Holloway, BA, PGCE
Mrs K Ibbett, BA, PGCE
Mrs E Jessup, BSc, MA
Mr W Jessup, BA Oxon, MA, MPhil
Mrs S Kuhrt, BA
Mrs A Lubikowski, BA, MPhil, PGCE
Dr J MacRae, MSc, PhD, QTS
Mrs J Mason, MA Oxon, PGCE
Miss A Morgan, Dip Tabla
Miss E Parker, BSc, MA
Mrs S Piegelin-Coles, Maître, PGCE, MA BLT
Mr S Powell, BSc, PGCE
Miss M Rahona-Solaz, BA Translation & Interpreting, QTS
Miss L Razzell, BA, LRAD, ARAD
Ms S Shah, PGDip, PGCE
Miss V West, BA, PGCE
Mr S Young, BSc, QTS

Visiting teachers:
Mrs S Pickles (*Needlework*)
Mrs R Downs (*Needlework*)
Mr M O'Shea (*Tennis*)

Founded in 1975, St James Senior School for Girls is a day school for 315 pupils from age 10–18. It is situated on a spacious site in Olympia, West Kensington, shared by its own Junior School. The Senior Girls' School provides an education which draws out and magnifies the unique talents innate in every individual. We provide an environment which enriches the intellectual, spiritual and physical development of the pupil in an atmosphere which supports unity and is conducive to the happiness of all. We inspire our pupils with a love for the finest aspects of human life so that they themselves develop the inner strength to live honest, dignified and magnanimous lives, employing their talents creatively for the benefit of humanity.

The school has strong spiritual and moral values, which lie at the heart of the education we offer.

Assemblies are conducted three times a week and are dedicated to spiritual nourishment as well as religious, social and cultural education. They include a wide range of presentations from visiting speakers, pupils and teachers.

Although the school draws much from the Christian faith and we have a school chaplain, our pupils are of many faiths and none. We support the principle that the spiritual search of humanity is one search and that it necessarily has many expressions, according to nature, inclination, time and place. We do not have a spiritual or religious doctrine of our own; our philosophical approach introduces our children to the best wisdom available so that they may be inspired by it. We offer a short period of quiet before and at the end of every activity. We also have a period of quiet for meditation, contemplation or silent prayer at the beginning and end of every day.

Our challenging and extensive curriculum provides intellectual, emotional, spiritual and physical nourishment and looks for balance with regard to these aspects of human nature. It is designed to encourage breadth and depth of understanding.

Whilst admission to the school is through a selective procedure, the school seeks to admit those candidates who are able and willing to make good use of the education offered. The school aims to foster creativity and intellectual curiosity, challenging its pupils to achieve excellence. Standards in public examinations are high: 100% of leavers proceed to Higher Education degree courses. 79% of these students achieve places at Russell and 1994 Group universities. Academic subjects are frequently set by ability.

The Curriculum offers appropriate education in PSHE, SMSC, Citizenship, Philosophy and Religious Studies. Emphasis is given to the cultivation of leadership training, public speaking and debating. Community Service runs throughout the school and is supported by a pupil Community Service Council. Career guidance is offered to all pupils from Years 8–13. All pupils engage in Sports, Singing and Dance. Drama, Music and ICT are also taught from Years 6–9.

Subjects available to GCSE: English (Language and Literature), French, Spanish, Latin, Greek, Sanskrit (St James Junior School pupils only), Maths, History, Geography, Physics, Biology, Chemistry, Art, Music, Drama. (The three sciences and Set 1 Maths take IGCSE examinations.) GCSE ICT will be available from 2012. Years 6 and 7 are taught General Science prior to commencing the three separate sciences in Year 8. Years 6 and 7 also receive lessons in needlework and the Art of Hospitality.

All subjects available at GCSE can be continued to A Level with the exception of Drama which becomes Drama & Theatre Studies. Additional A Levels include Economics, History of Art, Further Mathematics and Critical Thinking (AS only). In addition, Year 12 students are offered the opportunity to complete the Extended Project Qualification, a 5,000 word piece of research on a topic of their choice.

The Sixth Form. Most pupils stay on to complete their education in the Sixth Form. This is treated as a very distinct stage. Support and encouragement is given for the development of initiative and responsibility through leadership opportunities. The PSHE and SMSC programme is continued in order to provide support for personal development through a series of talks, debates and workshops. Emphasis is given to academic excellence and the cultivation of social awareness and, in particular, leadership skills are developed through assuming responsibility for younger pupils in the school. In Year 12 students are offered a community service project abroad (2009 South Africa Wilderness Project; 2010 World Challenge Expedition to Morocco; 2011 African Wilderness Project).

Creative Arts. Music, Drama and Dance are strong features of the school. There is a tradition of choral and solo singing, as well as instrumental music making. A fully-staged opera or musical is performed biennially in association with our brother school, St James Senior Boys' School (*My Fair Lady* in 2008 and *The Sound of Music* in 2010). There are three choirs and orchestras, several instrumental ensembles and girls are strongly encouraged to take up individual instruction with one of our visiting instrumental and/or vocal teachers. Many pupils participate in extra-curricular vocal or/and instrumental lessons. The latest dramatic pro-

ductions include the musical *The Railway Children* (Years 7 and 8), Shakespeare's *Romeo and Juliet* (Year 9) and *Daisy Pulls It Off* (Years 12 and 13). The Dance programme introduces pupils to a variety of dance forms: ballet, modern dance, ballroom and choreography. As well as extra-curricular lessons, pupils also have the opportunity to perform in the school's annual Dance Festival and Music, Speech, Debating and other artistic competitions.

Physical Education. Sports and games are an important part of school life. Lacrosse, Netball, Athletics, Gymnastics, Yoga, Pilates, Rounders, and Tennis are all offered within the curriculum. The Junior Sports' Leader qualification is offered as an option.

Extra-Curricular Activities. As well as a wide range of musical, sporting and other events, clubs include Art, Astronomy, Classics, Cookery, Dance, Drama, Fencing, Five-a-side soccer, History, Lacrosse, Netball, Rounders, Science and The Duke of Edinburgh's Award (Bronze, Silver and Gold awards). All girls attend the annual Activity Week with their own class at a variety of locations within and outside the UK.

Admission. For entry at 11+ girls sit the North London Independent Girls' Schools Consortium Entrance examination; at Sixth Form candidates are required to sit an entrance exam and to attain the necessary GCSE grades for A Level study. For occasional vacancies in Years 6, 8 and 9 candidates will need to take an entrance examination. All candidates are interviewed individually.

Fees per term (2011-2012). £4,360.

Bursaries. There are limited funds available for Bursary assistance. Awards are discretionary and based on full financial enquiry into parents' means by the Bursary Fund Committee. The funds are primarily to assist children already attending St James, but some help may be available to new parents in specific circumstances. Enquiries should be made in the first instance to the Bursar and completed application forms for the academic year 2012-2013 should be returned by Friday 6th January 2012.

Charitable status. The Independent Educational Association Limited is a Registered Charity, number 270156. It exists to provide education for children.

St Leonards-Mayfield School

The Old Palace, Mayfield, East Sussex TN20 6PH
Tel: 01435 874623 (Headmistress and Secretary)
          01435 874600 (School)
          01435 874642 (Admissions)
Fax: 01435 872627
e-mail: enquiry@mayfieldgirls.org
website: www.mayfieldgirls.org

At St Leonards-Mayfield School, girls will find the space to be themselves, within a challenging yet supportive environment. Mayfield girls learn how to combine rigorous academic study with a diverse range of activities beyond the classroom, while still finding the time to be still and know God. When they come to leave at the end of the Sixth Form, they will have matured into educated and independent young women, confident in their beliefs and prepared to make a positive difference in the world in which they find themselves, a force for good in responding to the challenges of the 21st century.

Of course, it is important to achieve the finest possible examination results, but the best independent learners know there is much more to education than simply achieving A grades. At Mayfield, we encourage girls to educate their mind, body, heart and soul. Every pupil has unique potential and, from the day she joins us, we support each girl to develop a love of knowledge, sound working habits and a responsibility for her own learning. In this way, she will become the best that she can be, academically, socially, physically and spiritually.

Governors:
Mr Nicholas Bagshawe, MA Oxon (*Chairman*)
Mrs Elizabeth Byrne Hill, BA, MA, PGCE (*Deputy Chairman & Chairman of Education Committee*)
Mr Michael Stevens, MA Oxon (*Deputy Chairman & Chairman of Finance Committee*)
Mrs Teresa Blaxland, BA
Sister Maria Dinnendahl, SHCJ, BA, MA Oxon, BA, Lic Phil
Mrs Karan Douglas, PGCEA
Mrs Amanda Dunn, BA, ACA
Mrs Sara Hulbert-Powell, BA
Ms Teresa Keogh, BA, PGCE, MA
Sister Judith Lancaster, SHCJ, BA, MTh, MA, PGCE
Mrs Maureen Martin, BA, PGCE
Sister Marie Quayle, SHCJ, BA, MSc, MA Oxon, PGCE
Dr Christopher Storr, KSG, MA, PhD, FRSA (*Chairman of Governance Committee*)

***Headmistress*: Miss A M Beary**, MA, MPhil Cantab, PGCE

Senior Managers:
Deputy Head (Academic): Miss D Rowe, BA Mus, MA Mus, NPQH, PGCE, CCRS
Deputy Head (Pastoral & Boarding): Mrs S Ryan BA, MA
Bursar: Lt Col A H Bayliss, MA Cantab, CEng, MICE
Head of Lower School: Mr P S Fisher, BA, MA, PGCE
Head of Middle School: Mrs S J Rothero, BEd, CertEd
Head of Sixth Form & Careers: Mr J Filkin, BA Oxon, MA, PGCE
Lay Chaplain: Miss P Cronin, MA
Senior Manager Organisation: Miss J P Eales, BEd Cantab, CertEd
Director of Development & Communications: Dr T Eaton, BA, MA, PhD

Teaching Staff:

Art:
Miss J Thackray, BA, PGCE (*Head of Department*)
Miss C Cossey, BA, QTS
Mr R Lamb, BA, MA
Mrs A Sivyour, BA, PGCE

Ceramics:
Mr A Topliss, BA, PGCE (*Head of Department*)
Mrs Y McFadyean, BA

Classics:
Mr K Rogers, BA, MSc, PGCE (*Head of Department*)
Miss D Downing, BA, MA
Mrs J King, BA, MA, PGCE

Drama & Theatre Studies:
Mrs J Upton, ALAM, LLAM, CertEd, PGCE (*Head of Department*)
Mrs H Halliday, Hon Dip

Economics & Business Studies:
Mr B McClelland, BSc, MSc, MPhil, PGCE (*Head of Department*)

English:
Mr J Filkin, BA Oxon, MA, PGCE (*Head of Department*)
Miss C Cox, BA, PGCE
Mrs N Evans, BA, PGCE
Mr M Harvey, BA

ESOL:
Mrs J Sandoval, MA, DipTEFLA (*Head of Department*)
Mrs S Balzarelli, BA, DipTEFLA
Mrs J Carter, BA, DipTEO, PGCE

Food & Nutrition:
Mrs S Rothero, BEd, CertEd (*Head of Department*)

Mrs C Davies, CNAA, BEd, PGCE
Mrs Y Nash, CB Dip

Geography:
Mr S Gough, BSc, PGCE (*Head of Department*)
Miss V Brown, BA, MA, MSc, PGCE
Mrs F Morris, BEd

History:
Miss N Clyma, BA, MA, RSA, CELTA, PGCE (*Head of Department*)
Mrs M Bushell, BA, PGCE

History of Art:
Mrs J Weddell, BA Arch, MA (*Head of Department*)

Information Technology:
Mr S Gough, BSc, PGCE (*Head of Department*)
Miss L Jackson, BA, QTS, Dip RSA
Mrs A Leschnikoff, CertEd

Learning Support:
Mrs J Bartlett, BA, Cert Ed (*Head of Department*)
Mrs P Bryer, HLTA
Mrs L Campbell, MA, CertEd, PGCE
Mrs K Daughtrey, CertEd

Mathematics:
Mrs A Pullinger, BSc, PGCE (*Head of Department*)
Miss J van Driesen, BA, MA
Miss J Eales, BEd Cantab, CertEd
Mrs L Motoc, BSc, PGCE
Mrs J Stone, BSc, MSc, PGCE

Modern Languages:
Mrs A C von Wulffen, MA Oxon, PGCE (*Head of Department*)
Mrs R E Boumediene, BA PGCE
Ms M Criado, BA, PGCE
Miss B d'Inverno, BA, PGCE
Mlle C Richard, BA, MA, MA, PGCE

Music:
Mr P Collins, GRSM, LRAM, ARCM, PGCE (*Director of Music*)
Miss H Woodruff, BA Mus, MA (*Assistant Director of Music*)
The Department also includes c20 visiting music teachers.

Physical Education:
Mrs H Hyde, BA, QTS (*Joint Head of Department*)
Mrs H Miller, BA, PGCE (*Joint Head of Department*)
Miss S Evans, BA, QTS
Mrs J Jones, BA, QTS
Miss S Mead, BA, QTS
Mrs F Morris, BEd
Mrs P Whitby, BA

Psychology:
Mrs P Tysh, BSc, PGTC (*Head of Department*)
Miss C Muckian, BA, PGCE
Mrs P Whitby, BA

Religious Studies:
Mr P Oxborrow, BA, MA, PGCE (*Head of Department*)
Mrs E Warnett, BA, MA, PGCE
Mr P Fisher, BA, MA, PGCE

Riding:
Miss J Barker, BEd, BHSII J, CertEd (*Director of Riding*)

Sciences:
Mrs L Varley, MA Oxon, PGCE (*Head of Sciences, Head of Physics*)
Mrs J Tayler, BSc, PGCE (*Head of Chemistry*)
Mrs K Blackman, BSc PGCE
Mrs J Gradon, BA, PGCE
Ms F Hussain, BSc, PGCE
Miss R Jackson, BSc Dunelm, PGCE
Miss T A Rakowska, BSc, PGCE

Mrs K Randolph, BSc, PGCE
Mr J Stacey, BSc, MSc, PGCE

Textiles:
Mrs T Budden, Dip Fashion Design & Construction (*Head of Department*)

Housemistresses & Medical Staff:
Leeds House: Mrs J Pirlot de Corboin, BSc, CCE, PGCE, QTS
Connelly House: Mrs J Roberts, HND, CertEd
St Dunstan's House: Mrs C Davies, CNAA, BEd, PGCE
School Doctor: Dr A Coates, BM, DROCG, Dip Therapeutics
Senior Nurses: Mrs D Streeter, RGN, Ms A Nikouei, RGN, RSCN

Pastoral Staff:
Years 7 & 8: Mr P Fisher, MA, MA, PGCE
Years 9, 10 & 11: Mrs S Rothero, BEd, CertEd
Years 12 & 13 Sixth Form: Mr J Filkin, BA Oxon, MA, PGCE
Transition Coordinator: Mrs F Morris, BEd

There are 400 girls enrolled, with 110 of these in the Sixth Form. Almost 30% of pupils are full or weekly boarders with many more flexi-boarding.

Organisation. There are three boarding houses: one for Years 7 and 8, one for Years 9, 10 and 11 and one for the Sixth Form.

Curriculum. In the first three years the curriculum seeks to establish a good foundation in the different disciplines, to encourage initiative, investigation, and many varieties of creative activity, and the growth of self-discipline and self-motivation. The core for GCSE comprises English Language, English Literature, Mathematics, a modern foreign language, Physics, Chemistry and Biology (either as three separate subjects, or in Science/Additional Science), and Religious Studies. Three further subjects may be chosen freely from fourteen options. Twenty-seven subjects are offered for AS and A2 Level. The importance of non-examination subjects is stressed, together with the need to develop inter-personal skills, to take responsibility for younger members of the school and those they help in the neighbourhood, and to achieve a proper balance between work and leisure. Virtually all proceed to higher education, over 95% to university.

The standard of Music is high. There are three choirs and one orchestra, and individual tuition is available in a large number of instruments. Teams and individuals compete at county, regional and national level in a wide variety of sports. The School is reigning NSEA National Schools Riding Champion, and has won the competition on six occasions.

The school has a music school and a concert hall which is used for both music and drama. The 14th century chapel is at the heart of the school life. There is an all-weather hockey pitch, an indoor heated 25-metre swimming pool, two riding arenas, stables, a gymnasium, a dance studio, tennis and netball courts, and playing fields. Sports include hockey, netball, tennis, rounders, athletics, swimming, gymnastics, volleyball, squash, sailing, golf, riding and more.

Admission. At 11+ via the School Entrance Examination; at 13+ via the School Entrance Examination or Common Entrance Examination; at 14 (exceptionally) on assessment and school report; at 16 (for Sixth Form Course) with at least six good passes at GCSE and report from present head.

Registration fee: £100 (£200 overseas).

Fees per term (2011-2012). Full Boarders £8,580, Day girls £5,540.

Scholarships. (*See Scholarship Entries section.*) Scholarships are offered for achievement and potential in academic subjects, choral singing, music, art, drama and sport.

Charitable status. St Leonards–Mayfield School is a Registered Charity, number 1047503. It exists to provide education for girls in keeping with its Catholic foundation.

St Margaret's School for Girls
Aberdeen

17 Albyn Place, Aberdeen AB10 1RU
Tel: 01224 584466
Fax: 01224 585600
e-mail: info@st-margaret.aberdeen.sch.uk
website: www.st-margaret.aberdeen.sch.uk

Founded in 1846.

School Council:
Councillor J Gifford (*Chair*)
Mr A Bannister, BA, CA
Mr S R Bertram, MA, CA, Dip BA
Dr C M Carden, BSc, DIC, PhD, CEng, MEI
Mrs J Craik
Professor J Harper, BSc, PhD, CChem, FRSC
Mr D Heslop, BSc Hons, MSc
Mr J C Leheny
Mr B R W Lockhart, MA, DipEd
Mrs L Mearns, MA Hons, CA, Assoc CIPD
Mrs M A M Ruddiman, LLB, Dip LP

Clerk to the Council: Mr G Brown, BSc, Dip H-WU, FCMI

***Head*: Dr Julie Land**, BSc Hons, PGCE, EdD

Deputy Head: Mrs S Lynch, MA Hons, PGCE (*Modern Languages*)

Senior Staff:
* *Head of Department*
§ *Part-time or Visiting*

Mr R Adair, BSc Hons, PGCE (**Chemistry*)
§Miss J Aitken, BEd (*Physical Education*)
Miss K Barsby, BSc Hons (**Physics*)
Ms S Brown, BEd Hons, ATCL (*Music, PSE*)
§Mrs A Bryce, BSc, PGCE (*Mathematics*)
Mrs S Chalmers, BA Hons, PGCE, QTS (*Modern Languages*)
Ms L Chellal, Licence d'Anglais Pau, Licence FLE Grenoble, PGCE (**Modern Languages*)
Miss K Cowie, BA Hons, PGCE (**Art and Design*)
Mrs E Crisp, BA Hons, CGeog, FRGS, PGCE (**Geography*)
Mr G Cunningham, MA Hons, PGCE (**History and Economics*)
§Mrs D Dale, MA (*English*)
Ms P Davey, BA, DipT (*Geography, *Modern Studies*)
Miss S Forgie, BA Hons, PGCE (*Modern Languages*)
§Mrs K Fowler, BEd Hons, CTS (*Physical Education*)
Mrs L Goodwin, BEd (**Speech and Drama*)
Mrs L Gurney, LTCL (*Music – Woodwind*)
§Mrs L Howitt, BSc (*Biology and Chemistry*)
§Mrs K Hudd, BA Hons (*History*)
§Mrs H Jennings, BD, PGCE (*RMPE and Philosophy*)
§Mrs J Johnson, DipDomSc, DipSEN (**Food Technology*)
Mrs A Leiper, MA Hons, DipEd (*English*)
§Mrs S Lynch, MA Hons, PGCE (*Modern Languages*)
Miss W Main, BA Hons, PGCE (**Latin & Classical Studies*)
§Mrs C Middleton BSc Hons, PGCE (*Biology and Physics*)
Mrs A Miller, BSc Hons, PGCE (**Biology*)
Mr R Minett, MA Hons, DipEd (*Modern Languages, Library*)
Mr I Murray, BSc (**ICT*)
Mrs K Norval, BEd Hons (**Physical Education*)

§Mrs C Ogg, BSc Hons (*Mathematics*)
Mr P Parfitt, BA Hons, MMus (**Music*)
Mrs N Pont, MA Hons, PGCE (*Mathematics*)
Mrs J Reid, BEd Hons (*Physical Education*)
Miss S Reid, BA, LTCL (*Music, Strings*)
§Mrs J Richardson, BA Hons, PGCE (*Art and Design*)
§Mrs J Robson, GRSC pt11, PGCE (*Science*)
Mrs J Slater, DipComm (**Business Mgt, Admin, Word Processing, Guidance*)
Mrs S Smith, BA Hons, PGCE (**Mathematics*)
§Mrs P Snape, BSc (*Chemistry, Biology, Careers*)
Mr J S Witte, MA Hons (**English*)

Junior Department:
Miss A M Bibby, DPE
Miss F Black, BEd Hons
Mrs C Bradbury, DPE
Mrs C Davenport, MA Hons
Ms A Dressel, BSc
Mrs L Easton, BEd
Mrs F King, BA Hons, QTS
*Miss A Lister, MA Hons, PGDE
§Mrs L Reilly, MA, CertEd
§Ms A Robertson, BEd Hons
Miss F Walker, MSc EPP, BSc Hons, PGDE
Mrs L Williams, BEd Hons

Classroom Assistants:
Mrs M Bentley
Mrs D Gregory, SVQ2 in Care
Mrs C Newcombe, BSc Hons, PGCE
Ms A Robertson, BEd Hons

Daffodil Nursery:
Miss W Fraser, HNC
Miss M McInnes, HNC Childcare and Education
§Mrs D Oswald, HNC Childcare and Education
*Mrs A Paterson, BEd, DipSEN (*Nursery Manager*)
Mrs C Spinelli, NNEB
Miss K Thomson, CCLD Level 3

Support for Learning:
*§Mrs L Williamson, MA, DPSE, SEN

Administrative Staff:
Bursar: Mr G Brown, BSc, Dip H-WU, FCMI
Assistant Bursar: Mrs M Raitt, FIAB
PA to Headmistress: Mrs G Smith
Admissions/Marketing: Mrs K McCulloch, BSc, MSc, CIM, DipM
Admissions: Miss A Fancett, MA Hons, MLitt
Receptionist: Mrs A Murray
Art Technician: Mr C McGeachie, BA Hons
ICT Technician: Mr C Morris, BSc Hons
Laboratory Technician: Miss K Mackie, ONC, HNC, Bio Sci
Reprographic Technician: Mrs S Ingram
Sports Coordinator: Mrs S Lowe, MA Hons, PGCE

After-School Care and Playground Supervision:
§Mrs S Butler, DipEd, BEd (*After-School Care*)
Mrs C Duncan, HNC (*Playground Supervisor/Auxiliary, After School Care Practitioner*)
Miss W Fraser, HNC (*After-School Care*)
§Mrs S Ingram (*Playground Supervisor*)
Mrs M Macdonald, HNC (*After School Care Practitioner*)
§Mrs C Newcombe, BSc Hons, PGCE (*Playground Supervisor*)
*Ms A Robertson, BEd Hons (*Manager*)
Miss K Thomson, CCLD Level 3 (*After-School Care*)

There are also visiting instrumental teachers for strings, brass and percussion and two modern language assistants for French and German.

Founded in 1846, St Margaret's School is the oldest all-through girls' school in Scotland and the Head is a member of the Girls' Schools Association, Scottish Girls' Schools Group and SLS. Education is provided for around 400 girls from Nursery to Sixth Year. The Nursery is within the main building, and boys and girls are admitted from the age of 3 years.

St Margaret's School is conveniently situated in the west end of Aberdeen. The school's excellent facilities include spacious, well-equipped science laboratories, dining room, art studio, an attractive music suite, a fine gymnasium, playing fields and a new pavilion at Summerhill. The school has three computer suites, and the whole school is networked.

Aims. We aim to provide a stimulating education for girls in an all-through school where each girl is encouraged to realise her potential in a friendly, caring atmosphere. The school also aims to provide public benefit through the advancement of education. We encourage staff and girls to contribute to the development of Scottish education.

Curriculum. Girls are prepared for Standard Grade, Intermediate 2, Higher and Advanced Higher examinations of the Scottish Qualifications Authority. National examinations can be taken for awards in music and drama.

The curriculum includes Art and Design, Biology, Chemistry, Classical Studies, Computer Studies, Drama, Economics, English (language and literature), Food Technology, French, Geography, German, History, Italian, Latin, Mathematics, Modern Studies, Music, Information Systems, Philosophy, Physics, Physical Education, Religious and Moral Education, Personal and Social Education and Spanish.

Girls are encouraged to take part in extra-curricular activities which include dance, swimming, drama, debating, computer club, science club, Scripture Union, junior and senior orchestra, woodwind ensemble, junior, senior and chamber choir, Duke of Edinburgh's Award Scheme, Young Enterprise, highland dancing, chess and Choi Kwang Do.

Admission. Girls are admitted to the School by informal or formal assessment.

Fees per term (2011-2012). Nursery (10 half sessions) £1,944; 1 Junior £1,944; 2 Junior £2,202; 3 Junior £2,763; 4 Junior £2,832; 5, 6 and 7 Junior £2,948; I to VI Senior £3,326.

These fees include SQA examination fees and all books and materials for nursery and early years classes; they are payable termly with an option to pay monthly. A reduction is made when three or more siblings attend at the same time.

Means-tested bursaries are available for entry to 6 and 7 Junior, I Senior, V and VI Senior.

Charitable status. St Margaret's School for Girls is a Registered Charity, number SC016265. It exists to provide a high quality education for girls.

St Margaret's School
Bushey

Merry Hill Road, Bushey, Herts WD23 1DT
Tel: 020 8416 4400
Fax: 020 8416 4401
e-mail: schooloffice@stmargarets.herts.sch.uk
website: www.stmargaretsbushey.org.uk

Founded 1749.
  Motto: *Sursum corda Habemus ad Dominuum*

Patron: Her Majesty The Queen

President: The Bishop of St Albans

Mr P Walton
Mrs J Herbert
Mrs S Shepherd
Miss K Bower
Revd W Gibbs

Staff:

***Headmistress*: Mrs L Crighton**, BA Hons Manchester,
   PGCE Cambridge, NPQH

Deputy Head: Mrs G Erdil, BSc Hons
Pastoral Deputy Head: Miss J Chatkiewicz, BA Wales,
   PGCE
Bursar: K Young, PhD, ARSM, DIC, BSc Eng Hons
Examinations Officer/Senior Teacher: Mr R Aniolkowski,
   BSc Leeds, PGCE

Art:
Mrs L Stewart, BA Hons Central St Martins College of Art,
   PGCE Goldsmiths
Miss K Kimber, BA Central St Martins College of Art,
   PGCE Middlesex

Careers:
Mrs B Blakemore, BA New York

Classics:
Ms C Garrow, BA Hons Newcastle Upon Tyne, PGCE

Drama:
Mrs E Janacek, BA CNAA Herts, BEd CNAA Herts
Miss P Mowll, CertEd, LLAM Teachers, ALAM Acting

English:
Mrs M Goodhew, BA London, TEFL Dip
Mrs R M Brennan, BEd Southampton
Mrs J Otlet, MA Hons Oxon, PGCE, Lic Phil et Lettres
   Brussels
Ms S Ahmed, BA Hons Essex, PGCE Homerton

Food Technology:
Mrs C Timms, BEd Bath

Geography:
Mr C Knox, BA Middlesex, PGCE, FRGS
Mrs J Faherty, TCert

History:
Mrs A Harper, BA Liverpool, PGCE
Miss J Chatkiewicz, BA Wales, PGCE

Information Technology:
Mrs G Ilott, CertEd Greenwich
Mr M A Hammond, MA Cantab, PGCE Dunelm, FRCO,
   LRAM

Mathematics:
Mr R Anghaee, BSc, MSc, PGCE
Mrs S Cohen, BSc Hons London, PGCE London
Mr B Haines BSc Essex, PGCE
Mr M A Hammond, MA Cantab, PGCE Dunelm, FRCO,
   LRAM

Modern Languages:
Miss A Corbach, MA London, BA Cologne, PGCE
Mrs C Hooper, BA Hons Sheffield
Ms P Holden, BSc Hons, PGCE
Ms G Baudet, Rennes, France, PGCE London
Miss S Charalambous, BA London

Music:
Mr I Hope, BMus Edin, PGCE, LTCL
Mr M A Hammond, MA Cantab, PGCE Dunelm, FRCO,
   LRAM
The Music Department is supported by a wide range of
   visiting peripatetic Music Teachers.

Physical Education:
Mrs D Pimlott, BEd Hons Brighton
Miss G Jackman, BSc Hons Brunel, PGCE Middx

Mrs J Faherty, TCert
Mrs F Hudson, BEd Hons Brighton

Religious Studies:
Ms K Roberts, BA Bangor, MA King's College London,
   PGCE
Mrs S Adams, BEd Bedford

Science:
Biology:
Miss V Jennings, BSc Hons London, PGCE Exeter
Miss S Branquinho, BA Durham, PGCE
Chemistry:
Mr D Anderson, BSc Port Elizabeth, BEd South Africa,
   PGCE
Mr S Dolan, BSc, PGCE
Physics:
Mr R Aniolkowski, BSc Leeds, PGCE
Mr P Ingram, BEd London, CertEd
Laboratory Technician: Mrs C Shah, Mrs B Rixon

Social Studies:
Mrs E Chaudhri, BA London, PGCE London
Mrs C Rees, BA Wales, MA Leicester
Miss S Smith, BSc Hons London, PGCE Middx

Learning Support:
Mrs A Baker, LSC

Speech & Drama
Coordinator: Miss P Mowll, CertEd, LLAM Teachers,
   ALAM Acting
Mrs F Lester, LLAM Teachers, LLAM Acting, Grad IPD
Mrs L St Hilaire, Speaking of Verse & Prose Gold, Acting
   Gold
Mrs A Watson-Picken, LCST, MCST, LGSM, LRAM
Ms K Woods, BA Hons, LLAM Acting, PGC Acting,
   PGCE Primary
Mrs P Shah, BA Hons
Mrs J Joseph, BSc Hons, LLAM Teachers, ALAM Hons
   Public Speaking, ALAM Recital, LTCL Effective
   Speaking
Mrs C Saunders, BA Hons, LLAM

Preparatory Department:
Head: Mrs C Brothers, MAEd, CertEd Bedford, AdvDipEd
Mrs L Franklin, BEd Maria Grey
Mrs J Lee-Bratt, BSc, Adv DipEd, CertEd Retford, Notts
Mrs J Thomson, CertEd Newcastle
Mrs T Walsgrove, BEd Sussex
Teaching Assistants:
Mrs R Garry
Ms L Morelli

Infant Department:
Head: Mrs S Kingsford, DipMus Aberdeen, MA Brunel
Ms V Seymour
Ms S Harvey, BEd Hertfordshire, PGCE
Teaching Assistants:
Mrs J Tabor, BA Manchester, PGCE
Mrs J Newall
Mrs L Ash, BA Hons Open, NQT Hertfordshire
Mrs S Hilton, BEd Hons

Senior Housemistress:
Mrs J Faherty, TCert
Assistant Housemistresses:
Mrs S Potter
Mrs S Hooper

Duke of Edinburgh's Award Scheme:
Mr S Dolan, BSc, PGCE

Catering Manager: Mr S Brown
Finance Manager: Mrs D Riordan
IT Manager: Mr M Graver, BSc Hons Middx, MBCS
Librarian: Mrs C Salmon, BA Econ Manchester, PGCE
Marketing Manager: Miss C Moyle

Medical Centre Sister: Mrs T Eales, RGN, ENB 998
Sports Centre Manager: Mr C Sneddon, BSc
Admissions Secretary: Miss G Morris
Bursary Secretary: Mrs J Curran
Finance Assistant: Mrs A Jenkins
Head's PA/School Secretary: Mrs S Wright
School Secretary: Mrs S Angell
Receptionists: Mrs A Smith, Mrs C McBride

St Margaret's provides a secure environment in which girls from 4 to 18 are enabled to develop to their full potential. A strong emphasis on pastoral care underpins a St Margaret's education which is rigorous and challenging, but also accessible. Small classes and highly professional staff lead to impressive public examination results at GCSE and A Level.

Founded in 1749 to educate the orphan children of the clergy, the School moved to its present site in 1896 where it has grown and developed into a thriving, multi-cultural community ideally located in rural surroundings, close to national and international transport links, preparing girls to play their part as active citizens of the 21st century.

The original main school building together with its chapel was designed by the Victorian architect Sir Alfred Waterhouse. New buildings have been added to the school complex and facilities have been considerably upgraded in recent years. There are two ICT suites and also modern Art, Technology and Careers facilities. The most recent building project is the new £3 million Sports Centre which includes a heated indoor swimming pool, sports hall, fitness centre and dance studio.

Although the majority of the pupils are day girls, the senior school admits full, weekly and occasional boarders which means that there is a busy, thriving community seven days a week. There is a wide range of sporting and cultural activities, for example, the Duke of Edinburgh's Award and the Young Enterprise Scheme as well as charitable fundraising drives. The school has close links with fellow Comenius project partners in Germany, Hungary, Portugal, Italy, Belgium, Poland and Norway, and there are regular field trips, outings and theatre visits. Other activities include choir, orchestra, speech and drama, drama, ballet and judo.

Fees per term (2011-2012). Senior and Lower School: Full Boarding £8,350; Weekly Boarding £6,075 (up to 3 nights), £7,110 (up to 5 nights); Day £4,500 Preparatory: Day £3,920 Transition £3,570 Infant £2,980.

Means-tested bursaries are available and discounts for members of the Forces and Clergy.

Scholarships. Academic and Music Scholarships are awarded at Year 7 and Sixth Form at the discretion of the Head. An Art Scholarship is also available in the Sixth Form.

St Margaret's Guild (Old Girls' Association). *Secretary*: Mrs J Wilson, 43 Chase Ridings, Enfield, Middx EN2 7QE. Guild Membership available to any old girl of St Margaret's School.

Charitable status. St Margaret's School Bushey is a Registered Charity, number 1056228.

St Margaret's School
Exeter
A Woodard School

147 Magdalen Road, Exeter EX2 4TS
Tel: 01392 491699 Headmistress/
         Admissions Secretary
         01392 273197 School Office
         01392 277132 Bursar
Fax: 01392 251402
e-mail: mail@stmargarets-school.co.uk

website: www.stmargarets-school.co.uk

Senior school girls-only, the Prep, Pre-Prep and Nursery welcome boys and girls (aged 3–11).

One of the Woodard Schools, St Margaret's aims to inspire pupils with a love of learning, of every kind, within a caring Christian environment. The school seeks to develop the potential of all pupils giving them the confidence to respond to the responsibilities and opportunities offered by society.

Chairman of Governors: Mr G Mulder, DIPL ING

Headmistress: Mrs S Cooper, MA Oxon, LTCL, PGCE, NPQH (*Classics*)

Deputy Headteacher: Mr L Bergin, BA Hull, PGCE, NPQH Manchester (*Business Studies, ICT*)

Deputy Headteacher: Dr Karen Marshall, BSc Bristol, PhD Cantab, PGCE (*Chemistry, ICT*)

Assistant Headteacher and Head of Sixth Form: Mrs B Hutchings, BA, PGCE (*English*)

Bursar: Mr D King, BSc, MAAT

Chaplain: Mrs J Frost, BA, PGCE

Headmistress's Secretary and Admissions Secretary: Mrs C Clapp

School Development Officer: Mrs J Benham

Foundation. St Margaret's was founded in 1902 and is a Woodard School.

Situation. St Margaret's is situated a mile from the City Centre in St Leonard's. The School consists of 7 large Georgian Houses and a Performing Art Centre. There is a Gym, Assembly Hall, specialist rooms and hard courts for tennis and netball. Playing fields are available in the locality for games. The Performing Arts Centre was opened in 1997, and the new Library in September 1998. There are 3 full IT Suites, four Science Laboratories (opened in 2003 by The Princess Royal) and a Home Economics Room (opened in 2001 by Gary Rhodes). The Nursery and Pre-Prep were opened in 2008 and the Arthouse and Sixth Form Internet Café in 2009.

Numbers. Total number of pupils 300. There are 60 pupils in the Sixth Form.

Admission. Entrance for the Senior School through to the Lower Sixth, is by the School's own examinations, held in the Spring Term prior to entry in September. For the Prep there are Assessment Tests which can be arranged at any time of year. Entrance to the Nursery and Pre-Prep is after a taster day and teacher observation.

Scholarships and Awards. (*See Scholarship Entries section.*)

Religious Life of the School. As a Woodard school, St Margaret's follows Christian principles of the Church of England and the school has a Chaplain. Children of different or no faith are welcome.

Inspection. October 2006: "pupils leave the school as confident, mature, friendly and lively young adults" and that "the pupils achieve very well academically" while the "care for pupils' welfare … is outstanding". Extra-curricular achievement was also judged "outstanding".

Curriculum. Full ranges of subjects are studied at GCSE, AS and A2 Levels. There are fully-equipped Science laboratories, Food and Information Technology centres. All girls take the ECDL course in computer literacy. French, Spanish and German are available at KS3, GCSE and A Level.

St Margaret's excels in music, art and drama. The choir has reached the finals of the BBC Radio 3 Choir of the Year Competition and the Chapel Choir has often won an Outstanding Performance Award at the National Festival of

Music for Youth. In 2008 St Margaret's joined all other Woodard Schools in the Birmingham Symphony Hall for Berlioz' *Te Deum*. Musical tuition (from over 18 visiting music teachers) is offered in any instrument.

The Drama department involves the whole school in its productions, *Daisy Pulls it Off!* and *We Will Rock You* being recent examples.

Games. Competitive netball, hockey, tennis, football and rounders are played. Gymnastics, dance and swimming are part of the curriculum and there is a range of sporting activities as girls move up the school, including rowing and trampolining.

Extra-Curricular Activities. There is a wide range of extra-curricular activities at St Margaret's including a thriving CCF. Very many girls are involved in The Duke of Edinburgh's Award scheme: in 2008–9 21 girls achieved their Duke of Edinburgh's Gold Award and in 2009 30 girls travelled to India as part of their Gold Award. Three teams usually compete in the Ten Tors Event. There are foreign exchange visits to Germany, Spain and France.

Careers Advice. A fully-stocked careers library with internet access, and guidance and information is available. There is a programme of work experience for Years 11 and 12 and opportunities for service to the community.

Fees per term (2011-2012). Senior £3,356–£3,395; Prep £2,781–£2,899; Pre-Prep £1,741–£1,899.

Charitable status. St Margaret's School Exeter Limited is a Registered Charity, number 1103316. It exists to provide education for girls (and boys in the Prep, Pre-Prep and Nursery).

St Margaret's School

18 Kidderpore Gardens, Hampstead, London NW3 7SR
Tel: 020 7435 2439
Fax: 020 7431 1308
e-mail: enquiry@st-margarets.co.uk
website: www.st-margarets.co.uk

Founded 1884.

Chair of Governors: Caroline Bradford

Principal: **Mr Mark Webster**, BSc, PGCE, NPQH (*Maths and Psychology*)

Deputy Principal: Ms Sarah Treagus, BA (*CPO, PE, Housemistress*)

Mrs P Atree, BEd, RSA Cert SpLD
Mr B Benson, CertEd, CSSD Dip Acting (*Drama*)
Mrs K Broughton, BA, MA, PGCE (*Art*)
Mr M Brown, Dip T (*ICT & Maths, Y5 Form Tutor*)
Ms K Collins. BEd (*Reception*)
Mrs S Dempster-Rivett, BSc, PGCE, HEA Cert (*Science, Careers Advisor, Pastoral Care Coordinator, Y7 Form Tutor*)
Mrs A Froggatt, BEd, BSc (*Art Teacher, Careers Advisor*)
Mrs F Gonzalez, BA, TFL, PGCE (*Spanish*)
Mr R Hartley, BA, PGCE (*History & Citizenship, Y9 Form Tutor*)
Mrs J Herman, BA, MA (*Y2*)
Ms C Hickey, BA, DipED (*PE*)
Mrs J Jefferys, Mont Dip, CertEd (*Y1, Learning Support Coordinator, Housemistress*)
Mrs R Johnson, BA QTS (*Y3*)
Mrs L Livermore, BA, PGCE, TESOL (*English, Y8 Form Tutor*)
Mr S Russell, BSc, MCC coaching, Dip Astronomy (*Science & Maths, Y10 Form Tutor, KS4 Coordinator, Examinations Officer*)
Ms J Steinberg, BA (*French*)
Mr M Urrestarazu, BSc, PGCE (*Mathematics*)

Mrs G Willford, BA QTS (*Y4 Form Tutor*)
Ms G Wilson, BA, PGCE (*Geography, Y11 Form Tutor, Learning Support Coordinator, Housemistress, DofE Coordinator*)
Mrs E Keenlyside, MA, PGCE, BA (*Music Coordinator*)

Bursar: Mrs S Beschizza
School Secretary/Admissions: Mrs L-A Scorgie

Age Range. 4–16.
Number in School. 150 Day Girls.
Fees per term (2011-2012). £3,074–£3,542. Compulsory extras: Books and outings.

St Margaret's is a small school situated in a quiet residential area of Hampstead, North London. In 2008/9 and 2009/10 the school topped the Sunday Times Small Independent School League Table.

Classes throughout the school are small, averaging 12 in the Junior School and 14 in the Senior School. Girls in Reception to Year 3 are taught mainly by their form teachers with specialist teachers for PE, French, ICT and Music. Specialist teaching increases in Years 4, 5 and 6 to include Art, Geography, History and Science. In Years 7–11 the girls are taught by specialist teachers for all subjects.

The girls enjoy a wide range of sporting activities at a number of local sites. Their after-school clubs include yoga, netball, football, tennis, cross-country, bicycle maintenance, self defence and choir. The girls play netball competitively against local schools. All girls take part in the *125 Things To Do Before You Leave St Margaret's* programme.

Girls take SATs at ages 7 and 11, and in Year 11 take 9 or 10 GCSE subjects. At 16 girls are prepared for Sixth Form entry. Former pupils are currently studying at Henrietta Barnett, Highgate, Channing, and Francis Holland amongst others.

A wide range of outings are organised to London galleries, museums and theatres. Girls in Year 10 undertake a week's work experience and trips abroad are organised to support the French and Spanish curriculum.

St Margaret's works hard to achieve high standards in work and discipline, while fostering a happy atmosphere in which girls feel involved and engaged. Their personal development is valued as highly as their academic.

Entry requirements: In class assessment to Year 4, thereafter by testing.

Charitable status. St Margaret's School (Hampstead) Ltd is a Registered Charity, number 312720. It exists as a charitable trust to provide a good education for girls with the emphasis on each girl fulfilling her own potential.

St Martha's

Camlet Way, Hadley Wood, Barnet, Hertfordshire EN4 0NJ
Tel: 020 8449 6889
Fax: 020 8441 5632
e-mail: admissions@saint-marthas.org.uk
website: www.st-marthas.co.uk

Governors and Trustees:

Chair of Governors: Mr Les Edgar

Mr Michael McCann	*Trustees*:
Mr Seamus O'Sullivan	Sister Cécile Archer
Sr Irene Brogan	Sister Christina O'Dwyer
Mrs Maureen Howie	Sister Janet Sinden
Mr Joseph Medayil	Sister Teresa Roseingrave
Mrs Eileen McDonald	
Mrs Maureen Zambra	

School Staff:

Headmaster: **Mr James Sheridan**, BSc, MA

Deputy Head: Sister T Roseingrave, CertEd, CTC

Chaplin: Fr T Seasman

Bursar: Mr S Rayner

Assistant Bursar: Mrs E Boonzaier, BEd, BCom, HDE

Director of Studies: Miss C Rouse, BA, PGCE

Assistant Heads:
Miss E Monchaux, BA, PGCE (*Curriculum*)
Dr M Wall, BSc, PhD, PGCE (*Curriculum*)

House Mistresses:
Miss K Maestranzi, BA, GTP (*Avila*)
Miss R McGonagle, BA, PGCE (*Siena*)
Miss D Mela, GLCM, ALCM (*Lisieux*)

* *Head of Faculty*

Art & Design:
Miss C Garrett, BA
Ms E Somerville, BA, PGCE
Mrs M Dixon (*Teaching Assistant*)

Business Studies and Economics:
*Mr J Boonzaier, BCom, HDE

Classics:
Miss K Maestranzi, BA, GTP

Drama:
*Miss R McGonagle, BA, PGCE
Miss L Taber, BA

English:
*Mrs D Williams, BA, MA, PGCE
Mr E Whitmore, BA, MLS, PGCE
Mr P Foley
Miss L Taber, BA

Geography:
*Mrs H Pestaille, BA, PGCE

History:
Miss I Saenz-Some, BA, PGCE
Mr P Foley

Home Economics:
Mrs B Rodgers, BA, GTP
Sister T Roseingrave, CertEd, CTC

Information Technology
*Mr J Boonzaier, BCom, HDE
Mr I Kay, BSc, ICM, GTP

Latin:
Mrs F Stamidou, BA, MA

Learning Resources:
*Mr E Whitmore, BA, MLS, PGCE

Mathematics:
*Mr J Boonzaier, BCom, HDE
Mr L Kasza, BEng, PGCE
Mrs M Platona-Basiel, BSc, PGCE
Mr R Hugill, BSc, PGCE

Modern Languages:
French:
*Mrs A Orr, BA, PGCE
Miss E Monchaux, BA, PGCE
Spanish:
Miss I Saenz-Some, BA, PGCE

Music:
Mrs M K Gil, BA, PGCE
Miss P Tham, BM

Physical Education:
Miss II Joncs

Psychology:
Mr P Hasell, BSc, MA, PGCE

Religious Education:
*Ms M Clancy, BA, PGCE
Mrs D Mela, GLCM, ALCM

Science:
*Mr R Odell, BSc, PGCE
Dr D Black, PhD
Mrs D Martin, BSc, PGCE, MSc
Dr M Wall, BSc, PhD, PGCE
Miss F Agrotis, Dip Med Tech (*Laboratory Technician*)

Sociology:
Mr P Hasell, BSc, MA, PGCE

Visiting Teachers:
Mrs V Charles (*LAMDA Speech & Drama*)
Miss A Henckel (*Singing*)
Ms A Renshaw (*Flute*)
Mr J Lee (*Drums*)
Mr I Cuthill (*Violin*)

Administration:
Ms F Watts (*School Secretary and Headmasters' PA*)
Mrs A Fitzpatrick, BA
Mrs M Keane, BA
Ms S Lamsley
Catering: The Brookwood Partnership
Information Technology Manager: Mr I Kay, BSc, ICM, GTP
Marketing and Communications: Mrs P Patel, BA
House Keeping: Mrs P Meally
Site Manager: Mr C Heaney
Groundsman: Mr D Meally
General Assistant: Mr J Pendlebury
General Assistant P/T: Mr P Mills
General Assistant P/T: Mr J Slawson
General Assistant P/T: Mr M Cork

Age Range. 11–18 Girls.
Number in School. 260 Day Girls.
Fees per term (2011-2012). £3,720.

St Martha's is an independent Catholic school for girls welcoming all denominations, faiths and nationalities into our community. Located in the leafy environs of Monken Hadley Common, we treasure our picturesque rural surroundings yet benefit from close public transport links by tube and rail to central London.

We are renowned as a warm and friendly school that believes a demanding and challenging ethos can go hand in hand with a caring and supportive atmosphere. Intellectual endeavour and hard work should be part of an exciting, stimulating and enjoyable environment that inspires achievement. St Martha's is in the top 100 independent schools for girls and places great emphasis on high academic standards which places us in the top 5% of independent schools in the UK for added value.

With the benefit of small classes, the particular talents of every girl are nurtured and developed by dedicated specialist teachers. Girls achieve well in exams and develop the skills and attitudes which enable them to work and study successfully.

Pastoral care and support are fundamental to ensuring the girls achieve their best in all areas of school life. St Martha's is a close-knit community where the girls are encouraged to look after each other. We are very proud of our girls' endeavours and achievements across the curriculum.

The girls also engage in an array of extra-curricular activities which we believe is vital to their development as a whole person and enables them to develop their self-esteem and confidence so that all their talents grow and flourish. Our clubs are designed not only to widen your daughter's experiences beyond the classroom but also to allow her to have fun with her peers.

St Martha's also provides a bus service and a shuttle service to and from local rail and underground stations. The routes available on the bus service are extensive and we are accommodating in trying to add new pick up points onto these routes.

Choosing a school for your daughter for the vital years of secondary education is an important and often difficult task, and so we want to provide you with every opportunity to visit and be welcomed by us. Please come along to see just what makes us so special and experience at first hand why so many parents are choosing St Martha's to educate their daughters.

Charitable status. Congregation of the Sisters of Saint Martha is a Registered Charity, number 233809.

Saint Martin's
Solihull

Malvern Hall, Brueton Avenue, Solihull, West Midlands B91 3EN
Tel: 0121 705 1265
Fax: 0121 711 4529
e-mail: mail@saintmartins-school.com
website: www.saintmartins-school.com

Motto: *The Grace of God is in Courtesy*
Founded 1941. Independent Day School for girls aged 2¾ to 18.

Board of Governors:
President: Baroness Joan Secombe, JP
Chair: Mr M Hope-Urwin, JP
Revd J Bradford, BA, MEd, FRSA
Mrs N S Bridgewater, JP
Ms E Butler
Miss A Davies, BSc, FCA, ATII, MSPI
Mrs P Harbour, MA
Dr S Madeley, MSc, PhD, JP
Mrs F de Minckwitz
Mr J Shepherd, FRICS

Clerk to the Governors and Bursar: Mr S Brown, BSc Loughborough

Head: Mrs J Carwithen, BSc, MA London, PGCE

Deputy Head: Mrs J Parker, BSc Reading, MA Nottingham, PGCE

Director of Studies & Head of Sixth Form: Mrs C Smith, BA Oxon, PGCE

Staff:

Art:
Mrs M Terry, BA University of Wales Newport, PGCE
Technician: Mrs S Le Resche

Business Studies and Economics:
Mr K Reeves, BA Lancaster, PGCE

Classics:
Mr K Carroll, BA Nottingham, PGCE
Mrs L Beaumont, BA Manchester, PGCE

Dance:
Ms J Felix

Drama:
Mrs J Plain-Jones, BA Hertfordshire, CertEd, LWCMD
  (*Speech and Drama*)

English:
Mrs C Inns, BA Kent, PGCE
Mrs R Speirs, BA Nottingham, PGCE
Mrs S Watton, BA Hull, PGCE

Food and Textiles:
Mrs J Fine, CertEd Gloucester College
Mrs J Massarella, BEd Bath College

Geography:
Mrs F Fowles, BA Dunelm, MSc Reading, PGCE
Miss C Bednall, BSc Cheltenham, MSc London, PGCE

History:
Mr M van Alderwegen, BA Leeds, MA Nottingham, PGCE
Mrs C Smith, BA Oxon, PGCE

Information Technology:
Mrs C Dance, BSc Keele, PGCE
Mrs A Short, BSc London, PGCE
Network Manager: Mr P Carlson, BS from St Paul TVI
Technician: Mr D Johnson

Learning Support:
Mrs F Franklin, BA Trinity & All Saints

Mathematics:
Mrs H Barber, BA York, PGCE
Mrs J Carwithen, BSc, MA London, PGCE
Mrs R Lawson, BEd Warwick
Mrs E Linford, BSc Salford, MSc Southampton, PGCE
Mrs A Short, BSc London, PGCE

Modern Languages:
Mr P Delaney, BA Exeter, PGCE
Mrs C Gibney, DUT Nancy, MIL, PGCE
Mrs I Jardon, DipIl, PGCE
Mrs C Mousset, BA, MA Merton College Oxford, PGCE

Music:
Mr P Allen, BA Liverpool, PGCE, ALCM
Mrs R Jenkins, BMus Birmingham, Dip Music Therapy,
  MA, GTP, ALCM
Cello: Mrs J Ludford, AGSM
Clarinet/Saxophone: Mrs K Moore
Drums: Mr J Bashford, BMus
Flute: Mrs A Thompson, BA, PGCE
Guitar: Mr M Whittaker, BMus
Piano: Mrs S Williamson, GRSM, ARCM
Piano/Keyboard: Ms L Hands
Singing: Mrs G Hartley, GBSM, ABSM
Violin/Viola: Mrs G Kirby, G Mus, PGCE, ALCM, LTCL

Physical Education:
Mrs H Burgess, BA Birmingham, PGCE
Mrs H Bradbury, AIST, MSTA
Mrs J Elston, CertEd Bedford College
Mrs T Gallagher, BEd Leeds
Mrs J Green, BSc Cheltenham and Gloucester, PGCE
Mrs S Trenchard, BEd London

Psychology:
Mrs M E Thompson, BSc Nottingham, PGCE

Religious Studies:
Mrs H Bryant, BA Dunelm, PGCE

Science:
Mrs B Ridley, BSc Wales, MAEd, PGCE
Mr N Bray, BSc Wales, PGCE
Mrs J Parker, BSc Reading, MA Nottingham, PGCE
Mrs S Parker, BSc Leicester, PGCE
Dr R L Parkin, BSc Coventry, PhD Glasgow, PGCE
Mrs A Short, BSc London, PGCE
Mrs J Waters, BSc Birmingham, PGCE
Technician: Miss D Gnych

Technology:
Mrs L Winnett, BEd Sheffield, CertEd
Technician: Mrs S Le Resche

Deputy Head (*Nursery to Year 6*): Mrs A Wilson, BEd Dunelm

Junior School (Years 4–6):
Deputy of Junior School: Mrs E Inglis, BEd
Mrs D Griffiths, BA Open, CertEd
Mrs T Marsh, BEd Bath College of Education
Mrs M Schofield, BA Dunelm, PGCE
Miss H Winn, LLB Manchester Metropolitan, PGCE
Teaching Assistant: Mrs J Crampton

Alice House *(Nursery–Year 3)*
Deputy of Alice House: Mrs McArthur, BA East London,
  PGCE
Mrs L Campbell, CertEd West Hill
Miss N L Ginns, BA Durham, PGCE
Mrs P Haynes, BEd Birmingham Polytechnic
Mrs V Higley, BEd Christ's & Notre Dame
Mrs E Pimlott, BSc Portsmouth, PGCE

Teaching Assistants:
Mrs S Coles
Mrs K Coley
Miss W Evans
Miss A Field
Mrs J Green
Mrs M Lee
Mrs S Sargent

Location. Saint Martin's is a well-established day school
for approximately 450 girls situated in a beautiful twenty-
acre site in the south of Solihull. Solihull is about 8 miles
from Birmingham and is on the edge of a rural district
within very easy reach of Warwick, Coventry, Leamington
Spa and the M42.

Buildings and Facilities. In addition to the main school
buildings which are attached to the very fine Grade II listed
Malvern Hall, there are separate, self-contained buildings
for the Preparatory and Junior Departments; the Sixth Form
is housed in renovated and extended listed buildings near to
the main school. The school has its own 25-metre indoor
swimming pool and an extensive synthetic sports pitch has
recently opened on the site. All playing fields, including tennis and netball courts, are on the premises and an exceptionally wide range of indoor and outdoor activities is offered.

The school enjoys well-resourced, specialist accommodation for teaching science, music, art, drama, ICT and technology.

Curriculum. Girls receive a broad academic education
with considerable opportunities for the development of individual interests and good academic standards are maintained. Emphasis is placed on hard work and independent
learning. Courses leading to GCSE examinations are offered
in all the usual subjects as well as ICT, Spanish, German,
Latin, Classical Civilisation, Art and Music and all girls are
required to continue with Mathematics, English Language,
English Literature, a modern language and all three sciences. Classes are not streamed, but some subjects are taught
in ability sets. In the Sixth Form, the majority of girls will
study four Advanced Subsidiary subjects in the first year
and complete three Advanced Level courses in the second
year chosen from the same range as is offered at GCSE, with
the addition of Economics, Business Studies, Psychology
and Critical Thinking. Virtually all Sixth Form students go
on to higher education and all senior pupils receive extensive careers education and advice and all take part in work
experience in Year 11 and the Lower Sixth.

Extra-Curricular Activities. Sport, music and drama
are all strong in school: plays and concerts are held throughout the year at all ages and a very large proportion of girls
study at least one instrument. A large selection of other
extra-curricular interests is catered for, such as calligraphy,
Young Enterprise and the Duke of Edinburgh's Award
Scheme. Clubs and societies are encouraged. There are
many visits to enrich the curriculum, including regular field
trips, and trips abroad to Merville, Iceland, Geneva, Italy and
New York among others.

Admission is by assessment for girls aged 5–10 and by
interview and examination for older pupils. Girls are admitted to the Sixth Form on the basis of GCSE results and interview.

Fees per term (2011-2012). Reception–Year 2 £2,530;
Year 3 £2,650; Years 4–6 £2,925; Senior School and Sixth
Form £3,485. Nursery: £37.52 per full day.

Scholarships. *(See Scholarship Entries section.)* A number of scholarships, including music and sports scholarships,
are awarded annually for admission at 11+ and scholarships
are awarded to girls entering the Lower Sixth or to enable a
girl in the school to complete her education.

Charitable status. Saint Martin's (Solihull) Limited is a
Registered Charity, number 528967. It exists to provide education for girls.

St Mary's School Ascot

St Mary's Road, Ascot, Berks SL5 9JF
Tel: 01344 623721 (Main Switchboard)
          01344 293614 (Admissions)
e-mail: admissions@st-marys-ascot.co.uk
website: www.st-marys-ascot.co.uk

Governing Body:
Chairman: The Hon Charles Martyn-Hemphill
Mr Jonathan Agnew
Mrs Oonagh Berry
Mrs Clare Colacicchi
Mr Peter Davis
Dr Andrew Gailey
Mr Patrick Gaynor
Mr George Jerjian
Mr Frank Morgan, BSc, PGCE, MEd
Professor Richard Parish
Miss Margaret Rudland, BSc
Mr Vincent Thompson

Trustees:
Chairman: Mr Geoffrey van Cutsem, FRICS
Mr Mark Armour
Baroness Sarah Hogg, MA
Sr Christina Kenworthy-Browne CJ, BA
Mrs Pauline Mathias
Mr Michael Milbourn
The Hon Mrs Olga Polizzi
Mr Brian Stevens

Management and Administration:

Headmistress: Mrs Mary Breen, BSc Exeter, MSc
  Manchester

Deputy Headmistress: Mrs Virginia Barker, BSc Reading,
  PGCE
Deputy Headmistress Boarding: Mrs Elizabeth Hewer, MA
  Cantab, PGCE
Director of Studies: Mr Michael Clennett, MA Oxon, MA
  London, Dip RE, PGCE
Head of Sixth Form: Dr Gareth Williams, BA Camb, MA
  Camb, DEd Cardiff

Bursar: Mr Giles Brand
Assistant to Bursar: Mrs Julie Osborne
Accountant: Mr Andrew Tidd
Assistant to Accountant: Mrs Sue Evans
Assistant to Accountant: Miss Chantal Morgan-Tolworthy
Caterer: Mr Cliff Atkinson
PA to the Headmistress: Mrs Phyllida Dewes, BA Leeds,
  MIPD
Registrar: Mrs Sandra Young
Assistant to the Registrar: Mrs Christine Holland
Recruitment Administrator: Mrs Nicola MacRobbie, LLB
  Southampton

Administrative Assistant: Mrs Christiane Scott, Lic Phil Zurich
Cover Supervisor: Mrs Michelle Vandenberg, BA Royal Holloway, PGCE
Lunch & Cover Supervisor: Mrs Sally McLachlan
Lunch & Cover Supervisor: Mrs Alain Heath
Development & Alumnae Director: Mrs Wanda Nash, BA, MEd
Assistant to the Development & Alumnae Director: Mrs Catherine Leneghan
School Secretary: Mrs Frances Green
School Receptionist: Mrs Sheila Hickmott
Sports Centre Weekend Supervisor: Mr Matt Davies
Housekeeper: Mrs Moyra Atkinson
Clerk of Works: Mr Terence Ford
Administrator to the Clerk of Works: Mrs Rebecca Johnson
School Doctor: Dr Gillian Tasker, MB BS, DRCOG
Senior Nursing Sister: Mrs Monica McGeown, RGN, SCM
Nursing Sister: Mrs Philippa Perera, RGN, RM
Nurse: Mrs Lesley Steele-Perkins, RGN, RM
CJ Chaplain: Sister Jane Livesey CJ, MA Cantab
Independent Listener: Mrs Marion Haycocks, HE Dip Counselling

Heads of House:
Mary Ward House: Mrs Brenda Vockings, BA Wales, BSA Surrey, PGCE
Babthorpe: Mrs Helena West, BA Surrey, PGCE
Bedingfeld:
Mr Tom Parsons, MA York
Mrs Katie Parsons, BA York, MA Warwick
Poyntz: Ms Roisin Toner, BA Cantab, MA London, PGCE
Rookwood: Mrs Helen Jansen, BEd Central School of Speech & Drama
Wigmore:
Mrs Valerie Hutchinson, BA Cork, Dip CompSc, DipEd HDGC
Mr Nigel Hutchinson, GBSM, ARCO, ARCM, LTCL

Residential Staff:

Miss E Cuff, BA East Anglia, CELTA	Miss K Horwood
	Mrs J Hunt
Miss Jane Bennett	Mrs B Lister
Mrs C Candappa	Mrs K Rabey
Mrs C Charman	Miss V Shipley
Mrs C Crane	Miss S Strongman
Mrs A Curtis, BA OU, BSc Anglia, FRGS	Miss V Swire
Mrs J Furneaux	Miss P Walker
Mrs B Grice	Mrs R Webb

Graduate Assistants:
Miss L Allen, BSc Edinburgh
Miss H Crumpton, BA Durham
Miss H Dunn, MA Edinburgh
Miss A Stollery, BSc Birmingham

Academic Departments:

Art and Design:
Mr M Mitchell, BA Bristol Polytechnic, PGCE (*Head of Department*)
Mrs D Farrell, BA Middlesex, BTEC Kent Inst Art & Design (*Textiles*)
Miss L Green, BA De Montfort, Reigate College of Art & Design, PGCE (*Art and Design*)
Miss S James, BA Plymouth, MA St Martins, PGCE
Mrs X Harrison, BA Wales, PGCE (*Ceramics*)
Miss H Oakden, BA Manchester, MA Courtauld (*History of Art*)
Mr T Parsons, MA York (*History of Art*)
Miss G Wigley, BA Coventry, MA Edinburgh (*Photography*)

Classics:
Mrs L Povey, BA Nottingham, MPhil London (*Head of Department*)
Mr M Clennett, MA Oxon, MA London, Dip RE, PGCE
Miss M Fisher, BA Wales, BA OU, ACCEG, PGCE
Ms A Wright, MA St Andrews

Drama:
Mr T Jelley, BA Surrey, MA Warwick, FRSA (*Head of Department*)
Mrs J Brayton, BA Lancaster
Miss B Carr, BA Southampton
Mr C Dexter (*Assistant Drama Technician*)
Mrs H Jansen, BEd Central School of Speech & Drama
Mrs A McNamara, BA Manchester, MA Ed
Mr I Warboys (*Rose Theatre Manager*)

English:
Mrs H Trapani, BA Leicester, MA Hong Kong, PGCE (*Head of Department*)
Miss D Borucka, BA York, MA York, PGCE
Mrs S Head, BA Nottingham, PGCE London
Mr T Parsons, MA York (*History of Art*)
Miss V Penn, MA Exeter, PGCE
Mrs L Waltho, BA, MLitt Newcastle

Humanities:
Mr M Clennett, MA Oxon, MA London Dip RE, PGCE
Mrs A Flamson, BSc Manchester Metropolitan, PGCE
Mrs E Hewer, MA Cantab, PGCE (*Geography*)
Mr D Hillman, BA Oxon, MSc London, PGCE (*Economics and Politics*)
Mrs K Holdich, MSc Kingston, PGCE
Mr A Knowles, BSc Liverpool, MSc Liverpool (*Geography*)
Mrs M Lake, BA Hatfield, PGCE (*History*)
Mr J Powell, BA Leeds, MSc London, PGCE (*Economics & Politics*)
Miss H Rider, BA Bath, PGCE (*History*)
Mr P Smith, BA Swansea, MA Warwick, PGCE (*Economics and Politics*)
Mrs B Vockings, BA Wales, BSA Surrey, PGCE (*Geography*)
Dr G Williams, BA Camb, MA Camb, DEd Cardiff (*Politics and History*)

Information & Communications Technology:
Miss B Hudson-Reed, BA Natal Univ, HDE, FDE (*Head of Department*)
Miss J Davis, BA Newcastle, PGCE, DipIT
Mrs V Hutchinson, BA Cork, DipComSc, DipEd, HDGC
Miss V Parsons, BSc Portsmouth
Mr A West

Mathematics:
Mrs R Davies, BEd Cantab (*Head of Department*)
Mrs V Barker, BSc Reading, PGCE
Mrs B Breedon, BEd Queen's Belfast, MSc Ulster
Mrs W Dutton, BSc Southampton, PGCE
Mrs L Matthews, BEd London
Mrs G Miles, BSc London, PGCE
Mrs E Whittaker, BA Wilhelms-Universität, Münster, PGCE

Modern Languages:
Mme E Cook, DEUG Licence Toulouse, AdvDip English Studies, PGCE (*Head of Department, French*)
Mrs R Cabrera, Lic en traducción Granada (*Spanish*)
Miss E Caretti, MA Milan, PGCE (*Italian*)
Mrs S Chasemore (*German Assistant*)
Mlle V Feuillet, DEUG Licence Maîtrise Sorbonne, PGCE (*French*)
Mlle E Eymin, DEUG Licence d'Anglais Toulouse, MA London, PGCE (*French*)
Mlle M Hervi, Licence Maîtrise Rennes, PGCE (*French*)
Miss S Martin (*French*)

Miss E Platts, BA Southampton, PGCE (*Spanish*)
Mrs S Webb, BA Cantab, PGCE (*German*)

Music:
Director of Music: Mr D Andrew, MA, BMus Oxford,
ARCO
Asst Director of Music: Mr N Hutchinson, ARCO, ARCM,
GBSM, LTCL
Dr J Brandon, MMus London, GBSM, ARCO, ARCM,
LTCL
Miss K-W Lee, MMus Royal College of Music
Ms J Chapman (*Secretary*)

Physical Education:
Miss G Eamer, BSc Coventry, PGCE (*Head of
Department*)
Miss J Brooker, BSc Gloucestershire
Mr A Flamson, BTEC Loughborough, CCA Exmouth
(*Head of Tennis*)
Mrs J Freeme, BEd Johannesburg, PGCE
Miss A Haylett, Dip Sports Psychology Newcastle College
Miss A Lloyd, BA Loughborough, PGCE
Miss L Lock, BSc Worcester, PGCE
Mrs Z Warboys (*Modern Dance*)
Mrs A Wright, BA OU, CertEd Chelsea College

Religious Education:
Mrs M-T Slater, BA London, PGCE, DPSE (*Head of
Department*)
Mr P Golden, BA Stirling, PGCE
Mr M J Hughes, PhB Rome, CertEd Birmingham
Sister Michaela Robinson CJ, CertEd London, PG
DipSpLD Dyslexia
Ms R Toner, BA Cantab, MA London, PGCE
Mrs H West, BA Surrey, PGCE
Mrs M Vandenberg, BA Royal Holloway, PGCE

Sciences:
Mrs P Shaw, BSc Leeds, PGCE (*Head of Biology*)
Mrs M Breen, BSc Exeter, MSc Manchester (*Physics*)
Mrs L Carlsson, BSc London (*Biology*)
Mrs A Curtis, BA OU, BSc Anglia, PGCE (*Biology*)
Mrs H Hesp, BSc Manchester, PGCE (*Physics*)
Mr N Jones, BSc Wales, MSc Wales, PGCE
Mr R Kernley, BSc London, PGCE (*Chemistry*)
Dr D Lampus, MSci Calgiari, PhD Nottingham. PGCE
(*Chemistry*)
Mrs J Lasouska, BSc Scranton University (*Biology*)
Mr D Riding, MPhys Sheffield, PGCE (*Physics*)
Miss C Roberts, MA Oxon, PGCE (*Chemistry*)
Mrs S Senior, BSc Durham, PGCE (*Physics*)
Mrs J Ford, ONC and HNC Med Lab Sciences
(*Technician*)
Mrs S Howard, BSc UMIST, MSc UMIST
Mrs L Weston, City and Guilds Cert (*Technician*)

Miscellaneous:
Librarian and Careers Officer: Mrs C Norvill, BA Lib,
CCEG
Reprographics: Mr R Liles
Examinations Officer: Mr M Hughes, PhB Rome, CertEd
Birmingham
Assistant Examinations Officer: Mlle V Feuillet, DEUG
Licence Maître Sorbonne, PGCE
Food Technology: Ms J Sherrard-Smith, BSc Westminster,
PGCE

Special Needs Coordinators:
Sr Michaela Robinson CJ, CertEd London, PGDipSpLD
Dyslexia
Mrs W Dutton, BSc Southampton, PGCE

Duke of Edinburgh's Award Scheme:
Head: Mrs A Wright, BA OU, CertEd Chelsea College
Mr P Edmunds, CertEd, MA Oxford Brookes

Mlle E Eymin, DEUG Licence d'Anglais Toulouse, MA
London, PGCE
Mr N Jones, BSc Wales, MSc Wales, PGCE

St Mary's School Ascot is a Roman Catholic boarding
school founded by the Religious of the Institute of the
Blessed Virgin Mary. St Mary's today is a self-governing,
self-financing school.

Founded in 1885, the school is set in 55 acres within easy
reach of London and Heathrow and close to the M4, M3 and
M25 motorways.

Numbers on roll. Boarders 367, Day pupils 13.

Age range. 11–18.

Method of Entry. 11+ and 13+ School's own examination and interview. There is a small entry at Sixth Form.

Scholarships and Bursaries. (*See Scholarship Entries
section.*)

Fees per term (2011-2012). Boarders £9,740, Day pupils
£6,930.

Curriculum. All pupils follow a broad curriculum to
GCSE including Religious Education, English, History,
Geography, Maths, Biology, Physics, Chemistry, French,
German, Italian, Spanish, Latin, Music, Drama, Art and
Design, Information Technology and Physical Education.
Tuition is also available in Piano, most String and Wind
Instruments, Ballet, Tap Dancing, Speech and Drama,
Ceramics and Craft activities, Tennis, Photography.

All pupils are prepared for GCSE at 16+ and typically
take 10 subjects.

Sixth Formers have a choice of 25 AS/A2 Level subjects
and normally study 5 AS subjects including Critical Thinking in the Lower Sixth year. Interview, CV and course choice
preparation is offered to all Upper Sixth including Oxbridge
candidates. They are encouraged to undertake some of the
many extra activities on offer and develop skills outside their
A Level curriculum. Sixth Formers also have their own tutor
who liaises closely with the Careers Specialist. Careers
advice forms an integral part of the curriculum. This is supported by work experience, work shadowing placements and
talks from external speakers, including Ascot Old Girls. The
majority of Sixth Formers go on to university, and preparation is offered to Oxbridge candidates.

The School is a member of ISCO (Independent Schools
Careers Organisation).

Religious Education is an integral part of the curriculum
and the chapel holds a central position in the life of the
school.

Sport. A varied programme is offered depending on age
group. It includes Netball, Hockey, Gym, Swimming,
Rounders, Tennis, Squash, Badmington and Athletics.

Purpose-built sports complex with sports hall, dance studio, squash courts and fitness suite.

Drama. New Performing Arts Centre which includes a
flexible auditorium with lighting catwalks and control room
with teaching facilities, fully-equipped drama studio and
make-up and dressing rooms.

Art, Music, Science, Modern Languages and English.
Specialist buildings are provided for all of these subjects and
all pupils are encouraged to develop their musical, artistic,
scientific and linguistic skills.

Libraries. State of the art library with fully integrated
information technology and access to school internet.

Other Activities. Senior pupils are encouraged to participate in Community Service Projects, and those interested
may enter the Duke of Edinburgh's Award Scheme. There is
a wide range of club activities for all ages, and, as a termly
boarding school, generous provision is made for evening
and weekend activities.

Charitable status. St Mary's School Ascot is a Registered Charity, number 290286. Its aim is to provide an excellent education in a Christian atmosphere.

St Mary's Calne

Calne, Wiltshire SN11 0DF
Tel: 01249 857200
Fax: 01249 857207
e-mail: office@stmaryscalne.org
website: www.stmaryscalne.org

Chairman of Governors: Mr S Knight, FRICS

Headmistress: Dr Helen Wright, MA Oxon, MA Leics,
   EdD Exeter, PGCE Oxon, FRSA, MIoD

Deputy Head: Mrs N Botterill, BSc Middlesex, MA
   London, PGCE Glasgow, NPQH, FRGS

Senior Master: Mr J Rothwell, MA Oxon

Director of Studies: Mrs C Strudwick, L-ès-L Sorbonne

Director of Development and Alumnae Relations: Miss L
   Leadbetter, BA Lancaster, PGCE Hull

School Chaplain: The Reverend P Giles

Director of Admissions and Marketing: Mrs C Depla, MA
   St Andrews

Bursar: Mr J McCausland, BA Deakin

St Mary's Calne is a boarding and day school of around
325 girls between the ages of 11 and 18. Approximately
80% board, and all take part in the full curriculum and extra-
curricular activities on offer.

When girls leave St Mary's, they are well-rounded, confident and ready to face all the challenges that lie ahead. All
girls go on to higher education and this transition is eased by
the 'pre-university experience' offered at St Mary's, facilitated by our Sixth Form Centre.

Throughout a girl's time at St Mary's, she is taught as an
individual and is supported continually by her personal tutor
who supervises her general welfare and academic progress
and gives her parents a clearly identified point of contact.

St Mary's has a forward-thinking curriculum that is continually developing in order to provide girls with an education that takes into account their individual interests and
ability levels. The curriculum offers breadth and depth,
intellectual stimulation and scope for creativity both inside
and outside the classroom. St Mary's encourages independent learning and motivates, challenges and inspires the
girls so that they become lifelong learners.

Girls consistently perform well in public examinations. In
2010, 91% of all A Level grades were A*–B and half of the
girls achieved A*–A grades in all of their examinations. We
look for girls who have potential and an eagerness to learn,
whatever their education before joining us.

There are many opportunities for leadership, community
service and extra-curricular activity which enhance and are a
key part of the curriculum. 80% of the girls play musical
instruments and the Chamber Choir has recently performed
in Italy, London, Paris and New York. Drama productions in
the theatre are exceptional and have transferred to both the
London stage, due to our unique relationship with RADA,
and the Edinburgh Festival Fringe. The school is currently
represented internationally, nationally and at county level in
sport, and all girls have access to our fitness suite and indoor
pool. Life at St Mary's is about much more than what goes
on in the classroom; the girls thrive in a safe, healthy and
happy atmosphere.

Fees per term (2011-2012). Boarding £9,898–£10,100,
Day £7,203–£7,350.

Scholarships. Scholarships available at main entry points
include Academic and All-Rounder, which are means-tested
and could be worth up to 40% of the fees; Music and Choral,
which receive free musical tuition, and Art, Drama and
Sport which are worth £1000 per annum. Exhibitions may

also be available to pupils showing outstanding ability in a
single subject. Foundation Scholarships are means-tested
and could be worth up to 100% of the fees.

All awards are retained to the end of Sixth Form and are
reviewed at regular intervals. Candidates who are successful
in gaining an award, but require greater remission in fees in
order to be able to take up their place may apply for a means-
tested Bursary.

Charitable status. St Mary's School (Calne) is a Registered Charity, number 309482 and exists for the education of
children.

St Mary's School
Cambridge

Bateman Street, Cambridge CB2 1LY
Tel: 01223 353253 Headmistress and School Office
Fax: 01223 357451
e-mail: enquiries@stmaryscambridge.co.uk
website: www.stmaryscambridge.co.uk

Founded in 1898 by the Religious Order of the Institute of
the Blessed Virgin Mary (IBVM), St Mary's School is an
independent Catholic Day and Boarding School for girls
aged 4–18, located close to the centre of Cambridge, in its
own grounds next to the beautiful University Botanic
Gardens. The School maintains a strong Catholic tradition
and ethos but welcomes and appreciates girls of every religious background or none.

Governing Body:
Chairman: Mrs D Wilkinson

Mrs J Bates	Mr W Matthews
Mr P Chamberlain	Mrs A McAllister
Mrs L Fairbrother	Mr F Morgan
Mrs A Hickling	Mr R Pearce-Gould
F P Leeming	Mr C Smart
Sr J Livesey CJ	Mrs S Varey

Clerk to the Governors and Bursar: Mr D Askew, AIIB,
   BA Hull

Headmistress: Miss Charlotte Avery, MA Oxon, MA
   London

Deputy Head (Community): Mr Richard Bird, BSc Hons
   Bath (*Physics*)
Deputy Head (Pastoral): Dr A Jackson, PhD Liverpool
   (*Chemistry*)
Deputy Head (Curriculum): Mr S Seidler, MBA Open
   University (*Religious Education*)

Teaching Staff:
Mr R Atkinson, BSc London (*Chemistry*)
Mr D Bennett, BA Cantab, MA Cantab (*Theology*)
Mrs V Bevan, BA Hons Australia, MA Cantab, MSc
   Edinburgh (*EFL*)
Mrs M Brown, MA St Andrews (*History*)
Mrs S Brown, MA Oxon (*Mathematics*)
Mrs A Chatterjee, PGCE London, BSc Hons London
   (*Biology*)
Mrs G Clifford, BA Winchester (*Art & Design*)
Ms J Cowan, BA Hons Cantab (*Geography*)
Mrs R d'Armada, BSc Manchester (*Mathematics*)
Ms K Darch, BA Hons King's College London (*French*)
Mrs K Dodsworth, MA Lampeter (*Theology*)
Miss J Earley, BA Northampton (*Physical Education*)
Mr T Edwards, BA Loughborough (*Mathematics*)
Mrs J Emmans, BA Hons West Surrey College of Art and
   Design (*Art & Design*)
Mrs J Essex, BSc Hons Bristol (*Mathematics*)
Mr P Fanourakis, BSc Dundee, MSc Cantab (*Mathematics*)

Miss A Fleming, BA Liverpool, MEd (*Religious Education*)
Ms L Fleming, BA Kent (*Physical Education*)
Mr D Gabbitas, MA Cantab (*Physics*)
Mrs H Garrett, MA Oxon (*English*)
Mrs S Gears, BA Hons Durham (*Director of Music*)
Mrs K Glencross, BA Cantab (*Mathematics*)
Dr C Goddard, MA Oxon, DPhil Oxon (*Classics*)
Miss S-E Godde, BEd Sydney (*Physical Education*)
Miss D Goodwin, BD Hons London (*Economics*)
Miss J Gregg, BA West Sussex Inst (*Physical Education*)
Mrs P Guy, MA Middlesex (*Language and Learning*)
Mrs E Hall, BSc Hons UMIST (*Mathematics*)
Miss M L Henham, BA Hons Cantab (*English*)
Mr J Hunnable, BA Hons Cantab (*Classics*)
Mrs H Jackson, BEd Nottingham (*Textiles*)
Miss S Jones, BA Hons Anglia Ruskin University (*Drama*)
Miss S Josiffe, BEd Bedford (*Physical Education*)
Mrs M Kakengi, BA Hons Evtek Institute (*Economics*)
Ms C Klimaszewska, CertEd Homerton (*Science*)
Dr G Klyve, DPhil Oxon (*Classics*)
Mrs A Ladds, BEd London (*Textiles*)
Mrs D Larman, BA London (*English*)
Miss N Lees, BA Hons Oxon (*Spanish*)
Mrs S Leighton-Scott, BA Wales (*Geography*)
Miss E Levy, BA Hons Cantab (*Music*)
Mr P Mallabone, BA Hons St Mary's College (*Religious Education*)
Miss K Marinho, BEng Hons Hertfordshire (*Information Technology*)
Mrs H Marmion, BA Hons Exeter (*German*)
Dr A McKinney, PhD Belfast, MTh Belfast, BA Hons (*Religious Education*)
Mr W Melville, BA Hons APU (*Art & Design*)
Dr G Miller, PhD Birmingham, BSc Manchester (*Physics*)
Ms S Mitchell, BA Hons Sheffield, MA York (*Psychology*)
Mrs P Nicholson, BA Liverpool (*Economics & Business Studies*)
Mrs C O'Connell, BEd Hons Brighton (*Physical Education*)
Ms M Overbury, BA Hons Kent, TEFL (*English*)
Mrs K Ratcliffe, BSc Natal, S Africa, MSc London (*Biology*)
Mrs L Reid, BA Hons Oxon (*English*)
Mr P Richards, BA, MA Nottingham (*History*)
Miss K Ring, BA Hons Wales (*English*)
Mrs D Russell, BSc Hons London, MSc London (*Physics*)
Mr M Scott, MA Oxon (*Science*)
Mrs T Shercliff, MA Cantab (*Science, Physics*)
Miss F Spore, MA Cantab (*Geography*)
Mrs S Vanderstay, Combined Hons Degree (*Drama*)
Dr C Walker, PhD London, BA Cantab (*German*)
Mrs C Williams, BSc St Andrews (*Chemistry*)
Mrs A Wilson, BA Hons Surrey (*Information Technology*)
Mrs S Wood, BA Hons Durham (*English*)

Nursing Staff: Mrs C Green, Mrs F Myers, Mrs M Brightwell

Boarding Staff:
Mrs S Bird (*Head of Boarding*)
Mrs A Crawford
Ms K Darch
Ms M Henham
Dr A McKinney
Ms H Pedlar (*Gap Student*)

Visiting Staff:
Mr Q Benziger (*Piano*)
Mrs S Blazeby (*Flute*)
Mrs L Britton (*Piano*)
Mr P Britton (*Piano*)
Mrs A Bury (*Flute, Clarinet*)
Mr D Carter (*Clarinet, Double Bass, Guitar*)
Ms A Daniels (*Singing*)
Mrs H Hymas (*Oboe*)
Mr J Landymore (*Saxophone*)
Ms A Mackenzie-Mills (*Singing*)
Ms G Oldham (*Cello*)
Ms R Platts (*Harp*)
Mr C Rutherford (*Trombone*)
Mrs R Stekly (*Speech & Drama*)
Mrs J Stevenson (*Violin*)
Mrs G Sutcliffe (*Violin*)
Miss S Tucker (*Speech & Drama*)
Mr A Vellacott (*Drums*)
Mrs K Weber (*Speech & Drama*)

Administrative Staff:
Head's PA: Mrs P Vallins
School Secretary: Mrs J Bauld
Director of Admissions & Marketing Strategy: Miss H Ison
Admissions Officer: Miss M Bottomley
Accountant: Mrs M Brown
Finance Assistant: Mrs K Simms
Accounts Secretary: Mrs J Doe
Careers Secretary: Mrs P Down
Marketing Officers: Miss C Westley, Miss L Beveridge
HR Manager: Mrs K Ross
HR Assistant: Mrs K Martin
Reprographics: Mrs S Law
Receptionist: Mrs C Turner, Mrs D Stutely
Domestic Bursar: Mrs S Heath
Catering Manager: Mr C Searle
Health and Safety Manager: Mr P Woods
Senior IT Technician: Mrs A Earl
IT Support Manager: Mr D Griffiths
Laboratory Technicians: Mrs M Crammond, Mrs E Miller, Mrs A Turpin
Site Maintenance: Mr E Knight, Mr N French

Admission. The School's main entry points are at 4+, 7+, 11+, 13+ and 16+. A few vacancies occur at other ages. Sixth Form entry is by examination and interview, conditional on 7 GCSE passes at A*–C, with B grade or above in those subjects to be studied at A Level.

Extra Subjects. Piano and Instrumental Music, Speech and Drama, and Dance.

Fees per term (2011-2012). Day Girls £4,230; Weekly boarding £7,840 inclusive; Full boarding £9,110.

Scholarships. Academic, Music, Art, Textiles, Drama, Performing Arts and Sport Scholarships are offered at 11+, 13+ and 16+. A Photography scholarship is also offered at 16+.

Curriculum. Within the setting of a Christian community the School provides an 'all-round' education, enabling each girl to realise her full potential. Students are prepared for GCSE, A Level, Oxbridge Entrance, and for other forms of higher education and professional training in a wide variety of careers. The curriculum includes Religious Education, English, History, Geography, Latin, French, German, Spanish, Mathematics, ICT, Physics, Chemistry, Biology, Art and Design, Textiles, Theatre Studies, Music, Drama, PE. Option schemes in Year 10 are arranged in such a way that each girl has a balanced programme without premature specialisation. In the Lower Sixth, students choose 4 subjects to study, making their choice from a total of 20 subjects. In the Upper Sixth, students continue their study of 3 or 4 subjects to A2 Level. All Sixth Formers follow an enrichment programme.

The School stands in its own grounds, close to the centre of Cambridge and adjoining the University Botanic Gardens. The complex of buildings contains Science laboratories, assembly halls, gymnasium, library, specialist rooms for Geography, Music, IT, Art, Textiles and Cookery.

Sixth Form Centre. The Sixth Form is housed in the newly refurbished 'Undercroft'. It provides the perfect setting for study and prepares students for life at university.

Sixth Formers also have their own ICT suite and two quiet study rooms.

Extra-Curricular Activities. The School provides a wide range of activities at lunch-times and after school – everything from Dance to Rowing and Arts Award, to The Duke of Edinburgh's Award Scheme and Young Enterprise Company.

Supervised Homework Club. Homework Club is available from 4–6 pm Monday–Thursday.

Boarding. We offer full as well as weekly boarding to pupils age 11+. Younger boarders share comfortable bedrooms (3–4 girls per room). Our weekly boarding facility is popular with both students and their parents as it offers the best of both worlds at school and at home.

Charitable status. St Mary's School, Cambridge is a Registered Charity, number 290180. It aims to promote and provide for the advancement of the education of children of any creed but particularly of the Roman Catholic faith.

St Mary's School
Colchester

Lexden Road, Colchester, Essex CO3 3RB
Tel: 01206 572544
Fax: 01206 576437
e-mail: info@stmaryscolchester.org.uk
website: www.stmaryscolchester.org.uk

Motto: *Scientia et Veritas*

Board of Governors:
Chairman: Mrs S Heath-Brook
Ms H Borgartz
Mr B Hogarth-Jones
Ms M Bell
Mr J Pendle
Mrs K Burns
Dr S Davidson
Mrs S Foakes
Mrs M Livingstone

Principal: **Mrs H Vipond**, BSc Hons Leeds, MEd Hatfield, CertEd, DipEd, NPQH

Vice-Principal: Mrs A Mullen, BEd Portsmouth, NPQH

Director of Studies: Mr P Burgoyne, BEd Anglia

Primary Head: Mrs E Stanhope, GMus Colchester, NPQH

Staff:
Mrs D Adamson, BA Brighton
Mr C Baalham, BEd Homerton, MSc Essex
Mr M J Barrett, CertEd S E Essex
Mr E W Black, BA Oxon, MA Keele
Ms G Boardman, BA Southampton
Ms D Booth, BA Middlesex, MA Goldsmiths
Mrs G Boyd, DipEd Moray House
Mrs A Bush, BEd Anglia
Mrs M Brown, CertEd Edge Hill
Mrs H Clayton-Grainger, BA Lancaster
Mrs K Daines, CertEd Walsall, DipEdSpN Cantab
Mr D Edwards, BSc Sheffield Hallam
Mrs L Gage, BEd Reading
Miss F Geraghty, BEd Edgehill
Mrs G Gerrard, GTCL, LTCL
Mrs L Gibbs, BA Chester
Mrs M Gowing, BA London
Mrs V Hall, BSc Essex
Mr J Hammersley, BA East Anglia
Mrs R Harries, BA London
Mr K Harris, CertEd Bognor Regis
Mrs D Hart, DipEd Bingley

Miss E Harvey, BA Lancaster
Miss E Hawkins, BEd De Montfort
Mrs V Heath, BEng Glasgow
Mrs A Heather, BA Coventry
Mrs J Johnson, BEd Brighton
Mrs C Kurzynski, BEd Anglia
Ms L Long, LLB Essex, PGCE Essex
Mrs K Margery, CertEd Eaton Hall
Mrs J Maydon, BEd Leicester
Mrs M Mitchell, BEd Chichester
Mrs L Murray, BSc Bucharest
Mrs V Nicholson, BEd Anglia
Mrs C J Parry-Jones, CertEd CNAA, FETC
Mrs L M Pendle, CertEd Cambridge
Mrs S Priestley, BA Keele
Mrs H Pritchard, BA Dunelm
Mrs R Robinson, BA Newcastle
Mrs D Rose, BEd Doncaster
Mrs S Ryan, BA Warwick, PGCE Herts
Mr J A Saunders, BA Wales
Mrs A Stopps, BSc Brighton, PGCE Brighton
Mrs S J Sutton, CertEd Sarum
Miss A Tew, BSc Hons Nottingham
Mrs L Taverner, CertEd Bedford
Mrs L Tilly, BA Stirling
Mr B Vidler, CertEd Exeter, DipEd Cantab
Mr N West, BA Griffith, Brisbane
Mrs S Wilding, BA Glamorgan

Visiting Staff:
Mrs M Blanchard, BA CNAA, LTCL (*Flute*)
Mrs F Hill, BA Mus Essex, LGSM, LTCL (*Woodwind*)
Mr A Johnson, BMus (*Guitar*)
Mr C Matthews, LLCM, CertMusicEd, TCL (*Brass*)
Mr T Parr, GMus CNAA, LTCL (*Piano, Singing*)
Ms C Simmons, LRAM (*Violin*)
Mrs G Watson, BA Colchester
Mr G Buck (*Percusssion*)
Mr Clark, BA Colchester

Bursar: Mr S Cooke
Finance Manager: Miss A Walker
Registrar: Ms S Gibson

History. St Mary's School was founded in the summer of 1908 and was originally based at St Mary's Terrace East on Lexden Road. It moved to its current premises, a Victorian house called Glen Mervyn, also on Lexden Road, in 1923. The neighbouring castle-style property, The Turrets, was purchased in 1974.

Due to the school's ongoing success and continued growth, another large Victorian residence was bought, three miles from the senior school, which became the base for the Lower School in 1982.

Lower School. Set in seven acres of grounds, St Mary's Lower School provides an idyllic environment for the girls to learn and play. In the grounds, an outdoor classroom has been constructed, which is perfect for nature, science and ecology studies.

As well as benefiting from a structured and stimulating curriculum, the girls also enjoy many extra activities. Our choir has been very successful in competitons and has sung at many prestigious venues, including the Barbican and the Royal Albert Hall. Excursions have included Buckingham Palace, Houses of Parliament and the Globe Theatre. Girls can enjoy a wide range of clubs including karate, netball and gardening.

St Mary's Kindergarten, for girls and boys aged from 2, was opened in 2011.

Senior School. Pupils enter the Senior School at Year 7 and enjoy a wide variety of subjects in accordance with the National Curriculum. Alongside the academic subjects, the students enjoy a wide range of activities and classes.

In PE, the girls participate in a variety of sports including netball, rugby, tennis, cross-country, basketball, football, hockey and athletics. St Mary's also has its own pony club which annually holds an interschool showjumping event.

In the Textiles department, students design and make their own creations which they model at our fashion shows. The pupils' artwork can be exhibited in our own 'Eat Your Art Out' Gallery in our dining room.

St Mary's also has a strong tradition of performing arts and music. Regular school productions mean that pupils of all ages have the opportunity to take part and learn new skills, from performing to production, and set construction, lighting and make up. Musical activities form a key part of school life, with choirs, orchestra and smaller instrumental groups performing at school functions and regular concerts for parents and friends.

The girls have the opportunity to enjoy travelling to many fascinating places: from history trips to the Somme to Skiing holidays. We have also visited a number of vibrant cities including Barcelona, Venice and Seville. The girls have the opportunity to take part in outdoor pursuits in central Spain, the Dordogne and the Pyrenees.

The St Mary's Experience. At St Mary's we pride ourselves on offering a remarkable educational experience where every girl is encouraged to achieve her very best. As an Independent Day School, situated in Colchester, we teach girls aged from 2–16 and our pupils benefit from a stimulating and diverse curriculum throughout their education. They are given the opportunity to participate in travel, sport, drama, the arts and community involvement, with the aim of enriching the school experience. This not only nurtures the girls' desire for learning, but also produces well-balanced, self-confident individuals, whose affinity with the school lasts a lifetime.

St Mary's School celebrates all of its students' successes, understanding how important this is to personal growth and development. The School focuses on the abilities of every child and the small class sizes provide the perfect environment for them to thrive. A recent Independent School Inspection praised the school for the outstanding quality of pastoral care. Our GCSE results consistently position us among the top local schools in the National League Tables and at the end of Key Stage 2 we have a significant number of girls gaining 11+ places.

Awards. St Mary's has twice been awarded the coveted Green Flag from the Eco Schools Initiative for its environmentally-friendly policies and is now aiming to be an ambassador school. Along with the Artsmark Gold Award and International School Award, St Mary's has also received Investors In People and Best Companies Awards. The Lower School has this year also been rewarded with Sing Up Platinum Award.

St Mary's School attributes its successes, large and small, to the School's ethos of embracing the modern world, while still retaining the traditions and family values that were so integral at its foundation.

Fees per term (2011-2012). Senior School: £3,255; Lower School: £1,650–£2,960.

Charitable status. St Mary's School (Colchester) Limited is a Registered Charity, number 309266.

St Mary's School
Gerrards Cross

Gerrards Cross, Buckinghamshire SL9 8JQ
Tel: 01753 883370
Fax: 01753 890966
e-mail: registrar@st-marys.bucks.sch.uk
website: www.stmarysschool.co.uk

Badge: *Ecce Ancilla Domini*
Founded by Dean Butler in 1872. Formerly at Lancaster Gate. Established in Gerrards Cross in 1937 as an Independent Day School catering for 330 day girls.

Governors:
Chairman: Mr D R Wilson, BA, FCA
Mrs C Bayliss, CertEd
Mr R J Burge
Mr D Campkin
Mrs C Eilerts de Haan, MSc ChemTech Ingenieur, PGCE
Mr N Hallchurch
Mrs P Hurd, NDD, ATC
Mr J Loarridge, OBE, RD, BA
Prof S Machin, MBChB, FRCP, FRCPath
Mr N Moss
Mrs H Phillips, FCA

Bursar: Mrs J Wilson, MBA

Headmistress: Mrs J Ross, BA Manchester

Deputy Headmistress: Dr J Ramsden, PhD, MSc UAE, BSc Hons Nottingham (*Physics*)

Middle School Tutor: Miss J H Miles, CertEd (*Mathematics*)
Upper School Tutor: Mrs S Vaughan, MA Oxford, PGCE (*Physics*)
Sixth Form Tutor: Mrs E Persaud, BA Hons Leicester, PGCE (*History, Careers*)

Senior House:
Miss S J Abbott, BA Hons Durham, PGCE (*Music*)
Mr M Adams, BSc Hons London, PGCE (*Physics and Chemistry*)
Miss F Alexander, BA Glasgow School of Art (*Art & Design*)
Mrs P Baggott, BPharm Hons Bradford, PGCE (*Science*)
Mrs E Beasley, BA Hons Cambridge (*Geography*)
Mrs L Burnhope, MA Theology Brunel (*Religious Education*)
Mrs J Cannon, BA Hons Newcastle, PGCE (*Spanish, French and Latin*)
Mrs M Christensen, Masters Law Nice, PGCE (*French*)
Mrs V Culmer, BA Hons Oxon, PGCE (*Drama*)
Mrs J Deadman, BEd Hons Exeter, PGCE (*Physical Education*)
Mrs J Dowling, HNC Microbiology (*Laboratory Technician*)
Mrs A Fitzpatrick, MA Hons Glasgow (*English*)
Mrs J V Giorgi, BA Hons Swansea, PGCE (*Geography*)
Mrs Z Glenister, BA Hons Newcastle upon Tyne, PGCE (*French and German*)
Miss T Hancock, HND Music/Theatre (*Speech & Drama*)
Mrs S Jones, MA Childrens Literature, BA Hons Reading, PGCE (*English*)
Mrs J L Kingston, BSc Hons Cardiff, MPhil Bath, PGCE (*Chemistry, Science*)
Miss C McKearney, MSc Hons Brunel (*Mathematics, InformationTechnology*)
Mrs S Moore, BEd Sussex (*Physical Education*)
Mrs A Morrison, TCert Auckland, New Zealand (*Design Technology, Numeracy*)
Mrs G Newman, GRSC Chemistry (*Laboratory Technician*)
Mrs E Roberts, CertEd Sheffield (*Home Economics*)
Mrs M Schwartz, BA Hons Leeds, PGCE (*Learning Support*)
Mrs J Shinnie, MSc Hons Bucks (*ICT Technician*)
Dr L Smith, PhD Surrey (*Mathematics*)
Miss H Snaith, MA Canterbury Christchurch (*Information Technology*)
Mrs C Stuart-Lee, MA Oxon, PGCE (*Learning Support Coordinator*)
Mr C Tucker, MA Oxon (*Mathematics*)

Mrs H Williams, BA Hons Cardiff, PGCE (*English and Media Studies*)
Mrs L Winter, BA Hons Nottingham, MBA (*Business Studies and Economics*)

Junior House:
Head of Department: Mrs A Maycock, BEd Hons Kingston (*General Subjects*)
Mrs S Brereton, BSc Leicester (*Combined Science*)
Mrs M Carney, BA Hons Galway (*Year 2 Class Teacher and French*)
Mrs R Galustian, BEd Hons Brunel, PGCE (*General Subjects and Religious Education*)
Miss K Gilliland, BEd PrimEd QTS De Montfort (*Physical Education*)
Mrs C Hargadon, BEd University of London Inst of Ed (*General Subjects and French*)
Mrs S Jenkins (*General Assistant, First Aider*)
Miss S Johnston, BA Ed Hons Exeter (*Mathematics and Design Technology*)
Mrs J Lukas, NNEB Cert (*Art, Nursery Teacher*)
Mrs H Mackinder, BA Hons PrimEd QTS Brighton (*General Subjects*)
Miss S Millar, NNEB (*Nursery Assistant*)
Mrs G Pierozynski, GRNCM, ARNCM, PGCE (*Music*)
Mrs J Redman, BA Hons (*General Subjects*)
Mrs J C Stone, BSc Hons Leicester, PGCE (*Science*)
Mrs C Wilson, ONC RSA, DipSpLD (*Learning Support*)

Visiting Staff:
Mr R Corden, ARCM, AI Kneller Hall (*Flute, Clarinet, Saxophone*)
Miss R Galustian, BACP (*School Counsellor*)
Miss K Harding, MA Hons, MPhil Cantab, LTCL (*Cello, Double Bass*)
Mrs J Holmes, BMus Hons, LRAM (*Piano*)
Mr J Keen, MIT (*Drumkit*)
Mrs J Miller, AISTD (*Ballet, Tap, General Dance*)
Miss J Stevenson, AGSM (*Singing*)
Mrs T Suggett, BA Hons Guildhall, PGDip Dist (*Singing*)
Mrs R Wheeler, ALCM, CT ABRSM (*Piano*)

Registrar & Headmistress's Secretary: Mrs C Pearcey

The School is situated in the attractive residential area of Gerrards Cross which is surrounded by beautiful countryside, 20 miles from London, close to the M25 and A40/M40, on the main bus routes and 10 minutes from the Railway Station.

The aim of the School is to provide an excellent academic and rounded education leading on to University for day girls between the ages of 3 and 18 and to enable each of them to develop their own talents and personalities in a happy, caring and disciplined environment, and to become successful, fulfilled adults.

Curriculum. Subjects offered include English Language and Literature, History, Geography, RE, Drama, Latin, French, German, Spanish, Italian, Business Studies, Economics, Information Technology, Mathematics, Chemistry, Biology, Physics, Music, Art, Home Economics, Key Skills, Gymnastics, Hockey, Netball, Tennis, Rounders, Football, Rugby, Swimming, Media, Personal, Social, Cultural and Health Care, Dancing and other sporting activities. Regular trips are made to places of educational interest, field courses are undertaken, foreign visits including a ski trip to the USA are arranged, and there is highly successful participation in The Duke of Edinburgh's Award Scheme and Young Enterprise. There is an excellent staff/pupil ratio.

Examinations. Girls are prepared for Entrance to the Universities and Colleges in all subjects; for the General Certificate of Education at AS, A2 and GCSE Level; RSA CLAIT Examinations, Associated Board Examinations in Music and examinations in Speech and Drama. Standardised tests are set at regular intervals in Junior House.

The Buildings are an attractive mixture of old and new and include 2 Libraries, Dining Hall, a Science Block with Laboratories and a Geography Room, a large open-plan Art Studio, a Home Economics Room, Textiles Room, 2 Computer Suites, a modern Sixth Form Centre, 2 Music Rooms, Drama Studio, Chapel and 2 Assembly Halls/Gymnasiums equipped to the highest standards. Junior House, in the grounds of the Senior House, comprises a Nursery and two modern purpose-built blocks, with a Science Laboratory, Hall, Gymnasium, Textiles/Art room and ICT suite. The lovely grounds include tennis and netball courts, a hockey pitch and an athletics lawn. A new Sport England full-size sports hall opened in 2009.

School Hours. The hours are 8.30 am – 3.40 pm. The School year is divided into 3 terms.

Reports. Full School Reports are sent to Parents at the end of each term and there are regular Parent/Staff meetings. The School also communicates with Parents via ParentMail.

Fees per term (2011-2012). £1,176–£4,260.

Scholarships are available at 7+, 11+ (including one for Music) and at 16+ in the Sixth Form. A means-tested Bursary scheme is in operation.

Charitable status. St Mary's School (Gerrards Cross) Limited is a Registered Charity, number 310634. It provides education for girls from Nursery to A level in a well-structured, academic and caring environment.

St Mary's School
Shaftesbury

Shaftesbury, Dorset SP7 9LP
Tel: 01747 854005 Head and Admissions
           01747 852416 School and Administration
           01747 851188 Bursar's Office
Fax: 01747 851557
e-mail: admin@st-marys-shaftesbury.co.uk
website: www.st-marys-shaftesbury.co.uk

Governors:
Major General Sir Sebastian Roberts (*Chair*)
Viscountess Asquith
Mr M Catchpole
Dr D J Ceiriog-Hughes
Mrs L Eeles
Sister Jane Livesey, CJ
Dr A-M May
Mr C McVeigh
Mrs B Quest-Ritson
Miss J Taylor

Management:

Head: Mr R James

Deputy Head: Mrs S Raffray
Director of Studies: Mr D Cohen
Bursar: Mr N M Peters
Head of Boarding: Mrs A Salmon
Senior Teacher & Registrar: Miss J Walker

Chaplain: Miss A Le Guevel
Resident Priest: Father Andrew Moore

Heads of School:
Mrs C Lane (*Head of Sixth Form*)
Mrs M Andow (*Head of Senior School*)
Mrs G Cork (*Head of Middle School*)
Mrs H Key (*Head of Lower School*)

Teaching Staff:
* Head of Department

Art & Design: Mrs J Hodge (*Art, Design*)
*Mrs J A Ridgway

Miss M Bridger (*Photography*)
Mrs D Sudlow (*Art, Design*)
Mrs J Tidbury-Coates (*Art Technician*)
Mrs K Banneel (*Art Technician*)

Business Studies:
Mrs M Reddyhoff

Careers:
Mrs C Lane (*Head of Guidance*)

Classics:
*Mr P Daley
Mrs D Clark

Drama:
Mr C J Sykes
Mrs S Holman

English:
*Ms R M R Brand
Mr D Cohen
Mrs S Holdaway
Mrs S Raffray
Mr C J Sykes (*Multiple Intelligences, G&T Coordinator*)

Geography:
*Mr P Davies
Mrs S Bramble

History:
*Mr T Goodwin
Mrs M Andow

History of Art:
Ms E Butterworth

ICT:
Mr J Pearce (*Network Manager*)
Mr A Hann (*ICT Technician*)
Mrs C Drew (*Subject Teacher*)
Mr C Norman (*Database Manager*)
Mr J Singleton (*Webmaster*)
Mr R Alexander (*ICT Technician*)

Mathematics:
*Mrs J Hall
Mr G Holdaway
Mr J O'Hare
Mrs D Kok
Mr A Rowden

Modern Languages:
*Mrs A Maclaine (*German, French*)
Mrs G Cork (*French*)
Mrs R Howcroft (*Spanish*)

Mrs A Lodder (*German, French*)
Mrs F M Rowland (*French*)
Mrs D Webb (*French, Spanish*)

Music:
*Miss D Radford (*Director of Music*)
Mrs S Pugh (*Head of Instrumental Music, Oboe, Recorder*)
Mr R James (*Piano*)
Miss S Williams (*Flute*)

Personal and Social Education:
Miss J Walker
Mrs A Salmon

Physical Education:
*Miss N Boyer
Mrs K Booth
Mrs C Collard
Mrs E James
Mrs B Roberts (*Pool Manager*)
Mrs A Salmon
Miss J Walker

Psychology:
Miss S Williams

Religious Education:
*Mrs J Bowe
Mrs C Lane
Mrs A Maclaine
Mrs S Raffray
Mrs Bramble
Miss A Le Gueval

Science:
*Mr P Rigby (*Physics*)
Dr G Caunt (*Biology*)
Mrs C Drew (*Chemistry*)
Mrs A Fearnley (*Chemistry*)
Miss S Flower (*Biology*)
Mrs D Kok (*Physics*)
Mrs V Rushton (*Biology*)
Mrs C Gray (*Science Technician*)
Mrs J Hill (*Assistant Lab Technician*)

Support Teaching:
Mrs R Davies (*Coordinator*)
Mrs Y Atkinson
Mrs H Hayward
Mrs J Kaskow
Miss Jo Maskell (*Learning Support Assistant*)
Mrs K McDonald
Mrs G Phillips
Mrs L Todd (*Learning Support Assistant*)
Dr H Vaughan

Examination Officer: Mrs D Clark
Librarian: Miss A Edmonds
Duke of Edinburgh's Award Scheme: Mrs M Reddyhoff
EAL & Portuguese: Mrs C Waddington

House Staff:

Head of Boarding: Mrs A Salmon

Givendale House:
Housemistress:
(*to be appointed*)
Assistants:
Mrs A Hannam
Mrs P Sealy

Harewell House:
Housemistress:
Mrs S Holman
Assistants:
Mrs S Shutler
Mrs E Samoluk

Hewarth House:
Housemistress:
Ms E Seal-Newman
Assistants:
Mrs S Hill
Mrs M Tomlinson

Nursing Staff:
Mrs L Fish, RN
Mrs P Hadley, RN
Mrs P Ross-Hurst, RN
Mrs S Savage, RN (*Head Nurse*)
Mrs K Webber, RN

Administration:
Mrs S Awdry (*Assistant to Registrar*)
Mrs K Condie (*Bursar's Assistant*)
Miss L Coffin (*School Office*)
Mrs K Keen (*Administration Assistant*)
Mrs M Gordon (*Accounts & Human Resources Bursar*)
Mrs L Gardiner (*Domestic Bursar*)
Mr F King (*Head Groundsman*)
Miss L Martin (*Accounts Assistant*)
Mrs E O'Sullivan (*School Office, Evenings/weekends*)
Mr R A Pitman (*Caretaker*)
Mrs J Sampson (*Head's PA*)
Miss D Williams (*Accounts Assistant*)

Visiting Staff:

Music:
Mrs K Alder (*Piano*)
Mrs D Binnington (*Piano, Singing*)
Mrs J Brookfield (*Flute, Piano*)
Mrs A Caunce, ARCM (*Piano*)
Mrs V Cross (*Singing*)
Mr J Gilbert (*Percussion*)
Mrs K Hawes (*Violin*)
Mr W Hawes (*Brass*)
Miss S Lockyer (*Clarinet, Saxophone*)
Mr S Lockyer (*Cello, Double Bass*)
Miss L Lowndes-Northcott (*Harp, Viola*)
Mr C Mahon (*Pipe Organ*)
Miss M Marton (*Singing*)
Mr D Mayo (*Acoustic/Electric Guitar*)
Mrs W Partridge, LTCL (*Classical Guitar*)
Mr D Price (*French Horn*)
Miss E Tolfree (*Clarinet, Saxophone, Bassoon*)

PE Coaching:
Miss T Carter (*Cross Country/Athletics*)
Mrs E Deuxbury (*Tennis*)
Mr I Griffin (*Tennis*)
Mrs V Peck (*Tennis*)

Speech and Drama:
Mrs S Holman
Mrs E Brown
Mrs H Earle
Mr S Earle

Mulwith House:
Housemistress:
Mrs A Salmon
Assistants:
Mrs B Roberts
Mrs E Hawkins

Newby House:
Housemistress:
Mrs D Whitehead
Assistants:
Mrs R Barrington
Mrs D Healy

Upper Sixth Boarding House:
Mary Ward House:
Housemistress:
Mrs D Webb
Assistants:
Mrs E Boote
Mrs T Richards

Founded in 1945, St Mary's School, Shaftesbury is an Independent Roman Catholic Boarding and Day School for girls. It is situated on the A30 just outside Shaftesbury and stands in its own grounds of 55 acres.

Numbers on Roll. 325 Girls (two-thirds boarders, one-third day).

Age Range. 11–18 years.

Admission. (*See Scholarship Entries section.*) The School has its own Entrance Examination held in January for 11+ and 13+ entry. Sixth Form entry is by testimonial and interview and is then conditional on 5 GCSE passes.

Fees per term (2011-2012). Year 7: Boarders £7,550, Day Girls £5,190. Years 8–13: Boarders £7,930, Day Girls £5,450.

Aims and Curriculum. The School aims to give girls as broad an education, both spiritual, personal, academic and extra-curricular, as possible, thus enabling each girl to realise her own strengths in the various areas and build on them. Religious education is an integral part of the curriculum throughout the School. During Years 7–9 all girls follow a common curriculum which includes Religious Education, English, History, Geography, French, Latin, Mathematics, Information Technology, Science, Art, Textiles, Music, Singing, PSE and PE. From Year 10 both the core curriculum (RE, English Language and Literature, Mathematics, One Modern Foreign Language and either Chemistry, Biology and Physics as separate science subjects or Science and Additional Science) and options, are arranged to ensure that each girl follows a balanced course suitable to her ability and interests.

The majority of girls remain for A Levels for which they have a choice of 22 subjects. The Sixth Form curriculum also includes RE, Information Technology, Desktop Publishing, General Studies and PE.

The School is a member of ISCO (Independent Schools Careers Organisation) and all girls receive individual careers advice from the Head of Guidance. All girls go on to some form of Higher Education and the majority to University.

Music. The Music Department is large and any orchestral instrument may be learned. In addition there are three school choirs, a chamber choir, orchestra and various instrumental ensembles. The last choir trip was to Rome.

Sport. Winter: Netball, hockey, cross country, swimming and waterpolo teams with a wide range of additional activities also available such as dance, badminton, volleyball. Summer: Swimming, tennis, rounders, athletics & waterpolo and also a range of other activities available to chose from. The School has its own Sports Hall, floodlit Astroturf and a 25m six-lane indoor swimming pool.

Extra subjects or activities. Speech and drama, ballet, riding, polo, tennis coaching, Duke of Edinburgh's Award, photography and a wide range of other Societies.

Charitable status. St Mary's School Shaftesbury Trust is a Registered Charity, number 292845. Its aims and objectives are to administer an independent Roman Catholic school for the education of children of any Christian denomination.

St Mary's
Worcester

Mount Battenhall, Worcester WR5 2HP
Tel: 01905 357786
Fax: 01905 351718
e-mail: head@stmarys.org.uk
website: www.stmarys.org.uk

Independent Day School for girls (aged 0 to 18) and boys (aged 0 to 7).

Headmistress: Mrs C Jawaheer, BA Hons, PGCE, DipEd, NPQH

Deputy Head: Mrs C Howe, BA Hons, PGCE

Head of Preparatory School: Mrs L Lister, CertEd

Mrs V Adams, BA Hons, MA, PGCE
Mrs E Amos, BSc Hons, PGCE
Ms J Bell, BSc Hons
Mrs S Brain, BSc Hons, PGCE
Miss G Cleary, BA Hons, PGCE
Mrs H Emerick BEd Hons
Mrs C Flannigan, BA Hons, PGCE
Mrs J Glazzard, CertEd
Mrs R Gunton BA Hons
Mrs H Holt, BEd, CertEd
Miss K Howarth, BA Hons
Mr A Howe, BSc Hons, PGCE
Mrs F Hudson, BA, LTCL, PGCE
Mrs J Hunt, BA Hons, PGCE
Miss R Lewis, BA, MA, PGCE
Mr J McCumisky, BA, MA, QTS
Mrs S Parry, BA Hons, PGCE, LTCL
Mrs S Ridge, BA Hons, QTS
Mrs M Robinson, BA Hons
Mrs C Rodgman, BEd Hons
Mr A Ross, BA Hons, PGCE
Mrs J Simpson BEd Hons
Mr G Stokes, BSc Hons, PGCE
Mrs N Thomas, BA Hons, MA, PGCE
Mrs M Thompson, BA, CertEd

Early Years Manager:
Mrs A Guida-Jones

Learning Support:
Mrs L Lane
Mrs L Wilson

PA to the Headmistress: Mrs Lorene Oliver

St Mary's is an independent day school offering a girls-only education from aged 4 through to 18 years together with a co-educational nursery housed in the former Stables.

We aim to prepare our girls of today to face the challenges of being women leaders of tomorrow. This aim continues the vision and spirit of our founder, Julie Postel, who sought to empower and equip young women to make their mark in the local and global community.

School life is focused around nurturing a girl's self-confidence, developing their intellectual curiosity and encouraging creative thinking. This is achieved within very small classes which allows for an extraordinary level of personal support and care.

Housed in an impressive Victorian mansion set in 15 acres of gardens and woodlands overlooking the Malvern Hills, the large school site is divided into three separate units: The Stables (3 months–4 years), the Preparatory School (4–11 years) and the Senior School (11–18 years).

The school has been sympathetically extended and updated to include up-to-date teaching facilities and resources. In addition the school has a 6.5 acre sports field as well as a dri-play hockey pitch, netball and tennis courts and three gymnasia.

The academic record of St Mary's is excellent helped by a vibrant academic coaching scheme. The school has been placed in the top 5% of schools for value-added score. Pupils are challenged and stretched to ensure they exceed their expectations and all girls go on to good universities including Oxford and Cambridge.

The school is an examination centre for the Associated Board of the Royal Schools of Music and LAMDA. Peripatetic teachers come into school to teach speech and drama, voice, pianoforte and a wide range of orchestral instruments.

There is a wide range of extra-curricular activities and clubs on offer at lunch time and after school: junior and senior orchestras and choirs, string groups, wind groups, recorder ensembles, speech and drama, modern dance club, judo, tennis, netball, hockey, athletics, science and engineering, art, design and technology, computer club, The Duke of Edinburgh's Award, Young Enterprise, computer club, chess club, debating etc.

Admission into the Preparatory School is based on a day visit and assessment. Admission to the Senior School and Sixth Form is based on successful performance in the entrance examination. A generous scholarship and bursary scheme is in place which includes two free places awarded each academic year.

Fees per term (2011-2012). Kindergarten (including lunch): £1,930 (full time), £430–£1,650 (part time 1–4 days), £320–£1,510 (part time 1–5 mornings); Preparatory School (including lunch): £1,875–£2,815; Senior School: £3,350 (Years 7–9 including lunch), £3,400 (Years 10 and 11 including lunch) £3,290 (Years 12–13 excluding lunch).

Swimming lessons are included in the fees for the Preparatory School.

Charitable status. St Mary's School Trust Worcester is a Registered Charity, number 1018889. Its purpose is the promotion of the Christian Education of girls from Nursery to University and boys up to Reception.

St Nicholas' School

Redfields House, Redfields Lane, Church Crookham, Fleet, Hampshire GU52 0RF
Tel: 01252 850121
Fax: 01252 850718
e-mail: headspa@st-nicholas.hants.sch.uk
website: www.st-nicholas.hants.sch.uk

Motto: *Confirma Domine Serviendo*

Chair of Governors: Mrs K Walker

Headmistress: Annette V Whatmough, BA Hons Bristol, CertEd

Deputy Head – Pastoral: Caroline Egginton, BEd Hons London

Deputy Head – Academic: Christine Moorby, BSc Hons Southampton, CertEd

Bursar: Caroline Taylor, MA Hons Edinburgh, CA

Assistant Staff:
Cherill Anderson, MA Cantab (*Modern Languages*)
Alison Audino, BEd Hons Bath (*Food Technology*)
Helen Barnes, BA Ed Hons Exeter (*Key Stage 2*)
Jenny Brackstone, BA Hons Nottingham, PGCE (*Key Stages 3 & 4*)
Nicky Brooks, BA Hons Exeter, PGCE (*Key Stage 2*)
Timothy Burns, BA Hons, CNAA (*Head of Art*)

Sarah Carter, BEd Hons Southampton (*Key Stage 2*)
Janet Coombe, BA Hons Manchester, PGCE (*Geography*)
Isabel Cook, BA Hons Southampton, PGCE (*Head of History*)
Barbara Edwards, BA Hons Sheffield, PGCE (*English*)
Susan Fitzhenry, MEd Johannesburg SA (*Chinese Mandarin*)
Amy Franke, BMus Hons Surrey, MMus (*Assistant Director of Music*)
Brenda Green, CertEd, CNAA (*Director of Sport*)
Maria Hadnett, BA Hons Manchester, PGCE (*Head of Drama*)
Rosalie Hague, BA Hons Lancaster, PGCE (*Head of English*)
Valerie Helliwell, BEng Hons Liverpool, PGCE (*Head of Mathematics, Examinations Officer*)
Laura Homer, BA Hons Wales, PGCE (*Key Stage 1*)
Lucy Hopkins Till, BA Hons Hull, PGCE (*Latin*)
Laura Johnson, BSc OU, CertEd (*Head of IT*)
Janice R King, BSc Hons London, PGCE (*Head of Biology*)
Alexandra Lawrence, MA Oxon, PGCE (*Head of Modern Languages*)
Julie Merker, BA OU, CertEd (*PE*)
Michelle Morgan, NNEB (*Nursery*)
Tessa Newton, BA Hons OU, PGCE (*Head of Junior Department*)
Helen Pasley, BEd Hons Lancaster (*Head of Curriculum Support*)
Tracy Perrett, BEd Sussex (*PE*)
Lee Render, BA Hons QTS Surrey (*Key Stage 1*)
Ann Rowe, MA Oxford Brookes, CertEd (*Head of Nursery*)
Lisa Ruffell, BA Hons QTS Surrey (*Key Stage 2*)
Patricia Semmens, BSc Hons Manchester, PGCE (*Key Stage 2*)
Paula Simpson, BSc Hons Bath, PGCE (*Textiles*)
Michelle Strevens, BEd, CNAA (*Key Stage 1*)
Julia Tiley, BA Hons QTS Kingston (*Foundation Stage/ Key Stage 1*)
Gail Tomblin, BSc Hons Loughborough, CertEd (*Mathematics*)
Jane Tomlinson, BA Hons London, PGCE (*Modern Languages*)
Frances van Heerden, BSc Natal, UED (*Science*)
Elizabeth Ward, BA Hons Leeds, PGCE (*Curriculum Support with English*)
Diane White, BA Hons Leeds, PGCE, LGSM (*Director of Music*)

Peripatetic Music:
Jonathan Baxter (*Drums*)
Zoë Belbin, BMus, PGdip TCM, GSMD, ABRSM (*Clarinet, Saxophone*)
Wendy Busby, BMus Hons (*Voice*)
Rebekah Duncalfe, BMus (*Violin*)
Rosemary Fox, BA Hons, BSc, Dip ABRSM (*Flute*)
Susan Gillis, PGDip Mtpp, ALCM, LLCM (*Piano*)
Sylvia Harper, BA Hons PGdip RCM Oboe
Neil Hickling, MMus, BMus (*Clarinet, Saxophone*)
Sally Hosken, GGSM, ARCM, DipEd (*Violin*)
Valerie Mitchell, LRAM (*Piano, Cello*)
Gail Mortley, LRAM, ARCM (*Voice*)
Alice Murray, BMus Hons (*Guitar*)
Virginia Pearson, Perf Cert RAM, LTCL, ARCM (*Guitar*)
Austin Pepper, ALCM (*Brass*)
Megan Pound (*Violin*)
Sally Pryce, BMus Hons RCM (*Harp*)
Angela Zanders, LTCL, BA Mus (*Piano*)

Administration:
Classroom Assistant: Tanya Negus
School Nurse: Sarah Watkins, RGN, NNEB
Payroll Clerk: Mary Wales

Headmistress's PA: Dawn Brown, FIPA
Marketing & Admissions Director: Clare Longfield, BA Hons Newcastle
School Secretary: Sarah Watkins
Accounts Secretary: Deborah Davies, Cert AAT London
Laboratory Technician: Michele Axton, BA Open Uni
Catering: Sodhexo Education Services Ltd
Maintenance: Peter Sleet, Peter White, Joseph Carrig, Stephen Turner
Caretaker: Robert Crail
Bus Driver: Timothy Hunt
Second Hand Uniform Shop: Jo Gibson
Librarian: Sarah Stokes

The School. St Nicholas' School is a small independent day school for girls aged 3–16 and boys 3–7. Founded in 1935 in Branksomewood Road, Fleet, the school moved to Redfields House, Redfields Lane, Church Crookham in 1996. Redfields House, a Victorian Mansion, is set in 27 acres of glorious parkland and playing fields.

Branksomewood, our Nursery and Infant department, retains the original name of the road where the school was founded. Being built of natural wood with a wonderful airy atmosphere this building gives light and space to our younger children, creating a calming environment in which they thrive. With an adventure playground set in the woods, a large hall fitted with PE equipment, overlooking the grounds and our experienced teaching staff, it is no wonder the children are so happy.

St Nicholas' junior department is based in Redfields House itself which keeps the charm of the old family house with its oak panelling and the senior department is located in the newer part of the school behind. All three departments have benefited from several building projects.

December 2000 saw the opening of the Olympic-size sports hall with netball and tennis courts showers, changing rooms and a viewing gallery. This has enhanced the sports lessons and enabled even more sports competitions as well as extra curricular activities. Badminton, tennis, netball, volleyball and basketball may be played throughout the year.

Spring 2006 saw yet another addition with the opening of the art, design technology and textiles centre, offering three spacious rooms with large work benches, and a kiln for pottery. By having this wonderful new building it opened an opportunity for the school to adapt the old art centre into several music practice rooms. Tuition in the violin, piano, guitar, harp, drums as well singing, woodwind and brass is offered.

November 2009 saw the grand opening of the performing arts centre. With raked seating for over 330, in the semi round, with an orchestra pit, concerts and plays are staged regularly. The drama department has in addition two studios.

Pupils come to St Nicholas' from Hampshire, Surrey and Berkshire. School buses operate from Farnham, Odiham, Fleet, Basingstoke, Camberley, Yateley, Aldershot and Farnborough. Situated just off the A287, Hook to Farnham road, junction 5 of the M3 is approximately 4 miles short away.

Religion. The school is a Christian foundation but children of other faiths are welcomed Assemblies are held each morning. Children are encouraged to show tolerance, compassion and care for others.

Curriculum. St Nicholas' offers an extended day, from 8 am to 6 pm. Academic standards are high and a balanced curriculum is offered. Small classes place greater emphasis on the individual and pupils are encouraged to achieve their full potential in every area of school life. The curriculum is kept as broad as possible until the age of fourteen when choices are made for GCSE. The option choices vary year by year depending upon the girls' abilities and talents. On average each girl sits ten subjects at GCSE. More than twenty subjects are offered at this level. A carefully structured personal development course incorporates a Careers programme. Our girls move confidently on to enter sixth form colleges or scholarships to senior independent schools. Choir, drama and music thrive within the school and there are frequent performances which enable the girls to develop self-confidence.

Physical Education. Pupils take part in inter-school and local district sports matches: hockey, netball and cross-country in winter; and tennis, athletics and swimming in summer. Rounders and lacrosse are also played.

Entry. Children may enter at any stage subject to interview, school report and waiting list. Scholarships and Bursaries are available. For 11+ candidates there is an entrance examination.

Fees per term (2011-2012). Nursery £1,362; Infants (Reception, Years 1 and 2) £2,725; Juniors (Years 3 to 6) £3,101; Senior School £3,701.

Further Information. The prospectus is available upon request from the Registrar. The Headmistress is pleased to meet parents by appointment.

Charitable status. St Nicholas' School is a Registered Charity, number 307341. It exists to provide high quality education for children.

St Paul's Girls' School

Brook Green, Hammersmith, London W6 7BS
Tel: School Office: 020 7603 2288
          Admissions: 0207 605 4882
          Business Director: 020 7605 4881
Fax: 020 7602 9932
          Business Director: 020 7605 4869
e-mail: admissions@spgs.org
website: www.spgs.org

Motto: '*Fide et Literis*'

The School is on the Foundation originally provided by Dean Colet in 1509 and is governed under the provisions of the Schemes of the Charity Commissioners dated 4 July 1879, and 16 June 1900. The Worshipful Company of Mercers are the trustees of the Foundation. The School was opened on 19 January 1904.

Governors:
Chairman: The Hon Timothy Palmer
Deputy Chairman: Dame Helen Alexander

Mr Mark Aspinall
Ms Kate Bingham
Mr Nicolas Chisholm MBE
Mr Christopher Sands Clayton
Mr Richard Cawton Cunis JP
Mrs Pauline Davies
Mr Michael de Giorgio
Ms Alice Hohler
Mr Daniel Houghton Hodson
Miss Judith Portrait

Appointed by The Mercers' Company in consultation with the University of Oxford:
Professor Dame Jessica Rawson

Appointed by The Mercers' Company in consultation with the University of Cambridge:
(*to be confirmed*)

Appointed by The Mercers' Company in consultation with the University of London:
Professor Charlotte Roueché

Clerk to the Governors: Mrs Menna McGregor

Head of Education: Mr Michael Marchant

High Mistress: Ms Clarissa M Farr, MA Exeter, PGCE

Deputy Head, Director of Studies:
Mrs Kate Clanchy, MA Cantab, MBA Insead (*Modern Languages*)

Deputy Head, Director of School:
Mr Paul Vanni, MA London (*Modern Languages*)

Director of Senior School:
Mrs Jenny Brown, BA Oxford (*English*)

Assistant Deputy Head, Director of Co-Curricular Education:
Mrs Su Wijeratna, BA Birmingham (*Geography*)

Ms Christelle Aguillon-Williams, DEA Poitiers (*Modern Languages*)
Miss Elizabeth Armstrong, MSc Lancaster (*Geography*)
Mr Stephen Arscott, BA Cantab (*Religious Studies*)
Mr Tim Askew, BA Oxon (*History and Religious Studies*)
Dr Howard Bailes, BA Adelaide, PhD London (*History*)
Miss Helen Barff, BA Goldsmiths College, MA Camberwell (*Art and Design*)
Revd Vanessa Baron, MA Cantab, BSc City (*Religious Studies*)
Dr Julia Barron, BA, MA, PhD University of Wales (*Modern Languages*)
Mr Wayne Barron, BA Cantab (*Classics*)
Miss Sandra Barth, BA Martin-Luther-Universität Halle-Wittenberg (*Modern Languages*)
Miss Mekhla Barua, BSc Warwick (*Mathematics*)
Mr David Benefer, BA Norwich School of Art (*Art and Design*)
Miss Carole Boothman, BA Liverpool (*Modern Languages*)
Miss Laurelle Borck, BA Waikato, NZ (*Physical Education*)
Miss Clare Brashaw, MA Leeds (*Art and Design*)
Mr Jonathan Bromley, BA Oxon (*History*)
Mr Spencer Buksh, BSc London (*Mathematics*)
Ms Elizabeth Coutts, MA Oxon (*History*)
Mr Ian Crane, BSc Durham (*Mathematics*)
Mr Nicholas Dakin, BA Birmingham (*English*)
Mr Alexander Daglish, BA Plymouth (*Art and Design*)
Mr Anthony Ellison, BSc Nottingham (*Chemistry*)
Miss Katherine Evans, BA London (*History of Art*)
Miss Kate Fisher, MA London (*Art and Art History*)
Miss Isabel Foley, BA London (*Drama*)
Miss Daniela Footerman, MA Oxon (*Mathematics*)
Miss Kate Frank, BA London, MA London (*Modern Languages*)
Mr Adrian Frost, MA Oxon (*Biology*)
Mrs Hannah Fussner, BA Oxon, MA Stanford, USA (*Learning Support*)
Miss Penelope Garcia-Rodriguez, BA Oviedo, Spain, MA London (*Modern Languages*)
Ms Blanche Girouard, BA Oxon (*Religious Studies*)
Dr Corissa Gould, BA Birmingham, MA Southampton, PhD London (*Music*)
Mr Roger Green, MA Kent (*Mathematics*)
Mr Chris Hack, MSci Cantab (*Physics*)
Mr Martin Hanak-Hammerl, BSc Graz, Austria (*Mathematics*)
Miss Emily Hardy, BA Cantab (*English*)
Miss Rachel Harris, BA Durham (*Geography*)
Dr Eilis Harron-Ponsonby, PhD, MSc, BA Cantab (*Chemistry*)
Miss Elizabeth Hodges, BA Wolverhampton Polytechnic, MA Royal College of Art (*Art and Design*)
Dr Anna Holland, BA Oxon, DPhil (*Classics*)
Miss Amy Hudson, MChem Oxon (*Chemistry*)
Mrs Ludmila Iakobachvili, MA Uralia (*Modern Languages*)
Dr Philip Jackson, BSc Sussex, PhD London (*Chemistry*)
Mrs Divya Kansagra, BSc University of Illinois, EdM Harvard (*Chemistry*)

Mrs Manuela Knight, BA Milan (*Modern Languages*)
Dr Kingston Koo, BSc Warwick, PhD London (*Physics*)
Mrs Nina Lau, BSc London (*Biology*)
Mr John Lee, BA Oxon, BA London (*Mathematics*)
Dr Kate Lee, BSc Witwatersrand, MSc Cape Town, PhD London (*Physics*)
Mrs Marika Lowe, BSc Sheffield Hallam (*Physical Education*)
Ms Silvana Marconini, Turin, Italy (*Modern Languages*)
Mr William Martin, MA Surrey (*Classics*)
Miss Lydia Mason, BA Durham (*English*)
Mr Paul McDonald, BA Oxon, MSc LSE (*Mathematics*)
Miss Katie McHugh, BA Maryland (*Physical Education*)
Mr Richard Michell, BA Bristol, MA Chelsea School of Art (*Art and Design*)
Dr Joanna Moriarty, BSc Birmingham, PhD Reading (*Biology*)
Mrs Irina Ninnis, BA Moscow and London (*Modern Languages*)
Miss Narelle O'Byrne, BPhysEd Otago, NZ (*Physical Education*)
Dr Jonathan Patrick, BA, DPhil Oxon (*English*)
Miss Emma Payler, BSc London (*Biology*)
Mr Tom Peck, BA Manchester (*History and Politics*)
Mr Matthew Reeve, BSc Newcastle (*Biology*)
Miss Katie Roberts, BA Cantab (*Modern Languages*)
Ms Leonie Rushforth, BA Cantab (*English*)
Ms Caroline Saunders BA London (*Music and Modern Languages*)
Mrs Alexandra Shamloll, MA Cantab (*Mathematics*)
Ms Holly Shao, BSc Hunan, China (*Modern Languages*)
Dr Clare Sharp, MA, DPhil Oxon (*Classics*)
Dr Marcin Slaski, BSc Krakow, PhD Krakow (*Physics*)
Mrs Kate Snook, MA, MPhil St Andrews (*History and Religious Studies*)
Miss Claire Suthren, BA Cantab (*Classics*)
Miss Rachel Tomlinson, BSc Durham (*Geography*)
Mr Michael Turner, BA Oxon (*Economics*)
Ms Paula Velez (*Modern Languages*)
Dr Sarah Wah, MA Leeds, DPhil Cantab (*English*)
Mrs Victoria Watkins, BA Lancaster (*English and Drama*)
Miss Mary Wenham, BA Oxon (*Modern Languages*)
Miss Sydne Wick, BA Queen's University of Charlotte (*Physical Education*)
Mr Gregory Wilsdon, BA Oxon, MBA Stanford, MA (*Classics*)
Ms Jane Zeng, BSc Guangzhan, China (*Modern Languages*)

Acting Director of Music:
Mr Mark Wilderspin, MA Oxon, MMus RCM London
Senior Music and Head of Keyboard:
Mr John York, AGSM, ARCM
Head of Singing:
Miss Heidi Pegler, BA Cardiff, LTCL
Head of Strings:
Miss Hilary Sturt, AGSM, ARCM (*Viola and Violin*)
Head of Wind & Brass:
Mr Angus Meryon, BMus, ARCM (*Woodwind*)
Music Department Manager:
Miss Emily Godfree, BA Exeter (*English*)

Miss Rose Andresier, LLCM, FRSA (*Guitar*)
Miss Charlotte Ansbergs, LRAM, DipRAM (*Violin*)
Mr Edward Barry, DipMus, LTCL (*Violin*)
Mrs Emily Bates, BA, MSTAT (*Alexander Technique*)
Mrs Jane Clark-Maxwell, BMus London, AKC, LTCL (*Singing*)
Miss Gillian Cracknell, LRAM (*Piano, Aural*)
Mr Matthew Dickinson, BA, GGSM (*Percussion, Drum Kit*)
Mr Harold East, GRSM, ARCM (*Piano*)
Miss Jane Fisher, LTCL, PGCE (*Flute*)

Miss Carolyn Fouthes, GRSM, LRAM, ARAM, DipAdv
Studies (*Singing*)
Miss Nicola-Jane Kemp, MA Cantab, MMus Opera,
RSAMD (*Singing*)
Mr Pete Kershaw, MA (*Guitar*)
Mr John Langley, BA (*Theory*)
Mr Mornington Lockett, BA (*Saxophone*)
Miss Naadia Manington, BMus, LGSM (*Jazz Piano,
Piano*)
Mr Andrew Mason, BMus (*Clarinet, Saxophone*)
Mrs Helen Mason, BMus RCM, PGDip Solo/Ensemble
RCM (*Horn*)
Mr Alexander Mobbs, BMus (*Double Bass*)
Dr Susan Monks, BEd, MA Mus, PhD (*Singing*)
Miss Catherine Morphett, BMus (*Clarinet*)
Miss Amanda Morrison, BA (*Singing*)
Ms Helena Mowat-Brown, ARCM (*Harpischord*)
Miss Helen Neilson, BSc, PGDipAdv RCM, MMus (*Cello*)
Ms Jessica O'Leary, BMus, DipCSM, LTCL, LRAM
(*Violin, Viola*)
Ms April Pierrot, MSTAT (*Alexander Technique*)
Miss Julie Ryan, ARCM (*Trumpet*)
Miss Rachel Shannon, MA Cantab, RAM (*Singing*)
Miss Erica Simpson, ARAM, ARCM (*Cello*)
Mr James Sleigh, ARCM, Hon ARAM (*Viola*)
Ms Louise Strickland, BMus, MMus, LGSMD (*Recorder*)
Mrs Sarah Stroh, BMus, Dip Dist RAM, LRAM (*Singing*)
Ms Shelagh Sutherland, ARAM, LRAM, STAT (*Piano,
Alexander Technique*)
Miss Emma Tingey, LWCMD, ACC PGDip (*Harp*)
Miss Judith Treggor, BMus Connecticut (*Flute*)
Ms Joanne Turner, DipRCM, ARCM (*Bassoon, Flute*)
Mr Simon Weale, MA Oxon, LGSM (*Piano and Organ*)
Miss Enloc Wu, ARCM, LRSM (*Piano*)
Mrs Fiona York, AGSM (*Piano*)

Business Director:
Mr Arnold Flanagan, Adv Dip BFM CIPFA

Registrar: Mrs Lindy Hayward, BA Open

Admissions Officer: Miss Jessica Dow, BA Exeter

Librarian: Mrs Linda Kelley, BA Manchester, MSc UCE

The main ages of admission are 11 and 16. There are 730
girls in the school, 215 being in the Sixth Form. The school
offers a balanced curriculum; both tradition and innovation
are valued. A strong core of academic subjects is combined
with Art, Design, Drama, Music, Information Technology
and Sport.

Girls are prepared for GCSE, AS and full A Level examinations and for university entrance. Girls go on to major universities in the UK or overseas, approximately 40% to
Oxford and Cambridge.

Sports facilities include a Sports Hall, a large heated
indoor swimming pool, lacrosse pitches and tennis and netball courts. The Library facilities are outstanding, as are
those for Music, centred on the Gustav Holst Singing Hall.
Drama takes place in the purpose-built Celia Johnson Theatre and Drama Studio. There is an ICT block with three
fully-equipped classrooms. Twelve Science laboratories are
housed in a separate Science block. There is a Sixth Form
centre with its own ICT facilities and relaxation areas,
together with a Careers suite. We are continually modernis-
ing and adding to these facilities: recently the Singing Hall
has been renovated to a very high standard.

Scholarships. (*See Scholarship Entries section.*)

Bursaries. *Junior Bursaries* (11+) to a value of up to full
fee remission based on proven financial need subject to
annual review are available. Candidates must be successful
in the 11+ Entrance Examination. The number of Junior
Bursaries available each year will vary.

Senior Bursaries (16+) to a value of up to full fee remission based on proven financial need subject to annual review

are available for candidates who have been successful in the
Senior School Entrance Examination and who are currently
in their final GCSE year at another school.

Fees per term (2011-2012). £5,842 including lunches,
excluding textbooks. The fee per term for girls entering at
16+ is £6,280.

Registration & Examination Fee £125.

Charitable status. St Paul's Girls' School is a Registered
Charity, number 1119613, and a Company Limited by Guarantee, registered in England, number 6142007. It exists to
promote the education of girls in Greater London.

St Swithun's School

Alresford Road, Winchester, Hants SO21 1HA
Tel: 01962 835700
Fax: 01962 835779
e-mail: office@stswithuns.com
website: www.stswithuns.com

The School was founded in 1884 and in 1931 moved to its
present attractive campus of 45 acres on the Downs on the
outskirts of Winchester.

The School aims to give a broad, balanced academic
education in which each girl has the opportunity to make
appropriate choices which will enable her to develop her
potential and give her the skills and confidence needed for
adult life.

A friendly and caring atmosphere prevails within a
framework of sensible discipline. Emphasis is placed on
Christian values and consideration for others.

It is a school for both Day Girls, Full and Weekly
Boarders and at present the Senior School (girls aged 11–18)
has 254 Day Girls and 217 Boarders. There is an adjoining
Junior School for girls aged 3–11 and boys from 3–7. years
(*see entry in IAPS section*).

Visitor: The Rt Revd Michael Scott-Joynt, Bishop of
Winchester

School Council:
Chairman: Mr J C Platt, FCA
The Mayor of Winchester (*ex officio*)
The Dean of Winchester (*ex officio*)
The Headmaster of Winchester College (*ex officio*)
Mrs M S Greenway, LLB
Dr M A Gruffydd Jones, MA, PhD
Mr P Martin, MA
Dr H M Mycock, BA, MSc, PhD
Mrs R Randle, BA, MA Ed
Mr M Reid, MA, FCA
Miss R L E Rothman, BA, ACA
Ms M Rudland, BSc, PGCE
Dr H R Trippe, BA, BMS, FFPHM, PGCE
Prof J M A Whitehouse, MA, MD, FRCPE, FRCR
Mr M Wilson, BA

Bursar and Clerk to the Council: Mr M G J Carter, FCMI

***Headmistress*: Ms J S Gandee**, MA Cantab

Deputy Headmistress: Mrs J Tomlinson, BA Kent, MA
Durham, PGCE York (*Religious Studies*)

Director of Studies: Mrs A Burns-Cox, BSc London, PGCE
Southampton

Chaplain: Revd Katrina Dykes, BA Bristol

Staff:

Religious Studies:
Miss J Cox, BA Birmingham, PGCE Birmingham

English:
Miss A Oliver, BA Warwick, PGCE Oxon

Mrs J Phillips, BA Oxon, PGCE Kings
Mrs N Young, BA Birmingham, PGCE
Miss J Askew, BA, DipEd NSW, Australia
Mrs D Burgess, MA Oxon, PGCE Cantab, DipPSE CNAA
Miss C Howard, BA, PGCE Leicester
Mrs S Clarke, BA Birmingham, MA Bristol Old Vic
Mrs A Hervey-Bathurst, BA, MA Cantab, PGCE

History:
Miss J Thomas, MA Oxford, MA London, PGCE Oxford
Dr S Burt, BEd Durham, MA, PhD Southampton
Mrs K Batten, BA West of England, PGCE Bristol

Geography:
Mr J Brown, BA, PGCE Birmingham
Mrs L Parsons, BSc Liverpool, PGCE
Mrs T Gill, BSc Brighton, PGCE Exeter

Economics:
Mrs J Campbell, BSc Plymouth State College, USA

Modern Languages:
Miss F Bolton, BA Oxford, PGCE Oxford
Mrs C Bewes, DEUG, Licence Maîtrise France, PGCE
   Southampton (*French*)
Mrs R Dhand, BA London, PGCE Southampton (*French*)
Mrs S Hayward, MA London, PGCE Durham (*German and
   French, Head of General Studies*)
Mrs C Glyn, MA Bochum, PGCE Durham (*German*)
Mrs M Grice, BA Germany, PGCE Southampton (*German*)
Miss N Lequang, Licence Spain, Maîtrise France, PGCE
   Bath
Mrs A Steer, MA Ed Frankfurt (*German*)

Classics:
Dr L Martin, MA, PhD Cantab, PGCE Southampton
Mrs P E Giles, BA Birmingham, PGCE Durham (*Careers*)
Mrs G Condell, BA Kings, PGCE Kings
Mrs C Webster, MA Oxford

Mathematics:
Mr S Power, BA Oxon, MSc Colorado, PGCE OU
Mrs C Bolger, BEng Exeter, PGCE Portsmouth, CEng,
   MIMechE
Mr P Debont, BSc Warwick, MSc Essex, PGCE Greenwich
Mrs H Greene, MA OU, BSc London, PGCE OU
Mrs C Thompson, BSc Exeter
Mr J Gillespie, BSc Durham, PGCE Loughborough
Mrs H Savoury, MEng UMIST, PGCE Nottingham
Mrs P Gennings, BSc Exeter, PGCE Cantab

Science:
Dr J Livy, BSc Liverpool, MSc, DIC, PhD London,
   CChem, MRSC (*Chemistry*)
Mr R Shah, BSc East Anglia, PGCE Southampton
   (*Chemistry*)
Mr A W J Smith, BSc Durham, PGCE Exeter (*Physics*)
Mrs P A Burley, BSc Swansea, PGCE Southampton
   (*Biology*)
Mrs S Evans, BSc London, MA OU, PGCE Bath (*Biology*)
Mr T Duncan, BSc, BEng Sydney, MEd Australia
Mrs H Fletcher, BSc, PGCE Bristol
Dr H Otter, PhD, BA, PGCE Cantab (*Science*)
Dr J Savillewood, BM, PGCE Southampton (*Chemistry*)

Design and Technology:
Mrs H Mitchener, BEng Exeter, PGCE Telford
Mr B Rood, BSc Bournemouth, PGCE Exeter

Careers:
Mrs A Campbell, BA Durham, DipRE Nottingham, PGCE
   Lancaster, CFPS Portsmouth, RSA DipTEFLA (*and
   Religious Studies*)
Miss J Webber, BA Wellington, NZ, Dip Teaching
   Christchurch, NZ, Cert Prof Studies CEG

Food Technology and Textiles:
Mrs N Sanvoisin, BSc, PGCE Cardiff

Mrs R Curry, BA Manchester, PGCE Worcester

Art:
Mrs K Ross, BA Surrey, PGCE Goldsmiths
Mrs P Larrington, BEd, MA Southampton (*and History of
   Art*)
Mrs L Mason-Smith, BA, MA, PGCE
Ms C Packer, BA London

ICT:
Mrs A Walker, BEd Leeds

Music:
Mr R Brett, MA, PGCE Cantab (*Director of Music*)
Miss J Richardson, MMus Perf, DRSAMD, RGN (*Head of
   Instrumental Studies*)
Mr R Patterson, MA, PGCE CfBT (*Head of Academic
   Music*)
Miss J Anderson, GRSM, LRAM, LTCL
Mr C Watkiss, GRSM, LRAM, PGCE
Mrs V Stenning (*Administrative Assistant*)

Visiting Music Staff:
Mr B Barasinski, Warsaw Acad, Dip RAM (*piano*)
Mrs G Slot, BMus, ALCM, LTCL (*piano*)
Mrs J Lloyd, ARCM, LGSM (*piano*)
Mr J Dickson, BMus Hons, LRAM (*jazz, piano*)
Mrs J Naylor, CertEd (*piano*)
Miss S Vysniauskiene (*piano*)
Dr N Wilkinson, MMus, ARCM, HonARAM (*piano*)
Miss K Murrelli, BA, MMus (*piano*)
Mrs J Kane, Dip RNCM (*violin*)
Mrs R Macdonald, ARCM (*violin*)
Mr T Nikolaev, MMus, BMus Hons GSMD (*violin*)
Mr M Mace, DipRAM (*violoncello*)
Mrs V Harding, BSc Sothampton (*violoncello*)
Mr M Frampton (*double bass*)
Miss S Pryce, MMus (*harp*)
Mr A Neville, ALCM (*guitar*)
Mr J O'Kane, LWCMD (*guitar*)
Mr R Morrow (*guitar*)
Ms R Miles, LTCL (*recorder*)
Miss L Burns, MA Hons, PGDip (*flute*)
Mrs A Roberts, BA London, PGCE Dundee (*flute*)
Mrs K Wills, GTC, LTGL, DipRAM (*flute*)
Mr A Collins, RA (*clarinet*)
Mrs S Mudd, ATCL (*oboe*)
Mrs J Paterson-Neild, BA (*saxophone*)
Miss E Innes, GGSM, AGSM Examiner to the GSMD
   (*bassoon and clarinet*)
Mrs F Brockhurst, ARCM (*French horn*)
Mr A Warren, BMus Hons, RCM, MMus, RCM
   (*trombone, tuba*)
Mr J Poore, GGSM, Dip Orch Studies (*trumpet*)
Mr J Evans (*drums*)
Mr D O'Neill, PG Cert Perf, BA Mus (*percussion*)
Mr J Evans (*drums*)
Ms K Fenech, PPRNCM, BMus, RNCM (*voice*)
Mrs M Allen, BMus, DipLRAM (*voice*)
Mr S Gallear (*voice*)
Mr B Gordon, LRAM, DipRAM (*voice*)
Mrs J Turner, MSAT (*Alexander Technique*)
Mrs J Bond, MSTAT, MGNI (*Alexander Technique*)

Drama and Theatre Studies:
Mrs T Spring, BA Hatfield, MA Middlesex, CertEd
   Birmingham
Mrs S Clarke, BA Birmingham, MA Bristol Old Vic
   Theatre School, GTP Chichester
Mrs G Oakley, BA East Anglia, PGCE Southampton

Visiting Staff:
Mrs M Armstrong, BA Bretton Hall
Ms J Wilson, BA North London, PGCE Oxon, LRAM,
   LLAM
Mrs L Funnelle

Learning Support:
Mrs M Hope, BEd, AdvDipEd, PGDipEd SpLD

Physical Education:
Mrs J Mackenzie, BSc Temple University, USA
Miss D Fenn, BSc, PGCE Swansea
Miss S Gilbert, BA, PGCE Chichester
Miss M Godfroy, BA Chichester, MSc, PGCE
Miss S Webb BSc Loughborough (*Teaching Assistant*)

Visiting Staff:
Mrs L Campbell (*Dance*)
Mrs L Goodhand (*Aerobics*)
Mrs F Brooks (*Pilates*)
Mrs F Brooks (*Aerobics*)
Miss C Pont (*Judo*)
Mr S Budden (*Karate*)
Mr A Cooke (*Fencing*)
Mrs P Francis (*Gym*)
Mr P Boyd-Leslie (*Tennis*)

IT:
Mr A S King, BEd Warwick, MITT (*Head of IT Services*)
Mr A Healey

Boarding Housemistresses:
Finlay: Miss J Webber
High House: Miss J Anderson
Hyde Abbey: Miss H Jones
Earl's Down: Mrs H Fletcher
Hillcroft: Miss T Mason
Le Roy: Mrs M Jervis

Day House Staff:
Caer Gwent: Mrs A Campbell
Venta: Mrs S Hayward
Davies: Mr R Shah
Chilcomb: Mrs C Bewes

Medical Staff:
Dr L Cole, MB BS, DRCOG
Mrs P May, RGN
Mrs E Oakley, RGN

Office Staff:
PA to The Headmistress: Mrs H Turner
Registrar: Ms A Davies, LLB Reading
Development Staff:
Development Director: Mr S Mayes, BA Northumbria
Development Manager: Mrs K Cairns, BA London, DipCIM, DipCAM
Communications Officer: Mrs M Kinder, BA Southampton
Old Girls Association Manager: Mrs J Brooker

Aim. The School aims to provide a well-ordered and supportive environment in which each girl is encouraged to fulfil her intellectual, physical and creative potential. Spiritual, moral and cultural development allows the girls to gain the knowledge and wisdom that will facilitate the lifelong continuation of learning and development. Importance is placed on girls gaining an understanding of themselves and on promoting self-esteem to allow them to embark on adult life positively and with the ability to contribute fully to society.

Location. The School is on a rural site in Winchester's 'green belt' but only a short distance from the city centre. It is easily accessible from Heathrow and Gatwick airports and is one hour from London by car (via the M3 motorway). There is a frequent train service to London Waterloo (one hour).

Curriculum. The curriculum is designed with an emphasis on flexibility and individual choice. All girls take English and Mathematics at GCSE Level and are given a free choice for their remaining 7 subjects from a selection of 19, the only conditions being that they should include at least one science subject and a modern foreign language. They are also encouraged to include at least one humanity, (History,

Geography, Religious Studies or Classical Civilisation) to ensure a breadth of knowledge and skills.

In the Sixth Form, girls are offered 24 subjects from which they choose 4. One of these will be normally followed to AS Level only while the remainder are taken through as full A Levels. Advice is given about the implications for their choice of university, degree course and career to ensure sensible combinations. Some girls choose to follow courses in subjects which are not offered at GCSE, eg Politics, Economics, History of Art. Over half the Sixth Form study at least one Science subject at A Level. To broaden their course further girls may take an additional subject to AS Level in the Upper Sixth and some will continue their 4 AS choices to full A Levels.

In addition, all Sixth Form girls take AS and A Level General Studies which, in its recognition of the connection between the various A Level disciplines, acts as a link between subjects. Contemporary, social, philosophical and political issues are explored through lectures, discussions, debates, visits and essays in a rolling programme which focuses in turn on music, science, technology, history of art, art and philosophy.

The curriculum is extended by exchange and educational visits to other countries.

Religion. The School is a Church of England foundation. There are close ties with Winchester Cathedral, where termly services and the annual Confirmation and Carol Services are held. A full-time Chaplain prepares girls for Confirmation and teaches in the School.

Music. The School has a strong musical tradition and there are frequent performances by the School choirs and orchestral groups. The Senior Choir sings Evensong in Winchester Cathedral twice a term, and chamber groups regularly enjoy success at national level.

Sports. There are extensive playing fields, a spacious modern sports hall and an impressive indoor swimming pool. Lacrosse players regularly attain national standard and a wide range of team and individual sports is offered.

Facilities. The original school building contains the main teaching rooms and libraries and has been extended and developed to provide specialist areas for Languages, Information Technology, Food and Textiles and Careers. The Science wing contains eight fully equipped laboratories, project rooms and a lecture theatre. In addition, there is an Art, Design and Technology Centre and a Performing Arts building was opened in 2003. This has a 600-seat main auditorium and two smaller performance spaces. A new Library, Careers and ICT facility was opened in 2007.

School Houses. There are 6 boarding houses and 4 day girl houses, each staffed by a housemistress and assistant who take pride in the high level of pastoral care offered to each girl. The Junior House is for girls aged 11 years who are then transferred to one of the Senior Houses after one year. They remain in the senior house until they have completed one year in the Sixth Form. The Upper Sixth House is for boarders and day girls together, with study bedrooms for boarders, study facilities for day girls and common rooms and galley for all.

Careers. Most girls continue to University, including Oxford and Cambridge, and all continue to some form of Higher Education and training. Each girl is counselled by one of our team of four Careers staff in a well-resourced department. Lectures and video presentations are organised frequently and a Careers Fair held annually.

Leisure Activities. There is an extensive range of extracurricular activities and an organised programme of visits and activities at the weekend. Girls participate in the Duke of Edinburgh's Award Scheme, Young Enterprise and local Community Service work. The Sixth Form runs a range of Societies including a Green Society, a Debating Society and a branch of Amnesty International. There are cookery, dressmaking, craft and engineering clubs and each year there are drama productions as well as regular drama activities. There is an annual visit to a Geographical/Outward Bound Centre in Wales, ski trips and water-sports holidays.

Health. The School Sanatorium forms part of the main buildings. It is staffed by qualified RGNs and visited by the School Doctor twice a week.

Entrance. Entry is by means of the Common Entrance Examination for Independent Schools. The majority of girls enter the Senior School at the age of 11 or 13 years, but girls are accepted at other ages, including the Sixth Form, subject to satisfactory tests.

Scholarships and Exhibitions. (*See Scholarship Entries section.*) These are awarded on the result of an examination at 11+ and 13+ and at entry to the Sixth Form. There are also Music Scholarships.

Fees per term (2011-2012). Senior School: Boarders £8,640; Day Girls £5,240. Junior School: £1,330–£3,430.

Charitable status. St Swithun's School Winchester is a Registered Charity, number 307335. It exists to provide education for girls aged 11–18 years.

St Teresa's School

Effingham Hill, Dorking, Surrey RH5 6ST

Tel: 01372 452037
Fax: 01372 450311
e-mail: info@stteresas.surrey.sch.uk
website: www.stteresasschool.com

Independent Day/Boarding School for 450 Girls aged 2–18 (Boarding 8–18), with Boys in the Nursery only.

A Different School for Every Girl

St Teresa's is a happy, thriving girls' boarding and day school with its own Preparatory School and Nursery. The Nursery is now co-educational. All departments of the school are responsive to the differing needs and latent talents of each individual girl, and each provides a warm and nurturing environment that recognises the girls as individuals with distinct personalities, needs and talents. St Teresa's is a flexible, 'can do' school that encourages every girl to explore her capabilities in her own way and provides whatever is necessary to support each girl's interests and passions, both in and beyond the classroom. The school has a broad ability intake but was placed 12th in the country for adding educational value in the January 2006 DfE Performance Tables (the last year Value-added scores were published for independent schools).

Chairman of the Governors: Mr Ian Wells

Acting Headmistress: **Mrs J Elburn**, BSc Hons, PGCE

Deputy Headmistress, Pastoral: Mrs J Elburn, BSc Hons, PGCE

Deputy Headmistress, Academic: Mrs V Low, BSc Hons, MA

Senior Teacher: Mrs J Gardner, BEd Hons, TCert

Senior Teachers: Mrs D Dixon, BSc Hons, PGCE

Bursar: Mr P Large, BA

Head of Sixth Form: Mrs K Kaur-Jansari, BA Hons, PGCE

Head of Boarding: Miss H Vose, BA Hons

Marketing Manager: Mr P Rennie, BSc Hons

Admissions Registrar: Mrs A Charles

Heads of Department:

Mr S Atkinson, BA Hons, MSc (*Biology*)

Ms J Bartlett, BA Hons, PGCE (*History*)

Miss J Bates, BA Hons, BEd Hons (*Food Technology*)

Mr G Beynon, BEd Hons, MA (*Mathematics*)

Mrs H Broadhurst, BSc Hons, PGCE (*Physics*)

Mr T Caister, GRSM, ARCM, PGCE (*Music*)

Mr M Collins, BA Hons, PGCE, MA (*Economics & Business Studies, Careers*)

Mrs S Coughlin, BA Hons (*Art & Design*)

Mr M Giles, BA Hons, PGCE (*Religious Studies*)

Mrs K Kaur-Jansari, BA Hons, PGCE (*ICT*)

Mrs S Knight, BSc Hons, PGCE (*Psychology*)

Mrs J Leeming, BSc Hons, PGCE (*Geography*)

Mrs K McGrath, BA Hons, PGCE (*English*)

Miss S G Nelson, BEd Hons (*Physical Education*)

Dr S Parish, BA Hons, MA. PhD, PGCE (*Chemistry*)

Miss A Ritchie, BA Hons, PGCE (*EAL*)

Mrs A Wilson, BA Hons, PGCE (*Performing Arts*)

Mrs N C Wilson, BA Hons, PGCE (*Modern Foreign Languages*)

Foundation. St Teresa's was established in 1928 on what was originally part of a manor site recorded in the Domesday Book. The present Georgian house, dating from 1799, is the centre of the Senior School, now greatly extended to provide modern facilities for its high level of education. Although founded as a Catholic school, the school welcomes girls from diverse backgrounds and different faiths.

In 1953, St Teresa's Preparatory School (*see entry in IAPS section*) was established at Grove House, in the village of Effingham, about 1½ miles away, but moved to brand new, purpose-built premises on the Senior School site in January 2009.

Location. Situated amid beautiful, rural surroundings, approximately 22 miles from London, St Teresa's is located in 48 acres of grounds amongst the Surrey hills. The M25 is only four miles away. Both Heathrow and Gatwick airports are half an hour's drive and there is a good train service to London (Waterloo) from Effingham Junction Station and London (Victoria) from Dorking.

Facilities. We are constantly investing in new facilities. A magnificent, new indoor swimming pool complex and an all-weather pitch were completed in 2003. Music, drama and the arts now benefit from a £3 million performing arts theatre hall, incorporating the latest sound and lighting technology and its own recording studio completed in September 2005. A New Nursery and Prep School was built on the senior school site in 2009 and a new Maths and English suite has just been completed in 2011. The next phase of development is to build a new Sports Hall.

Years 7–11. Entrance at 11 is based on success in the Entrance Examination. Scholarships are available (see below). It is school policy to maintain small classes so that each pupil's progress is closely monitored.

St Teresa's is well-equipped in every way for GCSE teaching and excellent examination results bear this out. 20 GCSE subjects are on offer and most girls take 10 subjects.

Individual tuition is available in a variety of subjects, including singing, most musical instruments, drama and a number of sporting activities. Parents receive reports regularly and they also have the opportunity to meet Staff on Parents' Evenings and are encouraged to approach the school whenever they feel it is necessary. Pastoral Care is provided at all levels by Form Tutors, Heads of Year and House Mistresses.

Sixth Form. As well as those who have come up through the school, every year St Teresa's Sixth Form welcomes girls from other schools. It has its own purpose-built accommodation in Magdalen House where girls live in a happy atmosphere in which high standards, responsibility and self discipline are encouraged. Currently 28 A Level subjects are on offer and each girl has a personal tutor. All girls follow a varied curriculum, in addition to their main examination subjects. The Lower Sixth all do one or two weeks of work experience and may also participate in the Young Enterprise Scheme and Voluntary Service. Almost all St Teresa's girls go on to higher education: many to top ranking universities; others to the best art schools, drama schools, and music colleges. Such is the school's reputation amongst top Art Colleges that girls regularly receive unconditional offers from all including University of Arts, London.

Dance and Drama. During the course of the year there are a number of productions enabling all year groups to participate. LAMDA examinations are taken by a high percentage of girls. Debating and Public Speaking is also an integral part of school life with notable successes in local and national competitions.

Music. St Teresa's has an excellent reputation for music. Standards are high with girls attending Saturday sessions at London music colleges, playing in county orchestras and bands, and in children's and youth orchestras at national level. Choirs, ensembles and individuals are entered for competitions and festivals with a high degree of success and there are annual choir trips to sing in prestigious venues across Europe – latterly Florence, Barcelona and Venice.

Sport. St Teresa's has a 5-acre Sports Field for athletics, field events and cricket, several tennis courts, an all-weather hockey pitch, an indoor swimming pool complex with Yoga/Pilates/Aerobics studio and a large sports hall. Hockey, netball and tennis are the main sports in which the school has won many titles locally and regionally, but numerous other sporting activities take place. Several girls hold national and international titles.

Boarding. St Teresa's offers full, weekly and flexi boarding in a happy relaxed atmosphere. Boarding facilities are first class with bright and attractive rooms. A full programme of weekend activities is provided. Extended day, weekly and flexi-boarding are also available to accommodate the varying requirements of parents and pupils.

Extra-Curricular Activities. Many extra-curricular activities are on offer including The Duke of Edinburgh's Award Scheme and World Challenge Expeditions. School trips at home and abroad and school exchanges play an important part in broadening the girls' outlook as well as affording cultural and social benefits.

Fees per term (2011-2012). Day Pupils: Senior £4,520–£4645. Includes lunch and most books/stationery and computer consumables. Boarding (additional fee): £2,745 (weekly), £3,360 (full).

Scholarships. Academic, Sport, Drama, Art and Music scholarships are available at 11+, 12+ and 13+ as well as in the Sixth Form.

Assisted Places. Three Assisted Places exist per year in the Senior School with means-tested fees remissions of up to 100%. One Assisted Place from Year 3 in the Prep School.

STOGA. St Teresa's Old Girls Association maintains links between the school and leavers.

FOST. Friends of St Teresa's is a flourishing parents' association which engages in fundraising through a variety of social events.

Prospectus. A fully illustrated prospectus is available on request or may be downloaded from our website.

Charitable status. St Teresa's School Effingham Trust is a Registered Charity. It exists to provide education for girls from 2 to 18 years.

Sheffield High School
GDST

10 Rutland Park, Sheffield S10 2PE
Tel:　　0114 266 0324
Fax:　　0114 267 8520
e-mail:　enquiries@she.gdst.net
website:　www.sheffieldhighschool.org.uk

Founded 1878.

Sheffield High School is part of the GDST (Girls' Day School Trust). The GDST is the leading network of independent girls' schools in the UK. As a charity that owns and runs 24 schools and two academies, it reinvests all its income in its schools. For further information about the Trust, see p. xxi or visit www.gdst.net.

Additional information about the school may be found on the school's website and a detailed prospectus is available from the school.

Chair of Local Governors: Mrs P Liversidge, OBE, DL, FREng, CEng, BSc Hons, DEng, DSc, UnivD, FIMechE, FCGI, FRSA

Headmistress: Mrs V A Dunsford, BA Manchester, NPQH

Deputy Head: Miss N Gunson, BSc, Huddersfield, MA Huddersfield

Senior Tutor: Miss H Thorneloe, BEd Liverpool John Moores

Head of Pastoral Care: Mrs R Bennett, BA York

Director of Studies: Miss J M Goodwin, BSc Leicester

Head of Sixth Form: Dr J Raymond, BA Lancaster, PhD Exeter

Head of Junior School: Mrs A Jones, BSc South Bank

School Business Manager: Mr S Mozley, BA Oxford

Number of Pupils. 1,010: 270 (Junior School), 540 (Senior School), 200 (Sixth Form)

The school was opened in 1878 and has occupied its pleasant site in the suburb of Broomhill since 1884. It draws its pupils from all parts of the city and from more distant rural and urban areas of Nottinghamshire, Derbyshire and Yorkshire, many travelling on special coaches organised by parents.

The Junior School, Senior School buildings and Sixth Form Centre are adjacent and share gardens, sports hall, hockey/rounders pitch, netball/tennis courts and a gymnasium on the site. An additional hockey and athletics field is situated a short bus ride from the school. In January 2007 the two-form entry Junior School acquired a new Infant building and ICT suite.

The infants and juniors have their own purpose-built libraries, a science room and art and music studios. The Junior School also provides a breakfast club from 7.45 am and supervised after-school care is available until 5.45 pm.

Recent additions to the Senior School include a new IT suite, Science laboratories, additional Art & Design studios, Music facilities, a Drama studio, two new libraries and a language media suite. A large £1 million extension to the Sixth Form Centre was completed in the summer of 2010 and now houses refurbished common rooms, teaching rooms and tutorial bases as well as a new learning resource centre which provides access to key study materials, laptop computers and a wealth of careers resources. There is a modern and bright café-diner as well as a decked outside eating areas for the students.

Curriculum. The usual Junior subjects are taught plus French, German, Spanish, Art, Computer Studies, Art/Technology, Drama, Music and PE. Most lessons are with form teachers but specialist staff teach older girls. In the Senior School, girls generally take 10 GCSE subjects from the range of usual options plus German, Greek, Latin, Drama, Spanish, Art and Design, Business Studies, Geology, Music and PE. Over 80% stay on to the Sixth Form and nearly all go on to Higher Education.

The school attaches great importance to the wide range of opportunities it offers and has received a string of prestigious national awards for the exceptional quality of its extra-curricular provision such as Arts Mark (Gold), GO4it, ICT Mark, Eco Schools Award and the International Schools Award. The school's sporting provision has also been commended nationally for its outstanding quality with teams in national finals last year in five different sports in addition to fielding national finals teams in film-making and debating. The School has over 50 lunchtime and after school clubs, which encourage excellence in sport, music, drama and art and offers the full Duke of Edinburgh's Award Scheme. A varied programme of residential trips and expeditions at home and abroad is offered, including Sport, Music and Art tours.

Fees per term (2011-2012). Senior School £3,336, Junior Department £2,397–£2,454.

The fees cover the regular curriculum, school books, stationery and other materials, most extra-curricular activities, but not school meals for Senior girls.

Scholarships and Bursaries. The GDST makes available to the School a substantial number of scholarships and bursaries. The bursaries are means-tested and are intended to ensure that the School remains accessible to bright girls who would profit from the education offered but who would be unable to enter the School without financial assistance.

A large range of scholarship and bursary support is provided at Sheffield High School. From Year 7, a number of prestigious Academic and Music Scholarships are provided each year with an additional means-tested HSBC Scholarship also available. In the Sixth Form, a range of Academic, Music, Art, Sport and Drama Scholarships are also made available to suitably talented girls.

Charitable status. Sheffield High School is part of The Girls' Day School Trust, which is a Registered Charity, number 306983.

Sherborne Girls

Bradford Road, Sherborne, Dorset DT9 3QN
Tel: Admissions: 01935 818224
          School: 01935 812245
          Bursar: 01935 818206
Fax: 01935 389445
e-mail: enquiry@sherborne.com
website: www.sherborne.com

Sherborne Girls, founded in 1899, provides an outstanding education for 11 to 18 year olds in the beautiful county of Dorset, and is proud of its extra-curricular programme and exceptional pastoral care. Girls are admitted at 11+, 12+, 13+ and into the Sixth Form. There are 406 girls, 376 Boarders, 30 Day girls. The International Baccalaureate Diploma is offered in addition to A Levels, which provides education tailored to each girl's needs. A close relationship with Sherborne School allows co-ed opportunities including some joint lessons in the Sixth Form, music, drama, activities, clubs and societies and social occasions. The schools have the same term dates. Scholarships and Bursaries are available.

Council:
Chairman: Mr S H Wingfield Digby, BSc, MBA
Mrs H Greenstock, MA
Mrs G M Blenkinsop, BSc
The Right Reverend T M Thornton, MA
Mr S J Mabey, MA, FCA
Mrs J Nicholson, BSc
Right Hon Oliver Letwin, MP
The Hon Mark Bridges, MA
The Right Reverend Dr Graham Kings, Bishop of Sherborne
Professor J M Brown, FRHistS
Mr D J Pow
Vice Admiral Sir Christopher Morgan, KBE
Mr A J C Palmer
Mrs S Tennant
Captain R J Fisher, RN
Mrs I Burke, MB BS, MRCGP, DRCOP, DCH

Mr R H Robson
Mr P Johnson, MA, FRSA
Mr O Stanley
Mr R W Strang
Mr R Pilkington, FRICS

Clerk to the Council: Mr S D Miller, MBA

Senior and Pastoral Staff:

Headmistress: Mrs Jenny Dwyer, BEd Hons Cantab

Bursar: Mr S D Miller, MBA
Deputy Head Academic: Mr W J Penty, BA Hons Bristol, PG Dip Sheffield
Director of Studies: Dr G P Oliver, PhD London, BA Cantab
Director of Sixth Form: Mr R MacNeary, BA Hons Cardiff, MA Winchester
Head of Pastoral: Mrs E Hattersley, BA Hons Dunelm

Chaplain: Revd Rebecca Ayers-Harris, BA Nottingham, Dip Theology, PGCE

Housemistresses of Boarding Houses:
Aldhelmsted East: Mrs E Poraj-Wilczynska, MSc Leicester, CertEd London (*PE*)
Aldhelmsted West: Mrs H Vanstone
Dun Holme: Mrs A Taylor, BA Amsterdam (*Languages*)
Wingfield Digby: Mrs I Morley-Smith, BSc Bath Spa (*English*)
Reader Harris: Miss R Brown, BSc London, PGCE Bath (*Science*)
Kenelm: Ms L Crampton, MEng Hull, PGCE Nottingham Trent
Mulliner: Mrs L Parsons, MA Southampton, CertEd Bishop Otter (*PHSE*)

Staff:
* *Head of Department*

Art and Design:
*Miss J Newman, BA Norwich, ATC London
Mrs J A Baker, BA Leeds, ATD
Mr M D Chapman, MA Birmingham, BA Sunderland
Ms A D Heron, BA Southampton
Mrs J Saurin, BA Sydney, MA Courtauld Institute, London
Mr T Taylor, CertEd Shoreditch College of Education
Mrs S H Wills, Dip Home Economics Aberdeen College (*Head of Fourth Forms*)
Miss T Farris, Leiths
Mr I McCarthy, BEng Leeds, PGCE
Mrs L Fosh, BA Arts Institute of Bournemouth, PGCE
Ms P Ellis, MA London, BA Courtauld Institute, London
Mr R MacNeary, BA Hons Cardiff, MA Winchester (*Director of Sixth Form*)

Classics:
*Miss S Jones, BA Toronto
Mrs R M Allen, BA Birmingham (*Head of Middle Fifth*)
Miss S Haslam, MA Cantab, PGCE

Drama and Theatre Studies:
*Mr S Hattersley, CertEd London Dip
Mr M Freestone, BA University of Natal
Ms J Moore, MA Warwick, BA Leicester, PGCE, DipEd Brighton

English:
*Mr P R Cantrell, BA Nottingham
Mrs N Alper, BA Birmingham, PGCE (*CAS Coordinator*)
Mrs P Golovchenko, CertEd, RSA Dip SpLD
Ms K Chapman, BEd Southampton
Ms J M Seegers, BA OU, PGCE
Mrs C J Stones, MA Bristol, BA OU, Cert TEFL (*Head of EAL, International Coordinator, Archivist*)
Mrs J Ward, BA OU, SpLD Dip, TESL Toronto, AMI Toronto, PGCE
Mr S P Wood, BA Oxon

Mrs J Trew, BSc Bath, Dip Hornsby Int Dyslexia Centre (*Head of Learning Support*)

Geography, Economics and Business Studies:
*Mrs E Morray-Jones, BSc Surrey
Revd Rebecca Ayers-Harris, BA Nottingham, Dip Theology, PGCE
Mr D Banks, BSc Cardiff, PGCE UWE
Miss J Burrow, BA Aberystwyth
Mrs A Dencher, BA Cambridge, MA Cambridge, PGCE
Mr P Richards, LLB Southampton, PGCE
Miss C Rule, BSc Hons Oxford Brookes

History:
*Miss C Valeur, BA London
Mrs R M Allen, BA Birmingham
Mrs S Francis, MA Oxon

ICT:
Mr S Jefferson, MA Cantab (*Duke of Edinburgh's Award*)

Mathematics:
*Mrs L Orton, BSc Hons Swansea, PCE
Mr M Crabtree, BSc Bath, PGCE
Miss J Davidson, BSc UMIST, PGCE
Mr R Lavender, BSc Dunelm, PGCE
Dr A Moore, BEng, PhD Bristol, MA Nottingham
Mr S Payne, BSc Kent, PGCE

Modern Languages:
*Mr M Felstead, MA Cantab
Mrs Y Bell, BA Birmingham
Mme M-D B Bonelli-Bean, Licence LLCE Paris
Mrs D Burgess
Miss L W Chen
Miss U Dedek
Mrs P J Fieldhouse, MA London, BA Rhodes, PGCE
Mrs D A Goldsack, BA Leeds
Mrs G Henderson, BA Exeter, PGCE
Dr G P Oliver, PhD London, BA Cantab
Mr W J Penty, BA Bristol, PGCE
Mlle C Petit
Mr A Orsorio, BA Nat Univ of Colombia, PGCE
Mr H Qaswari
Senora B Regaliza
Mrs R Rogerson, Zurich
Mrs A Taylor, BA Amsterdam

Music:
*Mr J M Jenkins, BA Dunelm, ARCO
Mr T J Urbainczyk, BA Dunelm (*Assistant Director of Music, Head of Strings*)
Mr S Clarkson, BMus Edinburgh, FRCO, ARCM (*Head of Academic Music*)
Miss Ana Manero (*Pianist in Residence*)
30 visiting teachers

Musical tuition in:
Flute, Double Bass, Clarinet, Saxophone, Percussion, Singing, Alexander Technique, Oboe, Cor Anglais, Bassoon, Bass, Electric Guitar, Baroque Recorder, Classical Guitar, Brass, Viola, Cello, Percussion, Piano and Harp.

Physical Education:
*Mrs N Matthias, BEd St Peter & St Mary, Cheltenham
Mr J Brooker, BA London
Miss K Hoffman, BA North Carolina
Mrs K Stringer, BEd Crewe & Alsager College of PE
Mr M Stringer, DipEd St Luke's, Exeter
Mr M Long (*Senior Tennis Coach*)

Religious Studies:
*Dr S D Loxton, PhD Seattle, BEd Sussex, MPhil Hull
Revd Rebecca Ayers-Harris, BA Nottingham, Dip Theology, PGCE
Miss K Pinsent, BA Durham, MSc Roehampton, PGCE
Mr P Woolway, BA Oxon, PGCE

Sciences:
*Dr J Ivimey-Cook, PhD Exeter
Miss P Abbott, BSc, Southampton
Mr D Buck, BSc London
Ms D B M Keating, BSc London, PGCE
Mr G Markham, BSc Dunelm, PGCE
Miss G Nelson, MSc East Anglia, BSc Dunelm
Mr P M Crabtree, BSc Leeds

Sanatorium Sister: Mrs A Watson
Director of Admissions: Mrs F Clapp, BSc London, PGCE Oxon
Librarian: Miss P A Deacon, MA Oxon (*Director of IB*)
Marketing Coordinator: Miss K Nutland, BSc Bath Spa, ACIM
Digital Marketing Coordinator: Miss J Seegers, BA OU, PGCE

Terms. Three terms of approximately 12 weeks each. Christmas holidays 4 weeks; Easter holidays 4 weeks; Summer holidays 8 weeks. Term dates are in common with those of Sherborne School.

Admission. (*See Scholarship Entries section.*) Common Entrance Examination to Independent Schools. Scholarship Examinations and interviews. The School's own entrance examinations where Common Entrance is not possible. Girls should be registered in advance and reports will be requested from their current school. For entry into the Sixth Form girls are required to gain 5 good passes in relevant subjects.

Registration fee £100. A deposit of £750 is required before entry (a term's fees for overseas pupils) and credited to the last term's bill.

Fees per term (2011-2012). Boarders £8,995–£9,450, Day Girls £6,540–£6,870.

Houses. There are five Houses for 13–17 year olds and one Upper Sixth House. 11 and 12 year old girls spend their first years together in a Junior House.

Religion. The School has a Church of England foundation, but it values the presence and contribution of members of all the Christian traditions and of other faiths. Regular services are held in the Abbey, some jointly with Sherborne School.

Examinations. Girls are prepared for GCSE, AS/A Levels and the International Baccalaureate Diploma. There is a wide choice of subjects to be studied. Some subjects at AS/A Level and IB are studied jointly with Sherborne School.

Games. Hockey and Lacrosse/Netball are played in the Michaelmas and Lent terms and Tennis, Rounders and Athletics during the Trinity term. Oxley Sports Centre in partnership with Sherborne Girls contains a 25m pool and state-of-the-art fitness suite. There are Squash Courts, floodlit Astroturf, Sports Hall, Dance Studio and Climbing Wall. Riding, Badminton, Cross-Country Running, Golf, Aerobics, Judo, Sailing, Trampolining are some of the alternative games.

Sherborne Old Girls Union (SOGU). All enquiries should be made to Ms Laura Windsor at the School, Tel: 01935 818329.

Prospective parents and their daughters are invited to the School for Open Mornings in the Spring and Autumn, or private visits by appointment. Please visit the school's website or telephone Admissions on 01935 818224 for further details.

Charitable status. Sherborne School for Girls is a Registered Charity, number 307427. It exists to provide education for girls in a boarding environment.

Shrewsbury High School
GDST

Senior School: 32 Town Walls, Shrewsbury SY1 1TN
Tel: 01743 494000
Fax: 01743 494039
e-mail: enquiries@shr.gdst.net
website: www.shrewsburyhigh.gdst.net

Prep School:
Old Roman Road, Shrewsbury SY3 9AH
Tel: 01743 494200
e-mail: enquiries@shr.gdst.net

Founded 1885.

Shrewsbury High School is part of the GDST (Girls' Day School Trust). The GDST is the leading network of independent girls' schools in the UK. As a charity that owns and runs 24 schools and two academies, it reinvests all its income in its schools. For further information about the Trust, see p. xxi or visit www.gdst.net.

The school's website and prospectus contain comprehensive information about the school. Shrewsbury High School has a Prep School for boys and girls a few minutes' walk from the Senior School. (*See also Prep School entry in IAPS section.*)

Chairman of Local Governors: Mrs S Quayle, TD, RGN, RGNT

Headmistress: **Mrs M Cass**, BA Exeter, MA EdMan Bath

Deputy Headmistress: Mrs H M Jones, BSc Liverpool

Head of Prep School: Mrs M Edwards, BEd Bedford, CertEd Primary Manchester

Head of Sixth Form: Mrs S Coppin, BSc Nottingham

Heads of Departments:

Art: Mr M Warner, BA Gwent
Biology: Mr B Brown, BSc Sheffield
Chemistry: Mr D Payne, BSc Exeter
Classics: Mrs J Lashly, MA Oxford
Drama: Mrs P Law, BA Manchester
Economics & Business: Mrs M Rumble, BA Staffordshire
English: Mr C Steare, BA Cambridge
Geography: Mr J High, BA Liverpool
History, Government & Politics: Mr G Niblock, BA Belfast
Home Economics: Miss L Hughes, BA Liverpool
ICT: Mr T Curtis, BSc West London Inst, Brunel
Mathematics: Mrs J Mills, BSc Cardiff
Modern Languages: Miss R Smith, BA Durham
PE: Mrs R Sadd, BA Manchester
PSHE: Mrs C Tonks, BA Westminster College
Physics & Science: Dr S Richards, PhD London
Psychology: Mrs M Morgan, BSc Open, MA Open
RE: Ms E J Thomas, BEd Polytechnic of Wales

School Business Manager: Mr J Harper, BSc, HFMA, ACMA
Admissions Officer: Mrs D Frost
Headmistress's PA: Mrs J Gittins
ICT Development Manager: Miss E Shaw
Network Manager: Mr L Hodgkinson, BA
Librarian: Mrs A Hale
Marketing & Development Manager: Mr B Jason, BSc Manchester, MBA Manchester Metropolitan, MCIM
School Doctor: Dr L Houghton, MBBS, DCH, DRCOG, MRCGP
School Nurse: Mrs L Steeple, SRN

Number of Pupils. 753: 496 girls in Senior School, 257 pupils in the Prep School.

Shrewsbury High School is a high-performing school and its reputation as the county's premier girls' day school remains as strong as ever. The Senior School, in the town centre, extends along the Old Town Walls with gardens sweeping down the hill to the banks of the River Severn.

The Senior School is for girls aged 11 to 18; the Prep School, a few minutes' walk away, takes boys from 3 to 13 and girls from 3 to 11. It is expected that girls in the Prep will move up to the Senior School at 11.

The school has invested considerably in areas such as Information Technology. Other recent investments include a new Sports Hall and classroom complex for the Senior School and a new Gym and classroom block at the Prep.

Curriculum. Alongside the academic subjects of the national curriculum, the school has excellent facilities for music, art and design, drama and sports. Public examination successes: 100% A Level pass rate for seven of the past eight years, with 91.7% of A Levels graded A*–C in 2010. GCSE: 67.5% achieving A*/A grades, 100% achieved at least 5 grades A–C.

The Prep boys regularly achieve scholarships to Senior Schools at 13+. In both 2010 and 2011 four boys gained scholarships to Shrewsbury School.

Sports in the Senior School include athletics, badminton, cricket, football, rugby, hockey, netball, rounders, swimming, tennis, rowing, canoeing, mountain-biking and volleyball. Opportunities exist for participation in debating, drama, Duke of Edinburgh's Award, music, public speaking, Amnesty, and Young Enterprise in the Senior School and ballet, judo, music, gym, crafts, ICT, chess and specialist speech and drama classes at the Prep.

Fees per term (2011-2012). Senior £3,434; Prep: Years 4–6 £2,797, Reception–Year 3 £2,489, Nursery according to sessions.

The fees cover the regular curriculum, school books, stationery and other materials, entry fees for public examinations, choral music, games, and swimming, but not optional extra subjects or school meals. Full details are in the prospectus.

Admissions Procedures. Full details are available from the Admissions Officer or on the school website.

Entrance Examinations. The 11+ Entrance Examinations are held in January. Sixth Form Scholarship Examinations are held in the Autumn Term of Year 11.

Open Days. Open Days are held from September to November each year, and also from January to March.

Scholarships and Bursaries. The GDST provides a substantial number of scholarships and bursaries. Bursaries are means tested and ensure that the school remains accessible to bright girls who would profit from private education, but who would be unable to enter the school without financial assistance. They are available for entry at 11+. In cases of financial need bursaries may be available after entry to the Senior School.

Several scholarships are available each year for internal and external candidates for entry at 11+ or in the Sixth Form. Music scholarships for entry at 11+ are also available. Entrants must reach Grade 5 or above with their first instrument.

Charitable status. Shrewsbury High School is part of The Girls' Day School Trust, which is a Registered Charity, number 306983.

South Hampstead High School
GDST

3 Maresfield Gardens, London NW3 5SS
Tel: 020 7435 2899
Fax: 020 7431 8022
e-mail: senior@shhs.gdst.net

website: www.shhs.gdst.net

Founded 1876.

South Hampstead High School is part of the GDST (Girls' Day School Trust). The GDST is the leading network of independent girls' schools in the UK. As a charity that owns and runs 24 schools and two academies, it reinvests all its income in its schools. For further information about the Trust, see p. xxi or visit www.gdst.net.

Local Governors:
Chairman: Mr J Rosefield, BA Oxon, MBA Harvard
Mrs C Brill, CertEd
Miss E Clements, BA, BArch, RIBA, FRSA
Prof R Jackman, MA Cantab
Mrs N Perlman, LLB
Prof A Stevens, MA Cantab, MSc, PhD
Mrs Madeline Trehearne, MA, BEd

***Headmistress*: Mrs J E Stephen**, BSc Leeds (*Chemistry*)

Deputy Heads:
Mr D Bradbury, MA Keele (*Mathematics*)
Mrs H Kay, BSc Sheffield, NPQH (*Mathematics*)
Mrs Claire Kelly, MA Cantab (*Politics and Psychology*)

Assistant Head:
Mr K C Blake, BSc Exeter, FRGS, CGeog (*Geography*)

Head of Sixth Form:
Miss C Stevenson, MA London, MA Edinburgh (*Classics*)

Senior School Staff:
Mrs J Arundale, BSc Lancaster (*Physics*)
Mr P Arundale, BSc Manchester (*Chemistry*)
Ms G Ashwell, DA Manchester
Mrs R J Banfield, BA Brighton (*Physical Education*)
Miss E J Bartlow, BSc Miami (*Geography and Religious Studies*)
Miss C Bateman, BHSc Leeds (*Biology and Religious Studies*)
Mrs V Boyarsky, BA Cantab, MPhil London (*History*)
Mr S Breen, BSc Limerick (*Product Design and Technology*)
Mr E Cabezas, BA Seville, Spain (*Spanish*)
Mrs J Coates, BA Bristol, MA Hawaii (*History*)
Miss A Cockerill, BA Durham (*Religious Studies*)
Miss I Condon, BA Manchester (*English*)
Mrs G Cooke, BA Brighton (*Physical Education*)
Mrs O Crossley-Holland, BA Oxon (*English*)
Dr B Davies, BA Open University, PhD London (*Mathematics*)
Dr M M Egan, BA UCL, MA Essex, PhD UCL (*Politics,History and Critical Thinking*)
Dr C Everall, BSc, PhD Southampton (*Physics with Astronomy*)
Mrs S Fanning, BSc London, Dip Arch RIBA (*Design & Technology*)
Mrs C Finley, CAPES Toulouse (*French and Spanish*)
Mr N Flower, BSc Open (*ICT and eLearning*)
Miss C Forsey, BMus, PGDip Royal College of Music (*Music*)
Mr K Fosbrook, BA Oxon (*Classics*)
Mrs L F Frank, BA York (*Mathematics*)
Miss R Furlonger, BA Oxon (*Classics*)
Mrs C E S Gibson, BSc Dunelm (*Mathematics*)
Mr B Harkins, MA Cantab, MA London (*English*)
Mr L Hearn, BSc Warwick, BSc Open, MSc Open (*Chemistry*)
Mrs D F Hugh, BA Manchester, MBA (*Modern Languages*)
Mr N Hunter, BA Liverpool, MA Goldsmiths College London (*Art*)
Mrs A S Johnson, BA Birmingham (*Religious Studies*)
Mr S Keeler, BSc Exeter, BSc Open, (*Psychology and Physics*)

Ms A Kennedy, BA Ulster, MA Philadelphia (*History of Art*)
Mrs E Keyte, MA Edinburgh, MSt Oxon (*English*)
Miss S G Lopez, BEd Edinburgh (*Physical Education*)
Miss H Lymburn, Sheffield Hallam (*Physical Education*)
Mr T McLaughlin, BA Oxon, MA University College London (*English*)
Mr S Mackintosh, MA Oxon (*Economics*)
Miss A Mobsby, BSc Wales (*Biology*)
Mrs P Morgan, MA Cantab (*History*)
Mr M Morley, BA Lancaster (*French and History*)
Mr J C R Morris, BSc Open (*Chemistry*)
Mr W Moss, BA Cardiff (*Art*)
Miss J Meyer, MA/BSc London (*German*)
Ms L O'Higgins, BSc Belfast (*Design & Technology*)
Mrs L Raitz, MA Cantab (*French*)
Miss J Reynolds, MA St Andrews (*Classics*)
Mr J Rowe, BEd, ALAM (*Drama*)
Mrs S Schildknecht-Birch, PGCE Institute of Education (*Modern Foreign Languages*)
Mr M Smeaton, BA Leeds (*Spanish*)
Ms V M Spawls, BSc Westminster (*Biology*)
Miss R J Stockdale, BHM Tasmania (*Physical Education*)
Mr N Stokes, BSc Imperial College (*Physics*)
Mrs R Stone, MMaths Oxon (*Mathematics*)
Mrs A Svoboda, BSc Imperial College (*Mathematics*)
Ms N Sweeney, MA Oxon (*Geography*)
Ms V Trinder, BA Leeds Met (*Art*)
Mr S Waygood, MA Victoria University of Wellington (*Philosophy and Mathematics*)
Mr D J Webb, MA Cantab, ARCO DipCHD, Barrister NP (*Music*)
Ms S Wilson, BA Oxon (*English*)
Dr C J Woodward, BSc, PhD London (*Biology*)

Science Technicians:
Mrs C I Ezike, BSc
Mrs A Weekes, HND
Mrs T Zabergia, BSc BA

Art Technician: Mr A Hennessey, BA

DT Technician: Mr J Parsotam

Language Assistants:
Mrs B Arnold
Miss L Pinana-Blanco

Librarians:
Ms M Ravetto-Wood
Mrs S Raitz (*Assistant Librarian*)

Junior School:
Head of Junior School: Mrs C Lough, MA Aberdeen
Deputy Head of Junior School: Miss L Szemerenyi, BSc Sussex

Miss A R Benjamin, CertEd Leeds
Mrs C Bercott, BA Middlesex
Ms V Croly, BA Exeter
Mrs M L Davenport, CertEd St Mary's
Miss Z Edwards, BA London
Mrs S Elian, BA Strathclyde
Mrs J Kirk, RAM Prof Cert, ARCM
Mrs S-J Lewis, BA London
Mrs J Lowen, BSc Leeds Metropolitan
Ms K Norton, MA Cantab
Miss N Scales, BA Oxford Brookes
Miss H Trembath, BSc Durham
Mrs L Young, BEd Bath
Mr M Weddell, BEng Brunel

Junior School Librarian:
Ms T Volhard, BA

Junior School Teachers' Assistants:
Ms E Bartunekova, NVQ Level 3
Miss I Pepel, NVQ Level 3

Mrs M Shakil, NVQ Level 3
Mrs S Suganthan, NVQ Level 4

Visiting Music Staff:
Piano:
Ms G Cracknell, LRAM
Mrs E Jones, LRAM
Mrs A Maneks, LRAM
Mr S Wybrew, BMus RCM

Strings:
Ms C Cohen, BMus, LRAM (*Violin, Chamber Music*)
Ms S Davis, BMus, MMus (*Cello, Theory*)
Mr R Fogg, BA (*Guitar*)
Mr J Gee (*Double Bass, Bass Guitar*)
Ms L Moore, BMus, LRAM, PPRAM (*Cello*)
Mr S Perkins, BMus, DipNCOS (*Violin, Viola, Chamber Music*)

Brass:
Ms D Calland, BMus, LRAM (*Trumpet*)
Mr D Clewlow, BA (*Trumpet, Trombone, Tuba*)

Woodwind:
Ms F Carpos, MMus, FTCL (*Bassoon*)
Miss S J Clarke, GGSM (*Clarinet, Saxophone, Theory*)
Ms K Corrigan, BA Dunelm, MMus (*Recorder*)
Mr I Judson, LWCMD ALCM (*Flute*)
Mr M Onissi, LTCL (*Saxophone*)
Miss E Tingey, LWCMD, ACC WCMD, TCM (*Oboe*)
Mr S West, GTCL, LTCL (*Saxophone*)

Percussion:
Mr T Marsden, BMus, MMus

Singing:
Mr V Kirk, ARCM, BMus London, LRAM
Mrs F McIntosh, BMus, PGDip RNCM
Ms M Phillips, BA York
Ms D Thomas, Dip Degree Cologne, PGDip RAM
Ms A Woodbridge, BSc Hons, Scholarship PG Adv Dip TCM

Support Staff:
Admissions Registrar: Ms P Karavla
Caretakers: Mr D Lacey, Mr R Clarke, Mr B Karavla
Deputy Heads' Secretary (Senior School): Mrs M Kleinman
Deputy Network Manager: Mr Y Lo, BSc
Finance Assistant: Miss A Halai, BSc
Finance Manager: Mrs B Quilantang BSc, CPA
Headmistress's Secretary: Mrs L Cripps
ICT Technician: Mr R Bateman
Junior School Administrative Assistant: Mrs H Shah
Junior School Secretary: Ms F Badham, BA
Receptionist: Ms J Douch
School Counsellor: Ms K Chessell, BA
School Nurse: Ms C Robinson, RGN
SIMS Data Manager: Mrs S Halai
Teacher Resource Officer: Mrs S Bell

The school was opened in 1876. It is situated close to the Finchley Road and Swiss Cottage underground stations and to Finchley Road and Frognal railway station. It is also easily reached by bus from central, north and north-west London.

In the Senior School there are 461 pupils, including 128 in the Sixth Form. There are 254 girls in the Junior School. Entry to the Junior School is at 4 and 7; entry to the Senior School is at 11; occasional vacancies arise at other ages and new girls are welcomed into the Sixth Form if they achieve the necessary entrance qualifications. Full details of the admission procedures are available from the school.

The Junior School occupies two large houses with gardens about 5 minutes' walk from the Senior School. The Senior School premises, which are also used at times by girls from the Junior School, include a 4 acre sports ground, large sports hall, theatre, library, and specialist teaching accommodation including three Art studios, Design Technology rooms, Music and Music Technology rooms, Science laboratories and a fully computerised Modern Languages laboratory. The school is fully networked and the computer rooms are equipped with a wide range of software. The school minibus is used for expeditions and games transport. Sixth Form students occupy a large house on the Senior School site and their common room has its own café and a kitchen, where they can prepare drinks and snacks. There is an extensive programme of visits and foreign exchanges, including work experience abroad.

The curriculum provides a wider general education and there is almost no specialism until the Sixth Form. The large compulsory "core" of subjects for GCSE includes three separate sciences or science with Additional Science, one modern foreign language and either History or Geography to which 2, 3 or 4 subjects are added. All girls in the Senior School prepare for GCSE and Advanced level examinations and all leavers go on to university. Pupils participate enthusiastically in an enormous number of extra-curricular clubs, societies and courses. Creativity in art, writing, music and drama is strongly encouraged at all stages. There are many orchestras, ensembles and choirs. Tuition in almost any instrument and singing can be arranged and girls are prepared for the examinations of the Associated Board of the Royal School of Music. Large numbers of pupils participate in the Duke of Edinburgh's Award Scheme and Young Enterprise Business Scheme.

Fees per term (2011-2012). Senior School £4,343, Junior School £3,379.

The fees cover the regular curriculum, games and swimming, but not school meals or instrumental/singing lessons. The fees for instrumental/singing lessons are detailed in the prospectus.

Scholarships and Bursaries. A number of scholarships and bursaries are available through the GDST to internal or external candidates for entry at 11+ or to the Sixth Form. The bursaries are means tested to ensure that the school remains accessible to bright girls who would benefit from our education but who would be unable to enter the school without financial assistance.

Charitable status. South Hampstead High School is part of The Girls' Day School Trust, which is a Registered Charity, number 306983.

Stamford High School

St Martin's, Stamford, Lincolnshire PE9 2LL
Tel: 01780 484200
Fax: 01780 484201
e-mail: headshs@ses.lincs.sch.uk
website: www.ses.lincs.sch.uk

Founded by Browne's Hospital Foundation, of Stamford, 1876.
Motto: *Christe me spede*

Chairman of the Governing Body: Malcolm Desforges, Esq

***Principal of the Stamford Endowed Schools*: S C Roberts**, MA

Vice-Principal, Head: Mrs Y L Powell, BEd, NPQH

Director of Studies: Mrs T E Griffiths
Director of Teaching and Learning: Mrs L A Johnson, BSc
Guidance Coordinator: Mrs A J Horton, BA
CPD & Marketing Coordinator: Mrs D E Evans, BA
Head of Careers: Mrs S Killgren, BSc
Head of Sixth Form: Mrs C A Hawkins, BSc
SES Chaplain: The Revd M Goodman, BA, BTh, MTh
Director of ICT: N A Faux, MA
Librarian: Mrs A Virgo

Teaching Staff:

Miss K Ainsworth, BA	Mrs L Holden, BSc
Miss K Allen, BSc, MSc	Miss L Hornby, BA
Mrs D Ashley, BA	Mrs J Husbands, BSc
Revd G B Austen, MA, MPhil	Mrs N Ingrams, GRSM RAM, LRAM
Mrs T R Bennie, BSc	Miss E L Jackson, BSc
P A Bowden, MA	Mrs A Johnson, MSc
Mrs C A S Boyfield, BA	Mrs A Johnstone, MA
Miss K Burghardt, BSc	Mrs B Joint, BEd
Mrs M L Cade, BSc	Miss E Kerbrat, BA, MA
Mrs L M Cannon, BSc	Mrs J Lewis-Gorman, BA
N S A Clift, BA	Mrs I M Matthews, BA
C Coles, MA	Mrs S Matthews, BA
A J Cox, BA	Mrs G Moss, BSc
Mrs A J B Cox, BA	Mrs E Mount, BEd
Dr A Crookell, BSc, PhD	Miss H Myles, BA
Mrs K Dexter, BA	Miss F Pace, BA
A J Elliott, BEd	Mrs A Rackham, BA
Mrs L Fisher, BA	Miss A D Reilly, BSc
Mrs Y Forman, BA	Mrs E Salt, BA
R M Gale, BA	Mrs V Saunders, BA
Mrs P A Galloway, RBTC	A Skailes, BA
P Galloway, BA, Drama Dip	Miss A Squibb
W Galloway	J Stewart-Greatorex, BEd
Mrs A P Gossel, BA	Mrs C Vie, BA
Miss J Hamphlett, BSc	Mrs N J Watson, BA
Miss E A Hardy, BSc	Mrs A Wenban, BA
G C Harman, BSc	G J Whitehouse, BEd
Mrs L Harte, BSc	C Williamson, BA
Dr T Hill, BSc, PhD	Mrs K Wilson, BEd
	Mrs V Wilson, MA

Music Department:

G E Turner, BA (*Director of Music*)
D McIlrae, BMus, HED (*Assistant Director of Music*)
S Chandley, CT ABRSM (*Head of Brass*)
D Leetch, MA, GRSM, LRAM (*Head of Strings*)
Mrs J E Roberts, GRSM, LRM, ARCM
N S Taylor, BA

Visiting Music Staff:

S Andrews (*Kit Drum/Percussion*)
F Applewhite (*Violin, Viola*)
J Aughton (*Flute*)
S Barber (*Organ*)
C Bell, BSc, LRAM, ARCM (*Guitar*)
Mrs M Bennett, LRAM, LTCL (*Singing*)
Mrs K Bentley, GTCL, LTCL (*Cello, Double Bass*)
F Black (*Singing*)
Mrs S Bond, GLCM, LLCM TD, FLCM (*Singing*)
G Brown, BMus (*Oboe, Pianoforte*)
Mrs H Brown, BA (*Clarinet*)
P J Casson (*Saxophone, Clarinet*)
Revd Mrs J Dumat, ARCM (*Clarinet*)
Mrs J Dustan (*Flute*)
J Forrow (*Classical Guitar*)
N Gray (*Electric Guitar*)
Mrs E Hanlon, ARMCM (*Pianoforte*)
Mrs J Lamb (*Pianoforte, Accordion/Keyboard*)
Mrs S Latham (*Violin, Viola*)
Mrs C Lee, LRAM (*Violin*)
Miss F Maclennan (*Pianoforte*)
Mrs M Maclennan, LRAM, ARCM (*Pianoforte*)
Mrs A McCrae (*Bassoon, Pianoforte*)
Mrs E Murphy, GTCL, LTLL, PGCE (*Violin, Pianoforte*)
D Price, LRAM (*Brass*)
Mrs G Spencer, CertEd, ACRM (*Pianoforte*)
Mrs A Sumner, CertEd, ARCM (*Pianoforte*)
Mrs E A Taylor, BA (*Violin, Viola*)
Mrs L Williamson, LTCC (*Pianoforte*)

Boarding:

Welland House:
Mr & Mrs A Cox (*Houseparents*)
Mrs M Tyers (*Assistant Housemistress*)
Mrs J Rose (*Assistant Housemistress*)

Park House:
Mrs J Sanford (*Resident Housemistress*)
Mrs S Johnson, Mrs W Hartley, Mrs J Rose (*Assistant Housemistresses*)
Mrs S Kavanagh (*Deputy Housemistress*)

Medical Officer: Dr J Barney, MBChB, DAvMed, DOccMED, MRCGP

Introduction. Stamford High School is one of three schools within the overall Stamford Endowed Schools Educational Charity, along with Stamford School (boys) and Stamford Junior School, the co-educational junior school.

Numbers and Boarding Houses. There are 633 girls aged 11–18 years including boarders. The main point of entry is at age 11 though applications are welcomed at any stage up to the Sixth Form. Girls who enter through the Junior School progress automatically on to the High School without further competitive entrance testing. Boarders are received from the age of 8 (in the Junior School). There are two Boarding Houses for girls including a Sixth Form Boarding House where the girls have single or shared study bedrooms. The School accepts full, weekly and three-night boarders.

Fees per term (2011-2012). Day £4,084; Full Boarding £7,452; Weekly Boarding £6,496; 3 Night Boarding £5,644.

These fees include all stationery, textbooks and games. School lunches for day girls are at additional charge.

Registration Fee £50. Acceptance Fee £250.

Extras. Individual music lessons, Speech and Drama, Dancing (Riding for boarders only).

Curriculum. The curriculum is designed to ensure all girls have a balanced educational programme up to age 16 thus avoiding premature specialisation. The National Curriculum is broadly followed but much more is added to the curriculum to make it stimulating and rewarding. Most girls are entered for at least 9 GCSE examinations and for GCE AS and A Level examinations leading to university entry. In partnership with Stamford School, all Sixth Form girls have access to the full range of A Level subjects offered across the two schools providing an exceptionally wide choice of 27 subjects.

Throughout their time in the school girls are prepared for the examinations of the Associated Board of the Royal Schools of Music in music and The London Academy of Music and Dramatic Art for speech and drama. There is much scope for creative activities in Music, Art and Drama and state-of-the-art facilities for Information & Communication Technology, including access to the Internet. The Director of Music for the Stamford Endowed Schools ensures that the Music Department works very closely with Stamford School providing access to a wide range of activities for orchestras, bands, Chapel Choir and choirs. There are joint drama productions and a Performing Arts Studio was opened in September 1995.

Sport and Physical Education include Hockey, Netball, Tennis, Swimming, Golf, Judo, Athletics, Volleyball, Basketball, Badminton, Trampoline, Gymnastics and Squash. There is a very full programme of extra-curricular activities including Olympic Gymnastics, Athletics and TaeKwonDo. There is a heated, indoor swimming pool, a Sports Hall and a floodlit artificial hockey pitch. The Duke of Edinburgh's Award Scheme operates at Bronze, Silver and Gold levels with a considerable number of girls taking part each year. There is a thriving, mixed CCF offering RN, Army and RAF sections. There are many school clubs and societies and a thriving weekend activity programme.

Entrance Examinations are held in January.

Scholarships. (*See Scholarship Entries section.*) Governors' Scholarships at 11+ and for the Sixth Form. Awards may be given for art, sporting, academic, all-round or musical ability and Bursaries up to full fees are available.

Charitable status. As part of the Stamford Endowed Schools, Stamford High School is a Registered Charity, number 527618. It exists to provide education for girls.

The Stephen Perse Foundation
(Perse Girls and The Stephen Perse Sixth Form College)

Union Road, Cambridge CB2 1HF
Tel: 01223 454700; 01223 454701 (Bursar)
Fax: 01223 467420
e-mail: office@stephenperse.com
website: www.stephenperse.com

Founded 1881.

Governors:
Dr G Sutherland (*Chairman*)

Lady Adrian	Councillor S Reid
Dr H D Allen	Mrs J Rigby
Mrs S Barlow	Mr A Ross
Mr C H W Birch	Professor B Sahakian
Dr M T Caleresu	Dr F Salmon
Professor C Carpenter	Ms N M Silverleaf
Mrs P Cleobury	Dr A Thomas
Dr A Crowden	Mrs R Wenham
Mr J Dix	

Clerk to the Governors: Mrs S Wall

Principal: Miss P M Kelleher, MA Oxon, MA Sussex

Vice-Principal: Dr H M Stringer, BA Hons Bristol, MA, DPhil Sussex (*History*)

Head of Senior School: Miss A Kilby, BA Hons, MA Cantab (*Classics*)

Director of Sixth Form: Mr S D Armitage, BA Hons Oxon, MPhil Cantab (*Geography*)

Director of Teaching and Learning: Miss B Pankhurst, BA Hons, MA Cantab, MA McMaster (*English*)

Senior School Staff (full-time):
* *Head of Department*

Miss J Allen, BPhEd Otago (**Physical Education*)
Miss E Anderson, BA Hons Edinburgh (**Art*)
Dr R Appleton, BA Hons Cantab, MPhil Oxon (**English*)
Ms H Barrell, CYGNET (*Drama, Year Head*)
Mrs C M Beadle, BA Hons York (*Chemistry, Year Head*)
Mr R Bett, BA Hons Loughborough, LTCL (**Design Technology*)
Mrs C Brown, BA Hons, MA Cantab (*History*)
Mrs T Churilina, Diploma of Higher Education Hons St Petersburg (*Russian*)
Mrs G Dambaza, BA Hons, MA Cantab (**Physics, *Science*)
Miss S Dickerson, BA Hons Leeds (*Spanish*)
Mr P Fannon, BA Hons, MSci, MA Cantab (*Mathematics*)
Mrs J Featherstone, BA Hons Durham (*Music*)
Miss C Freeman, BA Hons, MA Cantab (**German, *Modern Languages*)
Miss H Freeman, BA Hons, MA Cantab (*Geography*)
Mr W Frost, BA Hons Southampton (*Religious Studies and Philosophy*)
Miss D Gillanders, BA Hons Leicester (**Mathematics*)

Mrs B Horley, BA Hons Birmingham, MA OU (**Religious Studies and Philosophy*)
Mr D Hudson, BSc Hons Sussex, (*Physics, ICT*)
Mr S Jack, BA Hons, MA Cantab (**History*)
Miss S John, BSc UCL, MSc OU (*Chemistry*)
Miss R Johnson, BSc Hons Lancaster (*Biology*)
Ms H Kedie, BA Hons York (*English*)
Mlle J M Lambert, BA Hons, MA Cantab, DEA Amiens (*French*)
Miss R Lawrence, BA Hons Oxon (*Physics*)
Mrs L Lloyd, BA Hons, MA Oxon (*Biology*)
Mrs E Mack, BA Hons York (*English*)
Mrs C Mahey, M-ès-L Bordeaux, CAPES, Agrégation (**French*)
Miss F Mason, BEd Hons London (**Drama*)
Ms S McPhoenix, BA Cape Town, Dip RSA London (*English*)
Mr V Minei, BSc Hons OU (*Italian*)
Mrs P Moore, BA Hons Cagliari (**Italian*)
Mrs L Norman, BA Hons, MA Cantab (*Mathematics*)
Mme S Parente, BTS, MA ESIG Lyon (*French*)
Mrs J Paris, BSc Hons Leeds (**Chemistry*)
Mrs S Passmore, MEng Hons Edinburgh (*Physics*)
Mrs J Payne, BA Hons Cantab (*History, Year Head*)
Miss V Payne, BA Hons Nottingham (*Classics*)
Mr R Percival, BA Cantab, BA London, (*Mathematics*)
Mrs C Petryszak, BA Hons York (*Mathematics*)
Mrs E Pyle, BA Oxon, MSc Aberdeen (**Geography*)
Dr S Rahman, BSc Hons, PhD Salford (*Chemistry*)
Mrs R Rank, BSc Hons Exeter (*Physical Education*)
Mr A Reid, BA Hons Chelsea School of Art, MA Oxford Brookes (*Design Technology*)
Mr M Rudd, BA Hons, MA Oxon (**Music*)
Mrs J Reilly, BA Hons Sheffield Hallam, MA OU (**Spanish*)
Mrs C Ryan, DUEL, Licence Orleans (*French*)
Mr P Ryan, BSc Hons, MSc Manchester (*ICT*)
Mr P Seaman, BSc Eng Queen Mary's London (*Mathematics*)
Mrs A Smith, BSc Hons York (*Mathematics*)
Dr G Speller, BSc Hons London, MPhil, PhD Cantab (*Biology*)
Mrs A-M Stenson, BSc Hons Leeds Metropolitan, MEd Leeds, MBA Wellington (**ICT*)
Mr M Styles, BA Hons Brunel (*Physical Education*)
Mrs A Thompson, BA Liverpool, MPhil Oxon (**Classics*)
Miss C Toutoungi, BA Oxon (*English, Drama*)
Mr A Williams, BSc Hons Exeter (*Geography*)
Mrs S Williams, BSc Hons Manchester (**Biology*)
Mrs E Wilshaw, BA Sheffield Hallam (*Art*)
Mr B Woolley, BA Hons Oxon, MA, MPhil, Vet MB Cantab (*Mathematics*)
Mrs C Wren, BA Hons, MHist Warwick (*History*)

P.A to the Principal: Mrs V Farbon

Bursar: Mrs J Neild

The Senior School comprises over 470 girls between the ages of eleven and 16. At 16, students attend the co-educational Stephen Perse Sixth Form College set up by the school in 2008 with approximately 125 students in the sixth form. There are 63 full-time and 17 part-time teaching staff and 30 peripatetic music staff. The Junior School has approximately 130 girls between the ages of seven and ten with 11 full-time staff. Some Senior School staff also teach in the Junior School. The School's own entrance tests and interviews are held annually for applicants at 7+, 8+, 9+, 10+, 11+ and 13+. There is also regular entry at the Sixth Form stage, on the results of interviews and GCSE examinations. Entry to other year groups is by testing and interview if places are available. The Stephen Perse Foundation acquired Madingley Pre-Prep School in June 2010.

Fees per term (2011-2012). Pre-Prep £3,150; Junior School £3,975; Senior School £4,675; Sixth Form College £4,490.

Extras: Individual music lessons in most instruments, speech and drama.

Scholarships, Exhibitions and Bursaries. Academic Scholarships and Music Awards are available in the Senior School. Sixth Form Scholarships and Exhibitions are awarded on academic merit based on essays and interviews. Sixth Form Music and Art Scholarships are also offered. Bursaries are available for pupils throughout the School. Information about these may be obtained from the Bursar.

Senior School Curriculum. The School celebrates achievement in all aspects of school life. It offers a first-class, broad, well-balanced curriculum in a supportive and structured environment and provides opportunities and challenges for pupils to discover their talents and to reach their full potential. At Key Stage 3 there is a four-form entry; forms are unstreamed with setting in certain subjects. Pupils acquire knowledge and skills in a very wide range of subjects which retain the finest traditions and promote newer technologies. French, Latin and Spanish are taken in Year 7, and a new Modern Language (German, Italian or Russian) may be taken in Year 8. At GCSE the compulsory core consists of English, English Literature, Mathematics, French, Biology, Chemistry, and Physics (leading to a double or triple award). The options, of which girls choose three or four, include the second Modern Language, History, Geography, Religious Studies, Latin, Greek, Design and Technology, Information Technology, Art, Drama and Music. Pupils who sit French GCSE in Year 10 may take Mandarin Chinese in Year 11. Courses in Physical Education and General Religious Education continue throughout the Senior School, together with PSHE and Careers Guidance. Class excursions, fieldwork, foreign exchanges, clubs, activities, and cross-curricular theme days enrich the curriculum. International links are strong, with six modern languages taught, partner schools in Belgium, Finland and Hungary for a Year 9 Creative Arts project, and in Belgium, Germany, Italy and the Netherlands for a Year 10 Latin project. Several cross-curricular ventures have an international dimension. Drama, Music and Sport thrive both within and beyond the curriculum.

The Stephen Perse Sixth Form College. The School has established a sixth form college on a separate site offering A Level courses alongside the IB Diploma Programme.

AS/A2 courses are offered in the following subjects: English, Mathematics, Further Mathematics, Biology, Human Biology, Chemistry, Physics, Psychology, Economics, Geography, History, Religious Studies, Latin, Greek, French, German, Italian, Russian, Spanish, Design and Technology, Art, Music and Theatre Studies. Students have traditionally chosen to broaden their Sixth Form studies and can choose up to five subjects at AS in the first year, reducing to three or four A Levels in the second year.

For the IB Diploma Programme the following courses are offered at Higher and Standard Level: English, Latin, French, German, Italian, Russian, Spanish, Economics, Geography, History, Philosophy, Psychology, Biology, Chemistry, Physics, Mathematics, Theatre, Visual Arts.

All students take the IBDP Theory of Knowledge course and the Creative, Action and Service programme which offers sporting and leisure activities as well as cultural pursuits. European Work Experience is available for linguists and overseas visits extend the experience of other subjects.

The School is a member of ISCO and has links with Cambridgeshire Connexions. The extensive tutorial programme, including individual counselling, enables students to make informed choices about Higher Education and Careers.

Results. The results are consistently outstanding. In 2009, 89% of A Level results were graded A, 99% A–B and 99% A–C. At GCSE 66% of results were graded A*, 95% A*–A, and 99% A*–B.

Junior School Curriculum. The Junior School aims to nurture enthusiasm for knowledge and skills and to encourage imagination in a happy and secure environment. The curriculum includes English, Mathematics, Science, French, Spanish, History, Geography, Religious Studies, Information Technology, Design and Technology, Art, Music, Drama, Physical Education and PSHE. Recorder, violin, cello and speech and drama classes are available in addition to individual music and speech tuition. Staff develop cross-curricular projects and arrange outings both locally and further afield, including residential visits. The interests of pupils are also catered for in the range of clubs and societies.

Pastoral Care. Great emphasis is placed on pastoral care and the well-being of all pupils. Established pastoral structures support the pupils and foster personal development, responsibility and informed choice. Subject teachers and year staff care for the academic progress and individual welfare of each student.

Buildings and Facilities. The School is situated in the centre of Cambridge. Facilities include a Visual Arts Centre, well-equipped laboratories, language laboratory, computer rooms, a drama studio, a DT workshop, netball and tennis courts and hockey pitches, including an all-weather surface pitch. The Music Wing provides 18 individual teaching rooms. The Junior School building was refurbished in January 2001. The Senior School has just completed a major redevelopment of its hall and dining facilities, to include a two-storey building on the site of the previous School Hall. The Senior School opened a new library and learning resource centre in March 2008 and a specialist Visual Arts Centre in September 2008.

The Stephen Perse Sixth Form College, opened in September 2008, is a co-educational facility on Shaftesbury Road and includes disabled access to all areas.

Old Persean Guild. *Secretary*: Miss Claire Gould, c/o The Perse School for Girls, Union Road, Cambridge CB2 1HF.

Charitable status. The Stephen Perse Foundation is a Registered Charity, number 1120608, and a Company Limited by Guarantee, number 6113565.

Stonar School

Cottles Park, Atworth, Melksham, Wiltshire SN12 8NT
Tel: 01225 701740
Fax: 01225 790830
e-mail: office@stonarschool.com
website: www.stonarschool.com

Day and Boarding School for Girls aged 2–18 and Boys aged 2–11.

Governors:
Chairman: Mr Tim Holgate (*& Chair of Education Committee*)
Mr Angus Macpherson (*Chair of F&GP Committee*)
Mrs Mary Anderson
Mr David Haywood
Mrs Philippa Martin
Mr Colin Meeke
Mrs Janet Morgan
Dame Elizabeth Neville, DBE, QPM
Sir Michael Pitt
Mr Keith Robinson
The Venerable John Wraw

Bursar and Clerk to the Governors: Mr Peter Story

Headmistress: Mrs Elizabeth Thomas, BA Hons Lancaster, NPQH

Deputy Headmaster: Mr T Nutt, MSc, BSc Hons, PGCE

Senior Staff:
Mrs S Adams, MCLIP, MA (*Librarian, Careers*)
Mrs S Askew (*Learning Support*)
Miss N Barry, BSc Hons (*Physical Education*)
Mrs C Bennett, BA Hons PGCE (*Geography*)
Mrs H Brains, BA Hons PGCE (*Learning Support, Exams Officer*)
Mrs T Brain, BA Ed Hons (*English, Drama*)
Mrs J Brighouse, BA Hons, PGCE (*French, EAL, Houseparent of Ganbrook*)
Mr S Butler, BA Hons, PGCE (*History, Business Studies*)
Mrs L Carolan, BA Hons, PGCE (*Head of Art*)
Dr V Coote, BSc Hons, MSc, PhD, PGCE (*Physics*)
Mrs S Crouch (*Teaching Assistant*)
Mrs J Cross, BEd Hons (*SENCO, History of Art, Textiles*)
Mr A Curtis, BSc Hons, MSc, PhD (*Psychology, Careers*)
Mrs C Deans, MA, TEFL Dip (*Head EAL*)
Dr S Divall, MA, PhD, PGCE (*Director of Studies, Physics*)
Mr J Dyde, BA Hons, PGCE (*Head of English*)
Mrs H Dziedzic, BSc Hons, PGCE (*Head of Biology*)
Mrs A Fullalove, BA, MA, PGCE (*Mathematics, Learning Support*)
Mrs T Gates, BA Hons, PDSE (*Learning Support Teacher*)
Mr N Goodall, BA Hons, MMus PGCE (*Director of Music*)
Mrs D Harding, BEd (*Learning Support*)
Miss L Havranek, BA Hons, PGCE (*French, Spanish*)
Mrs N Hawkins, BSc Hons, MSc, PGCE (*Head of Boarding, Biology*)
Mrs J Helps, BEd, ADTS (*Head of Home Economics*)
Mrs M-P Jones, BA Hons (*French*)
Miss T Jones, BSc Hons, PGCE (*Physical Education, Houseparent of Curnow*)
Mrs L Kerbey, BA Hons (*History, EAL, Houseparent of Hart*)
Mrs P Lloret, BA Hons, PGCE (*Head of Modern Languages*)
Dr F Martinelli, BSc Hons, PhD (*Chemistry*)
Mrs L Medworth, MA, PGCE (*Mathematics*)
Mr R Miller, BA Hons (*Director of Sport and PE*)
Mrs R Morgan, BEd (*Mathematics*)
Mrs S Muir, BA, DipEd (*Head of History*)
Ms P Nix, BSc Hons, PGCE (*Head of Chemistry*)
Mr N Proud, BA Hons, MA, PGCE (*Head of Drama*)
Mrs A Rivers, BSc Hons, PGCE (*Head of Mathematics*)
Mrs S Scott-Moody, BSc Hons (*Learning Support Assistant*)
Mrs G Sherman, BSc, MCLIP, MBCS (*Head of ICT*)
Mrs L Smith, BSc Hons, PGCE (*Head of Geography*)
Mrs N Teasdale (*Physical Education, PSHE*)
Mrs K Watson, BA Hons PGCE (*English*)
Ms E West, BA Hons, MA, PGCE (*Art*)
Mrs P Willcox, BA Hons, PGCE (*Learning Support*)
Miss A Young, BSc Hons, PGCE (*PE*)

Preparatory School & Nursery Department:
Head of Prep: Mr M Brain, BSc Hons
Deputy Head of Prep: Mrs A Thethy, BEd

Mrs C Bath, CertEd (*Year 3 teacher*)
Mrs F Box, BEd, CertEd (*Year 1 teacher*)
Mrs G Johnson, TCert (*Year 2 teacher*)
Mrs S Musselwhite, BA, PGCE (*History*)
Mrs E Proud, BSc Hons, PGCE (*Year 5 teacher*)
Miss R Prosser, GRSM, PG Dip Early Music (*Music Coordinator*)
Mrs S van Gerwen, BA Ed Hons (*Head of Pre-Prep/Reception*)

Equestrian Centre:
Mrs J Storey, BHSI Regd, BE AcT, CertEd (*Director of Riding*)

Mrs D Pinfield, RSA Business/Secretarial (*Equestrian Centre Secretary*)
Miss D Jackson, BHSAI (*Yard Manager/Prep School Instructor*)
Mrs A Alderton, BHSIT, BHSSM (*Yard Manager/Instructor*)
Mrs J Dinsdale (*Yard Manager/Instructor*)
Miss J Chilcott (*Instructor*)

Ethos. Stonar is a centre of academic excellence for pupils, developing the talents and abilities of every individual and providing the breadth of opportunity to support and enable pupils of all abilities to achieve their potential across and beyond the formal curriculum. There is a positive work ethic and quality pastoral care. Curiosity, confidence and independence are encouraged so that pupils leave school well-equipped for the challenges of adult life and keen to contribute to the wider community.

From September 2011 co-education in the Prep School will be extended so that boys can continue through to Year 6. This step is a natural development which will build upon the success of co-education in the Early Years at Stonar and the wishes of so many current and prospective families for siblings to complete their prep education in the same school.

Curriculum. A talented and committed staff offers students a broad and flexible curriculum, with literacy and numeracy firmly at the centre of the junior school timetable and an individual choice from wide ranging options in addition to the core of Science, Maths, English, a foreign language and ICT at GCSE. AS and A2 courses can include Psychology, Photography, Business Studies, PE and IT.

Science is popular and Stonar has entered the Royal Aeronautical Society's human powered aircraft competition – the world's first female powered aircraft is expected to make a test flight in July 2012.

Results are good and students go on to university courses ranging from Medicine, Law and Accountancy to Geology, Veterinary Science and Music. Talented artists proceed to a variety of Art Foundation Courses. Young riders take up careers in eventing or go for the Equine Studies option. The BHSAI and a top-level Equestrian Competition Course are available in the Sixth Form.

Extra-curricular Activities. The Sports Hall, indoor Swimming Pool, Astroturf, Theatre, Music, brand new Sixth Form & Arts Centre and an internationally renowned Equestrian Centre offer first-class opportunities for sport, music, drama and riding. A timetabled tutorial period provides a rolling programme of careers advice, health education, study skills, first aid, self defence, citizenship and industrial awareness. In the Sixth Form, girls enjoy debating, dance, film studies, aerobics, Leith's Cookery Course and camping. The Duke of Edinburgh's Award scheme flourishes at Stonar.

Boarding. Boarders live in comfortable, family style houses. Each pupil has their own e-mail address for maintaining close contact with home, with the school's network extending into every academic building and boarding house. Pupils of any religion and of all nationalities are welcomed and can work towards IGCSE English, if this is not their first language.

Admission. Straightforward entrance procedures via Stonar entrance examinations, Common Entrance or school report at appropriate ages.

Fees per term (2011-2012). Prep Day £2,290–£3,510; Senior Day £4,245–£4,455; Prep Boarding £5,275; Senior Boarding £7,850.

Scholarships and Bursaries. (*See Scholarship Entries section.*) The school offers special Forces bursaries (for senior pupils) and scholarships for riding, sport, music, drama, art, academic excellence and for the good all-rounder.

Charitable status. Stonar School is a Registered Charity, number 309481.

Stover School

Newton Abbot, South Devon TQ12 6QG
Tel: 01626 354505 (01626 365279 out of hours)
         01626 331451 (Preparatory School)
         01626 335240 (Finance Office)
Fax: 01626 361475
e-mail: mail@stover.co.uk
website: www.stover.co.uk

Board of Governors:

Chair: Mrs C Walliker, BSc, MBA
Vice Chair:
Mr S Killick, ND Arb
Mrs C Whitehead

Members:
Mr H Akhtar
Mrs A Anning
Mrs M Batten, BScMr N Hole, BSc, RICS
Commodore B Key, BSc RN
Mr S Kings, BA Hons, MEd, PGCE
Mr P Moody, MA, BA, PGCE
Mr C Oliver
Mr D Wilson, ACIB

Honorary Members:
Mr R P Barlow, DL, FRICS
Professor R Hawker, OBE
Dr P J Key, OBE, MB, BS

Clerk to the Governors: Mr S J Drabble, BSc

Principal: Mrs Susan Bradley, BSc Hons, CBiol, MSB,
PGCE

Deputy Principal Senior School: Mrs K Veal, BEd Hons
Head of Preparatory School: Mrs C Coyle, BEd, MA
Director of Teaching & Learning: Dr J Stone, BSc, PhD,
HDipEd
Head of Sixth Form: Mr C Baillie, BSc Hons
Head of Boarding: Ms S Trainer, Dip Theol, CertEd
Director of Finance: Mr H Cummins, ACMA

Chaplain: Mrs F Wimsett, BA Hons, PGCE
Principal's PA: Miss J Warrender
Academic Secretary: Mrs S Simpkin
Registrar: Miss F White
Assistant Registrar: Mrs H Symons
Marketing Assistant: Miss R Littlefair
Senior School Secretary: Mrs B Lea
Preparatory School Secretary: Mrs F Martin
Finance Officer: Mrs G Hanbury
Finance Assistant: Miss L Lount
Finance Assistant: Mrs M Barnard

Academic Staff:
Ms P Absalom, BA Hons, PGCE (*Head of Drama*)
Dr D Allway, BSc, MSc, PhD (*Head of Science*)
Miss J Antenbring, BA Hons, CELTA
Mrs M Ayela, DEUG, Licence ES, PGCE (*Spanish*)
Mr C Baillie, BSc, PGCE (*Head of Sixth Form, Science*)
Ms A Barr, BEd Hons, HND, PG Dip (*Media Studies*)
Mr P Barter, BA Hons, PGCE (*Head of History*)
Mrs A Bate, BSc (*Science Technician*)
Miss C Bennett, BA Hons, PGCE (*Head of Art*)
Miss J Berry, BA, MA (*Speech & Drama*)
Mr C Brown, BA ODP (*Head of Physical Education,
Stover Preparatory School*)
Miss C Bulford, BEd (*Physical Education*)
Mrs A Butler, BSc, QTS (*Head of Home Economics*)
Mrs M Corby, BSc, DipEd (*Head of Mathematics*)
Mrs H Coyne, BA Hons (*Modern Languages*)
Miss T Craven, BA, QTS (*Head of Physical Education*)
Mrs E Creates, BA, MA, PGCE (*Head of Geography*)

Mrs L Decamville, BA Hons, CertEd (*Head of Access to
Curriculum in English*)
Mrs V Elce, BA, PGCE (*Geography*)
Miss E Evans, BA, PGCE (*Head of Modern Languages*)
Mrs G Fletcher, CertEd ITEC (*Home Economics*)
Mr G Forsyth, BA Hons, PGCE, TEFL (*English*)
Mrs K Gardner, BA Hons, PGCE (*History*)
Mrs S Griffin, BEd (*Senior Teacher Discipline*)
Mr J Haigh, BA, MA Hons (*Mathematics*)
Miss J Henwood, BSc Hons, PGCE (*Science*)
Mr R Holt, DipEd; FCP (*Mathematics*)
Mrs S Holt, BSc (*Mathematics*)
Mr S Lea, MMus, LTCL, GTCL, QTS (*Director of Music*)
Mrs E Machin, BA Hons, PGCE (*Director of ICT, Head of
ICT & Graphics*)
Mrs V Mackie, BSc Joint Hons, PGCE (*Biology*)
Mrs J Middleton, BA Hons, PGCE (*Head of English*)
Mrs N Milward (*Art Technician*)
Miss A Morgan, BSc (*Science*)
Ms A O'Donovan, BEd, ALCM (*Music*)
Mr S Pillinger, BA Hons, MA, PGCE (*Business Studies*)
Mrs E Rainsford-McMahon, BA Hons, MA (*Modern
Languages*)
Mrs A Richards, BSc Ed Hons PGCE (*Physics*)
Mrs N Rose, BEd (*Learning Support*)
Mrs C Simmons, BEd
Mrs H Skuckova, BA, PGCE (*Mathematics*)
Miss A Titterton, BA Hons (*Learning Support, PE*)
Ms S Trainer, Dip Theol, CertEd (*Head of Boarding; Head
of RE/PSHE*)
Mr D Veal, BA Hons, PGCE (*Science and Head of Senior
Boys, Physical Education*)
Mrs C Wightman, BA (*Art*)
Mrs H Wills, ALCM (*Music*)
Mrs F Wimsett, BA Hons (*RE, Chaplain*)

Visiting Staff:
Mr J Allnatt (*Double Bass*)
Mr J Baldwin (*Keyboard, Piano*)
Mrs A Brown (*Piano, Aural Training*)
Mr P Butcher (*Tennis Coach*)
Miss L Cordon, BMus Hons (*Recorder and Piano*)
Mr S Douglas (*Drum kit*)
Mrs S Farleigh, BA (*Voice and Flute*)
Mrs M Farley (*Percussion*)
Miss C Hayek (*Violin and Viola*)
Mr P Hill (*Guitar*)
Mr P Hurst (*Accompanist*)
Mr B Knight (*Tennis Coach*)
Mrs A O'Donovan (*Woodwind, Piano, Keyboard*)
Mrs S Oliver, BEd Hons (*LAMDA, Speech & Drama*)
Mrs E Rainsford-McMahon, BA Hons, MA, PGCE (*Piano*)
Mr T Unwin (*Jazz Piano*)
Mrs H Wills, ALCM (*Cello, Piano*)
Mr A Yang (*Mandarin*)
Mr S Young (*Brass*)

Stover Preparatory School:

Head of Preparatory School: Mrs C Coyle, BEd, MA

Mr M Appleby, DipEd, BEd, MA
Mrs K Austin, BA Hons QTS
Mr M Ayer, BSc Ed
Mr C Brown, BA Hons
Mrs J Cross, NNEB (*Nursery Coordinator*)
Mrs R Dawson, BA Hons, MA
Mr N Futrell, BA Hons
Mrs M Wolbold, NVQ3, EYCE
Mrs S Holmes, BA, PGCE
Mrs J Jamin, BEd Hons
Mrs I McIntosh, NNEB (*Nursery Coordinator*)
Mrs M Pallister, BEd
Mr K Perkins, BEd Hons
Mrs R Reynolds, BSc, PGCE

Mrs J Sanders, NNEB
Mrs L Smale, BA, PGCE
Mrs F Waring, CertEd, DELE
Mrs S Yonge, BA Ed

Nursery Assistants:
Mrs D Battershall
Mrs N Carey, NVQ3 (*Nursery Group Leader*)
Mrs K Freeman, NNEB

Residential Staff:
Miss L Johnson, BA Arts & Cultural Management, Visual
    Arts Practices; Dip Art & Design (*Housemistress*)
Mrs G Fletcher, CertEd, ITEC (*Housemistress*)
Ms S Trainer, Dip Theol, CertEd (*Head of Boarding*)

Each House also has attached Boarding Assistants:
Miss M Flint
Miss R Kaak

School Medical Officer: Dr D Milburn, MB BS
School Nurses:
Miss S Edworthy, RGN
Mrs C Palmer, RGN

"If you are looking for small class sizes, excellent results and a stunning school in beautiful, safe surroundings, look no further". The Good Schools Guide.

Stover School is one of the South West's leading schools, set in 64 acres of beautiful grounds; intentionally a small, friendly day and boarding school for both boys and girls from 3 years to 18. Stover enjoys the benefits of a rural location with an excellent transport network to the A38, railway station, airports and has its own heli-pad.

Stover's aim is to provide a supportive, nurturing environment enabling pupils to acquire excellent qualifications and the confidence to achieve their aspirations, pupils are happy; they thrive and flourish. We offer the best of both worlds; co-ed and single-sex teaching. Our record of achieving outstanding results at GCSE and A Level, is a testament to the hard work of the pupils and staff.

Stover provides a supportive, hardworking and purposeful atmosphere. Girls and boys are taught separately from Year 3 to Year 11 and together in our Nursery, Pre-Prep and Sixth Form. The emphasis is on regular work routines, independent learning, and a sense of community. Academic results are impressive and sit alongside our sporting achievements, musical talents and moral well-being. We offer an extensive extra-curricular programme, offering circus skills, web design, chess, golf, horse riding, Duke of Edinburgh's Awards, Ten Tors Training and many more. Overseas trips have included: World Challenge Trip to Botswana and Zambia, Art Trip to New York, Language trips to Paris and Barcelona, History trip to Flanders and Geography trips to Southern Italy, Costa Rica and California. Skiing and Watersports trips.

Stover has a thriving musical department, with choirs, orchestras, jazz band and ensembles offering plenty of opportunities to perform at school and at local festivals and concerts. We hold our whole school drama performance once a year and smaller plays throughout the year for younger pupils in both prep and senior school.

Within the grounds we have a dedicated Sixth Form Centre, where students have a individual study, recreational facilities and a kitchen. It is a strong, tight-knit community with a culture of hard working independent study.

Recent developments include a superb Art, Media and Photography Centre, and new Science Centre with four fully resourced laboratories and Mathematics Department upstairs.

Stover School is a dynamic and exciting place to be; parents can be assured that their child is receiving the best possible care enabling them to achieve their aspirations. We look forward to welcoming you to Stover School.

Examinations. Public examinations set by all examination boards are taken at GCSE Level and at A Level. Music examinations are set by the Associated Board of the Royal Schools of Music. Speech and Drama examinations are set by LAMDA.

Physical Education. Hockey, rugby, netball, football, rounders and cricket are the core team games. Individual sports include athletics, gymnastics, golf, tennis, badminton and cross country. Other sports throughout the year include adventure development, orienteering and dance.

The school has extensive grass pitches, six tennis courts (3 floodlit), a covered sports dome, a 3-hole short golf course, cross-country tracks and cricket nets. We run a full range of after-school sports clubs and fixture lists for both Senior and Prep.

Optional subjects. In addition to a wide variety of activities organised by Stover's own staff there are specialist peripatetic staff for instrumental and voice tuition, speech and drama, riding and golf and tennis coaching.

Fees per term (2011-2012). Preparatory School: Day: Reception–Year 2 £2,216, Year 3 £2,410, Years 4–5 £2,585, Year 6 £2,993. Boarding Years 3–6: £5,061 (weekly), £5,802 (full).

Senior School: Years 7–11: £3,497 (day), £6,122 (weekly boarding), £7,230 (full boarding); Years 12–13: £3,565 (day), £6,122 (weekly boarding), £7,298 (full boarding).

Entrance and Scholarships. Entrance assessments are sat by all prospective pupils from 7 years to 15 years either during a taster day or our entrance day in January. Scholarships are available at 7+, 11+, 13+ and 16+ in Academic, Art, Music and Sport. In addition means-tested Scholarships and bursaries are available, Laurus and Maurice Key Awards.

Health. Twenty four hours a day nursing care is provided by a team of SRNs and regular visits by a local GP.

Old Stoverites. *Secretary*: Mrs M Downey, c/o Stover School.

Charitable status. Stover School Association is a Registered Charity, number 306712. Stover School is a charitable foundation for education.

Streatham & Clapham High School GDST

42 Abbotswood Road, Streatham, London SW16 1AW
Tel: 020 8677 8400
             (Senior Department & Sixth Form Centre)
             020 8674 6912 (Junior Department & Nursery)
Fax: 020 8677 2001
e-mail: enquiry@shc.gdst.net
website: www.gdst.net/streathamhigh

Founded 1887.

Streatham & Clapham High School is part of the GDST (Girls' Day School Trust). The GDST is the leading network of independent girls' schools in the UK. As a charity that owns and runs 24 schools and two academies, it reinvests all its income in its schools. For further information about the Trust, see p. xxi or visit www.gdst.net.

Additional information may be found on the school's website and a more detailed prospectus may be obtained from the school.

Chairman of Local Governors: Mrs A Maryon-Davies

Acting Head: **Mr Richard Hinton**, BSc Hons, PGCE
Head from January 2012: Dr Millan Sachania, MA Cantab, MPhil, PhD, FRSA

Deputy Head: Mrs Ann Hooper, BSc Hons, PGCE

Head of Junior Department: Miss Louisa Burke, BEd
    Hons, MA Ed, PG Dip Psych

Head of Sixth Form: Mrs Veronica Mills, BSc, MSc, PGCE

Admissions Secretary: Mrs Phyllis Warner

Pupil numbers. Senior Department 400; Junior Department 190; Nursery 25.

Streatham & Clapham High School GDST is a happy and successful school situated on two sites. The school's vision is to provide a top-quality all-round education for girls in a considerate and supportive environment where diversity is embraced and celebrated. SCHS has some of the best facilities in South London and attracts pupils from a wide radius as well as from the immediate vicinity.

The Senior Department is surrounded by spacious grounds ("an oasis of green in South London") next to Tooting Bec Common. The school is easily accessible to local mainline stations at Balham and Streatham Hill, and to numerous bus services from Streatham High Road. Existing facilities include a magnificent Sports Hall, Art Studio and Fitness Centre. The Millennium Building (opened in 2003) provides a dedicated Sixth Form Centre, Music Suite and Recital Room, and an on-site all-weather hockey pitch and grass pitch were opened in 2009. The Junior Department and Nursery are based in nearby Wavertree Road and have large and well-equipped premises, including a new library and a spacious, specially designed indoor and outdoor area built specifically around the needs of the Nursery children.

Streatham & Clapham High School figures prominently in the National League tables and is consistently ranked top in the league tables for Lambeth schools. Girls in both the Junior and Senior Departments enjoy a relevant and practical curriculum, culminating in preparation for GCE examinations at GCSE and AS/A2 Level, and for entrance and scholarship examinations to Oxford and Cambridge.

A wide variety of sports is offered by both Departments; some of these take place in lunch time activity slots alongside arts and music clubs. Arts are strong, with orchestras, choirs and various musical groups, and the proximity to central London makes possible many excursions to concerts, as well as to museums, art galleries and theatres. Regular trips abroad are offered, including music and drama tours. Pupils can participate in the Duke of Edinburgh's Award Scheme and have substantial involvement with the local community, raising funds for charities and offering facilities for local use.

The school has an excellent reputation for pastoral care. Two sixth-formers are assigned to each class to support new entrants. Parents are kept in touch with their child's progress through regular feedback. In-depth reports are sent home twice each year, there are regular parents' evenings, and Effort and Attainment grades are issued routinely. Prefects and a Head Girl are elected by the staff and senior school members. Girls' successes are celebrated at assemblies. There is a School Council and effective provision for pupils requiring learning support.

Admission. There are five main stages for Admission: by assessment for the Nursery (3+ years), 4+ and 7+, by Entrance Examination at 11+ and at Sixth Form level. Occasional places sometimes arise at any age; interested parents are advised to contact the Admissions Secretary.

Fees per term (2011-2012). Senior School £4,203, Junior Department £3,270, Nursery £2,526.

The fees cover the regular curriculum, books, school meals for Juniors, stationery and other materials, choral music, games and swimming, but not optional extra subjects.

Bursaries. Bursaries, which are means tested and related to academic ability, are available at 11+ and at Sixth Form entry. Applications for bursaries at other levels can be made to the Head in cases of financial need. All requests are considered in confidence.

Scholarships. Scholarships are available to internal and external candidates at 11+ and at Sixth Form level. These are awarded according to academic talent and for art, sport, drama and music, covering a maximum of 50 per cent of the fees.

Charitable status. Streatham & Clapham High School is part of The Girls' Day School Trust, which is a Registered Charity, number 306983.

Sutton High School
GDST

55 Cheam Road, Sutton, Surrey SM1 2AX
Tel: 020 8642 0594
Fax: 020 8642 2014
e-mail: office@sut.gdst.net
website: www.suttonhigh.gdst.net

Founded 1884. Celebrated 125th Anniversary in 2009.

Sutton High School is part of the GDST (Girls' Day School Trust). The GDST is the leading network of independent girls' schools in the UK. As a charity that owns and runs 24 schools and two academies, it reinvests all its income in its schools. For further information about the Trust, see p. xxi or visit www.gdst.net.

A more detailed prospectus may be obtained from the school or downloaded at www.suttonhigh.gdst.net.

Chairman of The School Governing Body: Mrs Anne
    Pearcey

Head Teacher: Mrs B Goulding, BA London, BA
    Sheffield, MA Ed Mgt, NPQH

Deputy Head: Mrs K Crouch, BSc Leicester, NPQH

Assistant Head: Mrs E Nicholas, BA Bristol, PGCE

Head of Sixth Form: Mrs E Clark, BSc Econ Southampton

Head of Junior School: Mrs A Cooper, BEd Exeter

Deputy Head of Junior School: Mrs J Little, BSc OU,
    CertEd London

Administrative Staff:
School Business Manager: Ms E L Wilson, BSc
Marketing and Communications Manager: Mrs N New
Admissions Secretary: Mrs J Ward

Sutton High School, founded in 1884, is a member of the Girls' Day School Trust and provides continuity of education for girls from 3 to 18 years. It has a strong reputation for providing a broad, balanced education for all girls in a happy working environment. Distinguished former pupils include the novelist Susan Howatch, BBC correspondent Sue Littlemore, and Ruth Kelly, MP.

There are 710 girls in the school: 300 aged 3–11 years in the Junior School and 410 aged 11–18 years in the Senior School. The Sixth Form is 85 strong. Girls enter the school aged 3+, 4+, 11+, 13+ or 16 after taking the school's own entrance tests. With occasional places available throughout the school year. Open Mornings take place in the Autumn, Spring and Summer Terms when girls provide enthusiastic and informative tours of the school and the Head provides a welcoming talk and is available to answer questions. Further information and personal tours during the school day can be arranged by ringing the Admissions Secretary or e-mailing the school (j.ward@sut.gdst.net).

Aims and Values. Sutton High is a diverse community dedicated to enabling its pupils to develop their intellect and talents and a confidence to believe that their aspirations are achievable. From an early beginning, we encourage the girls to be honest, reliable and trustworthy. Academic rigour is valued at all stages and the focus in the classroom and beyond is on challenge, engagement and enjoyment. Learning is celebrated. The school has a well qualified and highly motivated staff, both teaching and non teaching. All members of the community are valued and given the opportunity to flourish in a caring and supportive ethos.

Our vision is that Sutton High gives girls;

- A rich and diverse curriculum in which they can achieve at all levels within a creative and vibrant atmosphere.
- The self confidence to be independent learners and achieve beyond the school environment.
- An enquiring and discriminating mind and a desire for knowledge.
- Respect for others.

We value the partnership which exists between school, parents and community and the part it plays in realising this vision.

Situation. The school occupies a central position in Sutton and is reached easily by train or bus from Dorking, Leatherhead, Epsom, Carshalton, Wallington, Worcester Park, New Malden, Wimbledon and Burgh Heath. A school bus services runs every morning from the Wimbledon area, picking up at 4 locations. A new school bus service will be launched in September, bringing girls to the school from Kenley, Purley, Coulsdon and Banstead. The school is only 5 minutes' walk from Sutton Station. The school has developed a specific green travel plan which is being supported by the London Borough of Sutton.

Facilities. The Junior and Senior Schools provide well-resourced accommodation for all major subjects. A large sports hall is located next to the indoor swimming pool and girls have access to astroturf pitches, netball and tennis courts. There is a dedicated music building and well-equipped art facilities. Summer 2010 will see the development of the sports hall and swimming pool complex. This project will see the enhancement of the existing facilities and the creation of a new dance and fitness suite.

The Sixth Form Centre – The Dene – provides the pupils with tutor rooms, ICT facilities, study areas, common rooms and a gym.

Curriculum. Girls are admitted to the Junior School from 3 years of age following an informal assessment and enter our Foundation Stage. The National Curriculum creates a framework for teaching and Key Stage 1 and 2 SATs are taken. In 2009, 100% of those sitting Key Stage 2 English SATs achieved Level 4 and above, 98% in Maths and 100% in Science. In Junior School there are many varied opportunities for extra-curricular activities including Music, ICT, Sport, Drama, Chess and Mandarin. Girls study French from 7 years of age and there is specialist teaching in many subject areas. Pre-school and after-school care is available form 7.30 am to 6.30 pm for all Junior School girls. Girls are encouraged to show kindness towards others, which is developed in our daily Act of Worship, our teaching, work in the local community and fundraising for charity. The school recognises the need for independent learning and homework is set regularly.

In the Senior School girls follow an enriched version of the National Curriculum in preparation for entrance to university and the professions. The school regularly sends students to Oxford, Cambridge and other top universities where girls successfully study a wide range of courses. In 2009, 4 girls received and accepted places at Oxbridge.

In Years 7–9 girls participate in a broad curriculum that, while encompassing Curriculum 2000, provides many extension opportunities. Two modern languages are studied from Year 7 and all girls study Latin from Year 8. It is a hallmark of the school that Science is taught as three distinct subjects by specialist teachers. At GCSE girls study 9 or 10 subjects including a core of English, ICT, IGCSE Mathematics, a Modern Language, Religious Studies and Sciences together with optional subjects from a wide range. Emphasis is placed on the use of ICT as a tool to enhance all aspects of

education. Wherever possible, cross-curricular opportunities are exploited, such as in the French and Geography residential visit to Lille for Year 8 girls. Careers advice is given from Year 7 and all girls are able to take extra lessons in Speech and Drama and Music. Each year over 300 girls pass the Poetry Vanguard and Guildhall Speech and Drama Examinations and over 100 pass the Associated Board and Trinity College Music Examinations.

In the Sixth Form, students benefit from teaching styles that are supportive but provide opportunities for independent study. Students currently take four or five AS/A2 Levels from a wide range of disciplines.In 2009, the girls achieved a 100% pass rate at A Level, 87.5% gained A or B grades with 100% taking up places at University.

Extra-Curricular Activities. Each year an excellent and varied programme of concerts, musicals, plays, art exhibitions and festivals in both Junior and Senior Schools enables members of the drama groups, choirs and orchestras to perform in public.

An elected committee of girls, led by the Head Girl and her deputy, contributes to the smooth running of the school. The Sixth Form also runs societies, produces musicals and concerts in aid of charity. In September 2009 a new House system was introduced in school with all girls being part of one of four houses.

Sport at Sutton High School is inclusive rather than exclusive and provides all abilities with an opportunity to take part in a team and represent their school. Many girls take part in swimming galas, Hockey, Netball, Gymnastics, Badminton, Rounders and Tennis matches, including all major county tournaments; several girls reach county and national squad level each year.

A wide variety of clubs and activities are provided for girls during the lunch break and after school. In addition, parents run the Otter and Centipede Clubs which offer sports and coaching sessions. Staff regularly arrange cultural visits to places as varied as New York, Paris and Yorkshire and an exchange programme is now in place with the Fachhöch Schule in Tübingen, Germany. The Junior School organises annual residential visits in Years 5 and 6.

A number of girls take part in Mathematics challenges and competitions with an excellent record of success. The school has a good reputation for debates and public speaking. In the Sixth Form girls form their own companies and compete in the Young Enterprise competition and have won the Sutton and Merton area 'Best Company' award in previous years.

Community Links. In addition to Harvest and Christmas parcel collections for the elderly, the whole school organises fundraising activities for their chosen charities.

The school has a thriving Parent Staff Association – Connections – which arranges school fairs each year and a range of social activities. Money raised by Connections has been used on many projects including the upgrading of performance facilities in both the Junior and Senior Schools and the creation of the new 'Tops and Tails' before and after school care facility.

Close links with a local boys' school have resulted in such productions as *Little Shop of Horrors*, *The Boyfriend*, *Grease*, *West Side Story*, and in 2010 *The Wedding Singer*.

Fees per term (2011-2012). Senior School: £4,239 (Years 7–11), £4,183 (Sixth Form); Junior School £3,254–£3,298, Pre-Reception £2,512.

The fees cover the regular curriculum, examination entry fees, school books, stationery and other materials, games and swimming, but not optional extra subjects or lunch. Details of the fees for extra subjects, including instrumental music, and Speech and Drama, are available from the school.

Scholarships and Bursaries. Following the ending of the Government Assisted Places Scheme, the GDST has made available to the school a substantial number of scholarships and bursaries. The bursaries are means tested and are intended to ensure that the school remains accessible to bright girls who would be unable to enter the school without financial assistance. At present there are, available to internal or external candidates, part-fee scholarships for entry at 11+ and for entry at 16+ into the Sixth Form. Performance Scholarships are awarded at 11+ in Sport, Music and Drama and in the Sixth Form for Music, Drama, Sport and Art.

Charitable status. Sutton High School for Girls is part of The Girls' Day School Trust, which is a Registered Charity, number 306983.

Sydenham High School
GDST

19 Westwood Hill, London SE26 6BL
Tel: 020 8557 7000
e-mail: info@syd.gdst.net
website: www.sydenhamhighschool.gdst.net

Founded 1887.
Sydenham High School is part of the GDST (Girls' Day School Trust). The GDST is the leading network of independent girls' schools in the UK. As a charity that owns and runs 24 schools and two academies, it reinvests all its income in its schools. For further information about the Trust, see p. xxi or visit www.gdst.net.

Additional information may be found on the school's website and a more detailed prospectus may be obtained from the school.

Chair of Local Governors: Ms S Bhavan

Headteacher: Mrs K E Pullen, BA Warwick, MA London, PGCE

Deputy Head: Dr C Laverick, BA Swansea, MEd OU, PhD Hull

Head of Junior School: Mrs B Risk, CertEd Salisbury, MEd Bath

Assistant Head Teacher: Mrs S J McLellan, BA Durham, PGCE

Head of Sixth Form: Miss B Pakey, BA Lancaster, PGCE

Pupil numbers. Senior School 450, Junior School 250.
For over 100 years, Sydenham High School has been committed to the fundamental aim of providing a first class education for girls – grounded in a tradition of academic rigour and focused on developing in our pupils the skills and confidence to face the challenges and enjoy the opportunities of life both in and beyond school.

Occupying the grounds of a Victorian mansion we enjoy an open, leafy setting in a location that is easily accessible by public transport. Our Junior School has its own recently refurbished facilities with ready access to those of the Senior School. The school is a distinctive blend of Victorian buildings and purpose-built accommodation refurbished to a high standard. Our facilities are impressive and include an extensive library with online facilities, two ICT suites and design technology centre. We have seven science laboratories, five of which have been recently refurbished. Our new Performing Arts Centre, featuring a new Theatre and Recital Hall, was opened in 2007.

Excellent on-site sports facilities comprise a Sports Hall and all-weather pitch, supplemented by extensive sports fields close by in Lower Sydenham. We produce fine sportswomen who compete in hockey, netball, tennis, and gymnastics to national level.

Curriculum. The school offers a broad curriculum, ensuring all our pupils are stimulated and excited by learning. English and maths provide a solid foundation while languages offered include French, German, Spanish and Latin. All students study biology, chemistry and physics. Creative and practical subjects include design technology, art, PE, music and drama. Humanities include History, Geography, Religious Studies and Classical Civilisation. All pupils receive a thorough grounding in ICT, taught as a discrete subject and confidently used as a cross-curricular tool.

In the Sixth Form, further mathematics, business studies, government and politics, ICT, theatre studies, PE and sociology are offered in addition to the normal range of AS and A Level courses. Specifically focused preparation for entry to prestigious universities, including Oxford and Cambridge, is provided. Our New Horizons Programme brings in speakers and takes students out to visit exhibitions and industry. Huge opportunities are available for leadership through the Community Leader Sports Award, Young Enterprise, sports teams, administering clubs, and an extended prefect system.

Students make informed choices of GCSE, AS and A Level subjects, supported throughout by specialist staff. Work in Careers and PSHE also informs the decision making process. 100% of our students are offered places at universities, while some take gap years abroad. The breadth of extra curricular opportunities encourages all pupils to broaden their interests and develop personal skills. Drama is popular with numerous clubs and productions at the Junior and Senior Schools. A diversity of opportunity for making music is available to pupils whatever their instrument or level of expertise. Highly qualified peripatetic staff teach instrumental lessons. Specialist music staff train school ensembles, orchestra and choirs which perform in, and beyond, the school on a regular basis. Involvement in the wider community is encouraged through our successful Duke of Edinburgh's Award Scheme and charity work.

Fees per term (2011-2012). Senior School £4,203, Junior School £3,270.
School fees include textbooks, stationery and other materials, choral music, PE and swimming, ISCO and Careers counselling. They do not include instrumental music, speech and drama, and after-school clubs.

Scholarships and Bursaries. *Entrance Scholarships*: The Girls' Day School Trust provides a number of scholarships each year for entry to the Senior School at 11+ and directly into the Sixth Form. Scholarships are awarded on academic merit and no financial means test is involved.

Bursaries: The GDST Minerva Fund provides bursaries which are means tested and intended to ensure that the school remains accessible to bright girls who would benefit from our education, but who would be unable to enter the school without financial assistance. Bursaries are awarded on the basis of financial need and academic merit. An application form can be obtained from the Admissions Secretary. It is recognised that occasions will arise when some form of short-term assistance is required – a small fund exists to help pupils taking public examinations in such cases.

Sydenham High School Scholarships: Art, music, drama and sports scholarships may be awarded on entry at 11+ in addition to our academic scholarships.

Charitable status. Sydenham High School is part of The Girls' Day School Trust, which is a Registered Charity, number 306983.

Talbot Heath

Rothesay Road, Bournemouth BH4 9NJ
Tel: 01202 761881
          01202 755402 Senior School Admissions
          01202 755417 Junior School Admissions
          01202 755419 Director of Finance
Fax: 01202 768155
e-mail: admissions@talbotheath.org
website: www.talbotheath.org

Motto: '*Honour before Honours*'

The School is an Independent School, founded in 1886 by private effort and transferred to Trustees in 1898 and is administered under a scheme drawn up by the Ministry of Education in 1903. It is a Church of England Foundation and pupils of all denominations are welcome. This School is committed to safeguarding and promoting the welfare of children and young people. The School is also committed to a policy of equal opportunity.

Governing Body:
Chairman: Mr G Exon
Vice Chair: Mrs C Norman
Dr T Battcock
Mrs M Day
Mr R Kennedy
Dr A Main
Mrs J Richardson
Rev Canon Dr C Rutledge
Mrs R Small
Mrs S Thomas, LLB
Mr D Townend

Head Mistress: **Mrs A Holloway**, MA Oxon

Heads of Faculty:
Mrs T Magrath, MA York (*English*)
Miss J A Barrett, MA Oxon (*Classics*)
Mrs J Hooton, BSc Hons Nottingham (*Mathematics*)
Mr A Hill, BMus Hons, FTCL (*Creative Arts & Technology*)
Mr M Gibson, BSc Hons Hull (*Science*)
Mrs H Chapleo, BSc Hons Kingston (*Humanities*)
Mrs K D Leahy, BA Hons London. MA Ed Open (*Head of Junior Department*)
Miss H Hardy, BEd Hons Exeter (*Physical Education*)
Miss E A Silvester, BA Hons Birmingham (*Modern Languages*)

Visiting teachers also attend for Piano, Violin, Violoncello, Double Bass, Flute, Clarinet, Oboe, Bassoon, Horn, Saxophone, Trumpet, Trombone, Tuba, Percussion, Singing, Dancing, Speech Training and Voice Production, English for foreign students, French, Spanish and German Conversation.

Medical Officer: Dr M Grainger
Director of Finance: Mrs J Cameron
Head Mistress's PA: Mrs I Richards
Office Manager/Admissions/HR: Mrs I Richards

There are some 302 girls in the Main School, of whom 62 are in the Sixth Forms. There is a Junior Department for about 147 girls between the ages of 7 and 11. The Pre-Preparatory department caters for 120 girls aged 3+ to 7.

Talbot Heath is among the longest-established schools in the Bournemouth area, with over a century of success. The school enjoys an attractive wooded site and outstanding facilities for Art, Drama, Music and the Sciences (new Art and Drama studios opened in September 2000, new Science Centre opened in March 1999) together with good ICT provision and extensive modern accommodation for a wide range of sports activities.

The school follows the best practice of the National Curriculum but does not undertake Key Stage testing at levels 1, 2 and 3.

Examinations. 21 subjects are offered to GCSE (including Core Subjects) and Advanced Level, and girls gain places at a variety of universities, including Oxford and Cambridge, or go on to other forms of higher education or professional training.

Admission. Girls are admitted into the Junior School by examination at 7 and above and into the Main School by examination at 11+, 12+ and 13+. The Entrance Examination is held annually in January and girls must be capable of working with those of their own age. Entry to the Pre-preparatory Department requires no examination.

Boarding Houses. St Mary's Boarding House is located in the School grounds, Miss Edwards being in overall charge.

Fees per term (2011-2012). Tuition: Senior School: £3,555; Junior School: £1,630–£2,900; Kindergarten according to sessions.

Boarding (in addition to Tuition Fees): £2,366 (full); £2,207 (weekly).

Scholarships and bursaries are available and there is also a discount for daughters of Service families and the clergy.

Charitable status. Talbot Heath is a Registered Charity, number 283708. It exists to provide high quality education for children.

Teesside High School

The Avenue, Eaglescliffe, Stockton-on-Tees TS16 9AT
Tel: 01642 782095
Fax: 01642 791207
e-mail: info@teessidehigh.co.uk
website: www.teessidehigh.co.uk

The School was founded in 1970 being an amalgamation of the Queen Victoria High School, Stockton-on-Tees, founded 1883 and the Cleveland High School, Eaglescliffe, founded 1939.

Board of Governors:
Chairman: Mr C G Neave, MA
His Honour Judge P J B Armstrong, MA Cantab
Mr R Anderson, BSc Hons
Mr C A S Atha, LLB
Mrs J Beeton, BEd Hons
Mrs C R J Chapman, FCA
Mrs A Greenwood
Mr D H Lister, JP, RIBA
Mr S Merckx, BSc, CEng
Mr R R Tindle, BA Hons, FCA
Miss E M Vane, CertEd
Mr C G Watson, BA Hons, PGCE

Acting Head: **Mr M K Wilkinson**, MA Cantab
Head from January 2012: **Ms Deborah Duncan**, MA, NPQH

Senior Leadership Team:
Mr G S Twist, BEd, BA, NPQH (*Head of Preparatory*)
Mrs K Mackenzie, BSc Hons Leeds (*Assistant Deputy Head*)
Miss N J Stephens, BA Hons York (*Assistant Deputy Head*)

High School Staff:
Mrs R Aitken, BSc Hons Edinburgh (*Psychology, Biology*)
Mr S C Atkinson, MSc, BEng (*ICT*)
Mr M D Bessey, BEd Hons De Montfort (*Boys' PE & Games*)
Mrs S Casey, BA Hons Hull (*History*)
Mrs K R Chamberlain, BA Hons Birmingham (*Geography*)
Mrs S Curtis, BA Open University (*Maths with ICT*)
Mrs H M Dey, BSc Heriot-Watt (*Mathematics*)
Miss J Duffy, MA Jt Hons Glasgow (*Senior Tutor; English*)
Mrs R Hancock, BA Hons York (*English*)
Mr J Harrington, BA Hons Newcastle (*French & German*)
Miss E Heather, MA Dunelm (*Art*)
Mrs S Jackson, BEd Hons (*Food/Nutrition & Textiles*)
Mrs R Kirk, BSc Newcastle, MSc Heriot-Watt (*Biology*)
Mrs S C M Low, BA Hons Sunderland (*French and German*)

Mrs E Machan, BA Hons Teesside (*HE & Technology*)
Mrs K McEndoo, MEd Hons Sheffield (*Food & Nutrition*)
Mrs S Parker, BA Hons Oxon (*Senior Sixth Form Tutor; English & Drama*)
Mr J Pollock, BSc Hons York (*Biology*)
Mrs K Rawlinson, BSc Reading (*Geography*)
Miss K A Rose, BA Hons Staffordshire (*Economics & Business Studies*)
Mr P Russell, MA Leeds (*History*)
Mrs V H Sherwood, MA Jt Hons St Andrews (*Classics*)
Mrs S Swalwell, BSc Hons Teesside (*Chemistry*)
Mrs J Thompson, BSc Hons Teesside (*IT*)
Mrs N Threadgold, BA Hons Leeds (*French and German*)
Miss V Turnbull, BSc Hons Gloucester (*Physical Education*)
Mrs G K Waddoup, BA Hons Dunelm (*German*)
Mr I Watson, BA Cantab (*Chemistry*)
Mrs G Wilson, BSc Hons York, MSc Birmingham (*Physics*)

Music Department:
Head of Music: Mr P A Laverick, BA Hons Welsh College of Music & Drama, PGCE

Mr S J Bone, CT ABRSM, GSMDP Hons (*Clarinet, Saxophone*)
Mrs S A Burniston (*Flute*)
Mrs B Bury, ARCM, LRAM, PGDipRNCM (*Piano*)
Mr P Collumbine (*Guitar*)
Mr S Ellerton (*Percussion*)
Mrs S Hunt (*Piano*)
Mr C J C Mackay, CertEd (*Brass*)
Mrs R Robinson, LGSM, DRSAM, DipCLCM (*Cello*)
Mr A Smith, GMus, PPRNCM (*Clarinet, Recorder*)
Miss E Smith, BMus (*Singing*)
Mr M Walton, BMus Hons RCM (*Violin, Viola*)

Speech & Drama:
Miss R Lewis, BA Hons Liverpool John Moores

Preparatory School:
Mrs H M Bennison, BEd Hons Southampton
Miss J Edwards, BEd Hons Liverpool
Mrs D Essex, BEd Dunelm
Miss R Farrell, BA Hons Southampton
Mrs C L Hatton, MA Teesside, CertEd
Miss T A Lockerbie, BA Hons York
Mr F I Maude, BA Hons Bradford
Miss H Pedley, BA Hons Durham (*PE & Games*)
Mrs J Todd, MA Dunelm (*Music*)
Mr D Winfield, BSc Hons Loughborough

Facilities Manager: Mr P J Herbert
Finance Manager: Mr M I Jones
Head of Marketing: Mrs H Mellor, BA Hons
Learning Resource Centre Manager: Miss R Ignirri, BA Hons Venice
Headmaster's PA & Admissions Registrar: Mrs S Brown

Teesside High School, set in 19 acres of outstanding landscaped grounds, is an independent school for boys and girls aged 3 to 18. The School operates a unique 'Diamond' system with opportunities for girls and boys to learn separately as well as develop socially by means of some classes and activities being organised on a single-sex basis, with others mixed. It is easily accessible by road and rail from North Yorkshire, County Durham and the Tees Valley. The facilities are extensive including specialist state of the art areas for Art, Music, IT, Technologies and the Sciences. The Sports facilities are particularly fine, including an indoor Sports Hall and Gymnasia together with spacious playing fields idyllically placed on the banks of the Tees.

The School has a fine academic tradition regularly featuring in local and national league tables. Pupils study French from Year 4 whilst later on a further foreign language and Latin can be taken from Year 7. The Sciences are taught as three separate subjects throughout the High School and at all stages a full range of subjects is offered.

The taught curriculum is supplemented with a rich and varied activities provision alongside opportunities for individual music tuition as well as Speech and Drama, Ballet and Dance. Outdoor pursuits and the Duke of Edinburgh's Award Scheme are popular with pupils from Year 10 upwards.

The recently refurbished Sixth Form Centre offers girls and boys an exciting pre University experience. Individual study areas together with teaching rooms, IT suite and conference facilities are complemented with a Sixth Form cafe: the Hot Spot. A full range of A Level subjects is offered and pupils are expected to move on to University. A structured careers programme from Year 7 enables students to make informed choices at all stages.

There are about 370 pupils on site, 130 in the Preparatory School (3+ to 11). Admission is normally at 3+, 5, 11, 13 and 16, but may be at other ages if vacancies occur. The School takes part in the Nursery Voucher Scheme. A Bursary System is in operation. There is a full range of Scholarships. Details of entry requirements are available on application.

Fees per term (from January 2011). Preparatory School: £1,402–£2,885. High School: £3,545.

Charitable status. Teesside High School Limited is a Registered Charity, number 527386. It is established to provide the highest possible standard of education for girls and boys.

Thornton College
Convent of Jesus and Mary

Thornton, Milton Keynes, Buckinghamshire MK17 0HJ
Tel: 01280 812610
Fax: 01280 824042
e-mail: registrar@thorntoncollege.com
website: www.thorntoncollege.com

Chair of Governors: Sister J M Cuff, RJM

Headmistress: **Miss A T Williams**

Deputy Headmistress: Mrs D Sheldon
Head of Junior School and Nursery: Sister M J O'Donohoe, RJM
Head of Boarding: Miss M Kelly
Bursar: Mr R A Inchley
Admissions Secretary: Mrs C Ballantyne
PA to Headmistress/Office Manager: Mrs L Tipping
School Secretary: Mrs L Try

Thornton College, Convent of Jesus and Mary, is a non-selective day and boarding school for girls aged 2½–16 years, with a nursery for boys and girls aged 2½–4+. The total number of pupils is 370, of which 55 are boarders.

Founded in 1917 by the Sisters of Jesus and Mary, Thornton College aims to provide a sound Christian education taking account of the aptitudes, aspirations and ability of each individual. We work in partnership with parents to develop the full potential of each child, both within the classroom and outside it. A Catholic foundation, girls of all denominations are warmly welcomed to Thornton.

School Mission Statement. 'To educate young people to meet the challenges of life courageously, to use their talents to the full and to live the values of Christ's Gospel.'

Location. Thornton College is situated in a rural location 5 miles from Buckingham and 11 miles from Milton Keynes. Whilst its setting is peaceful and secluded, Thornton College is close to excellent road, rail and air communications with Bedford, Northampton, Banbury and Aylesbury all within easy reach.

Extended Day 8 am – 8 pm. Crèche facilities provide after-school care for four to seven year olds and, from the age of eight, day pupils may stay for activities, supervised study and for supper.

Boarding Life. Girls are accepted as boarders from eight years of age (Year 4). Living in a relaxed, family atmosphere girls benefit from the constant companionship of other young people. Weekly and occasional boarding are popular options and GCSE pupils enjoy the privilege of individual study-bedrooms.

Academic Life. Classes are small; pupils receive individual attention and teaching is organised to allow each child personal success in all areas. Whilst keeping pace with the latest developments in education and the spirit of the National Curriculum, the best of traditional methods are employed in teaching literacy and numeracy skills.

Pupils enjoy a broad and balanced curriculum, which is both relevant and challenging. Highly qualified and committed staff bring wide-ranging knowledge and expertise to the classroom and pupils are encouraged to think for themselves and to become active learners.

We expect pupils to work hard at their studies and to participate fully in a wide range of extra-curricular activities. We equip our students to contribute effectively and responsibly to the community of which they are a part. Our pupils leave us prepared to meet future challenges and confident that they can make a difference to the world in which we live.

Our academic results are excellent and the majority of our girls go on to study A Level and progress to the University of their choice.

Careers Education and Guidance. Careers advice is provided throughout the Senior School. Delivered by our own careers staff and professional advisors, it is both up-to-date and informed. The Careers Library is well resourced and girls are encouraged to make full use of its facilities. Guest speakers are invited to talk to the girls about a wide variety of further education and careers options.

Time is set aside for group and individual counselling as girls prepare for GCSE options in Year 9 and for choice of sixth forms and further education courses in Year 11. Thornton girls are invariably offered the sixth form courses for which they apply, and each year a number obtain Scholarships or Exhibitions.

Extra-Curricular Activities. Pupils are encouraged to take part in a wide variety of extra-curricular activities. The school has an enthusiastic choir, orchestra and a number of instrumental groups that perform on special occasions within the school and in public. Drama is a popular activity at Thornton with many girls involved in the staging of large and small dramatic and musical productions. Dance is part of the PE curriculum and is offered as a GCSE subject and there are also opportunities for pupils to have lessons in ballet, tap and modern dance. Many pupils find pleasure and fulfilment in the creative arts. Girls may also choose to join a number of groups offering cooperative activity and fellowship. There are Art, Ceramics, Computer, French, Lace, Mathematics, Nature and Science clubs, Horse riding and an active Christian Union. A group of senior girls work on the writing, illustration and production of the termly 'Thornton Times'. The School also participates in the Duke of Edinburgh's Award Scheme. Senior girls engage in a wide variety of indoor and outdoor activities while working for the Bronze Award.

There are opportunities for pupils to have lessons in ballet, dance, drama, elocution and music with peripatetic staff. The instruments currently available for study are: Bassoon, Cello, Clarinet, Flute, Guitar, Piano, Saxophone, Singing and Violin.

Sport. Sport is recognised as a vital part of every girl's education. It holds an important place in the curriculum and

extra-curricular activities are plentiful. All pupils are encouraged to participate in individual activities and in team games. Not only do they gain immense enjoyment and a sense of achievement but also they develop the personal and social skills which come from team effort. We encourage each girl to recognise the importance of physical exercise as part of a healthy life-style.

Thornton boasts a magnificent sports hall, which is well equipped for gymnastics and indoor sports. The girls enjoy athletics, badminton, basketball, cross-country, dance, hockey, gymnastics, netball, swimming, tennis, trampoline and volleyball. There is a Gymnastics Club which gives displays and enters competitions. Outdoor games facilities are also excellent. There are two beautifully situated grass hockey pitches, six tennis courts, an outdoor swimming pool, and a further all-weather hockey pitch. The school offers a particularly strong fixture list. Every girl is offered the opportunity for competitive match play through the House system and House matches are always keenly contested.

Admission. Entrance is through interview with the Headmistress, satisfactory reports and availability of places. Prospective pupils spend a day in school with their peer group prior to the offer of a place.

Scholarships. Academic Scholarships of up to 50% are available for entry into Year 7. The scholarship examination for entry in September is held in March each year.

Fees per term (2011-2012). Day Pupil £2,260–£3,615; Weekly Boarder £3,760–£4,765; Termly Boarder £4,765–£5,925. Nursery fees range according to sessions required.

Friends of Thornton. All parents are automatically members of the parents' association, the Friends of Thornton. New parents are invited to a Cheese and Wine evening early in the school year where they have the opportunity to meet the Friends' Committee, other parents and members of the school staff.

Old Thorntonians Association. The Old Thorntonians can be contacted on oldthorntonians@aol.com and a reunion is held at Thornton College every May.

Charitable status. The Religious of Jesus and Mary is a Registered Charity, number 247358. Thornton College exists to provide education.

Tormead School

Cranley Road, Guildford, Surrey GU1 2JD
Tel: 01483 575101
Fax: 01483 450592
e-mail: registrar@tormeadschool.org.uk
website: www.tormeadschool.org.uk

Academically selective independent school for around 780 day girls from 4 to 18 years of age.
Founded 1905.

School Council:
Chairman: C W M Herbert, Esq, BSc Hons
Vice-Chairman: W T Gillen, Esq, MA

Governors:
Mrs J Bruton, BA, PGCE
J Dennis, Esq, DCAAE, AMIMI, OBE
Dr W R Ewart, BSc, PhD, FSB
Mrs R Harris, BA Hons, ACA
The Revd Dr J M Holmes, MA, PhD, VetMB, MRCVS
Dr C Kissin, MBChB, MRCP, FRCR
P J O'Keefe, Esq, RIBA, MCIOB, MIMgt
R Jewkes, Esq, BEng
Dr J Page, LLM,BSc, MB BS, MRCP, FRCR, MFFLM
D M Williams, Esq, BA, FCA

Bursar and Clerk to the Governors: Mr M O'Donovan, BA Canterbury

Headmistress: Mrs Christina Foord, BA, MPhil, PGCE Birmingham

Deputy Headmistresses:
Pastoral: Mrs D M Bendall, MA Ed Open, BSc, PGCE London (*Biology*)
Curriculum: Mr J Coles, BA Swansea, PGCE UEA (*Geography and IT*)

Senior School Staff:
* *Head of Department*

Mrs A Arnold, BA, PGCE Keele (*French/German*)
Mrs E M Atkinson, MA Cantab, PGCE London (**Sociology, History*)
Mrs G Averill, BA, PGCE London (*History*)
Mr T Ball, BEd Nottingham, FCSM (**Director of Music*)
Mrs L Balls, BA Chichester (*Physical Education*)
Miss D Bell, BA, PGCE Greenwich (*Physical Education*)
Mrs H Boczkowski, BSc Bath Spa (**Food Technology*)
Mrs E A Burton, BA, PGCE Birmingham (*Mathematics, Physical Education*)
Mrs P Chambers, BA London, MA Birkbeck College, CertEd London (**History*)
Mrs L A Chapple, BSc Manchester, PGCE Southampton, Dip Geosciences OU, Dip Molecular Science OU
Mrs S Clarke, MA Cantab, DipLib, MCLIP (*Senior Librarian*)
Mrs P Corbie, Cert Art & Design London College of Fashion and Clothing Technology (*Teacher in Charge of Textiles*)
Mrs S Culhane, BA Washington USA, PGCE Goldsmiths London (*English*)
Miss A Dalmont, BA Exeter, PGCE Oxford (*French and Spanish*)
Miss S E Darnton, MA Newcastle (**Art & Design*)
Mrs K R Dennison, BSc London, PGCE Leicester, Dip Psych London (**Psychology*)
Mrs C Don, MA Oxford, PGCE Surrey (*Mathematics*)
Mrs P Dreghorn, CertEd St Peter's Birmingham (**English*)
Mrs T A Dyer, BA Swansea, PGCE London (*Head of Upper School, Spanish, French*)
Mrs S Elmes, BA King's College, London, PGCE Cardiff (*Religious Studies*)
Mr R Ewbank, BA, PGCE Goldsmiths London (*Art, Technology, ICT*)
Mrs A Ferns MA Cantab (*Assistant Librarian*)
Mr M Ferry, BSc Bristol, PGCE. Reading (*Science*)
Mrs K Fletcher, BA UCL, CTEL, PGCE Trinity College London (*Classics*)
Mrs S M Gibbs, BSc Bangor, PGCE Nottingham
Mrs C Gibson Oxley, MSt Oxford, PGCE Oxford (*Head of Sixth Form*)
Mrs J Glazier, BSc Exeter, PGCE Gloucs (*Mathematics*)
Mrs A Haddock, MA Oxon, PGCE OU (*History, Sociology*)
Mrs S E Haddy, BSc Surrey (*Second in Charge of Mathematics, Assistant Timetabler*)
Mrs S Harrod Booth, MA Kingston, PGCE Cambridge (**Mathematics*)
Miss J Hansen, BA Pace University, New York, PGCE Cambridge (*Head of Lower School, Drama*)
Miss P Harris, BA Manchester Metropolitan, PGCE Manchester (*Teacher in Charge of Spanish, French*)
Mr P Heap, BA Hull, PGCE Manchester Metropolitan (*Teacher in Charge of Drama*)
Ms T Hetherington, BA Westminster, MA St Martin's College, PGCE Roehampton (*Art, 3D Studies*)
Miss J Hoffmann, BSc, PGCE Nottingham (*Mathematics*)
Mr T Hofmeyr, BA Cardiff, PGCE Oxford (*Religious Education*)

Mr M Holford, BMus Surrey, PGCE Roehampton, ARCO, LTCL (*Assistant Director of Music*)
Mrs S Jewkes (*Physical Education*)
Mrs S Jones, BSc Surrey, PGCE St Mary's College (*Geography*)
Mr J Kilfiger, BSc York (*Mathematics*)
Ms S Lane, BSc Bath, PGCE Bath Spa (**Economics*)
Miss M Langlet, MA Toulouse le Mirail, PGCE Oxon (*Teacher in Charge of French, Spanish*)
Mrs D Ledgerwood, MA Oxon, PGCE Reading (*Head of Chemistry*)
Dr M Lee, BSc, PhD UCL (**Geography*)
Mr J Lyng, MA London, BSc UMIST, PGCE Brunel (**Science *Physics*)
Mrs G M Mackay, BA, UED Rhodes (*English*)
Mrs M Meats, BSc Leicester, MSc Open, CertEd (**Biology*)
Miss J Odlin, BSc Murray USA (**Learning Support*)
Mrs M O'Brien, BA, HDEd PG Johannesburg, MA California (*Art & Design, Art History, Photography*)
Miss I Painter, BA Durham (*Classics*)
Mrs K Perkins, BA Surrey (*Physical Education*)
Mr A Philippi, BEd McGill Montreal (*Physical Education*)
Mr G Press, BSc, CertEd Brunel (*Teacher in Charge of Design and Technology*)
Mrs G Ralfe, BSc Aberystwyth, PGCE Exeter (*Geography*)
Mrs E Robinson, MA Oxon, PGCE York (*Spanish*)
Miss M Rudge, BA Southampton (*Physical Education*)
Mr J E Sykes, BAWestminster, MSc LSE (*Government & Politics, Geography, DofE*)
Mrs M-C Taylor, Cert D'Aptitude Pédagogique (*French*)
Mrs C Tee, BA South Bank, CertEd South Bank (*Food Technology*)
Mrs L Tidy, BA Chichester (**Physical Education*)
Ms M Graham, BEd Chichester (*Director of Gymnastics*)
Miss O Toubkin, MA York, BA Cantab, CertEd Leeds (*English, Oxbridge Coordinator*)
Ms S Travis, MA, PGCE Cantab (*Chemistry*)
Mrs R Wallace, BEd Cantab (**Religious Studies, *PSHE*)
Miss E Walshe, BSc Greenwich, PGCE Surrey (**Careers, Science*)
Mr J Watts, BEng Sussex (*Director of ICT*)
Mrs K R Ward-Close, BSc Birmingham, PGCE Durham (*School Administrator SMT*)
Mr K Wild, BA Bristol, PGCE Oxford Brookes (**Modern Foreign Languages, German*)
Mr P Wilkinson, MA Cantab, MSc UCL, MBA Brunel, CEng, CSci, MIChemE (*Science*)

Junior School Staff:
Head: Miss K Tuckwell, MA Bath, BSc York, PGCE Lincoln
Deputy Head: Mrs K Moulder, MA Kingston, BEd Avery Hill

Mrs E Alderman, BSc Leeds (*Class Teacher*)
Mrs G Blackburn, BSc Sussex, RSA Dip Helen Arkell Dyslexia Centre (*Special Educational Needs, Dyslexia*)
Miss M Colyer, BSc York, PGCE Cantab (*Year 5 Class Teacher*)
Mrs B E Deans, CertEd, DipEd Cantab (*Support Staff*)
Mrs S Doggett, NNEB Kingston (*Teaching Assistant*)
Ms C Harris, BA Kingston (*Year 3 Class Teacher*)
Mrs J J Fowler, BEd Wall Hall (*Year 1 Class Teacher, Extra-Curricular Activities Coordinator, KS1/Early Years Coordinator*)
Mrs H Frank-Keyes, BA Lancaster (*Teaching Assistant*)
Mrs S Heslop (*After-School Supervision*)
Mrs S Heighington, BEd Roehampton (*Year 5 Class Teacher*)
Mrs P Inskip, BSocSc, PGCE, CNAA (*Year 4 Class Teacher, Mathematics Coordinator*)
Mrs C Langley, BA Ed Exeter (*Year 5 Class Teacher, English Coordinator*)

Mrs C Mead, CertEd Brighton (*Year 5 Class Teacher, KS1/ Early Years Coordinator*)
Mrs J L Norman, MPhil Reading, BSc Nottingham (*Teaching Assistant*)
Mrs P Oldroyd, CertEd Reading (*Teaching Assistant*)
Mrs K Perkins, BA Surrey (*Physical Education*)
Mrs K Richards, BEd De Montfort (*Class Teacher*)
Mrs S Trott, BEd Reading (*Year 2 Class Teacher*)
Mrs S Vega, BA, PGCE Durham (*Music*)
Miss L Warden, BEd Hons Kingston (*Pre-Prep Class Teacher*)
Miss D Winter, BEd, CertEd Cambridge (*KS2 teacher*)

Registrar: Mrs C Scott
Headmistress's PA: Miss A Fardoe
Junior School Secretary: Mrs D Adams

Tormead is an academically selective independent day school for girls, aged 4 to 18. Founded in 1905, it stands in pleasant grounds, close to the centre of Guildford. The atmosphere is lively and the teaching stimulating and challenging. Standards and expectations are high and girls leave the school as confident, articulate and self-reliant young women, ready to meet the challenges of university and beyond. Almost all girls leave Tormead to read for degrees at the university of their choice. On average, 12% gain an Oxford or Cambridge place each year.

An extensive extra-curricular programme provides further challenge and opportunity. We believe that a breadth of interests, skills and initiative are an essential complement to academic success for the future lives of our pupils.

The school has a lively and active musical life with two orchestras, various chamber groups, ensembles and choirs as well as a highly popular and talented Jazz Band which has undertaken tours to various European countries. Drama, dance, public speaking and debating, Young Enterprise, The Wings of Hope Achievement Award, Schools Without Walls Scheme and Duke of Edinburgh's Award are all very well supported and sixth form girls are regularly selected to join the British Schools' Exploring Society's summer expeditions to such remote and far flung destinations as Greenland, Peruvian Amazon or Svalbard.

A wide range of sports is on offer and there is a busy programme of fixtures in Hockey, Netball, Rounders, Athletics and Swimming in all of which we compete with great success. Gymnastics has been a particular strength for some years with our teams competing successfully at national level; currently our U16 team are British Schools Champions and our U19 and U11 squad are National Floor and Vault Champions.

International links. We believe that an international outlook is important. We have a partner school in Wanyange, Uganda and an established programme of exchange visits with schools in France, Germany and Spain; and gap students from Australia and South America who each spend a year with us as staff assistants.

Fees per term (2011-2012). Pre-Prep £1,915, Years 1–2 £2,160, Years 3–4 £3,210, Year 5 £3,320, Year 6 £3,380, Years 7–13 £4,010.

Scholarships and Bursaries. Academic, Music and Art Scholarships are offered at 11+ and 16+. Bursaries are available at 11+ entry and are dependent on the level of parental income.

Tormead Old Girls' Association. *General Secretary::* Sally Hinkley, tel: 01603 720000, email: sally.hinkley@ btinternet.com.

Charitable status. Tormead Limited is a Registered Charity, number 312057. It exists to provide education for able girls.

Truro High School for Girls

Truro, Cornwall TR1 2HU
Tel: 01872 272830
Fax: 01872 279393
e-mail: admin@trurohigh.co.uk
website: www.trurohigh.co.uk

Founded 1880. Independent, formerly Direct Grant.

Governors:
President: The Rt Revd Tim Thornton, BA, Bishop of Truro
Chairman: Mr D Tandy, LLB Hons
Mrs J Abbotts, BA Hons, MEd, NPQH
Mrs N Bush, Dip Est Man, ASVA
The Honourable Mrs Evelyn Boscawen
Mr I Halford, MA Oxon
Mrs S Hall, BVet Med, MRCVS
The Very Revd Dr Christopher Hardwick, BA, MA, PhD
Mr R Hygate, FRICS
Mr J Nichols, MA Cantab, FRSA, FCollP
Mrs H O'Shea, BA Hons
Mr N Parsons, BMus Hons
Lieutenant Commander N Trefusis, RN, DL
Lady Vyvyan, BA Hons
Miss K Whitford, LLB Hons
Mrs M Wilson-Holt, MBChB, FRCA

Head: Mrs C A Pascoe, BSc Hons, MSc, NPQH

Deputy Head: Mrs F Matthew, BA Hons
Assistant Deputy Head: Mrs M Smith, BA Hons
Head of Sixth Form: Miss D Freeman, BEd Hons
Head of Preparatory School: Mrs A Miller, BSc Hons

Assistant Staff:
* *Head of Department*

Art, Design Technology and Food:
*Mr R E Hunter, BA Hons, ATC
Mrs W A Williams, BA Hons
Mrs L Williams, BSc Hons (*Food and Nutrition*)
Mrs S G Weiringa, BSc, MBA (*Textiles*)
Miss C Rowe, MA (*Art Technician*)

Business Studies/Economics:
*Mr J Brand, CertEd, BEd Hons, MA

Careers & Work Experience:
*Mr R E Hunter, BA Hons, ATC
Mrs L Williams, BSc Hons

Classics:
*Mrs S J Brown, MA Oxon
Mrs K Griffin, BA Hons

English and Drama:
*Mrs J A Holland, BA Hons
Mrs J A Lawrenson-Reid, BEd Hons
Mr I Tutin, BA Hons
Mr N Rendall, BA Hons
Mrs J Trewellard, BA Hons
Mrs S Bradbury, BA Hons, PgDip (*Speech and Drama peripatetic*)

Geography:
*Mrs J Rice, BA Hons
Miss S Morris, BA Hons

History:
*Mr G Ford, BA Hons

ICT:
Mr A Purchase, BSc Hons
Mr C Beechey-Newman, BSc Hons (*ICT Coordinator*)
Mrs B Clark, BSc Hons (*Data Manager*)

Mathematics:
*Mrs A Hanson, BSc Hons
Miss C Harding, BSc Hons
Miss C Lyle, BSc Hons
Mrs A Lamble, BSc Hons

Modern Languages:
*Mrs S Murley, BA Hons
Mrs M Smith, BA Hons
Mrs F R Matthew, BA Hons
Miss K Cox, BA Hons
Mrs K Griffin, BA Hons
Mrs F Ferris, BA Hons

Music:
*Miss F Eagar, BMus, ARCM, LRSM, FTCL, QTS

Peripatetic Music Staff:
Miss K Allen (*Singing*)
Mrs R Brenton (*Clarinet, Saxophone*)
Mrs T Carleston (*Oboe*)
Miss S Carpender (*Piano, Theory*)
Mrs Z Curnow (*Double Bass*)
Mrs J Edwards (*Violin, Viola*)
Mr G Graham (*Guitar*)
Ms F Hooper (*Flute*)
Ms J Kershaw (*Brass*)
Mrs H Mee (*Singing*)
Miss K Morse (*Flute*)
Mrs N Williams (*Guitar*)
Mr M Wilton (*Percussion*)

Physical Education:
*Mrs K Barbary-Redd, BEd Hons
Miss D Freeman, BEd Hons
Mrs J Barnfield, BEd Hons
Mrs G Tregay, CertEd

Preparatory Department and Nursery:
Head: Mrs A J Miller, BSc Hons
Mrs J Ellis, MEd
Mrs Y Simpson, BEd Hons
Mrs K A Roberts, BEd Hons
Miss H Mills, BEd Hons, MEd
Mrs E Symons, BA Hons
Mrs M Hendy, BA Hons
Miss T Kemp, NNEB (*Nursery Manager*)
Mrs G Redfearn, NVQ3
Mrs P Herbert, BA Hons (*Teaching Assistant*)
Mrs L Kingdon, NNEB (*Teaching Assistant*)
Mrs J Dick

Religious Philosophy & Ethics:
*Mr P J Mothersole, BA Hons, MA
Mrs L Williams, BA Hons
Mrs J Trewellard, BA Hons

Science:
*Mr M Patchett, BSc Hons
Mrs M Sharp, BSc Hons
Mr W Smith, BSc Hons
Mrs A Letheren, BSc Hons
Mrs C Hallam, BSc Hons
Miss E Bird, BSc Hons
Mrs E Hawken, BSc Hons (*Laboratory Technician*)

Special Needs:
*Mrs K Wood, SpLD, CCET Level A
Miss S Morris, BA Hons
Mrs A Letheren, BSc Hons

Librarian: Mrs V Rendell, BA Hons

Medical:
Dr C Newton, MB, ChB, MRCGP, DRCOG, DFFP, DCH
Mrs E Burnard, CertEd, SEN
Mrs G Tregay, CertEd

Bursar: Mr B Login, MA, MBA, FCIS, MBIFM

Estates Supervisor: Mr G Williams
Accountant: Mr M Brown
Assistant Accountant: Mrs D Tillgren
Headmistress's Secretary and Registrar: Mrs F Ellison
Bursar's Secretary and Lettings: Mrs S Stevens
School Secretaries: Mrs J Nisbet, Mrs K Bawden, Mrs C Shaw
Reprographics: Mrs S Boulter

Truro High School combines a Nursery and Preparatory Department of approximately 100 girls aged 3–11 (Nursery: boys and girls aged 3–5) and a Senior School of approximately 340 girls (aged 11–18). Boarding accommodation is provided from the age of 7. Entry is based on the school's own selection procedure and Scholarships and Bursaries are available.

A broadly based curriculum is provided to GCSE including Art, Religious Philosophy & Ethics, English, History, Geography, Latin, French, German, Spanish, Mathematics, Physics, Chemistry, Biology, Music, Art, Food and Nutrition, Textiles, Theatre Studies and Physical Education. Further subjects at AS/A2 in the Sixth Form are Business Studies/Economics, Classical Civilisation, and Economics alongside an Extended Project Qualification. A Careers Department exists to advise girls and parents on openings available over a wide field including entrance to Universities and other institutions of Higher Education. Music forms an important part of the curriculum and there are two orchestras, two very strong choirs, jazz band and numerous ensembles. The school has good facilities: six well-equipped Science laboratories, a new Modern Languages block with digital laboratory, a Studio Theatre, Textiles and Cookery rooms, three Information Technology suites, indoor heated swimming pool, tennis and netball courts and an all-weather hockey/athletics pitch. Pupils in the Sixth Form have their own Sixth Form Centre with individual cubicles for private study. Two outstanding boarding houses are located in the centre of the campus.

There is a wide range of extra-curricular activities and all pupils are encouraged to participate. The school enjoys good relationships with other schools in the neighbourhood.

Fees per term (2011-2012). Tuition: Nursery £1,475 (part time), £2,205 (full time); Pre-Prep £2,345; Prep £3,306; Senior School £3,536.

Boarding (in addition to Tuition fees): £3,107 (weekly), £3,185 (full).

Truro High School Old Girls' Association. *Membership Secretary*: Mrs M Inskip.

Charitable status. Truro High School for Girls is a Registered Charity, number 306577. It exists to give education to children.

Tudor Hall

Wykham Park, Banbury, Oxon OX16 9UR
Tel: 01295 263434
Fax: 01295 253264
e-mail: admissions@tudorhallschool.com
website: www.tudorhallschool.com

Motto: *'Habeo Ut Dem'*

Board of Governors:
Mrs B Polk (*Chairman*)
Mr C Dodson (*Vice-Chairman*)
Mr J W Lewis (*Chairman of Finance & General Purpose Committee*)
Mrs L A Mayne (*Chairman of Education Committee*)
Mr A T Brett
Miss C Duncombe
Mrs J Gloag

Miss H Holden-Brown, BA
Mr P C R Whittle
Mrs N Odey
Mr B T Gamble
Revd J Gardner
Mr R Wilson

Headmistress: **Miss W Griffiths**, BSc Wales, PGCE London (*Zoology*)

Deputy Headmistress: Mrs H A Granville, BA London (*History*)
Assistant Head Curriculum: Mrs A Johnson, BSc, PGCE Dunelm (*Chemistry*)
Assistant Head Pastoral: Ms R Tandon, BA Birmingham, PGCE Manchester Met
Assistant Head (Sixth Form): Mr I Edwards, BSc Newcastle, PGCE UEA
Deputy Head (Sixth Form): Mrs J Thorn, BA Reading, MSt Oxon (*Head of Classics*)

Staff:
Mrs J Adkins, BSc OU, CertEd Oxon (*Physical Education, Learning Support*)
Mr W Always, MPhys Oxon, PGCE Warwick (*Mathematics*)
Mrs G Armitage, BA Newcastle, PGCE Oxford (*Geography*)
Mrs C F Beecham, BA Exeter (*English*)
Mrs J Benlalam, BMus Hons Kings College, London, PGCE (*Music*)
Miss A Bennett, BSc Sheffield Hallam (*Netball*)
Mr P Bentley, CertEd Nottingham (*CDT Technician*)
Mrs S Bourne, BA Cantab, PGCE (*Classics*)
Miss A Brauer, BA Kent, PGCE Bedford (*Physical Education, PR Parents and Community*)
Mrs E Buckner-Rowley, BA Hons Portsmouth, PGCE Leeds (*Spanish*)
Mr P Carine, Outdoor Leadership Lancs, PGCE Keele (*Geography, Director of Outdoor Education*)
Mr A Christopher, MA Essex, BTEC Kingshurst, HND Coventry (*Drama*)
Mr B Clark, BA Dunelm, MSt Oxon (*Religious Studies*)
Mrs A Copham, BA Dunelm, PGCE Cambridge (*French*)
Mrs S A Craske, BA Oxon, PGCE Manchester Poly (*Art*)
Dr E Davies, BSc Edinburgh, PhD London (*Biology*)
Mrs C Dawson, RSA DipSpLD, BSc London, PGD PRM OU (*Head of Learning Support*)
Ms A Eastwood, OCR Dip SpLD, CertEd Newcastle (*Learning Support*)
Mr J Field, MA Oxon, BA Oxon, PGCE Oxon (*English*)
Mr J Galloway, BA Middlesex, PGCE London (*Religious Studies*)
Miss A J Gamble, BA London, MA London, CPE Law (*History/Politics*)
Miss E Gerrard, BA (*English*)
Mrs K Hadfield, BA Leeds, PGCE Canterbury (*Geography*)
Mrs J Haggarty, City & Guilds Cookery Aylesbury (*Practical Cookery*)
Mrs K Hart, BA Manchester, PGCE Birmingham (*Textiles*)
Miss S Holmes, BSc Birmingham, PGCE Nottingham
Mrs D Hughes, BA Cardiff (*German*)
Miss K Johnson, BA (*English*)
Mrs D Jones, BA Hons Sussex, PGCE Sussex, PGCE Sussex (*Art*)
Mr R L Jones, RAF Retd, CertEd, MIITTed, HNC Elec Eng
Mrs J Kelly, LTA Level 2 Coach, Netball Level 2 Coach
Mrs L Keyte, BA Nottingham, PGCE Warwick (*French*)
Mrs H Kidman, BA Portsmouth (*Textiles*)
Mr G Langer, BSc North Staffordshire, PGCE Oxon (*Physics & Combined Science*)
Mrs L Lea-James, BMus Hons, LTCL, ALCM Huddersfield, PGCE (*Director of Music*)

Mrs S Malpass, BSc Hons Sheffield, MSc Durham, PGCE London (*Biology*)
Mr R Moody, BSc Southampton, PGCE Southampton (*Mathematics*)
Doctor B Murphy, BA Hons Wales, MA Wales, PhD Wales, PGCE East Anglia (*History*)
Miss K Oatley, BA Durham, CELTA (*French*)
Miss S Orchard, MSc Liverpool, BSc, PGCE Loughborough (*Head of Science*)
Miss P Ozkan, DEUG & Licence d'Anglais France, PGCE Exeter (*Head of French*)
Miss K Peat, BA London, QTS (*Duke of Edinburgh's Award*)
Miss M Power, BA St Anselm College, USA (*Lacrosse*)
Mrs C Preston, BA Hons, PGCE Bangor (*Religious Education*)
Mrs R Pulvermacher, BA Hons Dunelm, PGCE UWE, (*SpLD Learning Support*)
Mr K Quinn, BA, PGCE Exeter (*p/t Economics*)
Mrs L Ravenscroft, LLM & LLB Birmingham (*History*)
Miss B Robinson, BEd, DipPE Worcs (*Dance*)
Miss S Rogers, BSc Hons Plymouth, PGCE Exeter (*Geography*)
Miss L Rowlands, BSc Plymouth, PCET UWCN (*Physical Education*)
Mr S Ryan, BA OU, CertEd Avery Hill (*Chemistry, Science*)
Mr G Sarwar, BSc Birmingham, PGCE Warwick (*Head of Mathematics*)
Mr J Stead, BA Cumbria, PGCE Cardiff (*Design Crafts*)
Mrs J Stephens, BA Hons London, PGCE Middlesex (*Drama & Theatre Studies*)
Mrs K Stobbart, BEd Teesside (*Spanish*)
Miss S Taylor, MPhil St Andrews, MA St Andrews (*Classical Studies*)
Miss H Thomas, BA Hons Bath, PGCE Coventry (*Modern Languages*)
Mrs J M Thorn, BA Reading, DPhil Oxford (*Classics*)
Mrs N Thurgur, MA Hertfordshire, BA South Africa (*Textiles*)
Miss R Tulloch, MA Courtauld Institute, BA York (*Head of History of Art*)
Mrs C E Varney, BEd Oxon (*Head of Business Studies*)
Mr N Watson, BEd Leeds (*Head of ICT*)
Miss R Wilson, BA Australia (*Physical Education*)
Miss V L Wormell, BA Loughborough, PGCE Brighton (*CDT*)

Health Centre:
Mrs H Bletchly, RGN (*Sister in Charge*)
Mrs J Bonham, RGN
Mrs Z Spring, RGN
Mrs J Stewart-Brown, RGN

Clerk to the Governors & Bursar: Miss H Jackson
Careers: Miss J Webb
Staff Coordinator: Miss K Martin
Registrar: Mrs P Drinkwater
Admissions Secretary/PR & Marketing: Ms S Wells
Headmistress's PA: Mrs F George
PA to Bursar: Ms T Tait
Senior Administrative Secretary: Mrs H Mascall
Senior Administrative Secretary: Mrs S Roberts
Receptionist: Mrs A Rutherford
Administrative Secretary: Mrs P Snowden
Administrative Secretary (Music): Mrs B Foley
Administrative Secretary (PE): Mrs R Knapman
Administrative Assistant: Mrs D Cook
Travel Secretary: Mrs C Thomas
Examinations Officer: Mrs S Berresford
Old Tudorians: Mrs J Huddart

Tudor Hall is an Independent Boarding School for Girls aged 11–18 years. The school was originally founded in

1850 and moved to Wykham Park in 1946. It is situated in spacious grounds 1½ miles from Banbury Station and is within easy access of London, Oxford and Stratford-upon-Avon – M40, Junction 11. This enables the girls to enjoy a wide range of cultural and educational activities.

The school accommodates approximately 246 boarders and 86 day girls. Its buildings comprise a 17th century and an 18th century manor with a modern purpose-built house for 78 Sixth Formers and extensive new facilities. These include laboratories for biology, chemistry, physics and general science; CDT workshop; 2 information technology rooms; language laboratory; modern languages and domestic science rooms; drama studio; music school; studios for art and pottery; textiles room; gym and sports hall. There are tennis and netball courts, a swimming pool, squash courts, astroturf and pitches for hockey, lacrosse and rounders. An extension to the Sixth Form block has recently been completed, with the original rooms undergoing extensive refurbishment.

The curriculum includes a full range of academic subjects and, where possible, outings and fieldwork are arranged. All girls begin Latin and French with Spanish or German. Italian, Ancient Greek, Mandarin and Russian are also available. Music and Drama are strongly encouraged. Girls are prepared for GCSE and Advanced Level GCE, and appropriate certificates in optional extra subjects. Girls may also take riding and dancing lessons. There is a library and a careers room where advice is given about university entrance and further training.

Admission is by Common Entrance at 11+ and 13+. Entry may also be made to the Sixth Form where all girls pursue courses leading to higher education or vocational training and they are treated as students. Those entering at 11 are accustomed to being away from home by being housed separately in a smaller environment. Girls are divided into four competitive Houses but residence is with their own age group.

Tudor Hall places great importance on having a friendly atmosphere, a lively and united spirit and high standards. Girls are expected to take an interest in a wide range of activities as well as following a broad educational programme. Involvement in the local community through the Duke of Edinburgh's Award and social service, and participation in events with other schools are encouraged. Debating and public speaking are strong and there is keen involvement in the Young Enterprise Scheme, Model United Nations and European Youth Parliament. Tudor Hall is an Anglican school but members of other religious groups are welcomed. There is a small chapel.

Scholarships and Bursaries. (*See Scholarship Entries section.*)

Fees per term (2011-2012). £8,900 for boarders; £5,725 for day pupils.

Wakefield Girls' High School

Wentworth Street, Wakefield, West Yorkshire WF1 2QS
Tel: 01924 372490
Fax: 01924 231601
e-mail: admissions@wghsss.org.uk
website: www.wgsf.org.uk

This is an Endowed High School under Management of the Governors of the Wakefield Grammar School Foundation established by Charter of Queen Elizabeth.

Motto: '*Each for All and All for God.*'

Governing Body:
The Governing Body, consisting of 13 co-opted Governors and 6 representative Governors, (including representatives

of the Universities of Leeds, Bradford, Sheffield and Huddersfield), is the Wakefield Grammar School Foundation.

Spokesman: Mr D Wheatley, BTech Hons, CEng

Clerk to the Governors: Mr L Perry, ACMA

* *Head of Department*
§ *Part-time*
‡ *Teaching Certificate*

Headmistress: Mrs G Wallwork, BA Manchester

Deputy Head, Academic: Mrs M K Davidson, BEd Queen's, MSc Ulster (*Mathematics*)

Deputy Head, Teaching and Learning: ‡Mr D J Eggleston, BA Nottingham, MEd Leeds (*Business Studies & Economics*)

Deputy Head, Pastoral: ‡Mrs J A Tingle, BEd Leeds Met (**Physical Education*)

Teaching Staff:
* *Head of Department*

‡Miss P M Applewhite, BEd Sussex (*Examinations Officer; Physical Education*)
‡Mr D A Baker, MA Oxon (*Science)
Mr S Besford (*Drama)
Mr B A Carlin, BSc Sheffield Hallam (*Design Technology*)
‡Mrs V E Carter, BA Leeds (*Classics)
‡Mr D S Collett, BSc Sheffield (*Physics)
Mrs A Craig, BSc Birmingham (*Chemistry*)
‡Mrs E A Cross, BA Manchester (*History & Classics*)
Mr J Cunningham, BSc Newcastle (*Mathematics*)
‡Dr M F Dabbs, BSc Swansea, PhD Keele (*Mathematics*)
Mrs V P Denison, PGDip Dyslexia Inst (*Learning Support*)
Dr S Duerden Brown, BSc Bradford, PhD (*Chemistry*)
Dr M Durrell (*Physics*)
Mr P Elmes, BEd Ripon & York St John (**Design Technology*)
‡Mrs S Fowler, BA Leicester (**General Studies; English*)
‡Mrs H M E Gill, BA Sheffield (*Learning Support*)
‡Miss J A Gore, BA Cardiff (*English; *Drama*)
‡Mrs R Gration, BEd Leicester (**Art & Design*)
‡Mrs D J Guthrie, BA Nottingham (*Modern Languages*)
‡Mrs D Hadfield, BA Open (*Mathematics)
Mr H J Hargreaves, BSc Birmingham (*Geography*)
Mrs S L Harrison (*English*)
Miss E Hawkridge, BA Leeds (*Textiles; Head of Main School Careers*)
‡Mrs R Hesmondhalgh, BA Edinburgh College of Art, MEd Leeds (*Art & Design*)
‡Mrs S Hotham, BA Leeds (*Modern Languages*)
‡Ms L J Hutchins, BA Wales (*Head of Guidance Information & Support; Head of Sixth Form; Geography*)
Miss E James (*Classics*)
Miss K L Kendall, BSc Leeds (*Biology*)
‡Dr J C Korosi, MB, BS, BSc St Thomas' Hosp Med Sch (*Biology)
‡Mr M Lassey, BA Leeds Metropolitan (*Information Technology*)
‡Mrs J Liddy, BSc Wales (*Biology*)
Mrs S Loftus (*English*)
‡Mrs E E MacGregor, BA Bedford College (*Physical Education*)
Dr L T McNamara, BA Lancaster, PhD (*English*)
Mr N Meredith, BA Cambridge, MMus Leeds (*Music*)
Mrs A J Murray, BA Leeds (*Modern Languages*)
Miss A O'Reilly, BA Birmingham (*History & Religious Studies*)
‡Mr S Paget, BA Christ Church College, Canterbury (*Information Technology*)
‡Miss J E Pick, BA Durham (*German)
Mrs F D Preston (*Music*)
‡Mrs K Preston, BSc Sheffield (**Information Technology*)

Mrs J L Rees, BSc Sheffield (*Mathematics*)
Mrs R Relano, Licenciatura Madrid (*Spanish and French*)
‡Mrs C Richards, BA Newcastle upon Tyne (*Classics*)
‡Mrs V C Riddle, BSc Sheffield (*Biology*)
‡Mrs K F Robinson, BA Leeds Metropolitan (*Physical Education*)
‡Mrs D Russell, BSc, MSc London (*Physics*)
‡Mrs J Sadler, BSc Salford (**Spanish*)
‡Mrs C Scott, BA Durham (*History & Classics*)
Mr R Sewell (*Business Studies & Economics*)
‡Mr A D Shaw, BA Leeds (**History*)
‡Mrs A Singleton, BA Newcastle upon Tyne, MEd Leeds (**English*)
Mrs L A Slack, BA (**Modern Languages*)
Mrs K Stothard (*Geography*)
Mrs S L Taylor (*Mathematics*)
‡Mr D J Turmeau, BEd Bristol, MA York, LRAM (*Foundation Director of Music*)
‡Dr M F Uttley, BSc London, MSc, PhD (**Chemistry*)
Mrs J Ward, CertEd Liverpool (*Food Technology*)
‡Mrs G E Woods, MA Oxon (*English*)
‡Mrs L Wraight, BA Leeds (**Geography*)
‡Mrs C J Young, BSc Newcastle, BA Open, MSc Sheffield (**Psychology*)

Head's Secretary: Mrs L Maddick

Librarian: ‡Ms J Waterhouse, BA Bretton Hall College, MSc

Junior School
Headmistress: Mrs D St C Cawthorne, BEd Sheffield, DipTEFL

Deputy Headmistress: Mrs A Sutcliffe, CertEd Ripon and York St John

Teaching Staff:
Mrs J Baldock, BEd Trent
§Mrs J Banks, CertEd Sheffield
‡Mrs J Bellhouse, BA Reading
Mrs E Boid, BSc London, PGCE
Mrs C Castle, BEd Lancaster
Mrs S H Charlesworth, BEd Leicester
Mrs L Cholewa, DLC TCert
Mrs J Craggs, BEd NE Wales
Mrs J M Cunningham, CertEd Leeds
Mrs D C Day, OCR CertSpLD
Mrs V P Denison, PGDip Dyslexia Inst (*Special Needs Coordinator*)
Mrs M E A Denton, CertEd Ormskirk
Mrs K Dickens, BEd Liverpool
Mrs J Earnshaw, BEd Hons Leeds
Miss K Fear, BEd Leeds Carnegie
Mr P Ganley, BA Leicester, PGCE
Mrs P Gibbons, BEd Brighton
Mrs G Halton, BEd Bretton Hall College
Mrs V Hutchinson, BEd Leeds
‡Mrs H Judge, BA London
‡Ms K T O'Malley, BSc, Bradford
Miss M M Potts, BEd Manchester
Mrs R Pye, BEd Leeds
Mrs J E Ratcliffe, CertEd, GBSM London, MA Open
‡Miss L Roberts, BA Leicester
Mrs P Rodgers, TCert Nottingham
Mrs A Simon, CertEd Kingston, DipSpLD
Mrs V A Smith, BA Birmingham
Mrs S J Stringer, BEd Leeds
Mrs A J Sugden, CertEd Alnwick Coll of Education
§Mrs S Turmeau, BEd Bristol
‡Mrs A M Walters, BA Leeds
Mrs A M Wimbush, BEd Cambridge

Secretary: Mrs B Milne

Visiting Instrumental Musicians:
Mr D Allen, MSc, GCLCM Grand Dip (*Guitar and Bass Guitar*)
Mr C J Bacon, GMus (*Brass*)
Mrs S T Bacon, GMus (*Flute*)
Miss Z Barker, BMus (*Clarinet and Saxophone*)
Mr D Beckley, BA, LTCL, FTCL, ARCM (*Brass*)
Miss L Berwin, GRSM, LRAM, PGCE (*Piano and Keyboard*)
Mr P Bingham (*Piano and Keyboard*)
Mr P Birkby, GCLCM, LRAM (*Percussion*)
Miss L Emms, BMus (*Percussion*)
Mr J Gibson, BA RNCM (*French Horn*)
Miss Z Glossop, LRAM (*Oboe*)
Mrs C Hall, DCLCM, LTCL (*Clarinet*)
Mrs E Hambleton, GNSM, LRAM, CertEd (*Piano and Keyboard*)
Mr D Heathcote, BSc, PhD, RSA, MD (*Voice*)
Mrs M B Hemingway, ALCM (*Piano and Keyboard*)
Mr G Hirst, LRAM, ARCM, LTCL, CertEd (*Saxophone and Clarinet*)
Miss A Holmes, BA, LTCL, CertEd (*Saxophone and Clarinet*)
Mr D G Lewis (*Percussion*)
Mrs J D Maunsell, GBSM, ABSM, DipNCOS (*Violin and Viola*)
Mr D Mitchell, BMus, MA (*Guitar*)
Mr T Moore, BMus, MA (*Piano and Organ*)
Mr I Naylor, BMus (*Cello and Double Bass*)
Mr R O'Connell (*Voice*)
Miss K Price, BMus, MMus, PGDipMus (*Voice*)
Mr M Roberts, LGSM, DPLM (*Clarinet and Saxophone*)
Mr M Ryal (*Bass Guitar*)
Mr J Storer, BA (*Guitar*)

Wakefield Girls High School was founded in 1878 and has a long tradition of providing an education of the highest quality.

The school aims to give good all round education to each pupil, encouraging academic excellence, nurturing talents, developing an individual's potential, and emphasising traditional values in a modern context. These aims are pursued within a happy and stimulating environment.

The school occupies an extensive site in a conservation area near the centre of Wakefield, and is easily accessible by road and rail from a wide area. The Georgian house in which it began has been adapted and extended over the years as numbers have grown. A steady programme of building and the acquisition of nearby property have enabled the school to anticipate and meet the needs of succeeding generations of pupils.

Specialist facilities exist for all subjects. Recent developments have included the new all-weather hockey astroturf, Creative Arts Centre, Sports Pavilion, the Science and Technology Centre and the Hartley Pavilion – a Sports and Assembly Hall.

The first phase of the Creative Arts development has produced two quite stunning buildings which have retained the features of Victorian Villas but have been transformed into bright modern purpose built accommodation.

Hepworth House, named after our illustrious Old Girl, the Sculptress Barbara Hepworth, will be the home of the Art Department and provides excellent space for both the Sixth Form and the lower school with specialist provision for pottery, sculpture, 3D, textiles and photography.

Cliff House contains the Economics and Business Studies Centre, the Careers Centre and has additional facilities for the Sixth Form.

The second phase of the Creative Arts development has provided a drama studio, design and technology laboratories, a textiles workshop, a recording studio and a new English department.

All ICT equipment has been up-graded and now includes video-conferencing. There are plans to enhance the provision in the school even more.

The pre-preparatory school, Mulberry House, was completed in 2001. The Junior School occupies its own premises on the main school campus and share its facilities and some specialist staff. (*For further details, see Junior School entry in IAPS section.*)

There is a very strong tradition of sporting excellence at local, county and National level. At the playing fields, a short distance away, there are tennis courts, cricket, hockey and netball grounds.

The creative and performing arts play an important part in the life of the school as do extra curricular activities, with over 80 currently available. The Duke of Edinburgh's Award is taken by large numbers.

Curriculum. The school offers a grammar school education. All girls follow a broad and balanced curriculum which keeps the widest possible range of options open until A Level when there is a choice of any combination of 28 A Level subjects. Languages are a major strength with French, German, Spanish, Italian, Russian, Latin and Greek available. Sciences are also very strong with all girls doing Biology, Physics and Chemistry at GCSE and over half taking Mathematics or a Science at A Level.

Public examination results in 2008 were superb. At GCSE 71% of grades were A* and A. Similar excellent results were achieved at A Level with another first division score of 79% of grades A and B. Most girls go on to university although some choose to go directly into management, the Forces or to RADA. There is a full Careers programme and well established links with industry.

The girls enjoy the best of both worlds. They benefit educationally from a single-sex environment but gain socially and culturally from the close cooperation with Queen Elizabeth Grammar School which has the same governing body. This means that there are many joint activities and some joint lessons at Sixth Form level.

School Hours. 8.45 am – 4.00 pm from Monday to Friday inclusive.

Admission. Boys and girls aged 3 to 7 years are admitted in order from the waiting list. Girls aged 7 years or older are admitted after passing an entrance examination. The main ages of entry are at 3, 7, 11 and 13 years. Some enter the school at 16 years to take A level courses; these girls need a suitable foundation of GCSE subjects.

Fees per term (2011-2012). Senior School £3,332; Junior School £2,499–£2,641; Pre-Preparatory and Nursery £2,419. Music lessons £185 for 10 lessons per term.

Scholarships and Bursaries. The Governors will consider providing a Foundation Award where the net parental income is less than £40,000 per annum.

11+ Peter Ogden Bursaries and Ogden Trust Sixth Form Science scholarships: two of these are awarded each year to help with fees up to 100%, uniform, travel costs and essential school trips.

Twelve Sixth Form Scholarships are awarded in recognition of academic work and GCSE results.

Charitable status. The Wakefield Grammar School Foundation is a Registered Charity, number 1088415. It exists to provide education for children.

Walthamstow Hall

Holly Bush Lane, Sevenoaks, Kent TN13 3UL
Tel: 01732 451334
Fax: 01732 740439
e-mail: registrar@walthamstowhall.kent.sch.uk
website: www.walthamstow-hall.co.uk

Walthamstow Hall is an Independent Day School for Girls in Sevenoaks, founded in 1838.

We take girls from 2½–11 years in Pre-Prep and Juniors and from 11–18 in Seniors.

We have an established history of preparing academically able girls for stimulating, purposeful and happy lives within and beyond school. We believe that every individual has huge potential and given the right opportunities, encouragement and inspiring teaching they develop an incredible range of skills and talents.

The Headmistress is a member of the GSA (Girls' Schools Association) and the Head of the Junior School is a member of IAPS (Independent Association of Prep Schools). (*see also Junior School entry in IAPS section*).

Governors:
Chairman: Ian Philip Esq, FCA

There are 15 school governors.

Headmistress: Mrs J Milner, MA Hons Oxford, PGCE Oxford

Senior Deputy Head: Mrs J Joynes, BA Hons Southampton, NPQH (*History and Politics*)
Deputy Head: Mr P M R Howson, BA Hons Plymouth, AST London (*English*)
Director of Studies: Mrs S F Cutter, BSc Hons 1st class London (*Head of Science and Chemistry*)
Head of Sixth Form: Ms E M Ancrum, MA Oxford, MPhil Hong Kong, PGCE London (*Economics and Business Studies*)
Head of Junior School: Mrs P A Austin, BA Hons London, LTCL Trinity College of Music, PGCE Brighton, NPQH

Senior School Assistant Staff:
* *Head of Department*

Miss V Bower-Morris, BA Hons Surrey, PGCE Goldsmiths (*Drama/Trinity Guildhall Drama*)
N Buckingham Esq, BA Hons Reading, MA Reading, PGCE London (*Classics*)
Miss K E Burtenshaw, BEd Westminster College, Oxford, Cert Ed (*Geography*)
Mrs J M Cox, MA Cambridge, PGCE Open University, ATCL (*Biology*)
Mrs A Earnshaw-Punnett, BA Hons Sheffield Hallam, QTS Canterbury Christ Church (*PE, ICT, *i/c Lacrosse, Charities Coordinator*)
Ms B d'Inverno, BA Hons Wales, PGCE Southampton (*i/c Spanish, Assistant Head of Lower School*)
Miss L Eden, BA Hons Surrey, PGCE King's College London (**ICT*)
Mrs C Evans, BA Hons Greenwich (*Design Technology*)
Mrs H Evernden, BA Hons York, PGCE York (*English*)
Mrs E Fairhead, BA Hons Oxford (*Classics*)
Mrs S C Fitzmaurice, BSc Hons Manchester, PGCE Manchester (*Biology*)
Mrs K Hofmann, MA Hons St Andrews, QTS (*MFL*)
Mrs L M Hogan, BSc Hons Durham, PGCE Durham (*Biology*)
Mrs M Holland, Dip Art & Design West Surrey College, PGCE Bristol (*Art*)
Mrs H A Hook, BA Hons Aberystwyth, PGCE Cambridge (*English*)
Mrs K M Howlett, BEd Hons Sussex (*PE, Head of Lower School, *i/c Swimming*)
Mrs C J Hughes, BA Hons West Surrey College of Art and Design, PGCE London (*Art*)
Mrs S L Isted, BA Hons Warwick, PGCE King's College (*Classics, Junior Careers*)
Dr P A Le Bas, MA Cambridge, DPhil Oxford, STB/STL Rome, PGCE St Mary's College (*Physics*)
Mr S Ledsham, MA Oxford, PGCE Sussex (*Physics*)
Mrs L A C Martin, BSc Hons Sheffield (*Mathematics, IT, Examinations*)

Miss S Mehaffey, MA, PGCE Edinburgh (*English*)

Mrs E H Morgan, BA Hons Hull, PGCE London (*Spanish, French*)

Ms A H Murphy, MA Oxford, PGCE East Anglia (*History, Politics, Oxbridge Coordinator*)

Ms A K Needham, MA Kent, CertEd Sussex (*Religious Studies, SINCO, GPR Coordinator*)

P J Newell Esq, GRSM Hons, ARCM, ARCO, MTC London (*Music*)

Dr R Peat, PhD, MA, BMus London (*Music, Assistant Head of Sixth Form*)

Mrs E Peters, BSc Hons Southampton, PGCE Southampton (*Mathematics*)

Mrs J A Robertson, MA Hons Cambridge, PGCE, MSc London (*Geography, *i/c Food & Nutrition*)

Mrs A Sherwen, BSc Hons London (*Biology*)

Mrs G M Smith, BA Nottingham (*Art*)

Mrs M C Smith, BA Hons Exeter (*French/German*)

Mrs C Solan, BA Hons London, PGCE Canterbury (*Art*)

D Swann Esq, BSc Hons Christ Church College, PGCE Christ Church (*Mathematics, ICT, DofE Coordinator*)

Miss B A Taylor, TCert PE Cambridge (*PE, Head of Middle School*)

Mrs L Thomas, BA Hons Wales, MA Open, PGCE Bristol (*History*)

Mrs S Whawell, BSc Hons Birmingham, PGCE Bristol, MSc Reading (*Mathematics*)

Mrs H Wiffen, BA Hons Trent University Ontario, BEd Queens University Ontario (*English*)

Dr S Wilkinson, DPhil Hons Oxford, PGCE King's College London (*Chemistry*)

S R Wilson Esq, BA Hons Sunderland, PGCE King's College London (*Sociology*)

Mrs C M Winder, BA Hons Exeter, MA Kent, PGCE Oxford (*English*)

Ms O Windle, MA, BA Hons USA (*History/Politics*)

Mrs M T Wood, BSc Hons Aberdeen, PGCE London (*Chemistry*)

Librarians:
Mrs H Evernden, BA Hons York
Mrs L White

Junior School

Deputy Head Teacher: Mrs A J Rotchell, BEd Hons Westminster College, Oxford

Director of Studies: Mrs P I Potter, BEd Southampton

Mrs N Armitage, BA Hons Nottingham, GTP

Mrs T A Ball, BSc Hons Essex (*Science Technician, Library*)

Ms N Briglia, BA Grad DipEd Australia

Mrs J Bullman, BEd Hons Manchester

Mrs K Caine, BTEC, PDC Cert Caring (*Classroom Assistant*)

Mrs G Cameron, Foundation Degree

Mrs L E Carter, BSc Hons Durham

Mrs C Clarke, NVQ3 (*After-School Supervisor*)

Miss E C Dargie, BEd Hons Christ Church College

Mrs L P Everitt, CertEd North Worcestershire College of Education

Mrs E Ferreira, BA South Africa, Dip P Ed

Miss S Harris, CertEd Lady Spencer Churchill College of Education, Oxford

Mrs N Hartley, BSc Hons, PG Cert, PG Dip Oxford Brookes, PGCE Cambridge (*Head of Pre-Prep*)

Mrs J D Haydock, CertEd Alsager College of Education

Mrs H E Malcolm, DipEd Aberdeen College of Education

Miss M R Murphy, BA Hons Swansea, PGCE Liverpool Inst of HE

P J Newell Esq, GRSM Hons, ARCM, ARCO, MTC London (*Music*)

Mrs K M B Pattison, BA Hons Keele, MEd Open University, PGCE Durham

Miss T Perry, NNEB Diploma

Miss A C Philip, BEd Hons Nottingham Trent

Mrs S Robinson, BSc Hons Herts, Dip Childcare

Mrs D Smith, SEN, NNEB

Mrs L Thompson, Montessori Gold Seal Dip

Mrs G M Watts, MA Hons St Andrews

Administrative Staff:
Bursar: N Wood Esq, MI Log
Registrar: Mrs S Timms, GIPD
External Communications and Alumnae Development: Mrs S Pelling, BA Hons Keele
Network Manager: Mrs E M Grant, BSc Hons Open University
PA to the Headmistress: Miss K Lippiatt
Junior School Secretary: Mrs W Fahy

Medical Centre:
Mrs C A Kirwan, RGN
Mrs L J Mottram, Dip Nursing Studies City University

Facilities. Walthamstow Hall is set in its own grounds within the town of Sevenoaks. Girls are taught in light and airy classrooms in buildings specifically designed for learning. All of our buildings are purpose built, from the 1882 Arts and Crafts main building through to the swimming pool complex opened in 2008, the new Maths Suite and Drama Studio opened in 2009, the new Music and Design Technology rooms opened in September 2010 and the new additional IT room and Student Entrance and Art Gallery opening at the end of 2011. The school also has its own theatre, science laboratories, libraries, sixth form centre, computer network, and the Erasmus Centre for Languages and Humanities.

Curriculum. Walthamstow Hall delivers an enriched grammar school curriculum which is innovative and flexible, facilitating breadth and individual choice, without sacrificing depth of study. This is brought to life with inspirational teaching.

All girls in their first three Senior School years (7, 8 and 9) follow a core curriculum of 17 subjects, with a second language being added in Year 8. As they progress through to public examinations the flexibility of the curriculum, enables girls to study a wide breadth of subjects rather than being shackled by restrictive subject blocks.

Subjects taught include Ancient Greek, Art, Biology, Business Studies, Chemistry, Classical Civilisation, Computer Studies, Design Technology, Drama, Economics, English, Fine Art, French, History, Geography, German, Government and Politics, Latin, Mathematics and Additional Mathematics, Music, the Global Perspectives and Research Project, Photography, Physical Education, Physics, Religious Studies, Sociology, Spanish, Textiles and Theatre Studies.

Girls are prepared for GCSE, IGCSE, AS, A2 Levels, Cambridge Pre-U and for entrance to universities (including a good proportion to Oxford and Cambridge). The record of success in public examinations is excellent.

Religious Teaching is interdenominational.

Extra-Curricular Activities. The high profile of the Performing Arts, Sports, trips, careers and study skills and personal development, together with our well developed pastoral system, provides further opportunity and support for every girl.

Our belief in sport for all enables both team players and individuals to find the sporting activities that suit them best. Our lacrosse, netball, swimming, athletics, judo, fencing, curling and tennis teams achieve highly at the many fixtures that they attend.

A good proportion of girls participate in the Duke of Edinburgh's Award scheme, Business enterprise, the school choirs and orchestra and Trinity Guildhall Drama.

Girls undertake voluntary service within the local community and the School is closely linked with the Union of

Girls' Schools for Social Service and gives its support to the settlement at Peckham.

Admission. Admission to the Junior School is by interview and tests suitable to the age group. Admission to the Senior School for 11 and 13 year olds is through the School's own entrance examinations and interview. Suitably qualified girls are admitted to the Sixth Form. Parents are warmly invited to visit the School.

Fees per term (2011-2012). Senior School: £5,080. Junior School: Kindergarten £235 per session (2–10 sessions per week); Reception to Year 2 £2,990, Years 3–6 £3,710.

Scholarships. Foundation Scholarships are awarded annually to the candidates who show the greatest academic potential in the school's own 11+ and 13+ entrance examinations.

The Erasmus Scholarship, the Darwin Scholarship, the Tanner Mathematics Scholarship and Sixth Form Academic Scholarships are awarded annually to the candidates who show the greatest academic potential in the school's own Sixth Form Scholarship Examination.

Music Scholarships are awarded annually at 11+ and at 13+.

In addition, 13+ Art, Drama and Sports awards are available.

The Lantern Award for Art is awarded annually to a Sixth Form candidate who demonstrates the greatest potential in art and textiles.

All awards are available to both internal and external candidates.

In addition, a generous means-tested bursary scheme in the Senior School provides financial help with school fees based on a family's financial circumstances. The scheme includes our Founders' Bursary, which pays nearly 100% of a pupil's school fees throughout their time at the school.

Charitable status. Walthamstow Hall is a Registered Charity, number 1058439. It exists to provide education for girls.

Westfield School

Oakfield Road, Gosforth, Newcastle-upon-Tyne NE3 4HS
Tel: 0191 255 3980
e-mail: westfield@westfield.newcastle.sch.uk
website: www.westfield.newcastle.sch.uk

Governors:
Chairman: Mrs O Forster
A C Coulson
Mrs J Keep
P C M Lewis
M Magowan
Mrs J Robson
D Ronn
Mrs S Ross
Mrs F Standfield
Dr D Younger

Headmistress: Mrs M Farndale, BA Hons London, PGCE Oxon, FRSA

Deputy Headteacher: Mrs D Thompson, MA Hons Cantab, PGCE

Assistant Head: S Ratcliffe, LLB Newcastle, BA Hons Wimbledon School of Art, MFA Cranbrook Academy of Art, Michigan

Assistant Head: G Wilson, BTL Canterbury NZ

Head of Sixth Form: Mrs E Wise, BA Hons Newcastle, PGCE

Art/Design:
S Ratcliffe, LLB Newcastle, BA Hons Wimbledon School of Art, MFA Cranbrook Academy of Art, Michigan
Miss K Dunn, BA Hons UWE, PGCE

Biology: Mrs S Vallance, BSc Hons London, PGCE

Careers: Mrs C Gaynor, BEd Hons Warwick, DipManSt Bristol

Chemistry: Mrs M Slack, BSc Leicester, PGCE

Drama/Theatre Studies: R Hersey, PDMus, AMus, PGCE

Business Studies: Mrs C Gaynor, BEd Hons Warwick, DipManSt Bristol

English:
Dr A Leng, BA Hons Reading, MA Reading, PhD
Miss E Baldwin, BA Hons Cantab, PGCE

Food & Nutrition:
Mrs P J Ford, BEd Hons Newcastle, CertEd

French:
Mrs F Boyce, BA Hons Salford, PGCE
Mrs S Dodds, BA Hons Durham, PGCE
Mrs E Wise, BA Hons Newcastle, PGCE

Geography:
Mrs D Thompson, MA Hons Cantab, PGCE
C Dunn, MA Hons Cantab

German: Mrs E Wise, BA Hons Newcastle, PGCE

History:
Miss J Patterson, BA Hons Northumbria, PGCE
Mrs S Gibson, BA Hons Wales, PGCE

Information Communication Technology:
Mrs C Lloyd, BA Hons, PGCE Liverpool

Mathematics:
Mrs A Whitfield, BSc, ACA, PGCE, Edinburgh
Mrs F Swift, BA Cantab, MEng Cantab, PGCE
Mrs K Wilkes, BSc Hons Northumbria, PGCE

Music:
G Wilson. BTL Canterbury NZ

Physical Education:
Mrs N Bolton, BSc Lancaster, PGCE
Miss J Harrison BSc Hons Manchester Met, PGCE

Physics:
Dr E Corbin, BA Oxon, MSc Newcastle, PhD Newcastle

Religious Studies:
S Shieber, BA Hons Durham, PGCE, MA

Science:
Miss R Riley, BSc Newcastle, PGCE

Spanish:
Mrs S Dodds, BA Hons Durham, PGCE

Additional Learning Support:
Mrs L Robertson, MA Hons Aberdeen, PGCE

Junior House:
Head: Mrs M Branson, BA Hons Leeds, PGCE Newcastle
Assistant Head: Mrs K Clappison, MA Hons Glasgow, PGCE

Teachers/Teaching Assistants:
Mrs N Alexanders, BA Hons Newcastle, PGCE
Miss J N Brown, BSc Hons Huddersfield, PGCE
Mrs F Collier, BA Hons Keele, PGCE
Mrs H Dean, BEd Hons Newcastle
Mrs S Hann, BA Hons Hull, PGCE
Mrs N Kyle, BA Hons Durham, PGCE
Mrs M Johnson, CertEd Eastbourne
Mrs K Meeson, BSc Hons Northumbria, PGCE
Mrs K Hickford

Miss G McKeating, BEd Hons York
Mrs L McNaught, BA Hons Staffs, NCFE2
Mrs T McQuade, NCFE Level ONC Dyslexia Level 3
Mrs A Rabey-Wilson, BA Hons London, PGCE
Mrs F Twaddle, NVQ3 Early Years
Mrs J Slack, BA Hons Hull, PGCE
Mrs A Winks, BEd Hons Newcastle

Visiting Staff:
Music:
B Alimohamadi, BA OU, LGSM, CertEd Newcastle
Mrs M A Huntingdon, BSc, FTCL, LRAM
Mrs P Green, BA Hons Newcastle, CT ABRSM
Miss L Mair, MMus
Miss H Sander, LTCL
Miss S Harrison, LTCL
J Radford
P Wight
Mrs E Brown
Dancing:
Miss G Quinn, RAD Int Children's Examiner, AdvTCert
   ARAD, MNCDTA
Mrs A Hall, MNCDTA
Miss L Toward
Tennis: Mrs F Twaddle, LTA Coach
Fencing: G Thompson, BFA County Coach
Gymnastics:
P Gleghorn, NPQH, BEd Hons, Senior Club Coach
Miss C Anderson, Assistant Coach

Bursar: Mrs S Easton, BA Hons, ACMA, CPFA
Domestic Bursar: Mrs D Oldroyd
Headmistress's Secretary: Mrs J Jokelson
School Secretary: Mrs J Stead
Junior House Secretary: Mrs C Park, BSc Hons Leeds
Laboratory Technician: J Beveridge
Examinations Officer: J W Hodgkins, BSc Hons Leicester,
   CertEd
Assistant Examinations Officer: Mrs J Stead
School Librarian: Mrs J Stead

Westfield is a day school for 380 girls aged 3+ to 18, in Junior and Senior Houses situated on one campus in a very pleasant wooded site of over 6 acres. The School's aim is an uninterrupted education, a high academic standard and a wide curriculum offering scope and stimulus for individual development. There is a vast range of extra curricular activities with particular emphasis on Sport, Outdoor Pursuits, Music, Art and Drama. The Duke of Edinburgh's Award Scheme has a high profile and all senior girls are encouraged to participate. In addition to a sound grounding in basic skills, Junior House (3–11) offers specialist teaching in Art, Craft, PE, French and Music. So that every child may be assured of individual attention class sizes are restricted to a maximum of 20. Frequently, classes are further divided into smaller units.

Senior house (11–18), has first rate classroom and laboratory facilities with excellent specialist accommodation for Home Economics and Music. A wide range of subjects is taught by specialists. Initially all girls have lessons in the traditional academic core subjects, in English, Mathematics, Geography, History, Science (taught as 3 separate subjects) and French, as well as in Music, Drama, PE, Food and Nutrition, ICT and Design. German and Spanish are introduced in the second year. Girls are encouraged to aim for breadth in their choice of subjects at GCSE. Most girls achieve 9 passes in the A–C range of the GCSE, a number with straight A and A* passes. There is a carefully structured programme of Careers and Personal and Social Education and a well developed pastoral system.

The Sixth Form occupies a cottage block in the grounds and is under the direction of the Head of the Sixth Form.

There is a full range of AS, A2 and other courses and girls are prepared for University and other Higher Education courses, including Oxbridge, as well as for other courses and for employment. The A level pass rate is always over 90%, ensuring for most girls a place in their first choice of institute of higher education.

Sixth Formers have considerable responsibility within the School in addition to their own thriving academic and cultural life.

Westfield is a member of Round Square, a worldwide association of schools which share a commitment, beyond academic excellence, to personal development and responsibility through service, challenge, adventure and international understanding. Girls from Westfield have the opportunity to attend the Annual International Conference and to participate in exchanges with member schools from all over the world, and in the Round Square International Service Projects in developing countries.

Westfield is totally committed to producing happy, self-confident, well-balanced young women who are international in their outlook and fully prepared to face life in the 21st Century.

Admission to Westfield is by interview and examination. While children of all faiths are accepted, the religious life of the school is based on Christian principles.

Fees per term (2011-2012). In Junior House fees range from £1,319–£2,778 and in Senior House are £3,547.

Scholarships are available at 11+ and 16+. Some bursaries are also available in cases of financial need.

Charitable status. Westfield School is owned and administered by the Northbrian Educational Trust Ltd, which is a Registered Charity, number 528143. It exists for the purpose of education.

Westholme School

Meins Road, Blackburn, Lancashire BB2 6QU
Tel: 01254 506070
Fax: 01254 506080
e-mail: principal@westholmeschool.com
website: www.westholmeschool.com

Governing Body:
Chairman: Mr K J Ainsworth, FGA
Deputy Chairman: His Honour E Slinger, BA

Mrs A Booth
Mr D J Berry, BA, FCMA, MIBM
Mr P Forrest, MRICS, FCIOB
Mrs A Gallacher
Mrs C Lamb
Mr B C Marsden, FCA
Miss J Panton, MA Oxon, FRSA
Mrs S-A Sharples
Professor R D Taylor, MA, LLM
Mr J R Yates, BSc

Clerk to the Governors: Mr J Backhouse, LLB Hons

***Principal*: Mrs Lillian Croston**, BSc Hons Dunelm,
   PGCE Cantab, ALCM

Vice-Principal: Mrs Anne Patefield, BSc Hons CNAA

Deputy Headteacher: Miss Nicola Edgar, BA Hons
   Liverpool, PGCE Liverpool

Assistant Headteacher (Pastoral): Miss Jude Entwistle, BA
   Hons Wolverhampton, PGCE, MISTC

Bursar: Mr J Henwood, BSc Hons, MA, FCMA

Westholme School comprises: Senior School for Girls and Sixth Form (Girls aged 11–18), Girls' Junior School (Girls aged 7–11), Boys' Junior School (Boys aged 7–11), Infant School (Boys and Girls aged 3–7), and Nursery (Boys and Girls from the age of 2).

Girls are guaranteed continuity of education through Westholme School to eighteen while boys are prepared for entry at 11 to the school of their parents' choice. A nursery for 2–3 year olds opened in October 2006.

There are 1,001 day pupils at Westholme: 593 girls in the Senior School and Sixth Form, 372 (237 girls, 135 boys) in the Infant and Junior Departments, and 36 boys and girls in the Nursery.

Westholme School, is administered by a Board of Governors which includes three nominated Governors representing current parents. Although the school is non-denominational, its Christian foundation is regarded as important, the emphasis being placed on the moral aspect of Christian teaching.

Senior School. The aim of the Senior School is to provide an atmosphere in which each girl can develop her abilities to the full and can excel in some field of activity. There is constant effort to widen interests and to instil a strong sense of individual responsibility. Most girls continue to the Sixth Form and then move on to Higher Education. Most pursue degree courses, a significant number at Oxford and Cambridge.

The Senior School offers an academic curriculum in English Language and Literature, Mathematics, Biology, Chemistry, Physics, Geography, History, French, German, Mandarin, Spanish, Food, Design, Information and Textiles Technology, Art, Business Studies, Classical Civilisation, Drama, Latin, Music, Ethics, Philosophy & Religion (EPR), Psychology, Sociology and Theatre Studies. Most of these subjects can be taken for the GCSE examination and at AS and A2 Levels; Oxbridge tuition is also offered.

Set in the countryside to the west of Blackburn, Westholme School offers excellent facilities. The premises have been regularly upgraded to give purpose-built accommodation for specialist subjects such as Art, Design and Information Technology and Music; seven modern laboratories support the three separate sciences. Sporting facilities include a sports hall, indoor swimming pool, brand new all-weather pitch and tennis courts and a large playing field with running circuit. The full-sized professional theatre opened in 1997, seats 700 and offers students outstanding production resources. The library has open-access multimedia giving students full research facilities. The Sixth Form wing opened in September 2003 complete with lecture theatre, common room, café and classrooms.

The Performing Arts are a special feature of the school. There are several school choirs and girls have the opportunity to learn a string, brass or wind instrument and to play in the school orchestras or wind ensembles. Extra-curricular drama includes the full scale spectacular musical, in the round productions, club and house competitions, while make-up and costume design are popular options at GCSE.

School societies and house teams meet on most days during midday break and girls are encouraged to participate in a variety of activities and in their house competitions. These provide younger girls with opportunities beyond the curriculum and older students with the chance to assume a leadership role.

Westholme Infant School, Westholme Girls' Junior School, Westholme Boys' Junior School. There is close cooperation between these schools and with the Senior School. A family atmosphere allows children to learn in a supportive and happy environment. Firm academic foundations are laid with the emphasis upon the basic skills of literacy and numeracy. Excellent facilities afford ample teaching space and resource areas; the Junior Schools (a Boys' Junior School, ages 7–11, was opened in September 2003) have three halls, music rooms and specialist provision for Information Technology. Extra-curricular activities include public speaking, orchestra, choir, sports, societies and school visits. Music and sport are taught by specialists and all Departments use the swimming pool, sports hall, athletics track and outdoor pitches at the Senior School.

Admission. Pupils usually enter the school in September. Entry to the Junior and Senior Schools is by examination, and to the Infant School by interview. The normal ages of entry are at 2, 3, 4, 7, 11 and 16.

In view of the demand for places, parents are advised to make an early application.

The Principal is happy for prospective parents to visit the school during normal working hours; appointments may be arranged through the Registrar, from whom application forms are available. Annual Open Days are held in October and other open days are held in the spring and summer terms.

Private coaches run from Accrington, Blackburn Boulevard, Bolton, Burnley, Colne, Chorley, Clitheroe, Darwen, Leyland, Preston, Standish, Ribble Valley, South Ribble, the Rossendale Valley and Wigan.

Fees per term (from January 2011). Senior School £2,864, Junior Schools £2,270, Infant School £1,803, Nursery £174 pw.

Scholarships are available at the Senior School for girls who show good academic ability and various Bursaries are available (means-tested).

Charitable status. Westholme School is a Registered Charity, number 526615. It exists for the education of children between the ages of 2 and 18.

Westonbirt

Tetbury, Gloucestershire GL8 8QG
Tel: 01666 880333
Fax: 01666 880364
e-mail: office@westonbirt.gloucs.sch.uk
website: www.westonbirt.gloucs.sch.uk

Governing Body:
Chairman: Mr D McMeekin, MBA
Vice-Chairman: Miss J Greenwood, BSc Hons, FRICS
Mr M Barrow, CBE
Mr R Boggis-Rolfe, MA Hons
Mrs S Castle, BSc Hons, RSA
Mr R Collinson, FCH, MBA, FCMC
Mr I Etchells
Mr H Falkenburg
Mr S Fisher, MA, FCA
Mrs J Jones, BA Hons, MA
Mrs P Leggate, BA Hons, MEd
Mrs H Metters, BSc Hons, PGCE
Mrs S Porter
Mrs A Scott, BA Hons
Mr J Squire
Mrs S Whitfield

Head: **Mrs M Henderson**, MA Hons St Andrews, PGCE Dunelm

Deputy Head: Mr M Gluning, BSc, PGCE Aberystwyth, MA Kingston

Chaplain: (*to be appointed*)

Heads of Department:

Art:
Mrs M Phillips, BA, FPSPhotog, CertEd Notre Dame, Liverpool

Business Studies:
Mrs A Sedman, BSc Dunelm, MSc Bath, PGCE UWE

Classics:
(*to be appointed*)

Drama:
Mrs C Crosbee, BA Hons Middlesex

Psychology:
Mr P Bolam, BSc

English:
Mrs D Browne, BA Hons University College Wales, PGCE
St Luke's Exeter

Geography:
Mrs N Gill, BA Hons Manchester, PGCE Cambridge

History:
Mrs A Cowell, MSc Leicester, BA Hons University
College Cardiff, PGCE Open

Food & Textiles Technology:
Mrs J Bell, BEd Hons Bath

Mathematics:
Mrs J Barlow, BSc Birmingham

Modern Languages:
Mrs C Rock, L-ès-L Université de Metz

Music:
Director of Music: Dr C Exon, BMus Hons, PhD
Birmingham, PGCE Southampton

Physical Education:
Ms H Siwek, BEd London

Religious Education:
(*to be appointed*)

Science:
Head of Physics: Dr J Stimpson, PhD Leicester, BSc
Leicester, PGCE Leicester
Head of Biology: Mrs S Barr, BSc, PGCE Leeds
Head of Chemistry: Mr M Gluning, BSc, PGCE
Aberystwyth, MA Kingston

Design Technology:
Mr J H M Sproule, CertEd London

Sanatorium Medical Officer: Dr A Walsh, MBChB,
DRCOG

Sisters:
Mrs S Bath, RGN, RMN
Mrs B Jansen-Van-Vuuren, RGN
Mrs Karen Haighton, BA Middlesex
Mrs Shirley Wyse, SRN

Housemistresses:
Badminton House: Miss G Fry, CertEd Birmingham
Beaufort House: Miss S Gould
Dorchester House: Miss S Gould
Holford House: Miss E Pollitt, BSc
Sixth Form: Mrs F Hudson, BA Hons Durham

Operations Director: Mr J Olver

Registrar: Mrs B Holley, BSc Hons Coventry

Location. Set in a Grade I listed, historic Cotswold mansion within over 200 acres of private parkland and gardens, Westonbirt School provides a peaceful, safe and inspiring setting for education, within easy reach of major motorways, rail networks and airports.

Philosophy. Founded in 1928, Westonbirt School offers all the advantages of a small rural girls' school, within a happy, caring community and an exceptionally beautiful setting. Subject teachers, personal tutors and pastoral staff work together to provide a supportive, nurturing environment, rather than the pressure of an academic hothouse. Consequently, both girls to whom academic success comes naturally and those who require more coaching and encouragement achieve their full potential, both academically and in extra-curricular activities. The 2011 Independent Schools Inspectorate (ISI) inspection report praised how *"Girls' overall achievement in Westonbirt School is excellent, academically, in their community service and in their outstand-*

ing personal development". The pursuit of fulfilling recreational activities is actively encouraged, as are healthy, close relationships between staff and pupils. The school remains predominantly boarding (65%) but day girls are welcome. Boarders and day girls mix together in the same houses and all enjoy the facilities associated with a full boarding school and a flexible approach to boarding.

The Curriculum. All pupils follow a broad, balanced course of study in line with the National Curriculum. The majority also learn at least two Modern Languages, Latin, Drama, Music, and all aspects of technology. A wide variety of sporting opportunities is also on offer.

Virtually all pupils go on to a good university or art college for a degree course to suit their long-term career ambitions.

In addition, girls follow a Lifeskills programme from Year 7 onwards. This comprehensive programme addresses specific issues relevant to their age. It incorporates and adds value to the six Key Skills identified by the Department for Education that will make them especially able to succeed in the world of work: communication, working with others, improving one's own learning and performance, numeracy, information technology and problem-solving.

Music, Speech and Drama. The performing arts thrive at Westonbirt. Most girls play at least one instrument and there are four very active and growing choirs and a school orchestra, plus a flute choir and Samba Band. Girls regularly take part in concerts and recitals at school and elsewhere. Musical instrument and singing lessons are timetabled for free periods wherever possible so that girls do not miss academic lessons.

Speech and Drama lessons and individual coaching are also very popular, and there are frequent opportunities for girls to take part in major school productions and to enter performing arts festivals. Many study for national qualifications such as LAMDA and ESB awards and take Drama and Theatre Studies to GCSE and A Level.

The Music and Drama departments closely collaborate on many productions.

Sport and Leisure. The main winter sports are lacrosse and netball, and the summer sports are tennis and athletics, but girls have the chance to learn to play many other sports also, including hockey, rounders and golf on the school's own private nine-hole golf course. There are excellent modern sports facilities on site (see Facilities below) and those keen on equestrian sports may take polo lessons at the nearby Beaufort Polo Club and use the local riding school. The school frequently enters teams in equestrian competitions.

Careers Advice. Westonbirt is an accredited Investor in Careers. This award is given only to schools whose careers advice is of the very highest calibre. The Deputy Head, Mark Gluning, plays a very active role in helping pupils choose the most appropriate public examination courses and to gain places at their preferred university. The school's work experience programme begins in Year 11 and continues into the Sixth Form.

Extra-curricular Activities. As well as organising frequent leisure outings at weekends, the school offers many extra-curricular activities with educational value in the broader sense. The school is an ardent supporter of the Young Enterprise Scheme in which participants set up and run their own business for a year and the school's company frequently wins awards. Under the Duke of Edinburgh's Award programme, many pupils pursue Bronze, Silver and Gold standard. The prestigious Leith's Certificate of Food and Wine is a popular sixth form option, and sixth formers may also have driving lessons timetabled for free periods. There are many interesting field trips and outings throughout the year. The 2011 ISI inspection report recognised how *"throughout, pupils' experiences are enriched by an excellent range of visits outside school"*. Recent overseas expeditions have included a sixth form trip to the 'Your Future in

Europe' conference in Paris, a ski trip to Italy and a World Challenge expedition to Southern Peru.

ELT (English Language Training). Although the vast majority of pupils are British, the school has a dedicated ELT Centre staffed by specialists for those whose first language is not English. The Centre offers individual and group coaching and self-help facilities. All overseas girls are taught in the mainstream school for all subjects except ELT, optimising their progress across the board and also ensuring effective integration with the rest of the pupils. The international contingent comes from all over the world, and the school respects and celebrates the cultural variety and cosmopolitan atmosphere that they bring to its community.

Learning Support. For those who need academic help, individual coaching can be arranged in all subjects. Pupils with learning difficulties such as dyslexia benefit from the superb Learning Support Department, and Westonbirt has an excellent track record of helping such girls achieve high academic standards and university entry.

Health Care. The school has its own Sanatorium constantly manned by experienced and sympathetic Sisters, supported by regular surgeries and an on-call service by the school's Medical Officer.

Spirituality. As a Church of England Foundation, Westonbirt School is underpinned by a strong Christian ethos, with morning prayers, evening vespers and Sunday services an important constant in the girls' timetable. Many girls choose to be confirmed, and all are expected to attend school worship as an act of school community, but pupils of other faiths are made to feel welcome and respected. Roman Catholics attend the local RC church regularly.

Facilities. Alongside the magnificent historic buildings at the heart of the school, there are excellent purpose-built facilities to provide for modern educational needs. The Francis Rawes Building includes spacious, airy art studios, well-equipped science laboratories, an extensive computer laboratory, enviable design and technology workshops, and a comfortable lecture theatre.

The school's private 210-acre estate includes extensive sports facilities. There are numerous outdoor pitches, courts and tracks immediately adjacent to the main school buildings, a nine-hole golf course, and the new £3 million Copland Sports Centre with extensive sports hall, with indoor swimming pool, aerobics and dance room and fitness suite.

The self-contained music school includes 22 rehearsal rooms plus the charming Victorian Camellia House, completely restored and refurbished to create a delightful venue for rehearsals and intimate recitals which will be at the heart of the proposed new Music School. There are two pipe organs, one in the Great Hall and one in the School Chapel.

The two-tiered Orangery Theatre, with adjacent Green Room and Rehearsal Room, provides a versatile venue not only for the performing arts but also for special events such as fashion shows, charity events and socials.

The younger girls eat, sleep and socialise within the magnificent setting of Westonbirt House, while Sixth Formers are accommodated in single study bedrooms with shared common rooms, set apart from the main school above the Classroom Courtyard, cleverly converted from the former Carriage House and Stable Block and providing an excellent halfway house to university life. A new modern accommodation block has recently been added due to growth in demand for Sixth Form places. The boarding areas were described by the ISI inspection report as "*attractive and welcoming*". All girls very much enjoy relaxing in the school's Grade I listed historic gardens.

Entrance Requirements. Girls normally join the school at 11, 12, 13 or 16, though they may do so at other ages in special circumstances. At 11+ and 13+ they must sit either the Common Entrance Examination or take the school's own entrance papers, attend an interview with the Headmistress, and provide a reference from their current school. Sixth

Form entrants must have a minimum of 5 GCSEs at grades A*–C including the subjects they intend to study.

Fees per term (2011-2012). Boarding (full & weekly) £7,990–£9,990; Day £5,350–£6,590. The fee is inclusive of tuition, board, lodging, stationery and laundry. Day girls may stay one night per week free of charge and on additional nights for a small fee. The school is renowned for its flexible approach to boarding.

Scholarships and Bursaries. Scholarships are awarded at 11+, 13+ and 16+ entry. Scholarships may be awarded for academic prowess, or for Drama, Art, Music or Sport, or any combination thereof, to a maximum of 25% of the annual tuition fees. Means-tested bursaries may be awarded wherever financial need is proven. Families of Serving Personnel in HM Armed Forces are entitled to a Services Reduction of between 10–20%, depending upon individual circumstances. For the daughters of the Clergy there is a reduction of up to 30% in fees, again depending upon individual circumstances. When sisters are at school together, a 5% reduction from net fees is made for the second sister and a 10% reduction from net fees for the third. Full details are available on request from the Registrar or the Operations Director.

Charitable status. Westonbirt School Limited is a Registered Charity, number 311715. It exists for the education of girls in mind, body and spirit.

Wimbledon High School
GDST

Mansel Road, London SW19 4AB

Tel:	020 8971 0900 (Senior School)
	020 8971 0902 (Junior School)
Fax:	020 8971 0901 (Senior School)
	020 8971 0903 (Junior School)
e-mail:	info@wim.gdst.net
website:	www.wimbledonhigh.gdst.net

Founded 1880.

Wimbledon High School is part of the GDST (Girls' Day School Trust). The GDST is the leading network of independent girls' schools in the UK. As a charity that owns and runs 24 schools and two academies, it reinvests all its income in its schools. For further information about the Trust, see p. xxi or visit www.gdst.net.

Additional information about the school may be found on the school's website. A prospectus may be obtained from the school.

Chairman of the Local Governors: Mrs B Rosewell, MSc

Headmistress: Mrs H Hanbury, MA Edinburgh, MSc Cantab

Deputy Head: Mrs J Mitchell, BSc Bristol

Deputy Head, Pastoral: Miss S Ferro, MA University College London, BA Oxon

Head of Junior School: Miss C Mitchell, MA Oxon

Director of Studies: Mr R Haythorne, MA Oxon

Pupil numbers. Junior School: 324 aged 4–11; Senior School: 580, including 152 in the Sixth Form.

Wimbledon High School combines academic strength with a firm belief that school should be a fun and exciting place in which to learn. Keen to create and embrace new opportunities in girls' education, the school has recently undertaken an entire review of its curriculum and has engaged its Years 10–13 students in a '6 is the best' project, to make WHS the best Sixth Form in London. Students respond to the challenges and responsibilities given them by setting and achieving their own goals. Results at A Level and GCSE are consistently extremely high and students are encouraged to participate in all aspects of school life within a vibrant and enriching extra-curricular programme. Activities include World Challenge, the Model United Nations, the Duke of Edinburgh's Award Scheme alongside music, drama, arts and sports as well as many smaller clubs and societies from Mah Jong to Basketball, that the girls often run themselves.

A secure framework of pastoral care ensures that students are given every chance to be themselves. For Headmistress Heather Hanbury, fostering intellectual resilience and encouraging risk-taking in girls are key aims. Students increasingly gain more responsibility as they move up through the school. Sixth Formers practise leadership through the School Council and by mentoring younger girls; there is a peer counselling service and older students help with Easter revision classes at local schools.

Junior and Senior Schools share one central Wimbledon site, with excellent facilities: a swimming pool and sports hall, Performing Arts Centre and a centre for design and technology. The playing fields are ten minutes' walk away at Nursery Road (the site of the original All England Lawn Tennis and Croquet Club) providing a full-size, all-weather hockey pitch and five netball/tennis courts. The school believes in nurturing all sporting talent and a fit and active lifestyle is encouraged.

The **Junior School** provides a creative and academic education in a happy and stimulating environment – bright, purpose-built accommodation, with specialist rooms for art, ICT and science. There is a balance of class and specialist subject teaching and girls are set clear and challenging targets for their learning. An enriched and extended National Curriculum is the foundation, with the school embracing the 'creative curriculum' encompassing various areas of learning at the same time; French is taught from Year 2. An after-school care programme offers flexibility to working parents.

The **Senior School** curriculum continues the breadth and balance with German or Spanish added alongside French in Year 7 and the addition of Latin in Year 8. Key Stage 3 also includes English and Drama, Mathematics, Combined Sciences (taught separately from Year 9); Humanities (Geography, History and Religious Studies), Art and Technology (including ICT); Music, PE and PSHE (Personal, Social and Health Education).

At Key Stage 4 all girls study English (Language and Literature), Mathematics, three separate sciences and ICT as well as PE, RS and PSHE (non-examined). The girls have a free choice of four other subjects, of which one must be a Modern Foreign Language, with the possibility of adding Classical Greek as a fifth.

In the **Sixth Form** students may choose from the same subjects as on offer at GCSE (except PE – compulsory in Year 12 but non-examined), plus Economics, History of Art, Psychology and Theatre Studies. In Year 12, most take four AS Levels; the majority continue with three A2s in Year 13. A range of enrichment activities is offered, including Critical Thinking and the EPQ. Students may participate in the Young Enterprise scheme. PSHE continues and a comprehensive programme of careers and university entrance advice is offered. Sixth Form House has been recently refurbished.

Admissions. 4+ girls are assessed in groups in a nursery-style environment; indication of a girl's potential is the key at this stage, rather than evidence of what has already been learnt.

7+ girls have a small group interview following formal assessments in English including comprehension and a story, mathematics and non-verbal reasoning.

For 11+ entry, as many applicants as possible are interviewed in the autumn term, prior to the entrance examination (in English, Mathematics and verbal reasoning) in January. The occasional entry examination has a Science paper.

16+ assessment comprises entrance exam and interviews. Offers of places are usually conditional upon GCSE A grades in their chosen AS subjects, and a minimum of seven B grades overall.

Fees per term (2011-2012). Senior School £4,343, Junior School £3,380.

The fees cover the regular curriculum, school books, choral music, games and swimming, but not optional extra subjects.

Scholarships and Bursaries. Academic scholarships are awarded to girls who do exceptionally well in the 11+ exam, worth 5% of the fees. There is also a music scholarship at 11+. At 16+, a separate academic scholarship exam can be taken and there are scholarships in Art, Drama, Music and PE, worth up to 10%. A 16+ science scholarship is worth up to 50%. Details and application forms available on request.

Bursaries take account of academic merit, but all are means tested. The maximum value is the full fee.

Charitable status. Wimbledon High School is part of The Girls' Day School Trust, which is a Registered Charity, number 306983.

Withington Girls' School

Wellington Road, Fallowfield, Manchester M14 6BL
Tel: 0161 224 1077
Fax: 0161 248 5377
e-mail: office@withington.manchester.sch.uk
website: www.withington.manchester.sch.uk

Independent (formerly Direct Grant)
    Founded 1890.
    Motto: *Ad Lucem*

Board of Governors:
Chair: Mrs E Lee, LLB
Mr D Illingworth, BA, FCA (*Hon Treasurer*)
Professor S B Furber, CBE, FRS, FREng, FBCS, CEng, MA, PhD
Mrs V Hempstock, BSc
Mr G Yeung, OBE, BA
Mr C E J Griffiths, MA
Mrs L Sabbagh, BA
Dr J Allred, MB, ChB, MRCGP, DRCOG, DFFP
Mr M Pike, LLB
Mrs F Lloyd
Mrs M McVeigh, MSc
Mrs V Turner, MA, Dip Arch
Miss S Johnson-Manning, GRSM, LRAM, ARCM

Headmistress: Mrs S E Marks, MA Oxon

Deputy Head: Mrs S J Haslam, BA Lancaster (*English*)

Director of Studies: Dr L Earps, PhD Southampton (*Chemistry*)

Bursar: Mrs S Senn, BSc Hull, ACA

Assistant Staff:
Mrs C Air, BA Oxon (*History*)
Mrs J Arthan, BSc Birmingham (*Biology*)
Mrs L D Bailey, BSc Newcastle (*Mathematics*)
Mrs J Baylis, BA Leeds (*Drama & Theatre Studies*)
Mr S Boddy, MA London (*Economics, Politics*)
Miss K L Browning, BA London (*Geography*)
Mrs J Buckley, BA Durham (*Geography*)
Miss C J Davies, MA Open University (*English*)
Miss J E Ellis, BA Bath (*German*)
Mrs M Ferrol, BEd Dunfermline College (*Physical Education*)
Mrs R Fildes, BA Liverpool (*Art*)

Miss S French, BA Manchester (*History*)
Mr K G Hodgson, BSc Sheffield (*Mathematics*)
Ms L Holden, BA Edinburgh (*Classics*)
Miss A R H Holland, BMus Birmingham (*Music*)
Mrs R Lindsay-Dunn, MSc Manchester (*Physics*)
Mr I McKenna, BA Manchester (*Religious Studies*)
Dr S E Madden, PhD Newcastle (*Biology*)
Ms J C Maher, BA Sheffield (*History*)
Dr E A Maisey, PhD London (*Chemistry*)
Mrs Y T Menzies, MA Salford (*French, German*)
Miss B O'Neal, MSc MMU (*Psychology*)
Mrs C Ositelu, DEA-ès-L Nantes (*French*)
Miss A Phillips, MA Manchester (*Mathematics*)
Miss J Richards, BA Liverpool John Moores (*PE & Games*)
Mrs E K Robinson, MA Cantab (*Classics*)
Mrs G E Sargent, BMus London (*Music*)
Mr V Sharples, BA London (*Religious Studies*)
Mrs G A Smith, BSc Nottingham (*Biology, Chemistry*)
Mr A Snowden, BSc Warwick (*ICT*)
Dr C Spinks, PhD Manchester (*Chemistry*)
Mr O Syrus, BA Oxon (*French, German*)
Mrs R Thompson, BA Birmingham (*Spanish*)
Dr D Verity, PhD Hull (*Physics*)
Dr C P G Vilela, PhD Lisbon (*Biology, Chemistry*)
Ms N A West, BA Manchester (*English*)

Junior Department:
Mrs E S K Burrows, MA St Andrews (*Year 6*)
Miss S J Davies, BA Nottingham (*Year 5*)
Mrs H Stallard, BA Newcastle-upon-Tyne (*Year 4*)
Mrs B Lowe, BSc Northumbria (*Year 3*)

Part-time Staff:
Mrs U Asim, BSc UMIST (*Science*)
Mrs J W Bowie, MA Dundee (*English, Psychology*)
Mrs L Bradshaw, BA Cantab (*Physics*)
Mrs F Cotton, BA Edinburgh (*Design & Technology*)
Mrs C E Edge, MA Leeds (*English*)
Mrs S E Fletcher, BEd Brighton (*Physical Education, Mathematics*)
Mrs P M Gavan, BA Open University (*Mathematics*)
Ms A Godwin, BA Oxon (*Spanish*)
Mrs S E Hamilton, MA Aberdeen (*Geography*)
Mrs J Healey, BSc Newcastle (*FTT*)
Mrs J Howling, MA Cantab (*Classics*)
Mrs A Humblet, BA University of Dijon (*French*)
Mrs J Johnson, BA London (*English*)
Mrs K Kelsall, BSc Northumbria (*PE & Games*)
Mrs V Kochhar, BSc Exeter (*Mathematics*)
Mrs R E Lamey, MEng Oxon (*Mathematics*)
Ms M Lopez, BSc Pennsylvania (*Spanish*)
Mrs J Manning, BA Newcastle (*History/Cover*)
Miss D J McGann, BA York (*English*)
Miss J McManus, BE Ireland (*ICT*)
Mrs Z Taylor, BA MMU (*Art*)
Dr E L Terrill, PhD Oxon (*Mathematics*)
Mrs J L Walker, BA Manchester (*History*)
Mrs J C Wallis, BA Leeds (*Politics*)

Librarians:
Mrs A Wells, BA, MCLIP Bolton
Mrs D Sutton, MA Manchester
Network Manager: Mr A Lockett, BSc Bradford
School Nurse: Mrs M McNeill, RGN
Examinations Officer: Dr Y E Walls, PhD Bangor
Development Director: Miss C Flynn, BA Durham
Development Officer: Mrs L Firth, MA Manchester

Administration:
PA to Headmistress: Mrs A Adshead
School Secretary: Mrs A Easton
Financial Secretary: Mrs L Bennett

Since its foundation in 1890, Withington has remained relatively small, with about 650 pupils, 90 of whom are in the Junior Department and 160 in the Sixth Form. This size allows a friendly, intimate environment together with a broad and balanced curriculum. Withington provides a wide range of opportunities for girls, helping them to achieve their potential, academically, socially and personally. Withington attracts pupils from a wide geographical area and from many different social and cultural backgrounds, producing a diversity in which the school rejoices.

The School's A Level and GCSE results have been consistently outstanding. Girls who gain a place as a result of the entrance examination take at least 10 GCSE subjects, 4 AS Levels, 3 or 4 A2 Levels together with A Level General Studies. Studies are directed towards knowledge for its own sake as well as towards University entrance, including Oxford and Cambridge. All the girls go on to Higher Education.

The School enjoys excellent facilities and has an ongoing programme of major developments. Recent projects have included a new classroom wing, new Science Laboratories, enhanced Language and Music facilities and a new Sixth Form Centre (2009).

Withington fosters all-round development and the academic work is complemented by an extensive range of extracurricular activities. Music is strong and very popular; there is a comprehensive range of choirs and orchestras, involving all age groups. Drama also thrives with regular productions including original works. Girls play a variety of sports, including hockey, lacrosse, netball, tennis, athletics, cricket and football. Pupils are regularly selected for county and national squads and there are regular sports tours within Europe and further afield. In addition to fixtures with other schools, games players compete within the school's House system. The four Houses, named after Withington's founders, also provide a focus for dramatic, musical and other activities.

The Duke of Edinburgh's Award and Young Enterprise Schemes, Model United Nations Conferences, voluntary work in the local community, Science and Mathematics Olympiads, residential activity weekends, foreign trips and local fieldwork all feature prominently in the school's provision. Numerous extra-curricular clubs and societies include Italian, photography, bridge, literature, debating, mosaics, robotics, aeromix, chess, fencing and dance. Awareness of the wider world is encouraged, girls participate in many fundraising activities and the School has special links with a hospital and two schools in Kenya and a school in Uganda. Each December a party of girls depart for community projects in The Gambia; in 2011 an expedition will also depart to Tanzania. Preparation for life after school starts early and involves a programme of careers advice, work experience and UCAS guidance.

Visitors are warmly welcomed at any time. Open Days are held in November. A number of means-tested Governors' Bursaries are awarded annually together with awards from various outside Trusts. Entrance at age 7–11 is by Entrance Examination, held in January, together with interview and report from current school. Admission to the Sixth Form is by interview and is conditional upon GCSE results.

The School engages in a number of projects with local State schools and has strong links with the local community. Withington was The Sunday Times Parent Power Top Independent Secondary School of the Year 2009/10.

Fees per term (2011-2012). Senior School £3,190, Junior School £2,380. LAMDA and individual instrumental music lessons are charged separately.

Charitable status. Withington Girls' School is a Registered Charity, number 526632. It aims to provide an exceptional quality of opportunity, to encourage independence of mind and high aspirations for girls from seven to eighteen.

Woldingham School

Marden Park, Woldingham, Surrey CR3 7YA
Tel: 01883 349431
Fax: 01883 348653
e-mail: registrar@woldinghamschool.co.uk
website: www.woldinghamschool.co.uk

Independent School for Girls aged 11–18.

Chairman of Governors: Mr Richard Stone, MA Cantab, FCA

Headmistress: Mrs J Triffitt, MA Oxon

Deputy Head: Mr N Waite, BSc Bristol

Bursar: Mr G Hunt

Registrar: Mrs L Underwood

Director of Pastoral Care: Mrs J Brown, BEd CNAA

Director of Studies: Mr D Murphy, BA, MSc, MPhil, DPhil Oxon

Assistant Head: Mr D Murtagh, BSc Southampton, MA London

Head of Sixth Form: Mrs F Kennedy, BA Oxon

Marketing & Development Director: Mrs C Saldanha, BA OU

Teaching Staff:
Mr S Baird, BSc Edinburgh (*Head of Geography*)
Mrs A Benton, BA Camberwell Art School, ATC London (*Head of Art*)
Mrs V Brown, BA Latvia (*Head of German*)
Mrs K Connor, BSc East Anglia (*Head of Physics*)
Mrs P Frisby, BA Keele, MA OU Adv Dip SEN (*Head of Learning Enhancement*)
Mr J Hargreaves, BA York (*Head of Music*)
Mrs A James, BSc UCL (*Head of Biology*)
Mrs A Lewis, BA equiv, MA equiv France (*Head of French*)
Mr R MacLean, BSc Cass, MSc Durham (*Head of Economics*)
Mrs L Mann, Dip Drama Middlesex (*Head of Drama*)
Mr A McGreevy, BSc Liverpool, MA IoE (*Head of ICT*)
Mrs Y Mulhern, BA Madrid, CertEd Oxford Brookes (*Head of Spanish*)
Miss A O'Neill, BEd London (*Head of Personal, Social & Health Education*)
Mr H Patterson, BA Bristol (*Head of History*)
Mrs K Payne, BA Dunelm (*Head of Politics*)
Mrs M Peake, BA Keele, MBA London Business School (*Head of Careers and Higher Education*)
Dr A Petzold, BA Manchester, DPhil Courtauld (*Head of Art History*)
Mr P Price, BSc UEA (*Head of Science*)
Mrs J Taylor, MA SOAS, London (*Japanese*)
Mrs J Tower, BEd CNAA (*Head of PE*)
Mrs J Vivian, BA Wales, MEd Newcastle (*Head of English*)
Mr D Wahab, BA Brighton (*Head of Design & Technology*)
Mrs M Walmsley, BA Birmingham (*Head of EAL*)
Miss R Williams, BA Twickenham (*Head of RE*)
Mrs E Williamson, BA Birmingham, MA Western Ontario, LLB London (*Head of Classics*)
Mrs C Sinclair, MA Oxon (*Head of Mathematics*)

Foundation. Founded in 1842 by the Society of the Sacred Heart, the school has been sited at Woldingham since 1945. Today, under lay management, Woldingham is part of the international network of Sacred Heart schools.

Woldingham is a leading independent Catholic girls' boarding and day school and provides a caring and supportive Christian community in which girls are happy, confident and inspired to meet challenges and to achieve excellence in whatever they choose to do. We encourage our girls to become independent, enquiring young women who forge lasting relationships, achieve academic success and become positive influences in the world they will enter.

Situation and Buildings. Woldingham is situated south east of London, inside the M25. The school is 35 minutes from London by train. Journey times to Gatwick and Heathrow airports are 20 and 45 minutes respectively. A stunning Jacobean house is the centre piece of the idyllic setting in a designated Area of Outstanding Natural Beauty. An intensive yet sympathetic buildings programme has now furnished the school with some of the most impressive facilities of any school or university in the country.

The Millennium Centre for the Performing Arts boasts state-of-the-art facilities. These include a 600-seat auditorium with orchestra pit, industry standard sound and lighting control rooms, scenery construction dock, wardrobe room for costume and prop construction and a fully-equipped studio theatre. In addition, the Centre hosts a Recital room, a Mac Suite, keyboard studio, String and Woodwind rooms, numerous practice rooms and an exceptional eight-track digital recording studio. The purpose-built Art department comprises two large 2D studios, facilities for printmaking and a superb 3D area equipped with a range of power tools and two kilns. Design Technology is taught in a fully-equipped workshop and studio, using state-of-the-art computer-controlled machinery. The Sports Centre includes a Sports Hall, 2 squash courts, fully-equipped Fitness Studio and a Dance/Gymnastics studio. In addition there are extensive outdoor playing areas, an indoor tennis dome, an indoor swimming pool and an all-weather pitch.

Boarding accommodation is impressive. Shanley House, the Upper Sixth centre, is a modern block with en-suite accommodation. Berwick House is the Lower Sixth centre and provides single room accommodation. All girls from Year 10 have single study bedrooms in Main House. Marden House is a small, friendly junior house with welcoming accommodation for the first two years. A major refurbishment during the Summer of 2011 has seen a further 4 classrooms built at Marden House, as well as a fully upgraded dining and kitchen area for students and staff.

Size. The school accommodates over 500 girls within the 11–18 age range, some 300 of whom are boarders. 60% of boarders are from families living in London and Home Counties and 10% come from overseas. Approximately 25% of the intake are of nationalities other than British; these students enrich the school by bringing to it an international dimension and outlook.

Pastoral Care. This is a key strength of the school. In each year care of the boarding side of the school life is the responsibility of the Head of Year, who acts in loco parentis and ensures that each girl is known and cared for as an individual. The Head of Year is assisted by a deputy and academic Tutors each of whom is responsible for the girls' individual guidance. Buddy schemes ensure that girls provide support for each other.

Curriculum. All girls take a common course for the first two years. Year 7 students take Latin and one of French, German or Spanish. In Year 9 girls are asked to choose three of their two creative subjects (Art, Music, DT and Drama) and two of their three languages. At this point Latin becomes an optional subject. Japanese becomes available as an option in Year 9.

It is expected that the majority of Years 10 and 11 girls will follow a total of 10 (occasionally 9) GCSE courses. The aim is to provide a broad and balanced curriculum for all up to the age of 16. All students take GCSE courses in English Language and Literature, Mathematics, Religious Education and at least one Modern Foreign Language. Science is also compulsory; most girls take it as a double GCSE subject, although a sizable minority sit separate papers in Biology, Chemistry and Physics. As options, girls are recommended to choose an overall combination of subjects which includes Geography or History, plus one creative or practical subject, including ICT and Physical Education. Health Education is studied by all students in Years 7–9, but is not examined. Students in all year groups have weekly PSHE sessions.

In the Sixth Form, girls study four AS Levels in the L6th and three A2 Levels in the U6th leading to three full A Levels and one AS qualification. A very small number of girls, usually those pursuing Further Mathematics, take five AS and four A2 Levels. Critical Thinking is available as a fifth AS subject for the more academically able students in the Lower Sixth. All students in the U6 follow a General Studies programme and a twelve week course called IDEAS, which helps to develop their research and presentation skills. All Sixth Formers have Physical Education lessons.

A Level pass rate is 100% with 85% A & B grades. The school bucks the national trend in uptake of Science, Economics and Mathematics. Girls also achieve outstanding results in Humanities and Languages. The School also has a Gifted and Talented Programme, a Tutor to the Scholars and an Oxbridge Coordinator in place to provide specialist support and guidance.

All leavers go to university or the equivalent, some to Oxbridge and many to Russell Group universities.

Careers Guidance. The School attaches great importance to careers guidance. There is a well-staffed and stocked Careers Room with a wide range of materials available, including computer programmes helping students identify strengths, interests and options.

Music. Woldingham is well known for its strong and lively tradition of music. Over half the students play a musical instrument; there is a full school orchestra, a string orchestra, two wind bands and three choirs. School musical productions, public concerts and the church's liturgical celebrations provide scope for a variety of talent and performance. A new Mac suite provides for Music Technology learning, as well as composition using the Sibelius package.

Drama. Drama is run by dedicated professionals and is very impressive here. Girls are involved in local and professional theatre and may go on to become specialists in their chosen field of Drama.

Art. Everyone takes Art for the first two years, developing creative and imaginative powers and acquiring a visual language, with the option to specialise at GCSE or A Level. On offer are drawing, painting, sculpture, ceramics, textile design, printmaking and photography. Our students visit St Ives and this provides an excellent opportunity for working with local artists in their studios, and also the Tate and Hepworth Museums there.

Sport. There is a full fixture list of inter-school matches and girls are regularly selected for County and National Competitions. Sports such as Pop Lacrosse, Water Polo and Body Combat are also offered.

International Exchanges. Close links exist with Sacred Heart schools abroad. There is an excellent exchange programme to France and Spain and an annual German trip.

Extra-Curricular Activities. Each term all boarders (and day girls who choose to do so) select options from the wide variety of indoor and outdoor activities available at weekends. Saturday morning features a packed programme of activities, "Saturday Active", run by professionals in their field. On offer is clay pigeon shooting, polo, fencing and cookery, amongst others. The Duke of Edinburgh's Award Scheme is well-established; participants, and other girls, are regular helpers at local hospitals and centres for disabled people. The vigorous Debating Society has a successful record of achievement in inter-school competitions. Theatre visits and other short outings are very popular; several overseas tours for different age groups complement work done in class. There is also an established CCF programme.

Exeats. Girls are allowed home most weekends from Saturday midday. There are two long weekends (from Friday evening) each term.

Health. There is an excellent Health Centre which has two resident nurses. Two doctors, a dentist and a physiotherapist attend regularly. There is a Health Education programme which emphasises healthy living. Our Wellness Centre provides support and a positive approach to matters of health.

Admissions. Main entry to Woldingham is via the Woldingham School examination in December for 13+, November for 11+ and October for 16+ applicants.

Students wishing to join the Sixth Form should be capable of taking at least four AS and three A2 courses and should have passed eight or more subjects at GCSE, 6 of which must be at least grade B, including Maths and English (grade A in Sixth Form options).

Applicants for occasional vacant places in other year groups are also required to sit the school's own entrance examination.

Scholarships. Academic, Art, Music, Drama and Sport scholarships are offered at 11+, 13+ and Sixth Form.

Fees per term (2011-2012). Boarders: £9,470; Day £5,925.

Charitable status. Woldingham School is a Registered Charity, number 1125376. It exists for the education of girls.

Wychwood School

74 Banbury Road, Oxford OX2 6JR
Tel: 01865 557976
Fax: 01865 556806
e-mail: admin@wychwood-school.org.uk
website: www.wychwood-school.org.uk

Staff List:

Headmistress: Mrs S Wingfield Digby, MA Oxon, PGCE

Deputy: Ms B Sherlock, BA, MEd

Mrs A Bennett-Jones, BSc, PGCE (*Mathematics*)
Miss J Bettridge, TESOLCert (*EFL, Dance*)
Ms M Bridgman, LDS (*Textiles*)
Miss V Castel, BEd Hons, OTT QTS (*Spanish, French*)
Mrs C Chalstrey, BA Hons, PGCE (*RS, History*)
Mrs C Collcutt, DEUG (*French*)
Mrs H Corkhill, BEd Hons (*History*)

Mrs S Cripps, MA Cantab, PGCE (*Chemistry*)
Mrs B Walster (*Music*)
Mrs L Doughton, BSc Hons, MA (*Biology*)
Mrs E Forrester, BSc Hons, PGCE (*Geography*)
Mrs B Stevens (*Mathematics*)
Mrs J Gregory-Newman, BA QTS, BSc (*Business Studies*)
Mrs G Hale, MA Cantab, PGCE (*English Support*)
Ms S Jones, BA Hons, PGCE (*Drama*)
Ms A Jones, BA Hons, PGCE (*Art & Design*)
Mrs P M Jones, BSc Hons, MTh, PGCE (*Physics*)
Mrs H Kirby, BA Hons, PGCE (*English*)
Mrs M Nash, BA Hons, PGCE (*Psychology*)
Miss R Odlin, BSc Hons, PGCE (*PE, Sports Studies*)
Mr M Pennington (*Photography*)
Miss B Sherlock, BA, MEd (*English*)
Mr G Singh, BSc Hons, PGCE (*ICT, Network*)
Mrs E Dean (*English*)
Mrs J Williams, BA Hons, PGCE, SRN, RSCN (*History of Art*)

School Secretary: Mrs S Grainger
Admissions Secretary: Mrs E Plint
Bursar: Mrs A E Drake-Brockman
Housemistress, Head of Boarding: Mrs L Henk
Assistant Housemistress: Miss R Dales
School Doctor: Dr K Howie, MA, BM, BCh, MRCGP, DRCOG, DGM, DCH
School Counsellor: Mrs M Davies

Wychwood School was established in 1897. It is a Charitable Trust set up for educational purposes and has 150 girls (ages 11–18), of whom about 50 are boarders. It offers small classes taught by qualified staff. Extra-curricular activities are a regular feature of the extended day and the school takes advantage of its central Oxford location.

Curriculum. All girls are expected to take up to 9 subjects at GCSE; most go on to work for AS and A2 and University entrance. The lower school curriculum includes: Religious Education, English, History, Geography, Mathematics, Biology, Physics, Chemistry, French, ICT, Textiles, Ceramics, Singing, Art, Photography, Dance, Music, Computing, PSE, Gymnastics, Spanish (from Year 9), Drama, Swimming and Games. Visiting staff teach other optional foreign languages and musical instruments; there is a school choir and chamber groups.

School Council. Day-to-day life is largely controlled by the School Council which meets weekly and consists of staff, seniors (elected by the school) and form representatives. This is a type of cooperative government, the matured result of a long series of experiments, which trains the girls to deal with the problems of community life and gives everyone, in greater or lesser degree according to her age and status, an understanding of, and a voice in, the rules necessary for a sensibly disciplined life.

Sixth Form. Members of the Sixth Form have considerable freedom yet play an active part in the life of the school. The choice of subjects at AS and A2 is wide, and classes are small and stimulating. Individual help with university applications and careers is a key feature of the Sixth Form. There are regular outside speakers and girls attend a variety of lectures, conferences, exhibitions and meetings. Their participation in school plays and concerts as well as School Council is greatly valued. Sixth Form girls may spend approximately 2 hours per week on community service. Optional computer courses are run after school. Sixth Form boarders have individual study bedrooms.

Conditions of Entrance. (*See Scholarship Entries section.*) A personal interview is usually essential between the Headmistress and both a parent and the pupil, though this may be waived where circumstances make it impossible. There is an entrance test to satisfy the staff that the girl will benefit from an education of this kind; the opinion of the girl's former school is also taken into account, particularly in relation to non-academic qualities. Scholarships are offered in creative arts, art, music, science and academic areas.

Fees per term (2011-2012). Boarders £6,250, Weekly Boarders £5,945, Day Girls £3,840.

Charitable status. Wychwood School is a Registered Charity, number 309684. It exists for the education of girls from the ages of 11 to 18.

Wycombe Abbey School

High Wycombe, Bucks HP11 1PE
Tel: 01494 520381
Fax: 01494 473836
e-mail: schoolsecretary@wycombeabbey.com
website: www.wycombeabbey.com

Founded in 1896.
Motto: *In Fide Vade*

Council:
President: The Rt Hon The Lord Carrington, KG, GCMG, CH, MC, JP, PC

Vice-Presidents:
Mrs C M Archer, BA
Mr W P W Barnes, MA
Mr A K Stewart-Roberts, MA
Mr A M D Willis, LLB, FCIArb

Chairman of the Council: Mr P P Sherrington, LLB, LLM, FCIArb

Lady Sassoon, MA
Mr P E B Cawdron, FCA
Mr Keith Oates, MSc, BSc Econ, LLD, DSc
The Rt Hon Sir Anthony May
Dr C A Seville, MA, BMus, LLM, PhD
Mr R N Strathon, MA, FRICS
Air Vice-Marshal T B Sherrington, CB, OBE
Mrs Penelope Lenon, BA
Mrs Gordon Hamilton, MA
Mrs Sue Singer, BA
Ms C Riley, MB, BA, MA, DBA
Miss Sue Carr, QC
Dr S V M Hordern, MBBS, BSc, MRCP, MD
Mr D P Lillycrop, LLB, FCMI
The Rt Revd Dr Alan Wilson, MA, DPhil, Bishop of Buckingham
Mrs Diana Rose, MA
Dr L Fawcett, MA, DPhil

Senior Management Team:

Headmistress: Mrs C L Hall, MA Oxon

Deputy Head: Mrs R Tear, BSc Exeter, PGCE London
Senior Housemistress: Mrs E C Best, BA Exeter
Director of Studies: Dr G Moodie, BA, MA, Dip Arts Otago, New Zealand, PhD Bristol
School Bursar and Clerk to the Council: Mr J C O Luke, CBE, BSc London
Development Director: Mrs B M Armitage, MInstF
Director of Admissions: Mrs S P Mathers, MA Open, PGCE London
Director of Higher Education and Careers: Miss E Boswell, MA Oxon, PGCE Roehampton

Senior Team (Curriculum):
Mrs R Tear, BSc Exeter, PGCE London (*Deputy Head*)
Dr G Moodie, BA, MA, Dip Arts Otago, New Zealand, PhD Bristol (*Director of Studies*)
Miss E Boswell, MA Oxon, PGCE Roehampton (*Director of Higher Education and Careers*)
Mr A Pawlowicz (*Director of IT*)

Miss K Fox, BA Hull, MA Cantab, QTS (*Head of Sixth Form and Clarence*)
Mrs S Jones, BSc Dunelm, PGCE Oxon (*Head of Science*)
Miss R A Keens, BEd IM Marsh College of PE Liverpool (*Director of Sport*)

Housemistresses Senior Team (Pastoral):
Senior Housemistress: Mrs E C Best, BA Exeter
Pitt: Miss L Aherne, BA Oxon, PGCE Exeter (*Geography*)
Rubens: Miss M Wrinch, BA UCL, MSc Reading, PGCE Oxford (*French and German*)
Airlie: Mrs P Harrison, CertEd Liverpool, MIPM (*Mathematics*)
Barry: Mrs A Spillman, BA Open, BSc Exeter, PGCE Greenwich (*Mathematics, Psychology*)
Butler: Mrs A Buxadé del Tronco, BA Southampton, PGCE Belfast, CPP Roehampton (*English, French, Spanish*)
Campbell: Dr A Yuasa, BA Oxon, PhD Reading, PGCE Cantab (*Music*)
Cloister: Mrs A Clee, BA Central England, QTS Wolverhampton (*ICT*)
Shelburne: Mrs S Jenkins, CertEd West Midlands, DipEd Reading, CPP Roehampton (*Physical Education*)
Wendover: Miss S B Lafford, BSc Bristol, PGCE London (*Biology*)
Junior House: Mrs S Stevens-Wood, BSc, PGCE Manchester (*Biology*)
Clarence Senior Academic Tutors:
Miss A Wallace, MA, MPhil Cantab, PGCE Oxon (*History*)
Dr J Ryder, MPhys Oxford, DPhil Oxford (*Mathematics*)

Chaplain: The Revd J Chaffey, MA Oxon, BA Dunelm

Heads of Department:
English: Mrs J M McPherson, BA Western Australia, MA Sydney, DipEd Edith Cowan, Australia
Mathematics: Mrs H Warnick, BA Oxon, PGCE West Sussex
Science & Physics: Mrs S Jones, BSc Dunelm, PGCE Oxon
Chemistry: Mrs Z Edwards, BSc St Andrews, PGCE Dunelm
Biology: Mr M Whiteley, BA Cantab, PGCE Canterbury
Modern Languages and French: Miss S Landsmann, Licence d'anglais La Sorbonne Nouvelle, PGCE Reading
German: Mrs N Wase, MA Cantab, MSc UCL, PGCE Oxford Brookes
Spanish: Ms E Pique, MA Langues Etrangères et Appliquées (Droit et Commerce) Montpellier, PGCE Cardiff
Classics: Miss S Lui, MA Oxon, PGCE Cantab
Religious Studies: Mrs A Khan, MA, PGCE Oxon
History: Dr S Tullis, BA DPhil PGCE Oxon, MLitt St Andrews
History of Art: Mr D Evans, BA Manchester
Geography: Mrs E King, BSc Lancaster, PGCE Cantab
Economics: Mrs J Sutcliffe, BA Tufts USA, PGCE Manchester
Information Technology: Mr A Porter, BSc, PGCE East Anglia, MA Reading, MBCS
Art, Design and Technology: Miss F Clark, BA Goldsmiths College London, PGCE London
Drama: Miss C Livesey, BEd Cantab, AGSM Guildhall
Director of Music: Mr L Tubb, BA Oxon, ABRSM
Director of Sport: Miss R A Keens, BEd IM Marsh College of PE, Liverpool
Head of Physical Education: Miss K Bennett, BSc, MSc Loughborough
Personal, Social, Health and Citizenship Education Coordinator: Mrs J Wright, BA Thames Valley, PGCE KCL, MA Brunel
Examinations Officer: Mrs L Armstrong-Smith
Director of Higher Education and Careers: Miss E Boswell, MA Oxon, PGCE Roehampton

Careers and Work Experience Coordinator: Mr P Kelly, BA Manchester, PGCE Exeter
Learning Support Coordinator: Mrs K J Kuhlmey, BA AKC London, PGCE Cantab
Librarian/Archivist: Mrs C Cunningham, BSc London, MSc Loughborough
Performing Arts Centre: Dr G Bates, BSc Bath, PhD Aberdeen

A full and up-to-date staff list can be seen on our website in the 'Contact' section.

Numbers on roll. 566 Girls: 530 Boarding; 36 Day Girls.
Age range. 11–18.
Aims. Wycombe Abbey aims to provide an education in the widest sense and our pursuit of academic excellence goes hand in hand with our commitment to pastoral care. We believe the welfare and happiness of every girl to be paramount. Each individual is encouraged to achieve her full potential; she receives first-class academic teaching and has the opportunity to discover and develop her talents – artistic, creative, musical, sporting. She also learns to take responsibility for herself and to have respect for others. It is an intrinsic part of the School ethos that girls care for each other and offer service to the community.

Location. Near the centre of High Wycombe, five minutes' drive from the M40.

Buildings. The School buildings are all within the extensive grounds of 160 acres which include playing fields, woods, gardens and a lake.

Boarding Houses. There is a Junior House for UIII. At LIV, girls move to one of nine Houses where they remain until the end of the Lower Sixth. In the final year all girls move to the Upper Sixth House where they are encouraged to prepare for university life.

Religion. Wycombe Abbey is a Church of England foundation with its own Chapel. All girls attend morning prayers and a Sunday Service. (Roman Catholic girls can attend Mass and Jewish girls may receive instruction from a Rabbi.) Christian principles inform the whole ethos of the School and a resident Chaplain oversees spiritual matters and plays a central role in pastoral care.

Curriculum. The Lower School curriculum includes the study of English, English Literature, History, Geography, Religious Studies, French, German, Spanish, Latin, Greek, Mathematics, Biology, Chemistry, Physics, Information Technology, Design and Technology, Art, Cookery, Drama, Music, Singing, Personal, Social and Health Education and PE. In the Sixth Form, Economics, History of Art, Classical Civilisation, Government and Politics, Psychology and Physical Education are also available. Critical Thinking AS is compulsory. Girls are prepared for the IGCSE, GCSE, AS and A2 Level examinations, Pre-U and for university entrance. Girls proceed to leading universities in the UK with about 35–40% going to Oxbridge and a handful to America.

Teaching facilities are very good and have been extended and upgraded over recent years.

Physical Education. The School has excellent outdoor facilities, including five lacrosse pitches, a full-size multi-purpose floodlit Astroturf pitch, an athletics track and twenty tennis courts which can be used for netball in the winter. The Davies Sports Centre is a state-of-the-art sports complex including a six-lane 25m swimming pool, well-equipped fitness suite and four glass-backed squash courts. Girls are taught lacrosse, netball, tennis, athletics, swimming, gymnastics and dance. A huge range of extra-curricular sports and activities is also available.

Music. There is a strong tradition of music-making with outstanding facilities for tuition and for recitals. About three-quarters of the girls study at least one musical instrument and are taught by a large team of visiting specialists who provide tuition in a wide range of instruments, including voice. There are many opportunities for performing in orchestras and ensembles. In addition, there is a strong tradition of singing; the Chapel choir plays a central role in Chapel worship and undertakes biennial overseas tours.

Drama. As well as Class Drama, GCSE and A Level Drama, extra-curricular Speech and Drama lessons are also available from Year 8 in groups of approximately six girls and from Year 10 in pairs or solo. LAMDA examinations take place in the fully-equipped 436-seater proscenium arch theatre and generally culminate in a Grade 8 Gold Medal in the final year. There are extra-curricular production opportunities at various points throughout the year, several girls annually get into the National Youth Theatre and alumnae include Naomi Frederick, Rachel Stirling and Polly Stenham.

Art, Craft, Design & Technology. Girls can pursue their interests in these subjects at weekends when the studios are open, as well as in curriculum time. Both our Artist-in-Residence and visiting artists provide workshops at weekends to give girls a broad experience in the subject.

Other Activities. A wide range of clubs and societies, usually led by girls, are very popular as are the numerous social events with leading boys' schools.

Fees per term (2011-2012). The fees for boarders are £10,200 (£7,650 for day boarders). They are inclusive and cover, in addition to the subjects and activities already mentioned, lectures, concerts, most textbooks and stationery.

Admission. Girls are admitted at the age of 11 or 13. Application should be made well in advance. The suggested procedure is given in the prospectus information booklet.

Sixth Form Entry: Competitive entry by examination for a limited number of places. Application must be made by the September preceding entry.

Scholarships. For details relating to Scholarships, please refer to the appropriate scholarship section.

Charitable status. The Girls' Education Company Limited is a Registered Charity, number 310638. Its aim is the provision of first class education for girls.

Wykeham House School

East Street, Fareham, Hampshire PO16 0BW
Tel: 01329 280178
Fax: 01329 823964
e-mail: office@wykehamhouse.com
website: www.wykehamhouse.com

Motto: *Vouloir C'est Pouvoir*

Trustees:
Chairman: Mr P D Jones, BA Hons Arch, DipArch, RIBA
Mrs L Hayes, BSc Hons (*Treasurer*)
Mr D Arthur
Dr F Baber, GP
Mr J Charles, BA Hons, BSc Econ, DipEd
Revd S Davenport
Mrs C A Freemantle, BEd Hons
Mr J B Fullarton, FCA
Mrs S Heaysman
Mr D Luckett, MBE, JP
Miss H A Tyler, LLB Hons
Mr G Wheeler, LLB Hons

Staff:
Headmistress: Mrs L R Clarke, BSc Hons, PGCE, PGDip Nottingham

Deputy Headmistress: Mrs J R Caddy, BEd Hons King Alfred's, Winchester
Head of Senior School: Miss H Wilson, BEd Hons Chichester Inst of HE
Head of Junior School: Mrs C Greenwell, BA Hons, PGCE King Alfred's, Winchester

Bursar: Mr D Bryant

Full-Time Staff:
Miss C Ball, NNEB
Mrs J Corrigan, BA Hons Chichester Inst of HE
Mr S Dearden, BSc Leeds, PGCE, Loughborough College
Mrs J Disley, BSc Hons Aberdeen, PGCE King's College, London
Mrs C Flack, BEd Hons Westminster College, Oxford
Mr P Gago, BEd, Hons Sunderland Polytechnic
Mrs A P Jones, BA Hons, PGCE Portsmouth
Mr D Jones, BMus Hons UCW Cardiff, QTS
Mr D Robertson, BA, Hons, PGDip Duncan of Jordanstone, PGCE Strathclyde
Mrs J Shaw, NVQ Level 3

Part-Time Staff:
Mrs A Bailey, BA Hons Exeter, MA Portsmouth, PGCE Bath
Mrs S Beacon, BA Hons Exeter, PGCE St Mary's College, Twickenham
Mrs J A Briggs, BA Open, PGCE LSU Southampton
Mrs J Bristowe, BEd Rolle College, Devon
Mrs S Cross, BA Hons, PGCE Reading
Mrs L Jones, CertEd Portsmouth, BA Hons Open
Mrs E Kay, CertEd LSU Southampton
Mrs G Kennard, BEd Hons Sussex
Mrs P Knight, BSc, PGCE Surrey
Mrs D Leighton, BA Hons Portsmouth, CertEd, CertEd FE London
Mrs K Lincoln, BA Hons Sunderland, PGCE Southlands College, Wimbledon
Mrs M I Menendez, MA, BA Oviedo, Spain, PGCE Portsmouth
Mrs C E Noyce, BSc Hons, PGCE Bristol
Revd C R Prestidge, BEd Hons West Sussex Inst of HE, BA Hons Open, Dip Ministry and Mission Surrey STETS
Mrs M Reverse-Hayes, Licence d'enseignments France, PGCE, MA Ed Southampton
Mrs A M Taylor, MA, PGCE St Andrews
Mrs J Thimbleby, BSc Hons Manchester, PGCE Southampton
Miss A Todd, BSc Hons Southampton, PGCE Portsmouth

Classroom Assistant:
Mrs J French

Visiting Staff:
Mr M Brown, PDip Composition and Music
Miss C Draycott, LLB Hons Middlesex, FE TCert Chichester College, DIP ABRSM Flute Perf
Mrs J Flatman, LRSM, BA Hons, PGCE
Mrs L Heathorn
Mrs L Knapman, LLAM
Mrs D Laycock (*Netball Coach*)
Miss K Richardson (*Asst Netball Coach*)
Mr G Walker

Headmistress's Secretary: Mrs L J Colbeck
School Administrator: Mrs M C Traynor
Assistant School Secretary: Mrs B M Rollo, NNEB

Wykeham House School in Fareham has a reputation for outstanding pastoral care, excellent results and a dedication to small class sizes and individual attention. A day school for girls aged 3 to 16 in the heart of Fareham, Wykeham House was praised in its most recent Independent Schools Inspectorate Report for its high standard of education and outstanding pastoral care. The report complimented the teachers and the girls alike on their hard work, creativity and sense of fun. The Nursery at Wykeham House has also received an outstanding self-review from Hampshire County Council.

The School's concept of education extends beyond the classroom with the aim of developing self-confident, self-disciplined and motivated girls. The excellent facilities at the School provide the opportunity to take part in art, music, drama, sport and other outdoor activities and emphasis is placed on courtesy and concern for others.

The Junior School (3 to 11 years) has an individuality of its own which contributes greatly to the School's atmosphere and the sense of community. All the usual activities which are taught at Primary level are covered by the Junior Curriculum. The teaching methods employed place an emphasis on the acquisition of the basic skills of Literacy and Numeracy. Full opportunities are given for creative work, self-expression and individual development.

The Foundation Stage, which incorporates the Nursery and Reception classes, is in its own self-contained unit within the School and provides a happy and caring environment for the girls. It has its own indoor and outdoor play areas, including an outdoor classroom, as well as having the advantage of being able to use the exceptional facilities at the School.

At the age of 9+ girls are introduced to a number of specialist teachers who teach across a wide curriculum leading to the 11+ Entrance. This helps to ensure a smooth transition to the Senior School.

The Senior School (11–16 years). The curriculum aims to maintain standards and yet recognises the need to keep apace of educational developments and modern teaching techniques. The Curriculum is under constant review by the Headmistress and the Staff Committee. Specialist rooms and well-equipped laboratories and computer facilities are available; a set of laptops is also available for use throughout the curriculum, as well as interactive whiteboards.

The subjects taught in the Senior School cover a broad curriculum leading to GCSE.

An options system is in existence from Year 9 but all pupils take English, Mathematics, a Modern Language, Science (either the separate subjects of Physics, Chemistry and Biology or as a double award) and a short course in RS, Philosophy and Ethics in their GCSE examinations. Private study periods are included in the option groups to encourage individual study skills and full use is made of the School Library and all girls study PSHE and have PE.

Visits are undertaken to theatres, museums, art galleries, and other places of interest. Field work is an integral part of the study of Humanities and in Science while Modern Language study involves visits to Europe. Lecturers and performers are invited to the School while the girls are encouraged to take part in Music, Art and Drama as well as other leisure pursuits.

Senior girls participate in the Duke of Edinburgh's Award Scheme. In this way they test their own initiative, discover fresh challenging pursuits, make new friends and become aware of the needs of others.

Many activities occur during lunch times and after school such as the mathematics workshop, computer clubs, games practices, school choirs, instrumental groups, dramatic productions, first aid, cookery and dancing.

A member of the staff is responsible for careers advice in the School and there is an extensive library of careers literature freely available. Each girl is interviewed and receives information and advice on her own choice of career from the local Careers Advisory Officer who visits the School. Close contact is maintained with local sixth form colleges, further education colleges and other schools in the area.

The pastoral system is organised on a House basis: the girls belong to four School Houses where the year groups mix socially and competitively.

Physical Education. The School supplements its Games facilities by hiring nearby local amenities.

Netball, Hockey, Tennis, Rounders and Athletics form the basis of the Senior Girls' Physical Education programme. Girls also have swimming lessons at the local pool.

Admission. Entry is by interview for the Infant Department and by assessment tests for the Junior School. Entry to the Senior School is through the School's own Entrance Examination in January.

Fees per term (2011-2012). Reception–Year 2 £2,400; Years 3–6; £2,600; Years 7–9 £3,300; Years 10–11 £3,400.

Nursery Fees: Wykeham House participates in the Early Years Extended Entitlement (Pathfinder) Scheme which provides 15 free hours of childcare per week. Any additional hours between 8.30 am and 3.30 pm are charged at £4.80 per hour. Employer childcare vouchers are also accepted subject to HMRC criteria.

Scholarships. (*See Scholarship Entries section.*) Information regarding Scholarships at 11+ are available on application from the School.

Charitable status. The Trustee of Wykeham House School Trust is a Registered Charity, number 307339. It exists to provide education for girls.

Entrance Scholarships

The Abbey School (see p 523)
Academic scholarships are available at point of entry to Senior School to top performers in the entrance exam at 11 or 13 and special Sixth Form Scholarship exam. Music, Drama, Sport, ICT and Art scholarships are also offered.

Abbot's Hill (see p 525)
Minor awards of 5–10% of fees. Scholarships are awarded based on entrance examinations results.

Badminton School (see p 528)
Scholarships and Bursaries are available for girls entering Badminton in Years 7, 9 and 12. Girls who are awarded scholarships, are also eligible to apply for a Bursary, to a maximum of 100% remission of fees.

There are major and minor academic scholarships worth up to 20% of fees, all-rounder scholarships worth up to 10% of fees, music scholarships worth up to 20% off fees and an art scholarship for Years 9 and 12 worth 20% of fees.

Closing date for scholarship applications is 20 October in the year prior to joining the Sixth Form and 1 December in the year prior to joining Years 7 or 9. Application forms can be requested by emailing admissions@badminton.bristol. sch.uk.

Bursaries are means-tested and awarded on the basis of parents' financial circumstances. Application forms are available by emailing admissions@badminton.bristol. sch.uk. Application dates are the same as for scholarship applications.

Benenden School (see p 531)
Academic Scholarships – Lower School Entry (11–13). Awards of up to 10% of fees available. The level of examination will be determined not by date of birth but by intended Form of entry (11+ for Fourth Form, 12+ for Upper Fourth, 13+ for Lower Fifth). The examinations are held in January preceding the date of entry.

Academic Scholarships – Sixth Form Entry. Examinations are held in November preceding entry in September. Candidates take three papers: a compulsory General Paper and two papers in subjects which they intend to study at A Level.

For further information, please contact the *Admissions Secretary*.

Blackheath High School (see p 534)
Several academic scholarships are offered every year. Academic scholarships are awarded on academic merit as measured by the entrance examination. Particulars of the examination are available from the Admissions Secretary.

Bruton School for Girls (see p 541)
Scholarships and Awards to recognise academic achievement and potential are offered on entry to the Senior School at 11+, 13+ and Sixth Form.

Casterton School (see p 544)
There are a number of scholarships at 11+, 13+ and Sixth Form entry – the categories are academic, art, music, drama, all round and sport. Scholarships may be supplemented by bursaries. For details of how to apply please contact the Registrar, e-mail: admissions@castertonschool.co.uk.

Channing School (see p 546)
Academic Scholarships and Exhibitions are offered at 11+ and 16+. All candidates are eligible. Scholarships are occasionally awarded for academic prowess within the school. Awards are also offered to Sixth Form entrants, based on 'mock' GCSE results and contribution to the school for internal candidates or on test papers and interviews for external candidates. Particulars and the current Sixth Form Prospectus may be obtained from the School.

The Cheltenham Ladies' College (see p 547)
A number of Academic, Art, Day Girl, Music or Sport Scholarships and other awards are made annually for girls of all ages.

Cobham Hall (see p 549)
The following Scholarships are offered annually:
For students entering at 11+ and 13+:
In all cases, Scholarships will be awarded as a result of performance in the school's own examinations, a full confidential report from the Head of the current school and an interview. Scholarships are awarded to candidates of outstanding ability in a particular subject or subjects.
Sixth Form Scholarships:
Scholarships are available to students entering the Lower Sixth and are awarded to candidates of outstanding ability in a particular subject or subjects. An informal interview is available to candidates unsure of their standard.
Scholarships are subject to annual review by the Headmaster.
Cobham Hall Awards are awarded to girls who, in the opinion of the school, would make a significant contribution to the all-round life of the school.
For further information contact the Registrar on 01474 823371.

Combe Bank School (see p 551)
Scholarships of up to half tuition fees at time of entry are awarded at 11+ and to the Sixth Form.
11+ Entry and Scholarship Paper in November followed by interview.
Sixth Form scholarships are awarded as a result either of Mock examinations and an assessment paper internally, or for external pupils, an interview and predicted GCSE results.

Downe House (see p 557)
Scholarships are awarded to recognise girls with strong academic, musical, artistic or dramatic potential from a variety of backgrounds and who will benefit from the overall education offered by Downe House.

All Academic, Art and Drama Scholars will receive recognition in the form of £1000 per annum remission in fees. Exhibitioners will receive a remission of £600 per annum.

Music Scholars will receive free tuition in two instruments, which may include the voice, up to a maximum of 30 lessons per year. Exhibitioners will receive free tuition in one instrument, up to a maximum of 30 lessons per year.

Candidates who are successful in gaining an award, but require greater remission in fees in order to be able to take up their place may apply for an Academic, Art, Music or Drama means-tested Bursary, as appropriate.

Academic Awards. The Olive Willis 13+ Scholarships, 12+ and 11+ Downe House Scholarships are awarded on the results of examinations and interviews with the Headmistress, Head of Upper School and Head of Lower School, held each year in January. In addition to these major awards, Exhibitions may be awarded in each age group. Further Minor Awards for excellence in specific fields may be made if candidates of sufficient merit present themselves. Candidates sit papers in English, Mathematics, Science, French (12+ and 13+ only), a General Paper, plus Latin (optional).

Sixth Form Scholarships are year round and candidates sit papers in two subjects of their choice, together with a General Paper. Candidates will also be required to undertake an interview with the Headmistress and Head of Sixth Form.

Age of entry will normally be in line with general entry, ie 11+, 12+, 13+ and Sixth Form (16+). Candidates must be under 12, under 13 or under 14 on the 1st September following the examination. Girls sitting for entry to the Sixth Form must be in the final year of their GCSE studies or equivalent.

Music Awards will be made on the results of auditions and aural tests held at Downe House in February each year

Art Awards will be made on the results of a girl's portfolio and a practical test held at Downe House in June each year.

Drama Awards will be made on the results of a one-hour written paper and a one-hour practical examination held at Downe House in May/June each year.

A number of *Head's Scholarships* may be awarded, at the discretion of the Headmistress, to reward outstanding all-round performers.

Sports Awards are made at 14+ to internal candidates.

For Music, Art and Drama awards junior candidates must be under 14 on the following 1st of September of the year of entry. Potential award holders are required to reach a satisfactory standard in the Common Entrance examinations for their age group before taking up their Award. Senior candidates (i.e. those entering the Sixth Form) must achieve Grade B or above in seven GCSE subjects before taking up their Award and at least an A/A* grade in the subjects they wish to pursue in the Sixth Form.

Edgbaston High School (see p 562)
Scholarships are available at 11+, including one for Music. They are awarded on the basis of performance in the entrance examination and in the case of Music there are additional written, aural and practical tests.

At 16+ there are further scholarships, offered in full or in part, to girls of outstanding ability. They include one for Music, one for Sport and one for the Arts. External candidates are examined by arrangement towards the end of the Autumn Term. Further particulars may be obtained from the School.

Farlington School (see p 564)
Scholarships are awarded on merit. There is no automatic fee reduction for scholarship awards; instead there is an automatic study support grant of £100 per term, rising to £200 in the Sixth Form, payable directly to the Scholar. Scholarships will be held for the duration of the girl's time at Farlington, subject to annual review.

There will be public recognition of Scholars and all girls who maintain their scholarships until they leave will be further acknowledged on their final Prizegiving Day. A monthly programme of Vive lectures is organised for Scholars.

Scholarships are available at three points of entry in the Senior School:

Entry into Year 7: Examination in January.
Academic, Music, Sport, Drama and Art Scholarships are available. Both internal and external candidates need to apply for all subject Scholarships. Candidates should be registered and entered by the last Friday in the preceding November. All girls who sit the Entrance Examination in January will automatically be considered for Academic Scholarships so there is no need to apply for these.

Entry into Year 9: Examination in January.
Academic, Music, Drama, Sport and Art Scholarships are available to both internal and external candidates who will need to apply in all cases. Candidates should be registered and entered by the last Friday in the preceding November.

Entry into the Sixth Form: Examination in November.
Academic, Music, Drama, Sport and Art Scholarships are available to both internal and external candidates who will need to apply in all cases. Candidates should be registered and entered by the first Monday in the November of Year 11 as the assessment will take place later that month.

Entrance Examination Day in 2012: Tuesday 3rd January.

Scholarship application forms may be obtained from the Registrar, Farlington School, Strood Park, Horsham, West Sussex RH12 3PN. Tel: 01403 254967 Fax: 01403 272258.

- Sports and Creative Arts scholarships are based on an assessment day held at HMSG in the Lent Term.
- Music scholarships are available on the basis of examinations, audition and interview, also in the Lent Term.

The entrance examinations for 13+ entry will be held in February and March 2012.

Farnborough Hill (see p 565)
Six Academic scholarships are offered for entry at 11+. One of these is reserved for a Roman Catholic student. In addition one Music scholarship, one Sports scholarship and one Art scholarship are awarded at 11+. There are also Bursaries for parents in need of financial assistance. Sixth Form scholarships are awarded for academic achievement, excellence in the performing arts, the creative arts and sports. An additional scholarship is awarded by Farnborough Hill Old Girls' Association.

Francis Holland School, Regent's Park (see p 567)
11+ entry: One Academic Scholarship of value up to 25% of the current school fee for seven years.

Sixth Form: Two Academic Scholarships of value up to 50% of the current school fee for two years.

Francis Holland School, Sloane Square (see p 568)
At 11+: 1 Academic and 1 Music scholarship, both up to the value of 25% of fees, are awarded.

Sixth Form: 4 Academic scholarships (3 internal, 1 external) up to the value of 50% of fees and 1 Music scholarship up to the value of 25% of fees are awarded for the two years leading to A Level.

Gateways School (see p 569)
The school has introduced a new programme of Scholarships which will be awarded through examination or assessment and interview depending on the type of scholarship applied for. Academic, Music, Drama, Sports, Exhibition and Foundation Scholarships will be awarded to pupils who demonstrate exceptional ability academically, in music, drama, and in sports. An Exhibition is awarded to a pupil who attains high standards across the curriculum and a Foundation Scholarship is awarded to able pupils who live close to the School. The value of the Scholarships will be up to a maximum of 30% of the tuition fee.

The Godolphin and Latymer School (see p 571)
Music scholarships are available on entry to Year 7 and in the Sixth Form. They are worth up to 50% of fees and include free tuition in one instrument.

An Art scholarship is available in the Sixth Form, again worth up to 30% of fees.

For all awards, candidates must satisfy the academic requirements of the school.

The Godolphin School (see p 573)
11+, 12+, 13+ and Sixth Form scholarships, worth up to 50% of the boarding fees, are awarded for outstanding merit and promise in academic work, music or sport. Art scholarships are awarded at 13+ and Sixth Form only. Further particulars may be obtained from the *Admissions Secretary*.

Greenacre School (see p 575)
Junior Scholarships are available for girls entering Year 3 in September 2012. Academic Scholarships, including the Founders' Scholarship, are awarded to girls on entry to the Senior School. Sports, Performing Arts and Creative Arts Scholarships are also awarded at 11+ and Sixth Form. Academic Scholarships are awarded at 16+.

Haberdashers' Monmouth School for Girls (see p 579)
Entry at 11+. A number of academic scholarships are awarded to the best candidates on the basis of the school's scholarship papers, interview and a report from the current school.

Music scholarships are available on the basis of examinations, audition and interview.

The entrance examinations for 11+ entry will be held in January 2012.

Entry at 13+ and 16+. In addition to academic scholarships, there are also Music, Sports and Creative Arts (art and drama) scholarships.

The entrance examinations for 16+ entry will be held in February 2012.

Further information may be obtained from the Admissions Registrar, Mrs Gloria Sheppard, Haberdashers' Monmouth School for Girls, Hereford Road, Monmouth, NP25 5XT. Tel: 01600 711104, e-mail: admissions@hmsg.co.uk.

Headington School (see p 583)

Awards for girls with exceptional Academic potential are made at 11+, 13+ and 16+. All awards are judged on merit with nominal financial benefit of £300 pa (with the exception of music awards, which comprise free tuition on one or two instruments). All scholarships may be augmented by bursaries following voluntary means testing, resulting in a significantly higher award of up to 100% of fees.

Hethersett Old Hall School (see p 589)

Scholarships open to internal or external candidates unless stated.

Year 7 Scholarships. Three types available: academic, creative and sporting. Academic Scholarships are awarded on the basis of examination and interview. Creative Scholarships are awarded on the basis of audition or practical test plus interview with the head of subject and the Headmaster. They can be taken in art, music or drama. Sporting Scholarships are awarded on the basis of ability trials held by the PE Department plus interview with the Head of PE and Headmaster. Applications and assessments are made in the January preceding September entry.

Years 7–10 Scholarships. Two Boarding Scholarships are available, worth 20% of the boarding fee, for girls entering the school in Years 7, 8, 9 or 10. They are awarded on the basis of examination and an interview exploring the contribution the candidate could make to school life. Applications and assessments are made in the January preceding September entry.

Sixth Form Scholarships. Two sorts are available for the two years of Sixth Form study; academic and citizenship. Academic Scholarships are awarded on the basis of examination and interview with a panel of senior staff and the Headmaster. Citizenship Scholarships are awarded on the basis of a letter outlining the contribution a candidate could make to school life and an interview with a panel of senior staff and the Headmaster. A Sixth Form Boarding Scholarship is also available, awarded on the criteria of either of the above. Applications and assessments are made in the November preceding September entry.

James Allen's Girls' School (see p 594)

Scholarships are awarded every year to girls of 11 years of age on entry to the School. There are also Scholarships on entry into the Sixth Form. Scholarships are awarded for academic ability, but are also available for Music and Art. All Scholarships are augmented by a means-tested element where there is need. Sports Exhibitions are awarded at 11+ each year which include family membership of the JAGS Sports Club. The School has also introduced its own scheme to replace the Government Assisted Places Scheme.

Kent College Pembury (see p 596)

The Senior School offers Academic, Music, Drama, Art and Sport scholarships to pupils entering at 11+, 13+ and 16+. A maximum of two practical scholarships may be applied for and these may be worth up to 10% of the tuition fees.

King Edward VI High School for Girls (see p 600)

Up to two full-fee Scholarships may be awarded on the results of the Governors' Admission Examination to girls entering the first year, with a maximum of 50% for any individual scholarship. These are independent of parental income and are normally tenable for 7 years.

The Lady Eleanor Holles School (see p 605)

11+ Entry: Academic Scholarships. At least four awards are offered each year. These are expressed as percentages of the full fee and will thus keep pace with any increases. Awards are likely to be for 10%, dependent on parental circumstances. The awards are based on performance in the

school's own Entrance Examination and subsequent interview.

Sixth Form Scholarships. A maximum of ten Scholarships worth 10% of fees (dependent on parental circumstances) over the two years of Sixth Form study are offered to internal and external candidates who sit the Sixth Form Entrance and Scholarship Examination in November of the year of proposed entry.

Governors' Bursaries. Candidates who sit entrance papers at any stage may be considered for a bursary award. These are means tested and subject to annual review.

Leicester High School for Girls (see p 609)

Bishop Williams Scholarships are awarded to girls in Year 7 who show outstanding academic promise.

Leweston School (see p 611)

Scholarships are awarded at 11+, 12+, 13+ and Sixth Form entry. Academic scholarships are available as well as awards in Music, Art, Drama and Sport and are offered as a result of examination and interview. Dates of examinations: Late November for Sixth Form scholarships, early February for others.

Further details and entry forms can be obtained from the Registrar, Leweston School, Sherborne, Dorset DT9 6EN.

Loughborough High School (see p 613)

The Governors offer a number of Scholarships at 11+ and 13+. The Scholarships are awarded on merit. In addition, some Governors' Awards are given at 16+. Further details of all these awards are available from the School.

Manchester High School for Girls (see p 616)

Entrance Scholarships: one or more Scholarships may be awarded for excellence in performance in the entrance tests taken at the age of 10 or 11 for admission to the Senior School in September. Such Scholarships will be awarded on merit only, not on the basis of parental income, and will provide part remission of fees.

Music, Sports and Dance Scholarships: details are available from the Registrar.

Manor House School (see p 618)

Academic scholarships are offered each year for entry to Year 7. The awards are based on performance in the school's own Entrance Examination, which is held in the January prior to entry, and interview with the Headmistress. Art, Drama, Music and Sports Awards may be awarded to girls who show outstanding talent in these areas.

Means-tested bursaries up to 100% may also be applied for.

Further details are available from the *Admissions Secretary*.

The Maynard School (see p 622)

Academic and Music Scholarships are available for senior school entry at 11+. Sixth Form Scholarships are available for Art, Music, Science and Sport, plus internal candidates can apply for an Academic Award, awarded to three students annually.

Moira House Girls School (see p 625)

Academic Scholarships are awarded annually for admission to Years 7, 9 and 12, and they are worth up to 35% of fees. Candidates take papers in English, Mathematics and Science, and are interviewed by the Principal.

In addition, the School offers Music, Art, Drama and Sport Exhibitions to candidates who are especially gifted in these disciplines, and these are awarded on the basis of an audition or practical assessment. Where appropriate, these awards may be supplemented with a Bursary.

Moreton Hall (see p 628)

A number of scholarships worth up to 10% of fees will be made to pupils at 11+, 12+, 13+ and 16+. Students may apply for more than one scholarship. Means-tested bursaries may be awarded up to the value of 100% of fees. Awards for Music, Drama, Art and for outstanding sporting talent are made at 11+, 12+, 13+ and 16+. For further details please contact the Principal.

The Mount School, York (see p 631)

Academic and Music scholarships are available for Year 7 entry; also Academic, Music, Drama, Art, and Sport scholarships in Year 9 and College (Sixth Form). A Scholarship is awarded for the duration of a girl's school career at The Mount up to and including College (Sixth Form). The value of awards is 5% of the current day fee (to which a means-tested bursary may be added which can be worth up to 100% of fees).

North London Collegiate School (see p 634)

A number of Scholarships, up to the value of 50% fees, are awarded each year on the results of the eleven year old entrance examinations and interviews.

Pipers Corner School (see p 647)

Scholarships are available for entry at 11+ into the Senior School in any one of the following areas: Academic, Art, Drama, Music and PE.

A limited number of Sixth Form Scholarships are also available at 16+.

Means-tested Bursaries are also available up to a maximum of 100% of day or boarding fees (including any Scholarship award).

The Jessie Cross Bursary – an award at 11+ for an all-rounder from a maintained primary school – is a means-tested bursary of up to 100% of fees.

Polam Hall (see p 648)

Academic Scholarships and Bursaries are offered at 7+, 11+, 14+ and 16+, with Music Awards at 11+, 14+ and 16+ and Sports at 16+. The maximum value of any scholarship is one-third remission of fees. Scholarships are awarded for academic excellence and for the promise or potential of academic excellence in the future. Examinations are held at the end of January for entry the following September. The 7+ Scholarship Assessments are held in June for entry the following September.

Bursaries are means-tested and awarded on merit.

Prior's Field (see p 651)

Academic Scholarships at 11+ and 13+ are awarded on the results of the Entrance Examination. These are valued at up to 20% of the current fees. Exhibitions for Academic Promise are also awarded for up to 10% of fees.

Applications must be with the school by the end of November of the year prior to entry.

Queen Anne's School (see p 656)

Scholarships are offered for entry at 11+, 13+ and 16+ and are awarded for excellence in one or more fields of the life of the school. Awards may be made in respect of Academic Excellence, All-Round Contribution, Art, Drama, Music or Sport.

Queen Margaret's School (see p 657)

Scholarships may be awarded to girls entering the school at any stage and are regularly reviewed. Academic, Art, Dance, Drama, Music and Sport awards are available.

The Red Maids' School (see p 666)

Open Scholarships can be awarded annually at 11+ for outstanding performance in the Entrance Examination. In addition discretionary Headmistress's Scholarships can be awarded to girls who perform particularly well in one area of the Entrance Examination. A Year 9 Scholarship may also be available annually for outstanding performance in the Entrance Examination.

Sixth Form Scholarships, awarded on merit in subjects of choice, are available to Red Maids and applicants from other schools wishing to join the Sixth Form. They are tenable for the two years of the Sixth Form.

Scholarships are not related to family income.

Redland High School (see p 667)

Scholarships are available for entry at Year 7 (11+), Year 9 (13+) and Sixth Form.

Academic, Art and Sport Scholarships. These are awarded annually to girls who display high academic potential at 11+, 13+ and for outstanding academic, artistic and sporting achievement at Sixth Form level. They are valued up to a maximum of half remission of fees and are awarded entirely on merit.

Music Scholarships. Scholarships are awarded to girls who are especially gifted in Music at Year 7 (11+), Year 9 (13+) and on entry to the Sixth Form. These are given irrespective of parental income and are valued up to a maximum of half remission of fees, or for free tuition on one or two instruments, as appropriate.

Bursaries are available.

A number of Bursary awards are available each year from Year 5 upwards to those girls who show good academic ability and whose parents are in need of financial help to meet fees. The John James Bristol Foundation enables the school to provide annual Bursary Awards in its name to girls residing in the City of Bristol.

Roedean School (see p 670)

Junior Scholarships: Examinations are held each January for candidates aged 11+, 12+ and 13+. Scholarships are worth 10% of fees.

Sixth Form Scholarships: Examinations are held each November for candidates aged 16+. Scholarships are worth 10% of fees.

Details of the scholarships may be obtained from the Admissions Manager.

The Royal Masonic School for Girls (see p 672)

Scholarships are offered by the School to encourage and reward excellence. Scholarships are awarded in recognition of outstanding achievement, or promise in a particular sphere, and involve financial support, not exceeding 25% of the annual fee.

A scholarship and bursary could run concurrently in the case of a scholar who needed financial assistance.

Awards are given in recognition of excellence at 11+ with regard to academic achievement in the entrance examination, Sport, All-Rounder potential and Music.

At 16+ awards are given for academic excellence, Music, Art, Sport and Performing Arts.

St Albans High School for Girls (see p 677)

Scholarships are offered annually at 11+ entry. These are awarded on academic merit shown in the entrance examinations and any subsequent interviews. The value of each Scholarship is up to 10% of the fees. Further Scholarships are offered on entry to the Sixth Form.

St Catherine's School, Bramley (see p 680)

11+ (Year 7)

Four Entrance Scholarships are available at age 11, awarded on the results of the Entrance Examination. Two scholarships are for 20% of the fees payable and the other two for 10% of fees payable. These run through the Middle School and are extended through the Sixth Form at the discretion of the Headmistress.

A Music Scholarship of 20% of the fees may be awarded annually to an 11+ candidate who shows exceptional musical talent. A second Music Scholarship of 10% of fees can be awarded in years where the field of applicants is particularly strong.

Upper 5 & Sixth Form (Year 11)

There are 8 internal and three external Academic Scholarships, one Sports Scholarship, one Music Scholarship, one Organ Scholarship and one Art Scholarship:

Margaret Kaye Scholarships: There are three scholarships of 20% of the fees payable awarded to run for three years (through Upper 5 and Sixth Form).

Sixth Form Scholarships: Five scholarships are available, each of 20% of the fees payable. Awards are based on performance in the Lower Fifth year, the results of the June examinations at the end of the Lower Fifth, and an interview. Parents of girls in the Lower Fifth are sent full details at the beginning of the Summer Term.

There are three *External Academic Scholarships*. Awards are based on the results of the Entrance Examination and an interview. Candidates interested in applying should contact the Registrar for details.

Clare Gregory Scholarship: This is awarded for sporting ability and is for 20% of the Day fees in the Sixth Form.

Music Scholarship. There is one Music Scholarship for a pupil entering the Sixth Form, to the value of 20% of the fees payable.

Organ Scholarship: There is also a Jennifer Bate Organ Scholarship with Guildford Cathedral offered in alternate years to girls who are already advanced organists. This award is typically for 20% of the fees payable, but may involve means-tested bursary assistance if appropriate.

Art Scholarship. There is one Art Scholarship for a pupil entering the Sixth Form, to the value of 20% of the fees payable. Further details can be obtained from the Head of Art.

Note: in each case the fees referred to are the fees payable by the parent for the term in question, whether boarding or day fees.

Music Awards. In addition there are Music Awards available for free Music Tuition on individual instruments. Further details can be obtained from the Director of Music.

St Francis' College (see p 685)
A number of Scholarships are awarded at 11+ and 13+ following the entrance examinations held in February. These vary in value between 20% and 50% of tuition fees and are awarded on overall Academic ability.

St Leonards-Mayfield School (see p 696)
Scholars are identified through a programme of examination and assessment and are expected to show a high degree of academic aptitude, or considerable talent in one or more of Art, Choral Singing, Drama, Music and Sport (including Riding) at the point of entering the School.

Scholarship Dates:

Fri 11 Nov: 16+ Entrance & Scholarship exams

Sat 12 Nov: 16+ Gifted & Talented Scholarship assessments

Fri 20 Jan: 11+ Entrance & Scholarship exams

Sat 21 Jan: 11+/13+ Gifted & Talented Scholarship assessments

Thu 26 & Fri 27 Jan: 13+ Scholarship exams

St Margaret's School, Bushey (see p 699)
Academic and Music Scholarships are awarded at Year 7 and Sixth Form at the discretion of the Head. An Art Scholarship is also available in the Sixth Form.

St Margaret's School, Exeter (see p 701)
St Margaret's wishes to attract and assist able children to join the School. Awards may be for academic ability, as well as for Music, Art, Drama and Sport and are based on entrance tests/auditions. Sixth Form Scholarships are awarded on merit, after exams/audition in the subject of a candidate's choice.

Bursaries are also available to assist pupils who would otherwise be unable to come to the school. Bursary applications are assessed on the basis of parental financial circumstances. If you would like further information about the financial and practical support St Margaret's provides, please contact, in the first instance, the Admissions Secretary on 01392 491699.

Parents who wish their child to considered for any of the Awards should complete the relevant section of the Pupil Registration Form. All awards are reviewed annually.

Entrance Exams (Senior School): January 2011.

Assessment tests for the Prep and Pre-Prep by arrangement.

Saint Martin's (see p 704)
A number of academic scholarships are offered each year for entry to the Senior School. Awards are made to candidates who show outstanding ability in the entrance examination and in interview.

Scholarships are also awarded annually to pupils entering the Sixth Form. Candidates are required to sit papers assessing a variety of skills and their potential for further study. Those who are shortlisted are interviewed by the Head and the Head of Sixth Form.

St Mary's School Ascot (see p 705)
At 11+ there are two Academic Scholarships available: the General Scholarship worth 5% of the boarding fees and the Mary Ward Exhibition worth 5% of the boarding fees.

At 13+ there is one General Scholarship available worth 5% of the tuition fees.

They are awarded on academic merit and interview based on the School's own entrance examination.

At 16+ there are two Academic Scholarships available: the General Scholarship worth 5% of the boarding fees and the Sixth Form Science Scholarship also worth up to 5% of boarding fees.

They are awarded on academic merit.

St Mary's School, Shaftesbury (see p 712)
11+ Academic, Sport, Music and Catholic Primary School scholarships are awarded.

13+ Academic, Music, Sport and Art scholarships are awarded.

Sixth Form Academic and Art scholarships are awarded.

Additional Head's Scholarships can also be awarded at 11+, 13+ and 16+.

All Scholarships offer up to 10% remission of day or boarding fees with a further 40% available by a means-tested bursary.

Scholarship Examinations take place in January.

St Paul's Girls' School (see p 716)
Junior Academic Scholarships (11+) of a value of £250 per annum are offered to up to four candidates who perform exceptionally well in the 11+ Entrance Examination.

Senior Academic Scholarships and Exhibitions of a value of £500 and £200 respectively are offered to present students on the basis of academic distinction demonstrated in a project completed at the end of the first year of AS Level Study.

The Ogden Trust Science Scholarship (16+) is a means-tested award which may be available to a successful senior candidate eligible for a bursary who is a British national entering the school and who is currently in her final GCSE year at a maintained school and who wishes to study Physics and Mathematics at A Level and at university.

St Swithun's School (see p 718)
Academic scholarships are available for day girls and boarders entering the School at 11+, at 13+ and to Sixth Form. The majority of scholarships are honorary, are not subject to means testing and carry no fee tuition subsidy. However, two academic scholarships (up to 25% of fees) may be awarded to external candidates on merit alone, at the discretion of the Headmistress.

Sherborne Girls (see p 723)
Academic Scholarships are offered at 11+, 12+, 13+ and 16+ annually as a result of examination and interview. There are also scholarships offered for outstanding promise in Music, Art and Sport.

All examinations are held in January apart from Sixth Form in November and All-Rounder (13+) in February. Award holders are offered scholarships up to a maximum of 25% of fees. Scholarships may be combined with bursarial support. Bursarial support (up to 100%) may be available in cases of demonstrable need.

Stamford High School (see p 727)
There are Governors' Scholarships and Bursaries available on entry. These are for Academic, Music, Art, Sporting and All-Round ability. For further particulars apply to the Head.

Stonar School (see p 730)
Academic, Music, Art, Sport, Drama, Riding and All-Rounder Scholarships are offered from Year 7. 11+ Scholarship Examinations are held in January each year and Sixth Form Scholarships by the end of the calendar year.

Tudor Hall (see p 742)
Academic 11+/13+ and 16+. These are awarded to candidates entering at 11+ or 13+ on the basis of their performance at Common Entrance and interviews. At 16+ awards are offered on the basis of interview, school report and examination. The value of the award is up to £1,000 per annum. These awards are intended for the support of the pupil's academic interests.

Music 11+/13+ and 16+. These are awarded on the basis of ability and potential at 11+, 13+ and 16+. The value of the award is up to £1,000 per annum to entrants who show outstanding musical ability. Music awards exist in the form of free tuition in one or more instruments for the duration of the student's time at the school.

Art 13+/16+. These are awarded on the basis of ability and potential either at 13+ or 16+. The value of the award is up to £1,000 per annum. These awards are intended for the support of the pupil's Art interests.

Dance 13+/16+. These are awarded on the basis of ability and potential either at 13+ or 16+. The value of the award is up to £1,000 per annum. These awards are intended for the support of the pupil's Dance interests.

Drama 13+/16+. These are awarded on the basis of ability and potential either at 13+ or 16+. The value of the award is up to £1,000 per annum. These awards are intended for the support of the pupil's Dramatic interests.

Sport 13+/16+. These are awarded on the basis of ability and potential either at 13+ or 16+. The value of the award is up to £1,000 per annum. These awards are intended for the support of the pupil's Sporting interests.

Bursaries are awarded to new and current parents who are in financial need.

Wychwood School. (see p 756)
At 11+ one Scholarship worth £1,200 pa and two Scholarships worth £600 pa are offered.

At 16+ one Scholarship worth £1,200 pa and one Scholarship worth £600 pa are offered, and one Science Scholarship worth £1,500 pa.

Academic Scholarship will be awarded on the results of the general entrance paper.

Wycombe Abbey School (see p 757)
Lower School Entry: A variety of Scholarship and Exhibition awards are available for candidates under 12 and under 14 on 1st September of the proposed year of entry.

Some awards are also available for candidates entering the Sixth Form.

For further information, please contact the Director of Admissions.

Wykeham House School (see p 759)
A number of Scholarships worth a fixed amount each year towards the cost of books, tenable for five years, are awarded each year based on good 11+ entrance results and interview.

Music and/or Performing Arts Scholarships

The Abbey School (see p 523)
Music scholarships, giving free tuition on up to two instruments, are awarded at point of entry following auditions.
Awards made to those with special talents in Drama.

Abbot's Hill (see p 525)
Music Scholarships of 5–10% of fees may be awarded.

Badminton School (see p 528)
Music Scholarships to a maximum of 20% remission of fees are available to all applicants. Auditions take place in January for girls entering Years 7 and 9 and November for girls entering the Sixth Form.

Benenden School (see p 531)
Lower School Entry (11–13): Awards of up to 10% of fees available. The examinations are held in January preceding the date of entry. Candidates should have reached the standard of Grade V (or equivalent) or show great potential. Those offering piano or singing as a principal study should be fluent in an orchestral instrument. Candidates will be required to do practical tests and will be interviewed; they are also required to show that they have reached the general academic standards of any entrant either by sitting qualifying papers, or by taking the academic scholarship examination.

Sixth Form Entry: Awards of up to 10% of fees available. Examinations are held in November preceding entry in September. The requirements for a Sixth Form Music Scholarship are very much the same as for Lower School candidates (see above entry), but candidates should have reached the standard of Grade VII (or equivalent). Candidates are also required to show that they have reached the general academic standard required of any entrant by taking two qualifying papers in subjects which they intend to study at Advanced Level.

For further information, please contact the *Admissions Secretary*.

Blackheath High School (see p 534)
Up to 2 Music Scholarships may be offered annually. Auditions are held following the entrance examination.

Bruton School for Girls (see p 541)
Music and Drama Scholarships include the Zhou Guang-Ren and Howard Music Exhibitions and Cumberlege Scholarship into the Sixth Form. The Besly and Palmer Music Awards are available to girls entering the School at 11+ and 13+.

Casterton School (see p 544)
A Music Scholarship or free tuition in one instrument may be awarded for each year of a girl's school career. These awards are based on auditions which are conducted by the Music Department staff and previous school reports. Internal candidates are assessed through examination, interview and staff recommendation.

Channing School (see p 546)
Academic and Music Scholarships and Exhibitions are offered at 11+ and 16+ entry. Music bursaries also awarded internally from Year 8 in the senior school. These cover lessons in school on one instrument for one year (renewable).

Combe Bank School (see p 551)
Music scholarships are awarded subject to a satisfactory performance on the academic papers. Candidates should be able to perform to Grade 3 or above. An audition will be mainly practical and designed to test musicianship and musical potential. Candidates are asked to play two contrasting pieces on their main instrument/voice, take some aural and sight reading tests, answer questions about their musical experience and offer one piece on their second instrument/voice. A Music Scholar will be expected to play a full and active part in the musical life of the school and be an ambassador for the subject among her peers.

Edgbaston High School (see p 562)
Two Music Scholarships are offered annually: one at 11+ and one at 16+. All scholarships can be combined with means-tested bursaries in cases of need. 11+ candidates must sit the main entrance test in January and then have written, aural and practical tests. Candidates at 16+ must attend an interview and sit a music examination in November. Further details may be obtained from the School.

Farlington School (see p 564)
Music and Drama Scholarships are available to both internal and external candidates entering Year 7, Year 9 and the Sixth Form.

Farnborough Hill (see p 565)
One Music scholarship is offered at 11+. Applicants are auditioned and the award is made on the basis of overall potential and likely contribution to the musical life of the school. Sixth Form scholarships are also awarded for excellence in the performing arts.

Francis Holland School, Regent's Park (see p 567)
11+ entry: One Music Scholarship of value up to 25% of the current school fee for seven years.

Sixth Form: One Music Scholarship of value up to 25% of the current school fee for two years.

Francis Holland School, Sloane Square (see p 568)
1 Music scholarship at 11+ up to the value of 25% of the fees.

1 Sixth Form Music scholarship up to the value of 25% of fees is awarded for the two years leading to A Level.

The Godolphin School (see p 573)
11+, 12+, 13+ and Sixth Form Music scholarships are awarded for outstanding merit and promise. Candidates for music awards should have attained at least Grade 4 at 11+ (Grade 6 at 13+) on one instrument. They are also expected to reach an acceptable academic standard.

Headington School (see p 583)
Awards for girls who demonstrate outstanding ability and further potential in Drama or Music are made at 11+, 13+ and 16+ (music only). Drama scholarships carry a nominal value of £300, and music scholarships may comprise tuition on one or two instruments. All scholarships may be augmented following voluntary means testing to result in awards of up to 100% of fees.

James Allen's Girls' School (see p 594)
Music Scholarships are available at 11+ and 16+. Candidates must satisfy the academic requirements of the school and pass an audition. Scholarships are on the same basis as academic scholarships but also include instrument tuition.

Kent College Pembury (see p 596)
Music and Drama scholarships are available each year for girls entering at 11+, 13+ and 16+.

The Lady Eleanor Holles School (see p 605)
Both Major and Minor Awards for Music are available at 11+ and 16+. These are likely to be for 10% and 7.5% respectively of fees (dependent on parental circumstances) and free tuition on one instrument. Candidates must satisfy academic requirements in entrance papers and attend on a further day for music auditions. Full details of requirements in these auditions are available from the school.

Leicester High School for Girls (see p 609)
A Music Scholarship is awarded at 11–18 available to all girls. An audition and interview is necessary.

Leweston School (see p 611)
Music and Drama Scholarships are offered at 11+, 12+, 13+ and Sixth Form entry. Dates of Auditions: Late November for Sixth Form candidates, early February for others.

Further details and entry forms can be obtained from the Registrar, Leweston School, Sherborne, Dorset DT9 6EN.

Loughborough High School (see p 613)
The Governors offer Music Scholarships to musically promising and talented pupils who are successful in the Entrance Examination. Auditions are held during the week preceding the Entrance Examinations.

The Maynard School (see p 622)
Senior School Music Scholarships and Exhibitions are awarded each year. Two Sixth Form Music Scholarships are awarded each year.

North London Collegiate School (see p 634)
A number of Music Scholarships, up to the value of 25% fees, are awarded each year.

Polam Hall (see p 648)
Music Awards are available at 11+, 14+ and 16+. A Minor Award normally involves free tuition in one instrument and a Major Award free tuition in two instruments. In exceptional cases some remission of fees may be made.

Prior's Field (see p 651)
Music Scholarships: First instrument, including voice, at approximately Grade 3 Associated Board standard at age 11+ is expected and candidates will be required to perform as part of their interview. Candidates with strength in one instrument only may apply. The scholarship is valued at up to 20% of fees at 11+, 13+ and for the Sixth Form.

Drama Scholarships may be awarded, valued at up to 20% of the current fees at 11+, 13+ and for the Sixth Form. Girls are required to perform on the day of the examination and take part in a practical workshop.

Applications for Scholarships must be with the school by the end of November of the year prior to entry.

Queen Margaret's School (see p 657)
For further information about Music and Drama Scholarships, please consult the school website or contact the Admissions Office. In addition to their scholarship, holders of music awards usually receive free tuition on two instruments. Auditions are held in the Spring Term.

The Red Maids' School (see p 666)
Music Scholarships are available and these cover a reduction of fees, or free tuition on one or two instruments, as appropriate.

Redland High School (see p 667)
Music Scholarships. Scholarships are awarded to girls who are especially gifted in Music at Year 7 (11+), Year 9 (13+) and on entry to the Sixth Form. These are given irrespective of parental income and are valued up to a maximum of half remission of fees, or for free tuition on one or two instruments, as appropriate.

St Albans High School for Girls (see p 677)
A number of Music Scholarships are offered annually at 11+ entry. Candidates who have first reached the required standard in the entrance examinations are asked to attend the Music School for auditions.

St Catherine's School, Bramley (see p 680)
A Music Scholarship of 20% of the fees may be awarded annually to an 11+ candidate who shows exceptional musical talent. A second Music Scholarship of 10% of fees can be awarded in years where the field of applicants is particularly strong.

There is one general Music Scholarship for a pupil entering the Sixth Form, to the value of 20% of the fees payable.

There is also a Jennifer Bate Organ Scholarship with Guildford Cathedral offered in alternate years to girls who are already advanced organists. This award is typically for 20% of the fees payable, but may involve means-tested bursary assistance if appropriate.

In addition there are Music Awards available for free Music Tuition on individual instruments.

Further details can be obtained from the Director of Music.

St Francis' College (see p 685)
One Music Scholarship is awarded annually up to the value of 50% of the tuition fees plus free tuition on two musical instruments.

Saint Martin's (see p 704)
A Music Scholarship is offered at 11+ which includes free tuition in one instrument.

St Mary's School Ascot (see p 705)
One Music Scholarship worth up to 5% of boarding fees and free tuition on two instruments is awarded annually to a pupil entering the School at 11+ or 13+. Candidates must have qualified to at least Grade V on the first study instrument at the time of application.

St Mary's School, Shaftesbury (see p 712)
Music Scholarships are available at 11+ and 13+.

St Paul's Girls' School (see p 716)
Junior Music Scholarships (11+) of the value of £100 per annum and free tuition in one instrument are awarded to up to four candidates on the basis of practical examination and interview.

Senior Music Scholarships (16+) of the value of £250 per annum and free tuition in two instruments are awarded on the basis of written and practical examinations and interview to up to two internal candidates and two external candidates. External candidates must be successful in the Senior School Entrance Examination.

St Swithun's School (see p 718)
Music awards (exhibitions) provide free tuition on up to two instruments. Means-tested music scholarships of up to 100% of school fees can be awarded each year to suitable candidates at 11+, 13+ and 16+.

Sherborne Girls (see p 723)
Music Awards (Junior and 16+): Major Awards of up to 25% of the current fees and Minor Awards of up to 20% (with free tuition in three instruments to a maximum of 2 lessons per week). Music Exhibitions offering free tuition. Further particulars may be obtained from Admissions.

Wychwood School (see p 756)
Two Music Scholarships are offered at ages 11+ or 16+ to cover instrument tuition. Candidates will be expected to play two prepared pieces on their instrument(s) and to do some sight reading and aural tests on the afternoon of the test day.

Wycombe Abbey School (see p 757)
Music Scholarships and Exhibitions of varying value are available to candidates under the age of 14 on 1st September of the proposed year of entry.

A Music Scholarship is also available to girls entering the Sixth Form.

For details, please contact the Director of Admissions.

Art and/or Design & Technology Scholarships

The Abbey School (see p 523)
Scholarships are available to those with special talents in Art and/or Design and ICT.

Abbot's Hill (see p 525)
Art Scholarships of 5–10% of fees may be awarded.

Badminton School (see p 528)
Art Scholarships to a maximum of 20% remission of fees are open to all applicants at 13+ and for Sixth Formers.

Benenden School (see p 531)
Art and Design: Awards of up to 10% of fees available. Examinations are held in January preceding entry in September. The examination for the Art Scholarship will consist of one hour on a set-piece drawing followed by an interview based on the candidate's portfolio on which particular emphasis will be placed for evidence of commitment and enthusiasm. Candidates are required to show that they have reached the general academic standard of any entrant by sitting two qualifying papers in subjects which they intend to study at Advanced Level.

Design and Technology: Awards of up to 10% of fees available. Scholarships are offered to girls who show exceptional promise and commitment in this area, supported by good academic results in the normal entry papers. Applicants will be asked to produce evidence of three kinds: a record or portfolio of previous work or achievements; a response to a challenge set at Benenden; and an interview.

Candidates will be asked to identify and research the main purposes of packaging and to design and make a suitable container for a given object. They will use non-specialist materials and processes such as paper, pencils, card, scissors, glue. Research might be prepared at home or in their school, but the task of designing and making would be executed at Benenden.

For further information, please contact the *Admissions Secretary*.

Blackheath High School (see p 534)
One Art Scholarship may be offered annually. Art assessments are held following the entrance examination.

Casterton School (see p 544)
Art and Design Scholarships may be awarded for each year of a girl's school career. These awards are based on assessments which are conducted by the Art Department staff and previous school reports. Internal candidates are assessed through examination, interview and staff recommendation.

Combe Bank School (see p 551)
Art scholarships are awarded on the basis of: satisfactory performance in the Entrance Examination; a reference from the Head of the applicant's current school; submission of a portfolio of work; attendance at a sketching/creative session in our Art Department.

Edgbaston High School (see p 562)
Art scholarships are available at 16+. Applications are assessed by interview and portfolio.

Farlington School (see p 564)
Art Scholarships are available to both internal and external candidates entering Year 7, Year 9 and the Sixth Form.

Farnborough Hill (see p 565)
One Art scholarship is offered at 11+. Applicants are tested and the award is made on the basis of overall potential and likely contribution to the artistic life of the school. Sixth Form scholarships are offered for excellence in Art and Design.

The Godolphin School (see p 573)
13+ and Sixth Form Art scholarships are awarded for outstanding merit and promise; candidates must present a portfolio. They are also expected to reach an acceptable academic standard.

Headington School (see p 583)
Awards for girls who demonstrate outstanding ability and further potential in Art are made at 11+ and 13+. All scholarships carry a nominal value of £300, but may be augmented following voluntary means testing to result in awards of up to 100% of fees.

James Allen's Girls' School (see p 594)
Art Scholarships are offered at 11+ and 16+ to girls who are successful in the Entrance Examination.

Kent College Pembury (see p 596)
Art scholarships are available at 11+, 13+ and 16+.

Leweston School (see p 611)
Art/DT Scholarships are offered at 11+, 12+, 13+ and Sixth Form entry. Dates of examinations: Late November for Sixth Form scholarships, early February for others. Candidates will be asked to bring a portfolio of work with them.

Further details and entry forms can be obtained from the Registrar, Leweston School, Sherborne, Dorset DT9 6EN.

The Maynard School (see p 622)
Two Sixth Form Art Scholarships are awarded annually.

Prior's Field (see p 651)
Art Scholarships are valued at up to 20% of current fees at 11+, 13+ and for the Sixth Form. Candidates are required to submit a sketchbook and two pieces of work. In addition, candidates will sit an examination and be interviewed by the Head of Creative Art.

Applications for Scholarships must be with the school by the end of November of the year prior to entry.

St Catherine's School, Bramley (see p 680)
There is one Art Scholarship for a pupil entering the Sixth Form, to the value of 20% of the fees payable. Further details can be obtained from the Head of Art.

St Mary's School Ascot (see p 705)
One Art Scholarship worth up to 5% of boarding fees is awarded annually to a pupil entering the School at 11+, 13+ or 16+.

St Mary's School, Shaftesbury (see p 712)
13+ and Sixth Form Art Scholarships are available.

St Paul's Girls' School (see p 716)
Senior Art Scholarships (16+) of the value of £250 per annum are offered up to two internal and two external candidates who are currently in their final GCSE year and who, if applying from another school, have previously been successful in the Senior School Entrance Examination. Candidates take part in a Saturday workshop and are also required to submit a portfolio.

Sherborne Girls (see p 723)
Art Awards (Junior and 16+): Major Award of up to 15% of the current fees and Minor Awards of up to 10%. Candidates will be required to bring a portfolio with them and would be asked to do some work in the Art Department whilst they are here.

Wychwood School (see p 756)
Two Creative Arts Scholarships are offered at age 11+ to candidates with outstanding ability in Music, Art or Creative Writing. One Scholarship worth £1,200 and the other £600.

English: Candidates are asked to bring six different pieces of writing, including poetry, a story and a description. These will be discussed with the Head of English.

Art: Candidates are asked to bring six artistic compositions or craft items which will be discussed with the Head of Art. A short unprepared task will be undertaken on the afternoon of the test day.

Wycombe Abbey School (see p 757)
One Art Scholarship for 11+ entrants and one for 13+ entrants, each worth up to 5% of the annual fee, are available. Candidates must be recommended for Scholarship by the Headteacher of their current school.

Sports and/or All-Rounder Scholarships

The Abbey School (see p 523)
Scholarships are available to those with special talents in Sport.

Abbot's Hill (see p 525)
Sports Scholarships of 5–10% of fees may be awarded.

Badminton School (see p 528)
All Rounder awards for good academic potential and aptitude in areas such as the creative or performing arts or sport are offered with 10% remission of fees.

Benenden School (see p 531)
Sports Scholarships. Awards of up to 10% of fees available. Scholarships are offered to girls who show exceptional promise and commitment in this area, supported by good academic results in the normal entry papers. Applicants will be asked to produce evidence of three kinds: a record or portfolio of previous work or achievements; a response to a challenge set at Benenden; and an interview. Candidates will undertake a test to measure levels of fitness, participate in a range of games to show physical ability and tactical awareness, and be given an opportunity to demonstrate their chosen specialism.

For further information, please contact the *Admissions Secretary.*

Bruton School for Girls (see p 541)
Sports and All-Rounder Scholarships include the Foundation Scholarships (11+), Hobhouse Exhibition (13+) and Cumberlege Scholarships (Sixth Form).

Casterton School (see p 544)
Sport Scholarships may be awarded for each year each year of a girl's school career. These awards are based on assessments which are conducted by the PE Department staff and previous school reports. Internal candidates are assessed through examination, interview and staff recommendation.

Combe Bank School (see p 551)
Sports scholarships are awarded to suitable candidates subject to a satisfactory performance on the academic papers. Candidates should be able to demonstrate: a high level in sport within their current school; likewise outside school, accompanied by Club references.

Edgbaston High School (see p 562)
A Sport Scholarship is available at 16+.

Farlington School (see p 564)
Sport Scholarships are available to both internal and external candidates entering Year 7, Year 9 and the Sixth Form.

Farnborough Hill (see p 565)
One Sports scholarship is offered at 11+. Applicants are tested and the award is made on the basis of overall potential and likely contribution to the sporting life of the school. Sixth Form scholarships are offered for excellence in sport.

The Godolphin School (see p 573)
11+, 12+, 13+ and Sixth Form Sports scholarships are available.

Headington School (see p 583)
Awards for girls who demonstrate outstanding ability and further potential in Sport are made at 11+, 13+ and 16+. All scholarships carry a nominal value of £300, but may be augmented following voluntary means testing to result in awards of up to 100% of fees.

Kent College Pembury (see p 596)
Sport scholarships are available at 11+, 13+ and 16+.

Leweston School (see p 611)
Sport Scholarships are offered at 11+, 12+, 13+ and Sixth Form entry. Dates of examinations: Late November for Sixth Form scholarships, early February for others.

Further details and entry forms can be obtained from the Registrar, Leweston School, Sherborne, Dorset DT9 6EN.

The Maynard School (see p 622)
There are two Sixth Form Sports Scholarships awarded annually.

Prior's Field (see p 651)
Sports Scholarships are valued at up to 20% of current fees at 11+, 13+ and for the Sixth Form. Candidates are required to take part in a practical assessment and interview with the Head of PE. A reference must also be submitted from their current school showing evidence of excellence in more than one sport or physical activity including achievements in team activities.

St Catherine's School, Bramley (see p 680)
Clare Gregory Scholarship: This is awarded for sporting ability and is for 20% of the Day fees in the Sixth Form.

Saint Martin's (see p 704)
A Sports Scholarship is offered at 11+.

St Mary's School Ascot (see p 705)
One Sports Scholarship worth up to 5% of boarding fees is awarded annually to a pupil entering the School at 13+.

St Mary's School, Shaftesbury (see p 712)
11+ and 13+ Sports Scholarships are available.

Sherborne Girls (see p 723)
All-Rounder Award (Junior): An award of up to 25% of the current fees. Candidates will sit papers in English, Mathematics and Science. The All-Rounder Award takes into account ability in two areas of activity outside of the classroom. Two All-Rounder Awards of up to 15% per annum may be awarded.

Sport Award: Candidates will offer one or more sports, preferably reaching county standard or higher. One award of up to 10% reduction of the current fees may be awarded per annum. Means-tested bursaries can raise considerably the effective amount of an award.

Bursaries/Educational Awards

The Abbey School (see p 523)
A means-tested bursary scheme (up to 100%) is in place to enable families who could not otherwise afford the fees to send their daughters to The Abbey School.

Badminton School (see p 528)
An Old Badmintonians scholarship is available for daughters/granddaughters of Old Badmintonians worth 15% remission of fees at Year 9.

The Baker Award for candidates currently studying at a girls' only prep school is also worth 15% remission of fees. Candidates will be considered for Academic or Art or Music.

Forces families in receipt of CEA receive 20% remission off fees.

Girls who are awarded scholarships, are also eligible to apply for a Bursary, to a maximum of 100% remission of fees.

Bursaries are means-tested and awarded on the basis of parents' financial circumstances. Application forms are available by emailing admissions@badminton.bristol.sch. uk. Application dates are 20 October preceding entry to the Sixth Form and 1 December for Years 7 and 9.

Bruton School for Girls (see p 541)
Governors' Exhibitions exist to support pupils from families who would find difficulty in affording the full fees.

Casterton School (see p 544)
Bursaries for the daughters of Clergy are available (as the school was originally founded for daughters of the clergy). In addition, there are a small number of bursaries for the daughters of schoolmasters and very substantial bursaries for children from a Services background.

Channing School (see p 546)
Bursaries up to 100% are offered at 11+ and 16+. Please see the website for further details.

The Cheltenham Ladies' College (see p 547)
Applications for bursaries, which range from 10% to 100%, are welcome from girls whose parents genuinely require some form of financial assistance in order to help their daughter join College. In 2010, 144 girls were on scholarships and 57 girls were on means-tested bursaries.

Edgbaston High School (see p 562)
A number of Bursaries at both 11+ and 16+ are available for candidates of good academic ability in financial need. They may cover part or full fees. Please apply to the Headmistress for further details.

Farlington School (see p 564)
The School offers means-tested Bursaries up to 100% of tuition fees for all prospective and current pupils from Year 5 upwards.

The main bursary award process is carried out in the first half of the Spring Term and applications, therefore, should be made in the second half of the preceding autumn term.

Subject to available funds, applications for bursaries will be considered at other times of the year, on a half-termly basis if parental circumstances change unexpectedly.

Francis Holland School, Regent's Park (see p 567)
The school is able to offer a limited number of bursaries at 11+ entry, of value of up to 100% of the current school fee. These bursaries are means tested and reviewed annually.

Francis Holland School, Sloane Square (see p 568)
3 up to full fees Bursaries are available at 11+ and one at 14+.

For daughters of Clergy there is a remission of one-third of the School Fee.

Gateways School (see p 569)
The school operates a means-tested bursary scheme.

The Godolphin School (see p 573)
Educational/Academic Awards
Six means-tested Foundation Bursaries worth up to 70% of the boarding fees, are available from time to time to boarding candidates from single parent, divorced or separated families who have been brought up as members of the Church of England.

Old Godolphin Bursary
A means-tested bursary, worth up to 50% of the boarding fees, is awarded from time to time by the Old Godolphin Association to the daughter of an Old Godolphin, either a girl of exceptional talent or an able, though not necessarily exceptional, girl who is in need of financial assistance.

Hethersett Old Hall School (see p 589)
Means-tested bursaries are available to enable pupils to attend the school who meet the entry criteria but who cannot afford the fees. These awards may be up to 100% of fees. They are limited in number and their award is discretionary.

Kent College Pembury (see p 596)
Fee assistance may be offered to those applying to the senior school. This fee assistance is for those girls who would benefit from all the school offers but whose parents cannot meet full fees. Such fee assistance is means tested on application.

Leicester High School for Girls (see p 609)
A limited number of bursaries is available throughout the school from Years 3–13.

The Maynard School (see p 622)
Means-tested Governors' Bursaries are available. Up to four Governors' Leaving Exhibitions are awarded in the Upper Sixth year.

There is also a generous sibling discount.

The Mount School, York (see p 631)
Members of the Society of Friends are assessed under the Joint Bursaries Scheme for Friends' Schools and according to need may be helped by other Friends' funds in addition to School funds.

Means-tested bursaries are also available for other candidates.

North London Collegiate School (see p 634)
Bursaries up to 100% are offered in cases of financial need.

Prior's Field (see p 651)
As part of widening access, bursaries are available at all points of entry and may be up to 100% fees. A Bursary of 10% of fees is awarded on the results of our own examination to the daughter of an Old Girl. Academic Bursaries for day places in the Sixth Form are awarded up to 95% of fees.

Queen Margaret's School (see p 657)
Means-tested bursaries are offered at all levels.

The Red Maids' School (see p 666)
Any student may apply for a School Bursary at the point of submitting an application for a place in the school. Bursaries are means tested in relation to family income and can be available up to 100%. For further details please contact the Bursar.

Redland High School (see p 667)
A number of Bursary awards are available each year from Year 5 upwards to those girls who show good academic ability and whose parents are in need of financial help to meet fees. The John James Bristol Foundation enables the school to provide annual Bursary Awards in its name to girls residing in the City of Bristol.

The Royal Masonic School for Girls (see p 672)
Bursaries enable suitable girls whose parents could not otherwise afford the fees to benefit from an education at The Royal Masonic School for Girls.

Bursaries are awards made to girls who reach the School's required standards but who require financial assistance to take up a place; these awards are subject to means testing, under a standard formula widely used within the independent sector, at the time the offer is made and biennially thereafter. The number of awards made in any one year will vary according to the quality and circumstances of candidates and the availability of funds.

Foundation Scholarships: Four Closed Scholarships, available only for girls who are the daughters of Freemasons, may be provided at 11+. The value of each of these is based upon a means test.

St Catherine's School, Bramley (see p 680)
Means-tested bursaries are available to external applicants which may cover up to 100% of the fees payable.

For further details please contact the Business Manager.

St Francis' College (see p 685)
Bursaries to assist parents of able girls may be awarded at the discretion of the Headmistress. Application for such assistance should be made to the Headmistress.

St Margaret's School for Girls, Aberdeen (see p 698)
Means-tested bursaries are available for entry to 6 and 7 Junior, I Senior, V and VI Senior.

St Mary's School Ascot (see p 705)
The Ascot Old Girls' Bursary is awarded annually to a daughter of an Old Girl entering the Sixth Form and is worth 30% of boarding fees.

St Swithun's School (see p 718)
Bursaries of up to 100% of school fees are available for girls who meet the School's entrance criteria, but are not scholars. All bursaries are subject to means-testing.

Wycombe Abbey School (see p 757)
A number of means-tested bursaries are available. Bursaries are held subject to the satisfactory conduct and progress of the recipient. Further particulars are obtainable from the Director of Admissions.

PART III
Schools whose Heads are members of the Society of Heads of Independent Schools

ALPHABETICAL LIST OF SCHOOLS

The following schools, whose Heads are members of both SHMIS and HMC, can be found in the HMC section:

Ackworth School	Reading Blue Coat School
Bedales School	Reed's School
Clayesmore School	Rydal Penrhos School
Cokethorpe School	St Columba's College, St Albans
Immanuel College	St George's College
The King's School, Ely	Seaford College
The King's School, Tynemouth	Shiplake College
Kirkham Grammar School	Silcoates School
Leighton Park School	Warminster School
Lincoln Minster School	Wisbech Grammar School
Lord Wandsworth College	Yarm School

The following schools, whose Heads are members of both SHMIS and GSA, can be found in the GSA section:

King Edward VI High School for Girls
Stover School
Teesside Preparatory & High School

GEOGRAPHICAL LIST OF SHMIS SCHOOLS

Individual School Entries

Abbey Gate College

Saighton Grange, Saighton, Chester CH3 6EN
Tel: 01244 332077
Fax: 01244 335510
e-mail: admin@abbeygatecollege.co.uk
website: www.abbeygatecollege.co.uk

Founded in 1977, Abbey Gate College is a co-educational day school for 494 boys and girls from 4–18 years of age. The school is set in beautiful grounds at Saighton Grange some three miles south of the City of Chester. The history of Saighton Grange goes back long before the Norman Conquest. However although most of the present building is Victorian and from 1853, the Grange was a residence of the Grosvenor family. Additional facilities include a large Sports Hall, playing fields and an Arts and Media Centre opened in March 2004 by HRH the Duchess of Gloucester. A purpose-built Art and Design & Technology Centre and new science laboratory were completed in Spring 2008 and opened by His Grace the Duke of Westminster. The completion of a modern Sixth Form Centre with purpose-built ICT, Careers, Social and Study facilities marked the culmination of the 30th Anniversary celebration in 2008. The Junior Department is sited at Aldford, a picturesque village only two miles from Saighton – facilities here include excellent playing fields and an ecology and wildlife area. The Juniors and Infants benefit from shared use of the senior site facilities and specialist staff that teach throughout the age range.

Motto: *Audentior Ito*

Visitor: His Grace The Duke of Westminster

Chairman of Governors: Mrs M Heywood, BA Hons

Head: Mrs L M Horner, BA Hons Birmingham

Deputy Head: D P H Meadows, BA Hons, PGCE (*History*)
Deputy Head: G Allmand, BSc Hons, PGCE (*Geography*)

Academic Staff:
A Austen, BSc Hons, PGCE (*Geography*)
S L Ball, PhD, MPhys, PGCE (*Physics*)
Miss J Bolton, BA Hons, PGCE (*Modern Languages*)
Miss K Burdon, BSc Hons, PGCE (*Mathematics*)
Mrs N Burton, BEd (*Art*)
M Cavallini, BSc Hons (*Mathematics*)
Mrs J Connor-Webb, MA, PGCE (*Modern Languages*)
C Cutler, BSc Hons (*Sport & Exercise Science, Psychology*)
Mrs S Dolan, BSc Hons, PGCE (*Biology/Chemistry*)
J P Gallagher, MA, DipEd (*Biology*)
Mrs V Goodwin, BMus Hons, PGCE
K Gray, BSc Hons, PGCE (*Geography, ICT*)
A P Green, BEd (*Physical Education*)
Mrs C Houghton, BA Hons, PGCE (*History*)
Mrs K Jackson, GTP, HDE (*English*)
Mrs J Jones, CertEd (*Home Economics and Careers*)
Mrs S J Kay, BSc Hons (*Mathematics*)
Mrs C Kingsley, BSc Hons, PGCE (*Mathematics*)
P Lincoln, MA, BA Hons, PGCE (*History and Politics*)
Mrs N Moses, BA Hons, PGCE (*English*)
Mrs S Parker, MSc, PGCE (*Geography*)
Mrs L Poyser, BSc, PGC (*Biology and Chemistry*)
D Rowett, BSc Hons (*Sports & Exercise Science*)
Mrs A Prestwich, PGCE (*Modern Languages*)
Mrs C Russell, MA, PGCE (*English*)
Mrs E Sanders, BA Hons (*Physical Education*)

Miss Z Shaughnessy, BA Hons, PGCE (*English*)
S F Smith, BA, CertEd, ARCM, LMusLCM (*Music*)
D I Stockley, MSc, PGCE (*Technology*)
Mrs S Storrar, BSc, PGCE (*Physical Education*)
M Tempest, BEng Hons, PGCE (*Materials Science/Eng*)
Mrs Z Walker, BA Hons (*Art*)

Part-time Staff:
Miss C Andrews, BA, PGCE (*Theatre and Performance*)
Mrs K Baty, MA, PGCE (*English*)
Mrs S Campbell-Woodward, BEd (*Modern Languages*)
Mrs J Dukes, BEd (*Music*)
Mrs C Faithfull, LRAM, ANEA
Mrs R Fitzhugh, BA Hons, PGCE
Mrs S Hall, BA Hons, QTS ATS (*Learning Support*)
Mrs F Kay, BSc Hons, PGCE (*Science*)
Mrs L L McMahon, BA Hons, PGCE (*Drama*)
Mrs M Pilkington, BA Hons, PGCE (*Art*)
Mrs P Selby, MA, PGCE (*Business Studies; Librarian*)
Mrs J Townsend, CertEd (*PE*)

Junior Department:
Head of Junior Department: Mrs R Findlay, BEd
P Butcher, BEd Hons
Mrs H Courtney, BEd Hons
Mrs J Dukes, BEd (*Music*)
Mrs J Gallagher, BSc Hons, PhD, PGCE
Mrs L Lake, BA, CertEd
Mrs W Richards, BEd Hons
Mrs C Travis, BA Hons
Mrs A Williams, BEd Hons
Mrs K Williams, BEd Hons
Mrs C Spreyer (*Classroom Assistant*)
Mrs G Foulkes (*Classroom Assistant*)

Musical Instruments Teaching:
Miss K Banerjee (*Piano*)
L Hardwick, BMus (*Drums*)
E Hartwell-Jones, BMus (*Singing*)
A Lewis, CT ABRSM, Adv DipMusTech (*Brass*)
G Macey (*Woodwind*)
Miss R Owen (*Clarinet, Flute*)
S A Rushforth (*Violin*)
P Williams (*Guitar*)

Speech and Drama: Mrs C Faithfull, LRAM, ANEA

Business Manager: A Bache
Finance Manager: Mrs P Rees
Finance Manager's Assistant: Mrs K Campion
PA to Headmistress: Mrs J E Gee
School Secretary: Mrs S Knowles
Admissions Officer: Mrs S Boyd
Receptionist: Mrs A McCleary
Junior Department Secretary: Mrs D Humphreys
Junior Receptionist: Mrs G Foulkes
Matrons: Mrs M Kirkaldie and Ms J Kenna

Aims. The College encourages its pupils to aim for academic success; we provide a framework where every pupil will have the opportunity to develop their full potential. Outside the world of academia our objective is also to introduce our boys and girls to a wide range of extra-curricular activities. In addition much emphasis is placed on good manners and discipline; this is a friendly, family school particularly aware of the values of moulding character in conjunction with the search for excellence in the classroom. We provide a caring environment; we are proud of the relationship between the teaching staff and their pupils; we encourage a love of learning and ensure that children feel safe, happy and eager to do their best.

Academic Programme. The College aims to provide children with a broad general education through GCSE, AS and A2 Levels, to university, or other forms of higher education. In Years 7 and 8 pupils study Art, Drama, English, French, German, Spanish, Home Economics, Geography, Geology, History, Mathematics, Music, Physical Education, PSHE, Textiles, Religious Studies, Science, Spoken English, Design & Technology, Information and Communication Technology.

In Years 10 and 11 an option scheme takes effect: within the core, all pupils study English, English Literature and Mathematics, a modern foreign language and at least two Sciences. Study skills are developed and all pupils participate in sport and a rolling PSHE programme. To support their academic curriculum, Year 10 undertake a week's work experience and Year 11 participate in a Development Course designed to build teamwork, self-confidence and leadership skills.

Option subjects for GCSE are taken from the following: Art, Biology, Chemistry, Design and Technology, Drama, French, Geography, German, History, Music, Physics, ICT, Spanish and PE.

In the Sixth Form AS and A2 Level subjects available (according to demand) are: Mathematics, Further Mathematics, English Literature, English Language, History, Government and Politics, Geography, Business Studies, Physics, Chemistry, Biology, French, German, Art, Music, Product Design, PE, ICT, Psychology and Theatre Studies. Sixth Form students follow a comprehensive PSHE programme, have the opportunity to study AS Critical Thinking and participate in sports.

In the Lower Sixth students may also join the Young Enterprise scheme which gives theoretical and practical knowledge of the business world. They enjoy an active community service programme. A number of outside speakers visit the school and regular trips to theatres, conferences or galleries are arranged. All the Lower Sixth students also attend a study skills and team building course in the Lake District in their first term which supports the transition from GCSE to A Level.

Music. The College is well known throughout Chester and North Wales for the outstanding quality of its music. The Chapel Choir has for several years undertaken week-long summer visits to Cathedrals in various parts of the country including Ely, Gloucester, St Albans, Ripon, Tewkesbury, Hereford, Winchester, Durham, York and Bath, as well as touring overseas: the USA in 2003; more recently, Italy in 2009 and Belgium in 2010. Annually, the Chapel Choir sings Evensong at St Paul's Cathedral or St George's Chapel, Windsor. The College also has a Concert Band, The Saighton Syncopators dance band, a modern Funk Band and a Barber Shop Group.

Many pupils of all ages take music lessons and with visiting staff are prepared for the Associated Board Examinations.

Drama. There are two major drama productions each year and these can be drama and musical. There is a whole-school production, a Key Stage 3 performance and GCSE and A Level plays. Pupils are also prepared for examinations in Speech and Drama and regularly enter local competitions with great success. All pupils in Years 7–9 participate in the English Speaking Board scheme within the English and Drama curriculum, helping to develop their confidence and public speaking skills. Year 6 Junior pupils also present a summer performance in their final term before moving into Year 7.

Sport. The College has extensive playing fields, tennis courts and a sports hall. The latter offers four badminton courts, five-a-side soccer, volleyball, basketball, netball, indoor hockey, tennis and cricket nets.

All pupils participate in physical education and games. Boys play rugby, soccer, cricket and tennis; girls play hockey, netball, tennis and rounders. Athletics is popular for both boys and girls and all sports provide full fixture lists for the various College teams. The local swimming pool is reserved each week for sessions with a fully-qualified instructor for the younger pupils.

The College competes in both Regional and National Independent Schools sports events, and has enjoyed great success in both athletics and swimming. Pupils are regularly sent for trials for Chester and District and County teams with players selected to represent Cheshire in hockey, cricket and rugby. There have been two soccer tours to Malta. The Hockey team toured South Africa in 2004 in conjunction with a large football squad and Germany in 2009. The school's Ski Racing team trains weekly and is involved in many competitions including the annual British Championships in France where individual and team performances have been impressive. A number of pupils already train with the English Schools Ski Squad. The equestrian team has gone from strength to strength and the college organises a local competition and sponsors a number of pony club or equestrian competitions.

Junior Department. Our Junior Department provides excellence in education with a broad based curriculum supported by a diverse extra curricular programme that gives children aged 4–11 a wide range of opportunities. These include choir, gymnastics, team games, Spanish, Belleplates, Ju jitsu, creative arts and drama to name but a few. There are frequent school trips and excursions that support the school experience, including a Year 6 residential outdoor and adventurous week at Glaramara in the Lake District.

Other activities. The College has a remarkable record of giving generously to Charities and the three Houses serve to raise money through sponsorship; Sixth Formers take a leading role in this. At weekends and during holidays many pupils take advantage of outdoor pursuits and many choose to follow the Duke of Edinburgh's Award Scheme; there are over 70 participants at all levels.

Admission. *Senior School*: Most pupils enter the College at age 11 following an Entrance Examination held in the Spring Term, although where occasional places occur in other year groups, assessments can be made mid year. Each pupil is allocated to one of the Senior School Houses; the house system encourages competition, community and positive attitudes through the allocation of home points.

Junior Department: Pupils are admitted to the Junior Department at Aldford by means of short assessment and interview at ages 7, 8, 9 and 10 dependent on spaces being available. It is expected that children already in this part of the school will move directly into the College at age 11 if they pass the Entrance Examination.

Infant Department: Entry at ages 4, 5 and 6 is also available. Reception places are limited and assessments are set up in January each year.

Sixth Form: Priority is given to existing pupils but places are offered to others and are conditional on good results at GCSE.

Scholarships. A number of academic scholarships are available following the results of the Entrance Examination. A comprehensive Bursary Scheme also operates at 11+ and Sixth Form entry offering places to pupils with proven ability or talents who would normally not be able to afford the school fees.

For musical talent awards are offered including Music Exhibitions at Year 7 and Sixth Form level and the Daphne Herbert Choral Scholarship. In addition there are sports awards available at 11+.

Fees per term (2011-2012). Tuition: Infant and Junior Departments £2,303; Senior School £3,367.

Old Saightonians. All pupils are encouraged to join the Old Saightonians' Association. Further details of the Association can be obtained from the Registrar at the College.

Charitable status. Deeside House Educational Trust is a Registered Charity. number 273586. It exists to provide co-education for children in the Cheshire, Wirral and North Wales areas.

Abbotsholme School
Derbyshire

Rocester, Uttoxeter ST14 5BS
Tel: 01889 594265 (admissions)
          01889 590217 (main number)
Fax: 01889 591001
e-mail: admissions@abbotsholme.co.uk
website: www.abbotsholme.com

Abbotsholme School was founded in 1889 by Dr Cecil Reddie and was the first of a series of new schools to have considerable influence on European education. Today Abbotsholme is a co-educational, non-denominational boarding, weekly boarding and day school for some 320 girls and boys aged 4 to 18.

President: Mr Nicholas Wilford, FRICS

Chair of Governors: Mr Mark Wells

Headmaster: Mr Steve Fairclough, MSc

Headmaster's PA: Mrs Julie Noon

Admissions Coordinator: Miss Jessica Ash

ISI Inspection. Following its latest inspection in May 2011 by the Independent Schools Inspectorate, Abbotsholme received another excellent report with many comments of "outstanding" and "excellent". The report stated that: *"Abbotsholme is exceptionally successful in achieving its aims. Pupils are empowered to find success… Achievement is excellent. The pupils' personal development is exemplary. Pupils embrace wholeheartedly the school's aspirations of courage, honesty, humility, integrity and respect."*

Ethos. Abbotsholme is a small, friendly school providing a modern, progressive education based on cooperation rather than competition, a compassion for others, and a whole-hearted respect for the environment. Abbotsholme is also a wholly inclusive school, where everyone in the community is valued for the individual contribution they make. We genuinely provide opportunities for self-discovery and personal development. This approach to education gives all our young people knowledge to facilitate success and achievement, commitment to nurture and care for the environment, challenges to build strength and test courage, cultural enrichment to widen perspective and responsibility for the needs of others. From this carefully planned curriculum emerge essential skills for life.

Location. Abbotsholme is located on the Staffordshire/Derbyshire border in a beautiful estate of some 140 acres on the banks of the River Dove in rural Derbyshire, close to the magnificent Peak District, easily accessible by road and rail and less than an hour away from three international airports.

Special Characteristics. Membership of the *Round Square* organisation (www.roundsquare.org) provides a strong international perspective. A worldwide and unique association of schools committed to personal growth and responsibility through service, challenge, adventure and international understanding, members share one aim – the full and individual development of every pupil into a whole person.

Our *outdoor education* programme is both well known and well regarded. Its pioneering principles inspired such organisations as the Outward Bound Movement, the United World Colleges and the Duke of Edinburgh's Award

Scheme. With adventures both close to home and internationally, it presents pupils with personal challenges, both physical and mental, and teaches them the importance of taking responsibility for themselves and others. Many pupils are involved in the Duke of Edinburgh's Award Scheme and all participate in summer camps and autumn hikes each year.

Abbotsholme is one of the very few schools in England to have a working *farm* upon which pupils are able to learn about animal husbandry and crop management and gain a healthy respect for the environment. In addition to the 70-acre farm, our British Horse Society approved *Equestrian Centre* is a popular place to be for our horse enthusiasts, who happily involve themselves in the upkeep of the stables and yard and can study for NVQ or BHS exams.

Music is a way of life at Abbotsholme. All pupils are encouraged to appreciate music in some way, either by learning to play an instrument or taking singing lessons or by simply attending some of the performances that are frequently organised. Both the orchestra and the choir comprise a mixture of staff and pupils, which fosters the special atmosphere so typical of Abbotsholme.

Drama flourishes, in and out of the classroom, with performances in the 120-seat theatre always oversubscribed. All pupils who are keen to be involved, whether on stage or behind the scenes, find regular opportunities to experience the fun and self-discipline characteristic of performance and improvised theatre.

The influence of the *Art* department is evident throughout school, where pupils' painting, drawing, pottery, ceramic, graphic design and 3D creations are permanently on display. In addition many pupils enjoy the facilities of the *Design and Technology* Department, which provides excellent opportunities for developing creative design into quality manufacture. Hours are also spent in the cutting edge *Film Studies* Unit, which enables pupils to design animation projects and create and edit film on computer, through digitisation.

We believe that the physical and mental disciplines of working together in a team are very important. *Sport* teaches the art of winning and losing with equally good grace, self-reliance and leadership, and the opportunities to compete are grasped by many of our pupils. Sports at Abbotsholme include: rugby, football, hockey, netball, tennis, swimming, athletics, squash, skiing, cross-country, horse riding, badminton and basketball.

Curriculum. Abbotsholme caters for a broad ability range. Academic standards are high with the majority of sixth formers going on to their first-choice university. Breadth and balance shape the curriculum, which aims to develop critical and creative thinking and self-discipline across a wide range of subjects at GCSE and A Level.

Activities. Abbotsholme firmly believes that a school should have a greater purpose beyond preparing students for College or University. As a result we seek not only to help all pupils realise their individual academic potential but also to develop in everyone a sense of responsibility for themselves and others through active participation within the community as well as a sense of adventure through challenges in and beyond the classroom. A comprehensive range of compulsory activities is integral to the curriculum, taking place on four afternoons a week. Each week's activities alternately include Outdoor Education and Farm/Conservation work, commitments to team sports, singers, and drama as well as a number of individual choices, including: art, bookworms, chess, debating, drama (major productions are staged every year), French for fun, music (including many concerts and recitals), Young Enterprise and Warhammer.

Home from Home. The boarding experience at Abbotsholme is a happy one, where staff and pupils know each other well and where every individual shares equal responsibility for the community's well being and progress. Small, friendly homes are run by resident houseparents as family units. Younger boarders share bright and comfortable dormitories in threes and fours whilst older pupils have single or shared study-bedrooms. A log cabin village has been added for sixth formers giving them opportunities to experience a greater degree of independence and privacy. Weekly boarding has become a popular option for families with busy lives and for our full boarders, a full programme of weekend activities provides plenty of choice and lots of fun, balancing academic work with social time. Our modern approach to boarding means that sleepover and flexi boarding are also options.

Facilities. These include: dedicated classroom areas, for each subject, including specialist science laboratories, art, music, design and IT centres (two suites), a purpose-built studio theatre for drama, film studies and films, a modern, multi-purpose sports hall, extensive playing fields and swimming pool, and a chapel, which combines as the venue for morning assembly as well as concerts.

Fees per term (2011-2012). Day £2,800–£6,285; Weekly Boarding £6,115–£7,730; Full Boarding £7,960–£9,225.

The Abbotsholmians' Club. The Club currently has some 2000 members and is run by a Committee of Old Abbotsholmians, elected yearly. Members receive regular mail-outs, which give contact addresses and details of the adventures of OAs, young and old. There are also regular invitations to events, to help them keep in touch with each other and with current developments at the school. An enormous amount of networking takes place between OAs, often facilitated by the Club, ensuring that friendships are sustained and memories are relived.

The Club operates a small Bursary fund specifically aimed at helping to educate sons and daughters of OAs at Abbotsholme.

Abbotsholme Arts Society. The School is host to one of the most respected concert presenters in the country. Although embracing jazz, poetry and drama performances, its core programme of chamber music has brought a Who's Who of big-name musicians to the school over the years – Ashkenazy, Brendel, Galway, Hough, the Amadeus Quartet to name just a few. Pupils are able to attend any of the Arts Society concerts free of charge.

Abbotsholme Parents' Association. Run by parents, for the benefit of parents, children and school, the Parents' Association (APA) aims to help new families settle in and become quickly familiar with Abbotsholme and all that it has to offer. Keen to promote active parental involvement in the school, members regularly organise social activities and fundraising events.

Charitable status. Abbotsholme School is a Registered Charity, number 528612. It exists to advance education and in particular to provide for children and young persons a broad, general education in accordance with the principles, traditions and aims developed since the school's foundation in 1889 by Dr Cecil Reddie.

Austin Friars St Monica's Senior School

Etterby Scaur, Carlisle, Cumbria CA3 9PB
Tel: 01228 528042
Fax: 01228 810327
e-mail: office@austinfriars.cumbria.sch.uk
        admissions@austinfriars.cumbria.sch.uk
website: www.austinfriars.cumbria.sch.uk

Austin Friars St Monica's is an independent co-educational day school, founded by members of the Order of St Augustine in 1951 and is one of the network of Augustinian schools across the world. Pupils of all denominations are welcome in the School, giving all the opportunity to embrace the Christian traditions on which the School is founded.

The School Motto is *"In Omnibus Caritas"*. The word "caritas" embraces so much more than the accepted English translation "charity": it is indeed a summary of all the virtues. Christian principles hold a central place in the life of the School with a pupil's faith creating a lively and effective influence on attitudes and activities.

The Senior School provides secondary education for 330 boys and girls aged 11–18. There are 160 children aged 4–11 in the brand new state-of-the-art Junior School and the purpose-built Pre-School has places for 24 children aged 3–4. (*For further details, see Junior School entry in IAPS section.*)

The School stands in its own grounds of 25 acres overlooking the historic City of Carlisle in North Cumbria. It is within easy reach of the M6 and there is excellent access to the North West and North East of England and to South West Scotland. There are also outstanding opportunities to take advantage of the cultural heritage of the area stretching back to Roman times and Hadrian's Wall, and for outdoor activities in the Lake District, Northumberland and north of the border in Scotland.

Austin Friars St Monica's School aims to foster the personal development of its pupils spiritually, academically, socially and physically to enable them to take their place creatively in society. The School has high expectations of its pupils and encourages them to develop their potential in a disciplined, happy, positive and productive atmosphere. Consequently, Austin Friars St Monica's School has established an enviable reputation for bringing out the best in each of its pupils. This means not only attaining high academic standards but realising sound spiritual and social values, self-discipline and the development of a sense of purpose for life.

The School is justifiably proud of its academic facilities, the breadth of its curriculum and its pupils' record in public examinations, which are among the best in the North of England. The School's highly qualified staff, the close attention to the individual pupils throughout their school careers and the nurturing of a positive attitude to work, ensure consistently good results and a sound preparation for higher education.

Both staff and pupils appreciate that school extends beyond the classroom and extra-curricular activities are a strong facet of Austin Friars St Monica's. The School is an excellent centre for developing new and existing interests and talents and offers numerous opportunities for participation in cultural and leisure activities and involvement in charitable work. Each year the School produces a musical/play and termly concerts. There are regular visits to theatres, concerts and galleries and school visits abroad. Qualified and enthusiastic staff provide coaching in team sports, and the School's record in inter-school competition is acknowledged far beyond Cumbria. Awards in the Duke of Edinburgh's Scheme are gained annually by a significant number of pupils, and other outdoor pursuits include climbing, fell walking and skiing.

The School has benefited from a large capital investment in the facilities over the last few years including: a new Sixth From Centre; a dedicated Learning Support unit; the installation of an all-weather pitch; a music recital, practice and classroom suite; new ICT facilities across the whole School; the Mendel building, a brand new science facility with 4 dedicated labs and technician rooms; and a state of the art Junior School (*see entry in IAPS section*).

The quality of pastoral care is one of the School's greatest strengths. All pupils belong to a tutor group, and the tutor who is the first point of contact for the students and parents. The Senior School is divided in to three Houses. A key feature and strength of the school, the House is central to the strong sense of a community which older and younger pupils mix freely; kindness, self-respect and respect for others are instantly evident.

Studies. The following subjects are available to GCSE and/or A Level: English, Latin, French, Spanish, History, Geography, Economics, Mathematics, Further Mathematics, Physics, Chemistry, Biology, Art, Music, Classical Civilisation, Religious Studies, General Studies, Design Technology, ICT, PE, Drama, Philosophy and Ethics, Psychology and Photography.

The size of classes is restricted so that each pupil may receive close attention and be taught as an individual. Reports are sent to parents four times a year. Sixth Formers are expected to learn to organise their time and their work in their own way. The dedicated Sixth Form Centre has a common room, a games room and two study rooms, allowing the pupils to develop a sense of independence while still under the care of the Head of Sixth Form and the rest of the staff. Specialist help is available for dyslexic pupils in the new Learning Support Centre.

The Learning Resources Centre is well equipped and designed for serious study, access of information and relaxation. The Centre's Librarian assists pupils in developing their information-handling skills and supervises the Careers Library.

Activities. The Junior and Senior Schools Choir and the Dramatic Society's annual production provide important extra-curricular activities (a musical is performed every other year). The School Orchestra and Swing Band are also very active. Extra tuition in piano, woodwind, brass, percussion and elocution is provided by peripatetic teachers, who also run ensemble classes for groups of wind, brass, strings and guitar. All this takes place in the dedicated music department.

Some 40 extra different extra-curricular activities are available to the students including Chess, Fell Walking, Photography, Public Speaking, Duke of Edinburgh's Award Scheme, Young Enterprise, and Rock Climbing. Pupils are encouraged to attend events outside the School in connection with their studies and interests. Outings are organised annually to both abroad and to places of interest in Britain. Situated as we are in an area which is rich in Roman History, there are endless opportunities for visiting and studying historical monuments. There are also trips to the Lakes, which are on the doorstep. Other extra curricular trips offer the opportunity to travel abroad for further study including trips to France, Iceland, Borneo and Spain.

Sport. The school has a full-sized astroturf which is utilised throughout the year. The range of sporting options available is vast: Rugby, Hockey, Netball, Cross-Country in winter; Athletics, Rounders, Cricket, Tennis in summer. Football, badminton, dance and fitness are all offered within the activities programme. The pupils regularly achieve county status in their various sports. Annual skiing trips take place in Europe and the USA.

Admissions. The Senior School adopts a three-form entry policy. The majority of places are offered at 11+ with a further entry at Sixth Form. Admissions at other ages are considered, subject to availability of places.

All pupils at 11+ sit the Senior School's entrance examination; entry to the Sixth Form is on the basis of performance at GCSE. At other levels, entry is on the basis of school reports and school-based assessment. The 11+ entrance examination takes place in January prior to entry the following September. Prospective pupils undertake an entrance examination assessing their abilities in English, mathematics and non-verbal reasoning. All prospective pupils are screened for specific learning difficulties.

Fees per term (2011-2012). £3,765 (Years 7–13). Fees are inclusive of lunches.

There is a reduction of 5% for brothers/sisters in the School at the same time. Bursaries are available.

Junior School. *For information about Austin Friars St Monica's Junior School, see entry in IAPS section.*

Travel. Carlisle is a main stopping point on the West Coast Mainline. The M6 motorway connects Carlisle with the South, the Midlands and North Wales, and there are excellent links to the east. The A74/M74 is the continuation of the M6 to Glasgow. There is easy access to International Airports. School bus services run from several of the surrounding areas.

An invitation to see the School and meet the Headmaster is extended to all those who write for information.

Charitable status. Austin Friars St Monica's School is a Registered Charity, number 516289. It exists for the purpose of educating boys and girls.

Bearwood College

Wokingham, Berkshire RG41 5BG
Tel: 0118 974 8300
Fax: 0118 977 3186
e-mail: headmaster@bearwoodcollege.co.uk
          Admissions:
          registrar@bearwoodcollege.co.uk
website: www.bearwoodcollege.co.uk

Bearwood College offers high-quality care and education to children aged from 3 months to 18 years through our Nursery, Pre-Prep, Prep and Senior Departments. With day pupils throughout the College and boarders from age 11 to 18, we are proud to engage each child in a wide range of experiences both in and beyond the classroom. Our expectations for effort, industry and achievement are high. Our focus is on personal success. Bearwood is a place where individuals thrive.

Bearwood's origins date back to 1827 and it was formerly the Royal Merchant Navy School. The College has a Church of England foundation, which also welcomes and respects those of other faiths. Only 35 miles west of London, near Wokingham in Berkshire, it is served by an excellent network of roads and railways. Heathrow airport is 40 minutes by car and Reading mainline station is only 15 minutes away. On entering the College grounds the convenient proximity to London is at once forgotten. The Mansion House was once the residence of John Walter II, the original nineteenth century owner of The Times newspaper. Newer buildings have been added over the years including a beautiful Theatre with a 350-seat auditorium.

The College is a member of the Association of Governing Bodies of Independent Schools (AGBIS) and the Headmaster is a member of The Society of Heads of Independent Schools (SHMIS).

Patron: Her Majesty The Queen.

President: HRH The Prince Philip, Duke of Edinburgh, KG, KT

Board of Governors:
Chairman: Mrs E Langley
M Bell
Mrs S R Cameron
Lieutenant Colonel C J Dawnay
Mrs A C Griffin
J Walter
M Watts

Headmaster: **S G G Aiano**, MA Cantab, PGCE, FRSA

Bursar: C H P Gillow, MA Oxon
Academic Deputy: G Penlington, BA, Dip Teach
Second Master: R P Ryall, BA, PGCE, FRGS

Teaching Staff:
* *Head of Department*

Arts:
H B Browning, BA, PGCE (*English and Film Studies*)
G D Penlington, BA, Dip Teach (*English*)
Mrs P Phillips, BA, Dip RSA, PGCE (*English, Drama*)
Ms B A Truman, BA, PGCE (*English*)
Miss N Madison, BA (*Theatre Studies*)
S Abery, BA, PGCE (**Art & Photography*)
Ms N Balfour, BA, PGCE (*Art & Photography*)
Ms G Joyce, BA, PGCE (*Textiles*)
C E Enston, BMus, FRCO, LRAM, Dip RAM (*Director of Music*)
R Frost, BA, PGCE (*Music & Geography*)

Humanities & Languages:
J R Talbot, BEd, BA (**Geography*)
R P Ryall, BA, PGCE, FRGS (*Geography*)
D Leese, BSc, PGCE (*Geography*)
Ms K Langford-Holt, BA, PGCE (**History*)
C R Kendall, BA, PGDT (*History*)
W J Nash-Wortham, BA, PGCE (**Business Studies*)
Miss J Jones, BSc, PGCE (**Modern Languages*)
Mrs C Ransom, BA, PGCE (*French, Spanish*)

Science & Technology:
M Ayoubi, MSc, PGCE (**Computing*)
G Swainston-Harrison, HDE EA (*Computing*)
S W Nichol, BSc, BEd (**Mathematics*)
D J Felstead, BSc, GTP (*Mathematics*)
Ms W Gosling, BEng, PGCE (*Mathematics*)
R Knight, BPhEd, Dip Teach (*Mathematics*)
C A Bell, CertEd (**Design & Technology*)
K Lovell, CertEd (*Design & Technology*)
Mrs S Nichol, BSc, PGCE (**Science*)
K N Buckler, BSc, QTS (*Physics*)
S King, BSc, QTS, MinstP, MIEE, FRAS (*Physics*)
R M Curtis, BSc, FETC, Adv DipEd (*Physics, Chemistry*)
Ms A Ellis, BEd (*Biology*)
D Leese, BSc, PGCE (*Biology*)
S Quinn, BSc, MSc (*Psychology*)

Sports:
Miss K Elsworth (**Girls' Games*)
J C Dance, BEd (**PE and Boys' Games*)

Study Support/ESOL:
Mrs P Bell, BA, Dip RSA (**Study Support*)
Mrs K Dain (*Study Support*)

Mrs J Michel, BSc Cert TESOL (**ESOL*)

Pastoral Staff:
Chaplin: S J King, BSc, QTS, MinstP, MIEE, FRAS

Boys' Housemasters:
Blake House (*Boarding*): D Leese, BSc, PGCE
Raleigh House (*Day*): R Knight, BPhEd, Dip Teach
Nelson House (*Day*): J Dance, BEd
Jellicoe House (*Juniors Day*): S Quinn, BSc, MSc

Girls' Housemistresses:
Drake House (*Boarding*): Mrs W Gosling, BEng PGCE
Grenville House (*Day*): Ms G Joyce, BA, PGCE

Matrons: Mrs T Greenham, Mrs M Simmonds

Medical Advisor: Ms M Agnew, BN, PGCert Nursing

Administrative Staff:
Registrar: Mrs D Birch
College Secretary: Mrs L Wood

Ethos. As the only co-educational day and boarding 'through school' within 15 miles, Bearwood College uniquely provides a stable yet evolving learning environment to meet the ever-changing needs of your developing child. Your child will gain great confidence from the College's ethos, staff and facilities throughout their school career. Age-appropriate pastoral care at every level ensures that personal development is supported, protecting childhood for younger pupils whilst fostering maturity in the upper years.

Academic Structure. At Bearwood College we expect your child to achieve his or her best. Each pupil works to an academic programme which is individually targeted and permanently monitored. It provides a structured, supported and demanding academic challenge appropriate to each pupil's capacity. The academic curriculum is based on and exceeds the guidelines of the National Curriculum. In the years up to GCSE, we provide a programme which offers choice, breadth of experience and the opportunity to develop particular academic skills.

A specialist Learning Support Unit is available for a limited number of suitable dyslexic pupils. ESOL lessons are similarly available for overseas pupils. An additional charge is made for these services.

During the GCSE years, each pupil is continually assessed, and set realistic fixed-date targets for improvement by the subject teachers, in order to maximise individual potential.

Sixth Form pupils are able to choose from a wide range of traditional subjects at A Level. They receive specialist attention in small teaching groups.

Pastoral. Day care and education is available for children from 3 months to 11 years. Once joining the Senior School the following day/boarding arrangements are available:

• Full boarding with continuous care and involvement for seven days a week.
• Weekly boarding with the chance to go home at weekends once College commitments have been fulfilled.
• Occasional or flexible boarding for limited or irregular periods to help busy parents.
• Day attendance, including Saturday mornings and one Sunday morning per term.

The House system
From the Prep School upwards the House system is at the core of virtually all College life outside the classroom. This arrangement provides all pupils with a contact for personalised pastoral care. It is the base for academic monitoring. It ensures a comfortable social environment and a structure within which games and many activities can thrive. The House is the focus of loyalty for the members.

Within the Senior School parents' first point of contact with the College on a day-to-day basis is the pupil's Houseparent. This is the person who pulls together all the different threads and weaves a coherent picture from the many strands of a pupil's varied existence at Bearwood College.

Houseparents are helped by their own team of House Tutors. The Tutor, who is an academic member of staff, assists in the general running of the House but is also in specific charge of a small group of tutees. Tutees meet with their own Tutors at least once a week. This may be for a personal chat about their progress, or a group tutorial. The House team is responsible for both encouraging and motivating those in their House to achieve their potential. All the Houses are supported by a skilled and dedicated group of ancillary staff the most important of whom are the Chaplain, the Medical Staff and the Matrons.

The Matrons are mainly responsible for the domestic arrangements but are also an important informal adult presence who may seem less official to those in need of a sympathetic ear.

Sport and Activities. All pupils take part in a wide range of games and activities outside the classroom. They enjoy a breadth of experience as well as being expected to discover specific areas in which to excel.

Everyone takes part in physical activities on most days. Sports and games give the pupils physical fitness, personal and team skills and recreation. They offer many opportunities to find a sense of achievement. On-site sports and activities on the extensive array of playing fields and facilities include all the usual field sports but in addition there are opportunities for: golf, equestrian sports, cycling and mountain biking, sailing, shooting, canoeing, to name but some.

Extra-curricular activities. Outdoor pursuits are encouraged at Bearwood. The pursuit of academic excellence is balanced by active encouragement of the pupils' extra-curricular involvement. The extensive grounds and lake are used for sailing, canoeing, mountain biking, camping, cross country and many other activities. Few schools can boast such a varied estate as that found at Bearwood College.

Combined Cadet Force. All pupils in the third and fourth forms of the Senior School join the Combined Cadet Force (CCF). Cadets learn self-reliance and teamwork, and develop their own leadership skills. The CCF also provides an unrivalled opportunity to experience outdoor pursuits. Two camps are held during holiday periods each year. The annual adventure training expedition provides boys and girls with the opportunity to experience environments that test and challenge their characters whilst under the supervision of highly qualified staff. Many cadets choose to continue their service in the cadet force during their fifth and sixth form years. At this time they take on the extra responsibilities of being senior cadets. The experience they gain from taking an active role in teaching and helping younger cadets provides a valuable insight into the qualities required from leaders.

The Duke of Edinburgh's Award Scheme. All pupils in the fourth year start the Duke of Edinburgh's Award at bronze level. This is organised partly in conjunction with the cadet force who help with the training for the expedition section. Senior pupils in the College are encouraged to continue with both silver and gold awards. The scheme provides pupils with an ideal opportunity to develop their own skills, fitness and commitment to others whilst fostering self-confidence and personal esteem.

Music. Music is part of the life of every pupil, non-specialist and specialist alike. Everyone participates in music events including the House Singing Competition and the Choral Society. There are regular informal and formal concerts given by instrumentalists and singers. All pupils are encouraged to take up instrumental and vocal lessons with our team of professional peripatetic musicians. A number of ensembles can be joined: the College Choir, the Chapel Choir, the Jazz Band, the Wind Band, the Dance Band and the Junior Ensemble. Regular visits to concerts and other musical outings take place.

Theatre and Drama. Our Theatre represents the very best that is available for the pursuance of music and dramatic arts. A busy programme of concerts, recitals and plays ensure that this 350-seat auditorium is continually in use. All pupils are encouraged to make a contribution to these productions. Performers from the College are supported by theatre technicians, lighting and sound engineers, stage crew and scenery builders. All have their part to play in the many productions.

Specialist tuition leading to LAMDA Speech and Drama grades and awards is available. These help to develop confidence and competence in acting, public speaking and general communication.

College Facilities. The Mansion House is the centre of the College around which all our other buildings are located. Historic rooms house modern facilities.

The Cook Library is situated in the former drawing room, one of the most beautiful rooms in the main mansion. It has a collection of both fiction and non-fiction books for loan and reference use. The library resource is further enhanced by networked computers with internet access. Pupils are encouraged to read daily quality broad sheet newspapers to keep abreast of current affairs, politics and news. This learning resource is run by a full-time Librarian and supports all areas of the curriculum as well as providing for recreational reading.

The need for modern technology is supported by a new computer resource suite. All departments in the College have networked PCs and wireless is available in some areas.

The range of facilities for pupils at Bearwood is extensive. A fully-equipped photographic suite, extensive sports pitches, a swimming pool, tennis courts, weights-training room, motor vehicle engineering workshop and rifle range are all found immediately adjacent to the main building.

The Pre-Prep and Prep Schools are located close to the main Victorian Mansion House, in a thoughtfully converted, listed coach house, known as Jellicoe House. The splendid surroundings of the wider campus combined with the intimate security of Jellicoe House allow children to explore, discover and learn in a safe and attractive setting.

The Nursery (3–5yrs) is adjacent to Jellicoe House in a purpose-designed building supplemented by a large Early Years unit for 0–3 year olds closer to the Mansion House. The Nursery enjoys unique facilities such as a trike track and access to the magnificent grounds.

Our grounds contain many additional features: two golf courses; a fifty acre lake and a well-equipped fleet of sailing dinghies, canoes and power boats; generous woodlands with a professionally-built obstacle course and fitness trail; a mountain bike course; stables and a skateboarding run.

Admission. Entry to the College is normally 0+, 3+, 5+, 11+, 13+ and the Sixth Form, but applications at other ages are accepted, subject to vacancies. Assessment is by interview, assessment and by Common Entrance where appropriate. Entry to the Sixth Form is normally conditional upon the achievement of a minimum of 5 GCSEs at C grade or above.

Fees per term (2011-2012). Nursery: £32.45 (half day session), £46.50 (short day), £59.50 (full day); Pre-Prep: £2,783 (Reception–Year 2); Prep School: £3,270 (Years 3–6). Senior School: Day £4,630 (Years 7–8), £5,455 (Years 9–13); Boarding £8,120 (Years 7–8), £9,360 (Years 9–13).

Charitable status. Bearwood College is a Registered Charity, number 285287, founded to provide education for young people.

Bedstone College

Bucknell, Shropshire SY7 0BG
Tel: 01547 530303
Fax: 01547 530740

e-mail: admissions@bedstone.org
website: www.bedstone.org

Bedstone College, founded in 1948, is a fully co-educational, independent, boarding and day school catering for children between the ages of 3 and 18 years. The school enjoys a beautiful 40-acre campus within an idyllic setting amongst the south Shropshire hills.

The school comprises the Pre-Preparatory Department (for children aged 3 to 7 years), the Junior School (for ages 8 to 11 years) and the Senior College (for ages 11 to 18 years), all integrated within one campus. Almost 65% of the pupils in the senior school are full boarders.

Bedstone offers a broad and balanced curriculum with over 17 subjects available at GCSE, AS and A2 Levels. Over 95% of sixth formers proceed to their first-choice University and Bedstone is consistently one of the top performing Shropshire Schools.

The College aims to fulfil the potential of every child wherever that potential may lie and, with a teacher:pupil ratio of 1:9, the smaller class sizes allow individual needs to be catered for. The well-qualified and highly-motivated staff believe that each child has a unique talent which it is their job to find and nurture.

Bedstone is very aware of the problems that learning difficulties, such as dyslexia, can cause and the highly-regarded learning support unit, led by its full-time director with the aid of fully-qualified staff, is central to the help provided.

Motto: *Caritas*

The Governing Body:
Chairman: Group Capt J Fynes, RAF (Retd)
Vice Chairman: Lt Col T Lowry

Members:
Mrs M Hughes, BA, DipEd   D J Owens, Esq, JP
E Dunphy   Mrs Y Thomas, BSc
J B P Jones, Esq   S Wright, Esq, LLB

Clerk to the Council and Bursar: A R Gore, Esq, AFA, FIAB, AIMgt

Headmaster: Mr David Gajadharsingh, BSc, PGCE, CPhys, MinstP, NPQH

Second Master: J Lynch, BA, PGCE, MA Ed

Houseparents:
Pearson House: Mr & Mrs B Chadderton
Rutter House: (*to be appointed*)
Bedstone House: Mr & Mrs C Braden
Wilson House: Mr & Mrs M Rozée

Day House Masters:
Mr J Lowe
Miss C Jenkins

Competitive Housemasters:
Hopton: Miss C Jenkins
Stokesay: Miss P Beresford-Webb
Wigmore: Mr J Lowe

Members of Common Room:
Mrs J Bartley, BA, PGCE (*Modern Languages*)
Miss P Beresford-Webb, CertEd, CT ABRSM, Dip RSCM (*Director of Music*)
C Braden, BEd, QTS PGDip Man (*Head of Design Technology*)
Mrs D Bradfield,CertEd, Cert SpLD (*English*)
Miss L Bullock, BA Hons, PGCE (*Geography, ICT & PHSE*)
B M Chadderton,BA, PGCE (*Head of Modern Languages*)
Miss E Davis, BA (*Head of Sport*)
D Fathers, BSc, PGCE, Cert CompSc (*Head of Physics*)
Miss A Flies, BA, PGCE, QTS (*Modern Languages*)

Dr A Foreman BSc Hons, PhD, PGCE (*Head of Science & Biology*)
Miss C Jenkins, BA Hons, MPhil, PGCE, Adv Cert TEFL (*Head of English*)
P Lloyd, BA Hons, PGCE, Dip TESOL (*Head of ESL*)
J Lowe, MA Hons, PGCE (*Learning Support*)
A Weston, MA QTS, CELTA (*Director of Studies, Head of History*)
D M Rawlinson, BSc, PhD, PGCE (*Head of Mathematics*)
D M Rozee, BSc, PGCE (*Head of Chemistry*)
J P Smith, BA (*Head of Art*)
J R Simpson, BA Hons, QTS (*Sports Studies & PE*)
I Spencer, BA Hons, PGCE (*Head of Business Studies*)
A A Whittall, BA, PGCE (*Mathematics*)

Preparatory Department:
Mrs J McPherson, CertEd (*Head of Preparatory Department*)
Mrs J Richards, BA Hons, PGCE, MA Ed
Mrs S Crabtree, BA

Pre-Prep Department:
Mrs M Savery, Dip Montessori
Mrs Z Semple, MA, PGCE
Mrs L Meredith, NNEB
Mrs R Rawlinson, MA, PGCE

Lay Chaplain: A C Dyball, MA Cantab, DipEd

Visiting Instrumental Teachers:
C Greene (*Woodwind*)
D Luke (*guitar*)
D Kirk (*drums*)
I Kennaway (*piano*)
K Norton (*piano*)
J Hymas (*strings*)

School Doctors:
Dr M Kiff
Dr A Lempert

School Sister: Mrs J M Fray, BSc, RGN
Catering and Domestic Supervisor: Mrs K Nichols
Transport Manager: Mr P Singh
IT Network Manager: F Jones
Headmaster's PA: Mrs P Davis
Director of Admissions & Marketing: Mrs C Reid-Warrilow
Accounts Administrator: P Downes
Accounts Clerk: Mrs S Gore

Character of the College. Many children who join Bedstone have done so because their parents feel that the individual strengths of their child have become lost within their current school; that the challenges and opportunities for fulfilling their child's unique talents do not exist, or that they wish for greater pastoral support and guidance for their child. Every parent knows that what they want is the education of the whole child – mind, body and spirit – and Bedstone provides that with its academic and extra-curricular programme coupled with its outstanding pastoral care and boarding ethos.

Family Education. There is a guarantee that once any member of a family is accepted at Bedstone, brothers and sisters will gain automatic entry by interview only. This is of immense value to parents who wish for all their children to be educated at the same school.

Accommodation. The main house, Bedstone Court, is a scheduled building of fine architectural merit and accommodates the Junior and Senior boys' houses. In addition it houses the administration, library, dining hall and sixth form club. The two girls' boarding houses are on the opposite side of the campus with the senior girls accommodated within a purpose built boarding house and the junior girls within the homely surroundings of an 18th Century house. All boarding houses have been completely refurbished. All boarding

Society of Heads of Independent Schools

houses have resident married staff as houseparents. The Science laboratories and classrooms are in modern buildings. There is seating for 300 people in the Rees Hall theatre. There is a modern well-equipped Sports Hall, Design Technology and Art Centre, a new music school opened in 2011, a Medical Centre with a resident RGN, a heated swimming pool and a wide range of additional facilities. There is also a social club for the Sixth Form. The College has a campus-wide wireless LAN.

Religious Education. Religious teaching at Bedstone is according to the tenets of the Church of England though other denominations are welcomed. Children, whose parents wish it, are also prepared for Confirmation by the Chaplain. The College enjoys a strong choral tradition and the Choir enjoys an excellent reputation.

Senior College Curriculum. From the First Form (Y7) to the Third Form (Y9) (when a number join from other Preparatory Schools) the subjects taught are: Religious Knowledge, English Language and Literature, History, Geography, French, Mathematics, Biology, Physics, Chemistry, Design Technology, Art, Music, Physical Education, Computer Studies and German.

In the Fourth and Fifth Forms, in addition to the Core Curriculum of English, French, Mathematics and the three Sciences, options are: History, Geography, Art, Business Studies, Music, German, Design Technology, Sports Studies and ICT.

Throughout the College, whenever possible, it is endeavoured to set classes in each subject so that every pupil may achieve the best of which they are capable. There is no "cramming" at Bedstone, but considerable effort is required from each pupil; and with the aid of close tutorial support, a well-qualified staff and high staff/pupil ratio, good progress and examination success are assured. AS and A2 courses are offered in English, History, Geography, French, German, Business Studies, Art, Music, Design Technology, Mathematics, Physics, Chemistry, Biology, Sports Studies and General Studies. The British Horse Society Assistant Instructor qualification may also be pursued in conjunction with 2 A Levels.

The College has its own learning Support unit and EAL is available for those who require it.

Careers. There are specific Careers staff and a well-resourced Careers Room. Bedstone makes full use of the Independent Schools' Careers Organisation and all members of the Fifth Form take the ISCO Psychometric tests and have the opportunity to undertake work experience.

Games and Physical Education. There are 15 acres of playing fields, with an excellent Sports Hall and a variety of netball, tennis and squash courts. The success of the boys and girls in physical activity at school, county and district level has been nothing short of remarkable.

Rugby, Athletics and Cricket are the main sports for the boys and Hockey, Netball and Athletics for the girls. A rotation system ensures that all pupils, to a greater or lesser degree, have their share of such activities as Basketball, Cross-Country running, Squash, Swimming and Tennis. Nor are the individualists forgotten. Horse-riding is popular and there are facilities for Fishing, Shooting, Badminton, Table Tennis and Mountain Biking, whilst the South Shropshire and Powys hills provide excellent opportunities for Duke of Edinburgh's Award activities.

Clubs and Activities. The Duke of Edinburgh's Award scheme flourishes and there is a wide range of out of class activity, including splendid dramatic and musical productions, debating, individual music tuition and an assortment of clubs to suit most tastes. Pupils are expected to know and observe all College rules and parents to cooperate in seeing that this is done. Prefects play an important part in the pastoral system of the College.

Bedstone Junior School & Nursery is for boys and girls aged 3 to 11 years. The school is housed in its own accommodation and yet shares all the facilities of the senior

school. Science, design technology, modern foreign languages, sport and music are all taught by subject specialists within specialist areas. The nursery school is based upon the Montessori system.

The Junior School is an integral part of the College and children find the transition to the Senior College seamless. Any child accepted within the Junior School is automatically accepted into the Senior College.

Scholarships. (*See Scholarship Entries section.*) For entry to the Senior College, there is a scholarship examination, held at the College on the first Saturday in March.

Fees per term (2011–2012). Senior: £4,085 (day), £7,410 (boarding). Junior: £2,960 (day), £4,875 (boarding). Pre-Preparatory: £1,400.

Old Bedstonian Society. *Hon Secretary:* Mr Frank Jones.

Charitable status. Bedstone College is a Registered Charity, number 528405. It is established for the education of young people.

Beechwood Sacred Heart School

Pembury Road, Tunbridge Wells, Kent TN2 3QD
Tel: 01892 532747
Fax: 01892 536164
e-mail: bsh@beechwood.org.uk
website: www.beechwood.org.uk

Beechwood is an independent school for boys and girls aged 3–18, with girls boarding from age 11–18. Of the 420 pupils, approximately 50 are boarders. Founded by the Society of the Sacred Heart, Beechwood has been a lay school since 1973; it retains a sound Catholic tradition whilst welcoming pupils from all nations and creeds.

The Nursery, Preparatory and Senior Schools are located in 23 acres of landscaped grounds overlooking open countryside, close to the centre of the historic town of Tunbridge Wells.

Beechwood Preparatory School has been a successful co-educational school for many years. A transition to co-education in the Senior School began in September 2008, with boys joining Year 7 for the first time. An additional intake of boys into Year 9 in September 2009 and into Year 12 in 2010, means that Beechwood will be fully co-educational by 2011.

Governors:
Mrs Marie-France Mason (*Chairman*)
Mr Drummond Abrams
Mr Peter Emmanuel
Dr David Findley, BSc, PhD (*Vice-Chairman*)
Mr Patrick Holland, BA Oxon
Lady Hilary Newman
Sister Moira O'Sullivan
Mrs Caron Peppard
Mr Michael Southern

Company Secretary and Clerk to the Governors: Mr Andrew Harvey

Head: Mr Nicholas Beesley, MA Oxon

Deputy Head: Mr Peter Fisher, MA, PGCE
Chaplain: Fr Peter Stodart
Curriculum Coordinator: Miss Lynda Wallens, BEd Hons

Staff:

Heads of Division:
Mrs Mary Allen, BSc Hons (*Junior Division*)
Mr Gary Hatter, MEd, PGCE (*Assistant Head of Junior Division*)
Mr Ivan Carson (*Assistant Head of Junior Division*)
Mrs Carol Mitchell, BA, PGCE (*Middle Division*)

Mr Michael Awdry, BA Hons, PGCE (*Senior Division*)

Heads of Department:
Mrs Olga Clarke, PGCE, Maîtrise MA, Licence/Deug BA
  (*Modern Languages*)
Mr Paul Cotton, BA Hons, PGCE (*Humanities*)
Mr Ian Harman, MSc, BEd (*Head of International
  Education*)
Mr Gary Hatter, MEd, PGCE (*Art & Design*)
Mrs Anne Hopper, BSc Hons, PGCE (*Science*)
Mrs Virginia Letchworth, PGCE, PGDipSLD Dyslexia
  (*Learning Support*)
Mrs Carol Mitchell, BA, PGCE (*Physical Education*)
Mrs Candy Prodrick, BD, PGCE (*Religious Education,
  PSHE*)
Mrs Diana Ringer, BSc Hons, PGCE, MSc (*Mathematics*)
Mr James Thomas, MA, FRCO, LRAM, PGCE (*Music*)
Mrs Sandy Truman, MA (*English & Drama*)

Preparatory School:
Head: Mrs Rachel Burton, BSc Hons, PGCE
Director of Studies: Mrs Teresa Cutts, MA Cantab, PGCE
KS1 Coordinator: Mrs Susan Judge, MRSC, CChem,
  PGCE

Head of Boarding: Mrs Cecilia Rejbakoz

Head's Secretary: Miss Liz Milner
Registrar: Mrs Sue Dyke

Beechwood is noted for its genuine family atmosphere. Consideration for others underpins the code of behaviour for all pupils, making Beechwood a happy, caring school with high standards being achieved through expectation, rather than prescription.

Curriculum. Small class sizes and teachers who are generous of their time, give the support and inspiration needed to ensure that all pupils do their best. For two years running Beechwood was the leading girls' school in Kent for value-added at GCSE in Government League Tables.

Beechwood provides a broad education. At Key Stage 3 all pupils take art, drama, music, cookery and design technology, along with the core subjects. Most subjects are taught in mixed-ability classes of boys and girls. Mathematics is setted from Year 7. French is studied in Year 7, with taster courses in German and Spanish in Year 8. In Year 9 all pupils study French and either Spanish or German which may be continued to GCSE and A Level.

Information Technology is provided as a cross-curricular discipline throughout the school. ICT skills are taught from an early age and the techniques acquired are quickly used as tools for projects, research and coursework in all areas of the school programme. There is a networked computer room and a wireless network provides Internet access from all classrooms, many of which have interactive whiteboards and digital projection.

At A Level, more than twenty subjects are offered including Theatre Studies, Further Mathematics, Business Studies, Photography, Psychology, Law, Home Economics and Textiles. The Sixth Form curriculum is enhanced by an enrichment course that includes Current Affairs, Art and Music appreciation and comprehensive Careers advice.

Sixth Formers are encouraged to show initiative and take responsibility. They have opportunities for leadership as prefects, and in organising activities for younger pupils. All leavers gain places at university on a wide range of courses.

The Learning Development Unit caters for pupils with dyslexia and other mild specific learning difficulties. It offers a comprehensive Study Skills Course at all levels, and coordinates programmes for gifted and talented pupils.

Examination Results. Its record in public examinations is particularly impressive for a non-selective school, with a pass rate (A*–C) of around 90% at GCSE and 100% at A Level. Beechwood regularly appears in the top 10% of schools nationwide in A Level league tables.

Sports. Pupils are encouraged to experience a wide variety of sports, the emphasis being on fun and participation. Recent successes include being Kent County Basketball Champions in four age groups. Sports facilities include hockey and football pitches, netball, basketball and tennis courts, heated swimming pool, gymnasium, badminton and volleyball courts.

Preparatory School and Nursery. Adjacent to the Senior School, the Preparatory School and Nursery provide a sound beginning for every child in a supportive, family atmosphere. The curriculum stimulates enquiry, academic standards being maintained through regular monitoring and assessment. French is studied from Year 1 and all pupils also enjoy cookery lessons. In addition, by sharing the facilities of the Senior School, pupils participate in a wide variety of sports and can represent the school in matches. Extra-curricular activities include chess, crafts, gardening and keyboard music making, and many pupils have instrumental music lessons.

Entry Requirements. The school is non-selective academically, selection being based on interview with the Headmaster, previous school report and confidential reference. All enquiries and applications should be addressed to the Registrar.

Fees per term (2011-2012). Full boarders £8,020; Weekly boarders £7,110; Day pupils £2,835–£4,835.

Scholarships. (*See Scholarship Entries section*.)

Charitable status. The Sacred Heart School Beechwood Trust Ltd is a Registered Charity, number 325104.

Bethany School

Curtisden Green, Goudhurst, Cranbrook, Kent
TN17 1LB
Tel: 01580 211273
Fax: 01580 211151
e-mail: registrar@bethanyschool.org.uk
website: www.bethanyschool.org.uk

The School was founded in 1866 by the Revd J J Kendon. It is a Charitable Trust administered by a Board of Governors, a member of the Association of Governing Bodies of Independent Schools.

Governors:
A Pengelly, MA, FRCS (*Chairman*)

Mrs R Bates	Dr R Hangartner, BSc, MB
D Boniface, MA, MSc	BS, MBA, FRCPath
Mrs C Bonnet	R M Harmer, BA, FCA
Mrs A Carboni, MA Cantab	Mrs W Hedges
Mrs A Culley, CertEd	S Hiscock
J M Fenn, LLB	C M Jackson, MA, MEP
M L Hammerton, BSc,	R J Pilbeam
MBA	G Radford

Bursar and Clerk to the Governors: S J Douglass

Staff:

Headmaster: M F Healy, BSc, HDipEd, NPQH

Deputy Headmaster: P Kilbride, MA

Assistant Head Academic: Mrs D Gale, BSc

Assistant Head Pastoral: A Sturrock, BA

Chaplain: The Revd P Bentham, MTh

Assistant staff:

Mrs S Alexander, BA	C Cooper, MSc
Miss K Berry, BA	Mrs E Cornell, BEd
Miss S Boyle, MDrama	C Coupland, MA
Mrs E Chrysanthou, BA	S Davies, BA
Mrs D Coley, MA	Mrs J Digby, BSc

Dr A Ducoulombier, BA, PhD	M Payne, BSc
Mrs K Harper, BSc	Miss R Rayner, BA
T P Hart Dyke, BA	Miss C Romero, MA
Mrs A Hodges, BSc	D Schooledge, BSc
Mrs G Hollman, CertEd	J Sheppard-Burgess, BSc
M W Hollman, BSc	G Simmons, BSc
Mrs F Johnson, CertEd PE	G Stubberfield, BA
Mrs A C Kelly, BA	M Thomas, BSc
A A Khan, BA	Mrs S Thompson, BA
Miss S King, BA	G K Thorpe, BA
Mrs K Lindsey, BSc	Mrs S Thorpe, BA
D Macdonald, BSc	J Vickerman, BSc
G Mourey, MA	Mrs J Wareham, BEd
Miss N Nixon, BA	Mrs A Wood, BEd
P Norgrove, BEd	Miss C Wood, BA
M D G E Norman, BEd	Mrs S Worby, MA
	Miss Z Zanger, BA

Medical Officer: Dr J N Watson, MBBS, MRCGP

Registrar: (*to be appointed*)

Headmaster's Secretary: Mrs L Lovelace

Bethany has 400 pupils, aged 11 to 18. 30% board on either a weekly or termly basis, with a varied weekend programme of activities available for termly boarders. A generous staff : pupil ratio of 1 : 8 ensures small classes and high quality pastoral care. Individuals are encouraged to develop their potential to the full in academic and all other respects. Most teaching takes place in modern classroom blocks, the result of an ongoing building development programme. Development in ICT has been a priority at Bethany: a wireless network enables pupils from Year 8 to use laptops across the curriculum. The Sixth Form House offers single study-bedrooms with en-suite facilities for the Upper Sixth boarders, study rooms for day pupils and communal facilities for both Upper and Lower Sixth Form students. In 2005 a new Dining Hall complex was opened. More recent additions to the facilities include a Science Centre (opened December 2008), a Food Technology Centre, a new Textiles Department and Modern Language classrooms.

Situation. The School occupies a scenic, 60-acre site in the Weald of Kent, easily accessible from most parts of South-East England, an hour from Charing Cross (Marden Station) and with easy access to Gatwick and Heathrow Airports, the Channel ports and Ashford and Ebbsfleet International stations.

Admission. The normal age of entry is at 11 or 13 by the School's Entrance Examination and at Sixth Form level based on predicted GCSE grades but the school welcomes students to the Bethany community at other stages if places are available.

Fees per term (2011-2012). Boarders £7,867; Day Pupils £5,040.

Scholarships. (*See Scholarship Entries section.*) Scholarships are awarded for Academic ability, Music, Art, Design Technology, Drama and Sport at years 7–9 and into Sixth Form. Children of members of HM Forces or Clergy receive at least 10% discount on full fees. Further means-tested bursaries are available.

Curriculum. The broad curriculum is based on the National Curriculum. The full range of subjects is taught including Information Technology from 11+ and Spanish from 13+. There are 20 GCE A Levels including Business Studies, Food Technology, Music, Photography, Textiles, Theatre Studies and Media Studies. The Double A Level in Business is also very popular and successful, as is the BTEC National Award in Sport. Almost all Sixth Form leavers proceed to degree courses at University.

Dyslexia. The Dyslexia and Learning Support Department, which enjoys an international reputation, has been supporting pupils of good-average intelligence for over 30 years.

Games and Activities. The School offers a wide range of sporting opportunities and enjoys an extensive fixture list, having established a long tradition of inter-school Sport. Facilities include a Sports Centre, climbing wall, fitness room, three squash courts, tennis courts, an outdoor heated swimming pool and a floodlit astroturf. There is a wide range of clubs and activities. The Duke of Edinburgh's Award Scheme is well established at Gold, Silver and Bronze levels.

Music. There are wide-ranging opportunities for instrumental tuition. There are sectional instrumental groups including: a Symphony Orchestra, Rock School, Jazz Band, Concert Band, Brass Consort and a Choir, all making use of the fine Music School with its recording studio and music technology area.

Careers. The School is a member of ISCO (Independent Schools Careers Organisation) and Careers Education is an important part of the Curriculum. Sixth Form students take part in the Coursefinder Analysis Scheme and receive detailed advice regarding Higher Education and Gap Year opportunities.

Chapel. The Chapel, built in 1878, is the focal point of School life and all pupils are expected to attend services. Confirmation classes are offered for those who wish to participate.

Charitable status. Bethany School Limited is a Registered Charity, number 307937.

Bournemouth Collegiate School
UCST

Senior School:
College Road, Bournemouth, Dorset BH5 2DY
Tel: 01202 436550
Fax: 01202 418030
e-mail: senior-admin@bournemouthcollegiateschool.co.uk

Prep School:
St Osmund's Road, Parkstone, Poole, Dorset BH14 9JY
Tel: 01202 714110
Fax: 01202 731037
e-mail: prep-admin@bournemouthcollegiateschool.co.uk

website: www.bournemouthcollegiateschool.co.uk

Chair of Governing Body: Mrs N Dunne

Principal: Mr Stephen Duckitt, MA, BEd, BSc, NPQH

Vice Principal: Mr Peter Harris, BSc Hons, PGCE

Head of Prep School: Miss Kay Smith, BEd, NPQH

Assistant Principal – Pastoral and Discipline: Mrs A Davies, BA Hons, PGCE

Assistant Principal – Teaching and Learning: Miss Kathy Castle, BA Hons, PGCE

Business Manager: Mr Jon Beale

The Best in Everyone
Bournemouth Collegiate School is a rapidly growing Senior School (day & boarding, 11–18) situated in excellent grounds in Bournemouth and a Preparatory School (day, 3–11) in spacious accommodation in Poole. With the sea and golden beaches only 5 minutes away, the school is well placed to deliver its extensive and exciting water sports programme.

As the only independent co-educational school offering through education from prep to sixth form in Bournemouth and Poole the school has responded to increased demand by offering more courses at GCSE and A Level. Parents and pupils are being attracted by the small classes, the excellent facilities and the school has enjoyed a significant investment in state-of-the-art ICT technology including the very latest ActivExpression kits which allow every pupil in every lesson to interact actively with the teacher. This enables staff to differentiate easily and to extend the most able, but at the same time to offer additional support for those who need it.

BCS has an exhaustive extra-curricular, sporting and music programme. We really believe in developing the potential of every pupil and are determined to get the best out of everyone.

Boarding (full, weekly or flexi) is very popular, and the newly refurbished boarding accommodation is spacious.

The school is a warm and engaging place, a visit is a must.

Fees per term (2011-2012). Prep School: £1,046–£2,934. Senior School: Day Students £4,070; Boarders £7,338.

Scholarships. (*See Scholarship Entries section.*) A number of scholarships may be available each year for students with all-round academic ability, or clear potential in either music, art, drama or sport. Internal and external awards may be available for Sixth Form candidates. Full details of these and other bursaries, including grants for children of ministers and lay members of the United Reformed and Congregational Churches, are given in the prospectus. Please contact the Registrar for a copy and details of special events for prospective parents and students.

Charitable status. The United Church Schools Trust is a Registered Charity, number 1016538.

Box Hill School

Mickleham, Dorking, Surrey RH5 6EA
Tel: 01372 373382
           01372 385002 (Registrar)
Fax: 01372 363942
e-mail: enquiries@boxhillschool.org.uk
website: www.boxhillschool.com

Warden: Vice-Admiral Sir James Weatherall, KCVO, KBE

Chairman of the Board of Governors:
Mr J M Banfield

Affiliations: SHMIS, Round Square, BSA, AGBIS, ISBA, AEGIS, BAISC, IBSC, DofE, NAGC

Headmaster: Mr Mark Eagers, MA Cantab, MA Bath

Bursar: Mr J Pratten

Registrar: Mrs K Hammond

Headmaster's PA: Mrs Sandy Watt

Box Hill School is a co-educational school, offering day and boarding places for 11–18 year olds. Set in forty acres of grounds, the school is situated in the heart of the Surrey countryside. We have a strong educational, artistic and sporting tradition, however, what makes us stand out is that we discover and nurture the talents and abilities of every student, so that they all achieve their potential – in the classroom, on the sports field or through interactions with other students.

Box Hill School is a proud founder member of the Round Square, an international organization of over 60 schools united by a set of 'IDEALS' : Internationalism, Democracy, Environmental concern, Adventure, Leadership and Service.

All the Houses at Box Hill School are small and friendly so that students never feel lost or overlooked. The single-sex Houses each board around 30–35 pupils. The majority of boarder rooms are doubles, particularly at Key Stage 4 and above. A central school dining room is provided. First-time Boarders are reassured by the family structure of our Houses

and find them easy to settle into. To strengthen the bond between students even further, Houses become teams for school-wide competitions. Full-time Boarders also enjoy a variety of outings at the weekend. An on-site medical centre is provided, staffed by two qualified nurses and two non-resident school doctors. Two non-compulsory weekend exeats are available each term for full boarders.

We provide strong pastoral support for each pupil, with every child being assigned to a House, complete with Houseparent, common room and kitchen. Each pupil is assigned to a personal tutor within their house – a member of teaching staff who supports their academic and pastoral development.

We believe that activities outside the classroom form an important part of education, and all students take part in weekly and termly activities. As well as this regular programme, junior years take part in expeditions around the UK twice a year. Students may also have the opportunity to participate in Round Square expeditions, carrying out community based activities in locations such as Peru, South Africa and India.

The school has an active Box Hill School Parents Association, comprised of supportive parents and friends of the school who maintain links with the local community as well as running social functions and fundraising events. Parents are strongly encouraged to join.

Special features of the School.
• International opportunities through Round Square membership
• IB World School
• Small classes and a high level of academic support
• Excellent pastoral care
• International Study Centre
• Weekly and termly activities for all students from a wide range of options

Courses offered. GCSE: Mathematics, English Language, English Literature, Biology, Chemistry, Physics, Geography, History, Business Studies, ICT, French, German, Spanish, Mandarin, Music, Art, Textiles, Drama, Physical Education.

IB: Art, Biology, Business Studies, Chemistry, Theatre, Economics, English, Visual Art, Geography, History, Mathematics, German, Russian, Japanese, Mandarin Chinese, Korean, French, Spanish, Music, Physics.

Sports. Athletics, basketball, cricket, football, hockey, netball, rounders, rugby and tennis. Horse riding, karate, judo, golf and tennis coaching are available by arrangement.

Drama, Music and Art. Art students gain excellent examination grades each year, with many going on to be accepted at major art schools. Our purpose-built Music School has greatly enhanced the already wide range of musical opportunities within school, including a choir, wind ensemble, string ensemble and numerous rock/pop bands. The school stages senior and junior plays each year and performed *Grease* in December 2010.

Fees per term (2011-2012). Years 7–11: Boarders £8,500; Weekly Boarders £7,155; Day Pupils £4,700–£4,925. Sixth Form: Boarders £8,750; Weekly Boarders £7,500; Day Pupils £5,200.

Scholarships. A variety of awards are offered for entry to Box Hill School; the latest information can be found on the school's website. Scholarships are available for those entering Years 7, 9 and the Sixth Form, under the following categories: Academic, Art, Expressive/Performing Arts, Sport, and All-Rounder. Bursaries are means tested and agreed between the Bursar and Headmaster.

Method of Entry. Entry is based on an interview with the Headmaster, two most recent reports from the pupil's present school, and written tests in Maths and English. Sixth Form entry is based on report, interview and GCSE predictions. For overseas pupils the interview may be waived. Main school entrance ages are 11, 13 and 16 years. Under normal circumstances, we like to meet prospective pupils and their parents or guardians – this also gives you an opportunity to have a look around our campus facilities.

Charitable status. Box Hill School Trust Limited is a Registered Charity, number 312082. It exists to promote the advancement of education.

Chetwynde School

Croslands, Ratings Lane, Barrow-in-Furness, Cumbria LA13 0NY
Tel: 01229 824210
Fax: 01229 871440
e-mail: info@chetwynde.cumbria.sch.uk
website: www.chetwynde.co.uk

Chairman of Governors: Dr G Murray, DObs, DCh, FRCGP

Senior Management Team:

Head of School: Mr Russell Collier, BSc Hons Leeds, PGCE, FRGS

Senior Teacher: Mrs P Curry, BEd Birmingham, TCert Worcs
Head of ICT: Dr A Amos, PhD, BSc Bristol, EMIIT MIBiol
Head of Primary School: Mr M Boyd, TCert Liverpool, ASA
Bursar: Mrs P Lightfoot

Administrative Staff:
PA to Head of School/Admissions: Mrs A Bell
Senior Administrator: Mrs S Young

Introduction. Chetwynde, a non-selective, co-educational, independent day school for 300 children aged from 3 to 18 years, was founded in 1936. It has charitable status administered by a Board of Governors. The school, although non-denominational, has a Christian ethos.

Location. The school, situated in the Furness Peninsula, is on the edge of the Lake District on the outskirts of the coastal town of Barrow-in-Furness. The school operates two minibuses to and from local villages and towns to the west and east.

Buildings and Facilities. The Senior and Primary Schools are housed in three main buildings set amongst gardens and woodland and adjacent to the school's large playing fields.

There are 4 purpose-built Science laboratories, 2 ICT areas, a Theatre, 2 Art rooms, a Library and Careers Resource Centre, Music rooms, a Sports hall, playing fields, courts and departmental resource areas. Substantial use is made of off-site sports facilities in the local area.

Curriculum. Chetwynde Primary School, comprises an Infant and Junior department catering for children aged 3–11 years. It is during these years that the solid foundations of future academic achievement are laid. The curriculum followed by Chetwynde Primary School is regularly reviewed and academic excellence is the school's main priority. However, particular attention is paid to meeting the individual needs and abilities of each pupil. Therefore, our aim in the early years at Chetwynde is to provide a secure and happy atmosphere within which children can develop into confident, well-balanced individuals with an enthusiasm for learning and a respect for others. We place considerable emphasis on moral, social, physical and aesthetic development as well as intellectual progress.

In Years 7–9 a wide range of academic subjects is taught: English, Mathematics, Biology, Chemistry, Physics, German, French, Spanish, Latin/Classical Studies, Art, Music, History, Geography, Religious Studies and ICT. The curriculum is traditional, but the subjects are taught with a full

awareness of new developments in teaching methods, and with an eye to catering for the varying levels of ability and need in any given class.

Pupils in Years 10 and 11 usually follow GCSE courses in ten subjects, including the core: English, Mathematics and Science; and also at least one Modern Foreign Language. GCSE Drama is offered as an extra-curricular subject. Balance in the curriculum is important and so the children are encouraged to maintain interests in such activities as sport, drama and music, along with their academic studies. Above all, children should enjoy life at school.

At Chetwynde the Sixth Form course leads to academic AS and A Levels. Academic work takes priority and the excellent standard is maintained by the high quality of teaching in the Sixth Form. We know our students well and there is a strong work ethic. The academic results are consistently excellent and students go on to study a wide range of disciplines at universities throughout the country including Oxford and Cambridge.

The Sixth Form play an important role in creating an ethos based on hard work, courtesy and participation. They provide a good example within the school as a whole and the school environment provides opportunities for students to develop their leadership skills and independence. There are positions of responsibility including the Head Boy and Head Girl as well as House Captains and Games Captains. The Sixth Form benefit from a varied sports and activity programme including mountain biking and outdoor pursuits. They also enjoy a range of cultural visits, for example to Berlin, New York and Beijing. Work experience is provided and modern languages students usually do theirs abroad.

Extra-Curricular Activities are very important in the school with an emphasis on participation, as you can see below:

Music is a very important aspect of the school with over 75% of pupils taking an active part in music making. Infant and Junior pupils benefit from a music specialist within the curriculum and there is a junior choir and junior orchestra. Several concerts are held during the year and there is a very popular House Music Competition which includes pupils from both junior and senior departments. There are several ensembles and pupils are encouraged to participate in these. The Music Department also contributes significantly to school productions which are held in both junior and senior departments.

Drama is included in the curriculum in Years 7 to 9 and is offered as a GCSE in Years 10 and 11 as an extra-curricular activity. There is at least one major production per annum involving pupils from across the school and members of the Drama Club and GCSE groups also perform in the RSC Shakespeare Festival as well as in additional drama evenings.

Sport. The school has a justifiably excellent reputation for sport at both junior and senior levels. In the last ten years the school has never failed to reach national finals in one sport or another. Junior swimmers are national record holders as Chetwynde is the only school to have reached the English National Swimming Championships for many years in succession, taking medals at every one. Senior netball teams, basketball teams and cross-country runners have all achieved distinction. Beyond this, of course, many individuals have gained county and north of England honours in football, rugby, cricket, rounders, tennis, orienteering etc. The emphasis is on participation and most children take part in something. The sport is run, not only by an excellent team of PE teachers and coaches but also by a large number of the teaching staff who support the extra-curricular programme.

Clubs and Activities include:

Senior: Senior Folk Group, Senior Choir, Chamber Group, String Orchestra Ensemble, Senior Orchestra, Senior Woodwind Ensemble, Senior Recorder Group, Senior Flute Group, Basketball, Chess Club, Computer Club, Croquet Club, Italian Club, Drama Club, Crossfire Christian Youth

Group, Science Club, Debating Society, Study Games Club, Dance Club, Dance Class, Duke of Edinburgh's Award Scheme.

Juniors: String Quartet, Composers Group, Junior Orchestra, Junior Choir, Engineers Club, Craft Club, Computer Club, Orienteering Club.

Chetwynde takes an active part in the community, attending and organising fundraising events and concerts for a wide range of local, national and international charities.

Fees per term (2011-2012). £2,400–£2,800. 5% sibling discount. The Government nursery grant scheme is in operation for 3 and 4 year old children.

Uniform. The uniform code is strict and the uniform itself is unique to the school and can only be purchased from the on-site school shop.

Admission. Pupils entering the Senior School sit an assessment test in the January prior to joining the school. A scholarship of one term's fees is offered to the pupil with the highest score in the entrance test and there are limited Assisted Places available throughout the school. A Governors Award Scheme is now in place for entrants at age 8, 11 and 16. This provides financial assistance to those who would otherwise be unable to afford to come to the school.

Charitable status. Our Lady's Chetwynde School Limited is a Registered Charity, number 1048501.

Claremont Fan Court School

Claremont Drive, Esher, Surrey KT10 9LY
Tel: 01372 467841
Fax: 01372 471109
e-mail: jtilson@claremont.surrey.sch.uk
website: www.claremont-school.co.uk

Head of Senior School: **Mr J Insall-Reid**, BSSc, DipT, BArch Hons

Head of Junior School: Mrs T Cruttenden, MEd, BEd, DipT

Situation. Claremont Estate is one of the premier historic sites in the country. The original house and the famous Landscape Garden were first laid out by Sir John Vanbrugh for the Duke of Newcastle early in the eighteenth century. Later Capability Brown built the present Palladian Mansion for Clive of India. For over a century Claremont was a royal residence and played an important part in Queen Victoria's early years. In 1930 the School acquired the Mansion and now owns 96 acres of peaceful parkland. Esher is only 16 miles from London and almost equidistant from Heathrow and Gatwick airports with access points onto the M25 within 3 miles.

General Information. Claremont Fan Court School is a co-educational school for pupils from 3–18 years. The School consists of the Lower Juniors for pupils aged 3–7 years, the Upper Juniors for pupils aged 7–11 years and the Senior School for pupils from 11–18 years.

At Claremont Fan Court School high personal expectations and moral values are established and developed within small classes in a happy, positive environment, free from the excessive pressures sometimes placed on young people today. This in turn leads to growth in confidence, independence, self-motivation and self-discipline.

Aims. To provide a broad and forward-looking curriculum in which pupils are encouraged to think independently to meet the demands of a rapidly changing world. A balanced education develops the whole child and prepares the pupils academically, morally and socially for their future adult lives. Pupils have the opportunity to discover where their individual interests and contributions lie, enabling each pupil to achieve his/her full potential. They know that all

their achievements, in whatever area they excel, are highly valued.

E-Learning. All pupils from Year 4 to Sixth Form have their own laptop. This is much more than 'laptops on desks'. The pupils use their laptops both in the classroom and for work at home. The laptops are not replacing traditional teaching methods where they are shown to be effective, but are providing flexible resources that will enrich and support the students' learning experience.

Curriculum. The School educational programme is based on National Curriculum guidelines but the expectation of pupil achievement far exceeds the national average. Junior School classes have between 16–20 pupils. It is vitally important that children are secure and happy so that effective learning can take place and well-qualified staff encourage active, structured learning. Pupils are expected to meet new social and educational challenges with confidence and perseverance. Emphasis is placed on the acquisition and development of skills in numeracy and literacy while providing a wide and varied range of subjects to stimulate the joy and wonder of learning. Subjects include English, maths, science, history, geography, religious studies, French, German, Spanish, design technology, ICT, art, music, drama and PE.

At the commencement of Senior School all pupils continue with the range of subjects offered in the Junior School and start German and Spanish. At GCSE all pupils take English Language, English Literature, maths, science and religious studies. The remainder of their subjects is chosen from a list, which includes French, German, Spanish, geography, history, technology, drama, art, PE and music.

Many pupils excel in the sporting arena, where they can develop talents through fixtures against other schools as well as in county or national school championships. Annual tours, both nationally and overseas, give an added dimension to pupils' sporting education.

Music, art and drama are also important aspects of the daily curriculum. All contributions are valued, whether they be leading, supporting or backstage roles, in order for the participants to be given every opportunity for creative thought and individual expression and to develop an awareness of self-worth.

Sixth Form. The Sixth Form at Claremont is a vibrant and vital part of the School. It aims to form a bridge between the years of compulsory schooling and the more independent years of Higher Education. The many responsibilities our students take on, including leadership and organisational roles, provide an all-round experience of special value to universities, colleges and employers.

A wide variety of subject options from the traditional to the more contemporary subjects of media studies, psychology, photography and music technology, is available to the Sixth Form. Students will usually study four or five AS subjects in Lower Sixth converting three or four of them through to full A Levels via the A2 examinations at the end of their second year of study.

At Sixth Form, Claremont also welcomes external students, who meet our entry requirements. The Sixth Form Centre provides recreation and study facilities and is housed in the historic surroundings of White Cottage, designed by John Vanburgh in 1715.

Careers. Pupils receive careers advice from Year 8 onwards. They participate in Industry Days where representatives from industry and commerce organise topical workshops. There is training in the formulation of effective CVs. Advice and guidance is given regarding UCAS applications and to those pupils who choose to take a gap year. Mock interviews are organised for pupils and conducted by external advisors.

Extra-Curricular Activities. Making individual choices in the learning programme and developing a wide range of interests are both necessary preparations for lifelong learning. All pupils are actively encouraged to participate in a wide variety of clubs and enrichment activities, including the Duke of Edinburgh's Award Scheme and offshore sailing.

Admission. The main intake of pupils occurs at 3, 4+, 7+, 11+ and Sixth Form. Places are offered subject to a pupil reaching the School's entry requirements. Applications for entry at other levels are welcome subject to a place becoming available.

Fees per term (2011-2012). Junior School: Nursery £1,360; Reception £2,618; Years 1–2 £2,720; Years 3–6 £3,500. Senior School: Years 7–8 £4,309; Years 9–11 & Sixth Form £4,550.

Scholarships. (*See Scholarship Entries section.*) We offer Academic Scholarships at Year 3, 7, 9 and Sixth Form, Music Scholarships from Year 7, 9 and Sixth Form, Art and Drama Scholarships for Sixth Form entry, and Sport Scholarships at Year 9 (internal) and Sixth Form.

Charitable status. The School is owned and run by an educational foundation with charitable status, Registered Charity number 274664.

Clifton High School

College Road, Clifton, Bristol BS8 3JD

Tel:	0117 973 0201 (School Office)
	0117 973 3853 (Finance)
Fax:	0117 923 8962
e-mail:	admissions@cliftonhigh.bristol.sch.uk
website:	www.cliftonhigh.bristol.sch.uk

Clifton High School, founded in 1877, is a co-educational independent school offering a first-class education to 515 pupils from nursery school class (rising 3s) to Sixth Form. Family boarders are accepted in the Sixth Form from the age of 16 years. Unique in Bristol, the school has adopted a Diamond Edge model where boys and girls are taught separately in core subjects in Years 7–9 before becoming fully integrated in Year 10 and above.

Governing Body (School Council):

President: Mr H Stebbing, BSc, FRICS, FBIFM, FRSA, FICPD
Vice-President: Miss L E Seager, MBA, BA

Mr J Caddy
Prof Selena Gray, BSc, MBCLB, MD, FRCP, FFPH
Mr A D Marval, BArch Hons, Dip Arch, RIBA
Mr J Smith, MA
Mr M Ursell
Mrs H Vaughan, BEng, CEng, MICE

***Head of School and Clifton High Sixth: Dr A M Neill**,* PhD, BSc Hons UCW Aberystwyth, PGCE

Head of Lower School: Mr A J Richards, MBE, BSocSc Hons Birmingham, PGCE

Director of Operations: Mr G Cowper, MSc Sheffield, BA Hons Warwick

Upper School Staff:
Deputy Head of Upper School: Mr G A Taylor, BA Hons York, PGCE
Assistant Deputy (Pastoral): Mrs S Archer, BSc Hons Brunel, PGCE
SENCO: Mrs G Pilgrim, BA Hons Reading, PGCE

* *Head of Department*

Art & Design:
*Mr P Ayers, MA Falmouth, BA Hons Cornwall, PGCE

Business Studies:
*Mr P G Jackson, BA Hons Westminster, PGCE

Careers:
*Mrs L M Broomsgrove, BSc Hons Exeter (*also Science and Enrichment*)

Classics:
*Mr M Psarros, BA Hons Wales, MA Bristol, C&G Teacher Training
Mr P Garland, BA Hons Exeter

Design & Technology:
Mr S Goldsmith, BSc Hons Birmingham (**Food Technology*)
Mrs W Bird, BSc Hons Bath, PGCE (*Food Technology*)
Miss E Warwood, BSc Hons Bolton, PGCE (**Textiles Technology*)
Mr J Noyce, BA Hons Manchester, PGCE (**Graphic Design also Information Technology*)

Drama:
*Mrs G Malpass, BA Hons London, Labon Dance Cert, PGCE (*also Theatre Studies*)
Mrs S Johnson-Martin, BA Hons Royal Holloway College London, PGCE

English:
*Mrs J P Pritchard, BA Hons Exeter, PGCE
Mrs S P Hosty, MA Kingston, Dip TEFL
Mrs S Swallow, MA Edinburgh, PGCE (*also Enrichment*)

Geography:
*Mrs L Giles, BSc Hons Loughborough, PGCE
Mrs H Ellerton, BSc Manchester, PGCE

Government and Politics:
*Mrs R Pullen, BSc Econ Hons Cardiff, PGCE (*also History*)
Mrs A Crossley MA London, BEd Hons (*also History, PSE and Enrichment*)

History:
*Mrs R Pullen, BSc Econ Hons Cardiff, PGCE (*also Government & Politics*)
Mrs A Crossley, MA London, BEd Hons (*also Government & Politics, PSE and Enrichment*)

Information Technology:
*Mr G A Taylor, BA Hons York, PGCE
Mr J Noyce, BA Hons Manchester, PGCE (*also Graphic Design*)

Mathematics:
*Mrs S Hargroves, BSc Hons King's College London, PGCE, Dip Inf Eng
Mr S Fawcus, BSc Hons, PGCE
Mrs D Jones, BSc Liverpool, PGCE

Modern Languages:
Dr E M Dand, PhD Bristol, PGCE (**French*)
Miss S Schiller, BA Hons, PGCE (**German*)
Mrs L Sobey, BA Hons Portsmouth, PGCE (**Spanish*)
Mrs P M Winter, BA Hons Durham, PGCE (*French*)

Assistants:
Mrs A Mebarki (*French*)
Miss I Horndl (*German*)
Ms S Roman de la Pena (*Spanish*)

Music:
*Mrs R Hindmarch, BMus Hons Manchester, PGCE (*Director of Upper School Music*)
Mrs M Johnson, BA Hons, MEd Cambridge, PGCE

Physical Education:
*Miss K Price, BEd Hons Sussex, Chelsea College of PE
*Mr C Collins, BA Hons UWIC, MA Bath, PGCE (*Head of Boys' Sport*)
*Mrs J Winn, CertEd Cambridge Bedford College of PE (*Head of Lower School Sport*)
Mrs D J Kingston, BEd Hons Cambridge, Bedford College of PE

Mrs V Williams, CertEd, Dip PE Bristol

Personal & Social Education:
*Mrs A Crossley, BEd Hons, MA London (*also
Government & Politics, History and Enrichment*)

Psychology:
Mrs V Papanikolaou, BA South Africa, HDipEd, QTS

Religious Studies:
*Mrs J Awolola-Hill, BEd, CertEd Birmingham (*also
Enrichment*)

Science:
Mrs S Archer, BSc Hons Brunel, PGCE (*Biology*)
Mrs L M Broomsgrove, BSc Hons Exeter, PGCE
  (*Chemistry also *Careers and Enrichment*)
Dr A Camacho, PhD Cardiff, BSc Hons Bristol, PGCE
  (*Physics*)
Mr C Gunter, BSc Hons Bristol, PGCE, MSc, AMRSC
  (*Physics also Examinations Officer*)
Miss L Brackenbury, BSc Hons Cardiff, PGCE
  (*Chemistry*)
Miss A Jones, BSc Hons Sheffield, PGCE (*Biology*)

Lower School Staff:
Head of Juniors and Assistant Head of Lower School: Mrs
  S Barker, BEd Hons UWE
Curriculum Coordinator: Mrs K Vinson, BA Hons
  Southampton, PGCE
Director of Lower School Music: Mr A Cleaver, BA Hons,
  Lincoln and Hull
SENCO: Mrs S Lloyd, BEd UWE, PGDip York, Cert
  Couns

Junior Department KS2:
Mrs F Barnard, BSc Hons Birmingham, PGCE
Mrs J Knott, BEd Bristol
Mr C Lowe, BA Ed Joint Hons Goldsmiths College
  London
Miss H Phillips, BEd Hons Winchester
Mr D J E Pye, BA Hons West London Inst of HE, PGCE
Mrs H Tabb, BA Hons QTS Surrey
Miss C Wise, BA Hons Bath Spa, PGCE

Preparatory Department KS1:
Head of KS1: Mrs J Lee, BA Hons Plymouth, PGCE
Mrs L Mitchell, BSc Hons Edinburgh, PGCE
Mrs A Roberts, BSc Hons Southampton, PGCE
Mrs S Willerton, BA Hons Bath Spa, PGCE

Foundation Stage:
Head of Foundation Stage: Mrs D Andrews, BSc Hons
  QTS Bath College, EYPS
Mrs J Denyer-Warr, BEd Hons UWE
Mrs J Sutcliffe, BA Hons Warwick, PGCE

Teaching Assistants:

Learning Support: Mrs B Williams, NNEB

Preparatory Department KS1:
Mrs S Bright, NVQ
Miss D Clark, HNC
Mrs L Ottley, BA Hons Kent, PGCE
Mrs V Owen, CertEd Bristol

Foundation Stage:
Mrs A Clancy, NNEB
Miss D Clements, NNEB
Mrs A Godshaw, NNEB
Mrs E Takle, NNEB

Visiting Staff:

Music:
Miss M Baker GTCL, LRAM, ALCM (*Clarinet and Piano*)
Mrs R Carpenter BMus (*Piano*)
Mr A Chetland (*Electric Guitar*)
Miss E-J Cormack (*Singing, Piano*)

Mrs J George, BA Hons LLCM (*Classical Guitar*)
Mr P Gittings, ARM, Dip RCM (*Oboe and Piano*)
Miss C Johnstone, BA, Dip NCOS (*Cello*)
Mr M Jones, BA Hons (*Percussion*)
Mr S Jones, BMus (*Upper Brass*)
Mrs K Skeet, BA Hons (*Violin & Viola*)
Mr A Stewart, BMus (*Lower Brass*)
Mrs L Tucker, AGSM (*Singing*)
Mrs R Whitworth, BSc Hons (*Violin*)
Miss L Beveridge, BMus, Dip ABRSM (*Flute*)
Ms N Willis, LTCL, ARCM, FTCL (*Saxophone*)
Mrs M Johnson, BA Hons, MEd Cambridge, PGCE
  (*Piano*)
Miss E Whitfield, BA Hons (*Bassoon*)

Speech & Drama:
Mrs S Johnson-Martin, BA Hons Royal Holloway College,
  PGCE

Tennis: Mr R Conway
Rugby: Mr J Buck
Tae Kwon Do: Mr D Chance
Trampolining: Mr O Monro
Hockey: Mrs E Morgan

Finance Office:
Accountant: Mr A Willford, BSc Hons Bristol, ACA
Fee Administrator: Mrs T Gajewski, BA Hons OU
Payroll: Miss T Nicholls
Transport & Lettings: Mrs H Warr

Admissions Registrar: Mrs K Bolton-Jones
PA to the Head of Upper School & Clifton High Sixth: Mrs
  T J Scales
PA to Head of Lower School: Mrs E J Hill
School Office Manager: Mrs J Rosser
School Office Assistant: Mrs E Freire-Baños, BA Hons OU
School Office Assistant: Mrs S Furlong
Head's Communications Manager: Mrs J Evans, BA Hons
  Lancaster, PGCE

IT Systems & Support:
Mr J Fülöp
Mr P Wilmott

School Librarians:
Mrs A Dobson, BA, MCLIP (*Head Librarian*)
Mrs J Scourse

Child Protection Officers:
Mrs S Archer (*Upper School*)
Mrs A Roberts (*Lower School*)

Examinations Officer: Mr C Gunter, BSc Hons Bristol,
  PGCE, MSc, AMRSC (*also Physics*)

Matrons:
Mrs S Clifton, RGN
Mrs E Shaw, RGN

School Counsellor:
Mrs P Telling, MSc Bristol

International Boarding Coordinator: Mrs Capucine
  Sha'Ban

Science Technicians:
Mr M Johnson, BA Hons Lancaster
Mrs H Power

Catering Manager: Miss C Wiltshire

Aims. The school is a community that places importance
on knowing each and every member – students, parents,
staff and old friends. High value is placed on the importance
of the individual. The school aims to inspire, support and
challenge the individual, enabling pupils to achieve their full
potential and excel at their particular talents. The school
believes that each and every student has a brilliance; within
an environment of high expectations, excellent teaching,

supportive staff and outstanding pastoral care the school aims to give pupils a rich and varied educational experience where they can realise that brilliance. The school believes that with the privilege of an excellent education comes responsibility, and they aim to send students out into the world who not only have a lifelong passion for learning but who are ready to make a real and positive contribution to society.

Facilities. The school occupies a splendid site in Clifton, near the Downs and Suspension Bridge. The facilities and accommodation are first class including an impressive science centre with seven laboratories, well stocked libraries and over 250 networked workstations with latest green technology implemented, a multimedia language laboratory, sixth form centre and a complex for the creative arts. Sports facilities include a heated 25m indoor swimming pool, gymnasium and floodlit netball courts on site. The offsite sports facilities, in partnership with Bristol University, include an indoor tennis centre (four courts), ten outdoor courts, two artificial turf hockey pitches and grass pitches for football, rugby and cricket.

Curriculum. Class sizes average 15 in the Lower School and 18 in the Upper School.

The *Lower School* offers an excellent academic, social and moral foundation.

The *Pre-Reception and Reception* Years follow the Foundation Stage curriculum, focusing upon: personal, social and emotional development; communication; language and literacy; problem solving, reasoning and numeracy; knowledge and understanding of the world; physical development and creative development. The children enjoy a myriad of experiences in a safe and stimulating environment. Recognition that they are "outstanding in every area" (Ofsted 2008), achievement of the Bristol Standard and accreditation by an Investors in Children quality assurance scheme, have all endorsed the splendid reputation of the Foundation Stage.

Years 1 and 2, working in an informal atmosphere within a structured framework, focus on high standards of literacy and numeracy, stimulating the children's minds through creative work and challenging projects. The curriculum also includes ICT, Science, History, Geography, Drama, Art, Music, PE, Swimming and Games. Pupils in Years 1 and 2 enjoy regular visits to a nearby Forest School throughout the year.

The *Junior Department* gives children a strong grounding in English, Mathematics, Science, ICT, History, Geography, Latin, Music, Art, Drama, Design Technology, Religious Studies, Gymnastics, Athletics and Games (Netball, Hockey, Rugby, Football, Tennis, Rounders and Cricket). French, Music, Swimming and PE are taught in the Junior Department by specialist teachers. Over 40 extra-curricular activities are on offer in the Lower School including Choirs, Orchestra, ICT, Speech and Drama, Dance and Art and Craft, together with a wide range of sports clubs providing for individual and team sports. Visiting speakers and regular trips to the local area and further afield enhance the curriculum in all departments. Children in the Junior Department also have the opportunity to enjoy overnight visits each year and there is a biennial ski trip.

After a successful first year of welcoming boys into its Sixth Form, the *Upper School* has taken further steps towards becoming fully co-educational throughout. In September 2009 boys were admitted into Years 7 and 9, and numbers of boys are continuing to grow in the Sixth Form. Boys are taught separately for English, maths, IT, sciences and French before becoming fully integrated in all subjects when they reach Year 10. This is known as the diamond edge model and Clifton High School is the only school in Bristol to adopt this approach. In Years 7 to 9 pupils study a broad and balanced curriculum. Subjects include English, Mathematics, Physics, Chemistry, Biology, ICT, History, Geography, Religious Studies, one or two modern languages (French, German, Spanish), Latin/Classical Studies Drama,

Music, Art & Design, Food, Graphic Design and Textiles, PE and Personal and Social Education (PSE). In Years 10 and 11, Physical Education and PSE form part of the general programme. For study at GCSE there is a common and balanced core of English, Mathematics, separate Sciences, a modern foreign language and ICT (Short Course), in addition to which pupils may select subjects based on their interests and career plans. The school has an excellent academic record at GCSE, AS and A Levels. Throughout the Upper School and Sixth Form pupils have a personal tutor who monitors their academic and social welfare.

The *Sixth Form*, which became co-educational in September 2008, is a thriving centre of excellence within the school. The students play an important part in the whole school community, developing their leadership skills with the younger pupils through a peer support scheme. Students have a free choice from over 20 A Level subjects including those offered at GCSE as well as Theatre Studies, Business Studies, PE, Further Mathematics, Government and Politics and Psychology. Almost all progress to university. The most able are encouraged to apply for Oxbridge entrance. All students applying for a place at Oxford in 2010 secured an offer. All Sixth Form students take part in an Enrichment Programme designed to offer a range of experiences and also have individual careers guidance sessions. All students have regular one to one tutorials. Sixth formers holding scholarships are encouraged to manage the *Forum* by producing an annual programme of debates and current affairs discussions and for inviting speakers in to the school to talk on specific topics of interest.

Family Boarding. Clifton High School offers a unique opportunity for Sixth Form students (especially those from overseas) to board, full-time or weekly, with families known to the school. The Family Boarding Coordinator acts as liaison officer and oversees the welfare of both the students and the host family. The 2009 Ofsted Inspection of the School's Family Boarding Facilities awarded the school "outstanding" in all areas.

Physical Education is a key part of the curriculum, not only for competitive sport, but for promoting a healthy lifestyle through the enjoyment of sport and exercise. In addition to the school's traditional sports of hockey, netball, football, rugby, swimming, athletics, rounders, cricket, tennis and gymnastics, specialist staff also teach a wide variety of other activities including squash, badminton, volleyball, basketball, water polo, and trampolining. Pupils regularly gain county and national honours.

Music and Drama. Virtually any instrument, including voice, may be studied, with some 50 per cent of pupils having individual lessons. Associated Board examinations are taken. There are opportunities to belong to orchestras, wind bands and choirs who perform in a variety of concerts. In Speech and Drama, a large number of pupils enter LAMDA examinations. Each year there is both a Lower and Upper School major production.

Charitable and Extra-Curricular Activities. Pupils have a strong sense of social responsibility and are actively involved in various local and national charity fundraising events. Annual collections amount to several thousand pounds. There is a lively extra-curricular activities programme both in the Lower and Upper sections of the school, responding to pupils' interests. There are over 20 clubs currently running including Science, Debating and Public Speaking, Christian Union, Astronomy and Mathematics. Pupils regularly take part in the Duke of Edinburgh's Award and World Challenge. There is a rich programme of trips both home and overseas.

Admission and Scholarships. Entry to the Lower School is by in-class assessment. Entry to the Upper School is dependent on the results of an entrance examination, Head's interview and school report. Pupils in Clifton High School Year 6 have automatic entry to Year 7. Academic scholarships are awarded each year at Year 7, 9 and Sixth Form level but there is flexibility. Some school assisted places are available in the Upper School. Music and sports awards are available at Year 7 and 9. Sports, performing arts and creative arts awards are also available in the Sixth Form. Further details are available from the School Admissions Registrar.

Fees per term (2011-2012). Tuition: Lower School £2,635–£2,655, Lunch £200; Upper School £3,780, Lunch £210. Family boarding (in addition) £3,015. Full details are available from the school.

Reductions for siblings concurrently in the school (except where fees are paid by an authority or bursary): 2nd – 5%; 3rd – 15%; 4th – 25%.

Charitable status. Clifton High School is a Registered Charity, number 311736. It exists to provide first-class education for pupils aged 3 to 18 years.

Concord College

Acton Burnell Hall, Shrewsbury, Shropshire SY5 7PF
Tel: 01694 731631
Fax: 01694 731389
e-mail: theprincipal@concordcollegeuk.com
website: www.concordcollegeuk.com

Concord College is a highly successful international boarding college providing GCSE and A Level courses. Set in 50 acres of Shropshire parkland, the College combines outstanding facilities with first-rate academic performance. The College is regularly rated in the top 20 schools in the UK. Students are cared for by a dedicated staff in a safe and beautiful environment. UK day and boarding students are also welcome at the College. Concord is a community that celebrates national and cultural diversity while students and staff are united by the wish to set high standards. The result is a happy and open community in which students are polite, articulate and conscientious without ever losing their sense of fun.

The College dates back to 1949 and moved to its present site in 1973. In 1983 it became a charitable trust. Over the years, students from over eighty countries have attended Concord.

Chair of the Governors: Dr Iain M Bride

Clerk to the Governors and Bursar: Mrs Barbara Belfield-Dean

Principal: **Neil G Hawkins**, MA Cantab, PGCE

Vice-Principal (*Summer School & Senior Master*): John Leighton, BSc, DipEd
Vice-Principal (*Academic*): Tom Lawrence, BA, PGCE
Vice-Principal (*Pastoral*): Jeremy Kerslake, MA
Head of Lower School: Mrs Gail Denham, BA

Registrar: Mrs Avril Randall

The College is a co-educational day and boarding school for students aged 13–19.
Number of students: 425 (approximately equal numbers of boys and girls) of whom over 380 are boarders.
Facilities. Facilities at Concord College are superb. Based around an historic Main Building, there are many new additions as well as medieval ruins within the grounds. There is a stunning Theatre and Music School, an excellent Sports complex, indoor swimming pool as well as an outstanding Science facility. Students eat their meals in the College Dining Room and select from a variety of international cuisine. Most students have individual study-bedrooms on campus, some with en-suite bathrooms. Students have a wide variety of facilities including a sports hall, internet café, social club and student kitchen.

Education. Teaching at Concord is undertaken in groups that average 16 at GCSE and 14 at A Level. Teachers are experts in their subjects.

At GCSE Biology, Chemistry and Physics are taught as separate subjects and emphasis is placed upon laboratory experience. Other compulsory subjects are Mathematics, English, Religious Studies and Physical Education. Optional subjects include Art, Business Studies, Geography, History, IT, Music, Spanish and Japanese.

At AS and A Level students normally study at least three A Levels and at least one further AS Level. Subjects include Art, Accounting, Biology, Chemistry, Chinese, Economics, English Language, English Literature, Geography, History, Law, Mathematics, Further Mathematics, Music, Photography, Physics and Spanish. All students who do not have GCSE English are expected to study English.

Lessons are taught in a variety of excellent classroom facilities. The new classroom block, The Jubilee Building, which opened in September 2010 houses the English and Mathematics departments in state-of-the-art classrooms.

In addition to their teachers, students have an individual tutor with whom they meet daily and who monitors their academic progress. Students also have a House Parent who is responsible for their well-being. Support is available to all students to develop their oral and discursive skills to ensure that they are able to express their ideas confidently especially at university interview.

Examination Results and University Entry. The College achieves excellent examination results with 93% A*/A/B at A Level in 2010, placing Concord comfortably within the top 20 schools in the UK according to The Times and The Financial Times league tables. The College is highly successful in placing students into UK medical schools and other top UK universities. In 2010 10 students won places at Oxford or Cambridge University, 29 at Imperial College, London and 15 at the LSE. 17 students went on to read Medicine at UK medical schools.

Selection for Entry. The college selects applicants upon the basis of interviews, school record and entry tests. Online tests are arranged for overseas applicants. Students can be accepted for entry at all ages.

Fees per annum (2011-2012). Full Boarding £26,550, Day £11,700. (Boarding fees are payable in 2 instalments.)

Scholarships and Bursaries. A fee reduction of up to 10% of full fees may be available to students who have a particularly strong academic background. For entrants to GCSE classes, scholarship entry tests are administered. General bursaries are also available on request: indeed the College has a 'needs blind' admissions policy for its day students.

Holidays. Half term holidays involve only a long weekend. The Christmas holiday is one month and Easter is only two weeks. There is a long summer vacation from the end of June until early September.

The college remains open at half term and during the Easter holiday (for students over the age of 16) and there is no additional charge for holiday accommodation and meals.

The School Day. Lessons run from 9 am to 4 pm Monday to Friday with Wednesday afternoon allocated to sport and to a trip to Shrewsbury for senior students. There is compulsory supervised study (prep) for two hours each evening Monday to Friday.

Saturday morning is used for whole-college testing. The public examination rooms are used for this purpose so that the rooms hold no fear for the students when the final public examinations are taken.

Reports to Parents. These are sent at half term in the first term and subsequently at the end of each term.

Clubs, Sports and Extra-Curricular Activities. Students at Concord can choose from a multitude of activities. Sports, music, dance and drama are all available in our own facilities. There is a Sports Hall, squash courts and gymnasium as well as outdoor facilities including football, athletics and tennis. A wealth of sporting activities is on offer ranging from archery to fencing and badminton to TaeK-wonDo. For dancers, there is a purpose-built dance studio where ballet, modern, latin and ballroom and streetdance clubs take place. Musicians can join the orchestra, wind or string groups. Choir and singing club can develop all levels of vocal talent. Many other activities are also offered ranging from bridge and chess to horse-riding and mountain-biking. Students take part in Concord's outdoor education programme and the Duke of Edinburgh's Award Scheme is also available. Whatever their talents, students are able develop them at Concord.

Charitable status. Concord College is a Registered Charity, number 326279. It exists to provide high quality education for secondary age students.

Dover College

Effingham Crescent, Dover, Kent CT17 9RH

Tel: 01304 205969
Fax: 01304 242208
e-mail: admissions@dovercollege.org.uk
website: www.dovercollege.org.uk

Dover College was founded in 1871 and occupies the grounds of the Priory of St Martin, a 24-acre site in the heart of Dover on the southeast coast of Kent. The site has been occupied for nearly 900 years and the College Close is surrounded by a number of impressive medieval buildings. Pupils still use the original Refectory, and the School Chapel is a fine 12th Century building. Another 20 acres of playing fields are nearby.

The College was granted a Royal Charter by His Majesty King George V in 1923 and the Patron of the College is the Lord Warden of the Cinque Ports.

We are the closest school to continental Europe, with easy access by Eurostar, Tunnel or Ferry. Dover Priory Station with its High Speed Link and good road links are within easy reach of the School making London 66 minutes away. London Heathrow and Gatwick airports are convenient by car.

Governors:
Members of the Council:
J T Sullivan, Esq (*Chairman*)
Revd Canon N P Nicholson (*Vice-Chairman*)

P Chadwick, Esq	M G Krayenbrink, Esq
M J Dakers, Esq	J G Ryeland, Esq
J P Gatehouse, Esq	C M Tomson, Esq
M V P H Harrington, Esq	T P Waggott, Esq
P A Koning, Esq	

Other Governors:
Mrs E J Abbotts	J N H Rice, Esq
Ms S Capito	Dr J Sedgwick, Esq
G A Conlon, Esq	J C H H Sinclair, Esq
S Devalia, Esq	Ms N F Sullivan
N J Drury, Esq	C H Thompson, Esq
R D S Foxwell, Esq	The Rt Revd S Venner
M Goodridge, Esq	P J Venning, Esq
C P Hare, Esq	D R Walter, Esq
A Lancaster, Esq	W T Westwater, Esq
H J Leslie, Esq	I S Wilmshurst, Esq
Ms K Rogers	

Headmaster: **Mr Gerry Holden**, MA St Andrews, FRSA

Deputy Head: Mrs Helen J Tresidder, BSc

Director of Studies: Mr D Ellerington, BSc, BA, MA

Head of Infant & Junior Department: Ms R Morley, BA Hons

Assistant Teaching Staff:
Mrs E Aylward, BA	Mr G R Hill, MA
Mr M Beere, BSc	Ms V Kitchen, BA Hons
Mrs L Binfield, BA	Mr C Lockyer, BMus
Mr D Brooks, BSc Hons	Mr G Mees, BA
Mr G Came, CEd	Mrs T Mills, NVQ
Mr R Chohan, BSc	Ms A Nicholas, BA
Mrs S Cook, Dip TEFL	Mrs J Palmer, MA
Mr J Dewick, BA Hons	Miss Y Ramadharsingh, BSc
Mrs F Donnelly, CertEd	Mrs E Repaska, MA
Mr P A H Donnelly, BA, DipTEFL	Mrs J Richardson, BA Hons
Mr P Driver, BA Hons Oxon	Mr N Roberts, BA
Mr D Fletcher, BA Hons Cantab, MA Cantab, PGCE	Mr T Root, BSc Hons
	Ms L Salter, MA
Mrs S E Eberlein, BEd	Miss J Single, BA
Mrs J Ellerington, Adv DipEd, PGCPSE	Mr B Smith, BSc
	Mrs E Smith
Mr B Fairclough, BA	Mr R G Spencer, MA, FRCO
Mrs I Gibbons, BSc Hons	Ms A Squire, Montessori TDip
Miss C Harland, BA Hons, Trinity Cert TESOL	Miss S Stow, BSc
Mrs J Harris, Adv CertEd	Ms T Taylor, BA, Dip de Cand
Ms D Hassan, CertEd	Mr P Wharton, MA
Mr C Henderson, BSc Hons, PGCE Phys Ed, PGCE Ed Mgmt	Mr P Young, BA

Bursar and Business Manager: Col P Barry
Business Development & Admissions Officer: Mrs G Degrange
Admissions Coordinator: Mrs S Powell
Headmaster's Secretary: Mrs V Henderson
Medical Officer: Dr Barley
Medical Centre Sisters: Mrs C Hunt, S Robinson, S May
IT Manager: Mr S Roberts

Co-education. Dover College (3–18) has been fully co-educational since 1975 and the 345 boys and girls are integrated at all levels. There are 120 boarders.

Organisation. The school divides into four parts: the Infants and Juniors from age 3–11, Priory from 11–13, Lower College from 13–16, and the Sixth Form. For Lower College and the Sixth Form there are four Houses, all situated on the College Close, two for boys and two for girls, all incorporating both day pupils and boarders.

Dover College's Infant and Junior School is housed in a spacious self-contained building within the beautiful grounds of Dover College and Priory has its own House accommodation.

Catering. The catering team provides delicious, healthy, well-balanced homemade food.

Curriculum. Infants and Juniors study a wide range of subjects. Great importance is placed upon literacy, numeracy, information technology and key skills. Pre-Reception children follow the Early Years "learn through play" curriculum. French is taught from Year 1. Fourth and fifth form pupils study between six and ten GCSE subjects, depending on their level of ability. The curriculum at this level is flexible, enabling pupils to have an academic curriculum designed to suit individual needs.

All pupils are given very careful guidance when making their GCSE level choices, by their Academic Tutor, Housemaster/Housemistress, the Careers Department and by the Director of Studies.

At all stages of a pupil's time at Dover College, progress is carefully monitored. Assessment periods occur regularly, during which pupils are graded for achievement and effort. A merit/demerit system operates for pupils up to 16 years.

Classes at Dover College are kept as small as possible. Class size up to GCSE are generally between 15–20 and at A level 10–15. Some A level sets are smaller.

Considerable emphasis is placed upon the breadth of education offered: music, art and drama are an integral part of the curriculum. All pupils participate in a variety of sports, with stress placed upon the development of leadership skills.

Sixth Form. The Sixth Form is overseen by a Head of Sixth Form and pupils are able to choose AS and A Levels from a list of over 20 subjects. Some BTEC subjects are also available (Sports, Health and Social Care, Travel and Tourism). Traditional academic subjects are provided, as are the practical subjects of art, design and technology, textiles, photography, drama and music.

Sixth Formers wear a distinctive uniform and are given more choice and freedom than junior pupils, being expected to respond positively to their treatment as young adults. A well-equipped Sixth Form Centre is used as a meeting place and social club.

The School's Careers Adviser works in close liaison with Connexions to plan, deliver and evaluate an integrated careers' education and guidance programme. This enables pupils to gain the necessary knowledge, skills and understanding in order to make informed career plans before attending the universities of their choice.

International Study Centre (ISC). The International Department was started in 1957 and backed at the time by members of NATO, although international boarding has a far longer history than this starting point. The International Study Centre provides intensive English courses for pupils whose first language is not English. These courses vary in length and the aim is to enable all pupils to integrate fully into the life of Dover College as soon as possible after their arrival.

Individual Support. There is an Individual Needs Department in which pupils with learning difficulties (eg Dyslexia) receive 1:1 tuition. Each pupil has a member of staff as a personal tutor. The tutor supervises his/her pupils' general academic progress.

Art and Technology. The Art Department is situated in a purpose-built accommodation. Fine Art, pottery, textiles and photography are all available. Examination results are always excellent both at GCSE and A Level.

The Technology Department shares the building with Art and is situated in a large, well-equipped, open-plan workshop. Pupils are encouraged to work with a range of materials (wood, plastic etc) and use CAD software. Design Technology is available at GCSE and A level. There are many opportunities for the students to use the workshop outside curriculum time. Design and Technology also thrives as an activity.

Music and Drama. Music plays a particularly important part in the life of the School. The well-equipped Music School was relocated onsite in January 2011 and opened by Julian Lloyd Webber. It comprises high-tech soundproof pods of various sizes for practice, classrooms and recital room. Extra-curricular activities are numerous. The Chapel Choir meets three times a week and is the backbone of the many concerts and services, but there are weekly rehearsals for the Choral Society, String group, Windband, Jazz band, and Madrigal group. There is a concert at the end of each term, held in the Refectory, and numerous informal concerts in a variety of locations. A House Music competition takes place annually.

Drama is a very active part of the cultural life of the School, as well as part of the Lower School curriculum; there is a major school production each year together with additional House productions. Drama is offered at A Level and GCSE.

Learning Resources Centre. It provides cutting-edge facilities and resources to all pupils, including Careers information.

Sport. The School's main playing fields are a short distance away; on site are tennis courts, an astroturf, basketball court and an excellent Sports Hall with a fitness suite. Sports include Athletics, Badminton, Basketball, Cricket, Cross Country, Running, Football, Hockey, Netball, Sailing, Tennis, Volleyball and various PE activities. Swimming takes place at the indoor swimming pool in the local leisure centre. Golf may be played on local courses and riding is also offered locally.

Extra-Curricular Activities. In addition to sport, pupils have the opportunity of taking part in a wide range of over 50 activities including Adventure Training, Art, Chess, Computing, Debating, Duke of Edinburgh's Award, Dancing, Fencing, First Aid, Language Clubs, Music, Photography, Wine Tasting, Stage Management and Technology. The London West End theatres are within easy reach and regular trips to a variety of productions are made.

Pastoral Care. All pupils benefit from a carefully designed system of outstanding pastoral care. Every Dover College student belongs to a House and Boarders are provided with comfortable accommodation in one of four boarding houses. All Sixth Formers have single study-bedrooms. A Housemaster or Housemistress, supported by a team of tutors, runs each House; it is their role to give pastoral support as well as supervising the pupils' academic progress.

Pupils have access to a fully equipped and professionally staffed Medical Centre, which can accommodate pupils overnight.

Religious Life. College has its own Chapel and is a Church of England school. All pupils are encouraged to respect each other's beliefs and faiths from a position of tolerance and understanding.

Entry. Pupils are typically admitted into the Senior School at 11, 13 or 16 but may come at any age. Most pupils join the College in September, but entry in January and April is possible.

Entry into the Infants and Juniors is by interview and an informal assessment carried out during a "Taster Day" at the school. The School has its own 11+ examination. 13+ pupils normally sit the Common Entrance at their own Preparatory School. Provision is made for direct entry into the Sixth Form for boys and girls. This is normally conditional upon GCSE results. Further information can be obtained from Admissions.

Fees per term (2011-2012). Junior Day £2,040–£3,050; Senior Day £3,555–£4,330; Senior Flexi Boarding £5,800–£6,900; Full Boarding £6,350–£8,650.

Scholarships. (*See Scholarship Entries section.*) Academic, Music, Art, Sports and All-Rounder Scholarships are available. The scholarships are offered at 11+, 13+ and 16+. Details can be obtained from Admissions.

Old Dovorian Club. *Secretary*: R Upton, Esq, c/o Dover College.

Charitable status. Dover College is a Registered Charity, number 307856. The School exists to develop confidence and individual talents.

d'Overbroeck's College

The Swan Building, 111 Banbury Road, Oxford OX2 6JX

Tel: 01865 310000 (Sixth Form)
          01865 302620 (Leckford Place 11–16)
Fax: 01865 552296 (Sixth Form)
          01865 302622 (Leckford Place 11–16)
e-mail: mail@doverbroecks.com
website: www.doverbroecks.com

Principal: **Sami Cohen**, BSc

Administrative Principal: Richard Knowles, MA, DPhil

Academic Head of Sixth Form: Alasdair MacPherson, MA
(*English**)

Academic Coordinator: Alastair Barnett, BA, PGCE
(*History**)

Head of Year 12: Carolyn Newton, BA, MPhil
(*Communication & Culture, Sociology**)

ISC Director: Helen Wood, MA, PhD, DTEFLA (*EAL**)

Head of Leckford Place: Mark Olejnik, BA, PGCE
(*History*)

Deputy Head of Leckford Place: Jane Cockerill, BA, MEd,
PGCE (*Music*)

Director of Studies, Leckford Place: Paul Wheeler, BSc,
PGCE (*Geography*)

Teaching Staff:
* *Head of Department or Departmental Coordinator*

Frank Adam, BSc, QTS (*Mathematics*)
Melinda Allan, BA, CELTA, DELTA (*EAL*)
Katie Amiri, BA, TESOL, TEFL (*EAL*)
Louise Arnould, BA, BTec (*Art*)
Rosie Astley, Froebel Dip, RSA SpLD (*Learning Support*)
Daniel Austin, BA (*EAL*)
Paul Baily, BA, CertEd (*Physics**)
Shanti Bharatan, MSc, PhD (*Biology*)
Gwenaelle Benson, BA, PGCE (*French*)
Ursual Boughton, BSc, PGCE, (*Mathematics*)
Christophe Brinster, M-ès-L (*French**)
Clare Cameron, BA, PGCE (*Business Studies*)
Chris Carter, BSc, PGCE (*Physics, Mathematics*)
Andrew Colclough, BA, MA (*Politics**)
Helen Cowley, BSc, PGCE (*Chemistry*)
Margaret Craig, BSc, FAETC, (*History of Art*)
Charles Currie, MPhys, PGCE (*Physics*)
Patricia Dass, MSc (*Psychology**)
Jon-Paul Davies, BSc, MA, PGCE (*Geography*)
Jing Ping Fan, BA, MA, PGCE (*Mandarin*)
Sylvia Fasel, MA (*French*)
Stephen Field, MA, PhD (*Chemistry*)
Julia Ford, BA (*Psychology*)
Andrew Gillespie, MA (*Business Studies*, Economics*)
Amy Godel, BA, PGCE (*Mathematics*)
Frances Godsal, BA, MA (*Drama & Theatre Studies*)
Anita Goriely, MS, PhD (*Mathematics*)
Nick Haines, MPhil (*Mathematics*)
Keiko Harada, MA (*Japanese*)
Simon Harrison, BA (*Economics*, Business Studies*)
James Holburn, MA CPE (*English*)
Christopher Holland, BA, MPhil (*English*)
Graham Hope, MA, DPhil (*Mathematics*)
Clare Horne, BSc, MA, DPhil, PGCE, PgDip
(*Mathematics*)
Margaret Horton, MA, PGCE (*History*)
Fizza Hussain, BA, PGCE (*Drama**)
Anna Irvine, BA, TESOL (*EAL*)
Adam Johnstone, MA, MSt (*Biology*)
Anne-Marie Jones, BSc, PhD (*Biology*)
Susanne Kreitz, PhD (*German**)
Pascale Lafeber, MA (*French*)
Jagjeet Lally, BA, MSc (*Economics*)
Andrew Latcham, BA, DPhil (*History, Politics*)
Abby Loebenberg, DPhil, MPhil (*Sociology*)
David Mackie, BA, MA, DPhil (*Classical Civilisation,
Philosophy*)
Christine Martelloni, MSc (*French*)
Susan McKendrick, BA, PGCE (*Music**)
Andrew McNeill, BSc, PhD (*Mathematics**)
Caroline McNicoll, BA (*History*)
Elina Medley, BA, MA, PGCE (*Photography*)
Alan Milosevic, BSc, PGCE (*Computing*)
Colin Murphy, BA, MSc (*Psychology*)

Jane Nimmo-Smith, BA (*Classics,* Ancient History**)
James O'Connor, BTEC HND (*Music Technology*)
Kate Palmer, BSc, PGCE (*Geography**)
Sharone Parnes BSc, LLB, LPC (*Law*)
Max Parsonage, BSc, PGCE (*Chemistry**)
Jill Partridge, BSc, PGCE (*Biology*)
Mark Piesing, BA, PGCE (*Communication Studies*)
Martin Procter, BA, PGCE (*Physical Education**)
Wendy Rawding, BA, PGCE (*Art & Design*)
Nick Reeves, MA Cantab, PGCE (*Art*, History of Art**)
Martine Renauld, M-ès-L, PGCE (*French*)
Angus Roberts, BA, PGCE (*Mathematics, Physics*)
Ruth Robinson, JP, BA, PGCE (*English*)
Ana Rodriguez Nodal, BA (*Spanish*)
Klaudia-Ines Schwenk, MA (*German*)
Simita Sem, BA, PGCE (*Law*)
Andrew Sheahan, BA (*Economics*)
Sarah Shekleton, BA, MA, PGCE (*Mathematics*, Leckford
Place*)
Mary Stephenson, BA, PGCE (*ICT*)
Oliver Stone, BA, PGCE (*Spanish**)
Tuncel Tack, BSc, PhD (*Chemistry**)
Jaimie Tarrell, BEd (*Biology**)
Emma Tinker, BA, MA, PhD (*Communication & Culture,
English, Film Studies*)
Oliver van Biervliet, BSc, PGCE (*Biology, Physical
Education*)
Natalie Vlachakis, BSc, MSc, (*Biology, Chemistry,
Science*)
Natalia Walker, BA (*Russian*)
David Wareham, BA, MA, TESOL (*EAL*)
Laurence Waters, City & Guilds (*Photography*)
Chris Webb, BEd, BTech, HND (*Design Technology*)
Louise Wheaton, BSc, PGCE (*Geography*)
Clare Wildish, BA (*Accounts*, Business Studies*)
Joanne Williams, BA, PGCE (*English*)
Helen Wilson, BA, PGCE (*Art*)
Martin Winstone, BA, MLitt (*History, Politics*)
Carly Wise, BA, PGCE (*Physical Education*)
Sharon Wyper, BA, PGATC, MA (*Art & Design*)
Edward Yeo, BA, PGCE (*Music*)

Sport & Extra-Curricular Activities:
Jo Kalies, BSc
Jonathan Richards, BSc (*Physical Education**)

Bursar: Peter Talbot, BEd

Registrar: Bridget Norton, BA

Accommodation Office:
Felisa Deas, BA
Rebecca Rue, BA

College Counsellor: Catherine Bech, BA

Principal's PA: Pat Harris

Age Range. 11–18. Day: age 11–16 (Leckford Place);
Residential and Day: age 16–18 (The Sixth Form).
Number in School. 435.
Fees per term (2011-2012). Tuition: £4,225 (Leckford
Place); £6,175 (Sixth Form). Accommodation: £1,850–
£3,175.

d'Overbroeck's is a co-educational school in Oxford for
pupils aged 11–18. We are fairly evenly divided between
residential and day students in the Sixth Form; but are day
only up to the age of 16.

Our academic approach is characterised by small classes
(maximum of 10 students per class in the Sixth Form and 15
up to GCSE) and a highly supportive and encouraging
approach that builds on each student's strengths and enables
outstanding academic achievements.

Teaching is highly interactive and seeks to generate
enthusiasm for the subject, sound academic skills and effective working habits – while at the same time providing a

thorough preparation for public examinations and ensuring that the learning experience is fun. The environment is friendly, stimulating and engaging with staff and students working together to achieve the best possible results.

A wide range of sporting and other extra-curricular activities is available to complement the learning in the classroom. Students can take part in numerous College events and performances as well as benefit from the wide range of educational, cultural and social activities which Oxford has to offer. We believe that happiness and success go hand in hand – and throughout the College we do our utmost to ensure that every student is given new opportunities to develop and is encouraged and rewarded – whether in the classroom, on stage or on the sports field.

Alongside academic achievement, there is a strong emphasis on personal development and on fostering a sense of individual responsibility, particularly in the Sixth Form. The fact the Sixth Form is on a different site allows us to offer a clear sense of progression from Year 11 with an approach appropriate to older students. Many students from other schools join us for direct entry into our Sixth Form.

We expect high standards of commitment and effort from our students and have a track-record of strong GCSE and A Level results, both in absolute terms and on a value-added basis. Students benefit from excellent teaching and a positive approach which enables them to maximise their potential. Last year, for example, our students achieved 62% grade As at A Level with around 25% of students gaining straight As in all their subjects. The overwhelming majority of students go on to university and we have an excellent record of success with entry including Oxford and Cambridge (usually 10% of the Upper Sixth), as well as medical, law and art schools.

Main Entry Points: age 11 and 13 into Leckford Place; direct entry into the d'Overbroeck's Sixth Form. Scholarships are available.

Ewell Castle School

Church Street, Ewell, Surrey KT17 2AW
Tel: 020 8394 3561 (admissions)
         020 8393 1413 (main office)
Fax: 020 8786 8218
e-mail: admissions@ewellcastle.co.uk
website: www.ewellcastle.co.uk

Ewell Castle, a day school, was built as a castellated mansion in 1814. The gardens and playing fields cover some fifteen acres and were once part of Nonsuch Park. The Senior School is accommodated at The Castle. The Junior School occupies two other premises in the village – Chessington Lodge, a Georgian house minutes from The Castle and Glyn House, the former Rectory to the parish church, opposite the Senior School. The school, which was founded in 1926, is registered as an educational charity and is administered by a Board of Governors, which is in membership of the Association of Governing Bodies of Independent Schools (AGBIS). The Principal is a member of the Society of Heads of Independent Schools (SHMIS) and the Head of the Junior School is a member of IAPS (The Independent Association of Prep Schools).

Chairman of the Governing Body: D C M Hill

Principal: A J Tibble, BSc, PGCE, NPQH

Head of Senior School: M Holder-Williams, MA, BA, PGCE, NPQH
Head of Junior School: Mrs H M Crossley, MA, BEd, CertEd

Deputy Head of Senior School: S D Bromley, BA, PGCE
Deputy Head of Junior School: Mrs S Laws, MA, BEd

Academic Staff:
* *Head of Department*

Mr J Aruliah, BA Hons, MA (*Mathematics*)
Miss K Ash, BA, PGCE (*Music, German*)
M Ashby, BSc, Grad Dip (*Physics*)
L Bader-Clynes, BA, RADA (**Drama*)
J Barnardo, BSc, MEd (*Information Technology, Mathematics*)
J C W Blencowe, BA, PGCE (**History, RS*)
Miss S L Brack, BA, PGCE (**Music*)
M Bradshaw BSc, Grad Dip (*Mathematics*)
Mrs C Buckley, BA, PGCE (*SENCo*)
S Casey, BA, BTEC (**Physical Education*)
Miss S Cronin, BBSt, PGCE (*Spanish, German*)
Mrs R Din, BSc, PGCE (*Biology*)
J J D'Souza, BSc, PGCE (*Business Studies, Psychology*)
C Fitzgibbon, BSc, PGCE (**Mathematics, *Psychology*)
J Grindrod, BA, PGCE (*Physical Education*)
Mrs D Hillman, BEd (*Religious Studies*)
Ms V Kennedy, MA, PGCE (*French, German*)
P Krause, BBus, DipEd (**Business Studies, *Government & Politics*)
D Laws, BA, PGCE (*Design Technology*)
S Leigh, BA, PGCE (*English*)
Miss E Lewis, BEd, PGCE (*History, Religious Studies, Government & Politics*)
Mrs E McManus, MA, BA, PGCE (*English*)
S Manley, BSc, PGCE (*Biology*)
Mrs E Morton, BA, PGCE (**Art & Design*)
K B Peto, BA, PGCE (*English, *PSHCE*)
Miss P Renouf, BA (*Drama*)
C H Roffey, BSc, PGCE (**Chemistry*)
N Saadallah, BA, PGCE (**French*)
V S Sandhu, BSc, PGCE (*Geography*)
Mrs N Scott, NVQ (*Learning Support*)
Mrs E Shepherd, BA (*Art & Design*)
V Singh, BSc, MTech (*Physics*)
Mrs C W Tapp, BA, PGCE (*Learning Support*)
Ms M Thomas, BSc, PGCE (*Chemistry*)
D P A Thompson, M des RCA, PGCE (**Design Technology*)
N Turk, BSc, GTP (*Physical Education*)
D Vijapura, BSc, PGCE (*Mathematics*)
Miss K Wallace, BA, PGCE (**English*)
Ms J Wilson, BSc, CertEd (**Information Technology*)

Junior School:
Miss H Albright, BEd
Mrs C Alford
Mrs T Blakeman, BEd
M Darlow, BEd
Mrs L Fisher, STAC
Mrs S Fowler, BSc, PGCE
Mrs D Goff, CertEd
Mrs P Hacker, BA, PGCE
Miss K Hewitt, BA
Miss C Leadbeter, MA, PGCE
Mrs C Leeds, NNEB, SEN
Mrs C Nightingale, BSc, PGCE
Mrs M Puri, CACHE Dip
Mrs A Rowe, BSc, CertEd
Miss H Seager
N J Tinkler, BA, PGCE
P E Young, BA, PGCE

Registrar & Principal's PA: Mrs D Bellenger
Bursar: G Holland
Assistant Bursar: Mrs M Kaegler
Clerk to Bursar: Mrs T Wilkins
School Secretaries: Mrs N Brown, Mrs J Dow, Mrs B Grierson
Head of Careers, School Counsellor: Mrs E Thomson-Coleman
Examinations Secretary: Mrs D Tibble

Development Officer: M J Coleman
Library Manager: Ms S Malost, BA
IT Management: M Szetela, DipEd

The school comprises approximately 550 pupils in total with 360 pupils in the Senior School and 190 pupils in the Junior School.

Buildings. The school is located on three sites within the village of Ewell, accommodating The Junior School (Chessington Lodge: co-educational 3–7 years; Glyn House: co-educational 7–11 years) and the Senior School (The Castle: boys 11–18 years). Academic departments are well resourced and accommodated. A new classroom block on The Castle site, scheduled for completion August 2011, will provide six new classrooms, purpose-built kitchen and dining/assembly area, Sixth Form cafeteria, cloakrooms and office accommodation. Other recent developments include: major refurbishment of the Library (The Castle), new hard play area (Glyn House) and establishment of new garden area (Chessington Lodge).

Aims and Values. The aim is to achieve potential and excellence over a broad field: in academic, in sport, and the arts, and in numerous other extra-curricular activities and aspects of school life. The cornerstone of this small school is the strong pastoral care system and Christian values upheld, which enable the school not only to achieve its main purpose but also to maintain high standards of discipline, conduct and appearance.

A highly qualified and committed staff achieve very impressive results at KS2, KS3, GCSE, AS and A Level from pupils with a range of abilities. The School has enjoyed particular success in public examinations in recent years, with record levels being achieved at GCSE and/or A Level.

Classes are small, averaging fifteen at the Senior School, where setting is also adopted in core subjects, and seventeen at the Junior School.

Organisation. The Junior School is co-educational and accepts pupils from three years. Most boys transfer to the Senior School at 11+. Girls are prepared for entry to other Independent and selective/non-selective schools at 11+. Many Sixth Form classes are shared with pupils from a local girls' school.

Curriculum. National Curriculum requirements are incorporated into Senior and Junior School schemes, though the broad and flexible curriculum extends beyond such criteria. Breadth at KS3 (11–13 years) is replaced at KS4 (14–16 years) by a core of Mathematics, English, Science and Religious Studies supplemented by a wide ranging option scheme covering the languages, arts, humanities and technologies. There is an increased range of subjects available at AS and A Level in the Sixth Form (17–19 years).

Work experience is undertaken by pupils in Year 11 (16 years). Specialist HE/Careers guidance is available from Year 9 within the Senior School.

After the Sixth Form the majority of pupils proceed to Universities and Colleges.

Extra-Curricular Activities. The principal sports are rugby, soccer and cricket. In addition there are numerous pursuits which include: athletics, badminton, basketball, fencing, sailing, skiing, squash, table tennis, and tennis. There is an extensive music and drama programme and other activities such as the Duke of Edinburgh's Award Scheme. Regular language, sports and field trips embarked for America, Austria, Belgium, France, Germany, Ireland, Italy and Spain in recent years.

The school benefits from a strong and active PTA.

Admissions. Boys and girls are admitted to the Junior School at the age of three. There are no entry requirements at this stage. Older children are invited to attend the school for a day's assessment, within a class, during which time they may undertake tests in English & Mathematics.

At the Senior School the standard points of entry are at 11+, 13+ and 16+. Subject to availability, there may be places at other levels. Entry requirements include interview, report from previous school and written assessments. At 13+ and 16+ the assessments may take the form of Common Entrance or GCSE respectively.

Visitors are welcome to the school on scheduled Open Days or by appointment. Individual assessments are held by arrangement. Scholarship assessments are undertaken in January each year.

Scholarships. Scholarships are available for pupils entering the school at 11+, 13+ and 16+. At 11+ awards are made on the basis of competitive examination/assessment in the designated category. In the case of 13+ and 16+ awards are likely to be made on the basis of Common Entrance and GCSE performance respectively. Awards are made for academic excellence and also in the categories of Art & Design, Performing Arts, Music, Sport and 'All-Rounder'.

Fees per term (2011-2012). Senior School £4,150, Junior School £1,220–£2,700.

Junior School. *For further information, see Ewell Castle Junior School entry in IAPS section.*

Charitable status. Ewell Castle School is a Registered Charity, number 312079. The aim of the charity is to achieve potential and excellence over a broad field: in academic, in sport, and the arts, and in numerous other extra-curricular activities and aspects of school life.

Farringtons School

Perry Street, Chislehurst, Kent BR7 6LR
Tel: 020 8467 0256
Fax: 020 8467 5442
e-mail: fvail@farringtons.kent.sch.uk
website: www.farringtons.org.uk

Board of Management for Methodist Schools.

Governing Body:
Chairman: Mr D Chaundler, OBE
Vice-Chairman: Mrs R L Howard, BSc, BA

Members:
Mr W Allen, FCIB
Reverend B Calvert
Mr D G Cracknell, LLB
Miss M Faulkner, BSc
Mr J Flannery
Mr S J Frankham
Mr T Harris, FRICS, FCIArb
Revd J Impey, BSc, MA
Dr H S Richardson, BA
Mr S Richardson
Mr G Russell, MA
Dr A G Williams, MB, MRCGP, DipPal Med
Mrs K York
Mr M Vinales

Bursar and Clerk to the Governors: Mrs J Niggemann

Headmistress: Mrs C James, MA Liverpool and London

Deputy Senior School: Mrs S Worth, BA Hons, PGCE
Deputy Junior School: Mrs S Wheeler, MA
Assistant Head Senior School: Mr J Attridge, BA Hons, PGCE
Assistant Head Senior School: Mrs J Baillie, BEd
Assistant Head Senior School: Mr M Phillips, BA Hons, PGCE
Chaplain: (*to be appointed*)
Registrar: Mrs F Vail (*Boarding*), Mrs J Grima (*Day*)

* *Head of Department*

English: PGCE
*Mrs V Denman, BA Hons,

Miss K Duncan, BA Hons, PGCE
Mrs S Worth, BA Hons, PGCE
Miss S Bliss, BA Hons, PGCE
Miss R George, BA Hons

Mathematics:
*Mr J Acford, BSc Hons, MA Education
Ms R Quinney, CertEd
Mrs I Haider, PGCE
Mrs E Lovell, MSc, PGCE
Mr M Sansom, BTech, PGCE, AdvDipEd

Science:
*Mrs C Crouser, BPE S Africa
Mr R H A Flack, BSc
Mrs P Drury, CertEd
Mrs M Raybould, BSc Hons
Mrs A Roberts, BSc Hons

Modern Languages:
*Mlle I Mosqueron, L-ès-L, PGCE
Mrs M Baron INSdP
Miss R Frances BA Hons, MA

Humanities:
Mr J Attridge, BA Hons, PGCE
Mrs J W S Baillie, BEd
Mrs S Bowman, BSc
Mrs A Harris, ICA
Mrs K Hodge, BSc Hons
Mr M Phillips, BA Hons, PGCE
Mrs J Pyle, CertEd

Technology:
Mrs G Allen, BA Hons, MA, PGCE
Mrs A Lowles, BA Hons
Mrs K Matthews, CertEd
Miss S Thorne, BEd
Mrs S Watson, BA Hons, PGCE
Miss A Fleming

ICT:
Mr J Gardner, BSc, MSc, PGCE

Music
*Mr G James (*Director of Music*)

Learning Support:
Mrs J Maynard, OCR Cert
Mrs A Vinales

Sport:
*Mr C Doyle, BEd
Miss N Hyde, BA Hons
Mrs G Ody, BEd Hons
Mr M Phillips, BA Hons, PGCE
Mrs J Wood, BEd Hons

Junior School:
Mrs L Knight, BEd, CertEd
Mrs W Reed, LTCL, CertEd
Miss V Bloomfield, CertEd
Miss J Cox, Bed Hons
Mrs J M Hook, BEd Hons
Mr M Dutton, BEd, CertEd
Mrs J Munro, DipEd
Mrs P Brookman, BA, JPED, BEd
Mrs L Long, BEd
Mrs C Williams, CertEd
Mrs L Hayes, CertEd, DipSpLD
Mrs J Cliff, MA, PGCE
Miss G Harvey, BEd, CertEd
Mrs K Kilgallon, CertEd
Mr T Ruffle, BEd, CertEd
Miss N Brett, BA Hons, PGCE
Miss S Cox, BA Hons, PGCE
Miss J Cox, BEd Hons
Miss E McCann, BA Hons
Mrs S Walker, BA Mus

Boarding Staff:
Mrs S Bowman
Mrs J Heighway
Miss M Xu

Nursery:
Miss N J Tetley, BA Hons (*Teacher in charge*)
Mrs E High, Dip in Pre School, NVQ3
Mrs J Wilkins, NVQ3

Farringtons School is situated in 26 acres of green belt land in Chislehurst, which provide attractive surroundings while still being within easy reach of London (20 minutes to Charing Cross), the South Coast and Gatwick (45 minutes) and Heathrow airport via the M25 (1 hour).

The School is committed to providing a first-class education for pupils of all ages in a caring community which supports all its members and helps each pupil to achieve his or her full potential both academically and personally. After school care is available until 6 pm.

The curriculum offered is that of the National Curriculum, with a wide range of GCSE and A Level subjects available. Nearly 100% of Sixth Form leavers customarily go on to degree courses at Universities or Higher Education Colleges. Academic standards are high from a comprehensive intake of pupils and in 2010 ran at 93% of all Year 11 pupils securing 5 or more A*–C grades and a 100% pass rate at A Level.

The excellent facilities include a Technology building, a large Sports Hall with Dance Studio and Weights Room, splendidly-equipped Science and Modern Language departments, well-stocked libraries, CD-ROM computers, Careers Room, new indoor heated swimming pool and extensive playing fields, as well as a School Chapel, where the School regularly comes together.

The main sports are netball, tennis, football, rugby, swimming and athletics, but badminton, volleyball and table tennis are also undertaken and other extra-curricular activities available include the Duke of Edinburgh's Award Scheme, Business Enterprise, various choirs and instrumental ensembles, gymnastics, jazz-dance, ballet, drama club, fencing, etc.

To obtain a prospectus and further information or to arrange a visit, contact the Registrar.

Fees per term (2011-2012). Day £2,920–£3,920, Weekly Boarding £7,050, Full Boarding £7,500.

Charitable status. Farringtons School is a Registered Charity, number 307916. It exists solely to provide a high-quality, caring education.

Friends' School

Saffron Walden, Essex CB11 3EB
Tel: 01799 525351
Fax: 01799 523808
e-mail: admissions@friends.org.uk
website: www.friends.org.uk

Clerk to the Board of Governors: Martin Dickinson

Head: Graham Wigley, BA, MA

Bursar: David Wood, ACIB
Deputy Head: Anna Chaudhri, MA
Assistant Head (Curriculum): ‡Eleanor Mackenzie Lambert, MEd, BSc, DipEnvSc
Assistant Head (Pastoral): Sarah Westerhuis, BEd
Head of Sixth Form: ‡John Searle-Barnes, BA, MA

Teaching Staff:
‡ *Holder of PGCE*

Art:
‡Serena O'Connor, BA
‡Phillip Richardson, DipAD, ATC
‡Matthew Miller, BA, BTEC

Business Studies:
Carolyn White, MEd, BEd

Careers:
Julie Anderson, BEd

Critical Thinking:
§‡Brigid Vousden, BA

Design Technology – Product Design:
‡Jessica Armitage, BA
‡Richard Twinn, BA

Design Technology – Food:
§Catherine Whyte, BEd

Drama:
‡Richard Smith, BA
Shelley Dowsett, BSc, GTP

English:
‡Gillian Kinnear, BA
‡Heather Carter, BA, MA
§Sue Lock, CertEd
§Joanna Matthews, BEd

ESOL:
‡Sarah Joseph, BA

‡Jane Henfrey, BA

Film Studies:
‡John Searle-Barnes, BA, MA

Geography:
‡Alison Ainsworth, BA
‡Hannah Sargent, MSc, BSc

History:
‡John Searle-Barnes, BA, MA
‡Charlotte O'Neill, BA
Jennifer Allwood, BEd

ICT:
§Carolyn White, BEd
Teresa Shepherd

Library:
Judith Brown, MA, BA

Mathematics:
Mark Caddy, PhD, BSc
‡Richard Moss, BTEC
‡Geoffrey Curtis, BSc
Carolyn White, MEd, BEd

Modern Languages:
‡Gisèle Searle-Barnes, Licence, MA
‡Peter Fasching, BA
§‡Jane Pearce, BA
‡Anna Chaudhri, MA

Music:
‡Gavin Greenaway, BA
Martin Wilson, BMus, ARCM, ALCM

Visiting Music Staff:
Mary Richardson, BA, PGCE, DipABRSM
Jason Meyrick, FTCL, LRAM, LTCL, Prof Cert
Alison Townend, BA, LLCM, LGSM, LTCL
Nicky Ogden, BA, PGCE, LRAM
Edward Dodge, MA, GRSM, ARMCM, PGCE
Philippa Hopewell, BSc, CT ABRSM
Steven Hynes, BTEC
Louis Thorne, BSc
Mark Townend, GRSM, LRAM, DipRAM
Sarah Clark, BTEC
Angela Lesslie, BMus, PGCE
Amy Klohr, BA, LRAM
Carla Robinson, LTCL

Physical Education:
Nicholas Batcheler, BEd, DipT
Jennifer Allwood, BEd
Raymond Mordini, BPHE
Shelley Dowsett, BSc, GTP

Religious Studies & PSHE:
§‡Helen Golden, BA

Science:
Christine Sleight, BEd, CPhys, MInstP
‡Joanne Walton, BSc
‡Philip Dant, BSc
§Julie Anderson, BEd
‡Eleanor Mackenzie Lambert, MEd, BSc, DipEnvSc
Raymond Mordini, BPHE

Speech & Drama:
Susan McConnel, BDS, ALAM, LRAM

Study Centre – Learning Support:
‡Heather Carter, BA, MA
Caryn Pepper
Heather Douglas, MSc
‡Brigid Vousden, BA, MPhil

House Staff:
Barbara Askew
Stephen Staerck, CertEd, Adv Dip Counselling & Welfare

Head of Junior School: Andrew Holmes, BEd, CertEd
Deputy Head: Sally Meyrick, BA

Junior Class Teachers:
‡Kate Richardson, BSc
Jacqueline Branch, CertEd
‡Jane Manley, BA
Deborah Ballingall, BEd
‡Sally Meyrick, BA

Infant Department & Early Years:
Sally Manser, CertEd (*Head*)
Lucy Nicholson, MA, PGCE
Claire Milner, BSc

Learning Support:
§Clare Gill, BA, Cert TESOL, PG Cert Dyslexia and Literacy

Nursery Coordinator:
Tiffany Johnson, NNEB

Friends' School is a co-educational day school for pupils ages 3 to 18 with boarding from age 11. We aim to realise the potential and talent of all pupils within a friendly but challenging environment. High standards of teaching and academic attainment are enriched by a broader framework of personal development.

At age 11 pupils finish the Junior School with excellent SATs results and are well prepared for their transition into the Senior School. Friends' is one of the top schools in the country to deliver a "value-added" education, improving achievement between age 11 and GCSE. We achieve this through small teaching groups with excellent, committed staff and a focus on academic progress and achievement within a framework of all-round development. Our supportive environment results in secure, happy students who succeed academically with internationally recognised qualifications and go on to a range of good British universities.

We are a small, family-orientated school with a strong and supportive community. Our pastoral care is excellent and our pupils receive high levels of individual attention. The School was founded in 1702 by the Religious Society of Friends (Quakers), Quakers believe that there is something of God in everyone. This belief influences all relationships within Friends' School and creates an environment where your child will be treated as an individual and integrated into the community. Individuality is cherished and pupils and staff show respect for the dignity of others.

We also seek to provide a broad foundation for your child's future, with a wide range of cultural and physical activities. We are known for our strong creative tradition in the performing arts, while our extensive playing fields, heated swimming pool and modern sports hall offer a wide range of sporting opportunities for all children.

We offer full and weekly boarding in three houses; Girls, Boys and the Sixth Form. House staff provide supportive and friendly environments where boarders are encouraged to take increasing amounts of responsibility and to contribute to the life of the Boarding House.

With excellent road and rail connections to London, Cambridge and Stansted Airport, access is easy both nationally and internationally.

Admission. (*See Scholarship Entries section*.) Open to Quaker and non-Quaker, determined by interview, an entrance test and school report.

Fees per term (from January 2011). Senior School: Full Boarding £6,550–£7,790, Weekly Boarding £6,045–£6,990, Day Pupils £4,830–£4,895. Junior School: Juniors £2,975–£3,145, Infants £2,350–£2,595, Reception £1,435–£2,195.

Charitable status. Friends' School Saffron Walden is a Registered Charity, number 1000981.

Fulneck School

Pudsey, Leeds, West Yorkshire LS28 8DS
Tel: 0113 257 0235
Fax: 0113 255 7316
e-mail: enquiries@fulneckschool.co.uk
website: www.fulneckschool.co.uk

Fulneck School was established on 1 September 1994 by the merger of Fulneck Boys' School and Fulneck Girls' School, both originally founded in 1753, by the Moravian Church (a very early Protestant Church which has two schools in England and many more abroad) as part of a settlement on the slopes of a valley within the Green Belt on the outskirts of Pudsey. Leeds and Bradford are both nearby and the School has easy access to the motorway network and airports.

The School is a registered charity and the Provincial Board of the Moravian Church is the Trustee of the School; the Governing Body provides a range of professional expertise. The school is a member of SHMIS and AGBIS.

The Governing Body:
Chairman of the Governors: L Everett
P Dean
L A Fairclough
Revd S Groves
Mrs V Hayton
Mrs M Rhead-Corr
C Robinson
D Scott
T R Smith
C J Stern
J Newman
Mrs L Sharp
Ms D Trayhurn

Principal: **T Kernohan**, BA Hons, MEd Leeds, PGCE

Vice-Principal: Mrs D M Newman, BEd Bedford

Head of Junior School: **D Goulbourn**, BA Hons Liverpool, PGCE

Bursar: R Haigh, HND, ACMA

Originally founded for the education of the sons and daughters of ministers and missionaries, the school nowadays provides an education for about 430 pupils from all backgrounds. Most of the pupils live in West Yorkshire and travel daily to School, but approximately 85 of them are boarders including some who board weekly and return home from Friday evening to Monday morning.

The School is co-educational and provides a modern, academic curriculum based on Christian principles. Fulneck Sixth Form offers 20 A Level subjects and the school has an outstanding record of success in public examinations. In 2011, Fulneck Sixth Form was named the Top Independent Boarding School in Leeds based on average A Level points per candidate. Class sizes rarely exceed 20 and most teaching groups are smaller; in the Sixth Form groups seldom exceed 10.

Buildings. The main buildings of the School are part of the original settlement, yet other buildings on the campus have been added over the years. Most recently these include a new Junior Library with ICT facilities, a new self-contained Sixth Form Centre, performing arts building and a totally refurbished teaching block. The boys' boarding accommodation was extended in the summer of 2008 with further extensions under way in 2011 involving both boarding houses. Extensive playing fields and tennis courts are located on the site, which adjoins Fulneck Golf Club, and looks over to the Domesday village of Tong.

Pastoral Care. The staff work closely and effectively together, sharing in the duties and recreational needs of the School. A senior Pastoral Tutor and two assistants look after the pupils' welfare. The School Nurse, who is medically qualified, and other house staff take care of the boarders in conjunction with the resident teaching staff and the Principal, who also lives on the campus. Weekly and flexi-boarding are offered in addition to full boarding.

Sport. Netball, Hockey, Football, Rugby, Cricket and Tennis are the main games of the School, but Athletics, Basketball, Badminton, Cross-Country running, Golf, Rounders, Swimming, Table Tennis and Martial Arts are all available to the pupils as part of a rapidly expanding programme of outdoor pursuits. Teams of various ages, in most sports, have full fixture lists with neighbouring schools. Dance classes are also run.

Activities. Music education is very strong with 2 choirs, 2 bands, a jazz group, a flute group, a rock band, and other orchestral groups. The Senior Choir performs often to the public. Drama is actively pursued with pupils involved in both lessons and Theatre Workshop productions.

There are a number of clubs and societies such as Art, Computer, Cooking, Golf, Orienteering, Hockey, Netball, Table Tennis, Theatre Workshop, Science, Gardening, Eco Friends and Martial Arts.

The Duke of Edinburgh's Award Scheme is available to pupils over the age of 14, together with a wide range of trips and residential visits, walking and skiing. The school has regularly participated in World Challenge expeditions.

Careers. The Careers teacher is on hand to advise, and the Library stocks most of the available literature on the whole range of courses and careers. All pupils complete a period of work experience at the end of Year 10.

Foundation Stage/Key Stage 1. This is housed within the main building and caters for children from the ages of 3 to 7.

Junior School (Key Stage 2). The Junior School is self-contained and caters for pupils from the ages of 7–11. Once a pupil is admitted he or she will usually progress into the Senior School, after examination at age 11. The Junior School has access to many of its own specialist facilities for Science, Art, Technology, Music, IT and Library, as well as to the Senior School sports facilities.

Learning Support Unit. Specialist staff provide help on an individual or small group basis to children with dyslexia or other learning differences. The Unit is CReSTeD approved and has repeatedly confirmed its 'DU' status, the highest grade awarded to mainstream schools.

Parents and Friends Association. There is a flourishing organization which acts as a fundraising body, and also supports the School in a variety of other ways. This is a living example of the belief that education is a partnership between home and school.

Admission. Admission to the school is welcomed at any age depending on the availability of places, although the main intake is at the ages of 3, 7 and 11. Direct entry to the Sixth Form is also possible. Means-tested academic bursaries and other scholarships are available.

Fees per term (2011-2012). Junior School Day: Nursery (mornings only) £1,225; Foundation Stage (full day) £1,990; Years 1 & 2 £2,160; Years 3–6 £2,680; Weekly Boarding: £4,930; Full Boarding £5,360; Flexi Boarding £38 per night. Senior School: Day £3,530; Weekly Boarding £5,960; Full Boarding £6,620; Flexi Boarding £39 per night.

Fulneck Former Pupils' Association. Mr D Robbins, Fulneck School, Pudsey, West Yorkshire LS28 8DS.

Charitable status. Fulneck School is a Registered Charity, number 251211. It exists to provide a traditional, Christian education for boys and girls between the ages of 3 and 18.

Halliford School

Russell Road, Shepperton, Middlesex TW17 9HX
Tel: 01932 223593
Fax: 01932 229781
e-mail: registrar@hallifordschool.co.uk
website: www.hallifordschool.co.uk

Halliford School was founded in 1921, moved to its present site in 1929 and was registered as a charity in 1966.

Brothers of existing pupils are usually accepted as long as they can benefit from a sound academic education. This policy creates a strong feeling of a family community and helps reinforce the close partnership that exists with parents.

Girls are admitted into the Sixth Form at Halliford.

The Governors are in membership of the Association of Governing Bodies of Independent Schools.

Governors:
K Woodward, QPM (*Chairman*)
C S Squire, FIHort (*Deputy Chairman*)
Mrs N F Cook, BA
M A Crosby, BSc, DipArch RIBA
R Davison, MA
W J Hargan, BSc
B T Harris, FIPD
Mrs T Harrison, BA
Mrs P A Horner, BA, LLB
A Lenoel
R J Parsons
Professor J P Phillips, BA, PhD, FRHS
P Roberts, BSc
Major General A P V Rogers, OBE, LLM, FRSA
Dr M Sachania

Headmaster: **Philip V Cottam**, MA Oxon, FRGS

Deputy Head: R C Talbot, BHum West London Inst, PGCE

Teaching Staff:
I P Bardgett, BA, PGCE
C Bartlett, BA, PGCE
P N Booth, BSc, MSc, PGCE
J E Carrington, BEng
G Cirillo, BA, PGCE
L Cupido, BEd
Mrs S Crosby, BSc, PGCE
N De Cata, CertEd
P Diamond, BEng, PGCE
Mrs D Duffy, BSc, MBA, PGCE
Dr J Dunlop, BSc, PhD, PGCE, NPQH, CPhys
Miss N Evans, BA, PGCE
Mrs K Gilbert, BEd
N Graham, BA, PGCE
Mrs R Greaves, BMus, PGCE
J Greggor, BA
M Gruner, BA
M Harris, BA, PGCE
Mrs P Heather, BSc, MSc, PGCE
D Henderson, BA, PGCE
Ms M Hodgson, BA, MA, PGCE
D Howard, BSc, PGCE
Mrs I Joce, BSc, PGCE
Mrs M Moon, BA
N Moseley, BA, MA, PGCE
A Nelson, BSc, CertEd, CM, DMS, MBA
J Newbery, BA
Dr R Singh, LLB, PhD, PGCE
S Slocock, BEd
Miss A Stowe, BA, PGCE
P A Sweeting, BSc
Mrs J Phelps, BSc
Miss D Weyman, BSc

J Willcox, BA, PGCE
Miss C Wilcockson, BA, PGCE

Part-time Staff:
Mrs K Beckerleg, BSc, PGCE
Mrs N F Cook, BA
Mrs S Regan, CertEd
B M Sunderji, MSc, DipEd, AFIMA, CMath, MIMA
Mrs A Wain, BA, PGCE
M Woolard, RSA Cert EFL

Visiting Staff:
Mrs S Blandford (*Trombone*)
I Brener (*Singing*)
W Brown (*Percussion*)
J Fryer (*Woodwind*)
Mrs H Head (*Piano*)
Miss A Law (*Strings*)
P Savides (*Guitar*)
S Tanner (*Piano*)

Administrative Staff:
Bursar & Company Secretary: P Godfrey, MA, BSc, CEng, CPhys, MIEE, MInstP
Registrar: Mrs D Milward
Headmaster's Secretary: Mrs J A Davies
Bursar's Secretary: Mrs L Gabb
Accounts: Mrs S O'Hara
School Administrator: Mrs F Clatworthy
Alumni Secretary: Mrs J Pollock
Librarian: Mrs S Lewin, BA
Marketing & Publicity: Mrs A Cottam, BA
Matrons: Mrs M Hammond, Mrs C Brooks
Lab Technicians: Dr V Harrison, BSc, PhD; Mrs S Luterbacker, M Green
IT Technicians: Mrs S Bryant, T Hext-Stephens
DT Technician: R Wiedemann
Teaching Assistant: P Hodgkinson

Visiting Chaplain: The Revd Christopher Swift, MA, Rector of Shepperton

Facilities. Halliford School is situated on the Halliford bend of the River Thames. The old house, a graceful eighteenth century building, which stands in six acres of grounds, is the administrative centre of the school. Some 500 yards from the school gate there are six additional acres of sports fields. Over the years there has been a steady development programme which has resulted in the addition of a Creative and Expressive Arts Block, a new classroom block housing four laboratories and a modern ICT department as well as bright and airy classrooms. In September 2001 the school opened an exciting new 320-seat theatre. Incorporated into this development is a kitchen, dining room and music practice facilities. In the Spring of 2003 three new classrooms and a new Science laboratory were added to the new teaching block. In September 2005 a new Sports Hall with new changing facilities, Library, Sixth Form Centre and additional classrooms were opened. The building of our new Music, Art and larger Sixth Form Centre began in June 2011, with the exciting completion scheduled for Autumn 2012.

Admission. There are 416 pupils on roll with a four-form entry at 11+ through Halliford's own entrance examination. There is a further entry at 13+ through Common Entrance and admission is possible at other times dependent on the availability of places. Entrance is by examination and interview.

Curriculum. During Years 7, 8 and 9 all boys study a broadly based curriculum which includes Drama, Religious Studies, PE and Careers.

In Year 8 Maths and Languages are set in four groups to provide even smaller group teaching. In Year 9 all subjects are divided into four groups whether set or not. At least nine subjects are taken at GCSE with the top Maths set taking GCSE a year early and then starting on AS Maths in Year 11. The most academic also start a Critical Thinking AS course in parallel with their GCSE course.

In the Sixth Form some 24 subjects are available at A/AS Level and all teaching is co-educational.

Games. Rugby, Football, Cricket, Athletics, Rowing, Basketball, Badminton, Tennis, Volleyball, Swimming and Golf are available. There is also a Climbing Club which makes use of the climbing wall in the new Sports Hall.

Pastoral Organisation. There are four Houses and pupils are tutored in House groups. Parents receive six communications each year on their son's progress and there is a Prep Diary which parents are requested to sign each week. Tutors are always willing to see parents and the Headmaster can usually be seen at very short notice.

Out of School Activities. These include a very successful Drama Department which mounts some eight productions a year including a major whole school production at the end of the Autumn Term. There are also lively Music and Art Departments.

There is a long list of clubs including Chess, Design, IT, Film, Creative Writing, Modern Languages, Science and Art. In addition there are Senior and Junior Debating and Academic Societies, a Philosophy Club and Interhouse Public Speaking and Unison Singing Competitions. The Duke of Edinburgh's Award is available as an additional activity.

School Council. Each Tutor group elects a representative to the School Council (19 members). This is not a cosmetic exercise and in recent times the School Council has effected real changes. Halliford believes that pupils do have good ideas which can be utilised for the well-being of the School as a whole.

Prospective Parents. In the Summer Term each year the School holds Open Days in March and May when the School is in session. In the Autumn Term the School holds an Open Day on a Saturday morning at the beginning of October and two days in November. Prospective parents are welcome at other times by appointment.

Fees per term (2011-2012). £3,807.

Scholarships and Bursaries. (*See Scholarship Entries section.*)

Old Hallifordians. *Chairman*: David Parsons, 25 Fir Tree Place, Church Road, Ashford Middlesex TW15 2PH.

Charitable status. Halliford School is a Registered Charity, number 312090. It exists to provide high-quality education.

Hampshire Collegiate School
UCST

Embley Park, Romsey, Hampshire SO51 6ZE
Tel: 01794 512206 (Senior School)
          01794 515737 (Junior School)
Fax: 01794 518737
e-mail: info@hampshirecs.org.uk
website: www.hampshirecs.org.uk

A word from the Principal: "Hampshire Collegiate School is really becoming quite astounding in multiple ways. There is a collective energy about our 130 acre campus which provides us the beautiful space to develop the 'best in everyone'. The energy comes from our sense that 'attitude is everything', and since our students love being sensational in all that they undertake, their winning attitudes are being expressed in sport, drama, music, and high academic outcomes. We are so fortunate to dwell within the childhood home of Florence Nightingale, and to unashamedly feed from her example and drive as an individual. We have a real forte for preparing students for optimal university and college placement, both in the Russell Group and Oxbridge, but also in colleges which are regarded as the very best in fields such as art and drama. In short, we are a school that is really going places; restless, dynamic and focused deeply on each individual and in bringing out the best in everyone."

D A d'Arcy Hughes, Esq (*Chairman*)
Professor M J Clark, BA, PhD (*Vice-Chairman*)
R Butler
Professor G Griffiths, BA, MSc, CEng, MIEE, FRGS, FSUT
Ms C Levy
Mr R Moody
Mrs D Moody, AILAM
Mrs V Perry, QT
Revd T Sledge
Professor T Thomas

Principal: **Hector MacDonald**, BSc, MA, CChem, CSci, FRMS, FRSC

Vice-Principal: Mrs T M Rogers, MA Ed, CertEd

Senior School
Head of Senior School: Mrs H Crawford, BSc, MIBiol
Deputy Head of Senior School: Mrs M Bateman, BA
Director of Studies: Mrs W E Martin, BSc
Head of Sixth Form: Mr M Laverty, BA
Boarding Housemaster: Mr P Carberry
Pastoral Leader Year 7 and 8: Mrs M Bateman, BA
Pastoral Leader, Years 9 to 11: Mr C D Cates, BSc

Heads of Years:
Mrs E Driver, BA
Mrs J Leighton, MA
Mr R Smith, BSc
Mr R Hay, BA
Mrs A James, CertEd

Director of Sports and Activities: Mr R Martin, BSc
Head of Music: Mr G Tinsley, BMus
Head of Drama: Mrs S Stevens, BEd
Head of Mathematics: Mr A D Pearce, BSc
Head of English: Mr S Bowyer, MA
Head of Science: Mrs L Miller, BSc
Head of Geography: Mrs N Spurr, BA
Head of History, Government and Politics: Dr R Foster, BA PhD (*Head of Palmerston House*)
Head of Art: Mrs J Pascoe, BA
Head of Design & Technology: Mr P Carberry
SENCO: Mrs H Garside, BA
Head of PSHE: Mrs D Birch, BA

Assistant Teaching Staff:
Miss E Boutcher-West, BA (*PE*)
Mr A J Brooks, BA (*Art, Head of Nightingale House*)
Mrs N Brown, BA (*Mathematics*)
Mr T Brittan, BSc (*Design Technology, PE*)
Mrs B Clark, BA (*Geography*)
Mrs S Cornforth, BSc (*Mathematics*)
Miss G Cornick (*Girls' Sport Coach*)
Mrs H Cunliffe, CertLibPrac (*Librarian*)
Dr M Davies, PhD (*Chemistry*)
Mrs J Ellis, BSc (*Science*)
Mrs A Gadsbey-Jones, BA (*English*)
Mrs S N Goodacre, BA (*French, German*)
Mr S Gordon, BA (*Mathematics*)
Miss C Hamstead, BSc (*Chemistry*)
Mrs S Hanson, BA (*Joint Head of Modern Languages, Spanish*)
Mrs S Haywood Smith, BSc (*ICT*)
Mr J Hillier, BA (*English*)
Mr P Hilton, BSc (*Head of ICT, Business Studies*)
Mrs M Jeffrey, BA (*Joint Head of Modern Languages, German*)
Mrs T Johnson, BA (*French*)
Mr N Joisce, BA (*PE, Director of Rugby*)
Mrs B Jones, BA (*Learning Support*)
Mr S Kent-Davies (*Music*)
Mr A Leatham, BA (*PE, Religious Studies*)

Miss D C Lulham, BA (*Head of Girls' Games*)
Mrs M Matlock, BA (*English*)
Mr G McInerney, BSc (*English*)
Mrs A Mole, MA (*EFL*)
Mrs R Ndhlovu, BA (*Spanish, French*)
Mr J Oldham, BA (*English*)
Mr C O'Sullivan, BA (*English*)
Mrs J Penfold, BA (*French, German*)
Dr M Price, PhD (*Chemistry/Physics, Head of Chichester House*)
Mr P Stanley, MA (*Drama*)
Mr I Stuart, BA (*English, i/c Cricket*)
Mr A Thickbroom, MA (*Chemistry, Maths*)
Dr N Thomas, PhD (*Biology*)
Mr J Thomson, BA (*Mathematics, Deputy Head of Sixth Form*)
Mr S Trodd, BA (*Subject Leader of Psychology, Physics*)
Mr R Watson, BA (*Design and Technology*)
Mrs A Wolfe, MA (*Learning Support*)

Junior School
Head of Junior School: Mrs T M Rogers, MA Ed, CertEd
Deputy Head, Academic & Pastoral: Mr G King, BA
Director of Studies: Mrs J Bell, BEd

Head of Key Stage One: Ms F Adams, BA Ed
Head of Art: Mrs M Coveney, BA
Head of Drama: Miss S Gordon, BEd
Head of Early Years: Mrs M Bower, BSc
Head of English: Mrs C Fletcher, BA
Head of Music: Mrs K Francis, BEd
Head of Science: Mrs Y Cooke, BSc
Head of Mathematics: Mr R Tarlton, MA, BEd
Head of Modern Foreign Languages: Mrs V Worden, MA (*French*)
Head of ICT: Mr P Shuttleworth

Assistant Staff:
Mr T Brittan, BSc (*Head of DT, KS2 Class Teacher*)
Mrs D Brown, BA Ed (*Learning Support Teacher*)
Miss L Burlinson (*Classroom Assistant*)
Mrs L Chandler, BAGA Cert (*Classroom Assistant*)
Mrs T Collins, NVQ2 (*Classroom Assistant*)
Mrs M Corlass, CertEd (*Classroom Assistant*)
Miss S Hardy, NNEB (*Early Years Team and Nursery Manager*)
Mr P Meaden, BA (*Educational Visits Coordinator, Teacher in Charge of Boys Games*)
Mrs K Tibble, NNEB (*Early Years Nursery Nurse*)
Mrs E Squires (*KS2 Teacher*)
Mrs S Sturgess (*Teaching Assistant and Learning Support*)
Mrs V Tozer, CertEd (*KS1 Class Teacher/Library*)
Mrs F Walker, BEd (*KS2 Class Teacher*)
Mrs F Winfield, CertEd (*SENCO*)

Visiting Teachers:
Mr R Armstrong, RMSM (*Percussion*)
Mrs M Bell (*Speech & Drama*)
Mr M Callow, Dip ABRSM (*Clarinet and Saxophone*)
Mrs P Glynn, DDME CertEd (*Classical Guitar*)
Mrs J Gover, ATCL, LTCL (*Flute*)
Mrs G Kuznicki, ALCM, LLCM (*Singing*)
Miss N Land, ALCM (*Violin & Viola*)
Mrs S Newman, GTCL, LTCL, CertEd (*Piano and Cello*)
Mr D Phaure (*Speech and Drama*)
Miss C Williams, BA Hons, CertEd (*Brass*)
Mrs M Williams (*Woodwind*)
Mr C Wickland, DipMus (*Electric Guitar*)
Mr P Wray (*Kit Percussion*)

Principal's PA: Mrs R Wells
Registrar: Mrs J Baird
Junior School Head's PA: Mrs J Piper
Deputy Bursar: Mrs L Rademaker, BCompt UNISA
Transport Manager & Finance: Mr B Dixon

Senior Matron: Mrs D Jarvis, RGNII
Assistant Matron: Mrs E Appleton, RGNII (*part-time*)
School Medical Officer: P J Burrows, BM, BCh, DObst, MRCP UK

Constitution. There are up to 750 pupils, with approximately 100 in the Sixth Form and 230 in the Junior School. Boys and girls are admitted at 11 and 13 by examination; and into the Sixth Form, at age 16, on GCSE results.

There are boarding places available for both boys and girls (11–18), and the whole School is divided into four houses. Day pupils and boarders are members of the same houses, thus obviating any feeling of division between boarding and day.

All senior pupils attend Assembly, often with Chapel and then commence six 55-minute lessons (with a twenty-minute morning break and an hour lunch break). Following the academic routine, every afternoon and at lunchtime, games or activities are organized allowing day pupils to depart between 4.00 pm and 5.00 pm having experienced the daily routine and ethos of a boarding school. Many day pupils opt to board in their senior years.

Junior School lessons are from 8.45 am to 3.15 pm for Nursery, with staggered finishes, then to 3.35 pm for KS2, followed, again, by voluntary activities every afternoon.

Curriculum. The Junior School follows the National Curriculum in the main and as a basis but seeks to go beyond this in many areas using imaginative teaching and innovative cross-curricular projects. The use of ICT is increasingly embedded throughout the curriculum. In addition French is taught together with Spanish in the older age groups. There is a wide range of after-school clubs including sport, art, performance and music activities.

The GCSE curriculum offers a choice of many subjects (including separate subject sciences) and careful note has been taken of those elements of the National Curriculum considered vital to personal development. All pupils study Spanish in Year 7, and continue with Spanish and French from Year 8. Each pupil must study a minimum of 1 foreign language to GCSE level. There is a wide range of subjects on offer. Most pupils take a minimum of 9 GCSE examinations.

More than 20 AS and A Level subjects are available.

Careers guidance is given by tutors from the earliest days, and is backed up by professional advice. Work experience is undertaken in the summer of Year 10.

Games and Activities. Rugby, Football, Cricket, Hockey, Rounders and Netball are the main games, with Cross-Country, Basketball, Swimming, Tennis, Athletics, Lacrosse and Golf among others in a supporting role.

The School has a strong games tradition, achieving representation at County level, and beyond, a reputation for drama and art and a thriving musical life.

The School has its own practice golf course, floodlit pitch, lake, and 7,000 sq ft Sports Hall, all-weather playing areas, tennis courts under lights and swimming pool.

All Senior School pupils are encouraged to attempt the Duke of Edinburgh's Award Scheme; there are several expeditions each year in the neighbouring New Forest, or in Wales, in the mountains; and abroad, including two ski trips.

In the Junior School Year 6 take part in a residential activity week in Normandy.

Admission Procedures. Admission to the Junior School is by informal assessment and a 'taster day' for younger pupils and, for the older pupils, interview with the Head Teacher, satisfactory reports and assessments in English and Mathematics.

An examination is set at 11 + and an interview expected, plus report from present school (often a State Primary School).

At 13+ HCS Entrance examination and an interview and report.

At 16+ an interview and report including details of GCSE success are expected.

Places are occasionally available in other age groups.

Examination and interviews may take place at any time during the twelve months preceding entry.

Details from the Registrar.

Scholarships, Exhibitions and Bursaries. (*See Scholarship Entries section.*) Awards are made for Academic ability, for Art, Music, Sport and Drama, and general All-Round contribution to the life of the School (including Sport) and Sixth Form.

Fees per term (2011-2012). Nursery: £1,023–£1,705 (mornings only), £2,382 (full time). Payment by Termly Direct Debit: Junior School £2,749–£3,070; Senior School: £4,438 (day), £7,345 (UK boarding) £8,048 (International Boarding).

There is a reduction for brother/sister and children of the Clergy, HM Forces and Teachers.

Location. Easily accessible from Southampton Airport (15 minutes), Southampton Parkway Railway Station (15 minutes) and M27 (5 minutes), HCS is 1½ miles north west of Romsey, on the Salisbury (A27) road. There is a railway station in Romsey.

Former Pupils. e-mail: HCSSociety@hampshirecs.org .uk.

Charitable status. The United Church Schools Trust is a Registered Charity, number 1016538. It exists to educate children.

Hipperholme Grammar School Foundation

Bramley Lane, Hipperholme, Halifax, West Yorkshire HX3 8JE

Tel: 01422 202256
Fax: 01422 204592
e-mail: hgsoffice@hgsf.org.uk
website: www.hgsf.org.uk

Hipperholme Grammar School Foundation was founded in 1648 by Matthew Broadley (former pupils are Brodleians).

The Foundation provides a small, caring setting in which children are educated to be the very best they can be. Alongside high academic standards, all children are provided with outstanding opportunities for their personal enrichment. A love of learning is developed alongside traditional values of politeness, good manners and strong moral code. The atmosphere that pervades through the school from Nursery to Sixth Form is welcoming yet challenging: all visitors to the schools are given a very warm welcome and all students are provided with a range of academic and personal development challenges.

Hipperholme Grammar School Foundation is a registered educational charity with a board of Governors.

Officers of the Board:
Chairman: Mr C D Redfearn, BSc, DMS, MBIM
Vice-Chair: Mr R Snowball

Foundation Contacts:
Headmaster: Dr John Scarth, BEd, PhD

PA to the Headmaster: Miss S Oxtoby
Bursar and Clerk to the Governors: Mr G Oliver

Grammar School Contacts:
Deputy Head: Mrs J Griffiths
Director of Studies: Mr P Rushton
Head of Lower School: Mrs J Sugden
Head of Upper School: Mr S Rose
Head of Upper Sixth: Mr M Hendry

Leadership & Personal Enrichment Coordinator: Mr R Griffiths

Junior School Contacts:
Headteacher: Mrs L Reynolds
Secretary: Mrs J Hall
Senior Teacher: Mrs C Roper
Sports Coordinator: Mr R Brighouse

Organisation. The Foundation is a co-educational day school comprising The Junior School, for children aged 3–11 years, and The Grammar School, for children aged 11–18 years.

Although founded in the nearby Coley Parish Church, the Foundation is not specifically a church school. It has a Christian ethos which pervades its life but which welcomes those of all faiths. Assemblies and end-of-term services (at Coley) are Christian, as is part of the GCSE Religious Education course, all of which are compulsory.

The pupil roll stands at around 400 pupils, with 15 in each Form in The Junior School and 40 in each year group in The Grammar School. The schools are small enough to ensure individual attention for all children, yet large enough to provide a full range of subjects to GCSE and A Level.

Pupil Welfare. A great strength of the two schools is a strong commitment to provide outstanding pastoral care. Our small teaching groups, individual attention, teachers who genuinely care and excellent relationships with parents enable all children to blossom and fulfil their potential. Where necessary, individual learning programmes are devised and learning support staff ensure children make excellent progress.

Teaching and Learning. Our teachers enjoy teaching: they are enthusiastic, dedicated and exceptionally caring. Our curriculum is broadly in line with the National Curriculum to Year 9, after which students choose from a range of subjects leading to GCSE and later to A Level.

Personal Enrichment. Our Personal Enrichment programme builds self-confident and well-balanced young people with strong leadership skills. A wide range of activities is provided, including sports, music and drama, as well as a varied outdoor education programme and The Duke of Edinburgh's Award Scheme.

Admission. Admission to The Junior School is non-selective and places are given following an interview with the Headteacher and individual assessments, if appropriate. Entry to The Grammar School follows an entrance examination, Junior School report and interview with the Headmaster. The Grammar School selects children for their personal qualities and desire to be at The Grammar School as much as academic performance. Entry to The Grammar School for other year groups depends on availability and admittance following a selection test and interview.

Fees per term (2011-2012). Nursery £17.50 per am/pm session; Reception to Year 6 £2,615; Grammar School £3,150.

The Foundation operates a number of schemes that enable parents to spread the cost of school fees throughout the year. School meals, transport and individual music tuition are charged separately.

Bursaries and Scholarships. A number of Scholarships are awarded for entry at both Year 7 and Year 12 (Lower Sixth) for academic, musical and sporting achievement. A new Choral Scholarship enables gifted choristers to benefit from a high-quality education whilst receiving excellent singing training. All Choral Scholars are also expected to attend Bradford Cathedral Choir. Discounts are available for siblings and children attending The Junior School children receive a generous fee reduction on transfer to The Grammar School. Bursaries are available throughout the school to families in financial need.

Charitable status. Hipperholme Grammar School Trust is a Registered Charity, number 517152. It exists to provide education of a high calibre for the boys and girls aged 3–18

of the area and to help those who cannot afford fees, to finance such education.

Hull Collegiate School
UCST

Tranby Croft, Anlaby, East Yorkshire HU10 7EH
Tel: 01482 657016
Fax: 01482 655389
e-mail: enquiries.hull@church-schools.com
website: www.hullcollegiateschool.co.uk

Governing Body: The Council of The United Church Schools Trust

Local Governing Body:
Mr K A Moffatt (*Chairman*)
Prof K Bardon
Revd Dr N D Barnes
Mr G Burnett
Mr B Evans
Mr P Grimwood
Mrs A Hales
Mr R Perry
Mr P Sexton

Headmaster: **Mr R Haworth**, MA Corpus Christi College Cambridge, PGCE, ADipEd

Head of Preparatory School: Mrs K A Williams, BEd Cantab

Deputy Heads:
Mr S F Jolly, BSc Durham, PGCE
Mr A D Norburn, BMus Birmingham, PGCE, LTCL, ALCM

Assistant Head (*Pastoral Care*): Mr C M Wainman, BA Leeds, PGCE
Assistant Head (*Learning*): Mrs C A Holt, BA York, PGCE, NPQH
Business Services Director: Mrs J A Garnett
Deputy Head of Preparatory School: Mrs J Plewes, BA Leeds, PGCE, NPQH

Senior School Staff:
Mrs C R Atkin, BA York, PGCE
Mrs A Asbury, Dip LAMDA, BA Hull, PGCE
Mr A S Birtchnell, BA Hons UWE Bristol, PGCE
Mme C S Blanc, Men Psych Nanterre, PGCE
Ms J E Blencoe, BA Hull, PGCE
Mrs K H Bloomfield, BA Hull, PGCE
Miss T E Burns, BA Manchester, PGCE
Mrs P J Carlisle, BEd Christchurch, Kent
Mr R J Chambers, BA Trinity & All Saints, Leeds
Miss A D Davis, BSc Birmingham, PGCE
Mr S M Doncaster, BA Leicester, PGCE
Miss J Dyer, BA York, PGCE
Mrs S A East, BEd Worcester College, MSc
Mrs G M Evans, BSc Leeds, PGCE
Miss C R Foreman, BA Hull, PGCE
Mrs S J Gibbs, BSc Leicester, PGCE
Mr B J Gilles, MA Oxon, PGCE
Mrs S Groves
Mrs J Grimley, BA Hull, PGCE
Mr A Harriott, BEng Lancaster, GTP
Mr M T Haughton, BA International Christian College, MA, PGCE
Mrs D Heads, BSc Hull, PGCE
Mr F S Henderson, BSc York St John, GTP
Mrs E J Holt, BA Manchester, PGCE
Mrs N J Holvey, BEd Sheffield City
Miss L Holvey, BA Manchester Metropolitan

Mrs M J Hugill, BSc UMIST, PGCE
Mrs P Jolly, MA Cantab, PGCE
Mrs S R Kelsall, BSc Bradford, PGCE
Mr M E Kirby, BEd Ripon & York St Johns
Mrs A Manton BSc Hull, PGCE
Mrs S L Maynard, BEd Leeds
Miss S McDowell, BA York, PGCE
Mr M Monaghan, BA Oxon, PGCE
Mr T E Norris, BSc Nottingham, PGCE
Mrs J K North, BA Trent Poly, PGCE
Mrs J Orlowska, BA Hull, PG Dip Lib
Mr C F Owen, BSc Liverpool, PGCE, MIBiol
Mrs C Palmer
Mr S D Pearce, BSc Portsmouth, PGCE, CBiol, MIBiol
Mrs V Pick, BA University of Wales, PGCE
Mr G Rogerson, BA Manchester Metropolitan, PGCE
Mr M E Roper, BSc Bradford, PGCE
Miss R H Spencer, BA Durham, PGCE
Mrs L P Stack, BSc Queen's Belfast, PGCE
Mr A Stather, CertEd Hull
Mrs M A Steigmann, BSc Hull, CPhys, MInstP
Mr G R Stephenson, BA Newcastle, PGCE, DipEd
Mr R G Tuck, BA Keele, ACA, PGCE
Mrs C M V Ullyart, DipAD Goldsmiths, MA, ATC
Mrs E J Wallis, BA Leeds, PGCE
Miss R D Willie, BSc Sheffield, PGCE
Mr A J Wilson, BA Humberside, PGCE
Mr J W Windeatt, BSc Hull, GTP
Ms E Witty, BA Hull, GTP

Preparatory School Staff:
Miss L Ballard, NNEB
Miss C E Barley, BA Hull, MCD, PGCE
Mrs A Broughton, Dip Pre-School Practice Level 3, Cert Learning Support Level 2
Mrs J Bousfield, CertEd Salisbury
Mrs L Burns, NVQ3 Child Care, C&G Learning Support Level 2
Mrs D Charlton, NVQ3
Mrs J Cooper, NVQ2
Mrs S Douthwaite
Mrs K Dent, BEd Durham
Mrs K Dewhirst, BSc Newcastle, PGCE
Mrs A Dinsdale, NNEB, HPSEB/BTEC HPS
Mrs L Grunner, BSc Hull, PGCE
Mrs J Hamilton, BA Hull, QTS
Mrs A Haworth, NNEB
Mrs R Hazel, MA Oxford, PhD, PGCE
Mrs D Hickman, NVQ2
Mr D Manners, GRSM, LRAM, ARCM, PGCE
Mrs J Maltby, BEd Leeds
Mrs A Manton, BSc Hull, PGCE, PG Dip SpLD
Mrs A Meltham, BA Sheffield, PGCE, MA Ed Open
Miss J Moorfoot, BSc Lincoln, PGCE
Mrs A Nicholls, BA Hons Lampeter, PGCE
Mr A North, BA Hons St Pauls, MSc, PGCE
Mrs J Purdy, CertEd Hull, BA DME
Mrs K Rogers, BA Hull, NNEB
Mrs H Silk, BA Hull, QTS
Mrs J Sowersby, NVQ2
Mrs S Smethurst, CertEd Liverpool
Mrs C Smith, BA Durham, PGCE, MBA
Mrs C Steele, NNEB
Mrs E Stewart, BEd Sheffield
Mrs J Taylor, DPP Level 3
Mrs C Wood, BSc York, QTS
Mrs V Young, NVQ3

Music:
Mrs E Ashmead, LRAM, Dip NCOS (*Cello*)
Miss L Bates BA (*Singing*)
Mr C Brown (*Guitar*)
Ms M Cross, ARCM, LGSM (*Flute, piano*)
Mrs R Dixon, MMus, BA, LRSM (*Clarinet, Saxophone*)

Miss C Holdich, BMus, Dip ABRSM (*Singing*)
Mr G Keenan (*Drum Kit*)
Mrs C Lyons, GRSM, LRAM, ARCM (*Piano*)
Dr R Mathieson, BA, PGCE, DPhil Oxon, BMus (*Piano*)
Mrs V McMunn, BA Oxon, PGCE (*Piano*)
Mrs S Newton, BA, LGSM (*Woodwind*)
Mr G Oglesby, ABSM (*Brass*)
Mr J Savory, BMus, ATCL (*Piano*)

Hull Collegiate School is a co-educational day school which educates 750 pupils from nursery age (the term in which they turn 3) to Year 13 (age 18).

Location and Facilities. Set in the Victorian country house of Tranby Croft, the school benefits from nine hectares of mature, landscaped grounds and is located approximately four miles to the west of Hull and one mile north east of the Humber Bridge. The Preparatory School is housed in a purpose-built facility which adjoins the Senior School and in 2005 a multi-million pound investment provided the school with state-of-the-art classrooms and science laboratories, an indoor sports hall built to Sport England standard, D&T workshops, a large open-plan art school and a café-style refectory. In 2007 the school opened the Wilberforce Centre housing spacious sixth form common and study rooms, a drama rehearsal room and further classrooms.

Inspection Report. The 2010 ISI report applauded the school's ethos, pastoral care and teaching, listing its key strengths as:

"The reflective and encouraging culture of the school provides an environment in which pupils thrive, becoming willing, independent learners.

The personal development of the pupils is excellent and is a significant strength of the school, meeting its aims to care for and respect pupils, and to nurture each individual.

Pupils respond to the school's high expectations of achievement, conduct and work.

The pupils are thoughtful and considerate of others, and the nurturing of these attitudes creates a happy atmosphere where they feel comfortable and secure."

Curriculum and Extra-Curricular Activities. The school has a history of consistently excellent academic results both at GCSE and A Level and boasts a very strong pastoral system, priding itself on preparing its pupils for entry to higher education. There is a wide choice of academic subjects available and the choice of extra-curricular activities is equally varied; participation in sport, music and drama is strongly encouraged, as the school plays a considerable amount of competitive sport and produces regular concerts and plays. There are many trips abroad every year, as well as numerous shorter visits to places of interest closer to home.

Admission. Hull Collegiate School welcomes pupils of a wide range of ability and all faiths. Admission is by pre-entry assessment, interview and report and subject to availability of a place. For further information please contact the Registrar.

Scholarships and Assisted Places. Academic scholarships are available at 11+, 14+ and 16+. Sport, art and music scholarships are also available for outstanding individuals who demonstrate a level of excellence and commitment to these areas.

Assisted places are available and the value of the award is calculated on a sliding scale that takes into account the financial position of both parents' income and assets. The maximum award is to the value of 85% of fees. Assisted places may only be awarded to a child entering the school in Year 7 or into the Sixth Form and are reviewed annually. Application forms may be obtained from the Registrar.

Fees per term (2011-2012). Reception, Years 1–2 £1,971; Years 3–4 £2,272; Years 5–6 £2,709; Years 7–13 £3,250. Lunch included Reception to Year 13. Kindergarten: £18 per session (morning or afternoon); First Steps £15 per session. Lunch: £5 per day.

Charitable status. Hull Collegiate School is a member of The United Church Schools Trust, which is a Registered Charity, number 1016538. It exists to provide education for boys and girls between the ages of 3 and 18 years.

Kingham Hill School

Kingham, Chipping Norton, Oxfordshire OX7 6TH
Tel: 01608 658999
Fax: 01608 658658
e-mail: admissions@kingham-hill.oxon.sch.uk
website: www.kingham-hill.oxon.sch.uk

Kingham Hill School is a thriving boarding and day school for 280 girls and boys from 11–18 years.
Motto: *In virum perfectum.*

Governors:
M Stanley-Smith (*Chairman*)

Mrs C Anelay	D Monro
Mrs V Ansah	D M Orton
Miss D Buggs	K Targett
M Cuthbertson	Mrs G R Thorne
The Revd R Cunningham	C Townsend
I Fry	The Revd S Wookey
Mrs B Goodwin-Hudson	

Headmaster: **Revd Nick Seward**, BEng, MA

Deputy Headmaster: A Evans, BA, BSc, MBA

Teaching staff:

D Ansley, BEng Hons	R Humphreys, BSc
L Baxter	Mrs E Jeffery, BA Hons,
D Beasant, BA Hons	PGCE
S Birnie	Miss H Jervis, BA Hons
Mrs G Boyd, BA, PGCE	R Jones, MMus, BH Hons
G Cape, DipEd	G Lane, BSc Hons
Dr P Carlin, BDS	Mrs S Lowe
Mrs J Chapman, BA Hons	M Metcalfe, BA, PGCE
Miss C Cleland, BEd Hons	R Owen, BEd Hons
T J Cottle, BEd	P Parmenter, CertEd
Mrs J Critchley, BA, MA	Mrs J Parmenter, CertEd
A Curwen, BA, MA Ed,	Miss S Parmenter, CertEd
MA	Mrs K Raccio, BSc, MA
Mrs A Curwen, BA Ed,	G Rees, BA Hons
MA Ed	D Ritchie, BA Hons
B Davis, BA, MA	Mrs K Ritchie, BSc, PGCE
Mrs K Davis, BA	B Sangster, BA, CertEd,
Mrs A Duckenfield	AdDipEd
K Ellerington, BSc Hons	Mrs C Slide
M Eyles, BSc Hons	N Stannard, BA Hons,
Mrs J A Fowler, BEng	PGCE
Hons, PGCE	Mrs J A Stodart-Cook, BA
R N Fox, BA, PGCE	Hons, DipM, PGCE,
Mrs R G Hayes, BA, PGCE	MSBT
Mrs C Heath, BEd Hons	Mrs I Swain, PGDip
Miss H Hiscox, BA, MA	SpecEd
Mrs G Holliday, BEd	

Chaplain: Revd A Savage, BTh, BSc, MSc
Deputy Chaplain: Miss D Moseley, PIA Theology, MA Ed
Honorary Chaplain: The Revd Canon Geoffrey Shaw, MA

Administration:
Bursar: Mrs A Kaye
Registrar: Mrs K A Harvey, BA Hons
Domestic Bursar: T D Smith
Headmaster's PA: Mrs J Cavan

Medical Officer: Dr D R Edwards, MB BS, DRCOG
Medical Centre: Mrs C Howes, Mrs E Barton

Beautifully situated, Kingham Hill has offered many generations of students the best possible opportunity to flourish, enjoying their formative years and becoming successful, responsible and well-rounded adults.

The Headmaster and his dedicated staff team ensure that the school's special qualities benefit all:

- Vibrant Christian ethos
- Superb pastoral care
- Academic excellence
- Value-added across the ability range
- Specialist department for dyslexia, dyspraxia and dyscalculia
- Excellent extra-curricular provision

Kingham Hill is an exceptional school with an inspiring history, stunning setting and ambitious plans.

We excel with able and average-ability students. Our record for enabling significant improvement in grades, achievement on the sports field and stage, and growth in all-round confidence, is superb.

We run an academic society – Octagon. The seven most able pupils from each year group sit with the master in charge and are challenged with extended studies, visits to public lectures, involvement in debates, etc. These students are expected to achieve outstanding results and go on to top universities.

The school's sporting facilities are superb and include: a leisure complex incorporating a pool, fitness suite and dance and drama studio; huge floodlit astroturf area; tennis and netball courts; sports hall; various grass pitches and athletics track; renowned assault course.

Kingham Hill School is situated on a beautiful 96-acre site in rolling Cotswold countryside. Oxford is just 24 miles away, Stratford-upon-Avon, 25 miles and London, one hour and twenty minutes by train.

Open Mornings: 15 Oct 2011; 4 Feb 2012; 12 May 2012
Assessment Days: 17 Nov 2011

Fees per term (2011-2012). Full Boarding: £6,500 (Years 7 & 8), £8,000 (Years 9–11), £8,360 (Sixth Form). Weekly Boarding: £6,300 (Years 7 & 8), £7,330 (Years 9–11), £7,700 (Sixth Form). Day: £4,500 (Years 7 & 8), £5,145 (Years 9–13).

SpLD tuition: £1,399, SpLD for Sixth Form: £700. ESOL tuition: £1,390. American Studies: £1,600.

Scholarships and Bursaries. The School is able to offer several categories of Scholarship: Art, Junior, Music, Organ, Performing Arts, Sixth Form and Sport. Generous Bursaries for sons and daughters of HM Forces personnel.

Charitable status. The Kingham Hill Trust is a Registered Charity, number 1076618, and a Company Limited by Guarantee, registered in England, number 365812. The school exists to provide education for girls and boys from 11 to 18.

Kingsley School
A Methodist Board School

Bideford, Devon EX39 3LY
Tel: 01237 426200
Fax: 01237 425981
e-mail: admissions@kingsleyschoolbideford.co.uk
website: www.kingsleyschoolbideford.co.uk

The school was created in January 2009 by the merger of Grenville College and Edgehill College.

Governors:
Chairman: Mrs Jennifer Wilson

Mrs Viv Ansell
Mr John Dare
Mrs Sue Fishleigh
Mrs Mary Gordon
Mr Richard Holwill
Mr John Hunkin
Mr Andrew Laugharne
Mr Alan Mead
Mr David Pinney
Mr Michael Portman
Dr John Prebble
The Hon John Rous
Mrs Anne Shirley
Mr John Tomalin
Mrs Liz West

Ex-officio:
Mr Graham Russell, Secretary to the Board of Management, Methodist Independent Schools
The Revd John Carne, Chairman of Plymouth and Exeter District of the Methodist Church

Headmaster: Mr Andy Waters, BEd, MA

Deputy Head (Pastoral) & Child Protection Officer: Mrs Sally Davies, BSc
Deputy Head (Curriculum): Dr Susan Ley, BSc, PhD
Senior Deputy Head & Head of Junior Departments: Mr Simon Woolcott, BSc, ARCS

Senior School Teaching Staff:
* *Head of Department/Subject*

Mr Chris Beechey, BA, MA, ACIEA (*History*)
Mrs Michele Borsten, BA, MA (*Drama*)
Mr Brown Cardoo (*PE & Games*)
Mr Matt Child (*Mathematics*)
Mr Peter Claridge, BEd, PGCPSE (*Dyslexia Dept, PE*)
Mrs Candy Collier (*Mandarin*)
Mr Simon Cullingham, BEd, DipSpLD, Cert TEFL (*Dyslexia Dept*)
Mrs Sally Davies, BSc (*Physics, Chemistry*)
Dr Jan Dawson, BSc PhD (*Chemistry*)
Mr Jon Dickinson, BA (*Art*)
Mr Brian Edge, BA (*Mathematics*)
Mrs Fo Edmonds, BA (*Vocational Studies, Careers Coordinator, Exams Officer*)
Mr Ian Holleran, BSc (*Science, *Physics*)
Father Steve Hunt, CA (*Chaplain, Outdoor Ed, *RS, PSHME*)
Mrs Sue Johnson, BSc (*Mathematics, Head of Years 7 to 9*)
Mrs Sarah Keirle, BSc (*Mathematics*)
Mr Richard Ker, BSc (*Design Technology*)
Mr Andy Lane, BEd, DipSpLD (*Head of Dyslexia Centre*)
Mrs Julie Lewis, BA (*Modern Foreign Languages*)
Dr Susan Ley, BSc, PhD (*Biology*)
Mr Alan Longman, CertEd (*Librarian*)
Mr Peter Lovett, BA (*English*)
Miss Kathryn Makepeace, BA (*English*)
Mr Simon Mathers, BSc (*Boys PE & Games, Science*)
Mrs Barbara Mingay, BEd, Adv Dip SEN (*Food Technology, PSHME, RS*)
Mr Matt Norris, BSc (*ICT, Science*)
Ms Diana Percy, BA, MEd, (*Psychology, *ESOL*)
Mrs Susan Roberts-Key, BEd, MA (*Mathematics*)
Mr Simon Robillard (*Music*)
Mrs Hilary Roome, BEd (*PE & Games*)
Mrs Linda Stella, BA (*Girls PE & Games*)
Miss Kat Timms, BA (*Art, PE*)
Mrs Sandrine Toubin-Whale, DEUG Licence, BA (*French*)
Mr Steve Whaley, BSc (*Geography*)
Mr Matt White, BA (*Mathematics, Music Technology*)
Mr Simon Woolcott, BSc, ARCS (*Biology, Head of Junior Departments*)
Mrs Pat Wright, BSc (*Chemistry*)

Junior School and Pre-School Teaching Staff:
Mrs Kim Curtis, BTEC Nat Diploma (*Pre-School Deputy Manager*)
Mr Richard Ker, BSc (*Design Technology*)
Mrs Emily King, BA (*Reception & Year 1*)
Mrs Meda Maynard, Montessori Teacher (*Pre-School Manager*)
Mrs Barbara Mingay, BEd, Adv Dip SEN (*Food Technology*)
Mrs Janet Minhinnett, BEd, MEd SEN (*Year 2*)

Mrs Linda Stella, BA (*PE & Games*)
Mrs Elaine Thorne, BA (*Year 4*)
Miss Kat Timms, BA (*Art*)
Mrs Sandrine Toubin-Whale, DEUG Licence, BA (*French*)
Mrs Emma Wilson, BA Ed (*Reception & Year 1*)
Miss Rachel Wilson, BA (*Years 5 & 6*)
Mrs Fiona Woolcott, BEd, DipSpLD, Cert Inclusive Ed,
    Cert TEFL (*Year 3*)

Leading Edge Nursery Staff:
Manager: Mrs Andi Fletcher-Cullum (Richards),
    Montessori Early Years Foundation Teacher, Further
    Education Teaching Certificate, NVQ4 Management,
    Business Management in Childcare, National Day
    Nurseries Inspector (*CP Officer, SENCO*)
Mr Mark Badham, BTEC Level 3 in Early Years
Miss Victoria Bath, NVQ4 Children's Care, Learning &
    Development
Miss Caylie Clayton, NVQ3 Children's Care, Learning &
    Development
Miss Louise Daff, Foundation Degree Arts & Early
    Childhood Studies
Miss Natasha Daniel, BTEC National Diploma Childcare
Miss Lucy Dewberry, NVQ3 Children's Care, Learning &
    Development (*Deputy Manager*)
Miss Claire Doran, Cache Diploma Level 3, NVQ4
    Childcare (*Deputy Manager, part time*)
Miss Victoria Fulford, Foundation Degree Early Childhood
    Studies
Miss Holly Glover, Cache Diploma Level 3 (*part time*)
Miss Rebecca Hill (*Trainee*)
Mrs Patricia Humphreys, Montessori Early Years Teaching
    Certificate
Miss Naomi Sherborne, NVQ2 Childcare (*trainee*)
Miss Tash Smith, BTEC National Award Level 3
Mrs Jenny White, Cache Diploma Level 3 (*part time*)

Registrar: Mrs Caroline Bailey, BSc
Head's PA: Mrs Anne Cadd
Finance & Resources Manager: Mr Andy Stevenson
Medical Centre:
Sister Sue Pittson, BSc, RGN, RScN
Mrs Debbie Barkley

Location. Kingsley School is situated in the market town of Bideford, an historic port beside the estuary of the River Torridge. The spectacular scenery of the North Devon coast is on our doorstep and there is easy access to the National Parks of Exmoor and Dartmoor. The North Devon link road, which passes close to Bideford, provides a direct route to the M5 motorway.

Organisation. Kingsley School is entirely co-educational and comprises a Senior School with approximately 250 pupils, aged 11 to 18 years, and a Junior School with approximately 70 pupils aged 2½ to 11 years, as well as a Nursery which offers wrap-around care for children from 3 months to 3 years old. The Grenville Dyslexia Centre, with a nationwide reputation for brilliant dyslexia provision, serves around 25% of the school's pupils.

Site and Buildings. Situated on a beautiful 25-acre site, the School has two Boarding Houses for boys and one for girls, all of which have immediate access to extensive playing fields, an all-weather hockey pitch, netball and tennis courts.

In recent years an ambitious programme of building has led to the provision of first-class facilities for science, ICT, drama, gymnastics, art and science. The Library provides an excellent environment for study, research and career guidance.

Curriculum. Senior School pupils study a core of subjects, including English, Mathematics, Biology, Chemistry, Physics, Modern Languages and Religious Studies. Subjects such as Geography, History, Art, Information & Communication Technology, Food & Nutrition, Textiles, Design &

Technology, Drama, Music, and Moral & Health Education complete the programme of study for years one to three.

For GCSE, in addition to the core subjects, other courses include Design & Technology, Food & Nutrition, Information & Communication Technology, Physical Education, Art, Business Studies, Statistics, Drama, Geography, History and Music.

In the Sixth Form there is a wide choice of AS and A Level subjects including English, Mathematics, Biology, Chemistry, Physics, Geography, History, Art, Design & Technology, French, German, Psychology, General Studies, Home Economics, Physical Education, Information & Communication Technology, Further Mathematics, Performance Arts and Music Technology.

In addition to these AS and A Level choices, GNVQ Business courses at Advanced Level (Vocational A Level) have proved both popular and successful.

Tuition in English for speakers of other languages is also available.

Sport and Physical Education. All pupils, girls and boys, are encouraged to participate in a large variety of sports including: rugby, hockey, netball, cross-country, athletics, cricket, dance, gymnastics, badminton, squash, volleyball, basketball, football, rounders, tennis, judo, swimming and health-related fitness. Rowing is fast becoming a very popular choice with both boys and girls. The Judo Academy has a unique link with the elite Team Bath, and the School's gymnasts and netball players are regular winners of national trophies.

Clubs and Activities. There is a 60+ range of extra-curricular activities which are organised and supervised by staff. Among the most popular are The Duke of Edinburgh's Award Scheme, the annual Ten Tors Expedition, electronics, computing, debating, art and music. A broad range of water sports is available, including rowing, sailing, canoeing, windsurfing, surfing and swimming. Skiing parties are organised each year together with other expeditions and field trips in the UK and abroad.

Musicals, plays and concerts are regularly presented in the school's purpose-designed theatre.

Careers. From Year 9 onwards, pupils are offered a planned programme of careers education and guidance as part of the tutorial programme. This is complemented by presentations from visiting professionals, visits to careers events and close contact with Careers advisers from Connexions Cornwall and Devon. All pupils have access to the latest careers information in the School Library.

Religion and Pastoral Care. In common with every Methodist Group School, Kingsley has a Christian ethos, and welcomes children of all religious denominations, as well as those without religious affiliation.

In addition to their Year Heads, all pupils have a personal Tutor who is responsible for monitoring their academic progress and personal well-being. For Boarders, care is also the responsibility of the Housemaster or Housemistress.

Admission. Boys and girls are admitted to the Junior School from the age of 2½ years. There are no formal tests.

Entry to the Senior School for pupils aged 11 and 12 years is by written tests in Mathematics, English and Science, as well as a verbal reasoning test. These requirements do not apply to pupils with recognised learning difficulties. In such cases, entry is by interview together with an up-to-date educational psychologist's report.

13+ admission is through the Common Entrance Examination or Scholarship Examination.

For older pupils, an interview together with a report from their present school is required.

Prospectus. The Kingsley School prospectus and DVD is available from the Registrar, Mrs Caroline Bailey, or online via the school's website.

Visitors are most welcome to tour the School by appointment.

Scholarships. (*See Scholarship Entries section.*)

Fees per term (2011-2012). Senior School: £7,400 (full boarders), £6,040 (weekly boarders), £3,650–£3,880 (day pupils including lunch).

Junior School: Day: £1,670 (Reception), £1,770 (Years 1 and 2), £2,230 (Years 3 and 4), £2,880 (Years 5 and 6). Boarding (from age 8): £4,810 (weekly), £5,990 (full).

Charitable status. Kingsley School, Bideford is a Registered Charity, number 306709.

Langley School

Langley Park, Norwich, Norfolk NR14 6BJ
Tel: 01508 520210
Fax: 01508 528058
e-mail: office@langleyschool.co.uk
website: www.langleyschool.co.uk

Langley School, formerly the Norwich High School for Boys, was founded in 1910. The School relocated from Norwich to Langley Park in 1946 and was renamed. It is the Senior School to Thorpe House Langley Preparatory School (*see entry in IAPS section*), and the business affairs of both schools are managed by a Council of Management as a non-profit making educational charity.

Langley admits boys and girls between the ages of 10 and 18 years to either day, weekly boarding or full boarding status. There are 533 pupils in the School, of whom around 100 are boarders.

Council of Management:

Chairman: Mrs Margaret M Alston, JP
Mr D J B Coventry, CA
Mr C E Self, FRICS, IRRV
Mrs C Smith
Mr C Townsend
Mr G Pritchard
Mr J Fuller
Mr R Hewitt
Mrs J Timmins
Mrs P Parker
Mrs M Philpott
Mrs J Anderson
Mr A Harmer
Mr S Rossall-Evans
Mr R Repper

Headmaster: **Mr D K Findlay**, BEd Exeter, NPQH

Senior Deputy Head (*Pastoral*): Mr M Rayner, BA Hons Leeds, PGCE Oxford
Deputy Head (*Academic*): Mr F Butt, BEng Hons Bath, PGCE Roehampton

Staff:

Science:
Mr J Clegg, BA Hons Hull, PGCE UEA
Dr C A Lowery, BSc, PhD Birmingham, PGCE UEA
Mr R E Holmes, MA, CertEd Mansfield College Oxford
Mr J A Pearman, BSc Hons, AKC, PGCE King's College London
Dr A Mason BSc, MSc, PhD MET University, PGCE UEA
Miss N Cowan BSc Hons, PGCE OU
Mr G Oclee-Brown, BA Hons University of Wales
Mr L Sitch

English & Drama:
Mr R Wood, BA Hons, MPhil, PGCE Liverpool
Mr J L McRobert, BA Jt Hons, PGCE Swansea
Mrs A Clarke, MA Hons Dundee, PGCE Swansea
Ms J Corser, BA, PGCE
Mr C McAllister
Mr J Aldridge

Mrs T Martin
Mrs S Cossey

Mathematics:
Mr W Baker, BEd Hons Manchester
Mr A Briggs, BA Hons OU, TCert
Mrs C A Feakes, BEd Worcester
Miss A Hanzelyova, MA Preston, QTS
Mrs K Skuse, BSc Hons UEA
Mrs L White, BSc Hons Swansea, PGCE Southampton
Mrs S Clegg

Languages:
Mr T J Batchelor, BA Hons Nottingham, PGCE Homerton
Mrs J L Skelton, BA Hons Oxford Brookes, PGCE Leeds
Ms A Konig, CertEd Coventry
Mrs L Holmes, BA Hons, PGCE UEA
Mrs M Ellwood, BA Hons Roehampton, PGCE
Mrs A Yandell, BA Hons Newnham College Cambridge, PGCE, Cert TEFL
Mrs J E Butt, BA Wolverhampton, Cert TEFL
Mrs D Harrington, BA Hons Durham, PGCE, RSA Dip TEFL
Mrs C Stewart, Cert Learning Support, Adult TCert
Mrs A Smith
Mr M Webb

Humanities:
Mr J Kempton, BA Hons Bristol, PGCE Bristol
Mr M Rayner, BA Hons Leeds, PGCE Oxford
Mr I Felton, BA Hons Portsmouth, PGCE UEA
Mrs G M Dover, BA UEA, PGCE St John's, York
Mrs K Lambert, BA Hons Sussex, PGCE Nottingham
Mr M Vanston, BSc Hons Sheffield, PGCE UEA
Mr D T Madgett, BA Hons, DipAcc City of London, PGCE Worc, Cert TEFL
Mr P Clark, BA Hons Northumbria, PGCE Sunderland
Mr S Read, LLB Cardiff
Mrs A Dain, BEd, MA, PhD, CertEd
Mr A Walker, BA Hons Brunel
Mr N Dyson
Mrs H Hanley
Mr T Kirkham

Art:
Mr J N Ogden, BA Hons, PGCE Lancashire
Mr R J Wheeler, CIC Hons Brighton
Miss H Stewart, BA Hons, PGCE
Mr S Robinson
Miss R Galer

Technology:
Mr F Butt, BEng Hons Bath, PGCE Roehampton
Mr S Daly, BEng Kingston, BA Greenwich QTS
Mr M J Holmes, BA, CertEd Brunel
Mr S Hughes, BA Hons Nottingham Trent
Mrs M Woolsey, CertEd Bath College of Educ
Mr D Innes, BA Hons Falmouth
Mr M Payne, BA Hons Warwick MA Leicester, PGCE
Mrs A Reynolds, BEd Hons Bristol

PE:
Mr C Greenhall, BA, PGCE Univ College, Wales
Mr C Cooper, PPC
Miss S Tea, BEd Hons De Montfort
Mrs C Vinsen
Mr T Malone

Music:
Mr A Stratford, BA Hons Huddersfield, PGCE Oxford Brookes
Mr R White, ATCL
Mr S Durant
Mr A Cronin
Mr J Stephens
Mr C Brady

Learning Support:
Mrs P Lightfoot, BA Hons, PGCE London, DipSpLD
Mr R Hull CertEd
Mrs R Hull
Mrs V Rickman
Mrs K Coulson
Mrs K Lamont

Bursar: Mr P J Weeks, BEd, CertEd, CertSpLD, MCollP

School Medical Officers:
Dr P Barrie, MBChB, DRCOG, DCH
Dr A Guy, FPCert, MB, BS

Headmaster's PA: Mrs C Mayes

Langley School aims to provide a framework within which each pupil will develop effective learning skills and will achieve their maximum academic potential. A happy, secure and well ordered environment is maintained in a beautiful country house setting with extensive grounds and playing fields, where individuals are encouraged to set their sights high. Their progress is monitored by a strong tutorial system to ensure that they follow a course of study that best suits their individual skills and needs. Langley pupils are encouraged to identify their talents and to use and develop them whilst contributing to a wide variety of new experiences that will help them acquire the values of honesty, enterprise, independence and social awareness. Small classes and a well organised House system help our children to sample these new experiences with confidence. They will learn to take personal and social responsibility and will get ample opportunities to develop leadership qualities. We hope to produce young people who will be prepared to meet the demands of a rapidly changing and demanding world which will require versatile, adaptable, receptive and confident citizens of the future.

Location and Facilities. Situated in some 100 acres of playing fields and wooded parkland south of Norwich, Langley benefits from good accessibility by road, rail, air and sea.

In recent years the school has been steadily expanding and its facilities have been substantially enhanced. Recent developments include a complete refurbishment programme for boarding facilities, a new floodlit Astroturf pitch, a new eleven-room Science Centre, a three-dimensional Art and Sculpture Studio, a multi-media suite for Modern Languages, a fully refurbished and extended Mathematics block and a multi-gym with fitness centre. In September 2010, a new state-of-the-art block of fifteen classrooms and four ICT rooms was opened, alongside the refurbishment of two other blocks.

Academic Curriculum. Syllabuses and schemes of work are designed to complement the National Curriculum and the Common Entrance Examination Syllabuses up to Year 9.

Lower School (10–13 years): All pupils in these years study English, Mathematics, French, German, Geography, History, Biology, Chemistry, Physics, Design and Technology, Drama, Art and Ceramics, Information Technology, Music, Physical Education and Religious Studies. A programme of Personal and Social Education includes study skills and careers guidance. Pupils are setted on ability in the core subjects while in other subjects streaming applies.

Middle School (14–16 years): All pupils are prepared for the GCSE examinations. The School is an examining centre for a number of Boards, and this enables staff to select those syllabuses which they believe are most appropriate to the needs of their pupils. All pupils study English, Mathematics and the Sciences. A variable number of additional subjects are selected which enables the most able pupil to study up to eleven subjects. A brochure on GCSE courses is available on request.

Most students in the Sixth Form will study 4 AS Levels in the Lower Sixth from a choice of 28 subjects and continue with three of these to A Level in the Upper Sixth. Other permutations of AS and A Levels are possible to suit students of varying ability.

Monitoring Academic Progress. High priority is given to the monitoring of each pupil's progress and is the specific responsibility of the Heads of Year with a team of tutors. A combination of complementary short, medium and long-term recording systems are in use. This permits effective communication between teachers, and between the School and the parent.

Extra-Curricular Activities. The school offers a wide choice of sports, artistic, musical, dramatic, scientific, technical and literary activities to enhance students life-long learning. In total there are more than 80 such activities operating daily throughout the week. All staff and students are required to contribute to this programme. The major team games are rugby, football, cricket, tennis, athletics, hockey and netball. Sailing, fencing, judo, squash, basketball, climbing, shooting and golf are but a few of the other options.

The School has a thriving CCF (Army, RAF and Navy sections) and encourages participation in the Duke of Edinburgh's Award Scheme.

The self-confidence which can be acquired through participation in music and drama is immeasurable. Consequently, the school promotes participation by all in dramatic and musical events at a class, house and school level. An Arts Umbrella programme offers the opportunity for pupils to experience the theatrical and musical productions in London and other centres.

Admission. Pupils will be considered for admission to Langley at 10+, 11+, 13+ and into the Sixth Form. Entry may be possible at other levels when vacancies permit and is conditional on an interview followed by detailed and satisfactory school reports. At Sixth Form level, satisfactory performance in GCSE is required.

Scholarships. (*See Scholarship Entries section.*) Competitive academic scholarships are awarded at 11+, 13+ and Sixth Form level. Music, Art, Drama, Design & Technology and Sports scholarships are also available.

Fees per term (2011-2012). Years 6–13: Boarders £7,715, Weekly Boarders £6,430, Day Pupils £3,795.

Generous family and Forces discounts are offered.

Further Information is available on the school's website. A School prospectus, Sixth Form brochure and GCSE brochure are available on application from the Headmaster's PA. Alternatively, you are invited to arrange to visit the school by telephoning the Headmaster's PA on 01508 522474.

Charitable status. Langley School is a Registered Charity, number 311270. It exists to provide a sound education for boys and girls.

LVS Ascot (The Licensed Victuallers' School)

London Road, Ascot, Berkshire SL5 8DR
Tel: 01344 882770
Fax: 01344 890648
e-mail: registrar@lvs.ascot.sch.uk
website: www.lvs.ascot.sch.uk

The School was founded in 1803 and has been co-educational from the outset. It is controlled by a Board of Governors on behalf of the parent charity, The Licensed Trade Charity.

Patron: Her Majesty The Queen

Director of Education: Mr I Mullins, BEd Hons, MSc, MBIM

Head of Senior School: **Mrs C Cunniffe**, BA Hons, MMus

Head of Junior School: Mrs H Donnelly, BA, BEd Hons

Deputy Head/Academic: Mr C Davis, BSc Hons, PGCE

Deputy Head/Pastoral: Mr C Seal, BA, PGCE

Asst Head/Director of Studies: Mr K Adams, BA Hons, PGCE, MA

Asst Head/Head of Sixth Form: Mr C Jenkins, BA Hons, PGCE

School Chaplain: Revd R F Walker, BSc Hons, BDThM

Heads of House:
Head of Guinness: Mr C Cunningham-Watson, BA
Assistant Heads of Guinness:
Mr B Hunt, BScHons, PGCE
Mr J Sullivan, BSc, PGCE
Head of Carlsberg: Mrs H Simpson, BA Hons
Assistant Head of Carlsberg: Mr D Simpson
Head of Bass: Mr G Blunt, BA Hons
Assistant Head of Bass: Mrs H Blunt
Head of Whitbread: Mrs H Miller, BSc Hons, PhD, MSc
Head of Courage: Mrs S Riley, BA Hons
Head of Bell's: Mr N Preston, BA Hons, MA
Head of Gilbey: Mrs D Lister, Dip Chd Dev & Psy, Cert Coun and Cert BSA

Child Protection Officer: Mrs R Sandford, BA Hons
Deputy Child Protection Officer: Mrs S Litherland, BA Hons, PGCE

* *Head of Department/Subject*

Art and Design:
*Mr P Cordeaux, BA Hons, PGCE
Mrs R Edwards, BEd
Mr T Hunter, BQ Hons, PGCE
Mrs S Litherland, BA Hons, PGCE
Mrs R Sandford, BA Hons

Business Studies/Economics:
*Mr R Sears, BSc BM
Mrs J Johnstone, BSc, H DipEd
Mrs S Ross, BA Hons, PGCE
Mr J Sullivan, BSc, PGCE

Design Technology:
*Dr P Hodges, PhD, MSc, BSc, PGCE
Mrs S Alder
Ms G Heuchel, BEd
Mrs K Rentell, BSc, PGCE
Mr J Swanepoel, BEd, MSS

Drama:
*Miss E Crowe, BA Hons
Miss S Gosney, BA Hons

English and Media Studies:
*Ms S Quant, BA Hons, MA, PGCE
Mr B Brown, BA, PGCE
Mr C Bryant, BA, PGCE
Miss C Macey, BA Hons, PGCE
Miss C Phippen, BA, PGCE
Ms N Rowley, BA, BEd
Mrs G Toms, BA Hons, PGCE
Mrs J Wren BA, PGCE

English as an Additional Language:
EAL Coordinator: Mr C Cunningham-Watson, BA Hons, MA, PGCE
Mrs P Bowley
Mrs W Brittaine, BA
Mrs S Carter
Mrs R Clegg
Mrs M Cook
Mrs C Dawson, BA

Mrs A Kawka-Olejnik, BA Hons, MA
Mrs G Makin BEd, ESOL
Ms S Natta, BA Hons, PGCE
Ms E Reynolds
Ms N Virdi
Mrs J Wadsworth

Geography:
*Mrs D Finch, BA Hons
Mr B Hunt, BSc Hons, PGCE
Mr C Jenkins, BA Hons, PGCE
Mr N Preston, BA Hons MA

History:
*Mr D Woolley, BA Hons, PGCE
Mrs T Bason, BA, PGCE
Mr C Cunningham-Watson, BA Hons, MA, PGCE
Mr P Moores, BA Hons
Mr C Seal, BA, PGCE

Information Technology:
*Mrs S Featherstone-Clark, BA Hons
Mrs K Southard, BSc, PGCE
Mr K Win, BSc Hons

Law:
*Mrs P Liverseidge, BSc

Learning Support:
*Mrs E Lawrence, OCR Dip SpLD, PGCE, BSc Hons
Mrs M Adams, Cert Ed, Teach Dip
Mrs C Child
Mrs R Hamblin, Cert Ed, Cert SLD
Mrs M Holloway, BEd
Mrs L Lunn, Cert Ed, Dip SLD
Mrs V Smith
Mrs L Spiller
Miss C White, BA, PGCE

Mathematics:
*Mr S Miller, BSc, PGCE
Miss L Betteridge, BSc, PGCE
Mr P Cantor, BSc Hons, PGCE
Mr N Collins, BSc Hons
Mr E Dennis, BA, PGCE
Mr N Funnell, BSc Hons, PGCE
Mr R Lawes, BA Hons, PGCE
Mrs H Miller, BSc Hons, PhD, MSc
Mrs S Scholefield, BSc Hons
Mr S Tomlin, BA Hons
Mr R Whiffen, MA, BA, PGCE
Mr K Win, BSc Hons

Modern Foreign Languages:
*Mrs A Roberts, BA Hons, PGCE
Mrs M Davies, BA Hons, PGCE (*German*)
Mrs E Meyer, Licence d'Anglais (*French*)
Mrs K Potter, BA Hons, PGCE (*Spanish*)
Mrs C Batt
Ms A Bokenda, Licence d'Anglais, PGCE
Miss E Dufloux
Mrs Y Farrelly, BA
Mrs E Limburn, BA Hons
Mr J Roszykiewicz, BA, PGCE
Miss E Sanchez-Escobar
Mrs G Wright, BA Hons, PGCE

Music:
Director of Music: Mr M Lister, ALCM, LTCL, LGSM, GCLCM
Mr D Gravett, BSc Hons
Mrs S Riley, BA Hons, ARCM
Miss C Smiga, BA, PGCE

Instrumental Staff:
Pianoforte: Mr J Chantrey, Mrs A Konjhodzic, Mrs K Stanley, Mrs G Tucker
Cello: Mr N Charlton

Woodwind: Mrs D Head, Mrs J Minns
Guitar: Mr J Clark, Mr K Jenkins
Percussion: Mr G Brown, Mr M Harrison
Singing: Mrs J Hatfield, Mr D Manners
Brass: Mr J Ellwood
Violin/Viola: Mrs M Bentley

Physical Education:
Director of Sport: Mr A Towse, BA Hons
Head of PE: Mrs L Towse, BSc Hons, PGCE
Mr T Andrews, BSc Hons, PGCE
Mr G Blunt, BA Hons
Miss E Bunyan, BA Hons
Miss C Heemskerk, BEd
Mr B McMurray, BSc Hons, PGCE
Miss A Murawska, BSc
Miss C Naalchigar, MSc
Miss K Pena, Dip PMT
Mr J Percy, BSc
Mr C Seal, BA, PGCE
Mr M Steele, BA Hons
Miss L Stevens, BA Hons, PGCE

Psychology:
*Mrs H Miller, BSc Hons, PhD, MSc
Mr R Ebbage, BSc, MSc
Mr B Stephenson, BSc, MA

Religious Studies:
*Mr B Padrick, BA
Revd R F Walker, BSc Hons, BDThM

Science:
*Mr G Cunningham, BSc Hons PGCE
Mr K Adams, MA, BA
Dr C Beswick, PhD, MSc, BScHons, PGCE
Mrs V Beswick, BSc Hons, PGCE
Mrs N Benimadho, BA Hons BPAED
Mrs L Chappell, BSc Hons
Mr S A Clark, BSc, PCGE
Mr C Davis, BSc Hons, PGCE
Mrs M Grant, BA
Mrs J Hopkins, BSc Hons, PGCE
Mr A Kemp, BSc, PGCE
Mrs S Lucas, BSc Hons, PGCE

Cover Teachers:
Mrs S Alder
Mr P Moores, BA Hons

Learning Resource Centre:
*Mrs S Bastone, ACLIP
Mrs S Buckerfield
Mrs A Harris
Mrs A Prahl
Mrs K Stokes

Medical:
Medical Officer: Dr Kade
Dr C McDonald
Mrs A Kew
Mrs J Webster, RN Child
Mrs L Wooldridge, RN

Technicians:
Design Technology: Mrs D Brophy, Mr T Withers
Theatre Manager: Mr K Morgan
Audio Visual: Mr G Makin
Science: Mr C Bushill, Mrs K Lavender, Mrs E Nicholson, Mr A Rentell

Junior School Teaching Staff:
Assistant Head of Junior School: Mrs L Rawlinson, BEd Hons
Miss H Buckett, BEd
Mrs E Earl, BEd
Mrs A Foster, BEd Hons
Mrs J Foster, BA Hons, PGCE, LTCL

Mr M Hamilton, BA Hons, QTS
Mrs A Hoddle, BEd Hons
Miss Z Hoddle, BA Hons
Mrs J Kraushar, BSc, Dip BA, QTS
Miss H Main, BA Hons, PGCE
Miss S Morrison
Miss N Mullins, BA Hons, PGCE
Miss K Pugh, BA Hons, PGCE
Mrs R Steel, BEd Hons
Mrs H Sexton, CEd
Mrs S Thomassen, OCR Cert SpLD
Mrs L Thomson, BSc Hons, PGCE
Miss L Williams, BSc Hons, PGCE

Junior School Teaching Assistants:
Mrs S Gould
Mrs M Hodgson
Mrs S Le Bellec
Mrs H Newman
Mrs S Parsons
Miss M Pospiech
Mrs S Seal
Mrs N Spackman
Miss S Taylor
Mrs H Wall

Administrative Staff:
Examinations Officer: Mrs S Chapman
Head of Senior School's PA: Mrs L Humphreys
Marketing: Mrs K Davies
Registrars: Mrs S Folley, Ms R Tocknell, BSc Hons
Senior School Secretaries: Miss H Austin, Mrs L Reddy
Senior School Reception: Mrs A Davies
Head of Junior School's PA: Mrs D Pearce
Junior School Administrator: Mrs V Smith

LVS Ascot is a co-educational day and boarding school for young people aged 4–18.

Numbers. Junior School 213, Senior School 748 (including 158 in Sixth Form), boarding approx 200

Organisation. Pupils aged 4 to 11 (Years R to 6) are taught in the Junior School, where they are taught in separate classes, each with a class teacher. Houses are used for sports and other competitions. Junior School pupils may board from Year 3 (age 7) and join a mixed House (Bass House), which is an integral part of the Junior School buildings.

Senior School pupils, aged 11 to 18 (Years 7 to 13), are placed in a tutor groups and a school House, with a tutor who monitors their pastoral care and oversees their academic performance. Students are taught in ability groups with a maximum class size of 20. Boarders are accommodated in four separate boarding Houses, each supervised by House Parents: Bass (Junior House) is mixed for pupils from Year 3 to Year 7; Carlsberg (girls' House) for pupils from Year 8 to Year 11; Guinness (boys' House) for pupils from Year 8 to Year 11; Gilbey (mixed Sixth Form House) for pupils in Years 12 and 13.

Location. LVS Ascot is north of the A329, close to Ascot Racecourse and Royal Windsor. The school is easily accessible from the M3, M4 and M25 motorways as well as Heathrow and Gatwick airports. The school bus service connects with trains at Ascot Station, as well many surrounding towns within a 20 miles radius.

Facilities. As the most modern boarding school in the UK, the purpose-built facilities, set in 26 acres of landscaped grounds, include: boarding accommodation and classroom blocks, a sports centre, indoor swimming pool, fully-equipped theatre and a music technology suite. LVS Ascot hosts over five-hundred networked computer workstations, with every classroom equipped with ICT resources for digital and interactive learning. Wireless networking provides additional facilities for centrally-managed student laptops, eBooks and other devices in a secure environment.

There is a dedicated Sixth Form Centre, and a Learning Resource Centre, that has an extensive range of books and journals.

Curriculum. The curriculum is broad and based on the national curriculum "plus". Pupils follow a common core curriculum of English, Mathematics, Science, one/two foreign languages, plus PE and PSHE. Science is taught as separate subjects. At GCSE, students select their choices from: Business Studies, Technology, Art & Design, Geography, History, Food Technology, Music, Drama, Media Studies, Economics, Physical Education, Computer Science, Spanish, German or French.

A wide range of A Level and vocational options are provided, including Mathematics, Physics, Chemistry, Biology, Music, Geography, History, Economics, Business Studies, English, Art & Design, Theatre Studies, Design & Technology, Media Studies, Photography, Psychology, French, Spanish, German, ICT, Computer Studies and Physical Education.

Games, etc. The school has superb indoor and outdoor facilities with a large Sports Hall, Dance Studio with ballet bars, a 25-metre swimming pool and a well-equipped gym as well as rugby, football and hockey pitches and tennis courts. The school has achieved considerable success in providing County, Regional and National standard players in a wide range of sports. Whilst all pupils play team games such as Rugby, Football, Cricket, Hockey, Tennis, Netball, Basketball or Athletics in their early years, the range of options widens as pupils become older to encourage fitness for life, with opportunities such as skiing skating and playing squash.

Clubs and Activities. LVS Ascot is an accredited Duke of Edinburgh's Award training centre and runs a vibrant and popular award scheme. Alongside this there is a range of co-curricular activities such as music ensembles, newspaper club, riding, canoeing, rowing, climbing, cookery, animation and film club.

Admissions. There is no entrance examination, reports are requested from a student's current school. All students are interviewed prior to acceptance. Prospective students and their families are welcome to visit the school. Dates of the regular Open Days are listed on the school's website. Personal tours can also be arranged by appointment.

Fees per term (2011-2012). Infants £2,665; Junior: £3,195 (Day), £6,820 (Boarding); Senior: £4,530 (Day), £5,010 (Extended Day), £8,080 (Full/Weekly Boarding); Sixth Form: £4,600 (Day), £8,080 (Full/Weekly Boarding).

Charitable status. The Licensed Victuallers' School is a Registered Charity, number 230011. It exists to provide education for boys and girls.

Longridge Towers School

Berwick-upon-Tweed, Northumberland TD15 2XQ
Tel: 01289 307584
Fax: 01289 302581
e-mail: enquiries@lts.org.uk
website: www.lts.org.uk

Motto: *Carpe Diem*

Board of Governors:
Chairman: Mr J Smithson
Vice-Chairman: (*to be appointed*)

Mr J Aynsley	Lord Joicey
Mr A Bell	Dr E Miller
Mrs J Coats	Mrs J McGregor
Lt Col (Retd) H Culley	Dr C Phillips
Mr J A Houston	Mr J Robertson

Headmaster: Mr T M Manning, BSc, PGCE

Deputy Head: Mr R Notman, BCom, PGCE

Head of Junior Department: Mrs S Maddock, BEd

Teaching Staff:
Ms D Bryden, BEd (*Junior Department*)
Mrs S Bullen (*Reception/EYFS*)
Mr M Caddick, BA, PGCE (*German*)
Miss G Campbell, BA, PGCE (*English*)
Miss L Cannon, BA, PGCE (*Art*)
Mrs R Caton, BA, QTS (*English*)
Mrs I Cheer, DTM, (*Music*)
Mrs B Chynoweth, MA, PGCE (*Junior Department*)
Mr R Davie, BSc, PGCE (*Mathematics, Computing*)
Mr I Dempster, BEd (*History, Games*)
Mr P Dodd, DIS, PGCE (*Mathematics*)
Mr R Glenn, BSc, PGCE (*ICT Coordinator*)
Mrs N Green, BA, PGCE (*EFL*)
Mrs C Krzysiak, BSc, PGCE (*Biology*)
Mrs L Lee, MA Ed, CertEd (*English, Drama*)
Miss K Martin, BA, PGCE (*Junior Department*)
Mrs J Masey, BSc, PGCE (*Science*)
Miss G Matthews, BSc, QTS (*Junior Department*)
Mr P McParland, BSc, MSc, PGCE (*Geography, Mathematics*)
Mrs L Monkman, BA, QTS (*Junior Department*)
Mrs H Notman, BSc, MSc, PGCE (*Head of Sixth Form, Economics*)
Mr A Phillips, BA, PGCE (*Boys Games, German, Sports Studies*)
Miss J Roberts, BEd (*Careers, PSHE, Psychology*)
Mr P Rowett, BA (*RE, History, Geography*)
Mrs K Rudge, BSc, PGCE (*Science*)
Mrs E Shaw, BA, PGCE (*Girls Games, Sports Studies*)
Mr A Skeen, BA (*Economics, Games*)
Mr A Skipper, BSc, PGCE (*Physics*)
Mr N Sumerling, BSc, PGCE (*Geography, History*)
Ms P Turner, MA, BSc, PGCE, AdvDip SEN (*Special Needs*)
Mrs F Weightman, MA, PGCE (*Modern Languages*)
Mr A Westthorp, BEng, PGCE (*CDT, Computing*)
Mrs K Westthorp, MA, PGCE (*French*)
Miss L Wood, BEd (*Girls Games, Sports Studies*)

Boarding Staff:
Mr G Hattle (*House Parent*)
Mrs S Hewitt (*House Parent*)
Mrs M Robson (*Senior House Parent/Resident Matron*)

Visiting Music Staff:
Mrs P Bonia
Mr R Cheer
Ms C Fish
Mrs M Rowland
Mrs C Smith
Mrs B Taylor
Mrs J Warren

Speech & Drama: Miss A Glasgow, BA

Medical Staff:
School Doctor: Dr S Ruffe
Matron: Mrs M Hattle, RGN

Administration:
Bursar: Mr S Bankier, BA, FCMA
Assistant: Mr D Burns
Head's Secretary: Mrs J Higgins
Reception: Mrs C Jobson
Site Manager: Mr L Caldwell
Catering Manager: Mrs C Krause

The school occupies a Victorian Mansion set in 80 acres of woodland in the beautiful Tweed Valley and enjoys excellent road and rail links with England and Scotland. Daily bus services operate within a radius of 30 miles from the school.

Longridge Towers, refounded in 1983 under its founder and President, the late Lord Home of the Hirsel, has grown from 113 pupils to nearly 300 pupils. It is probably unique in offering the close personal relationships between pupils, staff and parents which are only possible in a small school together with the facilities normally found in much larger schools, eg large sports hall, library, theatre, computer suites etc.

Specialities. Academic fulfilment is sought for all pupils and pass rates at GCSE and A Level exceed 90% and 95% respectively. It is usual for all Sixth Formers to be offered places at university. Sport figures strongly in the life of the pupils and over 20 each year gain representative honours at county and national level in a variety of sports, such as rugby, hockey, cross-country running, athletics, tennis and cricket. Art, Music and Drama are also very popular and successful activities. Almost half of the pupils take private instrumental lessons and the taking of grade examinations is encouraged.

Entry. The school caters for a wide spectrum of abilities among its pupils who are taught in small classes. Special provision is made for the needs of pupils with mild dyslexia and for the small proportion of pupils for whom English is their second language.

Assessments upon entry to the Junior and Senior Departments in Mathematics and English are diagnostic and have no fixed pass mark.

The school is divided into 2 departments, Junior and Senior, and caters for pupils throughout their school career, from four to eighteen years. Pupils may enter at any age provided that a vacancy exists. Classes are small with less than 20 pupils per teaching set, reducing to about half this in the Sixth Form.

Activities. Longridge Towers is a school where the development of the pupils outside the academic sphere is considered to be vital. Every afternoon there is an extensive Enrichment programme offering a wide range of activities including: archery, falconary, dance, karate, judo, drama, kick boxing, creative writing, wildlife and gardening, young engineers, science club, debating, along with many others. The major team games are rugby, hockey, tennis, cross-country running, athletics and cricket. Many senior pupils participate in the Duke of Edinburgh's Award Scheme. The musical activities within the school are varied and numerous. There are five Choirs, two Orchestras and various instrumental groups. No visitor to the school could fail to be aware of the variety and excellence of the artwork on display which includes clay modelling and photography.

Public Examinations. The school follows an enhanced version of the National Curriculum and enters pupils for Key Stage testing at Key Stages 1 and 2. Twenty-two subjects are offered at GCSE level, including Physics, Chemistry and Biology and 19, including Economics, Psychology, Sports Studies and Drama, are offered in the Sixth Form at A or AS Level.

Parents receive reports half-yearly and three-weekly Grade Cards ensure that they are kept up to date about their children's progress.

Boarding. The Boarding House and pastoral care are in the hands of resident non-teaching house parents. There is medical and dental care. Pupils have access to telephones and e-mail and may send or receive fax messages using the facilities in the school office. Boarders may attend on a weekly or termly basis from age 8 years onwards. At weekends the boarders participate in a wide range of activities.

Scholarships and Bursaries. Academic awards at various levels are available annually to pupils aged 8–14 and 16 (into Sixth Form). Music, Sports and All-Rounder Scholarships are also available.

Bursaries are available to children of serving members of the Armed Forces.

Bursaries are also available to pupils; the value of these is determined after consideration of a statement of parental income.

Fees per term (2011-2012). Full Boarders: £7,053 (Junior), £7,442 (Senior). Weekly Boarders: £5,922 (Junior), £5,922 (Senior). Day pupils: £2,338 (Junior age 4–7), £3,251 (Junior age 7–11), £3,653 (Senior age 11–18).

Charitable status. Longridge Towers School is a Registered Charity, number 513534. It exists to provide an academic education for boys and girls.

Milton Abbey School

Near Blandford, Dorset DT11 0BZ
Tel: 01258 880484
Fax: 01258 881194
e-mail: info@miltonabbey.co.uk
website: www.miltonabbey.co.uk

Visitor: Revd C W Mitchell-Innes, MA

Governors:
Chairman: J E A Barnes, BA
R D Barbour, FRICS
The Lady Elizabeth Barne
P H G Bradley, BA, BAI, ACA
¶A A B R Bruce of Crionaich
Mrs J C Dwyer, BEd
¶Captain N Hadden-Paton
P W McGrath, MA, MW
D P O'Brien, QC, MA
Mrs S Russell, LLB
M Sherwin, BSc
¶P M G Stopford-Adams, FSI, FPSI, DL
Sir Philip Williams, Bt, MA, JP, DL
S J Young, MC, JP, FRICS, DL

Clerk to the Governors: (*to be appointed*)
Finance Director: P Richardson

Headmaster: **G E Doodes**, MA

Deputy Headmaster: C N Staley, BA

* *Head of Department*
† *Housemaster/mistress*

Assistant Head (*Activities*): H A Mieville, BA, MA, DipEdMan
Assistant Head (*Pastoral*): †S Kibler, BA
Assistant Head (*Academic*): *M D Sharp, BA, MA

H Barnes, BA	*D E Lane, BSc
M Benjafield, BSc	*P Lord, BA, MA
J Bradbury, BA, MA, PhD	*Miss K Matthews, BA,
S J Brown, BSc	MEd
Mrs J Brown, BA	I Maxwell, BA
*Mrs S Burton, BA	F Million
F Channon, BA	*J D Milman, MA, DPhil,
Mrs E Charlton	CertEd, MIBiol
P Chichester, BSc, MSc	D Mohamed, BSc
Mrs S Church, BA	R P L Nicholson, CertEd
M S Clapper, BSc, HDipEd	Mrs C Peach, BA
N Cooke, BA	*M Phipps, BEd
Mrs R Dal Din, BSc	*A M Prior, BEd
*C Douchet, Maîtrise DP,	Mrs M Raindle, MSc,
LPC	BScEd
*†Mrs P Doubleday,	J Ratcliffe, BA
CertEd, RSA	*Mrs J Riley, BEd, CertEd
R Edwards, FIH	D Roberts, BSc
Mrs J Emerson, FIL	M J Sale, CertEd, DMS
†M Giles, BSc	F Shon, BA, MA, DPhil
Mrs C Hallam, CertEd,	Mrs C Stoot, CertEd
CertSpLD	A Stroud
D Jones	The Revd R Thomson, BA

P Timmis, BSc
Mrs L Unsworth, BA
M Watson, BSc
*Miss K P Wightman, BA

†M Williams
†F Wilson, BSc
†Mrs L Wingate-Grey
P W Wood, BA

Admissions Registrar: Mrs D Morant, BEd
Headmaster's PA: Mrs G Woolgar

Foundation. Milton Abbey was founded in 1954 and comprises 205 boys aged 13–18 and 25 Sixth Form girls. From September 2012 the School will be fully co-educational.

It aims to provide a Christian education, to develop individual potential as fully as possible and to furnish wide opportunities for the exercise of responsibility. Milton Abbey helps to produce pupils who mature into balanced adults. Boys and girls, who may find that a larger school environment drains their confidence, can be judged by their own capabilities and encouraged to achieve their maximum potential. The school provides a framework of rigorous kindness in a safe but stimulating environment with a well-qualified and enthusiastic team of teaching and pastoral staff who know each individual well.

Situation. The School lies in a wooded valley on the site of a Benedictine Monastery (founded 1,000 years ago) and a short distance from the picturesque village of Milton Abbas. The nearest towns are Blandford and Dorchester. The campus provides ample space for playing fields and a nine-hole Golf course.

Buildings. The two remaining buildings of the Monastery are the Great Abbey, which is now the School Chapel, and the Abbot's Hall around which a Georgian mansion was built by the Earl of Dorchester in 1770. Today these great buildings form a perfect partnership to fulfil the needs of a boarding school. Outside the mansion house, the modern facilities which are on a par with those of a much larger school include a Music school, Art Studio, Pottery, Technology/Computer building, 370-seat theatre, IT suite, rifle range, all-weather pitch, indoor heated 25-metre pool, cricket pavilion, Design Technology centre and a new Library.

Organisation. There are five boarding houses within the main building and a separate boarding house for girls. During the first year boys are housed in a dormitory of up to 4 boys. From the second year onwards the majority move into study-bedrooms for up to three occupants. In the Sixth Form pupils usually have single study-bedrooms. The School takes meals in the Abbot's Hall where the cafeteria service provides an informal atmosphere, but is well-disciplined.

Curriculum. All boys follow a broad and balanced curriculum up to GCSE. A boy is setted separately in most subjects, enabling him to work towards his academic goals at a comfortable pace. Most GCSE subjects are taken in year 10. Entry to the Sixth Form is dependent upon an interview, a literacy assessment test and team-building exercises with the Headmaster.

The Sixth Form offers a range of academic courses which incorporate traditional, bluechip ASs and A2s; vocational BTECs; and top-up GCSEs. Combinations are possible from: mathematics, further mathematics, physics, chemistry, biology, history, classical civilisation, English, French, Spanish, geography, religious studies, business studies, economics, art, music, music technology, design and technology, communication studies, drama, physical education; and these BTECs: Hospitality, Countryside Management, Sport and Exercise Science and Equine Studies.

Music. Individual tuition is available in all instruments, and in singing. A strong tradition of choral singing supports worship in the Abbey. Ensembles of all sorts perform music in a notably wide variety of styles.

Clubs and Societies. A wide range of interests and activities are encouraged in free time.

CCF and Community Service. The school's thriving CCF contingent has Royal Navy, Army and RAF sections, and enjoys close links with service establishments in the area. There are regular camps in the holidays. There are expeditions at home and abroad. Every weekend offers an opportunity for a pupil to choose from caving, climbing, sailing, windsurfing and canoeing. Most boys take part in the Duke of Edinburgh's Award Scheme. Community service is the alternative to the CCF.

Games. Christmas Term: Rugby, Football and Hockey. Easter Term: Hockey, Netball, Lacrosse and Cross-Country. Summer Term: Cricket, Athletics, Dinghy Sailing and Racing in Portland Harbour, Tennis and Rounders. All year round: Swimming, Squash, Rifle Shooting, Basketball, Golf, Polo, Fencing, Riding, Canoeing and Clay Pigeon Shooting.

Admission. The flexible curriculum and the small size of classes enable the school to cater effectively for a wide spread of ability. A few qualify through the Scholarship Examination held in May. The majority sit the Common Entrance Examination in June for entry in the following Autumn Term. An average of 50% in the Common Entrance ensures a place but the School is also prepared to consider a few candidates who seem unlikely to reach this standard because their academic progress has been uneven. Sixth Form assessment day in February.

Fees per term (2011-2012). Boarding £9,780, Day £7,350.

Scholarships. (*See Scholarship Entries section.*) Several Scholarships are awarded annually including ones for Academic, Music, Drama, Art, DT, Sailing and Sport. Bursaries may also be considered in cases of need.

Charitable status. The Council of Milton Abbey School Limited is a Registered Charity, number 306318. It is a charitable Trust for the secondary education of boys.

Newcastle School for Boys

Senior School:
34 The Grove, Gosforth, Newcastle-upon-Tyne NE3 1NH
Tel: 0191 255 9300
Fax: 0191 213 0973
e-mail: groveoffice@newcastleschool.co.uk

Junior School:
30 West Avenue, Gosforth, Newcastle-upon-Tyne NE3 4ES
Tel: 0191 285 1619
Fax: 0191 213 1105
e-mail: office@newcastleschool.co.uk

website: www.newcastleschool.co.uk

Chairman of Governors: P Mankin, BSc, ACA

Headmaster: L A Francis, BA

Deputy Head: D J Tickner, BA, MEd

Head of Sixth Form: G Hallam BSc

Head of Juniors: S Asker, BA

Head of Infants: Mrs S G P Woosnam, BEd

Bursar: Mrs J E Lightley, MA, ACA

Age Range. 3–18.
Number of Boys. 410.
Fees per term (2011-2012). £2,240 (Reception), £2,895 (Year 1 to Year 6), £3,495 (Year 7 and above).

Newcastle School for Boys is a young, forward-looking school created in 2005. It is now established as the only independent school in the North East providing continuous education for boys from ages 3 to 18. Situated on three sites in Gosforth, Newcastle upon Tyne, the Senior School site on The Grove covers 5 acres of playing fields and buildings that house Years 6 to Year 13. North of Gosforth High Street, a 10 minute walk, are two further sites that house the Junior and Infant Schools.

The school currently has over 400 pupils on role from Nursery to Year 13, with two classes per year group.

The academic curriculum starts in the Infants and provides boys with opportunities for stretch and challenge from the outset. This leads through the Juniors to GCSE and A Level qualifications in a wide range of disciplines at the Senior School.

Pastoral care is outstanding throughout the school and boys receive plenty of individual attention so that they grow in confidence and independence.

Newcastle School for Boys believes strongly in enhancing learning beyond the classroom and runs an extensive trips and visits programme with great emphasis being placed on this in the Junior and Infant departments. Residential and day visits are offered to all pupils from age 5 onwards and culminate in the Duke of Edinburgh's Gold Award expeditions in the Sixth Form.

Senior School. The Senior School starts at Year 6 (10+) and runs through to Year 13 (18+).

We generally run two classes per year group and offer an enhanced curriculum leading up to GCSE, where we offer 16 subjects.

The Senior School site has recently undergone an extensive programme of development to provide a new school hall, a large new teaching block incorporating Art and Technology facilities and a new purpose-built Sixth Form Centre.

The Senior School provides an extensive co-curricular programme including music, drama and a wide range of sports including a number of major overseas trips. The School enhances its sporting provision through the use of a number of excellent local facilities including South Northumberland Cricket Club, Northern Rugby Club and the 'Complete Football' training facilities at Newcastle Racecourse.

Sixth Form. The School has established a new Sixth Form offering students a wide choice from a traditional AS and A Level structure. True to our ethos, our Sixth Form offers a personal learning experience for the boys which provides the support they need to achieve their best possible academic and personal outcomes.

Through our own experienced teachers and through strong collaboration with Newcastle Church High School we are able to offer 22 subject choices at AS and A Level giving a full educational experience for all pupils.

This collaboration brings an extra dimension to the Sixth Form experience for the boys and joint activities and enrichment opportunities are arranged for NSB boys and girls from Church High School.

Entrance and Scholarship Examinations are offered in January for boys entering Year 7 (11+), Year 9 (13+) and Year 12 (16+). Entry at other points is possible following a full academic assessment and interview.

Newcastle School for Boys is committed to offering access to all potential pupils; means-tested assistance with fees is available for boys entering Year 5 and above.

Junior School. The well-established Nursery and Infant Department is housed in spacious accommodation to the west of Gosforth High Street and lays the foundations for everything which is to follow. A happy and safe environment is provided, where self-esteem and self-confidence are paramount. Throughout the Foundation Stage and Key Stage 1, the curriculum is a blend of the traditional and the innovative, and is designed to balance the need for adventure and fun, while maintaining progress in numeracy and literacy. Dedicated ICT lessons are taught from Year 1 and French is introduced from Year 2.

Breakfast Club and after-school clubs and activities provide full 'wrap-around' care and there is also provision for Holiday Club.

In the Junior Department (Years 3–5) the learning environment is tailored to the needs of the younger boys, taking into account their energy and enthusiasm for challenge and discovery. The boys are provided with opportunities to develop their individual academic talents and to pursue their creative goals. Excellence is also pursued in the sporting arena where boys have opportunities including soccer, rugby, cricket, golf and fencing.

Regular drama performances and musical productions encourage teamwork and build confidence from an early age.

Newcastle School for Boys encourages a strong partnership with parents and welcomes parental involvement in the classroom and through the Parents' Forum and the 'Friends of Newcastle School for Boys'.

Charitable status. Newcastle School for Boys is a Registered Charity, number 503975.

North Cestrian Grammar School

Dunham Road, Altrincham, Cheshire WA14 4AJ
Tel: 0161 928 1856
Fax: 0161 929 8657
e-mail: office@ncgs.co.uk
website: www.ncgs.co.uk

North Cestrian Grammar School was founded in 1951 to provide independent grammar school education for boys aged 11–16 with a co-educational Sixth Form. Since September 2008 the School has been fully co-educational.

As befits a School of 300 pupils attention to the individual is a reality, not an empty phrase. Over the years the School has acquired an enviable reputation for developing confidence and getting the best out of each child so that today's pupils come not only from the locality but from as far afield as North Manchester, Warrington, Macclesfield and the heart of rural Cheshire.

Board of Governors:

Chairman: Mr I T Parrott

Mr T D Brown	Mr J H Moss
Mr R Burdge	Dr A Pocklington
Mr D J Common	Mrs R Smart
Mrs S Forster	Mr N Swerling
Mr J-P Glaskie	Mr C D Wheeler
Mr D Merrell	Mr A Wong
Mr P F Morton	

Headmaster: D G Vanstone, MA

Deputy Head: N Dunn, BSc

Assistant Staff:

F I Barclay, BA	Mrs E Holmes, BSc
N G Brown, BA, MEd	P Robinson, BSc
M P Sharpe, BA	Mrs C Varney, DipComm
D J Bradley, MBE, MA	Mrs R Boyd, MA, BM
R W Horridge, BA	Mrs R Clifford, BSc
C W Robinson, BA, DipEd	Mrs P Patterson, BSc
R E Thompson, BSc	Mr A D Brown, BA
M Whittam, BA, ATD	Mr W H A Whittaker, BSc
S Cruxton, BA	Mrs E Evans, BA
Mrs G R Piatkiewicz, BEd	Mrs A Stevens, BCom
Mrs J James, BSc	Miss C Davies, BSc
Mrs L Facchin, BA	Mr J Raho, BSc
P Stobbs, BA	Miss E M A Klutz, BSc
K Jackman, BA	Mr P R Whittaker, BSc
A Boswell, BA	Mr P J Ware, BEd
A Heslop, BEng	

Dyslexia Specialists:
Mrs B Robson, MEd, TEFL, DipSLD, AMBDA

Mrs M Wheelan, MA, DipSpLD, AMBDA
Mrs R Clifford, BSc, MEd

Bursar: Mrs M Ratcliffe, AAT, CIMA
Librarian: Mrs Y Stevenson
Office Staff: Mrs C Brown, Mrs S M Roby

Facilities. The School is housed in fine modern buildings constructed around an imposing Victorian mansion. Continuing investment in school facilities has provided excellent teaching accommodation including five laboratories, a computer suite, technology wing and language laboratory. A splendid new Library and an impressive Assembly Hall have recently been completed; a six-laboratory science block opened at Easter 2010 and other recent additions include a Drama Studio, Sixth Form Common Room and Learning Support Centre. Art has special provision for ceramics and photography and there are specialist suites for most departments. In addition to a well-equipped and spacious sports hall, the 20-acre sports grounds provide pitches for soccer, hockey and cricket, alongside an athletics track and tennis courts.

Academic. The School aims to provide a balanced curriculum offering each pupil a broad range of subjects. High standards of academic work are expected with an emphasis on individual guidance. The majority of pupils are prepared for 9 GCSEs, but a small group are offered the chance to follow a restricted curriculum of 7 subjects within small teaching sets and with additional learning support. There is a wide and expanding range of A Levels for students to choose from in the Sixth Form. These include recently introduced options such as Sports Science, Information Systems and Music Technology. Most students secure places at University.

Junior pupils are taught in parallel classes. Specialist dyslexia and support staff are available to give individual assistance by private arrangement. From Year 10 there is some streaming, based upon ability in Maths and English, with a view to accelerating the pace for the most able whilst providing smaller teaching groups for those who need most attention. There is also a comprehensive PSE and Careers Programme.

North Cestrian has a reputation for individual support and personal development in both academic and social terms and "added value" is closely monitored through the use of NFER assessment. Extensive success in this area has been recognised both statistically and in the School's most recent ISI inspection report.

Extra-Curricular Activity. A wide range of extra-curricular activities aims to allow each pupil to excel in some area, thus building his confidence and self-esteem. North Cestrian has a strong sporting tradition and there is an extensive programme of inter-school fixtures. National and county honours have been gained in hockey, athletics, swimming, football and basketball. Regular holidays are offered both in Britain and abroad and the Languages Department conducts a series of annual foreign visits to strengthen European awareness. The Duke of Edinburgh's Award Scheme is well supported and there is a series of outdoor pursuit trips for junior pupils. Public speaking, board games, music, drama and an extensive charity programme are a reflection of the care taken to oversee the development of the whole pupil in a friendly and supportive family atmosphere.

Admission. There is a competitive examination in February for entry at 11+. Applications for other years are considered at any time and Sixth Form offers are made on the basis of predicted GCSE grades.

Bursaries. Bursaries based upon family income are made at the discretion of the Governors.

Fees per term (2011-2012). £2,767 (£8,301 per annum).

Location. The School is situated conveniently close to central Altrincham and there are few Manchester or Cheshire schools so easily accessible by either public or private transport. Ideally placed for mainline trains and buses which converge on Altrincham, the Metrolink provides a rapid link and regular service from Central Manchester whilst outlying districts are served by school coaches. Travel by car is equally easy as the School lies close to the A56 and within two miles of Junction 7/8 on the M56.

Further Information. A School Prospectus, Sixth Form Brochure and GCSE Options Booklet are available on the website or application to the School Office. Parents and their children are welcome at twice yearly Open Evenings held in November and January, but alternative arrangements for a personal interview and tour of the School at any reasonable time can be made through the Office.

Charitable status. North Cestrian Grammar School is a Registered Charity, number 525925. It exists for the purpose of educating children.

Oswestry School

Upper Brook Street, Oswestry, Shropshire SY11 2TL
Tel: 01691 655711
Fax: 01691 671194
e-mail: enquiries@oswestryschool.org.uk
website: www.oswestryschool.org.uk

Oswestry School, founded in 1407 by David Holbache and his wife Gwynhyfar, is one of the oldest non-denominational schools in England. The School is registered as a Charitable Trust and administered by a Board of Governors which is in membership with the Association of Governing Bodies of Independent Schools.

Governing Board:
Chairman: P T Wilcox-Jones
Vice-Chairman: B Morgan

M Bebb	R Morgan
P M Bracegirdle	Mrs A Morris
E Channon	I Payne
P D Edwards	J D Payne
Miss B Y Gull	The Revd S G Thorburn
Mrs E Hill	M J Thorpe

Headmaster: **D Robb**, MA, MEd

Deputy Head (Academic): T Jefferis, MSc, BSc, PGCE

Deputy Head (Pastoral): S Nancini, BA Manchester, PGCE, FAHE

Head of Sixth Form: N F Lambkin, BA Wales, MPhil Wales, PGCE

Oswestry School is a co-educational day and boarding school for pupils aged 4 to 18. Pupils are taught on two closely situated sites. The prep department, Bellan House, is situated in the town centre a short walk from the senior school. It takes children from Reception to Year 6 and is for children aged 4 to 10+ (those who will be 11 by 31st August). The senior school, located on the outskirts of the town, caters for Years 7 to 13, ages 11 to 18, both day and boarding.

Oswestry School moved to its present site in 1776, and its beautiful grounds and playing fields now occupy a site of 50 acres.

There has been an ongoing programme of building and refurbishment at Oswestry School for the last 600 years, and that will always continue. A Sixth Form boys' boarding house was completed in January 2006, a suite of classrooms in 2008 and boys' boarding accommodation (for 11–16 year olds) has recently been extensively refurbished. The School also has a 20-metre indoor heated swimming pool.

The School has a modern outlook but respects traditional values and is proud of its warm, caring 'family' atmosphere. Its distinctive ethos allows the School to give much individual care and attention to pupils and to motivate them as they make academic and personal progress.

Class sizes are small throughout the school and the teacher-pupil ratio is very generous, thus allowing every individual pupil to find the opportunity to excel. High-quality teaching enables each pupil to reach their academic potential regardless of ability.

Equally significantly, they acquire skills, confidence and leadership qualities through participation in a broad range of activities and by taking on a variety of responsibilities.

The School aims to maintain discipline and good manners in all aspects, and operates as a community which seeks to safeguard the rights of the individual. Each member of the community should have the chance to grow in knowledge and self confidence, encouraged by staff and pupils alike. School rules are based on the fundamental tenet that individuals need to recognise their own responsibilities to others and conduct themselves with self-discipline. Rules are enforced firmly but fairly.

The School motto is '*We learn not for school but for life*'.

Curriculum. The School aims to provide a broad general education up to GCSE with more specialised subjects in the Sixth Form. At present, the following subjects are taught to AS/A2 level: Art, Biology, Business Studies, Chemistry, Critical Thinking, Design Technology, English Literature, French, Geography, History, Information Communication Technology, Mathematics and Further Mathematics, Music, Philosophy, Physics, Psychology, Spanish, Sports and Physical Education.

Special provision is available for those with learning difficulties in a purpose-designed Learning Support Unit. Most of our pupils proceed to the Sixth Form and virtually all our Sixth Formers then move on to university. The School ensures that all Sixth Formers are prepared for the transition to university.

Boarders. Boarders are accommodated in three houses: School House for boys up to Year 11, Holbache House for Sixth Form boys and Guinevere House for girls. Guinevere House has an annexe attached for Sixth Form girls. Each house is headed by house parents who have overall responsibility for the welfare and general progress of the boarders.

School Chapel. The School Chapel, built in 1863, plays an important part in the life of the School. The School is non-denominational and services are as broadly based as possible within the Christian tradition. The School Chaplain has an important role in the pastoral structure of the School.

Games. The School has a strong tradition of participation in sports. All pupils are expected to participate in games unless medically exempt. Football, rugby, cricket, swimming, athletics and tennis are the main sports for boys while netball, hockey, rounders, football, swimming and tennis are available for girls. The School has extensive playing fields extending to some 30 acres and its own indoor swimming pool.

Out of School Activities. There is a wide range of extracurricular activities including music, art, photography, debating, chess, mountain biking, sailing, kayaking, canoeing, outdoor education, ballet, model making, swimming and computing. The School also has the Decimus Society which exists to promote all matters philosophical and to engage its members with the intellectual adventure of ideas. All boarders are encouraged to join at least two clubs.

CCF and Community Service. There is an active CCF contingent, membership of which is voluntary after two years' service; pupils can also pursue the Duke of Edinburgh's Award Scheme.

Admissions. Boys and girls are accepted into the Senior School from the age of 11, although applications are always considered for entry up to Year 10 and for Sixth Form. Scholarships are available at 9+, 11+, 13+ and 16+.

Registration fee: £50.

Fees per term (2011-2012). Day Pupils: £3,450 (Year 6), £4,000 (Years 7 and 8), £4,240 (Years 9–13). Weekly Boarding: £5,600 (Years 6–8), £6,800 (Years 9–13). Boarding: £6,245 (Years 6–8), £7,380 (Years 9–13).

Scholarships. The Governors offer a number of academic scholarships each year for conspicuously talented individuals, each of which remits up to 50% of the tuition fees. Scholarships are available at 9+, 11+, 13+ and 16+. Scholarships are also available in Art, Music and Sport.

Further details of all these Scholarships are available from the Headmaster.

Reductions for Services Families. Generous awards are available for children of Services personnel (when the child is in full-time education).

Old Oswestrians. Secretary: Tim Turner, who may be contacted via the school website.

Charitable status. Oswestry School is a Registered Charity, number 1079822. It exists to provide education for boys and girls.

Our Lady of Sion School

Gratwicke Road, Worthing, West Sussex BN11 4BL
Tel: 01903 204063
          01903 228638 (Admissions)
Fax: 01903 214434
e-mail: enquiries@sionschool.org.uk
          admissions@sionschool.org.uk
website: www.sionschool.org.uk

Our Lady of Sion School is a thriving town school, offering a complete education for boys and girls from 2½–18 (from Nursery through to University entrance), in a small family community. Our aim is to encourage each young person in our care to be the best that he or she possibly can, and to prepare children for adult life as citizens who can make a positive contribution to the world.

The school, founded in 1862, is one of eighteen schools worldwide established by the Sisters of the Congregation of Our Lady of Sion. It has enjoyed a long and quietly illustrious history, combining the very best of tradition with a forward-looking approach enabling the school to meet the educational challenges of the 21st century.

Mission Statement:

The Congregation of Sion is a Catholic Foundation, which works to foster mutual understanding between people of different religious and cultural traditions, through its communities in twenty-four countries of the world. The role of education in this work is vital.

Our Lady of Sion School aims to help young people of all faiths to reach their highest potential in a caring atmosphere.

Each boy and girl is encouraged to develop through all aspects of the school curriculum.

We encourage staff and students to engage in the wider community and to address issues vital to the future wellbeing of our society and the whole world.

Fostered in a climate that is permeated by the teachings of the Bible, the School's ethos is CONSIDERATION ALWAYS. All members of the School Community are encouraged to embrace the school motto.

Affiliations: SHMIS, ISA, ASCL, AGBIS, ISBA, CISC

Governors:
There are currently ten governors: four are Sisters of Sion, appointed by the Provincial of the Congregation of Sion, and the remainder are drawn from a range of backgrounds, bringing invaluable expertise in many key areas to the school.

Sr Mary Camilleri NdS
Sr Mary Cannon NdS
Mr M Caruana
Mrs K Henwood

Sr Brenda McCole NdS (*Provincial of the Sisters of Our Lady of Sion, UK and Ireland*)
Mrs C Reynolds
Sr Elise Saudan NdS
Mr M Spofforth (*Acting Chair*)
Mr N Thomas
Dr R Woodward-Court

School Management:

Headmaster: Mr M Scullion, JP, MA, BEd

Bursar: Mr G Miles, ACCA
Deputy Head, Senior School: Mrs P Starkey, BSc, PGCE
Deputy Head, Junior School: Mr J Summers, BA, PGCE

Senior School:

Senior Teachers, Heads of Faculties, Year Group Coordinators:

Mr J Arnold, BEd (*Faculty Head, Geography; Assistant Examinations Officer*)
Mrs J Baker, BEd (*Faculty Head, PE; Year Coordinator*)
Mr P Baker, BSc Econ, PGCE (*Head of History; Careers*)
Mrs A Coe, BA, PGCE (*Faculty Head, Modern Languages*)
Mr S Danes, BSc, PGCE (*PE; Head of House*)
Mrs J Freeman BA (*Drama; PSCHE; Year Coordinator*)
Mr M Hoarty, BSc, CertEd (*Senior Teacher; Faculty Head, Mathematics; ICT Timetabling; Head of House*)
Mrs J House, BEd (*PE; Games; Dance; Mathematics; Year Coordinator*)
Mrs J Monaghan, BA, PGCE (*Faculty Head, English; Head of House*)
Mrs A Paine, MA, PGCE (*Head of Art; PCSHE; Year Coordinator*)
Mr J Ramasami, BA, PGCE (*Religious Studies; Year Coordinator*)
Mr K Tilley, MSc, PGCE (*Senior Teacher; Faculty Head, Science; Chemistry; General Studies; Head of Sixth Form*)
Mrs A Whitchurch, BA, Dip Mus (*Senior Teacher; Director of Studies; Head of Music; PSCHE*)

Total number of Senior School Staff: 26 Full-time, 21 Part-time

Junior School Management Team:

Heads of Department:
Mr J Summers, BA PGCE (*Head of the Junior School*)
Miss S Dawson, NNEB (*Head of Nursery*)
Mr A Morgan, BSc, PGCE, MSc (*Form Teacher Year 6; Upper School Coordinator*)
Mrs S Sutherland, BA, QTS (*Form Teacher Reception; Lower School Coordinator*)

Total number of Junior School Staff: 11 Full-time, 10 Part-time

Our Lady of Sion is a fully co-educational school, taking boys and girls from age 2½ to 18 years. The school is divided into the Junior and Senior Schools, which are housed in separate buildings in close proximity to each other. The Early Years Nursery is located in purpose-built premises on the Junior school site. Currently there are 495 pupils on roll, including 69 pupils in the Sixth Form.

Admission to the Junior School at Key Stage 1 is at the discretion of the Deputy Head following the child's introductory visit and an interview with his/her parents. Key Stage 2 pupils will be tested in verbal, non-verbal and quantitative reasoning and English, as well as spending 2 days in the school.

Admission to the Senior School is on a selective basis, and is offered on attainment of acceptable results in written examinations in verbal, non-verbal and quantitative reasoning English, and French (for those who have already studied this subject), parent and pupil interview with the Headmaster and satisfactory references from previous schools. In the Sixth Form, admission for all pupils, both internal and external, is dependent upon GCSE results and satisfactory school reports. External candidates may be required to spend some time in school before the offer of a place is confirmed.

Fees per term (2011-2012). Senior School £3,225–£3,345; Junior School £2,100–£2,595. Nursery fees depend on number of days or half days attended. The school accepts the West Sussex Early Years Partnership Nursery Education Grant Scheme.

Curriculum. We pride ourselves on offering a balanced, relevant and flexible curriculum.

The Junior School works in close partnership with parents to ensure that children develop as individuals. A comprehensive curriculum enables all pupils to achieve their full potential, supported by highly qualified teachers. Pupils are taught in small groups and, in addition to the core subjects, French, Music, PE and Science are taught by specialist staff. Many after-school clubs and activities are offered, with supervision being available from 8.00 to 17.00.

In the Senior School, Years 7–9 pupils study a wide range of subjects, aimed at giving them a broad base from which to make their future choices. We offer 24 subjects at GCSE Level and 20 subjects at AS/A Level. Mathematics, English Language, English Literature, a Modern Language, Religious Studies and Science are compulsory at GCSE Level.

Languages: Pupils are required to take French, German, or Spanish at GCSE. French, German and Spanish are offered at A Level.

English Language and Literature are compulsory at GCSE. English Literature is offered at AS and A Level.

Science: All pupils take either the combined GCSE Dual Science award, or those interested in medical or similar careers may instead take Biology, Chemistry and Physics as separate subjects. Biology, Chemistry and Physics are offered at A Level.

ICT is taught across the curriculum as an integral part of each subject. We offer GCSE AS and A Level ICT.

Business Studies is offered at IGCSE, and at AS and A Level.

Law is offered at A Level.

Mathematics is compulsory at IGCSE, AS and A Level. Statistics is offered at GCSE.

General Studies is studied to AS Level by all members of the Sixth Form.

Geography is offered at GCSE, AS and A Level.

History: Modern World History is offered at GCSE and History at AS and A Level.

Design & Technology: Product Design is offered at GCSE and at AS and A Level.

Home Economics: Food and Nutrition is offered at GCSE.

Music: Every pupil is encouraged to discover and enjoy Music. Music is offered as a subject at GCSE, AS and A Level, with Music Technology being offered at AS and A Level. There is a vibrant extra-curricular music programme, which features regular formal and informal concerts. The Junior School award-winning Festival Choir performs several public concerts each year.

Drama and Performing Arts (Dance) are offered as GCSE options. Both departments aim to involve pupils actively in all aspects of drama and performance arts. Students can participate in productions, either by performing or being involved in vital backstage work. At least two major productions are staged each year, as well as performances of GCSE practical coursework.

Physical Education is offered at GCSE, AS and A Level.

Art and Design is offered at GCSE and Art at AS and A Level. The Art Department plays an integral part in supporting school events, providing exhibitions and display materials, and creating scenery and backgrounds for school music and drama productions.

Psychology is offered as an AS and A Level option.

Sport, Community Service and Clubs. Physical Education encourages a sense of fair play, sportsmanship and consideration, along with a positive attitude towards fitness and health. Activities range from traditional games, swimming galas and sports days to outdoor pursuits and ski trips.

The Duke of Edinburgh's Award Scheme is offered for pupils in Years 10 & 11.

Clubs include a full range of Music and Sporting lunchtime and after school practices, plus Art Club, Astronomy Club, Dance Club, Chess Club, Gym Club, Puzzle Challenge Club and Debating Society. In the Junior School, as well as Music and Sport activities, there is Animal Action, Art Club, Computer Club, and Italian or Spanish Language clubs as well as the Festival Choir and sport clubs.

School Life. *Uniform:* All pupils, except those in Nursery, are expected to wear the Sion School uniform. Sixth formers are allowed to wear their own (suitable) clothes.

Houses: There are three Houses, corresponding to form groups. Houses have their own prefects, and compete against each other in academic, sporting and extra-curricular events. The House Cup is awarded, termly in the Junior School and annually in the Senior School, to the House having the highest number of house points.

Heads of School and Prefects: The Head Boy and Head Girl are appointed by a selective process, which allows all Sixth Form pupils to put themselves forward as candidates. Prefects are appointed to take specific responsibilities within the school. Year 6 pupils in the Junior School are allocated monitor duties.

Spiritual and Community Life. Our Lady of Sion School is a Catholic Foundation with an ecumenical spirit and outlook. Our school's outlook is based on the ideals of tolerance and understanding, and we welcome children of different beliefs and backgrounds. We aim to create a strong educational community, promoting the highest academic standards and encouraging each child to develop to the best of their ability, while at the same time developing an atmosphere of mutual respect. We stress the importance of our awareness of the views, traditions and needs of others and the promotion of justice in the wider world. Religious Education and whole school assemblies are an integral part of the educational programme. The school community supports a number of charitable causes, recognising our role in the world around us.

Discipline. We encourage and promote the highest possible standards, for the benefit and growth of everyone in the school. In the Junior School, house points are awarded in recognition of good conduct, helpfulness or a high standard of achievement. Bullying, rough play or bad manners are not tolerated. In the Senior School, merit slips are awarded by the teaching staff to promote and publicise achievement, and encourage students to do their best. They can be awarded in recognition of good work, or for making a positive contribution to school life. We encourage our pupils to aspire to the highest standards of behaviour.

Charitable status. Our Lady of Sion School, Worthing is a Registered Charity, number 1121398. It exists to provide a high-quality education and spiritual framework for children and to prepare them for a positive role in the world.

Our Lady's Abingdon Senior School

Radley Road, Abingdon, Oxfordshire OX14 3PS
Tel: 01235 524658
Fax: 01235 535829
e-mail: office@olab.org.uk
website: www.olab.org.uk

In September 2009 boys were admitted to the school, which will become fully co-educational in 2013.

Board of Governors:
Chairman: Mr P F J Tobin, MA, FRSA

Governors:
Mr T Ayling MA Oxon
Mr J Cunliffe, MA Oxon
Dr A Colbrook, BSc, PhD
Mrs A Freeman, BEd
Dr T Hands, BA, AKC, DPhil
Mr D Heavens
Mr E McCabe, MA Oxon, MBA
Father J McGrath, STB, MA
Mr T Prosser, BSc, MSc, MBA, FIFireE
Mrs H Ronaldson
Ms J Shillaker, MA, LIM
Mrs M Shinkwin, BA, MA Ed, NPQH
Sr K Staunton, MA
Mr A Sullivan
Dr J R Woodman, MBChB, DipObst, MRCOG, DPhil Oxon
Mr I Yorston, MA
Institute Representative: Sr M Sheehy, RSM, BEd

Bursar & Clerk to the Governors: Mr S Hughes, BA Hons

Head: Mrs Lynne Renwick, BEd, NPQH

Deputy Head: Miss B Habayeb, MSc, PGCE

Second Deputy Head: Mr M Burke, BA Hons, PGCE, AdDipEd

Assistant Head: Mrs S Wales, BA Oxon, PGCE

Sixth Form Tutor: Mr M Burke, BA Hons, PGCE, AdDipEd
Year 11 Tutor: Mr P Hudson, BSc Hons, PGCE
Year 10 Tutor: Mrs K Rowe, CertEd
Year 9 Tutor: Mr M Gardiner, BSc Hons, PGCE
Year 8 Tutor: Mrs A Okeke, BSc Hons, MSc, PGCE
Year 7 Tutor: Miss F Gunn, LLB Hons, PGCE, MA

Heads of Departments:
Art: Mrs H Holden, BA Hons, MSt, PGCE
Business Studies: Mrs J Acutt, BA Hons, PGCE
Careers & PSHE: Mrs A Varney, BEd, CertEd
Classics: Miss P Smith, BA Hons Oxon
Drama: Dr E Moss, BA Hons, MA, PhD Loughborough
English: Miss M Hemingway, BA Hons, PGCE
Geography: (*to be appointed*)
History: Mrs J Mead, BA Hons, PGCE, MA
Home Economics: Mrs H Black, BA Hons, PGCE
Information Technology: Miss B Habayeb, MSc, PGCE
Mathematics: Mr R Ford, BSc, PGCE
Modern Languages: Mrs C Friend, MA Hons Oxon, MA, PGCE
Music: Mr J McKelvey, BA Hons, PGCE
Physical Education: Mrs M Barnett, BA Hons, QTS & Mr M Gardiner, BSc Hons, PGCE
Psychology: Mrs A Beasley, MA Hons, PGCE
Religious Studies: (*to be appointed*)
Science: Mr P Hudson, BSc Hons, PGCE
Special Educational Needs: Mrs L Barr, MSt, MA, BA, PGCE
Technology: Mr C Sephton, MSc, PGCE
Textiles: Mrs K Rowe, CertEd

Our Lady's Abingdon has a reputation for academic achievement coupled with strong support for the development of every pupil as an individual. The school was founded in 1860 by the Sisters of Mercy and retains their ethos of care and dedication to the teaching of Christian values. It provides for "each according to his/her needs" whether those needs be support for outstanding talents in music, sport, art, drama or academic subjects. The school encourages independence of thought and responsibility for one's own learning and behaviour. Our Lady's Abingdon, a Christian school in the Catholic tradition, welcomes pupils of all beliefs who wish to share its ideals and expectations.

The 2010 Inspection Report was most complimentary, noting in particular that:

"*Pupils achieve excellent results in a range of extra-curricular activities, especially in sport.*

Pupils make exceptional progress in their academic studies in relation to their ability profile.

Pupils' spiritual, moral, social and cultural development is excellent.

The outstanding pastoral care does much to ensure their safeguarding, and to foster their personal development and academic achievement."

Numbers. There are 370 pupils aged 11–18 in the Senior school and 110 pupils aged 3–11 in the Junior section, which is on the same site under its own headmaster, Brendan O'Neill.

Facilities and Buildings. Bright, spacious classrooms and an excellent library provide a pleasant ambience conducive to study and learning. The grounds surround both buildings, an attractive setting of lawns, flowerbeds and trees in which the pupils can relax during breaks. Sports facilities include a number of tennis courts, a sports hall with fitness room, hockey and athletics provision and a newly refurbished 25-metre indoor swimming pool. It has benefited recently from the creation of a new auditorium and library, the latest in ICT equipment, an extended Art department and additional Science laboratories. Music has new facilities for music technology to aid composition and to support the wide variety of instruments taught in the school.

Curriculum. The school teaches a balanced range of subjects both academic and practical during the first three years. Latin is a core subject. Pupils take 9 or 10 subjects at GCSE, including English, Mathematics, Science, Religious Studies and two modern languages. Options are chosen from the Humanities to Classics and Physical Education. Four subjects are studied in the Lower Sixth at AS, continuing with three at A2. 100% of the Sixth Form go on to Higher Education. There is also support for Special Educational Needs, and for pupils for whom English is not their mother tongue.

Extra-curricular activities. The school provides a wide programme of extra-curricular activities including drama, music, art, debating and many forms of sport. Rowing and sailing are particularly popular. Buses run later on three evenings of the week to accommodate these activities and to allow for supervised homework. There is also a strong commitment to local community schemes and an impressive record in the Duke of Edinburgh's Award Scheme and Young Enterprise. In 2011 the OLA Young Enterprise group won the award for Best Business Plan.

In 2008 OLA was one of only 508 schools to be accredited with the Department for Education's International School Award for the "outstanding work done by the staff and pupils". The school has gained the Eco-Schools Silver Award and is working towards the "Green Flag".

Fees per term (2011-2012). £3,756.

Admission. Through the school's own Entrance Examination at 11 and 13; Pupils require at least 5 GCSEs Grade B for entry at Sixth Form level. Pupils interested in entering the Sixth Form for whom English is a second language must in addition have achieved a minimum level of 6.5 in IELTS for each category. Pupils may join in any year if a place is available.

Pupils may apply for Scholarships for entry to Year 7 and the Sixth Form. Candidates may also apply for Bursaries which are awarded at the discretion of the Governors.

Charitable status. Our Lady's Abingdon Trustees Limited is a Registered Charity, number 1120372, and a Company Limited by Guarantee, registered in England and Wales, number 6269288.

Padworth College

Padworth, Reading, Berkshire RG7 4NR
Tel: 0118 983 2644
Fax: 0118 983 4515
e-mail: info@padworth.com
website: www.padworth.com

Founded 1963.

Padworth College is a co-educational boarding and day school for students aged 13–19 from the UK and all over the world. We aim to bring an informal tutorial-style atmosphere to school level education giving individual attention in very small classes underpinned by excellent pastoral care. The College's rural setting provides a peaceful and secure environment for study, yet the campus is within easy reach of the university town of Reading and just 45 minutes by road from Heathrow.

Board of Trustees:
John Crawshaw (*Chair*)
David Barnett-Roberts
Mike Hames
John Miller
John West
Jonathan Rawes

Senior Leadership Team:

Principal: Linde Melhuish, BA, MA, PGCE, NPQH

Director of Boarding and Studies: Neville Duckmanton, BA, MA, DipT, Dip EdMan
Director of International Study Centre: Belinda Sumner, CertEd, RSA Dip TEFLA
Director of Summer School: Arthur Shields, MA, CertEd
Bursar: James Wilson

Academic Staff:

Accounting:
Jane Joy, CertEd, RSA Dip

Art and Design:
Marianna Ziffo, BA, PGCE, Cert TEFLA

Biology:
Terna Newall, BSc, PGCE, Cert TEFLA

Business Studies:
Arthur Shields, MA, CertEd

Chemistry:
Sally Lightowlers, BSc, PGCE

Economics:
Michael Laizans, BA, PGCE

English:
Linde Melhuish, BA, MA, PGCE, NPQH
Debs Burnham, BA, PGCE

Geography and Environmental Studies:
Dr Alexander Mitlehner, BSc, MSc, PhD, PGCE

History and Politics:
Freddie Piper, BA

Information Technology and Computing:
Clive Trinder, BA, PGCE

Mathematics:
Antoinette van der Linden, BSc, DipT
Russell Bayliss, BA, MA, PGCE
Julie Ward, BSc, PGCE

Modern Languages:
Evelyn Ludbrook, BA, Dip Spanish (*Spanish*)
David Cleary, L-ès-L (*French*)

Music:
Ruth Jordan, BA, PGCE, TESOL

Physics:
Anthony Good, NDA, MA

Psychology:
Roxana Shields, BA, MA

UCAS, Careers and Examinations Officer:
Dr Alexander Mitlehner, BSc, MSc, PhD, PGCE

International Study Centre:
Belinda Sumner, CertEd, RSA Dip TEFLA (*Director of ISC*)
Heather Boraston, BA, PGCE, RSA Dip TEFLA
Sally Jeans, BA Hons, CELTA, CILIP
David Benedict, BA Hons, CELTA
Margaret Whitehead, SpLD, TEFL

Number of Students. 120.

Academic. Padworth aims to provide a well-balanced curriculum with a strong academic core. We offer a wide range of subjects at GCSE/IGCSE and AS/A Level as well as a one-year University Access programme in Business. In addition, the International Study Centre provides short and long-term English Language courses for overseas students of all abilities.

Our curriculum aims to contribute effectively to the intellectual, physical and personal attainment and development of our students, according to their age and ability range, to prepare students for the next stage of education, training or employment and to provide the skills needed for life-long learning.

Pastoral Care. Outstanding pastoral care is provided by our experienced resident house staff whose role is to guide and support students. House staff also organise a varied extra-curricular programme in the evenings and at weekends for students to make the most of school life. Many sports and clubs are offered and students participate in the Duke of Edinburgh's Award Scheme.

Facilities. Boarding students are accommodated in comfortable single or shared bedrooms with sitting rooms and kitchen facilities. The campus offers a range of sports facilities including an outdoor swimming pool and tennis, basketball and volleyball courts. Modern classrooms and specialist science laboratories are complemented by a well-equipped IT room, library and art studio.

Careers and Higher Education. Students are given individual careers counselling and guidance on their choice of course and university and support with the UCAS process.

Scholarships. A number of Academic Scholarships worth up to 50% of the fees are available for study at GCSE and A Level.

Admissions. Padworth welcomes students of a wide range of abilities. Admission is by interview and report from the previous school and subject to availability of a place.

A prospectus is available on request via the College's website or by telephoning the College on 0118 983 2644. Prospective parents and students are warmly invited to arrange a visit and an appointment to meet the Principal.

Fees per term (2011-2012). Day Students £3,950, Weekly Boarders £7,350, Full boarders £8,300.

Charitable status. Padworth College Trust Limited is a Registered Charity, number 325023, which exists to promote and provide for the advancement of education.

The Peterborough School
A Woodard School

Thorpe Road, Peterborough PE3 6AP
Tel: 01733 343357
          Bursar: 01733 355720
Fax: 01733 355710
e-mail: admin@thepeterboroughschool.co.uk
website: www.thepeterboroughschool.co.uk

The Peterborough School provides care and education for boys and girls aged 6 weeks to 18 years. It was founded in 1895 and welcomes pupils from a variety of faiths and cultures. The School, which has its own chapel and promotes the teaching of Christian principles, prides itself on excellent examination results and outstanding pastoral care.

School Council:
Chairman: Ms L Ayres, LLB
Mr C Beard
Dr D L Chinn
Mrs P Dalgliesh
Mrs L Frisby
Mrs K Hart
Canon R Hemingray, LLB
Prof C J Howe, MA, PhD, ScD, FLS
Mrs J M Mark
Mr S G Menon, MSc, MTech
Mrs E Payne
The Revd Canon B Ruddock
Mr D Sandbach, BA, FCA, D Ch A
Mr P Southern
Air Commodore MCG Wilson RAF Retd
The Senior Provost, The Woodard Corporation
The Rt Revd Robert Ladds, Assistant Provost, The Woodard Corporation

Head: **Mr A Meadows**, BSc Hons Manchester, NPQH

Deputy Headmistress: Mrs L Chambers, MA Oxford Literae Humaniores
Assistant Head, Head of the Preparatory Department: Mrs A-M Elding, MEd OU, BEd Hons Derby
Assistant Head, Head of Middle Years: Mrs A Axe, BA Hons Birmingham
Assistant Head, Head of Sixth Form: Mr C McManus, MA Ulster

Staff:
Mr S Awcock, BSc Hons De Montfort (*Head of Science, Physics*)
Mr K D Bingham, BA Hons Hull (*Preparatory Department*)
Mrs L Boyle Cert EYP (*Preparatory Department*)
Mr C Brocklesby, BA Hons Leicester (*Geography*)
Mrs K A Brown, BA Hons Oxford (*Mathematics*)
Miss S M Clarkson, BA Hons Cantab (*History*)
Mr G Cloke, BSc Reading (*Preparatory Department*)
Mrs L Coles, BA Hons Exeter (*French*)
Mrs P Cooper, BEd Cantab, DipEd Bedford (*PE*)
Mrs C Coulson, MSc OU (*Business Studies and ICT*)
Mrs K Davis, BSc Newcastle upon Tyne (*Chemistry*)
Mrs R Ditcher, BSc Hons Greenwich (*Preparatory Department*)
Ms T Doyle, MNATD (*Director of Creative Arts*)
Mrs R Elks, BA Hons Staffordshire (*Preparatory Department*)
Mrs J Evans, Licence Limoges (*French*)
Mrs S Fiddy, BEd Oxon (*Preparatory Department*)
Mrs E Foster, MA Oxon (*Mathematics*)
Mrs L Grinyer, BEd Hons Warwick (*English*)
Mrs O Guillet, BA Hons Loughborough (*English*)

Mrs R Hampson, BA Hons Derby (*Art, Textiles*)
Mr A Harwin, BA Hons Norwich (*Art*)
Mr A Jackson, BA Hons Warwick (*German*)
Mr C King, BSc Hons, CMath, MIMA Keele
  (*Mathematics*)
Mrs B A Laing, BA, DipRSA Drama Edinburgh (*Drama*)
Mrs G Mason, OND Hotel & Catering (*Food Technology
  & Preparatory Classroom Assistant*)
Miss R J Mayle, BA Hons Reading (*Geography*)
Mrs I McGregor, BA Hons Munich (*German*)
Mr D Moxon, BSc Hons UEL (*Psychology*)
Mrs A Poulain, BSc Hons Brunel (*Head of PE*)
Mr S M Roberts, BA Hons York (*Director of Sport*)
Ms S Robinson, BEd Hons Anglia (*Preparatory
  Department*)
Mrs P Samuels, LGSM (*Speech & Drama*)
Mrs A Skelton, BA Hons Bristol (*Preparatory Department*)
Miss J Smith, BA Hons Bedfordshire (*Physical Education*)
Miss L Smith, BEd Hons Wales (*Preparatory Department*)
Miss C L Steward, BA Hons UEA
Mrs A M J Taylor, MA Oxon (*Preparatory Department*)
Mrs S Ward, BSc Hons Leeds, PGCE (*Science*)

Music Department:
Mrs D M Culloty, BMus Hons, LGSM, PGCE (*Flute*)
Mrs E Hamilton-Box, BA Hons, LTCL (*Violin*)
Mrs Y Sandison, PPRNCM (*Singing*)
Mr I Stafford, BEd (*Choir Master*)
Mr A Steel, GTCLK, LTCL, A Mus TCL, ARCO
  (*Accompanist, Theory & Aural*)
Mr N Waldock, BA Hons (*Guitar and Drums*)
Mr I Winfrey, MSc, BSc, CTABRSM
Mrs J Wyndham-Hall, GGSM (*Brass*)

Boarding House:
Mr & Mrs S Crier (*House Parents*)
Mrs B Havenga, RGN, RM (*Matron*)

Administrative Officers:
Bursar: Mr C Charlton, BA Hons
Head's Secretary: Mrs A Field
Marketing Manager/Registrar: Mrs L Pengelly
Administration Assistant: Mrs J Farrow
Accounts: Mrs P Chapman/Mrs K Ross
Domestic Bursar: Mrs Z Clark
Estate Manager: Mr D Thornton
Laboratory Technician: Mrs A E Albon, BSc OU
Network Manager: Mr D Helstrip
Food Technology Technician: Mrs V Tobin
LRC Manager: Mrs C Thomson
Development Manager: Mrs J Hart
Receptionist: Mrs I Zizza
Teaching Assistant/After Care: Miss E Avison

Situation and Buildings. The School is located in beautiful secluded grounds, near the centre of Peterborough, 50 minutes by fast train from King's Cross and easily accessible by road from the A1 and A47. The elegant Victorian house which formed the original School is now the centre of a modern purpose-built complex of classrooms, well-equipped laboratories, Music School, Gymnasium, Art Block, Sixth Form Centre, Library and a modern ICT Suite. The Centre for Creative Arts, including Refectory Gallery and Drama Studio, was completed in September 2007 and building of the new Sports Facility will be complete for September 2012.

The Preparatory Department. Boys and girls are admitted into the Reception Class from the age of 3+. The National Tests are taken at Key Stage One and Two. The whole range of Key Stage subjects is covered in addition to a variety of other subjects and activities. Some subjects are taught by specialist staff from the Senior School. There is emphasis on academic standards, Physical Education, Music and Drama, with concerts or productions several times a year.

The Senior School. The curriculum of the main school is characterised by small classes and an emphasis on individual guidance and target-setting. A balanced programme leads to high achievement at GCSE in up to ten subjects. English, Mathematics, Science, Religious Education, Games and PE, remain compulsory throughout; Languages, History and Geography, Art (including Textiles), Music, Drama and Physical Education form the matrix of options. Unusually, both German and French are studied from Year 7.

Pupils are selected from the entrance examination and thereafter are in unstreamed tutor groups, although there is setting in Mathematics and Science.

The School has a modern ICT suite with state-of-the-art equipment. All classrooms are networked. ICT skills are central to the work of every department, and coordinated to allow the students to build up CLAIT certification in several modules by the end of Year 11.

There are specialist laboratories for all sciences.

In the Sixth Form students usually take four subjects at Advanced Subsidiary (AS) Level and three at A Level. In addition to studies for AS and A Level, student participate in a wider programme of activities within the curriculum. The School delivers the AQA Baccalaureate, which has a portfolio style with four main elements: three A Levels at its heart, a so-called 'Breadth' AS Level in Critical Thinking or General Studies, an Extended Project Qualification on a topic of the candidate's own choosing and the opportunity to catalogue and reflect upon the many Enrichment activities offered in the Sixth Form at the School.

As a School with pupils from Reception and children in the Nursery from 6 weeks and above, older pupils have many opportunities to develop a sense of involvement and responsibility, and carry out valuable service in the wider community of the city during the Sixth Form. Business sense is developed through the Young Enterprise scheme, in which the School is very successful.

The Nursery. The Peterborough School Nursery offers daycare for children aged from 6 weeks to 4 years. Optional lessons include French, Ballet and Little Kickers football.

Religion. Weekly Communion Services are held. Arrangements are also made for termly boarders to attend local churches, including Peterborough Cathedral, or to worship in the School Chapel on Sundays.

Music and Drama. The music of the School, in particular its choral tradition, is renowned and the School is benefiting from its new Centre for Creative Arts. Tuition in singing, piano and all orchestral instruments is available. Major theatrical and musical productions take place several times a year, and the School enjoys its links with theatres in the city. Standards are extremely high.

Games and Physical Education. The pupils achieve outstanding success in team and individual sports and athletics. Many pupils have represented the county, the region, and even England. The School estate is spacious with several pitches and all-weather courts. The many and varied sporting facilities of the city are within easy reach for swimming, rowing and major athletic events. The School will benefit from a major development of its sports facilities over the next academic year.

Extra-curricular Activities. Many clubs and societies operate in extra-curricular time, and field visits and excursions illuminate classroom work. Exchange schemes for French and German operate on an annual basis to Paris and Augsburg. Many pupils undertake the Duke of Edinburgh's Award Scheme at both Bronze and Gold levels, with outstanding success.

Fees per term (2011-2012). Senior School: £3,986 (day), £6,405 (weekly boarding), £7420 (termly boarding).

Preparatory Department: Day: £2,818 (Reception/Infants), £3,420 (Yrs 3–6); Boarding (Yrs 3–6): £6036 (weekly), £6,860 (termly). Lunches, breaktime snacks and all UK based educational trips and visits are included.

Scholarships. Academic, Art, Music and Sport are the main scholarships available to those entering Year 7. Please apply to the Registrar for more information.

Westwoodians' Association. Secretary: Mrs Julia Hart who is based at the School.

Charitable status. The Peterborough School Limited is a Registered Charity, number 269667. It is an independent school which exists to promote the education of children.

Pitsford School
formerly known as Northamptonshire Grammar School

Pitsford Hall, Pitsford, Northamptonshire NN6 9AX
Tel: 01604 880306
Fax: 01604 882212
e-mail: office@ngs-school.com
website: www.pitsfordschool.com

Governing Body:

Chairman: Mr J Kitchen

Mr M Adams	Lady Morton**
Mr S Frater	Mr A Ross
Mr D Hayton	Mr R Seward
Mr J Howard	Mrs J Tice**
Mr J Lockhart	Reverend S Trott
Mr K Melling	Ms J Wilkins

** *Foundation Governor*

Headmaster: **Mr N R Toone**, BSc, MInstP, FRSA

Deputy Head: Ms E Garcia Claremonte, BSc (*Chemistry*)

Mrs L E Brown, BA (*Junior School*)
Miss T Calnan, BEd (*Junior School*)
Mrs L A Chacksfield, BEd (*Girls Games and RS*)
Mme M H Conroy, BA France (*Junior School*)
Mrs J Cowie, BA (*Junior School*)
Mr M E Dean, BSc (*Physics*)
Mrs J M Drakeford, BSc (*Chemistry and Biology*)
Mme C R Filliol, BA (*Modern Languages*)
Mrs S E Goode, BSc Econ (*Junior School*)
Mr D A Hallowell, BEd (*History*)
Miss S M Jackson, BSc (*Chemistry*)
Mrs F Jeffrey, BA (*Junior School*)
Mrs L Jones, BA (*Junior School*)
Mr N J Leech, BSc (*Mathematics*)
Mrs J M Leeke, BSc (*Mathematics*)
Mr M J Lewis, BSc, FRGS, FRMetS (*Geography*)
Mrs L M Lyon, BEd (*Modern Languages*)
Mrs S E Matts, BSc, MA Ed, MIBiol, CBiol (*Head of Sixth Form, Biology*)
Ms M F McQuilkin, BA (*Art*)
Mrs M McNally, BA (*Geography and Girls' Games*)
Mr A J Moodie, BA (*Music*)
Mrs L M Peck, BEd (*Junior School*)
Mr J Saker, MA (*Modern Languages*)
Mr J Smorfitt, BA (*Economics*)
Mr C D Stanley, MA (*English*)
Mr C L Stoner, BSc (*Mathematics*)
Dr A Templeton, BSc, MSc, PhD (*Physics*)
Mr R P Tickle, BA, DipTh (*History and Religious Studies*)
Mr J A White, BA, DipTh (*English*)
Mrs C Whiting, MA (*ICT*)
Mrs J Willmott, BEd (*Junior School*)

Bursar: Mr C Bellamy
Development Director: Mrs L Rich
Registrar: Mrs K Cannon

Age Range. 3–18 Co-educational.
Number of Pupils. 440 boys and girls.
Fees per term (2011-2012). Kits (Pre-School): £1,498–£2,330 (inc lunch); Junior School: £2,263–£3,669, Senior School: £3,927. Lunches: £210 per term.

The School is set in 25 acres, four miles north of the county town. It was founded in 1989 and takes pupils from the age of 3 to 18. The School is constructing a new Junior School which is due for completion in January 2012. A full range of academic subjects through to GCSE, A Level and University entrance is taught. The curriculum draws on the best of the grammar school traditions of the past, makes them relevant to today's needs, and ensures that they are applicable to the demands of the future.

The School aims to educate the whole person and sets, expects and maintains high standards in all its disciplines and extra-curricular activities. Competition in both work and sport is encouraged and emphasis is placed on developing the highest personal and moral qualities. The School has not formed a particular connection with any one religious denomination, but strives to portray a living Christianity that reflects the whole range of denominations and it is sympathetic to other faiths. Assemblies, church services and religious education on the timetable ensure that moral and spiritual values underpin all the work. Pupils leave as mature, sensitive individuals with an excellent academic grounding, a high level of self-discipline and a broad range of skills.

Pupils usually join at the age of 11, entering Year 7 either from our Junior School or from other local schools. The School enjoys a strong academic reputation, which is complemented with effective pastoral support and a wide range of extra-curricular activities. Entry to the Senior School is selective; the academic curriculum is designed to cater for the upper 50% of the ability range and the selection criteria is based upon this. It is expected that all pupils will take 10 GCSEs before transferring to the Sixth Form at the end of Year 11.

The Sixth Form is structured to provide a stepping stone from the discipline of the Senior School to the demands of Higher Education. Each Sixth Form student has his or her own tutor, who is normally one of their A Level teachers. Sixth Formers take a full part in the life of the School and many have positions of responsibility.

The extra-curricular programme incorporates three elements: Service, Sports and Skills. In the main, these activities take place after school until 5.20 pm. The School currently has a junior percussion band, wind, string and guitar ensembles, two rock bands, a Senior and Junior choir and an emergent orchestra. A number of drama productions and concerts are staged every year.

The Junior School was established in 1991 to act as a bridge for pupils to enter the Senior School at 11. All pupils are taught by class teachers and in addition, receive specialist teaching in Games, Gymnastics, French, Information Technology and Music. The sports taught include Rugby, Hockey, Cricket, Rounders, Tennis, Cross-Country Running, Netball and Athletics. All pupils are taught to play the recorder and encouraged to read music. Many learn to play other instruments. All pupils take part in Drama lessons and many enjoy extra Speech lessons.

A number of means-tested bursaries are available each year. Consideration is given to any talents which an individual child may be able to offer the School. Usually, academic potential, sporting prowess or musical accomplishment will be required to support any application. Up to four 100% scholarships are available for talented individuals wishing to join our Sixth Form.

Further details can be obtained from the Registrar, Mrs Karen Cannon, on 01604 880306 or kcannon@ngs-school.com.

Charitable status. Northamptonshire Independent Grammar School Charity Trust Limited is a Registered Charity, number 298910.

Portland Place School
Alpha Plus Group

56–58 Portland Place, London W1B 1NJ
Tel: 020 7307 8700
Fax: 020 7436 2676
e-mail: admin@portland-place.co.uk
website: www.portland-place.co.uk

Portland Place School was founded in 1996 in response to demand in central London for a mixed school that provided for pupils from a broad range of backgrounds and abilities.

Headmaster: Timothy J Cook, BA

Deputy Head (*Pastoral*): Katherine Greenwood, BA London, PGCE (*Geography*)

Deputy Head (*Academic*): Philip Smyth, BSc Galway, PGCE (*Biology*)

Teaching Staff:
Simon Aaronson, BSc Perth Australia, BEd, MInstP (*Physics*)
Kamran Akhtar, MSc London, PGCE (*Mathematics*)
Clare Bacon, BA Hons Leeds Metropolitan, PGCE (*Physical Education*)
Thomas Barnes, MA Cantab, PGCE (*English*)
Catherine Brahams-Melinek, BA Durham, MA London, PGCE (*English*)
Richard Brightwell, BA York, PGCE (*Music*)
Sarah Brown, BA Hons St Mary's London (*English and Education*)
Colin Bryce, BSc Glasgow (*Physical Education*)
Debra Brown, BMus Manchester, PGCE (*Music*)
Juan Caballero, MA Seville, PGCE (*Spanish*)
Robert Chiodo, BA Hons Napoli, PGCE London (*Italian and French*)
Susan Court, BA, MEd Natal, SA, PGCE London (*English*)
Roger Dean, BEng London, MSc Imperial London, MSc Kent, PGCE (*Mathematics*)
Julie Dunkley, BSc London (*Physical Education*)
Danielle English, MSc Queen Mary London, MRSC, PGCE (*Chemistry*)
Elizabeth Ghojefa, MEd London, BA Brunel, PGCE (*Physical Education*)
Kirin Gill, BA Brunel, PGCE (*English*)
Caroline Guest, BA Newcastle, PGCE (*Geography*)
Elise Hartopp, BA Hons York, PGCE (*English*)
Lisa Hunt, MPhil, MA London, PGCE (*History*)
Claire Jabra, BA Hons Aberystwyth, PGCE (*Physical Education*)
Matthew Jones, BA London, PGCE (*Art*)
Paul Jones, BA Leeds, PGCE (*Media and Film Studies*)
Natalie Keen, BA Hons Manchester, PGCE (*English*)
Hina Kizilbash, BSc Brunel, MSc IOE London (*Child Development-Psychology*)
Thomas Lalande, BA Bordeaux, PGCE (*French and Spanish*)
Chad Macfarlane, BA Goldsmiths London (*Design and Technology*)
Adrian Martijono, BSc London PGCE (*Chemistry*)
Jamie McLoughlin, BSc Brunel (*Physical Education*)
Caroline McMeekin, BA Lancaster, PGCE (*Drama*)
Sarah Nelson, BA Cardiff, PGCE (*English*)
Teffany Osborne, BA London (*Art*)
Alissia Paris, MA Metz, PGCE (*French and Spanish*)
Emma Parker, BSc Manchester, PGCE (*Biology*)

Ruth Picado, BA Coruna Spain, PGCE (*Spanish*)
Lucy Price, MA Edinburgh, PGCE (*Classical Civilisation and History*)
Helen Richards, BSc Coventry, PGCE (*Geography*)
Scott Rider, BA Brunel, PGCE (*Physical Education*)
Amy Rogers, BA USA, MSc London, PGCE (*Business Studies and Economics*)
Graeme Rosie, BA Stirling, MA London, DipEd, PGCE (*Economics*)
Edna Scott, BSc Edinburgh, PGCE, GIBiol (*Chemistry*)
Sara Segerstrom, BEd Kalmar Sweden, PGCE (*Mathematics*)
Patrick Smullen, BSc Open, PGCE (*Biology*)
Parwez Soogund, MA London, PGCE (*Design and Technology*)
Phillip Stanway, BA Manchester Metropolitan, PGCE (*Physical Education*)
Alison Stringell, MA Slade, PGCE Goldsmiths (*Art*)
Sam Sugarman, BA Hons Lancaster, PGCE (*Drama*)
Steve Thompson, BSc Plymouth, PGCE (*Physics*)
Klaus Wehner, MA LCP (*Photography*)
David Wellings, MSc LSE, PGCE (*Business Studies*)
Virginia West, BSc Hons Sheffield, PGCE (*Mathematics*)
Heather Wilson, BA Leeds, PGCE (*English*)
Nader Yazdi, MSc Leeds, PhD UCL, MBA Imperial (*Mathematics and Computing*)

Visiting Music Teachers:
Nick Bentley (*Brass*)
Adam Blake (*Guitar*)
Zrinka Bottrill (*Classical Piano*)
Naomi Bristow (*Clarinet*)
Dan Ezard (*Bass*)
Peter Fraser (*Saxophone*)
Sam Jesson (*Drums*)
Siobhan Lavin (*Voice & Flute*)
Nicky Newman (*Voice*)
Mike O'Neill (*Jazz Piano*)
Charlotte Raven (*Cello*)
Balint Szekely (*Violin*)

Administration:
Imelda Rafter-Phillips (*Admissions Registrar*)
Sharon Wood (*Headmaster's Secretary*)
Clemmie Studd (*School Secretary*)
Amanda Murray (*School Manager*)
Yuki Abe (*Data Manager*)
Amanda Berrisford (*Librarian*)
Kim Wykes (*Laboratory Technician*)

Age Range. 9–18 Co-educational.
Number of Day Pupils. 275 Boys, 85 Girls.
Fees per term (2011-2012). Years 5 and 6: £4,970; Years 7–13: £5,225.
Aims and Philosophy. Portland Place is an inclusive and non-elitist school. We encourage pupils to excel in the arts, sport and in their academic studies. Discipline is firm, but compassionate. Our uniform is simple and functional. Teaching is structured. All teachers are not only specialists in their subjects, but are chosen for their ability to enthuse and draw out the best in all students at all levels. The relationship between teachers and pupils is courteously informal. We teach in small classes to offer every child individual attention. While we always strive for academic excellence, we never allow this to overshadow our dedication to nurturing natural intelligence or true potential. Each child's progress is followed through tests, homework and up to six reports a year. Parents are also encouraged to meet our staff to discuss any concerns at any time, as well as at a Parents' Evening every term. We are also a school in touch with the real world. The future of the children in our care comes first in all our decisions and the education every child receives is a journey to a successful later life.

Location and Buildings. Portland Place is ideally located right in the centre of the capital, less than five minutes' walk from Regent's Park (where much of the outdoor sporting activities take place) and ten minutes' walk from Oxford Circus. The school is housed in two magnificent Grade II* listed James Adam houses in Portland Place with a separate Art, Drama and Science building and a Senior School building close by in Great Portland Street. The buildings have been refurbished to an exceptionally high standard. Classrooms are supplemented by specialist rooms for drama, photography and computing.

Curriculum. The curriculum at Portland Place is developed from the English National Curriculum and offers a flexibility that puts the pupil first. Homework is supervised until 5.00 pm for those who want or require it and each pupil has a homework diary that details the homework programme for each week. Each child takes part in a comprehensive programme of physical education. Pupils in Years 5–9 have four PE sessions per week. Full advantage is taken of its central London location and excellent local facilities available. The outdoor programme takes place in neighbouring Regent's Park and includes athletics, hockey, football, rugby, tennis and cross-country. Indoor sports include basketball and fencing. Pupils represent the school in numerous matches against other London schools and in national tournaments. Class music is a compulsory part of the curriculum in Years 5–9 and all pupils are encouraged, if they do not already play one, to take up a musical instrument and take advantage of the team of visiting instrumental teachers.

Sport and Extra-Curricular Activities. Our central London position means that we have easy access to world class facilities. All children are encouraged to participate in an interesting and varied physical education programme. Portland Place School offers a wide range of popular sport including: Athletics, Basketball, Cricket, Cross Country, Fencing, Football, Hockey, Netball, Rounders, Swimming, Tennis and Rugby. Outdoor sports such as football, netball, tennis, cricket and athletics take place in Regent's Park less than a ten minute walk from the school. Indoor activities including basketball and fencing take place at the University of Westminster gym just minutes away in Regent Street. Swimming is at the Seymour Centre, and in the summer we have nets at Lords indoor school. Optional after-school sport activities abound with senior and junior clubs for matches held with schools across London and the UK.

There is a wide and expanding range of extra-curricular activities that are offered at the end of afternoon school. Whole school productions, concerts, chamber groups and small dramatic workshops take place throughout the year and clubs ranging from politics and debating to games and Christianity all thrive throughout the year. During the last week of the summer term all pupils take part in an Activities Week that includes outdoor adventure centres and overseas trips.

Admission. Entry to the school (usually at 9+, 10+, 11+, 13+ and Sixth Form) is by examinations in English and Mathematics and interview. Interviews for September entry are held in the Autumn term prior to entry and the school's entrance examination is in January.

Scholarships. There are five scholarships available for Year 7 (11+) candidates (Art, Music, Sport, Drama and Academic).

Governance. Portland Place School is part of the Alpha Plus Group of schools.

Princethorpe College

Princethorpe, Rugby, Warwickshire CV23 9PX
Tel: 01926 634200
Fax: 01926 633365
e-mail: post@princethorpe.co.uk

website: www.princethorpe.co.uk

The school, which has a Catholic foundation, was founded as a boys' school in 1957 in Leamington Spa by the congregation of the Missionaries of the Sacred Heart (MSC), moving to its present site, a former Benedictine monastery, in 1967. The College became co-educational in 1996, and in September 2001 formed a partnership with Crackley Hall School in Kenilworth in order to provide continuous education from 2 to 18 years. Both schools are members of an independent trust – the Warwickshire Catholic Independent Schools Foundation.

Chair of Trustees: Mrs Mary O'Farrell, BEd, QTS, CTC

Headmaster: Ed Hester, MA Oxon, PGCE (*Mathematics*)

Deputy Head – Academic: Dr Digby Carrington-Howell, BSc, MA Ed, Ed D, PGCE, NPQH (*Biology*)
Deputy Head – Pastoral: Mrs Susan Millest, BSc, PGCE, NPQH (*Physics*)
Assistant Head – Marketing and Operations: Alex Darkes, BEd (*Physics*)
Foundation Bursar, Company Secretary & Clerk to the Trustees: Edward Tolcher, BA, ACIB, ACMI
College Bursar: Mrs Anne Davey

Teaching Staff:
* *Head of Department*

Art:
*Paul Hubball, BA, PGCE (*also Photography*)
Mrs Susan Harris, BA, PGCE (*Head of Year 7*)
Mrs Rebecca Blunsom-Washbrook, BA, GTP

Careers:
*Mike Taylor, BA, PGCE (*also *Geography*)

Design and Technology:
*Frank Gahan, BEd, MA, CertEd, FCIEA (*also IT and Environment Manager*)
Mrs Charlotte Hetherington, BEng
Mrs Lesley McGaw, CertEd, GNVQ, ECDL
Mrs Sarah Sellars, BA, QTS

Economics and Business Studies:
*Kenneth Owen, BSc (*also Games*)
Peter Griffin, BA, PGCE (*Assessment and Examinations Manager*)

English:
*Christopher Kerrigan, BA, MA, PGCE
Mrs Lisa Challinor, BA, PGCE
Patrick Durkin, BA, MA (*also History*)
David Hare, BEd, Clait (*Head of Year 9*)
Mrs Emma Litterick, BA, PGCE, TESOL (*Teaching and Learning Coordinator and Foundation Cross Phase Coordinator*)
Ms Laura Nash, BA, PGCE
Mrs Helen Pascoe-Williams, BA, PGCE (*Coordinator of Provision for the Most Able*)
Dr Melanie Pope, BA, MPhil, PhD (*Second in English*)
Ms Vicky Roberts, BA, PGCE (*also Drama, Theatre Studies and Theatre Manager*)
Mrs Celia Scott, BA (*also Librarian*)

Geography:
*Mike Taylor, BA, PGCE (*also *Careers*)
Mrs Anne Allen, BSc, PGCE (*Assistant Head of Sixth Form; also Games*)
Jonathan Allen, BSc, PGCE (*also PE and Outdoor Education Coordinator*)
Ms Sarah Lucas, BSc, PGCE

History, Politics and Classical Civilisation:
*Dr Simon Peaple, BA, PhD, CGTC (*Competitive Universities Coordinator*)
Mrs Felicity Coulson, GMus, PGCE (*also Music*)

Patrick Durkin, BA, MA (*also English*)
Mrs Tracey Hester, BA Oxon, PGCE (*History and Politics*)
James Ridge, BA, PGCE (*History*)
Mrs Rachel Taylor, BA, QTS, IBT2 (*Classical Civilisation; also Latin*)

Information Technology:
*Indy Singh, BA, MSc, PGCE
Frank Gahan, BEd, MA, CertEd, FCIEA (*also *Technology and Environment Manager*)
David Smith, LLB, C&GAA, C&GIVA (*ICT Services Manager*)

Latin:
Mrs Rachel Taylor, BA, QTS, IBT2 (*Subject Leader Latin; also Classical Civilisation*)

Learning Development:
*Dr Gill Watkins, BSc, MA, PhD, PGCE
Mrs Elizabeth Dorfman, BA, DipSpLD

Mathematics:
*Michael Conroy-Hargreaves, BSc, PGCE
Mrs Karen Bannister, BSc, PGCE (*Sixth Form Mathematics Coordinator*)
Ms Sarah Biddle, BSc, PGCE
Mrs Tanya Cowan, BSc, PGCE (*KS3 Mathematics Coordinator*)
Ed Hester, MA Oxon, PGCE (*Headmaster*)
Mrs Sharon McBride, BSc, PGCE
Mrs Eileen Sharpe, BEd
Mrs Fenola Whittle, BEd

Modern Languages:
*Mrs Sarah Stewart, BA, PGCE, Cert TESOL (*French*)
Mrs Suzanne Ellis, BA, Cert TESOL (*Subject Leader German, French and TESOL*)
Mrs Stella Keenan, MA, PGCE (*Subject Leader Spanish*)
Mrs Carlota Medina Diaz, BA, PGCE (*Spanish*)
Mrs Caroline Perry, BA, PGCE, DEUG (*French*)
Mrs Margaret Robinson, BEd (*Head of Sixth Form; French, also General Studies*)
Mrs Brigitte Wood, CertEd (*French*)

Music:
Gil Cowlishaw, BMus (*Director of Music*)
Mrs Felicity Coulson, GMus, PGCE (*also History*)
Mrs Susan Olden, LRAM, ARCM, LLCM TD, AMus TCL, ALCM

Visiting Music Staff:
Thomas Abela (*Classical and Electric Guitar*)
Miss Victoria Ball, BA, PGCE (*Cello*)
Miss Alison Brierley, BA, GBSM, ABSM (*Clarinet, Bassoon, Piano, Keyboard and Theory*)
Mrs Felicity Coulson, GMus, PGCE (*Flute, Oboe, Clarinet, Saxophone and Theory*)
Mrs Wioletta Francis, MA (*Vocal Studies*)
Tim Howell (*Guitar*)
Andrew Hughes, ABSM (*Violin and Viola*)
Andrew Kristy, BSc (*Piano, Organ, Music Technology, Composing and Keyboard*)
Mrs Joanna Kunda, MA (*Vocal Studies and Music Theatre*)
Mrs Penny Matthews, Dip FSC, Dip LSP, Dip ASP (*Vocal Studies and Music Theatre*)
Adrian Moore, BA, ARCO (*Organ and Piano*)
Mrs Clare Rothwell, BMus (*Flute*)
Mrs Susan Shepherd, MA, ARCM, ARCO, LRAM, CertEd (*Piano*)
Alan Wickett (*Drum Kit*)
Peter Wraight (*Brass*)

Photography:
*Paul Hubball, BA, PGCE (*also *Art*)
Alex Darkes, BEd (*Assistant Head – Marketing and Operations; also Physics*)

Physical Education and Games:
*Neil McCollin, BA, QTS (*Foundation Director of Sport*)
Jonathan Allen, BSc, PGCE (*also Geography*)
Mrs Deborah Brookes, BA, QTS (*Joint *Girls' Games*)
Ms Louise Champion, BSc, PGCE (**Academic PE*)
Ms Sarah Cockayne, BA, PGCE
Colin Dexter, MAAT
Jonathan Fitt, BSc, PGCE (*Master in charge of Rugby*)
Stuart Friswell (*Rugby Coach*)
Mrs Emily Johnson, BA, PGCE (*Joint *Girls' Games*)
Mrs Christina McCullough, BA, QTS (*Head of Year 11; KS4 Coordinator*)
Bernard Moroney, CertEd
Symon Whitehouse

Psychology:
*Miss Clare Bishop, BSc, PGCE (*also Biology, Sociology and Games*)
Ms Rosie Hase, BSc (*also Games*)
Mrs Anila Patel, BA, PGCE (*also Sociology and General Studies*)

Religious Studies:
*Fr Alan Whelan, MSC, BA
Roderick Isaacs, MA Cantab, MA, CertEd (*Assistant Head of Sixth Form, also General Studies*)
Ian Lane, BA, PGCE (*also General Studies*)
Edward Smith, BA, PGCE (*also Games*)

The Sciences:
*Mrs Gill Smith, BSc, PGCE (**Chemistry*)
Miss Clare Bishop, BSc, PGCE (*Biology; also *Psychology*)
Dr Digby Carrington-Howell, BSc, MA Ed, Ed D, PGCE, NPQH (*Deputy Head – Academic; Biology*)
Alex Darkes, BEd (*Assistant Head – Marketing and Operations; Physics, also Photography*)
Philip Duckworth, BA, MA, PGCE (*Physics*)
Mrs Susan Millest, HNC, BSc, PGCE, NPQH (*Deputy Head – Pastoral; Physics*)
Ms Faye Roberts, BSc, MSc, PGCE (**Biology*)
Simon Robertson, BSc, PGCE (*Head of Year 10; Biology and Chemistry*)
Mrs Joanne Smith, MChem, PGCE (*Chemistry*)
Mrs Catherine Warne, BSc, PGCE (*House and Extra-Curricular Coordinator; Biology*)
Steve White, BSc, QTS (**Physics*)

Non Teaching Staff:
Chaplaincy Coordinator: Mrs Mary Benham
Finance Manager: Miss Francesca Borton-Wilkins
Marketing Manager: Mrs Melanie Butler, BA
Housekeeping: Mrs Cynthia Carpenter
Trainee Groundsman: Sam Cullinane
Registrar: Mrs Loretta Curtis
Assistant Matron: Mrs Helen Cutter
Senior Laboratory Technician: Mrs Ellen Davies, ONC
ICT Technician and Assistant Examinations Officer: Mrs Shellagh Dodds
Housekeeping: Lester Gibson
Estates Assistant: Jake Hall
Design and Technology Technician: Mrs Charlotte Hetherington, BEng
Headmaster's Personal Assistant and Office Manager: Mrs Carmel Hopkins
Foundation Estates Manager: Mark Johnson
Senior Matron: Mrs Maria Lawless, SEN
Estates Assistant: Gerry Lovely
Secretary/Receptionist: Miss Helen Morgan
Laboratory Technician: Mrs Angela Morris, CertEd
Groundsman: Joe Newton
Special Projects Officer: Mrs Gill Price
Groundsman: Tom Probert
Theatre Manager: Ms Vicky Roberts, BA, PGCE (*also English, Drama and Theatre Studies*)

Foundation Grounds Manager: Edward Robertson
ICT Technician: Jonathan Sant
Librarian: Mrs Celia Scott, BA (*also English*)
House Manager: Mrs Judith Southam
Uniform Shop Manager: Miss Naomi Taylor, BSc
Curriculum Coordinator: Dr Michael Tideswell, BSc, PhD, QTS
Catering Manager: Mrs Lesley Topham
ICT Manager: Robert Van Spelde
Estates Assistant: John Vasquez
Housekeeping: Mrs Judy Vick
Assistant to the Registrar: Mrs Elaine Warwick
Counsellor: Mrs Tina Watkins, MBACP Reg

Number in School. The school has about 800 day pupils from 11 to 18 years with 200 in the Sixth Form. An extensive network of private coaches transports pupils from a wide area.

Aims. The College provides a caring, Christian environment for children where their needs can be met and their talents, confidence and self-esteem developed. There is a healthy balance between freedom and structure and an emphasis on self-discipline through responsibility and trust, which develops confidence and independence.

The College draws on a rich tradition of Catholic teaching and the spirituality of the Missionaries of the Sacred Heart, whose ethos is central to its character and disciplinary system. In welcoming families of a variety of faiths, the school community is a living example of ecumenism. The College motto, *Christus Regnet* – let Christ reign – is a reminder of Christ's love, service, forgiveness and generosity of spirit.

Academic. A broad-based, stimulating curriculum satisfies a wide range of ability and fosters a love of learning. A favourable pupil-teacher ratio, permitting personal attention, contributes to impressive value-added achievements. High fliers are stretched and provided with intellectually challenging assignments, ensuring that they achieve at the highest possible levels. The curriculum is well supported by a magnificent library and ICT. Qualified specialists give tuition to dyslexic pupils.

Pupils in Years 7 to 9 have a broad-based curriculum which avoids early specialisation and usually go on to take nine or ten GCSEs.

Supervised homework and free extended day are offered until 6.00 pm.

The Sixth Form. A new £2.5m Sixth Form Centre opened at the end of 2007. Students in the Sixth Form are prepared for AS Level and A2 Level examinations after which the vast majority proceed to university. The Head of Sixth Form and the team of tutors monitor the academic progress of Sixth Formers through regular discussions with the students and their teachers. Visits to university Open Days, together with professional careers advice enables students to make the best choices about their next stage of education.

There is a strong emphasis on the acquisition of key skills and the education of the whole person. Sixth Formers are offered residential outward bound courses, training programmes and retreats which provide an opportunity for reflection and exploration, to develop a mature and balanced perspective. Guest lecturers, debates and theatre outings all enhance Sixth Form life.

All Sixth Formers enjoy privileges and have the responsibilities of leadership and example; certain members are elected to perform prefectorial duties. Prefects attend a leadership course and learn valuable management skills. They organise activities for younger pupils and chair the School Council, which offers a forum for lively discussion and gives the students an influential voice in the running of the College. Sixth Formers also act as Form Patrons, mentoring younger pupils and arranging outings for them. The House

Captains have a pivotal role in the organisation of inter-house events.

Careers. The Careers Advice Programme commences in Year 9 and regular tutorials are held concentrating on option subject choices and developing careers awareness. Interview technique is developed and students are assisted with work experience placements which are undertaken at the end of Year 10 and Lower Sixth.

Art & Design. A feature which immediately strikes all visitors to the College is the outstanding display of canvases. Superb examination results and successes in competitions are commonplace. The study of drawing, painting, graphics and ceramics are central and they are enhanced by using the work of great artists as stimulus material.

Technology includes Food, Graphics, Resistant Materials, Information and Communications Technology, Textiles and Electronics. Pupils can work with a variety of materials, realising their technical designs in the well-resourced workshops, which include CAD/CAM facilities.

Music and Drama. Music is studied by all pupils in their first three years and as an option at GCSE and A Level. The College choir gives regular performances and tours extensively overseas. Many pupils learn instruments and are encouraged to join the orchestra. Peripatetic staff offer tuition in most instruments. There are two well-equipped studios with digital recording facilities for Music Technology and there is an acclaimed Binns organ in the magnificent Chapel built by Peter Paul Pugin.

The College has a well-equipped theatre and regular productions are staged including pantomimes and revues, Shakespeare plays and adaptations from Dickens. Productions involve a large number of pupils and staff and provide an excellent way for pupils of different years to get to know each other. There are thriving Dance and Drama Clubs. Theatre Studies is offered in the Sixth Form.

Physical Education. All pupils participate in games and Physical Education classes. Physical Education can also be studied as an examination subject at GCSE and A Level. The major sports are rugby, netball, hockey, cricket, rounders, tennis and athletics; they are run in tandem with badminton, soccer, squash, basketball and trampolining. Off-site swimming and sailing are also available.

The Sports Centre has a sports hall, fitness gym and squash courts; a floodlit all-weather surface was laid in 2003. Extensive outdoor facilities include an internationally recognised cross-country course, tennis courts and over sixty acres of games pitches.

Extra-Curricular Activities. There is always a wide range of clubs, societies and activities such as art, board games, chemistry clinic, choir, computing, cookery, debating, drama, flight, history, jazz band, mathematics workshop, meditation, music workshop, orchestra, photography, Spanish, Warhammer, technology and textiles. The Duke of Edinburgh's Award Scheme, World Challenge and Outward Bound courses are also offered. The Arts Society provides a cultural programme of lectures, poetry evenings, music recitals and play readings.

Admission. Admission is by examination, usually towards the end of January, generally at 11 and 13 and at other ages as space allows. Students from other schools join the Sixth Form after their GCSE courses.

Scholarships. (*See Scholarship Entries section.*)

Fees per term (2011-2012). £3,118 excluding transport and meals. Instrumental tuition, external examinations and some targeted support for those with learning needs are charged as extras.

Charitable status. Warwickshire Catholic Independent Schools Foundation is a Registered Charity, number 1087124. It exists solely for the education of children.

The Purcell School

Aldenham Road, Bushey, Hertfordshire WD23 2TS
Tel: 01923 331100
Fax: 01923 331166
e-mail: info@purcell-school.org
website: www.purcell-school.org

The Purcell School is one of the world's leading specialist centres of excellence and has a national and international reputation in the education and training of exceptional young musicians. There are 184 pupils, boys and girls, aged from 9 to 18, with 79 in the Sixth Form. All pupils are means-tested on entry to the School and receive Scholarships under the Government's Music and Dance Scheme or from the School's Scholarship Fund.

Royal Patron: HRH The Prince of Wales

President: Sir Simon Rattle

Governing Body:
Mr Roy Cervenka (*Chairman*)
Ms Jenny Agutter, FRSA, Hon DLit
The Hon Mark Bridges, MA Cantab
Mr Andrew Carter, CMG, MA, FRCO, LRAM, ARCM
Mr Simon Channing, BA Cantab, ARCM
Mr Michael Garner, MA, FCA, FCT
Ms Janice Graham, ARCM, AGSMD, ACT Julliard
Mrs Brenda Hasler, BEd
Lady Jean McGregor
Mr Philip Newman, FCA, FRSA
Professor Sir Curtis Price, AM, PhD, Hon RAM, FKC, FRCM, FRNCM
Mr Martin Saunders, MA Cantab, FCA
Mr Peter van de Geest
Professor John Wass, MA, MD, FRCP
Mr David Woodhead, BA, FRSA

Headmaster: **Mr Peter Crook**, MA, BMus, FRSA, ARAM, ARCO

Deputy Head, Academic: Mr Paul Elliott, MA Hons Glasgow, PGCE
Deputy Head, Pastoral: Mrs Mary Pitkin, BSc Hons, CPhys, MInstP, HG Dip

Director of Music: Mr Quentin Poole, MA Cantab, FRAM
Assistant Director of Music: Mr Edward Longstaff, BMus, MMus, PGCE

Bursar: Miss Aideen McNamara, BA Hons

Head of Sixth Form: Miss Elizabeth Willan, BA Hons London, PGCE

Music Department:
Director of Music: Mr Quentin Poole, MA Cantab, FRAM
Assistant Director of Music: Mr Edward Longstaff, BMus, MMus, PGCE
Head of Academic Music: Mrs Miranda Francis, BMus Hons, LRAM, ARCM, PGCE
Head of Composition: Miss Alison Cox, GRNCM, DipAdvStdMus Comp, PGCE
Head of Jazz: Mr Simon Colam, BMus, LGSM
Head of Keyboard: Mr William Fong, GMus RNCM, PPRNCM
Head of Music Technology/IT: Mr Aidan Goetzee, MSc, GRSM, ARCM
Music Technology Assistant: Mr George Oulton
Head of Strings: Mr Charles Sewart, AGSM
Head of Wind, Brass, Percussion, Voice and Harp: Mr Kevin Hathway, ARCM, Hon RCM, FRCM
Accompanists:
Mrs Deborah Shah, ARCM

Mr Daniel King Smith, BMus, LRAM

Instrumental Staff:
Jazz Department:
Head: Mr Simon Colam (*Piano*)
Darren Altman (*Drums*)
Oliver Hayhurst (*Bass*)
Jacqui Hicks (*Voice*)
Carlos Lopez Real (*Saxophone*)
Steve Waterman (*Trumpet*)

Keyboard Department:
Head: Mr William Fong
Lidia Amorelli
Andrew Ball
Ronald Cavaye
William Fong
Rustem Hayroudinoff
Gareth Hunt
Emily Jeffrey
Jianing Kong
Alla Kravchenko
Ching Ching Lim
Pascal Nemirovski
Tessa Nicholson
Tatiana Sarkissova
Deborah Shah
Daniel King Smith
Clare Sutherland (+ *Harpsichord*)
Valeria Szervansky
Marissa Thornton-Wood
John Thwaites
Patsy Toh

Strings/Guitar Department:
Head: Mr Charles Sewart
Pal Banda (*Cello*)
Fiona Bonds (*Viola*)
Alexander Boyarsky (*Cello*)
Anna Cordova-Andreas (*Cello*)
Tony Cucchiara (*Violin*)
Evgueny Grach (*Violin*)
Ian Jewel (*Viola*)
Carmel Kaine (*Violin*)
Berent Korfker (*Violin*)
Francesco Mariani (*Guitar*)
Susie Meszaros (*Violin*)

Natalia Pavlutskaya (*Cello*)
Sadagat Mammadova-Rashidova (*Violin*)
Charles Sewart (*Violin*)
Carol Slater (*Violin*)
Neil Tarlton (*Double Bass*)
Nathaniel Vallois (*Violin*)

Wind, Brass, Percussion, Voice and Harp Department:
Head: Mr Kevin Hathway
Rachel Baldock (*Oboe*)
Daphne Boden (*Harp*)
Sarah Burnett (*Bassoon*)
Tony Cross (*Trumpet*)
Sue Dent (*Horn*)
David Fuest (*Clarinet*)
Kevin Hathway (*Percussion*)
Barbara Law (*Recorder*)
Tom Marandola (*Voice*)
Anna Pope (*Flute*)
Melanie Ragge (*Oboe*)
Tom Rainer (*Trumpet*)
Charlotte Seale (*Harp*)
Clare Southworth (*Flute*)
Stephen Wick (*Tuba*)
Rob Workman (*Trombone*)

Alexander Technique:
John Crawford
Jean Mercer

Choirs:
Marissa Thornton-Wood (*Lower School Choir*)
Joy Hill (*Middle School Choir*)
Edward Longstaff (*VI Form Choir*)
Quentin Poole (*Chamber Choir*)

Practice Supervisor and House Tutor:
Freya Jacklin, BA
Holly Reardon, BMus, MMus, MPerf
Katherine Smith, BMus

Academic Music Department:
Head: Mrs Miranda Francis, BMus Hons, LRAM, ARCM, PGCE
Simon Colam, BMus (*Jazz*)
Alison Cox, GRNCM, PGCE
Elaine Crook, BA, ARCM, PGCE (*Class Music*)
Aidan Goetzee, MSc (*Music Technology*)
Joy Hill, BEd Hons, MA, FRSA
Edward Longstaff, BMus, MMus (*Class Music*)
Quentin Poole, MA, FRAM
Marissa Thornton-Wood, BMus, MMus (*Class Music*)

Composition Department:
Head: Miss Alison Cox, GRNCM, PGCE
Haris Kittos, DMus, MMus, PGA, BMus, BA
Simon Speare, MA, ARCM
Joseph Phibbs, BMus, MMus

Academic Staff:
* *Head of Department*

Ms Nadine Sender, BA Hons, QTS (*Art)
Mr Panos Fellas, BSc Hons Surrey, MA ScEd (**Science/Physics*)

Mrs Mary Pitkin, BSc Hons, CPhys, MInstP (*Physics; PSHE*)

Mr David Chappell, MSc York, BSc London, PGCE Leeds (*Biology, *PSHE*)

Mr Peter Banks, BSc Hons Bangor, AMRSC (*Chemistry*)

Mrs Eva Andrusier, BA Hons Manchester, CertEd, CertTEFL (*EFL*)

Ms Katherine Higgins, BEd Hons Warwick, Dip TEFLA, MA TEFL, MSc (**EFL*)

Mr Andrew Leverton, BA Hons Tasmania, DipEd (**English*)

Mrs Sheila Young, BEd Glasgow, Dip SENCO Science (*English*)

Mrs Jocelyne Hazan, BA, MA Paris X (*French; Overseas Pupils Guardian Coordinator*)

Miss Elizabeth Willan, BA Hons London, PGCE (**French; Head of Sixth Form*)

Mrs Margaret Moore, BSc Hons, PGCE (*Geography*)

Ms Monica Lowenberg, BA Hons Sunderland, MA Sussex (*German*)

Mr Paul Elliott, MA Hons Glasgow, PGCE (**German; PSHE*)

Mr Darrell Pigott, BSc Hons Bradford, PGCE (**History*)

Mrs Cherry Trotter, BEd Hons (**Juniors*)

Mrs Sally-Ann Whitty, BA (*Learning Support Assistant*)

Mr Martin Whitfield, MSc, BSc, PGCE (*Mathematics*)

Mrs Yvonne Tagoe, BA Hons, MBA, PGCE (**Mathematics*)

Boarding Houses:
Avison: Mr and Mrs D Henderson
Gardner: Mr K Garner (*Acting Housemaster*), Ms Annette Cook (*Residential Matron*)
Graham Smallbone: Mrs R Branch
Sunley: Mr and Mrs J Francis
Day House: Mr D Pigott

Administration Staff:
PA to Headmaster/Office Manager: Mrs Gail Remfry, AIST, RSA
Office Administrators: Mrs Helen Gayle, Mrs Jannice Raw, Mrs Caroline Fletcher
Music Department Secretary & Registrar: Mrs Karen Gumustekin
Music Timetabler: Mrs Fiona Duce, BA Hons
Librarian: Mrs Diana Winny, Dip Cl St
Concerts and Recruitment Manager: Mrs Jane Hunt, BMus
Concerts Administrator: Miss Hannah James, BMus
Head of Fundraising and Development: Mr James Quinn, BA Hons
Development Department Assistant: Mrs Emma McGrath
Finance Officer: Ms Susan Pickard, MAAT
Computer Network and Telecommunications Manager: Mr Simon Kingsbury
Art Technician: Miss Lucy Jay, BA Hons
Lab Technician: Mrs Susan Pitts
Estates Assistant: Mrs Tina Stewart
House Keeper: Mrs Stella Rendle
Catering: Holroyd Howe Independent Limited
School Nurse: Mrs Hilary Austin, RGN
Pastoral Counsellor: Mrs Nikki Bennett
Physiotherapist: Mrs Sarah Upjohn, MA, MCSP

The Purcell School benefits from London's cultural and teaching resources. It offers exceptional opportunities to outstanding young musicians: the finest teachers, time and priority for musical activities, the opportunity to work with others of similar calibre and specialist education in an encouraging and balanced environment.

Music. At the heart of the very stimulating and challenging musical life of the School is an individually tailored programme for every pupil. There are Heads of Department for Academic Music, Composition, Jazz, Keyboard, Music Technology, Strings/Guitar and Wind/Brass/Percussion/Voice/Harp, and they are able to ensure that the balance between musical studies and academic work is finely-tuned to suit everyone, at each stage of their development.

The departments work closely together to provide as many links between them as possible, giving pupils a flexibility and breadth of experience that helps them adapt and flourish in their musical futures.

The world's leading musicians visit the School for masterclasses, recitals, courses and collaborative projects, enhancing the work of the fine instrumental, vocal and composition teachers who teach regularly for the School. The New Music Centre, opened in 2007, provides superb facilities in which much of the teaching takes place, as well as a warmly intimate Recital Room and a wealth of excellent equipment for composers and music technology pupils.

The School's busy Concerts Department provides a constant supply of opportunities to perform, from lunchtime concerts at School and in the surrounding area, to the most formal recitals around the UK and in the capital's leading venues. Pupils can audition for the chance to play concertos with the School's orchestras, to give solo and chamber music recitals at the Wigmore Hall and for many other prizes and special opportunities. Orchestras, choirs and ensembles of all kinds perform at School, throughout the UK and abroad, providing the ideal experiences for pupils to develop their talents to the full.

Of greatest interest to the staff is the development made by each pupil, year by year. Young musicians progress at different rates and at different times in their lives, so great care is taken to provide pupils with experiences and opportunities that are appropriate to their current stage of development.

Academic Curriculum. In addition to specialist musical training The Purcell School offers a full academic education of the highest quality to GCSE and Advanced Level. Examination results are outstanding.

Boarding. Pupils come from all over Britain and from all over the world. About 70% are boarders, all of whom live on the School campus.

The youngest pupils, aged between 9 and 13, live in Avison House. Sunley House (girls) is in the main School building. Graham Smallbone House (girls) and Gardner House (boys) are in a superb new building which opened in February 2011. Members of the Sixth Form can use their rooms for practice as well as for study. The Houses are run by a resident Housemaster/mistress respectively and there are also resident Deputy Hms.

Links between School and home are close and, with fax machines and e-mail, this is possible wherever in the world a pupil may live. In each half of the term there is an Exeat weekend when all pupils go home or to their guardian or to friends. There is also an extended half-term period in each of the three terms.

Admission. Entrance is by musical audition and interview. Further details and a prospectus are available from the Registrar, Mrs Karen Gumustekin, who will be pleased to answer queries (or see the School website).

The School has a principle of taking young musicians whose exceptional musical ability merits them a place.

Fees per term (2011-2012). Day £8,259; Boarding £10,562.

Government Aided places are available. Bursaries and Scholarships are also available for those not eligible for aided places.

Charitable status. The Purcell School is a Registered Charity, number 312855. It aims to offer specialist musical training, combined with an excellent general academic education, to children of exceptional musical ability.

The Read School
Drax

Drax, Selby, North Yorkshire YO8 8NL
Tel: 01757 618248
Fax: 01757 617432
e-mail: secretary@readschool.co.uk
website: www.readschool.co.uk

Chairman of Governors: R S Manock, LLM

Bursar and Clerk to the Governors: Mr P W Thompson,
  MA, DSBM, MInstAM

Head: Mrs B L McCrea, MA Cantab, NPQH

Deputy Head: J A Sweetman, BSc, PhD

Teaching Staff:
Mrs R A Ainley, MA (*Modern Foreign Languages,
  Business Studies*)
§Mrs P Anderson, BEd (*Junior School*)
Miss S Barbour, BA (*PE and Games*)
Miss J Bullock, BSc (*English Additional Language*)
§Ms S L Campbell, BSc (*Junior School*)
Mrs J Clark (*Brass instruments, Piano, CCF*)
Miss C Cross, BA (*English*)
B Garrard, BSc (*Head of PE and Games*)
Mrs E Gilmore, BA (*Head of MFL, Spanish, German*)
D I Gisbourne, BSc (*Director of ICT, Mathematics*)
Mrs H Haddock, BEd (*Lower Junior School*)
§Mrs H Hewson, BA (*English*)
Mrs C Howarth (*Lower Juniors*)
Mrs K Ives, BA (*French, Spanish*)
R S Kendrick, BA (*Mathematics, CCF*)
N L Marshall, BA (*Drama, English, Resident Tutor*)
J L Matthews, BSc (*Housemaster*)
D C McCrea, MEd (*Mathematics*)
Mrs S Morrell, BEd (*Religious Studies, PSHE
  Coordinator*)
Mrs A Oliver, BA (*Latin, French, Classical Studies; Exams
  Officer*)
Ms C M Palmer, BSc, MSc (*Assistant Head, Curriculum;
  Head of Mathematics*)
Mrs K E Patrick, PGDip Counselling, PGDip SEN, MA
  (*Head of Inclusive Learning*)
C S Patrick, BSc (*Specialist Tutor*)
M Raisborough, BEd (*Head of Junior School*)
§Mrs S Rothwell-Wood, BEd (*Design Technology,
  Graphics, Food*)
Mrs S Scholefield, BSc (*Head of Humanities*)
§Mrs E Stark, BSc, DipEd (*Biology, Chemistry*)
§R P Stark, BSc, DipEd (*Physics*)
J Staves, BSc, PhD (*Chemistry*)
Ms J Tate, BA (*Housemistress, Psychology*)
Mrs S A Tolman, CertMusEd (*Lower Juniors*)
Mr P Vasey, BA (*Business Studies, ICT, Resident Tutor*)
M A Voisey, BA (*Head of English, Head of Sixth Form*)
Mrs R M Wake, BA (*Upper Junior School*)
Mr P Whitcombe, BSc (*Head of Science*)
Mr R C Whyley, BA (*History, Boys' Games*)
§Mrs A Wightman, BA, LLB (*Upper Junior School*)
P Woodward, BA, MA (*Design Technology*)
§Mrs C M Wynne, BEd (*Junior School*)
Ms S A Yates, BA (*Art and Design, Tutor for Girls*)

Age Range. Co-educational 3–18 (Boarding 8–18).
Number in School. Total 320: Day 270, Boarding 50;
Boys 190, Girls 130.

The school is pleasantly situated in the rural village of
Drax and is very convenient for main rail (Doncaster, York)
and road access (M62, M18, A1). Manchester is the nearest
international airport (1½ hours distant). It is a relatively
small school where children are well known to each other
and to the staff.

The school has been a focal point for the education of
boys in the Selby–Goole area for over 340 years, first as
Drax Grammar School, and (since 1967) as The Read
School. The school is now co-educational, offering a wide
range of academic studies at GCSE and A Level, together
with a full programme of Sports, Drama, Music, CCF and
recreational activity. There is one class in each Junior
School year from Early Years to Year 5 and two in Year 6.
There are three classes in each of the Senior years (7–11).
There is a small Sixth Form (50 pupils) following AS and A
Level courses. High standards are expected in all aspects of
endeavour, and in behaviour and manners.

Facilities. In addition to the refurbished Edwardian buildings there continued to be steady developments in the facilities and accommodation throughout the 1980s and 1990s.
These include the fine Moloney Hall, Ramsker classrooms,
Sports Hall, Coggrave Building for the Upper Junior School
(Years 3–6), in addition to internal developments, especially
in the provision of IT. The Shipley Building for music and
mathematics opened in October 2002. The Lower Junior
School and girls' boarding accommodation are situated on
their own site in the village at Adamson House. New changing rooms have recently been completed and existing facilities refurbished. The dining room has been extended and
modernised, together with the kitchen facilities. In 2007 a
Multi-Use Games Area with Astroturf pitch was provided,
and in 2008, complete refurbishment of Norfolk House
(Boys' boarding) and the chemistry lab was undertaken, as
was the provision of a new Creative Arts Centre, for Art,
Design Technology and Food.

Fees per term (2011-2012). Boarders: £5,765–£6,600;
Day: £2,160–£3,060.

Sibling discount is available at a fixed sum of monetary
value equivalent to 5% of the basic fee on entry, applicable
to 2nd or subsequent children in the school at the same time.

Admission. An offer of a place in the school is made
after interview (and verbal reasoning and mathematics tests
for admission to the Senior School) and satisfactory report
from the pupil's current school.

Charitable status. The Read School is a Registered
Charity, number 529675. It exists to provide a proper education for boys and girls aged 3–18.

Rendcomb College

Cirencester, Gloucestershire GL7 7HA
Tel: 01285 831213
Fax: 01285 831331
e-mail: info@rendcomb.gloucs.sch.uk
website: www.rendcombcollege.org.uk

Rendcomb College was founded in 1920 by Noel Wills. It is
a member of the Association of Governing Bodies of Independent Schools and the Headmaster is a member of
SHMIS.

The Governors:
R Lane (*Chairman*)
Mrs P Hornby (*Vice-Chairman*)

Mrs S Arkle	H C W Robinson
E Daniels	Mrs L Singer
Mrs J Gunner	Major-General P G
A R Marchand	Williams
S D E Parsons	Major M T N H Wills, DL
Sir F Richards	R H Wills
The Ven H S Ringrose	

Headmaster: **R J Martin**, BA Hons

Deputy Headmaster: D Baker, BSc (*Mathematics*)

Assistant Head: Mrs D Dodd, BA (*English; Theatre Studies*)
Director of Studies,: D Illingworth, BSc (*Geography*)
Director of Sport: M Slark, BA (*Business Studies*)
Director of Music: (*to be appointed*)

* *Head of Department*

Housemasters/Housemistresses:
Park House:
Mrs K Coups (*PE & Lacrosse*)
M Coups (*Lacrosse Coach*)
Stable House:
P Bevans, BSc (**Physics*)
Mrs M Bevans BA (**Learning Support, SENCO*)
Lawn House:
Mrs A Ferreira
N Ferreira (*PE and Cricket Coach*)
Old Rectory:
A St J Brealy, BA (*Geography, Mathematics*)
Mrs A Brealy, BA (*Marketing*)
Godman House:
Mrs R E Fielding, BA (**German*)
Dr S Fielding
College House:
B L North, BA, BPhil (**French*)

Miss S Bell (*PE & Games, *PHSE*)
Ms A Berry, BSc (*Chemistry*)
P Brooke, BA (*English and *RE*)
S Clark, BSc, PGCE (**Mathematics*)
Mrs C Forshaw, BSc (*Mathematics*)
Mrs J Gibson, BSc, CChem, MRSC (**Chemistry, Physics, ICT*)
M H Graham, MA (**History, Librarian*)
Mrs L Gregory, BSc (*Mathematics, *Head of External Exams*)
Mrs G Harford, BSc (*Psychology*)
Miss M Harries, BA Manchester (*English*)
Mrs H Hill, BA (*Spanish*)
Mrs B Hughes, BA (**Design & Technology*)
P Jennings, BA (**English*)
Mrs M Kinson, BA (*History, Careers*)
Mrs M Lizana-Weeks, BA (*Spanish*)
Miss M Lucas (**Geography, Enviromental Coordinator*)
H Marsden BSc (*Sports and *DofE*)
Mrs S Mills, BA (*Drama*)
A O'Hanlon BA (**Art*)
Miss E Roffe, BA (*Art*)
J H Stutchbury, BSc (*Biology*)
Mrs J D Stutchbury, BA (**EFL*)
C Vuolo, BSc (*Chemistry and *PE*)
Mrs S White, BA (*German*)
F Whitham, BSc (*Physics*)
A Wilkes, BSc (*Mathematics, ICT*)

Junior School:
Head: M Watson, MA, BEd
Deputy Head: Anne Haas, BEd

J Arnold, BEd
Mrs F Auster, BSc, Cert Learning Support
Mrs A Barker, BA, PGCE
Mrs S Bischoff, BEd, BPhil
Mrs M Bleaken, BSc, PGCE
Mrs C Breare
Mrs A Brealy, BA, PGCE
P Colls, MA, BMus, ARCM, LTCL
Miss C Hayden, BA
Mrs K Hockey, BEd
A Lawrence, BA, PGCE
T Layton, BEd
Mrs B Lee, BA, PGCE, Hornsby Dip SLD
Mrs J Lee-Browne, LDAD, BS Dip, PGCE
Mrs L Louisson, PGCE

Mrs M Moore, MA, PGCE
Miss P Morrow-Brown, BA, PGCE
Miss C Rayner, BEd
Mrs D Walton-Smith, BA Hons, PGCE
Mrs L Watson, BEd

Nursery Staff:
Miss L Potter HND Early Years Childhood Studies
Mrs K Hardie, NVQ3

Games Coaches:
Miss A Ferebee
Mrs J Hill
N Ferreira
Mrs K Coups

Classroom Assistants:
Mrs K Burnip
Mrs K Cairns
Mrs S Liebenberg
Mrs N McKenna
Mrs J Major
Mrs J Scase

Bursar: Mrs E Sharman, BSc
Headmaster's PA: Mrs C Johnson
Junior School Headmaster's Secretary: Mrs J Nichols
Admissions Registrar: Miss E Hayward, BA
Marketing: (*to be appointed*)
Bursar's Secretary: Mrs C Endersby
Finance Manager: Mrs S Watkins
Finance Assistant: Mrs S Thomson
Reception: Mrs D Baker, Ms A Hardy
Network ICT Manager: M Harrison
Medical Officer: Dr S W Drysdale, MBChB, MRCP
Sister: Mrs J Rogers, GRN
Assistant Sister: Mrs L Wright, RGN

Visiting Music Staff:
P Anderson (*Brass*)
R Baggs (*Accompanist*)
Mrs S Blewett (*Flute*)
J Carter (*Head of Keyboard Studies, Piano*)
M Coldrick (*Drum Kit and Orchestral Percussion*)
P Colls (*Singing*)
Mrs M Cope (*Piano*)
P Cordell (*Electric Guitar*)
Mrs C de Burgh (*Woodwind*)
Miss P Crisp (*Piano*)
Mrs C Dukes (*Guitar*)
T Furness (*Recorder*)
Mrs L Gerrard (*Singing*)
Mrs R Howgego (*'Cello*)
J Morgan (*Clarinet and Saxophone*)
Ms J Orsman (*Upper Strings*)
Mrs N Philips (*Singing*)
Miss S Steele (*Piano*)
J Wright (*Organ and Piano*)

Situation and Buildings. Rendcomb overlooks the River Churn in the heart of the Cotswolds, five miles from Cirencester and ten miles from Cheltenham on the A435. It is easily accessible from the M4, A40 and M5. The College is set in 200 acres of beautiful parkland.

Numbers. There are 132 boys and 113 girls from 11 to 18 years, who either fully board, weekly board or are day pupils. Flexible boarding is available.

Admission. Pupils normally join at 11, 13 or 16 to enter the Sixth Form. The entrance examination for entry at 11 is taken at Rendcomb and comprises three papers: English, Mathematics and Verbal Reasoning. At 13, pupils are admitted by Common Entrance or Rendcomb Examination and at 16 by interview, school reports and GCSE results.

Character. Rendcomb is the right size for everyone to grow in confidence and ability. The College week is designed to combine academic studies with a wide variety of activities and sports.

We encourage pupils to achieve the best possible academic results and to find out what they are good at. We want them to care for other people and their surroundings, and to enter the world of work, of marriage and of family life, with confidence and sensitivity.

Rendcomb provides a stable, disciplined and structured way of life to sustain hard work, with fine opportunities for developing talent outside the classroom. Facilities for study and leisure are superb, helping prepare students for University and independent living.

Curriculum. Pupils are prepared for GCSE, AS and A2 Level examinations and for university entrance. They go on to a wide range of careers in the professions and services, commerce and industry, and in agriculture.

In the first two years there is a broad course of studies including Religious Studies, English, French, History, Mathematics, German, Geography, Music, Art, Spanish, Design & Technology, General Science, Drama, Games, PE, ICT and PSHE.

In the third year, Science is studied as separate subjects and all pupils study a short course GCSE in ICT.

In the fourth and fifth years pupils are offered a range of options and most take ten subjects at GCSE.

AS Level courses are provided in English, History, French, German, Geography, Business Studies, Mathematics, Further Mathematics, Physics, Chemistry, Biology, Psychology, Art, Music, Theatre Studies, and PE. Most pupils take four AS Levels. Three of these are continued in the second year of the Sixth Form to A2 Level.

University Entrance. A high level of academic achievement is maintained, and in recent years over 95% of leavers have gone on to Higher Education.

Careers. There is a Careers Section in our Library and our Sixth Form House which offer comprehensive current information on both careers and higher education and experienced staff are available for further information, consultation and advice.

Careers advice is available for all pupils throughout their stay at Rendcomb. It is particularly important when selecting subjects for GCSE and A level. Rendcomb uses the Centigrade System as part of the Higher Education Applications Procedure to assist Lower Sixth Form pupils in selecting universities and degree courses. All pupils will take part in an extensive cultural enrichment programme during their time in the Sixth Form.

Religious Education. Church Services take place on selected Sundays and during the week in the fine 16th Century Parish Church, which also serves as the church for the small village of Rendcomb. Pupils are required to attend a short service on two days in the week and boarders attend a Morning Service on Sunday. There is an annual Confirmation and the Chaplain is available as a listening ear to all members of the school.

Music, Art and Drama. The Arts Centre stands at the centre of the school site. It is equipped for Art, Music, Design & Technology, Pottery and Textiles.

Art is taught to all pupils for at least three of their years at Rendcomb and they may use the facilities at other times as an activity or for recreation. Special studios are dedicated to pupils studying AS/A Level Art and professional artists teach alongside the Head of Art to provide balanced, relevant and up to date teaching. Visits are undertaken to a wide range of art galleries.

There is a high standard of instrumental and choral performance. Individual tuition is available in all instruments and voice. There are many opportunities to play and sing throughout the year at Rendcomb and at other venues.

Plays are staged in the well-equipped fine Victorian Orangery including portable tiered seating. The Rendcomb site also lends itself to producing open air plays during the summer term. All kinds of productions are staged at Rendcomb from full scale performances involving large numbers of pupils and staff to the regular junior play, small plays and reviews produced by pupils. Recent productions include *Amadeus, We Will Rock You, Outside Edge, Guys and Dolls* and most recently, *Hairspray*. There are also performances by visiting companies and frequent trips to theatres in London, Stratford, Bristol, Oxford and Cheltenham.

Drama is offered at GCSE and Theatre Studies may be studied at A2 and AS Level.

Sport. The games fields are excellent and a large majority of members of the school represent Rendcomb at one or more sports in their age group. Recent tours include a Rugby Tour to Venice and a Hockey and Cricket Tour to Barbados.

An all-weather playing surface represents an important training advantage in hockey and tennis at Rendcomb; it complements the seven hard tennis courts already in use. There are two squash courts, four badminton courts in the sports hall, a heated open-air swimming pool and climbing wall. Football, water-sports, clay pigeon shooting and horse-riding are also popular.

Living Accommodation. Rendcomb has excellent accommodation for both boarders and day pupils. Most pupils in the Fourth Form and above have a comfortable single study bedroom and there are spacious Common Rooms and excellent social facilities. Sixth formers enjoy their own centre, with TV, Satellite TV, video, games room, dance area and bar.

Bursaries and Scholarships. (*See Scholarship Entries section.*) A number of means-tested Bursaries and Scholarships (Academic, Art, Music, Performing Arts and Sport) and a small number of Forces Scholarships are awarded each year at 11, 13 and 16 years of age. They are based on assessment of a pupil's potential and the value that we believe they will add to the life of the school. All awards are reassessed annually and are subject to satisfactory academic progress and behaviour. All cases are judged on their own merits and parents are invited to discuss their eligibility for a financial award with the Headmaster.

For further details apply to the Admissions Registrar on 01285 832306 or by email to admissions@rendcomb .gloucs.sch.uk.

Fees per term (2011-2012). Senior School: Boarding £6,390–£8,275, Day £4,580–£6,180.

Junior School: Day £1,920–£3,200; Year 6 Boarding Fee £1,140.

Fees are payable termly in advance, by the first day of term. The Governors reserve the right to charge interest at up to 2% per month on fees not paid by this date. For information on monthly and other payment schemes please contact the Bursar.

The premium for a pupil's personal accident insurance scheme is included.

The registration fee is £70 (Free online registration).

The Junior School. The Junior School opened in September 2000 and now has classes for three to eleven year olds.

For pupils in Nursery and Reception, the Curriculum is based on an extension of the Government's learning goals including social, emotional and physical development. Junior 1 and 2 are largely class teacher taught with Junior 3 to 6 operating a degree of subject specialism. A wide range of subjects are taught including ICT, Drama and French.

All pupils have the opportunity to represent the school in a variety of sporting fixtures and to participate in Music and Drama productions.

Each pupil's development is closely monitored and reports, grade cards and teacher meetings provide regular feedback to parents.

After-school clubs run Monday to Thursday, from Judo to Band, Nature Club to Computer Club. The use of College facilities by the Junior School, from the Astroturf to the Multimedia Suite, raises the standard of activities. The Junior School also has its own facilities including an adventure playground.

Enquiries should be directed to the Admissions Registrar on 01285 832306.

Charitable status. Rendcomb College is a Registered Charity, number 1115884. The aims and objectives of the Charity are the provision of boarding and day independent education.

Rishworth School

Rishworth, West Yorkshire HX6 4QA
Tel: 01422 822217 (Main School)
Fax: 01422 820911
e-mail: admissions@rishworth-school.co.uk
website: www.rishworth-school.co.uk

Rishworth is an exceptionally friendly, caring community, in which pupils are as strongly encouraged to rejoice in each other's achievements as to take pride in their own. The School succeeds in combining a disciplined environment with a relaxed and welcoming atmosphere.

While pupils are at Rishworth, we try to ensure that, in addition to the knowledge and skills acquired through academic study, they develop:

- A love of learning and the will to succeed.
- A sense of responsibility, self-discipline, purpose and fulfilment.
- A capacity for both self-reliance and cooperation.
- An appreciation of certain personal virtues and spiritual values, such as honesty, dependability, perseverance, commitment, humility and respect for others.

Visitor: The Most Reverend The Lord Archbishop of York

Honorary Governor: A J Morsley, Esq

The Governing Body:
Dr C A G Brooks, Esq (*Chairman*)
G C W Allan, Esq
Revd Hilary Barber
M W Gledhill, Esq
Mrs C Harris
E W Mitchell, Esq (*Vice Chairman*)
Mrs A K Riley, ACA
Mrs J C Slim
J G Wheelwright, Esq
T M Wheelwright, Esq
Mrs D M Whitaker, JP
J S Whittaker, Esq

Clerk to the Board of Governors: R M Schofield, BA, FCA

Teaching Staff:
* Head of Department

Headmaster: R A Baker, MA Cantab

Deputy Headmaster: P Seery, BSc, MEd (*Chemistry*)
Director of Administration: Mrs I Shelton, BA (*Art*)
Director of Studies: S Ogden, BSc Hons (*Geography, ICT*)
Director of Marketing & Registrar: Mrs S J Stamp, BSc Hons (*Geography*)
Head of Heathfield: A M Wilkins, BA, MA

T Anderson (*Sports Coach & Sports Club Manager, Games Teacher, Heathfield*)
Mrs M T Arbelo-Dolan, BA (*Spanish*)
Mrs R Aujla, BA (*Geography*)
Miss S Beesley, BTEC (*Out of School Care Deputy Manager & Foundation Stage Key Worker, Heathfield*)
P Bell, BA, MSc (*ICT*)
Mrs B Blackburn, BA (*Part-time Foundation Stage Teacher, Heathfield*)

C P Bouckley, BEd (*Deputy Head, ICT & DT Coordinator, Heathfield*)
Mrs H Bower, BSc (*PE & Sport, Mathematics, *Sport, Heathfield*)
Mrs J Bradley, LTCL, GTCL (*Music Coordinator, Heathfield*)
Mr C Brass, BSc Hons (*Infant Class Teacher, Heathfield*)
Mrs J Bridges (*Teaching Assistant, Heathfield*)
D Bullock, BEd Hons (*Drama*)
Mrs S Chatterton, BEd Hons (*Assistant Head Curriculum, Mathematics Coordinator, Junior Class Teacher, Heathfield*)
Ms R Chatwin, BSc (*Teacher i/c Physics, Science, Mathematics, Careers Coordinator, Assistant Boarding House Mistress*)
Miss F Choudhary, BSc (*Science, Assistant Boarding House Mistress*)
Mrs T Davidson, BA Hons, LTCL (*House Mistress of Wheelwright, Drama, Psychology, EFL*)
Mrs R C Davison, BA Hons (*English*)
J Drowley, BA, MEd (*Director of Boarding, Physical Education & Sport*)
M L Dunn, BA (*ICT, Design Technology, Assistant Housemaster*)
Ms K Foster, BSc Hons (*Part-time Foundation Stage Teacher, Heathfield*)
Mrs K Fraser, BA (*Art, Press Officer, Day House Area Mistress for Hanson House Year 11*)
Mrs S P Goldsmith (*EFL*)
Mrs E Gregory, BA (*Business Studies, *Economics, History*)
Mrs J Higgins, NNEB (*Teaching Assistant, Heathfield*)
C D Holmes-Roe, BA, MA (*History, RS*)
D I Horsfall, BSc (*Mathematics*)
Mrs J Hudson, BEd (*Learning Support Coordinator, Heathfield*)
Mrs V Hutchinson, BA Hons (*Junior Class Teacher, Heathfield*)
Mrs N I'Anson, BA (*Foundation Stage Teacher, Heathfield*)
P W Jones, MA Cantab (*Science Advisor, Teacher i/c Biology, Mathematics*)
Mrs A M Kellett-End, BA, PGCLD (*Coordinator of Learning Support*)
Mrs S Kiy, BA Hons (*Junior Class Teacher, French Coordinator, Heathfield*)
Dr J Ladds, MChem, PhD, MEd (*Science, Teacher i/c Chemistry*)
C Lewis, BA Hons (*Director of Music*)
S H J McGarry, BEng, MSc (*Science, Coordinator of Assessment, Teaching and Learning*)
Mrs L Meredith, BA, ARCM (*Music, English, EFL, Teacher i/c Provision for Academically Most Able*)
Mrs S Moore, BA (*English*)
D Newby, BTech (*Design Technology, Day House Area Master for Hanson Years 9 & 10*)
Miss L B Pots, BA (*Home Economics, Art, Design Technology*)
Mrs P Pritchard (*Teaching Assistant, Out-of-School Care Manager, Heathfield*)
Mrs C E Rhodes, BA (*Psychology, Staff Mentor for Management, Teaching & Learning*)
Miss E P Robinson, BA (*Art Coordinator, Heathfield*)
P I M Robinson, BEd (*Business Studies, Head of Sixth Form, UCAS & HE Coordinator*)
Mrs K Rose, BA Hons (*Junior Class Teacher, Sports Coordinator, Heathfield*)
Ms J Sheldrick, BSc (*Biology, Home Economics, Head of Lower & Middle School*)
Mrs S P Sheppard (*Librarian*)
M E Siggins, BA (*English, Coordinator of Enhanced Sixth Form Curriculum & General Studies*)
G M Smith, BA (*Modern Languages*)

Miss H E A Stembridge, BEd Hons (*Infant Class Teacher, Section Leader Early Years, Heathfield*)

Mrs G Sunderland (*Senior Teaching Assistant, Heathfield*)

A J Thomas, BSc (*Director of Physical Education and Sport*)

Mrs J Thompson, BA (**EFL*)

Miss L Timlin, MSc (*Mathematics, Day House Area House Mistress for Years 7 & 8*)

Miss L V Turner, BA, MA (*French, EFL*)

Miss D Van-Eda, BA (*Teaching Assistant, Heathfield*)

J Western, BSc (*Mathematics*)

Mrs A M R Wilby, BA (*Junior Class Teacher, English Coordinator KS2, Heathfield*)

M Wilson, BA (**History*)

Mrs L E Wood, BSc (*Physical Education & Sport, PSHCE Coordinator*)

Instrumental Music Teachers:

Mrs R K Burbidge

Mrs B Slade

C D Wood

Miss H Bywater

P Brown

J Moate

N Darwent

Ms P Thulborn

Administrative Staff:

Bursar: R M Schofield, BA, FCA

Assistant Bursar: Mrs A C Martin, BA

Admissions Officer: Mrs D Keeble

Headmaster's PA: Mrs D Keeble

Matron: Mrs D K Robinson

General organisation. Founded in 1724, Rishworth is a co-educational day and boarding school comprising a nursery for children from age 3, a Junior School, Heathfield, which has its own separate site where children are taught up to the age of 11, and the Senior School up to age 18. Rishworth is a Church of England foundation, but welcomes children of all faiths, or of none. Numbers stand at about 550 pupils, of whom over 100 are boarders.

Facilities and Location. Superbly located in 130 acres of a beautiful Pennine valley, the School has a mix of elegant older buildings and excellent modern facilities including a capacious sports hall with fitness suite, a separate, newly-redeveloped Sports Club with 25-metre indoor swimming pool and squash courts, a large expanse of games pitches, a music block, 3 modern ICT suites, wireless (and cabled) Internet and Intranet connection across the whole site, a Performing Arts Theatre, a centre dedicated to sixth-form study, freshly-refurbished boarding houses and newly-installed, state-of-the-art science laboratories.

Access to the School by road is easy, with the M62 within five minutes' drive. School buses run to the Halifax, Todmorden, Rochdale, Oldham and Huddersfield areas.

Welfare and Pastoral. The unusually high degree of attention afforded to pupils by small teaching groups, the careful monitoring of progress, coordinated pastoral support and a close working partnership with parents enables pupils to build on their strengths and allows specific needs to be addressed. Each boarding pupil is under the direct care of a Housemaster or Housemistress, who is ably supported by assistant staff in each boarding house.

Teaching. Taught by a dedicated staff of qualified specialists, the curriculum, both academic and non-academic, is broad and stimulating, and offers every pupil the chance to be challenged and to excel. A general curriculum, broadly in line with the National Curriculum, is followed until Year 9, after which pupils select GCSE options in consultation with their parents, tutors and subject teachers. AS and A2 options are also selected via consultation.

Support is given by qualified specialists for certain special needs including dyslexia and English where this is not the pupil's first language.

Broader Education. In order to help our pupils to become the confident, balanced and considerate young men and women we wish them to be, we encourage participation in a wide range of activities outside the classroom.

Sports are well appointed and well taught, and each term boys and girls enjoy excellent results. The School also has a justly high reputation in music and drama.

Other activities range from The Duke of Edinburgh's Award to golf, skiing, and many others.

Boarding. We have no dormitories. Boarders (from age 10 or 11, and sometimes age 9) are accommodated in individual study-bedrooms, almost all single or double occupancy, which allow pupils their personal space. These are located in spacious houses, overseen by house staff. The boarding houses have recently undergone major refurbishments which have ensured that the character of the historic buildings has been retained alongside the provision of top-rate modern amenities. A full programme of activities is arranged for the evenings and weekends, and there are good recreational facilities reserved for the boarders, including dedicated social areas.

Admission. Places in the Junior School, Heathfield, are given, subject to availability, on individual assessments appropriate to each applicant's age and previous education. Entrants for Rishworth at Year 7 are asked to sit the School's own entrance assessment, which also forms the basis for the award of scholarships.

Those who wish to join the School at other stages are assessed individually.

Fees per term (from April 2011). Reception to Year 2 £1,775; Years 3 to 6 £2,605; Years 7 & 8: £3,200 day, £6,495 full boarding, £5,900 weekly boarding; Years 9 to 13: £3,480 day, £7,090 full boarding, £6,460 weekly boarding. The School operates a number of schemes, including monthly payments, to ease the financial burden on parents.

Scholarships and Bursaries. (*See Scholarship Entries section.*) A number of scholarships are given for entrance at or after Year 7 for academic, musical, drama and sporting achievement. Substantial discounts are available for siblings of pupils in the School, for children of serving members of the Armed Forces and of ordained members of the Church of England. Bursaries may also be available in cases of financial need.

The Old Rishworthian Club maintains a fund for the grant of scholarships to children of ORs.

Charitable status. Rishworth School is a Registered Charity, number 1115562. It exists to provide education for boys and girls.

The Royal School Dungannon

1 Ranfurly Road, Dungannon BT71 6AS, Northern Ireland

Tel: 028 8772 2710
Fax: 028 8775 2845 Headmaster
         028 8775 2506 Bursar
e-mail: info@rsd.dungannon.ni.sch.uk
website: www.royaldungannon.com

Founded 1608.

Motto: *Perseverando* (*Excellence through Perseverance*)

Voluntary Grammar School (GBA)

Pupils: 654. Teachers: 41 full-time and 2 part-time.

Board of Governors:

Chairman: Mrs E Harkness, BL

Vice-Chairman: H McLean, LLB, MBA

Members:
Mrs J Archer
F Bain, BSc, MCOptom
D N Browne, MIB, MIMgt
G A Cooper, OBE, BSc, CEng, FICE, FCIWEM, FIEI,
    MConsE
J C M Eddie
R Eitel
Revd A J Forster, BA, BTh
M Girvan
Mrs I T Holmes, MBE, BSc, DASE
Prof D Jones, BSc Hons, PhD, DSc, CEng, CChem,
    FIMMM, FRSS, MRSC, MIEI, MPSNI
J W Hunniford, BA, MA, PGCE
The Revd K R Kingston, MA
Prof A E Long, BSc, PhD, DSc, CEng, FICE, MISE
Miss M E Macbeth, BSc
Lord Maginnis of Drumglass, PC
Dr D J Maguire, BDS
J C McCarter, BA, DipArch, RIBA
Dr H G McNeill, BA, MB, FFARCSW
R Patton, BA
A Ritchie, BSc, PGCE
The Very Revd Dr A Rodgers, MA, DD
Dr F Shields, KM, BBS, MFGPD UK
Mrs S Stewart
Revd A S Thompson, MA, BD
A T Turner, BSc, PGCE
Mrs J Williamson
K Wright, BEd, MEd, DASE
Miss J Garvin, BA, MEd, PGCE (*Co-opted*)
R J Clingan, BSc, MEd, PGCE (*Co-opted*)

Secretary to the Governors: The Headmaster

Headmaster: D A Burnett, BA, PhD

Teaching Staff:
* *Head of Department*
¹ *Head of Year*
² *Head of House*

Deputy Head: Miss V S J Garvin, BA, PGCE, MEd
Deputy Head: R J Clingan, BSc, MEd, PGCE

Senior Teacher: *G R Black, BSc, PGCE
Senior Teacher: *M A Batchelor, BEd, LRAM, LTCL
Senior Teacher: *Miss A E Chestnutt, BSc, MEd, PGCE

Senior Resident (*Boarding*): Miss D McCombe, BSc,
    PGCE

Mrs A Best, BA, PGCE
Miss G S Boyle, BSc, PGCE
*N J Canning, BEng, PGCE
*R E Chambers, BSc, PGCE
*Mrs W Y Chambers, BSc, PGCE
*¹Mrs M E Clingan, BA, ATD
Miss B Cummins, BA, PGCE
G Ferran, BSc, MA, PGCE
¹J R Graham, BA, MSc, PGCE
Miss C J Graham, BEd
*Mrs R L Hampton, BSc, PGCE
J W Hunniford, BA, MA, PGCE
*Mrs S J Jackson, BA, PGCE
Mrs P L Johnston, BSc, PGCE
¹Mrs C L Kerr, BA, PGCE
*P S Kerr, BA, PGCE
¹G S R Lucas, BSc, PGCE
²Mrs P L Matthews, BEd, PGCE
Mrs J S McCarthy, BSc, PGCE
M McDowell, BA, MA, PGCE
*K McGuinness, BSc, PGCE
*¹Mrs P McMullan, BEd, PGCTEd
*Miss H Montgomery, BSc, PGCE
*P G Moore, MA, PGCE, GC, TEFL
Mrs M P Napier, BA, MA, DipEd, ATCL

*²K D Patton, BEd
*Ms A M Prescott, BEd, MEd
Mrs E V Stitt, BA, PGCE
*²A S Ritchie, BSc, PGCE
*²Mrs D Robb, BSc, PGCE
Miss L Robinson, BSc, PGCE
*Mrs A R Straghan, BSc Econ, PGCE
A T Turner, BSc, PGCE
¹G T Watterson, MSc, PGCE
¹Miss C A Weir, BA, MA, PGCE
J W Willis, BEd
I A Wilson, BSc, PGCE

Chaplain: Revd P Boyd, DipTh

Administrative Staff:
Bursar: Mr D Wheeler, BSc Econ, FCA
Headmaster's Secretary: Mrs A Cullen
Reception Office Supervisor: Mrs P Williamson

Matrons:
Mrs M Willis, SRN (*Day*)
Mrs P Lucas (*Evening*)
Miss M Trainor (*Day*)
Miss R Nelson (*Evening*)
Mrs L A Mullen (*Cover for Evening*)

In 1608 James I made an order in Privy Council establishing six Royal Schools in Ulster of which Dungannon became, in 1614, the first to admit pupils. In 1983 plans were first drawn up to incorporate the neighbouring girls' grammar school and to use both campuses' excellent facilities for co-educational purposes. This development came to fruition in 1986. A £9 million building and refurbishment programme began in 2000 and was completed in 2003, providing very high-tech specialist accommodation in science, technology and IT. In 2007 an international standard Astro-turf hockey pitch was completed with flood lighting and four new all-weather tennis courts were opened.

For nearly four centuries the Royal School has aimed at providing an education which enables its pupils to achieve the highest possible standards of academic excellence and at developing each pupil into a mature, well-balanced and responsible adult, well-equipped for the demands of a highly complex and technological world.

There are four Houses which foster the competitive instincts and idiosyncrasies of young people. Pastorally, each year is supervised by a Form Master or Mistress who guides his/her pupils throughout the child's career in a caring school environment.

There is modern accommodation for 46 Boarders with boarding staff of nine teachers and five matrons. Girls and Boys are housed in separate wings of the modernised Old School building dating from 1789. The establishment of good study skills and practices is considered to be of crucial importance. The size of the School ensures that no child is overlooked in any way.

The extensive buildings are a mixture of ancient and modern, with recently opened technology and science accommodation. In the late 1980s a half million pound renovation provided new careers, music and girls' boarding facilities.

Eight well-equipped Science Laboratories, Audio/Visual Room, two Libraries, Sixth Form Centre and Study Rooms, Technology, two Music and Art Studios and two Information Technology Suites are supplemented by a Boarding Department housed in well-appointed accommodation. Boarders are able to make use of a wide range of facilities such as Sports Hall, Computer Laboratory, Multi-gym, Badminton Courts, Television Lounges and nearby facilities such as the local swimming pool and extensive parkland walks. Situated in its own spacious grounds in a quiet residential area of this rural town, the School is linked directly by motorway to Belfast (40 minutes), two airports, cross-Channel ferries and railway stations.

At A Level new subjects are offered such as Economics, Computing, Art and Food Technology; and in collaboration with partner schools, Media Studies, Psychology and Business Studies.

Pupils are prepared for GCSE and A Levels under all the major UK Examination Boards and there is a tradition of Oxbridge successes as well as a high rate of entry to the University of Ulster, Queen's University Belfast and other leading British Universities. In most years over 90% of the Upper Sixth Form proceed into Higher Education. Many of the School's overseas students have chosen to enrol at the Province's two Universities, such is their affection for Northern Ireland.

Apart from five nursing Matrons, the School is medically attended to by a team of doctors and dentists which gives Boarders first priority in calls. A major hospital is less than 30 minutes from the campus. Many co-curricular pursuits are encouraged during lunchtime or after school, such as Choir, Orchestra, Duke of Edinburgh's Award Scheme, Chess, Photography, Debating, Public Speaking and many more.

Alongside the School's academic achievements in both Arts and Sciences may be placed its record in the sporting world: in Rugby, Hockey, Cricket, Badminton, Shooting, Table Tennis and Tennis.

Fees per annum (2011-2012). Day: £135. Boarding: £12,835 (non-EC passport holders), £7,335 (EC passport holders).

Charitable status. The Royal School Dungannon is a Registered Charity, number XN46588 A. It was established by Royal Charter in 1608 for the purpose of education.

The Royal Wolverhampton School

Penn Road, Wolverhampton WV3 0EG
Tel: 01902 341230
Fax: 01902 344496
e-mail: mo@royal.wolverhampton.sch.uk
website: www.theroyalschool.co.uk

Motto: *Nisi Dominus Frustra.*

Patron:
His Royal Highnesss, The Earl of Wessex, KG, KCVO

Vice-Patrons:
The Countess of Lichfield
The Duke of Sutherland

Board of Governors:
P Hill, Esq, FCMA, MIMC (*Chairman*)
D Swift, Esq, BEd (*Vice-Chairman*)
R H Etheridge, Esq
P H Freeth, Esq, ACIB
P Gough, Esq, FRICS
Alderman R Hart
H V Hilton, Esq, LLB, ACIS
Mrs J Lawson, BA, ACIB
B Maybee, Esq, MA Oxon, JP
A T Sharp, Esq
Mrs B J Dixon
Prof S Chung, JP, FCIB, MRICS, FB Eng, FASI, MSc Dip Man
Mrs E P Hudson, LLB
A Rashid, Esq, JP, MA, MPhil
Dr S Suresh, BSc Eng, ME, PhD
D Jukes

Headmaster: **M Heywood**, BA, PGCE

Deputy Head (*Academic/Administrative*): Mrs D Bason, BEd, CertEd

Administrator, Clerk to the Governors and Secretary to the Foundation: D R Penn, BSc
Boarding Coordinator: D P Ireland, BEng Hons, PGCE
Lichfield House Parent: Mrs M Johanesen, BA Hons
Dartmouth Housemaster: M Taylor, BA Hons
Rogers Housemistress: Mrs R Ingerfield-Lapsley, BA Hons, PGCE
York House Parent: Mrs N Zhang

Senior School Staff:

Arts, Craft, Design & Technology:
M Allison, BA Hons, PGCE, BTec National Diploma (*Head of Art*)
P E Holliday, BEd (*Head of Design and Technology*)
Miss A M Atherton, BA, PGCE (*Head of Food Technology*)
Mrs L Fabre, BA Hons, PGCE

Business Studies:
C J Walker, BSc Hons, PGCE (*Head of Key Stage 3; Head of Business Studies*)
Ms J Tate, BA Hons, HND, MAAT, PGCE

English:
D P Boag-Munroe, CertEd, BA (*Head of English*)
Mrs A O'Grady, BA Hons

Geography:
Miss C Cadwallader, MSc, BSc (*Head of Geography, Head of Sixth Form*)

History:
M G White, CertEd (*Head of History & Religious Studies*)

Information Technology:
R Watkins, BSc Hons, PGCE (*Head of Information Technology*)
C Wilke-Zhang, BSc Hons, DIP

Mathematics:
A Long (*Head of Mathematics*)
D Ireland, BEng Hons, PGCE (*Boarding Coordinator*)
W Duckworth, BSc Hons, GTTP
Mrs D Bason, BEd, CertEd (*Deputy Head*)

Modern Languages:
Mrs A Goodlad, BA Hons, PGCE (*Head of Modern Languages*)
Mrs R Boden, BA Hons, PGCE

Physical Education:
G W Beckett, BSc Hons, PGCE, FIST, AISC (*Head of PE*)
Mrs R L Ingerfield-Lapsley, BA Hons, PGCE (*Head of Girls PE; Head of PSCHE/Careers, Rogers Housemistress*)
Miss A M Atherton, BA, PGCE
M Taylor, BA Hons (*Dartmouth Housemaster*)

Psychology/Sociology:
Miss C Martin, BSc, MSc (*Head of Psychology & Sociology*)

Science:
R C Bissell, BSc, PGCE (*Head of Science*)
Miss H Prosser, BSc, PGCE
Dr W Chhabra, MPhil, BSc, MSc, BA Ed
R Beardsmore, BSc Hons, PGCE
Mrs S Tappin, CChem, MRSC (*Laboratory Assistant*)

TEFL:
Miss J L Kyle, BA, PGCE

Junior School Staff:
R Alder, BA Hons, PGCE (*Year 4 Teacher*)
Mrs Cartwright, NVQ3 (*Pre-Prep Teaching Assistant*)
Mrs S Friday, BTEC (*Pre-Prep Teaching Assistant*)
Mrs Fox-Sipos, BEd, PGCE (*Year 5 Teacher*)
Miss C Galbraith, BA, PGCE (*Year 3 Teacher*)
Miss J Hall, BTEC, NVQ3, Cert EYP (*Year 2 Assistant*)

Mrs K Harris, BA Hons, PGCE (*Reception Teacher*)
Mrs J Higgins, NCFE Cert (*Year 3-4 Assistant*)
Mrs J Hocknull, BEd Hons, CertSpLd (*Special Educational Needs Coordinator*)
Mrs C Ireland, BA Hons, PGCE (*Teacher in charge of Junior School*)
Miss E Jackson, DCE Cert EYP (*Year 1 Assistant*)
Mrs K Jefferson, BEd Hons (*Year 2 Teacher, Head of Junior Library*)
Mrs K Newton, BA Hons, HBO Hons, PGCE (*Year 1 Teacher, Key Stage 1 Coordinator*)

Nursery:
Mrs S Lawrence, NNEB (*Head of Nursery*)
Mrs J Cooper, BTEC (*Nursery Nurse, Deputy SENCO*)
Mrs P Brannan (*Assistant*)
Miss L Butters, NVQ3 (*Nursery Nurse*)
Miss S Colley, BTEC (*Nursery Nurse*)
Mrs P Davies, NNEB (*Nursery Nurse*)
Mrs S Edwards, BTEC, FD (*Nursery Nurse*)
Miss L Fletcher, BTEC (*Nursery Nurse*)
Ms L Franklin, NVQ3 (*Nursery Nurse*)
Miss Z Hands, CACHE Level 3, CCLD Level 4 (*Nursery Nurse*)
Mrs D McKenzie, NVQ2 (*Assistant*)
Miss K Oram, BTEC 3 (*Nursery Nurse*)
Mrs S Page (*Assistant*)
Miss S Williamson (*Nursery Nurse*)
Miss R Woolley, NVQ3 (*Nursery Nurse*)
Mrs E Wood, BTEC EYP Open (*Nursery Nurse*)
Miss A Wylde BTEC EYP (*Nursery Nurse*)

Music Staff:
I Hackett, BMus Hons, PGCE (*Director of Music; Head of Key Stage 4*)
Mrs S Taylor, BA Hons, PGCE

Visiting Music Staff:
Miss C L Appleby, MA, BMus Hons (*Woodwind*)
N Aston, BMus Hons, Post Dip (*Woodwind*)
Mrs J Davis, LCM Hons (*Keyboard/London College of Music Rep*)
Miss A Finch, BMus, PG Dip (*Strings*)
Miss R Lakeland, CertEd, ALCM (*Singing/Harp*)
Mrs M Morton, GRSM, ARCM, LRAM, PGCE
B Perkins, ABSM (*Guitar*)
S Read, LGSM, ARCM, CertEd (*Brass*)
S Terry (*Keyboard/Drums*)
G Walker, BA Hons, ARCO, FRSA (*Piano*)

Administrative Staff:
Registrar: Mrs M Orton
Secretary to the Headmaster: Mrs J Edwards
Secretary to the Administrator: Mrs N Warmer/Mrs K Marsden
Junior School Secretary: Mrs A P Jackson
Administration Office Manager: Mrs D Hall, MAAT
Secretary: Miss J Chan, BA Hons, MA
Secretary: Ms K Hill
School Fees: Mrs M Wilkinson
Accounts Assistant: Mrs K Bastable
Receptionist: Mrs R Rollason
Resource Centre Manager: G Davies, BSc Econ
Head of International Office: Mrs L Penn

Medical Staff:
Dr D DeRosa, BSc, MB, CLB, MRCGP
Mrs C Dinham, RGN, RSCN
Mrs M Hadley, RGN
Mrs H Burrell, RGN

Estates Supervisor: D Brittain
Catering Manager: C Cooke

The Royal Wolverhampton School occupies a 28-acre site in a pleasant residential area to the west of Wolverhampton and provides an education for boys and girls aged 6 weeks to 19 years. The Royal Wolverhampton Junior School and The Young Royals' Nursery has approximately 200 pupils and the Senior School 250 pupils. Pupils can attend on a daily basis or as weekly, full or flexi boarders. The School can accommodate 170 boarders,from aged 10 years upwards.

Founded in 1850, the School is celebrating its 161st anniversary in 2011. The School was granted a Royal Charter by Queen Victoria in 1891. HRH The Earl of Wessex is our current Patron.

Facilities. The School has been transformed since its days as an orphanage and the elegant ivy-clad main school building has been continually updated and augmented with a number of substantial modern developments. Over the past ten years, the School has spent over £10 million on improvements to the buildings and equipment. Today, it offers tradition combined with modern facilities, including a brand new swimming pool and sports complex, a new sixth form centre and internet café, an art, craft and design centre, dining room and kitchens, a library, modern boarding houses, 5 refurbished science laboratories, 3 information technology suites and a floodlit astroturf. The most recent addition is the Baby Unit, opened in September 2010, which increased the Early Years Provision to a maximum of 135 children.

The School's boarding accommodation houses boys and girls separately according to their age. Younger children share with 2 or 3 others of the same age and pupils in the Sixth Form either have a single study-bedroom or a twin room. All boarding houses have a lounge as well as a kitchen and a launderette. Pupils are carefully supervised by the School's residential staff at all times. In the January 2009 Ofsted Boarding Inspection Report, the boarding provision was classified as "good" overall and "outstanding" in the category "Helping children achieve well and enjoy what they do".

The School's own catering staff serves a variety of meals to suit all tastes. A cooked lunch is provided for day pupils and boarders can enjoy breakfast, lunch and dinner. Special dietary requirements, for religious or medical reasons, can be accommodated.

Religion. The Royal Wolverhampton School has its own Chapel within the School grounds. This fine building forms a focus for School life, with daily assemblies and important events in the School calendar being held there. Although the School has a religious affiliation to the Church of England, it welcomes pupils of all religions. Staff will assist pupils of other religions in pursuing their beliefs during their stay at the School.

Pastoral Care. The well-being of all pupils in the School is of prime importance and pastoral care is a universally recognised strength. Both day and boarding pupils are allocated to "houses" under the guidance of a housemaster or housemistress. All pupils have a tutor responsible for overseeing their pastoral and academic welfare, although all staff are expected to take corporate responsibility for pupil welfare and pupils are entitled to consult any member of staff regarding matters of concern.

In case of illness, the School has a fully equipped sanatorium, which provides 24 hour healthcare.

Transport Links. The Royal Wolverhampton School is easily accessible by road, train and air. The school can arrange transfers from all major UK airports including Manchester, Birmingham, Heathrow and Gatwick. A daily school transport service is organised for pupils locally.

Curriculum. Use of IT is integral to the curriculum from Reception onwards. The Senior School is moving towards conducting the majority of its pupil work and reporting via a virtual learning environment.

The School offers a broad education at all levels, which is based on the National Curriculum. Recent additions to the curriculum include: French in the Nursery; Mandarin in Years 7 to 9; Sociology at GCSE; Psychology, Sociology and Photography at A Level; Photography and Electronics at AS

Level. Pupils in Year 10 study five compulsory subjects (English and English Literature, Mathematics, ICT and the Sciences) plus four optional subjects, out of a total of sixteen. Pupils of higher ability may take separate Sciences and additional Mathematics, both taught within the standard timetable. At the end of Year 11 all pupils take GCSE examinations.

At A Level students are advised on the quantity and type of subjects they should choose, bearing in mind their proposed university course and career. Twenty-two different A Level courses are available. The School has strength in a variety of areas and on six recent occasions pupils have finished in the top five in the UK in one of their A Level subjects.

Sixth Form. The School prides itself on the great care it takes in advising Sixth Form students on careers and universities. The School has direct links with many universities and students have the opportunity to discuss various options with representatives from Higher and Further Education. It is common for 100% of those students who wish to go to university to secure a place at the institution of their preferred choice.

In addition to the School's other facilities, which can be used by all pupils, Sixth Form pupils have their own study area, Sixth Form Centre and Internet Café where they can meet, study and relax.

Music and Drama. The School has an excellent reputation for its musical standards and is a recognised examination centre for the London College of Music. Our active Music Department, equipped with the latest technology, provides pupils with an opportunity to learn how to play 20 different instruments. In addition, pupils are encouraged to take part in the School's choir and to perform in a wide variety of events, including at the National Indoor Arena in Birmingham.

The Music Department organises regular Performing Arts festivals at which pupils of all ages perform. One of the highlights of the School calendar is the Variety Show, which presents the best of the School's dramatic and musical talents to parents and other guests.

The School supports the Mayor of Wolverhampton by providing musical evenings in order to raise money for the Mayor's charities.

Sport and Extra-Curricular Activities. The School aims to educate well-rounded individuals and a wide variety of extra-curricular activities are enjoyed by all pupils.

Pupils can choose from fifteen different sports and matches are frequently arranged both inter-house and against local schools. The School has a strong basketball team which has achieved major successes nationally.

The School launched an Elite Swimming Programme in conjunction with West Midlands Swimming and Sport England in September 2009. The Squad has already achieved Youth Olympic, European Junior and National success in the short time it has been open.

The School has a very strong Combined Cadet Force with Army and RAF sections. The shooting team has finished in the top ten in the UK in the RAF Assegai shooting competition for seven years in succession and regularly wins trophies in Army "March and Shoot" competitions. Pupils are also given the opportunity to participate in the successful Duke of Edinburgh's Award Scheme and various other community projects.

The School ethos promotes compassion towards those less fortunate than ourselves and considerable amounts of money are raised for local and national charities.

Entrance. The Senior School holds two entrance examinations each year for entry to Year 7, one in November and one in March. The minimum entry requirement for Sixth Form is five GCSE passes at Grade C or equivalent.

Entry to the Nursery and Baby Unit is throughout the year and entry to the Junior School usually takes place each September. Limited access is available at other time during the year by assessment.

Scholarships and Bursaries. (*See Scholarship Entries section.*) Scholarships may be offered to the pupils achieving the best grades in the entrance examinations. Sixth Form Scholarships are also available. The School awards a limited number of Music and Sports scholarships each year.

In addition the School can offer support via its Bursary Scheme. Foundation places are available for pupils facing difficult family circumstances and who fulfil the Foundation's criteria.

Fees per term (2011-2012). Senior School: Full Boarders £6,075–£8,540; Weekly Boarders £5,700–£6,865; Day Pupils £3,125–£3,985. Junior School: Boarders £5,900; Day Pupils £2,590–£3,245. Nursery £2,040–£2,240. Baby Unit £3,280. (Prompt payment discount available.)

Day fees include: lunch, textbooks, stationery, compulsory teaching materials and personal accident insurance cover. In addition to the above, boarding fees include: full board accommodation, laundry, dry cleaning, medical attention and nursing in the Sanatorium.

Boarding Fees include all meals, medical attention and nursing in the Sanatorium, text books, stationery and compulsory teaching materials. The fees also include the costs of any English as a Foreign Language (EFL) tuition that takes place during the lesson timetable for all students in years 10 and 11. If the Headmaster feels an individual student may require extra EFL tuition, this will be charged at £250 a term for each block of additional tuition. No charges for extra tuition will be made without parental agreement.

Day Fees include all text books, stationery and compulsory teaching materials. Junior School fees include lunch. Senior School lunches are a chargeable extra. Parents may choose one of the following options: (a) pre-pay for lunch by adding the sum of £132 to their fee invoice (this works out at approximately £2.20 a day for a two-course meal); (b) pay daily for their meals. There is a minimum charge of £2.75 a day which is payable in cash at the point of service.

The children of Serving Personnel in the Armed Forces receive a Bursary of £1,500 per term. The children of Old Royals receive a reduction of 25% off the basic fees and discounts are also available for siblings.

Old Royals' Association. The Association regularly organises reunions for former pupils. Founders' Day in June and Remembrance Sunday are also popular times for Old Royals and Old Rowans to return to the School. For further information, please contact Mr Mike Masters, 139 High Street, Coleshill, Birmingham B46 3AY; Tel: 01675 463093; e-mail: mike_masters@talk21.com.

Charitable status. The Royal Wolverhampton School is a Registered Charity, number 1092221. It exists solely to provide an education for children.

Ruthin School

Ruthin, Denbighshire LL15 1EE
Tel: 01824 702543
Fax: 01824 707141
e-mail: registrar@ruthinschool.co.uk
website: www.ruthinschool.co.uk

The School was originally founded in 1284. Refounded in 1574 by Gabriel Goodman, Dean of Westminster, the School was a centre of academic excellence in North Wales, and was granted a Royal Charter.

Motto: *Dei gratia sum quod sum*

Visitor: Her Majesty The Queen

Patron: Sir William Gladstone, Bt, KG, MA

Council of Management:
Chairman: J P Williams
A R Bale
Mrs T Kerrigan
Mrs J Oldbury
R N E Raven, JP, MA, MBE
J E Sharples
His Honour Judge I J C Trigger
Mrs S Willan, OBE

Principal: **T J Belfield**, MA Cantab

Head of School: I Welsby, BSc, MIBiol, PGCE, DipEd
Head of Pastoral Care: Ms J K Higham, MA, PGCE, CPE
Senior Housemistress: Ms S Morley, BEd

Assistant Staff:
N J R Blandford, BA, MA, PGCE
Mrs E T Brodzinska, LLB, MA, ELCOS
Mrs R Crowther, BA, PGCE
P J French, BSc, PGCE
Miss K A Goodey, MEd, TESOL, BEd, CETFLA
Dr G H Green, PhD
Dr M D Hannant, PhD, PGCE
J R Henry, BA, PGCE
D J Heywood, BA, PGCE
Mrs M Kenworthy, BSc, PGCE
Mrs T L Owen, BSc, PGCE
D A Owen Booth, BEd
I M Rimmer, BSc, PGCE
O Sammons, BMus, PGCE
Mrs E M Thomas, BA, PGCE, TEFL, AMBDA
Miss L Zhao, BA, PGCE

Visiting:
Mrs J Aldridge (*Violin*)
Mrs P Almond, CertEd (*Special Learning*)
Mrs G Bolton, GMus RNCM (*Piano*)
M Hamilton (*Guitar*)
M H L Hewer, MA Oxon, DipEd (*EAL*)
D Hughes (*Clarinet*)

Registrar and PA to the Principal: Mrs E L Eccles
Finance Administrator: Mrs L Evans
School Medical Officer: Dr G H Roberts
School Nurse: Mrs C Bland, RGN

The School. Ruthin School is co-educational with some 200 pupils in the School comprising 110 boarders and 90 day pupils. The emphasis is on academic excellence and providing an environment to gain our students entry to the very best universities in the UK and USA. Good manners, personal discipline and respect for others are of supreme importance, as is a thorough grounding in central subjects of the curriculum. We believe that social responsibility can be developed in a small community with a family atmosphere, comprising a wide range of academic and other talents. This is reflected in our entry policy. Ruthin School is committed to providing an education of the highest quality, endeavouring to develop the potential of all its pupils in all spheres of education. The pupils develop self-confidence through recognising and building upon their strengths as well as identifying and striving to improve their weaknesses. They are thus prepared to face the challenges of the changing world beyond school.

Organisation. Places (both day and full boarding) are offered to boys and girls from the age of 11.

The three boarding houses – Gladstone, Ellis and Wynne – have their own House system under the guidance of resident Housemasters.

Admission. The normal method of entry to the School is by interview, examination and reports.

Activities. A wide range of non-curricular activities is provided and has included car maintenance, fitness training, basketball, swimming, yoga, judo, TaeKwonDo, drama, rock climbing, sailing and canoeing, mountain biking, stage man-

agement, shooting, weight training, table tennis, badminton, conservation, gardening and tennis. Boys and girls are encouraged to participate in the Duke of Edinburgh's Award Scheme at the age of 14 until they have completed the Bronze Award; several go on to complete the Silver and a few aspire to the Gold Awards. A lively mix of traditional and contemporary musical and dramatic productions is a feature of the school year and half the pupils receive individual instrumental tuition from the professional music staff. A programme of excursions is organised for boarders in the evenings and at weekends and these are open to all pupils.

Bursaries and Awards. In addition to academic awards, remissions are available for siblings, children of members of the armed forces, and of Old Ruthinians.

Curriculum. A wide curriculum is offered and includes English, Mathematics, History, Geography, separate Biology, Physics and Chemistry, Art, Music, Design Technology, French, Mandarin and Spanish. PE and Business Studies are added at GCSE Level. Law and Economics are added at AS Level. Further Mathematics is taught in the Sixth Form.

An option scheme operates for Form 4, but English, Mathematics, Biology and Geography are compulsory. The BTEC in Public Service has been added as an option through the CCF.

Careers. Guidance begins in the Senior School and a comprehensive programme evolves through Forms 4 and 5 and the whole of the Lower Sixth is devoted to research and visits before university applications are made. All members of the Sixth Form who wish to enter university are successful. Work experience is undertaken in Form 4 and the Lower Sixth.

CCF. Pupils join either the Army or the RN Section at the end of their second year in the Senior School and may opt to continue membership in the Sixth Form. There are opportunities to attend courses and camps.

Games. Rugby, basketball, football, cross-country, netball, tennis and athletics all feature in the coaching programme. A new Sports Hall was opened in January 2004.

Fees per annum (2011-2012). Day £8,250–£11,750; Boarding £21,500. Fees are payable twice yearly, at beginning of August and February. British parents have the option to pay monthly by Direct Debit.

Transport. The School provides daily transport to and from the North Wales coast, Holywell and Mold. Transport is provided for boarders from Manchester and Liverpool airports to the School, at the beginning and end of each term.

Ruthin School Association. This parents' association of which all parents are members is very active and plays an important supportive role in the School community.

The Old Ruthinian Association fosters close links between past and present pupils of the School.

Charitable status. Ruthin School is a Registered Charity, number 525754. It exists to provide education for boys and girls.

Saint Augustine's Priory School

Hillcrest Road, Ealing, London W5 2JL
Tel: 020 8997 2022
Fax: 020 8810 6501
e-mail: registrar@staugustinespriory.org.uk
website: www.saintaugustinespriory.org.uk

Motto: '*Veritas*'

Chair of Governors: Professor Anne Hemingway, BSc, MBBS, FRCR, FRCP

Headmistress: **Mrs F J Gumley-Mason**, MA Cantab

Deputy Head Emeritus (*Examinations Officer*): Mr M J Strahan, BSc

Deputy Head (Curriculum & Compliance): Mr T Guilford, BA, Dip Fil
Deputy Head (Religious Life and Learning Environment): Mr D Walshe, BA
Junior Department Magistra: Mrs M Winslett, MA
EYFS Magistra: Miss E Keane, BA
School Bursar: Mr S F T Waas, BA

Heads of Subject Departments:
Art: Mrs B Maw, MEd
Biology: Dr J Wilson, PhD, BSc
Chemistry: Mr F Gaffney, MSc, MRSC (*Health and Safety Coordinator*)
Classics: Dr G Carleton, MA, PhD
Drama: Ms F Hagerty, BA, Dip LAMDA
English: Dr G Gill, MA, PhD (*Director of Sixth Form, Academic*)
Geography: Mrs C Wilson, BA
History: Miss P Trybuchowska, MA Oxon
IT: Mr S Gitlin, BSc
Mathematics: Mr S Bale, BSc
Modern Languages: Miss A Gandi, MA
Director of Music: Mr K Allen, BA, GRSM, LRAM, LTCI
Physical Education: Mrs M Bamford, BA
Physics: Mrs S Sampson, MSc (*Director of Sixth Form, Pastoral*)
Religious Studies: Mrs L McDermott, BA
Social Sciences: Mr P Murphy, BSc, MEd (*Director of Sixth Form, UCAS*)

Teaching Staff:
Miss L Akers, BSc (*Physical Education*)
Ms F Assemat, MA (*Modern Foreign Languages*)
Mrs A Bailey, BA (*English*)
Mrs J Bennet, MA Oxon (*Mathematics, SENCO*)
Mrs C Costello, BEd (*Prep Department*)
Mr D F Costello, BA (*Classics*)
Mr S Daughton, BA (*History*)
Mrs J Day, BEd (*Nursery*)
Ms M Dolan, BA (*Geography*)
Mr N Elder, BA (*English*)
Miss A Gambrill, BEd (*Junior Department*)
Miss F Gaynor, MSc (*Junior Department*)
Miss T Gibbs, BA (*RS*)
Mrs L Harley, BSc (*Biology*)
Ms G Hayden, MSc (*Science*)
Mr S Hullis, MA Oxon (*Classics*)
Mrs M Humphreys, BEd (*Junior Department*)
Miss E Jackson, BA, BTEC (*Nursery*)
Ms F Johnson, MA, ALCM (*Music*)
Mr M Khan, MSc (*Economics and Business Studies*)
Mrs T Lakomy, BSc (*Mathematics*)
Mrs P M Lyons, CertEd (*Art*)
Miss R MacDonald, BA (*Prep Department*)
Mrs K Madden-Crowe, BEd (*Junior Department*)
Dr I Maryniak, MA Cantab, PhD (*Russian*)
Mr M Maryniak, MSc, RSA Dip ALCM (*Music*)
Mrs P Mortimer, BEd (*Deputy Junior Department Magistra*)
Mrs B Ogley, BEd (*Junior Department*)
Mrs H Round, BA (*Junior Department*)
Mrs E Strahan, CertEd (*Junior Department*)
Mrs G Taher, BSc (*Psychology*)
Mr J Tizard, BSc (*Mathematics*)
Mrs N Drury, NNEB (*Nursery Assistant*)
Miss I Halton, NNEB (*Class Assistant*)
Mrs L Lubowiecka, Mont Dip (*Class Assistant*)
Mrs P O'Connell, DPP (*Class Assistant*)
Mrs L Sinton, NNEB (*Class Assistant*)
Mrs C Young, Mont Cert (*Class Assistant*)

Technicians:
Mrs J Kelly, HND, AIMS (*Sciences*)
Miss M Pobocha, MSc (*Sciences*)
Mrs L Yang, MSc (*IT*)

Administration:
Mrs C Cox, BSc Econ (*Display Coordinator*)
Mrs F Donovan (*Secretary for Juniors*)
Mrs J Hague (*PA to the Headmistress*)
Mrs F Jabra (*Almoner*)
Ms M King, BA (*Secretary for Seniors*)
Mrs J Lanek (*Domestic*)
Mrs M McPartlin (*Administration*)
Mrs J Reilly (*Bursar's Assistant*)
Mrs T Sumpter, RN (*School Nurse*)

Estate Staff:
Mr D Bamford (*Deputy Estate Factor*)
Mr A S Mason, BA (*Estate Factor*)
Mr C Mortimer, BSc (*Deputy Estate Factor*)
Mr I Smith (*Warden*)

St Augustine's Priory was founded in France in 1634 by Lady Mary Tredway to provide a haven where young English women could be provided with an Independent Education. Moving to Ealing in 1914–15, at its current location, the School follows the philosophy expounded by its Patron, St Augustine of Hippo, and known to every parent that is that children (and for that matter adults) achieve their best when they are happy. Pressurising girls yields very short term dividends. Our excellent results are achieved by stimulating the girls and passing on to them a joy in learning. This is far more effective and indeed much more fun for the teachers.

The School's success is firmly rooted in its readiness to adapt to change while retaining its unique identity and, by adhering to these ideals, we provide our girls with those skills which will enable them to face the future with confidence.

Our academic achievement is only part of our success.

The School has been in existence since 1634, so it is fair to say that St Augustine's knows how to educate girls.

Additional information may be found on the school's website and a more detailed prospectus may be obtained from the School.

Number of Pupils. There are approximately 500 girls aged from 4–18 (80 in the Sixth Form).

Location. The School is well served by public transport, with Hanger Lane, North Ealing and Park Royal Underground stations all within a ten minute stroll and Ealing Broadway Underground and main line station approximately 20 minutes' walk away. The School sits on top of Hanger Hill in an idyllic setting of thirteen acres, with views across to the South Downs. Buses stop near the entrance.

Admission. St Augustine's Priory is a unique and vibrant community, and the best way to understand it is to come and look around the school and importantly to meet our pupils, Headmistress and staff. During the application process we invite Parents to visit us at a series of Open Mornings during the Michaelmas Term. Admission to the Preps is via interview in the Michaelmas Term. Girls from St Augustine's Junior Department transfer automatically into the Senior School. The external candidates, typically about 100 for the 24 places available, sit the Entrance Examination in January. About 40 of these candidates are then called for interview with offers made based on personality and an assessment of what the girl and her family want from the school and can offer to it. We hold an Open Afternoon for prospective Sixth Formers and their parents during the Michaelmas Term, which is followed up by a Taster Day. The Taster Day allows prospective Augustinians to experience a day in the life of our School and get a feel for how they would fit in. Interviews are then conducted by the appropriate Heads of Department along with the Headmistress, and offers are sent out with conditional GCSE pass requirements. Occasionally places arise in other years. Once a completed Application Form is received, your daughter's name will be placed on the Applications Register appropriate for her age, and will be considered should a vacancy arise.

Religion. St Augustine's Priory is a Catholic Independent Day School for Girls. The Chapel is at the heart of school life and is used for daily assemblies, weekly Masses and as a place for moments of quiet reflection and prayer. Whilst most students are Catholic, we welcome girls from other religions and faiths and learn from them.

Pastoral Care. Children from all backgrounds and all races, with a wide range of gifts, make up the vibrant community which is St Augustine's. From their first day, girls become part of a family which respects the beliefs and customs of its members and learns to work together. When problems arise and questions need to be asked, we encourage a very personal approach. The Form Mistress has a special relationship with pupils, looking after their day-to-day needs and encouraging them to get the very best out of their time at school. It is to the Form Mistress that pupils and parents can look in the first instance for help and guidance.

Curriculum. We offer an extensive and balanced curriculum including PSHE, and offer 20 subjects at GCSE and 23 subjects at AS and A2 Level. Girls can take French and Spanish in Year 9 and Latin GCSE in Year 10, enabling them to pursue AS Level in these subjects pre Sixth Form. Girls are expected to take ten or more subjects at GCSE.

The Sixth Form and Careers. The Sixth Form facilities include a common room, kitchen and balcony overlooking the South Downs. The Head Girl and Deputy Head girls have their own offices.

Sixth Form students have the chance to take part in a range of additional activities to try out new sports or skills and meet people from other schools. Students also take part in a two-week work experience placement, when they are seconded to a variety of organisations, institutions and businesses to gain a practical insight into employment and areas of interest for future study.

We encourage girls to think about their next step and to make informed decisions at every stage of their development. The Sixth Form is supported by the Careers and UCAS Advisory Department providing advice and guidance. The Department works with the students to consider their many future options, assisting with university and course selection, preparation for Oxbridge and other university applications and subsequent interviews. This process is supplemented by an annual Careers Conference with guest speakers, mentors and experts in key fields invited in to speak and to offer advice and insight.

Working with the Directors of Sixth Form, every girl is encouraged to examine her own strengths and to explore possibilities suitable for her interests and personal abilities. Talks, conferences, seminars and courses, a visit to a Careers Fair and University Open Days, career profiling, as well as a well-stocked, up-to-date Careers library and the Internet, allow all our students to keep abreast of opportunities on offer.

All of this support builds on the guidance received throughout the school. When our girls leave here for university, they take with them not only impressive qualifications but also kindness, an understanding of, and the ability to adapt to, the world in which they live, the confidence to succeed in whatever they choose to do and above all, friendships which will last them through life.

Extra-Curricular Activities. Apart from Physical Education in the curriculum, the school also excels in its extremely popular after-school sports activities fielding winning teams in hockey, netball, swimming and cross country. Tennis, karate, football, ballet and gymnastics are all catered for after school.

Whilst Drama forms a part of the curriculum and is very strong here at St Augustine's we also stage an annual major production in the Spring which allows involvement by the whole Senior School.

Music is a particular strength with girls from Prep III to the Sixth Form being given the opportunity and encouragement to take any instrument they choose, from violin, cello and flute to harp, drums and guitar. If a girl is interested in a particular instrument we will try to find a teacher for her. As a result music flourishes throughout the school with girls taking part in lunchtime and after-school orchestras, music groups and choirs, and music tours abroad.

The Art is outstanding with the girls' work displayed throughout the school. An annual Art Exhibition is held each summer, and the department makes use of visits to the many theatres, museums and galleries in London.

The School is licensed as a Centre for The Duke of Edinburgh's Bronze, Silver and Gold Awards. Trips to Nepal, Borneo and China are recent examples of the girls' visits into the far flung reaches of the world with skiing trips for Juniors and Seniors, French student visits and Husky Sledging in Norway forming the basis of our recent European travels.

The School is no stranger to visits from Nasa rockets, military helicopters and rocket simulators. Augustinians learn to expect the unexpected.

Facilities. St Augustine's Priory offers superb amenities including a full-size floodlit all-weather astroturf pitch and floodlit competition-sized netball court set in stunning 13-acre grounds.

In addition to sporting facilities, our 13 acres include a dedicated Prep meadow, orchards, Sixth Form rose garden and croquet lawn. The brand new state-of-the-art Science Wing opened in 2007 with four laboratories and dedicated Senior and Junior music and drama rooms. A new Nursery block was completed in March 2011. To compliment this there are two IT suites, separate senior and junior libraries, music practise rooms, Senior and Junior Art rooms, a Sixth Form Art studio, Fifth Form Academy, dedicated Sixth Form areas and private studies, and Scriptorium. Kitchens are on site and the in-house Chef and catering staff serve fresh cooked lunches daily.

Fees per term (2011-2012). Preparatory Department £2,700, Junior Department £3,110, Senior Department £3,730.

Charitable status. St Augustine's Priory School Limited is a Registered Charity, number 1097781.

St Christopher School

Barrington Road, Letchworth Garden City, Herts SG6 3JZ
Tel: 01462 650850
Fax: 01462 481578
e-mail: school.admin@stchris.co.uk
          admissions@stchris.co.uk
website: www.stchris.co.uk

Fully co-educational from its foundation in 1915, St Christopher has always been noted for its friendly informality, breadth of educational vision, good academic standards and success in developing lifelong self-confidence. There are now some 516 pupils from rising 3 to 18. Boarders can start from age 11. There are full and weekly boarders. We aim for our young people to develop competence and resourcefulness, social conscience and moral courage, a capacity for friendship and a true zest for life.

The School was founded in Letchworth's infant Garden City by the Theosophical Educational Trust, whose object was to support schools 'where members of different faiths shall be encouraged to mix together and in this way learn a respect and tolerance for ideas other than their own'. The School in its present form developed under the Quakers, Lyn and Eleanor Harris and their son Nicholas from 1925 to 1980, and the same continuity of purpose was sustained by Colin Reid who retired in 2004. The School is now an educational charity conducted by a Board of Governors, all of whom have a close knowledge of the School.

Board of Governors:
Vernon McClure (*Chairman*)
Peter de Voil (*Vice-Chairman*)
William Armitage
Peter McMeekin
Meher Pocha
Veronica Raymond
Tom Routh
Helen Szirtes

Head: Richard Palmer, BEd, FRSA

Deputy Head: Emma-Kate Henry, BA
Director of Pastoral Care: Andy Selkirk, MBA, BSc, DipPhy
Director of Activities: Byron Lewis
Junior School Head: Paul Mason, BEd
Registrar: Pauline Barker

Teaching Staff:
Alison Bagg, BA (*Head of Mathematics*)
Lizzie Anstice-Brown, BA, MA (*Art/Artist In Residence*)
Sylvester Beecroft, BA, PGCE (*French, Examinations, Careers*)
Michael Clement, BEd, MEd (*Art, Arts Faculty Coordinator*)
Michael Collins, BA, MA, PGCE (*History, Politics*)
Wendy Cottenden, CertEd (*PE, Games, Head of Girls' PE*)
Chris Drayton, BSc (*Mathematics, Outdoor Pursuits*)
Denise Eades, BA (*Geography*)
Gavin Fraser Williams, BA, MA (*Design & Technology*)
Emma-Kate Henry, BA (*English*)
David Ilott, BA, DipEd (*Head of English, Head of EFL*)
Paul Kelly, BEd (*Head of PE*)
Andrew Lambie, BA, PGCE (*Chemistry*)
Samantha Lloyd, BSc, PGCE (*Biology*)
Penny Main, BA, MA, PGCE (*History, English*)
Liane May, BA, MA, PGCE (*English, Media Studies*)
Mario May, BA, MA, PhD, PGCE (*Head of History, Faculty Coordinator*)
Katy Miller, BA, PGCE (*Head of Geography*)
Isabelle Mills, Licence d'Anglais, PGCE (*French, Spanish*)
Linda Moore, BSc, PGCE (*Mathematics*)
William Norris, MPhil, BMus, AKC (*Assistant Director of Music*)
Angeles Ojeda, Licendiada (*Spanish*)
Andy Owen, BSc, PGCE (*Head of Science Faculty*)
Emma Roskilly BA, PGCE (*English, Media Studies*)
Andy Selkirk, MBA, BSc, DipPhy, PGCE (*Biology*)
Emma Semple, BA, MA, PGCE (*Head of Art*)
Cyrille Simon, Maîtrise (*Head of Modern Languages, French, Spanish*)
Liz Szarvas, BA (*History, English*)
Ben Wall, BSc, PGCE (*Head of Design & Technology*)
Linda Wallace, BSc, PhD, PGCE (*Biology, Chemistry*)
Ian Warder, MA, MSc, PGCE (*Mathematics*)
Terence Watson, BSc, PGCE (*Physics, Astronomy*)
Jenny White, BEd (*PE and Games*)
Richard White, BSc, PGCE (*Biology*)
Hamish Wilson, BA, MA (*Drama*)
Susan Woollard, BSc, MSc (*Psychology*)
Jonathan Wright, BSc (*PE, Games*)
Naz Yeni, BA, MA (*English, Drama*)

Junior School and Montessori Department:
Head: Paul Mason, BEd
Christine Percival, CertEd (*Senior Teacher*)
Bryan Anderson, BEd
Anne Holland, BA, PGCE
David Jackson, BA, PGCE
Adam McAndrews, BA
Carly Ougham, BA, PGCE
Louise Robb, BA, Dip Music
Sam Selkirk, BEd
Alyson Shiel, CertEd

Claire Slater, BEng, PGCE
Sally Wall, BA, PGCE

Lesley Edwards, HNC, AMI Asst Cert
Sarah Brown, Maria Montessori Diploma

Director of Music: Martin Goodchild, GRSM, LRAM, PGCE

Community Coordinator: Jane Edwards, BA
Librarian: Linda Aird, ALA
Performing Arts Technician: Robert Johnson
School Doctor: Carole Brookes, MBChB, DRCOG
School Nurse: Caroline Dorrington
Special Needs Tutor: Armande Fryatt, MA, BEd
Joint Heads of Special Needs:
Karen Hoyle, BA, Cert Dyslexia and Literacy
Liz Miller, BEd

Bursar & Clerk to the Governors: William Hawkes, MA

Boarding Staff:
Arundale: Chris and Cecilia Drayton, Angeles Ojeda, Adam McAndrews
Arunside: Malcolm and Pippa Hodgson

The School provides for children of average to outstanding ability. All who are admitted to the Montessori Nursery (for "rising 3" to 4 year olds) or to the Junior School (for 4 to 11 year olds) may continue through the Senior School, subject to performance. Entry to the Sixth Form is dependent on GCSE results and the ability to cope with the AS/A Level programme.

Academic Programme. The Montessori has its own very particular curriculum and is part of the Early Years Centre at St Christopher. Close attention is given to the transition to the Junior School which follows a programme which includes extensive enrichment built around the core elements of the National Curriculum. The Junior School offers small classes and a wide range of opportunities, including the use of specialist teachers and use of Senior School facilities. In the Senior School a wide-ranging programme continues to the age of 16, including the study of sciences to Double Award GCSE or GCSE in all three Sciences. In Modern Languages everyone in Year 10 visits one of our exchange schools in France or Spain. The creative and expressive arts are particularly encouraged and the School has been awarded the Arts Council Artsmark Gold award.

The Sixth Form. Although St Christopher is not a large school, the Sixth Form is a good size (generally numbering around 80) with excellent facilities in its Sixth Form Centre. 21 AS/A level courses are on offer with all the usual Arts and Science subjects and, in addition, Theatre Studies, Psychology, Economics, Media Studies and Design Technology. There is a lively extra-curricular programme.

Learning through experience. There is an emphasis on learning through experience both with regard to academic subjects and more generally. There are many opportunities for practical and community work and for Outdoor Pursuits. At the end of the Summer Term the timetable is suspended for all pupils to undertake an extended project, generally away from the School campus. Each year two groups of sixth formers visit development projects in the Indian desert province of Rajasthan. There are also long-standing international projects in Kosovo and Ladakh. As a result of these the School was awarded the International School Award by the Department for Education through the British Council. A new cookery centre is opening in September 2011.

A humane and global outlook. There is no uniform (except for games). All children and adults are called by their first names. Internationalist and green values are encouraged and the School was re-awarded the Eco-Schools Award in 2010. The School's diet has been entirely vegetarian from the foundation. People of different religions and of none feel equally at home; there is a significant period of silence in every assembly.

Self-Government. The informality of the School encourages openness: children speak up for themselves – and for others. Everyone, child and adult, is represented on the School Council which is chaired by an elected senior pupil. The elected Major Officials and Committees look after different aspects of community life.

Treating children as individuals. From the outset the School has sought to treat children as individuals. In consequence, the ethos is an encouraging one and suits children who enjoy a broad education and who will thrive in a non-competitive academic environment. In our Learning Centre individual and group help is available. We also deal individually with those of very high ability and children are placed "a year ahead" or "a year behind" according to their needs.

Creative and Performing Arts. The School has an excellent tradition in these areas and has fine purpose-built facilities that reflect this. There are several productions a year in the Theatre which has tiered seating and full technical resources. Similarly there are regular concerts and recitals in the Music Centre. A Music Technology Suite opened in 2007. In the Arts Centre there are studios for fine art, for design and for ceramics, together with individual Sixth Form work areas and a lecture theatre.

Technology and Computing. The School benefits from a modern ICT Centre; internal online resources for teaching and learning have been developed.

Clubs and Societies. There are plentiful activities for pupils to join in with, taking place after School and at weekends. Staff share their enthusiasms and pupils too can take the lead in their own areas of interest.

Health, Fitness and Physical Education. The diet has been vegetarian from the outset and considerable pride is taken in the catering. There is a resident nurse with relief staff on call. The PE programme is full and varied, making use of playing field, gym, sports hall, all weather surface and a 25m indoor swimming pool. Matches take place against many other schools.

Full collaboration with parents. The Parents' Circle was founded in 1921 and the School has throughout valued the close involvement of parents, who are welcome in the School not just for consultation about their children but also to take part in evening classes and in sharing the many performances and information evenings. We want parents to share in the education of their children and in the School community.

Boarders. There are up to 50 boarders living in 2 boarding houses. The provision for younger pupils has a strongly domestic feeling, with each under the supervision of resident house staff. The accommodation for sixth formers in a newly refurbished Sixth Form house is along student lines with almost all in single rooms. Most boarders go home each weekend on Friday evening and new weekly boarding arrangements and pricing reflect demand for, and benefits of, this service.

Day Pupils. Day pupils benefit from the residential nature of the community, sharing in the evening and weekend life and taking meals in the School when they wish. Sixth formers have their own study areas in the Sixth Form Centre.

Fees per term (2011-2012). Day Pupils £1,260–£4,990, Full Boarding £6,630–£8,830, Weekly Boarding £5,460–£6,760. There are discounts of 10% for second and subsequent children, so long as they have an older sibling in the School. A range of financial assistance is available.

Admission Procedure. The most usual ages of admission are at "rising 3" into the Montessori Nursery, at ages 4, 7, 8 or 9 into the Junior School, and at 11 or 13 into the Senior School. A number also enter at Sixth Form level. Our assessment procedure includes diagnostic tests and interview. Assessment for Years 7 and 9 entry takes place in January.

Situation and Travel. The School has an attractive 35-acre campus on the edge of the Garden City with excellent communications. The A1(M) is a mile away and London (King's Cross) is 35 minutes by train. Stansted Airport is 35 minutes and Heathrow 60 minutes by car.

Old Scholars. The Membership Secretary of the St Christopher Club is David Cursons who can be reached c/o The School. The Annual Reunion is held over a weekend each July.

Charitable status. St Christopher School is a Registered Charity, number 311062. It exists to provide education for boys and girls, aiming to treat all as individuals and to develop their proper self-confidence.

St Edward's School

Cirencester Road, Charlton Kings, Cheltenham, Glos GL53 8EY
Tel: 01242 538600
Fax: 01242 538610
e-mail: headmaster@stedwards.co.uk
website: www.stedwards.co.uk

Formed from two former Grammar Schools in 1987, St Edward's is a co-educational Catholic Day School for 11 to 18 year olds. Proud of its Roman Catholic foundation as the Carmelite Boys' School, Whitefriars, and the Girls' Convent School, Charlton Park, St Edward's is now lay-run and warmly welcomes all denominations. We have 435 pupils currently on roll, of whom 97 are in the Sixth Form. The School is set in 17 acres of beautiful grounds on the southern outskirts of Cheltenham. The site was originally King Edward the Confessor's Hunting Lodge and the main building dates from the 18th century. The School has a warm Christian ethos built on a firm Catholic foundation. There is a full-time Chaplain. The School promotes academic excellence and all-round cultural and physical development.

Motto: *Quantum Potes Aude*

Chairman of Trustees: Mr Peter Walsh

Headmaster: **Mr Paul Harvey**, MA

Organisation. On entry to the Senior School at age 11, the students are allocated to one of three Forms. They are taught in three or four teaching groups which are set by ability for the principal subjects. The pastoral system of the School is based on Sections for the different age groups, with Section Heads leading teams of Tutors. The Sixth Formers have their own Common Room, study area and 'Café 6'. As Prefects, they play a vital role in the life of the School.

Developments. The School opened the Abbott Building in the summer 2008, comprising a spacious new Refectory, state-of-the-art Drama Studio and additional teaching rooms. Older buildings were also refurbished as extra Art Studios & Photography Room, and a Careers Centre. In recent years there have also been: a CCF Headquarters, an additional Science Laboratory, and numerous classroom and Laboratory refurbishments.

Academic Curriculum. A broad range of subjects is offered up to GCSE, with 25 at A Level. During the first two years all pupils study Art, Drama, English, French, Geography, History, Information Technology, Latin (or Classical Civilisation), Mathematics, Music, Physical Education, Religious Studies, Science, Spanish, German and Technology (including Resistant Materials, Food and Textiles). In the third year, Science is studied as separate subjects: Biology, Chemistry and Physics.

The compulsory subjects for GCSE are English Language, English Literature, Mathematics, Religious Education, at least two Sciences (from Biology, Chemistry and Physics) and at least one Modern Language. Up to three further subjects are studied from: Latin, Classical Civilisation, French, German, Spanish, History, Geography, Music, Drama, Art, Design & Technology, PE, or Food Technology.

The A Level subjects offered are: Mathematics, Further Mathematics, English, History, Geography, Religious Studies (Philosophy & Ethics), Biology, Chemistry, Physics, French, German, Spanish, Latin, Classical Civilisation, Critical Thinking, Art (including Photography and Textiles), Music, Theatre Studies, Design Technology, Computing, Business Studies, Psychology and Physical Education.

Spiritual. There is a full-time Chaplain (shared with our Junior School). Every day starts with Prayers, whether in School Assembly or Form time. Whole School Masses and other liturgies are celebrated several times a term. The pupils go on spiritual 'away days' each year.

Careers. A specialist Higher Education Counsellor guides Sixth Formers through the university application process and there is a specialist Oxbridge Adviser. The School has had record numbers winning Oxbridge places over the last few years. In Year 11 pupils participate in a Work Experience week, and there is a Careers guidance programme for the lower Years.

Sport. The principal sports for boys are Rugby, Hockey, Soccer and Cricket; for girls Hockey, Netball and Rounders. The School also competes very successfully in Swimming, Tennis, Basketball, Athletics, Badminton, Golf and Cross-Country. There are regular sports tours, most recently to Australia and South Africa.

Facilities include four rugby pitches, three hockey pitches (including one synthetic-turf), cricket square, several tennis courts, two sports halls, a fitness centre and a large indoor swimming pool. A new cricket square has been created in association with Ryeworth Cricket Club.

Clubs and Activities. There is a thriving CCF Contingent with both Army and RAF sections. The Duke of Edinburgh's Award Scheme is also flourishing. There are two School Plays a year – recent productions have included: *A Midsummer Night's Dream*, *The Trojan Women*, and, for the younger pupils, *Arabian Nights*. As well as the Carol Service in Tewkesbury Abbey, there is a major concert held in the Pittville Pump Room featuring the School orchestra, jazz band and ensembles. Other societies range from Debating and Chess to Creative Writing and Bridge. Pupils are encouraged to take full advantage of the many activities which take place both at lunch time and after school. Supervised homework is available after school every day until 5.30 pm. Trips abroad are a major feature of school life, including: an annual Ski Trip; a tour of the Normandy Battlefields; a French Cuisine Trip; German, Spanish and French exchanges; a residential Art Course; trips to Iceland and Costa Rica; expeditions to Patagonia and Zambia.

Admission. The main entry to the Senior School is at age 11; the entry examination takes place in November. Pupils can also join the School at age 13 and into the Sixth Form.

Fees per term (2011-2012). £3,479–£4,078. Discounts are offered for the third, fourth and subsequent children. The Senior School offers means-tested Bursary-Scholarships for entry at age 11, a limited number of non-means tested Scholarships and also some Sixth Form Scholarships.

Junior School. St Edward's Junior School, with over 400 boys and girls aged 2½–11, is on a separate nearby site with its own extensive buildings and 40-acre grounds containing the main Sports Fields which are used by both the Senior and Junior Schools. It is very well equipped with its own Science Laboratories, new Library, Technology Room, Music Rooms etc. Admission to the Junior School is possible at any age depending on ability and the availability of places. With an emphasis upon sound learning of basics (French is studied from Kindergarten), yet with a broad range of opportunities, pupils are fully prepared for entry to the Senior School.

The Kindergarten, in a separate modern building, takes children from the age of 2½ and is open nearly all year round.

(*For further details, see entry in IAPS section.*)

Old Edwardians' Association. Secretary: Mrs P Hemming, St Edward's School, Cirencester Road, Charlton Kings, Cheltenham, Gloucestershire GL53 8EY.

Further information is available on the School's website. A School prospectus is available on request from the Headmaster's PA & Registrar. You are warmly invited to arrange a visit to the School by telephoning her on 01242 538600.

Charitable status. St Edward's School is a Registered Charity, number 293360. It exists to provide for the education of children of any creed with preference to those who are of the Roman Catholic faith.

Saint Felix School

Southwold, Suffolk IP18 6SD
Tel: 01502 722175
Fax: 01502 722641
e-mail: schooladmin@stfelix.suffolk.sch.uk
website: www.stfelix.co.uk

Founded 1897.
Motto: *Felix Quia Fortis*

Board of Governors:
Chairman: [1]Mr Nigel Johnson, BA
Vice-Chairman: Mr John Whyte
Mrs Margaret Angus, MSc, TCert
Mr Robin Fournel
Mrs Raewyn Hope-Cobbold
Mr Richard Turvill
Mrs Amorelle Hughes (*Parent Governor*)
Mr John Hunt (*Parent Governor*)
Mr Alan Burgess (*Company Secretary*)

Headmaster: Dr Simon R Letman, BA, MA Univ College of Wales, EdD UEA

[1] *PGCE/DipEd qualification*

Deputy Heads:
[1]Miss M F D'Alcorn, BA Hons Birmingham, MA UEA
Mrs J Campbell, CertEd, Adv Dip CSN Southampton

Senior School:

Art & Design:
Mrs S Bassett, BA Hons East London
Mr D Burns, BA Hons Birmingham
Mrs V Burns, BEd London

Business Studies:
[1]Mr M Surridge, BA Hons Warwick, MA Ed UEA
Mrs J Harlock, BA Hons Nottingham, MA De Montfort

Design Technology:
Mr R Kay, BEd Hons, DipEd Nottingham

Drama:
Miss K Maclean, BA Hons UEA, MA UEA
Miss C Franklin, MA Hons Glamorgan

English:
[1]Miss J Ashford, BA Hons Durham
Miss L J Branson, BA Hons OU, CertEd Bedford College
[1]Miss N Williamson, BA Hons Durham

English as a Foreign Language (EFL):
[1]Miss N Williamson, BA Hons Durham
Mrs S Hammond, BA Hons UEA
[1]Mrs J Poole, BA Hons De Montfort, CELTA, OCR Level 5 SpLD (*Dyslexia*)

Geography:
[1]Mr I McLean, BSc Hons UEA

History:
Miss J Anderson, BA Hons OU, CertEd Wales
[1]Miss M F D'Alcorn, BA Hons Birmingham, MA UEA
[1]Mrs J Camburn, BSc Hons Loughborough
Mrs R Sorapure, BA Hons Bangor

Home Economics:
Mrs J Anderson, BA Hons OU, CertEd Wales

ICT:
Mr T Ellard, HND Applied Physics, Grad Inst Physics
Mr M Grunnell, BEd Exeter

Latin:
Mr J Dodsworth, PhD Bath, BEd Hons Cantab

Mathematics:
Mr C Smith, BEd Nottingham Trent
Mr J Cowan BSc Hons Sheffield Hallam
Mrs M Westlake, BSc Queen Mary College, London

Modern Languages and EFL:
[1]Ms E Esteve, BA Hons, BMS
Miss F Hoareau, MA Université de la Réunion
Miss C Le, BA Hons Rheims

Music:
[1]Mr A Jenkins, BA Hons Welsh College of Music & Drama
Mrs V Wise, BMus, STD, PDO, PDM, LRSM, UPLM,
   RCMAC, ARCM, APC Nice

Photography:
[1]Ms L Roberts, BA Hons Leicester

Physical Education:
[1]Miss S Fenwick, BA Hons Warwick
Mrs J Greenacre, MA UEA, BEd Hons W Sussex
[1]Mrs G Kingstone, BSc Hons Exeter
Mrs G Nash, CertEd Sussex
Mrs L O'Connell, ASA Swimming Assistant, BSc Hons
   Exeter
[1]Mr T O'Connell, BSc Hons Exeter
Ms S Purchase, ASA Swimming Coach
Miss C Savage, BA Hons De Montfort
Mr B Collis
Mr N Brooker

Politics:
Mrs R Sorapure, BA Hons Bangor

Science:
Mr D Bryanton, BSc Hons Swansea, MA London (*Biology*)
[1]Mr A Hill, BSc Wales, MA OU (*Physics*)
Mr W Ryder-Davies, BA Dundee
[1]Mr D Swann, BSc Hons Sheffield (*Chemistry*)
Mrs M Westlake, BSc Queen Mary College, London

Technicians:
Mrs C Tyler
Mr M Miller

Careers & Sixth Form:
[1]Miss M F D'Alcorn, BA Hons Birmingham, MA UEA
[1]Miss J Ashford, BA Hons Durham

Learning Support:
[1]Mrs J Camburn, BSc Hons Loughborough
Mrs J Campbell, CertEd, Adv Dip CSN Southampton
   (*Junior School SENCO*)
[1]Mrs A Eastaugh, MA Hons Edinburgh, TEFL
[1]Mrs J Poole, BA Hons De Montfort, CELTA, OCR Level
   5 SpLD (*Dyslexia*)
Mrs P Webb, CertEd (*Junior School*)

Classroom Assistants:
Mrs J Grunnell
Mrs A Surridge

Chaplain: Mrs H Meldrum, BA Hons London

Librarian: Mrs C Thomas, BA Hons London, PG Dip,
   MCLIP

House Staff:

Head of Boarding: [1]Mr T O'Connell, BSc Hons Exeter
House Parents:
Mrs S Bland & Mr D Bland (*Gardiner House*)
Mr T & Mrs L Laughland (*Felix House*)
Mrs G Nash, CertEd Sussex (*Somerville House*)
Mrs L O'Connell, BSc Hons Exeter (*Fawcett House*)
[1]Mr T O'Connell, BSc Hons Exeter (*Fawcett House*)

House Matron: Mrs J Tindle

Sanatorium:
Sister A Carr, RGN
Sister Y Proctor, RGN
Nurse L Lewis, RGN

School Medical Officer: Dr M Niemeijer

Management Support:
Receptionist/School Secretary: Mrs G Robb
Registrar/Headmaster's Secretary: Mrs J Ellard
Assistant to the Registrar/Database Administrator: Miss M
   Bridgman
Bursar: Mr T Chapman
Assistant to the Bursar: Mrs E Mercer
Junior School & Early Years Learning Secretary: Mrs D
   Whittington
Bursary Assistants: Mrs L McIntyre & Mrs J Tracey
Press Officer: Miss E Hart

Junior School and Nursery:
Mrs K Barbrook (*Nursery Assistant*)
Mrs S Calver, CME, LTCL, LLCM (*Flute*)
Mrs J Campbell, CertEd, Adv Dip CSN (*Head of Junior
   School, Junior School SENCO*)
Mrs S Chambers, NNEB (*Nursery Assistant*)
Miss F Clarke, CCE, NNEB (*Classroom Assistant*)
Mrs I Cooke (*Nursery Assistant*)
[1]Mrs R Crane, BA Hons (*French*)
Miss K Craven, HNC, HND (*Teaching Assistant*)
Miss T Doy, CCE, DNN (*Nursery Supervisor*)
Mrs S Duckett, NNEB, CertEd (*Year Teacher, Key Stage 1
   Coordinator*)
Mrs A Evans, BA Hons (*Year Teacher*)
Miss C Franklin, MA Hons Glamorgan (*Drama*)
Mr D Goddard, BA Hons, MEd (*Year Teacher, Boys'
   Games, History*)
Mrs J Greenacre, MA UEA, BEd Hons W Sussex (*Girls'
   Games, Swimming*)
Miss S Greenfield, BEd (*Form Teacher, English
   Coordinator*)
Mr M Grunnell, BEd Exeter (*ICT, Mathematics*)
Mrs J Heal, Cert EYP Open FD Open (*Associate Teacher*)
Miss F Hoareau, MA Université de la Réunion (*French*)
Mrs J Hoddy, BEd UEA (*Year Teacher*)
Mrs A Horne, NVQ3, EYP (*Nursery Assistant*)
Mrs S Hunting (*Nursery Assistant*)
[1]Mr A Jenkins, BA Hons Welsh College of Music & Drama
[1]Mrs P Kinsella, BA Hons (*Year Teacher*)
Miss S Knights, CCLD, NVQ2, EYP (*Nursery Assistant*)
Mrs L Laughland, CCE, DNN (*Nursery Supervisor*)
Miss C Le, BA Hons Rheims (*French*)
Miss A Lee, EYCE, NVQ3, EYP (*Nursery Supervisor*)
Mrs G Nash, CertEd Sussex (*Sixth Form Somerville House*)
Mrs A Nunn (*Year Teacher, Art*)
Mrs L O'Connell, BSc Hons Exeter (*Swimming Teacher*)
Miss D Peck, BA Hons Worcester (*Nursery Nurse*)
Mrs J Proctor, NVQ3 (*Learning Support Assistant*)
Mr W Ryder-Davies, BA Dundee (*Science, Mathematics,
   Games*)
Mrs A Scriven, BTec Level 3 (*Teaching Assistant*)

Mrs A Watling, CCE, DNN (*Nursery Nurse*)
Mrs P Webb, CertEd (*Enhanced Learning*)
Mrs E Wilson, NNEB, CertEd (*Class Teacher, Early Years Foundation Coordinator*)
¹Mrs S Yates, BA (*Art Teacher p/t*)

Peripatetic Staff:
Mrs S Calver, CME, LTCL, LLCM (*Flute*)
Mr B Carben (*Woodwind*)
Mr M Chapman (*Guitar*)
Mrs C Cliff, DipEd Music (*Piano, Recorder, Cello*)
Mr M Dawson (*Squash*)
Miss A Evans, GRSM, ARCM, ATCL, MTC (*Piano, Singing*)
Mrs J Joliffe (*Judo Coach*)
Mrs E Lee, RAD, RTS (*Ballet/Dance*)
Mr T Marriott (*Drums*)
Mrs T Marriott, MIDA, SIPBE (*Ballet, Modern Dance*)
Mr J O'Toole (*Violin*)
Mrs S Pascall, LAMDA (*Speech & Drama*)
Mr R Simmons (*Brass*)
Mr P Stimpson (*Fencing*)
Mr D Strauss, GRSM, LRAM (*Piano*)
Mrs J Taylor, FTCL, GTCL Hons (*Cello*)
Mrs R Turner, LRAM (*Violin & Viola*)
Mr M Websdale (*Tennis*)
Mr R Whiley (*Guitar*)

Age Range. 1–18.
Number of Pupils. 430.
Saint Felix School was founded in 1897 and is set in 75 acres overlooking the Blyth Estuary near the picturesque town of Southwold in Suffolk. The extensive buildings are purpose built and well equipped.

As a co-educational day and boarding school Saint Felix offers boys and girls a broad and balanced curriculum from the age of 1 to 18. A through school from the Nursery (ages 1–6) to Junior (ages 7–11) through to the Senior School (ages 11–16) and then into the Sixth Form.

Academic. A well-structured timetable, and a broad and balanced curriculum, encourages children in the Junior School to achieve their personal best, both academically and socially. Small class sizes and specialist teaching staff ensure excellent SATS results together with happy, well-mannered and confident pupils.

In the Senior School, each individual child is encouraged to achieve the highest grade attainable, made possible by the expertise of committed, skilled and motivated teachers working in small class groups. A wide and distinctive range of subjects can be studied at GCSE, AS and A Level. Sixth Form students this year achieved 100% pass rate at A Level, enabling entry into many of the country's finest Art, Drama and Music colleges, and universities such as Cambridge. In addition the school's system of pastoral care ensures that children have continuous support and mentoring throughout their time at Saint Felix.

Music. Music is popular with over half taking peripatetic lessons. There is a variety of musical groups including chapel and chamber choirs, choral societies, orchestras as well as several chamber ensembles, eg piano trio, string quartets, jazz group and a rock band with electric guitar and drums especially popular. All pupils are encouraged to learn an instrument and lower Junior pupils learn the recorder. A 'Music in Residence' group encourages pupils to take up instruments. Music can be studied at GCSE and A Level. The department has 18 practice rooms and a performance area.

Sport. Facilities include a 25m indoor swimming pool, sports hall complex, squash courts, fitness suite and a 25-acre equestrian cross-country course.

A wide variety of sports are on offer including tennis, rugby, cricket, football, netball, hockey and rounders. Swimming is particularly strong throughout the school resulting in pupils competing in county, regional and national champi-onships and achieving national recognition. An extensive range of other sports is available including squash, sailing, basketball, fencing, table tennis, wall climbing and horse riding.

Arts. The school promotes the Arts with regular exhibitions and displays and eagerly-awaited school productions throughout the year. The combination of Art, Music and Drama is actively encouraged through an Arts Week. Photography and Art throughout the school is of a very high standard with excellent results at both GCSE and A Level. The new Silcox Theatre with a 200-seat capacity and state-of-the-art lighting and sound system further enhances the creative arts, one of the great strengths of Saint Felix.

Extra Curricular Activities. There is an extensive list of activities available. All pupils are actively encouraged to take part in the Duke of Edinburgh's Award Scheme. A similar scheme runs in the Junior school. The school day is extended to include activities. The Army Cadet Force is very popular.

Community. The school actively encourages the local community to get involved in school life and various clubs are closely linked to the school (Norwich City Football Club, Guides, Brownies, The Choral Society, Southwold Rugby, Netball and Tennis Clubs) enabling pupils to be involved in groups outside school.

Fees per term (2011-2012). Day: £2,052–£4,400; Boarding: £4,900–£6,225 (weekly), £6,450–£7,775 (full).

Scholarships. (*See Scholarship Entries section.*) The School offers Academic Scholarships of 50% maximum of fees and Exhibitions of 25% maximum on entry at 11+, 13+ or into the Sixth Form. The Hess Music Scholarship, for outstanding promise in music, is awarded annually, value 33% of the fees. Academic, Art, Drama, Music and Sport Scholarships at 16+ are also available. Forces Boarding School Allowance available.

Charitable status. Saint Felix School is a Registered Charity, number 310482. It exists to promote and advance education.

St George's School
Edgbaston

31 Calthorpe Road, Birmingham B15 1RX
Tel: 0121 625 0398
Fax: 0121 625 3340
e-mail: admin@sgse.co.uk
website: www.sgse.co.uk

Council:
Chairman: Mr Simon Topman, MBE
Mrs Gurjeet Bains, DLitt
Ms Catherine Canty, LLB
Mrs Sandra Carter
Mr Karl George, MBE
Mr Colin Goodier, MA Oxon
Mrs Linda Jones, BA Hons
Mr Jagdish Kumar, MBBS, FRCS, FACS
Dr Manju Kumar, BDS, MFGDP
Mrs Rosemary Plevey, BSc
Mrs Jennifer Uff, BA, CPFA

***Headmaster*: Sir Robert Dowling**, Kt

Director of Studies: Mr Geoffrey Thompson, BEd Hons Lancaster

Head of Sixth Form:
Mrs Vanessa Johnson, BA Hons Hull, PGCE
Mr Paul Ferris, BSc Hons QTS Brunel

Head of Learning Support: Mrs Carolyn Hayes, CertEd London, MA Ed (*SE/IE*), PGCert SEN Coordination

Upper School:

English:
Mrs Pia Abbott, BA Hons Kent, CertEd
Mr Stephen Abbott, BA Hons London, PGCE
Mrs Vanessa Johnson, BA Hons Hull, PGCE
Mrs Karen Parker, BA Hons Lancaster
Miss Josie Stinton, BEd Hons Birmingham
Mrs Helen Taylor, CertEd Liverpool, BEd Hons Liverpool

Mathematics:
Mr Ryan Bibb, BSc Hons York, PGCE
Mrs Balvinder Gill, BA Hons Bath, GTP
Mr Geoff Thompson, BEd Hons Lancaster (*Director of Studies*)
Mr Paul Richards, BSc Hons City GTP

Science:
Mrs Farin Dhanani, BSc Hons Aston, PGCE
Mr Matthew Bullock, BEng & Com Hons Birmingham, PGCE
Mr Paul Bullock, BSc Hons King's College London, PGCE
Mr David Lai, BSc Hons Lancashire, PGCE
Mrs Gillian Lyth, BSc Hons Aston, PGCE
Mr Michael Stewart, BSc Hons UCL
Dr Jane Thomas, PhD Bristol, PGCE
Mr Mark Williams, BSc Hons Bradford, PGCE

Information Technology:
Miss Jennifer Davis, BSc Hons Plymouth, PGCE
Mrs Michelle Fowler, BSc Hons Birmingham, PGCE

Business Studies:
Mr Martin Morgan, ACIB, PGCE Wolverhampton

Psychology:
Miss Danielle Fogg, BSc Hons Aston, PGCE

Modern Languages:
Mrs Tina Kenwood, BA Hons London, PGCE
Mrs Sue Sandys, AIL, MIL, PGCE
Ms Caroline Shuker, BSc Hons Aston, PGCE

Religious Studies:
Mrs Jane Kearey, MA Oxford, MA Carleton University, Canada

Government & Politics:
Mr Jonathan Yates, BA Hons York, PGCE, MA Lancaster

History:
Miss Sally Allder, BA Hons Essex, PGCE
Mrs Helen Reader, BA Hons Wolverhampton, PGCE
Mrs Eleanor Webster, BA Hons Leicester, PGCE

Geography:
Mr Richard Thomson, BA Hons Leeds, PGCE

Design Technology:
Mrs Michelle Harbott, BA Hons Wolverhampton, PGCE

Food Technology:
Mrs Corrine Roberts, BEd Hons, Dip RE/PSE

Art and Ceramics:
Miss Carla Webb, BA Hons De Montfort, PGCE
Miss Ursula Webster, BA Hons Brighton, PGCE

Music:
Mrs Sarah C Russell, MA Cantab, PGCE

Drama:
Mrs Pia Abbott, BA Hons Kent, CertEd

Physical Education:
Mr Paul Ferris, BSc Hons QTS, Brunel
Miss Ann Hollman, BSc Hons QTS, Brunel

Learning Support:
Mrs Debra Arnold, NVQ3 Child Care & Education
Miss Sally Coyne, NVQ1 Health & Social Care
Ms Roberta Davis, LLB Hons Birmingham

Mrs Katharine Dunn, BSc Hons Swansea, PGCE (*EAL*)
Ms Alison Fitchford
Miss Jennifer Hayes
Miss Jaspreet Kaur, BA Hons Cardiff
Mr Steven Kempson
Mrs Rubina Maher, NVQ2 Childcare
Mrs Wendy Nash, NVQ3 Early Years Care & Education
Mrs Sally Plotnek, CertEd Westhill College, Birmingham
Mrs Beverley Rance
Mrs Lindsey Reid, NNEB
Mrs Samina Sajawal
Mrs Jaqueline Sherlock
Mrs Ban Sikafi-Jawad, Dip HE Clinical Science, NVQ3 Childcare
Mrs Marieanne Stoke (*EAL*)
Mr Aarron Wynne, Cert Autism Awareness
Mrs Sandra Wynne

Lower School:

Head of Lower School:
Sir Robert Dowling, Kt

Lower School Staff:
Mr Jason Evans, BA Hons QTS Birmingham City
Miss Parminder Gill, ICS Dip Child Day Care
Ms Jo Goodyere, BEd Hons Exeter
Miss Rebecca Johnson, BEd Hons Newman University College
Mrs Marilyn Jones, NVQ3 Early Years Care & Education
Miss Sarah Matts
Mrs Lucy Merrell, BA Hons Lancaster
Miss Anna McGovern, BA Hons Newman University College
Miss Siobhan Pearson, BSc Hons UCE, PGCE
Mrs Sally Roberts, NNEB, Mont Dip
Mrs Patricia Tonks, BEd Hons Birmingham
Miss Denise Wood, NVQ3 Childcare & Education

Technical Staff:
Miss Lisa Allen, BSc King's College London, MSc Newcastle upon Tyne
Mr AdamMcCabe, MA Hons York
Mrs Julie Glover, Cert SocSci Open, Cert Hum Open

Finance Department: Mrs Jaqueline Elder
Head's PA: Mrs Maureen Fahy
Marketing & Admissions: Mrs Margaret Gough, CertEd Chelsea
Secretarial Assistants:
Mrs Natalie Williams (*Upper School*)
Ms Tracy Perry & Miss Annette Dodd (*Lower School*)
Caretakers: Mr Patrick Ryan, Mr Michael Bridgens
Groundsman: Mr David Evans

The school opened in September 1999 as the amalgamation of Edgbaston Church of England College for Girls and Edgbaston College. The School is co-educational and accepts pupils of all faiths. We pride ourselves on our warm family atmosphere where each child is known as an individual.

Entry to the upper school is selective and the majority of pupils expect and are expected to carry on their education post 19. Entry into the Lower School follows an informal interview.

The school is a listed building which has been sympathecially adapted to meet pupils educational needs.

Curriculum. The curriculum will provide each pupil with a broad education appropriate to their age and needs.

The overriding educational priority is to allow and encourage every pupil to be the best they can be.

The educational diet provides a wider range of subjects than required by the National Curriculum.

In the Sixth Form, which has its own centre, there is a wide breadth of subject choice. Sixth Form pupils provide various services to those in need in the local community.

Extra-Curricular Activities. Pupils take part in lunchtime and after-school activities. These include music, drama, and sports. Instrumental music, speech and drama, ballet and fencing lessons are provided as required.

Fees per term (2011-2012). £1,655–£3,255 (excluding lunch). Full details may be obtained on application to the School. We will be pleased to forward a copy of the prospectus and to arrange an opportunity for parents to visit the School to discuss their child's education with the Headmaster.

Charitable status. St George's School, Edgbaston is a Registered Charity, number 1079647. It exists to provide a quality education for boys and girls within the Birmingham area.

St James Senior Boys' School

Church Road, Ashford, Surrey TW15 3DZ
Tel: 01784 266 930
         01784 266 933 (Admissions)
Fax: 01784 266 938
e-mail: admissions@stjamesboys.co.uk
website: www.stjamesboys.co.uk

St James Independent School for Senior Boys, founded in 1975, is registered as an educational charity and is administered by a Board of Governors. The headmaster is a member of the Society of Heads of Independent Schools (SHMIS), the Independent Schools Association (ISA) and The International Boys' Schools Coalition (IBSC). These Associations require that excellence is assured by regular inspections by the Independent Schools Inspectorate which is itself monitored by Ofsted.

The school has 330 students – all boys, aged between 11 and 18. There is a small weekly boarding option.

The school has recently relocated from its riverside site in Twickenham and now resides in the magnificent Victorian building which once housed St David's School in Ashford, Surrey, set in 32 acres of grounds.

This move gives every boy the physical space necessary to develop his sporting, artistic and dramatic talents in addition to working in high-quality classrooms and state-of-the-art laboratories.

Chairman of Governors: Jeremy Sinclair

Headmaster: David Boddy, MA, DipJ, FIoD

Deputy Headmasters:
James Glover, BSc, CMath, FIMA, PGCE (*Mathematics*)
Koen Claeys, BA, GLSE Belgium (*French, German*)

Assistant Headmaster: David Hipshon, BA Hons, MPhil Cantab, PhD, PGCE (*History*)

Director of Studies: David Lacey, BA Mod, HDipEd, CPhys, MInstP (*Head of Science*)

Head of Sixth Form: Christian Daw BA Hons, PhB, STB, QTS (*Philosophy*)

Head of Years 9–11: David Beezadhur, BA Hons, MA, GTTP (*Ancient History*)

Head of Lower School: Koen Claeys, BA, GLSE Belgium (*French, German*)

Full-Time:
Penelope Andrews, BA, QTS (*French, German*)
Lucy Bailes, MA (*Chief Librarian*)
Kevan Bell, MA, MSc, BEd (*Sports Performance Director*)
James Carlyle, BA Oxon, PGCE (*Head of Classics*)
Christa Clark, BA, PGCE (*Mathematics*)
Christian Darwent, BSc, PGCE (*Geography*)
Richard Fletcher, BSc Hons, GTTP (*Head of Sport*)

Nic Lemprière, MA, PGCE (*English*)
Neil MacKichan, BSc Hons, PGCE (*Head of ICT, Computing*)
Pardeep Marway, BSc Hons, PGCE (*Science*)
Sam Moss, MA Hons, MLitt (*Classics*)
Elizabeth Munro, BA Hons, PGCE (*Science*)
Evelyn Murphy, BA, QTS (*Mathematics*)
Charles Neave, BA Melbourne, PGCE (*Head of English*)
Andrew Pilkington, BSc, PGCE (*Head of Geography*)
Virginie Quartier, BA, GLSE Belgium (*Head of French*)
Katerina Ridge, MSc, PGCE (*Science*)
Julia Russell, BSc Hons, QTS (*Art*)
Derek Saunders, BA Hons, PGCE (*Director of Music*)
Oliver Saunders, BA Hons, QTS (*Head of History*)
Mark Saunders, BA, HND Art & Design (*Head of Art*)
Yolanda Saunders, BA Hons, PGCE (*Classics*)
Lorraine Soares, MSc Hons, PGCE (*Science, Head of Chemistry*)
David Stollar, BA Hons, ATC (*Head of Sanskrit*)
Miriam Stollar, NNEB (*Sanskrit*)
Jessica Thomas, BA, QTS (*English and Geography*)
Joseph Verran, BSc, QTS (*Mathematics*)
Ben Wassell, BSc Hons, GTP (*Sports Science*)
Marie Wood, BA Hons, PGCE (*Head of Drama*)

Part-Time:
Jonathan Lewis, MA, LLB Hons, PGCE (*Law*)
Paul Ackford, MA (*Economics*)

Learning Support:
Talit Khan, BSc, PGCE (*Head of Learning Support*)
John Brook, LCST, MSc, BAF
Sarah-Jane Hipshon
Cora Wren, BA Hons
Caroline Moir, BSc Hons Psychology, Sp Lg Diploma

Boarding Staff:
Sam Moss, MA Hons, MLitt (*Houseparent*)
Isabel Moss, MA Hons (*Houseparent*)
Dominic Prendergast, BA Hons, PGCE (*Assistant Houseparent*)
James Johnson, BSc, PGCE (*Assistant Houseparent*)

Admissions Tutor: Colin Matten

Aims and Values. St James offers a distinctive education, uniting a philosophical approach to the development of life skills with academic excellence. The approach aims to unfold the twin powers of love and reason so that a boy may grow into a man who knows what he thinks, does what he says and is a friend to all.

The curriculum lays open the great cultures of East and West through Greek, Latin, Sanskrit and weekly lessons in Philosophy. Interest is also taken in the great scriptures of all traditions. The teaching of all the Sciences and Mathematics inspires a sense of the miraculous nature of the world in which we live, along with the desire to care for it. Meeting the finest examples of English literature, poetry, classical music, art, plus singing for all pupils, opens the emotional realm; while viewing History through the stories of great men and women gives boys a sense of the size of their human potential. Modern Languages, Geography, ICT, Drama, three afternoons of sport per week for every boy and an Adventure Pursuits programme, help ensure that the school day is rich in content and yet full of fun. It is important that every boy achieves more than he thinks is possible.

St James holds high expectations for its pupils. They are encouraged to discover the happiness that comes when we serve and care for the world, not just take from it; when we work to inspire harmony and cooperation among people of *all* faiths and cultures. The world is a challenging place, and St James tries to prepare its pupils to play leading roles. A quiet time for stillness and meditation is offered daily.

Academic Standards and Successes. Academic standards are high, but we also measure success to the extent that boys surpass their own expectations. 2010 results were: GCSE Pass Rate 100%, A*ABC 92%, 5+ A*ABC 96%; A Level Pass Rate 99%, A*ABC 86%.

Extra-Curricular Activities. Boys are offered an adventure pursuits programme designed to challenge the young men in terms of fitness, endurance, courage, leadership skills, service, self-esteem and confidence. Cadets (239 Para detachment), Duke of Edinburgh's Award Scheme, Skiing, Sailing Club, Climbing Club, Community Service and Task force are amongst the activities offered.

Philosophy. Each class throughout the school has one period of Philosophy per week. The boys are opened up to the great ideas relating to human values and relationships. Broadly, the themes prepare boys through different stages of development – Years 6 to 8: the correct use of mind, the power of attention; Years 9 to 11: aspiring to a great vision of Man and exploring human relationships and personal mastery; Years 12 to 13: living the philosophical life, making it practical, the importance of service.

Educational Trips. These are fairly regular and frequent for the Lower School, but there is an Activities Week in March when Year 7 visit Pompeii and Rome; Year 8 go to Greece to further their studies of Classical Civilisation; Year 9 stay in Paris for a week with French families, speaking the language and being introduced to French culture; and Year 10 spend some time in Lucca in Italy for leadership training and aspects of teamworking, then move on to Florence to study Renaissance art and architecture.

Meditation and Quiet Time. The importance of inner stillness is recognised in the school and the school day begins and ends with 10 minutes' meditation and reflection. Every lesson begins and ends in a quiet moment of stillness and rest.

Admissions. The standard entry is at 11+, 13+ and 16+. Boys applying for entry to Year 7 take an Entrance Exam in January and also are all interviewed by the Headmaster shortly afterwards. Boys are not judged solely on their exam results. At 13+, we favour the Common Entrance route, but the number of places available is dependent upon whether spaces have become available. We welcome applications to our Sixth Form at 16+. Good GCSE performance and satisfactory interviews will be the basis of selection.

Fees per term (2011-2012). £4,220. Weekly Boarding Fee: £1,800.

Open Days and Visits. Every year we hold two Open Days in early November. We also encourage parents to come and see the school in session. This takes the form of a two-hour tour around the school during normal classes, meeting staff and boys, witnessing some class lessons, hearing about the philosophical approach, having Q & A sessions and generally getting a good sense of the St James ethos.

Charitable status. The Independent Educational Association Limited is a Registered Charity, number 270156.

St John's College

Grove Road South, Southsea, Hampshire PO5 3QW
Tel: 023 9281 5118 (Upper School)
          023 9282 0237 (Lower School)
Fax: 023 9287 3603
e-mail: info@stjohnscollege.co.uk
website: www.stjohnscollege.co.uk

Founded in 1908 by the De La Salle Brothers, St John's seeks to provide an excellent all-round day and boarding education to boys and girls of all abilities. The school has a strong Christian ethos inspired by the teachings of St John Baptist De La Salle, the patron saint of teachers. Children of all Christian denominations, those of other faiths and those with no formal religious affiliation but who are in sympathy with the values of the school – all are welcome.

Chairman of Governors: Mr T Forer

Headmaster: **Mr G Best**, BA

Deputy Headmaster: Mr T Bayley, BSc, MA
Head of Lower School: Mr R Shrubsall, MA Ed
Head of Nursery: Miss A Utchanah
Senior Teacher (*Director of Studies*): Dr G D Goodlad, PhD, BA
Senior Teacher (*Boarding*): Mr M Renahan, BA
Senior Teacher (*Examinations*): Mr R Forshaw, BA

Heads of Department:
English: Mrs A Lowe, BA
Mathematics: Mrs A Cullum, BSc
Science: Mr A Martin, BSc
Art and Design: Mrs K Brown, BA
Design and Technology: Mr N Hayes, BA
Drama: Miss E Morley, BA
Economics & Business Studies: Mr L Rees, BSc
Geography: Mr P Hyde, BSc
Government & Political Studies: Dr G D Goodlad, PhD, BA
History: Mrs K Audsley, BA
Learning Support: Mrs L Gorham, BA, DipSpLD
Modern Languages: Mr G Walker, MA
Performing Arts: Miss E Morley
Physical Education: Mr A Tart, BA
Religious Studies: Mrs J Turner, BA, MA

Bursar: Mrs H Angel, MAAT

Head's PA/Admissions: Mrs J L Mengham

Number of Pupils. Boys 409, Girls 225, Boarders 122.

Situation. St John's day and boarding campus is located in the heart of Southsea, an attractive and thriving seaside suburb of Portsmouth. The College's 34 acres of sports fields are located on the outskirts of the city, with transport provided to and from that site.

Approach and Ethos. Academically, St John's is a non-selective school, its aim being excellence for every pupil according to their personal potential. All children who are able and willing to benefit from the curriculum provided are welcome to join the school community. The school's academic record – by all measures – is outstanding.

The pastoral care offered to boarders and day pupils is of very high quality. The commitment of the staff to the welfare and progress of each pupil is second to none. In return, honest effort and application is expected from the children – in order to meet the challenging standards set in academic work, sporting endeavour, behaviour and self-discipline.

Nursery. The Nursery occupies self-contained premises within the Junior (Lower) School. It has its own entrance and secure playground. The Nursery caters for children aged from two to four years and is open 51 weeks of the year. The children are actively involved in a carefully constructed pre-school programme. Great emphasis is placed on creative artwork, outdoor play and educational visits – as well as on acquiring foundation skills and concepts relating to numeracy and literacy.

Junior (Lower) School. The Lower School is also a self-contained unit within the main College campus. This enables younger children to make daily use of all the College's excellent facilities and to benefit in some areas from specialist tuition by Upper (Senior) School staff. The broadly-based curriculum incorporates and extends the National Curriculum. Great emphasis is placed on English, mathematics and science – which is taught in well-equipped laboratories. Musical talent is also carefully nurtured, with all pupils learning a musical instrument from the age of seven. The Lower School Choir and Orchestra provide opportunities for ensemble playing and performance.

Upper (Senior) School. The Senior School curriculum again incorporates and extends the National Curriculum. All subjects are taught by appropriately qualified specialists in well-resourced subject areas. A wide range of GCSE subjects is offered. Instrumental tuition is encouraged and the Upper School Choir and Orchestra are open to all pupils. Drama has a high profile within the school, with all pupils encouraged to be involved. Sport – principally rugby, cricket and netball – is strong at all levels. Pupils' progress in all areas is assessed formally each half-term, with formal examinations being held twice yearly.

Sixth Form. As they progress into the Sixth Form, older students are enabled and encouraged to become independent and self-motivated learners – in preparation for Higher Education. The teaching and pastoral staff continue to work closely with parents, who are kept fully informed of progress and achievement. A wide range of AS and A2 Level subjects is offered. The College ensures a good student/teacher ratio, allowing for close and constant monitoring of the performance and effort of each student. Preparation for Oxbridge entry is available. Students are also offered practice interviews for University and job applications and a full careers service.

Beyond the formal curriculum, a wide range of sporting, academic, dramatic, cultural and social activities is available. The Politics Society, administered predominantly by Sixth Form students, enjoys a national reputation.

Admission. Pupils are accepted and placed on the basis of a formal assessment and previous reports.

Fees per term (2011-2012). Lower School: £2,385–£2,540. Upper School: £3,100. UK Boarding £6,700, Overseas Boarding £7,150.

Occasional Boarding (including bed, breakfast, evening meal): £30 per day.

Music fees are extra.

Scholarships and Bursaries. Academic and other scholarships and bursarial awards are available.

Charitable status. St John's College is a Registered Charity, number 232632. It exists to provide excellent education and pastoral care to boys and girls.

St Joseph's College

Birkfield, Ipswich, Suffolk IP2 9DR
Tel: 01473 690281
Fax: 01473 602409
e-mail: registrar@stjos.co.uk
website: www.stjos.co.uk

A co-educational independent day school providing Christian education for 2–18 year olds with boarding facilities. High academic expectation and national achievement in sport, performing arts and community service.

Set in a beautiful wooded parkland site the College is situated just ten minutes' walk from Ipswich station or alternately just ten minutes' drive from the A12/A14 interchange.

Governing Body:
Chair: Mrs J Lea, MA
Vice Chair: Mr R Stace, LLB
Mr G Kalbraier, BSc, FRSA, FinstD, FIMgt
Mr P Clement, BSc Hons
Mr M Potter
Mr A Newman
Mrs C Lock
Dr P M Woods, BSc, MBBS
Mr S Davies, FREng, BSc, CEng, FIEE
Mr A Goulborn
Mr M Howes

Clerk to the Governors: Mrs J Blemings

Principal: Mrs S Grant, BMus Hons (*Music*)

Vice-Principals:
Mrs D Clarke, BA Hons (*MFL*)
Mr R Harris, BA Hons (*Geography*)

* *Head of Department*
§ *Part-time*

Senior School:
Mr P Andrew (*RE*)
Mrs J Bailey (*Geography*)
Mr A Bloore (**Technology*)
Mrs L Bloore (*Director of Music*)
Mrs A Bowden (*Food Technology*)
Mr H Bonnar (*§Mathematics*)
Mr R Bradford (*Mathematics*)
Mr C Branch (*PE & Games*)
Mr R Branch (*PE*)
Mr N Chandler (*History, Politics*)
Mr D Cole (*§Music*)
Mrs S Comley (*English, EAL*)
Miss R Crean (*History*)
Mr B Crisp (*Art*)
Mr M Davey (*Head of Sixth Form*)
Ms K Drake (**English Faculty, EAL*)
Miss H Ding (*§Dance*)
Mr D Edwards (*Business Studies & Economics*)
Mrs M Edwards (*§Food Technology*)
Mrs P Garnett (*§Primary Learning Support*)
Mrs V Harvey (**Creative & Performing Arts Faculty*)
Mrs K Higgins (*English, EAL, Media*)
Mr K Hirst (*§Science*)
Mr M Hockley (*§ICT*)
Dr T Hofmann (*Science*)
Miss D Holder (*Science*)
Mrs Z James (*Head of Nursery*)
Mrs B Jousiffe (*§PE & Games, EAL*)
Mr P Jousiffe (*KS4 Manager, D&T, Mathematics*)
Mrs J Lauder (*PE & Games*)
Mrs A Lee (*EAL, Chinese*)
Mrs S Lindridge (**Learning Support & Challenge*)
Dr J Ling (**Science*)
Mr C Long (*Science*)
Mrs J Marston (*§RE*)
Miss K Mayhew (*§Business Studies*)
Mr C McNicholas (*Director of E Learning*)
Mr A Miller (**Technology*)
Mr M Patterson (*Director of Sport*)
Mrs S Pearson (*German*)
Mr A Reavill (**Humanities Faculty*)
Miss A Rees (*English, EAL*)
Ms C Renshaw (*D&T*)
Mr G Richards (*Directory of Rugby, Head of Junior Boarding*)
Mrs J Rothwell (*French, Spanish, EAL*)
Mrs G Rowlands (*Spanish, French, CCF & Assistant KS3 Manager*)
Mrs J Scott (*History*)
Miss E Self (*Drama*)
Mrs M Simmonds (*French & KS3 Manager*)
Mr J Southgate (*Mathematics*)
Mrs M Stiles (*Geography*)
Mr P Twist (*Science*)
Mr N Walkinshaw (**Mathematics Faculty*)
Miss A Ward (*English GTP*)
Mr N Watson (*Mathematics*)
Mr G Weaver (*Year 2 Teacher*)
Mrs V Wood (*Reception Teacher*)
Mrs H Woodbridge (*EAL*)
Mrs A Woodgate (*English, EAL*)

Junior School:
Mrs J Apperley (*Year 6 Teacher*)
Miss A Brady (*Year 1 and Head of Early Years*)
Mrs S Crossley (*Year 6 Teacher*)
Mr M Davies (*Head of Primary Sport*)

Mrs C Gardiner (*Junior Teacher*)
Mrs P Garnett (*§Primary Learning Support Teacher*)
Mrs E Garstang (*Year 5 Teacher*)
Dr M Hine (*Head of Primary Education*)
Mrs L Ireland (*Year 4 and Advanced Skills Teacher*)
Mrs Z James (*Head of Nursery*)
Mrs M Mayne (*Infant Teacher*)
Miss S Mullins (*Year 3 Teacher*)
Mrs D Searle (*Year 6 Teacher*)
Mrs M Sharp (*Year 5 Teacher*)
Mr G Weaver (*Year 2 Teacher*)
Mrs V Wood (*Reception Teacher*)

Visiting Staff:
Miss M Dulgarn (*Piano*)
Mrs A Baker (*Piano*)
Ms S Maxwell (*Guitars*)
Mr G Gillings (*Percussion*)
Mr R Reavill (*Voice*)
Mrs Tinker (*Piano*)
Miss S Wilkinson (*Classroom Assistant*)

Administrative Staff:
Mr G Allen (*Facilities Manager*)
Mrs D Baber (*Business & Finance Manager*)
Mrs D Bickers (*Officer Manager*)
Mrs S Bosher (*Publications & Events Manager*)
Mr B Connell (*Head Groundsperson*)
Mrs J Debenham (*College Nurse*)
Mrs B Donovan (*Receptionist*)
Mrs S Gregory (*Registrar*)
Mr R Johnson (*Catering*)
Mr D Jones (*SSI, Boarding, CCF*)
Mrs L Leech (*Receptionist, Administration Junior School*)
Mrs E MacKay (*Reprographics/Library*)
Mr D McGinn (*Catering Manager*)
Sister Carmel (*College Chaplain*)
Mrs J Smith (*Head of Senior Girls' Boarding*)
Mrs P Walton (*HLTA*)
Mrs J Womble (*Principal's PA*)

Ethos. We believe that successful education depends upon a three-way partnership between the child, their parents and the College. Effective communication is at the heart of this, hence our extensive assessments and reporting system. We instil in our pupils a sense of responsibility, whilst encouraging self-reliance with a willingness to cooperate as part of a team.

St Joseph's prides itself on its pastoral care and the individual support and guidance it gives each child as he or she progresses through the school. This ethos, along with the pursuit of excellence, is reflected in all aspects of life at the College whether it is academic, sporting, cultural or spiritual.

Developments. In May 2006, St Joseph's College received a glowing inspection report, following a week-long ISI inspection by eleven inspectors. Their conclusions were that the College provides a well-rounded education of high quality and is committed to academic success within the context of fully developing all the talents and skills of its pupils. The report stated that "high standards of behaviour are the norm, pupils are contagiously enthusiastic about the educational opportunities offered by the school; examination results are a success story" and concluded that St Joseph's is a school which is "going places".

Never a school to rest on its laurels, further development and success have followed. Demand for places continues to rise and the school is expanding rapidly. In January 2008, the innovative new Junior school building was formally opened. This fascinating curved building with its Maltings-style wind-catcher towers provides a highly stimulating environment for pupils between 2 and 11 years of age and is resourced with the latest technological and physical resources.

Boarding. Although primarily a day school, we also offer flexible and full boarding facilities in family-run, spacious and warm boarding houses.

The College has two boarding houses, Senior 14–18, and Junior 11–14, which have undergone extensive modernisation to provide single study-bedrooms for the seniors and small, 3–4 bed rooms for the juniors.

Curriculum. The curriculum is designed to provide a broad and balanced education for all pupils from 2 to 18. Strong foundations in the core skills of reading, writing and numeracy, are laid down in the Infant Department. The Junior Section continues the process of preparing the children for their secondary education by concentrating further on the core skills. In addition to these subjects, Science, French, Music and PE are taught and the children are introduced to a wider curriculum, including Design and Technology, Art, History, Geography, RE, IT and Games.

The Senior School prepares pupils for entrance to universities, other forms of higher education and the professions. Pupils are set according to ability in certain subjects. In Years 7–9 the emphasis continues to be placed on the core subjects whilst developing knowledge, skills and experiences necessary for the GCSE courses. In addition to the mainstream subjects, all students follow an RE and PSHE course. Languages studied at the College include Mandarin, French and Spanish.

GCSE studies maintain a broad and balanced curriculum but with the introduction of a degree of specialisation. Mathematics, English Language and Literature, Double Science Award, a Modern Foreign Language and RE are compulsory. Once again core subjects continue to be set by ability.

To cater for developing interests and abilities there is a wide range of further choices from Graphics and Photography to Art, Dance and PE to Business Studies. In addition all students follow a short course GCSE in RE, which focuses on moral and current issues and combines with the PSHE course. PE and Sport complete the curriculum in the GCSE years.

The majority of our pupils continue into the Sixth Form to complete their A Level courses before going on to university. There is a wide range of subjects available in the Sixth Form and students choose 4 AS Level subjects for examination in the Lower Sixth, reducing to 3 A2s for completion in the Upper Sixth. General Studies are an integral part of the post-16 curriculum at the College, with a wide range of sporting and other leisure and cultural opportunities.

A Learning Support department operates throughout the College to provide support individually or in small groups particularly for Dyslexia and the more able child.

There is comprehensive careers guidance from Year 9 and extensive help with university admission in the Sixth Form.

Extra-Curricular Activities. Sport, Art, Music and Drama are strongly encouraged, together with participation in the CCF and The Duke of Edinburgh's Award scheme. A large number of extra-curricular clubs meet weekly. Regular ski trips, activity holidays and language exchanges are organised throughout the College.

Admission. Entry to the College is normally at 4+, 7+, 11+, 13+ and the Sixth Form, with applications for occasional vacancies at other ages. The entry process includes an interview, a test and a report from the applicant's previous school. For the Sixth Form, the test is replaced by GCSE results.

Fees per term (2011-2012). Nursery: £38.85 (per full session); Infants: £2,415; Juniors: £3,050 (day), £5,025 (weekly boarding), £5,690 (full boarding), £5,135 (overseas boarding). Senior School: £3,600–£4,075 (day), £6,195–£6,770 (weekly boarding), £6,485–£8,375 (full boarding).

Scholarships and Bursaries. The College offers a number of Academic Scholarships each year for different points of entry, as well as Scholarships for Music, Sport and

Drama. A number of bursaries are also available in cases of need. Please contact the Registrar for further information.

Charitable status. St Joseph's College is a Registered Charity, number 1051688. It exists to provide high quality education for children.

St Joseph's College

Upper Redlands Road, Reading RG1 5JT
Tel: 0118 966 1000
Fax: 0118 926 9932
e-mail: mailbox@stjosephscollegereading.co.uk
website: www.stjosephscollegereading.co.uk

Motto: *Optima Deo*

Patron: Rt Revd Crispian Hollis, Bishop of Portsmouth

Board of Governors:
Mr T Nickson (*Chairman*)
Sister Magdalena, Sisters of St Marie Madeleine Postel
Sister Helen, Sisters of St Marie Madeleine Postel
Dr Margaret Cross
Mrs Kate Firth
Miss K Gripton
Mr D Hallé
Mrs D Mason
Mr W Walker
Mrs H Buckle

Staff:

Headmistress: **Mrs Maureen T Sheridan**, BA Hons, CertEd, MA Ed, NPQH

Deputy Head & Head of Sixth Form: Mr N A Crean, BA Hons, NPQH

Head of Preparatory School: Mrs G Hope

Bursar: Mr R Vaux

PA to Headmistress and Registrar: Mrs D Kendrick

St Joseph's is an independent day school for pupils aged 3–18 years. The school was founded in 1894 by the Sisters of St Marie Madeleine Postel and welcomes pupils of all denominations and faiths. There are over 300 pupils on the school roll, making it large enough to offer a varied curriculum and excellent facilities but small enough to foster a strong sense of community.

St Joseph's is situated in the university area of Reading, convenient to the town centre and the M4. The Preparatory School is housed in a purpose-built complex, designed with the needs of small children in mind, which is adjacent to the Senior School campus. Classrooms and laboratories throughout the school are well equipped and within the grounds there is a full range of outdoor sporting facilities, including an indoor heated swimming pool.

At St Joseph's we work in partnership with our parents. We create an environment that is safe and happy, in which academic and social skills, individual talent and consideration of the needs of others are developed. We are justly proud of the achievements of our pupils, whether in the form of GCSE or A Level results or in seeing them grow in confidence and develop as young adults.

Curriculum. Tuition is organised in classes/tutorials/small groups. The average class size is 20 and there is a teacher/student ratio of 1:10.

Academic life at St Joseph's College is not confined to the National Curriculum, but this forms the basis of the school's teaching. Preparatory School pupils undertake Key Stages 1 and 2 testing in addition to regular monitoring. In the College the rigour of GCSE, AS and A Level requirements keep us close to the National Curriculum. For each Year Group there is regular testing with a Parents' Information Evening at the beginning of each academic year, plus two Consultative Evenings to discuss performance.

Academic standards are high and nearly all our Sixth Formers go on to higher education. In the summer 2010 examinations, a pass rate of 100% was achieved at A Level, with 80% Grades A*–B. In GCSE, 100% of pupils achieved five or more passes at Grades A*–C and 94% achieved 8 or more passes at Grades A*–C.

Artistic talent and practical skills are encouraged at all ages. Original and exciting work is produced in Art/Textiles, in CDT and Food Technology.

The school has a strong music and drama tradition. There are various orchestras, musical groups and choirs, regularly touring abroad, with the most recent visits being to Italy and Ireland, which included singing inside St Peter's Basilica in Rome, St Mark's Basilica in Venice and at Aras An Uachtarain in Dublin for the President of Ireland. The girls regularly give concerts and there are many opportunities to take part in Drama, Dance and Debating. The school has been awarded Artsmark Silver Status by the Arts Council of England.

Sport is an important part of life at St Joseph's. A full range of activities, from athletics and swimming to team games, is offered. Pupils are regularly chosen to represent their county in athletics, swimming, tennis and hockey.

Pastoral Care. Form Tutors form the backbone of the pastoral care system at St Joseph's. By developing an open and trusting relationship with their pupils, they can provide a receptive ear and the essential support and help that may be required.

Admission. Admission to the Preparatory School is by interview. Entry to the Senior School is by assessment, interview and a report from the pupil's previous school. Good GCSE grades, an interview, plus a report from the previous school, are required for admission to the Sixth Form.

Scholarships. (*See Scholarship Entries section.*) The school awards a number of scholarships each year. All candidates applying for entry into Year 7 are required to sit an entrance assessment and are automatically considered for an academic scholarship. These scholarships are reviewed annually up to the end of Year 11. Scholarships are also awarded for music, drama, sport and on entry to the Sixth Form. Bursaries are also available by application to the Governors.

Fees per term (2011-2012). Senior £2,980–£3,680; Preparatory £1,745–£2,515.

Charitable status. St Joseph's College Reading Trust is a Registered Charity, number 277077. It exists to promote and provide for the advancement of education of children and young persons.

Scarborough College

Filey Road, Scarborough, North Yorkshire YO11 3BA
Tel: 01723 360620
Fax: 01723 377265
e-mail: admin@scarboroughcollege.co.uk
website: www.scarboroughcollege.co.uk

Motto: *Pensez Fort*

Governors:
Dr J Renshaw (*Chairman*)
M Baines
Mrs G Braithwaite
A S Green
J M Green
Mrs L Griffin, BA Hons, BPhil (*Deputy Chairman*)
Mrs Z Harrison
R Marshall

Dr M Precious, MA, MPhil, DPhil
Dr I G H Renwick, MB BS
Dr C Rhodes
J Rowlands
P Worsley, QC, MA

Business Manager & Clerk to the Governors: Sqn Ldr T
    Fenton, MBE

Head: Mrs I Nixon, BA Hons York, MA Leeds, PGCE

Scarborough College is a co-educational day and boarding school for children aged 3–18. The College and its Junior School are on the same campus which is about a mile
from the centre of Scarborough and has fine views overlooking the South Bay of the town. Although the three boarding
houses are separate from the main campus, they are within
easy walking distance of the school.

Entry to the Senior School is at 11+ where children are
prepared for GCSE at the end of Year 11 and the International Baccalaureate in the Sixth Form.

For further up-to-date information on the school, please
visit the College's website.

For further details about Scarborough College Junior
School, see entry in IAPS section.

Fees per term (2011-2012). Senior School: £3,357–
£3,743 (day), £5,446–£6,139 (UK full and weekly boarding), £5,903–£6,543 (Overseas full and weekly boarding).
Junior School: £1,907–£3,064 (day).

Charitable status. Scarborough College is a Registered
Charity, number 529686.

Shebbear College

Shebbear, North Devon EX21 5HJ
Tel: 01409 282000
Fax: 01409 281784
e-mail: registrar@shebbearcollege.co.uk
website: www.shebbearcollege.co.uk

Shebbear College, set in 85 acres of healthy Devon countryside, was founded in 1841 by the Bible Christians. It is now
part of the Board of Management for Methodist Residential
Schools. It is fully co-educational for children between the
ages of 3 to 18 years. The secure, happy family atmosphere
at Shebbear, free from urban distractions, offers pupils full,
weekly, or occasional boarding and day education. We aim
to give our pupils self-confidence; we teach our pupils to be
self-disciplined and they leave the College with excellent
qualifications. Thus offering all our pupils "*A foundation for
life*".

Chairman of the Governors: Mr M J Saltmarsh

Headmaster: Mr R S Barnes, BA

Deputy Headmistress: Mrs A Farrell, MEd, BEd

Chaplain: Revd D Hull, MLitt, BTh Cantab

Bursar: Mr B Horn, ACMA, ACIS

Teaching Staff:
* *Head of Department or Subject Leader*

Mrs S Akers, CertEd (*Learning Support*)
Mr A Ashfield, MA, BA Hons (*Business Studies &
    Economics*)
Mrs P Back (*ESL*)
Mr A Barlow, BA (*Art*)
Mrs E Bearpark, LLB (*Mathematics*)
Mr A Bryan, CertEd
Mr I Burnett, BA
Mrs C Cardoo, BSc
Mr S Clewley, BSc (*Physics*)

Mr A Colville (*Biology*)
Dr S Crook, BSc, PhD (*Chemistry*)
Mrs A French
Mrs V Hale (*Food Technician*)
Miss S Ham, BSc (*Girls Games*)
Miss M Hily
Mrs D Jorgensen, BA (*Modern Languages*)
Mr M Langridge (*History*)
Mrs A Lofthouse
Mrs F Lovett, YTEFLA, CELTA
Mr M Newitt, BSc, FRGS (*Geography*)
Mr K Parker, GRSM (*Music*)
Mrs L Parker, GRSM, LRAM
Mrs S Pullin BA
Mrs K Purdew, CertEd
Mr M Rogers, MA (*Religious Studies*)
Mr A Steel, BSc (*Head of Boys Games*)
Mrs P Thomas, BA (*IT*)
Mr S Trask, BEng
Mrs J Welby, ALA (*Librarian*)

Senior House Staff (Boarding):
Mrs L Quirk, BSA (*Head of Boarding & Pastoral Care*)
Mr A Ashfield (*Pollard Houseparent*)
Mr B Harman (*Pyke Houseparent*)

Junior School Teaching Staff:
Mr B Harman, BSc (*Head of Junior School*)
Mrs J Burnett, BA
Mrs T Brock, BEd, HDipEd
Mrs F Goode, CertEd
Mrs D Jones, BA Ed, Certs SPCD
Mrs J Harman, MA, HDipEd

Kindergarten: Mrs J Biddlecoombe

Registrar: Mrs S Lindley
Marketing Coordinator: Miss E Burwood

Medical Department:
Dr A Aldoori, MBChB, MRCGP, FPCert
Sister R Light, SEN, RGN Dip Part 1

Visiting Music Staff:
Ms T Bennett
Mrs R Cornish
Mr A Davies
Mr G Goodwin
Mr J McAvoy
Mrs A Morphy
Ms H Riches
Ms R Slater-Lyons

Number in College. In the Senior School there are 276
pupils, of whom 81 are boarders, and a total of 77 pupils in
the Junior School.

Situation and Location. Shebbear College borders on
Dartmoor National Park and stands in 85 acres of unspoilt
countryside. It can be easily reached by main road and rail
links; only 40 miles west of Exeter and 40 miles north of
Plymouth. Both cities have their own regional and international airport.

Buildings. The main College buildings include Prospect
House, Lake Chapel, Beckly Wing, Shebbear College Junior
School, Science Department, Music School, Sixth Form
Centre, Language Centre and Sports Hall. There are 2 senior
boarding houses and 1 junior boys boarding house. (The jun-
ior girls have a separate area within the senior girls house).

In recent years there has been an impressive record of
school building projects. The latest work has been to build a
full-size all-weather-pitch and multi-gym. Work has commenced on a Junior School extension to open September
2011. All classrooms have interactive whiteboards.

Admission. The Kindergarten accepts children from the
age of 2½ where boys and girls are admitted to the Junior
School from the age of five. Entrance to the College at 11

years from other schools is by examination in January for entry in September. Pupils are also admitted at 13 or 14 after submitting Common Entrance Examination papers, but if they wish they may sit our own entrance papers instead. Entry into the Sixth Form is conditional upon GCSE performance.

Houses. Every pupil belongs to a House – Ruddle, Thorne or Way. These Houses organise activities and games competitions throughout the year. Our boarders also belong to an additional boarding house – Pollard House for senior boy boarders, Pyke House for junior boy boarders and Ruddle House for girl boarders – each having a Senior Houseparent and two assistants who "live-in". The House Tutors watch each child's progress academically as well as their general development.

Curriculum. All pupils at Shebbear College follow the National Curriculum until the age of 14. A wide choice of subjects is available in the following two years, leading to GCSE, but everyone is obliged to take English, Mathematics, Science and, usually, a foreign language. In the Sixth Form there is not only a wide choice of A2 and AS levels, but there is particularly flexible timetabling which enables students to mix Arts and Science subjects.

Sport. With more than 25 acres of playing fields, modern sports hall with multi-gym, squash courts, cricket nets, all-weather pitch, tennis and netball courts, and indoor climbing centre, pupils have the security to exercise within the school grounds confidently. The main games covered for the boys are rugby, football, hockey and cricket, in which we have fixtures with most of the major schools in the South West of England. For the girls, we have teams in netball, hockey, rounders and tennis. All pupils are also offered tennis, basketball, squash, athletics, cross-country, badminton, and table tennis. All pupils up to the 4th Form have one afternoon of games plus an additional one period of PE every week.

Music and Drama. Pupils are strongly encouraged to participate in music and drama. Our choir has over 40 members and our orchestra, which represents most instruments, also has over 40 members. Players perform regularly in concerts and instrumental ensembles. Every term candidates proudly achieve Honours and Distinctions with The Associated Board of the Royal School for Music. Also, every term, a theatrical production is performed to a very high standard.

Societies and Activities. All pupils participate in at least 4 afternoons a week of extra-curricular activities. This widens their interests and develops their self-confidence. The list of activities is endless and includes the usual and unusual. Many pupils enjoy getting involved with Ten Tors training, hill-walking, camping, sailing, canoeing, and surfing. The newly-formed Army Cadet Corp is proving to be very popular and many pupils are involved in the Duke of Edinburgh's Award scheme.

Careers. Careers advice is taken very seriously. Staff help our students prepare for their chosen career. The College is a member of ISCO. Individual attention is given at appropriate levels and a team of Old Shebbearians covering many professions visits the school regularly and helps with work experience and placement.

Scholarships. (*See Scholarship Entries section.*) Scholarships and Bursaries are offered.

Fees per term (2011-2012). Junior School: Day £1,720–£2,545, Weekly Boarding £3,955–£4,305, Full Boarding £4,815–£5,130. Senior School: Day £3,495, Weekly Boarding £5,460, Full Boarding £6,605.

Charitable status. Shebbear College is a Registered Charity, number 306945. It exists to provide high quality education for children.

Sibford School

Sibford Ferris, Banbury, Oxon OX15 5QL
Tel: 01295 781200
Fax: 01295 781204
e-mail: admissions@sibfordschool.co.uk
website: www.sibford.oxon.sch.uk

Founded 1842.

A Co-educational Independent Boarding (full/weekly) and Day School. Membership of SHMIS, BSA, AGBIS.

There are 443 pupils in the school aged between 3 and 18: 364 pupils in the Senior School and 79 pupils in the Junior School.

There are 44 full-time and 34 part-time teachers plus visiting staff.

Chair of School Committee: Seren Wildwood

***Head*: Michael Goodwin**, BA

Deputy Head: Maggie Guy, BA (*English*)

Senior School:
* *Head of Department*
§ *Part-time*

§Michael Ahmad, BA (*Music*)
§Charlotte Andrew, BA (*Classroom Assistant*)
Simon Baker, BSc Econ (*Geography)
Stephen Ball, BSc, MSc (*Mathematics*)
Derek Bottomley, BSc (*Mathematics*)
Angela Bovill, BEd, CertEd (**Horticulture, Countryside/ Environmental Sciences*)
Juan Casasbuenas (*Science*) (*Maternity Cover*)
Simon Chard, BA (*PE, Vocational Education*)
John Charlesworth, MA (*Director of Studies,* *Science)
Debra Collins, BSc (*Mathematics)
Lesley Cooley, BSc (*Classroom Assistant*)
Zoë Connor, BA, MA, AKC (**Religious Studies, Philosophy & Ethics*)
§Linda Denwood (*Food Technology*)
§Christopher Dudley, BA, MEd (*Economics*)
Debby Evans, CertEd PCE, Cert SpLD (*Dyslexia*) (**Information Technology*)
§Vanessa Evans, CertEd, Dip TS (*RS*)
§Claire Ferley, BSc, GTTP (*PE*)
§Richard Ferley (*PE*)
§Rebecca Flynn, BA, MA, CTEFL (*Psychology, EAL*)
Andrew Foakes, MA, BA (*English, Media*)
Andrew Glover, Dip SpLD, BA, Dip TEFL (*Dyslexia*)
Fay Godwin, BA, CertEd (*Dyslexia)
§Alan Greenslade-Hibbert, LLB (*EAL*)
Victoria Hall, BA (*English, Media, Careers, PSHE/ Citizenship*)
§Cath Harding, BSc (*Science*)
Susan Hinde, BSc (*Mathematics*)
§Susan Hirst, BA (*English*)
§Deborah Holroyd, BSc, MA Education (*Science*)
§Gillian Hughes, BA, Cert SpLD (*Classroom Assistant*)
Maria Jackson, BA, RADA, MA, PCGE (*Drama)
§Mary Kelly, Dip SpLD, AMBDA, FE & HE Teach Cert SpLD
Jane Kenehan (*Classroom Assistant, Dyslexia*)
Tracy Knowles, BA Ed (*Assistant Deputy Head, English, Activities Coordinator*)
§Jo Mayes (*EAL*)
Mary Memarzia, BA, MA (**Head of Sixth Form, Media Studies, English*)
Andrew Newbold, BSc, PhD (*Director of Studies (Examinations)* Science)
Lesley Norton, CertEd (*Textiles*)
Christopher Orr, BEd (*Business Studies, Careeers*)

Dolores Papin, Licence Anglais, Maîtrise Anglais (*Modern Foreign Languages*)
§Richard Phethean, BA, PGATC (*Ceramics*)
Alison Phillips, BA (*PE*)
Linda Phillips, BSc, MA (*Mathematics*)
Sally Pickering, BA (**EAL*)
§Matthew Platt, Grad Dip Music, LGSM Teaching Dip (*Music*)
Gracia Romano, BA (*Classroom Assistant*)
Anna Jo Righton, BA (*Director of Studies Teaching and Learning, *Humanities, History*)
Jeremy Ross, MA (*History*)
§Jonathan Seagroatt (*Music Technology, Woodwind*)
Sally Selwood, BSc (*Autism Support Worker*)
Deborah Simpkins, BA (*Modern Foreign Languages*)
§Iona Smith, MA (*Business Studies, PE*)
Michael Spring, BEd (**Expressive Arts Faculty*)
Penelope Spring, BA (**English*)
Victor Stannard, BA, BA Des (**Design & Technology*)
§Elizabeth Staple, BSc (*Geography*)
Laurence Suckling, BA, Cert TEFL (*ESOL*)
§Hazel Syks, BA (*SpLD*)
§Justine Tibbetts, NVQ (*Classroom Assistant*)
§Elizabeth Thomas, BA, ATCL, RADA, IDTA (*Dance*)
Alan Wallis, BSc (*Science*)
§Ginette Wheeldon (*Senior Classroom Assistant*)
Jayne Woolley, BA, TCert (*Discalculia*)
Emma Worsley (*Design Technology, Food Technology*)
§Joseph Zetter, CertEd (*Modern Foreign Languages*)

Junior School:
Patricia Howes, BSc (*Year 6*)
§Jane Kenehan (*Classroom Assistant*)
§Trudy Koochit, BA, CNAA, PGDip Mandarin, DipTEFL (*Year 1/2*)
§Amanda Levett (*Junior School*)
§Michael Maguire, BA (*Classroom Assistant*)
§Gill Newbold, TCert (*Dyspraxia, PE*)
§Sarah Newbould (*Classroom Assistant*)
Edward Rossiter, BSc, PG Dip Social Sciences (*Year 5*)
§Susan Sabin, CertEd, BEd, ALCM, Adv Dp Sp Needs (*Music*)
Alison Sayer (*Year 3*)
§Claire Solesbury (*Classroom Assistant maternity leave*)
§Hazel Sykes (*Classroom Assistant*)
Nicola Watson, BA (*Foundation Stage*)
Vanessa Zimmermann, BA, QTS (*Drama, Year 4*)

Visiting Staff:

Celia Bolton King	Greg Prosser
Richard Hamel	Martin Quinn
Ilone Jones	Hazel Rafter, RAF SoM
Lucy Mason, BMus	Miranda Ricardo
Clifford Pick, ABSM	Dittany Stirling
Peter Pontzen, BSc	Mickey Woodcock

Admissions Officer: Elspeth Gregory

Curriculum. Broad and balanced curriculum which reflects our view that while some may have talent for maths or history others may be gifted in the arts or horticulture. Renowned dyslexia tuition and support for a small number of pupils with other learning difficulties.

Junior School (age 3–11): a wide-ranging curriculum with an emphasis on outdoor education is provided to children in small groups. Literacy, numeracy, science and technology skills are emphasised alongside art, music, drama and PE. Enriched Curriculum in Year 6 with Senior School Staff. Specialist teachers help individual children with specific learning difficulties.

Senior School (age 11–16): all pupils follow courses leading to GCSE, in a curriculum expanding on the National Curriculum. Information Technology is introduced at an early age and the use of laptop computers is widespread.

Dyslexic pupils have special tuition in small groups on a daily basis. Highly regarded Specific Learning Difficulties (Dyslexic) Department provides specialised support within the timetable. Personal and Social Development runs through the school.

Sixth Form (age 16–18) students take A Levels and/or BTEC Diplomas. The Sixth Form curriculum leads to higher education, and offers a particularly wide range of opportunities for further study.

Overseas pupils are welcomed into the school community. English as an additional language is taught by ESOL qualified teachers.

Entry requirements. Admission to the Junior School, Senior School and Sixth Form is by interview and internal tests. Where applicable a report from the candidate's current school is required. No religious requirements.

Examinations offered. A Level, GCSE, BTEC Diploma, Associated Board Music Examinations, Oxford and Cambridge IELTS Examinations.

Academic and leisure facilities. Exceptional Performing & Creative Arts in purpose-built facilities, multi-purpose Sports Centre, squash courts, 25m indoor swimming pool, well-equipped Library and Information Technology Centres, Design Technology Centre, separate Sixth Form Centre, wide range of indoor and outdoor activities, 50 plus-acre campus set in beautiful North Oxfordshire countryside. Three boarding houses (for girls, boys and sixth form). Easy access to Stratford, Oxford, Cheltenham, Birmingham, London.

Religion. The School has a distinctive Quaker ethos. It welcomes pupils of all faiths, backgrounds and nationalities, encouraging in each of them genuine self-esteem in a purposeful, caring and challenging environment.

Fees per term (2011-2012). Full Boarders £7,402–£7,550, Weekly Boarders £6,894–£7,031, Day Pupils £3,811–£3,886.

Junior School: Day Pupils £2,421–£2,928.

The fee for a full term of learning support is £1,350.

Scholarships and Bursaries. The School offers general Academic scholarships and specific scholarships in Art and Music. A limited number of bursaries is offered to both Quaker and non Quaker children.

Charitable status. Sibford School is a Registered Charity, number 1068256. It is a company limited by guarantee under number 3487651. It aims to give all pupils a vehicle to educational and personal success.

Stafford Grammar School

Burton Manor, Stafford ST18 9AT
Tel: 01785 249752
Fax: 01785 255005
e-mail: headsec@staffordgs.plus.com
website: www.stafford-grammar.co.uk

Stafford Grammar School was founded in 1982 in response to demand for independent education in Stafford. The School, which is co-educational, is registered as an educational charity and the Board of Governors is in membership with the Association of Governing Bodies of Independent Schools.

Motto: *Quod tibi hoc alteri*

Patrons:
The Right Hon The Earl of Shrewsbury
The Lord Stafford
The Right Hon The Earl of Lichfield

Governing Body:
B K Hodges (*Chairman*)

J Archer, TD, FCIS, JP   B Baggott

Mrs S Flatters	Mrs P Pearsall
Dr A Kratz, BA, PhD	C Sproston
J Lotz, FRCS	Mrs H Watson Jones
R Nicholls	D White
D Pearsall	A Wright

Headmaster: **M R Darley**, BA

Deputy Head: M P Robinson, BA, DipEd Man

Senior Teacher: Mrs L I Robson, BA
Senior Teacher: Dr PA Johnson, BSc, PhD

Assistant Staff:

C Anderson, BSc	M J Jones, BSc
B Aston, BA	T Kirsch, BSc
Mrs E Ayirebi, BA	G R Lamplough, BMus
D R Beauchamp, BSc	Mrs A Lonsdale, BSc
Mrs R Beauchamp, BA	Miss L McConville, BSc
G Beckett, BSc	D Mole, BA
Mrs M Booth, BSc	Mrs P H Patrick, BSc
Mrs C L Clough, BA	Mrs E L Paton, BA
D Craig, BA, UED	Mrs B Robson, BSc
Dr F G Crane, BSc, PhD	G Robson, BSc
Mrs J A Fletcher, BA, ADB	Mrs A M Saxon, BEd, MA
Dr R Foster, BSc, PhD	Mrs F F Shakesheave, BSc,
S Godwin, MSc, BA	BA
R C Green, BA	Mrs D Shaughnessy, BA,
Mrs L J Griffiths, BA	MA
Miss H Hackett, BSc	J Smith, BA
L J Harwood, BEd	Mrs S Smith, BA
Mrs M M Hinton, BA	Mrs A J Taylor, BA
Mrs K Horsley, BA	L H Thomas, BA
A C Johnson, BSc	Mrs T Whyte, BSc, MSc

Chaplain: Prebendary R Sargent, MA

Bursar: J Downes

Headmaster's Secretary: Mrs S M Pickavance

Number in School. There are 415 pupils (11–18 years) of whom 227 are boys and 188 girls. There is a Sixth Form of around 100. Stafford Preparatory School has approximately 70 pupils.

Stafford Grammar School is housed in a fine Victorian manor house, designed by Augustus Pugin, standing in 40 acres of grounds with sports pitches, tennis courts and extensive additional specialist accommodation. Recent additions have included a sports hall and music centre, cafeteria, additional classrooms blocks, three ICT rooms, broadband internet and network access across the site and a mezzanine floor library. A new Science and Sixth Form Centre opened in 2007. Sixteen acres of sports land have recently been developed to further enhance outside sport provision.

Curriculum. In Year 7 and Year 8 all pupils follow a common course consisting of English, Mathematics, Science, French, German, Geography, History, Music, Art, Drama, Computing, Design, Technology, Religious Education and Physical Education. Year 9 sees Science divide into separate subjects.

Pupils in Years 10 and 11 study nine or ten subjects at GCSE: English (2), Mathematics, Science (IGCSE dual or triple award) and a language, together with three further subjects chosen from a whole range including humanities and practical subjects. Physical Education continues and Careers and Life Skills are introduced.

There is setting in Mathematics from Year 8, Science from Year 9 and English from Year 10. Other subjects are taught in mixed ability groups. Classes are kept small (maximum 20) so that pupils can receive individual attention.

In the Lower Sixth Form students study three or four A Level subjects (AS) leading to three or four A Level subjects (A2) in the Upper Sixth Form. Approximately 20 A Level subjects are available.

Creativity and the Arts. The School has an extensive Art and Design Department. Pupils' powers of observation and awareness are developed through practical skills and theoretical studies involving areas as varied as painting, printing, 3-D work, photography and textiles. There are frequent competitions and exhibitions of work as well as projects linked with other departments.

Music plays an important part in the life of the School. There is an orchestra, a concert band and choirs which perform on many occasions in musicals, church services and concerts. Ensembles, both instrumental and vocal, are encouraged. Pupils have the opportunity to learn to play a wide range of musical instruments with tuition provided by peripatetic teachers.

Drama enables pupils to gain confidence and self-understanding. It is particularly effective in the early years in the School. Two annual School Plays are major productions on the School's excellent stage and involve a large number of pupils.

Art and Drama are available at both GCSE and A Level.

Peripatetic LAMDA tuition is available from Grade 1 to Gold Medal (Grade 8). LAMDA students also attend local drama festivals.

Sport and Activities. Whilst competitive sport plays a prominent part in School life, the emphasis is also on preparation for future leisure time.

The School has outstanding sports facilities and the following sports are available: Soccer, Hockey, Rugby, Cricket, Tennis, Badminton, Basketball, Netball, Volleyball, Athletics, Gymnastics, Rounders, Table Tennis, and Health-related Fitness, as well as Swimming. The School has an extensive fitness suite.

The School plays a large number of matches against other schools, both state and independent, and is fully involved in local leagues. Individuals regularly secure places in Staffordshire and Midlands teams.

Our range of activities is deliberately wide since we believe that every child is good at something and that it is our job to discover and develop talent in any direction.

There are many Clubs and Societies of widely differing kinds and a large number of pupils are working for The Duke of Edinburgh's Award Scheme.

At present there are 15 inter-House competitions. These range from Technology to Public Speaking and from Football to Hobbies, and include some which are specifically for younger pupils.

The intention of these is not only to enable as many pupils as possible to represent their Houses, but also to stress that we value excellence in any area.

Pastoral Care. In its pastoral organisation, the School seeks to nurture the potential of every child giving both support and encouragement in an overt and practical way. The School is divided into three houses, the Head of House being the key figure in the academic and personal development of each child. Tutor groups are kept small and are based on the House to maintain continuity and to strengthen communal bonds. Tutors maintain strong links with each pupil using a programme of active tutoring which includes scheduled interviews. We place great emphasis on close contact with parents, believing that lack of progress and other problems are best addressed jointly and as early as possible.

In the Sixth Form a slightly different system operates. Although retaining the same House Tutor, the pupil will have a Form Tutor from a specialist team of Sixth Form Tutors. Additionally one of the Senior Teachers is attached to this team. Further to this is the opportunity for each pupil to choose a Personal Tutor with whom to build a special rapport.

Sixth Form. The Sixth Form is the ideal environment in which to foster confidence, responsibility, leadership, initiative and self-discipline.

The keynote of the Sixth Form is freedom with responsibility. At this stage pupils still need help in planning their time and in establishing good working habits, and the guidance of an understanding tutor can mean the difference between success and failure.

Careers. Considerable attention is paid to career advice, and there are frequent visits by speakers from industry and the professions. From Year 10 onwards, individual advice is given by our own careers staff, and pupils are also encouraged to consult the County Careers Service.

Religion. Although we welcome pupils of all faiths, or none, the School is a Christian foundation.

The School seeks to live by the Christian ideal, in particular by being a community in which members genuinely care about each other.

Admission. Entrance is by examination and interview in order to ensure that pupils have sufficient reasoning ability to be able to attempt GCSE in a reasonable range of subjects.

Entrance to the Sixth Form is by GCSE results and interview.

Scholarships and Bursaries. The Governors have allocated funds to enable pupils of exceptional ability or limited means to join the school.

Fees per term (from January 2011). Grammar School: £3,249 excluding lunch; Preparatory School (including lunch): Years 3 & 4 £2,801, Years 5 & 6 £2,912.

Stafford Preparatory School opened, in purpose-built accommodation, in September 2007 admitting pupils into Year 5 and Year 6. A Year 4 class was admitted in September 2008 and a Year 3 class in 2009. Stafford Preparatory School provides exciting opportunities for pupils to prepare for selective senior school education at Stafford Grammar School or elsewhere.

Charitable status. Stafford Independent Grammar School Limited is a Registered Charity, number 513031. It exists to provide education for children.

Stanbridge Earls School

Romsey, Hampshire SO51 0ZS
Tel: 01794 529400
Fax: 01794 511201
e-mail: admin@stanbridgeearls.co.uk
website: www.stanbridgeearls.co.uk

Number of Boys: 155 aged 11–18.
Number of Girls: 43 aged 11–18.

Governors:
D J Beeby (*Chairman*)
C P Bulman
J A Chandler
R Crockett
D Du Croz
J K Glen
P C Goodship
R P Grime

A J Knight (*Vice-Chairman*)
Mrs C Marsden
Mrs N J Moss
N Rogers
Mrs S Warner
M J Woodhall, FRICS

Bursar and Secretary to Governors: B R Taylor, Fellow ACCA

Headmaster: P J A Trythall, BA Stirling

Deputy Head Curriculum: D J Durnell, BSc, PGCE London
Deputy Head Pastoral: R J Bailey, BA Canterbury, CertEd, MEd Southampton

Assistant Staff:
† *House Master/Mistress*

Mr Robert J Bailey, MA Ed, BA Hons, PGCE (*Mathematics*)
Ms Marion B Adams, BSc, H DipEd, PG Dip Lit & Dys (*Life Skills*)
Mrs Alexandra Archer, BSc Hons, Cert MRCSLT (*Speech & Language Therapy*)

Mrs Kathyrn Barber, BA Hons (*English, Accelerated Learning Centre ALC*)
Miss Zoe Boyle, BA Hons (*Music*)
Miss Monica Cassidy, CertEd (*Auto Studies*)
Mrs Barbara Jean Coleman, CertEd, PG Dip SpLD (*ALC*)
Mrs Gillian Coppock, BA Hons, Dip OT (*Occupational Therapy*)
Mrs Mary Cornforth, BA Hons, PGCE (*Mathematics*)
Ms Angela Cryne, BA Hons, PGCE (*Junior School*)
Dr Patrick Dolan, BSc, PhD, PGCE (*Mathematics Learning Centre MLC*)
Mrs Alison Doherty, BA Hons, PGCE (*Media Studies*)
Mrs Caroline D'Urso, Dip Cert MRCSLT (*Speech & Language Therapy*)
Mr David J Durnell, BSc Hons, PGCE (*ICT*)
Mrs R J Eachus, BA, MRCSLT (*Speech & Language Therapy*)
Mrs Lynn Edwards, CertEd, PG Dip SpLD (*ALC*)
Mr Simon Elliott, BA Hons
Mr Reece Hancock, BEd (*Design & Technology*)
Mr James Hibberd (*Cricket*)
Dr Carys F Hughes, BSc Hons QTS (*Science, Biology*)
Miss Jean S Hughes, BA Hons, PGCE (*Modern Languages*)
Mrs Jane Johnston, Dip Ad Art/Design, Dip Ad Fashion/Textile (*Art & Design*)
Mrs Valerie Kelly, MSc, PGCE (*English*)
Ms Sarah Kinder, BSc (*PE*)
Ms Pamela Lake, BA Hons, PGCE (*Home Economics*)
Ms Paula Little, BEd, Cert Ad SEN, Dip Ad Ed SEN (*SENCo*)
Mrs Margaret Mackay, BEd, Dip BDA (*ALC*)
Ms Lisa Mann, BA Hons QTS (*Mathematics*)
Mrs Susan Martinelli, BSc (*Mathematics*)
Mrs Wendy L Molyneaux, BA Hons, BEd, Dip RSA SpLD (*ALC*)
Ms Nicola Morgan, BA Hons, PGCE (*English*)
Mrs Kay Morrish, BSc Hons
Dr Frank E Myszor, BA Hons, PhD, PGCE, Dip Ch Lit (*English*)
Mr Pierre Neethling, BA Hons, B HOD (*ICT, PE*)
Mrs Joanne Neudegg, BEd, Dip SpLD, AMBDA (*MLC*)
Mr Lance Nicholson, BA Hons, MA, CertEd (*Art & Design*)
Mr Gary Pearce, BA Hons, PGCE (*Business, Careers, †B House*)
Mr Paul C Pellatt, BA Hons, MA Ed, PGCE (*Geography, Leisure & Tourism*)
Ms Kate Percival, BA Hons, CertEd, PGCE (*MLC*)
Mrs Sarah L Puffitt, BEd, RSA TEFLA SpLD (*ESL*)
Mrs Kyria Richardson, BEd, PGCE (*Performance Studies; †C House*)
Mr Michael Roberts, BSc Hons (*Chemistry*)
Mr David Rose, BA Hons QTS (*Business/Citizenship*)
Ms Sue Rowe, BA Hons QTS (*MLC*)
Mr Christopher F Rowney, BA Hons, PGCE (*English, Media Studies; †A House*)
Mr Jonathon Stephens, BA Hons (*Junior School*)
Mrs Shelley Stevens, BSc Hons, Cert MRCSLT (*Speech & Language Therapy*)
Mr Grant Taylor, BEd Hons, MA SEN, Cert DPC (*PE; †D House*)
Mrs Diane Trotman, CertEd (*MLC*)
Mrs Alison J Visser, BA Hons, PGCE (*History*)
Dr Julie Wait, MEd, PLD, PG Dip, Dip RSA SpLD, CertEd TEFL (*ALC, ESL*)
Mr Nigel Warren, BEd Hons (*Maths*)
Mrs Sally Wesley, ACIB, BSc Hons, PGCE (*Mathematics, MLC*)
Mrs Helen Wheelwright, Joint Hons PGCE (*English, ALC*)

Visiting Staff:
Ms E Clark, BMus Hons (*Violin, Viola*)
Mr P M McKenna, BTec (*Drums*)

Mrs S Ormiston, BA Hons Cardiff, PGCE Reading (*Piano*)
Mr D Pruden (*Guitar*)
Mrs M Shearer, GTLC Hons, LTCL, PGCE (*Violin*)
Mr I T G Smith, AGSM with Distinction, PGCE Reading (*Brass*)
Miss R Weatherall, BA Hons Southampton, MSt Oxford
Miss M Williams, BA Hons, PGDip (*Woodwind*)

Houseparent, Goulds: Mrs F Callender
Houseparent, New House: Mrs P Jones
Houseparent, Agora Junior Boys: Mrs E Neethling, BA, HEd Soc Stellenbosch, SA
Houseparent, John Attlee: M Bernard, BEd
Houseparent, Cornock-Taylor: Mrs J Taylor
Houseparent, B Annex: Miss S-J Stanwyck, BSc
Houseparent, Forum: Mrs T Byfield

Administrative Staff:
Finance Officer: Ms J A Ramsay
Finance Assistant: Mr C Nunn
Headmaster's PA: Mrs A Cox
Medical Officer: Dr Scriminger
Registrar: Mrs A Spicer, BTec
Sister-in-Charge: Miss J L Thompson, RGN, RNS
School Nurses:
Mrs M Bavington, RGN
Mrs A O'Neill, RGN
Mrs N Atkins, RGN

Foundation and Purpose. Stanbridge Earls was founded in 1952 by Mr Anthony Thomas, the original Principal, and his wife with funds granted by the Graham Robertson Trust. The aim of this Trust was to encourage art, music and drama, and these activities have always played an important part in the life of the school. The school has over the years evolved its own special purpose, which is to offer parents a distinctive alternative to the large, traditional Independent Schools and to State Education.

It exists to serve those who are seeking a small and intimate school with a particularly high staffing ratio, individualised teaching methods and qualified additional staff for special needs English and Mathematics. The academic objectives are high GCSE grades for all, A Level for most, and entrance to university or other higher education for those capable of profiting from such courses. It is a particularly suitable school for boys or girls of good academic potential who, for one reason or another, have up to the time of entry not achieved that potential.

Special Needs. Since 1962 the school has been helping pupils with specific word-learning difficulties (dyslexia) and has a custom-built Accelerated Learning Centre where 16 qualified staff are able to help pupils overcome their problems on a one-to-one basis. Dyslexia is not seen as a reason for failure. The internationally-recognised specialist help, together with a whole school approach, means that success is not only possible but expected. There is also a well-established department to help those pupils who have a problem with Maths. Speech communication, EAL and Occupational Therapy are other specialisms on offer. CReSTeD rating "SP".

Entry. There is no entrance examination. The report of an Educational Psychologist may be required in some cases. In others, a pupil's current work may be asked for. A full confidential report must be received from the pupil's current Headmaster or Headmistress, to cover character, interests, ability at work, games or other skills.

Parents and child must attend the school for interview with the Headmaster prior to a 3-day trial period.

Curriculum. The curriculum covers all the basic academic skills and such further courses as can be offered from the skills and enthusiasms of the current staff, such as Automotive Studies. There are 20 subjects taught to GCSE Level. The following are taught at AS and A2 Level: English, History, Geography, Mathematics, Biology, Physics, Chemistry, Art, Textiles, Drama, Media Studies, Music, Design, French, Sports Studies, Leisure & Recreation, Business Studies and ICT.

In the Sixth Form, apart from the above subjects, there is also an emphasis on preparing students for adult life outside school.

Recreation. The school is unusually well equipped for its size for sport. There is a heated, indoor swimming-pool for all-year use, a sports hall, large motor vehicle workshop, a fitness suite, one squash court, two hard tennis courts and a normal games field. Soccer, rugger, cricket, tennis, badminton, basketball, netball, squash, swimming, athletics, TaeKwonDo, riding and golf are provided. A chain of small lakes offers fishing. Many hobbies are encouraged. There is no CCF or other cadet force but interested pupils join the ATC in Romsey and there is a Duke of Edinburgh's Award scheme.

Girls. At present there are 35 boarding places, but there is no limit to the number of day girls. The normal ages of entry is either 11 to 13 years for a full career or into the Sixth Form for A Levels.

Fees per term (2011-2012). Boarding – Foundation level: £8,920 (13+), £8,049 (11+). Day – Foundation level: £6,754 (13+), £6,158 (11+). Our fees are based on banding levels according to a pupil's needs. The figures quoted are at the base foundation level and the fees will be higher where the need is greater. Lessons on a musical instrument are extras.

Bursaries. All Bursaries are awarded on a means-tested basis.

Charitable status. Stanbridge Earls School is a Registered Charity, number 307342. It exists to provide education for boys and girls.

Sunderland High School
UCST

Mowbray Road, Sunderland SR2 8HY
Tel: 0191 567 7674
Fax: 0191 510 3953
e-mail: info.sunderland@church-schools.com
website: www.sunderlandhigh.co.uk

Junior School:
Tonstall House, Ashbrooke Road, Sunderland SR2 7JA
Tel: 0191 514 3278
Fax: 0191 565 6510

Co-educational Day School established by the United Church Schools Trust and opened in 1884.

Governing Body: The Council of the United Church Schools Trust

Local Committee:
Revd Canon S Taylor (*Chairman*)
D K Sherwood-Smith
V Ward
J Milne
R Brannigan
J Lee
P McLachlan
S Atkinson
M Lichfield
J May

Head: **Dr Angela Slater**, BA, PhD

Head of Junior School: Mr C Bulmer, MA Ed, NPQH, CertEd

Ann Bovill, CertEd, Dip Psych (*English, Learning Support*)
Helen Louise Bowerman, BSc, PGCE (*PE*)

Caroline Bowmer, MChem, PGCE (*Head of Science*)
Scott Brotherton, BSc, PGCE (*Biology, Chemistry*)
Joanna Bruce, BA, PGCE (*MFL*)
Judith Charalambous, BA PGCE (*Year 6, KS2 Coordinator*)
Emma Coxon, Level 3 (*Teaching Assistant*)
Jane Melrose Craven, BA Eng, BA MFL (*Media Studies, Head of Y10, i/c Teacher Induction*)
Anne Dargan, BEd (*Year 3, Literacy Coordinator*)
Michelle Diaz, HLTA (*HLTA*)
Valerie Dixon, MA, PGCE (*MFL Coordinator Junior School, MFL*)
Lee Ebblewhite, NVQ Level 3 (*ICT Technician*)
Allyson Eden, BSc Ed (*Year 1, SEN Coordinator*)
Diana Hudson Fearon, NNEB (*EYFS*)
David Whitfield Gardner, BSc, PGCE (*PE*)
Maxime Giron, Lic-ès-Lettres, PGCE (*French*)
Danielle Greest, BA, PGCE (*English, Drama, Head of Year 8*)
David Hair, BA, MA, PGCE (*Head of Art*)
Lynne Hallam, BA, MA, PGCE (*Head of MFL*)
Barbara Harrett, BA PGCE (*MFL*)
William Gordon Hedley, BSc, PGCE (*Head of Biology, Director of Studies*)
Joanne Hill, BA, PGCE (*Director of ICT*)
Joseph Alexander Hodson, BA, PGCE (*Mathematics*)
Susan Elaine Hope, BA, PGCE (*Religious Studies*)
Natalie Jewitt, BEd (*Reception, Numeracy Coordinator*)
Rhiannon Elizabeth Keating, BA, PGCE (*EYFS Coordinator*)
Sarah Kharko, Level 3 (*Teaching Assistant*)
Jenni Louise Little, BSc, PGCE (*PE*)
Lorna Ann Mason, CertEd (*Latin*)
Ian McDonough, BSc Ed, NPQH (*Year 5, Science Coordinator*)
Diane Elizabeth McVay, CertEd (*HLTA*)
Sarah Parker, NNEB Cert Level 3 (*EYFS*)
Colin George Peacock (*ICT Systems Manager*)
David Percy, BSc, PGCE (*Physics*)
Alison Phillips, BA, HLTA (*Learning Support, HLTA – Senior School*)
Rhodri Phillips, BA, PGCE (*Director of Sport*)
Joanne Porterfield (*EYFS*)
Gillian Miriam Prior, PGCE, BA (*Year 2, Deputy Head Junior School*)
Graham Prior, PGCE, BA (*Business Studies*)
Sharon Ann Probets, PGCE, BSc (*Mathematics*)
Tom Render, BEd, AMusTCL (*Music*)
Nathan Rich, BA, PGCE (*Year 6, Junior School Sport Coordinator*)
Jacqueline Robson, BA, PGCE (*Head of VI Form, SENCO, Head of HE*)
Margaret Mary Roddy, BA, PGCE (*Head of History, Head of Year 7*)
Colin Seadon, BA, PGCE (*Mathematics*)
Anthony David Smith, BA, PGCE (*Year 5, ICT Coordinator*)
Cherrylyn Summers, PGCE, BA (*Director of Music*)
Linda Taylor, BEd CertEd (*HE*)
Alan Robert Temple, BSc, PGCE (*Head of Maths*)
Julie Ann Thompson, BEd, CertEd (*Head of English, Head of Year 9*)
Margaret Walls (*Classroom Assistant, School Shop Manager*)
Ann Elizabeth Wayman, BA, CertEd (*Head of Geography, Head of Year 11*)
Philip Wayman, BSc, TechEd (*Head of DT*)
Andrew Wilkinson, BSc, PGCE (*Geography*)

Finance Administrator: Sarah Rachel Lindsay, AAT Level 4
Registrar & PA to Head: Elaine Margaret Martin
Senior School Secretary: Vanessa Charlton

Junior School Secretary: Cheryl Louise McArdle
Admin Assistant: Stephanie Simone Marshall, NVQ Level 2

The school is situated in the centre of the town close to the bus and railway stations. Pupils travel from Gateshead, Chester-le-Street, Washington, South Shields, Peterlee, Houghton-le-Spring and Durham. Transport services are good. School buses are organised from South Shields, Washington, Peterlee, Houghton-le-Spring and Durham.

The Junior School, for Nursery, Infant and Junior boys and girls, was opened by HRH The Princess Royal in May 1994. The building has specialist rooms for Science, Art, Computers and Music as well as a fully equipped Sports Hall. Outside sports facilities include a full sized, floodlit all-weather pitch and grass pitch. These sports facilities are shared by Junior and Secondary pupils for their games programme which includes hockey, netball, football, rugby, cricket, tennis, rounders and athletics. All boys and girls in the Junior School, including the Nursery, have swimming classes also.

The Nursery admits boys and girls on a full or part-time basis and prepares children for school through constructive educational play.

The Infant and Junior Departments provide a sound education for boys and girls. The special feature of the Infant and Junior programme is the Early Language Programme in which German is core curriculum for all pupils from the age of 4+. Junior School pupils enter the Senior School on the recommendation of the Head of Junior School, and they may take a scholarship test at that point. These scholarships are awarded on academic merit. There is also a music scholarship awarded at this stage.

The Senior School (Years 7 to 11) in Mowbray Road has three sites. The Centenary building provides excellent classrooms, four science laboratories and a networked Information Technology Room. The original building includes a fifth laboratory, a second networked Computer Room, library, art room, Design and Food Technology Centre, careers room and further classrooms.

Clifton Hall is especially equipped for Year 7 and Year 8 pupils. Each classroom is equipped with an interactive w/ board. There are specialist Music and Drama facilities. Langham Tower was acquired in 2004 and a newly built MUGA (Multi Usage Games Area) was completed in 2008.

ISI Inspection Report April 2011. The school achieved "outstanding" accolade with particular focus on excellent teaching, pastoral care and EYFS.

The Curriculum. The school is small enough for all pupils to be in close contact with the staff. Classes are limited in size and allow for teachers to deal with individual needs.

The Curriculum is designed to provide a broad education from 4+ to 18+, in line with the requirements of the National Curriculum. Pupils are encouraged to acquire the right qualifications for further study, an independence of spirit, a self awareness of their personal qualities and a sensitivity to the needs of others.

In the Junior School, core subjects are taught in forms with specialist subjects being added as pupils get older. German is taught to pupils from the age of 4+ as part of the school's European awareness policy.

In the Senior School, there are some twenty subjects which pupils study from the age of 11. Pupils receive guidance in Year 9 to enable them to make a wise and balanced choice of subjects for the GCSE courses. In Year 11 Work Experience is organised after the GCSE examinations.

Music, drama and sport are strongly encouraged as well as extra-curricular activities, including the Duke of Edinburgh's Award Scheme. Regular ski trips, activity holidays and visits abroad are organised for both junior and senior pupils.

The Sixth Form. The Sixth Form is housed in a separate Sixth Form Centre. Boys and girls are admitted to the Sixth

Form subject to a satisfactory standard at GCSE. Most students take four AS level subjects in Arts and/or Science, leading to three A2 levels. A General Studies programme is also offered. Extra courses, such as the CSLA and Young Enterprise, are part of the General Studies programme. All students are encouraged to help in the organisation of the school. Most students proceed to University and other areas of Higher Education. Scholarships are available on entry to the Sixth Form.

Admission. (*See Scholarship Entries section.*) Entry to the school is normally at 4+, 7+, 11+, 13+ and the Sixth Form, but applications at other ages are accepted, subject to vacancies. Entrance is partially selective and may include an interview, written tests and a reference from the applicant's previous school.

Fees per term (2011-2012). Infants £1,939; Juniors £2,373; Seniors (including the Sixth Form) £2,778. The fees include all books, stationery, equipment. Lunches are extra.

Foundation Assisted Places are also available.

Additional Subjects. Music, Speech, Karate, Dancing (Fees on request).

Charitable status. The United Church Schools Trust is a Registered Charity, number 1016538. It is a charitable trust existing to provide high quality education in keeping with the teaching of the Church of England.

Tettenhall College

Wood Road, Wolverhampton, West Midlands WV6 8QX
Tel: 01902 751119
Fax: 01902 741940
e-mail: head@tettcoll.co.uk
website: www.tettenhallcollege.co.uk

Tettenhall College was founded in 1863 by a group of Wolverhampton businessmen to provide a school for sons of nonconformists. Tettenhall is now co-educational and an interdenominational school, providing a quality education from nursery to university entrance.

There are about 400 pupils, of whom 65 are Boarders.

Motto: '*Timor Domini Initium Sapientiae*'

Governors:

Chairman: J F Woolridge, CBE, BSc

Vice-Chairman: Revd Prebendary G Wynne, MTh, BSc Soc, BD, AKC

Mrs C Baugh	Mrs V A Jones
P G Brough, BA	Mrs D Margetts
P H Creed	Mrs J Parker, SRP, MCSP,
Mrs L Cook, BA	JP
Mrs C Hammond, BA	G D H Sower, BA
Mrs H L Hawkins, FCIPD,	Miss M Whild, BA,
MSc	DipArch, RIBA

Headmaster: **M C Long**, BSc

Deputy Head: H R J Trump, BA

Teaching Staff:

J Bullock, BA	M T Jackson, BEd
P J Bullough, BA	Mrs A Y J Jarman, BA
T Clarke, BEng, MSc	Mrs P Jones, CertEd,
Mrs H Compain-Holt, MA	DipRSA SpLD
Mrs C Cooper, BSc	M L Lawley, MSc, PhD
R J Ellmore, BSc	S L Lawrence, BSc
P G Evans, BSc	R M Leighton, BA
A T Foster, BA	Mrs M Lofting, BA, MA
D E Groom, BA, BEd	Miss N F Minaker, BSc
Mrs E J Gwilt, BSc	Mrs A Nash, ACIB
J D Higgs, BA	Mrs V O'Neill, BSc
Ms C Hope, BEd	G J Raine, BA

Mrs A A Ridyard, BA	Mrs J L Taylor, C in E
Mrs R Samra-Bagry, BA	Miss M D Uttley, BA
Mrs D E Spencer, BEd	I F Wass, BEd
Mrs C A Squire, BA	Mrs C E Whiting, BSc,
Mrs D Stone, BA,	BEd
DipTEFL, MEd	C Woodward, BA, SpLD
Mrs K Stone, BA	

Head of Lower School: P J Kay, BA

Visiting Teachers:
11 staff provide Music tuition, 3 take pupils for individual learning support and 2 provide additional sports coaching.

Clerk to the Governors: M J Kilvert
Bursar: S Howard, FCMI, FIH
Personal Assistants to the Headmaster:
Marketing & Admissions: Miss A Addison
Administration: Mrs N Phelps

Medical Officers:
Dr J Bright
Dr A Williams

School Nurses:
Mrs C Wagstaff
Mrs S Philpott

Situation and Buildings. Three miles west of the centre of Wolverhampton in the old village of Tettenhall, the school stands in 33 acres of extensive gardens, woods and playing fields.

The original building contains the Boys' Boarding House, the Dining Hall, the Chapel and also Big School which is now the School Library. A new Girls' Boarding House was built in 1989.

The Towers, acquired from the Thorneycroft Estate in 1942, houses the Music Department and a fine theatre built in the nineteenth century. The Drive and Lower School buildings are new and purpose-designed.

The Maurice Jacks Building incorporates new Science laboratories, administrative offices, a staff common room and form rooms for Upper School.

Other amenities include a Sixth Form Centre, an Information Technology Network, an Art and Design Department, a Resources Room, a covered, heated Swimming Pool, a Sports Hall and courts for Netball, Tennis and Squash. There are two Cricket squares and playing fields for Rugby, Soccer, Hockey and Athletics.

Religion. Services in the College Chapel are interdenominational.

Entry. (*See Scholarship Entries section.*) The school accepts girls and boys. Entrance to the Upper School (age 11–18) is normally by way of assessment in Mathematics, English and Verbal Reasoning. Pupils at independent preparatory schools take the Common Entrance Examination. By arrangement with the Headmaster, pupils may be interviewed and tested according to their individual needs. Assessments are set by the Head of Lower School for pupils between the ages of 7 and 11. These can be taken in any term by appointment.

Organisation. Upper School (Years 7 to 11 and the Sixth Form) and Lower School (Years 3 to 6) are each divided into 4 Houses which compete in activities, work and games. The Drive School comprises a Nursery, Kindergarten, Reception and Years 1 and 2.

Upper School Curriculum. GCSE may be taken in the following subjects: Art, Biology, Business Studies, Chemistry, Electronics, English, French, Geography, German, History, Information Technology, Mathematics, Music, Physics, Physical Education, Religious Studies, Spanish and Statistics.

In the Sixth Form various combinations of subjects are possible, and AS and A Level courses offered include Art, Biology, Business Studies, Chemistry, Drama and Theatre Studies, Economics, Electronics, English, French, Geography, German, History, Law, Mathematics, Further Mathematics, Music, Physics, Physical Education, Psychology and Religious Studies.

Careers. Extensive advice is given by the Careers Teachers and the local Careers Service.

Societies and Activities. All pupils are encouraged to become fully involved in the life of the community and to play a part in the social and cultural organisations.

Pupils take part in the Duke of Edinburgh's Award Scheme, working for Bronze, Silver and Gold Awards.

Full facilities are provided for Badminton, Basketball, Chess, Computer Studies, Drama, Karate, Dance, Pottery and Table Tennis. There are numerous clubs and societies that meet regularly. Excursions are frequently arranged to places of special interest for those doing Business Studies, Geography, History, Science and Technology, and foreign journeys have, in recent years, regularly included visits abroad, sports tours and exchanges. School plays are produced each year; there is a house festival of Performing Arts and the Music Department is strong.

Lower School. Lower School is housed separately in a new, purposed-designed building opened in 2002. It shares a number of the facilities with Upper School and Upper School Staff help with games and specialist teaching.

Years 3 to 5 are taught mainly by their Form Teachers. Particular attention is paid to standards in Literacy and Numeracy. French is taught from the age of seven and German from Year 6.

Athletics, Cricket, Netball, Hockey, Rounders, Rugby, Soccer, Swimming and Tennis are the main sports and all pupils have PE and two afternoons of games each week. Extra-curricular activities include Badminton, Bridge, Chess, Computing, Dance, Drama and Table Tennis. Music and the playing of musical instruments are strongly encouraged.

The Drive School. The Drive, the pre-preparatory department for pupils aged 2 to 7 years, is accommodated within a new purposely designed building adjacent to The Towers. The emphasis is on the three Rs. The Humanities are approached through topic work; Science and Technology is experienced "hands on". Activities include Art and Craft, Music, PE, Dance and Swimming.

Fees per term (2011-2012). Year 7 and above: Boarders £7,680, Weekly Boarders £6,392, Day Boarders £4,658, Day Pupils £4,215. Below Year 7: Boarders £5,926, Weekly Boarders £4,809, Day Boarders £3,626, Day Pupils £3,194. The Drive School: £2,107–£2,765.

The Old Tettenhallians' Club. Correspondence should be addressed to Mr L N Chown at the College.

Charitable status. Tettenhall College Incorporated is a Registered Charity, number 528617. It exists to provide a quality education for boys and girls.

Thetford Grammar School

Bridge Street, Thetford, Norfolk IP24 3AF
Tel: 01842 752840
Fax: 01842 750220
e-mail: enquiries@thetfordgrammarschool.fsnet.co.uk
website: www.thetgram.norfolk.sch.uk

Refounded in the 17th century by Sir Richard Fulmerston, Thetford Grammar School can however show an unbroken roll of Headmasters from 1119 and traces its origins to the 7th century. In more recent times it was voluntarily controlled until, augmented by the adjacent girls' grammar school, it returned to independence in 1981. Today it is a two-form entry 3½–18 co-educational day school with 330 pupils drawn from a radius of 30 miles across the Norfolk/ Suffolk border. We seek to combine worthwhile academic standards with a tradition of care and support for the individual and commitment to the breadth of educational experience. A member of SHMIS (elected 1996) and AGBIS, the school is administered by the Governors of the Thetford Grammar School Foundation, acting as Trustees on behalf of the Charity Commission.

The Governing Body:

Chairman of Governors: Dr J E J Altham, MA, PhD
Vice-Chairman: Mrs L Hobden-Clarke
I M Clark
J G Crisp
Mrs M Eade
Mrs B Garrard, MA, BSc
T J Lamb, BSc Econ
Major T MacMullen, BA, TCD
P J Price, MBA
Dr G J Sigley
Mrs J M Sinclair
Mayor of Thetford (*ex officio*)
Cllr R Kybird, Breckland District Council (*co-opted*)

Bursar and Clerk to the Governors: Wing Cdr P J McGahan, MCMI, MInstLM

Headmaster: G J Price, MA Oxon

Deputy Head: Mrs K Elders, MA Nottingham
Director of Studies: J Mead, FRSA, CSci, CPhys, MInstP
Head of Junior School: Ms K A Dennis, MEd, BEd Melbourne
Head of Sixth Form: S G Spencer, MA Ed Open University, MCIL

Assistant Staff:
Mrs A Alecock, BA Manchester
A Bartley, BA Lancaster
Mrs T Beukes, BSc Stellenbosch SA
I M L Blundell, BSc UEA
S Braden, BSc RMCS Shrivenham
Mrs J Bull, BA Leicester
Miss H Butler, BA Sheffield
Mrs S Collins
Mrs R Dimminger, DipEd Zimbabwe
A M Durling, BA UEA, MCIL
Dr K Ellis, MBChB Leicester
Mrs J Fifield, BA University of Wales
M Foreman, BEd Nottingham
Miss F Foster, BA Warwick
M Glassbrook, BSc Northumbria
Mrs T E Granger, BSc Wolverhampton
M Hill, BA Bedfordshire
Ms G Irving, BA Essex
Mrs A Kingsnorth, BSc London
J A Law, BEd Loughborough
R Maringue, MA Clermont-Ferrand University
Mrs S Mears
Mrs L Perry, BA Sussex
Mrs A Poole, BA Open University, CertEd Dartford
Mrs H Pringle, BA Teesside Polytechnic
Mrs M Rolton, CertEd Bretton Hall
Mrs C Salt, BA Exeter
C M Shepherd, BSc Liverpool
Ms A Sherring, BA Camberwell
A J Shillings, MSci Bristol, PhD Cantab
S R Simpson, BSc Birmingham
Mrs D C Sims, BA EY Open
Dr M Stoppard, BA Nottingham, PhD UEA & City University
Ms C Stratford, BA York
Miss F Travers, BA Nottingham Trent
A Ward, BSc London
Mrs V S Webber, BA Open University
B Young, BA Cardiff

Librarian: Mrs J Settle

Teaching Assistants:
Ms J Blakemore
Mrs M Brooks

Visiting Music Staff:
Miss N Absolum (*Piano*)
Mrs F Brittain (*Flute & Oboe*)
M B Clarke, BA Sussex, MA Illinois (*Clarinet, Saxophone*)
Mrs K Harries, LLCM, FLCM (*Voice*)
Ms F Levy, LLCM TD, ALCM (*Violin*)
J Rowland (*Percussion and Jazz Piano*)
A H Salazar, GSMD, PGC, PG Ad Dip TCM (*Voice*)
D Scragg (*Brass*)
C Ward, BA (*Guitar*)
Mrs J G Weeks, GRSM, ARMCM (*Piano*)

Learning Support:
Mrs K E Jones, BSc Harper Adams, DipSpLD
Mrs P Ballard, BEd Southampton

Headmaster's Secretary: Mrs E Brooks
Senior School Secretary: Mrs C Reynolds
Junior School Secretary: Mrs I Cracknell
Accounts Secretary: Mrs S Summers

Buildings and Situation. Situated close to the centre of Thetford, the school occupies a well established site graced by several buildings of architectural interest and the ruins of a medieval priory. An active Development Programme has seen the impressive refurbishment of buildings to provide improved facilities, the most recent of these being a new Sixth Form Centre and Performing Arts Studio which has won a national architectural award. There are extensive playing fields with a refurbished pavilion within walking distance of the main buildings.

Organisation. Junior School pupils (3½–7 Goldcrest; 8–10 Junior Department) are taught primarily in their own premises with independent facilities. Older juniors, however, have contact with specialist teachers in several subject areas and benefit from similar integration into many other aspects of school life. Main School education from 11 follows a two or three-form entry pattern with setting in core subjects to GCSE. Sixth Form students, who have their own Common Room, play a full part in the life of the school.

Curriculum. Junior School teaching follows National Curriculum lines with strong emphasis on the English/Mathematics core and the range of specialist subjects in support. Music and Drama are important within the Department, while a full programme of PE and Games allows for the development of team sports and individual fitness.

Main School education through to GCSE is based on a common core of English, English Literature, Mathematics, a Modern Language (French or German) and the Sciences. Options allow students to develop skills and interests in History, Geography, RS, Business Studies, Languages, the Expressive Arts, Physical Education and Technology. IT is strongly represented across the curriculum. AS and A2 courses are offered in all these subjects, with the addition of Psychology. Mathematics and Science lead a strong pattern of results at this level and sixth form students proceed to university degree courses.

Sport and Extra-Curricular Activities. The life of the school extends widely from the classroom into sport, community service, dramatic and musical presentation; the lessons taught by the pursuit of excellence through individual commitment and teamwork are greatly valued.

Winter sports are Rugby, Soccer, Hockey, Netball and Cross-Country with Cricket, Tennis, Rounders and Athletics in the Summer. Popular indoor sports such as Basketball, Aerobics, Badminton, Volleyball and Gymnastics are also followed.

A majority of pupils take part in training for the Duke of Edinburgh's Award Scheme. Musically, a lively concert programme supports individual instrumental tuition and choral rehearsal while opportunities for theatre are provided termly by House and School productions.

A popular Activities Week is run biennially at the end of the Summer Term encompassing expeditions and foreign visits.

Admission. Admission into the Junior School follows a day in school with the appropriate year group during which an assessment is made. Admission into Main School is by formal examination with interview and school report. Sixth Form entrance is on the basis of interview and school report, with subsequent performance at GCSE taken into consideration. The main Entrance Examination is held in January but supplementary testing continues through the year. Full details from the Headmaster's Secretary.

Fees per term (2011-2012). £2,908 (Goldcrest), £3,231 (Junior Department), £3,516 (Main School) including books and tuition, but excluding uniform, lunches, transport, examination entry fees and some specialised teaching such as instrumental music lessons.

Scholarships and Bursaries. Within the limits of available funds the Governors are able to provide financial support with the fees in case of need. Such bursaries are based on a declaration of family income and can be up to 100% of the fees. They are available from Year 7 upwards. They are dependent of course on the pupil fulfilling the entrance requirements of the school. Scholarships of an honorary nature may be awarded to the top performers in the entrance examinations. Music scholarships are available on entry in Year 7 or 9 which will provide free instrumental or voice tuition. Scholarships are also available into the Sixth Form for both internal and external candidates. These can provide a reduction in fees for two years and are awarded as the result of a scholarship paper sat in January or in recognition of outstanding GCSE performance in the summer.

Details of all awards may be obtained from the Headmaster.

Charitable status. Thetford Grammar School is a Registered Charity, number 311263. It exists to provide education for boys and girls.

Tring Park School for the Performing Arts

Tring Park, Tring, Hertfordshire HP23 5LX
Tel: 01442 824255
Fax: 01442 891069
e-mail: info@tringpark.com
website: www.tringpark.com

Board of Governors:
Chairman: Mr Michael Geddes
Ms Elizabeth Adlington
Mrs Mary Bonar
Mrs Polly Dangerfield, BA Hons, ATD, MEd
Mr Michael Harper
Mr Mark Hewitt
Mr Jonathan Latham, BSc, MBA
Mrs Juliet Murray
Mrs Angela Odell
Mrs Venetia Wrigley

Principal: **Mr Stefan Anderson**, MA Cantab, ARCM, ARCT

Deputy Principal: Mr Anselm Barker, M St Oxon, BA Harvard

Director of Dance: Miss Rachel Rist, MA, FRSA
Deputy Director of Dance: Miss Teresa Wright, ARAD Adv, FISTD Cecchetti Branch Dip

Director of Drama: Mr Edward Applewhite, BA Hons

Deputy Director of Drama: Miss Heather Loomes, BA Hons

Director of Music: Miss Elizabeth Hewett, BMus Hons, PGCE, ALCM
Deputy Director of Music: Miss Helen Reynolds, BMus Hons, PGCE

Director of Musical Theatre Course: Miss Donna Hayward, FISTD
Deputy Director of Musical Theatre Course: Mr Simon Sharp, BA Hons, PGCE

Head of Performance Foundation Course: Miss Louisa Shaw
Head of Theatre Arts: Miss Elizabeth Odell

Director of Academic Studies: Mrs Helen Wells, BA, PGCE
Deputy Director of Academic Studies: Mrs Janet Allen, BSc Hons, MSc, PGCE

Marketing Manager: Mrs Miriam Juviler, ARAM, LRAM
Campaign Director: Mrs Jane Foy

Head of Learning Support: Dawn Sanders, CertEd, BEd Hons, MA EdMgt, PGCE, OCR Cert SpLD (*SENCO*)

School Administrator: Mrs Nicky Milne

Age Range. 8–19 years.
Number in School. Boarders: Boys 37, Girls 168. Day: 64.
Fees per term (2011-2012). Prep School: Boarders £6,890, Day £4,245. Aged 11–16: Boarders £9,100, Day £6,105. Sixth Form Entry: Boarders £9,735, Day £6,635. Sibling discount 10% of termly fees. Forces discount available on request.

Aided places are available under the Government's Music and Dance Scheme and Post 16 Dance and Drama Awards. School scholarships are available for Drama and Musical Theatre.

Tring Park School for the Performing Arts offers a unique opportunity for pupils from the age of 8 to 19 who show a particular talent in one or more of the Performing Arts, yet still wish to benefit from an excellent academic education to GCSE, IGCSE, BTEC and A Level.

Tring is a small market town situated 30 miles northwest of Central London, within easy travelling distance of the major international airports and motorways. Set in 17 acres of attractive and secluded grounds, the School is principally housed in a superb mansion, formerly the home of the Rothschild family. The school now boasts 5 superb Performance Studios.

Dance, Drama, Musical Theatre and Music are taught to the highest level and pupils perform regularly in our excellent modern theatre as well as at prestigious venues in London and the South East. Many pupils go on to enjoy successful performing careers. Academic achievements at GCSE and A Level enable many of our students to progress to Degree courses in higher education.

Whatever the career or course chosen, the fusion of natural talent, creativity and personality with sound teaching and direction produces young communicators, well-equipped to take the many opportunities that lie ahead.

Charitable status. The AES Tring Park School Trust is a Registered Charity, number 1040330. It exists to provide vocational and academic education.

Windermere School

The Lake District, Windermere, Cumbria LA23 1NW
Tel: 015394 46164
         International +44 15394 46164
Fax: 015394 88414

e-mail: admissions@windermereschool.co.uk
website: www.windermereschool.co.uk

A small and friendly school, with an emphasis on challenge through adventure and academic excellence.

Chairman of Governors: Peter Redhead

Head: **Mr Ian Lavender**, MA Oxford, BA Hons Oxford, NPQH

Deputy Head: Miss J Parry, MPhil, BSc Hons Liverpool, PGCE Manchester

Preparatory School:
Headmaster: Mr B C Freeman, BEd Hons Bristol
Deputy Head: Mr N Stanley, BA Hons, PGCE Charlotte Mason

Administrative Staff:
Bursar: Mr P Flint
Head's PA: Mrs J Jones
School Secretary: Mrs S Dougherty
Windermere Preparatory School Head's PA: Miss S Ingham
Head of Admissions: Mrs Jane Scott

Windermere School, is an independent co-educational boarding and day school, founded in 1863, and is an Educational Trust administered by a Board of Governors. It is divided into the Senior School (ages 11 to 18) and the Preparatory School (ages 2 to 11).

Located in the heart of the English Lake District National Park, our school offers a rich environment in which pupils can achieve academic and personal excellence. It has the beauty and tranquillity of a wooded campus overlooking the mountains and lake, along with a lakefront boathouse, beach and watersports centre. The amenities of the vibrant resort of Windermere are within minutes of the school. Even with its breathtaking location, the school has easy access to the motorway network, main rail lines and major airports.

Adventure activities and watersports opportunities are provided for each pupil with nationally recognised certificates from organisations including the Royal Yachting Association and the British Canoe Union. This combined with the rich literary and cultural heritage of the Lake District provides a unique setting for academic study and self-development; thus the motto Vincit qui se Vincit, *One conquers, who conquers oneself.*

The Senior School and Sixth Form is located on a mountainside campus overlooking the lake, with the Preparatory School campus and watersports centre nearby. The school owns over 100 acres in the Lake District National Park. There is a modern Sixth Form Boarding House with single and double study-bedrooms, plus a lodge-style Boys Boarding House with magnificent views south and west over Lake Windermere and the mountains, and a traditional girls dormitory in Browhead, formerly a private estate.

Numbers. There are approximately 375 pupils in total. The Senior School has approximately 284 pupils, of whom 50% are boarders. The size of the community has the advantage of providing a friendly atmosphere of understanding and fosters good staff-pupil relationships. Many members of the teaching staff hold additional qualifications in outdoor adventure. There is a 4-house system for competitions and games.

Curriculum. The curriculum offered at Windermere School reflects the belief that students should be exposed to as many opportunities as possible and leave the school as well-rounded individuals. It is tailored to the needs of each child, with small class sizes. Each pupil is provided with a personal tutor that stays with them throughout their years at the school, to oversee work on a daily basis and act as an advocate. GCSEs are spread over three years with some pupils entered into exams in Year 9. Sixth Form students undertake the internationally recognised International Baccalaureate Diploma which offers more options than A Levels. The school is also the only school in the UK to offer the International Baccalaureate Career Certificate which is a combination of diploma subjects and a BTEC in Sport and Adventure.

There are qualified staff and programmes in place for Special Educational Needs, English as an Additional Language, and Gifted and Talented pupils.

Music, Art, and Drama play an important part in the life of the school. There are two choirs, and individual instruction leading to chamber groups and orchestra. Students are prepared for the written and practical music exams of the Associated Board of the Royal Schools of Music. The school participates in regional Music Festivals. The Central School of Speech and Drama and LAMDA's examinations are also taken in Speech and Drama. Art, Pottery and Design Technology provide considerable scope and opportunity. The Art Studios contain facilities for History of Art and an Art History Library. Drama classes are included in the curriculum, and there are several productions staged each year.

Extra-Curricular Activities. Windermere School's watersports centre, Hodge Howe with over 160 metres of lakefront on the shores of Windermere, hosts a wide range of activities during the school's timetabled curriculum, and as part of the extra-curricular activity programme. The centre has accreditation from the British Canoeing Union and the Adventure Activities Licensing Authority, as well as being a Royal Yachting Association Teaching Centre. There are traditional competitive sports teams in hockey, netball, tennis, athletics and more. Many students play for regional and national teams, as well as for the school.

Service. Windermere School has a strong tradition of Community Service where pupils are active participants. The most high profile is Life Change South Africa with many staff and pupils travelling to South Africa each year to contribute to projects. The school supports many other charities including local Hospices, Young Carers, NSPCC, Save The Children Fund and works with regional Rotary Clubs.

Religion. The school is Christian in outlook and welcomes other denominations.

Medical. The health of the pupils is under the care of appointed school Doctors and a full-time nurse. There is a regular clinic, and dispensary twice daily.

Societies. More than 40 Clubs and Societies provide a variety of interests for out-of-school hours.

Uniform. Senior School – Girls wear blue kilt and striped blazer plus light blue blouses and optional navy jumper. Boys wear dark grey trousers, navy blue blazer, white shirt and school tie with optional navy jumper. Home clothes may be worn at weekends. The Sixth Form wear dark suits and they may wear home clothes in the evenings and at weekends.

Preparatory School – Girls wear blue kilt and striped blazer plus light blue blouses in the winter. In the summer the kilt is worn with a blue and white flowered short-sleeved blouse and blue sleeveless slipover. Boys wear grey trousers, pale blue shirts and sweater, the school tie and blazer.

Boarding. There is a strong boarding tradition at Windermere School that benefits the whole school community. Each Boarding House has live-in staff supervised by a House Mistress or House Master. Each evening, academic staff oversee prep and are available for extra tuition and advice. There are weekend activities both on campus and with staff-led excursions throughout the Lake District and beyond. It is a safe and caring extended family environment where pupils can excel both academically and personally.

Round Square. The School is a member of the international Round Square group of schools. Exchanges and Overseas Service Projects are regularly arranged between the schools involved in Australia, Canada, Germany, India, Switzerland, South Africa and USA and Brunei.

Preparatory School. The nearby Preparatory School is in the care of a Headmaster, and takes boarders from age 8, along with day children up to Year 6. There is also a Nursery School for children from age 2. The Preparatory school is fully integrated with the Senior School giving continuity of teaching programmes and use of joint facilities. (*For further details, see entry in IAPS section.*)

Entry. Pupils are accepted into the Senior School from Prep and Junior schools at age 11 or 13+, or by direct entry into the Sixth Form. In other circumstances students may be accepted at other times. In the Preparatory School, pupils are taken at various stages from Nursery onwards. Visitors are welcome at anytime during the year, and Open Days are held once a term.

Fees per term (2011-2012). *Autumn Term 2011*: Day (including lunch): £4,144 (Years 7–8), £4,589 (Years 9–11) Sixth Form £4,676. Boarding: £6,858–£7,956 (weekly), £7,245–£8,372 (full). *UK fees will increase by 1.5% at the start of each of the Spring and Summer Terms during 2012.*

International Students (all 3 terms): £8,500 (Years 7–8), £9,375 (Years 9–11), £9,375 (Years 12–13).

Discounts are available for Forces families eligible for the MOD Continuity of Education Allowance (CEA).

Scholarships. Academic, Performing Arts, Visual Arts and Sport Scholarships are available. For more information please visit the school's website or contact Admissions.

Charitable status. Windermere Educational Trust Limited is a Registered Charity, number 526973, with a mission to provide education of the highest quality.

The Yehudi Menuhin School

Stoke d'Abernon, Cobham, Surrey KT11 3QQ
Tel: 01932 864739
Fax: 01932 864633
e-mail: admin@yehudimenuhinschool.co.uk
website: www.yehudimenuhinschool.co.uk

The Yehudi Menuhin School was founded in 1963 by Lord Menuhin and is situated in beautiful grounds in the Surrey countryside, close to London and within easy reach of both Gatwick and Heathrow.

The School provides specialist music tuition in stringed instruments, piano and classical guitar to around 70 musically-gifted boys and girls aged between 8 and 19 and aims to enable them to pursue their love of music, develop their musical potential and achieve standards of performance at the highest level. The School also provides a broad education within a relaxed open community in which each individual can fully develop intellectual, artistic and social skills. We are proud that our pupils develop into dedicated and excellent musicians who will use their music to inspire and enrich the lives of others and into friendly, thinking individuals well equipped to contribute fully to the international community.

President: Daniel Barenboim
Vice-Presidents:
Sir John Burgh, KCMG, CB
A N Hollis, OBE, DFC
Barbara R-D Fisher, OBE
Sir Alan Traill, GBE, QSO
Governor Emeritus:
Daniel Hodson
Anne Simor
Music Patrons:
András Schiff
Steven Isserlis
Tasmin Little

Governors:
Chairman: Mr Richard Morris, MA Oxon, Hon FRAM,
   RCM, RNCM
Vice-Chairman: Mr Peter Willan, BSc Hons, MBA, FCMA
Mr Noël Annesley
Mr Clinton Askew
Mr Gavin Barrett
The Hon Zamira Menuhin Benthall
Prof Sebastian Forbes
Mr Oscar Lewisohn
Mrs Susan Mitchell
Mr Richard Nunneley, MBE, FCSI
Mr John Pagella
Mrs Alice Philips

Staff:

Headmaster: Dr Richard Hillier, MA Cantab, PhD,
   PGCE

Director of Music: Mr Malcolm Singer, MA Cantab
Director of Studies/Mathematics: Mr Richard Tanner, MA
   Oxon
Bursar: Dr Angela Isaac, PhD

Academic Staff:

Art & Craft: Mrs Patsy Belmonte, BA Hons
Biology & Science: Mrs Karen Lyle, BSc Hons, PGCE
Biology & Science: Mrs Jenny Dexter, BSc Hons, PGCE
English & Drama: Mr Joseph Bennett, MA Hons
French: Mrs Annie Perkins, M-ès-L, MA
German & Russian: Mrs Petra Young, MA
Spanish: Mrs Arantza Eyres, Inst of Linguists, CertEd
History: Mrs Sarah Howell, BA Hons, PGCE
Junior Subjects: Mrs Janet Poppe, BA Hons, PGCE
Mathematics: Mrs Sarah Lee, BSc
EFL: Mrs Hazel Brier, CertEd, MA TESOL
Chinese: Miss Jenny Chen, BEd
Japanese: Mrs Yoshiko Ohta, TJFL

Music Staff:

Violin:
Mrs Natalie Boyarskaya, Dip Solo Performance
Mr Simon Fischer, AGSM
Miss Akiko Ono, Dip Mus & Perf Arts, Vienna
Miss Claire Telford, PGDip Solo/Ens perf, BMus Hons
Miss Sara Struntz, MMus RCM, PGDip RCM, BMus
Miss Anna Harpham, BMus Hons
Miss Lisa Oberg, MMus RCM
Miss Diana Galvydyte, BMus, MMus

'Cello:
Miss Anna Menzies, BMus Hons GSMD
Mr Thomas Carroll, Cert Munich Hochschule

Bass:
Mrs Caroline Emery, LTCL, GTCL, CertEd

Piano:
Mrs Ruth Nye, DipMusPerf Melbourne Conservatory
Mr Marcel Baudet, Groningen Cons
Ms Mariana Izman, BMus Conservatorium van Amsterdam
Miss Mariko Brown, BMus Hons LGSM
Ms Zoe Mather, AGSM
Piano Assistant: Miss Janneke Brits BMus University of
   Rochester USA

Harpsichord:
Miss Carole Cerasi, Hon ARAM

Guitar:
Mr Richard Wright, GRSM Man, ARNCM

Coach Accompanist:
Mr Julian Dyson, ARCM, DipRCM Hons Perf & Tchng
Mr Nigel Hutchison, BMus Hons

Chamber Music:
Mr Ioan Davies, MA Cantab
Mr Malcolm Singer, MA Cantab

Senior Orchestra:
Mr Malcolm Singer, MA Cantab

Junior Orchestra:
Dr Oscar Colomina i Bosch, PhD RAM, MMus, BMus
   Hons GSMD

General Music:
Mr Malcolm Singer, MA Cantab
Mr John Cooney, BMus Hons
Mr Nathan Williamson, BMus, MMus Dist, MMus Arts
   Yale
Mr Damian leGassick, PG Dip Surrey
Dr Oscar Colomina i Bosch, PhD RAM, MMus, BMus
   Hons GSMD

Choral:
Mr Richard Hills, MA Oxon

Outreach:
Outreach Officer: Michaela Khatib, BEd Hons Cantab
Miss Claire Telford, PGDip Solo/Ens Perf, BMus Hons
Miss Sara Struntz, MMus RCM, PGDip RCM, BMus

Voice:
Miss Jenevora Williams, BA Hons, ARCM

Composition:
Mr John Cooney, BMus Hons, Cert Adv St RCM & GSMD
Miss Shu Wang, MMus GSMD

Alexander Technique:
Mrs Hannah Walton, NNEB, MSTAT

Pastoral Staff:
Housemistress: Mrs LucyAnn Curling, BA Hons, PGCE
Housemaster: Mr Joseph Bennett, MA Hons Edin
Matron: Mrs Anona Jones, SRN Dip Community School
   Nursing
Assistant Matron: Mrs Judi Brueton, RGN, RN Dip
   Counselling

Administrative Staff:
Headmaster's PA: Ms Angela Stockbridge, LRPS
Concert Secretary: Mrs Catharine Whitnall, MA Cantab,
   LTCL
Receptionist: Mrs Kim Anderson

Accounts:
Accountant: Mr Mark Armstrong, ACCA, BSc Hons
Bookeeper: Mrs Christine Feline

Menuhin Hall Staff:
Hall Manager: Ms Ambrosine Desoutter, BA Hons, LTCL
Technical Manager: Mr Brian Fifield
Box Office Manager: Mrs Penny Wright

Examinations Officer and School Archivist: Mrs Elaine
   Hillier, BA Hons
Marketing Manager: Ms Brenda Weller, BA Hons

Estate Manager: Mr Brian Harris
Housekeeper: Mrs Fiona Stevens

Music. At least half of each day is devoted to musical
studies. Pupils receive a minimum of two one-hour lessons
each week on their first study instrument and at least half an
hour on their second study instrument. Supervised practice
is incorporated into the daily programme ensuring that successful habits of work are formed. All pupils receive guidance in composition and take part in regular composers'
workshops and concerts. Aural training and general musicianship studies are included in the music curriculum. To
awaken feeling for good posture, training in Alexander
Technique is provided. GCSE and A Level Music are compulsory core subjects for all pupils.

Regular opportunity for solo performance is of central importance to the musical activity of the School, and pupils also perform chamber music and with the String Orchestra. Concerts are given several times each week within the School and at a wide variety of venues throughout the United Kingdom and overseas. The most distinguished musicians have taught at the school, including Boulanger, Perlemuter, Rostropovich and Perlman. Lord Menuhin visited the school regularly. Selection of pupils is by stringent audition which seeks to assess musical ability and identify potential. Special arrangements are made for applicants from overseas, who now account for almost half of the School's pupils.

The School opened a state-of-the-art Concert Hall in 2006 seating 315 with outstanding acoustics. Concerts and outreach programmes are now presented in this new facility. New Music Studios are planned for 2013.

Academic Studies and Sport. The curriculum is designed to be balanced and to do full justice to both the musical and the general education of each pupil. Academic studies including the understanding of art, literature and science are considered vital to the development of creative, intelligent and sensitive musicians. All classes are small with excellent opportunities for individual attention, and as a result GCSE and A level examination grades are high. To broaden their artistic and creative talents, all pupils work in a wide variety of artistic media including painting, ceramics, jewellery and textiles. Pupils from overseas with limited English receive an intensive course in the English Language from specialist teachers.

The extensive grounds allow plenty of scope for relaxation and sport, including tennis, badminton, football, running, swimming and yoga. A new swimming pool was opened in 2010.

An International Family. The international reputation of the School brings pupils from all over the world who find a happy atmosphere in a large musical family. Pupils live in single or shared rooms and are cared for by the resident House Staff, the Matron who is a qualified nurse, and the School Doctor. Special attention is paid to diet with the emphasis on whole and fresh food.

Fees and Bursaries. All pupils fully resident in the UK are awarded an Aided Place through the Music and Dance Scheme which is subsidised by the Department for Education (DfE). Parents pay a means-tested contribution to the school fees based on their gross income assessed on a scale issued by the Department for Education. Pupils from overseas pay full fees for two full calendar years until they acquire the residence qualification needed for support through the Music and Dance Scheme. The school has some bursary funds available to assist with fees for pupils who are not eligible for the Music and Dance Scheme.

Admission. Entry to the School is by rigorous music audition, and prospective pupils are auditioned at any time during the year. Candidates may audition at any age between 7 and 16, although most applicants are aged from 8 to 14.

Charitable status. The Yehudi Menuhin School is a Registered Charity, number 312010. It exists to provide musical and academic education for boys and girls.

Scholarships and Bursaries

Austin Friars St Monica's School (see p 778)
Bursaries are available at all levels.

Bearwood College (see p 779)
Open and Closed (British Merchant Navy and Old Royals) Scholarships can be awarded annually in Art, Drama, Music, Sport, General Academic Ability and Sixth Form Entry to those boys and girls reaching the required competitive standard in CEE or College Entry Tests. Sixth Form awards are made on GCSE Grades. A special fees package is available for HM Forces.

Discretionary Bursaries are available in cases of financial hardship.

Personal discussions with the Headmaster are very much encouraged. Full details from the Headmaster, Tel: 0118 974 8300; Fax: 0118 977 3186.

Bedstone College (see p 781)
Bedstone offers Academic, Sport, Music and Art scholarships at 11+/13+ and 16+ with the maximum award being 50% remission of fees. The school is also able to provide "top up" scholarships for exceptional pupils. Valuable Sixth Form scholarships are also available for successful GCSE candidates.

Forces fees discounts available upon request.

Beechwood Sacred Heart School (see p 783)
Scholarships are available at 11+, 13+ and 16+ in Academic, Music, Art, Sport and Drama. Major awards are up to 50% of the tuition fees and there are other minor awards. 11+ and 13+ Entrance and Scholarship Days take place in the Spring Term and 16+ in November. Further details are available from the Registrar.

Bethany School (see p 784)
Academic Scholarships are awarded based on performance in the Entrance Examination. Scholarships are also available in Art, Music, Sport, Design Technology and Drama at the main points of entry: Years 7 and 9 and into the Sixth Form. Further details available from the Headmaster. Members of HM Forces and the Clergy receive a 10% fee discount.

Bournemouth Collegiate School (see p 785)
Scholarships may be offered to pupils who join the school at 11, 12 or 13+. They are awarded to students with all-round academic excellence or special ability in music, art or sport.

A Sixth Form award may also be available.

Children of ministers and lay members of the United Reformed and Congregational Churches may be eligible for a bursary from the Milton Mount Foundation. A small number of assisted places (means-tested) may available for children entering the school in Year 7. Applications for assisted places must be received in the autumn term prior to entry.

Claremont Fan Court School (see p 788)
Academic Scholarships are offered at Year 3, to continue through to the end of Year 6, and at Year 7 and Year 9 to continue through to the end of Year 11. Offers are based on a written examination and interview. Sixth Form Academic Scholarships are offered for the two-year course with the minimum requirement of six Grade A passes at GCSE.

Music Scholarships are available for Senior School applicants. As a guide, scholarship candidates should be working at the following levels before applying: Year 7 – Grade 4, Year 9 – Grade 5, Sixth Form – Grade 6. Sixth Form Scholarships will be awarded for the two-year course. Year 7 and Year 9 Scholarships will be awarded through to the end of Year 11.

Both Art and Drama Scholarships are available to candidates applying for a Sixth Form place and are awarded for the duration of their two-year course. Applicants need to present a portfolio for Art which they will be asked to discuss at interview whilst those applying for Drama will

need to show evidence illustrating an active and ongoing involvement in drama and theatre.

Sports Scholarships are awarded for pupils of exceptional sporting ability. Sixth Form Scholarships are awarded for the two years of the course. Year 9 Scholarships are awarded through to the end of Year 11.

Dover College (see p 793)
Academic Scholarships are awarded by competitive examinations.

Scholarships for Music, Art, Sport and All-Rounder are available by competitive interview.

Scholarships are available to pupils at 11+, 13+ and 16+. Scholarships are not awarded to pupils in the Infant and Junior School.

Sibling Bursaries (10%) and Service Bursaries are automatically awarded. Members of HM Armed Forces and the Diplomatic Service who are eligible for the boarding allowance only pay a parental contribution of 10% of the full boarding fee.

Further details may be obtained on application to Admissions.

Friends' School (see p 798)
Scholarships are available to internal and external candidates.

Academic scholarships are available to applicants wishing to join Years 7 and 9. In addition, there are awards made for Art, Drama, Music and Sport.

Academic scholarships are available to those applicants wishing to join the Sixth Form.

Further details are available from the Admissions Secretary.

Friends' School is able to offer some assistance with fees in some cases. No application for a child who would benefit from the education that Friends' School provides should be discouraged solely on the grounds of financial need. Please contact the Bursar on 01799 525351 for further information.

Halliford School (see p 801)
The School offers up to six scholarships to the value of 10% of the annual school fees for entry at 11+. The scholarships are awarded for academic, artistic, musical and sporting excellence. All those taking the 11+ entrance examination will be considered for the academic scholarships. Means-tested Bursaries are available on application.

Sixth Form Scholarships and Bursaries: Three scholarships to the value of 10% of the annual school fees are available for external candidates showing excellence whether musical, artistic, dramatic or sporting. In addition there are means-tested Bursaries. These are available on application and are awarded either to support scholarships or to candidates with potential.

Hampshire Collegiate School (see p 802)
Scholarships and awards are available to both internal and external candidates at 11+, 13+ and 16+. An entrance examination takes place in January.

Scholarships of up to 50% of the fees in value may be awarded for Academic, Musical, Artistic, Dramatic, Sport and All-Round ability. Bursaries and Exhibitions of lesser value may also be awarded.

Sixth Form Scholarships are awarded on the basis of GCSE and all-round contribution (actual and potential) to internal and external candidates. These may all be worth up to 50% of the fee.

Kingsley School (see p 807)
Entrance Scholarships are offered annually at ages 11, 12 and 13 on the basis of the results of entrance tests held each January/February. A maximum of ten Academic Scholarship awards can be made each year; an exceptional candidate can receive an exceptional award. Awards are also available where candidates show outstanding ability in

Music, Art, Drama, Design & Technology, and/or Sport. Applications should be made to the Headmaster by the first week in January of the year of entry. Sixth Form Academic Scholarships are awarded on the basis of GCSE performance.

Langley School (see p 809)
Competitive academic scholarships are awarded at 11+, 13+ and at Sixth Form entry.

Two scholarships may be awarded in each Year group for each of the following categories: Art, Drama, Music Sport and Technology. We also offer an All Rounder Scholarship Award for academically bright students, who also have a flair in one or more of the non-academic areas.

Further details and a Scholarships application form may be obtained from the Headmaster's PA.

Milton Abbey School (see p 814)
Academic scholarships (held in May); Music, Drama, Art, DT, Sailing and Sport scholarships (held in February). Candidates must be under 14 on 1 September. Scholarships also awarded at Sixth Form entry level. Full particulars from the Admissions Office, e-mail: admissions@miltonabbey .co.uk.

Oswestry School (see p 817)
The Governors offer a number of academic scholarships each year for conspicuously talented individuals, each of which remits up to 50% of the tuition fees. Scholarships are available at 9+, 11+, 13+ and 16+. Scholarships are also available in Art, Music and Sport.

Further details of all these Scholarships are available from the Headmaster.

Princethorpe College (see p 826)
There is a variety of Scholarships available for particularly able or talented candidates ranging from Academic, Art and Music and All-Rounder. Additionally for the Sixth Form there are Academic Scholarships and Sport Scholarships.

Academic Scholarships: As a guide, there are eleven Academic Scholarships available. Three scholarships providing a reduction of one half of tuition fees, four scholarships providing a reduction of one third of tuition fees and four providing a reduction of one quarter of tuition fees may be awarded to external candidates aged 11+, 12+, 13+, or 14+.

In addition, Sixth Form Academic Scholarships, awarding a reduction of up to one half of tuition fees, are open to all external candidates who are expected to be top achievers at GCSE. A Sixth Form Scholarship examination is held in the middle of March each year.

Art Scholarships: One scholarship providing a reduction of one third of tuition fees and one scholarship providing a reduction of one quarter of tuition fees may be awarded to candidates aged 11+, 12+, 13+ or 14+. Candidates must submit a portfolio and attend an Art Scholarship day, usually in early January.

Further details and an Art Scholarship application form are available from the Registrar.

Music Scholarships: Instrumental and Choral
Four music scholarships may be awarded annually, either for instrumentalists or choristers. Two scholarships offer a reduction of one third of tuition fees and two offer a reduction of one quarter of tuition fees.

Additionally, one scholarship, providing a reduction of one half of tuition fees may be awarded to an organ scholar, either internally or externally.

Timing of auditions is usually staggered over a week in early January. Further details and a Music Scholarship application form are available from the Registrar.

Sixth Form Sport Scholarship: Senior Sport Scholarships, offering a reduction of up to one half of tuition fees, may be awarded to internal or external candidates entering the Sixth Form. Full details are available from the Registrar.

Rendcomb College (see p 831)
A number of means-tested Bursaries and Scholarships (Academic, Art, Music, Performing Arts and Sport) and a small number of Forces Scholarships are awarded each year at 11, 13 and 16 years of age. Further details from the Admissions Registrar on 01285 832306.

Rishworth School (see p 834)
Scholarships & Bursaries are available, the former on merit, the latter for demonstrable financial need. The extent to which these awards can be offered will also be determined by other factors, such as the School's own circumstances and the nature of a given cohort of applicants.

Scholarships may be awarded, up to a value of 50% of Tuition fees, for excellence in academic work, sport, music or drama. For Year 7 entry scholarships, applicants are formally assessed. For Year 12 entry, awards are made on the basis of an individual's past record (including examination results).

Most awards are made to applicants at these entry levels. However, suitable candidates at any stage will be considered.

For more information contact the Admissions Officer.

The Royal Wolverhampton School (see p 837)
Academic: Merit scholarships are available each year to pupils entering Senior School from Year 7 dependant on exam performance.

Music: A limited number of Music scholarships are available to pupils entering Senior School from Year 7. Such scholarships are awarded following an assessment. Future musical potential is also assessed.

Sports: The School offers a limited number of Swimming and Sports scholarships. Candidates will be expected to have achieved distinction in at least one sport and show potential for future development.

Sixth Form: Academic scholarships at Sixth Form level are normally awarded on the basis of GCSE grades. The amount of the award depends upon the academic ability of the pupil concerned.

Orphan Foundation: Orphan Foundation Scholarships are available to children who have lost one or both parents, whose father or mother is incapacitated through illness or who are from single or divorced families. A need for a boarding education normally has to be established. Foundation Scholarship entry forms are available from the Clerk to the Governors.

Awarding of such concessions takes full account of the Charity's requirement to deliver "public benefit".

For full details of Scholarships and Bursaries please contact The Registrar.

Saint Felix School (see p 845)
Saint Felix School seeks high-calibre candidates, who will contribute very positively and proactively to the life of the school community. The maximum award for an academic scholarship is 50% and for an exhibition 25% of the fees.

Academic awards at 11+ and 13+. All applicants will sit competitive academic examination papers. Awards will be made to high flying candidates, who demonstrate flair and the potential to excel in their academic studies. Exhibitions are awards given for candidates who show promise but do not attain the exacting standards demanded of scholars.

Examinations. Applicants for academic awards at 11+ and 13+ will sit examination papers in English, Mathematics, Science and Aptitude. Topics will be closely linked to those covered in Key Stages 2 and 3.

Performing Arts awards at 13+. Open to applicants who excel in at least two of the following disciplines: Drama, Dance, Music (including singing).

Sports Scholarships at 11+ & 13+. Candidates should offer a range of sporting talents. Pupils at 11+ should be playing at club level in at least one sport. Pupils at 13+ should have been selected for county/regional level sport and be playing at club level in at least one sport. There should be evidence of success in competitions and events for both age groups.

Tennis Scholarship at 13+. Candidates must have an LTA rating of at least 9.2, although applicants who do not possess a current rating may also be considered on the basis of their potential.

Music Scholarships for candidates in Year 5 to Year 10. These will be awarded on the basis of an audition, voice test and interview with the Director of Music and members of the Scholarship Selection Committee. Candidates will be asked to offer two instruments, one of which should be an orchestral instrument.

Margaret Isabella Gardiner Scholarship for candidates aged 11+ and 13+. Outstanding candidates may be eligible for this highly prestigious award, worth up to 75% of the fees. This scholarship will be awarded only to a candidate of sufficiently high calibre and not necessarily on an annual basis.

Sixth Form Scholarships and Exhibitions. Scholarships and exhibitions for Academic Studies, Art, Design & Technology (Phipps Award), Drama, Music and Sport are available for talented Sixth Form applicants, as the result of a competitive examination, trial or audition.

Full details of all awards, including Founder's Scholarships, Remissions and Swimming Scholarships may be obtained from the Registrar. Further information on Bursaries (available to current parents only) are available from the Bursar.

St Joseph's College, Reading (see p 853)
A number of scholarships are awarded each year. All candidates applying for entry into Year 7 are required to sit an entrance assessment and are automatically considered for an academic scholarship. These scholarships are reviewed annually up to the end of Year 11. Scholarships are also awarded for music, drama, sport and on entry to the Sixth Form.

Shebbear College (see p 854)
Scholarships up to the value of half fees are awarded as follows:

At 11+: All candidates take the Entrance and Scholarship Examination in February.

At 13+: The Scholarship Examination is held in the Spring Term. Awards are also made following Common Entrance Examination results.

For Sixth Form candidates, scholarships are awarded on the basis of interview, school report and GCSE performance.

Further details may be obtained from the Registrar.

Sunderland High School (see p 859)
Entrance Scholarships are available at 11+. These are awarded on academic ability and are worth up to 25% of the fees. Scholarships are also available to students wishing to join the School at 16+. These are awarded according to academic ability (interview and test).

A Music Scholarship worth 10% of the fees is available to pupils on entry to the School at age 11.

Foundation Assisted Places are available. A reduction in fees is also available to children of Clergy families and awarded by the United Church Schools Trust.

Tettenhall College (see p 861)
Lower School Awards and Upper School Scholarships may be offered to outstanding boys and girls from either state or independent schools. Sixth Form Scholarships are available for boys and girls joining the Sixth Form from Year 11 or after taking GCSE elsewhere.

Two Music Scholarships may be awarded with free tuition.

Reduction in fees for the children of the Clergy and members of HM Forces.

Society of Heads of Independent Schools

Additional Members

CHARLES JOHNSON
Headmaster
The Duke of York's Royal Military School, Dover, Kent CT15 5EQ
Tel: 01304 245024, e-mail: headmaster@doyrms.com
website: www.doyrms.com

DAVID WARD
Headmaster
Skegness Grammar School, Vernon Road, Skegness, Lincs PE25 2QS
Tel: 01754 610000, e-mail: admin@skegnessgrammar.lincs.sch.uk
website: www.skegnessgrammar.lincs.sch.uk

Additional Members Overseas

WENDY ELLIS
Principal
The British International School Bratislava, Peknikova 6, 841 02 Bratislava, Slovakia
e-mail: info@bisb.sk
website: www.bisb.sk

DR WALID EL-KHOURY
Principal
Brummana High School, PO Box 36, Brummana, Lebanon
e-mail: info@bhs.edu.lb
website: www.bhs.edu.lb

KOEN RINGOOT
Head
Leerwijzer School, Noordzeedreef 3, 8670 Oostduinkerke, Belgium
e-mail: info@leerwijzer.be
website: www.leerwijzer.be

JONATHAN HUGHES D'AETH
Headmaster
Repton School Dubai, Nad Al Sheba 3 & 4, PO Box 300331, Dubai, UAE
e-mail: info@reptondubai.org
website: www. reptondubai.org

VALERIE MAINOO
Head
The Roman Ridge School, PO Box GP 21057, Accra, Ghana
e-mail: enquiries@theromanridgeschool.com
website: www.theromanridgeschool.com

ADRIAN PALMER
Headmaster
St Andrew's Senior School Turi, Private Bag, Molo 20106, Kenya
e-mail: office@turimail.co.ke
website: www.standrews-turi.com

NIGEL FOSSEY
Headteacher
St George's International School, 11 rue des Peupliers, L-2328 Luxembourg
e-mail: info@st-georges.lu
website: www.st-georges.lu

Conference Members

STEPHEN MORRIS
Headmaster
The Cathedral School Llandaff, Cardiff Road, Llandaff, Cardiff CF5 2YH
e-mail: enquiries@cathedral-school.co.uk
website: www.cathedral-school.co.uk

PART IV
Schools whose Heads are members of the Independent Association of Prep Schools

ALPHABETICAL LIST OF SCHOOLS
UK

GEOGRAPHICAL LIST OF IAPS SCHOOLS
UK

IAPS Member Heads and Deputy Heads

Individual School Entries
UK

Abberley Hall

Worcester WR6 6DD
Tel: 01299 896275
Fax: 01299 896875
e-mail: john.walker@abberleyhall.co.uk
website: www.abberleyhallschool.co.uk

Chairman of Governors: The Hon David Legh

Headmaster: **J G W Walker**, BSc QTS University of Surrey

Assistant Headmaster: R Wesley, BEd Cheltenham

Age Range. 2–13.
Number of Pupils. Prep School: 197 (133 Boys, 64 Girls; 115 Boarders, 82 Day Pupils).
Pre-Prep & Nursery: 92 (57 Boys, 35 Girls).
Fees per term (2010-2011). Prep: Boarders £6,065, Day Pupils £4,525–£4,830. Pre-Prep: £1,330–£2,830.
Abberley Hall is co-educational. It is situated 12 miles north-west of Worcester, with easy access to the M5. It is a boarding school for boys and girls aged 8–13 years, and is set in 100 acres of gardens and wooded grounds amid magnificent countryside.

Pupils are prepared for all Independent Senior Schools. Although there is no entry examination, the school has a strong academic tradition with consistently good results in scholarships and Common Entrance, thanks to a highly-qualified staff, favourable teacher/pupil ratios and small classes. This also helps encourage the slower learners, for whom individual attention is available.

The school's facilities include an indoor swimming pool, a chapel, library, music school and concert studio; two new science laboratories, technology room, DT centre and extensively equipped computer centre; an art studio and pottery rooms; a multi-purpose hall with permanent stage, rifle range and climbing wall; a sports hall, hard tennis courts, a Ricochet court and ample playing fields for the major games and athletics, including a large Astroturf pitch. The school also owns its own French chalet where children go on three-week blocks for total immersion into the French language and way of life.

The pupils are also encouraged to take part in a wide range of hobbies and activities including archery, chess, fishing, golf, horse riding, fencing, model-making, printing, ballet, mountain-biking, woodwork and many more.

The school aims to combine a friendly atmosphere with the discipline which enables pupils to achieve their full potential and learn to feel responsibility for themselves and others.

Charitable status. Abberley Hall is a Registered Charity, number 527598. Its aim is to further good education.

The Abbey

Church Street, Woodbridge, Suffolk IP12 1DS
Tel: 01394 382673
Fax: 01394 383880
e-mail: office@theabbeyschool-suffolk.org.uk
website: www.woodbridge.suffolk.sch.uk/the_abbey

Chairman of the Governors: R Finbow, MA Oxon

The Master: **N J Garrett**, BA, PGCE
Head of Pre-Prep: Mrs J King, BEd

Age Range. Co-educational 4–11.
Number of Pupils. 330 Day pupils.
Fees per term (2011-2012). Pre-Prep £2,412; Prep £3,721.
Religious affiliation. Church of England (other denominations accepted).
Entry requirements. Entrance test according to age.
The Abbey is the Preparatory School for Woodbridge School for which boys and girls are prepared for entry. A small number of pupils go elsewhere. There is a highly qualified teaching staff of thirty, with additional visiting music and other specialist teachers. The academic record has been consistently good: scholarships are won regularly both to Woodbridge and to other schools. The teaching is linked to the National Curriculum and emphasis is placed on pupils reaching their full academic potential whilst also benefiting from a broad education. The school enjoys strong links with a number of European schools and exchange visits take place, and pupils learn four European languages. Music is regarded as an important part of school life with a large number of pupils receiving individual music lessons and in Year Four all pupils receive strings tuition as well as their class music lessons. In Games lessons boys play soccer, rugby, hockey and cricket and girls play netball, hockey and rounders. Children also have the opportunity to swim, play tennis and take part in athletics, cross-country, horse riding and sailing. In lunch breaks and after school, pupils are able to participate in a whole range of extra-curricular activities and hobbies.

The School is set in its own beautiful grounds of 30 acres in the middle of the town. As well as a fine Tudor Manor house, it has a well-planned and high-quality classroom and changing room block. Another major development includes a multi-purpose hall and classroom block. Recent developments have included an upgrade of Music, ICT, Art, DT and Science facilities. The grounds are extensive and include playing fields, an all weather surface games area and a science garden. The Pre-Prep Department is at Queen's House, situated within the Senior School's grounds, a short walk from The Abbey. Here the pupils enjoy spacious accommodation and excellent facilities.

Parents of Abbey pupils are eligible to join the Parents' Association and there is a close contact maintained between parents and school.

Charitable status. The Seckford Foundation is a Registered Charity, number 1110964. It exists to provide education for boys and girls.

Abercorn School

Infants: 28 Abercorn Place, London NW8 9XP
Tel: 020 7286 4785
Fax: 020 7266 0219
e-mail: a.greystoke@abercornschool.com

Lower Prep: The Old Grammar School, 248 Marylebone Road, London NW1 6JF
Tel: 020 7723 8700
e-mail: togs@abercornschool.com

Upper Prep: 7b Wyndham Place, London W1H 1PN
Tel: 020 7616 8989
website: www.abercornschool.com

High Mistress: **Mrs A Greystoke**, BA Hons
Headmaster: **Mr D Morse**, BSc, PGCE

Age Range. 2½ to 13+ Co-educational.
Number of Pupils. 390.
Fees per term (2010-2011). £2,495–£4,610. Fees include all extras, apart from lunch.

Abercorn School provides quality education in a happy caring atmosphere. Both branches are housed in gracious Victorian listed mansions. Children are in the senior building from age 6+.

Pupils flourish in the small classes (average size is 16) and the high degree of specialist teaching. As a result, the children achieve excellent entrance results to further schools, including St Paul's, North London Collegiate, South Hampstead High School and Westminster.

Before and after school care is available.

Aberdour School

Brighton Road, Burgh Heath, Tadworth, Surrey KT20 6AJ
Tel: 01737 354119
Fax: 01737 363044
e-mail: enquiries@aberdourschool.co.uk
website: www.aberdourschool.co.uk

The School is an Educational Trust run by a Board of Governors.

Chairman of the Governors: R C Nicol, FCA

Headmaster: **S D Collins**, CertEd

Deputy Headmistress: Mrs T Thomas, BEd Hons
Deputy Headmaster, Curriculum: G Clark, BEd Hons
Head of Pre-Prep: Miss A Reader, BA Hons

Age Range. 2–13.
Number of Pupils. 320 Day Boys and Girls.
Fees per term (2010-2011). £1,003–£3,712 fully inclusive.

Children are taken at 2 years old into the pre-preparatory department and transfer to the preparatory school at age 7. Children are prepared for all the major Senior Schools and many scholarships have been won. There is a school orchestra and a concert band as well as a large school choir. There are ample playing fields, two all-weather areas, a large sports hall and indoor heated swimming pool. There are two science laboratories and a design technology room. All the usual games are coached and the general character of the children is developed by many interests and activities.

Charitable status. Aberdour School Educational Trust Limited is a Registered Charity, number 312033. Its aim is to promote education.

Abingdon Preparatory School

Josca's House, Kingston Road, Frilford, Abingdon, Oxon OX13 5NX
Tel: 01865 391570
Fax: 01865 391042
e-mail: registrar@abingdonprep.org.uk
website: www.abingdon.org.uk/prep

The School was founded in 1956. In 1998 it merged with Abingdon School to become part of one charitable foundation with a single Board of Governors.

Chairman of the Governors: D P Lillycrop, LLB, FCMI

Headmaster: **C Hyde-Dunn**, MA Oxon, PGCE, MA Ed, NPQH

Age Range. 4–13.
Number of Pupils. 250 Day Boys.
Fees per term (2011-2012). £3,090–£3,975.

Main entry points are at age four and seven. Boys are prepared for senior school entrance examinations. A strong majority goes on to Abingdon School.

Abingdon Preparatory School is a thinking and learning school – as well as a teaching school. Pupils' needs are served by providing a happy and stimulating environment where the children are encouraged to develop self-reliance and a sense of responsibility. Considerable emphasis is placed on helping pupils to develop good working patterns together with sound organisational and learning skills.

The school opened stunning new facilities in September 2007, which include new classrooms, an art studio, sports hall and changing rooms. There has also been substantial refurbishment to many of the existing facilities such as the swimming pool, library, CDT and classrooms. Current facilities include new computer and science laboratories, a multipurpose hall, and a substantial music department.

Sport is a major strength of the school outside the classroom. The splendid amenities, which include an indoor swimming pool, thirty acres of playing fields and an adventure playground, enable every child to participate in a wide range of sports and activities. There are regular fixtures against local schools in the main school sports of rugby, football, cricket, tennis, and athletics. All pupils swim at least once a week. There is a range of after-school hobby clubs, which includes amongst many others, orchestra, choir, art, science, judo, golf, fencing, gardening, chess, computers and drama.

A regular number of academic, music, drama and all-rounder awards are gained every year – the majority to the senior school, Abingdon.

A large number of trips are organised for all year groups during the year and the oldest boys go abroad for a week on completing their Common Entrance examinations.

Charitable status. Abingdon School is a Registered Charity, number 1071298. It exists to provide for the education of children aged 4–18.

Aldenham Preparatory School

Aldenham Road, Elstree, Herts WD6 3AJ
Tel: 01923 851664
Fax: 01923 854410
e-mail: prepschool@aldenham.com
website: www.aldenham.com

Chairman of Board of Governors: J S Lewis, DL, FCIS

Head of Preparatory School: **Mrs V Gocher**, BA

Age Range. 3–11.
Number of Pupils. Total 164: 113 Boys, 51 Girls.
Fees per term (2011-2012). Prep: £3,674; Pre-Prep: £3,320; Nursery: £23.90 (per morning or afternoon session), £48.46 per day, £2,533 per term.

At Aldenham Preparatory School, we provide a warm, happy and nurturing environment where quality learning takes place and the needs of each individual child are fulfilled.

The Preparatory School is a co-educational day school encompassing the Nursery (3–4 years), the Pre-Prep Department (4–7 years) and the Prep Department (7–11 years). It forms an integral part of the main school which was established in 1597 and remains on the same glorious site, set in over 110 acres of countryside yet only 13 miles from the centre of London.

Our primary aim is to provide an excellent all round education, presenting all of our pupils with exceptional opportunities. The school is dedicated to ensuring the flexibility for each child to develop their own individual abilities, whether they are academic, creative or sporting. We offer high quality teaching from enthusiastic, motivated and caring staff.

An inspection commissioned by the Independent Schools Inspectorate (ISI) praised the school for being "... *a lively, happy community in which young children thrive. They benefit from a high standard of education and very good care in all year groups. Children's attitude to learning and their behaviour are exemplary. Relationships between children and staff are friendly and courteous.*"

We believe that the pastoral care at Aldenham is second to none, providing the children with a nurturing environment in which they flourish. We also place great importance on personal and social growth and strive to ensure that our pupils are confident and responsible members of the community.

Small class sizes (20 in the Pre-Prep and Prep) and expert teaching from an early age ensure that academic attainment is high. The requirements of the National Curriculum and preparation for entry into senior schools are blended into a broad based curriculum. This along with an excellent staff/pupil ratio enriches our children's learning and encourages them to work to the very best of their ability.

The accommodation for both Pre-Prep and Prep Departments is first class with pupils resident in newly purpose-built classrooms, having access to their own science and DT laboratory, library, music rooms and computer suite. We are also able to share the Aldenham School campus as a whole, enabling us to enjoy use of the extensive grounds and facilities, including the Sports Complex, Artificial Turf Pitch, Music School, Chapel, Dining Hall, and Theatre. (*For further information about the senior school, see Aldenham School entry in HMC section.*)

We have high expectations of all our pupils and encourage initiative, independence and self-confidence. We also insist on good manners and consideration for others, as a result there is a strong sense of community at Aldenham.

Entry is primarily at 3+, although there are also a number of places available at 7+.

Our excellent established Nursery facilities provide a structured lively and stimulating introduction to Aldenham School with morning and afternoon classes or full day care.

Charitable status. The Aldenham School Company is a Registered Charity, number 298140. It exists to provide high quality education and pastoral care to enable children to achieve their full potential in later life.

Aldro

Lombard Street, Shackleford, Godalming, Surrey GU8 6AS

Tel: 01483 409020 (Headmaster and Admissions)
        01483 810266 (School Office)
Fax: 01483 409010
e-mail: hmsec@aldro.org
website: www.aldro.org

Chairman of the Governors: M W Sayers

Headmaster: **David W N Aston**, BA, PGCE

   Age Range. 7–13.
   Number of Boys. 220: 40 boarders, 180 dayboys.
   Fees per term (2011-2012). Boarding: Form 3 £6,165, Forms 4–8 £6,685. Day: Form 3 £4,677, Forms 4–8 £5,197.

Aldro is a boys' boarding and day prep school set in a beautiful rural location yet within a mile of the A3 and 45 minutes of central London, Gatwick and Heathrow airports.

Aldro aims to offer boys an exceptional all-round education in a happy, purposeful community. It has a Christian foundation and this underpins the values and ethos of the school. Each school day starts with a short service in the lovely Chapel, beautifully converted from an eighteenth century barn.

The school is fortunate in having a spacious site including a lake and about 30 acres of playing fields. There are also four hard tennis courts, a squash court, two shooting ranges and a covered games area. The facilities are excellent and there has been much investment in new buildings over the past ten years. The Centenary Building opened in 2000 and houses most of the classrooms, the ICT centre, an outstanding library and, in the basement, changing rooms and a large common room. The Crispin Hill Centre incorporates a Music School, theatre and sports hall. Two science laboratories and the Art and Design Technology Centre have been developed in eighteenth century buildings either side of the Chapel. The Argyle Building including a new dining hall and kitchen was opened in late 2003. The dormitories in the main building have recently been refurbished. The boarders enjoy high quality pastoral care and a varied programme of activities in the evenings and at weekends.

In the classroom, there is a balance between the best traditional and modern approaches, whilst firm and friendly encouragement of each individual has led to an outstanding academic record of success at Common Entrance and Scholarship level. Thirty academic awards have been won in the last four years to leading schools such as Charterhouse, Eton, Sherborne, Winchester, Radley, Shrewsbury and Wellington College.

Aldro is committed to giving boys real breadth to their education and much emphasis is placed on extra-curricular activities. There are many opportunities for the arts, with a good record of success in Art and Music scholarships – 20 awards have been won in the past four years. Many boys learn musical instruments and there are three choirs, two orchestras and numerous ensembles. Drama also features prominently with several productions each year.

The major sports are rugby, soccer and hockey in the winter, with cricket in the summer. Athletics, tennis, swimming, cross-country running, squash and shooting are secondary sports and high standards are achieved. A huge range of activities are available including cubs and scouts, badminton, bottle digging, fly fishing and pétanque. The school has an enviable record for Chess with 8 teams winning National championships in the past five years.

Boys at Aldro are treated as individuals with talents to develop. They lead cheerful and purposeful lives, and are well-prepared for a wide range of leading senior schools.

'Bringing out the best in boys' is what Aldro has been achieving through the generations. There is a focus on excellence and achievement, whether that is in the classroom, music room or on the sports field. Aldro prepares boys for the rest of their lives.

Charitable status. Aldro School Educational Trust Limited is a Registered Charity, number 312072. It exists to provide education for boys.

Aldwickbury School

Wheathampstead Road, Harpenden, Herts AL5 1AD

Tel: 01582 713022
Fax: 01582 767696
e-mail: head@aldwickbury.org.uk
website: www.aldwickbury.org.uk

Chairman of Governors: S A Westley, MA

Headmaster: **V W Hales**, BEd Hons Exeter

Age Range. 4–13.
Number of Boys. Main School: 220 (including 35 weekly boarders). Pre-Prep: 100.
Fees per term (2011-2012). Day Boys: Pre-Prep £3,435–£3,540, Years 3–8 £3,750–£4,110. Weekly Boarding Fee: £975.

Aldwickbury is a day and boarding school set in 20 acres on the outskirts of Harpenden. Aldwickbury is a boys' school that focuses on boys' education, their growth and development. We allow them to flourish in an environment that challenges and stimulates them whatever their interests, passions or talents. Our teaching mixes traditional approaches together with modern ideas and methods; interactive whiteboards have been installed in all departments.

The school provides an extensive extra-curricular programme for the boys. Music, art and drama are well catered for with an emphasis on involvement as well as the desire for excellence. There are plays and concerts providing performance opportunities for all age groups, both formally and informally. A games session is held every day for all boys in Years 3–8 and teams in all the major sports at every level. The school has an excellent reputation at all sports and has had national recognition in skiing, swimming, athletics, tennis and soccer in recent years.

The school has excellent facilities based around a large Victorian House. Purpose-built teaching blocks, including a modern pre-prep department, ensure that the education is of a high standard. Other facilities include an indoor swimming pool, tennis courts, gymnasium, DT workshop and playing fields. Recent additions to the buildings have been a library, dining room and changing rooms.

The boys move onto a wide range of senior schools, both day and boarding. The recent results at Common Entrance, entry tests and scholarships have been a reflection on the good teaching that the boys receive.

The Pre-Preparatory Department is accommodated in a building opened in 2001.

Charitable status. Aldwickbury School Trust Ltd is a Registered Charity, number 311059. It exists to provide education for children.

All Hallows School

Cranmore Hall, Shepton Mallet, Somerset BA4 4SF
Tel: 01749 881600
Fax: 01749 880709
e-mail: info@allhallowsschool.co.uk
website: www.allhallowsschool.co.uk

Headmaster: **I A Murphy**, BA Hons (Durham), PGCE (Durham)

Age Range. 4–13 Co-educational.
Number of Pupils. 317. Boys: Boarding 38, Day 140. Girls: Boarding 33, Day 106.
Fees per term (2011-2012). Boarding £6,300, Day £4,225 (over 7), £2,250 (under 7). There are no compulsory extras.

True education is preparation for life in all its facets. It is all the better if it is also challenging, exciting, caring and great fun. We strive for the academic achievement of each individual to go hand-in-hand with spiritual growth, friendship, confidence, respect and a sheer love of live. Our children experience childhood in the truest sense.

All Hallows pioneered Catholic boarding co-education for preparatory school age children and the school continues to be very innovative and quite distinct being rated 'Out-

standing' in all categories by Ofsted in 2010 with no recommendations for improvement and overall by ISI in 2009.

Christian principles are integrated into daily life so that all faiths are welcomed into the life of this Roman Catholic foundation. Professionally qualified, energetic and family-orientated staff, many of whom reside in the school, provide for the academic and pastoral welfare of the children.

The school has a happy and deliberate mix of boarders and day pupils. Attractive flexibility exists between boarding and day arrangements. There is an extensive and innovative Activities Programme for all children each evening after school, with weekend and holiday highlights.

The school enjoys regional and national sporting success in rugby, hockey, cricket, tennis, trampolining and athletics, as well as regular competitive fixtures for children of all abilities against local opposition in the traditional team sports. Excellence within a framework of sport for all is our aim. Riding, golf and fencing are activities that are becoming increasingly popular. Our Tennis Academy carries an LTA Clubmark for excellence and is available to every child in the school as well as siblings and parents.

Music and the Arts thrive, ranging from the grace of the Chapel Choir to the creativity and performance of dance and drama. Exceptional facilities throughout the campus allow the children and staff to discover talent and develop potential. We are able to offer a specific environmental education, utilising the school's special outdoor teaching area and private wood. Our Junior children follow an outstanding Forest School curriculum.

All Hallows' independent status from any one particular senior school enables parents and the Headmaster to select the most appropriate senior school to suit a particular child's needs and talents. In the last few years we have sent pupils to over forty different schools. 2010 witnessed an impressive scholarship record, just under 40% of the leavers. We offer a range of scholarships and bursaries.

Charitable status. All Hallows is a Registered Charity, number 310281. The school is a Charitable Trust, the raison d'être of which is the integration of Christian principles with daily life.

Alleyn Court Preparatory School

Wakering Road, Southend-on-Sea, Essex SS3 0PW
Tel: 01702 582553
Fax: 01702 584574
e-mail: office@alleyn-court.co.uk
           admissions@alleyn-court.co.uk
           head@alleyn-court.co.uk
website: www.alleyn-court.co.uk

Headmaster: **Mr G R A Davies**, BA Hons, PGCE

Age Range. 2–11.
Number of Pupils. 320 Boys and Girls.
Fees per term (from April 2011). £1,880–£3,224 according to age.

Alleyn Court was founded in 1904 by Theodore Wilcox and is a non-selective, family-owned, co-educational day school, for children aged 2–11. The school is situated in beautiful grounds within the Thorpe Bay area of Southend and has an outstanding reputation for its breadth of curriculum and opportunities, academic achievement, sporting success (Essex County Cross-Country Champions for the third successive year), art and general all-round pastoral care. A happy and relaxed atmosphere and strong sense of community underpin the purposeful approach to school life and activities.

The school is split into three sections: two parallel Pre-Preparatory departments, located on the main school site in Thorpe Bay and on the original school site in Westcliff, offer an education based on Montessori principles for children aged 2–5 years in the EYFS; the Junior School is for Years 1–3 and the Senior School is for Years 4–6, with each class rarely rising above 20 children. Children are accepted for entry into any year group, providing that spaces are available.

Children are prepared for 11+ entry to the local selective grammar schools and for senior independent schools, with some successfully gaining scholarships. French is taught from age 4, with specialist teaching for Art, French, Music and PE from Year 1 upwards. All lessons in Years 5 and 6 are taught by subject specialists in dedicated subject rooms.

Academic facilities on the main school site include: library, fully-equipped science laboratory, modern computer suite with 21 workstations and an art studio. Part of the school site has recently been developed to create a Forest School and outdoor classroom to offer more practical and skill-based learning.

The school offers extensive provision for sport and extra-curricular activities, with a variety of clubs being offered whenever children aren't in the classroom – these occur and are well attended before and after school, as well as during morning and lunch breaks. The school offers the following sports: athletics, badminton, basketball, cricket, cross-country, dodgeball, football, hockey, rounders and rugby.

Sports facilities include: large, picturesque, onsite playing fields, sports hall, cricket nets, tennis courts, cross-country course and a newly renovated pavilion.

Other non-sporting clubs include: art, ballet, chess, debating, drama, DT, French, G&T core subjects, IT, jewellery, VR.

Scholarships and means-tested bursaries are available annually for pupils with academic, sporting, musical and artistic talent.

Alleyn's Junior School

Townley Road, Dulwich, London SE22 8SU
Tel: 020 8557 1519
Fax: 020 8693 3597
e-mail: juniorschool@alleyns.org.uk
website: www.alleyns.org.uk

Chairman of Governors: Prof the Lord Kakkar, BSc, PhD, FRCS

Headmaster: **Mark O'Donnell**, BA, PGDDes, MSc Arch, EdM Harv, PGDES Oxon

Age Range. 4–11.
Number of Pupils. 240 boys and girls.
Fees per term (2011-2012). £4,083–£4,250 including lunches, out of school visits and one residential trip per year for Years 3–6.

The school is part of the foundation known as 'Alleyn's College of God's Gift' which was founded by Edward Alleyn, the Elizabethan actor, in 1619.

Opened in 1992 to provide a co-educational Junior School for Alleyn's School and sharing the same excellent green site, Alleyn's Junior School provides a happy and lively environment in which well-motivated boys and girls follow a broad and academic education. Boys and girls work together with their teachers in a calm and structured way to develop their potential and self-confidence as they pursue the highest standards across a curriculum which embraces many opportunities for art, German, drama, music, French, ICT and a wide range of sports. Entry to the school is at 4+, 7+ and 9+. The overwhelming majority of children move on to Alleyn's senior school at 11+.

Within small classes and with a balance of class and specialist subject teaching, children are set clear and challenging targets for their learning. Children perform at above average level in KS1 and KS2 tests. The school enjoys a strong extra-curricular life offering children varied and exciting opportunities to extend their learning beyond the classroom.

Progress is carefully monitored and individual differences appropriately met. Competition has its place in the encouragement of the highest academic, artistic and sporting standards, but it is always tempered by an emphasis on values of thoughtfulness, courtesy and tolerance. All members of the school community are expected to maintain high standards in their behaviour, manners and appearance, showing pride in themselves and their school.

The school enjoys excellent support from its parent body. Regular meetings and reports keep parents informed of academic progress and pastoral matters and The Alleyn's Junior School Association works tirelessly to promote social cohesion within the school and to support the charity, sporting, dramatic and extra-curricular programmes. It also organises an After School Care scheme through which children can be supervised at school each day during term time until 6 pm.

Charitable status. Alleyn's College of God's Gift is a Registered Charity, number 1057971. Its purpose is to provide independent education for boys and girls.

Alpha Preparatory School

Hindes Road, Harrow, Middlesex HA1 1SH
Tel: 020 8427 1471
Fax: 020 8424 9324
e-mail: sec@alpha.harrow.sch.uk
website: www.alpha.harrow.sch.uk

Chairman of the Board of Governors: Mr A Bloom

Headmaster: **P J Wylie**, BA, CertEd

Age Range. 3–11.
Number of Pupils. 200 boys and girls (day only).
Fees per term (2011-2012). Inclusive of lunch, with no compulsory extras: Nursery £950–£2,000; Pre-Preparatory £2,640; Main School £2,890.

The School, situated in a residential area of Harrow, was founded in 1895, and in 1950 was reorganised as a non-profit-making Educational Charity, with a Board of Governors elected by members of the Company; parents of pupils in the School are eligible for membership.

The majority of children enter the Main School at the age of 4 by interview and assessment but there can also be a few vacancies for older pupils and here entry is by interview and/or written tests, dependent upon age.

There is a full-time staff of 16 experienced and qualified teachers, with additional part-time teachers in instrumental Music. The main games are Football and Cricket, with cross-country, athletics, tennis and netball. Extra-curricular activities include Piano and Violin instruction.

Religious education, which is considered important, is non-sectarian in nature, but follows upon the School's Christian foundation and tradition; children of all faiths are accepted.

Outside visits to theatres, concerts and museums form an integral part of the curriculum and during the Lent Term pupils in Year 6 visit the Isle of Wight.

Regular successes are obtained in Entrance and Scholarship examinations, with many Scholarships having been won in recent years.

The School has its own Nursery (Alphabets) for children aged 3 in the term of entry. Further details can be obtained from the Registration Secretary.

Charitable status. Alpha Preparatory School is a Registered Charity, number 312640. It exists to carry on the undertaking of a boys and/or girls preparatory school in Harrow in the County of Middlesex.

Altrincham Preparatory School

Marlborough Road, Bowdon, Altrincham, Cheshire WA14 2RR
Tel: 0161 928 3366
Fax: 0161 929 6747
e-mail: admin@altprep.co.uk
website: www.altprep.co.uk

Headmaster: Mr A C Potts, BSc

Age Range. 3–11.
Number in School. 320 Day Boys.
Fees per term (2010-2011). £2,060–£2,280.

Altrincham Preparatory School has been well known in the Manchester area for over 65 years and continues to maintain its high reputation for excellent academic, music and sporting achievements.

The School has a good pupil teacher ratio and offers a very wide range of academic subjects headed by the three main National Curriculum core subjects, English, Mathematics and Science.

The School has outstanding results to all the local independent grammar schools, particularly to Manchester Grammar School, as well as to a very wide range of other schools including the traditional senior independent schools where scholarships have been gained.

The School's sporting successes have been achieved on a national basis in rugby, soccer, athletics, cricket, tennis and swimming.

The School has an ongoing programme of improvement and development including, in 1996/7, the erection of a new purpose-built Junior School.

Amesbury

Hazel Grove, Hindhead, Surrey GU26 6BL
Tel: 01428 604322
Fax: 01428 607715
e-mail: enquiries@amesburyschool.co.uk
website: www.amesburyschool.co.uk

Chairman of the Governors: D Wenman

Headmaster: Nigel Taylor, MA

Age Range. 2–13.
Number of Pupils. Main School: 225 Day pupils. Pre-Preparatory Department: 100 Day pupils.
Fees per term (2010-2011). Day Pupils £3,715–£4,035, Pre-Prep £2,630.

Amesbury is a co-educational day school founded in 1870. The main building is unique, as the only school to be designed by Sir Edwin Lutyens, and stands in its own 34-acre estate in the heart of the Surrey countryside.

Classes are small guaranteeing individual attention. Study programmes currently lead to Common Entrance or senior school scholarship examinations at 11+ (for girls only) and at 13+ (for girls and boys). We have a proud tradition of academic, sporting and artistic achievement. The school has excellent purpose-built facilities.

For further information please contact the Headmaster's Secretary.

Charitable status. Amesbury School is a Registered Charity, number 312058. It exists to provide education for boys and girls. It is administered by a Board of Governors.

Appleford School

Shrewton, Nr Salisbury, Wiltshire SP3 4HL
Tel: 0800 135 7314
Fax: 01980 621366
e-mail: secretary@appleford.wilts.sch.uk
website: www.appleford.wilts.sch.uk

Headmistress: Lesley Nell, CertEd, Adv Dip Lang & Lit

Age Range. 7–13, Boarders from 7.
Number of Pupils. 34 (day), 59 (boarding). Girls 18, Boys 76.
Fees per term (2010-2011). Day £5,095; Boarding £7,521.

Founded in 1988, Appleford is a co-educational boarding and day specialist school for pupils aged 7–13. Teaching is in small groups.

Appleford School provides a stimulating, structured and varied curriculum for the dyslexic child, with the emphasis on literacy and numeracy skills.

Appleford offers a whole-school approach to Dyslexia:
• research-backed multi-sensory programmes designed to encourage increased self-confidence and self-esteem
• on site Speech and Language Therapy and Occupational Therapy
• qualified DfE teachers with a high ratio of specialist qualifications
• experienced and caring houseparents in friendly, structured boarding houses, encouraging the development of personal organisation and life skills within individual care plans
• an extensive games and fixtures programme, numerous challenging and exciting after-school activities from art to archery, cooking to croquet, putting to pottery. Judo, swimming and tennis also take place after school. Participation in music and drama is encouraged. There is a carefully planned and stimulating weekend programme for the full boarder.

Appleford is approved by the Council for the Registration of Schools Teaching Dyslexic Children (CReSTeD) and the Department for Education. It is a Corporate Member of the British Dyslexia Association.

Appleford's stated aim is to return the pupils to mainstream education as soon as possible and, since its foundation, over 80% of the children have achieved this goal. Some dyslexic pupils still need considerable support at senior school and advice is given on future placements. It is crucial that the foundations laid at Appleford are carefully and sympathetically built upon at the next stage of education.

Ardingly College Pre-Preparatory School – The Farmhouse
A Woodard School

Haywards Heath, West Sussex RH17 6SQ
Tel: 01444 893300
Fax: 01444 893301
e-mail: admin@ardingly.com
website: www.ardingly.com

Chairman of School Council: Mr J Sloane, BSc

Head: Mrs H Nawrocka, MSc, PGCE

Age Range. 2½–7 Co-educational.
Number of Pupils. 120 Day Boys and Girls.
Fees per term (2011-2012). Reception, Years 1 & 2: £2,395; Nursery (5 half days) £1,435; Nursery (5 full days)

£2,180; Pre-Nursery £17.50 per session or £43.50 per full day; Before and After-School Care available until 6.00 pm on school days.

The Farmhouse provides children with the perfect introduction to their education. Safely yet idyllically situated within the College estate, our Pre-Preparatory is housed within carefully restored Grade 2 listed Victorian farm buildings. We have full use of the College facilities, including swimming pool, sports hall, playing fields, chapel and full medical on-site care. The school grounds provide us with a wealth of resources for many different purposes.

We aim to lay the basic foundations – academic, social, physical and spiritual – upon which every child can build a sound education, all within a caring yet challenging and well-organised atmosphere.

The Farmhouse caters for children from 2½ to 3 years in our Pre-Nursery, 3 to 4 years in our Nursery and from 4 to 7 in the Pre-Preparatory classes.

The Pre-Preparatory children are taught in classes of about 16 pupils, whilst the Nursery may cater for up to 25 children (four sessions are compulsory, with full day available).

Our school is run from Monday to Friday. There are no boarding facilities at this age but a Before and After-School Care service is available.

After-school activities include Hockey, Country Dancing, Choir, Maths Club, Tennis, Chess, and Art Club.

All children have full use of the College swimming pool and a wide variety of sport is included in the curriculum.

French is taught from the age of 4 years.

The Farmhouse has its own qualified staff under the direction of the Headmistress and the School has access to specialist staff.

Charitable status. Ardingly College Limited is a Registered Charity, number 1076456. It exists to enable all boys and girls to develop their love of learning, academic potential and individual talents in a caring community which fosters sensitivity, confidence, a sense of service and enthusiasm for life.

Ardingly College Prep School
A Woodard School

Haywards Heath, West Sussex RH17 6SQ
Tel: 01444 893200
Fax: 01444 893201
e-mail: registrar@ardingly.com
website: www.ardingly.com

Chairman of School Council: Mr J Sloane, BSc

Headmaster: **Mr C B Calvey**, BEd Hons

Deputy Head: Mr J Castle, BEd

Age Range. 7–13.
Number of Pupils. Approximately 250. There are 20 weekly boarders and flexi-boarding is a popular option.
Fees per term (2011-2012). Day Pupils: £3,430 (Years 3–4), £4,250 (Years 5–6), £4,335 (Years 7–8), including meals. Weekly Boarding (in addition to Day Fees): £430–£1,290 (1–5 nights). Casual boarding: £40 per night.

Ardingly College Prep School is the Preparatory School for Ardingly College Senior School (*see entry in HMC section*). Boys and girls are admitted after they have reached the age of 7. Boarders from age 9.

Details of Scholarships available may be obtained from the Registrar.

The Prep School shares extensive grounds with the Senior School and benefits from the College's Chapel, Music School, Dining Hall, Design Technology Department, Gymnasium, a new Sports Hall, 25m indoor Swimming Pool, Squash Courts, Astroturf, Medical Centre (with 24 hour nursing cover) and school shop and it is organised as a separate unit. The Prep School has its own classrooms, Drama Studio, Library, Art Department (with pottery), new ICT suite, changing rooms and boarding accommodation.

Children are prepared for CE and PSS.

There are four live-in boarding staff, four resident Gappers and a full time Matron to look after the boarders.

A wide range of extra-curricular activities is encouraged. They include Study Skills, Drama Club (there are termly productions), Maths Club, Chess, Gardening, Leadership Challenge, Cookery, Board Games, Cubs, Riding, Art, various musical groups from Orchestra and strings to Jazz Band and plenty of sporting activities.

The Senior School boys concentrate on Football but Prep School boys will experience Rugby as well as Football. Girls play Netball and Rounders and both boys and girls enjoy Hockey, Athletics, Cross-Country, Cricket, Basketball and Squash. Ardingly College Prep School is an Activemark Gold school (Sport England recognised).

Children are streamed at the top end of the school and setted in core subjects. Prep is done at school. ICT is strong.

Religious Education is in accordance with the teaching of the Church of England.

Charitable status. Ardingly College Limited is a Registered Charity, number 1076456. It exists to provide high quality education for boys and girls aged 3–18 in a Christian context.

Ardvreck

Crieff, Perthshire PH7 4EX
Tel: 01764 653112
Fax: 01764 654920
e-mail: headmaster@ardvreck.org.uk
website: www.ardvreckschool.co.uk

Chairman of the Governors: A K Miller

Headmaster: **Richard Harvey**

Age Range. Co-educational 3–13.
Number of Pupils. Main School: 100 Boarders, 35 day. Pre-Prep 22. Nursery 12.
Fees per term (2010-2011). Main School: £5,665 (boarders), £3,770 (day); Pre-Prep £1,766.

Admission is by interview with the Headmaster. A Scholarship and several Exhibitions or Bursaries are awarded each year following a competitive examination in early March. Service Bursaries are also available.

Ardvreck stands in extensive grounds on the edge of Crieff, having been purpose built and founded in 1883. The School has a long tradition of providing academic excellence as well as outstanding achievement in sport and music. There are 17 full-time and 3 part-time members of the teaching staff and classes are no larger than 16. Health and domestic arrangements are under the personal supervision of the Headmaster's wife and she is assisted by four full-time Matrons – one of whom is the resident, qualified school Nurse.

The School Doctor visits regularly and dental and orthodontic treatment can be arranged if necessary.

Boys and girls are prepared for senior schools throughout Britain. In recent years, all have passed the Common Entrance to their schools of first choice and over 30 scholarships have been won in the past four years.

Rugby, Netball, Hockey, Cricket, Rounders and Athletics are the main games and on several Saturdays in the summer, pupils are provided with picnic lunches enabling them to explore the surrounding countryside, accompanied by members of staff, where they can study the wildlife, fish in one of the rivers or lochs, climb, sail or canoe. Other activities include Golf, Riding, Tennis and Shooting, a sport for which the School has a national reputation for excellence having won the UK Prep Schools Championship for the last fifteen years.

A modern and well-equipped Music School provides the best possible opportunities for music-making. There is an orchestra and choir both of which regularly achieve distinction at music festivals. Visiting music specialists teach a wide range of instruments including the Pipes. Music and Drama play an important part in the life of the School and a major production is staged annually with several smaller productions and numerous concerts taking place throughout the year.

There is a heated, indoor swimming pool (all children are taught to swim), an Astroturf surface for hockey, tennis and netball, and a superb sports hall.

Most full-time staff live within the School grounds and a special feature of Ardvreck is that there are two senior boarding houses – one for girls and one for boys – where pupils gain a little more independence and are encouraged to show greater personal responsibility in readiness for the transition to senior schools.

Many boarders live overseas and they are escorted to and from Edinburgh Airport; all necessary documentation can be handled by the School if required. Overseas pupils are required to have a guardian in the UK with whom they can stay during exeats.

Charitable status. Ardvreck School is a Registered Charity, number SC009886. Its aim is to provide education for boys and girls.

Arnold House School

1 Loudoun Road, St John's Wood, London NW8 0LH
Tel: 020 7266 4840
Fax: 020 7266 6994
e-mail: office@arnoldhouse.co.uk
website: www.arnoldhouse.co.uk

Chairman of the Board of Governors: A T N Warner Esq

Headmaster: **V W P Thomas**, BEd, MA

Age Range. 5–13.
Number of Boys. 250 (Day Boys only).
Fees per term (2010-2011). £4,900 including Lunch.

Arnold House is an independent day school for boys founded in 1905.

Most boys join the school after their fifth birthday. A few join at other ages.

The Arnold House website gives full details of recent developments in the school's curriculum and facilities. These include the complete refurbishment and extension of the main teaching facilities at Loudoun Road (2001) and the introduction of an innovative research and ICT based learning programme for pupils in Years 5 and 6 (2003). At the school's playing fields at Canons Park, Edgware, the existing pavilion hall has been adapted to become an auditorium seating 150 with a fully equipped stage and associated facilities (2007). The Canons Park Activity Centre has become an important addition to the excellent facilities at Loudoun Road.

Boys transfer to their chosen independent senior schools at the age of 13. Arnold House has an enviable record of success in placing each boy in the school that is right for him. More than half of the boys move on to the most sought-after London day schools: Westminster, St Paul's, Highgate, UCS, Mill Hill and City of London. Others transfer to renowned boarding schools: Eton, Winchester, Marlborough, Rugby, Harrow and Charterhouse have been popular destinations in recent years. Arnold House takes a long view of a boy's education. Academic breadth, a balance between

study, sport, music, the arts and activities together with excellent pastoral care constitute the foundations of the school's philosophy and success.

Charitable status. Arnold House School is a Registered Charity, number 312725. It exists to provide education for boys in preparation for transfer to senior independent schools at 13.

Arnold Lodge School

Kenilworth Road, Leamington Spa, Warwickshire CV32 5TW
Tel: 01926 778050
Fax: 01926 743311
e-mail: info@arnoldlodge.com
website: www.arnoldlodge.com

Principal: **Mr David H Williams**, BSc, CertEd

Age Range. 2 Years 8 months to 16.
Number of Pupils. 290 Co-educational.
Fees per term (2010-2011). £3,030 (Years 7–11), £2,945 (Years 5–6), £2,760 (Years 3–4), £2,395 (Reception–Year 2), Kindergarten: £35.90 (per full day), £19.90 (per half day).

Founded in 1864 and located in the heart of Leamington Spa, Arnold Lodge School is the only co-educational school in South Warwickshire educating girls and boys from Kindergarten to Year 11 (GCSE).

Teaching and learning at Arnold Lodge School is based on our belief that each child is special and brings to school widely different experiences, aptitudes and capabilities. We think that this individuality should be recognised, respected and developed. In order to make the most of each child's abilities and potential we provide a happy and confident environment to encourage excellence in every aspect of learning. We also give all children the opportunity to develop interests through field trips, cultural visits, music, dance, sport, drama, citizenship programmes and a wide range of lunch-time and after-school clubs.

At Arnold Lodge school we actively encourage children to become caring members of the school and society. We work hard to ensure that children and adults are valued and respected in all aspects of school life and expect our children to develop and demonstrate a responsible and caring attitude towards others both in and out of school.

Most children enter the school at Kindergarten during the term of their third birthday, thus enabling them to make a smooth transition in to the Reception class in the September following their fourth birthday. We do however welcome applications at any stage up to Year 10 provided there are spaces available.

Entrance exams are not required for entry to the school up to and including Year 6. Pupils entering the Senior School at Year 7 and beyond are required to pass an entrance exam which takes place in early January in addition to a 'taster day' and interview (in exceptional cases the entrance exam can be taken at other times of the year.)

An important part of the entry process to Arnold Lodge School for all pupils is a 'taster day'. A prospective pupil is expected to spend a full day at the school with pupils of their own age. In this way a child can get a good feel for the school and teachers can observe performance, social interaction with teachers and fellow pupils and the attributes he or she can bring to the school.

We offer academic awards for Year 3. Year 7 Scholarships are awarded for academic excellence, music, sport and art. These can be up to 50% of the school fees. Applicants for awards and scholarships from both within and outside the school are invited to attend an assessment morning which takes place in January.

Since the expansion of the school to GCSE in September 2008, our aim is to emulate our success as a Preparatory School where over 95% of our pupils gained a place at their first choice of senior school at 11+ and 13+. We will therefore be able to give every child the opportunity of gaining a place at the sixth form or college that will best suit their abilities, talents and aptitude.

Ashdell Preparatory School

266 Fulwood Road, Sheffield S10 3BL
Tel: 0114 266 3835
Fax: 0114 267 1762
e-mail: headteacher@ashdellprep.co.uk
website: www.ashdellprep.co.uk

Girls Day Preparatory.

Chairman of Council of Management: Ian Walker

Headmistress: **Mrs A B Camm**, BEd

Deputy Head: Mr L Guntrip, BEd

Age Range. 4–11 years.
Number of Pupils. 120 girls.
Fees per term (2010-2011). £2,590–£2,765.

Ashdell was founded in 1948, and whilst its traditional values of responsibility, respect and role in the community continue to be fundamental to our ethos, we love to have fun and realise that happiness at school is key to achieving a girl's potential, be it academic, artistic, personal or social.

Ashdell has an excellent reputation for academic success and for providing its pupils with a friendly, caring environment in which to flourish. We aim to develop each girls unique potential and are able to achieve this through small class sizes (average 17) and our careful attention to the basics. The school maintains a high pupil teacher ratio and the cosy atmosphere ensures that all children are well known and individual needs are catered for. We have programmes to support learning and to develop the talented or gifted child. Girls are prepared for entrance examinations to Independent Senior Schools at the age of 11.

Girls study a broad range of subjects including English, Mathematics, Science, French, ICT, Music, Swimming, Tennis, Drama, PE, Ballet, Pottery, Judo, Cookery and Woodwork. The School has an excellent music programme with a choir, orchestra, flute choir and string group. Individual lessons are offered in a variety of instruments and there are many opportunities for pupils to perform. The Prep School boasts excellent ICT, music and practice rooms, a science lab, art room and large gym. A rich Physical Education programme makes good use of local university sports facilities for swimming, netball, hockey and tennis.

Accommodated in a beautiful Victorian building our Pre-Preparatory Department caters for the 4–7 year olds. It has its own Art and Design Technology room, ICT facilities, garden and play area.

Snowdrops Pre-School opened in 2007 for boys and girls aged 3–5.

Meals are cooked in house by our own staff and pupils eat lunch in family style groupings. We offer a breakfast club which starts at 7.45 am and after-school care runs from 3.30 until 5.30 pm to cater for working parents.

Our fee schedule reflects our all inclusive policy but excludes individual music tuition and the many extra-curricular clubs such as gym, drama, cookery, art, and Spanish.

Charitable status. Ashdell Schools Trust Limited is a Registered Charity, number 529380. It was founded for the education of girls.

Ashfold School

Dorton, Aylesbury, Bucks HP18 9NG
Tel: 01844 238237
Fax: 01844 238505
e-mail: registrar@ashfoldschool.co.uk
website: www.ashfoldschool.co.uk

Chairman of Governors: Mr R Williams

Headmaster: **M O M Chitty**, BSc

Age Range. 3–13.
Number of Pupils. Age 7–13: 176 boys and girls (day pupils and weekly boarders). Pre-Prep (3–6 years): 104 boys and girls.
Fees per term (2010-2011). Weekly boarders £5,028; Day £4,300; Pre-Prep £1,095–£3,135.

Ashfold is housed in a magnificent Jacobean mansion set in thirty acres of parkland and playing fields in the heart of the countryside between Oxford and Aylesbury.

Ashfold aims to deliver confident and fully prepared young children ready to meet the challenges of their chosen secondary schools. Its emphasis remains upon the broadest possible education so, in addition to satisfying the academic requirements of preparing them for Common Entrance and Scholarship examination to Senior Independent Schools, every encouragement and opportunity is given to children to develop a wide range of sporting, musical (instrumental and choral), artistic, countryside and other interests (for many years National Clay Pigeon Champions). Children are also prepared, as required, for the LEA 11-plus examination to local grammar schools.

Ashfold is a small, close-knit Christian-based community, holding strong family values. With class sizes averaging just 14, the 36 mainly resident qualified staff are able to give each child the individual attention and encouragement they need. Recent developments include an ICT Centre, Performance Studio, new Library, Junior Department, expanded boarding wing and Astroturf pitches.

Charitable status. Ashfold School Trust is a Registered Charity, number 272663. It exists to provide a quality preparatory school education, academically and in other respects, for all the children entrusted to its care.

Ashford Friars Preparatory School
UCST

Great Chart, Ashford, Kent TN23 3DJ
Tel: 01233 620493
Fax: 01233 636579
e-mail: ashfordfriars@ashfordschool.co.uk
website: www.ashfordschool.co.uk

Co-educational Day School.

Chairman of School Council: Mr P Massey, MA

Head: **Mr R Yeates**, BA Hons

Age Range. 3–11.
Number of Pupils. 333: 158 Boys, 175 Girls.
Fees per term (2011-2012). Day: Nursery: £428 (one full day per week), £2,138 (full-time); Reception £2,138, Years 1 and 2 £2,458, Years 3–6 £3,644.

Ashford Friars Prep School is part of the United Church Schools Trust and as such has benefited from significant recent investment, including extensive refurbishment and new facilities. The school believes in the importance of focusing on the development of the individual through a broad education in which every child can find success whilst developing confidence, motivation, self-esteem and emotional intelligence.

A focus on pastoral care and the pursuit of excellence go together with high standards of discipline and a strong Christian ethos.

Situated in a rural setting, Ashford Friars Prep School lies in some 25 very attractive acres. The School enjoys both classroom-based and excellent specialist teaching with well-designed facilities for science, art, music, PE, ICT and design technology and has recently undergone a large investment development to bring the Pre-Prep School on site at the end of 2009. These new buildings provide 18 new classrooms, new kitchens, reception area, library facilities and a new hall. The School is fully networked and has exceptional provision for ICT with ACTIVboards in all classrooms, a computer room capable of accommodating entire classes and broadband access to the Internet throughout.

The thriving Nursery operates on a flexible basis and the school offers full, wrap-around care from 7.30 am to 6.00 pm for all our children. The school operates Mondays to Fridays. Holiday Clubs operate during school breaks.

Throughout the school, team sports include rugby, hockey, netball, football, rounders, athletics and cricket. Regular fixtures are held with other local schools. Children also participate in PE and swimming as part of their curricular programme.

An extensive range of co-curricular activities is provided, both at lunchtime and after school. Individual music tuition with a wide range of instruments is available. Music, drama, dance and public speaking are all important opportunities; productions and presentations are performed by all age groups to a high standard and take place throughout the year. The choir and orchestra meet regularly.

A programme of educational trips and visits provides a stimulating and important addition to the all-round education and development of the 'whole' child and the costs of these are included in the fees.

Children normally progress to Ashford Senior School (*see HMC entry*) without the need to take an entrance test unless they wish to sit scholarship exams. The Prep School has had considerable success in preparing children for scholarships to leading independent schools as well as other entrance tests including the 11+.

Charitable status. Ashford Friars Preparatory School is part of Ashford School and a member of The United Church Schools Trust, which is a Registered Charity, number 1016538.

Austin Friars St Monica's Junior School

Etterby Scaur, Carlisle, Cumbria CA3 9PB
Tel: 01228 528042
Fax: 01228 810327
e-mail: office@austinfriars.cumbria.sch.uk
        admissions@austinfriars.cumbria.sch.uk
website: www.austinfriars.cumbria.sch.uk

Chairman of Trustees: Revd Dr Peter Tiplady, MB BS, MRCGP, FFPHM, FRIPH

Headmaster: Mr C J Lumb, BSc, MEd, PGCE

Head of Junior School: Mrs F M Willacy

Age Range. 3–11.
Number of Pupils. Junior School: 132; Pre-School: 28.
Fees per term (2011-2012). Junior School: £1,825 (R–Year 2), £2,115 (Years 3–4), £2,480 (Years 5–6). Pre-School: £4.75 per hour, plus £1.55 for lunch.

Austin Friars St Monica's Junior School offers a wide and varied curriculum, which encourages academic achievement alongside sporting, musical, cultural and creative development, thus allowing each child's talents and potential to be fully pursued.

The importance of good primary education cannot be over emphasised and the Junior School commits itself to this purpose.

The teaching staff form a capable and highly motivated team totally dedicated to the aims and ethos of the School.

Pupils benefit from specialist teaching in subjects such as ICT, music, drama, modern languages and sports and games. Learning support is an integral part of the curriculum for those who will benefit.

Academically, the school has a fine reputation within the City of Carlisle and beyond, with a record of many scholarship successes at age 11.

Music, speech and drama have a high profile.

Annually Junior 1 (Year 3) pupils are given a musical instrument to learn and enjoy specialist tuition.

Juniors take LAMDA Verse and Prose Speaking Examination achieving consistently high grades.

Good use is made of the extensive grounds surrounding the school, including Astroturf, providing ample scope for PE lessons as well as hosting matches against local school teams.

A wide range of extra-curricular activities is offered from 4.00–6.00 pm, including history, chess, hockey, art, science, computing, young engineers, French, football and netball.

Due to the expansion of pupil numbers, a £3.1 million state-of-the-art Junior School was completed in February 2008.

The Junior School is an Ofsted registered provider of Free Nursery Education Entitlement for three and four year olds. Reception follows the Early Years Foundation Stage curriculum.

The Early Years Foundation Stage Pre-School occupies a spacious detached two-storey house, adjacent to the main School.

Set within its own grounds and bordered by a mature garden, the Pre-School provides pupils with excellent facilities, including an interesting garden bordered by mature trees and all-weather safe play area. The secure building and grounds offer parents an opportunity to educate children within a natural and comfortable setting.

The main aim of the Pre-School is to provide a caring and stimulating environment, endowing children with a positive attitude to learning which will serve them through their formative years. The Early Years Foundation Stage curriculum covers the six areas of learning. Through carefully-structured and well-planned, play-based activities pupils are encouraged to develop their own ideas and to learn sound spiritual and social values by being cooperative and aware of others. Pre-School pupils are taught to listen carefully, to make friends, share, take turns and be polite and to use good manners.

Admission. Children are admitted into the Pre-School in the three to four age range. 24 places are available per session.

Entry into the Junior School at all levels, except Kindergarten, is by formal assessment of English, mathematics and non-verbal reasoning; prospective pupils spend a taster day in School. All prospective pupils are screened for specific learning difficulties. Entry into Kindergarten is by interview and a taster afternoon.

Senior School. *For information about Austin Friars St Monica's Senior School, see entry in SHMIS section.*

Charitable status. Austin Friars St Monica's School is a Registered Charity, number 516289.

Avenue House School

70 The Avenue, Ealing, London W13 8LS
Tel: 020 8998 9981
Fax: 020 8991 1533
e-mail: school@avenuehouse.org
website: www.avenuehouse.org

Co-educational Day School.

Proprietor: Mr David Immanuel

Head: Mrs C M Self

   Age Range. 3–11.
   Number of Pupils. 120.
   Fees per term (2011-2012). £1,730–£2,975.
   Avenue House School provides a small, caring environment where children gain the confidence to flourish in all areas of the curriculum. Good manners, mutual respect and a caring community are prevalent at all times.
   Children are taught in small classes conducive to the development of an excellent work ethos and achieve high standards in academic subjects as well as an appreciation and understanding of Drama, Art, Music and Sport.
   Avenue House School does not test children on entry to Reception as we feel that each child develops at their own individual rate. All pupils are monitored and assessed individually throughout the year and meetings between parents and school are frequent as we believe a positive approach leads to excellence.
   Children have access to our own small library and gymnasium. The school has laptop computers with wireless broadband internet connection and whiteboards are installed throughout.
   Pupils are prepared for the competitive entrance examinations to the London Independent Day Schools.
   Avenue House School is proud of the many high standard musical and drama productions that are performed throughout the year from Nursery children to Year 6.
   Physical Education is an important part of our curriculum and all pupils go swimming every week. Children in the Nursery, Reception and Year 1 have Physical Education in our Gymnasium and small playground. From Year 2 the children have weekly sports lessons at Trailfinders Sports and Leisure Club. The traditional annual sports day for the whole school is also held here. We have a network of local schools with whom we play regular sports matches throughout the year.
   Extra curriculum activities form a valuable and key part of our education. Apart from the daily homework club other activities include football, drama, guitar, choir, ICT, art, tennis (Summer Term), ballet, Mad Science, French and gardening (Summer Term).
   Educational visits play an important role in helping children relate their class work to the real world. For this reason pupils are taken on outings each term where they can benefit from having first-hand knowledge of London and its surrounding areas. Children have the opportunity to go on residential trips which include The Black Mountains in Wales, Dorchester, Paris and the Isle of Wight.

Avenue Nursery & Pre-Preparatory School

2 Highgate Avenue, Highgate, London N6 5RX
Tel: 020 8348 6815
Fax: 020 8348 8123
e-mail: info@avenuenursery.com
website: www.avenuenursery.com

Principal: **Mrs Mary Fysh**

   Age Range. 3–7 Co-educational.
   Number of Pupils. 75.
   Fees per term (2011-2012). £2,000–£3,700.

Aysgarth School

Bedale, North Yorkshire DL8 1TF
Tel:01677 450240
Fax:01677 450736
e-mail:enquiries@aysgarthschool.co.uk
website:www.aysgarthschool.com

Chairman of Governors: The Marquess of Downshire

Headmaster: **C A A Goddard**, MA Emmanuel College
   Cambridge

Assistant Headmaster: P J Southall, BA Hull, PGCE St
   Mary's College, Twickenham

   Age Range. 3–13.
   Number of Pupils. 185. Pre-Prep Department: 65 boys and girls aged 3–8. Prep School: 125 boys aged 8–13.
   Fees per term (2010-2011). Boarders (full and weekly) £6,250, Day £4,870, Pre-Prep £1,960–£2,550.
   The Prep School is a boarding school for boys set in 50 acres of grounds in Wensleydale about 6 miles from the A1. It attracts boys from all over the UK, and boys go on to the country's leading independent senior schools, many of them in southern England. Some boys start as day boys or weekly boarders to enable them to adjust to boarding gently. For exeats, boys are escorted on trains from Darlington to the north and south and there are coaches to and from Cumbria and Lancashire.
   Boys of all abilities are welcomed and academic standards are high. All boys are prepared for Common Entrance and several gain scholarships. Before entry, each boy is assessed to ensure that any special needs are identified early and given fully integrated specialist help where necessary. Class sizes are typically around 12. There is a newly equipped computer centre and every teacher has a laptop to link to digital projectors and interactive whiteboards in most classrooms.
   The activities in which boys can participate are enormously varied. The facilities include a new heated indoor swimming pool, a modern sports hall, tennis, fives and squash courts, 17 acres of excellent playing fields and a floodlit all-weather pitch. Cricket, Soccer and Rugby Football are the main school sports, and there are opportunities to participate in a wide range of other sports. Music is one of the strengths of the school with more than 75% of boys playing a musical instrument and several boys have been awarded music scholarships. There are three choirs and the school musicians have regular opportunities to perform both in the school and locally. Each term different year groups produce a play or musical. Art and Craft and Design & Technology are taught by specialist teachers.
   The school has a fine Victorian chapel, and boys are encouraged to develop Christian faith and values in a positive, caring environment. Pastoral care is the first priority for all staff. The headmaster and his wife, a housemaster and his wife and three matrons, are all resident in the main building. A wide range of exciting activities in the evenings and at weekends ensure that boys are keen to board, and they are encouraged to do so particularly in their last two years as preparation for their next schools.
   The school aims to encourage boys to be well mannered and courteous with a cheerful enthusiasm for learning and for life and a determination to make the most of their abilities.

There is also a flourishing Pre-Prep Department including a Nursery for day boys and girls aged 3 to 8.

Charitable status. Aysgarth School Trust Limited is a Registered Charity, number 529538. Its purpose is to provide a high standard of boarding and day education.

Babington House Preparatory School

Grange Drive, Chislehurst, Kent BR7 5ES
Tel: 020 8467 5537
Fax: 020 8295 1175
e-mail: enquiries@babingtonhouse.com
website: www.babingtonhouse.com

Chairman of Governors: Mr T N Guise

Head: **Mrs S Harley**, LLB Hons, PGCE

Age Range. Girls 3–11, Boys 3–7.
Number of Pupils. 191: 123 Girls, 68 Boys.
Fees per term (2011-2012). £1,300–£3,520.

At Babington House Preparatory School we provide a happy, family atmosphere, where children can flourish, develop their academic potential and enjoy success in a wide range of other activities.

We believe that children learn best in a caring, friendly environment, where they feel valued as individuals and confident in themselves.

Our expectations are high, encouraging good behaviour, a strong work ethic and an awareness of the wider community. Pupils engage with each other with respect and an appreciation of diversity, following a curriculum designed to promote curiosity and stimulate a desire to learn about the world in which they live.

High-quality teaching effectively supports pupils to become creative and critical thinkers, who can employ different learning styles to improve their understanding.

We recognise that every child is unique and we greatly value the contribution they each have to make to our school. Babington House School pupils have a reputation for being articulate, enthusiastic and well-mannered.

The Preparatory School is housed in new purpose-built accommodation linked to the Senior School, thus ensuring close liaison and smooth transition between the two. We are proud of the exciting series of developments providing facilities to enhance the impressive standards for which our pupils have become known.

At each Key Stage our pupils achieve results for above the National Standards and are well prepared for the next stage of their education.

Charitable status. Babington House School is a Registered Charity, number 307914.

Bablake Junior School and Pre Prep

Junior School:
Coundon Road, Coventry, West Midlands CV1 4AU
Tel: 024 7627 1260
Fax: 024 7627 1294
e-mail: jhmsec@bablakejs.co.uk
website: www.bablakejuniorschool.co.uk

Pre Prep:
8 Park Road, Coventry, West Midlands CV1 2LH
Tel: 024 7622 1677
Fax: 024 7623 1630
e-mail: preprep@bablakejs.co.uk

Chairman of Governors: B Connor

Headmaster: **N A Price**, BA Hons, PGCE

Age Range. 3–11.
Number of Pupils. 300 Day Pupils.
Fees per term (2011-2012). £1,846–£2,313.

Bablake Junior School offers an outstanding environment for young people and all school relationships are exceptionally supportive. Pupils enjoy coming to school and are given broad opportunities to develop and learn. They acquire skills and interests that will equip them for life and their future learning.

We are a small school where people are nurtured as individuals. This helps them to achieve all that they are capable of academically, creatively and on the games field. Excellent learning support is offered to those failing to achieve their potential. Most of our pupils continue their education at Bablake until they complete their A Levels. (*See Bablake School entry in HMC section.*) Throughout the school we ensure they make the most of their abilities and the outstanding opportunities that exist here for them.

We follow a broad and balanced curriculum – lessons are interesting and our academic results exceptional. Our teachers' commitment to helping everyone achieve their potential is reflected in the support of our parents and the hard work our pupils put into their studies.

We encourage our pupils to take on many positions of responsibility within the school and to supplement this we spend some exciting times at various residential centres. This all helps the children's growing sense of themselves and their role within a community. A wide variety of other dramatic, cultural and sporting experiences help reinforce the learning experience.

All of our pupils receive expert coaching in sport and have the opportunity to take part in a wide range of activities. We share the swimming pool, games fields, sports hall and astroturfs with our Senior School and make use of Bablake's fantastic theatre and other specialist facilities. All achievement – academic, creative or sporting – is recognised and celebrated.

Admission to the Junior School is at age seven, or older if space exists, and all pupils have to pass an Entrance Exam. Scholarships and Bursaries are available.

Children may join the Pre Prep in the September after they turn 3. Cheshunt, Bablake Pre Prep, offers a happy, homely and stimulating environment. Considerate and caring preparation takes place for the challenges ahead.

Charitable status. Coventry School Foundation is a Registered Charity, number 528961. It exists to provide education for boys and girls.

Badminton Junior School

Westbury-on-Trym, Bristol BS9 3BA
Tel: 0117 905 5271
Fax: 0117 962 3049
e-mail: edavies@badminton.bristol.sch.uk
website: www.badminton.bristol.sch.uk

Chairman of Governors: Mrs Alison Bernays

Headmistress: **Mrs Emma Davies**, BA, PGCE

Age Range. 3–11.
Number of Girls. 114.
Fees per term (2011-2012). Day: £2,350–£3,470 inclusive of lunch. Boarding (from Year 5): £6,280–£6,550.

Educational Philosophy. The style of Badminton Junior School reflects the traditions of the Senior School – a combination of discipline and warmth. Children come to school to learn how to concentrate, how to think and how to get on with other people. This process happens best in a stimulating environment where high standards of work and behaviour are expected. A girl also needs a welcoming and friendly atmosphere so that she can feel emotionally secure and her own particular talents and abilities can blossom. Key notes in our philosophy are the development of self-confidence, respect for the individual and the nurturing of inquiring and critical minds.

Children are happiest when they are kept busy and so we try to create a balance between hard work in the classroom, plenty of physical exercise, a range of extra-curricular activities and opportunities for recreational play.

Facilities. The Junior School is well appointed with light airy classrooms, dedicated rooms for Art and Languages (French, German, Spanish and Latin), a new science laboratory, networked computer room, a library and an Assembly Hall/Dining Hall. There is a wonderful adventure playground used during break and lunch times.

The girls have use of the 25m indoor swimming pool, gymnasium and new all-purpose sports pitch which are all on site, and have expert coaching from the very beginning. There are excellent facilities for music which plays an important part both inside and outside the curriculum and for drama.

With our extended day facilities we aim to provide a warm and caring home from home to suit the needs of a variety of pupils and their parents. Every day clubs, such as gardening, cricket, drama, art or playground games, take place after school and girls are welcome to stay on for prep or late stay until 6 pm.

For further information on Badminton School, see entry in GSA section. A prospectus is available on request to Miss Karen Balmforth (admissions@badminton.bristol.sch.uk).

Charitable status. Badminton School Limited is a Registered Charity, number 311738. It exists to provide education for children.

Ballard School

Fernhill Lane, New Milton, Hampshire BH25 5SU
Tel: 01425 611153
Fax: 01425 622099
e-mail: admissions@ballardschool.co.uk
website: www.ballardschool.co.uk

The School is a non-profit making Educational Trust under a Board of Governors.

Chairman of the Board of Governors: Mr R Blake

Headmaster: **Mr Alastair J Reid**, MA Cantab, PGCE, NPQH

Age Range. 1½–16 Co-educational.
Number of Children. 560 day children.
Fees per term (2010-2011). Years 9–11 £3,791, Years 7–8 £3,654, Years 4–5 £3,597, Year 3 £3,437, Reception–Year 2 £2,114. Fees include the cost of School lunches.

The School is situated 2 miles from the sea and on the borders of the New Forest in its own very spacious grounds and woodlands.

Ballard School has key departments catering for the specific needs of the pupils. These departments include Early Years (1½–4), Pre-Prep (4–7), Prep (7–11), Middle (11–13) and Senior (13–16) sections.

There are over 60 qualified teaching staff plus a Learning Support Unit with 9 teachers. Academic results are excellent at all stages (7+, 11+, 13+ and GCSE) with many pupils gaining scholarships. The School offers a broad curriculum with further strengths in music, art, performing arts, and sport. More than 60 extra-curricular activities are offered.

Facilities are excellent, including 5 science laboratories, large art department, 4 computer suites, 3 libraries, large music department including a recording studio, technology laboratory, home economics laboratory, large sports hall, extensive playing fields, with tennis courts, netball courts, heated outdoor swimming pool and Performing Arts Centre.

The School has a Christian foundation and the aim of the School is to provide an all-round education where traditional values and standards are valued combined with facilities to prepare children for the 21st century.

Charitable status. Ballard School Ltd is a Registered Charity, number 307328. It exists for the education of children.

Bancroft's Preparatory School

High Road, Woodford Green, Essex IG8 0RF
Tel: 020 8506 6751
         020 8506 6774 (Admissions)
Fax: 020 8506 6752
e-mail: prep.office@bancrofts.org
website: www.bancrofts.org

Chairman of the Governors: S P Foakes, TD, DL, FCIB

Headmaster: **Christopher M Curl**, MA, BEd

Deputy Head: J P Layburn, MA, QTS
Assistant Head (Co-Curricular): M J Piper, BA Hons
Assistant Head (Academic): Mrs M Wright, BA Hons, PGCE, Cert SpLD

Age Range. 7–11.
Number of Pupils. 267 Day pupils: 150 girls, 117 boys.
Fees per term (2011-2012). £3,542.

Bancroft's Preparatory School was established in September 1990 in the attractive grounds of Bancroft's School in Woodford Green (*see entry in HMC section*) and became a member of IAPS in 2000. Academic results are excellent and places are much sought after – the school is heavily oversubscribed with numbers of registrations rising year by year.

The Prep School has its own distinct character within the Bancroft's community and has the advantage of being able to use excellent Senior School facilities including the Sports Hall, Music Facilities, Chapel, Catering Facility and Hard Play Area. The School is expanding: in 2009 an impressive new wing provided a further three classrooms, a performing arts studio for drama, music and dance, a science/design & technology room, a new front entrance and reception area as well as a children's adventure play area. This expansion has enabled the school to reduce its class sizes. By September 2011 the school will have three forms in each of its four year groups.

Built on a Christian foundation, the school seeks to provide an education enriched by a vibrant, cultural environment. Pastoral Care is seen as key and the happiness of all the children is fundamental to the ethos in which spiritual, moral, social and cultural development of the children are central and the school focuses on positive behaviour and rewards. Assemblies link with PSHE and focus on key values – such as treating others as they would like to be treated and going "the extra mile" for others. The school constantly seeks to encourage children to feel part of a happy and caring community.

Regular charity work is seen as very important and through it children gain an appreciation of the privileges and and advantages on offer to them. They also develop an understanding that there are others who are not as fortunate to experience these benefits, thereby instilling a sense of compassion for the world beyond Bancroft's. The Prep School wants its able pupils to have fun and "to sparkle" while they learn so that they will derive a lifelong love of learning.

The class teacher has a central role to play and there is an emphasis on specialised teaching, in the top two years, so that staff can pursue their subject passions to the benefit of the children. As well as establishing a strong academic base, the school is very much concerned with an holistic approach for each child – encouraging good manners, respect for others and a keen sense of humour. Children take part in a great variety of extra-curricular activities at lunch times, after school and at weekends. Older children are given the opportunity to take on responsibilities around the school – every child becomes a Monitor at some stage in their final year. The school hopes that the children will in time become successful adults who will make a difference in the 21st century.

Children are assessed for entry at the age of six/seven, visiting the school in small groups and tested in a friendly and low-key way by the Headmaster and Deputy Head. Once accepted they have guaranteed places in Bancroft's Senior School (on the same site) at the age of eleven. Academic standards are high with a broad, structured curriculum including French, Humanities, Critical Thinking, PSHE, Drama, Music, Games, Swimming, PE, Art & Craft and Design & Technology.

In 2010 the whole school, including the staff and many parents, performed (or assisted behind the scenes) in a spectacular and colourful production of Gilbert and Sullivan's comic opera *The Mikado* which was produced by the Headmaster and performed in two casts (half of the pupils in each) to four capacity audiences. This followed the previous whole school production of *Oliver!*

The curriculum and administration of the Prep School and Senior School are closely linked and the Headmaster of the Prep School is a member of the Senior Management Team of Bancroft's School.

In 2010 the Prep School was inspected and the school was delighted with the excellent report in which they were awarded the top grade in most areas. The full report can be read by visiting the ISI website: www.isi.net.

There is also a very positive and entertaining entry in the *Good Schools Guide* which gives a good flavour of the Bancroft's Prep School.

Charitable status. Bancroft's School is a Registered Charity, number 1068532. It exists to provide a rounded academic education for able children.

Barfield

Runfold, Farnham, Surrey GU10 1PB
Tel: 01252 782271
Fax: 01252 781480
e-mail: admin@barfieldschool.com
website: www.barfieldschool.com

The School is an Educational Trust, administered by a Board of Governors.

Chairman of Governors: Mr Mervyn Thomas

Head: **Mr Robin Davies**, BSc, PGCE

   Age Range. 2+–13 Co-educational.
   Number of Children. 250.
   Fees per term (2010-2011). Prep £3,770–£3,890, Pre-Prep £906–£2,760.
   Barfield, set in 12 acres of beautiful grounds, is a first-class IAPS Day Preparatory School for girls and boys. The Pre-Prep Department has an excellent reputation for high academic standards and caring staff. It enjoys all the facilities of the Prep School, which are based on one site, and

include a Cook House, Library, Auditorium, Music and Music practice rooms, ICT suite, Art and DT rooms.

The school has a flourishing PE and Outdoor Pursuits Department, with most major and minor sports covered. There is a magnificent indoor heated swimming pool and a Par 3 golf course. Children are encouraged to participate in a wide range of extra-curricular activities from Synchronised Swimming to Adventure Training. Activity courses are run throughout most of the school holidays and children aged 4 and above are eligible to attend.

Children, taught in small classes, are prepared for Common Entrance and Scholarship examinations, and for Grammar School entry. Visitors are always welcome – please contact Admissions.

Charitable status. Barfield is a Registered Charity, number 312085. It exists to provide a quality education for boys and girls.

Barlborough Hall School
Preparatory School to Mount St Mary's College

Barlborough, Chesterfield, Derbyshire S43 4TJ
Tel: 01246 810511
Fax: 01246 570605
e-mail: headteacher@barlboroughhallschool.com
website: www.barlboroughhallschool.com

Chairman of Governors: J Kelly, KSG

Headteacher: **Mrs W Parkinson**, BEd

   Age Range. 3–11 Co-educational.
   Number of Pupils. 247.
   Fees per term (2011-2012). £2,140–£2,851.
   Barlborough Hall School is a co-educational preparatory school in the Jesuit Catholic tradition, welcoming pupils aged 3–11 of all denominations. The preparatory school to nearby Mount St Mary's College (11–18), Barlborough is set in over 300 acres of parkland.

Barlborough became a school in 1939 and is built around an Elizabethan manor house which now houses many of the teaching rooms. In keeping with its Jesuit ethos, the school encourages children to develop their talents in many different areas: academic, social, spiritual and physical. There is a strong focus on the individual. Academically, pupils achieve success through small classes, low pupil to teacher ratios and setting from Preparatory (Year 3) onwards. Teaching facilities ensure that children receive a traditional preparatory school education and include a science laboratory, technology lab and ICT suite. Pupils learn French from Nursery onwards, and most pupils learn Latin in Elements II and I (Years 5 and 6).

All pupils receive pastoral care and academic tutoring through their form teachers, under the leadership of the Key Stage Coordinators. There is a clear sense of progression from Pre-Prep, situated in its own distinct area of the school with its own playground, to the Upper School, which allows pupils to develop greater independence while still being within a nurturing environment. There is a Jesuit chaplain who works closely with the teachers on the Chaplaincy team.

Emphasis is placed on developing the whole person, and the school enjoys an impressive reputation for its sport and music. There is an indoor heated swimming pool and extensive games fields, and pupils enjoy a wide range of sports, benefitting from professional teaching provided by staff from Mount St Mary's College. Barlborough Hall is well-established on the rugby, football, hockey and netball circuit and plays regularly against other schools. Many pupils learn instruments from skilled peripatetic teachers and the school's music teacher leads prize-winning choirs and an orchestra. Drama also flourishes, with a major production every year in the school's theatre.

There are many extra-curricular activities, allowing pupils to develop their interests in a wide range of fields. Pupils are encouraged to take part in at least two activities a week and have the option to attend Saturday school, where they are able to enjoy hobbies in a more relaxed environment or practise for team sports. The wide range of activities available includes Chess, Ballroom Dancing, Art, drama and touch typing. Pupils can also stay after school every evening to do homework under teacher supervision.

Admission to Barlborough Hall is by interview. Barlborough Hall pupils can automatically transfer at age 11 to the senior school, Mount St Mary's College. Further details and a prospectus can be obtained from the Headteacher's Secretary.

Charitable status. Mount St Mary's is a Registered Charity, number 1117998.

Barnard Castle Preparatory School

Westwick Road, Barnard Castle, Co Durham DL12 8UW
Tel: 01833 696032
Fax: 01833 696034
e-mail: secretary@barneyprepschool.org.uk
website: www.barnardcastleschool.org.uk

Chairman of Governors: Mr M McCallum

Headmaster: **Mr C F Rycroft**, BEd

Age Range. 4–11 years.
Number of Pupils. 201 girls and boys, including 25 boarders.
Fees per term (2011-2012). Prep: £4,944 (Boarders), £2,557 (Day). Pre-Prep: £1,683.

Barnard Castle Preparatory School is the Junior School of Barnard Castle School and offers an all round, high quality education for boys and girls aged between 4 and 11 years. The School offers both day and boarding places and is situated in a beautiful setting on the edge of a traditional English market town.

The campuses of the two schools are adjoining, allowing shared use of many excellent facilities. At the same time the Preparatory School is able to provide a separate, stimulating environment, with small classes, a wide range of extra curricular activities and an exciting school excursion programme. The school has recently benefited from an extensive building and refurbishment programme. This has included the construction of a new hall and greatly improved art, design, IT and library facilities.

The School is well served by a bus network system and supervision is given to those day children waiting for transport home. The boarders reside in a newly developed boarding house, which creates a warm and friendly environment supported by a full range of facilities including the School's medical centre.

Our Directors of Studies oversee a carefully designed, broad and balanced curriculum. Sport, drama and music occupy important places in the life of the School. All children have numerous opportunities to participate in each of these, as well as in a wide variety of other extra-curricular areas. The School also offers a qualified learning support service to those children who require further assistance.

Charitable status. Barnard Castle School is a Registered Charity, number 1125375. Its aim is the education of boys and girls.

Barnardiston Hall Preparatory School

Nr Haverhill, Suffolk CB9 7TG
Tel: 01440 786316
Fax: 01440 786355
e-mail: registrar@barnardiston-hall.co.uk
website: www.barnardiston-hall.co.uk

Headmaster: **K A Boulter**, MA Cantab, PGCE

Age Range. Co-educational 2–13.
Number of Pupils. Day 204, Boarding (full and weekly) 50.
Fees per term (2010-2011). Day Pupils £2,975–£3,810; Weekly Boarders £5,270; Full Boarders £5,715.

Barnardiston Hall, set in 16 acres of grounds on the borders of Suffolk, Essex and Cambridge, offers an individual all-round education for boys and girls, both day and boarding. High standards are achieved by small classes taught by graduate and teacher-trained staff, a caring approach and close liaison with parents.

The School has good facilities, including a Pre-Preparatory Block and Art Room complex, a very modern and well equipped computer room, assembly hall, tennis/netball courts, music room, science laboratory, library and extensive sports fields. For the boarders, the dormitories are bright, uncluttered and home-like.

The curriculum is designed to allow pupils to reach Common Entrance standards in the appropriate subjects. The best of traditional methods are mixed with modern ideas to provide an enjoyable and productive learning environment. French and computers are taught from the age of 3; Latin from age 7. The School is CReSTeD registered. It has received outstanding gradings in recent Ofsted reports for both welfare and education. Pupils go on to a wide range of secondary schools.

Sports in the Michaelmas and Lent Terms are hockey, swimming and cross-country/orienteering for all pupils, rugby for the boys and netball for the girls. During the Summer, all do athletics, cricket/rounders, and tennis/short tennis. U11 Girls are Suffolk Hockey Champions and the School National Champion in Orienteering.

There is a wide range of clubs and societies including 3 choirs, an orchestra, pet corner, recorders, chess, horse-riding, painting, drama, basketry, weaving, carpentry and science award. Ballet, speech and drama, piano, woodwind, brass, string and singing lessons are also offered.

Throughout the term, there are weekend activities for boarders (optional for day pupils) which include mountain walking. Derbyshire Dales at 6, Ben Nevis at 8, camping, visits to museums/historic buildings and other places of interest and theatre trips. There is an annual trip to Europe. Some pupils aged 7+ have reached Everest Base Camp.

Barrow Hills School

Roke Lane, Witley, Godalming, Surrey GU8 5NY
Tel: 01428 683639/682634
Fax: 01428 681906
e-mail: info@barrowhills.org.uk
website: www.barrowhills.org.uk

Chairman of the Governors: Mr Stephen Mulliner

Headmaster: **Mr Matthew Unsworth**, BEng Hons, PGCE

Age Range. 3–13.
Number of Pupils. 283.

Fees per term (2010-2011). £2,450–£3,900.

Barrow Hills is an Independent Catholic Day School for girls and boys between the ages of 3 and 13 years which warmly welcomes children from all denominations. It is set in 40 acres of attractive gardens and playing fields close to both Godalming and Haslemere. The main entry points are at age three, five, seven and eleven years. Our pupils are prepared for senior school entrance examinations including scholarships and Common Entrance to a range of day and boarding schools. We know that as a parent you wish your child to be very happy at school as well as having a wide range of outstanding educational opportunities. At Barrow Hills we fully recognise the importance of academic success but we also value each child's development and achievements in social skills, sport, art, music, drama and many other rewarding activities. The most recent inspection report notes the good teaching and the outstanding personal development of the pupils.

The children benefit from modern facilities including a science laboratory, two computer suites and an art & design centre that provides opportunities to study textiles, ceramics, food technology, multimedia and photography.

Music and drama are important aspects of school life and this is reflected in the dedicated music suite that the school has on offer.

There are regular drama productions and concerts for children of all ages using the school hall, chapel and outdoor stage. Most children study a musical instrument and there is a chapel choir, orchestra and wind band.

An impressive range of games is offered including rugby, netball, hockey, soccer, tennis, athletics and judo. The school has its own covered, heated swimming pool and Astroturf pitch.

There are strong links with excellent senior schools and many of our pupils have been awarded scholarships.

There is a broad range of extra-curricular activities available, including horse riding, cooking, dancing, craft, sport, chess, gardening, Lego and computers. Alongside this is a comprehensive programme of educational trips and visits throughout the year, including residential trips for all the children in the Prep Department.

Charitable status. Barrow Hills School Witley is a Registered Charity, number 1000190. It exists to provide high-quality education for both boys and girls.

Bassett House School

60 Bassett Road, London W10 6JP
Tel: 020 8969 0313
Fax: 020 8960 9624
e-mail: info@bassetths.org.uk
website: www.bassetths.org.uk

Motto: Quisque pro sua parte (From each to the best of his or her ability).

Chairman of Governors: Mr Anthony Rentoul

Head: **Mrs Andrea Harris**, BEd Lond, Mont Cert, CEPLF Caen

Age Range. 3–11 Co-educational.
Number of Pupils. 174.
Fees per term (2010-2011). Nursery (5 mornings) £2,100, Prep-Prep £4,144, Prep £4,332.

Bassett House School was founded in 1947. As a member school of the House Schools Group, it has two sister schools, Orchard House School in Chiswick and Prospect House School in Putney, both of which, like Bassett House School, take both boys and girls from the age of 3 or 4 until the time they leave for their next senior or, in some cases, intermediate preparatory schools. Bassett House takes children from age 3 to age 11. Entry is, in the younger years, non-selective. Aspects of the Montessori method are used in the Early Years. The school has some 160 pupils in eleven classes.

The school was built towards the end of the 19th century and what was originally designed as a large family house now provides classrooms that are spacious, brightly lit and well heated and ventilated. The entire building was substantially rebuilt in 2001 to a very high standard. The school premises include the church hall at St Helen's Church, just around the corner from 60 Bassett Road, providing an assembly hall with a stage and gymnasium, three classrooms, a kitchen and a garden. The main school building has a playground which doubles as a basketball or netball court.

Bassett House provides a thorough grounding in the usual educational subjects and the children are prepared for the entrance examinations to leading day and boarding preparatory schools. In recent years the entrance examination results to these schools have been excellent. The reason this school has enjoyed such a long track record of success is mainly due to its happy yet purposeful atmosphere... indeed, this is a hallmark of Bassett House: the school believes that only if a child is happy and actively wants to come to school will his or her potential in the widest sense be maximised. The school does not stint to obtain the very best staff and to support them with the best in resources. Within a friendly but nevertheless structured and disciplined academic environment, the school aims to bring out the best in every one of its children.

Beachborough

Westbury, Nr Brackley, Northants NN13 5LB
Tel: 01280 700071
Fax: 01280 704839
e-mail: office@beachborough.com
website: www.beachborough.com

The School is administered as a non-profit-making Educational Trust by a Board of Governors.

Chairman of Governors: H F Thuillier, BSc

Headmaster: **J F Whybrow**, BEd Exeter

Age Range. 2½–13.
Number of Children. Main School 180 (40% flexi boarding), Pre-Prep 100.
Fees per term (2011-2012). Day: £2,915 (Reception, Years 1 and 2), £4,205 (Years 3 and 4), £4,580 (Year 5–8). Weekly Boarding (4 nights): £5,105 (Years 3 and 4), £5,480 (Year 5–8). Nursery £246 per session per term. Occasional Flexi-boarding £28 per night.

The school is fully co-educational with a balanced mix of girls and boys throughout. The flourishing Pre-Prep takes children from 2½ years old with a Nursery Class allowing the youngest children to build up sessions during their first year. With an average class size of no more than 18, children are prepared for a wide range of Independent Senior Schools. A balance between work and play is achieved through the provision of a wide-ranging programme of co-curricular activities, coordinated by a Deputy Head, specifically appointed for this purpose.

The school occupies a fine Manor House in the small village of Westbury and enjoys 30 acres of grounds, playing fields and woodland. A major refurbishment programme of the boarding and teaching facilities in the prep school has recently been completed.

The Beachborough Association, run by parents and staff, arranges many events during the year.

Charitable status. Beachborough is a Registered Charity, number 309910. It exists to provide quality education for children.

The Beacon

Chesham Bois, Amersham, Bucks HP6 5PF
Tel: 01494 433654
Fax: 01494 727849
e-mail: office@beaconschool.co.uk
website: www.beaconschool.co.uk

Chairman of the Governors: W I D Plaistowe, Esq

Headmaster: **P Brewster**, BSc Hons, PGCE

Age Range. 3–13.
Number of Boys. 460.
Fees per term (2011-2012). Upper School (Years 5–8) £4,115–£4,400, Middle School (Years 3 & 4) £3,980, Lower School (Years 1 & 2) £3,085, Reception £2,735, Nursery £1,565–£2,735.

The Beacon is a Charitable Trust which provides education for some 460+ boys. Its buildings are a delightful blend of old and new; the school is centred around a 17th Century farmstead whose barns provide a lovely Dining Hall and a Library. Classroom accommodation is almost all purpose-built, and the excellent facilities include a large Sports Hall, Music Technology suite, ICT labs, Art Room, Design and Technology suite and a Modern Languages laboratory. As well as the 16-acre grass games field there is an Astroturf pitch for Hockey and Tennis, and a 20-metre outdoor Swimming Pool.

Most boys join the Nursery at age 3, or Reception at age 4. There are up to 24 boys in the Nursery, and two Reception classes with up to 20 boys in each. Each class teacher has an assistant. At age 5 and 6 the boys are based mainly with their form teacher in classes of up to 20. From age 7 class sizes are usually a maximum 20.

The aim of the school is to provide breadth of opportunity. The daily timetable contains a broad range of subjects, and there is a strong emphasis on participation in sport, music, drama, art and technology. There are teams for Rugby, Soccer, Hockey, Basketball, Cricket, Tennis, Swimming and Athletics. The Music Department has some 13 ensembles, including choirs, orchestras, wind band, brass, sax and guitar, with some 18 visiting teachers to cater for individual tuition.

The School's examination record is excellent, both at 11+ into Buckinghamshire Grammar Schools and at 13+ to senior independent day and boarding schools, with a number of academic, music, art and sports scholarships being won.

Charitable status. The Beacon Educational Trust Limited is a Registered Charity, number 309911. It exists to provide education for boys.

Beaudesert Park

Minchinhampton, Stroud, Gloucestershire GL6 9AF
Tel: 01453 832072
Fax: 01453 836040
e-mail: office@beaudesert.gloucs.sch.uk
website: www.beaudesert.gloucs.sch.uk

Chairman of Governors: R S Trafford, Esq, MA

Headmaster: **J P R Womersley**, BA, PGCE

Age Range. 4–13.

Number of Pupils. Weekly and Flexi Boarders 140, Day Boys and Girls 141, Pre-Prep Department 78.
Fees per term (2011-2012). Boarders £5,995, Day Fees £3,190–£4,605, Pre-Prep £2,325–£2,425.

The School was founded in 1908 and became an educational trust in 1968.

Beaudesert Park is a preparatory school for boys and girls from 4–13. The school is very well equipped with indoor and outdoor swimming pools, sports hall, art centre, design technology and music departments. There are also astroturf tennis courts and hard courts which are situated in beautiful wooded grounds. The school stands high up in the Cotswolds adjoining 500 acres of common land and golf course. Despite its rural location, the school is within half an hour of the M4 and M5 motorways and within easy reach of the surrounding towns of Gloucester, Cheltenham, Cirencester, Swindon, Bath and Bristol.

There is a strong academic tradition and all pupils are encouraged to work to the best of their ability. There is great emphasis on effort and all children are praised for their individual performance. Pupils are prepared for Common Entrance and Scholarship examinations. They are given individual attention in classes which are mostly setted not streamed. Over the last five years an average of 16 scholarships a year – academic, art, music, sport and technology – have been won to leading Independent Senior Schools. The staff consists of 42 full time teaching staff and 12 music teachers, all of whom take a personal interest in the children's welfare.

Good manners and consideration for others are a priority. Beaudesert strives to create a happy and purposeful atmosphere, providing for the talents of each child in a wide range of activities – cultural, sporting and recreational. There are thriving drama, art, pottery and music departments. Sporting activities include cricket, soccer, rugby, hockey, netball, rounders, tennis, swimming, athletics, golf, badminton, fencing, dance, judo, riding and sailing. A wide number of societies and clubs meet each week.

Charitable status. Beaudesert Park is a Registered Charity, number 311711. It exists to provide education for boys and girls in a caring atmosphere.

Bedford Girls' School Junior School

Cardington Road, Bedford MK42 0BX
Tel: 01234 361900
Fax: 01234 344125
e-mail: admissions@bedfordgirlsschool.co.uk
website: www.bedfordgirlsschool.co.uk

Foundation – The Harpur Trust.
"Let me keep an open mind so I understand as much as I can in my lifetime and not reach the limits of my imagination."

Chair of Governors: Mrs R Wallace, FRCS

Head of Bedford Girls' School: Miss J MacKenzie, MSc, BSc

Head of Bedford Girls' School Junior School: **Mrs C Royden**, MA

Age Range. 7–11.
Number of Pupils. 280 Girls.
Fees per term (2011-2012). £2,534.
A new beginning: a rich heritage. Bedford Girls' School is a new independent day school for girls aged 7–18. Formed by the merger of two distinct and respected schools, Dame Alice Harpur School and Bedford High School for

Girls, its new beginnings build firmly upon the long and rich heritage of the two schools that first opened their doors in 1882. Today it is our ambition that Bedford Girls' School will be an exceptional girls' school – continuing this long tradition of commitment to the education of young women.

Expanding horizons: raising expectations. Our philosophy is to be innovative, outward looking and open minded. We have unashamedly high standards and expectations across our school community. We look to each individual to act as an inspiring role model and bring a can do approach to their day. We foster connections within our local and international community, learning from the lives of those around us and developing sensitivity to culture and difference.

Learning for fun: learning for life. Our approach to learning is forward thinking, dynamic and vibrant. You can feel the energy and enthusiasm of the teaching and learning in the classroom and beyond. From Year 3 to Sixth Form it is our belief that learning should be exciting and spark a lifelong desire to engage in the wonder of the world around us.

An holistic approach: the right tools for the job. We are lucky to be part of the Harpur Trust Charity, one of the 200 largest charities in the UK. The Charity is committed to inspiring and supporting the people of Bedford and has been enriching lives by providing education, breaking down barriers and creating opportunities for over 400 years. This solid and stable backing ensures our future and means we are blessed with the funds to continue to innovate in our practice and invest in our resources.

Discover BGS: share in our vision. We invite you to get to know us better. Explore our website, or better still come and visit us – we hope your experience of Bedford Girls' School will inspire you to join us.

Admissions. Entry to the Junior School is on the basis of informal assessment and written tests.

Charitable status. Bedford Girls' School is part of The Bedford Charity (The Harpur Trust) which is a Registered Charity, number 204817.

Bedford Modern Junior School

Manton Lane, Bedford, Bedfordshire MK41 7NT
Tel: 01234 332513
Fax: 01234 332617
e-mail: info@bedmod.co.uk
website: www.bedmod.co.uk

Chairman of the School Committee: I McEwen, BPhil, MA, DPhil

Head of Junior School: **R Lynn**, BA, PGCE, MA

Age Range. 7–11 Co-educational.
Number of Pupils. 154 Boys, 76 Girls.
Fees per term (2011-2012). £2,596.

The Junior School is housed in its own separate buildings adjacent to the main school. Facilities include specialist rooms for Art and Science, ICT Centre, Design Technology Suite, library, designated Year 3 classrooms and play area and a superb state-of-the-art School Hall.

The whole site overlooks the School playing fields and the Junior School has extensive views over the Ouse Valley. Many of the Main School facilities are available to the Junior School, including full use of the playing fields, Sports Hall, Gymnasium, covered and heated Swimming Pool, Tennis Courts. The Main School Hall provides facilities for full-scale Drama productions and use is made of the Music School.

There is a strong Choral, Instrumental Music, Dramatic and Sporting tradition.

Pupils are admitted to the Junior School at 7, 8, 9 and 10, after taking tests in English and Maths, some of them on computer, in January each year. Pupils proceed automatically to the Main School at 11, unless special circumstances mean that this is inappropriate.

(*See Bedford Modern School entry in HMC section.*)
Charitable status. The Bedford Charity (The Harpur Trust) is a Registered Charity, number 204817. It includes in its aims the provision of high quality education for boys and girls.

Bedford Preparatory School

De Parys Avenue, Bedford MK40 2TU
Tel: 01234 362271/362274
Fax: 01234 362285
e-mail: prepinfo@bedfordschool.org.uk
website: www.bedfordschool.org.uk

Chairman of Governors: Professor Stephen Mayson, LLB, LLM, PhD, Barrister, FRSA

Headmaster: **C Godwin**, BSc, MA

Deputy Head: G J Wickens, MA

Age Range. 7–13.
Number of Boys. Dayboys 400, Boarders 18, Weekly Boarders 3.
Fees per term (2011-2012). Day £3,412–£4,471, Full Boarding £5,897–£7,004, Weekly Boarding £5,622–£6,728.

Bedford Preparatory School combines the two schools formerly known as the Preparatory School and the Bedford Lower School. An extensive building programme has been completed offering excellent facilities: three purpose-built and well-equipped Science Laboratories, an Art Studio, excellent computing resources, specialist teaching rooms, a new library and a spacious Assembly Hall.

Curriculum. Boys are prepared for the Bedford School 13+ Entrance Examination, which is allied to Common Entrance, but under normal circumstances boys transfer automatically. The curriculum is otherwise carefully tailored to match and prepare for the curriculum followed in the Upper School, and includes in addition to the usual subjects: French, Information Technology and Design/Technology from the age of 7 and Latin, Spanish and French from the age of 11.

The boys enjoy full use of the facilities available to Upper School pupils: the Recreation Centre, incorporating an excellent theatre, an indoor swimming pool and a large sports hall; the Technology Centre; superb playing fields, all-weather pitch and tennis courts. All the usual games are played to a high standard and boys are often selected to play in county or national teams.

Many boys play musical instruments, and orchestra and bands perform frequently. There are good School Choirs and selected boys sing alongside Upper School pupils in the Chapel Choir trained in the English Cathedral tradition. There are several theatrical productions each year in the theatre or hall, often in conjunction with girls from sister Harpur Trust Schools.

Boarding. Full boarders and a small number of weekly boarders live in the purpose-built Boarding House in the grounds of the Preparatory School. Boys are cared for by the Housemaster and his wife, two resident house-tutors and a full-time matron.

Pastoral Care. The progress and well-being of pupils are carefully monitored, and parental involvement and contact are maintained through reports and Parents Evenings and other formal and informal meetings. A competitive House system is in use.

Financial Assistance and Scholarships. Designed to open up new opportunities and bring out the best in every boy, Bedford's Access Award and Scholarship Scheme offers generous funding in recognition of academic potential to provide a wealth of opportunities for boys irrespective of background.

For more information please call our freephone helpline 0800 432 0084 or visit our website www.bedford-school.org.uk.

Charitable status. The Bedford Charity (The Harpur Trust) is a Registered Charity, number 204817. It aims to provide high quality education for boys.

Beechwood Park

Markyate, St Albans, Hertfordshire AL3 8AW
Tel: 01582 840333
Fax: 01582 842372
e-mail: hmsecretary@beechwoodpark.herts.sch.uk
website: www.beechwoodpark.herts.sch.uk

Chairman of Governors: D J Pirie, Esq, BSc, CEng, MICE

Headmaster: **Patrick C E Atkinson**, BSc, MIBiol, PGCE

Age Range. 2½–13.

Number of Pupils. 500: 54 boarders (aged 9–13), 258 day boys and 188 day girls (aged 4–13). In addition there are 44 pre-school children at the newly-acquired Montessori Nursery which is at a separate location less than one mile from the main school.

Fees per term (2010-2011). Day pupils: Senior £4,032 Junior £3,300, Reception £2,948. Boarders (in addition to day fees) £1,093. No compulsory extras

Beechwood Park occupies a large mansion, with a fine Regency Library and Great Hall, in 38 acres of surrounding grounds. Modernisation has added kitchens, changing rooms, Science laboratories, language rooms, Design Technology workshop, dormitories, gymnasium and sports facilities, including a large sports hall and two squash courts, hard tennis courts and two heated swimming pools. Three purpose-built classroom blocks house the Middle Department, Junior Forms and Reception classes. A Music Department has a music chamber and 14 practice rooms. More recently a Performance Hall and an all-weather pitch have been added.

Day pupils use private buses serving Harpenden, St Albans, Dunstable and the surrounding villages. Many subsequently convert to boarding under the care of the Housemaster, Mr O S C Bullock.

Maximum class size is 20; major subjects are setted. Qualified class teachers teach the Juniors; older children are taught by subject specialist graduates. There is a resident Chaplain. The Director of Music has a staff of visiting instrumentalists.

The number of scholarships gained each year and Common Entrance results affirm a high standard of work, against a background of every kind of worthwhile out-of-class activity. Music is distinguished.

Soccer, Rugby, Cricket, Golf, Hockey, Netball, Swimming and Athletics and an unusually wide range of minor sports are coached by well-qualified PE Staff.

Beechwood Park is a non-profit-making trust administered by governors of wide professional and educational experience.

Charitable status. Beechwood Park School is a Registered Charity, number 311068. It exists to provide education for boys and girls from 2½–13.

Beeston Hall School

West Runton, Cromer, Norfolk NR27 9NQ
Tel: 01263 837324
Fax: 01263 838177
e-mail: office@beestonhall.co.uk
website: www.beestonhall.co.uk

Chairman of Governors: D D Marris

Headmaster: **R C Gainher**, BSc Hons

Deputy Headmaster: A V L Richards, BSc, PGCE

Bursar: Mrs G Adams

Age Range. Co-educational 7–13 years.

Number of Pupils. 144: 80 Full Boarding, 64 Daily Boarding. 82 Boys, 62 Girls.

Fees per term (2011-2012). £6,571 Boarding, £4,913 Daily Boarding.

Beeston Hall was established in 1948 in a Regency house set in 30 acres in North Norfolk, close to the sea and surrounded by 700 acres of National Trust land. Beeston's reputation for being a happy, caring family school is in no small part due to the real sense of community which pervades throughout. The strength of the Pastoral Care system ensures that every child is closely watched over and cared for. Although there is no compulsory boarding, most of the children experience boarding before they leave, the majority moving on to boarding schools such as Ampleforth, Downe House, Eton, Gresham's, Harrow, Oakham, Oundle, Queen Margaret's York, Radley, Rugby, Stowe, Tudor Hall and Uppingham. In addition to the normal subjects, Art, Music, DT, ICT and Drama are all timetabled, providing the children with a wide curriculum and the opportunity to find an activity in which they can excel. The school enjoys great success at scholarship level, with 46 scholarships won in the last 4 years. Extra help is given on a one-to-one basis in English, Mathematics and French; a dedicated, professionally run Learning Support department emphasises the importance of the learning support work being carried into the classroom. There is a positive emphasis on the traditional values such as courtesy, kindness, industry and awareness of others, and at every stage of their education the children are encouraged to maximise their potential and think and act for themselves. Drama and Music are considered important for every child: each takes part in at least one play production each year. Three choirs and ten different music groups meet every week and over 90% of the school learn a musical instrument. The school is equally proud of its record on the sports field where all children are coached regardless of ability by a dedicated team of staff, and where all are, at some stage, given the opportunity to represent the school. It has a particularly impressive record in Rugby, Netball, Rounders, Cross Country, Hockey, Cricket, Athletics and Shooting, whilst a comprehensive activities programme provides opportunities to suit all tastes: camp craft, karate, dance, fencing, sailing, golf, debating, French cuisine, chess and archery, to name but a few.

The 2010 ISI Inspection Report comments on: "the rich educational experience provided the excellent pastoral care and support... the excellent relationships between staff and pupils... and the overall excellent curricular and extra-curricular provision."

Religious denomination: Mainly Church of England; 15% Roman Catholic.

Charitable status. Beeston Hall School Trust Limited is a Registered Charity, number 311274. It exists to provide preparatory education for boarding and day boys and girls.

Belhaven Hill

Dunbar, East Lothian EH42 1NN
Tel: 01368 862785
Fax: 01368 865225
e-mail: headmaster@belhavenhill.com
website: www.belhavenhill.com

Chairman of Governors: Mrs J W M Harper

Head Master: **I K MacAskill**, BEd Hons

Age Range. 8–13 Co-educational.
Number of Pupils. 66 boys, 59 girls. Boarders 105, Day 20.
Fees per term (2010-2011). Boarders £6,050, Day £4,200.
Religion. Non-denominational.

Founded in 1923 the school is beautifully situated in extensive grounds overlooking Belhaven Bay on the outskirts of Dunbar. Ideally placed just off the A1, it is close to both a mainline London-Edinburgh railway station and less than an hour to Edinburgh airport. Primarily a full boarding school with some day pupils, Belhaven Hill has a long tradition of providing an excellent all-round education before sending its pupils far and wide to all the leading public schools in both England and Scotland. These include Ampleforth, Downe House, Eton, Fettes, Glenalmond, Harrow, Loretto, Oundle, Queen Margaret's York, Radley, Rugby, Shrewsbury, Stowe, Strathallan and Uppingham. Eighteen committed and enthusiastic full-time members of staff work with small classes of between 10–16 pupils. There is ample opportunity for scholarship and extended work, resulting in a number of awards being gained every year. A strong learning support department with two dedicated, trained staff, provides one-to-one and small group tuition. The emphasis is on nurturing pupils' various talents and encouraging high standards in all that they undertake.

Belhaven Hill pupils are renowned for being happy children and this is in no small part due to the excellent pastoral care provided. Over half of the staff live on site and the policy of the governors has been to keep the school comparatively small in order to retain a family atmosphere. The boys are housed in the original main building and the girls in a newly-refurbished purpose-built house. The pastoral system revolves around the six patrols, with each pupil being looked after by their form teacher in the junior years and a personal tutor, higher up the school. Seven matrons take care of the children's health and the school doctor visits regularly.

The school has an excellent reputation for sport with Rugby, Netball, Hockey, Cricket, Rounders, Tennis and Athletics, making up the main part of the sporting programme. Swimming takes place all year round either in the school's heated outdoor pool or at a local indoor pool. Opportunities abound for a wide variety of other recreational activities: skiing, surfing, horse riding, golf on the adjacent links course, carpentry at a local renowned furniture makers and gardening for those who want to grow their own produce in the school's walled garden. Every sort of hobby and activity is practised and encouraged: debating, 'Mastermind', fly-tying, model-making, computer programming, cookery, chess, judo, modern dance and reeling.

Music and drama flourish at Belhaven and every child has ample opportunity to perform in regular concerts and productions throughout the year. A new state-of-the-art music building houses a vibrant department which caters for a wide range of instrumental ensembles and choirs. Over 90% of the children play one or more instruments, with specialist tuition provided by a team of visiting music staff.

The school is well resourced with purpose-built facilities, including a swimming pool, floodlit all-weather pitch, playing fields, sports hall, specialist music and art schools, attractive teaching rooms around a central pond, two ICT suites and recently refurbished common rooms.

Belhaven Hill may traditionally be less formal than many other schools but a high regard is paid to good manners and sensible conduct. Against a background of Christian values, pupils are expected to show consideration for others and to develop a sense of responsibility, with a view to making a positive contribution to society.

Fee concessions are available for third and fourth siblings and also children of members of the armed forces. Means-tested bursary support is available. For a prospectus and more information please contact the school secretary, Tessa Coleman.

Charitable status. Belhaven Hill School Trust Ltd is a Registered Charity, number SC007118. Its aim is to educate children in the full sense of the word.

Belmont
Mill Hill Preparatory School

The Ridgeway, Mill Hill, London NW7 4ED
Tel: 020 8906 7270
Fax: 020 8906 3519
e-mail: office@belmontschool.com
website: www.belmontschool.com

Chairman of the Court of Governors: Prof M R E Proctor, ScD, FRS

Head: **Mrs L C Duncan**, BSc, PGCE

Deputy Head (Pastoral): L Roberts, BA, PGCE
Deputy Head (Curriculum): Mrs R Alford, BEd

Age Range. 7–13.
Number of Pupils. Day: 238 Boys, 169 Girls.
Fees per term (2011-2012). £4,735.

Belmont is situated in the Green Belt on the borders of Hertfordshire and Middlesex, yet is only ten miles from central London. It stands in about 35 acres of its own woods and parkland and enjoys the advantages of a truly rural environment, but at the same time the capital's cultural facilities are easily accessible.

Belmont is part of the Mill Hill School Foundation; the Pre-Prep Grimsdell and Mill Hill School are situated less than a quarter of a mile away. Opened in 1912, Belmont takes its name from the original mansion built on the Ridgeway about the middle of the eighteenth century. Successive alterations and additions have provided a chapel, a gymnasium, music-rooms, science laboratories and a fully resourced ICT room, ample games fields, five all-weather cricket nets, two all-weather cricket pitches, and six hard tennis courts. A major building and refurbishment programme has recently been undertaken to provide a large new multi-purpose hall, junior classroom block, a new resources centre, design technology room, additional music teaching space and catering facilities.

Use is made of the five courts, and the indoor heated swimming-pool at Mill Hill School.

The School became co-educational in 1995 and 40% of the pupils are girls.

The usual age of entry is at 7 or 11 years, but 8, 9 and 10-year-olds are considered as vacancies occur. It is expected that most children will pass to Mill Hill at the end of Year 8, but some may be prepared for entry to other senior schools. Mill Hill has recently announced that the current Saturday school arrangements are due to end in September 2012 when weekly boarding will also become available.

There is a permanent teaching staff of 40, with 20 visiting teachers for Instrumental Music, supportive English and Mathematics, Ballet and Fencing. There is a full-time Matron and a visiting counsellor while the school's catering is entrusted to a national company.

The main games are Rugby, Soccer, Cricket, Hockey, Netball and Rounders, but minor sports also flourish, as do instrumental and choral music, drama, and many out-of-school activities. There are French exchanges with Belmont's 'twin' school in Rouen, and all the children take part in the Summer Activities Programme, which includes for senior children a Geography field trip and an outward bound week.

Charitable status. The Mill Hill School Foundation is a Registered Charity, number 1064758. It exists to provide education for boys and girls.

Belmont Grosvenor School

Swarcliffe Hall, Birstwith, Harrogate, North Yorkshire HG3 2JG
Tel: 01423 771029
Fax: 01423 772600
e-mail: admin@belmontgrosvenor.co.uk
website: www.belmontgrosvenor.co.uk

Chair of Governors: Mrs Frances Trowell

Head: **Mrs Jane Merriman**, BEd, MA, NPQH

   Age Range. 3 months–11 years Co-educational.
   Number of Pupils. 192.
   Fees per term (2010-2011). Main School £2,198–£2,600; Nursery £882–£2,198.
   Belmont Grosvenor School is set in 20 acres of beautiful countryside in Birstwith, near Harrogate.
   The school, for boys and girls up to the age of 11, has a warm and friendly atmosphere where children learn and grow both inside and outside the classroom. Belmont Grosvenor School provides everything that you would expect for a quality education for boys and girls aged 3 months to 11 years.
   The ethos of the School is characterised by the trusting and supportive relationships that exist between staff, children and parents. We create an environment that is safe and happy where academic and social skills, individual talents, consideration and sensitivity to the needs of others are developed. In this secure and friendly setting, learning becomes a pleasure and is its own reward. One of the school's greatest strengths is the continuity of education and care that it offers.
   It is not just school-aged children who benefit from Belmont Grosvenor's caring and nurturing environment – the school's Magic Tree Day Care Nursery cares for children from the age of three months. The nursery is divided into two main areas, one for the under twos and the other for the over twos. There is a smooth transition from the Magic Tree Day Care Nursery to the Early Years Department at Belmont Grosvenor.
   The school offers a firm academic foundation and develops the children as individuals, preparing them for the future. Sport, Music, Drama and Art are all essential elements in the balanced education enjoyed by the children at BGS.
   Children at Belmont Grosvenor School have access to specialist teachers and facilities and enjoy a wide range of extra-curricular activities, educational visits and residential trips.
   The school has undergone a series of improvements, including the opening of an outdoor classroom, amphitheatre and adventure trail as well as the redevelopment of the libraries and the introduction of interactive whiteboards and computer software enabling interactive teaching across each subject area. This allows us to deliver a broad curriculum to the highest standard with the children achieving well above National standards in KS1 and KS2 tests. The children are thoroughly prepared for transfer to secondary schools, where academic, music, sport and art scholarships are common.
   Plans for 2010 include the refurbishment of the school stage.
   Charitable status. Belmont-Birklands School Trust Limited is a Registered Charity, number 529584.

Belmont School

Feldemore, Holmbury St Mary, Dorking, Surrey RH5 6LQ
Tel: 01306 730852
Fax: 01306 731220
e-mail: schooloffice@belmont-school.org
website: www.belmont-school.org

Chairman of the Governors: Mr N Butcher

Headmistress: **Mrs H Skrine**, BA Hons Exeter, PGCE London, NPQH, FRSA

   Age Range. 2–13.
   Number of Pupils. 210 Boys and Girls: Day, Weekly and Flexible Boarding.
   Fees per term (2011-2012). Day Pupils: £3,760 (Years 3 to 8), £2,490 (Years 1 and 2), £2,220 (Little Belmont and Reception). Boarding supplement: £1,880.
   Founded in London in 1880, the School is now established in 65 acres of wooded parkland overlooking the picturesque village of Holmbury St Mary, between Guildford and Dorking. The main house, Feldemore, was completely refurbished in the early 1990s so that the school now boasts an historic building with a purpose-built interior. Outstanding facilities include a brand new Early Years building, impressive sports hall, a well-equipped theatre, two state-of-the-art computer suites, newly-refurbished Science lab and woodland adventure courses. These, together with our friendly, talented staff and confident, happy boys and girls, make Belmont the very best choice you could make for your child.
   We offer co-educational day education for boys and girls aged 2 to 13, and optional weekly boarding or flexible boarding arrangements. We prepare children for Common Entrance and Scholarship examinations to a wide range of schools, and will assist children in preparing for other Senior Schools that have their own admissions procedures.
   Here, every child matters and we look to develop children as individuals, seeking to inspire, to encourage self-esteem and to unfurl the hidden strengths of every boy or girl. There is a happy, industrious atmosphere and high expectations pervade throughout all aspects of school life. In addition, we have a challenging curriculum and an extensive array of extra-curricular opportunities which together are designed to captivate the imaginations of every boy and girl. Creativity is a particular strength of the school and pervades throughout the curriculum. The teaching staff is well qualified and healthy pupil : staff ratios have enabled us to develop a flexible setting system within a small school.
   The curriculum covers all the required Common Entrance subjects plus Drama, Art, DT, IT, Music, PSHCE, PE and Games. Sports include Netball, Rugby, Football, Hockey, Tennis, Swimming, Cricket, Athletics and Rounders depending upon the sex of the child.
   Children in Year 1 and above spend time in school prior to entry and this requires a half day or full day visit, depending on age. Further details can be obtained from the Registrar, Mrs Alison Owen.
   Charitable status. Belmont School (Feldemore) Educational Trust Limited is a Registered Charity, number 312077.

Berkhampstead School

Pittville Circus Road, Cheltenham, Glos GL52 2QA
Tel: 01242 523263
Fax: 01242 514114
e-mail: head@berkhampsteadschool.co.uk

website: www.berkhampsteadschool.co.uk

Chairman of Governors: Mrs R Hope

Headmaster: R P Cross, BSc Hons, PGCE

Age Range. 3–11 co-educational.
Number of Pupils. 250 day pupils.
Fees per term (2011-2012). Nursery Fees on request.
Pre-Prep: £1,839 (Reception), £1,865 (Year 1), £2,095 (Year 2). Prep: £2,282 (Year 3), £2,450 (Year 4), £2,565 (Years 5 and 6). Lunches: £200.

Berkhampstead School was founded over 60 years ago and continues to thrive today. Most of our pupils enter the school in the Nursery, which has its own team of teachers and nursery nurses and is situated in a purpose-built block that has recently been extended.

Parents comment on the wonderful, happy atmosphere and the stimulating environment that exists throughout the school.

Classes are small, never exceeding 18, and the curriculum is wide-ranging and offers many opportunities for individuals to develop their talents.

All major team sports are taught and a range of after-school sports clubs extend the activities offered. Gymnastics and swimming are core elements of the PE curriculum.

There are several choirs and bands and pupils have the opportunity to learn a variety of instruments in addition to their music lessons.

Drama is taught throughout the school and all pupils are involved in stage productions.

Art is another successful subject, and pupils are encouraged to enter local exhibitions.

The school has an enviable academic reputation, with over 20% of its pupils gaining Scholarships to many senior independent schools every year.

Pastoral care is also of a very high standard and a simple knowledge of Christ is woven gently into the life of the school.

In 2003 the Prep Department opened a new Art and Music block with extra classrooms and other facilities. A new Early Years centre opened in 2007.

Charitable status. Berkhampstead School is a Registered Charity, number 325018, which exists for the development of excellent education for children.

Berkhamsted Preparatory School

Kings Road, Berkhamsted, Hertfordshire HP4 3YP
Tel: 01442 358201/2
Fax: 01442 358203
e-mail: prepadmin@berkhamstedschool.org
website: www.berkhamstedschool.org.uk

Chairman of Governors: Mr P J Williamson

Principal: Mr M S Steed, MA Cantab, MA Nottingham

Head: Mr A J Taylor, BA, CertEd

Deputy Head: Mrs J L Howard, CertEd
Second Deputy: Mr D Brown, BA
Head of Pre-Prep: Mrs M Hall, BA, CertEd

Age Range. 3–11.
Number of Pupils. 225 boys, 222 girls.
Fees per term (2011-2012). Nursery: £1,170 (half day), £2,490 (full day). Preparatory: £2,930–£3,915.

Berkhamsted Preparatory School opened in September 1998 as a new co-educational school, offering first-class facilities for the 3 to 11 age group, in conjunction with the highest standards of teaching and educational development. All classes offer a happy, caring environment where children

are encouraged to investigate and explore the world around them. Classes at all levels have access to computers. Key features include a new multi-purpose hall, modern dining facilities, a full range of specialist classrooms (eg Science laboratory, 2 ICT suites) and nursery units. The Preparatory School also has use of Senior School facilities including extensive playing fields, tennis courts, a Sports Centre, a swimming pool and a 500-seat theatre.

A recent ISI Inspection Report (November 2009) noted pupils' attitudes to learning were excellent, that the children were happy, polite, well behaved and that their personal development was also excellent. High quality teaching was noted as a contributory factor to pupils' success.

Nursery. "Stepping Stones is an excellent nursery" *Ofsted report*.

Our Early Years department received an outstanding Ofsted inspection report in June 2008, and again in November 2009. The Stepping Stones department has provided nursery education for boys and girls aged 3 and 4 since 1991. It continues to grow in popularity with parents and is housed within a recently refurbished building, St David's House. A carefully structured curriculum encourages the development of basic skills with a broad and balanced programme of learning and play. Literacy and numeracy are taught from the entry class onwards and scientific thinking is developed through experiment and problem solving. Children are also encouraged to express themselves through art, music and drama.

Infants and Juniors. All children are encouraged to develop to their full potential and grow in confidence and independence. The School's general approach is progressive, while retaining traditional values and standards; courtesy and politeness towards others are expected at all times. Academic achievement is of great importance, but the emphasis on other activities such as sports and music ensures that pupils receive a well-rounded education.

At this level, literacy and numeracy are the key foundation skills, but subjects such as science, history, geography, religious studies, French, art, design, information technology, music and drama gain increasing prominence. Form teachers take overall responsibility for each child's social and academic progress and are supported by specialist teachers covering subjects such as science, music and sport.

A wide range of voluntary extra-curricular activities is offered at lunch-time, the end of the school day and on Saturday mornings, including art, drama, music and sport. Choirs and orchestras perform in concerts and services throughout the year and school teams compete successfully in a variety of sports.

Charitable status. Berkhamsted School is a Registered Charity, number 311056. It is a leading Charitable School in the field of Junior and Secondary Education.

Bickley Park School

24 Page Heath Lane, Bickley, Bromley, Kent BR1 2DS
Tel: 020 8467 2195
Fax: 020 8325 5511
e-mail: info@bickleyparkschool.co.uk
website: www.bickleyparkschool.co.uk

Chairman of Governors: Mr J S Tiley

Headmaster: P M Ashley, MBA, BA, CertEd

Age Range. Boys 3–13, Girls 3–4.
Number of Pupils. 380 Boys, 20 Girls.
Fees per term (2011-2012). From £1,510 (Nursery) to £4,115 (Boys in Years 7 & 8). There are no compulsory extras.

Bickley Park School, founded in 1918, occupies two sites in Bickley, the Prep at 24 Page Heath Lane and the Pre-Prep at 14 Page Heath Lane. The school has excellent modern facilities to complement the original Victorian buildings. Both sites are extremely attractive and the school's sports field is on the opposite side of the road.

The Nursery provides a very caring and stimulating environment for children to start their school lives. At Pre-Prep level, the children are cared for by a class teacher with the addition of specialist teaching for Music and Games. Classes are kept small with none exceeding 18 in total.

In the Prep Department, the children are introduced to more specialist teaching and setting for Mathematics, English, Science and French is introduced. The curriculum is broad with the emphasis being placed on encouraging the children to develop their potential to the full in a very caring environment. There is a wide range of extra curricular activities and a full sports programme. The major sports played are football, rugby and cricket, whilst athletics and tennis are also offered.

The majority of children leave at 13+ through the Common Entrance or Scholarship examinations whilst a small number leave at 11 to join local Grammar Schools.

The Parents Association, run by parents and staff, arrange events, both social and fundraising, during the year.

Visitors are made very welcome.

Charitable status. Bickley Park School Limited is a Registered Charity, number 307915. It exists to provide a broad curriculum for boys aged 3–13 and girls aged 3–4.

Bilton Grange

Dunchurch, Rugby CV22 6QU
Tel: 01788 810217
Fax: 01788 816922
e-mail: hmsec@biltongrange.co.uk
website: www.biltongrange.co.uk

The school is registered as an Educational Trust under the Charities Act and is controlled by a Board of Governors.

Chairman of Governors: J B Greenhalgh, Esq

Headmaster: **J P Kirk**, BSc, FRSA

Senior Staff:
Deputy Headmaster: Giles Tollit, BA Hons
Assistant Headmaster: Paul Nicholson, BA Hons, PGCE
Director of Studies: Philip Moore, BSc, MA, PGCE
Head of Pre Prep: Adrian Brindley, BSc, MA, PGCE

Age Range. 4–13.
Number of Pupils. 300 boys and girls of whom 50 are boarders. Preparatory (8–13 year olds): 180 pupils; Pre-Preparatory (4–7 year olds): 120 pupils.

Fees per term (from April 2011). Preparatory: Boarding £6,415, Day £4,605–£5,225. Pre-Preparatory: £2,730–£3,280.

Bursaries for those whose parents cannot afford full fees, for Service children, third child and scholarships are also available.

Bilton Grange School is one of the foremost co-educational prep schools in the country.

The school, which was established in 1887, prides itself on bringing out the very best in every child. Children are extremely happy at the school, and in a nurturing, inspiring and caring environment, children confidently find their true potential.

Bilton Grange offers a diverse range of opportunities all designed to support individual accomplishments. Here, children share common values of respect, awareness of others and courtesy. They are usually 'all-rounders', willing to take advantage of all the opportunities open to them – be it on the sports field, on an adventure weekend or in the classroom.

This sense of pride in the school was recently confirmed by external inspection. Bilton Grange was rated 'Outstanding' for quality of education, spiritual, moral, social and cultural development, facilities, boarding provision, leadership and management in the 2008 ISI inspection report. Ofsted boarding Inspectors also rated Bilton Grange as 'Outstanding'.

According to ISI Inspectors, "Pupils enjoy a rich childhood; they are articulate and imaginative, enthusiastic and confident, friendly and courteous. Outstanding provision begins in Reception and this is maintained throughout years 1 to 8. A quarter of all lessons observed by Inspectors were outstanding. The school provides an environment where pupils grow and blossom. The high calibre of the teaching staff has a direct bearing on the quality of education provided. The governance, leadership and management have transformed the school since the previous ISI inspection."

The school has 340 children aged 4–13 and is set in 160 secure acres of sports fields, woods, and landscaped gardens dominated by a 19th Century Pugin mansion. A Montessori Nursery school caters for the 3 to 4 years olds in morning and afternoon sessions.

Both full and flexible boarding are offered – with around 50 boarders divided equally between boys and girls.

Bilton Grange is not academically selective. Class sizes rarely exceed 16 and all classrooms are fitted with interactive whiteboards and the highest level of IT resources.

Children are entered for the Common Entrance Examination and Eton, Oundle, Rugby, Uppingham, Wycombe Abbey are the principal schools to which Bilton Grange children progress. Approximately 30% of Year 8 children win senior school awards in any one year.

Bursaries are available for children aged 7–11 in recognition of academic, music, artistic or sporting potential. Fee reductions of 90% are available subject to income. Bursary selection day takes place around the third Saturday in February.

Facilities include a 9-hole golf course, shooting range, theatre, indoor heated pool and chapel. Hockey is a particular strength of the school.

Music is also a very important part of school life and Bilton Grange is one of very few prep schools to have a CD of its own original music.

Out-of-school activities include international tours, outward bound activity, sporting and creative opportunities.

In 2008, parents rated the school very highly for providing a happy and secure environment, offering outstanding breadth of opportunity, having a talented, dedicated and friendly team of staff and offering excellent resources.

We encourage all prospective parents and children to visit the school to see and experience teaching and learning of the highest standards in an inspiring setting.

Charitable status. Bilton Grange Trust is a Registered Charity, number 528771. It exists to provide education for boys and girls.

Birchfield School

Albrighton, Wolverhampton WV7 3AF
Tel: 01902 372534
Fax: 01902 373516
e-mail: office@birchfieldschool.co.uk
website: www.birchfieldschool.co.uk

Chairman of the Governors: B Frankling

Headmaster: **Hugh Myott**

Age Range. 4–13.
Number of Pupils. 154 with weekly boarding. Preparatory (8–13 year olds) 95. Pre-Prep (4–7 year olds) 59.

Fees per term (2010-2011). Weekly boarding £5,550, Day: Years 3–8 £3,925, Year 2 £3,250, Juniors (Reception–Year 1) £2,420.

These are exciting times for Birchfield School. Girls joined Birchfield's reception class in September 2006 and have now progressed to Year 5. The last Independent Schools Inspectorate report in October 2007 described us as a *'very welcoming community with outstanding pastoral care and relationships'*.

Birchfield's academic staff consists of many subject specialists who operate from well-equipped classrooms and modern facilities such as a music suite, science laboratory, design and technology workshop and art studio, and library. There are two ICT suites with networked PCs.

Sport is a fundamental part of school life and with superb playing fields and a recently refurbished outdoor swimming pool, Birchfield enjoys an excellent sporting reputation. Birchfield also has a floodlit synthetic sports surface which is used for a variety of sports and by all age groups.

Birchfield also encourages self-expression through music, drama, art and design technology. Art is a considerable strength of the School. The Music Department holds regular concerts and our musicians have performed with professional bodies in major productions. The pupils are also involved in a wide-range of extra-curricular activities.

The school has a well-resourced Learning Enhancement department with two members of staff who provide excellent support for pupils with special educational needs. For those demonstrating strong academic prowess a scholarship form is in place during the final years.

In recent years senior pupils have achieved numerous scholarships and awards. One in three leavers at 13+ leaves with an award. There is a rich and challenging programme for pupils up to the age of 13, including the opportunity to board in the final years. When the time comes to say goodbye, senior pupils are prepared for entry into a wide range of independent senior schools and local grammar schools which suit best the individual's needs.

The headmaster's wife is actively involved in school life and there is a full-time school nurse. Birchfield has a fine reputation for its all-round holistic education.

Set in 20 acres of attractive grounds and playing fields, Birchfield School is close to Wolverhampton and Telford and boasts excellent transport links.

Co-educational nursery Prepcare (managed by Prepcare LLP) operates on the Birchfield School site and welcomes children from 6 weeks to 4 years old, all year round (except weekends and Bank Holidays) from 8.00 am until 6.00 pm.

Charitable status. Birchfield School is a Registered Charity, number 528420.

Birkdale Preparatory School

Clarke House, Clarke Drive, Sheffield S10 2NS
Tel: 0114 267 0407
Fax: 0114 268 2929
e-mail: prepschool@birkdaleschool.org.uk
website: www.birkdaleschool.org.uk

Chairman of Governors: Dr J R Goepel, MBChB, FRCPath

Head of Preparatory School: **C J Burch**, BA, PGCE

Age Range. 4–11.
Number of Boys. 267 day boys.
Fees per term (2011-2012). Pre-Preparatory Department £2,485; Preparatory Department £2,939. Lunch included.

Birkdale has grown and developed since the post war years into a school offering a continuous curriculum for boys aged 4 to 18 and girls in the Sixth Form.

This expansion led to the reorganisation of the school and in 1988 a new Preparatory School was established at Clarke

House, situated in a pleasant residential area near the University and close to the Senior School. The school has a firm Christian tradition and this, coupled with the size of the school, ensures that the boys develop their own abilities, whether academic or otherwise, to the full.

The Pre-Preparatory Department is accommodated in a self-contained wing of the school but enjoys full use of the well-resourced facilities of the Preparatory School. Specialist subject teaching across the curriculum starts at the age of 7 and setting in the core subjects in the final two years enhances, still further, the pupil teacher ratio.

The school has its own Matron and pastoral care is given high priority. Boys are encouraged to join a wide variety of clubs and societies in their leisure time. Music plays a significant part in school life, both in and out of the timetable. There is a large choir, brass band and orchestra and there are strong choral links with Sheffield Cathedral where many of the choristers are Birkdalians.

Cricket, Association and Rugby Football are played on the School's own substantial playing fields, which are within easy reach of the school. Instruction in Tennis and Judo are available as part of the extensive extra curricular programme.

The majority of boys pass into the Senior School.

Charitable status. Birkdale School is a Registered Charity, number 1018973, and a Company Limited by Guarantee, registered in England, number 2792166. It exists to provide education for boys.

Bishop's Stortford College Junior School

Maze Green Road, Bishop's Stortford, Herts CM23 2PH
Tel: 01279 838607
Fax: 01279 306110
e-mail: jsadmissions@bishopsstortfordcollege.org
website: www.bishops-stortford-college.herts.sch.uk

Chairman of Governors: P J Hargrave, BSc

Head: **J A Greathead**, BEd Bangor

Age Range. 4–13.
Number of Pupils. 58 boarders and 493 day pupils.
Fees per term (2011-2012). Full Boarders £5,011–£5,452; Overseas Boarders £5,159–£5,613; Weekly Boarders £4,961–£5,397; Day £3,569–£3,999; Pre-Prep £2,339. There are no compulsory extras.

Bishop's Stortford College is a friendly, co-educational, day and boarding community providing high academic standards, good discipline and an excellent all-round education.

There are 50 full-time members of staff, and a small number of Senior School staff also teach in the Junior School. Being on the same campus as the Senior School, many College facilities (design and technology centre, music school, sports hall, swimming pool, all-weather pitches, dining hall, medical centre) are shared. The Junior School also has its own buildings, with the main building containing multi-purpose Hall, laboratories, IT centre and classrooms and a more recent building containing library, art room and classrooms. An innovative, interactive science centre was opened in 2006.

The Junior School routine and curriculum are appropriate to the 7–13 age range, with pupils being prepared for Common Entrance and Senior Schools' Scholarships, although most children proceed to the College Senior School. There are 23 forms streamed by general ability and setted for Maths. High standards of work and behaviour are expected and the full development, in a happy and friendly atmosphere, of each child's abilities in sport and the Arts is actively encouraged. A strong swimming tradition exists and many of the Staff are expert coaches of the major games (rugby, hockey, cricket, netball, rounders, tennis and swimming). The choirs and orchestra flourish throughout the year, and two afternoons of Activities provide opportunities for pupils to participate in many minor sports, outdoor pursuits, crafts, computing and chess. Six major dramatic productions occur every year.

A Pre-Prep Department for 4–6 year olds was opened in 1995 and new purpose-built accommodation for the Pre-Prep opened in September 2005.

The Junior School is run on boarding lines with a six-day week and a 5 pm finish on four days with Wednesdays ending at 4 pm and Saturdays at 3 pm. The 7 and 8 year olds have a slightly shorter day and their own dedicated building.

Entry tests for 7, 8, 9, 10, 11 year olds are held each January; Academic, Music and Art Scholarships are available at 10+ and 11+, as are Bursaries.

Charitable status. The Incorporated Bishop's Stortford College Association is a Registered Charity, number 311057. Its aims and objectives are to provide high quality Independent Boarding and Day education for boys and girls from age 4 to 18.

Bishopsgate School

Englefield Green, Surrey TW20 0YJ
Tel: 01784 432109
Fax: 01784 430460
e-mail: headmaster@bishopsgate.surrey.sch.uk
website: www.bishopsgate-school.co.uk

Chairman of Governors: Mr A Taee

Headmaster: **A H Cowell**, BEd

Age Range. 2½–13.
Number of Pupils. 336.
Fees per term (2011-2012). £4,099 (Years 5–8), £2,675–£3,625 (Reception–Year 4); Nursery £1,149–£2,505 (full-time). Flexi-boarding is available for £30 per night.

Set in beautiful woodland, close to Windsor Great Park, Bishopsgate is blessed with a glorious learning environment. The heart of the school remains a large, Victorian house, but recent developments have included a multi-purpose sports hall, brand new classroom blocks for both Lower and Upper Schools, and an all-weather pitch. A new library and performing arts centre opened in 2007 and in 2010 a state-of-the-art Design Technology studio was added. Other specialist facilities include a Science laboratory, Art and Design studio, Music School, ICT suite and extensive playing fields.

Children may enter Bishopsgate from the age of 2½ into our cosy Pre-Nursery or at 3 into our Nursery. Our trained staff and well-equipped rooms ensure that each child is given the best possible start to life. There is a warm family atmosphere as we recognise how important it is for children to feel happy and secure. We place great emphasis on building a solid foundation of social skills and a love of learning, which will enable each child to settle confidently to school life. A wide variety of activities is on offer with plenty of opportunities for healthy outdoor learning.

Beyond Nursery, a class teacher remains at the core of each child's learning. Emphasis is placed on establishing a firm foundation in literacy and numeracy, but the curriculum is broad with a range of educational visits planned to enrich and extend the children's learning. Good use is made of our glorious grounds as a learning resource. The teaching of French, Music, PE, Singing and Dance is provided by specialist teachers.

Form-based teaching continues in Years Three and Four, but by Year Five all teaching is by subject specialists. Programmes of study in Upper School are full and varied, covering the traditional academic subjects as well as Art, Design, Music, Information and Communication Technology, PSHE and Physical Education. The children are prepared carefully for entrance to a range of senior schools and we are proud of our record of success. We prepare children for 11+ entry to senior schools, but we hope our children will remain with us to 13.

In Upper School, opportunities to represent the school in sports teams, plays, choirs and instrumental groups are all part of the 'Bishopsgate Experience'. In addition, a busy programme of extra-curricular activities ensures that all children have the opportunity to shine at something.

Music plays an essential part in the life of the school with many of our pupils enjoying individual music lessons. There are choirs and ensembles. Participation by children of all abilities, with ample opportunities to perform, is our aim. Dramatic productions, dance and public speaking events all provide additional occasions when the children can perform on stage.

Our vibrant Art and Design Department occupies a spacious studio equipped with a kiln for ceramics and a printing press for design projects. There is an annual art exhibition for both Lower and Upper Schools and the children's work is displayed proudly around the school and in our annual school magazine. There is a popular after-school Art club for children and regular workshops for parents.

Team Games, Rowing, Athletics, Dance, Tennis, Gymnastics, Judo, Tae Kwon Do, Swimming and much more are all included in a varied and exciting sporting programme within the school day. An extensive programme of inter-school fixtures is arranged each term and we like to see as many parents in support as possible! We like to win, but our priorities are participation, enjoyment and teamwork.

A prospectus and further details can be obtained from the School Office.

Charitable status. Bishopsgate School is a Registered Charity, number 1060511. It aims to provide a broad and sound education for its pupils with thorough and personal pastoral care.

Blackheath Nursery & Preparatory School

4 St German's Place, London SE3 0NJ
Tel: 020 8858 0692
Fax: 020 8858 7778
e-mail: info@blackheathprepschool.com
website: www.blackheathprepschool.com

Co-educational Day School.

Chairman of Governors: Mr Hugh Stallard

Headmistress: **Mrs P J Thompson**

Age Range. 3–11.
Number of Pupils. 191 Girls, 188 Boys.
Fees per term (2011-2012). Nursery: £1,640–£2,640; Reception–Year 2 £2,935; Years 3–6 £3,195.

The school is located in an attractive residential area close to Blackheath village, overlooking the heath itself and borders of Greenwich Park. The five-acre site includes attractive playing fields, cricket nets, tennis courts and two playgrounds, providing enviable sporting opportunities and room for children to play.

A rigorous refurbishment and building programme has resulted in an attractive learning environment. Lessons may take place in one of the 17 form rooms; in addition there are dedicated specialist rooms for Science, ICT, Art, DT, Maths and Music. A most attractive library encourages a real love of literature. A spacious multi-purpose hall and music suite have increased opportunities for music, drama, sport and leisure activities.

Most children join the school in the nursery at the age of three and progress through the Pre-Prep (4–7) and Prep (7–11) before leaving to transfer to selective senior schools. Academic standards are high and pupils are well prepared for selection at 11 and achieve consistent success in obtaining places at their first choice of grammar or independent senior school.

The form teacher of every class is responsible for the pastoral welfare of each child. In the Nursery and the Pre-Prep the key worker and the form teacher are primarily responsible for teaching the children. However, there is a strong emphasis on specialist teaching from the very beginning. Music, French, PE and dance are introduced in the nursery. As the children progress through the school, more specialist teachers are responsible for ICT, Drama, Design Technology, Maths, English and Science.

The quality of teaching has been recognised as one of the many strengths of the school. The dedicated and committed staff enjoy excellent relations with their pupils who achieve very good standards by the time they leave the school. Pupils display real pleasure in their learning.

The school positively encourages parental involvement in the daily life of the school. The strong ethos and vision of the school is underpinned by the considerable enthusiasm of all involved and by the very strong sense of community.

The Blue Coat School

Somerset Road, Edgbaston, Birmingham B17 0HR
Tel: 0121 410 6800
Fax: 0121 454 7757
e-mail: admissions@bluecoat.bham.sch.uk
website: www.bluecoat.bham.sch.uk

Founded 1722. Co-educational Day Preparatory School. Accredited by the Independent Schools Council.

Chairman of Governors: Professor J N Hay, DSc, BSc, PhD, CChem, FRSC

Headmaster: A D J Browning, MA Cantab, PGCE

Age Range. 2–11.
Number of Pupils. The total enrolment is 554 children. Pre-Prep has 260 girls and boys from 2–7 years, while Prep has 294 from 7–11 years.
There is a graduate and qualified full-time teaching staff of 39 and 6 part-time teachers, giving a teacher/pupil ratio of 1:12.
Fees per term (2011-2012). Pre-Prep: £2,235–£2,810; Prep: £3,320–£3,440. The fees quoted include lunches and morning and afternoon breaks. A range of some 50 activities may be taken as extras.
Assisted Places are available at reduced charges to children with a demonstrable need.
Scholarships are offered for academic and musical excellence at age 7.
The School is set in 15 acres of grounds and playing fields just 2 miles from the centre of Birmingham. Its well-designed buildings and facilities comprise the Chapel, the Administrative Building, the Prep Teaching Centre, the Pre-Prep Department, the brand-new Pre-School, sports pitches, tennis courts and a superb multi-purpose Sports Centre with a heated 25m swimming pool. After-school care is available. In Prep this is provided in two spacious, purpose-designed Houses.
Additional features include the Library Resource Centre and specialist facilities for Science, Art, Design and Technology, Music, Media Studies and ICT. All the classrooms

have an IWB, and the school is very well equipped with computers including laptops and Apple Macs.

Children are prepared for scholarships and examinations to prestigious local schools. The school enjoys particular success in the 11+ examinations to Birmingham's grammar schools and the schools of the King Edward VI Foundation. The National Curriculum is incorporated at Key Stages 1 and 2 as part of a wider academic structure.

The school places great emphasis on Music. The robed Chapel Choir is affiliated to the RSCM, and there are five further choirs and a significant number of instrumental groups. The school benefits from *Sibelius* software, used in the teaching of composition, and from a Steinway concert grand. Musicals, concerts and recitals feature in abundance, involving the great majority of the children. Over 250 instrumental lessons are given weekly.

The main sports are Hockey, Netball, Rounders, Rugby, Soccer, Cricket, Tennis, Athletics and Swimming. The teams enjoy considerable success in inter-school competitions and all children have the opportunity to develop their skills.

Extra-curricular activities include Gymnastics, Judo, Ballet, Drama, Sign Language, Speech Training, Chess and Dance. A Ski Trip, French Trip, excursions and field courses are available each year, together with a leadership training programme run in association with Outward Bound.

Charitable status. The Blue Coat School, Birmingham is a Registered Charity, number 528805. It exists to provide education of quality for children of Preparatory School age.

Blundell's Preparatory School

Milestones House, Blundell's Road, Tiverton, Devon EX16 4NA
Tel: 01884 252393
Fax: 01884 232333
e-mail: prep@blundells.org
website: www.blundells.org

Chairman of Governors: Mr P M Johnson, MA, FRSA

Headmaster: Mr A Southgate, BA Ed Hons

Age Range. 3–11 years.
Numbers of Pupils. Boys and Girls: Prep (aged 7–11) 146; Pre-Prep (aged 2½–7) 104.
Fees per term (2011-2012). Prep: £3,105–£3,135 (Lunch £245); Pre-Prep: £1,795–£2,290 (Lunch £210); Nursery: £612 (3 sessions, lunch £126), £204 per additional session (lunch £42).
Blundell's Preparatory School is a family school and all the staff adopt a personal interest in every child and work in partnership with the parents. The school places great emphasis on children being happy, secure and confident, thus offering individuals every opportunity to achieve their full potential within a caring family atmosphere.
The School has been established for over seventy years and is part of the Blundell's Charitable Trust. It enjoys its own separate site within the very extensive Blundell's campus. This rural setting is within easy reach of the market town of Tiverton and is conveniently placed less than ten minutes from the M5 motorway and Tiverton Parkway Station.
The School has an excellent reputation for providing the essentials. Sound academic standards are based on providing the core subjects of Maths, English and Science taught to an extremely high standard. Added to this is the bonus of a wide range of supplementary subjects, well taught by specialist teachers. The School has recently had a major redevelopment and a significant extension. This includes a fully-equipped Art & Design Centre and a new Food Technology Suite.

Drama, music and art flourish at Blundell's Preparatory School with all the children participating fully both in lessons and as part of extra-curricular activities. Specialist music teachers offer an extensive variety of different instruments. The Drama and Music department have their own dedicated facility.

The sports department has an enviable reputation of producing good all-round sporting pupils, as well as nurturing and extending those with talent. Amongst the sports offered are rugby, football, netball, hockey and cross-country in the winter and cricket, rounders, tennis, athletics and swimming in the summer. The Preparatory School has access to the extensive sporting facilities within Blundell's campus.

There is an comprehensive choice of extra-curricular activities offered to the pupils which includes ballet, chess, fencing, golf, choir, judo, environment club and woodwork.

Priority entrance to Blundell's is given to its Preparatory School pupils but the school's autonomous position ensures that, if wished for, the pupils are prepared for entrance, including scholarships, to a variety of other senior schools.

(See also Blundell's School entry in HMC section.)

Charitable status. Blundell's School is a Registered Charity, number 1081249. It exists to provide education for children.

Boundary Oak School

Roche Court, Wickham Road, Fareham, Hampshire PO17 5BL
Tel: 01329 280955
Fax: 01329 827656
e-mail: registrar@boundaryoak.co.uk
website: www.boundaryoak.co.uk

Chairman of Governors: Mr P Carden

Headmaster: **Stephen Symonds**, BA Ed Hons

Age Range. 2¾–13.
Number of Pupils. 23 Boarders, 114 Day Pupils.
Fees per term (2010-2011). Full Boarders £5,900–£6,240; Weekly Boarders £4,375–£5,550; Day Pupils: £2,490–£3,900 (Reception–Year 8), Nursery £1,170–£2,290 (all day).

The school was founded in 1918 and moved to Roche Court in 1960. A new 99 year lease was secured in 1994. The school is set in 22 acres of pleasant, self-contained grounds between Fareham and Wickham in Hampshire and enjoys extensive views of the countryside around.

The Nursery Department takes children from the age of 2¾ to rising 5 and this group is housed in a purpose-built centre offering the most up-to-date facilities. This department is structured to the needs of this age group and the day can extend from 8.00 am to either 12 noon or 5.30 pm.

The Pre-Prep Department has its own purpose-built buildings and other facilities within the school, and caters for children from rising 5 to 8 years of age.

At 8 years the children move to the Preparatory Department where they remain until they are 13+. Full, weekly and flexi boarding are offered to all from the age of 7 years and the school has a policy of admitting boarders in a flexible system that is of great benefit to all. Pupils are prepared for a wide number of independent schools throughout the United Kingdom in a friendly and caring environment.

Apart from the historic main house of Roche Court where the boarders live, there is the Jubilee Block of classrooms, two laboratories and a Geography room in a separate building, the Widley Block, Library and the Music Centre, which incorporates a computer centred music generating complex. The School has a new ICT Suite and a purpose-built Art and Design Technology Centre that incorporates work areas for Photography, Pottery and Carpentry. The school has a fine Assembly Hall that is also used for Drama and Physical Education.

As well as extensive playing fields with woods beyond for cross country, three new astroturf tennis courts and a netball court, there is an outdoor swimming pool and the indoor Fareham Pool is within very easy reach with our three minibuses.

Most sports are taught and there is a wide selection of clubs and activities run in the school for both day and boarding pupils including judo, horse riding, art, camp craft, chess and shooting.

For a copy of the prospectus and full details of scholarships, please apply to the Headmaster, or view us on the internet at www.boundaryoak.co.uk.

Charitable status. Boundary Oak School Trust Ltd is a Registered Charity, number 307346. It exists to provide education for boys and girls.

Bow, Durham School

South Road, Durham DH1 3LS
Tel: 0191 384 8233
Fax: 0191 384 1371
e-mail: bow@durhamschool.co.uk
website: www.durhamschool.co.uk

Chairman of Governors: A MacConachie, OBE, DL

Headmaster: **R N Baird**, BA, PGCE

Age Range. 3–11 Co-educational.
Number of Pupils. 130 Day Pupils (girls and boys).
Fees per term (2011-2012). £2,010 (Nursery), £2,360 (Reception, Years 1 & 2), £2,830 (Years 3–6).

Bow, Durham School (formerly Bow School) is Durham School's preparatory school and caters for girls and boys aged from 3 to 11. It has been situated on its present site, half a mile from the Senior School and overlooking the cathedral, since 1888. Bow has its own extensive facilities including a fully-equipped science laboratory, IT suite, sports hall and library. An extensive modernisation and improvement programme was completed in September 2006 when Bow became co-educational. Bow pupils are also able to use all the excellent facilities at the senior site, such as the swimming pool, all-weather sports surface, the chapel and the theatre.

Academic. Bow has a fine record of academic achievement over the years and results in externally-marked examinations, such as the Key Stage I and 2 tests, are regularly impressive. The overwhelming majority of pupils move into the Senior School at the age of 11 at which point a range of valuable awards are available. A high pupil-teacher ratio is maintained and small classes are considered vital as we seek to ensure that each child fulfils his or her academic potential.

Sport, Music and Drama. Bow has an outstanding tradition in competitive sport, many former pupils having represented their country. A wide range of sports is on offer to all pupils.

Music and drama form an integral part of life at Bow, with an active choir, ceilidh band and fiddle group performing regularly. In addition to their weekly class music lessons, each child has the opportunity to take part in a wide range of musical pursuits. Large numbers of pupils learn individual instruments and instruments are available for hire.

There are three drama productions each year. Pupils are encouraged to take part in these productions whether it is on the stage or behind the scenes.

Extra-Curricular Activities. Bow offers a wide range of extra-curricular activities which are seen as a vital ingredient in the daily diet of every Bow pupil. In addition further activities and hobbies are available as voluntary after-school clubs.

Admission. Admission is possible at any age and entry is based on an interview with the Headmaster and (if appropriate) an assessment test.

Adamson Scholarships are available at Years 3 and 4 and financial support in the form of bursaries can also be offered where necessary at any age. There are generous concessions for brothers and sisters and for children of the Armed Forces and the clergy.

Charitable status. Durham School is a Registered Charity, number 1023407. The aim of the charity is to advance education in the North-East.

Bradford Grammar Junior School
(Clock House)

Keighley Road, Bradford, West Yorkshire BD9 4JP
Tel: 01274 553742
Fax: 01274 553745
e-mail: chsec@bradfordgrammar.com
website: www.bgsjuniorschool.com

Chairman of the Board of Governors: Lady Lynne Morrison

Headmaster: **N H Gabriel**, BA, DipArch

Age Range. 6–11.
Number of Pupils. 125 boys, 73 girls.
Fees per annum (2011-2012). £8,210.
Bradford Grammar Junior School is located on the same site as the senior school, in the original seventeenth century manor house, Clock House. The manor house has been extended and refurbished and the thoughtful blending of the old with the new has created a school of style and spaciousness.

The school offers pupils a wide range of specialist facilities, including a swimming pool, theatre, instrumental music tuition, dedicated ICT and DT rooms and science laboratories. In Years 2, 3 and 4 the pupils are taught mostly by their form teachers, in Years 5 and 6 they are taught by specialist teachers within Clock House, though some specialist teaching from staff in the senior school also takes place in Art, Science, PE and Games. Modern foreign languages (French, German and Spanish) are taught from Year 4. The girls and boys are given a good grounding in all subjects, which prepares them well for what is required in the senior school.

Extra-curricular activities take place at lunchtime. There is a long tradition of excellence in sport, music and drama. Winter sports include rugby, netball, hockey, swimming, cross-country and football. In the summer children play cricket, rounders and take part in athletics and a variety of other sports.

The Junior School is a very busy place but pastoral care permeates all the school does. Our aim is to provide young boys and girls with a wide range of educational experiences and to develop the right attitude to learning so that they fulfil their potential, in a safe, friendly, tolerant and caring environment utilising all the resources and facilities the school has to offer.

Boys and girls can enter the school at the start of Years 2, 3, 4, 5 and 6 having satisfied our entrance requirements; an informal assessment for Years 2, 3 and 4 and an entrance examination for those joining in Years 5 and 6. Invariably most of our pupils transfer to the Senior School and the close relationship between the two schools enables us to make the transition as smooth as possible.

There are excellent transport links to the school along the Wharfe Valley and the Metro train station is a five-minute walk away; there is also a dedicated junior school bus serving the Aire Valley, thus putting the school within easy travelling distance from Skipton, Ilkley, Bingley and Keighley. The school also operates its own bus service from Huddersfield, Halifax and Leeds.

Charitable status. The Free Grammar School of King Charles II at Bradford is a Registered Charity, number 529113. It exists to provide education for children.

Brambletye

East Grinstead, West Sussex RH19 3PD
Tel: 01342 321004
Fax: 01342 317562
e-mail: admin@brambletye.com
website: www.brambletye.co.uk

Chairman of Governors: A J Hynard, Esq

Headmaster: **H D Cocke**, BA, CertEd Oxon

Age Range. 2½–13.
Number of Pupils. 292 co-educational day/boarding pupils.
Fees per term (2011-2012). Boarders £6,850, Day Pupils £4,980–£5,930, Pre-Prep £2,070–£2,680, Nursery £1,815 (5 full days).
Brambletye is an independent day and boarding Preparatory School for boys and girls aged 7–13 years, situated in beautiful grounds in rural Sussex. There is a Pre-Preparatory/Nursery department which takes boys and girls from the age of 2½ years to the age of 7 years.

Brambletye is a large country house in its own wooded estate of 140 acres, overlooking Ashdown Forest and Weir Wood Reservoir. The school stands one mile south of East Grinstead. Gatwick Airport is only 20 minutes by car and Heathrow is an hour away. London is 30 miles by road and 50 minutes by rail. There is escorted travel to and from London at the beginning of all exeat weekends and half-term holidays.

The school has outstanding academic, sporting, music, drama and arts facilities. These include a new modern classroom block, 2 redeveloped science laboratories, an up-to-date Arts Room and Design Technology workshop, an extensive Library, an ICT room, a large theatre and music rooms. There is also a Sports Hall, tennis and netball courts, two squash courts, a swimming pool, a golf course and several playing fields. We aim to produce happy, confident, well-rounded children who work hard, enjoy drama, games and music, play a part in some of the numerous societies and hobbies, and take a full share in the daily life of the school. These facilities in conjunction with high quality teaching staff, generate regular awards for the children from the schools that inherit them.

Brambletye has always been run along family lines, with a distinctive warm and friendly atmosphere. Traditional values such as high standards of manners and good behaviour provide a platform for academic and personal development. As a co-educational day and boarding school, pupils enjoy and benefit from living and working in a community. At weekends, there is a full programme of activities for the boarders and children are encouraged to make constructive use of their spare time. The environment is inspirational and pupils develop a love of learning which creates a positive interaction with the staff and a curiosity about the world around us.

The Nursery and Pre-Preparatory Department is situated in a self-contained purpose-built state-of-the art building. The main aim of the Department is to provide a secure, friendly and structured environment in which all children are encouraged to achieve their full potential and to develop at their own rate.

Children may join the Nursery class at the age of two and a half before progressing to Reception at four. Boys and girls transfer to the Preparatory Department at the age of seven. All children acquire the basic skills, while following the breadth of the National Curriculum. Religious Studies, Physical Education, Art, Music, Science and Technology are all integrated into the weekly timetable. Children have swimming lessons throughout the year in the indoor pool, and teachers from the Preparatory Department visit regularly to teach Music and to coach games. The Pre-Prep has an exciting School in the Woods project.

Enquiries about admissions, our scholarships and bursary programme are welcomed throughout the year. Brambletye offers generous discounts for Armed Services Families. Please contact the Headmaster's Secretary for a prospectus.

Charitable status. Brambletye School Trust Limited is a Registered Charity, number 307003. It aims to provide an all round education for the children in its care.

Bramcote School

Filey Road, Scarborough, North Yorkshire YO11 2TT
Tel: 01723 373086
Fax: 01723 364186
e-mail: info@bramcoteschool.com
website: www.bramcoteschool.com

Chairman of Governors: C Ryan

Headmaster: **A R A Snow**, BSc, PGCE

Age Range. Co-educational 3–13.
Number of Pupils. 44 boys, 42 girls.
Fees per term (2010-2011). Boarding £5,789, Day £2,177–£3,601.

Bramcote is a boarding and day preparatory school for boys and girls aged between 3 and 13 years. The school is set in its own grounds close to the sea on Scarborough's South Cliff. The school was founded on its present site in 1893 and became an Educational Trust in 1957, administered by a chairman and nine governors of wide professional and educational experience.

Recent developments have included the complete refurbishment of the boarding accommodation, improvements to the teaching facilities and a sports hall, which can be used as an indoor tennis court. The latest addition is the opening of a new Pre-Prep Department in 2006 and Nursery in 2010.

The curriculum is based on the Scholarship and Common Entrance requirements for major Independent Schools throughout the country. Although the experienced teaching staff of 14 ensures that the academic standards for which Bramcote has long held a high reputation are maintained, the school caters for children of mixed ability and classes are small with extra help available where needed by the school's qualified specialist.

Bramcote's facilities and position allow a wide range of extra-curricular activities in the evenings and at weekends. Facilities include the sports hall, a modern music and art centre, theatre, fully equipped computer room, indoor swimming pool and floodlit tennis court and play areas. Frequent visits are made to the theatre and concerts, whilst the seaside and nearby National Parks give opportunities for more adventurous pursuits such as orienteering, canoeing and rambling.

The school has excellent playing fields, where football, netball, rugby, hockey, rounders and cricket are played as major sports, with a wide variety of alternative opportunities including tennis, athletics, squash, dance, ballet, judo, golf, sailing and riding.

The school has a strong musical tradition and tuition is available for the full range of orchestral instruments and choir. The department is run by a Director of Music with 10 peripatetic staff and all pupils learn to play at least one musical instrument. The Chamber Choir visited Rome in 2007, Venice in 2009 and Salzburg in 2011.

Pastoral and health care is supervised by the Headmaster's wife and three assistant matrons.

For further information, parents are invited to write or to telephone the Headmaster or the school secretary for copies of a prospectus and current magazine or to arrange a visit to the school.

Charitable status. Bramcote School is a Registered Charity, number 529739. It exists to provide education for boys and girls.

Bramley School

Chequers Lane, Walton-on-the-Hill, Tadworth, Surrey KT20 7ST
Tel: 01737 812004
Fax: 01737 819945
e-mail: office@bramleyschool.co.uk
website: www.bramleyschool.co.uk

Chairman of Governors: Mr Michael Mason, LLB Hons RY

Headmistress: **Mrs P Burgess**, BEd Hons, MA, NPQH

Age Range. 3–11.
Number in School. 90 Girls.
Fees per term (2011-2012). £1,420–£3,105 including lunches.

Bramley was founded in 1945 as an independent pre-preparatory and preparatory day school and became an Educational Trust in 1972. A registered charity, the school is administered by a Trust Council and all income is used for educational purposes.

The strength of Bramley School lies in its commitment to developing happy, confident, self-motivated pupils with a lifelong love of learning. An excellent teacher/pupil ratio; a caring friendly atmosphere; highly qualified, specialised and enthusiastic staff, and a genuine concern for each child's welfare contribute to academic success. Bramley achieves excellent examination results at 11+ and many girls gain places and scholarships to prestigious senior schools within both the independent and maintained sectors. Alongside this, children are encouraged to develop their own interests and talents and a wide range of extra curricular activities are offered.

Throughout the school girls work in small classes, according to their age group, with particular attention being paid to meeting the specific needs of individuals. All children in the Pre-Preparatory Department are taught by dedicated class teachers who have full responsibility for their classes, whilst older children benefit from specialised teaching staff, for example in Mathematics, English, Science, ICT, Music, PE and Art. A specialist teacher teaches French from the age of 5. The Preparatory Curriculum is constantly being developed to keep abreast of educational changes in the National Curriculum, whilst retaining the excellence of well-tried methods.

The Little Bramley Nursery Department is an ideal starting point for school life with literacy and numeracy skills fostered through play in a safe and nurturing environment. Children from three years of age settle quickly and happily and the newly refurbished premises allow the early curriculum to take place outdoors as well as indoors.

Open Mornings take place in February, May and October; details can be found on the school website.

Charitable status. Bramley Educational Trust Limited is a Registered Charity, number 270046. Its aim is to provide an excellent educational establishment for 3–11 year old girls.

Brandeston Hall
Framlingham College's Preparatory School

Brandeston, Woodbridge, Suffolk IP13 7AH
Tel: 01728 685331
Fax: 01728 685437
e-mail: office@brandestonhall.co.uk
website: www.framlinghamcollege.co.uk

Chairman of Governors: A W M Fane, MA, FCA

Headmaster: **M K Myers-Allen**, BSc Hons, PGCE

Deputy Head: R Sampson, BA Hons, PGCE

Age Range. 2½–13 Co-educational.
Number of Pupils. 249: Boarders 70, Day 134; Pre-Prep 45, Nursery 23.
Fees per term (2011-2012). Boarding £6,525, Day £4,058 (inc lunch), Pre-Prep: Day £2,332 (inc lunch), Nursery: £35 (full day session inc lunch), £17 (half day session exc lunch).

Brandeston Hall is a leading preparatory school for 2½–13 year old boys and girls with full boarding, flexible boarding and day places. The school is located in an idyllic rural setting in East Suffolk, set in 27 acres of grounds on the banks of the River Deben.

All students are prepared for ISEB Common Entrance at 13 and it is worth noting that in the past 4 years all pupils leaving Brandeston have gained entry to the senior school of their choice, with the majority choosing to make the transition to Framlingham College (*see HMC entry*)

A recent ISI Inspection Report described the children at Brandeston as *unfailingly polite to visitors* and pupils' social, moral, spiritual and cultural development was described as *outstanding*.

The ISI Inspection Report also recognised the *excellent standard* of boarding at Brandeston, which was recently backed up with an Ofsted Inspection that described the provision of boarding and pastoral care as outstanding. The two boarding houses are warm and welcoming and are managed by experienced and caring Houseparents. Girl boarders share homely bedrooms in a purpose-built wing of the old stable block and boys are housed in comfortable, cosy bedrooms in the heart of the old manor house. Full-time boarders are often joined by their day friends for the wide range of Sunday activities on offer and flexible boarding is becoming increasingly popular.

Facilities include a modern library, an Arts Studio and Ceramics Centre, a specialist Music Room as well as full-size floodlit all-weather pitches (hockey/tennis/netball courts) and a nine-hole golf course. In addition pupils have use of the facilities at Framlingham College including the indoor swimming pool, theatre and Astroturf pitch.

Major games include rugby, hockey, cricket, netball, tennis, rounders and athletics. Skilled coaching is given and a full programme of matches is arranged at all levels in major and minor sports.

Music and Drama provide the perfect opportunity to star in a number of productions as well as performing in music recitals and attending drama workshops with visiting artists.

Pupils also enjoy many residential opportunities including camping trips throughout the UK, sports tours, adventure training camps and a biennial expedition to the Atlas Mountains. In addition Brandeston Hall has the use of a European Education Centre, Chateau de la Baudonnière, in Normandy, France. Senior pupils are encouraged to develop their French language skills as well as understanding and appreciating another culture.

The local parish church is situated within the school grounds and is used regularly by the school, providing a focus for community activities.

Scholarships are available for 11+ entrants in Music, Academic and Sports. An 'all rounder' Albert Memorial Scholarship is also available.

Charitable status. Albert Memorial College is a Registered Charity, number 1114383. It exists for the purpose of educating children.

Brentwood Preparatory School

Middleton Hall, Middleton Hall Lane, Brentwood, Essex CM15 8EQ
Tel: 01277 243333; Pre-Prep: 01277 243239
Fax: 01277 243340
e-mail: prep@brentwood.essex.sch.uk
          pre-prep@brentwood.essex.sch.uk
website: www.brentwoodschool.co.uk

Chairman of Governors: C J Finch, FRICS

Headmaster: **Mr K J Whiskerd**, BA

Head of Pre-Prep: Mrs S Wilson, BEd, CertEd

Age Range. 3–11.
Number of Children. Prep 241, Pre-Prep 152.
Fees per term (2011-2012). Nursery £1,787, Pre-Prep and Prep £3,571.

Brentwood Preparatory School and Brentwood Pre-Preparatory School have their own buildings and grounds quite distinct from Brentwood School (qv) but close enough to share the use of its chapel, indoor swimming pool, Sports Centre and all-weather pitch.

The co-educational Pre-Preparatory School, which opened in 1995, educates children from age 3 to 7 in a spacious building with very well-equipped classrooms. Entrance is by an informal assessment at age 3.

The Preparatory School is housed in elegant buildings and has its own spacious grounds and sports pitches. Entrance is at age 7 by an academically selective test; candidates come from a wide range of schools as well Brentwood Pre-Preparatory School. Small class sizes and a team of well-qualified teachers provide a caring and challenging environment. Specialist rooms for art, design technology, drama, French, ICT, music and science provide outstanding facilities and a stimulating environment in which children can thrive.

There is an extensive programme of house and inter-school sports matches. Three choirs, two orchestras and variety of ensembles perform regularly both in and out of school. Every child has the opportunity of taking part in a major drama production. There is a wide range of lunchtime and after-school clubs, and a late stay scheme for children to complete homework at school. Many day visits to museums and places of interest in London complement school-based work and children enjoy annual residential trips in the holidays.

The Preparatory School, which was founded in 1892, has a strong academic tradition and a reputation for providing an excellent all-round education. The vast majority of pupils transfer to the Senior School (founded in 1557) at age 11.

The Pre-Preparatory and Preparatory schools recently underwent an inspection by the ISI. The majority of the aspects in the report were judged as 'outstanding' or 'excellent' and all were rated good or better. The opening sentence of the conclusion provides the best summary of the inspectors' views: '*Both the Pre-Prep and the Prep are successful in achieving the aims of Brentwood School to provide a first class education for all its pupils*.' The 2008 report acknowledges the progress the schools have made since the last inspection in 2002, particularly the significant investment in ICT resources, the increase in facilities that the 'new' building has brought and the continuing improvement in academic standards.

Charitable status. Brentwood School (part of Sir Antony Browne's School Trust, Brentwood) is a Registered Charity, number 310864. It exists for the purpose of educating children.

Bricklehurst Manor

Stonegate, Wadhurst, East Sussex TN5 7EL
Tel: 01580 200448
Fax: 01580 200998
e-mail: office@bricklehurst.co.uk
website: www.bricklehurst.co.uk

Headmistress: **Mrs C Flowers**, CertEd, BEd Hons

Age Range. 3–11.
Number of Pupils. 146.
Fees per term (2010-2011). Kindergarten sessional; Years R, 1 and 2 £2,625; Years 3–4 £2,825, Years 5–6 £2,975.

Bricklehurst Manor was founded in 1959. It now operates as a co-educational school for boys and girls from 3 years old. Children are prepared for Common Entrance or equivalent standard entrance examinations at 11.

Bricklehurst stands in 3 acres of mature gardens and grounds. Previously a private house, the school retains many home-like characteristics, not least a friendly, family atmosphere which helps young children bridge the gap between home and school, and build up their confidence in the comfort and security of familiar surroundings.

The school has eight main classrooms and a purpose-built Kindergarten. The big panelled schoolroom is used for PE, Dancing, Drama, Music and any other activity requiring space. There is an Art/Science room, a reference library and a Music Room. Computers are used in all classrooms.

For outdoor playtime there is an orchard with an Adventure Playground, swings and sandpit. In the games periods the older children play hockey, netball, football, tag rugby, rounders and cricket; tennis coaching is available all year round and all the children learn to swim in our own heated and covered pool.

Curriculum. In the Kindergarten 3 and 4 year olds are given a happy introduction to school life learning to mix with others of the same age, to play contentedly together as one of a group, and generally to act in an orderly manner. Through using carefully structured equipment they also learn their letters and numbers, make a start at reading and gain simple number concepts.

From Reception Class onwards children stay all day. Gradually their curriculum is extended, subjects such as History, Geography, Scripture, Nature Study, Science and project work are introduced, and there are specialist teachers for Art and CDT, Drama and all musical activities. French is taught from Year 1 onwards. A variety of after-school activities is offered, including Spanish and Pottery. Mathematics is set from Year 3 and reasoning skills introduced from Year 4.

Bricklehurst has a reputation for sending children on to their next schools with a sensible attitude towards learning, and the ability to work independently and with enjoyment. A high standard of behaviour is expected, with emphasis on the gradual development of self-control, a sense of responsibility and real consideration for the needs of others.

Brighton College Prep School

Walpole Lodge, Walpole Road, Brighton, East Sussex BN2 0EU
Tel: 01273 704210
Fax: 01273 704286
e-mail: paprep@brightoncollege.net
website: www.brightoncollege.net

Chairman of Governors: Michael D L Chowen, DL

Headmaster: **Brian D Melia**, MA Cantab, PGCE

Deputy Heads:
Alison Hills, BEd
Neil Anderson, BEd

Headmistress of Pre-Prep: Joanna Williams, BEd

Director of Admissions: Caroline Ward Vine, BA

Age Range. 3–13.
Number of Pupils. Prep 285, Pre-Prep 204.
Fees per term (2011-2012). From £1,630 (Pre-Reception) to £4,994 (Year 8).

Brighton College Prep School is a co-educational school, which offers a broad curriculum taught to high standards by dedicated and energetic staff. The Pre-Prep School cares for children from 3–7 years in a modern, purpose-built building overlooking the playing fields of Brighton College. The Prep School is situated adjacent to the Senior School on its own site. The site is urban, but enjoys close proximity to the sea, the Downs and the vibrant sports and culture of Brighton, where an annual arts festival is held in May.

The excellent facilities provided by Brighton College are shared by the Prep School. These include the Chapel, swimming pool, a sports hall, two areas of playing fields, a purpose-built Performing Arts Centre and The Great Hall, which doubles as a large theatre for Prep School's annual senior musical. The Prep School itself has many specialist rooms including a well-equipped ICT suite, a large design technology room, art room, science laboratories, home economics room, library and hall. Art and DT are both key subjects on the timetable for all year groups.

Academic standards are high and are one of the foundations upon which school life is built, along with the broad range of subjects and activities. A variety of teaching methods is used – the key principle being that children enjoy their lessons and thus develop a love for learning. For details on assessment procedures and scholarships available at 13+, please contact the Director of Admissions.

The school also caters for able dyslexic pupils who are fully integrated into classes. The Dyslexia Centre attached to the school provides specialist teaching; dyslexic pupils are given extra support in small groups and may be withdrawn from French.

Sport is a very important part of the life at the school. Major girls' games are netball, hockey, athletics and rounders. Major boys' games are soccer, rugby, cricket and athletics. Swimming is on the curriculum for all pupils.

The Prep School is well known for its musical strength with a suite of specially designed music rooms and practice areas. Two orchestras, a concert band and three choirs are organised by the director of music and thirty-five visiting music teachers provide tuition for the large number of pupils who learn a wide variety of instruments including piano, violin, harp, saxophone, clarinet and drums.

Drama clubs and coaching are available for every year group and there are opportunities for children to perform during the academic year through assemblies, recitals, chapel services and also through annual drama productions and musicals.

The Brighton College School of Dance, based in the Performing Arts Centre, is thriving and many pupils attend classes on Saturdays and after school during the week.

The Prep School runs a large range of clubs and activities after school and at lunchtimes. There is a range of school bus routes. Further details on bus routes are available from the Director of Admissions.

Charitable status. Brighton College is a Registered Charity, number 307061. It exists to provide high quality education for boys and girls aged 3–18.

BGS Infants and Juniors

Elton Road, Bristol BS8 1SR
Tel: 0117 973 6109
Fax: 0117 974 1941
e-mail: recruitment@bgs.bristol.sch.uk
website: www.bristolgrammarschool.co.uk

Chairman of Governors: P Rilett, MBA, FCA

Headmaster: **Mr Peter R Huckle**, BA, MEd

Age Range. 4–11.
Number of Pupils. Boys 146, Girls 74 (all day children).
Fees per term (2011-2012). Juniors £2,456.75, Infants £2,417.75, Reception £1,997.75.

BGS Infants and Juniors is an independent co-educational day school. It was founded in 1900 and since 2010 has offered Infant as well as Junior provisions. The school occupies self-contained buildings on the same site as the Senior School, Bristol Grammar School (*see entry in HMC section*). Its own facilities include a Hall, Library, Music, Art, Science and technology rooms. Some facilities are shared with the Senior School, particularly the Sports Complex, Theatre and Dining Hall. The school now thrives on the happy and purposeful demands of approximately 220 girls and boys aged 4–11 years.

Entry into BGS Infants is by an informal assessment session. Entry for the Junior School is by test at seven or eight years old (and other age groups, subject to the availability of places) and thereafter to the Senior School at eleven by an examination in which the Junior School's record of success is outstanding. Peloquin bursaries are awarded annually and are means tested.

The school aims to provide a rich, broad and balanced curriculum while also maintaining a nurturing environment for children to flourish. BGS Infants and Juniors encourages all students to develop their own ideas, giving support so they gain skills and confidence, and offering challenges to stretch their thinking. Science and Music are taught by specialists to all pupils. Art and Drama are particularly encouraged and there are many clubs and activities including Craft, Cheerleading, Gardening, Fencing, Orchestra, Chess, many sports, outdoor pursuits and cookery. In addition all children in the Infant School take part in Forest School and have violin tuition.

A wide range of sports is offered to the pupils at the School's superb playing fields at Failand with its state-of-the-art sports pavilion. The impressive purpose-built sports hall on the main campus provides facilities for indoor and PE curriculum sport. Pastoral care is provided by the Form Tutors and Deputy Heads, supported by all teaching staff and the Headmaster. Form Tutors take a lead in ensuring that children are learning and progressing well. A prosperous House system produces many friendships between age groups, with peer aged buddies showing new pupils the ropes, making sure that things are running smoothly for them. This leads to a strong sense of family and community within the school owing much to the warm and trusting relationships between children with each other and with their teachers.

Charitable status. Bristol Grammar School is a Registered Charity, number 1104425. The object of the Charity is the provision and conduct in or near the City of Bristol of a day school for boys and girls.

Broadwater Manor School

Worthing, West Sussex BN14 8HU
Tel: 01903 201123
Fax: 01903 821777
e-mail: info@broadwatermanor.com
website: www.broadwatermanor.com

Headteacher: **Mrs E K Woodley**, BA Hons, CertEd

Head of Prep: Mr N Gunn, BA Hons, PGCE
Head of Nursery and Toddlers: Mrs C O'Rourke, BEd Hons & Mrs C Flower

Age Range. 2–13 Co-educational.
Number of Pupils. Day only: Prep 150, Pre-Prep 91, Nursery 63.

Girls occupy about 40% of the places throughout the school.

Fees per term (2011-2012). (inclusive) Prep (age 8–13) £2,800; Pre-Prep (age 4–8) £2,380; Nursery (age 2–4) £2,200 (full-time).

There are 19 full-time and 8 part-time teachers on the staff.

Pupils are prepared for entry to a variety of senior schools and scholarships are frequently gained. The school has a thriving musical tradition and a strong PE department. Soccer, Hockey, Netball, Tennis, Rounders and Athletics are all played. As well as computers in every classroom there is a well equipped Information Technology room. CDT is also a strong aspect of the school.

Brockhurst School

Hermitage, Newbury, Berkshire RG18 9UL
Tel: 01635 200293
Fax: 01635 200190
e-mail: info@brockmarl.org.uk
website: www.brockmarl.org.uk

Headmaster: **D J W Fleming**, MA Oxon, MSc

Age Range. 3 to 13.
Number of Boys. 154 Boys (including 74 Boarders).
Fees per term (2010-2011). Boarding £6,100, Day £4,330–£4,600. Pre-Prep School (Ridge House): £558–£2,750.

Established in 1884, Brockhurst is situated in 500 acres of its own grounds in countryside of outstanding beauty, but is only four miles from access to the M4. The school is located on the same site as Marlston House Girls' Preparatory School which occupies separate, listed buildings. Boys and Girls are educated separately, but the two schools join forces for drama, music and many hobbies. In this way, Brockhurst and Marlston House aim to combine the best features of the single-sex and co-educational systems: academic excellence and social mixing. The schools have built up a fine reputation for high standards of pastoral care given to each pupil within a caring, family establishment. (*See also entry for Marlston House School.*)

The Pre-Prep School, Ridge House, is a co-educational department for 75 children aged 3 to 6½.

Boys are prepared for entry to all Independent Senior Schools and there is an excellent scholarship record.

All boys play Soccer, Rugby, Hockey and Cricket and take part in Athletics, Cross Country and Swimming (25m indoor heated pool). Additional activities include Riding (own ponies), Fencing, Judo, Shooting (indoor rifle range) and Tennis (indoor court and three hard courts). Facilities for gymnastics and other sporting activities are provided in a purpose-built Sports Hall. The schools also have their own Château near Bordeaux where they practise their spoken French.

Music and art are important features of the curriculum and a good number of pupils have won scholarships to senior schools in recent years.

Where appropriate, pupils can be transported by members of staff to and from airports if parents are serving in the armed forces or otherwise working overseas.

Bromsgrove Preparatory School

Old Station Road, Bromsgrove, Worcs B60 2BU
Tel: 01527 579679
Fax: 01527 872618
e-mail: admissions@bromsgrove-school.co.uk
website: www.bromsgrove-school.co.uk

Chairman of Governors: S Towe, CBE

Headmaster: **Richard Evans**, BEd, Adv Dip Ed Man

Age Range. 7–13.
Number of Pupils. 474: 243 Day Boys, 174 Day Girls, 38 Boy Boarders, 19 Girl Boarders.
Fees per term (2011-2012). £3,050–£3,985 day, £6,085–£7,500 full boarding, £4,225–£5,370 weekly boarding. Forces Bursaries and, from 11+, scholarships are available.

Bromsgrove Preparatory School feeds the adjacent 900 strong Senior School. (*See Bromsgrove School entry in HMC section.*) The sites covering 100 acres offer exclusive and shared facilities, with over £23 million pounds having been invested in the last ten years. A new £2.5 million teaching block for Years 3, 4 and 5 was opened in 2005. More recent additions include a new science laboratory, refurbishment of the library, main hall and sports hall. Teachers working in both Senior and Preparatory Schools ensure continuity of ethos and expectation.

Academic, sporting and cultural facilities are extensive and outstanding.

Pupils are admitted at the age of 7+ with another substantial intake at 11+, but pupils including boarders are admitted throughout the age range up to 13. Admission to the school is by Entrance Test (English, Maths and VR) supported by a report from the current school. At the end of Year 6 pupils sit examinations which allow them to be guaranteed a place in Bromsgrove Senior School two years later. Pupils admitted at age 11 are also guaranteed entry to the Senior School.

The separate boys', girls' and mixed junior boarding houses are lively, homely environments where pupils are cared for by resident houseparents and a team of tutors. The school aims to make a boarder's first experience of life away from home enjoyable and absorbing. Prep School boarding is flourishing and plans are in place for a new boarding house.

Parents can choose either a five or six day week for their children. All academic lessons are timetabled from Monday to Friday with Saturdays offering an optional and flexible programme of activities and sports fixtures. The school has a national reputation in a number of sports.

The aim of the school is to provide a first-class education, which identifies and develops the potential of individual pupils, academically, culturally and socially. It prepares them to enter the Senior School with confidence.

In the Preparatory School there is a purposeful and lively atmosphere. Mutual trust, respect and friendship exist between staff and pupils. The high-quality and dedication of the teaching staff, favourable teacher/pupil ratio and regular monitoring of performance ensure that the natural spontaneity and inquisitiveness of this age group are directed purposefully. The pastoral care system, rated as 'outstanding' in the 2010 ISI Inspection, is rooted in the school's Christian heritage and firmly founded on the form tutor. It is designed to ensure that every pupil is recognised as an important individual and that their development is nurtured.

Charitable status. Bromsgrove Preparatory School is a Registered Charity, number 1098740. It exists to provide education for boys and girls.

Brontë House
The Junior School of Woodhouse Grove

Apperley Bridge, Bradford, West Yorkshire BD10 0PQ
Tel: 0113 250 2811
Fax: 0113 250 0666
e-mail: enquiries@brontehouse.co.uk
website: www.woodhousegrove.co.uk

Chairman of Governors: A Wintersgill, FCA

Headmaster: **S Dunn**, BEd

Age Range. 2½–11 Co-educational.
Number of Pupils. 327 Boys and Girls (including 8 boarders).
Fees per term (2011-2012). £6,300 (boarders), £5,775 (weekly boarders), £2,760–£3,100 (day). Ashdown Lodge: Nursery and Reception £2,300 (full day), £1,420 (half day), Years 1 & 2 £2,550.

These are graduated according to age. The day fee covers an extended day from 8 am to 6 pm; there are no extra charges for breakfast, tea and the majority of supervised activities after lessons.

The School is situated in its own grounds, a short distance from the Senior School, on the slopes of the Aire Valley at the edge of the urban area of Bradford and Leeds. The moors are within view and access to the Dales National Park and the international Leeds/Bradford Airport is swift.

The School is of Methodist foundation, but children of other denominations and faiths are willingly accepted. Morning assembly is run on broad ecumenical lines, and school services are held in the Chapel of Woodhouse Grove.

Normal entry is in September via the Entrance Tests held the previous January, but assessment and entry at other times in the year can be easily arranged if places are available. Academic, art and music scholarships may be awarded to children who display special merit, and the School offers bursaries. Entry to the Foundation and Key Stage 1 classes merely requires registration of the child. Part-time places are available in the Nursery. The Early Years Department offers holiday provision for all school holidays.

The work of all age groups is based on the National Curriculum; this is supplemented by a European Studies course in French, German and Spanish, plus a special emphasis on Music and Sport. Children automatically transfer to the senior school, Woodhouse Grove, and there is continuity of schooling from 3 to 18. Regular standardised testing takes place in all year groups, and the national Key Stage 1 and 2 Tests (for seven and eleven year olds) are taken. All staff, both full-time and visiting, are fully qualified. Individual tuition is encouraged in piano, string, wind and brass instruments and also in speech and drama, with the two choirs and orchestra participating regularly in assemblies and concerts. (Over 70% of the children learn to play an instrument). There is a Dyslexia Unit, run by specialist staff, for a maximum of 16 children of above average ability.

The curriculum includes compulsory physical education for all children. Those with ability and enthusiasm are coached in athletics, cricket, cross-country running, football, rugby, rounders, tennis and netball; there is a comprehensive fixture list with other schools in the area, and regular participation in local and regional tournaments. All children learn to swim; teaching and training takes place weekly in the full-size pool at Woodhouse Grove.

In addition to training sessions in sport, clubs and activities include art and craft, chess, computers, dance and model railway. Expeditions are made to the Dales and the Lake District, as are cultural outings into Bradford, Leeds and York. An annual ski trip takes place during the Easter holidays.

For a copy of the detailed prospectus, please apply to the Secretary.

Charitable status. Woodhouse Grove School is a Registered Charity, number 529205. It exists to provide education for children.

Brooke Priory School

Station Approach, Oakham, Rutland LE15 6QW
Tel: 01572 724778
Fax: 01572 724969
e-mail: info@brooke.rutland.sch.uk
website: www.brooke.rutland.sch.uk

Headmistress: **Mrs E S Bell**, BEd Hons

Age Range. 2.8 to 11 years (co-educational).
Number of Pupils. 230: 196 (age 4+ to 11); 34 (Nursery, age 2.8 to 4).
Fees per term (2010-2011). £2,250–£2,430.
Staff. There are 20 graduate and qualified members of the teaching staff.

Brooke Priory is a day Preparatory School for boys and girls. The school was founded in 1989 and moved into its own purpose-built building in February 1995. Since then it has doubled its classroom provision and established a fully-networked Computer Room, well-resourced Library and Drama Room.

Brooke Priory provides a stimulating, caring environment in which children are encouraged to attain their highest potential. Class sizes are optimally 16 in parallel forms and children are grouped according to ability in Mathematics and English.

The school delivers a broad and varied curriculum, where every child will participate in Art, Drama, French and Music. Over 50% of children in the Prep Department enjoy individual music lessons and are encouraged to join the Choir and Ensemble.

Brooke Priory enjoys a high success rate at Common Entrance and Senior Independent School Entry Examinations, with many children being awarded scholarships. With this solid foundation pupils move confidently on to their chosen senior schools.

Sport is an important part of the curriculum. Children swim weekly throughout the year and are coached in a wide variety of games by specialist staff. The main sports are Soccer, Rugby, Hockey, Netball, Cricket, Rounders and Athletics

The school offers a wide choice of extra-curricular activities.

Before and after school care is available.

Brooklands School

167 Eccleshall Road, Stafford ST16 1PD
Tel: 01785 251399

Fax: 01785 236987
e-mail: enquiries@brooklandsschool.com
website: www.brooklandsschool.com

Chairman of Council: Mr Robert Madders

Headteacher: **Mrs S Keenan**, BA Hons, MA

Age Range. 3 months–11 years.
Number of Pupils. 120.
Fees per term (2011-2012). Pre-School £2,050, Reception £2,410, Years 1–2 £2,710, Year 3 £2,800, Years 4–6 £3,050. Day Nursery according to sessions.

Brooklands is a thriving co-educational day prep school for 180 children aged 3 months to 11 years. Situated on the edge of the town it looks onto a delightful conservation area but is also only 1 mile from Junction 14 of the M6 affording excellent accessibility from within Stafford and the surrounding areas.

The philosophy of the school is to provide a secure, stimulating and structured environment where each child is encouraged to achieve as high an academic standard as possible whilst at the same time developing individual interests and talents in a wide range of areas. The children learn to live as happy and caring members of a school community, which values their personal contribution, and also the needs of others, all within a Christian framework.

A committed and enthusiastic staff of qualified teachers ensures that each child receives maximum individual attention in small class sizes.

Brooklands is well equipped with a Science Lab, Art and Design Centre, Music and Drama Suite, IT Suite and a brand new Early Years area with rooftop garden for outdoor education. The sports field enables us to provide an exciting mix of traditional boys and girls games throughout the year and all children from the age of 6 have the opportunity weekly to learn to swim at the Stafford Leisure Centre.

Our broad and dynamic curriculum gives each child the chance to flourish in many aspects of School life. Subjects taught are those required by the National Curriculum and for Entrance/Scholarship examinations to Senior Independent Schools. Opportunities to represent the School in sports teams, performing arts, choirs and instrumental groups are all part of the "Brooklands Experience".

The School recognises the importance of a child feeling happy, secure and motivated. The Form Tutor is of prime importance – overseeing the development of each child academically, socially and emotionally – but is supplemented with our 'House' system and care worker organisation. Close links with home provide even greater value to being part of the community as a whole. To help busy parents we provide early arrival care, including breakfast, from 8.00 am daily and a wide range of After School activities and child care are provided until 6.00 pm. The School and Day Nursery are open 49 weeks of the year with a dedicated Holiday Club running throughout the holiday periods.

Charitable status. Brooklands School is a Registered Charity, number 528616. It exists to provide quality education and care for boys and girls with bursarial help according to need.

Broomwood Hall

74 Nightingale Lane, London SW12 8NR
Tel: 020 8682 8800
Fax: 020 8675 0136
e-mail: broomwood@northwoodschools.com
website: www.broomwood.co.uk

Principal: Sir Malcolm & Lady Colquhoun

Head of Upper School: **Mrs C Jenkinson**

Age Range. Girls 4–13, Boys 4–8.

Number of Pupils. Lower School (4–8): 210 girls, 180 boys; Upper School (8–13): 210 girls.

Fees per term (2010-2011). £3,830 Lower School, £4,695 Upper School.

Broomwood Hall is an independent pre-prep and preparatory school for boys and girls from the ages of 4–8 (boys) and 4–13 (girls). Boys have an automatic right of entry at 8 to Northcote Lodge (day preparatory school on Wandsworth Common, in the same ownership as Broomwood Hall) subject to an interview with the Headmaster.

Broomwood Hall has expanded from 12 children to nearly 600 in five substantial Victorian Houses sprinkled round the south side of Clapham and Tooting Commons, but the school's approach and values have remained constant. Broomwood believes that a young child does not benefit from long drives across London (hence the catchment rule), that single-sex education works best after 8, and that the traditional virtues of self-discipline, a sense of responsibility and good manners are the core of a good education. The Upper School is unique in London in providing an education for girls specifically aiming for boarding at 13.

There are four separate sites: a pre-prep of 140 children at Garrad's Road SW16, another pre-prep of 250 – sub-divided into two neighbouring buildings – at 192 Ramsden Road and 50 Nightingale Lane, SW12. And finally, the Upper School – 210 girls aged 8–13 – based in the gracious Victorian mansion at 68–74 Nightingale Lane, SW12.

Teaching (in small groups) is strong throughout. Mixed-ability classes, but setting in maths and English. An extended day for the Upper School because homework is done at school. A variety of clubs – karate, mini-rugby, chess, pottery among many others – are on offer.

Art is particularly lively. Strong music, with two music lessons a week, a Chamber choir, wind ensemble and brass band. Lots of drama – everyone takes part in two productions a year. Netball, hockey, PE, football, touch rugby, athletics, cricket, rounders and tennis taught on site or nearby (five courts within walking distance), with inter-house competitions and external matches. Swimming at local baths, with swim squad once a week. Very good library. Sophisticated ICT, with state-of-the-art computers, interactive whiteboards, permanent high-speed internet connection and an email account for every child above class 2.

A Christian school with regular RE, morning assembly and church attendance once a week. Happy to welcome all faiths (special arrangements for Catholics to attend Mass and days of obligation), but all pupils must attend services. Pastoral care extremely well thought through at every level. From class 5 girls have a personal tutor (chosen by themselves), whom they meet weekly to discuss social and personal issues as well as work. The tutor liaises with parents, helps plan revision, sorts out friendships and writes reports. Social skills as important as academic ones and manners definitely a priority.

One compulsory, though much enjoyed, course is the weekly Leiths cookery lessons for girls in years 7 and 8. Lunches, prepared on site, are accompanied by the teachers for the younger children to ensure that table manners are observed and food is finished.

Entry requirements. Entry takes place in September following a child's fourth birthday. Admission is by personal interview with both parents and the child at the age of 3. Parents must live locally (Clapham/Battersea/Wandsworth/Tooting/Streatham).

Examinations offered. Boys' preparatory schools, girls' Common Entrance and Scholarship examinations at 11+ and 13+ (12+ where applicable) and London day schools' examinations. Pupils may also take Associated Board examinations (music).

Broughton Manor Preparatory School

Newport Road, Broughton, Milton Keynes MK10 9AA
Tel: 01908 665234
Fax: 01908 692501
e-mail: info@bmprep.co.uk
website: www.bmprep.co.uk

Chairman of the Governors: Mr Peter Squire, MA

Headmaster: **Mr Ross Urquhart**, BSc Hons, QTS

Age Range. 2 months – 11 years Co-educational.

Number of Pupils. 250.

Fees per term (2010-2011). Nursery (per week): £210 (babies under 1 year), £220 (1–2½ years). Pre-Preparatory: £3,100 (2½–5 years), £3,160 (6–7 years). Preparatory £3,380 (8–11 years).

Broughton Manor Preparatory School is purpose built with facilities which include a Science laboratory, ICT suite and a multi-purpose sports hall. Facilities at the Farm include a fitness room, weather station, outdoor classroom and a large pond to extend our environmental studies.

Opening hours are 7.30 am – 6.30 pm for 46 weeks per year which enable children of working parents to join play-schemes in school holidays and to be cared for outside normal daily school hours.

Staff are highly qualified and committed. Academic standards are excellent, with pupils being prepared for entry to senior independent schools locally and nationally and to grammar schools. Teaching is structured to take into account the requirements of the National Curriculum, with constant evaluation and assessment for each pupil.

Music and sport play an important part in life of the school. Concerts are held, and a wide variety of sports is played, with teams competing regularly against other schools.

The school aims to incorporate the best of modern teaching methods and traditional values in a friendly and busy environment where good work habits and a concern for the needs of others are paramount.

Bruern Abbey School

Chesterton House, Chesterton, Oxfordshire OX26 1UY
Tel: 01869 242448
Fax: 01869 243949
e-mail: headmaster@bruernabbey.org
website: www.bruernabbey.org

Chair of Governors: Mrs Sarah Austen, BA Hons

Headmaster: **Mr J Floyd**, MA, PGCE

Age Range. Boys 7–13.

Number of Pupils. 60.

Fees per term (2010-2011). Day £5,279, Boarding £6,411, Flexi Boarding £32 per night.

Bruern Abbey is situated in twenty acres of Oxfordshire countryside, ten miles north-west of Oxford and within easy commuting distance of London, from where a bus brings boys to school on Mondays – and takes them back on Fridays.

The School's raison d'être is to prepare boys who have dyslexia, or some other form of learning difficulty, or who, for whatever reasons, may not be flourishing at their present schools, for Common Entrance to the major English and Scottish independent senior schools. Bruern boys graduate to a range of independent schools, which have included in recent years, Winchester College, Tonbridge, Stowe, Harrow, Canford, Rugby, Gordonstoun, Shiplake, Milton Abbey and Uppingham.

Its purpose is to provide quality education in safe and pleasant surroundings, to ensure that the work of every child is recognised and appreciated, and to build confidence, in the firm belief that confidence is the key to academic success.

Bruern believes that it has found the right balance between the traditional and the progressive. All boys are permitted, and indeed, positively encouraged, to use a laptop, and for those who have difficulty in expressing themselves as swiftly or as coherently on paper as they do in speech, this proves a huge advantage. There is a focus on literacy and numerical work, with ten periods of English and Mathematics each week, but with little or no withdrawal, and small groups of rarely more than four or five boys taught by specialists in the field of dyslexia, dyspraxia and dyscalculia. Alongside the traditional, with boys climbing trees and building dens in the twenty acres of woodland, and sport every afternoon, are several examples of the cutting edge of education, the use of ICT across the range of the curriculum being just one.

The boarding accommodation and the care shown by staff are of the highest standard. This is reflected in the growing number of boarders. The School is steadfast in the teaching of traditional values, dear to all, and places an emphasis on good manners and self-discipline, and encourages boys to share their aspirations and their anxieties.

The Buchan School

Castletown, Isle of Man IM9 1RD
Tel: 01624 820481
Fax: 01624 820403
e-mail: secretary@buchan.sch.im
website: www.buchan.sch.im

Chairman of the Governors: N H Wood, ACA, TEP

Headteacher: **Mrs A Hope Hedley**, BEd Hons, NPQH

Age Range. 2–11.
Number of Pupils. 208 (113 boys, 95 girls).
Fees per term (2011-2012). Day £2,746–£3,582 according to age.

After more than a century of independence, mainly as a Girls' School, The Buchan School amalgamated, in 1991, with King William's College to form a single continuous provision of Independent Education on the Isle of Man.

As the Preparatory School to King William's College (*see entry in HMC section*), The Buchan School provides an education of all-round quality for boys and girls until the age of 11 when most pupils proceed naturally to the Senior School although the curriculum meets the needs of Common Entrance, Scholarship and Entrance Examinations to other Independent Senior Schools.

The school buildings are clustered round Westhill House, the centre of the original estate, in fourteen acres of partly wooded grounds. The whole environment, close to the attractive harbour of Castletown, is ideally suited to the needs of younger children. They are able to work and play safely and develop their potential in every direction.

Classes are small throughout, providing considerable individual attention. A well-equipped Nursery provides Pre-School education for up to 65 children. At the age of 5, boys and girls are accepted into the Pre-Preparatory Department. They work largely in their own building in bright, modern classrooms and also make use of the specialist Preparatory School facilities where they proceed three years later.

The School is particularly well-equipped with ICT facilities extending down to the Pre-Prep Department. There is a

Pavilion with fields marked out for a variety of team games and a multi-purpose area which is used for Netball, Tennis and Hockey.

There is emphasis on traditional standards in and out of the classroom, with an enterprising range of activities outside normal lessons. Music is strong – both choral and instrumental – and there is energetic involvement in Art, Drama, Sport.

The school strives for high academic standards, aiming to ensure that all pupils enjoy the benefits of a rounded education, giving children every opportunity to develop their individual talents from an early age.

Entry is usually by Interview and School report and the children may join The Buchan School at any time, providing there is space. The School is a happy, friendly community where new pupils integrate quickly socially and academically.

Charitable status. King William's College is a Registered Charity, number 615. It exists for the provision of high quality education for boys and girls.

Buckingham College Preparatory School

458 Rayners Lane, Pinner, Middlesex HA5 5DT
Tel: 020 8866 2737
Fax: 020 8868 3228
e-mail: office@buckprep.org
website: www.buckprep.org

Chairman of Governors: Mr Robert Brock

Headmaster: **Mr Laurence Smith**, BA Hons, MSc, LCP, PGDE, CertEd

Age Range. Boys 4–11.
Number of Pupils. 114.
Fees per term (2010-2011). £2,330–£3,050.

Buckingham College Preparatory School (BCPS) is a small 'family school' which offers its pupils a very high level of pastoral care. Indeed, an ISI Inspection found that: *"The overall provision for the pupils' spiritual, moral, social and cultural development is very good and is a strength of the school."*

With a maximum class size of 20 throughout the school, individual attention is thus assured.

The School also believes in forging a strong Parent/Teacher partnership so that parents feel as if they have a vital role to play in the education of their child. A thriving Parent/Teacher Association also organises as many as four major fundraising events during the academic year.

BCPS produces excellent academic results year in, year out, due to the expertise and professionalism of its dedicated and highly qualified teaching staff. Indeed, in 2010/2011 our Year 6 class of 17 pupils managed to gain no less than 51 offers to major Independent and Grammar schools. Moreover, in the past 11 years, the School has always managed to place every member of Year 6 in at least one of the prestigious Senior Independent Schools in the area – a remarkable achievement.

BCPS also prides itself in its results in other areas of the curriculum, namely Sport, Music and Drama.

Such is the enthusiasm for sport in the school that the PE/Games Department organises Inter-School competitions in Swimming and Cross-Country; we currently hold these two shields, as well as the Inter-School Football trophy. The School also competes in sports such as football, rugby, hockey and cricket at Under 9 and/or Under 11 levels. With a Judo squad of over 40 and a very comprehensive after-school programme of 16 sports and recreational pursuits, pupils at BCPS have every opportunity of developing their individual and social skills.

Music also plays a very important part in the life of the school with approximately 65% of pupils playing an orchestral instrument, some as young as 5. With an orchestra currently 35 strong and 7 peripatetic staff on call, it is not surprising that pupils frequently achieve examination results as high as Grade 6. Music scholarships are now a regular occurrence.

Drama holds a high profile at BCPS too, as the School presents four major productions in the academic year. The Expressive Arts Week, when pupils have the opportunity of participating in approximately 14 categories of events, is also a focal point of the academic year. Once again, Drama scholarships feature highly.

Charitable status. The E Ivor Hughes Educational Foundation is a Registered Charity, number 293623.

Burgess Hill School for Girls – Junior School

Keymer Road, Burgess Hill, West Sussex RH15 0EG
Tel: 01444 233167
Fax: 01444 243538
e-mail: registrar@burgesshill-school.com
website: www.burgesshill-school.com

Chairman of Governors: Mr C Bedwin, FCA

Head of Junior School: **Mrs H Miller**, BA

Age Range. Girls 2½–11.
Number of Pupils. 196.
Fees per term (2011-2012). £2,155–£3,780.

Burgess Hill School for Girls is a flourishing day and boarding school for girls between 2½ and 18 years. We welcome boys into our Nursery. The School is small enough that your child is known as an individual yet large enough to offer breadth, choice and opportunity. Pupils, teachers and parents work in partnership to make the most of the educational opportunities available.

Music, Sport, Art and Drama are all given high priority. There is an exciting programme of extra-curricular activities including Philosophy Club, Football, Water Sports and many more.

"The highly effective teaching and the excellence of the whole educational experience inspire a love of learning and exceptional motivation to achieve the highest possible standards in academic work, sport, drama and music."

Children learn from all that they experience and our Nursery provides an ideal environment in which youngsters can flourish and develop socially, emotionally and physically.

"The EYFS provision at Burgess Hill School is outstanding. The varied and rich curriculum enables children to enjoy their learning and achieve well."

When you visit our Junior School you will enter a warm and vibrant environment which buzzes with the sound of happy, enthusiastic and motivated young learners. The sense of community, the atmosphere in our School and the relationship between staff and pupils are invariably commented on by visiting parents. Small classes ensure that the teachers quickly get to know the girls and can focus on nurturing their individual talents, confidence and self-esteem.

"The quality of relations between staff and pupils is excellent. Respect and courtesy are evident and so is humour; relations are clearly warm and relaxed and there is an air of happiness and purpose."

All this is achieved in a friendly and focused environment. Our girls work hard, play hard and support each other in doing so. It is the norm to approach work with diligence

and commitment – excellent attributes for a successful future.

All this is achieved in a friendly and focused environment.

"The rich and stimulating educational experience, the high standard of the environment, the plentiful resources, the outstanding quality of display and the dedicated teaching, the excellent understanding of individual needs, all combine to encourage girls to develop their abilities and talents to the full."

All quotes taken from our ISI Inspection Report, March 2009.

Charitable status. Burgess Hill School for Girls is a Registered Charity, number 307001.

Butcombe
Clifton College Pre-Preparatory School

Guthrie Road, Clifton, Bristol BS8 3EZ
Tel: 0117 3157 591
Fax: 0117 3157 592
e-mail: apurnell@clifton-college.avon.sch.uk
website: www.cliftoncollegeuk.com

Chairman of College Council: T S Ross, MA

Headmistress: **Wendy E Bowring**, BEd HODS, ADB Ed, MEd, PhD

Age Range. 3–8.
Number of Pupils. 250 (150 day boys and 100 day girls).
Fees per term (2011-2012). £1,550–£3,420.

Butcombe is one of three schools that form Clifton College, independent in terms of running and organisation. However, it benefits from being governed by the same Council as the Preparatory School and Upper School, and enjoys the considerable advantages of sharing many of the College's extensive facilities. These include swimming pool, sports hall, gymnasium, multi-activity hall, Chapel and Theatre. The school is situated in two buildings either side of a superb playground with a variety of play equipment.

The school caters for children in the Foundation Stage (Nursery and Reception), Key Stage 1 (Y1 and 2) and Year 3, the first year of Key Stage 2. The nursery has up to 50 children on roll, with a staff-pupil ratio of 1-8. Attendance in the nursery may be either five mornings, three days or full-time. Morning sessions include lunch at no extra cost. Butcombe is a member of the Bristol Early Years Partnership and accepts the government's nursery grant for the majority of 3 and 4 year olds. The nursery staff are either qualified teachers or nursery nurses.

There are three classes of 16 children in Reception, each with a class teacher and teaching assistant, three classes in each of Year 1 and Year 2, and four classes in Year 3, where there is always a big intake. In all there are 20 full-time and 12 part-time staff. Qualified specialist class teachers deliver a topic-based curriculum, with specialist teachers for music, dance (ballet, jazz dance, tap), sports, French and IT. Piano and instrumental lessons are available from Year 2, and all children in Years 2 and 3 learn the recorder and sing in the choir. Some sports activity takes place every day.

Life at Butcombe is busy and challenging. Year 2 and 3 pupils may take part in a range of co-curricular activities at lunchtimes or after school, when around sixteen clubs and societies are held. These change termly, and may include a variety of sports, sewing, puppet-making, junior detectives, zoo club, chess etc. Termly services and concerts are held in the Chapel, and an annual musical is performed in the Redgrave Theatre. There is a full programme of visits and outings for all ages, including a youth hostelling trip for Year 3.

New investment sees the creation of an outdoor area leading from the reception classrooms. This is designed to give reception classes easy access to an outdoor space which they can use to extend and enhance their learning.

Another new provision is the creation of a Forest School at our Beggar Bush sports ground. All year groups at Butcombe from Nursery to Year 3 visit the school, and it provides a range of exciting outdoor experiences for the children, enabling them to learn, achieve and develop confidence through curriculum-linked activities and free exploration of the natural woodland.

Charitable status. Clifton College is a Registered Charity, number 311735. It provides boarding and day education for boys and girls aged 3–18.

Bute House Preparatory School for Girls

Bute House, Luxemburg Gardens, Hammersmith, London W6 7EA
Tel: 020 7603 7381
Fax: 020 7371 3446
e-mail: mail@butehouse.co.uk
website: www.butehouse.co.uk

Chairman of Governors: Mr S Wathen

Headmistress: Mrs S C Salvidant, BEd Hons London

Age Range. 4–11.
Number of Pupils. 314 Day Girls.
Fees per term (2011-2012). £3,970 inclusive of lunches.
Bute House overlooks extensive playing fields and is housed in a large bright modern building. Facilities include a science laboratory, art room, technology room, music hall, 2 drama studios, multi-purpose hall and a large well-stocked library. A well-qualified, enthusiastic and experienced staff teach a broad curriculum which emphasises both the academic and the aesthetic. Information Technology is an integral part of the curriculum and the school has a wireless network. The classrooms are all equipped with multimedia machines. Laptops are also widely used for individual or class work. Monitored access to the internet is available. French is taught from Reception, Spanish from Year 4 and Latin from Year 5.

Sports include swimming, gymnastics, dance, tennis, lacrosse, netball and athletics which are taught on excellent on-site facilities. Full use is made of all that London has to offer and residential trips further afield are also offered to older girls.

Girls are encouraged to take full part in the school life from an early age. There is a democratically elected School Council and regular school meetings run by the girls when all pupils are able to put forward their views as well as to volunteer for duties around the school. A wide variety of extra-curricular activities is available.

The school aims at academic excellence in a non competitive, happy environment where girls are encouraged to be confident, articulate and independent and where courtesy and consideration are expected. There is a flourishing Parents Association. Entry is by ballot at age 4 and by assessment at age 7.

Caldicott

Crown Lane, Farnham Royal, Bucks SL2 3SL
Tel: 01753 649300
Fax: 01753 649325

e-mail: office@caldicott.com
website: www.caldicott.com

Chairman of the Board of Governors: G Puttergill

Headmaster: **Simon Doggart**, BA

Age Range. 7–13.
Number of Boys. 130 Boarders and 120 Day Boys
Fees per term (2010-2011). Boarders £6,409, Day Boys: Middle School £4,716, Junior School £4,360.
Caldicott, founded in 1904, is an Educational Trust. The School is situated in 40 acres of grounds and playing fields adjacent to more than a thousand acres of permanent woodland. It is conveniently placed close to London between the M40 and the M4 and within 20 minutes of Heathrow Airport.

The school is forward-looking in its approach and the development of the buildings and playing fields is seen as a continuous process. The facilities are, therefore, modern, spacious, well-designed, well-maintained, and conveniently situated in and around the main building. They include a well equipped Technology Department and Computer Room, Music School, and an extensive Sports and Recreation centre which includes a Sports Hall and Squash Courts.

In September 2004 the Centenary Hall was finished giving the school excellent drama and concert facilities. In April 2008 the new Science Block was opened.

There is a high proportion of qualified teaching staff to boys. Classes are therefore kept as small as possible and each boy is able to receive individual help and attention. Our teaching methods combine what we believe to be the best in modern ideas with the more traditional ways we know to be indispensable. Throughout the school we insist on a high standard of work, and we offer all subjects necessary for the Common Entrance and Scholarship examinations to the Independent Senior Schools.

The school has a Christian ethos. The day begins with a short Chapel Service on most weekdays, and on Sundays parents are welcome to join in the Services.

All day boys are expected to board from the age of 11 for their last two years in preparation for boarding at their Senior Schools.

Much emphasis is placed on creative activities such as Music, Art, Design, Modelling, Photography and Drama, and through the tutorial system every boy is encouraged to use his leisure time sensibly.

The principal games are Rugby, Cricket, Football and Hockey. Other sporting activities include Squash, Swimming, Athletics, Tennis, Cross-country, Basketball and Gymnastics.

The prospectus is available on application to the Headmaster, who is always pleased to meet parents, discuss with them their sons' particular needs, and arrange for them to look around the school.

Charitable status. Caldicott is a Registered Charity, number 310631. Its purpose is to provide education for the young.

Cameron House

4 The Vale, London SW3 6AH
Tel: 020 7352 4040
Fax: 020 7352 2349
e-mail: info@cameronhouseschool.org
website: www.cameronhouseschool.org

Founded in 1980.

Principal: **Miss Josie Cameron Ashcroft**, BSc, DipEd

Headmistress: **Mrs Lucie Moore**, BEd Hons

Age Range. 4–11 Co-educational.
Number of Pupils. 120.
Fees per term (2010-2011). £4,595.

Based in a beautifully designed Edwardian building, just steps from London King's Road, Cameron House School prides itself on sending pupils to some of the most sought-after schools in the country.

At 11, boys go on to Colet Court, Latymer, Westminster Under and other day schools, and girls leave for St Paul's, Godolphin and City of London, as well as a number of other leading day and boarding schools.

The school is designed to be completely child-centred, modern and warm, creating the right atmosphere for learning. Yet it is not a hot house: its programme is designed to develop each child's personality and to stretch his or her individual talents. A high teacher/pupil ratio is essential to Cameron House's success. Excellent provision is made for children of exceptionally high IQ, or unusual ability, eg a Native French Speakers' Club, and Artists' Group.

The aim is to instil a firm sense of self, a passion for exploration and a freedom to express creativity, balanced by good manners, kindness and a selfless interest in others.

One of the first tasks is to foster a joy of reading, which Cameron House believes is the best foundation in each class. All pupils can access the school's own intranet, interactive whiteboards and the extensive computer suite.

From their earliest years, music, art and sport form an integral part of the children's school life and excellent local facilities allow the pupils to engage in a wide variety of sports. Unusually, a large majority of children learn karate, which builds physical confidence. Verbal communication skills are also developed, leading to English Speaking Board Examinations or Guildhall Examinations. Other popular clubs include Lunchtime Latin, Touch Typing, Tennis, Chess, Ballet, Tap and Fencing.

Three active choirs, as well as singing and percussion classes, composition and musical appreciation classes, and individual instrument lessons, lead to grade examinations of the Association Board of the Royal Schools of Music.

There is a genuinely open dialogue between parents and teachers, also fostered by The Friends of Cameron House. This contributes to the welcoming feel of the school. The Head of Cameron House is always delighted to give parents a tour of the school so that they can experience its special qualities for themselves.

Cargilfield

Barnton Avenue West, Edinburgh EH4 6HU
Tel: 0131 336 2207
Fax: 0131 336 3179
e-mail: admin@cargilfield.com
website: www.cargilfield.com

Chairman of the Board of Governors: Mrs Pamela Gray MA, Dip LE, FRICS

Headmaster: **Mr John Elder**, MA Hons Edinburgh, PGCE

Assistant Headmaster: Mr David Walker, BA Hons

Age Range. 3–13.
Number of Children. 315.
Fees per term (2011-2012). Boarding: £5,620 (full), £5,410 (weekly). Day Pupils: £4,050–£4,370, Pre-Prep £2,750, Nursery £2,750.

The School is ideally situated in spacious grounds five miles from the centre of Edinburgh, just off the A90 and close to Edinburgh Airport. The staff consists of 29 teach-ers, both full-time and part-time, a senior matron and one assistant matron. Pupils, who are taught in small groups (between 12 and 16), are prepared for all independent secondary schools: the majority of leavers move on to the major Scottish boarding and day schools, in particular Fettes, Merchiston, Loretto and Glenalmond, but a number go south of the border and, in recent years, children have gone to Ampleforth, Downe House, Eton, Harrow, Oundle, Radley, Rugby and Uppingham. Suitable candidates are encouraged to enter for Scholarships, and 84 awards have been gained in the last seven years, with a very strong showing in Classics (including Greek), Maths, English and Music. Recent Scholarship awards include Ampleforth (4), Eton (2), Fettes (16), Merchiston (5), Glenalmond (13), Oundle (3), Sedbergh (2), Shrewsbury (1) and Gordonstoun (1).

Rugby, Netball, Hockey, Cricket, Rounders, Tennis and Athletics make up the main part of the Games Programme and a wide variety of activities are organised, for example Skiing, mainly on the Hillend Dry Ski Slope, Riding, Sailing, Squash, Fencing, Judo, Archery, Swimming, Golf, Gymnastics, Climbing, Cookery and Chess. There is a very active Music Department: a thriving Pipe Band; Wind, Strings, Guitar, Flute groups and an Orchestra meets each week. There is both a Chapel Choir and a Junior Choir. The School is at the forefront of ICT with three suites serving both the Upper School and Pre-Prep. Other facilities include a lovely War Memorial Chapel, Theatre, new Science Department, two new classroom blocks, Music School, Girls' Boarding House, Art Studio, Design Workshop, and a superb multi-purpose Sports Hall; there are excellent playing fields and a floodlit Astroturf.

Our £2.5 million Pre-Prep and Nursery for boys and girls between the ages of three and eight feeds in directly to the Upper School. In the Upper School there are 60 boarders, but day children may board on a flexi-boarding system and all play a full part in the life of the School.

The pastoral system is centred on the Division Leader, Form Teacher and Tutor and we teach them about courtesy, appreciation of values (spiritual and social); we try to develop any talent and develop it to the full; we teach them about kindness, humour and honour.

Well-equipped games rooms offering snooker, table tennis, bar football and a host of board games and cosy and friendly bedrooms create a very strong family atmosphere. The staff have great fun here, the challenge of youth is ever present and although we have plenty of new buildings and equipment – the latest £5 million development was completed in 2009 – a boarding and day preparatory school is much more: to learn to help others, to enjoy ourselves; these are top priorities.

Fee concessions are offered for third and fourth siblings and also for children of members of the Armed Forces. Scholarships are awarded each year for Academic work, Drama, Art, Music and Sport. Means-tested Bursary support is available to all.

Charitable status. Cargilfield School is a Registered Charity, number SC005757. It is under a Board of Governors and is run on a non-profit-making basis; it exists solely to provide a first-class education for boys and girls.

Carrdus School

Overthorpe Hall, Nr Banbury, Oxon OX17 2BS
Tel: 01295 263733
Fax: 01295 263733
e-mail: office@carrdusschool.co.uk
website: www.carrdusschool.co.uk

Headmistress: **Miss S T Carrdus**, BA

Age Range. Boys 3–8, Girls 3–11, Nursery Class for children 3–4½.

Number of Day Pupils. 146 (126 girls, 20 boys)

Fees per term (from April 2011). £570–£2,985. Compulsory extras: Insurance £3.70; PTA membership £5.

Carrdus School is a day school for girls and a pre-preparatory school for boys. The large house stands in 11 acres of beautiful grounds.

The teaching staff consists of nine full-time qualified teachers and fifteen part-time specialists. Boys are given a good grounding for their preparatory schools and 7+ or 8+ entry exams. Girls take 11+ Common Entrance and all other 11 year old transitional tests. The school has an excellent record of success in examinations, regularly sending girls to many well-known independent senior schools. We also take National Curriculum KS1 and KS2 tests.

There is a heated outdoor swimming pool, two tennis courts and a purpose-built Sports Hall. Sport, music, drama and art are highly valued in our curriculum.

The aim of the school is to produce confident, well-disciplined and happy children, who have the satisfaction of reaching their own highest academic and personal standards. This is possible for an organisation run by teachers for children, flexible enough to achieve a balance between new methods of teaching and sound traditional disciplines.

Charitable status. Carrdus School is a Registered Charity, number 1140263.

Castle Court Preparatory School

The Knoll House, Knoll Lane, Corfe Mullen, Wimborne, Dorset BH21 3RF
Tel: 01202 694438
Fax: 01202 659063
e-mail: office@castlecourt.com
website: www.castlecourt.com

Chairman of the Governors: Michael J Cuthbertson, MA

Headmaster: Richard D P Stevenson, BA Hons, PGCE

Deputy Headmaster: Jeremy J Hett, BA

Age Range. 2½–13.

Number of Pupils. 266 (167 boys, 99 girls) including Pre-Prep, Reception and Badgers (Nursery).

Teaching Staff. 22 full time, 20 part time.

Fees per term (2010-2011). £2,375 (Reception to Year 2), £4,315 (Years 3 to 8). Nursery fees on application.

Castle Court is a day prep school for boys and girls aged 2½ to 13, situated in 35 acres of beautiful grounds and woodlands within easy reach of Bournemouth, Poole, Blandford, Dorchester and the Isle of Purbeck. A gracious Regency house forms the heart of the school and contains the reception rooms, dining rooms, offices and some of the junior classrooms, as well as the formal rooms used for entertaining parents and visiting school teams. The Badgers, Reception and Pre-Prep departments (for 2½ to 7 year olds) are all self-contained and, like the senior classrooms, are all purpose-built. There is a spacious hall for school plays, concerts, drama and gymnastics as well as school assemblies. There is a music department which includes classrooms and practice rooms, adjacent to the hall. A more recent extension has provided a light and attractive school library. A science and art complex provides laboratories, art studios, design and technology room and the central IT centre (although all classrooms are networked and the junior part of the school has their own banks of computers). Other new buildings include poolside sports changing rooms, an academic block with four classrooms, and office space, as well as smaller quieter rooms where individual learning support can be provided. There is an outdoor heated swimming pool and exten-

sive playing fields to include an all-weather synthetic hockey pitch, which is also used for tennis in the summer, as well as cricket practice.

To take full advantage of the fabulous site the school is also aiming to become an accredited Forest School, to ensure that the outdoor space is used fully in all the children's learning. This training will be completed by the beginning of 2011, although the teaching programme has already started across all areas of the school.

While Castle Court is a day school, from the age of seven children are able to stay on for tea and prep or explore various activities before going home at 5.45 pm. This is totally voluntary. Activities vary from term to term but include athletics, lego robotics, swimming, drama, dance, cookery, cross-country, chess, orchestra, band, choir, squash, rugby and reasoning. There is also a breakfast club, which is open from 7.45 am each day for children from Reception upwards.

The normal curriculum includes English, mathematics, science, French, Latin, history, geography, religious studies, information technology, design and technology, art, music, and sport, with speech and drama for some years. All the children are prepared for the Common Entrance or Scholarship exams to senior independent schools, as well as for entry to local grammar schools. The school has a strong musical tradition with its own Orchestra, Band, Choir and various ensembles. Sport also forms an important part in the life of the children with rugby, soccer, hockey and cricket for the boys, and netball, rounders and hockey for the girls, with athletics, cross-country, gymnastics, dance, swimming and tennis for all. There are opportunities for sailing instruction, riding and golf. Trips include visits to local places of interest, camping weekends, and expeditions to the continent.

Our goal at Castle Court is to provide an outstanding day education based upon strong Christian values, and ensure that all the children here do the best they can and find their natural talents.

A prospectus (with details of the school bus service if required) will be sent on application to the Admissions Secretary; further information may be found on our school website.

Charitable status. Castle Court School Educational Trust Limited is a Registered Charity, number 325028. It aims to provide a first class education for local children.

Caterham Preparatory School

Mottrams, Harestone Valley Road, Caterham, Surrey CR3 6YB
Tel: 01883 342097
Fax: 01883 341230
e-mail: prep-enquiries@caterhamschool.co.uk
website: www.caterhamschool.co.uk

Chairman of Governors: J W Bloomer

Head Teacher: H W G Tuckett, MA

Age Range. 3–11 years.

Number of Pupils. 276: 155 Boys, 121 Girls.

Fees per term (2011-2012). Pre-Preparatory £1,503–£2,522, Preparatory £3,219–£3,868. Lunch £180.

The School stands in 80 acres of grounds in the green belt on the slopes of the North Downs, approximately 1 mile outside Caterham.

In 1994 the School became co-educational and the Nursery and Pre-Prep Department provides excellent facilities for younger children joining the School.

The curriculum offers the normal range of subjects including Technology and Science in well equipped laboratories. In addition, French is taught from age 4. There is a full PE programme including Soccer, Netball, Cricket,

Rounders, Athletics, Tennis, Swimming and Gymnastics. Regular use is made of the new sports hall, astroturf and 25m indoor swimming pool.

Over 30 clubs and extra-curricular activities take place each week including Computer Club, Sailing, Drama, Short Tennis, Judo, Needlework, Choir, Orchestra and facilities for instrumental tuition.

All classrooms are equipped with their own multimedia computers and are fully networked with screened internet access. There is also a separate ICTSuite with 20 computers.

The Preparatory School enjoys close liaison with Caterham School, to which pupils normally proceed at age 11. In 1995 Caterham School became fully co-educational and a member of The United Church Schools Trust. This heralded an exciting series of developments providing the facilities for all pupils to continue achieving the high standards for which the School is well known.

Charitable status. Caterham School is an Associate School of the United Church Schools Trust and is a Registered Charity, number 1050847.

The Cathedral School Llandaff
A Woodard School

Llandaff, Cardiff CF5 2YH
Tel: 029 2056 3179
Fax: 029 2056 7752
e-mail: registrar@cathedral-school.co.uk
website: www.cathedral-school.co.uk

Chairman of the Council: Mr P S Davey

Headmaster: **S W Morris**, BA, MEd, PGCE

Age Range. 3–16 Co-educational, with plans to expand to Sixth Form.

Number of Pupils. 641 (426 Boys and 215 Girls), including 40 in Nursery, 123 in Infant Department.

Fees per term (2010-2011). Years 7 & above £3,290, Years 5 & 6 £3,055, Years 3 & 4 £2,690, Reception, Years 1 & 2 £2,280, Nursery £1,890.

A number of means-tested bursaries are available for children entering Year 7.

The Cathedral School Llandaff, with a 130 year tradition of academic excellence, is one of the leading independent schools in Wales, offering an outstanding and broad education to boys and girls throughout the age range.

During the last fifteen years the School has grown from a small preparatory school of 280 pupils to one of the leading co-educational establishments in Wales with 641 pupils.

This year the School is spending over £1 million on the development of its new Sports Pavilion, which opened in October 2010. This and previous investments continue to provide outstanding facililties, which benefit every pupil and greatly enhance the environment available to each child. The School's facilities include four science laboratories, five computer laboratories and a Design Technology department in the old boarding house, a fine purpose-built Music Department including a recording studio and practice rooms, a specially designed Drama centre for workshops and performances, a Sports Hall, on-site games fields and an impressive Nursery building with appropriate areas for work and play activities. The School will also open its new Art Studio this academic year. After-school activities happen daily and there is after-school care available until 6.00 pm. A beautifully restored school chapel is used daily for prayer, worship and contemplation.

Pupils at The Cathedral School Llandaff achieve outstanding GCSE results with the majority, if not all, of our students achieving 100% five or more A* to C grades.

In addition to the high academic standards, the School is well-known for its astonishing wide range of extra-curricular activities. Music (10 choirs and over 20 instrumental ensembles) is exceptionally strong and the School also provides choristers (boys and girls in two choirs) for Llandaff Cathedral. In Sport there are extensive opportunities for pupils both in terms of the traditional games (where competing teams have an outstanding record of success) and with regard to such activities as Rowing, Judo and Rock-climbing. In addition, pupils can opt for such diverse activities as Drama, Dance, Archaeology Club, Yoga, Chess, Outward Bound, Judo and Cookery.

The only way, however, to experience the true atmosphere of the School is to meet the pupils and staff and to see us in action. Visitors are warmly welcome either for an Open Day or on a normal working day.

Charitable status. The Cathedral School Llandaff Limited is a Registered Charity, number 1103522. It exists to provide a high standard of education for girls and boys with a caring Christian ethos.

The Cavendish School

31 Inverness Street, London NW1 7HB
Tel: 020 7485 1958
Fax: 020 7267 0098
e-mail: admissions@cavendish-school.co.uk
website: www.cavendishschool.co.uk

Chairman of Governors: Mrs M Robey

Head: **Mrs Teresa Dunbar**, BSc Hons, PGCE, NPQH

Age Range. 3–11.
Number of Children. 200 Day Pupils.
Fees per term (2011-2012). Reception–Year 6: £3,850; Nursery £1,915–£3,650 depending upon number of sessions. Fees include lunch and outings.

The Cavendish School is a small, friendly IAPS school for girls aged three to eleven and sibling boys aged three to seven. The school is situated near Regent's Park but still in the heart of Camden Town with its excellent public transport links. The Cavendish has a Christian ethos and welcomes pupils of all faiths.

Strong yet informal links between home and school are maintained and we pride ourselves on the high level of pastoral care and attention to each child's individual needs.

The school is non-selective at entry. We provide manageable class sizes and high teacher-pupil ratios so that the foundations of a good education and effective study habits are laid from the beginning.

Through a broad and balanced curriculum we provide personalised learning and much specialised teaching which allows our pupils to flourish and many gain entry and scholarships to top senior schools at 11+.

There is an extensive programme of extra-curricular activities, after-school care services and flexible arrangements for nursery-age pupils.

Our strengths in music, drama and art are reflected in the renewal of our Artsmark Gold in 2009 by Arts Council England. Class music is taught by specialists, instruction is available in a wide variety of instruments and we have a thriving orchestra and choirs.

The school is housed in well maintained Victorian buildings and a modern wing with purpose-built ICT facilities.

The school maintains close links with the local community in a variety of ways both charitable and educational.

Our most recent inspection report by the Independent Schools Inspectorate is very complimentary and well worth reading.

Charitable status. The Cavendish School is a Registered Charity, number 312727.

Chafyn Grove School

Salisbury, Wiltshire SP1 1LR
Tel: 01722 333423
Fax: 01722 323114
e-mail: office@chafyngrove.co.uk
website: www.chafyngrove.co.uk

Chairman of Governors: Annie Parnell

Headmaster: **Eddy Newton**, BA Hons, PGCE Cantab

Age Range. 3–13.
Number of Pupils. 323: 217 Boys, 106 Girls.
Fees per term (2011-2012). Boarding supplement £1,685. Day Children: Main School (Years 4–8) £4,710, Transition (Year 3) £3,565, Pre-Prep (Years R–2) £2,375, Nursery £16.80 per session.

Chafyn Grove is set in 14 acres of grounds on the edge of the historic city of Salisbury – just an hour and a half from London by road, with easy access to air and rail links. The children thrive in an ambitious academic environment, where good sports facilities; extensive Art, Music and Drama opportunities and a commitment to extra-curricular activities encourage your child to discover their interests and their strengths.

Chafyn Grove has a happy family atmosphere that is created by a caring pastoral system and a team of talented and committed teachers. Pupils at Chafyn Grove School enjoy a good relationship with our staff; there is mutual friendship and a healthy respect. Our children also develop good relationships with other pupils, whether younger or older. Assemblies, chapel and tutor time all foster an understanding of how people should treat one another.

We have a mix of day and boarding pupils. Our boarding enhances the sense of community and is all about making the most of your time at school, developing independence and making friends for life – our aim is to provide a caring and happy environment in which children thrive and grow. Our boarders benefit from a secure and homely atmosphere and are accommodated in cosy, brightly decorated dormitories, often creatively decorated with their own pictures and posters, their own bedding and of course a teddy or two! There is a full weekly activity programme for boarders as well as a full weekend programme where both boarding and teaching staff are fully involved with the children creating a strong bond between staff and pupils.

Small class sizes (maximum 16) and a commitment to high standards allow our pupils to perform impressively in the classroom. In 2010 all pupils achieved entry to the senior school of their choice and 11 Scholarships were awarded to Godolphin, Canford, Bryanston, Downside and Dauntsey's.

Pupils are also prepared for the 11+ entrance exam to the two Grammar Schools in Salisbury and a record number of Year 6 pupils made the grade this year with 4 girls and 10 boys winning places, although some opted to stay at Chafyn! Scholarships to Chafyn are awarded in Years 2, 4, and 6, and take place in February.

Our facilities include ten acres of playing fields, a large astroturf pitch, 25-metre heated swimming pool, 2 tennis courts, 2 squash courts, sports hall, music school, creative arts centre, two science laboratories and a computer centre. A library block with a computerised resource centre and 8 classrooms opened in May 2006. Construction of a new Pre-Prep building started in June 2011.

Charitable status. Chafyn Grove School is a Registered Charity, number 309483. It exists to provide an excellent education for children.

Cheam School

Headley, Newbury, Berkshire RG19 8LD
Tel: 01635 268381
         Registrar: 01635 267822
Fax: 01635 269345
e-mail: registrar@cheamschool.co.uk
website: www.cheamschool.com

The School, originally founded in 1645, is a charitable trust controlled by a Board of Governors.

Chairman of Governors: A F Gibbs, MA

Headmaster: **M R Johnson**, BEd College of St Mark & St John, Plymouth

Assistant Headmaster: T C Haigh, BA Birmingham, PGCE

Age Range. 3–13.
Number of Pupils. 90 boarders, 302 day children.
Fees per term (2011-2012). £7,550 Boarders; £3,195–£5,585 Day children.

The School became co-educational in September 1997. A merger with Inhurst House School, formerly situated at Baughurst, and which re-located to the Headley site in 1999, offers parents the opportunity for education from 3–13+ for their sons and daughters.

Bursaries are offered annually for 8 year olds.

Classes are small (maximum 18) and pupils are prepared for the major senior independent schools like Eton, Harrow, Radley, Marlborough, Sherborne, Wellington, Downe House, St Mary's Calne and Sherborne Girls' featuring frequently. Recent improvements include excellent facilities for Design Technology and Information Technology, a dedicated Science Building, a refurbished Chapel and Teaching Block, a Music School, a Sports Hall and much improved boarding facilities. Dormitories are comfortable, carpeted and curtained. A new Art & Design Centre and Pre-Prep classrooms and Assembly are due to open in September 2012.

Rugby, Soccer and Cricket are the major team games for boys; Netball, Rounders, Hockey and Lacrosse for girls. A heated outdoor swimming pool, 6 all-weather tennis courts and a 9-hole golf course in the extensive 80-acre grounds allow a wide range of other sports and pastimes to be enjoyed.

The School is situated half way between Newbury and Basingstoke on the A339 and is within easy reach of the M3 and M4 motorways and the A34 trunk route from Portsmouth, Southampton and Winchester to Oxford and the Midlands. London Heathrow Airport is within an hour's drive.

Charitable status. Cheam School Educational Trust is a Registered Charity, number 290143. It provides high-class education for boarding and day pupils; traditional values; modern thinking; education for the 21st century.

Cheltenham College Junior School

Thirlestaine Road, Cheltenham GL53 7AB
Tel: 01242 522697
Fax: 01242 265620
e-mail: ccjs@cheltcoll.gloucs.sch.uk
website: www.cheltenhamcollege.org

President of Council: The Revd J C Horan

Headmaster: **S Bryan**, BA, BSc Hons, PGCE

Age Range. 3–13.

Number of Pupils. 400 (50 boarders, 350 day boys and girls).

Fees per term (2011-2012). Boarders £5,241–£6,834; Day Boys and Girls £2,270–£5,130.

Cheltenham College Junior School is a co-educational preparatory school from 3 to 13. The Pre-Prep Department called Kingfishers is located in a separate purpose-built wing.

The school stands in a beautiful 15-acre parkland site near the centre of Regency Cheltenham; the town itself being well served by both motorway and rail networks. Excellent facilities include: all weather pitches, athletics track, squash courts, tennis courts, art block, computer centre, CDT centre, a large multi-purpose Assembly Hall, drama studio and music school. It also benefits from the senior school amenities including the stunning College Chapel, spacious sports complex with a 25m indoor swimming pool, floodlit astros and fully equipped Science classrooms.

The curriculum is wide and stimulating with all pupils being prepared for Common Entrance and Scholarship examinations. Apart from the normal academic subjects, all study Art, Music, PE, Information Technology, CDT and Drama. The excellent facilities are backed by a team of professional and dedicated teachers. French is taught from the age of 3 in Kingfishers, Latin from age 10.

A wide range of sports are available including: rugby, cricket, hockey, cross-country, netball, badminton, athletics, golf, gymnastics, squash, ballet, sailing, skiing, horse-riding, mountain biking, swimming, tennis and orienteering. Sporting skills are taught from an early age and include swimming for the whole school.

The school aims to give a well-rounded education in preparation for senior school. The environment is secure and caring with vast opportunities for pupils to fulfil their potential, from academic and sporting success to artistic and creative excellence. The boarding house aims to provide a 'home from home', with excellent pastoral care and a wide range of extra-curricular activities under the supervision of the House Parents. The boarding facilities themselves are large and airy, with plenty of pictures, toys and colourful duvets making the place warm and homely. Regular contact with parents is encouraged with exeats every third weekend. Progress reports are issued three times a term and either formal parent/teacher meetings are held or full reports issued at the end of each term.

Visitors are warmly welcomed and further information is available from the Registrar, Lucinda Roskilly, who arranges school tours, taster days and meetings for parents with the Headmaster.

Charitable status. Cheltenham College Junior School is a Registered Charity, number 311720. It exists to provide education for boys and girls.

Chesham Preparatory School

Two Dells Lane, Chesham, Bucks HP5 3QF
Tel: 01494 782619
Fax: 01494 791645
e-mail: secretary@cheshamprep.co.uk
website: www.cheshamprep.co.uk

Chairman of Governors: H H J Francis Sheridan

Head: **Mrs J Radcliffe**, BSc, PGCE

Age Range. 3–13.
Numbers of Pupils. 370 boys and girls.
Fees per term (from January 2011). £2,655–£3,770 (incl lunch).

Situated in the green belt on the Bucks/Herts border between Chesham and Berkhamsted Chesham Preparatory

School is just 20 minutes' drive using the A41 from Aylesbury or North Watford. Closer still are Amersham, The Chalfonts and Prestwood areas. Currently a school bus covers part of the Buckinghamshire catchments area.

Chesham Preparatory School, founded in 1938, is a co-educational, day school for boys and girls aged 4–13 years providing them with an outstanding education, excellent facilities and fabulous opportunities, in a wonderfully happy, exciting and supportive atmosphere. Children are nurtured, encouraged, challenged and rewarded; happiness and security are essential and the fear of failure is eradicated. Success is celebrated every step of the way and excellence is achieved across the curriculum.

There are almost 370 pupils across the school starting in Nursery, then Reception, an Early Years Foundation Stage (non-selective two-form entry point) through to Year 8. The other two main entry points are Years 3 (where an extra form is added) and 7 with an assessment and screening process, although pupils can join at any time, subject to availability of places. Many of our pupils leave at 11+ (after Year 6) to go on to Bucks grammar schools.

Chesham Preparatory School is proud to have achieved an overall "Excellent" rating in its 2010 ISI inspection (see our website for the Report).

To find out more or to arrange to visit the school, please visit our website www.cheshamprep.co.uk.

Charitable status. Chesham Preparatory School is a Registered Charity, number 310642. It exists to provide education for boys and girls.

Chigwell Junior School

Chigwell, Essex IG7 6QF
Tel: 020 8501 5721
Fax: 020 8501 5723
e-mail: admissions@chigwell-school.org
website: www.chigwell-school.org

Chairman of the Governors: C P de Boer, Esq

Head of the Junior School: **Mr S C James**, BA Hons, PGCE

Age Range. 7–13.
Number of Pupils. 329 Day Pupils.
Fees per term (2011-2012). £3,330–£4,846 inc Lunch/Tea.

The Junior School is housed in a purpose-built building on the same site as the Senior School only 10 miles from the heart of London. It shares the use of a wide range of activities and facilities including Chapel, Science laboratories, Music School, Arts and Technology Centre, Theatre, Gymnasium, Swimming Pool, Sports Hall and 70 acres of playing fields.

The curriculum and administration of the Senior and Junior Schools are closely linked.

Pupils sit a written test for entry to the Junior School and are normally admitted to the Senior School without further examination. (*See Chigwell School entry in HMC section.*)

Charitable status. Chigwell School is a Registered Charity, number 1115098. It exists to provide a rounded education of the highest quality for its pupils.

Chinthurst School

Tadworth, Surrey KT20 5QZ
Tel: 01737 812011
Fax: 01737 814835
e-mail: info@chinthurstschool.co.uk

website: www.chinthurstschool.co.uk

The School is an Educational Trust, administered by a Board of Governors.

Chairman of Governors: A Bisset, Esq

Headmaster: I D Thorpe, BA Ed, MA Ed

Deputy Headmasters:
P Mulhern, BEd
T Button, BEd

Age Range. Rising 3–13.
Number of Boys. 160.
Fees per term (2010-2011). Nursery (age Rising 3–4½) £1,200, Pre-Preparatory (age 4½–7) £2,420 (Lunch £210), Preparatory (age 7–13) £3,350 (Lunch £215).

The School is set in modern and attractive rural surroundings with spacious games facilities including a swimming pool and new astroturf area.

Boys are prepared for all Senior Independent Schools, by way of the Common Entrance or Scholarships. A very experienced and well qualified staff ensure a high standard is achieved both academically and on the games field. Chinthurst has a 'family' ethos, aimed at the achievement of high academic standards allied to a purposeful and active school life within a happy environment.

Charitable status. Chinthurst School is a Registered Charity, number 271160 A/1.

The Chorister School

Durham DH1 3EL
Tel: 0191 384 2935
Fax: 0191 383 1275
e-mail: headmistress@thechoristerschool.com
website: www.thechoristerschool.com

Chairman of Governors: The Dean of Durham, The Very Revd Michael Sadgrove

Headteacher: Mrs Y F S Day, BMus Cape Town, MMus London, GDL College of Law

Age Range. 3–13.
Number of Pupils. 219 (41 Chorister-boarders, 1 full/weekly boarder, 177 day pupils, including 69 in the Nursery and the Pre-Prep.) The school became co-educational in 1995 and there are girls in every year group.

Fees per term (2010-2011). Choristers (including piano lessons) £2,955, Full/Weekly Boarders £5,650, Day Pupils £3,275, Pre-Prep £2,430, Nursery £16 per half day session. Reductions are available for children of CofE clergy, serving members of the armed forces, children of former pupils and for younger siblings. Scholarships available at entry to Years 3 and 6 Fees are inclusive of all normal requirements; there are no compulsory extras.

The Chorister School is in an outstanding situation in a World Heritage Site tucked behind Durham Cathedral. Quiet and secluded it is a haven in the centre of Durham City. Whilst it is the school for the choristers who sing in the renowned Cathedral Choir over eighty per cent of pupils are not choristers.

Pastoral care is the responsibility of all members of staff. The needs of the boarders are attended to by a dedicated team led by the Housemistress, Housemaster and Headmistress. Before and After School Care is available from the Nursery onwards and there is a wide range of after-school activities including: Art, Embroidery, Choirs, Dance, Chess, Sports, Speech and Drama, Music Ensembles and World Challenge. Flexible boarding is also available.

Our curriculum introduces French from Pre-Prep level, where each of the classes has its own class teacher. In the Prep School class-teaching of the core curriculum is gradually replaced by subject-specialist teaching as children are prepared for Common Entrance and Scholarship examinations to senior schools. The school has a reputation for academic success,but cherishes all its pupils, whatever their academic attainment. The curriculum, which includes RE, PE, swimming, Art, Technology and Music, is designed to ensure that academic edge does not lead to academic narrowness.

Games are an important element in the curriculum. The Chorister School competes at various levels with other schools in athletics, cricket, netball, hockey, rounders, rugby, football and swimming. Badminton, volleyball, basketball, tennis, indoor football and netball (in our large Sports Hall) are also played. The Chorister School has its own sports fields, tennis court and play areas, and uses the indoor swimming pool at Durham School.

Individual instrumental music lessons are available in almost all instruments, and all pupils take class music in which they sing and learn about musical history, musical instruments, simple analysis and some famous pieces.

Entry is by English and Maths test graded according to age or by informal assessment during a 'taster' day, as seems best for the age of the individual child. Competitive voice trials for aspiring Choristers are held regularly.

Next School. Children move from The Chorister School to a wide range of maintained and independent secondary schools throughout the North East and further afield. The school advises and guides parents in the appropriate choice of next school and aims to secure a successful transition for every pupil. In the past ten years every child has won a place to the senior school of choice, with between 43%–72% winning an academic or subject scholarship or a competitive entry place.

Charitable status. The Chorister School and Durham Cathedral enjoy charitable status (exempt from registration) and the school exists to provide boarding education for the choristers of Durham Cathedral and day or boarding education for other children aged 3–13.

Christ Church Cathedral School

3 Brewer Street, Oxford OX1 1QW
Tel: 01865 242561
Fax: 01865 202945
e-mail: schooloffice@cccs.org.uk
website: www.cccs.org.uk

Governors: The Dean and Canons of Christ Church Cathedral

Headmaster: Martin Bruce, BA, MA, FCollP

Age Range. 3–13.
Number of Boys. About 21 boarders, all of whom are Cathedral Choristers (who must board) and 133 day boys.
Fees per term (2011-2012). Day boys £4,041 (including lunch); Pre-Prep £2,788 (including lunch); Cathedral Choristers £2,520–£2,783 (fees are subsidised by the Cathedral); Nursery £685–£1,775.

Christ Church Cathedral School is a day Preparatory, Pre-Preparatory and Nursery School for boys.

The School provides Choristers for the choirs of Christ Church Cathedral and Worcester College, and is governed by the Dean and Canons of Christ Church, with the assistance of lay members drawn from the city's professional community, some of whom are past or current parents.

It was founded in 1546 when provision was made for the education of eight Choristers on King Henry VIII's foundation of Christ Church on the site of Cardinal Wolsey's earlier foundation of Cardinal College. In the latter half of the nineteenth century, at the initiative of Dean Liddell, father of Alice Liddell, the inspiration for 'Alice in Wonderland', the boarding house was established at No 1 Brewer Street, and in 1892, during the Headship of the Reverend Henry Sayers, father of Dorothy L Sayers, the Italian Mediaeval scholar and creator of Lord Peter Wimsey, the present building was erected.

The School is centrally situated off St Aldates, and two hundred yards from Christ Church. It therefore not only enjoys the unique cultural background provided by Oxford itself, but also has the advantage of excellent recreational facilities on Christ Church Meadow. Buildings include a former residence of Cardinal Wolsey and the Sir William Walton Centre which contains a recital hall in addition to spacious classrooms.

Charitable status. Christ Church Cathedral School Education Trust is a Registered Charity, number 1114828.

Churcher's College Junior School

Midhurst Road, Liphook, Hampshire GU30 7HT
Tel: 01730 236870
Fax: 01428 722550
e-mail: ccjsoffice@churcherscollege.com
website: www.churcherscollege.com

Chairman of Governors: M J Gallagher, Esq, DipArch Hons, RIBA, MIOD, FIMgmt

Head: **Mrs S M Rivett**, CertEd, DipDrama London

Age Range. 4–11 Co-educational.
Number of Pupils. 228.
Fees per term (2011-2012). £2,450–£2,615 excluding lunch.

Churcher's College Junior School provides a happy, stimulating, safe and secure environment in which every child feels valued and is able to develop personally, socially and academically. Each child is nurtured and taught to hold a high regard for others and themselves.

We view education as a joint partnership between teachers, parents and pupils, and strive to develop a team spirit in which every member gives of their best. We hold high expectations of staff and pupils and aim to create an environment that values individuals, applauds success, strives to encourage questioning, lets pupils explore, be controversial and be special.

The Junior School is sited in Liphook approximately 8 miles from the College, but continues to have strong links with the Senior School in Petersfield.

The school is set in beautiful rural surroundings providing extensive grounds for sports practices, three separate playing areas and a nature garden. Latest computer technology, networked classroom computers and interactive whiteboards are all used by staff and pupils to enhance curriculum studies. The school has a fully-equipped ICT suite, science laboratory, dedicated music and art rooms and a Performing Arts wing.

The wider curriculum is valued, offering additional depth and scope in all subjects and pupils are encouraged to take part in a broad range of experiences both in and out of the classroom.

Churcher's College Junior School provides pupils with:

(a) a broad-based and challenging curriculum that enables all pupils to achieve their individual potential in all areas and caters for their individual abilities, needs and interests.

(b) a functional education in which pupils are able to develop transferable skills and a love of learning that will enable them to succeed in the ever-changing world.

(c) experiences of an aesthetic, creative and spiritual nature.

Teaching and learning activities cater for the varying needs of our pupils and allow all to achieve their full potential in a wide variety of areas – academic, creative, sporting, etc.

We maintain a broad and balanced curriculum in which pupils experience a wide range of activities to maximise their learning opportunities. Teaching is grounded in pupils past experiences and they are helped to see the importance of each area of study.

The school is seen as a continually evolving organisation and we constantly reflect upon practice as a means of self improvement.

Charitable status. Churcher's College is a Registered Charity, number 307320.

City of London Freemen's Junior School

Ashtead Park, Surrey KT21 1ET
Tel: 01372 822474 (Secretary)
          01372 822423 (Admissions)
Fax: 01372 822415
          01372 822416 (Admissions)
e-mail: admissions@clfs.surrey.sch.uk
website: www.clfs.surrey.sch.uk

Co-educational Day and Boarding School.

Chairman of Governors: J A Bennett

Head: **Mr Mark Beach**, BA Hons, AdvDipEd, MA Ed

Age Range. 7–13.
Number of Pupils. 360.
Fees per term (2011-2012). Tuition £3,624–£3,828.

City of London Freemen's Junior School was established formally in 1988 as an integral part of CLFS and it prepares girls and boys for entry to the Senior School in Year 9. It shares a magnificent 57 acre site in Ashtead Park, Surrey, where the many outstanding facilities are available to all pupils (*see separate entry in HMC section*).

With its broad based curriculum and modern purpose-built facilities, the Junior School offers a challenging and unique atmosphere for all new entrants. There is a Junior School Head with specialist teaching staff and a clearly defined academic and pastoral structure to ensure that all pupils know what is expected of them. On average there are about 17 pupils in each of the three parallel classes in each year group. In Year 7 the year groups rises to four classes. Junior pupils benefit greatly from seeing their Form Prefects, who are Sixth Formers from the Senior School, on a daily basis.

For the first four years, in Key Stage 2, Heads of Year work in liaison with the subject coordinators and the Heads of Senior School Departments to ensure that the programmes of work are compatible and progressive. The aim is to establish a secure foundation in traditional core subjects within a curriculum which will broaden experience and excite the imagination of each child. In Years 7 and 8 the teaching programme is managed by the Heads of the Senior School Departments using specialist teachers for all of the subjects. Whilst academic excellence throughout the Junior School is still a major aim, there is also a very full programme of extra curricular activities including drama, music and sports.

Fully integrated into whole school routines, the Junior School takes full advantage of Ashtead Park's facilities. Extensive playing fields, the floodlit all-weather pitch, the sports hall and the modern swimming pool ensure that the sports facilities available are second to none.

There are three Houses in the School providing pastoral care and supervision whilst also promoting healthy competition in many activities. In both the Senior and the Junior School outstanding work and good progress, inside and outside the classroom, are recognised by the award of appropriate merits and distinctions.

Admission to the Junior School is through entrance examination, interview and feeder school report. Progression to the Senior School is based on continuous assessment with no separate qualifying entrance test and as such is almost always automatic for Junior School pupils. Pupils are constantly reviewed and can be assured that they will move through to the Senior School with many familiar faces around them.

Clayesmore Preparatory School

Iwerne Minster, Blandford Forum, Dorset DT11 8PH
Tel: 01747 811707
Fax: 01747 811692
e-mail: prepadmissions@clayesmore.com
website: www.clayesmore.com

Chairman of Governors: Dr R Willis, MA, BM, BCh

Headmaster: Richard Geffen, BEd

Age Range. Rising 3–13 years.
Number of Pupils. 250 (Boarders 70, Day 180).
Fees per term (2011-2012). Boarders: £6,340 (Year 3), £6,949 (Years 4–8); Day Pupils: £2,538 (Pre-Prep), £4,834 (Year 3), £5,161 (Years 4–8).

Clayesmore Preparatory School was founded in 1929 at Charlton Marshall House by R A L Everett. In 1974 it moved to Iwerne Minster to occupy purpose-built premises close to Senior Clayesmore. A comprehensive development programme in recent years has provided the School with outstanding facilities for Sport, Music, Drama and the Arts, while the 62-acre parkland campus in one of the most beautiful parts of Dorset is the ideal environment for children to grow up in. In September 2008 a brand new state-of-the-art classroom building was opened. This comprises five classrooms which will accommodate Years 3 and 4 and two new Science laboratories.

Day children can join the new Pre-Preparatory Department at the start of the term they are 3, the youngest boarders usually arrive at the age of 8. Admission is normally by interview and report from a child's previous school. The School is fully co-educational.

Academic, Art, Music, Sporting and All Rounder Scholarships are offered each year, together with 11+ Continuity Scholarships for candidates intending to complete their Sixth Form education at Senior Clayesmore.

The school is particularly proud of its long association with HM Forces and offers a number of service bursaries. There are also children from expatriate families amongst the boarding community and the School is well versed in handling all the arrangements necessary for overseas travel.

The curriculum – with its strong emphasis on sound foundations – is typical of most good Prep Schools, but at Clayesmore each day is greatly enriched by the wide range of facilities and activities offered within the timetable. Younger children spend most of their time with their Form Teacher but by the age of ten all children are being taught by specialist subject teachers. In the Upper School the children are setted for Mathematics and English with some streaming taking place in Science, Humanities and Languages, which allows them to proceed at their own level and pace. Though the pressure of academic work increases as examinations approach, every child's programme includes a full range of Art, Music, ICT, Design Technology and Games and also gives time for play and relaxation.

The main games for boys are Rugby, Hockey, Football and Cricket; for girls Netball, Hockey, Tennis and Rounders. A well-equipped Sports Hall with a 25-metre heated pool, a floodlit all-weather hockey pitch and extensive playing fields give every opportunity for games to reach the highest standards. The School also enjoys considerable success at Athletics, Swimming and Orienteering. Many other minor sports are also available.

Many children learn instruments and music is held in high regard. The Chapel Choir has toured in Italy, France, Germany, USA, Spain and South Africa during the 90s and more recently Prague and France. The Prep School has two orchestras – sometimes three – and there are several instrumental ensembles. The Concert Band which draws the best woodwind, brass and percussion pupils from both schools is in hot demand in the locality and also tours abroad. Art, too, is very strong. The Prep School has its own Art Department with a separate pottery.

Boys and girls are prepared for Common Entrance and Senior School Scholarship examinations. The Prep School has an outstanding reputation for supporting pupils with dyslexia through its "all through" approach to teaching such pupils. All staff receive regular training so that the work of the Learning Support specialists is fully understood by the subject specialist staff and the form teachers. Communication is absolutely the key element in this.

Charitable status. Clayesmore School Limited is a Registered Charity, number 306214. It exists for the purposes of educating children.

Clevelands Preparatory School
GEMS Education

425 Chorley New Road, Bolton, Lancashire BL1 5DH
Tel: 01204 843898
Fax: 01204 848007
e-mail: clevelands@indschool.org
website: www.clevelandsprepschool.co.uk

Co-educational Day School.

Headteacher: Mrs L Parlane

Age Range. 2¾–11.
Number of Pupils. 173: 81 boys, 92 girls.
Fees per term (2010-2011). £2,025.

Clevelands Nursery and Preparatory School offers a traditional academic education in a caring, stimulating environment. The school and nursery department is open to boys and girls between the ages of 2¾ and 11 years.

We aim to give our pupils a stimulating and challenging curriculum linking strong, traditional values with the best of new educational initiatives. The range of experiences on offer ensures that our pupils have a broad curriculum which combines the National Curriculum with our own successful Educational programme. It also ensures that emphasis is placed on developing and celebrating each child's individual talents.

The school's family values are built on kindness, a sense of belonging, mutual respect and consideration of one another. The pupils spend each day in a happy, caring, work orientated environment in which their needs are prioritised and catered for by dedicated and highly qualified teachers.

Pupils have a proud record of academic success in entrance examinations and scholarships for entry into the leading day senior schools.

They also excel in other fields such as art, drama, music and sport. A significant number of pupils play at least one musical instrument.

Clevelands children compete successfully in local, regional and national sporting competitions.

Pupils are taught by specialist teachers from Nursery upwards. This teaching increases as the pupils move through the school.

Facilities at Clevelands include a fully networked Computer Suite. In the art /design and technology studio pupils can explore all media. The science laboratory is fully equipped with the latest technology. Our sporting facilities include a netball court and football pitch.

A myriad of extra-curricular activities takes place during lunchtimes and after school. A thriving programme of external Educational and Theatre visits exists as well as the opportunity for the children to encounter a variety of new and exciting experiences internally. Skiing trips take place annually.

Our pupils develop into well rounded, self-assured, competent young people who will meet the challenges of life with enthusiasm and vigour.

Before and after school care is available to all.

Most pupils enter the main school in September of any year, but the Headteacher is happy to consider requests for admission for children of any age during the academic year, should circumstances so warrant.

Entry to the Nursery is ongoing throughout the year as a child reaches the appropriate age.

Clifton College Preparatory School

Bristol BS8 3HE
Tel: 0117 3157 502
Fax: 0117 3157 504
e-mail: lwoodward@clifton-college.avon.sch.uk
website: www.cliftoncollegeuk.com

Chairman of College Council: T S Ross, MA

Head Master: **J Milne**, BA, MBA

Age Range. 8–13.
Number of Pupils. 375: 51 boarders, 324 day pupils.
Fees per term (2011-2012). Boarders £7,155, Weekly Boarders £6,625, Day Pupils £4,275–£4,670.

There is a full time teaching staff of 58, all of whom are qualified. A wide range of subjects is included in the normal curriculum.

The majority go on to the Upper School with whom there is cooperation on curriculum matters, but a number are prepared for and win scholarships to other schools. Over 60 awards have been won in the past three years. Pupils can be prepared for the Common Entrance examination to other schools.

The administration of the School is entirely separate from the Upper School, but some facilities are shared, including the Sports Hall and Indoor Swimming Pool, the Gymnasium, Chapel, Squash and Rackets Courts and 93 acres of playing fields, which include Astroturf pitches, a 3G pitch, an indoor Tennis and Netball Centre and, new for 2010, a water-based hockey pitch. The School has its own Art & Design Centre. The School possesses one of the most advanced Information Technology Centres in the West of England.

The House system operates for both boarders and day pupils. Three houses cater for the boarders, each under the supervision of a Housemaster or Housemistress assisted by wife or husband, house tutor and matron. The remaining five Houses cater specifically for day pupils. Boys and girls are in separate Houses, all recently renovated.

Out of school activities supplementing the main School games are many and varied, the aim being to give every child an opportunity to participate in an activity from which he or she gains confidence and a sense of achievement.

The youngest boys and girls (aged 3–8) work separately in the Pre-Preparatory School called Butcombe under the care of their own Head and teachers. (*See separate IAPS entry for Butcombe.*)

Charitable status. Clifton College is a Registered Charity, number 311735. It provides boarding and day education for boys and girls aged 3–18 years.

Clifton Pre-preparatory School

York YO30 6AB
Tel: 01904 527361
Fax: 01904 527304
e-mail: enquiries@cliftonprep.york.sch.uk
website: www.st-peters.york.sch.uk

Chairman of the Governors: P N Shepherd

Head: **Mr P C Hardy**, BA, PGCE

Age Range. 3–8 co-educational.
Number of Pupils. 97 boys, 75 girls.
Fees per term (2011-2012). Nursery (full time), Reception, Years 1 & 2: £2,268, Year 3: £2,355. Nursery Education Grant accepted for 3 and 4 year olds.

Clifton Pre-preparatory School is the Pre-prep of St Peter's School, York. The school has large modern buildings on the St Peter's School site which occupies 47 acres in the centre of York. A new synthetic outdoor play space and 25m 6-lane swimming pool have recently been built.

Curriculum. All aspects of the National Curriculum are covered but the syllabus at the school is broader and more challenging. Individual development in all subjects is a priority, particularly in literacy and numeracy. Small classes, individual attention and after-school activities enable high standards to be achieved.

Music and Drama. Nursery children have a session of music and movement, and all other classes have weekly lessons with a specialist teacher. From Year 2, children have the opportunity to learn to play the recorder, piano, violin or guitar at school. Each year there are opportunities for children to participate in performances to a wider audience. All classes have weekly drama lessons, and there is the opportunity for Y2 and Y3 to do speech and drama as an after school activity.

Sport and Extra-Curricular Activities. Physical Education starts in the Nursery. As children grow older, games and swimming are added. The pupils at Clifton Preparatory School have access to the Sports facilities at St Peter's School. Extra-curricular activities include gymnastics, board games, swimming club, country dancing, football club, short tennis, choir, drama, Art, Design and Technology Club and Computer Club.

Assessments. Throughout Nursery and Reception children work towards achieving the Early Learning Goals, culminating in the completion of the Foundation Stage Profile. Work is assessed continuously and children's progress is discussed at monthly staff meetings. There is ongoing communication between parents and staff through a reports system, invitations to visit the school and parent evenings.

After the recent ISI inspection, the inspectors reported that: "The School provides a high-quality education, which is outstanding in several important respects".

Charitable status. St Peter's School York is a Registered Charity, number 529740. It exists to provide education for boys and girls.

Cokethorpe Junior School

Witney, Oxfordshire OX29 7PU
Tel: 01993 703921

Fax: 01993 773499
e-mail: admin@cokethorpe.org
website: www.cokethorpe.org.uk

Chairman of Governors: Sir John Allison, KCB, CBE, FRAeS

Head: **Mrs C A Cook**, BEd Hons

Age Range. 4–11 Co-educational.
Number of Pupils. 140.
Fees per term (2011-2012). £3,425.
Staff. 13 full-time and 4 part-time qualified and enthusiastic staff teach the 10 classes.
Location. Cokethorpe Junior School is set in 150 acres of beautiful Oxfordshire parkland, two miles from Witney and ten from Oxford. It was established in 1994 and occupies the elegant Queen Anne Mansion House that is at the heart of Cokethorpe School. The Junior School retains its own identity, independence and distinct character, allowing the children to flourish, develop confidence and feel valued, whilst having the advantage of being part of a wider community with the Senior School.
Facilities. Whilst self-sufficient in most respects, the Junior School benefits from having access to the Senior School facilities, especially the all-weather pitches, Sports Hall and other sports facilities, performing arts, science laboratories, ICT resources and the splendid new Dining Hall. There is also a dedicated play area, library, art room and music room.
Aims. Cokethorpe Junior School is a small, friendly and caring school that places a large emphasis on its pastoral care, sense of community and family atmosphere. It aims to provide an insight into a world that is rich and varied, exciting and stimulating and puts its pupils on a journey of discovery. As they progress through the School they are equipped with the necessary academic and social skills to enable them to develop into confident children who are able to cope with all that school life offers. Children make the most of being in an environment which encourages them to aim higher, try harder, and expect more of themselves.
Curriculum. The Junior School offers a fully balanced curriculum with the focus on developing high standards and providing intellectual challenges. Children receive vital foundations for study in small classes and in a positive and purposeful learning environment. Whilst the National Curriculum is followed, the freedom to offer breadth is fully embraced. Trips and events support work done in the classroom and also help children meet the School's high academic, behavioural and social expectations.
Enrichment. Sport and The Arts play a strong part in the Junior School. Children participate in team sports on two afternoons a week, including competitive fixtures, and time is also found for other sports such as swimming, tennis, judo, golf, modern dance and ballet. There are drama productions each year where every child has a speaking or singing role. In addition they will have the opportunity to take part in concerts and recitals throughout the year. The dedicated art room is a riot of colour and creativity with displays decorating the corridors and classroom walls.
The School enjoys a particularly close relationship with parents and there is a strong Parents' Association.
Entry. There is no formal assessment for entry to the Reception or Year 1 although children will be invited to spend either the day or half day in school. For entry to Years 2 to 6, children are invited to an Assessment Day in the January before entry, during which they will complete an assessment appropriate to their age. Individual arrangements for assessment can be made throughout the academic year. Reports are also requested from the child's current school or nursery. Early registration is recommended as places are limited. The majority of pupils continue to Cokethorpe Senior School, with many being awarded scholarships every year. (*See Cokethorpe School entry in HMC section.*)

Charitable status. Cokethorpe Educational Trust Limited is a Registered Charity, number 309650.

Colet Court (St Paul's Preparatory School)

Lonsdale Road, London SW13 9JT
Tel: 020 8748 3461
Fax: 020 8746 5357
e-mail: hmpa@stpaulsschool.org.uk
website: www.coletcourt.org.uk

Chairman of Governors: Dr F C G Hohler, MA, DPhil

Headmaster: T A Meunier, MA, CChem, FRSC, PGCE

Deputy Headmaster: C G Howes, MA, PGCE

Age Range. 7–13.
Number of Boys. 436.
Fees per term (2011-2012). £5,017.
Colet Court, founded in 1881, is the preparatory school for St Paul's School (*see entry in HMC section*). Nearly all pupils at Colet Court transfer to St Paul's at 13. The two schools are in separate, but adjacent modern buildings on the south bank of the Thames, and share many amenities, including the dining hall, sports complex, design & technology workshops and playing fields. Colet Court has its own main teaching block, hall/theatre, library, art & design room, two computer rooms and music school. A drama studio and three science laboratories are situated in a separate building.
There is close consultation with St Paul's in matters of curriculum to ensure the benefit of continuity. Some members of staff teach in both schools. Boys are not specifically prepared for scholarships to senior schools other than St Paul's. Our aim is to give every pupil the opportunity to enjoy a broad education and a wide range of activities. Music, Art, Drama and Sport are all strong.
There are two Year 3 classes and four forms per year group from Years 4 to 8. Boys join the School at 7+ and 8+ and approximately 20 places are also available at 11+. Up to 10 of these places may be offered to pupils who sit an examination in Year 5 and defer their arrival for one year. This mode of entry is available to boys from maintained primary schools only. Entrance at all levels is by competitive examination and interview. Means-tested bursaries are available at all points of entry.
Charitable status. St Paul's School is a Registered Charity, number 1119619. The object of the charity is to promote the education of boys in Greater London.

Colfe's Preparatory School

Horn Park Lane, London SE12 8AW
Tel: 020 8463 8240 Prep
         020 8463 8266 Pre-Prep & Nursery
Fax: 020 8297 2941
e-mail: prep@colfes.com
website: www.colfes.com

Chairman of the Governors: Mr Ian Russell, MBE

Head of the Preparatory School: **Mr John Gallagher**, BA Hons, MBA

Age Range. 3–11.
Number of Pupils. 356 boys and girls.
Fees per term (2011-2012). Prep £3,546 (excluding lunch); Pre-Prep £3,345 (including lunch); Nursery and Reception £3,054 (including lunch).

Colfe's Preparatory School is a co-educational day school under the general direction of the Governors and Headmaster of Colfe's School (founded in 1652). It is academically selective, offers a broad curriculum and aims to provide an excellent all-round education. Children normally enter at the ages of 3, 4 or 7 although the occasional vacancy arises at other times.

The Preparatory School is housed in modern purpose-built accommodation with spacious and well-equipped classrooms. Small class sizes and a team of well-qualified teachers provide a caring and vibrant environment. Excellent library facilities and specialist accommodation for art and design, ICT and science provide boys and girls with a stimulating environment in which to learn. Full use is made of the school's swimming pool, sports centre, visual and performing arts centre and extensive on-site playing fields.

PE specialists teach a wide range of sports. There is an extensive programme of house and inter-school sports matches. A school choir, orchestra, strings group and numerous ensembles perform frequently both in and out of school. Drama productions normally take place each term. There is a wide range of after-school clubs on offer (over 50 each week for the 7–11 year olds) and a late school scheme until 6 pm. A very successsful Breakfast Club is in operation from 7.30 am until 8.00 am each day.

The school has a strong reputation in the local area for excellence within a friendly and caring atmosphere.

Charitable status. Colfe's School is a Registered Charity, number 1109650. It exists to provide education for children.

Colston's Lower School

Stapleton, Bristol BS16 1BA
Tel: 0117 965 5297
Fax: 0117 965 6330
e-mail: celiapullin@colstons.bristol.sch.uk
website: www.colstons.bristol.sch.uk

Chairman of Governors: D J Marsh

Head: Mrs C Aspden, MA, PGCE

Age Range. 3–11.
Number of Pupils. 230 Day Pupils.
Fees per term (from January 2011). Reception, Year 1 and 2 £1,970; Years 3 and 4 £2,490; Years 5 and 6 £2,755. Nursery: £27.15 per morning (8.30 am–12.30 pm incl lunch); £18.95 per afternoon (12.30–3.30 pm). Scholarships are offered from 7+.

Colston's Lower School is located in Stapleton village which is within the city of Bristol. It is less than one mile from Junction 2 of the M32 and therefore easily accessible from north Bristol and South Gloucestershire. In addition to its own specialist facilities for Science, ICT, Music, Design & Technology, Art and Games, the Lower School has full use of facilities at the neighbouring Upper School including 32 acres of playing fields.

At the end of Year 6 pupils move from the Lower to the Upper School (*see entry in HMC section*). They work in small classes on a broad curriculum that extends beyond the requirements of the National Curriculum, incorporating the full range of academic subjects together with French, German, Design and Technology, ICT, Art and Music. There is also a Learning Support Unit.

Music and Drama flourish in the Lower School, with a choir and orchestra, regular concerts, school plays and music competitions.

In addition to PE lessons there are two afternoons of Junior Games each week. The boys principally play rugby, hockey and cricket, and the girls play hockey, netball and

rounders. Pupils also enjoy opportunities to take part in football, tennis, swimming, athletics and badminton.

Colston's Lower offers a wide range of clubs and activities, and pupils are able to stay on at school under supervision for an extended day or start with Breakfast Club. There are numerous visits and trips including skiing and adventure activities.

Charitable status. Colston's School is a Registered Charity, number 1079552. Its aims and objectives are the provision of education.

Combe Bank Preparatory School

Combe Bank Drive, Sundridge, Kent TN14 6AE
Tel: 01959 564320
Fax: 01959 560456
e-mail: enquiries@combebank.kent.sch.uk
website: www.combebank.kent.sch.uk

Council of Management:
Chairman: Mr P Dickinson

Headmistress: Mrs Jane Abbotts

Head of Preparatory School: **Mrs S Walker**, BA Hons, CertEd

Age Range. Girls 3–11 (Boys in the Nursery).
Number of Pupils. 180.
Fees per term (2011-2012). £2,710–£3,740 (Nursery according to number of sessions).

Founded in 1924, Combe Bank Preparatory School is a flourishing independent girls' school that stands in 27 acres of gardens and grounds, on the Kent/Surrey borders within easy reach of the centre Sevenoaks. The school forms part of the Combe Bank School Educational Trust. (*See also Combe Bank School entry in GSA section.*

The Preparatory School is housed in an original stable block and affords a unique environment in which the children feel secure and comfortable. Specialist teaching rooms include those dedicated to ICT, French, Music, PE, Speech and Drama. The Hall includes a permanent stage with sound and lighting systems. The older girls have access to a purpose-built Technology Room and to the Senior School Science labs. The ICT suite, networked to all classrooms, allows full class access at any time.

EYFS Nursery classes are housed within the courtyard area, which has recently undergone refurbishment to provide first-class facilities for both indoor and outdoor activities, including a specially designed Secret Garden.

Beech Walk with its secure adventure play area gives the children greater freedom at break times. There are two playing fields and five outdoor tennis and netball courts. A purpose-built Jubilee Sports Hall allows for the teaching of multi-sporting activities and interschool fixtures. All pupils, including the Nursery, use the indoor heated swimming pool weekly throughout the year.

Academic standards are high. The girls between the ages of 7–11 are prepared for scholarship and entrance examinations. Girls sit the entrance examinations to the Senior School and compete with other potential Year 7 candidates for Academic, Art, Sports and Music Scholarships with high levels of success. Girls are also successfully prepared for the Kent Assessment Procedure at 11+ (100% pass rate for those girls recommended) and entrance into other independent schools.

Drama and Music flourish in the school. Girls have many opportunities to perform throughout their time in the Prep from large drama productions to musical ensembles. The majority of girls study at least one musical instrument from Year 3.

A highly dedicated staff team takes care of the academic, physical, pastoral and extra-curricular needs of the pupils. We are committed to academic excellence for all our pupils. We work together to raise the self-esteem of each child. We pay particular attention to the development of thinking skills and positively encourage independent learning. We actively promote the development of a strong home-school partnership through parent consultation, information evenings and a programme of INSET. We also recognise the impact of Music Speech and Drama, Art and sport in the life of the developing child. The school is distinguished by the high standard of pastoral care it offers. We nurture the individual.

Combe Bank is committed to safeguarding and promoting the welfare of children.

Charitable status. Combe Bank School Educational Trust Limited is a Registered Charity, number 1007871.

Copthorne School

Effingham Lane, Copthorne, West Sussex RH10 3HR
Tel: 01342 712311
Fax: 01342 714014
e-mail: office@copthorneprep.co.uk
website: www.copthorneprep.co.uk

Chairman of Governors: James Abdool

Headmaster: **C J Jones**, BEd Hons

Deputy Headmaster: A Hammond

Age Range. 2½–13.
Number of Boys and Girls. 300 (20 Boarders).
Fees per term (2010-2011). Day: Pre-Prep £2,395, Year 3 £3,225, Year 4 £3,535, Years 5–8 £4,055. Weekly Boarding £4,900. Occasional Boarding £25 per night.

Copthorne is a flourishing IAPS Prep School with approximately 300 boys and girls from 2½ to 13. The school has grown by over 40% within the last 3 years. Children are prepared for Independent School Scholarships or Common Entrance. In the last 3 years Copthorne children have been awarded 31 Scholarships or Awards to a variety of Senior Schools.

We believe that, in order to learn, children must be happy and feel secure in their environment. Copthorne Prep School is full of happy children and the environment is caring but still allows children the freedom to develop as individuals.

The school helps to develop each child's confidence, to raise self-esteem and to make children feel good about themselves. Nothing does this more than children enjoying success in all areas of school life. This is why Art, Music, ICT, DT, Drama and Sport are all just as important as the pursuit of academic excellence.

We provide opportunities for children to achieve success in all areas of the curriculum and we always celebrate their achievements.

We recognise that all children have talents, and every child is encouraged to realise their true potential, whatever that may be, in whatever area of school life.

We demand and set high standards, and our children respond by always giving of their best.

Put simply, our mission is to:

Develop **C**onfidence – Provide **O**pportunity – Realise **P**otential – in every single child.

The school is very proud of its history of over 100 years, and retains all the important traditions of the past whilst developing a very forward thinking approach. The children receive a "child-centred" education, where their individual needs come first, in an environment that is "parent-friendly", with very high levels of communication and pastoral care.

Charitable status. Copthorne School Trust Limited is a Registered Charity, number 270757. It exists to provide education to boys and girls.

Cottesmore School

Buchan Hill, Pease Pottage, West Sussex RH11 9AU
Tel: 01293 520648
Fax: 01293 614784
e-mail: schooloffice@cottesmoreschool.com
website: www.cottesmoreschool.com

Independent Co-educational Preparatory Boarding School.

Headmaster: **T F Rogerson**, BA, PGCE

Age Range. 4–13.
Number of Pupils. 100 Boys, 50 Girls.
Fees per term (2010-2011). Prep: £4,590 (Day), £6,270 (Boarding); Pre-Prep: £1,637–£2,183.

Cottesmore is a preparatory school offering Day, Weekly and Full Boarding. In September 2009 the school opened a Pre-Prep Department.

Cottesmore is situated a mile from Exit 11 of the M23, ten minutes from Gatwick Airport and one hour from Central London and Heathrow Airport.

Curriculum. Boys and girls are taught together in classes averaging 14 in number. The teacher/pupil ratio is 1:9. Children are fully prepared for Common Entrance and Scholarship examinations.

Music. The musical tradition is strong – more than 80% of children learn a variety of instruments; there are three Choirs, a School Orchestra and several musical ensembles.

Sport. The major games are Association and Rugby Football, Cricket, Hockey, Netball and Rounders. Numerous other sports are taught and encouraged. They include Tennis, Squash, Golf, Riding, Athletics, Cross-Country Running, Swimming, Windsurfing, Fishing, Boating, Gymnastics, Shooting, Judo and Archery. The School competes at a national level in several of these sports.

Recent Developments. Our Technology Centre houses a constantly developing Information Technology Suite, a Design Technology room for metal, woodwork, plastic and pneumatics, a Craft room, Kiln, two Science laboratories and Art Studio.

Hobbies and Activities. These include Pottery, Photography, Stamp Collecting, Chess, Bridge, Model-Making, Model Railway, Tenpin Bowling, Gardening, Rollerblading, Ballet, Modern Dancing, Drama, Craft, Carpentry, Printing, Cooking and Debating.

The boys and girls lead a full and varied life and are all encouraged to take part in as wide a variety of activities as possible. Weekends are a vital part of the school life and are made busy and fun for all.

Entry requirements. Entry is by Headmaster's interview and a report from the previous school. For a prospectus and more information, please write or telephone the Headmaster's Personal Assistant, Miss Janine Scola.

Coworth-Flexlands School

Valley End, Chobham, Woking, Surrey GU24 8TE
Tel: 01276 855707
Fax: 01276 856043
e-mail: secretary@coworthflexlands.co.uk
website: www.coworthflexlands.co.uk

Chairman of Governors: Mr Peter R Harris

Headmistress: Mrs Anne Sweeney, MA, DipEd

Age Range. Boys 3–7 years; Girls 3–11 years.
Number of Pupils. 141 day girls,11 day boys.
Fees per term (2010-2011). £1,295–£3,395.

If you are looking for a friendly, caring school where children hold on to their childhood and achieve high academic results in a relaxed setting, then Coworth-Flexlands is the school for you.

Situated in delightful rural surroundings on the outskirts of Chobham Common, and nestling in 13 acres of Surrey countryside, our lovely Edwardian house has been enhanced by a large, purpose-built extension, offering the best modern facilities.

On arrival you will immediately sense a happy, purposeful atmosphere and see classes engrossed in their studies or outside making use of our extensive grounds. Good-sized year groups provide lots of friends to play with and small teaching groups ensure that each child has the individual attention that they need to do really well academically. Our cheerful Learning Support department works closely with all the teachers to support those who need specific help and provide extended thinking skills for those who are particularly gifted.

In addition to all the usual National Curriculum subjects, Drama, Dance, Technology, Music, French, Art and Sport feature strongly in a broad curriculum, with our specialist teachers working with the children throughout the whole school to ensure progression and the best possible experience right from the word go. Classes enjoy outings and visits to enhance the curriculum and residential trips are arranged for the older children. For those who enjoy an extended day, we are open from breakfast at 7.30 am until 6 pm after tea, Clubs and Prep. Our extra-curricular activities include chess, dance, tennis, Rainbows and Brownies, orchestra, art, choir, gymnastics and Spanish and an after-school Homework Club for older children. There is a strong emphasis on pastoral care throughout the school and we are small enough for every child to be known to every teacher. In addition we have a thriving House system and the opportunities for children to contribute to school decision-making through the School Council and Eco Council.

We are particularly proud of our EcoSchool achievements, Gold Artsmark and our leavers for all obtaining places at the next schools of their choice, with many academic, Music and Art awards, both for our boys and girls.

There is an active Parents' Association which arranges many events throughout the year, adding to the lovely family feel as older and younger siblings come along and join in with us. Prospective parents are warmly invited to tour the school with the Headmistress. All enquiries and appointments should be made via the school secretary on 01276 855707.

Charitable status. Coworth-Flexlands School is a Registered Charity, number 309109 and Christian Foundation school, which welcomes pupils from all faiths. It exists to provide an excellent education and preparation for the next stage of schooling for all our pupils.

Craigclowan School

Edinburgh Road, Perth PH2 8PS
Tel: 01738 626310
Fax: 01738 440349
e-mail: headmaster@craigclowan-school.co.uk
website: www.craigclowan-school.co.uk

Chairman of Governors: James Bax, Esq

Headmaster: A R Rathborne

Age Range. 3–13.
Number of Pupils. 280: 140 boys, 140 girls; Pre-Prep 50.
Fees per term (2010-2011). £3,210.

Craigclowan is a co-educational, day school situated in 15 acres of its own ground on the outskirts of Perth. It is administered by a Charitable Trust.

Boys and girls are prepared for Common Entrance and scholarship for independent schools in both England and Scotland. In the recent past children have entered Glenalmond, Strathallan, Loretto, Merchiston Castle, Fettes, Gordonstoun, St Leonards, Ampleforth, Downe House, Sherborne, St Mary's Ascot, Malvern, Queen Margaret's York, Haileybury, Rugby, Stowe and Eton as a result of Common Entrance or Scholarship. In the last five years a total of 62 Scholarships have been gained covering academic, music, art, sport and all rounders.

Much attention is paid to each individual child in their preparation for academic success throughout the school and much energy is directed to a wide range of extra-curricular activities with games, music, drama, debating and art high on the list. The games played include rugby, hockey and cricket for boys, tennis, hockey and netball for girls, whilst everyone swims and takes part in athletics and skiing. Instrumental tuition takes in all the orchestral areas and children regularly participate in productions at the local Repertory Company. The children have won National Competitions in Rugby, Netball, Swimming, Skiing, Debating and Choir. Recent developments have included the construction of a dry ski slope, full-size astroturf for hockey and tennis and in September 2005 a one million pound classroom block.

The HMIE Inspection Report published in September 2004 gave significant praise to the school for the high standards achieved in key areas of school life. The major strengths identified by the Inspectors were:
- The school's positive ethos, including the strong partnership with parents.
- Attainment in English language.
- The high quality of pastoral care for pupils.
- The extensive range of extra curricular activities which provided opportunities for pupils to broaden their achievements.
- The commitment of staff and the polite, well motivated pupils.
- The quality of leadership provided by the Headmaster.

In addition, the Care Commission has inspected the Pre-school four times in the past three years, endorsing all that is being achieved within the Pre-school.

Charitable status. Craigclowan School Limited is a Registered Charity, number SC010817. It exists to promote education generally and for that purpose to establish, carry on and maintain a school within Scotland.

Cranford House Junior School

Moulsford, Wallingford, Oxfordshire OX10 9HT
Tel: 01491 651218
Fax: 01491 652557
e-mail: admissions@cranfordhouse.oxon.sch.uk
website: www.cranfordhouse.oxon.sch.uk

The School is a Charitable Trust run by a Board of Governors.

Chairman of the Governors: Mr R S Bray

Head of the Junior School: Mrs L Lawson, BA Hons, PGCE

Head of the Lower School: Mrs G Smeeton, BSc, QTS

Age Range. Girls 3–11, Boys 3–7.
Number of Pupils. 196.
Fees per term (2011-2012). £1,500–£3,675.
Children are admitted from 3 years old into the co-educational Lower School (pre-preparatory) which includes a purpose-built Nursery. Girls transfer to the Junior School (preparatory) at age 7.

Children are taught by specialist teachers for Music, Drama, PE, French and Religious Studies from the start of their time at Cranford. More specialist teaching is introduced in the Junior School to aid a smooth transition to Senior School education. In Form 3 there are two qualified teachers per class for English and Mathematics. All Junior pupils work in small ability groups for English and Mathematics to maximise achievement in these core subject areas. There is a full choir, chamber choir and orchestra and pupils are encouraged to take an active role in this as well as in school drama productions. A wide-reaching programme of extra-curricular clubs and activities ensures the all-round development of our pupils. Junior and Lower School pupils take part in sporting tournaments and competitions both at home and away. The curriculum includes a great number of curriculum+ activities and trips to enhance each child's learning experience in and out of the classroom.

Charitable status. Cranford House School Trust Limited is a Registered Charity, number 280883.

Cranleigh Preparatory School

Horseshoe Lane, Cranleigh, Surrey GU6 8QH
Tel: 01483 542058
Fax: 01483 277136
e-mail: fmjb@cranprep.org
website: www.cranprep.org

Chairman of Governors: J A V Townsend, MA

Head: M T Wilson, BSc

Age Range. 7–13.
Number of Pupils. 305 (50 Boarders, 255 Day).
Fees per term (2011-2012). Boarders £6,430; Day Pupils: £4,000 (Forms 1 & 2), £5,195 (Forms 3–6). These are genuinely inclusive and there are no hidden or compulsory extras.

The school stands in its own beautiful and spacious grounds of 35 acres. Cranleigh Preparatory School is a co-educational boarding and day school. A teaching staff of 40 enables classes to be small. The Head and his wife live in the school, as do the boys' boarding master and his family and the girls' housemistress and her family. They are fully involved with the health and happiness of the boys and girls, together with pastoral staff, including matrons. A great source of strength is the close partnership with Cranleigh School 'across the road'. The Preparatory School has use of Senior School sports facilities, including an indoor pool, artificial pitches, the stables and golf course.

The boys and girls are prepared for Common Entrance and many Scholarships are won. Through these exams about three quarters of the children move on to Cranleigh School and the remaining one quarter to a wide variety of other independent senior schools.

Boarding life is busy and fun. Pupils return home every week-end. There is also the opportunity to flexi board for two or more nights during the week.

The curriculum is broad, balanced and covers all and more than that laid down by the National Curriculum. The school teaches computing, and technological problem solving is encouraged. Art (including design, pottery, woodwork and various craft skills) and Music are included in the curriculum at all level. Individual instrumental lessons are available and peripatetic music staff teach at both schools.

There are choirs, orchestras, a band and several ensembles. Boys and girls are given every incentive to develop spare time interests and a choice of activities is built into the timetable.

The school is fortunate to have excellent facilities including a full-sized artificial pitch, a large sports and drama hall, a dance studio, a music school, very light airy classrooms and laboratories. The school has recently undergone a very large refurbishment programme and all facilities are extensive and modern. Boarding accommodation is bright and cheerful and fully modernised. Additions and improvements to the facilities are ongoing.

Rugby, football, hockey, netball, lacrosse, cricket, athletics, tennis, swimming, rounders, shooting, squash, cross country, basketball, fencing, riding, golf, Eton Fives, archery and badminton, are among the sports.

Normal entry age is at seven or eleven. Places are sometimes available in the intervening year groups.

Charitable status. Cranleigh School is a Registered Charity, number 1070856, whose Preparatory School exists to provide education for boys and girls aged 7–13.

Cranmore School

West Horsley, Leatherhead, Surrey KT24 6AT
Tel: 01483 280340
Fax: 01483 280341
e-mail: office@cranmoreprep.co.uk
website: www.cranmoreprep.co.uk

Chairman of Governors: The Very Revd Mgr J Scott, LCL, MCL

Headmaster: **M P Connolly**, BSc, BA, MA, MEd

Deputy Head: Mrs S Walker, CertEd
Assistant Head: T Hallett, BA Hons, QTS
Head of Pre-Prep: Miss M Kieran, CertEd

Age Range. 2½–13.
Number of Boys. 470 Day Pupils.
Fees per term (from January 2011). Nursery £1,375, Pre-Prep £3,065, Prep £3,690.

The School is situated midway between Leatherhead and Guildford, whilst Dorking and Woking are equally accessible.

There are 37 full-time members of staff, 16 part-time members and 19 visiting teachers for instruments in the Music department.

Our Nursery – Bright Stars at Cranmore – (2½–4 yrs) is co-educational with separate morning and afternoon sessions. It has its own dedicated accommodation which includes several classrooms and adjacent playground. The Junior Department of the school (4–8 yrs) offers all boys access to our tremendous resources including the sports hall, gymnasium, swimming pool and other sports and music facilities. Pupils enter the Senior Department at 8+ years and are taught by specialist subject teachers. At the end of National Curriculum Year 6 we create a Scholarship class and two parallel Common Entrance classes.

Boys are prepared for entry to a wide range of Independent Schools via the Common Entrance or Scholarship examination. We have an impressive track record in our pupils gaining academic, music, sport and all-rounder scholarships to a wide variety of prestigious schools.

A programme of investment over several years has given the school many outstanding facilities. These include a senior teaching block which comprises 3 large well-equipped science laboratories, 4 classrooms, a second ICT laboratory and a chapel. The gymnasium has been completely rebuilt, the swimming pool refurbished, 4 new astro tennis courts put in place and a large playground with playground furniture, all on a rubberised surface large enough to take two tennis courts, for 5-a-side football or 6-a-side hockey. There are 24 acres of playing fields, a sports hall (Badminton, Basketball, Cricket nets, Volleyball etc), 3 squash courts, a fitness room containing rowing machines and cross trainer treadmills, cross-country and athletics. In addition, another major development is our entrance hall, reception area, two libraries, art room and Design Technology room. In 2007 a second astroturf was completed and we opened a 6th Form common room.

School swimming and tennis teams compete in a wide variety of galas and tournaments. Inter-School and Inter-House competitions allow all boys to take part in organised games. Rowing, golf, tennis, ski clubs and many other sporting clubs operate through the term. There is also a Bridge Club, Technology Club, Board Games Club, etc, which occur weekly. A thriving chess club competes in a local schools' league and a number of honours have been won in recent years. The School has three ICT laboratories with the most up-to-date equipment.

A Drama, Speech and Music school incorporates a large Auditorium, two specialist teaching rooms and 7 practice rooms. Individual tuition in a wide variety of instruments is available; there are 2 orchestras, 8 choirs and various ensemble groups. A number of music scholarships are obtained each year.

Many other out-of-school activities are offered including skiing and rowing clubs. There are annual PGL, skiing and French holidays.

Many of the boys are Catholic although entry is open to boys of all denominations who are warmly welcomed.

Charitable status. Cranmore School, as part of the Diocese of Arundel & Brighton, is a Registered Charity, number 252878. It exists to provide education for children.

Crescent School

Bawnmore Road, Bilton, Rugby, Warwickshire CV22 7QH
Tel: 01788 521595
Fax: 01788 816185
e-mail: admin@crescentschool.co.uk
website: www.crescentschool.co.uk

Chairman of Trustees: Mr N Lines, ACIB

Headmaster: **Mr R H Marshall**, BSc Hons Wales, PGCE

Age Range. 3–11.
Number of Pupils. 156 Day Boys and Girls (69 boys, 87 girls).
Fees per term (2011–2012). £2,330–£2,520.

The Crescent School is an independent co-educational preparatory school for day pupils aged 4–11 years. In addition, there is a Nursery for children from the age of 3. The school was founded in 1947, originally to provide a place of education for the young children of the masters of Rugby School. Over the years the school has steadily expanded, admitting children from Rugby and the surrounding area. In 1988, having outgrown its original premises, the school moved into modern, purpose built accommodation in Bilton, about a mile to the south of Rugby town centre. The buildings provide large and bright teaching areas, with a separate annexe housing the Nursery and Reception classes. There are specialist rooms for Science, Art, Design Technology, ICT and the Performing Arts. In addition there is also a spacious Library and Resource Area. The multi purpose hall provides a venue for daily assemblies, large scale music making, is fully equipped for physical education and has all the necessary equipment to turn it into a theatre for school productions. The school is surrounded by its own gardens, play areas and sports field.

The requirements of the National Curriculum are fully encompassed by the academic programme and particular emphasis is placed on English and mathematics in the early years. All pupils receive specialist tuition in Information and Communication Technology, Music and Physical Education. Specialist teaching in other subjects is introduced as children move upwards through the school. Spanish is introduced in Reception, followed by French in Year IV and Latin in Year V. The pupils are prepared for the local 11+ examination for entry to maintained secondary schools, including local grammar schools, Common Entrance and specific entrance examinations also at 11+ for independent senior schools.

The performing arts are a particular strength of the school and lessons are given in speech and drama, singing, percussion, musical theory and appreciation and recorder playing. Instrumental lessons (piano, brass, woodwind and strings) are offered as an optional extra. There is a school choir, orchestra, brass, string and wind ensembles and recorder groups.

Charitable status. The Crescent School Trust is a Registered Charity, number 1120628. The object of the charity shall be the provision and conduct of a day school for children of the inhabitants of Rugby and the surrounding district.

The Croft Preparatory School

Alveston Hill, Loxley Road, Stratford-upon-Avon, Warwickshire CV37 7RL
Tel: 01789 293795
Fax: 01789 414960
e-mail: office@croftschool.co.uk
website: www.croftschool.co.uk

Principal: Mrs L K M Thornton, CertEd London

Chairman of the School's Council: A Wolfe, LLB

Headmistress: **Dr P A Thompson**, MA, DLitt, GRNCM, ARMCM, PGCE, FICPD, FRSA

Deputy Headmaster: Mr M Cook, BSc Hons, PGCE
Head of Prep: Mrs M Crocombe, BA Hons, PGCE
Head of Pre-Prep: Miss J Whitty, BA Ed Hons

Age Range. 2–11.
Number of Pupils. 484: 261 boys, 223 girls.
Fees per term (2011-2012). £495–£3,420.

The Croft is a co-educational day school for children from 2 to 11 years old, situated on the outskirts of Stratford upon Avon. Founded in 1933, the School occupies a large rural site with superb facilities and extensive playing fields, offering children some of the most exciting educational opportunities in the area. There is also a nature conservation area with lake.

A family-based school, The Croft provides specialist teaching in small groups, where good discipline and a wider knowledge of the world around us, both spiritual and geographical, is encouraged. Music, Sport and Drama each play an important part in the curriculum. The resulting high educational standards provide the all-round excellence which is at the heart of the School.

In May 2007, the School opened Mundell Court, a two-storey building which provides additional, spacious teaching areas for ICT, DT and Mathematics. It also incorporates a small-scale performance space. The concept underpinning the design is 'problem solving' and the development of thinking skills, vital for children in the 21st Century and beyond.

Children are prepared for 11+ entry either to the local Grammar Schools or Senior Independent Day Schools, or to go on to Boarding Schools.

Entrance requirements. Children can be accepted in the Nursery from the age of 2 years. Children above Reception age are assessed.

Crosfields School

Shinfield Road, Reading, Berks RG2 9BL
Tel: 0118 9871810
Fax: 0118 9310806
e-mail: office@crosfields.com
website: www.crosfields.com

Chairman of Governors: Mr R G Sutherland

Headmaster: **Mr J P Wansey**, BA, CertEd

Deputy Headmaster:
S C Dinsdale, MA Ed Open, BA Hons Chichester, FLCM, LTCL, LLCM, PGCE Open

Age Range. 3–13.
Number of Pupils. 506.
Fees per term (2011-2012). £2,465–£3,950 including lunches, school visits and after-school care. No compulsory extras.

Crosfields School is a co-educational day preparatory school based in Shinfield, Reading. It offers a first-class education with opportunities for all for boys and girls aged 3–13 years. Academically the school is excellent. Pupils progress quickly in small class sizes where they receive individual attention from dedicated teaching staff. Pupils move on to a range of senior schools and there have been a good number of scholarships and exhibitions in recent years and also an excellent record of entry to Reading School.

Facilities within the 40 acres of grounds are unrivalled at prep school level in the area, with a modern library, ICT suite, theatre and music complex, sports hall, indoor swimming pool, cricket nets and even a 6-hole golf course. The main sports for boys are Football, Rugby and Cricket with Netball, Hockey and Rounders for girls. Mixed football and tag rugby are played by both girls and boys and there is a wide range of extra-curricular hobbies and clubs from Year 3 upwards including Cookery, Golf, Drama, Judo, Dance and Fencing. A new Food Technology room opened in May 2009.

Crosfields' youngest members are enjoying the new Nursery class which opened in September for children aged 3+. It provides a happy and caring introduction to school life at Crosfields and a smooth transition to the Reception classes.

The school offers bursary awards of up to 100% of the fees at 11+ entry.

Charitable status. Crosfields School Trust Limited is a Registered Charity, number 584278. The aim of the School is solely to provide education for children between the ages of 3 and 13.

Culford Preparatory School

Culford, Bury St Edmunds, Suffolk IP28 6TX
Tel: 01284 729348
Fax: 01284 729183
e-mail: prepschool@culford.co.uk
website: www.culford.co.uk

Chairman of Governors: Professor R Swanston, DSc, FRICS, FCMI

Headmaster: **M Schofield**, BEd

Age Range. Co-educational 7–13.
Number of Pupils. 140 (Day), 40 (Boarders).
Fees per term (2011-2012). Day £3,135–£4,295, Boarding £6,160–£6,600.

Admission is by entrance examination at all ages, though the majority of pupils enter at age 7 or 11. Scholarships at 11+.

Culford Preparatory School has its own staff and Headmaster, but remains closely linked to the Senior School. This allows the School to enjoy a significant degree of independence and autonomy whilst benefiting from the outstanding facilities of the whole school, which is set on a site of 480 acres.

The Preparatory School is situated in its own grounds, within Culford Park. At the heart of the School is the quadrangle in the centre of which is the Jubilee Library. The two Science laboratories allow all children to benefit from specialist facilities and teachers. The pupils also enjoy splendid ICT facilities with the two dedicated ICT suites and the Prep School is fully networked with interactive whiteboards in all classrooms.

Beyond the quadrangle there are magnificent playing fields and a well equipped adventure playground. The pupils also benefit from Culford School Sports and Tennis Centre which offers a 25m indoor pool, cricket nets, squash courts, fitness suite, sports hall, specially designed climbing wall, floodlit Astroturf for hockey and tennis and a championship standard 4-court Indoor Tennis Centre which opened in 2009.

Pupils are given a thorough grounding in the essential learning skills of Mathematics and English and the curriculum broadens beyond the confines of the National Curriculum. Work in the classrooms is augmented by an extensive Activities Programme which offers pupils a wide range of opportunities and experiences. Music and drama play a significant part in school life with a variety of theatrical performances, choirs and ensembles (some in the new Studio Theatre) taking place throughout the year. Speech and drama lessons are also offered.

Boarders live in Cadogan House, a mixed boarding house located next to the School and overlooking the extensive playing fields and the adventure playground. There is a comprehensive programme of weekend activities and children are looked after by a team of dedicated staff under the direction of the Housemaster. There is a diverse programme of educational trips, both residential and day.

Religious affiliation: Methodist (pupils from other denominations are welcome).

Charitable status. Culford School is a Registered Charity, number 310486. It exists to provide education for boys and girls.

Cumnor House School
Cognita Schools Group

Boys School:
168 Pampisford Road, South Croydon, Surrey CR2 6DA
Tel: 020 8660 3445
Fax: 020 8645 2619
e-mail: admin@cumnorhouse.com
website: www.cumnorhouse.com

Girls School:
1 Woodcote Lane, Purley, Surrey CR8 3HB
Tel: 020 8668 0050
          Admissions: 020 8660 3445
Fax: 020 8660 9687
e-mail: admin.purley@cumnorhouse.com
website: www.cumnorhouse.com

Headmaster – Boys School: **P Clare-Hunt**, MA, CertEd

Headmaster – Girls School: P Kelly, DipEd

Age Range. Boys 4–13, Girls 4–11. Co-educational Nursery 2–4 years.

Number of Pupils. Prep & Pre-Prep: 400 Boys, 135 Girls. Nursery: 150.

Fees per term (2010-2011). £2,475–£3,210 (including lunch and school trips).

Cumnor House School for Boys is one of Surrey's leading Preparatory Schools. Pleasantly and conveniently situated, the School prepares boys for scholarships and common entrance examinations to leading senior independent schools and local grammar schools.

Scholarships have been won recently to Dulwich, Epsom, Westminster, Charterhouse, Tonbridge and the local senior independent schools, Whitgift, Trinity and Caterham.

Music, Art, Drama and Games play a large part in the life of the School and all contribute to the busy, happy atmosphere.

Choir, sports tours and matches, ski trips, regular stage productions and a broad spectrum of clubs and options, give the boys the opportunity to pursue a wide range of interests.

Religious denomination: Christian.

Entry requirements: Assessment test and interview.

Girls School. Cumnor House has at last responded to its parents' many requests for a girls school. They wanted their daughters to have the equivalent opportunities that their sons have enjoyed for many years. At Cumnor House School for Girls the aim is to provide excellence in education and a balanced and broad curriculum from nursery through to the age of 11 in a warm and caring environment.

Cumnor House School for Girls is a Preparatory School and its job is to do exactly that: prepare girls for their senior school education and indeed for life beyond.

Cumnor House School

Danehill, Haywards Heath, West Sussex RH17 7HT

Tel: 01825 790347

Fax: 01825 790910

e-mail: office@cumnor.co.uk

website: www.cumnor.co.uk

Chairman of Governors: S Cockburn, Esq, MA Oxon

Headmaster: **C St J S Heinrich**, BA Hons, PGCE

Deputy Headmaster: M N P Mockridge, BSc Hons, PGCE

Age Range. 4–13.

Number of Pupils. 365: 185 boys, 180 girls; 95 in the Pre-Prep; 60 boarders.

Fees per term (from April 2011). £6,275 (Boarding), £5,275 (Day); £2,790 (Pre-Preparatory).

We aim to provide a happy and purposeful atmosphere in which children learn to set themselves high standards. Individuality is encouraged and equal esteem is given to achievements in and out of class.

The School has a strong tradition of scholarship, and many awards have been won at a wide range of senior schools, primarily academic but also in art, music, sport, drama and technology.

Out of school we offer children many opportunities for sports and cultural activities. Girls and boys in the Prep school all play sport every day. Each term children are given a choice of 20 or so supervised hobbies, from which they choose three. Much music and drama takes place: 95% of pupils in the Prep school learn an individual instrument and the choirs perform regularly. There are two orchestras and a wind band, as well as much singing and ensemble work. Each Summer term 50 or more children are involved in the annual production of a Shakespearean play in our open air theatre. Our rebuilt Sussex barn is used as a Music School. A purpose-built theatre complex operates as a local arts centre for concerts, lectures, exhibitions and winter term plays. Set in 50 acres of fields and woodland, the school has a Sports Hall, four tennis courts and a heated outdoor pool, as well as a 25m indoor pool. Football, Rugby, Cricket, Netball, Hockey, Rounders and Athletics are all part of the sporting mix with 20 or so teams involved every Wednesday and/or Saturday. Old farm buildings have been converted into blocks for science, music, art, ICT and home economics whilst additions of new boarding wings, new kitchens and laundry are all recent. A new barn conversion in 2006 has provided 6 additional classrooms and a design technology centre and all classrooms have interactive whiteboards. The boarding staff includes a full-time qualified nurse. Boarding, entirely elective, is on a bi-weekly basis, allowing time for full weekends both at home and at school.

Charitable status. Cumnor House School Trust is a Registered Charity, number 801924. It exists for the advancement of education.

Dair House School

Bishop's Blake, Beaconsfield Road, Farnham Royal, Buckinghamshire SL2 3BY

Tel: 01753 643964

Fax: 01753 642376

e-mail: info@dairhouse.co.uk

website: www.dairhouse.org.uk

Chairman of Governors: Mr J O'Brien

Headmaster: **Mr Terence Wintle**, BEd Hons

Age Range. 3–11 Co-educational.

Number in School. 114 Day pupils.

Fees per term (2011-2012). £1,430–£3,040.

Located on the A355 at Farnham Royal we are conveniently placed for the Farnhams, Gerrards Cross, Beaconsfield, Stoke Poges and surrounding villages.

Dair House offers an exciting and personalised education to boys and girls from 3–11. We take pride in our warm, friendly, individual care, catering for each child's abilities. We provide our children with a firm sense of belonging and a sure foundation from the start in classes which are no larger than 16. The school has excellent facilities with a new ICT suite, a new dining room, new office, a recently updated library and Learning Support Department. Each class is fully resourced with interactive whiteboards and computers.

Dair House is situated in wonderful tree lined grounds with a large sports field, multi-purpose gym and all weather sports surface.

We offer a breakfast club from 8.00 am and an after-school tea club until 5.00 pm, as well as a plethora of lunchtime and after-school activities.

Charitable status. Dair House School Trust Limited is a Registered Charity, number 270719. Its aim is to provide 'a sure foundation from the start'.

Dame Bradbury's School

Ashdon Road, Saffron Walden, Essex CB10 2AL

Tel: 01799 522348

Fax: 01799 516762

e-mail: info@damebradburys.com

website: www.damebradburys.com

Dame Bradbury's is a co-educational day school, founded in 1525. It is an educational charity managed by a Board of Governors.

Chairman of Governors: Dr J Burch

Headmistress: Mrs J Crouch

Age Range. 3–11.
Number of Pupils. 265 Day Boys and Girls.
Fees per term (2011-2012). Nursery: £1,050 (mornings only), £950 (afternoons). A minimum of 3 nursery sessions a week is advised. Main school: Reception (4–5 years): £2,355 (mornings only), £2,820 (full time); 5–7 years £2,975; 7–11 years £3,200. Lunches £210. Bursaries are available.

Children are accepted from 3–11 years and are prepared for Common Entrance and entry into both independent and state schools.

A high teacher/pupil ratio is maintained and the fully qualified staff, augmented by part-time specialists and in the younger forms by teachers' assistants, work as a team to provide a stimulating educational environment. The curriculum is designed to give a broad general education of a high standard and covers the National Curriculum. French is introduced at the age of 3 and taught by a specialist. The school has a strong musical tradition and creative potential is encouraged in all the arts.

The spacious buildings provide room for the Nursery, large classrooms, a Performing Arts Theatre (created 2006), a multi-purpose Sports Hall (opened 2003), a well-equipped Science Laboratory and environmental garden with dipping pond (created 2007), a Teaching Garden (2008), a DT area, Music and Art Rooms, a spacious Library and Special Needs rooms and a main Dining Room. IT is fully integrated within the school with a wireless network, interactive whiteboards and an extensive Apple IT suite (opened in 2004). The School also runs a weekly Forest School in nearby woods.

There are spacious grounds and playing fields, 2 hard tennis/netball courts and an Astroturf court (September 2007). Physical Education features strongly in the curriculum and includes gymnastics, tennis, netball, football, rugby, hockey, cricket, athletics, rounders and swimming. There is an extensive programme of extra curricular activities which includes orchestra, choir, football, cricket, netball, drama, chess and philosophy.

The Headmistress will be pleased to provide further details and meet interested parents.

Charitable status. Dame Johane Bradbury's School is a Registered Charity, number 1070780. It exists to provide education for boys and girls.

Danes Hill

Leatherhead Road, Oxshott, Surrey KT22 0JG
Tel: 01372 842509
Fax: 01372 844452
e-mail: registrar@daneshillschool.co.uk
website: www.daneshillschool.co.uk

Chair of Governors: (*to be appointed*)

Headmaster: Mr William Murdock, BA, PGCE

Age Range. 3–13 co-educational.
Number of Children. 872.
Fees per term (2010-2011). £1,625–£4,504.

As a co-educational school, Danes Hill prepares boys and girls for Scholarship and Common Entrance examinations to senior schools. A high academic record (20 awards this year from a year group of 72) combines happily with a strong tra-

dition of sporting prowess to ensure that all children are exposed to a kaleidoscope of opportunity on a peaceful 55-acre site set well back from the main Esher-Leatherhead road. The Pre-Preparatory Department takes children from 3 to 6 years and is situated separately, but within easy walking distance of the Main School. There is a transport system available to take children both to and from school.

Extensive facilities include 2 state of the art IT suites, a science block with 4 fully-equipped laboratories and a new, high-tech Art and DT centre. Both Pre-Prep and Main School sites have covered swimming pools.

The curriculum is broad and a wide range of extra-curricular activity is encouraged. Languages are a particular strength of the school. All children learn French from age 3 and in addition choose German or Spanish in Year 4. All scholars and some Common Entrance pupils also study Latin, with Greek a further option and scholars are encouraged to sit one or more modern foreign languages at GCSE in their final year. Twenty-three children reached the final of the National Language Challenge recently.

Pastoral care and pupil welfare are closely monitored. The school's Learning Support Centre provides a high level of support both for those with specific learning difficulties as well as running a programme for the exceptionally gifted and talented.

Residential and day trips are seen as an essential part of the school experience. The school operates a well-established exchange programme with a German school, and there are language trips to centres in Spain and France. The annual Trips Week is a very special feature of the school calendar with over 500 children leaving the site to a range of residential destinations in the UK and abroad. There are also annual ski trips, as well as choir, rugby, netball and hockey tours.

Sport is a major strength and a team of 12 specialist games staff ensures that all the major sports are expertly coached. A floodlit astroturf pitch allows all-weather training and team spirit is valued alongside ability There are extensive programmes of inter-school fixtures for all age groups. Every child is encouraged to participate and in 2008-9 the school fielded 23 rugby, 28 football, 11 cricket, 16 netball and 21 hockey teams against other schools. We also arrange annual in-house games dinners for these teams and their parents to celebrate the end of each season. In-house Easter and Summer holiday activity courses are also very popular options with the pupils.

Former pupils are keen to stay in touch with the school. In 2004 a past pupils' society was founded, 'The Old Ravens', with over 3000 members on the database so far. A regular newsletter and a range of reunion dinners and events have proved extremely popular.

Charitable status. Danes Hill School (administered by The Vernon Educational Trust Ltd) is a Registered Charity, number 269433. It exists to provide high-quality education for boys and girls.

Daneshill School

Stratfield Turgis, Hook, Hampshire RG27 0AR
Tel: 01256 882707
Fax: 01256 882007
e-mail: office@daneshillprepschool.com
website: www.daneshillprepschool.com

Headmaster: Mr S V Spencer, CertEd, DipPhysEd St
    Luke's College, Exeter

Age Range. 2½–13.
Number of Pupils. Day Boys 118, Day Girls 122.
Fees per term (2011-2012). Nursery £1,550 (5 mornings); Reception & Year 1 £2,950, Year 2 & Year 3 £3,250,

Years 4–8 £3,650. Lunch included. There are no compulsory extras.

Founded in 1950, Daneshill has always prided itself on the collective qualities of its teaching staff and their ability to interact with pupils and deliver a stimulating learning experience.

Set in a beautiful, rural location close to the Hampshire-Berkshire border the School provides the perfect environment and atmosphere for each pupil to grow and prosper as an individual with a strong set of core values.

Academically the Daneshill curriculum has always maintained the expectations of the national curriculum while also offering so much more in respect of what we would regard as real education. Traditional values form the basis of a learning experience that engenders an enthusiasm for knowledge and encourages hard work as a means to academic success. This broadly-based curriculum also allows the development of high academic achievement to sit comfortably alongside our enthusiasm for pupils to become actively involved in all areas of the performing arts as well as the pursuit of sporting excellence.

Our aim has always been to develop enthusiastic learners who will make a strong contribution to their senior schools as good citizens and as pupils who are prepared to work hard in order to achieve success. This is certainly made easier by the children at Daneshill who possess a self-confidence and natural carefree joy which makes them a pleasure to teach. Each of them is a living testament to our belief that self-esteem is crucial to their development and success. We are also justifiably proud of the way our pupils exude courtesy, honesty, warmth and respect for others. They develop responsible attitudes to learning and life, and are a credit to themselves and their families.

Visitors to the School will be made very welcome and straight away they will experience the atmosphere that makes Daneshill unique.

Davenies School

Beaconsfield, Bucks HP9 1AA
Tel: 01494 685400
Fax: 01494 685408
e-mail: office@davenies.co.uk
website: www.davenies.co.uk

Chairman: S Dodds

Headmaster: **C Watson**, BEd, MA

Age Range. 4–13.
Number of Boys. 330 (Day Boys only).
Fees per term (2010-2011). £3,345–£4,270.

Davenies is situated in the heart of Beaconsfield, a Georgian town on the edge of the Chiltern Hills, close to the M40 and only thirty minutes from the centre of London by rail and car. Founded in 1940, the school aims to provide a broad education for day boys between the ages of 4 and 13. It enjoys a 'family' atmosphere, confident and courteous pupils and enthusiastic and committed staff.

The large site includes modern, airy classrooms, a purpose-built Science Laboratory, DT facility and Art Studio and a fully modernised IT Suite and Music Wing. A state-of-the-art Sports Complex incorporates an indoor swimming pool, Sports Hall and Performing Arts Centre. Boys are taught Rugby, Football, Cricket, Hockey, Athletics and Swimming and compete regularly against other schools.

Davenies follows a broad curriculum and there is a strong emphasis on numeracy and literacy from an early age. Specialist subject teaching begins in Year 3. French is taught from Year 1 and Latin from Year 6. There is an exciting array of over fifty extra-curricular activities each week which cater for individual interests; these include jazz band, moun-

tain biking, rock climbing, snowboarding, photography, electronics, cookery and media. The school also has its own Cub Pack.

Once they leave the Pre-Prep Department, the academic and pastoral welfare of the boys is undertaken by a network of form teachers. The Deputy Head and two of the Assistant Heads oversee the management of this care and ensure that regular, detailed communication with parents takes place, both formally and informally.

Some pupils move on to local Grammar Schools at the end of Year 6, although many choose to stay on to enjoy the hugely popular programme that Davenies offers its senior pupils before they move on to Senior Independent Schools at 13. As well as individual attention in the classroom, senior boys take part in the school's Senior Activity Programme (SAP) which introduces them to challenging, often unusual activities, whilst promoting team building and character development. SAP activities include paintballing, go-karting, sailing, skiing, water skiing and golf. Senior boys also have opportunities to go on skiing and adventure holidays, outward bound weekend and a wide variety of education trips. They also have the opportunity to participate in various sports tours, both at home and abroad.

Developing the whole individual is paramount at Davenies, where great emphasis is placed on the value of courtesy, good manners and consideration for others, encapsulated in the school's motto: 'singulus pro fraternitate laborans' (one working for the good of all).

Charitable status. Beaconsfield Educational Trust Ltd is a Registered Charity, number 313120. It exists to provide high standards and the fulfilment of each child's potential.

Dean Close Pre-Preparatory School

Lansdown Road, Cheltenham, Gloucestershire GL51 6QS
Tel: 01242 258079
Fax: 01242 258005
e-mail: squirrels@deanclose.org.uk
website: www.deanclose.org.uk

Chairman of Governors: Mrs P G Napier

Headmistress: **Dr C A Shelley**, BEd, PhD

Age Range. 2.9–7 Co-educational.
Number of Pupils. 178.
Fees per term (2011-2012). £2,280–£2,350.

The Pre-Preparatory School of Dean Close is a co-educational, Christian family school which occupies the same campus as Dean Close Preparatory and Dean Close School and is, therefore, able to share such outstanding facilities as the swimming pool, sports hall, tennis courts, theatre and art block.

The Pre-Preparatory School moved into a new, purpose-built school building opened by Lord Robert Winston in June 2004. The school has a large hall surrounded by classrooms on two floors. There are two playgrounds – one for the Nursery and Kindergarten and one for Reception and Years 1 and 2.

The curriculum within the Pre-Preparatory school offers a wide range of learning opportunities aimed at stimulating and nurturing a child's development and interests in an intellectual, physical, spiritual, social and emotional sense. Speech and Drama, Dance, Tennis, Music and Judo are available as extra-curricular activities. All children participate in Forest School, which teaches them about the trees and plants in the forest.

Charitable status. Dean Close School is a Registered Charity, number 1086829.

Dean Close Preparatory School

**Lansdown Road, Cheltenham, Gloucestershire
GL51 6QS**
Tel: 01242 258001
Fax: 01242 258005
e-mail: dcpsoffice@deanclose.org.uk
website: www.deanclose.org.uk

Chairman of Governors: Mrs P G Napier

Headmaster: The Revd Leonard Browne, MA

Age Range. 7–13.
Number of Pupils. 261: Boarding Boys 48, Boarding Girls 32, Day Boys 116, Day Girls 65.
Fees per term (2011-2012). Boarders £5,365–£6,795, Day Boarders £3,720–£5,255, Day Pupils £3,215–£4,750.

The Preparatory School of Dean Close is a fully co-educational, Christian family school which occupies the same campus as Dean Close School and is, therefore, able to share such outstanding facilities as the Chapel, swimming pool, theatre and extensive playing fields, including hard tennis courts, artificial astroturf hockey pitches and the new sports hall with indoor tennis, cricket nets, large gymnasium and dance studio.

Although the Preparatory School is administered by the same board of Governors, it has its own Headmaster and Staff. The Staff complement consists of 48 who either hold Degrees or Diplomas of Education, including a Director of Music and there is a team of excellent peripatetic musicians.

There are three boarding houses, each with resident Houseparents, 2 House Tutors and a resident matron.

The day pupils are accommodated in three purpose-built houses. Each is run by a Housemaster/Housemistress, assisted by house tutors.

The School follows a curriculum which embraces the National Curriculum and Common Entrance, preparing boys and girls for entry to the Senior School at 13+ by CE and internal transfer procedures. A few transfer to other senior independent schools.

The main games for boys are Rugby, Hockey and Cricket and for girls, Hockey, Netball, Cricket, Rounders and Tennis. Swimming, Athletics and Cross-Country Running are taught as well and use is made of the School's Covered Playing Area. Golf is available at a nearby course and Shooting is available in the school grounds.

Camping, Canoeing, Hill-walking and Orienteering are catered for and a wide range of activities is available including, among others, Trampolining, Badminton, Climbing, Computing, Cooking, Watercolour Painting and all forms of Dance. Special Activity courses are part of the curriculum.

There is a special music school and a purpose built hall for dramatic and orchestral performances. There is a separate Art, Pottery and Technology centre and a dining hall and kitchens.

The main classroom block consists of 10 specialist teaching rooms including 2 laboratories and a computer centre. This building is joined to the newest teaching block by the admin centre. This block has 7 purpose-built classrooms, together with day house facilities, the staff Common Room, a new Library and Art and Technology block.

The new purpose-built Pre-Prep School was opened in June 2004. (*See separate entry for Dean Close Pre-Preparatory School.*)

Charitable status. Dean Close School is a Registered Charity, number 1086829. It exists to provide education for children.

Denmead

Wensleydale Road, Hampton, Middlesex TW12 2LP
Tel: 020 8979 1844
Fax: 020 8941 8773
e-mail: secretary@denmeadschool.org.uk
website: www.denmeadschool.org.uk

Chairman of Governors: A J Roberts, CBE, BA, FRSA

Headmaster: M McKaughan, BEd

Age Range. Boys 3–11, Girls 3–7.
Number of Pupils. 220.
Fees per term (2011-2012). Kindergarten (3–4 years): £1,460 (mornings), £2,920 (all day). Pre-Prep (4–7 years): £3,130. Prep (7–11 years): £3,380 including lunch for full day pupils.

The School is situated in a quiet, leafy part of Hampton and is easily accessible by road and rail. The School merged with Hampton School in September 1999 to become the Hampton School Trust's preparatory school. Although there is still no expectation for pupils to select Hampton as their first-choice secondary school, at least 50 per cent on average each year transfer there. Both schools are served by the same Board of Governors and the Headmaster of Denmead now reports to the Headmaster of Hampton School. The amalgamation produces economies of scale from which Denmead benefits.

Boys now transfer to senior schools at 11+ rather than 13+. The Prep School is a two-form entry with 18 pupils per class, who are set for English, Maths and Reasoning. Since September 2004 Hampton has been offering Assured Places for 11+ entry. This is done from Year 2 through Denmead's ongoing programme of assessment of the boys and is also open to those starting in the Preparatory Department. Also, those boys who perform very well in the 11+ Hampton entry exams, but who do not gain an award from Hampton, will be considered for the W D James Award made by Denmead, which will be in the form of a reduction in the child's first term's fees at Hampton.

The Pre-Prep is housed on its own site in the homely atmosphere of two linked residential houses offering space and security. Rooms are well-appointed and there are 22 pupils per class. The Preparatory section which backs on to an attractive public park, boasts its own games field and purpose-built teaching facilities including a multi-purpose hall. Major school sports are Football, Rugby, Cricket and Athletics. An extensive programme of extra-curricular activities includes art clubs, chess, drama, judo, computing, Warhammer/Lego and a variety of minor sports. There is a School choir, an orchestra, and a flourishing tradition of drama. Individual music tuition is also provided.

Parents share in the life of the School as fully as possible and there exists a very active parents' association.

Please contact the School Office for a prospectus.

Charitable status. Denmead School is part of the Hampton School Trust, which is a Registered Charity, number 1120005. It exists to provide a school in Hampton.

Derwent Lodge
The Schools at Somerhill

Somerhill, Tonbridge, Kent TN11 0NJ
Tel: 01732 352124
Fax: 01732 363381
e-mail: office@somerhill.org
website: www.somerhill.org

Derwent Lodge is one of the three Schools at Somerhill under the care and control of The Somerhill Charitable Trust.

Chairman of Governors: Mr Philip Thomas

Principal: Mr J T Coakley, MA

Headmistress: **Mrs S Michau**, MA Oxon, PGCE

Age Range. Prep: Girls 7–11. Pre-Prep: Co-educational 3–7.
Number of Pupils. Prep: 144 Day Girls. Pre-Prep: 278 boys and girls.
Fees per term (2011-2012). Prep: £4,090.
Extras: individual music lessons, recreational outings, minibus service from Tunbridge Wells, West Malling and Brenchley area, residential study visits.

Derwent Lodge was founded in central Tunbridge Wells in 1952 and moved to its present parkland setting on the southern outskirts of Tonbridge in 1993.

The school is noted for its strong academic tradition and for its caring, happy atmosphere. High standards of work, manners and courtesy are expected of each girl. There are specialist facilities for science, art, music, IT and sport.

The curriculum is designed to give a stimulating and rich general education which will prepare pupils well for entry to the grammar or independent schools chosen by their parents. Pupils regularly gain scholarships to secondary schools.

An optional extended day is offered. There is a full programme of extra-curricular clubs and activities. Girls are offered residential visits to the Isle of Wight and France.

Admission to Derwent Lodge follows girls spending a taster day at the school for informal assessment before the offer of a place is confirmed. Girls from the pre-preparatory school at Somerhill may proceed to Derwent Lodge automatically.

Charitable status. The Somerhill Charitable Trust Limited is a Registered Charity, number 1002212. It exists for the purpose of providing education for children.

Devonshire House Preparatory School

2 Arkwright Road, Hampstead, London NW3 6AE
Tel: 020 7435 1916
Fax: 020 7431 4787
e-mail: enquiries@devonshirehouseprepschool.co.uk
website: www.devonshirehouseschool.co.uk

Headmistress: **Mrs S Piper**, BA Hons

Age Range. Boys 2½–13, Girls 2½–11.
Number in School. 580: 319 Boys, 261 Girls.
Fees per term (2011-2012). £2,455–£4,670.
Devonshire House School is for boys and girls from three to thirteen years of age and the School's nursery department, the Oak Tree Nursery, takes children from two and a half. The academic subjects form the core curriculum and the teaching of music, art, drama, computer studies, design technology and games helps to give each child a chance to excel. At the age of eleven for girls and thirteen for boys the children go on to their next schools, particularly the main independent London day schools.

Devonshire House pursues high academic standards whilst developing enthusiasm and initiative. It is considered important to encourage pupils to develop their own individual personalities and a good sense of personal responsibility. There is a wide variety of clubs and tuition is available in ballet, judo, fencing, speech and communication and in a range of musical instruments. High standards and individual attention for each child are of particular importance.

The School is located on the crest of the hill running into Hampstead Village and has fine Victorian premises with charming grounds and walled gardens.

Dolphin School

Hurst, Berkshire RG10 0BP
Tel: 0118 934 1277
Fax: 0118 934 4110
e-mail: omnes@dolphinschool.com
website: www.dolphinschool.com

Founded in 1970.

Headmistress: **Veronica Gibbs**, BSc, PGCE

Registrar: Mrs J Vernon

Age Range. 3–13.
Number of Pupils. 220: 126 Day Boys, 94 Day Girls.
Fees per term (2011-2012). Nursery: £1,668 (3 days), £2,224 (4 days), £2,780 (5 days); Reception £3,350; Years 1 and 2 £3,550; Years 3–8 £3,730.
"*An exciting, challenging, dynamic learning environment*" according to the 2004 ISI Inspection Report of Dolphin School. "*The warmth of the greeting everywhere is striking and genuine*", noted the Good Schools Guide review.

We believe that children have special gifts and talents, which too often remain hidden forever. Dolphin School offers an environment which encourages these gifts to flourish. Children leave Dolphin with confidence in themselves, a strong sense of individualism, the ability to adjust well in school and social situations, at least one area in which they can feel pride in their own achievement and a strong sense of curiosity and enjoyment in learning. Throughout life, in an ever more quickly changing world, they will have the skills and the confidence successfully to pursue their ambitions and interests and to lead happy and fulfilled lives.

Dolphin children are allowed to develop as individuals and encouraged to fulfil their various potentials in small classes under the careful guidance of specialist teachers. Abundant academic, artistic, social and sporting stimulation is provided through an extremely broad, well-rounded programme. We encourage lateral thinking and the ability to cross reference. Expectations for all children are high and academic rigour is a key component in all lessons.

Dolphin School provides the friendly, family atmosphere of a small school. All members of staff are actively concerned with the pastoral care of all the children, but each form teacher assumes special responsibility for the daily well-being and the overall progress of a very small group of children. In addition children in their final three years have a personal mentor. Class sizes average sixteen. Children learn both to talk and listen to each other, to evaluate and tolerate the opinions of others and to take pride in each other's achievements. They are also encouraged to accept responsibility and to develop their leadership abilities.

Courses offered. Children are taught by graduate specialists from age six in most subjects. In the early years we provide a firm grounding in English-based skills throughout all humanities subjects. French begins in Nursery, Latin in Year Five and German, Spanish and Greek in Year Seven. Laboratory science is taught from age seven. Mathematics, geography, history, ICT, classical studies, art, design technology, drama, music and PE are taught throughout the upper school. Architecture, astronomy, philosophy, thinking skills, religious education, current affairs, environmental studies and cultural studies are included in some years.

The "Dolphin Scheme" for teaching ICT is now used in more than 80 schools throughout Britain. It was invented and developed in our ICT Department. The subject is now integrated into all areas of the curriculum.

Activities. A unique strength of Dolphin School is our residential field trip programme in which all children participate from age seven. The work related to these trips forms major sections of all departmental syllabuses. Principal annual field trips visit East Sussex, Dorset, Ironbridge, North Wales, Northumbria, Normandy and Italy, while departments organise residential trips to Boulogne, York and Stratford. We also offer an extensive mountain-walking programme. We have a large number of trained British Mountain Leaders. Staff and children participate in a graded fell walking programme. Locations range from the Lake District and Brecon Beacons to Snowdonia and the Alps. We also organise sports tours and a "custom made" outward bound course.

We believe in 'hands-on' learning, whether in or outside the classroom, and children participate in a very wide range of day trips to museums, theatres, archaeological sites and many other venues.

Almost all costs associated with field, walking and day trips are included in the fees, as are lunch-time and after-school clubs which include: athletics, tennis, short tennis, judo, rounders, cricket, embroidery, computing, swimming, football, netball, gymnastics, craft, hockey, chess, cross country, rugby, art, table tennis, orchestra, windband, string group, choir, orienteering, gardening, cookery and drama.

We field teams at all levels in football, rugby, cricket, chess, netball, rounders, tennis, short tennis, swimming, cross-country, athletics, hockey and judo. We are well represented at county level.

Facilities. Our hall offers a splendid venue for school concerts and plays. We stage several major productions each year. Grounds include a swimming pool, all weather tennis courts and playing fields. Cricket matches are played at Hurst, a neighbouring county standard ground.

Entry. Nursery at age 3, Reception at age 4+, and throughout the Upper School as places become available.

Internal and external scholarships are available to children aged 10–13 in the performing arts, art, creative writing and sport. Academic bursaries are also available.

Examination results. Our examination results are outstanding and we regularly win major scholarships to senior independent schools, including St Paul's, Eton and Winchester. We have a thriving Old Delphinian organisation. Most past pupils gain good degrees and a high proportion attend Oxbridge colleges.

The Downs Malvern

Colwall, Malvern, Worcs WR13 6EY
Tel: 01684 544 100
Fax: 01684 544 105
e-mail: registrar@thedowns.malcol.org
website: www.thedowns.malcol.org

Chairman of Governors: Reverend Kenneth E Madden, BA, PGCE

Headmaster: **Alastair S Cook**, BEd Hons

Age Range. 3–13 years.
Number of Pupils. 150 boys, 100 girls.
Fees per term (2011-2012). Boarding £3,975–£6,136; Flexi-boarding £31.80 per night; Day £3,293–£4,636; Pre-Preparatory £1,931–£2,612; Early Years: £19.88 per am/pm session, £39.76 per day (8.30–3.30), £43.44 per day (8.30–5.00).

The Downs Malvern is a busy, vibrant and successful co-educational preparatory school for boarding and day children aged between 3 and 13 years, offering an outstanding education.

Located 3 miles west of Malvern, 4 miles east of Ledbury, 15 miles from the M5 motorway, on the main line from Paddington and served by Malvern College transport, the Downs is situated on the Herefordshire side of the Malvern Hills on a striking rural 55-acre campus in Colwall.

The Downs Malvern strives to exceed the confines of the National Curriculum in academic, as well as cultural, sporting and social accomplishments. The school offers a broad curriculum challenging the academically gifted and supporting those with special needs.

Last year the Pre-prep Department welcomed the Nursery pupils into their newly refurbished building and, after a seamless move over to the Prep Department at 7 years old, pupils will move on to Malvern College, or to their preferred senior school at 13 to complete their school education.

Year 8 pupils have moved on to a variety of independent senior schools on the basis of scholarship or Common Entrance examinations and, whilst the option to go on to a wide variety of independent schools is still there, the direction has changed. The Downs is the main feeder school for Malvern College and the emphasis in Years 7 and 8 is not only a preparation for scholarships and Common Entrance, but also to allow a smooth transition to the College academically and socially.

Sports, especially team games, are a significant part of the curriculum, as are Music and Art. 80% of the pupils learn to play a musical instrument. There is also a wide and expanding Hobbies programme that includes Railway Engineering as well as Speech and Drama, Dance, Design Technology and Art.

Boarding. The newly refurbished Boarding House provides a home for up to 60 boarders. Boarding can be full, flexi or a one-off experience with a published programme of evening and weekend activities. All boarders are looked after by a caring staff, dedicated to their welfare.

Facilities. There is a wide range of facilities including a 300-seat capacity Concert Hall, self-contained Music and Art buildings; new Science laboratories; a new Design and Technology suite, Pottery studio and wired computer network with whiteboards. A new sports complex is supplemented by an astroturf Hockey pitch, 3 Netball/Tennis courts and 55 acres of grounds set aside for games pitches, Forest School lessons and relaxation. The school has its own narrow gauge steam railway!

11+ Scholarships and Exhibitions are awarded to pupils who show academic excellence and/or who show academic competence as well as having a particular talent in Art, Music, Drama or Sport.

Bursaries are available offering assistance to parents subject to completion of a means test form.

Charitable status. The Downs, Malvern College Prep School, trading as The Downs Malvern, is a Registered Charity, number 1120616. It exists to provide education for girls and boys from 3–13 years.

The Downs School

Wraxall, Bristol BS48 1PF
Tel: 01275 852008
Fax: 01275 855840
e-mail: office@thedownsschool.co.uk
website: www.thedownsschool.co.uk

Chairman of Governors: A M J Currie

Head Master: **Marcus Gunn**, MA Ed, BA, PGCE

Age Range. 4–13.
Number of Pupils. 255: 165 boys, 90 girls.

Fees per term (2011-2012). £2,830–£4,400 including lunch.

The Downs School was founded in 1894 in a house near The Downs in Bristol. In 1927 it moved six miles due west to the idyllic country setting of Charlton House and in the Autumn of 2002, the School was bought from the late Lord Wraxall's estate.

The Downs is a co-educational preparatory school for children from 4 to 13 years old. The children enjoy an all-round education, achieving high academic standards and they are recognised nationally for their success in sport, particularly, rugby and hockey.

Through highly skilled teaching we create an exciting and stimulating environment for learning, and by developing the talents of each child we believe that every pupil can succeed. The children are encouraged to become independent thinkers and to use their own initiative with confidence. They are prepared for Common Entrance and scholarship examinations to a wide range of public and independent schools.

In the happy, caring Pre-Prep Department (from 4 to 7 years old) the girls and boys play imaginatively and grow in confidence. Each child is nurtured to establish a sound social and academic foundation for their future education.

The School has over 50 acres of playing fields, a sports hall, two astroturfs and an outdoor heated pool. The children play and compete in athletics, cricket, netball, rounders, rugby, rugby sevens, swimming and tennis. Outdoor pursuits include abseiling, caving and canoeing and a broad range of activities include cricket, ballet, cooking, sculpture and chess.

Major drama and musical productions, as well as more frequent informal music, poetry and drama evenings are staged throughout the year.

For further information or to arrange a visit to see the children at work and play, please contact The School Office on 01275 852008.

Charitable status. The Downs School is a Registered Charity, number 310279. It was established for the education of boys and girls aged 4–13.

Downsend
Cognita Schools Group

Leatherhead, Surrey KT22 8TJ
Tel: 01372 372311
Fax: 01372 363367
e-mail: admissions@downsend.co.uk
website: www.downsend.co.uk

Headmaster: F Steadman

Age Range. 2–13 co-educational.
Number of Pupils. Day: 580 (aged 6–13), 320 (aged 2–6).
Fees per term (2010-2011). Pre-Preparatory £755–£2,840, including lunch for full-time pupils and Early Bird and 'Little Lates' facilities. Preparatory: £3,120 (Year 2), £3,785 (Years 3–8), including lunch. Sibling discounts apply for more than one child in Reception or above.

Downsend is a co-educational day school for children aged between 2 and 13 years.

The main school stands on a pleasant, open site just outside the town, surrounded by its own playing fields and tennis courts. The Sports Complex includes a large indoor swimming pool and a new artificial pitch was completed in 2007. The newly styled library and the expanded, networked ICT provision, are available to support children's learning and development.

Pre-Preparatory (age 2 to 6). There are three co-educational pre-preparatory departments in Ashtead, Epsom and Leatherhead. Here pupils work in a small and friendly envi-

ronment, where they are encouraged to achieve their individual potential through a wide range of activities. Outings, sport, music and drama all play an important part in school life. French is enjoyed by Second Steps Nursery to Year 1 children. An extended day facility provides after-school care to 5.30 pm, which is especially useful for working parents. At 6, the majority of the children move on to the main Downsend site where they are joined by children from other local Independent and State schools.

Preparatory (age 6 to 13). Founded in 1918, Downsend is not only a traditional academic prep school which prepares children for Common Entrance, Scholarship and High School examinations, but also a thriving community where many other opportunities are provided.

The standard of work is high and the school is particularly proud of its scholarship record. Recently an average of 30 awards a year has been achieved.

There is a wide curriculum and the children study, in addition to the normal Common Entrance subjects, Art, Drama, Food Technology, Health Education, ICT, Music, Technology and Textiles. Parents are kept informed of their children's progress through regular parents' evenings and termly reports, and are welcome at all times to communicate with members of staff.

The school has a strong reputation for its music, with regular concerts throughout the year, and a large number of children learn a variety of musical instruments. Drama is equally important and there are several productions each year. Pupils can take part in a full range of sports not only in school but also at local, regional and national level. Regular visits occur outside school and trips abroad are also arranged.

A holiday care activity scheme, Downsend+, gives pupils access to exciting and absorbing workshops and courses, Masterclass coaching by professional sports people and thrilling days out. Run by qualified Downsend staff, this provision is available to children aged 5–13 from 8 am to 5.30 pm, including breakfast, lunch and tea as appropriate. Downsend Lodges+ is also available as a dedicated facility for children aged 2–5 at Leatherhead Lodge.

Dragon School

Bardwell Road, Oxford OX2 6SS
Tel: 01865 315400
Fax: 01865 311664
e-mail: admissions@dragonschool.org
website: www.dragonschool.org

Chairman of Governors: Chris Jones

Headmaster: John Baugh, BEd

Age Range. 4–8 (Dragon Pre-Prep), 8–13 (Dragon).
Number of Pupils. Day: 570 (371 boys, 199 girls); Boarders: 265 (195 boys, 70 girls).
Fees per term (2010-2011). Day £2,950–£5,440; Boarding £7,790.

The Dragon School, just north of Oxford city centre, enjoys a leafy setting on the banks of the River Cherwell. Traditional buildings, contemporary facilities and extensive playing fields are the setting for an exceptional all-round academic education for boarding and day pupils. Dragons are noted for a spirited informality and a confident, enthusiast approach to all they do. A culture of learning how to learn and the appreciation of effort of every kind, result in all-round academic, sporting and cultural excellence. A non-selective school, the Dragon regularly achieves an impressive list of scholarships and awards (37 in 2009) and children go on to the country's finest Independent Senior Schools.

A sizeable school, the Dragon is composed of small, friendly communities. A dedicated building for Year 4 (E block) with its own playground offers children a gentle introduction to a preparatory school that is large enough to grow with them. Boarding is the heart of the school where warm support and a caring ethos are enjoyed by boarders from the local community and around the world. Homely boarding houses of varying sizes provide a gradual transition to life at senior schools; a new additional house for girls opens in 2009/10.

The extensive curriculum is taught by highly qualified and individual staff whose innovative lessons and high standards led to the Dragon being deemed 'outstanding' on many fronts in its 2006 Inspection. A very strong sporting tradition is mirrored by rich creativity in drama, music and art.

Extra-curricular activities encompass games, languages, sports, debates, drama, music and much more. Dragons are seasoned travellers and many expeditions and trips are made to destinations ranging from local woodlands to Brazil and including Sri Lanka, Switzerland, South Africa and Morocco. There is a regular exchange programme with schools in New York and Tokyo.

The Dragon Pre-Prep Lynams is a short distance away in Summertown with its own staff and facilities for Reception and Years 1, 2 and 3. The Ofsted report for Reception was 'Outstanding'.

Bursaries of up to 95% of fees are offered for boarding or day places. Academic awards worth up to 20% of fees are also offered.

For further information or to arrange a visit please contact the Registrar on 01865 315405.

Charitable status. The Dragon School Trust Ltd is a Registered Charity, number 309676. It aims to provide education for boys and girls between the ages of 4 and 13.

Duke of Kent School

Peaslake Road, Ewhurst, Surrey GU6 7NS
Tel: 01483 277313
Fax: 01483 273862
e-mail: office@dukeofkentschool.org.uk
website: www.dukeofkentschool.org.uk

Chairman of the Governing Body: N J Ashman

Head: **Mrs J Fremont-Barnes**, MA Oxon, MEd

Age Range. 3–16 co-educational.
Number of Pupils. 235 including 15 full/part boarders.
The Duke of Kent School stands in magnificent surroundings in the Surrey Hills and is an excellent option for towns such as Guildford, Horsham and Dorking. It also serves a host of local villages and is within easy reach of Central London, the M25 and Heathrow and Gatwick Airports. It has been a highly successful Prep School for many years and from September 2009, has been admitting pupils into Year 9, subsequently taking them through to GCSE, so that the School is now offering Nursery, Pre-Preparatory, Preparatory and Senior education for pupils aged 3–16. Though predominantly a day school in total numbers, the School retains a small but thriving boarding section.

Our full-time qualified teaching staff has been preparing pupils for Common Entrance and Scholarship for many years to a wide range of distinguished senior schools. Alongside a number of new appointments, it is well placed to take our senior pupils through to their GCSEs in a choice of subjects and the overall quality of teaching staff is outstanding. The stable block and courtyard has become the new Boarding Village with a Housemaster and Boarding Supervisor living on site. Former dormitory space in the main school has been converted into new Art and Design

Technology studios and classrooms for the Senior School. Both Music and Art thrive in an energetic atmosphere that encourages pupils to excel. There are extensive playing fields, a heated and covered pool and all-weather tennis courts. A full-sized sports hall allows a wide range of indoor sports, including hockey and gymnastics. Facilities throughout the School, from Nursery upwards, have benefited from the expansion of the School's catchment area that has accompanied the extension of the age-range. Pastoral care and wide-ranging activities programmes ensure that all pupils are able to thrive in a broad sense, as well as achieving demanding academic targets.

Fees per term (2011-2012). Day Pupils £1,555–£4,525, Boarders £4,275–£6,640. Entrance scholarships are available for admission to the Main School for both day and boarding pupils. Special discounts are available for Service Boarders to supplement the CEA.

Charitable status. The Duke of Kent School is a Registered Charity, number 1064183.

Dulwich Prep London

42 Alleyn Park, Dulwich, London SE21 7AA
Tel: 020 8670 3217
Fax: 020 8766 7586
e-mail: registrar@dulwichpreplondon.org
website: www.dulwichpreplondon.org

The School was founded in 1885 and became a charitable trust in 1957 with a board of governors.

Chairman of Governors: Mr D Pennock

Headmaster: **M Roulston**, MBE, MEd

Age Range. Boys 3–13, Girls 3–5.
Number of Boys. 790 day boys, 20 girls, 25 weekly boarders (aged 8–13).
Fees per term (2011-2012). Tuition: Day boys £1,800–£4,862 (inclusive of lunch – there are no compulsory extras). Weekly boarders: £1,837 in addition to tuition fee.

Dulwich Prep London (formerly known as DCPS) is an independent prep school with a national reputation for excellence.

While we are essentially a boys' school, with about 810 pupils aged between 3 and 13, we start with the Nursery which also caters for girls. There are three other sections to the school: the Annexe (Years 1 & 2), the Lower School (Years 3 & 4) and the Middle & Upper Schools (Years 5–8). In addition we have a well-equipped boarding house set in 13 acres of grounds with tennis courts and playing fields. We are delighted to offer weekly boarding for up to 30 boys.

At 13+ our boys go on to more than fifty excellent day and boarding schools throughout the country. Alleyn's, Charterhouse, Dulwich College, Eton College, Marlborough College, Tonbridge, St Paul's, Wellington College, Westminster and Winchester College are just a selection of our leavers' destination schools. In the 2010-11 academic year our leavers gained more than 30 academic, musical, artistic and sporting scholarships and awards.

Situated in SE21, we have the very best in educational facilities. These include 4 science labs, a dedicated music school, a large sports hall, a studio theatre, 3 ICT suites, a superb art studio, a six-lane 25m swimming pool and more than 25 acres of playing fields, quite unique given our privileged location.

Some of the opportunities available to our pupils are:
• We run more than 25 sports teams each term with the top teams regularly doing well in national competitions. Recent sports tours include cricket to South Africa, football to Italy, swimming in the USA and rugby to Portugal.

- More than 700 individual music lessons take place every week and boys have opportunity to perform regularly in a range of groups and ensembles.
- Approaching 30 groups perform regularly in our own 300 seat concert hall. Many also appear on the programme for our gala concerts at prestigious venues such as The Royal Festival Hall and The London Palladium.
- We provide more than 100 clubs and extra-curricular activities, stimulating boys' intellectual and sporting interests.
- We run residential trips for pupils in Years 4–8 within the curriculum that are built in to the fee structure. 12 more trips, ranging from cultural visits to skiing, are offered during the holidays.
- Drama productions are staged annually from Reception to Year Six as well as an Upper School play in the spring.

Charitable status. Dulwich College Preparatory School Trust is a Registered Charity, number 312715. It exists to provide education for boys.

Dulwich Preparatory School

Coursehorn, Cranbrook, Kent TN17 3NP
Tel: 01580 712179
Fax: 01580 715322
e-mail: registrar@dcpskent.org
website: www.dcpskent.org

Chairman of Governors: D R M Pennock

Headmaster: **Mr Paul David**, BEd Hons

Age Range. 3–13.
Number of Boys and Girls. Day: 280 (Upper School), 200 (Little Stream), 64 (Pre-Prep).
Fees per term (2011–2012). Day: £4,635 (Years 5–8), £3,955 (Years 2–4), £3,000 (Year 1), Pre-Prep: £2,520 (full day), £1,575 (mornings). Boarders: £37.00–£40.50 per night.

The School, which is one mile from the country town of Cranbrook, has extensive grounds (50 acres) and offers a broad and varied education to boys and girls from 3 to 13+. To ensure that children receive the personal attention that is vital for this age range the School is divided up into three separate, self-contained, departments. These are Nash House (3–5 year olds), Little Stream (5–9 year olds) and Upper School (9–13 year olds). Each department has its own staff, teaching equipment, sports facilities, playgrounds, swimming pools, etc. Pupils are prepared for Common Entrance or Scholarship examinations to any school of their parents' choice, and there is a strong emphasis on up to date teaching methods. The wide scope for sporting activities – Football, Rugby, Cricket, Hockey, Netball, Rounders, Athletics, Cross-country, Swimming, Tennis – is balanced by the importance attached to Art, DT, Drama, ICT and Music. Over 200 pupils learn the full range of orchestral instruments. There are two Orchestras, Wind and Brass Bands, Jazz Band, and four Choirs. The boarders are divided into two houses, boys and girls, each under the care of House staff. The happiness of the boarders is a particular concern and every effort is made to establish close and friendly contact between the School and the parents. There is a flourishing Parents Association, and regular meetings are held between staff and parents.

The School is a Charitable Trust, under the same Governing Body as Dulwich College Preparatory School, London, although in other respects the two schools are quite separate. The link with Dulwich College is historical only.

Charitable status. Dulwich College Preparatory School Trust is a Registered Charity, number 312715. It exists for the provision of high quality education in a Christian environment.

Dumpton School

Deans Grove House, Wimborne, Dorset BH21 7AF
Tel: 01202 883818
Fax: 01202 848760
e-mail: secretary@dumpton.com
website: www.dumpton.com

Chairman of Governors: Mrs K Waterman

Headmaster: **A W Browning**, BSc, PGCE, MA Ed, CChem, MRSC

Age Range. 2½–13.
Number of Pupils. Girls and Boys: 209 (aged 7–13); 142 (aged 2½–7).
Fees per term (2011–2012). Prep School £4,267; Pre-Prep £2,383; Nursery (on application). Monday to Friday with some Saturday fixtures. All fees include meals. There are no compulsory extras.

In a beautiful rural setting, the school is nevertheless only one mile from Wimborne and there are daily school bus runs to and from the nearby towns of Bournemouth, Poole, Wareham, Ringwood and Blandford.

Despite record numbers in the school class sizes are small, averaging 16–17 in the Prep School and 16 in the Pre-Prep.

Children enjoy excellent teaching as well as incomparable opportunities for Music, Art, Drama and Sport in which the school excels. Dumpton is renowned for its caring approach in which every child is encouraged to identify and develop his or her abilities and personal qualities as fully as possible. It is a very happy and successful school and children regularly win scholarships to their Senior Schools or places at the local Grammar Schools. Over the past five years Dumpton pupils have been awarded over 100 scholarships to schools such as Bryanston, Canford, Clayesmore, Millfield, Talbot Heath and Sherborne.

Recent developments have included a new Science/Maths Block, a full-size Astroturf, a covered swimming pool, climbing wall and environmental area, complete with ponds, pontoons, beehives and pupil allotments.

For a copy of the prospectus, please apply to the Headmaster.

Charitable status. Dumpton School is a Registered Charity, number 306222. It exists to provide education for boys and girls.

Dunhurst
Bedales Junior School

Petersfield, Hampshire GU32 2DP
Tel: 01730 300200
Fax: 01730 300600
e-mail: jjarman@bedales.org.uk
website: www.bedales.org.uk

Chairman of Governors: A Redpath

Head: **Mrs J Grubb**, BA

Age Range. 8–13.
Number of Pupils. 195: 105 girls (77 day, 28 boarders), 90 boys (66 day, 24 boarders).
Fees per term (2011-2012). Boarders £6,860 Day: £5,370 (Years 5–8), £4,370 (Year 4).

Dunhurst, the Junior School of Bedales, was founded in 1902 and occupies a part of the Bedales estate. It follows the same general ethos as Bedales and is properly co-educational and non-denominational. The atmosphere is happy, relaxed, friendly and purposeful with a great amount of tolerance, trust and genuine rapport between teachers and pupils. There is much emphasis on personal responsibility and a sense of community.

Dunhurst aims to achieve high academic standards and follows a broad educational programme built around the "core" subjects of English, Mathematics and Science, but giving equal importance to Physical Education, Art, Pottery, Textiles, Workshop, Computing, Comparative Religion, Current Affairs, Geography, History, Dance, Drama and Music. In addition to Class Music for all, pupils' practice time for individual instruments is supervised and fitted into their daily timetable. The aim is to achieve breadth of opportunity and experience as well as the chance to achieve excellence in many different areas.

Matches against other schools take place regularly in Athletics, Cricket, Football, Hockey, Netball, Rounders, Rugby and occasionally Swimming and Tennis. A wide range of other sports and outdoor activities is also offered, including judo and golf.

Dunhurst makes full use of the first rate facilities at Bedales which include the Bedales "Olivier Theatre", a Sports Hall, an all-weather pitch and covered swimming pool. This and the similarity of ethos, makes for an easy transition for pupils moving from Dunhurst to the Senior School at the age of thirteen.

There is a strong boarding community at Dunhurst. Many of the older pupils are full boarders and provision is made for flexible boarding for day pupils.

Applicants for both boarder and day places sit residential entrance tests. The main points of entry are at 8+ and 11+. Entry at other ages is dependent on the availability of places.

For information about Dunannie, the Pre-Prep (3–8 years), see the Bedales entry in HMC section.

Charitable status. Bedales School is a Registered Charity, number 307332. It exists to provide a sound education and training for children and young persons of both sexes.

Durlston Court

Becton Lane, Barton-on-Sea, New Milton, Hampshire BH25 7AQ
Tel: 01425 610010
Fax: 01425 622731
e-mail: secretary@durlstoncourt.co.uk
website: www.durlstoncourt.co.uk

Chairman of Governors: Dr A Girling, BDS, LDSRCS

Headmaster: **D C Wansey**, MA Ed, CertEd

Age Range. 2–13 Co-educational.
Number of Pupils. 320 Day Pupils.
Fees per term (2010-2011). Kindergarten £21.50 per morning or afternoon session, £2,445 (Reception–Year 2), £3,670 (Year 3), £4,230 (Years 4–8).

Durlston Court Preparatory School, founded in 1903, is a happy and successful day school set in a beautiful campus with impressive facilities.

The school is committed to providing a first-class academic education within the framework of a broad curriculum. Music, Art, Sport and Drama are all strengths of the school and a wide range of clubs and activities is on offer.

Feeding many of the South's leading Senior Schools, Durlston has an enviable academic reputation. Small classes and dedicated teaching have resulted in excellent exam results. Scholarships are offered each year to pupils entering the school who can show Academic, Music, Artistic or Sporting Excellence. Scholarship exams take place at the end of January each year.

Bus services cover routes from the Beaulieu, Bournemouth, Brockenhurst, Christchurch, Ferndown, Ringwood, Lymington, Lyndhurst and Sowley areas.

Parents are most welcome to visit the school by making an appointment or by attending an Open Morning. They may also wish to take advantage of arranging for their child to spend a trial day at Durlston, without obligation.

Further details of the school are available by visiting the school's website or by contacting the Headmaster's Secretary by phone or e-mail, as above.

Charitable status. Durlston Court School is a Registered Charity, number 307325, which exists to provide quality education for children from 2–13 years.

Durston House

12 Castlebar Road, Ealing, London W5 2DR
Tel: 020 8991 6532
Fax: 020 8991 6547
e-mail: info@durstonhouse.org
website: www.durstonhouse.org

Chairman of Governors: A J Allen, MA, FCA

Headmaster: **N I Kendrick**, MA, BEd Hons

Deputy Head: W J Murphy, BA, DipTch
Director of Studies: Mrs A McIntyre, MA Cantab, PGCE
Head of Junior School: S W Perkins, BEd Hons
Head of Pre-Prep: Mrs H L Wyatt, MA, PGCE

Age Range. 4–13.
Number of Boys. 400 Day Boys.
Fees per term (2011-2012). £3,140–£4,100.

Durston House is an Educational Trust with charitable status. The school has a long history of academic success reflected in Scholarships won at many of the leading senior schools. The emphasis is on high standards of work and targets that are commensurate with each pupil's personal development.

Pre-Prep and Junior School (boys aged 4–8) cater for three classes of about sixteen boys in each year group. There is generous ancillary staffing and learning support for specific needs.

In Middle and Upper School (boys aged 9–13) the Headmaster is helped by a Deputy Head, a Director of Studies and a team comprising graduate specialist Heads of Department for English, Classics, Mathematics, Modern Languages, Science, ICT, History, Geography, Music, Art, Physical Education and Religious Studies.

Throughout the school there are Activities Programmes offering a wide range of cultural, recreational and sporting pursuits. Both playing field complexes have floodlit all-weather pitches and there has been much sporting success in recent years. Extensive use is made of local facilities, especially for drama and swimming. There are fixtures with other prep schools, full participation in IAPS events, and regular expeditions at home and abroad.

Entry assessment procedures take place some six months before boys are due to enter, which is usually in September at age 4, or later if there are vacancies. Durston House is currently seeking to increase its provision of bursaries for boys who would benefit from an education at the school.

Charitable status. Durston House School Educational Trust Limited is a Registered Charity, number 294670. Its aim is the provision and promotion of education.

Eagle House

Sandhurst, Berkshire GU47 8PH
Tel: 01344 772134
Fax: 01344 779039
e-mail: info@eaglehouseschool.com
website: www.eaglehouseschool.com

Chairman of Governors: Rear Admiral H A H G Edleston, RN

Headmaster: **A P N Barnard**, BA Hons, PGCE

Age Range. 3–13.
Number of Children. 293: 24 Boarders, 269 Day Children.
Fees per term (2011-2012). Main School: £6,350 (boarders), £4,740 (day pupils). Pre-Prep: £2,960. Nursery: £1,760 (5 mornings including lunch).

Eagle House was founded in 1820, and has been on its present site since 1886. The School is administered by a board of governors under the overall control of Wellington College.

Children are prepared for Scholarship and Common Entrance examinations to senior Independent Schools. There are 41 members of staff and two matrons. The average class size is 15.

The school is situated between Sandhurst and Crowthorne in over 30 acres of playing fields which include a large all-weather sports area, a Sports Hall, an indoor heated swimming pool, extensive woodlands, adventure playground and a small lake. The principal games are rugby, netball, hockey, soccer, rounders and cricket. Other sports include athletics, swimming, tennis, cross country, squash, judo, basketball, archery, golf, riding and badminton.

Much emphasis is placed on the Arts and there are excellent facilities for music, art, design and drama. Music scholarships are available for outstanding young musicians.

The school has its own chapel.

Recent major building works have provided a new classroom block, Art Centre and additional computer facilities.

Charitable status. Wellington College is a Registered Charity, number 309093. Eagle House School is owned by Wellington College and is part of the same charity registration.

Eaton House The Manor Girls' School

58 Clapham Common Northside, London SW4 9RU
Tel: 020 7924 6000
Fax: 020 7924 1530
e-mail: admin@eatonhouseschools.com
website: www.eatonhouseschools.com

Principal: Mrs H Harper

Headmistress: **Mrs Sarah Segrave**

Age Range. 4–11.
Number of Pupils. 140 Girls.
Fees per term (2010-2011). £3,975.

Eaton House The Manor Girls' School is a single-sex school, conveniently situated on Clapham Common, which offers an excellent education to girls aged 4–11. The Headmistress, Mrs Segrave, has a distinguished career as an educator with over 10 years experience as a Headmistress.

Our girls enter on a first-come, first-served basis, and all are encouraged to achieve their full potential in the academic, sporting and artistic fields. They are taught good manners and respect for others and themselves.

Each girl is treated as an individual; Eaton House The Manor Girls' School is intimate and nurturing, and offers state-of-the-art facilities in its new building, including a large gymnasium, library and ICT laboratory. The girls' school accommodates 140 girls in seven evenly-sized year groups.

Eaton House The Manor Pre-Preparatory School

58 Clapham Common Northside, London SW4 9RU
Tel: 020 7924 6000
Fax: 020 7924 1530
e-mail: admin@eatonhouseschools.com
website: www.eatonhouseschools.com

Principal: Mrs H Harper

Headmistress: **Mrs Philippa Cawthorne**

Age Range. 4–8.
Number of Pupils. 180 Boys.
Fees per term (2010-2011). £3,975.

The quality of an Eaton House The Manor education means that all of the boys leaving the Pre-Prep and Preparatory Schools go on to their first choice of senior school with several winning scholarships. Our approach, which teaches according to ability in small groups, means that we succeed in bringing out the best in each child, fostering a lifelong enthusiasm for learning and attaining the highest academic results. Pupils go on to the most prestigious independent schools including Eaton House The Manor Prep, Westminster Under School, Colet Court, Dulwich College Prep, Westminster Cathedral School, The Dragon School, Ludgrove and Summer Fields.

The curriculum at Eaton House The Manor Pre-Prep is traditional. Strong moral values and a concern for others are emphasised in the classroom and through the House system. Care is taken to develop each childs confidence, and instil a healthy pride in achieving personal goals as well as participating in team games and competitions.

Pupils are taught in a vibrant environment on an exceptionally large site opposite Clapham Common. A recent multi-million pound investment to extend and improve facilities means they benefit from the latest computer technology in the new ICT lab, lavish art and design rooms, an extended library and extremely good music facilities.

The children enjoy many day and weekend trips as part of the curriculum and are encouraged to take part in a host of extra-curricular activities. Displays, concerts and dramatic performances in the school theatre and gym always prove popular, as do the many parent vs pupils sporting events. Parents are encouraged to be closely involved in their children's education, and to take part in many of the children's activities.

Admission to Eaton House The Manor Pre-Preparatory School is non-selective and on a first-come, first-served basis. Parents wishing to enrol their children in the School are advised to register them at birth.

Eaton House The Manor Preparatory School

58 Clapham Common Northside, London SW4 9RU
Tel: 020 7924 6000
Fax: 020 7924 1530

e-mail: admin@eatonhouseschools.com
website: www.eatonhouseschools.com

Principal: Mrs H Harper

Head: **Mr J P Edwards**, BA Hons, MA

Age Range. 8–13.
Number of Pupils. 140 Boys.
Fees per term (2010-2011). £4,915.

The quality of an Eaton House The Manor education means that all of the boys leaving the Prep School go on to their first choice of senior school, with several winning scholarships. Our approach, which teaches according to ability in small groups, means that we succeed in bringing out the best in each child, fostering a lifelong enthusiasm for learning and attaining the highest academic results. Pupils go on to the most prestigious independent schools including Westminster, St Paul's, Eton, Harrow, Radley, Charterhouse, Marlborough and Dulwich College.

The curriculum at Eaton House The Manor Prep is traditional. Strong moral values and a concern for others are emphasised in the classroom and through the House system. Care is taken to develop each child's confidence, and instil a healthy pride in achieving personal goals as well as participating in team games and competitions. Every day, children at the Prep School enjoy a reading period after lunch and can attend a supervised homework club at the end of the day.

Pupils are taught in a vibrant environment on an exceptionally large site opposite Clapham Common. A recent multi-million pound investment to extend and improve facilities means they benefit from the latest computer technology in the new ICT lab, lavish art and design rooms, an extended library and extremely good music facilities.

The children enjoy many day and weekend trips as part of the curriculum and are encouraged to take part in a host of extra-curricular activities. Displays, concerts and dramatic performances in the school theatre and gym always prove popular, as do the many parent vs pupils sporting events. Parents are encouraged to be closely involved in their children's education, and to take part in many of the children's activities.

Entry to the Preparatory School is at 8 years of age by examination and interview. Places are offered at 7+ and 8+. Interviews occur a year before the child's projected start date, backed up by a report from their current Pre-Preparatory School.

Eaton Square School

79 Eccleston Square, London SW1V 1PP
Tel: 020 7931 9469
Fax: 020 7828 0164
e-mail: admissions@eatonsquareschool.com
website: www.eatonsquareschool.com

Headmaster: **Mr S Hepher>/B>**

Age Range. 2½–13 Co-educational.
Number of Pupils. 529: 280 boys, 249 girls.
Fees per term (2010-2011). Nursery £960–£4,050, Pre-Prep £4,950, Prep £5,120.

Entry. Early Registration for Nursery places, Early registration and assessment for Pre-Prep and Prep School admissions. Priority given to internal Nursery candidates.

Contact. *Pre-Prep & Prep*: Penelope Stitcher, Registrar, e-mail: admissions@eatonsquareschool.com.

Nursery: Rohan Kara, Assistant Registrar, e-mail: rohan.kara@eatonsquareschool.com.

Ethos. Eaton Square School is one of the few co-educational day schools in the heart of London offering nursery, pre-preparatory and preparatory education. The School maintains high standards and encourages in every child an enthusiasm for learning, good manners, self-discipline and, in all things, a determination to do their best and realise their potential. The ISI inspection (2005) indicated that personal development of pupils was a notable strength of the school. The School offers a stretching, challenging approach to learning that emphasises achievement and builds confidence. Great emphasis is placed on experiential learning including ski trips, classical tours of Rome and Pompeii, and a half term spent in a French château in Sauveterre in Year Seven.

Academic Life. The form teachers teach general subjects to their classes up to the age of 8. Thereafter, specialist subject teachers continue the curriculum in preparation for the Common Entrance Examinations for senior English Independent Schools, for girls at age 11 and boys at age 13. A wide range of subjects is encompassed in the curriculum, including English, Mathematics, Science, History, Geography, French, Latin, Art, Drama, Music and Physical Education. ICT is introduced from the age of 3 and it is an integral part of the syllabus. The various parts of the school are served by a school wide network, allowing pupils and staff to access their work from any computer. There is a computer suite in each of the three school buildings. In addition, all Prep School classrooms are equipped with interactive whiteboards and data projectors. The School also benefits from a new Art and Science block with separate Science laboratory and a wonderfully equipped Art, Design and Technology Studio.

Pupils are prepared for entry into both selective London day schools and leading boarding schools through London Day School examinations at 11+ and Common Entrance examinations at 13+.

Sport & the Arts. Sport and Physical Education include Swimming, Fencing, Gymnastics, Football, Rugby, Cricket and Tennis and the School has successful teams competing against other London schools. Music is a flourishing department within the School. Appreciation of music, singing, composition, music theory and recorder tuition are taught by specialists at all ages. There is an active School Choir, an orchestra and a variety of ensembles that rehearse throughout the week. Instruction in Music, Art and Design Technology is included for all children from Nursery School upwards, as part of the Curriculum. Individual Music lessons on a wide variety of instruments are available during the day and after school (for an additional fee) from Year 2 upwards. Drama is integrated within the curriculum and each child takes part in at least two public productions every year. The Prep School production for children in Years 4–8 is held at a West End Theatre during the Summer Term. The Art and Design room provides an outstanding resource and is equipped with a wide selection of facilities, including a kiln for ceramic work. Projects undertaken in Design and Technology include work with resistant materials, textiles, ceramics, electronics, mechanisms and computer control. The Art syllabus includes painting, drawing, printing, sculpture and sketchbook work.

Further information and a prospectus may be obtained from the Registrar.

Edenhurst Preparatory School

Westlands Avenue, Newcastle-under-Lyme, Staffordshire ST5 2PU
Tel: 01782 619348
Fax: 01782 662402
e-mail: headmaster@edenhurst.co.uk
website: www.edenhurst.co.uk

Headmaster: **N H F Copestick**, BSc University of St Andrews, CertEd The Queen's College, Oxford

Age Range. 3 months – 13 years.
Number of Pupils. 140 Boys, 120 Girls.
Fees per term (2010-2011). £2,438–£3,114.

A family-run day school established in 1961 by the present Headmaster's father.

The Victorian main building is set in a pleasant suburban area and boasts many purpose built additions, notably a well-equipped laboratory and an ITC centre.

Edenhurst has an enviable local reputation in preparing pupils for entrance examinations to local independent secondary schools and also for the Common Entrance 13+ Examinations. Results in National Curriculum tests have demonstrated consistently high standards of pupil achievement.

Particular strengths of the school include the music department which offers tuition in nine instruments. The orchestra and choir perform publicly many times throughout the year.

The new Full Day-Care Nursery offers places to babies from 3 months in a brand new centre providing quality care in an exciting yet safe environment.

Edge Grove

Aldenham Village, Radlett, Herts WD25 8NL
Tel: 01923 855724
Fax: 01923 859920
e-mail: headmaster@edgegrove.indschools.co.uk
website: www.edgegrove.co.uk

The school is a non-profit making Trust administered by a Board of Governors.

Chairman of Governors: N A Shryane, MBE, BA, MPhil

Headmaster: **M J Davies**, BA Hons, PGCE

Age Range. 3–13.
Number of Pupils. Day: 120 (Pre-Prep), 194 (Prep); Boarders 63.
Fees per term (2010-2011). Pre-Prep £1,525–£2,995; Day £3,600–£4,465; Boarding (weekly/full) £4,900–£6,095.

Edge Grove is situated in 28 acres of glorious Hertfordshire parkland. We are approximately 5 minutes' drive from both the M1 and M25 motorways and only 15 miles from Central London. Heathrow and Luton airports are 30 minutes' drive by car.

The Pre-Prep (Hart House) caters for children between the ages of 3 and 7 and is situated within the grounds, close to the main Preparatory school. The Early Years Department was moved into a new wing of the building in 2007. The children use many of the main Preparatory School's facilities. The main points of entry are at Nursery (3+) and Reception (4+).

Boys and girls normally join the Preparatory department, Edge Grove, at 7+ and all are prepared for the Common Entrance and Scholarship Examinations. Pupils are taught in co-educational classes and they move on to a wide variety of Senior Independent schools across the country. There is an excellent record of Scholarship and Common Entrance success; indeed, forty Scholarships were gained between 2005 and 2007. The Music, Art and Sport are also strong and there is a great range of extra-curricular activities on offer.

Facilities include a modern teaching block, purpose-built Pre-Prep, Science Laboratories, School Chapel, Music School and Sports Hall. We have two ICT suites and the school has further upgraded its ICT facilities to incorporate mobile trolleys of laptops. Edge Grove has two Art studios, a heated swimming pool and nine acres of games fields, as well as an artificial sports surface.

The main sports are Netball, Rounders and Hockey for girls and Football, Rugby, Cricket and Hockey for boys.

Swimming, Cross-Country, Archery, Tennis and Squash are also popular and are played by both boys and girls. Twenty-five pupils currently represent the county and the Region in a variety of different sports.

Charitable status. Edge Grove School Trust Ltd is a Registered Charity, number 311054.

Edgeborough

Frensham, Farnham, Surrey GU10 3AH
Tel: 01252 792495
Fax: 01252 795156
e-mail: office@edgeborough.co.uk
website: www.edgeborough.co.uk

Chairman of Governors: T Elliott, FCA

Headmaster: **C J Davies**, BA, PGCE

Age Range. 2–13.
Number of Children. Boarders 56, Day 201, Pre Prep 97, Nursery 54.
Fees per term (2010-2011). Upper Prep £4,475, Lower Prep £4,015, Pre Prep £2,745. Weekly Boarding £1,285.

Edgeborough is an independent school which focuses on the individual and offers a wealth of opportunities. The school's motto is *Carpe Diem*. Founded in 1906 in Guildford, Edgeborough moved to its current site, the beautiful Frensham Place, in 1939. With its 50 acres of mixed woodland and playing fields, Edgeborough offers a wonderful environment for children.

The school is distinctive in its setup and comprises of four departments: Nursery (2–4), Pre Prep (4–7). Lower Prep (7–10) and Upper Prep (10–13), all closely linked yet with their own character and individuality. This specialism enables us to tailor carefully the academic programme to the ages and stages of the pupils, and the aim is to provide an all-round education of high quality for all. From Edgeborough, boys and girls go to a wide range of top Independent Schools at 13+ via Common Entrance or Scholarship and we expect 20% of our pupils to gain scholarships and other awards in their final year.

As well as the spacious grounds and playing fields, the range of facilities is a strength of the school. They include well-equipped classrooms for all the departments, a stunning new Science and Technology Building, Art and Pottery Centre, fully-equipped Theatre with adjoining Dance and Drama Studio, large Sports Hall, floodlit Astroturf, heated Swimming Pool, Golf Course, Children's Farm and Adventure Playground. This enables the school to pursue a wide and varied programme of extra-curricular activities including sport, music, art and drama. In addition to the main sports of rugby, soccer, cricket, hockey, netball, rounders, lacrosse and athletics pupils can also participate in golf, basketball, badminton, tennis, swimming, climbing, gymnastics and canoeing. There are numerous school visits organised for the pupils, including a residential week in France, an annual ski trip, and sporting and cultural tours to South Africa.

Weekly or flexible boarding is a very popular option, and Edgeborough's distinctive warm and friendly atmosphere is rooted deep in its traditional family values of courtesy and care for the individual, developed over many years.

Entry to the school is by interview and informal assessment. Further information and a prospectus can be obtained from the Admissions Secretary.

'*Edgeborough provides an all-round education of high quality for all pupils.*'

Charitable status. Edgeborough Educational Trust is a Registered Charity, number 312051.

Elm Green Preparatory School

**Parsonage Lane, Little Baddow, Chelmsford, Essex
CM3 4SU**
Tel: 01245 225230
Fax: 01245 226008
e-mail: admin@elmgreen.essex.sch.uk
website: www.elmgreen.essex.sch.uk

Principal: **Mrs A E Milner**, BTech Hons, MSc, PGCE

Age Range. Co-educational 4–11 years.
Number of Day Pupils. 220: 115 Boys, 105 Girls.
Fees per term (from April 2011). £2,399.
Religious affiliation. Non-denominational.
Elm Green was founded in 1944 and enjoys a lovely rural
setting, surrounded by National Trust woodland.

Children enter in the September after their fourth birthday and in their final year are prepared for scholarships,
entry to other independent schools and for entry to maintained schools. Many of the pupils take the Essex 11+ and
the school has an excellent record of success in this examination.

The school maintains a high standard of academic education giving great emphasis to a secure foundation in the
basic subjects whilst offering a wide curriculum with specialist teaching in many areas.

Information technology and design technology form an
integral part of the curriculum and there are flourishing art,
music and PE departments. The school competes successfully in a wide range of sports – football, rugby, netball,
swimming, cricket, gymnastics, athletics, rounders and tennis.

There are many extra-curricular activities and all the children are encouraged to work and to play hard in order to fulfil their potential.

The school aims to foster intellectual curiosity and to
encourage individual and corporate work. Kindness and
thought for others are given a high priority.

The Elms

Colwall, Malvern, Worcestershire WR13 6EF
Tel: 01684 540344
Fax: 01684 541174
e-mail: office@elmsschool.co.uk
website: www.theelmsschool-colwall.co.uk

Founded 1614.

Chairman of the Governors: C F R Potter, OBE, MA

Head Master: **A Thomas**, BA Hons, PGCE

Age Range. 3–13.
Number of Pupils. Main School: 130: 80 Boys, 64 Girls.
89 boarders. Pre-Prep: 55.
Fees per term (2011-2012). Full board £6,655; Day
board £6,205; Pre-Prep (3–7) £2,350–£3,945. Fees are payable termly. There are no compulsory extras.

The Elms is run as a charitable, non-profit making company with a Board of Governors. Children are taken in the
Main School from the age of rising 8 and there is a Pre-Preparatory Department for 3–7 year olds.

An experienced staff and small classes ensure attention to
each pupil's special needs and a high academic standard is
maintained to CE and Scholarship levels. Small numbers
help to create a family atmosphere with comfortable accommodation and a resident Headmaster and staff.

Gardens, fields and woodland with stream in 150 acres
surround the school, beautifully set at the foot of the Malvern Hills, and include fine playing fields for Rugby, Association Football, Hockey, Cricket, Athletics, Netball and
Rounders. Facilities include a Sports Hall, Tennis Courts,
Laboratory, Computer Room, new teaching block, CDT
Centre and an Art Room with facilities for Pottery. There is
also a heated indoor swimming pool. The children manage a
small farming enterprise and many ride on school ponies or
bring their own.

Bursaries available for sons and daughters of Services
personnel, the Clergy and Teachers; there are also competitive awards.

Charitable status. The Elms (Colwall) Limited is a Registered Charity, number 527252. It exists to provide education for boys and girls.

The Elms
Junior School to Trent College

Derby Road, Long Eaton, Nottingham NG10 4AD
Tel: 0115 849 4942
Fax: 0115 849 4943
e-mail: elms.school@trentcollege.net
website: www.elmsschool.net

Chairman of Governors: C M McDowell, FCIB

Head: **K B Morrow**, BA Hons QTS, NPQH

Deputy Head: Mrs L Deller, BA Hons

Age Range. 3–11 co-educational.
Number of Pupils. 341: 197 Boys,144 Girls.
Fees per term (2011-2012). £2,500–£2,625.
The Elms was opened by Trent College in September
1999 and has since enjoyed considerable success. There is
two-form entry into the Reception Classes and three-form
entry into the Junior Classes in Year 3.

Located in beautiful grounds on the border of Nottinghamshire and Derbyshire, The Elms, Junior School to the
prestigious Trent College, is a thriving school for around
350 girls and boys, aged 2½ to 11. First class teaching,
excellent pastoral care and outstanding extra-curricular provision ensure we meet parents' highest expectations of a
quality education for their child.

Our superb academic standards are achieved through nurturing the social and emotional needs of our children.
Indeed, our recent ISI inspection report rated us amongst the
most successful schools nationally. Teaching and Learning,
Pupil Progress, Attitudes to Work, Leadership and Management were all found to be "excellent".

However, the emphasis at The Elms is not just on academic standards. Our philosophy, centred on educating the
whole child, nurtures all aspects of their character alongside
their academic progress. The Elms is a supportive and,
above all, happy environment for growing and learning. Our
focus is very much on the individual child, recognising their
specific talents and interests. Here at The Elms we seek to
develop mature and thoughtful children well versed in the
habits of good manners, who display care and consideration
for others and for their environment.

At The Elms the very fabric of the building is testament
to the extensive learning opportunities available to our children. Rooms dedicated to art and design, MFL, music, cookery, speech and drama and ICT are accessible to all our
children. We also have a superb award-winning library facility enjoyed by all our pupils. Moreover, our situation within
the grounds of a large Senior School means that we are able
to make use of other facilities not normally available to
smaller, discrete Junior Schools. We therefore have access to

Trent College's first-rate sports pitches, swimming pool, theatre and workshops, should they be needed.

In addition, some School buses shared with Trent College allow some of our older pupils to travel independently to and from school while our before and after school care systems provide extended day provision for busy families. Our children enjoy lunch in the superb dining facilities alongside teachers and pupils from Trent. The majority of our Year 6 pupils go on to Trent College for their secondary education. (*See Trent College entry in HMC section.*)

At the Elms we offer diverse enrichment outside the classroom as well as in it: meaningful trips and external speakers are frequent; sporting potential reaches beyond the School to regional and national competitions; music and drama play an intrinsic part of school life and we offer a wide range of extra-curricular clubs.

A very special community, our school offers inspirational teaching, a warm, friendly environment and the opportunity for every child to reach their personal best.

An Assisted Places Scheme is available in order to make our excellent education available to children from a variety of backgrounds. Please contact the Admissions Manager, Mrs Patricia Robinson, for more details.

Charitable status. Trent College is a Registered Charity, number 527180.

Elstree School

Woolhampton, Reading, Berks RG7 5TD
Tel: 0118 971 3302
Fax: 0118 971 4280
e-mail: registrar@elstreeschool.org.uk
website: www.elstreeschool.org.uk

The School is an educational trust controlled by a Board of Governors.

Chairman of Governors: Nicholas Bomford, Esq

Headmaster: **M J Sayer**, MA Cantab, PGCE

Deputy Headmaster: S C Bates, BEd, CertEd

Age Range. Boys 3–13, Girls 3–7.
Number of Pupils. Prep School (age 7–13): 190 boys (60 boarders, 130 day boys); Pre-Prep School (age 3–7): 70 boys and girls.
Fees per term (2010-2011). Boarders £6,825, Day Boys £5,300, Pre-Prep School £2,975.

Elstree is set in its own 150 acres in the beautiful Berkshire countryside, a quiet location but very accessible. The School moved to Woolhampton, between Reading and Newbury, in 1939, after nearly 100 years at Elstree, Hertfordshire. At the heart of the School is a magnificent Georgian house which has been modernized and extended. Facilities and accommodation are of a very high standard.

Elstree prepares boys for entrance to Britain's leading independent senior schools and has a fine Open Scholarship record. Boys play Football, Rugby, Hockey, Cricket and many other sports. Equal emphasis is given to an appreciation of music, art, drama and to life skills such as Information Technology.

Charitable status. Elstree School Limited is a Registered Charity, number 309101. It exists to establish, maintain and carry on schools for the education of boys and girls and to give such pupils general or specialised instruction of the highest class, and as an educational charity to promote education generally.

Eton End School

35 Eton Road, Datchet, Slough, Berkshire SL3 9AX
Tel: 01753 541075
Fax: 01753 541123
e-mail: admin@etonend.org
website: www.etonend.org

Chairman of Board of Governors: D Losse, Esq

Headmistress: **Mrs V M Pilgerstorfer**, BA Hons, PGCE

Age Range. Girls 3–11, Boys 3–7.
Number of Pupils. 205: 168 girls, 37 boys.
Fees per term (2011-2012). Nursery: £1,525–£2,450 (exc lunch); Pre-Prep £2,950–£3,150 (inc lunch); Prep £3,450–£3,690 (inc lunch).

The school is a day school set within six acres of spacious grounds. All the classrooms are purpose-built and modern, offering excellent facilities, including specialist rooms, eg art and craft, music, science laboratory, large library and IT suite. There is a large well-equipped gym, two hard tennis/ netball courts, a football and sports field. Boys are prepared for all preparatory schools in the area. Girls leave after the 11+ Entrance Examination often gaining Scholarships. Small classes allow each child to reach their maximum potential in a happy caring environment.

The school's origins lie in the traditions inspired by educationalist, Charlotte Mason, who founded the PNEU movement.

Charitable status. Eton End School Trust (Datchet) Limited is a Registered Charity, number 310644. The aim of the charity is to provide a well-balanced education for children whose parents wish them to attend Eton End School.

Eversfield Preparatory School

Warwick Road, Solihull, West Midlands B91 1AT
Tel: 0121 705 0354
Fax: 0121 709 0168
e-mail: enquiries@eversfield.co.uk
website: www.eversfield.co.uk

Chairman of Governors: Mrs E Owen

Headmaster: **R Yates**, BA, PGCE, LPSH

Age Range. 2¾–11 Co-educational.
Number of Pupils. 275.
Fees per term (2010-2011). £1,257–£2,900 according to age and inclusive of lunch, books and swimming lessons.

Eversfield is a Day Preparatory School on an attractive site in the centre of Solihull preparing boys and girls for entry to the leading Senior Schools in the West Midlands and beyond.

The curriculum values academic excellence and prepares pupils for National Curriculum Tests and 11+ examinations. At the same time it nurtures the creative, sporting, technical and social skills of each pupil. There are excellent facilities and opportunities for sports, music, the arts, and a varied programme of extra-curricular and holiday activities.

On-site facilities include specialist rooms for art, design & technology, science, cookery, music and information technology. Sporting facilities comprise a gymnasium, extensive playing fields, all-weather courts and a heated outdoor swimming pool.

The School encourages a strong sense of community where small classes, a well-ordered routine and good pastoral support help pupils to feel secure and develop their self-confidence. Eversfield promotes high moral standards and responsible attitudes based on clear and relevant Christian teaching.

Charitable status. Eversfield Preparatory School Trust Limited is a Registered Charity, number 528966. It is under the direction of a Board of Governors and exists to carry out the work of an Independent Preparatory School.

Ewell Castle Junior School

Glyn House, Church Street, Ewell, Surrey KT17 2AP
Tel: 020 8394 3579
Fax: 020 8394 2220
e-mail: enquiries@ewellcastle.co.uk
website: www.ewellcastle.co.uk

Chairman of Governors: D C M Hill

Principal: A J Tibble, BSc, PGCE, NPQH

Head of Junior School: **Mrs H M Crossley**, MA, BEd, CertEd

Deputy Head of Junior School: Mrs S Laws, MA, BEd

Age Range. 3–11.
Number of Pupils. 200 Boys and Girls.
Fees per term (2011-2012). £1,220–£2,700.

Ewell Castle Junior School is a co-educational day school, located on two sites in the heart of Ewell Village. Nursery to Year 2 pupils (3–7 years) are based at Chessington Lodge in Spring Street, while Years 3 to 6 (7–11 years) are based at Glyn House in Church Street, opposite the Senior School (360 boys, 11–18 years), with which a close liaison is maintained.

Those entering the Nursery may attend for a half-day (minimum three sessions per week) until they are ready for full-time education. There are no entry requirements for Nursery children, but older pupils attend the school for a day's assessment, which will include tests in Mathematics and English. Girls are prepared for local independent senior schools, whilst boys may proceed to the Senior School, for which a number of aided places and scholarships are available at 11+ entry. All pupils are prepared for entry at 11+ to selective state schools. The National Curriculum is incorporated within a broad curriculum.

The creative arts play an important part in school life. Apart from the timetabled music lessons, there is the opportunity for pupils to learn a variety of instruments under professional teachers. Drama productions take place regularly. Pupils' art work can be seen on display in the local community and is always to be found decorating the school walls. All pupils join in various sporting activities as part of the weekly curriculum. In addition, a wide variety of activities are available after school and during the holidays.

All pupils use the 5 acres of attractive gardens and playing fields at Glyn House for outdoor play and games lessons. In addition, Junior School pupils benefit from full access to the excellent sporting facilities, including a sports hall and playing fields, on the 15-acre site at The Castle. The main games are football, netball, cricket and tennis. There are also athletics and cross country events, including a school sports day. All pupils receive swimming instruction.

Outside speakers include police liaison officers and actors and authors who conduct workshops with pupils. A number of visits occur to places of interest which are relevant to a particular area of study. There are regular school visits abroad.

The school also enjoys close links with St Mary's Church, where regular assemblies are held throughout the year.

The Junior School aims to provide a caring, responsive and stimulating environment in which pupils are able to fulfil their potential. Hard work and high standards together

with courtesy and consideration to others are of prime importance.

Charitable status. Ewell Castle School is a Registered Charity, number 312079. It exists to provide education for boys and girls.

Exeter Cathedral School

The Chantry, Palace Gate, Exeter, Devon EX1 1HX
Tel: 01392 255298
Fax: 01392 422718
e-mail: reception@exetercs.org
website: www.exetercs.org

Chairman of Governors: The Dean of Exeter

Headmaster: **Stephen G Yeo**, BMus Hons, LTCL MusEd, NPQH

Age Range. 3–13.
Number of Pupils. 11 Boarders, 197 Day Pupils.
Fees per term (2011-2012). Day Pupils (excluding lunches): £1,861–£3,147. Boarding (in addition to Day fees): £1,999 (full), £1,777 (weekly).

Founded in 1159, the Cathedral School provides the Boy and Girl Choristers for Exeter Cathedral and educates 164 other pupils to the same high standard.

Entry is normally at 3 or 4 to the Pre-Preparatory Department or 7 or 8 years into the Prep School, though pupils may be accepted later. Entrance assessments for 7+ or later entry are by arrangement with the Headmaster.

Voice Trials for Choristers are held in February, or by arrangement, and successful applicants become probationers, upon completion of which they enter the Choir.

There are 18 scholarships available for Boy Choristers and probationers which can be worth up to 25% of the tuition fee. Scholarships of up to 20% are also available to Girl Choristers. Awards are also available to non-choristers, details of which can be given on application.

Pupils are prepared for Scholarship and Common Entrance to Independent and Maintained Senior Schools by a full-time staff of 17, assisted by other part-time teachers including 11 teachers of musical instruments.

There are no Saturday lessons, though day pupils sometimes join boarders in weekend or after school activities. The curriculum encompasses all National Curriculum and Common Entrance subjects, including Modern Foreign Languages, Latin and Greek.

In the Michaelmas Term, rugby football and netball are the team sports. Netball, soccer and hockey are played in the Lent Term. During the Trinity Term, cricket, rounders, athletics and swimming are all pursued competitively. Swimming takes place all year round.

Musical activities, including school choir, orchestra and ensembles for string, woodwind, brass and jazz instrumentalists are available to all pupils.

Daily morning worship takes place in the Cathedral or in The Chapter House led by the School Chaplain or Lay Pastor.

The buildings are located around the Close and include a Science Laboratory, a gymnasium and Kalendar Hall (the music and drama school), as well as a large portion of the 14th Century Deanery. There is a Food Technology Centre, Pottery and Design and Technology Department and Computer Centre.

For games, use is made of playing fields, swimming baths and other facilities situated short distances away in the city.

Charitable status. Exeter Cathedral School, as part of the Foundation of the Chapter of Exeter which is an ecclesiastical charity, is a Registered Charity and exists to provide education for boys and girls.

Exeter Junior School

Victoria Park Road, Exeter, Devon EX2 4NS
Tel: 01392 273679
Fax: 01392 498144
e-mail: admissions@exeterschool.org.uk
website: www.exeterschool.org.uk

Co-educational Day School.

Chairman of Board of Governors: Mrs B Meeke, LLB

Headmistress: **Mrs Alison J Turner**, MA

Age Range. 7–11.
Number of Pupils. 172: 119 Boys, 65 Girls.
Fees per annum (2011-2012). £9,150.

Exeter Junior School is housed in a spacious, Victorian building in the grounds of Exeter School. The close proximity of the Junior School to the Senior School enables the pupils to take full advantage of the facilities on site, which include a chapel, music centre, science laboratories, sports hall with dance studio, fitness suite and squash courts, outdoor heated swimming pool, playing fields, all-weather astroturf arena and tennis courts.

In addition to this the Junior School retains its own playground and green space, therefore giving the School a separate and clearly recognisable identity.

Liaison between Junior and Senior staff is a positive feature of this thriving Junior School.

The School aims to offer, in academic, cultural and sporting terms, the widest possible range of opportunities thus helping each pupil to identify the activities which will give the greatest scope for development and fulfilment in years to come. Music, drama, art, sport and expeditions all have an important part to play in the life of the school.

The majority of pupils enter the school at age 7 or 8, and entrance is by informal assessment in January. This includes a report from the child's previous school, classroom sessions in the company of other prospective pupils, and literacy, numeracy and general intelligence tasks.

Pupils are offered an academic programme which incorporates the National Curriculum model with the addition of French which is introduced from Year 3.

Specialist teaching is offered from the outset, with the additional support of Senior School staff in science, French, music and ICT.

A wide variety of clubs are available during the week including art & craft, Italian, calligraphy, football, hockey, netball, rugby, chess and drama. After-school care is available until 5.30pm.

(*For further information about the Senior School, see Exeter School entry in HMC section.*)

Charitable status. Exeter School is a Registered Charity, number 1093080. It exists to provide education for children.

Fairfield Preparatory School

Leicester Road, Loughborough, Leics LE11 2AE
Tel: 01509 215172
Fax: 01509 238648
e-mail: admin@lesfairfield.org
website: www.lesfairfield.org

Chairman of the Governors: H Michael Pearson, BA Econ, LLB, ACIS

Headmaster: **R Outwin-Flinders**, BEd Hons

Age Range. 4–11.

Number of Pupils. 253 Boys, 238 Girls (all day)
Fees per term (2010-2011). £2,502. Lunches and individual music lessons extra.

Fairfield School is the Preparatory School of the Loughborough Endowed Schools, the two Upper Schools being Loughborough Grammar School for Boys (*see HMC entry*) and Loughborough High School for Girls (*see GSA entry*).

The three Schools are governed by the same Governing Body and share a fine campus to the west of the Leicester Road, with their private roads free of through traffic.

The aim of Fairfield is to give a broad-based education appropriate for the needs of the children in our care. In the process, they will be prepared for their secondary education. For most this will mean either Loughborough Grammar School or High School, although some children move elsewhere.

Our intention is also to teach children how to live together in a community and to show respect for the property and feelings of others. We hope that time spent at Fairfield will be thoroughly enjoyable.

Whilst our children are prepared for entry to the Upper Schools, this is certainly not our only goal. In addition to all National Curriculum subjects French is taught and there are specialist rooms for ICT, Science and Music. Our Gymnasium is extremely well equipped.

The children are introduced to a wide variety of sporting and recreational activities. Team games are encouraged for the spirit of cooperation and working together which the School aims to foster. Activities of a more individual nature also play an increasing part in the life of the School. Winter games include Soccer, Netball, Cross-Country Running and Hockey. In the summer Cricket, Tennis, Rounders, Athletics and Short Tennis are played. The children swim throughout the year in the Endowed Schools' indoor, heated pool.

Music and Drama are considered very important areas of School life. In addition to class music lessons, children have the opportunity to receive tuition on a variety of musical instruments and many take advantage of this. The School Orchestras perform on a regular basis, there are also two Choirs, two Recorder Groups and numerous additional instrumental ensembles. The £4 million state-of-the-art whole school Music School opened in September 2006.

Music is coordinated by the new Loughborough Endowed Schools Director of Music and the music curriculum includes traditional music teaching, using extensive ICT in the modern facilities.

Dramatic productions play a major part in the life of the School. Here children are given the opportunity to express themselves and experience the excitement of performing before an audience.

There is a whole range of other activities in which children are given the opportunity to participate. Success and enjoyment in these invariably help to boost confidence and widen horizons generally.

Lunchtime and after-school clubs include Brownies, Cycling Proficiency, Drama, Pottery, Photography, Technology, Green Fingers Club, Latin and Mind Sports (Chess, Mini Bridge, Go), as well as the sporting and musical activities already mentioned.

The main ages for entry to the School are at 4+ and 7+ although a few places are available at other ages.

The examination for entry at 7+, 8+, 9+ and 10+ takes place in January each year whilst assessments for entry at 4+ take place in late January.

The Prospectus and further details can be obtained from the Registrar and the Headmaster will be happy to show prospective parents around the School and more information can be found on the school website www.lesfairfield.org.

Charitable status. Loughborough Endowed Schools is a Registered Charity, number 1081765, and a Company Limited by Guarantee, registered in England, number 4038033.

Fairstead House School

Fordham Road, Newmarket, Suffolk CB8 7AA
Tel: 01638 662318
Fax: 01638 561685
e-mail: secretary@fairsteadhouse.co.uk
website: www.fairsteadhouse.co.uk

Headmaster: Gareth Williams, BEd Hons

Age Range. Co-educational 3–11.
Number of Children. Day: 59 Boys, 63 Girls.
Fees per term (2011-2012). Nursery: from £740 (for a minimum of 3 sessions per week), lunches £1.80 per day; Main School: £2,520–£2,710 including lunches.

Fairstead House aims to excite each child's boundless sense of wonder, capture their natural enthusiasms and harvest a huge range of talents. A broad, balanced and exciting curriculum develops each pupil's full potential and ensures they are well prepared for the challenges of their next school. At Fairstead House, we are very proud of our friendly, caring and happy community with its unique family system and ethos. Over the years we have carefully nurtured this family atmosphere to provide our pupils with real leadership challenges, a sense of personal responsibility and the opportunities to grow into mature, intelligent and socially responsible individuals.

Staff: 9 full-time, 9 part-time. Classes are small and Pre-Prep children have the benefit of a teaching assistant in addition to the class teacher, enabling each child to receive individual help and attention. Extra help is available within the school for children experiencing difficulties in specific areas of the curriculum, or alternatively when a child requires further challenges. The broad and balanced curriculum emphasizes the value of creativity, be it in Art, DT, Music or Drama, as well as the pursuit of academic excellence. Many extra-curricular activities are offered along with pre-school and after-school care.

The progress of each child, both academic and social, is carefully monitored by means of ongoing assessment.

A continuous and ongoing programme of development has ensured the provision of first-class facilities throughout the school including a state-of-the-art Music & Drama Centre with specialist facilities, an ICT suite, a Science, Design & Technology room, an Eco Garden and an Astroturf play area.

A Bursary Fund is in place to help families in case of exceptional financial hardship and an academic scholarship is awarded to a child at 10+ for their final year. Scholarships in sport, music and drama are awarded to talented children entering school in Year 3 or 4.

Charitable status. Fairstead House School Trust Limited is a Registered Charity, number 276787. It exists to provide independent education for children.

The Falcons Schools
Alpha Plus Group

Boys School: 2 Burnaby Gardens, London W4 3DT
Tel: 020 8747 8393
Fax: 020 8995 3903
e-mail: admin@falconschool.com

Girls School: 15 Gunnersbury Avenue, London W5 3XD
Tel: 020 8992 5189
Fax: 020 8752 1635
e-mail: admin@falconsgirls.co.uk

Boys Prep School:
41 Kew Foot Road, Richmond, Surrey TW9 2SS
Tel: 0844 225 2211
Fax: 0844 225 2212
e-mail: prep@falconschool.com
website: www.falconschool.com

Head Teacher, Girls School: **Miss Joan McGillewie**

Head Teacher, Boys School: **Mr Gordon Milne**, BEd Hons, CertEd, MCollP, FRSA

Head Teacher, Boys Prep School: Mr Antony Shawyer, BSc Hons, PGCE, DipEd Man

Age Range. Boys School 3–7; Girls School 3–11; Boys Prep 7–13.
Number of Pupils. 188 Boys; 121 Girls; Boys Prep 270.
Fees per term (2011-2012). Boys School: £2,180–£4,370. Girls School: £1,974–£3,625. Boys Prep: £4,431.

The Falcons Schools enjoy a well-deserved reputation for excellence. Results to the leading London Day Schools are impressive, as too is the specialist teaching on offer throughout the schools. The schools provide a safe outdoor space for play and sport and a school hall for, gym, assemblies and lunch. Nearby sports facilities are used to enhance an exciting sports program. There are well-equipped libraries, music rooms, ICT suites, with a much-admired art and science facility. Our overriding emphasis is on achieving excellence in numeric and literacy whilst offering a broad and creative curriculum. The Falcons is a uniquely caring and stimulating environment, where learning is seen as fun and the pursuit of excellence is embraced by all.

Falkner House

19 Brechin Place, London SW7 4QB
Tel: 020 7373 4501
Fax: 020 7835 0073
e-mail: office@falknerhouse.co.uk
website: www.falknerhouse.co.uk

Principal: Mrs Flavia Nunes

Headmistress: **Mrs Anita Griggs**, BA Hons, PGCE

Age Range. Girls 4–11, Co-educational Nursery (ages 3–4).
Number of Girls. 190.
Fees per term (2011-2012). Main School £4,700, Nursery £2,350.

Falkner House provides a strong academic programme within a supportive family atmosphere. The broad curriculum taught by highly experienced staff results in girls achieving success at 11+ to top day and boarding schools.

Excellent facilities include a science laboratory, art room, IT centre, good libraries and large playground. The school has a strong musical tradition as well as an excellent sporting record. Pre/post school care is offered, as well as a wide range of after school activities.

Entrance at 4+ is by assessment and interview.

Falkner House Nursery caters for boys and girls aged 3–4 years. Extensive facilities and a team of specialist teachers create an ideal pre-school environment. Main school staff are on hand to enrich the Nursery School's curriculum.

Farleigh School

Red Rice, Andover, Hampshire SP11 7PW
Tel: 01264 710766

Fax: 01264 710070
e-mail: office@farleighschool.co.uk
website: www.farleighschool.com

Chairman of Governors: Michael Dawson

Headmaster: Fr Simon Everson

Age Range. 3–13. Boarding from age 7.
Number of Pupils. 75 Boarders (36 boys, 39 girls), 303 Day.
Fees per term (2010-2011). Boarders £6,565, Day £1,385–£5,045. 15% discount for Forces boarders. A junior boarding discount of 10% is offered for children in Years 3 to 6.

Originally founded in 1953 as a Roman Catholic boys' boarding school, Farleigh is now a fully co-educational boarding and day school which welcomes children of all faiths. Situated in a Georgian country house standing in 60 acres of magnificent parkland and landscaped woodland in the Test Valley of Hampshire, Farleigh is just over an hour from London and within easy reach of Southampton and London airports.

High standards are achieved both in and out of the classroom and excellent academic results are the norm, with leavers going to a large number of leading senior schools and many obtaining scholarships.

Farleigh has outstanding facilities, including a spacious and light Art and Design Technology building, three science laboratories, two well-equipped computer rooms with Apple Macs and PCs, a theatre with tiered seating, music suite, spacious recreation rooms, a fine Chapel, gymnasium, outdoor swimming pool, 22-metre heated indoor swimming pool, squash courts and purpose-built Pre-Prep and Kindergarten.

The teaching staff is complemented by a committed pastoral team including Year Heads, House Parents and two qualified matrons. Many staff are resident, giving the school a welcoming family atmosphere, often commented upon by visitors. A recent Ofsted inspection of the school's boarding provision reported that "Farleigh School offers a good standard of care, guidance and support to its boarding pupils."

The school provides a vibrant and active evening and weekend activity programme for boarders. Barbecue parties, 'pop stars' competitions, theatre trips, karaoke, quiz nights, bowling, Chinese takeaway nights, London museum visits are just some of the weekend events organised for pupils. Weekday activities include building dens in the woods, winter cricket nets, chess, community service, swimming, water polo, tennis, football, uni-hockey, board games, jewellery making, art and craft.

Drama, music and art have important places in school life. A programme of major drama and musical productions, and informal concerts weave variety into the school year and the children's artwork is always displayed around the school for all to see.

The major sports for boys are rugby, football, cricket, athletics and cross-country; for girls they are netball, hockey, rounders, athletics and cross-country. Swimming lessons and tennis coaching are available throughout the year.

Charitable status. Farleigh School is a Registered Charity, number 307340. It exists for the purpose of educating children.

Farlington Preparatory School

Strood Park, Horsham, West Sussex RH12 3PN
Tel: 01403 282566
Fax: 01403 272258
e-mail: baggsj@farlingtonschool.net
website: www.farlingtonschool.net

Chairman of Governors: M Simpkin, OBE

Headmistress: **Mrs Joy K Baggs**, BEd Hons, CertEd

Registrar: Mrs E V Healy

Age Range. 3–11.
Number of Girls. 200.
Fees per term (2011-2012). Tuition: £2,269–£4,054. Boarding (in addition to Tuition fees): £2,728 (weekly), £3,054 (full).

The Early Years Foundation Stage and Pre-Prep Departments at Farlington are housed in a new courtyard building opened in September 2008. This purpose-built accommodation comprises nursery, large infant classrooms, a library and two innovative play areas. The spacious hall and dining facilities are enjoyed by all of our Prep Pupils. The Junior School girls are also housed in purpose-built classrooms that mirror the architecture of the Mansion House in the School grounds. Younger children quickly feel at home in this close-knit community, and the older girls have the opportunity to learn responsibility and have status in "their" school by becoming prefects, house captains and stewards.

Early school days that are happy and secure, provide a sound basis for learning and for life. At Farlington, we aim to achieve high academic standards in our Preparatory School, with the emphasis on encouragement: we educate for confidence! The philosophy of the School is based on Christian ethics, but we also welcome girls from a wide range of religious and cultural backgrounds.

We have a staff of well-qualified and dedicated teachers. They form a wonderfully good-humoured team, who support fully the ethos of the School. Literacy and numeracy are the building blocks of education, and this is the basis of our teaching. Scientific skills are developed in a challenging way, using exploration and experiment, as well as practice and problem-solving.

We follow the National Curriculum, but offer far more in terms of subject content, and, of course, individual attention. As girls become older, they are taught most subjects by specialist teachers (for example French, Spanish, Latin, PE/Games, Drama, Music, Art). In Prep 6, Science is taught in the well-equipped laboratories in the Senior School. There is a strong emphasis on Music and individual tuition can be arranged for most instruments.

All girls can enjoy the beautiful 33-acre parkland setting for play and for learning.

The Prep School offers a wide range of extra-curricular activities which take place at lunchtimes and after school. These range from sporting clubs such as tennis, trampolining, golf and judo. Musical activities take place on a daily basis and include choir, orchestra, recorder groups and a samba band. We offer chess tuition, ballet, jazz dance and many more! Farlington Prep has its own Morris Dancing Side too! Although school finishes at 3.20 pm for girls in Reception to Prep 2, they can stay on at school until 5.00 pm supervised by members of staff.

The older girls finish their lessons at 3.45 pm and can do activities and supervised homework until 5.45 pm. Parents are encouraged to consult their daughters' teachers regularly and we hope that they will take an active part in their education. Parents are invited to join their daughters on educational outings and visits and they are keen supporters of junior teams. Farlington has a very active PTA and a Parents' Round Table (a focus group to develop ideas throughout the school).

Boarding is available to girls from the age of 9. Our Boarding House is friendly and run on family lines.

Prospective parents are always welcome to come and meet the Headmistress and have a tour of the School. Please telephone for an appointment and we will be delighted to forward a current prospectus.

Charitable status. Farlington Preparatory School is a Registered Charity, number 307048. It exists solely for the purpose of educating girls.

Felsted Preparatory School

Felsted, Essex CM6 3JL
Tel: 01371 822610
Fax: 01371 822617
e-mail: rmw@felstedprep.org
website: www.felsted.org

Chairman of the Governors: Mr J H Davies

Head: **Mrs J M Burrett**, BA Dunelm, MEd Cantab, PGCE

Deputy Head: T J Searle, BSc Loughborough, PGCE

Age Range. 4–13 Co-educational.
Number of Pupils. 339 day pupils (20 full time Boarders plus 80 flexi-boarders), plus 120 4–6 year olds in the Pre-Preparatory Department (Stewart House).
Fees per term (2011-2012). £3,720–£4,890; Pre-Preparatory: £2,575; Boarding £6,250.

The staff, excluding the Headmistress, consists of 50 full-time qualified teachers and there are additional part-time teachers for instrumental music and games. There are six matrons and two sisters in charge of the Medical Centre.

The Preparatory School, set in its own grounds, is separate from Felsted School itself, with all its own facilities, including a modern well-equipped library, an excellent theatre/assembly hall, music practice rooms, a new multi-purpose sports hall, open-air heated swimming pool and floodlit, multi-purpose, hard-play games area. Use is made of Felsted School's extra amenities at regular times so that small-bore rifle shooting, squash courts, indoor swimming, two Astroturf hockey pitches, a new state-of-the-art Music School and another indoor sports hall are also available to the pupils.

Rugby, football, netball, hockey, cricket, tennis, swimming, rounders, athletics and cross-country have been the major sports. Music plays an important part in the School's life, and there is an excellent Chapel choir. Regular instrumental, orchestral and rock concerts are given. The School has a deserved reputation for its drama productions, while Art, Design and Technology, and Computing are part of the weekly timetable. Out-of-class activities include public speaking and debating opportunities, horse riding, chess, fencing, golf, public speaking, aerobics, cookery and dance/ballet, among others.

Pupils joining at 11+ can be guaranteed assured transfer to Felsted School at 13, as can pupils of a similar age already at the Preparatory School, following successful completion of assessment tests. The majority of pupils proceed to Felsted School itself, but a number regularly move on to other major independent senior schools, having taken Common Entrance, and there is an excellent record of academic, art, music, sport, drama and Design & Technology scholarships. (*For further information about Felsted, see entry in HMC section.*)

Academic and Music Scholarships and Outstanding Talent Awards are open to pupils joining Felsted Preparatory School at ages of 11+ in the September of the year of entry depending on ability and financial circumstances. One 100% bursary is available each year to a child who meets the right criteria and is given at the discretion of the Head.

Charitable status. Felsted School is a Registered Charity, number 310870. It exists to provide education for boys and girls.

Feltonfleet School

Cobham, Surrey KT11 1DR
Tel: 01932 862264
Fax: 01932 860280
e-mail: office@feltonfleet.co.uk
website: www.feltonfleet.co.uk

Chairman of Governors: G D Ashbee

Headmaster: **P C Ward**, BEd Hons

Age Range. 3–13.
Number of Pupils. Nursery/Pre-Prep 72, Years 3–8 288, of whom 45 are Boarders.
Fees per term (2010-2011). Boarders £6,495; Day Pupils £3,220–£4,725; Nursery £1,720.

Feltonfleet School was founded in 1903 and became an Educational Trust in 1967. The School is situated in 20 acres of scenic grounds close to the M25 between Heathrow and Gatwick Airports. There are 50 full-time and 4 Gap Year members of the teaching staff. The School became fully co-educational in September 1994 and offers both weekly (Monday to Friday) boarding or day education, as well as a flexible boarding option. There is a flourishing, purpose-built Pre-Preparatory Department, Calvi House.

Ethos. It is the School's strongly held belief that if children are happy they will fulfil their potential, and by recognising the individual in a child this is more likely to happen, which is why it is committed to fostering a small school atmosphere centred on family values. The School does its best to place the children first, to meet each child's needs on an individual basis, to encourage and nurture the positive aspects of 'self': self-discipline, self-confidence, self-motivation, self-reliance and self-esteem. High-achieving children, irrespective of their real potential, are those who have a high self-esteem – without it very little can be achieved.

Pastoral. Caring for each other matters at Feltonfleet. From a child's first day, the adult community provides care, direction and confidence. The form tutor is the welcoming face on a daily basis and a secure link with daily routine, a familiar and reassuring presence, a trusted confidant and role model. Small classes make quality pastoral care much more certain. Once pupils join the Main School, the Head of Year provides further direction and guidance. The boarding house is run by two house parents, seven boarding house tutors and two matrons who promote the personal, family atmosphere on which Feltonfleet prides itself.

Entry. Children are admitted from the age of three into the Nursery in the Pre-Preparatory Department and, having moved into the Main School at the age of seven, are prepared for Common Entrance or Scholarship examinations to a wide range of independent senior schools. In the Main School there is a staff : pupil ratio of 9.5 : 1, with the average class size of 16.

For entry into the Main School pupils are required to sit an entrance assessment and interview. Academic, Art, Music, Drama, DT, All-Rounder and Sports Scholarships are offered at 11+.

Facilities. Well-equipped Science, Art, DT and ICT Departments, Library and Performing Arts Centre, where dramatic productions are performed by all year groups. The Pre-Prep, Calvi House, has recently undergone a major refurbishment with the addition of its own hall and ICT suite. Plans are in place for the building of a new swimming pool complex.

Sport. The Sports Department prides itself that is able to encompass both excellence and sport for all within a very busy prep school environment. All pupils receive high quality teaching and coaching in a variety of sports and activities in a positive and safe learning environment. Facilities include a magnificent sports hall, sports fields, two squash courts, cricket nets, floodlit courts for tennis, hockey, football and basketball, swimming pool and two shooting ranges (air weapon and .22 rifle).

Games played are rugby, football, hockey, netball, athletics and cricket.

Extra-Curricular Activities. The School has an active policy of preparing children for the challenges of today's world and an exceptional activities programme is offered to all pupils during the school day as often as possible. Pupils in the main school are offered the opportunity to attend residential activity courses as well as subject-related overseas trips. In the final two years pupils attend residential leadership courses. After Common Entrance examinations, Year 8 pupils take part in a varied programme of activities, lectures and trips in preparation for leaving Feltonfleet and moving on to their senior schools.

In recent years sporting teams have visited Belgium and Spain and the Drama Department has performed at the Edinburgh Fringe Festival.

Charitable status. Feltonfleet School Trust Limited is a Registered Charity, number 312070.

Fettes College Preparatory School

East Fettes Avenue, Edinburgh EH4 1QZ
Tel: 0131 332 2976
Fax: 0131 332 4724
e-mail: prepschool@fettes.com
website: www.fettes.com

Chairman of Governors: D B McMurray, MA

Chairman of Preparatory School Committee: Mrs J A Campbell

Headmaster: A A Edwards, BA Hons, PGCE

Age Range. 7–12.
Number of Pupils. 182 (52 boarders, 130 day pupils), 95 boys, 87 girls.
Fees per term (2011-2012). Boarders £6,560, Day Pupils £4,185, including all meals and textbooks.

Fettes Prep School lies within the Fettes College grounds – 80 acres of parkland in the heart of Edinburgh. Although housed in separate buildings about 200m away from the main Fettes College building, the Prep School has all the advantages of the excellent facilities of Fettes College but with the ability to be a complete campus in its own right. Due to expansion in the school roll, William House was completed in 2009 – a state-of-the-art teaching block with superb eco credentials.

Their HMIe inspection had superb results with both Fettes Prep and Fettes College deemed as 'sector-leading'.

The Boarding houses offer a safe, secure and happy environment within either a boys' or girls' house. The pastoral staff; housemaster, housemistress, matron and resident tutor, are of the highest calibre and dedicate themselves to creating a secure and happy home.

The curriculum is structured to reflect the strengths of the Curriculum for Excellence, the National Curriculum of England and Wales and IAPS guidance. A strong emphasis is placed on a sound and thorough grounding in the traditionally important subjects of Maths and English as well as specialists subjects such as Science, Art and Languages being taught by specialist teachers. Class sizes remain small to allowing individual attention for each child – the absolute maximum class size is 18.

Formal coaching is given to boys in rugby, hockey, athletics and cricket and to girls in hockey, netball, rounders, athletics and tennis. Each year pupils from the school represent their district in these sports as well as others. Swimming is also taught as are judo, fencing, squash and shooting. All

these take place in the new Westwoods Health Centre and newly-completed shooting range. There is an extensive activities programme with clubs ranging from knitting to flat water speed kayaking.

Music and Drama flourish. The School Choir and School Orchestra give concerts each term, and choirs and instrumental groups participate successfully in musical competitions. Year group concerts, too, are regularly held. Each year there is a large-production School Play, younger pupils produce their own pantomime, and shorter plays are performed in French and Latin. The art department continues to excel and every pupil within the school has their work displayed.

There are annual trips abroad to bring learning to life and other tours are regularly organised. All twelve year olds receive leadership training and the top two year groups are involved in a programme designed at the school to increase and improve skills in various areas including resourcefulness, initiative and personal challenge.

Entrance. Entrance at the age of seven, eight or nine is by assessment tests and at 10+, 11+ and 12+ by the Entrance examinations, taken in late Jan/early Feb. Scholarships are available at 11+ in music, academics and all-rounders. Music scholarships are available at other times. All scholarships holders automatically receive up to 10% of the fees with means-tested bursarial support available that can cover 95% of the fees.

Further information and a prospectus can be obtained from the Registrar (Tel: 0131 311 6744, e-mail: admissions@fettes.com) who will be very happy to arrange a visit.

Charitable status. The Fettes Trust is a Registered Charity, number SC017489. It exists to provide education for boys and girls.

Finborough Preparatory School

The Hall, Great Finborough, Stowmarket, Suffolk IP14 3EF
Tel: 01449 773600
Fax: 01449 773601
e-mail: admin@finborough.suffolk.sch.uk
website: www.finboroughschool.co.uk

Co-educational, Day and Boarding School.

Principal: Mr James Sinclair

Head of Preparatory School: **Mrs Stephanie Samuels**, BA Ed, DipMont, QTS

Age Range. 2½–11 years.
Number of Pupils. 85: 54 girls (7 boarders), 48 boys (8 boarders).
Fees per term (2011-2012). Day £2,290–£2,760, Full Boarding £5,255–£5,410, Weekly Boarding £4,225–£4,380.

Finborough Preparatory School is situated in 60 acres of its own playing fields, gardens and woodlands. Finborough Hall is an 18th Century manor house with modern extensions.

Classes are small, maximum 20, and often 10, taught by well-qualified staff. Subject specialists are used from year 3. The school teaches traditional values in education, manners and respect, whilst maintaining a friendly family atmosphere. Pride is taken in having pupils who are happy, and who benefit from staff whose mission is to help each child maximise his or her potential. The curriculum covers the full range of subjects, making full use of new facilities including art studio and Apple Mac suite.

The school offers a full sporting programme, a wide range of after-school and weekend activities, regular competition in art, speech and music, and a new on-site equestrian centre.

Full, weekly or occasional boarding is available from the age of 7, in a secure and friendly environment.

A thriving Parents Association organises social events for parents and children at least once a term.

The school is situated 2 miles west of Stowmarket, on the main London–Norwich railway line, and is a 5-minute drive from the A14.

(*See also Finborough School entry in ISA section.*)

Finton House

171 Trinity Road, London SW17 7HL
Tel: 020 8682 0921
Fax: 020 8767 5017
e-mail: admissions@fintonhouse.org.uk
website: www.fintonhouse.org.uk

Co-Founders: Terry O'Neill and Finola Stack founded Finton House in 1987.

Chair of Governors: Mr Mark Chilton

Headmaster: **Mr A E Floyd**, BSc, PGCE

Age Range. 4–11.
Number of Pupils. 109 Boys, 196 Girls.
Fees per term (2011-2012). £3,825–£4,150.
Entrance. No testing – first come/first served.
Exit. Boys at 8, 9, 10, 11 for both London Day and Prep. Girls at 11 for London Day and Boarding.

Strong policy of inclusion with a percentage of children with Special Needs. Employs a full-time Speech and Language Therapist, an Occupational Therapist and Special Needs Assistants. Aims to give an all-round education, developing the whole child with individual teaching to fulfil each child's potential. Music, Art and Sports are all taught to a very high standard. A stimulating environment which encourages all children to learn and gain confidence in their own abilities. Non-denominational but teaches a moral belief encouraging respect and self-discipline.

Charitable status. Finton House is a Registered Charity, number 296588. It exists to provide an broad, inclusive education for children.

Foremarke Hall
Repton Preparatory School

Milton, Derbyshire DE65 6EJ
Tel: 01283 707100
Fax: 01283 702957
e-mail: registrar@foremarke.org.uk
website: www.foremarke.org.uk

Chairman of Governors: J M Fry

Head: **R P Merriman**, MA, BSc Hons, FCollP

Age Range. 3–13.
Number of Pupils. 476: Boys: 42 boarders, 229 day; Girls: 24 boarders, 181 day.
Fees per term (2011-2012). Prep: £6,296 boarding, £4,741 day; Pre-Prep: Years 1 & 2 £2,858, Reception £2,578, Nursery £2,450 (full-time), £245 (part-time per session).

Foremarke Hall is under the control of the Governors of Repton School. Boys and girls are prepared for all Independent Schools but about two-thirds choose to continue to Repton.

The school is situated in a fine Georgian mansion surrounded by 50 acres of woods, playing fields and a lake. The facilities include all that the school requires including a new classroom building to house mathematics, three science laboratories, sophisticated computer technology with full time IT specialist, large art room with pottery facilities, Design Technology department, an extensive library run by a chartered librarian, an indoor competition sized swimming pool, a sports hall and a floodlit sports artificial turf surface.

An exciting £6.5m development started in July 2011 which will see an 18th Century quadrangle rebuilt on the site of former stable buildings. Phase 1 of The Quad development will house a contemporary Music School and four classrooms and is scheduled for opening Easter 2012 whilst Phase 1a, which will continue straight away, will accommodate eight classrooms. Phase 2 will comprise a new Art School and Design Technology Centre.

Great importance is attached to pastoral care where boarders have their own dedicated staff and space for themselves. There is an imaginative and varied programme of activities making most use of the grounds including outdoor pursuits. The games programme is extensive and includes athletics, cricket, football, rugby, hockey, rounders, swimming and tennis. We also have an extensive and varied after school activities programme.

We seek to bring out the most in every pupil, to provide a rounded education and a range of experience and skills that will be a preparation for life. We value our 'family atmosphere' and strong sense of community, the spacious grounds and happy environment.

Foremarke is situated in undisturbed countryside in the centre of England. It is easily reached by the M1, M42 and Birmingham and East Midlands airports.

Charitable status. Repton Preparatory School is a Registered Charity, number 1093165. It exists to provide high quality education for boys and girls.

Forest Preparatory School

College Place, Snaresbrook, London E17 3PY
Tel: 020 8520 1744
Fax: 020 8520 3656
e-mail: prep@forest.org.uk
website: www.forest.org.uk

Co-educational Day School.

Chairman of Governors: J W Matthews, FCA

Head: **Mrs E Garner**, BA Hons London, MEd Cantab

Age Range. 4–11.
Number of Pupils. 272.
Fees per term (2011-2012). £3,145–£3,647.

Forest Preparatory School is part of Forest School (HMC), with which it shares a 30-acre site at the foot of Epping Forest on the East London/Essex border. Its aims are to offer an education of high quality, and to encourage and develop each child academically, physically and creatively. From the age of 7, pupils are taught in single-sex classes, and at age 11 they proceed to the boys' and girls' sections of Forest School (*see separate entry in HMC section*).

Entry to the school is by selection at age 4 by means of informal assessment and, at age 7, by entrance examination.

The Pre-Prep Department is co-educational, with forms of 16 pupils who are taught predominantly by form teachers and supported by classroom assistants. Music, Drama and PE are taught by specialist teachers. From the age of 7, forms become single-sex and number around 22 pupils. Form teachers teach the main curriculum subjects, while specialists teach modern foreign languages – French, Spanish and German – ICT, music, drama, design and technology, physical education and games. In the final two years an element of setting is introduced in English and mathematics. Scholarship and music awards are available to pupils for entry at age 11 to the Boys' and Girls' Schools at Forest.

Sport and music are strengths of the school. The main sports played are football, cricket, netball and rounders, and teams compete locally and regionally. Athletics, swimming and cross-country are all coached to a high standard. The musical life of the school is enriched by its choirs, orchestra and several chamber groups, and all pupils in Years 2 and 4 are provided with free tuition in a musical instrument. There are endless opportunities for pupils to perform in concerts or recitals throughout the year, and Chapel services, form assemblies and school competitions provide occasions for public speaking and performance. Activities take place at lunchtime and after school, with a wide variety of extra-curricular clubs on offer. Breakfast club opens at 7.30 am, after-school care is available up to 6.00 pm, and an extensive school bus service is in operation.

Charitable status. Forest School, Essex is a Registered Charity, number 312677. The objective of the school is education.

Forres Sandle Manor

Sandleheath, Fordingbridge, Hampshire SP6 1NS
Tel: 01425 653181
Fax: 01425 655676
e-mail: office@fsmschool.com
website: www.fsmschool.com

Headmaster: **M N Hartley**, BSc Hons, PGCE

Age Range. 3–13.
Number of Pupils. Prep: 211 (half of whom are boarders, and half boys). Pre-Prep: 51 (all are day children, half are boys).
Fees per term (2010-2011). Prep: Boarders £6,460, Day pupils £4,735; Pre-Prep £1,050–£2,545.

Forres Sandle Manor is situated on its own beautiful 35-acre estate on the edge of the New Forest. The main school building is a large manor house and the grounds are perfect for children – extensive and well-maintained playing fields, woods, a stream and plenty of space for even the most active individual! Facilities include a fine multi-purpose hall, heated swimming pool, Technology Centre, a superb Coach House Art Studio, an astroturf and much more!

The School has a fine academic record and achieves an impressive number of Awards to Independent Senior Schools. There is an exceptionally dynamic teaching staff who teach in spacious, light classrooms and who prepare children for Common Entrance and scholarships at 13+ whilst delivering the National Curriculum wherever possible. It is our aim to develop in children a true enjoyment and involvement in their work and this is aided by our efforts to link various subjects together and to the wider world in general.

Music is an especially strong feature of the school with all children encouraged to play and to become confident in performance. Sport, too, is an important part of school life as are the extraordinary range of activities available to both boarders and day children. It is the school's policy to make weekends the best part of a thoroughly enjoyable week!

The Headmaster, his wife and family, are all fully involved in the school and it is the main aim of all who live and work at Forres Sandle Manor that the community be happy, confident and caring. Great care is taken to ensure the happiness of every child and to maintain the family atmosphere which has always been the basis of the school's tradition.

Charitable status. Forres Sandle Manor Education Trust Ltd is a Registered Charity, number 284260. It exists to provide high quality education for boys and girls.

Fosse Bank School

Mountains Country House, Noble Tree Road, Hildenborough, Kent TN11 8ND
Tel: 01732 834212
Fax: 01732 834884
e-mail: office@fossebankschool.co.uk
website: www.fossebankschool.co.uk

Chairman of Governors: Mr Miles Cavey

Head: **Mrs Gillian Lovatt-Young**, BEd, NPQH

Age Range. 3–11 Co-educational.
Number of Pupils. 115.
Fees per term (2010-2011). £460–£3,145.

Fosse Bank School and Pre-school, founded in 1892, offers an excellent academic education combined with a truly supportive, friendly and stimulating environment in which your child can learn, grow and flourish. Our school has a positive ethos which celebrates success and encourages each child to be the best that they can be. The importance of good manners is emphasised and our children have a reputation for being confident, articulate and well-behaved. The school has a strong family community and is located in a beautiful Grade II listed building, within 26 acres of parkland and boasting a range of wonderful facilities including a state-of-the-art ICT Suite, indoor heated swimming pool, tennis courts, sports hall and extremely well-resourced Pre-school. There are extensive playing fields and wooded areas with a pond for field-studies, and ample, safe parking.

Academic Studies. In the Pre-school and Foundation Stage we give the children a solid foundation based on the Early Years Foundations Stage Profile. Further up the school, we follow and extend the National Curriculum, offering broad, enriched learning experiences. ICT, Music, PE and French are taught by specialists so that high standards are achieved in all subject areas and the children are given frequent opportunities to perform and share their talents. Our children achieve excellent academic results accepting offers of places at selective state and independent schools every year. Our Kent 11+ results have been outstanding in recent years with over 90% of children who sit the test being offered Grammar School places at some of the best schools in Kent. Our Foundation Stage, Key Stage 1 and 2 SATs results are always well above the national standard of achievement.

Extra-Curricular. A wealth of activities are available both during and after school for all children, such as chess, sewing, cross-country running, ballet, football, choir, scuba diving, acrobatics and many others. A Late Club is available for siblings of children participating in clubs.

Entry Procedure. Fosse Bank is not academically selective at entry. All children are required to attend a Taster Day before a place may be offered. Dance scholarships and means-tested bursaries are available.

Charitable status. Fosse Bank New School is a Registered Charity, number 1045435.

The Froebelian School

Clarence Road, Horsforth, Leeds LS18 4LB
Tel: 0113 258 3047
Fax: 0113 258 0173

e-mail: office@froebelian.co.uk
website: www.froebelian.co.uk

Chair of Governors: Mrs R Richmond, LLB Hons

Headmaster: Mr J Tranmer, MA, PGCE, FCollP

Age Range. 3+ to 11+ years (3–4 years half days, optional afternoons).
Number of Pupils. 187 (92 boys, 95 girls).
Fees per term (2011-2012). £1,380–£2,070. Compulsory extras for full-time pupils, such as lunches and swimming, amount to approximately £182 per term.
Bursaries (income-related fee reduction) may be available.
Religious Affiliation: Christian, non-denominational.
Entry Requirements: Interview and assessment; written tests for older children.
Entry is usually at 3+, but limited places are sometimes available throughout the school.
Every child is respected as an individual and pupils are able to reach their full potential in the purposeful atmosphere of this caring, disciplined school. High standards are achieved in all areas of the school – academic work, creative arts, music, sport, behaviour and manners. Early progress in language and mathematics is sustained and broadened in the junior curriculum, which includes French, information and design technology, drama and outdoor pursuits.
The school enjoys an envied reputation for success in entrance and scholarship examinations at 11+. A flourishing Parent Teacher Association supports the school and a growing database helps to keep former pupils in touch.
Situated to the north-west of Leeds, and close to Bradford, the school is well served by major transport links. 'Wrap-around' care is available from 7.30 am to 6.00 pm in the form of Breakfast Club, Little Acorns and Homework and Activities Club and there is a holiday club during the breaks.
Charitable status. The Froebelian School is a Registered Charity, number 529111. It exists to provide education of the highest quality at affordable fee levels.

Garden House School

Turk's Row, London SW3 4TW
Tel: 020 7730 1652 (Girls)
        020 7730 6652 (Boys)
e-mail: info@gardenhouseschool.co.uk
website: www.gardenhouseschool.co.uk

Principal: Mrs J K Oddy

Headmistress (*Upper School*): **Mrs Kate Simon**, BA Hons, PGCE
Headmistress (*Lower School*): **Mrs Wendy Challen**, CertEd Froebel
Headmaster (*Boys' School*): **Mr Christian Warland**, BA Hons

Age Range. 3–11 Girls, 3–11 Boys.
Number of Pupils. 262 girls, 188 boys, taught in single-sex classes.
Fees per term (2010-2011). Kindergarten £3,330, Reception–Year 6 £5,500–£5,680. There is a 10% reduction for siblings.
Buildings and facilities. The School is housed in a charming, light and airy listed building. Original artwork hangs in every classroom, and facilities include libraries for different age groups, a ballet/performance/drama hall and dedicated science and art rooms.

The school has its own garden within the grounds of the Royal Hospital where children enjoy science lessons and attend a Gardening Club.
School drama productions are ambitiously staged at the Royal Court Theatre in Sloane Square.
Aims, ethos and values. Garden House provides a thorough and balanced education in a lively and purposeful environment. Our children achieve high academic results in a calm and constructive manner, being encouraged to have inquiring and independent minds. Emphasis is placed not only on academic, sporting and artistic ability but on manners and consideration to others. Our Kindness Code is adhered to and constantly re-emphasised.
Curriculum. Literacy, Numeracy, Science, History, Geography, Religious Education, French (from Kindergarten), Latin, ICT, PSCHE, Art, Drama, Singing and Music, Dancing, Fencing and Physical Education (netball, tennis, rounders, gymnastics, swimming, athletics, cricket, hockey, pop lacrosse, rugby and football). We have many sports squads, sports clubs and matches. Children with learning difficulties are catered for in small groups, taught by two full-time and many visiting specialist teachers. 80% of children learn at least one musical instrument. The school runs four choirs and a chamber orchestra.
A diverse range of after-school clubs include Spy Club, Touch-Typing, Mandarin, Chess, and Sculpture.
Benefiting from our central London location, visits to museums, galleries and churches form an essential part of the curriculum, as do annual field study and outward bound trips. Girls spend a week in France after Common Entrance and boys enjoy a camping expedition.
School Successes. Girls are prepared for the Common Entrance, with the majority leaving for the premier girls' schools, 60% to leading London senior schools, 40% to major boarding schools. Some boys leave us at 8, having been well prepared for entrance to leading London prep schools and 10% to top boarding preps. Other boys remain at Garden House, being educated to the age of 11. Our children achieve several scholarships each year.
Entrance. We encourage you to visit the school. Girls and boys join Garden House in the September after they reach 3 or 4 years of age. An Application Form can be obtained from the School Office and once completed, and returned with the relevant fee, your child's name is placed on the waiting list. Entry interview is held one year before entry. We look forward to welcoming you and your children to Garden House School.

Gatehouse School

Sewardstone Road, Victoria Park, London E2 9JG
Tel: 020 8980 2978
Fax: 020 8983 1642
e-mail: admin@gatehouseschool.co.uk
website: www.gatehouseschool.co.uk

Headmistress: Mrs Belinda Canham, JP, BA, PGCE

Age Range. 3–11 Co-educational.
Number in School. 300 Day Pupils.
Fees per term (2011-2012). £2,325–£2,860.
Gatehouse School is an Independent Co-educational School for girls and boys aged 3 to 11.
Founded by Phyllis Wallbank, in May 1948, in the gatehouse of St Bartholomew, the Great Priory Church near Smithfield London, the School was a pioneer of much that is now generally accepted in education. Gatehouse is based on the Wallbank plan whose guiding principle is that children of any race, colour, creed, background and intellect shall be accepted as pupils and work side by side without streaming or any kind of segregation with the aim that each child shall

get to know and love God, and develop their own uniqueness of personality, to enable them to appreciate the world and the world to appreciate them.

Gatehouse is now located in Sewardstone Road close to Victoria Park and continues to follow this philosophy.

The Nursery is accommodated in a large sunny space with its own outdoor play area. They follow a balanced curriculum of child-initiated and teacher-led activities.

Lower Juniors are taught most subjects by their own qualified teacher and assistant, but have French, PE and Music with a specialist teacher.

In Upper Juniors from the age of 7, teaching is by subject and is conducted by a highly qualified specialist staff. This is a special feature of Gatehouse and gives children from an early age, contact with subject specialists, not available to many children until secondary school.

Our classes average around 18 pupils.

We send children to schools such as City of London boys and girls, Forest, Bancroft's and Highgate. This year we won scholarships to these schools.

Charitable status. Gatehouse Educational Trust Limited is a Registered Charity, number 282558.

Gateway School

1 High Street, Great Missenden, Buckinghamshire HP16 9AA
Tel: 01494 862407
Fax: 01494 865787
e-mail: headteacher@gateway.bucks.sch.uk
website: www.gatewayschool-bucks.co.uk

Principal: **S J Y Wade**, MA, PGCE

Age Range. 2–12.
Number of Pupils. Day: 203 Boys, 146 Girls.
Fees per term (2011-2012). From £606 (Nursery one full day per week) to £3,032 (full-time).
• Montessori based Early Years Unit
• Flexible free entitlement for 3 and 4 year olds plus childcare vouchers
• High academic standard with a broad curriculum
• Wide range of sporting activities
• Extensive ICT provision
• Vibrant music department
• Day and overnight trips at home and abroad
• Provision from 8.00 am to 6.00 pm for 48 weeks pa.

Gayhurst School

Bull Lane, Gerrards Cross, Bucks SL9 8RJ
Tel: 01753 882690
Fax: 01753 887451
e-mail: gayhurst@gayhurstschool.eu
website: www.gayhurstschool.eu

Chairman of Governors: Mr P Cooke

Headmaster: **Mr A Sims**, MA Cantab

Age Range. 3–13.
Number of Children. 316.
Fees per term (2010-2011). £2,914–£3,702 inclusive of lunch for all pupils.

Gayhurst is a happy, thriving day school for boys and girls aged from three to 13, set in beautiful grounds. A purpose-built Nursery was opened in September 2008. Main entry points to the school are at Nursery, Reception, Year 3 and Year 7.

Gayhurst strives to give its pupils the best start in life. The school treats every child as an individual and provides a caring family environment and excellent facilities. From this foundation each child is given an opportunity to achieve their potential in academic, cultural and sporting pursuits.

The school has excellent academic results, both to local grammar schools and to the independent sector through scholarships or Common Entrance examinations in which Gayhurst has 100% record of success.

Facilities are first rate and there has been recent significant investment in the Junior School and in IT. The Senior School has been completely redeveloped in the last ten years. Gayhurst stands in a five-acre playing field with woodland and a further four-acre field beyond. An all-weather Astroturf pitch means that the widest range of sports are offered. Although the school has achieved many sporting successes, it has an inclusive attitude to sports and games with A to E teams participating in matches when possible.

Music and drama play an important part of the Curriculum with productions being wholly collaborative events where every child finds his or her strengths. A very high proportion of children choose to play musical instruments and take part in the many ensemble groups.

After-school and extra-curricular activities are wide-ranging and care for all interests, from chess, film-making and cookery to skiing, sailing and polo as well as Judo, gymnastics and ballet.

Charitable status. Gayhurst School Trust is a Registered Charity, number 298869.

Giggleswick Junior School

Giggleswick, Settle, North Yorkshire BD24 0DG
Tel: 01729 893100
Fax: 01729 893150
e-mail: juniorschool@giggleswick.org.uk
website: www.giggleswickschool.co.uk

Chairman of Governors: M H O'Connell, BA, FCA

Head: **M Brotherton**, BEd Hons, NPQH

Age Range. 3–11 Co-educational.
Number of Pupils. 80.
Fees per term (2011-2012). Boarders £5,410, Day Pupils £2,115–£4,410.

Giggleswick Junior School offers a co-educational day and boarding education within a secure, happy, family atmosphere. Day pupils are fully integrated into the life and ethos of the school. The Head and his family live on site and the Boarding Housemaster and his family live in the boarding house. There is an experienced team of academic staff and matrons to care for the children.

In its inspection report published February 2010, ISI adjudged both the Junior School and its Early Years Unit as 'outstanding' in every category and subheading, stating, "The school prepares pupils extremely well for the next stage of their education through an outstanding educational experience and through outstanding teaching".

There is a clear sense of purpose and development. Facilities are excellent: the Junior School and its Early Years Unit share a bright, modern, purpose-designed building with a full range of facilities, set within extensive grounds and playing fields. In addition to sharing Giggleswick's Swimming pool, Chapel, Food Technology, Design Centre, and all-weather pitch, a new sports hall was completed in 2005. Our ICT facilities, including email and supervised internet access, are constantly upgraded. The modern dining room serves particularly good food. The great majority of pupils progress to Giggleswick (*see HMC entry*).

In the centre of Britain, in the Yorkshire Dales, Giggleswick is within 75 minutes' drive of Manchester and Leeds, their airports and railway stations. Airport transfers are organised. The School also provides morning and evening bus services from Skipton, Grassington, Colne and Kirkby Lonsdale for the benefit of Day pupils.

Music and drama are integral to school life, as is participation in major team and individual sports and outdoor pursuits. The annual drama production is a highlight of the school year and involves all pupils from Year 1 through to Year 6. Pupils with particular educational needs are offered private individual or group lessons with the on-site specialists.

Visits and "taster" stays are warmly encouraged and contribute to new pupils' sense of involvement while part of the living school.

Charitable status. Giggleswick School is a Registered Charity, number 1109826. It exists to provide education for boys and girls.

Glebe House School

Cromer Road, Hunstanton, Norfolk PE36 6HW
Tel: 01485 532809
Fax: 01485 533900
e-mail: admin@glebehouseschool.co.uk
website: www.glebehouseschool.co.uk

Chairman of the Governors: Mr Chris Tyler

Headmaster: **J P Crofts**, BA, PGCE

Age Range. 6 months to 13 years.
Number of Children. 45 Boys, 48 Girls, Nursery 72.
Fees per term (2010-2011). Prep £4,185; Pre-Prep £2,790; Weekly boarding £4,915.
Glebe House School and Nursery was founded in 1874 as a preparatory school and is surrounded by 12 acres of playing fields.

The Junior School children are accommodated in a purpose-built building. The Senior School has specialist areas for all academic subjects and music, sport and drama are a significant part of a child's life at Glebe House. Our 25 metre indoor heated swimming pool, tennis and netball courts, adventure playground, gym, music school and performance hall all help to ensure that the core academic subjects are supported by a balanced and stimulating curriculum. Lessons finish at 3.30 pm (Pre-Prep), 4.10 pm (Prep) but breakfast club, after-school activities, cooked tea and supervised prep provide day care from 7.30 am to 6.30 pm.

Aims and Values. At the heart of Glebe House is our emphasis on supporting and valuing the individual. We encourage the traditional values of courtesy, consideration for others, self discipline and a desire to contribute to society.

Academic Life. We are committed to the achievement of high academic standards, harnessing the best of modern educational practice. Class sizes remain small and every child is encouraged to achieve their full potential. Close supervision, with one-to-one support where necessary, is maintained and progress is carefully monitored through regular standardised testing and classroom assessments. The broad curriculum both incorporates and exceed national requirements, including offering a second modern language in addition to French from year six. Glebe House enjoys a high success rate at Common Entrance and in Independent Scholarship Examinations and with this solid foundation our pupils move confidently on to a wide range of senior schools.

Sport and Activities. We offer a wide sporting programme aimed to encourage fitness and a healthy enjoyment of sport that will remain with the children for life. Rugby, hockey and cricket are the main sports for boys and hockey, netball and rounders for girls. We also encourage involvement in many activities including athletics, cross country, football, golf, swimming and tennis. The Glebe House Award Scheme encourages children to strive for high standards in acquiring skills that will prepare them for the future. We offer a wide range of activities during the summer holidays, including ballsports, swimming, craft, music and drama workshops, tennis, and sailing.

Pastoral Care and Boarding. Relations between children and staff are respectful but relaxed and the children know they are free to talk to all staff, one of the great advantages of a school this size. All pupils belong to one of three houses and have a tutor who sees them each morning and is the first point of contact for parents. Good communication is crucial and we operate an open door policy to parents. The school offers 35 weekly boarding places and flexibility in choosing from one to four nights.

Travel. Our minibus picks up in the morning and takes home at 4.15 pm and 6 pm to Kings Lynn and surrounding areas.

Further Information. Prospective parents and children are most welcome to contact the School Administrator to meet the Headmaster and tour the school.

Charitable status. Glebe House School Trust Limited is a Registered Charity, number 1018815.

The Gleddings Preparatory School

Birdcage Lane, Savile Park, Halifax, West Yorkshire HX3 0JB
Tel: 01422 354605
Fax: 01422 356263
e-mail: TheGleddings@aol.com
website: www.TheGleddings.co.uk

Headmistress: **Mrs P J Wilson**, CBE

Age Range. 3–11 Co-educational.
Number of Pupils. 191: 83 Boys, 108 Girls.
Fees per term (2010-2011). £1,185–£1,970.
"The Gleddings is very special. It is precious to several generations of families in the locality and beyond. We are now educating the children of our past pupils. We consider it a great privilege to do so.

The staff and I remember, all of the time, the trust that parents bestow in us. We promise our best efforts for every child.

Our academic results speak for themselves but The Gleddings is about much more than that. Our caring ethos is central to everything that we do and our intention is simply to make your children as successful as they can possibly be and as nice as they can possibly be."
Jill Wilson, Headteacher.

Glendower Preparatory School

87 Queen's Gate, London SW7 5JX
Tel: 020 7370 1927
Fax: 020 7244 8308
e-mail: office@glendower.kensington.sch.uk
website: www.glendowerprep.org

Chairman of Governors: Mr Rupert Harrison, LLB, LLM

Headmistress: **Mrs R E Bowman**, BA Warwick, PGCE

Age Range. Girls 4–11.

Number of Girls. 200.
Fees per term (2010-2011). £4,490.
Preparatory school for girls aged 4–11+ years. Pupils are prepared for the Common Entrance examinations and to the London Independent Day Schools at age 11.

French is taught throughout the school by a native speaker. Emphasis is laid on fluency and purity of accent. Science is taught in the purpose-built laboratory by a specialist, Latin is taught at age 10. ICT, Art and DT are included in the curriculum and taught in specialist rooms. All blackboards/whiteboards in KS2 classrooms have been replaced by plasma screens and every room has at least one computer.

In addition to class music lessons under a Director of Music, girls may learn piano, violin, recorder, viola, voice and flute; any other instruments by arrangement. Class drama is taught by a specialist and there are Drama Clubs for enthusiasts. Various club activities take place after school every day between 4pm and 5pm.

Physical Education includes Swimming, Netball, Gymnastics, Dance, Tennis and Athletics. The School values highly the close interest of parents, and staff are readily available by appointment as well as for regular Parent-Teacher discussion evenings.

The school had a successful ISI Inspection in 2005.

Charitable status. Glendower School Trust Limited is a Registered Charity, number 312717. It exists to provide high quality education for local girls.

The Godolphin Preparatory School

Laverstock Road, Salisbury, Wiltshire SP1 2RB
Tel: 01722 430652
Fax: 01722 430651
e-mail: prep@godolphin.wilts.sch.uk
website: www.godolphinprep.org

Chairman of the Governors: G Fletcher, Esq

Headmistress: **Mrs P White**, BEd

Age Range. 2½–11.
Number of Pupils. 80 Day Girls.
Fees per term (2011-2012). Full boarding £6,064, 5-day boarding £5,164, 3-day boarding £4,464; Day: Years 4–6 £3,564, Year 3 £2,836, Years 1–2 £1,851, Reception £1,845.

Godolphin Prep is a purpose-built, compact school for girls aged from two and a half to eleven. It is a mainstream academic school which focuses on the strengths of its pupils, values their potential as individuals and nurtures the girls to become caring members of society.

Many of the varied visitors to the school comment on the friendly atmosphere which they encounter. It is within such an environment that the girls are encouraged to have high expectations, good work habits and an active desire to take advantage of all that is on offer to them. Early specialist teaching across the curriculum is available from the age of 7, taught by people who are both dedicated and enthusiastic about their subjects. The high standard of teaching is reflected in the National Curriculum assessment results, as well as the scholarship awards gained by a significant number of pupils at eleven. There is an ambience of learning which comes from the 'work hard–play hard' ethic.

Courtesy and good manners are an implicit part of daily life at Godolphin; the basic precept is *'Never be the cause of another's unhappiness'*.

The school opened in 1993 as a part of the development plan of the Godolphin School. Following an inspection in 1996, which resulted in IAPS accreditation and then Department for Education registration two years later, the Prep has continued to thrive.

Godolphin Prep is a day school where outside interests are encouraged and weekends are perceived as family time, however, there is a programme of afterschool activities which creates opportunities for those who travel considerable distances to school by bus. This arrangement offers an element of choice which ensures that the girls develop as well-balanced individuals. Godolphin Prep will be introducing boarding for Years five and six in September 2011. The girls will be accommodated in bright and cheerful rooms and benefit from a tailor-made enrichment programme. There will also be a Breakfast club for day girls.

About 60% of the pupils move to the Godolphin School, following Common Entrance. Others move to boarding schools slightly farther afield or transfer to the local girls' grammar school.

Charitable status. The Godolphin School is a Registered Charity, number 309488. Its object is to provide and conduct in or near Salisbury a boarding and day school for girls.

Godstowe Preparatory School

Shrubbery Road, High Wycombe, Bucks HP13 6PR
Tel: 01494 529273
          01494 429006 Registrar
Fax: 01494 429009
e-mail: head@godstowe.org
website: www.godstowe.org

Motto: *Finem Respice*
Founded 1900.

Chairman of the Governors: A Kemp, BA Econ, ACA
(*Current Parent*)

Head: **Mr David Gainer**, BEd Hons London

Age Range. Girls 3–13, Boys 3–7.
Number of Pupils. Preparatory: 266 (boarding and day). Pre-Preparatory: 116.
Fees per term (2010-2011). Boarders £6,360, Day Children £2,780–£4,330. Nursery: £1,250–£2,500.

The School. Since its foundation in 1900, Godstowe Preparatory School has been at the forefront of education. It has a distinguished tradition as the first British boarding preparatory school for girls, in a foundation that includes Wycombe Abbey, Benenden and St Leonards.

Today, Godstowe is a flourishing boarding and day school with 380 pupils, enjoying an unparalleled academic reputation. It has a Pre-Prep department for boys and girls aged between three and seven, and a Preparatory School for girls from seven to thirteen years old. Class sizes are small allowing children to benefit from individual attention.

Academic Record. Godstowe enjoys an excellent and unparalleled academic reputation amongst British independent schools. Despite its non-selective entry policy, Godstowe consistently achieves unrivalled academic results. An average of 20 scholarships have been won each year for the last five years. By the age of nine, pupils are taught by specialists in 16 subjects across the curriculum. Language teaching includes French, Spanish and Latin. Sport, ICT, art and music are all outstandingly taught within first-rate facilities.

Boarding. Girls' boarding life is focused within three houses in the grounds, one of which is a dedicated junior house. Each has three resident staff and a warm and supportive atmosphere. A combination of professional and caring staff and beautifully refurbished accommodation ensures a safe and relaxing environment. Each house has its own garden and tennis court, reinforcing the feeling of 'going home' at the end of the school day. Weekends are packed full of activity and fun, with many weekly boarders often choosing to stay at School for the weekend.

The **Enrichment Curriculum** is an extended school day from 7.30 am to 7.30 pm, with some 50 after-school activities scheduled each week. The 'E-Curriculum' gives children the chance to try many exciting and challenging new pursuits including fencing, rock climbing, rowing, football and song writing. In addition, supervised homework sessions are offered every evening. Day children may join the boarders for breakfast and supper. Other than those sessions supervised by outside instructors all activities are offered free of charge. An Enrichment programme is also in place for Pre-Prep children.

Charitable status. The Godstowe Preparatory School Company Limited is a Registered Charity, number 310637. It exists to provide education and training for young girls and boys.

Grace Dieu Manor School

Grace Dieu, Thringstone, Leics LE67 5UG
Tel: 01530 222276
Fax: 01530 223184
e-mail: registrar@gracedieu.com
website: www.gracedieu.com

Chairman of Governors: Fr B E Cuddihy

Headmaster: **Mr C E Foulds**, BA University College, Swansea

Age Range. 3–13 Co-educational.
Number of Pupils. 350: Pre-Prep 132, Seniors 218.
Fees per term (2010-2011). £2,233–£3,344.

Grace Dieu, set in one hundred and twenty acres of grounds, is situated in the heart of the countryside. It is a co-educational Roman Catholic School, accepting children of all denominations and faiths from the age of 3. The School is divided into two departments, Pre-Prep (3–7) and Seniors (8–13+), each operating its own timetable. Entry is by interview and assessment.

The School has an excellent reputation academically, obtaining regular scholarships to local senior schools. Grace Dieu has a strong tradition in games and music and has its own indoor swimming pool and sports hall. There is a full programme of major sports (football, rugby, hockey, netball, rounders, cricket, tennis, swimming and athletics) as well as some minor sports (including volleyball and golf). The curriculum also includes Music and Drama, and school musicals are performed annually. Many children receive individual music tuition as an extra-curricular activity. A range of clubs operates during the lunch break or after school. There is an annual skiing trip, as well as an annual Jersey cricket tour and trip to France. Other tours for senior pupils also take place. The School offers before and after school care (8.00 am to 6.00 pm) at no extra charge. In addition, other activities for children are run on the premises during some holiday periods, though there is an extra charge for this service.

Charitable status. Grace Dieu Manor School is a Registered Charity, number 1115976. It exists to provide education for boys and girls.

The Grange
Monmouth Preparatory School

Hadnock Road, Monmouth NP25 3NG
Tel: 01600 715930
e-mail: thegrange@monmouthschool.org
website: www.habs-monmouth.org

Chairman of Governors: J B S Swallow, MA, FCA

Head: **Mrs E G Thomas**, BA

Age Range. 7–11.
Number of Pupils. 113 boys.
Fees per term (2011-2012). Boarding £6,050, Day £2,999.

The Grange provides the friendliness and close pastoral care of a small school together with the outstanding resources of a large school through its association with Monmouth School, a Haberdashers' school for boys aged 11 to 18. There are also strong links with the other schools in the area belonging to the family of Haberdashers' Monmouth Schools – Haberdashers' Agincourt School (for boys and girls aged 3 to 7), Inglefield House (for girls aged 7 to 11) and Haberdashers' Monmouth School for Girls (for girls aged 11 to 18). In their final year at The Grange boys take the General Entry Assessment for Monmouth School. Almost without exception there is a 100% pass rate and a significant number of boys gain scholarships and other awards – academic, music and sport. A wide and very popular extra-curricular programme combines with high academic achievement to provide a vibrant and stimulating educational experience. In 2011 independent research carried out by RSAcademics showed that the school was one of the very best they had surveyed in terms of how highly the parents regarded the school. Details are on the website.

Aims. The aims of The Grange are to provide an excellent education as the foundation for future achievement and to develop personal qualities of confidence, independence and social conscience.

Location. In February 2009 The Grange moved into brand new purpose-built premises on a Monmouth School site, situated next to Monmouth School Sports Complex with its own 25-metre swimming pool.

Facilities. Its new building has light, spacious, well-equipped classrooms, each of which opens out onto the play area, as well as a large hall, library, art studio, science laboratory, computer suite, music room and music studios. The Grange also has its own newly-equipped kitchens. The grounds provide a safe, spacious area for recreation, games and outdoor projects. In addition, The Grange shares the facilities of Monmouth School which include the School Chapel, large playing fields (25 acres), Sports Complex, new Sports Pavilion, Drama Studio and Performing Arts Centre – the Blake Theatre.

Staffing. 8 full-time and 9 part-time staff teach the 8 classes, in addition to peripatetic teachers and specialist coaches for extra-curricular activities.

Curriculum. The curriculum is broad and varied and takes account of, though is not constrained by, the National Curriculum. Subjects include English, Mathematics, Science, Information and Communication Technology, History, Geography, Religious Education, Art, Design Technology, Music, Physical Education, Games, Drama and French. Mandarin is added to the curriculum in Years 5 and 6. There is subject specialist teaching throughout. A part-time learning support teacher provides extra help on an individual or small group basis for boys who need it.

Extra-Curricular Activities. There is a full programme of activities which take place both in the lunch break and after school. These vary slightly according to the season though in any one year will include rugby, football, cricket, tennis, swimming, golf, cross-country running, string orchestra, wind band, choir, fencing, karate, art, gardening, modern foreign languages (including Mandarin), ICT and chess. There is a good record of boys playing at county and national level in rugby, cricket, fencing and chess.

Entry. Entry is usually at 7+ following assessment, though due to the larger new premises recruitment is currently across all year groups.

Charitable status. William Jones's Schools Foundation is a Registered Charity, number 525616. Its aims and objectives are to provide an all-round education for boys and girls at reasonable fees.

Grange Park Preparatory School

13 The Chine, Grange Park, London N21 2EA
Tel: 020 8360 1469
Fax: 020 8360 4869
e-mail: office@gpps.org.uk
website: www.gpps.org.uk

Day School for Girls.

Chair of Governors: Mr Nigel Barnes

Interim Head: **Mrs Bernadette McLaughlin**, BA Ed Hons

Age Range. 4–11.
Number of Girls. 95.
Fees per term (2010-2011). £2,780.
Grange Park Preparatory School is a long established, happy and successful school that provides a broad and stimulating education. It is situated in the pleasant residential area of Grange Park.

Hidden behind what was once a residential house lies a purpose built school with excellent facilities for the modern curriculum, including a fully-equipped ICT suite and facilities for science, art, design technology and pottery. There are two libraries, one for KS1 and the other for KS2. The younger children are taught PE and games within the school grounds. Years 5 and 6 make use of off-site facilities for netball and rounders/athletics. From Year 2 girls swim at a local pool.

Classes are small and the school has an excellent reputation for pastoral care and for nurturing the individual child.

We have a very broad curriculum and encourage excellence throughout, academically, in sport, art, dance and drama and in music.

In KS1 the children are taught mostly by form teachers with specialist teaching being introduced gradually in KS2. From Year 1 specialist teachers teach games, French, music and dance. Individual music tuition is available.

The girls are taught by experienced and well qualified staff.

The curriculum is enriched by a comprehensive programme of visits, which take advantage of the artistic and cultural opportunities of London, as well as local facilities for field studies. A ski trip takes place annually and Year 6 girls go on an outdoor pursuits weekend.

Girls are prepared for examinations for a wide range of secondary schools, both selective state schools and independent schools.

The school has a healthy eating policy. Lunches are cooked in school using only fresh ingredients. No processed food is used. There is always a vegetarian option and salads and fresh fruit are available daily.

The school is non-selective and places in Reception are offered after the Head has met with parents and daughters. Children taking up chance vacancies in other classes will be invited to spend a day in school to ensure they will fit into the class successfully.

Charitable status. Grange Park Preparatory School is a Registered Charity, number 268328.

The Granville School

2 Bradbourne Park Road, Sevenoaks, Kent TN13 3LJ
Tel: 01732 453039
Fax: 01732 743634

e-mail: secretary@granvilleschool.org
website: www.granvilleschool.org

Chairman of Governors: Mr R Campin

Headmistress: **Mrs Jane Scott**, BEd Hons Cantab

Age Range. Girls 3–11, Boys 3–5,
Number of Pupils. 200.
Fees per term (2011-2012). Nursery £1,490, Transition £2,562, Reception, Years 1 & 2 £3,020, Years 3 & 4 £3,415, Years 5 & 6 £3,845. Lunch included for Transition–Year 6.

Extras: Private Lessons: Pianoforte, Violin, Cello, Oboe, Clarinet, Flute £211 per term. Shared Lessons: Recorder £28.50, Ballet £56 per term.

The Granville School was founded on VE Day, 8th May 1945, with the Dove of Peace and Churchill's victory sign chosen to form the school crest.

The Granville is an exceptional school which combines the very best of a Prep school tradition with a vibrant, forward-looking outlook where change is embraced and innovation celebrated. Girls aged three to eleven, and boys aged three to four, thrive on individual attention and achieve their best in a happy, secure and stimulating environment. Our highly-qualified, specialist teachers make learning enjoyable, develop enquiring minds and raise levels of expectation.

The school maintains Christian principles and traditional values within a broad and stimulating curriculum. The Granville has a strong record of academic achievement and children are prepared for 11+ entry into independent schools and state grammar schools. Granville pupils excel in music, art, drama and sport. There is a wide range of extra-curricular activities available for all age groups and the school runs an early morning breakfast club.

The school is set in five acres of garden and woodland close to Sevenoaks Station. The original house and new buildings enable pupils to enjoy a high-quality learning environment with light and airy classrooms. The Granville has its own Indoor Heated Swimming Pool, a Sports Hall, Science Lab, Studio for Music and Drama, Art, DT and French rooms, a recently refurbished ICT Suite, individual teaching rooms and Junior and Senior Libraries. Outside facilities include three netball/tennis courts, sports/playing field and junior activity playgrounds.

Means-tested bursaries are available on request.

Charitable status. The Ena Makin Educational Trust Limited is a Registered Charity, number 307931. Its aim is to run any school as an educational charity for the promotion of education generally.

Great Ballard

Eartham, Chichester, West Sussex PO18 0LR
Tel: 01243 814236
Fax: 01243 814586
e-mail: admin@greatballard.co.uk
website: www.greatballard.co.uk

Headmaster: **D R Williams**, BA Hons, PGCE Cantab

Age Range. 2½–13 co-educational.
Number of Children. 195: 102 Boys, 93 Girls (including 77 in Pre-Prep and approx 35 Boarders).
Fees per term (2010-2011). Weekly Boarding £4,500, Day £3,300–£3,900, Pre-Prep £1,000–£2,275. The boarding fees for HM Forces are reduced by £150.

The school stands in 30 acres of wonderful countryside on the South Downs between Arundel and Chichester.

Children are prepared for the Common Entrance and Scholarship examinations to Independent Senior Schools, but the emphasis is on ensuring that all children achieve to their potential both in and out of the classroom. The average number of children in a teaching group in the main school is 14.

Outdoor activities include: Soccer, Rugby, Hockey, Cricket, Netball, Rounders, Tennis, Athletics, Swimming, Archery, Golf, Mountain Biking, Trampolining and Volleyball.

Facilities include: theatre, three main libraries, fully computerised science laboratories, main ICT suite and ICT facilities in all areas of the school, hall and dance/drama studio. There is an extensive range of clubs and activities organised both in and outside the school grounds.

There are also regular visits to a château in France for intensive language studies and Geography field work.

Children who show real potential in Art, Drama or Music are able to take advantage of excellence classes during the day.

Appreciation of Music is encouraged and a wide range of instruments is taught. There are three choirs and various ensemble groups, many of the children participate in local festivals and sit a range of musical exams. Importantly, all children perform and enjoy performing in regular concerts.

Drama is a timetabled subject and every child appears in a form play at some time during the year, some are on stage rather more frequently. LAMDA classes are also on offer.

Art is another strength of the school, many children build up portfolios of real quality to take to their next school and scholarships are won regularly. The constantly changing displays throughout the school are a testament to both the quality and the children's enthusiasm for Art.

While there is no compulsory Saturday school, there is a range of voluntary classes for the creative arts.

The Pre-Prep Department, for children aged 2½–7, is housed in a lovely walled garden area with plenty of space for play activities. The curriculum is delivered by well qualified, enthusiastic form teachers with extra input from Main School specialists in PE, Music and ICT.

There is an 'after hours' club for children from Nursery age upwards, enabling parents to work a full day.

Boarding remains popular and many children take advantage of the flexible arrangements. The boarding facilities have been redesigned and decorated, partly by senior children, with super results.

There is a rolling programme to continually update the impressive provision for ICT. There is an indoor heated pool and extensive fields. Plans for a new Sports Hall have again been turned down, but a new astro practice area has been provided.

Important though these facilities are, the happiness and safety of our children remain the top priority.

This is supported by the latest ISI Inspection report that states that "the quality of relationships between the pupils and staff is outstanding".

Number of Day Pupils. 138 boys, 64 girls.

Fees per term (2011-2012). Year 9 £3,193, Years 4–8: £3,777, Lunch £196; Reception to Year 3: £2,246–£3,095, Lunch £175.

Great Houghton Hall is a mainly Georgian house (Grade II) of architectural distinction. The school benefits from being easily accessible while providing delightful, secure, rural surroundings of 26 acres in a conservation area.

Great Houghton is a well-established school with many strengths, combining a very broad, inclusive approach with specialist expertise. The emphasis of the school is on the encouragement of the whole child: via assemblies that are Christian in ethos, in the classroom, on the games field, in relationships and through responsibilities. Children develop confidence and courtesy, self-discipline and self-knowledge in a happy, purposeful environment. Our most recent ISI inspection report observed that our pupils 'are notably well behaved, polite and hard working'.

Boys and girls join our 'outstanding' (Ofsted Report) Early Years department from age 3 months and from 2011 can continue up to GCSE. We also offer transfer to day or boarding, co-ed or single-sex Senior Schools at 13+ via Common Entrance or Scholarship. These include: the Bedford Schools, Bloxham, Kimbolton, Malvern St James, Northampton High School for Girls, Northamptonshire Grammar School, Oakham, Oundle, Rugby, Stowe, Uppingham and Wellingborough. Form teachers and subject specialists maintain high academic standards in line with and beyond the National Curriculum, supported where appropriate by an expert Special Educational Needs Department.

The buildings provide large, light classrooms, as well as a Science Laboratory, Theatre/Gymnasium, Library and dedicated facilities for ICT, Art, Pottery, DT and Music. The school places strong emphasis on performing and visual arts.

In addition to basketball, badminton, gymnastics and table tennis in the gym, the grounds offer an all-weather surface, tennis courts and excellent pitches for: rugby, netball, hockey, lacrosse, football, cricket, athletics and rounders. The range of extra activities includes: art, ballet, dance, band, chess, choir, choristers, cookery, drama, individual music tuition, instrumental groups, Girls' club, team training, golf, kayaking and skiing.

Nutritious lunches are cooked in the school kitchen, while breakfast and tea are available to fit in with parents' busy lives: we are open from 08.00 to 18.00. A lively programme of social events complements regular charity fundraising, directed amongst other worthy causes towards Outspan School, Kampala, Uganda, where we sponsor two pupils' education.

The school has a contemporary outlook and a traditional ethos.

Great Houghton School

Great Houghton Hall, Northampton NN4 7AG

Tel:	01604 761907
Fax:	01604 761251
e-mail:	office@ghschool.net
website:	www.ghschool.net

Founded in 1955.

Chairman of Governors: W Hughes

Joint Heads:
Mrs J E Lancaster-Adlam, BEd Hons, MEd Cantab, NPQH
Mr C Gibbs, BA, HDipEd

Age Range. 3 months –16 years.

Great Walstead School

Lindfield, Haywards Heath, West Sussex RH16 2QL

Tel:	01444 483528
Fax:	01444 482122
e-mail:	admin@greatwalstead.co.uk
website:	www.greatwalstead.co.uk

Chairman of the Board of Governors: J Lee

Headmaster: C Baty, BEd, DipT, CPP Boarding Hons, NPQH

Deputy Head (Academic): S Smith MSc, BSc Hons, CertEd
Deputy Head (Pastoral): J Sutherland, BEd

Age Range. 2½–13.

Number of Pupils. Boys: 21 Weekly Boarders, 129 Day Boys. Girls: 7 Weekly Boarders, 64 Day Girls. Pre-preparatory Dept: 76 boys, 53 girls, Nursery: 58 boys, 55 girls.

Fees per term (from January 2011). Day £2,160–£4,210. Weekly Boarding (in addition to Tuition): £320–£885 (1–4 nights).

In 1927, Mr R J Mowll, who founded his school in 1925, moved his pupils from Enfield to Great Walstead. He came to a Victorian country house set in over 260 acres of fields and woodland where children could both enjoy and learn from the unspoilt countryside around them.

From those beginnings, Great Walstead has developed into a thriving co-educational prep school, catering for children from 2½ to 13. It is a school which above all values children as people and regards it as vital that they develop their potential: in the academic sphere, in sport, in all things creative, socially and spiritually. The school stands for secure Christian values which provide an essential foundation for the whole of education and life. The school is built on strong values of Christian Faith, Success, Communication, Environment and Dedication.

The Nursery welcomes children from the ages of 2½ until it is time to enter the Pre-Prep at age 4. It provides a full, rich and varied nursery education and lays firm foundations in basic skills and understanding for future learning. The Nursery is open both mornings and afternoons to provide maximum flexibility of hours for children and parents.

The Pre-Prep covers the years from 4 to 7 within its own section of the school. It has its own library, ICT suite and playground. The aim here is to ensure that the foundation skills of reading, writing and maths which the National Curriculum endorses are taught and learnt while at the same time adding the breadth of interest which the staff are able to provide. For example children learn French, Computer skills, and have specialist PE and Music tuition.

Children enter the Junior School at 7, either from the Pre-prep or from other schools. For the next two years they will have a class teacher who supervises them closely for a good proportion of the day, but have specialist teachers for French, music, computers, art, craft, design technology and PE. They have games or outdoor activities each day and gradually learn to become more independent.

Children in the senior age group are taught by graduate specialist teachers for the most part and are prepared primarily for the Common Entrance examination and senior school scholarships at 13, but also for other examinations. In the past ten years over 100 scholarships to senior schools have been won and in the last three years over 50% of pupils gained scholarships to Senior schools. The Woodland Wing provides classrooms and subject rooms for the senior children. There are also two computer rooms (with 21 linked PCs), an extremely well-equipped Science laboratory, and a fine library.

269 acres of farmland, playing fields and woodland make many outdoor activities possible. The children build camps in the Summer term and the log cabin gives boarders an enjoyable chance to camp out! Woods activities such as Eco schools, Forest schools, Mudlarks, Woodlanders and Q-day are world famous at Great Walstead. The purpose-built Challenge Course gives enormous pleasure all the year round! In addition there are opportunities to go on expeditions.

The Art, Craft and Design Technology department is housed in old farm buildings which have been adapted to make fine modern workshops and studios. All children encounter all parts of the programme each year and in addition can gain further experience in their spare time.

The school's spacious grounds provide opportunities for a wide range of sports. All the year round swimming is encouraged using our own outdoor heated pool and local indoor pools. The superbly equipped sports hall and extensive outdoor facilities make it possible for a large number of different team games to be played as well as other more individual sports.

The school has a Learning Support department where staff with dyslexia training are able to give the extra support required by children who are referred to them and to provide training and techniques of learning that all need. It also helps children who need help in specific areas occasionally, but also the gifted and talented as well.

Music has long been a strength at Great Walstead. A high proportion of the children learn instruments in the Music School. They play in groups, bands and orchestras. Singing is encouraged. Music and drama often come together for performances. All children have opportunities to act. As well as major productions, there are shorter form plays with large casts.

The girls' and boys' boarding areas (which cater for weekly boarding only) provide a comfortable home under the care of a married couple assisted by other boarding staff. Matron (School nurse) sees to the health of all children in the school. The school provides 'The Keep' which allows flexible holiday, pre- and after-school care as well as other holiday activities to meet the needs of today's parents.

Parents are always made most welcome at the school. There is a thriving parents' organisation called FOGWA (Friends of Great Walstead Association) which provides a number of most successful social events and raises substantial sums for the benefit of the school.

Academic and Music Scholarships are offered at 7+, 8+, 9+, 10+ and 11+, and Sports Scholarships at 8+, 9+, 10+ and 11+.

Charitable status. Great Walstead School is a Registered Charity, number 307002. It exists to provide a good education on Christian foundations.

Greenfield

Brooklyn Road, Woking, Surrey GU22 7TP
Tel: 01483 772525
Fax: 01483 728907
e-mail: schooloffice@greenfield.surrey.sch.uk
website: www.greenfield.surrey.sch.uk

Chairman of Governors: Dr Geoffrey Smith

Headteacher: **Mrs Tania Botting**, BEd

Age Range. 3–11 years.
Number of Pupils. 61 day girls, 96 day boys.
Fees per term (2011-2012). £1,530–£3,562.

Greenfield is a non-selective co-educational school for children aged from 3 to 11 years. We aim to offer every possible opportunity for children to reach their full potential and recognise that all children have talents and strengths in many different areas. We are proud of our academic and non-academic successes and have a strong track record of achieving scholarships to a wide range of senior schools for music, art, sport, and academic excellence.

At Greenfield we believe that a happy child will learn. Therefore, we provide a secure and caring environment working closely with our parents, to enable the children to develop their confidence and self-esteem and prepare them for the next stage of their education and future.

We attach importance to traditional values, promoting courtesy, respect, tolerance, empathy, humility and consideration for others.

Greenfield has high standards but we also appreciate the need to strike a happy balance between work and play and the formal and informal. There is an excellent ratio of adults to children throughout the school enabling children to receive individual attention and children are often taught in small groups. Visitors are welcome to visit the school at any time and appointments can be made by calling the school office. To request a copy of the prospectus, please visit the school website or call the school office.

Charitable status. Greenfield is a Registered Charity, number 295145. It aims to offer an excellent all-round education to children of all abilities.

Gresham's Prep School

Holt, Norfolk NR25 6EY
Tel: 01263 714600
          01263 714575 Pre-Prep School
Fax: 01263 714060
e-mail: prep@greshams.com
website: www.greshams.com

Chairman of Governors: A Martin Smith

Headmaster: **J H W Quick**, BA Hons Durham, PGCE

Age Range. 3–13.
Number of Pupils. 374: Boarders 47, Day pupils 327.
Fees per term (2011-2012). Boarders £6,625, Day £5,050. Pre-Prep School: £2,525–£2,800.

Gresham's Prep School is part of the family of Gresham's Schools, which are located in the busy market town of Holt in a beautiful and tranquil part of North Norfolk. Some pupils enter the school from the Pre-Prep School, which is based on a separate site a quarter of a mile from the Prep School, but many others enter the school from elsewhere. Most pupils move on to Gresham's Senior School, but the school has a very good record of winning scholarships and gaining excellent Common Entrance results to other major Independent Schools.

The school has excellent facilities including extensive playing fields, an Art and Technology Centre, a Drama Hall and a modern and well-equipped Music School. Use of the Theatre, Chapel, two Astroturf pitches, swimming pool, sports hall and other excellent sports facilities is shared with the Senior School.

Boarders are accommodated in modern, comfortable bedrooms in Crossways House (girls) or Kenwyn House (boys). Flexible boarding is available and is extremely popular.

The school prides itself on the breadth of its curriculum. Sport, Drama and Music play an important part in the lives of all pupils. The school has built up a considerable reputation in these areas in recent years. There is a wide arrange of extra-curricular activities available in the evenings.

Above all the school wants children to enjoy the process of growing up and developing their talents to the full and to establish the strong roots that will help them become self assured and well balanced adults.

Entry Requirements. Entry is by assessment in Mathematics and English and the recommendation of the child's previous school. Entry is possible into all year groups. Scholarships and Bursaries are available for entry into Year 7.

Pre-Prep School. Co-educational, age 3–7, Day pupils only.

Headmistress: Mrs J Davidson

The Pre-Prep School is housed in the beautiful setting of Old School House. It is a vibrant and dynamic school that puts great emphasis on the development of the whole child as well giving children an excellent academic grounding.

Charitable status. Gresham's School is a Registered Charity, number 1105500. It exists for the purpose of educating children.

Grimsdell
Mill Hill Pre-Preparatory School

Winterstoke House, Wills Grove, Mill Hill, London NW7 1QR
Tel: 020 8959 6884
Fax: 020 8959 4626
e-mail: office@grimsdell.org.uk
website: www.grimsdell.org.uk

Co-educational Pre-Preparatory Day School.

Chairman of Court of Governors: Prof M R E Proctor, ScD, FRS

Head: **Mrs P E R Bennett-Mills**, CertEd

Age Range. 3–7.
Number of Pupils. 184: 111 Boys, 73 Girls.
Fees per term (2011-2012). £3,897 (full day), Nursery: £2,114 (mornings only), £1,793 (afternoons only).

Grimsdell is situated in the Green Belt on the borders of Hertfordshire and Middlesex but only ten miles from central London. It stands adjacent to Mill Hill School's 120 acres of land, enjoying the advantages of a rural environment. Grimsdell is part of the Mill Hill School Foundation. It provides a happy, secure and rich learning environment for boys and girls aged 3 to 7. Belmont, the Mill Hill Preparatory School, is less than a quarter of a mile away and educates pupils from 7 to 13, the majority of whom move on to the senior school, Mill Hill.

The boys and girls at Grimsdell learn through hands-on experience. With the support and guidance of professional, caring staff and excellent resources and equipment, each child is encouraged to reach their full potential. Our approach combines traditional skills of reading, writing and mathematics with the breadth and balance offered by an enhanced National Curriculum. Every pupil can enjoy many opportunities offered by learning through Science, Technology and Computing. They also gain much from Art, Drama, Music, PE and French lessons.

The school is housed in a large Victorian building with its own secure play areas and adventure playgrounds, taking advantage of further facilities on the Mill Hill site including sports fields, swimming pool and theatre.

The usual age of entry is at 3 and 4 years, but 5 and 6 year olds are considered as vacancies occur. It is expected that most children will pass to Belmont at the end of Year 2.

Charitable status. The Mill School Foundation is a Registered Charity, number 1064758. It exists to provide education for boys and girls.

Grosvenor School

Edwalton Grange, 218 Melton Road, Edwalton, Nottingham NG12 4BS
Tel: 0115 923 1184
Fax: 0115 923 5184
e-mail: office@grosvenorschool.co.uk
website: www.grosvenorschool.co.uk

Headmaster: **C G J Oldershaw**, BEd

Age Range. 6 weeks – 13 years.
Number of Pupils. 160 boys and girls.
Fees per term (2011-2012). £2,835–£3,145. Nursery: £195 (full week), £44 (full day, 7.30 am – 6 pm), £30 per session (morning or afternoon), £10 per early start (7 am), £10 per late pick-up (6.30 pm).

Founded in 1876, Grosvenor School is Nottingham's oldest and leading co-educational day Prep School based on a greenfield site in Edwalton, South Nottingham. It is easily accessible from Trent Bridge and the Nottingham Ring Road as well as surrounding villages and the Vale of Belvoir.

The School's history and foundation have ensured a supportive family atmosphere combined with high expectations. In order to prepare the modern child for life and education after Grosvenor, a broad curriculum is taught which goes beyond the academic. An example of this is the 'Grosvenor Challenge' leadership and skills programme, which builds confidence, resourcefulness and self-reliance.

Pupils are prepared for entry to all Independent Senior Schools and there is an excellent scholarship record in academia, sport, music and art.

Appropriate class sizes allow the Staff to get to know pupils well, build trusting relationships and identify individual strengths and needs.

To ensure the most effective learning, specialist teaching in Science, ICT, Music, French and PE is provided from Reception, with specifically equipped classrooms for the relevant subjects. Additionally, pupils from Year 2 receive specialist teaching in Art, Pottery, Design and Technology. In Year 5 and above, all lessons are taught by subject specialists to prepare the children effectively for their Senior Schools.

The main sports taught are Football, Swimming, Netball, Hockey, Cross Country, Cricket, Rounders and Athletics. Rugby, Golf and other sports are also offered or supported. There are weekly fixtures against both independent and maintained schools.

Music has long been a strength at Grosvenor, with the overriding majority of pupils studying at least one instrument in addition to their timetabled class music lessons. There are thriving junior and senior choirs, an orchestra and a samba band.

Every pupil takes part in a drama production every year.

Reading for pleasure is strongly encouraged. The Junior and Senior Libraries support this whilst providing a comprehensive set of reference books to aid study. The Reading Club is one of the many well supported after school clubs. Pupils take full advantage of this and the other extra-curricular activities on offer, of which there is a wide and varied range.

To assist parents, we provide before and after school care including a thriving breakfast club.

The Grange Nursery is on the School site and welcomes children from 6 weeks to 5 years. It provides a full and varied nursery education and lays the firm foundations in basic skills and understanding for future learning.

Overall Grosvenor offers a truly comprehensive education supported by the multitude of school clubs and regular expeditions and educational visits. In doing so, we aim to provide a value-added, bespoke education which will not only equip the children with an educated, enquiring mind but also with the experience and skills to become happy and well-rounded individuals.

"A traditional school for today's child."

Guildford High School Junior School
UCST

London Road, Guildford, Surrey GU1 1SJ
Tel: 01483 561440
Fax: 01483 306516
e-mail: guildford-admissions@church-schools.com
website: www.guildfordhigh.surrey.sch.uk

Chairman of Local Governing Body: Mrs L M Keat

Headmistress: **Mrs S J Phillips**, BA Hons Reading

Age Range. Girls 4–11.
Number of Pupils. 285.
Fees per term (2011-2012). Reception £2,681, Years 1 and 2 £2,632, Years 3–6 £3,587.

The Junior School at Guildford High School is situated on the same site as the Senior School. It is a modern, bright, self-contained school with the third floor especially designed for art, music, science, IT and the Library.

The girls normally start in the Reception classes (4 years) or at Year 3 (7 years), however, they are welcome in any year group depending on spaces available, and work their way through the Junior School with natural progression on to the Senior School at Year 7 (11 years).

The breadth and depth of the curriculum encompasses 15 fast paced subjects, with an embedded thinking skills programme. Three modern foreign languages are included, with Spanish starting in Year 1 for the five year olds. Music, drama and sport play an important part in the curricular and co-curricular programmes. Specialist teachers and resources are employed throughout the Junior School. Parents and teachers work closely together to ensure excellent differentiation and a nurturing environment with strong pastoral care.

Guildford High Junior School girls of all abilities and temperaments are confident, happy and well-prepared for entry to the Senior School. (*See Guildford High School entry in HMC section.*)

Charitable status. The United Church Schools Trust (to which Guildford High School belongs) is a Registered Charity, number 1016538.

The Haberdashers' Aske's Boys' Preparatory & Pre-Preparatory School

Butterfly Lane, Elstree, Herts WD6 3AF
Tel: 020 8266 1779
Fax: 020 8266 1808
e-mail: prepoffice@habsboys.org.uk
website: www.habsboys.org.uk

Chairman of Governors: Mr M Powell, BA

Head: **Miss Y M Mercer**, BEd, Adv Dip Ed

Deputy Head: Mr M G Brown, BSc

Age Range. Prep 7–11; Pre-Prep 5–7.
Number of Boys. Prep 210, Pre-Prep 70.
Fees per term (2011-2012). Pre-Prep £3,688; Prep £4,889.

The Preparatory School is housed in a delightful purpose-built building, on the same campus as the Main School. The boys are able to share the facilities and grounds of the Main School, the Sports Centre, the heated indoor Swimming Pool, the Music School and the Dining Room. The Pre-Prep School is located 6 miles north of the school at How Wood, near St Albans.

A broad and balanced curriculum is delivered. In addition, the Preparatory School offers a wealth of extra-curricular and holiday activities in which all boys are encouraged to participate.

Boys are admitted each September after assessments to the Pre-Prep at the age of 5+ and to the Prep at 7+. Boys are expected to move into the Main School at 11.

For further details, please see entry in HMC section.

Charitable status. The Haberdashers' Aske's Charity is a Registered Charity, number 313996. It exists to promote education.

The Hall

23 Crossfield Road, Hampstead, London NW3 4NU
Tel: 020 7722 1700
Fax: 020 7483 0181
e-mail: office@hallschool.co.uk
website: www.hallschool.co.uk

Chairman of Governors: C Lampard, Esq

Headmaster: **P J Lough**, MA Oxon, PGCE Dunelm

Age Range. 4–13.
Number of Pupils. 450 Day Boys.
Fees per term (2010-2011). £3,700–£4,252 (inclusive).
Founded in 1889, the school is on three sites within close proximity. The majority of boys join Reception or Year 1 at the age of 4 or 5, but a few places are occasionally available in later years. The average class size is 18.

In 2004 the Reception department was extensively refurbished and now provides excellent facilities.

The Junior School (Years 1–3) was extended recently and provides up-to-date computing, science and music facilities. The Senior School underwent a major programme of refurbishment in 2000/01 to give a new library, improved music, DT, pottery and computing facilities, and new changing rooms. Boys in the Junior School use the sports hall, located in the Senior School, and have lunch in the dining hall which serves the whole school.

From the Junior School, boys transfer to the Middle School for Years 4 and 5. During that time they make the transition from classroom based teaching to subject based teaching. Boys are taught by subject specialists from Year 5.

The Hall prides itself on the breadth of education it offers. Senior School boys study Life Skills, Art, Drama, Music, Pottery, ICT, Design Technology and Current Affairs within the timetable and there is a broad range of after-school activities. Music and Drama are considerable strengths within the school.

Team games, soccer, rugby and cricket are played mainly at the Wilf Slack Memorial Ground, and in recent years fencing has developed as a major sporting strength. Hockey, squash, athletics, golf and other sports are also offered.

The school is not linked with any particular senior school. Over half the boys proceed to London day schools, such as Westminster, St Paul's, Highgate, City of London and UCS, and others proceed to leading boarding schools such as Eton, Harrow, Winchester and King's Canterbury. In recent years numerous academic scholarships have been won at these and other schools. Other awards have been won in areas such as music and sport.

Means-tested bursaries are available at 11+, and a number of boys apply at this entry point from London primary schools.

The school was last inspected in October 2004 and the report may be found at www.isi.net.

Charitable status. The Hall School Charitable Trust is a Registered Charity, number 312722. It exists entirely for the purposes of education.

Hall Grove

London Road, Bagshot, Surrey GU19 5HZ
Tel: 01276 473059
Fax: 01276 452003

e-mail: office@hallgrove.surrey.sch.uk
website: www.hallgrove.co.uk

Headmaster: **A R Graham**, BSc, PGCE

Deputy Headmaster: I Adams

Age Range. 4–13.
Number of Children. Pre-Preparatory (age 4–7) 103. Preparatory (age 7–13) 231.
Fees per term (2010-2011). Pre-Preparatory £2,695; Preparatory: £3,400 (Years 3–5), £3,765 (Years 6–8). Fees inclusive of meals and all essential extras including field trips.

Hall Grove is a thriving co-educational school for 4–13 year olds. Weekly/Flexi boarding is offered for up to 12 pupils. The main entry ages are 4, 7 and 11. There is a separate nursery in the grounds for children from the age of 2.

The school was founded in 1957 by the parents of the current Headmaster. At its centre is a most attractive Georgian house set in beautiful gardens and parkland. Recent additions have provided some modern rooms and specialist teaching areas, an impressive computer facility and new classroom blocks. Despite this building programme, the character and atmosphere of a family home has been retained.

The academic standards are high and there is a very strong emphasis on Sport and Music. A wide range of activities flourish; woodwork, ceramics, food technology, drama and a host of major and minor sports including soccer, rugby, hockey, netball, rounders, cricket, tennis, athletics, swimming, golf, judo, basketball, badminton and dance. Riding and stable management is an added attraction.

The school day continues until 5.40 pm for Years 7 and 8 and older children may stay overnight on a regular basis. There is also provision for after-school care and a full programme of evening activities.

Hall Grove has its own residential field study centre situated on the South Devon coast called Battisborough House and there are many field trips and expeditions both in Devon and overseas. Battisborough is available for hire by other schools and can accommodate up to 30 in comfort.

Hallfield School

Church Road, Edgbaston, Birmingham B15 3SJ
Tel: 0121 454 1496
Fax: 0121 454 9182
e-mail: office@hallfield.bham.sch.uk
website: www.hallfieldschool.co.uk

Founded 1879.

Governing Body: The Hallfield School Trust

Chairman of Governors: K Uff, MA, BCL of Gray's Inn, Barrister

Headmaster: **J A Shackleton**, BEd, MA

Deputy Head: J P Thackway, BA Hons, PGCE

Age Range. 3 months to 11 years.
Number of Pupils. 513 Day Boys and Girls: Upper School (7–11 years) 204; Pre-Preparatory Department (2–7 years) 264; Hallfield *first* (3 months to 2 years) 45.
Fees per term (2010-2011). Hallfield *first* on application; Pre-Prep £2,350–£2,770; Upper School £3,294. Lunches are included in the fees.

The school is divided into three sections: Hallfield *first* for children aged 3 months to 2, the Pre-Preparatory Department for children aged 2 to 7 years and the Upper School for children aged 7 to 11 years.

The majority of pupils enter the School through Hallfield *first*. Direct entry into the Pre-Prep and Upper School is by means of an entrance test and interview. There is no automatic entry from Nursery to Pre-Prep and from Pre-Prep to Upper School. Children are appropriately assessed prior to the proposed move into either Pre-Prep or Upper School and are expected to perform at a level that will enable them to adjust to the new demands and expectations without difficulty.

The ethos of the School is outlined by our main school: "To act with courtesy and common sense at all times and to strive for excellence in all we do." High standards of work, dress, behaviour and courtesy are expected at all times.

Hallfield has achieved outstanding success in preparing pupils for entry to a variety of local day schools at the age of 11; a few pupils move on to boarding schools. Last year 77% of Year 6 pupils achieved a grammar school place. The wide curriculum satisfies and goes well beyond the demands of the National Curriculum.

The major sports are association football, rugby and cricket for boys; rounders, netball and tennis for girls. Other sports include athletics, swimming, gymnastics and basketball. The playing fields, which form part of the School grounds, provide sufficient space to accommodate all the major seasonal sporting activities. Music is given a high profile and many pupils learn musical instruments.

The School occupies a fine 20-acre site in a very pleasant area of the City. Classrooms are bright and well equipped and class sizes never exceed 20. Over the past twelve years an extensive development programme has added a range of new facilities to the original late Georgian buildings, including a purpose-built Nursery, six additional Pre-Prep classrooms, two impressive laboratories, Sports Hall, Music School, ICT suite, Art & Design room, sports pavilion and an all-weather pitch, as well as larger and refurbished classrooms for Upper School.

A wide range of extra-curricular activities is available. At the moment these include: art, athletics, ballet, badminton, basketball, brass ensemble, classics chess, chamber choir, cricket, cross-country, dance, debating, flute, choir, football, fun with maths, girls' games, Lego, string orchestra, school orchestra, science, speech and scrabble. During the Summer and Easter breaks there are also successful holiday clubs.

There is an active Parents' Association which organises a number of social events each year, as well as raising funds for equipment to enhance the education of children in the School. Pupils are encouraged to maintain their links with the School by joining the Old Hallfieldian Society.

Charitable status. Hallfield School Trust is a Registered Charity, number 528956. It exists for the purpose of providing education for children.

Halstead Preparatory School for Girls

Woodham Rise, Woking, Surrey GU21 4EE
Tel: 01483 772682
Fax: 01483 757611
e-mail: registrar@halstead-school.org.uk
website: www.halstead-school.org.uk

Chairman of Governors: Mr J Olsen

Headmistress: Mrs S G Fellows, BA Hons

Age Range. Nursery–11.
Number of Pupils. 215 Girls.
Fees per term (2010-2011). Nursery (flexible) from £756; Kindergarten to Year 2 £2,965; Years 3–6 £3,472.

At Halstead we believe passionately in the advantages of single-sex education for girls. We know that girls and boys develop at different rates and at Halstead we can gear all our teaching strategies to suit your daughter so that she makes the best possible progress.

Established in 1927 Halstead is situated in a leafy part of residential Woking. The main school building is a large Edwardian house to which modern facilities have been added including a purpose-built Pre-Preparatory Department, a new gym/performing hall and music room.

A happy, friendly atmosphere pervades giving the feel of a home with desks in.

Girls may join our Nursery in the term they are three years old. Parents may choose from a minimum of three sessions to five full days. From Reception pupils are full time. From age seven girls have the opportunity to stay after school to complete their homework three days a week.

Specialist teaching, motivated and happy pupils and high staff to pupil ratios ensure that all pupils make excellent progress. We offer a broad curriculum which includes two modern foreign languages, drama and dance as separate subjects. All pupils enjoy two music lessons a week and in Year 3 all pupils are given small group tuition for half a term in each of the following instruments: flute, clarinet, violin, cello, cornet and trombone. From the earliest age we want girls to enjoy sport so that good lifetime habits for physical recreation are established. We believe in 'sport for all' and all girls in Years 4–6 are given opportunities to represent the school in competitive matches.

Our school motto 'believe in yourself' underpins our aim to ensure girls are confident and know that through application and effort they can achieve. We have an outstanding record of getting girls into their first-choice senior school and as you can see from our honours board a large percentage of pupils gain scholarships.

We are an eco school and participation in the school council gives the pupils a real voice in school decision-making.

Outside the school day there are many optional extras such as Cricket, a Brownie pack, Yoga, Photography, Art and Craft workshops and many more. Breakfast Club and After School Care are available for a modest additional charge for all pupils from Nursery upwards.

Finally above all else we do all we can to ensure the girls really enjoy their time at Halstead.

Charitable status. Halstead (Educational Trust) Limited is a Registered Charity, number 270525. It exists to provide a high quality all-round education for girls aged 2+–11.

Hampshire Collegiate Junior School

UCST

Embley Park, Romsey, Hampshire SO51 6ZA
Tel: 01794 515737
e-mail: info@hampshirecs.org.uk
website: www.hampshirecs.org.uk

Chairman of the Local Council: Mr David d'Arcy Hughes

Principal: Hector MacDonald, BSc, MA, CChem, CSci, FRMS, FRSC

Vice-Principal & Head of Junior School: **Mrs T M Rogers**, MA Ed, CertEd

Age Range. 2½–11 Co-educational.
Number of Pupils. 220 Day Pupils: 112 Boys, 108 Girls.
Fees per term (2011-2012). Nursery: £1,023–£1,705 (mornings only), £2,382 (full time). Payment by Termly Direct Debit: Junior School £2,749–£3,070.

The school operates an extended day from 8.00 am to 6.00 pm offering comprehensive care to support busy, modern family living.

The school has its own Nursery (The Nightingale Nursery) taking children from 2½ years and is very flexible in session bookings to suit parents' working patterns and family life. The Nursery operates for 48 weeks of the year and there is also holiday cover for Reception Class, which can extend to Year and Year 2 pupils if there is sufficient interest.

Reception to Year 2 pupils enjoy small class sizes with an emphasis on careful monitoring of progress in the core subjects and early intervention in the event of any identified learning needs. A broad curriculum is offered, including French, Music, IT, DT and PE taught by specialists.

Within Years 3 to 6 the focus is on careful monitoring of progress and the development of potential in each child alongside preparation senior schooling and associated scholarships. The school seeks to provide, through small class sizes, teaching expertise and support staff, a broad education tailored to the individual needs of the children in the school. There is both a clear and effective learning support structure and policy to help children experiencing difficulties, as well as challenge those who are our most able children. The school has three clear aims:

- At HCS we focus on the individual
- We believe that every child has special qualities – it is our responsibility to define and refine these
- We support a broad vision of excellence for our children and our teachers

Throughout the school the children take part in Learning Outside the Classroom (LOC). This is part of the curriculum and introduces the children to learning experiences that engage them in finding out more about their environment, making use of the school orchards, allotments, an outdoor classroom and an amphitheatre, all within our 130 parkland grounds.

There is a strong tradition of musical achievement in the school with choir, an orchestra, and a rock band. Children compete in a wide range of sports within curriculum time and as part of the busy House and fixture programme. Drama is promoted via its inclusion within the weekly timetable for all children, annual LAMDA preparation and regular productions. Our annual art exhibition showcases artistic talent in the school and regular linked work with local artists encourages enthusiasm for the visual arts. Each year our 10 and 11 year olds undertake residential visits. Year 5 experience geographical studies and outdoor pursuits on the Isle of Wight, whilst Year 6 travel to a Normandy Château to experience a week's immersion in a wide variety of activities, all enjoyed in French.

The school seeks to achieve a high standard of academic achievement and to encourage attitudes of tolerance, adaptability, invention, persistence, responsibility, confidence, compassion, flexibility and creativity coupled with a lifelong love of learning and endeavour. Our last ISI inspection highlighted the personal development of pupils as 'outstanding'.

Charitable status. The United Church Schools Trust is a Registered Charity, number 1016538.

Handcross Park School

Handcross, Haywards Heath, West Sussex RH17 6HF
Tel: 01444 400526
Fax: 01444 400527
e-mail: info@handxpark.com
website: www.handcrossparkschool.co.uk

Where potential is nurtured and success is celebrated in a friendly learning environment.

Chairman of Governors: Mrs T J B Hutchings
Headmaster: G R Owton, BA QTS
Head of Nursery & Pre-Prep: Mrs T J Cuffley, MA, PGCE
Deputy Head: N K Cheesman, BSc, PGCE

Age Range. 2–13 Co-educational.
Number of Pupils. 268: Boys 148, Girls 120.
Fees per term (2010-2011). Nursery according to number of sessions, Pre-Preparatory: £2,800, Preparatory: £4,156 (Years 3–4), £4,769 (Years 5–8). Weekly Boarding: £5,588.

Handcross Park is a non-selective pre-preparatory and preparatory school, set in beautiful surroundings but conveniently located just off the A23 and close to Haywards Heath, Horsham, Gatwick and Crawley. The School provides a first-class education for children from 2 to 13 in a happy family atmosphere within a caring Christian framework.

The School unashamedly takes pride in the pursuit of excellence for all its pupils. Alongside academic endeavours staff believe ardently in educating children to become well-rounded, compassionate and articulate citizens.

The modern Nursery, situated in the Secret Garden and accommodated in well-designed and purpose-built classrooms, offers a wonderful environment in which to begin the exciting adventure of a child's school career. Activities are specially designed to help young minds investigate and find solutions for themselves and the cleverly planned classrooms allow children the opportunity to pursue interests both inside and outdoors. With an excellent staff to pupil ratio throughout the Early Years and small class sizes right the way through the school, the emphasis is on helping the individual to flourish as part of a supportive, vibrant and happy community.

Handcross Park has a proven academic record with many Year 8 pupils gaining scholarships to Senior Schools both locally and further afield and a 100% pass rate at Common Entrance. But as well as a deep and broad knowledge of the curriculum, pupils also develop an understanding of the role they can play in society as informed and caring citizens.

Alongside the provision of a high quality academic education for all children, the School's well-qualified, friendly staff focus on nourishing the creative, musical and sporting aptitudes of the pupils. With a vibrant Music Department, inspiring Art Studio, excellent sports coaching and facilities and well-equipped Science, IT and Design Technology Rooms, pupils are offered the best opportunities to foster and showcase their talents.

The 'home away from home' accommodation at Handcross Park has been refurbished, revamped and rejuvenated and early in 2008 received an excellent report following an Ofsted inspection. With a variety of activities to choose from the focus is on having fun in a structured environment. Both flexi and weekly boarding are available and are very useful elements in the package of flexible pre and after school care offered to parents.

From the Nursery through to Year 8 the School 'offers exceptionally supportive pastoral care for its pupils' and this, coupled with a focus on achieving high academic standards, 'results in confident and happy pupils who leave the school very well-prepared for the next stage in their education' (ISI Inspection Report 2007).

Charitable status. Newells School Trust is a Registered Charity, number 307038. Handcross Park School exists to provide a high-quality education to children aged 2 to 13.

Hanford School

Childe Okeford, Blandford, Dorset DT11 8HN
Tel: 01258 860219
Fax: 01258 861255

e-mail: office@hanford.dorset.sch.uk
website: www.hanford.dorset.sch.uk

Chairman of Governors: The Hon Mark Bridges, GCMG

Headmaster: **N S Mackay**, CertEd Zimbabwe

Age Range. 7–13.
Number of Girls. 100.
Fees per term (2011-2012). Boarders £6,400, Day Girls £5,300.

Hanford School, which was founded in 1947 by the Revd and Mrs C B Canning, is an early 17th Century manor house standing in about 45 acres and situated in the Stour valley, half way between Blandford and Shaftesbury. The amenities include a Chapel, Laboratories, a Computer Room, a Music School, an Art School, a Gymnasium, a Swimming Pool, a Handwork Room, two Netball/Tennis Courts (hard) and a covered Riding School. Pupils are prepared for entry to all Independent Senior Schools.

Charitable status. The Hanford School Charitable Trust Ltd is a Registered Charity, number 1001751.

Haslemere Preparatory School

Hill Road, Haslemere, Surrey GU27 2JP
Tel: 01428 642350
Fax: 01428 645314
e-mail: office@haslemereprep.co.uk
website: www.haslemereprep.co.uk

Chairman of Governors: Mr A Gardner

Headmaster: **P Wenham**, MA Cantab, PGCE

Age Range. Boys 2–13, Girls 2–4.
Number of Pupils. 154.
Fees per term (2011-2012). £2,515–£3,595. The school offers sibling discounts and Scholarships in academic subjects, sport and the arts.

Haslemere Preparatory School is committed to giving each individual boy the best possible start to his education.

The school is a boys' independent day school for 4 to 13 year olds, with a Nursery Department catering for boys and girls aged 2 to 4. The school is set in a stunning location, within walking distance of Haslemere town centre.

Academically it has an excellent reputation for producing well rounded, well mannered, confident young men. The majority of boys move on to senior schools such as the Royal Grammar School, King Edward's School, Churcher's College, Lord Wandsworth College, Portsmouth Grammar School, Charterhouse and Cranleigh. The school seeks to encourage all boys to find the best within themselves by creating a safe and stimulating environment in which they can learn. A highly dedicated and professional staff teaches a well balanced curriculum that includes not only the core subjects but also a wide range of extra-curricular activities. Each individual's performance is closely monitored. Class sizes are small, with a maximum of 16 boys in each. Minibus travel is provided from local areas and Haslemere railway station. After school care is provided until 6 pm. Haslemere Preparatory School encourages the active involvement of parents in achieving its pupils' success.

The school formed a federation with St Ives girls' school in January 2009 but remains committed to single-sex education.

For a prospectus, please contact the Headmaster's Secretary or visit www.haslemereprep.co.uk.

Charitable status. Haslemere Preparatory School Trust is a Registered Charity, number 294944.

Hatherop Castle Preparatory School

Hatherop, Cirencester, Glos GL7 3NB
Tel: 01285 750206
Fax: 01285 750430
e-mail: admissions@hatheropcastle.co.uk
website: www.hatheropcastle.co.uk

Chairman of Governors: Mr M StJ Parker, MA

Headmaster: **Mr P Easterbrook**, BEd

Age Range. 2½–13. Kindergarten/Transition 2½–4½.
Number of Pupils. 83 Boys, 107 Girls, including 21 Boarders (boarding from age 7).
Fees per term (2010-2011). £2,199–£3,660 (Day), £5,090–£5,370 (Boarding), Kindergarten/ Transition up to £2,355.

Founded in 1947, Hatherop Castle is a co-educational day and boarding prep school for children between the ages of 2½ and 13. Children are prepared for Common Entrance and Scholarship Examinations at 11+ and 13+; the children move on to a wide range of senior independent schools. Weekly boarders are accepted and the boarding facilities are homely and well furnished. A family atmosphere exists throughout the school. The curriculum spans a wide range of subjects and there is a great variety of sports and extra-curricular activities.

Set in 22 acres of beautiful Cotswold countryside, Hatherop Castle enjoys a superb setting and is a happy environment in which the pupils learn. The classes are housed in well-equipped rooms and the pre-prep and kindergarten/ transition have their own self-contained areas where the pupils enjoy playing and working in a welcoming and stimulating atmosphere. The ICT Suite impacts across the curriculum. New sports changing rooms with showers opened in March 2009. An Outdoor Classroom has been constructed in the grounds.

The report of the ISI Inspection in March 2010 can be viewed on the school website.

Charitable status. Hatherop Castle School Ltd is a Registered Charity, number 1125273. It exists for the education of children. Fundraising for home and overseas charities takes place throughout the year.

Hawkesdown House School

27 Edge Street, Kensington, London W8 7PN
Tel: 020 7727 9090
Fax: 020 7727 9988
e-mail: admin@hawkesdown.co.uk
website: www.hawkesdown.co.uk

Pre-Preparatory Day School for Boys.

Head: **Mrs C Bourne**, MA Cantab

Age Range. 3–8.
Number of Pupils. 130 Boys.
Fees per term (2011-2012). £4,095 (age 3), £4,440 (age 4), £4,700 (age 5–8).

The previous Head was the first Head of a free-standing pre-preparatory school to be elected to membership of IAPS (Independent Association of Prep Schools) and IAPS membership has continued under the leadership of the new Head, Mrs Claire Bourne.

Early literacy and numeracy are of prime importance and the traditional academic subjects form the core curriculum.

A balanced education helps all aspects of learning and a wide range of interests is encouraged. The School finds and fosters individual talents in each pupil. Boys are prepared for entry at eight to the main London and other preparatory schools. The Head places the greatest importance on matching boys happily and successfully to potential schools and spends time with parents ensuring that the transition is smooth and free of stress.

Sound and thorough early education is important for success, and also for self-confidence. The thoughtful and inspirational teaching and care at Hawkesdown House ensures high academic standards and promotes initiative, kindness and courtesy. Hawkesdown is a school with fun and laughter, where boys develop their own personalities together with a sense of personal responsibility.

The School provides an excellent traditional education, with the benefits of modern technology, in a safe, happy and caring atmosphere. Many of the boys coming to the School live within walking distance and the School is an important part of the Kensington community.

There are clear expectations and the boys are encouraged by positive motivation and by the recognition and praise of their achievements, progress and effort. Individual attention and pastoral care for each of the boys is of great importance.

Hawkesdown House has a fine building in Edge Street, off Kensington Church Street.

Religious Denomination: Non denominational; Christian ethos.

Parents who would like further information or to visit the School and meet the Head, should contact the School Office for a prospectus or an appointment.

The Hawthorns

Pendell Court, Bletchingley, Surrey RH1 4QJ
Tel: 01883 743048 (Prep); 01883 743718 (Pre-Prep)
Fax: 01883 744256
e-mail: admissions@hawthorns.com
website: www.hawthorns.com

Motto: *Love God, Love Your Neighbour*
The School is an Educational Trust controlled by a Board of Governors.

Chair of Governors: Mrs Z S Creighton

Headmaster: **T R Johns**, BA, PGCE, FRGS

Age Range. 2–13.
Number of Pupils. 540 Day Pupils.
Fees per term (2011-2012). From £570 (Nursery 2 mornings) to £3,705.

Founded in 1926 near Redhill, The Hawthorns moved in 1961 to the haven of its present impressive site, a Jacobean manor set in 35 acres below the North Downs, with a catchment area from East Grinstead to Coulsdon and Dorking to Westerham.

The prospectus and website reflect the rich and diverse nature of our School. Recent developments include an imaginative Pre-Prep building to complement The Nursery Ark, Sports and Swimming complex.

Boys and girls gain entry as day pupils between the ages of 2 and 13 and are prepared for the Common Entrance examination and/or Scholarships at 11+ and 13+. The curriculum, incorporating the National Curriculum, Common Entrance and Scholarship goals, blends modern and traditional methods with emphasis on thorough grounding in English, Maths, Science, ICT and Languages. In Music, DT, Art and Textiles specialist centres are very well equipped. The strong Music Department fields three choirs, an orchestra and a variety of ensembles, with a wide range of individual instrumental tuition available. Public recitals and regular

competition entries are encouraged, with good scholarship results. The co-educational commitment to PE and Games is of great importance with major sports including soccer, netball, rugby, hockey, pop-lacrosse, cricket, tennis, athletics and swimming. The grounds contain four sports areas, tennis courts, astroturf and 5 acres of woodland for outdoor pursuits. An extensive programme of extra-curricular activities is offered including sailing, high wires, squash, survival, model-making, film-making, fashion design, pet care and cooking.

A flourishing Parent/Toddler group runs during term time with Extended Day facilities and a comprehensive Holiday Activity Programme.

We believe firmly in hard work encouraging excellent results and providing breadth of opportunity. This includes trips, exchanges, and Schools of Swimming and Dance (open to the local community). Life Skills such as touch-typing, time management, teamwork, survival and service are all taught. Equal opportunities, enjoyment and success are sought for every child. "Happy children learn."

The staff consists of 40 full-time teachers, graduates or qualified in their particular field, and 31 part-time teachers. Mrs Johns oversees the domestic arrangements and personally supervises the children's health, aided by matrons. The school is a living, happy, working community and a visit is essential.

Charitable status. The Hawthorns Educational Trust Limited is a Registered Charity, number 312067. It exists to provide education for girls and boys of 2 to 13 years.

Hazelwood School

Wolfs Hill, Limpsfield, Oxted, Surrey RH8 0QU
Tel: 01883 712194
Fax: 01883 716135
e-mail: registrar@hazelwoodschool.com
website: www.hazelwoodschool.co.uk www.the-larks.co.uk

Chair of Governors: Mrs Jo Naismith, BA Hons, ACA

Head Teacher: **Mrs Maxine Shaw**, BSc Hons, PGCE, NPQH, EYPS

Age Range. 3 months–13 years.
Number of Pupils. 450 co-educational.
Fees per term (2010-2011). Day Pupils from £2,500 (Reception) to £4,130.

Founded in 1890, Hazelwood stands in superb grounds, commanding a magnificent view over the Kent and Sussex Weald.

Pupils enter at age 4 into the Pre-Prep or at 7+ to the Prep School, joining those pupils transferring from the Pre-Prep to the Prep School. Entry at other ages is possible if space permits. The Larks Nursery School, open all year round for children from 3 months to 4 years, opened in September 2009 on the Laverock site which offers unrivalled accommodation and facilities.

A gradual transition is made towards subject specialist tuition in the middle and upper forms. Pupils are prepared for the Common Entrance examinations at 11+ and 13+, and also for Scholarships to Senior Schools. Over 170 academic, all-rounder, sporting, music and art awards have been gained since 1995.

Extra-mural activity is an important part of every pupil's education. Excellent sports facilities, which include games fields, heated indoor swimming pool, gymnasium and many games pitches, tennis courts and other hard surfaces, allow preparation of school teams at various age and ability levels in a wide range of sports. A fully-equipped Sports Hall was completed in May 2004. Our aim is that every pupil has an opportunity to represent the School.

Art, Technology, Music and Drama are on the curriculum as well as being lively extra-mural activities. Our Centenary Theatre incorporates a 200-seat theatre, music school and Chapel. All our pupils are encouraged to play an instrument and join one of the music groups catering for all interests and abilities. Further extra-mural activities include tap, ballet and jazz dance, judo, art, gymnastics, warhammer, computing, modelling and chess.

Our pupils develop a curiosity about the world in which they live and a real passion for learning. Most importantly of all they become confident learners, mature and articulate individuals who love coming to school each day.

Charitable status. Hazelwood School Limited is a Registered Charity, number 312081. It exists to provide excellent preparatory school education for girls and boys in Oxted, Surrey.

Hazlegrove
King's Bruton Preparatory School

Hazlegrove, Sparkford, Yeovil, Somerset BA22 7JA
Tel: 01963 440314
Fax: 01963 440569
e-mail: office@hazlegrove.co.uk
website: www.hazlegrove.co.uk

Senior Warden: E W Thomas Esq, BA

Headmaster: **Richard Fenwick**, BEd, MA

Deputy Headmaster: Martin Davis, BEd

Head of Pre-Preparatory Department: Ellie Lee, BEd

Age Range. 2½–13.
Number of Pupils. 388 boys and girls of whom 99 are boarders. Preparatory (7–13 year olds) 308 pupils; Pre-Preparatory (2½–7 year olds) 80 pupils.
Fees per term (2011-2012). Preparatory: Boarders £5,310–£6,775 (fees are inclusive, there are no compulsory extras); Day pupils £3,730–£4,757. Pre-Preparatory: £2,347. Nursery: on application.
Scholarships and Bursaries. Academic Scholarships are available for entry at 7+ and 11+. Music and Sport awards and Armed Forces Bursaries to serving members are also available.

The school is located within a 200-acre park and is based around a country house built by Carew Hervey Mildmay in 1730. The entrance to the school is situated on the A303 at the Sparkford roundabout opposite the turning to Yeovil and Sherborne. The Preparatory School has a strong boarding ethos and was awarded "Outstanding" status by Ofsted 2010/2011. This is reflected in the full days and Saturday morning lessons from Year Four and the full range of activities for boarders and those day pupils who wish to join in during the evenings and at weekends.

Hazlegrove is a happy and purposeful school with an established tutor system. The curriculum provides a varied and exciting experience for pupils as they progress through the school and includes specialist taught Art, Design and Technology, Drama, Music and Outdoor Education. Specialist teaching is extended to all subjects from Year Five when Latin is also introduced. The main sports are Rugby, Hockey, Cricket, Netball, Rounders, Tennis, Athletics and Swimming. Squash, Golf, Horse Riding and Kayaking are also available amongst other activities.

Streaming and setting is introduced as pupils progress through the school with a scholarship stream in the top two years. Pupils are entered for Common Entrance or Scholarship Examinations. About half go to the senior school, King's School Bruton (*see entry in HMC section*). Others move on to major secondary schools such as Sherborne,

Sherborne School for Girls, Millfield, St Mary's Shaftesbury, King's College Taunton, Bryanston, Marlborough and Winchester. Between 15 and 20 scholarships and awards are gained by pupils each year. Extra support is available to those pupils who have specific learning difficulties or who are gifted.

Pupils have achieved considerable success at regional and national level in recent years through sport, in team and individual performances. In addition, the choir reached the finals of the BBC Radio 3 Children's Choir of the Year competition.

Hazlegrove has outstanding facilities. These include a comprehensive Computer Network, the Theatre, a Sports Hall, a 25m Indoor Heated Pool, two Squash Courts, the Design Centre and an extensive Music School. Outside, the extensive playing fields include a 6-hole Golf Course, hard Tennis Courts and two synthetic pitches.

Pastoral care for Boarders, which is overseen by the Headmaster's wife, is provided by three sets of House Parents, four Matrons and a Nurse. The school has considerable experience of meeting the needs of pupils whose parents are in the Services or who live and work overseas. Flexible boarding can also be arranged to meet individual needs.

The shop shop, which is on site, provides most necessary clothing and games kit.

Pre-Preparatory Department. Located in a purpose built facility within the grounds, the Pre-Preparatory Department provides a carefully structured curriculum which encourages the development of the basic skills within a balanced programme of learning and play. Full use is made of the Preparatory School facilities. After school care is available.

Recent developments in Pre-Prep include the introduction of the Forest School and specialist taught drama into the curriculum, a gardening area adjacent to the Rainbow Room and an extension of the climbing equipment in the playground. Elsewhere in the school the addition of a full-time tennis coach to the staff has ensured best use of the new hard tennis courts and synthetic surfaces. The mini-farm now has pigs, chickens and raised vegetable beds and the adventure playground has been refurbished with new equipment including timing devices so pupils can compete for the Tarzan award.

Charitable status. King's School, Bruton is a Registered Charity, number 1071997. It exists to provide education for children.

Headington Preparatory School

26 London Road, Headington, Oxford OX3 7PB
Tel: 01865 759400
Fax: 01865 761774
e-mail: admissions@headington.org
website: www.headington.org

Chairman of Board of Governors: Mrs H Batchelor, BSc

Headmistress: **Miss A J Bartlett**, BEd Hons London

Age Range. Girls 3–11.
Number of Pupils. 270.
Fees per term (2011-2012). Day: £1,119–£3,470. Boarding from age 9: Full boarding £6,979–£7,192; Weekly boarding £6,429–£6,652.

Headington Preparatory School occupies its own three-acre site just two minutes' walk from Headington School. The main building is a fine Victorian house, with several purpose-built additions, including a Foundation Stage Building for the Nursery and Reception classes and a new science block. The grounds comprise gardens, an adventure playground, a hockey pitch, netball court and a special children's garden for which pupils are responsible. The proximity of the Senior School means that Prep School girls can share their facilities, such as the Music School and sports facilities including a floodlit Astroturf pitch, and heated indoor pool, where Preparatory School pupils from the age of five swim weekly.

The Nursery and Reception classes lay the basis for the pupils' future education, developing confidence, curiosity and social skills, and gradually introducing simple reading, writing and mathematics. Also housed in purpose-built classrooms, the four Key Stage 1 classes build on previous learning, and a broad range of topics are gradually introduced. In Key Stage 2 the girls prepare for their eventual transition to secondary education. ICT is taught from the Nursery upwards by a specialist teacher, and French is introduced at age seven.

Throughout the school emphasis is placed on the breadth of education. There are a considerable number of after school clubs, ranging from Cross Country to Chess Club, a programme of visiting speakers and workshops for all age groups, as well as termly activities weeks. Numerous educational outings are offered, including a residential stay in France and an outdoor activity week in the UK. Drama plays an important role, with each year group staging an annual production. Most children learn at least one musical instrument and the Chamber Choir is highly acclaimed. The PE curriculum in Key Stage 2 includes hockey, netball, dance, gymnastics, swimming and rounders. Other sports, such as kwik cricket, judo, trampolining and fencing are optional after-school activities. After-school care is provided daily.

Entry to the school is by registration only until the age of seven. Thereafter candidates are invited to the school for a short assessment and informal interview. The main years of entry are at age 3 and 4 and then further up the school entry is subject to a place being available. The majority of pupils continue to Headington Senior School, with a number of girls being awarded scholarships every year. (*See Headington School entry in GSA section.*)

Charitable status. Headington School Oxford Limited is a Registered Charity, number 309678. It exists to provide quality education for girls.

Heath Mount School

Woodhall Park, Watton-at-Stone, Hertford, Hertfordshire SG14 3NG
Tel: 01920 830230
Fax: 01920 830357
e-mail: registrar@heathmount.org
website: www.heathmount.org

The school became a Trust in September 1970, with a Board of Governors.

Chairman of Governors: Mrs L Haysey

Headmaster: **R W Middleton**, MSc, BEd

Deputy Head: Mrs D J Mills, BA Hons

Age Range. 3–13.
Number of Pupils. Boys 215, Girls 215. Flexi/Sleepover boarding offered.
Fees per term (2011-2012). Boarding (1–4 nights): £475 –£1,600. Tuition: Years 3–8 £4,325–£4,475, Pre-Prep £3,355; Nursery £1,735–£2,900.

There is a reduction in fees for the second and subsequent children attending the School at the same time.

The School, situated five miles from Hertford, Ware and Knebworth, is at Woodhall Park – a Georgian mansion with 40 acres of grounds set in a large private park. A dedicated Nursery and Pre-Prep is situated in woods a short walk from the main house. The excellent sports facilities include a

sports hall, covered swimming pool, an all-weather pitch for hockey and tennis, netball courts and cricket nets. The main house contains an imaginatively developed lower ground floor housing modern science laboratories and rooms for art, pottery, textiles, film making, food technology and design technology. There is a further information technology room and well-stocked research and fiction libraries. The boys board in a wing of the main house and the girls in a dedicated house in the adjoining park. Resident boarding house parents provide a welcoming environment for both the boys and girls.

The School has an excellent record of scholarships to leading independent senior schools with 22 scholarships awarded in 2011.

Charitable status. Heath Mount School is a Registered Charity, number 311069.

Heatherton House School

Copperkins Lane, Chesham Bois, Amersham, Bucks HP6 5QB
Tel: 01494 726433
Fax: 01494 729628
e-mail: office@heathertonhouse.co.uk
website: www.heathertonhouse.co.uk

Chairman of the Governors: Mr David Bracey

Headmaster: **Mr P H Rushforth**, BEd, MA

Age Range. Girls 3–11.
Number of Pupils. 165 Girls.
Fees per term (2011-2012). £1,550–£3,600 inclusive of all but optional subjects.

Founded in 1912, the school is set in an attractive green and leafy location on the outskirts of Amersham.

Heatherton provides an excellent all-round education. Very high-quality facilities combined with an experienced staff of specialist teachers encourage each child's individual academic and emotional development. High standards are achieved across a broad curriculum with small classes (max 20), a caring ethos and a close relationship with parents.

Excellent results are produced at all stages of school performance tests: and at 11 pupils progress to both local independent girls' senior schools, often with scholarships, and Buckinghamshire grammar schools.

Musical, artistic and sporting talents flourish at Heatherton. A thriving orchestra, individual instrument lessons and many drama, ballet and music productions are an important part of life in a school year. Art and design skills are celebrated in display and exhibitions, both internally and externally. Each pupil is offered a wide range of sporting activities – swimming, netball, gymnastics, dance, athletics, tennis, pop lacrosse, hockey, with opportunities for cricket.

An extensive range of educational visits and activities in the UK and Europe are organised each year.

Charitable status. Heatherton House School Limited is a Registered Charity, number 310630. It exists to provide high quality education for girls.

Heathfield
The Junior School to Rishworth School

Rishworth, West Yorkshire HX6 4QF
Tel: 01422 823564
Fax: 01422 820880
e-mail: admin@heathfieldjunior.co.uk
website: www.rishworth-school.co.uk

Motto: '*Deeds Not Words*'

Chairman of the Board of Governors: Dr C A G Brooks

Head: **Mr A M Wilkins**, BA, MA

Age Range. 3–11 co-educational.

Number of Pupils. 170 day boys/girls and 50-place Foundation Stage Unit.

Fees per term (from April 2011). Reception–Year 2 £1,775; Years 3–6 £2,605.

Staffing. 10 full-time teaching and 5 part-time teaching; 2 NNEB staff and 6 teaching assistants; additional teaching support in Physical Education; 9 specialist peripatetic staff provide expert tuition in Music and the Arts.

Location. Heathfield stands in its own grounds and enjoys an outstanding rural position in a beautiful Pennine location with easy access via the motorways to Manchester and Leeds.

Facilities. Well-equipped classrooms; Foundation Stage Unit and purpose-built Infant classes; designated teaching rooms for Music, Drama, Art, Design Technology; modern ICT Suite; Library; a multi-purpose Hall for assemblies and productions; heated indoor swimming pool; netball court and football/rugby pitch; Pre/After School Care and Holiday School available.

Aims. To provide a stimulating and challenging environment in which individual attainment is nurtured, recognised and celebrated.

To ensure each child receives their full entitlement to a broad, balanced curriculum which builds on a solid foundation in Literacy and Numeracy.

Curriculum. An extensive programme of study which incorporates the Foundation Stage, Key Stage 1 and Key Stage 2. An emphasis on developing an independence in learning and analytical thinking through Literacy, Numeracy, Science, French, History, Geography, Religious Studies, Design Technology, Information and Communications Technology, Music, Art and Physical Education.

Extra-Curricular Activities. Drama, Choir, Orchestra, Brass, Recorder and String Groups, Steel Pans, Art, Board Games; Sports include Swimming, Rounders, Netball, Football, Rugby, Cross-Country, Cricket, Athletics, Hockey and Biathlon.

Extensive termly fixtures list of sports for boys and girls.

Each term there are plays and musical concerts incorporating most children in the School. Residentials include Outdoor Pursuits, Camping and Environmental Studies.

Charitable status. Rishworth School is a Registered Charity, number 1115562. It exists to provide education for boys and girls.

Hereford Cathedral Junior School

28 Castle Street, Hereford HR1 2NW
Tel: 01432 363511
Fax: 01432 363515
e-mail: enquiry@hcjs.org
website: www.hcjs.org

Established 1898.

Chairman of Governors: The Earl of Darnley

Headmaster: **T C Wheeler**, MA, BA

Age Range. 3–11.

Number of children. 312: 169 boys and 143 girls.

Fees per term (2011-2012). £1,330–£1,900 (Nursery), £2,320 (Reception–Year 2), £2,880 (Years 3–6).

The school is the Junior School for Hereford Cathedral School and has the same board of Governors. Games facilities, including the new sports hall opened in 2009, are shared and there is close cooperation between the two sections of the school, although the Junior School has its own specialist teaching staff.

Entry is generally via the Nursery or Reception but a number of children also enter at 7+ and above. Almost all children continue through to the senior school.

The school occupies listed Georgian and Medieval buildings in Castle Street at the East End of the Cathedral with facilities including specialist music rooms, a new Art and DT centre, an ICT suite and an extensive library. The Moat, a nine-classroom building to house the Pre-Prep, opened in 2003.

The quality of relationships between staff and children is a great strength and a positive and friendly atmosphere characterises the whole school. There is a full and broad curriculum with the school noted for the strength of its music, drama and games. French is taught from the age of 4.

The staff are well qualified and the maximum class size is 18. In the junior forms all subjects are taught by specialists.

Music plays an important part in the life of the school with the Cathedral Choristers being educated at the school and a team of over twenty peripatetic music teachers. There are two school choirs and an orchestra.

An extensive programme of clubs and activities is offered during lunchtime and after school aimed at giving all children opportunities to develop their talents. After school care is also available.

The games fields are on the banks of the River Wye with expert coaching being given in the main sports of cricket, football, rugby, hockey, netball, rounders, athletics and swimming.

There is an active PTA organising a wide programme of social and fundraising activities.

The Little Princess Trust founded in memory of former pupil, Hannah Tarplee, is based at the school and provides hair pieces for children who lose their hair through cancer treatment.

Charitable status. Hereford Cathedral School is a Registered Charity, number 518889. Its aims and objectives are to promote the advancement of education.

Hereward House School

14 Strathray Gardens, London NW3 4NY
Tel: 020 7794 4820
Fax: 020 7794 2024
e-mail: herewardhouse@btconnect.com
website: www.herewardhouse.co.uk

Headmaster: **Mr T W Burden**, BA

Age Range. 4–13.

Number of Pupils. 175 Day Boys.

Fees per term (2011-2012). £3,900–£4,475.

Hereward House provides a warm and welcoming atmosphere in which every child feels valued, secure and thrives. The school works hard to create a stimulating, purposeful and happy community, within which boys are encouraged and assisted to develop academically, morally, emotionally, culturally and physically. The school's aim is for boys to enjoy their school days yet at the same time be well prepared for the demands of Common Entrance and Scholarship examinations.

The school's academic success is built upon excellent teaching and the highly individual educational teaching programmes created to meet individual boy's needs. Great care is taken to ensure that a boy gains a place at the school which is right for him.

Boys are prepared for the Common Entrance and Scholarship examinations to highly sought after independent schools, both day and boarding. Two-thirds of boys proceed to London Day Schools, ie City of London, Highgate, St Paul's, UCS and Westminster, others to leading boarding schools such as Eton, Harrow, Radley, Rugby and Winchester. Scholarships and Awards have been won by our boys to several of the above schools.

The school takes pride in the breadth of education it offers. Music plays a major role in the boys' education. Approximately 90% of boys learn at least one instrument, most of them two or even three. There is a full school orchestra which gives a performance each term. Weekly tea-time concerts are held throughout the year.

Team Games play an integral part in the sports syllabus. We regularly field teams against other schools and have an enviable record of success in Cricket, Football and Cross-country running. Swimming, Hockey and Athletics are included in our sports programme.

Art, Pottery and Drama have a valued place in the syllabus. Chess, Fencing, ICT, Greek and Photography are among the clubs available to the boys.

Herries Preparatory School

Dean Lane, Cookham Dean, Berks SL6 9BD
Tel: 01628 483350
Fax: 01628 483329
e-mail: office@herries.org.uk
website: www.herries.org.uk

Chair of Governors: Miss N Coombs

Headmistress: Ms S Green, BSc Econ, PGCE

Age Range. 3–11 Co-educational.
Number of Pupils. 80 Day Boys and Girls.
Fees per term (2011-2012). £2,404–£2,824.
Herries has a delightful location alongside National Trust land and is close to Maidenhead and Marlow. Small class sizes enable each child to receive individual attention and to flourish in a secure environment. The curriculum is broad and balanced and there is a wide range of extra-curricular clubs including football coaching with Wycombe Wanderers, Gymnastics and Judo. Music and Dance lessons are available. Herries has a distinctive family atmosphere and happy pupils who progress to the grammar and independent secondary schools of their choice.

Curriculum. The National Curriculum is covered and we aim to teach beyond the levels expected of children in each age group. Class teachers deliver the core and foundation subjects while there is specialist teaching in KS2 Science, French, Music, PE, Swimming and Tennis.

Examinations. Children are assessed through the NFER testing scheme. Verbal reasoning test papers prepare children for the 11+ examinations taken by those seeking entry to the selective grammar schools.

Facilities. The Nursery occupies a purpose-built and spacious suite of rooms. ICT is taught in a specialist room with the latest computers and software. Class rooms are equipped with interactive Smart Boards and there is an excellent library. Games are played at the National Sports Centre at Bisham Abbey, only a few minutes away by coach. Swimming and tennis are based at Court Garden in Marlow. Athletics events are held at Braywick Sports Centre.

High March School

Beaconsfield, Bucks HP9 2PZ
Tel: 01494 675186
Fax: 01494 675377
e-mail: office@highmarch.bucks.sch.uk
website: www.highmarch.co.uk

Established 1926.

Chairman of the Governing Board: Mr C A E T Stevenson, MA Cantab

Headmistress: Mrs S J Clifford, BEd Hons Oxon, MA London

Age Range. Girls 3–11, Boys 3–4.
Number of Pupils. 292 day pupils.
Fees per term (2011-2012). £532–£3,675 inclusive of books, stationery and lunches, but excluding optional subjects.

High March consists of 3 school houses set in pleasant grounds. Junior House comprises Nursery and Key Stage 1 classes, ages 3–7 years, whilst Upper School covers Key Stage 2, ages 7–11 years. Class sizes are limited. There is a brand new 20-metre indoor heated swimming pool, which opened in September 2009. Other facilities include a well-equipped Gymnasium, as well as Science, Music, Art, Poetry, Design Technology, Drama, Information Technology rooms, and a Library.

High March is within easy reach of London, High Wycombe, Windsor and within a few minutes' walk of Beaconsfield Station.

Under a large and highly-qualified staff and within a happy atmosphere, the children are prepared for Common Entrance and Scholarships to Independent Senior Schools and for the 11+ County Selection process. All subjects including French, Latin, Music, Art, Technology, Speech and Drama, Dancing, Gymnastics, Games and Swimming are in the hands of specialists. Although the academic record is high, each child is encouraged to develop individual talents.

There is an Annual Open Scholarship to the value of one-third of the annual fee tenable for 3 years.

Highfield School

Liphook, Hampshire GU30 7LQ
Tel: 01428 728000
Fax: 01428 728001
e-mail: office@highfieldschool.org.uk
website: www.highfieldschool.org.uk

Chairman of Directors: W S Mills, Esq

Head: Mr Phillip Evitt, MA

Age Range. 8–13.
Number of Children. 235 (including 85 boarders).
Fees per term (2011-2012). Boarders £6,025–£6,725; Day Pupils £4,650–£5,675.

Discounts are available for siblings and Forces families. Means-tested Bursaries are available on application.

Location. 15 miles south of Guildford with easy access to London A3 and airports.

Highfield is a purpose built co-educational day and boarding school founded in 1907 set in 175 acres of superb grounds on the Hampshire/Sussex border.

The aim of the school is to provide children with a keen sense of their own individual identity and to help them to develop a sense of responsibility towards others and fulfil their potential in a happy and caring environment. Highfield children are encouraged to have high expectations, good work habits and a desire to benefit from all that the school offers.

Curriculum. Highfield children have a distinguished record of success at Common Entrance and Scholarships to all the major senior schools including Eton, Winchester, Marlborough, Bryanston, Canford, Wycombe Abbey, St Swithun's and Downe House.

Alongside the major academic subjects, French is taught from the age of 7 and Latin begins at 10. The broad curriculum includes ICT, PE and DT and the school's excellent tradition in music, drama and art is reflected in the number of scholarships gained.

The school has built outstanding new facilities for Science, ICT, Mathematics and English. An indoor swimming pool opened in 2005.

Sports and Activities. The major sports on offer are rugby, soccer, hockey and cricket for the boys, whilst girls play netball, lacrosse, hockey and rounders. All the children take part in athletics, swimming, tennis and cross country. Activities take place in the evenings and weekends and include judo, ballet, chess, golf, drama, modelling, pottery, sewing and story telling.

Highfield School

West Road, Maidenhead, Berks SL6 1PD
Tel: 01628 624918
Fax: 01628 635747
e-mail: office@highfieldprep.org
website: www.highfieldprep.org

Chairman of Governors: Mrs R Westacott

Head: **Ms Annie Lee**, BA, PGCE, MA

Type. Educational Charitable Trust Primary Day School with Kindergarten and Nursery.
Location. Town.
Number of Pupils. Approximately 160 Girls, 3 Boys.
Average Class Size. 18.
Maximum Class Size. 22.
Age Range. Girls 2½–11+.
Religion. Christian. Other denominations welcome.
Entry. By interview and/or placement test.
Aim. To provide an all-round education while maximizing individual potential. To engender in each pupil a love of learning which will endure for a life-time. The School follows the National Curriculum and prepares pupils for the Common Entrance Examination and other entry tests including 11+ Grammar School entry.
Prospectus. On request from the School Secretary.
Fees per term (2011-2012). Reception to Year 6: £2,465–£2,915 inc lunch; Nursery: £2,525 (full-time inc lunch), £263 per morning session.
Charitable status. Highfield School is a Registered Charity, number 309103. It exists to provide an all-round education for girls.

Highgate Junior School

Cholmeley House, 3 Bishopswood Road, London N6 4PL
Tel: 020 8340 9193
Fax: 020 8342 7273
e-mail: jsoffice@highgateschool.org.uk
          pre-prep@highgateschool.org.uk
website: www.highgateschool.org.uk

Chairman of Governors: J F Mills, Esq, MA, BLitt

Principal of Junior School: **S M James**, BA, MA

Principal of Pre-Preparatory School: Mrs D Hecht, DCE

Age Range. 3–11 Co-educational.
Number of Day Pupils. Junior (age 7–11): 320 boys and girls; Pre-Prep (age 3–7): 130 boys and girls.

Fees per term (2011-2012). Junior School: £4,850; Pre-Preparatory School: £4,580 (Reception–Year 2), £2,290 (Nursery).

Pupils are prepared for Highgate School only. (*See entry in HMC section.*)

Entry to the Pre-Preparatory School is by individual assessment for entry at 3+. Entry to the Junior School is by test and interview at the age of 7. Transfer to the Senior School is at 11+.

The Pre-Preparatory School and the Junior School are both housed in self-contained buildings, located in Bishopswood Road, N6.

The School is well situated close to Hampstead Heath and has excellent facilities as the result of an ongoing development programme. There are several acres of playing fields attached; the Mallinson Sports Centre (which includes a 25-metre indoor pool) is shared with the Senior School, and a newly completed all-weather sports pitch.

A broad and balanced curriculum is followed with art, drama, music, games, ICT and design technology all playing an important part.

Charitable status. Sir Roger Cholmeley's School at Highgate is a Registered Charity, number 312765. The aims and objectives of the charity are educational, namely the maintenance of a school.

Hilden Grange School
Alpha Plus Group

Dry Hill Park Road, Tonbridge, Kent TN10 3BX
Tel: 01732 351169
Fax: 01732 377950
e-mail: office@hildengrange.co.uk
website: www.hildengrange.co.uk

Headmaster: **J Withers**, BA Hons

Age Range. 3–13 Co-educational.
Number of Pupils. 300: 200 Boys and 100 Girls.
Fees per term (2011-2012). Prep School £3,880, Pre-Prep £2,995, Nursery: £40 per day, £26 per morning, £20 per afternoon. Lunches are provided at £195–£220 per term.

Hilden Grange is a friendly, unpretentious school with high standards of teaching and learning, conscientious pastoral care and strength in art, drama, music and sport.

We aim to bring out and develop the individual child's potential in the academic, creative, spiritual and physical areas. We expect our pupils to strive for high standards, to take pride in themselves and to gain satisfaction from their endeavours in an orderly and relaxed environment.

Though links are especially strong with Tonbridge and Sevenoaks boys and girls are prepared for all Independent Senior Schools and Grammar Schools at 11+ and 13+. We have an impressive record of success in this area. Examination results rank among the highest in Kent, and in 2009, all pupils gained entry to their chosen school at 13. Boys and girls who show special promise sit for scholarships to the school of their choice, and our track record in this area is excellent, with over 80 scholarships gained in the past ten years. Pupils benefit from specialist teaching in all subjects from Year 3, dedicated staff, and class sizes that average 16.

The School stands in about eight acres of attractive grounds in the residential area of North Tonbridge. Boys and girls are accepted into the Nursery at 3+ or at 4+ into the Pre-Preparatory Department within the school grounds, and at 7 into the main school. Two Scholarships of up to half fees are available annually for suitable candidates aged 7 to 10. Music Scholarships are also available. Tonbridge School Chorister awards are gained. At present there are eight Choristers.

There is an outdoor heated swimming pool, a Sports Hall with changing rooms and kitchen complex, a library and an

Art Studio. There are all-weather tennis courts, a Science Laboratory, a Music Room, and two Information Technology Rooms, with networks of personal computers with colour and laser printers.

The Headmaster, staff and children welcome visitors and are pleased to show them around the School.

Hilden Oaks School & Nursery

38 Dry Hill Park Road, Tonbridge, Kent TN10 3BU
Tel: 01732 353941
Fax: 01732 353942
e-mail: secretary@hildenoaks.co.uk
website: www.hildenoaks.co.uk

Chairman of Governors: Mrs C Phillips

Headmistress: Mrs S A Sunderland, MA, NPQH

Age Range. 3 months–11 years Co-educational.
Number of Children. 170.
Fees per term (2010-2011). 5 mornings: Nursery £1,475, Kindergarten £1,250, Transition £1,250. Reception £2,300, Forms 1 and 2 £2,650, Forms 3 and 4 £2,950, Forms 5 and 6 £3,150.

Hilden Oaks School, founded in 1919, became an Educational Trust in 1965. It is located in a quiet, residential area of north Tonbridge and the Trust owns all the land and buildings.

The Main School incorporates classrooms, the School Hall, a state-of-the-art ICT Suite and an extensive, welcoming Library. The Acorn Building incorporates Music and Drama facilities and also provides spacious rooms for the Nursery and the youngest children in the school. The Stable Block has been developed as a self-contained unit for Reception. The Salmon Building houses the Prep Department and specialist Science and Art rooms. The site is a pleasant, enclosed garden setting with hard and grassed playing areas for netball and five-a-side football. There is also a small, wooded section with a pond for field-studies.

Hilden Oaks prides itself on being a happy, family school where every child is helped and encouraged to develop their potential and independent learning in a caring, stimulating and purposeful environment. We maintain high academic standards while expecting good manners and consideration to others at all times. This is reflected in the active parents' association, close liaison between parents and staff and the school's close involvement with the local community.

In the Pre-School and Pre-Preparatory Departments, children are given a solid foundation upon which they can build, with additional specialist teachers for ICT, French, Music and PE. The Preparatory Department has specialist teachers for Science, ICT, French, Art, Music and PE. All forms are taught by form teachers for the core subjects.

Our pupils enjoy taking part in Music and Drama with regular opportunities to perform. They also enjoy competitive sport in house matches and against other schools. Extracurricular activities include Choirs, Drama, Art, ICT and Games. A late room operates for infants and juniors where children are provided with tea. Prep is supervised for the older children while the younger children can relax and play.

All pupils are prepared for both the Common Entrance examination at 11 and the 11+ examination for entry to grammar schools. Our results in these examinations, for Foundation Stage Profile assessments and for SATS at Key Stages 1 and 2, put us among the top schools in Kent.

Hilden Oaks offers a challenging and supportive environment designed to inspire children to life-long learning.

Charitable status. Hilden Oaks School is a Registered Charity, number 307935. It exists to provide education for children.

Hoe Bridge School

Hoe Place, Old Woking, Surrey GU22 8JE
Tel: Prep School: 01483 760018/760065
          Pre-Prep: 01483 772194
Fax: 01483 757560
e-mail: enquiriesprep@hoebridgeschool.co.uk
          enquiriespreprep@hoebridgeschool.co.uk
website: www.hoebridgeschool.co.uk

Co-educational Preparatory and Pre-Preparatory School.

Chairman of Governors: Ian Katté

Headmaster: N Arkell, BSc

Deputy Headmaster: G D P Scott, BEd Exeter

Head of Pre-Prep: Mrs Linda Renfrew, MA, PGCE

Age Range. 2½–14.
Number of Children. Prep 281, Pre-Prep 215.
Fees per term (2011-2012). Day: Prep £3,570–£4,135 (including lunch); Pre-Prep £580–£2,875 (including lunch).

Hoe Bridge School is on the outskirts of Woking, standing in its own grounds of 20 acres which affords admirable facilities for games and outdoor pursuits, including Rugby, Association Football, Cricket, Athletics, Netball, Hockey, Tennis and Swimming. A substantial part of the Grade II listed building has been restored and now houses a state of the art Music School, Art, Design Technology and Information Technology Centres. The Nursery unit is on the ground floor of this magnificent building and provides first class facilities for both indoor and outdoor activities. The recent refurbishment of the Sports Hall block has provided additional classrooms and 3 state-of-the-art science laboratories. The School's academic and sporting record is enviable.

Children between the ages of 7–14 are prepared for scholarship and common entrance requirements to all independent schools with all normal subjects, games and activities necessary for a child's development taught by experienced qualified staff.

The Headmistress of the Pre-Preparatory School is a member of the IAPS in her own right. Children may join the Pre-Prep from age 2½. The Nursery and Reception units offer children an excellent start to their Early Years Education with a structured programme of activities and experiences. Our experienced staff of teachers and assistants include games and music specialists. The Pre-Prep benefits from its own Hall fully equipped for gymnastics, a dedicated art room, interactive whiteboards and an ICT suite comprising 10 computers in addition to computers in all the classrooms. Children in Year 2 are well prepared for the curriculum of the Prep School and the transition to this department is eased by weekly games lessons with Prep staff and sample lessons each term in music, art and design.

Hoe Bridge School is an Educational Trust run by a Board of Governors whose members are drawn from parents, and the local community.

Charitable status. Hoe Bridge School is a Registered Charity, number 295808. It exists to provide a rounded education for children aged 2½–14.

Holme Grange School

Heathlands Road, Wokingham, Berkshire RG40 3AL
Tel: 0118 9781566
Fax: 0118 9770810
e-mail: school@holmegrange.org
website: www.holmegrange.org

Chairman of Governors: T Andrews, BA Hons

Head: **Mrs Claire Robinson**, BA, PGCE, NPQH

Age Range. 3–13 Co-educational.
Number of Pupils. 247: 104 girls, 143 boys.
Fees per term (2010-2011). Little Grange Nursery £1,555–£2,650, Pre-Preparatory £2,860, Prep: £3,660 (Years 3–4), £3,690 (Years 5–8), with an option to pay over 10 months. Reductions for second and subsequent children.

The School is a Day School receiving pupils from a wide catchment area and holiday care is available throughout the school holidays.

The School occupies a large country mansion, to which many additional facilities have been added, set in just over 20 acres of grounds comprising grass pitches, all weather surfaces and woodland walks for the children to explore. Specialist teaching and facilities for Music, Art and Technology, Dance, Performing Arts, Science, ICT and Sport enhance our provision and support the individual development of all our pupils.

Little Grange is an established Nursery for 3 year olds in its own safe, secure environment within the School grounds, providing flexible education either part or full day including lunch and tea. All children from age 3 may stay to 6.00 pm.

We are non-selective and both welcome and cater for pupils of a wide range of ability. We aim to foster confidence and a love of learning across the age range. Pupils are accepted from the start of the term in which they turn 3 providing continuous education until they take the Common Entrance or Scholarship examinations (Academic, Art, Music) for Senior Independent Schools. At both there is an enviable record of success.

The Headteacher is assisted by a highly qualified and experienced teaching staff with classroom assistants in the Pre-Prep and NNEB assistants in Little Grange. There is a Learning Support Department giving help to those children with special needs.

The School's policy is to set high standards, to establish good all-round personalities and to give inspiration for each pupil's life. Our aim is to create an environment where every child can thrive. We appreciate children's differences and respond to their individual needs.

We deliver a rounded education by providing opportunities in sport, the arts, languages, technology and a wide range of activities, maximising opportunities for success for all. We hope to inspire your child both in and outside of the classroom. At Holme Grange School, we foster self-reliance, self-discipline and self-confidence in a caring community where children gain interests and characteristics that give them a head start for life.

A broad curriculum is followed, embracing both the National Curriculum, and that currently required for the 11+ and 13+ Common Entrance Examinations. Maximum class size is 18; average size is 16, but fewer in Years 7 and 8.

The School is a Trust, administered by a board of Governors who have considerable experience in education and business.

Charitable status. Holme Grange Limited is a Registered Charity, number 309105. It exists to serve the local community in providing an all-round education for boys and girls.

Holmewood House

Langton Green, Tunbridge Wells, Kent TN3 0EB
Tel: 01892 860000
Fax: 01892 863970
e-mail: admin@holmewood.kent.sch.uk
website: www.holmewood.kent.sch.uk

Chairman of the Governors: M A Evans

Headmaster: **J D B Marjoribanks**, BEd Hons, Dip d'Et Fr

Deputy Headmaster: S A Gent

Age Range. 3–13.
Number of Pupils. 416 Boys and Girls.
Fees per term (2011-2012). Day Pupils: Years 3–8 £5,220, Pre-Prep £3,415–£3,950, Nursery £1,525–£2,290. There are reductions for third and fourth siblings, and children of Old Holmewoodians. Scholarships are available for those entering from primary schools.

The school was founded in 1945 as a boys' school. Girls were admitted in 1989 and we have been fully co-educational for many years. The school is a Charitable Educational Trust with a Board of Governors. Holmewood stands in over 30 acres of beautiful grounds on the Kent/Sussex border, just outside Tunbridge Wells, which is one hour by rail from London.

The pastoral side of the school is carefully set in place to ensure there is a member of staff responsible for every child. ISI Inspectors have described our pastoral care as *exemplary. The family atmosphere of the school is outstanding. Pupils have a strong sense of well-being and security.*

The breadth and quality of pupils' achievements are outstanding. Thanks to our highly qualified, dedicated and enthusiastic staff, Holmewood has an outstanding scholastic record in Common Entrance and Scholarship examinations. Despite being essentially a non-selective school, every year our Year 8s gain a large number of scholarships (Academic, Music, Art, DT, Drama and Sport) to senior schools. A strong Learning Support Department (ISI Inspection: *a strength of the school*) provides additional support for less able pupils.

Children follow a broad curriculum throughout the school. For example, French is taught from the Nursery; pupils have separate teaching of Physics, Chemistry and Biology from Year 6; Latin and Ancient Greek are available. Holmewood leads the way in the use of educational ICT. The school has 250 networked computers and four networked computer rooms. All classrooms have interactive whiteboards. Pupils have timetabled ICT lessons from Reception.

ISI Inspection: *Outstanding creative development is promoted in Art, Design Technology and Music. A wealth of extra-curricular activities enriches the experience of pupils.* An extensive activity programme is part of every school day. Expert coaching is given in a wide variety of sports and these include rugby, soccer, hockey, gymnastics, netball, cricket, tennis and table tennis, shooting, athletics, cross-country, golf, archery, fencing, judo, basketball, dance, squash, rounders and swimming. We regularly play at national level in most sports. There is a large Sports Hall, an indoor swimming pool, hard tennis courts, three squash courts, an astro surface hockey/football pitch and running track, and an indoor .22 shooting range.

Holmewood is an inspiring place for children. ISI Inspection: *Pupils clearly enjoy coming to school and revel in the opportunities the school provides.*

Our **Aims and Values** inform and underpin our policies, guidelines and practice:
- Consistent and high expectations for all.
- A broad and balanced curriculum, with a strong focus on teaching and learning.
- An emphasis on the examined subjects to ensure that pupils achieve the standard needed for entrance to their chosen senior schools and those with the potential have the opportunity to attain scholarship standard.
- Opportunities for pupils to experience a range of sports as well as extra-curricular activities and non-examined subjects.
- A culture of self review and school improvement.
- Sound procedures for planning and assessing the progress of pupils.
- A positive atmosphere and generosity of spirit.

- Self-esteem for everybody – a school where everyone feels valued.
- An ethos that celebrates achievement and recognises success.
- An environment that is attractive, calm, ordered, stimulating and promotes individual learning.
- Children who are highly motivated, fully involved in the life of the school, independent and who show initiative and self-discipline.
- A positive and purposeful partnership with parents.
- An effective team of teachers who are supportive of each other and prepared to try new ideas.
- An emphasis more on mutual cooperation than individual competitiveness, while accepting that there is a place for healthy competition.
- Valuing cultural diversity and enrichment.

Our whole school values are essentially Christian

- As a community – we value good discipline, independence of mind, mutual support and success for all.
- In our relationships – we value a caring approach, encouragement, good manners and generosity.
- On a personal level – we value integrity, effort, happiness and self-discipline.

Charitable status. Holmewood House is a Registered Charity, number 279267. It exists to provide education for boys and girls.

Holmwood House

Chitts Hill, Lexden, Colchester, Essex CO3 9ST
Tel: 01206 574305
Fax: 01206 768269
e-mail: headmaster@holmwood.essex.sch.uk
website: www.holmwood.essex.sch.uk

Headmaster: **Alexander Mitchell**, BA Hons, LLCM, PGCE

Age Range. 4½–13 Co-educational. Nursery School: 6 months to 4 years.
Number of Pupils. 334.
Fees per term (2011-2012). Boarders £6,086; Day Pupils £2,640–£4,693. All fees are inclusive; there are no compulsory extras. Nursery fees dependent on hours attended.

Holmwood House was founded in 1922 and stands in 26 acres of gardens and grounds only 2km from Colchester town centre. Children are prepared for the Common Entrance examination and for scholarships to senior independent schools.

The principal aim of the school is high academic standards and thus the Library and Resource Centre are deliberately at the centre of the school. The ICT facilities, networked to all classrooms and allowing two full classes access at any one time, support pupils' learning. Facilities include 20 acres of sports fields; large, well-equipped classrooms; five squash courts; indoor heated swimming pool; state-of-the-art sports hall; seven tennis courts (two covered); floodlit tarmac play area; 2 adventure playgrounds; a permanent stage with sound and lighting systems; Art School incorporating print and ceramic workshop; separate Music facilities. The majority of pupils study at least one musical instrument. There are four well-equipped science laboratories.

From the age of 8 each subject is taught by specialist teachers. French is taught from Year 1 onwards and exchange programmes are well established. Sport and the Arts receive many scheduled sessions of instruction in afternoons and evenings. Classes and compulsory games are all timetabled conventionally; so are some 'preps', but older pupils may do up to 4 'preps' a week in their own time to provide time for orchestra, chess, cookery and many other coached activities. Drama and music flourish particularly, from the large-scale production to the small musical ensemble. Children at Holmwood House are self-confident, self-disciplined and good time managers!

Holmwood House Nursery caters for children from 6 months to 4 years. A flexible service is offered so that children can attend either during Holmwood House term only, or for any number of different sessions and options. The Nursery is open for 48 weeks in the year.

Academic, Music, Art and Sports scholarships and bursaries are available for pupils aged 7+. Bursaries are also offered in certain cases of need to enable pupils to remain at or come to the school.

We would be pleased to send our prospectus and to welcome visitors to the school.

Holy Cross Preparatory School

George Road, Kingston-upon-Thames, Surrey KT2 7NU
Tel: 020 8942 0729
Fax: 020 8336 0764
e-mail: admissions@holycrossprep.co.uk
website: www.holycrossprepschool.co.uk

Headmistress: **Mrs S Hair**

Age Range. 4–11.
Number of Girls. 250.
Fees per term (2010-2011). £3,120 including lunch.
Location. The school is situated on a private estate in an attractive area of Kingston Hill.
Facilities. The building, the former home of John Galsworthy, is of both historical and literary interest and provides excellent accommodation for two classes in each year group through the school from Reception to Year Six. The school contains an assembly hall/gymnasium, dining hall, library, Design and Technology Centre, Music room, Computer room, TV/Drama room, Art room and 14 classrooms all with computers. A new building for the 6 Infant classes was opened in Spring 2001. A new Art room and and ICT room were developed and opened for the Summer Term 2003.

The 8 acres of grounds include two tennis/netball courts, hockey pitch, running track and three large playing areas which have play equipment, including adventure climbing frames. There is a nature trail and ecology area, together with a fountain within the ornamental lawns and a pond which is well used in science lessons.

Educational Philosophy. The school was founded by the Sisters of the Holy Cross, an international teaching order who have been engaged in the work of education since 1844. A sound Christian education is given in an Ecumenical framework. The children are happy, cared for and well disciplined. The emphasis is on developing the God-given gifts of each child to their fullest, in a stimulating, friendly atmosphere where high standards of work, behaviour and contribution to the well being of the school community are expected.

Curriculum. There is a broad and relevant curriculum providing a high standard of education. Specialist teaching in French, Music, Physical Education and Information Technology. The school has a first rate record of success in Common Entrance and in preparing pupils for Senior Independent, High and Grammar Schools. The varied extracurricular activities include ballet and dance, Speech & Drama, pottery, Art and Design, cello, piano, flute, clarinet, violin, guitar, sports, German, Technology, French, country dancing, tennis, origami and chess.

Charitable status. Holy Cross Preparatory School is a Registered Charity, number 238426. It is a Roman Catholic School providing excellence in Christian education to local children.

Homefield Preparatory School

Western Road, Sutton, Surrey SM1 2TE
Tel: 020 8642 0965
Fax: 020 8642 0965
e-mail: administration@homefield.sutton.sch.uk
website: www.homefield.sutton.sch.uk

"I don't believe we could have found a better school in the country to bring out the best in both our sons."

Chairman of Governors: T Jeans, BSc, FCA

Headmaster: **P R Mowbray**, MA Cantab

Age Range. 2½–13.
Number of Boys. 400.
Fees per term (2010-2011). Senior Department £3,190; Junior Department: 2nd & 3rd Years £2,700, 1st Year £2,290; Transition £2,150; Nursery: £2,060 (full day), £1,370 (mornings only). Lunches: £240 (Seniors and Juniors), £185 (Nursery and Transition).

Homefield is a Preparatory school for 400 boys aged 2½ to 13, and 50 staff, housed in an extensive purpose-built complex complemented by a spacious state-of-the-art Early Years Unit and a 2-acre adjoining playing field.

Rated by The Sunday Times Parent Power as *"Amongst the best performing schools in Greater London"*, Homefield School has cemented its powerful academic reputation by continuing to achieve a 100% pass rate at Common Entrance to 36 senior schools over the last 10 years. 23 awards for Art, Music, Sport, All-round and Academic achievements were won this year.

The school is renowned for its intimacy and family atmosphere, small class sizes, the fulfilment of individual potential, the openness of communication, the provision of specialist teaching at the earliest appropriate opportunity (French, ICT, Music and Sport from the Foundation stage), its commitment to best practice and its all-round academic, musical, dramatic, sporting and artistic achievements. The recent ISI inspection report states that "the boys are highly educated and their personal, social and cultural development is outstanding and complements the excellent programme of extra-curricular activities".

The school has county or national representatives in table tennis, squash, tennis, athletics, swimming, soccer, rugby, cricket and chess.

Awareness of others is encouraged and the pupils are involved in many fundraising charity events, raising over £9,000 last year.

Learning support is available for children with special needs. A wide range of opportunities is planned to extend gifted pupils such as World Class Maths, French National poetry and Regional French speaking competitions and the Townsend Warner History competition.

We offer academic, sporting, art and music scholarships as well as occasional bursaries.

Daily minibuses run to and from Wimbledon and other areas.

Breakfast and after school clubs are available.

Charitable status. Homefield Preparatory School Trust Limited is a Registered Charity, number 312753. It exists to provide education for boys.

Hordle Walhampton School

Lymington, Hants SO41 5ZG
Tel: 01590 672013
Fax: 01590 678498
e-mail: office@hordlewalhampton.co.uk
website: www.hordlewalhampton.co.uk

Chairman of Governors: N A McGrigor

Headmaster: **R H C Phillips**, BA Hons, CertEd, LGSM

Age Range. 2–13.
Number of Pupils. Boarding boys 28, Boarding girls 14, Day children 157, Pre-Prep 137.
Fees per term (2010-2011). Boarding £5,760; Day £3,180–£4,465; Pre-Preparatory £2,230; Kindergarten & Nursery (full-time) £1,762.50. The only extras are: Riding, individual Music, language support tuition and Expeditions.

Hordle Walhampton was established in 1997, following the merger of Hordle House and Walhampton. The School is one of the south coast's leading co-educational boarding and day Preparatory schools, situated on the edge of the New Forest, surrounded by 92 acres of playing fields, woodland and lakes, which are enjoyed by all the children for traditional games, sailing, riding, field studies, walks, free time and fun. There are excellent facilities for Art, Computing, Craft, Design Technology, Gymnastics and Woodwork; Music and Drama also play an important part in School life. A continuing programme of development has seen the creation of a Sports Hall, Performing Arts Centre, all-weather sports pitch and the complete renovation of the equestrian centre.

The aim of the School is to seek the good in the young and to educate the whole child in a caring, exciting and challenging community. The educational programme is broad, with equal importance attached to developing the intellectual, social, cultural, physical and spiritual faculties of each pupil. The academic results are excellent and this is achieved by employing well qualified, dedicated, caring Staff who teach in small, well resourced classes averaging 14 children. English and Maths are set throughout the school. Latin is taught to all children from Year 5. In Year 8 there is a special form to prepare pupils for 13+ scholarship examinations to Senior Schools. The majority of children leave after sitting their 13+ Common Entrance or Scholarship examinations to such schools as: Bryanston, Canford, Dauntsey's, Eton, Sherborne Boys and Girls, Marlborough, Millfield, St Swithun's and Winchester. Girls are also prepared for specific entry requirements to girls' schools.

There is a strong boarding ethos within the School with particular attention paid to weekends for which a varied and exciting programme is prepared each week. Facilities such as riding, sailing, computing, art and woodwork are available during the weekend. Full, weekly and flexi boarding are on offer to suit the needs of individual families. There are three boarding houses: the Lodge has boys and girls aged 7 to 10; Main House has boys aged 11 to 13, and the Clockhouse has girls aged 11 to 13. There is a strong boarding care team consisting of Houseparents, Assistant Houseparents and Matrons. The day children enjoy a full, all inclusive programme.

Hordle Walhampton aims to prepare each child for the demands and challenges of twenty-first century life by providing opportunities to grow in self-confidence, Christian standards and responsibilities and consideration for others. When children leave Hordle Walhampton it is hoped that they will be articulate, confident, self-motivated, considerate, generous and determined to give of their best to any enterprise with which they are involved.

Charitable status. Hordle Walhampton School Trust Limited is a Registered Charity, number 307330. It exists to provide high quality boarding and day education for boys and girls aged 2–13 years.

Hornsby House School

Hearnville Road, London SW12 8RS
Tel: 020 8673 7573
Fax: 020 8673 6722

e-mail: school@hornsby-house.co.uk
website: www.hornsby-house.co.uk

Chairman of Governors: Mr Charles Gotto

Headmaster: **Mr Jon Gray**, BA Ed Hons

Age Range. 4–11.
Number of Pupils. 184 Girls, 173 Boys.
Fees per term (2010-2011). £3,710 (Reception to Year 2), £3,980 (Years 3 to 6). Lunch included.

Hornsby House School was founded in 1988 by Professor Hornsby, with twenty children in a church hall in Clapham. It now comprises approximately 350 boys and girls and is sited in an Edwardian primary school enhanced by two new buildings. Hornsby House shares a local sports field with other local schools and plays football, rugby, cricket, netball and rounders.

Entry into Reception classes is unassessed and is on a first-come, first-served basis with priority being given to siblings.

A well-qualified teaching staff is supported by teaching assistants. The curriculum is based on the National Curriculum with emphasis on sport, music, art and drama. There is a wide variety of extra-curricular activities and an After School Care Club.

The school is very well resourced with new buildings providing specialist rooms for Art, Music, Science and a state-of-the-art ICT suite. Some teaching is done using interactive whiteboards. A well-stocked library provides a wide range of reference books and Internet access. Instrumentalists can join the orchestra, brass or flute ensembles and there are three choirs. Visits to theatres, museums and other places of interest all serve to broaden the curriculum.

To arrange a visit to see the children at work, please contact the Registrar.

Charitable status. Hornsby House Educational Trust is a Registered Charity, number 800284.

Horris Hill

Newtown, Newbury, Berks RG20 9DJ
Tel: 01635 40594
Fax: 01635 39586
e-mail: enquiries@horrishill.com
website: www.horrishill.com

Chairman of Governors: C J Ball, Esq

Headmaster: **G F Tollit**, BA Hons

Deputy Headmaster: F J Beardmore-Gray, BA Hons, PGCE

Age Range. 7–13.
Number of Boys. Boarders 100, Day 15.
Fees per term (2011-2012). Boarders: £7,250; Day £5,250. (No compulsory Extras.)

Horris Hill is one of the leading boys' prep schools in the UK. 115 boys live in the most spectacular grounds just south of Newbury; most are boarders, but we enjoy having our few dayboys. Small means that we know the boys and their parents very well and our latest Inspection Reports (see www.horrishill.com) emphasise the fact that pastoral care is outstanding. High expectations in everything ensure a first-class prep school education with confident, charming boys going on to the top independent schools. Most Horris Hill parents choose boys-only schools for the next stage and over half our boys go on to Winchester, Radley and Eton; the remainder going to Sherborne, Harrow, Milton Abbey, Shrewsbury, Bradfield, Marlborough and many others.

Busy weekends, high academic standards, superb music and art, brilliant sport make this a wonderful school to work in for both staff and boys. Come and see for yourselves.

Charitable status. Horris Hill Preparatory School Trust Limited is a Registered Charity, number 307331. It exists to prepare boys for the Senior Independent Schools.

Hunter Hall School

Frenchfield, Penrith, Cumbria CA11 8UA
Tel: 01768 891291
Fax: 01768 899161
e-mail: office@hunterhall.cumbria.sch.uk
website: www.hunterhall.co.uk

Chairman of Governors: Mr Tim Evans

Headmaster: **Dr F A Winzor**, BMet, PhD

Age Range. 3–11 co-educational.
Number of Pupils. 140.
Fees per term (2010-2011). £2,122.

Hunter Hall School has grown rapidly from its inception 24 years ago into a thriving and vibrant community, providing high quality education for children aged 3 to 11. Its location is idyllic, in imaginatively converted farm buildings on the outskirts of Penrith and only 2 km from the M6, providing easy access to the attractions of the Lake District and the north of England generally.

It is providing a range of experience that is important at Hunter Hall, and Staff recognise that effective learning can take place in a variety of situations. Within the classroom, creativity is emphasised, and the objective is to provide the children with the knowledge, skills and confidence to prosper, not only whilst at Hunter Hall, but also in the schools that they will subsequently join. In the Foundation Stage, the activities that are undertaken by the children, originating from their own interests and needs, then facilitated by the Staff. The aim is to stimulate curiosity, interest and excitement in learning, and to encourage self-discipline and develop confidence. These qualities extend as the children move through the school, with the emphasis on providing them with a range of skills to help them to recognise that they have the ability (and courage) to think. In addition, perseverance and co-operation are especially valued, creating a warm, friendly and almost tangible sense of community within the school.

The curriculum is broad, and specialist subject teaching is provided in Year 3 and above. Class numbers never exceed 20. Teaching facilities are very good, with ICT featuring prominently in learning. Pupils are encouraged to take responsibility for their own progress and to set themselves challenging targets.

Children at Hunter Hall spend a great deal of time outdoors and, indeed, beyond the school boundaries. The environment in the local area lends itself admirably to geographical and historical investigation, as well as providing an unrivalled stage for exploration and adventure. Participation in art, drama and music is extremely active, with extensive representation at local festivals. The variety and quality of sport that is on offer is equally remarkable, and Hunter Hall children have received wide-ranging recognition at local and even national level in recent years.

This is a happy school, in which a Christian ethos is present, but never over-dominant. Children (and their parents) and Staff enjoy spending time here and contributing to the development of the community.

Charitable status. Hunter Hall School Ltd is a Registered Charity, number 1059098.

Hurlingham School

122 Putney Bridge Road, Putney, London SW15 2NQ
Tel:　020 8874 7186
Fax:　020 8875 0372
e-mail:　office@hurlinghamschool.co.uk
website:　www.hurlinghamschool.co.uk

Headmaster: **Mr Jonathan Brough**, BEd Hons Cantab, NPQH

Age Range. 4–11 Co-educational.
Number of Pupils. 320.
Fees per term (2011-2012). £3,930–£4,160.
Location and Facilities. Hurlingham is a non-selective independent preparatory school in Putney, in very close proximity to Wandsworth Park. The modern and spacious building provides excellent facilities which include bright classrooms, a large gym and a dance and drama studio, as well as a science laboratory, art studio, ICT suite and several music rooms. Recreational space includes a large playground with climbing wall and a nature garden.

Ethos. The School's ethos is to provide a happy, secure atmosphere in which children flourish both academically and personally. Experienced and enthusiastic teachers provide opportunities for the children that strongly promote creativity and independence of thought, essential attributes for a child growing up in the 21st Century. Self-confidence, self-discipline, self-motivation, self-esteem and above all a thirst and enjoyment for learning are nurtured.

Academic. The curriculum is broad, with the aim of providing a balanced and rounded education in which every child is treated as an individual and is encouraged to make the most of their particular talents. The important skills of reading, writing and numeracy are given a high priority in everyday teaching; these are delivered through many exciting cross-curricular topics which bring the children's learning alive and allow them to make sense of the world around them. All children learn French from Reception onwards and Latin once they reach Form IV; pottery and philosophy are also greatly enjoyed across the school.

Sport. Hurlingham children are fit and healthy, and all boys and girls participate enthusiastically. Seasonal team games skills are taught in football, rugby, hockey, netball, cricket, rounders, gym and athletics. Numerous matches are organised with other local schools throughout the sporting year. Every Summer Term the whole school joins in the traditional Sports Day activities, and a family picnic lunch.

Music. Hurlingham has an excellent music department. The youngest children are encouraged to sing, play simple instruments and enjoy performing. For older pupils there are many opportunities to learn individual instruments, play in ensembles and participate in music concerts. There are two, very popular and talented, choirs.

Pastoral Care. Strong pastoral care is a very important feature of life at Hurlingham. All staff foster an intimate and welcoming environment centred on family values, with a clear focus on good manners and respect for one another. The House System, School Council and various pupil committees provide the children with wonderful opportunities to support each other and express their views about their own school.

Clubs. Children are encouraged to participate in a wide range of clubs which include: art, ballet, chess, drama, Japanese, karate, music, modern dance, pottery and science. Older children are able to do their homework in school at homework club.

Starting Out. Children begin their life at Hurlingham in our Early Years Department which, although contained within the school building, is a separate area allowing children to feel part of the whole school but not overwhelmed by it. The three parallel classrooms (divided according to the children's age) all have direct access on to the playground, thus enabling the teaching of the curriculum to extend outside. There is also a cosy Early Years Hall which provides space for all three forms to join together for group activities, regular access to computers and a quiet place for reading.

Entry. For entry to Reception there is no entrance test or interview. Places are offered in order of registration, although siblings, and those living within 1.2 km of the school, are given priority. Older children are invited to spend a day at Hurlingham and take part in lessons in order to assess their academic ability. Scholarships are available for children joining from 7+ onwards.

School Visits. Appointments should be arranged with the School Office. There is an underground car park which visitors are welcome to use.

Hurstpierpoint College Preparatory School
A Woodard School

Hurstpierpoint, West Sussex BN6 9JS
Tel:　　01273 834975 (Prep)
　　　　01273 835821 (Pre-Prep)
Fax:　　01273 836900
e-mail:　prepregistrar@hppc.co.uk
　　　　pre-prep.registrar@hppc.co.uk
website:　www.hppc.co.uk

Chairman of Governors: Rear-Admiral S Moore, CB

Head of Preparatory School: **Mrs H J Beeby**, BH, MA

Head of Pre-Prep: Mrs K M Finnegan, BEd

Age Range. 4–13 Co-educational.
Number of Pupils. Prep 261; Pre-Prep 81.
Fees per term (2011-2012). Prep: Years 7–8 £4,495, Years 4–6 £4,370, Year 3 £3,800. Occasional Boarding: £32.50 per night. Pre-Prep: £2,245–£2,415. There are no compulsory extras.

The Prep and Pre-Prep Schools of Hurstpierpoint College (*see entry in HMC section*) share a beautiful 140-acre campus with the College. Although both Schools operate independently of the Senior School, having their own timetable, staff, buildings and Heads, the schools work closely together to offer a first-class programme of education for boys and girls from the age of 4 to 18.

Hurst's Pre-Prep School for children aged 4–7 opened in 2001. It occupies a self-contained unit with reception area and well-equipped classrooms, with its own extensive, fenced hard and grass play areas. There are two classes in each year group.

The Prep School has joint use of many of the College's superb facilities (including 25m indoor swimming pool, fully-equipped modern CDT centre, theatre, drama and dance studios, music school, large sports hall, full-size Astroturf hockey pitch, tennis courts and squash courts). A new 15-classroom extension to the College teaching block in 2009 provided new accommodation for Prep School Years 7 and 8 along with the Senior School. New science laboratories for both schools open in 2011–12.

The aim of the schools is to provide an outstanding education in a secure and happy environment. The staff's overriding priority is to guide and inspire young people to develop their potential to the full, striving for the highest possible standards in the classroom, on the sports field, in the creative and performing arts and in a wide range of skills and activities.

The Prep School has a 5-day academic week and a Saturday afternoon match programme runs throughout the school year.

The academic programme is based around key assessment points in the Lent and Summer Terms of both Years 7 and 8 and pupils are set in as many subjects as possible. This provides a strong foundation for the GCSE programme which children begin when they enter the Senior School.

The Sports programme is extensive: Football, Netball, Rounders, Rugby, Cricket, Hockey, Squash, Swimming, Tennis, Basketball and Athletics. In addition there is a wide-ranging activity programme in place every day which caters for the interests of all pupils.

The Music, Drama and Dance Departments are also very strong; about half the pupils learn musical instruments. The Preparatory School choir performs at the weekly Chapel service. There are at least three musicals or plays each year involving many children throughout the School.

There is always one qualified person on the school site with responsibility for first aid. Prep School children are initially assessed in the School and staff will refer children to the College Medical Centre as necessary.

Each year a number of Awards are available: Academic and Sports awards are awarded at 11+ and Music awards are available at any stage. Awards may continue through to the Senior School.

Charitable status. Hurstpierpoint College is a Registered Charity, number 1076498. The College provides a Christian education to boys and girls between the ages of four and eighteen.

Ilford Ursuline Preparatory School

2–4 Coventry Road, Ilford, Essex IG1 4QR
Tel: 020 8518 4050
Fax: 020 8518 2060
e-mail: hroddy@ilfordursuline-prep.redbridge.sch.uk
website: www.ilfordursuline-prep.org.uk

Chair of Governors: Sister Anne Benyon OSU

Acting Head: **Mrs Joanne Walker**

Age Range. 3–11 Co-educational.
Number of Pupils. 245.
Fees per term (2011-2012). Nursery: £145 per week full-time inc lunch; £52 per week part-time inc lunch. Reception–Year 6 £2,500 inc lunch.

The Ilford Ursuline Preparatory School is a Roman Catholic day school in the trusteeship of the Ursuline Sisters. The Ursuline Sisters first came to England in 1862 settling at Forest Gate from where they established the school in Ilford in 1903 at 73, Cranbrook Road. The school has since flourished. Formerly part of the Ilford Ursuline High School, the Ilford Ursuline Preparatory School is now a fully independent school in its own right but continues to share close and valued links with the High School.

As a Catholic School we firmly believe that Religious Education is the foundation of the entire educational process. Prayers and liturgical celebrations are an important aspect of school life, unifying the hearts and minds of all associated with the school and ensuring we are all working to achieve the best possible education for the children in our care.

We provide a safe, secure and stimulating environment for our pupils to thrive. We recognise each child's unique value and are committed to encouraging self-esteem and developing each child's potential. We encourage the children to become independent learners by building on their curiosity and desire to learn and developing their skills, concepts and understanding.

While the school continues to set its own high standards, we complement these with the integration of the best of the National Curriculum. English, Mathematics, and Science form the core subjects together with History, Geography, French, Religious Education, Information Communication

Technology, Physical Education, Drama Art, Music and stimulating project work. The Performing Arts have a high profile in school and the children are regularly given the opportunity to develop their talents. Well-stocked libraries, audio-visual aids and a state-of-the-art specialist Information Communication Technology department are all available throughout the nursery and school.

We offer a wide range of extra-curricular activities including Sports, Ballet, Elocution and Choral Speaking, Irish Dancing, ICT, Chess and Latin. Individual instrumental tuition can be arranged for piano, violin, flute, clarinet and saxophone. There is a school choir and an orchestra.

All teaching staff are fully qualified, experienced and dedicated to the ideals of the school. They work in close partnership with parents to ensure that each child's special individual needs are recognised. In addition, we have the help of experienced general assistants. Our pupil:teacher ratio is excellent and we are able to engage in small group teaching.

Pre and after school care and a holiday club are available. A variety of structured activities is planned for the children enrolled and refreshments are provided.

Charitable status. The Ilford Ursuline Preparatory School is a Registered Charity, number 245661.

Inglefield House
Haberdashers' Monmouth School for Girls Preparatory School

Hereford Road, Monmouth NP25 5XT
Tel: 01600 711205
           01600 711104 (Admissions)
Fax: 01600 711118 (Admissions)
e-mail: admissions@hmsg.co.uk
website: www.habs-monmouth.org

A love of learning and an inquisitive, enthusiastic attitude to life are the cornerstones of our ethos, producing independent, confident girls who also have a very strong sense of responsibility and consideration of others. Girls at Inglefield House are happy and fulfilled, with a sense of fun and a sense of purpose.

Chairman of Governors: Mr J B S Swallow, MA, FCA

Head: **Mrs S Riley**, BSc Hons Swansea, PGCE Bristol

Age Range. Girls 7–11.
Number of Pupils. 124.
Fees per term (2011-2012). Day £3,142, Boarding £6,593.

Entrance to Inglefield House is selective, but great care is taken to look for potential, not just test performance.

A broad but balanced curriculum captures the imagination and allows girls to thrive in a variety of disciplines. Class-based teaching offers the core subjects of English, maths and science, supplemented by humanities, art, physical education, modern foreign languages, latin, music and drama. Specialist teachers in French, science, physical education and music ensure girls receive the finest tuition, while they are also able to make full use of the senior school facilities.

With encouragement and a high degree of personal attention, girls are given every opportunity to maximise their potential and achieve academic excellence. This forms just part of a school life which is vibrant, exciting and outward looking. Our location in the Wye Valley allows us to make educational trips to both Cardiff and Bristol with ease, as well as going further afield and organising residential trips which are highly effective in broadening horizons and increasing a sense of independence as girls move into Years 5 and 6.

The performing arts are a wonderful method of building self-confidence in the young girls at school. Individual music lessons, the school orchestra, choir and string sections offer a chance to flourish at music, while dance is taught both as part of PE and in extra-curricular dance clubs at lunchtime.

Bringing enjoyment and enthusiasm to sport is another of our central aims. Sport plays a big part in school life, with specialist PE teaching and a number of extra-curricular clubs every week. We look to nurture a love of team sports and to balance this with other activities which the girls can continue to enjoy into their adult lives.

There is a relaxed, warm relationship between children and staff, whether boarders or day girls. Boarding creates a real sense of community throughout Inglefield, where girls thrive in a safe, friendly environment which produces thoughtful, intelligent, compassionate girls who are well equipped for senior school life.

A high number of scholarships are awarded each year to girls moving on to the senior school. (*For further details see Haberdashers' Monmouth School for Girls entry in the GSA section.*)

Charitable status. William Jones's Schools Foundation is a Registered Charity, number 525616.

Ipswich Preparatory School

3 Ivry Street, Ipswich, Suffolk IP1 3QW
Tel: 01473 281302
Fax: 01473 400067
e-mail: prepregistrar@ipswich.suffolk.sch.uk
website: www.ipswich.suffolk.sch.uk

Chairman of Governors: Mr K Daniels, ACII, FPMI

Headteacher: **Mrs A H Childs**, BA QTS, PGC PSE, DipEd, MA

Age Range. 3–11.
Number of Pupils. 310.
Fees per term (2011–2012). Years 3–6 £3,067, Reception–Year 2 £2,786, Nursery £22.95 (per session).

The Preparatory School has its own staff and Head-teacher. It is located just across the road from the senior school (*see Ipswich School entry in HMC section*).

The school seeks to provide a learning environment which allows pupils to develop skills and personal qualities. The curriculum is planned to encourage the children to develop lively, enquiring minds and appropriate emphasis is placed on securing for each child a firm foundation of skills in literacy and numeracy. The broad, balanced curriculum offered provides a breadth of experience which is suitable for children of primary age. High academic standards are reached by the pupils, but in addition, they are encouraged to develop skills in music, art, drama and sport.

Children's happiness is considered essential and the School works closely with parents to ensure a partnership which provides the best possible care for all girls and boys.

The school enjoys the advantage of sharing Senior School facilities such as playing fields, sports hall, swimming pool, theatre/concert hall and the Chapel. The Prep School has its own Art, Design Technology, ICT and Science facilities.

Charitable status. Ipswich Preparatory School is part of Ipswich School, which is a Registered Charity, number 310493. It exists for the purpose of educating children.

James Allen's Preparatory School

East Dulwich Grove, London SE22 8TE
Tel: 020 8693 0374
Fax: 020 8693 8031

e-mail: japsadmissions@jags.org.uk
website: www.jags.org.uk/japs

Chair of Governors: Mrs Mary Francis, CBE, LVO, MA

Head: **Miss Finola Stack**, BA Hons, PGCE, Mont Dip

Age Range. Girls 4–11.
Number of Pupils. Day: 296 Girls (plus 31 Boys in Pre-Prep).
Fees per term (2010–2011). £3,824.

James Allen's Preparatory School (JAPS) is an independent day school for girls aged between 4 and 11.

We do not see primary education as being merely preparatory to secondary requirements but want the children to go forward at their own pace, benefiting from working together in small groups. With a well-devised and wide curriculum, the children reach high standards without the stress of blatant competition and are able to enjoy the many and varied facilities which we offer, particularly in sport, drama, music and art.

The school has an excellent staff/pupil ratio of approximately 1:10 and provides specialist teachers in Art, DT, ICT, Music, PE and Science. In French the children are taught from 4 years onwards using the immersion method.

The Pre-Prep School (for pupils aged 4–6) is housed in a beautiful Edwardian building. The Middle School (for pupils aged 7–11) is a large, modern building with a first-class Hall and Library, as well as specialist rooms for Science, ICT, DT and Art. Some facilities (the theatre, swimming pool and games fields) are shared with our senior school, James Allen's Girls' School.

JASSPA is the James Allen's Saturday School for the Performing Arts for pupils and siblings and other non-JAPS pupils. This is entirely voluntary and complements the week's activities: music lessons, dance and drama are all offered.

Pupils normally enter the school in the year in which they are 4 or 7 on 1 September. Assessments take place the preceding January. 36 places are available for 4+ entry and up to 20 places available for 7+ entry. At 11, girls normally progress to JAGS by means of an open competitive examination, where JAPS girls regularly win many scholarships. (*See JAGS entry in GSA section.*)

Charitable status. James Allen's Girls' School is a Registered Charity, number 1124853. The purpose of the charity is the conduct at Dulwich of a day school in which there shall be provided a practical, liberal and religious education for girls.

Keble School

Wades Hill, Winchmore Hill, London N21 1BG
Tel: 020 8360 3359
Fax: 020 8360 4000
e-mail: office@kebleprep.co.uk
website: www.kebleprep.co.uk

Chairman of the Board of Governors: Mrs R Davie

Headmaster: **G P McCarthy**

Age Range. 4–13.
Number of Boys. 220 Day Boys.
Fees per term (2011–2012). £3,270–£4,060.

As confirmed by the ISI Inspectors in September 2008, the warm and friendly atmosphere that exists at Keble ensures that the boys are well-motivated, keen to learn and able to mature at their own pace. Strong pastoral care is regarded as a key element in the boys' overall development and well-being, along with the encouragement of courteous and considerate behaviour.

The academic staff comprises 23 qualified graduate teachers, 5 classroom assistants and 2 Learning Support teachers. The buildings are well maintained and facilities are regularly updated. The school has an ambitious ICT development programme.

The average class size in the school is 15, although many classes are taught in half-groups and sets as the boys progress through the school. Boys follow the Foundation Stage in Reception. General subject teachers cover the academic curriculum in Years 1 to 4, with subject specialists following on from Year 5 onwards. The National Curriculum is used as a guide to curriculum development. Art, Music, PE, ICT, PSHE and Games are introduced at appropriate stages and are included within the timetable. Boys are encouraged to learn a musical instrument, sing in the choir, perform in plays and concerts, and play an active part in the wide range of sports on offer.

Football, rugby and cricket are the major team games. Further opportunities exist to participate in hockey, swimming, basketball, athletics, cross-country and tennis. There is a wide range of lunchtime and after-school activities and clubs, including drama, gardening and chess. There are also numerous educational outings and four residential trips.

Boys are not required to pass an assessment to gain entry into the school at Reception. Boys wishing to join the school at a later stage in Year 1 or above are assessed in order to ensure that they will fit comfortably into their new surroundings.

Boys are prepared for entry to senior independent schools through Common Entrance and Scholarship examinations at 13+. The school has a strong record of success in placing boys in the senior school which is right for them. In recent years, these schools include Aldenham, City of London, Haberdashers' Aske's, Highgate, Haileybury, Mill Hill, St Albans, St Columba's, University College and Westminster.

Charitable status. Keble Preparatory School (1968) Limited is a Registered Charity, number 312979. It exists to provide education for boys.

Kelly College Preparatory School

Hazeldon, Parkwood Road, Tavistock, Devon PL19 0JS
Tel: 01822 612919
Fax: 01822 612919
e-mail: admin@kellycollegeprep.com
website: www.kellycollegeprep.com

"Relationships between staff and pupils are outstanding and underpin the high quality of care, guidance and the personal development of pupils." ISI Inspection Report 2009.

Chairman of Governors: Mr D R Milford

Headmaster: **Mr M Foale**, BEd Hons, MSc

Age Range. 3–11.
Number of Pupils. 155.
Fees per term (2011-2012). Day: £1,995–£2,810 (lunch inclusive).

A well-established, co-educational day and boarding school for children from 3–11 years, Kelly College Preparatory School is situated in a beautiful rural setting on the western edge of Dartmoor National Park. It is half a mile from Kelly College and the market town of Tavistock.

The school's reputation is built on a friendly, family atmosphere with high standards. It is a happy and adventurous place, where the ethos is child-centred in an environment conducive to learning. Flexi, weekly and full boarding are available from the age of 8 years. Pupils are prepared for 11+ entry, including scholarship preparation, to a wide variety of Independent and State Secondary Schools. The majority move on to Kelly College or the local Grammar Schools.

The school is proud of its academic success. The curriculum is broad and varied, with subjects taught by specialist teachers from Year 4. French and swimming are timetabled weekly from Year 2.

Facilities include a new teaching block, two libraries, and separate Art/Design Technology, Music and French rooms. The school has extended its ICT provision, installing touch screen whiteboards and enlarging the ICT suite.

It has excellent sporting facilities both on site and at Kelly College, with access to their Astroturf, 25m indoor swimming pool and Adventure Centre. An extensive variety of sports and extra-curricular activities are on offer to pupils throughout the year and at times during the school holidays. These include horse riding, chess, art, dance and cookery. Individual music tuition is available. Residential trips are also organised for older pupils.

There is an active Parents' Association that organises numerous social and fundraising events throughout the year.

Further details and a prospectus are available from the School Secretary.

Charitable status. Kelly College Trust is a Registered Charity, number 306/716. It exists to provide education for boys and girls.

Kensington Prep School
GDST

596 Fulham Road, London SW6 5PA
Tel: 020 7731 9300
Fax: 020 7731 9301
e-mail: enquiries@kenprep.gdst.net
website: www.kensingtonprep.gdst.net

Founded in 1873.

Kensington Prep School is part of the GDST (Girls' Day School Trust). The GDST is the leading network of independent girls' schools in the UK. As a charity that owns and runs 24 schools and two academies, it reinvests all its income in its schools. For further information about the Trust, see p. xxi or visit www.gdst.net.

A more detailed prospectus may be obtained from the school or on the school's website.

Head: **Mrs P J F Lynch**, MA, PGCE

Age Range. 4–11 years.
Number of Girls. 280.
Fees per term (2011-2012). £4,061.

Since 1997 the School has been based in Fulham. The school is set in an acre of grounds and has large bright classrooms, a state-of-the-art hall/gymnasium, a beautiful library and specialist rooms for ICT, Art, Drama, Music, Science and Design Technology. The large playground provides fantastic play facilities, netball and tennis courts and a pond for environmental studies.

The school aims to provide an excellent, broadly-based but strongly academic curriculum. Independence, individuality and questioning thinkers are encouraged and the girls enjoy challenging and interesting work in a stimulating and caring environment, whilst being prepared for entry to leading boarding and day schools at 11+.

The School was named 'Independent Prep School of the Year' by the Sunday Times Parent Power for 2009-10 in recognition of its "consistently strong academic results, inspiring leadership and innovative curriculum".

Entry to the School is selective and the main entry points are at 4+ with a small intake at 7+. Occasional places do occur throughout the School from time to time.

Charitable status. Kensington Prep School is part of The Girls' Day School Trust, which is a Registered Charity, number 306983.

Kent College Nursery, Infant & Junior School

Vernon Holme, Harbledown, Canterbury, Kent
CT2 9AQ
Tel: 01227 762436
Fax: 01227 763880
e-mail: prepenquiries@kentcollege.co.uk
website: www.kentcollege.com

Chairman of Governors: D Shipton, CertEd Oxon, Dip
  MathsEd, Mathematical Assoc (*OC*)

Head Master: **A J Carter**, BEd Hons

(Full staff list can be found on the Kent College website.)

Age Range. 3–11 Co-educational.
Number of Pupils. Juniors (Day and Boarding) 116,
Infants 52, Nursery 20.
Fees per term (2011-2012). Juniors: Boarders £6,755
Day Pupils (including lunch): £4,468 (Years 4–6), £4,056
(Year 3). Infants: £3,144 (Years 1–2), £2,920 (Reception).
Nursery: £2,375 (5 full days).

The school is fully co-educational offering a broad, yet
balanced, curriculum appropriate to the educational and pastoral needs of the children in a happy atmosphere. Lessons
take place in bright, stimulating classrooms with specialist
rooms for science, ICT, drama, sports, music, art and design
technology.

Nursery pupils are admitted at age 3 and infants at the age
of 5 or, when appropriate, before their fifth birthday. There
is a further entry of juniors at age 7 (and at other ages if
there are vacancies). Children are prepared for entry to the
senior school (*see entry in HMC section*) to which many go
at the age of 11. In the process they are taught to think for
themselves and are given plenty of activity time to develop
their own interests within a structured environment that
encourages and develops community awareness and social
skills.

There is a small, comfortable boarding house within the
main building which can accommodate full and weekly
boarders as well as offering the opportunity for occasional
boarding to suit the needs of busy families. The school is
open between 7.45 am and 6.00 pm each day to allow parents to drop off early or collect late as required.

The school has a Dyslexia Unit which is designed to give
special support to children who experience this problem
whilst enabling them to integrate as fully as possible into the
normal school programme. The school offers an extended
day and weekend activity programme that is optional.

The 12 acres of ground were originally laid out by Sidney
Cooper RA. These idyllic surrounds have been adapted to
provide games fields and a heated swimming pool without
losing the varied character which makes them so suitable for
young children's activities.

Charitable status. Kent College, Canterbury is a Registered Charity, number 307844. The School was founded to
provide education within a supportive Christian environment and is a member of the Methodist Independent
Schools' Group.

Kent College Preparatory School
Pembury

Old Church Road, Pembury, Tunbridge Wells, Kent
TN2 4AX
Tel: 01892 820204
Fax: 01892 820214

e-mail: prepschool@kentcollege.kent.sch.uk
website: www.kent-college.co.uk

Chairman of Governors: Mr E Waterhouse

Headmistress: **Mrs A Lawson**, BEd Hons

Age Range. Girls 3–11.
Number of Girls. 212: 3 Boarders, 209 Day Girls.
Fees per term (2011-2012). Day Girls £2,443–£3,678,
Boarders £6,650. All fees include lunches. There are no
compulsory extras.

The school has its own purpose-built accommodation on
a beautiful 75 acre site, shared with Kent College Pembury
(Senior School), and benefits from facilities such as a 360-
seater state-of-the-art theatre, large sports hall, indoor
heated swimming pool with small learners pool, activities
hall, dining hall and dance studio.

The school believes that happy, confident children are
successful ones and the girls love coming to school. Academic standards are high, but it is never forgotten that there
is more to childhood and learning than examinations. Girls
are successfully prepared in small classes (average 16) for a
wide range of senior schools at age 11, but the school is not
a crammer.

The curriculum is broad and balanced, based on the
National Curriculum. All pupils benefit from specialist
teaching in swimming, dance, drama, ICT, PE and music,
with specialist French teaching from Nursery class.

Main intakes are in to the Early Years Department which
incorporates the Nursery and Reception classes for girls
aged 3–5. The department has its own wing of the School
with light, colourful and well-resourced classrooms and its
own outside playground areas. The Foundation Stage Curriculum is followed and by the end of the Reception year
some of the pupils will be working at the lower stages of Key
Stage One.

Performing arts is an important part of the curriculum
with opportunities for music, drama and dance at all ages.
Even the youngest pupils, aged 3, can do optional ballet lessons. The school has a choir and an orchestra and there are
regular concerts and drama productions. There is a good
range of sporting opportunities including The Kent College
Gymnastics Academy, netball, hockey, tennis, rounders,
cross-country, swimming, trampolining and athletics.

The school prides itself on providing an exciting and varied programme of over 35 clubs and activities and there is a
good ethos of participation. The curriculum is supported
with interesting trips and days out, and residential holidays
for Years 5 and 6. A variety of well-known authors have visited the school to run workshops.

An After School Care facility is available for girls in
Nursery upwards. Full and weekly boarders are accepted
from age 10, with flexi-boarders accepted from age 8. All
are part of a small, family-run Junior boarding house in
which girls have a secure, happy and homely environment.
Prospective boarders are invited to spend a day and overnight stay with us to give them a feel for the school. There is
a 20% discount for Forces' families.

Entry to Nursery, Reception, Years 1 and 2 are based on
availability of places. Pupils in Years 3–6 are required to sit
entry tests in English and mathematics. The Headmistress is
pleased to welcome visitors and to show them around the
school.

Charitable status. Kent College Pembury is a Registered
Charity, number 307920. It is a Christian school specialising
in girls' education.

Kew College

24–26 Cumberland Road, Kew, Surrey TW9 3HQ
Tel: 020 8940 2039
Fax: 020 8332 9945

e-mail: enquiries@kewcollege.com
website: www.kewcollege.com

Chairman of Governors: Mrs Karen Wyatt

Headteacher: **Mrs Anne Dobell**, MA Oxon, PGCE

Age Range. 3–11 Co-educational.
Number of Pupils. 277.
Fees per term (2011-2012). £1,770–£2,770.

Kew College was established in 1953 and was made into a charitable trust in 1985 by its founder, Elizabeth Hamilton-Spry, to ensure the long-term continuity of the school. The school's ethos is to ensure all pupils have an excellent grounding in the basics, but with a strong emphasis on areas such as art, music, drama and sport to develop the whole child.

Kew College's style is described as traditional, yet imaginative and the atmosphere is happy and lively with a team of enthusiastic, caring and dedicated staff to help fulfil each child's potential. Pupils enjoy excellent facilities including specialist ICT and science labs. The ISI inspection in October 2010 concluded that '*Pupils achieve well across the curriculum and extra-curricular activities, and standards are exceptionally high in all aspects of English and Mathematics. The quality of their reading, writing and mathematical skills is in advance of their years. Pupils also exhibit great creativity, particularly in art work. Pupils display enthusiasm for their lessons and good learning skills. Pupils' personal development and the school's arrangements for welfare, health and safety are outstanding. Pupils develop into exceptionally moral beings. Pupils leave the school as well-balanced personalities. The school is a caring community where pupils are thoughtfully and skilfully looked after by the pastoral care of the whole staff, which contributes strongly to their personal development.*' In the Early Years Foundation Stage the inspectors commented that '*Children are happy and secure and their needs are met well. Careful attention is given to children's welfare and safety; their exemplary behaviour and excellent personal development are strengths.*'

Beyond the core curriculum pupils enjoy participating in lively mixed-year clubs within school on Friday afternoons including graphic design, origami, Sudoku and table tennis. A wide range of weekly after-school clubs includes chess, computer, debating, fencing, German and jazz dance, with arts and crafts and little golfers for the younger pupils. There is also a school choir, wind band and string orchestra. The school takes full advantage of its London location for educational visits. There are residential field trips in Year 5 and Year 6. In their final term, Year 6 pupils enjoy a week-long stay at a chateau in France improving their language skills, cultural knowledge and doing outward bound team activities.

At 11+ pupils not only achieve places through competitive entrance examinations to selective London day schools but also win a good number of awards.

Charitable status. Kew College is a Registered Charity, number 286059.

Kew Green Preparatory School

Layton House, Ferry Lane, Kew Green, Richmond, Surrey TW9 3AF
Tel: 020 8948 5999
Fax: 020 8948 4774
e-mail: secretary@kgps.co.uk
website: www.kgps.co.uk

Chairman of Governors: Dr Helen Ireland

Headmaster: **Mr Jeremy Peck**

Age Range. 4–11 Co-educational.
Number of Pupils. 260.
Fees per term (2011-2012). £4,435.

This non-selective school is housed in an attractive building and grounds directly next door to the Royal Botanical Gardens. The front of the school overlooks Kew Green, which is used for games, and the back of the school has a good-sized playground which looks onto the River Thames.

KGPS, in a non-pressurised loving environment, produces excellent academic results, sending its pupils to London's best Independent Senior Schools.

The children are encouraged to use philosophy and ethical thinking throughout the curriculum which includes English, Maths, Science, French, RE, Music, Design & Technology, Games/PE, Computer Studies, Moral & Religious Education and Yoga. All Upper school children attend a Summer Term Residential Week where cross-curricular studies are applied in a non-urban environment.

There are many after-school clubs and sports activities and we have two choirs, an orchestra and rock band. Individual tuition is offered in piano, violin, brass, woodwind, cello, saxophone and singing.

An 8 am to 6 pm All-Day Care service is offered to parents at an extra charge.

The school is noted for its warm, happy atmosphere where parents play a full part in enriching the curriculum and social life. Off-site visits and guest workshops presented by noted visitors are a regular feature of education at Kew Green.

The school is always heavily over-subscribed and registration is recommended on the child's first birthday. A prospectus and registration form may be obtained from the School Secretary.

Kilgraston Preparatory School

Bridge of Earn, Perthshire PH2 9BQ
Tel: 01738 812257
Fax: 01738 813410
e-mail: headoffice@kilgraston.com
website: www.kilgraston.com

Day and Boarding School for Girls (day boys to age 9).

Chairman of Board of Governors: Mr Timothy Hall

Head: **Mrs Kathryn Ebrahim**, BSc Hons, PGCE

Age Range. Girls 2½–13, Boys 2½–9.
Number of Pupils. 120 Girls, 11 Boys.
Fees per term (2011-2012). Day £2,675–£4,350, Boarding £6,350.

Kilgraston Preparatory School and Nursery is the junior school for Kilgraston, a leading boarding and day school for girls in Scotland, and is co-educational up the age of 9 years. Located in its own building, the Preparatory School is surrounded by 54 acres of stunning parkland at Bridge of Earn, three miles from the centre of Perth, 45 minutes from Edinburgh and an hour's drive from Glasgow.

Admission to Kilgraston Preparatory School is by interview. Girls are able to progress into Kilgraston Senior School, or sit Common Entrance or scholarship exams for Kilgraston and other schools. The academic standard is high with all pupils completing the Preparatory School achieving a place in their senior school of choice.

Pupils are taught by class teachers until the age of nine (apart from PE, French, music and drama). Form teachers hold pastoral responsibility for the pupils and classes are small with provision for additional support needs. From age ten, the curriculum becomes more specialised with increasing input from specialised subject staff and use of the facilities in the Senior School. Pastoral care is the responsibility of a tutor. The Nursery too, benefits from senior school facilities such as the swimming pool, games hall, and theatre.

The core academic curriculum is enhanced by a wide range of co-curricular subjects. While academic excellence is a priority, pupils are encouraged to achieve excellence in every aspect of the wider curriculum. Classrooms are well equipped and modern IT facilities are spread throughout the school. Art, drama and music flourish and are an important feature of life at Kilgraston. Opportunities are provided throughout the year for pupils to perform in groups or as soloists and they compete successfully in local festivals. The girls have the opportunity to take LAMDA, Associated Board and Trinity examinations. There is an annual production involving all pupils.

Sports and recreation thrive within the superb Sports Hall, including a climbing wall. In April 2008 the magnificent indoor 25m Swimming Pool complex opened and the grounds incorporate 9 floodlit all-weather courts, playing fields and athletics track. The main sports are: hockey, netball, tennis, rounders, swimming and athletics with fixtures against other preparatory schools. The school has a an excellent skiing record and Kilgraston is the only school in Scotland with an equestrian facility on campus and also hosts the Scottish Schools Equestrian Championships each year at Gleneagles.

Kilgraston Preparatory School has a pastoral House system. Inter-House competitions and challenges in games, music and debating are serious fun. The family atmosphere in the newly refurbished boarding area, Butterstone, is enhanced by the wide range of weekend activities that make use of the superb local facilities and environment of Perthshire.

Charitable status. Kilgraston School Trust is a Registered Charity, number SC029664. It exists to develop a love of learning, a spirit of adventure and openness of heart.

Kimbolton Preparatory School

Kimbolton, Huntingdon, Cambs PE28 0EA
Tel: 01480 860281
Fax: 01480 861874
e-mail: prep@kimbolton.cambs.sch.uk
website: www.kimbolton.cambs.sch.uk

Chair of Governors: C A Paull

Headmaster: **R J Wells**, BEd, BA

Age Range. 4–11 Co-educational.
Number of Children. Approximately 320.
Fees per term (2011–2012). £2,705–£3,440 (including lunch).
Mission Statement. Within a friendly, caring environment, Kimbolton pupils are encouraged to develop the social responsibility and independence of thought to equip them for the challenges of a changing world.

Everyone has talent; the school aims to provide the opportunity for each individual to excel so that success can be celebrated and self-esteem enhanced.

Motto: *Spes Durat Avorum.*

To the west of Kimbolton village the Preparatory School is located within its own attractive grounds linked to the Senior School by means of a pathway, the 'Duchess Walk', the castle once being the home of Catharine of Aragon. It is partially housed in the old Kimbolton Grammar School buildings which date from 1876.

Boys and girls join the Preparatory School at four years of age. A purpose-built building (Aragon House) encompasses Reception, Year One and Year Two (Lower Prep). It is here that the children are educated in a safe, welcoming and happy environment. The younger children also use the facil-

ities on offer throughout the Preparatory School. The children automatically progress to the Upper Prep. The expectation is that the Year Six children progress to the Senior School. (*See entry in HMC section*)

Children may also join the School when places are available after assessment/examination and interview.

There is a programme in place for identified gifted and talented children.

The Preparatory School has, on its own site, a Dining Hall, Library, Computer Suite, Assembly Hall, Changing Rooms, Music Teaching and Practice Rooms, Science Room, Art and Design Technology Room, Sports Hall, Learning Support Unit and large, light and airy classrooms, all of which have recently been refurbished as a part of a rolling programme.

There is a full-time nurse on site.

Reception, Year 1 and Year 2 have two classes per year group and Years 3–6 have three classes. Each class has its own class teacher and there is a good deal of specialist teaching throughout the Upper Prep.

The outdoor facilities including the tennis and netball courts, athletics track, rounders fields, all-weather pitches, football, hockey and cricket pitches provide excellent facilities. The Swimming Pool located at the Senior School is used weekly by the Preparatory School.

The majority of children at KS2 have individual music lessons in addition to curricular class music. There are an extensive number of excursions, including an annual residential skiing excursion and many visitors and speakers visit the school thereby enriching the curriculum. There is an extensive range of extra-curricular activities.

Children may arrive for breakfast at 7.45 am and the Kim Club facility is available after school until 6.00 pm. Supervised Prep and an extensive list of activities and clubs are available after school.

We feel that children are given every opportunity to gain a first class education in a family orientated environment situated in superb surroundings. This allied with strong teaching in small class sizes prepares a child fully for the future.

The Preparatory School was inspected by ISI in 2005 and the Out of School care facility (Kim Club) by Ofsted in 2006.

Charitable status. Kimbolton School Foundation is a Registered Charity, number 1098586.

King Henry VIII Preparatory School

Kenilworth Road, Coventry CV3 6PT
Tel: 024 7627 1307
Fax: 024 7627 1308
e-mail: headmaster@khps.co.uk
website: www.khps.co.uk

Chairman of Governors: Mr Brendan Connor

Headmaster: **Mr Nicholas Lovell**, BA Hons, PGCE

Age Range. 3–11 Co-educational.
Number of Pupils. 500 Day Boys and Girls.
Fees per term (2011–2012). Reception–Year 2 £2,414 (inc lunch); Year 3 £2,467(inc lunch); Years 4–6 £2,313 (exc lunch).

King Henry VIII Preparatory School is part of Coventry School Foundation, which includes King Henry VIII Senior School and Bablake School (3–18).

The School is situated on two campuses a short distance from each other on the south side of Coventry.

The Swallows Campus, opposite Coventry Memorial Park, educates children aged 3–8 in classes of 16 (from Reception onwards). The campus occupies a beautiful 3½ acre site and has a wealth of facilities, including its own Swimming-pool, Sports Hall, Art & Design Centre, All-weather surface and Adventure Playground. Its main building dates to the 17th century. Most teaching is provided by class teachers, giving young children a continuity of approach and providing them with a key individual with whom to build a strong relationship and who will guide them through their daily studies. An increasing number of specialist teachers are provided as children progress through the infant years: Music from age 3, Games and Swimming from age 4 and Art & Design Technology from age 6. There is a strong family atmosphere and the aim is to provide children with a wonderful start to their education.

The Hales Campus is situated just down the road from Swallows and occupies a portion of the main King Henry VIII School site. The main building was purpose-built in 1997 and provides an excellent range of modern facilities for children aged 8–11. From Year 5 at this site children are taught by specialist teachers for all subjects in classes of 20. The Hales Campus has its own Sports Hall, Music Department, Library, Art & Design Room, Science Laboratory and playing areas. Some facilities are shared with the senior school, including Games fields and a 25 metre indoor swimming pool.

The School seeks to help its pupils to be happy, confident 'all-rounders'. Academic standards are high and entrance to the School, from the age of 5, is through academic assessment (ages 5–6) and examination (ages 7–10). Children joining the School at the ages of 3 or 4 are not academically selected and names may be registered from birth. The majority of children continue from King Henry VIII Preparatory School to King Henry VIII Senior School at age 11; however, children may sit entrance to a variety of other schools.

The Arts and Sport are very important aspects within the curriculum. The visual and performance Arts are specialist taught from the infant years. Music is strong, with children being able to learn a wide variety of musical instruments from an early age. Drama and performance are aspects of school life which flourish, with all children taking part in a variety of performances during their time at the School. A large number of performance opportunities are available each year.

Games are taught within the timetable from Reception onwards and competitive matches against other schools start in Year 2. The main sports for boys are Rugby, Football and Cricket; for girls Netball, Hockey and Rounders. Beyond the main team sports, there is a range of other sports that may be experienced, both within the timetable and as extra-curricular activities.

Scholarships are awarded from the age of 8, for academic subjects as well as the Arts and All-Rounder awards. Bursaries are available at entrance from Year 3 onwards (7+).

The School has a vibrant extra-curricular activities programme which may be accessed by pupils from Reception onwards, this includes both lunchtime and after school clubs. Before school care (from 7.45 am) and after school care (up to 6.00 pm) are available daily during term time, as well as voluntary Saturday morning sports. There is a full programme of care for children aged from 3–11, starting at 8.30 am and continuing until 5.30 pm, during every school holiday.

School trips and educational visits are regarded as an important aspect of each child's experience at the School. These include visits to local places of interest, usually associated with programmes of study, but also residential trips for each year group from the age of 7 onwards, one of which will be to the Coventry School Foundation manor house, Le Fousseau, in the Mayenne, France.

The School's motto *Confide Recte Agens* – have the courage to do what is right – lies at the heart of the School's ethos which encourages children to have the courage of their convictions. The School is a member of the Community of the Cross of Nails, thus having an association with Coventry

Cathedral. This stresses tolerance and understanding between people of different creeds and faiths. The School happily accepts children from various faiths and looks to build genuine understanding and tolerance between its pupils.

Overall the School seeks to help its children to be happy, confident people who enjoy learning.

Charitable status. Coventry School Foundation is a Registered Charity, number 528961. Its aim is to advance the education of boys and girls by the provision of a school or schools in or near the City of Coventry.

King's College School

West Road, Cambridge CB3 9DN
Tel: 01223 365814
Fax: 01223 461388
e-mail: office@kcs.cambs.sch.uk
website: www.kcs.cambs.sch.uk

The School is part of King's College and is administered by a Board of Governors.

Chairman of Governors: The Dean of King's College

Headmaster: N J Robinson, BA, PGCE

Deputy Heads:
Mrs K Richardson, BEd Lincoln
P Pillet, MA France

Age Range. Co-educational, age 4–13.
Number of Pupils. 365 day pupils, 35 boy boarders including 16 choristers.
Fees per term (2011-2012). Weekly Boarding: £6,340; Choristers: £2,115; Day Pupils: £4,090; Pre-Prep: £3,170.

The School is administered by Governors appointed by the Council of King's College, parents and teaching staff. King Henry VI's charter founding King's College in 1441 provided for Choristers and their education. In 1878 the School moved to its present site near the University library, across the river from the College. Over the years the facilities have steadily increased. The main house accommodates the catering facilities and boarding accommodation. A new Wiles Centre for Technology opened in June 1999 with first class facilities for ICT and DT. The Performing Arts Centre includes 16 new music rooms (opened in 2001) and a multi-purpose hall used for plays and concerts and also a fully-equipped gym. In 2010 an impressive new music wing was added to the department. A new classroom block called the "Briggs Building" was opened in May 2004 by the Duchess of Kent and it contains two very well equipped science labs, two maths classrooms, three modern language classrooms, two English classrooms and a new library. Sports facilities on site include two large playing fields, tennis courts and a heated outdoor swimming pool. A new floodlit astroturf field was laid in May 2005. Two new squash courts were built in 2010. The School also has the use of other nearby sports fields. The Pre-Prep has been expanded to accommodate two-form entry starting from September 2008.

The Headmaster is assisted by 36 full-time and 10 part-time teachers. There are 4 Matrons and a full-time Bursar and Assistant Bursar. There are 40 full- or part-time music staff. In 1976 girls were admitted as day pupils and the ratio of boys to girls is approximately 50:50 in the junior classes. In September 1981 the School started a small special centre for dyslexic children of good intelligence and there is now an excellent Learning Support Centre; auditory training and music play an important part, the children mix with their peers in normal classes, although some do not study French. Pupils are prepared for the Scholarship and Common Entrance examinations of the boys' and girls' Independent

Senior Schools. The school broadly follows the National Curriculum subjects, but also teaches French from the age of 4, Latin from 9, and Greek to some older children. The School has a tradition of winning numerous academic, art, music and sports awards annually.

Apart from choral and instrumental music (there are 2 orchestras of some 80 players in each and about 40 chamber groups), activities include Drama, Art, Craft, Pottery, Computing, DT, Gymnastics, PE, Chess, Science, RSPB Wildlife Explorers, Handwriting, Library, Model-making. Games include Rugger, Soccer, Hockey, Cricket, Netball, Rounders, Athletics, Tennis, Squash, Cross-Country and Swimming.

Bursaries. King's is pleased to offer a place at the School to a musical child at a Primary School on a means-tested bursary worth up to 100% of the school fees. The place will usually start from Year 3 or Year 4 and continue until the child leaves King's. This would suit a child with musical potential who would benefit from the wide musical provision offered at King's.

Further information about the School may be obtained from the Headmaster. Enquiries concerning Choristerships should also be addressed to him. Choristership Auditions take place annually, usually in October and January.

Charitable status. King's College School is part of King's College Cambridge, which is a Registered Charity, number 1139422. Its aim is to provide an excellent education for girls and boys of mixed ability aged 4 to 13.

King's College Junior School

Wimbledon Common, London SW19 4TT
Tel: 020 8255 5335
Fax: 020 8255 5339
e-mail: jsadmissions@kcs.org.uk
          HMJSsec@kcs.org.uk
website: www.kcs.org.uk

Chairman of the Governing Body:
J M Jarvis, QC, MA

Headmaster: Dr G A Silverlock, BEd Hons, MLitt, PhD

Age Range. 7–13.
Number of Boys. 460 (day boys only).
Fees per term (2011-2012). £4,660 (Years 3–4), £5,260 (Years 5–8).

The Junior School was established in 1912 as an integral part of KCS, to prepare boys for the Senior School. It shares with it a common site and many facilities, in particular the Music School, the Art, Design and Technology School, the Dining Hall, the Sports Hall, the swimming pool and extensive playing fields. For the rest, Junior School boys are housed in their own buildings. The Priory, rebuilt in 1980, contains twenty-three classrooms, including specialist rooms for languages, mathematics, history, geography, information technology and multimedia work. The youngest age groups have their own special accommodation in Rushmere, a spacious Georgian house whose grounds adjoin the Junior School. The School also has its own purpose-built library, science laboratories and well-equipped theatre and assembly hall.

The School is separately administered in matters relating to admission, curriculum, discipline and day to day activities. There are thirty-six members of staff in addition to those teaching in specialist departments common to both Schools.

The work and overall programme are organised in close consultation with the Senior School to ensure that boys are educated in a structured and progressive way from 7 to 18, having the benefit of continuity, while enjoying the range and style of learning that are best suited to their age.

Boys come from both maintained and pre-preparatory schools and are admitted at the age of 7, 8, 9, 10 or 11. Entry is by interview and examination.

Charitable status. King's College School is a Registered Charity, number 310024. It exists to provide education for children.

King's Hall School
A Woodard School

Kingston Road, Taunton, Somerset TA2 8AA
Tel: 01823 285920
Fax: 01823 285922
e-mail: schooloffice@kingshalltaunton.co.uk
website: www.kingshalltaunton.co.uk

Chairman of Governors: Roger Knight Esq, OBE, MA, DipEd

Head: Justin Chippendale, BSc Joint Hons

Age Range. 3–13+ Co-educational.
Number of Pupils. Preparatory (Years 3–8): 140 boys, 125 girls; 45 boarders. Pre-Prep (Nursery–Year 2): 45 boys, 45 girls.
Fees per term (2011-2012). Preparatory Day £2,350–£4,350, Full/Weekly Boarding £4,995–£6,435, Pre-Prep £1,725–£1,825.

King's Hall is set in a beautiful country location surrounded by National Trust farmland yet is only a couple of miles from the centre of Taunton with easy access to the M5 and less than two hours to London by train. It has all the characteristics of a traditional country preparatory school without being overshadowed by a senior school on the same site. This gives the children a pride in their school and visitors invariably comment upon the warmth and friendliness with which they are greeted. It is one of the Woodard Schools whose approach is based on the principles of the Church of England. The academic results are excellent. Sport, outdoor activites, music, art and drama are also strengths. Scholarships are available for pupils with exceptional ability. These are awarded at 11+ and continue at King's College, Taunton up to age 18. Others may join King's Hall through interview and assessment at any age after their third birthday (subject to availabilty of places).

King's Hawford

Worcester WR3 7SD
Tel: 01905 451292
Fax: 01905 756502
e-mail: hawford@ksw.org.uk
website: www.ksw.org.uk

Chairman of the Governors: D T Howell, Esq, BSc(Eng), FCA

Headmaster: J M Turner, BEd Hons, DipEd, ACP

Age Range. 2½–11.
Number of Pupils. 189 Boys, 143 Girls.
Fees per term (2011-2012). £1,913–£3,452.

King's Hawford is a junior school to the historic King's School, Worcester, and is set in thirty acres of parkland situated on the northern outskirts of Worcester. The school is accommodated within an elegant and recently refurbished Georgian house surrounded by well maintained playing fields, with tennis courts, a heated outdoor swimming pool, a multi-purpose sports hall and secure play area for younger children.

There are extensive opportunities for a wide range of extra curricular activities and there is a busy calendar of music, drama, sport, clubs. Sports include Rugby, Association Football, Cricket, Hockey, Netball, Rounders, Athletics, Tennis, Cross-Country and Swimming.

The Pre-Prep department accepts children from rising 3–6 and the Junior department from 7–11.

Charitable status. The King's School Worcester is a Registered Charity, number 1098236. It exists to provide a broad education for a wide range of children from rising 3–11 years.

King's House School

68 King's Road, Richmond, Surrey TW10 6ES
Tel: 020 8940 1878
Fax: 020 8939 2501
e-mail: head@kingshouseschool.org
website: www.kingshouseschool.org

The School was constituted an Educational Trust with a Board of Governors in September 1957.

Chairman of the Governors: Mr Simon Readhead

Head: **M Turner**, BA, PGCE, NPQH

Age Range. 3–13.
Number of Pupils. Senior Department 218 boys; Junior Department 176 boys; Nursery 54 boys and girls.
Fees per term (2010-2011). Reception and Year 1: £3,025; Years 2 and 3: £3,550; Senior Department £4,085 (all fees inclusive of lunch). Contact school for details of Nursery fees.

King's House is a Day Preparatory School for boys aged 4–13 on two sites in King's Road and boys and girls in its Nursery. Boys are prepared for entry by Scholarship or Common Entrance to all independent schools.

The School aims to provide a broad, balanced curriculum in a caring environment.

Charitable status. Kings House School Trust (Richmond) Limited is a Registered Charity, number 312669. It exists for the education of children.

King's St Alban's School

Mill Street, Worcester WR1 2NJ
Tel: 01905 354906
Fax: 01905 763075
e-mail: ksa@ksw.org.uk
website: www.ksw.org.uk

Chairman of the Governors: D T Howell, Esq, BSc Eng, FCA

Headmaster: **Mr R T Bellfield**, BEd

Age Range. 4–11 Co-educational.
Number of Pupils. 230.
Fees per term (2011-2012). Pre-Prep Dept £1,958–£2,211, Junior School £2,317–£3,287 excluding lunch.

Education is about far more than academic learning, although that is still our primary purpose. At King's St Alban's we aim to develop the whole child, encouraging each girl and boy to explore their capabilities, find fresh challenges and discover spheres in which they can excel.

King's St Alban's, an established school with a purpose-built Pre-Preparatory Department, is located near to Worces-ter Cathedral on a separate site adjacent to the Senior School. In the grounds stand the Chapel, the main buildings of the Junior School with the Pre-Preparatory Department on an adjacent, self contained site. The school has a large hall, a dedicated Science Laboratory, an IT suite, an Art and Technology Room, well-stocked Libraries and Music Rooms, all of which supplement the usual amenities of a preparatory school. In addition, use is made of Senior School facilities, which include an indoor Swimming Pool, a fully equipped Sports Hall, Dance Studio, Fitness Centre, the Music School, Playing Fields, and a purpose-built Theatre.

We work hard to discover talent and develop it to the full. Music, Art, Dance and Drama play an important part in the life of the school. King's St Alban's supports an Orchestra, Wind Band, Flute Choir and String and Recorder groups with most children playing at least one musical instrument. In the Junior School nearly all children are involved in the school's Choir and there is a smaller Chamber Choir. The annual Carol Service is held in the Cathedral with concerts and musical evenings held each term in the Theatre and Chapel. A major whole-school production is staged annually in the Theatre with several smaller workshop productions taking place during the year.

The staff comprises an equal balance of men and women, all of whom are experienced and well qualified. In addition there are various visiting music and sport specialists.

The main sports are Rugby, Netball, Soccer, Hockey, Cricket and Rounders with Swimming, Athletics, Cross-Country, Orienteering and Tennis also featured. Matches are arranged with other schools and excellence is sought, but participation of all girls and boys is the main objective. A thriving inter-House competition provides further opportunities for all to enjoy competition.

Beyond the classroom an extensive programme of after-school activities is available with opportunities varying each term, examples are Art & Craft, Science, Ball Skills, Latin, Chess and Life Saving. Children in Year 6 spend time each year at the school's Outdoor Activity Centre in the Black Mountains.

King's St Alban's is academically selective and pupils are expected to progress to the Senior School, subject to a satisfactory performance in their examinations at the age of 11. The assessment of candidates for the Junior School takes place in early February for entry in the following September. The tests cover English, Mathematics and Verbal Reasoning.

There are a small number of Scholarships and Bursaries available from the age of 7, as are Choral Scholarships for Cathedral Choristers.

Charitable status. The King's School, Worcester is a Registered Charity, number 1098236. It exists to provide high quality education for girls and boys.

Junior King's School

Milner Court, Sturry, Canterbury, Kent CT2 0AY
Tel: 01227 714000
Fax: 01227 713171
e-mail: head@junior-kings.co.uk
website: www.junior-kings.co.uk

Chairman of Governors: The Very Revd Dr R A Willis, BA, Dip Th, FRSA, Dean of Canterbury Cathedral

Headmaster: **Mr P M Wells**, BEd Hons

Age Range. 3–13.
Number of Pupils. 355 (72 Boarders; 199 Day Pupils; 84 Pre-Prep).
Fees per term (2011-2012). Boarders £6,790; Day Pupils £4,500–£5,005; Pre-Prep £2,950 (including meals).

The school, founded in 1879, is co-educational and is the Junior School of the King's School, Canterbury (founded AD579). The aims of the school are to provide excellent education tailored to encourage the broad development of each pupil, in a caring and supportive environment where children mix with ease, enjoy their learning, grow in confidence, and go on to fulfil their potential.

The school is structured into Pre-Prep (Early Years), Junior House (Years 3 and 4), Middle School (Years 5 and 6), and Upper School (Years 7 and 8), and a house team system operates across the whole school. This ensures educational and other activities are enjoyed amongst peers, and a sense of team spirit is encouraged through intra and inter-house competitions. The school's has a wide cultural perspective and attracts international applications and currently overseas pupils account for 7% of the roll.

The boarding community maintains a "family" feel, and weekends contain a variety of activities organised by the house parents. Throughout the school pastoral care has a high priority to ensure every child feels comfortable and happy, and able to develop their social skills.

The majority of the pupils move up to the King's School Canterbury through Scholarship or Common Entrance at 13+, though a few pass on to other independent schools or local grammar schools. Classes are kept sufficiently small (average 16) to allow plenty of individual attention and pastoral care, with additional support provided where appropriate. Academic standards are high and the record of success in Scholarships and Common Entrance is outstanding.

The school has a fine reputation for music, both instrumental and choral, as well as for art, design and drama. The school year includes a programme of concerts, recitals and exhibitions involving children of all ages. Pupils frequently gain awards to other schools.

For boys, cricket, soccer and rugby are the main team games, while girls play netball, hockey and rounders. Athletics, tennis and fencing are joint pursuits. There is a heated outdoor swimming pool for summer use.

A new sports hall was opened in 1998 and this is used for PE lessons, basketball, volleyball, badminton, and netball, as well as indoor hockey, soccer and tennis. There is canoeing on the River Stour, which runs through the grounds. Rowing and sailing take place on nearby lakes, and there is access to the King's School Recreation Centre in winter.

The school site covers 80 acres and contains a blend of the traditional and modern. The 16th century Tithe Barn has a fully-equipped stage. There is a modern design and technology centre, and a spacious, open-plan dining hall which also provides an attractive alternative venue for concerts and plays, as well as gastronomic delight!

In the last decade, eight new classrooms have been opened, the Library refurbished, the boarding facilities refurbished to a very high standard, and the Pre-Prep department, housed in the unique Oast House, has been extended by the addition of a new hall and classroom.

Charitable status. The King's School of the Cathedral Church of Canterbury is a Registered Charity, number 307942. It exists to provide education for boys and girls.

King's School Junior School
Ely

Ely, Cambs CB7 4DB
Tel:　01353 660732
Fax:　01353 665281
e-mail:　admissions@kings-ely.cambs.sch.uk
website:　www.kings-ely.cambs.sch.uk

Chairman of the Governors: R P Slogrove

Head: **R J Whymark**, BA Ed

Age Range. 7–13.
Number of Pupils. Boarders: 32 Boys, 11 Girls; Day: 146 Boys, 132 Girls.
Fees per term (2011-2012). Boarding £5,939–£6,268. Day £3,725–£4,064.

The Junior School has its own staff and its own new buildings are close to the main School. The facilities of the Senior School are freely available to Junior boys and girls.

There is a family boarding house for boys and girls up to the age of 13 and a separate boarding house for the boy choristers of Ely Cathedral who are all pupils in the Junior School. Each has its own Housemaster or Housemistress, assisted by House Tutors and experienced Matrons. Both houses have recently been refurbished and offer excellent boarding facilities.

During the school day all children are divided into four equal-sized co-educational 'houses' for pastoral and competitive purposes. Each of these 'houses' is staffed by a Housemaster or Housemistress and several House Tutors.

Entry to Junior School for boys and girls is through assessment tests and interview. The main two entry points are Year 3 (age 7) and Year 7 (age 11) but pupils may start in any year providing there is space. The main assessment weeks are in January, although it is common to assess for entry at other times of the year. Exceptional children for Year 7 entry may be invited to take the Junior School Scholarship examination. A broad preparatory school curriculum is followed and all pupils are prepared for the relevant transfer examination. While the great majority proceed to the Senior School in Year 9, pupils can also be prepared for other Independent Schools.

The main games for boys are Rugby, Cricket and Football, and for girls they are Netball, Hockey, Rounders and Tennis. Both boys and girls are involved in Athletics and Cross-Country Running. There is a Swimming Pool, a well-equipped Sports Hall, a full-size all-weather hockey/tennis area, and excellent playing fields. A wide-ranging programme of extra-curricular activities is also offered. All pupils have the opportunity to learn one or more of a wide variety of musical instruments. There are several Junior School Orchestras, and choral and ensemble music are taught. The Junior School musicians regularly tour abroad. The School has its own Music School and Technology Centre, and access to the Senior School's new £1 million Recital Hall and Music School. Years 7 and 8 enjoy a new £1.2m block of seven classrooms and a science laboratory, plus recreational and study facilities.

The School is also justly proud of its art and drama, which are taught in their own studios, and of its excellent computer facilities.

Charitable status. The King's School, Ely is a Registered Charity, number 802427. It exists for the provision of education.

King's Rochester Preparatory School

King Edward Road, Rochester, Kent ME1 1UB
Tel:　01634 888577
Fax:　01634 888507
e-mail:　prep@kings-rochester.co.uk
website:　www.kings-rochester.co.uk

Chairman of Governors: (*to be appointed*)

Headmaster: **R P Overend**, BA, FTCL, ARCM, FRSA

Age Range. 8–13.
Number of Pupils. 200.
Fees per term (2011-2012). Boarders £5,950, Day Pupils £3,590–£4,080 (including lunches).

Admission between 8+ to 12+ is by interview and report from present school as well as Entrance Examinations in English, Mathematics and Verbal or Non-Verbal Reasoning.

Scholarships are awarded (partly from the Cathedral, partly from the School) to Cathedral Choristers (boys only) and King's (30%) or Governors' Exhibitions (means-tested up to 100%) to those whose performance in the Entrance Examination merits it.

The Preparatory School is an integral part of the King's Rochester, founded in 604 AD by Justus, a Benedictine monk, the first Bishop of Rochester. The Cathedral is at the heart of the School's life with a weekly School service and every day the Choristers maintain the tradition of choral singing at the world's oldest Choir School. When the School is not in the Cathedral a religious assembly is held at the Preparatory School.

The School is a member of the Choir Schools' Association.

The School has been fully co-educational since 1993 and 30% are girls.

Set in the City, the Preparatory School building overlooks the Paddock, one of the School's playing fields. The teaching block consists of 12 classrooms, 2 Science Laboratories, a Computer Suite, Language Laboratory and a Library with over 6,000 volumes. Other facilities such as the Design and Technology Centre, Art Centre, Music School, Indoor Swimming Pool and Sports Halls are shared with the Senior School which virtually all pupils join following the internal Entrance Examination. Chadlington House, the purpose-built Pre-Preparatory School which educates pupils from age 3–8, and a Conference Centre are recent additions to the campus.

The Preparatory School has a small number of boarders who are housed either in School House for boys, or St Margaret's House for girls. Boarding, both full and weekly, is available for boys and girls from 11+.

The curriculum is broad and balanced. In Year 8 science is taught as three separate subjects, French and German are the modern languages, and Latin is taught to the A stream from Year 7. A full programme of CPSHE is given to all pupils. Individual educational support tuition and EFL is available if required.

All pupils enjoy the benefit of two full afternoons a week of Games in addition to a PE lesson for most year groups. Major sports include Rugby, Hockey, Cricket, Netball, Athletics, Rounders and Swimming. There is a wide range of extra-curricular activities at the end of the school day.

Choral and instrumental music is strong throughout the School. Many of our pupils learn one or more musical instruments and strong results are achieved in Associated Board examinations. Each year the Drama Club presents a play or musical held over three nights. Recently productions have required casts in excess of fifty and have been wonderful opportunities for pupils to show their dramatic and musical skills. Amongst latest productions have been "Olivia", "Bendigo Boswell", "Homer's Odyssey", "Under Milk Wood", "Bugsy Malone", "In Holland stands a House" and "Little Shop of Horrors".

Charitable status. King's School, Rochester is a Registered Charity, number 1084266. It is a Charitable Trust for the purpose of educating children.

Kingshott

St Ippolyts, Hitchin, Hertfordshire SG4 7JX
Tel: 01462 432009
Fax: 01462 421652
e-mail: pa2head@kingshott.herts.sch.uk
website: www.kingshottschool.co.uk

Chairman of Governors: Mr N Baker, QC

Headmaster: **I Gilmour**, BPrimEd, BEd Hons, MEd

Age Range. 3–13.
Number of Pupils. (All Day) Prep (7–13): 144 Boys, 66 Girls; Pre-Prep (4–7): 80 Boys, 39 Girls; Nursery (3–4): 13 Boys, 10 Girls.
Fees per term (2010-2011). (including Lunch) Nursery £1,545–£2,165, Pre-Prep £2,745, Prep £3,348.

Kingshott, founded in 1930, occupies a large Victorian building, with major recent classroom additions, in 14 acres of attractive grounds on the outskirts of Hitchin. Luton, Letchworth, Baldock, Stevenage, Welwyn and the A1(M) Motorway are all within a 10 mile radius. In September 2008 a new Middle School building opened for Years 3 to 5, the latest stage in the redevelopment of the school, which began with the new Pre-Prep building in 2004. September 2009 also saw the introduction of a nursery department.

Kingshott, a Charitable Educational Trust, with a Board of Governors, welcomes all denominations. Children are encouraged to make the best of individual potential – academic, creative, sporting – and to this end there is a happy friendly atmosphere, with strong emphasis on courtesy and self-discipline.

There are 40 full-time and 7 part-time qualified staff to teach 22 forms, varying in size from 11 to 22. Visiting Musicians teach a wide variety of instruments; there are a number of Orchestras and Choirs; Speech and Drama and Ballet are offered; field trips and educational visits form a regular feature of school life. All children from Year 4 up enjoy residential trips.

There is a strong and successful sporting tradition which includes Football, Rugby, Cricket, Hockey, Netball, Rounders, Tennis, Swimming, Cross-Country and Athletics. The School has its own covered, heated swimming pool, all-weather pitch, tennis court and hard play areas. Many pupils stay until 5.30 pm for Prep each evening, and there is opportunity for involvement in a wide variety of after-school Hobby activities. The School also offers a breakfast club and after-school care is also available until 5.30 pm for Pre-Prep pupils.

Girls were first admitted in 1983, and now constitute approximately 35% of the annual intake. Girls are able to continue their education at Kingshott until age 13, in line with the boys.

Academic, Music, Art and Sports Scholarships to Senior Independent Schools are gained each year, and Common Entrance results are very sound, with virtually all children accepted by their first choice schools.

Entry is by assessment, appropriate to age.

Registration for Nursery and Pre-Prep is advisable several years before required admission.

Charitable status. Kingshott School Trust Limited is a Registered Charity, number 280626. It exists to provide education for boys and girls.

Kingsmead School

Bertram Drive, Hoylake, Wirral CH47 0LL
Tel: 0151 632 3156
Fax: 0151 632 0302
e-mail: enquiries@kingsmeadschool.com
website: www.kingsmeadschool.com

Chairman of Governors: Barry L Hopkins, ACIB

Headmaster: **Mr M G Gibbons**, BComm, MSc, QTS

Age Range. 2–16.
Number of Pupils. 145 boys, 101 girls (Boarders: 9 boys, 9 girls).

Fees per term (2011-2012). Boarders £4,606–£5,657, Day Pupils £915–£3,157.

Academic, Music and Sports Scholarships are available at Year 7 entry. Scholarship and entrance examinations are held in January and March each year. Substantial Bursaries are available to the children of Clergy.

Kingsmead School was founded in 1904. It is in a rural setting with extensive playing fields on site, yet is easily accessible by road, rail and international airports. It has a strong Christian tradition, dedicated staff, a reputation for high academic standards, and a happy atmosphere.

The curriculum prepares pupils to go on to Grammar Schools at 11+, although the majority remain at Kingsmead until GCSE (age 16).

Facilities include two Computer Rooms, two well-equipped Science Laboratories, a large Gymnasium and an indoor heated swimming pool available throughout the year. There is a strong Choir and facilities are available to those wishing to learn a musical instrument. All children have the opportunity to perform in plays, musicals and concerts. The Centenary Building was opened on the campus in February 2003, containing state-of-the-art classrooms for History, Geography, Design Technology (DT), Information and Communications Technology (ICT), Art and French.

Up to the end of Key Stage 1 (Year 2), pupils are taught in their own rooms by Class Teachers. In the Junior Department (Key Stage 2) there is specialist teaching of certain subjects at the appropriate level. Thereafter pupils are based in a Form Room under the care of a Form Teacher but move to the different subject rooms for lessons. For spoken English and Drama, the School has enjoyed excellent results in the English Speaking Board and other examinations. At any level in the school, intelligent children with specific learning difficulties can be given a structured programme of remedial help by a specialist teacher at an extra charge.

Full, Weekly and Flexi Boarders are accepted from 7 years old and are in the care of the Boarding Team Leader and other members of the boarding staff. These, together with the Headmaster, Deputy and their wives, are all resident. Our boarders are accommodated in three family-sized houses – Bertram Lodge (boys), Meadway Cottage (girls) and Watts House (flexi-boarding). Boarders are met at Liverpool Lime Street Station or Liverpool or Manchester Airports.

Games offered include Football, Rugby, Cricket, Netball, Rounders, Hockey, Athletics, Tennis, and Golf.

Clubs include Ballet, Chess, Gymnastics, Judo, Scripture Union, Swimming, Sailing, Bushcraft, Archery and Dance.

Charitable status. Kingsmead School is a Registered Charity, number 525920.

Kingswood House School

56 West Hill, Epsom, Surrey KT19 8LG
Tel: 01372 723590
Fax: 01372 749081
e-mail: office@kingswoodhouse.org
website: www.kingswoodhouse.org

Founded in 1899, the school moved to its current site, a large Edwardian house in West Hill, Epsom, just outside the town centre in 1920. The school is an educational trust, overseen by a board of governors.

Chairman of Governors: Robert Austen, BScEng, CEng, MICE, MIHT

Headmaster: **Peter R Brooks**, MA, BEd Hons, CertEd

Age Range. Boys 3–13, Girls 3–7.
Number of Pupils. 204 day pupils.

Fees per term (2011-2012). Pre-Prep £2,730 (part-time Nursery payable by session). Junior 7+ upwards £3,520. Free after-school care provided until 5.00 pm.

Kingswood House is a thriving day preparatory school for boys aged 3–13 and girls aged 3–7. The school's reputation is based on a friendly and welcoming atmosphere, a positive and supportive ethos and successfully meeting the educational needs of all its pupils. Small classes facilitate individual attention from well-qualified teachers and allow pupils to learn in a relaxed, but stimulating and concentrated environment.

The broad aim of the school is to prepare boys for Common Entrance and Scholarships to senior school at age 13. Development of literacy and numeracy skills is the foundation of the curriculum. English, Maths, Science, History, Geography, French, Religious Education, PE, Music, Art, Design Technology and Information Technology make up the timetable. Study Skills and PSHE courses help prepare boys for senior school life and there is a Study Centre to supplement learning, with excellent provision for children with special educational needs. Kingswood House School is a member of CReSTeD (Council for the Registration of Schools Teaching Dyslexic Pupils) and NAGC (The National Association for Gifted Children).

The senior curriculum is determined by the Common Entrance syllabus with boys being prepared for a wide variety of local senior independent schools, including Epsom College, St John's, Ewell Castle, City of London Freemen's, Reed's, Box Hill and King's College, Wimbledon. Placing boys in the right senior school is of paramount importance and the teachers have wide experience in preparing boys for Common Entrance. There is an excellent success rate at 13+ Common Entrance, with a good proportion obtaining scholarships and awards.

The school prides itself on the quality of teaching, dedicated classrooms and resources provided for Art, Design Technology, Information Technology, Music and Science, all of which have been completely refurbished in the last few years. There are sporting facilities on site, with a playing field, astroturf surface, all-weather cricket nets, adventure playground and climbing wall. Pitches at Ashtead Cricket Club and Epsom College are also used.

Academic Scholarships are awarded at 7+. There are discounts for sons of teachers and fee reductions for second and subsequent boys. The school is registered for the Nursery Education Grant.

Charitable status. Kingswood House School is a Registered Charity, number 312044. It exists to provide educational support in the form of bursaries for the parents of children in need.

Kingswood Preparatory School

College Road, Lansdown, Bath BA1 5SD
Tel: 01225 734460
Fax: 01225 734470
e-mail: kpsreception@kingswood.bath.sch.uk
website: www.kingswood.bath.sch.uk

Chairman of Governors: Mr Colin Burns

Headmaster: **Mr Mark Brearey**

Age Range. 3–11.
Number of Pupils. 348: Prep: 102 boys, 86 girls; Pre-Prep: 96 boys, 64 girls. 16 Boarders.
Fees per term (2011-2012). Nursery, Reception, Years 1 and 2: £2,633 (Nursery part-day pro rata); Years 3–6: £3,048. Boarding: £6,003 (full), £5,042 (weekly).

Kingswood Preparatory School is the preparatory school for Kingswood School, Bath. It is part of the Kingswood Foundation and each year over 95% of pupils move on to

Kingswood School, through examination in January, at the end of Year 6.

Kingswood School is the oldest Methodist educational institution in the world, having been founded by John Wesley in 1748. Both Preparatory and the Senior Schools have extensive linked sites on Lansdown hill overlooking the world-famous city of Bath.

At Kingswood Preparatory School our aim is to create a happy, caring community based upon Christian principles in which all individuals can develop respect for themselves and for others.

We provide for the children a rich variety of academic, sporting and social experiences. By doing so we hope to give them the opportunity to develop their personalities and potential in an atmosphere of enthusiasm, enjoyment, security and care for fellow pupils.

As well as our regular Extra-Curricular Programme which currently contains fifty weekly options, the school offers regular opportunities to participate in Music, Drama and Sport. We are able to use certain senior school facilities such as the swimming pool, the astroturf hockey pitch and the theatre. The prep school shares 56 acres of playing fields with the seniors.

The prep school is situated in the splendid parkland setting of the Summerhill estate. Children of pre-preparatory age are educated in the modern, award-winning, purpose-built accommodation and the senior years in the main house, Summerhill. This fine mansion was designed by John Wood the Younger. Before it came into the schools possession in the 1950s it was the home of Ernest Cook, founder of the Ernest Cook Trust. The boarders live in High Vinnalls which offers all types of boarding to boys and girls aged between 7 and 11. Adjacent to the school and superbly situated in large gardens surrounded by woods and parkland, it has been acclaimed as a model for what boarding houses for young children should be like, in terms of its homely atmosphere and facilities. The school enjoys magnificent views over the City of Bath, and is situated only one and half miles from the centre.

There are 66 staff in all: 28 full-time and 6 part-time teachers, 8 ancillary support assistants and a further 20 part-time peripatetic staff.

Charitable status. Kingswood Preparatory School is a Registered Charity, number 309148. It exists for the purpose of educating children.

Knighton House

Durweston, Blandford, Dorset DT11 0PY
Tel: 01258 452065
Fax: 01258 450744
e-mail: enquiries@knighton-house.co.uk
website: www.knightonhouse.dorset.sch.uk

Chairman of the Governors: Lieutenant General Andrew Graham

Headmistress: **Mrs A Tremewan**, BA Hons, PGCE

Age Range. Girls 3–13, Boys 3–7.
Number of Girls. Boarders 58, Day Girls (including Flexi Boarders) 42; Pre-Prep and Nursery (co-educational) 39.
Fees per term (2010-2011). Boarders £6,500, Day £4,880, Pre-Prep £2,470, Nursery: £85–£200. There are no compulsory extras.

Established in 1950, Knighton House keeps pace with the expectations of the 21st century, whilst nurturing its unique traditional values. In a delightful country setting, the school provides a safe but challenging environment in which children can discover their strengths, take risks and make

friends. Boarding is entirely flexible and ponies and pets are all welcome.

The small classes and high staff/pupil ratio ensures individual attention. The scholarships and awards won from Knighton House reflect academic, musical, artistic and all-rounder prowess; there is a strong artistic and musical tradition. Team sports and Swimming have an all-year-round place in the timetable. There are many extra-curricular activities including riding from our own stables, triathlon, tetrathlon, dance, drama and outdoor environmental pursuits.

This careful balance of academic subjects and extra-curricular activities encourages all aspects of personal growth. The size of Knighton House ensures that each pupil is known by everyone; each girl has an identity and is respected for her individuality.

Knighton House feeds a wide range of senior schools, both co-ed and single-sex.

Charitable status. Knighton House School Limited is a Registered Charity, number 306316. It exists, principally, as a boarding school for girls.

The Lady Eleanor Holles School (Junior Department)

Burlington House, 177 Uxbridge Road, Hampton, Middlesex TW12 1BD
Tel: 020 8979 2173
       Registrar & Senior Department: 020 8979 1601
Fax: 020 8783 1962
e-mail: junior-office@lehs.org.uk
website: www.lehs.org.uk

Chairman of Governors: Mrs J Ross, BSc, CPFA

Head Mistress: Mrs G Low, MA Oxon

Head of Junior Department: **Mrs F Robinson**, BA Cardiff, MA King's College London

Age Range. 7–11.
Number of Pupils. 188 day girls.
Fees per term (2011-2012). £3,820.

The Lady Eleanor Holles School Junior Department is housed in its own separate building in one corner of the school's spacious thirty-acre grounds. Junior Department pupils make full use of the school's extensive facilities, such as a heated indoor 25m pool, Sports Hall and floodlit netball courts. (*See The Lady Eleanor Holles School's entry in the GSA section for more details.*) They also take advantage of a fleet of school coaches serving most of West London and Surrey.

The school is academically selective, with most girls joining in Year 3. Entrance exams in English and Maths are held the January before entry. The vast majority of Junior Department pupils are given guaranteed places in the Senior Department without having to take the Senior entrance exam.

The school's teaching is firmly based on the National Curriculum and there are specialist teachers for Science, Art, French, IT, Music and PE from the beginning. The school is very well resourced and staff use a wide variety of teaching styles and activities to ensure pace, stimulation and progression.

There is a wide range of extra-curricular activities so girls can develop their own interests and abilities, and all achievements and progress are valued and praised.

Extra-curricular clubs include Drama, Chess, Gardening and various Art, Music and Sports activities.

Whilst LEH is a broadly Christian foundation, it welcomes girls of all faiths, and none. School Assemblies, some of which are performed by the girls for their parents, may feature Hindu, Islamic Sikh or Jewish festivals and stories, as well as Christian.

In 2003, Burlington House, the home of the Junior Department, was the subject of a very extensive programme of extension and renovation, and now boasts superb facilities for a 21st-century education. Amongst the main improvements were four spacious new Practical Rooms for Art, DT and Science; two new Computer suites; a well-stocked and welcoming Library; and larger, brighter classrooms.

The staff work hard to establish and maintain a caring, supportive atmosphere in which girls feel confident to be themselves, to respect and care for everyone in the community, to be proud of their achievements and to persevere with things they find challenging. Pastoral care is a priority and we are proud of the happy, lively, hard-working pupils of the Junior Department.

Charitable status. Cripplegate Schools Foundation is a Registered Charity, number 312493. The Foundation is responsible solely for the Lady Eleanor Holles School, which exists to provide education to girls aged 7 to 18.

Lady Lane Park School and Nursery, Bingley

GEMS Education

Lady Lane, Bingley, West Yorkshire BD16 4AP
Tel: 01274 551168
Fax: 01274 569732
e-mail: secretary@ladylanepark.co.uk
website: www.ladylanepark.bradford.sch.uk

Headmistress: **Mrs Gill Wilson**

Age Range. 2–11 Co-educational.
Number of Pupils. 179 Day Pupils: 87 Boys, 92 Girls.
Fees per term (from January 2011). £2,086.25 (Lower Kindergarten–Form III), £1,964.75 (Form 4–Upper VI).

Lady Lane Park School is a member of the GEMS Education Group.

The school ethos is based on the development of the individual within a broad and challenging curriculum, and the firm belief that learning should be fun.

Our well qualified and dedicated staff combine professional expertise with commitment and understanding and our teaching methods are a balanced blend of the traditional and the very best in new ideas.

The life of the school is supported by our Governors' and Friends' committees, and we believe that the partnership between school and home is a very important one.

The emphasis is based on the laying of secure foundations in reading, writing, mathematical and scientific skills which are of the utmost importance for a child's development, and we believe in the importance of respect and care for each other and for the community.

A broad-based curriculum is reinforced by the National Curriculum and specialist teaching is provided in Science, Mathematics, ICT CDT, Music, Dance, Drama and Games.

French is introduced through songs and games and specialist teaching begins at the age of 5. Academic achievements are highly valued but we also aim for excellence in other spheres so that our children are encouraged to develop their talents with a positive and enthusiastic approach to school life.

Our teaching is enriched by out-of-school visits, both day and residential, which all help to extend and reinforce the children's experience and make learning fun.

Pupils are encouraged to take responsibility for themselves and for others and to actively contribute to the life of the school and the local environment.

Every child is given the opportunity to enjoy creative experiences and they are actively encouraged to fulfil their potential. Over 80% of our children study for theory and practical examinations in Music, Dance and Drama.

We have an excellent reputation in all aspects of physical education and children participate in a variety of sporting activities. We have a sports pavilion and large playing field – scope indeed for all our needs.

The friendly, yet competitive atmosphere is testament to team spirit and personal achievement.

Our well resourced and uniquely designed Science laboratory and DT facility provides an exciting environment where children learn through practical activities and experiments.

The dedicated computer room provides an introduction to word processing, databases, graphics, spreadsheets and Powerpoint presentations, and the networked system offers opportunities for group involvement. This up-to-date facility, with full Broadband Internet access, is a vital tool for all children in our forward-looking school. In addition, all our classrooms have an interactive whiteboard.

The whole school curriculum provides a coherent health education programme, including Personal & Social Development, which promotes children's self-esteem and social well-being.

Our Year 6 pupils achieve Life Saving awards in swimming, and undertake a programme of practical and written study resulting in a First Aid Certificate.

Environmental work enables children to work alongside specialists in many areas.

Lady Lane is Christian in attitude and welcomes children of all faiths. Our aim is to educate children to think for themselves, be confident in their abilities and take pleasure in the learning process as they prepare themselves for an exciting future.

Lambrook

Winkfield Row, Bracknell, Berks RG42 6LU
Tel: 01344 882717
Fax: 01344 891114
e-mail: info@lambrook.berks.sch.uk
website: www.lambrook.berks.sch.uk

Chairman of the Governors: Charles Donald, BA Hons, CDipAF

Headmaster: **J F Perry, BA Hons, PGCE**

Age Range. 3–13 Co-educational.
Number of Children. 450.
Fees per term (2010-2011). Boarding £5,601–£6,003; Day £4,658–£5,060; Pre-Prep £3,026–£3,157.

Lambrook is a co-educational boarding and day school for children aged 3 to 13. The school is situated at Winkfield Row, two miles from Ascot, six miles from Windsor and is easily accessible from the M4, M3 and M40 motorways. Heathrow is 30 minutes away by road.

The school has excellent facilities including a Science and IT Centre. We aim for high academic standards and prepare children for Scholarship and Common Entrance examinations to all major Senior Independent Schools. High quality teaching is provided in small classes and the school is set in a beautiful rural environment of some forty acres.

The school encourages a well-rounded education. Games, music and other cultural activities play an important part in the lives of the children. The boarding, in particular, is conducted in the spirit of a family atmosphere with a strong pastoral care system, in two boarding houses, with a very flexible approach ranging from occasional to weekly boarding.

The school has many day pupils who are attracted by the boarding ethos and the subsequent number of varied activities available. All pupils play a full part in the life of the school. The Pre-Prep Department opened in September 1993 and it has expanded rapidly with the nursery being added in January 2007. The Pre-Prep Building comprises eight very well resourced, modern classrooms, an enlarged library and a networked computer system.

Charitable status. Lambrook School Trust Limited is a Registered Charity, number 309098. Its purpose is to provide an excellent education for boys and girls.

Lancing College Preparatory School
A Woodard School

The Droveway, Hove, East Sussex BN3 6LU
Tel: 01273 503452
Fax: 01273 503457
e-mail: info@lancingprep.co.uk
website: www.lancingprep.co.uk

Chairman of Governors: Dr H O Brünjes, BSc, MBBS, DRCOG, FEWI

Headmaster: **A P Laurent**

Age Range. 3–13.
Number of Pupils. 210.
Fees per term (2010-2011). £1,045–£4,140.

Lancing College Preparatory School is situated in an enviable position in Hove overlooking the English Channel.

Much of our ethos is drawn from the fact that we are a Christian based school and central to this is the belief that children must feel happy and secure in their surroundings if they are to succeed. The school is run on family lines, each child being given a sense of their true worth as an individual but also as part of the family.

The school offers an excellent academic education with a modern curriculum preparing for the Common Entrance and Scholarship Examinations at the end of academic year eight. Central to our curriculum beliefs is the idea that all pupils have an area in which they can excel, and to that end we place huge importance on the teaching of Art, Drama, Music and Sport as well as all the subjects that you would expect to find in the National Curriculum.

We have a fully qualified staff of twenty five full and part time teachers who enjoy facilities including a fully equipped science laboratory, an art design and technology room, gymnasium, ICT suite and library. As well as extensive grounds there is an all weather area for the coaching of our main sports, cricket, football, rugby, hockey, netball, rounders and tennis.

Charitable status. Lancing College is a Registered Charity, number 1076483. It exists to provide education for boys and girls.

Lanesborough School

Maori Road, Guildford, Surrey GU1 2EL
Tel: 01483 880650
Fax: 01483 880651
e-mail: office@lanesborough.surrey.sch.uk
website: www.lanesborough.surrey.sch.uk

Chairman of Governors: Dr H J Pearson, OBE, MA, PhD, CMath, FIMA

Head: **Mrs C Turnbull**, BA Hons

Age Range. 3–13.
Number of Boys. 360 Day Boys.
Fees per term (2010-2011). Nursery £2,479, Reception–Year 1 £3,006, Years 2–3 £3,239, Years 4–8 £3,342.

Lanesborough is the Preparatory School of the Royal Grammar School and the choir school for Guildford Cathedral. Cathedral choristers qualify for choral scholarships.

The main entry points are Nursery, Reception and Year 3. Many of the pupils gain entry to the Royal Grammar School at age 11 or 13, whilst others are prepared for Scholarship and Common Entrance examination to senior independent schools at 13.

The School is divided into four houses for house competitions. Pastoral care and supervision of academic progress are shared by the Head, Housemasters, Form and subject teachers. Extra-curricular activities include art, chess, drama, computer club, judo, fencing, tennis, basketball, science and General Knowledge.

Music is a strong feature of the life of the school, which is a member of the Choir Schools Association. In addition to the Cathedral Choir, there are senior and junior choirs, an orchestra, wind and string groups. Private tuition by qualified peripatetic teachers is available in most instruments. There are music concerts and the School Carol Service at the Cathedral has achieved wide acclaim. Music Scholarships to Independent Senior Schools are gained each year.

Art plays an important part in the curriculum also, with boys receiving tuition throughout the school.

Games are association football, rugby football, cricket, athletics, swimming, basketball, hockey and badminton. There is a school field, gym and astroturf.

Regular school visits are undertaken to local places of interest. School parties also go abroad, eg for skiing and on cultural visits.

The pre-preparatory department (for boys aged 3–7 and including a Nursery unit) is housed in a separate building (Braganza), but shares many of the facilities of the senior part of the School.

There is an active Parents' Association.

Charitable status. Lanesborough is governed by the trustees of The Royal Grammar School of King Edward VI, Guildford which is a Registered Charity, number 312028. It exists for the purpose of educating boys in or near Guildford.

Lathallan School

Brotherton Castle, Johnshaven, Montrose, Angus DD10 0HN
Tel: 01561 362220
Fax: 01561 361695
e-mail: office@lathallan.com
website: www.lathallan.com

Chairman of Board of Directors: Mr Hamish Grant

Headmaster: **Mr Richard Toley**, BA Hons, MPhil, PGCE

Age Range. 6 weeks to 18 years.
Number of Pupils. 125 (72 boys, 53 girls) plus 50 in Nursery.
Fees per term (2010-2011). Tuition: Pre-Prep £2,855, Middle School £3,610, Upper School £4,091, Senior School £4,886. Weekly Boarding (in addition to Tuition): £1,170. Reductions for siblings and Services children. Scholarships and Bursaries available.

Lathallan School, situated in extensive spectacular grounds in a baronial castle overlooking the North Sea, began an exciting programme of re-development in 2003. In

2004 the existing nursery was refurbished and is now able to accommodate children and babies from 6 weeks for 50 weeks per annum. Recognising the growing demand for a senior school of the calibre of the existing preparatory school, the Board of Directors announced in 2004 that the school would begin to offer secondary education, adding one academic year at a time with an S6 class by September 2010. Sports facilities have been refurbished, the castle building adapted for senior teaching and a redevelopment of the site is under way to allow for school expansion.

High academic achievement, a wide-ranging choice of activities, strong pastoral care and happy children are fundamental ingredients in any description of a good school. Lathallan has all these and more – where family values are encouraged and all members of its community go about their daily tasks with a sense of fun and enjoyment. The school ethos is to foster independence and confidence, allowing children to achieve their full potential. Pupils are encouraged to develop existing skills but also to "step outside the comfort zone" and discover some hidden talents.

Weekly boarding is available and, unique to the local area, is our flexi-boarding system, where any pupil can opt to board on certain nights – either to suit the demands of busy family life or to join in one of the many extra-curricular activities which vary from term to term but include Pipe Band, cricket, athletics, cooking, football, Warhammer, Cycling Proficiency and creative writing. A daily bus services runs from both Aberdeen and Montrose. The school is capitalizing on its stunning rural coastal location by widening its focus on Outdoor Education and Environmental Studies.

Charitable status. Lathallan School is a Registered Charity, number SC018423. It exists to provide education of the highest standard for boys and girls.

Latymer Prep School

36 Upper Mall, Hammersmith, London W6 9TA
Tel: 0845 638 5700
Fax: 0845 638 5735
e-mail: mlp@latymerprep.org
website: www.latymerprep.org

Chairman of Governors: Professor R N Perham, MA, PhD, ScD, FRS

Principal: **Mr Stuart P Dorrian**, BA

Age Range. 7–11 Co-educational.
Number of Pupils. 163 Day Pupils.
Fees per term (2010-2011). £4,235.

Latymer Prep School, led by its own Principal, was granted independence by the Governors of the Latymer Foundation in 1995 – the Centenary Year of Latymer Upper School on its present site. Previously the Prep School had been run as a very successful department of the Upper School and the relationship remains an extremely close one with all children usually expected to proceed to the Upper School.

The school is academically selective and pupils are taught the full range of subjects following National Curriculum guidelines, but to an advanced standard. Classes are kept small (21) which allows for close monitoring and evaluation of each pupil's progress and well being.

The school is well resourced and has attractive facilities in two elegant period houses adjacent to the River Thames. Catering, sports and theatre facilities are shared with the Upper School.

A main feature of the school is its friendly and caring atmosphere which offers close pastoral support to each individual pupil. Academic achievement is strong, but in addition, all staff and pupils contribute to an extensive range of activities featuring Sport, Music, Art and Drama. The school has 3 large choirs and its own orchestra. Opportunities exist for all pupils to participate in concerts, plays, inter-school sporting events and an annual Project Week which includes a residential trip for the senior pupils in their final year.

The major sports are soccer, rugby, cricket, tennis, athletics, hockey and netball. There is also a thriving swimming club (the school has its own pool). Karate takes place after school as do chess, dance and drama.

There is a Parents' Gild and opportunities occur frequently to meet with staff socially. Visits for prospective parents occur throughout the year and can be arranged by telephoning for an appointment.

Charitable status. The Latymer Foundation is a Registered Charity, number 312714. It exists to provide an opportunity for able pupils from all walks of life to develop their talents to the full.

Laxton Junior – Oundle School

East Road, Oundle, Peterborough PE8 4BX
Tel: 01832 277275
Fax: 01832 277271
e-mail: info@laxtonjunior.org.uk
website: www.laxtonjunior.org.uk

Governors: The Worshipful Company of Grocers

Chairman: Mr Julian Tregoning

Headmaster: **Mr Mark Potter**, BEd Hons

Deputy Head: Miss Janet Bass

Age Range. 4–11.
Number of Children. 270 approximately.
Fees per term (2010-2011). £2,930–£3,210 (including lunches).

Opened in 1973 and part of Oundle School, Laxton Junior is a co-educational day school for children aged 4–11 years. In September 2002 Laxton Junior moved into a new building which caters for 280 pupils. The school has 14 forms of no more than 20 pupils, each with a fully qualified Form Teacher. The curriculum includes Art & Design, Computer Skills, French, Music, PE and Performing Arts as well as the major academic subjects. Emphasis has always been placed on the individual child and the importance of each doing their best at all times, according to their ability. Children are prepared for entrance examinations for Independent Senior Schools in the area; Kimbolton, Oundle, Oakham and Stamford Schools being the key schools.

The new building has a large multi-purpose hall which is used for PE, Music and Performing Arts as well as concerts, school plays and social events The school has its own games fields and netball courts plus all children receive swimming instruction each week in the Oundle School Pool. The main games are football, rugby, cricket, netball, rounders, hockey and athletics plus coaching in tennis.

In Year 2 all pupils have the opportunity to play the violin or cello as part of the curriculum. From Year 3 the recorder is introduced, plus additional time is given for choir, orchestra and learning other musical instruments. The school also has an Education Support Unit which monitors all pupils' development and helps individuals with specific difficulties.

The aims of the school are to encourage the formation of good work habits and good manners, to lay the foundations for the development of self-discipline, self-confidence and self-motivation and to offer the children the opportunity of experiencing the satisfaction of achievement.

The partnership of home and school in the education of the child is strongly emphasises and all parents are members of the Parents' & Friends' Association.

Laxton Junior School was inspected in March 2008. The report is available on the school website.

Charitable status. Oundle School is a Registered Charity, number 309921. It exists to provide education for boys and girls.

Leaden Hall School

70 The Close, Salisbury, Wilts SPI 2EP
Tel: 01722 334700
Fax: 01722 439269
e-mail: admin@leaden-hall.com
website: www.leaden-hall.com

Chairman: Mrs Sara Willan

Headmistress: **Mrs Julia Eager**

Age Range. Girls aged 3–11.
Number of Pupils. 261 Girls: 221 Day, 40 Boarders.
Fees per term (2010-2011). Day £2,290–£3,850, Boarding supplement £1,500.

Set in beautiful surroundings in Salisbury's Cathedral Close, Leaden Hall was once the home of the 'architect' of Salisbury Cathedral, Elias de Dereham.

Leaden Hall provides education for girls aged 3–11. We prepare children for the Common Entrance and the County 11+ examinations. We aim to give all girls self-confidence balanced with an awareness of others and a belief in themselves, so that entry to senior school follows naturally without fuss.

Our full, weekly and day boarding options give parents the flexibility to enable their daughters to take part in the many extra-curricular activities which ensure that our pupils flourish in a stimulating, happy and purposeful environment.

Charitable status. Leaden Hall School is a Registered Charity, number 309489. It exists to provide education for children.

Leehurst Swan School

19 Campbell Road, Salisbury SP1 3BQ
Tel: 01722 333094
Fax: 01722 330868
e-mail: registrar@leehurstswan.org.uk
website: www.leehurstswan.org.uk

Chairman of Governors: Mrs M Paisey, MBE

Headmaster: **Mr R N S Leake**, BSc, PGCE, CBiol, MIBiol

Age Range. 2–16 Co-educational.
Number of Children. 345.
Fees per term (2011-2012). Senior School £3,880; Prep School £2,195–£2,580; Pre-School £2,220.

Leehurst Swan is an Independent Day School, just 10 minutes' walk from Salisbury city centre. Originally a girls' school founded in 1914 under the name Leehurst and taken over in 1953 by the Sisters of La Retraite. In 1996 it was joined by the Swan School for Boys, a Prep School for boys aged 4–11 founded by Miss Swanton in 1933. The School was established as an Independent Charitable Trust in 1988.

The school is fully co-educational with over 350 children in the School: 150 children in the Prep School, 150 in the Senior School and 45 in the Pre-Prep. The School has small classes, a family atmosphere, and an environment that inspires and motivates pupils to achieve their best. The individual attention pupils receive reflects the ethos of Christian values and respect for the individual.

2010 saw the completion of the latest building project, the 'Walker Hall', a multi-purpose performance hall also providing new classrooms for the Music Department and outstanding facilities for Performing Arts.

The Pre-Prep welcomes children from the age of two. Set in a purpose-built building, nestling in a wooded glade, the Pre-Prep provides outstanding quality early years education and care in a safe and secure environment. The ethos is one of inclusion with parents as equal partners.

Pupils in the Prep School have specialist teaching in key subjects and use dedicated school facilities in 1CT, Science, Music, Art, and Design Technology. The children are prepared for 11+ examinations for entry into the local grammar schools and for entry into the Senior School.

In the Senior School the pupils normally pursue studies in ten GCSE subjects and academic results are excellent. The school equally values and nurtures creative and sporting talent awarding scholarships in these areas in addition to academic scholarships.

Individual lessons are arranged in a wide range of musical instruments leading to Associated Board examinations.

Leehurst Swan welcomes visitors to the school to come and see them at work and play.

Charitable status. Leehurst Swan Limited is a Registered Charity, number 800158. It exists to provide education for children.

Leicester Grammar Junior School

London Road, Great Glen, Leicester LE8 9FL
Tel: 0116 259 1950
Tel: 0116 259 1951
e-mail: friell@leicestergrammar.org.uk
website: www.leicestergrammar.org.uk

Chairman of Governors: I D Patterson, LLB

Headmistress: **Mrs M Redfearn**, BA Hons, PGCE

Age Range. 3–11 Co-educational.
Number of Pupils. 360.
Fees per term (2011-2012). £2,875 (Juniors), £2,756 (Infants).

Leicester Grammar Junior School was founded in 1992 when Leicester Grammar School Trust took over educational responsibility for Evington Hall, an independent school run by the Sisters of Charity of St Paul.

The school is a selective, co-educational day school with a Christian Foundation. It acts as the junior school to Leicester Grammar School and is the first stage in a continuous education from 3 years through to A Level. In September 2008 both the Junior and Senior schools relocated to a new purpose-built campus SW of the city of Leicester. Thus, the school now encompasses the full 3–18 age range on the one site.

The school provides a stimulating, disciplined, happy environment where each child is encouraged to aim for the highest standards in everything they do and take a full and active part in all aspects of school life. It operates as an extension of the family unit within which the staff act with firmness and fairness. Respect and consideration underpin school life. Pupils are encouraged to develop a caring and responsible attitude to others, leading to good manners and acceptable behaviour.

The children benefit from not only academic success and development but also from excellent musical, sporting and dramatic involvement within a broad and well balanced curriculum.

Music is a particular strength of the school and plays an important part in the life of every child. From the beginning as 3 year olds, children are taught by a music specialist. Pupils have the opportunity to learn a variety of instruments and there is a particularly strong Infant String Scheme; children as young as five or six years of age learn to play the violin or cello. The school orchestra and ensembles perform at festivals, concerts and assemblies. There are also many choral opportunities within the Junior and Infant choir which are often linked with Drama. A number of boys and girls are also members of the Leicester Cathedral choir and enjoy weekly training sessions with the Cathedral Master of Music.

In 2004 the school received the Sportsmark Gold Award in recognition of the quality of sport within the curriculum and extra curricular. The PE and Games provision aims to develop skills in team and individual games, gymnastics, dance, swimming and athletics. The main team games are rugby, football and cricket for the boys and netball, hockey and rounders for the girls. After-school clubs offer additional sporting opportunities such as tennis, badminton, table tennis and cross-country.

Charitable status. Leicester Grammar School Trust is a Registered Charity, number 510809.

Leweston Preparatory School

Sherborne, Dorset DT9 6EN
Tel: 01963 210790
Fax: 01963 210648
e-mail: enquiries@leweston.dorset.sch.uk
website: www.leweston.co.uk

Chairman of Board of Governors: Mr A May

Head Teacher: Mrs M Allen

Age Range. 2–11 Co-educational.
Number of Pupils. 83: 63 Girls, 20 Boys.
Fees per term (2011-2012). Nursery: £20.30 (1 x 3 hr session), Reception–Year 2 £2,595, Years 3–6 £3,695. Weekly Boarding £4,750, Full Boarding £5,495.

Setting. Leweston Preparatory School is an independent Catholic school for boys and girls with boarding provision for girls from age 7. The school is situated in forty-six acres of Dorset parkland three miles south of Sherborne and occupies an enviable setting in a skilfully converted former Coach House providing a unique range of bright spacious classrooms. The beautiful rural site is shared with Leweston School (girls 11–18 years) and the Preparatory School enjoys the benefit of many excellent facilities including a modern, well-equipped Design Technology Centre, an all-weather sports pitch, a heated swimming pool, a large sports hall, tennis courts and extensive playing fields. The parkland setting offers many opportunities for study and recreation.

Ethos. Traditional excellence in teaching is combined with modern facilities and resources in a stimulating, happy and purposeful Christian environment. The school motto 'Gaudere et Bene Facere' (Rejoice and Do Well) exactly reflects the importance of high academic standards together with artistic, musical and sporting excellence achieved in an atmosphere of joy and vibrancy. Each child is encouraged to develop individual talents within the caring and supportive school community. Small class sizes, a friendly family ethos, and traditional values of work and behaviour are appreciated by parents. Full and flexi boarding options provide flexibility for pupils to enjoy a wide variety of extra-curricular activities, whilst no Saturday morning school allows for rest and relaxation.

Curriculum. Programmes of study encompass the National Curriculum without being constrained by it. Basic subjects are taught to a high standard concentrating on literacy and numeracy acquisition in the early years before expanding into a broader curriculum in Years 3–6. Well qualified class teachers and specialist subject teachers foster independent learning and encourage the development of

problem solving and investigative skills in all areas of the curriculum. Academic standards are high and many pupils gain awards to senior school.

There is a strong tradition in the performing arts. Music, drama and dance are taught within the curriculum. A high percentage of pupils learn to play musical instruments and take additional drama. There is a school orchestra and choir and many opportunities throughout the year for performance and grade examinations in both music and drama. All pupils in Years 4–6 undertake English Speaking Board assessments. Individual and team sports are considered important as part of the healthy, active lifestyle and the school enjoys a particular reputation for hockey and cross-country. Art, Ceramics and Design Technology are taught by specialist teachers using the exceptional facilities in the Design Technology Centre.

Charitable status. Leweston School Trust is a Registered Charity, number 295175. It exists to provide for children a contemporary education in the Catholic tradition.

Lichfield Cathedral School

The Palace, The Close, Lichfield, Staffordshire WS13 7LH
Tel: 01543 306170
Fax: 01543 306176
e-mail: reception@lichfieldcathedralschool.com
website: www.lichfieldcathedralschool.com

Chairman of Governors: The Very Revd Adrian Dorber, Dean of Lichfield Cathedral

Headmaster: Mr M Chanter, MA, BSc Hons, PGCE

Age Range. 3–18.
Number of Pupils. 426 including up to 18 Cathedral choristers, approximately 45% girls, 22 boarders.
Fees per term (2010-2011). Day Pupils £2,235–£4,165; Weekly Boarders £4,325–£5,685; Full Boarders £4,950–£5,985. Instrumental Music Tuition: £197 per instrument.

Lichfield Cathedral School was founded in 1942 principally as a boarding school for the choristers of Lichfield Cathedral. Since that time it has grown considerably and in 1981 became a fully independent co-educational Preparatory and Pre-Preparatory Boarding and Day School for boys and girls between the ages of 3 and 13.

The school began providing secondary education in September 2005 for two classes in Year 7. The school will fill year by year, with a new Sixth Form expected in 2010.

The school currently occupies several buildings in the Cathedral Close, one being the magnificent 17th Century Palace, which was the home of the Bishops of Lichfield until 1952.

In September 2006, the Nursery and Pre-Prep departments moved to new premises in Longdon Green, just outside Lichfield. With the younger children being based in this wonderful six-acre site, with beautifully maintained, purpose-built classrooms, the current facilities in the Cathedral Close are being adapted into academic faculties and departments for the senior pupils, with the dedicated resources required for specialist learning across all subjects.

The link with the Cathedral remains strong with a weekly school service and all Cathedral Choristers board at the school on scholarships provided by the Dean and Chapter. A specialist Girl's Choir was launched in September 2006, with scholarships available from the school, and is already in great demand throughout the region. Academic scholarships are also offered along with all-rounder scholarships for sport, music, art/design, and drama.

Pupils are expected to attain a high standard in all areas of the curriculum. In addition to the academic curriculum, Music, Art, CDT, Drama and Dance are particular strengths and a wide range of Games and extra-curricular activities are also offered.

The general ethos of the School is that of a community where Christian values are upheld and, whilst most pupils are members of the Church of England, children of other denominations and religions are welcomed.

Parents are welcome to contact the school for a conducted tour and meeting with the headmaster or to attend the any of the school Open Mornings held throughout the year.

Charitable status. Lichfield Cathedral School is a Registered Charity, number 1078650. It exists to provide education for boys and girls.

Littlegarth School

Horkesley Park, Nayland, Colchester, Essex CO6 4JR
Tel: 01206 262332
Fax: 01206 263101
e-mail: office@littlegarth.essex.sch.uk
website: www.littlegarth.essex.sch.uk

Headmaster: **Mr Peter H Jones**, BEd Hons

Age Range. 2½–11.
Number of Pupils. Day: approx 156 Boys, 160 Girls.
Fees per term (2011-2012). £620–£2,800.

Set in 28 acres of glorious grounds in the beautiful Stour Valley, Littlegarth School was founded in 1940 in Dedham and moved to Horkesley Park in 1994. An accredited Independent School, Littlegarth offers a thorough and successful academic, cultural and sports education within a secure and friendly environment.

There is a flourishing Nursery Department where children are prepared for admission to the Pre-Prep, which they join at 4+, although children are accepted by assessment and interview at all levels, subject to space.

Littlegarth is proud of the broad curriculum offered. The school boasts small class sizes and a friendly atmosphere. French is taught from the age of 4, when specialist teaching is also provided in music and sport. Academic standards are high and progress is monitored closely at all times. Careful attention is given to children as they prepare for scholarships and entrance examinations to Independent Schools and local Grammar Schools. As the children move from the Pre-Prep, specialist teaching is given in each subject.

Music is one of the strengths of the school and a large percentage of our children learn at least one musical instrument as well as the recorder. School choirs perform in a number of local events and internal concerts are a regular feature of school life. A lunch-time Mandarin Club is open to children from Years 1–6.

The children participate in a wide range of sports throughout the year and the school promotes team participation for all children from the age of 8. As well as boasting a floodlit all-weather area, a substantial new sports hall and changing room complex has been built and a programme to level the sports fields has been completed. An exciting adventure playground has been erected next to the spacious play area.

The school produces many plays each year and strong drama links with the local community are being forged. As well as running the school library, parents are also actively involved in running a wardrobe department and there is a flourishing 'Friends of Littlegarth' parent body.

A wide variety of clubs, extra-curricular activity and pre and after school care are offered.

Charitable status. Littlegarth School Limited is a Registered Charity, number 325064. It exists to provide education for children.

Liverpool College Preparatory School

Queen's Drive, Mossley Hill, Liverpool L18 8BG
Tel: 0151 724 4000
Fax: 0151 724 6389
e-mail: sbuglass@liverpoolcollege.org.uk
website: www.liverpoolcollege.org.uk

Chairman of the Governors: Mr G N Wood, QC
Chairman of the Preparatory School Committee: Mrs M Mason

Head of the Preparatory School: **Mr S Buglass**, MEd Oxon, CertEd

Age Range. 3–11.
Number of Pupils. 281 boys and girls.
Fees per term (2011-2012). Nursery and Pre-Prep (ages 3–7): £1,995; Prep (ages 7–11): £2,585. Lunches £205.

Liverpool College is a co-educational day school set in 26 acres of beautiful wooded grounds. It is situated on the edge of Sefton Park in the conservation area of South Liverpool. The Preparatory School shares the site with the Senior Department, a successful day school of 600 pupils, aged from 11–18 years. However it has its own purpose built buildings and areas within the College.

The staff-pupil ratio (1:11) has encouraged the development of a broad based academic curriculum leading children through Early Years, Foundation Stage, Key Stages 1 and 2. There is breadth as well as depth to the curriculum and in addition to the core and foundation subjects, Modern Foreign Languages, ICT and Public Speaking and Debating are compulsory elements of the curriculum. A well qualified dyslexia specialist is available to assess and support children throughout the school and there is an effective Gifted and Talented programme in place.

Music is an important aspect of school life. There is a thriving choir, jazz orchestra, flute, saxophone, cello, violin, handbells, guitar and samba band groups and performances in school and in the local community are important features of school life.

Most children progress through to the Senior School at 11+ where the brightest have successfully competed for Scholarships. Children are also prepared for entry to other Senior Schools throughout the country.

An extensive extra-curricular programme encourages children to stay at school until 6 pm. Clubs include Judo, Soccer, Cookery, Natural History, Country Dancing, Gardening, Philosophy, Athletics, Drama, Orchestra, Choir, Tennis, Hockey, Cricket, Jewellery Making, Art and Dancing. There is also an after school homework club which enables children to be supervised up until 6 pm completing their homework with teaching staff support and participating in a range of interesting activities. A Breakfast Club operates between 7.45–8.30 am.

During their time in the school children have the opportunity to participate in the annual ski trip to Italy, language courses in France and Spain, Geography and Science field work in North Wales and outward bound activities in the Lake District and North Yorkshire.

There is a major commitment to sport and the facilities include extensive playing fields, an Astroturf playing surface and large Sports Hall and Fitness Suite. Specialist games staff teach the children rugby, cricket, netball, rounders, swimming, cross country, hockey, tennis and athletics.

Liverpool College has an Anglican Foundation, but children of all denominations and faiths are welcomed. The Chapel plays an important part in the life of the school, and twice a week they attend services there. The school is a caring community which places great importance on mutual respect and consideration for others. There is a strong and effective system of pastoral care.

Entry to the School. Children are assessed before entry and are assured of a place in the Senior School once accepted into the Preparatory School. Further details and a prospectus can be obtained from the Registrar.

Charitable status. Liverpool College is a Registered Charity, number 526682. It exists to provide education for boys and girls.

Lochinver House School

Heath Road, Little Heath, Potters Bar, Herts EN6 1LW
Tel: 01707 653064
Fax: 01707 620030
e-mail: registrar@lochinverhouse.herts.sch.uk
website: www.lochinverhouse.herts.sch.uk

Chairman of the Governors: Stuart Westley, MA

Headmaster: **Ben Walker**, BA Hons

Age Range. 4–13.
Number of Boys. 340 Day Boys.
Fees per term (2010-2011). £2,850–£3,734 no compulsory extras.

The academic staff consists of 36 qualified and graduate teachers, Laboratory and DT Technicians, ICT Systems Manager and Technician, classroom assistants and a Matron.

The school is situated in a pleasant residential area on the edge of green belt land in South Hertfordshire, and yet is conveniently placed for access to London. The heart of the school is a late Victorian house. The facilities are extensive and include a purpose built Pre-Prep Department, separate Sports Hall, Gymnasium & Theatre, Music Centre, Modern Languages and English Departments, two Science Laboratories and an Information Technology room equipped with a Network of PCs. All classrooms and offices contain PCs that are also part of the school's Intranet and have protected and supervised Internet access. The school has its own extensive playing fields on site.

Boys are prepared for Common Entrance and Scholarship examinations to a wide range of both day and boarding Independent Schools.

The major sports are Football, Rugby and Cricket together with Athletics and Badminton. All boys learn to swim whilst they are at the School and they have the opportunity to take part in a very wide range of sports and physical activities. This includes outward bound and there is an annual skiing holiday.

During their time at the school each boy will spend some time in France as this is an important and much valued part of the French Curriculum.

Music, Art, Design Technology and PE are part of the timetabled curriculum for all boys regardless of their age. The school encourages boys to learn musical instruments and currently two thirds of the children are doing so. There is a School Orchestra and choir, together with various instrumental groups.

The school is a non-profit making Educational Trust administered by a Board of Governors.

Charitable status. Lochinver House School is a Registered Charity, number 1091045. It aims to provide a quality education.

Lockers Park

Lockers Park Lane, Hemel Hempstead, Hertfordshire HP1 1TL
Tel: 01442 251712
Fax: 01442 234150

e-mail: secretary@lockerspark.herts.sch.uk
website: www.lockerspark.herts.sch.uk

Chairman of Governors: P D Nicholas, Esq

Headmaster: **D S Farquharson**

Admissions: C R Stephens, BA

Age Range. 5–13.
Number of Pupils. 149 Boys, of whom 45 are boarders.
Fees per term (2010-2011). Boarders £6,080, Day Boys £2,700–£4,895. No compulsory extras.

Further details are outlined in the prospectus, available on application.

Lockers Park is located in 23 acres of parkland above the town of Hemel Hempstead, only five miles from both the M1 and M25 motorways. It therefore lies within easy access of London (Euston 30 minutes) and all four of its airports; consequently the School is well accustomed to providing the necessary help and support to parents living both in Britain and abroad.

The main school building, purpose-built in 1874, is situated in grounds which are perfect for children, with well-maintained playing fields surrounded by woodland areas which easily occupy even the most active. There has been a steady process of modernisation over the past two decades and the School boasts first-class, all-round facilities: the Mountbatten Centre, which provides eight excellent specialist classrooms including a well-equipped ICT centre; an attached Science and Technology Building, which opened in July 2007, containing two spacious laboratories, technology classroom and fully-fitted workshop; an exceptional art and pottery centre and a well-resourced library.

Sports facilities are of a high calibre and include a fully-fitted sports hall, two squash courts, a heated swimming pool, two tennis courts, an all-weather sports surface and cricket nets, a shooting range and a nine-hole golf course.

Lockers is proud of its academic and musical records; its success in both scholarships and Common Entrance examinations to 45 different schools in the past ten years reflects this well. The average class size is 14 and the pupil:teacher ratio a very healthy 1:7. The Music Department is well known; encouragement is given to every boy to find an instrument which he will enjoy and most gain proficiency in at least one. There is a full orchestra, wind, brass and jazz bands, a string ensemble and two choirs. The number of senior school scholarships of all types awarded to Lockers Park is considered high.

Drama plays a large part in school life with at least one major production each year together with junior plays, school assembly productions, charades and public speaking debates.

At Lockers, there is a real family atmosphere, there is always someone to whom a boy can turn and great care is taken to ensure the happiness of every child. Boys are safe, happy, fit and well looked after. While day boys enjoy all the facilities and opportunities of a boarding school, boarding is fun; dormitories are warm and friendly rooms and opportunities for a variety of enjoyable weekend activities are immense. With day boys and boarders alike, great care is taken over the personal development of each individual.

Bursaries. Lockers Park is committed to offering financial help to deserving candidates, subject to financial resources. Bursarial help may be available up to 100% of fees in some circumstances.

Charitable status. Lockers Park School Trust Ltd is a Registered Charity, number 311061. It aims to provide an all round, high quality education on a non-profit making basis.

Longacre School

Shamley Green, Guildford, Surrey GU5 0NQ
Tel: 01483 893225
Fax: 01483 893501
e-mail: office@longacre.surrey.sch.uk
website: www.longacre.surrey.sch.uk

Headmistress: **Mrs Alexia Bracewell**, BA Hons, QTS, PCPSE

Age Range. 2½–11.
Number of Pupils. 200+ boys and girls.
Fees per term (2010-2011). £1,757–£3,486.

Are school days really the happiest days of your life? Many Longacre pupils would answer "Yes!" The cheerful and purposeful atmosphere at Longacre is apparent as soon as you enter the school. Here, children are valued as individuals and are encouraged to fulfil their potential in every facet of school life. Personal and social development is highly valued, enabling pupils to grow in confidence as they mature.

The Headmistress and her staff believe that children learn more effectively when they are happy, and that excellent academic results can be achieved without subjecting pupils to hothouse pressure. The fact that Longacre pupils gain a range of scholarships, and that they transfer successfully to senior schools of parental choice, shows that this approach is definitely working.

Academic progress is closely monitored and regularly tested. Small classes (maximum eighteen) enable pupils to be taught at an individual level, with increasing subject specialist tuition as children progress through the school. Alongside the core curriculum, Longacre offers a wide range of sporting opportunities, LAMDA lessons, stimulating off-site visits and exciting workshops. There are after school clubs every evening, ranging from Spanish to judo, and regular masterclasses for able pupils.

Set in a beautiful rural location on the outskirts of the picturesque village of Shamley Green, between Guildford and Cranleigh, the school offers a wonderful environment for young children. The school buildings comprise the original large 1902 house plus modern, purpose-built classrooms standing in nine acres of grounds. Facilities include sports fields, courts, gardens, woodland and an adventure playground.

Longacre is a community where parents are welcome. The school has a thriving and supportive PTA and parents are kept well informed about school events and their children's progress through a weekly newsletter, formal and informal meetings and written reports. The Headmistress and staff work closely with parents to ensure that their children are happy, successful and fulfilled.

To arrange a visit, please call 01483 893225. The Headmistress and her staff look forward to welcoming you to Longacre.

Lorenden Preparatory School

Painter's Forstal, Faversham, Kent ME13 0EN
Tel: 01795 590030
Fax: 01795 538002
e-mail: admin@lorenden.org.uk
website: www.lorenden.org.uk

Chairman of Governors: D Simmons

Headteacher: **Mrs P Tebbit**, CertEd, Adv Dip Prim Eng

Age Range. 3–11 Co-educational.

Number of Pupils. 120.
Fees per term (2010-2011). £1,060–£2,840.

Lorenden Preparatory School is situated in the village of Painter's Forstal near Faversham. Lorenden is very much a rural school. The school grounds form a well-enclosed and safe playing area and offer the children one of the most beautiful playgrounds in Kent. It is a small community of a hundred and twenty eager and happy children aged between 3 and 11, their committed parents and a staff of dedicated professional and inspiring teachers. Classes are small throughout the school.

We provide an excellent and all-round education, with emphasis on a solid foundation in the core subjects English, Maths and Science. Music, ICT, French, Art, Design Technology and the Humanities, Drama and Sport play an important part in the curriculum too.

There are Pre-Prep and Prep Department choirs, a string orchestra as well as individual music lessons. Speech and Drama are considered important and we have elocution lessons. There are opportunities for children to perform in drama productions, Kent Festivals and concerts.

We have a varied programme of visits and outings to enhance the curriculum.

Football, netball, hockey, rugby, cricket and rounders are the major sports. Athletics, swimming and fitness training are also in the curriculum. Our facilities have been significantly improved recently and now include a sports hall. Extra-curricular activities include a chess club, drama workshops, craft, sewing as well as a variety of sports clubs.

Children are well prepared for senior schools and local Grammar schools with the 11+ Entry.

Enquiries concerning places and admissions should be made to the secretary.

Charitable status. Lorenden School is a Registered Charity, number 1048805.

Loretto Junior School

North Esk Lodge, 1 North High Street, Musselburgh, East Lothian EH21 6JA
Tel: 0131 653 4570
Fax: 0131 653 4571
e-mail: juniorschool@loretto.com
website: www.loretto.com

Chairman of Governors: R L Martin, QC

Headmaster: **P Meadows**, MA

Age Range. 3–12.
Number of Pupils. 4 Boarders, 194 Day Pupils.
Fees per term (2011-2012). Full Boarding £5,865; Weekly Boarding £5,310; Day Pupils £2,085–£4,210.

Pupils can enter the Nippers at 3 and are prepared for entrance and scholarship examinations, mostly to Loretto at 12+. Weekly and flexi boarding is possible for pupils between the ages of 8 and 12. Scholarships and Bursaries are available for children aged 10 and over. There is one boarding house at Newfield. As well as the usual prep school facilities, the Nippers use the Loretto Computer Centre, Squash Courts, Fives Courts, Music School, Theatre, School Chapel, and the Sports Hall. The school enjoys a fine reputation for Rugby, Hockey, Cricket, Music, Drama and Art. Loretto has its own Art Gallery. A wide range of individual sports is coached. The staff are all University Graduates and each of the fourteen classes can accommodate up to 20 pupils. Pastoral care is of the highest quality. Catering is in the hands of an experienced Steward.

From an early age children are encouraged to use their initiative and accept responsibility.

Prospectus from the School.

Charitable status. Loretto School is a Registered Charity, number SC013978. It exists in order to educate young people in mind, body and spirit.

Loyola Preparatory School

103 Palmerston Road, Buckhurst Hill, Essex IG9 5NH
Tel: 020 8504 7372
Fax: 020 8505 5361
e-mail: office@loyola.essex.sch.uk
website: www.loyola.essex.sch.uk

Chairman of Governors: Mrs A M Fox

Headmaster: **P G M Nicholson**, BEd London

Age Range. 3–11.
Number of Boys. 190.
Fees per term (2010-2011). £2,635.

A Catholic day school for boys aged 3–11+ which welcomes all denominations – admission is possible at any stage. There are twelve full-time and five part-time staff.

Boys are prepared for entrance and scholarship examinations at 11+ to various Independent Senior Schools and to Grammar Schools in the maintained sector. In 2009 a 90% pass rate was achieved in 11+ procedures. The curriculum covers all the normal primary school subjects including German, science and computer studies. Music is taught throughout the school. There is a schola, choir and orchestra and tuition can be arranged in piano, strings, woodwind, brass and guitar. Sports include football, cricket, swimming, athletics and optional rugby. Early Years provision was found to be outstanding by Ofsted in June 2008.

The school prospectus is contained within its website. Parents are welcome to telephone to arrange tours of the school.

Charitable status. Loyola Preparatory School is a Registered Charity, number 1085079. The school is established in support of Roman Catholic principles of education.

Ludgrove

Wixenford, Wokingham, Berks RG40 3AB
Tel: 0118 978 9881
Fax: 0118 979 2973
e-mail: office@ludgroveschool.co.uk
website: www.ludgrove.co.uk

Chairman of Governors: The Earl of Rosslyn

Joint Headmasters:
S W T Barber, BA Durham, PGCE
A C T Inglis, BA Newcastle, PGCE

Age Range. 8–13.
Number of Boys. 185 Boarders.
Fees per term (2010-2011). £6,950.

Ludgrove stands in its own grounds of 130 acres. Boys are prepared for entry to Senior Independent Schools.

Charitable status. Ludgrove School Trust Limited is a Registered Charity, number 309100.

Lyndhurst House School

24 Lyndhurst Gardens, Hampstead, London NW3 5NW
Tel: 020 7435 4936
Fax: 020 7794 7124 (office hours)
e-mail: pmg@lyndhursthouse.co.uk
website: www.lyndhursthouse.co.uk

Headmaster: **A J C Reid**, MA Oxon

Age Range. 4–13.
Number of Day Boys. 160.
Fees per term (2011-2012). £4,175–£4,700 (excluding lunch and outings).

There is a full-time teaching staff of 19, with class assistants for Pre-Prep years, and part-time learning support. Entry is at 4+, or at 7+ following interviews and assessment. All boys stay to 13+, and sit the Common Entrance or Scholarship to the Independent Senior Schools, usually in London, but often outside. A broad foundation is laid in the junior classes, with subject specialisation commencing at 9+, and very small classes in the last three years. A full programme of games and other activities is pursued throughout. There are specialist rooms for Art and Science, housed in a fine Victorian building with large, well-lit, well-equipped classrooms, and a good-sized playground.

Lyndhurst School
The Junior School of Pocklington School Foundation

West Green, Pocklington, York YO42 2NH
Tel: 01759 321228
e-mail: office@lyndhurst-school.com
website: www.pocklingtonschool.com

Chairman of Governors: Mr C M Oughtred, MA, DL

Headmaster: **Mr I D Wright**, BSc Hons, PGCE, NPQH

Age Range. 4–11 co-educational.
Number of Pupils. 192: 92 Boys, 100 Girls.
Fees per term (2010-2011). Day Pupils: £2,000–£3,138. Full Boarders: £5,417. 5-day Boarders: £5,175.

Lyndhurst is part of Pocklington School (founded in 1514) but has its own staff and self-contained premises set amongst 64 acres of fields and open space on the edge of the market town of Pocklington, 12 miles east of York.

Lyndhurst has its own hall, library and specialist rooms for science, art and information communication technology.

Other excellent facilities such as the swimming pool, playing fields, astroturf pitches, the sports hall and performing arts centre are used jointly with Pocklington School.

There are two Junior boarding Houses, one for boys and one for girls. Each accommodates pupils from the age of 8+. Boarding is available as a full, a 5-day, or occasional option.

Class sizes are fewer than 16 for Pre-Prep and 18 or fewer pupils throughout the school.

An emphasis is placed on the core subjects of English, maths and science but history, geography, art and design technology, music, ICT, religious studies, French and Spanish also play a prominent part, together with swimming, PE and Games.

Initially forms are balanced in both gender and ability, with teachers taking care to ensure that individual children can progress at a pace according to need. From Year 5 onwards pupils are taught in ability groups in maths and English.

Most pupils transfer to Pocklington School at 11 following an entrance test and reports from Lyndhurst.

A wide range of sporting, cultural and other activities supports the curriculum. Pupils visit an outdoor education centre in the Yorkshire Dales, take part in fieldwork and leadership/team challenges and make full use of the excellent attractions in the area.

Games played include rugby, hockey, football, netball, cricket, tennis and rounders – with clubs and teams in athletics, swimming and trampoline also. PE and swimming form part of the weekly timetable for all pupils.

House competitions include music, art, drama, chess, creative writing, general knowledge and sport.

Extra activities take place at lunchtimes and after school and include art, computing, choir, drama, chess, dance, orchestra, trampoline, language clubs, swimming and team coaching.

Lyndhurst has a strong musical tradition with a successful choir and orchestra. Individual music tuition takes place throughout the age range.

Full use is made of the Arts Centre to perform in concerts, plays, sketches and musicals – some jointly with the senior school.

Charitable status. The Pocklington School Foundation is a Registered Charity, number 529834.

Magdalene House Preparatory School
Wisbech Grammar School

North Brink, Wisbech, Cambs PE13 1JX
Tel: 01945 586780
Fax: 01945 586781
e-mail: magdalenehouse@wgs.cambs.sch.uk
website: www.wgs.cambs.sch.uk/magdalene_house

Chair of Governors: Dr D Barter, MBBS, FRCP, FRCPCH, DCH

Headmaster: **Mr C E Moxon**, BA

Age Range. 4–11 co-educational.
Number of Pupils. 165 day pupils.
Fees per term (2011-2012). £2,430. Means-tested Bursary support is available.

Magdalene House Preparatory School, which caters for boys and girls from reception to year six, has doubled in size to over 165 pupils since its re-founding in 1997. Great emphasis is placed on reading, writing and numeracy, and the pupils follow a broad-based curriculum. The children have access to many of the excellent senior school facilities, including the science laboratory, sports hall and theatre. They also have their own library, a dedicated computer room and a light and spacious new hall. Specialist teaching is offered in science, music, design technology, physical education and games, information technology and drama. Many children receive peripatetic music lessons and there are three choirs. Opportunities for performance in drama and music, including class plays, assemblies and informal concerts, are regular features. In January the year six pupils sit an entrance examination for the senior school. (*See Wisbech Grammar School entry in HMC section.*)

Sporting opportunities abound and a full timetable of fixtures against other schools is arranged. The main boys' team sports are rugby, hockey and cricket, whilst the girls play hockey, netball and rounders. Members of the under 11 rugby and hockey teams enjoy an annual long weekend tour to North Yorkshire.

A varied after-school programme for both juniors and infants provides the opportunity to develop sports and leisure skills, as well as artistic and musical talents. A supervised homework club also runs each day.

Field trips, activity days at local museums and visits by theatre groups and outside speakers lie at the heart of the curriculum. Years four, five and six enjoy an annual week at an activity centre.

Generally children are admitted to the reception class at the beginning of the school year in which they reach the age of five, but entry into all year groups is possible at any stage of the year. All children registering are invited to spend part of a day in school when they are assessed in a manner appropriate to their age. Candidates for entry are also welcomed at all other stages of the junior school age range.

All enquiries should be made to the Secretary at Magdalene House Preparatory School.

Charitable status. The Wisbech Grammar School Foundation is a Registered Charity, number 1087799. It exists to promote the education of boys and girls.

Maidwell Hall

Maidwell, Northampton NN6 9JG
Tel: 01604 686234
Fax: 01604 686659
e-mail: thesecretary@maidwellhall.co.uk
website: www.maidwellhall.co.uk

Chairman of the Governors: R H Cunningham, Esq

Headmaster: **R A Lankester**, MA Cantab, PGCE

Age Range. 7–13.
Number of Pupils. 110 Boarders, 4 Day pupils.
Fees per term (2011-2012). £7,300 Boarding, £4,500 Day.

Maidwell Hall is a co-educational boarding school with some day pupils. Occupying a substantial 17th Century hall the school is situated in beautiful countryside and is characterized by its rural location and by 44 acres of grounds. It is a Christian school and the teachings of Jesus Christ are central to the moral and spiritual education of the children. Every Sunday morning the school worships in the parish church on the edge of the school grounds. The school aims to encourage all the children to discover and develop all their talents through the academic curriculum, the games programme, Music, Art, Drama and an impressive range of hobbies and activities. The school's happy atmosphere is based on a clear framework of rules and conventions with strong emphasis placed on good manners and a traditional code of behaviour and courtesy.

The school is organized as a 7 day-a-week boarding school with a comprehensive programme of club activities in the evenings supplemented by a choice of outings or school based free-time activities on Sundays. There is a weekly boarding option for Year 4. The children benefit greatly from the freedom and security of the school's spectacular grounds including its famous arboretum (wilderness) and its large lake for fishing and boating. Leave-outs occur every 2 or 3 weeks and run from Friday midday until Monday evening and each term contains a long half-term break. Pastoral care for the boarders is the direct responsibility of the Headmaster and his wife, the Housemaster and the team of Matrons and other residential staff. In addition each pupil has an individual tutor.

Pupils are prepared for Common Entrance to the major independent senior schools (typically Eton, Harrow, Oundle, Radley, Rugby, Shrewsbury, Stowe, Uppingham and Winchester) and every year several sit scholarships. In addition to core subjects all pupils study Art, Design, ICT, Latin, Music and Religious Studies and there are also timetabled lessons in PE, Swimming, PSHE, and Drama. There is a specialist carpentry shop which operates as a club activity.

The school has a strong reputation for sport. The major games for the boys are rugby, football, hockey and cricket and there are also matches against other schools in athletics, cross-country running, golf, squash, swimming and tennis. The major games for girls are hockey, netball, tennis and rounders. Teams are entered for riding events and the Pytchley hunt meets at the school every year. There is a successful school shooting team. In the Summer and Autumn there is sailing once or twice a week. In addition to impressive games pitches, sporting facilities include a multi-purpose sports hall with climbing wall, a squash court, a 6-hole golf course, astroturf, hockey pitch, tennis courts and a heated indoor swimming pool. There is particular emphasis on outward bound activities and leadership. There is a strong musical tradition and most pupils play one or two musical instruments; there is a thriving church choir and strings, wind and guitar groups. There are regular concerts throughout the year and each year there is a major school play.

Charitable status. Maidwell Hall is a Registered Charity, number 309917. It exists for the purpose of educating children.

Maldon Court Preparatory School

Silver Street, Maldon, Essex CM9 4QE
Tel: 01621 853529
Fax: 01621 853529
e-mail: enquiries@maldoncourtschool.org
website: www.maldoncourtschool.org

Head: **Mrs L F Guest**, BEd Hons

Age Range. 3–11 co-educational.
Number of Pupils. 130 Day Pupils.
Fees per term (from April 2011). £2,538.45 for the first child, with sibling discounts.

The school, founded in 1956, is a co-educational day school of seven classes. The school day begins at 8.45 am and finishes at 3.30 pm. There is an after-school facility available until 5.00 pm which incorporates homework classes and a variety of clubs. The Pre-Prep department welcomes children from the age of 3. Nursery Education Grants are available and the Pre-Prep is Ofsted registered. The school has the reputation of being a happy, friendly community with a family atmosphere.

Maldon Court's premises comprise the larger part of an eighteenth century town house, a separate four classroom block, separate toilets and a small assembly hall. The grounds consist of 2 playgrounds, gardens and adventure play areas. The premises are very convenient for the town centre. Sports grounds for association football, athletics, hockey and other activities are leased locally. There is a wide variety of after-school clubs including netball, cricket, gymnastics, rounders, athletics, and speech and drama. Swimming is undertaken throughout the year at a nearby sports centre. The school's sporting standard is high; over recent years it has won both national and regional awards in netball, football, swimming and athletics.

Approximately half the children leave the school for independent secondary schools, half enter the maintained sector. Maldon Court's scholarship and entrance record to the independent schools is excellent as is its eleven-plus success rate to Essex grammar schools. Close contact is maintained with both systems of education. Its curriculum covers and goes beyond the National Curriculum.

In 1975 a Parents' Association was formed. It is registered separately with the Charity Commission and has developed into an energetic and lively organisation.

The school had its most recent ISI Inspection in June 2008 where it was recognised that the curriculum and innovative teaching had contributed to the pupils' outstanding personal development.

Within the school motto of "Do it with thy might", the aims of Maldon Court are: to foster a love of learning in which the varied talents and life experiences of each pupil are recognised and valued; to provide a broad and stimulating curriculum through which pupils can flourish and become enthusiastic and independent learners, enabling them to reach their full potential; to promote the traditional values of kindness, respect and courtesy within a happy, nurturing atmosphere; to encourage a social awareness and respect for others through involvement in the local community; and to create confident and happy pupils, ready to face the challenges of the wider world. *ISI Inspection Report 2008*

The Mall School

185 Hampton Road, Twickenham, Middlesex TW2 5NQ
Tel: 020 8977 2523
Fax: 020 8977 8771
e-mail: admissions@mall.richmond.sch.uk
website: www.mall.richmond.sch.uk

Chairman of Governors: R J H Walker, BSc

Headmaster: **D Price**, BSc, MA, PGCE

Deputy Head: R H A Struck, BA Frankfurt, MA

Age Range. 4–13.
Number of Boys. 300 day boys.
Fees per term (2011–2012). £3,130 (under 8), £3,560 (over 8).

Established 1872, the School prepares boys for day and boarding Senior Independent Schools and is a charitable Trust. Boys are admitted at 4+, as well as at 7+ and 8+, and are taught by a well-qualified staff consisting of 26 full-time and 2 part-time members. The class size averages 20. There is a broad curriculum based on the CE syllabus, but including Art, DT, Music, and Drama, in addition to sport/PE. A number of awards are won each year (30/40 in the last 5 years, including top scholarships to London day schools).

Cricket, Rugby, Football, Swimming and Athletics are the main school games. The school has its own outstanding indoor swimming pool. Chess is optional. Music and Drama are warmly encouraged. There are 2 choirs and 2 orchestras with a large variety of ensembles and visiting teachers for piano, strings, guitar, woodwind and brass.

During the past 20 years of major redevelopment the school has been almost entirely rebuilt. In addition to bright modern classrooms, facilities include Science Laboratories and Music Department, IT suite, Library, and a sports hall. A new Creative and Performing Arts Centre opened in Spring 2010, providing a 200-seat theatre and large-sized Art and Design Technology studios.

A separate Junior department at Mall Infants, within five minutes' walk, is home to the youngest boys aged 4 and 5 years old.

A prospectus is available on application to the Headmaster's Secretary. Early application is advisable.

Charitable status. The Mall School Trust is a Registered Charity, number 295003. It exists to promote and provide for the advancement of the education of children.

Malsis School

Cross Hills, Nr Skipton, North Yorkshire BD20 8DT
Tel: 01535 633027
Fax: 01535 630571
e-mail: admin@malsis.com
website: www.malsis.com

Chairman of Governors: D A Johnson, Esq

Headmaster: **M R Peel**, BA Hons

Age Range. Co-educational 4–13.
Number of Children. Full Boarding 38, Daily Boarding 80.
Religious Denomination. Church of England. Other denominations welcome.

Fees per term (2010-2011). Boarding £5,825; Day: £4,460 Years 3–8; £2,480 Reception–Year 2.

About Malsis. Malsis is set in its own grounds of forty acres in the Craven District of North Yorkshire in an area of rare beauty near Skipton, Ilkley and the Dales but also within easy reach of the towns of the North of England, 15 miles from Leeds-Bradford airport and only fifteen miles from the M65 motorway. Approximately one-third of the children board and from Malsis move on to schools all over the country, in recent years to Ampleforth, Eton, Giggleswick, Glenalmond, Gordonstoun, Harrow, Oakham, Oundle, Queen Margaret's York, Radley, Repton, Rugby, Shrewsbury, Sedbergh, Stonyhurst, Uppingham and Windermere St Anne's. Scholarships for Academic, All-Rounders, Music, Drama, Art and Sport are won to many of these each year. The pastoral system is centred on the Personal Tutor and we teach the children about courtesy, appreciation of values (spiritual and social); we try to discover any talent and develop it to the full; we develop human qualities such as kindness, humour and honour. Mr and Mrs Peel live in the middle of the school and are very much the "parents" of the school.

All the main subjects are taught; Italian and Spanish are also on offer as activities. Information Technology, Design, Technology, Drama, Art and Cookery are part of the timetable. Reading and Handwriting are central to the children's education at Malsis, with reading periods every day. Extra help (free) is given in English, Mathematics and French; those with learning difficulties are looked after by trained staff.

There is particular emphasis on Art, Music, and Drama. Every child takes part in at least one drama production each year. There are separate boys (Chapel) and girls (Chamber) choirs which lead a regular Saturday morning service and also plenty of opportunities for children to perform. The school attends local music and drama festivals and children take part in many concerts. Music groups, including a Concert Band, meet each week. Groups visit local theatres, concert halls and places of interest.

Malsis has an excellent record in sport, regularly winning trophies far and near but more than that, nearly all the children play in a team and all children are coached games, whatever their ability. Rugby, Cricket, Cross-Country, Hockey, Netball, Swimming, Athletics, Rounders and Tennis are the main sports with Soccer an option for the smaller children. The school grounds include fifteen acres of pitches, an astroturf pitch (four all-weather tennis courts), a nine-hole golf course, a small grass athletics track, a beck, woods, a lake and a RAP (climbing) Tree. There is also a 3km long, professionally designed, mountain bike trail, accredited by the British Cycling Federation – the first school to have such a facility.

Malsis is generously equipped to meet the modern world of education: light, specialist teaching rooms including two Science Laboratories, Art Department, Design and Technology centre, IT centre, 18 room Music school, Sports Hall, Gymnasium, Indoor Swimming pool, a Theatre and a Chapel. Well-equipped games rooms offer snooker, table tennis, table-soccer and a host of board games. A varied activity programme is available each week with more than 70 activities on offer, ranging from hill walking, camping, archery, sailing, canoeing, shooting, basketball, badminton, judo, golf, cuisine, dance, fly-fishing, shotgun skills, bushchraft, photography, trampolining, and juggling to name but a few.

Pre-Preparatory Department. Years 1 and 2 are taught in the main school building. Reception Class is taught in its own self-contained building with outdoor learning areas, playground and access to the facilities enjoyed by the whole school.

Charitable status. Malsis School is a Registered Charity, number 529336. It exists to offer children a full, rounded education, promoting an environment that encourages young people to be purposeful in all that they do, to lead a well-balanced life, be charming in their dealings with all others and to develop a sense of modest style.

Maltman's Green

Maltmans Lane, Gerrards Cross, Bucks SL9 8RR
Tel: 01753 883022
Fax: 01753 891237
e-mail: office@maltmansgreen.com
website: www.maltmansgreen.com

Preparatory School for Girls.

Chairman: A M J Frost, Esq, JP, FRICS

Headmistress: **Mrs J Pardon**, MA, BSc, PGCE

Age Range. 3–11.
Number of Girls. 420.
Fees per term (2010-2011). £1,130 (half day Nursery) to £3,545.

Maltman's Green is a school for girls from 3 to 11. Our girls thrive, working hard and having fun. We believe in the pursuit of excellence whilst maintaining a sense of fun. Our girls are encouraged to take risks in all aspects of school life and are well known for their enthusiasm and confidence. We also nurture old-fashioned values such as courtesy, doing one's best, and respect for others.

Maltman's Green has exceptional facilities including two libraries, specialist teaching classrooms for science, ICT, design and art, music practice rooms, a sports hall and gym and safe and secure traditional playgrounds and a state-of-the-art six-lane indoor swimming pool as well as a new Discovery Garden.

There is plenty of open green space around the School. Sustainability is now at the heart of the School Development Plan and the school is successfully working towards Eco-School Status.

Inside, the classrooms are all bright and spacious, with colourful, ever-changing displays. The atmosphere is lively, challenging and happy.

Although we are a non-selective school, our girls have an outstanding track record of winning scholarships to top independent schools and of gaining entrance to the local grammar schools.

The creative and performing arts flourish at Maltman's. The school strongly believes that all children should be given the opportunity to develop their creativity and express themselves.

From Nursery, all girls enjoy specialist Music lessons twice a week. The nationally famous Maltman's Singers regularly reaches the top of national competitions.

All girls have weekly drama lessons from Reception to Year 6. The girls take part in a dramatic production every year.

In addition to the weekly lessons in Art and Design Technology, there are also numerous clubs.

All girls have a lesson of sport every day and, from Nursery. Our girls are frequently local, regional and national champions in swimming, gymnastics, tennis and several team sports.

We provide specialist learning support for girls with learning difficulties, such as dyslexia, and make time to help any girl who might slip behind. Specialist support is also provided for the very able and gifted girls.

Finally, the partnership with parents is not a cliché at Maltman's, but is a genuine joint approach to education. If your daughter knows what is expected of her and is given the expert support and care, and if you are kept informed and involved, the girls have every opportunity to achieve their best.

Charitable status. Maltman's Green School Trust Limited is a Registered Charity, number 310633. It exists to provide a high standard of education for young girls.

Manor Lodge School

Rectory Lane, Ridge Hill, Shenley, Herts WD7 9BG
Tel: 01707 642424
Fax: 01707 645206
e-mail: prospectus@manorlodgeschool.com
website: www.manorlodgeschool.com

Chair of Governors: Mr A Phipps

Head: **Mr G Dunn**, CertEd

Age Range. 3–11.
Number of Pupils. Nursery (age 3) 28; Infant Department (age 4–7) 173; Junior Department (age 7–11) 216.
Fees per term (2011-2012). Nursery £2,700; Infants £2,910; Juniors £3,330.

There are three forms of approximately 18 children in Years Reception to 6 inclusive. There are specialist teachers for French, PE, IT, CDT, Art and Music as well as numerous peripatetic teachers for brass, woodwind and strings. All staff are fully qualified.

The school consists of a 17th century house and the converted stables offer fifteen classrooms, a French Room, a DT Room and a beautiful hall. The classrooms are bright and well-equipped and the standard of work displayed is very high. The new conservatory across the EYFS has doubled the size of the classrooms and brought the outside in. We aim to provide excellent teaching within an environment characterised by a well balanced but friendly family atmosphere in which high standards of behaviour and good manners are encouraged and expected. We thus ensure that all pupils achieve their full potential and are prepared for entry to senior schools, both independent and state.

The cottage at the end of the drive has been completely refurbished and now houses a Nursery. The children must be siblings of pupils in the main school and are eligible to attend from the term in which they are three. The new dining room is complete and is a superb addition to the school. The Caterers, Brookwoods, provide a vast selection of fresh lunches, both vegetarian and meat based. The twelve acres of grounds include woodland, pitches, courts and play areas with climbing activity equipment and other outdoor toys. The children are offered a wide range of sporting activities including football, rugby, hockey, cricket, netball, rounders, swimming and athletics. Music plays an important part in the life of the school. There are several choirs, an orchestra and almost half the children in school learn an instrument. Music is of course linked into our Drama activities. Reception to Year 5 children take part in at least two performances a year, but in Year 6 a local theatre is hired for 10 days to give the children real theatre experience. Art is of a particularly high standard and the children use a variety of media, producing excellent original work.

Extra activities available at the school include chess, drama and ju-jitsu. There are numerous clubs run by the staff at lunchtime and after school until 4.15 pm or 5 pm, for example, sewing, calligraphy, football, rugby, cricket, netball, theatre, athletics and choir.

Charitable status. Manor Lodge School is a Registered Charity, number 1048874. The school exists to provide an education which will maximise the potential of the girls and boys in our care.

The Manor Preparatory School

Faringdon Road, Abingdon, Oxon OX13 6LN
Tel: 01235 858458
Fax: 01235 559593
e-mail: registrar@manorprep.org

website: www.manorprep.org

Chairman of the Governors: Mrs R Kashti

Headmaster: **Mr Piers Heyworth**, MA Oxon, PGCE

Age Range. Girls 2–11, Boys 2–7.
Number of Pupils. 370 Day: Girls 320, Boys 50.
Fees per term (2011-2012). £3,000–£3,860.

The Manor is a Charitable Trust. It is surrounded by spacious grounds and there are good facilities for indoor and outdoor games.

A well-qualified staff teach a full range of subjects. Boys are prepared for entry to preparatory schools and girls for the Common Entrance Examination for Girls Schools, or for entrance examinations to other senior schools.

The curriculum is broad. Science, Information Communication Technology, Art, Design, Music, Physical Education and Modern Languages are all taught by specialists. All subjects have specialist teaching in the final two years of the preparatory department.

Computers are used throughout the school to supplement the curriculum and ICT skills are taught in three specialist ICT suites. There are two school orchestras, two choirs and various instrumental groups. The chamber choir has performed at the Schools Prom at the Albert Hall. It is possible to learn almost any musical instrument as an optional extra.

Enthusiastic games teaching includes swimming throughout the year and skilled coaching in netball, football, tennis, athletics, rounders, badminton, tag rugby and lacrosse. Our netball team has reached the national final of the IAPS tournaments.

As an optional extra supervised after-school sessions run every day from 4.00–6.00 pm. Children are given tea before working or playing quietly and enjoying organised activities. There is also a very wide range of after-school clubs the children can join. A free Early Birds Club where children can be dropped off at school at 8.00 am is offered. Flexible nursery and pre-nursery sessions from age 2 are offered.

Bus transport is arranged for pupils travelling from surrounding areas.

The school promotes close cooperation between parents and teachers. Parents' Evenings are a regular feature. "The Friends of The Manor" association is run by parents to welcome new families and to support the school.

Charitable status. The Manor Preparatory School is a Registered Charity, number 900347. It exists to provide education for girls and boys.

The Marist Preparatory School

Kings Road, Sunninghill, Ascot, Berkshire SL5 7PS
Tel: 01344 626137
Fax: 01344 621566
e-mail: admissionsprep@themaristschools.com
website: www.themaristschools.com

Independent Catholic Day School for Girls.

Chair of Governors: Mrs M Cairns

Headteacher: **Miss Jenny Finlayson**, Adv Dip, BEd, MA

Age Range. 2½–11.
Number of Pupils. 230 girls.
Fees per term (2011-2012). £2,615–£2,775.
Mission Statement:
The aim of the school is to:
- provide a caring community where learning is guided by strong Christian values;
- promote excellence where all are encouraged to reach their full potential.

Strengths of the school:

- Early Years, infant and junior departments tailored to the specific needs of the girls at each stage of their education.
- Caring, well qualified and professional staff dedicated to developing happy, secure and stimulated girls.
- Curriculum designed to achieve all the foundation/early year learning goals.
- Able to offer a wide range of both academic and extra-curricular activities.
- High achievement in gym, ballet, art, judo, drama, choir and music.
- Strong emphasis on pastoral care, spiritual and personal development; care and consideration for others.
- Small class sizes to enhance individual progression and recognition.
- The school is renowned for its high standards regarding moral values, community spirit, respect and care. This is in line with the overall ethos of the Marist order which has a worldwide presence, providing a truly international dimension to a girl's education.
- Girls are taught to consider and help those less fortunate than themselves through involvement in a wide range of local, national and international charity projects.

The Marist Preparatory School is able to offer your daughter a complete and fulfilling education in the security of a single sex environment, from the age of 2½ to 11. We welcome all Christians and those supporting its ethos. We are renowned for our happy and caring ethos, where pastoral care is considered paramount. Your daughter will be treated as an individual and encouraged to achieve her full potential in every area. We have a strong academic record but we also place a strong emphasis on extra-curricular activities which help to develop important qualities such as self confidence, individual creativity and teamwork.

We also have a Senior School and Sixth Form on the same campus for girls aged 11–18. *For further details, please see the Marist Senior School entry in the GSA section.*

Charitable status. The Marist Schools is a Registered Charity, number 225485. The principal aims and activities of the Marist Schools are religious and charitable and specifically to provide education by way of an independent day school for girls between the ages of 2½ and 18.

Marlborough House School

High Street, Hawkhurst, Cranbrook, Kent TN18 4PY
Tel: 01580 753555
Fax: 01580 754281
e-mail: registrar@marlboroughhouseschool.co.uk
website: www.marlboroughhouseschool.co.uk

Marlborough House was founded in 1874 and is registered as an Educational Trust with a Board of Governors.

Chairman of Governors: J Hawkins

Headmaster: D N Hopkins, MA Oxon, PGCE

Deputy Head: P Tooze, BA, PGCE

Director of Studies: N Davidson, MA Oxon, PGCE

Age Range. 3–13 Co-educational.
Number of Pupils. 336.
Fees per term (2010-2011). Prep £4,605, Pre-Prep £2,310–£2,725, Nursery £795 (no compulsory extras). Flexi-boarding: £35 per night.

The School is fully co-educational creating a friendly, family atmosphere for children between the ages of 3 and 13.

Marlborough House is situated half a mile from the village of Hawkhurst in the beautiful countryside of the Kent/Sussex border. The fine Georgian house is set in 35 acres of superb gardens, playing fields, lawns and woodland. The School has a Chapel, Computer Centre, Sports Hall, Gym, superbly equipped Science Laboratory, Art, Pottery and Design Technology Department, Music Rooms, Swimming Pool, a .22 Rifle Shooting Range and all-weather games surfaces.

With our 40+ qualified teaching staff we aim to produce well motivated, balanced, confident children who know the value of hard work, and who will thrive in their next schools and the modern world beyond. Our classes are small and the children are prepared for all major Senior Schools, whilst those showing special promise sit scholarships.

Encouragement is given to each child to experience a wide variety of activities. In addition to the traditional sports of Cricket, Rugby, Soccer, Hockey, Athletics, Netball and Rounders, opportunities are provided for Music (with the opportunity to learn a wide range of instruments and join the orchestra and choir), Art (in many different media), Pottery, Drama, Ballet, Technology, Computers, Shooting, Tennis, Sailing, Golf, Swimming and Judo.

A copy of the Prospectus together with a Magazine will be mailed to prospective parents on application to the Registrar.

Charitable status. Marlborough House School is a Registered Charity, number 307793. It exists to provide education for children.

Marlston House School

Hermitage, Newbury, Berkshire RG18 9UL
Tel: 01635 200293
Fax: 01635 200190
e-mail: info@brockmarl.org.uk
website: www.brockmarl.org.uk

Headmistress: **Mrs C E Riley**, MA, BEd, CertEd

Age Range. 3–13.
Number of Girls. 169 Girls (including 65 Boarders).
Fees per term (2010-2011). Boarding £6,100, Day £4,330–£4,600. Pre-Prep School (Ridge House): £558–£2,750.

Established in 1995, Marlston House is situated in 60 acres of its own grounds in countryside of outstanding beauty, only four miles from access to the M4. The school is situated beside Brockhurst Boys' Preparatory school and occupies separate listed buildings. Boys and girls are taught separately, but the two schools join together for drama music and activities. In this way Brockhurst and Marlston House combine the best features of the single-sex and co-educational systems: academic excellence and social interaction. The schools are proud of the high standard of pastoral care established within a family atmosphere. (*See also entry for Brockhurst School.*)

The Pre-Prep School, Ridge House, is a co-educational department of Brockhurst and Marlston House Schools for 75 children aged 3–6 years, and is situated on the same site in new self-contained, purpose-designed accommodation.

Girls are prepared for entry to a variety of leading Independent Senior Schools through the ISEB Common Entrance and Scholarship Papers at 11+ and 13+.

All girls play Netball (outdoor and indoor courts), Hockey, Rounders and Tennis (outdoor and indoor courts) and take part in Athletics, Cross Country and Swimming (25m indoor heated pool). Additional activities include riding (own equestrian centre), fencing, judo, shooting (indoor rifle range), dance and ballet. Facilities for gymnastics and other sporting activities are provided in a purpose-built Sports Hall. The schools also have their own Chateau near Bordeaux where the pupils practice their spoken French as part of the Year 7 spoken French curriculum.

Music, Art/Design (newly built studios), Speech and Drama are important features of the curriculum and a number of girls have won scholarships and awards to senior schools in these subjects recently.

Transport is provided by the school to and from airports and between Newbury and Paddington stations. Pupils are accompanied by school staff to their destinations.

Mayfield Preparatory School

Sutton Road, Walsall, West Midlands WS1 2PD
Tel: 01922 624107
Fax: 01922 746908
e-mail: info@mayfieldprep.co.uk
website: www.mayfieldprep.co.uk

Administered by the Governors of Queen Mary's Schools.

Chair of Governors: Mrs J Aubrook

Headmaster: **Mr Matthew Draper**, BA, PGCE

Age Range. 2–11 Co-educational.
Number of Pupils. Day: 110 Boys, 88 Girls.
Fees per term (2011-2012). Main School £2,320; Pre-Nursery £1,395.

A co-educational day school for children aged 2 to 11+, set in a listed building with beautiful surroundings and playing fields. A purpose-built Science/Art building opened in November 2000.

The self-contained Nursery Department accepts children at 2+.

A fully qualified Staff with full-time ancillary support throughout KS1 ensures that the individual child receives maximum attention.

The main aim at Mayfield is to encourage intellectual excellence. Children experience a thorough grounding in literacy and numeracy skills.

Through stimulating courses of correctly-paced work the school specialises in the preparation of the children for Grammar and Independent School entrance examinations at 11+.

Our children achieve excellent results, but it is always borne in mind that the individual child's needs are met by matching achievement to potential. All children are expected and encouraged to develop daily in confidence and security.

We believe in a balanced curriculum, and at Mayfield practical and non-academic activities additionally provide interest and varied experiences in Sports, Art, Music, ICT, DT, Dance, Drama and Public Speaking.

Good manners are expected at all times, as well as a happy and whole-hearted participation in the life and studies offered by the school.

Micklefield School

10 Somers Road, Reigate, Surrey RH2 9DU
Tel: 01737 224212
Fax: 01737 248889
e-mail: office@micklefieldschool.co.uk
website: www.micklefieldschool.co.uk

Chairman of the Council: Mr A B de M Hunter, FCA

Headmistress: **Mrs L Rose**, BEd Hons, CertEd, DipPC

Age Range. Rising 3–11.
Number of Pupils. 272 (128 boys, 144 girls).

Fees per term (2011-2012). £905–£3,085. Lunches £165–£170.

'Micklefield recognised the individuality in my different twins and helped them realise their potential socially and academically.'

'Micklefield has helped my boys build confidence and self-esteem in a friendly and secure environment.'

'My children have flourished at Micklefield.'

These quotes from current and former parents sum up the very special education offered at Micklefield School. Established in Reigate 100 years ago, we offer small classes, taught by qualified staff and qualified subject specialists. We cater for boys and girls from the age of rising 3 up to the age of eleven, preparing them for Common Entrance and other examinations.

After-school care is available for children from Reception age.

In addition to the normal academic subjects, the curriculum includes design technology, information technology, dancing, drama, French, netball, tennis, athletics, swimming, football, rugby, cricket and uni-hoc. We have an excellent record in examinations for entrance to senior schools, twenty scholarships having been awarded in 2009.

Children enjoy academic success, take an active part in a variety of musical and theatrical activities and excel in sports. Dramatic productions and concerts provide opportunities for everyone to display their talents. We encourage participation in drama festivals, sports fixtures, the School's orchestra and choirs. Visits to concerts, theatres and museums are organised together with residential activity holidays for the older children.

A new nursery building was opened in 2006 which provides the younger children with a light, spacious learning environment, fully integrated with the main school. This new facility has up-to-date play equipment, computers and an outside play area. There is a dining room where professional caterers serve high-quality, healthy lunches. The school also has its own sports field within 250 yards in St Albans Road.

Visit the website or telephone for a prospectus on 01737 224212. Mrs Rose, the Headmistress, is always pleased to show prospective parents around by appointment.

Charitable status. Micklefield School (Reigate) Limited is a Registered Charity, number 312069. It exists to provide a first-class education for its pupils.

Millfield Preparatory School

Edgarley Hall, Glastonbury, Somerset BA6 8LD
Tel: 01458 832446
Fax: 01458 833679
e-mail: office@millfieldprep.com
website: www.millfieldprep.com

Chair of Governors: Sir J G Reith, KCB, CBE

Head: **Mrs Shirley Shayler**, MA, BSc Hons, PGCE

Age Range. 2–13.
Number of Boys and Girls. 140 Boarders, 300 Day Pupils.
Fees per term (2011-2012). Boarding £7,125, Day £2,234–£4,890.

The School is administered by the same Board of Governors and on the same principles of small-group teaching as Millfield Senior School (made possible by a staffing ratio of approximately 1 to 8) which ensures breadth and flexibility of timetable. It has its own attractive grounds of 185 acres some four miles from the Senior School, and its extensive facilities include games fields, art, design and technology centre, music school, science laboratories, sports hall, astroturf, gymnasium, golf course, tennis courts, equestrian centre on campus, 25 metre indoor swimming pool, three IT laboratories and chapel. The pupils also have access to some of the specialist facilities at Millfield Senior School including water based astro, Olympic-sized swimming pool, tartan athletics track and indoor tennis centre.

The Pre-Prep department, taking children from 2–7, moved onto the prep school site in 2004 so that the school now offers an education for children from ages 2–13, after which the majority of pupils transfer to Millfield. The small class sizes allow the individual pupil to be taught at his or her most appropriate pace. The range of ability within the school is comprehensive and setting caters for both the academically gifted and those requiring additional learning support.

The curriculum is broadly based and provides a balance between the usual academic subjects and the aesthetic, musical and artistic fields. Junior pupils study French, Year 6 French and Latin and there is a choice of French, Spanish and Latin from the age of 10 upwards. Children may choose either one or two foreign languages, dependent on ability. Science is taught throughout the school, and as three separate subjects from the age of 10.

There is a full games programme organised by qualified teachers of physical education, with the help of other staff. The programme includes Athletics, Badminton, Canoeing, Cricket, Football, Gymnastics, Hockey, Netball, Riding, Rounders, Rugby, Squash, Swimming, Tennis, Outdoor Pursuits and Multi-Sports to name but a few.

Over 90 different clubs are available. Nearly 300 pupils study musical instruments and there are 2 orchestras, 4 choirs and 14 musical groups.

Boys and girls are admitted from the age of 2 and up to the age of 12 and they come from many lands and widely differing backgrounds. Admission usually depends on interview, assessment and reports from the previous school. Assistance with fees in the form of awards may be available at certain ages to applicants for academic ability, sporting talent, musical, artistic, and skill in chess.

There are five boarding houses (three for boys and two for girls). Each house is under the care of resident houseparents and assistant house parents. The medical centre is staffed by 3 qualified nurses, and the School Doctor attends daily.

Charitable status. Millfield is a Registered Charity, number 310283. The Millfield Schools provide a broad and balanced education to boys and girls from widely differing backgrounds, including a significant number with learning difficulties, and many for whom boarding is necessary.

Milton Keynes Preparatory School

Tattenhoe Lane, Milton Keynes MK3 7EG
Tel: 01908 642111
Fax: 01908 366365
e-mail: info@mkps.co.uk
website: www.mkps.co.uk

Chairman of the Governors: Mr Peter Squire, MA

Headmistress: **Hilary Pauley**, BEd

Deputy Head: James Canwell

Age Range. Nursery 2 months–2½ years. Pre-Prep 2½–7 years. Preparatory Department 7+–11 years.
Number of Pupils. 450 Day Pupils.
Fees per term (2010–2011). Nursery (per week): £215 (babies under 1 year), £225 (1–2½ years). Pre-Preparatory: £3,160 (2½–5 years), £3,280 (6–7 years). Preparatory £3,640 (8–11 years).

Milton Keynes Preparatory School is purpose-built with facilities which include a Science laboratory, DT workshop

and large multi-purpose sports hall. Facilities at the Farm include a fitness room, weather station, ICT lab and a large pond to extend our environmental studies.

Opening hours are 7.30 am – 6.30 pm for 46 weeks per year which enable children of working parents to join playschemes in school holidays and to be cared for outside normal daily school hours.

Staff are highly qualified and committed. Academic standards are excellent, with pupils being prepared for entry to senior independent schools locally and nationally and to grammar schools. Teaching is structured to take into account the requirements of the National Curriculum, with constant evaluation and assessment for each pupil.

Music and Sport play an important part in the life of the school. Concerts are held, and a wide variety of sports is played, with teams competing regularly against other schools.

The school aims to incorporate the best of modern teaching methods and traditional values in a friendly and busy environment where good work habits and a concern for the needs of others are paramount.

The Minster School
York

Deangate, York YO1 7JA
Tel: 0844 939 0000
Fax: 0844 939 0001
e-mail: school@yorkminster.org
website: www.minsterschoolyork.co.uk

Chairman of Governors: The Dean of York, The Very Revd Keith Jones

Head Master: **Alex Donaldson**, MA St John's College, Cambridge, PGCE London, Cert ICT Cambridge

Age Range. 3–13 Co-educational.
Number of Pupils. Preparatory 111; Pre-Prep Department 69.
Fees per term (2010–2011). Upper School: £2,703. Pre-Prep: £1,758 (full day). Choristers receive a substantial Scholarship.

The Minster School was originally founded in 627 to educate singing boys. It is now a fully co-educational preparatory and pre-preparatory school, which includes a Nursery department. Recent Ofsted and ISI inspection reports highlighted the Nursery teaching and provision as 'excellent'. Teaching throughout the whole school was singled out as a particular strength and the achievement, attitude and behaviour of the pupils were warmly praised.

The Nursery and Pre-Prep departments are housed in their own accommodation with gardens, playgrounds and an ICT suite for junior pupils' use. French is taught from Year 2 upwards. In the prep school, teaching is delivered by well-qualified subject specialists. With computers in all classrooms, an IT suite, science lab, art room and DT suite the school is well equipped to deliver a broad curriculum. On our 8-acre sports fields games are taught by school staff and professional coaches. Regular fixtures for boys and girls teams are arranged throughout the year. The major sports are football, hockey, netball, cricket and athletics. In addition to the normal academic curriculum, there is a flourishing music department and all orchestral instruments are taught. Pupils' levels of musical achievement are very high though there are no academic or musical tests to join the school.

Lunch and after-school care are not charged as extras and a wide variety of extra-curricular activities is available – sewing, chess, ballet, fencing, judo, art and craft, modelmaking and sports clubs etc.

Of the 180 children in the School, 20 boys and 20 girls are choristers who sing the services in York Minster in return for a substantial scholarship. Pupils are prepared for Common Entrance and Senior Independent School Scholarships. Many children gain music, art and academic scholarships to their senior schools.

Moira House Junior School

Upper Carlisle Road, Eastbourne, East Sussex BN20 7TE
Tel: 01323 636800
e-mail: info@moirahouse.co.uk
website: www.moirahouse.co.uk

Chairman of School Council: Ms J A Jackson-Hill, BA Hons, FRSA

Head: **Mrs Linda Young**, CertEd, NPQH

Age Range. Girls 2–11, Boys 2–4.
Number of Pupils. 110.
Fees per term (2011-2012). £2,050–£3,740 (Day Pupils); £6,170 (Weekly Boarders); £6,640 (Boarders).

Moira House is set within 15 acres of attractively landscaped grounds, on the outskirts of the historic town of Eastbourne on the South Coast of England. Founded in 1875, Moira House welcomes girls from the age of two to eleven in the Junior School and boys in the Nursery, with full, weekly or flexi-boarding offered from the age of 9. The Junior School shares the site with the Senior School for girls aged eleven to eighteen. (*See entry in GSA section.*)

The Junior School aims to provide a broad and balanced curriculum and activity programme, ensuring equal access and opportunity so that children can celebrate and strive for excellence. We believe that children will learn if they feel happy and secure, and if their natural curiosity is aroused. They learn best when they are actively involved in the learning, with skilled teachers to guide them. As a school our aim is to provide an atmosphere and a richness of experience within which each child's unique qualities can flourish. Our emphasis is on the importance of individual development, helping each child to realise her maximum potential. We aim, therefore, to set high standards for each child so that they are constantly challenged to develop further their skills and understanding.

Curriculum. The Foundation Stage and National Curriculum form the basis of what is taught but with the flexibility of specialist teachers and creative learning and teaching strategies. The curriculum aims to develop critical and creative thinking and self-discipline. Education at this stage is a foundation for the future and as broad as possible, combining the modern technology of interactive whiteboards and an ICT suite with all areas of the curriculum. Teaching is in small groups and is strong throughout. The girls enjoy mixed-ability classes but are grouped according to ability in Maths.

EAL, SEN, Sport, Drama, French, Swimming and Music are all taught or supported to an exceptional level by specialists. The Junior School has three choirs and all the children are involved in productions, concerts and creative arts presentations across the year. Most of the children take individual music lessons on a variety of instruments.

PE and Swimming form part of the curriculum and the girls have been particularly successful in competitive challenges. The girls enjoy the facilities of a 50m heated indoor swimming pool, a sports hall and extensive playing fields and netball and tennis courts.

The school has recently created a wonderful outdoor classroom with a pond and large greenhouse where the children begin to understand how important their role is in looking after the natural environment in a more sustainable world.

Extra-curricular. The school offers a free daily Afternoon Activity Club until 6.00pm and there are a fleet of buses which can transport children to and from home each day.

A wealth of extra-curricular activities enriches the experience of the pupils. The activity programme includes Mandarin, Dance, Short tennis, TaeKwonDo, Trampolining, Gymnastics, ICT club, Environmental Studies club, Sewing club, Handbell ringing, String ensemble and a wide variety of sporting clubs.

Charitable status. Moira House Girls School is a Registered Charity, number 307072.

Monkton Preparatory

Combe Down, Bath BA2 7ET
Tel: 01225 837912
Fax: 01225 840312
e-mail: admin@monktonprep.org.uk
website: www.monktoncombeschool.com

Chairman of Governors: S Wilsher, BA Econ

Headmaster: **C J Stafford**, BA, CertEd

Deputy Head: M L Creeth, BEd

Director of Studies: M S Bray, BA, PGCE

Age Range. 2–13.
Number of Pupils. Boarders 51, Day Boys 142, Day Girls 86, Pre-Prep 117.
Fees per term (2011-2012). Boarders: £6,330 (Year 3), £6,632 (Years 4–6), £6,732 (Years 7–8). Day Pupils: £3,415 (Year 3), £4,019 (Year 4), £4,370 (Years 5–6), £4,722 (Years 7–8). Pre-Prep: £2,577–£2,762 (Kindergarten–Year 2). Nursery £26.37 per am session.

There are no extra charges except for learning a musical instrument and specialist activities like judo and dance. There are reductions in fees for the children of clergy and HM Forces. Scholarships are offered for those with all-round academic, musical, artistic, sporting ability at age 7 and 11. Interim awards are also given to pupils demonstrating outstanding ability.

The School became fully co-educational in September 1993 and has full flexi-boarding arrangements that cater for both boys and girls from the age of 7. It stands in its own grounds on a magnificent site with the city of Bath on one side and the Midford valley on the other. The buildings include a chapel, a modern classroom block, a theatre for drama and music with 12 music practice rooms, a sports hall, an indoor 25 metre pool and dance studio. The Coates Building incorporates an art studio, design technology workshop, a newly refurbished learning resource centre, seminar room and ICT suite. There are 20 acres of grounds, 3 tennis courts, a hard playing area, an adventure playground and a nature reserve. A new all-weather hockey pitch was opened in September 2009.

The School has a strong musical tradition and flourishing Art and DT Departments. There are two choirs, an orchestra, a band and various other instrumental groups. Drama also plays an important part in school life.

Rugby, Hockey, and Cricket are the major boys' games; Netball, Hockey and Rounders are the major girls' games. All pupils take part in Gymnastics, Swimming, Athletics and Cross-Country. Squash, Badminton, Dance, Judo, Basketball, Fencing and Horse-Riding are also available. There is a full programme of matches. All pupils take part in hobbies and activities sessions.

There are 29 fully qualified members of the teaching staff and others who are part time. In addition, the Pre-Preparatory Department, which works as a separate entity but shares many of the Preparatory School amenities, has 11 trained teachers, two nursery nurses and two assistants. Children join the Pre-Prep at two. The main entry to the Preparatory School is at seven plus, but the school accepts pupils who wish to join at a later stage.

Boys and Girls are prepared for Common Entrance and Scholarship exams to Independent Senior Schools. At least three-quarters of them proceed to the Senior School and a quarter to a wide range of other Independent Senior Schools. 90 Scholarships have been won in the past five years.

Over the years Monkton has educated many children from families who are working overseas, especially HM Forces families. We make special arrangements for them and are well used to meeting their various needs.

The School finds its central inspiration and purpose in its Christian tradition. The caring, family ethos is underpinned by a large number of resident staff, including the Headmaster and his wife.

Charitable status. Monkton Combe School is a Registered Charity, number 1057185. Its aim is to provide education for girls and boys aged 2 to 18, in accordance with the doctrine and principles of the Church of England.

Moon Hall School for Dyslexic Children

Pasturewood Road, Holmbury St Mary, Dorking, Surrey RH5 6LQ
Tel: 01306 731464
Fax: 01306 731504
e-mail: enquiries@moonhallschool.co.uk
website: www.moonhallschool.co.uk

Chairman of Governors: Mr David Baker

Headmistress: **Mrs Pamela Loré**, BA Hons Psych, MA Ed, DipSpLD

Age Range. 7–13.
Number of Children. Approximately 100.
Fees per term (2011-2012). Day Pupils £5,770; Boarding Pupils £7,450.
Religious denomination: Church of England.
Moon Hall School, Holmbury St Mary caters for boys and girls with SpLD. Accredited by CReSTeD (SP), it has a unique relationship with Belmont Preparatory School (*see separate entry*), sharing its site and excellent facilities. Uniform is common to both schools, and pupils are fully integrated at assembly, lunch and break. They also join together for sport/teams and in dramatic and musical productions.

MHS's specialist qualified, multi-disciplinary staff deliver a full curriculum to dyslexic children from 7 years. Pupils may transfer to Belmont classes when ready, usually into Year 7. They return for ongoing support, as required, up to age 13. Provision for these older children ranges from one 1:1 lesson per week to a complete curriculum in English, Mathematics and Typing (16 lessons). All are taught to touch-type and are successfully entered for OCR examinations normally taken by those aged 16+.

After Year 8 children may transfer to a number of suitable mainstream senior schools, or continue their education at Moon Hall College, our own Senior School located in Leigh, near Reigate.

Within the well-designed, purpose-built accommodation, classes contain a maximum of 14 children, subdivided for English and Mathematics. One-to-one tuition is available as needed. Literacy and numeracy teaching is structured and multi-sensory, incorporating material devised by acknowledged experts in the field. The Phono-Graphix Programme is employed at all levels. Study/Thinking Skills are an inte-

gral part of our teaching. Great emphasis is placed upon rebuilding self-esteem.

Entry requirements. A full report by an independent Educational Psychologist showing the child to be dyslexic and of at least average intelligence. Assessment and interview at MHS.

Charitable status. Moon Hall School is a Registered Charity, number 803481.

Moor Allerton School
GEMS Education

131 Barlow Moor Road, West Didsbury, Manchester M20 2PW
Tel: 0161 445 4521
Fax: 0161 434 5294
e-mail: office@moorallertonschool.manchester.sch.uk
website: www.moorallertonschool.com

Headmaster: **Mr P S Millard**, BA, MSc, NPQH

Age Range. 3–11 Co-educational.
Number of Pupils. 220 Boys and Girls.
Fees per term (2011-2012). Nursery/Reception (3–5 yrs) £2,375; Years 1–2 (age 6–7 yrs) £2,375; Years 3–6 (age 8–11 yrs) £2,495. (Fees are inclusive of lunch, milk and insurance, swimming, tennis tuition and 50% towards Junior Residential courses except the Ski Trip.)
Moor Allerton is a small independent day school, guided by Christian principles. All children are welcomed and encouraged to learn respect for differing cultures by living and working alongside those of other faiths and backgrounds, whilst maintaining their own identity. Although emphasis is placed on academic progress, games have traditionally been a way of fostering healthy competition and of teaching children to enjoy taking part; children are helped to learn how to win or lose graciously.

In the classroom children's progress is regularly monitored and they are encouraged and supported by a team of dedicated and committed teachers. Expectations of all children are high. Gifted children are challenged and stretched and support is given to children who have difficulties. Pupils receive appropriate preparation for entry at 11+ to Independent High Schools.

Music, Art and PE are important areas of the curriculum and sports played at the school include soccer, rugby, netball, cricket, rounders, tennis, swimming and athletics. We offer a wide range of extra-curricular activities, including: Drama, Ballet, Modern Dance, TaeKwonDo, Brazilian Football, Mandarin, Active Fun, French, Art Class, Cookery, Judo, Yoga plus musical tuition, including: percussion, flute, clarinet, guitar and piano.

There is After-School Care until 5.45 pm and Early Care from 07.45 am. Holiday Fun Clubs are offered during Summer, Easter and Whitsun Breaks.

Moor Park School

Ludlow, Shropshire SY8 4DZ
Tel: 01584 876061
Fax: 01584 877311
e-mail: head@moorpark.org.uk
website: www.moorpark.org.uk

Founded in 1964, Moor Park is a co-educational boarding and day school of Catholic foundation for children from 2½ to 13 years.

Chairman of Governors: Capt C Tuffley

Headmaster: **J R Bartlett**, BSc QTS Brunel University

Deputy Head & Headmistress of Lower School: Mrs J M Morris, CertEd

Age Range. 2½–13.
Number of Pupils. 263.
Fees per term (2010-2011). Boarding £4,600–£5,595, Day £1,685–£4,095

The school is built around a magnificent country mansion set in 85 acres of glorious Shropshire countryside. The school campus has a great sense of space, and pupils enjoy the playing fields, pasture, woodland and lake.

Facilities include a science/ICT block, art and design block, learning support department, sports hall, main hall/theatre, a delightful chapel and a heated pool.

The school has seen considerable investment in recent years with a new structure to the Lower School and remodelled Upper School campus with new classrooms. The Study Centre reflects our emphasis on independent learning and the Design Technology building would be the envy of many a senior school.

Fine facilities are nothing without people: the school is renowned for its warmth, its sense of community, its pastoral care, and the emphasis on the individual development of each pupil. There is breadth and depth of opportunity: the tally of scholarships and awards to senior schools – academic, artistic, musical, all-round is outstanding, with nearly 100 achieved in the last ten years.

All Boarding takes place in the main school house, under the care of houseparents and a team of matrons. Boarders may be full, weekly, half or flexi, and day pupils enjoy the opportunities, facilities, activities and pastoral care that such an infrastructure offers, during the week and at weekends. The success of our boarding provision is measured by an increase year on year in the number of children who board and their obvious enjoyment of the experience.

Charitable status. Moor Park School is a Registered Charity, number 511800, which exists to provide education for young people.

Moorfield School

Wharfedale Lodge, 11 Ben Rhydding Road, Ilkley, West Yorkshire LS29 8RL
Tel: 01943 607285
Fax: 01943 603186
e-mail: enquiries@moorfieldschool.co.uk
website: www.moorfieldschool.co.uk

Chairman of Governors: Mrs Lucy Clapham

Headmistress: **Jessica Crossley**

Age Range. 2–11.
Number of Pupils 110 Day Girls.
Fees per term (2010-2011). Nursery Unit (based on 5 mornings): £950 (preferred sessions pro rata). Main School £2,270. Lunches extra.
Staff: 10 full-time, 6 part-time.
Religious affiliation: Interdenominational.

Accommodated in a large house, Moorfield School is situated in a beautiful setting on the edge of Ilkley Moor. The School prides itself on its academic excellence and friendly, caring atmosphere, specifically for girls. It has a strong 'family' feel and lays particular emphasis on consideration for others in both in and beyond the school community. Independence and individuality are encouraged and confidence nurtured.

High standards of literacy and numeracy are the academic bedrock enabling all girls to enter well-respected senior schools at 11+. Success is also achieved in music, art, drama and sport with girls participating in a wide variety of local events. An all-round broad curriculum is followed with specialist teaching in small classes.

Excellent facilities include a purpose-built nursery unit, which gives girls a seamless education from rising 2 years, and a fully equipped IT suite, a newly refurbished music department and many specialist subject rooms. A full range of extra-curricular activities enables each girl to develop her interests; pre and after school care help busy families make the most of each day.

Moorfield is an Education Charitable Trust and the Headmistress is a member of IAPS.

Charitable status. Moorfield School Ltd is a Registered Charity, number 529112.

Moorlands School

Foxhill Drive, Weetwood Lane, Leeds LS16 5PF
Tel: 0113 278 5286
Fax: 0113 203 3193
e-mail: info@moorlands-school.co.uk
website: www.moorlands-school.co.uk

The School is an Educational Trust with a Board of Governors.

Chairman of Governors: Mr T Mulryne, MA, BEd, DPE

Headmaster: **John G Davies**, BA Hons, PGCE, DipRE

Age Range. 2–13 Co-educational.
Number of Pupils. 200 Day Boys and Girls.
Fees per term (2011-2012). Nursery £1,458–£2,567, Pre-Prep £2,584; Lunch £170. Upper School (Years 3–8) £2,891; Lunch £190.

The School was founded in 1898 and consists of day boys and girls who live in the city of Leeds and surrounding area.

The aim of the school is to develop the full potential of every child within a happy and caring environment fostered by small classes and the professional skills of a highly qualified staff. Strong links between the parents and the school are encouraged to facilitate the provision of an effective education.

Admission is by assessment and observation. Pupils are accepted at 2 years old for entry into the Nursery and are expected to progress through the school in preparation for entry to senior independent day and boarding schools. The school has a well developed specialist facility to provide assistance for pupils with any learning issue such as dyslexia or gifted children.

Blended with this traditional core of academic work is offered a comprehensive range of sporting activities and a wide range of musical and extra-curricular pursuits.

Religious affiliation: Undenominational.

Charitable status. Moorlands School is a Registered Charity, number 529216. It exists to provide children with the finest education possible, using the best resources in an environment of care.

Moreton Hall Preparatory School

Bury St Edmunds, Suffolk IP32 7BJ
Tel: 01284 753532
Fax: 01284 769197
e-mail: office@moretonhallprep.org
website: www.moretonhallprep.org

Chairman of the Board of Governors: Neil Smith

Headmaster: **S Head**, MA Cantab, PGCE, QTS

Age Range. 2¾–13.
Number of Pupils. Boys 63, Girls 41.
Fees per term (2011-2012). Boarding: £5,865 (full), £5,245 (weekly). Day: £2,345–£3,905.

Moreton Hall is a warm and welcoming school, set in an impressive historic building with 30 acres of attractive grounds. Its latest inspection (2011) assessed both the personal development of the children and their pastoral care as excellent. Sporting standards are high with daily games sessions. Rugby, soccer, hockey, cricket, netball, rounders and swimming form the major sports. There is an outdoor, heated swimming pool and a large sports hall. A second, indoor swimming pool and squash courts are available for use at the adjacent Health club.

The staff to pupil ratio is high with an average class size of 12 pupils. Some classes are setted in senior years to improve this ratio still further. Pupils are prepared for Scholarship or Common Entrance examination to the full range of Senior schools; prestigious Academic, Music and Sporting awards were all achieved in 2011. High importance is also placed upon Music and Drama. The majority of pupils learn a musical instrument and perform regularly in concerts; there are plays in each section of the school and weekly lessons in Speech and Drama available.

The school accepts boarders from the age of 8 and day pupils from the age of 2¾. Weekly and flexible boarding arrangements are also popular. The resident Housemaster and Housemistress are supported by the Headmaster, who also lives on site, and other staff in addition to gap students. Bury St Edmunds is five minutes away, Cambridge just over half an hour and London is under two hours by road or rail. The School can arrange transport to and from airports.

Moreton Hall has a Catholic tradition and welcomes children of all denominations. Financial support is available through bursaries or endowments.

For further information, please access our website or ring the office to arrange a visit or taster day.

Charitable status. Moreton Hall School Trust Limited is a Registered Charity, number 280927. It exists to provide high quality education for boys and girls.

Moulsford Preparatory School

Moulsford-on-Thames, Wallingford, Oxfordshire OX10 9HR
Tel: 01491 651438
Fax: 01491 651868
e-mail: headmaster@moulsford.com
website: www.moulsford.com

The School is a Charitable Trust controlled by a Board of Governors.

Chairman of the Board of Governors: Mr W Lazarus, FCA

Headmaster: **M J Higham**, BA, CertEd

Age Range. 4–13.
Number of Boys. 34 Weekly Boarders, 260 Day Boys.
Fees per term (2011-2012). Day Boys £2,950–£4,420, Weekly Boarders £5,540. These fees are all inclusive but individual coaching in music, judo, golf and fencing is charged as an extra.

The School has its own river frontage on the Thames, spacious games fields and lawns and is situated between Wallingford and Reading.

Boys are prepared for the Common Entrance and Scholarship examinations to the top independent schools in the country. An experienced and well qualified staff ensure that a high standard is achieved academically, musically, artistically and on the games field.

The principal games are rugby football, soccer, tennis and cricket. Other sporting activities include athletics, swimming, sailing, judo, golf and gymnastics. The school is proud of its fine academic and sporting reputation which has been built up over many years.

Charitable status. Moulsford Preparatory School is a Registered Charity, number 309643.

Mount House School

Tavistock, Devon PL19 9JL
Tel: 01822 612244 (Office)
         01822 619826 (Headmaster)
Fax: 01822 610042
e-mail: office@mounthouse.com (Office)
         hmsec@mounthouse.com (Headmaster)
website: www.mounthouse.devon.sch.uk

Chairman of the Governors:

Headmaster: **J R O Massey**, BSc

Deputy Headmasters:
H Walkington (*Pastoral*)
M Bassett (*Academic*)

Age Range. 3–13 Co-educational.
Number of Pupils. 192 (61 boarders, 85 day children and 46 Pre-Prep).
Fees per term (2011-2012). Boarders £5,569–£6,299, Day Children: Prep £3,231–£4,725, Pre-Prep £2,257–£2,392.

Mount House School is set in idyllic surroundings in fifty acres of playing fields, woodlands and gardens with lakes and streams. It is bordered on the west by over ½ mile of the River Tavy. Children are prepared for Common Entrance and Scholarship to the leading national Independent Schools. All the main subjects are taught throughout The School including Latin, Sustainable Design & Technology, Music, Art and Physical Education. Academic work is competitive. It is carefully monitored with regular Form Orders and Effort grades. High standards are expected and achieved.

A huge range of hobbies and activities is offered. There is a very happy atmosphere and particular attention is paid to good manners. There is a robed RSCM choir which leads the Chapel Services and sings in churches, cathedrals and senior schools from time to time. Most of the pupils learn a musical instrument. There are various musical groups and orchestras. The new music school complete with main music room and practice rooms was opened in 2001, and there is a hall with stage. There is a well-equipped Design & Technology Centre, 2 science laboratories, an outdoor heated swimming pool, a dedicated Art School and a farm raising livestock and growing vegetables for use in the school kitchens.

All the main sports are played and children are coached to a high standard. The fixture list includes schools in other parts of the country. There is a superb sports hall with facilities for a host of sports. The hall includes a full-size tennis court and two squash courts. An Astroturf pitch was opened in 2001. All pupils take part in the "Shackleton Award Scheme" which includes elements of community service, outward bound and first aid.

An exciting architect-designed Pre-Prep department was opened in the autumn of 1996 providing traditional teaching in small groups to children between the ages of 3 and 7 years old. The Pre-Prep has access to many of the Main School's facilities.

Charitable status. Mount House School Trust Limited is a Registered Charity, number 270147. It aims to provide high quality independent boarding and day education for boys and girls aged between 3 and 13.

The Mount Junior School

Dalton Terrace, York YO24 4DD
Tel: 01904 667500
Fax: 01904 667524
e-mail: registrar@mountschoolyork.co.uk
website: www.mountschoolyork.co.uk

Committee of Management:
Chair: Elisabeth Wilson

Head: **Mary Anderson**, CertEd

Age Range. 4–11 Girls only. Co-educational Day Nursery for age 3–4.
Number of Pupils. 135.
Fees per term (2011-2012). £2,950 Juniors (7 to 11 years); £2,220 Infants (4 to 7 years); £1,950 Nursery class.

The Mount School, York provides an exclusive 16-acre campus for its pupils to enjoy. Uniquely the only all-girls Quaker day and boarding school in the country, The Mount promotes the highest standards of education for girls aged 4 to 18. The Quaker ethos and caring family atmosphere can be seen in everyday life at The Mount. The Mount offers impressive facilities to live and work in, with a wide range of sports activities, music disciplines and artistic media. The School believes its pupils discover potential they never knew existed with pupils growing up at their own pace, free from the pressures of conformity and stereotypes, with support to take intellectual risks and to live adventurously.

The Junior School for girls aged 4 to 11 years is in the same grounds and shares many of the educational and recreational facilities. Academically the Junior School enjoys a renowned reputation for both the quality and commitment of its teaching staff, and for the results it produces at critically important stages of a child's education. We take even the smallest children to our Forest School in the school grounds where, through free play and structured activities, they learn to be adventurous, inquisitive and proud of success.

For further details about the Senior School, see entry in GSA section.

Charitable status. The Mount School (York) is a Registered Charity, number 513646.

Naima Jewish Preparatory School

21 Andover Place, London NW6 5ED
Tel: 020 7328 2802
Fax: 020 7624 0161
e-mail: secretary@naimajps.co.uk
website: www.naimajps.co.uk

Chair of Governors: Mrs Judy Dangoor

Headmaster: **Mr J W Pratt**, GRSM Hons, CertEd

Age Range. 2–11 Co-educational.
Number of Pupils. 175 girls and boys.
Fees per term (2010-2011). £1,425–£2,950.

Naima JPS is centred on the belief that an excellent secular education and strong Jewish grounding are mutually attainable. As such, our twin goals merge as we aspire to prepare our children for a successful life in society imbued with Torah values. We aim to provide a secular education on a par with the top national private schools with a curriculum that extends beyond the minimum guidelines provided by the National Curriculum. As a private school, we provide both the environment and teaching resources to monitor each individual, and to help children of all abilities to reach their full potential.

Naima JPS challenges all children, together with their parents, no matter what their level of religious observance, to pursue ongoing spiritual growth as individuals. We encourage children on their journey to spiritual maturity in a harmonious and nurturing community environment of tolerance, respect and care for one another.

The school has a one-form entry. Given that class sizes seldom exceed 22 and the favourable ratio of teachers and assistants to children – as little as 1:5 depending on the age and need – programmes of learning have the flexibility for differentiation. The school has a high number of particularly able children with specific intellectual gifts.

During the crucial early years at school it is important that children define themselves by things they can do well. Self-esteem, that essential by-product of success, empowers strength and gifts. Once children understand how their minds work, as they learn in many different ways, they can feel comfortable about entering any environment and mastering it. Children who truly understand, value and like themselves are better equipped to flourish and embrace fresh challenges. Confidence through success contributes to strong identities that welcome new horizons. Resiliency, discovery, independence and spiritual maturity are nurtured at all levels. At Naima JPS education is not about coveting garlands for the few, but ensuring that all children reach their full potential.

Charitable status. Naima JPS is a Registered Charity, number 289066.

The New Beacon

Brittains Lane, Sevenoaks, Kent TN13 2PB
Tel: 01732 452131
Fax: 01732 459509
e-mail: admin@newbeacon.org.uk
website: www.newbeacon.org.uk

Chairman of the Governors: Mr Charles Gordon

Headmaster: **Michael Piercy**, BA Hons

Age Range. 4–13.
Number of Boys. 400. Predominantly Day Pupils, but a small element of flexi-boarding is retained from Monday to Thursday.
Fees per term (2011-2012). £3,000–£3,870. Fees include lunches.

Boys are prepared for both grammar and independent schools, and enjoy considerable success at 11+ and 13+, with many achieving scholarships (including music, sport, art and drama) to a wide range of first-class senior schools.

The School divides into Senior, Middle and Junior sections in which boys are placed according to age and ability. Initiative is encouraged by organising the School into 4 houses or 'companies'. The well-equipped main School building is complemented by several modern, purpose-built facilities: separate Pre-Prep and Junior School buildings for boys aged 4–9; a Sports Hall with modern changing facilities; a Theatre; a heated indoor Swimming Pool; a centre for Art and Music; and modern facilities for Science and Technology. Soccer, Rugby Union and Cricket are the major games. During the summer months Tennis and Athletics are available. Swimming and Shooting are available all year round. A very extensive range of extra-curricular activities is offered (including many interesting and exciting trips) together with a programme of Pre and After School care.

Music, sport, art and drama at the School are highly regarded.

A limited number of music and academic bursaries are offered subject to means testing.

Charitable status. The New Beacon is a Registered Charity, number 307925. It exists to provide an all-round education for boys aged 4–13.

New College School

Savile Road, Oxford OX1 3UA
Tel: 01865 243657
Fax: 01865 210277
e-mail: office@newcollege.oxon.sch.uk
website: www.newcollegeschool.org

Governors: The Warden & Fellows of New College, Oxford

Headmaster: **N R Gullifer**, MA, FRSA

   Age Range. 4–13 years.
   Number of Boys. 140 Day Boys, including 22 Choristers.
   Fees per term (2011-2012). Reception £2,570, Year 1 £3,095, Years 2–4 £3,800, Years 5–8 £4,155, Choristers £1,478.

New College School was founded in 1379 when William of Wykeham made provision for the education of 16 Choristers to sing daily services in New College Chapel. Situated in the heart of the city, a few minutes' walk from the College, the school is fortunate in having the use of New College playing fields for sport and New College Chapel for school services.

The staff consists of some 20 full-time teachers and a full complement of visiting music teachers. Boys are prepared for the Common Entrance and Scholarship Examinations for transfer to independent senior schools at age 13. In the final year there is a scholarship form and a common entrance form. The school broadly follows the national curriculum subjects, but also teaches French, Latin, Design Technology and Greek.

A Saturday morning music education programme is followed by senior musicians. Games include soccer, hockey, cricket, rounders, athletics and rugby.

Music plays a major part in school life with orchestra, ensembles, concert and junior choirs and form concerts, in addition to individual tuition in a wide range of instruments.

Activities include archery, art, craft, pottery, design, chess, sport, computer, drama, gardening and science clubs. There is a Choral Society for parents.

Boys are admitted by gentle assessment to the Pre-Prep Department at 4 years and to the Prep School at 7 years. Potential Choristers are tested between the ages of 7 and 8 at annual voice trials.

New Hall Preparatory School

Boreham, Chelmsford, Essex CM3 3HS
Tel: 01245 236192
Fax: 01245 451671
e-mail: prep@newhallschool.co.uk
website: www.newhallschool.co.uk

Chairman of Governors: Professor Michael Alder, FRAgS, DL

Headteacher: **Mrs S H Conrad**, BA Hons Dunelm, PGCE, NPQH

   Age Range. 3–11 Co-educational.

Number of Pupils. 340.
   Fees per term (2011-2012). Day £2,512–£3,717; Boarding (from age 8) £5,003–£5,539. Fees shown include Prompt Payment Discount of £100 per term.

New Hall Preparatory School is a Catholic boarding and day school which welcomes all who are in sympathy with its ethos. The school caters for boys and girls aged 3–11 with full and flexi-boarding available from the age of 8. The school is located in the beautiful, spacious and historic grounds of New Hall School, Chelmsford.

New Hall Preparatory School offers a broad, balanced, differentiated curriculum which aims for academic excellence at all times. We believe that learning should be fun as well as rigorous and engaging as well as disciplined. Our curriculum is based upon the National Curriculum but is greatly enhanced by specialist subject teachers in Music, Recorders, Drama, French, Swimming, PE and in KS2, ICT and Latin. An Entrance Examination Programme is built into the curriculum in KS2 which introduces pupils to verbal reasoning skills and prepares them for future entrance examinations and scholarships. Our curriculum is enriched by inspiring speakers and outside visits and supplemented by a rich, varied programme of extra-curricular activities. As a Catholic School we are dedicated to helping each child to fulfil his/her true potential and to ensure that s/he becomes the very best s/he can be.

The school has outstanding facilities including: a purpose-built Pre-Reception class; a well-equipped library; a modern science laboratory; a state-of-the-art computer suite; a theatre; dedicated music rooms; a dance studio; 25m 6-lane indoor swimming pool; 10 floodlit tennis/netball courts; indoor sports hall; floodlit national standard Astroturf hockey pitch; athletics track; soccer, rugby and cricket pitches; a fitness suite.

Music and Sport play an important part in the life of the school. There are three choirs and a flourishing School Orchestra who take part in a number of competitions and festivals each year. Concerts and shows are regular features of the school calendar and Y6 take part in an annual end-of-year production. There are a number of sporting clubs and teams which regularly compete and enjoy successes in a variety of fixtures and competitions.

There is an excellent After School Care facility which provides fun, educational and structured activities in a safe, caring and informal environment. This is run by a dedicated team of After School Care staff.

Charitable status. New Hall School Trust is a Registered Charity, number 1110286.

Newbridge Preparatory School

51 Newbridge Crescent, Wolverhampton, West Midlands WV6 0LH
Tel: 01902 751088
Fax: 01902 751333
e-mail: office@newbridge.wolverhampton.sch.uk
website: www.newbridgeprepschool.org.uk

Chairman of Board: Mrs H M Hughes

Headmistress: **Mrs B Pring**, BEd, MEd, CertEd

   Age Range. Girls 2–11. Boys 2–7.
   Number of Pupils. 156.
   Fees per term (2011-2012). £1,537–£2,339 including dance, recorder, drama, gym, netball, singing, and swimming lessons.

Newbridge Preparatory School, founded in 1937, occupies a super site on the outskirts of Wolverhampton, convenient for parents travelling from Telford, Bridgnorth, Shropshire, and Stafford.

The school is divided into Lower School (Pre-Nursery–Year 2) and Upper School (Years 3–6). Upper School is housed in the main building which is a substantial house set in huge, beautiful mature gardens. There are specialist facilities in Art and Design, ICT, Science, Music and PE. The school has extensive netball and tennis courts.

Staff : pupil ratio is high. Specialist teaching takes place in Key Stage Two in English, Mathematics, Music, Science, PE, Dance and Drama. In Key Stage One: Dance, PE, Drama and Music.

Teaching Assistants work with highly qualified teachers in all classes.

Lower School enjoys a separate Nursery and a new building for Pre-Nursery–Year 2. There is a sports hall.

Children with Special Needs are well supported and nurtured.

Upper School girls take drama and enter ESB examinations. They also enter the annual local festival for Music and Drama.

The school offers an Early Morning Club, after-school care and a Holiday Club. It is a very popular school; there are waiting lists for many classes.

Standards are high in all areas of the curriculum – academic, PE and Music. Senior School results are excellent. Places are gained at local selective Independent and Maintained Schools but also Boarding Schools. Academic and Speech and Drama Scholarships are awarded. Once examinations are complete, Year 6 follow an exciting STAR (Spring Term Activities Refreshed) curriculum using and developing skills previously taught. Girls leave Newbridge well equipped to face the challenges of a Senior School.

Educational visits take place each term. Nursery children enjoy a six week Forest School experience. Residential visits occur in Years 3–6. The visits vary from outdoor activities and challenges, environmental study to a visit to France. Years 5 and 6 visit London for three days – this includes a guided tour, a theatre visit, Science Museum and a theatre workshop.

Emphasis is placed on traditional values, personal development and responsibility. The curriculum is very broad, including many opportunities in Sport, Dance, Drama and Music.

Our school mission statement is: Aiming High, Building Bridges and Preparing for Life.

Children are taught to do their best in all areas, strive for a challenge and succeed at their own level.

Emphasis is placed on self-discipline, inclusion, equal opportunity and respect.

Charitable status. Newbridge Preparatory School is a Registered Charity, number 1019682. It exists to advance the education of children by conducting the school known as Newbridge Preparatory School.

Newcastle Preparatory School

6 Eslington Road, Jesmond, Newcastle-upon-Tyne NE2 4RH
Tel: 0191 281 1769
Fax: 0191 281 5668
e-mail: enquiries@newcastleprepschool.org.uk
website: www.newcastleprepschool.org.uk

The School was founded in 1885 and is now a Charitable Trust with a Board of Governors.

Chair of Governors: Mrs C Wood

Head: **Margaret Coates**, BEd Oxon

   Age Range. 3–11.
   Number of Pupils. 280 Day Pupils (180 boys, 100 girls).

Fees per term (2010-2011). Reception & Year 1: £2,672, Years 2 & 3: £2,795, Years 4–6: £2,914.

The School is situated in a residential part of Newcastle with easy access from all round the area.

Newcastle Preparatory School is a fully co-educational day school for children aged 3 to 11 years. It is a warm, caring environment in which all pupils are encouraged to reach their full potential.

Children may join 'First Steps' at NPS from the age of 3 years. 'First Steps' is an exciting and colourful nursery with excellent resources and well qualified staff who look after the needs of each individual.

At age 4, children make the easy step into School where they experience many 'steps to success'.

The curriculum offered throughout school is broad and balanced so that children enjoy learning in a variety of ways. French is taught from the age of 4 with music and PE being taught by specialist teachers. As children progress through School they become independent learners, following a varied timetable and class sizes are small to provide individual attention.

Music is an important part of life at NPS. There is a choir and a lively swing band.

Sporting achievements too are very good. There is a purpose-built Sports Hall and a wide range of sport is offered with extra curricular activities including rugby, football, cricket, hockey, netball, athletics, tennis and swimming.

Also there are many clubs and activities to enrich the curriculum, eg Drama, Dance, Chess, Philosophy, Art, ICT, Design, Food Technology and there is an effective School Council as well as a Buddy System.

The variety of opportunities ensures that the children leave NPS well equipped for an easy transition into senior schools. The academic results are very good and the children receive an all-round education, so that they are confident, eager learners.

Charitable status. Newcastle Preparatory School is a Registered Charity, number 528152. It exists to provide education for boys and girls.

Newland House School

Waldegrave Park, Twickenham TW1 4TQ
Tel: 020 8865 1234
Fax: 020 8744 0399
e-mail: school@newlandhouse.net
website: www.newlandhouse.net

The School, founded in 1897, is a charitable Educational Trust with a Board of Governors.

Chairman of Governors: S Musgrave

Headmaster: **D A Alexander**, BMus, Dip NCOS

Deputy Headmaster: D S Arnold, BA

   Age Range. 4–13.
   Number of Pupils. 246 Boys, 149 Girls.
   Fees per term (2011-2012). Pre-Prep £3,100, Prep £3,480 (Lunches included).

Children are prepared for the Common Entrance and Scholarship examinations to Independent Schools. The school's main intakes are at the ages of 4 and 7. However, places do become available in other age groups throughout the school year.

The staff consists of 34 full-time teachers, 2 part-time teachers as well as 10 classroom assistants, mostly in the Pre-Preparatory department. In addition there are 15 visiting music staff who teach a variety of instruments. The School has 5 choirs, a concert band, several wind ensembles, 2 jazz bands and a string orchestra.

The main games are Rugby, Soccer, Cricket, Netball and Rounders. All children from the age of 7 have the opportunity to swim throughout the year.

The Main School has, in addition to 17 light and airy classrooms, a large gymnasium/assembly hall, dining room, separate senior and junior libraries and two well-equipped science laboratories. There is an Art and Design Technology block as well as a purpose-built Music block. The school has a substantial computer network, including a state-of-the-art computer suite and a control technology laboratory.

A separate Pre-Preparatory department, for children up to the age of 7, is also situated in Waldegrave Park.

A wide variety of extra-curricular activities is available.

Charitable status. The Newland House School Trust Limited is a Registered Charity, number 312670. It exists for the purpose of providing a good academic education in a friendly atmosphere.

Newton Prep

149 Battersea Park Road, London SW8 4BX
Tel: 020 7720 4091
Fax: 020 7498 9052
e-mail: admin@newtonprep.co.uk
website: www.newtonprep.co.uk

Chairman of Council: Dr Farouk Walji

Headmaster: **Mr N M Allen**, BA

Administration & Finance Manager: Mr P Farrelly

Age Range. 3–13.
Number of Pupils. 514: 235 Boys, 279 Girls.
Fees per term (2011-2012). £2,345–£4,950.
Average size of class: <20.
The current teacher/pupil ratio is 1:9.
Religious denomination: Non-denominational.

Newton Prep is a vibrant school which offers a challenging education for inquisitive children who are eager to engage fully with the world in which they are growing up. The school aims to:
• inspire children to be adventurous and committed in their learning;
• provide balance and breadth in all aspects of a child's education: intellectual, aesthetic, physical, moral and spiritual;
• encourage initiative, individuality, independence, creativity and enquiry;
• promote responsible behaviour and respect for others in a happy, safe and caring environment.

Entry requirements: Siblings are given first priority when allocating nursery places; other nursery places are awarded by lottery; children joining Reception are assessed individually. Older children spend up to three days in school, joining regular classes as well as undertaking tests.

Examinations offered: Entrance examinations to senior schools, Common Entrance and scholarships at 11, 12 and 13. Most children leave to go to London day schools though a significant minority leave to go boarding.

The school has expanded above and around the original Victorian building. The modern extension comprises a further sixteen classrooms, a multispace area, two gyms, a dining room, spacious art studios and an auditorium. The premises are bright and spacious. The school has an all-weather pitch which provides an ideal surface for hockey, netball, football, cricket and tennis. A generous area is devoted to a children's garden which they cultivate and use for nature study. In 2009, the library was refurbished and enlarged and three new science laboratories built. Three ICT suites are now grouped around the library which accommodates 16,000 books. Extra-curricular activities available

include: judo, fencing, yoga, ballet, modern dance, Mandarin Chinese, and speech and drama.

Norland Place School

162/166 Holland Park Avenue, London W11 4UH
Tel: 020 7603 9103
Fax: 020 7603 0648
e-mail: office@norlandplace.com
website: www.norlandplace.com

Headmaster: **Mr P Mattar**

Age Range. Girls 4–11, Boys 4–8.
Number of Children. 240.
Fees per term (2010-2011). £3,526–£4,356.

A Preparatory school founded in 1876 and still standing on the original site in Holland Park Avenue. Children are prepared for competitive London day schools and top rate boarding schools. The curriculum is well balanced with an emphasis on English, Mathematics and Science. Music, Art and Games are strong. The school contains a Library in addition to specialist Music, IT, Science and Art Rooms.

Early registration is essential.

Norman Court Preparatory School

Norman Court, West Tytherley, Salisbury SP5 1NH
Tel: 01980 862345
Fax: 01980 862082
e-mail: office@normancourt.co.uk
website: www.normancourt.co.uk

Chairman of Governors: Sir David Plastow

Headmaster: **P G Savage**, BA Hons

Deputy Head: Mrs J Kirkpatrick, MA

Age Range. 3–13.
Number of Children. Main School: 137: 60 Boarders (full and weekly, plus flexi), 77 Day. Pre-Preparatory Dept: 68.
Fees per term (2010-2011). Boarders and Weekly Boarders £6,635; Day Children £4,925; Pre-Preparatory £2,425.

Norman Court Preparatory School is a well established and flourishing co-educational boarding and day school located in idyllic surroundings between Salisbury, Andover and Winchester. The caring, friendly and approachable staff work closely together to inspire and motivate. The school enjoys superb facilities and the beautiful grounds lend themselves well to outdoor and adventurous pursuits.

The School's primary aim is to give children the opportunity to achieve their full academic and personal potential.

Norman Court is currently celebrating a very successful scholarship and public examinations season with Academic, Sports, Music, Art and All-Round Scholarship awards achieved to a variety of leading senior schools, together with successful candidates for local grammar schools.

The school can boast the latest information, communications and technology equipment, wonderful arts and music facilities, and unrivalled sports provision.

The boarding provision at Norman Court is excellent with a particular focus on stimulating weekend activities, good recreational facilities, and a home-from-home atmosphere. In a recent CSCI Inspection, the Inspectors confirmed that our children are clearly very happy to be boarding. Flexi boarding is very popular with many day children boarding regularly for one, two or even three nights each week.

The Pre-Preparatory Department has always been an extremely popular and flourishing establishment based in its own woodland setting, whilst benefiting from close proximity to the main building facilities. It is well equipped, spacious and an attractive environment in which to learn and play. Full use of the beautiful grounds is made and the school curriculum includes the Forest School programme.

To discover more about the choice we offer please contact the Registrar on registry@normancourt.co.uk or telephone on 01980 862345 today for the Norman Court prospectus. You can also find us at www.normancourt.co.uk, so do visit us and see us at work and play.

Charitable status. Norman Court School is a Registered Charity, number 307426. It exists to provide education for children.

Northbourne Park

Betteshanger, Deal, Kent CT14 0NW
Tel: 01304 611215 or 611218
Fax: 01304 619020
e-mail: office@northbournepark.com
website: www.northbournepark.com

Chairman of Governors: Professor Michael Wright, CBE, DL

Headmaster: **Edward Balfour**, BA Hons, PGCE

Age Range. 3–13 Co-educational.
Number of Pupils. 200 of whom approximately half are girls. There are approximately 50 boarders.
Fees per term (2011-2012). Boarders: £5,335–£6,105 (weekly), £5,725–£7,090 (full). Day Pupils: £2,535–£2,980 (Pre-Prep) £3,740–£4,490 (Years 3–8). Fees include customary extras and many extra-curricular activities.

Northbourne Park is a thriving, well established school committed to developing every child's full potential. Our unique environment ensures that children emerge confident, skilled and at ease with themselves and others.

Set in over 100 acres of beautiful parkland and woods, the school has easy motorway access to London, and to France/Belgium via Eurotunnel or ferry. The school provides a fortnightly bus service to central London and Eurostar service to Paris and Brussels, and school mini-buses serve the pupils locally.

Pupils achieve high academic standards, taught in small classes by an experienced and professional team. We offer a high quality education, which equips children for entry to senior school via Common Entrance or Scholarship, or to grammar school via the Kent Test.

The school has a long musical tradition and a recent ISI Inspection reported that 'pupils achieve high standards in music'. Children are encouraged to appreciate music in various ways, either through learning an instrument or joining the choir or orchestra, and gain great confidence by performing in various events throughout the year.

French is introduced from the age of 3, and we have a unique Anglo/French system with two classes of French children in the senior school, where Spanish is also taught.

A long established and well-reputed Learning Support Department, offers a wide range of SEN support including programmes for Dyslexia and social communication difficulties for children in the average plus range of abilities.

Sport and a wide range of extra-curricular activities play an important part of school life. Excellent pastoral care and a unique leadership programme encourage self-confidence and leadership skills. Boarders enjoy a home from home atmosphere, looked after by a caring and professional team. A very popular flexi-boarding service is also provided.

Some scholarships can be awarded for academic, music or sporting excellence. Sibling, HM Forces and Clergy dis-

counts are available. There is some Bursarial support available in cases of need.

Charitable status. Northbourne Park is a Registered Charity, number 280048. It exists to provide education for children.

Northcote Lodge

26 Bolingbroke Grove, London SW11 6EL
Tel: 020 8682 8888
Fax: 020 8682 8879
e-mail: northcote@northwoodschools.com
website: www.northcotelodge.co.uk

Day Preparatory School for Boys.

Principals: Sir Malcolm & Lady Colquhoun

Headmaster: **Mr J Hansford**

Age Range. 8–13.
Number of Pupils. 210 Boys.
Fees per term (2010-2011). £4,695.

Northcote Lodge was founded in 1993 and occupies a large mid-Victorian building overlooking Wandsworth Common, with its own grounds of over one acre.

The school is run along similar lines to a country prep school with a longer day at the end of which all 'homework' is done as prep at school. There is a broad and balanced curriculum leading to Common Entrance or scholarship to all major independent senior schools, usually boarding. Games are played, in one form or another, each day. Karate is on the curriculum and the school has a significant record of success in this field. There are thriving music and arts departments, frequent dramatic productions, a strong Chapel Choir and numerous extra curricular activities ranging from cookery to golf, debating to pottery, and model-making to basketball. The school has a state of the art computing system which is networked throughout the school.

There is a fully qualified and enthusiastic staff all of whom are totally committed to the aims and values of the school. There is a full-time Matron who shares responsibility with the Deputy Head for the pastoral care. During the first two years the boys have a form teacher and thereafter they are assigned to a tutor with whom they will stay until they leave.

We believe that in a disciplined and happy environment, boys will succeed academically and do not need to feel under constant academic pressure. They know that they are at school to work but it is crucial that they look on their time at school as an enjoyable experience. They will grow up all too soon; they must be allowed to be boys, to enjoy childhood and to mature at their own pace.

High standards are expected of the boys in every area of life at school. Manners, courtesy, self-respect and consideration for others are key values. Once a week the boys attend a service at the local Church. There is considerable value to be gained from being a member of a small and caring community where every boy has the opportunity to shine. A great emphasis is placed on developing self-confidence which is the key to success at school.

Entry Requirements. Entry is in September following their eight birthday, although places for older boys can sometimes become available. Admission is by means of assessment and interview when the boy is 7. Siblings have automatic right of entry into school or to nearby Broomwood Hall (our associate school for boys aged 4–8 and girls aged 4–13). Places are also sometimes available at 9+, 10+ and 11+. Parents should contact the school if interested in such a place.

Northwood College Junior School

Maxwell Road, Northwood, Middlesex HA6 2YE
Tel: 01923 845067
Fax: 01923 836526
e-mail: juniorschool@northwoodcollege.co.uk
website: www.northwoodcollege.co.uk

Chairman of Governing Council: Mr G Hudson

Head Mistress: **Mrs H Thaker**, BA Hons East London,
   PGCE North London

Age Range. Girls 3–11.
Number of Pupils. 350 Girls.
Fees per term (2011-2012). £2,750–£3,675.
Ethos. Our aim is to raise young women who know their
own minds and are creative and flexible thinkers, as well as
being able to achieve outstanding exam results. We are academically selective, but not narrowly exclusive. We value
girls for more than simple academic performance, because
our unique approach to advanced thinking skills means that
we can develop, stretch and challenge every single one of
them. We think that makes for an interesting and vibrant
school community – and it's what makes Northwood College special.
   Results show that Junior School girls reach standards far
above national norms for the age group. All National Curriculum subjects are taught, plus Latin and Drama. In addition,
girls in Year 3 to 5 study French and girls in Year 6 study
Spanish and German.
   Thinking Skills. Our approach to thinking skills is
another one of our defining characteristics. It sets Northwood College apart, and gives our girls an edge in the way
they approach any task or challenge. Our Thinking Skills
Programme is led by C J Simister, who has taught at Northwood College for many years and is a renowned expert,
author and consultant on cognitive development. Through
the programme, we ensure our girls start to understand and
develop the way they think from the day they join Nursery
through to the end of the Sixth Form. Over the years, they
build up their reasoning skills, improve their creativity and
acquire strategies for tackling complex problems and decisions. It gives them a life skill that will be as useful at university and in the workplace as it is at school.
   Pupil Well-being. We take the challenge of turning out
happy, confident and generous young women very seriously.
Northwood College creates an atmosphere in which courtesy, respect and self-respect thrive. Girls are taught to
understand and respect the other person's point of view and
to show good manners at all times. In keeping with this
ethos, the Junior School operates a system of recognition
and reward for good behaviour and attitude, as well as work.
   Come and visit us. The Junior School is housed in three
separate buildings including the recent addition of an Early
Years Centre which has been designed to allow for both
indoor and outdoor learning to take place in an exciting and
challenging environment.
   We enjoy showing parents and girls around Northwood
College. *For more information please see our entry in the
GSA section.*
   Charitable status. Northwood College Educational
Foundation Limited is a Registered Charity, number 312646,
which exists to provide high-quality education for girls.

Northwood Prep

Moor Farm, Sandy Lodge Road, Rickmansworth, Herts
WD3 1LW
Tel: 01923 825648

Fax: 01923 835802
e-mail: office@northwoodprep.co.uk
website: www.northwoodprep.co.uk

Founded as a private school in 1910 by Mr Francis Terry,
NP has a long history and proud traditions. It is still known
within the locality as "Terry's" after its founder. In 1954 it
became an educational charitable trust administered by a
Board of Governors.

Chairman of Governors: Dr O Bangham, BSc, MSc, PhD

Headmaster: **Dr Trevor Lee**, BEd Hons Exon, MEd Jesus
   College Cambridge, EdD Hull

Deputy Heads:
Mr Ian Rice, CertEd Carnegie, NPQH
Mr Andrew Crook, BA Lancaster, PGCE King's College
London

Age Range. 3–13.
Number of Pupils. 300 Day Boys.
Fees per term (2010-2011). £2,465 (Nursery full-time),
£3,637 (Reception, Years 1 and 2), £3,833 (Years 3–8).
   The School is located amidst 14 acres on a former farm in
an ideal park and woodland setting. The Grade II listed
buildings have been skilfully converted to provide a complete and unique range of classrooms and ancillary facilities.
The mediaeval Manor of the More, once owned by King
Henry VIII and used as a palace by Cardinal Wolsey, was
originally located within the grounds and provides some
interesting and historical associations.
   The School is divided into four sections: an off-site Nursery School for children aged 3+, the Junior School (Reception to Year 2), Key Stage 2 (Years 3–6) and Key Stage 3
(Years 7 and 8). These all have their own teaching areas
while making use of the same dining, games, extra-curricular and recreational facilities.
   Boys are admitted to the school after an assessment by
Heads of Section. The main entry is into Nursery at 3+ when
boys are admitted in the September after their third birthday.
Older boys may also be accepted further up the School if a
chance vacancy occurs. Boys are expected to remain until
the age of thirteen, being prepared for entry at that stage to
independent senior schools by way of Common Entrance.
The School has also built up a fine record of Scholarship
results over the years.
   Work of a traditionally high standard is expected of all
boys. The curriculum is interpreted as richly as possible and
includes Technology, Music, Art, Drama, Physical Education and Games. The School has modern teaching facilities
and the fully qualified and experienced staff is generously
resourced. The Sir Christopher Harding Building for Science and Technology, comprising two state-of-the-art laboratories, an ICT Suite and technology workshop was opened
in November 2000. A Learning Resource Centre was created in September 2001. A centre for the Performing Arts
was commissioned by Mr Kevin Spacey in April 2008 and a
music school was opened in May 2008. A nursery school
was opened in the grounds of Merchant Taylors' School in
April 2008. Additional sports changing facilities were
opened in February 2008. Additional classrooms have been
added as part of our centenary celebrations in 2010. A new
Centenary trail accommodates a range of outdoor learning
activities.
   Swift access to London by train from nearby Moor Park
Station means that staff often arrange for boys to visit places
of historical and cultural interest and attend concerts and
lectures.
   While the Christian tradition on which the life of the
School is based is that of the Church of England, boys from
all Christian denominations and other faiths are welcomed.
   There is an extensive programme of extra-curricular
activities in which all boys are encouraged to take part. A

key feature of the School's ethos is a strong tradition of caring, both for those within the community of the school, and those whom the boys can help through regular charitable activities.

Rugby Football, Association Football and Cricket are the principal team games. Tennis, Athletics, Judo and other sports are also coached. A fully equipped Sports Hall was opened in November 1996. The School has the benefit of a floodlit astroturf facility.

The School has a flourishing Parents' Association which arranges social and fundraising activities, and an active association for former pupils, The Old Terryers.

Charitable status. Northwood Preparatory School Trust (Terry's) Limited is a Registered Charity, number 312647. The aims of the charity are the education and development of boys aged 3–13.

Norwich School, The Lower School

Bishopgate, Norwich NR1 4AA
Tel: 01603 305791
Fax: 01603 629679
e-mail: L.School@norwich-school.org.uk
website: www.norwich-school.org.uk

Chairman of Governors: G H C Copeman, CBE, DL

Master of the Lower School: **J K Ingham**, BA

Second Master: R A Love, BSc

Director of Studies: C M W Parsons, BSc

Age Range. 7–11.
Number of Pupils. 164.
Fees per term (2011-2012). £3,696.

The Lower School is the Junior Day School for Norwich School (*see entry in HMC section*). It is delightfully located in the Cathedral Close, between the East End of the Cathedral and the River Wensum. The Cathedral Choristers are educated at Norwich School, which is a member of the Choir Schools' Association.

The Lower School provides depth and breadth of education through a challenging curriculum. It seeks to recognise, nurture and develop each pupil's potential within an environment which encourages all-round emotional, physical, social and spiritual growth and to foster positive relations between pupils, teachers and parents. The dedicated teaching staff is committed to providing a stimulating programme of active learning which has rigour and discipline but avoids unnecessary pressure.

With two forms in each of its four year groups, the Lower School is the ideal size for ensuring a lively environment within a warm family atmosphere. The main building has bright, spacious areas for activities and lessons. As well as the library, there are specialised facilities for science, art, technology and ICT. There is an excellent play area in addition to the adjacent, extensive playing fields.

A wide range of extra-curricular activities and school trips is offered. Music is a strong feature of school life. Many pupils choose to learn a musical instrument and participate in the various instrumental music groups. Rugby, netball, hockey, cricket, rounders and tennis are taught and the games programme is designed to encourage pupils of all abilities to enjoy games and physical activity.

The School aims to attract pupils who will thrive in a challenging academic environment and is therefore selective. Prospective pupils are assessed in English, mathematics and non-verbal reasoning. There is a two-form entry at 7+ and a small number of places is available each year at 8+, 9+ and 10+. The prospectus and application forms are available from the Admissions Registrar, Tel: 01603 728442.

The vast majority of pupils from the Lower School progress to the Senior School at age eleven, and the curriculum is designed to prepare the pupils effectively for the next stage of their Norwich School education.

Charitable status. Norwich School is a Registered Charity, number 311280.

Notre Dame Preparatory School

Burwood House, Cobham, Surrey KT11 1HA
Tel: 01932 869991
Fax: 01932 589480
e-mail: headmaster@notredame.co.uk
website: www.notredame.co.uk

Chairman: Mr Glen Travers

Headmaster: **Mr D S Plummer**, BEd Hons, DipHE, FRSA

Deputy Head: Miss M D'Aprano, BEd Hons, MA, CTC, FRSA

Age Range. Girls 2¾–11, Boys 2¾–5.
Number of Pupils. 340 Girls, 12 boys.
Fees per term (2011-2012). Nursery £1,150–£2,480; Reception £2,985, Prep 1 & 2 £3,255, Prep 3–6 £3,595.

Bursaries. A limited number of assisted places and bursaries are offered subject to income and asset tests.

Notre Dame Preparatory School has existed on its present site for over 70 years, but was founded by the Sisters of The Company of Mary, Our Lady, who have a four hundred year old tradition of excellence in education. The school has a strong pastoral care policy and welcomes children of all denominations.

The aim at Notre Dame Preparatory School is to identify individual potential. A rich and rewarding curriculum has been planned, encouraging each child to make the most of special talents.

Children can join the Nursery at 2¾ years. A broad and exciting curriculum exists for each Key Stage focussing on numeracy and literacy skills.

Girls progress through the Preparatory School and are prepared for entrance to the Senior School at 11. (*See Notre Dame Senior School entry in GSA section.*)

The School has an enviable local reputation, both for high academic standards and for the provision of a wide range of social, cultural and sporting amenities, including:

- an excellent ISI Inspection Report in 2011
- challenging scientific and technological programmes of study, with impressive laboratories
- modern computer system, with multiple internet access
- heated indoor swimming pool
- large Sports Hall, featuring gymnasium and indoor netball, soccer, badminton and tennis courts
- new Learning Resource Centre with library and video conferencing
- extensive grounds set in beautiful parkland
- golf, lacrosse, cross country, rounders, soccer, outdoor pursuits
- range of choirs, ensembles and orchestra ensure that music is enjoyed throughout the school. Choir tours to Belgium, Hungary, Bordeaux, Venice and Santiago de Compostela
- a brand new state-of-the-art theatre opening in September 2011

ISI Inspection 2011. Following an outstanding report in 2007, Notre Dame Preparatory School has continued to excel in all areas. '*The pupils' overall achievement from the EYFS onwards is outstanding and represents the successful fulfilment of the school's aim to strive for personal academic excellence.*' Every aspect of the school from learning and teaching to extra-curricular events was scrutinised and evidence confirmed that: '*Pupils follow a demanding and imaginative curriculum and are successful in entry to the senior schools of their choice, including the award of scholarships*' and '*Their personal development benefits from a carefully planned programme of personal, social and health education. Parents and pupils commend the wide range of clubs and opportunities outside the classroom*'. Teaching was again praised as being of the highest quality: '*Teachers know their pupils well and care is taken to ensure that they build on what they have already learnt. The pupils' successes are due, in large part, to the excellent teaching.*'

The school was particularly proud that the ethos of the school was reflected in the Inspectors' findings: '*Relationships between staff and pupils, and amongst the pupils themselves, are excellent. Parents appreciate the care provided for their children. Pupils are confident, caring and keen to celebrate the success of others. Pupils of all ages have outstandingly well-developed personal qualities. Excellent leadership and management are reflected in the pupils' outstanding overall achievement and personal development. The hallmark of the management is that nothing is left to chance, with meticulous attention to detail. Teamwork is of a high order.*'

Headmaster David Plummer said, "I am delighted that the school has once again been recognised for its many strengths, and so proud that the efforts of all in this community have contributed to a report on our beautiful school and fantastic girls that is even more glowing than the outstanding report of 2007 – we are forever looking forward to a bright future, starting with the imminent completion of our new 370-seat Elizabethan style Theatre".

This was echoed by the Chair of Governors who wrote to all staff to say, "This report is a credit to all and recognition of the effort everyone puts in. To be rated so highly in every area is an important external validation".

Demand for places has ensured school coaches serve a wide local area.

Prospectus. A fully illustrated Prospectus detailing the school's distinctive nature is available on request.

Charitable status. Notre Dame School Cobham is a Registered Charity, number 1081875. It exists to provide education for girls.

Notting Hill Preparatory School

95 Lancaster Road, London W11 1QQ
Tel: 020 7221 0727
Fax: 020 7221 0332
e-mail: admin@nottinghillprep.com
website: www.nottinghillprep.com

Co-Chairs of Governing Body:
John Mackay
John Morton Morris

Headmistress: **Mrs Jane Cameron**, BEd Hons

Age Range. 5–13 Co-educational.
Number of Pupils. 278.
Fees per term (2011-2012). £4,690.

Founded in 2003, NHP is a co-ed Prep School in the heart of Notting Hill, West London. It was created through the cooperation of parents and teachers and this partnership with parents is a cornerstone of the philosophy of the school. It operates on a split-site, Reception to Year 3 being housed in a fine Victorian School House and Years 4–8 in a magnificent new building providing, in addition, school hall/dining room, music room and music practice rooms, Science lab and ICT suite.

Our aim is to 'educate' children in the true sense of the word so that they develop an excitement and passion for learning. A broad-based curriculum ensures that academic subjects are balanced with ample time being dedicated to sport and subjects such as art, music and drama where the emphasis is on enjoyment and self-expression. Subjects are taught by specialist teachers in the Upper School, as are French, music, drama and PE from Reception. Latin is introduced in Year 5. Children are fully prepared for the competitive entrance examinations to London day schools and country boarding schools at 11+ and 13+.

Music and performance are particular features at the school, with creative staff producing original material for plays and concerts. There are two choirs and an orchestra and over two-thirds of the pupils learn a musical instrument.

A wide and varied sports programme using local facilities as well as our own on site gym ensures that children develop and perfect skills in the major sports (football, netball, hockey, rugby, cricket, athletics and swimming). Opportunities for displaying these skills are provided by frequent fixtures arranged with local schools.

Regular school trips enhance all aspects of the curriculum. Full use is made of the many and varied opportunities London offers to extend children's knowledge of their environment, their culture and their history.

NHP is noted for its open, friendly and happy atmosphere and its strong sense of being part of a wider community. Courtesy, kindness and appreciation of a diversity of talents, abilities and needs are defining values of the school's ethos.

The school is heavily oversubscribed and places are offered following a ballot. The School Secretary tries to keep waiting lists within reasonable limits.

Nottingham High Junior School

Waverley Mount, Nottingham NG7 4ED
Tel: 0115 845 2214
Fax: 0115 845 2298
e-mail: juniorinfo@nottinghamhigh.co.uk
website: www.nottinghamhigh.co.uk

Chairman of Governors: Paul Balen

Headmaster: **A R Earnshaw**, BA, QTS Lancaster

Age Range. 7–11.
Number of Boys. 159 Day Boys.
Fees per term (2011-2012). £2,965.

The Junior School is housed in purpose-built premises on the main school site, having its own Classrooms, ICT Suite, Library, Art Room, Science Laboratory, Dining Hall and Assembly Hall.

Entrance Assessments are held in January, based around the core subjects of Mathematics and English, including reading, along with some measures of general ability. The tests are all set at National Curriculum ability levels appropriate for each age group.

The Junior School has an experienced and well-qualified staff. The curriculum is designed for those who expect to complete their education at Nottingham High School. The subjects taught are Religious Education, English, Mathematics, History, Geography, Science, French and PSHE. Full provision is made for Music, Art, Design Technology, Information Communication Technology, Swimming, Physical Education and Games.

The Junior School has its own Orchestra and about 100 boys receive instrumental tuition. All Year 3 boys play an instrument of their choice. A Concert and School Plays are performed annually. A wide range of supervised activities and hobbies takes place during every lunch time.

School games are Association Football and Rugby with some Hockey and Cross Country in the winter, Cricket and Tennis in the summer.

A new Infant School, Lovell House, opened in September 2008 for boys in Reception, Year 1 and Year 2.

Charitable status. Nottingham High School is a Registered Charity, number 1104251. It exists to provide education for boys between the ages of 4 and 18 years.

Oakwood Preparatory School

Chichester, West Sussex PO18 9AN
Tel: 01243 575209
Fax: 01243 575433
e-mail: office@oakwoodschool.co.uk
website: www.oakwoodschool.co.uk

Headteacher: **Mrs G Proctor**, CertEd

Age Range. Co-educational 2½ to 11.
Number of Pupils. 290 Day boys and girls.
Fees per term (2011-2012). Pre-Prep £1,390–£2,835. Upper School £3,593–£3,901.

Oakwood was founded in 1912 and has grown into a thriving co-educational preparatory school.

Set in 160 acres of glorious park and woodland between the South Downs and the coast, Oakwood's home is a large Georgian country house.

The children learn in a wonderfully safe and spacious environment in the heart of beautiful Sussex countryside only three miles from Chichester. The school prides itself on its family atmosphere and the happiness of its children.

Oakwood is well-equipped with spacious classrooms, Science and Design Technology Studio, Art Room, Library, Music and Theatre Complex and ICT Centre. There is a Gymnasium and 3 floodlit tennis courts. The playing fields extend over nine acres, there is an indoor heated swimming pool and two adventure playgrounds.

The Pre-Prep, though fully integrated into the Oakwood community, enjoys its own spacious site with a safe and enclosed play area. The setting is particularly cosy and attractive, the classrooms having been sympathetically converted from a stable block.

There is a warm family atmosphere, as the school recognises the importance of children feeling happy and secure. Great emphasis is placed on building a solid foundation of social skills and a love of learning, thus enabling each child to settle confidently to school life.

There is a strong academic curriculum with small class sizes, ensuring that each child receives the closest possible attention. In Upper School, children are set for English and Mathematics. The curriculum is broad with each child's timetable including Design Technology, Science, Humanities, French, ICT, PE, Drama and Music.

Form tutoring is of prime importance, the form teacher overseeing the development of each child – academically, socially and emotionally. Contact with parents is frequent and encouraged.

Opportunities to represent the school in sports teams, plays, choirs and instrument groups are all part of the "Oakwood Experience".

Music is very much a part of Oakwood life. The children enjoy music lessons each week and there is every opportunity to learn an instrument. The school has three choirs, recorder ensembles, guitar groups, a mini orchestra and a wind band. Each term there is an Evening of Music, and there are major concerts every year for both Upper School and Pre-Prep. The summer term ends with a major musical. In addition, children are encouraged to perform in Assembly.

The Physical Education and Sports programme has an exciting mix to offer every child. Games are played three times each week and are coached by members of staff with an expertise and enthusiasm for their sport or by outside coaches.

In winter the boys enjoy a taste of all the major sports – Soccer, Rugby and Hockey, while the girls play Netball and Hockey. Karate, Fencing, Yoga, Dance and Ballet are also on offer to the boys and girls. In summer the boys play Cricket and the girls play Rounders, but the school also offers Swimming, Athletics and Tennis. An extensive programme of inter-school fixtures is arranged each term for A and B teams.

Early arrivals care, after school clubs and activities all ensure that busy parents can benefit from a flexible school day.

There is an excellent record of examination, scholarship and academic award success to a variety of senior schools.

Oakwood School

59 Godstone Road, Purley, Surrey CR8 2AN
Tel: 020 8668 8080
Fax: 020 8668 2895
e-mail: enquiries@oakwoodschool.org.uk
website: www.oakwoodschool.org.uk

Chairman of Governors: Dr Tony Newman-Sanders

Headmaster: **Mr Ciro Candia**, BA Hons, PGCE

Age Range. 2½–11 Co-educational.
Number of Pupils. 175.
Fees per term (2010-2011). £684–£2,290.
Charitable status. PACT Educational Trust Limited is a Registered Charity, number 1053810.

Old Buckenham Hall School

Brettenham Park, Ipswich, Suffolk IP7 7PH
Tel: 01449 740252
Fax: 01449 740955
e-mail: office@obh.co.uk
website: www.obh.co.uk

Chairman of Governors: M W Nicholls

Headmaster: **J Brett**, MA London, CertMusEd, FCollP

Deputy Headmaster: C C Schanschieff, BSc Ed Hons

Age Range. 3–13.
Number of Pupils. 131 Boarders; 79 Day Pupils; 33 Pre-Prep; 19 Nursery.
Fees per term (2010-2011). Full and Weekly Boarders £5,495–£6,495; Day £3,950–£4,950; Pre-Prep £2,460.

The School, founded in Lowestoft as South Lodge in 1862, moved in 1937 to Old Buckenham, Norfolk and in 1956 to Brettenham Park, Suffolk, 4 miles from Lavenham and 18 from Ipswich. It became an Educational Trust in 1967.

The pupils go on to a wide range of, mostly boarding, Senior Independent Schools via Common Entrance and Scholarship Examinations.

The Staff/Pupil ratio is approximately 1:9, giving an average class-size of 13. All members of Staff, including part-time Staff, contribute to the provision of a wide range of extra-curricular activities in which every child has a chance to participate. The major sports are Rugby, Hockey, Soccer, Netball, Cricket and Rounders, but all pupils also take part in Athletics and Swimming. In addition there are opportunities for Tennis (6 courts), Golf (9-hole course), Squash (2 courts), Table Tennis, Woodwork, Metalwork, Pets, Shooting, Photography, Dance and Archery. Art, Music and Drama particularly flourish.

The Main Building, an 18th Century mansion, stands in its own grounds of 75 acres of which some 25 are playing fields and 6 are woodland. In the past few years many building alterations and additions have been completed. In 1997 astroturf tennis courts were created and a purpose-built Pre-Prep Department opened in September 1998. A new girls' boarding house, new art studio and computer room opened in September 2001; four new classrooms opened in October 2003: Phase One of the School's Five Year Development Plan. A new multi-purpose hall was completed in October 2005 and a new science and music building is planned for completion by 2009.

A School Prospectus can be obtained on application to the Registrar.

Charitable status. Old Buckenham Hall (Brettenham) Educational Trust Limited is a Registered Charity, number 310490. It exists to provide education for boarding and day pupils.

The Old Hall School

Stanley Road, Wellington, Shropshire TF1 3LB
Tel: 01952 223117
Fax: 01952 222674
e-mail: enq@oldhall.co.uk
website: www.oldhall.co.uk

Chairman of the Governors: H W Campion, ACA, CTA

Headmaster: **M C Stott**, BEd Hons

Age Range. 4–11.
Number of Pupils. 239: 136 boys, 103 girls.
Fees per term (2010–2011). Kindergarten–Junior 2 (age 4–7) £2,153; Years 3–6 (age 7–11) £3,340.

Founded in 1845, The Old Hall School is a co-educational day school (4–11 years), which is housed in spectacular new premises, located alongside Wrekin College. The school offers first-class facilities; a double sports hall, 25-metre indoor swimming pool, Astroturf and grass pitches offer an excellent sports and games environment, whilst specialist music and drama areas help to promote high standards in the performing arts. A suite of specialist learning support rooms reflects the School's commitment to the needs of the individual. First-class facilities have also been created for pre-school care and the education of children from the age of three months.

The broad curriculum is enriched by a dedicated team of professionals who encourage pupils to fulfil their potential in a happy and secure environment.

Through the academic curriculum and caring pastoral system, the school aims to lay solid foundations in the development of well-motivated, confident and happy individuals who are always willing to give of their best on the road to high achievement.

Charitable status. Wrekin Old Hall Trust Limited is a Registered Charity, number 528417.

The Old Vicarage School

48 Richmond Hill, Richmond, Surrey TW10 6QX
Tel: 020 8940 0922
Fax: 020 8948 6834
e-mail: office@oldvicarage-richmond.co.uk
website: www.oldvicarage-richmond.co.uk

Chairman of Governors: Mr M Townsin

Headmistress: **Mrs G Linthwaite**

Age Range. 4–11.
Number of Pupils. 180 girls.
Fees per term (2011-2012). £3,015–£3,375.

The Old Vicarage school is a non-selective girls' prep school based in a beautiful Grade 2* listed "castle" on Richmond Hill. The School was established in 1881 and became a Charitable Educational Trust in 1973. Whilst retaining traditional values, there is a clear vision for the future and teaching and facilities combine the very best of the old and the new. Girls are admitted to the school into one of the two Reception forms in September following their fourth birthday. Older girls may be admitted further up the school if a vacancy arises, following a day spent at the school to ensure it is a good fit for them. Girls are expected to remain until the age of 11, being prepared for Common Entrance Examinations at 11+ and for entry to the London Day Schools. A good range of academic, sporting, drama and arts scholarships to senior schools has been awarded to girls over the years.

Work of a traditionally high standard is expected of the girls and they are challenged and supported in classes of 14 girls, encouraging self esteem and enabling them to fulfil their potential. Girls in the Lower School are taught by a Form Teacher, with some specialist input. Girls in the Upper School are taught by subject specialists who impart a real enthusiasm and love for their subject areas. They will also have a form tutor to provide the pastoral support the school is known for. A system of older buddies, prefects and the Student Council ensures that all girls feel an integral part of the school from the beginning.

Music and drama are active throughout the school. Individual music tuition is provided in a wide range of instruments and active choirs sing at numerous competitions and collaborations. All girls take part in at least one dramatic production a year, as well as in assemblies to which parents are invited.

The major sports are netball, hockey, rounders, athletics and swimming and the school has close access to state of the art facilities in the surrounding area as well as our own gym and playground. Girls compete in fixtures against other schools from Year 3 and have had notable successes in recent years in borough-wide championships.

Extra-curricular activities cater to a range of interests and include art, photography, sports, Adventure Service Challenge, computing, cooking, craft and drama clubs. All girls in the Upper School attend a residential trip to Sussex, Dorset, Oxfordshire or France and up to fifty join the biennial ski trip to Italy.

Charitable status. The Old Vicarage School is a Registered Charity, number 312671.

The Oratory Preparatory School

Goring Heath, Reading, Berks RG8 7SF
Tel: 0118 9844511
Fax: 0118 9844806
e-mail: office@oratoryprep.co.uk
          registrar@oratoryprep.co.uk
website: www.oratoryprep.org.uk

Chairman of the Board of Governors: M H R Hasslacher

Headmaster: **J J Smith**, BA, PGCE

Age Range. 3–13.
Number of Pupils. 400 (250 boys and 150 girls), including 50 full-time, weekly or flexi-boarders and 115 in the Pre-Prep department.
Fees per term (2010-2011). Boarders: £4,855 (weekly), £5,275 (full); Day £3,825; Pre-Prep: £2,200 (all day), £1,145 (am).

A Roman Catholic preparatory school, founded by John Henry Cardinal Newman, which prepares boys for The Oratory School and boys and girls for other independent senior schools. The OPS welcomes children of all denominations and faiths and aims to identify and develop their individual talents and gifts in all aspects of their school lives.

The well-qualified and experienced staff of 30 full-time and 40 part-time and visiting teachers and teaching assistants form a strong and supportive team who deliver a broad curriculum characterised by an unusually wide range of subjects, activities and sports. A friendly and secure environment fosters the welfare of every child. Spiritual and pastoral needs are met by the chaplain, a nursing sister, three matrons, and a large and dedicated team of boarding and day staff operating a comprehensive pastoral and academic tutorial system.

The school has an excellent record of achievement, with pupils gaining many academic, art, music, sports and all-rounder awards to The Oratory School and other major schools. Choral and instrumental music, drama and art play a major part in school life. The school is also very proud of its competitive success in rugby, rugby sevens (once national champions and three times runners-up, most recently in 2006), football, cricket, cross-country, hockey, netball and rounders as well as tennis, swimming, archery, squash, golf, badminton, basketball and table tennis. In addition there is an extensive range of activities to suit and stretch every child. The school also organises frequent educational, cultural and sporting tours, both within this country and overseas, to widen further pupils' horizons.

The school's facilities have been extensively developed, with a large theatre, sports hall, indoor swimming pool and trainer pool, all-weather tennis and hockey surfaces, as well as well-equipped science and art departments and a well-stocked library. The music school contains two large spaces for performance and class teaching and seven smaller practice rooms for individual tuition. ICT provision is considerable and forms an integral part of the educational experience offered. The thriving Pre-Prep department is housed in an attractive courtyard setting on the same site.

The school stands in its own 60-acre estate, high above the Thames and easily accessible by train and road (via the M4 from London and Heathrow airport).

Charitable status. The Oratory School Association is a Registered Charity, number 309112. It exists to provide general, physical, moral and religious education for boys and girls.

Orchard House School

16 Newton Grove, London W4 1LB
Tel: 020 8742 8544
Fax: 020 8742 8522
e-mail: info@orchardhs.org.uk
website: www.orchardhs.org.uk

Chairman of Governors: Mr Anthony Rentoul

Headmistress: **Mrs S A B Hobbs**, BA Hons Exon, PGCE, AMBDA Mont Dip

Age Range. Girls and Boys 3–11.
Number of Pupils. 260: 160 Girls, 100 Boys.
Fees per term (2010-2011). Nursery (5 mornings) £2,100, Pre-Prep £4,144, Prep £4,332.

Orchard House School, with Bassett House and Prospect House, is part of the House Schools Group. It provides an excellent all-round education for boys and girls from 3 to 11, preparing them for the competitive entry examinations for the London day and country boarding schools whilst maintaining a happy, purposeful atmosphere. In 2010 the school became fully co-educational with boys able to remain until 11, alongside the girls.

There is an emphasis on teaching traditional values tailored for children growing up in the 21st century. Uniform is worn and good manners are expected at all times. Children shake hands with the staff at the end of each day and are encouraged to take part, with the deputy head or headmistress, in describing the school to prospective parents and other visitors. Appetising lunches are provided and children are involved in growing vegetables and salad in the school garden.

The main premises were designed by the well-known architect Norman Shaw and built around 1880; the building is Grade 2 listed. The school enjoys a corner site in Bedford Park and the classrooms have good natural lighting as well as overlooking a large playground/garden. Additional classrooms and associated study areas have been gained through the acquisition of another attractive building within 5 minutes' walk of the main school.

Children aged 3 or 4 are admitted on a first come, first served basis. Occasional places higher up are filled following assessment. The Montessori method is used to deliver the Early Years Foundation Stage curriculum; at KS1 and KS2 the curriculum is based on the National Curriculum and the demands of the future schools. Specialist teachers are employed for many subjects and support teachers provide on-one or small group tuition where necessary. Staff turnover is low.

Orchard House is proud of the excellent results the children achieve at their future schools which include many of the most academic schools in this country. The school is within easy reach of St Paul's schools, Latymer Upper, Notting Hill & Ealing High School and Godolphin & Latymer and many pupils have taken up places at one of these schools. Links with boys' schools at 11+ will grow over the coming years.

The school boasts state-of-the-art ICT resources and attractive playgrounds/garden with an all-weather surface. The children make good use of additional local facilities to enhance their Sport and Drama lessons.

Orchard House participates in the Nursery Education Grant. There are occasional academic scholarships for children entering Year 4.

Orchard School

Higham Road, Barton-le-Clay, Bedfordshire MK45 4LT
Tel: 01582 882054
e-mail: admin@orchardschool.org.uk
website: www.orchardschool.org.uk

Chair of Governors: Mrs Louise Whitcombe

Head Teacher: **Mrs Anne Burton**, MEd Cantab, CertEd, HV SRN

Deputy Head: Miss Louise Burton, BEd Hons Cantab

Co-educational Day School.
Age Range. 4–9 years; Nursery for children aged 0–4.
Number of Pupils. Preparatory School 56; Nursery 50.
Fees per term (2011-2012). Tuition (inc lunch) £1,995. Breakfast Club £2 per day. After School Club (inc tea) £6.55 per day.

Orchard School is a Preparatory School for boys and girls situated on the outskirts of a large village in south Bedfordshire. The School has been established for 10 years, the Nursery for 20 years. Located in a beautiful setting the School and Pre-Prep is surrounded by rolling countryside with the abundance of wildlife that this brings. The Nursery has its own Deputy Head and specialist team. The children aged 0–3 are located in the charming setting of a Georgian house less than a mile from the main school.

At Orchard we aim to enable each child to value and strive for the highest levels of achievement, creating a culture of pride in success, one in which pupils are proud and have a strong sense of belonging. Praise and encouragement are the motivational tools we employ and we recognise that every child develops at their own pace.

Learning at Orchard is not compartmentalised; trust, motivation, interest, enjoyment as well as physical and social skills are as important as purely cognitive gains. Skillful and careful observations are undertaken across the Orchard teaching team and are key to helping the children learn.

The aim of the school is to develop a passion for learning – to be the best that I can be. We use praise and encouragement as the core motivating factors in school life and are pleased to have built a school of which pupils are proud and have a sense of belonging. We seek to encourage the moral, social and personal development of all pupils building their confidence and self-esteem.

The school boasts an excellent academic record with the majority of our pupils successfully entering the Harpur Trust schools in Bedford. The combination of a progressive, structured, yet genuinely friendly, family atmosphere creates an ideal environment for our children to thrive both academically and in other activities that they pursue.

Encouragement is given to each child to experience a wide range of activities. Music, choir, dance, philosophy and a comprehensive sporting programme including swimming and rugby are all included within the well-rounded curriculum we offer. Further opportunities from Spanish to craftwork, running and badminton to recorder are offered in addition via lunchtime and afterschool clubs. There are several visits a term across all year groups to complement topic learning and enhance the children's confidence and provide real-life context to topics being studied. For Years 3 and 4 we embark on residential trips to specialist adventure-based facilities. The children experience a range of activities including abseiling, kayaking and raft building to develop team spirit and confidence.

The School has historically been effective in building partnerships with parents on an individual basis. Together we encourage mutual respect and are mindful of our shared responsibilities. Orchard has had a very strong and supportive parent base and there is a well-established 'Friends of Orchard School' group who organise social gatherings as well as fundraising events which enhances our family-feel.

Orchard's pupils develop into well-motivated, balanced and confident children who are considerate to others, well-mannered, who know the value of hard work and who go on to excel at their next schools.

Orley Farm School

South Hill Avenue, Harrow on the Hill, Middlesex HA1 3NU
Tel: 020 8869 7600
Fax: 020 8869 7601
e-mail: office@orleyfarm.harrow.sch.uk
website: www.orleyfarm.harrow.sch.uk

The school is a Charitable Trust administered by a Board of Governors.

Chairman of Governors: Mr C J Hayfield

Headmaster: **Mr M Dunning**, BA, PGCE, FCollP

Age Range. 4–13 Co-educational.
Number of Pupils. 490 Day pupils, including 182 in Pre-Prep (age 4 to 7).

Fees per term (2011-2012). Years 5–8 £4,282; Years 3–4 £3,946; Pre-Prep £3,705 (inclusive of lunch).

Orley Farm School is in the fortunate position of being a London day school blessed with boarding school acreage and facilities. Founded in 1850, it has grown and developed to become one of the leading and largest co-educational prep schools in Greater London. Entry is by assessment at 4 years old and boys and girls transfer successfully to their senior schools. The academic journey of the children begins in Reception and ends in Year 6 for our girls and Year 8 for our boys. At the key assessment stages of five, seven, eleven and thirteen the standards achieved are high in relation to their ability. They enter a range of impressive senior schools – including St Paul's, North London Collegiate, Harrow, Westminster, St Helen's, Notting Hill and Ealing, Godolphin and Latymer, Westminster, Merchant Taylors', Northwood College, John Lyon, Haberdashers' Aske's Boys and Girls. Scholarships are regularly gained by our senior pupils – 16 in 2005-06, 12 in 2006-07, 15 in 2007-08, 13 in 2008-09, 15 in 2009-10 and 12 in 2010-11.

These results are achieved through the hard work of our talented pupils and the teaching of our staff, who were recently described as "effective overall and in many cases outstanding". With optimum class sizes of 20 (14 in Years 7 and 8) and a range of modern classroom and other facilities, the children are encouraged to make full use of all that is on offer at the School. Science laboratories and staffing permits specialist teaching from Year 4 onwards in this subject. In Years 7 and 8 the constituent subjects of Biology, Chemistry and Physics are taught separately by subject specialists. ICT provision has grown significantly in recent years and now all classrooms have appropriate interactive provision which is used in support of all areas of the curriculum. A separate and purpose built Music School enables the long tradition of musical excellence and involvement to continue. Over 200 individual music lessons take place each week and are supported by many musical groups and choirs. Our talented individual music teachers make full use of the music rooms and their combined efforts (pupils and teachers) bring us a regular feast of choral and instrumental music in our termly concerts and competitions.

Sport plays a very large part in our school life. We have over thirty six acres of land and full use is made of this in providing a venue for training and matches. The Autumn Term sees the girls playing netball and the boys football; the Spring Term brings out rugby for the boys and hockey for the girls; in the Summer Term the boys play cricket and the girls play rounders. In addition, tennis, cross-country, gymnastics, Fives and basketball also thrive through activities and matches. A Gym, Sports Hall and full-sized all-weather pitch enable our strong PE and Games Department to help our pupils develop their sporting talents.

This happy blend of curricular and extra-curricular comes together towards the end of the year in the great Orley Farm tradition of Expeditions Week. This is an occasion when all children from Year 4 and above leave the school for a variety of venues with their teachers and spend a week extending their curriculum and range of experiences. For most it is the highlight of their year.

An active Parents' Association ensures a strong bond between home and school and they organize an exciting series of events throughout the year fulfilling their goal of "fun, fundraising and feedback".

Entry to this exciting place of learning is by assessment. For further details contact the Registrar, Mrs Julie Jago.

Charitable status. Orley Farm School is a Registered Charity, number 312637.

Orwell Park

Nacton, Ipswich, Suffolk IP10 0ER
Tel: 01473 659225
Fax: 01473 659822
e-mail: headmaster@orwellpark.co.uk
website: www.orwellpark.co.uk

Chairman of Governors: David Wake-Walker, ARCM, LLCJ

Headmaster: **Adrian Brown**, MA Cambridge

Age Range. 3–13.
Number of Pupils. Main School: 210: 120 Boarders (46 girls, 74 boys); 90 Day Pupils (28 girls, 62 boys). Pre-Prep (age 3–7): 78 (32 girls, 46 boys).
Fees per term (2010-2011). Prep School: Full and Weekly Boarders: £6,380 (Form II and above), £5,740 (Form I); Day Pupils: £4,975 (Form II and above); £4,480 (Form I). Pre-Prep: Day Pupils: £1,770 (Nursery); £1,965 (Reception); £2,365 (PP1); £3,030 (PP2).

Flexible Boarding (ie 1–3 nights a week) is also possible – £34 per night.

Pupils are prepared for all Independent Senior Schools via the Scholarship or Common Entrance Examinations (71 awards in the last 5 years). The school has a thriving Pre-Prep School with two teachers who have recently been recognised as Key Practitioners in Outdoor Education.

The ratio of pupils to full-time staff is 9:1. The timetable is especially designed to be very flexible, with separate setting in most subjects, and the curriculum, both in and out of the class-room, is unusually broad. Children are encouraged to enjoy their learning and good learning support is offered. Thinking Skills and other opportunities for academic enrichment are also offered, including a weekly Young Einsteins session to challenge the older children. There are a host of extra-curricular activities (just under 100) run by permanent or visiting staff.

Over 90%of the school learn a musical instrument and the school has a number of orchestral and ensemble groups. A large number of children have been selected to play in IAPS Orchestras and 14 children are members of the 70-strong National Children's Choir. Drama is strong and all children have opportunities to perform regularly in school productions. All children take part in annual Reading and Public Speaking Competitions.

The very large Georgian style building and 110 acres of grounds (sandy soil) on the banks of the River Orwell have the following special features: 21 recently refurbished themed dormitories, 22 bright classrooms with modern audio-visual equipment, beautiful Orangery used as an Assembly and Lecture Hall, Computer and Maths work rooms, large Design Centre including metal, wood and plastic workshop plus electronics, mechanics, home economics, radio and model-making areas, Music Technology Room, Music Room, Band Room and 40 Practice rooms, 3 Laboratories plus associated areas, Library and Resources Centre, Art Room including large pottery area and kiln, Observatory with 10' Refractor Telescope, Photographic Room, 17 Games pitches and one Astroturf pitch, large Sports Hall with permanent stage, Climbing Wall, Games Room, large heated Swimming Pool, 3 Squash Courts, 5 Hard Tennis Courts, Nine-hole Golf Course (approx 1,800 yds), Assault Course, and Tuck and Book Shops.

Good coaching is given and, where appropriate, matches are arranged in the following sports: Association and Rugby Football, Hockey, Cricket, Tennis, Athletics, Squash, Golf, Sailing, Swimming, Badminton, Table-Tennis and Cross-Country Running. Emphasis is also placed on individual physical activities and we offer a wide range including Gymnastics, Fencing, Ballet, Canoeing, Sailing, Modern Dance, Abseiling, Karate, Riding, Shooting with .177 Air Pistols and Clay Pigeon Shooting. The school owns its own canoes and dinghies.

The School aims to introduce the pupils to a broad and varied set of experiences and opportunities. It tries to see that every activity, whether academic, sporting, social or character building, is properly taught using the best possible facilities and that each is conducted in an atmosphere which is friendly but disciplined. Core values include courage, compassion, commitment, compromise and courteous. Children are encouraged to feel comfortable taking risks and to be confident without being arrogant.

Charitable status. Orwell Park School is a Registered Charity, number 310481. It exists to provide education for boys and girls.

Packwood Haugh

Ruyton XI Towns, Shrewsbury, Shropshire SY4 1HX
Tel: 01939 260217
Fax: 01939 262077
e-mail: enquiries@packwood-haugh.co.uk
website: www.packwood-haugh.co.uk

Chairman of Governors: Dr J J Dixey

Headmaster: **N T Westlake**, LLB, PGCE

Deputy Heads
N R Jones, BEd, CertEd
Mrs S Rigby, BA, PGCE, Dip SpLD

Age Range. Co-educational 4–13.
Number of Children. 285. Boarding: 92 boys, 52 girls. Day: 63 boys, 38 girls. Pre-Prep 40.
Fees per term (2010-2011). Boarding £5,802, Day £3,600–£4,642, Pre-Prep (Acorns) £2,045. No compulsory extras.

Set in the heart of the Shropshire countryside, Packwood Haugh is a co-educational boarding (7–13) and day (4–13) school which aims to provide an excellent all-round education in a happy and caring environment. Children benefit from a wide range of academic, sporting, musical, artistic and cultural activities which encourage them to develop enquiring minds and an enthusiasm for learning. The school aims to foster an atmosphere of co-operation and understanding between pupils, staff and parents and to encourage good manners and consideration towards others at all times.

Packwood has always striven for academic excellence; class sizes are small (average 13) and children are prepared for all the major independent schools winning a number of academic, music, sports, art and all-rounder scholarships and awards each year.

The school's facilities are excellent: a new state-of-the-art sports hall was opened in 2007 allowing indoor tennis, four badminton courts, indoor cricket nets and five-a-side football. Incorporated in the building are fully-equipped CDT and Art departments and a linked computer suite. A 280-seat theatre was opened in 2004, in which regular music concerts and three major school plays are performed each year.

A new classroom block was opened four years ago. Other classrooms, within the main school buildings, also include three science laboratories and two further computer suites. A girls' boarding house is a short distance from the main building.

Packwood has a very strong sporting tradition. As well as a large area of grass playing fields, there is a full-size floodlit Astroturf pitch, an additional hard court area, 10 tennis courts, 2 squash courts, an indoor, heated swimming pool and a 9-hole golf course. In the winter terms the boys play rugby, soccer and hockey while the girls play hockey, netball and lacrosse. There is also cross-country running on a course within the grounds. In the summer the boys play cricket, the girls play rounders and all take part in tennis, athletics and swimming.

Additional facilities include a shooting range and an equestrian cross-country course as well as an adventure playground.

Charitable status. Packwood Haugh is a Registered Charity, number 528411. It exists to provide day and boarding education for boys and girls from the age of 4 to 13.

Papplewick

Windsor Road, Ascot, Berks SL5 7LH
Tel: 01344 621488
Fax: 01344 874639
e-mail: hm@papplewick.org.uk
         registrar@papplewick.org.uk
website: www.papplewick.org.uk

Chairman of Board of Governors: Brigadier (Retd) A R E Hutchinson, JP

Headmaster: T W Bunbury, BA University College, Durham, PGCE

Age Range. 6–13.
Number of Boys. 199: 146 boarders, 53 day boys.
Fees per term (2011-2012). Boarders £7,770; Day Boys: £4,450 (Year 2), £5,630 (Years 3–4), £5,965 (Years 5–6).

Papplewick is a day, weekly and full boarding school for boys with an exceptional Scholarship record to top Independent Schools. New Year 2 class from September 2010. Day boys do prep at school and come into board from the Summer term of Year 6. Happy, confident boys abound, and a modern, family-friendly approach to boarding is adopted. A daily transport service runs to/from West London, and being situated between M3 and M4, the school boasts easy access to London airports.

Papplewick exists to provide a high quality predominantly boarding education where – for all our academic, cultural and sporting success – the happiness of the boys come first.

Charitable status. The Papplewick Educational Trust is a Registered Charity, number 309087.

The Paragon
Junior School of Prior Park College

Lyncombe House, Lyncombe Vale, Bath BA2 4LT
Tel: 01225 310837
Fax: 01225 427980
e-mail: admissions@paragon.priorpark.co.uk
website: www.paragonschool.co.uk

Chair of Governors: Sister Jane Livesey, CJ, MA Cantab

Headmaster: Mr Titus Mills, BA Hons

Age Range. 3–11 years.
Number of Pupils. 162 Boys, 110 Girls.
Fees per term (2010-2011). Juniors £2,555; Age 5–7 £2,413; Under 5 £2,293 including lunches. Flexible sessions until five years (fees accordingly). Sibling discounts available. Registration Fee (non-refundable) £100.

19 experienced and qualified teachers.

The Paragon is an independent, co-educational day school based in a beautiful Georgian house situated a mile from the centre of Bath. The school is set in eight acres of beautiful grounds with woodland, conservation areas, lawns and streams. It's the perfect 'outdoor classroom' and we use it right across the curriculum. Following our recent merger with nearby Prior Park College, less than a mile away, we also enjoy regular access to their superb facilities.

Several factors help create the 'distinctive Paragon atmosphere'. One is undoubtedly the homely feel that comes from being based in a beautiful, former family home. Then there's our Christian ethos and strong pastoral care, as well as our belief that school at this age is about being stimulated and inspired, about laughter and spontaneity – in short, about having fun. We may be a private school and we certainly expect high standards of behaviour but we're anything but stuffy and grey.

We offer a broad curriculum taught in small classes by teachers with a real passion for their subject. Academic life at The Paragon cultivates a love of learning and encourages independent and creative thinking. Our results are impressive. Our children consistently achieve well above the national average and many Year 6 children win senior school scholarships. Our facilities include a library, large gymnasium/dining hall, ICT suite, nursery with secure indoor and outdoor play areas, art studio, modern languages and music rooms.

Sport is particularly strong at The Paragon. Our sports teams take part, with considerable success, in a wide range of tournaments and festivals. We also offer a vast range of sports clubs that all children can join regardless of ability. Prior Park College offers us an indoor swimming pool, astroturf and grass pitches, tennis courts, athletics track, sports hall, and dance studio.

The Paragon's extra-curricular programme is extensive. Staff run more than 40 lunchtime and after-school clubs that range from pottery and chess to conservation and Indian puppet making. The school also enjoys an enviable reputation for Music. All children receive weekly music lessons from a specialist teacher. In addition, visiting instrumental teachers offer tuition in a wide range of instruments. We offer an excellent choice of extra-curricular music activities including two orchestras, three choirs, a wind band, brass group, string ensemble, guitar group and a samba band.

The Paragon is proud of its consistently impressive academic results but we strive for much more than success in exams. We believe in developing the whole person – physically, spiritually, and emotionally as well as intellectually. As W B Yeats said: "Education is not filling a bucket but lighting a fire."

Charitable status. Prior Park Educational Trust is a Registered Charity, number 281242.

Parkside

The Manor, Stoke d'Abernon, Cobham, Surrey KT11 3PX
Tel: 01932 862749
Fax: 01932 860251
e-mail: enquiries@parkside-school.co.uk
website: www.parkside-school.co.uk

Chairman of Governors: C M East, ACII

Headmaster: D M Aylward, MA, BEd Hons

Deputy Heads:
D M Pulleyn, CertEd
Mrs H Sayer, BEd Hons

Age Range. Boys 2½–13. Co-educational Nursery.
Numbers. Day Boys 236, Pre-Prep 95, Nursery 85.
Fees per term (from January 2011). Day Boys £4,100, Pre-Prep £3,050, Nursery £308–£2,450.

Parkside was founded in 1879 and became a Charitable Trust in 1960. The School moved from East Horsley to its present site of over 40 acres in 1979, its centenary year. Since the move the Governors have implemented a continual development programme which has included a purpose built, well equipped Science Block, extending the main building to provide more Pre-Prep accommodation and a Music School with a large classroom and six practice rooms. A superb covered Swimming Pool and Sports Hall complex with an excellent stage for drama offers unrivalled facilities in the area. In addition, a £2m Classroom Block has been built recently to further enhance the facilities in the school. The Design Technology Department, Nursery and new ICT suite are housed in a delightful Grade II Listed Barn which has been completely and skilfully refurbished to provide spacious, well-lit classrooms and workshops. The Governors have plans in the near future to link a second Computer Room to the main network and further expand the Art and Music facilities.

The school is large enough to be flexible and offer setting in major subjects yet small enough for each pupil to be known and treated as an individual. On average there are 15 pupils in a Set and the teacher: pupil ratio is 1:8. All teaching staff are highly qualified and there is a low staff turnover. Each boy is a member of a House and this helps to stimulate friendly competition for work points and many other inter-house contests.

The National Curriculum is followed to prepare all boys for entry to Senior Independent Schools by Common Entrance and Scholarship examinations. All boys pass to their first choice Senior Schools and our results in these examinations are impressive. Over the past few years many Academic, Art, Music and Sporting Scholarships have been won. Our curriculum is broad based and all boys are taught Art, Music, PE and Technology in addition to the usual Common Entrance subjects. There are two School Choirs and a School Orchestra and over one third of the boys are receiving individual tuition in a wide variety of musical instruments. During the year, there are many opportunities for boys to perform in musical and dramatic productions.

The School has a fine sporting record and, over the past few years, many tournaments in different sports and at different age groups have been won. In addition, a number of boys have gone on to represent their County and Country in various sports. The main sports are football, hockey and cricket, but boys are able to take part in rugby, swimming, athletics, tennis, cross-country running, basketball and judo. An extensive Wednesday afternoon and After School Activity Programme (including supervised homework sessions) is available with over 40 different activities on offer, from gardening to kayaking, and horse-riding to golf. Many boys have also represented the school at a high level in chess. The beautiful estate and the River Mole, which runs through the grounds, are also used to contribute to the all round education each pupil receives both in and out of the classroom.

Unusually for a Preparatory School, Parkside has a large and active Old Boys Association which runs many sporting and social events during the year.

Further details and a prospectus are available on application to the Headmaster's Secretary.

Charitable status. Parkside School is a Registered Charity, number 312041. It exists to provide education for children between the ages of 2½ and 13 years.

Pembridge Hall School
Alpha Plus Group

18 Pembridge Square, London W2 4EH
Tel:　020 7229 0121
Fax:　020 7792 1086
e-mail:　contact@pembridgehall.co.uk

website: www.pembridgehall.co.uk

Head: **Mr B H Evans**, BEd

Age Range. 4½–11.
Number of Girls. 250.
Fees per term (2010-2011). £4,865.

Girls are prepared for entry into independent London day schools and for the Independent Schools Common Entrance examination.

The school aims to create a happy and contented atmosphere in which girls may learn to work with concentration and enthusiasm. The curriculum is designed to give a thorough grounding in English and Mathematics. The girls' interest and desire to learn are stimulated through History, Geography, Religious Instruction, French, Science, Music, Drama, Art, ICT and Physical Education. A wide range of after-school activities is also on offer.

Pennthorpe School

Rudgwick, Horsham, West Sussex RH12 3HJ
Tel:　01403 822391
Fax:　01403 822438
e-mail:　enquiries@pennthorpe.com
website:　www.pennthorpe.com

The School that puts the fun into the fundamentals.

Chairman of the Governors: Mr T Mullins, MBA, BA

Headmaster: **Mr M King**, BA Hons

Age Range. Co-educational 2–13.
Number of Pupils. 362 Day Pupils.
Fees per term (2011-2012). £464–£4,230.

Pennthorpe School in West Sussex lies close to the Surrey border, midway between Guildford and Horsham. The school is committed to high standards in all it does. Pennthorpe also recognises that putting the fun into the fundamentals of school life encourages the children to maximise their learning potential.

Pennthorpe has an outstanding record of 13+ Common Entrance successes, with a history of a 100% pass rate to first-choice schools stretching back as far as anyone can remember. In the last five years, more than a third of Pennthorpe's 13 year-old leavers have won over 70 academic scholarships or prestigious awards for music, art, sport or drama.

Many have also won all-rounder scholarships which reflects the school's commitment to developing its pupils into well-balanced youngsters, and it is this outlook, along with the principle of putting the fun into the fundamentals, that drives Pennthorpe forward.

Developing all-rounders means offering choice, and from the very earliest stages when the two year-olds join the Pennthorpe Kindergarten, the emphasis is on breadth, both academic and outside the classroom.

The Pennthorpe Sports Department offers a wealth of sporting activities and competitive opportunities: soccer, netball, rugby, hockey, rounders, cricket and athletics are regular features on the termly fixtures calendar, while gymnastics, climbing, judo, tennis, basketball, archery and many others are available as part of the huge range of after-school options.

Pennthorpe is committed to the Arts. From the age of five, every pupil enjoys weekly Performing Arts lessons in our own dance and drama studio. There are also specialist-taught music lessons for all; these, along with four choirs, an orchestra, individual instrumental tuition and termly concerts provide many performing opportunities.

With a separate Art & Design building (incorporating a computer suite), and a long-standing reputation for artistic excellence, Pennthorpe is also well equipped to fire the creative spirits of its pupils.

Complementing and building upon the classroom work, Pennthorpe's celebrated Flexiday programme of after-school activities aims to bring even more chances for every boy and girl to find their strengths and shine. Whether it is developing their computer skills, throwing a pot, scaling the climbing wall, or tapping to the rhythm in the dance studio, there's something for everybody.

A continuous programme of major capital investment is under way. A recently completed Pre-Prep building with 6 new classrooms, a state-of-the-art kindergarten and large multi-purpose hall has transformed the academic life of our younger pupils and plans are already laid for a new Performing Arts Centre. This is a school that never stands still!

If you would like to see how your child could thrive in this busy, happy and successful school, ask for a prospectus, visit our website (details above) and then book a visit: the Headmaster and all the staff and children will make you very welcome. There are two Open Mornings each term and the Headmaster is also happy to welcome parents for individual visits at any time.

Charitable status. Pennthorpe School is a Registered Charity, number 307043. It exists to provide an excellent education for boys and girls and to benefit the community.

Perrott Hill School

North Perrott, Crewkerne, Somerset TA18 7SL
Tel: 01460 72051
Fax: 01460 78246
e-mail: headmaster@perrotthill.com
website: www.perrotthill.com

Chairman of Governors: Lord Bradbury

Headmaster: **Mr R J Morse**, BEd Hons

Age Range. 3–13.
Number of Pupils. 111 boys and 91 girls, of whom 59 are full, weekly or flexi-boarders.
Fees per term (2011-2012). Boarders: £6,298 (full), £5,134 (weekly); Day pupils £1,406–£4,414.

Perrott Hill School is a co-educational day and boarding school and is registered as an Educational Trust. Set in 25 acres of beautiful grounds in the heart of the countryside, near Crewkerne on the Somerset/Dorset border, it is served by excellent road and rail networks.

Perrott Hill is a thriving country preparatory school where children settle quickly and learn in confidence. Class sizes are small, with an average of 15 children to a form; the pupils being streamed from Year 5 onwards. Staff are dedicated and highly qualified. Facilities now include an all-weather sports area, a purpose-built sports hall, a theatre, a DT/art school, a computer centre, a music school, games fields, swimming pool and woodland area.

The Montessori Nursery and Pre-Prep are housed within the converted stable courtyard next to the main school buildings, which gives the younger children their own safe, secure environment whilst allowing them to take advantage of the grounds and facilities of the Prep School.

Music, Drama and Art are taught within the timetable alongside core curriculum subjects. The choir and orchestra perform at charity concerts, in competitions and school functions. There are drama productions every term.

Teaching is class-based until Year 5 and subject-based in the upper school, where all lessons are taught by specialist teachers. French, Music, IT and PE, however, are taught by specialists throughout the school.

Each child, boarding or day, has his or her own pastoral and academic tutor, while the welfare of the boarders is supervised by Mr and Mrs Finch, the house master and house mistress. They are ably assisted by a dedicated and enthusiastic boarding staff (twelve of whom live on site).

Sport is played every day, and matches take place on most Wednesdays as well as on Saturdays for the senior part of the school. Emphasis is placed upon skills and team work, as well as the achievement of results. Games played include rugby, football, hockey, netball, cricket, tennis, rounders, swimming and cross-country running. The school takes part in national events, such as the IAPS Ski Championships, IAPS Sailing Regatta and the National Small Schools Rugby Sevens. Optional extras include fencing, carpentry, archery, karate, horse riding, ballet, modern dance, speech and drama, cookery, Spanish, golf and craft.

The school boasts an excellent academic record, with awards to major senior independent schools and success at Common Entrance. In the last 2 years the 62 children leaving school at the end of Year 8 have secured 32 awards to senior schools with scholarships being awarded for academic, artistic, sporting, dramatic, musical, equine and all-round ability.

Academic, music, sport, art, drama and all-rounder Scholarships are offered annually in February to children in Years 3–6.

The combination of countryside, space, a family atmosphere and a forward-looking academic programme creates an ideal environment for children to thrive both academically and in their leisure pursuits – we warmly invite you to come and see the school in action.

Charitable status. Perrott Hill School is a Registered Charity, number 310278. It exists to give high quality education to boys and girls.

The Perse Pelican Nursery and Pre-Preparatory School

92 Glebe Road, Cambridge CB1 7TD
Tel: 01223 403940
Fax: 01223 403941
e-mail: pelican@perse.co.uk
website: www.perse.co.uk

Chairman of Governors: Sir David J Wright, GCMG, LVO, MA

Headmistress: **Mrs S Waddington**, BSc, MA

Age Range. 3–7.
Number of Pupils. 145.
Fees per term (2011-2012). £3,580 (full-time – Reception, Year 1 and Year 2), £2,013 (Nursery – half day). From September 2011, Nursery children may attend up to 10 sessions each week (a full-time place). Each session attended above and beyond 5 sessions will be charge at no more than £35 per session per week.

The Perse Pelican Nursery and Pre-Preparatory School is set in its own grounds on the edge of the city centre.

The Board of Governors of The Perse Upper School oversees the management of the school.

At The Perse Pelican children work alongside a team of highly qualified and dedicated staff in bright, busy and superbly equipped surroundings. In this nurturing environment we are quickly able to identify strengths and areas for development and we provide every pupil with the best possible opportunities to enable them to achieve their full potential.

From their earliest days with us we enthusiastically support our pupils as they explore a wide range of opportunities. Activities are carefully planned to foster pupils' intellectual, emotional, creative and spiritual development. We encourage pupils to delight in discovery as well as their own increasing knowledge. They come to school eager to see what new challenges await them.

Always keen to move forward, the school embraces new technology and innovative ideas in education but traditional values remain steadfast. Perse Pelican pupils acquire a positive attitude to learning and a clear sense of right and wrong. They learn that each of us has a valid contribution to make and that all are valued members of the school community.

We recognise the special responsibility entrusted to us by parents and we particularly value the close partnership we establish with our families. Most pupils enter The Perse Pelican through the Nursery class, but a few places become available at the beginning of the Reception year. All pupils are screened prior to entry. We plan carefully for a smooth transition to the Perse Prep School.

Charitable status. The Perse School is a charitable company limited by guarantee (company number 5977683, registered charity number 1120654) registered in England and Wales whose registered office is situated at The Perse School, Hills Road, Cambridge CB2 8QF.

The Perse Preparatory School

Trumpington Road, Cambridge CB2 8EX
Tel: 01223 403920
Fax: 01223 403921
e-mail: prep@perse.co.uk
website: www.perse.co.uk

Chairman of Governors: Sir David J Wright, GCMG, LVO, MA

Head: **G R P Jones**

Age Range. 7–11.
Number of Pupils. 265.
Fees per term (2011-2012). £4,158.
The Perse Prep School is a co-educational preparatory school in Cambridge. It stands in its own grounds some 1½ miles away from the The Perse Upper School and is totally self-contained. Recent developments provided outstanding classroom and creative arts facilities.

The school aims to achieve high academic standards and a wide range of achievements in cultural, sporting and artistic endeavours. The depth of academic ability throughout the school allows intellectual curiosity to flourish and pupils thrive on challenges both inside and outside the classroom. Pupils enjoy each other's success and have the quiet confidence to be at ease with new ideas. As they grow we aim to develop the qualities of reliability, consideration for others, good manners and self-discipline which they need to complement their academic success. The school is in regular contact with parents and the Head of Pastoral Care works closely with form teachers to ensure the general well-being of pupils.

Excellent facilities enable us to offer a wide variety of sporting and recreational pursuits. The games programme (football, cricket, netball, athletics, tennis and hockey) is designed to encourage all pupils to enjoy games and physical exercise. The school is proud of its strong tradition in music, drama and the arts and the majority of pupils learn a musical instrument. There are choirs, two orchestras and numerous instrumental groups. Extra-curricular activities including badminton, chess, cookery, computing, cycling proficiency, drama, judo, school newspaper and PPES (Perse Prep Exploration Society) are also available. There is an annual adventure activity week for pupils in Year 6 and a Year 5 trip to France.

Pupils enter the Prep School each September. Places are awarded as a result of an examination held in January of the year of entry. The normal point of entry is Year 3, although there are sometimes a small number of places available in other year groups. Subject to having made satisfactory progress at the Prep School, pupils move to The Perse Upper School for Year 7.

Charitable status. The Perse School is a charitable company limited by guarantee (company number 5977683, registered charity number 1120654) registered in England and Wales whose registered office is situated at The Perse School, Hills Road, Cambridge CB2 8QF.

Pilgrims Pre-Preparatory School

Brickhill Drive, Bedford MK41 7QZ
Tel: 01234 369555
Fax: 01234 369556
e-mail: pilgrims@harpur-trust.org.uk
website: www.pilgrims-school.info

Chair of Governors: Mrs S Clark

Headteacher: **Mrs J Webster**, BEd Hons, EYPS

Co-educational Day School.
Age Range. 3 months–8 years.
Number of Pupils. 388: 199 Boys, 189 Girls.
Fees per term (2011-2012). £969–£2,630.
Pilgrims Pre-Preparatory School is the newest addition to the Harpur Trust family of schools. We opened in 2000 in spacious, purpose-built accommodation with extensive playing fields. Most of our children continue their education within the four other Harpur Trust schools.

Pilgrims is a vibrant, stimulating environment where we pride ourselves on providing a rich and varied curriculum that offers plenty of opportunities to develop each child's self-esteem and confidence, whilst giving the support to enable them to become independent learners and to achieve their full potential. We use the EYFS and the best of the National Curriculum, developing the curriculum further to meet the needs of our children. In addition, we take advantage of our experienced staff and excellent facilities to provide specialist weeks on a range of topics including Healthy Heart week, Art Week and Science Week. Good manners are valued and celebrated throughout the school.

Children are taught in small classes with specialist teachers. Emphasis is placed upon English and Mathematics to ensure that solid foundations are laid for success across the whole curriculum. School trips are arranged to a variety of local museums, wildlife centres and villages to further enrich the children's learning.

Academic standards are high and children who are identified as gifted and able are offered specific tuition in small groups to ensure their needs are met.

We have a strong music department with a successful choir and orchestra who regularly take part in the Bedfordshire Music Festival. Specialist music teaching begins in the toddler room and continues throughout the school. Individual instrumental tuition is available from Year 1 with over 60% of children learning one or more instruments.

We encourage the children to enjoy a healthy school life. Our menus are planned in conjunction with a nutritionist, and the children have a range of homemade biscuits, fruit and crudités provided for snacks each day. Sport is most important within the school; in addition to gymnastics, dance and outdoor games, from 2 years of age the children use our indoor swimming pool every week, and from Nursery they swim twice each week. Our tennis academy regularly produces county players.

The school is open 46 weeks a year with holiday clubs running outside term time. We also offer a huge range of after-school clubs and a breakfast club. Parents are welcomed into the school and work in partnership with the staff to create a warm, caring, purposeful and fun environment in which our children thrive.

Charitable status. Pilgrims Pre-Preparatory School is part of The Bedford Charity (The Harpur Trust) which is a Registered Charity, number 204817.

The Pilgrims' School

Winchester, Hampshire SO23 9LT
Tel: 01962 854189
Fax: 01962 843610
e-mail: info@pilgrims-school.co.uk
website: www.thepilgrims-school.co.uk

Chairman of Governors: The Very Revd James Atwell, Dean of Winchester

Headmaster: **P G Watson**, MA Hons, PGCE

Age Range. Boys 4–13.
Number of Pupils. 200 Boys (80 boarders/weekly boarders, 120 day boys). Pre-Prep: 54.
Fees per term (2010-2011). Boarders £6,230, Day boys £4,925, Pre-Prep £2,830.

The Governing Body consists of The Dean (Chairman) and delegated members of the Chapter of Winchester and the Headmaster and Bursar of Winchester College. Examinations for independent schools, with a significant number moving to Winchester College each year. Cathedral Choristers and Winchester College Quiristers are educated at the school and receive scholarships and bursaries up to the value of the full boarding fee together with free tuition in one musical instrument. All boys whether musical or not receive excellent academic and musical tuition, and the sporting tradition is equally strong. The school is noted for its happy family atmosphere, and a major recent building programme has ensured the highest standard of facilities possible. All enquiries about the school or singing auditions should be addressed to the Registrar.

Charitable status. The Pilgrims' School is a Registered Charity, number 1091579.

Pinewood

Bourton, Shrivenham, Wiltshire SN6 8HZ
Tel: 01793 782205
Fax: 01793 783476
e-mail: office@pinewoodschool.co.uk
website: www.pinewoodschool.co.uk

Headmaster: **Philip Hoyland**, BEd Exeter

Deputy Head: C J Acheson-Gray, BEd

Age Range. 3–13.
Number of Pupils. 237 Boys and Girls (80 flexi and 40 weekly boarders). Nursery and Pre-Prep: 110.
Fees per term (2011-2012). Day £2,450–£4,810 inclusive, with no compulsory extras. Weekly Boarding supplement: £1,175.

Pinewood is set in 84 acres of rolling countryside. The School offers a quality, family-based environment where children are encouraged to think for themselves and a strong emphasis is placed on self-discipline, manners, trust and selflessness. Resources include a purpose-built Music School and Junior Forms' Wing, a flourishing Pre-Prep and Nursery, Art and Design Workshops, Research and Reference Library and ICT Rooms.

Excellent academic results are achieved through a mixture of traditional and forward-thinking teaching within a happy, friendly and stimulating learning atmosphere. Outside trips are frequent and visiting speakers prominent. Music and drama are encouraged.

Sport is keenly coached and matches are played at all levels on our picturesque playing fields, which incorporate a nine-hole golf course. There is a wide range of activities and clubs both for day children and, in the evening, for boarders.

Pinewood is a school where staff, parents and children work together to find and realise the potential in every child.

Charitable status. Pinewood is a Registered Charity, number 309642. It exists to provide high quality education for boys and girls.

Plymouth College Preparatory School

St Dunstan's Abbey, The Millfields, Plymouth, Devon PL1 3JL
Tel: 01752 201352
Fax: 01752 201351
e-mail: prepschool@plymouthcollege.com
website: www.plymouthcollege.com

Chairman of Governors: D R Woodgate, BSc, MBA

Headmaster: **C D M Gatherer**, BA Keele

Age Range. 3–11 Co-educational.
Number of Pupils. 255.
Fees per term (2010-2011). Infant Department: Kindergarten £2,150, Reception £2,300, Years 1 & 2 £2,550. Junior Department: Years 3–4 £2,650, Years 5–6 £2,800.

Plymouth College Preparatory School is a co-educational school for children from 3–11 years. The school was founded in 1877 and is within a few minutes' drive of Plymouth College senior school.

The primary academic aim of the school is to prepare children for entry to Plymouth College at the age of 11, ensuring that they are articulate and have taken full advantage of an education designed to stimulate the development of each child both intellectually and socially.

There are thirty full-time and three part-time members of staff, including specialist teachers in Mathematics, English, Science, Information Technology, Design Technology, Geography, History, Art, Music and French. There is a wide range of extra-curricular activities.

There are two libraries, a computer room, a well-equipped laboratory, art room, music room and new sports centre.

Entry is by interview and assessment. Application forms can be obtained from the School Secretary and appointments to view the school are welcomed.

Charitable status. Plymouth College is a Registered Charity, number 1105544. It exists to help children fulfil their wish to achieve a higher standard of education.

Port Regis

Motcombe Park, Shaftesbury, Dorset SP7 9QA
Tel: 01747 857800
Fax: 01747 857810
e-mail: office@portregis.com
website: www.portregis.com

Chairman of the Governors: Mark A Vaughan-Lee

Headmaster: **Benedict H Dunhill**, BA Hons

Deputy Head: Kieron Peacock, MSc Leicester, CertEd & Phys Ed Madeley College, Staffs

Director of Studies: Michael J Jonas, MA London, BEd Durham

Age Range. 3–13.
Number of Pupils. Boarders: 252 (Boys 146, Girls 106); Day Boarders: 101 (Boys 44, Girls 57).
Fees per term (2011-2012). Boarders £7,450–£7,755 (no compulsory extras); Day Boarders £2,575–£5,995 (meals included). Weekly Boarding is available.

Port Regis is a well-established and highly regarded preparatory school set in 150 acres of beautiful Dorset parkland just outside the historic town of Shaftesbury. The main building is an Elizabethan-style mansion with elegant oak-panelled reception rooms and a splendid galleried Hall with a large feature-fireplace. The grounds encompass 35 acres of playing fields as well as extensive ancient woodland, gardens, lawns and a lake.

The school offers a purpose-built science, design and technology centre, a specialist teaching block for Arts subjects, a music school with recital hall, a 450-seat theatre, a new dining hall and kitchens, an astroturf hockey pitch, a nine-hole golf course, 13 tennis courts and a sports complex (including two Sports Halls) which serves as a National Centre for Junior Gymnastics with a 25-metre indoor heated swimming pool and the JM Upward Academic Centre, a striking modern building providing 14 spacious classrooms and resource rooms, which has been built using cutting-edge technology to provide heating and cooling without the burning of fossil fuels. There are also badminton and squash courts available. An equestrian centre is conveniently situated close to the School.

Younger pupils are accommodated in bright, cosy dormitories in the Mansion House, while the older pupils enjoy the comfort of splendid senior boarding houses. The boys' house has 60 individual study-bedrooms, each provided with its own washbasin, desk, cupboard and drawers. There are also two common rooms and separate kitchen areas as well as a generous provision of showers, baths and wcs. This house complements the senior girls' house, similar in design with 48 study-bedrooms, which was completed a few years ago.

A Pre-Prep and Nursery opened in September 1993 in the secure and beautiful environment of the Motcombe Park grounds with full use of the Prep School's facilities.

Each child's Tutor will, we hope, become a friend of the family as well as the child, especially since over 90 boarders have parents working overseas. Encouragement is given to each child to experience a wide variety of activities and develop skills where talent lies. Most staff live either on the estate or in the main building, so personal guidance and a family atmosphere has been created. Academic standards are high and children are prepared successfully for Common Entrance or Scholarship examinations. Learning Support is available for children with mild-to-moderate learning difficulties.

Extensive opportunities are provided for Music (about three-quarters of the School learn an instrument), Drama (there are up to six productions a year), and Art (in a wide choice of media), with Woodwork, Electronics, Riding, .22 Rifle Shooting, Karate, Gymnastics and Canoeing included in a list of over 70 hobby options. Major team games are Rugby, Hockey, Soccer, Netball, Cricket and Rounders. Inter-school, county and national standard competitions are entered. Home and abroad expeditions take place.

There are 56 full-time teaching staff, 16 visiting musicians, 4 State Registered Nurses, a Head of Boarding, an Assistant Head of Boarding, a Housemother, Houseparents and Matrons.

A prospectus may be had on application from the Headmaster, who would be delighted to welcome visitors to Port Regis. Next Open Morning: Saturday 8 October 2011.

Academic, Music, Gymnastic, Sport and All-Rounder entrance scholarships may be awarded annually. The School also has a wealth of experience in dealing with HM Services Families (approx 15% of pupils) and offers special awards to children of HM Services Families.

Charitable status. Port Regis School Limited is a Registered Charity, number 306218. It exists to provide an all-round education to the highest standard for boys and girls from the ages of 3 to 13.

The Portsmouth Grammar School Junior School

High Street, Portsmouth, Hampshire PO1 2LN
Tel: 023 9236 0036
Fax: 023 9236 4263
e-mail: juniorschool@pgs.org.uk
website: www.pgs.org.uk

Chairman of the Governors: B S Larkman, BSc, ACIB

Headmaster of the Junior School: P S Hopkinson, BA, PGCE

Deputy Headmaster: J Ashcroft, BSc, PGCE
Assistant Headmistress: Mrs E R Day, BA, CertEd
Assistant Headmistress: Mrs P Giles, BA, PGCE
Head of Nursery: Mrs L Johnson, BEd, PGDip Early Years

Age Range. 4–11. Nursery: 2¾–4.
Number of Day Pupils. 279 boys, 176 girls.
Fees per term (2011-2012). Reception, Years 1 and 2: £2,605. Years 3 and 4: £2,746. Years 5 and 6: £2,889. (Fees quoted include direct debit discount.)

The Junior School is an integral part of The Portsmouth Grammar School under the general direction of the Governors and Headmaster. Children from 4–9 years are educated within bright and spacious classrooms that occupy a discreet space on the Senior School site. The 9–11 year old pupils are educated in the historic original school building which stands in splendid isolation in close proximity to the Senior School site.

The Junior School's organisation is distinct under its own Headmaster, with 36 full-time, 10 part-time members of staff, and 17 learning support assistants.

The main entry is at 4+ and an additional class is formed at 7+. Pupils leave at 11 years, the majority moving on to The Portsmouth Grammar School Senior School.

Whilst emphasis is placed on literacy and numeracy there is a broad curriculum which includes; Science, Geography, History, Religious Studies, ICT, Modern Foreign Languages, Music, Design Technology, Art, Drama, Physical Education, Games and PSHE. In addition, many pupils receive tuition in a wide range of musical instruments.

The school also provides a wide choice of extra-curricular activities to all pupils. Currently over 30 different club activities are offered. The most recent innovations are a week's sailing instruction for all pupils in Year 4 and a French Trip for all pupils in Year 6. There are specialist rooms for Art and Craft, Music and Drama, plus a Science Laboratory and two Information Technology Centres. An innovative string scheme enables all seven year olds to experience a free term's tuition in learning the violin or 'cello.

Games include Association and Rugby Football, Netball, Hockey, Rounders, Cricket, Athletics, Tennis and Swimming. The Junior School has its own learner swimming pool and uses the Grammar School's excellent 16 acre playing fields at Hilsea, which include a Floodlit astro turf pitch.

It also has access to the Grammar School's Sports Hall, Music School and Theatre.

In September 2001 a Nursery School was opened offering up to 48 places in any one session. The architect designed building provides the children, aged from two years nine months, with exciting opportunities to learn through play and exploration. All staff have early years specialism, the Head of Nursery being a fully qualified primary teacher with Early Years expertise. The Nursery School offers provision for 45 weeks a year.

Charitable status. The Portsmouth Grammar School is a Registered Charity, number 1063732. It exists to provide education for boys and girls.

Pownall Hall

Carrwood Road, Wilmslow, Cheshire SK9 5DW
Tel: 01625 523141
Fax: 01625 525209
e-mail: headmaster@pownallhall.cheshire.sch.uk
website: www.pownallhall.cheshire.sch.uk

Chairman of the Board of Governors: Mrs Sue Page

Headmaster: **Mr Jonathan D Hall**, BEd Hons

Age Range. 2–11 Co-educational.
Number of Boys and Girls. 200 (Day Children)
Fees per term (2010-2011). £1,525–£3,095 (including lunch).

Pownall Hall, a preparatory day school for children aged 2 to 11 and set in its own beautiful and extensive grounds, has been established for over 100 years. It is situated on the north-western side of Wilmslow, 12 miles from Manchester and within easy reach of motorway, rail and air travel.

The school has a highly trained teaching staff, who prepare children for the Entrance Examinations to the Independent Day schools in the area. A thorough grounding is given in all academic subjects in line with the National Curriculum and an excellent mixture of traditional and modern techniques is used. In Key Stage 2 each major subject has specialist teaching staff and subject rooms including a fully equipped Science Laboratory, Maths, English, Information Technology and French rooms and, in addition, a computer-aided Library. French is taught from the age of six.

Pownall Hall School has two pre-school years with children entering the Nursery from the age of 2 and transferring to Kindergarten at the age of 3. From here the pupils then enter Reception and go through the school to Year 6 before deciding where to continue their education at the age of 11.

At Pownall Hall there is a generous staff to pupil ratio throughout the school which ensures that pastoral care is of a very high level and this also supports the children's learning of all abilities. Children are taught in small class sizes gaining from the individual attention they receive.

Great importance is attached to Sport, Music and Drama and the school has its own well equipped theatre where all children perform on stage during the year. Music is offered as part of the curriculum and also additionally as a full range of teaching with chances for the children to perform in and outside school. As well as subject specialist rooms with an outstanding range of specialist equipment, the newly-refurbished ICT suite gives the children an outstanding facility to bring their skills into the 21st century.

The facilities for sport are very impressive with the school having its own extensive grounds with a fully-equipped Sports Hall and both outdoor and indoor facilities for Netball and Tennis.

All children experience learning off site, with day and residential trips arranged. Children in Years 4 to 6 also experience outdoor pursuits at a range of well-equipped sites which enhance their learning experiences.

The school has received an outstanding inspection Report (2011).

Charitable status. Pownall Hall School is a Registered Charity, number 525929. It exists to provide education for boys and girls, aged 2–11 yrs.

The Prebendal School

54 West Street, Chichester, West Sussex PO19 1RT
Tel: 01243 772220
Fax: 01243 771821
e-mail: secretary.prebendal@btconnect.com
website: www.prebendalschool.org.uk

Chairman of Governors: The Dean of Chichester

Headmaster: **Mr T R Cannell**, MA Ed Man, BEd Winchester

Age Range. 3–13.
Number of Pupils. 153 (21 boarders, 132 day) with a further 80 in the Pre-Prep.
Fees per term (2011-2012). Boarders £5,560, Weekly Boarders £5,327, Day Pupils £4,112, Pre-Prep: £2,184–£2,511 (full day); Kindergarten £6.20 per hour. Compulsory extras: laundry and linen for boarders.

The School, which is co-educational, is governed by the Dean and Chapter of Chichester Cathedral with 6 lay members of the Board. It is the oldest school in Sussex and has occupied its present building at the west end of the Cathedral (though with later additions) for over 500 years. The Cathedral Choristers are among the boys educated at the School and they receive Choral Scholarships in reduction of fees. Annual Music and Academic Scholarships are open to boys and girls entering the school. Sibling Bursaries are awarded to brothers and sisters. Open and Music Scholarships to Independent Senior Schools are gained regularly.

There are excellent playing fields. Association Football, Hockey and Netball are played in the Christmas and Easter terms and Cricket, Athletics, Tennis and Rounders in the summer. A heated swimming pool is used for instruction in the summer term and there are two hard tennis courts.

A considerable number of children learn to play musical instruments and the School has 3 orchestras and numerous choirs and ensembles.

There are many optional extras and after-school clubs, for example Fencing.

'Occasional' boarding is available.

Charitable status. The Prebendal School is a Registered Charity, number 307370. Its aim is to promote education.

Prestfelde
A Woodard School

London Road, Shrewsbury, Shropshire SY2 6NZ
Tel: 01743 245400
Fax: 01743 241434
e-mail: office@prestfelde.co.uk
website: www.prestfelde.co.uk

Chairman of Governors: B Newman, MA, MBA, CEng, MIMechE, MIEE, FIOD

Headmaster: **M C Groome**, MA London, BEd Leeds

Age Range. 3–13.
Number of Pupils. 289 (5 boarders, 206 day pupils, and 83 children in Little Prestfelde).
Fees per term (2010-2011). Boarders £4,920. Day: Years 6–8 £3,850; Year 5 £3,820; Year 4 £3,650; Year 3 £3,130;

Year 2 £2,410; Year 1 £2,380; Reception £2,350; Nursery £1,220.

Pupils at Prestfelde are well known for their cheerful and purposeful attitude. The school aims to maximise the potential of every individual by providing them with significant opportunities for excelling academically, and in musical, sporting and dramatic performances. A well qualified, loyal, enthusiastic and dedicated staff form the backbone of the school's success. The use of subject specialist teachers for pupils from the age of eight adds greatly to the quality of the teaching and the enthusiasm of the pupils.

Prestfelde has excellent facilities. There has been an extensive building programme over recent years giving all age ranges the benefit of purpose built class and specialist teaching rooms. The school enjoys the benefits of thirty acres of delightful parkland playing fields on the edge of Shrewsbury. There are ample, well-maintained facilities for football, rugby, cricket, netball, rounders, lacrosse, tennis and swimming in a covered heated pool.

Although the school is non-selective, the academic standards of the school are excellent. Setting is used for pupils from the age of eight so that the curriculum meets the needs of all our children. Equally, pupils who require support have the benefit of an exceptionally successful learning support department. The great majority of pupils stay to thirteen, and talented pupils are encouraged to attempt scholarship exams to their chosen senior school. The school has an excellent reputation and 32 scholarships were gained this year to senior independent schools. 24 boys have gained academic scholarships to Shrewsbury School in the last four years with other academic awards to Repton, Moreton Hall, Wrekin College and Concord College. A number of boys and girls have gained music, art, sport and all-rounder scholarships.

Prestfelde is a Woodard School, with its own Chaplain and a clear stance in promoting spiritual and moral values within the school.

Charitable status. Prestfelde School is a Registered Charity, number 1102931. It aims to provide education for boys and girls.

Prince's Mead School

Worthy Park House, Kings Worthy, Winchester, Hampshire SO21 1AN
Tel: 01962 888000
e-mail: admin@princesmeadschool.org.uk
website: www.princesmeadschool.org.uk

Chairman of Governors: Mr B Welch

Headmistress: **Miss P Kirk**, BEd Exeter

Age Range. 3–11 co-educational.
Number of Children. 235 Day Boys and Girls.
Fees per term (2011-2012). £2,400–£3,935.
Established in 1949, Prince's Mead is a Day Preparatory School on the outskirts of Winchester. The school provides a balanced day and a purposeful atmosphere within which the children are encouraged to acquire sound working habits, an enthusiasm and zest for knowledge and a desire to achieve their full potential. The pleasures and responsibilities of school life are an integral part of development and we encourage cooperation, a responsible attitude and the confidence to work independently or within a group. The school is alive to the children's needs both now and in the future; the aim is to provide education for life.

Girls are prepared for Common entrance and Scholarships to a wide variety of Independent Schools. Boys are prepared for entry to local independent day and boarding schools at age 11. Results in Common Entrance and Senior School entrance examinations are consistently very good,

with a high percentage of pupils taking up places in Senior Schools having a strong national reputation.

The curriculum is built around the cores subjects and looks to provide education for the 21st Century. Music, Sport and a wide range of extra-curricular activities enhance and enrich development.

Bursaries (financial assistance) are available from Year 3 upwards.

Charitable status. Prince's Mead School is a Registered Charity, number 288675. It exists to provide education for boys and girls.

Prior Park Preparatory School

Calcutt Street, Cricklade, Wiltshire SN6 6BB
Tel: 01793 750275
Fax: 01793 750910
e-mail: officepriorparkprep@priorpark.co.uk
website: www.priorparkschools.co.uk

Chair of Governors: Sister Jane Livesey, CJ, MA Cantab

Head: **M Pearce**, BA Hons, PGCE

Age Range. 4–13.
Number of Pupils. 242 (45 Boarders, 197 Day; 133 Boys, 109 Girls).
Fees per term (2010-2011). Boarding £4,881–£5,737, Day Pupils £1,983–£4,104.

Prior Park Preparatory School is a thriving school situated in rural Wiltshire on the edge of the Cotswolds. Established in 1946, it forms part of the Prior Park Educational Trust with its senior school, Prior Park College in Bath. This year sees the opening of a new Pre-Prep department with significant investment in new facilities and resources for those children in Reception, Year 1 and Year 2 classes. Although only in its first year the Pre-Prep department has been launched with over 50 pupils.

Pupils are taught in small classes of between 10 and 20 and we accept pupils with a broad range of ability. Our broad based Pre-Prep curriculum gives children an excellent start to learning with French taught to the youngest pupils as well as an exciting programme of Forest School. The Prep school has an enviable programme of music, drama and art with pupils taking part in many local festivals to a high level. Our modern facilities include a large, sports hall, ICT suite with 20 flat screen computers, art studio with pottery kiln, music studio, extensive playing fields, new astroturf and 25m outdoor heated swimming pool. A wide ranging enrichment programme exists for both day and boarding pupils. Some of the most popular activities include judo, Irish dancing, golf, tennis, fencing, debating, chess, choir and orchestra, business enterprise, art, Eco club and archery.

Children have the chance to represent school in sports fixtures ranging from rugby and netball to swimming and athletics. Every year a few pupils are selected to play at County level. Regular foreign sports tours take place, the most recent being to Barbados, Jersey and Paris.

Our Learning Support Department is CReSTeD registered and offers support for pupils with mild to moderate dyslexia. We also support children who do not have English as their first language.

A strong boarding community lies at the heart of the school with a third of the pupils boarding from Year 3 (age 7). This includes both full and flexi-boarding. The school's philosophy towards boarding is to create a stable family atmosphere in which pupils feel happy and secure. Our most recent inspection highlighted the happy and caring atmosphere which pervades the whole school. Boarders are cared for by very experienced full time members of staff who live within the boarding houses. A range of activities is organised for boarders with pupils having a say in how they spend their free time. The trip out on Sunday is always one of the highlights of the week. We are located only just over an hour from several major airports as well as having excellent road and rail links to major cities.

A limited number of HM Forces bursaries is available.

Charitable status. Prior Park Educational Trust is a Registered Charity, number 281242.

Priory Preparatory School

Bolters Lane, Banstead, Surrey SM7 2AJ
Tel: 01737 366920
Fax: 01737 366921
e-mail: office@prioryprep.co.uk
website: www.prioryprep.co.uk

Chair of Governors: Mrs Serena Broad

Headmaster: **Graham D Malcolm**, BEd, MA, FRSA

Age Range. 2–13.
Number of Boys. 200 Day Boys.
Fees per term (2011-2012). Nursery £1,450–£1,985; Pre-Preparatory £2,425; Preparatory £3,275.

Priory is a small, friendly school where every boy is valued and contributes fully to the various activities organised in the school. A strong pastoral framework supports the boys' learning and enjoyment of what is on offer at Priory. Priory boys are happy boys.

The boys are prepared for the Senior Independent School selected by the parents in consultation with the Headmaster. The aim is to provide a sound, well-balanced course designed to prepare boys for a smooth transfer to their next school. The curriculum reflects this aim and in so doing includes all school games and physical activities as a normal and necessary part of every boy's life, irrespective of ability. Soccer, Rugby, Cricket, Athletics, Basketball and Swimming are coached extensively. Gymnastics is particularly strong. A multi-purpose Sports Hall greatly enhances the facilities, as does a large sportsfield. There is specialist accommodation for Art, Science and ICT and a library. There is a strong emphasis on Music and Drama.

The Pre-Preparatory Department is highly successful having had excellent inspection reports. The Preparatory School has also had excellent reviews in recent inspections, being cited as 'Outstanding' in every section (ISI Inspection 2011).

Although most boys are prepared for the Common Entrance Examination, a large number of Scholarships has been won in recent years. The essential groundwork of a good education lies in the experienced Pre-Preparatory Department which the School possesses. Traditional values, skills and standards run parallel with modern teaching methods and an extensive range of educational visits is arranged throughout the year.

Charitable status. The Priory School (Banstead) Trust Limited is a Registered Charity, number 312035. It exists for the education of boys aged two to thirteen years.

Prospect House School

75 Putney Hill, London SW15 3NT
Tel: 020 8780 0456
Fax: 020 8780 3010
e-mail: info@prospecths.org.uk
website: www.prospecths.org.uk

Chairman of Governors: Mr Anthony Rentoul

Headmistress: **Mrs D Barratt**, MEd Newcastle-upon-Tyne

Age Range. 3–11 co-educational.
Number of Pupils. 198 day pupils.
Fees per term (2010-2011). Nursery (5 mornings) £2,035, Reception–Year 2 £4,070, Year 3 £4,128, Years 4–6 £4,222.

Prospect House School occupies a large Victorian building in nearly an acre of grounds, including an all weather sports area, at the top of Putney Hill overlooking Putney Heath. There is a multi-purpose hall where assemblies, music recitals, gymnastics and drama productions take place. There are dedicated rooms for music, ICT and special needs with art, DT and science also having provision within the school.

Most children join the school at 3 or 4 years of age, although occasionally there are places for older children. Selection for entry at 3 is date of registration, with preference given to brothers and sisters of children already in the school. An equal balance of boys and girls is kept throughout the school and this is reflected in the staffing.

Although the school does not select at entry at age 3 or 4, the academic track record is strong. The curriculum includes all National Curriculum subjects, with the addition of French from the age of three. There are numerous specialist teachers and children from Nursery are taught by specialists for Music, PE, French and ICT. Children are prepared for a wide range of leading day and boarding schools for entry at 11 years of age, with some children taking academic, music and sport scholarships. There is a wide and varied sports programme with many fixtures against other preparatory schools and children from Year 3 upwards attend training sessions at a nearby sports ground under the guidance of qualified instructors.

The school was awarded 'Best Primary School' in the UK in 2009-10 for the teaching and use of ICT.

Clubs after school cater for many interests and visiting teachers also provide a wide range of individual music lessons. Children are regularly taken on educational visits to London and the surrounding area, with residential field study trips being undertaken in the final three years.

Quainton Hall School

Hindes Road, Harrow, Middlesex HA1 1RX
Tel: 020 8427 1304
Fax: 020 8861 8861
e-mail: admin@quaintonhall.org.uk
website: www.quaintonhall.org.uk

Chairman of Governors: Father David Clues, BD, PGCE

Headmaster: **Mr Edwin Brown**, BEd Hons Lancaster, MA London

Age Range. 3–13.
Number of Pupils. 200.
Fees per term (2010-2011). £2,675–£2,975.

Quainton Hall, which has had four Heads in its long history, is staffed by experienced and well-qualified men and women. There is a Nursery of 20 children from rising three to four. In 2006 this was acclaimed as "outstanding" by Ofsted. Nursery entrance is arranged through the School Office. Boys and girls are accepted into the Junior School from the age of 4+; the girls are prepared for transfer at 7+, while the boys move into the Middle School, where there is a further entry of boys at 7+. Additionally, candidates of prep school age are accepted into other classes, where space permits. Initially, parents are asked to submit a registration and the family is then invited to interview. Entry is by means of a short, friendly assessment and previous nursery/school report. Since the school's foundation in Harrow in 1897, a consistently high standard of work has been maintained, which is reflected in regular successes at 13+ in the competitive examinations for leading London schools (including Merchant Taylors', Haberdashers' and City of London) in Common Entrance and in entrance scholarships (for academic excellence, in Music, Drama, Art and Sport). Each year a small number of our Leavers go on to boarding schools, including Harrow.

The curriculum is broad and supportive and provides for lessons in Art, Drama, Technology and Music each week in addition to all the core subjects. French is begun at the age of seven, Latin is taken from the age of 10+ and German is offered as an additional Modern Language to the Seniors (12+). Dramatic productions are performed each year and there is an excellent tradition of choral and instrumental music. Over the years, many boys have played in children's orchestras and music scholarships are won regularly. Available to everyone is a wide and varied range of visits and expeditions, which include field trips, ski holidays, adventure weeks, visits to mainland Europe and numerous one-day outings to London and beyond. The school also takes very great pride in its extensive programme of extra-curricular activities. These occur both during the lunch hour and after school.

The Parents' Association (The Friends of Quainton Hall School) is very active and provides a range of social occasions for parents and staff through the year. In recent years, through their hard work and generosity, not least at the annual Christmas and Summer Fairs, the Friends have provided the school with a very great deal in terms of additional resources and equipment.

The school sets very great store by its sports provision. The games played include Athletics, Badminton, Basketball, Cricket, Cross-Country, Football, Hockey, Rugby, Swimming, Table Tennis, Tennis and Volleyball. We use our own indoor swimming-pool, our sports court and hall; home matches are played on green open spaces a few minutes from the school.

Quainton Hall, which belongs to the Shrine of Our Lady at Walsingham in Norfolk, has been a Church of England Educational Trust since 1944 and possesses its own Chapel. Candidates are presented for Confirmation if they and their parents wish. Our pupils come from the range of cultural and religious backgrounds to be found in North London and experience shows that this is a source of enrichment to the life and work of the whole school community.

Over the years, very considerable resources have been devoted to the ongoing development of the school; the most recent additions to the extensive facilities include four dedicated classrooms for our seven and eight-year-olds, a new Science Laboratory, a new School Library and a new Art Room. The self-contained Nursery with its garden attached provides an excellent start to school for our youngest pupils.

Charitable status. Quainton Hall School, under the Trusteeship of Walsingham College (Affiliated Schools) Limited, is a Registered Charity, number 312638. It exists to provide a sound education within a definite Christian framework.

Queen Elizabeth Grammar School Junior School

158 Northgate, Wakefield, West Yorkshire WF1 3QY
Tel: 01924 373821
Fax: 01924 366246
e-mail: admissions@qegsjs.org.uk
website: www.wgsf.org.uk

Spokesman for the Governors: Mrs M Waugh

Head: **Mrs L Gray**, CertEd, MA

Age Range. 7–11.

Number of Boys. 260 day boys
Fees per term (2011-2012). 7–8 years £2,499; 9–10 years £2,641. Fees include lunch.

QEGS Junior School is a friendly and fun community of 260 boys. The school has its own buildings and enviable facilities located adjacent to QEGS Senior School, and near to the City Centre of Wakefield. Pupils travel to the school each day from across South and West Yorkshire, with many taking advantage of the network of school buses and the close proximity to Wakefield Westgate station – a 10 minute walk away.

Boys can join the school in Years 3, 4, 5 and 6. Entry is by assessment, with the majority of Entrance Tests held in early February each year. Prospective parents and boys are very welcome to visit the School throughout the year as well as on the annual Information Mornings held in October and January.

Pastoral care is very strong within the School, with all boys encouraged to show exemplary friendship and sportsmanship whether in the classroom or on the sports pitch. Every boy's contribution to the school community is nurtured, recognised and valued by his peers and teachers.

There are 3 classes in each year group. In Years 3 and 4 the Form Teacher takes the majority of the classroom lessons, with significant involvement of specialist staff in subjects such as Science, Art, Games, Music, DT and ICT. Specialist teaching increases as a boy progresses through the School, which provides good preparation for transfer to the Senior School at Year 7.

Boys make full use of the range of the first-class teaching facilities, including the Music suite, Science lab, Design and Technology room with its own kitchen and the very well-equipped Learning Resources Library and ICT suite.

There is an excellent tradition of music, both choral and instrumental, in the School as there are two choirs, instrumental groups (jazz, brass and strings) and a Junior School orchestra. Choral Scholarships with Wakefield Cathedral are available.

The Junior School has its own playing fields, cricket nets and pavilion. The school also benefits from use of the Senior School all-weather Astroturf and athletics track. The major sports are rugby, cross country, swimming and rugby in the winter and athletics and cricket in the summer. Boys have timetabled PE, swimming or games every day, supplemented by many lunchtime and after-school sports clubs including football, martial arts, hockey and tennis.

There is an extensive programme of both inter-school and inter-house matches. The coaching of all games is undertaken entirely by specialist Junior School staff. The Junior School enjoys regular local and national success in many sports.

Each day there is a plethora of clubs and activities taking place – ranging from Art and Chess to Music and Movement or Gardening in the school's own kitchen garden and every boy is encouraged to take part and enjoy at least one club activity.

Charitable status. QEGS Junior School is part of The Wakefield Grammar School Foundation, which is a Registered Charity, number 1088415.

Queen Elizabeth's Hospital (QEH) – Junior School

Berkeley Place, Clifton, Bristol BS8 1JX
Tel: 0117 930 3087
Fax: 0117 929 3106
e-mail: juniors@qehbristol.co.uk
website: www.qehbristol.co.uk

Chairman of Governors: N J Tyrrell, BA

Junior School Headmaster: **M J Morris**, BEd, BA

Age Range. Boys 7–11.
Number of Pupils. 112 day boys.
Fees per term (2011-2012). £2,453. Fees include after-school care until 5.00 pm if required.

The QEH Junior School was opened in September 2007 and is located in gracious Georgian town houses in Upper Berkeley Place backing onto the Senior School which means it can share its first-class facilities including science, drama, music and sport. The cultural facilities of the city, such as the city museum and art gallery, are also on its doorstep.

Pupils travel to the school from across the region and there is a hub for public transport on the nearby Clifton Triangle. The school also offers timed parking facilities for parents in the adjacent West End multi-storey car park, to pick up and drop off pupils, at no extra cost.

As part of the only all-boys' school in the city, QEH Juniors is unique in Bristol. Being small, it focuses on the individual, fostering a love of learning whilst nurturing the interests and talents of each boy. In addition there is a wealth of extra-curricular and holiday activities available.

The school is a happy place with strong pastoral care, academic excellence, and high standards where the educational experience is designed to be relevant and meaningful for every single child. Each boy leaves recognising himself as a lifelong learner.

There is one class per Year group until Year 5 and Year 6 when there are two classes, each with a maximum of 20 pupils. Offers of places are subject to an entrance examination.

Boys can therefore enter in Year 3 or Year 5 though places occasionally become available in other Years. Boys are expected to move into the Main School at 11. (*See QEH entry in HMC section.*)

Charitable status. Queen Elizabeth's Hospital is a Registered Charity, number 1104871, and a Company Limited by Guarantee, number 5164477.

Queen's College Junior and Pre-Prep Schools
Taunton

Trull Road, Taunton TA1 4QP
Tel: 01823 272990 (Junior)
01823 278928 (Pre-Prep)
Fax: 01823 323811
e-mail: junior.sec@queenscollege.org.uk
website: www.queenscollege.org.uk

Chairman of Governors: Mr J N Birkett, FCIB, MSI

Head: **Mrs Tracey Khodabandehloo**

Age Range. 3–11.
Number of Pupils. Junior School: 153 of whom 15 are boarders. Pre-Prep: 46.
Fees per term (2011-2012). Junior: £3,535–£5,355 (boarders); £2,080–£3,430 (day). Pre-Prep: £1,690–£1,750. Nursery (per session): Morning £22, Afternoon £16.50, All day £37, After-School Care £6.80, Full time (per term) £1,490.

Queen's College is a co-educational boarding and day school on the outskirts of Taunton with fine views across the playing fields to the surrounding hills.

The Pre-Prep School educates pupils up to the age of 7; the Junior School educates pupils up to the end of Key Stage 2 (NC Year 6). Children aged 11+ will be admitted directly to the Senior School (*see Queen's College entry in HMC section*).

The Junior School is run as an independent unit but shares many of the excellent facilities of the adjacent Senior School. We aim to create a happy, caring atmosphere based on Christian values. For the boarders, especially, the School endeavours to provide a sympathetic background for a child's first venture away from home. We are well versed in settling pupils whose families have been posted abroad. Weekend activities for the boarding pupils are always fun and emphasis is made on creating a family-style, homely atmosphere in which they can relax and unwind. For every pupil, however, the aim of the School is to find areas in which each child can succeed, thereby developing the self-confidence which will help them achieve their potential.

The curriculum is organised in such a way as to promote all aspects of children's development. It allows each child to progress at an appropriate pace and to achieve satisfaction at an appropriate level.

The principal games are Rugby, Hockey and Cricket for the boys, Hockey, Netball and Rounders for the girls. Tennis, Swimming and Athletics matches also take place. Fullest use is made of the excellent sporting facilities of the School, particularly the Sports Hall, Tennis Courts, heated indoor Swimming Pool and floodlit Astroturf.

After-school activities include: Badminton, Cookery, Chess, Computer Club, Drama, Specialist Music Groups, Model Making, Origami, Puppets, Squash and Gymnastics. Also arranged at an extra charge are Dancing, Speech and Drama, and Riding. Pupils may attend local brownie, cub, guides and scout groups.

The Pre-Prep day school is in its own purpose-built building separated from the Junior School by the adventure playground.

To complete provision at Queen's College, there is a Nursery School for children aged 3–4 years. There are up to 18 places available on a sessional basis. After-school care is also provided for Nursery and Pre-Prep children. Parent and Toddler groups are also run on Tuesdays and Thursdays.

The Nursery and Pre-Prep environment is a happy and stimulating one with an informal atmosphere and high standards. We adhere broadly to the National Curriculum but enrich it, particularly in the core subjects. There is a full range of after-school activities.

Nearly all the children move on from one section of Queen's College to the next; there is no further qualifying examination. We offer parents and pupils continuity of education from the Pre-Prep, through the Junior School to the Senior School, with the school week running from Monday to Friday.

Charitable status. Queen's College, Taunton is a Registered Charity, number 310208. It exists for the purpose of educating children in a Christian environment according to the traditions of the Methodist Church.

Ramillies Hall School

Cheadle Hulme, Cheadle, Cheshire SK8 7AJ
Tel: 0161 485 3804
Fax: 0161 486 6021
e-mail: study@ramillieshall.co.uk
website: www.ramillieshall.co.uk

Principals:
Mrs A L Poole (*Bursar*)
Miss D M Patterson, BA, PGCE (*Head Teacher*)

Age Range. 6 months to 16 years.
Number of Children. Day: 77 boys, 15 girls. Nursery: 89 children.

Fees per term (2010-2011). Day pupils: £2,460 (Years 1–6), £2,675 (Years 7–9), £2,736 (Years 10–11). Nursery from £4.68 per hour.

Ramillies Hall, founded in 1884, is a small school for children aged 6 to 16 years. In our small classes (average 15 pupils) we bring together the best of traditional methods and modern multi-sensory teaching. We follow, and in some areas extend, the National Curriculum and offer a range of practical and vocational GCSEs along with the core subjects. Our well-structured learning programmes build confidence and encourage our pupils to become independent learners.

Our specialism is in dyslexia, dyspraxia and similar learning difficulties, and a high proportion of our pupils come to Ramillies for that reason. When they arrive, many children are lacking in self-esteem because of their previous experience of the education system. Our first task is often to find their strengths and build on them to increase their confidence. We offer tuition and support from specialist trained teachers in our Learning Support Department, to enable pupils to access the full curriculum. This has brought external recognition of our expertise in this field, with accreditation by CReSTeD (Council for the Registration of Schools Teaching Dyslexics). To maintain this, the School is subject to rigorous and regular inspection, and Ramillies is the only school in the Manchester area with the accreditation.

An extended day (until 5.50 pm, Mondays to Thursdays) enables us to offer a wide variety of sports and extra-curricular activities, and homework can be completed during this time under the supervision of a teacher.

Ramillies also has a Nursery, open from 8.00 am to 6.00 pm, Monday to Friday throughout the year, for babies and children up to school reception age. We are proud of our high standards of care, and our qualified and experienced staff provide a stimulating and exciting environment for our youngest children.

Easily accessible by road and rail, the School is set in its own spacious grounds with extensive playing fields and heated outdoor swimming pool.

For more information, visit our website as given above.

Ranby House School
A Woodard School

Retford, Nottinghamshire DN22 8HX
Tel: 01777 703138; Bursary: 01777 714391
Fax: 01777 702813
e-mail: office@ranbyhouseschool.co.uk
website: www.ranbyhouseschool.co.uk

Chairman of the School Council: C J D Anderson, MA

Headmaster: **D W T Sibson**, BA Ed Hons Durham

Age Range. 3–13 years.
Number of Pupils. 259: 137 boys, 122 girls, including 32 Full Boarders and 20 Flexi-Boarders.
Fees per term (2011-2012). Boarders £5,385, Day Children £3,680–£3,830, Pre-Prep (full-time) £2,290.

Ranby House School prides itself on its caring, happy and welcoming school community. Boarding and day pupils, boys and girls work and play hard, striving for excellence following the school's motto which is translated for twenty-first century children as 'Aiming High'. There is a purposeful yet friendly atmosphere; Ranby House is an exciting place to be at school.

The school is situated in 60 acres of outstanding countryside. The facilities inside and outside the classroom are excellent and include: a purpose-built Performing Arts Centre which houses a 330-seat Theatre and Music School; a large Sports Centre with Sports Hall and changing rooms;

two ICT suites to complement the school's fully-networked intranet; Design Technology Centre; Library; two Science Laboratories; outdoor, heated swimming pool; four floodlit all-weather netball/tennis courts; a new large outdoor adventure playground and extensive level playing fields.

At the centre of life in this Woodard School (see www.woodard.co.uk) is our modern Chapel. The teaching of Christian values helps the children to learn to live and respect one another within our community and also in the wider world through supporting a number of charities and good causes. Children from families of Christian faith, different faith or no faith are all welcome, and everyone attends Chapel services.

The purpose-built Pre-Prep Department takes children from 3 to 7 years after which they transfer to the Prep School for ages 7 to 13. At 13 the majority of pupils transfer to Worksop College, our senior school within Woodard Schools (Nottinghamshire) Ltd, although pupils are prepared for entry to a variety of independent senior schools.

Boys and girls may board from the age of 7 years. Spacious, colourful bedrooms, wholesome food and caring houseparents are important elements of the Ranby boarding experience. Boarding is flexible, and is dependent upon the needs of the individual family; full, weekly and casual boarding are all offered by the school.

Academic standards are high at Ranby House. In the last four years, a total of 57 Awards for academic, musical, sporting, art, all-round excellence and leadership have been gained by Ranbians transferring to their senior independent school. The school is non-selective and caters for children of all abilities including those with specific learning difficulties.

A wealth of extra-curricular opportunities is on offer and pupils are encouraged to take an active part in all aspects of school life. The school has strong traditions in sport, music and drama. Pupils are also encouraged to take on responsibility at all levels, on the School Council, the Eco Committee, as Librarians and as Year 8 Leaders.

The school is well-situated for road, rail and airport travel: just off the A1, and not far from the M1, there are also fast rail links (1½ hours from Kings Cross). Daily bus services are also run from the Retford, Worksop, Rotherham, Doncaster, Tickhill, Tuxford, Newark and Mansfield areas.

Worksop College is our senior school with the majority of our pupils moving on from Ranby House to Worksop College at age 13. Worksop College is about 4 miles from Ranby House and offers boarding and day education to boys and girls from ages 13–18. (*For further details see Worksop College entry in HMC section.*)

Charitable status. Woodard Schools (Nottinghamshire) Limited is a Registered Charity, number 1103326. It exists for the purpose of educating children.

Ravenscourt Park Preparatory School

16 Ravenscourt Avenue, Chiswick, London W6 0SL
Tel: 020 8846 9153
Fax: 020 8846 9413
e-mail: secretary@rpps.co.uk
website: www.rpps.co.uk

Chairman of Governors: Mr Kevin Darlington

Headmaster: **R C Relton**

Age Range. 4–11 co-educational.
Number of Pupils. 340 boys and girls.
Fees per term (2011-2012). £4,435.

This non-selective school provides education of the highest quality for boys and girls, preparing them for transfer to the best Independent Schools at 11 years of age. The Lower School caters for pupils aged 4–7 and is based in a large, Victorian house, formerly a vicarage. The Upper School, 7–11 years, enjoys purpose-built accommodation erected in 1996. The secure site includes a large play area and the school makes use of the extensive facilities of Ravenscourt Park which it adjoins. In September 2011 the newly expanded School will include a Theatre, a state-of-the-art Science laboratory and Art room.

The curriculum includes French, Music, Art and Craft, RE, Computer Studies and PE for all pupils in addition to the usual core subjects. In the Upper School the majority of subjects are taught by specialists. All Upper School pupils attend a Summer Term Residential Week where studies across the curriculum are applied to a non-urban environment.

There are many after school clubs and sports activities and we have two choirs and an orchestra. Individual tuition is offered in piano, violin, brass, woodwind, cello, saxophone, percussion and singing. Our Drama productions are a highlight of each school year.

An 8 am to 6 pm All Day Care service is offered to parents at an extra charge.

The school is noted for its warm, happy atmosphere where parents play a full part in enriching the curriculum and social life. Off-site visits and guest workshops presented by noted visitors are a regular feature of education at RPPS.

The school is always heavily over-subscribed and registration is strongly recommended on the child's first birthday. A prospectus and registration form may be obtained from the School Secretary.

The Red Maids' Junior School

Grange Court Road, Westbury-on-Trym, Bristol BS9 4DP
Tel: 0117 962 9451
Fax: 0117 989 8286
e-mail: juniors@redmaids.bristol.sch.uk
website: www.www.redmaids.co.uk

Chairman of Governors: Mrs J MacFarlane, BSc, MA

Headteacher: **Mrs G B Rowcliffe**, BEd Bristol

Age Range. 7–11.
Number of Girls. 120 Day Girls.
Fees per term (2011-2012). £2,305 plus lunches.

The Red Maids' Junior School occupies a wonderful new building including a library and ICT suite at the very heart of the school. There is a wonderful atmosphere for learning and a large garden for outdoor play. The lofty art and music studios inspire creativity and the large modern hall is a fabulous all-purpose space for whole school activities.

The school is equipped for approximately 120 girls aged 7–11 organised into six classes. In Years 3 and 4, each class is taught by their own class teacher for the majority of their timetable. In Years 5 and 6, girls are taught by more specialist teachers but we take care to ensure that they are nurtured within each year group unit. There are frequent opportunities built into the timetable for girls to work and make friends with children in all year groups. Since the girls know each other and every member of staff well, a strong community feeling is promoted within the school where girls can develop their confidence and self-esteem.

All the girls are encouraged to explore their individual talents and achieve their best through the school's broad and balanced curriculum, including Mandarin. Whole school planning is an essential feature of every subject area, ensuring continuity and progression; assessment is an integral

part of this. Year 6 girls sit National Curriculum Key Stage 2 Standard Assessment Tests in English, mathematics and science and results are very good indeed.

In addition there is a strong emphasis on the pastoral care of the children. Through school meetings and class activities, the school teaches a sense of good citizenship as girls are encouraged to share responsibility for the care of their community and their environment.

Close links are fostered between the Junior and Senior Red Maids through joint activities and visits. Pupils benefit from use of a science laboratory, extensive PE facilities including an all-weather pitch and the award-winning school lunches. At age 11, Junior Red Maids transfer to the Senior School (conditions apply) and achieve outstanding success in the entrance examination.

Extra-curricular activities are an essential part of every girl's school experience and there is a strong commitment to outdoor education.

The school enjoys close relationships with parents on a daily basis and generous support is offered to the school through a thriving Friends' Association.

Charitable status. The Red Maids' School is a Registered Charity, number 1105017. It has existed since 1634 to provide an education for girls.

Redcliffe School

47 Redcliffe Gardens, London SW10 9JH
Tel: 020 7352 9247
Fax: 020 7352 6936
e-mail: admissions@redcliffeschool.com
website: www.redcliffeschool.com

Chairman of the Board of Governors: Simon Lalor

Headmistress: **Mrs Susan Bourne**, BSc, PGCE

Age Range. Boys 2½–8, Girls 2½–11.
Number of Pupils. 160 Day Pupils (60 boys, 100 girls)
Fees per term (2011-2012). £4,010. Nursery: £2,300 (morning class), £1,535 (afternoon class), £3,850 (full day).

Easily accessible from all parts of central and West London, Redcliffe is a small, friendly school with highly motivated, confident and happy children. Emphasis is placed on a good combination of hard work and plenty of fun within a framework of discipline and good manners. The balanced curriculum includes Mathematics, English, History, Geography, Science, IT, Art and Craft, Scripture, Current Affairs, Music, Physical Education and Drama. French is taught throughout the school. Individual attention encourages the pursuit of high academic standards and we are proud that our children gain places at their first choice of senior or prep school, including Colet Court, Sussex House, St Philip's, Downe House, Benenden, Queen's Gate, Godolphin and Latymer and Francis Holland. Every class has some form of Physical Education each day; in the gym or playground, local netball court or park. All pupils participate in a wide range of sports and activities including: rugby, hockey, cricket and swimming. After school activities include cookery, ballet, computer skills and drama. Music is strength of the school with visiting instrumental staff and a high standard of performance. Parents are encouraged to be involved with the school through Open Assemblies, Parents' Discussion Groups, the Parents' Committee and regular meetings with the teachers.

Redcliffe Robins is our nursery class for children between the ages of 2½ and 4 years with a specialist Montessori-trained teacher and access to all of Recliffe's resources and facilities to help prepare the children for entry to the main school. Each day has a balanced timetable of language work, mathematical skills, art and craft, music, drama and PE with ample opportunity for structured free play and the development of social skills.

Children are assessed at three years of age for entry to the main school at four. Entry for subsequent years by test. Tours of the school are held weekly during term-time by appointment with the school office.

Charitable status. Redcliffe School Trust Ltd is a Registered Charity, number 312716. It exists to provide a high standard of education for children within a caring environment.

Reddiford School

38 Cecil Park, Pinner, Middlesex HA5 5HH
Tel: 020 8866 0660
Fax: 020 8866 4847
e-mail: office@reddiford.org.uk
website: www.reddiford.org.uk

Chairman of Governors: Mr F C Flood

Head: **Mrs J Batt**, CertEd, NPQH

Age Range. 2¾–11.
Number of Pupils. Day: 142 Boys, 108 Girls; Nursery: 32 Boys, 24 Girls.
Fees per term (2010-2011). Nursery: £1,245 (mornings only), £2,210 (all day), Nursery plus £2,660, Reception £2,890, Years 1–2 £2,910, Years 3–6 £2,980.

Reddiford School has been established in Cecil Park, Pinner since 1913. Whilst the school maintains its Church of England status, children from all faiths and cultures are welcomed. Throughout the school the ethos is on respect for one another. Reddiford prides itself on being a town school based in the heart of Pinner; a few minutes' walk from local transport facilities.

Reddiford possesses a fine academic record, preparing its pupils for entrance at 11+ into major independent schools, many at scholarship level. There is a high teacher pupil ratio ensuring small classes leading to a friendly caring environment where all children are valued.

The early years department is situated in its own building and caters for children from 2 years nine months to rising 5 years. It offers a stimulating and attractive environment where children are encouraged to be independent and active learners. The nursery follows the foundation stage profiling which incorporates the six areas of learning. There is a choice of full or half day provision.

The pre-prep department builds on the knowledge and skills acquired in the nursery placing the emphasis on developing confidence and the ability to learn and work independently and with others. The pre-prep department has its own computer suite and interactive whiteboards in classrooms. There is specialist teaching in French, Music and PE from reception upwards and all children are taught to swim.

In the prep department children are taught by specialist teachers in properly resourced subject rooms. There is a fully-equipped science laboratory, dedicated art and music rooms and an ICT suite. Pupils are prepared for entry to the many prestigious senior schools in the area, a process which involves consultation with parents from an early stage.

There is an extensive programme of extra-curricular activities throughout the school including: sports (football, cricket, netball, gymnastics), languages (French, Spanish, Mandarin), art, science, sewing, and ballet. We also offer before and after school care, with a prep club for older children.

Entry to the nursery is possible in any term once a child has reached 2 years and 9 months. Most children move from the nursery to the main school at 4+, but there are spaces for other applicants in the reception classes. An assessment day for these places is held in January for September entry. Means-tested bursaries may be available.

Charitable status. Reddiford School is a Registered Charity, number 312641. It exists to provide education for boys and girls.

Redland High School for Girls Junior School

Redland Court, Bristol BS6 7EF
Tel: 0117 924 5796
e-mail: admissions@redlandhigh.com
website: www.redlandhigh.com

Chairman of Governors: Mr P J F Breach, BA, FCA, ATII, ACT, IIMR

Head: **Mr J P Eyles**, BEd Bath Spa, MEd Bristol

Age Range. 3–11.
Number of Girls. 150.
Fees per term (2011-2012). Nursery £19 per half day; Reception, Years 1 & 2 £2,100; Years 3–6 £2,400.

Redland High Junior School is situated in two Victorian houses close to the Senior School in a very pleasant residential area of Bristol. The School is easily reached from the surrounding districts.

Children are taught by well qualified and highly motivated teachers who are very well supported by a number of excellent classroom assistants.

The School aims to provide each child with the opportunity to develop fully her particular talents within a stimulating and supportive environment. We try to create a friendly, family atmosphere within which high standards are expected in all areas of the curriculum.

While emphasis is placed on numeracy and literacy, children also respond to high expectations in science, ICT, drama, history, geography, RE, art, PE and modern languages. Music is a particular strength of the school with most pupils learning to play an instrument or joining in choral or orchestral activities. Our curriculum embraces the principal areas of study appropriate for Primary School education. It is based on the National Curriculum requirements and the Early Learning Goals for the Under Fives. However, we aim to give our pupils more than these minimum requirements so that they have a head start when they reach senior school. Our high standards and expectations ensure that the brighter pupils can be stretched to their full potential, whilst those who need extra help get additional support.

There are a number of extra curricular activities available, including outdoor pursuits (canoeing, abseiling etc), orienteering, judo, computer clubs, netball, short tennis, recorder groups, dance and art clubs.

During each school year there are a number of educational visits and workshops. Most of these visits are a way of enabling pupils to consolidate knowledge acquired in lessons. Other outings are of a more cultural nature and often include visits to concerts and theatres. Pupils are encouraged to nominate and support charities, and each term sees an event designed to raise money for the chosen charity.

When our pupils reach 11 they are ready to move on. Most girls move on to our Senior School where they experience new challenges and choices. The girls from the Junior School are well prepared and ready to embrace the next stage of their education with enthusiasm and confidence.

Charitable status. Redland High School for Girls is a Registered Charity, number 311734. It exists to provide education for girls.

Reigate St Mary's Preparatory and Choir School

Chart Lane, Reigate, Surrey RH2 7RN
Tel: 01737 244880
Fax: 01737 221540
e-mail: hmsec@reigatestmarys.org
website: www.reigatestmarys.org

Chairman of Governors: Mr Alan Walker

Headmaster: **Marcus Culverwell**, MA Ed

Age Range. 3–11.
Number of Pupils. 290 pupils (190 boys, 100 girls).
Fees per term (2010-2011). Kindergarten £1,366 (mornings), £2,732 (whole day); Reception to Year 2 £3,078, Years 3–6 £3,623.

Reigate St Mary's is an independent day school for boys and girls aged 3–11. It is the nursery and junior school of Reigate Grammar School. Set in 15 acres of beautiful parkland and sports fields. We are proud of our reputation as a lively, happy, family friendly school where each child is encouraged and known as an individual.

Reigate St Mary's aims to provide an education of considerable depth and breadth within a disciplined, happy and caring environment, incorporating a tradition of choral excellence and Christian values. All pupils are encouraged to be ambitious, to reach the best standards they can in their academic studies, in sport, in art, in music and in other performing arts. The school aims to engender a love of learning, a zest for life and to develop a caring and understanding attitude towards other people. The school places a very high value on good relationships and developing inter-personal skills in our pupils to enable them to become responsible, adaptable, independent people in a changing world. At Reigate St Mary's we believe that all children should feel valued for who they are, not just for what they achieve.

As a member of the Choir Schools' Association Reigate St Mary's is one of only a small number of schools, not attached to a cathedral or college, which maintain a traditional choir of boys and men under the direction of a Master of Choristers. The choir sings regular school and church services with a repertoire of music from the 16th Century to the present day. Entrance to the choir is by voice trial, and choral scholarships are offered by the Godfrey Searle Choir Trust.

RGS Springfield

Britannia Square, Worcester WR1 3DL
Tel: 01905 24999
Fax: 01905 27957
e-mail: springfield@rgsw.org.uk
website: www.rgsw.org.uk

Chairman of Governors: R A Ingles

Headmistress: **Mrs M Lloyd**, BEd CNAA

Age Range. 2½–11 Co-educational.
Number of Pupils. 133.
Fees per term (2011-2012). £1,780–£3,144.
Introduction from the Headmistress. "Welcome to a small school with a big heart.

First steps in education can be a daunting prospect. At RGS Springfield we work hard to provide a warm and caring environment where traditional values count and children and parents feel they are part of a nurturing and supportive family.

My own daughters were pupils here before I joined as headmistress and my husband and I chose the school for its unique blend of academic, sporting and creative excellence and a home-from-home atmosphere.

Our smaller size means that everyone knows each other and we work in real partnership with parents, making all our children feel secure and contented.

I look forward to welcoming you to the family."

Overview. RGS Springfield is the co-educational junior school for RGS Worcester (*see HMC entry*). The school educates children between the ages of 2 and 11 and is situated within a large, beautiful Georgian Town House and gardens in the centre of Worcester.

In 2009 an extensive refurbishment was undertaken to restore and develop the original historic site, Springfield, providing excellent modern facilities including art, design technology, science and ICT rooms alongside large, airy and warm well-equipped classrooms.

The school is set in six acres of maintained grounds and offers fantastic games facilities and outdoor space, including an extended Forest School, Walled Garden and Paddock Play Area.

High academic standards are expected as the children are prepared to enter RGS Worcester at 11. There is a wide range of extra-curricular activities on offer and, while the school is noted for academic, creative and sporting excellence, it is of the greatest importance that the children are encouraged to be kind, considerate and well-mannered.

Charitable status. The Royal Grammar School Worcester is a Registered Charity, number 1120644.

RGS The Grange Worcester

Grange Lane, Claines, Worcester WR3 7RR
Tel: 01905 451205
Fax: 01905 757917
e-mail: grange@rgsw.org.uk
website: www.rgsw.org.uk

Chairman of Governors: R A Ingles

Headmaster: **G W Hughes**, BEd Hons

Age Range. 2½–11 Co-educational.
Number of Pupils. 325.
Fees per term (2011-2012). £1,950–£3,102.
Introduction from the Headmaster: "Welcome to a nurturing school with a big personality.

Giving a child the best possible foundations for a bright future is a true privilege. Our fantastic facilities give pupils tremendous scope for achieving the academic, sporting and creative excellence that we encourage. Just as important is the safe, secure and caring framework that we provide, giving children the support and self-belief they need to make their own individual strides forward.

I get huge satisfaction from seeing each one cross barriers and shine in a way that is uniquely theirs and with two children myself, I know the pride parents feel when they see their child thriving.

I look forward to helping your child thrive too."

Overview: RGS The Grange is the co-educational junior school for RGS Worcester (*see HMC entry*). The school educates children between the ages of 2 and 11 and is situated in open countryside three miles north of Worcester in Claines.

In 2004 a multi-million pound extension was added to the original country house, The Grange, providing excellent modern facilities including specialist art, design technology, science and ICT rooms alongside large, airy, well-equipped classrooms.

The school is set in 48 acres of grounds and offers exceptional games facilities and outdoor space, including a full-sized floodlit Astroturf, cricket pavilion, wilderness garden and adventure play area.

High academic standards are expected as the children are prepared to enter RGS Worcester at 11. There is a wide range of extra-curricular activities on offer and, while the school is noted for academic, creative and sporting excellence, it is of the greatest importance that the children are encouraged to be kind, considerate and well-mannered.

Charitable status. The Royal Grammar School Worcester is a Registered Charity, number 1120644.

The Richard Pate School

Southern Road, Leckhampton, Cheltenham, Glos GL53 9RP
Tel: 01242 522086
Fax: 01242 524035
e-mail: hm@richardpate.co.uk
website: www.richardpate.co.uk

Chairman of Trustees: D Barnes, Esq

Headmaster: **R A MacDonald**, MEd, BA

Deputy Heads:
Mrs S Wade
P Lowe

Age Range. 3–11 Co-educational.
Number of Pupils. 300 (approximately an equal number of boys and girls).
Fees per term (2011-2012). Nursery: £900 (5 mornings), £1,200 (any 3 full days), £1,600 (any 4 full days), £1,950 (5 full days). Preparatory: £2,050 (Reception), £2,200 (Year 1), £2,350 (Year 2). Junior: £2,450 (Year 3), £2,550 (Year 4), £2,725 (Year 5), £2,850 (Year 6).

Hot lunches are provided and included in the fees, except for 'mornings only' nursery.

The School, occupying an 11½ acre semi-rural site at the foot of the Cotswold escarpment, is part of the Pate's Grammar School Foundation which is a charity founded by Richard Pate, a Recorder of Gloucester, in 1574.

It is a non-denominational Christian school which in its present form began in 1946. The aim of the school is to provide a high academic standard and continuity of education up to the age of 11 years. The curriculum is broadly based with strong emphasis being attached to music, art, drama and sport, for these activities are seen as vital if a child's full potential is to be realised.

Facilities include a music centre with individual practice rooms; a fully equipped computer suite; an all-weather astroturf with floodlights and an enclosed pond for environmental studies. There is also a specialist wing with science labs, language suite and art studio. After-school care is available through until 5.30 pm.

At present the School is divided into three sections: Nursery 3–4½ years; Preparatory Department 5–7 and Junior 7–11. Entrance is dependent upon the availability of places but most pupils join the school at the commencement of the Nursery, Preparatory or Junior Departments.

No entry tests are taken by younger pupils but interviews and selective tests are used for assessing pupils aged 6 years and upwards. A small number of 7+ scholarships are awarded each year.

The teaching takes full account of national curriculum guidelines with children in the upper part of the school following the normal preparatory school curriculum leading to Common Entrance and Scholarship at 11+. Pupils leave at age 11 for local Grammar Schools and a variety of independent secondary schools, particularly those in Cheltenham.

The Headmaster is assisted by two deputies and 18 fully qualified teachers including specialists in Latin, French, History, Art/Design, Science, Music and Learning Support. The School employs music and dance teachers, who prepare children for participation in various competitions, in particular the Cheltenham Festival.

Charitable status. The Pate's Grammar School Foundation is a Registered Charity, number 311707.

Richmond House School

170 Otley Road, Leeds, West Yorkshire LS16 5LG
Tel: 0113 2752670
Fax: 0113 2304868
e-mail: enquiries@rhschool.org
website: www.rhschool.org

Chairman of the Board of Governors: Mr D Stubbs

Headmistress: **Mrs Jane Disley**, BA Hons

Age Range. 3–11.
Number of Day Pupils. 236 boys and girls.
Fees per term (2010-2011). Nursery: £1,461 (half days only), £2,281 (full time). Reception–Year 6: £2,281. Lunches: £155.

Richmond House School is an independent co-educational preparatory school providing a high standard of education for children aged 3 to 11 years within a happy, stimulating, family environment.

At Richmond House School, a team of dedicated staff is committed to giving each child the opportunity to develop into confident, hard-working and successful individuals.

All pupils are given the chance to learn and achieve across a broad range of activities and subject areas and the talents of each child are nurtured. The breadth of activities offered aims to challenge pupils, build self-confidence and lead pupils to discover new interests and skills.

The School boasts outstanding 11+ exam success with pupils having their choice of senior school and a substantial number being awarded scholarships.

In addition to strong academic credentials, Richmond House School is committed to providing all pupils with the opportunity to excel in other areas. The School is situated in 10 acres of land, providing excellent sports facilities and offering pupils a wide range of sports to choose from. The School also provides specialist teaching in Music, Art, Design Technology, Information Communication Technology, Languages and Science.

Pastoral Care is an important aspect of school life at Richmond House School. There is a Deputy Head Teacher responsible for leading Pastoral Care who works closely with staff, pupils and parents to ensure the well-being and progress of all pupils.

Excellent Pre and After School Care are available for busy families.

Charitable status. Richmond House School is a Registered Charity, number 505630. It exists to provide high quality education for boys and girls aged 3–11 years.

Rickmansworth PNEU School

88 The Drive, Rickmansworth, Herts WD3 4DU
Tel: 01923 772101
Fax: 01923 776268
e-mail: office@rickmansworthpneu.co.uk
website: www.rickmansworthpneu.co.uk

Chairman of Governors: Miss C Smith, MA Hons

Headmistress: **Mrs S Hayes**, BA Hons, PGCE

Age Range. 3–11.
Number of Pupils. 140 Girls.
Fees per term (2011-2012). £840–£3,150.

The PNEU School in Rickmansworth is a Preparatory School for girls aged 3–11 years, which achieves excellent results across the board (but particularly at 11+) in an atmosphere which feels both comfortable and familiar. PNEU girls aspire to be the best that they can and to that end, we offer a wide curriculum and begin specialist teaching in French, Science, Music and PE at Reception.

Girls join the school at age three, and can choose to stay for as much (or as little) of the school day as they like, while they are in Nursery in order that the transition to school is made as easy as possible for them. Early Years pupils enjoy the freedom of our beautiful garden whilst also having access to the Sports Hall, the IT suite and the Library. Older girls are encouraged to develop their dramatic talents by putting on plays, concerts and assemblies for parents each term. Science is taught in our new Science Lab and the school has enjoyed phenomenal success in the Haileybury Science challenge (first place in 2010), the Eton Young Voices Festival, Maths challenges and Thinking Skills days.

PNEU sports teams play harder and more competitively because we place an emphasis on cooperation and responsibility as well as giving all girls the chance to play on a team.

PNEU staff are strongly committed to the school's ethos and work hard to ensure that pupils have high expectations of themselves, enjoy learning and become responsible and responsive individuals. Our classrooms are bright, modern and airy and our facilities first class in a site which combines the benefits of an urban setting with the freedom of a wonderful garden.

The school's excellent record at Secondary Transfer means that girls leave us at 11 to join one of the first class maintained or independent schools which have come to value the calibre of PNEU girls.

Charitable status. The Rickmansworth PNEU School is a Registered Charity, number 311075. It exists to provide an enjoyable education that will develop the full potential of each child.

Riddlesworth Hall Preparatory School

Nr Diss, Norfolk IP22 2TA
Tel: 01953 681246
Fax: 01953 688124
e-mail: rhps@riddlesworthhall.com
website: www.riddlesworthhall.com

Headmaster: **Mr P I Cochrane**, CertEd

Age Range. Girls 2–13, Boys 2–13. Girls Boarding from age 7–13. Boys boarding from age 7–13.
Number of Pupils. 17 Boarders, 72 Day, 12 Nursery.
Fees per term (2011-2012). Full Boarders £5,845; Weekly Boarders £5,500; Day: Years 3–8 £3,490, Nursery–Year 2 £2,450. (Nursery sessions will be pro rata.)

Riddlesworth Hall, situated in a magnificent country house on the Norfolk/Suffolk border, provides an excellent all-round education. The aim is to develop each child's potential to the full in all areas – academic, sport and creative arts. The boys and girls are prepared for Common Entrance and Scholarship examinations to independent senior schools.

Riddlesworth Hall has excellent art and pottery studios, science, domestic science and technology laboratories, a computer room, music and drama rooms and a refurbished gymnasium. French is taught from Reception. A range of sports is taught to all levels and good-quality teams are regularly produced.

The care of the children is in the hands of the Headmaster and his wife who are resident, supported by a team of matrons.

The school enjoys CreSTeD status and is specifically staffed to welcome dyslexic children. IEPs are prepared for these children, who enjoy all the benefits of full integration into main school activities.

Extras include speech and drama, ballet and riding. There is a very active music department with choirs, orchestra, various ensembles and a recorder group. Senior school music, drama and academic scholarships have been recently achieved.

There is a wide variety of clubs and activities including skiing, dance, ball skills, gym and cookery. A feature of Riddlesworth Hall is its Pets Corner which houses a variety of small animals brought from home and permanently resident at school.

Self-reliance, self-discipline, and tolerance are encouraged, and good manners are expected.

Ripley Court School

Rose Lane, Ripley, Surrey GU23 6NE
Tel: 01483 225217
Fax: 01483 223854
e-mail: head@ripleycourt.co.uk
website: www.ripleycourt.co.uk

Chairman of Governors: P Armitage, BA, FCA

Headmaster: **A J Gough**, BSc UED, MA

Deputy Headmaster: D M Cockerill, BA Hons

Age Range. 3–13 Co-educational.
Number of Day Pupils. 252: Main School (age 7–13) 160; Little Court (age 4–7) 68; Nursery (age 3+) 24.
Fees per term (2011-2012). Main School £3,295–£3,680; Little Court £2,600–£2,675; Nursery £2,450 full-time (part-time pro rata).

The School is a Charitable Trust and offers bursarial scholarships and bursaries on a means-tested basis. Pupils are prepared for Common Entrance and Scholarship Examinations for all the Boys' and Girls' Senior Independent Schools. There is a high academic standard and many Scholarships are won including some for Sport, Music and Art, but there is no cramming: PE, Music, Art and Craft are a part of every child's timetable with opportunities in orchestral, choral and dramatic productions. Facilities include a library, science laboratories, a gymnasium, a computer suite, and art, music and hobbies rooms. There are 20 acres of playing fields. Games and sports are Football (Association and Rugby), Hockey, Netball, Cricket, Tennis (2 hard, 2 grass courts), Athletics, Rounders, Volley-ball, Stoolball; Swimming and Life Saving are taught in a large, covered, heated swimming pool.

Little Court is the Pre-Prep Department which also uses the main playing field, swimming pool and gymnasium. The "Ark" Nursery uses all school facilities and nursery children receive tuition in French, music, swimming and dance.

School transport serves Woking, Pyrford and West Byfleet.

Charitable status. Ripley Court School is a Registered Charity, number 312084. It aims to educate children and prepare them well for adult life.

Ripon Cathedral Choir School

Whitcliffe Lane, Ripon, North Yorkshire HG4 2LA
Tel: 01765 602134
Fax: 01765 608760
e-mail: admin@cathedralchoirschool.co.uk
website: www.cathedralchoirschool.co.uk

Governors:
Members of the Chapter of Ripon Cathedral and Lay
 Governors

Headmaster: **Mr Christopher McDade**, BA Hons,
FCollT, PGCE, LTCL

Deputy Head: Mrs K Coram, NPQH, BA Open, CertEd
London

Age Range. 3–13.
Number of Pupils. 84.
Fees per term (2010-2011). Full Boarders £4,848;
Weekly Boarders £4,467; Day Pupils: Year 4 and above
£3,535, Years 2–3 £2,610, Year 1 £2,330, 2nd Year Foundation £2,025, 1st Year Foundation: sessional rates. 10%
reduction for children of Service families, and a 5% reduction for siblings.

There are 16 Choristers who can be full or weekly boarders or day pupils and who have gained a 50% choral scholarship by a Voice Trial, and another 70 day, boarding and
weekly boarding pupils. Members of the Girls' Cathedral
Choir enjoy a reduction of 20% of the termly fee if they
attend the Choir School. The school is fully co-educational.
Children are accepted into Pre-Prep from the age of 3 and
move into the main school at the age of seven.

The school gives children a first-class academic education in small classes in a supportive family atmosphere.
There are spacious facilities for indoor and outdoor sport,
and art, drama and IT are greatly encouraged. Music is
exceptionally strong. The school is attractively situated on
the edge of the city of Ripon in a very pleasant and semi-
rural area. The boarding accommodation is secure and
friendly and has recently been upgraded and significantly
improved.

Charitable status. Ripon Cathedral Choir School is a
Registered Charity, number 529583. It exists to provide non-
profit making full-time education for the boy choristers of
Ripon Cathedral, and for other children.

Rockport School

**Rockport Road, Craigavad, Holywood, Co Down
BT18 0DD, Northern Ireland**
Tel: 028 9042 8372
Fax: 028 9042 2608
e-mail: info@rockportschool.com
website: www.rockportschool.com

Chairman of the Governors: Mr Michael Burke

Headmistress: **Ms C A Osborne**, BEd

Age Range. 3–16.
Number of Pupils. 105 Girls, 75 Boys.
Fees per term (2011-2012). Day: £2,800–£3,800, Pre-
Prep (from age 3) £1,450–£2,500. Boarding (in addition to
Day fee): £1,100–£1,250 (4 nights).

Rockport School is the only independent preparatory and
senior School in Northern Ireland. It is situated in twenty-
five acres of beautiful surroundings, overlooking Belfast
Lough, and prides itself in its happy atmosphere.

Rockport is a child-centred school and caters for the individual. It provides a well-balanced, rounded education for
children from 3 to GCSE. Pupils are made to feel they have
something valuable to contribute – whether in the classroom, in music and drama, on the sports field or elsewhere.

Rockport aims to give each pupil the capacity and confidence to live in an uncertain world – to encourage the pupils
to work hard, to take a pride in achievement, to accept
responsibility and to show concern for others. In the pursuance of these aims, Rockport is fortunate in having a dedicated and experienced staff, excellent teacher pupil ratios, a
wide range of facilities and an extensive range of extra curricular activities.

Staff and parents work closely together for the common
good of the children. There is an active Parent Teacher Association which meets each term. Funds are raised for the
school, but regular Educational Evenings are also arranged.

Normal entry points are 3, 8 and 11.

Charitable status. Rockport School Limited is a Registered Charity, number XN48119. It exists to provide education for boys and girls.

Rokeby

George Road, Kingston-upon-Thames, Surrey KT2 7PB
Tel: 020 8942 2247
Fax: 020 8942 5707
e-mail: hmsec@rokeby.org.uk
website: www.rokebyschool.co.uk

Maxim: *Smart, Skilful and Kind*

Chairman of the Governors: Mr Charles Carter

Headmaster: **Mr J R Peck**

Age Range. 4–13.
Number of Boys. 370.
Fees per term (2010-2011). Pre-Prep £2,825–£3,385;
Prep £3,865–£4,110 (including lunch, books and all com-
pulsory extras).

Rokeby has an outstanding record of success in Common
Entrance and Scholarships to leading Independent Schools.
Boys are accepted at 4+ to the Pre-Prep and at 7+ to the Prep
School. There is a number of scholarships available to the
Prep School at 7+.

Science is taught in two well-equipped Laboratories.
There is a large Computer Room and a very spacious Art
and Design Technology Centre. Soccer, Rugby, and Cricket
are played while other sports include Swimming, Athletics,
Hockey and Basketball. There are two large Halls and an
Astroturf. A full activities programme is available for boys
from Chess Club to Golf. The Music Department provides
Orchestra, Ensembles and two Choirs and there are fourteen
visiting peripatetic teachers, who work within a sound-
proofed music block.

There is a number of educational school trips arranged as
well as trips overseas, including Italy, Greece and Skiing.
The school operates a bus service to the Wimbledon and
Putney areas.

Charitable status. Rokeby Educational Trust Limited is
a Registered Charity, number 312653. It exists to provide an
excellent education for boys aged 4–13.

Rose Hill School

Coniston Avenue, Tunbridge Wells, Kent TN4 9SY
Tel: 01892 525591
Fax: 01892 533312

e-mail: admissions@rosehillschool.co.uk
website: www.rosehillschool.co.uk

Chairman of Governing Body: Mr Alan Baker

Headmaster: **P D Westcombe**, BA, PGCE

Deputy Head: G J Coventry, BSc, CertEd Loughborough

Age Range. 3–13.
Number of Pupils. 175 Boys, 139 Girls.
Fees per term (2011-2012). £3,980 (over 7 years); £2,890 (under 7 years); £1,575–£1,785 (3 years old).

The school is situated in seventeen acres of beautiful grounds adjacent to the green belt, but within five minutes of the centre of the town. A superb Pre-Preparatory building was opened in 1991, followed by a new ICT centre. A Sports Hall was completed in 1998 and a new dining room and kitchen in 1999. Facilities also include an outdoor heated swimming pool and 6-hole golf course. A new block, comprising six classrooms, library and changing rooms, was completed in 2003 and linked to a superb Theatre and Creative Arts Centre in September 2008. An astroturf pitch was completed in 2010.

Children are prepared for Common Entrance and Scholarship entry to Independent Senior Schools and for competitive entry into local grammar schools at 11+ and 13+. Small classes ensure individual attention and the fulfilment of academic challenge. The School prides itself on its friendly and personal approach to pupils and parents.

Sport and the Creative Arts are highly valued. Hockey, Soccer, Rugby, Netball, Cricket, Rounders and Athletics are the main team games supported by a range of individual sports. There is a junior and senior Choir, a School Orchestra and many children receive instrumental tuition. Two major drama productions occur every year.

A full range of extra-curricular clubs, including Cubs and Brownies, ensures breadth of experience. Within a secure environment, based on clear Christian principles, children are encouraged to meet new challenges with confidence.

Charitable status. Rose Hill School is a Registered Charity, number 270158. It aims to provide a high quality education to boys and girls aged 3–13.

Rose Hill Westonbirt School

Tetbury, Gloucestershire GL8 8QG
Tel: 01666 881400
Fax: 01666 881391
e-mail: rosehill@rhwestonbirt.co.uk
website: www.rhwestonbirt.co.uk

Chairman of Governors: Mr D McMeekin, MBA

Headmaster: **Mr N Shaw**, MA, BA Hons, PGCE

Deputy Head: Mr G Barrett, BSc Hons, GRTP, QTS

Age Range. 3–11.
Number of Pupils. 120 day pupils.
Fees per term (2011-2012). £2,160–£3,225.

Rose Hill Westonbirt School is a preparatory school for boys and girls age 3–11.

Location. The school's idyllic setting in 210 acres of beautiful rural park and woodland in Gloucestershire (shared with Westonbirt School, an independent boarding and day school for girls) allows pupils the freedom to play and explore in a safe and natural environment, developing imagination and confidence. The school is located close to the village of Tetbury and is within half an hour of the M4 and M5 and within easy reach of the surrounding towns of Cirencester, Gloucester, Swindon, Bath and Bristol.

Philosophy. Rose Hill Westonbirt is committed to enhancing children's broader personal development, as well as preparing them for senior independent, grammar and secondary maintained schools. The 2011 Independent Schools Inspectorate (ISI) inspection report praised how Rose Hill Westonbirt is *"successful in meeting its aims to encourage every pupil, educating the whole child and celebrating the individual"*. The school fosters a strong family and Christian ethos. This combination of care and overriding sense of community creates a happy, secure and stimulating environment in which the boys and girls thrive.

The emphasis of the staff is on achieving the highest academic standards whilst encouraging participation in a full programme of sport and creative activities such as art, drama, and music.

Rose Hill Westonbirt pupils receive specialist coaching in a wide variety of games using the exceptional sporting facilities. These include a 25-metre swimming pool, well-maintained pitches, netball and newly-resurfaced tennis courts. The boys play rugby, football, hockey and cricket and the girls' main sports are hockey, netball and rounders. During the inter-house competitions mixed teams participate in these sports. Both girls and boys take part in track and field athletics, swimming, tennis, golf and cross-country activities.

Rose Hill Westonbirt School is accredited by Forest Schools and successfully incorporates an Outdoor Education Programme into the curriculum. Pupils enjoy one double lesson per week in the spinney, where children are encouraged to explore the unique environment in order to support and develop their learning.

The school has a formidable Music Department and pupils have at least two periods of singing and music per week. Many children learn an instrument with tuition from peripatetic teachers who cover instruments in the string, brass, percussion and wind disciplines. Children are encouraged to take part in regional and national festivals and recently won top awards at the 2011 *Cheltenham Festival of Performing Arts*.

School results are on a par with the best prep schools and the school also does well in national rankings and assessments generally. The 2011 ISI inspection report praised the teaching at the school – *"Teachers at Rose Hill Westonbirt know their pupils very well and provide high-quality support and guidance, enabling the pupils to learn and understand effectively."* When pupils leave Rose Hill Westonbirt School at 11+, they are fully prepared for entrance/scholarship exams or Common Entrance exams, and they have acquired an excellent educational foundation and are happy, accomplished and caring persons motivated to make the best of their prospects wherever they go.

Charitable status. Westonbirt School Limited is a Registered Charity, number 311715. It exists to provide quality education in a demanding world.

Rosemead Preparatory School

70 Thurlow Park Road, Dulwich, London SE21 8HZ
Tel: 020 8670 5865
Fax: 020 8761 9159
e-mail: admin@rosemeadprepschool.org.uk
website: www.rosemeadprepschool.org.uk

Headteacher: **Mrs C Brown**, CertEd, DipEd, RSADipSpLD

Age Range. 3–11.
Number of Pupils. Day: 152 Boys, 164 Girls.
Fees per term (from January 2011). £2,865–£3,040.

Rosemead is a well-established preparatory school with a fine record of academic achievement. Children are prepared for entrance to independent London day schools at age 11 years, many gaining awards and scholarships. The school has a happy, family atmosphere with boys and girls enjoying a varied, balanced curriculum which includes maths, English, science, French, information and communication technology, arts and humanities. Music and drama are strong subjects with tuition available in most orchestral instruments and various music groups meeting frequently. A full programme of physical education includes gymnastics, most major games, dance and (from age 6) swimming. Classes make regular visits to places of interest. Three residential field studies courses are arranged for the junior pupils along with various school holidays. Main entry to the school is at Nursery (age 3), following informal assessment, and at National Curriculum Year 3, following a formal assessment. The school is administered by a board of governors elected annually by the parents.

All religious denominations welcome.

From September 2009 a small number of bursaries will be available from Year 3.

Charitable status. Rosemead Preparatory School (The Thurlow Educational Trust) is a Registered Charity, number 1186165. It exists to provide a high standard of education in a happy, caring environment.

Rowan Preparatory School
UCST

6 Fitzalan Road, Claygate, Esher, Surrey KT10 0LX
Tel: 01372 462627
Fax: 01372 470782
e-mail: office@rowan.surrey.sch.uk
website: www.rowan.surrey.sch.uk

Rowan is part of the United Church Schools Trust which is an educational trust controlled by a Board of Governors and chaired by Lord Carey. In addition Rowan has a Local Governing Body, who play an active, supportive role in the school.

Chairman of the Local Governing Body: Mr Alastair
   Spencer

Headteacher: **Mrs Kathy Kershaw**, CertEd

Age Range. 2–11 (Pre-Preparatory age 2–7, Preparatory age 7–11).
Number of Pupils. 270 Day Girls.
Fees per term (2010-2011). Nursery (5 mornings) £1,202; Kindergarten (5 mornings) £1,568; Reception–Year 6 £2,933–£3,759.

The school is located on two sites very close to each other in a leafy part of Claygate. Rowan Brae accommodates the Nursery and Pre-Prep and Rowan Hill, the Prep. Both sites have benefited from extensive refurbishment in recent years and the purpose-built Nursery was opened in September 2005. Breakfast club is available to assist working families.

The Brae, under the leadership of its own Head, Mr James Tilly, has a warm and caring atmosphere and many of the classrooms have been purpose built; they all have up to date IT facilities including interactive whiteboards. The playgrounds, with separate area for Nursery and Kindergarten, are packed with Early Years activities, toys and climbing equipment. At the Hill, the girls move around the classrooms, which are well equipped for the relevant subject with interactive whiteboards in all classrooms. There is also an excellent new ICT Suite, which was funded by the very supportive parents association, The Friends of Rowan. Again the Hill has well-equipped playgrounds and adventure walkways. There is a wooded area, The Spinney, which is held in great affection by the girls.

Admission in the Early Years is non-selective. Early registration is advisable if a place in the pre-prep is to be assured. Entry at other stages requires a satisfactory level of attainment in basic skills and this is determined through participation in a variety of activities rather than through rigorous testing. The girls move seamlessly from Rowan Brae (KS1) to Rowan Hill (KS2) without additional assessment.

Girls are prepared for entry to a wide variety of Senior Independent Day and Boarding Schools. There is an excellent record of girls gaining places at their senior school of choice, including each year a number of girls being offered music, sports, art or academic scholarships. A special programme for Year 6 girls is organised in the summer term to prepare them for moving on to their respective schools. This programme includes PSHE and citizenship studies, life skills and community service.

Rowan offers a broad-based curriculum of work so that each pupil is able to develop her own talents and maximize her potential. The school welcomes visiting speakers and performers to enhance the curriculum. Day trips are also included in each term and the annual residential trips to Sayers Croft, Marchants Hill, The Isle of Wight and France are both popular and highly educational in content. In addition, a wide variety of clubs are offered before and after school and at lunchtimes and include: drama, African drumming, gymnastics, chess, music, art, science, foreign languages and a host of sports and musical activities.

Rowan has an excellent Music Department with all girls singing in a choir and playing the recorder. In addition, three-quarters of girls at the Hill play a further instrument with lessons timetabled during and outside the school day. There are various ensembles, which the girls can also join in preparation for the orchestra. The latest initiative where all girls play the violin or cello at Year 1 has encouraged the girls' musical abilities and enhanced performance throughout the prep school.

The school has an excellent sporting record, especially in swimming and gymnastics (where national standard is reached), netball, hockey and pop lacrosse to mention but a few.

Rowan is very proud of its art, providing stunning displays around both the Brae and the Hill expressing the girls' individuality and excellent capabilities.

With small classes on both sites and strong pastoral care it is Rowan's aim to provide the essential early grounding in a happy, stimulating and secure environment where every child's needs are catered for.

The 2007 ISI Inspection commented that:

"Rowan is outstanding in achieving its aim of providing excellent quality education in a warm, caring, supportive atmosphere, in which all girls can achieve whatever their ability."

"… where it is perfectly acceptable to be yourself and where individual success is recognised a every level."

"Rowan is an exceptionally happy place, distinguished by the strongly positive relationships between all members of its community, where girls enjoy a genuine sense of childhood", strongly supporting the school's mantra that Rowan is an outstanding school for girls.

There is a thriving 'Old Girls' association. Rowan celebrated its 75th Anniversary in May 2011. A prospectus is available on request and prospective parents are asked to make an appointment to view the school during a normal working day, and to attend one of the Open Mornings held each term. The school welcomes girls for Taster and Activity Days.

Assisted places are available and details are available upon request from the school Registrar.

Charitable status. Rowan Preparatory School is a member of The United Church Schools Trust, which is a Registered Charity, number 1016538.

Royal Russell Junior School

Coombe Lane, Croydon, Surrey CR9 5BX
Tel: 020 8651 5884
Fax: 020 8651 4169
e-mail: juniorschool@royalrussell.co.uk
website: www.royalrussell.co.uk

Patron: Her Majesty The Queen

Chairman of Governors: K Young

Headmaster: J Thompson, BA QTS St Mary's University College, Twickenham

Age Range. 3–11.
Number of Pupils. 152 Boys, 133 Girls.
Fees per term (2011-2012). Upper Juniors (Years 3–6) £3,500, Lower Juniors (Reception–Year 2) £2,865, Nursery £1,265–£2,865.

The Junior School stands on a magnificent wooded campus extending to over 100 acres, which it shares with the Royal Russell Senior School (11–18 years). (*See Royal Russell School entry in HMC section.*)

The school is well served by road, tram and rail links and is one of the few co-educational schools in South London.

There is a fully-qualified teaching staff of 28. The school has a broad curriculum which seeks to blend the highest standards of academic work with a wide range of extra-curricular activities. There are opportunities for all pupils to participate in football, netball, hockey, rounders, cross-country and cricket as team sports, and as individuals to be coached in athletics, swimming, tennis, and table tennis. There is an extensive fixture list of matches against other schools. Artistic development extends to include full dramatic and musical productions, and many pupils learn musical instruments. All forms of art, design and technology are actively encouraged. There are excellent teaching facilities which are complemented by an Assembly Hall, a Sports Hall, Gymnasium, Science Laboratories, Music School, Art Room, Computer Suite, School Chapel and a Performing Arts Centre with a 200-seat auditorium. Our stunning indoor swimming pool offers a 25m main pool, learner pool and function room. All Junior School pupils receive weekly swimming lessons from qualified instructors.

The majority of the pupils join the school at 3+ or 7+, and are prepared for transfer to the Senior School at 11+. Candidates for entry to the Infants and Early Years are interviewed informally, while all other entrants sit assessments in English, Mathematics and Cognitive Ability appropriate to their ages.

Prospective parents are very welcome to come and meet the Headmaster and to tour the school, and should telephone for a prospectus in the first instance.

Charitable status. Royal Russell School is a Registered Charity, number 271907. It exists solely to provide education to girls and boys.

Rudston Preparatory School

59/63 Broom Road, Rotherham, South Yorkshire S60 2SW
Tel: 01709 837774
Fax: 01709 837975
e-mail: office@rudstonschool.com
website: www.rudstonschool.com

Co-educational Day School. The school is a charitable educational trust with a Board of Trustees.

Chairman of Trustees: Mr N H Morton, FCIEH
Principal: Mrs Lynda J Sharpe, CertEd

Age Range. 2–11 years.
Number of Pupils. 117 Boys, 105 Girls.
Fees per term (2011-2012). Age 4–11: £2,070; Pre-School: £40 per day.

There are 18 members of staff.

Our small classes, combined with a wide curricula, flexibility in organisation, detailed attention to the acquisition of skills and personal consideration of each individual's ability, help to ensure that the highest standards are achieved.

The school offers a range of subjects including English, Mathematics, Sciences, Design Technology, French, Latin, Music and Computer Studies, Drama, History, Geography, Art, Religious Education, Personal and Social Education, and Physical Education.

Pupils are prepared for extrance examinations to other schools. We have an excellent reputation for gaining successful results.

Pupils are expected to maintain a good code of conduct at all times; courtesy and consideration for others are an intrinsic part of school life.

Charitable status. Rudston Preparatory School is a Registered Charity, number 529438. It exists to provide education for boys and girls.

Runnymede St Edward's School

North Drive, Sandfield Park, Liverpool L12 1LE
Tel: 0151 281 2300
Fax: 0151 281 4900
e-mail: contact@runnymede-school.org.uk
website: www.runnymede-school.org.uk

Choir School to Liverpool Metropolitan Cathedral
Motto: *Viriliter Age – Be of good courage*

Chairman of Governing Body: Dr J Myerscough, BSc, PhD, MInstP, CPhys

Headteacher: Mr B Slater, BA, HDipEd, NPQH

Age Range. 3–11.
Number of Pupils. 128 Day Boys, 109 Day Girls.
Fees per term (2011-2012). £2,021–£2,131.

Runnymede St Edward's School offers a broad balanced education in a welcoming, caring Christian environment, while preparing pupils for selective and non-selective secondary education. The school, which includes a Nursery Department, occupies a number of spacious buildings including Runnymede, a former Victorian mansion.

The School is a member of the Catholic Independent Schools Conference as well as the Association of Junior Independent Schools.

The National Curriculum is followed and pupils are entered for Key Stage 1 and 2 Tests. Emphasis is placed on positive attitudes through the provision of merit-based rewards for excellent work and effort. Above all, children are given every opportunity to discover their own self-worth and happiness through a sense of achievement and fulfilment.

Pupils are encouraged to recognise their own abilities and to appreciate those of others. They are urged to pursue goals which will lead to the achievement of high standards in all aspects of school life. Girls and boys are encouraged to participate fully in a challenging and varied curriculum to ensure that their potential is fully explored.

Facilities include the Nursery, classrooms, 2 assembly halls, library, computer suite, science laboratory, art and design unit, music department and secure play areas. In addition there are sports pitches, running track, floodlit astroturf, sports hall, gymnasium, swimming pool and dining hall. Field trips, residential activities, education and theatre trips are regular activities.

Alongside its excellent academic and sporting facilities, Runnymede is the Choir School to the Metropolitan Cathedral of Christ the King, Liverpool. Music plays a very important part in the life of the school which has its own choir and orchestra. The school is also fortunate in being able to provide after-care facilities every day from the end of school until 6.00 pm and a breakfast club that operates from 8.00 am daily.

Standards of discipline are high and good manners and courtesy are regarded as essential. In a recent ISI Inspection the quality of the school's Pastoral Care was identified as "outstanding".

Prior to entering Runnymede at Nursery level, potential pupils – both boys and girls – are expertly assessed by our Early Years staff, in order to establish whether the individual child is developmentally ready for Nursery education. Parents are invited to attend this assessment and, if successful, the child will enter the School through the Nursery. Here they will spend their first year and attain their fourth birthday.

Pupils are admitted to other age groups within the School as and when vacancies occur. Entry is as a result of a day assessment carried out by the School staff, combined with a report received from the child's current Headteacher. Assessment of pupils' progress is an important feature of the school.

The Headteacher and staff consistently aim to enhance the role played by parents in the life of the school. The support of parents is fundamental to pupils' development and the school values highly the shared responsibility between home and school based on clear understanding between pupils, teachers and parents. Parents are kept regularly informed of their child's progress through reports and parents' meetings.

Further information regarding all aspects of Runnymede can be found in the Prospectus, copies of which are available from the Admissions Officer.

Rupert House School

90 Bell Street, Henley-on-Thames, Oxon RG9 2BN
Tel: 01491 574263
Fax: 01491 573988
e-mail: office@ruperthouse.oxon.sch.uk
website: www.ruperthouse.org

Chairman of Governors: C Barker, OBE, BA Hons

Headmistress: **Mrs N Gan**, MA Ed, FRSA

Age Range. Girls 4–11, Boys 4–7.
Number of Pupils. Girls 176, Boys 59.
Fees per term (2010-2011). £1,340–£3,185 (inclusive).

Rupert House School, a Charitable Trust, is a day preparatory school for girls aged 4–11 and boys aged 4–7. The school is set in its own large garden in the centre of Henley-on-Thames. The pre-preparatory school is housed in a purpose-built unit and the older children work in a large Georgian House. Specialist facilities include a laboratory, art room, French room, music studio, IT suite and learning support room. There are all-weather games facilities on the site and a sports ground within a short walk.

The staff are fully qualified and experienced. They aim to give a sound and stimulating education in the basic subjects required for 11+ Common Entrance but are concerned also with the wider curriculum. Extra-curricular activities, which can include maths club, martial arts, golf, Latin, gymnastics, swimming, art, craft, football, hockey and computers, are

offered after school hours. Individual music lessons in piano, string and wind instruments are offered as an extra.

Within a disciplined framework, where courtesy and consideration are expected, there is a friendly, family atmosphere in which the individual nature of each child is respected. The pupils are encouraged to match their performance to potential and to meet all challenges with enthusiasm and determination. There are regular consultation evenings and twice yearly reports. Parents may consult the Headmistress at any time by appointment.

Care is taken to ensure that pupils are well prepared for transfer to a school suited to their academic ability and personal qualities. In recent years girls have gained admission to well respected Independent Senior Schools and boys to excellent Prep Schools.

Charitable status. Rupert House School is a Registered Charity, number 309648. It exists to provide quality education for boys and girls.

Russell House School

Station Road, Otford, Sevenoaks, Kent TN14 5QU
Tel: 01959 522352
Fax: 01959 524913
e-mail: head@russellhouse.kent.sch.uk
website: www.russellhouseschool.co.uk

Headmistress: **Mrs Alison Cooke**, BA Hons Oxon, CertEd, LGSM, NPQH

Age Range. Co-educational 2–11+.
Number of Pupils. Boys 100, Girls 100.
Fees per term (2011-2012). Nursery Department (mornings) £1,660, Transition £1,685, Reception £2,790, Years 1–3 £3,155, Years 4–6 £3,625 (including lunch).

Russell House is a small, friendly school for boys and girls aged from 2 to 11.

We have a reputation for achieving excellent academic results while at the same time maintaining a friendly, caring and inclusive atmosphere where every child has access to every activity.

Many of our pupils are successful in the 11+ examination, gaining entry to the local grammar schools, and others pass on to independent schools such as Sevenoaks. We have a consistently strong record in gaining scholarships, both academic and music.

Academic excellence at the school goes hand in hand with an ethos which encourages individuality, self-expression and the curiosity to learn.

The school is careful to cultivate a calm, happy atmosphere and there is also a strong emphasis on building skills for the future and developing a sensitive awareness of the world beyond the school.

Rydal Penrhos Preparatory School

Pwllycrochan Avenue, Colwyn Bay, North Wales LL29 7BP
Tel: 01492 530381
Fax: 01492 539720
e-mail: prep@rydal-penrhos.com
website: www.rydal-penrhos.com

Chairman of Governors: Mr D Rae

Headmaster: **Roger McDuff**, BEd Hons, MA

Age Range. 3–11.
Number of Pupils. 214 (113 boys, 101 girls).

Fees per term (2011-2012). Day: Pre-Prep £1,860–£2,265, Prep £2,300–£2,660.

Rydal Penrhos Preparatory School is a welcoming, vibrant school for young boys and girls aged 3 to 11 years.

Ethos. As a Christian school with a Methodist foundation, it seeks to provide a firm but sympathetic moral framework in which care, support, respect, tolerance and responsibility for oneself and for others is accepted as fundamental. The School has a strong family atmosphere and concern for every aspect of a child's development. Parental support is encouraged and welcomed.

Environment. Set on a 12-acre site, the magnificent school building offers breathtaking views to the sea across playing fields and woodland. Maximum advantage is taken of the coastal aspect, the close proximity of the Snowdonia National Park and rich historic and cultural resources in the locality.

Curriculum. The School curriculum is very broad and is based on the National Curriculum, teaching being mainly class-based from the ages of 3 to 8 and subject-based from 8 to 11, with input from subject specialists throughout. All children also have the opportunity to develop their special interests and skills through a varied programme of extra-curricular activities.

Opportunities. Although the syllabus has rigorous academic elements, specialist provision is available within the School for those with learning difficulties. Sport, Music, Drama, Art, Design and Information Technology feature strongly and provide real opportunities for every child to explore and develop individual talents, not always expressed through academic work. Most pupils proceed through to Rydal Penrhos Senior School (*see entry in HMC section*).

Bursaries and Awards to the Senior School are offered at 11+. Parents appreciate the educational continuity between the junior and senior schools and the integrated curriculum ensures a smooth transition between the Schools.

Facilities at the Preparatory School are excellent, including science laboratories, an Information Technology suite, art studio, Design Technology room, gymnasium and a 25m indoor swimming pool. The large multi-purpose hall with stage provides for dance, drama, gymnastics and regular musical and dramatic productions. An orchestra, and wind and string groups are formed from those pupils taking tuition in a wide range of instruments, and choral singing is also of a high standard. The School has an excellent reputation for both girls' and boys' sport.

The pupils make full use of the superb astroturf and sports hall at the Senior School.

Positive Reinforcement. Discipline is clear and fair. Staff make sure that pupils know how they are doing and take particular care to praise them for good work.

Playscheme/Holiday Club. A holiday club is also run by staff for many weeks of the school holidays.

Location. The Headmaster, colleagues and pupils assure visitors of a warm welcome at the school, which is easily accessed from the A55.

Charitable status. Rydal Penrhos is a Registered Charity, number 525752. It exists to provide education for boys and girls.

Age Range. 3–11.

Number of Pupils. 118 Boys, 143 Girls.

Fees per term (from January 2011). Tuition: Foundation Stage: £1,620 (full day), £895 (half day); Pre-Prep £1,810–£2,570; Junior School £3,110. Boarding (excluding tuition): £3,595 (full), £3,150 (weekly). Lunch: Pre-Prep £155, Junior School £215.

Ryde School Assisted Places/Scholarships are awarded annually for pupils entering Year 5.

The school provides a good, civilised environment that does well academically for a wide range of ability. The pupils are well-motivated and work hard with evident enjoyment in both lessons and activities. By paying careful attention to all aspects of school life, pupils are able to flourish within a supportive community. In this environment, where regular contact between parents and staff is considered to be of paramount importance, children develop confidence and happily give of their best.

Ryde Junior School caters for children aged 3–11 years. Fiveways, just across the road from the main site, is home to the Foundation Stage and Early Years. Through creative and imaginative teaching in new purpose-built classrooms, a sound foundation of key skills is established. At the end of Key Stage 1 pupils are ready to move to the 'senior' part of the Junior School, having already benefited from some specialist teaching in the Junior School. Here they continue to receive the support of a well qualified and dedicated staff, enjoying a full range of specialist facilities including a recently upgraded ICT facility comprising 20 PCs with Internet access, a Creative Centre, Science Laboratory, Music room and Theatre.

A broad, balanced and rich curriculum is followed. This is based on the National Curriculum but is greatly enhanced. A wealth of trips and outings is offered, enriching the curriculum still further, making use not only of the beautiful sites on the Island, but on the mainland and abroad. Pupils are encouraged to develop their full range of talents, with Music, Drama and Sports enjoying equally high profiles. The school maintains a consistently successful record in all areas of team and individual sports. The major sports offered are: Athletics, Cricket, Cross-Country, Hockey, Netball, Rounders, Rugby, Soccer, Swimming and Tennis, with fixtures being arranged both locally and on the mainland (at no extra charge). There is a full and wide ranging programme of clubs and activities (which changes each term) during lunchtime and after school, offering something for everyone.

Our Senior School is on the same campus, enabling us to benefit from the use of a Sports Hall and pitches. Careful liaison between the staff and induction days in the summer term effect a smooth transition for our pupils to the Senior School (*see entry in HMC section*).

The Junior School has a small number of weekly and full boarders who, together with Senior School boarders, have use of the range of facilities available at the Bembridge campus, situated in some 100 acres on a beautiful cliff top site approximately six miles from Ryde. Transport is provided to and from the school during the week.

Charitable status. Ryde School with Upper Chine is a Registered Charity, number 307409. The aims and objectives of the Charity are the education of boys and girls.

Ryde Junior School

Queen's Road, Ryde, Isle of Wight PO33 3BE
Tel: 01983 612901
Fax: 01983 614973
e-mail: juniorhead@rydeschool.org.uk
website: www.rydeschool.org.uk

Chairman of the Board of Governors: R J Fox, MA, CMath, FIMA

Head: **H Edwards**, BSc, PGCE

Rydes Hill Preparatory School

Rydes Hill House, Aldershot Road, Guildford, Surrey GU2 8BP
Tel: 01483 563160
         01483 578472 (Admissions)
Fax: 01483 306714
e-mail: enquiries@rydeshill.com
         admissions@rydeshill.com

website: www.rydeshill.com

Chairman of the Governors: Bernard Stevens, Esq

Headmistress: **Mrs Stephanie Bell**, MA Oxon

Age Range. Girls 3–11, Boys 3–7. Nursery class for children 3–4.
Number of Day Pupils. 160.
Fees per term (2010–2011). £915–£3,115. Compulsory extras: Lunch £175, Stationery £45. Extra Subjects: Pianoforte, Clarinet, Flute, Violin £155; Speech and Drama, Elocution £50; Ballet £50.

Rydes Hill Preparatory School is situated in a beautiful Georgian house with magnificent Library, vaulted Dining Hall, and recently restored Victorian Conservatory. Facilities also include a large Science Laboratory, interactive whiteboards in all preparatory classes and a new IT suite.

This Catholic school welcomes children from all denominations and offers an exceptional start, academically and socially.

Rydes Hill achieves outstanding academic results. Experienced and dedicated teachers encourage self-esteem and give pupils a strong educational foundation. Year after year the school's excellent Key Stage 2 SATs results ensure that Rydes Hill is ranked in the top echelon of preparatory schools nationally and many pupils are awarded scholarships at leading senior schools. Sport, IT, Art and Music are taught by specialist teachers. Every pupil performs in one of the school's yearly productions and the creative arts are a major strength of the school.

Rydes Hill's ISI Inspection Report 2007 concluded, "Rydes Hill aims high for its pupils and they flourish. All aspects of the school's work are good and some are outstanding. In a calm, caring and purposeful environment, with major strengths in aspects of pastoral care, the school achieves remarkable academic success".

Rydes Hill offers a wide range of extra-curricular activities and an extended school day is available from 8:00 am to 5:30 pm every day, if required. Supervised homework sessions are also offered every day.

Charitable status. Rydes Hill Preparatory School is a Registered Charity, number 299411. It exists to ensure excellence in all aspects of education.

The Ryleys

Alderley Edge, Cheshire SK9 7UY
Tel: 01625 583241
Fax: 01625 581900
e-mail: info@theryleys.com
website: www.theryleys.com

Founded 1877.

Chairman of Governors: W T C Smith

Headmaster: **P G Barrett**, BA, CertEd

Age Range. 2½–11/13.
Number of Pupils. 206 Day Boys, 64 Day Girls.
Fees per term (2011–2012). Nursery: £1,115 (half day), £1,720 (full day); Reception, Years 1–3 £2,698; Years 4–6 £3,028; Years 7 and 8 £3,085.

The Ryleys School is situated in Alderley Edge, a rural village just 15 miles south of the city of Manchester, within easy reach of the motorway and rail networks and close to Manchester Airport.

The School is an Educational Trust with an active and forward-thinking Board of Governors. The staff consists of 19 highly-qualified full-time teachers and 7 part-time. There are also 8 Classroom and Nursery assistants. In the Junior

section of the school (Reception to Year 2) class teachers are responsible for delivering the majority of the curriculum while in the Middle School (Years 3 and 4) children are introduced to subject specialist teaching while retaining the class teacher format. In the Senior School (Year 5 to Year 8) all subjects are taught by subject specialists. Pastoral care in the Senior School is maintained by personal tutors. The thriving and successful Nursery School is staffed by qualified teachers.

Children are thoroughly prepared for entry via examination into Independent Day Schools at 11 and 13 or into Boarding Schools at 13 via the Common Entrance or Scholarship examinations. The school has an excellent academic record.

The extensive curriculum consists of English, Mathematics, Science, French, History, Geography, Scripture, Design Technology, Information Technology, Art, Music and Physical Education and provides an outstanding foundation for the children's future schooling. German or Spanish is offered to children in Years 7 and 8. Each subject is taught in a fully-equipped subject room and there is a computerised library. Other facilities include a Sports Hall, Music Department, Craft and Woodwork Centre, a large outdoor heated Swimming Pool, an Astroturf playing area and 8 acres of playing fields.

Various extra-curricular sports and activities are on offer including chess, computing, music, woodwork, basketball, badminton, table tennis, golf etc.

Football, Rugby, Cricket, Athletics, Hockey, Rounders and Netball are the main team games and there is an extensive fixture list of matches against other schools at various ages. The school has undertaken sports tours to Italy and Spain in the last few years and there is an annual skiing trip to Europe or North America. Outdoor pursuits are encouraged and the school organises a regular expedition to Rua Fiola in Scotland.

Music is another of the school's great strengths with well over 130 children receiving individual instrumental tuition from a highly-qualified staff of 9 visiting teachers. The school has a fine reputation for its concerts and musical productions. These performances take place on a full proscenium stage and every child is involved in one of the four productions each year. There are three choirs involving over 70 children.

Art, too, is of a notably high standard with children sitting for various scholarships and awards.

The domestic and catering arrangements and the health and welfare of the children are under the direct supervision of Mrs Barrett, the Headmaster's wife.

Children are accepted into the school at various ages providing places are available and are assessed upon entry so that the correct educational provision can be made in order to ensure that each pupil achieves his/her full potential. Bursaries are available.

The school places great emphasis upon such personal qualities as good manners and consideration for others.

Charitable status. The Ryleys School Limited is a Registered Charity, number 525915. It exists to provide a quality education for children from 3 to 13 years of age.

St Albans High School for Girls – Wheathampstead House

Wheathampstead House, Codicote Road, Wheathampstead, Hertfordshire AL4 8DJ
Tel: 01582 839270
Fax: 01582 839271
e-mail: WHOffice@stalbans-high.herts.sch.uk
website: www.stahs.org.uk

Chairman of School Council: Mrs J F Boulton, MRICS

Head of Wheathampstead House: Miss G M Bradnam,
BEd, MA Ed Mgmt, NPQH

Age Range. Girls 4–11.
Number of Pupils. 312.
Fees per term (2011-2012). Reception (age 4) £3,220,
Years 1 and 2 (age 5–6) £3,395 (inc Lunch); Years 3–6 (age
7–11) £3,395 (exc Lunch).

The Preparatory School for St Albans High School for
Girls is a very popular, academically selective school, with a
welcoming family atmosphere, offering outstanding pastoral
care. St Albans High School is uniquely placed in being able
to offer all the advantages of a continuous education in two
very different settings. From the ages of 4–11, the girls have
the freedom to grow and develop in an attractive rural environment, before moving on to the more urban setting of the
Senior School, close to the heart of the City of St Albans.

The Preparatory School, Wheathampstead House, is set
in 18 acres of grounds, within the village of Wheathampstead. The extensive site includes play areas, an adventure
playground, woods and an outdoor learning classroom.

The curriculum extends beyond the National Curriculum
in all year groups; French is taught from Year 3. State-of-
the-art facilities support innovative teaching and the development of independent, creative thinkers, who are confident
in the use of new technologies. There are specialist rooms
for Science, Art, DT and ICT with a very extensive library.
Pupils at the Preparatory School use the school swimming
pool located at the Senior School.

It is a happy, exciting and busy school with a wide variety
of activity days and educational visits throughout the school
year. There is an extensive range of clubs including Science,
Art, Speech and Drama, Puzzles, Dancing, Sports, Orienteering through to Latin, Mandarin and Spanish. Music is a
real strength of the school and there are plenty of orchestras,
bands and choirs. Enrichment groups extend and support
learning and there are opportunities for highly talented
pupils to join with Senior School girls for Music and Sport
events.

The School provides a supportive, challenging and creative environment, where girls work hard, are very successful academically and enjoy learning. It provides support for
mild dyslexia and mild dyspraxia, all screened in Year 3.

Charitable status. St Albans High School for Girls is a
Registered Charity, number 311065.

St Ambrose Preparatory School

**Wicker Lane, Hale Barns, Altrincham, Cheshire
WA15 0HE**
Tel: 0161 903 9193
Fax: 0161 903 8138
e-mail: stambroseprep.admin@traffordlearning.org
website: www.stambroseprep.org

Chairman of Governors: Mr Mark Holland

Headmaster: Mr Michael Lochery

Age Range. Boys 3–11, Girls 3–4.
Number of Pupils. 160.
Fees per term (2011-2012). £2,065.

St Ambrose Preparatory School is situated in a very
attractive, peaceful location in the heart of Cheshire, within
convenient reach of Manchester Airport, rail links and an
extensive motorway network, including the M56, M60, M6
and M62. This Roman Catholic school warmly welcomes
pupils of other Christian denominations, other Faiths and
those with no religious background. A broad, balanced curriculum is offered in a happy, secure environment and all are

helped and encouraged to attain the highest academic standards.

There are three departments in the school: Early Years for
3 to 5 year olds, the Infant Department for 5 to 7 year olds
and the Junior Department catering for boys between 7 and
11. All enjoy modern, airy classrooms in purpose-built
accommodation. The main building was erected in 1990 and
extended in 1994. A further building development, completed during 2009, provides a new hall, music room and
changing rooms.

Boys generally join the school in the Nursery, Reception
or at the beginning of the junior years and all receive an
excellent grounding academically, socially and morally. The
vast majority of pupils move on to St Ambrose College,
which shares the same site, having passed the Entrance
Examination at 11+. (The College is to be completely rebuilt
within the next two years and will enjoy the most up-to-date
facilities.)

St Ambrose has an outstanding sporting tradition and
encourages enjoyment and excellence in soccer, rugby, tennis, cricket, cross-country and athletics, making full use of
the nine acres of sports fields. There is an extensive list of
fixtures which continues throughout the year and sports
courses are held during most holidays.

Music provides many exciting opportunities to perform
and excel. An impressive team of peripatetic staff support
both curricular and extra-curricular activities. Good, enthusiastic singing is nurtured at all levels. The computer suite is
regularly upgraded, offering a wide selection of software
and restricted access to the internet for research. Many trips
and visits are arranged including a residential stay for Year 6
pupils at an outdoor adventure camp. French is taught
throughout the Infant and Junior Departments.

Charitable status. The Congregation of Christian Brothers is a Registered Charity, number 254312.

St Andrew's School

Meads, Eastbourne, East Sussex BN20 7RP
Tel: 01323 733203
Fax: 01323 646860
e-mail: office@androvian.com
website: www.androvian.co.uk

Chairman of the Governing Body: Admiral Sir Ian Forbes,
KCB, CBE

Head: S Severino, BA Hons, PGCE

Age Range. 2–13.
Number of Pupils. 269 (Prep School), 151 (Pre-Prep and
Nursery).
Fees per term (2011-2012). Boarders £6,500; Weekly
Boarding £5,810; Day Children: £4,610 (Years 4–8), £4,185
(Year 3), Pre-Prep £2,645. Nursery sessions: please enquire
at the school for session costs and EYEE discounts.

Situated in twelve acres of grounds at the foot of the
South Downs, St Andrew's, founded in 1877, has a highly
qualified teaching staff and children are taught in classes
with a maximum size of 20 and an average number of
approximately 16. A number of children in the Upper
School are boarders and the school operates a popular
scheme of 'Sleepover' boarding allowing day children to
stay during the week on a flexible basis on any night or
nights they wish.

The Head is supported by a Deputy Head, a Head of Pastoral Care and a strong management team. All children in
the school have a Form Teacher or Form Tutor who is
responsible for their pastoral welfare and academic progress.
Each section of the school has its own Head (Pre-Prep, Junior, Middle and Senior), who coordinates, together with the

Academic Director and Head of Pastoral Care, the overall pastoral and academic work of the staff.

In addition to the expanse of playing fields, St Andrew's benefits from its own indoor swimming pool and a well-equipped gymnasium. There are three computer suites equipped with up-to-date software and hardware including a wireless network connection and interactive whiteboards. The equipment in the Pre-Prep suite is designed specifically for children from 3 to 7 years of age. Other facilities include a modern purpose-built music block, an extensively equipped research and resource centre, a chapel and a creative arts centre with an art studio and design and technology facilities. The school strongly encourages music and drama and more than two-thirds of the children play instruments and participate in orchestras, bands and choirs. As well as Music, Drama is a timetabled subject and plays take place every term.

From the age of nine, children are taught by subject specialists. French is taught from the age of five and Latin is introduced from the age of 9. Children are introduced to working on computers at the age of two. The breadth of the curriculum means that, while the requirements of the National Curriculum are fulfilled, the children are able to experience a variety of other stimulating activities.

Accelerated sets exist from Year 5 to provide more challenging opportunities for those who are academically gifted. Academic, music, drama, sport and all-rounder awards have been achieved to many major senior schools and over the past five years more than 150 scholarships have been won by St Andrew's pupils. The school amalgamated with Eastbourne College in 2010 and approximately half the leavers each year progress there. Where necessary, extra Specific Needs teaching is provided as well as ESL support for those who require it.

There is a wide range of activities on offer. The Co-Curricular programme, which runs for children in Years 5 to 8, offers opportunities for all children to develop areas of interest and strength or to discover new ones. Each activity offered has its own educational objectives and challenges designed to improve children's skills and broaden their horizons. An extensive programme of after-school activities has always been a strong feature of St Andrew's. This starts at the Pre-Prep and runs through to Year 8. The school also operates various activity weeks during the school holidays and courses, which are run by our own staff, include art, rugby, football, swimming, tennis, netball and hockey.

The school's strong sporting reputation manifests itself in national honours regularly achieved in many different sports. Specialist coaches are employed to teach the skills required for all to enjoy participating in team games and opportunities are available to anyone wishing to represent the school.

Charitable status. Eastbourne College Incorporated is a Registered Charity, number 307071. The aim of the Charity is the promotion of Education.

St Andrew's School

Buckhold, Pangbourne, Reading, Berks RG8 8QA
Tel: 0118 974 4276
Fax: 0118 974 5049
e-mail: admin@standrewspangbourne.co.uk
website: www.standrewspangbourne.co.uk

The School is an Educational Trust controlled by a Board of Governors.

Chairman of Governors: H C C Jones, Esq

Headmaster: **Dr D Livingstone**, BSc, PhD, NPQH

   Age Range. 3–13. Weekly Boarding from age 7.

Number of Pupils. 300 including weekly boarders.

Fees per term (2011-2012). Boarders £5,460; Day Pupils £2,740–£4,600. Nursery from £1,300 (5 mornings).

The School is fully co-educational and set in over 50 acres of private wooded estate and parkland.

The Curriculum includes all the traditional CE and Scholarship subjects and there is emphasis on Music, Speech and Drama and Modern Languages. Study Skills are an important part of the senior pupils' timetable and Information Technology is well resourced.

Academic and Sporting standards are high.

Charitable status. St Andrew's (Pangbourne) School Trust Limited is a Registered Charity, number 309090. It exists to provide education for boys and girls.

St Andrew's School

Horsell, Woking, Surrey GU21 4QW
Tel: 01483 760943
Fax: 01483 740314
e-mail: hmsec@st-andrews.woking.sch.uk
            admin@st-andrews.woking.sch.uk
website: www.st-andrews.woking.sch.uk

Chairman of Governors: Mr Andrew Douglas

Headmaster: **Mr Adrian Perks**, MSc

Deputy Head: Mrs Sarah Marsh, BEd Hons

   Age Range. 3–13 co-educational.
   Number of Pupils. Total: 304 Day pupils. Pre-Prep and Nursery 169.
   Fees per term (2011-2012). Prep £3,505–£4,200. Pre-Prep £1,020–£2,970.
   Average Class Size: 15.

St Andrew's School was founded in 1937 and is an established, respected and thriving co-educational prep school, set in 11 acres of grounds within a quiet residential area approximately half a mile from Woking town centre. The School seeks to create a nurturing and happy environment of trust and support in which all pupils are encouraged and enabled to develop their skills, talents, interests and potential to the full – intellectually, physically and spiritually, regardless of social circumstances, age or religion.

Within St Andrew's walls children feel secure and confident and are highly motivated to perform to the best of their ability in all aspects of school life. They are competitive without losing sight of their responsibility to share and they are justifiably proud of their school and their own personal achievements. In a world of changing values, self-confidence and a solid grounding are essential building blocks for life. St Andrew's hopes to provide all their children with this basic foundation as they prepare for the bigger challenges that follow. Children are prepared for entrance and scholarship exams to a wide range of independent senior schools and there are specialist teaching facilities for all subjects including science, ICT, music and art. The curriculum is broad and the school places great emphasis on music, sport and the arts.

St Andrew's is very proud of its excellent on-site facilities including sports pitches, tennis courts, cricket nets and a newly refurbished swimming pool. We are very fortunate to enjoy the benefits of carefully designed school grounds that incorporate facilities to meet the needs of the children's physical and social development. There is a sports hall, tennis and netball courts, heated swimming pool and ample grounds for games (11 acres). Main school games are football, hockey, cricket, netball and rounders. Other activities include rugby, cross-country running, swimming, tennis and athletics.

Children can be supervised at school from 8 am and, through our extensive after-school activities programme for Year 3 and above, until 6/6.30 pm most evenings during the week. There is also an after-school club from 4 pm to 6 pm (chargeable) for Pre-Prep and Year 3 children.

Children are assessed for entry into Year 2 and above. The school has a number of scholarships and bursaries available at 7+ and 11+.

Charitable status. St Andrew's School is a Registered Charity, number 297580, established to promote and provide for the advancement of education of children.

S Anselm's

Bakewell, Derbyshire DE45 1DP
Tel: 01629 812734
Fax: 01629 814742
e-mail: headmaster@anselms.co.uk
website: www.sanselms.co.uk

The School is an Educational Trust.

Chair of Governors: Mrs N Weston

Headmaster: **S C Northcott**, MA Hons (Marlborough College and St Andrews)

Age Range. 4–13.
Numbers. Prep School (age 7 to 13) 90 boys, 80 girls. Pre-Prep (age 4 to 7) 50 boys and girls.
Fees per term (2010-2011). Boarders £6,070. Day: Prep £4,120–£5,170; Pre-Prep £2,660.

At S Anselm's we strive to create pupils who are good citizens, children who are kind and respectful and who are known for their friendliness and self-confidence.

We firmly believe the formative years are the most important and we work hard to bring out the best in each and every child in our care.

There are no academic entry requirements at S Anselm's but at 13 many of our boys and girls go on to senior school with a scholarship which is a tribute to the quality of the teaching at the school.

The school is proud of its outstanding academic record but life at S Anselm's is about much more than results alone. As a prep school with a strong boarding tradition we understand how important it is to make the evenings and weekends happy and fulfilling times too.

Over half of our pupils choose to board and during their last few years at the school virtually all the children are full boarders. The girls live in three separate houses, which are the homes of the housemistresses and their husbands. The boys live in the main school, sleeping in small, comfortable dormitories.

There is a high standard of pastoral care and a happy, family atmosphere is created by the resident housemaster and his wife and the matrons.

The school site comprises a modern, light and airy collection of buildings, set in 18 acres of beautiful countryside in the heart of the Peak District National Park. Facilities include a large sports hall, a purpose-built theatre, a computing centre, an extended library, and a state-of-the-art indoor swimming pool and common room complex.

S Anselm's has magnificent sporting facilities. There are extensive playing fields, tennis courts and an indoor swimming pool. The school enjoys sporting success in many different disciplines and S Anselm's teams achieve national recognition, being represented at the IAPS Finals regularly.

Most children learn a musical instrument and there are several choral and instrumental ensembles. There are more than 50 extra activities on offer, ranging from golf and sailing to Brownies and pottery.

The key to the school's outstanding record of success is the quality of teaching and the small class sizes which ensure that S Anselm's pupils get a great deal of individual attention. In recent years we have enjoyed record number of scholarships to many of the best senior schools such as Ampleforth, Malvern, Oundle, Rugby, Uppingham, Cheltenham Ladies' College, Shrewsbury, Repton, Winchester, Oakham and Sedbergh.

We aim to produce self-motivated children with enquiring minds but we never lose sight of the fact that competition must be tempered by consideration for others.

Charitable status. S Anselm's is a Registered Charity, number 527179. Its purpose is to carry on the education of children of either sex or both sexes.

St Anthony's Preparatory School
Alpha Plus Group

90 Fitzjohns Avenue, Hampstead, London NW3 6AA
Tel: 020 7435 3597 (Junior House)
          020 7435 0316 (Senior House)
          020 7431 1066 (Admissions)
Fax: 020 7435 9223
e-mail: headmaster@stanthonysprep.org.uk
website: www.stanthonysprep.org.uk

Headmaster: **P M Keyte**, MA Oxon

Age Range. 5–13.
Number of Boys. 290 Day Boys.
Fees per term (2010-2011). £4,315–£4,435 including lunches.

Founded in the 19th century and set in the heart of Hampstead village, St Anthony's is an academic IAPS preparatory school for boys between the ages of 5 and 13. It is Roman Catholic but welcomes boys of other faiths. The majority of boys transfer at 13, via scholarship or CE, to leading independent senior schools including Westminster, University College, Radley, St Paul's, Mill Hill, Highgate, Harrow, Eton, City of London, Ampleforth.

The school accommodation consists of two large Victorian houses in close proximity. Both have their own grounds and separate playgrounds. There are eight forms in the Junior House, where boys range in age from five to nine, and eight forms in the Senior House, where boys range in age from nine to thirteen. The Senior House has a specialist Design and Technology room, a Music room, a Computer room, a Science laboratory and a swimming pool. Games fields are close by.

All boys receive Religious Education lessons twice a week. The course, which centres on Catholic beliefs and practices, but includes aspects of other faiths, is followed by all pupils. The school's spiritual dimension is regarded as highly important and it exists within a liberal and inclusive atmosphere. Catholic pupils attend mass about three times each term.

The school curriculum is stimulating and challenging and, for example, it is possible for boys to study seven foreign languages. All pupils must study three, including French and Mandarin from Year 1. The arts have an important place in the school with a majority of boys learning to play a musical instrument and all boys involved in drama. Sport is a further strength of the school with some pupils achieving success on a national stage.

St Anthony's retains a slightly bohemian tradition with former pupils making their mark in the fields of rock music and art. Recently, four pupils won prizes in national competitions for creative writing.

The school works hard to instill in its pupils a sense of social responsibility and charity fundraising is a feature of school life. A former pupil was recently awarded the Gusi

Peace Prize (Asian equivalent of the Nobel) and the school has just financed the building of a kindergarten for a school in southern India. Much work is also done with local charities.

St Aubyns School

76 High Street, Rottingdean, Brighton, East Sussex BN2 7JN
Tel: 01273 302170
Fax: 01273 304004
e-mail: office@staubyns-school.org.uk
website: www.staubynsschoolbrighton.co.uk

A co-educational Preparatory and Pre-Prep School founded in 1895.

Chairman of the Governors: T R Prideaux, Esq

Headmaster: **S Hitchings**, MA Oxon

Deputy Headmaster: S M Greet, BEd Hons

Age Range. 3–13.
Number of Pupils. 200 day and weekly boarding children.
Within the Prep Department a number of the pupils board, some on a weekly basis from Monday morning until Friday evening, others as flexi-boarders on a regular night a week or on an occasional basis giving the school 24 hours' notice of the intention to board. This flexible arrangement suits many families and is a splendid introduction to boarding.
Fees per term (2010-2011). Day Pupils: Prep £3,275–£4,630, Pre-Prep £1,730–£2,270. Weekly Boarding supplement £850.
St Aubyns is a happy and friendly school which firmly believes in the traditional values that encourage self-discipline, good manners, and consideration for others.
St Aubyns has an excellent academic record, preparing children for a wide range of Senior Schools. Each year an impressive number of scholarships is gained by our Leavers (at 13+). Entry is by assessment on a Taster Day and report, although the school is non-selective. Academic, Music, Drama, Dance and Sports scholarships are available for children aged 7 to 11.
St Aubyns offers a carefully balanced, very broad curriculum which allows each individual child's talents to grow. The school is situated in the delightful seaside town of Rottingdean. The campus of 11 acres offers a wide range of facilities including a large sports hall, squash court, all-weather tennis court, heated outdoor swimming pool, spacious art room and modern, well-equipped Science and Design Technology laboratories. In January 2000 a large, state-of-the-art ICT Centre with twenty two linked computers and an 85-seat theatre were opened. In 2001 a spacious well-equipped Library was opened, providing a large quiet space for study and open access for all children to a wide range of fiction and non-fiction. As a Christian community, services are held daily in the beautiful timber lined Chapel.
Cricket, netball, lacrosse, soccer, rugby, hockey, rounders and athletics are the major games, plus a wide selection of minor games such as fencing, swimming, tennis and basketball. The Activities Programme offers children over 27 different clubs including drama, dance, art, LAMDA, model making, board games and chess.
We attach a great deal of importance to the children's cultural development. Our "Arts Express Programme" encompasses music, art, drama and dance. The children have regular Arts Express whole-day workshops.
St Aubyns is three miles from Brighton and less than an hour by train from London. Gatwick Airport is 40 minutes away and the journey to Heathrow takes about 85 minutes. For day pupils, there is minibus transport from a wide catchment area.
In September 2002 a Nursery Unit was opened. This now has 25 3–4 year olds and has recently been re-housed.
Charitable status. St Aubyns School Trust Limited is a Registered Charity, number 307368. It exists to provide an excellent all round education for boys and girls aged 3–13.

St Aubyn's School

Bunces Lane, Woodford Green, Essex IG8 9DU
Tel: 020 8504 1577
Fax: 020 8504 2053
e-mail: school@staubyns.com
website: www.staubyns.com

The School was founded in 1884 and is governed by a Charitable Trust.

Chairman of the Governors: D Shah, BSc Econ, FCA

Headmaster: **Gordon James**, MA

Deputy Head: Marcus Shute, BEd

Age Range. 3–13+.
Number of Children. 500 Day.
Fees per term (from April 2011). £1,328 (Nursery) to £3,263 (Seniors) fully inclusive.
St Aubyn's provides an all-round preparatory education for children aged 3–13. The school is non-selective at its main point of entry for children aged 3 and 4. There are assessment tests for older children, principally at ages 7+ and 11+.
Key characteristics of the school include: well-qualified, dedicated staff; small classes (generally no more than 21); a teacher:pupil ratio of 1:13. Younger children are also supported by nursery nurses and teaching assistants (in the Nursery the staff:child ratio is 1:6). A full-time qualified nurse deals with all medical issues and emergencies.
The school offers a wide-ranging curriculum within a traditional framework, encompassing all National Curriculum and Common Entrance requirements. French is taught from 4+ and Latin from 10+. French, Music and PE are specialist-taught from an early age. All subjects are specialist-taught from Year 6.
Children progress to a range of independent and state schools at 11+ and 13+. Pupils gain a range of scholarships at both 11 and 13. Recent awards include several academic scholarships as well as awards in Sport, Technology, Music and Drama. In 2011 a total of 20 awards were gained by a total of 13 children.
The school is pleasantly situated on the borders of Epping Forest, yet is close both to the North Circular and the M11. There are four departments within the school: Nursery (3+); Pre Prep (4+, 5+, 6+); Middle School (7+, 8+, 9+) and Seniors (10+, 11+ and 12+) and each has its own base and resources. Facilities are extensive with 8 acres of grounds, large Sports Centre, an all-weather pitch, fully-equipped Performing Arts Centre and Music School, Science Laboratory, Art and Design Base, a Library and two IT Suites. A computer network runs throughout the school. Games include soccer, cricket, hockey, tennis, netball, athletics and swimming, all coached to a high standard.
The Director of Music leads a thriving department, with a school orchestra and various instrumental groups and choirs. Children are regularly involved in performances both within and outside the school. The school has gained Arts-mark status for its provision for Music, Dance, Drama and Art. St Aubyn's has also gained the British Council's International School Award.

St Aubyn's School is a registered charity. All income from fees is for the direct benefit of its pupils. Two scholarships are available at 11+. The primary criterion for the award of a scholarship is academic ability, though special talent in music, technology, art, sport, etc may be taken into account. There is a bursary scheme at 7+. The school has Investors in People status.

Charitable status. St Aubyn's (Woodford Green) School Trust is a Registered Charity, number 270143. It exists to provide education for children.

St Bede's

Bishton Hall, Wolseley Bridge, Nr Stafford ST17 0XN
Tel: 01889 881277
Fax: 01889 882749
e-mail: admin@saintbedes.com
website: www.saintbedes.com

(Under the patronage of His Grace the Archbishop of Birmingham)

Headmaster: C W H Stafford Northcote, BA Hons
Headmistress: Miss H J A Stafford Northcote, BSc Hons

Age Range. 3–13.
Number of Pupils. 74 Boys and Girls.
Fees per term (2010-2011). £4,000 Boarders and Weekly Boarders, £2,000–£3,300 Day Pupils. Compulsory Extras Nil.

St Bede's is a Catholic Preparatory School, in which other faiths and denominations are welcomed.

St Bede's was founded in 1936 by the parents of the current headmasters. Since then, the Northcote family has educated young people as additions to their own family, treating each child with care and respect. This has helped to create an educational atmosphere unlike any other.

Bishton Hall is a Grade II* listed Georgian Mansion, surrounded by 25 acres of beautifully kept gardens and woodland and 7 acres of professionally levelled playing fields. The school has its own Chapel, hard tennis courts, indoor heated swimming pool, gymnasium/theatre and science laboratory. Situated on the edge of Cannock Chase, this rural setting provides children with a happy and safe environment in which to learn.

Pupils are prepared for all Independent Schools and many Scholarships have been won.

There is a teaching staff of 12, with visiting teachers for violin, brass instruments and guitar. A specialist Drama Teacher teaches Performing Arts to a highly proficient standard.

The Craft, Design and Technology Centre incorporates metal work and metal casting, carpentry, pottery, enamelling, jewellery making, computers, art and stone polishing.

Tennis, Rugby, Cricket, Rounders, Hockey, Netball and Volleyball are played in season.

The Headmistress is personally responsible for the health and welfare of the children. Individual care is taken of each child and good manners and consideration for others insisted upon. An acknowledged feature of the School is its family atmosphere.

For further particulars, please contact the School Office.

St Bede's Preparatory School

Duke's Drive, Eastbourne, East Sussex BN20 7XL
Tel: 01323 734222
Fax: 01323 746438
e-mail: prep.school@stbedesschool.org

website: www.stbedesschool.org

Co-educational day and boarding school with Nursery and Pre-Prep departments.

Chairman of Governors: Anthony Meier, CB, OBE

Headmaster: Nicholas Bevington, BA Hons

Deputy Head: Gordon Ferguson, BSc Hons

Age Range. 3 months–13 years Co-educational.
Number of Pupils. 392: Prep 270 (176 boys, 94 girls), Pre-Prep 59, Nursery 63. Boarders: 20 boys, 10 girls.
Fees per term (2010-2011). Boarding £2,070 (in addition to Tuition); Tuition: Prep £3,535–£4,425, Pre-Prep £2,695. Nursery Prices per session.

St Bede's, founded in 1895, is situated in Eastbourne, on the South Coast with spectacular views of the sea. It takes five minutes to reach the beach from the school and the principal playing fields are in a wide natural hollow nestling in the South Downs.

Boarders sleep in cosy bedrooms in a house that has a real family feel and are looked after by dedicated and caring staff. Both winter and summer weekends are filled with an exciting variety of activities and special celebrations take place on the children's birthdays.

Pupils are prepared for Common Entrance and the more able are tutored to sit scholarships to independent senior schools. Approximately 98% of pupils choose to continue their education at St Bede's Senior School (*see HMC section entry*).

St Bede's offers academic, sport, music, dance, art and drama scholarships and bursaries for children from the ages of 9 to 12 years.

Pupils from the age of 4 are given Information Technology lessons at least once a week in a Computer Centre which is constantly updated to keep at the forefront of educational technology. French and Music, Short Tennis and other Sports are also introduced to children in this age group.

New science laboratories and classrooms were opened four years ago. In September 2009 a beautiful new building overlooking the sea and housing new kitchens and dining room and eight new classrooms opened.

February 2010 saw the Nursery and Pre-Prep moving into bespoke accommodation and since September 2009 the Nursery has operated for 50 weeks a year with a holiday club for Pre-Prep pupils operating outside of term time. Babies from three months old can join the Nursery.

The Art and Design and Technology Departments are both very strong, opening for after-school activities to encourage young talent. Music also plays an important role at St Bede's. There is a thriving orchestra and the majority of pupils learn one or more instruments, with children as young as six playing in recorder groups. Informal concerts take place during the school year and there are also several choirs.

Drama forms an integral part of the school. The Pre-Prep produces a Christmas play and there are frequent productions throughout the year for older children to take part in. From age 7 some children join the Legat Junior Dance programme. Entry is by audition.

Sport at St Bede's is taken seriously. Boys play soccer, rugby, hockey, cricket, tennis and athletics and the major sports for girls are netball, hockey, rounders, athletics, cricket and tennis. All the pupils use the indoor 20-metre swimming pool. The fixture list is very comprehensive and, whilst the top teams enjoy a high standard of coaching and performance, special emphasis is placed on ensuring that the other teams also have the opportunity to play matches against other schools. The Matt Sports Hall covers two indoor tennis courts and is used to house a huge variety of sports. Wet weather activities include badminton, basketball and table tennis.

There is a Learning Support department staffed by qualified learning support staff which can cater for pupils who require additional or particular support. The school also has an EAL centre which is run by highly trained and experienced staff. Gifted children are placed on a Curriculum Enhancement Programme to maximise their potential.

On Monday and Thursday afternoons and every evening after school the pupils are encouraged to participate in an extensive range of activities. In all there are over fifty activities on offer each week which range from fencing to cookery and basketball to art master classes. Day pupils who stay late for activities enjoy supper with the boarders and often sleep over a few nights each week.

The school runs a comprehensive coach and minibus service locally and transport to and from Gatwick and Heathrow airports is arranged by the transport department.

Entry to St Bede's is by interview.

Charitable status. St Bede's School Trust Sussex is a Registered Charity, number 278950. It exists to provide education for boys and girls.

St Benedict's Junior School

5 Montpelier Avenue, Ealing, London W5 2XP
Tel: 020 8862 2050
Fax: 020 8862 2058
e-mail: jssecretary@stbenedicts.org.uk
website: www.stbenedicts.org.uk

Governing Body:
The Abbot & Community of Ealing Abbey, assisted by a lay Advisory Body.

Headmaster: **Mr R G Simmons**, BA Hons, PGCE

Age Range. Boys and Girls 3–11.
Number of Pupils. 304.
Fees per term (2011-2012). £3,620.

Our ethos is firmly based in the Benedictine Catholic tradition, and the pastoral and spiritual care of our pupils is central to all that we do. It is the School's mission to '*teach a way of living*' that goes beyond the acquisition of formal academic qualifications and ensures a holistic approach to education from the Nursery through to Sixth Form. Boys and Girls enjoy the very best of a Catholic independent education, with strong links maintained with the monastic community of Ealing Abbey.

St Benedict's provides a stimulating academic education within a broad, balanced and progressive curriculum. Great importance is placed on achievements in Art, Design Technology, Drama, Information and Communications Technology, Music and Sport. In addition, we offer a wide range of co-curricular activities, including Choir and Orchestra, Dance, Eco Gardening, Fencing, Ju Jitsu, and Swimming. High-quality teaching, exceptional pastoral care, small classes and a broad curriculum ensure that all pupils have the opportunity to achieve their potential. Interactive whiteboards are present in every classroom and the Library is very well-resourced.

Girls and boys are taught together throughout their time at St Benedict's (3–18), with the exception of traditional single-sex sports. Specialist teachers provide tuition in French, Information and Computing Technology, Science, Music and Art Design Technology. Excellent academic results across the School are matched by equally impressive value-added scores, reflecting the strong and effective partnership between pupils, parents and the staff. We rejoice in the successes of all of our pupils.

The natural points of entry in the Junior School and Nursery are at 3+, 4+ and 7+. Entry is possible at other ages subject to the availability of places.

Charitable status. St Benedict's is a Registered Charity, number 242715.

St Bernard's Preparatory School

Hawtrey Close, Slough, Berkshire SL1 1TB
Tel: 01753 521821
Fax: 01753 552364
e-mail: registrar@stbernardsprep.org
website: www.stbernardsprep.org

Headmistress: **Mrs M B Smith**, CertEd, NPQH

Age Range. 2½–11 co-educational.
Number of Pupils. 220.
Fees per term (2010-2011). £2,030–£2,500.

St Bernard's Preparatory has a unique ethos. We are a Catholic school, teaching the Catholic faith and living out the Gospel values which are shared by all faiths and are the foundation of all our relationships and the daily life of our school. We welcome and embrace children of all faiths and we recognise and celebrate our similarities and differences, developing mutual respect, understanding and tolerance.

We recognise the value and uniqueness of each individual, both child and adult. We celebrate the talents and gifts of each child and enable them to develop to their full potential spiritually, morally, academically, socially and physically. Our children are happy, courteous, confident, articulate young citizens, committed to the ideal of service to others.

We work in partnership with parents, recognising that they are the first and best educators of their child. We consider ourselves to be very privileged that parents have entrusted us with the care and education of their child. We ensure that parents are kept fully informed of their child's progress.

We are committed to offering a broad, balanced, creative and challenging curriculum, enriched by experiences and opportunities which enhance and consolidate the learning process. Small class sizes enable our team of highly qualified, caring, committed and enthusiastic teachers to be responsive to the needs of the individual child ensuring continuity and progression for all our children. We have developed a wide and varied range of after-school activities which broaden the curriculum and enrich the children's lives. Children are encouraged to develop new skills.

We are proud of our reputation as a school with a strong ethos and nurturing pastoral care coupled with academic excellence reflected in consistently outstanding results in local and national tests.

Our school motto 'Dieu Mon Abri' meaning 'God is my Shelter', is an inspiring reminder of God's love for each one of us. The three swords represent 'Love, Work and Prayer' which underpin and permeate the life of our school.

St Catherine's Preparatory School

Bramley, Guildford, Surrey GU5 0DF
Tel: 01483 899665; Senior School: 01483 893363
Fax: 01483 899669
e-mail: schooloffice@stcatherines.info
website: www.stcatherines.info

Chairman of the Governing Body: Mr Peter J Martin, BA, FRGS, FCCA

Headmistress: Mrs Alice Phillips, MA Cantab

Head of Preparatory School: **Mrs Kathleen Jefferies**,
BSc Bridgewater, Massachusetts, PGCE
From January 2012: Miss Naomi Bartholomew, MA
London, BEd Cantab

Age Range. 4–11.
Number of Pupils. 260 Day Girls.
Fees per term (from January 2011). Pre-Prep 1 £2,350,
Pre-Prep 2 £2,845, Pre-Prep 3 £3,355; Prep School £3,965.

Girls are accepted from the age of 4 to 11 when they take
the Entrance Examinations for entry to Senior Schools.

Charitable status. St Catherine's School Bramley is a
Registered Charity, number 1070858, which exists to provide education for girls in accordance with the principles of
the Church of England.

St Cedd's School

178 New London Road, Chelmsford, Essex CM2 0AR
Tel: 01245 354380/392810
Fax: 01245 348635/392815
e-mail: info@stcedds.org.uk
website: www.stcedds.org.uk

Chairman of Governors: Mr L Bartle

Head: **Dr P A Edmonds**, EdD, MEd, BEd Hons

Deputy Head: Mr A J Lowe-Wheeler, BA, CertEd, Cert
ICT, AICTT

Age Range. 3–11 Co-educational.
Number of Pupils. 463+ Day.
Fees per term (2011-2012). £2,440–£2,625 including
lunch.

St Cedd's School, founded in 1931, exists to provide independent education for boys and girls of 3–11. The school
prides itself on combining a traditional emphasis on literacy
and numeracy with a broad and balanced curriculum.

PE, Music, Art, French, Swimming and Recorders appear
on the timetable from Year 2, International Studies is taught
in Years 5 and 6, and Spanish is introduced in Year 6. Music
is a particular strength. The school has links with Chelmsford Cathedral, where the choir performs at Choral Evensong twice a term, and is a member of the Chelmsford
Choral Foundation.

The grounded confidence the pupils have as a result of
differentiated teaching and learning in a happy and supported environment, where children have fun and are
encouraged to take risks, results in great personal achievements across the expansive academic curriculum. This is
supplemented by a wonderful programme of sport, drama
and art. Such provision leads to successful entry and excellent preparation for scholarships to pupils' first-choice
schools, whether that is within the state or independent sector or grammar school entry.

Breakfast Club from 07.30–08.10 and a thriving after-
school club until 18.15 provide wrap-around care.

Charitable status. St Cedd's School Educational Trust
Ltd is a Registered Charity, number 310865. It exists to provide education for boys and girls.

Saint Christina's RC Preparatory School

25 St Edmund's Terrace, London NW8 7PY
Tel: 020 7722 8784
Fax: 020 7586 4961
e-mail: secretary@saintchristinas.org.uk

website: www.saintchristinas.org.uk

Headteacher: **Miss Nathalie Clyne Wilson**, BA Hons,
PGCE

Age Range. Girls 3–11, Boys 3–7.
Number of Pupils. 162 girls, 50 boys.
Fees per term (2011-2012). £3,075 (inclusive).

Saint Christina's was founded in 1949 by the Handmaids
of the Sacred Heart of Jesus. At Saint Christina's, children
experience the joy of learning and the wonder of God and
His Creation. Our purpose at Saint Christina's is to create an
environment where children enjoy learning and where each
individual experiences respect and acceptance enabling
them to become the balanced person they are called to be.

As a School we take pride in the excellent examination
results which we achieve. We value most of all our strong
sense of community. We seek to ensure that children feel
appreciated for themselves as individuals as much as their
achievements. We believe that confidence can only grow in
an atmosphere of trust and safety.

Boys are prepared for entrance tests for day and boarding
schools.

Girls are prepared for Common Entrance Examination
and entrance exams to day and boarding schools.

The School is purpose built in a pleasant location within
a short walk of Primrose Hill and Regent's Park. Prospective
parents are warmly invited to visit the School.

Charitable status. Saint Christina's is a Registered Charity, number 221319.

St Christopher's School
Hampstead

32 Belsize Lane, Hampstead, London NW3 5AE
Tel: 020 7435 1521
Fax: 020 7431 6694
e-mail: admissions@st-christophers.hampstead.sch.uk
website: www.st-christophers.hampstead.sch.uk

Preparatory school for girls.

Chairman of Governors: Graham Hinton, BSc, MIPA

Headmistress: **Mrs S A West**, BA, PGCE, MEd

Deputy Headmistress: Mrs C Carty

Age Range. 4–11.
Number of Girls. 235 Day Pupils.
Fees per term (2010-2011). £3,723 inclusive of lunch
and all outings, except residential.

The School employs a fully qualified teaching staff of 16
full-time, 6 part-time, and 7 peripatetic music teachers.
Strong emphasis is placed on music. There are three choirs,
quartets, ensembles and 2 orchestras; instrumental lessons
are arranged within the school timetable. Whilst maintaining
high standards in numeracy and literacy, the curriculum provides a wide range of subjects including art, science, computer studies, design and technology, French, Spanish,
drama, chess, gymnastics and games.

Extra-curricular activities over the year include art,
dance, debating, drama, football, gym, language, Mandarin,
netball, science, sewing, striking/fielding games and yoga.

All applicants are assessed for entry. 100% means-tested
scholarships are available, as well as 50% bursaries. The
girls are prepared for entrance examinations to the major
London day schools and for 11+ Common Entrance to
boarding schools.

Charitable status. St Christopher's School (Hampstead)
Limited is a Registered Charity, number 312999. It exists to
provide education for girls.

St Christopher's School
Hove

33 New Church Road, Hove, East Sussex BN3 4AD
Tel: 01273 735404
Fax: 01273 747956
e-mail: hmsec@stchristophershove.org.uk
website: www.stchristophershove.org.uk

Chairman of Governors: Mr A J Symonds, FCIS

Headmaster: **Mr C J Wheeler**, BA Hons, PGCE

Age Range. 4–13 co-educational.
Number of Pupils. 230.
Fees per term (2011-2012). £2,300–£3,319.

Since its foundation in 1927, St Christopher's School has expanded to become a highly successful academic preparatory school, located in the middle of Brighton & Hove, England's youngest and most vibrant city.

St Christopher's School aims to provide a traditional academic education within a supportive family environment where individual talents are developed to produce confident, articulate and well-balanced children. Pupils regularly obtain top academic scholarships and awards for art, music, drama and sport. St Christopher's is a Member of the Brighton College Family of Schools and 11+ Continuation Scholarships to Brighton College are available.

Entry to the School is virtually non-selective at 4+ and by examination and interview at 8+ and 11+. Places are occasionally available in other age groups. In the Lower School, pupils are taught mainly by their form teachers. Particular emphasis is placed upon reading, writing and mathematics, but the curriculum is broad and a wide range of subjects is taught by specialist teachers, including French, Mandarin, Latin, science, music, art, ICT, PE and games.

Pupils move into the Middle School in Year 4, where the curriculum reflects the syllabuses of the Common Entrance and Brighton College Academic Scholarship Examinations. Formal homework is introduced at this stage. In the Upper School (Years 7 and 8), all subjects are taught by specialists, who make full use of the interactive ICT suite, music technology suite, science laboratory, art studio and library. A variety of educational day trips, an annual residential visit to France and sports trips ensure that children receive a broad and stimulating educational experience.

In addition to football, netball and rounders, the School has an enviable record of success at rugby at local and county level. The musical life of St Christopher's is enriched by three choirs and the choice of a wide variety of instrumental and vocal tuition. A wide range of extra-curricular activities is on offer. After-school care is available until 5.30 pm each evening.

The Headmaster is always delighted to welcome prospective parents. Please contact the Registrar to arrange a visit.

Charitable status. St Christopher's School, Hove is a member of the Brighton College Family of Schools, which is a Registered Charity, number 307061.

St Columba's College Preparatory School

King Harry Lane, St Albans, Hertfordshire AL3 4AW
Tel: 01727 862616
Fax: 01727 892025
e-mail: headofprep@st-columbas.herts.sch.uk
website: www.stcolumbascollege.org

Chairman: Mrs G Cummings, JP

Head: **Mrs R Loveman**, BSc

Age Range. 4–11.
Number of Pupils. 255 Boys.
Fees per term (2011-2012). Prep 4–6 £3,360, Prep 3 £3,065, Reception–Prep 2 £2,898 including personal accident insurance. Additional charges are made for coaches and consumables.

The Prep School is an academically selective Catholic Day School which strives to create a welcoming community in which each boy is valued as an individual and endeavours to promote positive relationships based on mutual respect and understanding. There is a rigorous academic curriculum with an extensive range of extra curricular opportunities. A full curriculum and sports programme is offered at Key Stage 1 and 2.

Admissions at age 4 and 7 years. Entry requirements of the school is by assessment; at age 7+ assessment is via maths, mental arithmetic, perceptual reasoning, creative writing and reading; at age 4 assessment takes place informally using a standardised test and in context in a classroom situation. Subjects include: English, Mathematics, Science, Drama, RE, French, History, Geography, IT, PE, Games, Music, Art and Design Technology.

Examinations: Pupils progress at 11+ to St Columba's College on the same site, or to other senior schools.

Academic facilities include: modern form rooms with specialist facilities for Science, IT, ADT, Music, PE, Games, RE and French, and a professionally staffed extensive library.

Sports facilities include: Rugby/Football pitches, Cricket nets and square. There is access to a swimming pool and athletics track.

There are means-tested bursaries at Prep level and a number of scholarships available to Prep School boys on entry to St Columba's College. These include academic and music scholarships.

(*See also St Columba's College entry in HMC section.*)

Charitable status. St Columba's College is a Registered Charity, number 1088480. It exists to provide a well-rounded Roman Catholic education for pupils from 4–18 years of age.

St Dunstan's College Junior School

Stanstead Road, London SE6 4TY
Tel: 020 8516 7225
Fax: 020 8516 7300; 020 8516 7399 (Bursary)
e-mail: rscard@sdmail.org.uk
website: www.stdunstans.org.uk

Chairman of Governors: ¶Sir Paul Judge

Head of Junior School: **Miss J H Bate**

Age Range. Co-educational 3–11.
Number of Pupils. Pre-Preparatory (3–7) 120, Preparatory (7–11) 130.
Fees per term (2011-2012). Nursery £2,561, Pre-Preparatory £3,261, Preparatory £3,479–£4,263. Fees include lunch.

The Junior School is an integral part of St Dunstan's College and prepares boys and girls for the Senior School (age 11–18) (*see entry in HMC section*). It shares with it a common site and many facilities. In particular the Music Centre, Refectory, Great Hall, Sports Hall, indoor Swimming Pool and playing fields increase the opportunities for all pupils in curricular and extra-curricular activities. For other work the Junior School pupils have their own buildings. The Pre-Preparatory Department is located in a Victorian house which has been beautifully converted for the specific needs of the 3–7 year olds. The Preparatory Department has its own teaching area with a library, ICT Suite, art room and activity room.

We provide an excellent all-round education with special emphasis upon the development of a high level of literacy and numeracy. The curriculum is also designed to promote learning and appreciation of Science, Humanities, Music, Art, Design and Technology, Information Technology, Drama, Languages and Study Skills. Games and Physical Education play an important part in the growth and development of each pupil and the children follow an extensive programme of activities. The children's learning is enhanced by a variety of visits and residential school journeys.

Boys and girls are encouraged to take part in various clubs and activities after school hours and at lunch times. Opportunities range from music, art and sport groups to ICT and drama.

A caring and friendly environment is provided by small class sizes and a dedicated team of well-qualified class teachers and support staff. In addition to being taught many subjects by their class teacher, Preparatory Department pupils have the advantage of being educated by specialists in Art, Music, Languages, Physical Education and Games.

An effective strong partnership exists between the home and school and parents are encouraged to participate in their children's education and the life of the Junior School. Regular contact is maintained between school and the home to ensure that parents are aware of their child's academic and social progress.

Boys and Girls are admitted at all ages from 3+ to 10+ but principally at 3+ and 4+ (Nursery and Reception) and at 7+ (Year 3).

Charitable status. St Dunstan's Educational Foundation is a Registered Charity, number 312747. It exists to provide education for boys and girls.

St Edmund's Junior School
Canterbury

Canterbury, Kent CT2 8HU
Tel: 01227 475600
Fax: 01227 471083
e-mail: juniorschool@stedmunds.org.uk
website: www.stedmunds.org.uk

Chairman of Governors: M C W Terry, FCA

Master of the Junior School: R G Bacon, BA Durham

Age Range. 3–13.
Numbers of Pupils. 262 (Boarders: School House 15, Choir House 30); Day Pupils: Boys 128, Girls 89.
Fees per term (2011-2012). Junior School: Boarders £6,185, Weekly Boarders £5,636, Choristers £6,084, Day pupils £4,333. Pre-Prep: Forms 1 & 2 £3,070, Reception £2,656, Nursery £2,163 (mornings only £1,215).

Pupils may enter at any age from 3 to 12. Boarding begins at the age of 8.

The Junior School is closely linked with the Senior School (*see entry in HMC section*) but is run as a separate entity, working to the Common Entrance Examination and Independent Schools Scholarship Examination. The Junior School uses some Senior School specialist staff, particularly in the teaching of Science, Music, Art, Technology and shares with the Senior School such amenities as the Chapel, concert theatre, sports hall and swimming pool. There is a full-time school Chaplain. Domestic arrangements, including health and catering, are under centralised administration.

The Canterbury Cathedral Choristers, who are St Edmund's pupils, live in the Choir House which is under the care of a married Housemaster and is situated in the precincts of Canterbury Cathedral.

Scholarships and bursaries. Academic, music, drama, sport, and all-rounder awards are available for applicants aged 11. Cathedral choristerships are available for boys from age 7. Fee concessions are also available as detailed in the Senior School entry in HMC section.

Charitable status. St Edmund's School Canterbury is a Registered Charity, number 1056382. It exists to educate the children in its care.

St Edmund's School

Portsmouth Road, Hindhead, Surrey GU26 6BH
Tel: 01428 609875
Fax: 01428 607898
e-mail: registrar@saintedmunds.co.uk
website: www.saintedmunds.co.uk

Chairman of Governors: Mrs J Alliss

Headmaster: **A J Walliker**, MA Cantab, MBA, PGCE

Age Range. Boys and Girls 2–13.
Number of Pupils. Prep School: Flexi Boarders and Day Pupils 159. Pre-Prep and Nursery: 80.
Fees per term (2010-2011). Prep: Day Pupils £3,859–£4,879; Weekly Boarding Fee £995; Pre-Prep £2,871; Nursery from £632 (two mornings).

The fees are inclusive of all ordinary extras, laundry, games, swimming, lectures, optional Saturday activities etc.

St Edmund's, the 132 year-old prep school in Hindhead, now welcomes girls from age 2–13. The introduction of girls, which took place in September 2008, has happened with the minimum of disruption and fuss. The Headmaster Adam Walliker comments: "I think the key to it is that our school was always cut out for co-education. We're an intimate, 'family' kind of school. The presence of girls has simply amplified those qualities."

"I like St Ed's. It's a school I fit into." These words, from one of our children, capture much of what we strive to do at St Edmund's: to instil in every child a sense of self-esteem and belonging by building on their own talents, opening their eyes to new ones and giving them focused and personal support whenever it's needed.

Academically, it is an approach that continues to pay dividends, with our pupils going on to wide range of senior schools, both boarding and day. Yet of equal importance are the discoveries, excitements and good old-fashioned fun that St Edmund's creates inside our 40 beautiful acres. These include an immaculate 9-hole golf course, indoor pool and astro pitch, and a wealth of activities ranging from cooking and the chapel choir to campfire building and language master-classes. A thriving and optional Saturday morning school activity programme is allowing us to introduce a greater breadth of ideas and new experiences.

We also offer an unusually flexible boarding option, from one-off nights to regular weekly boarding. Scholarships and means-tested bursaries are available.

Charitable status. St Edmund's School Trust Limited is a Registered Charity, number 278301. Its aim is the education of children.

St Edward's Junior School

London Road, Charlton Kings, Cheltenham, Glos GL52 6NR
Tel: 01242 538900
Fax: 01242 538901

e-mail: headmaster@stedwardsjunior.co.uk
website: www.stedwards.co.uk

Co-educational Day School.

Chairman of Governors: Mr P Walsh

Headmaster: Mr S McKernan, BA Hons, MEd, NPQH

Age Range. 1–11 years.
Number of Pupils. 455.
Fees per term (2011-2012). £1,889–£2,925.

St Edward's Junior School is an independent co-educational Catholic Foundation welcoming pupils of all denominations from 1 to 11 years. We provide a supportive family atmosphere in which pupils are encouraged to develop their individual potential – academic, social, physical, creative and spiritual – in preparation for their secondary education. The school is situated on the edge of Cheltenham in forty acres of beautiful parkland. Our facilities are truly exceptional and give our pupils opportunities for practical experience rarely available in a junior school, as well as enabling us to provide an unusually wide range of after-school activities.

Our Kindergarten is open all year round and provides a secure and stimulating introduction to school life.

St Edward's Junior School has established an excellent relationship with the local community and with many regional and national organisations through the leasing and lending of its buildings and grounds to a miscellany of educational, religious, cultural, social and sports clubs, groups and organisations.

The facilities at both Schools are available throughout the year both during term time and holiday periods.

Charitable status. St Edward's School is a Registered Charity, number 293360. It exists to provide for the education of children of any creed with preference to those who are of the Roman Catholic faith.

St Edward's School

64 Tilehurst Road, Reading, Berkshire RG30 2JH
Tel: 0118 957 4342
Fax: 0118 950 3736
e-mail: admin@stedwards.org.uk
website: www.stedwards.org.uk

Chairman of Governors: Mrs S Pellow

Principal: G Mottram, HDipEd SA, MA Ed, NPQH

Vice-Principal: **D A Cumming**, MEd, BA, CertEd

Age Range. 4–13.
Number of Boys. 170 day boys.
Fees per term (2011-2012). £2,380–£3,055. Dayboarding (until 5.55 pm): £575 (Reception, Years 1 & 2), £500 (Years 3–8). There are no compulsory extras.

St Edward's School, situated on the west side of Reading, Berkshire, is a small independent day preparatory school for boys aged 4 to 13, founded in 1947.

St Edward's prides itself on being a small, caring prep school. Traditional values of good manners, respect for others and an excellent understanding of right and wrong make for a very positive environment in which to grow up. Our boys leave us as bright, happy, well-rounded and confident individuals, ready to make the most of their time at their chosen senior school.

The 'Outstanding' Pre-Prep department accepts boys from 4 and offers a caring and positive environment in which children can thrive and learn.

The Prep School's curriculum is broadly based and incorporates the best of the National Curriculum, but we seek to offer more, and in greater depth.

Boys study English, Maths, Science, French, History, Geography, RS, Music, Art, Design Technology, PSE and PE. Drama, Study skills and Latin are optional, depending on year groups.

On entry to the prep school at 7+, the boys are taught for the bulk of the time by one teacher, with specialist teaching for Mathematics, Science, Information Technology, Music, PE and Sport.

In subsequent years the boys are taught exclusively by subject specialists, and are placed in one of two sets within the year group for the core curriculum subjects. Acknowledging the increasing future importance of foreign languages, spoken French is introduced at age 4.

The curriculum also includes *Information and Communications Technology* which is taught as a skill in its own right. The school computers, which are networked together with permanent internet access, are in regular daily use across the curriculum.

The boys are prepared for 13+ entrance to Independent Senior Schools, either by the Common Entrance examination, or by Scholarship. The school has had a fine record of winning Scholarships throughout its history, including success at Reading Grammar School.

St Edward's promotes sound and clearly defined moral values in a learning environment where boys work together enjoying the challenge and rigour of quality teaching. Each child is treated as an individual and strives to achieve their potential whether in academia, sport or the arts.

Charitable status. St Edward's and Highlands School Ltd is a Registered Charity, number 309147.

St Faith's School

Trumpington Road, Cambridge CB2 2AG
Tel: 01223 352073
Fax: 01223 314757
e-mail: info@stfaiths.co.uk
website: www.stfaiths.co.uk

Chair of Governors: Mrs E Mimpriss, CertEd

Headmaster: N L Helliwell, MA, BEd Hons

Deputy Head: Mrs L M Dennis, BEd Southampton

Age Range. 4–13.
Number of Pupils. 536.
Fees per term (2011-2012). £3,245–£4,090.

St Faith's, founded in 1884, is a co-educational day school set in extensive and attractive grounds on the south side of Cambridge, approximately one mile from the city centre. It is situated close to the A10 and M11 and the Park and Ride facilities and operates a school minibus from the Trumpington Road Park and Ride site to the school each morning. Boys and girls enter the school at age 4 and stay until they are 13. Interviews and assessments for places occur throughout the year and scholarships are available at 7+.

St Faith's is very highly regarded in Cambridge. It is valued for the breadth of its curriculum, the attractiveness of its surroundings, the warmth of its family feeling and for the commitment of its staff. The children are encouraged to develop their talents to the full by following a curriculum which is broadly based and rigorous in its requirement. Classes are small. Teaching in the early years is principally class based, while, from Year 5, pupils work with specialist subject teachers. St Faith's prides itself on the pastoral care of the children, which operates through a House-based tutorial system. The school's principal aim is to ensure that the children feel safe, secure and happy. Learning happily is a natural extension of this.

The facilities and educational resources at St Faith's are up to the minute and excellent. The recently completed Keynes building has provided enviable facilities for the teaching of Design and Technology, Information and Communication Technology and Music and the Ashburton building houses science and drama as well as a hall equipped with computer equipment and a mixing desk for sound and lighting. In addition to the excellent sports facilities on site, the school has the use of the nearby Leys Sports Hall and the Astroturf.

St Faith's has an excellent sporting tradition with rugby, netball, hockey, cricket, tennis, rounders, football and athletics being the main outdoor games. Basketball, cross-country running and other games are also organised, but on a less formal basis. Our sports programme involves inter-House competitions and a strong fixture list with numerous matches against other schools. Music and drama are also important at St Faith's and the school has a flourishing music department with the emphasis placed upon enjoyment as well as good performance. Pupils are able to participate in class and whole school concerts and a large number of instrumental groups, choirs and the school orchestra perform regularly. Drama is timetabled for all forms; there are performances of plays or musicals by each Year group throughout the year and the standard of performance is high.

Extra-curricular activities range from chess, reading, art and model making to more energetic sporting pursuits. In addition there are Play Clubs and Multi-Activity Courses during the holidays and team-building activity holidays, language trips and a ski trip for older children. Late Stay facilities operate and families wishing to miss the Cambridge traffic are able to enjoy breakfast in the school's dining room from 07.30 each morning.

St Faith's is part of The Leys and St Faith's Foundation and although each year approximately half of the children move on to The Leys at the end of Year 8, others prepare for entry to a variety of schools, mainly independent, many of them with scholarships.

Charitable status. The Leys and St Faith's Schools Foundation is a Registered Charity, number 311436. The aim of the charity is the provision of first-class education.

St Francis School

Marlborough Road, Pewsey, Wilts SN9 5NT
Tel: 01672 563228
Fax: 01672 564323
e-mail: admissions@st-francis.wilts.sch.uk
website: www.st-francis.wilts.sch.uk

Chair of Governors: Mrs S Soar

Headmaster: B L Brown, MA, BA Hons, PGCE

Age Range. 2–13.
Number of Boys and Girls. 265: 144 Boys, 121 Girls.
Fees per term (2010-2011). Reception–Year 8: £2,196–£3,267 including lunch. Nursery £219 per session.

St Francis is a charitable trust with a board of governors that includes The Deputy Head of Marlborough College. The School is situated in the lovely Vale of Pewsey some five miles south of Marlborough. Its grounds border the Kennet and Avon Canal.

The School is co-educational and takes children from the age of 2 to 13. It is a day school with pupils travelling from a wide area of mid-Wiltshire; a daily minibus service operates from Marlborough and Devizes.

Small classes giving every child the opportunity to fulfil his or her full potential are a feature of the school. Staff ensure that they are very positive and encouraging in their teaching. Should a child be found to need some form of spe-

cific learning assistance then appropriate help will be given. The facilities are constantly being improved. The new Burden Block comes with Library, Design Technology room, specialist rooms for English, French and Geography, as well as three new form rooms.

The curriculum is delightfully diverse enabling the pupils to have, for instance, CDT, Pottery, Drama, Computing and Swimming all in their normal weekly timetable. French is taught from the age of three. The majority of the pupils take up individual musical tuition and a wide range of instruments is available. Latin is an option in senior school.

Results are excellent. The pupils are mainly entered for the local senior schools, St Mary's Calne, Godolphin, Dauntsey's, Marlborough College, Stonar and Warminster, but scholarships and common entrance are also taken for boarding schools further afield. Awards are regularly achieved to all of the aforementioned.

Please write, telephone or fax for a prospectus, or ask to visit and tour round the school. The Headmaster will be happy to oblige.

Charitable status. St Francis is a Registered Charity, number 298522. It exists solely to provide education for boys and girls.

St Gabriel's School
Junior Department

Sandleford Priory, Newbury, Berkshire RG20 9BD
Tel: 01635 555680
Fax: 01635 555698
e-mail: info@stgabriels.co.uk
website: www.stgabriels.co.uk

Chairman: Mr N Garland, BSc Hons

Principal: **Mr A Jones**, LTCL, LWCMD

Head of Junior Department: **Mr P Dove**, BA Hons, PGCE

Age Range. Girls 3–11, Boys 3–7.
Number of Pupils. 180.
Fees per term (2011-2012). £3,085–£3,640.

The Pre-Prep and Junior departments at St Gabriel's are situated adjacent to the Senior School in 54 acres of parkland on the southern outskirts of Newbury.

Girls are accepted from the age of 3 to 11 years and boys from 3 to 7 years. Entry to the Pre-Prep Department is non-selective. Entry to the Junior Department is by assessment. Maximum class size is 20 pupils.

The majority of girls progress through to the Senior School at the age of 11, at which point entry is by entrance examination and interview. (*For further information about the Senior School, see St Gabriel's School entry in GSA section.*)

Subjects taught in the Junior Department include English, Mathematics, Science, Art, Drama, Humanities (History, Geography), ICT, Modern Foreign Languages (French, Spanish, Italian, Mandarin), Music, PE, Religious Studies, Technology (Textiles, Food Technology, Design Technology) and Thinking Skills.

The excellent range of facilities includes a multi-discipline sports hall, digital theatre, dance studio, junior science laboratory and library. All Junior Department ICT lessons take place in the state of the art ICT and MFL block.

Sport plays an important and integral role in the life of the school and there is a comprehensive fixtures list for each year group. Gymnastics, Dance, Netball, Hockey, Cross-Country, Tennis, Rounders and Athletics are included in the curriculum for all pupils. Swimming takes place during the Summer Term in the outdoor heated swimming pool.

Music holds an equally high profile. As well as curriculum Music lessons, there is a wide range of extra-curricular music-making for all pupils with an interest in the subject. Many pupils learn instruments in school and they are given numerous opportunities to perform at concerts ranging from informal lunchtime events to major end-of-term extravaganzas.

In addition, pupils are offered a wide range of extra-curricular activities, including Ballet, Climbing, Cricket, Drama, Creative Writing, ICT Club, German, Cookery, Samba, Binca, Puppet Making, Painting on glass, Jazz Dance, Chess, Bridge, Art Club, Recorder, Choir, Training Orchestra, Music Theory, Gym Club, Film Making Club, Gardening Club and Science Club.

Charitable status. The St Gabriel Schools Foundation is a Registered Charity, number 1062748. It exists to provide education for girls from age 3–11 and for boys from age 3–7.

St George's College Junior School

Thames Street, Weybridge, Surrey KT13 8NL
Tel: 01932 839400
Fax: 01932 839401
e-mail: JSHead@st-georges-college.co.uk
website: www.st-georges-college.co.uk

Chairman of Board of Governors: Mrs K Quint

Headmaster: **A J W Hudson**, MA Cantab, PGCE, NPQH

Age Range. 3–11.
Number of Pupils. 590.
Fees per term (2011-2012). Nursery: £1,350 (mornings only); £2,200 (full days). Reception–Year 2 £2,550; Years 3–6 £3,500. Lunches £210.

St George's College Junior School is a fully co-ed Roman Catholic Day School and all pupils attending the Junior School normally belong to one of the mainstream Christian traditions. The School was established in 1950 by a Religious Order of Priests and Brothers known as "The Josephites" who maintain a keen interest in the future of the School. Only pupils who are aged three are admitted into the Nursery.

While the majority of the pupils at the school come from around North Surrey, some 13% of the pupils are from countries as far away as Australia, New Zealand, Hong Kong, South Africa, Brazil, Canada, USA as well as from most European countries including Russia. The School operates a very extensive bus service and an option for parents using cars to drop off their children at either the Junior or Senior School.

In September 2000 the Junior School moved from its previous co-located site with St George's College one mile down the road to its present 12½ acre site on the outskirts of Weybridge close to the River Thames. Since then a £1.5 million refurbishment programme has been completed involving the upgrading of most of the classrooms, the science teaching room, the library, the music room, playground equipment, an Astroturf pitch, cricket nets and the creation of a school wide computer network including two computer resources rooms, one with 25 computers with an interactive whiteboard which is networked, as well as three other rooms, each with 10 networked computers. In 2006, a new Development Launch has focused on providing a new 'state of the art' Nursery classroom (now complete), and a totally refurbished Kitchen and Dining Area, called 'The Mulberry Hall', opened in January 2008.

The Junior School has a genuinely happy atmosphere in which every pupil is respected and treated as an individual. The headmaster considers the staff, pupils and parents to be constituent parts of an extended family. The School has always placed great emphasis on the importance of maintaining excellent channels of communication between members of staff, parents and pupils.

The size of classes ensures that the School is a learning community by creating the correct balance between pupil interaction and pupil-teacher contact. The pupils in the top two years of the School are taught by subject specialists. French is offered to all pupils from Year 1. The School was described in its recent ISI report (2011) as having pupils whose "personal qualities are excellent and the emphasis on promoting the values of the Josephite tradition results in pupils who are well mannered, polite and welcoming".

All pupils are assessed on entry and when they leave at the end of Year 6 nearly all transfer to St George's College. Over 150 scholarships, including music scholarships, have been won by pupils in Year Six since 1989.

While the pursuit of academic excellence is highly valued, the Mission Statement of the School stresses the importance of pupils having high personal self-esteem as well as emphasising the importance of their religious, spiritual, social and physical development. The School requires its pupils to have high moral values especially those of its school motto "Honesty and Compassion".

The Junior School has four Houses which compete against each other across a wide range of activities inside and outside the classroom including Music, Public Speaking and Chess.

Extra-curricular and other enrichment activities are, likewise, considered to play an important role in the educational development of children. The extensive range of activities includes dance (ballet, modern and tap), gymnastics and clubs based on the academic subjects taught in the School, for example the Young Scientist Club. Pupils are taken to places of educational interest regularly including theatre, music and art trips and there is an annual book week during which pupils meet and listen to visiting authors and storytellers.

Considerable emphasis is placed on the Creative and Performing Arts. Pupils have dance lessons throughout the school with specialist ballet and tap dance lessons being a compulsory part of curriculum for all pupils up to the end of Year Reception. The School stages six major drama productions a year. All children from Year 2 have two lessons of music each week. Children in Year 2 learn the violin and recorder as part of the music curriculum. There is an Orchestra, Jazz Band, Chapel Choir and Year 3 Choir which rehearse on a weekly basis as well as Violin, Brass, Guitar and Recorder ensembles. Individual music lessons are very popular with about 50% of the children in Years 2–6 learning at least one additional instrument. Concerts happen at least once every term. The School has recently invested in the provision of a newly refurbished music room; as a result, music lessons are now supported by the use of the latest computer-based technology. Pupils have achieved considerable success at Public Speaking Competitions and achieve a very high level of attainment in their external Spoken English, Lamda and instrumental music exams.

Apart from its own sports facilities on site comprising an artificial sports pitch, netball and tennis courts, a sprung floor gymnasium and a swimming pool, the School has the use of 20 acres of outstanding sports facilities at the College including three floodlit netball/tennis courts, a floodlit artificial surface for hockey about to be completely refurbished, a four-court indoor tennis centre, three floodlit French clay courts, a sports hall and gym, three cricket squares, a tartan athletics track and six large grass fields.

The Under 9 boys' mini-rugby team won the National Prep School finals in 2003 and 2009; in 2008 they got through to the semi-finals. The Under 10 rugby team got through to the semi-finals of the National Prep Schools Finals in 2004 and into the Nationals again, as U11s, in 2005 as did their successors in 2006. The School has reached the Under 11 Boys National Mini-Hockey Finals 11 times since

1989, becoming National Champions of England six times and runners-up three times. The girls won the Under 11 National Mini-Hockey Finals in 2000 and came fourth overall in 2006 and 2008. They also won the IAPS National Hockey Championships in 2002, 2003 and were South East Champions in 2007; in 2008 and 2009 they became South of England champions. The girls reached the Under 11 IAPS Netball Finals in 2000 and 2011 and came third in 2004; they also got through to the Netball Nationals in 2006 and 2008. Tennis and Fencing are very popular Saturday morning activities. The School organises a major netball tournament for girls and a tennis festival for boys each year. There is an annual residential outward bound adventure holiday for the pupils in Year Six.

School lunches are compulsory from Reception Year, are prepared on site and eaten in the dining rooms which can seat 320 people. The School offers a free supervised homework facility each weekday evening during term time until 4.45 pm for those children in Reception and Years 1 and 2. Children in Years 3–6 can sign up for clubs which continue until 5.00 pm.

For the last few years the school has usually had more applications for places than it can accommodate in all year groups. When vacancies do occur, pupils are admitted if they meet the School's entry criteria and successfully complete an assessment day at the School as well as receiving a satisfactory report from the current school where this is appropriate. Priority is afforded to siblings and Roman Catholics.

Charitable status. St George's College, Weybridge is a Registered Charity, number 1017853. The aims and objectives of the charity are the Christian education of young people.

St George's School

Windsor Castle, Windsor, Berks SL4 1QF
Tel: 01753 865553
Fax: 01753 842093
e-mail: enqs@stgwindsor.co.uk
website: www.stgwindsor.co.uk

Patron: Her Majesty The Queen

Visitor: The Lord Chancellor

Chairman of the Governors: The Dean of Windsor

Headmaster: **A A Salmond Smith**, BA Hons, PGCE

Age Range. 3–13 Co-educational.
Number of Pupils. 400 (30 boarders).
Fees per term (2011-2012). Boarders £5,850–£6,005, Day Pupils £3,930–£4,405, Choristers (Boarding) £2,830, Pre-Prep £2,655–£3,011, Nursery £1,115–£1,385.

St George's School was established as part of the foundation of the Order of the Garter in 1348 when provision was made for the education of the first choristers. In 1893 the School moved into the Georgian building of the former College of the Naval Knights of Windsor situated between the mound of the Castle and the Home Park. Expansion followed with the admission of supernumerary (non-chorister) pupils. Extensions were made to the buildings in 1988 and 1996, the latter of which allowed for the opening of a Pre-Preparatory Department and Nursery. Girls were admitted to the School for the first time, entering both the Pre-Prep and the main School. A new Middle School building was opened in Spring 2006.

St George's School boasts a long tradition of musical and academic excellence alongside lively art and drama. It is well equipped for games having beautiful playing fields in the Home Park, an indoor swimming pool, a tennis and netball court and gymnasium. The whole School building has undergone a recent refurbishment which has included the creation of a Design and Technology Workshop and the updating of an Information Technology Room fully on line.

The School pursues the highest standards whilst retaining a relaxed and friendly atmosphere. There is a strong sense of pastoral care and a high pupil staff ratio. Communications are excellent: two stations, the M25, M3, M4 and M40 are all close by and Heathrow is just twenty minutes away.

Charitable status. St George's School, Windsor Castle is a Registered Charity, number 1100392. Its purpose is the education, either as boarding or day pupils, of children of pre-preparatory and preparatory school age and of the choristers who maintain the worship in the Queen's Free Chapel of Our Lady, St George and St Edward the Confessor in Windsor Castle.

St Helen's College

Parkway, Hillingdon, Middlesex UB10 9JX
Tel: 01895 234371
Fax: 01895 619818
e-mail: info@sthelenscollege.com
website: www.sthelenscollege.com

Headmaster: **Mr D A Crehan**, ARCS, BA, BSc, MSc, CPhys
Headmistress: **Mrs G R Crehan**, BA, MA, PGCE

Age Range. 3–11 co-educational.
Number of Pupils. 350 Day Pupils.
Fees per term (2011-2012). £1,490–£2,455.

The aims of St Helen's are to develop as fully as possible each child's academic potential, to provide a wide, balanced, stimulating and challenging curriculum, and to foster true values and good character based on moral and spiritual principles. The children enjoy a purposeful and happy 'family' atmosphere and are taught by committed professional teachers.

Children are prepared for independent senior schools and local grammar schools, and records of success are very good indeed. In addition to the academic subjects, sport, music and drama play an important part in the lives of the children.

A wide range of extra-curricular activities is offered, and pupils enjoy outings, day and residential, to many places of interest. There is an after-school club and summer school, and a holiday club which runs throughout the year.

St Hilary's School

Holloway Hill, Godalming, Surrey GU7 1RZ
Tel: 01483 416551
Fax: 01483 418325
e-mail: registrar@sthilarysschool.com
website: www.sthilarysschool.com

Chair of Governors: Mrs V J Gillman, DMS, MCMI

Headmistress: **Mrs S Bailes**, BA Hons, MA, PGCE

Age Range. Girls 2–11, Boys 2–7.
Number of Pupils. 270 Day Pupils.
Fees per term (from January 2011). (including lunch) Reception £2,650, Year 1 £2,850, Years 2 £3,350, Years 3 £3,450, Years 4–6 £3,850. Nursery £24 per session (one session being single morning or single afternoon) with lunch extra.

"Overall the quality of the provision is outstanding. Children flourish within the stimulating environment of the nursery. They benefit from their own dedicated base area, but also from spending time with the three and four-year-olds during play and activities. Excellent procedures ensure children's individual needs are met well and all children are included within the wide range of challenging activities. Children benefit from an exceptional outdoor area, which is used as an extension to the indoor learning environment. The nursery has very good systems to ensure consistency and continuous improvement within provision, for example, through regular in-house training opportunities." *Ofsted Early Years Inspection Report, December 2009.*

"The quality of pupils' learning and achievement is excellent. Pupils are well educated; the school fulfils its aim to support and nurture high expectations. Pupils of all abilities achieve highly in all aspects of their learning. They are articulate, show independence of thought and have well-developed literacy skills." *ISI Interim Inspection Report, November 2010.*

The School is situated in beautiful grounds, with an all-weather pitch, brand new indoor sports building, tennis and netball courts, a large playing field and separate quiet play area with a Trim Trail. Use is made of nearby facilities – the sports centre at Prior's Field School and swimming pool at Charterhouse.

In 1927 Miss Marjorie Hiorns founded St Hilary's and it became a Charitable Trust in 1966 with a board of Governors. The Headmistress is an active member of IAPS (The Independent Association of Prep Schools), an organization which guarantees high standards for parents.

As Headmistress, Mrs Susan Bailes remarks: "Our aim is to provide a happy, secure environment and to unlock a love of learning, which will last for ever". As Inspectors confirmed, "Learning in class is complemented by a wide range of extra-curricular activities. Pupils are well prepared for the next stage in their education. They look forward to their senior school with confidence, both in their academic foundations and their ability to form firm friendships with peers and positive relationships with adults".

The School bases its values on firm Christian principles and regularly raises funds for Charities including Save the Children and Canine Partners. A School Council in the Upper School involves children in democratic elections for representatives and decision-making with meetings to discuss ways in which the School can be improved. In addition St Hilary's is an 'Eco School' with pupils and staff actively engaged in caring for the environment in their daily lives.

The school has an excellent Foundation Stage with a purpose-built Nursery and spacious classrooms, specialist teaching in Upper School, Gym/Hall with stage and separate dining room, Music wing, an Art and D&T Studio, a Performing Arts room, well-stocked Library and modern ICT suite and equipment to support and promote individuals' learning.

Charitable status. St Hilary's is a Registered Charity, number 312056. It exists to provide education for children.

St Hilda's School

High Street, Bushey, Hertfordshire WD23 3DA
Tel: 020 8950 1751
Fax: 020 8420 4523
e-mail: secretary@sthildasbushey.co.uk
registrar@sthildasbushey.co.uk
website: www.sthildas-school.co.uk

Chairman of Governors: Mrs B Batten, MA

Headmistress: **Mrs T S Handford**, MA, BSc QTS

Age Range. 3–11.
Number of Pupils. 150 Day Girls. Boys in Kindergarten.
Fees per term (2011-2012). £1,715–£3,222. Compulsory extras: Lunches £218.

St Hilda's is an Independent Day School for girls, although boys are accepted into the Early Years. It was founded in 1918 and has occupied its present 5-acre site since 1928. The Victorian house at the centre of the site has been continually improved, adapted and extended to provide an excellent educational environment. This includes a nature garden area, tennis courts, a covered heated swimming pool, a large all purpose hall, science laboratory, technology laboratory and computer suite. We teach a wide range of subjects to a high academic standard in a secure and happy environment in which every pupil can develop their academic and personal potential. We offer a broad and challenging curriculum in which art, drama and music play an important role. French is taught from Reception and Latin is introduced at the appropriate stage. There is a wide range of extra-curricular activities, including Ballet, Tap and Short Tennis; also after school clubs including Art and Drama. An after school care facility is available until 6 pm Monday to Friday during term time.

Charitable status. St Hilda's School is a Registered Charity, number 311072. It exists to provide education for girls.

St Hilda's School

Dovecote Lane, Horbury, West Yorkshire WF4 6BB
Tel: 01924 260706
e-mail: head@sthildasschool.org.uk
website: www.silcoates.org.uk

Chairman of Governors: Mr John Payling, MA, ACA

Headteacher: **Mrs Ruth Grunwell**

Age Range. 0–7 Co-educational.
Number of Pupils. 165.
Fees per term (2011-2012). £1,970.

St Hilda's is an IAPS school where children are able to blossom and grow in a stimulating learning environment 51 weeks of the year. Children may attend St Hilda's from birth in a specialized birth to 3 years Unit and then move seamlessly through the school until they transfer to Silcoates Junior School at age 7.

Our mission at St Hilda's is to promote the highest quality teaching and learning to help each individual child achieve and be valued for their achievement and effort. We expect every child at St Hilda's School to feel happy, confident and secure in their environment and that through the guidance of adults, reach their full potential.

St Hilda's has a long and enviable reputation of achievement where children make very good progress, confidently and with enjoyment. The school occupies a beautiful Grade II listed former convent in the centre of Horbury. The picturesque setting of the former convent provides a safe and stimulating learning environment in which children can truly flourish. The school offers space both inside and outside where children prepare for their aspirations and goals. Separate specially equipped play areas for the younger and older child ensures that learning continues outside and is valued and stimulating. A team of dedicated experienced teachers and staff works closely with parents to ensure that all pupils reach their full potential. Small class sizes and lots of space enable the children to receive the care and attention they deserve.

The school has a strong academic tradition and a purposeful atmosphere permeates each class. Our belief is that children should be exposed to a broad up-to-date curriculum which is enriched and enhanced to ensure the pupils are interested and challenged by all we offer.

Our recent Independent Schools Inspectorate inspection reported that:

"The quality of care that staff devote to the well-being of the pupils at every stage is outstanding"
"behaviour is exemplary"
"Children have confidence in their ability to learn"
St Hilda's offers flexible care for all the children to help parents. Out of School Care facilities include breakfast clubs from 8 am to care until 6 pm in the evenings. A Holiday club with activities and outings operates during the school holidays between the hours of 8 am and 6 pm. For our younger children, up to the age of 3 years we offer flexible care packages daily from 8 am to 6 pm.

Charitable status. The Silcoates School Foundation is a Registered Charity, number 529281.

St Hugh's

Woodhall Spa LN10 6TQ
Tel:　　01526 352169
Fax:　　01526 351520
e-mail:　sthughs-schooloffice@btconnect.com
website:　www.st-hughs.lincs.sch.uk

Chairman of Governors: C R Wheeldon, Esq

Headmaster: **S G C Greenish**, BEd

Age Range. 2–13.
Number of Pupils. 194+. Boarders: 48 boys, 36 girls. Day: 31 boys, 26 girls. Pre-Prep: 14 boys, 13 girls. Nursery: 26 children.
Fees per term (2011-2012). Boarding £5,300–£5,400; Day £3,690–£4,045; Pre-Prep £2,190.
St Hugh's School was founded by the Forbes family in 1925, became a Charitable Trust in 1964 and has continued to prosper over the years administered by a forward-thinking Governing Body.

Today the School is fully co-educational, offering both day and boarding places. The Headmaster is assisted by 20 qualified and experienced teachers, a Bursar, Catering Manager and 3 Matrons. Through its Headmaster the School is a member of IAPS (The Independent Association of Prep Schools) as well as the Boarding Schools' Association.

Boys and girls are prepared for the Common Entrance and Scholarship examinations. The School's academic record is good, with regular awards being gained to major Independent Schools, as well as places in Lincolnshire Grammar Schools. Children with special learning needs are treated sympathetically within the mainstream, with support from specialist staff. The aim of the School is to give every child a good all-round education and to discover and develop his or her own particular talents.

The major school games for boys are rugby, hockey and cricket, and for girls netball, hockey and rounders. Both boys and girls can also enjoy cross-country, tennis, athletics and swimming. There is an annual Sports Day. All children have PE each week with time set aside for instruction in gymnastics and swimming. Skills in games such as basketball and badminton also form the basis of these lessons.

The school lays heavy emphasis on extra-curricular activities, sport of various kinds, music, the visual arts and drama. All teachers are expected to help in some way with this. There is also a strong and continuing Christian tradition at St Hugh's, where children are encouraged to consider what they believe and develop a faith of their own within the context of regular acts of Christian Worship.

The school has excellent facilities including a modern sports hall, an assembly hall with stage and lighting, a heated indoor swimming pool, extensive playing fields, a fine library, dedicated classrooms and a large Music, Design and ICT studios. The facilities are continually being updated and added to.

Boarders are accommodated in two well-appointed Houses under the close supervision of the resident matrons and the Headmaster and his wife. Dormitories and common rooms are bright and cheerful and recognition is given to the importance of children having a place where they can feel at home and relaxed at the end of the day. Contact with parents and guardians is well maintained. Every half term is punctuated by an exeat weekend and arrangements are made for boarders whose parents live abroad. Minibus transport for day pupils is provided from Boston, Louth and Skegness.

The Pre-Preparatory department caters for approximately 40 children, aged from 4 to 7, and is located in its own building with separate play area and staff.

The Nursery for children between 2 and 4 is attached to the Pre-Prep and accommodates approximately 45 children.

Half-fee bursaries are available for the sons and daughters of clergymen. There are also reductions for brothers and sisters as well as bursaries for the children of service personnel. The fees are fully inclusive.

Charitable status. St Hugh's School (Woodhall Spa) Limited is a Registered Charity, number 527611. It exists to provide a high standard of education and care to pupils from the age of 2 to 13.

St Hugh's

Carswell Manor, Faringdon, Oxon SN7 8PT
Tel:　　01367 870700
Fax:　　01367 870707
e-mail:　headmaster@st-hughs.co.uk
　　　　registrar@st-hughs.co.uk
website:　www.st-hughs.co.uk

Chairman of Governors: J M Guillum Scott

Headmaster: **A J P Nott**, BA Hons, PGCE

Age Range. 3–13.
Number of Pupils. 307: 20 Weekly Boarders, 191 Day Pupils (of whom many flexi board); Pre-Prep 96. (Boy-Girl ratio approximately 3:2, both boarding and day).
Fees per term (2010-2011). Upper School: Boarders £5,760, Day £4,810; Middle School: Boarders £5,400, Day £4,445; Pre-Prep £2,835–£3,095. (All fees inclusive, with no compulsory extras.)
The School's main building is a fine Jacobean house with extensive grounds. Boys and girls are prepared for Common Entrance and Scholarship examinations to senior independent schools. The school is organised into four departments: Nursery (3–4), Pre-Prep (4–6), Middle School (7–8) and Upper School (9–13). Careful liaison ensures a strong thread of continuity throughout the school. The main entry points are at 3, 4, 7 and 11.

We are non-selective and both welcome and cater for pupils of a wide range of ability. We aim to foster confidence and a love of learning across this range: an impressive scholarship and CE record and the provision of integral specialist support both bear testimony to our inclusive approach. The arts and sport feature strongly and pupils are encouraged to develop their talents and interests as broadly as possible.

St Hugh's is described by the Good Schools Guide as a school which "personifies what is best in prep school education".

Charitable status. St Hugh's is a Registered Charity, number 309640. It exists to provide a centre of excellence for the education of children.

St Ives School

Three Gates Lane, Haslemere, Surrey GU27 2ES
Tel: 01428 643734
Fax: 01428 644788
e-mail: admin@stiveshaslemere.com
website: www.stiveshaslemere.com

Chairman of Governors: Mr T Plant

Headmistress: **Mrs L Shaikh**, MA, BA Hons, PGCE

Age Range. Girls 2–11, Boys 2–5.
Number of Children. 150 (Day).
Fees per term (2011-2012). Reception & Year 1 £2,100, Year 2 £2,675, Years 3–4 £3,275, Years 5–6 £3,800. Lunch included.

St Ives is a Preparatory Day School situated within half a mile of the centre of Haslemere and stands in its own attractive and spacious grounds of eight acres.

The school aims to provide a broad and balanced curriculum whilst retaining academic excellence, and a traditional prep school education is combined with the best of modern teaching methods. Each child is encouraged to work hard in a secure, relaxed and happy environment. Individual needs are catered for and high standards of manners, discipline and appearance are encouraged. Classes are small and in addition to class teachers, qualified teaching assistants are provided in each of the Pre-Prep classes. Specialist teaching throughout the school in core subjects, ICT, Art, French and PE enables each child to fulfil her potential.

Our children are prepared for a variety of senior schools and we are very proud of our strong academic achievements. Whilst the basic skills of Numeracy and Literacy are at the heart of our curriculum, the girls also enjoy a wide range of experiences and opportunities.

Competitive sport is played in good spirit with an emphasis on enjoyment, involvement and working together whilst attaining high standards. The school enjoys regional and national sporting success and a large variety of extra-curricular activities is offered including speech and drama, ballet, instrumental lessons and tennis coaching. Annual residential field studies are organised for the upper school and a ski trip is normally organised on alternate years for the Easter holidays.

The school is well resourced including Maths and IT suites, purpose-built Nursery, Pre-Prep classrooms, Science, Art and Music rooms. Two new netball courts and enlarged grassed areas have enhanced the sporting facilities.

Girls are prepared for the Common Entrance and senior school examinations at 11+ and the school has a good record for gaining scholarships to a wide range of well known senior independent schools. St Ives' full independence from any senior school enables parents and the Head to select the most appropriate senior school for their child.

The St Ives bus provides a daily service, the route currently covering the Haslemere, Liphook, Hindhead, Grayshott, Churt and Frensham areas.

Entry at 7+ is by interview with the Head and a trial day at the school. Scholarships are available for entry into Year 3, the number and value of the awards varying from year to year.

For a copy of the prospectus please apply to the Registrar.

Charitable status. St Ives School is a Registered Charity, number 312080. Its aim is the advancement of education for girls.

St John's Beaumont

Priest Hill, Old Windsor, Berkshire SL4 2JN
Tel: 01784 432428
Fax: 01784 494048
e-mail: admissions@stjohnsbeaumont.co.uk
website: www.stjohnsbeaumont.org.uk

Chairman of Governors: M C Brenninkmeyer

Headmaster: **G E F Delaney**, BA Hons, PGCE

Age Range. 3½–13.
Number of Boys. 290 (60 Full and Weekly Boarders; 230 Day Boys).
Fees per term (2011-2012). Boarding £7,480, Weekly Boarding £6,460, Day Boys £3,360–£4,930, Pre-Preparatory (Nursery–Year 1) £2,600.

St John's is a Jesuit School. Classes are small, and boys can receive individual attention according to their needs and abilities. Although following the Common Entrance syllabus for senior independent schools, St John's also promotes the National Curriculum and boys are assessed at Key Stages 1 and 2, audited by the Local Education Authority. Boys are prepared for entry to some of the top independent schools in the country and have won many scholarships in recent years.

The school was purpose built in 1888 by J F Bentley and stands in spacious grounds on the edge of Windsor Great Park, with extensive facilities for outdoor sports. It has a large gymnasium and considerable sports fields. Several facilities have been opened in recent years, including two ICT suites, technology block science and art block, music school, concert hall and 25-metre indoor swimming pool. A new purpose-built sports complex was opened by HM The Queen in October 2009. Wireless technology is available in classrooms enabling access to individual laptops and there are interactive whiteboards in all classrooms. On top of their daily curriculum schedules, each member of staff offers an extra activity after school. These include chess, drama, art, and various sports. Games are played every day and the school particularly excels at rugby, cricket, tennis and swimming. The school's swimming pool is also used by other schools and the local community.

The boys have daily opportunity for religious practice, as well as formal instruction and informal guidance.

An illustrated prospectus is available from the Headmaster, who is always pleased to meet parents and to show them round the school.

Charitable status. St John's is a Registered Charity, number 230165. It exists to provide education for boys.

St John's College Lower School

Albany Road, Southsea, Hampshire PO5 2AB
Tel: 023 9282 0237
Fax: 023 9287 3603
e-mail: info@stjohnscollege.co.uk
website: www.stjohnscollege.co.uk

Chairman of Governors: Mr T Forer

Head Master: **Mr R A Shrubsall**, MA Ed

Age Range. Co-educational 2–11 years.
Fees per term (2011-2012). Day: £2,385 (Reception, Years 1 & 2), £2,435 (Years 3 & 4), £2,540 (Years 5 & 6). UK Boarding £6,700, Overseas Boarding £7,150.

St John's College is an independent school founded to provide an academic education in a Christian environment.

The College is fully co-educational, day and boarding, with over 600 pupils and students ranging in age from 2 to over 18. We offer a continuous range of education, starting in the Nursery and progressing in the Lower and Upper schools to the Sixth Form. We are a Catholic foundation but welcome pupils of all faiths and also those with no religious beliefs.

The Lower School is a self-contained unit but located on the main College campus. The Lower School enjoys the use of many excellent facilities: a sports centre, theatre, computer suite, library, science laboratory and music room. The attractive site is complemented by 34 acres of well maintained playing fields, located on the outskirts of the city.

A broadly balanced and extended curriculum is offered, encompassing all aspects of the National Curriculum at Key Stages 1 and 2. Close staff liaison ensures a smooth automatic transition for pupils into the Upper School at age 11. The Early Years Foundation Stage is covered in Nursery and Reception Year.

The Lower School has a fine academic, musical and sporting tradition and there are a wide range of extra-curricular clubs which run during lunchtimes and after school. Educational and character-building residential trips are offered at holiday times.

St John's is a family school committed to developing the whole person, but at the very heart of all that we do is teaching and learning. Our academic record is a very good one and the commitment of our staff to each pupil is outstanding.

A prospectus and further details are available from the Admissions Secretary.

St John's College School

75 Grange Road, Cambridge CB3 9AA
Tel: 01223 353532 Headmaster
          01223 353652 Admissions Secretary
          01223 272701 Bursar
Fax: 01223 355846
e-mail: shoffice@sjcs.co.uk
website: www.sjcs.co.uk

Chairman of Governors: The Reverend Mr Duncan Dormor

Headmaster: **K L Jones**, MA Gonville and Caius College Cambridge

Age Range. 4–13.
Number of Children. 460 girls and boys (including 20 Chorister and up to 30 Non-Chorister boy and girl boarders).
Fees per term (2011-2012). Choristers £6,485; Day Boys and Girls (4–13) £3,268–£4,106 according to age. Bursaries available for Choristers.
Profile. St John's prides itself on the quality of the academic and pastoral care it provides for each child. Through relaxed and friendly relations with children in a well-structured environment rich with opportunity; through close monitoring of progress; through communication and cooperation with parents; through expert staffing and, above all, through a sense of community that cares for the strengths and weaknesses of each of its members, St John's has consistently achieved outstanding results exemplified by over 70 scholarships during the last three years. Whilst its Choristers maintain the tradition of choral services and tour the world, St John's status as an Expert Centre for ICT, and other innovations, ensure the school's commitment to the future.
Entry. At 4–7 by parental interview; at 7–12 by parental interview, report from previous school and, as appropriate, assessment.
Curriculum. The curriculum surrounds the core of formal skills teaching with a breadth of enrichment and extension for each child's talents. In addition to the usual subjects including specialist taught DT, ICT, Art, Music, Dance and Drama, and PE for all pupils, the following are also available: French (from 8+), Latin (optional from 10+), Greek (optional from 11+), Spanish (optional from 11+). Pupils prepared for CE and Scholarship examinations. Philosophy was introduced into the curriculum this year.
Leavers. Virtually all go to senior independent day or boarding schools. The School works closely with parents to assist them in finding the best school for their child.
Consultation. Tutorial system (1 teacher to 10 pupils) with daily tutorial session timetabled. Half yearly academic assessments, end of year examinations, termly Parents' Evenings and weekly staff 'surgery' times.
Sports. Athletics, Badminton, Basketball, Cricket, Cross Country, Football, Golf, Gymnastics, Hockey, Netball, Real Tennis, Rounders, Rowing, Rugby, Short Tennis, Squash, Swimming, Table Tennis, Tennis. All games are timetabled and therefore given significant status. All major sports strong.
Activities. Numerous clubs including Art, Chess, Dance, Drama, Pottery, Sketching, Design Technology, Craft, Information Technology, Maths games and puzzles, Magic, Touch-typing, Cycling Proficiency, General Knowledge, Debating, Poetry, Sewing and Wardrobe. College Choir of international status, Chamber Groups, Orchestras, School Chapel Choir, Junior Chamber Choir, Parents' Choir, Major theatrical productions, eg The Ragged Child, The Tempest, and theatrical opportunities for all children. A range of visits relating to curriculum plus French, Classics, skiing and outward bound trips.
Facilities. School on two sites with facilities used by all pupils. *Byron House (4–8).* Outstanding facilities including Science, DT Centre, two large suites of networked PCs, computerised Library, Drama Studio, Gym, Hall, and specialist Music wing.
Senior House (9–13). Design Technology Centre, two Information Technology Centres, Drama Studio, computerised Library, Music School, Theatre, School Chapel and use of St John's College Chapel for school carol and special services. Sports Hall with indoor Cricket nets, multi-purpose Gym and Indoor Pool. Athletics track, playing fields with brand new astroturf hockey pitch and tennis courts. The space left vacant in the old boarding house to become a new library of the 'old school' kind with wood and bookshelves and ladders and armchairs and reading lamps. Other improvements will include new science labs, new technology rooms, new classrooms, new lecture space, all-weather multi-sport court, gardens and covered outdoor spaces. This should be completed by 2012.
Boarding. From age 8. Girl and boy boarders form an integral part of life at St John's and benefit from all the School's facilities whilst living in the homely, caring atmosphere of a brand new Boarding House which was completed in Spring 2011. These improved facilities include recreation areas, a library, TV, table tennis and use of all Senior House facilities. Day boarding and 'Waiters' facilities allow the School to be flexible to the needs of parents and children alike.
Charitable status. St John's College School is part of St John's College Cambridge, which is a Registered Charity, number 1137428.

St John's International School

Broadway, Sidmouth, Devon EX10 8RG
Tel: 01395 513984
Fax: 01395 514539
e-mail: contact.stjohns@iesedu.com
website: www.stjohnsdevon.co.uk

Headmistress: **Mrs Angela Parry-Davies**, BEd Hons

Age Range. 2–16.

Number of Pupils. Main School 200, of whom 40–50 are Boarders. The Nursery (up to 5 years) has 50 children. Girl/boy ratio 50:50.

Fees per term (2010-2011). Day: £1,980–£3,020; Boarding: £4,580–£5,700. There are no compulsory extras.

St John's is one of the few fully independent, co-educational preparatory day and boarding schools in the South West and caters for children between the ages of two and thirteen. The School (a Charitable Trust) is owned by The International Education Systems (IES) and situated in substantial buildings and grounds above the small seaside town. The School aims to ensure that all pupils have the benefit of a fulfilling and rounded education and gives children every opportunity to develop their individual talents from the earliest age.

The Headmistress believes that children who are able to relate to a happy family community achieve the best results. This contributes to sound attitudes towards academic work and the many oft of school activities that are available to every child. The success of this positive attitude towards education is seen by looking at the results the School has enjoyed over the years. St John's School cares about the child as an individual and the strong team of experienced staff is able to devote a great deal of time to each pupil.

The small classes (the staff pupil ratio is at present 1:10) enjoy bright, cheerful, well equipped classrooms with the additional advantage of overlooking stunning sea views. Interest is sport is high and the School in addition to playing fields, has an extensive sports centre with an indoor swimming court and a 20 metre swimming pool. The School encourages all pupils to take an active role in music and with its own specialist Music School, there is a high number of pupils learning individual instruments. Art facilities include a pottery studio and pupils enjoy a wide range of media in the Art School. The small, but well-equipped drama studio also converts to a small cinema and is popular with boarding pupils.

The school caters for children who suffer from dyslexia with qualified specialist teachers (BDA). The school is CReSTeD registered.

As well as regular 11+ passes to the local Grammar School, each year pupils win a number of scholarships to independent secondary schools. Academic results are of the highest standard.

Charitable status. St John's School Trust (Sidmouth) Limited is a Registered Charity, number 274864. It exists to provide education for children.

St John's-on-the-Hill School

Tutshill, Chepstow, Monmouthshire NP16 7LE

Tel: 01291 622045
Fax: 01291 623932
e-mail: registrar@stjohnsonthehill.co.uk
website: www.stjohnsonthehill.co.uk

Chairman of Governors: I Fielder

Headmaster: **N A Folland**, BSc Hons, PGCE

Age Range. Co-educational 3 months to 13+ years.
Number of Pupils. 302.
Fees per term (2011-2012). Boarders £5,175. Day £3,265–£3,675. Pre-Prep £2,225–£2,400. Nursery and Early Years Department (half or full day sessions) £19.25 per session.

St John's-on-the-Hill is a co-educational day and boarding preparatory school with a pre-prep and day nurseries situated in extensive, attractive grounds on the border of Monmouthshire and Gloucestershire, overlooking Chepstow Castle and the beautiful Wye Valley. Served by an excellent motorway system, just 3 miles from the old Severn Bridge,

the school also has its own minibus network covering Newport, Usk, Monmouth, Ross-on-Wye and the Forest of Dean area.

St John's offers Day Nursery care to children from 3 months to pre-school. There are two Day Nurseries in Chepstow, one at the school site and one at the Racecourse, with a third Nursery at Celtic Springs, Newport.

St John's aims to provide a consistently high standard of care and education for children aged between 3 months and 13+ years.

Latest Developments. A new purpose-built teaching block for the pre-prep and new nursery at the school site in Tutshill. The pre-prep building includes six classrooms each with direct access to an outdoor play area in addition to an assembly hall and a large indoor play area for both Foundation stage and Key Stage 1 children. The Tutshill Nursery is divided into three main areas of learning by age. Other shared facilities within the Nursery include a superb indoor soft play room, a light, bright dining area and a large 'messy' craft room designed for all ages of children to enjoy.

Discovering and developing individual talent. The family atmosphere ensures that even the youngest child feels a sense of belonging. Each child is valued and there is time to cater for the needs of all. A high standard of teaching and small class sizes, combined with first-class facilities, ensure boys and girls can develop both their academic ability and character to the full. Emphasis is on mutual respect, integrity and the need to discover and develop individual talents, whether they are creative, intellectual or athletic.

Celebrating achievement. Children are encouraged to develop skills and achieve success across the curriculum. Sport, Art, Design Technology, Music and Performing Arts are therefore an important part of school life. Children are encouraged to be creative from an early age and to take part in regular drama productions either front or backstage. All Year 3 children benefit from recorder and violin lessons as part of the music curriculum. Traditional and modern choral music is a particular strength within the school. The St John's choristers perform regularly at weddings and special events within the community whilst also leading school services.

St John's values achievement both in and out of the classroom. The aim of the sporting programme is to ensure that all children develop a love of both team and individual sport and to understand the importance of losing gracefully and winning modestly.

A varied outdoor education programme enhances each child's personal and social development. The school also offers a wide range of non-academic activities and after-school clubs. These may include archery, cookery, golf, horse-riding, and chess.

St John's has a specialist Learning Support Department and welcomes children across the ability range.

The school aims to ensure that each child has the opportunity to participate in almost everything, to go on achieve their individual best in all areas and to celebrate success individually and collectively. St John's encourages a sense of community where each child feels secure, significant and responsible, able to play a full part in the life of the school.

Scholarships and Bursaries. Scholarships and awards are made for academic, music, sporting and dramatic ability. HM Forces bursaries are also available.

Boarding at St John's. Children can board from the age of 7 on a full, weekly, or 'flexi' basis. The boarding house is family-run and has a friendly, homely atmosphere. The accommodation is spacious and fully modernised to provide a comfortable secure home environment.

A varied programme of weekend outings and activities is offered to the many boarders who remain at St John's throughout the term.

Building on Tradition. St John's holds sound traditional values whilst embracing the best of modern approaches. The environment at St John's is stimulating in its breadth of opportunity and yet personal in its size.

Creating the Future. On leaving St John's, children enter a wide range of senior schools of their choice and with more than 100 senior school scholarships awarded to St John's children in the last five years, the school is justifiably proud of its scholarship record and senior school links.

Charitable status. St John's-on-the-Hill and Brightlands School Trust Limited is a Registered Charity, number 312953, founded for the education of children.

St John's School

Potter Street Hill, Northwood, Middlesex HA6 3QY
Tel: 020 8866 0067
Fax: 020 8868 8770
e-mail: office@st-johns.org.uk
website: www.st-johns.org.uk

Chairman of Governors: J Armstrong, Esq

Headmaster: **C R Kelly**, BA, PGCE Durham University

Assistant Headmaster: S Robinson, BSc, PGCE Loughborough

Age Range. 3–13.
Number of Boys. 400 Day Boys (Prep 260; Pre-Prep and Nursery 140).
Fees per annum (2011-2012). Prep £11,750, Pre-Prep £10,870 and Nursery £7,970.

Facing South, on a 35-acre site, we have outstanding views over London. Since the Merchant Taylors' Educational Trust took the School under its wing, impressive development has taken place. St John's has gained a gymnasium and changing block, two science laboratories, a six classroom Pre-Prep Department and a junior classroom block. Another major development provided an Assembly Hall/Theatre, an Art Studio, Design & Technology Workshop, ICT Centre and a new Music Department. At the same time, other areas of the School were refurbished creating specialist teaching areas for English, French, History, Geography and Mathematics. We also acquired an area of grassland and woodland for ecological and environmental study, to add to our extensive playing fields and formal gardens.

We opened a new, purpose-built Nursery in 2003. This major extension of our pre-preparatory department included an Information Technology Suite and Library. At the same time extra play areas, including an 'indoor quiet area', were created. Most recently a large, all-weather multi-purpose sports area was constructed. We have just completed installing drainage and irrigation on our four rugby pitches and athletics track. Part of this project includes the creation of a small Golf Course.

Most of the boys enter the School at either the age of three into the Nursery or at four into the Pre-Prep and there is a separate entry into the Main School at seven. St John's has an excellent record of success in scholarship and senior school entrance examinations. Boys are prepared for all independent schools, however, our links with Merchant Taylors' School, Northwood, are particularly strong.

Although the School was originally a Church of England foundation, boys of all religions and denominations are welcome.

Charitable status. St John's School, part of the Merchant Taylors' Educational Trust, is a Registered Charity, number 1063738. It exists for the purpose of educating boys.

St Joseph's In The Park School

St Mary's Lane, Hertingfordbury, Hertfordshire SG14 2LX
Tel: 01992 581378
Fax: 01992 505202
e-mail: admin@stjosephsinthepark.co.uk
website: www.stjosephsinthepark.co.uk

Chair of Governors: Mr Andy Wodhams

Headmaster: **Mr Neil Jones**, BSc, MSc, PGCE

Age Range. 3–11 Co-educational.
Number of Pupils. 173.
Fees per term (2011-2012). Nursery (minimum 5 sessions) £1,766, Kindergarten (minimum 7 sessions) £2,344, Pre School (full-time) £3,211, Infants £3,276, Juniors £3,337, Woodlands Learning Support Centre £4,749.

St Joseph's In The Park is a single-form entry, co-educational school for children between the ages of 3 and 11 years. Founded in 1898, it is one of the oldest Independent Schools in area.

Set within 40 acres of Hertingfordbury Park on the outskirts of Hertford, St Joseph's In The Park has not only a celebrated reputation for valuing support for learning and high academic standards, but also a particularly outstanding tradition in pastoral care.

Through each Key Stage the children experience an exciting curriculum. The core focus on Literacy and Mathematics is supported by a themed approach to the Foundation Subjects.

A school that thrives on values and tradition can also boast an environment that permits children to develop and learn in a contemporary educational setting which includes:

- an extended day starting with Breakfast Club at 7.45 am;
- an outdoor heated swimming pool, sports field and large, multi-purpose hall for drama, dance, concerts and sports;
- the Woodlands Learning Support Centre, established in 1998, providing differentiated education for children between Years 3 and 6 who need extra learning support;
- Wednesday afternoon "Kaleidoscope" activities which extends the curriculum and includes horse riding, skiing, outdoor pursuits, creative arts, digital media & thinking skills;
- three choirs and an orchestra, ensuring that music is enjoyed throughout the school;
- a dedicated ICT room, site-wide wireless network, laptops used across the Junior Classes and Interactive Whiteboards in every classroom;
- extensive woodland set within beautiful parkland.

A prospectus which further illustrates the distinctiveness of the school is available on request.

Charitable status. St Joseph's In The Park School is a Registered Charity, number 1111064.

St Lawrence College Junior School

Ramsgate, Kent CT11 7AF
Tel: 01843 572912
Fax: 01843 572913
e-mail: hjs@slcuk.com
website: www.slcuk.com

Chairman of the Council: Mr David W Taylor, MA Oxon, PGCE, FRSA

Head: **Mr Simon J E Whittle**, BA Hons, PGCE

Age Range. 3–11.

Number of Pupils. 190 boys and girls, a few of whom are boarders.

Fees per term (2011-2012). Boarders £6,639, Day £2,018–£3,247.

St Lawrence College Junior School offers a supportive, caring environment, based on traditional Christian values, in which children are given every opportunity to fulfil their potential. Academic expectations are high, but realistic and open-minded. Personal attention is given within small classes where talents are recognised and needs are catered for. There is a strong belief that education, in its truest sense, is measured not just in a student's exam results but by its ability to open young people's minds.

Most pupils transfer to the Senior School at 11+, and scholarships are regularly earned. There is also an excellent record of success at securing places in the highly-selective local grammar schools.

The Junior School is based in an attractive Victorian building in a peaceful corner of the 150-acre St Lawrence College campus. Its own independent facilities include a Music Department and Performance Hall, two fully-networked ICT Suites, adventure playgrounds, tennis courts and spacious playing fields. These have recently been enhanced by the opening, in September 2009, of a new Science Lab and Art Studio. Membership of the wider College community gives pupils the best of both worlds, and they are able to share many of the Senior School's excellent specialist facilities. Boarders are accommodated in the splendid new Kirby House, an ultra-modern, eco-friendly development which opened its doors in January 2007.

A wide range of extra-curricular opportunities includes sports such as football, rugby, hockey, cricket, lacrosse, rounders, netball, basketball, athletics, cross-country running, swimming and dance. There are plenty of fixtures against other schools, but, most importantly, children learn the value of fitness, cooperative teamwork and good sportsmanship. There is a proud musical tradition, and plenty of scope for drama and the creative arts. Some Activities take place at the end of the school day, but most are concentrated into the popular, informal Saturday morning programme.

St Lawrence's Christian heritage underpins all that the Junior School stands for. An atmosphere of trust and mutual respect is based on kindness, forgiveness and consideration for others. There is a strong emphasis placed on thoughtful conduct, courtesy and good manners, and on endowing young people with a clear sense of moral responsibility.

Charitable status. The Corporation of St Lawrence College is a Registered Charity, number 307921. It exists to provide education for boys and girls.

St Leonards-New Park

St Andrews, Fife KY16 9QJ
Tel: 01334 472126
Fax: 01334 476152
e-mail: slnp@stleonards-fife.org
website: www.stleonards-fife.org

Chairman of the St Leonards Council: James Murray

Headmaster: **Andrew Donald**, BSc Aberdeen

Age Range. 5–12.
Number of Pupils. 180 (85 girls, 95 boys).
Fees per term (2011-2012). £2,647 (Years 1–5), £2,967 (Years 6–7).

St Leonards–New Park in St Andrews is the co-educational preparatory school of St Leonards. Formed as a result of a merger between the St Leonards Junior and Middle Schools and New Park in 2005, the school is administered by the St Leonards Council and educates children between the ages of 5 and 12, from Year 1 to Year 7.

Pupils are prepared for entry to St Leonards Senior School. With specialist teachers and small class sizes, children benefit from individual attention. In addition to a strong academic tradition, drama, music, art, ICT and PE are included in the timetable.

Outside the classroom, a wide variety of sports are available; netball, rugby, hockey, lacrosse, tennis and cricket being the main team activities. Tuition in golf, judo and swimming is also offered. Outdoor education activities include water sports. There are also classes in Scottish Country Dancing and ballet.

Charitable status. St Leonards School is a Registered Charity, number SC010904. It exists to provide education to children between the ages of 5 and 19.

St Margaret's Preparatory School

Curzon Street, Calne, Wiltshire SN11 0DF
Tel: 01249 857220
Fax: 01249 857227
e-mail: office@stmargaretsprep.org.uk
website: www.stmargaretsprep.org.uk

Chairman of Governors: Mr S Knight, FRICS

Headmistress: **Mrs K E Cordon**, GLCM, LLCM TD, ALCM

Age Range. 3–11.
Number of Pupils. 202 Day: 125 girls, 77 boys.
Fees per term (2011-2012). £1,557–£3,330.

St Margaret's is an IAPS day preparatory school for boys and girls aged 3 to 11 based in Calne, Wiltshire.

The St Margaret's curriculum comprises an extensive range of activities, designed to promote not only learning, but also personal growth and development. It is based upon the subjects of the National Curriculum which are delivered, in the main, by class teachers, all of whom are experts in the relevant ages. This is then enhanced, not only by specialist tuition in Sport, Music, Latin, ICT and Modern Foreign Languages, but also the extensive extra-curricular programme, designed to enrich every child's experience whilst at the school; this includes the 'hidden curriculum' – what the children learn from the way they are treated and how they are expected to behave. It is important that the pupils to grow into positive, responsible adults who can work and cooperate with others, whilst at the same time developing their knowledge and skills in order to achieve their true potential.

Sport plays an important part at St Margaret's and the school is fortunate to share a 25-acre site with St Mary's, Calne. Consequently, the children benefit from a wide range of facilities not usually available to preparatory school pupils. These include a 25m indoor swimming pool where all children from Kindergarten to Year 6 have weekly swimming lessons, in addition to being able to take advantage of the various swimming clubs. Every child enjoys up to five timetabled sessions of sport in school each week; these include swimming, PE and Games. The main games for the boys are rugby, hockey and cricket and for the girls, netball, hockey and rounders. St Margaret's competes with other schools in Bath, Wiltshire Oxfordshire and Somerset at various inter-school matches and festivals throughout the year. Other sports activities include tennis, football, cross-country and athletics. All children are encouraged to improve their physical co-ordination and to compete with confidence on the games field.

The Performing Arts have a high profile and there are Music and Drama opportunities at every age group. The children are encouraged to enter for external examinations, as well as competing in local festivals and their success rate is high. There is a comprehensive performance programme in place, which is enjoyed by both performers and spectators alike!

St Margaret's is extremely proud of their pupils' academic achievements. The children are thoroughly prepared for entrance examinations to senior schools and St Margaret's has an impressive record of success in academic and specialist subject scholarships, as well as consistently gaining entry to first-choice schools.

The St Margaret's children have access to a wonderful Chapel, theatre, well equipped medical centre and dining hall. They enjoy lunch every day in the dining hall, which is freshly prepared by the catering team, using locally sourced, organic produce.

St Margaret's has an ethos that is based on 'traditional values combined with an innovative approach', providing a happy environment for all children in a friendly, caring community. Within this context, the school hopes that boys and girls will learn the value of hard work and how to accept discipline and responsibility.

Charitable status. St Mary's School (Calne) is a Registered Charity, number 309482. It exists to provide education for boys and girls.

St Martin's Ampleforth

Gilling Castle, Gilling East, York YO62 4HP
Tel: 01439 766600
Fax: 01439 788538
e-mail: headmaster@stmartins.ampleforth.org.uk
website: www.stmartins.ampleforth.org.uk

Chairman of the School Governors: Mr P B R Houghton

Headmaster: **Mr Nicholas Jonathan Higham**, BEd Hons (Leeds)

Age Range. 3+ to 13+ years.
Number of Pupils. 180 (60 Boarders, 120 Day Children).
Fees per term (2011-2012). Boarding £6,422; Day £2,226–£4,129.

St Martin's Ampleforth is a boarding and day preparatory school which takes boys and girls from the age of 3+ years and prepares them for Common Entrance and Scholarship examinations. It is expected most of the pupils will enter Ampleforth College at 13+.

St Martin's Ampleforth is based in a 14th century castle with spacious and secluded gardens, 18 miles north of York and close to the North Yorkshire Moors National Park.

All Faiths are made most welcome in this Benedictine school. The Chaplaincy team is led by a monk of Ampleforth Abbey and includes an Anglican priest.

The highest academic standards are aimed for, within a broad and challenging curriculum. Each pupil's ability is taken into account. Very able children are provided for and coached for scholarships to Ampleforth College and other leading independent senior schools, whilst those with learning difficulties, including dyslexia, are given qualified specialist help. Each form of approximately 15 children has a tutor responsible for overall progress and pastoral support. Setting is in place from Year 6 and beyond.

There is a striking variety of extra-curricular pursuits including horse-riding, chess, golf, judo, drama, swimming and debating. The School has an enviable reputation for games and fields highly successful teams in rugby, netball, cricket, rounders, hockey, track and field and cross-country running.

Music is strong. Typically, 80% of pupils learn musical instruments and perform regularly. The School provides the trebles for the acclaimed Ampleforth College Schola Cantorum and there is an increasingly successful girls' Schola too. A performing arts centre has recently been built which enhances the current provision for choral and instrumental performance as well as fostering drama throughout the school.

Parents are considered part of the School community. They are welcome at any time, especially for matches, other organised events and, of course, for Mass on Sundays and feast days.

Facilities include a sports hall, ICT room, all-weather cricket nets, a 9-hole golf course and all-weather floodlit astroturf. A programme of refurbishment of the boarding accommodation started in July 2008. The extensive grounds, including woods, lakes and gardens, combine a sense of space and freedom with unrivalled beauty.

Academic, all-rounder, choral and music scholarships, up to the value of 15% of fees, are available each spring for children under the age of 11. Bursaries are available.

Daily transport is provided to and from Pickering, Malton, Kirkbymoorside, Easingwold, York and Helmsley.

Charitable status. St Martin's Ampleforth, as part of the St Laurence Trust, is a registered charity, number 1063808 and exists to provide education for boys and girls.

St Martin's School

40 Moor Park Road, Northwood, Middlesex HA6 2DJ
Tel: 01923 825740
Fax: 01923 835452
e-mail: office@stmartins.org.uk
website: www.stmartins.org.uk

Chairman of Governors: Roy Jakes

Headmaster: **David T Tidmarsh**, BSc Hons, PGCE

Age Range. 3–13.
Number of Boys. 400 Day Boys.
Fees per term (2010-2011). Main School £3,760; Pre-Prep £3,425; Kindergarten £1,250 (mornings). Bursaries are available, details on request.

St Martin's aims to provide boys aged 3–13 with the breadth of education and experience necessary for them to realise their full potential in a safe and friendly environment. An enthusiastic staff of 40 experienced and well-qualified teachers maintains high academic standards and provides broad sporting, musical and cultural opportunities. The atmosphere is friendly and lively with great emphasis on pastoral care.

The School, which is an Educational Trust, administered by a Board of Governors, prepares boys for entry to all the Independent Senior Schools. Forty-eight Scholarship awards have been won to senior schools during the last five years. The School, which is in a pleasant residential area, stands in 12 acres of grounds. Facilities include a Kindergarten and separate Pre-Preparatory building; two Science Laboratories; a Performing Arts Centre; a Sports Centre including an indoor swimming pool; a playground; two ICT suites; an Art Studio with facilities for Design Technology; 3 Tennis Courts.

ICT, Art, DT, and Music are included in the curriculum for all boys, and a large proportion of the boys in the School learn a musical instrument. There is a varied after-school activity programme for boys to pursue their interests.

There is a pre-school and after-school club from Kindergarten age upwards enabling parents to work a full day.

The School is divided into Patrols for competitions in work and games, and senior boys make a responsible contribution towards the running of the School. Boys are taught football, rugby, cross-country running, hockey, cricket, swimming, athletics and tennis. The school has a fine reputation in inter-school matches.

Charitable status. St Martin's (Northwood) Preparatory School Trust Limited is a Registered Charity, number 312648. It exists to provide education for boys.

St Mary's Junior School
Cambridge

2 Brookside, Cambridge CB2 1JE
Tel: 01223 311666
Fax: 01223 472168
e-mail: juniorschool@stmaryscambridge.co.uk
website: www.stmaryscambridge.co.uk

Chairman of Governors: Mrs D Wilkinson

Headmistress: **Mrs D O'Sullivan**, MEd Cantab, BCommHDE

Age Range. 4–11.
Number of Pupils. 189 Day Girls.
Fees per term (2010-2011). Reception, Years 1 and 2: £2,570; Years 3 and 4: £3,070; Years 5 and 6: £3,190. All fees are excluding lunches, which are charged at £155 per term.

Staff: 17 full-time; 18 part-time; 6 part-time music staff.

At St Mary's Junior School, we are proud of our unique, friendly and homely atmosphere. Each child is nurtured and understood by the caring staff, who take the time to listen and discuss. Small class sizes facilitate this further. In our all-girls environment, the classroom is a quiet place where concentration and hard work are easily facilitated. Children are encouraged to question and to investigate. Each child learns to understand her own potential and her needs. The children are given appropriate opportunity for one-to-one learning within our personalised approach.

Our week is well balanced from the point of view of academic, physical, pastoral and spiritual guidance. Children who arrive early in the morning are encouraged to take part in meaningful tasks. After school hours children are offered a good variety of activity clubs and after school care extends to 6 pm.

Girls are selected by interview at age 4+ to 7 years, and by an examination and interview from age 7+. The children progress to St Mary's Senior School at age 11, which provides a seamless transition for an education from ages 4 to 18.

The school maintains a strong Catholic tradition and ethos but welcomes and appreciates girls of every religion, or none.

Please come and visit St Mary's Junior School and experience our happy learning environment. If you are seriously considering our school for your child, she is welcome to come and have some taster sessions with children of her age. We look forward to meeting you.

Charitable status. St Mary's School, Cambridge is a Registered Charity, number 290180.

St Mary's School
Hampstead

47 Fitzjohn's Avenue, London NW3 6PG
Tel: 020 7435 1868
Fax: 020 7794 7922
e-mail: enquiries@stmh.co.uk
website: www.stmh.co.uk

Chairman of Governors: Mrs Marion Jeffrey

Headmistress: **Miss A M Rawlinson**, MA Hons, Dip Tchng

Age Range. 2½–11.
Number in School. 270 Girls, 28 Boys. Nursery: 35 Girls, 17 Boys.
Fees per term (2010-2011). Nursery £1,924; Kindergarten to Year 6 £3,600.

Surrounded by mature woodland and gardens, unmatched by any other school in the area, St Mary's has been established in Hampstead since 1926. Founded by the Institute of the Blessed Virgin Mary as a Roman Catholic School for Girls, the school remains true to the ideals of the IBVM foundress, Mary Ward who believed in the provision of a thoroughly grounded academic and spiritual education as a foundation for an enriched and confident adulthood.

The school has a thriving Pre-Nursery, Nursery and Pre-Prep for girls and boys. Boys are prepared for transfer to popular London Boys Preparatory Schools at the age of 7 years.

The girls are prepared for Common Entrance and the entrance examinations for top London Senior Schools. They transfer at the age of 11 years, many gaining awards and scholarships.

In addition to a broad curriculum, a wider range of activities is seen as essential to the rounded development of a healthy child. Importance is attached to physical education, drama and the arts. Extra curricular classes include Speech and Drama, Ballet and Tap. There is a school orchestra, choir and a chapel choir. Tuition is offered for many musical instruments. School trips abroad are arranged for older children.

There is an enthusiastic and dedicated staff of 40 experienced and well qualified teachers. There are specialist staff for Science, French, Art, Design and Technology, Music, PE and Special Needs. St Mary's aims to develop and fulfil the maximum potential of each child and this objective is fostered within a happy and caring environment which recognises the needs and importance of children of all abilities.

Bursaries are available (100%). Contact the Bursar for further details.

Charitable status. St Mary's School, Hampstead is a Registered Charity, number 1006411. It exists to provide education for girls and boys. It is managed by a majority of Lay Trustees and Governors.

St Mary's Preparatory School
Melrose

Abbey Park, Melrose, Roxburghshire TD6 9LN
Tel: 01896 822517
Fax: 01896 823550
e-mail: office@stmarysmelrose.org.uk
website: www.stmarysmelrose.org.uk

Founded 1895.

Chairman of Governors: Mr G T G Baird

Headmaster: **William J Harvey**, BEd Hons

Age Range. 2–13 co-educational.
Number of Pupils. 150.
Fees per term (2010-2011). Pre-Prep £3,250, Prep £4,200.
Curriculum. A healthy variety of subjects including traditional core studies reflecting both the Scottish "Curriculum for Excellence" and the England and Wales National Curriculum (English, Maths, Science, Computer Studies, French, Geography, History, Classics, Latin, RE, Art and

Music, Drama). The School's intention is to provide a genuinely nourishing environment allowing for the development of the whole child.

Entry requirements. Application by letter or telephone, followed by a visit to the school, if possible, and a tour guided by senior pupils. All pupils can be offered an 'In-day' to help with placement.

Examinations offered. Common Entrance to Scholarship for independent senior schools in Scotland and England.

Academic, sports, games and leisure facilities. Classroom computers, Science Laboratory and a big open Art Room. Theatre-Arts and Assembly Hall for concerts and drama. Spacious games pitches supporting a strong tradition in rugby, cricket, hockey, netball and rounders. There is a cross-curricular Study Support Programme for talented and gifted children as well as for children with Specific Learning Difficulties.

Religious activities. Morning Assembly with hymn-singing and readings, stressing pupil participation and contribution through drama and music.

Charitable status. St Mary's School, Melrose is a Registered Charity, number SC009352. Its aim is to provide education for primary school children.

St Michael's School
Barnstaple

Tawstock Court, Barnstaple, North Devon EX31 3HY
Tel: 01271 343242 School Office
Fax: 01271 346771
e-mail: mail@st-michaels-school.com
website: www.st-michaels-school.com

Chairman of Governors: Mr Mark Parkhouse

Headmaster: **Mr Philip Foley**, BA Hons

Age Range. 3 months – 13+.
Number of Pupils. 250 Day Boys and Girls.
Fees per term (2011-2012). £1,890–£3,700.
St Michael's was founded in 1832 and moved to North Devon in 1940. St Michael's is set in 30 acres overlooking the beautiful Taw valley. The Headmaster is a member of IAPS. The School is a Charitable Trust administered by a Board of Governors.

The teaching staff are all qualified and include a Director of Music, Director of Sport and a specialist in Information Technology.

Excellent academic results are achieved in small classes, quite often from boys and girls of modest initial ability. Modern languages form an important part of the very wide curriculum. Children are prepared for all Independent Senior Schools, and Scholarships and other Awards are regularly gained.

Facilities include Science Laboratories, a Computer Suite, a Design and Technology Centre and a spacious Art Room. There is also a Sports Hall and Squash Court. Children also learn to swim in the heated pool. PE forms part of the curriculum and Hockey, Squash, Badminton, Athletics, Netball, Rounders and Tennis are played as well as Rugby, Soccer and Cricket. Tuition is available in all musical instruments.

Scholarships are offered termly for children between the ages of 7 and 11 and credit is given for outstanding sporting or musical ability.

Charitable status. The St Michael's Charitable Trust is a Registered Charity, number 272464. It exists to provide high quality education for local boys and girls.

St Michael's Preparatory School

La Rue de la Houguette, St Saviour, Jersey, Channel Islands JE2 7UG
Tel: 01534 856904
Fax: 01534 856620
e-mail: tm@stmichaels.je
website: www.stmichaelsschool.je

Headmaster: **Richard de Figueiredo**, BA, CertEd

Deputy Head: C P Cook, MA, AdvDipEd

Age Range. 3–13.
Number of Pupils. 203 Boys, 146 Girls.
Fees per term (2011-2012). Pre-Prep £2,683–£2,999; Forms 1 and 2 £3,784; Form 3 £3,822; Form 4 £4,096; Forms 5 and 6 £4,116. Lunch £265.

Boys and girls are prepared for scholarship and entrance to all Independent Senior Schools. Hockey, rugby football, soccer, gymnastics, netball, rounders, cricket, athletics and tennis are taught on spacious playing fields with pavilion and hard tennis courts which adjoin the school. The school also has a purpose-built Sports Hall (4 badminton court size), indoor swimming pool and gymnasium.

Recent additions to the school's facilities include Court House comprising 3 Senior Humanities classrooms, a Gym/Dance studio and a new DT room.

The school has computer, art and technology suites in addition to networked computers in every classroom. A large variety of clubs and hobbies function within the school and many out-of-door activities, including surfing, sailing and photography, are enjoyed by the children. Music, drama and art, which includes pottery, are all encouraged and a wide range of musical instruments are taught. There are two school choirs and two orchestras. The senior choir regularly competes in the choral competitions around the country.

For senior children there is an annual Activities Week. Year 6 have overnight trips to neighbouring islands and France, while Year 7 go to Brittany and Year 8 to the south of France. Each winter a party of children ski in Switzerland. Regular tours are made to Guernsey and England for sporting fixtures.

Care, consideration, courtesy and good manners are important aspects of behaviour that the school holds dear.

The academic and physical development, in addition to the spiritual, moral and cultural growth, of the whole child is the main aim of the school and every child is encouraged to do "a little better" than anyone thought possible.

St Michael's Preparatory School

198 Hadleigh Road, Leigh-on-Sea, Essex SS9 2LP
Tel: 01702 478719
Fax: 01702 710183
e-mail: info@stmichaelsschool.com
website: www.stmichaelsschool.com

Chairman of Governors: The Revd Robin Eastoe

Head: **Mr S Tompkins**, BSc Hons Sunderland, PGCE Leeds, MA York

Age Range. Co-educational 3–11 years.
Number of Pupils. 270 day pupils (153 boys, 117 girls).
Fees per term (2010-2011). £1,170–£2,330.
St Michael's is a Church of England Preparatory (IAPS) School founded in 1922 to provide a sound academic education based on Christian principles, with children welcomed

from other Christian traditions and faiths. The school has its own Chapel.

The school is situated in a good residential area in Leigh-on-Sea within easy reach of public transport. London is accessible by rail and Fenchurch Street Station is approximately 40 minutes away.

The curriculum offered is broad, balanced and geared towards the different age groups within the school and it aims to contribute to the intellectual, physical, creative, social and spiritual development of each child. All the children, from Nursery through to Form 6, receive specialist teaching in Music, French and PE with additional specialist teaching in the Prep department. Pupils are prepared for the end of Key Stage standardised attainment tests, 11+ entry to local grammar schools and Entrance or Scholarship examinations for independent schools. High academic standards are achieved throughout the school and the children thrive in a happy but disciplined environment.

St Michael's has a dedicated and well-qualified staff. Class sizes are small to enable personal attention to be given. The school is well resourced with many specialist areas. Nearby playing fields are used for Games. There is a wide range of extra-curricular activities available, with Music and Drama as particular strengths.

Visits to the school are warmly welcomed.

Charitable status. St Michael's Preparatory School is a Registered Charity, number 280688. It exists to provide education.

St Michael's Prep School
Otford

Otford Court, Row Dow, Otford, Kent TN14 5SA
Tel: 01959 522137
Fax: 01959 522137
e-mail: office@stmichaels.kent.sch.uk
website: www.stmichaels-otford.co.uk

Chairman of Governors: Gordon Owen, Esq, CBE

Headmaster: **K S Crombie**, BSc

Deputy Head: D Sinclair

Head of Pre-Prep Department: Mrs M Stephens

Age Range. 2–13 Co-educational.
Number of Pupils. 460.
Fees per term (2011-2012). £310–£3,845.

St Michael's is a thriving, friendly school in a superb setting. We offer a fully co-educational, all-round preparatory education of the highest standard in a caring, family community. With a generous staff to pupil ratio and small classes, St Michael's achieves excellent results at every stage. Boys and girls share all activities; everyone is encouraged to try their best and to take part, perform and enjoy every aspect of school life.

The school's Christian roots support its modern ethos. St Michael's was founded in 1872 by London vicar Arthur Tooth who used his own fortune to create a school. The simple, egalitarian style of the founder has strong echoes today in a community where children from a wide variety of backgrounds and every faith are welcome.

St Michael's provides a unique environment for learning and enjoyment. The distinguished Victorian architecture of the original estate has been thoughtfully extended and upgraded. Spacious facilities for learning now include modern science, music, drama and art rooms, a large sports hall and splendid indoor 25m swimming pool. The school's wonderful wooded grounds on the slopes of the North Downs provide outdoor inspiration and extensive space for exploration, sport and play. They are also a truly memorable back-

drop to a well-balanced education which allows every pupil to flourish.

The school prepares pupils for senior independent schools and local grammar schools (at 11+ and 13+) and has a proven academic record with many pupils gaining prestigious awards. It also has a high reputation for music, games (rugby, cricket, soccer, netball, hockey and athletics), drama and art.

A thriving Nursery, Kindergarten and Pre-Prep Department is self-contained and housed in the converted stable block, together with additional purpose-built facilities. Children play in the secure environment of the old walled garden, which has recently been equipped with an adventure playground.

An extensive out of school extra-curricular activity programme is offered to all pupils on a weekly basis and all classes participate in an integral programme of visits, workshops and field trips.

An active Parents and Friends Association is a strong supporter of the school and the Old Michaelian Society is one of the longest established in the Prep School world.

Charitable status. St Michael's is a Registered Charity, number 1076999. It exists to provide education for boys and girls.

St Neot's Preparatory School

Eversley, Hook, Hampshire RG27 0PN
Tel: 0118 973 2118
Fax: 0118 973 9949
e-mail: office@st-neots-prep.co.uk
website: www.st-neots-prep.co.uk

Chairman of Governors: Mr P Smith

Headmaster: **J Gear**, BEd Hons

Age Range. 3 months–13 years co-educational.
Number of Pupils. 26 weekly boarders, 10 flexi-boarding places, 215 Main School, 91 Lower School, 21 Nursery, 29 Crèche.
Fees per term (2011-2012). Boarders: £5,625; Day pupils: Years 4–8 £4,540, Year 3 £3,345, Reception–Year 2 £2,740, Nursery £8.25 per hour, Tiny Tuskers £5.80 per hour.

The school is situated on the border of Hampshire, Surrey and Berkshire in its own 70-acre peaceful site, comprising many grass pitches, all-weather surfaces and woodland. There is a mixed staff of 83 spread over the child age range of 3 months to 13 years. Overall staff ratio is about 1:9.

All curriculum subjects are taught; streaming exists from Year 5 and exams are sat at all appropriate ages and stages; some children are prepared for Senior School scholarships and all-rounders awards and about 30 have been gained in the last 3 years. A very broad range of other activities is available, music, art, ICT, drama, PE to name but a few and all of these, as with the academic subjects, are taught by subject specialists.

As well as the wide provision of sports facilities for all ages and stages, the school has its own enclosed swimming pool, a rifle range and golf course. Constant development of these facilities over the last few years has meant that matches can be played by all children, either boys or girls, in all year groups. A wide-ranging sports enrichment programme is also offered.

Facilities include a beautiful Boarding House, extended Dining Room enabling family service meals for all children and a 70m × 50m astroturf pitch. The Nursery and Crèche are housed in an eco-friendly, carbon-neutral building, with facilities for 60 children and 10 staff, and its own gardens and play area.

The school aims to ensure that all pupils receive the best possible training for life in a hard working, but happy family atmosphere, based on Christian practice and principles.

Charitable status. St Neot's (Eversley) Limited is a Registered Charity, number 307324. The aim of the Charity is to try to provide the best all-round education possible to as many pupils as possible, with bursarial help according to need.

St Olave's Preparatory School

106–110 Southwood Road, New Eltham, London SE9 3QS
Tel: 020 8294 8930
Fax: 020 8294 8939
e-mail: office@stolaves.org.uk
website: www.stolaves.org.uk

Chairman of Governors: M D Ireland, Esq

Headmaster: **Mr James Tilly**, BA Hons QTS

Age Range. 3–11.
Number of Pupils. 217 Day Boys and Girls.
Fees per term (2011-2012). Pre-Prep £1,272–£2,540; Reception & Year 1 £2,680; Years 2–6 £2,900.

Founded in 1932, St Olave's is a day preparatory school for girls and boys aged 3–11 years. A fully qualified and committed teaching staff prepares children for entry to local Grammar and Independent Senior Schools.

The aim of the school is to offer a warm and caring environment in which each child can thrive and be happy knowing that each is accepted for who they are. All achievements both great and small are acknowledged and celebrated. A Christian ethos permeates the pastoral life of the school, where care for others through thoughtful and responsible behaviour is expected. Praise and encouragement, rather than punishment and restriction, are emphasised and relationships between staff and pupils are relaxed and friendly. A close partnership with parents is sought.

The children in the Lower School are taught in mixed-ability classes where each child's progress is carefully monitored by the Form Teacher. In the Upper School the children are set across the year group for Mathematics. Individual differences are appropriately met, with the very able and those with mild learning difficulties receiving additional support where this is thought beneficial. The school is noted for the broad curriculum it offers and for its excellent achievements in Music and Drama. A range of sporting activities is taught as part of the curriculum and there is a wide range of after school clubs and activities. Music and PE are taught by specialist teachers from the age of three and French is introduced at 6 years old. The classrooms are equipped with computers and there is a networked suite which supports all areas of the curriculum. A specialist ICT teacher teaches all year groups from Reception to Year 6. Interactive whiteboards are used in the Upper School classrooms.

St Olave's feeds a wide range of secondary schools and parents are given help in choosing the school most appropriate to meet the needs of their child.

Charitable status. St Olave's School is a Registered Charity, number 312734. It exists to provide high quality education for boys and girls.

St Olave's School, York
The Prep School of St Peter's School, York

York YO30 6AB
Tel: 01904 527416
Fax: 01904 527303
e-mail: enquiries@st-olaves.york.sch.uk
website: www.st-peters.york.sch.uk

Chairman of the Governors: P N Shepherd

Master: **A Falconer**, BA, MBA

Deputy Head: D S Newman, MA, PGCE

Age Range. 8–13 co-educational.
Number of Pupils. 183 Boys, 121 Girls.
Fees per term (2011-2012). Day £3,256–£3,938. Boarding: £6,631 (Years 7 & 8), £6,011 (Year 6). Flexi boarding is available. Fees are fully inclusive.

St Olave's was founded in 1876. With its own halls, music school, practical subjects workshops, sports hall and magnificently appointed specialist teaching rooms, St Olave's enjoys some of the best facilities for a prep school of its type.

The school puts praise, encouragement and pastoral care of the individual as its highest priority. There is a demanding wide curriculum from the earliest age with specialist subject areas – modern foreign languages, information technology, science and music amongst others – being taught by specialist teachers from Year 4. Progress is monitored through a regular system of effort grades, and attainment is measured through internal and externally moderated tests.

Boarding is a flourishing aspect of the school with an extension to accommodate more girls in what is now a co-educational House under the constant care of resident House parents and their own family. Weekly and flexi boarding are now also available. There are also five Day Houses.

Music plays an important part in the life of the school with 22 music teachers, two orchestras, a wind band and 14 ensembles playing and practising weekly. Over 200 pupils learn individual instruments, and all are encouraged to join larger groups. Sport has an equally high profile where rugby football, hockey, cricket, netball, tennis and swimming are major sports. Athletics, cross-country running, squash, badminton, basketball and volleyball are also available for all. The boys have won the National Schools' Seven-a-Side rugby tournament four times in the last eight years. The school has 23 tennis courts, a new synthetic pitch and 24m 6-lane swimming pool.

Drama has an increasing profile with a newly-refurbished theatre and out-of-school activities flourish through such clubs as science society, chess, Mandarin, climbing, art and trampoline. The three modern languages – French, German and Spanish – organise holidays and exchanges with the appropriate country.

The vast majority of boys and girls move on to St Peter's and are not required to take the Common Entrance examination.

Entrance examinations are held in January/February each year, and tests can also be arranged at other times. Entry is possible in all years. Means-tested bursaries are available from 11.

Charitable status. St Peter's School York is a Registered Charity, number 529740. It exists to provide education for boys and girls.

St Paul's Cathedral School

New Change, London EC4M 9AD
Tel: 020 7248 5156
Fax: 020 7329 6568
e-mail: admissions@spcs.london.sch.uk
website: www.spcs.london.sch.uk

Chairman of Governors: The Dean of St Paul's Cathedral,
   The Rt Revd Graeme Knowles, AKC

Headmaster: **Mr Neil R Chippington**, MA, FRCO

   Age Range. 4–13 Co-educational.
   Number of Pupils. Boarding Choristers 40, Day Boys
121, Day Girls 88, Pre-Prep 65.
   Fees per term (2011-2012). Choristers £2,398; Day
Pupils £4,145; Pre-Prep £3,850.
   There have been choristers at St Paul's for over nine centuries. The present school is a Church of England Foundation dating back over 100 years and is governed by the Dean
and Chapter of St Paul's Cathedral. The broadening of educational expectations and the challenge of curricular developments led the Dean and Chapter to agree to expand the
school in 1989 by admitting non-chorister day-boys for the
first time; a decision which continues to enrich the life of the
school and Cathedral. In September 1998, the school admitted girls as well as boys into its new pre-prep department for
4–7 year olds. The school became fully co-educational in
September 2002. It offers a broad curriculum leading to
scholarship and Common Entrance examinations. In the
first three years the work is tailored to individual needs bearing in mind the wide variety of educational backgrounds
from which pupils come. The school has an excellent record
in placing pupils in the senior schools of their choice, many
with music scholarships. Every opportunity is taken to make
use of the school's proximity to museums, libraries, galleries, theatres and the numerous attractions which London has
to offer.
   The 40 chorister boarders are housed on the Cathedral
site and are fully integrated with the day pupils for all their
academic studies and games. The choristers' cathedral choral training offers them a unique opportunity to participate
in the rich musical life of St Paul's and the City.
   The school was rehoused in the 60s in purpose-built premises on the eastern end of the Cathedral site. A refurbishment project added a new music school, art room, IT room,
three pre-prep classrooms and games rooms to the existing
facilities which include a hall/gymnasium, science laboratory, common room and a TV/video room. All pupils are
encouraged to play a musical instrument (most pupils play
two) and there are music and theory lessons with school
orchestras and chamber groups.
   A wide variety of games is offered including field sports
at local playing fields and weekly swimming lessons. The
children have their own playground and the use of the hall
for indoor games and gymnastics.
   Admissions procedure. Prospective pupils of 7+ years in
September are given academic tests in Mathematics and
English, usually in January of the previous academic year.
   Pre-Prep children are assessed in an informal play situation in the November prior to entry.
   Voice trials and tests for chorister places are held in February, May and October for boys between 6½ and 8½ years
old.

St Peter and St Paul School

Brambling House, Hady Hill, Chesterfield, Derbyshire
S41 0EF
Tel: 01246 278522
e-mail: head@spsp.org.uk
website: www.spsp.org.uk

Chairman of Board of Trustees: Mr John Edwards

Headmaster: **Mr Andrew Lamb**, CertEd

   Age Range. 4–11 years.
   Number of Pupils. 130.
   Fees per term (2011-2012). £2,273–£2,404.
   Laughter, self-esteem, family, being cherished, awe and
wonder, security, opportunity, preparation, independence
and success are all part of the St Peter and St Paul School
experience.
   The school is set in 12 acres of park and woodland in
walking distance of the town centre. The school has undergone enormous changes since 2002 under the current Headmaster, including joining the ranks of IAPS in 2006. As well
as the school itself which caters for children from 4 to 11,
there is a flourishing Nursery run by Children 1st in partnership with the school. This enables provision to be made for
care and education throughout the year from birth to 11.
There are no formal entry requirements and a number of
bursaries are available.
   Through five simple aims that involve us being dedicated
to providing the best education, the best standard of care, the
best opportunities, the best possible preparation for life for
children while at the same time providing exceptional value
for parents we are able to achieve our mission of providing a
challenging and supportive environment where every child
is valued as an individual and can reach their full potential.
   Combining traditional teaching methods, family values,
care from 7.30 am to 6 pm in a safe, secure and happy environment ensures that all our children meet with success. Our
modern facilities designed to provide the greatest opportunities for children help us to achieve our aims.
   The school's academic standard is exceptionally high and
pupils are prepared for entry to a range of both independent
and state schools. Recently pupils have gained a variety of
awards to independent schools.
   The school has a dedicated staff team who provide the
children with stimulating and enjoyable learning experiences. Whether in the classroom, on the games field, in the
concert hall or on the school stage, staff give all children the
opportunity to shine. Our unique Life Skills programme has
been designed to develop skills in teamwork and leadership
as well as to enable children to make healthy life style
choices. We live in an ever-changing world and the programme also involves managing and coping with change.
Within the programme children experience such activities as
Indoor Climbing, Orienteering, First Aid, Aerobic Dance,
Archery and much more.
   While achieving our aims, our pupils develop honesty,
good manners, confidence, independence, motivation, the
ability to succeed as well as the value of helping others.
   Never being satisfied and always expecting a lot from
both children and staff ensures that the school continues to
thrive and develop in this modern world.
   Charitable status. The St Peter and St Paul School Trust
is a Registered Charity, number 516113.

St Peter's School

Harefield, Lympstone, Nr Exmouth, Devon EX8 5AU
Tel: 01395 272148

Fax: 01395 222410
e-mail: hmoffice@stpetersprep.co.uk
website: www.stpetersprep.co.uk

Chairman of Board of Reference: G P Dart

Headmaster: N G Neeson, BEd Hons Glasgow, NPQH

Chairman: C N C Abram, BEd St Luke's College, Exeter

Finance Director: J R Middleton, BSc Hons London, ACIB

Age Range. 3–13.
Number of Pupils. 167 Boys, 108 Girls (265 day, 10 weekly boarders).
Fees per term (2011-2012). Weekly Boarders £5,196, Senior Day Pupils £3,450, Junior Day Pupils £3,131, Pre-Prep Pupils £2,333, Nursery £2,014.

St Peter's is an independent prep school, established in 1882, offering day and weekly boarding for children aged 3 to 13. It is committed to traditional prep school values with a modern approach and prides itself on its warm, family atmosphere.

The Independent Schools Inspectorate report from October 2008 found that '*The Educational Experience at St Peter's is outstanding*' and that '*leadership and management are highly successful ... reflected in the good standards achieved, the pupils' outstanding personal development and the fulfilment of the school's ethos and aims*'. Weekly and Flexi boarding was highlighted by Inspectors as being '*outstanding as close as possible to the model of really good home life*'.

Set in 28 beautiful acres overlooking the Exe estuary, the school provides a friendly and safe environment. It offers small class sizes and provision from 8 am to 6 pm. There is a holiday activity programme and a school bus service, which covers Exeter, East Devon and the Teign Valley.

St Peter's has a long and successful history of recognising that every child is unique and is inspired to learn in a different way. The caring staff nurture the children as individuals, encouraging each one to become independent, creative, resourceful and confident with a strong sense of community.

St Peter's enjoys an excellent Scholarship and Common Entrance record and prides itself on maintaining high academic standards while retaining balance and breadth in the curriculum. French, PE and Music is taught by specialists throughout the whole school and there are specialist subject teachers for all subjects from Year 5 onwards. The school is not selective and caters for pupils of wide-ranging abilities, from those taking scholarships in curriculum areas such as academics, sport, art and music to those who require more support.

Flourishing Music and Drama Departments provide scope for all pupils to perform individually and combine their talents in acting, singing or working as technicians. Lessons in Brass, Strings, Woodwind, Piano, Guitar, Percussion, Singing and Speech & Drama are offered.

The Games programme is reinforced with a strong fixtures list at all age levels for boys and girls. St Peter's is proud of its successful games record, with IAPS champions in athletics, badminton, hockey, squash and tennis.

Since 2000, the school's progressive development plan has introduced new classrooms in the junior and senior schools, a new science laboratory, and refurbishment of the library and sports hall.

St Piran's

Gringer Hill, Maidenhead, Berkshire SL6 7LZ
Tel: 01628 594302
Fax: 01628 594301
e-mail: registrar@stpirans.co.uk
website: www.stpirans.co.uk

Chairman of Governors: Mr Edward Parrott
Headmaster: J Carroll, BA Hons, BPhilEd, PGCE, NPQH

Age Range. 3–13 Co-educational.
Number of Pupils. 360 day pupils.
Fees per term (2010-2011). £510–£3,830.

St Piran's is a thriving co-educational IAPS day school with approximately 360 pupils aged from to 3 to 13. The school is set amid 10 delightful acres just to the north of Maidenhead town centre. In 2005 we celebrated our bicentenary, having been founded as a small school in Blackheath, London in 1805.

Class sizes are small. Boys and girls benefit from individual attention in all subjects. They are provided with a wide range of exciting opportunities both inside and outside the classroom. Numerous trips to castles and museums, theatres and shows, history re-enactments, geographical fieldwork and religious sites extend the children's understanding of the world around them. In addition to the academic subjects, pupils take part in a wide range of other activities each week. These include music and art as well as pursuits as diverse as riding, website design, technology, cycling and even fishing.

Academically, the school supports a broad curriculum at all levels in the school. French starts with our youngest classes where confidence in the spoken language is encouraged. By Year 6 we are introducing Latin and Spanish. The children enjoy specialist teaching in art, games and PE, ICT, swimming and music from an early age. By the age of 10, all lessons are taught by extremely well qualified subject specialists. We support children with their entrance exams at 11+ to Grammar Schools or other independent schools, and also the children who stay with us to 13 who take Common Entrance and Scholarship exams to independent senior schools. Our results over the years have been excellent, supporting our desire to encourage independent thinkers, confident individuals and strong leaders of the future.

The main sports that pupils take part in are rugby, soccer, netball, hockey, cricket, rounders and swimming. The school has its own indoor swimming pool and large sports hall. St Piran's also has a dance studio and pupils are encouraged to take an active part in the performing arts. We are blessed with wonderful facilities which serve to enhance the varied sports programmes that we offer the children at all levels.

The school has its own Leadership programme and regular visits off site are arranged for all the children, including residential trips.

Pupils may enter the school at any age, although the main intakes occur at Nursery, Year 3 and Year 7. Scholarships and bursaries may be offered after assessment. Please contact the school and an appointment can be arranged to talk to the Headmaster about financial support.

The school is proud of its outstanding record of achievement and the fully rounded education that it provides within a friendly caring atmosphere. We are proud of our Christian tradition and family ethos which foster high expectations and successful, happy children.

Children and parents are warmly invited to visit St Piran's to see for themselves the excellent facilities that we offer and to meet some of the staff and pupils.

Charitable status. St Piran's School Limited is a Registered Charity, number 309094.

St Pius X Prep School

200 Garstang Road, Fulwood, Preston, Lancashire PR2 8RD
Tel: 01772 719937
Fax: 01772 787535
e-mail: enquiries@st-piusx.lancs.sch.uk
website: www.stpiusx.co.uk

Chairman of Governors: P Clegg

Headmistress: **Miss B Banks**, MA

Age Range. 2–11.
Number of Children. 250 Day Girls and Boys.
Fees per term (2011-2012). Main School £2,150, Nursery £190 per week.

The School is administered as a non-profit-making educational trust by a Board of Governors, providing education from 2–11. The children are prepared for entrance examination to independent schools and local high schools. The school has an excellent record of scholarships to senior schools and SATS results at KS1 and KS2. The school has a large Nursery division which covers the EYFS in recently-refurbished Nursery rooms. The school is in four acres of its own grounds in a pleasant suburb of Preston. All preparatory curriculum subjects covered.

Sports taught are Association Football, Cricket, Tennis, Hockey, Netball, Rugby, Table Tennis, Rounders, Athletics and Cross-Country.

Ballet, piano, clarinet, flute, violin, guitar and singing lessons are some of the optional extras offered. The school has a recently-built junior extension which houses a thriving music centre.

Charitable status. St Pius X School is a Registered Charity, number 526609. Its purpose is to equip the children with an outstanding academic and social education in a Catholic Christian environment, which will enable them to achieve their full potential – the school welcomes pupils of all faiths.

Saint Ronan's

Water Lane, Hawkhurst, Kent TN18 5DJ
Tel: 01580 752271
Fax: 01580 754882
e-mail: info@saintronans.co.uk
website: www.saintronans.co.uk

Chairman of Governors: Mr Robin Dalton-Homes

Headmaster: **W E H Trelawny-Vernon**, BSc Hons

Deputy Head (Pastoral): T Fox
Deputy Head (Academic): G Vincendeau

Age Range. 3–13 fully co-educational.
Number of Children. 320.
Fees per term (2010-2011). Day £2,748–£4,711. We also operate a flexi-boarding system (£31 per night) which can be tailored to individual needs.

Saint Ronan's is a family school as it has been since it was started in Worthing in 1883. It occupies a fine Victorian Mansion set in 247 acres of beautiful Weald of Kent countryside. There are numerous games pitches, hard tennis courts, golf course and a swimming pool as well as a hundred acre wood.

By deliberately remaining small the school has developed a unique and special atmosphere in which staff and children work together to achieve their aims. Our small size helps the transition from home to school and a maximum class size of 16 enables children to gain confidence and interact positively with their peers and the staff.

Academically we have an excellent pass rate at CE and many pupils gain Scholarships to major senior independent schools such as Eton, Sevenoaks, Benenden, Tonbridge, Harrow, King's Canterbury and Eastbourne; we also prepare children for entry to local Grammar Schools and boast an enviable record here too.

Music and art play a vital role at Saint Ronan's. We have two choirs: the Chamber choir and the Chapel choir, and over two thirds of the children learn at least one musical instrument. We have an excellent orchestra and ensembles for most instruments. Music is thriving and Scholarships to Eton and King's Canterbury are amongst recent notable achievements. The art department is flourishing and the children have the option to learn pottery and woodwork in addition to their timetabled art lessons. In 2009, we obtained four Art Scholarships to Senior schools.

The major sports at Saint Ronan's are rugby, football, hockey, cricket and netball but we also offer coaching in athletics, tennis, swimming, dance, rounders, judo, golf, archery, fencing, lacrosse and cross-country.

The Pre-Prep is very much part of the school, in both location and ethos, and is a thriving and dynamic department taking children from 3 to 7.

In 2006 we opened a new Nursery, Pre-Prep, Music school and IT suite. Our swimming pool has been renovated and there are many new and exciting projects afoot, including the opening of a new Sports Hall in 2010.

Charitable status. Saint Ronan's School is a Registered Charity, number 1066420. It exists for the advancement of education of its children.

St Swithun's Junior School

Alresford Road, Winchester, Hants SO21 1HA
Tel: 01962 835750
Fax: 01962 835781
e-mail: office.juniorschool@stswithuns.com
website: www.stswithuns.com

Established 1884. Girls day preparatory school with pre-preparatory boys. Church of England.

Chairman of Governors: Mr J C Platt, FCA

Headmistress: **Mrs P Grimes**

Age Range. Girls 3–11, Boys 3–7.
Number of Pupils. 169 Girls, 9 Boys. Average class size 24. Pupil/teacher ratio 12:1.
Fees per term (2011-2012). Nursery: £1,330 (mornings), £2,660 (all day); Reception, Years 1 & 2 £2,655; Years 3–6 £3,430.

Profile. St Swithun's Junior School shares a spacious 45-acre campus with the Senior School on the Hampshire Downs and is an independent day school for approximately 200 girls and boys. Girls are aged 3–11 and boys are aged 3–7.

The Junior School ethos centres around the belief that education should awaken a spirit of wonder and discovery in children. In a stimulating environment staff aim to foster an eagerness to learn, to strive and to achieve, indeed to release the potential of each pupil – academically, creatively, on the sports field and at play.

The school encourages pupils, parents and staff to be part of a caring community committed to the nurture and encouragement of every individual. It is important to us that our pupils develop a sense of their own worth whilst demonstrating consideration and courtesy for others. Like the Senior School, St Swithun's is a Christian foundation and its ethos is reflected in the school's values and relationships.

Facilities are first-class and include specialist classrooms for Science, Art and Technology, Music and IT. There is a purpose-built Performance Hall and Sports Hall and the Nursery and Reception classrooms were rebuilt in 2005.

Entry. At 3.

Curriculum. Usual subjects taught plus French, Art, Technology, Drama, ICT, Music and PE, with due regard for National Curriculum requirements.

Leavers. Boys leave for various preparatory schools, including The Pilgrims' and Twyford. Girls go on to a range of senior independent schools including St Swithun's Senior School.

Consultation. Biannual reports, regular Parents' Evenings and PTA.

Sports. Gymnastics, Hockey, Netball, Rounders, Tennis, Short Tennis, Swimming, and Athletics.

Activities. These include Tennis, Art, Drama, Gymnastics, Judo, Science, Cookery, Swimming, Football and Dance.

Musical concerts and productions are regularly held and two annual field study trips and regular visits take place.

Special needs. Qualified Learning Support teacher.

Charitable status. St Swithun's School Winchester is a Registered Charity, number 307335.

St Teresa's Nursery and Preparatory School

Beech Avenue, Effingham Hill, Dorking, Surrey RH5 6ST
Tel: 01372 453456
Fax: 01372 451562
e-mail: prepinfo@stteresas.surrey.sch.uk
website: www.stteresasschool.com

Motto: *Gaudere et bene facere*

Chairman of Governors: Mr I Wells

Acting Headmistress: Mrs J Elburn, BSc Hons, PGCE

Head of Preparatory School: **Mrs M A Arnal**, BA, MSc, PGCE

Age Range. Girls 2+–11 with Co-educational Nursery; Boarding from 8+.

Number of Pupils. 100 girls (including some boarders).

Fees per term (2011-2012). Tuition: Nursery £230 per am/pm session, £2,395 (full-time); Reception £2,395; Years 1–2 £2,640; Years 3–4 £3,295; Years 5–6 £3,580. Full day fees include lunch. Boarding (in addition to Tuition fees): £2,745 (weekly), £3,360 (full).

Nestling in an area of outstanding natural beauty in the Surrey hills, St Teresa's Preparatory School provides a happy and stimulating environment where all girls thrive.

In close partnership and open communication with parents, the school creates a solid foundation for your daughter's future, equipping her with the knowledge and self-confidence to stretch and fulfil her potential. Girls are accepted from age 2 and prepared for Senior School, both St Teresa's Senior and a range of other schools.

We offer an exciting and extensive Curriculum, allowing girls to develop strong literacy, numeracy, ICT and social skills. Wellbeing and Relaxation classes complement the plethora of extra-curricular activities on offer, both intellectual and physical. Specialist core subject teachers and Modern Linguists deliver dynamic lessons in a bright airy and spacious environment. We enjoy a 48-acre site along with our Senior School as well as a state-of-the-art Theatre, Performing Arts centre and Swimming Pool. Our beautiful Chapel is a quiet place for reflecting and prayer as well as the spiritual centre of our community. Our Choir and Drama excel as part of this setting and Music provision is superb.

St Teresa's Nursery Plus embraces both boys and girls in an equally attractive Early Years setting. Facilities are first rate and the Curriculum expands learning and play in readiness for big school. Exposure to modern languages, Science, Sport, Music, Dance, Gym and Swimming fill young lives with wonder and achievement along their learning journey. The Garden offers a chance to grow fruit, flowers and vegetables and nurture wildlife and birds.

St Teresa's offers an extended day for all age groups and a supervised homework club until 6 pm. Boarding facilities are on offer from Year 4 including our popular occasional overnight options. We welcome all faiths and none, but ask that you accept our Catholic values of love, honour and respect for each person in our school.

A fully illustrated prospectus is available both on our website and from our Office.

Charitable status. St Teresa's School Effingham Trust is a Registered Charity, number 1095103.

Salisbury Cathedral School

1 The Close, Salisbury, Wilts SP1 2EQ
Tel: 01722 555300
Fax: 01722 410910
e-mail: headsec@salisburycathedralschool.com
website: www.salisburycathedralschool.com

Founded in 1091. Co-educational Preparatory, Pre-Preparatory and Choir School.

Chairman of Governors: The Dean of Salisbury

Head Master: **P M Greenfield**, BEd

Age Range. 3–13.

Number of Pupils. Preparatory: 142 boys and girls (42 boarders); Pre-Prep Department 46 boys and girls.

Fees per term (2011-2012). Pre-Prep: Nursery £17 per am session, £14.50 per pm session, £2,204 (Reception, Years 1 & 2), £3,557 (Year 3). Preparatory School: £4,275 (day), £6,245 (boarding).

The school was founded in 1091 and is situated in the former Bishop's Palace on a 25 acre site in the beautiful Cathedral Close. There is a self-contained Pre-Prep Department for boys and girls between the ages of three and seven. A new boarding house opened in April 2002.

High academic standards, excellent music and drama. Many scholarships are gained to senior schools. Although the main thrust of the academic work leads towards examinations at 13+, some children sit the 11+ tests for the local Grammar Schools. The school also has a fully qualified Individual Needs team.

Facilities include: refurbished science laboratory, IT centre, music technology room, gymnasium, large all-weather pitch, extensive playing fields, heated outdoor swimming pool.

Talented sports staff coach all the major team sports and there are regular fixtures.

There are many after-school clubs open to all children in the Preparatory School. (Quality before and after school care is available for children in the Pre-Prep). The boarding house staff operate an "open door" policy to parents, organise many outings and activities and have achieved an enviable reputation for running a truly happy and caring boarding house.

For a prospectus and/or to arrange a visit to the school, please telephone or visit our website.

Charitable status. Salisbury Cathedral School is a Registered Charity, number 309485. It exists to provide high quality education for children.

Sandroyd School

Rushmore, Tollard Royal, Salisbury, Wiltshire SP5 5QD
Tel: 01725 516264
Fax: 01725 516441
e-mail: office@sandroyd.com

website: www.sandroyd.org

Chairman of Governors: W R Hillary, Esq, FRICS

Headmaster: M J S Harris, BSc, PGCE

Age Range. 3–13 co-educational.
Number of Pupils. 106 boarders, 93 day, plus 30 in Pre-Prep, The Walled Garden.
Fees per term (2010-2011). Boarding £6,710, Day £5,610. Year 3: Boarding £5,340, Day £4,100. Pre-Prep £2,390, Nursery: £25.50 (per morning), £44.00 (all day).

Sandroyd is a co-educational boarding and day school set in 700 acres of beautiful parkland in the heart of the Cranborne Chase on the Wiltshire/Dorset border.

The facilities which the school has to offer are second to none. They include an indoor swimming pool, all-weather hockey/tennis surfaces, cross-country riding course, squash court, extensive games fields and access to a golf course and driving range. Pets such as ponies, ferrets, rabbits and hamsters are welcome.

On the academic side high standards are expected and achieved. The children are prepared for Common Entrance and Scholarships to all the leading independent senior schools and further awards have been won in recent years for Art, Music, Sport and all-round ability. A specialist Learning Support department is in place to assist those who need extra help with their studies. The school is well known for the excellence of its music, both choral and instrumental and a new theatre caters for the many productions which the pupils put on throughout the year across all age-ranges.

Generous bursaries are offered annually.

Visitors are always welcome to meet the Headmaster and to look round the school and its exceptional grounds.

Charitable status. Sandroyd School Trust Limited is a Registered Charity, number 309490. It exists for the purpose of providing education.

Sarum Hall School

15 Eton Avenue, London NW3 3EL
Tel: 020 7794 2261
Fax: 020 7431 7501
e-mail: office@sarumhallschool.co.uk
website: www.sarumhallschool.co.uk

The School, which has a Christian (Church of England) foundation, is an educational trust with a Board of Governors.

Chairman of Governors: Mr B Gorst

Headmistress: Mrs Christine Smith, BA Open, CertEd, RSA SpLD

Age Range. 3–11.
Number of Pupils. 175 Day Girls.
Fees per term (2010-2011). £2,350–£3,900 including lunch.

Founded in 1929, the school has, since 1995, been housed in new purpose-built premises which provide excellent, spacious facilities, including a large playground, gym, dining room and specialist art, IT, music and science rooms. Recently a French room, changing room, multi-purpose room and three individual music teaching rooms have been added.

Girls are prepared for senior London day schools and for 11+ Common Entrance. Girls entering at age 3 are not assessed, but those joining from Year 1 will be tested in English and maths. The school is ambitious for its girls and believes that in a caring, supportive and imaginative environment, every girl can achieve her potential. They are encouraged to develop a love and interest of learning for itself and awareness that their success in all fields is dependent on their own efforts. Consequently the school has a well established record of scholarship and examination success.

A broad curriculum is followed and a major investment in IT ensures that each girl has access to the latest technology. A comprehensive games programme, which takes place on site, ensures that girls have the opportunity to experience a variety of sports. Strong emphasis is placed on music, art, design and drama. Woodwind, violin, piano, cello and singing are offered. There are also two choirs, an orchestra and ensemble groups. Other extra-curricular activities include stage combat, football, Mandarin, theory of music, craft, games and yoga.

Charitable status. Sarum Hall School is a Registered Charity, number 312721. Its purpose is education.

Scarborough College Junior School

Filey Road, Scarborough, North Yorkshire YO11 3BA
Tel: 01723 380606
Fax: 01723 380607
e-mail: juniorschool@scarboroughcollege.co.uk
website: www.scarboroughcollege.co.uk

Chairman of the Governors: Dr John Renshaw

Head of School: D Davey, BEd Hons

Age Range. 3–11 Co-educational.
Number of Pupils. 110.
Fees per term (2011-2012). Tuition: Years 5–6 £3,064, Years 3–4 £2,850, Years 1–2 £2,404, Reception £1,907. Pre-School: £17.50 (per half-day session), £33.50 (full day with lunch).

Wrap-around School Care (3–7 year olds) is all-inclusive. Holiday Clubs (8 am to 6 pm) operate throughout the main school holidays (closed for Christmas and Easter): £14 per half day, £25 per full day.

Scarborough College Junior School dates back some 80 years when it started life as a boys' preparatory school: Lisvane. In February 2000, Lisvane re-located to the main Scarborough College campus.

The Junior School now occupies superb purpose-built premises affording striking views over Oliver's Mount, the South Bay and Scarborough Castle. Facilities include a self-contained pre-school, early years and junior suites, an administration unit together with a school hall and a fully dedicated design and technology/art workshop. All classrooms are equipped with television, video/DVD and radio-cassette/CD equipment. Interactive whiteboards are being installed and all classroom computers are networked to the schools' two ICT suites with intranet and Internet facilities. The Junior School shares many impressive resources and amenities with the Senior School: science laboratories, drama studio, main sports/drama hall, Music School, sports fields, a full-size all-weather pitch and school minibuses.

The breadth of opportunity on offer does not detract from the solid grounding pupils receive in the core subjects. Class teaching – with thoughtfully introduced specialist support where this is advantageous – is the pattern until Year 4. This is then advanced by full subject specialist teaching in the last two years, in readiness for transfer to the Senior School. The full complement of well-qualified staff ensures a generous teacher-pupil ratio. Provision is further enhanced by a SENCO who oversees the school's learning support unit in conjunction with Hull Dyslexia Action.

The standard of pastoral care at the school is very high. The Junior School seeks to nurture well-rounded, confident and competent pupils who are ready for the challenges of secondary education at Scarborough College.

Seaford College Prep School
Wilberforce House

Lavington Park, Petworth, West Sussex GU28 0ND
Tel: 01798 867893
Fax: 01798 867802
e-mail: wilberforce@seaford.org
       jmackay@seaford.org
website: www.seafordprep.org

Seaford College Prep School (Wilberforce House) is an integral part of Seaford College with its own buildings, playground and corporate organisation. Wilberforce House is named after Samuel Wilberforce, the son of the anti-slavery campaigner William Wilberforce. Samuel is buried in the grounds of the School's chapel. The School is set in a magnificent 400-acre site adjacent to the South Downs National Park.

Chairman of Governors: G Sinclair

Head of Prep School: **R W Stather**, BA Hons, PGCE

   Age Range. 7–13 Co-educational.
   Number of Pupils. 161.
   Fees per term (2011-2012). Day: £2,455–£4,125 (Years 3–6), £4,325 (Years 7 & 8). 4-day Boarding: £5,275 (Year 6), £5,480 (Years 7 & 8).
   The school is the Prep School for Seaford College and has the same board of governors. There is very close cooperation between the two schools and there are many shared facilities such as the games fields, the recently refurbished Music School and the catering facilities.
   The Prep School educates boys and girls from the age of 7 and the vast majority of children continue their education at Seaford College until 16 or 18. The main entry points for the Prep School are at 7+ and 11+ although children are welcome to join the school at any age.
   The school aims to nurture a love of learning through a broadly based curriculum and classroom activities are often complemented by day and residential visits. In Years 3, 4 and 5, the majority of lessons are taught by form teachers with subjects such as Music, French, PE/Games and Design and Technology taught by specialist staff. From Year 6 upwards all subjects are taught by specialist staff, many of whom also teach in the Senior School. All classrooms are equipped with interactive whiteboards while a Special Educational Needs Coordinator oversees the school's learning support provision which further enhances learning and achievement. The majority of children complete their homework in school and the school day finishes at 5.20 pm.
   Boarding provision, from Year 6 upwards, is an important aspect of life in the school with the aim being to be as flexible as possible in order to meet parents' and pupils' needs as well as providing a warm and caring home-from-home atmosphere.
   Pupils are able to benefit from the impressive range of games facilities on site, including an astroturf hockey pitch, swimming pool and a 9-hole golf course, with practice greens and driving range as well as the services of a golf professional. Expert coaching is provided in the main sports of football, rugby, hockey, cricket, netball, rounders, tennis, athletics and swimming. The school also has excellent facilities for music, art and design and technology.
   The standard of pastoral care is high and the school has its own Chaplain who takes a weekly assembly in the school chapel. The Prep School aims to treat each pupil as an individual and to establish the firm foundations necessary for success in the Senior School and beyond. (*See Seaford College entry in HMC section.*)
   Charitable status. Seaford College is a Registered Charity, number 277439.

Seaton House School

67 Banstead Road South, Sutton, Surrey SM2 5LH
Tel: 020 8642 2332
Fax: 020 8642 2332
e-mail: office@seatonhouse.sutton.sch.uk
website: www.seatonhouse.sutton.sch.uk

Headmistress: **Mrs V Rickus**, MA, BEd

   Age Range. Girls 3–11, Boys 3–5.
   Number of Pupils. Main School 130; Nursery 35.
   Fees per term (2010-2011). £893–£2,530.
   Seaton House School was founded in 1930 by Miss Violet Henry and there is a strong tradition of family loyalty to the school. The School aims to provide children with a thorough educational grounding to give them a good start in their school lives and to instil sound learning habits in a secure, disciplined but friendly atmosphere. Boys are prepared for admission to a number of pre-preparatory schools and the girls are prepared for various entrance examinations at 11+, both in the London Borough of Sutton and those required by independent day schools. Our highly qualified and committed staff create a stimulating learning environment and small classes ensure that all children have the necessary individual attention and encouragement to achieve the highest standards.
   We follow the broad outlines of the National Curriculum with generous provision for Music, French and Physical Education. There is a School Orchestra and Choir and, each year, all children have the opportunity to take part in dramatic productions. School sports teams enjoy considerable success when they compete regularly against neighbouring schools and each Spring we host our own Netball Tournament. Years 5 and 6 have the opportunity to experience outdoor pursuits during their annual week's residential course. The School has excellent Library and ICT resources, while the range of extra-curricular activities offered is extremely varied, complementing the established provision of after-school care.
   Pastoral care is of the highest calibre with form staff taking a keen interest in all their pupils. Courtesy, good manners and kindness are expected as the norm and children are encouraged to develop initiative, independence and confidence. There is a strong house system in the main school which stimulates good community awareness.
   The prospectus is available upon request and the Headmistress is always happy to meet parents and arrange for them to look around the School.
   Charitable status. Seaton House School is a Registered Charity, number 800673. It exists to provide education for children.

Sedbergh Junior School

Danson House, Loftus Hill, Sedbergh, Cumbria LA10 5RX
Tel: 015396 22295
Fax: 015396 22296
e-mail: hmsjs@sedberghschool.org
website: www.sedberghjuniorschool.org

Chairman of Governors: Hugh M Blair

Headmaster: **Mr Scott G Carnochan**, BEd

   Age Range. 4–13 Co-educational.
   Number of Pupils. 125.
   Fees per term (2011-2012). Day £2,175–£4,190, Full Boarding £5,565–£6,300, Weekly Boarding £5,150–£5,980.

Sedbergh Junior School was opened in 2002 and since that time has become well known as a very friendly and caring school catering for pupils with a wide range of skills and interests. Pupils come from a variety of backgrounds, schools and nurseries. SJS caters for local day pupils, full-time boarding pupils from the UK and overseas and every possible combination of day, weekly and occasional boarding is available in order to meet the needs of parents.

Entrance Exams and Scholarships. Entrance to the school is by assessment and entrance exam. Pupils can start at any age from 4–13. A number of scholarships are available for pupils aged 8 and over.

Subjects. Small class sizes enable pupils to receive individual attention in all subjects. There is a concentration on Maths and English in the early years but Science, Art, Languages, History, Geography, Classics, Music, ICT and Design and Technology form important parts of the curriculum.

Parental involvement. Parents are a crucial component of the school. There are formal Parents Evenings arranged providing opportunities to have one-to-one discussions with individual teachers; termly reports are written for each pupil and the form teachers and subject teachers are happy to discuss any issues at any time.

Sport. Girls: traditional team sports of hockey and netball in the Michaelmas Term. After Christmas, netball and cross-country running become the main sports and in the Summer Term the focus is on tennis, rounders and athletics.

Boys: Sedbergh is renowned for its rugby and has gained numerous regional and national titles. After Christmas rugby is replaced by soccer, hockey, cross-country and rugby 7s. In the Summer Term cricket, athletics and tennis are the main sports.

The Performing Arts. Music and drama are a very important part of school life. Lunchtime practices, individual lessons, concerts, musicals and plays all contribute to a varied and rich programme for the pupils.

Extra-Curricular Activities. There is a variety of trips throughout the year including skiing trips, French trips, History and Geography field trips and for the younger children visits to the local Scarecrow Festival at nearby Wray, and visits to museums such as the Leeds Armouries.

Open Days and Visiting. The school organises three Open Days per year (details are on the website) and visits can be arranged at any time by ringing the School Secretary.

Charitable status. Sedbergh School is a Registered Charity, number 1080672.

Sevenoaks Preparatory School

Godden Green, Sevenoaks, Kent TN15 0JU
Tel: 01732 762336
Fax: 01732 764279
e-mail: admin@theprep.org.uk
website: www.theprep.org.uk

Headmaster: **Philip Oldroyd**, BA, PGCE

Deputy Head: Luke Harrison, BA Hons, PGCE

Head of Pre-Prep: Marjorie Shea, CertEd

Age Range. 2½ to 13.
Number of Children. 220 Boys, 170 Girls.
Fees per term (2010-2011). Nursery & Kindergarten £265 per session; Reception £2,525, Years 1–2 £2,925, Years 3–8 £3,580.

Founded in 1919 Sevenoaks Prep School stands on a spacious 19-acre site of playing fields and woodland bordering the 1,000-acre Knole Estate. We welcome girls and boys from three to thirteen years of age. Our small class sizes and

family atmosphere enables us to build special relationships with the children and their parents.

The curriculum is tailored to the needs of the pupils and their future aspirations. Whilst due regard is paid to the National Curriculum, our children are taught to the highest standard achievable by the individual. To this end our teachers enhance their Programmes of Study to ensure that every pupil is motivated, challenged and prepared for 11+ or 13+ entry tests to local Grammar schools or via Common Entrance Examinations and Scholarships to Independent schools. Our academic achievements are consistently high and our pupils compete successfully for academic, music and other scholarships.

Throughout the school all classes regularly participate in a programme of visits, workshops and field trips to support their learning. Education at Sevenoaks Prep is for life not just the classroom – it is the balance of academic study and co-curricular projects that prepare the children for life.

The school comprises the Pre-Prep (Nursery–Form 2), and the Prep School (Forms 3–8).

Nursery and Kindergarten are staffed by teachers who are specially qualified in Early Years education, with a high teacher to pupil ratio. The education provided is specifically designed to match each child's needs, so that child-initiated play and teacher-directed activities are thoughtfully planned and carefully balanced.

Full-time education starts in the Reception class and from this point, through Forms 1 and 2, class teachers and their assistants provide a rich and stimulating environment where curiosity and enthusiasm to learn are fostered.

On entering the Prep School in Form 3 class teaching is continued for core subjects, with specialist teaching for Drama, Languages, Music, ICT, PE and Games. By the age of eleven, our pupils are taught by specialist teachers in all subjects whilst each class continues to have a form teacher who monitors their progress. Forms 7 and 8 are the senior school years and this is reflected in the teaching and levels of responsibility offered to the children. At Sevenoaks Prep they are at the top of the school they know, rather than the bottom of another, usually much larger, that they do not know. Heads of our destination schools say that children from the Prep enter Form 9 as rounded individuals confident both academically and socially.

Facilities include a large multi-purpose sports hall, a brand new state-of-the-art drama and music suite as well as a brand new childrens restaurant and kitchen. Our location provides a useful and natural extension to our teaching facilities and provide a vast playground, where children are trusted and encouraged to explore safely.

The school provides after-school care until 6 pm each evening and the extra-curricular activities are extensive. The school is supported by an active Social Events Committee who regularly arrange social events for parents to meet each other and raise money for the school.

Sherborne Preparatory School

Acreman Street, Sherborne, Dorset DT9 3NY
Tel: 01935 812097
Fax: 01935 813948
e-mail: registrar@sherborneprep.org
website: www.sherborneprep.org

Chair of Governors: Mr P Jones

Headmaster: **P S Tait**, MA, FRSA

Age Range. 2–13.
Number of Boys and Girls. 268 (Pre-Prep 66, Prep 202).
Fees per term (2010-2011). Boarders: £6,165–£6,450. Day: Nursery £1,235–£1,445; Pre-Prep £2,435; Prep:

£3,675 (Year 3), £4,505 (Years 4–8). Assistance available for Forces families.

Sherborne Prep School is an independent co-educational day and boarding school for children aged 2–13 years. Founded in 1885, the School is set in twelve acres of attractive grounds and gardens in the centre of Sherborne and is well served by road and rail links. Although fully independent, it enjoys a long and close association with its neighbours, Sherborne School and Sherborne Girls.

The Pre-Prep Department is housed in a fully equipped and purpose-built classroom block, with experienced and well-qualified staff providing an excellent ratio of teachers to children.

The Prep School (Years 3–8) offers a broad education, leading to Common Entrance and Scholarship examinations in the penultimate and final year groups. There is a strong emphasis on languages, art and design technology and in independent learning. Over the last few years our pupils have won a large number of scholarships and awards to leading independent schools, including Sherborne School, Sherborne Girls, Bryanston, Sedbergh School, Taunton School, Wells Cathedral School, Abingdon School, Monmouth School, St Swithun's School, St Mary's Shaftesbury, Milton Abbey, Canford School, King's College Taunton and Leweston School.

Following the opening of a new six-classroom block in 2003, the School has also completed a complementary wing housing a further four classrooms and new Art Room. In Years 3–6, the curriculum has been modified to foster independent learning through the teaching of a broader enquiry-based curriculum with an emphasis on study and thinking skills, designed to meet the individual learning styles of the pupils, and the teaching of languages, including Spanish and Mandarin.

The School's ISI report in November 2006 was outstanding and praised the School for its success in many areas, notably in developing independent learning and positive attitudes to work and study. The Ofsted Inspection Report for Boarding in 2010 was also outstanding.

Charitable status. Sherborne Preparatory School is a Registered Charity, number 1071494. It exists to provide an all-round education for children.

Shrewsbury High Prep School
GDST

Old Roman Road, Shrewsbury, Shropshire SY3 9AH
Tel: 01743 494200
Fax: 01743 494213
e-mail: enquiries@shr.gdst.net
website: www.shrewsburyhigh.gdst.net

Shrewsbury High Prep School was formed in 2007 by combining the Junior Department of Shrewsbury High School for girls with Kingsland Grange Prep School for Boys. The school accepts boys and girls from age 3 to 11 (for the girls) or 13 for boys.

Head: **Mrs M Edwards**, BEd Bedford, CertEd Primary Manchester

Deputy Head (*curriculum*): R J Lloyd, BEd Madeley College

Deputy Head (*pastoral*): Miss C James, BA Hons University of Central England

Age Range. Girls 3–11, Boys 3–13.
Number of Pupils. 257.

Fees per term (2011-2012). £2,489 (Reception–Year 3), £2,797 (Years 4–6), £3,466 (Years 7–8 boys). Nursery according to sessions.

Shrewsbury High Prep is located a few minutes' walk from the town centre and Shrewsbury High School's Senior School and occupies a delightful 13-acre woodland site with ample space and superb facilities. It is close to the A5 ring road and Shrewsbury School.

Facilities include three classroom blocks, the most recent of which opened in 2008, comprising a Gymnasium, Science laboratory and Design and Technology workshop.

Small class sizes are employed throughout the school to ensure as much individual attention as possible. The four to eight year-old pupils have a class teacher responsible for teaching and pastoral care. Subject specialists are introduced from the age of eight years. The school curriculum is continually upgraded and developed to meet the modern needs of education whilst still employing tried and tested traditional learning methods. The boys move on to senior independent schools at 13+, mostly by way of Common Entrance or Scholarship examinations, while at 11+ most girls move up to the renowned Shrewsbury High School Senior School. On average 75% of boys move on to Shrewsbury School each year. In both 2010 and 2011, four boys gained scholarships to Shrewsbury School.

We supplement the academic subjects with a timetable of Design and Technology, Art, Music, Drama and Information Technology. The vast majority of pupils study a musical instrument. We have a School choir and our boys supply the treble voices for the Shrewsbury School Choir. The main sports are Soccer, Rugby and Cricket for the boys and Netball, Rounders and Hockey for the girls. Athletics, Swimming and Cross-Country Running also feature for all pupils. Additional activities include Chess, Outward Bound, Canoeing, Mountain-biking and Tennis. These take place at lunchtimes and after school, within an extended school day.

Annual trips abroad include a French Adventure trip, French City visit and a Ski Trip. Extra-curricular visits and invited speakers/performers are a normal part of the school life. Pupils take English Speaking Board examinations, and regularly take part in Festivals of Poetry and Verse Speaking with great success. There is an annual musical and dramatic production.

Charitable status. Shrewsbury High School is part of The Girls' Day School Trust, which is a Registered Charity, number 306983.

Shrewsbury House

107 Ditton Road, Surbiton, Surrey KT6 6RL
Tel: 020 8399 3066
Fax: 020 8339 9529
e-mail: office@shspost.co.uk
website: www.shrewsburyhouse.net

Chairman of the Governors: A Weiss

Headmaster: **K A Doble**, BA, PDM HR, PGCE

Deputy Head: S Ford, BEd Hons, DipIT

Age Range. 7–13.
Number of Boys. 294 Day Boys.
Fees per term (2010-2011). £4,560.

Shrewsbury House was founded in 1865, and moved to its present site in 1910. In 1979 it became an Educational Trust and is administered by a Board of Governors.

Boys are admitted from 7 years of age and are prepared for entry at 13+, either by Scholarship or Common Entrance, to any of the Independent Senior Schools. There are 33 full-time staff, as well as visiting music staff and a French assistant.

The School aims to provide both an academic and broad education; to give a comprehensive preparation for the various examinations required by independent Senior Schools; to develop sound work attitudes and habits; to promote spiritual, moral, social and cultural development and to advance individual development, including instilling self-esteem, confidence and wholeheartedness.

The School is particularly committed to offering every boy a truly broad education. Regardless of his ability – not only on the academic side but also on the non-academic – every boy is taught/coached by someone with expertise. The aims are to foster and discover talents, to aid boys to fulfil them, and, for those not so talented in a pursuit, to give them nevertheless a chance to develop an interest in and/or enjoyment for it. To this end, for instance: every boy is in a team with its own coach; every boy who wishes to be individually tutored in Music may be (currently over 80% learn at least one musical instrument); every boy may be in at least one concert each year and every boy is in a play every year (there are 6 plays a year).

The School is fortunate in its extensive land, including on-site playing fields. The main building is Victorian; its interior has been adapted, furnished and decorated for modern educational needs. There is a covered heated swimming pool, further playing fields and a floodlit all-weather playing surface.

Facilities are constantly being updated and improved. In 2004/5 the following facilities were added: a new Music centre, a new Theatre, a new Dining hall, a new Library and Resources room, a new Pottery room, a new Technology room, 2 new Science Laboratories, a new Art room and 8 further new Classrooms. In 2008 the school completed a two-year programme of installing computer equipment in every desk.

The main sports are Association Football, Rugby Football and Cricket. At the same time boys are encouraged to try a variety of the more individual sports such as Swimming, Tennis, Squash and Scuba Diving. In addition, there is ample opportunity for boys to discover other abilities and talents through activities in Music, technical activities and Drama.

Shrewsbury Lodge. In 2009 Milbourne Lodge Junior School merged with Shrewsbury House to become its Pre-Preparatory School and was renamed Shrewsbury Lodge (*see Shrewsbury Lodge entry*).

Charitable status. Shrewsbury House School Limited is a Registered Charity, number 277324. It seeks to provide the best possible learning environment for boys aged between 7 and 14 who have the potential for above-average academic achievement.

Shrewsbury Lodge School

22 Milbourne Lane, Esher, Surrey KT10 9EA
Tel: 01372 462781
Fax: 01372 469914
e-mail: admin@shrewsburylodge.com
website: www.shrewsburylodge.com

Chairman of Governors: A Weiss

Headmistress: **Mrs G Hope**, BEd, CertEd

Age Range. 3–7 years.
Number of Children. 130 Co-educational.
Fees per term (2011-2012). £2,254–£3,571.

Shrewsbury Lodge is an independent day school for boys and girls aged from 3 to 7 years. It is the Pre-Prep School for Shrewsbury House, the prestigious Preparatory School for boys in nearby Surbiton.

We aim to develop the whole child within an environment of academic excellence. High standards of success are achieved through individual attention, provided by highly qualified professionals in a nurturing and caring family atmosphere. We create a secure, purposeful and happy atmosphere where the children learn positive attitudes to work and play, and develop self-confidence and a respect for others.

We welcome children from different faiths and ethnic backgrounds. Together we respect our many differences. Our curriculum sets out to encourage the diverse talents of the children fostering intellectual, physical, cultural moral and spiritual development.

Shrewsbury Lodge has extensive facilities including modern purpose-built classrooms, a well-stocked library, a hall, a gym, a heated swimming pool, as well as specialist facilities for ICT, Art, Design and Technology and Music. There is a soft surface playground with climbing frames and a variety of outdoor equipment. The school also owns a large sports field.

When children leave us, they are equipped for the next stage of their education, having acquired sound work habits and a caring attitude. Pupils are prepared for entry to a number of Prep schools, although the majority of the boys move on to Shrewsbury House. (*See separate entry.*)

Charitable status. Shrewsbury House School Trust is a Registered Charity, number 277324. It exists to provide education for children.

Silcoates Junior School

Wrenthorpe, Wakefield, West Yorkshire WF2 0PD
Tel: 01924 885276
e-mail: adrianboyer@silcoates.org.uk
website: www.silcoates.org.uk

Chair of Governors: Mrs M C Chippendale, BSc

Headmaster: **A P Boyer**, BEd

Deputy Head: J C Clewarth, BEd Hons, MEd

Age Range. 5–11.
Number of Pupils. 220.
Fees per term (2011-2012). £1,970–£3,020.

Silcoates Junior School is part of the Silcoates School Foundation. The Junior School and the Senior School are on the same campus and share many facilities, which include the chapel, sports hall, indoor swimming pool, music school, playing fields and specialist subject areas for science, design technology and information technology.

Music and drama feature prominently in the life of the school. There is a Junior School Choir, and concerts and musical evenings are held throughout the year, with a major dramatic production staged annually.

There are eleven full-time members of the teaching staff, all of whom are experienced and well qualified. The Junior School is able to call upon the use of specialist teachers from the Senior School for PE, games, French and music. In addition, there are various visiting music specialists.

With over 50 acres of playing fields, we are able to teach a range of sports, which include: rugby, netball, football, cricket, rounders, athletics and cross country and swimming.

There is also a wide range of activities in which pupils can participate at lunchtimes and after school. These include ICT, chess, drama, recorders, orchestra, swimming and sewing. We also utilise residential camps in the Lake District at weekends and in the school holidays for other outdoor activities.

Boys and girls are accepted through an entrance assessment and then the pupils are expected to enter Senior School at the age of 11. There is no entrance examination for pupils entering the Senior School, subject to satisfactory progress having been made by the end of Key Stage 2. (*See Silcoates School entry in HMC section.*)

Charitable status. The Silcoates School Foundation is a Registered Charity, number 529281. It aims to provide a first-class education for boys and girls.

Skippers Hill Manor Preparatory School

Five Ashes, Mayfield, East Sussex TN20 6HR
Tel: 01825 830234
e-mail: info@skippershill.com
website: www.skippershill.com

Headmaster: **T W Lewis**, BA Exon, PGCE London

Age Range. 4–13.
Number of Pupils. 133 Day Pupils.
Fees per term (2011-2012). Reception £2,220, Year 1 £2,590, Year 2 £2,750, Year 3 £4,120, Year 4 £4,150, Years 5 to 8 £4,185.

The school was founded in 1945 and is set in the beautiful Weald of Sussex in grounds covering 32 acres. A dedicated, qualified staff of twenty prepare children for Grammar Schools and Senior Independent Schools' Common Entrance and Scholarship examinations. Classes are small and individual attention, thereby, guaranteed.

Facilities include a well-stocked library, gymnasium, individual music room, ICT suite, all-weather multi-purpose courts and a covered heated swimming pool.

The main games are hockey, rugby, football and cricket for boys; netball, rounders and cricket for girls. Swimming, gymnastics, ballet and athletics are also given prominence. Leisure pursuits include judo, pottery, arts and crafts, vocal training and instrumental music. The Choir and Orchestra are flourishing.

The school is interdenominational in approach and its aim is to help each pupil towards the ultimate goals of self-discipline, common courtesy and the ability to cope with a rapidly changing world. Moreover, happiness is a prime factor in achieving these goals. A happy child is a successful child.

Smallwood Manor Preparatory School
A Woodard School

Uttoxeter, Staffs ST14 8NS
Tel: 01889 562083
Fax: 01889 568682
e-mail: enquiries@smallwoodmanor.co.uk
website: www.smallwoodmanor.co.uk

Custos: S Varley

Headmaster: **M Harrison**, BA Hons, MA, PGCE

Age Range. 2–11.
Number of Pupils. 87 Boys, 77 Girls.
Fees per term (2011-2012). £2,520–£3,230.

Smallwood Manor is a co-educational Nursery and Day School for children aged 2 to 11, set in 50 acres of beautiful woods and parkland just south of Uttoxeter on the Staffordshire/Derbyshire border.

The aims of the school are:
• To ensure that every child enjoys coming to school and that each individual's potential is fully realised.

• To educate the whole child so that academic achievement goes hand in hand with developing spiritual, cultural and physical maturity.
• To emphasise traditional Christian values of good manners and responsible behaviour.
• To provide a stimulating programme of activities to encourage children to develop skills and interests, which will make their school careers successful and rewarding.
• To lay a firm foundation for further education.

As a Woodard School Smallwood has strong ties with Denstone College and has enjoyed an excellent reputation for preparing children for 11+ Entrance Examinations and Scholarships. Smallwood has a fine reputation for sport. Facilities include a covered heated swimming pool, a gymnasium and two hard tennis courts. Rugby, Hockey, Football and Netball are the main winter games; Cricket and Rounders are the main summer games. There is a whole range of clubs and activities after school including Cookery, Art and Crafts, Chess, Board Games and Computers.

Smallwood has a fine modern Chapel and a choir which sings regularly in Music Festivals and local churches. Each child learns the violin for a year and the school has a string group and wind band. Four children currently sing in the National Children's Choir of Great Britain.

Charitable status. Smallwood Manor Preparatory School Limited is a Registered Charity, number 1102929. It aims to provide a Christian education for boys and girls aged 2 to 11.

Solefield Preparatory School

Sevenoaks, Kent TN13 1PH
Tel: 01732 452142
Fax: 01732 740388
e-mail: admissions@solefieldschool.org
website: www.solefieldschool.org

Chairman of the Governors: Mr R Clewley

Headmaster: **D A Philps**, BSc

Age Range. 4–13.
Number of Boys. 170.
Fees per term (2010-2011). £2,730–£3,360 including lunch.

Solefield is a Day Preparatory School for boys from 4 to 13. The school was founded in 1948 and is situated in Solefields Road on the south side of Sevenoaks. The main building is a large town house containing classrooms, kitchen and the school office. The facilities have been increased considerably to include the Science Block, School Hall, Art Room, Dining Room, Junior Classrooms and Changing Rooms. A Music School has recently been built, along with a Library and ICT block opened in April 2008. The grounds contain the main school buildings and a large floodlit playground. The playing fields are a short walk from the school. A qualified and graduate staff prepare boys for entry to Independent Senior and Grammar Schools. Solefield has a strong tradition of academic excellence. Emphasis is placed on teaching the 3 R's in a caring yet well-structured atmosphere with close contact maintained between parents and teachers.

The curriculum includes French, Spanish, Latin, Music, Drama, Art, PE and a number of club activities. Cricket, Soccer and Rugby are the principal games.

Enquiries concerning places and admissions should be made to the Registrar.

Charitable status. Solefield School is a Registered Charity, number 293466. It aims to provide a high quality education to boys aged 4–13.

Sompting Abbotts

Church Lane, Sompting, West Sussex BN15 0AZ
Tel: 01903 235960
Fax: 01903 210045
e-mail: office@somptingabbotts.com
website: www.somptingabbotts.com

Principal: Mrs P M Sinclair

Head Master: **T R Sinclair**, BA

Age Range. 3–13 Co-educational.
Number of Pupils. 190.
Fees per term (2010-2011). Day £2,470–£3,165 (including lunches).

Set in a magnificent site on the edge of the South Downs, Sompting Abbotts overlooks the English Channel with views towards Beachy Head and the Isle of Wight. The imposing Victorian House has some 30 acres of sports fields, woodlands, gardens and activity areas.

The aim of the school is to provide a well-balanced education in a caring environment, recognizing and developing the individual needs of each child, so that maximum potential academic achievement may be gained. Within the community of the school an emphasis is laid on the cultivation of courtesy, self-discipline and respect for one another in order to engender a happy atmosphere.

The school has a vibrant Pre-Preparatory Department, which includes lively Early Years classes. In the Preparatory Department well-equipped Science Laboratory and Computer Room are enjoyed by all ages. The Art and Drama departments offer wide scope for creativity, and peripatetic teachers provide tuition for a range of musical instruments.

South Lee School

Nowton Road, Bury St Edmunds, Suffolk IP33 2BT
Tel: 01284 754654
Fax: 01284 706178
e-mail: office@southlee.co.uk
website: www.southlee.co.uk

Chairman of the Governors: Mr A Holliday

Headmaster: **Mr Derek Whipp**, MA, CertEd

Age Range. 2–13.
Number of Pupils. 300 Boys and Girls.
Fees per term (2011-2012). £2,450–£3,030 including lunches.

South Lee enjoys an excellent reputation for its friendly, family atmosphere. The school provides a stimulating and caring environment where children have every opportunity to learn and develop. From an early age, pupils are taught the traditional subjects, emphasising mathematics, science and English but within a wider curriculum that incorporates the use of the latest developments in technology and educational resources.

The school is situated close to the A14, has purpose-built, modern classrooms and specialist teaching areas. Sport is an important part of the curriculum and the school has the use of excellent local facilities

South Lee offers its pupils opportunities for self-expression and individual development through study of the Arts, drama, music and a broad range of outdoor, sporting and extra-curricular activities.

The **Nursery**, which caters for children from 2 to 4 years of age, makes learning a fun experience from the very start.

The **Pre-Prep** is essentially class-based, though specialist staff teach French, music, ICT and Physical education.

The **Prep School** is well staffed with experienced teachers. The full range of academic subjects is taught, encompassing the national curriculum and preparing pupils for the Common Entrance 13+ examination.

Charitable status. South Lee exists to educate children from 2–13 years of age. Control is vested in a Board of Governors, the majority of whom are current parents. The school is run as a non-profit making Limited Company and is a Registered Charity, number 310491.

Spratton Hall

Spratton, Northampton NN6 8HP
Tel: 01604 847292
Fax: 01604 820844
e-mail: office@sprattonhall.com
website: www.sprattonhall.com

Chairman: G N Underwood, Esq, FRICS

Head Master: **S J Player**, MA

Deputy Head: S J S Clarke, BA

Age Range. 4–13+ Co-educational.
Number of Pupils. 409.
Fees per term (2010-2011). Prep £3,400–£3,600, Pre-Prep £2,650. Fees include stationery, lunch, all academic books and most extra-curricular activities.

Set in 50 acres of Northamptonshire countryside, Spratton Hall is a fully co-educational day school for 4 to 13 years old.

Through highly skilled teaching we create an exciting and stimulating environment for learning, and by developing the talents of each child we believe that every pupil can succeed. The children are encouraged to become independent thinkers and to use their own initiative with confidence.

In the happy, caring Pre-Prep Department (from 4 to 7 years old) the girls and boys play imaginatively and grow in confidence. Each child is nurtured to establish a sound social and academic foundation for their future education.

Spratton has an enviable record of success at Common Entrance. Scholarships and awards are frequently won to many of the leading Independent Senior Schools.

The children enjoy a truly all-round education, achieving high academic standards as well as being recognised nationally for their success in sports and the Arts.

There are excellent facilities for Music, Art and Drama together with a new Library and Media Centre. A wide variety of concerts, productions and exhibitions are enjoyed by all age groups throughout the year.

This year a new Sports Dome has been completed, the Science laboratories, catering facilities and Dining Hall have been completely refurbished and Smart boards have been installed into classrooms.

The extensive playing fields together with the new Jubilee Sports Dome, two all-weather surfaces and a full-size floodlit Astroturf enable all pupils to enjoy a range of sports including rugby, hockey, cricket, netball, rounders, athletics, cross-country and tennis with the Dome allowing for indoor tennis, badminton, gymnastics, dance and ballet.

In November 2010 Spratton Hall's successes were confirmed by an 'excellent' and 'outstanding' school inspection report in every respect by the Independent Schools Inspectorate.

For further information or to arrange a visit to see the children at work and play, please contact The Registrar on 01604 847292 or e-mail afj@sprattonhall.com.

Charitable status. Spratton Hall is a Registered Charity, number 309925. It exists to provide education for boys and girls.

Spring Grove School

Harville Road, Wye, Kent TN25 5EZ
Tel: 01233 812337
Fax: 01233 813390
e-mail: office@springgroveschool.co.uk
website: www.springgroveschool.co.uk

Chairman of Governors: Mr Robert Balicki

Headmaster: **Mr W J B Jones**, BMus Hons, PGCE

   Age Range. 2–11 Co-educational.
   Number of Pupils. 230.
   Fees per term (2010-2011). £1,100–£3,125.
   Spring Grove is a co-educational Day Preparatory School from 2 to 11. The school was founded in 1967 and is situated on the outskirts of the beautiful village of Wye. The main building is a large Edwardian house and contains classrooms and the school office. The facilities have been increased considerably to include the Science Block, School Hall, Art Room, Music Room, Dining Room, Junior Classrooms and Changing Rooms. A new computer room and network is now in operation. The grounds contain the main school buildings and 15 acres of playing fields. Qualified and graduate staff help prepare the children for entry to Independent Senior and Grammar Schools. Spring Grove has a strong tradition of academic excellence. Emphasis is placed on innovative and creative teaching in a caring yet well-structured atmosphere with close contact maintained between parents and teachers.
   The curriculum includes Music, Drama, Dance, Art and Design, PE and a number of club activities. Cricket, Soccer, Rugby, Hockey, Netball and Rounders are the principal games.
   Enquiries concerning places and admissions should be made to the Secretary.
   Charitable status. Spring Grove School 2003 is a Registered Charity, number 1099823.

Staines Preparatory School

3 Gresham Road, Staines, Middlesex TW18 2BT
Tel: 01784 450909
Fax: 01784 464424
e-mail: registrar@stainesprep.co.uk
website: www.stainesprep.co.uk

Co-educational Day School.

Chairman of Governors: Mr M Bannister

Headmaster: **P Roberts**, BSc

   Age Range. 2½–11.
   Number of Pupils. 200 Day Boys, 125 Day Girls.
   Fees per term (2011-2012). £1,400–£2,905.
   Throughout its history SPS has maintained a reputation for high standards of education and care. The School aims for all pupils to attain their potential within a secure and happy environment and strives to produce boys and girls who are confident, honest, considerate and courteous.
   The School believes in traditional values but is committed to providing the very best in terms of modern facilities and educational methods.

The School's philosophy of '*Educating Today's Children for the Challenges of Tomorrow*' is highlighted by the outstanding achievements of former SPS pupils in their secondary schools, with many attaining positions of responsibility as well as enjoying academic, sporting, musical and artistic success.
   The curriculum is based upon the National Curriculum with a sharp focus on the acquisition of literacy and numeracy skills. However, it is given additional breadth by the inclusion of French from Year 2 and Latin/Classical Studies in Years 5 and 6. Sport plays an important role at SPS and there is a regular programme of fixtures against other preparatory schools. Whilst the School believes in competitive sport and has won a number of local tournaments in soccer, netball, cricket and swimming in recent years, it also believes that as many pupils as possible should be given the opportunity to play in matches at various levels. Development of abilities in the Arts is also considered highly important with opportunities provided throughout the School both in the classroom and as extra activities. Subject specialist teaching commences in Year 4 following a series of assessments at the end of Year 3. A regular programme of trips and visits enhance the curriculum and the annual Ski Trip, trip to Melun and Field Trip are much enjoyed.
   The Jubilee Wing along with the new Library and ICT Suite indicate the School's commitment to providing the very best facilities as well as in education. In addition to the general teaching classrooms there are special facilities for Science, Art, Design and Technology and Special Needs. Hard surfaced playground areas, all-weather floodlit court and the adjoining playing fields provide ample space for sport and recreation.
   The School welcomes contact with parents and has a flourishing Friends Association whose activities strengthen the links between home and school. SPARKS, the School's Child Minding facility, operates from 7.30 am and remains open until 5.30 pm and is available for pupils of all ages.

Stamford Junior School

Stamford, Lincolnshire PE9 2LR
Tel: 01780 484400
Fax: 01780 484401
e-mail: headjs@ses.lincs.sch.uk
website: www.ses.lincs.sch.uk

Stamford Junior School, along with Stamford High School (girls) and Stamford School (boys), is one of three schools in the historic market town of Stamford comprising the Stamford Endowed Schools Educational Charity. The schools are under a single Governing Body and overall management and leadership of the Principal and allow continuity of education for boys and girls from 2 to 18, including boarding from age 8. Each school has its own Head and staff.

Chairman of Governors: Malcolm Desforges, Esq

Principal of the Stamford Endowed Schools: S C Roberts, MA

Headmistress: **Miss E M Craig**, MA

   Age Range. 2–11.
   Number of Children. 334.
   Fees per term (2011-2012). Day £3,228; Full Boarding £5,728; Weekly Boarding £5,192; Three Night Boarding £4,564.
   The Junior School educates boys and girls up to the age of 11 (including boarders from age 8), when boys move on to Stamford School and girls to Stamford High School.

Admission from the Junior School to the two senior schools is based on progress and without further entrance testing.

The Junior School occupies its own spacious grounds, bordering the River Welland, overlooking the sports fields and open countryside, the boarding houses, the sports hall, floodlit artificial hockey pitch and the swimming pool on the same site. It is on the south west outskirts of Stamford within easy reach of the A1.

Entry to the School is according to registration at 4+ and assessment and interview in all other age groups.

The attractive and varied curriculum is designed to establish firm foundations in oracy, literacy and numeracy whilst providing excellent opportunities for music, drama, art and design and for acquiring technical and physical skills. The aims of the school are to develop the talents and potential of all the children.

There are 26 full-time staff, with specialist teachers in physical education, swimming, art and music, and visiting teachers offering a variety of sports, dance, speech and drama.

There is a purpose-built nursery in the grounds of the school – the Earlybird Nursery – offering first-class care and early learning for children aged 2–4.

Boarding. The co-educational Boarding House (St Michael's) is run in a homely, family style under the experienced leadership of Mr and Mrs Phillips. Boys and girls are accepted as full or weekly boarders from the age of 8. Occasional or flexi-boarding is accommodated where possible and according to family need. A full programme of activities takes place at weekends so that boarders enjoy a rich and varied week.

Stockport Grammar Junior School

Buxton Road, Stockport, Cheshire SK2 7AF
Tel: 0161 419 2405
Fax: 0161 419 2435
e-mail: sgs@stockportgrammar.co.uk
website: www.stockportgrammar.co.uk

Chairman of Governors: R L E Rimmington, BA, FCA

Headmaster: **L Fairclough**, BA

Age Range. 3–11.
Number of Pupils. 365: 198 boys, 167 girls.
Fees per term (2011-2012). £2,382, plus lunch.

Entry is mainly at 3+ and 4+ following assessment, with occasional places available at other ages. Stockport Grammar Junior School is a happy school, where children are encouraged to develop their strengths. A broad curriculum is taught and academic standards are very high. There are specialist facilities and teaching in science, ICT, physical education, music, art and design technology. A large number of pupils learn to play a musical instrument and tuition is available for many orchestral instruments. French is taught throughout. All children have a weekly swimming lesson in the School's pool. Both infant and junior children can choose to join in the numerous lunch-time and after school clubs and activities.

The Junior School and the Senior School share the same site. The vast majority of pupils move into the Senior School at 11, having passed the Entrance Examinations. (*See also Stockport Grammar School entry in HMC section.*)

Hockey, netball, football, cricket and athletics are the main sports. Swimming, tennis, rounders, cross-country and rugby are also offered. There is a full range of sporting fixtures and regular music and drama productions. All junior pupils have the opportunity to participate in residential visits, which include outdoor pursuits.

Before and after school care is available and holiday play schemes are run at Easter and in the summer.

Facilities are excellent. In addition to specialist teaching rooms, which include a computer room and a science laboratory, there are extensive playing fields, a large all-weather area, new sports hall and drama theatre.

Charitable status. Stockport Grammar School is a Registered Charity, number 1120199. It exists to advance education by the provision and conduct, in or near Stockport, of a school for boys and girls.

Stonar Preparatory School

Cottles Park, Atworth, Melksham, Wiltshire SN12 8NT
Tel: 01225 701762
Fax: 01225 790830
e-mail: office@stonarschool.com
website: www.stonarschool.com

Chairman of Governors: Mr C Beard

Headmaster: **Mr M Brain**, BA Ed Hons Exeter

Age Range. Girls 2–11, Boys 2–7.
Number of Pupils. 123.
Fees per term (2010-2011). Day £2,180–£3,510, Boarding £5,030.

Stonar Prep School is a vibrant and exciting place to be. We pride ourselves on our genuinely small classes which enable us to offer individual care for girls and boys. Happy children are the feature of our school rather than an added extra, as we strive to develop everyone's confidence in a secure and caring atmosphere. Uniquely for a school of our size we are blessed with outstanding facilities in a beautiful environment; we make the most of these to offer a wide-reaching curriculum abounding with purpose and new experiences.

There are plenty of clubs and sports coaching on offer throughout the year, including Judo, Football, Ballet, Orchestra, Trampoline, Gymnastics and Yoga, plus all the traditional team sports and riding lessons.

Boarders are welcomed from 8 years and upwards. They live in a warm and cosy farmhouse known as Fuller House, where they are looked after by a House Parent and her assistant. Weekends are lively and there are plenty of trips and activities for the girls.

Stonar Pre-Prep is for girls and boys aged 2–7. The children begin their 'Early Years' in Nursery before progressing through the transition stage of Kindergarten and on into the Reception class and more formal learning. The Pre-Prep is a lively and exciting area of the school where small groups allow genuine individual attention to be given to each child at this most crucial developmental stage. A wide variety of experiences is enabled through our excellent facilities and generous staff ratios.

Stonar Prep and Pre-Prep benefit from the excellent facilities shared with the senior school, set in 80 acres of parkland and gardens. These include a range of grass and all-weather and sports pitches, a multi-purpose indoor sports hall, indoor heated swimming pool, music school, theatre, brand new art facility and of course Stonar's renowned equestrian centre which has stabling for up to 60 horses, indoor and outdoor arenas and 4 levels of cross country courses.

Minibuses operate throughout Wiltshire and South Gloucestershire and the Prep School provides a free before and after-school club with breakfast available for those who require it.

Charitable status. Stonar School is a Registered Charity, number 309481.

Stonyhurst St Mary's Hall
Preparatory School for
Stonyhurst College

Stonyhurst, Lancs BB7 9PU
Tel:　　01254 826242
Fax:　　01254 827136
e-mail:　admissions@stonyhurst.ac.uk
website:　www.stonyhurst.ac.uk

Chairman of Governors: Kevin Ryan

Headmaster: **L A Crouch**, BA, MA, PGCE

Chaplain: Fr A Howell, SJ

Age Range. 3–13 (Boarders from age 8).
Number of Pupils. Day 186, Boarding 62.
Fees per term (2011-2012). Day £2,162–£4,310; Weekly Boarding £5,530; Full Boarding £6,410.

St Mary's Hall, Stonyhurst, provides a co-educational preparatory education in the Jesuit Catholic tradition for boarders (age 8–13) and day pupils (age 3–13). Stonyhurst, founded in 1593, is one of the oldest Jesuit schools in the world, and the College and Preparatory School are set within two thousand acres of outstanding natural beauty.

The children receive a high quality rounded education. St Mary's Hall has its own outstanding teaching facilities and resources for all preparatory subjects, including French and Latin, and also enjoys the benefit of very extensive games fields, a sports hall, a fully equipped modern theatre, shared use with the College of a large indoor swimming pool, and (2001) one of the finest all-weather pitches in the North. St Mary's Hall has a national reputation for rugby, but at the same time many boys' and girls' sports flourish, as do a wide variety of cultural pursuits including drama and music. Many educational and recreational excursions take place both at home and abroad. The School's Scholarship record is excellent, with 50 awards being gained to Stonyhurst College in the last five years.

All pupils receive pastoral care and academic tutoring through their Class teachers and Playroom (Head of Year) Staff, who meet regularly to monitor closely pupils' progress. Early Years and Key Stage 1 pupils are taught in their own purpose-built building. The teaching staff are also closely supported by a resident Chaplaincy team, which leads the largely lay staff in the religious life of the School. Pupils of other denominations are also welcome at St Mary's Hall.

Boarders are also under the care of the resident Housemistress and her husband, supported by a resident pastoral team, including the Headmaster and other teaching staff. The boarders enjoy a stimulating and wide-ranging programme of lunchtime, evening, and weekend activities. St Mary's Hall, like Stonyhurst College, provides a seven-day a week boarding environment, one in which the day pupils are able to participate to a great extent if they wish.

The main sports played are Rugby, Cross Country, Netball, Rounders, Hockey, Cricket, Athletics and Tennis. The wide range of extra-curricular activities available for the children in their recreational time includes Chess, Model Making, Camping (Summer), Art, Photography, Fencing, Gymnastics, Computing, Theatre Workshop, Modern Dance, Ballet, and Skiing.

Admission to St Mary's Hall of pupils from age 3 to 10+ is by previous school report (where applicable) and interview. At 11+ there is also an entrance test. Academic Scholarships are also awarded at 11+, as is an annual music scholarship. Under normal circumstances all pupils proceed to the College at 13+.

Further details and a prospectus may be obtained from the Headmaster's Secretary.

Charitable status. St Mary's Hall is a Registered Charity, number 230165. It exists to promote Catholic Independent Jesuit Education within the Christian Community. It also runs its own registered, pupil-led charity, Children for Children, which raises funds for a school in Zimbabwe and other worthy causes.

Stormont

The Causeway, Potters Bar, Herts EN6 5HA
Tel:　　01707 654037
Fax:　　01707 663295
e-mail:　admin@stormont.herts.sch.uk
website:　www.stormont.herts.sch.uk

The school is administered by a Council of Management.

Chairman of Council of Management: Mr J H Salmon, FCA

Headmistress: **Mrs M Johnston**, BA Hons, PGCE

Age Range. 4–11.
Number of Pupils. 170 Day Girls.
Fees per term (2011-2012). £3,170–£3,325 (including lunch). There are no compulsory extras.

The School was founded in 1944 and has occupied its attractive Victorian House since then. There is a spacious, bright, purpose-built Lower School Building, which adjoins the Assembly Hall and Dining Room. Old stables have been converted to provide well-equipped rooms for Art, Pottery, Design Technology, Science and French. A Millennium Building houses a Drama/Music Studio and an Information and Communications Technology Suite. The school has two tennis courts and a playground. It has use of a two-acre playing field and a swimming pool. A well-equipped Sports Hall was opened in the Summer Term 2009.

Well-qualified and experienced staff prepare the girls for entry to a wide range of senior schools at the age of eleven.

Charitable status. Stormont School is a Registered Charity, number 311079. It exists to establish and carry on a school where children may receive a sound education.

The Stroud School

Highwood House, Romsey, Hampshire SO51 9ZH
Tel:　　01794 513231
Fax:　　01794 514432
e-mail:　secretary@stroud-romsey-sch.co.uk
website:　www.stroud-romsey.com

Chairman of Governors: Mr G B Gibbs

Headmaster: **A J L Dodds**, MA Cantab, DMS

Deputy Head: Mrs J E Gregory, BEd Hons King Alfred College, CertEd Whitelands College

Director of Studies: Mrs M Freemantle, CertEd

Age Range. 3–13.
Number of Pupils. 318: 182 Boys, 136 Girls.
Fees per term (2011-2012). Upper School £4,280, Middle School £3,850, Pre-Preparatory £2,610, Nursery £6 per hour.

Stroud is a co-educational day school for children aged 2 years 9 months to 13 years. Pupils are prepared for entrance to senior Independent or Grammar Schools.

The School stands on the outskirts of Romsey in its own grounds of 20 acres, which include playing fields, a full-sized sports hall, a heated outdoor swimming pool, tennis courts, riding arena, lawns and gardens. The main team games for boys are cricket, hockey, rugby and soccer, and for girls hockey, rounders and netball. Both boys and girls play tennis.

Music and drama play an important part in the life of the School. A wide variety of instruments is taught and children are encouraged to join the school orchestra. Each year there is a musical production and the Carol Service is held in Romsey Abbey.

The Stroud School Association, run by the parents, holds many social activities and helps to raise money for amenities, but its main function is to generate goodwill.

A new Early Years building was completed in 2007.

The Study Preparatory School

Wilberforce House, Camp Road, Wimbledon Common, London SW19 4UN
Tel: 020 8947 6969
Fax: 020 8944 5975
e-mail: wilberforce@thestudyprep.co.uk
website: www.thestudyprep.co.uk

Chairman of Governors: Mr C Holloway

Headmistress: **Mrs Susan Pepper**, MA

Age Range. 4–11.
Number of Girls. 320 (approximately).
Fees per term (2011-2012). £3,395.

The Study Preparatory School provides a happy and stimulating learning environment for girls from 4 to 11 on two very attractive and well-equipped sites close to Wimbledon Common.

The girls enjoy a rich diversity of experiences, both in and out of the classroom. Each girl is encouraged to do her best academically. Music, sport, drama, public speaking and a varied clubs programme play an important part, while guest speakers, fundraising events and school trips all help the children to understand important issues beyond the school gates. Good manners and consideration for others are encouraged at all times. Girls leave at 11+, very well prepared for the next stage of their education, with a zest for learning and many happy memories.

The Study has an assisted places scheme for girls aged 7+. For details contact Joint Educational Trust (JET) on 020 3217 1100.

Charitable status. The Study (Wimbledon) Ltd is a Registered Charity, number 271012. It exists to provide education for girls from 4 to 11.

Summer Fields

Mayfield Road, Oxford OX2 7EN
Tel: 01865 459204
Fax: 01865 459200
e-mail: admissions@summerfields.com
website: www.summerfields.com

Chairman of Governors: E A Davidson, QC, MA

Headmaster: **David Faber**, MA Oxon

Age Range. 7–13.
Number of Boys. 220 boarders and 30 day.
Fees per term (2011-2012). £7,256 Boarding, £5,619 Day, £3,739 7+ Day Boys.

Set in 70 acres of delightful grounds which lead down to the river Cherwell and yet only a few miles from the city

centre, Summer Fields is often known as Oxford's *Secret Garden*.

The School has always had a strong academic reputation. In 2011, Summerfieldians secured 15 scholarships and awards to top independent schools including Charterhouse, Eton, Radley, St Edward's and Wellington. Each year, boys pass Common Entrance to their first-choice senior schools including Eton, Harrow, Radley, Winchester, Stowe, St Edward's, Abingdon, Magdalen College, etc.

Huge emphasis is placed on providing the highest standards of pastoral care – this was noted and highly praised in the 2009 ISI inspection report. Each boy has a personal tutor, who is responsible for his academic progress and social welfare and will be in regular contact with the boy's parents. The boarders live in comfortable Lodges within the school grounds and are looked after by an experienced and dedicated husband and wife team of Lodgeparents. More than 90% of the staff live on site, making a significant contribution to school life both in and out of the classroom.

The Music, Art, Drama, Design Technology, ICT and Sport departments are all impressive. The Choir has recently sung in Westminster and Christ Church Cathedrals and at Keble, Magdalen and New College, Oxford. They also regularly tour abroad, most recently visiting Belgium in May 2011. At least one Drama production takes place every term in the Macmillan Theatre with DVDs available of the major productions. Every summer an Art Exhibition of boys' work is held at the School and is open to the public.

The facilities are outstanding, including a fine library, theatre and chapel; purpose-built classrooms; Art, Design & Technology, Music and ICT Centres and a magnificent Sports Hall, with squash and Eton fives courts, a shooting gallery and swimming pool. In 2011, Summer Fields build a new Astroturf and tennis courts and new all-weather cricket nets, to add to the extensive outdoor facilities including a nine-hole golf course, an adventure playground and an outdoor swimming pool. A huge range of sports, activities and hobbies is on offer throughout the week and at weekends.

100% scholarships and bursaries are available.

For further information or to arrange a visit, please contact Mrs Christine Berry, Tel: 01865 459204.

Charitable status. Summer Fields is a Registered Charity, number 309683.

Sunningdale School

Dry Arch Road, Sunningdale, Berks SL5 9PY
Tel: 01344 620159
Fax: 01344 873304
e-mail: headmaster@sunningdaleschool.co.uk
website: www.sunningdaleschool.co.uk

Headmaster: **T A C N Dawson**, MA, PGCE

Deputy Headmaster: W Brooks

Age Range. 8–13.
Number of Boys. 100.
Fees per term (2011-2012). Boarding £5,995 (no compulsory extras).

Sunningdale is a small, mainly boarding school of around 100 boys. The unique family atmosphere means that the boys feel happy and secure and as a result are able to achieve their full potential. Our aim is to find each boy's strengths and give him the opportunity to shine in different areas of school life.

Our academic record speaks for itself, with scholarships gained on a regular basis to senior schools. The structure of our forms means that boys move through the school at their own pace, constantly challenged or supported where necessary.

Three quarters of the boys play at least one musical instrument; many play two or even three. The chapel choir sings on Sundays and occasionally at old boys' weddings and there is a pipe band which plays on Sports Day and at other events. As well as other drama productions we produce a musical each year in which every boy appears. The art department puts on a large exhibition every year and often wins awards at senior schools.

We have a good reputation on the sports field and one of the benefits of being a small school is that almost all the boys get to represent the school in a team. This does wonders for their confidence. There is a wide range of activities on offer from judo to juggling, clay pigeons to clay modelling.

The school has a strong boarding ethos and boys can weekly board in their first year. Weekends are packed with activities to keep the boys stimulated and entertained.

Sunninghill Preparatory School

South Court, South Walks, Dorchester, Dorset DT1 1EB
Tel: 01305 262306
Fax: 01305 261254
e-mail: secretary@sunninghill.dorset.sch.uk
website: www.sunninghillprep.co.uk

Chairman of Governors: Mr P Rodgers, BSc Hons

Headmaster: **Mr A P Roberts-Wray**, BA Hons, PGCE

Age Range. 3–13.
Number of Children. Nursery (3–5) 16 girls, 14 boys; Pre-Prep (5–8) 19 girls, 23 boys; Main School (8–13) 57 girls, 40 boys.
Fees per term (2010-2011). £2,400–£3,238. There are no compulsory extras, but a cooked lunch costs £195 per term. Nursery: £587.80 (based on 5 sessions per week, inclusive of Early Years Grant).

Sunninghill is a co-educational day school. There are 16 full-time and 7 part-time fully qualified staff.

Founded in 1939, Sunninghill became a Charitable Trust in 1969. It moved to its present site in January 1997 and has its own swimming pool, tennis courts and extensive grounds. Children are prepared for the Common Entrance examination to any Independent Senior School, and those with particular ability may be entered for scholarships. Over the years the school has attained many academic successes, but the broad curriculum also includes drama, art, craft, music and physical education.

Games are played on four afternoons a week and these include hockey, netball, lacrosse and rounders for the girls, and hockey, rugby, association football and cricket for the boys. In the summer term both boys and girls participate in athletics, swimming and tennis.

Out-of-school activities include choir, LAMDA, ballet, Outdoor Pursuits, and Swimming. There is a flourishing Parents' Association, which ensures that parents and staff get to know each other and work together for the good of the children and the School.

The prospectus is available on request.

Charitable status. Sunninghill Preparatory School is a Registered Charity, number 1024774. It exists to provide education for boys and girls.

Sunny Hill Preparatory School
Bruton School for Girls

Sunny Hill, Bruton, Somerset BA10 0NT
Tel: 01749 814400

Fax: 01749 812537
e-mail: info@brutonschool.co.uk
website: www.brutonschool.co.uk

Chairman of Governors: Mr D H C Batten

Head of Preparatory School: **Mrs Helen Snow**, BEd

Age Range. Day places for Girls and Boys aged 2–7. Day and Boarding places for Girls aged 8–11. No Saturday school.
Numbers of Pupils. 70.
Fees per term (2011-2012). Day: £3,100–£3,200 (Preparatory School), £1,550–£2,065 (Pre-Preparatory School), £18.75 per session (Nursery).
Boarding (from Year 4): £5,635–£5,735 (full), £5,110–£5,210 (weekly boarding), £47.00 per day (casual boarding).
Ethos. Sunny Hill Prep aims to create a happy, caring and vibrant atmosphere where children build strong academic foundations and develop personal confidence. Pupils are encouraged to think of others in a community based on mutual respect.
Location. Situated in 40 acres in beautiful countryside, the school is conveniently located on the Somerset, Wiltshire and Dorset borders with easy access to the A303. It shares the campus with the senior school and pupils benefit from specialist teachers and facilities.
Curriculum. A carefully structured and broad curriculum, delivered using an exciting variety of teaching and learning styles ensures good foundations are laid and high standards are achieved by all. Pupils thrive on a rich mix of activities – including themed curriculum weeks, imaginative topic work and educational visits – all encouraging curiosity and a love of learning. Food Technology modules are an integral part of Years 5 and 6 DT work. Creative and enthusiastic teachers inspire and stretch pupils. Pupils are nurtured by an excellent system of pastoral care. Children in the Nursery and Reception classes follow the Early Years Foundation Stage curriculum with emphasis on learning through play.

A love of creative and performing arts is encouraged as are opportunities to perform – facilities include a modern theatre and an amphitheatre. Other facilities include a new library, an outdoor activity trail and a meadow. There is a wide variety of extra-curricular activities, for example horse riding, photography and yoga.
Sport. Hockey, netball, rounders, gymnastics, tennis, swimming and athletics are integral to the curriculum taught by specialist PE teachers. Facilities include an astroturf pitch, dance studio and heated outdoor swimming pool. Pupils participate in inter-school competitions and in addition pupils can try activities such as riding, indoor rowing, dance and trampolining.
Boarding. A high standard of care and comfort is provided in a self-contained junior boarding house with well-equipped facilities and grounds. In the evenings and at weekends, pupils enjoy a full programme of activities.
Spiritual Life. The school has a Christian ethos and welcomes pupils from all faiths or none.
Medical Care. The school has its own medical centre with a qualified nursing Sister.
Charitable status. Bruton School for Girls is a Registered Charity, number 1085577, and a Company Limited by Guarantee.

Surbiton High Boys' Preparatory School

UCST

3 Avenue Elmers, Surbiton, Surrey KT6 4SP
Tel: 020 8390 6640
Fax: 020 8255 3049
e-mail: surbiton.prep@surbitonhigh.ucst.co.uk
website: www.surbitonhigh.com

Chair of Local Governing Body: Mr Ruairidh Hogg
(*Acting*)

Head: **Miss C Bufton**, BA Wales, PGCE Kingston

Age Range. 4–11.
Number of Pupils. 135 day boys.
Fees per term (2011-2012). £2,626 (Reception); £2,578 (Years 1–2); £3,510 (Years 3–6). A reduction in fees applies when two or more children from the same family attend the Preparatory and either the Junior or Senior Girls' Schools. Reductions are also made for children of members of the Clergy.

Established in 1862 the School became the Boys' Preparatory School of Surbiton High School and thus part of the United Church Schools Trust in 1987. Situated in a large Victorian Villa in Avenue Elmers the school shares the facilities offered at the Senior School including access to those in the Surbiton Assembly Rooms and Hinchley Wood Playing Fields.

Boys join the school at 4+ (Reception) although places in other forms are occasionally available. The School is single-form entry and at the 11+ stage all pupils take Entrance Examinations to their chosen Senior School.

At Surbiton High Boys' Preparatory School we have contact with some 20 Senior Schools in South-West London and North Surrey. All of these schools have strong academic traditions and reputations and those in the maintained sector are established selective Boys' Secondary Schools. Regularly the boys' success in entrance examinations allows the opportunity to choose between three or more senior schools and many pupils gain scholarship awards.

The Boys' Preparatory School follows an enhanced National Curriculum combining traditional values with the best of modern methods. A high standard of written and practical work is expected. Languages, Music and Physical Education are taught by specialist teachers throughout the school.

In addition to the computer suite, each classroom has its own interactive whiteboard and laptops are available for use and facilitated through a wireless network.

Teaching is frequently supported by visits to outside venues and by visits from speakers, theatre groups and musicians. Further opportunities to develop interests are provided by a wide range of extra-curricular activities.

The development of a thirty-acre complex at Hinchley Wood allows the boys access to floodlit tennis areas, playing fields and an Astroturf playing surface.

At Surbiton High Boys' Preparatory School we work with parents to ensure that each child develops intellectually, physically, socially, morally and spiritually into a confident, happy individual. The boys are introduced to a variety of different experiences in a secure, caring and stimulating environment. The natural curiosity of every child is fostered and developed within a traditional academically based environment. We hope, thus, to encourage a positive attitude towards education and develop boys' self-motivation.

Charitable status. Surbiton High Boys' Preparatory School is governed by The United Church Schools Trust, a Registered Charity, number 1016538.

Surbiton High Junior Girls' School

UCST

95–97 Surbiton Road, Kingston-upon-Thames, Surrey KT1 2HW
Tel: 020 8546 9756
Fax: 020 8974 6293
e-mail: surbiton.juniorgirls@surbitonhigh.ucst.co.uk
website: www.surbitonhigh.com

Chair of Local Governing Body: Mr Ruairidh Hogg
(*Acting*)

Head: **Miss C Bufton**, BA Wales, PGCE Kingston

Age Range. 4–11.
Number of Pupils. 241 Day Girls.
Fees per term (2011-2012). £2,626 (Reception); £2,578 (Years 1–2); £3,510 (Years 3–6). Sibling discount applies to families with 2 or more children in the School and for children of members of the Clergy.

The main age of entry is at 4+, with a second intake joining the School at the age of 7, however the school does admit girls at other age groups dependent on the availability of places. We have approximately 24 girls in a class.

The Junior Girls' School is in an urban location on the edge of Kingston upon Thames. The Junior School building is spacious, well planned and well resourced. In addition to the classroom accommodation there is a Library, Hall/Gym, Computer Room, Music Studio, Drama Studio, and a large Science/Art laboratory.

The School is cabled and networked with interactive whiteboards in all classrooms and also has a wireless network to facilitate the laptops available for use. The boards enable the curriculum to be taught with the most up-to-date resources and methods, keeping the pace and stimulus appropriate for children of today.

Our curriculum is based on the National Curriculum with an emphasis laid on the acquisition of proficient English, mathematical and scientific knowledge and skills. We retain a broad and balanced curriculum with Languages, Music and PE being taught to all girls from the age of 4 by specialist teachers. As the girls move through Years 3 and 4 a more subject-specialist approach is employed and by the time girls reach Year 5 all subjects are taught in this way. This is a gentle introduction for the girls to the expectations of a range of teachers and a Senior School type of organisation.

The curriculum is enhanced through visitors, trips and excursions and the girls take part in residential experiences from Year 3.

In Music and Drama there are many opportunities for performing. The girls present Form Assemblies for the School and their parents, who are invited to attend. There is a range of concerts, musicals and plays throughout the year for pupils of all ages. The girls perform eagerly and confidently, displaying a wonderful range of talents.

One of the strengths of the School is its pastoral care. which is reflected in the warmth of its atmosphere. We try to ensure that we give each child social, emotional and academic support and opportunities for growth. The successful School Council and 'pupil voice' is another way in which this strength can be identified. The girls leave Surbiton High Junior Girls' School as contented, articulate and capable young ladies ready for the challenges of Senior School life.

The School has beautiful playing fields at Hinchley Wood nearby on a 33-acre site, to which the girls are transported by coach for their lessons. There are School teams for Netball, Tennis and Rounders and a thriving after school Ski Club where the children can soon reach extremely high standards. We have national champions at Junior level.

Charitable status. Surbiton High Junior Girls' School is governed by The United Church Schools Trust, a Registered Charity, number 1016538.

Sussex House

68 Cadogan Square, London SW1X 0EA
Tel: 020 7584 1741
Fax: 020 7589 2300
e-mail: schoolsecretary@sussexhouseschool.co.uk
website: www.sussexhouseschool.co.uk

Chairman of the Governors: John Crewe, Esq

Headmaster: **Nicholas Kaye**, MA Magdalene College Cambridge, ACP, FRSA, FRGS

Deputy Headmaster: Paul Schmieder, BEd Leeds, MA Southampton

Age Range. 8–13.
Number of Boys. 182.
Fees per term (2011-2012). £4,960.

Founded in 1952, Sussex House is situated in the heart of Chelsea in a fine Norman Shaw house in Cadogan Square. Its Gymnasium and Music School are housed in a converted chapel in Cadogan Street. The school is an independent charitable trust. At Common Entrance and Scholarship level it has achieved a record of consistently strong results to academically demanding schools. The school enjoys its own entirely independent character and the style is traditional yet imaginative.

There is a full-time teaching staff of 22. Creative subjects are given strong emphasis and throughout the school boys take Music and Art. Team sports take place at a nearby site and the school's football teams have an impressive record. Cricket is the main summer sport and there are opportunities for tennis, swimming, basketball, indoor football and indoor hockey. All boys have physical education classes and Sussex House is a centre of excellence for fencing and its international records are well known.

Cultural and creative activities play a major role, including theatrical productions in a West End theatre, a major annual exhibition of creative work featuring large-scale architectural models and an annual competition of poetry written by boys. There is a strong bias towards music and an ambitious programme of choral and orchestral concerts. A large number of pupils play musical instruments and there is an impressive record of music awards to senior schools. The school provides a range of sporting and cultural trips.

The school has a Church of England affiliation. There is a school chaplain and weekly services are held in St Simon Zelotes Church, Chelsea. Boys of all religions and denominations are welcomed.

Charitable status. Sussex House is a Registered Charity, number 1035806. It exists to provide education for boys.

Sutton Valence Preparatory School

Church Road, Chart Sutton, Maidstone, Kent ME17 3RF
Tel: 01622 842117
Fax: 01622 844201
e-mail: enquiries@svprep.svs.org.uk
website: www.svs.org.uk

Chairman of Governors: B F W Baughan, Esq

Head: **Richard Johnson**, LLB, PGCE

Age Range. 3–11.
Number of Day Pupils. Prep (7–11): 182 boys, 159 girls. Pre-Prep (3–6): 83 boys, 59 girls.
Fees per term (2011-2012). £1,240–£3,690 (exclusive of lunch).

The school is fully co-educational with its own Pre-Prep department housed in a new purpose-built facility. We have specialist Art, Science and ICT facilities and a new Library. The United Westminster Schools Foundation provides valuable resources and support.

The school is situated in 18 acres of countryside overlooking the Weald and includes a hard and grass play areas, heated outdoor swimming pool, 4 hard tennis courts, a Sports Hall, a 13-acre games field and a full-size Astroturf.

Classes are small throughout the school. The 40 teaching staff are all well qualified and there is an extensive peripatetic staff for music. Special needs are addressed by the SENCO and 3 part-time teachers. The Kindergarten to Year 2 classes all have qualified classroom assistants.

We provide an excellent all round education, with an emphasis on a solid foundation in the core subjects of English, Mathematics, Science and ICT. Languages, Music, Drama, Art, Design Technology and Sport play an important part in the curriculum too.

There is a wind band, string orchestra, quartets and a choir, the best of whom sing with our senior school choir. There are many opportunities for children to perform in drama productions and in concerts.

We have a varied programme of visits and outings to further the children's experience.

Cricket, Football, Hockey, Netball, Rugby and Rounders are the major sports. Athletics, Swimming and Cross Country are also in the curriculum. The proximity of the senior school, Sutton Valence, allows the children to benefit from their staffing and facilities, including the use of the Sports Hall and the new indoor swimming pool. Extra-curricular activities include chess club, art, 5-a-side football, gymnastics, drama, craft, croquet, science club, ballet and judo.

The school is a Christian foundation. Assemblies and the use of the local church are an important facet of our lives. We have a Chaplain for both prep and senior school.

Children are prepared for our senior school, Sutton Valence, the local Grammar schools and other independent schools with an 11+ entry.

Charitable status. United Westminster Schools Foundation is a Registered Charity, number 309267. It exists to provide education for boys and girls.

Swanbourne House School

Swanbourne, Milton Keynes, Buckinghamshire MK17 0HZ
Tel: 01296 720264
Fax: 01296 728089
e-mail: office@swanbourne.org
website: www.swanbourne.org

The School is a Charitable Trust, administered by a Board of Governors.

Chairman of Governors: J Leggett

Joint Heads: **S D Goodhart**, BEd Hons; **Mrs J S Goodhart**, BEd Dunelm

Age Range. 3–13.
Number of Pupils. Prep: 148 Boys, 119 Girls (full/weekly boarders 21, flexi-boarders 27). Pre-Prep: 49 Girls, 55 Boys. Nursery: 14 Girls, 28 Boys.
Fees per term (2011-2012). Full/Weekly boarding £6,275; Day: Prep £4,895, Pre-Prep £2,790, Nursery £1,290 –£2,290.

The house, which was once the home of the Cottesloe family, is a Grade II listed building, standing in 40 acres of wooded grounds and commanding extensive views of the surrounding countryside. Swanbourne has been described by Gabbitas Guardianship as 'a school you would just dream of'. The School has just celebrated its 90th Anniversary.

There are 40 full-time members of teaching staff, many of whom are resident. They are assisted by several peripatetic specialist teachers. The well-being of the boarders is in the hands of a resident Housemaster and his wife: they are assisted by our daily RGN staff and an Assistant Housemaster and Assistant Housemistress.

A strong musical tradition has been established. There are three choirs, an orchestra and various ensembles. Musical concerts are held throughout the school year and all pupils are encouraged to participate in drama and the Inter-House music competition. The school has its own chapel.

Boys and girls are prepared for entry to independent senior schools, usually at 13+, with 30 Common Entrance passes and 18 scholarships awarded last year. The majority of boys and girls go on to leading senior independent schools, where the pass rate in recent years has been 100%. From age 9, pupils are taught by specialist teachers in well-equipped subject rooms. There are 2 Modern Language Laboratories and all senior pupils have the opportunity to spend a week in France.

The more practical side of the Curriculum is fully catered for in the Fremantle Hall of Technology. Art, Design Technology, Science and Information Technology are taught in this attractive building: more than 200 computers are in use throughout the school. We have two computer rooms and intranet into every classroom.

The Pre-Preparatory Department occupies an Elizabethan Manor House, adjoining the school grounds. Whilst retaining a separate identity, the younger children are able to use the Main School facilities throughout the year.

A House system operates to encourage healthy competition in work and games. The Housemasters and Housemistresses have a special responsibility and concern for the welfare of the children in their House.

For boys, the main school games are Rugby, Hockey, Football and Cricket, and for girls Hockey, Netball and Rounders. Coaching and matches are also arranged in Athletics. Both winter and summer Tennis is played. Further opportunities include Cross-country, Judo, Dance and Squash. A very wide range of extra-curricular activities is available in the evenings, at weekends and on certain afternoons. Tennis and Golf facilities are excellent.

The Bridget More Hall offers outstanding facilities for Drama, Music and PE. Other facilities include a rifle range, an indoor swimming pool, two astroturf pitches, and a squash court. There are various holiday sports clubs and time to offer camping and outward-bound activities, such as canoeing, climbing, riding, skiing and leadership training.

School Prefects are taught to foster a caring concern for the well-being of every member of our community.

Children are prepared for Senior Independent Schools through lectures and workshops on international education, drugs, first aid and senior school life. All leavers at 13+ take part in a residential week of outdoor education. Our Leadership Training is first-rate and has led to the regular winning of all-rounder scholarships and the Gordonstoun Challenge.

Scholarships are awarded for 11+ entry to the School for talent in Art, Sport, Academic or any combined area. The deadline for this is February.

Bursaries are available for Forces Families.

Charitable status. Swanbourne House School is a Registered Charity, number 310640. It seeks to provide a continuous structured education for children aged 3–13 years.

Taunton Preparatory School

Staplegrove Road, Taunton, Somerset TA2 6AE
Tel: 01823 703307; Admissions: 01823 703303
Fax: 01823 703308
e-mail: tps.enquiries@tauntonschool.co.uk
website: www.tauntonschool.co.uk

Chairman of the Governors: Mrs Jane E Barrie, OBE, BSc, ARCS, FSI

Headmaster: **Mr Jimmy M H Beale**, BSc

Age Range. 2–13.
Number of Pupils. Day 409; Boarders 31.
Fees per term (2011-2012). Prep: Boarders £3,705–£6,715; Day £2,225–£4,185. Pre-Preparatory & Nursery (full-time) £1,925.

Taunton Preparatory School is the Preparatory School of Taunton School (q.v.) and shares its aim to prepare young people to shape a changing world in the 21st century. The School offers a broad and balanced education in a friendly, Christian community, in which pupils can develop their talents and interests. Classes and academic sets are small, allowing close personal attention to each child. All children are encouraged to mix easily with each other and with adults, and it is a principle of the School's teaching that learning is best achieved through the fostering of enthusiasm and the development of an enquiring mind. Kindness and courtesy are highly prized qualities.

The Preparatory School was almost entirely rebuilt in 1994 to provide outstanding academic, cultural and athletic facilities. The new teaching facilities include 4 dedicated Science laboratories, Art, Design Technology and IT suites, a well-resourced library and spacious classrooms. A second Junior Art/Technology room, a further ICT suite and a new library are recent additions.

Boarding care of a high standard is provided & the School prides itself on its high standards of catering and individual care for all its pupils. Full and weekly boarding are on offer. An ambitious weekend programme of activities is organised. The School welcomes pupils from overseas and provides specialist support within the Junior International Group. The school enjoys close links with the Armed Services – a generous Bursary scheme is well established.

Music, Drama and Dance are highly valued and the School received Artsmark Gold accreditation in 2008. There is a large Orchestra, three choirs, and specialist groups for strings, jazz and brass. Over 200 children now learn at least one instrument. There is an annual choir tour abroad – to Prague in 2010.

Sporting facilities at Taunton School are quite exceptional. The Preparatory School enjoys its own Sports Centre comprising an indoor heated 25 metre Swimming Pool and Sports Hall. The main boys' games are Rugby, Hockey and Cricket whilst girls are offered Netball, Hockey, Tennis and Rounders. All-weather playing surfaces and extensive grass pitches are available within the campus.

The wide curriculum is supported by a full programme of extra-curricular activities which include Dance, Board Games, Canoeing, Chess, Computing, Debating, Drama, "Green" club, Modelling and Pottery. The School is a keen supporter of the Scout movement.

A thorough grounding is given in core subjects and all children learn three modern languages during their time in the School. The requirements of the National Curriculum are met by enthusiastic and committed staff. There are scholarships at 11+ and 13+ (for entry to the Senior School). Art, Sports, Music and All-Rounder Scholarships and Awards are also offered. There are a number of ministerial bursaries and awards at 11+.

There is a purpose-built Nursery and Pre-Prep, which enjoys its own excellent classrooms, hall, library, computers and recreational facilities and has full access to the Preparatory School's Sports Centre. Each class teacher is supported by a nursery nurse.

A comprehensive prospectus is available from The Admissions Secretary.

Charitable status. Taunton School is a Registered Charity, number 1081420. It exists to provide a high standard of education for children.

Taverham Hall

Taverham, Norwich, Norfolk NR8 6HU
Tel: 01603 868206
Fax: 01603 861061
e-mail: enquire@taverhamhall.co.uk
website: www.taverhamhall.co.uk

Chair of Governors: Mrs Sharon Turner

Headmaster: **M A Crossley**, NPQH, BEd Hons

Deputy Headmaster: J Worrall, BSc, Dip Teach

Age Range. 1–13.
Number of Pupils. 271: Prep 129, Pre-Prep 65, Nursery 52, Toddlers 25.
Fees per term (2011-2012). Weekly Boarding £5,195; Day (including lunch): Prep £3,195–£4,015; Pre-Prep £2,745–£2,995.
Nursery (per session): £27.00 (morning), £42.00 (all day), Lunch £1.95 per day. The Nursery is open all year round.

Taverham Hall is a co-educational IAPS independent day and flexi/weekly boarding school which caters for girls and boys aged 1–13 years old.

The school was inspected by Ofsted in January 2010 and the Independent Schools Inspectorate (ISI) team in November 2010. The ISI Inspection report described the Pre-Prep department and Prep School as providing '*an excellent all-round education.*' '*The well-planned, wide-ranging and stimulating curriculum enables all pupils to reach high standards in relation to their age and ability.*' Furthermore, both inspections rated the Early Years Provision as '*outstanding*'.

Taverham Hall School is a modern, forward thinking school which offers children time, space and freedom to grow through a focus on personalised learning whilst placing significant emphasis on the pastoral side of each child's development. A dedicated team provides a supportive and nurturing environment for all children in our care.

Every child is different and how pupils learn is just as important to us as what they learn. Our aim is to help children find the confidence they need, to become the best they can be.

The Pre-Prep Department for children aged 4–7 years, provides purpose-built modern classrooms with state-of-the-art interactive whiteboards. Our Reception year has much to offer. Class sizes are small and therefore, unlike most other schools, a member of staff will hear your child read every day. We use creative, hands-on methods to introduce that all-important formal learning. All classes are structured around the National Curriculum and close individual monitoring allows us to set appropriate challenges at each key stage. In Year 2 children begin to learn conversational French which is taught by a specialist teacher. Children develop academically and socially at a pace commensurate with their ability.

We also believe that learning should always be fun and our extensive 100 acres of enclosed school grounds allow for a huge range of learning environments. Outdoor learning takes place through our innovative Forest School programme – where practical and problem-solving skills are stretched as well as enabling children to take an increasingly investigative and independent approach to learning.

Educational trips and activity weeks are further opportunities to try out new skills. In addition, our Pre-Prep (ages 4–7) and Prep (ages 7–13) school pupils share the school's modern Sports Hall, indoor swimming pool and extensive playing fields. All children are encouraged to have healthy bodies as well as healthy minds.

Pastoral care is the cornerstone of the school and all children have a class teacher in Years 3 and 4. A form tutor takes full responsibility for their academic and pastoral development from Year 5 and above with tutor groups no larger than 15. With the added advantage of flexi or weekly boarding facilities and a wide range of after-school activities, such as canoeing, riding, blogging, karate, table tennis, rock band, around the world and creative writing, everyone contributes to the sense of community which extends throughout the school. The matrons and other staff together with the Head, his wife and young family reside within the school and its grounds, providing a supportive and nurturing environment for the popular flexi-boarding option. Our enormously dedicated and enthusiastic team take great pride in their partnerships with pupils and parents alike.

Over sixty scholarships have been won in the past decade. The chapel choir (which is one of 3 choirs at the school) has performed in Prague, Florence and Salzburg in recent years and children have gained national and county honours in sport. A love of music is instilled from a young age with children in our Pre-Prep department being able to sing in our Pre-Prep Choir as well as the opportunity to try out new instruments and undertaking private tuition lessons. '*Their spiritual and cultural development is enhanced by inspirational experiences in art and music*' – ISI Report November 2010.

Small class sizes and a rich broad curriculum gives pupils, however varied their abilities, the opportunity to achieve academic success through recognition of learning styles and personalised target setting. Numerous opportunities to participate and perform in whole school performances; public and individual events exist as well as exciting tours and trips to expand their horizons. Our pupils are encouraged to make decisions for themselves; have respect for one another, make friendships, be polite and develop their social skills. Specialist subject teaching takes place from Year 2 in certain subjects and is in every subject from Year 5.

All are given the chance to represent the school in competitive weekly fixtures against other schools and have access to some outstanding in-house facilities: an indoor swimming pool, a sports hall, tennis and netball courts, rugby, cricket, rounders and hockey pitches and the use of an adjacent astroturf. In addition, they can let off steam on our own zip wire and ropes course or simply have fun building dens and climbing trees within our grounds at break times.

The school's own in-house catering team ensures that pupils enjoy a healthy and varied diet in the school's Dining Hall with their teachers. Everything is cooked and prepared on the premises and the menus vary daily. Specific dietary requirements are catered for and also prepared on site.

Taverham Hall School is multi-denominational and promotes the spiritual, moral, social and cultural development of pupils of all faiths and nationalities. Daily assemblies are Christian in their nature and offer the opportunity for reflection and consideration of values, beliefs and principles, held in common by all faiths.

Recent developments have included a modern sports hall, ICT suite, refurbished DT Centre and the installation of dual-purpose interactive whiteboards throughout the whole school.

Charitable status. Taverham Hall is a Registered Charity, number 311272. It exists for the purpose of educating children.

Terra Nova Preparatory School

Jodrell Bank, Holmes Chapel, Cheshire CW4 8BT
Tel: 01477 571251
Fax: 01477 571646
e-mail: registrar@terranovaschool.co.uk
website: www.terranovaschool.co.uk

Chairman of Governors: P A Johns

Headmaster: **Andrew Lewin**, BA Hons, PGCE

Deputy Head: Mark Mitchell, BSc, PGCE

Age Range. 3–13.
Number of Pupils. 273 Day Pupils: 156 Prep, 117 Pre-Prep; Flexi Boarders: 55.
Fees per term (2010-2011). Prep: Day £2,900–£3,900, Flexi Boarding £30 per night, Weekly Boarding £90 per week. Pre-Prep: £2,450*. Nursery: £1,200* (*Free Early Education Entitlement for three and four year olds).

Terra Nova is a happy, family school set in 35 acres of fine grounds in the heart of the Cheshire countryside. The school is 5 minutes from Junction 18 of the M6 and 25 minutes from Manchester Airport.

Boys and girls are prepared for entry at both 11+ and 13+ to a wide variety of Day, Grammar and Boarding Senior Schools. The school enjoys an excellent academic reputation and its pupils have won over 86 scholarships and awards in the last ten years. Each child experiences a broad curriculum including Music, Art, PE, ICT and Design Technology. The experienced and hard-working staff inspire and challenge pupils. Class sizes are kept small to ensure that each child receives the attention they need in order to focus on their strengths and work on their weaknesses.

The grounds and buildings include a multi-purpose Sports Hall and Performing Arts Centre, Tennis Courts (both hard and grass surfaces), specialist Art and Pottery Department, Music School, Science Laboratory, Language Lab, Design & Technology facilities and ICT Suite. A new Nursery was opened in 2004 and the classrooms for five, six and seven year olds refurbished and enlarged. In addition there is a fully-staffed Library and heated covered Swimming Pool. Music is taught at all levels and every child is given the opportunity to learn a musical instrument. The school has a number of choirs, as well as various instrumental ensemble groups and an orchestra.

The family atmosphere and friendliness found in the boarding house make it an exceptionally happy place. A range of boarding options are available in the newly refurbished dormitories including weekly and flexi boarding.

The main winter sports for girls are hockey and netball and in the summer tennis, rounders, athletics and swimming. The boys play rugby and soccer in the two winter terms and cricket, tennis, athletics and swimming in the summer. Additionally, the school enjoys a strong reputation for athletics and cross-country. A wealth of after school clubs are available including activities such as judo, badminton, volleyball, cooking, chess, riding, golf, dance and gymnastics. Terra Nova also boasts its own Cub pack.

The Pre-Preparatory Department is housed in a separate building adjoining the main school site but enjoys the benefits of many of the main school facilities. Transfer from the Pre-Preparatory to the Preparatory department of the school is smooth and natural, undertaken in a climate of strong pastoral care.

An after-school and holiday club (Tembos) together with very flexible boarding arrangements meets the need of today's busy working parent.

Bursaries may be available in cases of genuine hardship. The school, which is in its 113th year, became a charitable trust in 1955.

For more information visit www.terranovaschool.co.uk.

Charitable status. Terra Nova School Trust Limited is a Registered Charity, number 525919. It is dedicated to all round educational excellence for children.

Terrington Hall

Terrington, York YO60 6PR
Tel: 01653 648227
Fax: 01653 648458
e-mail: office@terringtonhall.com
website: www.terringtonhall.com

Chairman of Governors: Mrs K Willink

Headmaster: **M J Glen**, BA, PGCE Dunelm

Age Range. 3–13 years.
Number of Children. 150: 80 boys, 70 girls (Boarding 15, Day 135).
Fees per term (2010-2011). Boarding: £5,335. Day: £3,765 (Years 5–8), £3,710 (Year 4), £3,515 (Year 3), £2,315 (Year 2), £2,185 (Year 1), £2,065 (Reception & Nursery). There are no compulsory extras.

Terrington is a co-educational school situated in beautiful countryside in the Howardian Hills (an area designated to be of Outstanding Natural Beauty) some fifteen miles from the City of York.

Terrington is busy and vibrant seven days a eek but all activities are available to day pupils, many of whom convert to boarding in their final years in preparation for the next stage of their education.

Terrington prepares pupils for all the leading independent schools in the North and further afield and is particularly proud of the twenty scholarships and exhibitions won by its pupils in the last three years.

The school enjoys excellent sporting facilities, with eight acres of playing fields, tennis courts, indoor heated swimming pool and Sports Hall. All major sports are played and, in addition, Athletics, Cross Country, Fencing, Gymnastics, Judo, Riding, Orienteering, Sailing, Canoeing and Clay Pigeon Shooting are available. There is an extensive outdoor education programme with all children learning to canoe/kayak. The school has its own climbing wall.

Teaching facilities are modern and well-equipped and they include a Computer Suite, two Science Labs and a Middle School Block. Music, Art and Drama all form an important part of the curriculum. Tuition is available for most instruments and children can be prepared for Associated Board exams. There are two choirs and a very successful Wind Band, which has recently toured overseas. There are at least two major drama productions each year.

The School Chaplain is the local Rector and boarders attend the village Church most Sundays. Each day starts with a short act of worship.

The Headmaster, his wife and children live in the school and the pupils are very much part of an extended family. A wide range of activities is followed at weekends and full use is made of the surrounding countryside. Parents are fully involved in the life of the school and there is a flourishing social committee.

The school welcomes children whose parents live overseas and an escort service is provided to collect and deliver the children from airports at the beginning and end of term. There is a bus service to the Salisbury area available at half-terms.

A number of Entrance Scholarships are available for children under eleven and there are Bursaries for sons and daughters of Clergy and HM Forces Personnel.

Charitable status. Terrington Hall is a Registered Charity, number 532362. It exists to provide a quality education for boys and girls.

Thorngrove School

The Mount, Paintings Lane, Highclere, Newbury, Berkshire RG20 9PS
Tel: 01635 253172
Fax: 01635 254135
e-mail: admin@thorngroveschool.co.uk
website: www.thorngroveschool.co.uk

Headmaster: **Mr Adam King**, BA Hons QTS Leeds, PGCAE

Age Range. 4–13 Co-educational.
Number of Pupils. 201 Day Pupils.
Fees per term (2011-2012). Forms 1–3 £3,360; Form 4–5 £3,750; Forms 6–9 £4,150.

Thorngrove School was founded in 1988 by Connie and Nick Broughton and is a co-educational day preparatory school for children aged 4 to 13 years. The purpose-built facilities are set in former farmland in the village of Highclere, 5 miles south of Newbury and 12 miles north of Andover. Children are prepared for Common Entrance at 13+, from where their paths lead to a wide range of senior day and boarding schools.

The school is set in 25 acres of beautiful, Hampshire countryside. The extensive games fields provide numerous rugby, football and hockey pitches. In addition to this there is an astro and two further hard courts which are used for tennis and netball. A multi-purpose hall was opened by Robert Hardy in 2007. This provides a wonderful space for music concerts and drama productions as well as indoor PE and games. Either side of the hall are four classrooms and changing facilities. We have a large IT suite and many of the classrooms have interactive whiteboards. There is a dedicated music room in the Senior Block with several practice rooms. The Science laboratory is fully equipped. The Art room is well resourced and in addition to our Head of Art, we currently have an 'Artist in Residence'. Our well-stocked library is located centrally in the main building and we have a full-time librarian. All classrooms are modern, light and airy and some have direct access to the outside. In 2010 a D&T centre was created in the old nursery.

Thorngrove offers a unique environment where children can grow and learn independently. We value our intimate and friendly community, and the benefits that it brings; we are proud of our small class sizes and the individual attention we are able to offer to each of our pupils. The school has a relaxed yet purposeful atmosphere, where working relationships between staff and pupils flourish. We are forward thinking in our approach – ready to adapt to change and technological advancement, whilst at the same time remaining true to traditional values. Pupils are assessed continuously, and parents are always welcome to discuss their children's progress with staff on a regular basis or at parents' meetings. Above all, our aim is that all our pupils should reach their potential in terms of confidence, creativity and achievement.

Thorpe House School

Oval Way, Gerrards Cross, Bucks SL9 8QA
Tel: 01753 882474
         01753 885535 Kingscote Pre-Preparatory School
Fax: 01753 889755
e-mail: office@thorpehouse.co.uk
website: www.thorpehouse.co.uk

Chairman of the Governors: Mr Richard Coward, MA

Headmaster: **Mr A F Lock**, MA Oxon, PGCE

Kingscote Pre-Preparatory School and Nursery:
Headmistress: Mrs F Davies

Age Range. 7–16. Kingscote 3–7.
Numbers of Boys. 233 Day Boys. Kingscote: 100.
Fees per term (2011-2012). £3,525–£4,225. Kingscote: Reception £2,710, Years 1 & 2 £2,825, Nursery £1,350–£2,170.

Thorpe House was founded in 1923 and registered as a Charitable Trust in 1986.

The School is staffed by a Headmaster, 24 full-time teachers, 5 part-time teachers and 13 peripatetic staff. There are 16 classrooms, 2 Science Laboratories, Library, Gymnasium, networked Computer room, Design Technology department, Art room, Music room and 4 Music Practice rooms. The School has its own open-air heated swimming pool, 7 acres of playing fields, tennis court and pavilion. All Saints' Church stands next to the main building, and is regularly used by the school. In addition to the three traditional major games of rugby, soccer and cricket, swimming and athletics are taught. Out-of-school activities include tennis, golf, judo, skiing, sailing, chess and a variety of clubs and societies. The School's examination record is very strong and boys predominantly go on to the local grammar schools at 11, or stay on to take GCSE at 16, although some move on to independent senior schools at 13 via the Common Entrance or scholarship examinations.

Kingscote Pre-Preparatory School and Nursery is situated adjacent to Thorpe House in its own grounds. Boys normally spend 3 or 4 full years there before transferring to the main school at 7+. (*For further details see entry in ISA section.*)

The Schools provide a continuous education for boys from 3 to 16. The provision for boys to stay on for Years 9 to 11 was introduced in September 2006.

Charitable status. Thorpe House School Trust is a Registered Charity, number 292683. It exists to provide education to boys.

Thorpe House Langley Preparatory School and Nursery

7 Yarmouth Road, Thorpe St Andrew, Norwich, Norfolk NR7 0EA
Tel: 01603 433055
Fax: 01603 436323
e-mail: office@thlps.co.uk
website: www.thlps.co.uk

Chairman of the Governors: Mrs M Alston, JP

Headmaster: **S B Marfleet**, BSc Hons, MSc, PGCE

Age Range. 2–11 co-educational.
Number of Pupils. 323.
Fees per term (2011-2012). £1,890 (Reception–Year 2), £2,290 (Years 3, 4 and 5), £2,670 (Year 6). Nursery (per session): £33 (full day), £22.50 (half day).

The school is situated in 10 acres of gardens, woodlands and playing fields and is close to the city centre. Facilities include an indoor swimming pool, fully-equipped gymnasium, a large sports hall, dance studio, library, art studio, cookery room, science laboratory, IT suite and technology workshop. The entire site is networked with secure internet access.

Pupils are taken from the age of 2 into Nursery or at age 4 into Reception Class. Entry into school thereafter is dependent upon availability and follows a trial day and receipt of a satisfactory report from the previous school.

Children are prepared for many schools, but principally for entry to Langley School at the age of 11+. (*See Langley*

School entry in SHMIS section.) Qualified and experienced staff maintain a purposeful academic atmosphere, but there is a friendly and caring family environment where children can discover individual talents and abilities so that they will be well prepared for the secondary stage of their education. A broad curriculum is followed, and classes rarely exceed 16. English, Mathematics, Science and ICT form the core of the curriculum, but from Year 3 subject specialists teach Design Technology, Art, Drama, French, Music and Humanities.

Hockey, rugby, soccer, netball, cricket, rounders and tennis are the main team games. Activities operate at the end of the school day and offer the chance for children to try numerous other sports, music and drama activities, including sailing, ten pin bowling, dry slope skiing, archery, golf, orienteering, karate, and so on. The school is particularly strong at chess with many pupils representing the county and country.

There is a fine tradition of drama and public speaking. There are drama productions for each section of the school every year and a Summer Concert which involve every child in the school. We participate in local speech, drama and music festivals and children are taught and entered for LAMDA examinations. There are numerous performance opportunities for music and drama.

Experienced and qualified staff also run the Nursery, which caters for 2 to 4 year olds. It is well equipped and has its own secure play area. Nursery hours are flexible and a child-minding service is offered after school hours. The Nursery has been Ofsted inspected and is a registered provider under the government scheme. It is open during school term time and for much of the holidays.

Charitable status. Langley School is a Registered Charity, number 311270. It exists to provide a sound education for boys and girls.

Tockington Manor

Washingpool Hill Road, Tockington, Bristol BS32 4NY
Tel: 01454 613229
Fax: 01454 613676
e-mail: admin@tockingtonmanorschool.com
website: www.tockingtonmanorschool.com

Chairman of Governors: P E H Smith

Headmaster: **R G Tovey**, CertEd Oxon

Age Range. Boys and Girls aged 2–13+.
Number of Pupils. 20 Boarders, 80 Day, 65 Infants, 80 Nursery.
Fees per term (2010-2011). Boarders £5,450 (inclusive); Day £3,440–£3,997 (including meals); Lower School £2,445. Nursery from £22 per session.

The school stands in its own 27 acres of parkland some 10 miles north of Bristol, close to the Severn Bridge and M4/M5 motorways, allowing easy access to road, rail and air links.

Boys and girls in the Preparatory School are prepared via the Scholarship or Common Entrance examinations for a wide range of independent schools. A highly qualified staff has ensured continuous success at these levels. The Headmaster's wife, who is also qualified to teach, takes a full part in school activities. Boarders accepted from age 7. Daily transport service to local areas.

The main school games are soccer, rugby, cricket, athletics, cross country, swimming (large indoor heated pool) and tennis (all weather courts). Girls play hockey, netball and rounders. Ballet, riding, archery and a wide variety of other activities are available in all terms, and children are encouraged to take part in music and drama. A feature of the sum-

mer term is an outdoor activity week, known as Tockington Tramps, leading to some nights at camp for senior children.

The Lower School has small classes for children aged 4–7, who share the facilities of the Prep School, and provides a stimulating environment. The Nursery for children aged 2–4 is well equipped with toys and games, has an extensive outdoor play area and aims to lay the foundations of independence and academic learning.

The excellent buildings, which stand in an attractive setting facing the games field, have been increased over the years.

Reductions in fees are offered for brothers/sisters and sons/daughters of Service personnel.

Tormead Junior School

Cranley Road, Guildford, Surrey GU1 2JD
Tel: 01483 796073
Fax: 01483 450592
e-mail: registrar@tormeadschool.org.uk
website: www.tormeadschool.org.uk

Chairman of Governors: C W M Herbert, Esq, BSc Hons

Head of Junior School: **Miss K Tuckwell**, BSc York, PGCE Lincoln, MA Bath, NPQH

Age Range. Girls 4–11.
Number of Girls. 205.
Fees per term (2011-2012). £1,915–£3,380.

Of all the gifts a girl can receive, none has more lasting value than a first-rate education, at a school in which she will be happy and successful. We believe this is achieved at Tormead. We encourage each girl to develop her talents to the full, instilling a life-long love of learning. The curriculum offers breadth and challenge, and ensures that each girl gains a fine foundation to her education – providing her with core skills and knowledge that will stand her in good stead for the future. Academic expectations are high but our aim is to achieve this through stimulating, enjoyable and well-taught lessons in a happy, friendly and relaxed school.

Entry is selective at age 4 and 7 by assessment. When space is available, entrance at all other year groups is considered. When the girls come for assessment into the Reception class they are invited to a 'Party' and we hope this provides an environment where we can see the potential for learning in the girls, whilst they enjoy a selection of fun activities. As the girls get older, assessment becomes more academically based. All the junior girls sit the entrance examination for the senior school and have priority on places over the external candidates.

The school prides itself on its high academic standards and expectation of the girls whilst ensuring teaching and learning is 'fun' including many first-hand experiences. The Early Years Foundation stage and National Curriculum are extended and enriched by skilled, enthusiastic staff. French is taught from Year 2 and Latin is added to the girls' timetable in Year 5. All girls enjoy specialist teaching in music, games and gymnastics and from Year 2 also in Design Technology. The ICT curriculum gradually builds up the skills of the girls, and by the end of the Junior School they are confidently using computers as a tool for learning in other subjects. SEN provision is provided on an individual needs basis, is not an issue in school and holds no stigma.

The girls enjoy numerous opportunities to be involved in extra-curricular activities. The aim of the school is to offer a comprehensive range of activities to allow each girl to find something during the week that she would like to participate in and so develop her talents in this area, regardless of their ability. Girls with a particular talent are taken on further in their chosen activity with additional practices. Extra-curricular activities (in addition to sports) include; art, LAMDA,

Jazz band, instrumental ensembles, two orchestras, two choirs, gardening, computers, cookery and board games.

All the girls enjoy specialist teaching in all aspects of PE including swimming and gymnastics. All sport except swimming is catered for by facilities on the Junior or Senior School site and includes the use of the sprung floor gymnasium. The school enjoys success at the highly competitive GISGA gymnastics competition. The girls have regular fixtures in numerous sports, throughout the year, with neighbouring schools. The ethos of the school means that all girls have an opportunity to be involved in sporting (in fact, all) extra-curricular activities regardless of their ability. There are high expectations of behaviour both in and outside the classroom, but as this is the accepted norm the need for strong discipline is rare. When there are difficulties with friendships the girls know to seek help and all concerns are taken seriously by staff. Time is given to ensure any problem is resolved in a fair and lasting manner.

There are numerous opportunities during the year when parents enjoy seeing their girls 'in action'; weekly sporting fixtures, termly informal music concerts, an annual open afternoon, carol service, nativity, formal concert and summer play. In addition, parents help in the library, and organise special class social events.

Charitable status. Tormead Limited is a Registered Charity, number 312057.

Tower House School

188 Sheen Lane, East Sheen, London SW14 8LF
Tel: 020 8876 3323
Fax: 020 8876 3321
e-mail: secretary@thsboys.org.uk
website: www.thsboys.org.uk

Chairman of Governors: Mr Jamie Forsyth

Headmaster: **Mr G Evans**, BSc, MA, PGCE

Age Range. 4–13.
Number of Boys. 180.
Fees per term (2011-2012). Reception and Year 1 £3,345, Years 2 and 3 £3,695, Senior School £3,795 (including residential trips and all school lunches).

Tower House is a day school established in 1931. The school stands in its own grounds and is conveniently situated near a number of bus routes and the local station.

Entry is at the age of 4+. Admission of boys after the age of 4+ depends very much on the availability of places. There is an entry test at this later stage and the Deputy Head interviews all boys.

The school prepares boys for Common Entrance and Scholarships to appropriate Independent Senior Schools.

The staff is fully qualified and includes specialists in art, music and games, which together with drama play an important part in the school curriculum. In addition to the full time staff, there are visiting teachers for piano, violin, woodwind, brass and guitar.

The school is well supplied with modern teaching aids, including computers. There is a well-equipped science laboratory, an art and technology room, library, and an ICT Room.

The principal games are rugby, soccer and cricket. Other sports include athletics, cross country, squash, swimming, tennis and water sports. There are many fixtures arranged with other schools.

A prospectus is available on application to the School Secretary.

Charitable status. Tower House School is a Registered Charity, number 1068844.

Town Close House Preparatory School

14 Ipswich Road, Norwich, Norfolk NR2 2LR
Tel: 01603 620180 (Prep)
          01603 626718 (Pre-Prep)
Fax: 01603 618256 (Prep)
          01603 599043 (Pre-Prep)
e-mail: admissions@townclose.com
website: www.townclose.com

Chairman of Governors: Mr Richard Beck, BA, LLM

Headmaster: **G R Lowe**, BEd Nottingham

Age Range. 3–13 Co-educational.
Number of Pupils. Prep 280, Pre-Prep 185.
Fees per term (2011-2012). £2,260–£3,540 including lunch and all single-day educational excursions. No compulsory extras.

Town Close House was founded in 1932 and became a Charitable Trust in 1968. The School is fully co-educational and is situated on a beautiful wooded site near the centre of Norwich. This location gives all our girls and boys space and freedom, and contributes substantially to our reputation as an outstandingly happy school.

There are altogether 50 full-time and 7 part-time members of staff. Together, we aim to produce well-motivated, balanced, confident children, who are caring and sociable and who know the value of hard work. Our classes are small and the children are prepared for all major senior schools, whilst those showing special promise sit scholarships.

The School's facilities include a well-equipped science laboratory, an indoor heated swimming pool, a new high specification sports hall completed in July 2009 and a new performance hall completed in January 2010. A modern teaching centre stands at the heart of the School, containing a large, well-equipped library, an art room and 16 purpose-built classrooms.

Our Nursery and Reception classes follow the Foundation Stage curriculum, an important element of which is outdoor learning. Children progress through a broad and varied programme of activities with a strong emphasis on the development of personal and social skills and on establishing positive attitudes to learning and to school life. Swimming and music are taught by specialist teachers, while the rest of the curriculum is delivered by class teachers, ably supported by well-qualified teaching assistants. The Nursery is purpose-built and the children play an important part in the life of the Pre-Prep Department.

Throughout the children's time at Town Close we pay particular attention to the teaching of good handwriting and spelling. Whilst recognising the importance of ICT, we value these traditional core skills very highly. Our ICT provision is extensive. We aim for all our children to become confident and proficient users of ICT. Our Pre-Prep pupils use a range of children's software in the computer rooms to develop key skills. Prep Department children build on these skills using more professional based software, either in the computer room or on the set of mobile tablets. All sections of the School have filtered access to the internet across our growing network. The School Intranet contains interactive activities, images, lesson material and links to carefully selected websites. Interactive whiteboards are used throughout the School to support the curriculum.

Town Close has an excellent academic and sporting reputation, but music, art, drama and a wide range of extra-curricular activities, trips and expeditions form a valuable part of what we offer, and provide the balance essential for a full and rounded education. Activities take place during the lunch hour, after school, and occasionally at week-ends. In terms of music, the School has an orchestra, a variety of choirs and a wide range of ensembles. All children are encouraged to perform and concerts take place regularly.

Physical Education plays an important part in the development of each child, be they in the Nursery or in Year 8. Emphasis is placed on fostering healthy exercise, as well as encouraging a positive, competitive attitude, individual skills and teamwork. As well as providing all the usual opportunities for the major sports (rugby, netball, hockey, cricket and athletics), coaching is offered in many other minor sports.

A copy of our prospectus is available on request, while a visit to our website will provide a fuller picture of the School, including a sight of our most recent inspection report.

Charitable status. Town Close House Educational Trust Limited is a Registered Charity, number 311293. It exists to provide education for children.

Truro School Preparatory School

Highertown, Truro, Cornwall TR1 3QN
Tel: 01872 272616
Fax: 01872 222377
e-mail: enquiries@truroprep.com
website: www.truroprep.com

Chairman of the Governors: Mr G Rumbles

Headmaster of Truro School: Mr P K Smith, MA Cantab, MEd, FRGS

Headmaster of Preparatory School: **Mr M J Lovett**, BA Ed

Head of Pre-Prep: Mrs A Allen, CertEd

Age Range. 3–11.
Number of Pupils. 269: 153 Boys, 115 Girls.
Fees per term (2011-2012). Prep (including lunch): £3,515 (Years 5–6), £3,450 (Years 3–4). Pre-Prep (including lunch): £2,650 (Years 1 and 2), £2,600 (Nursery and Reception).

Optional extras: Individual music lessons, fencing, dance, judo.

Truro School Prep was opened as Treliske School in 1936 in the former residence and estate of Sir George Smith. The school lies in extensive and secluded grounds to the west of the cathedral city of Truro, three miles from Truro School. The grounds command fine views of the neighbouring countryside. The drive to the school off the main A390 is almost 800 metres and Truro Golf Course also surrounds the school, so producing a campus of beauty and seclusion.

The keynote of the school is a happy, caring atmosphere in which children learn the value of contributing positively to the school community through the firm and structured framework of academic study and extra curricular interests. The approach is based firmly in Christian beliefs and the school is proud of its Methodist foundation.

Building development has kept pace with modern expectations and Truro School Prep has its own large sports hall, an indoor heated swimming pool, a design and technology workshop with a computer room adjoined and purpose-built Pre-Prep.

The games programme is designed to encourage all children, from the keenest to the least athletic, to enjoy games and physical exercise. Our excellent facilities and the diverse skill of our staff enable us to offer a rich variety of sporting and recreational pursuits. There are over 20 popular clubs and activities run each week from 4.00 pm to 5.00 pm.

There is a strong school tradition in music and drama and the arts. Children may choose to learn a musical instrument from the full orchestral range. Each year the November con-

cert, with Truro School, allows the school to show the community the excellent talents, which flourish in both schools.

Close links are maintained with the Senior School and nearly all pupils progress through at age 11 on the Headmaster's recommendation to Truro School which is the only Independent Headmasters' and Headmistresses' Conference School in Cornwall (*see entry in HMC section*).

The prospectus and further details can be obtained from the Headmaster's Secretary, and the Headmaster will be pleased to show prospective parents around the school.

Charitable status. Truro School is a Registered Charity, number 306576. It is a charitable foundation established for the purpose of education.

Twickenham Preparatory School

Beveree, 43 High Street, Hampton, Middlesex TW12 2SA
Tel: 020 8979 6216
Fax: 020 8979 1596
e-mail: office@twickenhamprep.co.uk
website: www.twickenhamprep.co.uk

Chairman of Governors: Mr D Howell, BA, FRGS

Headmaster: **D Malam**, BA Hons Southampton, PGCE Winchester

Age Range. 4–13.
Number of Pupils. Boys 151, Girls 120.
Fees per term (2011-2012). £2,890–£3,125 plus £155 lunch.

Originally founded as a private school in 1932 and re-founded in 1969, the school is now a limited company with charitable status.

Boys are prepared for Common Entrance Examinations and girls for entrance examinations to independent senior schools. Able pupils take scholarships and the academic standard of the school is high.

The staff is graduate and class sizes are approximately 18. Children are admitted at 4 years old. Girls leave at 11+ and boys at 13+.

The school, which is housed in a Grade II listed building in the Hampton conservation area, is well equipped to cover the full range of subjects. Emphasis is on individual attention and developing each pupil to their full academic potential.

There is a purpose-built pre-prep block, gymnasium, dining and changing facilities. Grounds and playgrounds have also been developed. A new Music department is about to be built.

The school is a friendly and happy community where there is a clear non-sectarian Christian tradition, though pupils of all faiths are accepted.

Football, rugby, cricket, netball and rounders are the main team games and pupils swim regularly from Year 1 to Year 6. Athletics, tennis, squash, golf and other sports are also coached. Music and drama play a large part in school with full scale productions and concerts annually, involving all pupils. Individual instrumental lessons are taught by visiting specialists and there are many varied after school activities.

Charitable status. Twickenham Preparatory School is a Registered Charity, number 1067572. It exists to provide education for boys and girls.

Twyford School

Winchester, Hampshire SO21 1NW
Tel: 01962 712269

Fax: 01962 712100
e-mail: registrar@twyfordschool.com
website: www.twyfordschool.com

Chairman of Governors: Mr S P Kelly

Headmaster: **Dr S J Bailey**, BEd, PhD, FRSA

Age Range. 3–13.
Number of Children. 361. Main School: 258 (161 boys, 97 girls, 61 weekly and flexi boarders); Pre-Prep: 103 (54 boys, 49 girls).
Fees per term (2011-2012). £6,625 (boarding), £5,260 (day), £4,220 (Year 3). No compulsory extras. Pre-Prep: £1,480–£2,690. Bursaries are available.

Twyford School is situated at the edge of the beautiful South Downs just two miles from the historic city of Winchester and the M3. Twyford is a family school that aims to offer an all-round top-rate education with a Christian ethos. Boarding is central to life at Twyford. Most pupils start as day pupils, but by the end of their last year over 80% are weekly boarding through the school's flexi-boarding system, which makes an excellent preparation for their move to senior school. The contrast between the modern facilities (classrooms, laboratories, music school, creative arts and ICT block, swimming pool and sports centre) and the Victorian chapel and hall creates a rich and stimulating environment.

The school regularly achieves scholarships – 47 awards (academic, art, design, sport and music) in the last 5 years – to major senior schools such as Winchester College, St Swithun's, Canford, King Edward VI Southampton, Harrow, Pangbourne College, Wycombe Abbey, Radley and Sherborne.

Charitable status. Twyford School is a Registered Charity, number 307425. It exists to provide education for children.

Unicorn School

238 Kew Road, Richmond, Surrey TW9 3JX
Tel: 020 8948 3926
Fax: 020 8332 6814
e-mail: registrar@unicornschool.org.uk
website: www.unicornschool.org.uk

Chairman of Governors: Mrs Vicky Hastings

Headmistress: **Mrs Roberta Linehan**, BA, PGCE Queen's Belfast

Age Range. 3–11.
Number of Children. 169 Day Pupils: 79 boys, 90 girls.
Fees per term (2011-2012). £1,860–£3,405.

Unicorn is a Parent-owned school founded in 1970 and the Headmistress is a member of IAPS. Situated opposite Kew Gardens, the school occupies a large Victorian house and converted coach house with a spacious, well-equipped playground and garden.

The school has free and unrestricted access to Kew Gardens and the sports facilities at the nearby Old Deer Park are utilised for games and swimming.

There are 9 full-time teachers, supported by 13 part-time assistants and specialist teachers, with visiting teachers for music, individual tuition and clubs. Classes average 21 children.

Unicorn aims to give children firm foundations and a broad education. A variety of teaching methods are used and the children are regularly assessed. Importance is placed upon the development of the individual and high academic standards are achieved. The main point of entry is to nursery at 3+ and the majority of children stay the full eight years.

Children are prepared for entry at 11+ to the leading London Day Schools, as well as a variety of boarding schools.

There is a specialist ICT room and networked computers in every classroom. At nine years old all children take an intensive touch-typing course. In addition, there is a Science and Design Technology suite with interactive whiteboard technology in most classrooms.

The curriculum includes Drama, French (from age 5), Art and Music – with individual music lessons offered in piano, violin, cello, clarinet, saxophone, flute, guitar and trumpet, as well as singing. Recorder groups, choirs, chamber groups, an orchestra and wind band also flourish.

In addition to the major games of football, rugby, hockey, netball, cricket, rounders and athletics, there are optional clubs for tennis, squash, badminton, ice skating, golf, riding, sailing and self-defence. Other club activities include arts and crafts, calligraphy, cookery, ICT, fabric design, film club, gardening, lego robotics, mosaic, papier mache, pottery and sewing. There are regular visits to the theatre as well as to the museums and galleries of Central London. All children, from the age of seven upwards, participate in residential field study trips.

An elected School Council, with representatives from each age group, meets weekly. A weekly newsletter for parents is produced.

A happy, caring environment prevails and importance is placed on producing kind, responsible children who show awareness and consideration for the needs of others.

Charitable status. Unicorn School is a Registered Charity, number 312578. It exists to provide education for boys and girls.

University College School – Junior Branch

11 Holly Hill, Hampstead, London NW3 6QN
Tel: 020 7435 3068
Fax: 020 7435 7332
e-mail: juniorbranch@ucs.org.uk
website: www.ucs.org.uk

Chairman of Council of Governors: The Rt Hon Sir Brian Leveson, MA, LLD Hon

Headmaster: **K J Douglas**, BA, BSc, CertEd

Age Range. 7–11.
Number of Boys. 240.
Fees per term (2011-2012). £4,930.

The School was founded in 1891 by the Governors of University College, London. The present building was opened in 1928, but retains details from the Georgian house first used. It stands near the highest point of Hampstead Heath and the hall and classrooms face south. Facilities include a Science Laboratory, Library, Drama Studio, Music and Computer Rooms, and a Centre for Art and Technology. Boys receive their Swimming and PE lessons in the pool and Sports Hall at the Senior School, 5 minutes' walk away. The Junior School has full use of the 27 acres of playing fields on games days.

Boys enter at 7+ each year and they are prepared for transfer to the Senior School at 11+. (*See entry in HMC section.*)

Charitable status. University College School, Hampstead is a Registered Charity, number 312748. The Junior Branch exists to provide education for boys aged 7+ to 11 years.

University College School – The Phoenix

36 College Crescent, Hampstead, London NW3 5LF
Tel: 020 7722 4433
Fax: 020 7722 4601
e-mail: thephoenix@ucs.org.uk
website: www.ucs.org.uk

Chairman of Council of Governors: The Rt Hon Sir Brian
   Leveson, MA, LLD Hon

Headmistress: **Miss Caroline Froud**, BEd

   Age Range. 3–7 Co-educational.
   Number of Pupils. 140.
   Fees per term (2011-2012). £1,530–£4,170.
   At The Phoenix, we firmly believe that happiness and
self-esteem are the keys to success in every pupil's learning
journey. The well-qualified and highly-supportive staff
accompany each child on a voyage of educational and social
discovery during the first years of school life.
   The Phoenix School joined the UCS Foundation of
Schools in 2002 and fully supports the aims and ethos of
UCS: intellectual curiosity and independence of mind are
developed, self-discovery and self-expression are fostered
and a cooperative and collaborative approach to learning is
of great importance.
   For every child in our care, we provide a continuously
positive and creative learning environment that allows the
individual the opportunity to develop personal qualities and
talents. We are able to cater for up to 140 pupils aged 3–7 in
our well-resourced classrooms. At the end of Year 2, both
girls and boys transfer to a range of local independent
schools. Whilst it is hoped that most boys will transfer to the
Junior Branch of UCS this is not automatic and is subject to
meeting the required standard in the entrance examination.
(*See separate Junior Branch entry.*)
   Charitable status. The Phoenix School Limited is a Registered Charity, number 1098657.

Upton House School

115 St Leonard's Road, Windsor, Berkshire SL4 3DF
Tel: 01753 862610
Fax: 01753 621950
e-mail: info@uptonhouse.org.uk
         registrar@uptonhouse.org.uk
website: www.uptonhouse.org.uk

Chairman of the Council: Mr D R Llewellyn, BA, DipEd

Headmistress: **Mrs Madeleine Collins**, BA Hons, PGCE
   Oxon

   Age Range. Girls 2–11 years, Boys 2–7 years.
   Number of Pupils. 240 Day: 170 Girls, 70 Boys.
   Fees per term (2011-2012). £1,535–£3,995 (inclusive).
   The aim of Upton House is to foster a happy and stimulating environment in which each child can prosper academically, socially and emotionally. The school will prepare all
children for their continuing education and enhance their
awareness of the world in which they live.
   Upton House School was founded in 1936 by benefactors
and has evolved over the years to provide a well-equipped
environment where children can thrive. The extensive facilities include music rooms, state-of-the-art ICT suite, science
laboratory, two libraries, a fully-equipped gymnasium, a
drama studio and purpose-built food technology room. The
school aims to motivate every child to develop their poten-

tial to the full in a happy, lively and caring community. We
believe in the importance of small classes taken by well-
qualified, caring members of staff. In our broad, inclusive
curriculum the children are taught from Nursery by subject
specialists. They have the opportunity to benefit from the
best possible teaching, and to be inspired by teachers who
love their subjects and who are able to get the best from their
pupils. Boys are prepared for entry to preparatory schools in
the area at 7+. Girls leaving gain places at a wide range of
senior schools and regularly win scholarships (in the last 5
years on average 20% of Form 6 girls have gained scholarships).
   Entry is non-selective and means-tested bursaries (up to
100%) are available for those entering the school.
   We provide care from 8.00 am in Early Birds until the end
of the official teaching day. Children are able to enjoy a late
programme until 5.45 pm from the age of 3 years old
upwards. A wide variety of clubs are offered in the late programmes as well as teacher-supervised prep.
   We have an active PTA who organise many fundraising
events through the year and help forge close links between
the school and parents.
   Charitable status. Upton House School is a Registered
Charity, number 309095. It exists to provide an excellent all-
round educational foundation for boys and girls.

Ursuline Preparatory School
Wimbledon

18 The Downs, Wimbledon, London SW20 8HR
Tel: 020 8947 0859
Fax: 020 8947 0885
e-mail: admissions@ursuline-prep.merton.sch.uk
website: www.ursuline-prep.merton.sch.uk

A Catholic Independent day school.

Chair of Governors: Mr Francis Bacon

Headmistress: **Mrs Anne Farnish**, BA Hons

   Age Range. Girls 3–11, Boys 3–4.
   Number of Pupils. 200+.
   Fees per term (2011-2012). £1,645–£2,690.
   Our school has a strong academic, musical and sporting
tradition, producing excellent results in the Pre-Prep and
Prep Departments. Our new Nursery Cottage Development
(including Early Years' Art Studio, Astro play area and garden allotments) opened in September 2010 and caters for
boys and girls from 3 years of age. Boys then leave the
school to take up Reception places at Donhead Catholic
Prep. New developments include an exciting Design Art studio, Performing Arts Room and Music practice rooms for
girls from age 5, as well as sick bay and disabled access.
Pupils are introduced to Modern Foreign Languages at age
3; PE, French, Art and Music are all taught by specialist
teachers. ICT is integrated throughout the curriculum. There
are extensive out-of-school activities including choirs,
orchestra, chess, football, drama, ballet, jazz dance, sailing,
science club, sewing and Spanish. Residential trips are organised in Years 4, 5 and 6 to a field study centre and France
respectively. Hot organic lunches and snacks are provided by
our business partners "Out to Lunch".
   Girls aspire to many selective independent schools at age
11 years; some also transfer to our Catholic Ursuline High
School.
   The school is regularly inspected by ISI and Ofsted. In its
most recent Ofsted inspection the Early Years provision was
rated 'Outstanding' in all areas.
   We are a thriving IAPS Prep School with a vibrant Catholic ethos.

Charitable status. Ursuline Preparatory School Wimbledon Trust is a Registered Charity, number 1079754.

Victoria College Preparatory School

Jersey, Channel Islands JE2 4RR
Tel: 01534 723468
Fax: 01534 780596
e-mail: admin@vcp.sch.je
website: www.vcp.sch.je

Chairman of Governors: C Barton

Headmaster: **Russell Price**, BSc, MPhil

Age Range. 7–11.
Number of Boys. 293 Day Boys.
Fees per term (2011-2012). £1,440 (inclusive).
Victoria College Preparatory School was founded in 1922 as an integral part of Victoria College and is now a separate School under its own Headmaster, who is responsible for such matters as staffing, curriculum and administration. The Preparatory School shares Governors with Victoria College whose members are drawn from the leaders of the Island of Jersey with a minority representation from the States of Jersey Education Committee. Members of staff are all experienced and well-qualified teachers, including specialists in Music, Dance, Art, PE, French, Science and Technology. Entry to the Prep School is at 7 and boys normally leave to enter Victoria College at the age of 11. The school games are cricket, soccer, athletics, swimming, hockey, cross-country and rugby. Sporting facilities are shared with Victoria College. Special features of the school are sport, drama, music and a high standard of French. Many visits, both sporting and educational, are arranged out of the Island.

A separate Pre-Preparatory School (5 to 7 years) is incorporated in a co-educational school situated at the Jersey College for Girls' Preparatory School and offers places for boys whose parents wish them to be educated at both Victoria College and the Preparatory School. Candidates for Pre-Prep entry should be registered at the Preparatory School of the Jersey College for Girls, St Helier, Jersey.

Vinehall

Near Robertsbridge, East Sussex TN32 5JL
Tel: 01580 880413
Fax: 01580 882119
e-mail: office@vinehallschool.com
website: www.vinehallschool.com

Chairman of Governors: Mr D W Chivers

Headmaster: **Richard Follett**

Age Range. 2–13.
Number of Children. 292: 34 boarders, 258 Day Children, 99 Pre-Preparatory and Nursery.
Fees per term (2011-2012). Day Pupil: Years 3–5, £4,705, Years 6–8 £4,820; Boarder: Years 3–5 £6,175, Years 6–8 £6,290; Pre-Prep: Reception, Years 1 & 2 £2,600, Nursery: 5 full days £2,440 or pro rata: 1 full day £488, 1 morning £330, 1 afternoon £158.
The School prepares boys and girls for a variety of senior schools. It has been designated a Christian School and has both day and boarding pupils.
The School's scholastic record over the past five years has been extremely good, with scholarships having been won to

schools such as Benenden, Eastbourne College, Eton, King's Canterbury, Lancing, Sevenoaks, Sherborne, Tonbridge and Winchester. The School has excellent teaching facilities with science laboratories, a computer room and a superb pre-preparatory department built in 1996. In September 2000 a Resources Centre and Library was completed at the heart of the main teaching block.

All the creative and performing arts are encouraged and the School has a wonderful theatre, built in 1991, which seats 250. The performing arts are a strength of the School. Most of the children learn musical instruments and regular plays and concerts are performed, both by the children and by visiting international musicians to the School's concert series.

The School stands in its own grounds of some 48 acres, and has a 9-hole golf course, as well as extensive playing fields, tennis courts, an indoor heated swimming pool and a well-equipped sports hall. A new floodlit, all-weather pitch was opened in 2009. Pupils can reach very high levels in a variety of sports.

Woods and gardens provide an excellent setting for all kinds of outdoor recreations.

The boarders are cared for by residential houseparents along with matrons. All staff have an involvement in the varied boarding activity programme at weekends and evenings. Boarding is full, although there are regular exeats. Many pupils take the option of occasional boarding nights.

Charitable status. Vinehall School is a Registered Charity, number 307014. It exists to provide a secure, quality education, in particular for those in need of residential schooling.

Wakefield Girls' High School Junior School

2 St John's Square, Wakefield, West Yorkshire WF1 2QX
Tel: 01924 374577
Fax: 01924 231602
e-mail: admissions@wghsjs.org.uk
website: www.wgsf.org.uk

Spokesman: Mr D Wheatley

Head Mistress: **Mrs D St C Cawthorne**, BEd

Age Range. Girls 3–11, Boys 3–4.
Number of Pupils. All day pupils: 390 girls, 25 boys.
Fees per term (2011-2012). Nursery and Pre-Preparatory Department £2,419; Lower Juniors (7–8 year olds) £2,499; Upper Juniors (9–10 year olds) £2,641. Lunch included.
Instrumental lessons: £185 (10 lessons per term).
The Governors of the High School are shared with Queen Elizabeth Junior and Senior Schools (for boys) situated nearby. Close links are enjoyed between all four schools.
The school is extremely well resourced and enjoys an excellent reputation for high academic standards, caring pastoral system and numerous extra curricular activities.
The Nursery Department takes children full-time at the age of three, in order of registration. It is housed in its own spacious, stimulating and secure surroundings. The well-planned environment and an appropriate mix of formal and informal education allows for the social, physical and educational development of each individual child. The Nursery Department ensures that preparation and progression to Reception, at the age of four, is an exciting and natural transition.
Pre-Prep girls (aged 4–7) are housed in Mulberry House and enjoy a child-centered learning environment. Boys move to Queen Elizabeth Grammar School Junior School at the age of 4. At the age of 7 the girls move into the Junior

School. The Lower Junior girls are taught in St John's House and the Upper Juniors in a building with access to Science Laboratories, a Lecture Theatre and other Senior School facilities. The girls move into the Senior School at the age of 11.

The school aims to give a good all-round education to each pupil, encouraging academic excellence, emphasizing traditional values, nurturing talent and developing an individual's potential. Entrance is by examination from the age of 5 with the main Entrance Examination being held in February. In addition to the Head, a team of 32 dedicated and enthusiastic full-time teachers care for the children and encourage them in all aspects of school life. There are also many teaching assistants, three secretaries and other ancillary staff.

The school is a Christian foundation but with no particular denominational bias. Assemblies take place each day. The faiths of all members of the community are respected and valued.

The curriculum covers a wide range of subjects, including all of those prescribes by the National Curriculum, but the emphasis remains on numeracy and literacy. Music and physical education are natural parts of the curriculum and play important roles in the life of the school. A spirit of sensible competition is encouraged and the school teams and choirs enjoy success in local tournaments and festivals. All classrooms, the ICT Suite, Science/Mathematics Room, Music, Library and resource areas are well equipped. All classrooms have an interactive whiteboard. Closeness to the Senior School makes it possible to share teaching staff, resources and specialist areas. The curriculum is further enriched by a variety of clubs and societies, in-school workshops and educational outings. The children are encouraged to think of others less fortunate than themselves and money is raised for a variety of charities.

Parental involvement is welcomed and participation both in the classroom and extra-curricular activities appreciated. Social and fundraising events are organised by the Friends of St John's House, the school's PTA. All children stay to lunch which is cooked on the premises. Before and after school care is available to parents for a small additional charge.

Charitable status. The Wakefield Grammar School Foundation, founded in 1591, is a Registered Charity, number 1088415. It exists to provide an excellent education for your children.

Walthamstow Hall Junior School

Bradbourne Park Road, Sevenoaks, Kent TN13 3LD
Tel: 01732 453815
Fax: 01732 456980
e-mail: registrar@ @walthamstowhall.kent.sch.uk
website: www.walthamstow-hall.co.uk

Chairman of Governors: Ian Philip, Esq, FCA

Head of the Junior School: **Mrs P A Austin**, BA Hons London, LTCL Trinity College of Music, PGCE, NPQH

Day School for Girls.
Age Range. 2½–11.
Number of Girls. 220.
Fees per term (2011-2012). Kindergarten £235 per session (2–10 sessions per week); Reception–Year 2 £2,990, Years 3–6 £3,710.

Walthamstow Hall Junior School offers a quality education for girls from 2½–11 years. It has a vibrant Pre-Preparatory department with flexible Kindergarten sessions. A well-planned programme of education brings out the potential of each child as she progresses through the Junior School. A broad curriculum is enriched with many extra-curricular activities and clubs. Girls are well prepared for a range of

senior schools and have won awards to prestigious independent schools, including Walthamstow Hall Senior School, Sevenoaks and Benenden. Many choose to take advantage of the opportunity of an 'all through' education. Entry to our Senior School is from 11+, 13+ and 16+ with Awards, Scholarships and bursaries offered on merit. Equally, our track record at 11+ assessment is excellent. Walthamstow Hall was founded in 1838 and is one of the oldest girls' schools in the country with a fascinating history. It has built a reputation for 'all-round' excellence and achievements by girls are outstanding. Over recent years, many new facilities have been added including new nursery classrooms, a new library with computerised lending facility and a new science laboratory. Girls have access to the Senior School facilities including 'Ship Theatre', art rooms, interactive science block, extensive sports grounds and swimming pool. The school is situated in the centre of Sevenoaks within easy reach of road and rail networks. Minibuses operate from surrounding towns and villages.

Warminster Preparatory School

Vicarage Street, Warminster, Wiltshire BA12 8JG
Tel: 01985 224800
Fax: 01985 218850
e-mail: prep@warminsterschool.org.uk
website: www.warminsterschool.org.uk

Co-educational, Day & Boarding.

Chairman of Governors: R Payn, MA Oxon

Headmaster: **D A H Edwards**, BEd, MA

Age Range. 3–11 co-educational.
Number of Pupils. 170.
Fees per term (2011-2012). Day: Reception £2,165; Years 1 & 2 £2,335; Years 3 £2,760; Year 4 £3,080; Years 5 & 6 £3,465. Boarding: £5,855.

Conveniently situated on the edge of Salisbury Plain with easy access to London and the South-West, Warminster Prep is a thriving school with a friendly, family atmosphere. Together with our Senior School, we make up Warminster School, providing exciting, high-quality education for children from 3 to 18 years old.

Fully-qualified and dedicated teaching staff deliver a vibrant and stimulating curriculum enriched with many trips and theme days. Our teaching in the Prep School is rich and varied in its styles to suit the diverse variety of children who thrive in our inclusive and holistic environment. We have Learning Support for those who may need it and an 'Able & Talented' club to ensure that all our children are achieving their potential in a supportive and caring atmosphere.

The curriculum is broad and balanced reflecting an ethos that values the development of skills and achievement in all subjects and areas of school life. Whilst the pursuit of excellence in core subjects is very important, Art, Sport, Music, Drama and Technologies are also vital areas in building confidence and self-esteem. Scholarships are available for academic Years 3 and 5 as well as for Years 7 and 9 in the Senior School.

Totally flexible boarding arrangements exist for children from 7 years upwards within our attractive Prep School boarding house; Golspie. Under the auspices of our experienced, dedicated Matron and House Parents, children enjoy a very high standard of Pastoral care with weekend trips and outings being a highlight of the week. A number of children are full boarders, but weekly and hotel boarding are very popular with, and a cost-effective service for, busy working parents. The Boarding Schools Allowance is available for serving members of HM Forces.

Sport is an important part of life at Warminster Prep, with a busy programme of inter-school fixtures in Rugby, Soccer, Hockey and Cricket for boys, and Hockey, Netball and Rounders for girls. In the summer term, children also swim and enjoy Tennis and Athletics.

Warminster Prep School has a strong creative tradition in the Arts; performing art in Music, Speech and Drama, visual art in a wide range of media including sculpture and fired clay.

The Prep (and Pre-Prep) School is well-equipped with its own catering and Dining Hall, modern fully-equipped Science lab, ICT suite, sports pitches, astroturf, Art and DT studio, well-equipped stage, tennis courts, Music and practice rooms and Library. This is in addition to the superb facilities we share with our adjacent Senior School such as the Swimming pool, Senior Library, Chapel and Sports Hall. The new Courtyard Nursery was opened in 2007 and provides superb accommodation for the Early Years Foundation Stage. The Nursery is oversubscribed and parents are advised to register for places in plenty of time.

We provide, for Day and Boarding children, a wide choice of clubs and activities. These augment our timetabled curriculum and ensure that children can develop their individual tastes and interests alongside more traditionally academic abilities. We include opportunities for foreign travel with our French Trip and Ski Trip.

Interested parents are invited to ring the Headmaster's Secretary for a prospectus and to arrange a visit and free taster-day.

For information about the Senior School, please see entry in HMC section.

Charitable status. Warminster School is Registered Charity, number 1042204, providing education for boys and girls.

Warwick Junior School

Myton Road, Warwick CV34 6PP
Tel: 01926 776418
Fax: 01926 776478
e-mail: enquiries@warwickschool.org
website: www.warwickschool.org

Chairman of Governors: R M Dancey, MA

Head of Junior School: **G R G Canning**, BA, PGCE

Age Range. 7–11.
Number of Pupils. 243 boys.
Fees per term (2011-2012). Tuition: £2,686 (7+), £3,049 (8+/9+), £3,415 (10+).

The School is the Junior School of Warwick School. The Junior School is situated on a site on the outskirts of Warwick Town adjacent to Warwick Senior School. The buildings are contained within a four-acre site and enjoy the use of the Sports and other facilities of Warwick Senior School. A new extension to the school, providing six classrooms and a library, was completed in May 2002. A programme of refurbishment in the existing Junior School building was completed in September 2002 and this includes new ICT and DT rooms.

The aim of the School is to provide a good general education based on Christian principles. Academic standards are high and in particular participation in a range of activities is encouraged. Each pupil is encouraged to develop his own personality and to realise his own potential.

The curriculum gives a good grounding in English, Mathematics, Science, Technology, ICT, History, Geography, Religious Education, French, Art, Music, Drama and PE. Many sporting activities are available on the fifty acre campus of Warwick School, which includes a sports hall and indoor swimming pool. Rugby and Soccer are the main winter sports, with Cricket in the summer, plus Athletics, Swimming, Tennis, Squash and Cross Country.

The School's creative activities, dramatic productions and musical performances provide a useful focus in the development of many talents within the School.

Warwick Junior School provides a programme of learning support. This support is available for boys with specific learning difficulties such as dyslexia or dyspraxia and for those who need just a "little extra help" in any area.

Extended day facilities are available until 5.30 pm when pupils can either do their homework or enrol in the activity programme.

Boys are prepared for the Entrance Examination to Warwick Senior School at age 11. The majority of pupils who leave Warwick Junior School gain a place in the Senior School at Warwick. (*See Warwick School entry in HMC section*)

Charitable status. Warwick Independent Schools Foundation is a Registered Charity, number 1088057. It exists to provide quality education for boys.

Warwick Preparatory School

Bridge Field, Banbury Road, Warwick CV34 6PL
Tel: 01926 491545
Fax: 01926 403456
e-mail: info@warwickprep.com
website: www.warwickprep.com

Chairman of the Governors: Mrs V Phillips

Headmaster: **Mr M Turner**, BA Hons, PGCE, NPQH

Age Range. Boys 3–7, Girls 3–11.
Number of Children. 106 Boys, 338 Girls.
Fees per term (2010-2011). Nursery: £2,354 (full time). Lower School (4–6 years) £2,727; Middle and Upper Schools (7–11 years) £3,014. (Lunch included)
Instrumental music tuition optional extra.

Warwick Preparatory School is an Independent School, purpose built in 1970 on a 4½ acre site on the outskirts of Warwick. It is part of the Warwick Independent Schools Foundation, which includes Warwick School and the King's High School for Girls.

The Prep School has 40 teachers and 25 nursery nurses, teaching assistants and technicians, with specialist tuition in Art, French, Science, Music, Drama, DT, Physical Education and Information Technology.

Boys and girls are admitted from the age of 3+, subject to the availability of places. At the age of 7 the boys sit the competitive entry examination for admission to the Junior Department of Warwick School, whilst the girls normally remain with us until they are 11.

Entry to both Warwick School and King's High School is by competitive examination and boys and girls at the Prep School are prepared for this. Girls are also prepared for the Common Entrance and any other appropriate examinations for their secondary education.

Early registration is advised if a place in the Pre-Preparatory Dept is to be ensured. Entry to the School at the age of 7 and later requires a satisfactory level of attainment in the basic skills and may be competitive.

Charitable status. Warwick Independent Schools Foundation is a Registered Charity, number 1088057.

Waverley School

Waverley Way, Finchampstead, Wokingham, Berkshire RG40 4YD
Tel: 0118 973 1121
Fax: 0118 973 1131
e-mail: waverley@cfbt.com
website: www.waverleyschool.co.uk

Chairman of the Board of Trustees: J Harwood, Esq

Principal: **Nigel Woolnough**, BA Hons, MSc, PGCE, RSA Prep, Cert TEFL

Age Range. 3–11 years.
Number of Pupils. 134 Day pupils (76 boys, 58 girls).
Fees per term (2010-2011). Reception–Year 6: £2,200–£2,679 (including lunch). Nursery: according to sessions attended.

Waverley is a co-educational day school, founded in 1945 and now part of CfBT Education Trust.

In September 1997 Waverley School relocated to new purpose-built premises just south of Wokingham. This prestigious development in a superb location offers children outstanding opportunities in and out of the classroom. A new Art, Science and Technology suite opened in 2002.

Waverley's curriculum provides children with a solid foundation, particularly in the areas of literacy and numeracy. An excellent network of computers provides outstanding opportunities for Information and Communications Technology. All subjects of the National Curriculum are taught, with the addition of French from Reception. Team games include soccer, rugby, netball, cricket and rounders. Swimming and athletics are included in the physical education programme. Children's self-confidence is developed through their involvement in drama. Music, both choral and instrumental, is a particular strength of the School.

Waverley School welcomes visiting specialists for French, Swimming, Piano, Violin, Clarinet, Flute, Guitar, Ballet, Judo, Chess, and Speech and Drama. There is specialist help for pupils with specific learning difficulties.

Waverley successfully prepares boys and girls for entrance to Independent Senior Schools and Reading's grammar schools at 11+. An integral Nursery offers a carefully balanced introduction to the School, and ensures both social and educational continuity from 3–11 years.

Waverley School offers an extended day and year facility and a full and active clubs programme.

There is also a thriving Friends' Association.

Charitable status. Waverley School is a Registered Charity, number 309102. It exists to provide education for boys and girls between 3 and 11.

Wellesley House

Ramsgate Road, Broadstairs, Kent CT10 2DG
Tel: 01843 862991
Fax: 01843 602068
e-mail: office@wellesleyhouse.net
website: www.wellesleyhouse.org

Chairman of the Governors: T M Steel, Esq

Headmaster: **S T P O'Malley**, MA Hons, PGCE

Age Range. 7–13.
Number of Pupils. 80 Boys, 59 Girls.
Fees per term (2010-2011). Boarding £6,650; Day £5,200; Year 3 Day: £4,700.

Location. The school, which is run by an Educational Trust, stands in its own grounds of 20 acres and was purpose-built in 1898.

Trains run hourly from Victoria Station, London with a high-speed rail link from St Pancras which takes as little as 1 hour 15 minutes or under two hours by road. At the beginning of each term, and at exeats, the school operates coach services between Broadstairs and London via the M2 services and also Birchanger services on the M11 via Brentwood. The school also operates a minibus at exeats and half-terms to Charing, near Ashford, and Benenden.

Facilities. The school has a science and technology building, which includes modern science laboratories, an ICT laboratory and a craft room. Other facilities include a library, an indoor heated swimming pool, four hard tennis courts, two squash courts, a modelling room, art room, a music wing, a .22 shooting range and separate recreation rooms, all of which are in the school grounds. There is a spacious sports hall. The main team games are cricket, Association and rugby football, hockey, netball and rounders. Tuition is also given in squash, shooting, fencing, golf, tennis, archery, judo and swimming. Ballet, tap, modern dancing, riding and sailing are also available.

A special feature of the school is that boys between the ages of 7 and 9 live in a junior wing. This is linked to the main school but self-contained under the care of resident house staff and a resident matron.

The girls live in a separate house, The Orchard, within the school grounds, under the care of a housemaster and his wife.

Education. Boys and girls are prepared for all independent senior schools. Those who show sufficient promise are prepared for scholarships and the school has a fine record of success on this front with a third of leavers gaining scholarships in recent years. The curriculum is designed to enable all children to reach the highest standard possible by sound teaching along carefully thought out lines to suit the needs of the individual.

The Headmaster and his wife are assisted by 23 teaching staff.

Charitable status. Wellesley House and St Peter Court School Education Trust Ltd is a Registered Charity, number 307852. It exists solely to provide education to boys and girls.

Wellingborough Preparatory School

Wellingborough, Northants NN8 2BX
Tel: 01933 222698
Fax: 01933 233474
e-mail: prep-head@wellingboroughschool.org
website: www.wellingboroughschool.org

Chairman of the Governors: J J H Higgins

Headmaster: **R J Mitchell**, BEd

Deputy Headmaster: R W H Smith, BEd

Age Range. 8–13.
Number of Pupils. 167 Boys, 156 Girls.
Fees per term (2011-2012). £3,923 (lunches included).

The School is the Preparatory School of Wellingborough School (a registered charity). Girls and boys are admitted from 8 years old. The Preparatory School is self-contained with its own teaching centre, Library, Science Laboratory and Computer Suite. Music, sports and design technology facilities are shared with the Senior School.

The School offers a broad, well-balanced curriculum with Foundation Scholarships available at 11+ and Entrance Scholarships at 13+.

The School enjoys a strong sporting reputation which combines a desire for excellence with a 'sport for all' ethos. Games played are rugby, football, and cricket for the boys. Hockey, netball and rounders are the games played by the girls. The children are also able to represent the school at athletics, tennis and cross-country. There is an Equestrian Team whose fixture list continues to grow.

The creative arts are highly valued, with termly drama productions and a flourishing Art Department that has exhibited nationally. The School boast two orchestras and a wide variety of groups and ensembles. All the pupils have an opportunity to learn a brass instrument in Y5 as well as learning composition and keyboard skills in other year groups. There are around 50 to 60 after-school activities to choose from during the week, as well an optional Saturday Morning Activities programme which includes such activities as; film club, .22 shooting, Karate, fencing, golf, street dance, athletics and tennis.

The School is organised into six Clubs. Each Club is headed by a member of staff who oversees the academic and social progress of the girls and boys within their club.

The children work in a stimulating environment. The School aims for the pupils to become successful learners, confident individuals and responsible citizens, with parents working together in partnership with the School in the education of their children.

Charitable status. Wellingborough School is a Registered Charity, number 309923. It exists to provide education for girls and boys.

Wellington Junior School

South Street, Wellington, Somerset TA21 8NT
Tel: 01823 668700
Fax: 01823 668708
e-mail: junior@wellington-school.org.uk
website: www.wellington-school.org.uk

Chair of Governors: Mr D R Wheeler, BSc, FCA

Headmaster: **Mr Adam Gibson**, BSc, PGCE, NPQH

Age Range. 3–11 Co-educational.
Number of Pupils. 270.
Fees per term (2011-2012). Day: £1,587–£2,957; Year 6 Boarding £6,000; Year 6 Weekly Boarding £4,800.

Wellington Junior School opened in September 1999 in purpose-built accommodation designed to provide one of the most modern and stimulating educational environments for young children anywhere in the country. Throughout the planning and design stages, the architects worked closely with experienced educational consultants to ensure that Wellington Junior School meets all the educational, recreational, social and aesthetic needs of its pupils.

Wellington Junior School provides an education of unrivalled quality which both complements and enhances the national reputation of Wellington School and enables us to deliver educational excellence for pupils from nursery level through to university entrance.

The School Chapel is central to the ethos of the school and the School Chaplain visits the Junior School weekly. At Wellington traditional Christian values combine with the best of modern innovation to give children the best possible of starts in a wonderfully happy and purposeful atmosphere. Boarding options are available from Year 6.

Classes are limited to a maximum of 20 pupils. Each class in Nursery and Reception operates the keyworker system with support assistants working alongside the teacher.

In all other classes specialist support is available to help gifted children as well as to support those in difficulty.

Encouragement and reward systems promote hard work and good behaviour.

The superb facilities include:
- eighteen purpose-designed, modern classrooms;
- a large, attractive school hall;
- the most modern and up-to-date educational resources and computers;
- an extremely well resourced library;
- landscaped grounds, including an architect-designed playground and recreational area;
- a visitors' reception area.

Situated in South Street, immediately opposite the Senior School, the Junior School has full access to the Princess Royal Sports Complex, rugby pitches, tennis courts, purpose-built netball courts, hockey pitches, including an all-weather hockey pitch, cricket pitches, athletics track. Specialist teaching in ICT, French, music, science and sport means that these are integral parts of our curriculum – as are art, dance and drama. Pupils enjoy success in these and many other areas.

There is an extensive clubs programme each afternoon and a holiday club catering for 3–8 year olds during the holiday period. Aftercare facilities operate each evening to accommodate working parents.

A comprehensive prospectus is available from the Headteacher's PA.

Charitable status. Wellington School is a Registered Charity, number 310268.

Wellow House School

Wellow, Nr Newark, Notts NG22 0EA
Tel: 01623 861054
Fax: 01623 836665
e-mail: wellowhouse@btinternet.com
website: www.wellowhouse.notts.sch.uk

Chairman of the Governors: John Pearce

Headmaster: **Peter Cook**, BEd

Age Range. 3–13.
Number of Pupils. 142.
Fees per term (2011-2012). Pre-Prep pupils £2,070; Day pupils £3,365–£3,565; Boarding pupils £4,480. Fees include meals and normal extras.

Wellow House School was founded in 1971 by the Stewart General Charitable Trust. Since 1994 it has been managed as an educational charity by the Directors and administered by a Board of Governors. This co-educational school has an established reputation for high academic standards, a successful sporting record, broad cultural interests and a happy family atmosphere. Weekly and occasional boarding has become an increasingly popular means of encouraging self-reliance within a supportive community and as a preparation for senior school and university.

The teaching staff of 8 men and 13 women is well qualified and experienced. A distinctive teaching style places great emphasis on the rapport between teacher and pupil in small classes, without slavish reliance on worksheets and textbooks. Each pupil maintains a file of notes, as a record and for reference. All take pride in honest hard work, confidence through encouragement, courtesy and fair discipline, and a strong sense of belonging. The thriving house points' system encourages much voluntary study and is the basis of the disciplinary process.

The Headmaster, Matron and Boarding Parents look after the boarders. They are assisted by a team of resident and non-resident tutors, one of whom oversees the evening activity programme. Qualified Catering Manager and Matron supervise the pupils' boarding, catering and medical needs. There are visiting teachers for instrumental tuition, table tennis, judo and drama.

The school is attractively set in 20 acres of parkland and playing fields on the fringe of the Sherwood Forest village of Wellow. There is easy road access to this heart of Nottinghamshire from Worksop and Sheffield to the north, Mansfield and Chesterfield to the west, Nottingham and Grantham to the south, and Lincoln and Newark to the east. Newark lies on north-south and east-west main line rail routes.

A continuous programme of development has provided purpose-built classrooms, science laboratory, networked computer room, music rooms, library, assembly hall and dining hall to add to the original country house. The boarding accommodation was refurbished in 1997 and 2000 with further refinements and updates in 2006 to 2008. Recent additions to the school include studios for art and ceramics and a sports hall with indoor cricket nets. There is an indoor heated swimming pool, an all-weather cricket net, and an all-weather tennis court. The Pre-Prep classes are housed in their own building, which was totally refurbished and extended in September 2006 and is surrounded by play-time facilities. There are close links with the village church.

Children enter the school after an interview visit and a trial day at any age from 3 to 11+ – the oldest often transferring from primary schools. Six Entrance Scholarships may be awarded annually and Bursaries can give financial assistance. Pupils are prepared for Common Entrance and Scholarships to a wide range of Senior Independent Schools, both boarding and day, and there is a continuous programme of assessment and reporting.

There is a broad physical education programme, with school matches in Rugby, Netball, Soccer, Hockey, Cricket, Rounders, Cross Country, Swimming and Tennis. The school is renowned for its pupils' prowess in Archery and Table Tennis. Weekend and holiday expeditions for Outdoor Pursuits in the Peak District, Yorkshire, Scotland and beyond are popular.

There is encouragement to participate in Natural History, the Visual Arts, Dance, Drama and Music, and more than half of the pupils learn a musical instrument. Most are involved in the much enjoyed regular concerts.

The school provides activity week cover during the holiday periods on Monday, Wednesday and Friday in the Pre Prep (to include pupils in Y3 and Y4). The Prep run activity weeks for 7–13 year olds for 2 full weeks in the summer.

Charitable status. Wellow House School is a Registered Charity, number 528234. It exists solely to provide a high standard of all-round education for children aged 3 to 13 years.

Wells Cathedral Junior School

8 New Street, Wells, Somerset BA5 2LQ
Tel: 01749 834400
Fax: 01749 834401
e-mail: juniorschool@wells-cathedral-school.com
website: www.wells-cathedral-school.com

Chairman of Governors: The Very Revd John Clarke, MA, BD (*Dean of Wells*)

Head of the Junior School: **Mrs K Schofield**, BA Hons, NPQH

Age Range. 3–11 years.
Number of Boys and Girls. 200: 102 Boys and 98 Girls.
Fees per term (2011-2012). Boarders £6,745, Day £3,868; Pre-Prep £2,079; Nursery £19.14 per 2 hour, 35 minute session.

The Junior School is made up of the Pre-Prep department (age 3–7) and the Junior School (age 7–11). Pupils accepted into the Junior School normally make a smooth transfer to the Senior School at 11 and academic and music scholarships are awarded.

Academic Work. The Junior School prepares children for the academic work in the senior school and takes part in the national tests at the end of KS 1 & 2 however the school is not restricted by the demands of the National Curriculum. The aim of the school is to ensure sound academic standards within a friendly and stimulating environment.

Children are assessed regularly for both academic achievement and effort, and parents have many opportunities to meet staff and receive information on their child's progress.

Pastoral Care. The form teacher is responsible for the pastoral care of pupils; in addition each pupil is allocated to a House which has an assembly once a week. Work and sports competitions take place in houses and pupils are able to develop a good relationship not only with their own peer group but with pupils from across the Junior School.

Creativity. Set in beautiful grounds just to the north of the Cathedral, pupils from the school provide the boy and girl choristers at the Cathedral. In addition, a number of pupils are specialist musicians enjoying the expert tuition of the music department at the school which is one of the four in England designated and grant-aided by the Government's Music and Dance Scheme. Scholarships are available for both the choristers and the musicians.

Drama, music and dance are considered vital activities to bring out the best in children. A full programme of concerts, both formal and informal, takes place during the year for all age groups as well as big productions and small year group dramas. The school takes its production to the Edinburgh Festival in alternate years and it has established drama exchange links with schools in other European countries.

A whole school arts week each summer allows all aspects of creativity to come to the fore for every pupil. Themes have included the Caribbean, Somerset and China; pupils experience workshops in the areas of art, dance, drama and music. Regular exhibitions and performances are a feature of the school. The school has received the Artsmark Gold award from Arts Council England.

Sport. The school has many of its own facilities and it is able to share some, such as the sports hall, astroturf pitch and swimming pool, with the senior school which is on the same site. Pupils experience a wide range of activities on the games field. Sport is played to a high standard with rugby, netball, hockey, cricket, swimming, athletics and gymnastics being the main sports. A full programme of inter-school matches and house matches is available for all pupils in Year 3 to 6. Many clubs and societies run at lunchtimes or after school.

Charitable status. Wells Cathedral School is a Registered Charity, number 310212. It has existed since AD 909 to provide education for its pupils.

West Hill Park

St Margarets Lane, Titchfield, Hants PO14 4BS
Tel: 01329 842356
Fax: 01329 842911
e-mail: admin@westhillpark.com
website: www.westhillpark.com

Chairman of Governors: The Lord Poole

Headmaster: **A P Ramsay**, BEd, MSc

Age Range. 2½–13.
Number of Pupils. Prep School (age 7–13): 25 Boarders (10 girls, 22 boys); 150 Day Pupils (59 girls, 91 boys). Pre-

Prep (age 4–7): 61 boys, 48 girls. Nursery (age 2½–4): 13 boys, 14 girls.

Fees per term (2010-2011). Prep School: Day £3,970–£4,875, Boarding supplement £1,500. Pre-Prep: £2,885; Nursery according to sessions.

At West Hill Park pupils are prepared for Scholarships and Common Entrance to all Independent Schools.

The main building is Georgian, originally a shooting lodge for the Earls of Southampton, and provides spacious and comfortable boarding accommodation for boys and girls under the supervision of resident Houseparents. Resident matrons and a qualified school nurse complete the Boarding team. Also in the main building are the administrative offices, the Library, the Dining Hall and the Assembly Hall with fully equipped sound and lighting equipment and stage. Further excellent facilities include the Art Centre, the Music School, a 25m heated indoor Swimming Pool, a fully equipped Sports Hall, the Design and Technology Centre, 2 Science Laboratories, the Information Technology Centre, the French, History, Maths and Geography Departments with Interactive Whiteboards, the purpose built Pre-Prep Department and the Nursery Department. West Hill Park stands in its own grounds of nearly 40 acres on the edge of Titchfield village. There are sports fields, 5 hard, 3 grass and 5 Astro tennis courts, a floodlit Riding School, a floodlit Astroturf, a cross-country course and in summer a nine hole golf course.

There are 28 fully qualified members of the teaching staff. 13 members of staff are resident, either in the main building or in houses in the school grounds, giving a great sense of community to the school.

A tutorial system monitors the individual child's well being on a weekly basis and there is a strong pastoral care system. There is a wide range of activities available in order to encourage children to develop individual skills and talents; choirs, orchestra, dance, aerobics, carpentry, judo, ballet, drama, golf, life-saving, computer club, string group, squash, chess, sailing, fly fishing, riding on school ponies and Brownies, as well as the more intensive training available in the Swim Squad, Tennis Squad and other sporting clubs. The Boarders enjoy many expeditions at weekends as well as fun events at school, such as orienteering, theatre workshops, cycle marathons and games evenings.

Games played include soccer, rugby, football, cricket, hockey, tennis, athletics, netball and rounders.

Charitable status. West Hill School Trust is a Registered Charity, number 307343. It exists to educate children.

West House School

24 St James Road, Edgbaston, Birmingham B15 2NX
Tel: 0121 440 4097
Fax: 0121 440 5839
e-mail: secretary@westhouseprep.com
website: www.westhouseprep.com

Chairman of Governors: S T Heathcote, FCA

Headmaster: **A M J Lyttle**, BA Hons Birmingham, PGCE Birmingham, NPQH

Age Range. Boys: 4–11 years; Co-educational Nursery: 12 months to 4 years.

Number of Pupils. A maximum 200 boys aged 4–11 (Reception to Year 6) plus 90 boys and girls aged 12 months–4 years.

Fees per term (2011-2012). 4–11 year olds: £2,280–£3,265 according to age. The fees include lunches and break-time drinks. Under 4: fees according to number of sessions attended per week. Fee list on application.

West House was founded in 1895 and since 1959 has been an Educational Trust controlled by a Board of Gover-

nors. The school has a strong academic reputation and pupils are regularly awarded scholarships to senior schools at 11+. The well-qualified and experienced staff provides a sound education for boys of all abilities. The National Curriculum has been adapted to suit the aptitudes and interests of pupils and to ensure that it provides an outstanding preparation for entry into selective senior schools. Pupils are taught in small classes which ensures that they receive much individual attention. Specialist help is available for children with Dyslexia or who require learning support. Music teachers visit the school to give individual music tuition.

The school occupies a leafy five-acre site a mile from Birmingham city centre. As well as the main teaching blocks there are two well-equipped science laboratories and a sports hall.

The Centenary Building, opened in 1998, accommodates the art and design technology department, ICT room and senior Library. Extensive playing fields, two all-weather tennis courts and all-weather cricket nets enable pupils to participate in many games and sports. Pupils also enjoy a wide range of hobby activities, and drama and music play important roles in school life.

The school is open during term time between 8 am and 6 pm. On-site Holiday Clubs are run by members of staff during the holidays.

Charitable status. West House School is a Registered Charity, number 528959. It exists to provide education for boys.

Westbourne House

Shopwyke, Chichester, West Sussex PO20 2BH
Tel: 01243 782739
Fax: 01243 770759
e-mail: office@westbournehouse.org
website: www.westbournehouse.org

Chairman of the Governors: J P L Perry, FCA

Headmaster: **Martin Barker**

Age Range. 3–13.
Number of Pupils. 469: Boarders 124; Day 186; Pre-Prep 159.
Fees per term (2011-2012). Boarders £5,685; Day £4,640; Pre-Prep £2,750.

Westbourne House School was founded in 1907 and became a Charitable Trust in 1967. It has been co-educational since 1992. There is a well-qualified teaching staff of 54, plus 26 visiting music staff and 38 support staff; all play important roles in the care of the children. The School has a strong boarding ethos.

Situated in a beautiful parkland setting of 100+ acres, Westbourne House offers a warm, happy environment, which fosters learning and development. Pupils are prepared for the Common Entrance and many Scholarships (31 in 2011) have been won at an impressive list of Senior Independent Schools in recent years; virtually all children go on to their first-choice school at 13+. Individual academic progress is carefully monitored and the school has recently invested in the latest database technology to enhance this process. The average class size (16) allows for plenty of individual attention, differentiation and pastoral care. The broad curriculum includes the full quota of academic subjects as well as Music, Art, Design Technology, Ceramics, Food Technology, Drama, Physical Education & Games, and Information Technology. Individual Needs, as well as the Gifted & Talented, are nurtured by a highly-qualified SENCO.

Children are encouraged to discover their talents within the wide range of activities on offer, with the aim of developing these talents to the full. Westbourne enjoys a proud record of sporting achievement and the children have access to excellent facilities: extensive playing fields, including a new astroturf pitch, host the major sports (football, rugby, hockey and cricket for boys; netball, hockey, pop lacrosse and rounders for girls) and the children also engage in swimming (25 metre indoor heated pool), squash (3 courts), tennis (16 courts), as well as golf, fencing, judo and dance (new dance studio). A large, well-equipped Sports Hall caters for indoor sports. Music is outstanding: the children enjoy excellent facilities and teaching, with a wide range of instruments, orchestras, bands and choirs on offer. All children are encouraged to perform from an early age. Art and Technology are housed within the original stable block of the Georgian house, providing a delightful environment for the children to develop their creative skills. Drama is encouraged through a number of productions involving most of the children.

An extensive building programme has been undertaken in recent years. A new Junior Teaching block for Years 3, 4 and 5 was built in 1997, a purpose built Science Department in 1999 and a Theatre seating 300 was completed in 2001. A new Dining Room, catering facilities and three new classrooms were completed in 2004, as were improvements to the library and recreational facilities. A new dance studio (2008) and full-size astroturf all-weather surface (2009) have recently been added. Development in 2011 included a new 30-acre lake on the school grounds for rowing, sailing and canoeing, as well as Pre-Prep extensions to accommodate 3-form entry.

Charitable status. Westbourne House is a Registered Charity, number 307034.

Westbourne School

60 Westbourne Road, Sheffield S10 2QT
Tel: 0114 266 0374
Fax: 0114 263 8176
e-mail: admin@westbourneschool.co.uk
website: www.westbourneschool.co.uk

Chairman of the Governors: Mr M P Loxley

Headmaster: **John Hicks**, MEd Kingston, BEd Hons Exeter

Age Range. 4–16.
Number of Pupils. 357 day pupils, boys and girls.
Fees per term (2011-2012). £2,450–£3,460.
The fully co-educational School, founded in 1885, is an Educational Trust with a Board of Governors, some of whom are Parents. The number of entries is limited to maintain small classes of around 16 with a staff/pupil ratio of less than 1:10.

The Junior School is housed in a specially designed and equipped building, staffed by qualified and experienced teachers. Music and Games are taught by specialists from Y1. Specialist Science and Technology are introduced from Y4 (8+), as well as specialist teaching in Information Technology, Art and Design, and RE. French, Science and Computers are introduced from the age of 4.

In the Junior School, some lessons are taught by specialists in Subject Rooms. There is also a Science Laboratory and ICT, Art and Music Rooms, Fiction and Reference Libraries, and a Hall with Stage.

The Senior School provides teaching to GCSE from Year 7 to 11 up to age 16. It has its own campus immediately adjacent to the Junior School. A new, adjacent building opened for Y7 and Y8 pupils in September 2007. The school has a 3-form entry in Y7 with a scholarship class. External and internal scholarships are taken in January of Y6. All children are setted in Maths and English from Year 5. A Virtual Learning Environment is in place from Y5.

A high standard of work is maintained – the main aim being to bring out the best in every pupil according to their ability. A few pupils are entered for Common Entrance and Independent School Scholarships, but 95% move to Westbourne Senior School. There is also a Department catering for those with Specific Learning Difficulties. Great emphasis is laid on courtesy and a mutual respect for each other.

Art, Music and Drama are strongly encouraged throughout the school, with regular concerts, plays and art exhibitions. Tuition in several instruments is available.

The main sports are Rugby, Football, Hockey, Cricket, Athletics, Netball, Rounders and Cross-Country Running with regular matches against other schools. There are also opportunities for Short Tennis, Swimming, TaeKwonDo, Basketball, Volleyball, Fencing, Skiing, Badminton, Climbing, Golf and Scuba Diving.

Breakfast (at an extra cost) is available from 7.45 am and, while the length of day depends on the age of the child, there are after-school facilities for all pupils until 5.30 pm, with the older pupils able to stay until 5.15 pm. There is no school on Saturdays.

Charitable status. Westbourne School is a Registered Charity, number 529381. It exists to provide education for boys and girls.

Westbrook Hay

London Road, Hemel Hempstead, Herts HP1 2RF
Tel: 01442 256143/230099
Fax: 01442 232076
e-mail: admin@westbrookhay.co.uk
website: www.westbrookhay.co.uk

Chairman of Governors: John Stevens

Headmaster: **Keith D Young**, BEd Hons Exeter

Age Range. Boys 3–13, Girls 3–11.
Number of Pupils. Day: 195 Boys, 100 Girls.
Fees per term (2010-2011). £2,320–£3,900. Flexi-Boarding £32 per night.

Westbrook Hay is a thriving independent school which educates boys and girls from rising 3–13 years. The school's beautiful location boasts 26 acres of parkland overlooking the Bourne valley in Hertfordshire, and its location just off the A41, between Berkhamsted and Hemel Hempstead, enables easy access to all major routes. This unique setting offers a secure environment, within which children explore and enjoy all that childhood has to offer.

Through visionary teaching in small classes and with a wonderful mixture of purpose built facilities and historic surroundings, our children achieve excellent results, enjoy a broad curriculum, and have the all-important confidence to succeed.

Classes are small and each individual is encouraged and helped to achieve their potential. Individuality, honesty, a sense of humour and self-reliance are attributes which are stimulated and valued in this most friendly school, which maintains a caring, family atmosphere.

Lower and Middle School departments prepare children from rising three to eight for entry into the Upper School. Children in Years 3 and 4 are class taught primarily by their form teacher, before a move to a subject-based curriculum in Year 5. The academic focus is provided by the goals of the Common Entrance and Scholarship examinations as most children go on to independent senior schools. All children follow the National Curriculum subject areas and in many cases extend them.

The facilities of the school have benefited from significant recent improvements including a £2 million lower school building, an art studio with pottery kiln and a two new fully equipped Information Technology rooms.

Extensive playing fields give ample room for rugby, soccer, hockey, cricket, golf, rounders and athletics. All-weather netball and tennis courts and a heated swimming pool are complemented by a purpose built Sports Hall which provides for badminton, table tennis, cricket nets, five-a-side football, gymnastics and a galaxy of other indoor sports.

A breakfast club, after school care and a school bus service are also offered to accommodate the needs of working parents.

Charitable status. Westbrook Hay School is a Registered Charity, number 292537. It exists to provide education for boys and girls.

Westminster Abbey Choir School

Dean's Yard, London SW1P 3NY
Tel: 020 7222 6151
Fax: 020 7222 1548
e-mail: headmaster@westminster-abbey.org
website: www.westminster-abbey.org

Chairman of Governors: The Dean of Westminster

Headmaster: **J H Milton**, BEd

Age Range. 8–13.
Number of Boys. Up to 38 all chorister boarders.
Fees per term (2010-2011). £2,021 inclusive of tuition on two instruments. Additional bursaries may be available in cases of real financial need.

Westminster Abbey Choir School is the only school in Britain exclusively devoted to the education of boy choristers. Boys have been singing services in the Abbey since at least 1384 and the 34 boys in the school maintain this tradition.

Westminster Abbey Choir School is a special place, offering boys from eight to thirteen a unique and exciting opportunity to be a central part of one of our great national institutions. Boys sing daily in the Abbey and also take part in many special services and celebrations both in the UK and abroad.

The small size of the school, the fact that all boys are boarders and the high proportion of staff who live on the premises, allow the School to have an extended family atmosphere.

A full academic curriculum is taught by specialist staff and boys are prepared for the Common Entrance and academic scholarship examinations; most boys win valuable scholarships to secondary independent schools when they leave at 13.

Music obviously plays a central part in the school. Every boy learns the piano and at least one orchestral instrument and there are 15 visiting music teachers. Concerts, both inside and outside school, are a regular feature of the year.

Besides music and academic lessons there is a thriving programme of other activities and there are many opportunities for boys to develop interests outside music.

Sports played include football, cricket, rugby, athletics, hockey, sailing, canoeing and tennis.

Entry is by voice trial and academic tests; further details are available from the Headmaster, who is always please to hear from parents who feel that their son might have the potential to become a chorister.

Charitable status. Westminster Abbey is a Registered Charity, number X8259. It is a religious establishment incorporated by Royal Charter in 1560.

Westminster Cathedral Choir School

Ambrosden Avenue, London SW1P 1QH
Tel: 020 7798 9081
Fax: 020 7630 7209
e-mail: office@choirschool.com
website: www.choirschool.com

President: The Most Reverend Vincent Nichols, Archbishop of Westminster

Chairman of Governors: John Gibbs

Headmaster: **Neil McLaughlan**, BA Hons

Age Range. 7–13.
Number of Boys. 150 (27 Choristers, 123 Day Boys).
Fees per term (2010-2011). Chorister Boarders £2,375; Day Boys £4,665.

Founded in 1901, Westminster Cathedral Choir School is a Day Prep School and Boarding Choir School concerned with the development of the whole person. Choristers must be Roman Catholic, but Day Boys of all denominations are welcome.

The school forms part of the precincts of Westminster Cathedral and enjoys such facilities as a large playground and a Grade 1 listed Library. The school has recently undergone a £1.3 million refurbishment, including a brand new playground and boarding facilities.

In the top two years, if there are sufficient candidates, boys are taught in three groups in order to prepare them to sit scholarships as well as the two tiers of the Common Entrance examination. Boys regularly win Academic and Music Scholarships to the major independent senior schools.

Choristers and Day Boys alike achieve a high level of music making. The Choristers sing the daily capitular liturgy in the Cathedral and are regularly involved in broadcasts, recordings and tours abroad. There is also a Day Boy Choir, two orchestras and a substantial programme of chamber music. Boys can learn the piano and any orchestral instrument in school.

The major sports played at the Choir School include football, rugby and cricket and the boys travel to Vincent Square, Battersea Park and the Queen Mother Sports Centre for Games.

There is a wide range of extra-curricular activities available including: chess, computing, debating, fencing, football, judo, drama and a Saturday rugby club.

The school is justly famed for its fantastic food!

Assessment for Choristers is by academic assessment and voice trial, generally in November and February. Day Boy assessments are held in January.

Charitable status. Westminster Cathedral Choir School is a Registered Charity, number 1063761. It exists to provide a musical education for Roman Catholic boys.

Westminster Under School

Adrian House, 27 Vincent Square, London SW1P 2NN
Tel: 020 7821 5788
Fax: 020 7821 0458
e-mail: under.school@westminster.org.uk
website: www.westminsterunder.org.uk

Chairman of Governors: The Very Revd J R Hall, The Dean of Westminster

Master: **Mrs E A Hill**, MA

Deputy Master: D S C Bratt, BA York

Age Range. 7–13.

Number of Boys. 265 (day boys only).

Fees per term (2011-2012). £4,892 (inclusive of lunches and stationery).

The Under School is closely linked to Westminster School, sharing the same Governing Body, although it has its own building overlooking the beautiful school playing fields in Vincent Square. The school is extending its premises in September 2011 and refurbishing the current site.

Boys are prepared, though not exclusively, for Westminster through the Common Entrance examinations and "The Challenge", Westminster School's scholarship examinations. Most boys proceed to Westminster, but entry into the Under School does not guarantee a place at the "Great School". Each year some boys will go on to Eton or similar schools.

There is a strong musical tradition at the Under School, with a junior and senior choir, an orchestra, and string, brass and jazz groups. There is a specialist suite of art rooms with facilities for all kinds of creative activity and the art department organises competitions in photography and model-making. There are other competitions each year in public speaking, creative writing, chess and Scrabble.

Games are played on the school grounds adjacent to Adrian House in Vincent Square and although football and cricket are the main sports, there are opportunities to participate in athletics, basketball, cross-country, hockey, rugby, swimming and tennis.

20 new boys are admitted at each entry point (7+, 8+ and 11+) in September. Means-tested bursaries are available at 11+, as are music scholarships, and many boys apply at this entry point from London primary schools.

Charitable status. St Peter's College (otherwise known as Westminster School) is a Registered Charity, number 312728. It exists to provide education for boys.

Westville House School

Carter's Lane, Middleton, Ilkley, West Yorkshire LS29 0DQ

Tel: 01943 608053

Fax: 01943 817410

e-mail: westville@epals.com

website: www.westvilleschool.co.uk

Chairman of Trustees: Mr A N Brown

Headmaster: **Mr C A Holloway**, BA Hons, PGCE

    Age Range. 3–11.

    Number of Pupils. 128.

    Fees per term (2011-2012). £1,465–£2,540.

Westville House is a preparatory school for girls and boys aged 3–11, situated in glorious countryside just outside the town of Ilkley in West Yorkshire. It was founded in 1960 as an extension of the owner's family and, although the school has grown since then, the family atmosphere has been retained to this day.

Children join the Pre-Preparatory department at three where outstanding courses are offered in the Foundation years. They move into the Preparatory department at seven, where specialist teaching is introduced in all subjects and preparation begins for entry to senior schools at age eleven. The school offers a broad and stimulating curriculum and has an outstanding academic record with awards gained annually at all the local independent senior schools.

As well as the broad curriculum on offer, there are many other areas of strength within the school. Drama begins at an early age and there are regular performances by children of all ages. Visiting specialist staff also prepare children for the Guildhall Speech and Drama examinations and for performances at local Festivals. Music is a vital part of the life of the school. Children perform regularly in concerts from an early age and many learn instruments individually. The school orchestra and choir perform regularly at Festivals and in Church services. Sport is also an important part of school life and teams play against other schools at rugby, football, cricket, rounders, athletics, swimming and cross-country running. Trips into the community are a regular and important feature of school life, taking advantage of the wealth of facilities in the area.

The school has a staff of fifteen well-qualified and experienced teachers. The family atmosphere within the school means that all the children are well-known to them and they combine just the right blend of firmness and fun to bring out the best in each individual child.

Charitable status. Westville House School is a Registered Charity, number 1086711.

Wetherby Pre-Preparatory School
Alpha Plus Group

11 Pembridge Square, London W2 4ED

Tel: 020 7727 9581

Fax: 020 7221 8827

e-mail: learn@wetherbyschool.co.uk

website: www.wetherbyschool.co.uk

Headmaster: **Mr Mark Snell**, BA Hons, PGCE

    Age Range. Boys 4–8.

    Number of Pupils. 241.

    Fees per term (2010-2011). £4,865.

Wetherby School overlooks the beautiful Gardens of Pembridge Square where the boys are fortunate to play every day. Whilst proud of its academic attainments for London Day School entry at 7+ and 8+ and top Boarding Schools, the priority is in producing happy, confident and resourceful boys. The curriculum is well balanced, with excellent sport, music and art opportunities including specialist teaching rooms for art, ICT, library and music. There is also a wide range of extra-curricular activities available. Wetherby operates a non selective admissions procedure; registration is at birth.

Wetherby Preparatory School
Alpha Plus Group

48 Bryanston Square, London W1H 2EA

Tel: 020 7535 3520

Fax: 020 7535 3523

e-mail: admin@wetherbyprep.co.uk

website: www.wetherbyprep.co.uk

Headmaster: **Mr Nick Baker**, BA Hons, PGCE

    Age Range. Boys 7–13.

    Number of Pupils. 280.

    Fees per term (2011-2012). £4,965.

The school's motto, *Participes Civitatis* (being part of a community), exemplifies life at Wetherby Preparatory School. Boys, teachers and parents work closely together to create a unique educational experience. The quality of communication with parents and a strong PTA demonstrate the high level of partnership and cooperation at the school.

Every boy at Wetherby Prep finds the opportunity to shine, be it for academic scholarship, sporting excellence, choral or instrumental accomplishment or involvement in the vast array of clubs offered. This is not a school for an apathetic boy: enthusiasm, application and self-motivation are applauded and actively encouraged.

Wetherby Prep boys experience a varied and challenging academic curriculum. Boys enjoy their lessons and core subjects of Maths, English and Science are strongly emphasised. With subject-specialist teaching from Year 5 onwards, boys are educated by experienced and enthusiastic teachers, guiding them forwards and preparing them for the 13+ Common Entrance examinations.

Classroom learning is enhanced regularly by guest speakers and wide-ranging visits. All boys participate in an annual residential excursion, ranging from outdoor pursuits to language and other study trips.

Some boys spend their lunchtimes debating and discussing matters relating to the school, as part of the School Council, whilst others enjoy a variety of games or "downtime" at either the Seymour Leisure Centre or the parks nearby, depending on the weather. The lunch menu includes a choice of hot and cold dishes, cooked on site, and includes numerous themed days for breakfast and lunch. Good table-manners and healthy eating are clearly promoted.

Sport enjoys a high profile at Wetherby Prep, with two Games afternoons a week, as well as PE, Swimming and Upper-School Rowing classes. In addition, boys can develop their skills and learn new ones by attending after-school clubs including football training, cricket nets and fencing. Numerous fixtures and tournaments against other schools are held, along with eagerly awaited inter-house competitions.

White House Preparatory School

Finchampstead Road, Wokingham, Berkshire RG40 3HD
Tel: 0118 978 5151
Fax: 0118 979 4716
e-mail: office@whitehouse.wokingham.sch.uk
website: www.whitehouse.wokingham.sch.uk

Chairman of Governors: Mr R H Higson, BSc, MRPharmS, MIHM

Headmistress: **Mrs S J Gillam**, BEd Cantab

Age Range. 2½–11 years Co-educational.
Number of Pupils. 100 day pupils.
Fees per term (2011-2012). £807–£2,895.

White House takes pride in offering high levels of academic achievement within a warm and friendly community. Founded on Christian principles, the school seeks to teach care and courtesy. Our visitors frequently comment on the friendly, purposeful and happy atmosphere. Small classes enable teachers to meet the needs of each individual. The school aims to develop the full potential of each child through a wide range of activities and opportunities.

Girls and boys are accepted from 2+ to 11 years of age and are prepared for entry to a range of senior schools.

The school stands in its own attractive grounds on the edge of Wokingham. The excellent facilities include a multi-purpose Hall, ICT Suite, Science/Technology Department, Music Department and Art Studio. Sport is promoted and pupils have regular swimming lessons in the Summer Term. There is a purpose-built Nursery designed around the needs of the youngest children.

All children are given access to a broad and stimulating curriculum augmented by specialist teaching in PE, Music, Science, Technology and French. Children take part in a wide range of extra-curricular activities including drama, ballet, tap, choirs, orchestral groups, golf, tennis and sporting fixtures. Individual music lessons are offered in piano, flute, clarinet, stringed instruments and voice. Active learning is encouraged through visits and a variety of events throughout each year.

White House is able to meet the needs of busy parents too. The school offers an extended day which allows children to be cared for from 8.00 in the mornings and up to 6.00 pm. Children can attend a variety of clubs or play activities.

Special links with Luckley-Oakfield School mean that a number of pupils choose to continue their education close by through to the age of 18.

Charitable status. The White House Preparatory School Trust is a Registered Charity, number 1112529. The school is a Christian school, established and maintained for the purpose of providing high quality education based on Christian principles for children aged 2–11.

Widford Lodge

Widford Road, Chelmsford, Essex CM2 9AN
Tel: 01245 352581
Fax: 01245 281329
e-mail: admin@widfordlodge.org.uk
website: www.widfordlodge.org.uk

Principal: Mrs Louise Williams

Head Master: **S C Trowell**, BHum Hons, PGCE London

Age Range. 2½–11 years.
Number of Pupils. Prep 111; Pre-Prep 89; Pre-School Nursery: varies according to number of sessions.
Fees per term (from April 2011). Pre-Prep £2,021.30, Main School £2,638.80. All fees include lunch, textbooks, stationery, etc.

Widford Lodge is a co-educational day school situated on the southern fringe of Chelmsford. Founded in 1935 the school aims to provide an all-round education within a happy, caring environment. Children are encouraged to enjoy their time at school, while also learning a sense of responsibility and a positive approach to their role in school and the wider community.

An enthusiastic staff prepare the children for grammar school via the 11+, entrance into senior independent schools through examination or scholarship and local secondary schools. A combination of form tutors, subject specialists and small classes ensure a good academic standard. The curriculum is broadly based and aims to develop a variety of interests, academic, aesthetic and sporting. The school has a well-equipped computer suite and the children are encouraged to use their IT skills in many different ways.

The main part of the school stands in 5 acres of wooded grounds that include an outdoor Swimming Pool, a Floodlit Tennis Court, Cricket Nets, Science Laboratory and Design Technology Centre. There is plenty of space for the children to play and to use their imagination. The school also owns 9 acres of playing fields.

The children have the opportunity to play cricket, netball, rugby, hockey, soccer, athletics, swimming, cross-country, tennis, golf and rounders. Although a small school we are proud of our sporting tradition, which is underpinned by our belief that sport is for all and is ultimately played for fun.

Music, drama and art are all encouraged and a wide range of musical instruments are taught. There is a busy school choir and an annual concert.

There are many after-school activities which the children are encouraged to get involved in, as well as the opportunity to do their prep, supervised by a teacher, until 5.30 pm.

Wilmslow Preparatory School

Grove Avenue, Wilmslow, Cheshire SK9 5EG
Tel: 01625 524246
Fax: 01625 536660
e-mail: secretary@wilmslowprep.co.uk
website: www.wilmslowprep.co.uk

Day School for Girls founded 1909.

Chairman of Board of Trustees: Mr Rudgard

Headmaster: **Mr P H Reynolds**, BA Hons, PGCE, MEd
    Exon

Age Range. 3–11.
Number of Pupils. 124 Day Girls.
Fees per term (2011-2012). £765–£2,850 (lunches extra).

The School is registered as an Educational Trust. It is purpose built and is situated in the centre of Wilmslow in its own spacious grounds. The facilities include an Assembly Hall, new Sports Hall, a Science Room, Computer Room with networked PCs, an Art Room and Kindergarten Unit, a Classroom Block for 5–8 year olds and two well-stocked libraries. There is a Tennis/Netball Court, a Sports field with its own stand-alone Sports Hall, and ample play areas.

The School aims to provide wide educational opportunities for all girls. It has a long established excellent academic record and caters for a wide variety of entrance examinations to Independent Senior Day and Boarding Schools.

Wilmslow Preparatory School offers a variety of activities which include Music, Art and Drama. Principal sports include gymnastics, netball, hockey, tennis, athletics and swimming.

There are sixteen qualified and experienced teachers on the staff.

Charitable status. Wilmslow Preparatory School is a Registered Charity, number 525924. It exists to provide full-time education for pupils aged between 5 and 11, and part-time or full-time education to kindergarten children from the age of 3.

Winchester House School

High Street, Brackley, Northants NN13 7AZ
Tel: 01280 702483
Fax: 01280 706400
e-mail: office@winchester-house.org
website: www.winchester-house.org

Chairman of Governors: K H Fowler

Headmaster: **M S Seymour**, BA

Age Range. 3–13.
Number of Children. 363: Boarding Boys 49; Day Boys 176; Boarding Girls 29; Day Girls 109.
Fees per term (2011-2012). Preparatory: Boarders £5,385–£6,795 inclusive, Day £4,080–£5,145. Pre-Prep: £2,360–£2,965.

Winchester House School is a fully co-educational independent day and boarding Preparatory School.

Winchester House School sits in its own 18 acres of sports fields and gardens in the market town of Brackley, midway between Oxford and Northampton and close to the borders of Buckinghamshire, Oxfordshire and Northamptonshire. Lying just 10 minutes from the M40 it is within easy reach of both Heathrow and Birmingham airports.

The boys and girls are taught by dedicated specialist teachers with a pupil:staff ratio of 8:1. Children in the middle and upper school are placed in streamed sets for all academic subjects and potential scholars are carefully prepared for the scholarship examinations to all major independent senior schools. Over the last few years, excellent examination results have included a significant number of awards to Senior Schools.

Many children enter the school in the nursery or reception classes while others join Year 3 at seven years old. The day children and the boarders follow the same timetable during the day and many convert from day to either weekly or full boarding during their time at the school. The school operates two minibus services for day-children in the local area.

Winchester House has magnificent facilities that include an extensive information and communication technology suite, well-equipped art and design studios, a well-stocked library and dedicated science laboratories. Sports facilities include numerous rugby, hockey and cricket pitches, tennis courts, a heated swimming pool, squash courts, a rifle range, and a fully fitted sports hall with indoor cricket nets. The Seligman building, opened in 2005, provides six new classrooms, a performing arts studio and new music practice rooms.

Winchester House is dedicated to a fully rounded education. In addition to the academic timetable, extensive instrumental music teaching and team sports, a broad range of further activities is offered. Activities include brass group, chamber choir, chess, cookery, dance, drama, gymnastics, golf, judo, maypole dancing, mountain biking, orchestra, rambling, rowing, speech & drama and war games. Recent major dramatic productions have included the musicals Bugsy Malone and Captain Stirrick.

The school is also committed to teaching leadership skills to all pupils. This takes place both on the school grounds and on expeditions in the UK and Europe. Winchester House is the first prep school to introduce such a programme to all its pupils under the banner 'Learn to Lead' in conjunction with World Challenge Expeditions Ltd.

Charitable status. Winchester House School Trust Limited is a Registered Charity, number 309912. It aims to provide education for boys and girls between the ages of 3 and 13.

Windermere Preparatory School
Preparatory School of Windermere School

Windermere, Cumbria LA23 1AP
Tel: 015394 43308
Fax: 015394 46803
e-mail: admissions@windermereschool.co.uk
website: www.windermereschool.co.uk

Chairman of Governors: Mr Peter Redhead

Headmaster: **Mr B C Freeman**, BEd Hons, PGDip

Type of School. Co-educational Day and Boarding School.
Age Range. 2–11.
Number of Pupils. 76 girls, 55 boys.
Fees per term (2011-2012). *Autumn Term 2011*: Day (including lunch): Pre-School £2,101 (5 days full-time), Reception £2,153, Years 1–2 £2,885, Years 3–6 £4,144. Boarding: £6,858 (weekly), £7,245 (full). Discounts are available for Forces families eligible for the MOD Continuity of Education Allowance (CEA). Government Nursery Education Grants accepted. *UK fees will increase by 1.5% at the start of each of the Spring and Summer Terms during 2012.*

International Students (Years 3–6): £8,500 (all 3 terms).

The Purpose of the School. Windermere School and Windermere Preparatory School promote academic excellence and challenge through adventure. It has an international outlook which develops courageous, responsible and inspiring individuals. Windermere Preparatory School is an Independent Preparatory School for boys and girls from 2–11 years, set in 17 acres of grounds in the heart of the English Lake District, and a lakeside watersports centre.

Adventure activities and watersports opportunities are provided for each pupil with nationally recognised certificates from organisations including the Royal Yachting Association and the British Canoe Union. This combined with the rich literary and cultural heritage of the Lake District provides a unique setting for academic study and self-development; thus the motto Vincit qui se Vincit, *One conquers, who conquers oneself.*

The school aims to ensure that children enjoy the excitement of learning, and benefit from their outstanding location, where adventure skills support academic confidence. Individuality is praised and encouraged. It has a friendly and family-like atmosphere, where children are given the opportunity to use the great outdoors as an inspirational classroom. The school has its own Adventure! Programme built into the daily curriculum.

Academic Ethos. Windermere Preparatory School offers an enhanced curriculum which has science at its core, and includes French in Year 1. Children learn presentation skills and hold regular exhibitions to showcase their work. There are spacious classrooms – most with spectacular views of the lake and fells. All Form Tutors are specialist primary teachers and there is both Extension Learning through the Gifted and Talented programme and Special Educational Needs support. The majority of pupils achieve results well ahead of the national average in the Standard Attainment Tests at seven and eleven years, and are successful in winning places at Windermere School or other secondary schools in the UK or abroad. Subject specialists teach Art, Drama, Dance, French, Games, Design and Technology, Music, Physical Education, and the unique Adventure! lessons. There are progressive camping trips, first on the school grounds, and when children are older, on staff-led expeditions throughout the Lake District.

Sport for All. Windermere Preparatory School offers a wide range of challenging and competitive sports, available every day after school. They are taught by specialist staff and include Athletics, Judo, Badminton, GymClub, Cricket, Dance (tap, jazz, modern, ballet), Fell walking, Football, Netball, Rounders, Sailing, Swimming, Tennis, Tag Rugby, Rugby, Adventure Club, Dens, Kayaking, Canoeing, Hockey, Adventure Playground, Gymnastics, and Cross-Country Running.

Clubs and Activities. *The Arts*: Art Club, Choir, ICT, Video Club, Drama, Infant Cookery, Individual Music lessons including piano, strings, woodwind, brass and guitar, Le Club Francais, Library, Orchestra, Recorder groups, Craft Club.

Uniform. Girls wear blue kilt and striped blazer plus light blue blouses in the winter. In the summer the kilt is worn with a blue and white flowered short-sleeved blouse and blue sleeveless slipover. Boys wear grey trousers, pale blue shirts and sweater, the school tie and blazer.

Pastoral and Boarding. Windermere Preparatory School accepts boarders from the age of eight. They reside at Windermere School just minutes away. The boys reside in Langdale House, and the girls reside in Browhead with children in their age group. There are qualified Housemasters and Housemistresses to offer care and supervision. All meals are provided, along with laundry and transportation by dedicated school drivers. There are after school, early evening and weekend activities, as well as supervised prep with academic staff available for advice and assistance at all times.

Leadership and teamworking skills are continually developed and there is a thriving School Council and House System. Thoughtfulness towards others, and a strong ethos of service and contribution towards society are all part of the Windermere Preparatory School spirit.

Charitable status. Windermere Educational Trust Limited is a Registered Charity, number 526973. It exists to provide education of the highest quality.

Windlesham House School

Washington, Pulborough, West Sussex RH20 4AY
Tel: 01903 874700
Fax: 01903 874702
e-mail: office@windlesham.com
website: www.windlesham.com

Chairman of Governors: Lucinda Williams, BA Hons, PGCE

Head: **Richard Foster**, BEd Hons

Age Range. 4–13.
Number of Pupils. 366: 226 boarders (128 Boys, 98 Girls), 140 day (84 Boys, 56 Girls).
Fees per term (2011-2012). Prep £4,365–£7,025; Little Windlesham £2,545–£2,960.

Windlesham nestles in 65 glorious acres of the South Downs and is within easy reach of London and both Gatwick and Heathrow airports. It is a co-educational boarding school from which children go on to a wide variety of senior schools. Above all it is a happy, family-centred school where children and adults live and work together in a unique and purposeful atmosphere. There is a very strong pastoral care system in place that ensures every child feels secure and happy no matter how far from home they may be. The last ISI Inspection report highlighted the excellence of the school's pastoral care and the provision for boarding; other areas of excellence included the school's ICT facilities and extra-curricular activities programme. In its recent Ofsted Boarding Inspection (June 2010) the overall quality of the school's boarding provision was rated 'Outstanding'.

Our curriculum is very broad and this, together with our talented and creative staff, enables us to place great emphasis on the individual development of each child, academically, socially and emotionally. Our academic standards are high, in line with and beyond the National Curriculum and we gain numerous scholarships to senior schools each year.

We have a very wide range of activities on offer, from karate and archery to silk painting and rug making and we have a strong reputation on the sports field. The opportunity exists for children to develop the sports they enjoy, whilst the less sporting child can pursue other activities and hobbies. Innovative drama and musical productions play a very important part in the life of the school. Our weekend arrangements are flexible and we provide a full programme of well-organised activities, many of an outward bound nature.

Windlesham gives children the opportunity to achieve the unexpected; the school is renowned for producing extremely happy, confident and well-balanced young people.

Little Windlesham opened in 1997 and provides a broad and varied education for 4–7 year olds. It is situated in a separate and well-designed unit, from which it can also make use of the impressive facilities of the main school. The curriculum is tied in with the main school so that children can follow a structured programme throughout their time in the school.

Charitable status. Windlesham House School is a Registered Charity, number 307046. It exists to provide education for girls and boys aged 4–13.

Winterfold House

Chaddesley Corbett, Worcestershire DY10 4PW
Tel: 01562 777234
Fax: 01562 777078
e-mail: linda@winterfoldhouse.co.uk
website: www.winterfoldhouse.co.uk

Chairman of Governors: Mrs M Chapman, MA

Headmaster: **W C R Ibbetson-Price**, MA, NPQH

Age Range. 3–13 Co-educational.
Number of Pupils. 350 Day Boys and Girls.
Fees per term (2011-2012). Preparatory £3,200–£3,650; Pre-Prep £2,175–£2,390; Kindergarten: £29 per day (inc Nursery Education Funding), £43.90 per day (excluding Nursery Education Funding).

Winterfold is centered around a spacious Georgian house set in nearly 40 acres of attractive grounds, surrounded by beautiful and unspoilt Worcestershire countryside. However, we are only half an hour from the centre of Birmingham, Worcester is just 10 miles away, and we are a mere 10 minutes from the M5 and M42.

Winterfold is a Roman Catholic co-educational day preparatory school but children of all faiths are warmly welcomed and made to feel valued members of the community.

The school has an excellent academic record at all levels including National Curriculum Key Stage Tests, Common Entrance and Scholarship. Children are prepared for entrance to both local independent day schools (such as RGS Worcester, Holy Trinity, King's Worcester, and the King Edward's schools in Birmingham) and to independent schools of national renown (such as Shrewsbury, Cheltenham Ladies' College, Malvern College, Stonyhurst, Ampleforth Cheltenham College and Bromsgrove). We have a highly regarded Learning Support Unit which provides one to one help for children with specific learning difficulties such as dyslexia. In the last 3 years our children have gained 69 scholarships to senior schools.

Winterfold places a great emphasis upon educating the whole child and aims to produce well rounded and confident boys and girls with high moral standards and good manners. In order to develop self-belief we encourage every child to achieve success in some area and thus the school fields a great number of teams and not just in the main sports of rugby, soccer, cricket, netball, hockey and rounders; but also in the minor sports which include fishing, golf, archery, tennis, swimming, athletics, basketball, fencing, judo, chess and shooting. There are also a large number of clubs and societies and regular visits to theatres and concerts and other places of educational interest which gives fullness and breadth to the educational experience.

In recent years there has been considerable investment into the school which has seen the development of a new sports hall, ICT suite, entrance hall and offices, classrooms, a chapel, library and three adventure playgrounds. A brand new classroom block has just been completed, with eight new classrooms, Science labs and Art and CDT rooms. A new Performing Arts Centre is currently under construction and will be completed for 2012.

Charitable status. Winterfold House School is a Registered Charity, number 1063133. It exists solely to provide education for boys and girls.

Witham Hall

Witham-on-the-Hill, Bourne, Lincolnshire PE10 0JJ
Tel: 01778 590222
Fax: 01778 590606

e-mail: heads@withamhall.com
website: www.withamhall.com

The school was founded in 1959 and was formed into an Educational Trust in 1978.

Chairman of Governors: Mr J W Sharman

Headmaster: **Mr A C Welch**, BEd

Age Range. 4–13.
Number of Pupils. Boys: 65 boarders, 16 day pupils. Girls: 55 boarders, 17 day pupils. Pre-Prep aged 4–8: 76 pupils.
Fees per term (2010-2011). Boarders £5,210, Day pupils £3,820 Pre-Prep £2,330.

The school is situated in a country house setting in the village of Witham on the Hill. There are all the usual amenities of a preparatory school.

There is a teaching staff of 35 and there are visiting teachers for instrumental music. The maximum class size is 16.

The school has a full musical life – most of the children learn one instrument or more. There are two bands and four choirs.

Games are played on most days of the week throughout the year. There is a full fixture list of games, for both boys and girls, with other schools at both senior and colts level including rugger, soccer, cricket, hockey, netball, rounders, athletics, cross-country, tennis and squash. In 2008, the school has built an Olympic size all-weather Astroturf and an additional four tennis courts and three netball courts to augment the current facilities. Our 9-hole golf course provides a challenging course for pupils and parents alike and our squash court has much usage. In 2009 the school built a brand new Pre-Prep playground with train, boat, equipment and a giant totem pole.

The school has a multi-purpose hall. The hall provides an indoor tennis court, four badminton courts, basketball courts, an indoor soccer and hockey pitch, indoor cricket nets and a general covered play area.

A purpose-built Pre-Prep block was opened in 1998 to house the growing Pre-Prep department and a purpose-built Prep block was built in 2000. A further Pre-Prep building was completed in September 2002 and The Stimson Hall, a purpose-built hall/theatre was completed in February 2006. The school has seen a huge growth in numbers and in almost every year group early registration is recommended.

Charitable status. Witham Hall School Trust is a Registered Charity, number 507070. It exists for the purpose of educating children.

Woodcote House

Windlesham, Surrey GU20 6PF
Tel: 01276 472115
Fax: 01276 472890
e-mail: info@woodcotehouseschool.co.uk
website: www.woodcotehouseschool.co.uk

Headmaster: **Henry Knight**, BA, PGCE

Age Range. 7–13.
Number of Boys. 105 (80 boarders, 25 day).
Fees per term (from April 2011). £6,300 (Boarding), £4,675 (Day). No compulsory extras. Annual Scholarship Day in March.
Location. Originally a Coaching Inn on the old London to Portsmouth Road, Woodcote enjoys a beautiful, rural setting in 30 acres of grounds. The school is easily accessible, being only 25 miles from London via the M3 (Junction 3), 25 minutes from Heathrow and 40 minutes from Gatwick.

Pastoral Care. Woodcote House has been owned and run by the Paterson family for over 75 years. They have recently promoted Henry Knight to be the new Headmaster and he, along with his wife Susannah and their three young children, will maintain the strong family ethos for which Woodcote has become so well known. With a settled and committed staff, most of whom live on site with their own families, Woodcote provides an exceptionally caring and supportive environment for both Boarders and Day Boys. A strong emphasis is placed on manners, consideration and respect for others. The school has its own Chapel in the woods and parents are welcome to Sunday services, as well as to school matches on Wednesdays and Saturdays (after which legendary Match Teas are served), so there is plenty of opportunity to see their boys and talk to staff and fellow parents.

Academic. There are two forms in each year group, with an average of 10 boys in each class, enabling the staff to offer all boys an enormous degree of individual attention. With SEN and EFL teaching also available, academic standards are high and the school is proud of its 100% Common Entrance and excellent Scholarship record. Woodcote boys go on to a wide variety of independent senior schools and Mr Knight takes particular care in assisting parents to choose the right school for their son.

Music and Drama. 80% of boys learn at least one musical instrument, and the young and innovative Director of Music has ensured that it is considered 'cool' to be in the excellent choir. There is an orchestra and a jazz band and the school holds regular concerts so that the boys are comfortable with public performance, both individually and as part of a group. The school produces a Junior and a Senior Play each year, in which all boys are involved one way or another.

Sports. Rugby, football, cricket and hockey are coached to a high standard and there are teams at all levels of age and ability, with a high success rate for a small school. Individual sports include tennis (the school has five courts), swimming, athletics, golf, judo, riding, squash, rifle-shooting and polo.

Hobbies and Free Time. With 'prep' done first thing in the morning, there are numerous opportunities for the boys to pursue hobbies after lessons and games, and each member of staff offers a 'club' during Hobbies Hour on Wednesday afternoons. These activities are also available at weekends, along with the traditional activities of 'hutting' (camp building in the woods), 'cooking' (frying potatoes on camp fires), and overnight camping in the grounds. Boys are also offered the opportunity to be involved in the CCF. Boys are encouraged to read and have a quiet time after lunch each day for this as well as before lights out in the evening.

Ethos. The school motto, "Vive ut Discas et Disce ut Vivas" (Live to Learn and Learn to Live), embodies the school's aim to give all boys a love of learning and to discover and nurture their individual talents in a happy and positive atmosphere.

Woodford Green Preparatory School

Glengall Road, Woodford Green, Essex IG8 0BZ
Tel: 020 8504 5045
e-mail: admin@wgps.co.uk
website: www.woodfordgreenprep.co.uk

The School is an Educational Charity, controlled by a Board of Governors.

Chairman of Governors: Mr D Paterson

Head: **Mrs J Hart**, BEd, MSc, Adv Dip RE

Age Range. 3–11.

Number of Pupils. 384 (Boys and Girls).
Fees per term (2010-2011). £2,200; Nursery £1,545.

The School provides a broad well-balanced curriculum and the overall standard is extremely high. The School has an outstanding record of success in 11+ examinations to Senior Independent and Grammar Schools and demand for places far outstrips availability. Parents are advised to make a very early application to the school.

Means tested Bursaries, of up to 100% of the full fees, are available for 7+ entry.

Charitable status. Woodford Green Preparatory School is a Registered Charity, number 310930.

Wycliffe Preparatory School

Stonehouse, Gloucestershire GL10 2LD
Tel: 01453 820470
Fax: 01453 825604
e-mail: prep@wycliffe.co.uk
website: www.wycliffe.co.uk

Chairman of Trustees: Mrs G E Camm, BSc Hons

Headmaster: **A Palmer**, MA, BEd

Age Range. 2–13.
Number of Pupils. Nursery: 79 pupils; Preparatory: 93 boarding, 308 day pupils.
Fees per term (2011-2012). Day £1,870–£3,865 (Lunch £200), Boarding £4,925–£6,270.

Wycliffe Preparatory School is a co-educational day, boarding and flexi-boarding school from 2 to 13 years. The School is administered by the Governors' Advisory Body and the Trustees of Wycliffe (*see Wycliffe College entry in HMC section*), but is a separate unit with its own Headmaster and full-time staff of 30 teachers (all qualified), house staff and matrons.

A range of Scholarships, both academic and non-academic, are offered by competition annually. There are also bursaries available for children from HM Forces families. The vast majority of our pupils go on to the Senior School – however, pupils are prepared for Common Entrance Examinations to all schools.

Wycliffe is committed to fostering individual learning in all areas of the curriculum and pupils benefit from small class sizes with a high teacher to pupil ratio. One of Wycliffe's aims is to cultivate each pupil's unique talents and to bring out the best in its pupils by creating a supportive learning environment which promotes individual achievements in all fields. Specialist teachers ensure outstanding teaching delivery across the curriculum and a wide variety of extra-curricular activities enables the school to offer a fully-rounded education designed to develop confidence and self-esteem.

There is also a dedicated CReSTeD registered SEN Department which supports children who have weaknesses in some areas of the curriculum. The school not only promotes success in the classroom, but prides itself on enabling every child to do well, whether on the sports field, in one of the many drama or musical productions or by taking part in the annual Art exhibition, hosted at the Senior School.

Academic excellence is something pupils are encouraged to attain and many of our able pupils, across a range of talents, have been encouraged to join the government's Gifted and Talented Register. This attests to the high-achieving nature of many of our students and the school's ability to nurture this. In the spring of 2007 Wycliffe celebrated being the first UK independent school to be awarded the NACE (the National Association for Able Children in Education) Challenge Award title across every one of the six stages of education – from Lower Prep right through to A Level.

The Preparatory School continues with its programme to improve facilities and has recently opened a dedicated Year 8 Centre, complete with classrooms and common room, a new Reception, Years 1 and 2 teaching block which is situated on the Prep campus and the extension of the boys' and girls' boarding houses by a further 16 beds. The school also boasts a new all-weather pitch, refurbished Years 3 and 4 classrooms, swimming pool, art studio and craft workshop, extensive playing fields, tennis courts, sports hall, studio theatre and music school, two science laboratories, four computer rooms, a covered playground and cafeteria-style dining room. The Preparatory School uses the College Chapel, Medical Centre and state-of-the-art Sports Centre.

The boarding houses are in the care of House staff and there are members of staff with particular responsibility for the welfare of day pupils. Vegetarian and other dietary specialities can be catered for.

As well as the usual range of sport, drama and music, there are clubs, activities and opportunities for outdoor pursuits. A number of holiday trips are also arranged, including an annual exchange with an independent school in Florida, team building activity in Wales and a trip to Paris, organised by the languages department.

Charitable status. Wycliffe College Incorporated is a Registered Charity, number 311714. It is a co-educational boarding and day school promoting a balanced education for children between the ages of 2 and 18.

Yardley Court
The Schools at Somerhill

Somerhill, Tonbridge, Kent TN11 0NJ
Tel: 01732 352124
Fax: 01732 363381
e-mail: office@somerhill.org
website: www.somerhill.org

Chairman of Governors: Mr Philip Thomas

Headmaster: **John Coakley**, BA Hons, PGCE, MA

Age Range. Prep: Boys 7–13. Pre-Prep: Co-educational 3–7.

Number of Pupils. Prep: 250 Day Boys. Pre-Prep: 278 boys and girls.

Fees per term (2011-2012). Prep: £4,175 inclusive of lunch. There are no compulsory extras.

Yardley Court is one of the three Schools at Somerhill. From a co-educational Pre-Prep of some 270+ children, the seven year old boys join Yardley Court and the girls join our sister school, Derwent Lodge. All three schools are housed in a magnificent Jacobean mansion set within 150 acres of beautiful parkland. Thus we are able to offer single sex education in the classroom but very much within a co-educational setting.

Yardley Court was founded in 1898 and moved to the Somerhill estate in 1990. We prepare boys for Common Entrance and Scholarships to senior independent schools in the immediate vicinity such as Tonbridge and Sevenoaks and also to schools further afield. Boys are also prepared for 11+ and 13+ entrance to the very strong Grammar Schools in our area. Sound foundations are the basis of all the academic teaching with particular emphasis placed on the core subject of Mathematics, English, Science and French.

Music plays an important part in school life with most boys participating in some way, either through the choirs, the orchestra or in solo or group instruction in a wide range of instruments.

The parkland and woods adjoining the school together with our purpose built playing fields provide an excellent environment for both sport and play. A strong sports programme centres around Soccer, Rugby, Cross-country, Cricket, Tennis and Athletics. All the boys are given the opportunity to represent the school. Further sporting pursuits include Golf, Basketball and Swimming. The school also encourages participation in a wide range of clubs and activities.

A new multi-purpose hall opened in April 2002 and an astroturf pitch in 2003. A new dining room and an indoor swimming pool opened in 2009 have greatly enhanced our facilities.

Charitable status. The Somerhill Charitable Trust Limited is a Registered Charity, number 1002212. It exists to provide education for children.

Yarlet School

Yarlet, Nr Stafford ST18 9SU
Tel: 01785 286568
Fax: 01785 286569
e-mail: headmaster@yarletschool.org
website: www.yarletschool.org

Chairman of the Governors: R D Montgomerie

Headmaster: **Mr Ian Raybould**, BEd Hons, ALCM

Age Range. Co-educational 2–13.

Number of Pupils. 172 pupils: 87 Girls and Boys in the Preparatory School (aged 7 to 13) and 85 Girls and Boys in the Nursery and Pre-Preparatory School (aged 2 to 7).

Fees per term (2011-2012). £2,025–£3,375. Flexi boarding available (Thursday and Friday nights) at £25 per night.

Established in 1873, Yarlet stands in 33 acres of grounds in unspoilt open countryside 5 miles north of Stafford. The school offers small classes, qualified teachers, excellent facilities and a warm, friendly environment conducive to learning. All teachers keep fully abreast of the National Curriculum guidelines to Key Stage 3 and beyond.

Pupils have access to the wide range of facilities which include a modern Science Laboratory, an Information Technology Centre, a CDT Centre, a purpose-built Art Studio and an indoor Sports and Performance Hall; and extensive outdoor facilities which include a heated swimming pool, four playing fields (for football, rugby, hockey, cricket and athletics), three tennis courts, a netball court, an all-weather Astroturf pitch (for football, hockey and netball), and a large Adventure Playground close to the Pre-Prep.

Club and extra-curricular activities are a strong feature of Yarlet and include art (painting, sculpture and pottery), model-making, music, drama, French culture, chess, photography and fishing.

Yarlet has high expectations of all its children. Children are prepared for entry to a wide variety of senior schools and their achievements in both Key Stage tests and Common Entrance examinations are a source of great pride, as too is the fact that many children leave with a Scholarship award from their Senior School.

Charitable status. Yarlet is a Registered Charity, number 528618. It exists to provide education for boys and girls from 2 to 13.

Yarm Preparatory School

Grammar School Lane, Yarm, Stockton-on-Tees TS15 9ES
Tel: 01642 781447
Fax: 01642 787425
e-mail: prepschool@yarmschool.org
website: www.yarmschool.org

Chair of Governors: Ms C Evans, MA, MBA, ARCM

Head: **W J Toleman**, BA

Age Range. 3–11.
Number of Pupils. 340 Boys and Girls.
Fees per term (2011-2012). Preparatory School £2,669–
£2,953; Early School/Nursery £2,096–£2,132; Early School/
Nursery (for children qualifying for Nursery Grant) £1,436.
Lunches are extra.

Yarm Preparatory School is a co-educational day school
which educates children from 7–11 years of age (3–7 within
the Early School and Nursery).

Ethos. The Preparatory School is well known as a
friendly and stimulating environment that encourages children to flourish educationally whilst also developing valuable social abilities and leadership skills. Through the broad
variety of extra-curricular activities, children come to excel
in sport and music as well as a wide range of other pastimes.

Organisation. Pastoral care is based on both a year group
and a House system. Every pupil belongs to one of four
Houses. Houses exist to promote competitions, sporting
events, charity and fundraising etc. Pupils have opportunities to represent their form as Form Captains, who also serve
on the School Council.

Curriculum. The Preparatory School curriculum is
based upon the National Curriculum, although it offers
greater breadth and depth in many subject areas. In addition
to the core curriculum of English, mathematics and science,
full weight is given to both history and geography, whilst
subjects such as design technology, ICT, art, music, religious
education, PSHE, PE and games are fully catered for. Children are also taught French from age 3. Whilst form teachers
deliver much of the core curriculum, subject specialist
teachers are employed to cover many areas of the curriculum.

Games and Activities. The Preparatory School hosts a
whole range of sports. However, rugby and hockey are the
school's main winter games. Soccer and netball are played
during the Spring Term, followed by cricket, athletics and
rounders in the summer. In addition, cross-country is also
pursued at inter-school level throughout the year. There are
many school activities including music, dance, drama, orienteering, chess, swimming, badminton, gardening, modelling, crafts, pottery, ICT and quizzes which are timetabled to
take place during two lessons, at lunchtimes and after school
each week. These activities change at least termly.

Music. The Preparatory School boasts many musical
groups, choirs, choristers and a variety of traditional and
modern ensembles with well over half of the school learning
an instrument.

Educational Visits. A varied programme of educational
day visits is undertaken by all year groups to enrich the curriculum, using the locality as a resource. From age 7, pupils
have the opportunity to participate in residential trips,
including visits to Whitby, York, Robinwood, Ru'a Fiola and
Saint-Omer, France.

Admission. Entry to the Preparatory School is by assessment which may be carried out at any time of the year if
places are available. Pupils are prepared for entry to the
Senior School, sitting transfer papers in January before the
September in which they transfer. The results of transfer
papers are considered in conjunction with ongoing assessment information made available by teachers in the Preparatory School.

Open Days. The Early School and Preparatory School
hold Open Mornings each year, normally in October, January and May. Prospective parents are encouraged to attend at
least one Open Morning as this gives excellent opportunity
to look around the school at leisure, view the new facilities,
see our development plans and chat with staff. Visits are,
however, welcome at any time.

Religion. The school is an inter-denominational community but follows Christian traditions and ethos.

Charitable status. Yarm School is a Registered Charity,
number 1093434. It exists to provide education for boys and
girls from 3–18.

Yarrells Preparatory School

Yarrells House, Upton, Poole, Dorset BH16 5EU
Tel: 01202 622229
Fax: 01202 620870
e-mail: enquiries@yarrells.co.uk
website: www.yarrells.co.uk

Headmistress: **Mrs N A Covell**, BA, MSc

Deputy Head: P Brady, BEd Hons

Age Range. 2–13.
Number of Pupils. 220 Boys and Girls.
Fees per term (2010-2011). £138–£3,463.

Ethos. Yarrells School offers a unique environment for
the early development of intellectual, artistic and sporting
potential. Only minutes from Bournemouth and Poole,
Yarrells occupies a late Georgian country house surrounded
by woods, gardens, playing fields, tennis courts and covered,
heated swimming pool. The atmosphere is warm and
encouraging while a rigorous approach is taken to the maintenance of each child's highest standards. A well-qualified
and committed staff work with the Headmistress to ensure
careful character building and maximum academic performance. The school seeks to identify and develop children's
gifts and abilities in such a way that the children grow in
self-knowledge, self-discipline and self-confidence.

Curriculum. The classes are small and learning is
designed to meet individual requirements. From Nursery up,
the school follows a detailed curriculum based on the
National Curriculum, the Common Entrance Syllabus
(where appropriate) and the school's own demands, which
emphasise the mastery of basic skills from an early age. The
normal subject range is taught throughout and by specialists
from the age of 8/9. The children start learning French from
4 years of age. Parents are invited to discuss their child's
progress regularly with staff and are also sent termly written
reports.

All children have curricular tuition in Art, Music (singing
and instrumental), Drama and Dance. There are Recorder
Ensembles, a Wind Band, Choir, Choral Societies and an
Orchestra. There is a broad PE programme that includes
swimming, tennis, football, rugby, netball, rounders, hockey
and cross-country. Science, Investigational Mathematics,
Design and ICT are areas of study given good accommodation in the timetable. The school is active until 5.45 pm each
weekday evening for those children from age 7 who elect to
stay for supervised prep and a range of activities which
include football, cross-country, ballet, extra swimming and
tennis, tap and modern dance, art, drama and music.

Senior Success. Yarrells School has an excellent record
of success in Entrance Examinations and Scholarship
Awards to senior schools. Most children go on to Grammar
Schools or to Senior Independent Schools.

Summer Holiday Activity Weeks. During the summer
holidays, Yarrells offer Summer Activities Weeks, which are
led by the Deputy Head, for children aged 3 to 13. These are
attended by pupils of Yarrells as well as non-pupils. These
weeks are packed with sport, music, drama, craft and good
company. Activities are timetabled depending on children's
ages.

Eco. As an Eco School Yarrells has been awarded a
Green Flag Award by Eco School. Yarrells is deeply committed to developing a sustainable environment. Through
studies across the curriculum and links with parents, the
whole community participates in environmental activities:
recycling and re-using, gardening, composting, caring for
wildlife and conserving energy.

Yateley Manor Preparatory School

51 Reading Road, Yateley, Hampshire GU46 7UQ
Tel: 01252 405500
Fax: 01252 405504
e-mail: office@yateleymanor.com
website: www.yateleymanor.com

The School is an Educational Trust controlled by a Board of Governors.

Chairman of Governors: Stephen Sharp

Headmaster: **Robert Williams**, MA Hons Edinburgh, PGCE Bedford

Age Range. 3–13.
Number of Pupils. Pre-Preparatory and Nursery: 110 boys, 66 girls. Main School: 204 boys, 115 girls.
Fees per term (2011-2012). £1,425–£3,860. Fees are inclusive of all normal activities, extended supervision from 8.00 am until 6.30 pm, meals and residential field trips for Years 5, 6, 7 and 8.

Yateley Manor is a warm, lively, forward-looking school where traditional values are fused with modern methods and a sense of fun. It is a day, co-educational preparatory school, founded in 1947, occupying a nine-acre site containing attractive playing fields, sports pitches and adventure play areas. The original Victorian building houses administration and a continuing building programme has provided attractive modern facilities including a new Nursery, many classrooms, science laboratories, a swimming pool and a sports hall. Investment in information technology is also a strong feature.

Children are encouraged to enjoy learning and are challenged to do their best and to find achievement as measured against their own capabilities whether in academic circles, in sport or in the arts. Children are encouraged to explore without fear of failure, to have a sense of curiosity in the world around them and to develop into happy and confident people. Because the school believes in educating the whole person the enormous range of activities is included within the school fees.

Small classes averaging 16, individual attention, stable staff and excellent facilities, have all led to impressive examination results and scholarships to senior schools. Yateley Manor is independent of any senior school so pupils proceed to a wide variety of local independent schools, and to many further away.

A network of School coaches serves the surrounding areas including, Camberley, Church Crookham, Frimley, Fleet, Hartley Wintney, Hook and Odiham. There is an informal screening assessment for entry to the school and the most common entry points are at 3 into the Nursery, at 4 into Reception, and at 7 into the main school. Children are welcome to join at all other ages and many do.

Charitable status. Yateley Manor is a Registered Charity, number 307374. It is dedicated to providing the highest quality education for children of the local community.

York House School

Redheath, Croxley Green, Rickmansworth, Herts WD3 4LW
Tel: 01923 772395
Fax: 01923 779231
e-mail: yhsoffice@york-house.com
website: www.york-house.com

Founded in 1910, York House School is a non-profit making Educational Trust with a Board of Governors.

Chairman of the Governors: Mrs G Noach

Headmaster: **P R MacDougall**, BEd Hons

Age Range. Boys 3–13, Girls 3–7. Move to co-education commenced in September 2009. Now taking girls up to and including Year 2 September 2011.
Number of Children. All are Day pupils: 150 Prep, 70 Pre-Prep, 40 Kindergarten.
Fees per term (2011-2012). £3,615 including lunch. Kindergarten dependent upon days/hours.

York House School is a well-established, innovative and forward-looking school located in a Queen Anne country house standing in 47 acres of the Hertfordshire countryside. The Headmaster is assisted by a fully-qualified and caring staff. Our extended day arrangements enable pupils to attend early morning clubs and after school clubs between 7.45 am and 6.00 pm (see our website for costs).

The school's aim is to encourage children to achieve the highest academic results in a happy atmosphere while promoting self-discipline and caring for others.

The school has excellent facilities which include a multi-purpose hall and theatre, Library, state-of-the-art computer suite, a modern Pre-Prep and Kindergarten opened in 2001. In 2005 a new Junior School, Science Laboratory, Art Design and Technology Rooms were opened. The music centre is large with practice rooms and a new music computer suite.

Sporting facilities are excellent with 15 acres of playing fields for cricket, rugby, soccer, and athletics as well as a 25-metre indoor heated swimming pool.

Pupils are prepared for Common Entrance and Independent Schools Scholarships. There is a Pre-Preparatory Department for children from age 4 to 6+ and a Kindergarten for children from rising 3 to 5.

Charitable status. York House School is a Registered Charity, number 311076. It exists for the purpose of achieving educational excellence.

Independent Association of Prep Schools
Overseas Members

ALPHABETICAL LIST OF SCHOOLS

GEOGRAPHICAL LIST OF SCHOOLS

Individual School Entries
Overseas Members

Aiglon College Junior School

CH-1885 Chesières-Villars, Switzerland
Tel: 00 41 24 496 6141
Fax: 00 41 24 496 6142
e-mail: junior@aiglon.ch
website: www.aiglon.ch

Chairman of Governors: Mark Elliott

Headmaster: **Didier Boutroux**, L-ès-L, M-ès-L (Nancy)

Age Range. 9–13.
Number of Pupils. Boys 35, Girls 35, Boarders 55, Day Children 15.
Fees per annum (2011-2012). Day: CHF 39,000–43,350; Weekly Boarding: CHF 52,200–56,250; Full Boarding: CHF 58,650–65,100.
Setting. The Aiglon College Junior School provides a warm family atmosphere in the beauty and peace of the Swiss Alps for children from all over the world – with around 25 different nationalities. The intimate and caring community spirit encourages self-discipline, thought for others and joy in learning. Aiglon College Junior School's buildings and life are kept quite separate from those of the Senior school. However, it shares part of the campus of Aiglon College, and follows the principles of the founder, John Corlette. Ultimately we aim at ensuring a smooth and well-prepared transition into the Senior School.
Pastoral Care. Having a place of their own allows us to concentrate on issues most significant to this age group, such as creating and developing good habits in a positive and encouraging environment. Our main goal is to create a caring environment and, through carefully chosen experiences, build up the whole person and develop the many talents that all our pupils possess. We also aim at making the transition from Junior to Senior School a comfortable one. Learning to live and grow up with peers, listening to each other, and acquiring a taste for discovery and independence within a supportive environment; all these skills contribute, using moral and spiritual beliefs in a constructive way, to the foundation of a healthy attitude towards the challenges of teenage life. Moral principles are developed within school "meditations" (morning assemblies) especially and spiritual life is encouraged in chapel services.
Curriculum. The school also offers an ESL programme for all non-English speakers aged 9–12. The Junior School curriculum includes English, Maths, French, Science, Geography, History, Art, Music, Physical Education, Drama, Religious Studies and ICT. Strong pastoral care and individual attention allows for a curriculum which has its roots in the British National Curriculum but caters for the international diversity of our recruitment. The Learning Support department aids children with special learning needs and tests all children on a yearly basis.
Sports and expeditions. Sports and "expeditions" form an essential component of a well-rounded approach to the development of our children's personality and character. There is a range of sports teams to choose from and we encourage full participation. "Expeditions" take place at weekends and activities include walking, map reading and orienteering, cycling, canoeing, gorge walking and rock climbing. Children participate in camping, hiking or skiing "expeditions" under expert and qualified supervision. Apart from learning to enjoy and understand nature, being outdoors together, come rain or shine, reinforces children's team spirit and respect for each other and their environment as they learn to live a little closer to nature!
Extra-curricular activities. There is a wide variety of extra-curricular activities called "Options", which encompass sports, art and craft activities, music clubs, choir and bands, as well as quieter pastimes.
Further information. Further information may be obtained from the Headmaster or the Director of Admissions.
Aiglon College is a non-profit making organisation, accredited by ECIS.

The Alice Smith School Primary Campus

2 Jalan Bellamy, 50460 Kuala Lumpur, Malaysia
Tel: 00 603 2148 3674
Fax: 00 603 2148 3418
e-mail: klass@alice-smith.edu.my
website: www.alice-smith.edu.my

Chairman of Governors: Sue Bamford

Director of School: Valerie Thomas-Peter, MA Ed, BEd, ADES

Principal, Primary Campus: **Kate Fuller**, BA, QTS, NPQH

Age Range. 3–11.
Number of Pupils. 780 (Pre-School to Year 6).
Fees per term (2011-2012). Pre-School RM8,420, Reception RM11,855, Years 1–2 RM12,450, Years 3–6 RM12,800.
Location. The Alice Smith Primary School at Jalan Bellamy is situated in a beautiful area adjacent to the Royal Palace, just 10–15 minutes from the major residential suburbs on the west side of the capital.
Facilities. The Primary School offers a specialised learning environment and benefits from the following facilities:
• Well-resourced, air-conditioned classrooms and large shared year group learning areas
• Gymnasium
• 3 Libraries
• Design & Technology Room
• Multi-purpose Hall
• Hard and grassed playing areas
• 20m swimming pool
• Playground with climbing frames
• 3 ICT suites
• New purpose-built Years 5 and 6 Block
• New purpose-built Years 3 and 4 Block
Curriculum. We offer a rigorous British education in an international context while celebrating the culture and natural environment of our hosts, the people of Malaysia. The English National Curriculum enables us to develop the essential knowledge, skills and concepts our international students need in a broad programme that encompasses English, Mathematics, Science, Design Technology, Information Technology, Modern Foreign Languages (from Year 4), History, Geography, Music, Drama and Physical Education.
Children have specialist teachers for Music, Physical Education, Learning Support, Foreign Languages and Swimming. All classes carry a maximum of 22.

The school undertakes the NCT assessments in Years 2 and 6 and the non-statutory NCT tests for Years 3, 4 and 5. Standards and expectations are high and regular In-service Training and Inspections are undertaken with UK based Inspectors/Advisory teams.

Staff. At the heart of a good school is the staff, both teaching and non-teaching. Our teaching staff are well qualified, caring and experienced professionals, recruited mainly from the UK.

All classes benefit from a full-time assistant in addition to the class teacher.

Extra-curricular programme. Our main curriculum is enhanced by a full programme of extra-curricular sporting, performance and cultural activities. Older children are regular participants in National and International expeditions, competitions and trips, while our younger students participate in frequent visits to local places of interest. A busy Saturday Sports programme ensures children have recreational opportunities on many Saturdays throughout each term. An intensive after-school swim programme exists for a Torpedoes Club, who train 5 evenings a week.

Aravon Preparatory School

Old Conna House, Bray, Co Wicklow, Ireland
Tel: 00 353 1 282 1355
Fax: 00 353 1 282 1242
e-mail: aravon@indigo.ie
website: www.aravon.ie

The oldest school of its kind in Ireland, Aravon was founded in 1862.

It is a Charitable, Educational and Scientific Trust administered by a Board of Governors.

Principal: **Mr K W J Allwright**

Location. Aravon is located 2.5 km from Bray, approximately 19.5 km south-east of Dublin City and three-quarters of an hour from Dublin Airport.

The house stands on an elevated site overlooking 15 acres of terraced lawns and playing fields. It is surrounded by mature woodland and an 18 hole Championship golf course.

The school has seven newly-built classrooms, independent from the main building.

Pupils. Inter-Denominational, Co-Educational, Day Preparatory School (from 4 to 12 years). Pre-School Montessori (3–4 years), and Extended Day available from 1–5.30 pm.

Syllabus. All pupils are prepared for entry to Irish Secondary and all independent senior schools. The Irish National Curriculum is followed.

The range of core subjects taught at Infant level is extended to encompass additional French, Junior Science, Mathematics, English, History, Geography, RE and Recorder from Forms I to III, Experimental Science (Physics, Chemistry and Biology) Forms IV to VI. In addition each form averages two periods of Art per week.

Outings to Theatres and Concerts are considered an integral part of the English and Music curricula, developing an early appreciation of Literature and the Arts. Outings are also arranged throughout the year by the Geography, History and Science Departments, and the Languages Department has cultural exchanges with overseas schools.

Science. Large, well equipped laboratory. General Science is taught in Forms I to IV and Experimental Science – Physics/Chemistry/Biology in Forms V to VI.

Computers. Computer studies are a part of the curriculum for all pupils. There is a well-equipped computer room and all classes are equipped with their own computer on the network. There are seven interactive whiteboards.

Languages. Irish and French from Junior Infants to Form VI. Annual Exchanges with a school in Bourg en Bresse for senior pupils, and several days in an Irish speaking area of Ireland. Bi-annual trip to Gaeltacht school is undertaken in top classes.

Drama. Drama is an integral part of language teaching and there is also a major school production every year and each child is involved in some way in productions through the year.

Special Needs. Full time professional Remedial help is available as an extra for those pupils who require it.

Music. School Orchestra, Chamber Groups, Senior and Junior Choirs. A wide range of musical instruments is taught: Flute, Oboe, Clarinet, 'Cello, Violin, Viola, Piano, Guitar, Recorders and Percussion.

Sports. Hockey, rugby, cricket, tennis, football, basketball, athletics, netball, PE, cross-country running, swimming. The school has a large astroturf area for hockey/tennis/football/netball, in addition to grass rugby/hockey/cricket pitches.

Aravon has a 25-metre outdoor pool for Summer use, but also avails of 25-metre indoor facilities where swimming takes place throughout the school year.

Extras. Horse-riding, Ballet and Modern Dance, Music, Carpentry, Tennis coaching, Wood turning (4 lathes).

Parent Teachers Association. Aravon has an active and enthusiastic PTA and a School Development Committee.

Fees per annum (2010-2011). Junior Infants €4,500; Senior Infants €5,600; Form 1 €6,750; Form 2 €7,100; Senior (Forms 3–6) €8,350. There are three terms in the school year.

Charitable status. Aravon School Limited is a Registered Charity, number 59277. It exists to provide education for children from the age of 3 to 12+.

The Banda School

PO Box 24722, Nairobi 00502, Kenya
Tel: 00 254 20 8891220 / 8891260 / 3547828 /
            2603929 / 5000728 / 9
            Mobiles: 00 254 20 0726-439909 / 0737-563438
Fax: 00 254 20 8890004
e-mail: bandaschool@swiftkenya.com
website: www.bandaschool.com

Chairman of Governors: Mr D G M Hutchison

Headmaster: **Mr M D Dickson**, BA Hons Worcester

Deputy Head: Miss W Rutter, CertEd Leeds

Age Range. 1–13.

Number of Children. 420 (Day and Weekly Boarding).

Fees per term (2010-2011). Tuition: Kshs 322,500 (Years 3–8 including lunches). Weekly Boarding: Kshs 90,000 in addition to Tuition Fees. Sliding fee scale Year 2 and below.

The School was founded in 1966 by Mr and Mrs J A L Chitty. It is 9 miles from Nairobi and stands in its own grounds of 30 acres adjacent to the Nairobi Game Park. Boys and girls are admitted in equal numbers and are prepared for Independent Senior School Scholarship and Common Entrance Examinations to leading secondary schools in Kenya, South Africa and the UK. The Staff consists of 40 teachers with the vast majority being graduates. The teacher-pupil ratio is about 1:10.

Facilities include a modern Weekly Boarding House, new Pegasus Pre-Prep building, Science laboratories, ICT rooms, Art room, Music rooms, Hall with well-equipped stage, two Libraries, Junior Art Room and a Dance Studio, specialist rooms for Mathematics, French, History and Geography, Design Technology, audio-visual room, Astroturf, two

Squash courts and a six-lane 25-metre Swimming Pool with three diving boards.

Sports include Rugby, Football, Hockey, Cricket, Tennis, Swimming, Netball, Rounders, Athletics, Sailing, Squash and Cross-Country. A wide range of other activities including Instrumental lessons and Dancing is also available. Music, Art and Drama are an important part in the life of the school.

Braeburn Mombasa International School
Primary School

PO Box 83009, 80100 Mombasa, Kenya
Tel: 00 254 20 2026156
Mobile: 00 254 723 846878
e-mail: primaryheadteacher@braeburnmombasa.co.ke
website: www.braeburn.com

Primary Headteacher: Mr W Sawyer

Age Range. 3–11 Co-educational
Number of Pupils. 113.
Fees per term (2010-2011). Tuition: Kshs 38,000–138,000. Transport to and from school: Kshs 17,300. School meals: Kshs 15,000. Weekly boarding (Monday–Thursday): Kshs 114,550. The uniform can be purchased from the school store.

Situated in Shanzu on the North Coast of Mombasa, the school follows the National Curriculum of England and Wales, and all pupils sit the Statutory Attainment Tests (SATs) issued from the UK at the end of Key Stages 1 and 2.

The pupil/teacher ratio is approximately 1:16 with trained Class Assistants for the Early Years and Key Stage 1 classes.

In addition to the British curriculum subjects, all pupils learn French and Kiswahili from Year 2 to Year 6. Pupils are with their Class Teachers most of the day but go to specialists for Languages, ICT, Music, PE and Games. They are encouraged to use the Library for research as well as reading.

Learning support is provided for pupils with Special Educational Needs and, because we have so many nationalities, we have to cater for children who start with little or no English.

Classrooms are large and well ventilated in a rural setting surrounded by coconut palms. As well as sports fields the children have a grassed play area. The family atmosphere and pastoral care of the pupils are crucial to our ethos and parents are encouraged to be involved.

School begins at 07.55 and finishes at 14.50. Optional after–school activities run from 15.00–16.00. The Early Years Unit (Playgroup, Nursery and Reception) finishes at 12.00. Homework is formally set from Year 3 upwards from half an hour (Y3) to one hour (Y6) per night. This is to encourage pupils to develop good study habits for later on.

Comprehensive reports are issued at the end of every term and parents are formally invited to meet with teachers once a term.

Sport, music and drama are important aspects of the school ethos with cricket, rounders and athletics in the first term, hockey and swimming in the second and rugby, netball and soccer in the third. Cross-country running, tennis and basketball are also included in our valuable after-school activities which take place every day.

We are an ABRSM and LAMDA practical examinations centre as we have many talented young musicians and actors and we stage two musical productions each year.

For more information, please visit our website at www.braeburn.com.

Braeburn School

PO Box 45112-00100, Gitanga Road, Lavington, Nairobi, Kenya
Tel: 00 254 20 3872300-2
Fax: 00 254 20 3872310
e-mail: scott.webber@braeburn.ac.ke
website: www.braeburn.com

Headteacher: Mr Scott Webber

Age Range. 3–13.
Number of Pupils. 642.
Fees per term (2010-2011). Tuition: Kshs 109,200–270,700.

Braeburn is the largest British Curriculum School in Kenya, catering for children from over 70 nationalities.

At Braeburn School, our children come first. We believe that it is our responsibility to provide opportunities for all children, from the Early Years to Year 8, to excel academically and socially. Our school is a community and we recognise that each individual is important and has a valuable contribution to make towards the quality of life enjoyed by the people within it. We continually stress the importance of honesty, trust, fairness and self-discipline, mutual respect and self-esteem. We endeavour to encourage and praise good behaviour and help all children to appreciate that this is the normal expectation.

In Early Years, the curriculum is based on the "Early Learning Goals". Here we have two classes for 3–5 year-olds in 2 age groups, a dedicated play area, daily morning Nursery class, full-day provision for Reception Class, afternoon Crèche facilities. The children start learning Music, PE and Swimming and also have library time and cooking.

Our school follows the British National Curriculum. Our teaching is a combination of whole class, group and individual teaching with more specialised teaching in the subject areas of ICT, French, Swimming, PE and Music. We have a learning support team that works with individual children or small groups within a class or year group. Core subjects are: English, Mathematics, Science and Information Communication Technology (ICT). Foundation subjects are: French, History and Geography, Religious Education, Art & Design Technology, Music & Drama, Personal, Social & Health Education (including Sex Education), PE and Swimming.

Beyond the primary years, we extend into Key Stage 3 (Year 7 and Year 8). Our students enjoy the expertise of subject-based teachers as well as the pastoral support of a form tutor.

At Braeburn, we enjoy excellent facilities and resources. We have a well-stocked and up-to-date library, a centre for music, 2 computer suites, a design technology workshop, science laboratories, an art room and a fine arts and ceramics room. We also boast 2 wonderful theatres seating 120 and 420 people respectively.

Provision for sports is superb. A good-size playing field complements 3 swimming pools, 3 squash courts, 2 tennis courts, a dance studio and a large indoor sports hall.

A large and varied programme of extra-curricular activities is offered. Various martial arts, ballet, origami, squash, golf, horse riding and sailing are but a few of the activities available at lunch time, after school and at weekends.

The British International School, Cairo

The Junior School

Km 38, Alexandria Road, Beverly Hills, Cairo, Egypt
Tel: 00 202 3827 0444
Fax: 00 202 3857 1720
e-mail: info@bisc.edu.eg
website: www.bisc.edu.eg

Chairman of Governors: Mr Yasser Hashem

Head of Junior School: Mr Michael Higgins, BEd Hons, MA

Age Range. 3–11 Co-educational.
Number of Pupils. 547.
Fees per term (2010-2011). £2,254–£2,646.
The Junior School of The British International School, Cairo (BISC) is situated alongside its Senior School within a new purpose-built 65,000 square metre campus on the western outskirts of Cairo, having relocated from the School's former city centre position in the summer of 2008. BISC, founded in 1976, is the oldest established of Cairo's British international schools and is academically selective with a strong tradition of excellent academic results. The Junior School has its own dedicated and spacious classroom buildings within the whole school campus, including a large library and multimedia learning centre, science laboratory, art and design technology centres and multi-purpose hall. All classrooms are equipped with interactive 'smart' boards and computer facilities. The Junior School also shares with the Senior School a large sports hall, a gym, a 50-metre and learner swimming pools, several playing fields, an athletics track, outdoor tennis and basketball courts, and a 670-seat theatre.

The British National Curriculum is taught throughout the School and all staff are UK qualified and experienced teachers. Arabic and French are taught by qualified native speakers. Best UK educational practice is also maintained through the School's continuing professional development programme for all staff.

The school's aims are included in its mission statement: to be a first-class school preparing pupils who will eventually progress to positions of leadership in life; to provide a stimulating British education with an appreciation and understanding of Egyptian culture and Arabic; to ensure equal opportunities for pupils to develop their full intellectual, aesthetic, emotional, physical and moral potential; and to provide a broadly based education within a supportive pastoral environment, with the best possible resources and facilities. BISC seeks to foster mutual respect and tolerance and to teach essential human values such as honesty, loyalty, compassion and charity. The positive values promoted at BISC connect to those of families, the local community and the wider world, and embrace a commitment to international co-operation and understanding.

The School has over 40 nationalities represented amongst its pupil body and as such there is no affiliation to any one particular religious system. The School places a strong emphasis on moral education, both within the Personal, Social and Citizenship curriculum programme and in terms of all aspects of the life of the School. Values that characterise and permeate BISC also include a commitment to respect for others' beliefs. Regular assemblies involve participation of all pupils. The pupils' voice and developing sense of responsibility is also expressed within regular meetings of the Pupil Council and other pupil positions such as within the School's House Captaincy system.

The School's pursuit of excellence in education is also expressed in the provision of a wide programme of sporting, cultural, and artistic pursuits for all pupils, both within and as additional to the main curriculum. Concerts, choral productions and drama performances feature in every term and the Junior School has its own dedicated specialist staff for music, drama, PE and modern foreign languages, in addition to its teams of Key Stage class teachers. Junior School pupils throughout Foundation and Key Stages One and Two also enjoy regular opportunities for off-site educational visits. As pupils progress into KS2 these include Humanities trips to Luxor and El Alamein, and overseas trips in Mathematics and Sports competitions. Inter-school sporting and cultural events also take place with other schools in Cairo and Alexandria.

Learning, teaching and pastoral care structures in the Junior School are child-centred. Great importance is attached to the close monitoring of all pupils' academic progress and pastoral well being, and their progress as successful, confident and responsible learners. Regular pupil reports, parent conferences, presentation evenings and opportunities for both formal and informal meetings are all part of the natural rhythm of BISC. There is also an active PTA through which parents encourage and run many family social events, and also help to promote the wider community links of the School. Open Days for prospective parents to view the School are also held each term.

In addition to IAPS membership, BISC is also in membership of COBIS, BSME, and AGBIS. The School's most recent Inspection was undertaken by the Independent Schools Inspectorate (ISI) in November 2008, and this Report is viewable on the ISI and BISC Websites.

BISC is constituted as a not-for-profit organisation of the British International Schools Society, whose elected Board members are all current parents of the School.

The British School – Al Khubairat

P O Box 4001, Abu Dhabi, United Arab Emirates
Tel: 00 971 2 446 2280
Fax: 00 971 2 446 1915
e-mail: registrar@britishschool.sch.ae
website: www.britishschool.sch.ae

A member of HMC, IAPS and COBIS.

Chair of Governors: Mrs Julie Richards, MA EdMgt

Principal: Mr Paul Coackley

Head of Primary: Mr Mark Yeowell

Head of Secondary: Mr Stephen Rogers

Age Range. 3–18.
Number of Pupils. 892 Boys, 890 Girls (all day).
Fees per term (2010-2011). Nursery: AED10,395; Reception–Year 6: AED13,480; Years 7–13: AED18,100.
The school's overriding aim is to provide education for English speaking children "in accordance with the best teaching practices, in order to enable children to qualify for normal subsequent education in the United Kingdom within their own age groups, without disadvantage". There is an extensive exra-curricular programme in which sport, music and drama figure prominently. In order to maintain and enhance the school's high standards, all classes are taught by fully-qualified British trained and experienced teachers and the school is inspected on a three-yearly cycle. The recent ISI report of March 2011 deemed the school excellent in all aspects of its work.

All the buildings are fully air-conditioned, light and spacious. Facilities are outstanding and will be further improved by the current building programme. Our Primary department comprises of 34 classrooms with additional central activity areas. We also have modern electronic libraries, computer suites, assembly/gymnasium halls, specialist music rooms, specialists rooms for French, Arabic and Special Education Needs. Our Secondary Department caters for students up to and including Sixth Form. Accommodation includes a sports hall, gymnasium, 8 laboratories, 3 Design Technology workshops, 4 ICT suites, 3 Art rooms, a range of Music rooms, a 330-seat theatre, a library, Sixth Form facilities and a range of academic classrooms. Students access top universities in the UK and worldwide as well as an extensive range of top independent and state schools in the UK.

The school is self-supporting, financed by fees paid by parents for the education of their children. It operates as a 'not for profit' concern, the funds being used only for the school's purposes. The British Ambassador appoints several Board members and the Ambassador's representative sits on the Board.

The British School of Brussels
Primary School

Leuvensesteenweg 19, 3080 Tervuren, Belgium
Tel: 00 32 2 766 04 35
Fax: 00 32 2 767 80 70
e-mail: juniors@britishschool.be
website: www.britishschool.be

Patron:
Her Excellency the British Ambassador to the King of the Belgians

Chairman of the Board: Mr Ian Backhouse

Principal: Mrs Sue Woodroofe, BA Hons, NPQH

Vice-Principal & Head of Primary School: **Ms Carole Denny**, MA, BA Hons, PGCE

Age Range. 1–11 Co-educational.
Number of Pupils. 600.
Fees per annum (2011-2012). €13,200–€22,550.
Introduction. The development of the whole child is at the heart of BSB's primary education programme. Learning in the Primary School is about developing personal, emotional and social skills as well as being an intellectual and academic process. We aim to help children find their voice – their own unique, personal significance. We encourage them to think about what their contribution will be in the world – how they will try to make a difference as responsible and engaged members of the school community as well as citizens of the world.

BSB has high expectations for all its learners. In the Primary School we pride ourselves on knowing each child as an individual in order to help them make progress. Learning opportunities are planned so that all students are challenged appropriately. Above all, we are interested in the learning process – learning how to learn and how to apply skills and knowledge across an ever-increasing spectrum of experience. From the earliest age we ensure that children have an enjoyable experience of school and are motivated to learn and improve. This positive attitude is supported by a team of highly professional teachers who are themselves engaged in lifelong learning and model effective habits of mind.

Curriculum. The curriculum is based on that of the National Curriculum for England adapted to reflect the needs of an increasingly international and multi-cultural student body and to capitalise upon the opportunities of being in Belgium at the heart of Europe. We aim to build on the children's background knowledge and experience to equip them with the skills, strategies and a love of learning that will inspire them to succeed whatever the next step on their educational journey. The Primary Senior Management Team

works to ensure coherence, consistency, continuity and progression across the whole primary age range.

Facilities. The Primary School enjoys excellent resources and provides a stimulating and varied environment. The children are spread geographically across the school campus, housed in three buildings.

We seek not only to provide an environment which promotes achievement in learning, but also one of warmth, security and care. The School was purpose-built and laid out to be both light and spacious. Our visitors frequently comment not only on the beautiful site and these excellent facilities but also on the warm and happy atmosphere which infuses the School. This complements the purposeful working environment and enables our children's learning development to flourish.

As the children move through the age groups they have access to well-resourced classrooms (including computers in every classroom and interactive boards in teaching rooms), dedicated computer suites, a fully equipped gymnasium, differentiated playgrounds, the main 240-seat School Theatre for drama productions, a spacious hall, the School playing field, an art, design and technology room, well-stocked libraries and smaller classrooms for Additional Educational Needs. Rooms are also provided for English as an Additional Language (EAL) and French teaching.

"Kindercrib" is our own crèche with full-time or part-time availability for children between the ages of 1 to 3 providing a caring and stimulating pre-school environment situated in a separate villa next to the School.

(*See also British School of Brussels entry in HMC section.*)

The British School in The Netherlands
Junior School Diamanthorst

Diamanthorst 16, 2592 GH, The Hague, The Netherlands
Tel: 00 31 (0)70 315 7620
Fax: 00 31 (0)70 315 7621
e-mail: junior.diamanthorst@britishschool.nl
website: www.britishschool.nl

Chairman of Governors: Mr P Bayliff

Headteacher: **Mr Paul Ellis**

Age Range. 3–11 Co-educational.
Number of Pupils. 350.
Fees per annum (2011-2012). Foundation Stage €12,510, Years 1–2 €12,630, Years 3–6 €12,750.

The Junior School Diamanthorst is a place where children can thrive and grow, develop and study, play and perform and, above all, discover the enjoyment of learning. We aim to help children understand the value of both work and leisure and encourage them to become confident, happy individuals.

The site is located in a residential area in the north of The Hague. The facilities include a Media Library Centre, Food Technology Room, Hall/Gym, Design Technology Room, Wild Garden, Dance/Drama Studio, IT suite and Music Room. All classrooms are equipped with interactive whiteboards and computers. The school has a wireless network system throughout.

The learning programme includes the three core subjects Mathematics, English and Science, together with the foundation subjects, geography, history, design and technology, art & music, information technology and PE with the addition of Dutch from entry into the School and taster courses in French, German and Spanish from Year 5.

Our Foundation classes follow the English Foundation Curriculum with particular emphasis on acquiring literacy, numeracy and social skills.

In Key Stages 1 and 2 specific schemes of work outline the progressive skills and knowledge which are taught, and all work is closely monitored to ensure that pupils are making progress matched to their abilities. In the case of children who display unusual talent or ability, extension material is given to motivate and challenge their intellectual growth. All children enjoy a variety of experiences, visiting places of interest in the immediate locality, performing in dance, drama and choral activities and engaging in a wide range of extra-curricular programmes.

As children progress through the Junior School subject teaching becomes more defined, especially in the core subjects of English, Mathematics and Science. Children are carefully prepared for the subject-orientated approach evident in the Senior School where they are expected to become more independent in the planning and completion of tasks and time management.

The British School of Paris
Junior School

2 rue Hans List, 78290 Croissy sur Seine, France
Tel: 00 33 1 34 80 45 90
Fax: 00 33 1 39 76 12 69
e-mail: junior@britishschool.fr
website: www.britishschool.fr

Chairman of Governors: Mr P Kett

Headmaster: Dr Steffen Sommer

Head of Junior School: **Mr J Hornshaw**

Age Range. 3–11 Co-educational.
Number of Pupils. 400.
Fees per annum (2010-2011). €10,000–€18,296.

The Junior School caters for pupils aged 3–11 and is located very close to the Senior School along the leafy banks of the river Seine. This brand new facility opened in September 2010; there are 35 classrooms accommodating up to 480 pupils, as well as 4 bespoke classrooms and 2 activity areas that are dedicated to our foundation stage/nursery section. The school was specifically designed to meet the educational and social welfare needs of junior school pupils. It is bristling with new technology and up-to-the-minute IT facilities to assist the pupils' learning and development. The British School of Paris's philosophy of education permeates throughout the Junior School and has at its core the goal of unlocking the potential of all students, by identifying strengths and supporting areas of development, while having fun and enjoying happy and strong social relationships. Studies are based on the British National Curriculum with emphasis on English, Maths and Science, and of course, the French language. Various sports, music, drama and many other extra-curricular activities are also provided.

For further details and applications, please contact the Registrar, e-mail registrar@britishschool.fr.

The British School in Tokyo

Shibuya Campus (Nursery–Year 3):
1-21-18 Shibuya, Shibuya-ku, Tokyo 150-0002, Japan
Tel: 00 81 03 5467 4321
Fax: 00 81 03 5467 4322

Showa Campus (Years 4–13):
Showa Women's University 5th Bldg 3F & 4F, 1-7-57
Taishido, Setagaya-ku, Tokyo 154-8533, Japan
Tel: 00 81 03 3411 4211
Fax: 00 81 03 3411 4212
e-mail: admissions@bst.ac.jp

website: www.bst.ac.jp

Head of School: **David Williams**

Head of Primary School: Sue Aspinall

Head of Secondary School: Chris Nicholls

Age Range. 3–18 Co-educational.
Number of Pupils. 650.
Fees per annum (2011-2012). Yen 1,860,000 (Nursery), Yen 2,050,000 (Reception–Year 13).

The British School in Tokyo is the only British school in Japan. Our unique position provides our pupils with unprecedented opportunities for academic achievement within a Japanese context. The best of British education is our aim, with all children being offered the stimuli to reach their full potential within the School's disciplined and caring environment. Set this aim in the context of one of the most exciting and vibrant cityscapes in the world and it is easy to see why our pupils are the beneficiaries of a truly memorable educational experience.

The BST is an independent co-educational two-site day school, offering a high quality English National Curriculum education. The School is a non-profit organisation; administered by a Board of Trustees representing the British and international community in Tokyo. Being a British School, the majority of pupils are from the UK, but pupils from all nationalities are welcome, provided that each child, relative to age, is fluent in English. There are on average over 30 nationalities represented within the School community.

The ethos of a busy 'community' school is reflected in the high degree of parental involvement. Parents are encouraged to play a full and active role in school, offering support in the classrooms, on educational visits and on residentials and through the activities of the PTA and Parent Advisory Group.

The British School Tripoli

PO Box 6122, Tripoli, Libya
Tel: 00 218 21 4772452
Fax: 00 218 21 4779133
e-mail: office@britishschooltripoli.com
website: www.britishschooltripoli.com

Headmaster: **Mr Alistair Bond**

Age Range. 3–14 Co-educational.
Number of Pupils. 230.
Fees per term (2010-2011). Nursery: £1,100 plus Libyan Dinars 1,675, Primary: £2,100 plus Libyan Dinars 2,575, Secondary: £2,600 plus Libyan Dinars 2,775.

The British School Tripoli was founded in 1968 with the support of the British Embassy. It is managed by a Governing Body which comprises seven elected parents and two co-optees. The British Ambassador is the school's Patron.

The school is a non-profit making organisation and does not receive financial assistance (other than donations for specific Projects) from any of the multi-national companies based in Libya.

The school prides itself on being warm and friendly whilst ensuring the highest standards of teaching and learning.

The school is located on Shara Ahmed Jezi between two arterial highways, Gargaresh Road and the Gurji Road, on the west side of the city. The school occupies four large spacious detached villas with an adjoining hall/gym and has a large playground with play equipment to the rear.

The Curriculum is based on the English National Curriculum. The Literacy and Numeracy Strategies have been adopted for Years 1-6 age groups. Foundation subjects are taught through the EYFS, with an increasing emphasis on cross-curricular themes throughout the school, including Key Stage 3. Children in Years 1–9 are taught conversational Arabic and French. All class teachers must be UK trained and are supported by specialist teaching in PE, Art, DT, Music, Arabic and French. The school emphasises the whole curriculum and celebrates the achievements of its students.

The school's PTA is proactive in organising activities for parents and children in the school community. An Autumn Fair is held every year and money raised is used to buy new, or refurbish existing, resources.

In accordance with Libyan Law the school does not admit Libyan national children.

The school primarily serves the British community although applications are accepted from Commonwealth, European Union and other countries. A maximum class size of 22 has been set for all classes. All children are required to pass a basic competency test in English before being accepted into the school.

Brookhouse International School
Preparatory School

PO Box 24987, Langata, Nairobi 00502, Kenya
Tel: 00 254 20 2430 260-3
Fax: 00 254 20 2430 269
e-mail: info@brookhouse.ac.ke
website: www.brookhouse.ac.ke

Preparatory School Headteacher: **Ms Michelle Forsyth, BA, PGCE**

Age Range. 2–13 Co-educational.
Number of Pupils. 300 boys and girls, including 30 boarders.
Fees per term (2010-2011). Tuition: Kshs 100,000–300,000 (includes lunch, but excludes transport). Transport to and from school: Kshs 30,000. Boarding: Kshs 225,000 in addition to Tuition Fees.

Established in 1981 in a leafy suburb of Nairobi about 10 minutes from the city centre, Brookhouse Preparatory School is an independent co-educational day and boarding school accredited by the Council of International Schools. Brookhouse benefits from a purpose-built "castle-style" building design that ensures a physical environment for children that is truly inspirational. The school delivers an adapted form of the British National Curriculum, catering mainly for the professional, business and diplomatic communities of the East African region. Brookhouse balances traditional values with an innovative approach to the curriculum. Our philosophy as a Round Square international member school focuses on respect for each child as an individual and the development of leadership through service to others. The school features small classes, and a particular focus on the core areas of numeracy, literacy and computer literacy. The average class size is 15.

With more than 40 nationalities represented on the student roll, the school prides itself on fostering tolerance and understanding, and promotes a diverse programme of extra-curricular activities, sports and clubs to ensure the development of the whole child. Teachers are recruited from both UK and East Africa and average nearly fifteen years of classroom experience. They are carefully selected for their ability to provide both a challenging academic environment and a caring pastoral network of support for each child.

Situated on a thirteen-acre campus adjacent to Nairobi National Park, the school has on-site co-educational boarding accommodation. Academic facilities include a 'space station' computer laboratory, purpose-built science and home science laboratories, a three-storey library, Fine Art and Music studios, and a world-class performance theatre where regular drama and musical productions are staged. All classrooms are computer networked, and students have supervised e-mail and internet access. A Learning Support Unit caters for students with Special Educational Needs (SEN) and for students who have English as an Additional Language (EAL) backgrounds, as well as providing an Academic Extension Programme (AEP) for highly able pupils.

Sporting facilities include a gym and aerobics studio, swimming pool, indoor sports centre for tennis and basketball and irrigated playing fields to ensure a year round quality playing surface. A varied programme of team and individual sports are available.

The English School
Kuwait

PO Box 379, 13004 Safat, Kuwait
Tel: 00 965 2563 7205/7206
Fax: 00 965 2563 7147
e-mail: registrar@tes.edu.kw
website: www.tes.edu.kw

Sponsor: M A R Al-Bahar

Chair of the Governing Committee: Colonel John Ensor

Headmaster: **J A Allcott**

Age Range. 2–13.
Number of Pupils. 609.
Fees per annum (2010-2011). Nursery (PreKG and KG) KD1,580; Pre-Preparatory (Rec, Year 1 and Year 2) KD2,320; Preparatory (Years 3–8) KD2,765.

The English School, founded in 1953 under the auspices of the British Embassy, is the longest established school in Kuwait catering for the expatriate community. The School operates as a not-for-profit, private co-educational establishment providing the highest standards in education for children of Pre-Kindergarten to Preparatory School age. The School is registered with the United Kingdom Department for Education (DfE No 703 6052) and the Headmaster is a Member of the Independent Association of Prep Schools. TES is an Accredited Member of BSME. Uniquely in Kuwait, the language of the playground is English. The roll is predominantly British, as are the resources and texts. With the exception of foreign language teachers, the teaching staff are predominantly British and qualified in the United Kingdom. The number of pupils in the School continues to increase although the average class size remains around 20. The School is housed in well-resourced and spacious, fully air-conditioned premises in a pleasant residential suburb of Kuwait City.

The curriculum is British, contemporary and aiming for the best of traditional standards being sought within a broad-based structure. Class teachers are supported by specialist coordinators in Art, Design and Technology, Information Technology, Music, Library and PE and Games. Music is taught to all ages and French is introduced from Year 4. The National Curriculum for England and Wales is used as the core for the curriculum. Formal End-of-Key Stage assessment takes place in Years 2 and 6. In addition the pupils are prepared for entrance tests to other schools including, where appropriate, Common Entrance Examinations at 11+, 12+ and 13+, and scholarship examinations.

Responsibility for the School is vested in the Governing Committee whose members serve in a voluntary capacity.

The School provides a learning environment within which children develop their individual capacity for achievement to its fullest potential. Each individual is directed towards self-discipline and respect for himself/herself and for others. Strong emphasis is placed on academic study, together with a wide range of non-academic activities to provide a balance. The School aims to ensure that, by achieving standards equivalent to those of competitive private and State schools in Britain, our pupils are well prepared for the subsequent stages of their academic development whether in Britain, Kuwait or elsewhere in the world.

In the first instance application for enrolment should be made online via the website – please see drop-down menu: Parents, Enrolment, Online Registration Form.

The Registrar will confirm receipt of the Online Registration Form. If there are places in the Year requested, the Registrar will ask for copies of current academic reports and arrange a date for the child/children to be assessed. At the time of the assessment a tour of the school and facilities will be offered.

Grimwade House

67 Balaclava Road, Caulfield Victoria 3161, Australia
Tel: 00 61 3 9865 7800
Fax: 00 61 3 9865 7888
e-mail: grimwade@mgs.vic.edu.au
website: www.mgs.vic.edu.au

Chairman of School Council: Professor R G Larkins, AO, MBBS Melb, MD Melb, PhD Lon, LLD Hon Melb

Head: **Mr Andrew Boyd**, DipT, BEd, MEdPA Monash, MACE

Age Range. 5–12.
Number of Children. 680 girls and boys, all day pupils.
Fees per term (from January 2011). Prep–Year 6: A$4,860 ($19,440 per annum). There are four terms to the school year.

Grimwade House, the co-educational junior school of Melbourne Grammar, is located in Caulfield, about seven kilometres from the Senior School and Wadhurst. It opened as a school in 1918, following the gift of a fine old Victorian home, "Harleston", to Melbourne Grammar by the Grimwade family.

Grimwade House has its own Chapel, Assembly Hall, two Libraries, two Art and Craft areas, a Science Laboratory, Music School, PE Centre including an indoor pool and gymnasium, playgrounds and modern classrooms.

A full-time qualified staff of 50 teach a core curriculum including English, Mathematics, Science, Art, Technology, Religious & Values Education, Music, Physical Education and Mandarin Chinese. Computers are used at all levels and notebook computers for each student are an integral part of the curriculum in Years 5 and 6. There are also a School Counsellor, Chaplain and Learning Strategies teachers. The emphasis is on learning as a positive and challenging experience.

The School has its own orchestra and choir as well as many smaller instrumental and choral groups. Sporting activities include Australian Rules Football, soccer, hockey, cross country, athletics, aerobics, netball, cricket, basketball, tennis, snowsports and swimming.

All students in Years 5 and 6 attend the School Camp at Woodend, some 80 kilometres from Melbourne.

Hillcrest Preparatory School

PO Box 24282, Karen 00502, Nairobi, Kenya
Tel: 00 254 (0)20 883914/16/17
Fax: 00 254 (0)20 883920
e-mail: admin_prep@hillcrest.ac.ke
website: www.hillcrest.ac.ke

Chairman of Governors: (*vacant*)

Head: **Mrs Karen Morey**, MA, DipSpLD

Age Range. 6–13 Co-educational.
Number of Pupils. 171.
Fees per term (2010-2011). Kshs 193,000–275,000, excluding transport and lunches.

Hillcrest School was founded in 1965 by Mrs Elizabeth Node with Mr Frank Thompson as Founding Headmaster. It is located on an attractive, purpose-built, 20-acre campus next to our Secondary School in Karen/Langata.

Boys and girls are accepted from the age of 6 and they follow a broad and extensive curriculum which prepares them for Common Entrance Examinations. Some children transfer to UK Independent Secondary Schools but the majority enter the equivalent in Kenya, Hillcrest Secondary School, which prepares pupils for IGCSE and A Levels. Entry to the Senior School is achieved after successfully writing either Common Entrance or the Hillcrest Secondary examination. A thriving Kindergarten of 50, called Forestcrest, opened on site in September 2001.

The school has an International flavour and its pupils are drawn from the Diplomatic and United Nations community, expatriate families on contract, and Kenyan residents. The friendly spirit and strong communication network that exists between staff, pupils and parents are of particular note. There are 18 fully qualified teachers, 60% are Honours Graduates recruited from the UK. The average form size is 18 and the teacher:pupil ratio of approximately 11:1 allows for considerable individual attention and learning support.

Hillcrest offers a wide range of extramural activities each week including dance, TaeKwonDo, sub-aqua, instrumental tuition, tennis, basketball, flight simulation and scouting.

Field trip studies are offered to the Coast and Rift Valley and outdoor pursuits are strongly encouraged. These include climbs of Mount Longonot and Kenya, up-country farm visits and water activities trips to Lake Naivasha. Charitable fundraising activities are also regularly organised by pupils for underprivileged children.

The school's Inter-House Competitions are a focal point of each term. House Chieftains play an important role in welcoming new pupils, monitoring behaviour and promoting a competitive spirit. Cricket, Rounders, Hockey, Rugby, Netball and Swimming are taught and a full fixtures programme is arranged each term with other Preparatory Schools.

Hillcrest is also well-known for the quality of its drama productions, choir performances and standard of artistic display throughout the school. Our principle aim is to nurture pupils' individual talents and produce well-balanced children who actively contribute to all academic, aesthetic and sporting activities in a caring and family-like atmosphere.

Jerudong International School
Junior School & Middle School Divisions

PO Box 1408, Bandar Seri Begawan BS8672, Negara Brunei Darussalam
Tel: 00 673 2 411000
Fax: 00 673 2 411010

e-mail: enrol@jis.edu.bn
website: www.jis.edu.bn

Jerudong International School (for Kindergarten to Year 13) is a British international day and boarding school located near the University of Brunei Darussalam in Jerudong, Brunei, just five kilometres from the capital city of Bandar Seri Begawan.

Principal & CEO: **Andrew J Fowler-Watt**, MA Cantab

Head of Junior School: **Karen Mehta**, BEd Hons Leeds

Head of Middle School: **Ian Mehta**, BSc Hons Exeter

Age Range. 2–18.
Number of Pupils. 1,473 (Junior School, Nursery to Year 5: 376; Middle School, Years 6–8: 348; Upper School, Years 9–11: 457; Sixth Form, Years 12–13: 292).
Fees per annum (2011-2012). Nursery: B\$7,656–\$9,500, Kindergarten: B\$10,236–\$12,200, Reception to Year 7: B\$15,312–\$18,700, Year 8–11: B\$16,104–\$20,000, Year 12 and 13: B\$16,848–\$20,500. Boarding: B\$17,688–\$23,500. (£1 = 3BN\$).
Facilities. Built in 1997, JIS has excellent facilities that are shared with the secondary school. There is a gymnasium which incorporates a dance studio and a fitness room. The fifty-metre swimming pool is shaded and pupils enjoy the use of tennis and netball courts. There is a well-stocked library with computer access and three additional computer suites exclusively for Junior and Middle Schools. Science, design technology, art, food technology and music are taught in dedicated rooms. The playground areas are extensive and shaded in some areas.
Curriculum. At JIS much emphasis is placed on academic achievement. Children are expected to work hard and achieve very high standards, but the school is not selective at this level. Children transfer to the Middle School at the end of Year 5. The pastoral system is well developed. Much support is given to parents relocating to Brunei and the problems of expatriate life are well understood. Since August 2005 the school has had both a nurse and a counsellor.

All pupils have a class teacher for most of their studies. There are specialist teachers in Design and Technology, ICT, Art, Music, Malay, French, Urdu and Physical Education. Mandarin is taught by a native speaker. Pupils follow the British National Curriculum and the International Primary Curriculum. From 2011, the School will introduce the International Baccalaureate Diploma in addition to A Levels in the Sixth Form. The school is proud to welcome parents and children of all nationalities. Teachers are predominantly from the UK and Australia, whereas pupils are from more than forty different countries.

The extra-curricular programme offers pupils the opportunity to take part in a variety of activities. Music, Art and Sport are all strong. Children acquire good social and communication skills and learn to cooperate with others. There is a lively sporting programme and opportunities to compete locally and internationally at the games organised by the Federation of Independent Schools of South-East Asia (FOBISSEA). There is an After School Care Centre for children who cannot be collected immediately at the end of the school day.

Kenton College

PO Box 30017, 00100 Nairobi, Kenya
Tel: 00 254 20 4347000/4347532/4347371
Fax: 00 254 20 4347332
e-mail: admin@kenton.ac.ke
website: www.kentonschoolnairobi.com

Chairman of the Governors: C H Banks, Esq

Headmistress: **Mrs M Cussans**, BA, PGCE, MA

Age Range. 6–13 Co-educational.
Number of Pupils. 250.
Fees per term (2011-2012). Kshs 350,000.
Founded in 1924 and transferred to purpose built accommodation in 1935, Kenton College is one of the oldest schools in the country. Situated in its own secluded grounds of 35 acres, at an altitude of nearly 6000 feet, some three miles from the centre of one of Africa's most cosmopolitan capitals, Kenton is an oasis of calm amidst the rapidly sprawling urban development of the city of Nairobi.

Kenton College is an independent co-educational preparatory school, entry to which is open to both boys and girls of any race or religious persuasion, who have had their sixth birthday before the beginning of the school year in September. Most pupils remain seven years with us and leave in the July following their thirteenth birthday for senior schools in the UK, Kenya or South Africa, having followed a syllabus in the senior part of the school leading to the ISEB Common Entrance Examination. Kenton pupils frequently obtain scholarships to UK or Kenyan senior schools.

The school is based on a strong Christian foundation which is reflected in the warm and caring environment provided for its pupils, wherein positive encouragement is given towards any aspect of school life. Considerable emphasis is placed on character building, discipline and good manners, within a relaxed and happy atmosphere.

We aim for high academic achievements by offering a full curriculum in which the best of traditional and modern approaches are employed. The British National Curriculum provides the framework for our teaching throughout the school. Use is made of specialist subject teaching rooms in the senior school, to which recent additions are a Modern Languages suite, a Design Studio and two Computer rooms. There are two Science laboratories, a well-stocked Library, a 300 seat Assembly Hall with large stage, and a purpose-built Music Studio.

The academic day is balanced by opportunities for drama and music for all, together with a wide variety of sports and extra-curricular activities. Traditional British sports are played using our first class facilities which include three tennis courts and a heated swimming pool.

Many pupils opt for extra activities such as riding, ballet, karate, music tuition, tennis or swimming coaching, speech and drama awards. Sailing in the school boats on Lake Naivasha is available a few times each term. Trips to facilities found in an international city are combined with expeditions and fieldwork in the unrivalled Kenyan countryside.

Academic subjects are taught by a staff complement of local and expatriate teachers numbering 25. Full use is made of accomplished musicians for music tuition, while recognised Kenyan sportsmen assist with games coaching. The average class size is 18, with 20 the maximum.

King's College School, La Moraleja

Paseo de Alcobendas 5, 28109 La Moraleja, Madrid, Spain
Tel: 00 34 916 585 540
Fax: 00 34 916 507 686
e-mail: info.lamoraleja@kingscollege.es
website: www.kingscollege.es

King's College School La Moraleja opened in September 2007. It is a co-educational day school and one of three King's Group schools in Madrid, the first of which was founded in 1969. The Headteacher is an international member of IAPS, while the school is a member of COBIS.

The school is governed by the King's Group Board of Directors and the School Council. These governing bodies are composed of distinguished members from the business and academic communities.

Headteacher: **Harry FitzHerbert**, BA Hons Nottingham, PGCE London

Deputy Headteacher: June Donnan, BA Hons Ulster, MEd OU

Technical Director: Maria Dolores Oñoro, Diplomada Magisterio Madrid

Head of Admissions: Andrew Moore

Age Range. 2–14 Co-educational.
Number of Pupils. 470.
Fees per term (2011-2012). €1,871–€3,070 excluding lunch and transport.

This is a day school which caters for children of approximately 20 nationalities between the ages of 2 and 14 years (Nursery to Year 9). Pupil enrolment is approximately 470 boys and girls and there are 30 fully qualified British staff, and four qualified Spanish language teachers.

The aim of the school, like its sister schools in Madrid, is to deliver "A British Education in Spain for Europe and the World" – to provide students with an excellent all-round education while fostering tolerance and understanding between young people of different nationalities and backgrounds. The modern on-site facilities include a library, ICT centre, laboratory, music rooms, multi-purpose sports surface, gymnasium and infirmary.

At the age of fourteen, at the end of National Curriculum Year 9, pupils transfer to the school in Soto de Viñuelas to complete their final four years of study. (*See King's College entry in HMC section.*)

Location. This new purpose-built school is situated in La Moraleja, one of the most highly regarded residential areas in Madrid. The site is well connected to the city, just off the A1 and a short walk from the La Moraleja Metro station. There is an optional bus service for pupils to the city of Madrid and its outlying residential areas and all routes are supervised by a bus monitor.

Curriculum. Pupils follow the English National Curriculum (leading to (I)GCSE, GCE AS and A Level examinations once pupils transfer to Soto de Viñuelas). There are Induction English Classes for children over the age of 7 who need to improve their English. There are also Beginners' Spanish Classes for international children joining the school. All pupils learn Spanish and some will follow the Spanish Baccalaureate from the age of 16 (Y12) in Soto de Viñuelas.

Activities. There are choirs and musical ensembles, which participate in events throughout the year. Pupils are encouraged to explore their capabilities in the areas of music and the arts from a very early age.

Sports play an important role at the school and pupils are encouraged to take part in tournaments and local competitive events, in addition to their normal PE classes. School football and basketball teams compete in the local Alcobendas Leagues and pupils also take part in inter-school championships in athletics and cross-country.

There is a programme of optional classes (some of which take place at Soto de Viñuelas) which includes horse riding, ballet, judo, Spanish dancing, swimming, tennis, tuition in various musical instruments, performing arts, chess, language clubs and craft workshops.

Admission. Pupils wishing to enter Year 3 and above are required to sit entrance tests in English and Mathematics and to present copies of recent school reports, while younger candidates (Nursery to Year 2) are screened by our Educational Psychologist.

Further information may be obtained from The Head of Admissions, Mr Andrew Moore: andrew.moore@kingsgroup.org.

Lagos Preparatory School

36–40 Glover Road, Ikoyi, Lagos, Nigeria
Tel: 00 234 1 727 2804
          00 234 702 908 9556
e-mail: admin@lagosprepikoyi.com.ng
          headteacher@lagosprepikoyi.com.ng
website: www.lagosprepikoyi.com.ng

Headmaster: **Mr Graham Stothard**

Age Range. 2–13 Co-educational.
Number of Pupils. 320.
Fees per term (2010-2011). £1,000–£2,500.

Our school is an international 13+ preparatory school delivering the British National Curriculum to over 300 pupils of 17 different nationalities. English is the medium of all tuition. The majority of the school's 95 staff is Nigerian with the school having its full legal quota of expatriate teacher colleagues, from the UK; South Africa and India. Each of the 20 classes has a graduate teacher, who also possesses the PGCE qualification, and an assistant teacher. All assistant teachers are graduates, many working towards the PGCE. Y2 classes and below also have a class assistant and a Nanny working in them. The school is located in Ikoyi that part of Lagos regarded as the prime residential area of the city. Our new purpose-built premises opened in September 2010. Parents and all stakeholders have high academic and social aspirations for their children. The school has a selective admissions policy.

Approximately 65% of children are Nigerian nationals therefore in order to acknowledge their cultural identity and heritage, clear evidence exists of using local exemplars to supplement programmes of study. This is further witnessed by the programme of pre and after school clubs and in the many school visits the children undertake. The school's senior leadership team are primarily focused on 'quality first teaching' across the whole school and this is reflected in our mission statement. We acknowledge parental aspirations for their children through a continual drive for reflective practices both within and outside the classroom. There is regular monitoring of the quality of teaching and learning, the school learning environment and pupil progress via homework and termly testing (including optional and 'statutory' SATs).

There is an active PTA which in addition to raising substantial amounts of money to assist in purchasing additional resources for the school, provides a most useful and constructive link with the Headmaster around everything from individual parental concerns through to strategic whole school development matters. In keeping with the school's mission statement it maintains a proactive stance in relation to community links. We are a main sponsor of the charity African Child Development Initiative (ACDI) and as such we assist them in developing and running a new community school (The Premier Foundation School) in Makoko village, Lagos. Our school has a very active CPD programme and performance management system for all staff. One member of the SLT is responsible for this crucial area of development. Over the last few years a significant number of graduate teachers and assistant teachers have undertaken distance learning PGCE course with the University of Sunderland, with much success.

In the Lent term 2010 the school became the World's first international school to achieve the Every Child Matters Standards Award. In addition to membership of the Independent Association of Prep Schools, pending publication of our recent ISI inspection the school hopes to become an accredited member of the Council of British International Schools – the first British school in Africa to achieve this status.

Maadi British International School

4th District, Zahraa El-Maadi, Next to Wadi Degla Sporting Club, Cairo, Egypt
Tel: 00 20 2 2705 8671/2/3/4/5
Fax: 00 20 2 2705 8679
e-mail: mbis@mbisegypt.com
website: www.mbisegypt.com

Headmaster: **Gerard L Flynn**, BPhil Newcastle, CertEd

Deputy Head: G McInroy

Age Range. 2–13.
Number of Pupils. Preparatory (age 4–13): 300 boys and girls. Early Years (age 2–4): 60 boys and girls.
Fees per term (2011-2012). Preparatory: £2,674–£3,074 (Registration: one term's fee payable once only). Early Years: £1,338–£1,604 (Registration: £200).

MBIS is an International Preparatory School situated in Maadi, a suburb of Cairo favoured by expatriates. Approximately 50% of pupils are British; the remaining 50% represent over 30 nationalities. The school follows the English National Curriculum and all its assessment requirements including end of Key Stage 1 and 2 testing. All teaching staff are UK graduate teachers, in the main recruited directly from Britain. In each class there is a teaching assistant working alongside the class teacher. Specialist teachers are employed for French, Arabic, ICT, Music, Physical Education and Special Needs. The school has a non-class based 'able child' coordinator and a full-time SRN.

The school relocated to purpose-built premises in September 2004; these offer an indoor 25m swimming pool, a superbly equipped theatre, large ICT suite, food technology and Science discovery rooms. There are also spacious outdoor facilities.

The school is inspected by Ofsted registered inspectors on a regular cycle. It is a member of the European Council of International Schools (ECIS).

There is a thriving programme of extra-curricular activities which is as varied as horse riding and calligraphy. Piano, guitar, drums and violin lessons are available as an after-school activity.

Children undergo an assessment before admission. This is to ensure that the school can meet the individual needs of the child. This process can be bypassed if current school reports are available and forwarded to the Headteacher.

There is a very strong PTA which benefits all pupils and their parents.

The overall aim of the school is to deliver a high quality British education in a caring and stimulating environment.

Prospective parents are requested to contact the Headteacher and he would be particularly pleased to show any parents visiting Cairo around the school.

The school is a 'not for profit' organisation registered as a non-governmental organisation (NGO) with the Egyptian Ministry of Social Affairs, with a charter to educate foreign children. The school's Board of Directors is made up of parents who have children in the school with the addition of up to three invited governors which at present includes HM Consul in Cairo.

Pembroke House

PO Box 31, 20116 Gilgil, Kenya
Tel: 00 254 (0)20 231 2323
         00 254 (0)734 480 439
e-mail: headmistress@pembrokehouse.sc.ke
website: www.pembrokehouse.sc.ke

Chairman of Council: Mr Richard Fernandes

Headmistress: **Mrs Deborah Boyd-Moss**, MA Cantab, PGCE

Age Range. 6–13.
Number of Pupils. 80 boy boarders, 75 girl boarders.
Fees per term (2011-2012). KShs 435,000 (UK£3,295).

The school was founded in 1927 and is presently owned and administered by the Kenya Educational Trust Limited. It is situated in over 40 hectares of well-maintained grounds in the Rift Valley at 2,000 metres and is 120 kms from Nairobi. The climate is sunny throughout the year affording many opportunities for an extensive education.

Facilities include the Chapel, Swimming Pool, Music School, two Libraries, Art and Design Technology Centre, Computer Room, two Squash Courts and tennis courts and access to a neighbouring Golf Course, and a multi-purpose sports hall. The school has a well-equipped Surgery on site.

The main sports are Cricket, Hockey, Rugby, Rounders and Netball with Tennis, Swimming, Athletics, Squash, Golf, Horse Riding, Sailing, Soccer, Shooting and TaeKwonDo on offer as well.

A full range of clubs and various extras, including individual music instruction, are also offered. Drama is strong with several productions put on each year.

Children are admitted from six years as full boarders and are prepared, through the British Curriculum, for the ISEB Common Entrance Examinations which qualifies them for entry to Independent Senior Schools in the UK and South Africa as well as Kenyan schools. The School usually gains numerous academic scholarships and awards each year in addition to music and sports awards. The Learning Support Facilities at Pembroke House have been developed over many years and now provide essential help for those who require such assistance. The school currently has children from seven different countries including the United Kingdom.

The average number of pupils in each form is 16, and there are 26 fully qualified members of teaching staff plus two qualified Nurses, a Cateress, an Estate Manager, Registrar and a Bursar.

Pembroke has an excellent reputation for work, games and activities. The Headmistress's aim is to continue to produce confident, polite boys and girls of upright character who will give of their best in all spheres of life, in school and beyond. This is the best preparation for life.

Peponi House

PO Box 23203, Lower Kabete, Nairobi 00604, Kenya
Tel: 00 254 20 4184998, 4180583, 4183453,
         734881255, 722202947
Fax: 00 254 20 4180159
e-mail: secretary@peponihouseschool.co.ke
website: www.peponihouseschool.co.ke

Headmaster: **R J Blake**, BSc Hons, PGCE, NPQH

Age Range. 6–13.
Number of Pupils. 325 boys and girls, all day.
Fees per annum (2011-2012). Kshs 1,086,000.

Founded in 1986, Peponi House has grown to become one of the leading preparatory schools in East Africa. The attractive and spacious site in Lower Kabete houses all that a thriving prep school requires to get the very best out of the children, both in and out of the classroom.

We are a multi-cultural community which encourages respect for self and others. Our emphasis is on excellence, through a broad, balanced education which aims to maximise the potential of each pupil as a whole person. To this end, we have outstanding facilities including a 25-metre swimming pool, three hard tennis courts, purpose-built Art and Design Technology rooms and networked PCs in all rooms. We have two fully-equipped science laboratories and a new music school is in the process of being built. The school libraries and ICT room occupy an area that is central to the school both geographically and philosophically. These facilities help to complement the excellent work that the children and staff carry out in the well-resourced classrooms. Our extensive use of interactive whiteboards has resulted in the school being elected as a SMART Showcase School.

Whilst always striving for academic excellence, it is central to Peponi's philosophy that education is not limited to the classroom. In addition to the numerous scholarships to senior schools that our pupils have won in the last three years, we have had notable successes in sport, music, art and drama. Peponi teams have won competitions at a national level, with many individuals going on to represent their country.

We follow the British National Curriculum but this is seen very much as a framework for extension. In addition to the core subjects of Literacy, Numeracy, Science and ICT, pupils in the Junior School (Years 2 to 4) also have lessons in Music, PE and Games, Swimming, Art and DT, tennis and, from Year 3, French. Junior children are taught these subjects by specialist teachers while the class teachers deliver the core subjects and humanities. All children are taught in a way that best suits their individual needs and some children do require additional support. This is carried out by our Learning Support teachers who will help children either individually or in small groups. Our special needs teachers also play a vital role in advising colleagues as to the strengths and weaknesses of particular children so that teaching can be differentiated to suit everyone.

In Year 5, children are taught Humanities and English by their form teachers, who also play a vital pastoral role in preparing the children for life in the senior school. In Year 6, all subjects are delivered by subject specialists. The sciences are taught separately and there is an option for children to study Kiswahili, Spanish or Latin.

We also have a wide and varied range of extra-curricular activities. Seniors have activities twice a week and Juniors once a week.

Our music department flourishes and will shortly move into new purpose-built accommodation. In addition to twice-weekly class music lessons, the children have the opportunity to play in the orchestra or in one of the ensembles, or sing in either the Junior or Senior Choir. As well as the two major school concerts during the year, all children have the opportunity to perform in front of their peers and parents at our termly "Tea-Time Concerts". The Christmas and Easter Services are another chance for our choirs to perform and all the children are encouraged to take part in the plays that are staged in December, March and June.

We have children from many different cultures and ethnic backgrounds and we encourage understanding and above all respect for each other. We are a Christian School and the ethos of "Love one another" is a recurring theme in our Thursday services, but we are proud of our multi-faith society where children learn to appreciate and value their differences as well as their similarities.

The school's motto "A School of Many Nations, a Family of One" encapsulates all that we hold most dear. First and foremost, we are a school and the academic side of things lies at the heart of all that we do. However, we are also a family and that makes itself very clear in the day to day life of the school. We have an open door policy with our parents and encourage them to be very active in their support of what we do, either through our energetic PTA or through close consultation with the staff.

At Peponi House, we believe that our role as educators is to give our children the best possible foundation for what lies ahead. We are, after all, a preparatory school and excel-lent preparation is what we set out to achieve. By the time they leave us, our pupils will be confident young adults who are ready to face the future with poise and self-belief.

The Roman Ridge School

No 8 Onyasia Crescent, Roman Ridge, Accra, Ghana
Tel: 00 233 302 780456/780457
Fax: 00 233 302 780458
e-mail: enquiries@theromanridgeschool.com
website: www.theromanridgeschool.com

Postal Address:
PO Box GP 21057, Accra, Ghana

Co-educational Day School.

Governors:
Chairman: Mr Frank B Adu Jnr, BA Hons, MBA
Chair, Academic Board: Dr Joyce Aryee, BA Hons,
    PGCert Public Administration

Principal: Mrs Valerie Mainoo

Age Range. 4–18.
Numbers of Pupils. 230 Boys, 232 Girls.
Fees per term (2010-2011). Junior School (Reception–Class 6): US$1,450; Senior School (Forms 1–5) US$1,750; Sixth Form US$1,850.

Established in September 2002, The Roman Ridge School aims to provide the very best of British Education whilst being firmly rooted in Ghanaian life and culture. The school is a unique facility in Ghana as it offers small class sizes (18), individual pupil attention, a family atmosphere, firm discipline, emphasis on good manners, a sound Christian foundation, a caring environment and a full programme of Sports and extra-curricular activities.

The school is noted for its Special Needs and Individual Learning Programmes as well as its dedication to all other pupils including the high ability learners and scholars. Pupils are carefully monitored and assessed regularly in order to achieve academic success, and, parents are encouraged to help in this process.

All teaching is initially based on the English National Curriculum for the Foundation Course and Key Stage One, after which the pupils progress to the 11+ examination, then take the full range of academic subjects at the 13+ Common Entrance & the IGCSE Courses with the Cambridge Board. The school has begun its A Level programme and offers a comprehensive range of Courses.

There are thirty classrooms at present, three ICT suites, a Multimedia Centre with a Language lab, two up-to-date Libraries with full audio-visual facilities, junior & senior Science Labs, a Dance Studio, a specialised Art Room and a climbing wall. A modern clinic is on site staffed by a qualified SRN.

Pupils play Football, Netball, Hockey, Basketball and Rounders and also enjoy a very successful Swimming programme. Scouting is also provided throughout the school for Beavers (6–8), Wolf Cubs (8–11), Scouts (11–16) and Senior Scouts (16+). Pupils keenly attend visits and trips to various places of interest including the Slave Forts, Game Parks, a jungle canopy walk and the Volta Lake.

At weekends, the school offers a full range of Adventure Activities including Mountain-Biking, Canoeing, Climbing, Hiking, Camping and Orienteering which are all led by fully qualified UK instructors.

During the very full school day the pupils take part in many activities such as Choirs, Music Lessons (Piano and Guitar), Drama, Karate, Traditional Drumming and Dancing, and the school has its own Skittle Alley. School productions and concerts take place at the end of each term.

The school is open on Saturdays for extra work programmes, swimming, games, music lessons, art and computer clubs, and special events.

Pupils thrive in The Roman Ridge School and are reluctant to go home at the end of the day.

St Andrew's Preparatory School

Private Bag, Molo 20106, Kenya
Tel: 020 2025709
           020 722209750
           020 735337736
e-mail: office@turimail.co.ke
website: www.standrewsturi.com

Chair of Governors: Mrs Anne Aliker

Headmaster: Mr Paddy Moss

Age Range. 5–13.
Number of Pupils. 229: 122 Boys, 107 Girls.
Fees per term (2011-2012). Boarding: KSh367,000–KSh427,000.

St Andrew's Preparatory School, Turi, is an international, multicultural, Christian boarding school offering British Curriculum education of the highest standard. The School aims to provide a happy, stimulating, well-rounded educational experience for children. Pupils are encouraged to grow into well-educated, confident, self-disciplined young adults with the potential to be future leaders.

The Prep School together with its Senior School is situated 200 km north west of Nairobi on a beautiful 300-acre estate at an altitude of over 2,000 metres, where the climate is both healthy and invigorating.

Pupils are accepted from the age of 5 and follow the British National Curriculum and then the Common Entrance Syllabus which prepares them for entry to St Andrew's Senior School and to other independent senior schools in Britain or elsewhere.

The original School, founded in 1931, was destroyed by fire in 1944. It was completely rebuilt and is superbly designed and equipped as a modern purpose-built preparatory school. There are subject rooms for English, Mathematics, French, History, Geography and Science laboratories. A special needs teacher gives individual attention to those with learning difficulties in the well-equipped Learning Success Centre. Information Technology is an integral part of the curriculum throughout the School and many classrooms are equipped with interactive white boards and data projectors. An exceptionally large Hall is used for physical education, plays, concerts and large functions. The average size of classes is 14.

Sports form a key part of school life at St Andrew's School. The grounds and playing fields are extensive. Boys play cricket and rugby; girls play rounders and netball; all play football, hockey, tennis and take part in athletics and cross-country. There are seven school tennis courts and a heated swimming pool, as well as a riding school on site where pupils of all abilities are taught by qualified instructors.

The School has a strong musical tradition. In addition to the many and varied opportunities for music within the curriculum over 80 pupils opt for specialist instrumental tuition in a wide range of instruments. Many of these pupils work towards ABRSM examinations. There are also several specialist music groups who practice and perform together and the Junior and Senior choirs.

A large and well-equipped Art Studio as well as Design Technology and Food Technology rooms allow pupils to express themselves creatively. A wealth of arts and crafts, hobbies and outdoor pursuits are actively encouraged. The School has its own Chapel and aims to give a practical Christian education in a community with high standards and in a supportive family atmosphere.

All staff live within the estate. The teaching staff are all qualified and are committed to the Christian ethos of the School.

St Andrew's Senior School offers a three-year course to IGCSE examinations with excellent academic results, and thereafter students can opt for A Levels at the incorporated St Andrew's College. The School has the same Board of Governors, but its own Headmaster, teaching staff and Management Team.

St Catherine's British School

**Leoforos Sofokli Venizelou 77, Lykovrissi, Athens
GR 141 23, Greece**
Tel: 00 30 210 2829 750/1
Fax: 00 30 210 2826 415
e-mail: info@stcatherines.gr
website: www.stcatherines.gr

Chairman of Governing Body: Mr Stavros Taki

Headmaster: Mr Peter Armstrong, MA

Deputy Heads:
Dr S Bond (*Head of Upper School*)
Mrs P Zoulias (*Head of Lower School*)

Age Range. 2½ to 18.
Number of Children. 400 boys, 400 girls (day pupils only).
Fees per annum (2011-2012). Range from €8,050 in the Nursery up to €13,040 for Year 13.

The School was founded in 1956 by the late Sir Charles Peake, British Ambassador at the time in Athens and Lady Catherine Peake. Originally concerned with the education of British and Commonwealth children resident in Greece, it now teaches pupils from 52 nationalities. Priority is given to British and Commonwealth children. The teaching staff of 85, including the Headmaster, are mainly British except for language teachers. The School is administered by a Governing Body of 12 persons selected by the British, Canadian and Australian Ambassadors.

St Catherine's teaches the full programmes of study for the National Curriculum of England and Wales from Foundation Stage through to the end of Key Stage 3. Children are prepared for all types of British and Commonwealth senior education; attention is also given to children who wish to sit Common Entrance Examinations. In Years 10 and 11 (at 14–16 years of age) pupils study for examinations in IGCSE (Cambridge Board). Students in Years 12 and 13 (ages 16–18) undertake the International Baccalaureate Diploma Course. Greek, Latin, French, German and Spanish are offered at various stages. There is a strong tradition of music, drama and dance. In addition to a programme of some 30 extra-curricular activities per week, the school offers The Duke of Edinburgh's International Award Scheme and London Academy of Music and Dramatic Arts (LAMDA) examinations.

The School is situated out of central Athens, near to the elegant northern suburbs of Kifissia and Ekali, in an attractive environment, including sports facilities, courts and a large heated, open-air swimming pool. The grounds and property are entirely owned by the school. Classes are usually over-subscribed and waiting lists exist in most of the lower school classes – early application for places is advised.

Charitable status. St Catherine's British Embassy School is a Registered Charity, number 313909. It aims to provide high-quality education to children from the British,

Commonwealth and International communities resident in Athens.

St Paul's School

Rua Juquiá 166, Jardim Paulistano, CEP 01440-903, São Paulo, Brazil
Tel: 00 55 11 3087 3399
Fax: 00 55 11 3087 3398
e-mail: spshead@stpauls.br
website: www.stpauls.br

Chairman of the Board of Governors: Mr David Bunce

Headmaster: Mr Crispin Rowe, BA

Head of Preparatory School: Ms Siobhain Anita Allum

Head of Pre-Preparatory School: Dr Anne d'Heursel-Baldisseri

Age Range. 3–18.
Number of Pupils. 1,052: Pre-Preparatory 244, Preparatory 388, Senior 420.
Fees per annum (2011-2012). Pre-Prep and Prep School R$46,392 (approx £18,394); Senior School R$59,856 (approx £23,733).

St Paul's School was founded in 1926 and is an independent non-denominational school. It is *the* British School in the São Paulo area, although there are some other English-speaking international schools. St Paul's is situated in the leafy and affluent residential area aptly named *Jardins*.

The Board of Governors is appointed by Trustees of the British Community, and includes parents of current or former pupils, a representative of the British Commonwealth and Community Council, ex-officio members and the Headmaster. Her Majesty's Ambassador to Brazil is the Honorary President. St Paul's is co-educational with a School roll of 1000 pupils from 3 to 18 years old. There are approximately 30 different nationalities in School. The teaching staff totals 140; around 80 are British or Anglo-Brazilians. The aim of the School is to provide an education for British children in São Paulo, Anglo-Brazilians, Brazilians and other nationalities. The curriculum offered in the Pre-Preparatory and Preparatory Schools follows the spirit of the National Curriculum, with pupils sitting Key Stage 2 Examinations before entering the Senior School. Pupils then prepare for IGCSEs in Forms 4 and 5, and the International Baccalaureate Bilingual Diploma Programme in the Sixth Form. Pupils normally go on to universities in the UK and in the United States, as well as to universities in Brazil.

All members of staff are expected to contribute to the Extra-curricular Activities Programme, which includes an extensive range of activities after School. Each part of the School has its own floor in the main building: the Pre-Preparatory School is a self-contained unit on the ground floor, the Preparatory School is situated on the middle floor and the Senior School on the top floor. The general impression when entering the School is that of any other modern British school – it just happens to be in Brazil.

The School has gone through an interesting and challenging period in its development. Classrooms have been refurbished to the highest standards, up to date Science facilities have been installed and the computer provision is complete with over 300 PCs networked on site. The recently refurbished Library has over 32,000 items on its database, and the best selection of magazines and newspapers in town. The School has an impressive Art Centre, a spacious Theatre and Drama Studio, Music rooms, excellent Sports facilities as well as underground parking. New Dining facilities, a Sixth Form Centre and a Chapel were inaugurated in May 2001. Air conditioning was installed throughout the main teaching block in 2007.

The School is a busy, hardworking place and standards are high. In 1995 the School underwent a full HMC Inspection, the first overseas school so to do, and emerged with great credit. A second full inspection took place in 1999; again there was much praise. A further inspection, by members of South America's Latin American Heads' Conference (LAHC), took place in April 2007. Once again, the school was warmly commended. St Paul's School is seen as one of the foremost academic establishments in Latin America, capable of holding its own with the best in the UK.

St Saviour's School, Ikoyi
Lagos, Nigeria

54 Alexander Avenue, Ikoyi, Lagos, Nigeria
Tel: 00 234 1 8990153
Fax: 00 234 1 2700255
e-mail: info@stsavioursschikoyi.org
website: www.stsavioursschikoyi.org

Chairman of Board of Trustees: Mr L N Mbanefo, SAN

Head Teacher: Ms A Tempest, CertEd, BEd, MEd

Age Range. 4–11 Co-educational.
Number of Pupils. 320.
Fees per term (2008-2009). Naira 350,000.

A truly rounded education is a preparation for life. Grounded on our core values, St Saviour's seeks to provide an education that is challenging, relevant, exciting and delivered in a caring and thoroughly professional manner. We look, unashamedly, for academic achievement in each pupil alongside equal progress in spiritual growth, friendship, independence, confidence and some appreciation of their place in the world and their responsibilities towards others.

Christian principles are integrated into the daily life of the school which is an Anglican foundation. Children of a number of denominations and faiths attend the school and are warmly welcomed. Parents are welcomed as part of the learning cycle; communication with them is regular and their support of the school is exceptional.

The school follows the English National Curriculum, integrates elements of our equatorial location into our curriculum and is excellently resourced. Currently, SATs are taken at Y2 and Y6. ICT facilities are outstanding and enhance the process of learning throughout the school on a daily basis. A mix of Class Teachers and Subject Teachers deliver an exciting and challenging programme every day. There are 7 Nigerian and 7 expatriate Class Teachers in our two-form entry, Reception / Foundation 2 – Y6.

The school has developed and renewed its own sports facilities over the past few years and now has its own 25m swimming pool and extensive sports field, including football pitch and running track as well as informal play areas. Routinely, about 30 extra-curricular Clubs operate after school each week and they are very well supported. Events such as Assemblies, Independence Day, Foundation, KS1 and KS2 Productions, Sports Day, International Week, Flower Show, Fun Day and Harvest Festival add greatly to the school's character. Our support of local orphanages flows from monies raised at some of these events.

Pupils leave the school from Y6 to leading Secondary schools in Lagos and Nigeria. About 20% leave to attend outstanding independent schools in the UK, where they prove to be excellent ambassadors of the holistic education they have received at St Saviour's.

PART V
Schools whose Heads are members of the Independent Schools Association

ALPHABETICAL LIST OF SCHOOLS

The following school, whose Head is a member of both ISA and HMC, can be found in the HMC section:

The Grange School

The following schools, whose Heads are members of both ISA and GSA, can be found in the GSA section:

Alderley Edge School for Girls	St Dominic's High School for Girls
Dodderhill School	St Dominic's Priory School
Highclare School	St James Senior Girls' School
Hollygirt School	St Margaret's School
St Catherine's School, Twickenham	St Martha's

The following schools, whose Heads are members of both ISA and SHMIS, can be found in the SHMIS section:

Abbey Gate College	Our Lady of Sion School
Bedstone College	Pitsford School
Bournemouth Collegiate School	Portland Place School
d'Overbroeck's College	Princethorpe College
Halliford School	St Edward's School
Hull Collegiate School	St James Senior Boys' School
LVS Ascot (The Licensed Victuallers' School)	Stafford Grammar School
North Cestrian Grammar School	Tring Park School for the Performing Arts

The following schools, whose Heads are members of both ISA and IAPS, can be found in the IAPS section:

Abercorn School	Pilgrims Pre-Preparatory School
Alleyn Court Preparatory School	Reddiford School
Gatehouse School	Rosemead Preparatory School
Gateway School	St Edward's Junior School
Hatherop Castle Preparatory School	Shrewsbury Lodge School
Leehurst Swan School	The Study Preparatory School
Littlegarth School	Wilmslow Preparatory School

GEOGRAPHICAL LIST OF ISA SCHOOLS

Individual School Entries

Abbey College Manchester
Alpha Plus Group

5–7 Cheapside, King Street, Manchester M2 4WG
Tel: 0161 817 2700
Fax: 0161 817 2705
e-mail: admin@abbeymanchester.co.uk
website: www.abbeymanchester.co.uk

Principal: **Ms L Elam**

Age Range. 15–18.
Number of Pupils. 225.
GCSEs, A Levels and One Year Retakes
An independent school with a college environment
* Year 11, Lower Sixth and Upper Sixth entry
* Very small classes (an average 7 students in each) ensure excellent progress
* Unique one year GCSEs and A Levels for those sitting for the first time or retaking
* High levels of personal support and individual responsibility gives good preparation for university life
* Expert advice is delivered for entry onto all university courses leading to strong relationships with the top universities in Britain
* City centre location means students benefit from the unlimited arts, business, science, sports and music resources on offer

Flexible learning programmes mean that students can join at any time during the academic year, not just September.
Fees per annum (2011-2012). GCSE/A Level Two Year course: £10,800. One Year GCSE Retake/Year 11 Transfer course: £9,990 (6-9 subjects), £2,160 (1-4 subjects). One Year A Level Retake course: £5,350 (1 subject), £10,000 (2 subjects), £14,500 (3 subjects).

Abbey Gate School

Clare Avenue, Hoole, Chester CH2 3HR
Tel: 01244 319649
e-mail: abbeygateschool@talk21.com
          headteacher.abbeygateschool@live.co.uk
website: www.abbeygateschool.org.uk

Head: **Mrs S M Fisher**, CertEd Birmingham

Age Range. 3–11.
Number in School. Day: 77 Boys and Girls.
Fees per term (2010-2011). £1,950–£2,100.
Abbey Gate School, founded in 1910, is a small, caring Christian community, comprising around 80 children and a dedicated, well-qualified staff. The pastoral care of children is a priority.

It offers a broad and well-balanced curriculum and has a proven tradition of academic success both locally and nationally, as well as a growing reputation for excellence in the performing arts. Tuition is offered in a variety of musical instruments and in speech & drama and dance. Some scholarships and bursaries are available.

Specialist help is available for children with specific learning difficulties.

Extra-curricular activities include chess, Scottish country dancing, ballet, modern dance, a variety of sports, recorder consorts, choir and orchestra, and ICT clubs.

A forward-looking school, it aims to create exciting and challenging opportunities to develop academic, creative and physical skills, to produce confident and self-disciplined young people of the future. Excellent links have been established with the local community and with other schools in the area, both independent and maintained.

School opens at 8 am and has an After-School Club until 6 pm each day. A thriving holiday club operates throughout most holiday periods.

Abbotsford Preparatory School
GEMS Education

211 Flixton Road, Urmston, Manchester M41 5PR
Tel: 0161 748 3261
Fax: 0161 746 7961
e-mail: pshiels@abbotsford-prep.trafford.sch.uk
          secretary@abbotsford-prep.trafford.sch.uk
website: www.abbotsfordprepschool.co.uk

Head: **Mrs P Shiels**

Age Range. 4 months to 11 years.
Number in School. Day: 44 Boys, 50 Girls.
Fees per term (2011-2012). £1,450–£1,953.
Established one hundred years ago, this school sends children to State Grammar schools as well as the major Independent schools in the North West. Although the success rate is exceptionally high, children are not crammed but encouraged to achieve their full potential and leave us as pleasant, confident, well-rounded individuals.

The school is a well-equipped building, with specialist areas for Science, Art/Technology and Information Technology, which are second-to-none for this age group. The new, fully-enclosed outdoor multi-purpose hard area has been greatly enhanced with an astroturf surface and the school also has a large indoor sports hall.

Children may start at 4 months old, part-time or full-time, in our newly opened 24-place nursery. It is fully equipped and run by well-qualified staff. Children have the option of remaining in the nursery until school age or moving into our Pre-School at 3 years of age. All children from Pre-School upwards use the computer suite and learn a foreign language.

In the main school, besides the full range of primary subjects there is a range of extra-curricular activities, which include sport, drama, music, art and wildlife. The curriculum is enhanced and supported through regular trips. All KS2 children are offered the opportunity to take part in annual Adventure Holidays. Staff take great pride in the standard of the children who leave the school.

In our last ISI Inspection we were rated 'Outstanding' in all areas. You may read the full report on our website.

Abingdon House School
Alpha Plus Group

Broadley Terrace, London NW1 6LG
Tel: 0845 2300426
Fax: 020 7361 0751

e-mail: ahs@abingdonhouseschool.co.uk
website: www.abingdonhouseschool.co.uk

Headmaster: **Mr N J Rees**, NPQH, MA, PGCE, DipRSASpLD

Age Range. 5–13 Co-educational.
Number of Pupils. 50.
Fees per term (2011–2012). £8,295.

In September 2011 the school relocated to a refurbished Victorian school in London NW1 on four levels with facilities to educate 90 pupils aged between 5–13 years of age.

Abingdon House School provides a whole-school approach for pupils who are diagnosed with a specific learning difficulty early in their education and who would respond well to intense intervention for a period of time.

Pupils with 'disabilities', such as dyslexia, dyspraxia, speech and language delays, and social and communication difficulties, ADD/ADHD, are admitted. Suitability of children for admission is determined by multi-disciplinary screening conducted over two days and the receipt of assessment reports. Pupils may join the school at any stage if a place is available.

Our teaching environment is based on understanding a child's individual needs, nurturing a child's academic and social development and caring for a child's well-being. The environment is therefore warm and friendly and we are committed to every child.

We aim to prepare the children for a return to mainstream schooling through: the provision of a holistic and individually tailored education programme, a whole-school teaching regime of small classes with teaching assistants, therapists and trained staff using a range of teaching strategies and by maintaining an appropriately low pupil to teacher ratio. A number of pupils have integrated successfully into a number of London day schools.

Each pupil has an IEP (Individual Education Plan). Each target aims to be SMART (a specific, measurable, achievable, realistic target).

The change in the pupil's self-esteem is marked and almost immediate. A Prize Giving is held each term so that pupils are given the opportunity for their efforts and achievements to be recognised and celebrated on a regular basis.

We offer a full curriculum. PE/Games take place on a weekly basis at school or in Holland Park. Reading, Literacy and Maths lessons are ability grouped to enable pupils to progress as soon as they are ready. After-school clubs are offered twice a week.

Home/School Diaries form an important link between home and school. We value teamwork and the partnership between parents and staff.

ACS Cobham International School

Heywood, Portsmouth Road, Cobham, Surrey KT11 1BL
Tel: 01932 867251
Fax: 01932 869789
e-mail: CobhamAdmissions@acs-schools.com
website: www.acs-schools.com

Head: **Thomas Lehman**

Age Range. 2–18.
Number in School. Day: 771 Boys, 598 Girls; 96 Boarders.
Tuition Fees (2011–2012) per semester (2 semesters). £3,175–£10,410.

Boarding Fees (2011–2012) per semester (2 semesters). In addition to tuition fees: 7 day £7,810 (grades 7–13); 5 day £5,705 (grades 7–13).

Founded in 1967 to serve the needs of international and local families, ACS International Schools now educates 2,600 students aged between 2 and 18, from more than 70 countries, at three London area campuses in England. All our schools are non-sectarian and co-educational.

The success of the programme at ACS Cobham is based on teamwork, collaboration, and the broad participation of its international community. All students are treated as unique individuals, with equal potential to make a positive contribution to the school. The goal is to instill an enthusiasm for lifelong learning and a sense of global awareness in each student, along with the necessary skills to prepare them for the challenges and changes which lie ahead.

The academic programme offers both the International Baccalaureate (IB) Diploma and Advanced Placement (AP) courses, creating a curriculum that meets the needs of a broad international student body. ACS graduates have established a tradition of attaining excellent exam results, enabling them to continue their studies at top universities around the world, including the US and UK.

Situated on 128 acres approximately 30 minutes by train from Central London, ACS Cobham enrolls over 1,300 students. Exceptional facilities include an Early Childhood village; purpose-built Lower, Middle, and High School buildings; gymnasium and cafeteria complex and a Dormitory. All Lower, Middle and High School buildings have separate classrooms, science labs, libraries, computer labs, art and music studios and an Interactive Learning Centre.

ACS Cobham offers extensive and varied extracurricular clubs and community service activities both locally and internationally, which encourage students to participate in the richness of school life. Students also participate in international theatre arts programmes, maths, literature and music competitions in the UK and across Europe.

The campus sports programme runs three seasons fielding teams in soccer, volleyball, cross-country, basketball, rugby, swimming, dance, tennis, track & field, baseball, softball and golf. Sports facilities include six tennis courts, an Olympic-sized track, playing fields for soccer, rugby and baseball, a six-hole golf course, and a state-of-the-art Sports Centre with 25-metre competition indoor swimming pool, basketball/volleyball show courts, dance and fitness studios, and a café.

The Dormitory provides a home-away-from-home for 110 students, aged 12–18. Boarders share ergonomically designed two-person rooms with ensuite facilities and internet connections; there are student lounges, kitchens, computer and study rooms. Six full-time Dormitory houseparents and over ten resident teaching staff ensure an active yet well-considered programme of pastoral care, friendship and advisor groups, house activities and weekend trips.

The admissions team is available throughout the year to answer questions, book campus visits, and assist families through the enrolment process. Students are accepted in all grades throughout the year.

ACS Egham International School

Woodlee, London Road (A30), Egham, Surrey TW20 0HS
Tel: 01784 430800
Fax: 01784 430626
e-mail: EghamAdmissions@acs-schools.com
website: www.acs-schools.com

Head of School: **Mr Jeremy Lewis**

Age Range. 2–18.
Number in School. Day only: 324 Boys, 292 Girls.
Tuition Fees (2011-2012) per semester (2 semesters).
£3,130–£9,995.

Founded in 1967 to serve the needs of international and local families, ACS International Schools now educates 2,600 students aged between 2 and 18, from more than 70 countries, at three London area campuses in England. All our schools are non-sectarian and co-educational.

ACS Egham offers all three International Baccalaureate (IB) programmes – the IB Primary Years Programme (3–11), the IB Middle Years Programme (11–16) and the IB Diploma Programme (16–18). These programmes share a common philosophy and common characteristics: they develop the whole student, helping them to grow socially, physically, aesthetically, and culturally; and provide a broad and balanced education that includes science and the humanities, languages and mathematics, technology, physical education, and the arts.

This academic programme challenges students to fulfil their potential, and offers a broad-based selection of courses and levels to meet individual needs and interests. An important characteristic of ACS Egham is individual attention to students' needs facilitated by an exceptionally well-qualified, experienced, and sympathetic faculty; many of whom are IB examiners, moderators, and teacher trainers. The success of our programme is reflected in our IB Diploma pass rate over the last six years, which has enabled our graduates to continue their studies at top universities around the world, including the US and UK.

Situated on a 20-acre campus approximately 25 miles from central London, ACS Egham enrols more than 600 students. The school has purpose-built computer labs, libraries, spacious classrooms, playgrounds and sports fields. To further enhance the teaching programme there is a 21st century Visual Arts & Design Technology Centre and a new Science wing.

ACS Egham runs small class sizes which afford a greater opportunity for individual attention and support for various learning styles so that students are encouraged and challenged accordingly. Child Study Teams meet with individual student's teachers, administrators and parents, to ensure that every child is appropriately challenged and supported. A Language Coordinator assists families in organising native language lessons after-school or, if possible, during the school day.

ACS Egham offers extensive and varied extracurricular clubs and community service activities both locally and internationally, which encourage students to participate in the richness of school life. Students also participate in international theatre arts programmes, maths, literature and music competitions in the UK and across Europe. The Campus sports programme runs three seasons fielding teams in soccer, volleyball, cross-country, basketball, rugby, swimming, dance, tennis, track & field, baseball, softball and golf.

The admissions team is available throughout the year to answer questions, book campus visits, and assist families through the enrolment process. Students are accepted in all grades throughout the year.

ACS Hillingdon International School

Hillingdon Court, 108 Vine Lane, Hillingdon, Middlesex UB10 0BE
Tel: 01895 259771
Fax: 01895 818404
e-mail: HillingdonAdmissions@acs-schools.com
website: www.acs-schools.com

Head of School: **Ginger G Apple**

Age Range. 4–18.
Number in School. Day only: 329 Boys, 286 Girls.
Tuition Fees (2011-2012) per semester (2 semesters).
£4,585–£9,745.

Founded in 1967 to serve the needs of international and local families, ACS International Schools now educates 2,600 students aged between 2 and 18, from more than 70 countries, at three London area campuses in England. All our schools are non-sectarian and co-educational.

The ACS Hillingdon philosophy:

- encourages a positive attitude toward education and life-long learning
- provides meaningful educational experiences that enable students to acquire and apply knowledge, concepts, and skills
- helps each student realise his/her academic, creative, and physical potential
- provides opportunities for students to understand, appreciate, and develop sensitivity for other cultures
- encourages participation in community service, and support of local and international charities
- promotes a partnership with parents to meet the needs of students, and offer programmes that addresses issues associated with a highly mobile population
- promotes students to become lifelong learners in a global community

The academic programme offers both the International Baccalaureate (IB) Diploma and Advanced Placement (AP) courses, creating a curriculum that meets the needs of our entire international student body. IB scores rank it among the highest achieving schools in the UK, enabling graduates to continue their studies at top universities around the world, including the US and UK.

The campus is situated on an 11-acre estate less than 15 miles from central London. A door-to-door busing service covers much of London. ACS Hillingdon accepts over 600 students aged between 4 and 18. The campus combines Grade II listed stately mansion with a modern wing housing classrooms, computer labs, an integrated IT network, libraries, cafeteria, gymnasium, auditorium, and the Harmony House Centre for international music which houses a digital recording studio, rehearsal rooms, practice studios and a computer lab for music technology.

The campus has on-site playing fields, tennis courts and playgrounds, and off-site playing fields for soccer, rugby and track. Local swimming and golf facilities are also used by our students. The sports programme runs three seasons fielding teams in soccer, volleyball, cross-country, basketball, rugby, swimming, dance, tennis, track & field, baseball, softball and golf.

ACS Hillingdon also offers extensive and varied extracurricular clubs and community service activities both locally and internationally, which encourage students to participate in the richness of school life. Students also participate in international theatre arts programmes, maths, literature and music competitions in the UK and across Europe.

The admissions team is available throughout the year to answer questions, book campus visits, and assist families through the enrolment process. Students are accepted in all grades throughout the year.

Adcote School

Little Ness, Shrewsbury, Shropshire SY4 2JY
Tel: 01939 260202
Fax: 01939 261300
e-mail: secretary@adcoteschool.co.uk
website: www.adcoteschool.co.uk

Chairman of Board of Governors: Mr T Morris, BSc

Headmaster: **Mr G Wright**, BA, MA, PGCE, NPQH

Age Range. 4–18.

Number in School. 170 Girls.

Occupying a distinguished country house designed by Norman Shaw RA in 1879 and set in 27 acres of landscaped parkland, Adcote is a thriving day and boarding school for girls aged 11–18 with a Junior School for girls aged 4–11. There is also a Montessori nursery on site, "Happy Faces", with c 70 pupils enrolled.

Curriculum. Experienced and dedicated teaching professionals are the essence of Adcote's success. Small class sizes make individual attention a reality. Specialist learning support is always available and similarly, expertise in challenging the gifted and talented pupils ensures that all the girls fulfil and exceed their potential in at least one field of study. Perhaps Adcote's greatest achievement is the variety and breadth of education that it provides for its pupils. Adcote produces confident, enquiring and well-rounded girls who are equipped to play full and constructive roles in an ever-changing society.

Performing Arts. The School places great emphasis on Music, Dance, and Drama as well as a range of other activities. All the performing arts are included in the core curriculum to age 14, and thereafter voluntarily. Instrumental playing is much encouraged, and there are extra-curricular workshops in dance and drama, and performances several times a year.

Activities. All girls participate in a wide range of activities, including rowing, trampolining, Chinese language and culture, gardening and horse riding. Sport plays an important part in the life of the school. The school regularly plays hockey, netball, rounders and tennis, with gymnastics being particularly strong. Outward bound programmes also play an important part of life at Adcote, as do interesting weekend activities, and trips away from school. There is an interesting programme of weekly activities for boarding students.

Pastoral Care. Despite its imposing exterior, Adcote is proud of its welcoming, friendly and unpretentious reputation. The school's size means that the children, staff and parents really get to know each other. There is a tangible sense of community, creating a warm and enabling atmosphere. Boarders are looked after by the Housemistress and her resident staff, and all girls have a personal tutor, responsible for individual welfare and academic progress. Great importance is attached to understanding the individual and developing personal abilities so that girls meet the demands of the modern world with confidence and good judgement.

Fees per term (2011-2012). Day Girls: £1,428–£4,105; Weekly Boarders: £4,640–£6,657; Full Boarders: £5,276–£7,287.

Reductions are made in fees of second and subsequent sisters. Bursaries are available for children from the clergy or from Forces families. There are scholarships for academic excellence. The School welcomes applications from girls whose parents cannot afford the fees in full or in part. In line with our aim as a Charity to provide public benefit the school offers means-tested bursaries to outstanding pupils who would not otherwise be able to benefit from the education we provide. The School offers a wide range of discretionary and means-tested bursaries each year to pupils.

A prospectus and further details may be obtained from the Admissions Secretary: admissions@adcoteschool.co.uk.

Charitable status. Adcote School Educational Trust Limited is a Registered Charity, number 528407.

Alton Convent School

Anstey Lane, Alton, Hampshire GU34 2NG
Tel: 01420 82070
Fax: 01420 541711
e-mail: enquiries@altonconvent.org.uk
website: www.altonconvent.org.uk

Motto: *Vita dulcedo spes nostra salve*

Chairman of Governors: Mr Kevin Ryan

Headmistress: **Mrs S E Kirkham**, BA Hons, MA

Age Range. Girls 3–18, Boys 3–11. The Garden House Nursery: Girls and Boys 6 months – 3 years.

Number in School. Day: Girls 438 Boys 102.

Fees per term (2011-2012). Preparatory £3,005, Senior School £3,600. Nursery (daily charge): 6 months–2 years £52.50; 2–3 years £55.50; 3+ £67 (EYE grants applicable).

Alton Convent School, situated in north east Hampshire, is an independent Catholic day school welcoming pupils from all faiths. It has a stimulating, friendly community promoting mutual tolerance, courtesy, care for others, a sense of self worth and personal discipline. Inspectors recently noted that pupils' personal development is excellent and a strength of the school, enhanced by excellent pastoral care integral to the school's ethos. Pupils are happy, confident, courteous and articulate. There is excellence of pupils' achievements, learning, attitudes and basic skills. High standards are fostered by good quality teaching, excellent monitoring and a changing, varied curriculum. Visitors comment on the calm, happy, purposeful working environment.

The Garden House Nursery, a purpose-built facility, is open 51 weeks a year from 8.00 am to 6.00 pm. It takes babies from 6 months and EYE grants are applicable. The quality of provision is rated as 'outstanding'.

Entry at the beginning of the prep school is non-selective but entry to the senior school is by entrance examination taken in January for September entry. Whilst academically selective, we seek to admit pupils in sympathy with our ethos who will flourish in our community. The curriculum is broad and balanced for all ages with a wide range of science, sports, languages, and expressive arts. Academic standards are high, with pupils encouraged to think for themselves and take responsibility for their own development. Boys and girls are prepared for entry into their senior schools. Senior girls take an average ten GCSEs and continue to A Level in our Sixth Form, selecting five AS subjects with three or four subjects continued to A2 Level.

Inspectors recently affirmed that A Level performance is impressive and above the national average for girls in maintained and selective schools for the last three years, and results at GCSE are also well above national averages. Girls progress to prestigious universities.

Co-curricular activities include a wide range of competitive sporting opportunities, artistic activities and study workshops. Musical and dramatic opportunities are strong in both schools, with thriving choirs, orchestras, ensembles, jazz group and drama productions. All pupils are encouraged to become involved in the major music and drama productions: additional tuition in sport, dance, and music is offered. Art is strong and has been recognised nationally in various awards. The school has retained its Gold status for the Artsmark Award marking the high expectations and provision offered in the school.

Parents have regular opportunities for consultation with staff. Open Mornings, newsletters and the school website keep parents up to date. The school is noted as having a clear vision for the future.

A range of school scholarships and means-tested bursaries are available in Years 3, 7 and 12.

Charitable status. The Alton Convent School Charity is a Registered Charity, number 1071684.

Argyle House School

19/20 Thornhill Park, Tunstall Road, Sunderland, Tyne & Wear SR2 7LA
Tel: 0191 510 0726
Fax: 0191 567 2209
e-mail: info@argylehouseschool.co.uk
website: www.argylehouseschool.co.uk

Head: **Mr C Johnson**

Age Range. 2½–16.
Number in School. 210 Boys and Girls.
Fees per term (2011–2012). £1,850–£2,240.

Argyle House School was established in 1884 as a small independent day school for boys and girls, situated in the centre of Sunderland. Students travel from all parts of the region, by our buses, or local forms of transport. The school has maintained its high standards of academic achievement, whilst catering for a wide variety of abilities.

At Argyle House, we believe in the individual, and work with him or her to enable the achievement of each student's potential. This is due to attention to detail by fully qualified and dedicated staff, who help to mould the individual into a well-mannered and accomplished young individual, who will be able to meet future challenges.

Small class sizes and a friendly environment facilitate learning, but not all work is academic, as the school takes an active part in many sporting leagues, both within the school, and locally with other schools. We aim to offer all the facilities of a much larger school, whilst remaining at present student levels to keep the intimacy and friendliness of a smaller school, for both parents and students.

Arts Educational Schools London

Cone Ripman House, 14 Bath Road, Chiswick, London W4 1LY
Tel: 020 8987 6600
Fax: 020 8987 6601
e-mail: pupils@artsed.co.uk
website: www.artsed.co.uk

Founded in 1919.

Interim Headmaster: **Mr Greg Beavis**

Age Range. 11–18 Co-educational.
Number in School. Day: 114 Girls, 41 Boys.
Fees per term (2011–2012). £3,830.

"The UK's Leading Specialist Performing Arts Institution in Academic Achievement" Sunday Times, Parent Power 2007.

100% A Level Pass Rate and outstanding GCSE results.

The Arts Educational Schools London are committed to developing to the full the potential of each and every pupil. High quality vocational, academic and social education, in a warm, friendly, caring environment, ensures that our pupils feel challenged and fulfilled throughout the whole of their exciting careers at the school.

The school has been educating young performing artists since 1919, and there is no comparable school in the UK. Dancers learn to act and sing, actors learn to sing and dance, musicians learn to do more than play their instruments well, and everyone has the opportunity to be grounded in the visual arts, languages, humanities, sciences, and mathematics.

From Year 7 all pupils follow a course leading to eight or nine GCSEs. All pupils have access to the outstanding performance facilities, rehearsal rooms, proscenium and studio theatres. At Year 12 pupils follow a course of four AS Levels, leading to three or four A Levels, whilst receiving outstanding training in dance, drama, music and musical theatre.

In addition, students in Year 12 can opt to take a BTEC in Musical Theatre, using all the expertise and excellence of the professional Musical Theatre Department with the academic reputation and pastoral guidance of the Secondary School. It aims to develop skills in Dance, Singing and Acting so that students start to develop a foundation as a 'triple threat performer' as well as continuing with academic studies to A Level standard.

Former Students of the schools include: Julie Andrews, Samantha Barks, Sarah Brightman, Darcey Bussell, Martin Clunes, Joan Collins, Adam Cooper, Bonnie Langford, Jane Seymour, Hugo Speer, Summer Strallen and Will Young.

Admission is at 11+ and 16+ and occasionally at other ages if places become available.

Charitable status. The Arts Educational Schools is a Registered Charity, number 311087. It exists solely for educational purposes.

Ashton House School

50–52 Eversley Crescent, Isleworth, Middlesex TW7 4LW
Tel: 020 8560 3902
Fax: 020 8568 1097
e-mail: principal@ashtonhouse.com
website: www.ashtonhouse.com

Principal: **Mr S J Turner**, BSc

Head Teacher: **Mrs M Grundberg**, MA, PGCE

Age Range. 3–11.
Number in School. Day: 70 Boys, 75 Girls.
Fees per term (2011–2012). £2,162–£2,996.75.

Founded 1930. Proprietors P A, G B & S J Turner. Entry by interview and assessment. Prospectus on request.

Modern and traditional methods combined ensure that a firm foundation in basic skills is gained within the Infant Department with which to undertake confidently the widening Junior curriculum.

Specialist teaching throughout the school in Music, Information Computer Technology, Physical Education and French are major strengths. Peripatetic music by arrangement in seven instruments.

Sports: netball, rounders, football, cricket, swimming, hockey and basketball.

Excellent record of examinations success for entry to top Independent Day Schools.

Ayscoughfee Hall School

Welland Hall, London Road, Spalding, Lincs PE11 2TE
Tel: 01775 724733
Fax: 01775 769669
e-mail: admin@ahs.me.uk
website: www.ahs.me.uk

Head: **Mr B G Chittick**, MA, BEd

Age Range. 3½–11 co-educational.
Number of Pupils. 146 Day Pupils: 71 Boys, 75 Girls.
Fees per term (2011-2012). £1,460–£1,840.

Founded in 1920, Ayscoughfee Hall School is centred around a beautiful Georgian family home. A purpose-built extension complements the already spacious accommodation. The School houses a Kindergarten, Infant and Junior Departments and has further developed its facilities to include enlarged classrooms, a dedicated Science/Art Room, a Music Department, changing facilities for PE and Games and a Foreign Language Room.

The guidelines and principles of the National Curriculum are followed in all subjects but go far beyond the basic requirements in order to give each child a broader, more varied understanding. Academic standards are high and progress is well monitored throughout the school. The vast majority of pupils are successful in the Lincolnshire County Council selection examination and progress to secondary selective school education very well equipped to tackle all subjects. The curriculum is continually reviewed and upgraded if necessary with advice from the subject coordinators.

Computers are routinely used in every classroom and pupils receive weekly, dedicated ICT tuition in our up-to-date ICT suite. Interactive whiteboards are also used as a teaching aid throughout the school.

The School excels with its music and drama productions over the academic year, in which all children perform in front of their parents and guests.

French is taught from Reception Class, whilst Russian is offered as after-school tuition.

The school competes successfully in local and regional sports activities, including football, rugby, hockey, netball, cross-country and athletics.

There is a thriving programme of extra-curricular activities, including sport, drama, cookery, poetry, textiles, choir, instrumental groups and ICT. A wide variety of educational visits is offered, with the older children having the opportunity to participate in alternate foreign and activity holidays, accompanied by the staff. Furthermore, regular visits by professional groups and individuals take place in school.

As a small school with classes limited to 20, we aim to provide a happy and caring environment where the individual child may flourish. We are proud of our academic standards but we also strive to give a broad and balanced education. Above all, we want our boys and girls to use and develop their different gifts and to enjoy the success this brings.

Charitable status. Ayscoughfee Hall School Limited is a Registered Charity, number 527294. It exists to provide education for boys and girls.

Babington House School

Grange Drive, Chislehurst, Kent BR7 5ES
Tel: 020 8467 5537
Fax: 020 8295 1175
e-mail: enquiries@babingtonhouse.com
website: www.babingtonhouse.com

Headmistress: **Mrs D Odysseas-Bailey**, BA Hons, PGCE

Age Range. Boys 3–7+, Girls 3–16.
Number in School. Day: 68 Boys, 196 Girls.
Fees per term (2011-2012). £1,300–£4,390.

A day school that is frequently No. 1 in the London Borough of Bromley league tables. Praised by the ISI for achieving outstanding academic success at all key stages and providing exemplary pastoral care. The school has a friendly atmosphere, set in a pleasant suburban area. Full range of courses for examinations at all levels. Most boys

transfer to selective independent schools. Schools Curriculum Award. ISA Excellence Award. Investors in People fourth exemplary reaccreditation. "Outstanding" in all areas of school (ISI report November 2010).

Specialist facilities for Computing – Information Technology, Music, Art, Business & Communications, and Textiles.

Small classes: Maximum size 20 pupils. Careers guidance by specialists.

Wide range of sports (Athletics, Swimming, Tennis, Netball, Gymnastics, Trampoline, Table Tennis and access to fitness centre in Senior School) and extra-curricular activities (Drama, gym club, choir, ballet, tap, funky street dance, clay modelling, golf, yoga, elocution and instrumental tuition).

Charitable status. Babington House School is a Registered Charity, number 307914. It exists to provide exemplary education.

Beech Hall School

Tytherington, Macclesfield, Cheshire SK10 2EG
Tel: 01625 422192
Fax: 01625 502424
e-mail: secretary@beechhallschool.freeserve.co.uk
website: www.beechhallschool.org

Chairman of Board of Governors: Mr E McGrath

Head: **Ms G Yandell**

Age Range. 6 months–16 years.
Number of Pupils. 241.
Fees per term (2010-2011). Infants £2,095, Transition £2,490, Junior School £2,920, Senior School £2,980. Lunches and snacks are a compulsory extra charged at £150 per term.

Kindergarten, Infant, Junior and Senior departments offer education between 8.30 am and 4.00 pm with further supervised sporting and leisure activities available until 5.00 pm. If required, there is supervised care up until 6.00 pm for all children.

Beech Hall is a co-educational Day school situated in spacious and attractive grounds with extensive playing fields, a heated outdoor swimming pool and many other facilities.

Boys and girls are prepared for entry to a wide variety of Independent Schools and local Independent Day Schools. Classes are kept small – the school has a maximum class size policy of 20 pupils – making individual attention possible in every lesson.

There is a very popular Kindergarten and Reception department, consisting of children between the ages of 6 months and 6 years under the care of their own specialist teachers. These classes were started with the objective of giving boys and girls a good grounding in reading, writing and arithmetic.

Beech Hall aims to provide a sound all-round education and children are encouraged to sit for academic, music and art scholarships. There is a school choir, a high standard of drama and the children produce their own school magazine.

Rugby, Association football, hockey and netball are played in the winter terms. The school also has a good cross-country course. In the summer, cricket, athletics, rounders and tennis. Swimming is taught throughout the year. Other activities include squash, badminton and ju-jitsu.

The school is situated off the main Stockport–Macclesfield road, within easy reach of Manchester International Airport and the M6 and M62 motorways.

Further details and illustrated prospectus are obtainable from the school or via the school's website.

Charitable status. Beech Hall School Trust Limited is a Registered Charity, number 525922. It exists to provide education for boys and girls.

Beech House School

184 Manchester Road, Rochdale, Lancashire OL11 4JQ
Tel: 01706 646309
e-mail: info@beechhouseschool.co.uk
website: www.beechhouseschool.co.uk

Headmaster: **Mr Kevin Sartain**, BSc Hons, PGCE, Dip Spo Psy, CBiol, FIBiol

Age Range. 2–16 Co-educational.
Number of Pupils. 259.
Fees per term (2011-2012). £825–£1,754.
The school is a wholly independent co-educational day school for boys and girls aged 2 to 16 years. Founded in 1922, it comprises a Lower Preparatory Department for children aged 2 to 6 years, and an Upper Preparatory Department for children aged 7 to 11 years and a Senior Department for those aged 11 to 16 years based at Manchester Road.

The aim of the school is to blend the best of traditional education with the skills and resources of the modern system to ensure that pupils' talents are exercised to the full. To this end, class sizes are kept small, with 20 or fewer pupils per form at preparatory level and 16 or fewer in each secondary class. The school upholds traditional values and behaviour, providing a secure, caring and academically challenging environment. This gives Beech House its unique character as a 'family-centred school'.

The Lower Preparatory Department is an integral part of the main school but is housed in its own self-contained unit at Broadfield Stile. It overlooks the delightful gardens and open play area of Broadfield Park. Pupils are admitted to the Nursery during the course of the term in which they attain the age of three. It is usual then for natural progression to take place through the rest of the school in line with age and ability.

The Upper Preparatory and Senior Departments enjoy the benefit of two Science Laboratories and pupils from the age of seven years and upwards spend time each week in this specialist facility under the direction and guidance of fully-qualified Science teachers. The school also has its own Lending, Reference and Careers Libraries as well as Art and Design, Information and Communication Technology and Craft, Design and Technology facilities, which allow pupils to work with a variety of materials including electronics and textiles. A new music room and Sports Hall have just opened. The school has its own sports field. These facilities have been installed to provide opportunities for developing skills relevant to modern life and all pupils enjoy 'hands on' experience.

The curriculum is designed to flow from the grounding in the Nursery Department through to the upper sections of the school, culminating in external examinations at 16 years of age. Some pupils are not necessarily set by their chronological age and are fast tracked. These pupils are allowed to sit their external examinations early.

Bishop Challoner School

228 Bromley Road, Shortlands, Bromley, Kent BR2 0BS
Tel: 020 8460 3546
Fax: 020 8466 8885
e-mail: office@bishopchallonerschool.com
website: www.bishopchallonerschool.com

Headteacher: **Ms Karen Barry**, BA, MA, PGCE, NPQH

Age Range. 2½–18.
Number in School. 420 Day Pupils.
Fees per term (from April 2011). Seniors £3,012, Juniors £2,410, Infants £2,173, Nursery £450–£2,147.
This is a Roman Catholic Independent Co-educational School with Nursery, Infants and Junior Sections 2½–11 years and a Senior School section 11–18 years.

The School includes a percentage of non-Catholics.

The School curriculum includes all National Curriculum subjects and others leading to GCSE and A Levels. Admissions to the Senior School at any age follows the successful completion of an entrance examination and an interview with the headteacher.

Charitable status. Bishop Challoner School is a Registered Charity, number 235468. It exists to provide education for boys and girls.

Bowbrook House School

Peopleton, Nr Pershore, Worcs WR10 2EE
Tel: 01905 841242
Fax: 01905 840716
e-mail: enquiries@bowbrookhouseschool.co.uk
website: www.bowbrookhouseschool.co.uk

Headmaster: **Mr C D Allen**, BSc Hons, CertEd, DipSoc

Age Range. 3½–16.
Number in School. Day: 127 Boys, 56 Girls.
Fees per term (2010-2011). £1,650–£2,680.
Bowbrook House is set in 14 acres of picturesque Worcestershire countryside yet within easy reach of Worcester, Pershore and Evesham. The school caters for the academic child and also those of average ability, who can benefit from the small classes. All pupils are able to take full advantage of the opportunities offered and are encouraged to participate in all activities. As well as the academic subjects, the school has a flourishing art department, a computer room, hard tennis courts and an open air swimming pool in addition to extensive games fields.

The Pre-Prep department of 3½–8 year olds is a self-contained unit but enjoys the use of the main school facilities.

Whilst stressing academic achievement, the school aims to provide a structured and disciplined environment in which children of all abilities can flourish, gain confidence and achieve their true potential. The small school size enables the head and staff to know all pupils well, to be able to accurately assess their strengths and weaknesses it enables each pupil to be an important part of the school and to feel that their individual attitudes, behaviour, efforts and achievements are important.

There is an extended school day from 8.15 am to 5.30 pm, with supervised prep sessions. There is also an extensive and varied extra-curricular programme run by specialist coaches from basketball, gym and dance to kick-boxing and fencing.

Brabyns Preparatory School
GEMS Education

34/36 Arkwright Road, Marple, Stockport, Cheshire SK6 7DB
Tel: 0161 427 2395
Fax: 0161 449 0704
e-mail: admin@brabynsprepschool.co.uk
website: www.brabynsprepschool.co.uk

Head: **Mr L Sanders**, BEd

Age Range. 3–11 years.
Number in School. Day: Boys 57, Girls 72.
Fees per term (2010–2011). £1,435–£1,953.

Brabyns Preparatory School is an independent school offering education for children from Nursery age to 11 years old, accommodated in two large Edwardian houses which have been sensitively redesigned to provide for the needs of the children while retaining a sense of warmth and security.

Specialist facilities include Hall/Gym, Nursery, ICT Suite, Art room and Science Laboratory.

Children are taught in small classes throughout the school. The broad curriculum is based on the requirements of the National Curriculum and children are prepared for examinations to the Local Independent Grammar Schools. Brabyns has an excellent record of successful entrants to these schools.

Our pre-school provision starts in Nursery where pupils embark upon the Foundation Station Curriculum. Children are accepted from the half term in which they have their third birthday. Planned and directed activities led by qualified teachers and Nursery Nurses provide rich and challenging learning experiences. The current pupil staff ratio in the Foundation Stage is 1:6. Pupils receive a sound foundation in basic skills and socialisation preparing the way to the more structured academic work in Reception. The school curriculum from Year 1 to Year 6 is linked to the National Curriculum, but preparation for the independent schools examinations becomes increasingly important.

Braeside School for Girls

130 High Road, Buckhurst Hill, Essex IG9 5SD
Tel: 020 8504 1133
Fax: 020 8505 6675
e-mail: enquiries@braesideschool.co.uk
website: www.braesideschool.co.uk

Headteacher: **Mrs G Haddon**, BA Hons, PGCE

Age Range. 3–16.
Number in School. 208 Day Girls.
Fees per term (2011–2012). £1,330–£3,305.

Braeside School was founded in 1944 by Marjory Wakefield. She championed educational partnership between home and school, reflecting the Parents National Education Union principles which had underpinned her own training as a teacher.

Choosing the right school for your daughter is not easy. Changes in education and the way that these are interpreted by schools can mean that it is hard to find a school that combines traditional values and high standards of discipline with excellent teaching in a stable and caring environment. At Braeside our well-qualified staff share the common goal of educating, enhancing and empowering pupils throughout their years at Braeside so that at 16, when they leave us, our girls are confident, outgoing, well-educated individuals.

In the GCSE league tables, published in *The Times* in 2011, Braeside was listed in the ten top performing schools in Essex and the fact that four of the top ten schools listed, including ourselves, were all-girl schools is clearly a positive indicator for single-sex education.

At Braeside School our small community allows everyone to feel valued. We consider the needs of every student as they move through the school, providing the necessary challenge and opportunity for each individual at different stages of their lives, so that they can achieve their academic potential.

Our Early Years Department welcomes girls from the age of 3 and focus is on the six learning areas. The Department

was judged by Ofsted in its last inspection to be 'outstanding' in all areas. We fully understand the issues of maturity linked to birthdays and operate a flexible programme of activities within our Lower Kindergarten and Kindergarten classes to meet all educational needs.

Infant and Junior class teachers are supported by specialist teachers in French, Music, ICT and PE and have the benefit of dedicated Music and Art rooms and an ICT suite.

At Braeside Senior School a combination of the best in traditional and contemporary teaching methods in a full range of subjects can be seen. Class sizes are small and some subjects are delivered in half class groups with correspondingly successful grades being achieved at GCSE. Academic class work is well balanced by activities such as sport, music and drama; enhancement programmes for enrichment of the curriculum are well established. Citizenship is taught throughout the school and is linked to community events.

Whilst the modern world gives girls enormous opportunity to develop rewarding professional lives, it also poses difficulties in creating a workable home/life balance. We try to equip all our pupils with the ability and confidence to make informed choices about their lives at every stage of the learning process.

Entry, at every age apart from 3 and 4, is by test and interview.

Bredon School

Pull Court, Bushley, Nr Tewkesbury, Gloucestershire GL20 6AH
Tel: 01684 293156
Fax: 01684 276392
e-mail: enquiries@bredonschool.co.uk
website: www.bredonschool.org

Headmaster: **J A Hewitt**, MBA, BA

Director of Education: Mrs S Webb, BEd Hons, Dip SpLD

Age Range. 4–18.
Number in School. 240. Boarders: 77 Boys, 25 Girls. Day: 106 Boys, 32 Girls.
Fees per term (2011–2012). Day £1,945–£5,285. Weekly boarding £5,705–£8,135. Full Boarding £5,855–£8,290.

Bredon School is situated in magnificent rural surroundings and delivers a broad based education centring upon individual attention and personal recognition. Bredon provides a broad academic curriculum at all Key Stages through to GCSE and A Level. In addition Bredon offers extensive vocational programmes at Foundation, Intermediate and Advanced levels. Class sizes average 10–12 and teacher/pupil ratio 1:7. Bredon also has a thriving School Farm.

Selection is by potential not just attainment and specialist support is available to pupils with learning difficulties through the specialist Access Centre. Bredon educates the whole child through sound realistic academic provision, sympathetic pastoral care, regular leadership challenges and a varied sports programme.

Bridgewater School

Drywood Hall, Worsley Road, Worsley, Manchester M28 2WQ
Tel: 0161 794 1463
Fax: 0161 794 3519
e-mail: admin@bwslive.co.uk
website: www.bridgewater-school.co.uk

Chairman of Governors: Mr A T Miller, BEd Hons, DASE

Head Teacher: **Mrs J A T Nairn**, CertEd Distinction

Age Range. 3–18 Co-educational.
Number of Pupils. 504: 279 Boys, 225 Girls.
Fees per term (2010-2011). £2,120–£2,833. Lunch is included.

Bridgewater School is a co-educational, independent day school for pupils aged between 3 and 18 years. Established as a boys' school in 1950 and having moved to its present, delightful, semi-rural setting soon afterwards, the school has since grown considerably – admitting girls and developing a sixth form. We draw pupils from the immediate locality, but also from a much wider area, well served as we are by the motorway network and by other major road links.

Bridgewater is by design not a large school. This enables us to provide small classes and high levels of attention to the needs of individual pupils. We seek to maximise education attainment all through a child's development, not least in the years of external examinations at GCSE and A Level.

In addition to its academic goals Bridgewater seeks to retain the intimate atmosphere it has had since its inception. We greatly value our capacity to offer provision across the full age range, from the nursery years to university entrance, for families wanting this continuity of individual attention for their children.

At the same time, however, pupils must look outward to the wider community and to the society in which they will live as adults. We see it as an integral part of Bridgewater's role to foster high standards of behaviour and self-discipline, as well as to develop an awareness of personal and social responsibility. Vital, too, are the many activities which take place outside the classroom – sport, music, drama clubs and societies, language exchange visits and outdoor activity breaks to name but a sample of the range available.

Entrusting your child's education to a school is a very big decision. We are mindful of our responsibility to justify a parent's decision to send their child to us, and of the need for that child's education to be a partnership between school and home. We aim, by the end of this partnership, to produce rounded, articulate young people who are well prepared for the challenges of adult and business life.

The School governors, staff and pupils share a sense of excitement about Bridgewater's future. The school has developed rapidly in recent years, with splendid new buildings and facilities and a considerable increase in pupil numbers. We have a commitment to continual development and improvement. If you have not yet visited us then may we recommend that you do so soon. We would be delighted to meet you and to show you how much Bridgewater School has to offer you and your child.

Charitable status. Bridgewater School is a Registered Charity, number 1105547.

Bronte School

Mayfield, 7 Pelham Road, Gravesend, Kent DA11 0HN
Tel: 01474 533805
Fax: 01474 352003
e-mail: enquiry@bronteschool.co.uk
website: www.bronteschool.co.uk

Headmaster: **Mr R A Dyson**, BA, CertEd

Age Range. 4–11.
Number in School. 120 Day Pupils: 70 Boys, 50 Girls.
Fees per term (2011-2012). £2,438 (£40 discount for those paying on or before first day of term). Compulsory extras: Swimming from Year 1.

Bronte is a small, friendly, family-orientated, co-educational day school serving Gravesend and surrounding vil-

lages. The children are taught in small classes and are prepared for all types of secondary education. In 1999 the school moved to its present building which has since been expanded to accommodate specialist teaching rooms. A broadly-based curriculum and an extensive number of activity clubs provide the children with every opportunity to develop their individual interests and abilities.

Entry is preferred at 4 following a parental visit to the school and an interview with the Head. Children joining at a later stage are assessed informally prior to entry.

Buckingham College School

Hindes Road, Harrow, Middlesex HA1 1SH
Tel: 020 8427 1220
Fax: 020 8863 0816
e-mail: enquiries@buckcoll.org
website: www.buckcoll.org

Headmaster: **S H Larter**, BA Hons, PGCE

Age Range. Boys 11–18, Girls 16–18.
Number in School. Day: 86.
Fees per term (2011-2012). £3,218–£3,733. Compulsory extras: Lunches.

Buckingham College is an independent secondary school for boys aged 11–18, and girls aged 16–18.

Founded in 1936, it is a member of the E Ivor Hughes Educational Foundation.

Students are prepared for 16 GCSE and 13 GCE A Level examinations. The Sixth Form is conducted on tutorial lines, preparing small groups of pupils for A levels. There is a full range of games and physical education activities.

The school aims to provide a well disciplined and happy community based on Christian principles in which each pupil may play an active and satisfying part. Classes are small – under 20 – and there is a wide range of sports.

Admission is by way of an individual entrance test and interview.

Scholarships are available on merit.

Charitable status. The E Ivor Hughes Educational Foundation is a Registered Charity, number 293623. It exists to provide education for children.

Buxlow Preparatory School

5/6 Castleton Gardens, East Lane, Wembley, Middlesex HA9 7QJ
Tel: 020 8904 3615
Fax: 020 8904 3606
e-mail: buxlow.head@happychild.co.uk
           buxlow.admin@happychild.co.uk
website: www.buxlowschool.com

Headteacher: **Mrs Ann Baines**, CertEd

Age Range. 4–11 Co-educational.
Number of Pupils. 90.
Fees per term (2010-2011). £2,295.

Cambridge Centre for Sixth-form Studies (CCSS)

1 Salisbury Villas, Station Road, Cambridge CB1 2JF
Tel: 01223 716890
Fax: 01223 517530

e-mail: enquiries@ccss.co.uk
website: www.ccss.co.uk

Principal: **Mr Stuart Nicholson**, MA, MBA, PGCE, NPQH, CPhys

Age Range. 15–21.
Number in School. 210.
Fees per term (2011-2012). Boarding £6,137–£9,847; Day £2,272–£5,982.

CCSS offers a unique and individual approach to learning, building a relationship of mutual respect between students and staff and developing self-confidence within each student.

CCSS is one of the UK's leading independent sixth-form colleges, specialising in A Level and GCSE courses, and preparing students for entry into the best universities in the UK and abroad.

We have 210 students aged from 15 to 21. Half of them stay in our boarding accommodation and the other half are day students. CCSS is a happy, purposeful and vibrant place with a wide range of sporting, cultural and social activities available.

The College is based in the exciting university town of Cambridge, close to the railway station and a 50-minute train ride from London, with easy connections to international airports.

Teaching: The teaching at CCSS is a collaborative and shared learning experience, which fosters focus and motivation, and creates a very productive and exciting schooling environment and experience for every student at the College. The informality and strength of working relationships lead to a bond of loyalty between students and staff, and the trust and independence that students have at the College give them freedom to make the right choices and decisions for them in their learning.

Classes at CCSS are less than half the average for the independent sector in the UK and much smaller than in state schools. The average class size at CCSS is five pupils so everyone gets the attention they need.

As well as group classes, all A Level students have additional 'one-to-one' sessions in each subject. These tutorials allow students and teachers to work together on areas of uncertainty or interest, analysing examination questions and discussing outstanding answers and the strategy for creating these answers.

Preparation for university: CCSS prides itself on being a college offering a "pathway to university" giving their students support and guidance to ensure that they are well prepared in all aspects of the university application, from personal statement writing and interview practice to university visits and careers workshops. Work experience can also be arranged to strengthen and enhance university applications.

The success of the CCSS students means that the great majority go on to university in the UK or elsewhere, with many enjoying success at Cambridge, Oxford, LSE and other top universities in subjects ranging from international business to law and medicine.

Charitable status. The Cambridge Centre for Sixth Form Studies is a Registered Charity, number 1084601.

Cambridge Tutors College

Water Tower Hill, Croydon, Surrey CR0 5SX
Tel: 020 8688 5284
Fax: 020 8686 9220
e-mail: admin@ctc.ac.uk
website: www.ctc.ac.uk

Principal: **Mr Mario Di Clemente**, BA, PGCE

Age Range. 15–19 Co-educational.
Number of Pupils. 260.
Fees per annum (2011-2012). £16,650–£20,295.

Since 1958 Cambridge Tutors College has offered high-quality education to young people from the United Kingdom and from across the world. Fundamental to the College's ethos is small group teaching – no group is larger than 9 – and regular testing – students take a test in every subject every week. This combination of small classes and sympathetic testing has proved to be highly successful in giving students the confidence to succeed.

The College's most recent ISI Inspection report in 2011 was outstanding.

The College has grown over the years, both in size and reputation, but still offers the individual attention that can only be gained in a small school. Most of its students are studying A Levels and their achievements, year-on-year, are impressive. The average A Level pass rate (A–E) for the last 5 years is 99% (A/B 80%). Over 70% of leavers gain entry into their first-choice university with Russell group destinations such as Oxbridge, LSE, UCL, Imperial and Warwick among the most common. The College runs a fast-track 1-year GCSE programme too, catering for students from 15+.

Situated in a pleasant parkside location by Park Hill in South Croydon, CTC is just a few minutes' walk from the town centre, East Croydon station and bus and tram routes. It is close to London, just 15 minutes by train, but surrounded by parkland and quiet residential streets.

Facilities and resources at CTC are modern and extremely well-appointed – all subjects have specialist resources and the Osborne Centre, opened in 2003, offers state-of the-art ICT technology as well as a comfortable library and reading room and a lecture theatre. An all-day café provides a wide variety of fresh food and drinks.

The College's welfare provision includes a team of trained professionals and all students have a personal tutor. Sporting and social activities take place each week and students are encouraged to take part. There is a good selection of clubs and societies that students can join, and trip and visits take place to places such as Euro Disney Paris, Edinburgh and London attractions.

Last summer's crop of A Level results was again outstanding, with a 99% pass rate, 79% A/B, and 59% at grade A*/A. Individual successes were remarkable: half of all students gained 3 or 4 A*/A grades with 5 students going on to Oxford or Cambridge.

Charitable status. Cambridge Tutors Educational Trust Limited is a Registered Charity, number 312878.

Canbury School

Kingston Hill, Kingston-upon-Thames, Surrey KT2 7LN
Tel: 020 8549 8622
Fax: 020 8974 6018
e-mail: head@canburyschool.co.uk
website: www.canburyschool.co.uk

Founded in 1982, Canbury School is a co-educational independent day school. It is non-denominational.

Head: **Mr R F Metters**, BEd

Age Range. 11–17.
Number in School. 65 day children.
Fees per term (2011-2012). £4,440.

Curriculum. We cover a full range of GCSE subjects, most pupils taking a total of eight or nine.

Entry requirements. There are tests in English and Mathematics. The Headmaster interviews each candidate. A trial day or two at the school can be arranged prior to entry.

Subjects offered. In Years 7, 8 and 9 we emphasise English, Mathematics and Science in line with the requirements of the National Curriculum. Our extended curriculum includes Spanish, Geography, History, Information Technology, Art, Design & Technology, Drama, PE and Games, Music, and Personal, Social and Health Education. Later, Physics, Chemistry and Biology are taken as doubly-certificated GCSE subjects. Individual arrangements can be made for pupils to prepare for GCSE in Japanese, German, Chinese and other languages. Business Studies is offered in Years 10 and 11 as an option leading to the GCSE.

Facilities. IT computer facilities are accessible to all pupils. There is an excellent art room. Pupils are transported to a wide range of sports facilities within the Borough.

Canbury School is different in placing emphasis on small classes. No class has more than 18 pupils. Full concentration is placed on bringing out the talents of each pupil. Pupils participate in the school council which makes decisions in some areas of school life.

Charitable status. Canbury School is a Registered Charity, number 803766. It exists to provide education to a broad range of children including some of various nationalities who stand to benefit from being in a small school.

Carleton House Preparatory School

145 Menlove Avenue, Liverpool L18 3EE
Tel: 0151 722 0756
Fax: 0151 737 1408
e-mail: info@carletonhouse.co.uk
website: www.carletonhouse.co.uk

Chair of Governors: Dr Peter Edwards

Head Teacher: **Mrs A Daniels**, BA Hons, PGCE

Age Range. 3+–11 Co-educational.
Number in School. 150.
Fees per term (2010-2011). £1,976 inclusive of lunch, day trips, French/Spanish lessons and personal insurance cover.

Located in the leafy suburbs of south Liverpool, Carleton House is Merseyside's leading co-ed Preparatory School (*Times Parent Power 2009*). It is a Catholic school that welcomes children of all denominations.

They can because they think they can truly embodies the spirit of Carleton House. Our school is a lively, vibrant community that gives its pupils a first-class education for the 21st century.

Small class sizes (we endeavour to keep to a maximum of 22) and a high ratio of teaching staff to pupils enable the well-qualified and experienced staff to provide individual attention in a friendly, caring atmosphere. We nurture the development of the whole child – academically, spiritually and in the sporting and cultural aspects of their lives. Through excellent teaching and the close relationship that exists between school and home, our pupils are challenged, encouraged and supported to achieve their very best.

The implementation of all ten National Curriculum subjects ensures a broad, well-balanced curriculum is followed, but great importance is given to Maths and English as success in these subjects is central to development in other areas. Additional specialist teaching is provided for children requiring support in the basic subjects.

French has been successfully introduced in all classes including Reception with Spanish in the upper years.

All children receive music lessons and individual piano and guitar lessons are also available.

Emphasis is placed on high academic standards with children being prepared for a variety of Entrance examinations

at 11 and more than 90% of pupils gain places at selective schools of their choice.

A wide range of sports and extra-curricular activities is offered to both boys and girls, including football, netball, cricket, rounders, swimming, chess, quiz, singing and speech choir. The children compete in local sporting events as well as choral festivals.

Theatre and educational visits are encouraged along with a residential trip to the Lake District, and Shropshire for older pupils, which provide field and adventure activities that help build confidence and self-esteem.

Close contact with parents is promoted through regular parent/teacher meetings and reports on pupils progress.

A thriving Parent Teacher Association provides social functions for parents while raising funds for extra equipment.

After-school provision is provided by the 'Kids Club'. This operates daily from 3.30 pm until 6.00 pm and school is open from 8 am for early drop-offs.

Parents are welcome to visit the school by appointment. Further information available from the Head Teacher.

Charitable status. Carleton House Preparatory School is a Registered Charity, number 505310. It exists to provide education for boys and girls.

Castle House School

Chetwynd End, Newport, Shropshire TF10 7JE
Tel: 01952 811035
Fax: 01952 810022
e-mail: admin@castlehouseschool.co.uk
website: www.castlehouseschool.co.uk

Chairman of Governors: Dr Martin Deahl

Headmaster: **Richard Walden**, MA Hons Downing College Cambridge, CertEd, MEd Hons, FCollP

Type of School. Co-educational day preparatory school.
Age Range. 2–11.
Number of Pupils. 105: 55 girls, 50 boys.
Fees per term (2011-2012). £1,899–£2,179.

Castle House is a friendly day preparatory school with a family feel. It is small enough for everybody to know and be known by everybody else, but offers a full and busy programme.

The school aims to bring the best out of every pupil by providing opportunities to excel and developing confidence to try.

Much importance is attached to the children being kind and considerate to each other, in the belief that happy children work best. We develop positive and courteous behaviour.

Since 1980 the school has been a charitable trust, run by a board of governors with varied talents and local interests. It was founded in 1944 by Miss Zellah Pitchford. The current head is the fourth.

The school's Georgian house, set in delightful gardens, is in the conservation area of Newport in east Shropshire. It serves urban and rural areas, including west Staffordshire, Market Drayton, Eccleshall, Telford and Shifnal.

Pupils are prepared for entrance exams to independent schools and to local grammar schools of which the two in Newport are unique in Shropshire. There is an excellent record of passes and scholarships, from a mixed ability intake, with children achieving their potential and beyond.

The curriculum covers all major subjects, and Art, DT, French, Music, Spanish, ICT, PE, Games, Swimming, Gymnastics and Drama. RE and assemblies are Christian, but non-denominational, encouraging all to join in.

Our flourishing educational nursery, CHerubS, for two to four year olds, is open all year from 8.00 am to 6.00 pm.

Holiday care is available all day for children up to eleven, every holiday.

A rich range of after-school activities includes build-it, art, crafts, choirs, computers, gymnastics, chess, radio, football, netball, short tennis, cricket and rounders.

Matches are played in traditional team games, cross-country and swimming. Particular success has been achieved in schools' gymnastics, with girls' teams winning silver medals at national level in GISGA (independent schools) competitions. Boys' teams have three times won national under 9 titles and the school team has twice won the BSGA under 11 mixed teams Floor and Vault national title. The teams are ISA national champions.

We see education as a cooperative venture with parents. There are regular progress reports and feedback meetings. Parents are encouraged to bring their concerns to the teachers. There is a lively Parents' Association.

Further information can be obtained on our website or by telephoning the Registrar at the school.

Charitable status. Castle House School Trust Ltd is a Registered Charity, number 510515. It exists for the provision of high quality education for boys and girls.

CATS Cambridge

Round Church Street, Cambridge CB5 8AD
Tel: 01223 314431
Fax: 01223 467773
e-mail: enquiries@catscambridge.com
website: www.ceg-uk.com

Principal: **Dr Glenn Hawkins**, BSc, PhD, MBA

Age Range. 14–19+.
Number of Students. 268.
Fees per term (2011-2012). Tuition: £4,450–£8,765; Accommodation: £2,200–£3,330; .

CATS Cambridge is a top independent school offering Pre:Programme, A Level, University Foundation, Academic English and Summer School programmes.

The location of our college, in the historic heart of Cambridge between the Cambridge Union and St John's College, enhances the lives of our cosmopolitan student body who benefit from the city's academic tradition and lively student community.

Our results are outstanding. In 2009 38% of our students achieved an A grade at A Level at CATS Cambridge – 42% above the UK national average, and 72% of University Foundation students achieved offers from the Times Top 30 universities.

We offer a wide selection of study pathways and subjects, including over 30 A levels selected to meet the diverse needs of our students, alongside additional study skills support and brain training for our gifted and talented cohort.

Students are taught in small groups of up to ten and able, stimulating and enthusiastic tutors help develop study skills and examination technique. Situated on the same campus, Cambridge School of Visual & Performing Arts runs a highly-regarded Art Foundation course in preparation for entry to Art Colleges. The school also offers a Drama Foundation course (in association with RADA) – the only one of its kind in the UK.

Much of our student success lies in our personalised learning approach. We encourage a shared commitment to learning and offer a wide programme of study skills coaching sessions, including language support, memory enhancement, mind mapping and speed reading.

Our Students benefit from free and unlimited supplementary tuition, regular personal tutor meetings, and Higher Education advice that results in offers from the best universities in the UK and Overseas, such as Cambridge University, The London School of Economics and Imperial College London.

We are experts in welcoming international students to our College and a comprehensive support network is in place that includes pre-arrival information, airport transfers, a College induction, campus tour and tutor introduction, help setting up a UK bank account, registering with a doctor and native language tutors.

Students can choose from a range of accommodation and Homestay options, varying in size and cost. All our residences are supervised, safe and secure and located within easy reach of the campus offering single, shared and en-suite bedrooms, catered or self-catered and fully-furnished communal areas and wireless internet.

Chase Academy

Lyncroft House, St John's Road, Cannock, Staffordshire WS11 0UR
Tel: 01543 501800
Fax: 01543 501801
e-mail: info@chaseacademy.com
website: www.chaseacademy.com

Principal: **Mr M D Ellse**, MA, CPhys, MInstP, PGCE

Age Range. 3–18.
Number in School. 8 Boarders, 204 Day.
Fees per term (2011-2012). Day: £904–£3,108, Boarding £4,100–£7,200.

Independent day and boarding school for boys and girls from nursery to A Level.

Formerly a convent, founded in 1879, the senior school was added in 1980.

Extensive modern school on spacious urban site. New science, sport, technology, computing, language facilities. New Music School. Extensive sports facilities, including 3 floodlit astroturf pitches.

Academic work. Small classes allow attention to the individual student. The National Curriculum is shadowed throughout. Common core up to Year 9. GCSE, AS and A2 Level in: English, Mathematics, Physics, Chemistry, Biology, Design and Technology, Business Studies, History, Geography, French, German, Physical Education, Music, Drama, Art, Dance, Accounting, Latin.

Boarding. Delightful modern rooms, half of which are single study-bedrooms. The associated International College makes provision for overseas students who need to learn or improve their English.

Dyslexia. Support for intelligent dyslexics from a Dyslexia Institute trained teacher and within the small classes.

Sport. Football, cricket, hockey and netball are the principal sports with school facilities for tennis, volleyball and basketball.

Music and Drama. A strong team of professional performers and first-rate teachers producing big uptake in the performing arts.

School day. 08.50–15.50. Prep until 16.45. Facilities for early drop-off and late pick-up.

Chilton Cantelo School
Cognita Schools Group

Chilton Cantelo, Yeovil, Somerset BA22 8BG
Tel: 01935 850555
e-mail: info@chiltoncanteloschool.co.uk
website: www.chiltoncanteloschool.co.uk

Headmaster: **Dr John M Price**, BSc, PhD

Age Range. Co-educational 7–16.
Number of Pupils. 241 Boys, 144 Girls; 149 Boarding, 236 Day.
Fees per term (2010-2011). Preparatory Department: £2,550 (day), £4,995 (boarding). Senior School: £3,300 (day), £6,445 (boarding).

Set in and around an imposing 18th Century manor house and 20 acres of grounds, four and a half miles from both Sherborne and Yeovil, Chilton Cantelo school offers a genuine all-round education designed to develop each pupil's potential. This co-educational boarding and day school provides exceptional value for money. Fees start at an unbelievable £2,550 with no additional charges for meals, books or extra tuition.

In this idyllic, safe setting with a very strong sense of community and a care and concern for every individual, children develop into the best possible versions of themselves.

Central to the school's ethos is highlighting and attempting to meet the individual needs of each and every pupil. The small class sizes enable children to learn and develop their confidence so that they leave us having become well-rounded individuals who possess the academic credentials and skills to meet the challenges of the modern world.

Boarders go on all-inclusive trips most weekends, and the school has recently opened a stunning new girls boarding house to enhance its boarding provision.

The main strength of the School, in addition to small teaching groups, impressive academic results and an extremely broad curriculum, is our experience and success at affording each pupil a great deal of individual attention.

Results at GCSE are exceptional. Over 88% of the Year 11 cohort achieved 5 or more A*–C grades This is a school that is moving forward and with the backing of parent company, Cognita Schools, exciting times lie ahead. You will be hard pressed to find an independent school that offers better value for money.

A prospectus may be obtained from the School and prospective parents are encouraged to visit. Please telephone the Admissions Secretary to arrange an appointment.

Claires Court Schools

1 College Avenue, Maidenhead, Berkshire SL6 6AW
Tel: 01628 411470; Registrar: 01628 411472
Fax: 01628 411466
e-mail: registrar@clairescourt.com
website: www.clairescourt.com

Principals:
H StJ Wilding, BA, MCIM, FRSA (*Bursar*)
J T Wilding, BSc, FRSA

Head of Claires Court: J M Rayer, BSc, PGCE
Head of Ridgeway: J C Watkins, BEd, CertEd
Head of College: Mrs L Green, CPhys, MInstP, BSc, PGCE

Age Range. 3–18.
Number of Pupils. 602 Boys; 277 Girls. Sixth Form: 76 Boys, 38 Girls.
Teaching Staff. 75 full time, 36 part time, 20 visiting.
Fees per term (2011-2012). £2,310–£3,945.

Claires Court Schools is a school on three sites – Claires Court (Senior Boys), Ridgeway (Junior Boys) and College (Co-ed Nursery, Girls to 16 and Co-ed Sixth Form). The ethos of the Schools lies in the provision for its pupils of a broad and thorough education in all senses so that in time the challenges of the future will be met with confidence.

A rich and full programme of study and activity leads to academic success, sports accomplishment and cultural fulfilment, within a firm structure based on friendship and self discipline. All pupils follow an enhanced National Curriculum and participate in the main sports for boys and girls.

Ridgeway (boys 4+ to 11) is situated to the west of the town centre in its own extensive grounds which include a purpose-built sports hall. The classroom accommodation has been considerably extended to provide additional space for art and science.

At 11+ boys transfer to Claires Court which is located near Boulters Lock in a pleasant residential area of the town. Here the facilities include a technology wing housing science laboratories as well as facilities for art, ICT and technology. The Nicholas Watson Sports Centre opened in March 2003 with an extended gallery area for physiological testing and fencing development planned. A wide range of subjects are offered at GCSE as well as PSCHE and careers advice being available.

The College, based close to the town centre of Maidenhead, has its own pleasant grounds housing a covered year round heated swimming pool, tennis courts and its own sports grounds. The Nursery based here is co-ed for children from 3 to 4+ years from where girls transfer into the main school at College and boys to Ridgeway. As with Claires Court, a wide range of subjects is available for study at GCSE together with quality facilities for all subjects throughout the age range.

The Sixth Form is co-ed with boys and girls transferring from Claires Court and College as well as accepting external candidates. A wide range of A Level subjects is available for study with considerable pastoral, higher education and careers guidance available.

All parts of the School participate in extensive after school activities programmes and whilst boys and girls are academically taught on separate sites, they meet for many social, extra curricular and aesthetic activities.

The School is multi denominational. A prospectus containing further information may be obtained from the School or the website and prospective parents are always welcome to visit. Open Mornings are held throughout the year.

Colchester High School
Cognita Schools Group

Wellesley Road, Colchester, Essex CO3 3HD
Tel: 01206 573389
Fax: 01206 573114
e-mail: info@colchesterhighschool.co.uk
website: www.colchesterhighschool.co.uk

Principal: **Mr David Young**, MEd, BSc Hons, BA Hons, PGCE

Age Range. 2½–16 Co-educational.
Number in School. Day: 440.
Fees per term (2011-2012). £2,365–£3,205 incl lunch to Year 2 only.
Assistance with fees: Discount for Siblings & Scholarship available.
Entry requirements: Assessment test and satisfactory report from previous school.

The atmosphere in the school is friendly and purposeful, and all pupils receive close individual direction to reach the best standard each one of them can achieve. Many pupils join the school on personal recommendation.

There is a flourishing Nursery Department, where girls and boys are prepared for entrance into the Preparatory Department. A full range of GCSEs is taught by specialist staff in the Senior Department, with classes averaging 16 in number and some subjects having sets of about 10 students.

An Art & Technology Wing gives excellent facilities for CDT, Electronics, Art, Music, Sciences and ICT and a new Performing Arts Centre.

Pupils of all ages enjoy a wide variety of clubs and activities for Sport, with impressive achievements at regional and national level. Music and Drama are also strong features of the school, with frequent performances by the choir and orchestra and a major production each year.

Pupils with specific learning difficulties are given extra help by the school's Learning Support Unit.

To book a visit or request a Prospectus please contact the Registrar.

Religious Affiliation: Non-denominational.

Collingwood School

Springfield Road, Wallington, Surrey SM6 0BD
Tel:	020 8647 4607
Fax:	020 8669 2884
e-mail:	headmaster@collingwoodschool.org.uk
website:	www.collingwoodschool.org.uk

Headmaster: **Mr C R T Fenwick**, BA Hons, MA

Age Range. 2–11 Co-educational.
Number in School. Day: 150.
Fees per term (2010-2011). £1,160–£2,170 (reduction for siblings).

Collingwood was founded in 1929 and became an Educational Trust in 1978.

The aims of the School are to give each child a firm educational foundation upon which to build a successful future. In the Nursery, happy children learn number work, the rudiments of reading and writing, the love of books and enjoy their music and movement activities. The 4/5 year olds in the Kindergarten are reading, writing short stories, investigating scientific and mathematical problems, or striving to express themselves in French.

This excellent introduction gives them a head start in their studies in later classes, and the many scholarships and entrance successes to State Selective and Independent Senior Schools reflect the teaching abilities of the well-qualified staff.

However, Collingwood is not only concerned with academic success. Drama, Singing, Orchestra, Violin, Keyboard, Woodwind, Brass, Percussion, Piano and Recorder lessons, together with Chess Club, Design Technology Club, Football Club (with an ex-Premier League Footballer), Athletics Club, Gym Club, Hockey, Rounders, Netball, Tennis, Cricket and Swimming, broaden and enhance the pupils well-being and knowledge.

A truly all-round education is what Collingwood provides for boys and girls between the ages of 2 and 11 years.

Pre-school and after-school care clubs available.

For a prospectus, details of examination results and to arrange a visit, please telephone 020 8647 4607. You will be made most welcome.

Charitable status. Collingwood School Educational Trust Ltd is a Registered Charity, number 277682. It exists to promote and foster a sound educational foundation for girls and boys aged 2–11 years.

Coopersale Hall School

Flux's Lane, Epping, Essex CM16 7PE
Tel:	01992 577133
Fax:	01992 571544
e-mail:	info@coopersalehallschool.co.uk
website:	www.coopersalehallschool.co.uk

Headmistress: **Miss Kaye Lovejoy**, CertEd, BEd Hons

Age Range. 2½–11.
Number in School. 275 Day Pupils.
Fees per term (from January 2011). £960–£2,935.
Entry requirements. Interview and assessment.
Location. Just off Stewards Green Road, close to M11 and M25 routes.

Coopersale Hall School is a thriving, caring local independent school with a high standard of academic achievement and a wide range of activities.

The School offers small class sizes and specialist teachers for ICT, Science, PE, Sport, Music and Drama. We provide a high standard of education and enjoy success in Entrance Examinations at 11 years to a wide choice of Secondary Schools.

We encourage our pupils to develop self-confidence and to take on roles of responsibility as they move up through the school. Creativity is nurtured within a disciplined environment and traditional values such as self-discipline are promoted to maximise our pupils' effectiveness in an ever-changing world.

Coopersale Hall is situated in a large country house that is pleasantly situated on the outskirts of Epping. The School has its own private road and stands in some seven acres of landscaped garden and playing fields.

Copthill School

Barnack Road, Uffington, Stamford, Lincolnshire PE9 3AD
Tel:	01780 757506
e-mail:	mail@copthill.com
website:	www.copthill.com

Headmaster: **Jonathan Teesdale**, BA Hons, PGCE

Age Range. Co-educational 2–11 years.
Number of Pupils. 300: Main School (age 4+ to 11): 240; Nursery and Pre-School (age 2 to 4): 60.
Fees per term (from January 2011). £2,350–£2,540.
Aim. To give pupils the opportunity to fulfil their potential in happy and stimulating surroundings. High academic standards offering a thorough grounding in basic educational values. Copthill has strong family values and a warm, welcoming atmosphere.
Location. Purpose-built, modern facilities set within 350 acres of farmland, including river and woodland. 2 miles from Stamford and the A1 and 15 miles from Peterborough.
School Day. Monday to Friday. School Day – 8.40 am to 3.30 pm. Creche hours – 8.00 am to 6.00 pm. 25 clubs per week, finishing at 4.30 pm. Breakfast and Tea available.
Facilities. IT Centre, Library, Languages Suite, Science Laboratory, Sports Hall, extensive playing fields and outdoor facilities. High quality catering facilities offering delicious, nutritionally balanced meals.
Pastoral Care. In addition to their forms, pupils from Year 5 onwards are also placed in small tutor groups in which their progress is closely monitored in preparation for senior school entrance. There is a genuine 'open door policy' throughout the School. Parents' Evenings and reports given twice a year.
Curriculum. A modern curriculum based on the National Curriculum. Combines traditional and innovative teaching methods. Learning support offered where a specific need has been assessed.
Music, Speech & Drama. Music and Drama are taught as part of the curriculum. Regular drama productions encourage all pupils to participate. Pupils can also receive expert individual tuition and perform at school concerts, assemblies and in local music and drama festivals.

Sport. Athletics, Cricket, Football, Hockey, Netball, Cross-Country, Rounders, Rugby, Swimming, Tennis. All pupils encouraged to be in teams.

Future Schools. Pupils leave Copthill at 11 years old with great confidence and the ability to think for themselves. Copthill is a truly independent primary school, offering thorough preparation to a wide variety of state and independent senior schools, both local and national, and achieving a large number of scholarships and awards.

Crackley Hall School

St Joseph's Park, Kenilworth, Warwickshire CV8 2FT
Tel: 01926 514444
Fax: 01926 514455
e-mail: post@crackleyhall.co.uk
website: www.crackleyhall.co.uk

Headteacher: **Mr Robert Duigan**, BComEd, MEd

Co-educational Nursery and Junior School
Age Range. 2–11 years.
Number in School. 182 (97 boys, 85 girls).
Fees per term (2011-2012). Junior School: £2,175–£2,432. Nursery: £170 per week (full time).

Crackley Hall is a co-educational independent Catholic day school which welcomes members of all denominations. The school is part of the Warwickshire Catholic Independent Schools Foundation and is the Junior School to Princethorpe College.

Situated on the outskirts of Kenilworth, Crackley Hall occupies a pleasant and safe setting with playing fields a short distance across the road. An extended day facility is offered; pupils may be dropped off from 7.50 am and can stay at school until 6.00 pm. Nursery attendance times are flexible.

Crackley Hall bases its care for individuals on the sound Christian principles of love and forgiveness; children become strong in the understanding of themselves and others. There is a keen sense of community between pupils, staff and parents. We encourage fairness, freedom, friendship and fun.

Small class sizes promote individual attention. The curriculum is based on national guidelines, but pupils are encouraged to achieve well beyond these targets. During the early years, great emphasis is placed on developing key skills in reading, writing, speaking, listening, mathematics and science. The learning of tables and spellings is actively developed through simple homework tasks. Specialists teach Art, Design Technology, French, Music, Games, ICT and RE. Pupils have access to up-to-date networked ICT facilities in their own classrooms and there are several mobile laptop-based units.

Football, rugby, cricket, hockey, netball, tennis, athletics, swimming, rounders, trampolining and judo are all available. There is a strong and thriving music department and all pupils together with members of the choir, choral group and orchestra participate in concerts and stage productions to enrich their learning and to build confidence and self-esteem. Pupils have the opportunity to study a wide range of individual instruments under the guidance of a team of peripatetic staff and specialist teachers offer classes in music theatre, speech and drama and dance. Other activities are offered before and after school as well as during lunch breaks including art, chess, craft, ICT, gardening, steel band, food and textiles.

Admission is through interview with the Head, assessments in English and Mathematics, and a taster day at the school. We also ask for a reference from the child's current school. The admission information is considered as a whole so that as accurate a picture as possible of the child can be obtained. The pastoral elements are as important to us as academic ability.

Parents are welcomed into school for Friday morning assembly when the children's good work is celebrated. An active Parent Teacher Association organises social and fundraising events. Pupils are encouraged to maintain their links with the school by joining the Past Pupils' Association.

Charitable status. Warwickshire Catholic Independent Schools Foundation is a Registered Charity, number 1087124. It exists solely for the purpose of educating children.

Cransley School

Belmont Hall, Great Budworth, Nr Northwich, Cheshire CW9 6HN
Tel: 01606 891747
Fax: 01606 892122
e-mail: admin@cransleyschool.org.uk
website: www.cransleyschool.org.uk

Head: **Mrs Geraldine Gaunt**, BA, PGCE

Age Range. Girls 3–16, Boys 3–11.
Number in School. Day: 151 Girls, 21 Boys.
Fees per term (2010-2011). £1,208–£2,753. Compulsory extras: Lunches £105–£202.

Cransley School near Great Budworth is a very special place. Set in the midst of the beautiful Cheshire Countryside, it has a warm, friendly atmosphere in which all students are encouraged to fulfil their potential. Well-qualified, dedicated staff work hard to make the 'Cransley Experience' a rewarding, happy one. Small class sizes and a positive environment encourages academic success at every level.

GCSE results are always good. This year again 100% of our final year students achieved at least 5 GCSEs at grades A*–C and all went onto A Level studies in the Sixth Forms of their choice. In fact we were ranked as the 5th small Independent School in the country by the Sunday Times Parent Power Survey 2010.

Life is never dull at Cransley. There is a wide variety of extra-curricular activities available throughout the school – there are three choirs, a thriving orchestra and regular drama performances. Students have a choice of clubs – gymnastics, gardening, languages, football and rugby to name but a few. There are many sporting opportunities and Cransley teams regularly compete against other schools in the area.

Cransley students enjoy many visits to enrich the curriculum. We also play hosts to visiting theatre groups. We offer residential opportunities – groups have been overnight in London for theatre and museum visits; GCSE Geography students visit the Lake District; activity weekends are particular favourites for both Senior and Junior Department pupils; foreign travel is also on the menu. Recently groups have been on a French Exchange, as well as visiting New York, Lake Garda, Amsterdam and Rome.

Cransley also has a thriving PTA – they organise regular events throughout the year which raise valuable funds to support staff and students and also offer a fantastic opportunity for parents to get to know each other.

Crowstone Preparatory School

Westcliff School: 121/123 Crowstone Road, Westcliff-on-Sea, Essex SS0 8LH
Tel: 01702 346758
Fax: 01702 390632
e-mail: info@crowstoneprepschool.com
website: www.crowstoneprepschool.com

Sutton School: Fleet Hall Lane, Shopland Road,
Rochford, Essex SS4 1LL
Tel: 01702 540629
Fax: 01702 540629

Headmaster: **J P Thayer**, TCert London

Age Range. 2½–11.
Number in School. Day: 95 Boys, 65 Girls.
Fees per term (2010-2011). £1,251.90–£2,621.50
excluding lunch and insurance.

Crowstone Preparatory School is an independent day
school for boys and girls between the ages of three years and
eleven years.

The aim of the school is to obtain the highest possible
achievement from each individual pupil in a happy relaxed
atmosphere in all areas of school work.

We are especially concerned in providing extra stimulus
for children of high ability but also provide extra facilities
for slower learners.

Dagfa School Nottingham

57 Broadgate, Beeston, Nottingham NG9 2FU
Tel: 0115 913 8330
Fax: 0115 913 8331
e-mail: head@dagfaschool.notts.sch.uk
website: www.dagfaschool.notts.sch.uk

Head: **Mrs Jane Le Poidevin**, BEd Hons, NPQH

Age Range. 3–16.
Number in School. Day: Boys 160, Girls 80.
Fees per term (2010-2011). £2,214–£2,848.

Dagfa School is situated in pleasant gardens in a quiet
neighbourhood adjacent to University Park, and it enjoys
easy access from all areas of the city and county. Small
classes are taught by caring and dedicated staff, creating a
purposeful learning environment where individual talents
flourish.

A wide curriculum is provided, which includes the
National Curriculum but leaves time available for other
important aspects, such as an early introduction to foreign
languages. Results are very good at all stages, and pupils
also learn to be caring and thoughtful towards others.

Daiglen School

68 Palmerston Road, Buckhurst Hill, Essex IG9 5LG
Tel: 020 8504 7108
Fax: 020 8502 9608
e-mail: admin@daiglenschool.co.uk
website: www.daiglenschool.co.uk

Perstare et Praestare – Persevere and Excel

Head Teacher: **Mrs M Bradfield**, BA, CertEd, DipNatSci

Age Range. 3–11.
Number in School. 152.
Fees per term (2011-2012). £2,115–£2,465, sibling discount available. Extras: Lunch, swimming (juniors), drama
(infants).

Daiglen School is a small preparatory school which provides a happy and secure environment for all pupils. Kindness to others is valued above all, and pupils are polite and
considerate with each other as well as with adults. We have a
strong sense of family and community, underpinned by
warm supportive relationships and mutual respect, which

ensures that all pupils are valued and given the chance to
shine.

Confident children relish challenge and the school promotes a culture of excellence. We celebrate individual and
group successes as children learn the importance of pursuing their ambitions with determination and perseverance.
They are inspired to do well both by the infectious enthusiasm of their excellent teachers and by the example of older
children who become their role models. Our pupils flourish
in this environment and leave as caring, confident, articulate
and well-mannered young people, fully prepared for the next
stage in their journey through life. We are justifiably proud
of our pupils' academic achievements, as well as those on
the sports field and other areas, and a good proportion leave
with scholarships to selective independent and state secondary schools.

Founded in 1916, Daiglen School is rich in history and
tradition. The school is built around an elegant Victorian
house with much of its stained glass and cornices intact.
Modern features include a purpose built gymnasium/hall, art
room, science laboratory and ICT suite. It is pleasantly situated on the borders of Epping Forest and is well served by
public transport.

Inspection: Daiglen School was inspected in September
2010 and received the highest accolades from the Independent Schools Inspectorate. The team praised Daiglen in
glowing terms, awarding the highest possible rating in areas
that include pupils' all-round achievement, personal development and the quality of teaching, and declaring the
school's Early Years Foundation Stage setting to be outstanding in every respect. The full report is available to read
on our website.

Choosing a school is arguably the most difficult decision
you will make for your child, and one which will have the
greatest consequences in his or her life. Most of our pupils
come to Daiglen on personal recommendation from parents
of past or present pupils. We encourage a close and mutually
supportive partnership with parents. To find out more about
us, you can visit our website or make arrangements to visit
the school; you will receive a warm welcome.

Charitable status. The Daiglen School Trust Limited is
a Registered Charity, number 273015.

Davies Laing & Dick
Alpha Plus Group

100 Marylebone Lane, London W1U 2QB
Tel: 020 7935 8411
Fax: 020 7935 0755
e-mail: dld@dld.org
website: www.dldcollege.co.uk

Principal: **Mr David Lowe**

Age Range. 15+ Co-educational.
Number of Pupils. 380 Day.
Fees per annum (2010-2011). £16,400.

Davies Laing and Dick (DLD) is a co-educational London day school accepting pupils from the ages of 15+. There
are over 320 students in the Sixth Form studying A Levels
from a choice of 40 subjects. Two thirds are doing A Levels
in the normal way over a two-year period. Another large
group joins DLD at the start of Upper Sixth. There are no
subject restrictions at A Level. GCSE courses are taught
over a one-year period so pupils are able to join at the beginning of Year 11. The average class size is 6. Supplementary
lessons in English as a foreign language are taken by 6% of
the student body.

DLD is housed in two linked buildings in Marylebone,
both newly refurbished and very well equipped buildings.
There are three laboratories, two IT classrooms, a library for

private study with an IT annexe, a GCSE study area, an eighty-seat theatre which is also used to screen films. There is a recording studio and a film edit suite. Many classrooms are equipped with interactive whiteboards. Students are able to access work done in class, teachers' notes and homework assignments remotely via the DLD Virtual School.

Extra-curricular activities include sport, DLD youth theatre, set design, film making, the DLD house band, concerts, French club, life drawing classes, fundraising and Activities Week, which takes place at the end of June. The school day finishes at 4.40 pm; most activities take place after this.

While the atmosphere at DLD is more informal than in mainstream independent schools, rules regarding academic performance are strictly enforced. Those who do not hand in work on time are required to attend Supervised Study at the end of the day. Lateness to lessons is not tolerated. There are fortnightly tests in each subject and three weekly reports. Parents receive five reports each year and there are two parents' evenings.

The teaching staff are highly qualified and chosen not just for their expertise but also for their ability to relate positively to young people. The college aims to make learning interesting, active and rigorous. While clear guidelines are very important to ensure pupils establish a good working routine, the college believes strongly that pupils respond best when there is a culture of encouragement. Effort, progress, achievement and courtesy are regularly acknowledged and formally rewarded.

Derby Grammar School

Rykneld Hall, Rykneld Road, Littleover, Derby DE23 4BX
Tel: 01332 523027
Fax: 01332 518670
e-mail: headmaster@derbygrammar.co.uk
website: www.derbygrammar.co.uk

Headmaster: **Mr R D Paine**, BA, PGCE

   Age Range. Boys 7–18, Girls 16–18.
   Number in School. 300.
   Fees per term (2011-2012). £2,593 (Years 3–4), £2,875 (Years 5–6), £3,593 (Years 7–13).
   Derby Grammar School has a Christian foundation and seeks to promote Christian values whilst respecting those from other faiths. We admit pupils of above-average ability and believe that intellectual endeavour and hard work in the classroom and outside should be at the heart of an exciting, challenging and stimulating environment that inspires all pupils to succeed. The School has established a proven success record in public examinations and university entry. The size of the School ensures that all pupils know each other and are supported by the teaching staff, with all the pupils' individual needs addressed. Dedicated and inspiring teachers teach a wide range of subjects in small classes. In our community the pupils are taught to take responsibility for their own actions, to develop leadership qualities, to learn self-respect and concern for others. A variety of extra-curricular work helps the pupils to boost their self-confidence and gives all of them the chance to take part. In their time with us, we aim to produce articulate and confident young men and women, who have enjoyed their schooling, are confident in relationships and can go on to higher education with the skills needed to do well. The School aims to continue its development and building programme to ensure that current and future students have the opportunity to work in a stimulating environment.
   Charitable status. Derby Grammar School is a Registered Charity, number 1015449. It exists to educate children.

Ditcham Park School

Petersfield, Hampshire GU31 5RN
Tel: 01730 825659
Fax: 01730 825070
e-mail: info@ditchampark.com
website: www.ditchampark.com

Head Teacher: **Mr A P N Rowley**, BSc Hons

   Age Range. 4–16.
   Number in School. Day: 177 Boys, 172 Girls.
   Fees per term (2011-2012). £2,262–£3,776 excluding lunch.
   Situated high on the South Downs, the School achieves excellent results in a happy purposeful atmosphere.
   Charitable status. Ditcham Park School is a Registered Charity, number 285244R. It exists for educational purposes.

The Dixie Grammar School

Market Bosworth, Leicestershire CV13 0LE
Tel: 01455 292244
Fax: 01455 292151
e-mail: info@dixie.org.uk
website: www.dixie.org.uk

Headmaster: **Mr J R Wood**, MA Cantab, PGCE

   Age Range. 3–18.
   Number in School. Grammar School: 160 boys, 200 girls; Junior School: 91 boys, 71 girls.
   Fees per term (2010-2011). Grammar School £2,970, Junior School £2,160–£2,480, Pippins Nursery £199.25 per week.
   The Dixie Grammar School, a medieval foundation, was closed in 1969, but re-founded as an independent school in 1987. Its Junior School opened three years later. The Grammar School occupies a site in the heart of the quiet country town of Market Bosworth, the attractive early nineteenth-century main school building overlooking the market square. The school has over thirty acres of playing fields just outside the town. The Junior School is just under three miles away at Temple Hall in Wellsborough, where it enjoys a spacious site surrounded by countryside. The schools are served by six bus routes, with a free shuttle service between the two sites.
   Both schools are selective and have academic achievement as their central aim. Music, drama, sport and service are also an integral part of the education offered. Both schools have an inter-denominational Christian basis. The relative smallness of the schools ensures that they combine great friendliness with excellent discipline, providing a secure and well-ordered framework in which children can confidently achieve their full potential.
   The Grammar School offers academic, music, art, sports and sixth form scholarships.
   Charitable status. The Leicestershire Independent Educational Trust is a Registered Charity, number 514407. It exists to provide a grammar school education.

Egerton Rothesay School

Durrants Lane, Berkhamsted, Herts HP4 3UJ
Tel: 01442 865275
Fax: 01442 864977

e-mail: admin.dl@eger-roth.co.uk
website: www.eger-roth.co.uk

A School with a Difference

Headteacher: **Mrs N Boddam-Whetham**, BA Hons, PGTC

Age Range. 5–16 years: Main School 9–16 years; Springboard 5–11 years; Rainbow, Speech and Language Centre 5–11 years.
Number in School. 122 boys, 58 girls.
Fees per term (2011-2012). £4,562–£6,495 (lunches included).

When you visit Egerton Rothesay in Berkhamsted you soon see that it is a school that is different.

ERS aims to provide an exciting and relevant educational experience for pupils who need that little bit more support from their school.

It focuses especially on students who have found, or would find, it difficult to make progress and succeed within another school – perhaps because of an earlier, negative, educational experience or perhaps because of a specific learning difficulty, such as dyslexia or dyspraxia or a speech and language difficulty. If your child has other educational difficulties the school may also be able to help with these.

Children come with a variety of learning styles and use is made of a wide range of teaching strategies in order to match these. The school provides additional levels of support both in the classroom and on an individual basis, varying to suit the need of the child.Throughout the school children are taught in small classes to match their need for support, to the level of teaching and support staff provided. In addition there are also two special groups with a specific focus: Rowan (a base for senior aged pupils with complex needs) and The Rainbow Centre (for children, up to Year 6, with speech and language difficulties).

To help with ongoing child assessment, and again to ensure the correct matching of need and assistance given, the school has an Educational Psychologist who works closely with parents, pupils and staff.

Every child at Egerton Rothesay is seen as a unique person and an individual student. The school aims to make an excellent contribution into the life of each one ensuring that they can be supported in the way that they personally need to maximise their individual learning potential.

The school wants more than just to deliver a curriculum and has a learning skills approach throughout the school – aiming to prepare students not just for school and exams but for life in today's complex society and an ever changing world of work.

A child can often be able and talented in one aspect of the curriculum yet find it difficult to make good progress in another. Some students will need support for the duration of their time in school whilst others may only need a short amount of support to address a specific problem or to give a boost.

All activities takes place within an environment offering exceptional pastoral care and spiritual development that is driven and informed by the school's Christian foundation.

Transport: Egerton Rothesay is also more than just a local school – students travel to the school from all directions, many using the comprehensive bus service that the school runs over a 35-mile radius.

If you think this may be the right type of school for your child you can obtain more information from the Registrar on 01442 877060 or visit the website at www.eger-roth.co.uk.

Elmhurst School

44–48 South Park Hill Road, South Croydon, Surrey CR2 7DW
Tel: 020 8688 0661
Fax: 020 8686 7675
e-mail: office@elmhurstschool.net
website: www.elmhurstschool.net

Principal: H J Wickham, MA

Age Range. 4–11.
Number in School. 210 Boys.
Fees per term (2010-2011). £2,360–£2,835 (including lunches and ISC Personal Accident Insurance).

Elmhurst School (established 1869) prepares boys for entry to such prestigious schools as Whitgift, Trinity, Dulwich College and Caterham and possesses an enviable record of academic success.

Equally important is the wide ranging curriculum designed to encourage boys to make the most of their talents and strengthen their weaknesses in a structured but friendly family environment. An extremely well equipped and flourishing computer department, together with active participation in educational visits and drama, foster interest in technology and creativity. A wide variety of sports is encouraged, including participation in Soccer, Cricket, Rugby, Athletics, Gymnastics, Tennis, Swimming and Golf.

Elmhurst accepts boys at the age of four, with occasional vacancies arising in other year groups.

Fairfield School

Fairfield Way, Backwell, Bristol BS48 3PD
Tel: 01275 462743
Fax: 01275 464347
e-mail: secretary@fairfieldschool.org.uk
website: www.fairfieldschool.org.uk

Headteacher: **Mrs Lesley Barton**, BA Hons, PGCE

Age Range. 3–11.
Number in School. 58 Boys, 63 Girls.
Fees per term (2011-2012). Nursery (full-time), Reception, Years 1–2 £2,215; Years 3–6 £2,435.

Fairfield is an independent day school for boys and girls aged 3–11. The school was founded in 1935 and aims to provide a broad, traditional education. We encourage each child to maximise his or her potential through creating a family ethos in which children feel happy, secure and valued. A fundamental aspect of our ethos is our commitment to small classes, usually of 18–20. Fairfield offers a broad and balanced curriculum, informed by the National Curriculum. Teachers and visiting coaches provide a wide range of extracurricular lessons including music, dance, sport, drama and creative activities. Pupils are prepared for entry into all local independent senior schools as well as for the local maintained sector schools.

For further details please apply to the School Secretary.
Charitable status. Fairfield PNEU School (Backwell) Limited is a Registered Charity, number 310215.

Fairley House School

Junior Department:
220 Lambeth Road, London SE1 7JY
Tel: 020 7803 3170
Fax: 020 7620 1069

Senior Department:
30 Causton Street, London SW1P 4AU
Tel: 020 7976 5456
Fax: 020 7976 5905
e-mail: office@fairleyhouse.org.uk

website: www.fairleyhouse.org.uk

Principal: **Jacqueline Murray**, BA Hons, MEd, MSc,
DipPsychol, RSA Dip SpLD

Head of Junior Department: Ann Osborn, CertEd, BEd,
RSA Dip SpLD, DPSE SEN

Head of Senior Department: Michael Taylor, BA Hons,
PGCE, FRGS

Age Range. 5–14.
Number of Pupils. 157 (121 Boys, 36 Girls).
Fees per term (2010-2011). £8,750.
Fairley House School is a school for children with specific learning difficulties, dyslexia and dyspraxia. The aim of the school is to provide intensive support to help children to overcome difficulties, coupled with a full, rich curriculum designed to bring out children's strengths and talents. Most children return to mainstream schooling after two to three years. Fairley House School was founded in 1982 for children aged 6–12 by Daphne Hamilton-Fairley, a speech and language therapist. She set up the school with the intention of integrating education with therapies (speech and language, occupational) normally only obtainable through the health service. This integration is one of the many things that sets us apart as a specialist day school for children with specific learning difficulties.

We emphasise the development of the whole child, helping him or her to gain confidence and self-esteem through an encouraging and nurturing ethos. The children have plenty of opportunities to develop sound academic and social skills and to become independent. At Fairley House, everyone succeeds.

Ferndale Preparatory School
Cognita Schools Group

5–7 Bromsgrove, Faringdon, Oxon SN7 7JF
Tel: 01367 240618
Fax: 01367 241429
e-mail: info@ferndaleschool.co.uk
website: www.ferndaleschool.co.uk

Headmaster: **Mr Andrew Mersh**, BEd Hons

Age Range. 3–11 years.
Number in School. Day: 53 Girls, 51 Boys.
Fees per term (2010-2011). £2,295 (Nursery), £2,435 (age 4–7), £2,575 (age 7–11).
Ferndale is a small, thriving co-educational prep school, occupying pleasant Georgian buildings in the historic market town of Faringdon. Its size means that each child receives individual attention and in its family atmosphere pupils find a secure and supportive environment where confidence burgeons and exceptional results are achieved.

There is no formal test, but an interview, with a "taster" day may help ensure that a child is appropriately placed. Entry is age 3 into the Nursery and in succeeding years subject to place availability. Ferndale welcomes children of all faiths, though broadly Christian values underpin an ethos where social responsibility and habits of courtesy and consideration for others are much in evidence.

Ferndale has a remarkable record of success in entrance to schools of first choice, amongst them several in the highest league. Scholarships and other awards have regularly been won at target schools from Cheltenham to Abingdon

and from Bath to Oxford, while places have also been gained at Grammar and other maintained schools.

In recent years most of our boys have been offered places at Abingdon School or Magdalen College, Oxford; our girls have mainly gone to the School of St Helen & St Katharine or Our Lady's Convent in Abingdon. Other schools have included Oxford High, Headington, Wychwood, Cokethorpe, Grittleton House, Pate's Grammar, King Edward's Bath, Warneford, Farmor's, Faringdon, Rendcomb and Kingham Hill.

The arts flourish at Ferndale. Music and the visual arts are strong, and drama and dance are highly regarded. Games from rugby and netball to chess are another success story and a wide range of extra-curricular activities includes such activities as art, football, gardening, rugby, ICT and swimming at Faringdon's Leisure Centre.

At Ferndale there are specialist rooms for music, art, science and ICT which perfectly complement the homely, child-friendly classrooms in the original buildings; these also house a custom-designed nursery department. The school employs its own chef who provides excellent and varied lunches with an impressive range of choices.

Finborough School

The Hall, Great Finborough, Stowmarket, Suffolk
IP14 3EF
Tel: 01449 773600
Fax: 01449 773601
e-mail: admin@finborough.suffolk.sch.uk
website: www.finboroughschool.co.uk

Principal: Mr James Sinclair

Head of Senior School: **Mr Stephen Banks**, BA Hons,
PGCE

Head of Preparatory School: Mrs Stephanie Samuels, BA
Ed, DipMont, QTS

Age Range. Co-educational 2½–18.
Number of Pupils. Boarders 59, Day 167.
Fees per term (2011-2012). Full Boarding £5,255–£7,050, Weekly Boarding £4,225–£5,655. Day £2,290–£3,535. The Montessori Nursery has its own fee structure. Termly fees are fully inclusive of all meals, educational materials and extended day care for day pupils. Flexible and occasional boarding facilities for day pupils are available at additional cost.

Location. Finborough School is two miles west of Stowmarket, which is on the main London-Norwich line and is 5 minutes' drive from the A14. The school operates a local bus service for day pupils.

Facilities. Founded in 1977, the School moved to its present site in 1980 since when it has consistently reinvested in improved facilities, including a new Art Studio and Apple Mac suite. Well-maintained playing fields and hard courts for tennis, netball and basketball. The woodland provides an adventure playground, camping site and a stretch of river for canoeing and fishing. An equestrian centre has been opened with a floodlit arena.

Aims. By acknowledging each pupil as an individual and by nurturing their individual talents, our aim is to prepare them for life after school. The School Development Plan allows for planned growth to around 400 pupils in total. The number permits retention of our small school family atmosphere whilst providing a unit where viability will allow the provision of first-rate facilities in all areas.

Education. Classes are small, with an average of 15 pupils and are taught by highly-qualified professional staff. The curriculum covers the full range of traditional subjects, as well as technology and ICT through to GCSE and A Level. All pupils receive trained advice on careers and university entry.

Examination results are good, reflecting not only pupil ability but their hard work and the expertise and commitment of teaching staff.

Music, Drama and Art. Pupils receive expert tuition and perform at School concerts, assemblies, and in the local music and drama festivals. A wide range of instrumental tuition is available at additional cost. The School regularly has successes in Art competitions and a wide range of work is displayed around the premises.

Sport. Competitive but well-mannered – Rugby, Netball, Hockey, Soccer, Rounders, Cricket, Golf, Cross-country, Athletics, Swimming, Tennis etc.

Entry. Following application, previous schools reports and school references are received and interview arranged. All candidates attend trial sessions for 2 or 3 days before making up their minds about the school. Entry tests in Mathematics and English are taken during trial days.

General. Day pupils can be accommodated from 8.00 am to 5.30 pm and there is no Saturday school. A weekly assembly in the village church is an important social as well as spiritual occasion.

The Firs School

45 Newton Lane, Chester CH2 2HJ
Tel: 01244 322443
Fax: 01244 400450
e-mail: admin@firsschool.org
website: www.firsschool.net

Headmistress: **Mrs M A Denton**, CertEd

Age Range. 3–11 Co-educational.
Number in School. 228: 148 Boys, 80 Girls.
Fees per term (2011-2012). £440–£2,330.

The Firs School is an independent co-educational primary school set in attractive grounds about a mile and a half north of the city of Chester. It was founded in 1945 by Mrs F A Longman.

The aim of the Firs is to help children achieve their academic potential in the context of a caring environment based upon Christian principles. Children of all faiths are welcome and we respect and learn from their beliefs and cultures. Our strengths lie in the individual attention we are able to give, a carefully planned curriculum and an effective partnership with parents. Specialist teaching for dyslexia and other educational needs is available. We have a proven record of success in preparing children for entrance to local independent and state schools. The school is well resourced with a continuous programme of investment, including our technology and pottery rooms.

Whilst placing great emphasis on the core subjects, our curriculum is enhanced through the teaching of French, Spanish, gardening club, the opportunity for sport and the quality of our provision of art and music throughout the school.

Our objective is to encourage the development of the whole child so that each will leave The Firs School with an understanding of the wider world and an awareness of his or her responsibility to others.

Firwood Manor Preparatory School
GEMS Education

Broadway, Chadderton, Oldham OL9 0AD
Tel: 0161 620 6570
Fax: 0161 626 3550

e-mail: admin@firwoodmanor.org.uk
website: www.firwoodmanor.org.uk

Head: **Mr D Robinson**, BEd Hons

Age Range. 2¾–11 Co-educational.
Number of Pupils. 130.
Fees per term (2010-2011). £1,950 plus £160 for lunch.

Firwood Manor Preparatory School opened in September 2002 and is an independent, co-educational day school for children aged from 2¾ to 11 years. It is situated on Broadway in Chadderton, Oldham close to the beginning of the A627M. This location makes it very accessible from a number of places in Greater Manchester and Lancashire, including Bury, Rochdale, North Manchester and Ashton. It is also an easy dropping-off point for parents who commute to work. The school is open from 7.30 am to 6.00 pm to care for your child.

The school is being developed through teamwork, close interaction, open communication and collaborative planning and has a hard working, dedicated, well-qualified and experienced staff.

At Firwood Manor we are very aware of our responsibility to provide children with the very best educational possibilities and to optimise the opportunities for children to reach their full potential, so that their years of primary education culminate in the maximum appropriate outcomes.

Our exceptional facilities certainly help us to realise these aims. They include a fully equipped nursery, purpose built classrooms from Reception to Year 6, specialist rooms for Science and Art, Design and Technology, an ICT suite, a hall for sport, gymnastics, dance, music and drama, extensive grounds with facilities for football, hockey and netball and on-site catering facilities.

The starting point of every teacher is the infinite worth of each child. Every day our aim is to provide each and every child with exciting and challenging learning experiences, which are both traditional and innovative.

Our children are encouraged to be independent, confident, responsible and compassionate with a strong sense of purpose and self-discipline. They have a love of learning for its own sake with enquiring minds and the ability to freely express their likes and dislikes. We aim to give them opportunities to develop skills to enable them to be good team players, to solve problems, both academically and in their daily lives, and to enable them to manage change, risk and uncertainty. And above all, they have a strong belief in themselves and in what they can achieve.

Forest Park Preparatory School

Lauriston House, 27 Oakfield, Sale, Cheshire M33 6NB
Tel: 0161 973 4835
Fax: 0161 282 9021
e-mail: post@forestparkschool.co.uk
website: www.forestparkschool.co.uk

Headteacher: **Mrs H S Gee**, BEd Hons

Age Range. 3–11.
Number in School. 71 Day Boys, 59 Day Girls.
Fees per term (2010-2011). £1,720–£1,880.

Forest Park occupies a pleasant site in a quiet road surprisingly close to the centre of Sale, easily accessible from motorways and surrounding areas.

The school aims to discover and develop each child's particular abilities by offering a varied curriculum in a stimulating and happy atmosphere. Forest Park has a good pupil teacher ratio and offers a wide range of subjects with priority given to the traditional disciplines of English, Mathematics and Science. Pupils from three years of age are taught

Information Technology by specialist staff. Swimming is taught from the age of five and games offered are Football, Cricket, Lacrosse, Netball, Tennis and Hockey. Pupils are taught French from an early age, the older children having the opportunity to visit a language study centre in France.

The confidence and social ease one expects of a private education is a product of the school. Our aim is to develop skills and knowledge through a habit of hard work in a secure and happy environment within a disciplined framework. The school prepares pupils for all independent grammar school examinations and has an excellent record in this respect.

The school prides itself on strong links and communication with a most supportive Parents' Association.

Forest Preparatory School

Moss Lane, Timperley, Altrincham, Cheshire WA15 6LJ
Tel: 0161 980 4075
Fax: 0161 903 9275
e-mail: headteacher@forestschool.co.uk
website: www.forestschool.co.uk

Headmaster: **Mr R Hyde**

Age Range. 2–11.
Number in School. Day: 90 Boys, 95 Girls.
Fees per term (2011-2012). £1,779–£1,998.
A co-educational school set in spacious grounds with high academic standards and an enviable reputation for its care of the individual.

Working within a happy environment, the children experience a traditional approach to education both in the subject disciplines and the high expectations of good behaviour.

The Infant Department ensures the children have a thorough understanding of reading, writing and number work. The Junior curriculum is very broad and includes all curriculum areas whilst special attention is given to those subjects which the children require for entry to the senior schools.

Small classes, a friendly atmosphere and extra-curricular activities ensure the children achieve their full potential and are well prepared for future schooling.

Francis House Preparatory School

Aylesbury Road, Tring, Hertfordshire HP23 4DL
Tel: 01442 822315
Fax: 01442 827080
e-mail: info@francishouseschool.co.uk
website: www.francishouseschool.co.uk

'Combining the best of the past with the excellence of today for a very bright future.'

Chairman of Board of Governors: Mr Ron Busby

Head: **Mrs Helen Stanton-Tonner**, BEd

Type of School. Co-educational Day School
Age Range. 2–11.
Number of Pupils. 117: 51 boys, 66 girls.
Fees per term (2011-2012). £680–£2,580.
Francis House is a family school for boys and girls aged 2–11 where emphasis is placed on the following:
• A happy and disciplined environment
• Teaching of the highest quality
• Encouragement to develop a sense of responsibility and independence
• A high standard of politeness and consideration for others

• High quality pastoral care

Francis House is situated in an attractive elevated position in Tring. It is easily accessible from the A41 and our pupils travel from Aylesbury, Hemel Hempstead, Berkhamsted, Dunstable, Leighton Buzzard and the surrounding villages. The school is housed in two purpose built buildings and is surrounded by beautiful grounds, gardens, playing fields and tennis courts.

Here at Francis House we are a dedicated team working in partnership with parents to develop the potential of the whole child in a happy and caring community.

Francis House offers all of its pupils a wealth of opportunities. Education is about exploring and engaging every child's imagination in order that he or she will reach their full potential. Self-esteem is so important, particularly in the learning and growing up process and at Francis House praise and positive feedback provide the basis upon which every child can build, develop and grow educationally, and emotionally.

The joy of human nature is that we are all different and at Francis House each child is treated as an individual; everyone's strengths are recognised and celebrated.

Frewen College

Brickwall, Northiam, Nr Rye, East Sussex TN31 6NL
Tel: 01797 252494
Fax: 01797 252567
e-mail: office@frewencollege.co.uk
website: www.frewencollege.co.uk

Principal: **Mrs Linda Smith**, BA, PGCE, PGC Asp Synd

Age Range. 7–17 Co-educational (Boarding from age 8).
Number in School. Full Boarders: 15 boys, 3 girls; Weekly Boarders: 22 boys, 5 girls; Day: 40 boys, 20 girls.
Fees per term (2011-2012). Day £5,400–£7,055; Full and Weekly Boarding £7,792–£9,794.
Frewen College is a small friendly independent specialist school catering principally for children with Specific Learning Difficulties (dyslexia, dyspraxia, dyslcalculia) and related speech and language and sensory integration problems. We also accept a small number with Asperger's Syndrome if we feel they will fit in and enrich the school environment. We are inspected by Ofsted and rated 'Outstanding'.

The school adopts a holistic approach to teaching, designed to enhance pupils' confidence and self-esteem, allowing them to build on their strengths while learning to cope with their difficulties. Each pupil has a comprehensive Individual Education Plan in each subject (described by CReSTeD as 'exemplary') so that teaching can be tailored to individual needs. About half the children have statements of special educational need and are funded, currently by 18 different LEAs. Services children are also welcome.

The move to co-educational status has proved popular with the number of girls increasing each year. Boarding for girls was introduced in September 2009 and has already been extended. Boarding is run very much like an extended family, with bedrooms of 1–4 pupils, all with en-suite facilities, and numbers have more than doubled in the past 4 years. Catering is 'in house', and rated by all-comers as 'excellent'! A very wide range of recreational activities is available, and transport is provided to and from London each weekend.

Juniors have the benefit of a separate school adjacent to the main site, where our recent Ofsted Inspection found 'a particularly high standard of education'. Frewen Juniors has an outstanding reputation for the performing arts, enjoys modern IT facilities, and a popular adventure playground.

Frewen College has excellent facilities, based around a historic house located in 60 acres of playing fields, gardens and parkland. Educational provision includes two modern IT suites, a drama workshop, food and nutrition kitchens, pottery, music and music practice rooms, CDT workshop and an art studio. English lessons are supplemented by intensive daily reading sessions.

Outdoor facilities include a large open-air swimming pool, tennis and basketball court, all-weather five-a-side and hockey pitch, fitness suite, as well as extensive playing fields. Our cricket pitch is rated one of the best village pitches in the County. We also have access to another 100 acres of ancient parkland for cross-country runs, camping, and orienteering. All Year 9 pupils are entered for the Duke of Edinburgh's Award Scheme. A new addition to the facilities is a mountain bike trail.

All classroom staff have specialist dyslexia training. We are Department for Education approved, a supporting corporate member of the BDA, and rated 'Dyslexia Specialist Provision' by CReSTeD.

Charitable status. The Frewen Educational Trust Limited is a Registered Charity, number 307019.

Fyling Hall School

Robin Hood's Bay, Near Whitby, North Yorkshire YO22 4QD
Tel: 01947 880353
Fax: 01947 881097
e-mail: office@fylinghall.org
website: www.fylinghall.org

Headmaster: **Mr Ken James**

Age Range. 4–18.
Number of Pupils. Boarders: Boys 68, Girls 47, Day: Boys 39, Girls 40.
Fees per term (2011-2012). Day: £1,900–£2,600; Weekly Boarding: £4,700–£5,500;   Full   Boarding: £4,900–£5,900.

Fyling Hall School is one of the oldest recognised co-educational schools in the country. It occupies a spectacular coastal setting within the North York Moors National Park. Pupils may safely enjoy freedom in this beautiful and peaceful rural area.

The buildings centre on a grade two listed Georgian country house in delightfully landscaped gardens incorporating an outdoor theatre overlooking Robin Hood's Bay. Recent expansion has included two new boarding houses, science laboratories and dining room in addition to the purpose-built Junior School. We have also built a spacious multi-functional sports hall and an astroturf recently.

The school is intentionally small due to its desire to educate pupils as individuals. The advantageous pupil-teacher ratio encourages effective learning. The teaching is along traditional lines with an emphasis on 'doing one's best' within a supportive yet challenging environment. A broadly based and well resourced curriculum is followed which reflects recent national initiatives, particularly in the scientific and information technology fields. A wide range of GCSE and A Level courses are offered.

Fyling Hall is a closely knit society with an emphasis on proactive pastoral care and a real sense of communal responsibility. The chief feature is a spirit of confidence and cooperation between staff and pupils in an atmosphere which is natural for growth.

There is no entrance examination but an interview and a report from the current school are integral parts of the admission process.

Many of the pupils stay to join the Sixth Form, where privilege and responsibility present a balance and are a useful preparation for university life.

The school takes advantage of its natural surroundings in the provision of numerous extra-curricular activities. Fyling Hall has its own ponies and these constitute a much loved part of school life. Climbing, Karate, Duke of Edinburgh's Award and Riding are all popular. The main games are rugby, hockey, cricket and tennis, each with a full fixture list. Music enjoys a good reputation and individual tuition is available in all the usual musical instruments.

Robin Hood's Bay is remarkably accessible despite its rural splendour. Nearby Whitby and Scarborough are both railheads. Teesside Airport and the ferry port of Hull, with their frequent continental connections, are both easily reached. An experienced Secretary is able to advise on all travel arrangements.

Academic standards are high, but other abilities are valued, and aided by the small size of classes it is hoped that all pupils can be encouraged to achieve their maximum potential.

Charitable status. Fyling Hall School Trust Ltd is a Registered Charity, number 507857. It exists for the provision of high quality education for boys and girls.

Gads Hill School

Higham, Rochester, Kent ME3 7PA
Tel: 01474 822366
Fax: 01474 822977
e-mail: admissions@gadshillschool.org
website: www.gadshill.org

Headmaster: **Mr D G Craggs**, BSc, MA, FCollP, FRSA

Age Range. Co-educational 3–16.
Number in School. 370.
Fees per term (2011-2012). £2,398–£3,139.
Entry requirements. Interview and assessment.
Aim. To provide a good all-round education, to build confidence, establish friendships, to reward success (however small) and to ensure our students leave as mature, self-reliant young people who depart Gads for the career or University placement of their choice.

Kindergarten (3–6 years). From the very early years in Kindergarten the children are encouraged to learn through play, music and drama. Basic letter and number work is introduced within the nursery and reception class as the children concentrate on the Early Learning Goals. In Year 1 and Year 2 they largely follow Key Stage One of the National Curriculum although in addition; from Reception upwards, all of our children are taught French and also Information and Communications Technology.

Junior School (7–11 years). Our Junior School curriculum seeks to build upon the children's undaunted love of adventure. Literacy, Numeracy and Humanities continue to be taught by Form Tutors however, the children begin to benefit from more lessons delivered by specialist tutors particularly in French, Information Technology, Design & Technology, RE, Games and Drama.

Senior School (11–16 years). Senior School concentrates very much on the preparation for GCSE success and our classes are kept to a maximum of 20 children per class. This way the children benefit from smaller class sizes and consequently our tutors get to know each child as an individual and this enables them to provide the right level of support and assistance. This goes a long way to helping them achieve their goals for GCSEs and A levels.

Location. Gads Hill School is centred on the former home of Charles Dickens and is surrounded by beautiful grounds, playing fields and countryside. It is a few minutes' drive from the A2 and M2, with good access to the Medway Towns, Dartford and Gravesend.

Curriculum. At Gads we largely follow the National Curriculum although we place a strong emphasis on "communication" with all of our children benefiting from lessons in French, Information and Communications Technology and Drama as well as English. Senior School children progress to take GCSEs in English, English Literature, Maths, French, Design & Technology, Combined Science (Double Award), Geography and GNVQ ICT (4 GCSEs).

Sports and Activities. We concentrate very much on team games (rugby, hockey, soccer, netball, cricket, athletics and rounders) to ensure that our children learn the values of team work and communication. In the Kindergarten and Junior Schools all students take part in weekly swimming lessons. Because of our small class sizes almost all of our children have the opportunity to represent the school in competitive fixtures against other schools. Gad's Hill also has a thriving Combined Cadet Force. Students join the CCF in Year 8 and take part in weekly training sessions as well as termly field days and an annual camp. The CCF allows children to experience fantastic outdoor pursuits, adventurous training and leadership courses and is essentially about doing something different and challenging. Gad's Hill pupils are also able to take part in a variety of after-school activities. These range from academic pursuits to a variety of other sports and Performing Arts.

Charitable status. Gads Hill School is a Registered Charity, number 803153. It exists for the purpose of educating children aged 3–16.

GEMS Bolitho School

Polwithen Road, Penzance, Cornwall TR18 4JR
Tel: 01736 363271
Fax: 01736 330960
e-mail: enquiries@bolithoschool.co.uk
website: www.bolithoschool.co.uk

Head: **Mr Clive Keevil**

Co-educational Day and Boarding School.
Age Range. 4–18 years.
Number of Pupils. Boys: 16 Boarders, 89 Day; Girls: 16 Boarders, 74 Day.
Fees per term (2011-2012). Day £2,145–£4,620; Weekly Boarding £5,576–£7,392; Full Boarding £6,332–£8,198. Lunch for Day Pupils £195.

GEMS Bolitho School is a small, co-educational school catering for pupils of all ages and for day pupils, weekly and full boarders. It deservedly has a national and international reputation for its pioneering and forward-looking approach. Distinctive educational features include: an accelerated national curriculum strategy, whereby pupils take the Key Stage 2 and 3 SATs tests a year early; there is a bilingual section, unique to the UK, where pupils can take around 30% of the syllabus through the medium of French; in the sixth form, students take the internationally prestigious International Baccalaureate – welcomed and recognised by all UK universities, all EU and USA universities, and most other universities worldwide. Set sizes average 12 for children between the ages of 5 years old and 13 years old. Above all, however, the school is a very happy school indeed.

The school's stated aim is to 'bring out the potential of every child and to offer a rounded education that aims at the highest academic standards'. At the heart of the school's philosophy lies the belief that children have extraordinary potential in a great many directions. If this potential is not realised during childhood, it fades; if it is identified and nourished, a child can be galvanised into a dynamic and motivated personality. If a child is to receive a genuinely rounded education, then it must hold that art, drama, music and sports should be embedded firmly into the curriculum –

and this the school has done. In addition, there are a great many clubs, activities, outings and expeditions catering for all age groups.

The school prides itself on its European and international outlook. International students from all over the world are warmly welcomed and encouraged to apply. Penzance, in Cornwall, is the warmest locality of the UK. It is also one of the safest and most beautiful parts of the country. This not only attracts pupils of excellence: the location, combined with the school's strong reputation, attracts large numbers of applications for teaching posts, and in consequence the teaching at the school is genuinely excellent.

GEMS Hampshire School

15 Manresa Road, Chelsea, London SW3 6NB
Tel: 020 7352 7077
Fax: 020 7351 3960
e-mail: hampshire@indschool.org
website: www.ths.westminster.sch.uk

Early Years Section:
5 Wetherby Place, London SW7 4NX

Principal: **Mr Arthur Bray**, CertEd

Age Range. 3–13.
Number in School. Day: 150 Boys, 150 Girls.
Fees per term (2010-2011). £3,300–£4,633.

From January 2009, the Pre-Preparatory and Preparatory section made a successful move to a new site at 15 Manresa Road, London SW3. The school spent three years working on the refurbishment of the Grade 2* listed building, which was originally built as a Library in 1890. The building has state-of-the-art facilities for the children which are sympathetically integrated with its original architectural features.

A broad-based and balanced curriculum is provided. Children are given every opportunity to develop individual talents as fully as possible – a broad range of academic subjects being supported by a high level of instruction in music, art, physical education and drama. Children are encouraged to study the history and development of their environment by means of regular visit to museums, art galleries, exhibitions and places of interest.

The School has been successful in preparing pupils for examination and scholarship entry into leading day and boarding senior independent schools. Great emphasis is placed on developing each child's individual talents.

Fully qualified and experienced teachers provide a high standard of tuition in all aspects of the curriculum.

Pupils start French from the age of three and senior forms attend an annual study visit to France, as an integral part of the French syllabus.

The School also offers a home-to-school bus service, after-school care and multi-activity holiday courses.

GEMS Sherfield
GEMS Education

Sherfield-on-Loddon, Hook, Hampshire RG27 0HT
Tel: 01256 884800
Fax: 01256 883172
e-mail: info@sherfieldschool.co.uk
website: www.sherfieldschool.co.uk

Executive Principal: **Professor Pat Preedy**

Head of Seniors: Olwen Wright
Head of Primary: Karen Chard

Age Range. 3 months – 18 years Co-educational.
Number in School. 525 Day Pupils.
Fees per term (2011-2012). £2,576–£4,630.

We offer a first-class academic education within a forward-looking and enriched curriculum to pupils aged from 3 months to 18 years from 7.30 am to 6.00 pm for 48 weeks of the year. Provision includes a range of holiday activities so that pupils can continue to extend and develop their talents.

Teaching methods are a blend of the traditional and the very best of new ideas, based upon research and an understanding of how the brain develops and functions. Along with the core subjects for all pupils there is a range of options to meet the needs of each individual student. The flexible approach allows some students to take examinations early if appropriate. Our Sixth Form offers a range of subject choices within the International Baccalaureate Diploma Programme, which is studied in Years 12 and 13.

Sherfield also offers an Extended Learning Programme. The pupils can choose from a vast range of academic, sport and practical subjects such as chess, mandarin, photography, and gymnastics.

Setting high standards, developing self-discipline and meeting the needs of each individual pupil ensures that each child meets their full potential. As part of the school's commitment to achievement they offer outstanding opportunities for talented individuals. Scholarships are offered in sports, music, arts and academic excellence for pupils at Year 7 and upwards.

Sherfield TV, available to view or download from the Sherfield website, provides vital information about the school to parents, the community and the media.

Sherfield prides itself on not just specialising in one area, but in all aspects of academic and sporting life. The focus is on fulfilling its motto of 'Roots to Grow and Wings to Fly'.

Gidea Park College

2 Balgores Lane, Gidea Park, Romford, Essex RM2 5JR
Tel: 01708 740381
Fax: 01708 740381
e-mail: office@gideaparkcollege.co.uk
website: www.gideaparkcollege.co.uk

Headmistress: Mrs Susan Gooding, BA Hons Dunelm

Age Range. 2½–11 Co-educational.
Number in School. 197 Day Pupils.
Fees per term (2011-2012). £2,500.

An established Preparatory school founded in 1924, the current Directors are the grand-daughters of the founders.

The main building, a substantial Georgian/Victorian house, accommodates the 7–11 year old children, the school library, assembly room and IT room plus the kitchens. In separate outside classrooms, bounded by lawns and playgrounds, is the small Pre-school unit and accommodation for 4–7 year old pupils.

All children are known and treated as individuals with specific talents which are valued and developed. Likewise, identified areas needing extra help and encouragement are recognised.

The broad-based curriculum is delivered by highly qualified, full-time classroom staff using traditional methods, assisted by qualified support staff.

Results in selection procedures at 11+ are of a consistently high standard with scholarships and places awarded at local Independent and Grammar Schools. Our KS1 and KS2 National Assessment Testing reveals standards above the National expectations.

All National Curriculum areas are covered using whole-class teaching methods. Latin and German are introduced in the higher year groups.

A school choir performs on formal occasions and visits local care homes to sing.

Local facilities are used for PE, swimming and games lessons. Our House system fosters team spirit and enables each individual to participate in a variety of inter-house competitions as well as inter-school events.

The school has a Christian Foundation and strong links with our local parish church. However, within our diverse community those of other faiths are welcomed and their beliefs respected and festivals celebrated. Our pupils are encouraged to think of others less fortunate than themselves and arrange a variety of fundraising events for charity.

The staff supervise an early Morning and After School Club for the convenience of working parents. Those staying relax and then complete homework assignments giving quality time for parents and children at home.

New parents are made welcome by our thriving Parents' Association and encouraged to join in the various social events arranged providing a friendship base for them whilst at the school. Their fundraising provides extra equipment and fun occasions for the children.

We encourage all prospective parents to visit the school prior to applying so they may see classes in action and have an opportunity to ask any questions. We consider the partnership between pupils, parents and school to be of paramount importance in enabling each child to reach his/her potential.

Gosfield School

Halstead, Essex CO9 1PF
Tel: 01787 474040
Fax: 01787 478228
e-mail: enquiries@gosfieldschool.org.uk
website: www.gosfieldschool.org.uk

Chair of Governors: Mr Peter Sakal

Principal: **Dr Sarah J Welch**, MA, PhD

Age Range. 4–18 Boys and Girls.
Number in School. Boarders 12, Day 175.
Fees per term (2011-2012). Day £2,480–£4,180; Boarding: £4,830– £5,230 (5 nights), £5,625–£6,995 (7 nights).

Founded in 1929, Gosfield occupies a gracious, listed country house which was built in 1870 for Lady Courtauld. The school is set in a glorious 110 acre estate which borders ancient woodland and is a haven for wildlife and rare species. There are conservation areas and nature trails within the grounds.

Recent building developments include a Sports Hall, IT Suite and an all-weather sports surface. Boarding accommodation has also been completely upgraded.

The school is deliberately small in numbers and provides a caring family atmosphere in which every pupil will be able to develop his or her own potential to the full. Classes are small, and standards are high. The system of personal tutors ensures that every child's needs are properly looked after both in academic work and in the sporting and cultural activities in which the school encourages all pupils to participate.

There is a wide range of activities including sports, music, drama and conservation work. The programme changes termly and provides something for everyone. There are no weekend lessons.

The school day is from 8.30 am to 3.50 pm with Infants finishing at 3.00 pm. On Monday–Thursday there are after-school games and activities which run until 4.50 pm. All our pupils are encouraged to participate in these activities. On Friday school ends at 3.50 pm. Games fixtures are all in midweek.

The whole structure – daily and weekly – aims to be flexible and helpful to parents and pupils. The school sees education as a partnership, so parents are always welcome to visit, to talk to staff, and to be involved in the school's activities.

Gosfield is situated in rural North Essex only 20 miles from Stansted Airport and thirty miles from the M25. The nearest town, Halstead, is a mile away and the nearest station is just fives miles away at Braintree.

There is a daily minibus service to and from Chelmsford, Sudbury, Braintree and Colchester.

Charitable status. Gosfield School is a Registered Charity, number 310871. It exists to provide education for boys and girls.

Grangewood Independent School

Chester Road, Forest Gate, London E7 8QT
Tel: 020 8472 3552
Fax: 020 8552 8817
e-mail: admin@grangewoodschool.com
website: www.grangewoodschool.com

Head: **Mrs Bim Amokeodo**, BEd Hons

Age Range. 3–11.
Number in School. 50 boys, 31 girls.
Fees per term (2010-2011). £1,160–£1,495.

Grangewood is a Christian Day School which welcomes children from any faith background. We offer a secure, friendly and caring environment in small classes where children can achieve their potential.

Charitable status. Grangewood Educational Association is a Registered Charity, number 803492.

Greenbank School

Heathbank Road, Cheadle Hulme, Cheadle, Cheshire SK8 6HU
Tel: 0161 485 3724
Fax: 0161 485 5519
e-mail: headmistress@greenbankschool.co.uk
website: www.greenbankschool.co.uk

Headmistress: **Mrs Janet Lowe**, CertEd

Age Range. 6 months–11 years.
Number in School. Day: 87 Boys, 61 Girls. Daycare: 70.
Fees per term (2011-2012). £1,280–£2,175.

Greenbank is an independent co-educational school for pupils aged three to eleven years. A separate Nursery, open fifty weeks of the year, cares for babies and children from six months to four years old.

Greenbank School was founded in 1951 by Karl and Linda Orsborn. Since 1971 the School has been administered by an Educational Trust and is registered with the Department for Education.

Greenbank is situated within extensive grounds, comprises a mixture of traditional and modern buildings including an IT Suite and Library, separate play areas for Foundation, Infant and Junior children, playing fields with a cricket pavilion, an Astroturf area and netball court. 2009 saw the opening of state-of-the-art Science, Art and Music classrooms within a new administration building.

The school day begins at 8.45 am and ends at 3.30 pm, however we provide wraparound care from 7.30 am until 6.00 pm. The school also runs activity and sports clubs in the holidays.

Through its varied curricula and extra-curricular activities the School provides pupils with the opportunity of expanding their natural abilities to the full. Music, drama,

sport, computing and educational visits are some of the activities which play their part in providing a well-rounded programme of education. We strive to meet the social, emotional and intellectual needs of all pupils and the success of this philosophy is proven by the consistently outstanding examination results throughout the school, particularly at age eleven.

Charitable status. Greenbank School Limited is a Registered Charity, number 525930.

Greenfields School

Priory Road, Forest Row, East Sussex RH18 5JD
Tel: 01342 822189
Fax: 01342 825289
e-mail: admissions@greenfieldsschool.com
website: www.greenfieldsschool.com

Headteacher: **Mr G Hudson**

Age Range. 3–18.
Number in School. Day: 56 Boys, 30 Girls. Boarding: 18 Boys, 8 Girls.
Fees per term (2010-2011). Day £695–£3,521, Boarding (in addition to Tuition): £3,437 (Juniors), £2,757 (Seniors).

Greenfields has a fresh approach to education. It is a co-educational, non-denominational day and boarding school situated on the Ashdown Forest with 11 acres of its own woodland at the edge of the Sussex village of Forest Row.

The school offers a friendly, caring and safe environment, with a relaxed yet focused study environment. This is created by the study methods used that teach students what the barriers to study are and HOW to study and thereby help students to achieve success and a high degree of self-confidence, motivation, an enjoyment of study, and most important of all, an ability to continue studying successfully throughout life – it creates an ability to study independently and do research – students are well prepared for further education and work.

There is a high level of open communication between students and staff that helps to prevent failure, bullying or drugs.

Every student is individually programmed and targeted to ensure each one achieves the success they are capable of.

The classes are small and an excellent curriculum, providing core subjects and peripheral studies, is available up to GCSE and Advanced Levels.

A "qualifications" department exists for checking that students have fully understood each step of their studies, and also provides extra help for any student having any trouble in class. There is also an "ethics" department that helps to resolve any personal problems the student may have.

The pre-school has Montessori trained staff who use Montessori materials to ensure the best foundation for the rest of a student's education.

Entry is by tests for literacy and numeracy. There is a pre-entry section for those who need a short programme to catch up and be ready to join their correct class.

Extensive building work that started in 2002 has modernised the whole site and created new boarding bedrooms, new science labs, art room, maths and English purpose-built rooms and a large study room/library.

Trains take under an hour from London to East Grinstead, which is a ten minute car ride from the school. Gatwick Airport is a twenty minute car ride away.

Charitable status. Greenfields Educational Trust is a Registered Charity, number 287037. The object for which the trust is established is the advancement of education.

The Gregg School

Townhill Park House, Cutbush Lane, Southampton SO18 2GF
Tel: 023 8047 2133
Fax: 023 8047 1080
e-mail: office@gregg.southampton.sch.uk
website: www.gregg.southampton.sch.uk

Chairman of Board of Trustees: Mr John W Watts, MCIPS, MILT, AIGEM

Headteacher: **Mrs S Sellers**, MSc, BSc Hons, PGCE

Age Range. 11–16 years.
Number in School. 318.
Fees per term (2011-2012). £3,320.

The Gregg School is situated to the east of Southampton and set in 23 acres of beautifully landscaped grounds. The School, which currently has 318 students on roll, has a unique family atmosphere, and an excellent reputation for its outstanding pastoral care. A high value is placed on identifying and developing each child's individual talents and abilities, and small classes, taught by experienced and dedicated staff, ensure that every student has the opportunity to achieve their very best.

A broad and balanced curriculum is supplemented by a wide range of extra-curricular clubs and activities, ranging from orienteering to off-road buggy building.

The School's music and drama departments provide a host of opportunities for students to perform to a range of audiences, and the School regularly achieves success in sporting disciplines at both city and county level.

A comprehensive transport service is provided for students living within a 15 mile radius of the School.

Our Trust Partner, St Winifred's School, offers a high-quality educational experience for children aged 2–11.

The Grove Independent School

Redland Drive, Loughton, Milton Keynes, Buckinghamshire MK5 8HD
Tel: 01908 690590
Fax: 01908 694043
e-mail: office@groveindependentschool.co.uk
website: www.groveindependentschool.co.uk

Principal: **Mrs Deborah Berkin**

Age Range. 3 months – 13 years Co-educational.
Number of Pupils. 218.
Fees per term (2011-2012). £3,876. Nursery: £877 per month.

Hale Preparatory School

Broomfield Lane, Hale, Cheshire WA15 9AS
Tel: 0161 928 2386
Fax: 0161 941 7934
e-mail: mail@haleprepschool.com
website: www.haleprepschool.com

Headmaster: **J Connor**, JP, BSc, FCP

Age Range. 4–11.
Number in School. Day: 98 Boys, 84 Girls.
Fees per term (2010-2011). £1,875.

Hale Preparatory School is a completely independent, co-educational school for children from the age of 4 to 11.

The conclusion of the 2008 ISI Inspection Report states: "Hale Preparatory School outstandingly fulfils its aims and aspirations and meets the needs of all its pupils. It supports a positive and supportive learning environment within a caring, family atmosphere in which all school staff, parents and pupils work to a common purpose. Pupils are very well cared for and enjoy close relationships with members of staff: their personal development is outstanding."

Pupils, in maximum class sizes of 16, enjoy a wide curriculum including French, Spanish, drama and ethics. An extensive range of extra-curricular activities is on offer including ski and outdoor pursuit holidays and regular theatre visits.

The Hammond School

Hoole Bank House, Mannings Lane, Chester CH2 4ES
Tel: 01244 305350
Fax: 01244 305351
e-mail: enquiries@thehammondschool.co.uk
website: www.thehammondschool.co.uk

The Hammond School is accredited by the Independent Schools Council and CDET (Council for Dance Education and Training), and caters for a wide range of talents and interests. The Hammond has a place amongst the leading schools specialising in the field of dance, drama and music providing pupils with an education and training at the highest level in all aspects of the curriculum.

A number of funded places are available for talented dance students through the Music and Dance Scheme and the DADA Awards.

Head: **Mrs M Evans**, BA, MA, PGCE, NPQH, FRSA

Age Range. 11–19.
Number in School. 73 Boarders, 154 Day Pupils.
Fees per term (2010-2011). £3,286 for education only. Boarding £2,333.
Education Department takes girls and boys from 11 years to GCSE level.
Drama Department takes girls and boys from 11 years joining the Education Department with additional Drama.
Dance Department takes girls and boys from 11 years joining the Education Department with a Vocational Dance training.
Music Department takes girls and boys from 11 years joining the Education Department with additional Music.
Sixth Form takes boys and girls into the Education Department to study for A/AS Levels, also BTEC in Performing Arts (Acting), as well as those wishing to specialise in Dance, Musical Theatre and Drama.

Full boarding is available.

Outreach Programme. The School is acknowledged for its commitment to the community and its varied outreach projects include:
• Hammond Dance Associates – Specialist classes for talented children, selected by audition, 9–16 years.
• Paul Nicholas School of Acting – weekend drama classes for 4–16 year olds.
• The Hammond's Easter and Summer schools, working with participants drawn from the community.
For a prospectus apply to The Secretary.

Haresfoot School

Chesham Road, Berkhamsted, Herts HP4 2SZ
Tel: 01442 872742
 01442 866269 (Happy Hares Day Nursery)
e-mail: haresfootschool@btconnect.com
website: www.haresfoot.herts.sch.uk

Head: Mrs S Jaspal

Age Range. 5 months–11 years Co-educational.
Number in School. 150.
Fees per term (2011-2012). £882–£3,090 (excluding lunch).

Haresfoot Preparatory School is set in a tastefully converted Georgian coach house and stables in seven acres of grass and woodland, conveniently located on the Herts-Bucks border, 10 kms from the M25 and Ml motorways, at the Chesham exit of the A41. It has a walled garden and specialist art, pottery and music rooms, science room and a large new Sports Hall. Haresfoot provides a beautiful, safe environment – the ideal place for children's gifts to be nurtured.

A co-educational independent preparatory school, established for 21 years, Haresfoot is a caring, vibrant community. It endeavours to create an extended family atmosphere where happy children enjoy learning and each child is encouraged to reach his or her full potential. The school offers a broad-based, stimulating education, including Spanish and French, Music, Drama, Dance, Sport, Sciences and Art. Children progress to the next stage of their education and into the world beyond, making the most of their strengths and achieving at the highest possible levels across the curriculum. Because of our small numbers, adults have time to listen and appreciate each child as a unique person. The children learn to communicate confidently with people of all ages. They excel in many areas of our broad curriculum and many progress to Grammar school and selective entry independent schools.

There is a wide variety of after-school clubs and children participate in many day and residential trips. Before- and after-school clubs provide wrap-around care from 8 am to 5.45 pm, with homework supervision where required. There are extended-day holiday clubs through many of the school holidays, offering Sport, Drama, Art and other activities.

Happy Hares Day Nursery (0–4+ years) is open 51 weeks per year from 7.30 am to 6.30 pm, and is situated on the school site. Children can join the Haresfoot Family from 5 months of age at Happy Hares, moving on at around 2½ years into Haresfoot's Pre-school, which is just next door. They gradually build up their sessions in Pre-school at their own individual pace. They can return to Happy Hares for the rest of the day. Alternatively, children can join Pre-school at around 2½ years. Happy Hares caters for children up to the September that they begin in Reception (when they can use the school's out of hours clubs).

Harvington Prep School

20 Castlebar Road, Ealing, London W5 2DS
Tel: 020 8997 1583
Fax: 020 8810 4756
e-mail: admin@harvingtonschool.com
website: www.harvingtonschool.com

Headmistress: Mrs Anna Evans, BA Hons, PGCE

Age Range. Girls 3–11, Boys 3–4.
Number in School. 179 Girls, 10 Boys (in nursery).

Fees per term (2010-2011). £1,950–£3,330. Fees include lunch and a snack at break. No compulsory extras.

The School was founded in 1890 and made into an Educational Trust in 1970. Harvington is known for its high standards and happy atmosphere. Classes are small so that individual attention can be given by qualified and experienced staff. An academic education is offered preparing girls for senior school entrance examinations. The school continues to improve specialist facilities and also to provide a mixed nursery class for 3–4 year olds.

It is close to Ealing Broadway station and a number of bus routes.

Prospectus available from the Secretary.

Charitable status. Harvington School Education Trust Ltd is a Registered Charity, number 312621. It aims to subscribe to traditional values in behaviour and academic standards in a happy environment; to encourage a high standard of academic achievement for girls across a broad range of abilities; to encourage girls to develop their potential to the full, both in personal and academic terms; and to create an environment in which pupils will want to learn.

Hawley Place School

Fernhill Road, Blackwater, Camberley, Surrey GU17 9HU
Tel: 01276 32028
Fax: 01276 609695
e-mail: office@hawleyplace.com
website: www.hawleyplace.com

Principals: **Mr T G Pipe**, MA and **Mrs M L Pipe**, L-ès-L

Age Range. 2–16.
Number in School. 370 Day Pupils.
Fees per term (2010-2011). Juniors (Reception to Year 4) £2,640; Seniors (Years 5 to 11) £3,300.

Hawley Place is a small school based around an old country residence set in 17 acres of grounds. The beautiful setting provides an ideal learning environment, where kindness, courtesy and consideration are fostered in all pupils.

Maintaining a high quality of teaching and learning is our main concern. Well qualified staff, working with enviably small groups, enable us to recognise individual needs more quickly and meet them more effectively. Examination results at GCSE level are consistently above the national average and most pupils take ten subjects or more.

We offer a broad and balanced curriculum to cover all National Curriculum subjects. With the development of the single market economy we feel it important to offer pupils two foreign languages from the age of 11 to facilitate possible study or work abroad later. Moreover, French is introduced to Nursery pupils and continued through the Junior section of the school. A third foreign language is available for able linguists.

We believe in and practise the "Pursuit of Excellence" both inside and beyond the classroom. Physical education constitutes an integral part of the curriculum and sporting activities form part of a broad extra-curricular programme. Pupils are also regularly involved in music and drama rehearsals for school productions, the Debating Society, the French Club and local Art and Literature Competitions, as well as a considerable amount of charity work.

We hold our annual Open Morning in the Autumn Term and the School Entrance Examination in the Spring Term. Several Scholarship Awards are available each year for outstanding academic ability and for special talents in particular fields such as Modern Languages, Art, Music, Drama and Physical Education. The School runs its own Assisted Places Scheme.

We are successful at Hawley Place because pupils, parents and staff work together in partnership with good cooperation and communication. Full details and a prospectus may be obtained from the School Secretary. We look forward to your visit. Our door is always open.

Heathcote School

Eves Corner, Danbury, Essex CM3 4QB
Tel: 01245 223131
Fax: 01245 224568
e-mail: enquiries@heathcoteschool.co.uk
website: www.heathcoteschool.co.uk

Head of Prep School: **Mr P Ewan**, BEd Hons Keele, CertEd

Head of Pre-Prep: **Miss H Petersen**, BA Open University

Age Range. 2–11+.
Number in School. 60.
Fees per term (2011-2012). £2,330.
Founded in 1935, Heathcote School has achieved a high reputation as a school where every child matters. It is a small, family school that encourages excellence in all areas. However, there is room in this happy school for children of all abilities and parents can be sure that their child's education, at all levels, will be designed to develop their particular potential.

Children may start in our Nursery from 2 years old. We offer wrap-around care from 7.30 am to 6.00 pm and have many extra-curricular activities.

Specialist subject teachers ensure the success of the high teaching standards expected at this school. Many children are prepared for scholarships, entrance examinations and the Essex Selective Schools Examination at 11+. A very high pass rate is attained in these examinations.

Pupils are expected to show courtesy and consideration at all times and encouraged to develop self-discipline and pride in themselves and their environment. Parents are asked to support the school in this. Regular consultations with parents are held and the Head Teachers are always available for any discussions that parents consider necessary. We have an active and dedicated "Friends of Heathcote School" who regularly hold social events and raise funds for charity and for the school.

For more information please contact us or visit our website.

Heathfield School

Wolverley, Kidderminster, Worcestershire DY10 3QE
Tel: 01562 850204
Fax: 01562 852609
e-mail: info@heathfieldschool.co.uk
website: www.heathfieldschool.co.uk

Headmaster: **R H Brierly**, BEd

Age Range. 3–16. Baby Unit for children 3 months plus.
Number in School. 272 Day pupils.
Fees per term (2011-2012). £1,896–£3,143. Pre School: £14.50 per session, £20 per half day, £30.45 per full day.
Heathfield is a co-educational day school, governed by an Educational Trust. The School is situated in spacious grounds in a green belt area north of Kidderminster, within easy reach of the West Midlands conurbation.

The curriculum is broadly based and pupils are prepared for GCSE. We also prepare children for the Entrance Examination for local senior schools at 11+ and for the Common Entrance Examination at 13+. The majority of pupils in our Junior School move up to our own Senior School at 11+. Classes are small. Careers guidance is available to senior pupils.

The school is strong in Drama, Music, Art and sport. A wide variety of team and individual sports is offered with some pupils achieving regional and national standards.

Prospectus available from Headmaster's Secretary.

Charitable status. Heathfield Educational Trust is a Registered Charity, number 1098940. It exists to provide excellent educational opportunities at a reasonable cost.

Hemdean House School

Hemdean Road, Caversham, Reading, Berks RG4 7SD
Tel: 0118 9472590
Fax: 0118 9464474
e-mail: office@hemdeanhouse.co.uk
website: www.hemdeanhouse.co.uk

Headmistress: **Mrs J Harris**, BSc, PGCE

Age Range. Girls 2½–16; Boys 2½–11.
Number in School. 120 Girls, 60 Boys.
Fees per term (2011-2012). £1,900–£2,570.
Founded in 1859, Hemdean House is a school where traditional educational concepts are highly valued. We look for personal achievement in academic and other spheres, responsible behaviour and consideration for others. We aim to develop the varied talents of each and every child within our structured and caring environment; individual attention has high priority. Small classes help us to achieve our aims. We believe that school and family should work together and have opportunities to meet.

The school is organised and operated as one complete unit; many of the specialist staff teach in both the Senior and Junior schools.

The self-contained Nursery unit offers children aged 2½–4 the opportunity to begin the learning process and to develop their skills in a secure and happy environment.

We follow the National Curriculum throughout the school; Mathematics, Science, Information Technology, the Humanities and the Expressive Arts, Modern Languages, Technology and Physical Education are taught throughout the age range. French lessons begin at age 5 and recorder lessons begin at age 7 and many children learn at least one other musical instrument. Drama and Public Speaking, Music and Art head a wide range of extra-curricular activities. For the working parent, after-school and holiday care are available if required.

Examination results including GCSE and National Curriculum Key Stage Tests are excellent with pupils achieving well in excess of the national average. Over the last five years an average of 86% of our GCSE grades were A* to C.

The school has always been committed to Christian ethics and values, but all faiths are welcomed and understanding and appreciation of the beliefs of others is encouraged.

The most recent inspection report made some of the following statements:

Hemdean House School provides outstanding pastoral care throughout the school, where pupils are educated well and achieve their full academic potential.

The pupils are friendly, forthcoming and assured, their manners are excellent, and their behaviour throughout the school is exemplary.

Teachers know their pupils extremely well and this creates a happy, supportive environment in which the pupils thrive.

Nursery children are curious and eager to investigate.

The school successfully builds confidence and self-esteem in pupils.

Admission. Assessment during a day or half-day spent in school according to age. An entrance exam is taken by prospective Year 7 pupils. Scholarships and bursaries are available throughout the school.

Charitable status. Hemdean House is a Registered Charity, number 309146. Its aims include academic achievement, the development of every pupil's potential, Christian values and care for others.

Herne Hill School

The Old Vicarage, 127 Herne Hill, London SE24 9LY
Tel: 020 7274 6336
Fax: 020 7924 9510
e-mail: enquiries@hernehillschool.co.uk
website: www.hernehillschool.co.uk

Head Teacher: **Mrs Jane Beales**

Age Range. 3–7.
Number in School. 260 boys and girls.
Fees per term (2011-2012). £1,545–£3,510.

Herne Hill School has much to offer – caring and enthusiastic staff, happy and confident children, and excellent results at 7+ years. Main entry is into the Nursery at 2+ years, the Kindergarten at 3+ (both in order of registration, with priority given to siblings) and the Reception at 4+ (after an informal interview).

The school is well known as an oasis of happy learning and as the largest feeder into the Dulwich Foundation Schools. It is situated in an Old Vicarage and a spacious new building set within half acre grounds, which include a bark playground in the old orchard.

Since its foundation in 1976, Herne Hill School has focused on Early Years education and thereby developed a strong expertise in making the critical transition from Nursery to School seamless. Children joining the Nursery or Kindergarten can avoid the disruption of a 4+ change and have continuity for up to five years in what are arguably their most important formative years. Children joining in Reception also benefit from the smooth progression from a play-based learning approach to more structured lessons.

"Herne Hill School for love, care and an excellent education" encapsulates the school philosophy that love, nurture and a caring environment foster the children's self-confidence, sense of achievement and happiness, thereby stimulating their curiosity and desire to learn. The school's atmosphere lives this philosophy. It is a caring, friendly and fun place, and at the same time there is an air of achievement, respect and discipline. In addition, its co-ed nature and non-selective admissions policy in Nursery and Kindergarten enables it to build a wonderfully diverse community.

The curriculum is finely balanced to take account of each child's individual needs as well as the requirements of the 7+ entry tests – and to make learning fun! It is designed to develop the skills of independent learning and to sustain the children's innate joy of learning. Music, drama, gym, dancing and French are emphasised and taught by specialists.

The latest ISI inspection report delivered a strong endorsement of the school's ethos, staff, curriculum, *modus operandi* and infrastructure. The inspectors summarised their findings as follows: "High-quality teaching effectively supports pupils' very good personal development and enables them to achieve results which are far above national standards."

The school's website contains relevant information about life at the school, its curriculum, the destination of its leavers and some useful links.

Heywood Preparatory School

The Priory, Corsham, Wiltshire SN13 0AP
Tel: 01249 713379
Fax: 01249 701757
e-mail: principals@heywoodprep.com
website: www.heywoodprep.com

Principals: **M Hall**, BSc Hons; **P Hall**, BA Hons

Age Range. 2–11 Co-educational.
Number in School. Day: 90 Boys, 70 Girls. Nursery 45.
Fees per term (2010-2011). £1,885–£2,160. Lunches £190.

Heywood Preparatory School in Corsham has a well-established reputation for academic excellence combined with a high standard of pastoral care.

A major expansion was completed in 1998 comprising a multi-purpose hall for gymnasium activities, plays, concerts and individual music lessons, together with improvements in cloakroom and dining facilities. A fully-equipped ICT Suite was added in the summer of 2000.

Class sizes at Heywood are kept to a maximum of 16 to allow teachers to give as much individual attention as possible to each child. Progress is monitored by weekly tests and termly examinations with a full report to parents at the end of each term.

The recorder is taught to 6 and 7 year olds and a wide range of musical instruments taught on an individual basis leading to Associated Board Examinations. A high standard of Speech Training with tuition for examinations is available. French is taught throughout the main school and Nursery. Swimming is an integral part of the curriculum.

Girls games are netball, hockey, tennis, athletics and rounders. Boys play rugby, football, cricket, tennis, athletics and rounders. Other activities available are chess, orchestra, judo, cycling proficiency, sewing and cookery.

Heywood is a co-educational school from 4 to 11 years. Pupils go on to all the major independent senior schools in the area, many of them having gained academic, music or sports scholarships.

It has its own year-round Nursery School, called Wigwam, which takes children from 2 years and prepares them for entry to either the main school or state schools at four or sometimes five years old.

Highclare School

10 Sutton Road, Erdington, Birmingham B23 6QL
Tel: 0121 373 7400
Fax: 0121 373 7445
e-mail: abbey@highclareschool.co.uk
website: www.highclareschool.co.uk

Founded 1932.

Chair of Governors: Mrs L Flowith

Head: **Mrs M Viles**, BA Hons Nottingham, MEd, PGCE Cambridge

Age Range. 18 months to 18 years Co-educational.
Number of Pupils. 700.
Fees per term (2011-2012). £1,495–£3,395.
Location. The School is situated on three sites on the main road (A5127) between Four Oaks, Sutton Coldfield and Birmingham. The Senior Department (girls and boys in Year 7 from September 2011, becoming fully co-educational in 2015) and co-educational Sixth Form, is on direct train

and bus routes from Birmingham City Centre, Tamworth, Lichfield and Walsall as well as being serviced by our own buses. There are two Primary Schools, known as Highclare Woodfield and Highclare St Paul's. Wrap-around care operates from 7.30 am until 6.00 pm for the parents who require it, including holiday cover. The ethos of the school lies in the encouragement of individual excellence for each pupil and outstanding pastoral care.

Organisation. Four departments:

Nursery and Preparatory Department (age 18 months to 7 years, Girls and Boys). The Nursery caters for children from 18 months to 3 years and although an independent unit it has the support of facilities and resources of the Preparatory Department. French is taught from Reception.

Junior Departments (age 7+ to 11 years, Two Co-educational Departments). The Junior Departments, with classes of up to 22 pupils, follow National Curriculum guidelines. Pupils also have the benefit of specialist tuition in French, PE and Music. Other foundation subjects are taught by subject and by class teachers. Entry by School's own assessment procedure.

Senior Department (age 11 to 16, Girls and Boys). The full curriculum is covered at KS3. At GCSE all students study English Language and English Literature, Mathematics, Science and Additional Science, with the opportunity for some to study separate sciences, and a modern foreign language, either French, German or Spanish with a wide choice of options. In addition pupils also study PSHCE and take the ECDL qualification in Information Technology. Physical Education also forms an important part of the curriculum. Through a wide programme of enrichment activities every child has the opportunity to enjoy activities beyond the academic. Entry by School's own assessment procedure.

Co-educational Sixth Form (age 16+). The Sixth Form is co-educational and accepts external candidates as well as pupils transferring from Highclare Senior School. A wide range of A Level subjects is available for study with considerable pastoral, higher education and careers guidance available. The timetable is structured to meet the individual requirements of each student.

All parts of the School participate in extensive lunchtime and after-school activities.

The School is multi-denominational. Further information may be obtained from the School or the website and prospective parents are always welcome to visit. Open mornings are held throughout the year.

Charitable status. Highclare School is a Registered Charity, number 528940.

Highfield Priory School

Fulwood Row, Fulwood, Preston, Lancashire PR2 5RW
Tel: 01772 709624
Fax: 01772 655621
e-mail: schooloffice@highfieldpriory.co.uk
website: www.highfieldpriory.co.uk

Headmaster: **Mr J Duke**

Age Range. 6 months–11 years.
Number in School. Day: 130 Boys, 96 Girls.
Fees per term (2010-2011). £2,070.

Highfield is set in 8 acres of landscaped gardens, woodlands and playing fields and is a co-educational preparatory school for children aged 6 months to 11+ years. It is fully equipped with its own established nursery and prepares children for all Independent, Grammar and Senior Schools in Lancashire, for which it has an excellent academic record. Class numbers average 20 and children are taught by fully qualified and experienced staff. Recent additions to the

school include a classroom block, multi-purpose sports hall, a music centre, infant/nursery wing and dining room. A new library and ICT suite opened in 1994, a new CDT centre in November 2005 and in October 2006 a new Science Laboratory. The school has strong musical and sporting traditions. Highfield holds Sport England's Activemark Gold Award, National Association Of Gifted Children Gold Star Status and 'Healthy School' status.

We offer an extended day from 7.15 am until 6.00 pm. Extra-curricular activities include Ballet, Gardening, Choir, Design, Dance, Judo, Public Speaking, Chess, Spanish, Cookery and Instrument Tuition. The school is well supported by an enthusiastic Parents Association. A prospectus is available on application to the Headmaster.

Charitable status. Highfield Priory School is a Registered Charity, number 532262. It exists to provide independent education to all children between the ages of 6 months and 11 years within Preston and surrounding areas for all who wish to participate and to provide access to the community at large to all sporting, musical and artistic provision within the school.

Highfields School

London Road, New Balderton, Newark,
Nottinghamshire NG24 3AL
Tel: 01636 704103
Fax: 01636 680919
e-mail: office@highfieldsschool.co.uk
website: www.highfieldsschool.co.uk

Headteacher: **Mrs C L Fraser**, BEd Hons

Age Range. 3–11.
Number in School. Day: 65 Boys, 65 Girls.
Fees per term (2011-2012). £2,350 including lunch. Nursery £17.75 per half day session.

Highfields School is situated within 14 acres of quiet parkland and sports field. It provides a happy, lively, caring community that allows the children to experience a sense of pride and fulfilment that comes from working to their full potential. Basic subjects need to be mastered but children learn to react in different ways and need to be treated as individuals. Personal responsibility, initiative, good manners and smart appearance are encouraged and developed.

Children enter a structured course of Nursery Education in the term in which they reach the age of three. Children enter the Reception Class before their fifth birthday and proceed through the School in year groups. Each class is taught by its own teacher in the basic subjects. The maximum class size is twenty-four, with the average being nineteen. All members of staff are fully qualified and specialist teachers assist with Music, PE and Games throughout the School. Support teachers are available to help individuals or small groups with specific learning difficulties.

The curriculum is balanced and broadly based with the emphasis on English, Mathematics and Science. The full range of National Curriculum subjects is covered in order that the varying interests and skills of the children may be fully developed.

All children are encouraged to be creative and exhibit a delight in learning. There are ample opportunities for speech and drama, ballet and music with recorder ensembles, choir and an orchestra. Peripatetic staff offer lessons in saxophone, violin, cello, flute and clarinet. The School offers a wide range of extra curricular activities and sports teams compete against local authority and independent schools. Highfields has fully qualified staff who teach tennis, hockey, cricket, football, rugby and netball. The School holds an Activemark Gold Award. All children have a swimming lesson each week.

Highfields has an excellent academic record sending pupils to local selective independent schools and to Grammar Schools in Lincolnshire through 11+ entry.

The School is administered by a Board of Governors, including parent governors.

Charitable status. Newark Preparatory School Company Limited is a Registered Charity, number 528261. It exists to provide and further the education of children.

Hill House School

Fifth/Sixth Avenue, Auckley, Near Robin Hood Airport, Doncaster, South Yorkshire DN9 3GG
Tel: 01302 776300
Fax: 01302 776334
e-mail: info@hillhouse.doncaster.sch.uk
website: www.hillhouse.doncaster.sch.uk

The School is an Educational Trust with a Board of Governors.

Chairman of Governors: Mrs E Paver

Principal: **David Holland**, MA Cantab

Age Range. 3–18.
Number of Pupils. 510 Day Pupils: 250 Boys, 260 Girls.
Fees per term (2010-2011). £2,202–£3,148 according to age. Fees include lunch and most extras.

Children enter the School at 3 years of age via Nursery where structured play and learning are the order of the day. Much care and thought is given to the preparation for transition to the Lower School at 4+, the Middle School at 7+ and the Senior School at 11+. As children progress through the School there is a gradual change to subject based teaching in specialist rooms, in preparation for GCSEs at 16. The School curriculum correlates closely with the National Curriculum. Music, Drama, Art and Sport play an important part in the life of the School. Throughout the year over 60 academic, recreational, musical and sporting activities per week are also offered in extra-curricular time. The major sports undertaken include rugby, soccer, netball, hockey, cricket, tennis, athletics and rounders. There are two orchestras and three choirs within the school. Drama productions and concerts are undertaken on a regular basis. Residential trips are made at most age levels, including a number of overseas tours.

The whole school, formerly working on two sites, moved to a new campus in 2008, and is now based in the converted former Officers' Quarters of RAF Finningley.

Charitable status. Hill House School Limited is a Registered Charity, number 529420. It exists to provide nursery, primary and secondary education to boys and girls aged 3–18.

Hillcrest Grammar School

Beech Avenue, Stockport, Cheshire SK3 8HB
Tel: 0161 480 0329
Fax: 0161 476 2814
e-mail: headmaster@hillcrest.stockport.sch.uk
website: www.hillcrest.stockport.sch.uk

Headmaster: **J D Williams**, BSc, PGCE

Age Range. 3–16.
Number in School. Day: 130 Boys, 130 Girls.
Fees per term (2010-2011). £1,873–£2,570. No compulsory extras.

Hillcrest is a charitable educational trust and comprises Senior, Preparatory and Pre-Preparatory Schools.

Our primary aim is to maximise the potential of each individual and progress, both academic and social, is monitored with great care at all levels of the School. Good communication between School and Home is especially important and the Headmaster and the staff are readily accessible at short notice. We make no apology for stressing traditional values such as mutual respect, good manners and self-discipline.

Classes are small and are taught by fully qualified and experienced staff. Sixteen GCSE courses are currently offered and excellent facilities include more than seventy multimedia PCs accessible to all, the Art & Design Centre, a first-class sports hall and all-weather tennis/netball courts. There is a wide range of musical, sporting and extra-curricular activity. Because we are a relatively small community both boys and girls have every opportunity to be more prominent in a wide range of pursuits than would be the case in larger schools.

At 11+ children are prepared for entry not only to our own Senior School but also to larger independent and state schools. At 16+ most pupils progress to Sixth Form courses either at State Colleges or HMC Schools. Parents are most welcome to visit us in order that they may appreciate the happy working atmosphere of the school. Admission is by annual 11+ entrance examination and by interview and individual assessment for other age groups. A limited number of means-tested Bursary places are available each year at both Preparatory and Senior Schools.

Charitable status. Hillcrest Grammar School is a Registered Charity, number 525928. It exists to provide education for boys and girls.

Hopelands Preparatory School

38 Regent Street, Stonehouse, Gloucestershire GL10 2AD
Tel: 01453 822164
Fax: 01453 827288
e-mail: enquiries@hopelands.org.uk
website: www.hopelands.org.uk

Chairman of Governors: Mr R D James

Head: **Mrs Sheila Bradburn**, BA Hons, PGCE

Age Range. 3–11 Co-educational.
Number of Pupils. 73.
Fees per term (2010-2011). £1,725–£2,065.
Charitable status. Hopelands Preparatory School is a Registered Charity, number 1007707.

Howe Green House School

Great Hallingbury, Bishop's Stortford, Herts CM22 7UF
Tel: 01279 657706
Fax: 01279 501333
e-mail: info@howegreenhouseschool.co.uk
website: www.howegreenhouseschool.co.uk

Headmaster: **Mr G R Gorton**, BA, PGCE

Age Range. 2–11 years.
Number in School. 158.
Fees per term (2010-2011). Kindergarten £1,859, Infants £2,382, Juniors £2,953.

Howe Green House offers an education of the highest quality in the widest sense. Facilities are excellent being sited in 8 acres of countryside adjacent to Hatfield Forest. It is a single-stream school which works broadly to the National Curriculum, offering additional French, Music, Drama and Sport. There is a strong parental involvement within the school whereby parents are actively encouraged to be part of their childrens education. The school is seen as a community which fosters an understanding of children's development within both school and home. Children sit external examinations to senior schools both boarding and day and have been highly successful.

Entry to the school is mainly via Acorns Nursery but children are considered for entry to the Junior School by assessment and interview.

Charitable status. The Howe Green Educational Trust Ltd is a Registered Charity, number 297106. It exists to promote and provide for the advancement of education for the public benefit and in connection therewith to conduct a day school for the education of boys and girls.

Hulme Hall Grammar School

Hulme Hall Road, Cheadle Hulme, Stockport, Cheshire SK8 6LA
Tel: 0161 485 3524/0161 485 4638
Fax: 0161 485 5966
e-mail: secretary@hulmehallschool.org
website: www.hulmehallschool.org

Co-educational, Independent and Accredited.

Headmaster: **Philip Marland**, BSc Hons, MA, PGCE

Age Range. 2–16.
Number in School. 300.
Fees per term (2011-2012). £1,500–£2,780.
Junior School. We cater for girls and boys from 2 to 11 years in our Nursery, Kindergarten, Infant and Junior classes. At every stage of the learning process, we provide a caring and stimulating environment.

Given excellent resources, small classes and teachers of high calibre, children derive considerable satisfaction from their school work and experience no difficulty in realising their academic potential.

Senior School (11–16 years). The school is well staffed and equipped to deliver a curriculum covering a wide range of academic, creative and practical subjects. An extensive choice of GCSE and other external examination options enables pupils at Key Stage 4 to target optimum qualifications reflecting their personal choice of programme. The staff are consistent in the emphasis they place upon the encouragement of pupils who respond with a highly conscientious approach to their studies, which in turn ensures steady progress and excellent results.

Communication between school and home is given high priority and the regular issue of reports enables parents to monitor closely their child's educational development. At the age of 16, almost all pupils continue with A Level studies.

The school operates its own fleet of coaches, offering an extensive network of services covering a 15 mile radius of the school.

For further information please contact the School Secretary.

Charitable status. Hulme Hall Educational Trust is a Registered Charity, number 525931. The school aims to promote personal, moral, social and academic development of all pupils.

Hurst Lodge School

Bagshot Road, Ascot, Berkshire SL5 9JU
Tel: 01344 622154
Fax: 01344 627049
e-mail: admissions@hurstlodgesch.co.uk
website: www.hurstlodge.co.uk

Principal: **Miss V S Smit**, BSc Hons

Age Range. Girls 3–18; Boys 3–11. Weekly Boarding from age 9.
Number in School. Day: 23 Boys, 189 Girls; 17 Weekly Boarders.
Fees per term (2010-2011). Weekly Boarding £7,015; Senior Day £4,310; Junior Day £3,580; Pre-Prep £2,850.

Hurst Lodge is a small, well established day and boarding school successfully combining an academic, performance and creative education. We aspire to help our students realise their potential by encouraging learning for life and celebrating all achievements equally.

Small teaching groups ensure high standards, individual attention and excellent pastoral care.

We have a strong dyslexia department.

Hurst Lodge offers a wide breadth of academic and vocational subjects to GCSE and A Level. We specialise in Drama, Music and Dance at all levels.

Students have Form and Personal Tutors to ensure a high level of pastoral care and support.

The Sixth Form is small, offering traditional A Levels, a mixture of A Levels and vocational ballet, modern, tap and jazz or BTECs in Performing Arts and Early Years Education.

Hurtwood House School

Holmbury St Mary, Dorking, Surrey RH5 6NU
Tel: 01483 279000
Fax: 01483 267586
e-mail: info@hurtwood.net
website: www.hurtwoodhouse.com

Headmaster: **C Jackson**, BEd

Age Range. 16–18.
Number in School. 300 (150 girls, 150 boys).
Fees per term (2011-2012). £11,200–£12,880.

Hurtwood House is the only independent boarding school specialising exclusively in the Sixth Form. It concentrates on the 16–18 age range and offers students a caring, residential structure and a commitment to a complete education where culture, sport, friendship and a full range of extra-curricular activities all play an important part. Hugely successful across the whole range of academic subjects, Hurtwood House is also widely recognised as having the best Creative and Performing Arts and Media departments in the country and is therefore especially attractive to aspiring actors, directors, film directors, dancers, singers, artists and fashion designers.

Many students now want to leave the traditional school system at 16. They are seeking an environment which is structured and safe, but which is less institutional and better equipped to provide the challenge and stimulation which they are now ready for, and which is therefore better placed to develop their potential. They also require teaching methods which will prepare them for an increasingly competitive world by developing their initiative and encouraging them to think for themselves.

Hurtwood House has 300 boys and girls. It is a small and personal school, but it is a large and powerful sixth form which benefits from having specialised A level teachers. The examination results put Hurtwood House in the top independent school league tables, but it is equally important to the school that the students develop energy, motivation and self-confidence.

In short, Hurtwood House is a stepping-stone between school and university for students who are all in the same age group and who share the same maturity and the same ambitions.

The school is situated in its own grounds high up in the Surrey Hills and offers excellent facilities in outstandingly beautiful surroundings.

Ibstock Place School

Clarence Lane, London SW15 5PY
Tel: General Enquiries: 020 8876 9991
Headmistress's PA: 020 8392 5802
Bursar's Office: 020 8392 5804
Registrar: 020 8392 5803
Fax: 020 8878 4897
e-mail: office@ibstockplaceschool.co.uk
website: www.ibstockplaceschool.co.uk

Chairman of Governors: Michael Gibbins, LVO, FCA

Headmistress: Mrs Anna Sylvester-Johnson, BA Hons, PGCE

Deputy Headmaster: Mr Huw Daniel, BSc Hons London, PGCE

Second Master: Mr Keith Birch, BA Hons Queensland, MA, DipEd

Head of Pastoral Care: Dr Trevor Addenbrooke, BEng, AGCI Imperial, MSc, DIC, PhD

Heads of Houses:
Miss Katie Callaghan, BA Loughborough
Mr Andrew Copeman, BA Newcastle, MSc
Mr Charles Janz, MA Oxon
Mr Samuel Robinson, BA Sussex

Head of Preparatory Department: Miss Diana Wynter, BA, CertEd

Head of Kindergarten: Miss Maggie Smith, BEd Northumberland

Age Range. 3–18 Co-educational.
Number in School. 880: 460 Boys, 420 Girls.
Fees per term (2011-2012). £2,035–£5,185 (including lunches).

Ibstock Place School, founded in 1894, is located in spacious grounds adjacent to Richmond Park with easy access to Putney, Barnes, Richmond and Hammersmith. The school offers a balanced education combining a traditional academic curriculum with modern educational developments.

The school has grown and prospered with significant building development in recent years. The school has a new Sports Hall, a 200-seat performance hall for music and drama, a new dining room with upgraded catering facilities, and a new Preparatory building. The school has a swimming pool and eight acres of playing fields on site. The new Senior School building was opened in January 2011 and comprises 18 classrooms, 6 laboratories and a new Library at this popular school in SW London.

The Kindergarten, the Preparatory Department and the Senior School remain distinctive and are housed separately, so that each child benefits from a small school ambience, but the younger pupils gain from the facilities enjoyed by the Senior School.

The Senior School, age 11–18, offers a full range of Arts, Science and Technology subjects and all pupils follow a core curriculum in line with national requirements and with many opportunities for enrichment. Extra curricular emphasis is placed on sports, drama and music, with recent expeditions to China, USA and Iceland, and there is an outstanding programme of outdoor education. There is a wide range of after-school clubs as well as the Duke of Edinburgh's Award scheme. There are excellent links with the local community.

The Sixth Form opened in September 2005 with a breadth of A Level Options and a flexible blocking system which allows considerable opportunity to include science and arts subjects at A2. The school is a member of ISCO and all pupils receive guidance by experienced staff. All pupils are supported by a strong and effective pastoral system which produces well balanced and socially accomplished young people.

Priestman House, the Froebel Kindergarten (age 3–6), and **Macleod House**, the Preparatory Department (age 6–11) provide a rich and stimulating environment, with a wide range of curricular activity carefully planned to maximise each child's abilities and talents.

Entry to the school is by assessment for children aged 5 and 6 and by examinations in Mathematics, English and Reasoning at 7 and 11 and subject to a satisfactory report from the entrant's current school, and by date of registration for entry into the Nursery and Reception.

The prospectus is available from the Registrar and Open Mornings are held regularly by appointment. Occasional places may arise from time to time.

Charitable status. Ibstock Place School is part of the Incorporated Froebel Educational Institute which is a Registered Charity, number 312930R. It exists to provide high quality education for boys and girls.

International College, Sherborne School

Newell Grange, Sherborne, Dorset DT9 4EZ
Tel: 01935 814743
Fax: 01935 816863
e-mail: reception@sherborne-ic.net
website: www.sherborne-ic.net

Principal: **Dr C Greenfield**, MA, MEd

Age Range. Co-educational 11–17 (Boarding 11–17).
Number in School. 150 boarders: 100 boys, 50 girls.
Fees per term (2011-2012). £11,000.

The International College at Sherborne was set up by Sherborne School in 1977. It has grown to become a separate institution and is now separately recognised by the Department for Education and the Independent Schools Association.

The College aims to be the best starting point for children from non-English speaking, non-British educational backgrounds who wish to join the British educational system. Students normally stay at the College for one academic year. During this time the College aims to equip each student to take his or her place successfully at a traditional British independent boarding school.

While the full academic curriculum is provided, all teachers of all subjects at the International College are trained or qualified in teaching English as a foreign language. Each student is prepared for any appropriate public examinations, for example GCSEs and IGCSEs, Common Entrance or Cambridge English language examinations. Each year the group taking GCSEs records very impressive results – in 2009, over 87% of the entries achieved A–C grades.

The College has no entry requirements and no entry examinations for most courses. All students are non-native speakers of English, and some are complete beginners in English. However, the popular one-year GCSE/IGCSE course requires all applicants to have at least lower-intermediate standard English (IELTS 4+).

The College is housed in a purpose-built campus close to the centre of Sherborne. Its boarding houses are nearby. Students are taught in classes of up to eight.

The College is also a member of the Boarding Schools Association, the European Council of International Schools and the British Association of International Study Centres. The College is also accredited by the British Council.

Charitable status. Sherborne School is a Registered Charity, number 1081228. The College is part of the Sherborne School educational charity which exists to provide education to school-aged children.

The Italia Conti Academy of Theatre Arts

Italia Conti House, 23 Goswell Road, London EC1M 7AJ
Tel: 020 7608 0047/8
Fax: 020 7253 1430
e-mail: admin@italiaconti.com
website: www.italiaconti.com

Principal: Mrs A Sheward

Head: **Mr C K Vote**, BA, DipEd

Age Range. 10–16.
Number in School. Day: 99.
Fees per term (2010-2011). £3,652.

Throughout the 95 years the Academy has been preparing young people for successful careers in the performing arts it has been aware that the profession expects excellent standards of education and training of its new entrants. Today's Producers and Directors demand that performers entering the industry be versatile and be able to take direction within the theatre, television or film studio.

The five courses offered by the Academy seek to expose students to a wide range of disciplines and techniques in the Dance, Drama and Singing fields working in the mediums of stage, television and recording studio under the careful tuition of highly qualified professional staff.

The courses are as follows:

The Theatre Arts School. For 10 to 16 year olds providing a balanced traditional academic education leading to ten GCSEs with broadly based vocational training in dance, drama and singing. Sixth Form Studies within the Performing Arts Course allows two GCE A levels to be studied alongside a full professional dance, drama and singing theatre arts course. Accredited by the ISA.

Performing Arts Course. A three year course for students aged 16+. Accredited by the National Council for Dance Education and Training. Leading to the Award of National Diploma in Professional Dance (Musical Theatre).

One Year Singing Course. From age 16. Drama & Dance Award Scholarships are available for this Course.

BA Hons Musical Theatre Course.

Entry Requirements. Entry for all the above courses is by audition and assessment.

In addition to the above the Academy offers part-time Saturday classes to children aged 3½ to 18 years in Dance, Drama and Singing. Entry is by interview. Also offered is a Summer School, one week Performing Arts or Drama courses for those aged 9 to 19.

Charitable status. The Italia Conti Academy Trust is a Registered Charity, number 290261. It exists to promote education in the Performing Arts through both teaching and the provision of scholarships.

King Alfred School

Manor Wood, North End Road, London NW11 7HY
Tel: 020 8457 5200
Fax: 020 8457 5249
e-mail: kas@kingalfred.org.uk
website: www.kingalfred.org.uk

Head: **Mrs Dawn Moore**, MA London

Age Range. 4–18.
Number in School. Primary: approx 320; Secondary: approx 308.
Fees per term (2011-2012). Reception, Years 1–2 £3,915, Years 3–6 £4,510, Middle & Upper School £4,720.

King Alfred School is unique among independent schools in North London. Apart from being all-age (4–18), co-ed and strictly secular, it takes in a wide range of ability as opposed to its academically selective neighbours in the private sector. About 30% of the pupils receive support from the Special Needs department.

KAS's beginnings are unusual: it was founded (in 1898) by a group of Hampstead parents and its large governing body comprises only current and ex-parents. Visitors tend to comment on the pretty site (on the edge of Hampstead Garden Suburb), the "villagey" layout (carefully preserved by a succession of architects), and the friendly atmosphere – this is a no-uniform establishment and all are on first-name terms. The recent purchase of property across the road has enabled the school to extend classroom facilities.

Academic results are consistently impressive and constantly improving and almost 100% of the KAS Sixth Form go on to university or Art Foundation courses or music colleges and conservatoires. The School relishes the opportunity to work with children of all abilities and to stimulate the best from all of them.

Bursaries for the Sixth Form and Year 7 are available.

Charitable status. King Alfred School is a Registered Charity, number 312590. It exists to provide quality education for boys and girls.

Kings Monkton School

6 West Grove, Cardiff CF24 3XL
Tel: 029 2048 2854
Fax: 029 2049 0484
e-mail: mail@kingsmonkton.org.uk
website: www.kingsmonkton.org.uk

Principal: **Mr N D B Dorey**, MA Cantab

Age Range. 3–18.
Number in School. 300.
Fees per term (2010-2011). £1,999–£2,606.

Kings Monkton School is a co-educational day school for children from nursery age right up to university entrance. The school is administered by a board of governors as a registered charity, dedicated to the sole aim of providing an education of excellence.

Kings Monkton is one of South Wales's oldest independent schools, having educated generations of local pupils since its foundation in 1870. The school prides itself on its consistent record of academic success, its system of pastoral care and its relations with parents. Pupils are drawn from a wide catchment area including Cardiff, the Vale of Glamorgan, the Valleys and Monmouth. The school is housed in purpose-built accommodation in the centre of Cardiff, close to Queen Street station and to all amenities.

Kings Monkton's primary school has small classes in which young children can receive individual care and guidance. Pupils follow a well-balanced curriculum, designed to develop and stimulate young minds to the full. Entry for infant children is by informal assessment, whilst junior pupils are tested in Mathematics, English and Reasoning before being offered a place.

In the secondary school, pupils pursue a wide curriculum with their progress being carefully monitored and receive strong pastoral support throughout their adolescent years. All pupils are encouraged to strive for high standards in their work and to contribute to the well-being of the community to which they belong. Entry to the secondary school is by interview and testing with scholarships available at 11+, 13+ and 16+.

In the school's A Level college, students are taught in small tutorial groups and in addition to their academic studies participate in a number of other activities including Young Enterprise as part of the school's philosophy of giving its pupils a thorough preparation for life. The minimum entry requirements to the College are five GCSE passes at grades A–C.

In 2003 the school opened its new purpose-built sixth form centre with upgraded facilities for physics, technology and music.

The school became part of the CfBT Education Trust, one of the top 20 charities in the UK, in 2008. This has opened up immense opportunities for the further development of the school, its staff and its pupils.

Charitable status. Kings Monkton School is a Registered Charity, number 525759.

Kingscote Pre-Preparatory School

Oval Way, Gerrards Cross, Bucks SL9 8PZ
Tel: 01753 885535
Fax: 01753 891783
e-mail: office@kingscoteschool.info
website: www.kingscoteschool.info

Headmistress: **Mrs F Davies**

Age Range. 3–7 years.
Number of Boys. 130.
Fees per term (2011-2012). Nursery: Autumn Term £1,350 (5 sessions), Spring Term £1,900 (7 sessions), Summer Term £2,170 (8 sessions). Reception £2,710, Years 1 & 2 £2,825.

Kingscote School was established in 1964 as the pre-preparatory school for Thorpe House. The primary aim of the Kingscote curriculum is to provide a thorough grounding in reading, writing and arithmetic. Mornings are spent learning 'the basics' and in the afternoons the boys become involved in a variety of activities – project work, music, PE and games, art, cookery and ICT.

Kirkstone House School

Baston, Peterborough, Lincolnshire PE6 9PA
Tel: 01778 560350
Fax: 01778 560547
e-mail: info@kirkstonehouseschool.co.uk
website: www.kirkstonehouseschool.co.uk

Co-Principals: **Mrs B K Wyman, Mr E G Wyman, Mr J W R Wyman**

Head: **Mrs C Jones**

Age Range. 5–16.
Number in School. 196: 111 boys, 85 girls.
Fees per term (2010-2011). £1,896–£2,831.

Kirkstone House prides itself on being a caring, supportive school that embraces a 'whole child' approach at all times. There are high aspirations for pupils and the school aims to provide the highest quality of education through all years. In an atmosphere characterised by its supportive nature and sense of community, pupils are helped to recognise and fulfil their unique potential.

The school caters for the full academic range and there is a very well established Special Needs Department which supports pupils with a range of needs including dyslexic pupils.

The curriculum is wide with emphasis being placed on pupil choice at GCSE. A wide range of GCSEs and BTEC courses is offered.

Classes are small and pupils and staff know each other well. There is a wealth of extra-curricular subjects on offer including The Duke of Edinburgh's Award and a thriving Youth Theatre.

Kirkstone's unique 60-acre site of woodlands and lakes has specific scientific interest and is used for environmental and land-based study.

Knightsbridge School

67 Pont Street, London SW1X 0BD
Tel: 020 7590 9000
Fax: 020 7589 9055
e-mail: admissions@knightsbridgeschool.com
website: www.knightsbridgeschool.com

Headmaster: **Mr Magoo Giles**

Age Range. 4–13.
Number in School. 350.
Fees per term (2011-2012). £4,095–£4,995.

Knightsbridge School is a preparatory school offering a broad, balanced and challenging curriculum to prepare both boys and girls for entry to senior day and boarding schools.

Pupils are encouraged to play hard, work hard in the Junior School and work hard, play hard in the Senior School, and make the most of every opportunity open to them to achieve their full potential. They are taught all National Curriculum subjects to a high standard, and modern languages from nursery age upwards.

The school fosters a strong sense of community, and provides a supportive and warm environment. Small classes, overseen by highly qualified, dynamic and enthusiastic staff, will ensure that boys and girls benefit not only academically but also personally. By developing their self-esteem and confidence they will grow into happy, independent all-rounders of healthy body and healthy mind.

Located in the heart of Central London, the school is housed in two magnificent mansions. The premises have undergone an extensive renovation and upgrade programme. Teaching facilities include well-equipped and modern classrooms, a new science laboratory, an information and communication technology suite, music rooms, and a performing arts studio and a new library, as well as a fully catered kitchen and dining area.

Sports facilities include a gymnasium on site and the diverse and challenging sports programme makes use of local venues such as Burton's Court, Battersea Park, St Luke's recreational grounds, the Queen Mother Sports Centre and Hyde Park.

Entry to Knightsbridge School is by informal interview of both parents and children at the appropriate level. Prospective boys and girls for Year 1 and above will be expected to spend a day of assessment at the school in their relevant year group, and a report from the Head of the applicant's current school will be required.

Charitable status. Knightsbridge School Education Foundation is a Registered Charity, number 1120970.

The Knoll School

Manor Avenue, Kidderminster, Worcestershire DY11 6EA
Tel: 01562 822622
Fax: 01562 865686
e-mail: info@knollschool.co.uk
          head@knollschool.co.uk
website: www.knollschool.co.uk

Headmaster: **N J Humphreys**, BEd Hons

Age of Children. Co-educational 3 months–11 years.
Number in School. Day: 77 Boys, 42 Girls.
Fees per term (2010-2011). £543–£2,380.

The Knoll School was founded in 1917 and became an Educational trust in 1966. It continues to be a popular co-educational day school for children from 3 months to 11 years.

Our First Steps Nursery, which was officially opened by Dr Richard Taylor MP in 2003, is open 50 weeks a year from 8 am to 6 pm. Children from the age of 3 months now benefit from the caring, family environment for which the Knoll School is well known.

We have high expectations of our pupils in all aspects of their education. Under the guidance of an experienced and caring staff a stimulating and challenging school life is achieved which enables our children to reach their true potential.

The school has a busy calendar incorporating drama, music and sporting events. The children also benefit immensely from educational outings and visiting guest speakers. Extra curricular activities play an important part in school life and pre/after school care from 8 am to 6 pm benefits many parents.

Following the opening of the main school new wing in September 1997, our facilities are excellent. We are proud of our children's achievements, particularly those of Year 6 in gaining places at top independent schools in the area, and attaining scholarships.

Charitable status. The Knoll School Educational Trust Limited is a Registered Charity, number 527600.

Lady Barn House School

Schools Hill, Cheadle, Cheshire SK8 1JE
Tel: 0161 428 2912
Fax: 0161 428 5798
e-mail: info@ladybarnhouse.stockport.sch.uk
website: www.ladybarnhouse.org

Headmistress: **Mrs S Yule**, BA Hons, PGCE

Age Range. 3–11.
Number in School. Day: 247 Boys, 199 Girls.
Fees per term (2010-2011). Nursery £1,736 (all day), KS1 and KS2 £1,983. Lunch £130.

W H Herford, minister and educational pioneer, founded the school in 1873. His vision was to establish a co-educational school that promoted happiness, academia, whilst embracing a Christian ethos. Today, Herford's vision still drives our thriving, family-orientated community. Boys and girls flourish, learning side by side, in an exceptional educational setting.

We combine the latest educational thinking with tried and tested traditional methods. Pupils are gradually nurtured and developed so that they can confidently face their future with knowledge, understanding and the ability to be independent. Music, sport, drama, languages, outdoor adventure and a wide range of other clubs, trips and residential visits enhance our curriculum.

Pupils are prepared and supported for their 11+ entrance exams; they then move on to the best and most appropriate senior schools.

Lady Barn House School is a truly special educational institution where each and every pupil experiences success and reaches their potential. It remains one of the North West's most prestigious independent primary schools.

The School is a Charitable Trust. Bursaries are available at Year 2 and Year 3.

Charitable status. Lady Barn House School Limited is a Registered Charity, number 1042587. It exists to provide education for boys and girls.

Ladymede School
GEMS Education

Little Kimble, Aylesbury, Buckinghamshire HP17 0XP
Tel: 01844 346154
Fax: 01844 275660
e-mail: office@ladymede.com
website: www.ladymedeschool.bucks.sch.uk

Head Mistress: **Mrs Carole Hawkins**, BA, PGCE

Age Range. 3–11 Co-educational.
Number in School. Day: 52 Girls, 53 Boys.
Fees per term (2010-2011). £1,310–£2,680.

Ladymede, founded in 1939, is a co-educational day school for pupils aged 3–11 years set in beautiful grounds at the foot of the Buckinghamshire Chilterns.

We aim to provide a happy, supportive and purposeful environment in which children learn to set themselves high standards and become independent learners. Good manners and traditional values, incorporating respect for oneself and others, are fundamental to life at Ladymede.

In small classes (maximum 20) children experience a broad balanced curriculum enriched by residential and day trips and specialist teaching in French, German, Spanish, ICT, Music, Science and PE. The well-qualified and caring staff are able to offer individual attention.

All Day Care from 7.45 am to 6.30 pm is an important part of Ladymede, as are the flexible Nursery sessions, a Toddler Group (18 months–3 years) and a wide range of extra-curricular clubs which run at lunchtime and after school.

At 11 our articulate, confident pupils enter selective grammar schools, a variety of independent schools and some local state schools. They are prepared for entrance into both sectors (11+ and Common Entrance).

Lime House School

Holm Hill, Dalston, Nr Carlisle, Cumbria CA5 7BX
Tel: 01228 710225
Fax: 01228 710508
e-mail: lhsoffice@aol.com
website: www.limehouseschool.co.uk

Headmaster: **N A Rice**, MA, BA, CertEd

Age Range. 3+–18+. Boarders from age 9.

Number in School. Day: 40 Boys, 38 Girls; Boarding: 65 Boys, 45 Girls.

Fees per term (2010-2011). Boarding £4,750–£5,950; Day £1,500–£2,750.

Compulsory extras: Activities, Laundry.

Lime House School is a fully independent co-educational boarding and day school for pupils aged 3½ to 18. Our aim is to ensure that each pupil achieves his or her potential both academically and socially, with each child treated individually. Our pupils are cared for in a safe rural environment and every possible attempt is made to ensure that they develop confidence and self-esteem. Boarding is available to all pupils, with the majority being full boarders.

Foreign students whose first language is not English add to the cosmopolitan atmosphere of the school. They are prepared for Cambridge English examinations and follow the same curriculum as all other students.

Games and sport form an important part of school life. All students participate and a wide range of team and individual sports is offered. Most pupils take games to GCSE level, with many continuing to A Level.

We would welcome a visit to our school to see it in action. Simply contact the school and we will arrange a time convenient for you.

Lingfield Notre Dame

Lingfield, Surrey RH7 6PH
Tel: 01342 833176
e-mail: office@lingfieldnotredame.co.uk
website: www.lingfieldnotredame.co.uk

Headmaster: **Mr Richard Bool**, BA, MBA

Age Range. 2½–18.

Number in School. 333 in Junior School; 502 in Senior School.

Fees per term (2011-2012). £1,170–£3,315.

Entry. Junior School: by assessment from Reception year upwards, subject to vacancies.

Senior School: at 11+ and 13+ by Entrance Examination, interview and report from previous school. At 16+ by 6+ GCSEs at A grade, and interview.

Scholarships. Academic, Music and Sporting Scholarships and Bursaries are offered to the top candidates in the 11+ and 13+ Entrance Examination. Scholarships are also available for the Sixth Form.

Curriculum. In the Junior School the usual primary subjects are taught, including French, Dance, Speech and Drama. In the Senior School a wide curriculum of academic and practical subjects is offered to GCSE and A Level. The National Curriculum is incorporated throughout the school.

Reports and Consultations. In the Junior School, written reports are sent home every term. In the Senior School, detailed written reports are sent home once a year and interim report sheets are issued at appropriate stages throughout the year. Parent/Teacher interviews are held annually. Parents are always welcome to discuss progress with the appropriate Head of Year. There is a well developed pastoral system.

Leavers. The majority of pupils in the Junior School progress to the Senior School. Ninety percent of Sixth Form leavers go on to further education courses at University, including Oxbridge, resulting in a wide variety of careers.

Sport. In the Junior School sports include Gym, Golf, Hockey, Cricket, Football, Dance, Netball, Swimming, Karate, Rounders and Short Tennis.

In the Senior School, Tennis, Netball, Trampolining, Rounders, Fitness Suite, Volleyball, Gymnastics, Dance, Swimming, Basketball, Rugby, Football, Hockey, Squash, Badminton, and Athletics are all played.

Annual Ski Trips are arranged for Senior School pupils.

Extra-Curricular Activities. In the Junior School, the following are a few of the activities offered: Choir and Orchestra, Language Clubs, Cookery, Sewing, Technology, Squash, Computer, Drama, Gardening, Art and Craft, and Eco Club.

In the Senior School an extensive range of activities is offered including Duke of Edinburgh's Award Scheme, Outward Bound, Drama, Music and Science Clubs, Public Speaking, Chef's Club, Sports fixtures, Choir, Orchestra and Ensembles.

In the Sixth Form a wide programme of activities is arranged such as Salsa Dancing, Ballroom Dancing, Self Defence, Car Maintenance, Orienteering, Cooking, Youth Parliament, Debating, Public Speaking, Critical Thinking, Safe Driving Talks plus an extensive range of outside speakers.

In addition, the School has participated in expeditions to destinations near and far.

Religious Services. Regular school, house, form and year assemblies are held. Interdenominational services are held.

Lingfield Notre Dame transferred to a lay management in 1987. It maintains its Christian ethos and welcomes students and staff of all faiths, and of none. Its philosophy is based on a strong belief in the development of the whole person. The school has a tradition of providing a caring, friendly and disciplined environment.

Charitable status. Lingfield Notre Dame is a Registered Charity, number 295598. It exists to provide education.

Loreto Preparatory School

Dunham Road, Altrincham, Cheshire WA14 4GZ
Tel: 0161 928 8310
Fax: 0161 929 5801
e-mail: info.loretoprep@btconnect.com
website: www.loretoprep.co.uk

Headteacher: **Mrs Rosemary Hedger**, BA Hons

Age Range. Girls 3–11, Boys 3–7.

Number in School. 163 Day Girls.

Fees per term (2011-2012). £1,690.

Loreto Preparatory School, founded in 1909, is a modern, purpose-built school (1971), standing in pleasant grounds and offering an all-round education by well-qualified staff. Religious education and moral training are central to our teaching, based on Gospel principles. Our recent ISI Inspection stated that the school "maintains its traditional values, yet incorporates some modern thinking in the curriculum".

Music plays an important part in the life of the school. All aspects of class music are taught by a specialist. We have a school orchestra, and private individual lessons are available in most instruments. The children's dramatic ability and interest are developed through class lessons, theatre visits and regular productions. Gymnastics, swimming, netball and athletics, taught by a PE specialist, rate high in our physical education programme and the school participates fully in local and national competitions.

Our ICT facilities are excellent and include a computer suite and interactive whiteboards in every class. There is a well-stocked, computerised library, allowing pupils to select, issue and return their own books.

The Junior curriculum has been extended to include Latin, Chinese and touch typing. We offer a wide range of extra-curricular activities.

Of equal importance is social development and each child is encouraged to reach his or her full potential and to care for others.

Loreto is a Catholic independent school and is one of many Loreto schools built on the foundations laid by Mary

Ward, foundress of the Institute of the Blessed Virgin Mary, according to the vision of St Ignatius of Loyola.

Visits to the school are welcome by appointment. Admission at 3+ is usually by interview and by interview and Entrance Examination for those wishing to join at 7+. The school is also registered with Trafford's Sure Start Early Years. Pupils eligible under the scheme receive up to 5 free sessions.

Charitable status. Loreto Preparatory School is a Registered Charity, number 250607.

Lucton School

Lucton, Leominster, Herefordshire HR6 9PN
Tel: 01568 782000
Fax: 01568 782001
e-mail: admissions@luctonschool.org
website: www.luctonschool.org

Headmistress: Mrs Gill Thorne, MA, BA Hons, PGCE, LLAM

Age Range. 6 months–19 years.
Number in School. 285.
Fees per term (2010-2011). Day £1,755–£3,430, Boarding £5,675–£7,315.

Pupils at Lucton School benefit from small classes, a friendly atmosphere and an idyllic rural location. Pupils are provided with an excellent all-round education which aims to bring out the full potential of each individual. There are extensive sports facilities and a good mix of day pupils, weekly boarders and full boarders.

Subjects taught to GCSE include English language and literature, mathematics, biology, chemistry, physics, information technology, French, Spanish, German, history, geography, business studies, religious education, design & technology, art, music, drama and PE/games. Most pupils sit GCSE examinations in ten subjects. Lucton School has a strong academic record and an established tradition of getting the best possible results from each pupil.

All the above GCSE subjects, plus many more, are available in the Sixth Form at AS and A2 Levels. The Sixth Form is housed in a brand new sixth form centre, created in 2005, including a new senior library and another new IT suite.

Founded in 1708, the school is set in a safe, healthy and attractive location in 45 acres of beautiful Herefordshire countryside. Facilities on site include junior and senior libraries, science laboratories, ICT rooms, design and technology workshop, tennis courts, new indoor swimming pool, games field and equestrian centre. Fourteen different sports are offered; the school achieved a Sportsmark Gold award in 2002. Boarding pupils are housed in a modern building and all have individual rooms.

Admission can take place at any time of the year by interview and assessment. Prospective pupils are always invited to spend a trial day in the school without obligation. Examinations for academic scholarships are held in January each year.

Lucton School is a member of the Boarding Schools' Association.

Charitable status. Lucton School is a Registered Charity, number 518076.

Lyndhurst School

36 The Avenue, Camberley, Surrey GU15 3NE
Tel: 01276 22895
Fax: 01276 709186

e-mail: office@lyndhurstschool.co.uk
website: www.lyndhurstschool.co.uk

Head: Stephen G Yeo, BMus Hons, LTCL (MusEd), NPQH

Registrar: Mrs Lesley Howlett

Age Range. 2–11.
Number in School. Day: 87 Boys, 79 Girls.
Fees per term (2011-2012). £2,425–£2,930.

Boys and girls are accepted from the age of 2 into the happy and friendly Nursery Department. From here until they leave the school at the age of 11½, every care is taken to realise the full potential of each child. The Headmaster's wife looks after the welfare of the children.

The School maintains a high academic standard but children of all abilities are welcomed and are taught in a sympathetic environment.

Music and drama play an important role in the life of the School and swimming is part of the weekly curriculum.

Sports and activities offered include football, basketball, badminton, hockey, cricket, netball, rounders, judo, gymnastics, tennis and rugby.

Most children enter their senior schools at 11½ and Lyndhurst has an enviable record of exam successes over the years.

Entry to the School can be at any age if there is a vacancy. At least one internal scholarship is awarded annually for academic achievement, and one external when there is a place available.

Lyonsdown School

3 Richmond Road, New Barnet, Hertfordshire EN5 1SA
Tel: 020 8449 0225
Fax: 020 8441 4690
e-mail: enquiries@lyonsdownschool.co.uk
website: www.lyonsdownschool.co.uk

Headmistress: Mrs Lynn Maggs-Wellings, BEd

Age Range. Girls 3–11, Boys 3–7.
Number of Pupils. 210.
Fees per term (2011-2012). Pre-Reception: £1,027–£1,863; Reception–Year 2 £2,372; Years 3–6 £2,610.

Lyonsdown School has built on its past inheritance since its foundation in 1906, to embrace the needs of education for children of the 21st Century. Pupils are nurtured by our well-qualified, experienced and caring staff who help them to maximise their potential. The school has a tradition of high academic standards and achievements within a broad curriculum.

The personal development of each child is a high priority. A wide variety of extra-curricular activities allows pupils to extend their experiences and learn new skills.

A balanced academic, physical and cultural education, together with a high level of pastoral care, enables pupils to grow and look forward to being part of the modern world.

Entry into Pre-Reception and Reception is non-selective. Pupils are considered for entry at other ages if places become available.

We aim to allow each child to move easily into the next stage of their education by preparing them for schools which best suit their needs.

Charitable status. Lyonsdown School Trust Ltd is a Registered Charity, number 312591.

Mander Portman Woodward (MPW)
London

90–92 Queen's Gate, London SW7 5AB
Tel: 020 7835 1355
Fax: 020 7259 2705
e-mail: london@mpw.co.uk
website: www.mpw.co.uk

Principal: **Steven Boyes**, BA, MSc, PGCE

Age Range. 14–18.
Number in School. Day: 279 Boys, 256 Girls.
Fees per term (2011-2012). £5,926–£7,362.
Mander Portman Woodward (MPW) is a co-educational London day school accepting pupils from the first year of GCSE onwards. Approximately 100 new pupils join each year at the start of the sixth form. We offer a very wide range of subjects (39 at A Level and 23 at GCSE) and there are no restrictions on subject combinations at A Level. At all levels the absolute maximum number of pupils in any one class is eight.

The school has completely refurbished its Queen's Gate premises with modern facilities tastefully blended in with the traditional architecture of the buildings. There are six well equipped laboratories for Science subjects and specialist studios for Art, Ceramics, Photography and Media Studies. The school also has extensive facilities for independent study, including two supervised reading rooms and an internet library.

There is a range of compulsory extra-curricular activities for GCSE pupils, including sport, and a variety of voluntary extra-curricular activities is offered at A Level. In keeping with our founding principles, our primary focus at all age levels is on academic goals. Entry into the sixth form is dependent on a student's academic record and performance at interview. Almost all pupils proceed to university after leaving, with about 20 each year going to read Medicine. Over the past four years an average of 7 of our full-time pupils each year have won places at the Universities of Oxford or Cambridge.

We insist on strict punctuality in the attendance of lessons and the submission of homework and there is a formal system of monthly examinations in each subject throughout a pupil's career at the school. This system is designed to ensure that sensible, cumulative revision becomes a study habit not only at school but also later on at university. We require pupils to have a strong commitment to academic discipline but our reputation is based on having created a framework in which pupils can enjoy working hard. The environment is friendly, the teachers experienced and enthusiastic and the atmosphere positive and conducive to success.

Manor House School

South Street, Ashby-de-la-Zouch, Leics LE65 1BR
Tel: 01530 412932
Fax: 01530 417435
e-mail: enquiries@manorhouseashby.co.uk
website: www.manorhouseashby.co.uk

Chairman of the Governors: Mr R Bayliss

Acting Head: **Mrs E A Scrine**, BA Hons, PGCE, MEd

Age Range. 4–16.
Number of Pupils. 147: 75 Boys, 72 Girls.

Fees per term (2010-2011). From £1,833 (Kindergarten) to £2,666, including meals.
Manor House is an independent co-educational school for children ranging in age from 4 to 16. It is situated in a magnificent setting between the impressive ruins of Ashby Castle and the ancient Parish Church, and is within easy reach of Derby, Leicester, Birmingham and Nottingham.

The school caters for mixed ability children with a maximum class size of twenty and one class per year group.

From the age of 8 children have access to the school's fully-equipped Science Laboratory, Computer Suite, Art Room, and two libraries. Children are taught French from the age of 5 and German from the age of 11. A wide range of extra-curricular activities is also on offer, as well as a Breakfast Club and an After-School Club.

The school has a wide reputation for both its academic achievements and its genuinely friendly and happy atmosphere. We deliver a curriculum that stimulates and challenges children to produce their best. We also provide an environment where children can develop self-discipline, responsibility, and self-motivation with a respect for others.

Charitable status. Manor House School is a Registered Charity, number 527859. It exists to provide education for boys and girls.

Maple Hayes Hall School for Dyslexics

Abnalls Lane, Lichfield, Staffordshire WS13 8BL
Tel: 01543 264387
Fax: 01543 262022
e-mail: office@dyslexia.gb.com
website: www.dyslexia.gb.com

Principal: **Dr E N Brown**, PhD, MSc, BA, MSCME, MINS, AFBPsS, CPsychol

Headmaster: Dr D J Brown, DPhil, MEd (Psychology of SpLD), MA Oxon, PGCE

Age Range. 7–17.
Number in School. 120 Day Boys and Girls.
Fees per term (2011-2012). £4,313–£5,832.
Maple Hayes is a specialist independent day school approved under the 1996 Education Act as a co-educational school for children of average to very high intelligence who are not achieving their intellectual potential by normal teaching methods.

This school is under the direction of Dr E Neville Brown whose work in the field of learning strategies has achieved international recognition and includes a major breakthrough in the teaching of dyslexic children. Attention is paid to the individual child by teaching the basic literacy and numeracy skills required for the child to benefit from a full curriculum, (with the exception of a foreign language) including the three sciences to GCSE level. The school had an excellent Ofsted report.

The very favourable teacher-pupil ratio of 1:10 or better ensures a high standard of educational and pastoral care. The children's learning is under the supervision and guidance of a qualified educational psychologist.

Mark College

Mark, Highbridge, Somerset TA9 4NP
Tel: 01278 641632
Fax: 01278 641426
e-mail: markcollege@priorygroup.com
website: www.priorygroup.com

Principal: Mrs Michelle Whitham Jones

Vice Principal: Mrs Sharon Bowden

Age Range. 10–19.
Number in School. Boarding: 46 Boys, 3 Girls; Day: 22 Boys, 1 Girls.
Fees per term (2010-2011). Boarding £8,566; Weekly Boarding £8,219; Day £5,884.

Mark College is a Department for Education and CReSTeD approved school for boys and girls diagnosed as having dyslexia, dyspraxia and language disorders. The College offers a full curriculum with specialist help so that boys and girls enter for 6 to 8 GCSEs, BTECs or other examinations in their fifth (Year 11) year. GCSE results are good.

Accommodation, including a full sized sports hall, is of a high standard. The College is well resourced and the atmosphere is relaxed and purposeful.

The College's provision for mathematics is recognised internationally, and its English provision involves the use of the latest work in information technology.

After a very good Ofsted report, the College received a commendation and was listed in the HMCI Annual Report, described as a "significant achievement" by the Secretary of State. Mark College is a Beacon school. It received the ISA "Award for Excellence" in May 2000. In 2003 the College was awarded a Sportsmark with Distinction. The latest Ofsted report (2011) commented on the high standard of education, the outstanding sports provision and the high quality of personal care afforded to the students by the staff. The Ofsted care inspection in 2011 gave the overall judgement of "good".

The Sixth Form allows pupils to gain further independence skills whilst studying for A Levels.

Mayville High School

35 St Simon's Road, Southsea, Hants PO5 2PE
Tel: 023 9273 4847
Fax: 023 9229 3649
e-mail: enquiries@mayvillehighschool.com
website: www.mayvillehighschool.com

Mayville High School – Excellence through nurture

Head teacher: Mr Martin Castle

Age Range. 2 years 9 months–16 years.
Number in School. Day Pupils: 254 Boys, 224 Girls.
Fees per term (2011-2012). £1,882–£2,761.

Mayville High School can offer your child a place from the age of 2 years 9 months to 16 years. Our close-knit community is divided into the Early Years, Pre-Prep, Junior and Senior Schools. We have a renowned Dyslexia Unit, recognised by CReSTeD, and offer a Gifted and Talented Programme. Our pupils star in numerous ways, and the Mayville family includes pupils, teachers, parents, carers and grandparents.

Mayville, a co-educational day school in Southsea, Hampshire was founded in 1897. There is a strong emphasis on traditional skills, yet Mayville adopts innovative teaching methods to help promote your child's learning. Our size is our strength, big enough to offer pupils a wide range of opportunities, we are small enough to truly treat and know each pupil as an individual.

Mayville provides a learning environment where your child is able to achieve their goals. At Mayville we want children to feel secure and valued: this enables them to take advantage of every opportunity, whether it be academic, social, physical, creative or spiritual.

Mayville sets high standards in all areas. Small class sizes encourage academic success. Boys and girls are taught separately throughout, to best meet their individual learning styles. Over the years Mayville pupils have consistently achieved high standards in GCSE examinations. Flexible teaching, varied resources, support and extension programmes coupled with high expectations help to meet the needs of each individual learner. Art, drama, dance, music and sport play an important part in school life, the latter now enhanced by new playing fields. There are a number of clubs and after-school activities. There is something available to interest everyone.

Nursery (2 years 9 months–3+ years). At "the Cottage" children feel cherished and secure in "a home from home" environment. Our Nursery has also been awarded the much-coveted Flying High for Early Years Accreditation that stamps a seal of excellence on the care we provide.

When you leave your child at Nursery for the first time you want them to be cared for as they would at home. In our cosy bright building with its own playground and garden children are nurtured by qualified Early Years staff. Children sit down together at lunchtime and enjoy freshly cooked nutritious meals. Close proximity to the seafront and local amenities means children are taken out for trips, weather permitting. Our Nursery is open 50 weeks of the year 8 am–6 pm.

Pre-Prep Dept (3+–7 years). Kestrels and Lower I classes are where children make a smooth and natural transition from nursery or home to school. It also provides an early start to literacy and numeracy, and a wide range of activities designed to help them become active and independent learners. In Key Stage One (5–7 years) the curriculum widens to include science, geography, history and ICT as separate subjects. All pupils in Pre-Prep benefit from use of the the school's halls for drama, dance and PE. French and Music are taught throughout the Department.

Junior and Senior Schools. The Junior School accepts boys and girls from the age of 7+. We offer bright airy surroundings, a caring yet disciplined environment and small class sizes. While a strong emphasis is placed on the traditional skills of reading writing and numeracy, children in the Junior School enjoy a varied curriculum. Pupils are taught to appreciate that education is as much about attitudes and values, as it is about academic and sporting success. In the senior school this ethos continues, and pupils are given a wide range of opportunities to excel in: academic, creative, sporting and social. Pupils at KS3 follow a full curriculum. This includes thinking skills and first aid, and also study skills seminars. It is Mayville's policy to enter all pupils for their GCSE providing they have completed the course of study and the coursework. Therefore our results, which have been well above the national average for the past ten years, are a true reflection of the efforts of staff and pupils.

At Mayville we believe that confidence is the central building block to success in future life. Our commitment to Global Rock Challenge and membership of our own St John Ambulance cadet unit, allows pupils to develop teamwork and leadership skills. At Mayville we celebrate the many successes of our pupils and encourage their competitive spirit. With three houses, there are a number of inter-house competitions which also promote this. Trips to local, national and international locations are encouraged to broaden the experiences begun in the classroom.

Transport. There are good public transport links into the city from the surrounding areas. School minibuses pick up pupils from the local ferry terminals and train stations.

If you would like a prospectus, to book a tour of the school with the Head teacher, Mr Castle, or to find out about our taster days, please telephone the school or visit our website. Applications for the January 2012 Entrance Assessments are being accepted for intake in September 2012. Scholarships are available from Year 2.

Charitable status. Mayville High School is a Registered Charity, number 286347. It exists to provide a traditional education to children from a wide range of academic backgrounds within a caring environment.

Mead School

16 Frant Road, Tunbridge Wells, Kent TN2 5SN
Tel: 01892 525837
e-mail: meadschool@hotmail.co.uk
website: www.meadschool.info

Headmistress: Mrs A Culley

Age Range. 3–11.
Number in School. 190.
Fees per term (2010-2011). Kindergarten £1,499; Infants £2,759; Juniors £3,056.

The Mead is an independent, co-educational preparatory school situated in the centre of Tunbridge Wells. We prepare children for both Kent Selection into Grammar School and for Common Entrance to a wide range of Independent Schools at 11+.

We aim to create a happy, secure and enthusiastic atmosphere in which every individual can develop his or her all round potential and thereby become well motivated, interesting and hard working members of society.

Academic standards are high and based on National Curriculum requirements. Strong emphasis is placed on individual attention and close cooperation between school and parents is encouraged.

We offer a broad range of extra-curricular activities: sport, drama, music, ballet, judo, swimming.

A copy of our Prospectus and outstanding recent ISI report are available on request.

The Moat School

Bishop's Avenue, Fulham, London SW6 6EG
Tel: 020 7610 9018
Fax: 020 7610 9098
e-mail: office@moatschool.org.uk
website: www.moatschool.org.uk

Chair of Governors: Richard Simmons, CBE

Headteacher: Abigail Gray, BA Hons, PGCE, Cert SpLD

Co-educational Day School.
Age Range. 11–16.
Number of Pupils. 71 Boys, 23 Girls.
Fees per term (2011-2012). £8,050.

Set within the historic conservation area of Fulham Palace, The Moat School is a specialist school for secondary-age SpLD pupils. Mainstream in structure and specialist in nature, The Moat caters successfully for the needs of pupils with specific learning difficulties. Alongside the curriculum, the school also offers expertise in speech and language therapy, occupational therapy and a school counsellor.

All teachers complete a post-graduate BDA approved course in teaching students with SpLD within their first 2 years of appointment. Qualified Learning Support Assistants accompany pupils throughout their lessons at Key Stage 3, where class sizes are a maximum of 10. Class sizes are even smaller at Key Stage 4.

Multi-sensory teaching is combined with advanced IT provision, each pupil being provided with a laptop computer for use in school and at home. Touch-typing is taught in Year 7 and there is a state-of-the-art wireless network which enables staff and pupils to access the school intranet with its wide range of learning resources and data, as well as the internet.

At Key Stage 3, pupils follow a mainstream curriculum (with the exception of foreign languages) before selecting their GCSE options alongside the core subjects of English, Mathematics and Single or Dual Award Science. The Moat offers excellent facilities for learning, with a suite of Design Technology workshops offering state-of-the-art facilities for Food Technology, Resistant Materials and Graphics. Art, Music, Drama, ICT and Business Studies each have dedicated studios or specialist classrooms.

The Moat has an extensive enrichment programme of extra-curricular activities designed to widen experience and develop self-confidence. In drama, all Year 9 pupils take part in an annual Shakespeare play and there are several productions and workshop performances each year. The Moat's proximity to the River Thames enables pupils to experience rowing as a sport, swimming is popular and 2011 saw the introduction of Martial Arts. The Duke of Edinburgh's Award encourages pupils to test their own limits and each summer students in Years 7, 8 and 9 make a residential visit to an outdoor activity centre to develop independence and leadership skills.

Charitable status. The Constable Educational Trust is a Registered Charity, number 1068445. It exists to establish and support The Moat School so that it can provide education and opportunity for SpLD learners (dyslexic & dyspraxic).

Moffats School

Kinlet Hall, Bewdley, Worcs DY12 3AY
Tel: 01299 841230
Fax: 01299 841444
e-mail: office@moffats.co.uk
website: www.moffats.co.uk

Head: Mark Daborn, MA, ARICS, QTS

Age Range. 4–13+.
Number of Children. 67.
Fees per term (2010-2011). Boarding £4,700, Day £1,212–£2,920.

Moffats is a co-educational boarding and day school in a Grade 1 historic house set in its own hundred acres of park and farmland, a glorious environment a mile from any public road. There are equal numbers of boys and girls who share the same opportunities and responsibilities in all activities. We are proud of our record since 1934, but this is not limited to academic awards or A grades in the Common Entrance Examination. Our joy and satisfaction is in bringing out the best in every child. Their achievements in speech and drama are outstanding. All usual games are coached, including athletics and cross-country running with conspicuous successes at inter-school and national levels. With our own stables riding is professionally taught to half the school. Annual sailing camp with ten boats. Weekends and spare time are filled with a multitude of activities. Moffats is a truly family school; the personal touch of members of the same family which founded Moffats ensures the well-being and happiness of all the children in their care.

Moorland School

Ribblesdale Avenue, Clitheroe, Lancashire BB7 2JA
Tel: 01200 423833
Fax: 01200 429339
e-mail: jhicks@moorlandschool.co.uk
website: www.moorlandschool.co.uk

Principal: Mrs J Harrison, BA Hons, CertEd, NLP

Age Range. 3 months – 16 years.
Number of Pupils. 144 including 33 boarders.

Fees per term (2010-2011). Day: £1,743–£2,370; Full Boarding: £4,877–£6,325; Weekly Boarding: £4,674–£5,954.

Admission to Moorland. Parents and children are encouraged to visit the school to meet the Principal and see the school in action. Boarding or Day children are also welcome to attend Moorland for a one or two day 'taster visit'.

The success of the school owes much to our small class sizes which helps to build a special relationship between teacher and pupil producing excellent results.

Pastoral care is well managed and Moorland offers a range of activities, clubs, competitions and school visits to give each child every opportunity to take part and be challenged.

Kindergarten & Nursery. As well as having its own indoor softplay area, the nursery also has a large outdoor play area within its extensive grounds, with unbroken views over Waddington Fell. The Nursery's superb layout of colourful rooms and equipment make it an ideal and exceptional learning environment.

Junior School. The Preparatory Department takes children between the ages of 4 and 11. The children have their own play area and IT suite and benefit from using the facilities of the Senior School such as science laboratories and sports hall.

The children follow Key Stages 1 and 2 of the National Curriculum with particular emphasis on numeracy and literacy. Our small class sizes allow every child to read to the Teacher on a daily basis. French is also included in the Junior curriculum.

The Senior School follows the criteria set down in the National Curriculum. We enter our pupils for the Standard Attainment Tests and for GCSE at the end of Key stage 4.

Options for GCSE are chosen at the end of Year 9, and parents and pupils are fully consulted to ensure that the best possible choice is made for the future.

Football at Moorland. Our FA approved coach, Charles Jackson, is one of the UK's most innovative and well-respected football coaches. He teaches to a Premier League standard. He has worked at Moorland since November 2002. He also worked at the Manchester United Advanced Coaching Centre up to July 2005 and is now the Under 14 academy technical skills Development Coach at Blackburn Rovers' Brockhall training site. He spends 4 days per week at Moorland School teaching children from age 4–16.

Pastoral Care. At Moorland children benefit from continuous pastoral support within a friendly family environment. By day, teaching staff provide continual support within small classes. Evening and weekend care is undertaken by the teaching staff and House Parent team.

More House School

Frensham, Farnham, Surrey GU10 3AP
Tel: 01252 792303
            Admissions: 01252 797600
Fax: 01252 797601
e-mail: schooloffice@morehouseschool.co.uk
website: www.morehouseschool.co.uk

Headmaster: **B Huggett**, BA Hons, QTS, FSB

Age Range. 9+ to 18.
Number in School. Boarders: 103 Boys, Day: 293 Boys.
Fees per term (2011-2012). Full Boarding £6,550–£8,220; Weekly Boarding £5,935–£7,590; Day £3,770–£5,285.

More House School occupies a unique position in helping boys with specific learning difficulties in that multi-sensory remediation is applied across the curriculum, through carefully targeted and maintained intervention, and extra help is available in our Learning Development Centre, so that proper support is always available and individual needs met.

It is approved by the Department for Education and has been listed by CReSTeD in their Specialist Schools category. No school can help every child, so we have a very careful selection assessment to ensure that we really can help those who finally enter the school.

Founded over 70 years ago, the school prides itself in using the best modern practice to increase confidence and make children feel valued, happy and to fulfil their potential at GCSE, AS, A Level and other public examinations.

Boarding is run by caring staff and is situated in lovely grounds with plenty of opportunities for outdoor pursuits. Our activities programme, which offers 18 options each day, encourages all day boys and boarders to make good use of their leisure time. There is a strong sense of community.

There is an ongoing building programme and the facilities are very good in all departments.

Ofsted described More House as "an excellent school offering an outstanding education".

We have a comprehensive information pack, and always welcome visitors. Why not ring us?

Charitable status. More House School is a Registered Charity, number 311872. A Catholic foundation, open to all, helping boys to succeed.

Moyles Court School

Moyles Court, Ringwood, Hampshire BH24 3NF
Tel: 01425 472856/473197
Fax: 01425 474715
e-mail: info@moylescourt.co.uk
website: www.moylescourt.co.uk

Headmaster: **G Meakin**, BSc, MA, PGCE

Age Range. 3–16.
Number in School. Boarders: 27 boys, 17 girls. Day: 57 boys, 47 girls.
Fees per term (2011-2012). Boarders: £5,684–£7,083; Senior Day: £3,845–£3,913; Junior Day £1,806*–£3,667; Nursery: £4.70 per hour (Early Years Pathfinder Scheme Funding available*).

Moyles Court is a small and successful co-educational boarding and day school for children from 3 to 16 years. A strong pastoral ethos with traditional family values supports a broad and balanced curriculum. Academic achievement is very good. In 2010 the GCSE pass rate at grades A*–C was 86% with 100% pass rate overall; 30% of all grades were A*/A.

The school is administered by a Board of Governors and is registered as an Educational Charitable Trust. The trust has passed the Charity Commission Public Benefit Test.

The school is situated two miles north east of Ringwood in beautiful grounds on the edge of the New Forest, surrounded by heath, woodlands and streams. The fourteen acres provide ideal playing areas for the children and they use these extensively in their free time.

At Moyles Court, we aim to enthuse and encourage children of all academic abilities to maximise their potential in preparation for the challenging and competitive world, which lies outside the security of home and school. Education means development of the 'whole' person and this is the aim at Moyles Court.

It is the school's policy to follow the National Curriculum, within which a comprehensive range of GCSE subjects are offered. The National Curriculum is enriched in the Junior School by the International Primary Curriculum.

Moyles Court has a thriving sporting and outdoor education programme. An extensive selection of extra-curricular activities is available throughout the year including the Duke of Edinburgh's Award Scheme.

Discounts apply for Service families. Sibling discounts, Scholarships and Bursaries are available. Admission is through personal interview with the Headmaster, report from previous school and a taster day at Moyles Court, during which Literacy and Numeracy assessments are conducted.

For further details visit the website at www.moyle-scourt.co.uk or contact Chris Young, Admissions Secretary. A warm welcome awaits you.

Charitable status. Moyles Court School is a Registered Charity, number 307347.

The Mulberry House School

7 Minster Road, West Hampstead, London NW2 3SD
Tel: 020 8452 7340
e-mail: info@mulberryhouseschool.com
website: www.mulberryhouseschool.com

Headteacher: **Ms Julie Kirwan**

Age Range. 2–7 Co-educational.
Number of Pupils. 198.
Fees per term (2011-2012). £2,820–£5,233.
The Mulberry House School is an established independent school for 2–7 year olds, offering a stimulating and caring environment that meets the needs of individuals, while preparing them for the next stage of their schooling at 4+ or 7+. Extended day, full and part time places available. To attend an Open Evening, please visit the Register section of the website www.mulberryhouseschool.com.

Mylnhurst Preparatory School & Nursery

Button Hill, Woodholm Road, Ecclesall, Sheffield S11 9HJ
Tel: 0114 236 1411
Fax: 0114 236 1411
e-mail: enquiries@mylnhurst.co.uk
website: www.mylnhurst.co.uk

A Catholic Foundation Welcoming Families of All Faiths – maximising the potential of your children through partnership within a challenging and supportive Catholic Christian Community.

Headmaster: **Mr C P Emmott**, BSc, MEd

Age Range. 3–11 Co-educational.
Number of Pupils. 179.
Fees per term (2011-2012). £2,525.
Situated in extensive private grounds, Mylnhurst provides a state-of-the-art teaching environment supported by our outstanding school facilities, which include a 25m pool, dance studio, sports hall and Apple Mac suite.

With a strong emphasis on school-parent partnership, Mylnhurst embraces your high expectations and ensures each child benefits from an exciting and stimulating curriculum.

Be assured of a very warm welcome and the opportunity to work closely with our committed and talented staff. So, whether it be an informal chat or a school open day, we look forward to sharing our vision with you and discussing the exciting future of your children.

Charitable status. Mylnhurst Limited is a Registered Charity, number 1056683.

New Eccles Hall School

Quidenham, Nr Norwich, Norfolk NR16 2NZ
Tel: 01953 887217
Fax: 01953 887397
e-mail: admin@neweccleshall.com
website: www.neweccleshall.com

Headmaster: **R W Allard**, CertEd

Age Range. 5–18.
Number in School. 70 Boarders, 110 Day.
Fees per term (2010-2011). Day £2,025–£3,320, Boarding £4,880–£5,760.
The school offers:
- Excellent standard of teaching in small classes.
- Curriculum that covers the national requirements and more.
- Caring for the pupil as an individual is at the centre of the school's ethos.
- Large country estate providing a perfect learning environment.
- Exceptional games facilities combined with an extensive leisure programme.
- Successful Individual Teaching Unit for Specific Learning Difficulties.
- Happy relaxed atmosphere for teaching and learning.
- Attractive and comfortable boarding accommodation.
- Learning respect for each other considered essential.
- Length of the day suits working families.
Visitors to the school are welcome when the school is in session.

Newlands School

Eastbourne Road, Seaford, East Sussex BN25 4NP
Tel: 01323 490000
Fax: 01323 898420
e-mail: enquiries@newlands-school.com
website: www.newlands-school.com

Head: **Mandy Johannson**

Age Range. 0–18 years.
Number of Pupils. 157.
Fees per term (2011-2012). Tuition: £2,033–£3,630. Boarding (in addition to Tuition fees): £2,675. Overseas Pupils: £7,500 (including Boarding and Tuition).
Newlands provides a quality education from birth to 18 years on a 17-acre campus in a pleasant coastal town surrounded by an area of outstanding natural beauty.

Newlands has good communication links with Gatwick (37 miles), Heathrow (78 miles) and London (65 miles). The school runs a door-to-door mini-bus service for day pupils. Boarders are escorted to airports and stations.

Your Child is Unique! Our emphasis at Newlands is to enable each individual to thrive, confident to be themselves, in a nurturing and happy environment. We encourage active, hands on, fun learning, with pupils fully involved in decision-making.

Classes are small and pupil progress is monitored carefully, closely involving parents and pupils.

Curriculum. Pupils from Reception to Y6 follow the Creative Learning Journey framework, which is skill-based, topic-linked active learning. Pupils from Y7–Y11 follow the National Curriculum and GCSEs. In September 2012 we re-open our Sixth Form for A Levels.

Facilities. Both arts and sciences flourish. An exceptional textiles, photography and art department produce consistently high standards, a very well equipped art studio, two photography labs with dark room and textiles studio. Science labs, IT media rooms, a recording studio and music technology department stimulate high-quality opportunities and standards.

17 acres of grounds include excellent sporting facilities: football pitches, indoor swimming pool, three hard surface tennis courts, purpose-built sports hall. Cricket, hockey, rugby, football, athletics, volleyball, tennis, swimming, rounders are all offered.

Educational Support Unit. We offer additional support for students with dyslexia in our Educational Support Unit with specialist staff. This incurs additional costs for parents who wish to buy into it.

Norfolk House School

Norfolk Road, Edgbaston, Birmingham B15 3PS
Tel: 0121 454 7021
Fax: 0121 454 7021
e-mail: norfolkhs@aol.com
website: www.norfolkhouseschool.co.uk

Headmistress: **Mrs H Maresca**, BEd

Age Range. 3–11.
Number in School. 155.
Fees per term (from April 2011). £1,731–£2,262.
Norfolk House School is a Christian Independent day school situated in the pleasant suburb of Edgbaston and is ideally located for pupils and parents all over Birmingham and the surrounding areas.

The school aims to provide individual attention to each pupil, thus enabling each child to fulfil his or her potential. Small class sizes and favourable pupil:teacher ratios (average 17:1) culminate in the best possible academic results. Many pupils move on to the various King Edward Schools, or to other Grammar Schools or senior Independent Schools as the direct result of the high standards achieved at Norfolk House.

The syllabus is designed to give each child a general academic education over a wide range of subjects – in line with the National Curriculum; the requirements of the Eleven Plus and the various Entrance Examinations are also taken into consideration.

In addition to education, Norfolk House School aims to instil in each child good manners, consideration and respect for others, and recognition of personal responsibility. Norfolk House is a small school with an emphasis on caring and traditional values, yet forward thinking in outlook. It is a happy school with high attainment, competitive fees and a family atmosphere.

Norfolk House School

10 Muswell Avenue, Muswell Hill, London N10 2EG
Tel: 020 8883 4584
Fax: 020 8883 4584
e-mail: admissions@norfolkhouseschool.org
website: www.norfolkhouseschool.org

Headmaster: **Mr Mark Malley**, BA Ed Hons

Age Range. 4–11 Co-educational.
Number of Pupils. 154.
Fees per term (2011-2012). £3,285.
Norfolk House School is a leading London Preparatory School for boys and girls aged 4–11.

The school takes great pride in its happy and warm environment, where each and every pupil is valued and supported. Pupils at Norfolk House are nurtured and guided through school life; we aim to stimulate and inspire our children and to develop their interests.

We ensure our curriculum is interesting and stimulating as well as broad and balanced. We want our pupils to be excited about lessons and fully engaged in all of school life. We strive to offer personalisation to our learning programmes; our pupils are involved in their own learning and our older children conference regularly with their teachers to set realistic learning targets. Self and peer evaluation of work are both well embedded in our curriculum and our pupils are always aware of what they need to do to achieve next steps, and are well supported in this.

Norfolk House has unashamedly high academic standards. We are a non-selective school but our pupils achieve very impressive results.

The school is generously staffed and this is reflected in the individual attention pupils receive at school. We have an excellent support system for pupils whom require extra help as well as those whom benefit from extension activities.

Sport is taken very seriously at Norfolk House. Our pupils spend two afternoons a week dedicated to sport. Pupils are largely taught by sport specialists who offer further sports clubs after school. Younger pupils are taught general ball skills and in the summer have dedicated tennis lessons. They also enjoy gymnastic lessons and athletics lessons. Pupils start swimming lessons from the age of six and have these each year until they leave. Older pupils are exposed to a wide range of sports including gymnastics, cross country, athletics, tennis, netball, football, cricket and rounders.

Normanhurst School

68–74 Station Road, Chingford, London E4 7BA
Tel: 020 8529 4307
Fax: 020 8524 7737
e-mail: info@normanhurstschool.co.uk
website: www.normanhurstschool.co.uk

Headmistress: **Mrs Claire Osborn**, BA Hons, PGCE

Age Range. 2½–16.
Number in School. 240 Day Pupils.
Fees per term (from April 2011). £1,515–£3,745.
Entry requirements. Interview and assessment.
Location. In the centre of a tree-lined suburban street with good parking, two minutes from a mainline British Rail station and from a far-reaching bus terminus.

Normanhurst School is a thriving, caring, local independent school with a warm, friendly atmosphere and a wide range of activities offered. The School boasts a high standard of academic achievement with excellent SATs and GCSE results.

We encourage our pupils to develop self-confidence and to take on roles of responsibility as they move up through the school. Creativity is nurtured within a disciplined environment and traditional values such as self-discipline are promoted to maximise our pupils' effectiveness in an ever-changing world.

The School offers small class sizes and a wide range of core and optional subjects up to GCSE, including English, Science, Maths, French, Spanish, Design Technology, Art, History, Geography, ICT, Business Studies, PE, Sport, Music and Drama.

Numerous clubs are provided to strengthen the important social aspect of schooling. These include Football, Netball, Gymnastics, Chess, French, Cross-country, Dance, and ICT. Homework club and Teatime club are available to all pupils, while tuition on various musical instruments takes place either as an extra-curricular activity during the day or after school.

The North London International School

6 Friern Barnet Lane, London N11 3LX
Tel: 020 8920 0600
Fax: 020 8211 4605
e-mail: admissions@nlis.org
website: www.nlis.org

Headmaster: **Mr David Rose**, BA, CertEd, MA Ed

Age Range. 2–19.
Number in School. 414 Boys and Girls.
Fees per term (2010-2011). £1,075–£5,160.
The North London International School provides a secure, well-ordered and happy environment with the learning process at its core, offering the finest possible education for all pupils in order for them to reach their full potential. Serving a cosmopolitan and diverse North London community, great importance is attached to respect, understanding and empathy with everyone's cultures, religions and backgrounds. Emphasis is placed on development of the individual student with academic, artistic, sporting, creative, practical and social skills being encouraged and individual talents nurtured. Every child has a spark of genius, we aim to ignite it!

Students follow the International Baccalaureate curriculum, starting at aged 3 with the Primary Years Programme, moving onto the Middle Years Programme at age 11 and the International Baccalaureate Diploma Programme at age 16. The programmes are designed to encourage the development of learning skills and to meet a child's academic, social, physical, emotional and cultural needs. Through enquiry-based learning and various disciplines, subject interrelatedness is accentuated, preparing students for the pre-university Diploma Programme. Within the programme students must study six subjects, a research project, leading to a 4000 word essay, The Theory of Knowledge course, and Creativity, Action, Service (CAS). The CAS programme is a fundamental part of the Diploma programme, requiring students to participate in 150 hours of activities both in and out of school.

The Quest Programme is designed for students who need help developing strategies to assist them to study effectively. Through one-to-one tuition from specialist staff in skills such as effective reading, time management, planning of work and revision and exam techniques, students can reach their full potential, further enhanced by the school's teacher-student ratio.

Entry requirements. Students are accepted for entry at any time throughout the school year.

Kindergarten and Lower School (ages 2–11): Students are invited to attend for half a day and may be asked to complete a basic assessment.

Upper School (ages 11–16): Students attend an interview with the Head of the school, are invited to visit the school for a day and may be required to complete a basic assessment.

Entry to the Upper School is automatic for students in the Lower School.

Upper School (ages 16–19): Diploma programme applicants are invited for interview with the programme coordinator. Students would be expected to have 5 or 6 GCSE passes, with B, A or A* grades for subjects to be studied at Higher Level. Students arriving from overseas without GSCE qualifications need to demonstrate a sound academic background and understanding of English. The school is able to offer a Foundation Year to students whose command of the English language or subject area knowledge is not sufficient to enable them to start the full programme, including specialist English as an Alternative Language support.

Any decision regarding the offering of a place to a prospective student from overseas who is unable to visit for interview or assessment, will be made by the Head of the respective department, referring to school reports and scholastic references.

Examinations offered. Key Stages 1, 2 and 3; GCSE; International Baccalaureate.

Facilities. The school has dedicated IT, music, art and Design Technology facilities for all students. The commitment to the use of Information and Communications Technology in all subject areas is highlighted by IT and graphics suites, individual student home drives and email accounts, student dedicated laptops and wireless network.

Music tuition is incorporated into the curriculum with the addition of individual lessons in a wide variety of instruments such as piano, guitar, drums, saxophone and violin with composition and singing also available. The school has a number of bands and groups with varying styles from jazz to rock and regular concerts highlight the very real talent within the student body.

Student's physical development is considered as important as academic development and the school's sports fields provide excellent facilities for football, cricket, athletics, hockey, tennis and softball. The school's hall, playgrounds and local amenities are also utilised to offer further activities such as basketball, badminton, squash, swimming, table tennis, ice-skating and skiing. Matches and tournaments between local schools are regular fixtures.

The school's close proximity to central London allows for numerous trips to the capital's museums, galleries and theatres. A variety of overseas trips are offered, both academic and leisure, including France, Spain, skiing and our sister school, The Dwight, in New York while Diploma students are given the opportunity to attend the Model United Nations conferences at The Hague.

Scholarships and Bursaries. A number of scholarships are offered each year to students with a high ability in academic, sporting, musical or artistic areas. For students wishing to enter the Diploma Programme, a scholarship award of up to 30% will be considered for candidates who show a high level of academic achievement. Bursaries are considered on application.

Northease Manor School

Rodmell, Lewes, East Sussex BN7 3EY
Tel: 01273 472915
Fax: 01273 472202
e-mail: office@northease.co.uk
          pa2headteacher@northease.co.uk
website: www.northease.co.uk

Chairman of Governors: David Boys

Head: **Mrs C Harvey-Browne**, BA, PGCE

Type of School. Co-educational day and weekly boarding school.
Age Range. 10–17.
Number of Pupils. 98: 20 Girls, 78 Boys.
Fees per term (2010-2011). Day £6,472, Boarding £8,850.

Northease Manor School is a co-educational special school for pupils, aged ten to seventeen, who have specific learning difficulties. It caters for both weekly boarders and day pupils. It is approved by the Department for Education and is accredited by CReSTeD. It is set in the South Downs with Grade II listed buildings.

It provides a holistic approach to Specific Learning Difficulties within small teaching groups and provides on-site access to Speech and Language Therapy and Occupational Therapy. Most of the staff have specialist qualifications and benefit from in-house training.

Northease caters for potentially able pupils who have not realised their true potential at previous schools due to their Specific Learning Difficulties which normally results in a deficit in literacy skills but sometimes in numeracy skills as well. They receive full access to the National Curriculum and benefit from an intensive multi-sensory input which provides for all their literacy and language needs. Detailed pastoral support is given to enable pupils to feel secure and become independent learners. Everything that happens at the school is geared to the needs of the child and to ensure that each pupil experiences success in order to raise self-esteem and self-confidence.

In July 2007, Ofsted described Northease Manor as "an excellent school" that gave "outstanding value for money" and where "progress that pupils make is outstanding". A CReSTeD Inspection concluded that "the school has a clear and focused objective to remain one of the best schools in its field".

The ethos of the school is based upon respect for the individual and the celebration of success and achievement. All pupils have abilities and talents and it is the school's role to enable every pupil to discover and develop these talents. Pupils are encouraged to "work hard, play hard" and to have a sense of ownership. It is "our school" and everybody contributes to its well-being and development. High standards of behaviour are expected, with the onus on partnership between pupils and adults. Mistakes are seen as part of the learning process.

Charitable status. Northease Manor School Trust Ltd is a Registered Charity, number 307005. It exists for the provision of high-quality education for pupils with Specific Learning Difficulties.

Notre Dame Preparatory School

147 Dereham Road, Norwich, Norfolk NR2 3TA
Tel: 01603 625593
Fax: 01603 444139
e-mail: info@notredameprepschool.co.uk
website: www.notredameprepschool.co.uk

Chairman of Governors: Mr Philip Hook

Headmaster: **Mr K O'Herlihy**, BA, HDipEd

Age Range. 3–11 Co-educational.
Number of Pupils. 130 Day.
Fees per term (2010-2011). £1,635–£1,815.

Notre Dame Prep School was originally founded by the Sisters of Notre Dame de Namur in 1865. The school transferred to its present site in 1971 and is now a Company with charitable status. The school maintains the traditions and the spirit of the Sisters of Notre Dame and the former name and uniform.

As a Catholic school the school and staff endeavour to nurture a love of God through Jesus Christ in all the children. The school has an ethos of love and care and embraces children of all faiths.

Children are treated as individuals, respected, nurtured and encouraged to embrace and fulfil their potential in all areas of school life. We have excellent links with High Schools in both the maintained and independent sectors.

The school achieves well above average results in external tests and has a strong academic reputation. Children are prepared for entry to selective independent schools on request. Subjects include English, Maths, Science, ICT, Design and Technology, Art, Geography, PE, History, Music, RE, French and Personal, Social and Health Education.

The school has a strong musical tradition and has a wide range of extra-curricular musical activities on offer including Choir, Music Ensemble, Recorder, Piano, Guitar, Flute, Violin, Saxophone and Clarinet lessons.

Sports include Football, Cricket, Rugby, Netball, Hockey, Tennis and Swimming.

The school has a wide range of extra-curricular activities including Ballet, Speech and Drama, Chess, ICT, Arts and Crafts, Sailing, Skiing and Golf.

We have an After School Activities Club which runs until 5.40 pm which includes help with homework, tea and games.

Charitable status. Notre Dame Preparatory School (Norwich) Limited is a Registered Charity, number 269003.

Oakfield Preparatory School

125–128 Thurlow Park Road, Dulwich, London SE21 8HP
Tel: 020 8670 4206
Fax: 020 8766 6744
e-mail: cdecisneros@oakfield.dulwich.sch.uk
           (Admissions)
           info@oakfield.dulwich.sch.uk
           (General Enquiries)
website: www.oakfield.dulwich.sch.uk

Principal: **Mrs Jane Stevens**, BA Hons, PGCE, NPQH

Age Range. 2–11.
Number in School. Day: 227 Boys, 184 Girls.
Fees per term (2011-2012). £350–£2,807 including lunch.

Oakfield School was founded in 1887 and is today a modern co-educational prep school which prepares children for the entrance examinations of London and countrywide independent senior schools. These senior schools base their 11+ entrance exams on English and Maths and it is these core subjects that form the basis of the Oakfield curriculum, but not to the exclusion of French, Humanities, Science, the Arts and Computing.

The School is arranged into three groups, the Nursery (age 2–3) (full time or half day), Foundation Years and Year 1 (age 3–6) and Years 2–6 (age 6–11). Each age group has its own self-contained building and facilities. The School site of nearly three acres allows space for play and games and older children use the nearby playing field where all normal games are played. Children aged five to eight swim once a week under instruction.

Entry to the Nursery is by informal assessment. Once accepted the child will progress automatically into the Foundation Years and Main School. Entry at 3+ and 4+ is also by assessment and children should have a good idea of colours, shapes, matching, sorting and simple counting. Entry at 5+ and 7+ follows an informal assessment and observation in a class setting.

Prospective parents – and children – would be very welcome to visit Oakfield during a school day.

Oakhill College

Wiswell Lane, Whalley, Clitheroe, Lancashire BB7 9AF
Tel: 01254 823546
Fax: 01254 822662
e-mail: enquiries@oakhillcollege.co.uk
website: www.oakhillcollege.co.uk

Chairman of Governors: Mr Tony Baron

Principal: **Mrs Carmel Riley**, BA, PGCE, MA

Age Range. 2–16 Co-educational.
Number of Pupils. 229 pupils.
Fees per term (2010-2011). Pre-Prep (Reception–Year 2) £1,986; Prep (Years 3–6) £2,238; Upper School (Years 7–11) £3,076. Nursery: £33.00 per day.

Oakhill College is a small, independent Roman Catholic day school, warmly welcoming all faiths. We provide a Catholic education for school life and beyond for children of all abilities aged 2–16. We are committed to providing a happy, safe and stimulating education within a family environment.

We seek to develop spiritual awareness; encourage a sense of self-worth; challenge students to achieve; instil mutual respect and understanding; and teach the value of service to others.

We are a family community where honesty, humour and commitment help us to achieve these aims.

Oakhill College has excellent teaching facilities within a mixture of traditional and new buildings which include the extensive sporting facilities of Oakhill Academy. The large grounds offer attractive seating areas, all-weather pitches, playing fields and a nature trail along a small stream through woodlands.

The curriculum at Oakhill College is broad and well balanced with pupils being offered a range of subjects for GCSE including individual award sciences, French, Spanish, Latin, Music, Art, ICT and Business Studies. All pupils in Year 10 take part in the Duke of Edinburgh's Bronze Award and some go on to complete the Silver Award in Year 11. There is an extensive programme of educational visits for all of the year groups and a wide range of extra-curricular activities offered. The main sports played at Oakhill are Tennis, Badminton, Football, Netball, Hockey, Basketball, Cross Country Running and Orienteering.

We encourage parents and their children to visit the school, meet the Principal and experience school life for two or more taster days. Scholarships are available for entry into Year 7 and awarded following the Entrance Examination in the Easter Term prior to Senior School entry. Bursaries are also available.

Charitable status. Oakhill College Charitable Trust is a Registered Charity, number 1048514.

Oakhyrst Grange School

Stanstead Road, Caterham, Surrey CR3 6AF
Tel: 01883 343344
Fax: 01883 342021
e-mail: office@oakhyrstgrangeschool.co.uk
website: www.oakhyrstgrangeschool.co.uk

Headmaster: **Mr A Gear**, BEd

Age Range. 4–11.
Number in School. Day Boys and Girls: 142.
Fees per term (2011-2012). £1,059–£2,343.

Oakhyrst Grange School is an independent, co-educational preparatory day school for boys and girls between 4 and 11 years.

The School was established in 1950 and moved to its present premises in Stanstead Road in 1957. Since September 1973 the School has been administered by a non-profit making trust.

Standing in five acres of open country and woodland and surrounded by the Green Belt, the School enjoys a fine position amongst the Surrey Hills.

The school has a wide and imaginative curriculum, which includes traditional teaching combined with innovative ideas. Small class sizes, an excellent teacher/pupil ratio, enable pupils to work at their own rate and capabilities whilst being encouraged to meet new challenges.

Our pupils secure the offer of places at prominent senior schools, including scholarships and awards across the range of academic, all-rounder, music, sports and art.

There are many sporting opportunities offered and particularly high standards have been reached in cross-country, swimming, football, judo and athletics where ISA National level has been achieved. The pupils compete in many inter house, inter school and area competitions. The school also has its own heated indoor swimming pool, all weather tennis, netball, hockey and 5-a-side court, sports pitch, cross-country course and gymnasium.

Extra curricular music lessons are offered and much music making also takes place as part of the normal school timetable. The school has an orchestra in addition to clarinet, violin and trumpet ensembles and a choir, all of whom perform regularly.

In addition to the curriculum the pupils can enjoy an extensive range of clubs and activities throughout the week.

Academic excellence is encouraged and achieved, every child is expected to attain his or her individual potential. The School helps children to develop into caring, thoughtful and confident adults.

Charitable status. Oakhyrst Grange School Educational Trust is a Registered Charity, number 325043. It exists to provide an all-round education, to give the children success and the best possible start.

Oaklands School

8 Albion Hill, Loughton, Essex IG10 4RA
Tel: 020 8508 3517
Fax: 020 8508 4454
e-mail: info@oaklandsschool.co.uk
website: www.oaklandsschool.co.uk

Headmistress: **Mrs Pam Simmonds**, MA Oxon, BSc

Age Range. 2½–11 Co-educational.
Number in School. 248 Day Pupils.
Fees per term (from January 2011). £1,600–£2,995.

Oaklands is a long-established preparatory school, founded in 1937, and delightfully situated in extensive grounds on the edge of Epping Forest. It provides a firm foundation for girls and boys aged 2½ to 11. Great care is taken in preparing pupils for entrance examinations to their next schools.

A broad curriculum is offered, with early emphasis on literacy and numeracy, ensuring high standards, and great importance is placed on fully developing each child's potential in a secure and caring atmosphere. We have small class sizes and specialist teachers for Science, French, Music, PE, Dancing, ICT, Sport and Drama. A wide range of extra-curricular activities is offered and an after-school care club operates until 5 pm. The school has now established a reputation for excellent dramatic productions. Individual music tuition is available, including piano and woodwind instrumental lessons, and singing lessons.

Oaklands is a friendly, happy school where children can enjoy learning and take pride in both their own success and the achievements of others. In addition to the attainment of high standards, pupils build personal qualities of confidence, self-reliance and respect for others, in preparation for the challenges and opportunities of the modern world.

The Old School
Henstead

Toad Row, Henstead, Nr Beccles, Suffolk NR34 7LG
Tel: 01502 741150
Fax: 01502 741150
e-mail: office@theoldschoolhenstead.co.uk
website: www.theoldschoolhenstead.co.uk

Headmaster: **Mr I R Griffin**, BA Hons

Age Range. 4½–11.
Number in School. 90 Day Boys and Girls.
Fees per term (2010-2011). £1,615–£2,335.
The Old School, Henstead offers a traditional style of education in a caring family environment. It is well staffed with small classes. Children are prepared for entrance examinations to all local senior schools, many winning scholarships. The curriculum is broad and balanced with facilities for Music, ICT, Science, Pottery, Art & Drama and Physical Education and Games. There is a wide variety of after-school clubs on offer as well as care before school starts.

The school is an Educational Trust; it is in membership of ISA.

Charitable status. The Old School Henstead Educational Trust Limited is a Registered Charity, number 279265. It exists to provide education for boys and girls.

OLCS – Our Lady's Convent School

Gray Street, Loughborough, Leics LE11 2DZ
Tel: 01509 263901
Fax: 01509 236193
e-mail: office@olcs.leics.sch.uk
website: www.olcs.leics.sch.uk

Headteacher: **Mrs Patricia Hawley**, BA, PGCE

Age Range. Girls 3–18, Boys 3–11.
Number of Pupils. 390.
Fees per term (2011-2012). Nursery £2,372, Infants £2,585, Juniors £2,715, Seniors £3,241.
OLCS is a Catholic day school that extends a warm welcome to children of all faiths and denominations. It educates girls from 3 to 18 and boys from 3 to 11. The focus is very much on the individual child and their personal progress and achievement at all levels. Our next Open Day would be an excellent time to see our Senior and Primary School Departments in action on a normal working day, view our facilities and meet our Headteacher.

At all stages of their education, our students receive individual attention in guaranteed small classes. They are helped, encouraged and supported rather than pressured, stretched and not stressed. Academic achievement is high at all levels. In 2010, Year 13 achieved a pass rate of a 100% with 83% of students gaining A to C grades, whilst Year 11 had a 100% pass rate with over 95% of students achieving grades A* to C. A wide variety of GCSE and A Levels is offered in the Senior department. Learning Support is excellent for all students in all areas. 99% of our students go on to university to study a wide range of subjects. In addition there are numerous cultural, musical and sporting activities. Music and Drama have a high profile in the school; for instance, this year junior and senior musicians have participated in a whole-school Cabaret Production, and girls have taken part in the national Shakespeare Festival. A wide variety of extra-curricular activities is on offer. The school suc-cessfully participates in The Duke of Edinburgh's Award and Young Enterprise schemes.

The school is a registered charity and its policy is to continually enhance the facilities available to our students and to improve our service to them and their parents. All departments are well resourced and ICT facilities are excellent and updated regularly. Our most recent developments include a refurbished and re-equipped Early Years/Infant Department, play and recreation areas and library for primary children, and a refurbished sixth form suite.

The School campus is an attractive walled area; an oasis of calm, near the centre of Loughborough. Open Days are held during working school days and visitors continually note the happy classroom environment and the mutual respect between students, staff and visitors. Some of our students are with us from 3 to 18 but others are very welcome to join at other stages of their education.

The Pelican Club provides before and after school care for a small additional cost.

For further information visit our website www.olcs.leics.sch.uk.

Charitable status. Our Lady's Convent School is a Registered Charity, number 1110802.

The Park School

Queen's Park South Drive, Bournemouth BH8 9BJ
Tel: 01202 396640
Fax: 01202 392705
e-mail: office@parkschool.co.uk
website: www.parkschool.co.uk

Headmaster: **Mr Andrew D Edwards**, BA Hons

Age Range. 3–11.
Number in School. Day: 150 Boys, 130 Girls.
Fees per term (from April 2011). £1,780–£2,525.
The Park is a co-educational junior day school occupying a quiet location overlooking Queens Park Golf course in a pleasant residential area near the town centre.

Pupils are taught in small classes in a caring, happy environment. The school is geared principally towards academic achievement although we do provide special help for a limited number of children with specific learning difficulties. The emphasis is on nurturing individual and academic progress whilst fostering a positive ethos and the development of the all-round child. This covers not only work in the classroom but also all other aspects of school life: games, music, the Arts and many practical activities. Pupils are prepared for entry to Senior Independent Schools and to the local Grammar Schools through their tests at 11+ years. Many children gain scholarships to Senior Independent Schools.

Most pupils start aged 3+ years but there are occasional vacancies at other ages. Offer of a place is made only after prospective pupils have been formally assessed.

Parents with pupils in our Nursery classes can take advantage of our extended working day and the longer school terms should they so wish.

Park School for Girls

20–22 Park Avenue, Ilford, Essex IG1 4RS
Tel: Office: 020 8554 2466
             Bursar: 020 8554 6022
Fax: 020 8554 3003
e-mail: admin@parkschool.org.uk
website: www.parkschool.org.uk

Headmistress: **Mrs E Gallagher**, BA Hons, PGCE

Age Range. 3–16.
Number in School. 150 Day Girls.
Fees per term (2011-2012). Nursery £1,900, Prep School £2,142, Senior School £2,833.

The School is situated near Valentine's Park in Ilford. It is convenient for road, rail and Central Line tube services.

Our basic aim is to provide a full educational programme leading to recognised external examinations at the age of 16.

We create a caring, well-ordered atmosphere. Our pupils are encouraged to achieve their full academic and social potential. The well-qualified staff and the policy of small classes produce well above the national average GCSE results. The majority of our sixth form enter university and the professions.

In addition, the staff and I stress the development of each child as a whole person. We expect every girl to strive for self-confidence in her ability to use her talents to the full and to respect individuality. She is encouraged to make decisions and to accept responsibility for her own actions. The poise that comes from good manners and correct speech, we consider to be highly important. Honesty, reliability, courtesy and consideration for others are prime factors in the educative system.

Interested parents are welcome to visit the school, where the Headmistress will be pleased to answer their queries.

Charitable status. Park School for Girls is a Registered Charity, number 269936. It exists to provide a caring environment in which we develop our pupils' potential to the full.

The Park School
Yeovil

The Park, Yeovil, Somerset BA20 1DH
Tel: 01935 423514
Fax: 01935 411257
e-mail: admin@parkschool.com
website: www.parkschool.com

Head: **Mrs J Huntington**, ARAM, GRSM, LRAM, CPSEd

Age Range. 3–18 Co-educational.
Number in School. 251: 122 Boys, 129 Girls. 28 Boarders.
Fees per term (2011-2012). Day £1,750–£3,030 (including lunch); Weekly Boarding £5,620–£5,990; Full Boarding £5,860–£6,260.

The Park School, Yeovil is an Independent day and boarding school founded in 1851. It aims to provide a sound education based on Christian principles. It is a non-denominational Evangelical Christian school and has strong connections with a number of different local churches.

The School is pleasantly situated near the centre of Yeovil with easy access to surrounding towns and villages, from which day pupils are drawn, and to the main line station, Yeovil Junction, for London Waterloo. There is also a rail connection to Bristol and Weymouth from Yeovil, Pen Mill station. Transport to London Heathrow and other airports is arranged for boarders travelling abroad.

The School buildings consist of an interesting historic listed building, which has been sympathetically upgraded, and modern additions. Recent developments include the establishment of four ICT rooms, a refurbished Sports Hall, a Sixth Form building and a floodlit all-weather Sports field.

Pupils flourish in a friendly, caring environment where, in small classes, they benefit from well-qualified staff. There is a wide and varied curriculum which encourages each pupil to develop their own abilities and interests to the full. In line with the National Curriculum guidelines, senior pupils choose from a range of subjects at GCSE and A Level, including: English, RE, History, Drama, Geography, French, German, Mathematics, Science, Art, Music, Design Technology, Food Technology, ICT, Sports Studies and English for overseas pupils. Physics, Chemistry and Biology are studied as separate Sciences. Chinese and Spanish are offered subject to demand. Additional subjects studied at A Level include: Business Studies, Sports Studies, Further Mathematics and Psychology.

Physical Education is also an essential part of the curriculum. Pupils participate in a varied programme of sporting activities including: Athletics, Badminton, Basketball, Cricket, Football, Gymnastics, Hockey, Netball, Squash, Swimming, Tennis, Table Tennis, Volleyball and Cross-Country. Many Senior pupils also take part in the Duke of Edinburgh's Award Scheme as well as Young Enterprise.

A wide range of musical instruments are taught by the Director of Music and visiting staff. There are School Choirs and an Orchestra as well as a jazz band, rock group and a baroque ensemble. Music and drama productions are regular features of School life.

Boarders live in a newly refurbished, purpose-built School House. Many students occupy single study-bedrooms. They are cared for in a homely, family atmosphere by resident houseparents aided by assistants. At weekends a variety of interesting activities is available. On Sundays all boarders are encouraged to attend the church of their choice.

Academic standards in the School are high with The Park being consistently well placed in the GCSE league tables. However, the School is not rigidly selective and pupils are encouraged to develop their talents as individuals with extremely favourable pupil/teacher ratios.

The school offers scholarships which may be given for academic, music, art, sport or drama ability. These are awarded by examination and interview in January of each year for entry to Years 4, 7, 9 and Sixth Form. Bursaries are available for children of those parents who are engaged in full-time Christian work or are members of HM Forces. In addition bursaries are available for parents on low incomes.

Charitable status. The Park School (Yeovil) Limited is a Registered Charity, number 310214. It exists to provide Christian education and care for children aged 3–18 years.

Peterborough & St Margaret's School

Common Road, Stanmore, Middlesex HA7 3JB
Tel: 020 8950 3600
Fax: 020 8421 8946
e-mail: psm@psmschool.org
website: www.psmschool.org

Headmistress: **Mrs S Watts**, BA Hons, PGCE

Age Range. Girls 4–16 with Nursery for boys and girls aged 2½+.
Number in School. 150 Day Pupils.
Fees per term (2010-2011). Nursery £2,450, Juniors £2,310–£3,044, Seniors £3,435.

Peterborough & St Margaret's School, or PSM as it is affectionately known, is situated on a picturesque, wooded site between Stanmore and Bushey Heath. It was founded over a hundred years ago and combines traditional attitudes and values with high expectations and excellent academic results. Boys are welcome in the nursery. Part of a Christian Foundation, it values the enrichment of the community by other faiths and cultures.

Education is for life and choosing the right school is one of the most important decisions parents make. Learning should be enjoyable and here at PSM we aim to make it so, whether the pupils are spending their first day in the nursery or studying for their GCSE examinations.

Because there is only one form per year group, no girl gets lost in the crowd. This is a small, 'family' school, where pupils and staff all know each other. The Junior Department offers a friendly, caring environment, so important to children as they begin their school life. Some staff teach throughout the age groups – specialist teachers teach Drama, Music, French, and ICT from The Early Years Foundation Stage onwards – so the younger ones not only benefit from their expertise but get to know many of the teachers before reaching the Senior Department.

Having followed the EYFS in the nursery and reception, the girls are ready to start to follow the Key Stage 1 National Curriculum in Year 1. Small classes enable staff to support and challenge all girls on an individual basis. We aim to help them discover their talents and give them the maximum opportunity to develop, both intellectually and creatively.

Success breeds more success and involvement in music, drama, sport and a whole range of extra-curricular activities, as well as residential visits beginning in Year 5, gives them a confidence that bears fruit in their academic studies as well. At PSM every child has the chance to shine.

The Year 10 and 11 girls are treated as 'sixth formers', with all the associated positions of responsibility and privileges. They rapidly grow into their roles, becoming more responsible and mature than girls of the same age who will have to wait a couple of years for such opportunities. They are then ready to spread their wings and move on to neighbouring sixth forms, often winning scholarships, as a transition to university. They leave Peterborough & St Margaret's confident, capable, courteous and compassionate young women with a secure grounding for life.

Bursaries and scholarships are available.

Charitable status. The E Ivor Hughes Educational Foundation is a Registered Charity, number 293623. It exists to provide education for children.

Polwhele House School

Truro, Cornwall TR4 9AE
Tel: 01872 273011
e-mail: office@polwhelehouseschool.co.uk
website: www.polwhelehouse.co.uk

Headmaster: **Alex McCullough**, BA Hons, PGCE

Age Range. 3–13+.
Number in School. 131 Day; 6 Boarding.
Fees per term (2011-2012). Day: £450–£3,615 Lunch £155–£175; Flexi Boarding (1–4 nights per week): £358–£1,340.

Polwhele House is a beautiful and historic listed building, set in 30 acres of garden, playing fields, park and woodland. The school enjoys a glorious and secure environment only 1¼ miles from the Cathedral.

Uninterrupted education is provided for boys and girls during those important early years from three to thirteen. There is flexible attendance for under-fives who are taught by qualified teachers in Nursery and Reception. The Pre-Preparatory School has an established reputation for high levels of care and excellent teaching.

Although mainly a day-school, weekly boarding, day boarding, 'sleepovers' and after-school care are growing in popularity. The boarders live in the Main House in comfortable surroundings which include a TV lounge, en-suite facilities, quiet areas and garden. The well-being and happiness of each child is the top priority.

This flourishing family school has had a continual programme of development, building and refurbishment since 1976 when the Pre-Prep School was opened. In 1994 new quality accommodation was built and equipped for art and craft, design technology, sciences, languages and ICT. In 1992 an equestrian centre was provided for pupils and riding is professionally taught. In 2008 a new atrium was added to the Pre-Prep School.

The school combines modern teaching methods with the best of traditional values. The social development of the child is carefully nurtured to help them to become confident, considerate and polite young people. Polwhele House values each child and a strong team of skilled and caring staff are able to devote a great deal of time to every pupil in small classes.

Drama flourishes with each child participating in at least one of eight productions a year. Music is an important part of the school life with all pupils singing, and the majority playing an instrument. There are Truro Cathedral Choristerships for boys and Polwhele House Music Scholarships for girls. All the usual team games are coached and there are regular outstanding successes in athletics and cross-country running at school, county and national levels.

Polwhele House is a Christian, non-denominational school and assembly is considered to be an important part of the day. The school motto is 'Karenza Whelas Karenza', Cornish for 'Love Begets Love'. Boys and girls share the same opportunities and responsibilities in all areas of school life.

The school has a fine record of academic achievement. There is a wide variety of sporting and extra-curricular activities to bring out the best in every child. Pupils are prepared for a broad range of schools, and win numerous scholarships, bursaries and exhibitions to Senior Independent Schools every year.

Mr McCullough takes great pleasure in meeting prospective parents and showing them around personally. Polwhele House is not just a school, more a way of life.

Prenton Preparatory School

Mount Pleasant, Oxton, Wirral CH43 5SY
Tel: 0151 652 3182
Fax: 0151 653 7428
e-mail: enquiry@prentonprep.co.uk
website: www.prentonprep.co.uk

Headteacher: **Mr M T R Jones**

Age Range. 2½–11.
Number in School. Day: 47 Boys, 61 Girls.
Fees per term (from January 2011). £1,750 Infants; £1,835 Juniors; from £819 part-time in FS.
Founded in 1935.

Prenton Preparatory School is a co-educational day school for children aged 2½–11 years, situated about a mile from Junction 3 of the M53.

The building is a large Victorian house which has been carefully converted into the uses of a school. There is a large playground and gardens. Facilities include an ICT/Science block and an Art block and Pre-School outdoor play area are recent additions to the school.

The children benefit from small classes and individual attention in a disciplined environment which enable them to realise their full potential.

The school offers a wide range of academic subjects with emphasis on the three main National Curriculum core subjects: English, Mathematics and Science. French is taught from an early age.

Children are prepared for entrance examinations to county, independent and grant-maintained grammar schools, gaining above average pass rates.

Child care facilities are available from 8 am to 6 pm. Clubs are provided at lunchtime and after school. They include football, cricket, computers and technology, karate, swimming, gymnastics, ballet, netball, music group, handchimes and musical instruments.

Priory School

Sir Harry's Road, Edgbaston, Birmingham B15 2UR
Tel: 0121 440 4103/0256
Fax: 0121 440 3639
e-mail: enquiries@prioryschool.net
website: www.prioryschool.net

Chairman of Governors: Mr S Gilmore, LLB

Headmaster: **Mr Jonathan Cramb**, BA Hons, PGCE MEd

Age Range. 6 months – 16 years.
Number in School. 371.
Fees per term (2011-2012). £2,335–£3,675.
The school, founded on its present site in 1936 by the Sisters of the Society of the Holy Child Jesus, stands in 17 acres of parkland in the pleasant suburb of Edgbaston, only 2 miles from the centre of Birmingham. The school has extensive playing fields, excellent astroturf tennis courts, athletics facilities and football and cricket pitches. There are coaches running to and from school and frequent bus services to all parts of the city.

The school has an excellent Nursery on site which offers care for 51 weeks per annum and accepts children from the age of 6 months. All pupils are able to remain in After Care until 6.00 pm if parents so wish.

The school has a culturally diverse pupil community, based on catholic values, but welcomes all faiths. Pupils are taught by specialist teachers from the age of 9 and in the Senior School the curriculum is broad and balanced and pupils benefit from small class sizes and individual attention enabling the to make excellent progress in their academic development.

The school, whilst remaining proudly multi-ability, is justly proud of the academic achievements of the pupils. A wide range of subjects is available for GCSE, with good facilities, including well-equipped Science Laboratories, Language Resources rooms, Information Technology facilities, Sports Centre, Performing Arts Suite and Learning Resources Centre. The school offers support for children with special needs, particularly dyslexia, and has a purpose-built learning enrichment centre with specially qualified staff.

A wide range of extra-curricular opportunities are offered in both Prep. and Senior School. These currently include photography, debating, chess, Duke of Edinburgh's Award scheme to name just a few. Private tuition is also offered in Speech, singing and a wide range of musical instruments.

Entry to the school is by interview, assessment and day visit. Scholarships are awarded at 11+. Bursaries may be awarded in cases of special need.

Parents are warmly welcomed into the school to discuss individual needs. Full details prior to the visit may be obtained from the Admissions Registrar.

Charitable status. Priory School is a Registered Charity, number 518009.

Putney Park School

Woodborough Road, London SW15 6PY
Tel: 020 8788 8316
Fax: 020 8780 2376

e-mail: office@putneypark.london.sch.uk
website: www.putneypark.london.sch.uk

Headmistress: **Miss Sarah Mostyn**, BSc, MA

Age Range. Girls 4–16, Boys 4–8.
Number in School. Day: 40 Boys, 180 Girls.
Fees per term (2011-2012). Upper School £4,072; Lower School £3,565. Extras: Individual music lessons, ballet, EFL, lunches, school bus.

Putney Park School was established in 1953 and is now in the second generation of the Tweedie-Smith family ownership. The aim of the school is personal success and academic achievement in a happy atmosphere.

The school provides pupils with a happy and secure environment. Small classes of around 10 to 12 pupils ensure that no pupil is overlooked, and that each child is able to reach their full potential.

Pupils are offered a broad curriculum to enable them to develop their creativity and individual talents to their full potential. Pupils thrive in the caring and supportive environment. Good manners and initiative are encouraged. We are a mixed-ability school and we pride ourselves on being a strong learning community. We boost pupils' self-esteem regardless of academic ability and produce confident, articulate individuals ready for the challenges and opportunities that lie ahead. To achieve this, teachers are chosen for their qualifications, their experience and their understanding of the needs of the pupils. Small class sizes ensure that pupils are given the maximum individual attention and encouragement to reach the highest standards possible.

The school is situated in a Conservation Area and consists of four delightful Edwardian houses with a welcoming family atmosphere. The gardens are attractively landscaped with both play and seating areas. We offer a variety of sports taking advantage of the extensive facilities at the Bank of England Sports Ground together with rowing at Barn Elms. Both inter-school and inter-house matches take place frequently.

Children are accepted from four years old into Reception. The school prepares boys for entry to other schools including Colet Court, King's College, Wimbledon and Shrewsbury House at 7+ and 8+. Girls are prepared for entry to other schools, particularly Bute House, Latymer, Putney High, Surbiton High and Wimbledon High at 7+ and 11+. The Upper School includes Year 6 to Year 11. There is an examination for entry to Year 7.

Girls take between eight and eleven GCSEs which must include English and Mathematics with the option of Core Science and Additional Science or the separate sciences – Biology, Chemistry and Physics.

Optional subjects at GCSE include English Literature, Art, Drama, French, Geography, Home Economics: Child Development, Home Economics: Food, History, Music, Physical Education and Spanish. In addition there is the opportunity to take the ECDL (European Computer Driving Licence) in ICT.

Our careers programme reflects the importance we attach to the development of the individual skills and talents of all pupils. At the end of Year 11 all pupils are welcomed into a wide range of schools and colleges including Putney High, Surbiton High and Wimbledon High.

Academic excellence is achieved at GCSE with a five year average of 37% A and A* grades. This is probably unique for a mixed ability school and reflects the quality of the teaching. We are a CReSTeD school and pride ourselves on our dyslexic pupils' successes.

Queen Ethelburga's Collegiate Foundation

Thorpe Underwood Hall, York YO26 9SS
Tel: 01423 333330
Fax: 01423 333754
e-mail: info@QE.org
        pj@QE.org
website: www.QE.org

Co-educational Day and Boarding School.

Chairman of Governors: Brian R Martin, FCMI, FInstD, FFA

Headmaster: **Steven Jandrell**, BA

Head of The Faculty: **Mrs Denise Willis**, MA, CertEd

Age Range. 3 months–18 years.
Number of Pupils. 771: 126 day boys, 143 day girls, 235 boy boarders, 263 girl boarders.
Fees per term (2010-2011). Day: £1,183–£3,320; Boarding: £6,750–£9,512 (UK students), £8,230–£11,535 (International students).

Queen Ethelburga's is located at Thorpe Underwood, situated between Harrogate and York. The College is co-educational, for students in the age range 11 to 19. The Faculty provides more vocational/professional courses and courses for students who need support in the English Language and is for students aged 14 to 19 and Chapter House Preparatory School has children up to age 11. The schools are supported by the Queen Ethelburga's Charitable Foundation which provides many bursaries, scholarships and awards, and investment in the yearly capital projects.

The campus is exceptional. Set in 100 acres of manicured country park in the Vale of York, the Foundation maintains an excellent quality of provision with huge investments in the last 10 years. Set around a Grade 2* Listed country house there are Science, Modern Language, Art and Technology suites, together with Sports Hall, excellent floodlit pitches for Rugby, Hockey and Football, floodlit tennis courts and a swimming pool. The Equestrian Centre is probably unique in Europe with stabling for 60 horses, an Olympic-size indoor arena and acres of all-weather floodlit arenas. Many students take advantage of the Foundation Riding Award, which allows students to bring their own horses to school with free livery. Planned projects include a second, and much larger Sports Hall, additional Classroom areas, extra sports facilities and Sixth Form Boarding and Leisure Accommodation. There will also be a new Art, Fashion and Design Technology area and extensive library provision.

We are proud that we have been able to maintain a broad access school with students obtaining very good academic results. The overriding ethos is "to be the best that I can with the gifts that I have". The College and Faculty offer a broad ranging curriculum up to GCSE based around the NC, with small classes and a wide range of extra curricular activities. Sixth Form students have the choice of 22 different A Levels, IB and BTech.

Boarding is based around three boys' houses and three girls' houses with excellent facilities including most bedrooms being en suite and equipped with TV, hi-fi, telephone and other modern electrical equipment (albeit on timers). The strong pastoral care is centred on House Parents and Tutors, who work closely with the Heads of Year and the Head of Pastoral Care.

Entry is via our own entrance examination and interview with the Headmaster. Applicants are expected to have achieved the equivalent of at least Level 4 at Key Stage 2, Level 5 at Key Stage 3, at least 4 B Grades and 2 C Grades

for the College and have attained at least 4 GCSE passes at C Grade and above for the Faculty. The Foundation contributes over £1,000,000 each year in awards for academic excellence, sport, music, drama, equestrian and many others. All boarders of HM Forces families attract a Forces Bursary of 20%.

Charitable status. Queen Ethelburga's College Foundation is a Registered Charity, number 1012924.

Raphael Independent School

Park Lane, Hornchurch, Essex RM11 1XY
Tel: 01708 744735
Fax: 01708 722432
e-mail: admin@raphaelschool.com
website: www.raphaelschool.com

Headmistress: **Mrs J Lawrence**, BEd Hons

Age Range. Co-educational 4–16.
Number of Pupils. Day: 100 boys, 50 girls.
Fees per term (2010-2011). £1,650–£2,600.
Entry requirements. Interview for Early Years and Infants. Informal assessment for Juniors. Entry Tests in English and Maths for Seniors.
Aims. To develop the academic, social, artistic and sporting potential of each individual within a caring and welcoming school community.
To foster respect for each other within a multi-cultural school.
To offer a broad range of educational visits and extra-curricular activities.
Location. Raphael is a ten minute walk from Romford Main Line Station, and a fifteen minute drive from the A12 or A127 junctions of the M25.
School day. Infants from 8.40 am, Juniors until 3.25 pm and Seniors until 4.00 pm. Our After School Club looks after pupils until 5.45 pm.
Curriculum strengths. ICT, French and Spanish, English and Drama, Maths.
Sport. We believe in competitive sport, and we offer Soccer, Rugby, Netball, Cross-Country, Swimming, Cricket and Tennis amongst others.
A prospectus containing further information may be obtained from our Office Manager, Carolyn Carter, and all prospective parents are most welcome to visit the school.

Rastrick Independent School

Ogden Lane, Rastrick, Brighouse, West Yorkshire HD6 3HF
Tel: 01484 400344
Fax: 01484 718318
e-mail: info@rastrick-independent.co.uk
website: www.rastrickschool.co.uk

Headmistress: **Mrs S A Vaughey**

Age Range. 0–16 co-educational.
Number of Pupils. 200.
Fees per term (2011-2012). £2,075–£2,560.
Rastrick Independent educates and cares for pupils from birth to sixteen years. We follow a full National Curriculum up to GCSE.
The school boasts excellent academic results: 15 consecutive years with 100% pass rate at 11+and 100% A*–C grades at GCSE. The school was voted 68th nationally in The Times Parent Power 2008.

We believe this success is rooted in our ethos of caring for the individual, providing exciting learning and a stimulating environment and having a highly qualified and motivated staff team. The curriculum is balanced with emphasis on Sports and The Arts. We have a strong musical tradition. We welcome children of all faiths and are fully inclusive. We are the Northern Centre for CHI (Children of High Intelligence), yet specialise in the excellent provision for special needs, especially dyslexia.

We open all the year round from 7.30 am until 6.30 pm. The school is happy and vibrant and is an obvious choice for working parents where children are safe and secure in an environment which they love.

Red House School

36 The Green, Norton, Stockton-on-Tees, Cleveland TS20 1DX

Tel: 01642 553370
Fax: 01642 361031
e-mail: headmaster@redhouseschool.co.uk
website: www.redhouseschool.co.uk

Chairman of Governors: Mr Vinay Bedi

Headmaster: Mr A R W Taylor, BSc, MSc, CBiol, MSB

Deputy Head (*Nursery & Infant School*): Miss Joanna Everington

Age Range. 3–16.
Number in School. Approx 201 girls and 237 boys.
Fees per term (2010-2011). Nursery and Infant School £1,950, Prep £2,250–£2,380, Senior £2,610. Lunches: £190.

Red House School is a 3–16 co-educational, independent day school of about 440 students. Founded over 80 years ago the School is situated in a very pleasant location around the Village Green in Norton which is on the northern edge of the Teesside Conurbation.

Our commitment to pupils and parents is summarized below:

*   To provide a happy, stimulating and well disciplined environment in which children succeed.
*   To encourage each child to reach their full potential and strive for excellence in all areas of school life.
*   To develop pupil's self-esteem so that they have the confidence to use their individual talents, skills and knowledge effectively.
*   To develop their skills of communication, analysis and independent thinking so that children are equipped to be lifelong learners prepared for a rapidly changing society.
*   To develop a positive partnership between staff, parents, pupils and the wider community.

The school is based on two sites. The Nursery and Infant school (Pre-Nursery to Year 3) is housed in and around "The Old Vicarage", a beautiful listed building. This site was further developed in 2004 with the construction of purpose-built nursery facilities, additional classrooms and the redevelopment of 'The Barn' to provide an assembly hall and dining room. There is an ICT suite and all classrooms have interactive whiteboards. Close links are maintained with the Preparatory and Senior Schools.

The Preparatory and Senior schools, Years 4–11, are housed on the Main School site. The original Victorian building has been augmented over the years with purpose-built sports and assembly halls, classrooms and laboratories. The school has its own playing fields, including tennis courts. ICT is well developed within the teaching and learning across the school. Ambitious plans to further improve the facilities at the Senior School are in place.

Although a selective school, Red House caters for pupils with a wide range of abilities and backgrounds. Small class sizes means that teaching can be tailored to the needs of the individual child allowing them to reach their full potential. All pupils take 9 or 10 subjects to GCSE. Results at GCSE have been consistently amongst the best, if not the best, of any school within the area. In 2010 all pupils achieved 7 or more passes at GCSE Grade A–C, including Maths and English; 70% of all passes were at A*/A. The academic side of the school is balanced by an extensive programme of games and activities. Pupils have regularly achieved representational honours at county, regional and national level.

Charitable status. Red House School Limited is a Registered Charity, number 527377. It exists to provide education for children and for the advancement of education for the benefit of the community.

Redcourt – St Anselm's

7 Devonshire Place, Oxton, Birkenhead, Wirral CH43 1TX

Tel: 0151 652 5228
Fax: 0151 653 5883
e-mail: admin@redcourt.wirral.sch.uk
website: www.redcourtstanselms.com

Chairman of Governors: Mr J Sullivan

Headmaster: Mr K S Davey, MA, PGCE

Age Range. 3–11 Co-educational.
Number of Pupils. 260.
Fees per term (2010-2011). £1,588.

Redcourt – St Anselm's is an inclusive school welcoming all children of all abilities. There is no formal entrance examination. Prospective pupils are invited into Redcourt for a day's visit. During the day, Staff will assess the level at which the visiting child is currently working. However, most children join at nursery level. Our aim is to provide each and every child with a sound academic education in an environment which is explicitly Christian and where discipline and care go hand in hand. We endeavour to be aware of each child as an individual and we seek to encourage the development of the whole person. The school operates in an open and friendly manner, becoming something of a second home for its pupils.

The core national curriculum subjects plus RE, History, Geography, Art and Design, PE and Games, Music, ICT and French form the basis of what is taught. Children are prepared for the eleven plus and entrance examinations to grammar and selective independent schools. Last year all children in Prep 6 transferred to Grammar Schools.

Charitable status. Redcourt St Anselm's is part of the Congregation of Christian Brothers which is a Registered Charity, number 254312.

Riverston School

63–69 Eltham Road, Lee Green, London SE12 8UF

Tel: 020 8318 4327
Fax: 020 8297 0514
e-mail: office@riverstonschool.co.uk
website: www.riverstonschool.co.uk

Principal: Professsor D M Lewis, MBA Ed, DMS, FRSA

Headteacher: Mrs S E Salathiel, CertEd

Director of SEN: Mr J Allen, MEd, NPQH

Age Range. 1–16.
Number in School. Day: 226 Boys, 100 Girls.

Fees per term (2011-2012). £2,381–£3,680.

Since 1926 Riverston School has enjoyed a well-earned reputation for its work with children of all abilities especially those requiring learning support. The School's aim is to help all pupils maximise their potential – whatever that may be and in whichever area of the curriculum most interests them – in a truly child-centric, family-orientated environment.

Riverston has the capabilities, facilities, understanding, commitment and determination to help boys and girls with a wide range of learning difficulties – yet remains a mainstream school enabling the majority of pupils to achieve exemplary GCSE and vocational results.

Riverston has a remarkable track record in helping its pupils exceed expectations.

Rochester Independent College

Star Hill, Rochester, Kent ME1 1XF
Tel: 01634 828115
Fax: 01634 405667
e-mail: admissions@rochester-college.org
website: www.rochester-college.org

Co-Principals:
Pauline Bailey, HND, PgDip, MA
Alistair Brownlow, MA Hons, MPhil
Brian Pain, BSc Hons, PGDip

Age Range. 11–19 Co-educational.
Number of Pupils. 185 (including 45 boarders).
Fees per term (2010-2011). Day: £3,330–£4,500; Boarding: £7,906.

Rochester Independent College is a progressive alternative to conventional secondary education with a happily distinctive ethos. Accepting day students from the age of 11 and boarders from 16 the focus is on examination success in a lively, supportive and informal atmosphere. Students are encouraged to be themselves and achieve exam results that often exceed their expectations. There is no uniform, no bells ring and everybody is on first name terms. The average class size is eight. Our January 2008 Ofsted report judged that "the quality of education is outstanding".

Students enjoy being here and are treated as young adults. We encourage them to search for their own answers, to voice their opinions, to think critically, creatively and independently. They leave not only with excellent examination results but with enthusiasm for the future and new confidence about themselves and their education.

Personal Tutors work closely with students on all courses to give advice about course combinations and help students to ensure that their courses are designed to meet the requirements of university entrance. With such small class sizes individual attention is not only available, it's practically inescapable.

The College has particular academic strengths in Science and Mathematics and the Creative and Visual Arts including Film, Photography and Media.

The College's reputation for academic excellence is founded on almost 25 years experience of rigorous teaching. Students come to us for a variety of reasons and from many different backgrounds. We are not academically selective; our only entrance qualification is an honest determination to work hard. Our results however are always ranked among the best of the academically selective and students secure places at top UK universities. Direct entry into any year group is possible and the College also offers intensive one year GCSE and A Level courses as well as retake programmes. International students benefit from specialised English Language teaching support.

The College Halls combine the informality of a university residence with the supervision and pastoral support appropriate for young adults. The College offers students the opportunity to thrive in an atmosphere of managed independence and acts as a stepping stone between school and university. All accommodation is on campus and in either single or double rooms. All rooms have a direct dial telephone and a computer with internet connection.

Rookwood School

Weyhill Road, Andover, Hants SP10 3AL
Tel: 01264 325900
Fax: 01264 325909
e-mail: office@rookwood.hants.sch.uk
website: www.rookwood.hants.sch.uk

Headmistress: **Mrs L Whetstone**, MA, BA Hons, PGCE

Age Range. Co-educational 3–16 with Boarders from age 8.
Number in School. 300: 159 girls, 130 Boys, plus 11 in Nursery.
Fees per term (2011-2012). Boarding £6,276–£7,345; Day £2,492–£4,104. Nursery £8.40 per hour; Early Years Education Funding accepted.

Recently described by the Independent Schools Inspectorate as a place *'where pupils flourish'*, Rookwood is a highly successful Independent Day & Boarding School nurturing children from their first steps in the nursery all the way through to their GCSEs. Known for its strong pastoral care and family atmosphere, Rookwood prides itself on its ability to develop the individual, ensuring each child is given every opportunity to achieve their full potential. Indeed, despite its non-selective entry system, Rookwood consistently produces strong academic results; 42% of all GCSEs sat in 2010 were awarded an A*/A with 91.5% of all pupils achieving at least 5 GCSEs at grades A–C – testament to Rookwood's small class sizes and dedicated teaching.

Set in 8 acres of private grounds Rookwood has an impressive range of amenities including a £2 million state-of-the-art sports hall, a lovely outdoor swimming pool, excellent art and science facilities and a wonderful purpose-built Pre-Prep (currently deemed educationally *'Outstanding'* by the ISI). Music and Drama thrive at Rookwood with every child encouraged to take part and the Physical Education department is equally busy, with several pupils advancing to represent their favourite sports at national level.

In addition to its many tangible achievements Rookwood remains dedicated to developing courteous and caring pupils with a strong sense of right and wrong and a natural respect for those around them – just one of the reasons why the school's boarding houses run so smoothly. A stone's throw from the main site, Rookwood boarders enjoy a unique 'home- from-home' experience. Family-style meal times, experienced and supportive boarding staff and busy weekends all combine to ensure that Rookwood's boarders receive the very best of care.

As the ISI recently observed, pupils at Rookwood *'take great pride in their school and the value placed on everyone's contribution'*. They would be delighted to show you around and prospective pupils and parents are warmly invited to attend one of Rookwood's open days (please see website for latest information). Alternatively, if you require any further information or would like to make an individual appointment, please do not hesitate to contact the Registrar directly.

Admission is by school reports and individual visits.

Charitable status. Rookwood School is a Registered Charity, number 307322. It exists to provide education for children.

Roselyon School

Par, Cornwall PL24 2HZ
Tel:　　01726 812110
Fax:　　01726 812110
e-mail:　secretary@roselyonschool.com
website:　www.roselyonschool.com

Head: Mrs Hilary Mann, MBA, BEd

Age Range. 2½–11.
Number in School. Day: 44 Boys, 59 Girls.
Fees per term (2011-2012). £2,515.
Roselyon School, formerly the Victorian manor house in the village of Par, near St Austell, stands in 5 acres of beautiful woodland. A new multi-purpose gymnasium and hall recently built in the centre of the campus has added greatly to the school's facilities. Roselyon is fully co-educational, taking pupils in the full time Nursery from 2½ and joining the Main School from 5–11.

The school is proud of its academic strengths and excellent examination results to local senior independent schools. It offers a broad curriculum, a variety of sports, music and drama and has an extensive range of extra curricular activities.

Academic and Music Scholarships and Bursaries are available for pupils in Years 3 to 6, and assessments are usually taken in the Summer Term.

Roselyon is a small, friendly school where a warm family atmosphere is maintained by the committed team of caring staff.

Charitable status. Roselyon School Limited is a Registered Charity, number 306583. It exists to provide quality education to boys and girls.

Ruckleigh School

17 Lode Lane, Solihull, West Midlands B91 2AB
Tel:　　0121 705 2773
Fax:　　0121 704 4883
e-mail:　admin@ruckleigh.co.uk
website:　www.ruckleigh.co.uk

Headmistress: Mrs B M Forster

Age Range. 3–11.
Number in School. Day: 120 Boys, 105 Girls.
Fees per term (2011-2012). £849–£2,468.
Ruckleigh is an independent day school offering education to boys and girls between the ages of 4 and 11 with a Nursery Department catering for children from the age of 3.

Although a high standard of work is expected this is related to the individual child, and the school is able to provide opportunities within a wide range of academic ability. Each child has every chance to develop his or her talents to the full, often resulting in achievements beyond initial expectations.

The comparatively small classes mean that every child is well known individually throughout the school creating a friendly environment.

Pupils are guided into habits of clear thinking, self-reliance and courtesy. Sound practical judgement, sensitivity towards the needs of others, and a willingness to "have a go" are the qualities that the school seeks to promote.

Rushmoor School

58–60 Shakespeare Road, Bedford MK40 2DL
Tel:　　01234 352031
e-mail:　admissions@rushmoorschool.co.uk
website:　www.rushmoorschool.co.uk

Chair of Governors: G M Bates, OBE, JP

Head Teacher: I M Daniel, BA, NPQH

Age Range. Boys rising 3–16, Co-educational rising 3–11.
Number in School. 280 Day Pupils.
Fees per term (2011-2012). £1,720–£3,050.
Rushmoor has grown and improved by investing greatly to provide excellent facilities. In September 2006 a major new building was opened which comprises a second ICT suite, Art rooms, Library, Drama studio, and an additional eight classrooms. In September 2011 we will be opening a Food Technology facility and we have just completed the new cricket facility.

At Rushmoor we appreciate the importance of selecting the right school for your son or daughter; childhood is something which can be experienced only once. With this in mind, and the belief that children learn best when they feel happy and secure, we aim to develop in our pupils a lifelong interest in learning – one which encompasses the full range of intellectual, cultural, artistic and sporting achievements of our society.

We believe in individual care and attention. Visitors to the school are impressed by the friendly, positive attitude of the pupils and their energetic sense of purpose. The staff are caring and understanding, yet know the importance of effort and personal discipline in enabling pupils to achieve the highest academic standards.

At Rushmoor we ensure that all children have opportunities to develop their intellectual, physical and creative gifts, across a broad and balanced curriculum. Children in Reception and Junior classes benefit greatly from a wide range of specialist teachers.

We emphasise the individual, recognizing that all children are different and value each child in their own right. Encouraging children to develop their strengths improves their self-esteem, enabling them to find their role in the community. We promote children's personal development, encouraging lively and enquiring minds, respect for others and a high regard for truth. The stability of continuous education, spanning the ages 3–16 years, is a major factor in helping us achieve this.

At Rushmoor we pride ourselves on our ability to integrate children with Specific Learning Differences within main stream school life. We believe that every child should be allowed to embrace any aspect of the curriculum. Enabling children to receive support without undermining their confidence amongst their peers is of primary importance.

Rushmoor has a fine reputation in sport and boasts a highly successful record with many pupils gaining county and national honours. Children have also gained much success in national and local drama competitions and festivals.

Prospective parents and children can tour the school at any time and 'taster days' can be arranged. Come and experience our caring ethos which enables our children to develop the confidence and flexibility which allows them to face the demands of modern life. To view our excellent inspection report please visit our website.

Charitable status. Rushmoor School Limited is a Registered Charity, number 307530. It exists to provide education.

Sackville School

Cognita Schools Group

Tonbridge Road, Hildenborough, Kent TN11 9HN
Tel: 01732 838888
Fax: 01732 836404
e-mail: office@sackvilleschool.com
website: www.sackvilleschool.com

Headmaster: **Mr Peter S Lane**

Age Range. 11–18.
Number in School. 185.
Fees per term (2010-2011). £3,945.

Sackville School is situated in Hildenborough, midway between Tonbridge and Sevenoaks. The school is set in 28 acres of magnificent parkland and the main building dates from the 1860s. The school has three modern laboratories, two dedicated Computer Rooms, an impressive Sports Hall, Art and Design Suites, as well as the usual range of specialist teaching rooms.

The philosophy of the school is based on the individual and their unique learning needs. By concentrating on excellence, and by treating every child as a wonderfully unique individual, the school ensures that each child has the opportunity to fulfil their true potential, and develop their gifts and talents at all levels. Students achieve excellent GCSE results and the Sixth Form offers a wide range of A Level courses, plus Young Enterprise and various life-enriching opportunities.

Sackville students are cheerful, confident children who work hard and enjoy aiming high and achieving their very best – they are expected to take a full part in the life of the school. The Head and staff encourage a warm, friendly working atmosphere, whilst promoting pride in achievement. Every student is valued, and their talents recognised, by the Head and staff.

The full range of academic, cultural and sporting activities are offered and all students are encouraged to try all activities. All major team games, and minor sports, are played and Sackville students have represented their County as well as National Squads. The school has a lively Music Department and over three quarters of the students are engaged in music making. The Creative Arts are particularly well represented. Art is exceptionally strong and Drama has a growing reputation for excellence. The Activities programme is an integral part of the school day and includes Orchestra, Choir, Duke of Edinburgh's Award, Drama, Golf, Film Unit, Table Tennis, Boules, Fishing, Archery, Self Defence, Community Service, Shooting, Ceramics, Computing, Photography and many other activities.

The school fosters the qualities of honour, care for others, thoughtfulness and tolerance. The Head is always delighted to show parents, and their sons and daughters around, and to discuss the educational opportunities available at Sackville.

Sacred Heart School

Swaffham, Norfolk PE37 7QW
Tel: 01760 721330/724577
Fax: 01760 725557
e-mail: info@sacredheartschool.co.uk
website: www.sacredheartschool.co.uk

Headteacher: **Sister Francis Ridler**, FDC, BEd Hons, EYPS

Age Range. 3–16 Co-educational.
Number in School. 55 Day Pupils, 12 Girl Boarders.

Fees per term (2011-2012). Boarders: Termly £6,150, Weekly £4,750–£5,075; Day: £2,250 (Juniors); £3,000–£3,350 (Seniors).

Assistance with fees: Academic, Music, Art, Sport, All Rounder (Boarder) Scholarships for Year 7 (11+). Some bursaries available.

Entry requirements: Non-selective, Assessments, School Report and Interview.

Religious Affiliation: Roman Catholic (other denominations welcome).

Staff: 19 Full Time, 8 Part Time, 7 Learning Support.

The Sacred Heart School was founded by the Daughters of Divine Charity in 1914. The Sisters and lay staff work together to provide a safe and caring environment where Christian values are upheld.

Principally a day school, the school is now co-educational. Pupils study for eight to eleven GCSEs gaining consistently high A–C grades. At 16, the pupils have gained the confidence and self-possession which makes them much sought after by all Sixth Form Centres and other Independent Schools. There is a limited number of boarding places for girls aged 8–16 as well as the opportunity for flexi-boarding.

All pupils are encouraged to develop their gifts in Music, Drama, Art and Sport, and the School has a fine record of success in all these areas.

Facilities include a Sports Hall, Swimming Pool and Arts Centre with Theatre, Art and Music Rooms and a Pottery Workshop.

A very active Parents' Association, loyal past pupils and parents network, together with highly-qualified Staff provide the energy, enthusiasm and friendly atmosphere which characterises the school community.

Before and after school care is available and Nursery Vouchers are accepted.

Charitable status. The Daughters of Divine Charity is a Registered Charity, number 237760.

Sacred Heart School

Mayfield Lane, Durgates, Wadhurst, East Sussex TN5 6DQ
Tel: 01892 783414
Fax: 01892 783510
e-mail: admin@sacredheartwadhurst.org.uk
website: www.sacredheartwadhurst.org.uk

Chairman of Governors: Father Kevin Gaskin

Head Teacher: **Mrs Hilary Blake**

Age Range. 3–11 Co-educational.
Number of Pupils. 110.
Fees per term (2011-2012). £2,010.

Sacred Heart School is a small independent Catholic primary school and Nursery, nestling in the heart of the Sussex countryside.

We welcome boys and girls from 3–11 and with pupil numbers around 100 we have the opportunity to know each child individually, to recognise and encourage their strengths and support them in overcoming areas of difficulty.

Our pupils enjoy a high degree of academic success, regularly obtaining places at their first choice of school, including passes at 11+ and Scholarships.

Courtesy and care for each other are important values nurtured at Sacred Heart School where children play and work well together.

Charitable status. Sacred Heart School, as part of the Arundel and Brighton Diocesan Trust, is a Registered Charity, number 252878.

St Anne's Preparatory School

154 New London Road, Chelmsford, Essex CM2 0AW
Tel: 01245 353488
Fax: 01245 353488
e-mail: headmistress@stannesprep.essex.sch.uk
website: www.stannesprep.essex.sch.uk

Headmistress: **Mrs F Pirrie**, BSc, PGCE

  Age Range. 3+–11+.
  Number of Children. 160.
  Fees per term (2011-2012). £2,000–£2,110.
  St Anne's is a co-educational day school, with its own excellent nursery facility. Established in 1925, the school is conveniently situated in the centre of Chelmsford. The building is a large Victorian house, which has been carefully converted into the uses of a school. Extensive lawned areas, astroturf, playground and Nursery play area provide ample space for both recreation and games lessons. In addition, older pupils benefit from the use of the excellent sports facilities at the nearby Essex County Cricket Club.
  The children benefit from small classes and individual attention in a disciplined but happy environment, which enables them to realise their full potential. Provision is made in the school for the gifted as well as those pupils less educationally able. Classrooms are bright and well equipped and the teachers are chosen for their qualifications, experience and understanding of the needs of their pupils.
  St Anne's combines modern teaching with the best of traditional values. The school maintains a high standard of academic education giving great emphasis to a secure foundation in the basic subjects whilst offering a wide curriculum with specialist teaching in many areas.
  Examination results at both KS1 and KS2 levels are excellent and many pupils gain places at the prestigious Grammar and Independent schools in the county.
  The school offers a wide range of extra curricular activities and an excellent after-care facility is available for all age groups. St Anne's is rightly recognised for its friendly and supportive ethos. Parents are particularly supportive of all aspects of school life. Visitors are always welcome.

St Christopher's School

6 Downs Road, Epsom, Surrey KT18 5HE
Tel: 01372 721807
Fax: 01372 726717
e-mail: office@st-christophers.surrey.sch.uk
website: www.st-christophers.surrey.sch.uk

Headteacher: **Mrs A Thackray**

  Age Range. 3–7.
  Number in School. 140.
  Fees per term (2011-2012). £2,535 whole-day (including lunch), £1,290 half-day.
  St Christopher's School (founded in 1938) is a co-educational nursery and pre-preparatory school for children from 3–7 years.
  Set in a quiet residential area a short distance from the centre of Epsom, famous for the annual Derby and horse racing traditions, it has attractive secure grounds with gardens and play areas.
  St Christopher's main purpose is to support children and parents through the early years of education. We offer a carefully managed induction programme to school life and, subsequently, a broad and challenging education within a happy, caring and secure family environment. Above all we aim to offer your child the best possible start to their education.
  The children are prepared to enter a wide range of Surrey schools and we maintain a very high pass rate in a variety of entrance tests.
  Breakfast Club opens at 8 am and After-School Care is available until 6 pm Monday to Friday. There are also a number of after-school clubs.
  St Christopher's enjoys the support of an active parents association that organises a wide variety of social and fundraising events.
  For further information and a prospectus please contact the school. Parents are welcome to visit the school by appointment with the Headteacher.
  Charitable status. St Christopher's School Trust (Epsom) Limited is a Registered Charity, number 312045. It aims to provide a Nursery and Pre-Preparatory education in Epsom and district.

St Christopher's School

Mount Barton, Staverton, Totnes, Devon TQ9 6PF
Tel: 01803 762202
Fax: 01803 762202
e-mail: office@st-christophers.devon.sch.uk
website: www.st-christophers.devon.sch.uk

Headmistress: **Mrs Victoria Kennington**

  Age Range. 3–11 Co-educational.
  Number of Pupils. 100.
  Fees per term (2011-2012). Nursery: £225 per am/pm session; Reception £2,000; Years 1–6 £2,200.
  St Christopher's School is a proprietorial school owned by Mrs Jane Kenyon, the Principal, and Mr Gregory Kenyon, the Bursar. It is a non-selective school with a Christian ethos. Admission is on completion of a Registration Form by the child's parents or guardians. We are a small, co-educational Prep School providing for children aged 3 to 11 years.
  St Christopher's was established in 1991 and moved to its present site at Staverton in 1993. The school occupies 19th Century stables and barns converted to provide a delightful setting in which to learn, surrounded by the beautiful South Hams countryside.
  At St Christopher's we treat your son or daughter as an individual, striving to discover their needs and abilities while giving them security and a sense of belonging to the community of the school family. In preparing children not only for the next stage of education, but for the wider world, we aim to provide solid foundations based on a clear Christian ethos, resulting in sound values and the ability to make clear judgements. Education is a team effort. We need and expect strong support from home. The family atmosphere at St Christopher's encourages a happy, cooperative approach including parental access to the teaching staff on an informal basis. Our formal reporting system lies in providing short quarterly reports two or three times a term and a full subject-based report at the end of each term. Formal parents' evenings are held in the Autumn and Summer Terms.
  All pupils are prepared for entrance to Secondary Education and great care is taken to ensure that their transfer to the next stage of education is as smooth and positive as possible. The School has a long record of successfully preparing pupils for 11+ Entrance Examinations to the excellent local grammar schools and Common Entrance Examinations to Independent Senior Schools.

St Christopher's School

**71 Wembley Park Drive, Wembley Park, Middlesex
HA9 8HE**
Tel: 020 8902 5069
Fax: 020 8903 5939
e-mail: stchris.admin@happychild.co.uk
website: www.happychildschools.co.uk

Headteacher: **Mrs Alison McNeill**

Age Range. 4–11.
Number in School. 48 Boys, 27 Girls.
Fees per term (2010-2011). £2,295–£2,415. Discount for siblings 10%.
Entry requirements: Interview and Assessment.

St Christopher's School, a large Victorian building on Wembley Park Drive, offers a caring family atmosphere coupled with an equal emphasis on good manners, enthusiastic endeavour and academic excellence. The School, a Christian foundation dating from 1928, welcomes children of all faiths and cultures.

Caring and supportive staff provide a well-structured, disciplined and stimulating environment in which children are nurtured and encouraged to develop the necessary skills – academic, social and cultural – so that when they leave us at the age of 11 they can be certain of future success. All children at St Christopher's are equal and we emphasise the qualities of equality, justice and compassion. Children benefit from a curriculum that offers both breadth and depth, an activity programme that teaches skills and develops talents, and a pastoral programme that develops social responsibility.

The full range of academic subjects is taught based on an enriched National Curriculum. Sports and Music are seen as central elements in school life with sports matches, regular concerts and an annual carol service. In addition there is a variety of clubs and activities both at lunchtime and after school; these include First Aid, Cookery, Drama, Art, Computing, Spanish, Needlework, Recorders, Choir, String Quartet, Orchestra and Games.

Children are prepared for the full range of examinations at 11 years. In 2011 9 scholarships were awarded.

Recent leavers have gained entry to a wide range of excellent schools including Haberdasher's Boys and Girls, Merchant Taylors', Northwood College, Heathfield, St Helen's, North London Collegiate, City of London Boys and Girls, Henrietta Barnet, Queen Elizabeth's Boys Barnet, JFS, St Albans, UCS, Aldenham, Watford Grammar Boys and Girls, Royal Masonic Rickmansworth, John Lyon, Dr Challoner's, Beaconsfield High and South Hampstead High.

St Christopher's offers both Pre-School and After-School Care.

Please phone for an appointment to view the school. We look forward to welcoming you.

St Clare's, Oxford

139 Banbury Road, Oxford OX2 7AL
Tel: 01865 552031
Fax: 01865 513359
e-mail: admissions@stclares.ac.uk
website: www.stclares.ac.uk

Principal: **Mrs Paula Holloway**, BSc, PGCE, MSc Oxon, DipPM

Age Range. 15–19 Co-educational.
Number of Students. 260.

Fees per term (2011-2012). Boarding £9,757–£10,053, Day £5,948.

St Clare's is an international college founded in 1953 with a mission "To advance international education and understanding", something it has been doing successfully ever since. The College embraces internationalism and academic excellence as core values. It is a coeducational day and residential college which has been offering the International Baccalaureate Diploma for over 30 years, longer than any other school or college in England.

Students from over 40 countries study at St Clare's with a core group of British students. The atmosphere is informal and friendly with an equal emphasis on hard work and developing personal responsibility. Each student has a Personal tutor who oversees welfare and progress.

Most students are enrolled for the full IB Diploma. St Clare's has an especially wide range of subjects on offer at Higher and Standard level and, in addition, currently teaches 28 different languages. The College takes a small number of transfer students each year. For students not yet ready to begin the IB Diploma, a PreIB course is offered with regular entry points throughout the year. There is an extensive programme of social, cultural and sporting activities and students are encouraged to take full advantage of the opportunities that Oxford provides.

The College also runs a highly successful IB Institute providing introductory refresher and revision courses for students. St Clare's is also authorised to run IB workshops for teachers.

St Clare's is located in an attractive residential area which is part of the North Oxford Conservation Area. It occupies 26 large Victorian and Edwardian houses to which purpose-built facilities have been added. These include a beautiful library building (over 35,000 volumes, an IT suite and a Careers and Higher Education Information Centre), four science laboratories, art and music studios, dining room and the popular Sugar House café. Students live in College houses close to the central campus under the care of residential staff.

The College welcomes applications from students irrespective of gender, race, colour, religious belief or national origin. Entry is based on academic results, interview and confidential school report. There is a competitive scholarship and bursary programme awarded by examination, interview and group exercises.

St Clare's had a highly successful ISI inspection in March 2008; the full Report can be accessed via the College website.

Charitable status. St Clare's, Oxford is a Registered Charity, number 294085.

St David's College

**Justin Hall, Beckenham Road, West Wickham, Kent
BR4 0QS**
Tel: 020 8777 5852
Fax: 020 8777 9549
e-mail: StDavids@dial.pipex.com
website: www.stdavidscollege.com

Principal: **Mrs A Wagstaff**, BA Hons London

Head Teachers:
Mrs A Peters, CertEd
Mrs G Talley, CertEd

Bursar: Mrs R Smith, MA Hons Edinburgh, ACA

Age Range. 4–11.
Number in School. Day: 93 Boys, 63 Girls.
Fees per term (2011-2012). £2,095–£2,145. Reduction in fees for all siblings.

A full-time staff of nine teachers, all fully qualified, is supplemented by ten part-time specialist teachers. Entry is by interview and informal test. Pupils are prepared for entrance to independent schools at age 11, as well as for the Kent grammar schools and for places at the London Boroughs of Bexley, Bromley and Sutton selective schools. Many scholarships and awards are gained each year. The school offers before and after-school care.

Speech and Drama, Clarinet, Dance, Flute, Music Theory, Piano, Recorder, Solo Singing, Recorder, Trumpet and Violin lessons are available. Sports include Athletics, Cricket, Cross-Country, Football, Hockey, Netball, Rounders, Swimming and Tennis. There is a Chess Club and a School Orchestra.

There are separate infant and junior schools, set within extensive and beautiful grounds. The school is positioned close to bus routes and to the mid-Kent and Hayes railway line, and is within easy reach of Bromley South and East Croydon stations.

The Principal and Head Teacher are always pleased to show the school to visitors.

St David's School

23–25 Woodcote Valley Road, Purley, Surrey CR8 3AL
Tel: 020 8660 0723
Fax: 020 8645 0426
e-mail: office@stdavidsschool.co.uk
website: www.stdavidsschool.co.uk

Headmaster: **Mr Vincent Fox**, BEd Hons, MA

  Age Range. 3+–11.
  Number in School. 151 Day: 76 boys, 75 girls.
  Fees per term (2010-2011). £1,300–£2,375 (including lunch).
  St David's School, derived originally from a Church of England foundation, believes in training children to be tolerant and supportive of one another within school and caring in their concern for others in a wider perspective.
  The children study all the usual academic subjects including Information and Communications Technology, Design Technology and Science. French is taught from the Infant classes and throughout the Juniors, and Latin is an optional language in Year 6. Small classes allow for much individual attention so that the children may develop to their full potential. The success of this ethos is demonstrated by the excellent results in selective entry to local Grammar Schools and in the Entrance Examinations to independent secondary schools where scholarships are frequently gained.
  The school is fortunate to own very adequate games facilities despite a suburban setting and the children do well in competitive events. Music, Art and Drama are considered to be fundamental to the development of character and the leadership qualities they encourage. There is a flourishing choir and orchestra.
  St David's participates fully in the Government Nursery Vouchers scheme.
  Charitable status. St David's (Purley) Educational Trust is a Registered Charity, number 312613. It aims to provide a quality education for boys and girls from 3+ to 11 years old. Bursaries are awarded in cases of financial hardship.

St Gerard's School
Bangor

Ffriddoedd Road, Bangor, Gwynedd LL57 2EL
Tel: 01248 351656
Fax: 01248 351204

e-mail: sgsecretary@st-gerards.org
website: www.st-gerards.org

Chairman of the Governing Body: Mrs L Lynch
Headteacher: **Miss Anne Parkinson**, BA

  Age Range. 3–18.
  Number in School. Day: 109 Boys, 122 Girls.
  Fees per term (2010-2011). £1,750–£2,650.
  Founded in 1915 by the Congregation of the Sisters of Mercy, this Catholic, co-educational school is now a lay trust. The school welcomes pupils of all denominations and traditions and has an excellent reputation locally. It has consistently attracted a high profile in national league tables also.
  Class sizes in both junior and senior schools ensure close support and individual attention in order to enable all pupils to achieve their full academic potential, within an environment which promotes their development as well-rounded individuals with a keen social conscience.
  The curriculum is comprehensive – pupils in the senior section usually achieve 9/10 good GCSE grades, going on to A Level and to university.
  Charitable status. St Gerard's School Trust is a Registered Charity, number 1001211. It exists to promote Catholic education in this area of Wales.

St Hilda's School

28 Douglas Road, Harpenden, Hertfordshire AL5 2ES
Tel: 01582 712307
Fax: 0871 714 5579
e-mail: office@sthildasharpenden.co.uk
website: www.sthildasharpenden.co.uk

Headmistress: **Mrs C Godlee**, BMus Hons, PGCE

  Age Range. 2½–11.
  Number in School. 180 approx.
  Fees per term (2011-2012). £2,880 (Forms II to VI including lunch), £2,850 (Reception & Form I including lunch), Nursery: £240–£2,160 (including lunch if appropriate).
  St Hilda's School, situated in a residential site of 1¼ acres, has its own swimming pool, hard tennis/netball court and adjacent playing field. It also has a fully-equipped stage, a suite of music rooms and a dedicated computer room.
  A broad, well-balanced curriculum covering the requirements of the National Curriculum prepares girls for the Common Entrance and other senior independent school entrance examinations. Girls also enter State secondary schools if desired. Latin and French are taught.
  A prospectus is available on application to the School Secretary.

St Hilda's School

15 Imperial Avenue, Westcliff-on-Sea, Essex SS0 8NE
Tel: 01702 344542
e-mail: office@sthildasschool.co.uk
website: www.sthildasschool.co.uk

Head: **Mrs S O'Riordan**, BA Hons, PGCE

  Age Range. Girls 3–16, Boys 3–11.
  Number in School. 120 Day Pupils.

Fees per term (2011-2012). Early Years: £2,112. Nursery Funding available. Years 1–11: £2,499–£3,150 excluding lunches. Compulsory extras: Textbooks.

St Hilda's is a small Independent School taking both girls and boys from the age of 3 up to 11. It is the only all-girls Independent Senior School in the Southend area, taking girls from 11 to 16.

At St Hilda's School we aim to maximise every child's gifts and talents in a safe and stimulating environment. To do this we offer a high quality education, based on the National Curriculum, which will maximise our pupil's potential. The success of this is shown by the excellent academic results throughout the school in SATs, 11+ selection test and GCSE results. In 2010 90% of our Year 11 pupils gained 5 or more GCSEs at Grades A*–C.

In the Infant and Junior Schools, pupils are taught the core subjects by their Form teachers; however they have an increasing number of specialist staff to further enhance their learning.

French is taught throughout the school from Early Years to Year 11, while pupils in the Senior school also study German. Spanish is offered after school to pupils from the age of 7.

Despite being a small school, we have a reputation for sporting excellence with pupils competing at school, borough, county, regional and national level in netball, cross-country running and athletics.

The Drama Department puts on a range of shows during the year for all ages, and every year a significant number of the pupils gain medals and cups at the Southend and Leigh Drama Festivals.

The Learning Development Department provides support for all pupils who are identified as needing additional help with their studies. This help is provided both in the classroom, and as additional individual or small group lessons.

While providing a 21st century education, the School recognises the importance of traditional values and actively promotes a caring and supportive environment for the pupils. They are also encouraged to learn to value others and make a positive contribution to the community in which they live, and the wider world. As a result of this caring ethos pupils develop a strong sense of personal value and personal aspiration which they take through to their adult lives.

Prospectus available on application to the Secretary.

St James Junior School

Earsby Street, London W14 8SH
Tel: 020 7348 1794
Fax: 020 7348 1790
e-mail: admissions@stjamesjunior.org
website: www.stjamesjuniors.co.uk

Chair of Governors: Mr Jeremy Sinclair

Headmistress: **Mrs Catherine Thomlinson**, BA Hons

Age Range. Boys 4–11+. Boys can then transfer to St James Senior Boys' School (*see entry in SHMIS section*) or other senior schools.

Girls 4–10+. Girls then transfer to Year 6 at St James Senior Girls' School (*see entry in GSA section*).
Number in School. 115 Boys, 138 Girls.
Fees per term (2011-2012). £3,800.

St James provides an inspiring education. The Junior School is situated on a large Central London site and the beautiful Victorian building provides an Assembly Hall/Theatre, Gym and large airy classrooms. The playground has a climbing wall and pretty cloister gardens.

The curriculum is imaginatively and carefully balanced and, together with the impressive level of commitment from the teaching staff, high academic standards of reading, writ-

ing and arithmetic are achieved and above all a love of knowledge. Art, Drama and Music are taught with enthusiasm and results are outstanding; children sing daily and morning assemblies bring joy and a sense of unity throughout the school.

An interest and knowledge in that which is common to all traditions is cultivated. Every class has a weekly Philosophy lesson during which they explore virtues such as consideration, friendship and truthfulness. The school's philosophy curriculum is available on the website, together with curriculum details of all subjects taught.

Team sports, gymnastics or athletics are played daily and full use is made of good facilities both within school and locally. After-school clubs offer a rich choice of activities including Ballet, French, Cricket, Netball, Rugby and Yoga.

Creative residential holidays are organised each year for children in the Upper Junior School (7+ years) to places such as New Barn in Dorset, Chartres in France and to Northumberland, where History, Geography and Geometry become a living experience and time is enjoyed out of London with their friends and teachers.

Boys and girls are taught separately with frequent joint activities such as plays, concerts and outings. Educating the children about the environment is part of the school's wider curriculum. The Reception classes are involved with the Forest Schools programme and from Year 3 the children visit Minstead Study Centre in Hampshire, where they learn about the enviroment and look after livestock.

The obvious happiness of the children flows from the full education offered and a level of attention and care from teachers that has become a St James trademark.

Charitable status. The Independent Educational Association Limited is a Registered Charity, number 270156. It exists to provide education for boys and girls.

St James' School
A Woodard School

**22 Bargate, Grimsby, North East Lincolnshire
DN34 4SY**
Tel: 01472 503260
Fax: 01472 503275
e-mail: enquiries@saintjamesschool.co.uk
website: www.saintjamesschool.co.uk

Head Teacher: **Mrs S M Isaac**, BA, PGCE

Age Range. 2–18.
Number in School. Boarders: Boys 23, Girls 17. Day: Boys 133, Girls 118.
Fees per term (2011-2012). Tuition: Prep School: Nursery (full time) £1,783 to Year 6 £2,285. Senior School Day Pupils: £3,530. Boarding: £1,940 (weekly), £2,255 (termly).

St James' School, Grimsby provides an excellent day and boarding education for children aged 2 to 18 years. The School is co-educational and a fully incorporated Member of the Woodard Corporation.

The Preparatory School (2 yrs to 11 yrs), including a fantastic Day Care and Nursery, is set well away from the main road within beautiful grounds. The School offers a traditional Prep School education, where discipline, manners and respect are promoted. The School has an excellent academic record and Grammar School pass rate (with an 11+ course incorporated into Year 5, outside of school hours). The School also has individual education plans for every child.

The Senior School (11 yrs to 18 yrs) offers both GCSE and A Level courses, with the majority of Sixth Form going on to Universities and a large number of students completing GCSEs early.

Both the Prep School and the Senior School offer a wide range of sporting and musical activities and the high standards of Pastoral Care and firm anti-bullying policies are evident throughout.

The School offers academic scholarships and also bursaries for Choristers and candidates within the Academy Girls' Choir (both subject to voice trials).

The School operates a morning bus service calling in at villages from the Louth and Brigg areas.

Charitable status. St James' School is a Registered Charity, numbers 529765 and 1099060. It exists to provide education for boys and girls.

St John's School

Stock Road, Billericay, Essex CM12 0AR
Tel: 01277 623070
Fax: 01277 651288
e-mail: registrar@stjohnsschool.net
website: www.stjohnsschool.net

Headteacher: **Mrs Fiona Armour**, BEd Hons

Age Range. 3–16.
Number in School. Day: 202 Boys, 168 Girls.
Fees per term (from January 2011). £1,432–£3,427.

St John's is a caring, but dynamic, day school situated in almost 8 acres of its own grounds and backing onto Lake Meadows Park.

The curriculum is a traditional one which embraces new educational innovations based on the requirements of the National Curriculum, and extends to include a wide range of options at GCSE.

Children work within a safe and disciplined environment studying a broad curriculum. Both traditional and modern teaching methods are used to prepare pupils for Key Stage Two, the Essex County 11+ Selection Examination, and GCSEs.

Attention is paid to both the social and academic development of all pupils and this is reflected in the outstanding results at both 11+ and GCSE, with the School currently ranked 7th in the county at GCSE. There are good facilities for rugby, football, basketball, hockey, netball, tennis, athletics, badminton, gymnastics and swimming.

Other activities include fencing, karate, LAMDA awards, the Duke of Edinburgh's Award Scheme, dancing, skiing, first aid training and community service. Foreign travel is encouraged with pupils travelling to Canada, USA, Spain, Bulgaria, France and Italy, as well as extensive British locations.

The first phase of our brand new state-of-the-art School is now fully operational. This now matches the high standard and quality of education we offer, in addition to enhancing our sporting facilities, which are both excellent and extensive. We offer an extended day from 8 am to 6 pm as well as Holiday Clubs.

The School goes beyond the classroom and looks at the whole person, someone who is highly motivated, with self-respect, respect for others, good manners, and the ability to "light up the room", and make others hear what they have to say.

The school aims to educate its pupils to be mature, responsible and confident in a happy, supportive and friendly environment. Our pupils want to learn and this is totally reflected in our results.

St Joseph's Convent School

59 Cambridge Park, Wanstead, London E11 2PR
Tel: 020 8989 4700
Fax: 020 8989 4700
e-mail: enquiries@stjosephsconventschool.co.uk

Chair of Governors: Mrs Ann Ross

Headteacher: **Ms Christine Glover**

Age Range. 3–11.
Number in School. 172 Day Girls.
Fees per term (2010-2011). £1,735.
Charitable status. Institute of Our Lady of Mercy is a Registered Charity, number 290544.

St Joseph's Park Hill School

Padiham Road, Burnley, Lancashire BB12 6TG
Tel: 01282 455622
Fax: 01282 435375
e-mail: parkhillschool@aol.com
website: www.parkhillschool.co.uk

Chairman of Governors: Mr Ed Morgan

Head Teacher: **Mrs A Robinson**

Age Range. 3–11 Co-educational.
Number of Pupils. 122.
Fees per term (2011-2012). £1,670.

St Joseph's was founded by the Sisters of Mercy in 1913 and has operated from its present site since 1957.

It is a small school with a warm, friendly atmosphere where the children are known personally by all the staff. We have a broad, enriched curriculum which provides many activities and opportunities, both sporting and musical. The children enjoy their learning experience and are encouraged to do their best, achieving excellent results.

The Catholic ethos permeates all areas of the school. Pupils learn to care for each other, and respect different cultures. We welcome children from all faiths.

The school has the benefit of extensive grounds, and offers a before and after school service as well as a 4-week summer school.

Charitable status. St Joseph's School is owned by The Institute of our Lady of Mercy which is a Registered Charity, number 290544.

St Joseph's Preparatory School

Rookery Lane, Trent Vale, Stoke-on-Trent, Staffs ST4 5RF
Tel: 01782 417533
Fax: 01782 849327
e-mail: enquiries@stjosephsprepschool.co.uk
website: www.stjosephsprepschool.co.uk

Chair of Governors: Mr D Harding

Head: **Mrs S D Hutchinson**, BEd

Age Range. 3–11 Co-educational.
Number of Pupils. 150 Day Pupils.
Fees per term (2011-2012). £1,550–£2,048.
Charitable status. The Congregation of Christian Brothers is a Registered Charity, number 254312.

St Joseph's School

St Stephens Hill, Launceston, Cornwall PL15 8HN
Tel: 01566 772580
Fax: 01566 775902

e-mail: registrar@stjosephscornwall.co.uk
website: www.stjosephscornwall.co.uk

Headmaster: Mr G M Garrett, BEd, BA, CMath, CSci

Age Range. Girls 3–16, Boys 3–11.
Number in School. Day: 27 Boys, 155 Girls.
Fees per term (2010-2011). Day: £1,995–£3,135.

St Joseph's School, Launceston is an Independent Day School for boys and girls from 3–11 years and senior girls from 11–16 years, although from September 2010 the senior department will be opening its doors to boys for the first time. The school is an ecumenical educational community, open to members of all faiths, in which Christian values are the cornerstone, and truth the essence of school life.

St Joseph's has a truly unique atmosphere. The school's size means that it is possible to keep sight of strong family values, which gives children the confidence necessary to succeed, and to allow both staff and pupils to work happily together. Due to the high teacher-pupil ratio (average 1:14), St Joseph's is able to encourage each pupil to reach his or her full potential through positive encouragement and commendation.

The school provides a good academic education for all, regardless of ability and background, with a wide variety of extra-curricular activities to provide balance and insight into opportunity. It offers equal prospects to all and inspires them to respond positively to challenges through encouragement and commendation. In last year's examinations, 95% of candidates gained at least six GCSEs at grades A*–C. This is a remarkable achievement as St Joseph's is a non-selective school. Pupils do not sit an Entrance Examination and places are offered at interview with the Headmaster.

National Honours have been gained in many areas including athletics, swimming, textiles, cookery and music. The senior chamber choir is a "flagship" choir for the South West, having appeared on both local and national television. The choir has also participated in the finals of the Music for Youth Festival at the Royal Festival Hall, London. In July 2009 the senior chamber choir will be travelling to Spain on a Concert Tour.

Recent new facilities include refurbished Nursery Department, two new Science Laboratories, an ICT suite and conference facilities. Scholarships are offered at 7+ in the Junior Department and Academic and Specialist Scholarships at 11+ in Music and Sport. Bursaries and Governors' Awards are considered on an individual basis. An extensive daily bus service allows pupils from a wide area of Devon and Cornwall to attend St Joseph's.

For further details please contact the Registrar or visit our website.

Charitable status. St Joseph's School is a Registered Charity, number 289048. It exists to provide education for girls and boys.

St Joseph's School

33 Derby Road, Nottingham NG1 5AW
Tel: 0115 941 8356
Fax: 0115 952 9038
e-mail: office@st-josephs.nottingham.sch.uk
website: www.st-josephs.nottingham.sch.uk

Headteacher: Mr Brendan O'Grady, BA, CertEd

Age Range. 1–11 years.
Number in School. 90 Boys, 60 Girls.
Fees per term (2010-2011). £2,275 (Main School Reception to Year 6). Nursery fees on application.

A co-educational day school providing the very highest standards to children of all abilities. Children receive individual attention in small classes. The curriculum is planned to encourage children to develop lively, enquiring minds with emphasis on literacy and numeracy. Music and Drama have a high profile in the school.

Sports include Football, Netball, Cricket, Rounders, Tag Rugby, Swimming and Squash.

Extra-curricular activities include Karate, Dance, Speech and Drama, Chess, Piano, Drums, Violin and Guitar.

It provides a happy and caring environment in which children can develop their full potential both socially and academically. The school is Roman Catholic but welcomes children of all faiths.

Charitable status. St Joseph's School Nottingham is a Registered Charity, number 1003916.

St Margaret's Preparatory School
Cognita Schools Group

Gosfield Hall Park, Gosfield, Halstead, Essex CO9 1SE
Tel: 01787 472134
Fax: 01787 478207
e-mail: admin@stmargaretsprep.com
website: www.stmargaretsprep.com

Headmistress: Mrs B Y Boyton-Corbett

Age Range. 2–11.
Number of Pupils. Day: 131 Boys, 124 Girls.
Fees per term (2010-2011). £2,430–£2,885.

St Margaret's is an ISA accredited school which specializes in the needs of children from 2 to 11 years. Academically, we provide excellence beyond the National Curriculum, stretching each child to the best of their individual ability, but not at the expense of a full and varied childhood. Although we regularly gain academic, music, art and sports scholarships to Senior schools, the emphasis is on an all-round education, encompassing the academic needs, enriching aspects such as social integration and encouraging other interests of each individual. Typically, a child at St Margaret's will have two afternoons a week of coached sport as well as a PE lesson, extra coaching sessions at lunchtime for the keen and able, and numerous after-school clubs. These clubs encompass a whole range of activities including fencing, archery, all major sports, speech and drama, martial arts, ballet, country dancing, chess, Forensic Science – the list goes on. They are regarded as an important and integral part of school, broadening their horizons. With a purpose-built ICT Suite and Art Studio, along with Music Rooms, Science Lab and gymnasium, the children have every opportunity to excel in their chosen sphere.

Naturally, the school has choirs, ensembles, an orchestra and numerous concerts and plays throughout the year. There are trips to Art Galleries, concerts, museums, as well as taking part in Festivals, competitions and local events.

Our extensive curriculum provides the children with the social confidence and academic ability to achieve their potential.

St Martin's Preparatory School

63 Bargate, Grimsby, N E Lincolnshire DN34 5AA
Tel: 01472 878907
e-mail: secretary@stmartinsprep.com
website: www.stmartinsprep.com

Headmaster: Mr S Thompson, BEd

Age Range. 2–11.

Number in School. Day: 65 Boys, 70 Girls.
Fees per term (2011-2012). £1,440–£1,840.

St Martin's was founded in 1930. It aims to foster an interest in learning from an early age. A fully qualified and dedicated staff ensure that a high standard in Primary School subjects is attained throughout the school. French is taught from the age of 4. Children are taught in small classes and great attention is given to individual development. Specialist teaching is available for children with specific learning difficulties.

Our purpose-built Kindergarten and Infant block is a modern building full of light and colour, which enhances the already excellent education provided by the school.

Girls and boys are prepared for Common Entrance and the 11+ examination. The vast majority of children transfer to the local Grammar schools. The school offers a range of clubs, including Yoga, Art, Football, Netball, Boules, Chess, Table Tennis, Computer and Drama. The school has an orchestra and two choirs. A happy and friendly atmosphere prevails throughout the school.

St Michael's School

Bryn, Llanelli, Carmarthenshire SA14 9TU
Tel: 01554 820325
Fax: 01554 821716
e-mail: office@stmikes.co.uk (Office)
          bursar@stmikes.co.uk (Bursar)
website: www.stmikes.co.uk

Headmaster: **D T Sheehan**, BSc Hons, PGCE

Age Range. 3–18.
Number in School. 423: 213 boys, 210 girls.
Fees per term (from January 2011). Tuition: Preparatory School £1,575–£2,410; Senior School £3,190–£3,485. Sibling allowances available. Boarding per annum (2011-2012): Years 7–9 from £18,800, Years 10–11 (GCSE) from £19,600, Sixth Form (A Level) from £22,200.

St Michael's is very much in the pattern of the small well-disciplined grammar schools. The school has a traditional approach to learning, which does not mean it lives in the past, but places emphasis on the importance of **hard work** and **homework** in the school curriculum. The high academic standards of the school are reflected in the National League Tables. In August 2010/11 the school was ranked in The Times Top 60 Co-Educational Schools in the UK at GCSE and A Level.

The school's boarding house, Park House, is a handsome and historic mansion set in an acre of grounds in the village of Llangennech, just 10 minutes from the school site. It has been totally refurbished to a high standard of comfort and attractiveness, and so provides a bright, cheerful and secure environment, where every pupil feels safe, happy and protected. Pupils are accommodated in well furnished and equipped, single or shared study-bedrooms. The house provides spacious recreation rooms and pleasant grounds in which pupils may relax, play or watch TV.

No school can build up such a strong reputation without a competitive, but well-disciplined atmosphere and a highly-qualified and dedicated staff. This is where we feel St Michael's is particularly fortunate.

We have well-equipped computer laboratories where pupils have access to a computer each from 3 years of age. Languages taught in the school are French, Spanish, Welsh and Chinese (Mandarin).

Apart from its academic basis, the school is proud of the wide range of games and activities, which include horse riding, fencing, archery and ski instruction. Pupils from Year 10 onwards can also take part in the Duke of Edinburgh's Award Scheme to Gold Award standard.

Speech, Drama and Music are strongly emphasized in the school and all pupils sit the early LAMDA examinations and can go on to achieve gold medal standard at school. We have a large choir and school orchestra and pupils may take music examinations at GCSE and A Level.

One of the main reasons for the school's success is the thorough grounding that pupils receive in the 'basics' – English, Mathematics, Computing and Science in the school's Preparatory Department.

We have enjoyed outstanding sporting success over the last few years in netball, rugby, football, tennis, cricket and athletics.

Every pupil is encouraged to develop his / her full potential whether in academic work or in all the extra-curricular activities and games that are offered.

St Nicholas House School

Yarmouth Road, North Walsham, Norfolk NR28 9AT
Tel: 01692 403143
Fax: 01692 403143
e-mail: office@stnicholashouse.com
website: www.stnicholashouse.com

Headmaster: **Mr C J A Wardle**, BA Hons, CertEd

Age Range. 3–11 co-educational.
Number of Pupils. 90.
Fees per term (2010-2011). £1,340.

St Nicholas House School is a small caring happy environment where children are encouraged to try their best and provided with the opportunity to thrive.

In small classes children benefit from a wide and varied curriculum giving a solid grounding and foundation in English and Maths, in addition to history, geography, art, craft, RE and ICT. Subject specialists teach French and Music from Reception to Year 6. In addition Peripatetic teachers offer a wide variety of musical instruments, speech and drama, dancing and singing.

Children are encouraged to try as many activities as possible through Clubs and after-school activities such as skiing, golf and chess. Sport plays an important part in the curriculum and in a child's time in the school, they will have the opportunity to try football, hockey, swimming, netball, cricket, rounders and short tennis in addition to seasonal sports.

The school enjoys an excellent success rate in entrance examinations to Senior independent schools obtaining numerous academic, sporting and drama scholarships.

Please telephone for an appointment to come and see us at work and play.

St Nicholas School

Hillingdon House, Hobbs Cross Road, Old Harlow, Essex CM17 0NJ
Tel: 01279 429910
Fax: 01279 450224
e-mail: office@saintnicholasschool.net
website: www.saintnicholasschool.net

Headmaster: **Mr K M Knight**, BEd Hons, MA, NPQH

Age Range. 4–16.
Number in School. 400 Day Pupils: 200 Boys, 200 Girls.
Fees per term (from April 2011). £2,260–£3,040.

St Nicholas School was founded in 1939 and is situated in a delightful rural location. St Nicholas combines a fresh and enthusiastic approach to learning with a firm belief in traditional values.

The academic record of the school is excellent, reflected in high pupil success rates in all competitive examinations. The dedicated team of staff involves itself closely with all aspects of pupils' educational progress and general development. High standards of formal teaching are coupled with positive encouragement for pupils to reason for themselves and develop a high degree of responsibility.

Main sports include Hockey, Netball, Tennis, Football, Rugby, Cricket, Swimming, Athletics and Gymnastics. Optional extras include Ballet, Individual Instrumental lessons, Spanish and Speech and Drama classes.

Recent building developments include a magnificent new Junior Department building, Infant Department building, Theatre, Science and Technology Centre, Junior Library, swimming pool and Sports Hall.

Charitable status. St Nicholas School (Harlow) Limited is a Registered Charity, number 310876. It exists to provide and promote educational enterprise by charitable means.

St Peter's School

52 Headlands, Kettering, Northamptonshire NN15 6DJ
Tel: 01536 512066
Fax: 01536 416469
e-mail: info@st-peters.org.uk
website: www.st-peters.org.uk

Headmistress: **Mrs M Chapman**, BA Hons, PGCE

Age Range. 2½–11.
Number in School. Day: 72 Boys, 69 Girls.
Fees per term (2010-2011). £957–£2,431.

Established in 1946, St Peter's is a small day school set in pleasant grounds on the outskirts of Kettering. It offers a sound education for boys and girls aged 2½ to 11. Pupils are thoroughly prepared for entry into their senior schools and a high rate of success in Entrance and Scholarship Examinations is regularly achieved. In addition to fulfilling the requirements of the National Curriculum the school emphasises the importance of Music, Art, Sport and Information Technology in its programme. French is introduced at Nursery.

St Peter's School is a lively, friendly school with a strong family atmosphere where children are encouraged to develop to the full their individual strengths and talents. It aims to promote, through Christian teaching, a respect for traditional values, a sense of responsibility and a concern for the needs of others.

Charitable status. St Peter's School is a Registered Charity, number 309914. It exists to maintain and manage a school for boys and girls in the town of Kettering.

St Philomena's Preparatory School

Hadleigh Road, Frinton-on-Sea, Essex CO13 9HQ
Tel: 01255 674492
Fax: 01255 674459
e-mail: generalenquiries@stphilomenas.com
website: www.stphilomenas.com

Co-educational Day School.

Chair of Governors: Mr Richard Whybrew

Headmistress: **Mrs Bernadette Buck**, CertEd

Age Range. 3½–11.

Number of Pupils. 140: 73 girls, 67 boys.
Fees per term (2011-2012). £1,640–£1,950.

St Philomena's is situated in a pleasant coastal area close to the beach. The school is dedicated to providing sound education based on Gospel values of the Whole Child within a Christian environment. Children flourish in the tangible family atmosphere throughout the school

Very good attitudes to learning are promoted for the mixed ability intake. Pupils strive for high academic standards and have achieved a very good record in 11+ selection examinations for both the grammar schools in the maintained sector and secondary schools in the independent sector.

Staff are fully qualified, experienced and dedicated professionals who communicate well with parents. Very high standards in pupil behaviour are maintained – pupils are caring and courteous with each other and towards adults.

There is a wide range of extra-curricular activities including sports clubs, science club, Scrabble, chess, needlework, nature, art, cycling proficiency and ICT. Tuition is offered for a wide range of musical instruments including, piano, violin, drums, guitar, flute, clarinet, trumpet, saxophone as well as individual singing. Music lessons with a music specialist take place throughout the school and there are recorder lessons for whole classes. There are weekly swimming lessons and French and Spanish lessons available from 4+. The school choirs and drama groups have achieved outstanding success in local and national competitions in recent years.

Emphasis is given to physical education. There are representative teams for football, hockey, cricket, rounders, netball, cross country and swimming. Tennis is taught to the senior children.

All children are encouraged to speak confidently and to express themselves clearly. All children from 7+ participate in an annual oral communication assessment adjudicated externally. Parents are invited to regular concerts, plays, class presentations and class assemblies.

Further developments have recently included a school chapel, an ICT suite, and after-school care.

Charitable status. St Philomena's Preparatory School is a Registered Charity, number 298635. It exists to provide Roman Catholic children and those of other denominations with the opportunity to reach the highest possible standards in every area of school life.

St Piran's School

14 Trelissick Road, Hayle, Cornwall TR27 4HY
Tel: 01736 752612
Fax: 01736 759446
e-mail: pirans@btconnect.com
website: www.stpirans.net

Headteacher: **Mrs Carol A de Labat**, BEd Hons, CertEd

Age Range. 3–16.
Number of Pupils. 70.
Fees per term (2010-2011). £1,560–£2,000.

Established in 1988, St Piran's Preparatory School is set in attractive and well-maintained premises, which, at present, house around seventy children, aged between three and sixteen. It is a friendly, well-ordered community with a positive ethos where pupils make good friendships with each other and relate well to staff. Pupils are treated with respect and valued equally. They have a clear sense of right and wrong. There is a good sense of community within the school and new pupils are quickly made to feel welcome. The school places a strong emphasis on good manners and politeness.

The curriculum is broad and balanced and helps to prepare the children for the next stage in their education. A wide variety of after school and lunchtime clubs provide additional activities and experiences for pupils of all ages. Educational visits to local places of interest and an annual residential visit (for Year 5 and up) further enrich the curriculum.

From Years Five and Six there is greater emphasis on subjects being taught by specialists. Class size remains low with the maximum class size being twelve. Well-qualified, conscientious and hard-working staff teach children in a supportive learning environment. Children are given the opportunity to explain their ideas and be involved in activities. There is a very well-equipped and effectively-organised computer suite, which ensures that the children are at the cutting edge of modern technology.

Our Year 10 pupils are our first GCSE cohort and they are achieving impressive results in their modular examinations.

The Ofsted Inspection for Early Years Provision in 2006 found our Foundation Stage to be 'outstanding in all areas'.

St Teresa's School

Aylesbury Road, Princes Risborough, Buckinghamshire HP27 0JW
Tel: 01844 345005
Fax: 01844 345131
e-mail: office@st-teresas.bucks.sch.uk
website: www.st-teresas.bucks.sch.uk

Acting Head: **Mrs J Draper**

Age Range. 3–11.
Number in School. Day: 80 Boys, 60 Girls. Nursery School: 11 Boys, 13 Girls.
Fees per term (2011-2012). £2,436 (first child), £2,278 (siblings).

Compulsory extras: swimming and lunch.

St Teresa's School is primarily a Catholic School, but is open to boys and girls of all religions or none.

A full programme of clubs includes cricket, rounders, tennis, football, netball, cross-country, athletics, swimming, chess, choir, orchestra and others.

A well-qualified and caring staff prepares the children for independent and state senior schools. The school has an excellent academic record of achievement and our pupils leave as confident and well-mannered individuals.

The children are encouraged to live out the school motto, *Fidelity* – faith in God, faith in others and faith in oneself.

Charitable status. St Teresa's is a Registered Charity, number 310645. It exists to provide a broad education enfolded by the Catholic faith.

St Winefride's Convent School
Shrewsbury

Belmont, Shrewsbury, Shropshire SY1 1TE
Tel: 01743 369883
Fax: 01743 369883
e-mail: stwinefridesschool@postmaster.co.uk

Headmistress: **Sister M Felicity**, BA Hons

Age Range. 4+–11. Nursery: 3+–4.
Number in School. Day: 73 Boys, 105 Girls.
Fees per term (from April 2011). £1,115–£1,165.

St Winifred's School

17–19 Winn Road, Portswood, Southampton SO17 1EJ
Tel: 023 8055 7352
Fax: 023 8067 9055
e-mail: office@stwinifreds.southampton.sch.uk
website: www.stwinifreds.southampton.sch.uk

Chairman of Board of Trustees: Mr John W Watts, MCIPS, MILT, AIGEM

Headmistress: **Mrs C A Pearcey**, BEd

Age Range. 2–11 Co-educational.
Number of Pupils. 100.
Fees per term (2011-2012). £2,175 (Lunch £140).

St Winifred's is a small school, on a pleasant, urban road in central Southampton, close to the university. It exists to make *the most of Individual Talent – nurturing every child*. The school caters for children aged 4–11; the nursery takes children from age two, including those receiving nursery grants. The school provides care from 8.00 am until 6.00 pm for pupils aged three upwards.

The school aims to provide for the whole child through a varied curriculum, with a wide programme of study and opportunities to develop all aspects of every pupil's talents. The core subjects, English, Maths and Science, as well as the development of ICT skills are at the centre of learning throughout the school. Pupils are encouraged and helped to develop a disciplined approach to personal study skills at all ages. Group and class activities help everyone to experience cooperative work and gain useful understanding of others skills and feelings.

Details of the curriculum can be found on our website. A structured academic program is covered by all age groups. This is delivered by specialist staff that enable every pupil to achieve their potential. Continuous assessment and tests prepare the upper school pupils for their entrance exams and for further achievement at secondary school.

The school provides regular feedback about pupils' progress at Parents' Evenings and through reports. Regular newsletters are sent to parents informing them of events the pupils are involved in as well as activities happening within the school. Parents are encouraged to be involved in their children's education where ever possible.

The school is proud of its achievements in music, drama, games, swimming and dance. As well as our own two indoor hall spaces and playground, the school takes advantage of The Gregg School's sporting facilities. Weekly games, swimming and gym/dance sessions with qualified staff are provided, as well as a variety of after-school activities.

Upper school pupils gain valuable experience whilst preparing for Trinity College Effective Communication examinations. Each year many pupils achieve distinctions and merits but, most importantly, all gain much personal satisfaction and confidence that will help them in later life.

Further opportunities are provided, through extra-curricular activities, to develop pupils' individual talents and personal strengths and interests. Monthly Achievement Assemblies celebrate individual and group interests in and out of school as well as focusing on pupils Endeavour and Courtesy within school. These are an opportunity for every individual to learn their own self-worth.

For taster days and further information, please contact the school secretary or visit our website.

Charitable status. The Gregg and St Winifred's Schools Trust is a Registered Charity, number 1089055.

St Wystan's School

High Street, Repton, Derbyshire DE65 6GE
Tel: 01283 703258
Fax: 01283 703258
e-mail: head@stwystans.org.uk
website: www.stwystans.org.uk

Headmaster: **Mr P Soutar**, BEd

Age Range. 2½–11.
Number in School. Day: Boys 60, Girls 62.
Fees per term (2010-2011). £2,045–£2,185. Compulsory extras: Lunch £217.

A small number of scholarships are offered for 7+ entry to Year 3.

Situated in the historic village of Repton, only a short distance from Burton-on-Trent and the city of of Derby, St Wystan's is ideally placed to serve a wide catchment area. Both Nottingham and Uttoxeter are within 25 minutes of the school, though the majority of pupils come from Derby, Burton and surrounding villages.

St Wystan's prides itself on a family atmosphere in which every child can grow in confidence and develop to his or her full potential as an individual. Great emphasis is placed on courtesy and good manners and a pastoral system, centred on the four school houses, promotes a caring environment and develops teamwork and commitment.

Academic expectations are high, though the school serves a wide ability range. Small classes enable the children to receive individual attention and work at a pace appropriate to their ability. As a free-standing junior school, St Wystan's prepares pupils for a large number of senior schools and pupils have won a significant number of academic, sport and music scholarships recently.

The pre-school department provides a nursery, headed by a fully qualified teacher and a reception class which both accept pupils on government subsidised "Early Years" places. The main school covers Key Stages 1 and 2 but is not restricted by the National Curriculum, offering a broad range of subjects and a blend of form teacher based teaching at the lower end and subject specialist teaching further up the school.

St Wystan's enjoys an excellent reputation in music and sport, with pupils progressing to regional and national championships, recently in football, swimming, cross-country and athletics. Many pupils have instrumental tuition and there is a thriving school choir and orchestra, together with a broad range of other extra-curricular activities.

St Wystan's runs a very popular pre-school and after-school care facility. Children can be delivered to school from 7.30 am and looked after at school until 6.30 pm.

Charitable status. St Wystan's School (Repton) Limited is a Registered Charity, number 527181. It exists to provide a quality education for boys and girls.

Salesian College

Reading Road, Farnborough, Hampshire GU14 6PA
Tel: 01252 893000
Fax: 01252 893032
e-mail: office@salesiancollege.com
website: www.salesiancollege.com

Headmaster: **Mr Patrick A Wilson**, BA Hons, MA, CertEd

Age Range. Boys 11–16 years; Co-educational Sixth Form.

Number in School. 625.
Fees per term (2011-2012). £2,950.

Salesian College at Farnborough in Hampshire was founded in 1901 and is an Independent Catholic Grammar School of about 600 students aged 11 to 18 years. Members of all Christian faiths are welcomed into the school which is part of a worldwide organisation of educational foundations run by the Salesians, a religious Order founded in the last century in Italy by St John Bosco specifically for the formation of young people, spiritually, academically, culturally, physically and emotionally. This continues to be our aspiration for each student.

Our aim is to send out from the school at 18 years young men and women who are confident without being arrogant, comfortable with themselves and all those around them, good Christians, honest citizens, and good individuals, well equipped to take their place in, and make a significant contribution to society.

This is achieved by the use of The Preventive System of Education promoted by St John Bosco and based on the three principles of Reason, Religion and Kindness. These principles encourage the students to develop a strong sense of responsibility and a caring attitude towards each other and the Community at large.

Academic achievements at GCSE and A Level, and sporting achievements are outstanding and highly valued. The friendliness and mutual respect that exist between staff and pupils provides a family and Christian ethos conducive to good order, confidence and scholarship.

The recent ISI Inspection report stated: "*Salesian College produces well-educated, confident, courteous and kind young men and women who are ready to take on responsibility and to serve*". The new co-educational Sixth Form has enhanced this.

We regard education to be a tripartite process involving the school, the family and the student and in order to produce the desired result all three must work in harmony.

Public speaking, music, orchestra, chess, drama and debating all flourish and there are many other extra-curricular activities.

The school has its own chapel, chaplaincy and resident chaplain.

Prospective parents are always welcome to make an appointment to visit the College while in session. Please see our website for up-to-date details.

Charitable status. Salesian College Farnborough Limited is a Registered Charity, number 1130166. It exists to provide education in North East Hampshire and neighbouring counties.

Salterford House School

Salterford Lane, Calverton, Nottinghamshire NG14 6NZ
Tel: 0115 965 2127
Fax: 0115 965 5627
e-mail: office@salterfordhouseschool.co.uk
website: www.salterfordhouseschool.co.uk

Headmistress: **Mrs M Venables**, CertEd

Age Range. 2½–11.
Number in School. Main School 170: 89 Boys, 81 Girls. Kindergarten and Pre-Prep 59: 30 Boys, 29 Girls.
Fees per term (2010-2011). £1,860–£1,880.

Salterford House is situated in rural Nottinghamshire, in a woodland setting and aims to provide a happy, family atmosphere with small classes, in order to equip children academically and socially to cope with the demands of any type of education which might follow.

Although the school is mainly Church of England, all faiths are accepted. 75% of pupils go on to senior independent schools such as Nottingham High Schools NGHS, Trent College and Hollygirt.

Sports include Cricket, Tennis, Swimming, Rounders, Football, Golf and Skiing.

The school produces 3 concerts a year and there is a recorder Group and Choir. Individual tuition in Speech and Drama, Piano, Woodwind, Guitar and Percussion is available.

A dyslexia teacher is employed to give individual lessons to children with dyslexia problems.

All classrooms are equipped with computers.

Staff are easily available for discussion. Regular contact is maintained with parents via Parents Evening and newsletters.

Sancton Wood School

2 St Paul's Road, Cambridge CB1 2EZ
Tel: 01223 359488
Fax: 01223 471703
e-mail: head@sanctonwood.co.uk
website: www.sanctonwood.co.uk

Headmaster: **Mr Richard J Settle**, BA, PGCE

Age Range. 1–16 Co-educational.
Number of Pupils. 103.
Fees per term (2010-2011). £1,024–£3,198.
Sancton Wood School was founded in 1976 by Mrs Jill Sturdy, initially for the education of her 9 adopted children. It has expanded in every subsequent year and now occupies 3 sites in central Cambridge. The current headmaster was most recently Dean of Gonville and Caius College, Cambridge, the post occupied by Mrs Sturdy's husband, the Revd John Sturdy, until his death in 1996.

The school has an overwhelmingly generous, "family" atmosphere, with 14 pupils per class at KS1, 15 per class at KS2 and 16 per class at KS3 and KS4. Nonetheless, the school is selective and expectations of academic achievement, as well as of the quality of relationships, are very high. The aim of the school is to send motivated, mature, kind and qualified young people into sixth form education.

Scarisbrick Hall School

Southport Road, Ormskirk, Lancashire L40 9RQ
Tel: 01704 880200
Fax: 0845 505 7890
e-mail: enquiries@scarisbrickhallschool.co.uk
website: www.scarisbrickhallschool.co.uk

Headteacher: **Ms S C O'Connor**

Age Range. 0–17.
Number of Pupils. 306.
Fees per term (2011-2012). Reception £1,595, Years 1–2 £1,925, Years 3–6 £2,140, Years 7–9 £2,775, Years 10–12 £3,060. Nursery £18 per am/pm session.

The essential elements of Scarisbrick Hall School are: the daily efforts of staff to provide an ambience where spiritual and cultural gifts can develop, the quality of teaching in the classroom, and the commitment of staff to extra-curricular activities.

The school follows the guidelines of the National Curriculum, but enhances these through an impressive selection of options to present a breadth and depth for all the pupils. The aim is to provide equal opportunities for all and to cater for the needs of the individual.

Throughout the school the size of classes is restricted to approximately 20 so that each pupil may receive close attention and be treated as an individual, encouraged to develop his/her abilities to the full in a friendly, caring environment.

High standards are set and expected from the pupils, with the emphasis on self-discipline. The school rules have been compiled from principles which are necessary for good order. The utmost importance is attached to the cultivation of good manners and consideration for others.

The Headteacher and staff consider the school as a partner with parents in the education of their children.

Shapwick School

Shapwick Prep (age 6–13):
Mark Road, Burtle, Bridgwater, Somerset TA7 8NJ
Tel: 01278 722012
Fax: 01278 723312
e-mail: prep@shapwickschool.com

Shapwick Senior & Sixth Form (age 13–19):
Shapwick Manor, Shapwick, Bridgwater, Somerset TA7 9NJ
Tel: 01458 210384
Fax: 01458 210111
e-mail: senior@shapwickschool.com
          sixthform@shapwickschool.com
website: www.shapwickschool.com

Joint Headmasters:
D C Walker, BA Hons, **J P Whittock**, CertEd

Age Range. 6–19.
Number in School. Boarders: 83 boys, 27 girls; Day: 39 boys, 13 girls.
Fees per term (2010-2011). Boarders £6,120–£7,029, Day £4,670–£4,889.
Shapwick is a specialist school for boys and girls whose education would otherwise be impaired by dyslexia. The School provides a caring and supportive atmosphere, staffed by specialist teachers across a wide curriculum offering the structured help needed by students who have dyslexia. Students take up to 8 GCSE subjects and the aim is to teach to their strengths whilst their weaknesses are being overcome and their confidence grows. Supplementary courses, such as Study Skills, Keyboard Skills, and careers advice are also taken. The School has a full range of specialist classrooms, including four laboratories, computing rooms, design centre, art rooms, library, sports hall, recreation room and games field. Students are involved in a wide range of extra curricular activities, the Duke of Edinburgh's Award, and games fixtures, to complement the formal curriculum.

Prospective entrants need an Educational Psychologist's report diagnosing dyslexia and at least average intellectual potential together with a current Head's report, and interview.

Sherborne House School
GEMS Education

39 Lakewood Road, Chandler's Ford, Hants SO53 1EU
Tel: 023 8025 2440
Fax: 023 8025 2553
e-mail: info@sherbornehouse.co.uk
          enquiry@sherbornehouse.co.uk
website: www.sherbornehouse.co.uk

Head: **Mrs Heather Hopson-Hill**, BEd Hons

Age Range. Girls and Boys from 2¾–11.
Number of Pupils. 250 (all day pupils).
Fees per term (2010-2011). £795–£2,700 including lunches. Nursery Grants (vouchers and salary sacrifice schemes) available for 3–4 year olds.

Sherborne House School, founded in 1933, takes children from Chandler's Ford, Winchester, Romsey, Southampton and the surrounding villages.

Sherborne House occupies an attractive four-acre site within the Hiltinbury area of Chandler's Ford. Boys and girls between 2 and 11 years of age are admitted through informal assessment. Scholarships in academic subjects, art, sport and music are available.

We have an enviable reputation for excellent Common Entrance and SATs results and regularly secure scholarships to established senior schools. Our outstanding results are achieved as a result of highly qualified staff, small classes and specialist learning support. Our broad curriculum emphasises literacy, numeracy and science but not at the expense of other subjects. Performing Arts is a particular strength of the school, with all children being encouraged to perform in both musical and dramatic activities, with additional peripatetic lessons are offered on a wide range of instruments. Art and CDT are taught in a specialist craft facility and all classrooms have interactive whiteboards to support work undertaken in the IT suite. A wide variety of sports is offered, including soccer, rugby, cricket, netball, hockey, short tennis, basketball and volleyball and the school has an extensive fixtures programme. French is offered from Nursery and Spanish is added to the curriculum in the upper school. Sherbourne House also provides a strong Learning Support network for those with special needs and individual programmes are drawn up and delivered by our SENCO in collaboration with the appropriate teaching staff. School trips and workshops and specialists curriculum days are arranged for all children as are residential visits for Key Stage 2 pupils. A wide range of after-school activities and clubs is also available.

At Sherborne House we believe that a child's self-esteem is paramount. We expect children to work and play and we take pride in our multi-sensory teaching methods, high but realistic expectations and our broad, engaging curriculum to accelerate our pupils' learning. The pastoral care at Sherborne House is outstanding and the pupils are confident, disciplined, purposeful and happy.

School hours: The school day runs from 8.40 am to 3.30 pm (pre-prep) and 3.55 pm (prep). Additional supervised care is available from 7.45 am until 6.00 pm.

We are always delighted to show prospective parents around the school and have regular Open Days.

Sherrardswood School

Lockleys, Welwyn, Hertfordshire AL6 0BJ
Tel: 01438 714282
Fax: 01438 840616
e-mail: mimram@sherrardswood.herts.sch.uk
website: www.sherrardswood.herts.sch.uk

Headteacher: **Mrs L E Corry**

Age Range. 2–18.
Number in School. Day: 207 Boys, 162 Girls.
Fees per term (2010-2011). £2,680–£4,435.

Sherrardswood, founded in 1928, is a co-educational day school for pupils aged 2–18. The School is set in 25 acres of attractive parkland two miles north of Welwyn Garden City. The Junior Department is housed in a fine 18th century building whilst the Senior Department occupies a purpose-built facility. Games fields, tennis courts and woodlands trail are available on the Lockleys site for both departments.

Entry to the school is by interview or by interview and examination according to age. A broad curriculum is offered to GCSE level and a wide range of A Level subjects is available.

A range of sport and extra-curricular opportunities is available, both within the school day and out of school hours. There is a commitment to a caring environment within a disciplined framework and the opportunity to develop qualities of self-discipline and responsibility.

The recent ISI inspection confirmed that Sherrardswood is achieving its aims and that the quality of education and pastoral care is outstanding.

Charitable status. Sherrardswood School is a Registered Charity, number 311070. It exists solely to provide independent education for boys and girls aged 2–18.

Shoreham College

St Julian's Lane, Shoreham-by-Sea, West Sussex BN43 6YW
Tel: 01273 592681
Fax: 01273 591673
e-mail: info@shorehamcollege.co.uk
website: www.shorehamcollege.co.uk

Headmaster: **J Stearns**, BSc, MA, PGCE, NPQH

Age Range. 3–16.
Number in School. 308 Day Boys, 126 Day Girls.
Fees per term (2011-2012). £2,450–£3,950.

Founded in 1852, the College is a Charitable Trust and is sited to the east of Shoreham in a Tudor manor house supplemented by modern buildings set in spacious grounds.

Shoreham College has a non-selective entry policy and all pupils are prepared for GCSE Examinations. There is a very favourable teacher/pupil ratio and a well-qualified and experienced staff. Particular care is taken to help pupils in their career choice.

The main games are soccer, rugby and cricket as well as athletics, squash, badminton, tennis and swimming. There is an active CCF and thriving Music Department, both choral and instrumental.

The School offers a caring community with a proper balance between straightforward discipline and friendly relationships.

Charitable status. Shoreham College (The Kennedy Independent School Trust Limited) is a Registered Charity, number 307045. It exists to provide high quality education for local boys and girls.

Silcoates Sunny Hill

7 Wrenthorpe Lane, Wrenthorpe, Wakefield WF2 0QB
Tel: 01924 291717
Fax: 01924 291717
e-mail: sunnyhillhead@silcoates.org.uk
         adrianboyer@silcoates.org.uk
website: www.silcoates.org.uk

Chair of Governors: **Mrs M C Chippendale**, BSc

Headmaster: **A P Boyer**, BEd

Foundation Leader & Early Years Programme Manager:
    Mrs H Lindenmayer

Age Range. 2–5.
Number in School. 60 Boys and Girls.
Fees per term (2011-2012). £1,970.

The dedicated teaching team sees the school as an enlarged family unit, constantly seeking to provide a happy environment where young children can develop naturally as individuals and gain the confidence necessary to realise their full potential both socially and academically. The basic concepts of literacy and numeracy are taught in small classes within the Early Years Foundation Stage Curriculum and great attention is paid to cultivating responsible social attitudes in an exciting and energetic atmosphere.

Silcoates Sunny Hill is part of the Silcoates School Foundation and has access to its excellent sports facilities and resources. All children are then able to enter Silcoates Junior School at the end of Reception.

Charitable status. The Silcoates School Foundation is a Registered Charity, number 529281. It exists to provide education for boys and girls.

Slindon College

Slindon, Arundel, West Sussex BN18 0RH
Tel: 01243 814320
Fax: 01243 814702
e-mail: registrar@slindoncollege.co.uk
website: www.slindoncollege.co.uk

Headmaster: **I Graham**, BEd, MA

Age Range. 8–16.
Number in School. 40 Boarders, 40 Day Boys.
Fees per term (2011-2012). Boarders £8,470, Day Boys £4,975–£5,290.

A small school for approximately 100 boys whose classes have a maximum of 12 pupils. The National Curriculum is followed where appropriate and in Years 4–9 a broad-based, balanced curriculum is provided. GCSE courses include PE, photography, art, music and design technology – all practical based and "hands-on". BTEC Food Skills & Horticulture also offered. The excellent Learning Support Department helps boys with specific learning difficulties, including dyslexia and ADD/ADHD.

A wide range of extra-curricular activities is offered, including car mechanics, farm club and stagecraft.

The school is non-denominational but has firm links with the local Anglican church.

Some bursaries are available and discount is available for Service families and second sons.

Charitable status. Slindon College is a Registered Charity, number 1028125. It aims to provide for the academic, social and personal development of each boy in a caring and purposeful environment.

Snaresbrook College Preparatory School

75 Woodford Road, South Woodford, London E18 2EA
Tel: 020 8989 2394
Fax: 020 8989 4379
e-mail: office@snaresbrookcollege.org.uk
website: www.snaresbrookcollege.org.uk

Headteacher: **Mrs L J Chiverrell**, CertEd

Age Range. 3½–11.
Number in School. 160.
Fees per term (2011-2012). £2,183–£2,918.

Snaresbrook College is an Independent day school for boys and girls aged from 3½ to 11 years. Founded in the 1930s, the school occupies a substantial Victorian building,

once a large private family home – a fact that contributes to the strong community spirit within the school. We aim to cultivate an intimate, caring family atmosphere in which children feel secure and valued. Most children join the school at age 3½ and stay with us until they reach 11 when they leave for their senior schools.

We provide a rounded primary education covering every aspect of your child's early development. The curriculum is designed to prepare pupils for senior independent and grammar school entrance and scholarship examinations. The curriculum includes Mathematics, English, Science, Social Studies, ICT, Art, DT, Music, Drama, French, PE/Games and PSHE. Latin and Swimming are introduced in the Juniors. Year 6 undertake the Adventure Service Challenge in preparation for The Duke of Edinburgh's Award undertaken at senior school.

At age 11, we find that Snaresbrook children are confident, cheerful and courteous, with a good sense of community and a readiness to care for each other and the world around them. They have learned how to work in the ways that suit them best, are receptive to teaching and are well prepared for the next stage of their education and development.

We see ourselves as joint trustees, with parents, of the young lives in our care, bearing equal responsibility for their happiness, well being and development.

Southbank International School
Hampstead Campus
Cognita Schools Group

16 Netherhall Gardens, Hampstead, London NW3 5TH
Tel: 020 7243 3803
Fax: 020 7727 3290
e-mail: admissions@southbank.org
website: www.southbank.org

Principal: **Helen O'Donoghue**

Age Range. 3–11.
Number in School. Day: 111 Boys, 99 Girls.
Fees per term (2011-2012). £4,160–£6,400.

Southbank International School was founded in 1979 by a group of educators in order to provide a challenging academic environment for students from around the world, aged 3 to 19. There are three campuses. The Hampstead campus serves the age range 3 to 11. Students receive tuition through the International Baccalaureate Primary Years Programme (PYP) and transfer to the Westminster campus at age 11. Southbank uses London as a classroom – taking full advantage of the cultural riches of the city. The campuses have students representing 73 nationalities, and the school is noted for its friendly and inclusive atmosphere.

Southbank was the first UK school to offer the International Baccalaureate curriculum to students of all ages. The IB PYP is inquiry-based and uses a cross-curricular approach. It includes the core subjects as well as Spanish, IT, art, music and Suzuki violin/cello. In the IB Middle Years Programme (MYP) offered at the Westminster campus, French and design technology are added to the core subjects begun in the Primary. The emphasis is on skills development and students are prepared for the High School and the IB Diploma Programme (16–18/19 years).

Southbank Hampstead is housed in a purpose-built building with a library, an IT centre, art and music rooms, a multi-purpose hall, and a playground. The door-to-door bus service covers a wide area of central and north London.

English is the language of instruction, but English as an Additional Language (EAL) is also offered throughout the school. Southbank attracts well-qualified and internationally experienced teachers.

Admission is based on previous school records and satisfactory references, as well as suitability of the candidate for the curriculum offered.

Southbank International School
Kensington Campus
Cognita Schools Group

36–38 Kensington Park Road, London W11 3BU
Tel: 020 7243 3803
Fax: 020 7727 3290
e-mail: admissions@southbank.org
website: www.southbank.org

Principal: **Mark Case**

Age Range. 3–11.
Number in School. Day: 108 Boys, 105 Girls.
Fees per term (2011-2012). £4,160–£6,400.
Southbank International School was founded in 1979 by a group of educators in order to provide a challenging academic environment for students from around the world, aged 3 to 19. There are three campuses. The Kensington campus serves the age range 3 to 11. Students receive tuition through the International Baccalaureate Primary Years Programme (PYP) and transfer to the Westminster campus at age 11. Southbank uses London as a classroom – taking full advantage of the cultural riches of the city. The campuses have students representing 73 nationalities, and the school is noted for its friendly and inclusive atmosphere.

Southbank was the first UK school to offer the International Baccalaureate curriculum to students of all ages. The IB PYP is inquiry-based and uses a cross-curricular approach. It includes the core subjects as well as Spanish, IT, art, music and Suzuki violin/cello. In the IB Middle Years Programme (MYP) offered at the Westminster campus, French and design technology are added to the core subjects begun in the Primary. The emphasis is on skills development and students are prepared for the High School and the IB Diploma Programme (16–18/19 years).

Southbank Kensington is housed in a large Victorian villa in Notting Hill with a library, an IT centre, art and music rooms, a multi-purpose hall, and a playground. The door-to-door bus service covers a wide area of central and north London.

English is the language of instruction, but English as an Additional Language (EAL) is also offered throughout the school. Southbank attracts well-qualified and internationally experienced teachers.

Admission is based on previous school records and satisfactory references, as well as suitability of the candidate for the curriculum offered.

Southbank International School
Westminster Campus
Cognita Schools Group

63–65 Portland Place, London W1B 1QR
Tel: 020 7243 3803
Fax: 020 7727 3290
e-mail: admissions@southbank.org
website: www.southbank.org

Principal: **Terry Hedger**

Age Range. 11–18/19.
Number in School. Day: 173 Boys, 159 Girls.
Fees per term (2011-2012). £6,900–£7,520.
Southbank International School was founded in 1979 by a group of educators in order to provide a challenging academic environment for students from around the world, aged 3 to 19. There are three campuses with Hampstead and Kensington teaching the International Baccalaureate Primary Years Programme (PYP) to 3–11 year olds and Southbank Westminster offering the Middle Years Programme (MYP) and the IB Diploma Programme for 16–18/19 year olds. The campuses have students representing 73 nationalities.

Southbank was the first UK school to offer the International Baccalaureate curriculum to students of all ages. In the MYP (11–16 years) at Westminster, French and design technology are added to the core subjects begun in the Primary School. The MYP links traditional subject areas to one another through a holistic framework. The emphasis is on skills development and students are prepared for the IB Diploma Programme (16–18/19 years), where they choose six subjects from six subject groups: Language A1 (a literature course in the student's first language); Second Language; Individuals and Societies (history, business and management, geography); Experimental Sciences (biology, chemistry, physics); Mathematics and Computer Science; The Arts (visual arts, film studies, theatre arts).

Southbank Westminster is conveniently located in central London near Regent's Park with good transportation nearby. Facilities at Westminster include five science labs, a computer lab, a hall/theatre, cafeteria, art and music rooms, and two libraries served by networked computers. The door-to-door bus service covers a wide area of central and north London.

English is the language of instruction, but students may also study their native language: currently 17 languages are offered as first or second languages. English as an Additional Language (EAL) is also offered throughout the school. Southbank attracts well-qualified and internationally experienced teachers.

Admission is based on previous school records and satisfactory references, as well as suitability of the candidate for the curriculum offered.

All students progress to universities mainly in the UK, but also around the world.

Stanborough School

Stanborough Park, Garston, Watford, Hertfordshire WD25 9JT
Tel: 01923 673268
Fax: 01923 893943
e-mail: registrar@spsch.org
website: www.spsch.org

Head of Secondary School: **Mr R Murphy**, BSc, MA Ed

Head of Primary School & Nursery: **Mrs K Hanson**

Age Range. 3–18.
Number in School. 234 girls and boys (boarding and day).
Fees per term (2010-2011). Boarding: £2,919–£3,979; Tuition: £1,621–£3,234.
Stanborough School, housed in attractive parkland, is a Christian independent school for boys and girls of all faiths between the ages of three and eighteen. Boarding is available for children who are at least 11 years of age.

It aims to give an education which fosters the growth of the whole person and is small enough for each student to remain an individual and not lose his or her personal identity. It has a warm, friendly atmosphere supported by firm yet kindly discipline providing a milieu in which pupils may develop their abilities and personal qualities to the full.

Charitable status. Stanborough School is a Registered Charity, number 1044071.

Steephill School

off Castle Hill, Fawkham, Longfield, Kent DA3 7BG
Tel: 01474 702107
Fax: 01474 706011
e-mail: secretary@steephill.co.uk
website: www.steephill.co.uk

Head Teacher: **Mrs Caroline Birtwell**, BSc, MBA, PGCE

Age Range. 3–11 co-educational.
Number of Pupils. 113.
Fees per term (2010-2011). £1,440–£2,400.

Steephill School is a very successful School based on its academic, sporting and musical achievements. In 2009 it had 80% entry into selective schools, winning many awards at the Gravesham Musical festival, and numerous successes at inter-school sports.

The School believes in high-quality teaching within a disciplined but relaxed atmosphere. The School holds traditional values and beliefs; working with and supporting each other is an important part of the ethos. There are close links with the church opposite the School. Four services per year are held there and the Rector takes a fortnightly assembly. The setting is very rural despite being only a few minutes' drive from the M2 and 5 miles from the M20 and M25. The School enjoys beautiful views of the countryside with very little traffic nearby.

The classes are a maximum of 16 and with only 120 pupils in the School, there is a close liaison between all members of the school community: children, staff, family members and governors. Parents are welcomed into the School and work closely with the teachers. There is regular feedback to parents on children's progress. Parents are also active in Friends of Steephill School, the Parents Association to provide social and fundraising activities.

The 2006 ISI report said that "pupils are at the heart of everything the School does". This begins from the time the children join the School aged 3½ in the Nursery to when they leave at age 11. The curriculum is designed to support all abilities to achieve academically and in all the broader aspects of education such as drama, the arts and sports. Information Technology has been developed well over the last few years and is being continually updated.

There is a large selection of extra-curricular activities at lunchtime and after school. Our Gardening Club is one of the more popular together with the choir, instruction on musical instruments, dance and football. We are very fortunate to have large grounds with a superb sports field, despite being a small school.

There is also a care facility both before and after school so we are open from 8 am to 5.30 pm.

Charitable status. Steephill School is a Registered Charity, number 803152.

Stoke College

Stoke-by-Clare, Sudbury, Suffolk CO10 8JE
Tel: 01787 278141
Fax: 01787 277904
e-mail: office@stokecollege.co.uk
website: www.stokecollege.co.uk

Headmaster: **J Gibson**, BA, CertEd

Age Range. 3–16+ Co-educational.
Number in School. Total 230: 131 Boys, 99 Girls. Boarders: 5 Boys, 1 Girl.
Registration Fee. £50.
Fees per term (2010-2011). Day: £2,375–£3,698. Weekly Boarding: £5,145–£5,971.

Stoke College provides a broad, balanced and relevant curriculum up to GCSE. Weekly boarders or day pupils enjoy a caring environment in an idyllic rural situation with small classes yielding excellent results in public examinations. The College has a strong tradition in athletics and cross-country and in Music and Drama. The school benefits from a new Sports/Assembly Hall, Junior School Teaching Block, Technology Rooms, a Performing Arts Centre, a swimming pool, hard tennis courts and a Nursery Department. The College aims to develop the individual's strengths and to produce a well rounded young adult to take his or her place in society.

Charitable status. Stoke College is a Registered Charity, number 310487. It is devoted to providing a full and relevant education to its pupils.

Stratford Preparatory School

Church House, Old Town, Stratford-upon-Avon, Warwickshire CV37 6BG
Tel: 01789 297993
Fax: 01789 263993
e-mail: secretary@stratfordprep.co.uk
website: www.stratfordprep.co.uk

Motto: *Lux et Scientia*

Principal: **Mrs C Quinn**, MBA, BEd Hons

Headmaster: Mr Neil Musk, MA, BA Hons, PGCE

Age Range. Preparatory School 4–11 years. Montessori Nursery School 2–4 years.
Number in School. Main School: 55 Boys, 64 Girls; Nursery School: 10 Boys, 20 Girls.
Fees per term (2010-2011). Junior School £2,675; Infant School £2,450; Nursery School: £2,300 (full-time), £1,225 (5 mornings), £1,100 (5 afternoons). Compulsory extras: Lunch £125.

Stratford Preparatory School is situated in the heart of the historic town of Stratford-upon-Avon. The Preparatory school opened in September 1989 and has developed around a large town house. An additional detached house within the school's grounds provides accommodation for the Reception and Nursery children, a gymnasium, a science room and design and technology room.

The Nursery implements the Montessori philosophy of learning which encourages a structured learning environment. French and ballet are taught from the age of 2 years.

The main school offers a broad balanced learning plan adapted to the individual needs of the children using traditional teaching methods and with specific reference to the National Curriculum. All children are entered for the 11+ and independent school entrance examinations.

The school offers a high level of pastoral care and attention to personal development.

Physical education facilities include: sailing, swimming, football, cricket, tennis, netball, rounders, ballet and athletics.

There are opportunities for the children to learn a variety of musical instruments. The school has two choirs and an orchestra.

Reduction in fees is offered for families with two or more children in Main School.

The Headmaster is pleased to provide further details and meet prospective parents.

Study School

57 Thetford Road, New Malden, Surrey KT3 5DP
Tel: 020 8942 0754
Fax: 020 8942 0754
e-mail: info@thestudyschool.co.uk
website: www.thestudyschool.co.uk

Principal: Mrs Susan Mallin, CertEd, FRSA

Headmistress: **Miss Joanna Knight**, BA Hons

Age Range. 3–11 Co-educational.
Number in School. Day: 78 Boys, 65 Girls.
Fees per term (2011-2012). Nursery (mornings only) £1,328, Reception & Year 1 £2,612, Years 2–6 £2,991. Additional Nursery afternoon sessions available each day of the week: £204 per afternoon per term. All fees include a cooked school lunch. The school belongs to the Early Years Funding Scheme for 3 and 4 year olds.

Since 1923 we have successfully given our children a firm foundation in reading, writing and number skills, whilst also teaching French, music, art and games. Science, geography, history, technology and ICT play an important part in the curriculum, with interactive whiteboards in every classroom.

Small classes allow us to stretch the most able pupils, whilst giving all our children individual attention.

Popular After School Clubs include Football, Art, Computer, Drama, Dance, Chess and Cookery. Individual instrumental music tuition is also available. We have After School Care until 6.15 pm. All classes go on a school trip once a term and Years Five and Six attend residential activity and field study courses.

We provide a caring and stimulating atmosphere in which our children thrive. After Year Six they leave us to enter such schools at King's College, Wimbledon, Kingston Grammar School, Hampton School, the High Schools at Wimbledon, Sutton, Putney and Surbiton, and both Tiffin Schools.

Please visit our website: www.thestudyschool.co.uk.

The Swaminarayan School

260 Brentfield Road, Neasden, London NW10 8HE
Tel: 020 8965 8381
Fax: 020 8961 4042
e-mail: admin@swaminarayan.brent.sch.uk
website: www.swaminarayan.brent.sch.uk

Chairman of Governors: Mr Piyush Amin

Headteacher: **Mr Mahendra Savjani**, BSc

Age Range. 2½–18.
Number of Pupils. 490: 274 boys, 216 girls.
Fees per term (2011-2012). £2,425–£3,399.
The Swaminarayan School was founded in 1991 by His Holiness Shree Pramukh Swami Maharaj to provide education along the lines of independent British schools, whilst reinforcing Hindu culture and tradition. It is a non-profit making co-educational school for children aged two and a half to eighteen years.

The school admitted its first eighty or so Prep School pupils in September 1992 and the Senior School took its first intake the following September. Now there are well over 485 pupils in the school and already students from the school have gained admission to Oxford, Imperial, Warwick, UCL, LSE and King's.

Since those early days excellent progress has been made in all areas. The most striking aspect that always attracts comment from visitors is the purposeful atmosphere, both in

classrooms and throughout the school. Teachers are able to help pupils achieve their full potential because of the generous staffing ratio, excellent behaviour of pupils and commitment from parents.

Resources and premises have also improved beyond recognition with modern libraries and computer rooms for each school. Former students from those early days dropping in to meet their teachers are amazed by the transformation!

On the curriculum front, the school has taken up the most desirable elements of the National Curriculum while developing the best practices of independent education. The cultural subjects unique to the school give it a special dimension – students have lessons in the Indian Performing Arts up to Year 8 and all students study Gujarati and Religious Education in Hinduism up to GCSE level.

In addition to their timetabled LAMDA lessons, PE lessons and club afternoons, pupils are encouraged to take part in a range of extra-curricular activities such as public speaking, sports, drama, dance and much more. An extensive programme of instrumental lessons, both Indian and European, is also on offer to all pupils. The school arranges regular day trips to museums, parks and other places of educational interest. The Duke of Edinburgh's Award Scheme and residential outings such as the annual ski trip are also a feature of the school. Whilst continuing to deliver a value based, broad and balanced curriculum, the school excels academically. Each year its excellent GCSE and A Level results put it at the top end of Brent Performance tables. In The Daily Telegraph list of top independent schools published in January 2011 the school was ranked 4th in the country.

Nearly twenty years of vision, investment and hard work from trustees and governors, teaching and non-teaching staff as well as parents and pupils have made this a school to be proud of. The next ten years will see the school reaching even greater heights.

Charitable status. The Akshar Educational Trust is a Registered Charity, number 1023731.

Sylvia Young Theatre School

1 Nutford Place, London W1H 5YZ
Tel: 020 7258 2330
Fax: 020 7724 8371
e-mail: info@sylviayoungtheatreschool.co.uk
website: www.syts.co.uk

Principal: Mrs Sylvia Young, OBE

Headteacher: **Ms Frances Chave**, BSc, PGCE, NPQH

Age Range. 10–16.
Number in School. Day: Boys 75, Girls 145. Weekly boarding is available with host families at an additional cost.
Fees per term (2011-2012). Junior Department £3,120, Years 7, 8 and 9 £4,125, Years 10 and 11 £4,230. Fees include a compulsory school lunch.

The School has a junior department (Year 6 only) and a secondary department (Years 7–11). We aim to provide an appropriately balanced academic and vocational experience for our students. We are proud of the caring and well disciplined environment that prevails and promotes a very positive climate of individual success.

Academic subjects are delivered by highly qualified staff to the end of Key Stage 4.

GCSE Examination subjects include English, English Literature, Mathematics, Science, Additional Science, Art, Drama, Expressive Arts, Music, Media Studies, Spanish and History.

Theatrical training is given by experienced professional teachers. Pupils are prepared for examinations in Speech and Drama – LAMDA (London Academy of Music and Dramatic Art). Entry is by audition with academic ability assessed.

Thornlow Preparatory School

Connaught Road, Weymouth, Dorset DT4 0SA
Tel: 01305 785703
Fax: 01305 780976
e-mail: headmaster@thornlow.co.uk
website: www.thornlow.co.uk

Head: **Mr R A Fowke**, BEd Hons

Age Range. 3–13 Co-educational.
Number of Pupils. 70 Boys and Girls.
Fees per term (from January 2011). £2,290–£2,340.
Thornlow Preparatory School is a must on any visiting list in order to appreciate fully the unique blend of teacher dedication and expertise that produces a happy, caring atmosphere. A highly qualified staff and small teaching groups ensure that any child's unique potential is nurtured to the full.

On the cultural and extra-curricular front, Thornlow certainly lives up to its motto of "preparing children for life's horizons", for not only is music a strong feature with a wide range of instruments being taught, but there is also a thriving culture of drama.

Another special feature is the Sailing, which takes place twice a week in the safe confines of Portland Harbour.

The well equipped Nursery Unit has en-suite facilities and enjoys the support of an NNEB.

In addition, Thornlow has a brand new ICT Room, Science Laboratory, Art Room, Library and Cooking Room.

Thorpe Hall School

Wakering Road, Thorpe Bay, Essex SS1 3RD
Tel: 01702 582340
Fax: 01702 587070
e-mail: sec@thorpehall.southend.sch.uk
website: www.thorpehall.southend.sch.uk

Headmaster: **A Hampton**, BA Hons, LTCL, MEd, NPQH

Age Range. 2–16 years.
Number in School. Approximately 345 girls and boys.
Fees per term (2010-2011). £2,003–£2,960.
Thorpe Hall School is a co-educational independent day school, pleasantly situated on green belt land on the outskirts of Southend-on-Sea, Essex. The buildings are modern and purpose-built.

Communications to London are good via the A13 and A127 and the Liverpool/Fenchurch Street railway lines. The nearest station is approximately 10 minutes' walk.

Founded in 1925, the school has been educating children for 80 years and consistently achieves excellent academic results at Key Stage 1, 2, 3 and GCSE with special emphasis being placed on the traditional values of good manners, behaviour, dress and speech.

On Monday, Tuesday and Thursday each week the school day is extended by one hour to enable all children to access library and computer facilities as well as having the opportunities to participate in Sport, Music, Drama, Mathematics and French or simply to do their homework in a suitable and supervised environment.

Refurbishments in Science, Modern Languages, Information Systems and the Resources Centre have greatly enhanced the learning opportunities for all pupils.

A new building was recently completed, which houses a Theatre, Technology rooms, an extra ICT suite and an excellent Modern Art area. These new facilities ensure that Thorpe Hall School has the most modern, up-to-date and technologically advanced facilities of any independent school in South East Essex.

Thorpe Hall School has an orderly, disciplined and caring ethos that caters for the social and academic needs of children – Pre-Nursery, Nursery, Reception, Infant, Junior and Senior – not only between the hours of 9 am to 4 pm but also offers sporting opportunities in golf, tennis, karate, netball, horse riding and football at weekends and during holiday times. Youngsters have the opportunity to join our Beavers, Cubs and Scout groups while senior pupils can become involved in the Duke of Edinburgh's Award Scheme.

The Charitable Trust status enables fees, which are very competitive, to be kept to a minimum. Nursery vouchers are accepted and some bursaries are available. The School is regularly inspected by the Independent Schools Inspectorate.

Charitable status. Thorpe Hall School is a Registered Charity, number 298155. It exists to provide good quality education for boys and girls in South East Essex.

Tower College

Rainhill, Merseyside L35 6NE
Tel: 0151 426 4333
Fax: 0151 426 3338
e-mail: rjoxley@lineone.net
website: www.towercollege.com

Principal: **Miss R J Oxley**

Age Range. 3–16.
Number in School. Day: 258 Boys, 269 Girls.
Fees per term (2010-2011). £1,671–£1,965.
Tower College is a non-denominational Christian Day School housed in a beautiful Victorian mansion set in 11 acres.

Our emphasis is on academic excellence and good behaviour. We have a strong musical tradition.

Seven coaches cover a 25-mile radius including South Liverpool, Widnes, Warrington, Runcorn, St Helens, Prescot, Rainford and Ormskirk. Breakfast and after school clubs are available.

Academic and music scholarships are available.

Charitable status. Tower College is a Registered Charity, number 526611. It aims to provide a sound education based on Christian beliefs, with an emphasis on good behaviour and academic excellence.

The Towers Convent School

Upper Beeding, Steyning, East Sussex BN44 3TF
Tel: 01903 812185
Fax: 01903 813858
e-mail: admin@towers.w-sussex.sch.uk
website: www.towers.w-sussex.sch.uk

Headmistress: **Mrs Carole Baker**, BEd, MA

Age Range. Girls 2–16, Boys 2–8.
Number in School. 326 including 20 boarders.
Fees per term (2011-2012). Weekly Boarders: £4,185–£4,480; Day Pupils £2,250–£2,920.
The Towers, a Roman Catholic boarding and day school for girls 2–16 and boys 2–8 years in the healthy and beautiful setting of the South Downs, is owned by a Community of Sisters. At the heart of The Towers Community is Christian love; all people of whatever race, colour, creed or status are welcome, and have equal worth and opportunity. We aim to celebrate the dignity of each individual pupil. Our motto

"Always Faithful" upholds the qualities of honesty and trust, responsibility, self-discipline and forgiveness. Pupils are encouraged to achieve their full potential in everything they do, developing a love of learning and seeking "wholeness". Technology and Science subjects are a particular strength, and the school has three times won the Whitbread Prize for GCSE results. The GCSE pass rate is consistently high and reflects a quest for high academic standards. There is a keen interest in Music and Drama and a major musical is produced annually. The school has again won the coveted Sportsmark Award, witness of a fine sports tradition, especially in tennis, where the school has won the Sussex Shield five times; netball and gymnastics are also very strong.

Find enjoyment and fulfilment at affordable fees!

Charitable status. The Towers Convent School is a Registered Charity, number 229394. It exists to provide quality education for girls and boys.

Trevor-Roberts School

55-57 Eton Avenue, London NW3 3ET
Tel: 020 7586 1444
Fax: 020 7483 1473
e-mail: trsenior@trevor-robertsschool.co.uk

Headteacher: **Mr Simon Trevor-Roberts**, BA

Age Range. 5–13 Co-educational.
Number in School. 169 Day Pupils: 100 boys, 69 girls.
Fees per term (2010-2011). £3,550–£4,200.
Trevor-Roberts School was founded in Hampstead in 1955 by the headmaster's late father and moved to its present site in 1981. The school is made up of two departments but operates as one school and occupies two adjacent much-adapted late Victorian houses in Belsize Park. In addition to on-site facilities, the school makes use of nearby playing fields and a leisure centre swimming pool.

Central to the education provided is the school's aim for all pupils to become happy and confident individuals who fulfil their potential. Strong emphasis is placed on personal organisation and pupils are encouraged to develop a love of learning for its own sake. In a happy, non-competitive atmosphere, pupils are well cared for and teachers' responses are tailored to the individual needs of pupils. It is the School's strong belief that much can be expected of a child if he or she is given self-confidence and a sense of personal worth and does not feel judged too early in life against the attainment of others.

High success rates throughout the school are achieved through small classes, individual attention and specialist teachers. The standards achieved enable almost all pupils to gain places in their first choice of school at either 11+ or 13+ into the main London day schools and academically selective independent boarding schools. In recent years a number of pupils have been awarded academic and music scholarships to these schools. The school aims to make pupils prepared for this process and give them the confidence to enjoy the academic challenges they will be offered.

The school provides a broad range of curricular and extra-curricular activities, contributing to pupils' linguistic, mathematical, scientific, technological, social and physical development in a balanced way. Aesthetic and creative development is strongly encouraged through art, drama and music. In the Senior Department the syllabus is extended to include Classical History, Latin and Greek. The curriculum is enriched at all stages by a variety of one-day educational visits as well as by residential trips for Years 6–8 for activity weekends, geography field trips and visits to France.

A range of extra-curricular activities and sporting opportunities, appropriate for boys and girls of all ages, is offered on two afternoons a week and after school. The school's

founder believed passionately in music and drama as a means of developing pupils' confidence and self-esteem and both subjects are a strong feature of the school today. All classes prepare and perform two drama performances each year in which every pupil has a speaking part.

Pupils thrive in a caring family atmosphere where the emphasis is on individual progress and expectation, and where improvement is rewarded as highly as success. It has a broadly Christian tradition, but welcomes pupils of all faiths and of none.

Trinity School

Brizes Park, Ongar Road, Kelvedon Hatch, Brentwood, Essex CM15 0DG
Tel: 01277 374123
Fax: 01277 373596
e-mail: enquiries@trinityschool.ac
website: www.trinityschool.ac

Headmaster: **Mr Rob Whitaker**, MA Cantab, DMS, PGCE

Age Range. 3–18 co-educational.
Number of Pupils. 105.
Fees per term (2011-2012). £1,152–£1,860 .
Trinity School is situated in Brizes Park, a 73-acre site of magnificent parkland on the outskirts of Brentwood. An elegant Georgian mansion houses the senior section while the primary section is in modern classrooms in a beautifully landscaped walled garden.

Trinity School has a distinctively Christian ethos, and aims for its pupils to develop as grounded and successful individuals. The academic results at GCSE and A Level are consistently strong, and sporting achievements, especially in table tennis, are excellent. Most pupils go on to gain good university degrees and then proceed to top jobs and careers. Many former students regularly give back to the school in various ways as a thank you for all they received here.

The school has a warm family atmosphere with many of the parents fulfilling roles in teaching, administration and support. The school is closely linked to Trinity Church, Brentwood, and one of the secrets of its success is the principle established from its foundation that the pupils should find the same standards in the school, the church and the home. This has produced happy, secure and well-motivated children who have a strong sense of service as well as a platform for success throughout life.

Charitable status. The school is a Registered Charity, number 1112705.

Trinity School

Buckeridge Road, Teignmouth, Devon TQ14 8LY
Tel: 01626 774138
Fax: 01626 771541
e-mail: enquiries@trinityschool.co.uk
website: www.trinityschool.co.uk

Headmaster: **Mr Tim Waters**, MA, MSc Oxon

Age Range. 3–19.
Number in School. Boarders: 80 Boys, 50 Girls. Day: 196 Boys, 164 Girls.
Fees per term (2011-2012). Boarders: £6,455–£7,305. Day: £2,185–£3,385. No compulsory extras.
Trinity is a joint Roman Catholic and Anglican school, although it has a non-denominational intake of pupils. Trinity is a co-educational school, with boarders from 7+, and

day pupils from 3. Entry to the School is by assessment and interview of the younger pupils, and entrance test and interview for the older pupils.

The School promotes good discipline with a friendly caring family atmosphere, within small classes, where individual potential is encouraged to develop to the full.

The School offers excellent facilities in a very attractive environment with panoramic views of Lyme Bay. The School has embarked on an ambitious building and development programme, spending in excess of £6 million in recent years. Facilities include a Design Technology building, assembly hall, IT laboratories, a Music Centre, a Science and Resources block, a Food Technology Centre and en-suite boarding accommodation for Sixth Formers. New indoor tennis facilities and a 25m heated swimming pool were completed in the summer of 2002. In 2005 8 new classrooms and a new Art Centre were completed.

Academic results are excellent, and there is a thriving programme of over thirty extra-curricular activities including many different sports.

The curriculum has also undergone development and expansion: recently Music, Spanish, Drama, Design Technology and Physical Education have been added to a full GCSE programme. Part One intermediate GNVQs in Business and Information Technology introduced in September 2000. Post-16. Various approaches exist dependent on the needs of the individual. Over 20 AS and A2 levels are offered and AVCE courses are available at intermediate and advanced level. The School has a strong Careers Department and a Programme for Health and Personal Relationships.

Trinity is close to the M5 motorway and a mainline railway station and runs daily buses to local towns. There are nearby airports at Exeter and Plymouth.

Links have been developed with Europe and an exchange system operates with Germany and trips are undertaken to France. Pupils also attend the School from a wide variety of other countries, but the intake of overseas students never exceeds 15%.

Academic, sporting, musical and drama bursaries and scholarships available. Generous Bursaries are available for children whose parents are members of the Armed Forces or the Police Force.

Charitable status. Trinity School is a Registered Charity, number 276960. It exists to provide education for children and students aged 3–19+.

Ursuline Preparatory School

Great Ropers Lane, Warley, Brentwood, Essex CM13 3HR
Tel: 01277 227152
Fax: 01277 202559
e-mail: headmistress@ursulineprepwarley.co.uk
website: www.ursulineprepwarley.co.uk

Headmistress: **Mrs Pauline Wilson**, MSc

Age Range. 3–11.
Number in School. Day 160.
Fees per term (2010-2011). £1,435–£2,680.

Founded in the early 1930s, the Ursuline Preparatory School enjoys a reputation as a happy family school, where pupils strive to give of their best in all areas of school life. Consequently, much emphasis is placed on encouraging the children to develop to the full their individual talents and interests, as well as fostering in each pupil a strong sense of well-being, self-reliance and team spirit. This is achieved by the frequent use of praise, by adherence to an agreed policy of consistent and fair discipline, and by the high standards, moral code and caring attitudes deriving from the strongly Catholic ethos which underpins the life of the whole school.

The Ursuline Preparatory School has well qualified and very experienced teachers and support staff. It is committed to offering to all its pupils the distinct advantages of a broad and balanced curriculum. This includes following the National Curriculum, in addition to affording many other opportunities such as the provision of French and Information Technology to all children from 4 years upwards, Swimming Lessons, and also Extension classes where this is deemed appropriate.

A comprehensive range of extra-curricular activities are offered to the pupils. These are often taught by specialist staff and include subjects such as Theatre Club, Art Appreciation, Computing, German, Chess, and Speech and Drama as well as many Instrumental Classes and Sporting Activities, with which the School has considerable success in gaining individual and team awards at competition level.

The School successfully prepares children for entry to local and national independent schools, Grammar Schools or local Secondary Schools, including the Ursuline High School.

The relatively small size of the School allows for very close contact between staff, pupils and parents and provides each child with the opportunity to fulfil his or her academic potential. The pupils are encouraged to follow their own interests and to develop a sense of self-confidence and self-worth which will hopefully remain with them throughout their lives, allowing them to reflect the school motto: *A Caring School that strives for excellence.*

Charitable status. The Ursuline Preparatory School is a Registered Charity, number 1058282. It exists to provide Roman Catholic children and those of other denominations with the opportunity to reach the highest individual standards possible in every area of School life.

Vernon Lodge Preparatory School

School Lane, Stretton, Near Brewood, Staffordshire ST19 9LJ
Tel: 01902 850568
Fax: 01902 850568
e-mail: info@vernonlodge.co.uk
website: www.vernonlodge.co.uk

Proprietor/Principal: Mrs D Lodge, CertEd, FCollP Hons, Cert Montessori

Headteacher: **Mrs P Sills**, CertEd, BEd Birmingham, RSACertSpLD

Age Range. Kindergarten 2+–4+, Prep School 4+–11.
Number of Children. 80.
Fees per term (2011-2012). £1,970–£2,330.

Situated in a lovely country garden, Vernon Lodge with its small classes provides individual attention and a happy atmosphere. We are a very active school with pupils participating in music, LAMDA, drama, ballet and dance, and sporting events; our all-weather court and playing field enables pupils to participate in tennis, football, netball, rounders and athletics. Pupils are offered swimming lessons and enjoy entering swimming galas.

The Early Years Department provides young children with an excellent foundation to learning. In our well equipped Kindergarten and Lower Prep class, children flourish as they enjoy a creative curriculum where they are stimulated and encouraged to develop reading, writing and number work which are introduced as a natural progression.

We make no apology for our traditional teaching methods, in fact we are proud of them as, together with up to date resources, excellent results of passes and scholarships to senior schools are achieved each year.

Our facilities have expanded over recent years. There is a well-equipped IT suite and interactive whiteboards in classrooms; a purposely designed library and music room provides the opportunity for personal study.

All pupils learn French and visits to France are offered where pupils may visit a French school and various places of interest giving 'hands-on' experience. There are also Youth Hostel weekends in the UK which are always enjoyed.

The popularity of Vernon Lodge School and Kindergarten is evident from its wide catchment area: children travel from Wolverhampton, Stafford, Cannock, Telford, Newport and the surrounding villages.

Virgo Fidelis Preparatory School

147 Central Hill, Upper Norwood, London SE19 1RS
Tel: 020 8653 2169
Fax: 020 8771 0317
e-mail: office@vfps.org
website: www.vfps.org

Headmistress: **Mrs C A Baines**, BA, MBA, FRSA

Age Range. 3–11.
Number in School. Day: 200 Boys and Girls.
Fees per term (2010-2011). £1,650–£2,430.
The school is a Roman Catholic Foundation with a strong ecumenical outlook. Pupils are received from various religious backgrounds. Emphasis is placed on the pursuit of good educational standards and on the development of personal responsibility.

Charitable status. Our Lady of Fidelity at Upper Norwood, London is a Registered Charity, number 245644. The general objects of the Trust are Religious and Charitable in connection with the advancement of the Roman Catholic Faith in England and Wales.

Vita et Pax Preparatory School

6A Priory Close, Green Road, Southgate, London N14 4AT
Tel: 020 8449 8336
Fax: 020 8440 0483
e-mail: vitaetpax@lineone.net
website: www.vitaetpax.co.uk

Chair of Governors: Mrs Jaisa Hugill

Headteacher: **Mrs Margaret O'Connor**, BEd Hons, MSc

Co-educational Day School.
Age Range. 3–11 years.
Number of Pupils. 110 Boys, 81 Girls.
Fees per term (2011-2012). £2,225.
Vita et Pax Preparatory School has a strong family atmosphere. The staff work in close partnership with parents and children to provide a happy and well balanced place of learning where everyone is valued and cared for.

Our School, founded in 1936 by the Olivetian Benedictine Sisters, has evolved under lay headship into a modern environment preparing tomorrow's citizens for tomorrow's challenges whilst maintaining the spirit of ecumenism, which was the foundation on which the Sisters built the School.

The programme of study in Nursery and Reception classes follows the Foundation Stage curriculum, while Years 1 to 6 are linked to the National Curriculum. Additionally, pupils are prepared for transfer to independent and maintained schools. The school was judged to be outstanding in all respects by Ofsted in our Early Years Inspection Report 2008.

Though academic success is important, pupils are nurtured to develop their own talents and interests.

Our aim is that pupils, with the support of our highly qualified and dedicated staff, become confident and considerate members of the wider community.

Charitable status. Vita et Pax School (Cockfosters) Ltd is a Registered Charity, number 281566. It exists to promote and provide for the advancement of education of infant and junior school age children.

The Webber Independent School
GEMS Education

Soskin Drive, Stantonbury Fields, Milton Keynes, Bucks MK14 6DP
Tel: 01908 574740/574753
Fax: 01908 574741
e-mail: registrar@wis.gemsedu.co.uk
website: www.webberindependentschool.co.uk

Principal: **Mrs Sue Vig**

Vice-Principal: Mrs Hilary Marsden

Age Range. 3–18.
Number in School. 236: 156 boys, 80 girls.
Fees per term (2010-2011). Early Years (ages 3–5) £1,298–£2,552; Years 1 and 2 (ages 6/7) £2,591; Years 3 and 4 (ages 8/9) £2,682; Years 5 and 6 (ages 10/11) £2,879; Years 7–13 (ages 12–17) £3,457.

The Webber Independent School offers quality, all-ability independent co-educational day schooling for pupils aged 3–18 years. There is a policy of non-selective entry and core subjects are taught according to ability. The School is located in private grounds, on a single site, close to the centre of Milton Keynes.

The School equips pupils with the relevant skills to contribute to, and thrive in, the local community and wider world. With international pupils from families posted to Milton Keynes on professional secondments, we have a breadth of personnel, cultural influences and perspectives beyond our size and location. Our pupils benefit from a wide range of intellectual, sporting and social opportunities. These encourage them to attain the very highest standards they can achieve, academically and in the areas of leadership, presentation, motivation and communication.

The Webber Independent School offers:
- High educational standards
- Close care and attention in small classes
- Excellent pastoral support
- Superb learning support department
- Before and after school care (8 am to 6 pm)
- Holiday clubs
- Healthy food cooked on the premises
- Minibus transport within Milton Keynes and to outlying towns and villages

The 2008 ISI Inspection report concluded that "the School is successful in its aim of providing a family atmosphere in which everybody is valued as an individual and is encouraged to reach their full potential within a disciplined yet caring atmosphere".

Please visit the School website to find out more, to play the School video (in English and Japanese) and to download a prospectus.

West Lodge School

36 Station Road, Sidcup, Kent DA15 7DU
Tel: 020 8300 2489
Fax: 020 8308 1905
e-mail: info@westlodge.org.uk
website: www.westlodge.org.uk

Chairman of Governors: Mr A Ridge

Head Teacher: **Mrs Susan Webb**, MA

   Age Range. 3–11.
   Number of Pupils. 160 Day Boys and Girls.
   Fees per term (2011-2012). £1,540–£2,570.
   West Lodge was founded in 1940 and is now an educational trust. The main building is an extended Victorian house, well adapted to use as a school, whilst still retaining its homely atmosphere. Facilities include a fully equipped gymnasium, astroturf, science/and art room, music rooms and a computer suite.

   There are eight classes of 21 pupils within the school, one class in each year group from Nursery through to Year 6. The staff-pupil ratio is extremely high and the children are taught in smaller groups by specialist teachers for many subjects. The school is open from 8.15 am and an after school crèche facility is available until 5.30 pm.

   The school has a strong academic tradition and a purposeful atmosphere permeates each class. The National Curriculum is at the core of the school's curriculum, but it is enhanced and enriched by the inclusion of a wider range of subjects. These include: English, mathematics, science, French, information technology, design technology, history, geography, religious education, music, art and craft, games, physical education, swimming and drama.

   Great emphasis is placed on a thorough grounding in basic learning skills, with literacy and numeracy seen as key elements in the foundation upon which future learning will be built. Particular care is taken to extend the most gifted children and support the less able. The school has a consistent record of a high level of entry to independent schools and local authority selective schools.

   Music has a particularly high profile within the school and all of the children are encouraged to develop their talents. Well-qualified peripatetic staff give both group and individual lessons and children of all ages are encouraged to join the school orchestras. Concerts and dramatic performances are staged regularly and parents are warmly invited to attend.

   The school promotes a caring attitude between all its members and aims to help each child towards the achievement of self-control and self-discipline. The Head Teacher and the class teachers know each of the 163 children well and the excellent pastoral care is a chief feature of the school.

   Home-school links are strong and the open door policy gives parents immediate access to members of staff should worries occur. The school also has strong contacts with the local community.

   Extra curricular activities are given the highest priority and clubs run each afternoon after school. Regular school outings form part of the curriculum for all children, the older pupils enjoying residential visits.

   Charitable status. West Lodge School Educational Trust is a Registered Charity, number 283627. It exists for the provision of high quality education for boys and girls between 3 and 11 years.

Westbourne School

4 Hickman Road, Penarth, Vale of Glamorgan CF64 2AJ
Tel: 029 2070 5705
Fax: 029 2070 9988
e-mail: enquiries@westbourneschool.com
website: www.westbourneschool.com

Headmaster: **Mr K W Underhill**, BA Ed Hons

   Age Range. 3–17.
   Number in School. 110 Boys, 60 Girls.
   Fees per term (2010-2011). £1,710–£3,295 (payable in advance). Fees include textbooks, sporting activities and examination charges.

   We are an Independent Co-educational day school for children from Nursery age to Sixth Form, with continuity in teaching methods throughout the School, and a stable context for study. From September 2008 we will be delivering the IB Diploma Programme in a brand new Sixth Form Building. A wide and flexible range of subjects is offered at GCSE, and results are consistently excellent. The staff is well-qualified and settled and pupils are known individually to all teachers and also to the Headmaster; education takes place in a happy, family-like environment.

   A disciplined, caring context is maintained and ample opportunity is given for a variety of sporting activities.

   Entry into Year 12 is based on GCSE Results and a Headmaster's Interview; entry into Year 9 is by Common Entrance at which a 50% pass is required. Otherwise entrance is by interview and two day induction.

   Penarth is a small seaside town on the outskirts of Cardiff, and pupils are normally drawn from Penarth, Sully, Cardiff, Barry, Cowbridge and the Vale of Glamorgan. There is a convenient train service to Penarth and the School has minibuses running each day from The Vale of Glamorgan, Cowbridge, Barry and Cardiff.

Westward School

47 Hersham Road, Walton-on-Thames, Surrey KT12 1LE
Tel: 01932 220911
Fax: 01932 220911
e-mail: admin@westwardschool.co.uk
website: www.westwardschool.co.uk

Principals: Mr & Mrs David Townley

Headmistress: **Mrs Shelley Stevenson**, BEd Hons

   Age Range. 3–11 Co-educational.
   Number of Pupils. 145.
   Fees per term (from April 2011). £916–£1,985.

Whitehall School

117 High Street, Somersham, Cambs PE28 3EH
Tel: 01487 840966
Fax: 01487 840966
e-mail: office@whitehallschool.com
website: www.whitehallschool.com

Headmaster: **Mr Sean Peace**, BA Ed Hons

   Age Range. 3–11 years.
   Number in School. 90 Day children: 43 boys, 47 girls.
   Fees per term (from April 2011). £1,609–£2,083.

Whitehall School is situated in a pleasant village with easy access to both Cambridge, St Ives and Huntingdon.

The buildings comprise a 1920s house and an 18th century Coach House. There are pleasant grounds with mature trees and garden play areas. Founded in 1983, the school offers the benefit of small tuition groups usually containing up to 16 children. The school has a good academic record (see website) and offers a broad curriculum including French, Swimming (own pool) and Drama.

Windrush Valley School

The Green, London Lane, Ascott-under-Wychwood, Oxfordshire OX7 6AN
Tel: 01993 831793
Fax: 01993 831793
e-mail: info@windrushvalleyschool.co.uk
website: www.windrushvalleyschool.co.uk

Headmaster: **Mr G A Wood**, MEd, TCert, DipSpEd, ACP, FCollP

Age Range. 3–11 Co-educational.
Number of Pupils. 130.
Fees per term (2011-2012). £1,945.

Windrush Valley School is a lively, happy community in which boys and girls thrive. Its rural location provides access to all the amenities of a beautiful Cotswold village including the 12th century church and playing fields. The school is non-selective; admission is by interview with the Headmaster. Before- and after-school care extend the school day from 8 am to 6 pm with a wide range of after-school clubs/societies. The small number of children with special educational needs are taught under the supervision of specialist staff. The school plays competitive sports in a wide range of games. Class groups are organised on a chronological age basis and the curriculum exceeds the requirements of the National Curriculum. Excellent examination results enable pupils to achieve their first choice of school on transfer to secondary education.

Woodlands School
Great Warley

Warley Street, Great Warley, Brentwood, Essex CM13 3LA
Tel: 01277 233288
Fax: 01277 232715
e-mail: info@woodlandsschools.co.uk
website: www.woodlandsschools.co.uk

Headmistress: **Mrs B Harding**

Age Range. 3–11.
Number in School. 127: 60 boys, 67 girls.
Fees per term (2011-2012). £2,360–£3,760.

Admission is by interview.

Woodlands School at Great Warley is set in attractive, spacious grounds, with excellent facilities for outdoor activities. The school also uses the extensive facilities of our sister school at Hutton Manor.

It is the School's principle aim to ensure that all the children are happy and secure and are as successful as possible. They are encouraged to work hard and to show kindness and consideration to their peers. The resulting ethos of the School is one of warmth, support and mutual respect.

The School provides an exciting learning experience which enables the pupils to achieve full academic potential and to develop qualities of curiosity, independence and fortitude. Classes are small. The school aims to develop high levels of self-esteem and a good attitude to learning. The School has an excellent record in public examinations. Pupils are highly successful in gaining places at the schools of their choice. Examination results in Music and LAMDA are also excellent.

A varied programme of team and individual sports aims to offer something for everyone.

There is a strong music tradition and a variety of dramatic and musical concerts and productions are staged throughout the year for children of each age group.

Modern languages are taught to a very high standard, with French introduced at the age of 3 and Spanish, in addition, from 7 years old.

Pastoral care is a major feature. An 'Open House' policy is in place for parents, which results in any concern being dealt with promptly and effectively.

It is the School's view that the education of the whole child is the most important priority and is confident that the learning experience it provides is fun, truly stimulating and memorable.

Woodlands School
Hutton Manor

428 Rayleigh Road, Hutton, Brentwood, Essex CM13 1SD
Tel: 01277 245585
Fax: 01277 221546
e-mail: info@woodlandshutton.co.uk
website: www.woodlandsschools.co.uk

Head Teacher: **Mrs Paula Hobbs**, BEd

Age Range. 3–11 Co-educational.
Number of Pupils. 118.
Fees per term (2011-2012). £3,160–£4,305.

PART VI
Schools in membership of the
Council of British International Schools

Member Schools

Africa

Kenya

Hillcrest Secondary School
PO Box 24819, Karen 00502, Nairobi, Kenya
e-mail: admin@hillcrest.ac.ke
website: www.hillcrest.ac.ke

Headteacher: Ian Stamp

Nigeria

Lagos Preparatory School
36–38 Glover Road, Ikoyi, Lagos, Nigeria
e-mail: admin@lagosprepikoyi.com
website: www.lagosprepikoyi.com

Headmaster: Graham Stothard

(*See entry in IAPS section*)

Asia

Brunei Darussalam

Jerudong International School
PO Box 1408, Bandar Seri Begawan BS8672, Negara
Brunei Darussalam
e-mail: office@jis.edu.bn
website: www.jis.edu.bn

Principal & CEO: Andrew J Fowler-Watt, MA Cantab

(*See entry in IAPS section*)

China

The British School of Beijing
Sanlitun Campus:
5 Xiliujie, Sanlitun Road, Chaoyang District, Beijing
100027, China

Shunyi Campus:
South Side, No.9 An Hua Street, Shunyi District, Beijing
101318
e-mail: info@britishschool.org.cn

website: www.britishschool.org.cn

Principal: Mike Embley

The British School of Guangzhou
983-3 Tonghe Road, Nanhu, 510515 Guangzhou,
Guangdong Province, China
e-mail: info@bsg.org.cn
website: www.bsg.org.cn

Head Teacher: Mark Thomas

Japan

The British School in Tokyo
1-21-18 Shibuya, Shibuya-ku, Tokyo 150-0002, Japan
e-mail: admissions@bst.ac.jp
website: www.bst.ac.jp

Head of School: David Williams

Vietnam

ABC International School
2 1E Street, KDC Trung Son, Binh Hung, Binh Chanh,
Ho Chi Minh City, Vietnam
e-mail: abcintschoolss@vnn.vn
website: www.theabcis.com

Headmaster: Mr Gary Benfield, BEd Hons, MIMgt

Central and South America

Costa Rica

The British School of Costa Rica
PO Box 8184, 1000 San José, Costa Rica
e-mail: britsch@racsa.co.cr
website: www.thebritishschoolofcostarica.com

Director General: David Lloyd

Europe

Belgium

The British International School of Brussels
163 Avenue Emile Max, 1030 Brussels, Belgium
e-mail: schooloffice@bisb.org
website: www.bisb.org

Headteacher: Stephen Prescott, BEng, PGCE, MA
   EdMgt

British Junior Academy of Brussels
83 Boulevard St Michel, 1040 Brussels, Belgium
e-mail: bjabrussels@yahoo.com
website: www.bjab.org

Head Teacher: Diane Perry

The British School of Brussels
Leuvensesteenweg 19, 3080 Tervuren, Belgium
e-mail: principal@britishschool.be
admissions@britishschool.be
website: www.britishschool.be

Principal: Mrs Sue Woodroofe, BA Hons, NPQH

(*See entry in HMC section*)

St Paul's British Primary School
Stationsstraat 3, Vossem, 3080 Tervuren, Belgium
e-mail: secretary@britishprimary.com
website: www.britishprimary.com

Headteacher: Brett Neilson

Czech Republic

Park Lane International School
Norbertov 3, Praha 6, Czech Republic
e-mail: info@parklane-is.com
website: www.parklane-is.com

Director: Barbara Lubaczewska

The Prague British School
K Lesu 2, 142 00 Praha 4, Czech Republic
e-mail: info@pbschool.cz
website: www.pbschool.cz

Managing Director: Michael Bocan

Riverside School
Roztocka 9, Sedlec, 160 00 Prague 6, Czech Republic
e-mail: administration@riversideschool.cz
website: www.riversideschool.cz

Director: Peter Daish

Denmark

Rygaards School
Bernstorffsvej 54, 2900 Hellerup, Denmark
e-mail: admin@rygaards.com
website: www.rygaards.com

Principal: Charles Dalton

France

The British School of Paris
38 Quai de l'Ecluse, 78290 Croissy-Sur-Seine, France
e-mail: registrar@britishschool.fr
website: www.britishschool.fr

Headmaster: Dr Steffen Sommer

(*See entry in HMC section*)

Mougins School
615 Avenue Dr Maurice Donat, Font de l'Orme, BP 401, 06251 Mougins Cedex, France
e-mail: information@mougins-school.com
website: www.mougins-school.com

Headmaster: Brian Hickmore

Germany

Berlin British School
Dickensweg 17-19, 14055 Berlin, Germany
e-mail: info@berlinbritishschool.de
website: www.berlinbritishschool.de

Headteacher: Graham Lacey

Independent Bonn International School
Tulpenbaumweg 42, 53177 Bonn, Germany
e-mail: ibis@ibis-school.com
website: www.ibis-school.com

Headmistress: Irene Bolik

Greece

Campion School
PO Box 67484, Pallini, Athens 153 02, Greece
e-mail: dbaker@campion.edu.gr
website: www.campion.edu.gr

Headmaster: Stephen W Atherton, MA Oxon, MSc Open, LRSM, ARCO

St Catherine's British School
PO Box 51019, Kifissia GR 145 10, Greece
e-mail: info@stcatherines.gr
website: www.stcatherines.gr

Headmaster: Peter Armstrong, MA

(*see entry in IAPS section*)

Italy

The New School Rome
Via della Camilluccia 669, 00135 Rome, Italy
e-mail: info@newschoolrome.com
website: www.newschoolrome.com

Headteacher: Domini MacRory

St George's British International School
Via Cassia La Storta, 00123 Rome, Italy
e-mail: Secretary@stgeorge.school.it
website: www.stgeorge.school.it

Principal: Martyn Hales

(*See entry in HMC section*)

St Louis School
Via Caviglia 1, 20139 Milan, Italy
e-mail: info@stlouisschool.com
website: www.stlouisschool.it

Director of Primary & Middle School: Luciana Vescovi

Sir James Henderson School
Via Pisani Dossi 16, 20134 Milan, Italy
e-mail: info@ @sjhschool.com
website: www.sjhschool.com

Principal: Dr Carlo Ferrario

Luxembourg

St George's International School Luxembourg
11 rue des Peupliers L-2328, Luxembourg
e-mail: info@st-georges.lu
website: www.st-georges.lu

Headteacher – Secondary: Nigel Fossey
Headteacher – Primary: Heather Duxbury

Netherlands

The British School of Amsterdam
Anthonie van Dijckstraat 1, 1077 ME, Amsterdam,
Netherlands
e-mail: j.light@britams.nl
website: www.britishschoolofamsterdam.nl

Principal: John Light

The British School in The Netherlands
Boerderij Rosenburgh, Rosenburgherlaan 2, 2252 BA
Voorschoten, Netherlands
e-mail: principal@britishschool.nl
website: www.britishschool.nl

Principal: Martin Coles

(See entry in HMC section)

Norway

British International School of Stavanger
Gauselbakken 107, N-4032 Stavanger, Norway
e-mail: principal@biss.no
website: www.biss.no

Principal: Anne Howells, BA, PGCE, CertEd

Poland

Poznan British International School
Ul Darzyborska 1A, 61-303 Poznan, Poland
e-mail: office@pbis.edu.pl
website: www.pbis.edu.pl

Principal: Danuta Koscinska

Romania

British School of Bucharest
42 Erou Iancu Nicolae Street, 077190 Voluntari, Ilfov
County, Romania
e-mail: office@britishschool.ro
website: www.britishschool.ro

Headteacher: Jo Puddy-Wells

International British School of Bucharest
Str Agricultori Nr 21, Sector 2, Bucharest, Romania
e-mail: office@ibsb.ro
website: www.ibsb.ro

Head of School: Ciprian Tiplea, BSc, MSc

Slovenia

British International School of Ljubljana
Trg 9, Maja 1, Sl-1000, Ljubljana, Slovenia
e-mail: jeremy.hibbins@britishschool.si
website: www.britishschool.si

Headmaster: Jeremy Hibbins

Spain

Aloha College
Urb El Angel, Nueva Andalucia, 29660 Marbella,
Malaga, Spain
e-mail: info@aloha-college.com
website: www.aloha-college.com

Headteacher: Elizabeth Batchelor

The British School of Alicante
Glorieta del Reino Unido 5, 03008 Alicante, Spain
e-mail: info@bsalicante.com
website: www.bsalicante.com

Head Teacher: Derek Laidlaw, DipT Mus, NPQH

British School of Gran Canaria
Crta Tafira a Marzagán s/n, El Sabinal, 35017 Las
Palmas de Gran Canaria, Spain
e-mail: hardes@bs-gc.net
website: www.bs-gc.net

Head: Steven Hardes

The International School of Catalunya
Passeig 9, La Garriga, 08530 Barcelona, Spain
e-mail: info@iscat.es
website: www.iscat.es

Director: Alan Roberts

King's College
The British School of Madrid
Paseo de los Andes 35, 28761 Soto de Viñuelas, Madrid,
Spain
e-mail: info@kingscollege.es
website: www.kingscollege.es

Head: Elaine Blaus, BA Hons, PGCE

(See entry in HMC section)

Sierra Bernia School
Apartado 121, La Caneta s/n San Rafael, 03580 Alfaz Del
Pi, Alicante, Spain
e-mail: sierraberniaschool@gmail.com
website: www.sierraberniaschool.co.cc

Headteacher: Duncan Allan

Sweden

British International Primary School of Stockholm
Östra Valhallavägen 17, S182 68 Djursholm, Sweden
e-mail: borgen@britishinternationalprimaryschool.se
website: www.britishinternationalprimaryschool.se

Principal: **Carl Hutson**

Switzerland

Aiglon College
CH-1885 Chesières-Villars, Switzerland
e-mail: info@aiglon.ch
website: www.aiglon.ch

Head Master: **Richard McDonald**, MA Oxon, PGCE

Geneva English School
36 route de Malagny, 1294 Genthod, Geneva, Switzerland
e-mail: gesadmin@iprolink.ch
website: www.geneva-english-school.ch

Headmaster: **Stephen Baird**

Turkey

The British Embassy Study Group
Sehit Ersan Caddesi 46/A, Çankaya 06680, Ankara, Turkey
e-mail: admin@besg.org
website: www.besg.org

Head Teacher: **Dawn Akyürek**, BA Hons, PGCE

The British International School, Istanbul
Dilhayat Sokak No 18, Etiler, Istanbul 34337, Turkey
e-mail: bisadmin@bis.k12.tr
website: www.bis.k12.tr

Secondary School Director: **William Bradley**

Pre School & Primary School Director: **Richard I'Anson**

Middle East

Egypt

The British International School, Cairo
PO Box 137, Gezira 11211, Cairo, Egypt
e-mail: info@bisc.edu.eg
website: www.bisc.edu.eg

Principal: **Simon O'Grady**

(*See Junior School entry in IAPS section*)

Maadi British International School
4th District, Zahraa El Maadi, Cairo, Egypt
e-mail: mbis@mbisegypt.com
website: www.mbisegypt.com

Headteacher: **Gerard Flynn**

(*See entry in IAPS section*)

United Arab Emirates

The British School – Al Khubairat
P O Box 4001, Abu Dhabi, United Arab Emirates
e-mail: principal@britishschool.sch.ae
website: www.britishschool.sch.ae

Principal: **Paul Coackley**

North America

United States of America

The British International School of New York
20 Waterside Plaza, New York, NY 10010, USA
e-mail: info@bis-ny.org
website: www.bis-ny.org

Headmaster: **William T Phelps**

INDEX OF ALL SCHOOLS